Volume 1
Western and Frontier
Film and Television Credits

Western and Frontier Film and Television Credits
1903–1995

compiled by
HARRIS M. LENTZ III

VOLUME 1

Section I: Actors and Actresses
Section II: Directors, Producers and Writers

McFarland & Company, Inc., Publishers
Jefferson, North Carolina, and London

British Library Cataloguing-in-Publication data are available

Library of Congress Cataloguing-in-Publication Data

Lentz, Harris M.
    Western and frontier film and television credits : 1903–1995 /
compiled by Harris M. Lentz III.
       p.   cm.
    Includes bibliographical references and indexes.
    Contents: v. 1. Section I. Actors and actresses. Section II.
Directors, producers and writers—v. 2. Section I. Film index.
Section II. Television index.
    ISBN 0-7864-0158-3 (set : 45# alk. paper).—
ISBN 0-7864-0217-2 (v. 1 : 45# alk. paper).— ∞
ISBN 0-7864-0218-0 (v. 2 : 45# alk. paper)
    1. Western films—Catalogs. 2. Motion picture actors and
actresses—Credits. 3. Motion picture producers and directors—
Credits. 4. Television actors and actresses—Credits.
5. Television producers and directors—Credits. I. Title.
PN1995.9.W4L383   1996
016.79143'6278—dc20   95-43360
                                                 CIP

Manufactured in the United States of America

McFarland & Company, Inc., Publishers
  Box 611, Jefferson, North Carolina 28640

To Tony Pruitt, Fred Davis, and
all the fine folks at the Memphis Film Festival

CONTENTS

VOLUME 1

ACKNOWLEDGMENTS

Special thanks go to Larry Tauber, Bud Greene, Tony Pruitt, Bobby Matthews and Kent Nelson for long conversations to determine what exactly constitutes a Western. Thanks also to Jeffrey Fisher for digging up information on death dates of many performers. Also thanks to Fred Davis and the fine folks at the Memphis Film Festival, Bill Anchors at Epi-Log, Francis M. Nevins, for the *Judge Roy Bean* information, and all my friends at Fred P. Gattas Co. and Berretta's Spike and Rail. I am also grateful to Kim Brown, Mikki Patterson, Louis & Vickie Berretta, Jay Kelley, Maggie Trafford, Bettye Dawson, Mark & Nina Heffington, Paul Geary, Dave Andrews, Doy L. Daniels, Jr., Andrew Smith, Forrest J Ackerman, Kim Love, Boyd Magers, Anne Taylor, Scott Graves, Tracey Patterson, Joy Martin, Pam Gaia, John Hoffman and Tom Walters.

I would also like to thank the people involved in making Western films who have so graciously shared their memories with me in the past several years. These include Gene Evans, Lash LaRue, Peggy Stewart, the late Sunset Carson, Pedro Gonzalez-Gonzalez, Linda Stirling, James Best, James Drury, the late James Griffith, Russell Johnson, the late Jane Nigh, the late Jim Brown, Tommy Farrell, Myron Healey, Ben Johnson, Jeff Corey, Pauline Moore, Elena Verdugo, Jane Addams, the late Richard Martin, Hank Penny, the late Slim Andrews, Sheb Wooley, Don Reynolds, Bob Terhune, Peter Breck, Barbara Fuller, John Mitchum, Robert Rockwell, Ed Kemmer, Jan Merlin, Frankie Thomas, Jr., Beverly Garland, Virginia Crowley, Eleanor Stewart, Betty Lynn, Terry Moore, Chris Alcaide, the late Claude Akins, S. Newton Anderson, Keith Andes, the late Chuck Connors, Edd Byrnes, Efrem Zimbalist, Jr., Myrna Dell, Penny Edwards, Donald Curtis, the late Aneta Corsaut, Ed Kemmer, Keith Larsen, Tommy Ivo, Lucille Lund, Richard Anderson, Gary Gray, Audrey Totter, the late John Lupton, the late John Pickard, Irish McCally, Donald May, the late Hal Smith, Frank Thomas, Jr., Plato Skouras, Russ McCubbin, Johnny Western, and Elaine Riley.

PREFACE

From 1903's *The Great Train Robbery* to 1995's *Buffalo Girls*, the American West has been one of the most popular topics on film and television. During the silent era, Westerns were perhaps the most successful type of films, establishing such performers as Bronco Billy Anderson, Tom Mix, William S. Hart and Colonel Tim McCoy as heroes both on and off the screen. The Western remained popular during the 1930s and 1940s, from major epics featuring such stars as John Wayne, Randolph Scott and Errol Flynn, to the singing cowboys exemplified by Gene Autry, Roy Rogers and Eddie Dean, to the second feature B-Westerns with Hopalong Cassidy, The Three Mesquiteers, Sunset Carson and Lash LaRue. The West was also the setting for many successful serials during this period, and the genre remained popular through the early fifties. While the number of Western films sharply declined in the later part of the decade, television filled the void. Westerns accounted for the majority of successful shows on television during the late 1950s and early 1960s. Such shows as *The Lone Ranger*, *Wagon Train*, *Maverick*, *Rawhide* and *Have Gun Will Travel* dominated the airwaves. *Gunsmoke* and *Bonanza* proved so successful they remained on air for twenty and fourteen seasons respectively. But by the early 1970s virtually all television Westerns were off the air, and the few Western films being produced were the "spaghetti" Westerns from Europe, which established Clint Eastwood as a major star. The genre was largely dormant throughout the next decade, though remained fondly remembered by its numerous fans. A resurgence of interest in the Western began with the successful television mini-series *Lonesome Dove* in 1989. Once again the Western was a popular subject in Hollywood with such films as *Dances with Wolves*, *Tombstone* and *The Unforgiven*, and television series such as *Dr. Quinn,*

Medicine Woman and *Legend*. One hopes that interest will remain high to provide for another generation of fans the tales of "those thrilling days of yesteryear."

The purpose of this work is to provide the reader with a comprehensive listing of Western and Frontier film and television series and the creative talent involved in their production. A traditional Western generally takes place in the American West during the latter half of the 19th century and the early years of the 20th Century. The genre is populated by cowboys and Indians, wagon trains and settlers, desperadoes and Texas Rangers, and other figures, both historical and fictional, who were involved in the expansion of the United States' borders to the Pacific Ocean. I have also included what I term Frontier films in order to include those films which were not strictly Westerns, but contained many of the Western conventions. Therefore films dealing with the Alaskan gold rush, the Royal Canadian Mounted Police, Daniel Boone, and *The Last of the Mohicans* will be found in this work.

The first section of the book contains the actors and actresses listing. I have listed performers and their dates of birth and death, when that information could be ascertained. This is followed by a chronological listing of their film credits, including title, date and character name. The performer's television credits are then listed with series title, episode title and date, and character name. The names of European stars were often Anglicized in film credits. I have generally listed the performer under the name they were best known by and have cross-referenced other names under which they performed.

The second section contains the directors, producers and writers listing (including original authors of many films). I have limited the depth of credits to these roles as I felt that they, along

1

with the actors, were the individuals primarily responsible for the creation of the films. Unlike science fiction or horror films, the make-up artist or special effects director is typically of lesser importances in the Western. The individual entries are listed in the same format as the actors and actresses section.

The third section is the Film Index. Each film is listed alphabetically with year of release, country of release (if other than the United States), production credits and cast and character information. I have noted serials as such and have indicated the number of chapters the serial contained. I have also listed the titles of the individual chapters of each serial. I have also indicated a short sound film when a film is under thirty minutes in length. I did not indicate the length of silent films prior to 1929. A great many of these films are unfortunately lost and credit information is sometimes sketchy. I have also included alternate titles by which the film has been known and have cross-referenced these titles.

The final section is the Television Index. I have attempted to include every Western television series accompanied by its regular cast. This is followed by an episode index of each individual episode, containing episode title, original airing date, and cast and character names. I believe this to be the most comprehensive listing of Western television series yet compiled, though cast information of some syndicated programs is limited. The chronological scope of this book reaches from the very first Westerns through the end of the 1994-95 television season (approximately June 1995). I utilized many sources in the compilation of this work, and these can be found in the References section. I particularly recommend Bill Anchor's *Epi-Log* magazine for further information on many television series. Thomas Weisser's *Spaghetti Westerns—The Good, the Bad and the Violent* is an invaluable reference on Euro-Westerns of the 1960s and 1970s, and Larry Langman's *A Guide to Silent Westerns* is especially comprehensive. *Classic Images* and Boyd Magers' *Western Clippings* are also highly recommended publications for those interested in Western films and their performers.

I have made this work as complete as possible and have done my best not to confuse the credits of William Boyd, William "Stage" Boyd and Bill "Cowboy Rambler" Boyd, Pat O'Malley and J. Pat O'Malley, and the Charles Kings, James Masons and Chief Thunderclouds, but with any work of this size undoubtedly mistakes and omissions have occurred. As always, any additions, corrections, or comments from the readers are welcome.

Harris M. Lentz III
Bartlett, Tennessee
Fall 1995

REFERENCES

Books

The Academy Players Directory. Beverly Hills, Calif.: Academy of Motion Picture Arts and Science, 1978–1995.

Adams, Les, and Buck Rainey. *Shoot-Em-Ups*. New Rochelle, N.Y.: Arlington House, 1978.

Anderson, Robert. *The Kung Fu Book*. Las Vegas, NV: Pioneer Books, 1994.

Barabas, SuzAnne, and Gabor Barabas. *Gunsmoke*. Jefferson, NC: McFarland, 1990.

Brooks, Tim. *The Complete Directory of Prime Time TV Stars*. New York: Ballantine Books, 1987.

Buscombe, Edward, ed. *The BFI Companion to the Western*. New York: Atheneum, 1988.

Calder, Janni. *There Must Be a Lone Ranger*. London: Hamish Hamilton, 1974.

Cline, William C. *In the Nick of Time: Motion Picture Sound Serials*. Jefferson, NC: McFarland, 1984.

Corneau, Ernest N. *The Hall of Fame of Western Film Stars*. North Quincy, MA: Christopher Publishing House, 1969.

Dimmitt, Richard Bertrand. *An Actors Guide to the Talkies*. Metuchen, NJ: Scarecrow, 1967. Two volumes.

Erickson, Hal. *Syndicated Television*. Jefferson, NC: McFarland, 1989.

Eyles, Allen. *The Western*. London: Tantivy Press, 1975.

Frayling, Christopher. *Spaghetti Westerns*. London: Routledge & Kegan Paul, 1981.

French, Philip. *Westerns*. New York: Viking Press, 1973.

Friar, Ralph, and Natasha Friar. *The Only Good Indian... The Hollywood Gospel*. New York: Drama Book Specialists, 1972.

Garfield, Brian. *Western Films*. New York: Rawson Associates, 1982.

Gianakos, Larry James. *Television Drama Series Programming: A Comprehensive Chronicle, 1947–1959*. Metuchen, NJ: Scarecrow, 1980.

_____. *Television Drama Series Programming: A Comprehensive Chronicle, 1959–1975*. Metuchen, NJ: Scarecrow, 1978.

_____. *Television Drama Series Programming: A Comprehensive Chronicle, 1975–80*. Metuchen, NJ: Scarecrow, 1981.

_____. *Television Drama Series Programming: A Comprehensive Chronicle, 1980–82*. Metuchen, NJ: Scarecrow, 1983.

_____. *Television Drama Series Programming: A Comprehensive Chronicle, 1982–84*. Metuchen, NJ: Scarecrow, 1987.

_____. *Television Drama Series Programming: A Comprehensive Chronicle, 1984–86*. Metuchen, NJ: Scarecrow, 1992.

Goldberg, Lee. *Unsold Television Pilots, 1955–87*. Jefferson, NC: McFarland, 1990.

Hansen, Patricia King, ed. *The American Film Institute Catalog: Feature Films, 1911–20*. Berkeley: Univ. of California Press, 1988.

_____, ed. *The American Film Institute Catalog: Feature Films, 1931–40*. Berkeley: University of California Press, 1993.

Hardy, Phil. *The Western*. Woodstock, NY: Overlook Press, 1991.

Hilger, Michael. *The American Indian in Film*. Metuchen, NJ: Scarecrow, 1986.

Holland, Ted. *B Western Actors Encyclopedia*. Jefferson, NC: McFarland, 1988.

Katz, Ephraim. *The Film Encyclopedia*, 2d edition. New York, HarperPerennial, 1994.

Krafsur, Richard P. *American Film Institute Catalog: Feature Films, 1961–70*. New York: R.R. Bowker, 1976.

Lahue, Kalton C. *Continued Next Week*. Norman: University of Oklahoma Press, 1964.

_____. *Riders of the Range*. New York: Castle Books, 1973.

_____. *Winners of the West: The Sagebrush Heroes of the Silent Screen*. New York: A.S. Barnes, 1970.

Langman, Larry. *A Guide to Silent Westerns*. Westport, CT: Greenwood Press, 1992.

Lenburg, Jeff, Joan Howard Maurer, and Greg Lenburg. *The Three Stooges Scrapbook*. Secaucus, NJ: Citadel Press, 1982.

McDonald, Archie P., ed. *Shooting Stars*. Bloomington: Indiana University Press, 1987.

McNeil, Alex. *Total Television*. New York: Penguin Books, 1991.

Maltin, Leonard, ed. *Movie and Video Guide 1995*. New York: Signet Books, 1994.

Marill, Alvin H. *Movies Made for Television*. Westport, CT: Arlington House, 1980.

Monaco, James. *Who's Who in American Film Now*. New York: Zoetrobe, 1988.

Munden, Kenneth W., ed. *American Film Institute Catalog: Feature Films, 1921–30*. New York: R.R. Bowker, 1971.

Nash, Jay Robert, and Stanley Ralph Ross. *The Motion Picture Guide*. 10 vols. Chicago: Cinebooks, 1985.

Oliviero, Jeffrey. *Motion Picture Players' Credits*. Jefferson, NC: McFarland, 1991.

Parks, Rita. *The Western Hero in Film and Television*. Ann Arbor: UMI Research Press, 1982.

Parrish, James Robert. *Actors' Television Credits 1950–1972*. Metuchen, NJ: Scarecrow, 1973.

_____. *The Hollywood Death Book*. Las Vegas, NV: Pioneer Books. 1992.

_____, and Michael R. Pitts. *The Great Western Pictures*. Metuchen, NJ: Scarecrow, 1976.

_____, and _____. *The Great Western Pictures II*. Metuchen, NJ: Scarecrow, 1988.

Perry, Jeb H. *Variety Obits*. Metuchen, NJ: Scarecrow, 1980.

Pitts, Michael R. *Western Movies*. Jefferson, NC.: McFarland, 1986.

Ragan, David. *Who's Who in Hollywood, 1900–1976*. New Rochelle, NY: Arlington House, 1976.

Rainey, Buck. *Saddle Aces of the Cinema*. New York: A.S. Barnes, 1980.

Rothel, David. *The Gene Autry Book*. Madison, NC: Empire Publishing, 1988.

_____. *The Roy Rogers Book*. Madison, NC: Empire Publishing, 1987.

Singer, Michael. *Film Directors*. Beverly Hills, CA: Lone Eagle, 1990.

Stewart, William T., Arthur F. McClure, and Ken D. Jones. *International Film Necrology*. New York: Garland, 1981.

Terrace, Vincent. *Encyclopedia of Television Series, Pilots and Specials, 1937–1973*. New York: Zoetrope, 1986.

_____. *Encyclopedia of Television Series, Pilots and Specials, 1974–1984*. New York: Zoetrope, 1986.

Truitt, Evelyn Mack. *Who Was Who on the Screen*, 3d edition. New York: R.R. Bowker, 1983.

Tuska, Jon. *The American West in Film*. Westport, CT: Greenwood Press, 1985.

Walker, John, ed. *Halliwell's Filmgoer's and Video Viewer's Companion*, 10th edition. New York: HarperPerennial, 1993.

Weiss, Ken, and Ed Goodgold. *To Be Continued...* New York: Bonanza Books, 1972.

Weisser, Thomas. *Spaghetti Westerns—The Good, the Bad and the Violent*. Jefferson, NC: McFarland, 1992.

West, Richard. *Television Westerns: Major and Minor Series, 1946-1978*. Jefferson, NC: McFarland, 1987.

Willis, John, ed. *Screen World*. New York: Crown Publishers, 1971–1994.

Woolley, Lynn, Robert W. Malsbary & Robert G. Strange, Jr. *Warner Bros. Television*. Jefferson, NC: McFarland, 1985.

Periodicals

Classic Images (Muscatine, Iowa), 1985–.

The Commercial Appeal (Memphis, Tenn.), 1930–.

Epi-Log (Dunlap, Tenn.), 1990–95.

Epi-Log Journal (Dunlap, Tenn), 1992–94.

The Hollywood Reporter (Hollywood). 1933–.

Motion Picture Guide Annual (Evanston, Ill.), 1986–.

Motion Picture Herald (New York), 1919–68.

The New York Times (New York), 1925–.

TV Guide (Radnor, Penn.), 1953–.

Variety (New York), 1930–.

Section I

ACTORS AND ACTRESSES

Aaker, Lee (1943-). Films: "Arena" 1953 (Teddy Hutchins); "Hondo" 1953 (Johnny); "Take Me to Town" 1953 (Corney); "Destry" 1954 (Eli Skinner); "Ricochet Romance" 1954 (Timmy Williams). ¶TV: *The Adventures of Rin Tin Tin*—Regular 1954-59 (Rusty); *The Lone Ranger*—"The School Story" 1-20-55.

Aames, Willie (1960-). TV: *Gunsmoke*—"P.S. Murry Christmas" 12-27-71 (Tom), "A Quiet Day in Dodge" 1-29-73 (Andy Ballou).

Aaron, Victor. Films: "Geronimo: An American Legend" 1993 (Ulzana).

Abbass, Pam. Films: "Bronco Billy" 1980 (Mother Superior).

Abbiana, Franco. Films: "Price of Death" 1972-Ital. (Jeff Plummer).

Abbott, Alan. Films: "Halleluja and Sartana Strikes Again" 1972-Ger./Ital.

Abbott, Blanche. Films: "The Forfeit" 1919 (Nan Tristam).

Abbott, Bud (1895-4/24/74). Films: "Ride 'Em, Cowboy" 1942 (Duke); "The Wistful Widow of Wagon Gap" 1947 (Duke Eagan); "Lost in Alaska" 1952 (Tom Watson).

Abbott, Dorothy (1920-12/5/68). Films: "Gunfight at the O.K. Corral" 1957 (Girl); "Sergents 3" 1962 (Mrs. Collingwood).

Abbott, Frank (1879-2/2/57). Films: "The Wild Bull's Lair" 1925 (Yuma).

Abbott, John (1905-). TV: *Gunsmoke*—"Professor Lute Bone" 1-7-56 (Professor Lute Bone), "The Tragedian" 1-23-60 (Edward Vanderman); *Have Gun Will Travel*—"Shot by Request" 10-10-59 (Ainslee); *The Rifleman*—"The Vision" 3-22-60 (Dr. Hennekin); *Bonanza*—"Gabrielle" 12-24-61 (Zachariah); *The Outlaws*—"Buck Breeson Rides Again" 1-25-62 (Murtry); *Destry*—"Deputy for a Day" 4-3-64 (Jake Weatherby); *Laredo*—"Jinx" 12-2-65 (Irwing); *Iron*

Horse—"Death Has Two Faces" 12-23-67 (Burris); *Wild Wild West*—"The Night of the Simian Terror" 2-16-68 (Dr. Von Liebig).

Abbott, Philip (1923-). TV: *Gunsmoke*—"How to Kill a Friend" 11-22-58 (Ben Corder), "Tobe" 10-19-63 (Frank Abels); *Black Saddle*—"Client: Jessup" 4-18-59 (Lon Jessup); *Hotel De Paree*—"Sundance and the Man in the Shadows" 4-15-60 (Gilmer); *Stoney Burke*—"The Contender" 10-1-62 (Royce Hamilton); *Empire*—"The Tiger Inside" 2-12-63 (Sid Keller); *Bonanza*—"The Toy Soldier" 10-20-63 (James Callan); *Rawhide*—"No Dogs or Drovers" 12-18-64 (Ben Dennis).

Abdullah, Joe. TV: *Sergeant Preston of the Yukon*—"Blind Justice" 1-17-57 (Indian Joe); *Tales of Wells Fargo*—"The Gunfighter" 11-17-58 (Sheriff Welch); *Wagon Train*—"The Hunter Malloy Story" 1-21-59 (Radford).

Abdullah, Mohammed. Films: "Africa—Texas Style!" 1967-U.S./Brit. (Witch Doctor).

Abel, Walter (1898-3/26/87). Films: "The Indian Fighter" 1955 (Capt. Trask).

Abelar, Michael. TV: *Wild Wild West*—"The Night of the Torture Chamber" 12-10-65 (Guard); *Iron Horse*—"Grapes of Grass Valley" 10-21-67 (Jed).

Abellira, Remi. TV: *Big Hawaii*—Regular 1977 (Kimo Kalahani).

Abel, Albert. Films: "Banjo Hackett: Roamin' Free" TVM-1976 (Rudolph, the Bettor).

Abineri, John (1928-). TV: *Masterpiece Theatre*—"The Last of the Mohicans" 1972 (Chingachgook).

Abraham, F. Murray (1939-). Films: "Dream West" TVM-1986 (Abraham Lincoln).

Abrams, Jack. Films: "The Dawn of Understanding" 1918 (Parson Davies).

Abril, Dorothy (1897-4/28/77). Films: "The Love Mask" 1916 (Estrella).

Abril, Victoria. Films: "Comin' at Ya" 1981-Ital. (Abilene).

Ace, Rosemary. TV: *Death Valley Days*—"The Luck of the Irish" 4-21-57, "Fifty Years a Mystery" 11-11-57.

Acker, Jean (1893-8/16/78). Films: "The Blue Bandanna" 1919 (Ruth Yancy); "The Round Up" 1920 (Polly Hope); "Braveheart" 1925 (Sky-Arrow).

Acker, Sharon (1935-). Films: "Hec Ramsey" TVM-1972 (Nora Muldoon); "The Hanged Man" TVM-1974 (Carrie Gault). ¶TV: *Wild Wild West*—"The Night of the Sedgewick Curse" 10-18-68 (Lavinia Sedgewick); *Lancer*—"The Gifts" 10-28-69 (Tiffany Mumford); *Alias Smith and Jones*—"The Fifth Victim" 3-25-71 (Rachel Carlson); *Gunsmoke*—"Trafton" 10-25-71 (Terese Farrell).

Ackerman, Bettye (1928-). TV: *Bonanza*—"Second Chance" 9-17-67 (Estelle); *Gunsmoke*—"The Golden Land" 3-5-73 (Zisha).

Ackerman, Walter (1881-12/1/38). Films: "Man of the Forest" 1926 (Deputy); "Aflame in the Sky" 1927 (Desert Rat); "Bride of the Desert" 1929 (Solomon Murphy).

Ackroyd, David. Films: "The Mountain Men" 1980 (Medicine Wolf).

Acord, Art (1890-1/4/31). Films: "Back to the Prairie" 1911; "A Deputy's Honor" 1911; "The White Medicine Man" 1911; "Custer's Last Fight" 1912; "The Indian Massacre" 1912; "The Invaders" 1912; "The Claim Jumper" 1913; "A Western Romance" 1913; "The Awakening" 1915; "Buck Parvin and the Movies" 1915; "Buck's Lady Friend" 1915 (Buck Parvin); "Buckshot John" 1915 (Jordan); "Cattle Queen's Romance"

1915; "Film Tempo" 1915; "A Life at Stake" 1915; "Man-Afraid-of-His-Wardrobe" 1915; "This Is the Life" 1915; "Under Azure Skies" 1915; "When the Fiddler Came to Big Horn" 1915; "The Cactus Cyclone" 1916; "Curlew Corliss" 1916; "A Man's Friend" 1916; "Margy of the Foot-hills" 1916; "A Modern Knight" 1916; "The Return" 1916; "Sandy, Re-former" 1916; "Water Stuff" 1916; "Headin' South" 1918; "The Fighting Line" 1919; "The Kid and the Cow-boy" 1919; "The Wild Westerner" 1919; "Call of the West" 1920; "The Cowboy's Sweetheart" 1920; "The Fiddler of the Little Big Horn" 1920; "The Mayor of Gopher Hole" 1920; "The Moon Riders" 1920-serial; "Out West" 1920; "Ranch and Range" 1920; "Vulture of the West" 1920; "The Call of the Blood" 1921; "The Cowpuncher's Comeback" 1921; "The Fightin' Actor" 1921; "A Ranch Romeo" 1921; "The Show-down" 1921; "The White Horseman" 1921-serial; "Winners of the West" 1921-serial (Arthur Standish); "Come Clean" 1922; "Go Get 'Em Yates" 1922; "The Gypsy Trail" 1922; "In the Days of Buffalo Bill" 1922-serial (Art Taylor); "The Lone Hand" 1922; "Matching Wits" 1922; "A Race for a Father" 1922; "The Ranger's Reward" 1922; "Ridin' Through" 1922; "The Scrapper" 1922; "Tracked Down" 1922; "Unmasked" 1922; "The Ore-gon Trail" 1923-serial; "Fighting for Justice" 1924 (Bullets Bernard); "Looped for Life" 1924 (Buck Dawn); "The Call of Courage" 1925 (Steve Caldwell); "The Circus Cy-clone" 1925 (Jack Manning); "Pals" 1925 (Bruce Taylor); "Three in Exile" 1925 (Art Flanders); "The Wild Girl" 1925 (Billy Woodruff); "Lazy Light-ning" 1926 (Rance Lighton); "The Man from the West" 1926 (Art Louden); "The Ridin' Rascal" 1926 (Larrabie Keller); "Rustlers' Ranch" 1926 (Lee Crush); "The Scrappin' Kid" 1926 (Bill Bradley); "The Set-Up" 1926 (Deputy Art Stratton); "The Silent Guardian" 1926 (Jim Sul-livan); "Sky High Coral" 1926 (Jack McCabe); "The Terror" 1926 (Art Downs); "Western Pluck" 1926 (Ari-zona Allen); "Hard Fists" 1927 (Art Alvord); "Loco Luck" 1927 (Bud Harris); "Set Free" 1927 (Side-Show Saunders); "Spurs and Saddles" 1927 (Jack Marley); "The Western Rover" 1927 (Art Hayes); "His Last Battle" 1928; "The Texas Battler" 1928; "Two Gun O'Brien" 1928; "The Arizona Kid" 1929 (Bill Strong/the Arizona Kid); "Bullets and Justice" 1929; "Fighters of the Saddle" 1929 (Dick Weatherby); "Flashing Spurs" 1929; "An Oklahoma Cowboy" 1929; "Pur-sued" 1929; "The White Outlaw" 1929 (Johnny Douglas, the White Outlaw); "Wyoming Tornado" 1929.

Acosta, Armando. Films: "Deadly Trackers" 1973.

Acosta, Carmelita. TV: *Raw-hide*—"El Hombre Bravo" 5-14-65 (Tia).

Acosta, Enrique (1870-5/22/49). Films: "Don Q, Son of Zorro" 1925 (Ramon); "Whispering Sage" 1927 (Old Pedro); "The Texan" 1930 (Sixto); "The Prescott Kid" 1934 (Servant); "Twilight on the Rio Grande" 1947.

Acosta, Gregorio. Films: "The Scalphunters" 1968 (Scalphunter).

Acosta, Rodolfo (1920-11/7/74). Films: "Pancho Villa Returns" 1950-Mex. (Martin Corona); "Horizons West" 1952 (General Escobar); "City of Badmen" 1953 (Mendoza); "Hondo" 1953 (Silva); "San Antone" 1953 (Chino Figueroa); "Wings of the Hawk" 1953 (Arturo); "Drum Beat" 1954 (Scarface Charlie); "Pas-sion" 1954 (Salvador Sandro); "Ban-dido" 1956 (Sebastian); "The Proud Ones" 1956 (Chico); "Apache War-rior" 1957 (Marteen); "Trooper Hook" 1957 (Chief Nanchez); "From Hell to Texas" 1958 (Bayliss); "Flam-ing Star" 1960 (Buffalo Horn); "Walk Like a Dragon" 1960 (Sheriff Mar-guelez); "The Last Rebel" 1961-Mex. (Three Fingers Jack); "One-Eyed Jacks" 1961 (Rurales Officer); "Posse from Hell" 1961 (Johnny Caddo); "The Second Time Around" 1961 (Rodriguez); "How the West Was Won" 1962 (Desperado); "Savage Sam" 1963 (Bandy Legs); "Rio Con-chos" 1964 (Bloodshirt); "The Re-ward" 1965 (Patron); "The Sons of Katie Elder" 1965 (Blondie Adams); "Return of the Seven" 1966-Span. (Lopez); "Stranger on the Run" TVM-1967; "Young Billy Young" 1969 (Mexican Officer); "Flap" 1970 (Storekeep); "Run, Simon, Run" TVM-1970 (Manuel); "The Mag-nificent Seven Ride" 1972 (Juan De Toro). ¶TV: *Have Gun Will Travel*—"Strange Vendetta" 10-26-57, "Show of Force" 11-9-57 (Pedro Valdez), "Hunt the Man Down" 4-25-59 (John Wildhorse), "Fandango" 3-4-61 (Sanchez); *Sheriff of Cochise*—"Gold Is Where You Find It" 11-29-57; *Zorro*—"The Secret of the Sierra" 3-13-58 (Perico); *Cheyenne*—"Stand-off" 5-6-58 (Lobos), "The Rebellion" 10-12-59 (Luis Cardenas), "Day's Pay" 10-30-61 (Luis Boladas); *Jeffer-son Drum*—"Bandidos" 6-13-58 (Mendoza); *Rawhide*—"Incident of the Power and the Plow" 2-13-59 (Chisera), "Incident at Superstition Prairie" 12-2-60 (Ossolo), "Incident of the Hostages" 4-19-63 (Arapahoe Leader), "Incident at Gila Flats" 1-30-64 (Del Latigo); *Sugarfoot*—"Small Hostage" 5-26-59 (Rafael); *The Rebel*—"Yellow Hair" 10-18-59 (San-tanta); *The Texan*—"The Reluctant Bridegroom" 11-16-59; *Bronco*—"La Rubia" 5-17-60 (Tomas Fierro); *Tales of Wells Fargo*—"Tanoa" 10-28-61 (Red Knife); *Maverick*—"Poker Face" 1-7-62 (Sebastian Bolanos); *The Vir-ginian*—"The Mountain of the Sun" 4-17-63 (Yaqui Leader); *Great Ad-venture*—"The Death of Sitting Bull"/"Massacre at Wounded Knee" 10-4-63 & 10-11-63 (Lieutenant Bullhead); *The Travels of Jaimie McPheeters*—"The Day of the Tin Trumpet" 2-2-64 (Joe Oswego); *Death Valley Days*—"A Book of Spanish Grammar" 4-18-64 (Valdez), "The Other White Man" 11-15-64 (Running Wolf); *Bo-nanza*—"A Knight to Remember" 12-20-64 (Juan);, "All Ye His Saints" 12-19-65 (Lijah), "Yonder Man" 12-8-68 (Matar), "El Jefe" 11-15-70 (Sheriff Vicente Aranda); *The Big Valley*—"The Way to Kill a Killer" 11-24-65 (Rico); *Daniel Boone*—"The Thanks-giving Story" 11-25-65 (Gabriel), "Grizzly" 10-6-66 (Running Fox); *Iron Horse*—"Cougar Man" 10-24-66; *Laredo*—"Scourge of San Rosa" 1-20-67 (Luis); *The High Chaparral*—Reg-ular 1967-71 (Vaquero); *The Out-casts*—"The Stalking Devil" 4-7-69 (Chief Frente).

Acquanetta (1920-). Films: "Callaway Went Thataway" 1951 (Na-tive Girl).

Actman, Jane (1949-). Films: "Last of the Mohicans" TVM-1977 (Alice Morgan).

Acuff, Eddie (1908-12/17/56). Films: "The Devil's Saddle Legion" 1937; "Guns of the Pecos" 1937 (Jeff Carter); "Rhythm of the Saddle" 1938 (Dixie Erwin); "Days of Jesse James" 1939; "Rough Riders' Round-Up" 1939 (Tommy); "Buck Benny Rides Again" 1940 (Truck Driver); "Shooting High" 1940 (Andy Car-son); "Texas Rangers Ride Again" 1940 (Stenographer); "Bad Man of Deadwood" 1941; "Robin Hood of the Pecos" 1941 (Sam Starr); "They Died with Their Boots On" 1941 (Cpl. Smith); "Bells of Capistrano" 1942 (Sign Poster); "San Antonio" 1945 (Gawking Cowboy); "Bad Bas-comb" 1946 (Corporal); "Heldorado" 1946 (Shooting Gallery Attendant); "Bells of San Angelo" 1947 (Bus

Driver); "Bandits of Dark Canyon" 1947 (Farraday); "The Sea of Grass" 1947 (Cattleman); "Swing the Western Way" 1947; "Wyoming" 1947 (Homesteader); "Smoky Mountain Melody" 1948; "Song of Idaho" 1948 (Hash Brown); "The Timber Trail" 1948 (Telegraph Operator).

Acuff, Roy (1903-11/23/92). Films: "Daredevils of the West" 1943-serial (Red Kelly); "Cowboy Canteen" 1944; "Smoky Mountain Melody" 1948 (Roy Acuff); "Home in San Antone" 1949.

Adair, Alic. Films: "Desperado: Avalanche at Devil's Rider" TVM-1988 (Rachel Slaten).

Adair, Phyllis. Films: "Wild Horse Valley" 1940 (Ann Kimball); "Billy the Kid's Fighting Pals" 1941 (Ann); "Land of Hunted Men" 1943; "Riders of the Dawn" 1945 (Penny); "Gunning for Vengeance" 1946.

A'Dair, Robert (1900-8/10/54). Films: "Chief White Eagle" 1912; "Empty Saddles" 1937 (Ezra Biggers).

Adair, Robyn. Films: "A Soldier's Furlough" 1912; "The Uprising" 1912; "Across the Desert" 1915; "On the Border" 1915; "Boots and Saddles" 1916 (George Ferris); "The Yellow Bullet" 1917 (Fred Fowler); "An Adventure on the Mexican Border" 1918.

Adair, Virginia. Films: "Western Firebrands" 1921 (Mildred Stanton).

Adams, Abigail (1922-2/13/55). Films: "Colorado Serenade" 1946 (Lola).

Adams, Arthur. TV: *Cowboy in Africa*—"Fang and Claw" 10-30-67 (Ebawa), "The Quiet Death" 2-19-68 (Inspector Ebawa); *Wild Wild West*—"The Night of the Sedgewick Curse" 10-18-68 (2nd Desk Clerk).

Adams, Ashby. TV: *Adventures of Brisco County, Jr.*—"Deep in the Heart of Dixie" 11-5-93 (U.S. Attorney Breakstone), "AKA Kansas" 12-17-93 (U.S. Attorney Breakstone).

Adams, Betty. *see* Adams, Julia.

Adams, Brooke (1949-). Films: "The Daughters of Joshua Cabe Return" TVM-1975 (Mae). ¶TV: *Black Bart*—Pilot 4-4-75 (Jennifer).

Adams, Caitlin (Nira Barab) (1950-). TV: *Nichols*—"Where Did Everybody Go?" 11-30-71 (Mabel Zimmerman).

Adams, Carol. Films: "Bad Man of Deadwood" 1941 (Linda); "Ridin' on a Rainbow" 1941 (Sally).

Adams, Caroll. Films: "The Hallelujah Trail" 1965 (Simons).

Adams, Casey (Max Showalter) (1917-). Films: "The Return of Jack Slade" 1955 (Billy Wilcox); "Dragoon Wells Massacre" 1957 (Phillip Scott). ¶TV: *Gunsmoke*—"Mavis McCloud" 10-26-57 (Barney Wales); *Stagecoach West*—"The Guardian Angels" 6-6-61 (David Harkness); *Empire*—"The Earth Mover" 11-27-62 (Hobart Muncey).

Adams, Claire (1898-9/25/78). Films: "Speedy Meade" 1919 (Alice Hall); "Riders of the Dawn" 1920 (Lenore Anderson); "The Killer" 1921 (Ruth Emory); "Man of the Forest" 1921 (Helen Raynor); "The Mysterious Rider" 1921 (Columbine); "Do and Dare" 1922 (Juanita Sanchez); "Just Tony" 1922 (Marianne Jordan); "When Romance Rides" 1922 (Lucy Bostil); "Brass Commandments" 1923 (Ellen Bosworth); "Stepping Fast" 1923 (Helen Durant); "The Night Hawk" 1924 (Celia Milton); "Oh, You Tony!" 1924 (Betty Faine).

Adams, Constance (1893-7/17/60). Films: "Where the Trail Divides" 1914 (Mrs. Rowland).

Adams, Doc. Films: "Son of Zorro" 1947-serial.

Adams, Dorothy (1900-3/16/88). Films: "The Shepherd of the Hills" 1941 (Elvy Royal); "Unconquered" 1947 (Mrs. Bront); "The Cariboo Trail" 1950 (Nurse); "Montana" 1950 (Mrs. Maynard); "Fort Osage" 1952 (Mrs. Winfield); "The Broken Star" 1956 (Mrs. Trail); "Johnny Concho" 1956 (Sarah Dark); "The Buckskin Lady" 1957 (Mrs. Adams); "The Big Country" 1958 (Hannassey Woman); "Gunman's Walk" 1958 (Mrs. Stotheby). ¶TV: *Frontier*—"The Devil and Doctor O'Hara" 2-5-56 (Mrs. Noonan); *Gunsmoke*—"Cow Doctor" 9-8-56 (Mrs. Pitcher), "Born to Hang" 11-2-57 (Mrs. Glick); *Wagon Train*—"The Bernal Sierra Story" 3-12-58 (Lorrie); *Trackdown*—"The Unwanted" 5-13-59 (Widow Harper); *The Law of the Plainsman*—"The Hostiles" 10-22-59; *The Rebel*—"The Hunted" 11-6-60 (Mrs. Colburn); *Bonanza*—"The Long Night" 5-6-62.

Adams, Ed. Films: "Desperado" TVM-1987; "Gunsmoke: To the Last Man" TVM-1991 (Billy Wilson); "Gunsmoke: The Long Ride" TVM-1993 (Tebbel).

Adams, Eddy. Films: "Road Agent" 1941 (Lewis).

Adams, Edie (1929-). Films: "Evil Roy Slade" TVM-1972 (Flossie).

Adams, Ernie (1885-11/26/47). Films: "The Pony Express" 1925 (Shorty); "Where the Worst Begins" 1925; "Hair Trigger Baxter" 1926 (Shorty Hills); "The Valley of Bravery" 1926 (Valet); "The Gay Defender" 1927 (Bart Hamby); "Men of Daring" 1927 (Ace); "Nevada" 1927 (Scah Burridge); "The Virginian" 1929 (Saloon Singer); "The Fighting Legion" 1930 (Jack Bowie); "Shadow Ranch" 1930 (Joe; "The Storm" 1930 (Johnny); "Fair Warning" 1931 (Jordan); "The Phantom of the West" 1931-serial; "Beyond the Rockies" 1932 (Blinky); "Broadway to Cheyenne" 1932 (Gangster); "One-Man Law" 1932 (Stubb); "Breed of the Border" 1933 (Joe Shaw); "Fighting with Kit Carson" 1933-serial; "Galloping Romeo" 1933 (Andy); "The Ranger's Code" 1933 (Nat the Bat); "The Law of the Wild" 1934-serial (Raymond); "The Prescott Kid" 1934 (Red Larson); "Annie Oakley" 1935 (Wranglers); "The Last of the Clintons" 1935; "The Miracle Rider" 1935-serial (Stelter); "Ruggles of Red Gap" 1935 (Dishwasher); "Square Shooter" 1935 (Wilson); "Trails End" 1935 (Lefty); "Code of the Range" 1936 (Spooky); "Hopalong Cassidy Returns" 1936 (Benson); "Rio Grande Romance" 1936 (Oscar Lampson); "Rose of the Rancho" 1936 (Bus Boy); "Three on the Trail" 1936 (Idaho); "Arizona Gunfighter" 1937 (Grizzly Barr); "Bar Z Bad Men" 1937 (Pete); "Come on Cowboys" 1937; "Danger Valley" 1937 (Old Timer); "Dodge City Trail" 1937 (Dillon); "Gun Lords of Stirrup Basin" 1937 (Red); "The Gun Ranger" 1937 (Wally Smeed); "Hopalong Rides Again" 1937 (Keno); "Law of the Ranger" 1937 (Zeke); "Lightnin' Crandall" 1937 (Texas); "The Old Wyoming Trail" 1937 (Cattle Rustler); "Range Defenders" 1937 (McTavish); "Ridin' the Lone Trail" 1937 (Peters); "Two-Fisted Sheriff" 1937 (Sheriff Rankin); "Wells Fargo" 1937 (Miner); "California Frontier" 1938 (Barclay); "Colorado Kid" 1938 (Pibben Tucker); "Cowboy and the Lady" 1938 (Rodeo Rider); "Durango Valley Raiders" 1938; "Gun Packer" 1938 (Stage Driver); "Land of Fighting Men" 1938; "Law of the Plains" 1938 (Cook); "Man's Country" 1938 (Caleb Hart); "Mexicali Kid" 1938 (Carl); "The Painted Trail" 1938 (Nosey); "The Purple Vigilantes" 1938 (Blake); "Rollin' Plains" 1938 (Cain Moody); "The Texans" 1938 (Confederate Soldier); "Thunder in the Desert" 1938 (Tramp); "West of Cheyenne" 1938 (Shorty); "Where the Buffalo Roam" 1938 (Bert); "Down the Wyoming Trail" 1939

(Limpy Watkins); "Frontier Pony Express" 1939; "The Lone Ranger Rides Again" 1939-serial (Doc Grover); "The Man from Sundown" 1939 (Shorty Bates); "Overland with Kit Carson" 1939-serial; "The Phantom Stage" 1939 (Stage Guard); "Song of the Buckaroo" 1939; "Sundown on the Prairie" 1939 (Blackie); "Texas Stampede" 1939; "Trigger Pals" 1939 (Pete); "Union Pacific" 1939 (Gen. Sheridan); "The Dark Command" 1940 (Wiry Man); "The Fargo Kid" 1940 (Bush Cleveland); "The Man from Tumbleweeds" 1940 (Shifty Sheldon); "Out West with the Peppers" 1940 (Telegraph Operator); "Riders from Nowhere" 1940 (Manny); "West of Carson City" 1940 (Snicker Joe); "Along the Rio Grande" 1941; "Bad Man of Deadwood" 1941; "Bury Me Not on the Lone Prairie" 1941; "The Pinto Kid" 1941 (Ed Slade); "Riders of Death Valley" 1941-serial (Cactus Pete); "Road Agent" 1941 (Jake); "Roaring Frontiers" 1941; "Robbers of the Range" 1941 (Greeley); "Westward Ho-Hum" 1941-short; "Bandit Ranger" 1942; "Cactus Makes Perfect" 1942-short (Stumpy); "The Lone Prairie" 1942; "Riding the Wind" 1942 (Jones); "Stagecoach Buckaroo" 1942 (Blinky); "Valley of Vanishing Men" 1942-serial; "West of Tombstone" 1942; "Beyond the Last Frontier" 1943 (Kincaid); "Hail to the Rangers" 1943 (Latham); "Sagebrush Law" 1943; "Ghost Guns" 1944; "Girl Rush" 1944 (Dave); "Marshal of Gunsmoke" 1944 (Nuggett); "Outlaws of Santa Fe" 1944; "Raiders of Ghost City" 1944-serial; "Raiders of the Border" 1944 (Whiskey); "Along Came Jones" 1945 (Townsman); "Frisco Sal" 1945 (McKinney); "The Fighting Frontiersman" 1946; "King of the Forest Rangers" 1946-serial (Hiram Bailey); "The Lawless Breed" 1946; "Law Comes to Gunsight" 1947; "Robin Hood of Monterey" 1947; "Son of Zorro" 1947-serial (Judge Hyde); "Trail Street" 1947 (Eben Bowen); "Trailing Danger" 1947; "Yankee Fakir" 1947 (Charlie); "Return of the Badmen" 1948 (Leslie, the Townsman).

Adams, Fay. Films: "A Daughter of the Sioux" 1925 (Trooper Kennedy); "Tonio, Son of the Sierras" 1925 (Captain Stannard).

Adams, Gloria. Films: "Natchez Trace" 1960 (Liza).

Adams, Henry. Films: "The Sea of Grass" 1947 (Gambler).

Adams, Hugh Allen. Films:

"Whispering Smith" 1916 (Clerk in Superintendent's Office); "The Painted Desert" 1931.

Adams, Jane (Poni Adams) (1926-). Films: "Code of the Lawless" 1945 (Julie Randall); "Salome, Where She Danced" 1945 (Salome Girl); "Trail to Vengeance" 1945 (Dorothy); "Gunman's Code" 1946; "The Lawless Breed" 1946; "Rustler's Roundup" 1946 (Jo Fremont); "Gun Law Justice" 1949; "Western Renegades" 1949 (Judy Gordon); "The Girl from San Lorenzo" 1950 (Nora); "Law of the Panhandle" 1950 (Margie Kendal); "Outlaw Gold" 1950 (Kathy). ¶TV: *The Cisco Kid*—"Boomerang" 1-20-51; *Wild Bill Hickok*—"Silver Stage Holdup" 10-16-51.

Adams, Jeb Stuart. Films: "Once Upon a Texas Train" TVM-1988 (Billy).

Adams, Jessie. Films: "Montana" 1950 (Rancher's Wife).

Adams, Jimmy (1890-12/19/33). Films: "The Tabasco Kid" 1932-short.

Adams, Julia (Betty Adams, Julie Adams) (1926-). Films: "The Dalton Gang" 1949 (Polly); "Crooked River" 1950 (Ann); "Fast on the Draw" 1950 (Ann); "Hostile Country" 1950 (Ann Greene); "Marshal of Heldorado" 1950 (Ann); "West of the Brazos" 1950 (Ann); "Bend of the River" 1952 (Laura Baile); "Horizons West" 1952 (Lorna Hardin); "The Lawless Breed" 1952 (Rosie); "The Treasure of Lost Canyon" 1952 (Myra Wade); "The Man from the Alamo" 1953 (Beth Anders); "The Stand at Apache River" 1953 (Valerie Kendrick); "Wings of the Hawk" 1953 (Raquel); "Slim Carter" 1957 (Clover Doyle); "The Gunfight at Dodge City" 1959 (Pauline); "Tickle Me" 1965 (Vera Radford); "The Trackers" TVM-1971 (Dora Paxton). TV: *Zane Grey Theater*—"Man of Fear" 3-14-58 (Julie Brand), "The Tall Shadow" 11-20-58 (Nora Pepson); *Yancy Derringer*—"Return to New Orleans" 10-2-58 (Amanda Eaton); *Maverick*—"The Brasada Spur" 2-22-59 (Belle Morgan), "The White Widow" 1-24-60 (Wilma White); *The Alaskans*—"Doc Booker" 12-6-59 (Clara); *Cheyenne*—"Gold, Glory and Custer—Prelude" 1-4-60 (Irene Travers), "Gold, Glory and Custer—Requiem" 1-11-60 (Irene Travers); *The Rifleman*—"Nora" 5-24-60 (Nora Sanford); *Wrangler*—"The Affair with Browning's Woman" 8-25-60 (Eve Browning); *Tate*—"The Mary Hardin Story" 9-21-60 (Mrs. Hardin); *Bonanza*—"The Courtship"

1-7-61 (Helen Layton); *The Outlaws*—"Return to New March" 6-22-61 (Juill Ramsur); *The Virginian*—"No Drums, No Trumpets" 4-6-66 (Marian); *The Big Valley*—"Target" 10-31-66 (Edna Wesley), "The Emperor of Rice" 2-12-68 (Janet Masters).

Adams, Kathryn (1894-2/17/59). Films: "The Shooting of Dan McGrew" 1915 (Lou Maxwell); "Riders of the Purple Sage" 1918 (Masked Rider-Millie); "True Blue" 1918 (Ruth Merritt); "Molly Cures a Cowboy" 1940-short; "Arizona Cyclone" 1941 (Elsie); "Bury Me Not on the Lone Prairie" 1941; "Rawhide Rangers" 1941 (Joan).

Adams, Kathy. TV: *Gunsmoke*—"Obie Tater" 10-15-55 (Ella).

Adams, Ken. Films: "Flashing Guns" 1947 (Dishpan); "Prairie Express" 1947 (Pete).

Adams, Lillian. Films: "The Wild and the Innocent" 1959 (Kirk). ¶TV: *The Rebel*—"The Captive of Tremblor" 4-10-60 (Squaw); *The Big Valley*—"A Noose Is Waiting" 11-13-67.

Adams, Madeleine. TV: *Dirty Sally*—"Wimmen's Rights" 3-15-74 (Ida).

Adams, Mae. Films: "The Hidden Law" 1916 (Mildred Holmes).

Adams, Mary (1908-1/30/73). Films: "Bugles in the Afternoon" 1952 (Woman); "Rebel in Town" 1956 (Grandmaw Anstadt). ¶TV: *Gunsmoke*—"Tape Day for Kitty" 3-24-56 (Nettie); *The Adventures of Rin Tin Tin*—"Homer the Great" 4-20-56 (Mrs. Mack); *Sergeant Preston of the Yukon*—"The Rookie" 9-20-56 (Alice Burns).

Adams, Mildred. Films: "Their Compact" 1917 (Verda Forrest).

Adams, Nick (1931-2/7/68). Films: "Strange Lady in Town" 1955 (Billy the Kid); "The Last Wagon" 1956 (Ridge); "Fury at Showdown" 1957 (Tracy Mitchell). ¶TV: *Zane Grey Theater*—"Sundown at Bitter Creek" 2-14-58 (Lynn Parsons), "A Thread of Respect" 2-12-59 (George Pelleti); *Wagon Train*—"The Marie Dupree Story" 3-19-58 (Tonio), "The Traitor" 12-13-61 (Sam Upton); *Trackdown*—"The Winter Boys" 4-11-58 (Luke Crane), "The Gang" 2-25-59 (Will Hastings), "The Trick" 4-15-59 (Deal Jackford); *Wanted—Dead or Alive*—"The Martin Poster" 9-6-58 (Andy Martin); *Cimarron City*—"Twelve Guns" 11-1-58 (John Hartman, Jr.); *Yancy Derringer*—"The Night the Russians Landed" 1-29-59

(Duke Alexis); *Tales of Wells Fargo*—"The Tired Gun" 3-30-59 (Ira Watkins); *The Rebel*—Regular 1959-61 (Johnny Yuma); *Rawhide*—"Corporal Dasovik" 12-4-64 (Corporal Dasovik); *Wild Wild West*—"The Night of the Two-Legged Buffalo" 3-11-66 (Prince), "The Night of the Vipers" 1-12-68 (Sheriff Dave Cord); *The Monroes*—"Gun Bound" 1-25-67 (Dave); *Hondo*—"Hondo and the Apache Kid" 10-13-67 (the Apache Kid), "Hondo and the Apache Trail" 12-22-67 (the Apache Kid).

Adams, Paige. TV: *Have Gun Will Travel*—"The Long Weekend" 4-8-61 (Peggy Collins).

Adams, Peggy. Films: "Salt of the Earth" 1917 (Marjorie Kincaid).

Adams, Peter (1917-1/8/87). Films: "Bullwhip" 1958 (Parnell). ¶TV: *Wyatt Earp*—"Bat Masterson Again" 4-17-56; *Zorro*—"The New Commandante" 3-20-58 (Magistrado Captain Arturo Pollidano), "The Fox and the Coyote" 3-26-58 (Arturo Pollidano), "Adios, Senor Magistrado" 4-3-58 (Arturo Pollidano); *Have Gun Will Travel*—"Treasure Trail" 1-24-59; *Rawhide*—"Incident at Red River Station" 1-15-60 (Lieutenant Shaw), "Incident of the Running Man" 5-5-61, "The House of the Hunter" 4-20-62 (Burt Wells); *Man from Blackhawk*—"Remember Me Not" 9-9-60 (Harrison Elwood); *Gunslinger*—"Johnny Sergeant" 5-4-61 (Beau Dunning); *The Virginian*—"The Fortunes of J. Jimerson Jones" 1-15-64 (Duncan St. John); *Custer*—"The Raiders" 12-27-67 (Major Benteen).

Adams, Phil. Films: "Buck and the Preacher" 1972 (Frank).

Adams, Poni. see Adams, Jane.

Adams, Ray. Films: "Adventures of Red Ryder" 1940-serial (Hall).

Adams, Reetsy. Films: "The Kid Ranger" 1936 (Mary as a Child).

Adams, Richard. Films: "It Happened Out West" 1937; "Advance to the Rear" 1964 (Courier). ¶TV: *The Texan*—"The Marshal of Yellow Jacket" 3-2-59 (Dell), "No Love Wasted" 3-9-59, "The Telegraph Story" 10-26-59 (Conners), "End of Track" 12-21-59.

Adams, Ritchie. Films: "The Hunting Party" 1971-Brit./Ital./Span. (Owney Clark).

Adams, Sam (1871-3/24/58). Films: "The Golden West" 1932 (Mike).

Adams, Stanley (1915-4/27/77). Films: "Black Patch" 1957 (Drummer); "Trooper Hook" 1957 (Salesman); "Valerie" 1957 (Dr. Jackson); "Saddle the Wind" 1958; "North to Alaska" 1960 (Breezy); "Nevada Smith" 1966 (Storekeeper); "Machismo—40 Graves for 40 Guns" 1970 (Granger); "The Great Gundown" 1977 (Buck). ¶TV: *Wild Bill Hickok*—"Town Without Law" 2-23-53; *My Friend Flicka*—"The Golden Promise" 1-6-56; *Gunsmoke*—"Indian White" 10-27-56 (Ross), "Spring Team" 12-15-56 (Bartender), "He Who Steals" 5-29-65 (Charlie Rath); *Tales of the Texas Rangers*—"Cattle Drive" 10-30-58 (Sally); *Maverick*—"Betrayal" 3-22-59 (Link); *Rawhide*—"Incident of the Druid's Curse" 1-8-60; *Riverboat*—"That Taylor Affair" 9-26-60 (Captain Morgan); *Tales of Wells Fargo*—"Rifles for Red Hand" 5-15-61 (Sam Tustin); *The Deputy*—"The Legend of Dixie" 5-20-61 (Dixie Miller); *The Rifleman*—"Outlaw Shoes" 4-30-62 (Dr. Carter); *Have Gun Will Travel*—"Cream of the Jest" 5-5-62 (Caleb Musgrove); *Wide Country*—"Who Killed Edde Gannon?" 10-11-62 (George Root); *Wagon Train*—"The Emmett Lawton Story" 3-6-63 (Monte West), "The Sam Pulaski Story" 11-4-63 (Jersey), "The Trace McCloud Story" 3-2-64 (Merlin the Great), "The Stark Bluff Story" 4-6-64 (Judge Pike), "The Jarbo Pierce Story" 5-2-65 (Samuel); *Bonanza*—"The Pure Truth" 3-8-64 (Sheriff Tate); *The Legend of Jesse James*—"The Widow Fay" 12-20-65 (Blake); *Laredo*—"Quarter Past Eleven" 3-24-66 (Bartender); *Pistols 'n' Petticoats*—"No Sale" 9-24-66 (Jed Timmons), 10-8-66 (Jed Timmons); *Death Valley Days*—"The Lady and the Sourdough" 10-8-66 (Tom Despo); *The Monroes*—"Wild Bull" 2-15-67; *Lancer*—"The Experiment" 2-17-70.

Adams, Stella (1883-9/17/61). Films: "The Whirlwind" 1933 (Ma Reynolds); "Tonto Kid" 1935 (Landlady).

Adams, Ted (1890-9/24/73). Films: "Cavalier of the West" 1931 (Lee Burgess); "Cyclone Kid" 1931 (Joe Clark); "God's Country and the Man" 1931 (Romero); "Rider of the Plains" 1931 (Parson); "The Ridin' Fool" 1931 (Boston Harry); "Battling Buckaroo" 1932 (Pedro); "Beyond the Rockies" 1932 (Emory); "Ghost Valley" 1932 (Gordon); "Human Targets" 1932 (Deputy); "Wyoming Whirlwind" 1932; "Man of Action" 1933 (Deputy Ted Adams); "War on the Range" 1933; "Gunfire" 1935 (Alex McGregor); "His Fighting Blood" 1935; "Hopalong Cassidy" 1935 (Hall); "Law of the 45's" 1935 (Rentel); "Lawless Borders" 1935; "Border Caballero" 1936 (Buff Brayden); "The Crooked Trail" 1936 (Estaban Solano); "Custer's Last Stand" 1936-serial (Barney/Buffalo Bill); "Song of the Gringo" 1936 (Evans); "Three on the Trail" 1936 (Jim Trask); "Toll of the Desert" 1936 (Tegue); "Trail Dust" 1936 (Joe Wilson); "Undercover Man" 1936 (Ace Pringle); "Arizona Gunfighter" 1937 (Wolf Whitson); "Boss of Lonely Valley" 1937 (Slim); "Desert Phantom" 1937 (Salizar); "The Gambling Terror" 1937 (Sheriff); "Guns in the Dark" 1937 (Manuel Menendez/Rusty Walker); "Heart of the West" 1937 (Saxon); "Lawless Land" 1937 (Clay Wheeler); "Rustler's Valley" 1937 (Taggart); "Smoke Tree Range" 1937 (Gil Hawkins); "Sudden Bill Dorn" 1937 (Montana); "Colorado Kid" 1938 (Sheriff Bill Hannon); "Desert Patrol" 1938 (Apache Joe); "Durango Valley Raiders" 1938 (Lobo); "Gunsmoke Trail" 1938; "Lightning Carson Rides Again" 1938; "The Lone Ranger" 1938-serial (Drake); "Pals of the Saddle" 1938 (Henry C. Gordon); "Six-Gun Trail" 1938; "Code of the Cactus" 1939 (Thurston); "Crashing Thru" 1939 (Eskimo Pete); "El Diablo Rides" 1939; "Fighting Mad" 1939 (Leon); "Fighting Renegade" 1939 (Link Benson); "Henry Goes Arizona" 1939 (Buzz Sawyer); "In Old Montana" 1939; "Mesquite Buckaroo" 1939 (Luke Williams); "Outlaw's Paradise" 1939 (Slim Marsh); "The Pal from Texas" 1939 (Ace Brady); "Riders of the Sage" 1939 (Poe Powers); "Six-Gun Rhythm" 1939 (Sheriff); "Smoky Trails" 1939 (Chief); "Straight Shooter" 1939 (Brainard); "Texas Wildcats" 1939 (Reno); "Three Texas Steers" 1939 (Steve); "Trigger Fingers" 1939 (Jeff); "Trigger Pals" 1939 (Harvey Kent); "Billy the Kid Outlawed" 1940 (Sam Daly); "Billy the Kid's Gun Justice" 1940 (Sheriff); "Frontier Crusader" 1940 (Jack Trask); "Gaucho Serenade" 1940 (E.J. Jenkins); "Gun Code" 1940 (Sheriff Kramer); "Law and Order" 1940 (Walt Daggett); "Phantom Rancher" 1940 (Collins); "Pinto Canyon" 1940 (D.A. Farley); "Pioneer Days" 1940 (Slater); "Riders from Nowhere" 1940; "Riders on Black Mountain" 1940 (Pete); "Riders of Pasco Basin" 1940 (Magee); "Sky Bandits" 1940; "Trail of the Vigilantes" 1940; "Wild Horse Range" 1940; "Wild Horse Valley" 1940 (Baker); "Wyoming" 1940 (Brother); "Billy the Kid" 1941 (Buzz Cobb); "Billy the Kid's Range War" 1941

(Sheriff); "The Lone Rider Ambushed" 1941 (Deputy); "The Lone Rider in Frontier Fury" 1941; "Riders of Death Valley" 1941-serial (Hank); "The Royal Mounted Patrol" 1941 (Pete); "Thunder Over the Prairie" 1941 (Dave Wheeler); "Along the Sundown Trail" 1942; "Billy the Kid Trapped" 1942 (Sheriff Masters); "Billy the Kid's Smoking Guns" 1942; "Fighting Bill Fargo" 1942 (Vic Savage); "King of the Stallions" 1942; "Law and Order" 1942 (Sheriff); "The Mysterious Rider" 1942; "Outlaws of Boulder Pass" 1942; "Overland Stagecoach" 1942; "Rolling Down the Great Divide" 1942 (Martin); "The Sundown Kid" 1942 (Jim Dawson); "Cattle Stampede" 1943; "Daredevils of the West" 1943-serial (Silas Higby); "Hail to the Rangers" 1943 (Schuyler); "The Kid Rides Again" 1943 (Sheriff); "Saddle Leather Law" 1944; "Swing, Cowboy, Swing" 1944; "Bells of Rosarita" 1945; "Gentleman from Texas" 1946; "Red River Renegades" 1946; "Shadows on the Range" 1946; "Silver Range" 1946; "Stagecoach to Denver" 1946 (Sheriff); "Trigger Fingers" 1946; "Tumbleweed Trail" 1946 (Alton Small); "Under Arizona Skies" 1946; "Buffalo Bill Rides Again" 1947 (Sam); "Code of the Saddle" 1947; "Flashing Guns" 1947 (Ripley); "Gun Talk" 1947 (Tim); "The Last Round-Up" 1947; "Law Comes to Gunsight" 1947; "Prairie Express" 1947 (Lem); "Raiders of the South" 1947; "Range Beyond the Blue" 1947 (Henry Rodgers); "Son of Zorro" 1947-serial (Cody); "Song of the Wasteland" 1947; "Under Colorado Skies" 1947 (Doc Thornhill); "Valley of Fear" 1947; "Vigilantes of Boomtown" 1947 (Sheriff); "Back Trail" 1948 (Frazer); "Buckaroo from Powder River" 1948 (Les Driscoll); "Check Your Guns" 1948 (Laswell); "Crossed Trails" 1948 (Laswell); "Dangers of the Canadian Mounted" 1948-serial (Meggs); "Frontier Agent" 1948; "Gunning for Justice" 1948; "Overland Trails" 1948; "Quick on the Trigger" 1948 (Martin Oaks); "The Sheriff of Medicine Bow" 1948; "Across the Rio Grande" 1949 (Sloan); "Deputy Marshal" 1949 (Telegrapher); "Gun Runner" 1949 (Danny); "Haunted Trails" 1949; "Navajo Trail Raiders" 1949 (Sheriff Robbins); "Outlaw Country" 1949 (Frank Evans); "Shadows of the West" 1949 (Davis); "Stallion Canyon" 1949 (Wolf); "Arizona Territory" 1950; "Hills of Oklahoma" 1950 (Sam); "I Killed Geronimo" 1950 (Walt Anderson); "Law of the Panhandle" 1950

(Fred Kendal); "Abilene Trail" 1951 (Sheriff); "Night Riders of Montana" 1951 (Connors); "The Vanishing Outpost" 1951 (Detective); "Kansas Territory" 1952 (Hank). ¶TV: The Cisco Kid—"Newspaper Crusade" 5-5-51, "Freight Line Feud" 6-2-51, "Performance Bond" 6-30-51.

Adams, Willie. Films: "Natchez Trace" 1960 (Buck).

Adamson, James (1896-1/29/56). Films: "The Lone Cowboy" 1934 (Railroad Porter).

Adderley, Julian "Cannonball" (1928-8/8/75). TV: Kung Fu—"Battle Hymn" 2-8-75 (Trim Delavalle).

Addobbati, Giuseppe. see MacDouglas, John.

Addy, Wesley (1913-). Films: "Four for Texas" 1964 (Trowbridge).

Ades, Daniel (1938-5/30/92). Films: "The Missouri Breaks" 1976 (John Quinn). ¶TV: Wild Wild West—"The Night of the Ready-Made Corpse" 11-25-66 (Pellargo #1); Gunsmoke—"The Newcomers" 12-3-66 (Vasquez); The High Chaparral—"Tiger by the Tail" 2-25-68 (Rafael).

Adez, Sally. Films: "Chato's Land" 1972 (Moira Logan).

Adiarte, Patrick. TV: Bonanza—"Warbonnet" 12-26-71 (Swift Eagle).

Adler, Bud. Films: "Sam Whiskey" 1969 (Pete).

Adler, Charles. Films: "Looped for Life" 1924 (Sheriff); "Mark of the Spur" 1932 (Sleepy).

Adler, Fay. Films: "My Little Chickadee" 1940 (Mrs. Pygmy Allen).

Adler, Jay (1896-9/23/78). Films: "Man with the Gun" 1955 (Cal); "Saddle the Wind" 1958 (Hank); "Seven Guns to Mesa" 1958 (Ben Avery); "Curse of the Undead" 1959 (Bartender). ¶TV: Sheriff of Cochise—"Fire on Chiricahua Mountains" 11-2-56 (Prisoner #1); Wanted—Dead or Alive—"Bounty on Josh" 1-25-61 (Ferris).

Adler, Luther (1903-12/8/84). Films: "The Tall Texan" 1953 (John Tinnen). ¶TV: Hec Ramsey—"The Detroit Connection" 12-30-73 (Victor Bordon).

Adler, Robert. Films: "My Darling Clementine" 1946 (Stagecoach Driver); "Fury at Furnace Creek" 1948 (Leverett Henchman); "Green Grass of Wyoming" 1948 (Joe); "Yellow Sky" 1948 (Jed); "Broken Arrow" 1950 (Lonergan); "Ticket to Tomahawk" 1950 (Bat); "Two Flags West" 1950 (Hank); "Rawhide" 1951 (Billy Dent); "The Outcasts of Poker Flat"

1952 (Vigilante); "Return of the Texan" 1952 (Foreman); "City of Badmen" 1953 (Barney); "Powder River" 1953 (Pike Kendrick); "The Silver Whip" 1953 (Man in Tom's Posse); "Broken Lance" 1954 (O'Reilly); "The Tall Men" 1955 (Wrangler); "Fury at Showdown" 1957 (Alabam); "The True Story of Jesse James" 1957 (Sheriff Trump); "Valerie" 1957 (Lundy); "The Bravados" 1958 (Tony Mirable); "Three Thousand Hills" 1959 (Godwin); "Warlock" 1959 (Foss); "Bandolero!" 1968 (Ross Harper). ¶TV: My Friend Flicka—Regular 1955-56 (Ben); Bonanza—"The Mission" 9-17-60 (O'Hara), "Cut-Throat Junction" 3-18-61, "The Lady from Baltimore" 1-14-62, "The Miracle Worker" 5-20-62, "She Walks in Beauty" 9-22-63, "Enter Thomas Bowers" 4-26-64; The Tall Man—"A Bounty for Billy" 10-15-60 (Driver); Rawhide—"Incident of the Running Man" 5-5-61; Have Gun Will Travel—"Bandit" 5-12-62 (Sheriff); Laramie—"The Long Road Back" 10-23-62; Gunsmoke—"Abe Blocker" 11-24-62 (Emmett); Temple Houston—"The Town That Trespassed" 3-26-64 (Townsman); The Big Valley—"Down Shadow Street" 1-23-67 (Stage Driver); Daniel Boone—"The Bait" 11-7-68 (Driver), "The Return of Sidewinder" 12-12-68 (Equerry), "The Landlords" 3-5-70.

Adolfi, John (1888-5/11/33). Films: "The Kentuckian" 1908.

Adoree, Andre. Films: "Escape from Red Rock" 1958 (Guard).

Adoree, Renee (1898-10/5/33). Films: "West of Chicago" 1922 (Della Moore); "The Eternal Struggle" 1923 (Andree Grange); "The Flaming Forest" 1926 (Jeanne-Marie); "Tide of Empire" 1929 (Josephina).

Adorf, Mario (1930-). Films: "Taste of Violence" 1961-Fr.; "Massacre at Marble City" 1964-Ger./Ital./Fr. (Matt Ellis); "Apache Gold" 1965-Ger. (Santer); "Major Dundee" 1965 (Sgt. Gomez); "Sunscorched" 1966-Span./Ger. (Abel Dragna); "A Sky Full of Stars for a Roof" 1968-Ital. (Harry); "Drop Them Or I'll Shoot" 1969-Fr./Ger./Ital.; "Last Ride to Santa Cruz" 1969-Ger./Fr.; "Deadlock" 1970-Ital./Ger./Isr. (Charles Dumm).

Adrian, Iris (1913-9/17/94). Films: "Go West" 1940 (Mary Lou); "Lady from Cheyenne" 1941 (Chorus Girl); "Calaboose" 1943; "Alaska" 1944; "The Singing Sheriff" 1944 (Lefty); "The Wistful Widow of Wagon Gap" 1947 (Dance Hall

Hostell); "The Paleface" 1948 (Pepper); "Tough Assignment" 1949 (Gloria); "Trail of the Yukon" 1949 (Paula); "The Big Trees" 1952; "Carson City" 1952; "Scandalous John" 1971 (Mavis); "The Apple Dumpling Gang" 1975 (Poker Polly). ¶TV: *Wild Bill Hickok*—"Counterfeit Ghost" 8-11-53.

Adrian, Jane. Films: "Gunfire" 1950 (Flo); "Snow Dog" 1950 (Red Father). ¶TV: *The Marshal of Gunsight Pass*—Pilot 1950 (Ruth).

Adrian, Lillian. Films: "The Dangerous Coward" 1924 (Conchita); "Way of a Man" 1924-serial.

Agar, John (1921-). Films: "Fort Apache" 1948 (Lt. Michael "Mickey" O'Rourke); "She Wore a Yellow Ribbon" 1949 (Lt. Flint Cohill); "Along the Great Divide" 1951 (Billy Shear); "Woman of the North Country" 1952 (David Powell); "The Lonesome Trail" 1955; "Star in the Dust" 1956 (Sheriff Bill Jordan); "Flesh and the Spur" 1957 (Luke/Matthew Random); "Ride a Violent Mile" 1957 (Jeff); "Frontier Gun" 1958 (Jim Crayle); "Cavalry Command" 1963-U.S./Phil. (Sgt. Norcutt); "Law of the Lawless" 1964 (Pete Stone); "Stage to Thunder Rock" 1964 (Dan Carrouthers); "Young Fury" 1965 (Dawson); "Johnny Reno" 1966 (Ed Tomkins); "Waco" 1966 (George Gates); "The Undefeated" 1969 (Christian); "Chisum" 1970 (Patton); "Big Jake" 1971 (Bert Ryan). ¶TV: *Rawhide*—"Incident at the Buffalo Smokehouse" 10-30-59 (Lou Grant), "Incident of the Slavemaster" 11-11-60 (Mike Anderson); *Bat Masterson*—"Farmer with a Badge" 5-18-61 (Sam Phelps); *Lawman*—"The Witness" 6-24-62 (Jim Martin); *Death Valley Days*—"Pioneer Doctor" 1-23-63 (Dr. Edwards); *The Virginian*—"Walk in Another's Footsteps" 3-11-64 (Raine), "The Mustangers" 12-4-68 (Joe Williams); *Branded*—"$10,000 for Durango" 11-28-65 (Sheriff); *Hondo*—"Hondo and the Judas" 11-3-67 (Frank James).

Agee, James (1910-5/16/55). Films: "Face to Face" 1952 ("The Bride Comes to Yellow Sky" segment—the Prisoner).

Agnew, Robert (1899-11/8/83). Films: "The Valley of Doubt" 1920 (Tom); "Three Who Paid" 1923 (Hal Sinclair).

Agostini, Franco. Films: "Raise Your Hands, Dead Man ... You're Under Arrest" 1971-Ital./Span. (Frank Bamba).

Agren, Janet (1950-). Films:

"Sometimes Life Is Hard, Right Providence?" 1972-Ital./Fr./Ger.

Aguglia, Mimi (1885-7/31/70). Films: "The Outlaw" 1943 (Guadalupe); "Unconquered" 1947.

Aguilar, George. Films: "Ulzana's Raid" 1972; "The Mystic Warrior" TVM-1984 (Kungi Yuha Leader). ¶TV: *The Life and Times of Grizzly Adams*—"The Unholy Beast" 4-20-77 (Grey Wind).

Aguilar, Pedro. Films: "The Scalphunters" 1968 (Kowa).

Aguilar, Tony (1924-). Films: "The Undefeated" 1969 (Gen. Rojas).

Agutter, Jenny (1952-). Films: "China 9, Liberty 37" 1978-Ital./Span./U.S. (Catherine).

Aherne, Brian (1903-2/10/86). Films: "A Bullet Is Waiting" 1954 (David Canham). ¶TV: *Wagon Train*—"The Bruce Saybrook Story" 11-22-61 (Lord Bruce Saybrook); *Rawhide*—"The Gentleman's Gentleman" 12-15-61 (Woolsey).

Aherne, Pat (1901-9/30/70). TV: *Sergeant Preston of the Yukon*—"The Skull in the Stone" 11-7-57 (Anthony Colville).

Ahn, Philip (1905-2/28/78). Films: "Roaring Timber" 1937 (Ah Sing); "Tex Rides with the Boy Scouts" 1937 (Sing Fong); "One-Eyed Jacks" 1961 (Uncle); "Kung Fu" TVM-1972 (Master Kan). ¶TV: *Wild Bill Hickok*—"Jingles Wins a Friend" 4-28-53; *The Californians*—"Death by Proxy" 3-18-58 (Choo); *Have Gun Will Travel*—"Hey Boy's Revenge" 4-12-58, "The Hatchet Man" 3-5-60; *Jefferson Drum*—"The Cheater" 5-23-58 (Charles Wong); *Lawman*—"The Intruders" 12-7-58 (Wong); *The Adventures of Rin Tin Tin*—"The Ming Vase" 3-13-59 (Hop Sing); *Bonanza*—"The Fear Merchants" 1-30-60, "Day of the Dragon" 12-3-61 (Kam Lee), "Pink Cloud Comes from Old Cathay" 4-12-64 (Wang Sai); *The Rebel*—"Blind Marriage" 4-17-60 (Quong Lee); *Wanted—Dead or Alive*—"Payoff at Pinto" 5-21-60 (Tom Wing); *Stoney Burke*—"The Weapons Man" 4-8-63 (the Zen Master); *Wild Wild West*—"The Night the Dragon Screamed" 1-14-66 (Quong Chu); *Laredo*—"The Bitter Yen of General Ti" 2-3-67 (Captain Wong Lee); *Kung Fu*—Regular 1972-75 (Master Kan).

Ahren, George. Films: "Overalls" 1916 (Flap-Jack).

Ah-Tee-Ha, Princess. Films: "Circle of Death" 1935 (White Fawn).

Aidman, Charles (1925-11/7/93). Films: "Hour of the Gun" 1967 (Horace Sullivan); "Tell Them Willie Boy Is Here" 1969 (Benby); "Dirty Little Billy" 1972 (Ben Antrim); "The Barbary Coast" TVM-1975 (Lieutenant Tully). ¶TV: *Have Gun Will Travel*—"Twenty-Four Hours to North Fork" 5-17-58 (Tom Barton), "Return to Fort Benjamin" 1-30-60 (Lieutenant Graham), "The Search" 6-18-60 (Harper); *The Californians*—"Mutineers from Hell" 9-30-58 (Coffin), "Crimps' Meat" 1-27-59 (Joe Ryan); *Gunsmoke*—"Stage Holdup" 10-25-58 (Verd), "Unwanted Deputy" 3-5-60 (Vince Walsh), "About Chester" 2-25-61 (Dack), "The Money Store" 12-30-68 (Ray Jarvis), "The Intruders" 3-3-69 (Riley Sharp); *Wanted—Dead or Alive*—"Competition" 1-31-59 (Meadows), "Estrelita" 10-3-59 (Jake Pringle); *Trackdown*—"The Samaritan" 2-18-59 (Starbuck); *Colt .45*—"The Confession" 4-26-59 (Arthur Sibley); *Black Saddle*—"Client: Neal Adams" 5-9-59 (Luke Morley), "Murdock" 11-13-59 (Murdock); *Zane Grey Theater*—"Confession" 10-15-59 (Watson Cooke); *Fury*—"The Big Leaguers" 10-17-59; *Wichita Town*—"Ruby Dawes" 1-6-60 (Wes Barker); *Riverboat*—"Fight at New Canal" 2-22-60 (Frank Paxton); *Rawhide*—"Incident at Sulphur Creek" 3-11-60 (Waltzer), "The Blue Sky" 12-8-61 (Bert Pearson); *Wagon Train*—"The Amos Gibbon Story" 4-20-60 (Amos Gibbon), "The River Crossing" 12-14-60 (Colonel Buckner), "The Janet Hale Story" 5-31-61 (Whit Martin); *Johnny Ringo*—"The Stranger" 5-19-60 (Jeffrey Blake); *The Outlaws*—"Ballad for a Badman" 10-6-60 (Drew Craven); *Bonanza*—"The Rival" 4-15-61 (Jim Applegate); *The Rebel*—"Ben White" 5-28-61 (Ben White), "The Executioner" 6-18-61 (Ferguson); *The Tall Man*—"Shadow of the Past" 10-7-61 (Ben Wiley); *Laramie*—"The Jailbreakers" 12-19-61 (Gil Martin); *Wide Country*—"Who Killed Edde Gannon?" 10-11-62 (John Nieman); *The Virginian*—"The Devil's Children" 12-5-62 (Sam Hicks), "No War for the Warrior" 2-18-70 (William T. Webb); *A Man Called Shenandoah*—"The Siege" 12-13-65 (Andrew Stiles); *The Road West*—"The Lean Years" 10-3-66 (Lucius Franklin/Lloyd Franklin); *The High Chaparral*—"The Champion of the Western World" 2-4-68 (Paddy O'Bannion); *Wild Wild West*—Regular 1968-69 (Jeremy Pike); *The Outcasts*—"The Bounty Children" 12-23-68 (Dan Forrest); *Hec Ramsey*—"Scar

Tissue" 3-10-74 (Will Bannister), "Only Birds and Fools" 4-7-74 (Clyde Harris); *Nakia*—"A Matter of Choice" 12-7-74 (Barrows); *Kung Fu*—"The Last Raid" 4-26-75 (Dr. Cooper).

Aiken, Elaine. Films: "The Lonely Man" 1957 (Ada Marshall).

Aiken, Hugh. Films: "High Lonesome" 1950 (Art Simms).

Ainslee, Marguerite. Films: "Firebrand Jordan" 1930 (Peggy Howe).

Ainslee, Mary. Films: "When the Daltons Rode" 1940 (Minnie).

Ainsworth, Cupid (1901-8/18/61). Films: "Gold Mine in the Sky" 1938 (Jane Crocker).

Ainsworth, Phil. Films: "The Man from Funeral Range" 1918 (Freddie Leighton).

Ainsworth, Sidney (1870-5/21/22). Films: "The Branding Iron" 1920 (Jasper Morena); "Doubling for Romeo" 1922 (Pendleton).

Ainsworth, Virginia. Films: "The Avenging Arrow" 1921-serial; "White Eagle" 1922-serial; "Yankee Speed" 1924 (Inez La Velle); "Rustlers of Red Dog" 1935-serial.

Aitken, Spottiswoode (1868-2/24/33). Films: "The Angel of Contention" 1914; "The Outlaw's Revenge" 1916 (Federal Officer); "Evangeline" 1919 (Benedict); "Fighting Through" 1919 (Colonel Dabney Carr); "Rough-Riding Romance" 1919 (King); "Dangerous Love" 1920 (the Father); "Nomads of the North" 1920 (Old Roland); "Man of Courage" 1922 (Stephen Gregory); "The Snowshoe Trail" 1922 (Herbert Lounsbury); "The White Messenger" 1922; "Lure of the Yukon" 1924 (Sourdough McCraig); "The Power of the Weak" 1926 (the Father).

Akins, Claude (1918-1/27/94). Films: "Bitter Creek" 1954 (Vance Morgan); "The Burning Hills" 1956 (Ben Hindeman); "Johnny Concho" 1956 (Lem); "Joe Dakota" 1957 (Aaron Grant); "The Lonely Man" 1957 (Blackburn); "Rio Bravo" 1959 (Joe Burdette); "Yellowstone Kelly" 1959 (Sergeant); "Comanche Station" 1960 (Ben Lane); "A Distant Trumpet" 1964 (Seely Jones); "Incident at Phantom Hill" 1966 (Krausman); "Return of the Seven" 1966-Span. (Frank); "Ride Beyond Vengeance" 1966 (Elwood Coates); "Waterhole No. 3" 1967 (Sgt. Henry Foggers); "Butch Cassidy and the Sundance Kid" 1969 (Bank Teller); "The Great Bank Robbery" 1969 (Slade); "Flap" 1970 (Lobo); "Lock, Stock and Bar-

rel" TVM-1971 (Punck Logan); "Man Called Sledge" 1971-Ital./U.S. (Hooker); "Dream West" TVM-1986 (Tom Fitzpatrick); "The Gambler Returns: The Luck of the Draw" TVM-1991 (Teddy Roosevelt). ¶TV: *Gunsmoke*—"Word of Honor" 10-1-55 (Harry), "Greater Love" 12-1-56 (Jed Butler), "The Cabin" 2-22-58 (Hack), "He Learned About Women" 2-24-62 (Solis), "The Way It Is" 12-1-62 (Ad Bellem), "Innocence" 12-12-64 (Art McLane), "Bad Lady from Brookline" 5-1-65 (Sy Sherne), "Snap Decision" 9-17-66 (Marshal Clint Tucker), "Ladies from St. Louis" 3-25-67 (Worth Sweeney), "The Predators" 1-31-72 (Howard Kane); *My Friend Flicka*—"Rogue Stallion" 11-25-55, "The Little Secret" 12-2-55 (Keenak), "Lock, Stock and Barrel" 4-6-56 (August Hoskins); *Frontier*—"The Ten Days of John Leslie" 1-22-56 (Bud); *Zane Grey Theater*—"Courage Is a Gun" 12-14-56 (Collins), "Man Unforgiving" 1-3-58 (Sheriff Adam Prescott), "Ransom" 11-17-60 (Comanchero), "Jericho" 5-18-61 (Chuck Wagner); *Have Gun Will Travel*—"The Great Mojave Chase" 9-28-57 (1st Gunman); *Wagon Train*—"The John Cameron Story" 10-2-57, "The Roger Bigelow Story" 12-21-60 (Wes Varney), "The Selena Hartnell Story" 10-18-61 (Will Cottrell); *The Restless Gun*—"Thicker Than Water" 12-9-57 (Rafe Marlow), "The Gold Buckle" 12-30-57 (Lex Springer), "Melany" 3-2-59; *Jim Bowie*—"A Grave for Jim Bowie" 2-28-58 (Criminal); *Cheyenne*—"The Long Search" 4-22-58 (Sheriff Bob Walters); *Schlitz Playhouse of the Stars*—"Way of the West" 6-6-58 (Gus Garner); *Bronco*—"The Besieged" 9-23-58 (Dirk Baggot); *Yancy Derringer*—"Gallatin Street" 10-9-58 (Tobey Cook), "Collector's Item" 3-26-59 (Toby Cook); *Tales of Wells Fargo*—"The Most Dangerous Man Alive" 11-10-58 (John Leslie Nagel), "The Hand That Shook the Hand" 2-6-61 (John L. Sullivan), "The Dodger" 10-7-61 (Rake); *The Rifleman*—"The Safe Guard" 11-18-58 (Floyd Doniger), "Meeting at Midnight" 5-17-60 (Tom Benton), "Strange Town" 10-25-60 (Bletch Droshek); *Maverick*—"Burial Ground of the Gods" 3-30-59 (Paisley Briggs); *Bat Masterson*—"The Death of Bat Masterson" 5-20-59 (Jack Fontana); *The Texan*—"Cattle Drive" 9-28-59, "Border Incident" 12-7-59; *Riverboat*—"Escape to Memphis" 10-25-59 (Jarrett Sutton), "Duel on the River" 12-12-60 (Beaudry Rawlins); *Rawhide*—"Incident of the Druid's

Curse" 1-8-60 (Jim Lark), "Incident of the Lost Idol" 4-28-61 (Clete Manson), "The Sendoff" 10-6-61 (Karse), "Incident of the Four Horsemen" 10-26-62 (Ben Kerran), "Incident at Quivira" 12-14-62 (Sergeant Parker), "Incident of the Rusty Shotgun" 1-9-64 (Aloysius Claybank), "Walk into Terror" 10-5-65 (Jerry Boggs); *Laramie*—"Death Wind" 2-2-60 (Tom Cole), "Queen of Diamonds" 9-20-60 (Jim Dark), "Among the Missing" 9-25-62 (Sheriff Tyler Shaw), "Trapped" 5-14-63 (Walker); *Bonanza*—"Desert Justice" 2-20-60 (Marshal Dowd), "The Mill" 10-1-60 (Ezekiel), "Sam Hill" 6-3-61 (Sam Hill), "The Deserter" 10-21-62 (Col. Edward J. Dunwoody); *The Law of the Plainsman*—"The Question of Courage" 2-25-60 (Sheriff Cliff Shaw); *Overland Trail*—"Fire in the Hole" 4-17-60 (Jumbo); *Wanted—Dead or Alive*—"Prison Trail" 5-14-60 (Jack Kelly); *The Alaskans*—"The Silent Land" 5-15-60 (Constable Watts); *The Rebel*—"The Waiting" 10-9-60 (Tom Hall); *Death Valley Days*—"Splinter Station" 10-19-60 (Caleb); *The Tall Man*—"Night Train to Tularosa" 11-5-60 (Dan Rees); *Klondike*—"Swoger's Mules" 11-21-60 (John Conrad); *The Deputy*—"Lorinda Belle" 6-24-61 (Jason Getty); *Frontier Circus*—"The Balloon Girl" 1-11-62 (Powcheek); *The Outlaws*—"Charge!" 3-22-62 (Thompson); *Empire*—"Ride to a Fall" 10-16-62 (Joe Horvath), "65 Miles Is a Long, Long Way" 4-23-63 (Joe Horvath); *Wide Country*—"Straightjacket for an Indian" 10-25-62 (Bullriver); *The Virginian*—"West" 11-20-62 (Lump), "The Laramie Road" 12-8-65 (Hezikiah); *The Dakotas*—"The Chooser of the Slain" 4-22-63 (Tom Doucette); *Great Adventure*—"The Death of Sitting Bull"/"Massacre at Wounded Knee" 10-4-63 & 10-11-63 (Father Franz); *Destry*—"The Solid Gold Girl" 2-14-64 (Rafe Collins); *Branded*—"The Vindicator" 1-31-65 (Ned Travis); *Daniel Boone*—"A Place of 1000 Spirits" 2-4-65 (Toka); *A Man Called Shenandoah*—"Obion-1866" 10-25-65 (Fordy Brown); *The Big Valley*—"The Brawlers" 12-15-65 (Callahan); *The Legend of Jesse James*—"The Colt" 1-17-66 (Harte); *Laredo*—"Limit of the Law Larkin" 1-27-66 (Cotton Buckmeister), "The Treasure of San Diablo" 2-17-66 (Buck Buckmeister), "Hey Diddle Diddle" 2-24-67 (Cotton Buckmeister), "A Question of Guilt" 3-10-67 (Cotton Buckmeister), "Walk Softly" 3-31-67 (Cotton Buckmeister; *The Monroes*—"Ride with Terror" 9-21-66

(Bud Chapel); *The Guns of Will Sonnett*—"The Guns of Will Sonnett" 9-8-67 (Turnbaugh); *Hondo*—"Hondo and the Gladiators" 12-15-67 (Brock); *Hec Ramsey*—"The Mystery of the Yellow Rose" 1-28-73 (Bert McCabe); *The Oregon Trail*—"Trapper's Rendezvous" 10-12-77 (Lemus Harker).

Alaimo, Marc. Films: "No Man's Land" TVM-1984 (Clay Allison); "The Gambler, Part III—The Legend Continues" TVM-1987 (Bob Butler); "Rio Diablo" TVM-1993 (Jud Everly). ¶TV: *Gunsmoke*—"The Iron Man" 10-21-74 (Kane); *Paradise*—"The Return of Johnny Ryan" 12-2-89 (Sheriff Fry).

Alamo, James. Films: "The Bearcat" 1922 (Henry).

Alaniz, Rico. Films: "California Conquest" 1952 (Pedro); "The Fighter" 1952 (Carlos); "Column South" 1953 (Trooper Chavez); "Conquest of Cochise" 1953 (Felipe); "Wings of the Hawk" 1953 (Capt. Gomez); "Jubilee Trail" 1954 (Spaniard); "The Siege at Red River" 1954 (Chief Yellow Hawk); "Stagecoach to Fury" 1956 (Miguel Torres); "Toughest Gun in Tombstone" 1958 (Fernandez); "The Magnificent Seven" 1960 (Sotero). ¶TV: *Death Valley Days*—"The Saint's Portrait" 10-11-54 (Miguel); *The Lone Ranger*—"Enfield Rifle" 1-13-55; *The Adventures of Rin Tin Tin*—"Rin Tin Tin Meet's O'Hara's Mother" 2-17-56 (Big Elk), "The Invaders" 12-14-56 (Don Valdez); *Loretta Young Show*—"The Wise One" 3-26-56 (Proprietor); *Wyatt Earp*—Regular 1956-59 (Mr. Cousin), "The Schoolteacher" 3-11-58 (Esteban), "Death for a Stolen Horse" 1-13-59 (Joe Riva), "The Scout" 3-1-60 (Tahzay); *Tales of Wells Fargo*—"Rio Grande" 6-3-57 (Sebastian), "Portrait of Teresa" 2-10-62 (Lopez); *26 Men*—"Border Incident" 11-5-57; *Maverick*—"Plunder of Paradise" 3-9-58 (Fernando); *Walt Disney Presents*—"Elfego Baca" Regular 1958-60 (El Sinverguenza); *Have Gun Will Travel*—"Pancho" 10-24-59 (Paul Rancher); *Bronco*—"Rendezvous with a Miracle" 2-12-62 (Rico Cardido); *Gunsmoke*—"Extradition" 12-7-63 & 12-14-63 (El Pinon), "The Jackals" 2-12-68 (Young Padre), "Zavala" 10-7-68 (Blacksmith); *Bonanza*—"The Campaneros" 4-19-64 (Pacheco), "Decision at Los Robles" 3-22-70 (Ricardo); *The Big Valley*—"Legend of a General" 9-19-66 & 9-26-66; *The Monroes*—"Ordeal by Hope" 10-19-66 (Renegade Leader); *The High Chaparral*—"The High Chaparral" 9-10-67 (Ricardo),

"The Firing Wall" 12-31-67 (El Gato), "The Lion Sleeps" 3-28-69 (Armando), "Fiesta" 11-20-70; *Wild Wild West*—"The Night of the Jack O'Diamonds" 10-6-67 (Chico), "The Night of the Winged Terror" 1-17-68 & 1-24-68.

Alba, Luz. Films: "Daughter of the West" 1949 (Wateeka).

Alba, Maria (-6/24/92). Films: "Hell's Heroes" 1930 (Carmelita); "West of the Pecos" 1934 (Dolores).

Alba, Orpha. Films: "The Square Shooter" 1920 (Minerva Doolittle).

Alba, Ricardo. Films: "Wings of the Hawk" 1953 (Ramon).

Albaicin, Rafael. Films: "The Savage Guns" 1961-U.S./Span. (Gonzales); "Navajo Joe" 1966-Ital./Span. (Bandit); "El Condor" 1970 (Officer); "Charley One-Eye" 1973-Brit. (Mexican Leader).

Albeck, J. Frederik. Films: "The True Story of Jesse James" 1957 (Jorgenson).

Albee, Josh. Films: "Jeremiah Johnson" 1972 (Caleb). ¶TV: *Gunsmoke*—"P.S. Murry Christmas" 12-27-71 (Michael), "Eleven Dollars" 10-30-72 (Chad).

Alberghetti, Anna Maria (1936-). Films: "The Last Command" 1955 (Consuela); "Duel at Apache Wells" 1957 (Anita Valdez). ¶TV: *Wagon Train*—"The Conchita Vasquez Story" 3-18-59 (Conchita Vasquez).

Alberni, Luis (1886-12/23/62). Films: "The Santa Fe Trail" 1930 (Juan Castinado); "The Big Stampede" 1932 (Sonora Joe); "The California Trail" 1933 (Commandante Emilio); "The Last Trail" 1933 (Pedro Gonzales); "The Man from Monterey" 1933 (Felipe); "Let Freedom Ring" 1939 (Tony).

Albers, Hans (1892-7/24/60). Films: "Water for Canitoga" 1939-Ger.

Albert, Eddie (1908-). Films: "The Dude Goes West" 1948 (Daniel Boone); "Oklahoma!" 1955 (Ali Hakim). ¶TV: *Zane Grey Theater*—"Stage to Tucson" 11-16-56 (Bide Turley), "A Fugitive" 3-22-57 (Sam Barlow), "A Gun for My Bride" 12-27-57 (Jed Wiley), "The Vaunted" 11-27-58 (Jess Matson); *Wagon Train*—"The John Darro Story" 11-6-57 (John Darro), "The Kurt Davos Story" 11-28-62 (Kurt Davos); *Laramie*—"Glory Road" 9-22-59; *Riverboat*—"The Unwilling" 10-11-59 (Dan Sampson); *Frontier Circus*—"The Hunter and the Hunted" 11-2-61 (Dr. Jordan); *Tales of Wells Fargo*—"A Fist-

ful of Pride" 11-18-61 (Bonzo Croydon); *The Virginian*—"Impasse" 11-14-62 (Cal Kroeger); *Wide Country*—"The Judas Goat" 2-21-63 (Duke Donovan); *Rawhide*—"The Photographer" 12-11-64 (Taylor Dickson); *Kung Fu*—"Blood of the Dragon" 9-14-74 (Dr. Baxter).

Albert, Edward (1951-). TV: *Paradise*—"Birthright" 3-8-91 (Robert Carroll); *Dr. Quinn, Medicine Woman*—"Where the Heart Is" 11-20-93 (Dr. William Burke).

Albert, Elsie (1888-10/7/81). Films: "Refuge" 1915.

Albert, Susan. TV: *The Legend of Jesse James*—"The Dead Man's Hand" 9-20-65 (Dobie Bedford); *Daniel Boone*—"Thirty Pieces of Silver" 3-28-68 (Susan).

Albertini, Giampiero. Films: "Return of Sabata" 1972-Ital./Fr./Ger. (McIntock); "Halleluja to Vera Cruz" 1973-Ital. (General Miguel).

Albertson, Frank (1909-2/29/64). Films: "The Plainsman" 1936 (Young Soldier); "When the Daltons Rode" 1940 (Emmett Dalton). ¶TV: *My Friend Flicka*—"Rough and Ready" 3-9-56 (Roosevelt); *Sugarfoot*—"Misfire" 12-10-57 (Sheriff Crabtree), "The Canary Kid" 11-11-59 (Judge Mortimer Hall), "Angel" 3-6-61 (Sheriff Boyce); *Zane Grey Theater*—"Welcome Home a Stranger" 1-15-59 (Lane Fullerton); *The Californians*—"Bella Union" 1-20-59 (Charley Tuttle); *Lawman*—"The Return" 5-10-59; *The Restless Gun*—"The Englishman" 6-8-59 (Lacey); *Wanted—Dead or Alive*—"The Tyrant" 10-31-59 (George Elkins), "To the Victor" 11-9-60 (Mike Strata); *Bronco*—"The Masquerade" 1-26-60 (Keene), "The Equalizer" 12-18-61; *Colt .45*—"Strange Encounter" 4-26-60 (General Devery); *Cheyenne*—"The Long Rope" 10-3-60 (Jornny Kent); *Maverick*—"Epitaph of a Gambler" 2-11-62 (Harvey Storey); *Bonanza*—"A Passion for Justice" 9-29-63 (Sam Walker); *Destry*—"Big Deal at Little River" 3-20-64 (Alex Whitney).

Albertson, Grace Gillern. Films: "Fancy Pants" 1950 (Dolly). TV: *Circus Boy*—"The Pawnee Strip" 4-14-57 (Sarah); *Wanted—Dead or Alive*—"The Most Beautiful Woman" 1-23-60 (May).

Albertson, Jack (1910-11/25/81). Films: "Lock, Stock and Barrel" TVM-1971 (Brucker). ¶TV: *Sheriff of Cochise*—"Closed for Repairs" 11-30-56 (Greenbriar Merritt); *Have Gun Will Travel*—"High Wire" 11-2-57,

"Out at the Old Ball Park" 10-1-60 (Mayor Whiteside); *Klondike*—"Sure Thing, Men" 11-28-60 (Eskimo Eddie); *Riverboat*—"Listen to the Nightingale" 1-2-61; *Lawman*—"The Unmasked" 6-17-62 (Doc Peters); *The Slowest Gun in the West* 7-29-63 (Carl Dexter); *Death Valley Days*—"Sixty-Seven Miles of Gold" 2-2-64 (Pearlman); *Pistols 'n' Petticoats*—10-1-66 (O'Brian); *Bonanza*—"A Girl Named George" 1-14-68 (Enos Blessing), "The Sound of Loneliness" 12-5-72 (Jonathan May); *Here Come the Brides*—"A Man and His Magic" 12-4-68 (Merlin); *The Big Valley*—"The Battle of Mineral Springs" 3-24-69 (Judge Ben Moore); *The Virginian*—"The Girl in the Shadows" 3-26-69 (Doc Watson); *Gunsmoke*—"Danny" 10-13-69 (Danny Wilson), "One for the Road" 1-24-72 (Lucius Prince), "Cowtown Hustler" 3-11-74 (Moses Darby); *Daniel Boone*—"Run for the Money" 2-19-70 (Shem Sweet); *The Men from Shiloh*—"With Love, Bullets, and Valentines" 10-7-70 (Billy Valentine); *Alias Smith and Jones*—"Jailbreak at Junction City" 9-30-71 (Judge Hanley).

Albertson, Lillian (1881-8/24/ 62). TV: *The Cisco Kid*—"Church in Town" 5-17-52, "The Haunted Stage Stop" 3-7-53, "Doorway to Nowhere" 9-26-53.

Albertson, Mabel (1900-9/28/ 82). Films: "The Hangman" 1959. ¶TV: *The Californians*—"Panic on Montgomery Street" 1-14-58; *Have Gun Will Travel*—"Les Girls" 9-26-59 (Mme. Chalon); *Rawhide*—"Incident of the Dancing Death" 4-8-60 (Kalla); *Gunsmoke*—"Long, Long Trail" 11-4-61 (Gody), "Kate Heller" 9-28-63 (Kate Heller); *Bronco*—"Rendezvous with a Miracle" 2-12-62 (Mother Maria), "A Dollar's Worth of Trouble" 5-15-66 (Madame Adella); *The Tall Man*—"G.P." 5-19-62 (Kate Baines); *Wild Wild West*—"The Night of the Bottomless Pit" 11-4-66 (Mrs. Grimes); *The Rounders*—12-13-66 (Abbey Marstow); *Daniel Boone*—"Take the Southbound Stage" 4-6-67 (Mrs. Abigail Adams); *The Virginian*—"Big Tiny" 12-18-68 (Ma Lacey).

Alberty, Karl Otto. Films: "Man from Oklahoma" 1965-Ital./Span./ Ger.; "Day of Anger" 1967-Ital./Ger.

Albin, Andy (1908-12/27/94). Films: "Gun Fight" 1961 (Jonathan). ¶TV: *Bat Masterson*—"License to Cheat" 2-4-59 (Eddie); *Wyatt Earp*—"Frontier Surgeon" 1-19-60 (Tinkham Brown), "Johnny Behan Falls in Love" 2-14-61 (Limpy Davis); *Zane*

Grey Theater—"The Ox" 11-3-60; *Rawhide*—"Incident of the Slavemaster" 11-11-60; *The Deputy*—"Lorinda Belle" 6-24-61 (Zack Martinson); *Gunsmoke*—"Miss Kitty" 10-14-61 (Proprietor), "Extradition" 12-7-63 & 12-14-63, "Stage Stop" 11-26-66 (Charlie Woodson); *The Tall Man*—"The Girl from Paradise" 1-13-62 (Farmer); *Tales of Wells Fargo*—"Chauncey" 3-17-62 (Uncle Joe); *Bonanza*—"Twilight Town" 10-13-63.

Albright, Hardie (1903-12/7/ 75). Films: "Carolina Moon" 1940 (Wheeler); "Men of the Timberland" 1941; "Sunset in El Dorado" 1945 (Cecil Phelps). ¶TV: *Gunslinger*—"Road of the Dead" 3-30-61 (Barber); *Rawhide*—"Incident of the Phantom Burglar" 4-14-61 (Ben Wallace), "The Black Sheep" 11-10-61 (Verterinarian); *Laramie*—"Wolf Cub" 11-21-61; *Gunsmoke*—"The Ditch" 10-27-62 (Pickett), "Killer at Large" 2-5-66 (Storekeeper); *Iron Horse*—"High Devil" 9-26-66 (Wilson); *The Monroes*—"Gold Fever" 12-14-66.

Albright, Lola (1925-). Films: "Sierra Passage" 1951 (Ann); "The Silver Whip" 1953 (Waco); "Treasure of Ruby Hills" 1955 (May); "Pawnee" 1957 (Meg); "Oregon Passage" 1958 (Sylvia Dane); "Seven Guns to Mesa" 1958 (Julie Westcott); "The Way West" 1967 (Rebecca Evans). ¶TV: *Screen Director's Playhouse*—"Arroyo" 10-26-55 (Nancy Wheeler); *Gunsmoke*—"The Reed Survives" 12-31-55 (Lucy Hunt); *Rawhide*—"Incident of the Banker" 4-2-64 (Maribelle Ashton-Warner), "The Gray Rock Hotel" 5-21-65 (Lottie); *Wagon Train*—"Those Who Stay Behind" 11-8-64 (Leonora Parkman); *Bonanza*—"The Search" 2-14-65 (Ann), "A Bride for Buford" 1-15-67 (Dolly); *Branded*—"Mightier Than the Sword" 9-26-65 (Ann Williams), "Cowards Die Many Times" 4-17-66 (Ann Williams), "Kellie" 4-24-66 (Ann Williams); *Laredo*—"Above the Law" 1-13-66 (Lilah Evans); *Cimarron Strip*—"The Beast That Walks Like a Man" 11-30-67 (Stacey Houston).

Albright, Jr., Wally (1925-). Films: "The Conquerors" 1932 (Twin); "End of the Trail" 1932 (Timmy Travers); "Smoky" 1933 (Junior Cowboy); "The Cowboy Star" 1936 (Jimmy); "Old Louisiana" 1937 (Davey); "Roll Along, Cowboy" 1937 (Danny Blake); "Mexicali Rose" 1939 (Tommy).

Alcaide, Chris (1922-). Films: "Cripple Creek" 1952 (Jeff); "Junction City" 1952 (Jarvis); "The Kid from Broken Gun" 1952 (Matt Fal-

lon); "Smoky Canyon" 1952 (Lars); "The Black Dakotas" 1954 (Burke); "Massacre Canyon" 1954 (Running Horse); "The Outlaw Stallion" 1954 (Truxton); "Overland Pacific" 1954 (Jason); "Gunslinger" 1956 (Joshua Tate); "Day of the Bad Man" 1958 (Monte Hayes). ¶TV: *The Adventures of Kit Carson*—"Trouble in Sundown" 12-4-54; *Tales of the Texas Rangers*—"Uranium Pete" 10-1-55 (Clinton Hollister), "Hail to the Rangers" 12-17-55 (Slade), "Trail Herd" 11-10-57 (Ben Thomas); *Gunsmoke*—"Doc's Revenge" 6-9-56 (Clem Maddow), "Kitty's Outlaw" 10-5-57 (Cowboy), "Grass" 11-29-58 (Ned Curry), "Big Man" 3-25-61 (Mike); *Broken Arrow*—"Passage Deferred" 10-30-56 (Brown Eagle), "Hired Killer" 3-4-58 (John Brett); Bronco—"The Silent Witness" 3-10-59 (Brutus Traxel); *Sugarfoot*—"Trail's End" 11-12-57 (Clay Horton); *Maverick*—"Stampede" 11-17-57 (Tony Cadiz); *Zane Grey Theater*—"A Gun for My Bride" 12-27-57 (Nate Evers), "Threat of Violence" 5-23-58 (Clay Culhane), "The Accuser" 10-30-58 (Deputy Sheriff); *Have Gun Will Travel*—"The Bostonian" 2-1-58 (Bill Whitney), "Justice in Hell" 1-6-62 (Big Fontana), "The Eve of St. Elmo" 3-23-63 (Brock March); *The Californians*—"The Street" 3-25-58 (Gordon); *Man Without a Gun*—"Teen-Age Idol" 9-27-58, "Hero" 5-9-59; *Trackdown*—"Deadly Decoy" 11-14-58 (Cass Desmond); *The Texan*—"The Peddler" 1-26-59 (Wade Clinton), "Image of Guilt" 9-21-59 (Tubbs), "Presentation Gun" 4-4-60 (Deputy Luke Smith); *The Rifleman*—"The Trade" 3-10-59 (Hamp Ferris), "Obituary" 10-20-59 (Panama Billings), "A Case of Identity" 1-19-60 (Lon Perry), "A Time for Singing" 3-8-60 (Spence Hadley), "Meeting at Midnight" 5-17-60 (Schroeder), "Dead Cold Cash" 11-22-60 (Ben Casper), "The Wyoming Story" 2-7-61 & 2-14-61 (Ross), "The Journey Back" 10-30-61, "Squeeze Play" 12-3-62 (Dave Rankin); *Rawhide*—"Incident of the Dry Drive" 5-22-59 (Gates), "Incident of the Arana Sacar" 4-22-60 (Pagan), "Inside Man" 11-3-61 (Roy Craddock); *Wanted—Dead or Alive*—"Estrelita" 10-3-59, "Chain Gang" 12-12-59 (Cree Colter); *Black Saddle*—"The Long Rider" 10-16-59 (Bill Logan); *The Law of the Plainsman*—"Blood Trails" 11-5-59 (Wolf), "Calculated Risk" 12-31-59 (Dan), "Amnesty" 4-7-60 (Conroy); *Shotgun Slade*—"Freight Line" 11-17-59; *Lawman*—"The Shelter" 12-27-59 (Ben Moray),

"Cold Fear" 6-4-61 (Lou Quade); *Laramie*—"Death Wind" 2-2-60 (Will Brent), "Three Roads West" 10-4-60 (Greg), "The Sunday Shoot" 11-13-62; *Bonanza*—"Escape to the Ponderosa" 3-5-60 (Captain Bolton), "The Boss" 5-19-63 (Gus Hanna), "The Deed and the Dilemma" 3-26-67 (Blake); *The Deputy*—"The Choice" 6-25-60 (Fred Tanner); *Tales of Wells Fargo*—"Forty-Four Forty" 2-29-60 (Notch Duggin); *Two Faces West*—"The Prisoner" 2-6-61; *Klondike*—"The Hostages" 2-13-61 (Grayson); *Stagecoach West*—"The Remounts" 3-14-61 (Rob); *The Tall Man*—"The Liberty Belle" 9-16-61 (Joe Durango); *Frontier Circus*—"The Clan MacDuff" 4-26-62; *Cheyenne*—"The Quick and the Deadly" 10-22-62 (Harry Thomas); *The Dakotas*—"Thunder in Pleasant Valley" 2-4-63 (Merric); *Death Valley Days*—"The Man Who Died Twice" 12-22-63 (Jules Reni); *Destry*—"Ride to Rio Verde" 4-10-64 (Ace); *Daniel Boone*—"Tekawitha McLeod" 10-1-64 (Flathead Joseph), "The Prisoners" 2-10-66 (Noah Pierce); *Branded*—"Leap Upon Mountains…" 2-28-65 (Karp), "This Stage of Fools" 1-16-66 (John F. Parker); *A Man Called Shenandoah*—"The Locket" 11-22-65 (Frank Abbott); *The Big Valley*—"Legend of a General" 9-19-66 & 9-26-66 (Marshal Ralston), "Hide the Children" 12-19-66 (1st Horse Thief), "Ladykiller" 10-16-67, "Hell Hath No Fury" 11-18-68 (Ryan); *Hondo*—"Hondo and the Ghost of Ed Dow" 11-24-67 (Selby).

Alcaide, Mario (1926-4/22/71). TV: *U.S. Marshal*—"The Reservation" 10-18-58; *Have Gun Will Travel*—"The Scorched Feather" 2-14-59 (Robert Ceilbleu); *The Texan*—"Stampede" 11-2-59 (Yellow Hawk), "The Reluctant Bridegroom" 11-16-59 (Yellow Hawk), "Showdown at Abilene" 11-9-59 (Yellow Hawk); *Overland Trail*—"Daughter of the Sioux" 3-20-60 (Bloody Hand); *The Outlaws*—"A Day to Kill" 2-22-62 (Carlos Vincente); *Bonanza*—"Five into the Wind" 4-21-63 (Robert de Sorto); *Great Adventure*—"The Testing of Sam Houston" 1-31-64 (Too-Chee-La); *Daniel Boone*—"Daughter of the Devil" 4-15-65 (Russ Kresson); *Laredo*—"Lazyfoot, Where Are You?" 9-16-65 (Lazyfoot); *Gunsmoke*—"Fandango" 2-11-67 (Lorca); *Wild Wild West*—"The Night of the Jack O'Diamonds" 10-6-67 (Fortuna); *The Men from Shiloh*—"The Best Man" 9-23-70 (Cristobal), "Mark of Death" 1-4-67 (Poza).

Alcaraz, Eduardo. Films: "Zorro, the Gay Blade" 1981 (Don Jose).

Alcayde, Rafael. Films: "The Last of the Fast Guns" 1958 (Alcaide); "Ten Days to Tulara" 1958 (Colonel); "Villa!" 1958 (Don Alfonso).

Alcorn, Cherokee. Films: "Whistling Bullets" 1937 (Karl).

Alda, Rutanya (1945-). Films: "Pat Garrett and Billy the Kid" 1973 (Ruthie Lee).

Alden, Debra. Films: "Code of the West" 1947 (Ruth).

Alden, Eric (1908-2/28/62). Films: "The Cowboy Star" 1936 (Leading Man); "Bad Man from Red Butte" 1940 (Brady); "Northwest Mounted Police" 1940 (Constable Kent); "Unconquered" 1947; "The Paleface" 1948 (Bob); "Pony Express" 1953 (Miller); "Last Train from Gun Hill" 1959 (Craig's Man). TV: *The Lone Ranger*—"High Heels" 11-17-49; *The Rebel*—"The Champ" 10-2-60 (Sheriff).

Alden, Joan. Films: "Call of the Heart" 1928 (Molly O'Day).

Alden, Mary (1883-7/2/46). Films: "The Good Bad Man" 1916 (Jane Stuart); "Honest Hutch" 1920 (Mrs. Hutchins); "The Eagle's Feather" 1923 (Delia Jamieson).

Alden, Norman (1924-). Films: "The Great Bank Robbery" 1969 (the Great Gregory); "The Trackers" TVM-1971 (Dilworth). TV: *Circus Boy*—"The Marvelous Manellis" 11-21-57 (Pierre Manelli); *The Adventures of Rin Tin Tin*—"The Foot Soldier" 10-10-58 (Black Claw), "The Luck of O'Hara" 4-3-59 (Black Cloud); *Bonanza*—"Breed of Violence" 11-5-60 (Poke), "The Friendship" 11-12-61 (Teller); *Wyatt Earp*—Regular 1961 (Johnny Ringo); *Lawman*—"The Four" 10-1-61 (Charley); *The Rifleman*—"The Anvil Chorus" 12-17-62 (Duff); *The Dakotas*—"Sanctuary at Crystal Springs" 5-6-63 (Jim Barton); *The Travels of Jaimie McPheeters*—"The Day of the Taboo Man" 10-27-63 (Broken Mouth); *Temple Houston*—"The Law and Big Annie" 1-16-64 (Carlton Owens); *Rango*—Regular 1967 (Captain Horton); *The Big Valley*—"Guilty" 10-30-67 (Jeff Bowden); *Gunsmoke*—"Death Train" 11-27-67 (Purlie Loftus), "Wonder" 12-18-67 (Deke Franklin), "The Night Riders" 2-24-69 (Berber), "Lynch Town" 11-19-73 (Tom Hart); *The Guns of Will Sonnett*—"The Secret of Hangtown Mine" 12-22-67 (Clay); *Iron Horse*—"Death Has Two Faces" 12-23-67 (Benton); *Kung Fu*—"A Praying Mantis Kills" 3-22-73 (Sheriff Crossman); *Young Dan'l Boone*—"The Game" 10-10-77 (Marcus Digby).

Alden, Richard. Films: "The Canadians" 1961-Brit. (Billy); "The McMasters" 1970 (Lester).

Alderman, John (1933-1/12/87). Films: "Hot Spur" 1968; "Mr. Horn" TVM-1979; "Kung Fu: The Movie" TVM-1986. TV: *Gunsmoke*—"The Patsy" 9-20-58 (Dave Thorp); *Wanted—Dead or Alive*—"The Looters" 10-12-60 (Chum), "Dead Reckoning" 3-22-61 (Wade Taggert); *Iron Horse*—"Sister Death" 4-3-67 (Dinsmore).

Alderson, Erville (1882-8/4/57). Films: "The Bad Man" 1930 (Hardy); "The Dawn Trail" 1930 (Denton); "The Lash" 1930 (Judge Travers); "Haunted Gold" 1932 (Benedict); "To the Last Man" 1933 (Judge); "The Fighting Code" 1934 (Joshua La Plante); "Square Shooter" 1935 (Doc Wayne); "Ramona" 1936 (Doctor at Hacienda); "Wells Fargo" 1937 (Marshal); "Wild and Woolly" 1937 (Deacon); "Gold Is Where You Find It" 1938 (Cryder); "Out West with the Hardys" 1938 (Deputy); "Henry Goes Arizona" 1939 (Dr. John Clemens); "Jesse James" 1939 (Old Marshal); "The Man from Dakota" 1940 (Commandant); "Rangers of Fortune" 1940 (Mr. Ellis); "Santa Fe Trail" 1940 (Jefferson Davis); "When the Daltons Rode" 1940 (District Attorney Wade); "Bad Men of Missouri" 1941 (Mr. Adams); "Last of the Duanes" 1941 (Zeke); "Lady from Cheyenne" 1941 (Fairchild); "Arizona Trail" 1943 (Dan Trent); "Oklahoma Outlaws" 1943-short; "Tall in the Saddle" 1944; "Along Came Jones" 1945 (Bartender); "Canyon Passage" 1946 (Judge); "The Sea of Grass" 1947 (Station Agent); "Unconquered" 1947; "Blood on the Moon" 1948. TV: *The Lone Ranger*—"Gold Train" 3-16-50.

Alderson, John (1916-). Films: "The Last Stagecoach West" 1957; "Shoot-Out at Medicine Bend" 1957 (Walters); "No Name on the Bullet" 1959 (Ben Chaffee); "Deserter" 1970-U.S./Ital./Yugo. (O'Toole); "The Duchess and the Dirtwater Fox" 1976. TV: *Stories of the Century*—"Last Stagecoach West" 1954 (George Bryson); *You Are There*—"The Gunfight at the O.K. Corral" 11-6-55; *Gunsmoke*—"General Parsley Smith" 12-10-55 (Ed Nash), "Sweet and Sour" 3-2-57 (Ab Laster), "Blind Man's Bluff" 2-23-63 (Canby); *Cheyenne*—"Quicksand" 4-3-56 (Beef Simpkins); *Zane Grey Theater*—

"Death Watch" 11-9-56 (Corporal Durkin); *Boots and Saddles*—Regular 1957-59 (Sergeant Bullock); *The Californians*—"Sorley Boy" 2-25-58 (Sorley Boy McDonald), "The Marshal" 3-11-58 (Slater), "Bridal Bouquet" 6-10-58 (Dolph Parker); *Have Gun Will Travel*—"Duel at Florence" 10-11-58, "The Mark of Cain" 1-13-62 (Doggett), "Caravan" 2-23-63; *The Texan*—"Return to Friendly" 2-2-59 (Swede Yocum), "Badman" 6-20-60 (Jake); *Maverick*—"Passage to Fort Doom" 3-8-59 (Ben Chapman), "Benefit of Doubt" 4-9-61 (Zindler), "The Art Lovers" 10-1-61 (Captain Bly); *Colt .45*—"Queen of Dixie" 10-4-59 (the Captain); *Laramie*—"The Run to Rumavaca" 11-10-59 (George Crystal); *Wagon Train*—"Trial for Murder" 4-27-60 & 5-4-60; *Bonanza*—"The Countess" 11-19-61 (Montague), "Five Sundowns to Sunup" 12-5-65 (Gwynedd); *Tales of Wells Fargo*—"Who Lives by the Gun" 3-24-62 (Gage); *Death Valley Days*—"From the Earth, a Heritage" 12-13-64 (Joe Meek), "Hugh Glass Meets the Bear" 6-11-66 (Hugh Glass), "An Organ for Brother Brigham" 7-16-66 (Hank Butterford), "The Kid from Hell's Kitchen" 11-12-66 (John Tunstall); *Wild Wild West*—"The Night of the Falcon" 11-10-67 (Clive Marchmont); *The Guns of Will Sonnett*—"Look for the Hound Dog" 1-26-68 (Sheriff), "Alone" 2-9-68 (Officer); *Cowboy in Africa*—"A Man of Value" 2-26-68 (Baron).

Aldin, Eric. TV: *Have Gun Will Travel*—"The Poker Friend" 11-12-60.

Aldon, Mari (1929-). Films: "Distant Drums" 1951 (Judy Beckett). ¶TV: *Tales of Wells Fargo*—"Deadwood" 4-7-58 (Beth Hollister), "That Washburn Girl" 2-13-61 (Nora Washburn); *Yancy Derringer*—"Mayhem at the Market" 1-22-59 (Celest Duval); *The Deputy*—"Final Payment" 3-19-60 (Priscilla Groat); *Laramie*—"The Protectors" 3-22-60 (Celie Rawlins); *Man from Blackhawk*—"The Montreal Story" 5-13-60 (Mrs. Stoddard); *Wagon Train*—"The Jeremy Dow Story" 12-28-60 (Hester Millikan); *Bonanza*—"The Fighters" 4-24-66 (Ruby Keely).

Aldrich, Charles T. Films: "Lady from Cheyenne" 1941 (Leo).

Aldrich, Charlie. Films: "Ballad of a Gunfighter" 1964 (Amigo).

Aldrich, Fred (1904-1/25/79). Films: "Mrs. Mike" 1949 (Louis Beauclaire), "Lost in Alaska" 1952 (Bearded Prospector).

Aldrich, Mariska (1881-9/28/65). Films: "The Cherokee Strip" 1937 (Big Wife); "Bar Buckaroos" 1940-short.

Aldrich, Roma. Films: "Frontier Fury" 1943 (Stella Larkin).

Aldridge, Kay (1917-1/12/95). Films: "Shooting High" 1940 (Evelyn Trent); "Daredevils of the West" 1943-serial (June Foster).

Aldridge, Victoria. TV: *Wagon Train*—"The John Wilbot Story" 6-11-58 (Amy Broxton); *The Rifleman*—"The Sharpshooter" 9-30-58 (Waitress).

Alejandro, Miguel (1958-). Films: "Yuma" TVM-1971 (Andres) ¶TV: *The High Chaparral*—"Fiesta" 11-20-70 (Beto).

Aleong, Aki. Films: "Buckskin" 1968 (Sung Li). ¶TV: *The Californians*—"The Lost Queue" 10-29-57 (Lee Sing); *Wyatt Earp*—"China Mary" 3-15-60 (Li Kung); *The Virginian*—"Ah Sing vs. Wyoming" 10-25-67 (Ah Sing).

Aletter, Frank (1926-). TV: *Wide Country*—"The Girl from Nob Hill" 3-8-63 (Mott); *The Quest*—"Welcome to America, Jade Snow" 11-24-76.

Alexander, Annette. Films: "Natchez Trace" 1960 (Emily Goodrich).

Alexander, Ben (1922-7/5/69). Films: "The Lady of the Dugout" 1918 (the Son); "Blue Streak McCoy" 1920; "Frivolous Sal" 1925 (Benny Keene); "The Vanishing Frontier" 1932 (Lucien Winfield); "Western Gold" 1937 (Bart); "The Dark Command" 1940 (Sentry); "Man in the Shadow" 1957 (Ab Begley).

Alexander, Clarke. TV: *Maverick*—"Duel at Sundown" 2-1-59 (Sheriff), "The Sheriff of Duck 'n' Shoot" 9-27-59 (Jonah), "The Goose-Drownder" 12-13-59 (Hurley); *Have Gun Will Travel*—"The Fifth Man" 5-30-59 (Bartender); *Bonanza*—"The Sisters" 12-12-59.

Alexander, Clifford (1891-3/2/65). Films: "With Hoops of Steel" 1919 (Will Whittaker).

Alexander, Denise (1945-). TV: *Stoney Burke*—"The Mob Riders" 10-29-62 (Arlette Hughes); *The Virginian*—"Impasse" 11-14-62 (Mildred Kroeger).

Alexander, Edward (1888-8/15/64). Films: "North of '53" 1917 (Jack Barrow).

Alexander, Frank "Fatty" (1879-9/8/37). Films: "Cyclone Jones" 1923 (Fatty Wirthing).

Alexander, Fred. Films: "Young Fury" 1965 (Pony).

Alexander, James (1902-1/31/61). Films: "Treasure of Ruby Hills" 1955 (Burt). ¶TV: *Wild Bill Hickok*—"Ghost Town Lady" 1-27-53, "Blind Alley" 2-24-53

Alexander, James. TV: *Wild Wild West*—"The Night of the Jack O'Diamonds" 10-6-67 (Gregorio).

Alexander, Jane (1939-). Films: "A Gunfight" 1971 (Nora Tenneroy); "This Was the West That Was" TVM-1974 (Sarah Shaw); "Calamity Jane" TVM-1984 (Martha "Calamity Jane" Canary).

Alexander, John (1897-7/13/82). Films: "The Ghost Rider" 1935 (Sheriff); "Fancy Pants" 1950 (Teddy Roosevelt); "Winchester '73" 1950 (Jack Rider); "Untamed Frontier" 1952 (Max Wickersham); "One Foot in Hell" 1960 (Sam Giller).

Alexander, Katherine (1901-1/18/81). Films: "Sutter's Gold" 1936 (Mrs. Anna Sutter); "The Vanishing Virginian" 1941 (Marcia Marshall).

Alexander, Richard "Dick" (1903-8/9/89). Films: "The Fightin' Comeback" 1927 (Red Pollack); "The Lone Star Ranger" 1930 (Jim Fletcher); "Rough Waters" 1930 (Little); "Hurricane Horseman" 1931 (Bull Carter); "Sunrise Trail" 1931; "Daring Danger" 1932 (Bull Bagley); "Law and Order" 1932 (Kurt Northrup); "One-Man Law" 1932 (Sorenson); "The Sunset Trail" 1932 (One Shot); "Texas Bad Man" 1932 (Gene); "Two-Fisted Law" 1932 (Zink Yokum); "The Sundown Rider" 1933; "Cowboy Holiday" 1934; "The Fighting Code" 1934 (Olson); "The Law of the Wild" 1934-serial (Salter); "Born to Battle" 1935; "The Cowboy and the Bandit" 1935 (Scarface); "Coyote Trails" 1935 (Mack Larkin); "Fighting Shadows" 1935 (Maddigan); "Riding Wild" 1935 (Jim Barker); "The Unconquered Bandit" 1935; "Drift Fence" 1936 (Seth Wilson); "Everyman's Law" 1936 (Barber); "Roarin' Guns" 1936 (Bull Langdon); "Wild Brian Kent" 1936 (Phil Hanson); "Mystery Range" 1937 (Lupe Bardes); "Outlaws of the Prairie" 1937 (Rufe Lupton); "Two-Fisted Sheriff" 1937 (Bull); "Zorro Rides Again" 1937-serial (Brad Dace/El Lobo); "Feud of the Trail" 1938; "The Mysterious Rider" 1938 (Hudson); "Santa Fe Stampede" 1938; "Renfrew on the Great White Trail" 1938 (Doc Howe); "Six Shootin' Sheriff" 1938 (Big Boy); "Where the Buffalo Roam" 1938 (Sellers); "Where the West Begins" 1938 (Barnes); "Destry Rides Again" 1939 (Cowboy); "Frontier Marshal" 1939 (Curly Bill's

Man); "The Kansas Terrors" 1939 (Miguel); "Union Pacific" 1939 (Card Player); "Covered Wagon Days" 1940; "The Dark Command" 1940 (Sentry); "Death Rides the Range" 1940; "Son of Roaring Dan" 1940 (Big Taylor); "Wyoming" 1940 (Gus); "Boss of Bullion City" 1941 (Steve); "Forbidden Trails" 1941; "Lady from Cheyenne" 1941 (Man); "Man from Montana" 1941 (Kohler); "Riders of Death Valley" 1941-serial (Pete); "Code of the Outlaw" 1942; "In Old California" 1942; "Raiders of the Range" 1942; "Romance on the Range" 1942; "The Return of the Rangers" 1943; "Boss of Boomtown" 1944 (Yuma); "Gunsmoke Mesa" 1944 (Frank Lear); "Oklahoma Raiders" 1944 (Duggan); "Raiders of the Border" 1944 (Steve); "Riders of the Santa Fe" 1944 (Biff Macauley); "Spook Town" 1944; "Trigger Trail" 1944 (Waco); "Flaming Bullets" 1945; "His Brother's Ghost" 1945; "Renegades of the Rio Grande" 1945 (Pete Jackson); "Salome, Where She Danced" 1945 (Shotgun); "Canyon Passage" 1946 (Miner); "'Neath Canadian Skies" 1946; "North of the Border" 1946; "Jesse James Rides Again" 1947-serial (Clem Williams); "The Marauders" 1947; "Northwest Outpost" 1947 (Large Convict); "Unconquered" 1947 (Slave); "The Dead Don't Dream" 1948 (Duke); "False Paradise" 1948; "Loaded Pistols" 1948; "Silent Conflict" 1948 (1st Rancher); "Lust for Gold" 1949 (Man); "Rimfire" 1949 (Weber); "Silver Canyon" 1951 (Luke Anders); "Night Stage to Galveston" 1952; "Pack Train" 1953; "A Perilous Journey" 1953 (Crying Miner); "Flesh and the Spur" 1957 (Bartender); "Requiem for a Gunfighter" 1965. ¶TV: *The Lone Ranger*—"Trouble Waters" 3-9-50, "Pardon for Curley" 6-22-50; *The Gene Autry Show*—"Gun Powder Range" 10-29-50, "Fight at Peaceful Mesa" 11-19-50; *Wild Bill Hickok*—"Blacksmith Story" 1-1-52; *The Rifleman*—"Smoke Screen" 4-5-60, "The Martinet" 11-8-60 (Swensen).

Alexander, Tommy. TV: *Gunsmoke*—"Ex-Con" 11-30-63 (Kid), "Jonah Hutchison" 11-21-64 (Franklin Hutchison); *Wagon Train*—"The Whipping" 3-23-64.

Alexis, Demetrius (1905-3/12/73). Films: "Don Dare Devil" 1925 (Parader).

Alfonso, Jose. Films: "Behind the Mask of Zorro" 1965-Ital./Span. (Don Esteban).

Alford, Phillip. Films: "Shenandoah" 1965 (Boy Anderson); "The In-

truders" TVM-1970. ¶TV: *The Virginian*—"A Time of Terror" 2-11-70 (Joe).

Alicia, Ana (1956-). Films: "The Sacketts" TVM-1979 (Druscilla).

Alighiero, Carlo (1931-). Films: "The Moment to Kill" 1968-Ital./Ger.; "The Five Man Army" 1969-Ital. (Gutierrez).

Allan, Anthony. Films: "Out West with the Hardys" 1938 (Cliff Thomas); "The Kid from Texas" 1939 (Bertie Thomas).

Allan, Hugh (1903-). Films: "Sin Town" 1929 (Silk Merrick).

Allard, Shirlee. Films: "The Fargo Phantom" 1950-short; "Gold Strike" 1950-short.

Allardt, Arthur. Films: "The Gun Men of Plumas" 1914; "The Sheriff's Story" 1914; "The Hidden Children" 1917 (Capt. Jean de Contrecoeur); "The Midnight Stage" 1919 (Pasquale).

Allbritton, Louise (1920-2/16/79). Films: "The Doolins of Oklahoma" 1949 (Rose of Cimarron).

Alleman, W.A. Films: "The Fighting Stranger" 1921 (Winthrop Ayre).

Allen, Alfred (1866-6/18/47). Films: "A Yoke of Gold" 1916 (Luis Lopez); "Fighting Mad" 1917 (Eldorado Smith); "Follow the Girl" 1917 (Martinez); "The Eagle" 1918 (Mining Official); "The Grand Passion" 1918 (Ben Mackey); "Nobody's Wife" 1918 (Sheriff Carew/Alec Young); "Tongues of Flame" 1918 (Sheriff Dunn); "Winner Takes All" 1918 (Saul Chadron); "A Pistol Point Proposal" 1919; "Riders of Vengeance" 1919; "The Sleeping Lion" 1919 (Col. Doharney); "O'Malley of the Mounted" 1921 (Big Judson); "The Sage Hen" 1921 (John Rudd); "Desert Driven" 1923 (Yorke); "The Miracle Baby" 1923 (Dr. Amos Stanton); "Shootin' for Love" 1923 (Jim Travis); "Bustin' Thru" 1925 (John Merritt); "The Outlaw Dog" 1927 (Henry Jordan); "Under the Tonto Rim" 1928 (Dad Denmeade); "Sunset Pass" 1929 (Amos Dabb).

Allen, Alta. Films: "Daring Chances" 1924 (Agnes Rushton); "The Set-Up" 1926 (Thora Barton).

Allen, Ariane. Films: "Galloping Dynamite" 1937 (Jane Foster).

Allen, Arthur (1881-8/25/47). Films: "Rangers of Fortune" 1940 (Mr. Prout).

Allen, Audrey (1946-). Films:

"Valley of the Dancing Widows" 1974-Span./Ger.

Allen, Barbara. Films: "Oklahoma Justice" 1951; "Stagecoach Driver" 1951; "Dead Man's Trail" 1952; "Fort Osage" 1952; "The Homesteaders" 1953 (Jenny).

Allen, Barbara Jo (Vera Vague) (1904-9/14/74). Films: "Melody Ranch" 1940 (Veronica Whipple); "Cowboy Canteen" 1944 (Vera); "Girl Rush" 1944 (Suzie Banks); "Mohawk" 1956 (Aunt Agatha). ¶TV: *Maverick*—"The Rivals" 1-25-59 (Mrs. Mallaver), "A Tale of Three Cities" 10-18-59 (Hannah Adams).

Allen, Beatrice. Films: "Fangs of Fate" 1925 (Azalia's Mother).

Allen, Betty. Films: "The Redhead from Wyoming" 1953 (French Heels).

Allen, Chad (1974-). TV: *Dr. Quinn, Medicine Woman*—Regular 1993- (Matthew Cooper).

Allen, Chris (1869-11/7/55). Films: "Deadshot Casey" 1928; "Man from Music Mountain" 1938; "The Blazing Sun" 1950; "Gene Autry and the Mounties" 1951.

Allen, Corey (1934-). TV: *The Restless Gun*—"Friend in Need" 1-13-58 (Art Hemper); *Gunsmoke*—"Ma Tennis" 2-2-58 (Ben Tennis); *Trackdown*—"The Young Gun" 2-7-58 (Tom Summers); *Have Gun Will Travel*—"Gun Shy" 3-29-58 (Chuck); *Rawhide*—"Incident of Fear in the Streets" 5-8-59 (Mel Mason); *The Rebel*—"The Hostage" 6-11-61 (Yancey Dagget); *Lawman*— "The Lords of Darkness" 12-3-61 (William Lord); *The Dakotas*—"The Chooser of the Slain" 4-22-63 (Clen Biglow); *Bonanza*—"The Roper" 4-5-64; *The Loner*—"Escort for a Dead Man" 12-18-65 (Drake).

Allen, Dave (1885-1/3/55). Films: "Little Joe, the Wrangler" 1942 (Miner).

Allen, David. Films: "The Chisholms" TVM-1979 (Squire Bailey). ¶TV: *The Chisholms*—3-29-79 (Squire Bailey).

Allen, Edwin H. (1885-8/13/42) Films: "The Law of the West" 1912.

Allen, Elizabeth (1934-). Films: "Cheyenne Autumn" 1964 (Miss Guinevere Plantagenet). ¶TV: *Tales of Wells Fargo*—"Threat of Death" 4-25-60 (Ilona); *Stoney Burke*—"Kelly's Place" 4-15-63 (Kelly); *The High Chaparral*—"The Glory Soldiers" 1-31-69 (Capt. Ellie Strong).

Allen, Estelle (1893-7/14/40). Films: "Overalls" 1916 (Peggy Malone).

Allen, Ethan (1882-8/21/40). Films: "The Border Legion" 1930 (George Randall); "Alias the Bad Man" 1931 (Sheriff); "The Two Gun Man" 1931 (Sheriff); "Flaming Lead" 1939 (Sheriff); "Riders of the Black River" 1939; "The Singing Cowgirl" 1939 (Sheriff Teasley); "The Stranger from Texas" 1939 (Taylor); "The Taming of the West" 1939 (Judge Bailey); "Trigger Pals" 1939 (Sheriff); "Water Rustlers" 1939 (Tim Martin).

Allen, Gary. Films: "The Wicked Die Slow" 1968 (the Kid); "The New Maverick" TVM-1978 (Dobie); "The Night Rider" TVM-1979 (Donald White, the Hotel Clerk). ¶TV: *The Texan*—"The Widow of Paradise" 11-24-58 (Nathan Crawford).

Allen, Harry (1883-12/4/51). Films: "The Silent Hero" 1927 (Blinky); "In Old California" 1929 (Sgt. Washburn); "Headin' North" 1930 (Smith); "Texas Pioneers" 1932 (Corporal); "The Fourth Horseman" 1933 (Charlie); "Stand Up and Fight" 1939 (Engineer); "Buckskin Frontier" 1943 (McWhinny).

Allen, J.J. Films: "The Bearcat" 1922 (Jake Hensen).

Allen, Jr., Joe (1918-11/9/62). Films: "Gunfighters of the Northwest" 1954-serial (Fletcher Stone).

Allen, Joel. Films: "The Man from Black Hills" 1952 (Bates); "The Maverick" 1952 (John Rowe). ¶TV: *Wild Bill Hickok*—"Cry Wolf" 10-7-52.

Allen, Jonelle (1944-). TV: *Dr. Quinn, Medicine Woman*—Regular 1993- (Grace).

Allen, Joseph (1872-9/9/52). Films: "Told in the Rockies" 1915.

Allen, Judith (1913-). Films: "The Thundering Herd" 1934 (Milly Fayre); "Boots and Saddles" 1937 (Bernice Allen); "Git Along, Little Dogies" 1937 (Doris); "It Happened Out West" 1937 (Anne Martin); "Texas Trail" 1937 (Barbara Allen); "I Shot Billy the Kid" 1950; "Train to Tombstone" 1950 (Belle).

Allen, Lester (1891-11/6/49). Films: "Klondike Kate" 1942 (Duster Dan).

Allen, Lillian. Films: "Saddle Mates" 1928 (Mrs. Saunders).

Allen, Mark. Films: "The Gambler Wore a Gun" 1961 (Dex Harwood); "How the West Was Won" 1962 (Colin). ¶TV: *Wanted—Dead or Alive*—"Reckless" 11-7-59, "Death, Divided by Three" 4-23-60 (Blacksmith), "The Showdown" 10-26-60; *Man from Blackhawk*—"A Matter of Conscience" 12-11-59 (Borchard); *Bonanza*—"The Outcast" 1-9-60 (Garth); *Riverboat*—"Fort Epitaph" 3-7-60 (Sergeant Matthews); *Pony Express*—"The Killer" 3-23-60 (Marshal Stahl); *Gunsmoke*—"No Chip" 12-3-60 (Grant Dolan); *Empire*—"Stopover on the Way to the Moon" 1-1-63 (Carl); *The Travels of Jaimie McPheeters*—Regular 1963-64 (Matt Kissel); *A Man Called Shenandoah*—"Plunder" 3-7-66 (Man with Rifle); *Lancer*—"The Fix-It Man" 2-11-69; *Kung Fu*—"King of the Mountain" 10-14-72 (Postmaster).

Allen, Marty (1922-). TV: *The Big Valley*—"The Jonah" 11-11-68 (Waldo Diefendorfer).

Allen, Maude Pierce (1887-4/24/60). Films: "Cowboy Millionaire" 1935 (Henrietta Barclay); "Whispering Smith Speaks" 1935 (Mother Roberts); "Secret Valley" 1937 (Mrs. Hogan); "The Painted Desert" 1938 (Yukon Kate); "Let Freedom Ring" 1939 (Hilda); "Adventures of Red Ryder" 1940-Serial (the Duchess); "Danger Ahead" 1940 (Mrs. Hill).

Allen, Melvin F. (1933-). TV: *The Rifleman*—"Miss Bertie" 12-27-60 (Wrangler); *The Big Valley*—"Palms of Glory" 9-15-65 (Morgan), "Target" 10-31-66, "Hide the Children" 12-19-66 (Lounger), "Price of Victory" 2-13-67, "Guilty" 10-30-67 (Marty).

Allen, Penelope (1943-). Films: "Doc" 1971 (Mattie Earp).

Allen, Rex (1922-). Films: "The Arizona Cowboy" 1950 (Rex Allen); "Hills of Oklahoma" 1950 (Rex Allen); "Redwood Forest Trail" 1950 (Rex Allen); "Trail of Robin Hood" 1950; "Under Mexicali Stars" 1950 (Rex Allen); "Rodeo King and the Senorita" 1951 (Rex Allen); "Silver City Bonanza" 1951 (Rex Allen); "Thunder in God's Country" 1951 (Rex Allen); "Utah Wagon Train" 1951 (Rex Allen); "Border Saddlemates" 1952 (Rex Allen); "Colorado Sundown" 1952 (Rex Allen); "The Last Musketeer" 1952 (Rex Allen); "Old Oklahoma Plains" 1952 (Rex Allen); "South Pacific Trail" 1952 (Rex Allen); "Down Laredo Way" 1953 (Rex Allen); "Iron Mountain Trail" 1953 (Rex); "Old Overland Trail" 1953 (Rex Allen); "Red River Shore" 1953 (Rex Allen); "Shadows of Tombstone" 1953 (Rex Allen); "The Phantom Stallion" 1954; "For the Love of Mike" 1960 (Rex Allen); "Tomboy and the Champ" 1961; "Legend of Lobo" 1962 (Narrator); "Secret of Navajo Cave" 1976. ¶TV: *Frontier Doctor*—Regular 1958-59 (Dr. Bill Baxter); *The Men from Shiloh*—"Tate, Ramrod" 2-24-71.

Allen, Ricca (1863-9/13/49). Films: "Speedy Meade" 1919 (Mrs. Buck Lennon); "Redskins and Redheads" 1941-short.

Allen, Ricky. Films: "Plunderers of Painted Flats" 1959 (Timmy Martin). ¶TV: *The Texan*—"The Widow of Paradise" 11-24-58 (Joey Crawford).

Allen, Robert (1906-). Films: "Fighting Shadows" 1935 (Bob Rutledge); "Law Beyond the Range" 1935 (Johnny Kane); "The Revenge Rider" 1935 (Chad Harmon); "Rio Grande Ranger" 1936 (Bob); "The Unknown Ranger" 1936 (Bob Allen); "Law of the Ranger" 1937 (Ranger Bob Allen); "Ranger Courage" 1937 (Bob Allen); "The Rangers Step In" 1937 (Bob Allen); "Reckless Ranger" 1937 (Bob Allen/Jim Allen); "Death Valley Rangers" 1944 (Ranger).

Allen, Rusty. Films: "Black Spurs" 1965 (Sadie's Girl).

Allen, Sam (1861-9/13/34). Films: "The Conflict" 1921 (Orrin Lakin); "The Son of the Wolf" 1922 (Father Roubeau); "The Virginian" 1923 (Uncle Hughey); "The Timber Wolf" 1925 (Joe Terry); "Call of the Klondike" 1926 (Burt Kenney); "Man Rustlin'" 1926 (Pop Geers); "Black Jack" 1927 (Ed Holbrook); "Death Valley" 1927 (the Father); "Burning Brides" 1928 (Dr. Zach McCarthy); "Cowboy Counsellor" 1933 (Hotelkeeper); "The Last Round-Up" 1934 (1st Miner).

Allen, Sian Barbara (1946-). Films: "Billy Two Hats" 1973-Brit. (Esther). ¶TV: *Bonanza*—"Ambush at Rio Lobo" 10-24-72 (Teresa Burnside); *Alias Smith and Jones*—"Six Strangers at Apache Springs" 10-28-71 (Sister Grace); *Gunsmoke*—"The Bullet" 11-29-71, 12-6-71 & 12-13-71 (Allie).

Allen, Slim. Films: "A Western Wooing" 1919; "Western Grit" 1924 (Slim Burrows); "The Human Tornado" 1925 (Sheriff Cutter).

Allen, Ta-Ronce. TV: *Kung Fu*—"The Well" 9-27-73 (Juliet Brown), "The Last Raid" 4-26-75 (Juliet).

Allen, Tex. Films: "Vengeance and the Woman" 1917-serial.

Allen, Todd. Films: "Silverado" 1985 (Deputy Kern); "Wyatt Earp" 1994 (Sherm McMasters). ¶TV: *Paradise*—"Bad Blood" 2-1-91 (Paul Forrester).

Allen, Valerie (1934-). Films: "Pardners" 1956 (Dance Hall Girl).

¶TV: *Walt Disney Presents*—"Elfego Baca" Regular 1958-60 (Lucita Miranda); *The Texan*—"The Taming of Rio Nada" 1-11-60 (Anne Banner), "Sixgun Street" 1-18-60 (Anne Banner), "The Terrified Town" 1-25-60 (Anne Banner); *Bat Masterson*—"The Prescott Campaign" 2-2-61 (Catherine Guild); *Gunsmoke*—"The Dreamers" 4-28-62 (Annie); *Bonanza*—"Invention of a Gunfighter" 9-20-64 (Olive).

Allen, Victor. Films: "Fast and Fearless" 1924 (Sheriff Hawkins); "Rainbow Rangers" 1924 (Frank Owens); "Don X" 1925 (Pecos Pete); "Vic Dyson Pays" 1925 (Madden); "Lawless Trails" 1926 (Mojave Kid); "The Outlaw Dog" 1927 (Sheriff); "The Sonora Kid" 1927 (Sheriff); "Greased Lightning" 1928 (Jack Crane); "The Trail of the Horse Thieves" 1929 (Sheriff); "The Mysterious Avenger" 1936 (Posse); "Come on Cowboys" 1937.

Allen, III, Vernett. TV: *The Travels of Jaimie McPheeters*—Regular 1963-64 (Othello).

Allen, W.J. Films: "The Devil's Bowl" 1923 (Jim Sands).

Allen, Winifred. Films: "The Long Trail" 1917 (Mitchette Dubois).

Allende, Fernando. Films: "The Alamo: 13 Days to Glory" TVM-1987 (Almonte).

Allgood, Sara (1883-9/13/50). Films: "The Man from Texas" 1947 (Aunt Belle); "Sierra" 1950 (Mrs. Jonas).

Allison, Jean (1929-). Films: "Bad Company" 1972 (Dixon's Mother). ¶TV: *Have Gun Will Travel*—"The Last Laugh" 1-25-58 (Nora Borden); *The Californians*—"Mutineers from Hell" 9-30-58 (Rosie), "Crimps' Meat" 1-27-59 (Millie); *Maverick*—"The Jail at Junction Flats" 11-9-58 (Madame Higgins); *Rough Riders*—"The Nightbinders" 11-20-58 (Jan); *Trackdown*—"Day of Vengeance" 11-28-58 (Eileen); *Lawman*—"The Posse" 3-8-59 (Beth Hunter); *The Law of the Plainsman*—"A Matter of Life and Death" 10-15-59, "Clear Title" 12-17-59; *Rawhide*—"Incident at Jacob's Well" 10-16-59 (Melissa Calvin); *Wanted—Dead or Alive*—"Reckless" 11-7-59, "Bounty on Josh" 1-25-61 (Carol Frazer); *Bronco*—"The Last Resort" 11-17-59 (Flora Waters), "Death of an Outlaw" 3-8-60 (Susan McSween), "The Last Letter" 3-5-62; *Wagon Train*—"The Felezia Kingdom Story" 11-18-59 (Angela); *Johnny Ringo*—"Die Twice" 1-21-60 (Lydia Hackett); *Riverboat*—

"Fight at New Canal" 2-22-60 (Tracy Paxton); *Bonanza*—"The Avenger" 3-19-60 (Sally); *Tombstone Territory*—4-1-60 (Hope Jensen); *The Alaskans*—"A Barrel of Gold" 4-3-60 (Rose Stevenson), "The Ballad of Whitehorse" 6-12-60 (Yukon Kate); *Tate*—"Before Sunup" 8-17-60 (Della); *The Westerner*—"Mrs. Kennedy" 10-28-60 (Mrs. Kennedy); *Tales of Wells Fargo*—"The Killing of Johnny Lash" 11-21-60 (Francine); *The Rifleman*—"Flowers by the Door" 1-10-61; *Wyatt Earp*—"Johnny Behan Falls in Love" 2-14-61 (Minna Marlin); *The Outlaws*—"The Bill Doolin Story" 3-2-61 (Edith); *Bat Masterson*—"Ledger of Guilt" 4-6-61 (Lorna); *Laramie*—"The Dynamiters" 3-6-62 (Sarah Hodding), "Badge of Glory" 5-7-63; *Gunsmoke*—"Kitowa!" 2-16-70 (Martha Vail), "The Town Tamers" 1-28-74 (Martha); *Hec Ramsey*—"A Hard Road to Vengeance" 11-25-73 (Grace Lambert).

Allison, May (1895-3/27/89). Films: "The Buzzard's Shadow" 1915 (Alice Corbett); "The Hidden Children" 1917 (Lois de Contrecoeur); "The Promise" 1917 (Ethel Manton).

Allman, Elvia (1905-3/6/92). TV: *Wagon Train*—"The Donna Fuller Story" 12-19-62 (Sabrina), "The Melanie Craig Story" 2-17-64.

Allman, Sheldon (1924-). Films: "Hud" 1963 (Thompson); "The Sons of Katie Elder" 1965 (Judge Harry Eyers); "Nevada Smith" 1966 (Sheriff). ¶TV: *The Restless Gun*—"Take Me Home" 12-1-58 (Mr. Thomas), "The Way Back" 7-13-59; *Gunsmoke*—"The Coward" 3-7-59 (Bill), "Ash" 2-16-63 (Murdock), "The Magician" 12-21-63 (Banks), "Song for Dying" 2-13-65 (Cory Lukens), "A Noose for Dobie Price" 3-4-68 (Skeets Walden), "Lobo" 12-16-68 (Badger); *Maverick*—"The Witch of Hound Dog" 11-6-60 (Ox Sutliff), "Dutchman's Gold" 1-22-61 (Vern Tripp); *Death Valley Days*—"3-7-77" 12-14-60 (Sheriff Cal Cornell), "The Fighting Sky Pilot" 4-25-65; *Lawman*—"Firehouse Lil" 1-8-61 (Louis Vesuto), "The Break-In" 5-21-61 (Walt Hudson), "By the Book" 12-24-61 (Teakwood); *Cheyenne*—"Duel at Judas Basin" 1-30-61 (Charlie Lutz), "The Beholden" 2-27-61 (Elijah McGuire); *The Rebel*—"The Pit" 3-12-61 (Hunk); *Bronco*—"The Equalizer" 12-18-61 (Billy Doolin); *Laramie*—"Badge of Glory" 5-7-63 (Sam Logan); *The Dakotas*—"A Nice Girl from Goliah" 5-13-63 (Velie); *The Travels of Jaimie McPheeters*—"The Day of the Pawnees" 12-22-63

& 12-29-63 (Tod Bullard); *Bonanza*—"The Gentleman from New Orleans" 2-2-64 (Betts); *Temple Houston*—"The Town That Trespassed" 3-26-64 (Cutter); *Daniel Boone*—"Goliath" 9-29-66 (Caleb Smith), "The Dandy" 10-10-68.

Allport, Christopher. Films: "The Chisholms" TVM-1979 (Franz Schwarzenbacher). ¶TV: *The Chisholms*—4-16-79 (Franz).

Allwyn, Astrid (1909-3/31/78). Films: "Reno" 1939 (Flora McKenzie).

Allyn, William. TV: *Jim Bowie*—"Hare and Tortoise" 11-22-57 (Andre Roman); *Maverick*—"The Rivals" 1-25-59 (Livingston); *The Virginian*—"Vengeance Is the Spur" 2-27-63.

Allyson, June (1917-). TV: *Zane Grey Theater*—"Cry Hope! Cry Hate!" 10-20-60 (Stella).

Almanzar, James. Films: "Charro!" 1969 (Sheriff Ramsey); "Pony Express Rider" 1976 (Puddin); "The Apple Dumpling Gang Rides Again" 1979; "The Sacketts" TVM-1979. ¶TV: *Temple Houston*—"Seventy Times Seven" 12-5-63 (Nate Hollister); *Gunsmoke*—"Honor Before Justice" 3-5-66 (Barking Dog), "The Wrong Man" 10-29-66 (Morell), "Saturday Night" 1-7-67 (Hounddog), "The Wreckers" 9-11-67 (Indio), "The First People" 2-19-61 (Mako), "The Scavengers" 11-16-70 (Ogana), "Kitty's Love Affair" 10-22-73 (Clel); *Iron Horse*—"Broken Gun" 10-17-66 (Jordan), "Welcome for the General" -2-67 (General Sherman); *The Monroes*—"War Arrow" 11-2-66; *The High Chaparral*—"Shadows on the Land" 10-15-67 (Soldado), "The Assassins" 1-7-68 (Soldano), "Survival" 1-14-68 (Soldano), "The Hair Hunter" 3-10-68; *Cimarron Strip*—"Whitey" 10-19-67 (Rosario); *Here Come the Brides*—"Here Come the Brides" 9-25-68, "And Jason Makes Five" 10-9-68 (Canada), "Letter of the Law" 10-30-68 (Dupre), "None to a Customer" 2-19-69 (Canada).

Alonso, Chelo. Films: "The Good, the Bad, and the Ugly" 1966-Ital.; "Run Man, Run" 1967-Ital./Fr.; "Night of the Serpent" 1969-Ital.

Alonso, Maria Conchita (1957-). Films: "James A. Michener's Texas" TVM-1995 (Lucia).

Alonso, Mercedes. Films: "Gunfighters of Casa Grande" 1965-U.S./Span. (Maria); "Jesse James' Kid" 1966-Span./Ital. (Dorothy); "Three from Colorado" 1967-Span.

Alonzo, John. Films: "The Long Rope" 1961 (Manuel Alvarez); "Terror at Black Falls" 1962; "Invitation to a Gunfighter" 1964 (Manuel). ¶TV: *Cheyenne*—"Winchester Quarantine" 9-25-61 (Rico); *Temple Houston*—"Last Full Moon" 2-27-64 (Long Maned Pony); *Destry*—"Ride to Rio Verde" 4-10-64 (Jose); *Wild Wild West*—"The Night of the Golden Cobra" 9-23-66 (Sarcan), "The Night of the Surreal McCoy" 3-3-67 (Lightnin' McCoy).

Alper, Murray (1904-). Films: "Two in Revolt" 1936 (Andy); "Down Mexico Way" 1941 (Flood); "Moonlight and Cactus" 1944 (Slugger)."Devil's Canyon" 1953 (Driver/Guard); "The Outlaws Is Coming!" 1965 (Chief Battlehorse). ¶TV: *Wild Bill Hickok*—"Behind Southern Lines" 6-26-51, "Border City" 11-13-51, "Mexican Gun Running Story" 1-8-52, "The Kid from Red Butte" 8-26-52; *Maverick*—"Hadley's Hunters" 9-25-60 (Gus).

Alpert, David. Films: "The Charge at Feather River" 1953 (Griffin); "The Moonlighter" 1953; "The Redhead from Wyoming" 1953 (Wally Beggs). ¶TV: *Annie Oakley*—"The Tomboy" 7-17-54 (Fred Hutton).

Alphin, Patricia. Films: "Western Whoopee" 1948-short; "Six Gun Music" 1949-short; "West of Laramie" 1949-short.

Alsace, Gene (Rocky Camron, Buck Coburn) (1902-6/16/67). Films: "Guns for Hire" 1932; "Fighting Shadows" 1935 (Tim McCoy's Double); "Gunsmoke on the Guadalupe" 1935; "Moonlight on the Prairie" 1935; "Range Warfare" 1935; "Gun Smoke" 1936 (Steve Branning); "Song of the Saddle" 1936 (Marty); "Trailin' West" 1936; "Treachery Rides the Range" 1936 (Scout Blackbourne); "Blazing Sixes" 1937; "The California Mail" 1937 (Jake); "Guns of the Pecos" 1937; "Land Beyond the Law" 1937; "The Overland Express" 1938; "Arizona Frontier" 1940 (Bisbee); "Adventures of Red Ryder" 1940-serial (Deputy Lawson); "The Golden Trail" 1940 (Bat Toles); "Pals of the Silver Sage" 1940; "Rainbow Over the Range" 1940 (Bart); "Take Me Back to Oklahoma" 1940 (Red); "Arizona Bound" 1941; "The Driftin' Kid" 1941; "Dynamite Canyon" 1941 (Capt. Grey); "The Gunman from Bodie" 1941; "Lone Star Law Men" 1941 (Brady); "The Pioneers" 1941 (Sheriff); "Ridin' the Cherokee Trail" 1941 (Bat); "Riding the Sunset Trail" 1941 (Pecos Dean); "Rollin' Home to

Texas" 1941; "Wanderers of the West" 1941 (Bronco); "Western Mail" 1942 (Rod); "Where Trails End" 1942; "Outlaw Trail" 1944 (Sheriff Rocky Camron); "Sonora Stagecoach" 1944 (Rocky); "Song of Old Wyoming" 1945 (Ringo); "Wildfire" 1945 (Buck Perry); "Romance of the West" 1946 (Chico); "White Stallion" 1947 (Rocky Cameron); "The Fighting Stallion" 1950 (Lem); "Callaway Went Thataway" 1951 (Cowboy).

Alton, Kenneth. TV: *Gunsmoke*—"Indian White" 10-27-56 (Cowboy); *Have Gun Will Travel*—"The Long Night" 11-16-57; *Bat Masterson*—"Trail Pirate" 12-31-58 (Hyde); *MacKenzie's Raiders*—Regular 1958-59.

Alvarado, Don (1904-3/31/67). Films: "Night Cry" 1926 (Pedro); "Captain Thunder" 1931 (Juan Sebastian); "A Demon for Trouble" 1934 (Galindo); "Rio Grande Romance" 1936 (Jack Carter); "Rose of the Rancho" 1936 (Don Luis Espinosa); "Rose of the Rio Grande" 1938 (Don Jose de la Torre).

Alvarado, Jose. Films: "The Last Round-Up" 1947; "The Big Sombrero" 1949; "The Cowboy and the Indians" 1949.

Alvarez, Angel. Films: "Damned Pistols of Dallas" 1964-Span./Ital./Fr.; "Django" 1966-Ital./Span.; "Navajo Joe" 1966-Ital./Span. (Oliver Blackwood); "Fury of Johnny Kid" 1967-Span./Ital.; "The Mercenary" 1968-Ital./Span. (Notary).

Alvin, John (1917-). Films: "San Antonio" 1945 (Pony Smith); "Cheyenne" 1947 (Single Jack); "Under Colorado Skies" 1947 (Jeff); "The Bold Frontiersman" 1948 (Post); "Two Guys from Texas" 1948 (Jim Crocker); "Kentucky Rifle" 1956. ¶TV: *The Lone Ranger*—"Bullets for Ballots" 5-11-50, "The Black Widow" 8-24-50, "Trouble at Black Rock" 2-8-51, "The New Neighbor" 12-18-52; *Tales of Wells Fargo*—"Cow Town" 12-15-58 (Joe Rivers); *Rawhide*—"Incident of the Big Blowout" 2-10-61, "A Woman's Place" 3-30-62; *Bronco*—"Yankee Tornado" 3-13-61 (Jim March); *The Rifleman*—"Skull" 1-1-62 (Applegate).

Alyn, Kirk (1910-). Films: "The Man from the Rio Grande" 1943 (Tom Traynor); "Overland Mail Robbery" 1943 (Tom Hartley); "Call of the Rockies" 1944; "Forty Thieves" 1944 (Jerry Doyle).

Alzamora, Armand. Films: "Sergents 3" 1962 (Caleb); "Duel at Diablo" 1966 (Ramirez); "Barquero"

1970 Lopez); "Something Big" 1971 (Luis Munos). ¶TV: *Death Valley Days*—"The Last Bad Man" 12-16-57; *Tales of Wells Fargo*—"Desert Showdown" 9-14-59 (Yaqui Kid); *Wyatt Earp*—"The Fugitive" 11-17-59 (Francisco Vasquez); *Bonanza*—"El Toro Grande" 1-2-60 (Eduardo), "The Roper" 4-5-64; *Wichita Town*—"Seed of Hate" 1-27-60 (Indian); *Maverick*—"A Flock of Trouble" 2-14-60 (Basco); *Wagon Train*—"The Don Alvarado Story" 6-21-61 (Bartholomeo), "The Michael Malone Story" 1-6-64 (Dr. Perez); *Lawman*—"The Vintage" 1-21-62 (Antonio Lazarino); *Empire*—"Stopover on the Way to the Moon" 1-1-63 (Luis); *The Legend of Jesse James*—"South Wind" 2-14-66 (Clell Miller); *Nichols*—"The Siege" 9-23-71 (Raoul).

Amann, Betty. Films: "The Trail of the Horse Thieves" 1929 (Amy Taggart); "In Old Mexico" 1938 (Janet Leeds).

Amarilla, Florencio. Films: "El Condor" 1970 (Aguila); "Chino" 1973-Ital./Span./Fr. (Little Bear).

Amber, Audrey. *see* Ambesi, Adriana.

Ambesi, Adriana (Audrey Amber). Films: "Joe Dexter" 1965-Span./Ital. (Laura); "Ringo's Big Night" 1966-Ital./Span.; "The Tall Women" 1966-Austria/Ital./Span. (Betty); "10,000 Dollars Blood Money" 1966-Ital. (Dolores); "Stranger in Paso Bravo" 1968-Ital.

Ambler, Jerry. Films: "Beyond the Purple Hills" 1950; "Fort Defiance" 1951 (Cheyenne); "Bronco Buster" 1952.

Ameche, Don (1908-12/6/93). Films: "Ramona" 1936 (Alessandro). ¶TV: *Alias Smith and Jones*—"Dreadful Sorry, Clementine" 11-18-71 (Diamond Jim Guffy).

Amelio, Sonia. Films: "The Wild Bunch" 1969 (Teresa).

Amendola, Tony. Films: "The Cisco Kid" CTVM-1994 (Washam).

American Horse, Chief. Films: "Tomahawk" 1951 (Indian).

American Horse, George. Films: "Dream West" TVM-1986 (Chief); "Outlaws" TVM-1986 (Indian Tracker); "The Gambler, Part III—The Legend Continues" TVM-1987 (Sitting Bull); "Son of the Morning Star" TVM-1991.

Ames, Allyson (1940-). TV: *Maverick*—"Three Queens Full" 11-12-61 (Lou Ann); *The Virginian*—"The Exiles" 1-9-63; *Stoney Burke*—"King of the Hill" 1-21-63 (Nancy); *Gunsmoke*—"The Kite" 2-29-64

(Clara Cassidy); *Wagon Train*—"The Race Town Story" 10-11-64 (Julie).

Ames, Amanda. Films: "Geronimo" 1962 (Mrs. Burns). ¶TV: *The Rifleman*—"The Hangman" 5-31-60, "The Silent Knife" 12-20-60, "The Executioner" 5-7-62 (Ruth).

Ames, Ed (1929-). Films: "Gunsmoke: One Man's Justice" TVM-1994 (Waco). ¶TV: *The Rifleman*—"Quiet Night, Deadly Night" 10-22-62 (Lee Coyle); *Redigo*—"Lady War-Bonnet" 9-24-63 (John Talltree); *The Travels of Jaimie Mc-Pheeters*—"The Day of the Pawnees" 12-22-63 & 12-29-63 (Kennedy); *Daniel Boone*—Regular 1964-68 (Mingo).

Ames, Florenz (1926-85). Films: "Man with the Gun" 1955 (Doc Hughes); "Texas Lady" 1955 (Wilson); "Fastest Gun Alive" 1956 (Joe Fenwick). ¶TV: *Broken Arrow*—"The Conspirators" 12-18-56 (Emperor Norton); *Gunsmoke*—"The Last Fling" 3-23-57 (John Peavy).

Ames, Floyd. Films: "Triple Action" 1925 (Servant); "The Love of Paquita" 1927.

Ames, Heather. TV: *Overland Trail*—"The O'Mara's Ladies" 2-14-60 (Mimi); *Bat Masterson*—"The Big Gamble" 6-16-60 (Angelita); *The Virginian*—"Ring of Silence" 10-27-65 (Lisa).

Ames, Jimmy (1909-8/14/65). Films: "River Lady" 1948 (Logger); "Silver River" 1948 (Barker); "Calamity Jane and Sam Bass" 1949 (Blacksmith).

Ames, Joyce. TV: *Gunsmoke*—"Kitowa!" 2-16-70 (Melissa Vail).

Ames, Judith. Films: "Arrowhead" 1953; "Ricochet Romance" 1954 (Betsy Williams); "Oregon Passage" 1958 (Marion); "Gunfighters of Abilene" 1960 (Alice). ¶TV: *Broken Arrow*—"The Mail Riders" 9-25-56 (Terry Wilson); *Tales of Wells Fargo*—"A Time to Kill" 4-22-57 (Ellen), "Special Delivery" 3-31-58 (Maud Kimball); *The Californians*—"The Avenger" 10-15-57, "A Turn in the Trail" 2-17-59 (Madge Dorsett); *Trackdown*—"The Farrand Story" 1-10-58 (Jenny Krail), "The House" 3-21-58 (Melinda Curry); *Zane Grey Theater*—"The Stranger" 2-28-58 (Martha Bream), "The Homecoming" 10-23-58 (Ellen Larkin); *Wagon Train*—"The Dan Hogan Story" 5-14-58 (Mary Hogan), "The Ben Courtney Story" 1-28-59 (Nora Courtney); *Wyatt Earp*—"Remittance Man" 11-4-58 (Doris Burns); *Wanted—Dead or Alive*—"The Corner" 2-21-59, "An-

gels of Vengeance" 4-18-59 (Sarah Buchanan); *Cimarron City*—"The Unaccepted" 2-28-59 (Emmy Barton); *The Texan*—"Badlands" 5-11-59 (Beth Kincaid).

Ames, Leon (1903-10/12/93). Films: "Man of Conquest" 1939 (John Hoskins); "The Marshal of Mesa City" 1939 (Sheriff Jud Cronin); "Ambush" 1950 (Major Beverly); "Cattle Drive" 1951 (Mr. Graham). ¶TV: *The Men from Shiloh*—"The Animal" 1-20-71 (Judge Fitzroy).

Ames, Lionel (1930-). TV: *Sergeant Preston of the Yukon*—"The Rebel Yell" 10-10-57 (Iggy); *Tales of Wells Fargo*—"Alias Jim Hardie" 3-10-58 (Cliff Harmon).

Ames, Rachel (1931-). TV: *Wyatt Earp*—"A Murderer's Return" 1-5-60 (Phoebe McKean); *Laramie*—"A Sound of Bells" 12-27-60 (Jenny); *Stagecoach West*—"Songs My Mother Told Me" 2-21-61, "The Root of Evil" 2-28-61 (Cecilia Barnes); *Wagon Train*—"The Saul Bevins Story" 4-12-61 (Jan Harley), "The Eli Bancroft Story" 11-11-63, "The Trace McCloud Story" 3-2-64 (Florence); *The Virginian*—"Death Wait" 1-15-69 (Mary Kincaid).

Ames, Ramsay (1919-). Films: "Beauty and the Bandit" 1946; "The Gay Cavalier" 1946; "The Vigilante" 1947-serial (Betty Winslow).

Ames, Virginia. Films: "The Mother of the Ranch" 1912; "Broncho Billy's Sentence" 1915.

Amidou (1942-). Films: "Buddy Goes West" 1981-Ital.

Amis, Suzy (1958-). Films: "The Ballad of Little Jo" 1993 (Little Jo).

Amman, Lukas (1912-). Films: "Day of Anger" 1967-Ital./Ger. (Judge Cutchel).

Amont, Duane. Films: "The Bounty Killer" 1965 (Ben Liam).

Amor, Carlos. Films: "Ramona" 1928 (Shepherder).

Amos, John (1941-). Films: "Bonanza: The Next Generation" TVM-1988 (Mr. Mack).

Amrani, Gabi. Films: "Madron" 1970-U.S./Israel (Angel).

Amsterdam, Morey (1912-). TV: *Jim Bowie*—"Choctaw Honor" 1-3-58 (Pinky); *Gunsmoke*—"Joe Phy" 1-4-58 (Cicero Grimes); *Have Gun Will Travel*—"The Moor's Revenge" 12-27-58 (Lucien Bellingham).

Anakorita. Films: "The Sacketts" TVM-1979. ¶TV: *Bonanza*—"Decision at Los Robles" 3-22-70

(Maria); *Daniel Boone*—"How to Become a Goddess" 4-30-70 (Dawn).

Anchoriz, Leo (1932-). Films: "Finger on the Trigger" 1965-Span./Ital./U.S. (Ed Bannister); "Seven Guns for the MacGregors" 1965-Ital./Span. (Santillana); "Kill Them All and Come Back Alone" 1967-Ital./Span. (Deker); "Up the MacGregors!" 1967-Ital./Span. (Maldonado); "I Came, I Saw, I Shot" 1968-Ital./Span.; "The Magnificent Bandits" 1969-Ital./Span.; "A Bullet for Sandoval" 1970-Ital./Span. (the Padre); "Three Musketeers of the West" 1972-Ital.; "What Am I Doing in the Middle of the Revolution?" 1973-Ital.; "Cipolla Colt" 1975-Ital./Ger.

Andelman, Julie. TV: *Kung Fu*—"Night of the Owls, Day of the Doves" 2-14-74 (Lisa).

Anders, Donna. TV: *Laredo*—"The Sweet Gang" 11-4-66.

Anders, Dusty. TV: *The Californians*—"The Painted Lady" 1-13-59 (Julie); *Wyatt Earp*—"Silver Dollar" 2-2-60.

Anders, Laurie. Films: "The Marshal's Daughter" 1953 (Laurie Dawson).

Anders, Luana (1940-). Films: "Evil Roy Slade" TVM-1972 (Alice Fern); "When the Legends Die" 1972 (Mary Redmond); "The Missouri Breaks" 1976 (Rancher's Wife); "Goin' South" 1978 (Mrs. Anderson). ¶TV: *The Restless Gun*—"Jody" 11-4-57 (Lucy Anne); *Cimarron City*—"Child of Fear" 1-17-59 (Nancy Tucker); *The Rifleman*—"Shivaree" 2-3-59 (Lisabeth Bishop); *Sugarfoot*—"The Avengers" 5-12-59 (Nature Girl); *Lawman*—"The Swamper" 6-5-60 (Ellie); *Rawhide*—"Incident of the Running Man" 5-5-61 (Maddy Trager); *Bonanza*—"Forever" 9-12-72 (Julie).

Anders, Merry (1932-). Films: "The Dalton Girls" 1957 (Holly Dalton); "Five Bold Women" 1960 (the Missouri Lady); "Young Jesse James" 1960 (Belle Starr); "The Gambler Wore a Gun" 1961 (Sharon Donovan); "The Quick Gun" 1964 (Helen Reed); "Tickle Me" 1965 (Estelle Penfield); "Young Fury" 1965 (Alice). ¶TV: *Cheyenne*—"Big Ghost Basin" 3-12-57 (Sherry Raven), "The Long Rope" 10-3-60 (Ruth Parma); *Sugarfoot*—"Brannigan's Boots" 9-17-57 (Katie Brannigan), "Outlaw Island" 11-24-59 (Sally Ormand); *Broken Arrow*—"Smoke Signal" 12-10-57 (Amy Breece); *Tales of Wells Fargo*—"The Tall Texan" 4-27-59 (Laurie);

Maverick—"The People's Friend" 2-7-60 (Penelope Greeley), "The Town That Wasn't Threre" 10-2-60 (Maggie Bradford), "Destination Devil's Flat" 12-25-60 (Marybelle McCall), "Three Queens Full" 11-12-61 (Cissie); *Bonanza*—"Bitter Water" 4-9-60 (Virginia); *Bronco*—"Winter Kill" 5-31-60 (Francy Owens), "Ordeal at Dead Tree" 1-2-61 (Lucy Follett); *Death Valley Days*—"Way Station" 5-2-62 (Abby Jefferson), "The Vintage Years" 1-30-63 (Lorna Erickson); *The Virginian*—"A Man Called Kane" 5-6-64 (Donna).

Anders, Richard. TV: *The High Chaparral*—"The Long Shadow" 1-2-70 (Deacon); *Bearcats!*—12-23-71 (Cadwell).

Anders, Rudolph (1902-3/27/87). Films: "Under Nevada Skies" 1946 (Alberti) ¶TV: *The Rebel*—"Land" 2-21-60 (Frank Gottwald); *Hotel De Paree*—"Sundance and the Cattlemen" 5-13-60 (Barnaby).

Andersen, Elga (1936-12/7/94). Films: "Johnny Colt" 1966-Ital. (Caroline).

Andersen, Suzy. Films: "Two Gunmen" 1964-Span./Ital. (Stella Rattison); "Fifteen Scaffolds for the Killer" 1968-Ital./Span.

Anderson, Anne. TV: *Bronco*—"Riding Solo" 2-10-59 (Orissa Flynn); *Lawman*—"The Bandit" 5-31-59 (Jenny Gibbons).

Anderson, Audley (1885-12/19/66). Films: "Outlaw's Son" 1957 (Egstrom).

Anderson, Augusta. Films: "The Bandit and the Baby" 1915; "Ruggles of Red Gap" 1935 (Mrs. Wallaby).

Anderson, Barbara (1945-). Films: "Bonanza: The Next Generation" TVM-1988 (Annabelle Cartwright). ¶TV: *The Virginian*—"The Challenge" 10-19-66 (Sarah Crayton); *The Road West*—"Pariah" 12-5-66 (Susan Douglass), "Never Chase a Rainbow" 3-6-67 (Barbara); *Laredo*—"The Other Cheek" 2-10-67 (Delia Snilly).

Anderson, Bridgette. TV: *Gun Shy*—Regular 1983 (Celia).

Anderson, Carol. Films: "Rough Night in Jericho" 1967 (Claire).

Anderson, Charles E. "Cap" (1882-3/24/56). Films: "The Boss of Copperhead" 1920; "Bullet Proof" 1920 (Bandit); "Overland Red" 1920 (Boggs); "Runnin' Straight" 1920; "West Is Best" 1920; "The Conflict" 1921 (Ovid Jenks); "The Fox" 1921 (Rollins); "The Night Horsemen" 1921 (Jerry Strann); "The Wallop" 1921 (Applegate); "Catch My Smoke"

1922 (Sheriff); "The Love Gambler" 1922 (Curt Evans); "Under Pressure" 1922; "A California Romance" 1923 (Steve); "Brass Commandments" 1923 (Bannock); "The Huntress" 1923; "Snowdrift" 1923; "The Scrappin' Kid" 1926 (Hank Prince); "The Terror" 1926 (Blair Hatley); "Border Cavalier" 1927 (Beaver Martin); "The Rambling Ranger" 1927 (Sam Bruce); "Spurs and Saddles" 1927 (Hawk); "Clearing the Trail" 1928 (Dan Talbot); "The California Mail" 1929 (Butch McGraw); "The Lariat Kid" 1929 (Scar Hagerty); "Spurs" 1930 (Pecos); "The Galloping Kid" 1932; "Texas Bad Man" 1932 (Jim); "The Fourth Horseman" 1933 (Caleb Winters); "Call of the Wild" 1935 (4th Poker Player); "Red River Valley" 1936; "Let Freedom Ring" 1939 (Sheriff Hicks); "Queen of the Yukon" 1940 (Old Timer); "The Westerner" 1940 (Hezekiah Willever); "The Ox-Bow Incident" 1943 (Posse); "My Darling Clementine" 1946 (Townsman).

Anderson, Christian (1939-). TV: *Wild Wild West*—"The Night of the Fatal Trap" 12-24-65 (Mike Dawson); *Bonanza*—"Destiny's Child" 1-30-66 (Hunter), "Little Girl Lost" 11-3-68 (Driver), "The Deserter" 3-16-69 (Turner).

Anderson, Claire (1896-3/23/64). Films: "The Fly God" 1918 (Mrs. Aliers); "The Rider of the Law" 1919 (Roseen); "The Meddler" 1925 (Dorothy Parkhurst).

Anderson, Cornie. Films: "Round-Up Time in Texas" 1937 (Namba).

Anderson, Dave. Films: "Jesse James Rides Again" 1947-serial (Sam).

Anderson, Donna J. TV: *The Travels of Jaimie McPheeters*—Regular 1963-64 (Jenny); *Gunsmoke*—"The Other Half" 5-30-64 (Nancy Otis).

Anderson, Dusty (1921-). Films: "Singing on the Trail" 1946.

Anderson, Eddie (1905-2/28/77). Films: "Buck Benny Rides Again" 1940 (Rochester).

Anderson, Ernest (1912-). TV: *Laredo*—"Lazyfoot, Where Are You?" 9-16-65 (Bartender); *Rango*—"The Daring Holdup of the Deadwood Stage" 1-20-67 (Preacher).

Anderson, Eve. Films: "Perils of the Wilderness" 1956-serial (Donna Blane).

Anderson, Floyd. Films: "The Kingfisher's Roost" 1922 (Dan McGee).

Anderson, George (1891-8/28/

48). Films: "Union Pacific" 1939 (Tunnel Engineer); "Hidden Gold" 1940 (Ward Ackerman).

Anderson, Gilbert M. "Broncho Billy". (1884-1/20/71). Films: "The Great Train Robbery" 1903; "Western Stage Coach Hold Up" 1904; "Life of an American Cowboy" 1906; "The Bandit Makes Good" 1907; "The Best Man Wins" 1909; "Black Sheep" 1909; "The Heart of a Cowboy" 1909; "His Reformation" 1909; "The Indian Trailer" 1909; "Judgment" 1909; "A Maid of the Mountains" 1909; "A Mexican's Gratitude" 1909; "The Ranchman's Rival" 1909; "The Road Agents" 1909; "Shanghaied" 1909; "The Spanish Girl" 1909; "A Tale of the West" 1909; "A Western Maid" 1909; "Away Out West" 1910; "The Bad Man's Christmas Gift" 1910; "The Bad Man's Last Deed" 1910; "The Bandit's Wife" 1910; "The Bearded Bandit" 1910; "Broncho Billy's Redemption" 1910; "The Brother, the Sister and the Cowpuncher" 1910; "Circle C Ranch Wedding Present" 1910; "The Cowboy and the Squaw" 1910; "The Cowboy's Sweetheart" 1910; "A Cowboy's Vindication" 1910; "The Cowpuncher's Ward" 1910; "The Deputy's Love" 1910; "The Desperado" 1910; "The Dumb Half-Breed's Defense" 1910; "The Fence at Bar Z Ranch" 1910; "The Flower of the Ranch" 1910; "The Forest Ranger" 1910; "The Girl and the Fugitive" 1910; "The Girl on Triple X Ranch" 1910; "An Indian Girl's Love" 1910; "The Marked Trail" 1910; "The Mexican's Faith" 1910; "The Millionaire and the Ranch Girl" 1910; "The Mistaken Bandit" 1910; "An Outlaw's Sacrifice" 1910; "Pals of the Range" 1910; "Patricia of the Plains" 1910; "The Pony Express Rider" 1910; "The Ranch Girl's Legacy" 1910; "The Ranchmen's Feud" 1910; "The Ranger's Bride" 1910; "The Sheriff's Sacrifice" 1910 (Sheriff Egan); "The Silent Message" 1910; "The Tenderfoot Messenger" 1910; "Trailed to the West" 1910; "Under Western Skies" 1910; "The Unknown Claim" 1910; "A Vein of Gold" 1910; "Western Chivalry" 1910; "A Western Woman's Way" 1910; "A Westerner's Way" 1910; "Across the Plains" 1911; "At the Break of Dawn" 1911; "Bad Man's Downfall" 1911; "The Bad Man's First Prayer" 1911; "The Border Ranger" 1911; "Broncho Billy's Adventure" 1911; "Broncho Billy's Christmas Dinner" 1911; "Broncho Billy's Last Spree" 1911; "Carmenita, the Faithful" 1911; "The Cattle Rustler's Father" 1911; "The Cattleman's Daughter" 1911; "The

Cowboy's Mother-in-Law" 1911; "The Corporation and the Ranch Girl" 1911; "The Count and the Cowboys" 1911; "The Cowboy Coward" 1911; "The Cowpuncher's Law" 1911; "The Desert Claim" 1911; "The Faithful Indian" 1911; "The Forester's Plea" 1911; "Forgiven in Death" 1911; "A Frontier Doctor" 1911; "A Gambler of the West" 1911; "The Girl Back East" 1911; "The Girl of the West" 1911; "The Hidden Mine" 1911; "The Indian Maiden's Lesson" 1911; "An Indian's Sacrifice" 1911; "The Lucky Card" 1911; "The Millionaire and the Squatter" 1911; "The Mountain Law" 1911; "On the Desert's Edge" 1911; "The Outlaw and the Child" 1911; "The Outlaw Deputy" 1911; "The Outlaw Samaritan" 1911; "A Pal's Oath" 1911; "The Power of Good" 1911; "The Prospector's Legacy" 1911; "The Puncher's New Love" 1911; "The Romance on Bar Q Ranch" 1911; "The Sheriff" 1911; "The Sheriff's Brother" 1911; "The Sheriff's Chum" 1911; "The Sheriff's Decision" 1911; "Shootin' Mad" 1911; "Spike Shannon's Last Fight" 1911; "The Stage Driver's Daughter" 1911; "A Thwarted Vengeance" 1911; "The Tribe's Penalty" 1911; "The Two Fugitives" 1911; "The Two-Gun Man" 1911; "The Two Reformations" 1911; "A Western Girl's Sacrifice" 1911; "A Western Redemption" 1911; "What a Woman Can Do" 1911; "Alkali Bests Broncho Billy" 1912; "An Arizona Escapade" 1912; "The Bandit's Child" 1912; "The Boss of the Katy Mine" 1912; "Broncho Billy and the Bandits" 1912; "Broncho Billy and the Girl" 1912; "Broncho Billy and the Indian Maid" 1912; "Broncho Billy and the Schoolmarm's Kid" 1912; "Broncho Billy and the Schoolmistress" 1912; "Broncho Billy for Sheriff" 1912; "Broncho Billy Outwitted" 1912; "Broncho Billy's Bible" 1912; "Broncho Billy's Escapade" 1912; "Broncho Billy's Gratitude" 1912; "Broncho Billy's Heart" 1912; "Broncho Billy's Last Hold-Up" 1912; "Broncho Billy's Love Affair" 1912; "Broncho Billy's Mexican Wife" 1912; "Broncho Billy's Narrow Escape" 1912; "Broncho Billy's Pal" 1912; "Broncho Billy's Promise" 1912; "The Cattle King's Daughter" 1912; "A Child of the Purple Sage" 1912; "Child of the West" 1912; "The Dance at Silver Gulch" 1912; "The Dead Man's Claim" 1912; "The Deputy and the Girl" 1912; "The Deputy's Love Affair" 1912; "The Desert Sweetheart" 1912; "The Foreman's Cousin" 1912; "The Indian and the Child" 1912; "An Indian Sun-

beam" 1912; "An Indian's Friendship" 1912; "The Little Sheriff" 1912; "The Loafer" 1912; "Love on Tough Luck Ranch" 1912; "A Moonshiner's Heart" 1912; "The Mother of the Ranch" 1912; "The Oath of His Office" 1912; "On El Monte Ranch" 1912; "On the Cactus Trail" 1912; "On the Moonlight Trail" 1912; "An Outlaw's Sacrifice" 1912; "The Ranchman's Trust" 1912; "The Prospector" 1912; "The Ranch Girl's Mistake" 1912; "The Ranch Girl's Trial" 1912; "The Ranchman's Anniversary" 1912; "The Ranchman's Trust" 1912; "A Road Agent's Love" 1912; "A Romance of the West" 1912; "The Sheepman's Escape" 1912; "The Sheriff's Inheritance" 1912; "The Sheriff's Luck" 1912; "The Shotgun Ranchman" 1912; "The Smuggler's Daughter" 1912; "A Story of Montana" 1912; "The Tenderfoot Foreman" 1912; "Their Promise" 1912; "The Tomboy on Bar Z" 1912; "Under Mexican Skies" 1912; "Western Girls" 1912; "Western Hearts" 1912; "A Western Legacy" 1912; "A Wife of the Hills" 1912; "A Woman of Arizona" 1912; "The Accusation of Broncho Billy" 1913; "Across the Great Divide" 1913; "Across the Rio Grande" 1913; "At the Lariat's End" 1913; "Belle of the Siskiyou" 1913; "Bonnie of the Hills" 1913; "Borrowed Identity" 1913; "The Broken Parole" 1913; "Broncho Billy and the Express Rider" 1913; "Broncho Billy and the Maid" 1913; "Broncho Billy and the Navajo Maid" 1913; "Broncho Billy and the Outlaw's Mother" 1913; "Broncho Billy and the Rustler's Child" 1913; "Broncho Billy and the Schoolmarm's Sweetheart" 1913; "Broncho Billy and the Sheriff's Kid" 1913; "Broncho Billy and the Squatter's Daughter" 1913; "Broncho Billy and the Step-Sisters" 1913; "Broncho Billy and the Western Girls" 1913; "Broncho Billy Gets Square" 1913; "Broncho Billy Reforms" 1913; "Broncho Billy's Brother" 1913; "Broncho Billy's Capture" 1913; "Broncho Billy's Christmas Deed" 1913; "Broncho Billy's Conscience" 1913; "Broncho Billy's Elopement" 1913; "Broncho Billy's First Arrest" 1913; "Broncho Billy's Gratefulness" 1913; "Broncho Billy's Grit" 1913; "Broncho Billy's Gun-Play" 1913; "Broncho Billy's Last Deed" 1913; "Broncho Billy's Mistake" 1913; "Broncho Billy's Oath" 1913; "Broncho Billy's Reason" 1913; "Broncho Billy's Secret" 1913; "Broncho Billy's Sister" 1913; "Broncho Billy's Squareness" 1913; "Broncho Billy's Strategy" 1913; "Broncho Billy's Ward" 1913; " Broncho Billy's

Way" 1913; "The Call of the Plains" 1913; "Children of the Forest" 1913; "A Cowboy Samaritan" 1913; "The Crazy Prospector" 1913; "The Dance at Eagle Pass" 1913; "The Daughter of the Sheriff" 1913; "Days of the Pony Express" 1913; "The Doctor's Duty" 1913; "The Edge of Things" 1913; "The End of the Circle" 1913; "The Episode of Cloudy Canyon" 1913; "The Greed for Gold" 1913; "The Heart of a Gambler" 1913; "The Housekeeper of Circle C" 1913; "The Influence on Broncho Billy" 1913; "The Kid Sheriff" 1913; "The Last Roundup" 1913; "The Last Shot" 1913; "Love and the Law" 1913; "The Making of Broncho Billy" 1913; "The Man in the Cabin" 1913; "The Miner's Request" 1913; "A Montana Mix-Up" 1913; "The Naming of the Rawhide Queen" 1913; "The New Schoolmarm of Green River" 1913; "The New Sheriff" 1913; "The Ranch Feud" 1913; "The Ranch Girl's Partner" 1913; "The Ranchman's Blunder" 1913; "The Redeemed Claim" 1913; "The Redemption of Broncho Billy" 1913; "A Romance of the Hills" 1913; "The Rustler's Spur" 1913; "The Rustler's Step-Daughter" 1913; "The Sheriff and the Rustler" 1913; "The Sheriff of Cochise" 1913; "The Sheriff's Child" 1913; "The Sheriff's Honeymoon" 1913; "The Sheriff's Son" 1913; "The Sheriff's Story" 1913; "The Sheriff's Wife" 1913; "The Story the Desert Told" 1913; "The Struggle" 1913; "The Tenderfoot Sheriff" 1913; "This Life We Live" 1913; "Three Gamblers" 1913; "The Trail of the Snake Band" 1913; "The Two Ranchmen" 1913; "Two Western Paths" 1913; "The Western Law That Failed" 1913; "A Western Sister's Devotion" 1913; "Where the Mountains Meet" 1913; "Why Broncho Billy Left Bear County" 1913; "A Widow of Nevada" 1913; "The Arm of Vengeance" 1914; "The Atonement" 1914; "Broncho Billy a Friend in Need" 1914; "Broncho Billy and the Bad Man" 1914; "Broncho Billy and the Gambler" 1914; "Broncho Billy and the Greaser" 1914; "Broncho Billy and the Mine Shark" 1914; "Broncho Billy and the Rattler" 1914; "Broncho Billy and the Red Man" 1914; "Broncho Billy and the Settler's Daughter" 1914; "Broncho Billy and the Sheriff" 1914; "Broncho Billy and the Sheriff's Office" 1914; "Broncho Billy Butts In" 1914; "Broncho Billy—Favorite" 1914; "Broncho Billy—Guardian" 1914; "Broncho Billy—Gunman" 1914; "Broncho Billy—Outlaw" 1914; "Broncho Billy Puts One Over" 1914; "Broncho Billy

Rewarded" 1914; "Broncho Billy the Vagabond" 1914; "Broncho Billy, Trapper" 1914; "Broncho Billy Wins Out" 1914; "Broncho Billy's Christmas Spirit" 1914; "Broncho Billy's Close Call" 1914; "Broncho Billy's Cunning Way" 1914; "Broncho Billy's Dad" 1914; "Broncho Billy's Decision" 1914; "Broncho Billy's Double Escape" 1914; "Broncho Billy's Duty" 1914; "Broncho Billy's Fatal Joke" 1914; "Broncho Billy's Indian Romance" 1914; "Broncho Billy's Jealousy" 1914; "Broncho Billy's Judgment" 1914; "Broncho Billy's Leap" 1914; "Broncho Billy's Mission" 1914; "Broncho Billy's Mother" 1914; "Broncho Billy's Punishment" 1914; "Broncho Billy's Scheme" 1914; "Broncho Billy's Sermon" 1914; "Broncho Billy's True Love" 1914; "Broncho Billy's Wild Ride" 1914; "The Calling of Jim Barton" 1914; "The Cast of the Die" 1914; "Dan Cupid, Assayer" 1914; "A Gambler's Way" 1914; "The Good for Nothing" 1914 (Gilbert Sterling); "The Hills of Peace" 1914; "The Interference of Broncho Billy" 1914; "The Night on the Road" 1914; "Red Riding Hood of the Hills" 1914; "Single-Handed" 1914; "The Squatter's Gal" 1914; "The Story of the Old Gun" 1914; "Strategy of Broncho Billy's Sweetheart" 1914; "The Tell-Tale Hand" 1914; "Through Trackless Sands" 1914; "The Treachery of Broncho Billy's Pal" 1914; "The Warning" 1914; "The Weaker's Strength" 1914; "What Came to Bar Q" 1914; "Andy of the Royal Mounted" 1915; "The Bachelor's Baby" 1915; "The Bachelor's Burglar" 1915; "Broncho Billy and the Baby" 1915; "Broncho Billy and the Card Sharp" 1915; "Broncho Billy and the Claim Jumpers" 1915; "Broncho Billy and the Escaped Bandits" 1915; "Broncho Billy and the False Note" 1915; "Broncho Billy and the Land Grabber" 1915; "Broncho Billy and the Lumber King" 1915; "Broncho Billy and the MacGuire Gang" 1915; "Broncho Billy and the Parson" 1915; "Broncho Billy and the Posse" 1915; "Broncho Billy and the Vigilante" 1915; "Broncho Billy Begins Life Anew" 1915; "Broncho Billy Evens Matters" 1915; "Broncho Billy Misled" 1915; "Broncho Billy, Sheepman" 1915; "Broncho Billy Steps In" 1915; "Broncho Billy Well Repaid" 1915; "Broncho Billy's Brother" 1915; "Broncho Billy's Cowardly Brother" 1915; "Broncho Billy's Greaser Deputy" 1915; "Broncho Billy's Love Affair" 1915; "Broncho Billy's Marriage" 1915; "Broncho Billy's Parents" 1915; "Broncho Billy's Protege" 1915;

"Broncho Billy's Sentence" 1915; "Broncho Billy's Surrender" 1915; "Broncho Billy's Teachings" 1915; "Broncho Billy's Vengeance" 1915; "Broncho Billy's Word of Honor" 1915; "The Burglar's Godfather" 1915; "A Christmas Revenge" 1915; "The Convict's Threat" 1915; "The Escape of Broncho Billy" 1915; "The Face at the Curtain" 1915; "Her Return" 1915; "His Regeneration" 1915; "His Wife's Secret" 1915; "The Indian's Narrow Escape" 1915; "Ingomar of the Hills" 1915; "The Little Prospector" 1915; "The Other Girl" 1915; "The Outlaw's Awakening" 1915; "The Revenue Agent" 1915; "Too Much Turkey" 1915; "An Unexpected Romance" 1915; "The Western Way" 1915; "The Book Agent's Romance" 1916; "Broncho Billy and the Revenue Agent" 1916; "Humanity" 1917; "Naked Hands" 1918; "Shootin' Mad" 1918 (Broncho Billy); "Red Blood and Yellow" 1919 (Jack/Jim); "The Son of a Gun" 1919 (the Son of a Gun); "The Bounty Killer" 1965 (Old Man).

Anderson, Gus. Films: "Flying Lariats" 1931 (Sheriff); "Riders of the Cactus" 1931 (Ranger Captain).

Anderson, Herbert (1917-6/11/94). Films: "Night Passage" 1957 (Will Renner). ¶TV: *Rawhide*—"Incident of the Rusty Shotgun" 1-9-64 (Sheriff Burr); *Gunsmoke*—"Trip West" 5-2-64 (Elwood Hardacre); *Daniel Boone*—"Thirty Pieces of Silver" 3-28-68 (Wyman).

Anderson, James (Kyle James; Kyle Anderson) (1921-9/14/69). Films: "Along the Great Divide" 1951 (Dan Roden); "The Duel at Silver Creek" 1952 (Rat Face Blake); "Hellgate" 1952; "The Last Musketeer" 1952 (Russ Tasker); "Arrowhead" 1953 (Jerry August); "The Great Jesse James Raid" 1953 (Jorrette); "Drums Across the River" 1954 (Jed Walker); "At Gunpoint" 1955 (Barlow); "The Marauders" 1955 (Louis Ferber); "Seven Angry Men" 1955 (Thompson); "The Violent Men" 1955 (Hank Purdue); "Friendly Persuasion" 1956 (Poor Loser); "Fury at Gunsight Pass" 1956 (O'Neil); "The Rawhide Years" 1956 (Deputy Wade); "Running Target" 1956 (Strothers); "The Big Land" 1957 (Cole); "The Ballad of Cable Hogue" 1970 (Preacher); "Little Big Man" 1971 (Sergeant). ¶TV: *The Gene Autry Show*—"The Lawless Press" 1-25-52, "Ruthless Renegade" 2-8-52; *The Cisco Kid*—"The Census Taker" 6-7-52, "The Lowest Bidder" 4-4-53, "Sundown's Gun" 4-18-53, "Choctaw Justice" 12-26-53; *The Ad-*

ventures of Rin Tin Tin—"The Star Witness" 12-9-55; *Gunsmoke*—"Magnus" 12-24-55 (Lucifer Jones), "The Do-Badder" 1-6-62, "The Violators" 10-17-64 (George Hewitt), "The Bounty Hunter" 10-30-65 (Cowboy), "The Wrong Man" 10-29-66 (Harmon), "Vengeance" 10-2-67 & 10-9-67 (Hiller), "Blood Money" 1-22-68 (Jesse Hill); *My Friend Flicka*—"Wind from Heaven" 2-3-56; *Loretta Young Show*—"The Wise One" 3-26-56 (Burton); *Circus Boy*—"White Eagle" 11-25-56 (Taylor); *Zane Grey Theater*—"No Man Living" 1-11-57 (Tatum), "Back Trail" 2-1-57 (Lomax), "Man in the Middle" 2-11-60 (Waco); *Maverick*—"The Long Hunt" 10-20-57 (Whitey), "Prey of the Cat" 12-7-58 (1st Deputy), "Maverick at Law" 2-26-61 (Wooster); *Colt .45*—"Young Gun" 12-13-57 (Jeff Lanier), "Don't Tell Joe" 6-14-59 (Shift Wilson); *The Restless Gun*—"The Gold Star" 5-19-58 (Bill Coughan); *Jefferson Drum*—"The Post" 7-4-58 (Ritter); *Rawhide*—"Incident West of Lano" 2-27-59, "Incident of the Running Man" 5-5-61, "The Black Sheep" 11-10-61 (Sheriff), "The Enormous Fist" 10-2-64 (Sheriff); *The Californians*—"Stampede at Misery Flats" 3-17-59 (Piute); *The Texan*—"No Place to Stop" 4-27-59 (Crockett), "Rough Track to Payday" 12-28-59, "The Invisible Noose" 5-16-60; *Laramie*—"Death Wind" 2-2-60 (Troy Thomas), "Ride the Wild Wind" 10-11-60 (Dallas), "Ladies Day" 10-3-61, "The Jailbreakers" 12-19-61, "Vengeance" 1-8-63, "The Violent Ones" 3-5-63 (Benson); *The Rifleman*—"The Grasshopper" 3-1-60; *Bonanza*—"The Avenger" 3-19-60, "The Dark Gate" 3-4-61, "Little Man—Ten Feet Tall" 5-26-63 (Al); *The Westerner*—"School Days" 10-7-60; *Have Gun Will Travel*—"Vernon Good" 12-31-60 (Codilene), "The Last Judgment" 3-11-61; *Lawman*—"The Break-In" 5-21-61 (Ed Hill); *Frontier Circus*—"Stopover in Paradise" 2-22-62 (Hobey); *Empire*—"A Place to Put a Life" 10-9-62 (Dusty Rhodes); *The Virginian*—"West" 11-20-62 (Otie); *The Dakotas*—"Sanctuary at Crystal Springs" 5-6-63 (Stan Barton); *Temple Houston*—"Letter of the Law" 10-3-63 (Vint Harrod); *Branded*—"Now Join the Human Race" 9-19-65 (Lieutenant Garrett), "Nice Day for a Hanging" 2-6-66 (Frank Allison); *Iron Horse*—"The Man from New Chicago" 11-14-66 (Jim Nations); *The Guns of Will Sonnett*—"Of Lasting Summers and Jim Sonnett" 10-6-67 (Sheriff); *The Legend of Jesse James*—"Vendetta" 10-25-67 (Wallace).

Anderson, Jean (1908-). Films: "Robbery Under Arms" 1958-Brit. (Ma).

Anderson, John (1922-8/7/92). Films: "Last Train from Gun Hill" 1959 (Salesman at Bar); "Geronimo" 1962 (Burns); "Ride the High Country" 1962 (Elder Hammond); "The Hallelujah Trail" 1965 (Sgt. Buell); "Scalplock" TVM-1966 (Standish); "Welcome to Hard Times" 1967 (Ezra/Isaac Maple); "Day of the Evil Gun" 1968 (Capt. Addis); "Five Card Stud" 1968 (Marhsal Dana); "The Great Bank Robbery" 1969 (Kincaid); "Heaven with a Gun" 1969 (Asa Beck); "A Man Called Gannon" 1969 (Capper); "Young Billy Young" 1969 (Frank Boone); "Soldier Blue" 1970 (Col. Iverson); "The Animals" 1971 (Sheriff Allan Pierce); "Man and Boy" 1971 (Stretch); "Molly and Lawless John" 1972 (Sheriff Parker); "Banjo Hackett: Roamin' Free" TVM-1976 (Moose Matlock); "Bridger" TVM-1976 (President Andrew Jackson); "Peter Lundy and the Medicine Hat Stallion" TVM-1977 (Alexander Majors); "The Deerslayer" TVM-1978 (Hutter); "Donner Pass: The Road to Survival" TVM-1978 (Patrick Breen); "Dream West" TVM-1986 (Brigadier General Brooke). ¶TV: *Wyatt Earp*—Regular 1956-58 (Virgil Earp); *You Are There*—"The End of the Dalton Gang" 5-12-57 (Powers); *Zane Grey Theater*—"Episode in Darkness" 11-15-57 (Roy Kelsey), "The Man from Yesterday" 12-22-60 (John Duncan); *Trackdown*—"End of an Outlaw" 11-29-57 (Sam Bass), "Toss Up" 5-20-59; *Gunsmoke*—"Buffalo Man" 1-11-58 (Ben Siple), "Stage Holdup" 10-25-58 (Yermo), "Annie Oakley" 10-24-59 (Dolliver), "The Cousin" 2-2-63 (Cheevers), "Gold Mine" 12-25-65 (Pa Gibbijohn), "The Raid" 1-22-66 & 1-29-66 (Les McConnell), "Mail Drop" 1-28-67 (Roberts), "A Matter of Honor" 11-17-69 (Jess Fletcher), "Roots of Fear" 12-15-69 (Amos Sadler), "Mirage" 1-11-71 (Lemuel), "Kimbro" 2-12-73 (Adam Kimbro); *Tales of Wells Fargo*—"The Renegade" 5-12-58 (Charles Mason), "The Quiet Village" 11-2-59 (Sheriff), "Reward for Gaine" 1-20-62 (Colonel Bledsoe); *Have Gun Will Travel*—"Twenty-Four Hours to North Fork" 5-17-58 (Fred Cooley), "Something to Live For" 12-20-58 (Martin Wheeler), "First, Catch a Tiger" 9-12-59 (Dunne); *The Californians*—"Hangtown" 11-18-58 (Reed Bullard); *The Rifleman*—"The Retired Gun" 1-20-59 (Owney), "Shivaree" 2-3-59, "The Hawk" 4-14-59 (Eli Flack), "The Patsy" 9-29-59 (Sully Hobbs), "Day of the Hunter" 1-5-60 (Cass Callicot), "Mail Order Groom" 1-12-60 (Jess Prophet), "Shotgun Man" 4-12-60 (John Beaumont), "Face of Yesterday" 1-31-61 (Hank Clay), "The Journey Back" 10-30-61 (Will Temple), "The Wanted Man" 9-25-62 (Sam Gibbs), "Incident at Line Shack Six" 1-7-63 (Gangling); *Rough Riders*—"End of the Track" 3-5-59 (John Healey), "Ransom of Rita Renee" 6-11-59 (Matt Kane); *Yancy Derringer*—"Outlaw at Liberty" 5-7-59; *Black Saddle*—"Client: Vardon" 5-30-59 (Clyde Wicker); *The Law of the Plainsman*—"Appointment in Sante Fe" 11-19-59 (Clyde Santee), "Endurance" 1-14-60, "Jeb's Daughter" 4-14-60 (Jeb Wickens); *Bonanza*—"House Divided" 1-16-60, "Rain from Heaven" 10-6-63 (Tulsa Weems), "The Fence" 4-27-69 (Sam Masters); *Overland Trail*—"High Bridge" 2-28-60 (Marshal); *Lawman*—"Left Hand of the Law" 3-27-60 (Lloyd Malone), "Dilemma" 10-30-60 (Harry Carmody), "Hassayampa" 2-12-61 (Hassayampa Edwards); *Bronco*—"Legacy of Twisted Creed" 4-19-60 (Andy Sturdevant); *Wanted—Dead or Alive*—"The Inheritance" 4-30-60 (Deputy Sheriff Fix); *The Rebel*—"Paint a House with Scarlet" 5-15-60 (Ezra Taber); *Johnny Ringo*—"The Derelict" 5-26-60 (Cartwright); *Man from Blackhawk*—"The Money Machine" 6-10-60 (Craig); *The Westerner*—"School Days" 10-7-60 (Lath Ritchie); *Laramie*—"The Long Riders" 10-25-60 (Ed McKeever), "Siege at Jubilee" 10-10-61, "The Perfect Gift" 1-2-62, "A Grave for Cully Brown" 2-13-62 (Sobey), "Bad Blood" 12-4-62 (Leo McCall), "The Violent Ones" 3-5-63 (Bob Blayne); *The Outlaws*—"Starfall" 11-24-60 & 12-1-60 (Simon Shaw); *Death Valley Days*—"A Girl Named Virginia" 12-28-60 (Jim Reed), "The Law of the Round Tent" 4-11-64; *Bat Masterson*—"The Court Martial of Major Mars" 1-12-61 (Major Liam Mars); *Frontier Circus*—"The Hunter and the Hunted" 11-2-61 (Carl); *Cheyenne*—"Retaliation" 11-13-61 (Thackeray Smith); *The Tall Man*—"Night of the Hawk" 3-3-62 (Maj. Jud Randolph); *Alcoa Premiere*—"Second Chance" 3-13-62 (Heber Greshon); *The Virginian*—"Throw a Long Rope" 10-3-62 (Major Cass), "Day of the Scorpion" 9-22-65 (Adam Tercell), "Harvest of Strangers" 2-16-66 (Jeremiah Chilton), "An Echo of Thunder" 10-5-66 (Sam Murrel), "Bitter Autumn" 11-1-67 (Sam McLain), "Home to Methuselah" 11-26-69 (Seth James); *Stoney Burke*—"Spin a Golden Web" 11-26-62 (Bruce Austin), "To Catch the Kaiser" 3-11-63 (Foster Fowler); *Redigo*—"Horns of Hate" 11-19-63 (Lee Cresco); *Rawhide*—"Incident at Hourglass" 3-12-64 (Captain Rankin), "The Retreat" 3-26-65 (Major Cantwell); *A Man Called Shenandoah*—"Survival" 9-20-65 (Sheriff Haley); *The Big Valley*—"Boots with My Father's Name" 9-29-65 (Matt), "The Guilt of Matt Bentell" 12-8-65 (Matt Bentell); *The Legend of Jesse James*—"The Hunted and the Hunters" 4-11-66 (Moss Canby); *The Road West*—"Road to Glory" 2-20-67 (Major Perry); *Iron Horse*—"Five Days to Washtiba" 10-7-67 (Olsen); *Cimarron Strip*—"Whitey" 10-19-67 (Arn Tinker); *Dundee and the Culhane*—11-15-67 (Kintpaush); *Lancer*—"Blood Rock" 10-1-68 (Sheriff); *Here Come the Brides*—"A Man's Errand" 3-19-69 (Silas); *Bearcats!*—12-30-71 (Judge O'Brien); *Hec Ramsey*—"The Mystery of Chalk Hill" 2-18-73 (Gabe Rawlins), "Dead Heat" 2-3-74 (Harry Munson), "The Road to the Cradle" 11-7-69 (Gentleman Harry); *Kung Fu*—"Blood Brother" 1-18-73 (Benjamin Dundee), "Cross-ties" 2-21-74 (Youngblood); *The Quest*—"Shanklin" 10-13-76 (Harper); *Bret Maverick*—"The Vulture Also Rises" 3-16-82 (General Frye).

Anderson, Judith (1898-1/3/92). Films: "Pursued" 1947 (Medora Callum); "The Furies" 1950 (Florence Burnett); "A Man Called Horse" 1970 (Buffalo Cow Head). ¶TV: *Wagon Train*—"The Felezia Kingdom Story" 11-18-59 (Felezia Kingdom).

Anderson, Kyle. see Anderson, James.

Anderson, Loni (1944-). Films: "The Gambler V: Playing for Keeps" TVM-1994 (Fanny Porter).

Anderson, Mary (1859-5/29/40). Films: "By Right of Possession" 1917 (Kate Saxon); "The Divorcee" 1917 (Wanda Carson); "Sunlight's Last Raid" 1917 (Janet Warned); "Johnny, Get Your Gun" 1919 (Ruth Gordon); "Vanishing Trails" 1920-serial; "The Half-Breed" 1922 (Evelyn Huntington).

Anderson, Mary. Films: "Passage West" 1951 (Myra Johnson). ¶TV: *Tombstone Territory*—"Shoot Out at Dark" 1-8-58 (Doris); *The Californians*—"The First Gold Brick" 1-6-59 (Dora Morgan); *Lawman*—"The Actor" 5-27-62 (Martha Carson); *The Travels of Jaimie McPheeters*—"The Day of the Toll Takers" 1-5-64 (Hannah Devlin).

Anderson, Melissa Sue (1962-). Films: "Little House on the Prairie" TVM-1974 (Mary Ingalls). ¶TV: *Little House on the Prairie*—Regular 1974-82 (Mary Ingalls).

Anderson, Jr., Michael (1943-). Films: "The Glory Guys" 1965 (Martin Hale); "Major Dundee" 1965 (Tim Ryan); "The Sons of Katie Elder" 1965 (Bud Elder); "The Daughters of Joshua Cabe" TVM-1972 (Cole Wetherall); "Shootout in a One-Dog Town" TVM-1974 (Billy Boy). ¶TV: *Stoney Burke*—"Gold-Plated Maverick" 1-7-63 (David Latimer); *The Legend of Jesse James*—"Put Me in Touch with Jesse" 9-27-65 (Cass Pritchard); *The Monroes*—Regular 1966-67 (Clayt Monroe).

Anderson, Mignon (1892-2/25/83). Films: "Beating Back" 1914; "The Claim" 1918 (Kate MacDonald); "The Shooting Party" 1918; "The Midnight Stage" 1919 (Mary Lynch); "The Secret Peril" 1919; "Cupid's Brand" 1921 (Neva Hedden).

Anderson, Nellie. Films: "Little Red Decides" 1918 (Mrs. Jones).

Anderson, Nick. see Zamperla, Nazareno.

Anderson, Richard (1926-). Films: "The Vanishing Westerner" 1950 (Jeff Jackson); "Across the Wide Missouri" 1951 (Dick); "Escape from Fort Bravo" 1953 (Lt. Beecher); "The Gunfight at Dodge City" 1959 (Dave); "The Ride to Hangman's Tree" 1967 (Steve Carlson); "Macho Callahan" 1970 (Senior Officer); "The Honkers" 1972 (Royce). ¶TV: *Zane Grey Theater*—"Black Is for Grief" 4-12-57 (Sheriff Bates), "Medal for Valor" 12-25-58 (Adam Stewart); *Jefferson Drum*—"The Lawless" 7-18-58 (Varner); *Zorro*—"The Practical Joker" 12-11-58 (Ricardo Del Amo), "The Flaming Arrow" 12-18-58 (Ricardo Del Amo), "Zorro Fights a Duel" 12-25-58 (Ricardo Del Amo), "Amnesty for Zorro" 1-1-59 (Ricardo Del Amo); *The Rifleman*—"One Went to Denver" 3-17-59 (Tom Birch), "The Lariat" 3-29-60 (Lariat Jones), "Miss Bertie" 12-27-60 (Duke Jennings), "Flowers by the Door" 1-10-61 (Jason Gowdy), "Milly's Brother" 4-23-62 (Harry Chase), "The Bullet" 2-25-63 (Griff); *Wagon Train*—"The Matthew Lowry Story" 4-1-59 (Matthew Lowry); *The Law of the Plainsman*—"Cavern of the Wind" 4-21-60 (Lee Talent); *Stagecoach West*—"The Land Beyond" 10-11-60 (Cole Dawson); *Wanted—Dead or Alive*—"Three for One" 12-21-60

(Tom), "Epitaph" 2-8-61 (Sheriff Jim Kramer); *Redigo*—"The Crooked Circle" 10-22-63 (Tom Walker); *Gunsmoke*—"Jonah Hutchison" 11-21-64 (Samuel Hutchison), "The War Priest" 1-5-70 (Gregorio), "The Guns of Cibola Blanca" 9-23-74 & 9-30-74 (Coltraine); *Death Valley Days*—"Kate Melville and the Law" 6-20-65 (Judge Lander); *The Big Valley*—"Last Train to the Fair" 4-27-66 (Travers), "The Disappearance" 11-6-67 (Mel Trevor), "Fall of a Hero" 2-5-68 (Nathan Springer), "The Long Ride" 11-25-68 (Hen Matson), "Alias Nellie Handley" 2-24-69 (Warden Garreck); *Cimarron Strip*—"The Legend of Jud Starr" 9-14-67; *Bonanza*—"Showdown at Tahoe" 11-19-67 (Jamison Fillmore); *Wild Wild West*—"The Night of the Headless Woman" 1-5-68 (Commissioner James Jeffers); *Daniel Boone*—"For Want of a Hero" 3-6-69 (the Sergeant); *Alias Smith and Jones*—"Never Trust an Honest Man" 4-15-71.

Anderson, Richard Dean (1950-). TV: *Legend*—Regular 1995 (Ernest Pratt/Nicodemus Legend).

Anderson, Rick. Films: "King of Dodge City" 1941 (Judge Lynch); "Riders of the Badlands" 1941 (Sheriff Taylor); "Cowboy Serenade" 1942; "The Lone Star Vigilantes" 1942 (Lige Miller); "Prairie Gunsmoke" 1942; "Thunder River Feud" 1942 (Colonel).

Anderson, Robert G. "Bob" (1890-). Films: "The Foreman of the Bar-Z Ranch" 1915; "The Gold Dust and the Squaw" 1915; "Pals in Blue" 1915; "Cyclone Smith Plays Trumps" 1919; "The Phantom Fugitive" 1919; "Tempest Cody Flirts with Death" 1919; "Tempest Cody Hits the Trail" 1919; "Tempest Cody Rides Wild" 1919; "Under Pressure" 1922; "The Eternal Struggle" 1923 (Olaf Olafson); "West of the Pecos" 1945 (Gambler); "Gold Strike" 1950-short; "Gunfire" 1950 (Bob Ford); "Winchester '73" 1950 (Bassett); "Silver City" 1951 (Rucker); "Cripple Creek" 1952 (Muldoon); "The Lawless Breed" 1952 (Wild Bill Hickok); "Untamed Frontier" 1952 (Ezra McCloud); "Born to the Saddle" 1953; "Take Me to Town" 1953 (Chuck); "The Outlaw Stallion" 1954 (Martin); "Fury at Gunsight Pass" 1956 (Sam Morris); "Showdown at Abilene" 1956 (Sprague); "The Phantom Stagecoach" 1957 (Varney); "The Tall T" 1957 (Jace); "Buchanan Rides Alone" 1958 (Waldo Peek); "The Left-Handed Gun" 1958 (Hill); "The Gambler Wore a Gun" 1961 (Tray

Larkin); "Stagecoach to Dancer's Rock" 1962 (Carl "Whip" Mott); "Advance to the Rear" 1964 (Steamer Captain); "Young Billy Young" 1969 (Gambler). ¶TV: *Gunsmoke*—"Matt Gets It" 9-10-55 (Jim Hill), "The Blacksmith" 9-17-60 (Tolman), "Big Man" 3-25-61 (Mike Boatwright), "Hung High" 11-14-64 (Burke); *My Friend Flicka*—"Act of Loyalty" 12-8-55, "Old Danny" 3-2-56 (Hank Miller); *Frontier*—"The Well" 4-8-56 (Lane), "A Somewhere Voice" 5-6-56 (Lou); *Zane Grey Theater*—"The Lariat" 11-2-56 (Rack Williams); *Colt .45*—"One Good Turn" 11-29-57 (Cranly); *Wyatt Earp*—"One-Man Army" 1-7-58 (Drum Denman), "The Mysterious Cowhand" 10-14-58 (Tim Corkle); *Bat Masterson*—"The Treasure of Worry Hill" 12-3-58 (Richard Woodman); *Tales of Wells Fargo*—"Lola Montez" 2-16-59 (Zach), "The Dowry" 7-10-61 (Constable Willets); *Wagon Train*—"The Annie Griffith Story" 2-25-59 (Blade Griffith), "The Nancy Davis Story" 5-16-62 (Rafer); *Have Gun Will Travel*—"Commanche" 5-16-59 (Sam Dolan); *Wichita Town*—"The Night the Cowboys Roared" 9-30-59 (Aeneas MacLinahan), "Drifting" 10-28-59 (Mac Linehan); *Rawhide*—"Incident of the Thirteenth Man" 10-23-59 (Gene Matson); *Pony Express*—"Replacement" 3-30-60; *The Texan*—"The Nomad" 4-18-60 (Fraiser); *Cheyenne*—"Two Trails to Santa Fe" 10-28-60 (Jones), "One Way Ticket" 2-19-62 (John Warren); *Two Faces West*—"The Proud Man" 12-26-60 (Amos Johnson), "The Lesson" 5-22-61; *Bonanza*—"Cut-Throat Junction" 3-18-61; *Bronco*—"Ride the Whirlwind" 1-15-62 (Len Peters); *Empire*—"The Convention" 5-14-63 (Mackey); *Laramie*—"The Road to Helena" 5-21-63; *Redigo*—"The Crooked Circle" 10-22-63 (Pat Royal), "Papa-San" 11-12-63 (Clayton); *Daniel Boone*—"The Returning" 1-14-65 (Donovan), "The Young Ones" 2-23-67 (Sam Ogilvie), "A Matter of Vengeance" 2-26-70; *F Troop*—"Corporal Agarn's Farewell to the Troops" 10-5-65 (Bob Colton); *A Man Called Shenandoah*—"Obion-1866" 10-25-65; *The Legend of Jesse James*—"Benjamin Bates" 2-28-66 (Sheriff); *Death Valley Days*—"The Firebrand" 4-30-66 (General Kerany), "The Taming of Trudy Bell" 12-6-69; *The Rounders*—9-6-66 (Ez Bernstein).

Anderson, Roger. Films: "Cattle Queen" 1951 (Lefty); "Rancho Notorious" 1952 (Red).

Anderson, S. Newton (1953-).

TV: *Maverick*—"A Rage for Vengeance" 1-12-58 (Sanderson); *The Virginian*—"The Golden Door" 3-13-63 (Larson); *Bonanza*—"Ride the Wind" 1-16-66 & 1-23-66 (Gus), "The Clarion" 2-9-69 (Sam); *Cliffhangers*—"The Secret Empire" 1979 (Kalek).

Anderson, Stanley. Films: "Son of the Morning Star" TVM-1991 (Ulysses S. Grant).

Anderson, Stuart. Films: "Texas Across the River" 1966 (Yancy Cottle). ¶TV: *The Virginian*—"The Horse Fighter" 12-15-65 (Strafton), "That Saunders Woman" 3-30-66 (Billy Conklin); *Laredo*—"Finnegan" 10-21-66 (Kid Case); *Bonanza*—"The Gentle Ones" 10-29-67 (Trask); *Cimarron Strip*—"The Roarer" 11-2-67.

Anderson, Thomas (1906-). Films: "The Legend of Nigger Charley" 1972 (Shadow).

Anderson, Warner (1911-8/26/76). Films: "Oklahoma Outlaws" 1943-short; "Trial by Trigger" 1944-short; "Bad Bascomb" 1946 (Luther Mason); "Only the Valiant" 1951 (Trooper Rutledge); "Santa Fe" 1951 (Dave Baxter); "The Last Posse" 1953 (Robert Emerson); "Drum Beat" 1954 (Gen. Canby); "The Yellow Tomahawk" 1954 (Major Ives); "A Lawless Street" 1955 (Hamer Thorne); "The Violent Men" 1955 (Jim McCloud); "Rio Conchos" 1964 (Col. Wagner). ¶TV: *Death Valley Days*—"The Stranger" 3-15-60 (John Gaunt).

Andersson, Bibi (1935-). Films: "Duel at Diablo" 1966 (Ellen Grange).

Andes, Keith (1920-). Films: "Pillars of the Sky" 1956 (Capt. Tom Gaxton). ¶TV: *Have Gun Will Travel*—"The Piano" 11-11-61 (Franz Lister); *The Rifleman*—"The Debit" 3-5-62 (Renolds); *Death Valley Days*—"Paid in Full" 1-3-65 (Col. Rob Hunter); *Branded*—"Price of a Name" 5-23-65 (Roy Harris); *Daniel Boone*—"The Williamsburg Cannon" 1-12-67 & 1-19-67 (Beb Moore); *Gunsmoke*—"Matt's Love Story" 9-24-73 (Starcourt).

Andre, Annette (1939-). TV: *Whiplash*—"Storm River" 8-12-61, "Dark Runs the Sea" 9-2-61; *The Guns of Will Sonnett*—"The Sins of the Father" 2-23-68 (Leah).

Andre, Carl (1905-3/20/72). Films: "The Paleface" 1948 (Horseman); "Streets of Laredo" 1949 (Townsman); "Colt .45" 1950; "Dallas" 1950 (Cowpuncher); "Carson City" 1952; "The Charge at Feather River" 1953 (Hudkins); "Thunder Over the Plains" 1953; "Tall Man Riding" 1955; "The Violent Men" 1955 (Dryer).

Andre, Carole (1953-). Films: "Face to Face" 1967-Ital.; "Here We Go Again, Eh Providence?" 1973-Ital./Fr./Span. (Countess Pamela de Ortega).

Andre, Dorothy. Films: "Wildcat of Tucson" 1941; "Callaway Went Thataway" 1951 (Girl); "Cattle Queen of Montana" 1954. ¶TV: *The Roy Rogers Show*—"False Faces" 2-5-56.

Andre, E.J. (1908-9/6/84). Films: "Showdown" 1963; "The Shakiest Gun in the West" 1968; "The Duchess and the Dirtwater Fox" 1976. ¶TV: *Wagon Train*—"The Patience Miller Story" 1-11-61 (Mr. Wise), "The Geneva Balfour Story" 1-20-64; *Whispering Smith*—"Dark Circle" 9-4-61 (Philo); *Bonanza*—"The Long Night" 5-6-62, "A Passion for Justice" 9-29-63, "The Trouble with Trouble" 10-25-70 (Judge), "Shanklin" 2-13-72 (Yost); *Rawhide*—"Abilene" 5-18-62 (Doctor); *The Virginian*—"The Man Who Couldn't Die" 1-30-63 (Alex), "A Slight Case of Charity" 2-10-65; *The Dakotas*—"The Chooser of the Slain" 4-22-63 (Judge Langford); *Temple Houston*—"The Siege at Thayer's Bluff" 11-7-63 (Judge Diversey); *Wild Wild West*—"The Night of the Howling Light" 12-17-65 (Superintendant), "The Night of the Doomsday Formula" 10-4-68 (Prof. Crane); *Daniel Boone*—"The Accused" 3-24-66 (Peterson); *The Legend of Jesse James*—"Wanted: Dead and Only" 5-2-66 (Judge Dawson); *Iron Horse*—"Right of Way Through Paradise" 10-3-66; *The Road West*—"Long Journey to Leavenworth" 10-17-66 (Willard); *Laredo*—"The Last of the Caesars—Absolutely" 12-2-66 (Silversmith); *Shane*—"The Great Invasion" 12-17-66 & 12-24-66 (Bullhead O'Reilly); *The Big Valley*—"The Lady from Mesa" 4-3-67 (Sam Williams); *Death Valley Days*—"Along Came Mariana" 5-27-67 (Domingo); *The Guns of Will Sonnett*—"Look for the Hound Dog" 1-26-68, "Joby" 11-1-68; *Gunsmoke*—"A Noose for Dobie Price" 3-4-68 (Joe Katcher), "Eleven Dollars" 10-30-72 (Jeb Spender); *Lancer*—"Devil's Blessing" 4-22-69; *The High Chaparral*—"Spokes" 9-25-70 (Trapper); *Nichols*—"Ketcham Power" 11-11-71 (Ed); *The Chisholms*—3-1-80 (Caleb Ives).

Andre, Gaby (1937-8/9/72). Films: "Sign of Zorro" 1964-Ital./Span.

Andre, Lona (1915-). Films: "The Mysterious Rider" 1933 (Dorothy); "Border Brigands" 1935 (Diane); "Under the Pampas Moon" 1935 (Girl); "Custer's Last Stand" 1936-serial (Belle Meade); "Lucky Terror" 1936 (Ann Thornton); "The Plainsman" 1936 (Southern Belle); "Trailing Trouble" 1937 (Patience Blair); "Ghost Valley Raiders" 1940 (Linda Marly).

Andrece, Alyce. TV: *Bonanza*—"The Lady and the Mountain Lion" 2-23-69 (Jan).

Andrece, Rhae. TV: *Bonanza*—"The Lady and the Mountain Lion" 2-23-69 (Janice).

Andreeff, Starr. Films: "Outlaws" TVM-1986 (Bambi).

Andreoli, Annabella (1939-). Films: "The Five Man Army" 1969-Ital. (Perla).

Andress, Ursula (1936-). Films: "Four for Texas" 1964 (Maxine Richter); "Red Sun" 1971-Fr./Ital./Span. (Cristina); "Mexico in Flames" 1982-Rus./Mex./Ital. (Mabel Dodge).

Andreu, Simon (1941-). Films: "I Do Not Forgive … I Kill!" 1968-Span./Ital.; "Bad Man's River" 1971-Span./Ital./Fr. (Angel); "Those Dirty Dogs!" 1973-U.S./Ital./Span. (Angelo Sanchez); "Triumphs of a Man Called Horse" 1984 (Gance).

Andrews, Dana (1909-12/17/92). Films: "Kit Carson" 1940 (Capt. John C. Fremont); "Lucky Cisco Kid" 1940 (Sgt. Dunn); "The Westerner" 1940 (Bart Cobble); "Belle Starr" 1941 (Major Thomas Crall); "The Ox-Bow Incident" 1943 (Donald Martin); "Canyon Passage" 1946 (Logan Stuart); "Three Hours to Kill" 1954 (Jim Guthrie); "Smoke Signal" 1955 (Brett Halliday); "Strange Lady in Town" 1955 (Dr. Rork O'Brien); "Comanche" 1956 (Read); "Town Tamer" 1965 (Tom Rosser); "Johnny Reno" 1966 (Johnny Reno); "Take a Hard Ride" 1974-Ital./Brit./Ger. (Morgan).

Andrews, David. Films: "Wild Horses" TVM-1985 (Dean Ellis); "Wyatt Earp" 1994 (James Earp).

Andrews, Edward (1914-3/9/85). Films: "Tension at Table Rock" 1956 (Kirk); "Trooper Hook" 1957 (Charlie Travers); "The Fiend Who Walked the West" 1958 (Judge Parker); "The Man from Galveston" 1964 (Hyde); "The Over-the-Hill Gang" TVM-1969 (Mayor Nard Lundy); "The Intruders" TVM-1970 (Elton Dykstra); "Lacy and the Mississippi Queen" TVM-1978 (Isaac

Harrison). ¶TV: *Cheyenne*—"The Argonauts" 11-1-55 (Duncan); *The Outlaws*—"The Waiting Game" 1-19-61 (Veckser); *Rawhide*—"Incident at Rio Salado" 9-29-61 (Ben Andrews), "Incident of the Querencias" 12-7-62 (Lije Crowning); *Frontier Circus*—"The Race" 5-3-62 (Duke Felix Otway); *Bonanza*—"Song in the Dark" 1-13-63 (Johnson), "Rock-a-Bye, Hoss" 10-10-71 (Bert); *Temple Houston*—"The Man from Galveston" 1963 (Hyde); *Gunsmoke*—"Malachi" 11-13-65 (Ethan Harper); *Wild Wild West*—"The Night of the Braine" 2-17-67 (Mr. Braine); *The Guns of Will Sonnett*—"What's in a Name?" 1-5-68; *The Kowboys*—Pilot 7-13-70 (Mayor); *Alias Smith and Jones*—"The McCreedy Bush" 1-21-71 (Ralph Peterson); *Barbary Coast*—"Irish Coffee" 10-13-75 (Grimes); *The Life and Times of Grizzly Adams*—1-11-78 (Marvin).

Andrews, Laverne (1915-5/8/67). Films: "Moonlight and Cactus" 1944 (Laverne).

Andrews, Lloyd "Slim" (1906-4/3/92). Films: "Breed of the West" 1930; "Arizona Frontier" 1940 (Slim Chance); "Cowboy from Sundown" 1940 (Judge Pritchard); "The Golden Trail" 1940 (Slim); "Pals of the Silver Sage" 1940 (Cactus); "Rhythm of the Rio Grande" 1940; "Take Me Back to Oklahoma" 1940 (Slim); "The Driftin' Kid" 1941; "Dynamite Canyon" 1941 (Slim); "The Pioneers" 1941 (Slim); "Ridin' the Cherokee Trail" 1941 (Slim); "Riding the Sunset Trail" 1941 (Jasper Raines); "Rollin' Home to Texas" 1941 (Slim); "Wanderers of the West" 1941 (Slim); "Cowboy Serenade" 1942; "The Cyclone Kid" 1942 (Pop Smith); "The Lone Rider and the Bandit" 1942; "The Sombrero Kid" 1942 (Panamint); "The Dead Don't Dream" 1948 (Jesse Williams); "Buffalo Bill in Tomahawk Territory" 1952 (Cactus).

Andrews, Lois (1921-4/4/68). Films: "Western Heritage" 1948 (Cleo); "Rustlers" 1949 (Trixie).

Andrews, Mark. TV: *Laramie*—"The Dynamiters" 3-6-62 (Dave Boyd).

Andrews, Maxine (1918-10/21/95). Films: "Moonlight and Cactus" 1944 (Maxine).

Andrews, Nancy (1921-7/29/89). TV: *Pistols 'n' Petticoats*—"A Crooked Line" 9-17-66 (Ma Turner).

Andrews, Patty (1920-). Films: "Moonlight and Cactus" 1944 (Patty).

Andrews, Stanley (1891-6/23/69). Films: "Nevada" 1935 (Cawthorne); "Wanderer of the Wasteland" 1935 (Sheriff Collishaw); "Drift Fence" 1936 (Clay Jackson); "The Texas Rangers" 1936 (Henchman); "White Fang" 1936 (Sergeant Drake); "Wild Brian Kent" 1936 (Tony Baxter); "The Bad Man of Brimstone" 1937 (Clergyman); "High, Wide and Handsome" 1937 (Lem Moulton); "Forbidden Valley" 1938 (Hoke Lanning); "The Lone Ranger" 1938-serial (Mark Smith); "The Mysterious Rider" 1938 (William Bellounds, Foreman); "Prairie Moon" 1938 (Frank Welch); "Shine on Harvest Moon" 1938 (Jackson); "Racketeers of the Range" 1939; "Union Pacific" 1939 (Dr. Harkness); "Brigham Young—Frontiersman" 1940 (Hyrum Smith); "Geronimo" 1940 (Presidential Advisor); "King of the Royal Mounted" 1940-serial (Tom Merritt, Sr.); "Kit Carson" 1940 (Larkin); "Mark of Zorro" 1940 (Commanding Officer); "Rainbow Over the Range" 1940 (Slim Chance); "The Westerner" 1940 (Sheriff); "In Old Colorado" 1941 (George Davidson); "North to the Klondike" 1942 (Jim Allen); "Valley of the Sun" 1942 (Major); "Canyon City" 1943 (Alfred Johnson); "Daredevils of the West" 1943-serial (Colonel Andrews); "In Old Oklahoma" 1943 (Mason); "The Ox-Bow Incident" 1943 (Bartlett); "Riding High" 1943 (Reynolds); "Tucson Raiders" 1944 (Governor); "Vigilantes of Dodge City" 1944; "Code of the Lawless" 1945 (Chad Hilton, Sr.); "The Daltons Ride Again" 1945 (Walters); "Trail to Vengeance" 1945 (Sheriff); "Bad Bascomb" 1946 (Colonel Cartright); "God's Country" 1946; "Smoky" 1946 (Rancher); "The Fabulous Texan" 1947; "The Michigan Kid" 1947 (Sheriff); "Robin Hood of Texas" 1947 (Mr. Hamby); "The Sea of Grass" 1947 (Sheriff); "Trail Street" 1947 (Ferguson); "The Adventures of Frank and Jesse James" 1948-serial (Jim Powell); "Last of the Wild Horses" 1948 (Ferguson); "The Man from Colorado" 1948 (Roger); "Northwest Stampede" 1948 (Bowles); "The Paleface" 1948 (Commissioner Emerson); "Panhandle" 1948 (Tyler); "The Return of Wildfire" 1948 (Pop Marlowe); "Sinister Journey" 1948; "The Valiant Hombre" 1948 (Sheriff Dodge); "Brimstone" 1949 (Mr. Winslow); "Brothers in the Saddle" 1949; "Cheyenne Cowboy" 1949-short; "The Last Bandit" 1949 (Jeff Baldwin); "Tough Assignment" 1949 (Patterson); "Trail of the Yukon" 1949 (Rogers); "The Arizona Cowboy" 1950 (Jim Davenport); "Across the Badlands" 1950 (Sheriff Crocker); "Copper Canyon" 1950 (Bartender); "Mule Train" 1950 Chalmers); "The Nevadan" 1950 (Deputy Morgan); "Outcast of Black Mesa" 1950 (Sheriff Grasset); "Salt Lake Raiders" 1950 (Head Marshal); "Short Grass" 1950 (Pete); "Streets of Ghost Town" 1950 (Sheriff); "Trigger, Jr." 1950 (Rancher Wilkins); "Two Flags West" 1950 (Col. Hoffman); "Under Mexicali Stars" 1950 (Announcer); "West of Wyoming" 1950 (Simon); "Al Jennings of Oklahoma" 1951 (Marshal Slattery); "Hot Lead" 1951 (Warden); "Saddle Legion" 1951 (Chief Layton); "Silver Canyon" 1951 (Maj. Weatherly); "The Texas Rangers" 1951 (Marshal Goree); "Utah Wagon Train" 1951 (Sheriff); "Vengeance Valley" 1951 (Mead Calhoun); "Fargo" 1952; "Kansas Territory" 1952 (Governor); "Lone Star" 1952 (Man); "The Man from Black Hills" 1952 (Pop Fallon); "Montana Belle" 1952 (Marshal Combs); "Thundering Caravans" 1952 (Henry Scott); "Waco" 1952 (Judge); "Canadian Mounties vs. Atomic Invaders" 1953-serial (Anderson); "El Paso Stampede" 1953 (Marshal Banning); "Ride, Vaquero!" 1953 (Gen. Sheridan); "Dawn at Socorro" 1954 (Old Man Ferris); "Southwest Passage" 1954 (Constable Bartlett); "Treasure of Ruby Hills" 1955 (Garvey); "Frontier Gambler" 1956; "Star in the Dust" 1956 (Ben Smith); "The Three Outlaws" 1956. ¶TV: *The Lone Ranger*—"High Heels" 11-17-49, "The Man with Two Faces" 2-23-50, "Drink of Water" 10-26-50, "Two Gold Lockets" 2-15-51, "Delayed Action" 11-6-52, "The School Story" 1-20-55; *The Gene Autry Show*—"Blackwater Valley Feud" 9-3-50, "Doublecross Valley" 9-10-50, "The Sheriff of Santa Rosa" 12-24-50, "T.N.T." 12-31-50 (Colonel Towne), "Cold Decked" 9-15-53 (Ben Tansey), "Rio Renegades" 9-29-53, "Santa Fe Raiders" 7-6-54, "Sharpshooter" 8-3-54, "Civil War at Deadwood" 9-14-54, "Outlaw Warning" 10-2-54; *The Cisco Kid*—"Stolen Bonds" 7-28-51, "Protective Association" 9-8-51; *Sky King*—"The Geiger Detective" 11-4-51; *The Range Rider*—"Outlaw Pistols" 4-5-52; *Death Valley Days*—Regular 1952-65 (the Old Ranger); *Wild Bill Hickok*—"Ambush" 1-13-53, "The Gatling Gun" 5-5-53; *Annie Oakley*—"Annie Finds Strange Treasure" 3-6-54, "The Tomboy" 7-17-54 (Mr. Trumbull),

"Western Privateer" 9-30-56 (Dan Peddicord), "Desperate Men" 2-24-57 (Chet Osgood); *The Roy Rogers Show*—"Doc Stevens' Traveling Store" 7-25-54; *Tales of the Texas Rangers*—"Shorty Sees the Light" 9-10-55, "The Shooting of Sam Bass" 10-15-55 (Marshal MacDonald), "The Black Eyes of Texas" 12-31-55 (Will Thompson), "The Hobo" 1-28-56 (Sheriff); *The Adventures of Rin Tin Tin*—"Rusty Goes to Town" 11-25-55 (Travis), "The Third Rider" 3-16-56 (Sheriff), "The Silent Witness" 3-29-57 (Ed Whitmore), "Apache Stampede" 3-20-59 (Silas Clarkson); *Fury*—"Joey Saves the Day" 12-10-55 (Doc Fullmer); *Judge Roy Bean*—"Outlaw's Son" 1-1-56 (Tutt Clemens); *Wyatt Earp*—"The War of the Colonels" 4-10-56 (Col. Wade); *Circus Boy*—"Corky and the Circus Doctor" 10-21-56 (Pop Warren), "The Masked Marvel" 12-9-56 (Sheriff); *Maverick*—"The Long Hunt" 10-20-57, "The Savage Hills" 2-9-58 (Sheriff Gait).

Andrews, Tige (1923-). TV: *Gunsmoke*—"Gone Straight" 2-9-57 (Mike Postil), "The Jackals" 2-12-68 (Santillo); *Sheriff of Cochise*—"Mechanic" 10-11-57 (Sam); *Zorro*—"The Iron Box" 1-15-59; *The Big Valley*—"Wagonload of Dreams" 1-2-67 (Bodos); *Dundee and the Culhane*—10-18-67 (Nicasio); *Barbary Coast*—"An Iron-Clad Plan" 10-31-75 (Phineas T. James).

Andrews, Tod (1920-11/6/72). Films: "They Died with Their Boots On" 1941 (Cadet Brown); "Hang 'Em High" 1968 (Defense Attorney). ¶TV: *Death Valley Days*—"Yankee Confederate" 10-26-60 (Parker), "The Great Diamond Mines" 3-9-68 (Ralston); *Gunsmoke*—"The Love of Money" 5-27-61 (Myles Cody); *Frontier Circus*—"Karina" 11-9-61 (Jeff Andrews); *Rawhide*—"The Devil and the Deep Blue" 5-11-62 (Holt).

Andrews, William. *see* Forrest, Steve.

Androsky, Carole (1941-). Films: "Little Big Man" 1971 (Caroline).

Angarola, Richard. Films: "Hang 'Em High" 1968; "The Undefeated" 1969 (Petain); "Jeremiah Johnson" 1972 (Lebeaux); "The Master Gunfighter" 1975 (Don Santiago). ¶TV: *Death Valley Days*—"Tribal Justice" 12-22-59 (Quanah Parker), "The Man Who Planted Gold in California" 5-23-70 (Haraszthy); *Man from Blackhawk*—"Portrait of Cynthia" 1-29-60 (Jacques DeVries); *Bonanza*—"Marie, My Love" 2-10-63;

Cimarron Strip—"The Hunted" 10-5-67 (Padre), "Knife in the Darkness" 1-25-68; *The High Chaparral*—"The Doctor from Dodge" 10-29-67 (Jacques Dubois); *Daniel Boone*—"Fort New Madrid" 2-15-68 (Captain Miro), "The Fleeing Nuns" 10-24-68 (Monet); *Wild Wild West*—"The Night of the Spanish Curse" 1-3-69 (Allesandro); *Gunsmoke*—"Kitowa!" 2-16-70 (Quinchero); *How the West Was Won*—Episode Two 2-7-77 (Chief Claw).

Angel, Heather (1909-12/13/86). Films: "Bold Caballero" 1936 (Lady Isabella Palma); "Daniel Boone" 1936 (Virginia Randolph); "The Last of the Mohicans" 1936 (Cora Munro); "Western Gold" 1937 (Jeannie Thatcher). ¶TV: *Lawman*—"The Grubstake" 4-16-61 (Stephanie Collins); *The Guns of Will Sonnett*—"A Fool and His Money" 3-8-68 (Miss Barlow).

Angela, Mary. TV: *Here Come the Brides*—"Wives for Wakando" 1-22-69 (Sylvia), "A Dream That Glitters" 2-26-69; *Gunsmoke*—"The Badge" 2-2-70 (Bea).

Angel, Mikel. Films: "Tell Them Willie Boy Is Here" 1969 (Old Mike).

Anglim, Sally. Films: "The Thundering Trail" 1951 (Betty-Jo).

Angold, Edith (1895-10/4/71). Films: "Tough Assignment" 1949 (Mrs. Schultz).

Angus, Hal. Films: "The Little Sheriff" 1912; "An Outlaw's Sacrifice" 1912; "The Smuggler's Daughter" 1912; "A Woman of Arizona" 1912.

Angus, Katherine. Films: "Just Squaw" 1919; "The Flame of Hellgate" 1920 (Hotel Proprietress).

Anhalt, Edward (1914-). Films: "Hour of the Gun" 1967 (Denver Doctor).

Aniston, John. TV: *The Virginian*—"Ride the Misadventure" 11-6-68 (Frank West).

Ankers, Evelyn (1918-8/28/85). Films: "North to the Klondike" 1942 (Mary Sloan); "Pierre of the Plains" 1942 (Celia Wellsby); "Last of the Redmen" 1947 (Alice Munro); "The Texan Meets Calamity Jane" 1950 (Calamity Jane). ¶TV: *Cheyenne*—"The Gamble" 1-28-58 (Robbie James).

Ankrum, Morris (Stephen Morris) (1897-9/2/64). Films: "Hopalong Cassidy Returns" 1936 (Blackie); "Trail Dust" 1936 (Tex Anderson); "Borderland" 1937 (Loco); "Hills of Old Wyoming" 1937 (Andrews); "North of the Rio Grande" 1937 (Henry Stoneham/Lone Wolf);

"Rustler's Valley" 1937 (Randall Glenn); "Buck Benny Rides Again" 1940 (2nd Outlaw); "Cherokee Strip" 1940 (Hawk Barrett); "Knights of the Range" 1940 (Gamecock); "The Light of Western Stars" 1940 (Nat Hayworth); "The Showdown" 1940 (Baron Rendor); "Three Men from Texas" 1940 (Bruce Morgan); "The Bandit Trail" 1941 (Red); "Border Vigilantes" 1941 (Dan Forbes); "Doomed Caravan" 1941 (Stephen Westcott); "In Old Colorado" 1941 (Joe Weller); "Pirates on Horseback" 1941 (Ace Gibson); "Road Agent" 1941 (Big John Morgan); "The Round Up" 1941 (Parenthesis); "Wide Open Town" 1941 (Jim Stuart); "The Omaha Trail" 1942 (Job); "Ride 'Em, Cowboy" 1942 (Ace Anderson); "Barbary Coast Gent" 1944 (Alec Veeder); "Gentle Annie" 1944 (Gansby); "The Harvey Girls" 1946 (Rev. Claggett); "The Sea of Grass" 1947 (Crane); "Bad Men of Tombstone" 1949; "Colorado Territory" 1949 (U.S. Marshal); "Short Grass" 1950 (Hal Fenton); "Along the Great Divide" 1951 (Ed Roden); "The Redhead and the Cowboy" 1951 (Sheriff); "Fort Osage" 1952 (Arthur Pickett); "Hiawatha" 1952 (Igaoo); "The Man Behind the Gun" 1952 (Bram Creegan); "The Raiders" 1952 (Thomas Ainsworth); "Arena" 1953; "Devil's Canyon" 1953 (Sheriff); "Fort Vengeance" 1953 (Crowfoot); "The Moonlighter" 1953 (Prince); "Apache" 1954 (Dawson); "Cattle Queen of Montana" 1954 (J.I. "Pop" Jones); "Drums Across the River" 1954 (Ouray); "The Outlaw Stallion" 1954 (Sheriff Fred Flummer); "Silver Lode" 1954 (Zachary Evans); "Southwest Passage" 1954 (Doc Stanton); "Taza, Son of Cochise" 1954 (Grey Eagle); "Three Young Texans" 1954 (Jeff Blair); "Two Guns and a Badge" 1954 (Sheriff Jackson); "Vera Cruz" 1954 (Gen. Aguilar); "Chief Crazy Horse" 1955 (Red Cloud/Conquering Bear); "The Silver Star" 1955 (Childress); "Tennessee's Partner" 1955 (the Judge); "The Desperados Are in Town" 1956 (Mr. Rutherford); "Fury at Gunsight Pass" 1956 (Doc Phillips); "The Naked Gun" 1956; "Quincannon, Frontier Scout" 1956 (Col. Conover); "Walk the Proud Land" 1956 (Gen. Wade); "Drango" 1957 (Calder); "Hell's Crossroads" 1957 (Wheeler); "Badman's Country" 1958 (Mayor Coleman); "Frontier Gun" 1958 (Andrew Barton); "The Saga of Hemp Brown" 1958 (Bo Slauter). ¶TV: *Fireside Theater*—"Man of the Comstock" 11-3-53 (Joseph Goodman); *The Adventures* of Rin Tin Tin—"Farewell to Fort Apache" 5-20-55, "The Secret Weapon" 4-11-58 (Chief Red Eagle), "The General's Daughter" 9-19-58 (Brig. Gen. Jack Lawrence), "The Foot Soldier" 10-10-58 (Yellow Wolf); Wyatt Earp—"Trail's End for a Cowboy" 12-6-55 (Collin); Cheyenne—"The Traveler" 1-3-56 (Roden), "White Warrior" 3-11-58 (Matt Benedict), "Incident at Dawson Flats" 1-9-61 (Cyrus Dawson); Jim Bowie—"The Beggar of New Orleans" 1-11-57 (Gabriel Durand); Boots and Saddles—"The Obsession" 10-3-57 (Surgeon Major); Sugarfoot—"The Strange Land" 10-15-57 (Cash Billing); Tombstone Territory—"Revenge Town" 11-6-57 (Mayor), 11-6-59 (Mine Owner); Tales of the Texas Rangers—"Trail Herd" 11-10-57 (Col. Cole Bryson); Maverick—"Naked Gallows" 12-15-57 (Joshua Haines), "The Marquesa" 1-3-60 (Judge Mason Painter); Have Gun Will Travel—"The Hanging Cross" 12-21-57, "Deliver the Body" 5-24-58 (Max Bruckner); MacKenzie's Raiders—Regular 1958-59; Wagon Train—"The Tobias Jones Story" 10-22-58 (Michael Folsom); 26 Men—"Manhunt" 12-16-58; Northwest Passage—"Dead Reckoning" 1-16-59; Frontier Doctor—"Sabotage" 1-17-59; The Rifleman—"Shivaree" 2-3-59 (Aaron Pelser), "The Actress" 1-24-61 (Jacob Black); Death Valley Days—"The Talking Wire" 4-21-59 (Phillips); Rawhide—"Incident of Fear in the Streets" 5-8-59 (Dr. Jackson), "Incident of the Broken Word" 1-20-61 (Dr. Morgan); Man from Blackhawk—"Portrait of Cynthia" 1-29-60 (Martin Randolph); The Texan—"Thirty Hours to Kill" 2-1-60; Gunsmoke—"The Bobsy Twins" 5-21-60 (Merle Finny); Tales of Wells Fargo—"That Washburn Girl" 2-13-61 (Jonas Coe); Bronco—"Guns of the Lawless" 5-8-61 (Gilbert Groves); Bonanza—"The Gamble" 4-1-62.

Anna-Lisa (1934-). TV: Sugarfoot—"Man Wanted" 2-18-58 (Ellie Peterson); Maverick—"The Judas Mask" 11-2-58 (Karen Gustavson); Bronco—"Brand of Courage" 12-16-58 (Sister Theresa); Black Saddle—Regular 1959 (Nora Travers); Wagon Train—"The Sam Livingston Story" 6-15-60; Gunsmoke—"The Blacksmith" 9-17-60 (Gretchen); Laramie—".45 Calibre" 11-15-60 (Louisa Clark); Bonanza—"The Savage" 12-3-60 (White Buffalo Woman); Death Valley Days—"The Hat That Huldah Wore" 6-25-66 (Huldah Sanson).

Annese, Frank. TV: Outlaws—"Independents" 3-21-87 (Crown).

Ann-Margret (1941-). Films: "Stagecoach" 1966 (Dallas); "The Train Robbers" 1973 (Mrs. Lowe); "The Villain" 1979 (Charming Jones).

Ansara, Michael (1922-). Films: "Only the Valiant" 1951 (Tucsos); "Brave Warrior" 1952 (the Prophet); "The Lawless Breed" 1952 (Gus); "Three Young Texans" 1954 (Apache Joe); "Gun Brothers" 1956 (Shawnee); "The Lone Ranger" 1956 (Angry Horse); "Pillars of the Sky" 1956 (Kamiakin, the Indian Chief); "Last of the Badmen" 1957 (Kramer); "Quantez" 1957 (Delgadito); "The Tall Stranger" 1957 (Zarata); "... And Now Miguel" 1966 (Blas); "Texas Across the River" 1966 (Chief Iron Jacket); "Guns of the Magnificent Seven" 1969 (Colonel Diego); "Powderkeg" TVM-1971 (Paco Morales); "Shootout in a One-Dog Town" TVM-1974 (Reynolds); "The Barbary Coast" TVM-1975 (Diamond Jack Bassiter); "Kino, the Padre on Horseback" 1977. ¶TV: The Lone Ranger—"Trouble at Black Rock" 2-8-51; Broken Arrow—Regular 1956-58 (Cochise); The Adventures of Rin Tin Tin—"Yo-o Rinty" 10-12-56 (Tioka); Hawkeye and the Last of the Mohicans—"Hawkeye's Homecoming" 4-3-57; Frontier Doctor—"The Outlaw Legion" 11-15-58; The Rifleman—"The Indian" 2-17-59 (Sam Buckhart); Zane Grey Theater—"The Law and the Gun" 6-4-59 (Fitzgerald); The Law of the Plainsman—Regular 1959-60 (Sam Buckheart); The Rebel—"The Champ" 10-2-60 (Docker Mason); The Westerner—"Hand on the Gun" 12-23-60; Wagon Train—"The Patience Miller Story" 1-11-61 (North Star), "The Adam MacKenzie Story" 3-27-63 (Adam MacKenzie); Tales of Wells Fargo—"Moneyrun" 1-6-62 (Colonel Peralta); Wide Country—"A Devil in the Chute" 11-8-62 (Jay Brenner); Rawhide—"Incident at Rio Doloroso" 5-10-63 (Alfredo Maldenado), "Incident of Iron Bull" 10-3-63 (Joseph/Iron Bull), "Canliss" 10-30-64 (Don Miguel); Branded—"The Bounty" 2-21-65 (Capt. Thomas Frye); The Virginian—"The Showdown" 4-14-65 (Marshal Merle Frome), "High Stakes" 11-16-66 (Paul Dallman); A Man Called Shenandoah—"Rope's End" 1-17-66 (Adam Lloyd); Daniel Boone—"The Search" 3-3-66 (Sebastian Drake), "The Enchanted Gun" 11-17-66 (Red Sky); Gunsmoke—"Honor Before Justice" 3-5-66 (Gray Horse), "The Returning" 2-18-67 (Luke Todd); Iron Horse—"Big Deal" 12-12-66 (Gillingham Conner); The

Road West—"A War for the Gravediggers" 4-10-67 (Serafin); Cowboy in Africa—"The Kasubi Death" 4-1-68 (Ernst Rolf); Here Come the Brides—"Wives for Wakando" 1-22-69 (Wakando); The High Chaparral—"For the Love of Carlos" 4-4-69 (Alberto Ruiz); Lancer—"Lamp in the Wilderness" 3-10-70 (Curley); Nakia—"The Dream" 11-23-74 (Howard Gray Hawk); Centennial—Regular 1978-79 (Lame Beaver).

Anson, Laura (1892-7/15/68). Films: "The Call of the Canyon" 1923 (Beatrice Lovell).

Anthony, Jack (1901-2/28/62). Films: "The Fighting Hombre" 1927 (Sheriff); "Gun-Hand Garrison" 1927; "Ridin' Luck" 1927; "Tom's Gang" 1927 (Bill Grimshaw); "Wild Born" 1927; "The Texas Tornado" 1928 (Bill Latimer).

Anthony, Larry. TV: Wild Wild West—"The Night of the Tartar" 2-3-67 (Detective); Cimarron Strip—"The Beast That Walks Like a Man" 11-30-67.

Anthony, Mark. TV: Death Valley Days—"The Jolly Roger and Wells Fargo" 2-4-67 (Lloyd Stevenson), "The Saga of Dr. Davis" 3-18-67 (Tad).

Anthony, Tony (1937-). Films: "A Stranger in Town" 1966-U.S./Ital. (the Stranger); "The Stranger Returns" 1967-U.S./Ital./Ger./Span. (the Stranger); "Stranger in Japan" 1969-Ital./U.S./Jap. (the Stranger); "Blindman" 1971-Ital. (Blindman); "Get Mean" 1975-Ital.; "Comin' at Ya" 1981-Ital. (H.H. Hart).

Anthony, Walter. Films: "The Stranger from Arizona" 1938 (Sandy).

Anton, Ronny. TV: Wagon Train—"The Matthew Lowry Story" 4-1-59 (Benjamin).

Antonelli, Laura (1946-). Films: "Man Called Sledge" 1971-Ital./U.S. (Ria).

Antonio, Jim (1934-). TV: Alias Smith and Jones—"Shootout at Diablo Station" 12-2-71 (Harry).

Antonio, Lou (1934-). TV: Have Gun Will Travel—"The Tender Gun" 10-22-60; Gunsmoke—"Outlaw's Woman" 12-11-65 (Harve Kane), "Prairie Wolfers" 11-13-67 (Rich), "O'Quillian" 10-28-68 (Curt Tynan), "The Gold Mine" 1-27-69 (Smiley), "The Long Night" 2-17-69 (Mace); The Virginian—"The Inchoworm's Got No Wings at All" 2-2-66 (Niles); The Road West—"The Eighty-Seven Dollar Bride" 4-3-67 (Mike Kerkorian); Bonanza—"In Defense of Honor" 4-28-68 (Davey);

Here Come the Brides—"Land Grant" 11-21-69 (Telly), "To the Victor" 2-27-70 (Telly).

Antonio, Marco. see Arzate, Marco Antonio.

Antrim, Harry (1884-1/18/67). Films: "The Devil's Doorway" 1950 (Dr. C.O. MacQuillan); "The Lion and the Horse" 1952 (Cas Bagley); "The Bounty Hunter" 1954 (Dr. Spencer); "A Lawless Street" 1955 (Mayor Kent); "Gunmen from Laredo" 1959 (Judge Parker). ¶TV: *Wild Bill Hickok*—"Meteor Mesa" 6-16-53; *DuPont Theater*—"The Texas Ranger" 4-9-57 (Station Master); *Colt .45*—"Gallows at Granite Gap" 11-8-57; *Sugarfoot*—"Brink of Fear" 6-30-58 (Mr. Logan); *Rawhide*—"Incident of the Thirteenth Man" 10-23-59 (Ted); *Have Gun Will Travel*—"The Trial" 6-11-60; *Lawman*—"The Mad Bunch" 10-2-60 (Doc Shea), "Dilemma" 10-30-60 (Dr. Shea); *Bonanza*—"The Trail Gang" 11-26-60; *The Tall Man*—"Legend of Billy" 12-9-61 (Clerk), "An Hour to Die" 2-17-62 (Doc Hogan).

Anza, Andy. Films: "Son of a Gunfighter" 1966-U.S./Span. (Fuentes); "Cry Blood, Apache" 1970 (Crippled Indian).

Aoki, Tsuru (1892-10/18/61). Films: "Desert Thieves" 1914; "Love's Sacrifice" 1914.

Apfel, Oscar (1879-3/21/38). Films: "The Valley of Hunted Men" 1928 (Dan Phillips); "The Spoilers" 1930 (Struve); "The Texan" 1930 (Thacker); "Rainbow's End" 1935 (Neil Gibson, Sr.); "Sutter's Gold" 1936; "Rustler's Valley" 1937 (Clem Crawford).

Apone, John. TV: *Gunsmoke*—"Crowbait Bob" 3-26-60 (Ace); *The Westerner*—"The Courting of Libby" 11-11-60.

Appel, Sam (1871-6/18/47). Films: "Whispering Smith" 1916 (Regstock); "The Light of Western Stars" 1918 (Gomez); "Two Kinds of Women" 1922 (Crowdy); "The Girl of the Golden West" 1923 (Pedro Micheltorena); "Under a Texas Moon" 1930 (Pancho Gonzalez); "Yankee Don" 1931; "Under the Pampas Moon" 1935 (Bartender); "Hi Gaucho!" 1936; "Ramona" 1936 (Servant); "Rose of the Rancho" 1936 (Vigilante); "Twenty Mule Team" 1940 (Proprietor); "Down Mexico Way" 1941.

Appleby, Dorothy (1906-8/9/90). Films: "The King of the Wild Horses" 1933 (Wanima); "North of Nome" 1936 (Ruby Clark); "Stagecoach" 1939 (Dancing Girl); "Rockin' Through the Rockies" 1940-short (Tessie).

Applegate, Christina (1972-). TV: *Father Murphy*—"A Horse from Heaven" 11-24-81 (Ada).

Applegate, Hazel (1886-10/30/59). Films: "His Regeneration" 1915.

Applegate, Royce D. (1940-). TV: *The Life and Times of Grizzly Adams*—4-26-78 (Corp. Mullaney); *Centennial*—Regular 1978-79 (Holmes); *Paradise*—"A House Divided" 2-16-89 (Mulligan).

Appleton, Elinor. Films: "Yankee Fakir" 1947 (Jenny).

Appleton, Kathryn. Films: "Way of a Man" 1924-serial.

Applewhite, Ric (1897-5/29/73). TV: *Wanted—Dead or Alive*—"The Medicine Man" 11-23-60, "Bounty on Josh" 1-25-61.

Appling, Bert (1871-1/14/60). Films: "Beyond the Shadows" 1918 (Semcoe Charlie); "Desert Law" 1918 (Deputy); "The Grand Passion" 1918 (Red Pete Jackson); "The Light of Western Stars" 1918 (Sheriff Hawes); "The End of the Game" 1919 (Sheriff); "Gun Magic" 1919; "The Jaws of Justice" 1919; "A Man's Fight" 1919 (Callahan); "A Western Wooing" 1919; "Just Pals" 1920 (Brakeman); "The Vengeance Trail" 1921 (Broncho Powell); "Western Firebrands" 1921 (Pete Carson); "Danger" 1923 (Norton); "The Devil's Twin" 1927 (Sheriff); "Hands Off" 1927 (Bull Duncan); "Men of Daring" 1927 (Lone Wolf); "Wizard of the Saddle" 1928 (Kirk McGrew).

Arabeloff, Sergei. Films: "The Girl of the Golden West" 1938 (Jose).

Aragon, Tita. TV: *Annie Oakley*—"Annie Rides the Navajo Trail" 11-18-56 (Little Rider); *The Adventures of Rin Tin Tin*—"The Invaders" 12-14-56 (Juanita Estaban); *Jim Bowie*—"Ursula" 2-14-58 (Teresa de Veramendi).

Aranda, Angel. Films: "Bullets Don't Argue" 1964-Ital./Ger./Span. (Logan Clanton); "The Hellbenders" 1966-U.S./Ital./Span. (Nat); "And the Crows Will Dig Your Grave" 1971-Ital./Span. (Don Parker); "Dallas" 1972-Span./Ital.

Arau, Alfonso (1939-). Films: "The Wild Bunch" 1969 (Herrera); "Scandalous John" 1971 (Paco Martinez); "Posse" 1975 (Peppe); "Where the Hell's That Gold?!!!" TVM-1988 (Indio). ¶TV: *Gunsmoke*—"Survival" 1-10-72 (Mando); *Bonanza*—"Customs of the Country" 2-6-72 (Simon).

Arbuckle, Andrew (1887-9/21/39). Films: "The White Man's Courage" 1919 (Valentino); "The Spider and the Rose" 1923 (the Priest); "The Dangerous Coward" 1924 (David McGuinn); "The Fighting Boob" 1926 (Old Man Hawksby).

Arbuckle, Roscoe "Fatty" (1887-6/29/33). Films: "The Under-Sheriff" 1914; "Fatty and Minnie He-Haw" 1915; "Out West" 1918; "The Round Up" 1920 (Slim Hoover).

Arbus, Allan (1918-). Films: "The Electric Horseman" 1979 (Danny). ¶TV: *Here Come the Brides*—"A Wild Colonial Boy" 10-24-69 (Denis); *Bret Maverick*—"Horse of Yet Another Color" 1-5-82 (Phineas Swackmeyer).

Arcaro, Flavia (1876-4/8/37). Films: "The Plunderer" 1915.

Archainbaud, George (1890-2/20/59). TV: *Gunsmoke*—"Indian White" 10-27-56 (Citizen).

Archer, Anne (1947-). Films: "The Honkers" 1972 (Deborah Moon); "The Mark of Zorro" TVM-1974 (Teresa); "The Last of His Tribe" TVM-1994 (Mrs. Kroeber). ¶TV: *Alias Smith and Jones*—"Shootout at Diablo Station" 12-2-71 (Ellen Lewis).

Archer, Harry. Films: "Mixed Blood" 1916 (Bluootch White); "The Red Ace" 1917-serial; "The Joyous Troublemaker" 1920 (Under Butler); "Beating the Game" 1921.

Archer, John (Ralph Bowman) (1915-). Films: "Flaming Frontier" 1938-serial (Tom Grant); "Overland Stage Raiders" 1938 (Bob Whitney); "Colorado Territory" 1949 (Reno Blake); "High Lonesome" 1950 (Pat Farrell); "Best of the Badmen" 1951 (Curley Ringo); "Santa Fe" 1951 (Clint Canfield); "The Big Trees" 1952 (French LeCrois); "Rodeo" 1952 (Slim Martin); "Decision at Sundown" 1957 (Dr. Storrow); "Apache Rifles" 1964. ¶TV: *Cheyenne*—"Test of Courage" 1-29-57 (Colonel Wilson), "Home Is the Brave" 3-14-60 (Prescott); *The Californians*—"Little Lost Man" 12-3-57 (Clint), "J. Jimmerson Jones, Inc." 4-1-58 (Jim Maston); *Zane Grey Theater*—"The Freighter" 1-17-58 (Ad Masters); *Broken Arrow*—"War Trail" 4-8-58 (Major Stone); *Laramie*—"The Run to Rumavaca" 11-10-59 (Arnold Demeistre); *Riverboat*—"Fight at New Canal" 2-22-60 (Dunnigan); *Colt .45*—"Phantom Trail" 3-13-60 (Joe Holman); *Tales of Wells Fargo*—"The Outlaw's Wife" 3-28-60 (Pete), "That Washburn Girl" 2-13-61 (Dean

Chase), "Who Lives by the Gun" 3-24-62 (Grant Reynolds); *Wagon Train*—"The Prairie Story" 2-1-61 (Matt), "The Sandra Cummings Story" 12-2-63 (Jonathan); *The Tall Man*—"The Reversed Blade" 2-4-61 (Ben Webster); *Maverick*—"The Devil's Necklace" 4-16-61 & 4-23-61 (Major Reidinger); *Bonanza*—"The Jacknife" 2-18-62 (Mathew Grant), "The Last Haircut" 2-3-63, "The Dilemma" 9-19-65 (Powell), "Ballad of the Ponderosa" 11-13-66 (Dave Sinclair), "The Crime of Johnny Mule" 2-25-68 (Prosecutor); *Temple Houston*—"The Guardian" 1-2-64 (Adam Ballard); *The Virginian*—"Girl on the Glass Mountain" 12-28-66 (Connally).

Archer, Mel. Films: "Winchester '73" 1950 (Bartender); "Distant Drums" 1951 (Pvt. Jeremiah Hiff).

Archibek, Ben. Films: "Desperate Mission" TVM-1971 (Frankie).

Archuletta, Arline. Films: "The Last Round-Up" 1947.

Archuletta, Beulah. Films: "The Searchers" 1956 (Look). ¶TV: *Wagon Train*—"A Man Called Horse" 3-26-58.

Archuletta, James. Films: "Wyoming" 1947 (Indian Boy).

Ardell, Alice. Films: "Ruggles of Red Gap" 1935 (Lisette); "Songs and Bullets" 1938 (Jeanette Du Mont).

Arden, Edwin (1864-10/2/18). Films: "The Eagle's Nest" 1915 (Jack Trail).

Arden, Elaine. Films: "Headin' East" 1937 (Penny).

Arden, Eve (1912-11/12/90). Films: "Last of the Duanes" 1941 (Kate); "Curtain Call at Cactus Creek" 1950 (Lily Martin). ¶TV: *Laredo*—"Which Way Did They Go?" 11-18-65 (Emma Bristow).

Arden, Jane (1905-3/21/81). Films: "The Escape" 1926 (Flossie Lane).

Ardia, Pinuccio. Films: "10,000 Dollars Blood Money" 1966-Ital.; "Get the Coffin Ready" 1968-Ital.

Ardigan, Art. *see* Ortego, Artie.

Ardisson, Georges. Films: "Massacre at Grand Canyon" 1963-Ital.; "May God Forgive You ... But I Won't" 1968-Ital. (Cjamango); "Django Challenges Sartana" 1970-Ital. (Sartana); "Gold of the Heroes" 1971-Ital./Fr. (Doc).

Ardoin, Voorhies J. TV: *Wagon Train*—"The Gabe Carswell Story" 1-15-58; *The Restless Gun*—"Take Me Home" 12-29-58 (Fowler), "The Way Back" 7-13-59; *Colt .45*—"Appoint-ment in Agoura" 6-7-60; *The Outlaws*—"Blind Spot" 3-30-61 (the Weasel).

Arena, James. Films: "Hot Spur" 1968 (Jason O'Hare).

Arena, Maurizio (1933-11/22/79). Films: "Terror of Oklahoma" 1961-Ital.

Arenas, Miguel (1902-11/3/65). Films: "The Legend of the Bandit" 1945-Mex. (Isabel's Father).

Arenas, Paco. Films: "Ten Days to Tulara" 1958 (Chris).

Arent, Eddi. Films: "Treasure of Silver Lake" 1963-Fr./Ger./Yugo. (Castlepool); "Last of the Renegades" 1966-Fr./Ital./Ger./Yugo. (Lord Castlepool); "Winnetou and Shatterhand in the Valley of Death" 1968-Ger./Yugo./Ital.

Argo, Victor. TV: *Kung Fu*—"The Chalice" 10-11-73 (Diaz).

Aris, Ben (1937-). TV: *Branded*—"Romany Roundup 12-5-65 & 12-12-65 (Lazar).

Arizmendi, Yareli. Films: "The Cisco Kid" CTVM-1994 (Rosa).

Arkansas Johnny. Films: "Wheels of Destiny" 1934; "Western Courage" 1935.

Arkin, Alan (1934-). Films: "Hearts of the West" 1975 (Kessler).

Arledge, John (1906-5/15/47). Films: "Two in Revolt" 1936 (John Woods).

Arlen, Ghia. *see* Ghia, Dana.

Arlen, Richard (1900-3/28/76). Films: "The Enchanted Hill" 1926 (Link Halliwell); "Under the Tonto Rim" 1928 (Edd Denmeade); "The Virginian" 1929 (Steve); "The Border Legion" 1930 (Jim Cleve); "The Light of the Western Stars" 1930 (Dick Bailey); "The Santa Fe Trail" 1930 (Stan Hollister); "Caught" 1931 (Lieutenant Tom Colton); "The Conquering Horde" 1931 (Dan McMasters); "Gun Smoke" 1931 (Brad Farley); "The Mine with the Iron Door" 1936 (Bob Harvey); "Secret Valley" 1937 (Lee Rogers); "Call of the Yukon" 1938 (Gaston Rogers); "Man from Montreal" 1940 (Clark Manning); "Men of the Timberland" 1941; "The Big Bonanza" 1944 (Jed Kilton); "Buffalo Bill Rides Again" 1947 (Buffalo Bills); "The Return of Wildfire" 1948 (Dobie); "Grand Canyon" 1949 (Mike Adams); "Kansas Raiders" 1950 (Union Captain); "Silver City" 1951 (Charles Storrs); "Flaming Feather" 1952 (Showdown Calhoun); "Hidden Guns" 1956 (Sheriff Young); "Warlock" 1959 (Bacon); "Cavalry Command" 1963-U.S./Phil. (Sgt. Heisler); "Law of the Lawless" 1964 (Bartender); "The Shepherd of the Hills" 1964 (Old Matt); "Black Spurs" 1965 (Pete); "The Bounty Killer" 1965 (Ridgeway); "Town Tamer" 1965 (Dr. Kent); "Young Fury" 1965 (Sheriff Jenkins); "Apache Uprising" 1966 (Capt. Gannon); "Johnny Reno" 1966 (Ned Duggan); "Waco" 1966 (Sheriff Billy Kelly); "Fort Utah" 1967 (Sam Tyler); "Hostile Guns" 1967 (Sheriff Travis); "Red Tomahawk" 1967 (Telegrapher); "Buckskin" 1968 (Townsman). ¶TV: *Wanted—Dead or Alive*—"Rope Law" 1-3-59 (Damon Ring, Sr.); *Lawman*—"The Gunmen" 2-15-59 (Kurt Monroe), "Last Stop" 1-3-60 (Bill Jennings), "The Man from New York" 3-19-61 (Fred Stiles); *Yancy Derringer*—"A State of Crisis" 4-30-59 (Gen. Morgan); *Bat Masterson*—"Death and Taxes" 11-26-59 (John Minor), "The Price of Paradise" 1-19-61 (Sheriff Rainey); *Branded*—"Coward Step Aside" 3-7-65 (Hatton).

Arlen, Roxanne (1931-2/22/89). Films: "Slim Carter" 1957 (Cigarette Girl). ¶TV: *Cheyenne*—"One Way Ticket" 2-19-62 (Flo); *Rango*—"The Daring Holdup of the Deadwood Stage" 1-20-67 (Stella).

Arling, Charles. Films: "The Border Wireless" 1918 (Herman Brandt); "The Ranger" 1918 (Red Haggerty); "Who Knows?" 1918 (Hank Weaver/Dr. Raymond Pratt); "Wagon Tracks" 1919 (the Captain); "Blue Streak McCoy" 1920 (Howard Marlowe); "The Vengeance Trail" 1921 (Lady Killer Larson); "When Romance Rides" 1922 (Bostil).

Arliss, Dimitra (1932-). Films: "This Was the West That Was" TVM-1974.

Armendariz, Pedro (1912-6/18/63). Films: "Fort Apache" 1948 (St. Beaufort); "The Three Godfathers" 1948 (Pedro "Pete" Roca Fuerte); "Border River" 1954 (General Calleja); "The Wonderful Country" 1959 (Gov. Cipriano Castro).

Armendariz, Jr., Pedro (1930-). Films: "Guns for San Sebastian" 1967-U.S./Fr./Mex./Ital. (Father Lucas); "The Undefeated" 1969 (Escalante); "Chisum" 1970 (Ben); "Macho Callahan" 1970 (Juan Fernandez); "Hardcase" TVM-1972 (Simon Fuegus); "The Magnificent Seven Ride" 1972 (Pepe Carral); "Deadly Trackers" 1973 (Blacksmith); "The Soul of Nigger Charley" 1973 (Sandoval); "Old Gringo" 1989 (Pancho Villa); "Bandidos" 1991-Mex. (Priest); "Tombstone" 1993 (the

Priest); "The Cisco Kid" CTVM-1994 (Montano).

Armenta, Phillip. Films: "Vigilantes Are Coming" 1936-serial (Dark Feather); "The Girl of the Golden West" 1938 (Long Face); "The Lone Ranger" 1938-serial (Dark Cloud).

Armetta, Henry (1888-10/21/45). Films: "The Plunderer" 1915 (Pedro); "The Desert's Price" 1925 (Shepherd); "In Old Arizona" 1929 (Barber); "Men of America" 1933 (Tony Garboni); "Romance of the West" 1935-short.

Armida. Films: "Border Romance" 1930 (Conchita Cortez); "Under a Texas Moon" 1930 (Dolores); "Wings of Adventure" 1930 (Maria); "Under the Pampas Moon" 1935 (Rosa); "Border Cafe" 1937 (Dominga); "Rootin' Tootin' Rhythm" 1937 (Rosa Montero); "Bullets and Ballads" 1940; "Bad Men of the Border" 1945; "South of the Rio Grande" 1945 (Pepita); "The Gay Amigo" 1949 (Rosita).

Armitage, Gordon. Films: "Canadian Mounties vs. Atomic Invaders" 1953-serial (Ed Olson).

Arms, Russell (1929-). Films: "The Fighting Vigilantes" 1947 (Trippler); "Stage to Mesa City" 1947; "Loaded Pistols" 1948 (Larry Evans); "Quick on the Trigger" 1948 (Fred Red); "Smoky Mountain Melody" 1948 (Kid Corby); "Tornado Range" 1948 (Dorgan); "Sons of New Mexico" 1949 (Chuck Brunton). ¶TV: *Have Gun Will Travel*—"Death of a Gunfighter" 3-14-59 (Will Haskel), "The Revenger" 9-30-61 (Major Ralph Turner); *Buckskin*—"I'll Sing at Your Wedding" 5-4-59 (Ethan Comstock); *Rawhide*—"Incident of the Arana Sacar" 4-22-60 (Joel Belden), "Deserter's Patrol" 2-9-62 (Marshal), "Incident at Hourglass" 3-12-64; *Gunsmoke*—"Bad Sheriff" 1-7-61 (Hark).

Armstrong, David. Films: "Heller in Pink Tights" 1960 (Achilles).

Armstrong, Herb. Films: "Gun Street" 1961 (Jeff Baxley). ¶TV: *The Rifleman*—"The Actress" 1-24-61; *Empire*—"Down There, the World" 3-12-63 (Colby); *Gunsmoke*—"The Drummer" 10-9-72 (Sayers); *Bret Maverick*—"The Rattlesnake Brigade" 4-27-82.

Armstrong, Louis (1900-7/6/71). Films: "Courtin' Trouble" 1948; "Cowboy Cavalier" 1948; "Outlaw Brand" 1948; "The Rangers Ride" 1948.

Armstrong, Margaret. Films: "Annie Oakley" 1935 (Mrs. Oakley);

"Western Jamboree" 1938 (Mrs. Gregory).

Armstrong, R.G. (1917-). Films: "From Hell to Texas" 1958 (Hunter Boyd); "No Name on the Bullet" 1959 (Asa Canfield); "Ten Who Dared" 1960 (Oramel Howland); "Ride the High Country" 1962 (Joshua Knudsen); "He Rides Tall" 1964 (Josh McCloud); "Major Dundee" 1965 (Rev. Dhalstrom); "El Dorado" 1967 (Kevin MacDonald); "The Ballad of Cable Hogue" 1970 (Quittner); "The McMasters" 1970 (Watson); "J.W. Coop" 1971 (Jim Sawyer); "The Great Northfield, Minnesota Raid" 1972 (Clell Miller); "Hec Ramsey" TVM-1972 (Ben Ritt); "My Name Is Nobody" 1973-Ital. (Honest John); "Pat Garrett and Billy the Kid" 1973 (Deputy Ollinger); "Boss Nigger" 1974 (Mayor); "Last Ride of the Dalton Gang" TVM-1979 (Langdon Sanford); "The Legend of the Golden Gun" TVM-1979 (Judge Harrison Harding); "The Shadow Riders" TVM-1982 (Sheriff Miles Gillette); "Independence" TVM-1987 (Uriah Creed); "Red Headed Stranger" 1987 (Sheriff). ¶TV: *Zane Grey Theater*—"The Sharpshooter" 3-7-58 (Sheriff Fred Thompson), "Let the Man Die" 12-18-58 (Sheriff Les Houghton); *Have Gun Will Travel*—"Killer's Widow" 3-22-58, "The Manhunter" 6-7-58 (S.J. Lovett); *The Californians*—"The Street" 3-25-58 (Malone); *Jefferson Drum*—"Law and Order" 5-9-58 (Kreiger); *Texas John Slaughter*—Regular 1958-61 (Billy Soto); *The Rifleman*—"The Sharpshooter" 9-30-58 (Sheriff Tomlinson), "The Marshal" 10-21-58; *Bronco*—"The Turning Point" 10-21-58 (Rev. Hardin); *Sugarfoot*—"The Hunted" 11-25-58 (Clay Calhoun), "The Giant Killer" 3-3-59 (Lou Stoner); *The Texan*—"Desert Passage" 12-1-58 (Cliff Clifford), "Letter of the Law" 3-23-59 (Aldridge); *Lawman*—"The Brand Release" 1-25-59 (Gabe Dallas), "Battle Scar" 3-22-59 (Ben Rogers); *Black Saddle*—"Client: Dawes" 1-31-59 (Ben Dawes); *Maverick*—"The Saga of Waco Williams" 2-15-59 (Col. Karl Bent), "The People's Friend" 2-7-60 (Wellington Cosgrove); *Rawhide*—"Incident of the Dog Days" 4-17-59 (Enoch Talby), "Incident of the One Hundred Amulets" 5-6-60 (Burke), "Incident of the Lost Woman" 11-2-62 (Gantry Hobson), "Six Weeks to Bent Fork" 9-28-65 (Sheriff Keeley); *Wanted—Dead or Alive*—"The Tyrant" 10-31-59 (Asa Wynter); *Bonanza*—"The Diedeshiemer Story" 10-31-59 (Andrew

Holloway), "The Horse Breaker" 11-26-61 (Nathan Clay), "The Last Mission" 5-8-66 (Col. Keith Jarell); *Cheyenne*—"Alibi for a Scalped Man" 3-7-60 (Angus Emmett), "The Return of Mr. Grimm" 2-13-61 (Grimm); *The Westerner*—"School Days" 10-7-60 (Snell Davidson); *Laramie*—"License to Kill" 11-22-60 (Sam Jarrad), "Run of the Hunted" 4-4-61 (Jud), "The Jailbreakers" 12-19-61 (Dawson), "Time of the Traitor" 12-11-62 (Vic Prescott); *The Tall Man*—"Bitter Ashes" 12-3-60 (Neal Bailey); *Wyatt Earp*—"Casey and the Clowns" 2-21-61; *Bat Masterson*—"No Amnesty for Death" 3-30-61 (Marshal MacWilliams); *Gunsmoke*—"Indian Ford" 12-2-61 (Captain Benter), "With a Smile" 3-30-63 (Major Creed), "The Lady" 3-27-65 (Jud Briar), "Which Doctor" 3-19-66 (Argonaut Modnercan), "Stranger in Town" 11-20-67 (Carl Anderson), "Disciple" 4-1-74 (Ransom); *Frontier Circus*—"Coals of Fire" 1-4-62 (Uriah Foster); *Tales of Wells Fargo*—"Winter Storm" 3-3-62 (Hanson); *Wagon Train*—"The Charley Shutup Story" 3-7-62 (John Muskie), "The Shiloh Degnan Story" 11-7-62 (General Kirby); *Wide Country*—"Don't Cry for Johnny Devlin" 1-24-63 (Charlie Devlin); *The Virginian*—"The Small Parade" 2-20-63 (Ben Winters), "The Girl on the Pinto" 3-29-67 (Frederick Harley); *Death Valley Days*—"Birthright" 5-30-65 (Bundage); *The Big Valley*—"My Son, My Son" 11-3-65 (Wally Miles); *Daniel Boone*—"The Wolf Man" 1-26-67 (Jarvis), "The Flaming Rocks" 2-1-68 (Joseph Garth); *Cimarron Strip*—"The Battleground" 9-28-67 (William Payne); *Custer*—"War Lance and Saber" 10-11-67; *The Guns of Will Sonnett*—"The Turkey Shoot" 11-24-67 (Collin Atwood); *Lancer*—"Foley" 10-15-68 (Gant Foley); *Here Come the Brides*—"The Deadly Trade" 4-16-69 (Lijah); *The High Chaparral*—"Wind" 10-9-70 (Henderson); *Alias Smith and Jones*—"The Bounty Hunter" 12-9-71.

Armstrong, R.L. "Tex" (1925-3/10/78) Films: "The Rare Breed" 1966 (Barker); "J.W. Coop" 1971 (Tooter Watson); "Ulzana's Raid" 1972; "The Missouri Breaks" 1976 (Bob). ¶TV: *Kung Fu*—"Alethea" 3-15-73 (Clancy Pratt), "Ambush" 4-5-75 (Man).

Armstrong, Robert (1890-4/20/73). Films: "Man of Conquest" 1939 (Jim Bowie); "The Kansan" 1943 (Malachy); "Belle of the Yukon" 1944 (George); "Royal Mounted Rides Again" 1945-serial (Price); "The Sea of Grass" 1947 (Floyd McCurtin);

"The Paleface" 1948 (Terris); "Return of the Badmen" 1948 (Wild Bill Doolin); "Sons of New Mexico" 1949 (Pat Feeney). ¶TV: *Cheyenne*—"The Traveler" 1-3-56 (Merrick); *Broken Arrow*—"Justice" 11-27-56 (Insp. Higgins); *Tales of Wells Fargo*—"The Prisoner" 2-17-58 (Red), "Lady Trouble" 4-24-61 (Jess Walden); *Have Gun Will Travel*—"The Hanging of Roy Carter" 10-4-58 (Sidney Carter); *Cimarron City*—"The Town Is a Prisoner" 3-28-59 (Josh Matthews); *26 Men*—"The Unwanted" 3-31-59; *Wagon Train*—"The Estaban Zamora Story" 10-21-59 (Roy Daniels); *Lawman*—"The Hardcase" 1-31-60 (Lacy Grant), "The Catcher" 12-4-60 (Frank Fenway); *Sugarfoot*—"The Long Dry" 4-10-60 (Big Bill Carmody); *The Alaskans*—"Sign of the Kodiak" 5-29-60 (John Coleman); *Laramie*—"The Lost Dutchman" 2-14-61 (Sheriff); *Rawhide*—"Incident Before Black Pass" 5-19-61 (Cal Stone).

Armstrong, Todd (1939-4/12/93). Films: "Scalplock" TVM-1966 (Dave Tarrant); "Thunder at the Border" 1967-Ger./Yugo.; "A Time for Killing" 1967 (Lt. Prudessing). ¶TV: *Gunsmoke*—"The First People" 2-19-61 (John Eagle Wing), "9:12 to Dodge" 11-11-68 (Johnny August); *Nakia*—"The Driver" 11-2-74 (Walberg).

Armstrong, Vaughn. Films: "Triumphs of a Man Called Horse" 1984 (Captain Cummings). ¶TV: *Adventures of Brisco County, Jr.*—"AKA Kansas" 12-17-93 (Major).

Armstrong, Will (1868-7/29/43). Films: "Red Fork Range" 1931 (Sgt. O'Flaherty).

Arnall, Red (and the Western Aces). Films: "Blazing Across the Pecos" 1948.

Arnaz, Desi (1917-12/2/86). TV: *The Men from Shiloh*—"The Best Man" 9-23-70 (El Jefe).

Arnaz, Jr., Desi (1953-). Films: "Billy Two Hats" 1973-Brit. (Billy).

Arner, Gwen. TV: *The New Land*—Regular 1974 (Molly Lundstrom).

Arness, James (1923-). Films: "Sierra" 1950 (Little Sam); "Wagonmaster" 1950 (Floyd Clegg); "Wyoming Mail" 1950 (Russell); "Cavalry Scout" 1951 (Barth); "Hellgate" 1952 (George Redfield); "Horizons West" 1952 (Tiny); "Hondo" 1953 (Lennie); "The Lone Hand" 1953 (Gus Varden); "Many Rivers to Cross" 1955 (Esau Hamilton); "The First Traveling Saleslady" 1956 (Joel Kingdon);

"Gun the Man Down" 1957 (Rem Anderson); "Alias Jesse James" 1959 (Matt Dillon); "The Macahans" TVM-1976 (Zeb Macahan); "The Alamo: 13 Days to Glory" TVM-1987 (Jim Bowie); "Gunsmoke: Return to Dodge" TVM-1987 (Matt Dillon); "Gunsmoke: The Last Apache" TVM-1990 (Matt Dillon); "Gunsmoke: To the Last Man" TVM-1991 (Matt Dillon); "Gunsmoke: The Long Ride" TVM-1993 (Matt Dillon); "Gunsmoke: One Man's Justice" TVM-1994 (Matt Dillon). ¶TV: *The Lone Ranger*—"A Matter of Courage" 4-26-50; *Gunsmoke*—Regular 1955-75 (Marshal Matt Dillon); *How the West Was Won*—Regular 1977-79 (Zeb Macahan).

Arness, Jenny Lee. TV: *Gunsmoke*—"The Glory and the Mud" 1-4-64 (Amy), "Aunt Thede" 12-19-64 (Laurie).

Arness, Virginia. TV: *Gunsmoke*—"The Reed Survives" 12-31-55 (Gypsy).

Arngrim, Allison (1962-). Films: "I Married Wyatt Earp" TVM-1983 (Amy); "Little House on the Prairie: Look Back to Yesterday" TVM-1983 (Nancy Oleson); "Little House: Bless All the Dear Children" TVM-1984 (Nancy Oleson). ¶TV: *Little House on the Prairie*—Regular 1974-81 (Nellie Oleson).

Arngrim, Stefan (1955-). Films: "The Way West" 1967 (Billy Tadlock, Jr.). ¶TV: *Gunsmoke*—"By Line" 4-9-66 (Jock); *The Virginian*—"The Gauntlet" 2-8-67 (Jimmy Keets); *Here Come the Brides*—"Man of the Family" 10-16-68 (Tommy).

Arnold, Bert. Films: "The Rough, Tough West" 1952 (Jordan MacCrea). ¶TV: *The Lone Ranger*—"The Squire" 11-9-50.

Arnold, Denny. TV: *Gunsmoke*—"The Deadly Innocent" 12-17-73 (Slim).

Arnold, Eddy (1918-). Films: "Hoedown" 1950 (Eddy Arnold).

Arnold, Edward (1890-4/26/56). Films: "Sutter's Gold" 1936 (John Sutter); "Let Freedom Ring" 1939 (Jim Knox); "Lady from Cheyenne" 1941 (Cork); "Big Jack" 1949 (Mayor Mahoney); "Annie Get Your Gun" 1950 (Pawnee Bill).

Arnold, Jessie (1877-6/10/71). Films: "Mixed Blood" 1916 (Lottie Nagle); "Tennessee's Pardner" 1916 (Kate Kent); "Rough and Ready" 1918 (Estelle Darrow); "Hard Hombre" 1931 (Mrs. Patton); "Whistlin' Dan" 1932 (Horty); "Sundown Valley" 1944 (Mom Johnson); "Lawless

Empire" 1946 (Mrs. Murphy); "Trail Street" 1947 (Jason's Wife).

Arnold, Joanne. Films: "Son of Paleface" 1952 (Dance-Hall Girl); "The Great Jesse James Raid" 1953 (Brunette). ¶TV: *Wild Bill Hickok*—"The Avenging Gunman" 7-29-52.

Arnold, Phil (1909-5/9/68). Films: "Hollywood Barn Dance" 1947 (Toppitt); "Deadline" 1948; "The Comancheros" 1961. ¶TV: *Maverick*—"A Rage for Vengeance" 1-12-58 (Porter), "Alias Bart Maverick" 10-5-58 (Man); *Wagon Train*—"The Elizabeth McQueeney Story" 10-28-59; *The Big Valley*—"Image of Yesterday" 1-9-67; *Pistols 'n' Petticoats*—1-21-67 (Sad Owl); *Cimarron Strip*—"The Last Wolf" 12-14-67; *Hondo*—"Hondo and the Gladiators" 12-15-67 (Impresario).

Arnold, Phillip (1909-5/9/68). Films: "Buzzy and the Phantom Pinto" 1941; "Buffalo Bill Rides Again" 1947 (Scratchy).

Arnold, Rick. Films: "The Black Whip" 1956 (Red Leg); "Ballad of a Gunfighter" 1964. ¶TV: *Rawhide*—"Incident of the Judas Trap" 6-5-59.

Arnold, William (1883-7/20/40). Films: "Gun Smoke" 1931 (Mugs Maransa); "Call of the Wild" 1935 (1st Faro Player); "The Overland Express" 1938 (Henry Furness).

Arnt, Charles (1908-8/6/90). Films: "Rhythm on the Range" 1936 (Steward); "In Old Oklahoma" 1943 (Joe); "Roaring Guns" 1944-short; "Saddle Pals" 1947 (William Schooler); "Masked Raiders" 1949 (Doc); "The Great Sioux Uprising" 1953 (Gist); "The Miracle of the Hills" 1959 (Fuzzy). ¶TV: *The Rifleman*—"The Sharpshooter" 9-30-58 (Wes Tippert); *The Californians*—"The Long Night" 12-23-58 (Doc Folden); *Black Saddle*—"Client: Northrup" 3-14-59 (Burnett); *The Texan*—"No Place to Stop" 4-27-59 (Old Man Blackstone), "The Mountain Man" 5-23-60 (Ed Kingman); *Maverick*—"Maverick Springs" 12-6-59 (Charley Peters), "Dade City Dodge" 9-18-61 (Mason); *Sugarfoot*—"A Noose for Nora" 10-24-60 (Judge Lawson).

Arper, Clarence. Films: "Salomy Jane" 1914 (Col. Starbottle); "The Lily of Poverty Flat" 1915 (Cal Starbottle); "The Heart of Juanita" 1919 (Rev. Daniel Stiggens); "The Flame of Hellgate" 1920 (Sheriff).

Arquette, Cliff (1905-9/23/74). TV: *F Troop*—"Our Brave in F Troop" 3-30-67 (Gen. Sam Courage).

Arquette, Lewis. TV: *Paradise*—

"Ghost Dance" 11-24-88 (Mr. Sinclair), "A Private War" 1-5-89 (Sinclair).

Arquette, Rosanna (1959-). Films: "Silverado" 1985 (Hannah); "Son of the Morning Star" TVM-1991 (Elizabeth "Libby" Custer).

Arrants, Rod. TV: *Paradise*— "Shield of Gold" 4-12-91 (John Wolcott).

Arriaga, Simon. Films: "The Hellbenders" 1966-U.S./Ital./Span.; "Navajo Joe" 1966-Ital./Span. (Monkey); "Three from Colorado" 1967-Span.; "The Mercenary" 1968-Ital./Span. (Simon); "Rattler Kid" 1968-Ital./Span.; "Companeros" 1970-Ital./Span./Ger.; "What Am I Doing in the Middle of the Revolution?" 1973-Ital.

Arruza, Carlos (1924-5/20/66). Films: "The Alamo" 1960 (Lt. Reyez).

Arselle, Carmen. Films: "Four Hearts" 1922 (Marion Berkley); "Canyon of the Fools" 1923 (Incarnacion).

Arslan, Sylvia. Films: "Great Stagecoach Robbery" 1945; "Sheriff of Cimarron" 1945 (Little Girl).

Arteaga, Mario. Films: "The Young Land" 1959; "The Man Who Shot Liberty Valance" 1962 (Henchman); "Bite the Bullet" 1975 (Mexican).

Arthur, Carol (1935-). Films: "Blazing Saddles" 1974.

Arthur, Indus (-1984). Films: "Alvarez Kelly" 1966 (Melinda). ¶TV: *Wild Wild West*—"The Night of the Bars of Hell" 3-4-66 (Jenifer McCoy); *The Virginian*—"An Echo of Thunder" 10-5-66 (Margaret Lundee).

Arthur, Jean (1905-6/19/91). Films: "Biff Bang Buddy" 1924 (Bonnie Norton); "Bringin' Home the Bacon" 1924; "Fast and Fearless" 1924 (Mary Brown); "The Powerful Eye" 1924; "Thundering Romance" 1924 (Mary Watkins); "Travelin' Fast" 1924 (Betty Conway); "Drug Store Cowboy" 1925 (Jean); "The Fighting Smile" 1925 (Rose Craddock); "A Man of Nerve" 1925 (Loria Gatlin); "Tearin' Loose" 1925 (Sally Harris); "Thundering Through" 1925 (Ruth Burroughs); "Born to Battle" 1926 (Eunice Morgan); "The Cowboy Cop" 1926 (Virginia Selby); "Double Daring" 1926 (Marie Wells); "The Fighting Cheat" 1926 (Ruth Wells); "Hurricane Horseman" 1926 (June Mathews); "Lightning Bill" 1926 (Marie Denton); "Twisted Triggers" 1926 (Ruth Regan); "Under Fire" 1926 (Margaret Cranston); "Winners of the Wilderness" 1927 (Woman); "Stairs of Sand" 1929 (Ruth Hutt); "The Silver Horde" 1930 (Mildred Wayland); "The Plainsman" 1936 (Calamity Jones); "Arizona" 1940 (Phoebe Titus); "A Lady Takes a Chance" 1943 (Mollie Truesdale); "Shane" 1953 (Marion Starrett). ¶TV: *Gunsmoke*—"Thursday's Child" 3-6-65 (Julie Blane).

Arthur, Johnny (1883-12/31/51). Films: "It Happened Out West" 1937 (Thaddeus Cruikshank); "Jeepers Creepers" 1939 (Peabody).

Arthur, Karen (1941-). TV: *Wild Wild West*—"The Night of the Running Death" 12-15-67 (Gerta).

Arthur, Louise. Films: "Moon Over Montana" 1946. ¶TV: *Death Valley Days*—"Little Washington" 9-9-53; *Wyatt Earp*—"The Englishman" 2-21-56; *Wagon Train*—"The Davey Baxter Story" 1-9-63 (Mrs. Forbes).

Arthur, Maureen (1934-). TV: *Branded*—"Mightier Than the Sword" 9-26-65 (Teddi Stafford).

Arthur, Robert (1925-). Films: "Green Grass of Wyoming" 1948 (Ken); "Yellow Sky" 1948 (Bull Run); "The Desperados Are in Town" 1956 (Lenny Kesh); "Three Violent People" 1956 (One-Legged Confederate Soldier). ¶TV: *The Lone Ranger*—"Trouble for Tonto" 7-20-50, "Ranger in Danger" 10-30-52.

Arutt, Cheryl. Films: "Davy Crockett: Rainbow in the Thunder" TVM-1988 (Young Ory Palmer/Delia).

Arvan, Jan (1913-5/24/79). Films: "Gunfighters of Abilene" 1960 (Miguel); "Noose for a Gunman" 1960 (Hallop); "Frontier Uprising" 1961; "Winchester '73" TVM-1967. ¶TV: *Frontier*—"The Voyage of Captain Castle" 2-19-56 (Santa Ana); *The Adventures of Rin Tin Tin*—"The Indian Hater" 1-11-57 (Stone Wolf), "Corporal Carson" 5-3-57 (Pointed Spear), "Border Incident" 3-28-58 (Juarez), "Running Horse" 10-24-58 (Chief Running Horse); *Zorro*— "Zorro Rides to the Mission" 10-24-57 (Nacho Torres), "The Ghost of the Mission" 10-31-57 (Nacho Torres), "Zorro's Romance" 11-7-57 (Nacho Torres), "Garcia's Sweet Mission" 12-12-57 (Nacho Torres); *Broken Arrow*—"Renegades Return" 12-3-57 (Akara); *Gunsmoke*—"Overland Express" 5-31-58 (Station Man); *Jefferson Drum*—"The Hanging of Joe Lavetti" 8-1-58 (Joe Lavetti); *The Restless Gun*—"Ride with the Devil" 5-18-59 (Don Tomas Verdes); *Wanted—Dead or Alive*—"A House Divided" 2-20-60, "Barney's Bounty" 3-29-61 (Sam); *Wagon Train*—"The Albert Farnsworth Story" 10-12-60, "Weight of Command" 1-25-61, "The Pearlie Garnet Story" 2-24-64; *Gunslinger*—"Road of the Dead" 3-30-61 (Jiminez); *Rawhide*—"Incident at Rio Salado" 9-29-61 (Don Andreos Marcos); *Empire*—"The Fire Dancer" 11-13-62 (Pete Twist); *The Virginian*—"The Man from the Sea" 12-26-62 (the Mayor); *Laredo*—"The Callico Kid" 1-6-66, "The Treasure of San Diablo" 2-17-66 (Padre Anselmo), "Road to San Remo" 11-25-66, "The Short, Happy Fatherhood of Reese Bennett" 1-27-67; *Pistols 'n' Petticoats*—2-18-67 (Burnt Rope); *Custer*— "Massacre" 10-4-67; *The High Chaparral*—"Shadows on the Land" 10-15-67 (Perez); *Lancer*—"The Gifts" 10-28-69 (Clerk); *Bonanza*—"Cassie" 10-24-71 (Jensen).

Arvidson, Linda (1884-7/26/49). Films: "The Greaser's Gauntlet" 1908; "The Red Girl" 1908; "The Stage Rustler" 1908; "The Vaquero's Vow" 1908; "Comata, the Sioux" 1909; "Leather Stocking" 1909; "The Broken Doll" 1910; "Over Silent Paths" 1910; "In the Days of '49" 1911; "The Gambler of the West" 1914 (Mabel Grey).

Arvin, William. TV: *Great Adventure*—"The Testing of Sam Houston" 1-31-64 (Jackson's Aide); *Gunsmoke*—"Journey for Three" 6-6-64 (Adam Gifford); *Death Valley Days*—"Hero of Fort Halleck" 6-27-65 (Lt. Harper).

Arzate, Marco Antonio (Marco Antonio). Films: "Chuka" 1967 (Hanu); "The War Wagon" 1967 (Wild Horse); "The Scalphunters" 1968 (Scalphunter); "Soldier Blue" 1970 (Kiowa Brave).

Ash, Sam (1884-10/20/51). Films: "Robin Hood of El Dorado" 1936 (Arriga); "Wells Fargo" 1937 (Man with Beaver Hat); "Stand Up and Fight" 1939 (Teamster); "Union Pacific" 1939 (Engineer); "Konga, the Wild Stallion" 1940 (Fisher); "Bells of Rosarita" 1945; "King of the Forest Rangers" 1946-serial (Citizen); "Saddle Pals" 1947; "Along the Great Divide" 1951 (Defense Counsel); "The Big Sky" 1952.

Ashbrook, Daphne. Films: "Longarm" TVM-1988 (Pearl).

Ashby, Linden. Films: "8 Seconds" 1994 (Martin Hudson); "Wyatt Earp" 1994 (Morgan Earp).

Ashdown, Isa. TV: *Wild Bill*

Hickok—"The Lady Mayor" 7-10-51, "The Lady School Teacher" 10-2-51, "Grandpa and Genie" 5-20-52, "Ghost Town Lady" 1-27-53; *Annie Oakley*—Semi-Regular 1954-57 (Elroy).

Ashdown, Nadene. Films: "Toughest Man in Arizona" 1952 (Jesse Billings); "Frontier Gambler" 1956. TV: *Wild Bill Hickok*—"The Doctor Story" 7-1-52 (Susie); *The Lone Ranger*—"Uncle Ed" 3-3-55.

Ashe, Martin. TV: *Iron Horse*—"The Pembrooke Blood" 1-9-67 (Tom); *The Big Valley*—"A Noose Is Waiting" 11-13-67 (Martin Erskine); *Bonanza*—"The Survivors" 11-10-68 (Major Anderson).

Ashe, Warren (1903-9/19/47). Films: "Deerslayer" 1943 (Harry March).

Asher, Max (1880-4/15/57). Films: "Mike and Jake in the Wild West" 1913; "The Tender-Hearted Sheriff" 1914; "At Devil's Gorge" 1923 (Tobias Blake); "Riders of the Range" 1923 (Red Morriss); "Trigger Finger" 1924 (Mackhart's Deputy); "Beyond the Rockies" 1926 (Mayor Smithson); "Avenging Fangs" 1927 (Sheriff); "Galloping Fury" 1927 (Freckles Watson); "Trigger Tricks" 1930 (Mike); "Rider of Death Valley" 1932 (Citizen); "Crashing Broadway" 1933 (Bozo).

Ashkenazy, Irvin. Films: "Davy Crockett and the River Pirates" 1956 (Moose). ¶TV: *Walt Disney Presents*—"Davy Crockett"—Regular 1954-55 (Moose).

Ashley, Edward (1904-). Films: "The Great Scout and Cathouse Thursday" 1976 (Nancy Sue). ¶TV: *Jim Bowie*—"The Alligator" 12-6-57 (Armand de Rivnac); *The Texan*—"The Telegraph Story" 10-26-59 (Darrell Stanton); *Maverick*—"The Marquesa" 1-3-60 (Knobby Ned Wingate), "The Iron Hand" 2-21-60 (Nobby Ned Wingate); *Bonanza*—"The Last Trophy" 3-26-60 (Lord Dunsford).

Ashley, Elizabeth (1939-). Films: "Rancho Deluxe" 1975 (Cora Brown); "Stagecoach" TVM-1986 (Dallas). ¶TV: *Stoney Burke*—"Tigress by the Tail" 5-6-63 (Donna Weston); *The Men from Shiloh*—"The West vs. Colonel MacKenzie" 9-16-70 (Faith).

Ashley, Herbert (1874-7/23/58). Films: "Rhythm on the Range" 1936 (Brakeman); "Belle Starr" 1941.

Ashley, Joel (1921-85). Films: "The Broken Star" 1956

(Messendyke); "Ghost Town" 1956 (Sgt. Dockery); "Rebel in Town" 1956 (Doctor); "Warlock" 1959 (Murch). ¶TV: *The Cisco Kid*—"Schoolmarm" 1-23-54; *Tales of the Texas Rangers*—"The Atomic Trail" 11-19-55 (Fred Douglas); *Gunsmoke*—"The Big Broad" 4-28-56 (Nate Bannister), "Chester's Mail Order Bride" 7-14-56 (Linus), "No Indians" 12-8-56 (Jake), "The Constable" 5-30-59 (2nd Cowboy), "The Wake" 12-10-60 (Harry); *The Adventures of Rin Tin Tin*—"Hubert Goes West" 5-18-56 (Hugh Marsh); *The Lone Ranger*—"The Courage of Tonto" 1-17-57; *Annie Oakley*—"The Dutch Gunmaker" 2-17-57 (John Reed); *Boots and Saddles*—"The Marquis of Donnybrook" 12-26-57 (Boone); *Zane Grey Theater*—"Man Unforgiving" 1-3-58 (Sam Baker); *The Restless Gun*—"Dragon for a Day" 9-29-58 (Sheriff Berryman); *Have Gun Will Travel*—"A Score for Murder" 11-22-58 (Jack Martin), "The Unforgiven" 11-7-59 (Caterall); *Wagon Train*—"The Flint McCullough Story" 1-14-59 (the Captain); *Black Saddle*—"Client: Steele" 3-21-59 (Barnes), "The Last Word" 1-23-58; *Bonanza*—"The Outcast" 1-9-60; *Daniel Boone*—"The Long Way Home" 2-16-67 (General Harmer).

Ashley, John (1934-). Films: "Hud" 1963 (Hermy); "Smoke in the Wind" 1975 (Whipple). ¶TV: *Jefferson Drum*—"Arrival" 4-25-58 (Tim Keough), "A Matter of Murder" 7-11-58 (Vardo); *Frontier Doctor*—"Elkton Lake Feud" 5-16-59; *The Deputy*—"The Wild Wind" 9-19-59 (Trooper Nelson); *Wagon Train*—"The Amos Gibbon Story" 4-20-60, "The Abel Weatherly Story" 1-2-63 (Fratelli); *Death Valley Days*—"The Hold-Up Proof Safe" 10-4-61 (Sandy); *Wild Wild West*—"The Night of the Watery Death" 11-11-66 (Lt. Keighley).

Ashley, Mary. TV: *Wild Wild West*—"The Night of the Circus of Death" 11-3-67 (Prescilla Goodbody).

Ashley, Peter. TV: *Gunsmoke*—"Cale" 5-5-62 (Will Archer).

Ashlock, Jesse. Films: "Song of the Sierras" 1946; "Ridin' Down the Trail" 1947; "Song of the Wasteland" 1947.

Ashton, Sylvia (1880-11/18/40). Films: "Buck's Lady Friend" 1915; "Overalls" 1916 (Widow Malone); "Johnny, Get Your Gun" 1919 (Aunt Agatha); "While Satan Sleeps" 1922 (Mrs. Bones).

Askam, Earl (1898-4/1/40). Films: "Silver Spurs" 1936 (Durango); "Trail Dust" 1936 (Red);

"Empty Saddles" 1937; "Thunder Trail" 1937 (Flinty); "Pride of the West" 1938 (Dutch); "Red River Range" 1938 (Morton); "Allegheny Uprising" 1939 (Jim's Man); "Union Pacific" 1939 (Bluett); "The Light of Western Stars" 1940 (Sneed); "Pioneers of the West" 1940 (Mac).

Askew, Luke (1937-). Films: "Will Penny" 1968 (Foxy); "Night of the Serpent" 1969-Ital.; "The Culpepper Cattle Company" 1972 (Luke); "The Great Northfield, Minnesota Raid" 1972 (Jim Younger); "The Magnificent Seven Ride" 1972 (Skinner); "Pat Garrett and Billy the Kid" 1973 (Eno); "This Was the West That Was" TVM-1974; "Mackintosh & T.J." 1975 (Cal); "Posse" 1975 (Krag); "The Invasion of Johnson County" TVM-1976 (Deputy Sheriff Brooks); "The Quest" TVM-1976 (Luke); "Wanda Nevada" 1979 (Ruby Muldoon); "Kung Fu: The Movie" TVM-1986 (Sheriff Mills); "Frank and Jesse" TVM-1995 (Lone Rider). ¶TV: *The High Chaparral*—"Shadow of the Wind" 1-10-69 (Johnny Ringo); *Bonanza*—"Kingdom of Fear" 4-4-71 (Hatch); *Bearcats!*—12-30-71 (Greer); *How the West Was Won*—"Hillary" 2-26-79 (Bowdin).

Askin, Leon (1907-). Films: "Carolina Cannonball" 1955 (Otto); "Guns for San Sebastian" 1967-U.S./Fr./Mex./Ital. (Vicar General). ¶TV: *The Restless Gun*—"The Shooting of Jett King" 10-28-57 (Ollie Rowan); *Daniel Boone*—"Benvenuto ... Who?" 10-9-69 (Roquelin).

Aslin, Edna. Films: "The Cowboy and the Outlaw" 1929 (Bertha Bullhead); "The Invaders" 1929; "Riders of the Rio Grande" 1929 (Barbara Steelman); "A Texas Cowboy" 1929; "Breezy Bill" 1930 (Barbara Pennypincher); "Arizona Trails" 1935; "Defying the Law" 1935 (Edna Francis); "The Phantom Cowboy" 1935; "Trails of Adventure" 1935; "Western Racketeers" 1935 (Molly Spellman).

Asner, Edward (1925-). Films: "El Dorado" 1967 (Bart Jason); "Skin Game" 1971 (Plunkettt). ¶TV: *The Outlaws*—"The Dark Sunrise of Griff Kincaid" 1-4-62 (Keef); *The Virginian*—"Echo from Another Day" 3-27-63 (George Johnson); *Stoney Burke*—"Tigress by the Tail" 5-6-63 (Kapp); *Gunsmoke*—"Hung High" 11-14-64 (Sergeant Wilks), "The Whispering Tree" 11-12-66 (Redmond); *A Man Called Shenandoah*—"The Verdict" 11-1-65 (Sam Chance); *Iron Horse*—"The Prisoners" 12-30-67 (Ned Morley); *Wild Wild West*—"The Night of the Amnesiac" 2-9-68 (Furman Crotty); *Here Come the Brides*—"The Firemaker" 1-15-69 (Belter), "The Legend of Big Foot" 11-14-69 (Matt).

Ast, Pat (1942-). Films: "The Duchess and the Dirtwater Fox" 1976 (Dance Hall Girl).

Astaire, Fred (1899-6/22/87). Films: "The Over-the-Hill Gang Rides Again" TVM-1970 (the Baltimore Kid).

Astar, Ben. Films: "Fort Ti" 1953 (Francois Leroy).

Asther, Nils (1897-10/13/81). Films: "Alaska" 1944.

Asti, Adriana (1933-). Films: "Zorro" 1974-Ital./Fr.

Astin, John (1930-). Films: "Evil Roy Slade" TVM-1972 (Evil Roy Slade); "The Brothers O'Toole" 1973. ¶TV: *Maverick*—"The Town That Wasn't Threre" 10-2-60 (Joe Lambert); *Destry*—"The Infernal Triangle" 5-1-64 (Pete Daley); *Wild Wild West*—"The Night of the Tartar" 2-3-67 (Count Nikolai Sazanov); *Sheriff Who?*—Pilot 9-5-67 (Roy Slade); *Gunsmoke*—"Hard Luck Henry" 10-23-67 (Hard-Luck Henry); *Death Valley Days*—"The Gold Mine on Main Street" 5-11-68 (Jesse Martin); *Bonanza*—"Abner Willoughby's Return" 12-21-69 (Abner Willoughby); *The Men from Shiloh*—"Jump-Up" 3-24-71 (Slick); *Adventures of Brisco County, Jr.*—Pilot 8-27-93 (Prof. Albert Wickwire), "No Man's Land" 9-10-93 (Prof. Albert Wickwire), "Socrates' Sister" 9-24-93 (Prof. Albert Wickwire), "Senior Spirits" 10-15-93 (Prof. Albert Wickwire), "Iron Horses" 11-19-93 (Prof. Albert Wickwire), "High Treason" 5-13-94 & 5-20-94 (Prof. Albert Wickwire).

Astin, Mackenzie (1973-). Films: "Iron Will" 1994 (Will Stoneman); "Wyatt Earp" 1994 (Young Man on Boat).

Astor, Camille (1896-9/16/44). Films: "The Regeneration of the Apache Kid" 1911; "The White Medicine Man" 1911; "The Bandit's Mask" 1912; "A Message to Kearney" 1912; "The Old Stage Coach" 1912; "The Rancher's Failing" 1913; "Chimmie Fadden Out West" 1915 (the Duchess).

Astor, Gertrude (1887-11/9/77). Films: "Cheyenne's Pal" 1917; "The Girl Who Wouldn't Quit" 1918 (Stella Carter); "Tapering Fingers" 1919; "What Am I Bid?" 1919 (Diana Newlands); "The Branding Iron" 1920 (Betty Morena); "Broadway or Bust" 1924 (Mrs. Dean Smythe); "The Ridin' Kid from Powder River" 1924 (Kansas Lou); "The Reckless

Sex" 1925 (Lucile Dupre); "Border Brigands" 1935 (Big Carrie); "Northern Frontier" 1935 (Mae); "The Mysterious Avenger" 1936; "Empty Saddles" 1937 (Eloise Hayes); "Wells Fargo" 1937; "Montana" 1950 (Woman); "At Gunpoint" 1955 (Woman); "The Oklahoman" 1957 (Woman); "The Man Who Shot Liberty Valance" 1962.

Astor, Mary (1906-9/25/87). Films: "Don Q, Son of Zorro" 1925 (Dolores de Muro); "Rose of the Golden West" 1927 (Elena); "The Lash" 1930 (Rosita Garcia); "Brigham Young—Frontiersman" 1940 (Mary Ann Young); "Desert Fury" 1947 (Fritzie Haller). ¶TV: *Zane Grey Theater*—"Black Is for Grief" 4-12-57 (Sarah Simmons); *U.S. Marshal*—"My Sons" 4-11-59 (Amy); *Rawhide*—"Incident Near the Promised Land" 2-3-61 (Emma Cardwell).

Atcher, Leota. Films: "Hail to the Rangers" 1943 (Bonnie Montgomery).

Atcher, Robert Owen (1914-10/30/93). Films: "Hail to the Rangers" 1943 (Bob Atcher).

Atchison, Tex. Films: "Gun Law Justice" 1949; "Gun Runner" 1949.

Atchley, Hooper (1887-11/16/43). Films: "The Santa Fe Trail" 1930 (Marc Collard); "Arizona Terror" 1931 (Captain Cole Porter); "Branded Men" 1931; "Clearing the Range" 1931 (Lafe Kildare); "Near the Trail's End" 1931; "Sundown Trail" 1931 (George Marsden); "Fighting for Justice" 1932 (Trout); "Gold" 1932 (Peter Kramer); "Local Bad Man" 1932 (Joe Murdock); "Spirit of the West" 1932 (Matt Ryder); "Drum Taps" 1933; "The Dude Bandit" 1933 (Al Burton); "Scarlet River" 1933 (Clink McPherson); "Gun Justice" 1934 (Sam Burkett); "The Prescott Kid" 1934 (Bonner); "Speed Wings" 1934 (Crandall); "The Westerner" 1934 (Wayne Wallace); "The New Frontier" 1935; "The Outlaw Deputy" 1935 (Howger); "Sagebrush Troubador" 1935 (Henry Nolan); "Roarin' Lead" 1936 (Hackett); "The Old Barn Dancer" 1938 (Maxwell); "Mountain Rhythm" 1939 (Daniels); "Saga of Death Valley" 1939; "Adventures of Red Ryder" 1940-serial (Treadway); "The Gay Caballero" 1940 (Sheriff McBride); "Geronimo" 1940 (George Boutwell); "Honky Tonk" 1941 (Senator Ford); "King of the Texas Rangers" 1941-serial (Porter); "In Old California" 1942; "Black Hills Express" 1943 (Jason Phelps); "In Old Oklahoma" 1943.

Ates, Roscoe (1895-3/1/62).

Films: "Billy the Kid" 1930 (Old Stuff); "Come on, Danger!" 1932 (Rusty); "Rainbow Trail" 1932 (Ike Wilkins); "Renegades of the West" 1932 (Dr. Fawcett); "The Cheyenne Kid" 1933 (Gaby Bush); "Scarlet River" 1933 (Ulysses Mope); "God's Country and the Woman" 1937 (Gander Hopkins); "The Great Adventures of Wild Bill Hickok" 1938 (Snake Eyes); "Riders of the Black Hills" 1938 (Sheriff Brown); "Three Texas Steers" 1939 (Sheriff Brown); "Cowboy from Sundown" 1940 (Gloomy Day); "Rancho Grande" 1940 (Tex); "Meet Roy Rogers" 1941-short; "Bad Men of Missouri" 1941 (Lafe); "Robin Hood of the Pecos" 1941 (Guffy); "Colorado Serenade" 1946 (Soapy Jones); "Driftin' River" 1946 (Soapy); "Stars Over Texas" 1946 (Soapy); "Tumbleweed Trail" 1946 (Soapy); "Wild West" 1946 (Soapy); "Range Beyond the Blue" 1947 (Soapy); "Shadow Valley" 1947 (Soapy); "West to Glory" 1947 (Soapy); "Wild Country" 1947 (Soapy); "Black Hills" 1948 (Soapy); "Check Your Guns" 1948 (Soapy); "The Hawk of Powder River" 1948 (Soapy); "Prairie Outlaws" 1948; "Thunder in the Pines" 1948 (Whiskers); "The Tioga Kid" 1948 (Soapy); "Tornado Range" 1948 (Soapy); "The Westward Trail" 1948 (Soapy); "Hills of Oklahoma" 1950 (Dismal); "The Stranger Wore a Gun" 1953 (Milt Hooper); "Those Redheads from Seattle" 1953 (Dan Taylor); "The Sheepman" 1958. ¶TV: *The Marshal of Gunsight Pass*—Pilot 1950 (Deputy); *The Cisco Kid*—"The Census Taker" 6-7-52; *Annie Oakley*—Semi-Regular 1954-57 (Curley Dawes); *Wagon Train*—"The Sacramento Story" 6-25-58 (Placer Pete); *The Adventures of Rin Tin Tin*—"Sorrowful Joe Returns" 2-1-57 (Jorgenson); *The Restless Gun*—"The Painted Beauty" 1-5-59 (Juniper Dunlap); *Maverick*—"Gun-Shy" 1-11-59 (Barfly), "Two Beggars on Horseback" 1-18-59 (Kibitzer), "Two Tickets to Ten Strike" 3-15-59 (Barker), "Hadley's Hunters" 9-25-60 (Albert); *Lawman*—"The Visitor" 3-15-59 (Old Timer), "The Gang" 3-29-59 (Ike), "The Stranger" 1-17-60; *Buckskin*—"A Well of Gold" 3-16-59 (Harrison); *Tales of Wells Fargo*—"Long Odds" 12-14-59 (Renton), "Long Odds" 6-27-60 (Renton); *Sugarfoot*—"Man from Medora" 11-21-60 (Barber); *Whispering Smith*—"Three for One" 7-3-61 (Sheriff).

Athens, Vi. Films: "Cowboy from Lonesome River" 1944; "Saddle Leather Law" 1944.

Atherton, William (1946-). Films: "Grim Prairie Tales" 1990 (Arthur); "Frank and Jesse" TVM-1995 (Allan Pinkerton). ¶TV: *Centennial*—Regular 1978-79 (Jim Lloyd).

Athloff, Charles. Films: "Hills of Peril" 1927 (Ezra).

Atienza, Edward (1924-). TV: *The Outlaws*—"The Fortune Stone" 12-15-60 (Fescu).

Atkinson, Frank (1890-2/23/63). Films: "Smoke Lightning" 1933 (Alf Bailey).

Atkinson, George (1877-5/1/68). Films: "The Crimson Canyon" 1928 (Abner Slade).

Atkinson, Jack. Films: "Stampede" 1936 (Hodge).

Atterbury, Ellen. TV: *Have Gun Will Travel*—"Blind Circle" 12-16-61 (Mrs. Madison); *The Rounders*—9-27-66 (Pearl).

Atterbury, Malcolm (1907-8/23/92). Films: "Man Without a Star" 1955; "Dakota Incident" 1956 (Bartender); "The Rawhide Years" 1956 (Paymaster); "Reprisal!" 1956 (Luther Creed); "Stranger at My Door" 1956 (Rev. Hastings); "The Dalton Girls" 1957 (Mr. Sewell, the Bank Manager); "Fury at Showdown" 1957 (Norris); "Badman's Country" 1958 (Buffalo Bill Cody); "From Hell to Texas" 1958 (Hotel Clerk); "Rio Bravo" 1959 (Jake); "Hell Bent for Leather" 1960 (Gambie); "Cattle King" 1963 (Clevenger). ¶TV: *Gunsmoke*—"Matt Gets It" 9-10-55 (Bird), "Yorky" 2-18-56 (Seldon), "Brush at Elkador" 9-15-56 (Liveryman), "The Cover-Up" 1-12-57 (Jed Bates), "Milly" 11-25-61 (Bart Glover), "The Boys" 5-26-62 (Professor Eliot), "Take Her, She's Cheap" 10-31-64 (Duggan Carp), "My Brother's Keeper" 11-15-71 (Cob); *Ford Theater*—"Sudden Silence" 10-10-56; *DuPont Theater*—"The Texas Ranger" 4-9-57 (Conductor); *Wagon Train*—"The John Darro Story" 11-6-57, "The Riley Gratton Story" 12-4-57 (Bixby), "The Julia Gage Story" 12-18-57, "The Jessie Cowan Story" 1-8-58 (Bixby); *Fury*—"The Renegade" 11-9-57 (Steve Cruthers); *Schlitz Playhouse of the Stars*—"Way of the West" 6-6-58 (Johnson); *Rawhide*—"Incident of the Power and the Plow" 2-13-59 (Will Morton), "Encounter at Boot Hill" 9-14-65 (Jarvis); *Have Gun Will Travel*—"Shot by Request" 10-10-59 (Sheriff); *Bonanza*—"The Sisters" 12-12-59 (Ol' Virginny), "The Unwritten Commandment" 4-10-66

(Willard Walker); *Man from Blackhawk*—"The Savage" 1-15-60 (Seth Miles); *The Texan*—"Thirty Hours to Kill" 2-1-60; *The Tall Man*—"A Bounty for Billy" 10-15-60 (Jagger); *The Westerner*—"Dos Pinos" 11-4-60 (Andy), "Treasure" 11-18-60; *Stagecoach West*—"The Guardian Angels" 6-6-61 (Joshua Jessop); *A Man Called Shenandoah*—"The Siege" 12-13-65 (Judge Evans); *Daniel Boone*—"Requiem for Craw Green" 12-1-66 (Thaddeus Hill); *Laredo*—"The Other Cheek" 2-10-67 (Ernest Snilly); *The Guns of Will Sonnett*—"Home Free" 11-22-68 (Asa Campbell).

Atwater, Barry (1918-5/24/78). Films: "Man from Del Rio" 1956 (Dan Ritchy); "The Hard Man" 1957 (George Dennison); "The True Story of Jesse James" 1957 (Attorney Walker); "Alvarez Kelly" 1966 (Gen. Kautz); "Return of the Gunfighter" TVM-1967 (Lomax). ¶TV: *Frontier*—"The Shame of a Nation" 10-23-55, "Romance of Poker Alice" 12-11-55; *Gunsmoke*—"Robin Hood" 2-4-56 (Mr. Bowen), "How to Kill a Woman" 11-30-57 (Jesse Daggett), "The Coward" 3-7-59 (Ed Eby), "Doc Judge" 2-6-60 (Brice Harp), "The Innocent" 11-24-69 (Yewker); *Zane Grey Theater*—"Blood in the Dust" 10-11-57 (Gunman); *Have Gun Will Travel*—"The Reasonable Man" 1-11-58; *Bat Masterson*—"Trail Pirate" 12-31-58 (Egan); *Black Saddle*—"Client: Mowery" 3-28-59 (Coley Dakins), "Client: Brand" 5-16-59 (Brand); *Bronco*—"School for Cowards" 4-21-59; *Cheyenne*—"Gold, Glory and Custer—Prelude" 1-4-60 (Col. George Custer), "Gold, Glory and Custer—Requiem" 1-11-60 (Col. George Custer); *The Rebel*—"Absolution" 4-24-60 (Colonel Morgan), "The Executioner" 6-18-61 (Chief Leblanc); *Shotgun Slade*—"Crossed Guns" 9-19-60 (Phillips); *Riverboat*—"The Water of Gorgeous Springs" 11-7-60 (Gould Jennings); *Lawman*—"The Unmasked" 6-17-62 (Carter Banks); *Empire*—"The Four Thumbs Story" 1-8-63 (Dr. Forsythe); *Wagon Train*—"The Cassie Vance Story" 12-23-63, "The Barbara Lindquist Story" 10-18-64 (Frazer); *Rawhide*—"Corporal Dasovik" 12-4-64 (Chief), "Crossing at White Feather" 12-7-65; *Bonanza*—"Five Sundowns to Sunup" 12-5-65 (Merrick); *Wild Wild West*—"The Night of the Camera" 11-29-68 (Gideon Stix); *Lancer*—"The Fix-It Man" 2-11-69 (Bonell); *Kung Fu*—"Night of the Owls, Day of the Doves" 2-14-74 (Kyle Thurmond).

Atwater, Edith (1912-3/14/86).

Films: "Ride a Northbound Horse" 1969; "True Grit" 1969 (Mrs. Floyd); "Mackintosh & T.J." 1975. ¶TV: *The Legend of Jesse James*—"One Too Many Mornings" 11-22-65 (Sarah Todd); *Bonanza*—"The Night Virginia City Died" 9-13-70 (Roberta).

Atwill, Lionel (1885-4/22/46). Films: "Raiders of Ghost City" 1944-serial (Alex Morel).

Auberjonois, Rene (1940-). Films: "McCabe and Mrs. Miller" 1971 (Sheehan); "The Wild Wild West Revisited" TVM-1979 (Capt. Sir David Edney); "Longarm" TVM-1988 (Gov. Lew Wallace); "The Ballad of Little Jo" 1993 (Streight Hollander).

Aubert, Lenore (1918-). Films: "The Prairie" 1947 (Ellen Wade).

Aubrey, Danielle. TV: *Wagon Train*—"The Elizabeth McQueeney Story" 10-28-59; *Laramie*—"Double Eagles" 11-20-62 (Marie Duval); *Bonanza*—"Three Brides for Hoss" 2-20-66 (Yvette).

Aubrey, Jimmy (1887-9/2/83). Films: "The Gold Hunters" 1925 (Shorty); "Call of the Klondike" 1926 (Bowery Bill); "A Gentleman Preferred" 1928 (Bill Jenkins); "Code of Honor" 1930 (Nosey); "The Lonesome Tail" 1930 (Tenderfoot); "The Sheriff's Secret" 1931; "Forty-Five Calibre Echo" 1932; "Lariats and Sixshooters" 1933; "Border Guns" 1934 (Doctor Wilson); "The Border Menace" 1934 (Sheriff); "A Demon for Trouble" 1934 (Killer); "Fighting Hero" 1934 (Cowboy); "Loser's End" 1934 (Dick); "Potluck Pards" 1934; "Rawhide Mail" 1934 (Mike); "Terror of the Plains" 1934 (Henchman); "The Way of the West" 1934 (Jim, the Bartender); "West on Parade" 1934; "Courage of the North" 1935 (Constable Jimmy Downs); "Coyote Trails" 1935; "Defying the Law" 1935 (Jake Palmer); "The Judgement Book" 1935 (Ed Worden); "The Laramie Kid" 1935 (Convict); "The Phantom Cowboy" 1935 (Ptomaine Pete); "Rio Rattler" 1935; "Silent Valley" 1935; "Six Gun Justice" 1935; "Tracy Rides" 1935 (Cowboy); "Aces and Eights" 1936 (Lucky); "Fast Bullets" 1936 (Jake); "Gun Grit" 1936 (Murphy); "Lightning Bill Carson" 1936 (Pete); "Ridin' On" 1936; "Roamin' Wild" 1936; "Stormy Trails" 1936 (Shives); "Too Much Beef" 1936 (Shorty Rawlins); "The Traitor" 1936 (Bus Driver Slim); "Vengeance of Rannah" 1936; "Danger Valley" 1937; "The Idaho Kid" 1937 (Gunman); "Law of the Ranger" 1937; "Moonlight on the Range"

1937; "Knight of the Plains" 1938; "The Painted Trail" 1938; "Phantom Ranger" 1938 (Telegraph Operator); "The Rangers' Roundup" 1938; "Six-Gun Trail" 1938; "Songs and Bullets" 1938; "West of Rainbow's End" 1938 (Postmaster); "Frontier Marshal" 1939 (Cockney); "Mesquite Buckaroo" 1939; "Smoky Trails" 1939 (Cookie); "Covered Wagon Trails" 1940 (Denton); "The Kid from Santa Fe" 1940 (Henry Lupton); "Pinto Canyon" 1940 (George); "Pioneer Days" 1940 (Guard); "Wild Horse Valley" 1940 (Shag Williams); "Law of the Wolf" 1941; "Riding the Sunset Trail" 1941 (Jim Dawson); "Along the Sundown Trail" 1942; "Billy the Kid Trapped" 1942; "Boot Hill Bandits" 1942 (the Drunk); "Border Roundup" 1942; "Outlaws of Boulder Pass" 1942; "Bad Men of Thunder Gap" 1943; "Fighting Valley" 1943; "The Haunted Ranch" 1943; "Law of the Saddle" 1943; "My Friend Flicka" 1943; "Raiders of Red Gap" 1943; "The Renegade" 1943; "Wild Horse Rustlers" 1943 (Deputy); "Blazing Frontier" 1944; "Death Rides the Plains" 1944; "The Drifter" 1944 (Sheriff Perkins); "Oath of Vengeance" 1944; "Outlaw Roundup" 1944; "The Pinto Bandit" 1944; "Trail of Terror" 1944; "Ghost of Hidden Valley" 1946 (Tweedle); "Thunder Town" 1946 (Peter Collins).

Aubuchon, Jacques (1924-12/28/91). Films: "Gun Glory" 1957 (Sam Winscott); "September Gun" TVM-1983 (Father Jerome). ¶TV: *Gunsmoke*—"The Guitar" 7-21-56 (Short), "The Roundup" 9-29-56 (Ray Torp), "Bank Baby" 3-20-65 (Bert Clum), "The Sharecroppers" 3-31-75 (Linder Hogue); *The Restless Gun*—"Strange Family in Town" 1-20-58 (Johann Hoffman); *Trackdown*—"The Witness" 1-24-58 (Payette), "The House" 3-21-58 (Ben Steele); *Zane Grey Theater*—"License to Kill" 2-7-58 (Mayor Danforth); *Northwest Passage*—"The Assassin" 11-16-58 (Lt. Joseph Sarat); *Bat Masterson*—"River Boat" 2-18-59 (King Henry); *Have Gun Will Travel*—"Incident at Borasca Bend" 3-21-59 (Judge Wessen), "The Campaign of Billy Banjo" 5-28-60 (Billy Banjo), "Squatter's Rights" 12-23-61 (Moriarity); *Wanted—Dead or Alive*—"The Kovack Affair" 3-28-59 (Peter Kovack); *Rawhide*—"Incident at Spanish Rock" 12-18-59 (Juan Carroyo), "A Woman's Place" 3-30-62 (Prof. Daniel Pearson); *The Law of the Plainsman*—"The Comet" 1-21-60 (Jordan); *Hotel De Paree*—"Hard

Luck for Sundance" 2-19-60 (Harry Holcombe); *Johnny Ringo*—"The Reno Brothers" 2-25-60 (Collins/Carter Scarrbro); *Man from Blackhawk*—"The Sons of Don Antonio" 4-22-60 (Don Antonio); *Maverick*—"Dutchman's Gold" 1-22-61 (the Dutchman); *Cheyenne*—"Duel at Judas Basin" 1-30-61 (Pike Hanson); *The Outlaws*—"The Bill Doolin Story" 3-2-61 (Jones); *Sugarfoot*—"Stranger in Town" 3-27-61 (Harry Bishop); *Wide Country*—"A Cry from the Mountain" 1-17-63 (Mikla Szradna); *The Virginian*—"The Final Hour" 5-1-63 (Antek); *Daniel Boone*—"The Sound of Fear" 2-11-65 (William "Toff" Dunston); *Laredo*—"Limit of the Law Larkin" 1-27-66 (Judge Ike Macallam), "Hey Diddle Diddle" 2-24-67 (Morgan); *F Troop*—"Yellow Bird" 10-20-66 (Gideon D. Jeffries); *Kung Fu*—"Barbary House" 2-15-75 (French), "Flight to Orion" 2-22-75 (French), "The Brothers Cain" 3-1-75 (French), "Full Circle" 3-15-75 (French); *Barbary Coast*—"An Iron-Clad Plan" 10-31-75 (Roszack); *The Quest*—"Seventy-Two Hours" 11-3-76 (Mayor).

Audley, Eleanor (1905-11/25/-91). Films: "The Second Time Around" 1961 (Mrs. Trask). ¶TV: *Jim Bowie*—"The Select Females" 11-23-56 (Miss Peabody); *Wagon Train*—"The Millie Davis Story" 11-26-58 (Mrs. Winton), "The Kitty Allbright Story" 10-4-61 (Mother Allbright), "The Cassie Vance Story" 12-23-63; *Have Gun Will Travel*—"The Day of the Bad Men" 1-9-60 (Cynthia Palmer), "Squatter's Rights" 12-23-61 (School Teacher), "The Debutante" 1-19-63 (Mrs. Quincy); *Man from Blackhawk*—"Remember Me Not" 9-9-60 (Comtesse de Villon); *The Big Valley*—"The Brawlers" 12-15-65 (Mother Callahan); *Pistols 'n' Petticoats*—"No Sale" 9-24-66 (Mrs. Teasley), 10-8-66 (Mrs. Teasley), 12-31-66 (Mrs. Teasley), 1-14-67 (Mrs. Teasley).

Audran, Stephane (1939-). Films: "Eagle's Wing" 1979-Brit./Span. (the Widow).

Auer, Florence (1880-5/14/62). Films: "The Kentuckian" 1908; "The Tavern-Keeper's Daughter" 1908; "Silver Lode" 1954 (Mrs. Elmwood). ¶TV: *Wild Bill Hickok*—"The Fortune Telling Story" 4-22-52.

Auer, Mischa (1905-3/5/67). Films: "The Last of the Mohicans" 1932-serial; "The Western Code" 1932 (Chapman); "The Gay Desperado" 1936 (Diego); "Destry Rides Again" 1939 (Boris Callahan); "Trail

of the Vigilantes" 1940 (Dmitri Bolo). ¶TV: *Desilu Playhouse*—"Ballad for a Badman" 1-26-59 (Baron Von Zigler).

August, Adele. Films: "Apache Ambush" 1955 (Ann). ¶TV: *Cheyenne*—"Julesburg" 10-11-55 (Jeremy Barnes).

August, Edwin (1883-3/4/64). Films: "The Fugitive" 1910; "The Squaw's Love" 1911; "A Tale of the Wilderness" 1912; "On Burning Sands" 1913; "Old California" 1914; "The Two-Gun Man" 1914; "Romance of the West" 1930 (Chuck Anderson).

August, Tammy. *see* O'Grady, Lani.

Aumont, Tina (Tina Marquand) (1946-). Films: "Texas Across the River" 1966 (Lonetta); "Man: His Pride and His Vengeance" 1967-Ital./Ger. (Carmen); "Brothers Blue" 1973-Ital./Fr.

Aureli, Andrea. *see* Ray, Andrew.

Austin, Alan. TV: *Maverick*—"Relic of Fort Tejon" 11-3-57 (Tommy Norton); *Wanted—Dead or Alive*—"Barney's Bounty" 3-29-61 (Rake).

Austin, Blackie. TV: *26 Men*—"Cross and Double Cross" 10-28-58; *Wanted—Dead or Alive*—"No Trail Back" 11-28-59, "Man on Horseback" 12-5-59.

Austin, Carmen. TV: *Cheyenne*—"The Rebellion" 10-12-59 (Carla); *Gunsmoke*—"The Jackals" 2-12-68 (Mexican Girl).

Austin, Charles (1881-1/14/44). Films: "Blind Man's Bluff" 1927; "Wild West Whoopee" 1931.

Austin, Charlotte (1933-). Films: "Pawnee" 1957 (Dancing Fawn).

Austin, Frank (1877-5/13/54). Films: "The Desert Demon" 1925 (Dad Randall); "Moccasins" 1925 (John Avery); "Code of the Northwest" 1926 (Sandy McKenna); "The Drifter" 1929 (Seth Martin); "The Range Feud" 1931 (Jed Biggers); "Outlaws of the Prairie" 1937 (Doctor); "Wells Fargo" 1937 (Toothless Miner); "Texas Stampede" 1939 (Doctor); "West of Abilene" 1940 (Doctor); "Riders of Death Valley" 1941-serial (Chuckawala Charlie); "Twilight on the Trail" 1941 (Steve); "The Sea of Grass" 1947 (Station Agent); "Trail Street" 1947 (Farmer); "Arizona Territory" 1950 (Assayer).

Austin, Gene (1900-1/24/72). Films: "Songs and Saddles" 1938 (Gene Austin); "My Little Chickadee" 1940 (Gene Austin).

Austin, George. Films: "The Secret of Black Mountain" 1917 (George Cooper); "The Circus Cyclone" 1925 (Joe Dokes).

Austin, Jane. Films: "Butch and Sundance: The Early Days" 1979 (Daisy Mullen).

Austin, Jere (1876-11/12/27). Films: "Pure Grit" 1923 (Jim Kemp); "Sundown" 1924 (John Burke); "The Cowboy and the Countess" 1926 (Bozarri); "The Demon" 1926 (Bat Jackson); "The Desperate Game" 1926 (Mel Larrimer).

Austin, Leslie. Films: "Jamestown" 1923 (John Rolfe).

Austin, Lois (1909-4/26/57). Films: "Down Texas Way" 1942 (Stella); "Silver River" 1948 (Lady); "Night Stage to Galveston" 1952 (Mrs. Wilson).

Austin, Marie. Films: "Trail to Gunsight" 1944 (Clementine); "Boss of Boomtown" 1944 (Minerva); "Sing Me a Song of Texas" 1945.

Austin, Pam (1942-). Films: "Evil Roy Slade" TVM-1972 (Betsy Potter). ¶TV: *Lawman*—"Jailbreak" 6-10-62 (Little Britches); *Wagon Train*—"The Molly Kincaid Story" 9-16-63 (Merrybell); *The Virginian*—"It Takes a Big Man" 10-23-63 (Judy), "Girl on the Glass Mountain" 12-28-66 (Donna); *Wild Wild West*—"The Night of the Whirring Death" 2-18-66 (Priscilla Ames).

Austin, Vivian (Vivian Coe). Films: "Adventures of Red Ryder" 1940-serial (Beth Andrews); "Boss of Boomtown" 1944 (Dale Starr); "Trigger Trail" 1944 (Ann Catlett); "Twilight on the Prairie" 1944.

Austin, William (1884-6/15/-75). Films: "The Cowboy King" 1922 (Wilbur); "Ruggles of Red Gap" 1923 (Mr. Belknap-Jackson); "The Flaming Forest" 1926 (Alfred Wimbledon); "West of Broadway" 1926 (Mortimer Allison); "One Hour of Love" 1927 (Louis Carruthers); "Renfrew of the Royal Mounted" 1937 (Constable Holly).

Autry, Alan. Films: "Proud Men" TVM-1987 (Brian).

Autry, Gene (1907-). Films: "In Old Santa Fe" 1934 (Gene Autry); "Mystery Mountain" 1934-serial (Cowboy); "Melody Trail" 1935 (Gene Autry); "The Phantom Empire" 1935-serial (Gene); "Sagebrush Troubador" 1935 (Gene Autry); "The Singing Vagabond" 1935 (Captain Tex Autry); "Tumbling Tumbleweeds" 1935 (Gene Autry); "Comin' Round the Mountain" 1936 (Gene Autry); "Guns and Guitars" 1936

(Gene Autry); "Oh, Susanna!" 1936 (Gene Autry); "The Old Corral" 1936 (Gene Autry); "Red River Valley" 1936 (Gene Autry); "Ride, Ranger, Ride" 1936 (Gene Autry); "The Singing Cowboy" 1936 (Gene Autry); "The Big Show" 1937 (Gene Autry/Tom Ford); "Boots and Saddles" 1937 (Gene Autry); "Git Along, Little Dogies" 1937 (Gene Autry); "Public Cowboy No. 1" 1937 (Gene Autry); "Rootin' Tootin' Rhythm" 1937 (Gene Autry/the Apache Kid); "Round-Up Time in Texas" 1937 (Gene Autry); "Springtime in the Rockies" 1937 (Gene Autry); "Yodelin' Kid from Pine Ridge" 1937 (Gene Autry); "Gold Mine in the Sky" 1938 (Gene Autry); "Man from Music Mountain" 1938 (Gene); "The Old Barn Dancer" 1938 (Gene Autry); "Prairie Moon" 1938 (Gene Autry); "Rhythm of the Saddle" 1938 (Gene Autry); "Western Jamboree" 1938 (Gene Autry); "Blue Montana Skies" 1939 (Gene); "Colorado Sunset" 1939 (Gene Autry); "Home on the Prairie" 1939 (Gene); "In Old Monterey" 1939 (Gene Autry); "Mexicali Rose" 1939 (Gene); "Mountain Rhythm" 1939 (Gene Autry); "Rovin' Tumbleweeds" 1939 (Gene Autry); "South of the Border" 1939 (Gene Autry); "Carolina Moon" 1940 (Gene Autry); "Gaucho Serenade" 1940 (Gene); "Melody Ranch" 1940 (Gene); "Rancho Grande" 1940 (Gene Autry); "Ride, Tenderfoot, Ride" 1940 (Gene Autry); "Rodeo Dough" 1940-short; "Shooting High" 1940 (Will Carson); "Back in the Saddle" 1941 (Gene Autry); "Down Mexico Way" 1941 (Gene Autry); "Meet Roy Rogers" 1941-short; "Ridin' on a Rainbow" 1941 (Gene Autry); "Sierra Sue" 1941 (Gene Autry); "The Singing Hill" 1941; "Sunset in Wyoming" 1941 (Gene Autry); "Under Fiesta Stars" 1941 (Gene Autry); "Bells of Capistrano" 1942 (Gene Autry); "Call of the Canyon" 1942 (Gene Autry); "Cowboy Serenade" 1942 (Gene Autry); "Heart of the Rio Grande" 1942 (Gene Autry); "Home in Wyomin'" 1942 (Gene Autry); "Stardust on the Sage" 1942 (Gene Autry); "Sioux City Sue" 1946 (Gene Autry); "The Last Round-Up" 1947 (Gene Autry); "Robin Hood of Texas" 1947 (Gene); "Saddle Pals" 1947 (Gene); "Trail to San Antone" 1947 (Gene Autry); "Twilight on the Rio Grande" 1947 (Gene Autry); "Loaded Pistols" 1948 (Gene Autry); "The Strawberry Roan" 1948 (Gene Autry); "The Big Sombrero" 1949 (Gene Autry); "The Cowboy and the Indians" 1949 (Gene Autry); "Riders in the Sky" 1949

(Gene); "Riders of the Whistling Pines" 1949 (Gene); "Rim of the Canyon" 1949 (Gene Autry); "Sons of New Mexico" 1949 (Gene Autry); "Beyond the Purple Hills" 1950 (Gene Autry); "The Blazing Sun" 1950 (Gene Autry); "Cow Town" 1950 (Gene Autry); "Indian Territory" 1950 (Gene Autry); "Mule Train" 1950 (Gene); "Gene Autry and the Mounties" 1951 (Gene Autry); "Hills of Utah" 1951 (Gene Autry); "Silver Canyon" 1951 (Gene Autry); "Texans Never Cry" 1951 (Gene Autry); "Valley of Fire" 1951 (Gene Autry); "Whirlwind" 1951 (Gene Autry); "Apache Country" 1952 (Gene Autry); "Barbed Wire" 1952 (Gene Autry); "Blue Canadian Rockies" 1952 (Gene Autry); "Night Stage to Galveston" 1952 (Gene); "The Old West" 1952 (Gene); "Wagon Team" 1952 (Gene Autry); "Goldtown Ghost Raiders" 1953 (Gene Autry); "Last of the Pony Riders" 1953 (Gene Autry); "On Top of Old Smoky" 1953 (Gene); "Pack Train" 1953 (Gene Autry); "Saginaw Trail" 1953 (Gene Autry); "Winning of the West" 1953 (Gene Autry); "Alias Jesse James" 1959 (Gene Autry). ¶TV: *The Gene Autry Show*—Regular 1950-55 (Gene Autry).

Avalon, Frankie (1940-). Films: "The Alamo" 1960 (Smitty); "Guns of the Timberland" 1960 (Bert Harvey). ¶TV: *Rawhide*—"Incident at Farragut Pass" 10-31-63 (Billy Farragut).

Avalos, Luis (1946-). Films: "The Gambler V: Playing for Keeps" TVM-1994. ¶TV: *Ned Blessing: The Story of My Life and Times*—Regular 1993 (Crecencio).

Avenetti, Phillip. Films: "The Soul of Nigger Charley" 1973 (Pedro). ¶TV: *The High Chaparral*—"Surtee" 2-28-69; *Bonanza*—"The Hunter" 1-16-73 (the Mexican).

Averill, Arnold. Films: "Heart of the North" 1938 (Whipple).

Avery, Brian (1940-). Films: "Journey to Shiloh" 1968 (Carter Claiborne). ¶TV: *The Virginian*—"Girl on the Glass Mountain" 12-28-66 (Paul).

Avery, Charles (1873-7/23/26). Films: "A Western Romance" 1913; "The Fighting Ranger" 1925-serial; "The Rambling Ranger" 1927 (Seth Buxley); "The Western Rover" 1927 (Hinkey Hall).

Avery, Emile. Films: "Run of the Arrow" 1957 (Gen. Grant).

Avery, Phyllis (1924-). TV: *Zane Grey Theater*—"The Unrelenting Sky" 10-26-56 (Peg Howard); *Broken Arrow*—"The Teacher" 11-19-57 (Teacher); *Trackdown*—"Look for the Woman" 12-6-57 (Charlotte); *Rawhide*—"Incident in No Man's Land" 6-12-59 (Ann Macauley); *The Rifleman*—"The Baby Sitter" 12-15-59 (Leona Bartell); *The Deputy*—"Queen Bea" 2-20-60 (Beatrice Vale); *Tate*—"The Reckoning" 8-24-60 (Lulie); *Laramie*—"Ride into Darkness" 10-18-60 (Mae), "The Fugitives" 2-12-63 (Myra); *Have Gun Will Travel*—"The Man Who Struck Moonshine" 3-24-62 (Sylvia); *The Virginian*—"If You Have Tears" 2-13-63 (Martha Clain); *Daniel Boone*—"The Renegade" 9-28-67 (Martha Jimson).

Avery, Ted. Films: "Little Big Horn" 1951 (Pvt. Tim Harvey).

Avery, Tol (1915-8/27/73). Films: "Buchanan Rides Alone" 1958 (Simon Agry). ¶TV: *Maverick*—"According to Hoyle" 10-6-57 (George Cross), "Rope of Cards" 1-19-58 (John Cloan), "Yellow River" 2-8-59 (Sawyer), "Maverick Springs" 12-6-59 (John Flannery), "Last Wire from Stop Gap" 10-16-60 (Hulett), "Maverick at Law" 2-26-61 (Cyrus Murdock), "Poker Face" 1-7-62 (George Rockingham); *Colt .45*—"Circle of Fear" 3-7-58 (Archer Belgarde), "Queen of Dixie" 10-4-59 (Barnes); *Bronco*—"Quest of the Thirty Dead" 10-7-58 (Mohler), "Moment of Doubt" 4-2-62 (Turlowe); *Sugarfoot*—"Devil to Pay" 12-23-58 (Big Jim Case); *Lawman*—"The Posse" 3-8-59 (Bliss Carter); *Cheyenne*—"Outcast of Cripple Creek" 2-29-60 (Ab Murchison); *Tales of Wells Fargo*—"Treasure Coach" 10-14-61; *Bonanza*—"The Miracle Worker" 5-20-62 (Dr. Moore), "The Jury" 12-30-62 (Breese), "Ponderosa Matador" 1-12-64 (Troutman), "Justice Deferred" 12-17-67 (Judge), "Trouble Town" 3-17-68 (Almont), "What Are Pardners For" 4-12-70 (Bradley); *The Virginian*—"If You Have Tears" 2-13-63 (Coroner), "That Saunders Woman" 3-30-66 (Rutledge); *Temple Houston*—"Gallows in Galilee" 10-31-63 (Ed Bascombe); *Laredo*—"It's the End of the Road, Stanley" 3-10-66 (Millburn W. Willburn); *Death Valley Days*—"The Resurrection of Deadwood Dick" 10-22-66 (Frank Brenner), "Doc Holliday's Gold Bard" 12-31-66 (Walter Benson); *F Troop*—"The Ballot of Corporal Agarn" 10-27-66 (Derby Dan McGurney); *Iron Horse*—"Explosion at Waycrossing" 11-21-66 (J.J. Sedley); *Rango*—"It Ain't the Principle, It's the Money" 3-31-67 (Colonel); *Wild Wild West*—

"The Night of the Avaricious Actuary" 12-6-68 (Asa), "The Night of the Tycoons" 3-28-69 (Mr. Gorhan).

Avery, Val (1924-). Films: "Last Train from Gun Hill" 1959 (Bartender); "The Magnificent Seven" 1960 (Henry); "Hud" 1963 (Jose); "The Hallelujah Trail" 1965 (Denver Bartender); "The Dangerous Days of Kiowa Jones" TVM-1966 (Morgan); "Nevada Smith" 1966 (Buck Mason); "Hombre" 1967 (Delgado). ¶TV: *Zane Grey Theater*—"Proud Woman" 10-25-57 (Carson); *Gunsmoke*—"Cows and Cribs" 12-7-57 (Joe Nadler), "Twenty Miles from Dodge" 4-10-65 (Dorner), "The Lure" 2-25-67 (Trent), "A Man Called Smith" 10-27-69 (Bull); *Bonanza*—"Breed of Violence" 11-5-60 (Sheriff Kincaid); *Tales of Wells Fargo*—"Town Against a Man" 1-23-61 (Frank "Bully" Armstrong); *Have Gun Will Travel*—"The Gold Bar" 3-18-61 (Throckton); *Rawhide*—"Incident of the Blackstorms" 5-26-61; *Daniel Boone*—10-14-65 (Watowah); *The Virginian*—"Harvest of Strangers" 2-16-66 (Sunderland); *Wild Wild West*—"The Night of the Whirring Death" 2-18-66 (John Crane), "The Night of the Cadre" 3-24-67 (Warden Primwick), "Night of the Bubbling Death" 9-8-67 (Bad Logan); *Laredo*—"Road to San Remo" 11-25-66 (Sheriff Daniels); *Lancer*—"Julie" 10-29-68 (Wade); *Nichols*—"Wings of an Angel" 2-8-72 (Jasper), 3-7-72.

Avila, Enrique (1932-). Films: "Savage Pampas" 1966-U.S./Span./Arg. (Petizo); "Kitosch, the Man who Came from the North" 1967-Ital./Span.; "The Man Who Killed Billy the Kid" 1967-Span./Ital.

Avonde, Richard. Films: "Snow Dog" 1950 (Phillippe); "Oklahoma Justice" 1951; "Dead Man's Trail" 1952; "The Gunman" 1952; "Outlaw Women" 1952 (Frank Slater); "Waco" 1952 (Pedro); "Wild Horse Ambush" 1952 (Jalisco); "Fangs of the Arctic" 1953; "Savage Frontier" 1953 (Cherokee Kidd); "Shadows of Tombstone" 1953 (Deputy Todd); "Vigilante Terror" 1953. ¶TV: *Wild Bill Hickok*—"Outlaw Flats" 10-9-51, "Monster in the Lake" 8-12-52; *The Cisco Kid*—"Freedom of the Press" 9-27-52; *The Lone Ranger*—"El Toro" 5-7-53, "The Perfect Crime" 7-30-53; *The Roy Rogers Show*—"The Outlaws of Paradise Valley" 11-8-53, "The Kid from Silver City" 1-17-54, "The Lady Killer" 9-12-54; *Death Valley Days*—"Little Papeete" 11-25-53; *The Gene Autry Show*—"Law Comes to Scorpion" 10-22-55, "Feuding Friends"

11-26-55; *Tales of the Texas Rangers*—"The Devil's Deputy" 1-7-56 (Beau Morgan); *Brave Eagle*—"The Gentle Warrior" 1-25-56; *Sergeant Preston of the Yukon*—"Skagway Secret" 2-16-56 (Capt. Arnold); *The Adventures of Rin Tin Tin*—"Wagon Train" 11-23-56 (Bat Colby); *Jim Bowie*—"The Swordsman" 12-14-56 (Count De Nivernais), "Spanish Intrigue" 2-8-57 (Raul Guzman); *Circus Boy*—"The Remarkable Ricardo" 1-20-57 (Ricardo); *Wyatt Earp*—"The Vultures" 3-19-57 (Lawrence Younger); *Tales of Wells Fargo*—"Kid Brother" 5-23-60 (Le Main).

Avram, Chris (1931-). Films: "Man Called Django" 1971-Ital.; "Thunder Over El Paso" 1972-Ital./Span. (Santo); "California" 1976-Ital./Span. (Nelson).

Axton, Hoyt (1938-). Films: "Smoky" 1966 (Fred); "Desperado: Avalanche at Devil's Rider" TVM-1988 (Sheriff Ben Tree). ¶TV: *Bonanza*—"Dead and Gone" 4-4-65 (Howard Mead); *Iron Horse*—"Right of Way Through Paradise" 10-3-66 (Slash Birney).

Axzell, Evelyn (1890-5/11/77). Films: "The Hell Cat" 1918 (Wan-o-Mee).

Axzelle, Carl (1881-10/30/58). Films: "Driftin Sands" 1928.

Axzelle, Violet. Films: "The Dawn Trail" 1930 (Molly).

Ayars, Ann (1919-2/27/95). Films: "Apache Trail" 1943 (Constance Selden). ¶TV: *The Virginian*—"Brother Thaddeus" 10-30-63 (Sister St. Luke).

Aye, Maryan (1906-7/21/51). Films: "Montana Bill" 1921; "The Vengeance Trail" 1921 (Grace Winwood).

Ayer, Eleanor. TV: *Rawhide*—"Incident of Fear in the Streets" 5-8-59 (Mandy).

Ayer, Harold (1916-). TV: *Laredo*—"The Land Grabbers" 12-9-65; *Daniel Boone*—"The Kidnaping" 1-22-70.

Aylesworth, Arthur (1883-6/26/46). Films: "Call of the Wild" 1935 (2nd Miner in Dawson); "The Arizona Raiders" 1936 (Andy Winthrop); "King of the Pecos" 1936 (Hank Matthews); "Rose of the Rancho" 1936 (Sheriff James); "Sandflow" 1937 (Tex); "Wells Fargo" 1937 (Southern Orator); "Gold Is Where You Find It" 1938 (Rancher); "Drums Along the Mohawk" 1939 (George); "Frontier Marshal" 1939 (Card Player); "Jesse James" 1939 (Tom); "The Oklahoma Kid" 1939 (Judge

Morgan); "The Return of the Cisco Kid" 1939 (Stage Coach Driver); "Brigham Young—Frontiersman" 1940 (Jim Bridges); "Northwest Passage" 1940 (Flint, the Innkeeper); "Santa Fe Trail" 1940 (Abolitionist); "The Westerner" 1940 (Mr. Dixon); "Last of the Duanes" 1941 (Cannon); "Sin Town" 1942 (Sheriff Bagby).

Ayres, Agnes (1898-12/25/40). Films: "Sacred Silence" 1919; "The Inner Voice" 1920.

Ayres, John. Films: "The Halliday Brand" 1957. ¶TV: *Sergeant Preston of the Yukon*—"Underground Ambush" 4-25-57 (Inspector Graves), "Gold Rush Patrol" 1-16-58 (Inspector), "The Criminal Collie" 2-27-58 (Inspector).

Ayres, Lew (1908-). Films: "The Capture" 1950 (Vanner); "New Mexico" 1951 (Capt. Hunt). ¶TV: *Zane Grey Theater*—"The Unrelenting Sky" 10-26-56 (Clint Howard), "A Man to Look Up To" 11-29-57 (Jud Lester), "The Scar" 3-2-61 (Jesse Martin); *Frontier Justice*—Host 1958; *Laramie*—"Time of the Traitor" 12-11-62 (Dr. Samuel Mudd); *Gunsmoke*—"The Prodigal" 9-25-67 (Jonathan Cole); *The Big Valley*—"The Disappearance" 11-6-67 (Sheriff Roy Kingston), "Presumed Dead" 10-7-68 (Jason Fleet); *Here Come the Brides*—"One Good Lie Deserves Another" 2-12-69 (Matthew Muncey); *The Men from Shiloh*—"The Price of the Hanging" 11-11-70 (Judge Markham); *Kung Fu*—"The Vanishing Image" 12-20-74 (Beaumont); *Outlaws*—"Madrid" 2-7-87 (Timothy Wade).

Ayres, Sydney (1879-9/9/16). Films: "Heart of John Barlow" 1911; "How Algy Captured a Wild Man" 1911; "The Rival Stage Lines" 1911; "The Peacemaker" 1912; "Rose of San Juan" 1913; "The Pote Lariat of the Flying A" 1914; "True Western Hearts" 1914; "On Desert Sands" 1915.

Azzara, Candy (1945-). Films: "Hearts of the West" 1975 (Waitress).

Babatunde, Obba. TV: *Adventures of Brisco County, Jr.*—"AKA Kansas" 12-17-93 (Mongoose).

Babcock, Barbara (1937-). Films: "Day of the Evil Gun" 1968 (Angie); "Heaven with a Gun" 1969 (Mrs. Andrews); "Far and Away" 1992 (Nora Christie). ¶TV: *Best of the West*—"Frog Gets Lucky" 1-7-82; *Dr. Quinn, Medicine Woman*—Regular 1993- (Dorothy Jennings).

Babich, Frank. Films: "Barquero" 1970 (Roland).

Baca, Charles. Films: "Showdown" 1973 (Martinez).

Bacall, Lauren (1924-). Films: "The Shootist" 1976 (Bond Rogers).

Baccala, Donna (1945-). TV: *Gunsmoke*—"Blood Money" 1-22-68 (Elenya Skouras); *Cimarron Strip*—"The Greeners" 3-7-68 (Ruth Arlyn); *The Big Valley*—"A Passage of Saints" 3-10-69 (Emilena Grant); *The High Chaparral*—"A Time to Laugh, a Time to Cry" 9-26-69 (Mercedes).

Bach, Vivi (1937-). Films: "Bullets Don't Argue" 1964-Ital./Ger./Span. (Agnes).

Bachelor, Stephanie (1924-). Films: "Springtime in the Sierras" 1947 (Jean Loring); "Sons of Adventure" 1948 (Laura).

Bacigalupi, Louis (1910-8/6/66). Films: "The Talisman" 1966 (Isaac).

Backes, Alice (1923-). Films: "The Glory Guys" 1965 (Mrs. Poole). ¶TV: *Gunsmoke*—"Tail to the Wind" 10-17-59 (Cora), "Owney Tupper Had a Daughter" 4-4-64, "Sweet Billy, Singer of Songs" 1-15-66 (Widow Folsome); *The Law of the Plainsman*—"Passenger to Mescalero" 10-29-59; *The Rifleman*—"Mail Order Groom" 1-12-60 (Isabel); *The Virginian*—"The Accomplice" 12-19-62; *Wagon Train*—"The Link Cheney Story" 4-13-64 (Ada Meecham); *The Big Valley*—"Deathtown" 10-28-68; *Lancer*—"The Experiment" 2-17-70.

Backlinie, Susan. Films: "Grizzly and the Treasure" 1975 (Eve).

Backman, George. TV: *Daniel Boone*—"Empire of the Lost" 9-16-65 (Lt. Stuart Morris), "The Williamsburg Cannon" 1-12-67 & 1-19-67 (Major Ferguson), "The Man" 10-16-69 (Addison).

Backus, Anthony. Films: "Calamity Jane and Sam Bass" 1949 (Deputy).

Backus, Georgia. Films: "Shut My Big Mouth" 1942 (Woman); "Copper Canyon" 1950 (Martha Bassett); "Apache Drums" 1951 (Mrs. Keon); "Mark of the Renegade" 1951 (Duenna Concepcion).

Backus, Jim (1913-7/3/89). Films: "The Naked Hills" 1956 (Willis Haver); "The Wild and the Innocent" 1959 (Cecil Forbes); "Advance to the Rear" 1964 (Gen. Willoughby); "The Cockeyed Cowboys of Calico County" 1970 (Staunch). ¶TV: *Maverick*—"Three Queens Full" 11-12-61 (Joe Wheelwright); *Daniel Boone*—"The Scrimshaw Ivory Chart" 1-4-68 (Will Scataway); *Wild Wild West*—"The Night of the Sabatini Death" 2-2-69 (Fabian Swanson); *Alias Smith and Jones*—"The Biggest

Game in the West" 2-3-72 (J.P. Sterling); *Gunsmoke*—"Brides and Grooms" 2-10-75 (the Rev. Mr. Sims).

Baclanova, Olga (1899-9/6/74). Films: "Avalanche" 1928 (Grace Stillwell).

Bacon, Irving (1893-2/5/65). Films: "Alias the Bad Man" 1931 (Simpson); "Branded Men" 1931 (Ramrod); "Fighting Caravans" 1931 (Barfly); "The Lone Cowboy" 1934 (Zeke); "West of the Pecos" 1934 (Wes); "Powdersmoke Range" 1935 (General Storekeeper); "Wanderer of the Wasteland" 1935 (1st Bartender); "Arizona Mahoney" 1936 (Smoky); "Drift Fence" 1936 (Windy Watkins); "Hopalong Cassidy Returns" 1936 (Peg Leg Holden); "Rhythm on the Range" 1936 (Announcer); "The Texas Rangers" 1936 (David's Father); "The Texans" 1938 (Pvt. Chilina); "The Arizona Wildcat" 1939 (Jailor); "The Oklahoma Kid" 1939 (Hotel Clerk); "The Return of Frank James" 1940 (Man at Wagon Sale); "Ride on, Vaquero" 1941 (Baldy); "They Died with Their Boots On" 1941 (Salesman); "Western Union" 1941 (Barber); "The Great Man's Lady" 1942 (Parson); "The Spoilers" 1942 (Hotel Proprietor); "The Desperadoes" 1943 (Dan Walters); "In Old Oklahoma" 1943 (Ben, the Telegraph Operator); "King of the Cowboys" 1943 (Deputy Alf Cluckus); "Under Western Skies" 1945 (Sheriff); "Saddle Pals" 1947 (Thaddeus Bellweather); "Adventures in Silverado" 1948; "Albuquerque" 1948 (Dave Walton); "Sons of New Mexico" 1949 (Chris Dobbs); "Desert of Lost Men" 1951 (Skeeter Davis); "Rose of Cimarron" 1952 (Sheriff); "Devil's Canyon" 1953 (Abby's Guard); "Fort Ti" 1953 (Sgt. Monday Wash); "Kansas Pacific" 1953 (Casey); "Black Horse Canyon" 1954 (Doc); "At Gunpoint" 1955 (Ferguson); "Run for Cover" 1955 (Scotty); "Dakota Incident" 1956 (Tully Morgan); "Hidden Guns" 1956 (Doc Carter); "Ambush at Cimarron Pass" 1958 (Stanfield); "Fort Massacre" 1958 (Charlie). ¶TV: *Wild Bill Hickok*—"Prairie Flats Land Swindle" 5-6-52, "The Iron Major" 4-21-53; *Tales of the Texas Rangers*—"Trail Herd" 11-10-57 (Henry Waterman); *Maverick*—"Shady Deal at Sunny Acres" 11-23-58 (Employee), "The Sheriff of Duck 'n' Shoot" 9-27-59 (Andrews), "A Flock of Trouble" 2-14-60 (Honest Donald McFadden); *Wagon Train*—"The Millie Davis Story" 11-26-58 (Pete Bailey); *Laramie*—"Hour After Dawn" 3-15-60 (Elmer).

Bacon, James (1914-). Films: "More Wild Wild West" TVM-1980 (Wheelman).

Bacon, John. Films: "Guns for Hire" 1932; "The Lone Ranger" 1938-serial (Rancher).

Bacon, Lloyd (1890-11/15/55). Films: "Broncho Billy and the Card Sharp" 1915; "Broncho Billy and the Lumber King" 1915; "Broncho Billy Begins Life Anew" 1915; "Broncho Billy Misled" 1915; "Broncho Billy's Cowardly Brother" 1915; "The Burglar's Godfather" 1915; "A Christmas Revenge" 1915; "The Feud" 1919 (Ben Summers); "Square Deal Sanderson" 1919 (Will Bransford/Barney Owen); "Wagon Tracks" 1919 (Guy Merton); "Hands Off" 1921 (Ford Wadley).

Bacon, Ruth. Films: "Springtime in the Rockies" 1937 (Peggy).

Bacon, Shelby. Films: "Corpus Christi Bandits" 1945 (Moonlight); "Surrender" 1950 (Georgie).

Bad Bear, Chief. Films: "Tomahawk" 1951 (Indian).

Bad Bear, Ina. Films: "Dirty Dingus Magee" 1970 (Old Crone).

Badalo, Francisco. Films: "Companeros" 1970-Ital./Span./Ger. (Gen. Mongo).

Baddeley, Hermionie (1908-8/19/86). Films: "The Adventures of Bullwhip Griffin" 1967 (Irene Chesney).

Badessi, Giancarlo. Films: "Blood and Guns" 1968-Ital./Span.; "Night of the Serpent" 1969-Ital.; "Halleluja to Vera Cruz" 1973-Ital.

Badger, Clarence (1880-6/17/64). Films: "The Lady Doctor of Grizzly Gulch" 1915.

Baer, Buddy (1915-7/18/86). Films: "The Big Sky" 1952 (Romaine); "The Marshal's Daughter" 1953; "Jubilee Trail" 1954 (Nicolai Gregorovitch Karakozeff); "Hell Canyon Outlaws" 1957; "Once Upon a Horse" 1958 (Beulah's Brother); "Ride Beyond Vengeance" 1966 (Mr. Kratz). ¶TV: *Sky King*—"The Wild Man" 6-15-52 (LeTourneau); *Cheyenne*—"Big Ghost Basin" 3-12-57 (Mocassin Joe); *Circus Boy*—"The Gentle Giant" 6-16-57; *Have Gun Will Travel*—"High Wire" 11-2-57 (Bolo); *Gunsmoke*—"Never Pester Chester" 11-16-57 (Stobo); *Wagon Train*—"The Dan Hogan Story" 5-14-58; *Rawhide*—"Incident at El Crucero" 10-10-63 (Big Will Cornelius).

Baer, John. Films: "Arizona Manhunt" 1951 (Deputy Jim Brown); "Indian Uprising" 1951 (Lt. Whitley);

"The Battle at Apache Pass" 1952 (Pvt. Bolin); "Riding Shotgun" 1954 (Hughes). ¶TV: *Screen Director's Playhouse*—"Arroyo" 10-26-55 (Dude); *Trackdown*—"End of an Outlaw" 11-29-57 (Jim Murphy); *Wanted—Dead or Alive*—"The Medicine Man" 11-23-60 (Jim Lansing); *Temple Houston*—"Miss Katherina" 4-2-64 (Frank McGuire); *The High Chaparral*—"A Hanging Offense" 11-12-67 (Sergeant); *Gunsmoke*—"Patricia" 1-22-73 (Johnny's Father), "The Iron Blood of Courage" 2-18-74 (Nichols).

Baer, Mary (1910-12/9/72). Films: "Singing Guns" 1950 (Mother).

Baer, Max (1909-11/21/59). Films: "Buckskin Frontier" 1943 (Tiny); "Skipalong Rosenbloom" 1951 (Butcher Baer); "Utah Blaine" 1957 (Gus Ortmann); "Once Upon a Horse" 1958 (Ben). ¶TV: *The Lone Ranger*—"The Law and Miss Aggie" 4-11-57.

Baer, Jr., Max (1937-). Films: "A Time for Killing" 1967 (Sgt. Luther Liskell) ¶TV: *Maverick*—"Bundle from Birtain" 9-18-60 (Brazos), "A Bullet for the Teacher" 10-30-60 (Cowboy), "Kiz" 12-4-60 (Ticket Taker); *Cheyenne*—"The Beholden" 2-27-61 (Bert McGuire), "The Frightened Town" 3-20-61 (Callow); *Sugarfoot*—"Angel" 3-6-61 (Frank).

Baer, Parley (1914-). Films: "Comanche Territory" 1950 (Boozer); "Drango" 1957 (Randolph); "The Adventures of Bullwhip Griffin" 1967 (Chief Executioner); "Day of the Evil Gun" 1968 (Wilford); "Young Billy Young" 1969 (Bell); "The Over-the-Hill Gang Rides Again" TVM-1970 (the Mayor); "Skin Game" 1971 (Mr. Claggart); "The Incredible Rocky Mountain Race" TVM-1977 (Farley Osmond); "True Grit" TVM-1978 (Rollins); "Rodeo Girl" TVM-1980 (Doc Tanner). ¶TV: *Fury*—"The Horse Coper" 10-29-55 (Piggott); *Trackdown*—"The Toll Road" 1-31-58 (Ronald Desmond); *Zane Grey Theater*—"Make It Look Good" 2-5-59 (Clem Doud); *Black Saddle*—"Client: Starkey" 2-7-59 (Ed Gunther); *The Rifleman*—"A Matter of Faith" 5-19-59 (Walter Mathers), "A Friend in Need" 12-25-61 (Neff Parker); *The Texan*—"Blue Norther" 10-12-59 (Drummer); *Have Gun Will Travel*—"Tiger" 11-28-59 (Ellsworth), "Hobson's Choice" 4-7-62 (Sam Thurber), "Genesis" 9-15-62 (Reston); *Rango*—"The Daring Holdup of the Deadwood Stage" 1-20-67 (Wilkins); *Bonanza*—"Thunderhead Swindle"

4-29-61 (Jack Cunningham), "No Less a Man" 3-15-64 (Armistead). "The Emperor Norton" 2-27-66 (Harry Crawford); *Wagon Train*—"The Hobie Redman Story" 1-17-62 (Clyde Montgomery), "The Mavis Grant Story" 10-24-62 (Maitland), "The Eli Bancroft Story" 11-11-63; *Frontier Circus*—"Calamity Circus" 3-8-62 (Sheriff); *The Virginian*—"Woman from White Ting" 9-26-62 (Senator), "A Bad Place to Die" 11-8-67 (Pat Magill); *Laramie*—"The Fortune Hunter" 10-9-62; *The Slowest Gun in the West* 7-29-63 (Collingswood); *Rawhide*—"Incident at El Crucero" 10-10-63 (Bryant); *Temple Houston*—"The Third Bullet" 10-24-63 (Sheriff Beckman), "The Town That Trespassed" 3-26-64 (Claude Spanker); *Walt Disney Presents*—"Gallegher" 1965-67 (Mayor); *F Troop*—"The 86 Proof Spring" 12-14-65 (Colonel Watkins); *Death Valley Days*—"The Great Turkey War" 3-26-66 (Horace Greeley); *Laredo*—"Like One of the Family" 3-24-67 (Alcott); *The Guns of Will Sonnett*—"Join the Army" 1-3-69 (Gilbey); *The Outcasts*—"How Tall Is Blood?" 5-5-69 (Bannerman); *The Men from Shiloh*—"Last of the Comancheros" 12-9-70 (Banker); *Kung Fu*—"An Eye for an Eye" 1-25-73 (Dr. Gormley); *How the West Was Won*—Episode Three 2-14-77 (Sheriff Aames), "The Forgotten" 3-19-79.

Baer, Russell. Films: "Pioneer Woman" TVM-1973 (Jeremy Sergeant).

Baffert, Al. Films: "Park Avenue Lodger" 1937; "Gold Raiders" 1951 (Utah); "The Storm Rider" 1957 (Blackie); "Escape from Red Rock" 1958.

Bagdad, William (1921-11/20/75). TV: *The High Chaparral*—"Mi Casa, Su Casa" 2-20-70 (Juan).

Bagdasarian, Ross (1920-1/16/72). Films: "Viva Zapata!" 1952 (Officer); "Three Violent People" 1956 (Asuncian).

Baggott, King (1879-7/11/48). Films: "The Man from the West" 1912; "Hello Trouble" 1932; "Secrets" 1933.

Bagni, John (1910-2/13/54). Films: "King of the Royal Mounted" 1940-serial (Higgins); "King of the Texas Rangers" 1941-serial (Slater); "Heldorado" 1946 (Johnny); "The Far Frontier" 1949 (Rollins).

Baguez, Salvador. Films: "The Iron Mistress" 1952 (Mexican Artist); "Viva Zapata!" 1952 (Soldier); "The Americano" 1955 (Capt. Gonzales);

"The First Texan" 1956 (Veramendi); "The Hired Gun" 1957 (Domingo Ortega); "From Hell to Texas" 1958 (Cardito). ¶TV: *The Cisco Kid*— "Mad About Money" 3-22-52; *The Californians*—"Mr. Valejo" 1-28-58 (Don Mariano Valejo); *Bonanza*— "The Spanish Grant" 2-6-60, "The Fugitive" 2-4-61 (Gomez), "Look to the Stars" 3-18-62, "The Genius" 4-3-66 (Jesus); *Wanted—Dead or Alive*—"Triple Vise" 2-27-60 (Bartender).

Bail, Chuck. TV: *The Texan*— "The Sheriff of Boot Hill" 6-1-59 (Lou); *Bat Masterson*—"The Reluctant Witness" 3-31-60 (Tod Mason); *Wanted—Dead or Alive*—"The Voice of Silence" 2-15-61 (Wally Brice); *Gunsmoke*—"Perce" 9-30-61 (Withers); *The Big Valley*—"Forty Rifles" 9-22-65, "The Guilt of Matt Bentell" 12-8-65 (Donlon), "Under a Dark Sea" 2-9-66 (Catlin), "Last Train to the Fair" 4-27-66 (Mel), "The Velvet Trap" 11-7-66, "Last Stage to Salt Flats" 12-5-66, "Day of the Comet" 12-26-66 (Wilgus); *Laredo*—"Enemies and Brother" 2-17-67; *Daniel Boone*—"The Traitor" 11-2-67, "The Flaming Rocks" 2-1-68, "To Slay a Giant" 1-9-69; *The High Chaparral*— "Shadow of the Wind" 1-10-69 (Curly Bill), "A Fella Named Kilroy" 3-7-69 (Beri); *Bonanza*—"Mrs. Wharton and the Lesser Breeds" 1-19-69 (Reese), "To Stop a War" 10-19-69 (Ike Kels), "The Grand Swing" 9-19-71 (Kale); *Kung Fu*—"Dark Angel" 11-11-72 (1st Tough), "Forbidden Kingdom" 1-18-75 (2nd Guard).

Bailey, Buck. Films: "Satan's Cradle" 1949 (Rocky); "Fence Riders" 1950; "Over the Border" 1950 (Ford).

Bailey, Carmen. Films: "Rustlers' Paradise" 1935 (Dolores Romeros, the Ranch Owner); "Under the Pampas Moon" 1935; "Ramona" 1936 (Servant); "California Frontier" 1938 (Dolores Cantova); "Drifting Westward" 1939 (Nicki).

Bailey, Charles. Films: "The Boiling Point" 1932 (Gonzales).

Bailey, David (1933-). Films: "Up the MacGregors!" 1967-Ital./Span. (Gregor MacGregor). ¶TV: *Cimarron Strip*—"The Judgment" 1-4-68.

Bailey, Gail. Films: "Stallion Canyon" 1949 (Laramie).

Bailey, G.W. Films: "The Capture of Grizzly Adams" TVM-1982 (Tom Quigley); "Rustler's Rhapsody" 1985 (Peter). ¶TV: *How the West Was One*—Episode Two 2-7-77 (Ivie),

Episode Three 2-14-77 (Ivie); *Legend*—"Legend on His President's Secret Service" 5-2-95 (President Ulysses S. Grant).

Bailey, Harry (1880-8/9/54). Films: "Beyond the Sacramento" 1940 (Storekeeper); "Geronimo" 1940 (3rd Politician).

Bailey, Jack (1908-2/1/80). TV: *Gunsmoke*—"Noose of Gold" 3-4-67 (Ben Leary), "A Matter of Honor" 11-17-69 (Judge Brooker); *The Monroes*—"Ghosts of Paradox" 3-15-67 (Crick).

Bailey, Joe. Films: "Cattle Queen" 1951 (Blackie Malone); "The Redhead from Wyoming" 1953 (Jack).

Bailey, Polly (1882-8/25/52). Films: "Return of the Badmen" 1948 (Mrs. Webster).

Bailey, Raymond (1904-4/15/80). Films: "The Return of Jack Slade" 1955 (Professor). ¶TV: *Gunsmoke*—"General Parsley Smith" 12-10-55 (General Parsley Smith), "The Big Con" 5-3-58 (Shane); *My Friend Flicka*—"When Bugles Blow" 5-18-56; *Zane Grey Theater*—"Back Trail" 2-1-57 (March Beckworth), "Trial by Fear" 1-20-58 (Baker), "Pressure Point" 12-4-58 (Ed Fowler); *Union Pacific*—"Deadline" 10-4-58; *The Rifleman*—"The Photographer" 1-27-59 (Col. Jess Whiteside); *Have Gun Will Travel*—"Lady on the Stagecoach" 1-17-59 (Clyde Barnes), "Charley Red Dog" 12-12-59 (John Staffer); *Yancy Derringer*—"Mayhem at the Market" 1-22-59 (Col. Duval); *Black Saddle*—"Client: Robinson" 2-21-59 (Walter Griggs); *Bronco*—"The Burning Spring" 10-6-59 (General Miles); *Bonanza*—"The Last Hunt" 12-19-59 (Sumner Kyle), "The Miracle Worker" 5-20-62 (Sam Blanchard), "The Beginning" 11-25-62; *Wagon Train*—"The Charlene Brenton Story" 6-8-60 (Jim Brenton), "The Lizabeth Ann Calhoun Story" 12-6-61 (Major Hanley); *The Texan*— "Mission to Monteray" 6-13-60 (Consul Wade); *Bat Masterson*— "Death by Decree" 12-22-60 (Justice Bradshaw); *Texas John Slaughter*— "Frank Clell Is in Town" 4-23-61 (Mark Morgan); *Laramie*—"The Fatal Step" 10-24-61, "The Runt" 2-20-62.

Bailey, Richard. Films: "Riders of the Northwest Mounted" 1943; "The Desert Horseman" 1946 (Sam Treadway); "Galloping Thunder" 1946; "The Marauders" 1947 (Oil Driller); "Ambush" 1950 (Lt. Tremaine); "Outcast of Black Mesa" 1950 (Andrew Vaning).

Bailey, Sherwood (1923-8/6/87). Films: "The Big Stampede" 1932 (Pat Malloy); "The Mysterious Rider" 1933 (Sheriff Arnold, Jr.).

Bailey, William Norton (1886-11/8/62). Films: "Speedy Meade" 1919 (Cal Merchant); "The Phantom Foe" 1920-serial; "Against All Odds" 1924 (Tom Curtis); "The Desert Hawk" 1924 (Tex Trapp); "Bustin' Thru" 1925 (Harvey Gregg); "The Desert Flower" 1925 (Jack Royal); "The Flaming Forties" 1925 (Desparde); "Fighting Jack" 1926 (Jack Rhodes); "Lightning Bill" 1926 (William H. Williams); "Ranson's Folly" 1926 (Lt. Crosby); "The Stolen Ranch" 1926 (Sam Hardy); "The Fighting Three" 1927 (Steve Clayton); "Burning Brides" 1928 (Jim Black); "The Flyin' Cowboys" 1928 (James Bell); "Man in the Rough" 1928 (Jim Kane); "The Lone Patrol" 1928; "Fighting for Justice" 1932 (Colorado); "The Lone Avenger" 1933 (Sam Landers); "Thunder Mountain" 1935 (Cliff Borden); "Rhythm of the Saddle" 1938; "Code of the Saddle" 1947; "Robin Hood of Texas" 1947; "Back Trail" 1948; "Courtin' Trouble" 1948 (Curtis); "False Paradise" 1948; "Silver Trails" 1948 (Chambers); "Across the Rio Grande" 1949 (Sheriff); "Brand of Fear" 1949; "Son of a Badman" 1949 (Brad Burley); "Trail's End" 1949 (Sheriff); "West of El Dorado" 1949 (Sheriff); "Cody of the Pony Express" 1950-serial (Chet); "Gunfire" 1950 (Officer); "Lightning Guns" 1950 (Luke Atkins); "Al Jennings of Oklahoma" 1951 (Robert Kyle); "Cattle Queen" 1951 (Warden); "Three Desperate Men" 1951 (Buckboard Driver); "Tall Man Riding" 1955; "Gunfight at the O.K. Corral" 1957. ¶TV: *Maverick*—"A Rage for Vengeance" 1-12-58 (Doctor), "Diamond in the Rough" 1-26-58 (Banker).

Bain, Barbara (1932-). TV: *Empire*—"Hidden Asset" 3-26-63 (June Bates); *Wagon Train*—"The Fenton Canaby Story" 12-30-63 (Lucy).

Bain, Sherry (1947-). Films: "Wild and Wooly" TVM-1978 (Jessica) ¶TV: *Bearcats!*—9-16-71 (Rose).

Bainbridge, Phyllis. Films: "Covered Wagon Trails" 1930 (Wanda Clayton); "O'Malley Rides Alone" 1930 (Joyce McGregor).

Bainbridge, Sherman. Films: "His Squaw" 1912; "An Indian Legend" 1912; "The Green Shadow" 1913; "An Indian's Honor" 1913; "The Law of the Range" 1914; "The Trail Breakers" 1914; "The Dawn Road" 1915; "The Ghost Wagon" 1915 (David Fairchild); "In the Sunset Country" 1915; "The Superior Claim" 1915.

Bainbridge, William H. (1853-10/24/31). Films: "The Desire of the Moth" 1917 (Col. Vorhis); "The Promise" 1917 (D.S. Appleton); "The Savage" 1917 (Michael Montague); "Under Handicap" 1917 (John Crawford); "Hands Down" 1918 (Dan Stuyvesant); "Hungry Eyes" 1918 (Dudley Appleton); "Desert Gold" 1919 (Jim Belding); "His Back Against the Wall" 1922 (Henry Welling).

Baine, Hollis. Films: "Buffalo Bill Rides Again" 1947 (Rankin).

Bainter, Fay (1891-4/16/68). Films: "The Virginian" 1946 (Mrs. Taylor).

Baird, Harry (1931-). Films: "Colt in the Hand of the Devil" 1972-Ital.; "Trinity and Sartana Are Coming" 1972-Ital. (Trinity); "Those Dirty Dogs!" 1973-U.S./Ital./Span. (Washington Smith); "Four Horsemen of the Apocalpyse" 1975-Ital. (Wilson).

Baird, Jeanne (1936-). Films: "Black Spurs" 1965 (Mrs. Nemo). ¶TV: *Northwest Passage*—"The Long Rifle" 11-23-58 (Martha Ramsey); *Bonanza*—"The Legacy" 12-15-63 (Jeanie).

Baird, Jimmy. TV: *Fury*—Regular 1955-60 (Rodney "Pee Wee" Jenkins); *My Friend Flicka*—"Rebels in Hiding" 3-30-56 (Silver Fawn); *Ford Theater*—"Sudden Silence" 10-10-56 (Billy); *Zane Grey Theater*—"Return to Nowhere" 12-7-56 (Andy); *The Lone Ranger*—"Christmas Story" 12-20-56; *The Restless Gun*—"Multiply One Boy" 12-8-58 (Dudley Higgins); *Lawman*—"The Bandit" 5-31-59 (Bob), "9:05 to North Platte" 12-6-59 (Joey Buckner); *Maverick*—"Royal Four-Flush" 9-20-59 (David Mason); *Man from Blackhawk*—"A Matter of Conscience" 12-11-59 (Johnny); *Rawhide*—"The Hostage Child" 3-9-62 (Arnee); *The Travels of Jaimie McPheeters*—"The Day of the Homeless" 12-8-63 (Bains).

Baird, Phillip. TV: *Tombstone Territory*—11-27-59 (Ron Browning); *Bat Masterson*—"The Inner Circle" 12-31-59 (John Scott Powers).

Bairstow, Scott. "White Fang 2: Myth of the White Wolf" 1994 (Henry Casey). ¶TV: *Lonesome Dove*—Regular 1994- (Newt Dobbs Call).

Bakalyan, Richard (1931-). TV: *Bat Masterson*—"Double Trouble in Trinidad" 1-7-59 (Sam Teller); *U.S. Marshal*—"Trigger Happy" 10-31-59

(Joe Savage); *Hotel De Paree*—"A Rope Is for Hanging" 11-6-59 (Rob); *The Deputy*—"The Big Four" 11-14-59 (Billy the Kid); *Wanted—Dead or Alive*—"Angela" 1-9-60 (Harry Quint); *Johnny Ringo*—"The Raffertys" 3-3-60 (Lee Rafferty); *The Tall Man*—"Tiger Eye" 12-17-60 (Tiger Eye); *The Rebel*—"The Threat" 2-12-61 (Bart Vogan), "The Calley Kid" 5-21-61 (the Calley Kid); *Lawman*—"The Trojan Horse" 12-31-61 (Eggers); *Laramie*—"Broken Honor" 4-9-63 (Mel Doleman); *Wagon Train*—"The Sam Pulaski Story" 11-4-63 (Muscles); *Branded*—"The Richest Man in Boot Hill" 10-31-65 (Roy Barlow); *The Monroes*—"Night of the Wolf" 9-14-66 (Grad); *Gunsmoke*—"The Hanging" 12-31-66 (Teems), "A Matter of Honor" 11-17-69 (Billy Holland); *Hondo*—"Hondo and the Judas" 11-3-67 (Cole Younger); *Cimarron Strip*—"Nobody" 12-7-67 (Colly Sims).

Baker, Art (1898-8/26/66). Films: "Prairie Moon" 1938 (Arthur Dean); "Silver River" 1948 (Maj. Wilson); "Massacre River" 1949 (Col. James Reid); "Only the Valiant" 1951 (Capt. Jennings).

Baker, Benny (1907-9/20/94). Films: "Wanderer of the Wasteland" 1935 (Piano Player); "Drift Fence" 1936 (Jim Traft); "Rose of the Rancho" 1936 (Hillbilly Boy); "Paint Your Wagon" 1969 (Haywood Holbrook); "Scandalous John" 1971 (Dr. Kropak); "Jory" 1972 (Jordan). ¶TV: *Cheyenne*—"The Brand" 4-9-57 (Tulliver); *Maverick*—"Point Blank" 9-29-57 (Mike Brill); *Lawman*—"Parphyrias Lover" 11-19-61 (Dave); *F Troop*—"Dirge for the Scourge" 10-19-65 (Pete), "El Diablo" 1-18-66 (Pete), "Will the Real Captain Try to Stand Up" 5-10-66 (Pete).

Baker, Betty. Films: "The Galloping Gobs" 1927 (Mary Whipple); "Skedaddle Gold" 1927 (Wande Preston); "The Painted Trail" 1928 (Betty Winters); "The Trail Riders" 1928; "Trailin' Back" 1928; "Bar L Ranch" 1930 (Gene Polk).

Baker, Bob (1910-8/29/75). Films: "Courage of the West" 1937 (Jack Saunders); "Black Bandit" 1938 (Don/Bob Ramsay); "Border Wolves" 1938 (Rusty Reynolds); "Ghost Town Riders" 1938 (Bob Martin); "Guilty Trails" 1938 (Bob Higgins); "The Last Stand" 1938 (Tip Douglas/the Laredo Kid); "Outlaw Express" 1938 (Bob Bradley); "Prairie Justice" 1938 (Bob Randall); "The Singing Outlaw" 1938 (Scrap Gordon); "Western Trails" 1938 (Bob Mason); "Chip of

the Flying U" 1939 (Dusty); "Desperate Trails" 1939 (Clem Waters); "Honor of the West" 1939 (Bob Barrett); "Oklahoma Frontier" 1939 (Tom Rankin); "The Phantom Stage" 1939 (Bob Carson); "Bad Man from Red Butte" 1940 (Gabriel Hornsby); "Riders of Pasco Basin" 1940 (Bruce Moore); "West of Carson City" 1940 (Nevada); "Meet Roy Rogers" 1941-short; "Overland Mail" 1942-serial (Young Bill Cody); "Wild Horse Stampede" 1943 (Cliff Tyler); "Mystery Man" 1944 (Bar 20 Boy); "Oklahoma Raiders" 1944.

Baker, Bonita. Films: "Outlaws' Highway" 1934 (Stella).

Baker, Carroll (1935-). Films: "Giant" 1956 (Luz Benedict II); "The Big Country" 1958 (Patricia Terrill); "How the West Was Won" 1962 (Eve Prescott); "Cheyenne Autumn" 1964 (Deborah Wright); "Captain Apache" 1971-Brit./Span. (Maude).

Baker, Diane (1938-). Films: "The Dangerous Days of Kiowa Jones" TVM-1966 (Amelia Rathmore); "Baker's Hawk" 1976 (Jenny Baker). ¶TV: *Wagon Train*—"The Alice Whitetree Story" 11-1-64 (Alice Whitetree); *The Big Valley*—"By Fires Unseen" 1-5-66 (Hester Converse); *The Virginian*—"Linda" 11-30-66 (Linda Valence), "A Love to Remember" 10-29-69 (Julie Oakes); *Bonanza*—"A Woman in the House" 2-19-67 (Mary Farnum Wharton), "Cassie" 10-24-71 (Norma); *The Men from Shiloh*—"Nan Allen" 1-6-71 (Nan Allen).

Baker, Dora. Films: "Rough Going" 1925 (Mother Burke).

Baker, Dottie Bee. Films: "The Rainmaker" 1956 (Belinda).

Baker, Eddie (1897-2/4/68). TV: *Laramie*—"The Killer Legend" 12-12-61.

Baker, Elsie (1893-8/16/71). Films: "Three Hours to Kill" 1954 (Woman). ¶TV: *The Cisco Kid*—"Quiet Sunday Morning" 12-5-53, "Young Blood" 1-16-54.

Baker, Fay. TV: *Jim Bowie*—"A Fortune for Madame" 10-18-57 (Charlotte De Vaux); *Wyatt Earp*—"Bad Woman" 12-31-57 (Marie Burden); *Have Gun Will Travel*—"Lady on the Stagecoach" 1-17-59 (Lydia Grayson).

Baker, Floyd "Silver Tip" (1887-3/15/43). Films: "The Riding Tornado" 1932; "The Phantom Thunderbolt" 1933; "Riders of Destiny" 1933; "Between Men" 1935 (Johnson); "Border Vengeance" 1935; "Powdersmoke Range" 1935; "Wagon

Trail" 1935; "Westward Ho" 1935; "Frontier Justice" 1936; "Oh, Susannah!" 1936; "Arizona Gunfighter" 1937; "Left Handed Law" 1937; "The Durango Kid" 1940 (Townsman).

Baker, Frank (1894-12/30/80). Films: "Lash of the Whip" 1924 (Frank Blake); "Red Blood and Blue" 1925 (Bill Gronn); "Scar Hanan" 1925 (Edward Fitzhugh Carstowe); "Call of the Heart" 1928; "A Romeo of the Range" 1928; "Run of the Arrow" 1957 (Gen. Lee); "Two Rode Together" 1961 (Capt. Malaprop).

Baker, Joby (1934-). Films: "The Adventures of Bullwhip Griffin" 1967 (Bandido Leader). ¶TV: *Wagon Train*—"The Bettina May Story" 12-20-61 (Nathan May); *Frontier Circus*—"Mighty Like Rogues" 4-5-62 (George Washington Jukes); *Gunsmoke*—"Call Me Dodie" 9-22-62 (Ky); *The Loner*—"The Oath" 12-4-65 (Billy Ford); *F Troop*—"La Dolce Courage" 11-24-66 (Mario Marcucci); *Death Valley Days*—"The Saga of Dr. Davis" 3-18-67 (Davis).

Baker, Joe Don (1936-). Films: "Guns of the Magnificent Seven" 1969 (Slater); "Wild Rovers" 1971 (Paul Buckman); "Junior Bonner" 1972 (Curly Bonner); "Shadow of Chikara" 1978 (Wishbone Cutter). ¶TV: *Gunsmoke*—"Prime of Life" 5-7-66 (Woody Stoner), "The Reprisal" 2-10-69 (Tom Butler); *Lancer*—"The High Riders" 9-24-68 (Day Pardee), "Cut the Wolf Loose" 11-4-69 (Santee), "Shadow of a Dead Man" 1-6-70 (Harner); *Bonanza*—"The Real People of Muddy Creek" 10-6-68 (Luke Harper); *The Big Valley*—"Lightfoot" 2-17-69 (Tom Lightfoot); *The High Chaparral*—"The Hostage" 3-5-71 (Yuma).

Baker, Kenny (1912-8/10/85). Films: "The Harvey Girls" 1946 (Terry O'Halloran).

Baker, Lynn. Films: "Billy Jack" 1971 (Sarah).

Baker, Ray. Films: "Silverado" 1985 (McKendrick).

Baker, Rex "Snowy" (1884-12/3/53). Films: "The Fighting Breed" 1921 (Brian O'Farrell); "Fighter's Paradise" 1924; "The Kid from Texas" 1939 (Umpire).

Baker, Silver Tip. *see* Baker, Floyd "Silvertip".

Baker, Stanley (1928-6/28/76). Films: "Zorro" 1974-Ital./Fr. (Colonel Huerta)

Baker, Tom (1940-9/2/82). TV: *The Virginian*—"Requiem for a Country Doctor" 1-25-67 (Deputy);

Iron Horse—"Steel Chain to a Music Box" 11-18-67 (Cal).

Baker, Virginia. TV: *Gunsmoke*—"The Gentleman" 6-7-58 (Boni Damon), "Kitty's Love Affair" 10-22-73 (Mrs. Colby); *Dirty Sally*—4-12-74 (Martha).

Bakewell, William (1908-4/15/93). Films: "The Great Meadow" 1931; "Speed Wings" 1934 (Jerry Ahearn); "King of the Mounties" 1942-serial (Hal Ross); "King of the Bandits" 1947 (Capt. Mason); "The Capture" 1950 (Tobin); "Wells Fargo Gunmaster" 1951 (Charlie Lannon); "When the Redskins Rode" 1951 (Appleby); "Davy Crockett, King of the Wild Frontier" 1955 (Tobias Norton). ¶TV: *The Cisco Kid*—"Face of Death" 2-16-52, "Lost City of the Incas" 3-29-52; *Walt Disney Presents*—"Davy Crockett"—Regular 1954-55 (Major Tobias Norton); *Tombstone Territory*—"Fight for a Fugitive" 6-4-58 (Walt Dickerson); *Maverick*—"Maverick Springs" 12-6-59 (Desk Clerk); *The Virginian*—"The Fatal Journey" 12-4-63 (Sam); *Bonanza*—"The Greedy Ones" 5-14-67 (Henshaw), "Trouble Town" 3-17-68 (Slatter).

Bakey, Ed (1925-5/4/88). Films: "Heaven with a Gun" 1969 (Scotty Andrews); "Barquero" 1970 (Happy); "Wild Rovers" 1971 (Gambler); "The Godchild" TVM-1974 (Shaw); "The White Buffalo" 1977 (Ben Corbett); "Hot Lead and Cold Feet" 1978 (Joshua); "The Gambler" TVM-1980 (Eli); "Bret Maverick" TVM-1981 (Lyman Nickerson). ¶TV: *The Big Valley*—"The Time After Midnight" 10-2-67 (Corell), "Shadow of a Giant" 1-29-68 (Floyd Stryder), "The Battle of Mineral Springs" 3-24-69 (Burt Simpson); *Dundee and the Culhane*—11-1-67 (Amber); *Gunsmoke*—"Death Train" 11-27-67 (The Rev. Mr. Bright), "The Night Riders" 2-24-69 (Farmer), "Bohannan" 9-25-72 (Goody Stackpole); *The Guns of Will Sonnett*—"Sunday in Paradise" 12-15-67 (Homer Blessing), "One Angry Juror" 3-7-69 (Jellicoe); *Cimarron Strip*—"Without Honor" 2-29-68; *Bonanza*—"The Survivors" 11-10-68 (Hake), "Speak No Evil" 4-20-69 (Louby Sains), "The Initiation" 9-26-72 (Lumis); *Lancer*—"The Experiment" 2-17-70; *The High Chaparral*—"New Hostess in Town" 3-20-70 (Bates), "Only the Bad Come to Sonora" 10-2-70 (Jubel); *Kung Fu*—"The Centoph" 4-4-74 & 4-11-74 (Bloom); *Bret Maverick*—"The Not So Magnificent Six" 3-2-82 (Tulsa Jack).

Bakke, Brenda. TV: *Young Riders*—"The Peacemakers" 1-19-91 (Alice); *Ned Blessing: The Story of My Life and Times*—Regular 1993 (the Wren); *Adventures of Brisco County, Jr.*—"Ned Zed" 3-13-94 (Frances McCabe).

Bakunas, A.J. (1951-9/22/78). Films: "The Apple Dumpling Gang Rides Again" 1979.

Bal, Henry K. Films: "The Mystic Warrior" TVM-1984 (Siyo Breed).

Bal, Jeanne (1928-). TV: *Riverboat*—"Listen to the Nightingale" 1-2-61; *Bonanza*—"The Saga of Whizzer McGee" 4-28-63 (Melissa); *Wagon Train*—"Alias Bill Hawks" 5-15-63 (Alice Wells).

Balaban, Bob (1945-). TV: *Legend*—Pilot 4-18-95.

Balaski, Belinda. Films: "Proud Men" TVM-1987 (Nell). ¶TV: *The Cowboys*—"Requiem for a Lost Son" 5-8-74 (Obie Graff).

Balbo, Ennio. Films: "Day of Anger" 1967-Ital./Ger. (Turner).

Balch, Joseph "Slim" (1898-1/30/67). Films: "The Westerner" 1934 (Bucking Horse Rider); "Hollywood Cowboy" 1937 (Slim); "Racketeers of the Range" 1939; "Sunset Pass" 1946 (Posse Man); "Son of Zorro" 1947-serial.

Baldassare, Raf. Films: "Gunfight at High Noon" 1963-Span./Ital.; "Magnificent Three" 1963-Span./Ital.; "Shadow of Zorro" 1963-Span./Ital.; "A Fistful of Dollars" 1964-Ital./Ger./Span.; "Seven Guns from Texas" 1964-Span./Ital.; "Seven Hours of Gunfire" 1964-Span./Ital.; "Jesse James' Kid" 1966-Span./Ital.; "Outlaw of Red River" 1966-Ital.; "Relentless Four" 1966-Span./Ital.; "Rojo" 1966-Ital./Span.; "A Stranger in Town" 1966-U.S./Ital.; "The Stranger Returns" 1967-U.S./Ital./Ger./Span.; "Three from Colorado" 1967-Span.; "All Out" 1968-Ital./Span.; "Between God, the Devil and a Winchester" 1968-Ital./Span.; "Cry for Revenge" 1968-Ital./Span.; "Great Silence" 1968-Ital./Fr.; "Hour of Death" 1968-Span./Ital.; "The Mercenary" 1968-Ital./Span. (Mateo); "Pistol for a Hundred Coffins" 1968-Ital./Span.; "Canadian Wilderness" 1969-Span./Ital.; "Dead Are Countless" 1969-Ital./Span.; "Man Who Cried for Revenge" 1969-Ital./Span.; "Quinta: Fighting Proud" 1969-Ital./Span.; "Stranger in Japan" 1969-Ital./U.S./Jap.; "Arizona" 1970-Ital./Span.; "Dig Your Grave, Friend…Sabata's Coming" 1970-Ital./Span./Fr.; "Sartana Kills Them All" 1970-Ital./

Span.; "And the Crows Will Dig Your Grave" 1971-Ital./Span.; "Blindman" 1971-Ital. (Mexican General); "Hey Amigo! A Toast to Your Death!" 1971-Ital.; "Prey of Vultures" 1973-Span./Ital.; "Drummer of Vengeance" 1974-Brit./Ital.; "Get Mean" 1975-Ital.

Balding, Rebecca (1949-). TV: *Paradise*—"Crossroads" 1-26-89 (Mary McBride), "The Secret" 2-8-89 (Mary McBride), "A Matter of Honor" 4-8-89 & 4-15-89 (Mary McBride), "The Plague" 12-9-89 (Mary McBride), "Dust on the Wind" 4-28-90 (Mary McBride).

Baldini, Renato. Films: "Among Vultures" 1964-Ger./Ital./Fr./Yugo.; "Man from Canyon City" 1965-Span./Ital.; "Dynamite Joe" 1966-Ital./Span.; "Last of the Renegades" 1966-Fr./Ital./Ger./Yugo. (Col. J.F. Merril); "Woman for Ringo" 1966-Ital./Span.; "I Am Sartana, Your Angel of Death" 1969-Ital./Fr.; "Dick Luft in Sacramento" 1974-Ital.

Baldra, Charles (1899-5/14/49). Films: "Fighting Thru" 1930; "Secret Menace" 1931; "Lawless Valley" 1932; "The Western Code" 1932; "Fighting Hero" 1934 (Henchman); "Fighting Through" 1934 (Singer); "Wheels of Destiny" 1934; "The Dawn Rider" 1935 (Henchman); "Five Bad Men" 1935; "Gallant Defender" 1935; "His Fighting Blood" 1935; "Lawless Range" 1935; "Paradise Canyon" 1935; "The Rider of the Law" 1935; "Stormy" 1935; "The Last of the Warrens" 1936; "The Lawless Nineties" 1936 (Tex); "Outlaws of the Prairie" 1937 (Outlaw); "Cattle Raiders" 1938 (Outlaw); "The Old Barn Dance" 1938; "Prairie Moon" 1938; "The Man from Texas" 1939 (Deputy); "The Border Legion" 1940; "Colorado" 1940; "Pioneers of the West" 1940; "The Ranger and the Lady" 1940; "The Trail Blazers" 1940; "The Phantom Cowboy" 1941; "Ridin' the Cherokee Trail" 1941.

Balducci, Franco. Films: "The Tramplers" 1965-Ital. (Pete Wiley); "Black Tigress" 1967-Ital.; "Day of Anger" 1967-Ital./Ger.; "Death Rides a Horse" 1967-Ital.; "Time of Vultures" 1967-Ital.; "A Long Ride from Hell" 1968-Ital.; "Night of the Serpent" 1969-Ital.

Balduzzi, Dick (1928-). Films: "Zorro, the Gay Blade" 1981 (Old Man) ¶TV: *Here Come the Brides*— "Here Come the Brides" 9-25-68, "And Jason Makes Five" 10-9-68, "Lovers and Wanderers" 11-6-68, "The Log Jam" 1-8-69, "The Wealthiest Man in Seattle" 10-3-69 (Butch).

Baldwin, Adam. Films: "Wyatt Earp" 1994 (Tom McLaury).

Baldwin, Alan. Films: "Undercover Man" 1942 (Bob Saunders).

Baldwin, Alec (1958-). Films: "The Alamo: 13 Days to Glory" TVM-1987 (Col. William Travis).

Baldwin, Ann. Films: "Wall Street Cowboy" 1939 (Peggy Hammond); "Rancho Grande" 1940 (Susan Putnam).

Baldwin, Beau. Films: "Rhythm on the Range" 1936 (Cuddles).

Baldwin, Bill (1913-11/17/82). TV: *The Virginian*—"The Devil's Children" 12-5-62, "The Death Wagon" 1-3-68; *Wagon Train*—"The Kate Crawley Story" 1-27-64.

Baldwin, Curley. Films: "Fighting Back" 1917 (Alama Sam); "Desert Law" 1918 (Buck); "Little Red Decides" 1918 (Foreman); "Wolves of the Border" 1918; "Law of the 45's" 1935 (Deputy Sheriff); "Lawless - Borders" 1935; "Blazing Justice" 1936.

Baldwin, Peter (1931-). Films: "The Tin Star" 1957 (Zeke McGaffey).

Baldwin, Ralph. Films: "Hands of a Gunman" 1965-Ital./Span.; "Four Gunmen of the Holy Trinity" 1971-Ital.

Baldwin, Stephen. Films: "Posse" 1993 (Little J); "8 Seconds" 1994 (Tuff Hedeman). ¶TV: *Young Riders*—Regular 1990-92 (Billy Cody); *Legend*—"Mr. Pratt Goes to Sheridan" 2-25-95 (Johnny Siringo).

Baldwin, Walter (1889-1/27/77). Films: "Frontier Marshal" 1939; "They Died with Their Boots On" 1941 (Settler); "Tall in the Saddle" 1944 (Stan); "Rhythm Round-Up" 1945; "Trail to Vengeance" 1945 (Jackson); "Albuquerque" 1948 (Judge); "The Man from Colorado" 1948 (Tom Barton); "Rachel and the Stranger" 1948 (Callus); "Return of the Badmen" 1948 (Muley Wilson); "Calamity Jane and Sam Bass" 1949 (Doc Purdy); "The Gay Amigo" 1949 (Stoneham); "Rough Riders of Durango" 1951 (Cricket Adams); "Ride, Vaquero!" 1953 (Adam Smith); "Destry" 1954 (Henry Skinner); "Stranger on Horseback" 1955; "Oklahoma Territory" 1960 (Ward Harlen); "Cheyenne Autumn" 1964 (Deborah's Uncle). ¶TV: *The Californians*—"The First Gold Brick" 1-6-59 (Asa Warren); *Wagon Train*—"Trial for Murder" 4-27-60 & 5-4-60; *Gunsmoke*—"Fandango" 2-11-67 (Old Man); *Lancer*—"Glory" 12-10-68 (Storekeeper).

Balenda, Carla (1925-). Films: "Outlaw Women" 1952 (Beth Larabee); "The Phantom Stallion" 1954.

Balgobin, Jennifer. Films: "Straight to Hell" 1987-Brit. (Fabienne).

Balin, Ina (1937-6/20/90). Films: "The Comancheros" 1961 (Pilar); "Charro!" 1969 (Tracy); "Desperate Mission" TVM-1971 (Otilia). ¶TV: *Stoney Burke*—"Child of Luxury" 10-15-62 (Sutton Meade); *Bonanza*—"Devil on Her Shoulder" 10-17-65 (Sarah Reynolds); *The Loner*—"To the West of Eden" 1-1-66 (Trina Lopez); *Alias Smith and Jones*— "Miracle at Santa Marta" 12-30-71 (Margaret Carruthers).

Balk, Martin. TV: *The Adventures of Rin Tin Tin*—"The New C.O." 2-14-58 (Torredo); *Have Gun Will Travel*—"Gun Shy" 3-29-58, "The Silver Queen" 5-3-58; *Jefferson Drum*—"The Outlaw" 6-20-58 (Roland Greer).

Ball, Frank. Films: "Fighting Champ" 1932 (Fred Mullins); "The Forty-Niners" 1932 (MacNab); "The Man from New Mexico" 1932 (Mr. Langton); "Mark of the Spur" 1932 (Agent); "Scarlet Brand" 1932 (John Walker); "Galloping Romeo" 1933 (Sheriff); "The Ranger's Code" 1933; "When a Man Rides Alone" 1933 (Jack Davis); "The Star Packer" 1934; "Between Men" 1935 (Gentry Winters); "Big Calibre" 1935 (Father); "The Courageous Avenger" 1935 (Davis); "Desert Trail" 1935; "The New Frontier" 1935; "Rainbow Valley" 1935; "Brand of the Outlaws" 1936 (Doctor); "The Fugitive Sheriff" 1936 (Prospector); "The Kid Ranger" 1936 (Ben Brokaw); "The Last of the Warrens" 1936; "Rogue of the Range" 1936 (Express Agent); "Sundown Saunders" 1936 (Manning); "Undercover Man" 1936; "Valley of the Lawless" 1936 (Amos Jenkins); "Arizona Gunfighter" 1937 (Dan Lorimer); "Bar Z Bad Men" 1937 (Judge); "Boothill Brigade" 1937 (Murdock); "Border Phantom" 1937 (Hartwell); "Desert Phantom" 1937; "The Gambling Terror" 1937 (Garet); "The Gun Ranger" 1937 (Judge); "Law of the Ranger" 1937; "Lawless Land" 1937 (Bill); "Reckless Ranger" 1937; "The Red Rope" 1937 (Pop Duncan); "Ridin' the Lone Trail" 1937 (Randall); "Trail of Vengeance" 1937 (Steve Warner); "The Trusted Outlaw" 1937 (Sheriff); "Colorado Kid" 1938 (Judge Smith); "Durango Valley Raiders" 1938; "The Feud Maker" 1938 (Ben Harbison); "In

Early Arizona" 1938; "Paroled to Die" 1938 (Judge).

Ball, George. Films: "Men of the Plains" 1936 (Billy Sawyer); "Rogue of the Range" 1936 (Jim Mitchell).

Ball, Lucille (1911-4/26/89). Films: "Valley of the Sun" 1942 (Christine Larson); "Fancy Pants" 1950 (Agatha Floud).

Ball, Robert. Films: "Zachariah" 1971 (Stage Manager). ¶TV: *Bonanza*—"Child" 9-22-68 (Clerk), "The Big Jackpot" 1-18-70 (Henny).

Ball, Suzan (1933-8/5/55). Films: "Untamed Frontier" 1952 (Lottie); "War Arrow" 1953 (Avis); "Chief Crazy Horse" 1955 (Black Shawl).

Ball, Vincent (1923-). Films: "Robbery Under Arms" 1958-Brit. (George Storefield).

Ballantine, Carl (1917-). Films: "The Shakiest Gun in the West" 1968 (Swanson). ¶TV: *Laredo*—"Hey Diddle Diddle" 2-24-67 (Lemuel Beamish); *The Men from Shiloh*—"The Politician" 1-13-71 (Matt).

Ballard, Ray (1929-). Films: "The Cockeyed Cowboys of Calico County" 1970. ¶TV: *The Alaskans*—"The Ballad of Whitehorse" 6-12-60 (Bailey); *Bat Masterson*—"High Card Loses" 11-10-60 (Clerk); *Laredo*—"The Treasure of San Diablo" 2-17-66 (Dandy Davis); *Kung Fu*—"The Passion of Chen Yi" 2-28-74 (Prison Cook).

Ballard, Shirley (1927-). TV: *Shotgun Slade*—"Flower on Boot Hill" 8-9-60 (Kate); *Bonanza*—"Cut-Throat Junction" 3-18-61; *The Rebel*—"Two Weeks" 3-26-61 (Ann Galt); *Tales of Wells Fargo*—"A Quiet Little Town" 6-5-61 (Meg Prescott); *Death Valley Days*—"A Matter of Duty" 4-4-62 (Indiana); *Wide Country*—"Who Killed Edde Gannon?" 10-11-62 (Fay McHugh); *Stoney Burke*—"The Scavenger" 11-12-62 (Suzan).

Ballew, Robert. TV: *Gunsmoke*—"Killer at Large" 2-5-66 (Grange), "The Well" 11-19-66 (Jim Grady).

Ballew, Smith (1902-5/2/84). Films: "Roll Along, Cowboy" 1937 (Randy Porter); "Western Gold" 1937 (Bill Gibson); "Hawaiian Buckaroo" 1938 (Jeff Howard); "Panamint's Bad Man" 1938 (Larry Kimball); "Rawhide" 1938 (Larry Kimball); "Gaucho Serenade" 1940 (Buck Benson); "Drifting Along" 1946 (Smith Ballew); "Under Arizona Skies" 1946; "Tex Granger" 1948-serial (Blaze Talbot); "I Killed Geronimo" 1950 (Lt. Furness).

Ballin, Mabel (1887-7/24/58). Films: "Laughing Bill Hyde" 1918 (Alice); "Beauty and the Bad Man" 1925 (Cassie); "Code of the West" 1925 (Mary Stockwell); "Riders of the Purple Sage" 1925 (Jane Withersteen).

Balsam, Martin (1919-). Films: "Hombre" 1967 (Mendez); "The Good Guys and the Bad Guys" 1969 (Mayor Wilker); "Little Big Man" 1971 (Allardyce T. Merriweather); "Cipolla Colt" 1975-Ital./Ger. (Lamb). ¶TV: *Have Gun Will Travel*—"In an Evil Time" 9-13-58 (Brother), "Saturday Night" 10-8-60 (Marshal Brock); *Rawhide*—"Incident at Alabaster Plain" 1-16-59 (Father Fabian); *Zane Grey Theater*—"Lone Woman" 10-8-59 (Sam Butler); *Wagon Train*—"The Whipping" 3-23-64 (Marcy Jones).

Balsam, Talia. Films: "Calamity Jane" TVM-1984 (Jean).

Bamber, Judy. TV: *Pony Express*—"The Station Keeper's Bride" 3-2-60.

Bamby, George. Films: "Shadow Valley" 1947; "Tornado Range" 1948; "South Pacific Trail" 1952.

Bancroft, Anne (1931-). Films: "The Last Frontier" 1955 (Corinna Marston); "Walk the Proud Land" 1956 (Tianay); "The Restless Breed" 1957 (Angelita). ¶TV: *Zane Grey Theater*—"Episode in Darkness" 11-15-57 (Isabelle Rutledge).

Bancroft, George (1882-10/2/56). Films: "The Deadwood Coach" 1924 (Tex Wilson); "Teeth" 1924 (Dan Angus); "Code of the West" 1925 (Enoch Thurman); "The Pony Express" 1925 (Jack Slade); "The Rainbow Trail" 1925 (Jake Willets); "The Splendid Road" 1925 (Buck Lockwell); "The Enchanted Hill" 1926 (Ira Todd); "White Gold" 1927 (Sam Randall); "Stagecoach" 1939 (Sheriff Curly Wilcox); "Northwest Mounted Police" 1940 (Jacques Corbeau); "When the Daltons Rode" 1940 (Caleb Winters); "Texas" 1941 (Windy Miller).

Bane, Holly (Michael Ragan) (-8/25/95). Films: "Hoppy's Holiday" 1947 (Ace); "Jesse James Rides Again" 1947-serial (Tim); "Song of the Wasteland" 1947; "Carson City Raiders" 1948 (Joe); "Dangers of the Canadian Mounted" 1948-serial (Garson); "Night Time in Nevada" 1948 (Mort Oakley); "Overland Trails" 1948; "Renegades of Sonora" 1948; "The Return of Wildfire" 1948 (Dirk); "Brand of Fear" 1949; "The Far Frontier" 1949 (Rocco); "Ghost

of Zorro" 1949-serial (Larkin); "Grand Canyon" 1949 (Rocky); "Red Desert" 1949 (Barton); "Riders of the Dusk" 1949 (Gus); "Roaring Westward" 1949 (Bart); "Cow Town" 1950; "Desperadoes of the West" 1950-serial (Bryant); "Fence Riders" 1950; "Over the Border" 1950 (Duke Winslow); "Ready to Ride" 1950-short; "Six Gun Mesa" 1950; "Storm Over Wyoming" 1950 (Scott); "West of Wyoming" 1950 (Chuck); "The Dakota Kid" 1951 (Marker); "Don Daredevil Rides Again" 1951-serial (Miller); "Texans Never Cry" 1951 (Rip Braydon); "Montana Belle" 1952 (Ben Dalton); "Springfield Rifle" 1952 (Red); "Target" 1952 (Higgins); "Arrowhead" 1953; "Canadian Mounties vs. Atomic Invaders" 1953-serial (Reed); "Ride Clear of Diablo" 1953 (Jim); "Son of Belle Star" 1953 (Earl); "Bitter Creek" 1954 (Joe Verango); "Rage at Dawn" 1955; "Tall Man Riding" 1955; "Frontier Gun" 1958 (Tanner); "Stagecoach to Dancer's Rock" 1962 (Ben Wade); "Gunpoint" 1966 (Zack). ¶TV: *The Lone Ranger*—"Barnaby Boggs, Esquire" 2-2-50, "Bullets for Ballots" 5-11-50, "The Black Widow" 8-24-50; "Danger Ahead" 10-12-50, "The Silent Voice" 1-11-51, "Through the Wall" 10-9-52, "Ghost Canyon" 12-27-56; *The Gene Autry Show*—"Doublecross Valley" 9-10-50, "The Raiders" 4-14-51, "Double Barrelled Vengeance" 4-21-51, "The Million Dollar Fiddle" 10-1-55; *The Cisco Kid*—"Haven for Heavies" 5-19-51, "Phony Sheriff" 6-16-51, "Uncle Disinherits Niece" 7-14-51, "The Puppeteer" 1-19-52, "Canyon City Kit" 3-1-52, "Sky Sign" 12-6-52, "Marriage by Mail" 1-3-53; *Wild Bill Hickok*—"Tax Collecting Story" 8-7-51, "The Doctor Story" 7-1-52 (Malone); *The Roy Rogers Show*—"The Train Robbery" 2-3-52, "Go for Your Gun" 11-23-52, "Bad Company" 12-27-53 (Ira Logan), "The Land Swindle" 3-14-54 (Tom Sherman); *Wyatt Earp*—"Killing at Cowskin Creek" 2-14-56 (Roy Blake), "Shootin' Woman" 1-1-57 (Hogan), "The Time for All Good Men" 6-4-57 (Clay Allison), "Ballad and Truth" 3-4-58 (Mike Denby), "His Life in His Hands" 3-22-60 (J.B. Ayers), "Behan's Double Game" 3-29-60 (J.B. Ayres); *Annie Oakley*—"Annie Rides the Navajo Trail" 11-18-56 (Sergeant Yorkton); *Zane Grey Theater*—"Badge of Honor" 5-3-57 (Sam Gibson), "This Man Must Die" 1-24-58 (Bartender); *Tombstone Territory*—"Guns of Silver" 11-27-57 (Billy Hooter); *Wagon Train*—"The Clara Beauchamp Story" 12-11-57 (Soldier); *Maverick*—"Trail West to Fury" 2-16-58 (1st Johnny Reb); *Wanted—Dead or Alive*—"Fatal Memory" 9-13-58 (Cowpoke); *The Texan*—"A Quart of Law" 1-12-59, "Traildust" 10-19-59; *Bonanza*—"The Paiute War" 10-3-59, "The Spanish Grant" 2-6-60 (High Card Smith), "The Mission" 9-17-60 (Kelly), "The First Born" 9-23-62 (Miner), "Ponderosa Matador" 1-12-64 (Saloon Keeper), "Pink Cloud Comes from Old Cathay" 4-12-64, "The Reluctant Rebel" 11-21-65 (Burkhart); *Rawhide*—"Incident of the Thirteenth Man" 10-23-59 (Clem Jackson), "Incident of the Gallows Tree" 2-22-63 (Pete), "Incident at El Crucero" 10-10-63 (Eddie Cornelius), "Incident at Gila Flats" 1-30-64 (Corporal Rokka); *Fury*—"Man-Killer" 10-31-59; *Colt .45*—"Impasse" 1-31-60, "Strange Encounter" 4-26-60 (Sergeant Quinn); *Laramie*—"Queen of Diamonds" 9-20-60 (Abel Reeves); *Frontier Circus*—"The Smallest Target" 10-12-61 (Bill Poster); *Gunsmoke*—"The Search" 9-15-62 (Frank); *Daniel Boone*—"The Aaron Burr Story" 10-28-65 (the Leader), "The Symbol" 12-29-66 (Butcher); *Laredo*—"A Matter of Policy" 11-11-65 (Hawk), "No Bugles, One Drum" 2-24-66 (Jonesy), "A Double Shot of Nepenthe" 9-30-66; *The Legend of Jesse James*—"Benjamin Bates" 2-28-66 (Prisoner); *The Monroes*—"Ride with Terror" 9-21-66 (Luke); *Iron Horse*—"The Prisoners" 12-30-67 (Cantley).

Bang, Joy (1946-). TV: *The Kowboys*—Pilot 7-13-70 (Smitty).

Bank, Douglas. TV: *Have Gun Will Travel*—"Fragile" 10-31-59 (Duck).

Banke, Richard. TV: *Walt Disney Presents*—"Daniel Boone" 1960-61 (Squire Boone).

Banks, Emily. Films: "The Plainsman" 1966 (Louisa Cody); "Gunfight in Abilene" 1967 (Amy Martin). ¶TV: *Cowboy in Africa*—"Stone Age Safari" 10-16-67 (Dr. Anne Marlow); *Wild Wild West*—"The Night of the Avaricious Actuary" 12-6-68 (Arden Masters); *Death Valley Days*—"Biscuits and Billy the Kid" 11-1-69.

Banks, Joan. TV: *Wanted—Dead or Alive*—"Fatal Memory" 9-13-58 (Clara Hood); *Zane Grey Theater*—"Legacy of a Legend" 11-6-58 (Melanie Fleming); *Rough Riders*—"The Wagon Raiders" 6-4-59 (Norah Eddiman).

Banks, Jonathan (1946-). Films: "Timerider" 1983 (Jesse) ¶TV: *Best of the West*—"They're Hanging Parker Tillman" 10-15-81 & 10-22-81 (Hombre).

Banks, Perry (1877-10/10/34). Films: "The Land o' Lizards" 1916 (Dave Moore); "Overalls" 1916 (Harrison Warren); "Snap Judgment" 1917 (Smiling Jed Baldwin); "Six Feet Four" 1919 (Old Man Adams).

Banks, Zack. TV: *Wild Wild West*—"The Night of the Firebrand" 9-15-67 (Pierre); *Cimarron Strip*—"Whitey" 10-19-67.

Banky, Vilma (1898-3/18/91). Films: "The Winning of Barbara Worth" 1926 (Barbara Worth).

Bannen, Ian (1928-). Films: "Deserter" 1970-U.S./Ital./Yugo. (Crawford); "Bite the Bullet" 1975 (Norfolk).

Banner, Jill (1946-8/7/82). Films: "The Stranger Returns" 1967-U.S./Ital./Ger./Span. (Caroline).

Banner, John (1910-1/28/73). Films: "Callaway Went Thataway" 1951 (Headwaiter); "The Wonderful Country" 1959 (Ben Turner). ¶TV: *The Lone Ranger*—"Damsels in Distress" 6-8-50; *Cimarron City*—"I, the People" 10-11-58 (P.B. Minscher); *The Adventures of Rin Tin Tin*—"Grandpappy's Love Affair" 11-14-58 (Baron Cartifle); *The Virginian*—"The Small Parade" 2-20-63; *Wide Country*—"The Quest for Jacob Blaufus" 3-7-63 (Doctor); *Alias Smith and Jones*—"Don't Get Mad, Get Even" 2-17-72 (Otto).

Banning, Leslye. Films: "Renegades of the Sage" 1949 (Ellen Miller); "Cactus Caravan" 1950-short; "Black Hills Ambush" 1952 (Sally); "Stagecoach to Fury" 1956 (Ann Stewart).

Bannister, Harry (1888-2/26/61). Films: "Girl of the Golden West" 1930 (Jack Rance).

Bannister, Monica. Films: "The Cowboy and the Blonde" 1941 (Maybelle).

Bannon, Jack (1940-). Films: "Little Big Man" 1971 (Captain). ¶TV: *Daniel Boone*—"The Secret Code" 12-14-67, "The Printing Press" 10-23-69, "The Kidnaping" 1-22-70; *Lancer*—"Blood Rock" 10-1-68; *Here Come the Brides*—"The Fetching of Jenny" 12-5-69.

Bannon, Jim (1911-86). Films: "Riders of the Deadline" 1943 (Tex); "Renegades" 1946 (Cash Dembrow); "Dangers of the Canadian Mounted" 1948-serial (Christopher Royal); "Frontier Revenge" 1948 (Brant); "The Man from Colorado" 1948 (Nagel); "Trail to Laredo" 1948; "Ride, Ryder, Ride" 1949 (Red Ryder); "Roll, Thunder, Roll" 1949 (Red Ryder); "Cowboy and the Prizefighter" 1950 (Red Ryder); "The Fighting Redhead" 1950 (Red Ryder); "Jiggs and Maggie Out West" 1950 (Snake Bite); "Canyon Raiders" 1951; "Lawless Cowboys" 1951 (Jim Bannon); "Nevada Badmen" 1951; "Ridin' the Outlaw Trail" 1951 (Ace Conley); "Sierra Passage" 1951 (Jud Yorke); "Stagecoach Driver" 1951; "Wanted Dead or Alive" 1951; "Rodeo" 1952 (Bat Gorman); "The Great Jesse James Raid" 1953 (Bob Ford); "Jack Slade" 1953 (Farnsworth); "War Arrow" 1953 (Capt. Roger Corwin); "They Came to Cordura" 1959 (Capt. Raltz). ¶TV: *The Lone Ranger*—"Devil's Pass" 5-25-50, "The Courage of Tonto" 1-17-57, "Mr. Trouble" 3-8-51, "The Prince of Buffalo Gap" 4-4-57, "The Banker's Son" 5-16-57; *The Gene Autry Show*—"The Breakup" 11-5-50, "Twisted Trails" 11-12-50, "Talking Guns" 8-10-54, "Civil War at Deadwood" 9-14-54; *The Range Rider*—"Stage to Rainbow's End" 9-2-51, "Outlaw Territory" 5-17-52, "The Badmen of Rimrock" 9-13-52, "Marked for Death" 11-8-52; *Wild Bill Hickok*—"The Sheriff Was a Redhead" 7-15-52; *The Adventures of Champion*—Regular 1955-56 (Uncle Sandy); *Annie Oakley*—"Flint and Steel" 10-14-56 (Frank Jessup); *The Adventures of Rin Tin Tin*—"Along Came Tubbs" 5-24-57 (McCoy); *Maverick*—"Stage West" 10-27-57 (Matson); *Wyatt Earp*—"Mr. Buntline's Vacation" 11-19-57 (Lt. Warden), "Truth About Gunfighting" 11-18-58 (Lanigan); *Tales of Wells Fargo*—"Doc Bell" 1-6-58 (Curly), "Bob Dawson" 4-20-59 (Marshal); *Zorro*—"Death Stacks the Deck" 2-13-58 (Carlos Urista); *Sergeant Preston of the Yukon*—"The Criminal Collie" 2-27-58 (Dirk); *Fury*—"The Bounty Hunters" 2-22-58 (Lane), "A Fish Story" 3-8-58 (Warden Lane); *Jefferson Drum*—"A Very Deadly Game" 5-30-58 (Tay Beloin); *Buckskin*—"Miss Pringle" 10-16-58 (Nate); *Wagon Train*—"The Beauty Jamison Story" 12-17-58 (Rancher); *Bat Masterson*—"Trail Pirate" 12-31-58 (Sheriff); *Wide Country*—"The Quest for Jacob Blaufus" 3-7-63 (Red Pickens); *Daniel Boone*—"The King's Shilling" 10-19-67 (Larkin), "They Who Will They Hang from the Yardarm If Willy Gets Away?" 2-8-68 (Lieutenant Parker), "Minnow for a Shark" 1-2-69 (Corporal).

Bara, Nina (1925-8/15/90). Films: "Black Hills" 1948 (Chiquita).

Bara, Theda (1892-4/7/55). Films: "Gold and the Woman" 1916 (Juliet De Cordova).

Barab, Nira. *see* Adams, Caitlin.

Baragrey, John (1918-8/4/75). Films: "Tall Man Riding" 1955 (Cibo Pearlo); "Pardners" 1956 (Dan Hollis). ¶TV: *Cimarron City*—"Have Sword, Will Duel" 3-14-59 (Grand Duke Nicolai).

Baral, Eileen. TV: *Wagon Train*—"The Brian Conlin Story" 10-25-64 (Sara), "Little Girl Lost" 12-13-64 (Robin); *Bonanza*—"Found Child" 10-24-65 (Lisa); *The Big Valley*—"A Flock of Trouble" 9-25-67 (Gayle); *Lancer*—"Splinter Group" 3-3-70 (Tillie).

Baratto, Luisa (Louise Barrett). Films: "Payment in Blood" 1968-Ital. (Manuela).

Barbar, Newton. Films: "All Around the Frying Pan" 1925 (Ruddy Logan); "The Ridin' Streak" 1925 (Gus Dokes).

Barbara, Paola (1912-10/1/89). Films: "Sign of Coyote" 1964-Ital./Span.; "Relentless Four" 1966-Span./Ital.; "Killer Goodbye" 1969-Ital./Span.; "Man Called Sledge" 1971-Ital./U.S. (Jade).

Barbeau, Adrienne (1949-). Films: "Blood River" TVM-1994 (Georgina).

Barber, Bobby. Films: "King of the Texas Rangers" 1941-serial (Eduardo); "Vigilantes of Boomtown" 1947 (2nd Sparring Partner); "Lost in Alaska" 1952 (Chief); "Pardners" 1956 (Townsman).

Barbi, Vincent (1912-). Films: "Machismo—40 Graves for 40 Guns" 1970 (Harris Gang Member).

Barbier, George (1864-7/19/45). Films: "The Broken Wing" 1932 (Luther Farley); "Sunset Pass" 1933 (Judge); "Under the Tonto Rim" 1933 (Weston); "The Return of Frank James" 1940 (Ferris, the Judge).

Barboo, Luis. Films: "God Forgives—I Don't" 1966-Ital./Span.; "Between God, the Devil and a Winchester" 1968-Ital./Span.; "Cowards Don't Pray" 1968-Ital./Span.; "Cry for Revenge" 1968-Ital./Span.; "One After Another" 1968-Span./Ital.; "Piluk, the Timid One" 1968-Ital.; "Rattler Kid" 1968-Ital./Span.; "Dead Are Countless" 1969-Ital./Span.; "Killer Goodbye" 1969-Ital./Span.; "Arizona" 1970-Ital./Span.; "Montana Trap" 1976-Ger.

Barclay, David. *see* O'Brien, Dave.

Barclay, Don (1892-10/16/75).

Films: "The Lion's Den" 1936 (Paddy Callahan); "Treachery Rides the Range" 1936 (Cpl. Bunce); "Border Phantom" 1937 (Lucky); "Outlaw Express" 1938 (Andy Sharpe); "Thunder in the Desert" 1938 (Rusty); "The Oklahoma Kid" 1939 (Drunk); "My Darling Clementine" 1946 (Opera House Owner); "Whispering Smith" 1948 (Dr. Sawbuck).

Barclay, Jerry. Films: "Valerie" 1957 (Mingo); "Gun Fever" 1958 (Singer); "Gunmen from Laredo" 1959 (Jordan Keefer). ¶TV: *Colt .45*—"Showdown at Goldtown" 6-14-60 (Tip Cooper); *Rawhide*—"Incident of the Music Maker" 5-20-60 (Fran Zwahlen); *Lawman*—"Cold Fear" 6-4-61 (Bert Quade); *Bronco*—"One Evening in Abilene" 3-19-62 (Clay); *The Dakotas*—"Trouble at French Creek" 1-28-63 (Weems); *Bonanza*—"The Last Haircut" 2-3-63 (Cal).

Barclay, Joan (Geraine Grear). Films: "Feud of the West" 1936 (Molly Henderson); "The Kid Ranger" 1936 (Mary Brokaw); "Men of the Plains" 1936 (Laura Long); "Phantom Patrol" 1936 (Doris McCloud); "Ridin' On" 1936 (Gloria O'Neill); "West of Nevada" 1936 (Helen Haldain); "The Glory Trail" 1937 (Lucy Strong); "The Trusted Outlaw" 1937 (Betty); "Lightning Carson Rides Again" 1938 (Sally); "Pioneer Trail" 1938 (Alice); "The Purple Vigilantes" 1938 (Jean McAllister); "The Singing Outlaw" 1938 (Joan McClain); "Two-Gun Justice" 1938 (Nancy Brown); "Whirlwind Horseman" 1938 (Peggy Radford); "The Gentleman from Arizona" 1939 (Georgia); "Outlaw's Paradise" 1939 (Jessie); "Six-Gun Rhythm" 1939 (Joan Harper); "Texas Wildcats" 1939 (Molly Arden); "Billy the Kid's Range War" 1941 (Ellen); "Billy the Kid's Roundup" 1941; "Bandit Ranger" 1942; "Billy the Kid's Smoking Guns" 1942; "Sagebrush Law" 1943.

Barclay, Martha. Films: "Across the Plains" 1928 (Sally Howard).

Barclay, Per. Films: "El Condor" 1970 (Convict); "Bad Man's River" 1971-Span./Ital./Fr. (Reverend); "Doc" 1971 (Clanton Cowboy); "Valdez Is Coming" 1971 (Bartender).

Barclay, Stephen (1918-2/2/94). Films: "Pride of the Plains" 1944 (Kenny Revere); "Vigilantes of Dodge City" 1944; "Don't Fence Me In" 1945 (Tracy); "Fool's Gold" 1946 (Bruce Landy); "Landrush" 1946 (Caleb Garvey); "Where the North Begins" 1947.

Barcroft, Roy (1902-11/28/69).

Films: "Flaming Frontier" 1938-serial; "The Frontiersman" 1938 (Buster Sutton); "Heroes of the Hills" 1938 (Robert Beaton); "The Stranger from Arizona" 1938 (Thane); "Crashing Thru" 1939 (Green); "The Man from Texas" 1939 (Drifter); "Mexicali Rose" 1939 (McElroy); "The Oregon Trail" 1939-serial (Colonel Custer); "Renegade Trail" 1939 (Stiff Hat Bailey); "Riders of the Frontier" 1939 (Ed Carter); "Silver on the Sage" 1939 (Ewing); "Bad Man from Red Butte" 1940 (Hank); "Deadwood Dick" 1940-serial; "Hidden Gold" 1940 (Hendricks); "Ragtime Cowboy Joe" 1940 (Putt Lewis); "Rancho Grande" 1940 (Madden); "Santa Fe Trail" 1940 (Engineer); "The Showdown" 1940 (Bowman); "Stage to Chino" 1940 (Dude Elliott); "Trailing Double Trouble" 1940 (Jim Moreland); "West of Carson City" 1940 (Bill Tompkins); "Winners of the West" 1940-serial; "Yukon Flight" 1940 (Lodin); "The Bandit Trail" 1941 (Joel Nesbitt); "Jesse James at Bay" 1941 (Vern Stone); "King of the Texas Rangers" 1941-serial (Ross); "The Masked Rider" 1941 (Luke); "Outlaws of the Cherokee Trail" 1941; "Pals of the Pecos" 1941 (Keno Hawkins); "Riders of Death Valley" 1941-serial (Dirk); "Riders of the Badlands" 1941 (Capt. Martin); "Sheriff of Tombstone" 1941; "They Died with Their Boots On" 1941 (Officer); "West of Cimarron" 1941; "White Eagle" 1941-serial; "Wide Open Town" 1941 (Red); "Below the Border" 1942; "Dawn on the Great Divide" 1942 (Loder); "Land of the Open Range" 1942 (Gil Carse); "The Lone Rider in Cheyenne" 1942; "Old Chisholm Trail" 1942 (Ed); "Pirates of the Prairie" 1942; "Ridin' Down the Canyon" 1942 (Lafe Collins); "Romance on the Range" 1942 (Pete); "Silver Queen" 1942 (Dan Carson); "Stardust on the Sage" 1942 (Murphy); "Sunset on the Desert" 1942 (Nelson); "Sunset Serenade" 1942 (Bart Reynolds); "Valley of Vanishing Men" 1942-serial (Luke); "West of the Law" 1942; "False Colors" 1943 (Sheriff Clem Martin); "Bordertown Gunfighters" 1943 (Jack Gattling); "Calling Wild Bill Elliott" 1943; "Canyon City" 1943 (Jeff Parker); "Carson City Cyclone" 1943 (Joe Newman); "Cheyenne Roundup" 1943 (Slim Layton); "Hands Across the Border" 1943; "Hoppy Serves a Writ" 1943 (Tod Colby); "In Old Oklahoma" 1943; "The Man from the Rio Grande" 1943 (Ace Holden); "Overland Mail Robbery" 1943 (David Patterson); "Raiders of Sunset

Pass" 1943 (Lefty Lewis); "Riders of the Rio Grande" 1943 (Sarsaparilla); "Sagebrush Law" 1943; "Six Gun Gospel" 1943; "The Stranger from Pecos" 1943 (Sheriff); "Wagon Tracks West" 1943 (Laird); "The Big Bonanza" 1944 (Don Pendleton); "Cheyenne Wildcat" 1944; "Code of the Prairie" 1944 (Professor David Larson Graham); "Firebrands of Arizona" 1944 (Deputy Ike); "Hidden Valley Outlaws" 1944; "The Laramie Trail" 1944; "The Lights of Old Santa Fe" 1944 (Ken Ferguson); "Marshal of Reno" 1944; "Sheriff of Sundown" 1944 (Jack Hatfield); "Stagecoach to Monterey" 1944; "Tucson Raiders" 1944; "Along the Navajo Trail" 1945 (Rusty Channing); "Bells of Rosarita" 1945 (Maxwell); "The Cherokee Flash" 1945; "Colorado Pioneers" 1945; "Corpus Christi Bandits" 1945 (Wade Larkin); "Dakota" 1945 (Poli's Driver); "Lone Texas Ranger" 1945; "Santa Fe Saddlemates" 1945; "Sunset in El Dorado" 1945 (Buster Welch); "The Topeka Terror" 1945 (Ben Jode); "Trail of Kit Carson" 1945; "Wagon Wheels Westward" 1945; "Alias Billy the Kid" 1946 (Matt Conroy); "Home on the Range" 1946 (Clint Baker); "My Pal Trigger" 1946 (Hunter); "The Phantom Rider" 1946-serial (Marshal); "Plainsman and the Lady" 1946 (Cowboy); "Stagecoach to Denver" 1946 (Big Bill Lambert); "Sun Valley Cyclone" 1946; "Along the Oregon Trail" 1947 (Jake Stoner); "Bandits of Dark Canyon" 1947 (Jeff Conley); "The Fabulous Texan" 1947 (Standifer); "Jesse James Rides Again" 1947-serial (Frank Lawton); "Last Frontier Uprising" 1947 (Boyd); "The Marshal of Cripple Creek" 1947 (Link); "Oregon Trail Scouts" 1947 (Bill Hunter); "Rustlers of Devil's Canyon" 1947 (Clark); "Son of Zorro" 1947-serial (Boyd); "Springtime in the Sierras" 1947 (Matt Wilkes); "Vigilantes of Boomtown" 1947 (McKean); "The Wild Frontier" 1947 (Lon Brand); "Wyoming" 1947 (Sheriff Niles); "The Bold Frontiersman" 1948 (Smiling Jack); "Desperadoes of Dodge City" 1948 (Homesteader); "Eyes of Texas" 1948 (Vic Rabin); "The Gallant Legion" 1948; "Grand Canyon Trail" 1948 (Dave Williams); "Madonna of the Desert" 1948 (Buck Keaton); "Marshal of Amarillo" 1948 (Ben); "Oklahoma Badlands" 1948 (Sanders); "Old Los Angeles" 1948 (Clyborne); "Renegades of Sonora" 1948; "Sons of Adventure" 1948 (Bennett); "Sundown in Santa Fe" 1948; "The Timber Trail" 1948 (Bart); "Down Dakota

Way" 1949 (H.T. McKenzie); "The Far Frontier" 1949 (Bart Carroll); "Frontier Marshal" 1949 (Flint Fleming); "Ghost of Zorro" 1949-serial (Hank Kilgore); "Hellfire" 1949; "Law of the Golden West" 1949 (Clete Larrabee); "Outcasts of the Trail" 1949 (Jim Judd); "Pioneer Marshal" 1949 (Clip Pearson); "Powder River Rustlers" 1949 (Bull Macons); "Prince of the Plains" 1949 (Regan); "Ranger of Cherokee Strip" 1949 (Mark Sanders); "San Antone Ambush" 1949 (Roberts); "Sheriff of Wichita" 1949 (Sam Stark); "South of Rio" 1949 (Lon Bryson); "The Arizona Cowboy" 1950 (Slade); "Code of the Silver Sage" 1950 (Hulon Champion); "Desperadoes of the West" 1950-serial (Hacker); "Gunmen of Abilene" 1950 (Brink Fallon); "The James Brothers of Missouri" 1950-serial (Ace Marlin); "The Missourians" 1950 (Nick Kovacs); "North of the Great Divide" 1950 (Banning); "Rock Island Trail" 1950 (Barnes); "Rustlers on Horseback" 1950 (Leo Straykin); "Salt Lake Raiders" 1950 (Brit Condor); "The Savage Horde" 1950 (Fergus); "Surrender" 1950 (Deputy); "Under Mexicali Stars" 1950 (Hays Lawson); "The Vanishing Westerner" 1950 (Sand Sanderson); "Vigilante Hideout" 1950 (Muley Price); "Arizona Manhunt" 1951 (Pete Willard); "The Dakota Kid" 1951 (Turk); "Desert of Lost Men" 1951 (Link Rinter); "Don Daredevil Rides Again" 1951-serial (Douglas Stratton); "Fort Dodge Stampede" 1951 (Pike Hardin); "In Old Amarillo" 1951 (Clint Burnside); "Night Riders of Montana" 1951 (Brink Stiles); "Pals of the Golden West" 1951 (Ward Sloan); "Rodeo King and the Senorita" 1951 (Steve Lacey); "Utah Wagon Train" 1951 (Driscoll); "Wells Fargo Gunmaster" 1951 (Brick Manson); "Black Hills Ambush" 1952 (Bart); "Border Saddlemates" 1952 (Steve Baxter); "Captive of Billy the Kid" 1952 (Plute); "Desperadoes' Outpost" 1952 (Jim Boylan); "Leadville Gunslinger" 1952 (Chet/Pete Yonker); "Montana Belle" 1952 (Jim Clark); "Oklahoma Annie" 1952 (Curt Walker); "Old Oklahoma Plains" 1952 (Arthur Jensen); "Ride the Man Down" 1952 (Russ Schultz); "South Pacific Trail" 1952 (Link Felton); "Thundering Caravans" 1952 (Ed Brill); "Wild Horse Ambush" 1952 (Big John Harkins); "Bandits of the West" 1953 (Bud Galloway); "Down Laredo Way" 1953 (Cooper); "El Paso Stampede" 1953 (Floyd Garnett); "Iron Mountain Trail" 1953 (Mate Orrin); "Marshal of Cedar

Rock" 1953 (Henry Mason); "Old Overland Trail" 1953 (John Anchor); "Savage Frontier" 1953 (William Oakes); "Shadows of Tombstone" 1953 (Mike); "The Desperado" 1954 (Martin Novack); "Man with the Steel Whip" 1954-serial (Sheriff); "Two Guns and a Badge" 1954 (Bill Sterling); "Man Without a Star" 1955 (Sheriff Olson); "Oklahoma!" 1955 (Marshal); "The Spoilers" 1955 (the Marshal); "Gun Brothers" 1956 (Sheriff Jergen); "The Last Hunt" 1956 (Barfly); "Domino Kid" 1957 (Ed Sandlin); "The Last Stagecoach West" 1957; "Escort West" 1959 (Doyle); "Ten Who Dared" 1960 (Jim Baker); "Six Black Horses" 1962 (Mustanger); "Billy the Kid vs. Dracula" 1966 (Marshal Griffin); "Gunpoint" 1966 (Dr. Beardsley); "Texas Across the River" 1966 (Cy Morton); "The Way West" 1967 (Masters); "Bandolero!" 1968 (Bartender); "Monte Walsh" 1970 (Saloon Proprietor). ¶TV: *Cowboy G-Men*—"Ghost Town Mystery" 4-4-53, "Sidewinder" 5-2-53; *Stories of the Century*—"Last Stagecoach West" 1954 (Pa Ketchum); *Wyatt Earp*—"Rich Man's Son" 12-13-55 (Jim Grimes), "The Manly Art" 1-21-58, "The Bounty Killer" 9-30-58 (Moyer); *Fury*—"Stolen Fury" 1-28-56 (Jep); *My Friend Flicka*—"Lock, Stock and Barrel" 4-6-56 (Jud Hoskins); *Annie Oakley*—"The Waco Kid" 10-28-56 (Deacon McCanles); *The Lone Ranger*—"The Avenger" 1-10-57; *Zane Grey Theater*—"The Necessary Breed" 2-15-57 (Cal Neuman), "Never Too Late" 2-4-60 (Rady Smith), "So Young the Savage Land" 11-20-60 (Mike); *Circus Boy*—"Corky's Big Parade" 3-24-57 (Matt Flint); *Have Gun Will Travel*—"A Matter of Ethics" 10-12-57 (Sheriff), "Killer's Widow" 3-22-58 (Rancher), "Commanche" 5-16-59 (Sergeant Barsky), "The Haunted Trees" 6-13-59 (Flannigan), "The Tax Gatherer" 2-11-61 (Lewt Cutter), "The Long Weekend" 4-8-61 (Shep Montrose), "The Hanging of Aaron Gibbs" 11-4-61 (Marshal), "Lazarus" 1-20-62 (Jake Trueblood), "Be Not Forgetful to Strangers" 12-22-62 (Simon), "Face of a Shadow" 4-20-63; *Sheriff of Cochise*—"The Promise" 11-22-57 (Doc Shuman); *Maverick*—"The Jeweled Gun" 11-24-57 (Cattleman), "The Thirty-Ninth Star" 11-16-58 (Marshal); *Trackdown*—"The Town" 12-13-57 (Marshal Kent); *Death Valley Days*—"Birth of a Boom" 2-3-58 (Jim Butler), "The Wild West's Biggest Train Holdup" 5-2-65 (Sheriff Jackson), "Halo for a Badman" 4-

15-67 (Mayor Engley); *Tales of Wells Fargo*—"Deadwood" 4-7-58 (Sheriff), "The Rawhide Kid" 3-16-59 (Sheriff Turner), "Forty-Four Forty" 2-29-60 (Olseen); *26 Men*—"Legacy of Death" 4-29-58, "The Bells of St. Thomas" 5-13-58, "The Last Rebellion" 11-4-58, "The Hasbeen" 3-24-59, "Tumbleweed Ranger" 6-2-59; *Rough Riders*—"Strand of Wire" 12-18-58 (John Ames); *Wanted—Dead or Alive*—"The Legend" 3-7-59, "The Voice of Silence" 2-15-61 (Frank Hagen); *The Deputy*—"Proof of Guilt" 10-24-59; *The Texan*—"Stampede" 11-2-59, "Showdown at Abilene" 11-9-59; *Tombstone Territory*—12-11-59 (Flint Anson); *Shotgun Slade*—"Barbed Wire" 1-12-60; *Gunsmoke*—"Say Uncle" 10-1-60 (George Farr), "Ben Toliver's Stud" 11-26-60 (Jake Creed), "Bad Seed" 2-4-61 (Asa Trent), "Cotter's Girl" 1-19-63 (Cotter), "Once a Haggen" 2-1-64 (Pop), "Jonah Hutchison" 11-21-64 (Roy), "Circus Trick" 2-6-65 (Roy), "Thursday's Child" 3-6-65 (Roy), "Honey Pot" 5-15-65 (Roy), "Outlaw's Woman" 12-11-65 (Jonas), "The Returning" 2-18-67 (Jonas), "O'Quillian" 10-28-68 (Roy), "Mannon" 1-20-69 (Roy); *Gunslinger*—"Border Incident" 2-9-61 (Taggert); *Laramie*—"The Debt" 4-18-61 (Cotter), "Badge of the Outsider" 5-23-61 (Doc Longley), "The Renegade Brand" 2-26-63; *Frontier Circus*—"The Smallest Target" 10-12-61 (Pete Andrews), "Winter Quarters" 11-23-61 (Gore); *Rawhide*—"Judgment at Hondo Seco" 10-20-61 (Casey), "Incident at Alkali Sink" 5-24-63 (Stanton), "Incident at Confidence Creek" 11-28-63 (Sheriff), "Walk into Terror" 10-5-65 (Adams); *Lawman*—"Change of Venue" 2-11-62 (Luke Tannant); *Bonanza*—"Crucible" 4-8-62, "The Cheating Game" 2-9-64, "The Lonely Runner" 10-10-65 (Frank), "Peace Officer" 2-6-66 (Deputy Hacker); *The Rifleman*—"Outlaw Shoes" 4-30-62 (Mr. Stevens); *Empire*—"The Fire Dancer" 11-13-62 (Charlie Hooper); *The Virginian*—"The Small Parade" 2-20-63, "Sue Ann" 1-11-67 (Tait); *Laredo*—"The Golden Trail" 11-4-65 (Deputy), "Jinx" 12-2-65 (Marshal Ezzard Speaks); *Wild Wild West*—"The Night of the Howling Light" 12-17-65 (Sikes); *A Man Called Shenandoah*—"Run, Killer, Run" 1-10-66 (Drew Narramore); *The Road West*—"Charade of Justice" 3-27-67 (George Reap); *Cimarron Strip*—"The Legend of Jud Starr" 9-14-67; *Iron Horse*—"Leopards Try, But Leopard's Can't" 10-28-67 (Dan Barrington).

Bard, Ben (1893-5/17/74). Films: "Arizona Wildcat" 1927 (Wallace Von Acker).

Bard, Katherine (1917-83). TV: *Gunsmoke*—"Widow's Mite" 5-10-58 (Ada Morton); *The Rifleman*—"The Trade" 3-10-59 (Beth Landis); *The Big Valley*—"My Son, My Son" 11-3-65 (Jenny Miles).

Bardem, Raphael. Films: "Seven Guns for the MacGregors" 1965-Ital./Span. (Justice Garland).

Bardette, Trevor (1902-11/28/77). Films: "Borderland" 1937 (Col. Gonzales); "In Old Mexico" 1938 (Col. Gonzales); "Let Freedom Ring" 1939 (Gagan); "The Oklahoma Kid" 1939 (Indian Jack Pasco); "Overland with Kit Carson" 1939-serial (Arthur Mitchell); "Stand Up and Fight" 1939 (Mob Leader); "The Dark Command" 1940 (Hale); "Santa Fe Trail" 1940 (Agitator); "Three Faces West" 1940 (Clem Higgins); "Virginia City" 1940 (Fanatic); "Wagons Westward" 1940 (Alan Cook); "The Westerner" 1940 (Shad Wilkins); "Winners of the West" 1940-serial (Raven); "Young Buffalo Bill" 1940 (Emilio Montez); "Doomed Caravan" 1941 (Ed Martin); "Red River Valley" 1941; "Romance of the Rio Grande" 1941 (Manuel); "Wild Bill Hickok Rides" 1942 (Sam Bass); "Apache Trail" 1943 (Amber); "Deerslayer" 1943 (Chief Rivenoak); "Law of the Badlands" 1945-short; "Marshal of Laredo" 1945; "The Last Round-Up" 1947 (Indian Chief); "The Marshal of Cripple Creek" 1947 (Tom Lambert); "Ramrod" 1947 (Bailey); "The Sea of Grass" 1947 (Andy Boggs); "Wyoming" 1947 (Timmons); "Adventures in Silverado" 1948; "Black Eagle" 1948 (Mike Long); "The Gallant Legion" 1948; "Marshal of Amarillo" 1948 (Frank Welch); "The Paleface" 1948 (Horseman); "Smoky Mountain Melody" 1948; "Sundown in Santa Fe" 1948; "Apache Chief" 1949 (Big Crow); "The Blazing Trail" 1949 (Jess Williams); "Hellfire" 1949 (Wilson); "Renegades of the Sage" 1949 (Miller); "San Antone Ambush" 1949 (Wade Shattuck); "Sheriff of Wichita" 1949 (Ira Flanders); "The Wyoming Bandit" 1949 (Wyoming Dan); "Broken Arrow" 1950 (Stage Passenger); "Hills of Oklahoma" 1950 (Hank); "The Palomino" 1950 (Brown); "Fort Dodge Stampede" 1951 (Sparkler McCann); "Fort Savage Raiders" 1951 (Old Cuss); "Gene Autry and the Mounties" 1951 (Raoul Duval); "The Texas Rangers" 1951 (Telegraph Operator); "Lone Star" 1952 (Sid Yoakum); "Montana Terri-

tory" 1952 (Lloyd Magruder); "The San Francisco Story" 1952 (Miner); "Ambush at Tomahawk Gap" 1953 (Sheriff); "Bandits of the West" 1953 (Jeff Chadwick); "A Perilous Journey" 1953 (Whiskered Miner); "Red River Shore" 1953 (Frank Barlow); "Thunder Over the Plains" 1953 (Walter Morgan); "Destry" 1954 (Sheriff Joe Bailey); "Johnny Guitar" 1954 (Jenks); "The Outlaw Stallion" 1954 (Rigo); "The Man from Bitter Ridge" 1955 (Walter Dunham); "Rage at Dawn" 1955 (Fisher); "Run for Cover" 1955 (Paulsen); "The Rawhide Years" 1956 (Captain); "Red Sundown" 1956 (Sam Baldwin); "Dragoon Wells Massacre" 1957 (Marshal Bill Haney); "The Hard Man" 1957 (Mitch Willis); "Shoot-Out at Medicine Bend" 1957 (Sheriff); "The Saga of Hemp Brown" 1958 (Judge); "The Raiders" 1964 (Uncle Otto Strassner); "MacKenna's Gold" 1969 (Old Man). ¶TV: *My Friend Flicka*—"The Settler" 1-27-56 (Sam Hunter); *Frontier*—"The Voyage of Captain Castle" 2-19-56 (Sam Houston); *Wyatt Earp*—"The Desperate Half-Hour" 2-28-56 (Osborne), "The Sharpshooter" 1-29-57 (Rufe Hawes), "Four" 5-27-58 (Crump Elliot), "The Bounty Killer" 9-30-58 (Elzey Rash), Regular 1959-61 (Old Man Clanton); *Cheyenne*—"West of the River" 3-20-56 (Ed), "Lone Gun" 12-4-56 (Amarilo Ames), "The Young Fugitives" 10-23-61 (Lige), "Day's Pay" 10-30-61 (Clem McCracken), "Indian Gold" 10-29-62 (Charlie Feeney); *20th Century Fox Hour*—"Gun in His Hand" 4-4-56 (Willis); *Ford Theater*—"Sudden Silence" 10-10-56 (Jordan); *Broken Arrow*—"The Captive" 10-23-56 (Whittier), "Conquistador" 10-8-57; *Zane Grey Theater*—"Time of Decision" 1-18-57 (Jed Curtis); *The Lone Ranger*—"A Harp for Hannah" 1-31-57; *Sheriff of Cochise*—"Grandfather Grandson" 2-11-57 (Carter); *Maverick*—"Hostage!" 11-10-57 (Inspector Marvin), "Benefit of Doubt" 4-9-61 (Bert Coleman); *Trackdown*—"The Toll Road" 1-31-58 (Dr. Wilson); *Jim Bowie*—"Bad Medicine" 4-18-58 (Nitakechi); *The Restless Gun*—"Hiram Grover's Strike" 5-12-58 (Enoch Wilson), "Peligroso" 12-15-58 (Grant Fisher); *Rough Riders*—"The Maccabites" 10-16-58 (John Schroeder); *Man Without a Gun*—"Wire's End" 12-20-58 (Simon); *Union Pacific*—"Lost Boy" 2-28-59; *The Texan*—"Letter of the Law" 3-23-59 (Pop Koller); *Tales of Wells Fargo*—"Terry" 4-6-59; *Gunsmoke*—"Kangaroo" 9-26-59 (Slim), "Small Water" 9-24-60

(Finn Pickett), "The Wreckers" 9-11-67 (Clete Walker), "Death Train" 11-27-67 (Conductor), "McCabe" 11-30-70 (Conductor); *Hotel De Paree*—"Vein of Ore" 10-16-59 (D.J. Hobbs); *Have Gun Will Travel*—"Jenny" 1-23-60 (Carruthers), "A Head of Hair" 9-24-60 (Chagra), "The Road" 5-27-61 (Hensoe); *The Rebel*—"The Unwanted" 1-31-60 (Amister), "The Threat" 2-12-61 (Sheriff Ike Howard); *Bronco*—"A Sure Thing" 1-22-62 (Dutch Vandervort); *Laramie*—"The Runaway" 1-23-62 (Ezra Watkins); *Wagon Train*—"The Levi Hale Story" 4-18-62 (Pete Rudge), "The Lily Legend Story" 2-13-63 (Sheriff Lund), "The Antone Rose Story" 5-22-63 (Henry Ludlow); *Bonanza*—"The Way Station" 10-29-62 (Jesse), "The Toy Soldier" 10-20-63 (Scotty); *A Man Called Shenandoah*—"The Locket" 11-22-65 (the Trader).

Bardine, Mabel. Films: "Rough and Ready" 1918 (Bess Brown).

Bardot, Brigitte (1934-). Films: "Viva Maria" 1965-Fr./Ital. (Maria Fitzgerald O'Malley); "Shalako" 1968-Brit./Fr. (Countess Irini Lazaar); "The Legend of Frenchie King" 1971-Fr./Ital./Span./Brit. (Frenchie King).

Bare, Bobby. Films: "A Distant Trumpet" 1964 (Cranshaw).

Bari, Lynn (1917-11/20/89). Films: "The Return of the Cisco Kid" 1939 (Ann Carver); "Kit Carson" 1940 (Dolores Murphy); "The Man from Texas" 1947 (Lee Bixbee). ¶TV: *Screen Director's Playhouse*—"Arroyo" 10-26-55 (Hattie Mae Warren); *Walt Disney Presents*—"Elfego Baca: Elfego Baca, Attorney at Law" 2-6-59 (Mrs. Simmons); *Bronco*—"Hero of the Town" 6-2-59 (Amy Biggs); *Overland Trail*—"Perilous Passage" 2-7-60 (Belle Starr); *The Law of the Plainsman*—"The Matriarch" 2-18-60 (Constance Valeri); *Death Valley Days*—"Trial at Belle's Springs" 5-23-64 (Belle Wilgus).

Barjac, Sophie. TV: *Bordertown*—Regular 1989 (Dr. Marie Dumont).

Barker, Jr., Alfred. "The Cowboys" 1972 (Singing Fats). ¶TV: *Bonanza*—"The Initiation" 9-26-72 (Billy Newton).

Barker, Bob (1924-). TV: *Bonanza*—"Denver McKee" 10-15-60 (Mort).

Barker, Bill. Films: "Revolt at Fort Laramie" 1957 (Hendrey).

Barker, Florence (1891-2/15/13). Films: "The Gold Seekers" 1910; "A Knot in the Plot" 1910; "Over Silent Paths" 1910; "The Tenderfoot's Triumph" 1910.

Barker, Jess (1911-84). Films: "The Daltons Ride Again" 1945 (Jeff); "Senorita from the West" 1945; "Kentucky Rifle" 1956; "The Peacemaker" 1956 (Ed Halcomb).

Barker, Lex (1919-5/11/73). Films: "Unconquered" 1947 (Royal American Officer); "Under the Tonto Rim" 1947 (Deputy Joe); "Return of the Badmen" 1948 (Emmett Dalton); "The Battles of Chief Pontiac" 1952 (Kent McIntire); "Thunder Over the Plains" 1953 (Capt. Bill Hodges); "The Yellow Mountain" 1954 (Andy Martin); "The Man from Bitter Ridge" 1955 (Jeff Carr); "The Deerslayer" 1957 (the Deerslayer); "War Drums" 1957 (Mangas Coloradas); "Treasure of Silver Lake" 1963-Fr./Ger./Yugo. (Old Shatterhand); "Apache Gold" 1965-Ger. (Old Shatterhand); "The Desperado Trail" 1965-Ger./Yugo. (Old Shatterhand); "Pyramid of the Sun God" 1965-Ger./Ital./Fr. (Dr. Karl Sternau); "Half Breed" 1966-Ger./Yugo./Ital. (Shatterhand); "Last of the Renegades" 1966-Fr./Ital./Ger./Yugo. (Old Shatterhand); "A Place Called Glory" 1966-Span./Ger. (Brenner); "Who Killed Johnny R.?" 1966-Ital./Span. (Dillon); "Old Shatterhand" 1968-Ger./Yugo./Fr./Ital. (Old Shatterhand); "Winnetou and Shatterhand in the Valley of Death" 1968-Ger./Yugo./Ital. (Old Shatterhand).

Barkley, Lucille. Films: "Frenchie" 1950 (Dealer); "Arizona Manhunt" 1951 (Clara Drummond). ¶TV: *Death Valley Days*—"The Big Team Rolls" 5-23-55.

Barlow, Reginald (1866-7/6/43). Films: "Red Blood of Courage" 1935 (Mark Henry/Pete Drago); "The Last of the Mohicans" 1936 (Duke of Newcastle); "O'Malley of the Mounted" 1936 (Commissioner); "It Happened Out West" 1937 (Middleton); "Heritage of the Desert" 1939 (Judge Stevens); "New Frontier" 1939 (Judge Lawson); "Rovin' Tumbleweeds" 1939 (Higgins); "Wall Street Cowboy" 1939 (Bainbridge); "Law of the Northwest" 1943 (Jean Darcy).

Barnes, Binnie (1905-). Films: "The Last of the Mohicans" 1936 (Alice Munro); "Sutter's Gold" 1936 (Countess Elizabeth Bartoffski); "Frontier Marshal" 1939 (Jerry); "In Old California" 1942 (Lacey Miller); "Barbary Coast Gent" 1944 (Lil Damish); "The Dude Goes West" 1948 (Kiki Kelly).

Barnes, Eddie. Films: "Honor of the Range" 1934 (Charlie).

Barnes, George (1890-11/18/49). Films: "The Great Train Robbery" 1903.

Barnes, Jane. Films: "Melody Trail" 1935 (Helen); "Frontier Justice" 1936 (Ethel Gordon).

Barnes, Joanna (1934-). Films: "The Purple Hills" 1961 (Amy Carter); "The War Wagon" 1967 (Lola). ¶TV: *Maverick*—"Ghost Riders" 10-13-57 (Mary Shane), "The Burning Sky" 2-23-58 (Mrs. Baxter), "Lonesome Reunion" 9-28-58 (Abigail Taylor), "The Resurrection of Joe November" 2-28-60 (Felice De Lassignac), "Arizona Black Maria" 10-9-60 (Daphne Tolliver); *Cheyenne*—"Devil's Canyon" 11-19-57 (Alice Claney), "Dead to Rights" 5-20-58 (Adelaide Marshall); *Colt .45*—"Ghost Town" 2-21-58 (Kate Henniger); *Man from Blackhawk*—"Remember Me Not" 9-9-60 (Colette); *Stagecoach West*—"The Outcasts" 3-7-61 (Ruby Sanders); *Laramie*—"The Barefoot Kid" 1-9-62 (Ruth), "War Hero" 10-2-62 (Lucy Barton); *Have Gun Will Travel*—"Penelope" 12-8-62 (Penelope Lacey); *Empire*—"Down There, the World" 3-12-63 (Neva Bradford); *Alias Smith and Jones*—"How to Rob a Bank in One Hard Lesson" 9-23-71 (Janet Judson), "Miracle at Santa Marta" 12-30-71 (Mrs. Hanley).

Barnes, Pinky. Films: "Fighting Caballero" 1935; "Cavalry" 1936; "Desert Guns" 1936 (Morgarn); "The Singing Buckaroo" 1937.

Barnes, Priscilla (1955-). Films: "The Wild Women of Chastity Gulch" TVM-1982 (Dr. Maggie McCulloch).

Barnes, Rayford (1925-). Films: "Hondo" 1953 (Pete); "Red River Shore" 1953; "The Stranger Wore a Gun" 1953; "The Desperado" 1954 (Ray Novack); "Wichita" 1955 (Hal Clements); "The Burning Hills" 1956 (Veach); "Stagecoach to Fury" 1956 (Zick); "The Young Guns" 1956 (Kid Cutler); "Gun Glory" 1957 (Blondie); "Fort Massacre" 1958 (Moss); "Lone Texan" 1959 (Finch); "North to Alaska" 1960 (Gold Buyer); "Thirteen Fighting Men" 1960 (Sgt. Yates); "Young Jesse James" 1960 (Pitts); "Guns of Diablo" 1964 (Dan Macklin); "Shenandoah" 1965 (Horace); "The Hunting Party" 1971-Brit./Ital./Span. (Crimp); "Cahill, United States Marshal" 1973 (Pee Wee Simser); "Breakheart Pass" 1976 (Bellew); "The Wild Women of Chastity Gulch" TVM-1982 (Russell). ¶TV: *Wild Bill Hickok*—"Buckshot Comes

Home" 11-25-52; *The Roy Rogers Show*—"Bad Neighbors" 11-21-54 (Mack Houston), "Outcasts of Paradise Valley" 1-9-55 (Will Clements); *Fury*—"Joey and the Stranger" 12-1-56 (Biff), *Colt .45*—"Small Man" 11-15-57 (Brent Nelson); *Tombstone Territory*—"Shoot Out at Dark" 1-8-58 (Laredo); *Northwest Passage*—"Fight at the River" 9-14-58 (Fessler); *Have Gun Will Travel*—"The Road to Wickenberg" 10-25-58 (Sol Goodfellow), "Something to Live For" 12-20-58 (Harleigh Preston), "The Shooting of Jesse May" 10-20-60 (Sim Lenzer), "Long Way Home" 2-4-61 (Deputy), "The Revenger" 9-30-61 (Jelly Wilson), "Face of a Shadow" 4-20-63 (Canning); *The Adventures of Rin Tin Tin*—"Deadman's Valley" 11-7-58 (Taggart Jersey), "Apache Stampede" 3-20-59 (Joad Horn); *Tales of the Texas Rangers*—"Desert Fury" 11-20-58 (Eddie Temple); *Maverick*—"Passage to Fort Doom" 3-8-59 (Frank), "Last Stop: Olivion" 2-12-61 (Dave Lyme), "The Devil's Necklace" 4-16-61 & 4-23-61 (Corporal Sean Cassidy); *Wyatt Earp*—Regular 1959-61 (Ike Clanton); *Laramie*—"The Lawbreakers" 10-20-59 (Marcy), "The Lost Dutchman" 2-14-61 (George Lake), "Widow in White" 6-13-61 (Birch), "Fall into Darkness" 4-17-62 (Jack Frances); *The Law of the Plainsman*—"Passenger to Mescalero" 10-29-59; *Gunsmoke*—"Til Death Do Us" 1-16-60 (Puggy Rado), "Kitty Shot" 2-11-61 (George Helm), "Big Man" 3-25-61 (Harry), "Wagon Girls" 4-7-62 (Lee), "Carter Caper" 11-16-63 (Flack), "No Hands" 2-8-64 (Jess Ginnis), "Old Man" 10-10-64 (Harve Litton), "Danny" 10-13-69 (Carl Bahlman), "Alias Festus Haggen" 3-6-72 (Grebbs), "Kitty's Love Affair" 10-22-73 (Dowel); *The Deputy*—"Meet Sergeant Tasker" 10-1-60 (Charlie); *Bat Masterson*—"Bullwhacker's Bounty" 2-16-61 (Ed Twister); *Rawhide*—"Incident of the Woman Trap" 1-26-62 (Grieve); *Bonanza*—"A Hot Day for a Hanging" 10-14-62, "The Marriage of Theodora Duffy" 1-9-73 (Shaw); *Wide Country*—"The Girl from Nob Hill" 3-8-63 (Yost); *The Travels of Jaimie McPheeters*—"The Day of the Reckoning" 3-15-64 (Dan Macklin); *The Virginian*—"Two Men Named Laredo" 1-6-65 (Bojo Sanders), "Blaze of Glory" 12-29-65 (Smith); *Laredo*—"Meanwhile, Back at the Reservation" 2-10-66 (Fred Chaney); *Daniel Boone*—"Onatha" 11-3-66 (Millard Church); *Iron Horse*—"Through Ticket to Gunsight" 11-28-66 (Captain Miles); *The Big Valley*—

"Image of Yesterday" 1-9-67, "Shadow of a Giant" 1-29-68, "Hell Hath No Fury" 11-18-68 (Carl); *Death Valley Days*—"A Man Called Abraham" 3-11-67 (Cassidy); *The Guns of Will Sonnett*—"A Bell for Jeff Sonnett" 9-15-67 (Jack Collins), "Time Is the Rider" 1-10-69 (Chihuahua); *Cimarron Strip*—"The Roarer" 11-2-67, "Sound of a Drum" 2-1-68; *The High Chaparral*—"The Kinsman" 1-28-68 (Gurney), "Trail to Nevermore" 10-31-69 (Lippert); *Lancer*—"Blood Rock" 10-1-68; *The Outcasts*—"Gideon" 2-24-69 (Hank); *Nichols*—"The One Eyed Mule's Time Has Come" 11-23-71, 3-7-72; *Kung Fu*—"Night of the Owls, Day of the Doves" 2-14-74 (Sheriff Bryce); *The Quest*—"The Buffalo Hunters" 9-29-76 (Timmons); *Adventures of Brisco County, Jr.*—Pilot 8-27-93 (Sherman Paulson), "Crystal Hawks" 11-12-93 (Sherman Paulson).

Barnes, T. Roy (1880-3/30/37). Films: "A Regular Scout" 1926 (Steve Baxter); "The Unknown Cavalier" 1926 (Clout Pettingill).

Barnes, V.L. (1870-8/9/49). Films: "Crossed Trail" 1924 (George Moran); "The Fighting Cheat" 1926 (Doctor); "Hidden Valley" 1932 (McCord).

Barnes, Walter. Films: "Oregon Passage" 1958 (Sgt. Jed Erschick); "Westbound" 1959 (Willis); "Among Vultures" 1964-Ger./Ital./Fr./Yugo. (Baumann); "Apache Gold" 1965-Ger. (Bill Jones); "Duel at Sundown" 1965-Fr./Ger. (Mr. McGow); "Rampage at Apache Wells" 1965-Ger./Yugo. (Campbell); "The Big Gundown" 1966-Ital. (Brokston); "Half Breed" 1966-Ger./Yugo./Ital. (Mac); "Garter Colt" 1967-Ital./Span./Ger.; "Clint the Stranger" 1968-Ital./Span./Ger. (Walter Shannon); "The Greatest Robbery in the West" 1968-Ital. (Key Jarrett); "The Moment to Kill" 1968-Ital./Ger. (Bull); "Cahill, United States Marshal" 1973 (Sheriff Grady); "High Plains Drifter" 1973 (Sheriff Sam Shaw); "The Gun and the Pulpit" TVM-1974; "Mackintosh & T.J." 1975; "Another Man, Another Chance" 1977-Fr. (Foster); "Bronco Billy" 1980 (Sheriff Dix). ¶TV: *Zane Grey Theater*—"A Time to Live" 4-5-57 (Gus), "The Stranger" 2-28-58 (Bartender); *Death Valley Days*—"Thorn of the Rose" 6-16-57; *Colt .45*—"Final Payment" 11-22-57 (Mace Bluestone); *Cheyenne*—"Top Hand" 12-31-57 (Chris Barstow); *Have Gun Will Travel*—"The Five Books of Owen Deaver" 4-26-58 (Mason Enfield); *Gunsmoke*—"Ches-

ter's Hanging" 5-17-58 (Jack Haney), "Thoroughbreds" 10-18-58 (Burke); *Maverick*—"The Belcastle Brand" 10-12-58 (1st Outlaw); *Bronco*—"Four Guns and a Prayer" 11-4-58 (Dan Banner); *Rough Riders*—"Double Cross" 1-22-59 (Marshal Kenyon); *Bat Masterson*—"River Boat" 2-18-59 (Paulson); *Bonanza*—"Anatomy of a Lynching" 10-12-69 (Will Griner), "Long Way to Ogden" 2-22-70 (Emmett J. Whitney), "Top Hand" 1-17-71 (Weatherby), "Bushwacked" 10-3-71 (Sheriff Truslow); *The High Chaparral*—"Spokes" 9-25-70 (Bartender); *Alias Smith and Jones*—"The Man Who Murdered Himself" 3-18-71; *Kung Fu*—"The Elixir" 12-20-73 (Sheriff); *Father Murphy*—"Outrageous Fortune" 11-9-82 (Sheriff Bunch).

Barnett, Chester (1885-9/22/47). Films: "Salt of the Earth" 1917 (Dr. Wallace Hyde).

Barnett, Griff (1884-1/12/58). Films: "The Lone Ranger" 1938-serial (Rancher); "Santa Fe Stampede" 1938; "The Lone Ranger Rides Again" 1939-serial (E.B. Tuly); "Arizona" 1940 (Sam Hughes); "Frontier Vengeance" 1940 (Joel Hunter); "Gangs of Sonora" 1941; "Lady from Cheyenne" 1941 (Man); "Outlaws of the Cherokee Trail" 1941; "Shadows on the Sage" 1942 (Steve Jackson); "The Sombrero Kid" 1942; "Stardust on the Sage" 1942; "Death Valley Rangers" 1944; "Duel in the Sun" 1946 (the Jailer); "The Gunfighters" 1947 (Bonner); "The Michigan Kid" 1947; "Unconquered" 1947 (Brother Andrews); "Fury at Furnace Creek" 1948 (Appleby); "The Doolins of Oklahoma" 1949 (Deacon Burton); "Sierra" 1950 (Dr. Robbins); "Cattle Drive" 1951 (Conductor O'Hara); "Passage West" 1951 (Papa Ludwig); "The Treasure of Lost Canyon" 1952 (Judge Wade).

Barnett, Vince (1902-8/10/77). Films: "Heritage of the Desert" 1932 (Windy); "Man of the Forest" 1933 (Little Casino); "Sunset Pass" 1933 (Windy); "Boots of Destiny" 1937 (Acey Deucy); "Trailing Trouble" 1937; "Overland Mail" 1939 (Porchy); "Ride 'Em, Cowgirl" 1939 (Dan Haggerty); "The Singing Cowgirl" 1939 (Kewpie); "Water Rustlers" 1939 (Mike); "Heroes of the Saddle" 1940 (Constable); "Sierra Sue" 1941; "The Phantom Plainsmen" 1942 (Deputy Short); "Stardust on the Sage" 1942 (Haskins); "Thundering Trails" 1943; "The Virginian" 1946 (Baldy); "Gas House Kids Go West" 1947 (Steve); "Loaded Pistols" 1948

(Sam Gardner); "Thunder in the Pines" 1948 (Bernard); "Deputy Marshal" 1949 (Hotel Clerk); "Border Treasure" 1950 (Pokey); "Mule Train" 1950 (Barber Mulkey); "Carson City" 1952 (Henry); "Springfield Rifle" 1952 (Cook); "Outlaw Queen" 1957; "The Quiet Gun" 1957 (the Undertaker). ¶TV: *Tales of the Texas Rangers*—"Edge of Danger" 10-23-58 (Harry Sanders); *Cimarron Strip*—"Nobody" 12-7-67 (Willy).

Baron, Emma. Films: "Arizona Colt" 1965-Ital./Fr./Span.; "A Long Ride from Hell" 1968-Ital.

Baron, Lita. Films: "Jesse James' Women" 1954 (Delta); "The Broken Star" 1956 (Conchita); "Red Sundown" 1956 (Maria). ¶TV: *Frontier Doctor*—"South of the Rio Grande" 4-18-59; *The Texan*—"Quarantine" 2-8-60 (Dolores), "Buried Treasure" 2-15-60 (Dolores), "Captive Crew" 2-22-60 (Dolores), "The Governor's Lady" 3-14-60 (Lita Moreno); *Death Valley Days*—"The Water Bringer" 4-23-66 (Maria Martinez), "The Gold Mine on Main Street" 5-11-68 (Danita).

Barondes, Elizabeth. TV: *Adventures of Brisco County, Jr.*—"Mail Order Brides" 12-10-93 (Meg).

Barr, Byron (1917-11/3/66). Films: "Down Dakota Way" 1949 (Steve Paxton); "Covered Wagon Raid" 1950 (Roy Chandler).

Barr, Leonard (1903-11/22/80). Films: "Evil Roy Slade" TVM-1972 (Randolph).

Barr, Tony. Films: "Daughter of the West" 1949 (Yuba).

Barrat, Robert H. (1889-1/7/70). Films: "Massacre" 1934 (Dawson); "Moonlight on the Prairie" 1935 (Buck Cantwell); "The Last of the Mohicans" 1936 (Chingachgook); "Trailin' West" 1936 (President Abraham Lincoln); "The Barrier" 1937 (John Gale); "God's Country and the Woman" 1937 (Jefferson Russett); "The Bad Man of Brimstone" 1938 (Hank Summers); "Forbidden Valley" 1938 (Ramrod Locke); "The Texans" 1938 (Isaiah Middlebrack); "Allegheny Uprising" 1939 (Professor); "Bad Lands" 1939 (Sheriff Bill Cummings); "The Cisco Kid and the Lady" 1939 (Jim Harbison); "Colorado Sunset" 1939 (Doc Blair); "Heritage of the Desert" 1939 (Andrew Naab); "Man of Conquest" 1939 (Davy Crockett); "The Return of the Cisco Kid" 1939 (Sheriff McNally); "Union Pacific" 1939 (Duke Ring); ; "Go West" 1940 (Red Baxter); "The Man from Dakota" 1940

(Parson Summers); "Northwest Passage" 1940 (Humphrey Towne); "Riders of the Purple Sage" 1941 (Judge Dyer); "American Empire" 1942 (Crowder); "Girl from Alaska" 1942 (Frayne); "Dakota" 1945 (Mr. Stowe); "San Antonio" 1945 (Col. Johnson); "Wanderer of the Wasteland" 1945 (Uncle Collinshaw); "Sunset Pass" 1946 (Curtis); "The Fabulous Texan" 1947 (Dr. Sharp); "The Sea of Grass" 1947 (Judge White); "Relentless" 1948 (Ed Simpson); "Bad Men of Tombstone" 1949 (Sheriff); "Canadian Pacific" 1949 (Cornelius Van Horne); "The Doolins of Oklahoma" 1949 (Heck Thomas); "The Baron of Arizona" 1950 (Judge Adams); "Davy Crockett, Indian Scout" 1950 (Lone Eagle); "The Kid from Texas" 1950 (General Lew Wallace); "Riders of the Range" 1950 (Sheriff); "Distant Drums" 1951 (Gen. Zachary Taylor); "Denver and Rio Grande" 1952 (Haskins); "Cow Country" 1953 (Walt Garner); "Tall Man Riding" 1955 (Tucker "Tuck" Ordway). ¶TV: *The Restless Gun*—"The Last Grey Man" 2-23-59 (General).

Barret, Liz. Films: "Killer Kid" 1967-Ital. (Mercedes); "Two Pistols and a Coward" 1967-Ital.; "Long Day of the Massacre" 1968-Ital.

Barreto, Gil. Films: "Joe Kidd" 1972 (Emilio). ¶TV: *The Virginian*—"The Mountain of the Sun" 4-17-63.

Barrett, Claudia. Films: "The Old Frontier" 1950 (Betty Ames); "Rustlers on Horseback" 1950 (Carol Reynolds); "Night Riders of Montana" 1951 (Julie Bauer); "Desperadoes' Outpost" 1952 (Kathy); "Seven Ways from Sundown" 1960 (Gilda); "Taggart" 1964 (Lola). ¶TV: *The Cisco Kid*—"The Raccoon Story" 11-15-52, "Vendetta" 11-14-53; *Wild Bill Hickok*—"Mountain Men" 2-3-53; *The Lone Ranger*—"Colorado Gold" 12-9-54; *The Roy Rogers Show*—"The Showdown" 5-22-55 (Ellen Corbin), "Ranch War" 10-23-55 (Susan Wagner), "Treasure of Paradise Valley" 12-11-55 (Maybelle); *Death Valley Days*—"Gold Is Where You Find It" 1-28-56, "Stagecoach Spy" 2-17-59 (Lee Whipple); *Fury*—"The Baby" 4-7-56 (Martha Stanhope); *Schlitz Playhouse of the Stars*—"Flowers for Jenny" 8-3-56; *Tales of Wells Fargo*—"Ride with the Killer" 12-2-57 (Emily Handsfelt); *The Californians*—"Panic on Montgomery Street" 1-14-58 (Judith); *Rough Riders*—"Paradise Gap" 4-16-59 (Sister Loretta); *Colt .45*—"Alibi" 4-12-60 (Janice Benson).

Barrett, Curt (and the Trails-

men). Films: "Drifting Along" 1946; "Galloping Thunder" 1946; "Gentleman from Texas" 1946; "Gunning for Vengeance" 1946; "That Texas Jamboree" 1946; "Raiders of the South" 1947; "Shadows of the West" 1949 (Singer). ¶TV: *Rawhide*—"Incident of the Thirteenth Man" 10-23-59, "Gold Fever" 5-4-62, "Incident of the Swindler" 2-20-64; *The Virginian*—"The Man from the Sea" 12-26-62.

Barrett, Edith (1913-2/22/77). TV: *Northwest Passage*—"The Witch" 2-13-59 (Reba Morris).

Barrett, Leslie. TV: *Maverick*—"Maverick Springs" 12-6-59 (Mr. Mason); *Man from Blackhawk*—"The Money Machine" 6-10-60 (Webb).

Barrett, Louise. *see* Baratto, Luisa.

Barrett, Majel (1932-). Films: "Westworld" 1973 (Miss Carrie). ¶TV: *Bonanza*—"Gift of Water" 2-11-62 (Mrs. Ganther), "Three Brides for Hoss" 2-20-66 (Annie Slocum); *Here Come the Brides*—"Lovers and Wanderers" 11-6-68 (Tessa).

Barrett, Paul. Films: "Under Strange Flags" 1937 (Denny de Vargas); "The Singing Cowgirl" 1939 (Rex Harkins).

Barrett, Stan. TV: *Hondo*—"Hondo and the Singing Wire" 9-22-67 (Diamond), "Hondo and the Apache Kid" 10-13-67 (Running Wolf), "Hondo and the Judas" 11-3-67 (Del Harker).

Barrett, Tony (1916-11/16/74). Films: "Under the Tonto Rim" 1947 (Patton); "Wild Horse Mesa" 1947 (Jim Horn); "Guns of Hate" 1948 (Wyatt); "Western Heritage" 1948 (Trigg). ¶TV: *The Adventures of Rin Tin Tin*—"Rin Tin Tin Meets Mister President" 10-21-55, "The Courtship of Marshal Higgins" 9-27-57 (Cleg Compson).

Barrey, Christopher. TV: *Rawhide*—"Incident of the Pied Piper" 2-6-64; *Gunsmoke*—"Caleb" 3-28-64 (George).

Barri, Barta (1911-). Films: "Son of a Gunfighter" 1966-U.S./Span. (Esteban).

Barrie, Barbara (1931-). Films: "Giant" 1956 (Mary Lou Decker). ¶TV: *The Virginian*—"The Small Parade" 2-20-63 (Ellen Beecher); *Rawhide*—"Mrs. Harmon" 4-16-65 (Elizabeth Harmon).

Barrie, Judith. Films: "The Last Frontier" 1932-serial (Rose Matland); "Hidden Gold" 1933 (Nora).

Barrie, Mona (1909-). Films: "Dawn on the Great Divide" 1942 (Sadie Rand).

Barrier, Edgar (1907-6/20/64). Films: "Adventures in Silverado" 1948; "The Stand at Apache River" 1953 (Cara Blanca); "Silver Lode" 1954 (Taylor). ¶TV: *Broken Arrow*— "The Conspirators" 12-18-56 (Chenoweth); *Zorro*—"The Man from Spain" 4-9-59 (Don Cornelio Esperon), "Treasure for the King" 4-16-59 (Don Cornelio Esperon), "Exposing the Tyrant" 4-23-59 (Don Cornelio Esperon), "Zorro Takes a Dare" 4-30-59 (Don Cornelio Esperon); *The Rebel*—"Take Dead Aim" 3-6-60 (Bianco), "Don Gringo" 11-20-60 (Don Diego).

Barrier, Ernestine (1909-2/13/89). Films: "The Vanquished" 1953 (Mrs. Colfax). ¶TV: *Colt .45*— "Decoy" 1-31-58 (Dona Rita); *Bat Masterson*—"To the Manner Born" 10-1-59 (Mrs. Dwight Chancellor).

Barringer, Stephen. TV: *Laramie*—"The High Country" 2-6-62 (Matt), "The Dynamiters" 3-6-62 (Peter Hodding), "Bad Blood" 12-4-62 (Skip).

Barris, Harry (1905-12/13/62). Films: "Cowboy from Brooklyn" 1938 (Louie).

Barriscale, Bessie (1884-6/30/65). Films: "Rose of the Rancho" 1914 (Juanita); "Two-Gun Betty" 1919 (Betty Craig); "Secrets" 1933 (Susan Carlton).

Barron, Baynes (1917-82). Films: "California Conquest" 1952 (Ignacio); "Ambush at Cimarron Pass" 1958 (Corbin). ¶TV: *Sky King*—"Fish Out of Water" 12-9-51, "The Silver Grave" 12-30-51 (Sinclair Mason); *Wild Bill Hickok*—"Sheriff of Buckeye" 6-30-53; *Death Valley Days*—"A Killing in Diamonds" 11-21-55; *Tales of the Texas Rangers*—"Blazing Across the Pecos" 12-3-55 (Buckshot Roberts), "The Rough, Tough West" 12-10-55 (Jordan), "Gypsy Boy" 11-24-57 (Jed Kincaid); *Annie Oakley*—"The Dutch Gunmaker" 2-17-57 (Al Jensen); *The Lone Ranger*—"Two Against Two" 3-21-57, "Ghost Town Fury" 3-28-57; *Circus Boy*—"The Fortune Teller" 6-9-57 (Florenzo); *The Adventures of Rin Tin Tin*—"The Southern Colonel" 10-18-57 (Ed Graves); *Jefferson Drum*—"The Captive" 11-6-58 (Sawyer); *The Restless Gun*—"The Cavis Boy" 6-1-59 (Sheriff Hyde); *Tales of Wells Fargo*—"Clay Allison" 6-15-59 (Ned Taggert), "Moneyrun" 1-6-62 (Scorpio); *The Rifleman*—"The Spiked Rifle" 11-24-59, "The Deserter" 3-15-60 (Kirk); *Laramie*—"The Protectors" 3-22-60 (Sheriff); *Two Faces West*—"The Sure Thing" 7-3-61 (Reynolds);

Gunsmoke—"Perce" 9-30-61 (Vicks), "Deadman's Law" 1-8-68 (Newt); *Branded*—"I Killed Jason McCord" 10-3-65; *Bonanza*—"Dark Enough to See the Stars" 3-12-67 (Marshal).

Barron, Jim (1923-). TV: *Hawkeye and the Last of the Mohicans*—"The Contest" 11-13-57; *Hudson's Bay*—"His Name Was Choctaw" 2-22-58 (Choctaw), "The Accounting" 3-1-58 (Ed Taylor), "The Celebration" 4-5-58 (Carson), "Fort Caribou" 4-19-58 (Pat Gallagher).

Barron, Richard. Films: "Yukon Manhunt" 1951 ¶TV: *The Cisco Kid*—"Thunderhead" 4-5-52, "Bell of Santa Margarite" 4-19-52.

Barron, Robert (1880-1971). Films: "Back in the Saddle" 1941 (Ward); "King of the Texas Rangers" 1941-serial (Blake); "Boss of Hangtown Mesa" 1942 (Flash Hollister); "Overland Mail" 1942-serial (Charles Darson); "Cheyenne Roundup" 1943 (Judge Hickenbottom); "The Man from Thunder River" 1943; "The Return of the Rangers" 1943; "West of Texas" 1943 (Bert Calloway); "Boss of Boomtown" 1944 (Brett); "Guns of the Law" 1944; "Gunsmoke Mesa" 1944 (Bill Moore); "Spook Town" 1944; "Both Barrels Blazing" 1945; "Song of Old Wyoming" 1945 (Dixon); "The Caravan Trail" 1946 (Remo); "Terror Trail" 1946; "The Vigilante" 1947-serial (Prince Amil).

Barros, Esmeralda. Films: "Evan Django Has His Price" 1971-Ital./Span.; "Man Called Django" 1971-Ital.; "God Is My Colt .45" 1972-Ital.

Barrows, George (1913-10/17/94). Films: "They Died with Their Boots On" 1941; "Belle Starr's Daughter" 1948; "The Outlaw's Daughter" 1954 (Rick); "The First Traveling Saleslady" 1956 (Meat Packer); "The Fastest Guitar Alive" 1958; "The Jayhawkers" 1959; "Donner Pass: The Road to Survival" TVM-1978. ¶TV: *Wild Bill Hickok*—"Lumber Camp Story" 3-11-52, "The Gorilla of Owl Hoot Mesa" 9-23-52, "Town Without Law" 6-23-53; *The Lone Ranger*—"Colorado Gold" 12-9-54; *The Texan*—"Desert Passage" 12-1-58; *Frontier Circus*—"The Patriarch of Purgatory" 11-30-61 (Clint); *Rawhide*—"The Child Woman" 3-23-62; *F Troop*—"Reach for the Sky, Pardner" 9-29-66 (Pecos).

Barrows, Henry A. (1875-3/25/45) Films: "The End of the Trail" 1916 (Harvey Gordon); "Fighting Blood" 1916 (Tom Gray); "The Man from Bitter Roots" 1916 (T. Victor Sprudell); "The Captain of the Gray Horse Troop" 1917 (Sen. Bris-

bane); "The Sunset Trail" 1917 (Vernon Treloar); "The World Apart" 1917 (Jack King); "The Girl Who Wouldn't Quit" 1918 (Roscoe Tracy); "Hungry Eyes" 1918 (Jack Nelda); "The Footlight Ranger" 1923 (David Marsh); "The Return of the Riddle Rider" 1927-serial; "Burning Brides" 1928 (Ed Wilson).

Barrows, James (1853-12/7/25). Films: "The Untamed" 1920 (Joe Cumberland); "The Old Fool" 1923 (Grandad Steele); "Shadows of the North" 1923 (Ezra "Pancake" Darby).

Barry, Barta. Films: "Cavalry Charge" 1964-Span.; "Left Handed Johnny West" 1965-Span./Ital.; "Dynamite Joe" 1966-Ital./Span.; "Savage Pampas" 1966-U.S./Span./Arg. (Priest); "The Man Who Killed Billy the Kid" 1967-Span./Ital.; "White Comanche" 1967-Ital./Span./U.S. (Sheriff Logan); "Dead Are Countless" 1969-Ital./Span.; "Red Sun" 1971-Fr./Ital./Span. (Sheriff); "The Man Called Noon" 1973-Brit./Span./Ital. (Mexican).

Barry, Baby Charlene. Films: "Trails End" 1935 (Mary Jane Moorehead); "Riddle Ranch" 1936 (Betty).

Barry, Donald "Red" (1912-7/17/80). Films: "Fugitive from Sonora" 1937 (Keeno Phillips/Dave Winters); "Days of Jesse James" 1939 (Jesse James); "Saga of Death Valley" 1939 (Tim Rogers/Jerry); "Wyoming Outlaw" 1939 (Will Parker); "Adventures of Red Ryder" 1940-serial (Red Ryder); "Frontier Vengeance" 1940 (Jim Sanders); "Ghost Valley Raiders" 1940 (Tim Brandon); "One Man's Law" 1940 (Jack Summers); "Texas Terrors" 1940 (Bob Milborune); "The Apache Kid" 1941 (Pete Dawson); "Desert Bandit" 1941 (Bob Crandall); "Kansas Cyclone" 1941 (Jim Randall); "A Missouri Outlaw" 1941 (Cliff Dixon); "The Phantom Cowboy" 1941 (Lawrence); "Two-Gun Sheriff" 1941 (the Sundown Kid/Bruce McKinnon); "Wyoming Wildcat" 1941; "Arizona Terrors" 1942 (Jim Bradley); "The Cyclone Kid" 1942 (Johnny Dawson); "Jesse James, Jr." 1942 (Johnny Barrett); "Outlaws of Pine Ridge" 1942 (Chips Barrett); "The Sombrero Kid" 1942 (Jerry Holden); "Stagecoach Express" 1942 (Dave Gregory); "The Sundown Kid" 1942 (Red Tracy/Red Brannon); "Black Hills Express" 1943 (Lon Walker); "California Joe" 1943 (Lt. Joe Weldon); "Canyon City" 1943 (Terry Reynolds/the Nevada Kid); "Carson City Cyclone" 1943 (Gilbert Phalen); "Days of Old Cheyenne" 1943 (Clint

Ross); "Dead Man's Gulch" 1943 (Tennessee Colby); "The Man from the Rio Grande" 1943 (Lee Grant); "Death Valley Rangers" 1944 (Johnny); "Outlaws of Santa Fe" 1944 (Bob Hackett/Bob Conray); "The Tulsa Kid" 1940 (Tom Benton); "Bells of Rosarita" 1945; "Out California Way" 1946; "Plainsman and the Lady" 1946 (Feisty); "Madonna of the Desert" 1948 (Tony French); "The Dalton Gang" 1949 (Larry West); "Red Desert" 1949 (Pecos Kid); "Square Dance Jubilee" 1949 (Don); "Tough Assignment" 1949 (Dan Reilly); "Border Rangers" 1950 (Bob Standish); "Gunfire" 1950 (Fenton/Frank James); "I Shot Billy the Kid" 1950 (Billy); "Train to Tombstone" 1950 (Len Howard); "Jesse James' Women" 1954 (Jesse James); "Untamed Heiress" 1954 (Spider Mike); "The Twinkle in God's Eye" 1955 (Dawson); "Seven Men from Now" 1956 (Clete); "Gun Duel in Durango" 1957 (Larry); "Born Reckless" 1959 (Oakie); "Warlock" 1959 (Edward Calhoun); "Walk Like a Dragon" 1960 (Cabot); "Buffalo Gun" 1961 (Murdock); "Law of the Lawless" 1964 (Tuffy); "Convict Stage" 1965 (Marshal Karnin); "Fort Courageous" 1965 (Capt. Howard); "Town Tamer" 1965 (Deputy); "War Party" 1965 (Sgt. Chaney); "Alvarez Kelly" 1966 (Lt. Farrow); "Apache Uprising" 1966 (Henry Belden); "Fort Utah" 1967 (Harris); "Hostile Guns" 1967 (Johnson); "Red Tomahawk" 1967 (Bly); "Bandolero!" 1968 (Jack Hawkins); "The Shakiest Gun in the West" 1968 (Rev. Zachary Grant); "Shalako" 1968-Brit./Fr. (Buffalo); "The Cockeyed Cowboys of Calico County" 1970 (Rusty); "Dirty Dingus Magee" 1970 (Shotgun); "Rio Lobo" 1970; "Junior Bonner" 1972 (Homer Rutledge); "Boss Nigger" 1974; "From Noon to Three" 1976 (Outlaw Leader); "Hot Lead and Cold Feet" 1978 (Bartender); "Kate Bliss and the Ticker Tape Kid" TVM-1978 (Devery's Foreman). ¶TV: *Stories of the Century*—"Milt Sharp" 12-9-55; *Sergeant Preston of the Yukon*—"Ten Little Indians" 4-18-57 (Harvey Brand); *Colt .45*—"The Mirage" 1-10-58 (Capt. Thane), "Mantrap" 2-14-58 (Percival), "Arizona Anderson" 2-14-60, "Phantom Trail" 3-13-60 (Stevens); *Sugarfoot*—"Bullet Proof" 1-21-58 (Tanner), "The Canary Kid" 11-11-59 (Arkansas), "The Return of the Canary Kid" 2-3-59 (Arkansas), "The Trial of the Canary Kid" 9-15-59 (Arkansas); *Cheyenne*—"Dead to Rights" 5-20-58 (Shorty Jones); *Have Gun Will Travel*—"The

Road to Wickenberg" 10-25-58 (Tom Goodfellow); *Maverick*—"Betrayal" 3-22-59 (Sheriff), "The Sheriff of Duck 'n' Shoot" 9-27-59 (Fred Leslie), "The Resurrection of Joe November" 2-28-60 (Willie Safron), "Arizona Black Maria" 10-9-60 (Dishonest Abe), "Last Stop: Olivion" 2-12-61 (Smith); *Lawman*—"The Senator" 5-17-59 (Shorty), "Belding's Girl" 4-3-60 (Jim Gaylor), "Hassayampa" 2-12-61 (Dusty McCade), "The Stalker" 10-29-61 (Jess Schaeffer); *Bronco*—"Shadow of a Man" 5-19-59 (Cookie Meyers), "Destinies West" 2-26-62 (Stumpy); *Laramie*—"The General Must Die" 11-17-59 (Cowly), "Broken Honor" 4-9-63 (Dave Byrnie); *Bat Masterson*—"The Pied Piper of Dodge City" 1-7-60 (Luke Short); *Rawhide*—"Incident of the Running Man" 5-5-61 (Grist); *Alcoa Premiere*—"Second Chance" 3-13-62 (Wes Holbrook); *Wide Country*—"The Girl in the Sunshine Smile" 11-15-62 (Roy); *Gunsmoke*—"The Renegades" 1-12-63 (McIver), "Shadler" 1-15-73 (Dobson); *The Virginian*—"The Golden Door" 3-13-63, "Run Quiet" 11-13-63 (Dugan), "The Black Stallion" 9-30-64 (Slaughter), "The Claim" 10-6-65 (Man), "Doctor Pat" 3-1-67 (Charles Coulter), "Silver Image" 9-25-68 (Hutton); *Bonanza*—"The Saga of Squaw Charlie" 12-27-64 (Bud), "A Time to Step Down" 9-25-66 (Temple); *F Troop*—"Don't Look Now But One of Our Cannons Is Missing" 9-21-65 (Colonel Donnell); *The Legend of Jesse James*—"1863" 3-28-66 (Daniels); *Laredo*—"Leave It to Dixie" 12-30-66 (Sam Dixie); *Pistols 'n' Petticoats*—1-21-67 (Colonel Malloy); *Wild Wild West*—"The Night of the Bogus Bandits" 4-7-67 (Rainey), "The Night of the Sabatini Death" 2-2-69 (Farnsworth/Harry Borman); *Hondo*—"Hondo and the Singing Wire" 9-22-67 (Sergeant Daniels); *Cimarron Strip*—"The Blue Moon Train" 2-15-68 (Kedge); *Daniel Boone*—"A Touch of Charity" 2-27-69 (Amos Brown); *Barbary Coast*—"Mary Had More Than a Little" 1-2-76 (Paddington).

Barry, Eddie. Films: "Reckless Courage" 1925 (Slim Parker); "The Sagebrush Lady" 1925 (Harmony Hayden); "Red Blood" 1926 (Donald Custer).

Barry, Fern (1909-9/9/81). TV: *Maverick*—"Stage West" 10-27-57 (Ella Taylor); *The Rifleman*—"The Woman" 5-5-59, "The Horse Traders" 2-9-60; *Rawhide*—"Incident of the Dust Flower" 3-4-60; *Wyatt Earp*—"Shoot to Kill" 10-18-60.

Barry, Gene (1922-). Films: "Those Redheads from Seattle" 1953 (Johnny Kisco); "Red Garters" 1954 (Rafael Moreno); "Forty Guns" 1957 (Wes Bonnell); "The Devil and Miss Sarah" TVM-1971 (Rankin); "Ransom for Alice!" TVM-1977 (Harry Darew); "The Gambler Returns: The Luck of the Draw" TVM-1991 (Bat Masterson). ¶TV: *Hallmark Hall of Fame*—"The Lonely Path" 11-8-53 (John Charles Fremont); *Bat Masterson*—Regular 1958-61 (Bat Masterson); *Paradise*—"A Gather of Guns" 9-10-89 (Bat Masterson).

Barry, Ivor (1919-). TV: *Hudson's Bay*—"Sally MacGregor" 2-15-58 (the Director), "The Drummer Boy" 3-22-58 (Governor); *Bonanza*—"Home from the Sea" 5-1-66 (Morgan), "The Initiation" 9-26-72 (Preacher); *Daniel Boone*—"First in War, First in Peace" 10-13-66 (President Washington), "Beaumarchais" 10-12-67 (British Commandant), "Minnow for a Shark" 1-2-69 (Commodore Morrison); *Laredo*—"A Prince of a Ranger" 12-9-66 (Frollo); *Kung Fu*—"The Passion of Chen Yi" 2-28-74 (Poindexter); *Father Murphy*—"The Adoption" 2-23-82 (Charles).

Barry, Joe (1924-7/8/74). Films: "Man with the Gun" 1955 (Dade Holman). ¶TV: *Jim Bowie*—"A Night in Tennessee" 4-25-58 (Doug Dawson).

Barry, Leon (Leon Bary) (1880-1954). Films: "The Galloping Kid" 1922 (Fred Bolston); "Suzanna" 1922 (Pancho); "Bucking the Barrier" 1923 (Luke Cavendish); "The Grail" 1923 (Sam Hervey); "The King of the Wild Horses" 1924 (Billy Blair); "The Lightning Rider" 1924 (Ramon Gonzalez).

Barry, Patricia (1922-). TV: *Gunsmoke*—"The Cabin" 2-22-58 (Belle), "Shooting Stopover" 10-8-60 (Laura), "Albert" 2-9-70 (Kate Schiller); *Maverick*—"Prey of the Cat" 12-7-58 (Kitty Stillman), "Two Beggars on Horseback" 1-18-59 (Jessamy Longacre); *Sugarfoot*—"The Giant Killer" 3-3-59 (Doreen Bradley); *Yancy Derringer*—"Thunder on the River" 3-12-59; *The Rifleman*—"Three-Legged Terror" 4-21-59 (Schoolteacher), "The Woman" 5-5-59 (Adele Adams), "A Time for Singing" 3-8-60 (Laurie Hadley); *Laramie*—"The Star Trail" 10-13-59 (Evie); *Bronco*—"Every Man a Hero" 2-23-60 (Amy Carter); *Rawhide*—"Incident of the Champagne Bottles" 3-18-60 (Susan Parker), "Incident of the Married Widow" 3-1-63 (Abigail); *Tales of Wells Fargo*—"Dealer's Choice" 5-2-60 (Phyllis Randolph); *The Outlaws*—"Rape of Red Sky" 10-27-60 (Aimie), "No More Pencils—No More Books" 3-16-61 (Laurie Palmer); *Zane Grey Theater*—"The Scar" 3-2-61 (Beth Martin); *The Tall Man*—"Where Is Sylvia?" 9-23-61 (Sylvia); *Frontier Circus*—"Quick Shuffle" 2-1-62 (Amy); *The Virginian*—"The Judgment" 1-16-63 (Alice Finley); *Destry*—"The Nicest Girl in Gomorrah" 3-13-64 (Sarah Sprague); *Iron Horse*—"The Golden Web" 3-27-67 (Helen); *The High Chaparral*—"The Widow from Red Rock" 11-26-67 (Melanie Cawthorne); *The Guns of Will Sonnett*—"The Hero" 12-29-67 (Alice Butler); *Alias Smith and Jones*—"Six Strangers at Apache Springs" 10-28-71 (Lucy Fielding).

Barry, Viola (1894-4/2/64). Films: "The Chief's Daughter" 1911; "Evangeline" 1911; "The Indian Vestal" 1911; "John Oakhurst—Gambler" 1911; "McKee Rankin's '49" 1911; "The Squatter's Child" 1912.

Barry, Wesley (1906-4/11/94). Films: "Bob Hampton of Placer" 1921 (Dick); "His Own Law" 1924; "Border Romance" 1930 (Victor Hamlin); "Mexicali Kid" 1938 (Mexicali Kid).

Barrye, Emily (1896-12/15/57). Films: "Fast and Fearless" 1924 (Blanca); "The Bloodhound" 1925 (Betty Belleau); "Border Intrigue" 1925 (Rita); "The Bonanza Buckaroo" 1926 (the Maid); "Speedy Spurs" 1926 (Witch).

Barrymore, Diana (1921-1/25/60). Films: "Frontier Badman" 1943 (Claire).

Barrymore, Drew (1975-). Films: "Bad Girls" 1994 (Lilly Laronette).

Barrymore, Ethel (1879-6/18/59). Films: "The Secret of Convict Lake" 1951 (Granny).

Barrymore, John Blyth. TV: *Kung Fu*—"Barbary House" 2-15-75 (Zeke Caine), "Flight to Orion" 2-22-75 (Zeke Caine), "The Brothers Cain" 3-1-75 (Zeke Caine), "Full Circle" 3-15-75 (Zeke Caine).

Barrymore, John Drew (John Barrymore, Jr.) (1932-). Films: "High Lonesome" 1950 (Cooncat); "The Sundowners" 1950 (Jeff Cloud); "Winchester '73" TVM-1967 (the Preacher). TV: *Wagon Train*—"The Ruttledge Munroe Story" 5-21-58 (Ruttledge Munroe); *Rawhide*—"Incident of the Haunted Hills" 11-6-59 (Tasunka), "Corporal Dasovik" 12-4-64 (Private Harry Eccles); *Gunsmoke*—"One Killer on Ice" 1-23-65 (Anderson), "Seven Hours to Dawn" 9-18-65 (Mace Gore); *Wild Wild West*—"The Night of the Double-Edged Knife" 11-12-65 (American Knife); *The Road West*—"This Savage Land" 9-12-66 & 9-19-66 (Stacey Daggart); *Dundee and the Culhane*—"The Turn the Other Cheek Brief" 9-6-67 (Royal Bodie); *Kung Fu*—"A Dream Within a Dream" 1-17-74 (Alex McGregor).

Barrymore, Lionel (1878-11/15/54). Films: "The Chief's Blanket" 1912; "Heredity" 1912; "The Massacre" 1912; "My Hero" 1912; "Three Friends" 1912; "The Battle at Elderbrush Gulch" 1913; "Just Gold" 1913; "A Misunderstood Boy" 1913; "The Ranchero's Revenge" 1913; "The Stolen Treaty" 1913; "The Sheriff's Baby" 1913; "Strongheart" 1914; "The Quitter" 1916 (Happy Jack Lewis); "A Yellow Streak" 1915 (Barry Dale); "The Splendid Road" 1925 (Dan Clehollis); "The Yaqui Cur" 1913; "Let Freedom Ring" 1939 (Thomas Logan); "The Bad Man" 1941 (Uncle Henry Jones); "Duel in the Sun" 1946 (Sen. McCanles); "Lone Star" 1952 (Andrew Jackson).

Barrymore, William. *see* Bullock, Boris.

Barselow, Paul (1922-). TV: *Rawhide*—"Incident of the Painted Lady" 5-12-61 (Clerk), "The Gentleman's Gentleman" 12-15-61; *Tales of Wells Fargo*—"The Dodger" 10-7-61 (Happy); *Maverick*—"A Technical Error" 11-26-61 (Ferguson); *Bonanza*—"Crucible" 4-8-62; *The Virginian*—"Big Day, Great Day" 10-24-62; *Gunsmoke*—"Twenty Miles from Dodge" 4-10-65 (Banker); *Wild Wild West*—"The Night of Miguelito's Revenge" 12-13-68; *The Big Valley*—"The Battle of Mineral Springs" 3-24-69 (Joe); *Father Murphy*—"False Blesing" 2-9-82 (Emmett).

Bartel, Paul (1938-). Films: "Posse" 1993 (Mayor Bigwood).

Bartell, Harry. Films: "Johnny Concho" 1956 (Sam Green). TV: *Gunsmoke*—"Doc's Revenge" 6-9-56 (Ben Bartlett), "Cain" 3-9-57 (Cain Vestal), "The Deserter" 6-4-60 (Jed), "The Do-Badder" 1-6-62, "I Call Him Wonder" 3-23-63 (Colonel), "Kate Heller" 9-28-63 (Gus), "Scot-Free" 5-9-64 (Harper), "Honey Pot" 5-15-65 (James Riley), "Honor Before Justice" 3-5-66 (Elias Franklin); *Have Gun Will Travel*—"A Score for Murder" 11-22-58 (Nick Talbot), "First, Catch a Tiger" 9-12-59 (Mordain); *Bonanza*—"The Sun Mountain Herd" 9-19-59 (Winnemucca); *Laramie*—"Day of Vengeance" 1-19-60 (Ernie Polk); *Tales of Wells Fargo*—"The Canyon" 2-1-60 (Fred Kimball); *The Rebel*—"In Memory of a Son" 5-8-60 (Charlie Burton); *The Texan*—"Twenty-Four Hours to Live" 9-5-60; *Branded*—"Elsie Brown" 2-14-65 (Mayor); *Wild Wild West*—"The Night the Wizard Shook the Earth" 10-1-65 (Prof. Neilsen), "The Night of the Flaming Ghost" 2-4-66 (Will Glover).

Bartell, Richard (1897-7/22/67). Films: "Battling Marshal" 1950; "The Vanquished" 1953. TV: *Wanted—Dead or Alive*—"The Medicine Man" 11-23-60 (Man); *Bonanza*—"Sam Hill" 6-3-61 (Hathaway); *Gunsmoke*—"Cody's Code" 1-20-62 (Hank), "Ash" 2-16-63 (Harry); *Rawhide*—"Incident of the Reluctant Bridegroom" 11-30-62 (Man).

Barth, Ed (1931-). TV: *Cimarron Strip*—"Broken Wing" 9-21-67.

Bartha, John Janos. Films: "Man from the Cursed Valley" 1964-Ital./Span.; "Hands of a Gunman" 1965-Ital./Span.; "Relentless Four" 1966-Span./Ital.; "Rojo" 1966-Ital./Span.; "Big Ripoff" 1967-Span./Ital.; "Kill Them All and Come Back Alone" 1967-Ital./Span.; "Killer Caliber .32" 1967-Ital.; "This Man Can't Die" 1968-Ital. (Melin); "The Dirty Outlaws" 1971-Ital.; "His Name Was King" 1971-Ital.; "Tequila" 1974-Ital./Span.

Barthelmess, Richard (1897-8/17/63). Films: "Scarlet Days" 1919 (Alvarez, a Bandit); "Ranson's Folly" 1926 (Lt. Ranson); "The Lash" 1930 (Francisco Delfino); "The Spoilers" 1942 (Bronco Kid Farrell); "Massacre" 1934 (Joe Thunder Horse).

Bartlett, Bennie. Films: "The Texas Rangers" 1936 (David); "Adventures of Don Coyote" 1947 (Ted); "Gas House Kids Go West" 1947 (Orvie); "Dig That Uranium" 1956 (Butch). TV: *The Cisco Kid*—"Church in Town" 5-17-52.

Bartlett, Bonnie (1935-). TV: *Gunsmoke*—"The Foundling" 2-11-74 (Maylee Baines), "In Performance of Duty" 11-18-74 (Agnes Benton); *Little House on the Prairie*—Regular 1974-77 (Grace Edwards).

Bartlett, Cal. Films: "Joshua" 1977; "Bonanza: Under Attack" TVM-1995 (Sheriff); "Maverick" 1994 (Riverboat Poker Player). TV: *The Virginian*—"The Drifter" 1-29-64 (Dolan), "The Showdown" 4-14-65 (Bobb Landers); *Bonanza*—"The Hostage" 9-27-64 (Len); "The Unseen Wound" 1-29-67 (Garrett); *Father Murphy*—"Stopover in a One-Way Horse Town" 10-26-82 (Marshal Robinson).

Bartlett, Charles. Films: "At Old Fort Dearborn" 1912; "The Girl from Golden Run" 1912; "The Massacre of Santa Fe Trail" 1912; "A Red Man's Love" 1912; "Trapper Bill, King of the Scouts" 1912; "The Genius of Fort Lapawal" 1913; "The Fate of a Squaw" 1914; "Kidnapped by Indians" 1914; "The Paleface Brave" 1914; "Don Desperado" 1927 (Aaron Blaisdell).

Bartlett, Hall (1922-9/8/93). Films: "The Paleface" 1948 (Handsome Cowboy); "Navajo" 1952 (Indian School Counsel).

Bartlett, Martine (1925-). TV: *The Big Valley*—"The Guilt of Matt Bentell" 12-8-65 (Cinda Bentell); *The Virginian*—"One Spring Like Long Ago" 3-2-66 (Maggie McKinley).

Bartlett, Richard (1925-). Films: "Hiawatha" 1952 (Chunung); "The Lonesome Trail" 1955; "The Silver Star" 1955 (King Daniels).

Bartlett, W.A. Films: "The Fighting Stranger" 1921 (Laughing Bill).

Barto, Dominic (1930-). Films: "A Man from the East" 1974-Ital./Fr. (Monkey).

Bartold, Norman (1928-5/28/94). Films: "Westworld" 1973 (Medieval Knight) ¶TV: *Gunsmoke*—"The Sodbusters" 11-20-72 (Darga), "Jessie" 2-19-73 (Sheriff).

Barton, Anne. Films: "Pawnee" 1957 (Mrs. Brewster); "The Left-Handed Gun" 1958 (Mrs. Hill); "The Way West" 1967 (Mrs. Moynihan); "The Great Northfield, Minnesota Raid" 1972 (Clell's Wife). TV: *Gunsmoke*—"Prairie Happy" 7-7-56 (Quiet One), "The Gypsum Hills Feud" 12-27-58 (Liza Peavy), "Scot-Free" 5-9-64 (Millie Scot), "Doctor's Wife" 10-24-64 (Mrs. Boake); *Zane Grey Theater*—"Village of Fear" 3-1-57, "Killer Instinct" 3-17-60 (Ann Bigger); *Have Gun Will Travel*—"The Long Hunt" 3-7-59 (Mrs. Ordey); *Black Saddle*—"Client: Northrup" 3-14-59 (Louise Northrup); *Laramie*—"Hour After Dawn" 3-15-60 (Sarah); *The Deputy*—"Day of Fear" 12-17-60 (Gail Nathan); *Tales of Wells Fargo*—"The Angry Sky" 4-21-62 (Helen Lowell); *Cimarron Strip*—"Nobody" 12-7-67 (Sarah).

Barton, Dan. TV: *The Adventures of Rin Tin Tin*—"Connecticut Yankees" 11-4-55; *The Roy Rogers Show*—"Ambush" 1-15-56, "Johnny Rover" 6-9-57 (Johnny Rover); *Zane Grey Theater*—"Village of Fear" 3-1-57, "The Stranger" 2-28-58 (Garth), "The Accuser" 10-30-58, "Heritage" 4-2-59 (Crower); *The Lone Ranger*—"Clover in the Dust" 3-7-57; *Cheyenne*—"Incident at Indian Springs" 9-24-57 (Jim Ellis); *Trackdown*—"Right of Way" 1-17-58 (Phil Ballard); *Tombstone Territory*—"Strange Vengeance" 4-9-58 (Frank Callaway); *Death Valley Days*—"Price of a Passport" 3-3-59 (Pattie); *The Texan*—"Blue Norther" 10-12-59 (Pony Sloan); *Have Gun Will Travel*—"Ambush" 4-23-60 (Daniel); *The Rebel*—"Berserk" 12-18-60 (Frank Maggio); *The Virginian*—"Vengeance Is the Spur" 2-27-63.

Barton, Finis. Films: "My Pal, the King" 1932 (Gretchen); "Secret Patrol" 1936 (Ann); "Stampede" 1936 (Dale Milford).

Barton, George (1897-9/21/55). Films: "Bells of Rosarita" 1945; "Lost in Alaska" 1952.

Barton, Gregg. Films: "West to Glory" 1947 (Barrett); "Massacre River" 1949 (Frank); "Beyond the Purple Hills" 1950 (Ross Pardee); "The Blazing Sun" 1950 (Trot Lucas); "Mule Train" 1950 (Keg Rollins); "Texas Dynamo" 1950 (Luke); "Distant Drums" 1951 (Pvt. James Tasher); "Gene Autry and the Mounties" 1951 (Sgt. Stuart); "Silver City Bonanza" 1951 (Hank); "Valley of Fire" 1951 (Blackie); "Whirlwind" 1951 (Bill Trask); "Apache Country" 1952 (Luke Thorn); "Dead Man's Trail" 1952; "The Gunman" 1952; "The Maverick" 1952 (George Pane); "Montana Belle" 1952 (Deputy Stewart); "Wagon Team" 1952 (Gandy); "The Command" 1953 (Capt. Forsythe); "Last of the Pony Riders" 1953 (Dutch Murdoch); "Law and Order" 1953 (Wingett); "The Moonlighter" 1953; "Saginaw Trail" 1953 (Lin Oakes); "Winning of the West" 1953 (Clint Raybold); "Drums Across the River" 1954 (Fallon); "Gunfighters of the Northwest" 1954-serial (Hank Bridger); "Man with the Steel Whip" 1954-serial (Stanton); "Masterson of Kansas" 1954 (Sutton); "Riding with Buffalo Bill" 1954-serial (Bart); "Two Guns and a Badge" 1954; "The Far Country" 1955 (Rounds); "The Man from Laramie" 1955 (Fritz); "Backlash" 1956 (Sleepy); "Blazing the Overland Trail" 1956-serial (Captain Carter); "Raw Edge" 1956 (McKay); "Joe Dakota" 1957 (Tom Jensen); "Good Day for a Hanging" 1958 (Frank); "Man from God's Country" 1958 (Colonel); "Toughest Gun in Tombstone" 1958 (Leslie); "Lone Texan" 1959 (Ben Hollis); "The Gun Hawk" 1963. ¶TV: *The Gene Autry Show*—"Gold Dust Charlie" 7-30-50, "Silver Arrow" 8-6-50, "The Doodle Bug" 8-13-50, "Double Switch" 8-27-50, "The Raiders" 4-14-51, "Double Barrelled Vengeance" 4-21-51, "Frontier Guard" 10-13-51, "Killer's Trail" 10-27-51, "The Lawless Press" 1-25-52, "Ruthless Renegade" 2-8-52, "Bullets and Bows" 3-2-52, "The Sheriff Is a Lady" 3-23-52, "Cold Decked" 9-15-53, "Santa Fe Raiders" 7-6-54, "Johnny Jackaroo" 7-13-54, "The Hold-Up" 12-14-52, "The Hoodoo Canyon" 8-17-54, "The Carnival Comes West" 8-24-54, "Battle Axe" 8-31-54, "Boots and Ballots" 9-25-54, "Outlaw Warning" 10-2-54, "Saddle Up" 12-3-55, "Ride, Rancheros" 12-10-55, "The Rangerette" 12-17-55; *The Lone Ranger*—"Drink of Water" 10-26-50, "The Outcast" 1-18-51, "The Woman in the White Mask" 5-12-55, "The Cross of Santo Domingo" 10-11-56, "The Twisted Track" 11-29-56, "Mission for Tonto" 5-2-57; *Wild Bill Hickok*—"The Dog Collar Story" 7-17-51, "Ex-Convict Story" 11-20-51, "Sagebrush Manhunt" 11-11-52, "Great Obstacle Race" 3-3-53, "Angel of Cedar Mountain" 7-28-53; *The Roy Rogers Show*—"Jailbreak" 12-30-51, "The Desert Fugitive" 2-24-52, "The Minister's Son" 3-23-52, "Pat's Inheritance" 11-11-53, "Bullets and a Burro" 11-15-53, "The Deputy Sheriff" 2-7-54, "End of the Trail" 1-27-57 (Joe Phillips), "Brady's Bonanza" 3-31-57; *The Range Rider*—"Marshal from Madero" 1-24-53; *The Cisco Kid*—"The Caution of Curley Thompson" 5-2-53, "Gold, Death and Dynamite" 2-13-54; *Annie Oakley*—"The Tomboy" 7-17-54 (Crane), "Flint and Steel" 10-14-56 (Boyd Spencer), "Annie and the Bicycle Riders" 7-8-56 (Saunders); *Tales of the Texas Rangers*—"Horseman on the Sierras" 1-14-56 (George Webster), "Hardrock's Dilemma" 11-3-57, "Double Reward" 12-15-57 (Quigley); *My Friend Flicka*—"Refuge for the Night" 4-20-56; *Wyatt Earp*—"Hunt the Man Down" 5-3-56, "Nineteen Notches on His Gun" 12-11-56 (Dutch Henry), "The Frame-Up" 6-3-58 (Red Smith), "Juveniles—1878" 3-10-58 (Greasy Murkin); *Sergeant Preston of the Yukon*—"Last Mail from Last Chance" 5-31-56 (Bowker), "Treasure of Fifteen Mile Creek" 8-2-56 (Shanto); *Zane Grey Theater*—"Until the Man Dies" 1-25-57 (Roy Boggs); *26 Men*—"Incident at Yuma" 11-19-57, "Parrish Gang" 4-1-58,

"Bounty Hunter" 4-15-58, "Dead or Alive" 3-17-59; *The Restless Gun*—"The Woman from Sacramento" 3-3-58 (Sheriff Collins), "The Red Blood of Courage" 2-2-59 (Broky Jake Thomas); *Colt .45*—"The Manbuster" 4-4-58 (Marshal); *Fury*—"The Claim Jumpers" 4-5-58 (Gregg); *Jefferson Drum*—"The Hanging of Joe Lavetti" 8-1-58 (Yance Meeker); *The Texan*—"Desert Passage" 12-1-58, "Rough Track to Payday" 12-28-59, "The Invisible Noose" 5-16-60 (Posse Leader); *Rawhide*—"Incident at Dangerfield Dip" 10-2-59 (Fiske); *Bonanza*—"The Fear Merchants" 1-30-60; *Maverick*—"Hadley's Hunters" 9-25-60 (Boggs); *Laramie*—"Riders of the Night" 3-7-61 (Frank), "Run of the Hunted" 4-4-61, "The Runt" 2-20-62, "Justice in a Hurry" 3-20-62, "The Renegade Brand" 2-26-63; *Wagon Train*—"The Lisa Raincloud Story" 10-31-62 (Tabor); *Death Valley Days*—"The Firebrand" 4-30-66 (Stockton).

Barton, Irene. TV: *Death Valley Days*—"Claim-Jumpin' Jennie" 7-21-56 (Jennie), "The Capture" 4-14-57 (Keepo).

Barton, James (1890-2/19/62). Films: "The Shepherd of the Hills" 1941 (Old Matt Matthews); "Yellow Sky" 1948 (Grandpa); "The Naked Hills" 1956 (Jimmo McCann); "Quantez" 1957 (Minstrel); "The Misfits" 1961 (Old Man in the Bar). ¶TV: *Hotel De Paree*—"A Fool and His Gold" 11-13-59 (Cully Jackson); *The Rifleman*—"The Legacy" 12-8-59 (Matt "Pop" Simmons); *Frontier Circus*—"The Clan MacDuff" 4-26-62.

Barton, Joan (1925-5/77). Films: "Lone Star Moonlight" 1946; "Romance of the West" 1946 (Melodie); "Angel and the Badman" 1947 (Lila); "Strange Gamble" 1948.

Barton, Joe (1883-7/5/37). Films: "The Lone Cowboy" 1934 (Junkman).

Barton, Larry (1909-). Films: "The Black Lash" 1952 (Judge); "The Frontier Phantom" 1952. ¶TV: *Gunsmoke*—"The Moonstone" 12-17-66 (Bartender).

Barton, Michael. Films: "Black Hills Ambush" 1952 (Clay Stewart); "South Pacific Trail" 1952.

Barton, Phil. Films: "I Killed Wild Bill Hickok" 1956 (Poncho).

Barton, Robert "Buzz" (1914-11/20/80). Films: "The Boy Rider" 1927 (David Hepner); "The Slingshot Kid" 1927 (Red Hepner); "The Bantam Cowboy" 1928 (David "Red" Hepner); "The Fightin' Redhead" 1928 (Red Hepner); "The Little Buckaroo" 1928 (David "Red" Hepner); "Orphan of the Sage" 1928 (David "Red" Hepner); "The Pinto Kid" 1928 (David "Red" Hepner); "Rough Ridin' Red" 1928 (David "Red" Hepner); "Wizard of the Saddle" 1928 (Red Hepner); "Young Whirlwind" 1928 (David "Red" Hepner); "The Freckled Rascal" 1929 (Red Hepner); "The Little Savage" 1929 (Red Robbins); "Pals of the Prairie" 1929 (Red Hepner); "The Vagabond Cub" 1929 (David "Red" Hepner); "Breed of the West" 1930 (Jim Sterner); "Canyon Hawks" 1930 (George Manning); "The Lone Defender" 1930-serial (Buzz); "Cyclone Kid" 1931 (Buddy Comstock); "Flying Lariats" 1931 (Buzz); "The Mystery Trooper" 1931-serial; "Riders of the Cactus" 1931 (Buzz); "Wild West Whoopee" 1931 (Human Targets" 1932 (Buzz Dale); "Fighting Pioneers" 1935 (Splinters); "Gunfire" 1935 (Danny Blake); "Powdersmoke Range" 1935 (Buck); "The Reckless Buckaroo" 1935; "Saddle Aces" 1935; "Tonto Kid" 1935 (Wesley Fritch); "Feud of the West" 1936 (Six-Bits); "The Riding Avenger" 1936 (Tony); "Romance Rides the Range" 1936 (Jimmy Morland); "In Early Arizona" 1938; "Mexicali Kid" 1938; "Phantom Gold" 1938 (Pedro); "Rolling Caravans" 1938 (Jim Rankin); "Lone Star Pioneers" 1939 (Chuck); "Silver on the Sage" 1939; "The Kid from Santa Fe" 1940; "Wild Horse Valley" 1940 (Joe).

Barty, Billy (1910-). TV: *Circus Boy*—"Meet Circus Boy" 9-23-56 (Little Tom), "The Fabulous Colonel Jack" 9-30-56 (Little Tom); *Rawhide*—"The Prairie Elephant" 11-17-61 (Shorty).

Bary, Leon. *see* Barry, Leon.

Barzell, Wolfe (1903-2/14/69). TV: *Zorro*—"Welcome to Monterey" 10-9-58; *Rawhide*—"Incident at Spanish Rock" 12-18-59 (Julio); *Have Gun Will Travel*—"The Uneasy Grave" 6-3-61 (Figaro Panziera); *Wild Wild West*—"The Night of the Dancing Death" 11-5-65 (Landgrave); *Bonanza*—"Ride the Wind" 1-16-66 & 1-23-66 (Bornstein).

Basch, Harry (1926-). Films: "Scalplock" TVM-1966; "A Man Called Gannon" 1969 (Ben). ¶TV: *Gunsmoke*—"Noose of Gold" 3-4-67 (Milt Agnew); *Daniel Boone*—"The Witness" 1-25-68, "Big, Black and Out There" 11-14-68 (Jesse Watts); *Bonanza*—"The Initiation" 9-26-72 (Prosecutor); *Nakia*—"The Driver" 11-2-74 (Cook).

Basehart, Richard (1915-9/17/84). Films: "Canyon Crossroads" 1955 (Larry Kendall); "For the Love of Mike" 1960 (Father Phelan); "The Savage Guns" 1961-U.S./Span. (Steve Fallon); "Bounty Man" TVM-1972 (Angus Keough); "Chato's Land" 1972 (Nye Buell). ¶TV: *Zane Grey Theater*—"Medal for Valor" 12-25-59 (David Manning); *Rawhide*—"The Black Sheep" 11-10-61 (Tod Stone); *Gunsmoke*—"Captain Sligo" 1-4-71 (Captain Aron Sligo); *How the West Was Won*—Episode Two 2-19-78 (Colonel Flint), Episode Three 2-26-78 (Colonel Flint), Episode Four 3-5-78 (Colonel Flint).

Baseleon, Michael (1925-10/9/86). Films: "A Man Called Horse" 1970 (He-Wolf). ¶TV: *Here Come the Brides*—"Land Grant" 11-21-69 (Stephanos), "To the Victor" 2-27-70 (Stephanos); *The High Chaparral*—"The Forge of Hate" 11-13-70 (Two Pony); *Nichols*—"The Dirty Half Dozen Run Amuck" 10-28-71 (Willy Brownfur).

Basham, Tom. Films: "The Cockeyed Cowboys of Calico County" 1970 (Traveler); "Squares" 1972. ¶TV: *The Virginian*—"Nora" 12-11-68 (Sergeant Keller), "Rich Man, Poor Man" 3-11-70 (Jess).

Basie, Count (1904-4/26/84). Films: "Blazing Saddles" 1974 (Count Basie).

Baskin, Elya. Films: "Butch and Sundance: The Early Days" 1979 (Bookkeeper).

Baskin, William "Tiny". Films: "Good Day for a Hanging" 1958 (Man). ¶TV: *Branded*—"Nice Day for a Hanging" 2-6-66 (Tiny).

Basquette, Lina (1907-9/30/94). Films: "The Dude Wrangler" 1930 (Helen Dane); "Arizona Terror" 1931 (Katherine Moore); "Hard Hombre" 1931 (Senora Isabel Martinez); "Mounted Fury" 1931 (Nanette LeStrange); "Hello Trouble" 1932 (Janet Kenyon); "Rose of the Rio Grande" 1938 (Anita).

Bass, Bobby. Films: "Tom Horn" 1980 (Corbett's Bodyguard). ¶TV: *Alias Smith and Jones*—"How to Rob a Bank in One Hard Lesson" 9-23-71; Barbary Coast—"Crazy Cats" 9-15-75 (Forbes).

Bassett, Joseph. Films: "The Redhead from Wyoming" 1953 (Man); "Robbers' Roost" 1955 (Stud); "Tall Man Riding" 1955 (Will); "Johnny Concho" 1956 (Bartender). ¶TV: *The Roy Rogers Show*—"False Faces" 2-5-56, "Smoking Guns" 3-3-56; *Have Gun Will Travel*—"Show of Force" 11-9-57,

"Death of a Gunfighter" 3-14-59 (Charlie Pitt); *Gunsmoke*—"Innocent Broad" 4-26-58 (Aaron Saxon); *Tales of the Texas Rangers*—"Traitor's Gold" 10-2-58 (Jim Rhodes); *The Rifleman*—"Duel of Honor" 11-11-58 (Nat Gilkey), "The Grasshopper" 3-1-60; *Wrangler*—"A Time for Hanging" 8-11-60 (Ed Brady); *Death Valley Days*—"The White Healer" 11-30-60 (Geronimo); *The Deputy*—"The World Against Me" 11-26-60 (Boyd); *Wyatt Earp*—"The Shooting Starts" 4-18-61 (Jack Tyler).

Bassett, Ned. Films: "Rustlers' Ranch" 1926 (Sheriff Collins).

Bassett, Roy E. Films: "Idaho" 1925-serial; "The Terror of Bar X" 1927 (Sheriff).

Bassett, Russell (1846-5/2/18). Films: "Young Wild West Leading a Raid" 1912.

Bassett, William H. (1935-). TV: *Wild Wild West*—"The Night of the Arrow" 12-29-67 (Lt. Carter); *Here Come the Brides*—"Wives for Wakando" 1-22-69 (Willard), "The Deadly Trade" 4-16-69; *The Outcasts*—"The Long Ride" 4-28-69 (Travers); *Bonanza*—"Decision at Los Robles" 3-22-70 (Jed Walker).

Bastedo, Alexandra (1946-). Films: "Draw" CTVM-1984 (Bess).

Bastion, Yvonne. Films: "Fury of the Apaches" 1966-Span./Ital.; "Savage Gringo" 1966-Ital.

Baston, Jack (1892-5/3/70). Films: "Chain Lightning" 1927 (Campan); "The Circus Ace" 1927 (Kirk Mallory); "The Branded Sombrero" 1928 (Charles Maggert); "Hello Cheyenne" 1928 (Buck Lassiter); "Gunfire" 1935 (Lafe Hutchins).

Batanides, Arthur. Films: "Evil Roy Slade" TVM-1972 (Lee). ¶TV: *Tombstone Territory*—"Apache Vendetta" 12-11-57 (Tee-A-Hah); *Maverick*—"Comstock Conspiracy" 12-29-57 (Brock); *Colt .45*—"Split Second" 3-14-58 (Frank Fowler); *Zorro*—"The Runaways" 1-8-59 (Lazaro); *Rawhide*—"Incident of the Valley in Shadow" 11-20-59 (Beckstrom), "Incident Before Black Pass" 5-19-61 (Gypsy); *Riverboat*—"Landlubbers" 1-10-60 (Shag Ryan), "Devil in Skirts" 11-21-60 (Matt Jennings); *The Deputy*—"The Truly Yours" 4-9-60; *Wanted—Dead or Alive*—"Vendetta" 4-9-60 (Allan Stokes); *Bonanza*—"Dark Star" 4-23-60 (Spiro), "The Futivie" 2-4-61 (Pablo); *Stagecoach West*—"Three Wise Men" 12-20-60 (Boone); *The Rifleman*—"The Wanted Man" 9-25-62 (Littleboy

Sherman); *Great Adventure*—"The Pathfinder" 3-6-64 (Gomez); *Gunsmoke*—"The Violators" 10-17-64 (Harve Foster), "Taps for Old Jeb" 10-16-65 (Feeter Kreb); *Wild Wild West*—"The Night of the Dancing Death" 11-5-65 (Marius Ascoli), "The Night of the Gypsy Peril" 1-20-67 (Scullen), "The Night of the Death-Maker" 2-23-68 (Sergeant), "The Night of Miguelito's Revenge" 12-13-68 (Philo); *A Man Called Shenandoah*—"The Bell" 12-20-65 (Larson); *Death Valley Days*—"The Firebrand" 4-30-66 (Varella); *Cimarron Strip*—"The Hunted" 10-5-67 (Woods); *Daniel Boone*—"Readin', Ritin', and Revolt" 3-12-70 (Chief Tekwatana).

Bateman, Charles. TV: *Maverick*—"Black Fire" 3-16-58 (Cousin Jeff); *Yancy Derringer*—"A State of Crisis" 4-30-59; *Rawhide*—"Incicdent of a Burst of Evil" 6-26-59; *Two Faces West*—Regular 1960-61 (Marshal Ben January/Dr. Rick January); *Temple Houston*—"Last Full Moon" 2-27-64 (Bowman); *Bonanza*—"The Pressure Game" 5-10-64 (Rick), "Found Child" 10-24-65 (Jim); *The Virginian*—"The Girl from Yesterday" 11-11-64 (Neal Fairburn); *Death Valley Days*—"The Wild West's Biggest Train Holdup" 5-2-65 (Jim Brand); *Daniel Boone*—"The Tamarack Massacre Affair" 12-30-65 (Major Lorne); *Barbary Coast*—"Sauce for the Goose" 10-20-75 (Woodie).

Bateman, Jason (1969-). TV: *Little House on the Prairie*—Regular 1981-82 (James).

Bateman, Victory (1866-3/2/26). Films: "Captain Fly-By-Night" 1922 (Senora).

Bates, Alan (1934-). Films: "Silent Tongue" 1993 (Eamon McCree).

Bates, Barbara (1925-3/18/69). Films: "Salome, Where She Danced" 1945 (Salome Girl); "The Secret of Convict Lake" 1951 (Barbara Purcell); "The Outcasts of Poker Flat" 1952 (Piney); "Apache Territory" 1958 (Jennifer Fair).

Bates, Ben. Films: "Banjo Hackett: Roamin' Free" TVM-1976 (Logger). ¶TV: *Gunsmoke*—"The Fourth Victim" 11-4-74 (2nd Matt).

Bates, Blanche (1873-12/25/41). Films: "The Border Legion" 1918 (Joan Randall).

Bates, Florence (1888-1/31/54). Films: "Hudson Bay" 1941; "Belle of the Yukon" 1944 (Viola); "San Antonio" 1945 (Henrietta); "River Lady" 1948 (Ma Dunnigan); "The San

Francisco Story" 1952 (Sadie).

Bates, Granville (1882-7/8/40). Films: "The Kill-Joy" 1917 (the Crab); "The Plainsman" 1936 (Van Ellyn); "Wells Fargo" 1937 (Bradford, the Banker); "Cowboy from Brooklyn" 1938 (Pop Hardy); "Gold Is Where You Find It" 1938 (Nixon).

Bates, Jeanne (1918-). Films: "Sundown Valley" 1944 (Sidney Hawkins); "Trooper Hook" 1957 (Ann Weaver); "Blood Arrow" 1958 (Almee). ¶TV: *Gunsmoke*—"Night Incident" 10-29-55 (Mrs. Wyatt), "Smoking Out the Nolans" 11-5-55 (Mrs. Nolan); *My Friend Flicka*—"The Unmasking" 4-13-56 (Mary Anderson); *The Lone Ranger*—"The Cross of Santo Domingo" 10-11-56; *The Restless Gun*—"Jody" 11-4-57 (Millie), "Strange Family in Town" 1-20-58 (Greta Hoffman), "Gratitude" 6-16-58, "No Way to Kill" 11-24-58 (Mary Jepson), "Better Than a Cannon" 2-9-59 (Ana); *Buckskin*—"The Trial of Chrissy Miller" 7-31-58 (Alice); *Tales of Wells Fargo*—"The Dealer" 12-29-58 (Florence Peel), "The Train Robbery" 10-12-59 (Amy); *Wagon Train*—"The Dick Richardson Story" 12-31-58 (Erna Logan), "The Estaban Zamora Story" 10-21-59, "Weight of Command" 1-25-61 (Hester), "The Nancy Palmer Story" 3-8-61 (Mrs. MacGregor), "The Frank Carter Story" 5-23-62 (Mrs. Casper); *Have Gun Will Travel*—"The Taffeta Mayor" 1-10-59 (Harriet Morrow); *Cimarron City*—"Child of Fear" 1-17-59 (Amy Shaw); *Rawhide*—"Incident of the Power and the Plow" 2-13-59 (Henny Morton), "Incident at Tinker's Dam" 2-5-60; *Bonanza*—"The Sun Mountain Herd" 9-19-59 (Stella Harris); *Riverboat*—"The Faithless" 11-22-59 (Sara); *Zane Grey Theater*—"The Sunday Man" 2-25-60; *Laramie*—"The Track of the Jackal" 9-27-60 (Sarah Campbell); *Wyatt Earp*—"The Fanatic" 11-22-60 (Selma Grant); *The Slowest Gun in the West* 7-29-63 (Wife); *The Chisholms*—3-1-80 (Abigail).

Bates, Jimmie. Films: "The Wistful Widow of Wagon Gap" 1947 (Jefferson Hawkins).

Bates, Kathryn (1877-1/1/64). Films: "The Texas Rangers" 1936 (School Teacher); "Hands Across the Rockies" 1941.

Bates, Leslie (1877-8/8/30). Films: "Skyfire" 1920 (Pete Lamoose); "Belle of Alaska" 1922 (Dugan); "Big Stakes" 1922 (Bully Brand); "Blood Test" 1923; "Triple Action" 1925 (Blackie Braxton); "Blue Blazes" 1926 (Buck Fitzgerald); "The Iron Rider"

1926 (Sheriff); "The Texas Streak" 1926 (Pat Casey); "The Glorious Trail" 1928 (Horse-Collar Keller); "Lure of the West" 1928; "The Fighting Legion" 1930 (Fred Hook); "Mountain Justice" 1930 (Abner Harland).

Bates, Tom (1864-4/11/30). Films: "The Parson of Panamint" 1916 (Crabapple Thompson); "Two Kinds of Women" 1922 (Jose); "Don Mike" 1927 (James Kelsey).

Batson, Susan. TV: *Gunsmoke*— "The Sisters" 12-29-69 (Sister Blanche).

Battaglia, Rik (1927-). Films: "The Desperado Trail" 1965-Ger./Yugo. (Rollins); "Legacy of the Incas" 1965-Ger./Ital.; "Pyramid of the Sun God" 1965-Ger./Ital./Fr.; "Sheriff Was a Lady" 1965-Ger.; "Black Jack" 1968-Ital.; "Old Shatterhand" 1968-Ger./Yugo./Fr./Ital. (Dixon); "Shoot, Gringo ... Shoot!" 1968-Ital./Fr.; "This Man Can't Die" 1968-Ital. (Vic Graham); "Winnetou and Shatterhand in the Valley of Death" 1968-Ger./Yugo./Ital.; "Duck, You Sucker!" 1971-Ital. (Santerna); "Gold of the Heroes" 1971-Ital./Fr. (Major); "Hey Amigo! A Toast to Your Death!" 1971-Ital.; "Deadly Trackers" 1972-Ital.; "Genius" 1975-Ital./Fr./Ger.; "Man Called Blade" 1977-Ital.

Battier, Robert (1887-12/16/46). Films: "Rollin' Home to Texas" 1941.

Battista, Aurora. Films: "One Against One ... No Mercy" 1968-Span./Ital.; "Twenty Thousand Dollars for Seven" 1968-Ital.

Battista, Lloyd (1937-). Films: "Stranger in Japan" 1969-Ital./U.S./Jap.; "Chisum" 1970 (Neemo); "Blindman" 1971-Ital. (Domingo); "Get Mean" 1975-Ital.; "James A. Michener's Texas" TVM-1995 (Gen. Santa Anna). ¶TV: *Bonanza*—"The Stalker" 11-2-69 (Jake); *The Men from Shiloh*—"Crooked Corner" 10-28-70 (Embry).

Baucom, Bill. TV: *Judge Roy Bean*—"Sunburnt Gold" 10-1-55 (Little Ben Haney), "Gunman's Bargain" 1-1-56 (Little Sam), "The Defense Rests" 6-1-56 (Bank Clerk); *Wyatt Earp*—"Shootin' Woman" 1-1-57 (Perkins), "The Peacemaker" 9-23-58 (Banker).

Bauer, Belinda (1956-). Films: "Timerider" 1983 (Clair Cygne).

Bauer, Jaime Lyn (1949-). Films: "Where the Hell's That Gold?!!!" TVM-1988 (Brandy). ¶TV: *Young Riders*—"Star Light, Star Bright" 12-15-90 (Sarah).

Baugh, Sammy (1914-). Films: "King of the Texas Rangers" 1941-serial (Sergeant Tom King, Jr.).

Baumont, Frances. Films: "Rough Ridin'" 1924 (Rosalind Nolan).

Baur, Elizabeth (1948-). TV: *Lancer*—Regular 1968-70 (Teresa O'Brien); *Daniel Boone*—"Noblesse Oblige" 3-26-70 (Virginia).

Bavier, Frances (1905-12/6/89). Films: "Bend of the River" 1952 (Mrs. Prentiss); "Horizons West" 1952 (Martha Hammond). ¶TV: *The Lone Ranger*—"Sawtelle Saga's End" 3-24-55; *Wagon Train*—"The Sister Rita Story" 3-25-59 (Sister Joseph); *Sugarfoot*—"The Trial of the Canary Kid" 9-15-59 (Aunt Nancy); *Rawhide*—"Incident of the Dust Flower" 3-4-60.

Baxley, Barbara (1927-6/7/90). TV: *Have Gun Will Travel*—"Killer's Widow" 3-22-58 (Lucy Morrow), "Full Circle" 5-14-60 (Lily Leighton); *The Texan*—"The Edge of the Cliff" 10-27-58 (Ruth McKnight).

Baxley, Jack (1884-12/10/50). Films: "Wells Fargo" 1937 (Knick-Knack Vendor); "Cowboy and the Lady" 1938 (Rodeo Rider); "The Arizona Wildcat" 1939 (Wells Fargo Clerk); "A Tornado in the Saddle" 1942; "Along Came Jones" 1945 (Rancher on Street); "Song of the Sierras" 1946; "The Last Round-Up" 1947; "The Kid from Gower Gulch" 1949.

Baxley, Jane. Films: "Riders of the Dawn" 1945 (Doc).

Baxley, Paul. TV: *Maverick*— "The War of the Silver Kings" 9-22-57; *Buckskin*—"Annie's Old Beau" 4-13-59 (Whitey); *The Restless Gun*—"Lady by Law" 5-11-59 (Will); *The Tall Man*—"Bitter Ashes" 12-3-60 (Willliams); *Wagon Train*—"The Myra Marshall Story" 10-21-63, "The Sandra Cummings Story" 12-2-63, "The Link Cheney Story" 4-13-64; *The Travels of Jaimie McPheeters*—"The Day of the Haunted Trail" 1-26-64 (Tracey); *The Virginian*—"The Black Stallion" 9-30-64 (Hogan); *Laredo*—"The Golden Trail" 11-4-65 (Ike).

Baxter, Alan (1908-5/8/76). Films: "Santa Fe Trail" 1940 (Oliver Brown); "Bad Men of Missouri" 1941 (Jesse James); "The Prairie" 1947 (Paul Hover); "Ticket to Tomahawk" 1950 (Kit Dodge, Jr.); "Three Violent People" 1956 (Lorna Hunter Saunders); "The True Story of Jesse James" 1957 (Remington); "Face of a Fugitive" 1959 (Reed Williams);

"Welcome to Hard Times" 1967 (Jack Millay); "Paint Your Wagon" 1969 (Atwell); "Chisum" 1970 (Gov. Axtell). ¶TV: *The Restless Gun*—"The Torn Flag" 5-5-58 (George Frazier); *The Rifleman*—"The Boarding House" 2-24-59 (Sid Fallon); *Tales of Wells Fargo*—"The House I Enter" 3-2-59; *Wagon Train*—"The Swift Cloud Story" 4-8-59 (Jeb Harcourt); *Rawhide*—"Incident at Dangerfield Dip" 10-2-59 (J.B. Kincaid); *Bronco*—"Bodyguard" 10-20-59 (Frank Kelton); *The Alaskans*—"Winter Song" 11-22-59 (Lee Bannister); *The Deputy*—"Marked for Bounty" 4-2-60 (Mort Harch); *Colt .45*—"Chain of Command" 4-5-60 (Colonel Bealey); *Sugarfoot*—"Blue Bonnet Stray" 4-26-60 (Vance O'Connel); *Cheyenne*—"The Long Rope" 10-3-60 (Reed Moriarty); *Wyatt Earp*—"Miss Sadie" 12-20-60 (Ben Roberts); *Maverick*—"Flood's Folly" 2-19-61 (Judge John Scott); *The Tall Man*—"Death or Taxes" 5-27-61 (Fallon); *Gunsmoke*—"Long, Long Trail" 11-4-61 (Farmer), "Lover Boy" 10-5-63 (Ab Fisher); *Have Gun Will Travel*—"Man in an Hourglass" 12-1-62 (Dr. Moody); *The Virginian*—"The Old Cowboy" 3-31-65 (Northrup), "The Deadly Past" 9-20-67 (Walt Adams); *The Loner*—"Widow on the Evening Stage" 10-30-65 (Driscoll); *Branded*—"Romany Roundup 12-5-65 & 12-12-65 (Sheriff); *The Legend of Jesse James*—"The Lonely Place" 2-21-66 (Sheriff Pat Davis); *Wild Wild West*—"The Night of the Flying Pie Plate" 10-21-66 (Sheriff Ned Briggs); *Daniel Boone*—"Onatha" 11-3-66 (John Ruth); *The Monroes*—"Gold Fever" 12-14-66 (Stargis); *Bonanza*—"The Bottle Fighter" 5-12-68 (Becker), "The Witness" 9-21-69 (Jim).

Baxter, Anne (1923-12/12/85). Films: "Twenty Mule Team" 1940 (Jean Johnson); "Smoky" 1946 (Julie Richards); "Yellow Sky" 1948 (Mike); "The Outcasts of Poker Flat" 1952 (Cal); "The Spoilers" 1955 (Cherry Malotte); "Cimarron" 1960 (Dixie); "The Tall Women" 1966-Austria/Ital./Span. (Mary Ann); "Stranger on the Run" TVM-1967 (Valverda Johnson); "Fools' Parade" 1971 (Cleo). ¶TV: *Wagon Train*—"The Kitty Angel Story" 1-7-59 (Kitty Angel); *Riverboat*—"Race to Cincinnati" 10-4-59 (Ellie Jenkins); *Zane Grey Theater*—"Hand on the Latch" 10-29-59 (Laura Fletcher); *The Loner*—"One of the Wounded" 10-16-65 (Agatha Phelps); *Cowboy in Africa*—"Search for Survival" 10-9-67 (Erica Holloway); *The Virginian*—"Nora" 12-11-68 (Nora Carlton); *The Big Valley*—"The

Twenty-five Graves of Midas" 2-3-69 (Hannah).

Baxter, Eugene. Films: "The Cimarron Kid" 1951 (Tilden).

Baxter, George (1905-9/10/76). Films: "Son of Billy the Kid" 1949 (Jim Thorn); "Prairie Roundup" 1951 (Jim Eaton); "Gun Battle at Monterey" 1957. ¶TV: *Wild Bill Hickok*—"The Gatling Gun" 5-5-53; *Wyatt Earp*—"Dull Knife Strikes for Freedom" 5-7-57 (Judge); *Maverick*—"Diamond in the Rough" 1-26-58 (Vincent); *Sergeant Preston of the Yukon*—"The Criminal Collie" 2-27-58 (Logan McAlestor).

Baxter, John. TV: *Wyatt Earp*—"Juveniles—1878" 3-10-58 (Deputy Walt), "Wells Fargo Calling Marshal Earp" 12-29-59 (Smiley), "John Clum, Fighting Editor" 4-12-60; *Bat Masterson*—"Double Trouble in Trinidad" 1-7-59 (Lead Guard), "Flume to the Mother Load" 1-28-60 (Curt); *The Big Valley*—"Guilty" 10-30-67 (Alex).

Baxter, Louise. Films: "Colorado" 1915 (Kitty Baxter).

Baxter, Warner (1889-5/7/51). Films: "A Son of His Father" 1925 (Big Boy Morgan); "Drums of the Desert" 1927 (John Curry); "Ramona" 1928 (Alessandro); "In Old Arizona" 1929 (the Cisco Kid); "Romance of the Rio Grande" 1929 (Pabloe Wharton Cameron); "The Arizona Kid" 1930 (the Arizona Kid); "Cisco Kid" 1931 (the Cisco Kid); "The Squaw Man" 1931 (Capt. James Wynnegate/Jim Carsten); "Under the Pampas Moon" 1935 (Cesar Campo); "Robin Hood of El Dorado" 1936 (Joaquin Murrieta); "The Return of the Cisco Kid" 1939 (the Cisco Kid).

Bay, Sarah. *see* Neri, Rosalba.

Bay, Susan (1943-). TV: *A Man Called Shenandoah*—"The Lost Diablo" 1-24-66 (Conchita Roberts).

Bay, Tom (1901-10/11/33). Films: "The Better Man Wins" 1922 (Dr. Gale); "The Dead Line" 1926 (Snake Smeed); "The Devil's Gulch" 1926 (Heavy); "The Fighting Boob" 1926 (Bowers); "The Valley of Bravery" 1926 (Jim Saunders); "Tearin' into Trouble" 1927 (Johnnie); "White Pebbles" 1927 (Happy Bill); "Desperate Courage" 1928 (Col. Halliday); "The Devil's Tower" 1928 (Dutch Haynes); "Lightnin' Shot" 1928; "Mystery Valley" 1928; "The Painted Trail" 1928 (Badger James); "The Trail Riders" 1928; "Trailin' Back" 1928; "Code of the West" 1929; "Fighters of the Saddle" 1929 (Pete); "The Fighting Terror" 1929;

"The Lone Horseman" 1929; "The Oklahoma Kid" 1929; "Pioneers of the West" 1929 (Bull Bradley); "Fighting Thru" 1930; "Parting of the Trails" 1930 (Lucky Hardy); "The Fighting Sheriff" 1931 (Sam); "Freighters of Destiny" 1932 (Heavy).

Bay, Vivian. Films: "Code of the West" 1929 (Phyllis).

Bayless, Francis. Films: "A Texas Steer" 1915 (Mrs. Brander).

Bayley, Wilson. Films: "Sandy Burke of the U-Bar-U" 1919 (Sheriff Quinlan).

Baylor, Hal (Hal Fieberling) (1918-). Films: "Fort Osage" 1952; "River of No Return" 1954 (Drunken Cowboy); "Outlaw Treasure" 1955; "The Burning Hills" 1956 (Braun); "The Comancheros" 1961 (Comanchero); "The Cheyenne Social Club" 1970 (Lady of Egypt Barkeep); "One Little Indian" 1973. ¶TV: *The Lone Ranger*—"Mission Bells" 9-21-50, "Bad Medicine" 12-7-50, "The Silent Voice" 1-11-51, "Tenderfoot" 11-25-54; *Wyatt Earp*—"Mr. Earp Becomes a Marshal" 9-6-55 (Bill Thompson), "Mr. Earp Meets a Lady" 9-13-55 (Bill Thompson), "Bill Thompson Gives In" 9-22-55 (Bill Thompson), "One" 4-15-58 (Sam Wilson), "Two" 4-29-58 (Sam Wilson), "Three" 5-13-58 (Sam Wilson), "The Bounty Killer" 9-30-58 (Callum); *Gunsmoke*—"Hack Prine" 5-12-56 (Lee Trimble), "Now That April's There" 3-21-64 (Grody), "Rope Fever" 12-4-67 (Luke Summers), "The Gang" 12-11-72 (Toke), "The Boy and the Sinner" 10-1-73 (Boomer), "Thirty a Month a Found" 10-7-74 (Railroader); *Cheyenne*—"Lone Gun" 12-4-56 (Rowsy Shane), "Outcast of Cripple Creek" 2-29-60 (Turk Moylan); *Fury*—"Nature's Engineers" 2-2-57 (Bob Thomas); *Wagon Train*—"The Honorable Don Charlie Story" 1-22-58, "Alias Bill Hawks" 5-15-63 (Lester Cole); *Have Gun Will Travel*—"The Prize Fight Story" 4-5-58 (Bryan Sykes), "Bob Wire" 1-12-63; *Jefferson Drum*—"$50 for a Dead Man" 11-13-58 (Ben Grotcher); *The Californians*—"The Long Night" 12-23-58 (Jake), "Act of Fait" 5-26-59; *Lawman*—"The Gunmen" 2-15-59 (Harlin Smith), "The Man Behind the News" 5-13-62 (Mort Peters); *Maverick*—"The Sheriff of Duck 'n' Shoot" 9-27-59 (Bimbo); *The Texan*—"Blue Norther" 10-12-59 (Dobe Bisbee), "Cowards Don't Die" 11-30-59; *Laramie*—"Bare Knuckles" 12-8-59 (Cowboy Hill), "Riders of the Night" 3-7-61 (Beamer), "The Runaway" 1-23-62 (Samson), "The

Fugitives" 2-12-63 (Hub); *Hotel De Paree*—"Sundance and the Bare-Knuckled Fighters" 1-8-60 (Whitel Adams); *Bonanza*—"The Stranger" 2-27-60 (Tom Cole), "Breed of Violence" 11-5-60 (Clegg), "The Ride" 1-21-62 (Stewart), "The Saga of Whizzer McGee" 4-28-63 (Big Red), "A Man to Admire" 12-6-64 (Ev Durfee), "Shining in Spain" 3-27-66 (Drummer), "Old Charlie" 11-6-66 (Jack Barker), "Six Black Horses" 11-26-67 (Tierney), "The Stronghold" 5-26-68 (Kelty). "An Earthquake Called Callahan" 4-11-71 (Shad Willis); *The Alaskans*—"A Barrel of Gold" 4-3-60 (Corporal Thomas); *Bat Masterson*—"Debt of Honor" 9-29-60 (Eli Fisher); *The Deputy*—"The Challenger" 2-25-61 (Titan); *The Rifleman*—"Short Rope for a Tall Man" 3-28-61 (Charlie Crown); *Gunslinger*—"Johnny Sergeant" 5-4-61 (Big Red); *Tales of Wells Fargo*—"Incident at Crossbow" 2-3-62 (Hondo); *Death Valley Days*—"Miracle at Whiskey Gulch" 5-16-62 (Ben Poole), "The Resurrection of Deadwood Dick" 10-22-66 (Hughie Snow), "The Other Cheek" 11-16-68 (Hardy); *Rawhide*—"Incident of the Hunter" 9-28-62 (Jenkins), "Incident of the Querencias" 12-7-62 (Jenkins), "Incident at El Toro" 4-9-64 (Jenkins), "Hostage for Hanging" 10-19-65 (Cousin Will); *Wide Country*—"What Are Friends For?" 10-18-62 (Burt Carter); *The Dakotas*—"Mutiny at Fort Mercy" 1-21-63 (Bone); *The Virginian*—"Ride a Dark Trail" 9-18-63 (Fiske), "Man of the People" 12-23-64 (Sergeant Costello), "We've Lost a Train" 4-21-65, "The Brothers" 9-15-65 (Jobie), "Paid in Full" 11-22-67 (Bert); *Temple Houston*—"Ten Rounds for Baby" 1-30-64 (Con Morgan); *Daniel Boone*—"The Sisters O'Hannrahan" 12-3-64 (Cyrus Ballard); *A Man Called Shenandoah*—"The Siege" 12-13-65 (Driscoll); *Laredo*—"Above the Law" 1-13-66 (Mott), "One Too Many Voices" 11-18-66; *The Road West*—"Long Journey to Leavenworth" 10-17-66 (Alex); *Pistols 'n' Petticoats*—11-5-66 (Roy); *The Big Valley*—"Price of Victory" 2-13-67; *Iron Horse*—"Sister Death" 4-3-67 (Sergeant Greer); *The Guns of Will Sonnett*—"The Natural Way" 9-29-67, "A Fool and His Money" 3-8-68, "Home Free" 11-22-68; *Kung Fu*—"The Squaw Man" 11-1-73 (Sam Blake); *Barbary Coast*—"Guns for a Queen" 10-6-75 (Bystander), "Arson and Old Lace" 11-14-75 (Paddy Mulddon).

Bayne, Beverly (1895-8/18/82). Films: "Their Compact" 1917 (Mollie Anderson); "God's Outlaw" 1919 (Ruth Heatherly).

Bazlen, Brigid (1944-5/25/89). Films: "How the West Was Won" 1962 (Dora Hawkins).

Beach, Brandon (1879-11/22/74). Films: "Under Western Stars" 1938 (Senator Wilson); "Mountain Rhythm" 1939; "Oklahoma Terror" 1939 (Reynolds); "Return of the Bad-men" 1948 (Conductor); "A Perilous Journey" 1953 (Ad Lib).

Beach, Guy (1887-10/31/52). Films: "North of the Border" 1946; "Plainsman and the Lady" 1946 (Bookkeeper); "Singin' in the Corn" 1946 (Judge); "Smoky" 1946 (Sheriff); "Trail Street" 1947 (Doc Evans); "Trail of the Yukon" 1949 (Matt Blaine); "High Noon" 1952 (Fred). ¶TV: *Wild Bill Hickok*—"Lost Indian Mine" 12-11-51.

Beach, John. Films: "Trail Dust" 1936 (Hank); "Hopalong Rides Again" 1937 (Pete); "Hills of Old Wyoming" 1937 (Saunders); "North of the Rio Grande" 1937 (Clark); "Rustler's Valley" 1937 (Sheriff Boulton); "Texas Trail" 1937 (Smokey); "Bar 20 Justice" 1938 (Dennis); "Borderland" 1937 (Bailey); "The Frontiersman" 1938 (Quirt); "Heart of Arizona" 1938 (Sheriff Hawley); "Heroes of the Hills" 1938 (Crane); "Overland Stage Raiders" 1938; "Partners of the Plains" 1938 (Mr. Benson); "Blue Montana Skies" 1939 (N.W.M. Corporal); "The Cisco Kid and the Lady" 1939 (Stevens); "Home on the Prairie" 1939 (Tom Ross); "The Lone Ranger Rides Again" 1939-serial (Hardin); "Mexicali Rose" 1939 (Brown); "Ghost Valley Raiders" 1940; "Son of Roaring Dan" 1940 (Steve).

Beaird, Barbara (1948-). Films: "Flaming Star" 1960 (Dotti Phillips). ¶TV: *Wild Bill Hickok*—"Runaway Wizard" 6-9-53; *Death Valley Days*—"Old Blue" 4-7-59 (Arabella); *Rawhide*—"Incident of the Fish Out of the Water" 2-17-61 (Margaret Favor), "The Bosses' Daughter" 2-2-62 (Maggie Favor); *Wagon Train*—"The Will Santee Story" 5-3-61 (Wendy Santee).

Beaird, Pamela (1942-). TV: *My Friend Flicka*—Regular 1955-56 (Hildy Broeberg); *Jim Bowie*—"Thieves' Market" 3-29-57 (Bridget O'Brien); *Circus Boy*—"Royal Roustabout" 9-26-57 (April).

Beal, Frank (1862-12/20/34). Films: "Playing It Wild" 1923 (Wetherby, the Painter); "Soft Boiled" 1923 (John Steele); "Hook and Ladder" 1924 (Captain Smoky Joe Drennan); "Romance Ranch" 1924; "The Best Bad Man" 1925 (Mr. Swain); "The Golden Strain" 1925 (Major Denniston); "A Man Four-Square" 1926 (Wallace Roberts); "Galloping Fury" 1927 (Jasper Thornby); "The Danger Rider" 1928 (Warden Doyle); "The Big Diamond Robbery" 1929 (George Brooks); "Senor Americano" 1929 (Don Manuel); "Cimarron" 1931 (Louis Venable); "The Phantom Thunderbolt" 1933 (Mr. Oldham); "Sunset Pass" 1933 (Judge).

Beal, John (1909-). Films: "Border Cafe" 1937 (Keith Whitney); "Ten Who Dared" 1960 (Maj. John Wesley Powell). ¶TV: *Bonanza*—"The Diedeshiemer Story" 10-31-59 (Philip Diedeschiemer); *The Alaskans*—"The Bride Wore Black" 4-10-60 (Cass Wilson).

Bean, Orson (1928-). TV: *Dr. Quinn, Medicine Woman*—Regular 1993- (Loren Bray).

Beard, Matthew "Stymie" (1925-1/8/81). Films: "Two Gun Man from Harlem" 1938 (Jimmy Thompson); "The Return of Frank James" 1940 (Mose, the Bellboy); "Belle Starr" 1941 (Young Jake).

Bearpaw, Cody. Films: "Oklahoma Crude" 1973 (Indian). ¶TV: *Alias Smith and Jones*—"The Clementine Incident" 10-7-72.

Beasley, Barney. Films: "Desert Vengeance" 1931 (Chuck); "Arizona Cyclone" 1934; "Rawhide Mail" 1934; "The Sundown Trail" 1934; "The Cyclone Ranger" 1935 (Outlaw); "Fighting Pioneers" 1935; "Gun Play" 1935 (Pete); "The Last of the Clintons" 1935; "North of Arizona" 1935 (Barney); "The Vanishing Riders" 1935.

Beatty, May (1881-4/1/45). Films: "Union Pacific" 1939 (Mrs. Morgan).

Beatty, Ned (1937-). Films: "The Life and Times of Judge Roy Bean" 1972 (Tector Crites). ¶TV: *Gunsmoke*—"The Hiders" 1-13-75 (Karp).

Beatty, Robert (1909-3/3/92). Films: "The Spikes Gang" 1974 (Sheriff).

Beatty, Warren (1938-). Films: "McCabe and Mrs. Miller" 1971 (John McCabe).

Beauchamp, Richard. TV: *Zorro and Son*—Regular 1983 (Sergeant Sepulveda).

Beauford, Tonya. Films: "Desert Mesa" 1935 (Sally Kent).

Beaulieu, Andrea. Films: "The Night Rider" 1920 (Julian Marbolt).

Beaumont, Harry (1888-12/22/66). Films: "How the Boys Fought the Indians" 1912.

Beaumont, Hugh (1909-5/14/82). Films: "Callaway Went Thataway" 1951 (Mr. Adkins); "The Last Outpost" 1951 (Lt. Fenton); "Overland Telegraph" 1951 (Brad); "Bugles in the Afternoon" 1952 (Lt. Cooke); "Wild Stallion" 1952 (Capt. Wilmurt); "Night Passage" 1957 (Jeff Kurth). ¶TV: *The Lone Ranger*—"The Godless Men" 1-29-53; *My Friend Flicka*—"One Man's Horse" 9-30-55; *Tales of Wells Fargo*—"Jesse James" 7-1-57 (Jesse James); *Wagon Train*—"The Pearlie Garnet Story" 2-24-64 (Jed Halleck); *The Virginian*—"Girl on the Glass Mountain" 12-28-66 (Maguire), "With Help from Ulysses" 1-17-68 (Charles Martin), "Nora" 12-11-68 (Major James Carlton).

Beaumont, Leon. Films: "Pioneer Trail" 1938 (Joe); "The Law Comes to Texas" 1939 (Jeff).

Beaumont, Lucy (1864-4/24/37). Films: "Sandy Burke of the U-Bar-U" 1919 (Widow Mackey); "The Last of the Duanes" 1924 (Mother); "The Fighting Failure" 1926; "The Ridin' Demon" 1929 (Mrs. Riordan).

Beauvy, Nicolas (1958-). Films: "Shoot Out" 1971 (Dutch Farrell); "The Cowboys" 1972 (Four Eyes). ¶TV: *The Virginian*—"The Death Wagon" 1-3-68; *Bonanza*—"The Initiation" 9-26-72 (Ron).

Beaver, Jim. Films: "El Diablo" TVM-1990 (Spivy Trick); "Gunsmoke: To the Last Man" TVM-1991 (Deputy Rudd); "Gunsmoke: The Long Ride" TVM-1993 (Blacksmith).

Beavers, Louise (1902-10/26/62). Films: "Sundown Trail" 1931 (Jenny); "West of the Pecos" 1934 (Mauree); "Belle Starr" 1941 (Mammy Lou); "The Vanishing Virginian" 1941 (Aunt Emmeline); "Barbary Coast Gent" 1944 (Bedelia); "Colorado Sundown" 1952 (Mattie).

Beban, Jr., George. Films: "The Fabulous Texan" 1947 (Dick Clayton).

Becher, John C. (1915-9/20/86). TV: *Wyatt Earp*—"Santa Fe War" 12-2-58 (Sheriff Ben Johnson).

Beck, Billy. Films: "The Girl Called Hatter Fox" TVM-1977. ¶TV: *Branded*—"I Killed Jason McCord" 10-3-65, "Kellie" 4-24-66 (Mouse); *Gunsmoke*—"Wishbone" 2-19-66 (Tonkin).

Beck, Ethel. Films: "Gun Grit" 1936 (Jean).

Beck, James (1932-8/6/73). Films: "40 Guns to Apache Pass"

1967 (Higgins). ¶TV: *Texas John Slaughter*—Regular 1958-61 (Burt Alvord); *Gunsmoke*—"The Coward" 3-7-59 (Jack Massey); *Johnny Ringo*—"The Reno Brothers" 2-25-60 (Chris Reno); *The Outlaws*—"The Bill Doolin Story" 3-2-61 (Red Buck); *Stagecoach West*—"The Remounts" 3-14-61 (Clete); *Bonanza*—"The Lonely House" 10-15-61 (Gavin), "The Quest" 9-30-62 (Dave Donovan), "The Roper" 4-5-64 (Dolph), "The Medal" 10-26-69 (Walt); *Laramie*—"The Confederate Express" 1-30-62 (Luke Kerrigan), "Double Eagles" 11-20-62 (Easy), "Naked Steel" 1-1-63 (Lee Christy); *Tales of Wells Fargo*—"Winter Storm" 3-3-62 (Eddie Pierce); *Rawhide*—"Incident of the Dogfaces" 11-9-62 (Marker); *The Virginian*—"Shadows of the Past" 2-24-65 (Dink Gar); *Branded*—"McCord's Way" 1-30-66 (Bill Tomlin); *Hondo*—"Hondo and the Apache Kid" 10-13-67 (Sergeant Highton), "Hondo and the Mad Dog" 10-27-67 (Sergeant Highton), "Hondo and the Sudden Town" 11-17-67 (Sergeant Highton).

Beck, Jennifer. TV: *Father Murphy*—"Knights of the White Camelia" 2-2-82, "The Accident" 12-28-82 (Henrietta); *Paradise*—Regular 1988-92 (Claire Carroll Cord).

Beck, John. Films: "When Romance Rides" 1922 (Van); "The Devil's Bowl" 1923 (Andy Walker); "General Custer at the Little Big Horn" 1927 (Gen. George Armstrong Custer); "Little Big Horn" 1927 (Gen. George A. Custer); "Billy the Kid" 1930 (Butterworth); "The Spoilers" 1930 (Hansen); "Battling with Buffalo Bill" 1931-serial; "Dynamite Ranch" 1932 (Sheriff); "The Man from Arizona" 1932 (Sheriff Hartman); "Everyman's Law" 1936 (Pike); "Hopalong Cassidy Returns" 1936 (Robert Saunders); "King of the Pecos" 1936 (Clayborn, Sr.); "Wild and Woolly" 1937 (Purist); "Jesse James" 1939 (Turnkey); "Twenty Mule Team" 1940; "When the Daltons Rode" 1940 (Native).

Beck, John (1946-). Films: "The Silent Gun" TVM-1969 (Billy Reed); "Lawman" 1971 (Jason Bronson); "Lock, Stock and Barrel" TVM-1971 (Micah Brucker); "Pat Garrett and Billy the Kid" 1973 (Poe); "Sidekicks" TVM-1974 (Luke); "The Call of the Wild" TVM-1976 (John Thornton). ¶TV: *Lancer*—"Chad" 1-20-70 (Chad Lancer), "Dream of Falcons" 4-7-70 (Chad Lancer); *Gunsmoke*—"Kitowa!" 2-16-70 (Albert Vail), "The Tycoon" 1-25-71 (Moody Fowler), "The Busters" 3-10-75

(Mitch Hansen); *Bonanza*—"What Are Pardners For?" 4-12-70 (Luke); The Buffalo Soldiers—Pilot 5-26-79 (Col. Frank "Buckshot" O'Connor); *Nichols*—Regular 1971-72 (Ketcham); *How the West Was Won*—"The Scavengers" 3-12-79 (Clay Wesley); *Paradise*—"Hard Choices" 1-12-89 (Matthew Grady), "Squaring Off" 5-13-89 (Matthew Grady), "Dangerous Cargo" 1-20-90 (Matthew Grady).

Beck, Kimberly (1956-). TV: *The Virginian*—"The Return of Golden Tom" 3-9-66 (Laura).

Beck, Michael (1948-). Films: "Triumphs of a Man Called Horse" 1984 (Koda); "Houston: The Legend of Texas" TVM-1986 (Jim Bowie).

Beck, Thomas (1909-9/23/95). Films: "White Fang" 1936 (Hal Burgess).

Beck, Vincent (1928-7/24/84). TV: *Gunsmoke*—"Outlaw's Woman" 12-11-65 (Coley Martin); *Daniel Boone*—"Gabriel" 1-6-66 (Gabriel Lajeune); *Bonanza*—"The Pursued" 10-2-66 & 10-9-66 (Grant Carbo); *Iron Horse*—"Hellcat" 12-26-66 (Lanker); *Wild Wild West*—"The Night of the Pelican" 12-27-68 (Corporal Simon); *Alias Smith and Jones*—"The Great Shell Game" 2-18-71.

Becker, Ken. Films: "The Rainmaker" 1956 (Phil Mackey); "True Grit" 1969 (Farrell Parmalee). ¶TV: *Gunsmoke*—"Joe Phy" 1-4-58 (Cowboy), "Cody's Code" 1-20-62 (Kim Kroger); *Tales of the Texas Rangers*—"Jace and Clay" 12-5-58 (Kit Brady); *Lawman*—"The Wayfarer" 6-7-59 (Treb Cates), "The Swamper" 6-5-60 (Greg Thatcher); *Hotel De Paree*—"Sundance and the Blood Money" 1-1-60 (Eaton); *Wanted—Dead or Alive*—"Tolliver Bender" 2-13-60; *Bonanza*—"Bitter Water" 4-9-60 (Tucker); *Man from Blackhawk*—"Incident at Tupelo" 4-29-60 (Jeff).

Becker, Pauline. Films: "The Arizona Catclaw" 1919 (Amelia Young).

Becker, Terry. Films: "The Oregon Trail" TVM-1976 (William Thorpe). ¶TV: *Gunsmoke*—"The Big Broad" 4-28-56 (Emmett Fitzgerald); *Cimarron City*—"The Beauty and the Sorrow" 2-7-59 (Ezekiel); *Rawhide*—"Incident of the Thirteenth Man" 10-23-59 (Seth Warner), "The Backshooter" 11-27-64 (Burt); *Bonanza*—"A Hot Day for a Hanging" 10-14-62 (Shukie).

Becker, Tony. Films: "The Alamo: 13 Days to Glory" TVM-1987 (George Taylor). ¶TV: *The Oregon Trail*—Regular 1977 (William Thorpe).

Beckett, Scotty (1929-5/10/68). Films: "The Bad Man of Brimstone" 1937 (Sammy Grant); "Wells Fargo" 1937 (Young Nick); "Days of Jesse James" 1939 (Buster Samuels); "The Royal Rodeo" 1939-short; "The Vanishing Virginian" 1941 (Joel Yancey); "The Oklahoman" 1957 (Messenger at Ranch).

Beckley, William (1930-). TV: *Daniel Boone*—"The Desperate Raid" 11-16-67.

Beckman, Henry (1921-). Films: "The Glory Guys" 1965 (Salesman); "The Stalking Moon" 1969 (Sgt. Rudabaugh); "The Undefeated" 1969 (Thad Benedict); "Death Hunt" 1981 (Luce); "Blood River" TVM-1994. ¶TV: *Laramie*—"The Turn of the Wheel" 4-3-62; *Gunsmoke*—"Quint Asper Comes Home" 9-29-62 (Duff), "Uncle Sunday" 12-15-62 (Uncle Sunday Meachem), "Cowtown Hustler" 3-11-74 (Thaddius McKay), "The Guns of Cibola Blanca" 9-23-74 & 9-30-74 (Dr. Rhodes); *Have Gun Will Travel*—"Beau Beste" 10-13-62 (Hogan); *Wild Wild West*—"The Night of the Torture Chamber" 12-10-65 (Governor Bradford/Sam Jamison), "The Night of the Vicious Valentine" 2-10-67 (Paul J. Lambert); *Rango*—"It Ain't the Principle, It's the Money" 3-31-67 (Sheriff); *Death Valley Days*—"Along Came Mariana" 5-27-67 (Franklin); *The Virginian*—"A Bad Place to Die" 11-8-67 (Corey); *Custer*—"The Raiders" 12-27-67 (Claude Ostler); *Iron Horse*—"The Prisoners" 12-30-67 (Dr. Thompson); *Here Comes the Brides*—Regular 1968-70 (Clancey); *Bonanza*—"Child" 9-22-68 (Charlie Matson), "A Time to Die" 3-21-71 (Dr. Phelps); *Nichols*—"The Dirty Half Dozen Run Amuck" 10-28-71 (Murphy); *The Life and Times of Grizzly Adams*—2-8-78.

Beckwith, Mildred. Films: "The Crimson Dove" 1917 (Nevada).

Becwar, George (1917-7/9/70). TV: *The Rebel*—"He's Only a Boy" 2-28-60 (Bartender), "Berserk" 12-18-60 (Stevens), "Jerkwater" 1-22-61 (Dainer).

Beddoe, Don (1898-1/19/91). Films: "The Taming of the West" 1939; "Beyond the Sacramento" 1940 (Warden McKay); "Konga, the Wild Stallion" 1940 (Fred Martin); "The Man from Tumbleweeds" 1940 (Governor Dawson); "Texas Stagecoach" 1940 (Tug Wilson); "West of Abilene" 1940 (Forsyth); "Texas" 1941 (Sheriff); "Shut My Big Mouth" 1942 (Hill); "Black Bart" 1948 (J.T. Hall); "Beyond the Purple Hills" 1950

(Amos Rayburn); "Young Daniel Boone" 1950 (Charlie Bryan); "Man in the Saddle" 1951 (Love Bidwell); "Rodeo King and the Senorita" 1951 (Bill Richards); "The Big Sky" 1952 (Horse Trader); "Blue Canadian Rockies" 1952 (Cyrus Higbee); "Carson City" 1952 (Zeke Mitchell); "The Iron Mistress" 1952 (Dr. Cuny); "Cow Country" 1953 (Joe); "Jubilee Trail" 1954 (Mr. Maury, the Hotel Manager); "River of No Return" 1954 (Ben); "Wyoming Renegades" 1955 (Horace Warren); "The Rawhide Years" 1956 (Frank Porter); "Shoot-Out at Medicine Bend" 1957 (Mayor); "Bullwhip" 1958 (Judge); "Toughest Gun in Tombstone" 1958 (David Cooper); "Warlock" 1959 (Dr. Wagner); "Texas Across the River" 1966 (Mr. Naylor). ¶TV: *The Lone Ranger*—"The Condemned Man" 12-11-52; "Rendezvous at Whipsaw" 11-11-54; *Death Valley Days*—"Black Bart" 11-8-54; "Lady of the Press" 12-29-59 (Emmett); *My Friend Flicka*—"The Accident" 11-4-55; *Broken Arrow*—"The Trial" 1-22-57 (Silas Baldwyn); "The Missionaries" 1-29-57 (Silas Baldwyn); *Sheriff of Cochise*—"Grandfather Grandson" 2-11-57 (Mr. Wilkins); *Circus Boy*—"Counterfeit Clown" 4-7-57 (Judge Josh Simmons); *Maverick*—"Rope of Cards" 1-19-58 (Price); "Kiz" 12-4-60 (Fire Chief Thorpe); "Triple Indemnity" 3-19-61 (Dr. Whalen); *Wagon Train*—"The Bernal Sierra Story" 3-12-58; *The Restless Gun*—"The Suffragette" 3-24-58 (Henry Peabody); "The Battle of Tower Rock" 4-28-58 (Rome Madden); *Colt .45*—"The Manbuster" 4-4-58 (Ticket Agent); *Bronco*—"Backfire" 4-7-59 (Bert Daley); *Lawman*—"The Bandit" 5-31-59; "The Promoter" 2-19-61 (Simon Rodgers); *Cheyenne*—"Trial by Conscience" 10-26-59 (Judge Pruett); *The Alaskans*—"The Challenge" 1-24-60 (Reed); *Have Gun Will Travel*—"The Ledge" 2-13-60 (Stebbins), "The Uneasy Grave" 6-3-61 (Marshal); "The Mark of Cain" 1-13-62 (Wagner); *Laramie*—"Duel at Parkison Town" 12-13-60 (Dr. Sweeny); "The Confederate Express" 1-30-62 (Doctor); *The Texan*—"Buried Treasure" 2-15-60; *Rawhide*—"The Peddler" 1-19-62 (Hood); "Incident of the Rusty Shotgun" 1-9-64 (Minister); *The Tall Man*—"Quarantine" 3-17-62 (Doc Beckett); *Bonanza*—"The First Born" 9-23-62 (Stan Perkins); *Temple Houston*—"The Third Bullet" 10-24-63 (Simpson); *Gunsmoke*—"Deputy Festus" 1-16-65 (Halligan); *Wild Wild West*—"The Night of the Druid's Blood" 3-

25-66 (Prof. Robey); *F Troop*—"The West Goes Ghost" 10-13-66 (Hermit); *Pistols 'n' Petticoats*—12-3-66 (Doc Holliday); *Laredo*—"Like One of the Family" 3-24-67 (Colonel Willingham).

Bedelia, Bonnie (1946-). TV: *The High Chaparral*—"The Deceivers" 11-15-68 (Tina); *Bonanza*—"The Unwanted" 4-6-69 (Lorrie Mansfield), "Forever" 9-12-72 (Alice Harper); *The New Land*—Regular 1974 (Anna Larsen).

Bedell, Lew. Films: "Slaughter Trail" 1951 (Hardsaddle).

Bedford, Barbara. Films: "The Last of the Mohicans" 1920 (Cora Munro); "The Big Punch" 1921 (Hope Standish); "Arabia" 1922 (Janice Turner); "Out of the Silent North" 1922 (Marcette Vallois); "Step on It!" 1922 (Lorraine Leighton); "Romance Land" 1923 (Nan Harvess); "The Spoilers" 1923 (Helen Chester); "The Whipping Boss" 1924 (Grace Woodward); "Tumbleweeds" 1925 (Molly Lassiter); "The Cavalier" 1928 (Lucia D'Arquista); "Smoke Bellew" 1929 (Joy Gastrell); "The Lash" 1930 (Lupe); "Desert Vengeance" 1931 (Anne Dixon); "The Mine with the Iron Door" 1936 (Carrie Daily); "Senor Jim" 1936 (Mona Cartier); "Go West" 1940 (Baby's Mother).

Bedoya, Alfonso (1904-12/15/57). Films: "The Treasure of the Sierra Madre" 1948 (Gold Hat); "Streets of Laredo" 1949 (Charley Calico); "Man in the Saddle" 1951 (Cultus Charley); "California Conquest" 1952 (Jose Martinez); "The Stranger Wore a Gun" 1953 (Degas); "Border River" 1954 (Captain Vargas); "Ricochet Romance" 1954 (Alfredo Gonzales); "Ten Wanted Men" 1955 (Hermando); "The Big Country" 1958 (Ramon).

Bee, Molly (1939-). Films: "Corral Cuties" 1954-short.

Beebe, Marjorie. Films: "Hills of Peril" 1927 (Sophia); "The Cow-Catcher's Daughter" 1931-short; "The Fighting Deputy" 1937 (Peaches); "Lost Ranch" 1937 (Minnie); "Orphan of the Pecos" 1937 (Mrs. Barnes).

Beecher, Bonnie. TV: *The Road West*—"Road to Glory" 2-20-67 (Hope Trask); *Gunsmoke*—"Nitro!" 4-8-67 & 4-15-67 (Anne Gilchrist); *Cowboy in Africa*—"The Red Hand of Michael O'Neill" 2-5-68 (Deirdre O'Neill).

Beecher, Janet (1884-8/6/55). Films: "Man of Conquest" 1939

(Mrs. Lea); "The Gay Caballero" 1940 (Kate Brewster); "Mark of Zorro" 1940 (Senora Isabella Vega); "The Parson of Panamint" 1941 (Mrs. Tweedy); "Men of Texas" 1942 (Mrs. Sam Houston); "Silver Queen" 1942 (Mrs. Forsythe).

Beecher, Robert. Films: "Shoot Out at Big Sag" 1962. ¶TV: *Laredo*—"The Sweet Gang" 11-4-66 (Abel Sweet).

Beecher, Sylvia. Films: "Beyond the Sierras" 1928 (Rosa).

Beekman, Bobby. TV: *Death Valley Days*—"Nevada's Plymouth Rock" 3-10-56; *The Rebel*—"Dark Secret" 11-22-59 (Larry); *Wagon Train*—"The Clayton Tucker Story" 2-10-60.

Beer, Jacqueline (1932-). TV: *Maverick*—"Diamond in the Rough" 1-26-58 (Henriette); *Sugarfoot*—"The Royal Raiders" 3-17-59 (Yvette Marveux); *The Alaskans*—"The Seal Skin-Game" 2-21-60 (Jacqueline St. Clair); *Bronco*—"Manitoba Manhunt" 4-3-61 (Celeste Powell), "Until Kingdom Come" 3-26-62 (Duchess Eugenia); *Daniel Boone*—"Gabriel" 1-6-66 (Heloise Jolliet).

Beery, Bucklind. Films: "Macho Callahan" 1970; "Rodeo Girl" TVM-1980 (Marsh). ¶TV: *Bonanza*—"Honest John" 12-20-70 (Luke); *Kung Fu*—"The Ancient Warrior" 5-3-73 (Gil).

Beery, Harry. Films: "The Way of the West" 1934; "Timber Terrors" 1935 (Inspector).

Beery, Jr., Noah (1916-11/1/94). Films: "Mark of Zorro" 1920; "Heroes of the West" 1932-serial (Noah Blaine); "Fighting with Kit Carson" 1933-serial (Nakomas); "Rustlers' Roundup" 1933 (Danny Brand); "Sunset Pass" 1933 (Marshal Blake); "The Trail Beyond" 1934 (Wabi); "Devil's Canyon" 1935; "Five Bad Men" 1935 (Gene Taggart); "Stormy" 1935 (Stormy); "Zorro Rides Again" 1937-serial (J.A. Marsden); "Forbidden Valley" 1938 (Ring Hazzard); "Bad Lands" 1939 (Chile Lyman); "The Carson City Kid" 1940 (Warren); "The Light of Western Stars" 1940 (Poco); "Twenty Mule Team" 1940 (Mitch); "Riders of Death Valley" 1941-serial (Smokey); "Dudes Are Pretty People" 1942 (Pidge); "Overland Mail" 1942-serial (Sierra Pete); "Calaboose" 1943; "Frontier Badman" 1943 (Jim); "Prairie Chickens" 1943; "The Daltons Ride Again" 1945 (Ben Dalton); "Under Western Skies" 1945 (Tod); "Indian Agent" 1948 (Redfox); "Red River" 1948 (Buster McGee); "The Doolins of

Oklahoma" 1949 (Little Bill); "Davy Crockett, Indian Scout" 1950 (Tex); "The Savage Horde" 1950 (Glenn Larrabee); "Two Flags West" 1950 (Cy Davis); "The Cimarron Kid" 1951 (Bob Dalton); "The Last Outpost" 1951 (Sgt. Calhoun); "The Texas Rangers" 1951 (Buff Smith); "Wagons West" 1952 (Arch Lawrence); "War Arrow" 1953 (Sgt. Augustus Wilks); "Wings of the Hawk" 1953 (Orozco); "The Black Dakotas" 1954 (Gimpy Joe Woods); "The Yellow Tomahawk" 1954 (Tonio); "White Feather" 1955 (Lt. Ferguson); "Fastest Gun Alive" 1956 (Dink Wells); "Jubal" 1956 (Sam); "Decision at Sundown" 1957 (Sam); "Escort West" 1959 (Jamison); "Guns of the Timberland" 1960 (Blackie); "Incident at Phantom Hill" 1966 (O'Rourke); "Journey to Shiloh" 1968 (Sgt. Mercer Barnes); "Heaven with a Gun" 1969 (Garvey); "The Cockeyed Cowboys of Calico County" 1970 (Eddie); "Sidekicks" TVM-1974 (Tom); "The Spikes Gang" 1974 (Jack Bassett); "The Capture of Grizzly Adams" TVM-1982 (Sheriff Hawkins). ¶TV: *Circus Boy*—Regular 1956-58 (Uncle Joey); *Rawhide*—"Incident at Chubasco" 4-3-59 (Arkansas); *Riverboat*—Regular 1959-61 (Carney); *Wagon Train*—"The Jonas Murdock Story" 4-13-60 (Jona Murdock), "Path of the Serpent" 2-8-61 (Rudy Blaine), "The Kate Crawley Story" 1-27-64 (Stump Beasley); *Wanted—Dead or Alive*—"El Gato" 2-22-61 (El Gato), "Barney's Bounty" 3-29-61 (Barney Durant); *Wide Country*—"A Guy for Clementine" 9-27-62 (Barney Hamlin); *Death Valley Days*—"The Train and Lucy Tutaine" 3-13-63 (Abel); *Great Adventure*—"The Death of Sitting Bull"/"Massacre at Wounded Knee" 10-4-63 & 10-11-63 (Jervis); *Temple Houston*—"Toll the Bell Slowly" 10-17-63 (Bailey); *Gunsmoke*—"Prairie Wolfer" 1-18-64 (Nate Guthrie), "Honor Before Justice" 3-5-66 (John Two-Bears); *Bonanza*—"Lothario Larkin" 4-25-65 (Lothario Larkin), "The Crime of Johnny Mule" 2-25-68 (Johnny Mule); *Branded*—"Now Join the Human Race" 9-19-65 (Major Lynch); *Laredo*—"A Taste of Money" 4-28-66 (Ezekial Fry); *The Monroes*—"Lost in the Wilderness" 11-30-66 (Alkali Tom); *The Virginian*—"Long Journey Home" 12-14-66 (Simpson), "You Can Lead a Horse to Water" 1-7-70 (Baxter); *Hondo*—Regular 1967 (Buffalo Baker); *Lancer*—"Devil's Blessing" 4-22-69 (Hamlin); *The High Chaparral*—"Too Many Chiefs" 3-27-70 (Hannibal); *The Men from

Shiloh—"Follow the Leader" 12-2-70 (Morgan); *Alias Smith and Jones*—"Something to Get Hung About" 10-21-71.

Beery, Sr., Noah (1882-4/1/46). Films: "The Squaw Man" 1918 (Tabywana); "In Mizzoura" 1919 (Jo Vernon); "Johnny, Get Your Gun" 1919 (Town Marshal); "The Fighting Shepherdess" 1920 (Mormon Joe); "Mark of Zorro" 1920 (Sergeant Pedro); "The Sagebrusher" 1920 (Sim Gage); "Bob Hampton of Placer" 1921 (Red Slavin); "The Call of the North" 1921 (Galan Albret); "Belle of Alaska" 1922 (Wade Harkin); "Good Men and True" 1922 (S.S. Thorpe); "I Am the Law" 1922 (Sgt. Georges Mardeaux); "The Call of the Canyon" 1923 (Haze Ruff); "Dangerous Trails" 1923 (Insp. Criswell); "Quicksands" 1923 (Silent Krupz); "The Spider and the Rose" 1923 (Maitre Renaud); "The Spoilers" 1923 (Alex McNamara); "To the Last Man" 1923 (Colter); "When Law Comes to Hades" 1923; "Heritage of the Desert" 1924; "North of '36" 1924 (Slim Rudabaugh); "The Wanderer of the Wasteland" 1924 (Dismukes); "The Light of Western Stars" 1925 (Brand); "The Thundering Herd" 1925 (Randall Jett); "The Vanishing American" 1925 (Booker); "Wild Horse Mesa" 1925 (Bud McPherson); "The Enchanted Hill" 1926 (Jake Dort); "False Feathers" 1929 (Parson); "Billy the Kid" 1930 (Barrett); "Under a Texas Moon" 1930 (Jed Parker); "Riders of the Purple Sage" 1931 (Judge Dyer); "The Big Stampede" 1932 (Sam Crew); "Cornered" 1932 (Red Slavens); "The Devil Horse" 1932-serial (Canfield); "Fighting with Kit Carson" 1933-serial (Kraft); "Man of the Forest" 1933 (Clint Beasley); "To the Last Man" 1933 (Jed Colby); "The Thundering Herd" 1934 (Randall Jett); "The Trail Beyond" 1934 (George Newsome); "The Bad Man of Brimstone" 1938 (Ambrose Crocker); "The Girl of the Golden West" 1938 (the General); "Panamint's Bad Man" 1938 (King Gorman); "Mexicali Rose" 1939 (Valdes); "Adventures of Red Ryder" 1940-serial (Ace Hanlon); "Pioneers of the West" 1940 (Judge Platt); "The Tulsa Kid" 1940 (Montana Smith); "A Missouri Outlaw" 1941 (Sheriff Dixon); "The Devil's Trail" 1942; "Outlaws of Pine Ridge" 1942 (Honest John Hollister); "Overland Mail" 1942-serial (Frank Chadwick); "Pardon My Gun" 1942 (Judge); "Carson City Cyclone" 1943 (Judge Phalen); "Barbary Coast Gent" 1944 (Pete); "Gentle Annie" 1944 (Hansen); "Sing Me a Song of Texas" 1945.

Beery, Wallace (1885-4/15/49). Films: "The Last of the Mohicans" 1920 (Magua); "The Mollycoddle" 1920 (Henry Von Holkar); "The Round Up" 1920 (Buck McKee); "The Last Trail" 1921 (William Kirk); "I Am the Law" 1922 (Fu Chang); "The Man from Hell's River" 1922 (Gaspard the Wolf); "The Sagebrush Trail" 1922; "The Eternal Struggle" 1923 (Barode Dukane); "The Great Divide" 1925 (Dutch); "The Pony Express" 1925 (Rhode Island Red); "Stairs of Sand" 1929 (Guerd Larey); "The Bad Man of Brimstone" 1938 (Trigger Bill); "Stand Up and Fight" 1939 (Captain Boss Starkey); "The Man from Dakota" 1940 (Sgt. Barstow); "Twenty Mule Team" 1940 (Skinner Bill Bragg); "The Bad Man" 1941 (Pancho Lopez); "Jackass Mail" 1942 (Marmaduke "Just" Baggott); "Barbary Coast Gent" 1944 (Honest Plush Brannon); "Bad Bascomb" 1946 (Zeb Bascomb); "Big Jack" 1949 (Big Jack Horner); "Wyoming" 1940 (Reb Harkness).

Beggs, Hagan (1937-). Films: "The Last Gunfighter" 1961-Can.; "Sally Fieldgood & Co." 1975-Can. ¶TV: *Cowboy in Africa*—"The Man Who Has Everything" 12-4-67; *Here Come the Brides*—"The Firemaker" 1-15-69 (Davey Hingle), "The Wealthiest Man in Seattle" 10-3-69 (Claude).

Beggs, James. TV: *Gunsmoke*—"Killer at Large" 2-5-66 (Jace).

Beggs, Pat. Films: "The Devil's Gulch" 1926 (Bill Griggs); "Man Rustlin'" 1926 (Smude Perkins).

Begley, Ed (1901-4/28/70). Films: "Saddle Tramp" 1950; "Wyoming Mail" 1950 (Haynes); "The Lady from Texas" 1951 (Dave Blodgett); "Lone Star" 1952 (Sen. Anthony Demmett); "Firecreek" 1968 (Preacher Broyles); "Hang 'Em High" 1968 (Cap'n Wilson); "The Silent Gun" TVM-1969 (John Cole). ¶TV: *Empire*—"Ballard Number One" 10-2-62 (Dan Ballard); *Wagon Train*—"The Sam Spicer Story" 10-28-63 (Reno Sutton); *The Virginian*—"The Invaders" 1-1-64 (Mike Tyrone), "Chaff in the Wind" 1-26-66 (Micah Ellis); *Rawhide*—"Piney" 10-9-64 (Piney); *Bonanza*—"The Other Son" 10-3-65 (Clint Watson), "A Time to Step Down" 9-25-66 (Dan Tolliver); *Gunsmoke*—"Taps for Old Jeb" 10-16-65 (Jeb Crater), "Mr. Sam'l" 2-26-68 (Mr. Sam'l); Wild Wild West—"The Night of the Infernal Machine" 12-23-66 (Judge M'Guigan); *The High Chaparral*—"Follow Your Heart" 10-4-68 (Ben Lynch).

Begley, Jr., Ed (1949-). Films: "Showdown" 1973 (Pook); "Goin' South" 1978 (Mr. Haber).

Behrens, Bernard. Films: "Another Man, Another Chance" 1977-Fr. (Springfield).

Behrens, Frank (1919-12/15/86). TV: *Stoney Burke*—"Color Him Lucky" 4-1-63 (Perry Clark).

Behrens, William. Films: "Whispering Smith" 1916 (Bartender); "The Railroad Raiders" 1917.

Behrle, Fred (1891-5/20/41). Films: "Ride 'Em, Cowgirl" 1939 (Deputy Sheriff).

Beir, Fred (1927-6/3/80). Films: "Damned Pistols of Dallas" 1964-Span./Ital./Fr.; "Fort Courageous" 1965 (Sgt. Lucas). ¶TV: *Maverick*—"Passage to Fort Doom" 3-8-59 (Lee Granger), "Epitaph of a Gambler" 2-11-62 (Sheriff Ed Martin); *Sugarfoot*—"The Twister" 4-14-59 (Roy Cantwell); *The Deputy*—"Like Father" 10-17-59 (Brad Vantage); *Wanted—Dead or Alive*—"Man on Horseback" 12-5-59 (Merv Bascomb); *The Rebel*—"A Grave for Johnny Yuma" 5-1-60 (Simon); *Bonanza*—"Badge Without Honor" 9-24-60 (Jason Blaine); *The Outlaws*—"The Waiting Game" 1-19-61 (Adams); *Bronco*—"Guns of the Lawless" 5-8-61 (Joe Spain); *Wagon Train*—"The Daniel Clay Story" 2-21-62 (John Cole), "The Naomi Kaylor Story" 1-30-63 (Blucher); "The Luke Grant Story" 6-1-60 (Reverend Peters); *A Man Called Shenandoah*—"The Imposter" 4-4-66 (Tim O'Rourke); *The Big Valley*—"The Velvet Trap" 11-7-66 (Jack Floyd); *The Virginian*—"A Love to Remember" 10-29-69 (Ord Glover); *Kung Fu*—"The Third Man" 4-26-73 (Jim Gallagher); *Barbary Coast*—"Guns for a Queen" 10-6-75 (Arthur).

Bejarano, Julia. Films: "The Lone Defender" 1930-serial (Duenna Maria); "Cowboy Holiday" 1934; "The Prescott Kid" 1934 (Juanita).

Bekassy, Stephen (1915-). Films: "The Pathfinder" 1952 (Col. Brasseau); "Woman of the North Country" 1952 (Andre Duclos); "The Light in the Forest" 1958 (Col. Henry Bouquet). ¶TV: *Maverick*—"Hostage!" 11-10-57 (Andrew Devereaux); *Tombstone Territory*—"A Bullet for an Editor" 11-13-57 (Raoul de Moreney); *Rough Riders*—"The Duelists" 10-23-58 (Andre Leroux); *Bat Masterson*—"A Matter of Honor" 4-29-59 (Anton Von Landi), "Flume to the Mother Lode" 1-28-60 (Emile Ba-

role); *The Rifleman*—"The Princess" 1-8-62.

Belafonte, Harry (1927-). Films: "Buck and the Preacher" 1972 (Preacher).

Belasco, Art (1888-11/8/79). Films: "Honky Tonk" 1941 (Pallbearer); "Jackass Mail" 1942 (Miner).

Belasco, Leon (1902-6/1/88). TV: *Maverick*—"The Art Lovers" 10-1-61 (Cosmo Nardi).

Belasco, Walter (1876-6/21/39). Films: "Judge Not, or the Woman of Mona Diggings" 1915 (Barkeeper).

Belcher, Alice (1880-6/21/39). Films: "The Cowboy Kid" 1928 (Lilly Langdon).

Belcher, Charles (1872-12/10/43). Films: "Mark of Zorro" 1920; "The Devil's Gulch" 1926 (Max Crew).

Belfield, Richard (1873-1/2/40). Films: "Galloping On" 1925 (Banker Brown).

Belford, Christine (1949-). Films: "Pocket Money" 1972 (Adelita); "The Gambler" TVM-1980 (Eliza); "Outlaws" TVM-1986 (Maggie). ¶TV: *Alias Smith and Jones*—"Bushwack!" 10-21-72 (Ellie Alcott); *Outlaws*—Regular 1986-87 (Maggie Randall).

Bel Geddes, Barbara (1922-). Films: "Blood on the Moon" 1948 (Amy Lufton). ¶TV: *Riverboat*—"Payment in Full" 9-13-59 (Missy).

Bell, Charles. Films: "Wyoming" 1928 (Chief Big Cloud).

Bell, Charles Alvin. TV: *Maverick*—"The White Widow" 1-24-60 (Joe Barnes), "The Maverick Line" 10-20-60 (Bandy); *Lawman*—"The Old War Horse" 10-9-60 (Man).

Bell, Cynthia. Films: "Those Redheads from Seattle" 1953 (Connie Edmonds).

Bell, Frank. Films: "Gun Lords of Stirrup Basin" 1937 (Hub Stockton).

Bell, Genevieve (1895-10/3/51). Films: "Union Pacific" 1939 (Kate).

Bell, George (1898-10/2/69). Films: "Too Much Beef" 1936 (Tracey Paine); "Son of Zorro" 1947-serial (Deputy #3); "Shoot-Out at Medicine Bend" 1957.

Bell, Hank (1892-2/4/50). Films: "The Last Straw" 1920 (Pat Webb); "Don Quickshot of the Rio Grande" 1923 (Henchman); "Gold and Grit" 1925 (Sheriff); "The Pony Express" 1925 (Townsman); "Ace of Action" 1926; "Double Daring" 1926 (Lee Falcon); "The Scrappin' Kid"

1926 (Slim Hawks); "The Terror" 1926 (Sheriff); "Twin Triggers" 1926 (the Law); "Between Dangers" 1927; "Code of the Cow Country" 1927 (Red Irwin); "Saddle Mates" 1928 (Tim Mannick); "The Fighting Terror" 1929; "The Last Roundup" 1929; "'Neath Western Skies" 1929 (Wildcat Riley); "Billy the Kid" 1930; "Breed of the West" 1930 (Sheriff Cole); "Near the Rainbow's End" 1930; "Shadow Ranch" 1930; "Trails of Danger" 1930 (Hank); "The Man from Death Valley" 1931; "Partners of the Trail" 1931; "Pueblo Terror" 1931 (Hank); "Beyond the Rockies" 1932 (Whiskey Bill); "The Big Stampede" 1932; "Fighting Champ" 1932; "Ghost City" 1932 (Blacksmith Joe Meeker); "Guns for Hire" 1932; "Law and Order" 1932; "Law of the West" 1932 (Dad Carruthers); "Lawless Valley" 1932; "The Man from Arizona" 1932; "The Riding Tornado" 1932; "Single-Handed Sanders" 1932; "South of Sante Fe" 1932 (Member of Stone's Gang); "Texas Pioneers" 1932; "Whistlin' Dan" 1932; "Wyoming Whirlwind" 1932; "Young Blood" 1932 (Deputy Sheriff); "Come on Tarzan" 1933; "The Dude Bandit" 1933; "Fargo Express" 1933; "Outlaw Justice" 1933; "Sagebrush Trail" 1933; "Terror Trail" 1933 (Smith); "The Trail Drive" 1933; "The Whirlwind" 1933; "Blue Steel" 1934 (Stage Driver); "The Dude Ranger" 1934; "The Fiddlin' Buckaroo" 1934; "Fighting Through" 1934 (Hank); "Gun Justice" 1934; "Honor of the Range" 1934; "The Law of the Wild" 1934-serial; "The Red Rider" 1934-serial; "Smoking Guns" 1934; "Thunder Over Texas" 1934; "The Westerner" 1934; "Wheels of Destiny" 1934; "The Arizonian" 1935; "Border Brigands" 1935 (Sisk); "Border Vengeance" 1935; "Cheyenne Tornado" 1935 (Sheriff); "Circle of Death" 1935; "Lawless Riders" 1935; "The Man from Guntown" 1935; "North of Arizona" 1935 (Barfly); "The Outlaw Deputy" 1935; "Rustlers of Red Dog" 1935-serial; "The Silver Bullet" 1935; "Thunderbolt" 1935 (Chuck); "Trails End" 1935 (Ranch Hands); "Westward Ho" 1935 (Mark Wyatt); "Comin' Round the Mountain" 1936 (Ranch Hand); "End of the Trail" 1936 (Hank); "Lucky Terror" 1936 (Hank); "The Phantom Rider" 1936-serial; "The Plainsman" 1936; "Red River Valley" 1936; "Roarin' Guns" 1936; "The Texas Rangers" 1936 (Ranger); "Too Much Beef" 1936 (Tucson Smith/Johnny Argyle); "Dodge City Trail" 1937 (Red); "Goofs and Saddles" 1937-short (Character); "North of the Rio Grande" 1937; "One Man Justice" 1937; "Outlaws of the Prairie" 1937 (Jim); "Thunder Trail" 1937 (Barfly); "Two-Fisted Sheriff" 1937; "Two Gun Law" 1937 (Cookie); "Valley of Terror" 1937 (Sheriff Judson); "Wild West Days" 1937-serial; "Border Wolves" 1938; "Call of the Rockies" 1938 (Rankin); "Cattle Raiders" 1938; "Colorado Trail" 1938 (Tombstone Territory); "Flaming Frontier" 1938-serial; "The Girl of the Golden West" 1938 (Deputy); "Gun Law" 1938; "The Lone Ranger" 1938-serial (Rancher); "Renegade Ranger" 1938 (Barfly); "Rio Grande" 1938 (Hank); "South of Arizona" 1938 (Hank); "West of Santa Fe" 1938 (Hank); "Chip of the Flying U" 1939; "The Fighting Gringo" 1939 (Outlaw); "Frontier Pony Express" 1939; "Oklahoma Frontier" 1939 (Corporal); "Overland with Kit Carson" 1939-serial; "Rough Riders' Round-Up" 1939 (Patrolman Kit Grant); "Silver on the Sage" 1939; "Spoilers of the Range" 1939 (Sheriff Hank); "The Taming of the West" 1939 (Marshal Bates); "Teacher's Pest" 1939-short; "Texas Stampede" 1939 (Hank); "The Thundering West" 1939 (Tucson); "Westbound Stage" 1939; "Western Caravans" 1939 (Hank); "The Carson City Kid" 1940; "Covered Wagon Trails" 1940 (Sheriff); "My Little Chickadee" 1940; "Oklahoma Renegades" 1940; "Pioneers of the Frontier" 1940 (Harper); "Prairie Law" 1940; "Riders of Pasco Basin" 1940; "Rocky Mountain Rangers" 1940; "Stage to Chino" 1940; "Trail of the Vigilantes" 1940; "Twenty Mule Team" 1940 (Barfly); "The Westerner" 1940 (Deputy); "Young Bill Hickok" 1940; "Young Buffalo Bill" 1940; "Border Vigilantes" 1941 (Liveryman); "Down Mexico Way" 1941; "Jesse James at Bay" 1941; "Nevada City" 1941; "North from the Lone Star" 1941; "The Pinto Kid" 1941 (Hank); "The Return of Daniel Boone" 1941; "Riders of the Timberline" 1941; "Roaring Frontiers" 1941; "The Shepherd of the Hills" 1941 (Man with Mustache); "Tonto Basin Outlaws" 1941; "White Eagle" 1941-serial; "Wrangler's Roost" 1941; "Billy the Kid Trapped" 1942; "The Great Man's Lady" 1942; "Heart of the Golden West" 1942; "Rock River Renegades" 1942; "Shut My Big Mouth" 1942 (Stagecoach Driver); "The Silver Bullet" 1942; "The Sombrero Kid" 1942; "South of Santa Fe" 1942; "Stagecoach Buckaroo" 1942; "Valley of the Sun" 1942 (Shotgun); "Cattle Stampede" 1943; "Cowboy Commandos" 1943; "The

Haunted Ranch" 1943; "The Law Rides Again" 1943 (Sheriff); "Man from Music Mountain" 1943 (Dobe Joe); "Overland Mail Robbery" 1943; "The Ox-Bow Incident" 1943 (Red); "Raiders of Sunset Pass" 1943 (Old Cowhand); "Wagon Tracks West" 1943; "Blazing Frontier" 1944; "Boss of Boomtown" 1944; "Code of the Prairie" 1944 (Jim, the Stage Driver); "Firebrands of Arizona" 1944 (Townsman); "Mystery Man" 1944 (Deputy Ed); "San Fernando Valley" 1944; "Along Came Jones" 1945 (Posse); "Bells of Rosarita" 1945; "The Cherokee Flash" 1945; "Flame of the Barbary Coast" 1945 (Cabby); "Great Stagecoach Robbery" 1945; "Rough Riders of Cheyenne" 1945; "Salome, Where She Danced" 1945 (Cowhand); "Stagecoach Outlaws" 1945; "Sunset in El Dorado" 1945; "The Topeka Terror" 1945 (Stage Driver); "Plainsman and the Lady" 1946 (Yard Master); "Rustler's Roundup" 1946 (Rancher); "Three Troubledoers" 1946-short (Sheriff); "Cheyenne Takes Over" 1947; "The Sea of Grass" 1947 (Sam Hall)."The Gallant Legion" 1948; "Loaded Pistols" 1948; "The Plunderers" 1948; "Tornado Range" 1948; "The Last Bandit" 1949; "Red Desert" 1949 (State Driver); "Copper Canyon" 1950 (Man); "Fancy Pants" 1950 (Barfly); "Gunslingers" 1950 (Hollister); "Over the Border" 1950 (Sheriff); "Montana Belle" 1952 (Bartender).

Bell, Ivan. TV: *F Troop*—Regular 1965-67 (Duddleson).

Bell, James (1891-10/26/73). Films: "My Friend Flicka" 1943 (Gus); "Black Eagle" 1948 (Frank Hayden); "Roughshod" 1949 (Pa Wyatt); "Streets of Laredo" 1949 (Ike); "Arizona Manhunt" 1951 (Sheriff White); "Buckaroo Sheriff of Texas" 1951 (Tom "Grampa" White); "The Dakota Kid" 1951 (Sheriff Tom White); "Red Mountain" 1951 (Dr. Terry); "Ride the Man Down" 1952 (John Evarts); "Wild Horse Ambush" 1952 (Sheriff Tom White); "Devil's Canyon" 1953 (Dr. Betts); "The Last Posse" 1953 (Will Romer); "Riding Shotgun" 1954 (Doc Winkler); "A Lawless Street" 1955 (Asaph Dean); "Lay That Rifle Down" 1955 (Mr. Fletcher); "Stranger on Horseback" 1955 (Vince Webb); "Texas Lady" 1955 (Cass Gower); "A Day of Fury" 1956 (Doc Logan); "Tribute to a Badman" 1956 (L.A. Peterson); "The Lonely Man" 1957 (Judge Hart); "The Tin Star" 1957 (Judge Thatcher); "The Oregon Trail" 1959 (Jeremiah Cooper); "Posse from Hell" 1961 (Benson). ¶TV: *Wild Bill

Hickok*—"Trapper's Story" 3-18-52; *Zane Grey Theater*—"The Freighter" 1-17-58 (Judge Garrison); *Wanted—Dead or Alive*—"Eight Cent Record" 12-20-58; *Lawman*—"The Captives" 1-11-59 (Doc Stewart); *The Texan*—"The Peddler" 1-26-59 (Mr. Webb); *Tales of Wells Fargo*—"The Cleanup" 1-26-59 (Sheriff Pete Haney); *The Rebel*—"The Scavengers" 11-8-59 (Old Man); *Cheyenne*—"Riot at Arroyo Soco" 2-1-60; *Colt .45*—"Alibi" 4-12-60 (Coroner Andrew Karp); *The Deputy*—"Lucifer Urge" 5-14-60 (Rab Stebbins); *Wagon Train*—"The Luke Grant Story" 6-1-60 (Reverend Peters); *Have Gun Will Travel*—"The Trial" 6-11-60, "Bob Wire" 1-12-63 (Anderson); *Stoney Burke*—"Bandwagon" 12-17-62 (Paul Grayson); *Bonanza*—"The Jury" 12-30-62 (Olson), "A Dime's Worth of Glory" 11-1-64; *Temple Houston*—"Toll the Bell Slowly" 10-17-63 (Dr. Davis Carter).

Bell, Joseph. Films: "That Devil Quemado" 1925 (Ned Thatcher).

Bell, Kay. Films: "Those Redheads from Seattle" 1953 (Neil Edmonds). ¶TV: *Tales of the Texas Rangers*—"Home in San Antone" 10-22-55 (Cece Prudy), "Jail Bird" 10-29-55 (Jim Hackett).

Bell, Leonard. TV: *Jim Bowie*—"Silk Purse" 12-27-57 (Placide Presuette); *Wrangler*—"Encounter at Elephant Butte" 9-15-60 (Sheriff); *Wanted—Dead or Alive*—"Three for One" 12-21-60 (Ken Hunter), "Dead Reckoning" 3-22-61 (Ollie Prescott); *Tales of Wells Fargo*—"The Repentant Outlaw" 5-29-61 (Sheriff Wills).

Bell, Marjorie. see Champion, Marge.

Bell, Michael. Films: "Blue" 1968 (Jim Benton); "Go West, Young Girl" TVM-1978 (Nestor). ¶TV: *Here Come the Brides*—"A Christmas Place" 12-18-68 (Roger); *The Big Valley*—"Joshua Watson" 1-20-69 (Charlie); *The Quest*—"Prairie Woman" 11-10-76 (Dub Dailey).

Bell, Rex (1903-7/4/62). Films: "The Cowboy Kid" 1928 (Jim Barrett); "The Girl-Shy Cowboy" 1928 (Joe Benson); "Taking a Chance" 1928 (Joe Courtney); "Wild West Romance" 1928; "Battling with Buffalo Bill" 1931-serial (Dave Archer); "Broadway to Cheyenne" 1932 (Breezy Kildare); "The Man from Arizona" 1932 (Kent Rogers); "Crashing Broadway" 1933 (Tad Wallace); "Diamond Trail" 1933 (Speed Morgan); "The Fighting Texans" 1933 (Randolph Graves); "The Fugitive" 1933 (Joe "Lefty" Keyes); "Lucky Larrigan" 1933 (Craig "Lucky" Larrigan);

"Rainbow Ranch" 1933 (Ed Randall); "Fighting Pioneers" 1935 (Lt. Bentley); "Gunfire" 1935 (Jerry Dunbar); "Saddle Aces" 1935 (Brandon); "Tonto Kid" 1935 (Paul Slauson, the Tonto Kid); "Law and Lead" 1936 (Jimmy Sawyer); "Men of the Plains" 1936 (Jim Dean); "Stormy Trails" 1936 (Tom Storm); "West of Nevada" 1936 (Jim Lloyd/Jim Carden); "The Idaho Kid" 1937 (Idaho/Todd Hollister); "Dawn on the Great Divide" 1942 (Jack Carson); "Tombstone, the Town Too Tough to Die" 1942 (Virgil Earp); "Lone Star" 1952.

Bell, Jr., Rex. Films: "Stage to Thunder Rock" 1964 (Shotgun); "Young Fury" 1965 (Farmer).

Bell, Rodney (1916-8/3/68). Films: "Montana Belle" 1952 (Hotel Clerk); "The Missouri Traveler" 1958 (Herb Davis). ¶TV: *Wanted—Dead or Alive*—"Bad Gun" 10-24-59, "The Twain Shall Meet" 10-19-60; *Wichita Town*—"Bought" 1-13-60 (Dixon); *Tales of Wells Fargo*—"The Killing of Johnny Lash" 11-21-60 (L.L. Jones); *Rawhide*—"Incident of the Reluctant Bridegroom" 11-30-62 (Barber), "Incident of the Pied Piper" 2-6-64 (Clarence).

Bell, Spencer (1887-8/18/35). Films: "The Outlaw Dog" 1927 (Snowball Black).

Bell, Tobin. Films: "The Quick and the Dead" 1995 (Dog Kelly).

Bell, Tom (1932-). TV: *The Virginian*—"Johnny Moon" 10-11-67 (Johnny Moon).

Bellamy, Anne. Films: "Westworld" 1973 (Middle-Aged Woman). ¶TV: *Wyatt Earp*—"Old Slanders Never Die" 1-31-61.

Bellamy, Madge (1903-1/24/90). Films: "Blind Hearts" 1921 (Julia Larson); "The Call of the North" 1921 (Virginia Albret); "Do It Now" 1924; "The Iron Horse" 1924 (Miriam Marsh); "The Golden Strain" 1925 (Dixie Denniston); "The Reckless Sex" 1925 (Mary Hamilton); "Gordon of Ghost City" 1933-serial (Mary Gray); "Wild Brian Kent" 1936 (Brian Kent); "Northwest Trail" 1945.

Bellamy, Ned. Films: "Gunsmoke: The Last Apache" TVM-1994 (Captain Harris). ¶TV: *Father Murphy*—"The Robber" 12-14-82 (Floyd).

Bellamy, Patsy. Films: "Lightning Range" 1934 (Dorothy Horton).

Bellamy, Ralph (1904-11/29/91). Films: "Men of Texas" 1942 (Major Lamphere); "The Professionals" 1966 (J.W. Grant); "Charlie Cobb: Nice Night for a Hanging" TVM-1977 (McVea); "Testimony of Two Men" TVM-1977 (Dr. Jim Spaulding). ¶TV: *Zane Grey Theater*—"Stars Over Texas" 12-28-56 (Joel Todd); *Rawhide*—"Judgment at Hondo Seco" 10-20-61 (Judge Quince), "The Pursuit" 11-9-65 (Dickson); *Death Valley Days*—"The Vintage Years" 1-30-63 (Daniel Quint); *Gunsmoke*—"Rope Fever" 12-4-67 (Sheriff Bassett); *The Virginian*—"The Saddle Warmer" 9-18-68 (Jeremiah).

Bellaver, Harry (1905-8/8/93). Films: "Stage to Tucson" 1950 (Gus Heyden). ¶TV: *Trackdown*—"The Trail" 2-28-58 (Michael Doyle); *Wanted—Dead or Alive*—"Bad Gun" 10-24-59 (Curly Bill); *Man from Blackhawk*—"Death at Noon" 1-8-60 (Jonah); *Sugarfoot*—"Fernando" 2-16-60 (Corky McCoy); *Annie Get Your Gun* 3-19-67 (Sitting Bull); *Daniel Boone*—"A Matter of Blood" 12-28-67 (Teduskan).

Bellflower, Nellie. TV: *Gunsmoke*—"Cowtown Hustler" 3-11-74 (Sally).

Bellin, Thomas. Films: "The Young Country" TVM-1970 ¶TV: *The Virginian*—"Siege" 12-18-63 (Sam Oliver), "Two Men Named Laredo" 1-6-65 (Clint); *Alias Smith and Jones*—"Jailbreak at Junction City" 9-30-71.

Bellinger, Roberta. Films: "West of the Rio Grande" 1921 (Mrs. Nawn).

Bellini, Cal. Films: "Little Big Man" 1971 (Younger Bear); "Little House on the Prairie" TVM-1974 (Brave); "Law of the Land" TVM-1976 (Tom Condor); "Scott Free" TVM-1976 (Little Lion); "Go West, Young Girl" TVM-1978 (Chato); "The Mountain Men" 1980 (Cross Otter). ¶TV: *The Cowboys*—"The Indian Givers" 5-1-74 (Wa-Cha-Ka); *Kung Fu*—"The Predators" 10-5-74 (Hoskay); *Young Dan'l Boone*—"The Salt Licks" 9-26-77 (Red Eagle); *Big Hawaii*—"Sun Children" 9-28-77 (Joe Minho).

Bellis, Dick. Films: "Shoot-Out at Medicine Bend" 1957. ¶TV: *Cheyenne*—"The Long Rope" 10-3-60 (Young Cheyenne).

Bellwood, Pamela (1951-). Films: "The Wild Women of Chastity Gulch" TVM-1982 (Sarah) ¶TV: *Big Hawaii*—"Sarah" 11-23-77.

Belmar, Henry (1849-1/12/31). Films: "The Desert Man" 1917 (Razor Joe).

Belmont, Joseph "Baldy" (1875-5/16/39). Films: "Prowlers of the Night" 1926 (Sheriff Brandon); "Trailin' West" 1936 (Old Man).

Belmont, Virginia. Films: "Girl Rush" 1944 (Troupe Member); "Nevada" 1944; "Prairie Express" 1947 (Peggy Porter); "Courtin' Trouble" 1948 (Carol); "Dangers of the Canadian Mounted" 1948-serial (Bobbie Page); "Oklahoma Blues" 1948 (Judy); "Overland Trails" 1948; "The Rangers Ride" 1948; "Silent Conflict" 1948 (Rene Reichards).

Belmore, Cy. Films: "Double Action Daniels" 1925 (the Kid).

Belmore, Harry (1882-9/8/36). Films: "The Web of the Law" 1923 (Buck Barbee); "Payable on Demand" 1924 (Martin Selby); "Double Action Daniels" 1925 (the Hotel Keeper); "Tearin' Loose" 1925 (Stubb Green); "Triple Action" 1925 (Pancho); "Speedy Spurs" 1926 (Doctor); "Twisted Triggers" 1926 (Cook); "Pals in Peril" 1927 (Hank Bassett).

Belmore, Lionel (1868-1/30/53). Films: "West Wind" 1915; "Sting of the Lash" 1921 (Ben Ames); "The Galloping Kid" 1922 (Five-Notch Arnett); "Iron to Gold" 1922 (Sheriff); "Out of the Silent North" 1922; "Quicksands" 1923 (Ring Member); "Winners of the Wilderness" 1927 (Governor Dinwiddie); "The Yellowback" 1929 (McDougal); "The Last of the Mohicans" 1936 (Patroon); "The Red Rope" 1937.

Beltran, Alma. Films: "Jubilee Trail" 1954 (Servant Girl); "Dragoon Wells Massacre" 1957 (Station Agent's Wife); "The Deerslayer" TVM-1978; "El Diablo" TVM-1990 (Old Woman). ¶TV: *Wild Bill Hickok*—"Missing Diamonds" 3-17-53; *Colt .45*—"One Good Turn" 11-29-57 (Maria Valdez); *Bonanza*—"El Toro Grande" 1-2-60 (Maria Teresa); *The Tall Man*—"Sidekick" 12-23-61 (Maria); *Lancer*—"Warburton's Edge" 2-4-69 (Cantina Owner); *Gunsmoke*—"Manolo" 3-17-75 (Engrace).

Beltran, Ray (1892-10/17/67). Films: "The Cowboy and the Indians" 1949; "Flaming Star" 1960 (Indian).

Beltran, Robert. Films: "The Mystic Warrior" TVM-1984 (Ahbleza the Adult); "El Diablo" CTVM-1990 (El Diablo).

Belushi, John (1949-3/5/82). Films: "Goin' South" 1978 (Hector).

Benaderet, Bea (1906-10/13/68). Films: "Plunderers of Painted Flats" 1959 (Ella). ¶TV: *The Restless Gun*—"Mme. Brimstone" 5-4-59 (Mme. Brimstone).

Bender, Russ (1910-8/16/69). Films: "Badlands of Montana" 1957 (George); "No Name on the Bullet" 1959; "Walk Tall" 1960 (Col. Stanton); "The Purple Hills" 1961 (Deputy Sheriff). ¶TV: *Wyatt Earp*—"Young Guns" 3-26-57 (Hanford Craig), "Plague Carrier" 12-9-58 (Lem Evans); *Jim Bowie*—"The Pearl and the Crown" 4-5-57 (Capt. Gunderson); *Broken Arrow*—"The Assassin" 4-23-57 (Marshal), "Bad Boy" 1-21-58 (Marshal); *Trackdown*—"The Reward" 1-3-58 (Sheriff John Kemp); *Maverick*—"Trail West to Fury" 2-16-58 (Doctor); *Telephone Time*—"Trail Blazer" 4-1-58 (Matt Heller); *Wanted—Dead or Alive*—"Shawnee Bill" 10-4-58, "Die by the Gun" 12-6-58 (Sam), "Journey for Josh" 10-5-60; *Rough Riders*—"The Governor" 11-6-58 (Col. Rayford); *Rawhide*—"Incicdent of a Burst of Evil" 6-26-59, "Incident of the Captive" 12-16-60, "The Little Fishes" 11-24-61 (Gilmore); *Cheyenne*—"Prisoner of Moon Mesa" 11-16-59; *Hotel De Paree*—"Sundance and the Black Widow" 4-1-60 (Willie), "Sundance and the Good-Luck Coat" 5-6-60 (Willie); *The Tall Man*—"The Lonely Star" 10-8-60 (Townsman); *Have Gun Will Travel*—"The Siege" 4-1-61 (Doctor); *The Virginian*—"The Devil's Children" 12-5-62; *Laramie*—"The Wedding Party" 1-29-63 (Red Wheeler); *Bonanza*—"Calamity Over the Comstock" 11-3-63 (Walt), "Enter Thomas Bowers" 4-26-64, "Logan's Treasure" 10-18-64, "The Running Man" 3-30-69 (Garvey); *Gunsmoke*—"Gold Mine" 12-25-65 (Sheriff).*Cimarron Strip*—"Whitey" 10-19-67; *The Big Valley*—"Top of the Stairs" 1-6-69.

Bendix, William (1906-12/14/64). Films: "Streets of Laredo" 1949 (Wahoo Jones); "Law of the Lawless" 1964 (Sheriff Ed Tanner); "Young Fury" 1965 (Blacksmith). ¶TV: *Wagon Train*—"Around the Horn" 10-1-58 (Captain Cobb); *Riverboat*—"The Barrier" 9-20-59 (Vance Muldoon); *Overland Trail*—Regular 1960 (Fred Kelly).

Bendixsen, Mia (1964-). TV: *Gunsmoke*—"The Convict" 2-1-71 (Penny Wilson).

Benedict, Billy (1906-). TV: *Maverick*—"A Rage for Vengeance" 1-12-58 (Denver Porter).

Benedict, Brooks (-1/1/68). Films: "Ranson's Folly" 1926 (Lt. Curtis); "The Cowboy Kid" 1928 (Trig Morgan); "Gun Smoke" 1931 (Spot Skee); "Zorro Rides Again" 1937-serial (Starcroft); "Out California Way" 1946 (Cameraman).

Benedict, Greg. TV: *Maverick*—"Marshal Maverick" 3-11-62 (Keno), "One of Our Trains Is Missing" 4-22-

62 (Tim Hardesty); *Lawman*—"Sunday" 4-15-62 (Jim Young).

Benedict, Kingsley (1878-11/27/51). Films: "Judge Not, or the Woman of Mona Diggings" 1915 (Clarence Van Dyne); "Lone Larry" 1917; "Number 10, Westbound" 1917; "The Plow Woman" 1917 (Surgeon Fraser); "The Human Target" 1918; "The Stampede" 1921 (Beauty Anders); "Riders of the Plains" 1924-serial; "White Thunder" 1925 (Reverend Norris).

Benedict, Paul (1938-). Films: "Jeremiah Johnson" 1972 (Reverend).

Benedict, Richard (1916-5/25/84). Films: "The Arizona Ranger" 1948 (Gil). ¶TV: *Jim Bowie*—"Jim Bowie and His Slave" 11-30-56 (Policeman); *Circus Boy*—"Death Defying Donzetti" 5-12-57 (Donzetti); *Tales of the Texas Rangers*—"Gypsy Boy" 11-24-57 (Dave Brock), "Midway Kewpie" 10-16-58; *Wyatt Earp*—"Loyalty" 2-7-61 (Briscoe).

Benedict, Steve. Films: "The Cowboys" 1972 (Steve). ¶TV: *Bonanza*—"First Love" 12-26-72 (Henry).

Benedict, Val. Films: "The Wild and the Innocent" 1959 (Richie). ¶TV: *Zane Grey Theater*—"Man Unforgiving" 1-3-58 (Clint); *Gunsmoke*—"Laughing Gass" 3-29-58 (Cloud Marsh); *Maverick*—"Shady Deal at Sunny Acres" 11-23-58 (Cowhand); *Man Without a Gun*—"The Gun from Boot Hill" 3-28-59.

Benedict, William "Billy" (1917-). Films: "Ramona" 1936 (Joe Hyar); "Timber Stampede" 1939 (Tiny Tim); "Adventures of Red Ryder" 1940-serial (Dan Withers); "Legion of the Lawless" 1940 (Edwin); "Melody Ranch" 1940 (Slim); "My Little Chickadee" 1940 (Lem the Schoolboy); "Prairie Law" 1940; "Stage to Chino" 1940; "In Old Cheyenne" 1941 (Vendor); "Jesse James at Bay" 1941; "Home in Wyomin'" 1942; "Valley of Hunted Men" 1942; "The Ox-Bow Incident" 1943 (Greene); "Bowery Buckaroos" 1947 (Whitey); "Riders of the Pony Express" 1949; "The Hallelujah Trail" 1965 (Simpson); "Bonanza: The Next Generation" TVM-1988. ¶TV: *Wild Bill Hickok*—"Sheriff of Buckeye" 6-30-53; *Tales of Wells Fargo*—"End of the Trail" 10-20-58 (Pringle); *The Rifleman*—"Smoke Screen" 4-5-60; *Branded*—"Cowards Die Many Times" 4-17-66 (Hogan); *Gunsmoke*—"Old Friend" 2-4-67 (Gus); *Hondo*—"Hondo and the Apache Kid" 10-13-67 (Willie), "Hondo and the Mad Dog" 10-27-67 (Willie),

"Hondo and the Sudden Town" 11-17-67 (Willie); *The Guns of Will Sonnett*—"Chapter and Verse" 10-11-68; *Alias Smith and Jones*—"Dreadful Sorry, Clementine" 11-18-71.

Benet, Brenda (1945-4/7/82). TV: *Daniel Boone*—"The Matchmaker" 10-27-66 (Princess Little Fawn); *Iron Horse*—"Banner with a Strange Device" 2-6-67 (Kitty Clayborne); *The High Chaparral*—"The Lion Sleeps" 3-28-69 (Anita); *Death Valley Days*—"The King of Uvalde Road" 4-25-70 (Chela); *The Men from Shiloh*—"The Town Killer" 3-10-71 (Susan Masters); *Father Murphy*—"The Adoption" 2-23-82.

Benge, Wilson (1875-7/1/55). Films: "A Gentleman Preferred" 1928 (Dobbs).

Bengell, Norma. Films: "The Hellbenders" 1966-U.S./Ital./Span. (Claire); "I Do Not Forgive ... I Kill!" 1968-Span./Ital. (Lucy).

Benham, Elsa. Films: "Rough Ridin'" 1924 (Mary Ross); "Fighting with Buffalo Bill" 1926-serial; "The Iron Rider" 1926 (Anita Nelson Parsons); "Code of the Cow Country" 1927 (Helen Calhoun); "The Menace of the Mounted" 1927; "The Two Fister" 1927; "Western Courage" 1927.

Benjamin, Paul (1938-). Films: "Deadly Trackers" 1973 (Jacob); "Friendly Persuasion" TVM-1975 (Swan Stebeney).

Benjamin, Richard (1938-). Films: "The Stranger Wore a Gun" 1953; "Thunder Over the Plains" 1953 (Sgt. Shaw); "Riding Shotgun" 1954 (Blackie); "Westworld" 1973 (Peter Martin).

Bennett, Alma (1904-9/16/58). Films: "Thieves' Clothes" 1920; "Flaming Hearts" 1922; "Smiling Jim" 1922 (Louise Briggs); "Without Compromise" 1922 (Nora Foster); "The Grail" 1923 (Susie Trammel); "Man's Size" 1923 (Jessie McRae); "Three Jumps Ahead" 1923 (Annie Darrell); "The Light of Western Stars" 1925 (Bonita).

Bennett, Barbara (1906-8/8/58). Films: "Black Jack" 1927 (Nancy Blake).

Bennett, Belle (1891-11/4/32). Films: "A Ticket to Red Horse Gulch" 1914; "A Deal in Indians" 1915; "Ashes of Hope" 1917 (Gonda); "The Bond of Fear" 1917; "The Devil Dodger" 1917.

Bennett, Billie (1874-5/19/51). Films: "Fighting Cressy" 1920 (Mrs. Dabney); "Crossing Trails" 1921 (Mrs. Warren); "Blood Test" 1923;

"Call of the Mate" 1924; "Crossed Trail" 1924 (Alice Dawson); "The Fighting Smile" 1925; "Galloping Jinx" 1925 (Aunt Martha); "The Wyoming Wildcat" 1925 (Blendy Betts); "The Sonora Kid" 1927 (Aunt Marie).

Bennett, Bruce (1906-). Films: "Land of Fighting Men" 1938 (Fred Mitchell); "The Lone Ranger" 1938-serial (Bert Rogers); "Blazing Six Shooters" 1940 (Winthrop); "West of Abilene" 1940 (Frank Garfield); "Frontier Fury" 1943 (Clem Hawkins); "Cheyenne" 1947 (Ed Landers); "Silver River" 1948 (Stanley Moore); "The Treasure of the Sierra Madre" 1948 (Cody); "The Younger Brothers" 1949 (Jim Younger); "The Great Missouri Raid" 1951 (Cole Younger); "The Last Outpost" 1951 (Jeb Britten); "Robbers' Roost" 1955 (Herrick); "Hidden Guns" 1956 (Stragg); "Love Me Tender" 1956 (Maj. Kincaid); "The Three Outlaws" 1956; "Three Violent People" 1956 (Harrison); "Daniel Boone, Trail Blazer" 1957 (Daniel Boone); "Flaming Frontier" 1958-Can. (Capt. Jim Hewson). ¶TV: *Fireside Theater*—"Man of the Comstock" 11-3-53 (Bill Stewart); *Stories of the Century*—"Quantrill and His Raiders" 4-22-55; *Tales of Wells Fargo*—"Scapegoat" 5-5-58 (Clyde Bender); *The Texan*—"The Man with the Solid Gold Star" 10-6-58 (Jim Caldwell); *Laramie*—"Hour After Dawn" 3-15-60 (Con Creighton); *Branded*—"I Killed Jason McCord" 10-3-65 (Archie Fletcher); *The Virginian*—"Yesterday's Timepiece" 1-18-67 (Silas Graham), "The Gauntlet" 2-8-67.

Bennett, Catherine (1901-10/11/78). Films: "The Devil's Bowl" 1923 (Helen Hand); "The Wild Bull's Lair" 1925 (Eleanor Harbison).

Bennett, Charles (1891-2/15/43). Films: "The Outlaw" 1913; "Rosalind at Red Gate" 1919.

Bennett, Constance (1905-7/24/65). Films: "Code of the West" 1925 (Georgie May Stockwell); "Sin Town" 1942 (Kye Allen); "Wild Bill Hickok Rides" 1942 (Belle Andrews).

Bennett, Edna (1900-6/9/76). Films: "Cowboy Commandos" 1943 (Katie).

Bennett, Enid (1893-5/14/69). Films: "A Desert Wooing" 1918 (Avice Bereton); "Partners Three" 1919 (Agnes Cuyler); "The Bad Man" 1923 (Mrs. Morgan Pell).

Bennett, Fran. Films: "The Far Horizons" 1955; "Giant" 1956 (Judy Benedict). ¶TV: *Colt .45*—"Rebellion" 12-20-57 (Laura Killian).

Bennett, Frank (1891-4/29/57). Films: "The Last Card" 1915.

Bennett, Gertrude. Films: "Call of the West" 1930 (Kit); "The Westerner" 1940 (Abigail).

Bennett, Helen. Films: "Royal Mounted Rides Again" 1945-serial (Madame Mysterioso).

Bennett, Joan (1910-12/7/90). Films: "The Texans" 1938 (Ivy Preston).

Bennett, Joe (1889-8/31/67). Films: "Faith Endurin'" 1918 (Vic Dryer); "The Feud" 1919 (Cal Brown); "The Gamesters" 1920 (Harvey Blythe); "The Terror" 1920 (Phil Harland); "The Night Horsemen" 1921 (Dr. Byrne); "The Breed of the Border" 1924 (Red Lucas); "Flashing Spurs" 1924 (Butch Frazier); "Trigger Finger" 1924 (Bob Murtison); "Cold Nerve" 1925; "Men of Daring" 1927 (David Owen); "Shooting Straight" 1927 (Tom Hale); "Somewhere in Sonora" 1927 (Bart Leadley); "Straight Shootin'" 1927 (Tom Hale); "The Valley of Hell" 1927 (Anita Garvin); "Wolf's Trail" 1927 (Bert Farrel); "The Shepherd of the Hills" 1928 (Ollie); "The Lariat Kid" 1929 (Pecos Kid).

Bennett, Kathy. TV: *Maverick*—"The Money Machine" 4-8-62 (Jacqueline Sutton); *Cheyenne*—"Man Alone" 10-15-62 (Julie Burns).

Bennett, Lee (1911-10/10/54). Films: "Song of Old Wyoming" 1945 (Waco); "The Caravan Trail" 1946; "Colorado Serenade" 1946 (Mr. Timble); "Driftin' River" 1946 (Tucson Browne); "Stars Over Texas" 1946 (Waco-Bert); "Wild West" 1946 (Butler); "The Last Round-Up" 1947 (Goss); "Coroner Creek" 1948 (Tip Henry); "Prairie Outlaws" 1948; "The Tioga Kid" 1948 (Tucson); "The Daltons' Women" 1950; "The Dakota Kid" 1951 (Cole White); "Three Desperate Men" 1951 (Dick Patten).

Bennett, Leila. Films: "Sunset Pass" 1933 (Hetty Miller); "Wagon Wheels" 1934 (Hetty Masters).

Bennett, Linda. TV: *Zane Grey Theater*—"Miss Jenny" 1-7-60 (Cora); *Empire*—"The Earth Mover" 11-27-62 (Fay Saunders); *Bonanza*—"Lothario Larkin" 4-25-65 (Francine).

Bennett, Marjorie (1895-6/14/82). Films: "Silver River" 1948 (Large Woman); "Two Flags West" 1950 (Mrs. Simpkins); "Ricochet Romance" 1954 (Mrs. Harvey); "Lay That Rifle Down" 1955 (Mrs. Speckleton); "Shoot-Out at Medicine Bend" 1957; "A Thunder of Drums" 1961 (Mrs. Yates); "Four for Texas"

1964 (Miss Ermaline); "The Man from Galveston" 1964 (Mrs. Warren); "Billy the Kid vs. Dracula" 1966 (Mrs. Ann Bentley). ¶TV: *Wild Bill Hickok*—"Tax Collecting Story" 8-7-51; *Sergeant Preston of the Yukon*—"All Is Not Gold" 5-10-56 (Martha Brown); *Buckskin*—Regular 1958-59 (Mrs. Newcomb); *The Californians*—"One Ton of Peppercorns" 5-12-59 (Aunt Hatty); *Wagon Train*—"The Elizabeth McQueeney Story" 10-28-59, "The Melanie Craig Story" 2-17-64; *Maverick*—"Maverick and Juliet" 1-17-60 (Mrs. Montgomery); *Temple Houston*—"The Man from Galveston" 1963 (Mrs. Warren); *Rawhide*—"Incident of the Banker" 4-2-64 (Old Lady); *F Troop*—"Reunion for O'Rourke" 3-8-66 (Ella); *The Virginian*—"The Mustangers" 12-4-68 (Soapie).

Bennett, Mark. TV: *Death Valley Days*—"The Man Who'd Bet on Anything" 2-11-56 (Abe Curry); *Fury*—"Joey and the Stranger" 12-1-56 (Rocky).

Bennett, Mickey (1915-9/6/50). Films: "The Vanishing West" 1928-serial.

Bennett, Ralph (1878-3/29/59). Films: "Border Badmen" 1945 (Deputy Spencer).

Bennett, Raphael "Ray" (1895-12/18/57). Films: "Battle of Greed" 1934 (Bates); "The Devil's Saddle Legion" 1937 (Sheriff Gornman); "Drums of Destiny" 1937 (Jenkins); "Forlorn River" 1937 (Bill Hall); "Old Louisiana" 1937 (Flint); "Public Cowboy No. 1" 1937; "Raw Timber" 1937 (Jim Hanlon); "Texas Trail" 1937 (Brad); "The Lone Ranger" 1938-serial (Taggart); "The Old Barn Dancer" 1938 (Buck); "Prairie Moon" 1938 (Hartley); "Range War" 1939; "Texas Stampede" 1939 (Zack Avery); "Hidden Gold" 1940 (Fleming); "Knights of the Range" 1940 (Bill Heaver); "The Man from Tumbleweeds" 1940 (Powder Kilgore); "Texas Renegades" 1940 (Snipe); "Thundering Frontier" 1940 (Ed Filmore); "Doomed Caravan" 1941 (Pete Gregg); "Gauchos of El Dorado" 1941 (Monk); "The Medico of Painted Springs" 1941 (Ed Gordon); "A Missouri Outlaw" 1941; "The Return of Daniel Boone" 1941 (Lach Kilgrain); "Robbers of the Range" 1941 (Daggett); "Romance of the Rio Grande" 1941 (Carver); "Call of the Canyon" 1942; "Lawless Plainsmen" 1942 (Set McBride); "The Spoilers" 1942 (Clark); "Cattle Stampede" 1943 (Stone); "The Kansan" 1943 (Messenger); "The Renegade" 1943; "Cyclone Prairie Rangers" 1944; "Dead or Alive" 1944; "Death Rides the Plains" 1944 (Ben Dowdey); "The Drifter" 1944 (Simms); "Marshal of Gunsmoke" 1944 (Spike); "Raiders of the Border" 1944 (Harsh); "Trail to Gunsight" 1944 (Bert Nelson); "Flame of the West" 1945 (Rocky); "Gun Smoke" 1945; "The Navajo Trail" 1945; "Return of the Durango Kid" 1945; "Rustlers of the Badlands" 1945; "Galloping Thunder" 1946; "The Gay Cavalier" 1946; "Gun Town" 1946 (Nevada); "The Haunted Mine" 1946; "Under Arizona Skies" 1946; "Heaven Only Knows" 1947 (Freel); "Prairie Raiders" 1947; "Frontier Revenge" 1948 (Deuce Rago); "Northwest Stampede" 1948 (Barkis); "The Dalton Gang" 1949 (Gorman); "Red Canyon" 1949 (Pronto); "Rimfire" 1949 (Barney); "Fancy Pants" 1950 (Secret Service Man); "Winchester '73" 1950 (Charles Bender); "Apache Drums" 1951 (Mr. Keon); "The Thundering Trail" 1951 (Ed West); "The Black Lash" 1952 (Rago); "The Man from Black Hills" 1952 (Hugh Delaney); "Springfield Rifle" 1952 (Commissioner); "Untamed Frontier" 1952 (Sheriff Brogan); "Waco" 1952 (Bull Clark); "The Great Sioux Uprising" 1953 (Sgt. Manners); "Powder River" 1953 (Richards); "The Redhead from Wyoming" 1953 (Wade Burrows); "Giant" 1956 (Dr. Bornehohm). ¶TV: *The Lone Ranger*—"The Tenderfeet" 11-10-49, "Jim Tyler's Luck" 2-16-50, "The Star Witness" 8-17-50; *The Gene Autry Show*—"Head for Texas" 7-23-50, "Ghost Town Raiders" 10-6-51, "Silver Dollars" 10-20-51; *Wild Bill Hickok*—"Tax Collecting Story" 8-7-51; *The Cisco Kid*—"Robber Crow" 11-24-51, "Spanish Dagger" 1-5-52; *The Roy Rogers Show*—"Flying Bullets" 6-15-52, "Death Medicine" 9-7-52, "Violence in Paradise Valley" 11-2-55; *Gunsmoke*—"Greater Love" 12-1-56 (Hank).

Bennison, Louis (1884-6/9/29). Films: "Oh, Johnny!" 1918 (Johnny Burke); "High Pockets" 1919 (High Pockets Henderson); "Sandy Burke of the U-Bar-U" 1919 (Sandy Burke); "Speedy Meade" 1919 (Speedy Meade).

Benny, Jack (1894-12/26/74). Films: "Buck Benny Rides Again" 1940 (Jack Benny). ¶TV: *The Slowest Gun in the West* 7-29-63 (Chicken Farnsworth).

Benson, Carl. TV: *Have Gun Will Travel*—"The Teacher" 3-15-58 (Jackson Breck); *Wyatt Earp*—"China

Mary" 3-15-60 (Tuker); *The High Chaparral*—"It Takes a Smart Man" 10-23-70.

Benson, Clyde. Films: "The Girl Who Wouldn't Quit" 1918; "A Daughter of the Wolf" 1919 (M. Pomgret); "The Sheriff's Son" 1919 (Dan Meldrum).

Benson, Lucille (1922-2/17/84). Films: "Wanted: The Sundance Woman" TVM-1976 (Elsie). ¶TV: *Bonanza*—"Search in Limbo" 2-20-72 (Mrs. Melody); *How the West Was Won*—"Luke" 4-2-79.

Benson, Robby (1956-). Films: "Jory" 1972 (Jory).

Bentley, Bob (1895-4/19/58). Films: "Fool's Gold" 1946 (Barton).

Bentley, Irene (1904-11/23/65). Films: "Smoky" 1933 (Betty Jarvis); "Frontier Marshal" 1934 (Mary Reid).

Bentley, John (1916-). Films: "The Singer Not the Song" 1961-Brit. (Chief of Police).

Benton, Anne. Films: "Flaming Star" 1960 (Dorothy Howard). ¶TV: *The Law of the Plainsman*—"The Hostiles" 10-22-59 (Girl); *Bonanza*—"The Guilty" 2-25-62 (Caroline).

Benton, Curtis (1885-9/14/38). Films: "The Siren" 1917.

Benton, Dean. Films: "Cowboy Millionaire" 1935 (Clerk); "Thunder Mountain" 1935 (Steve Sloan).

Benton, Gene. TV: *Gunsmoke*—"The Cook" 12-17-60 (Waiter), "Reprisal" 3-10-62 (Green), "Chester's Indian" 5-12-62 (Waiter); *Rawhide*—"Incident Near the Promised Land" 2-3-61; *The Travels of Jaimie McPheeters*—"The Day of the Pawnees" 12-22-63 & 12-29-63 (Frisbee).

Benton, Steve (1897-8/4/76). Films: "Riders of the Whistling Pines" 1949.

Benton, Suzanne (1947-). TV: *The Virginian*—"A Bad Place to Die" 11-8-67 (Lila Standish); *Gunsmoke*—"The Sharecroppers" 3-31-75 (Av Marie Pugh).

Benussi, Femi (1948-). Films: "Death Walks in Laredo" 1966-Ital./Span.; "Born to Kill" 1967-Ital. (Lauri Waldman); "Duel in the Eclipse" 1967-Span.; "Time of Vultures" 1967-Ital.; "Rattler Kid" 1968-Ital./Span.; "Finders Killers" 1969-Ital.; "Quintana: Dead or Alive" 1969-Ital./Span. (Virginia); "Stranger and the Gunfighter" 1973-Ital./Span./Hong Kong.

Ben-Victor, Paul. Films: "Tombstone" 1993 (Florentino). ¶TV: *Ad-*

ventures of Brisco County, Jr.—"Wild Card" 4-8-94 (Joey).

Beradino, John (1918-). Films: "Seven Men from Now" 1956 (Clint); "Wild Heritage" 1958 (Arn). ¶TV: *Wild Bill Hickok*—"Golden Rainbow" 12-9-52; *The Cisco Kid*—"Extradition Papers" 9-12-53, "Son of a Gunman" 10-10-53, "Roundup" 4-17-54; *The Lone Ranger*—"The Sheriff of Smoke Tree" 9-20-56; *Annie Oakley*—"Annie Rides the Navajo Trail" 11-18-56 (Gorman); *Broken Arrow*—"Legacy of a Hero" 2-26-57 (Choleno), "Rebellion" 3-5-57 (Choleno), "Turncoat" 4-15-58 (Charro); *Colt .45*—"The Three Thousand Dollar Bullet" 11-1-57 (John Modoc); *Tombstone Territory*—"Shoot Out at Dark" 1-8-58 (Frank Leslie); *Jefferson Drum*—"Prison Hill" 12-4-58 (Johnny Cracker); *Cimarron City*—"A Respectable Girl" 12-6-58 (Sam Jethro); *Tales of Wells Fargo*—"The Counterfeiters" 12-8-58 (Kendall), "The Border Renegade" 1-2-61 (Virgil McCready); *Zane Grey Theater*—"Bury Me Dead" 12-11-58 (Garth Redfern); *Schlitz Playhouse of the Stars*—"A Tale of Wells Fargo" 12-14-58 (Harrigan); *Have Gun Will Travel*—"Juliet" 1-31-59 (Nelson Pike); *Northwest Passage*—"The Deserter" 2-27-59 (Steve Warner); *The Texan*—"The Marshal of Yellow Jacket" 3-2-59 (Duke Ellis), "Blue Norther" 10-12-59 (Sebe Bisbee); *Bronco*—"The Belles of Silver Flat" 3-24-59 (Turk Hansen); *Rough Riders*—"Hired Gun" 4-23-59 (Dane); *Maverick*—"Mano Nera" 10-23-60 (Giovanni Marchese); *Lawman*—"Dilemma" 10-30-60 (Walt Carmody).

Beranger, George (Andre de Beranger) (1893-3/8/73). Films: "The Good Bad Man" 1916 (Thomas Stuart); "The Half Breed" 1916 (Jack Brace); "Mixed Blood" 1916 (Carlos); "Tiger Rose" 1923 (Pierre); "Beauty and the Bad Man" 1925 (L.I.B. "Liberty" Bell); "Hollywood Roundup" 1938 (Hotel Clerk).

Berard, Roxane. TV: *Maverick*—"Game of Chance" 1-4-59 (Countess de Barot), "Royal Four-Flush" 9-20-59 (Liz Bancroft/Countess de la Fontaine), "The Resurrection of Joe November" 2-28-60 (Veronique De Lassignac), "Diamond Flush" 2-5-61 (Danielle de Lisle); *Colt .45*—"The Man Who Loved Lincoln" 5-3-59 (Adah Menken); *Zorro*—"The Fortune Teller" 6-18-59 (Lupita); *Have Gun Will Travel*—"Les Girls" 9-26-59 (Cecile), "The Fatalist" 9-10-60 (Rivka Shotness), "A Drop of Blood" 12-2-61 (Rivka Shotness); *The*

Deputy—"The Hidden Motive" 1-30-60 (Louise Spencer); *Johnny Ringo*—"The Raffertys" 3-3-60 (Emily Rafferty); *Rawhide*—"Incident of the Last Chance" 6-10-60 (Marcia Eaton); *Bronco*—"Moment of Doubt" 4-2-62 (Petra); *Tales of Wells Fargo*—"The Wayfarers" 5-19-62 (Ada Parker).

Berben, Iris. Films: "Companeros" 1970-Ital./Span./Ger. (Lola).

Bercutt, Sharon. Films: "Flaming Star" 1960 (Bird's Wing).

Beregi, Oscar (1876-10/18/65). Films: "The Flaming Forest" 1926 (Jules Lagarre).

Beregi, Jr., Oscar (1918-11/1/76). Films: "The Oregon Trail" 1959 (Ralph Clayman); "North to Alaska" 1960 (Captain). ¶TV: *Bat Masterson*—"The Disappearance of Bat Masterson" 3-10-60 (Herman the Great); *Have Gun Will Travel*—"An International Affair" 4-2-60 (Hengst), "Vernon Good" 12-31-60; *The Virginian*—"A Portrait of Marie Valonne" 11-6-63 (Robaire); *Wild Wild West*—"The Night of the Glowing Corpse" 10-29-65 (Dr. Jean Paul Ormont), "The Night of the Running Death" 12-15-67 (Col. Diebold), "The Night of the Cossacks" 3-21-69 (Petrusky); *Death Valley Days*—"A City Is Born" 1-29-66 (Dutch Yaeger), "The Day All Marriages Were Cancelled" 12-3-66 (Charles Meyer).

Berenger, Tom (1949-). Films: "Butch and Sundance: The Early Days" 1979 (Butch Cassidy); "Rustler's Rhapsody" 1985 (Tex O'Herlihan); "The Avenging Angel" TVM-1995 (Miles).

Beresford, Evelyn (1881-1/21/59). Films: "Buffalo Bill" 1944 (Queen Victoria); "Annie Get Your Gun" 1950 (Queen Victoria).

Bergen, Candice (1946-). Films: "Soldier Blue" 1970 (Cresta Marybelle Lee); "The Hunting Party" 1971-Brit./Ital./Span. (Melissa Ruger); "Bite the Bullet" 1975 (Miss Jones).

Bergen, Constance. Films: "Big Boy Rides Again" 1935 (Nancy Smiley); "Too Much Beef" 1936 (Ruth Brown); "High, Wide and Handsome" 1937 (Singer).

Bergen, Frances. TV: *Yancy Derringer*—Regular 1958-59 (Madame Francine).

Bergen, Polly (1930-). Films: "Warpath" 1951 (Molly Quade); "Arena" 1953 (Ruth Danvers); "Escape from Fort Bravo" 1953 (Alice Owens). ¶TV: *Wagon Train*—"The Kitty Allbright Story" 10-4-61 (Kitty Allbright).

Berger, Mel (1932-). TV: *Bonanza*—"The Flapjack Contest" 1-3-65 (Big Ed).

Berger, Senta (1941-). Films: "The Glory Guys" 1965 (Lou Woodward); "Major Dundee" 1965 (Teresa Santiago).

Berger, William (1928-93). Films: "Cisco" 1966-Ital. (Cisco); "Ringo's Big Night" 1966-Ital./Span. (Jack Balman); "Face to Face" 1967-Ital.; "Death Knows No Time" 1968-Span./Ital. (Sheriff Johnny Silver); "Sartana" 1968-Ital./Ger. (Lasky); "Today It's Me … Tomorrow You!" 1968-Ital.; "Man Who Cried for Revenge" 1969-Ital./Span.; "No Room to Die" 1969-Ital. (Everett Murdoch); "Sabata" 1969-Ital. (Banjo); "Sartana in the Valley of Death" 1970-Ital. (Lee Calloway); "They Call Him Cemetery" 1971-Ital./Span. (Duke); "Colt in the Hand of the Devil" 1972-Ital. (Butch Brown); "Fasthand" 1972-Ital./Span. (Macedo); "On the Third Day Arrive the Crow" 1972-Ital./Span. (the Crow); "Kung Fu Brothers in the Wild West" 1973-Ital./Hong Kong; "Son of Zorro" 1973-Ital./Span.; "Yankee Dudler" 1973-Ger./Span. (Doc Hollidan); "Keoma" 1975-Ital./Span.; "California" 1976-Ital./Span.; "Tex and the Lord of the Deep" 1985-Ital.; "Django Strikes Again" 1987-Ital./Span./Ger.

Bergerac, Jacques (1927-). Films: "Thunder in the Sun" 1959 (Pepe Dauphin). ¶TV: *Daniel Boone*—"The Desperate Raid" 11-16-67 (LeGrandce).

Bergere, Lee. Films: "Dream West" TVM-1986 (Papa Joe Nicolett). ¶TV: *The Alaskans*—"The Bride Wore Black" 4-10-60 (Jack Hawley); *Wanted—Dead or Alive*—"Surprise Witness" 11-2-60 (Carlos); *Bonanza*—"The Dowry" 4-29-62 (Ricardo Fernandez); *Wagon Train*—"The Mary Beckett Story" 5-9-62 (Alex Lamont); *Pistols 'n' Petticoats*—1-14-67 (Pirandello Lovelace); *Wild Wild West*—"The Night of the Colonel's Ghost" 3-10-67 (Col. Wayne Gibson); *Death Valley Days*—"By the Book" 5-4-68 (Culverwell).

Bergh, Jerry. Films: "Hittin' the Trail" 1937 (Jean Reed); "Mystery Range" 1937 (Jennifer Travis).

Bergman, Richard. Films: "Bonanza: The Next Generation" TVM-1988. ¶TV: *Father Murphy*—Regular 1981-82 (Father Parker).

Bergmann, Alan (1925-). TV: *Bonanza*—"Home from the Sea" 5-1-66 (Gilly Maples), "Mark of Guilt"

12-15-68 (Gort); *Wild Wild West*—"The Night of the Ready-Made Corpse" 11-25-66 (Claudio Antille/Murphy); *The Big Valley*—"Court Martial" 3-6-67 (Macklin); *The High Chaparral*—"A Hanging Offense" 11-12-67 (Major Anderson).

Berkeley, George (1921-2/1/92). Films: "The Law vs. Billy the Kid" 1954 (Tom O'Folliard). ¶TV: *The Adventures of Rin Tin Tin*—"The Lonesome Road" 6-4-55 (Bucky); *Daniel Boone*—"Be Thankful for the Fickleness of Women" 9-19-68.

Berkeley, Lynne. Films: "Songs and Saddles" 1938 (Carol Turner).

Berkeley, Xander. Films: "Straight to Hell" 1987-Brit. (Preacher). ¶TV: *Adventures of Brisco County, Jr.*—"Riverboat" 10-1-93 (Brett Bones).

Berkes, John (1895-7/5/51). Films: "Cowboy Serenade" 1942; "Canyon Passage" 1946 (Man in Hallway); "Station West" 1948 (Pianist); "Branded" 1951 (Tattoo). ¶TV: *The Lone Ranger*—"High Heels" 11-17-49.

Berle, Milton (1908-). Films: "Evil Roy Slade" TVM-1972 (Harry Fern). ¶TV: *F Troop*—"The Great Troop Robbery" 10-6-66 (Wise Owl); *The Big Valley*—"A Flock of Trouble" 9-25-67 (Josiah Freeman).

Berliner, George. Films: "The Lonesome Tail" 1930 (Crabb).

Berlinger, Warren (1937-). Films: "Wanted: The Sundance Woman" TVM-1976 (Sheriff). ¶TV: *Desilu Playhouse*—"The Hanging Judge" 12-4-59 (George); *Gunsmoke*—"Wonder" 12-18-67 (Ed Franklin); *Young Maverick*—"Clancy" 11-28-79 (Doyle).

Berman, Edward. Films: "The Broken Spur" 1921 (John Dexter).

Berman, Shelley (1926-). TV: *Rawhide*—"The Peddler" 1-19-62 (Mendel J. Sorkin).

Bermudez, Richard. TV: *Buckskin*—"The Greatest Man in History" 1-5-59 (Pancho Garces); *Have Gun Will Travel*—"The Exiles" 1-27-62 (Lupo).

Bernard, Arthur. TV: *Cimarron Strip*—"The Battleground" 9-28-67; *Lancer*—"Lifeline" 5-19-70.

Bernard, Barry (1924-6/24/88). TV: *Circus Boy*—"The Fortune Teller" 6-9-57 (Bumps).

Bernard, Butch. TV: *My Friend Flicka*—"A Good Deed" 10-21-55; *Wagon Train*—"The Rex Montana Story" 5-28-58 (Timmy).

Bernard, Crystal. TV: *Hot Prospects*—Pilot 7-31-89 (Lorelei); *Paradise*—"A Proper Stranger" 11-11-89 (Laura Clark).

Bernard, Dorothy (1890-12/14/55). Films: "Black Sheep" 1912; "The Female of the Species" 1912; "Goddess of Sagebrush Gulch" 1912 (the Sister); "A Tale of the Wilderness" 1912; "A Chance Deception" 1913; "The Sheriff's Baby" 1913; "The Stolen Treaty" 1913; "Fighting Blood" 1916 (Evie Colby).

Bernard, Harry (1878-11/4/40). Films: "Ruggles of Red Gap" 1935 (Bartender); "North of the Rio Grande" 1937; "Roll Along, Cowboy" 1937 (Shep); "Way Out West" 1937 (Man Eating at Bar); "Konga, the Wild Stallion" 1940 (Jury Foreman); "Out West with the Peppers" 1940 (Checker Player).

Bernard, Joseph (1923-). Films: "Wells Fargo" 1937 (Customer). TV: *The Big Valley*—"Rimfire" 2-19-68 (Kusack); *Here Come the Brides*—"The Eyes of London Bob" 11-28-69.

Bernard, Joseph E. (1880-10/18/58). Films: "Wild and Woolly" 1937; "Twenty Mule Team" 1940; "Thundering Hoofs" 1942 (Hank); "Raiders of San Joaquin" 1943 (Jim Blake); "Frontier Gal" 1945 (Dealer); "Pirates of Monterey" 1947 (Doctor); "The Sea of Grass" 1947 (Homesteader); "Silver River" 1948 (River Boat Captain).

Bernard, Ray. *see* Corrigan, Ray.

Bernard, Sam (1889-7/5/50). Films: "Tumbledown Ranch in Arizona" 1941 (Nick); "The Big Sombrero" 1949.

Bernard, Sue (1948-). Films: "Machismo—40 Graves for 40 Guns" 1970 (Julie).

Bernard, Tom. Films: "Yankee Fakir" 1947 (Tommy). ¶TV: *The Cisco Kid*—"Church in Town" 5-17-52.

Bernardi, Herschel (1923-5/9/86). Films: "The Man from Button Willow" 1965 (Voice). ¶TV: *Bonanza*—"The Smiler" 9-24-61 (Clarence Bolling).

Bernath, Shari Lee. Films: "The Fiend Who Walked the West" 1958 (Janie); "The Jayhawkers" 1959 (Marthe). ¶TV: *Tales of Wells Fargo*—"Treasure Coach" 10-14-61 (M'liss); *The Virginian*—"The Small Parade" 2-20-63.

Bernay, Lynn (1931-). TV: *Telephone Time*—"Trail Blazer" 4-1-58 (Mary); *Rough Riders*—"Gunpoint Persuasion" 4-30-59 (Margaret Tolen); *Wagon Train*—"The Elizabeth McQueeney Story" 10-28-59.

Bernoudy, Jane (1893-10/28/72). Films: "Lasca" 1913; "The Sheep Herder" 1914.

Berns, Wally (1929-). Films: "The Apple Dumpling Gang" 1975 (Cheating Charley).

Bernstein, Milton. Films: "The Last of the Fast Guns" 1958 (James Younger); "Ten Days to Tulara" 1958 (Teniente).

Berrell, George W. (1849-4/20/33). Films: "The Committee on Credentials" 1916; "Mountain Blood" 1916; "The Three Godfathers" 1916 (Tim Gibbons); "Double Suspicion" 1917; "The Golden Bullet" 1917; "The Man from Montana" 1917 (Dad Petzel); "Straight Shooting" 1917 (Sweetwater Sims); "Swede Hearts" 1917; "The Wrong Man" 1917; "As the Sun Went Down" 1919 (Piety Pete); "Hell Roarin' Reform" 1919 (Mr. Jenkins); "The U.P. Trail" 1920 (Slingerland); "The Fire Eater" 1921 (Dad McCarthy); "Tracks" 1922 (Phillip Carlson); "The Everlasting Whisper" 1925; "The Trail Rider" 1925 (Uncle Boley); "Black Jack" 1927 (Judge); "The Girl in the Garrett" 1927.

Berry, Eleanor. TV: *Death Valley Days*—"Alias James Stuart" 11-1-61 (Mrs. Stuart), "Coffin for a Coward" 2-6-63 (Ann Carter); *Bonanza*—"The Trouble with Amy" 1-25-70 (Mrs. Eads), "The Rattlesnake Brigade" 12-5-71 (Emily Fancher).

Berry, Ken (1933-). Films: "Guardian of the Wilderness" 1976 (Zachary Moore). ¶TV: *Rawhide*—"A Time for Waiting" 1-22-65; *F Troop*—Regular 1965-67 (Captain Wilton Parmenter), "Milton, the Kid" 12-1-66 (Kid Vicious); *The Life and Times of Grizzly Adams*—"The Fugitive" 2-23-77 (Will Boker).

Berryman, Michael (1948-). Films: "The Gambler, Part III—The Legend Continues" TVM-1987.

Bert, Margaret. Films: "Vengeance Valley" 1951 (Mrs. Calhoun). ¶TV: *The Roy Rogers Show*—"Outcasts of Paradise Valley" 1-9-55 (Hannah Salem).

Berte, Genevieve. Films: "The Galloping Devil" 1920 (Elsie Gray); "The Struggle" 1921 (Norma Day); "The Gold Grabbers" 1922; "So This Is Arizona" 1922 (Peggy Newton); "Trail's End" 1922 (Molly).

Berthier, Jack. Films: "Colorado Charlie" 1965-Ital./Span. (Sheriff Bill Danders); "Sheriff with the Gold" 1966-Ital./Span. (Sheriff Jeff Randall).

Berti, Aldo. Films: "Stranger in Sacramento" 1964-Ital.; "Django, A Bullet for You" 1966-Span./Ital.; "Go with God, Gringo" 1966-Ital./Span.; "Ramon the Mexican" 1966-Ital./Span.; "A Stranger in Town" 1966-U.S./Ital.; "Big Ripoff" 1967-Span./Ital.; "Born to Kill" 1967-Ital. (Dodge); "Blood at Sundown" 1967-Span./Ital.; "Once Upon a Time in the West" 1968-Ital.; "The Reward's Yours, the Man's Mine" 1970-Ital.; "Sartana in the Valley of Death" 1970-Ital.; "The Dirty Outlaws" 1971-Ital. (Jonat); "Hey Amigo! A Toast to Your Death!" 1971-Ital.; "Mallory Must Not Die" 1971-Ital. (Stone); "Death Played the Flute" 1972-Ital./Span.; "Gunmen and the Holy Ghost" 1973-Ital.

Berti, Dehl (1922-11/26/91). Films: "Apache Warrior" 1957 (Chikisin); "Seven Alone" 1974 (White Elk); "Scott Free" TVM-1976 (George Running Bear); "Last of the Mohicans" TVM-1977. ¶TV: *Wild Bill Hickok*—"Good Indian" 8-4-53; *Sergeant Preston of the Yukon*—"Dog Race" 12-8-55, "Justice at Goneaway Creek" 2-9-56 (Johnny Johnson); *Loretta Young Show*—"The Wise One" 3-26-56 (William); *The Adventures of Rin Tin Tin*—"The Indian Hater" 1-11-57 (Black Cloud), "The Warrior's Promise" 1-25-57 (Tolque), "O'Hara Gets Culture" 3-8-57, "Bitter Bounty" 3-14-58 (Palo), "The Secret Weapon" 4-11-58 (Katawa); *Jefferson Drum*—"$50 for a Dead Man" 11-13-58 (Cocopah Brave); *Tombstone Territory*—"Marked for Murder" 3-20-59 (Stu Regan); *Rough Riders*—"The Promise" 4-2-59 (Blackie); *The Texan*—"No Place to Stop" 4-27-59 (Jackson), "Johnny Tuvo" 5-30-60 (Mouse Murphy), 9-12-60 (Jim Teach); *Bat Masterson*—"No Funeral for Thorn" 10-22-59 (Tobe Pruitt), "The Fourth Man" 4-2-61 (Gant Barth); *Wyatt Earp*—"Wells Fargo Calling Marshal Earp" 12-29-59 (Joe); *Two Faces West*—"The Return" 10-24-60; *Gunsmoke*—"The Ditch" 10-27-62 (Waco); *Lancer*—"Cut the Wolf Loose" 11-4-69; *Bonanza*—"Shanklin" 2-13-72 (Ritter); *Born to the Wind* 1982 (One Feather); *Paradise*—Regular 1988-91 (John Taylor).

Berti, Marina (1928-). Films: "Hatred of God" 1967-Ital./Ger.; "The Stranger Returns" 1967-U.S./Ital./Ger./Span. (Ethel).

Berto, Juliet (1947-1/10/90). Films: "Guns" 1980-Fr. (Margot).

Bertram, Vedah (1892-8/27/12). Films: "The Bandit's Child" 1912; "Broncho Billy and the Indian Maid"

1912; "Broncho Billy and the School-marm's Kid" 1912; "Broncho Billy Outwitted" 1912; "Broncho Billy's Escapade" 1912; "Broncho Billy's Gratitude" 1912; "Broncho Billy's Last Hold-Up" 1912; "Broncho Billy's Pal" 1912; "The Deputy's Love Affair" 1912; "The Loafer's Mother" 1912; "A Moonshiner's Heart" 1912; "On the Cactus Trail" 1912; "The Ranch Girl's Mistake" 1912; "A Road Agent's Love" 1912; "The Smuggler's Daughter" 1912; "Under Mexican Skies" 1912; "Western Hearts" 1912; "A Wife of the Hills" 1912.

Bertram, William (1880-5/1/33). Films: "Big Rock's Last Stand" 1912; "Trapper Bill, King of the Scouts" 1912; "Truth or Fiction" 1915; "Bond of Blood" 1916; "The Long Chance" 1922 (Sam Singer); "The Smoking Trail" 1924; "Fangs of Fate" 1925 (Judge Harcourt); "Twisted Triggers" 1926 (Jim Regan); "Under Fire" 1926; "The Boss of Rustler's Roost" 1928 (Sheriff Drain); "Spurs" 1930 (Indian Joe); "God's Country and the Man" 1931; "Lightnin' Smith Returns" 1931 (Sheriff); "The Mystery Trooper" 1931-serial; "The Riding Kid" 1931 (Mark Perdue); "Trails of the Golden West" 1931.

Bertrand, Rafael. Films: "The Professionals" 1966 (Fierro).

Besch, Bibi (1942-). Films: "Peter Lundy and the Medicine Hat Stallion" TVM-1977 (Emily Lundy). ¶TV: *How the West Was Won*—"The Innocent" 2-12-79 (Cora Johnson); *Paradise*—"A Gathering of Guns" 2-17-90 (Maggie Atwater).

Besser, Joe (1907-3/1/88). Films: "Two-Gun Lady" 1956 (Doc M'Ginnis); "Plunderers of Painted Flats" 1959 (Andy Heather). ¶TV: *The Gene Autry Show*—"The Million Dollar Fiddle" 10-1-55.

Besserer, Eugenie (1868-5/28/34). Films: "The Cowboy's Adopted Child" 1911; "It Happened in the West" 1911; "One of Nature's Noblemen" 1911; "The Regeneration of the Apache Kid" 1911; "A Child of the Wilderness" 1912; "The End of the Romance" 1912 (Jezebel); "The Last of Her Tribe" 1912; "The Little Indian Martyr" 1912; "Opitsah" 1912; "Sergeant Byrne of the N.W.M.P." 1912; "Me an' Bill" 1914; "Twisted Trails" 1916; "Scarlet Days" 1919 (Rosie Nell); "To the Last Man" 1933 (Granny Spelvin).

Best, George. Films: "The Land Just Over Yonder" 1916 (F.W. McAlpin).

Best, James (1926-). Films:

"Comanche Territory" 1950 (Sam); "Kansas Raiders" 1950 (Cole Younger); "Apache Drums" 1951 (Bert Keon); "The Cimarron Kid" 1951 (Bitter Creek); "The Battle at Apache Pass" 1952 (Cpl. Hassett); "City of Badmen" 1953 (Gig); "Column South" 1953 (Primrose); "Seminole" 1953 (Cpl. Gerard); "They Rode West" 1954 (Lt. Finlay); "Seven Angry Men" 1955 (Jason); "Last of the Badmen" 1957 (Ted Hamilton); "Cole Younger, Gunfighter" 1958 (Kit); "The Left-Handed Gun" 1958 (Tom Folliard); "Cast a Long Shadow" 1959 (Sam Mullen); "Ride Lonesome" 1959 (Billy John); "The Quick Gun" 1964 (Scott Grant); "Black Spurs" 1965 (Sheriff Elkins); "Shenandoah" 1965 (Carter); "Firecreek" 1968 (Drew); "Run, Simon, Run" TVM-1970 (Henry Burroughs); "Winchester '73" 1950 (Crater). ¶TV: *The Gene Autry Show*—"The Hold-Up" 12-14-52, "The Hoodoo Canyon" 8-17-54 (Ray Saunders); *Death Valley Days*—"Million Dollar Wedding" 1-31-55, "The $275,000 Sack of Flour" 11-7-62 (Ruel Gridley), "Sixty-Seven Miles of Gold" 2-2-64 (Jimmy Burns), "Hero of Fort Halleck" 6-27-65 (Jim Campbell); *Frontier*—"The Texicans" 1-8-56 (Ben Reed), "Out from Taos" 6-24-56 (Jason Cartwright); *Buffalo Bill, Jr.*—"Death of Johnny Ringo" 5-19-56; *Zane Grey Theater*—"The Three Graves" 1-4-57 (Pyke Dillon); *West Point*—"Dragoon Patrol" 5-10-57; *Trackdown*—"Marple Brothers" 10-4-57, "The Mistake" 4-18-58 (Bob Ahler), "Sunday's Child" 11-21-58 (Joe Sunday); *Have Gun Will Travel*—"The Long Night" 11-16-57 (Cowhand), "A Quiet Night in Town" 1-7-61 & 1-14-61 (Roy Smith); *Tombstone Territory*—"Guilt of a Town" 3-19-58 (Mitt Porter); *The Restless Gun*—"Jebediah Bonner" 9-22-58 (Jim Kenyon); *Bat Masterson*—"Stampede at Tent City" 10-29-58 (Joe Best), "Dakota Showdown" 11-17-60 (Danny); *Wanted—Dead or Alive*—"Sheriff of Red Rock" 11-29-58 (Stoner), "Six-Up to Bannack" 1-10-59 (Luke Perry); *Black Saddle*—"Client: Nelson" 5-2-59 (Ben Travers); *Wagon Train*—"The Andrew Hale Story" 6-3-59 (Garth English), "The Colonel Harris Story" 1-13-60 (Bowman Lewis), "The Clayton Tucker Story" 2-10-60 (Art Bernard); *Laramie*—"The Lawbreakers" 10-20-59 (Dallas), "Company Man" 2-9-60 (Ben Leach), "The Runaway" 1-23-62 (Johnny Best); *Pony Express*—"The Story of Julesburg" 3-9-60 (Bart Gentry); *G.E. Theater*—"Aftermath" 4-17-

60 (Hardy Couter); *The Texan*—"Killer's Road" 4-25-60 (Clay Kilby); *Overland Trail*—"Escort Detail" 5-22-60 (Frank Cullen); *The Rebel*—"Night on a Rainbow" 5-29-60 (Ted Evans), "Deathwatch" 10-23-60 (Abel Waares); *Stagecoach West*—"High Lonesome" 10-4-60 (Les Hardee), "The Arsonist" 2-14-61 (Jack Craig), "The Dead Don't Cry" 5-2-61 (Mike Pardee); *Bonanza*—"The Fugitive" 2-4-61 (Carl), "The Legacy" 12-15-63 (Page), "The Price of Salt" 2-4-68 (Sheriff Shaler); *Whispering Smith*—"The Hemp Reeger Case" 7-17-61 (Hemp Reeger); *The Rifleman*—"The Day a Town Slept" 4-16-62 (Bob Barrett); *Bronco*—"Then the Mountains" 4-30-62 (Banton); *Cheyenne*—"Satonka" 10-1-62 (Ernie Riggins), Sweet Sam" 10-8-62; *Rawhide*—"Incident at Spider Rock" 1-18-63 (Willie Cain), "Incident of the Rawhiders" 11-14-63 (Brock Quade), "Incident at El Toro" 4-9-64 (Fuller); *The Virginian*—"Say Goodbye to All That" 1-23-63 (Hank), "Letter of the Law" 12-22-65 (Curt Westley); *Gunsmoke*—"With a Smile" 3-30-63 (Dal Creed), "The Glory and the Mud" 1-4-64 (Sam Beal), "Charlie Noon" 11-3-69 (Charlie Noon); *Temple Houston*—Regular 1963-64 (Bill Gotch); *Redigo*—"Little Angel Blue Eyes" 10-29-63 (Les Fay); *Destry*—"Go Away, Little Sheba" 3-27-64 (Curly Beamer); *Daniel Boone*—"The Devil's Four" 3-4-65 (Jethroe Wyatt); *Iron Horse*—"High Devil" 9-26-66 (Chico); *The Guns of Will Sonnett*—"Meeting at Devil's Fork" 10-27-67 (Rake Hanley), "Robber's Roost" 1-17-69 (Harley Bass); *Lancer*—"Goodbye, Lizzie" 4-28-70 (Clayt); *Centennial*—Regular 1978-79 (Hank Garvey); *How the West Was Won*—"Luke" 4-2-79 (Sheriff Gruner).

Best, Willie (1916-2/27/62). Films: "West of the Pecos" 1934 (Jonah); "Annie Oakley" 1935 (Cook); "The Arizonian" 1935; "Two in Revolt" 1936 (Eph); "Gold Is Where You Find It" 1938 (Helper); "Prairie Papas" 1938-short; "Lady from Cheyenne" 1941 (George); "West of the Rockies" 1941-short; "The Kansan" 1943 (Bones); "The Red Stallion" 1947 (Jackson); "South of Caliente" 1951 (Willie).

Bestar, Barbara. Films: "Navajo Trail Raiders" 1949 (Judy Clark); "Man with the Steel Whip" 1954-serial (Nancy Cooper). ¶TV: *Death Valley Days*—"Halfway Girl" 11-22-54; *Wyatt Earp*—"John Wesley Hardin" 11-1-55 (Mrs. Hardin), "Shoot to Kill" 10-8-57, "Wyatt Earp's Baby" 4-25-61 (Christine Trask).

Beswicke, Martine (1941-). Films: "A Bullet for the General" 1966-Ital. (Adelita); "John the Bastard" 1967-Ital. (Antonia).

Bethew, Herbert. Films: "A Son of the North" 1920; "Under Northern Lights" 1920 (Abner Lee); "The Cherokee Strip" 1926.

Bethune, Ivy. Films: "The Legend of Earl Durand" 1974. ¶TV: *Kung Fu*—"King of the Mountain" 10-14-72 (Jenny McCoy), "The Last Raid" 4-26-75 (Mrs. Wright); *Father Murphy*—Regular 1981-82 (Miss Tuttle).

Bethune, Zina (1945-). TV: *Lancer*—"Chad" 1-20-70 (Callie); *Gunsmoke*—"A Family of Killers" 1-14-74 (Jonnalee Simpson).

Bettger, Lyle (1915-). Films: "Denver and Rio Grande" 1952 (Johnny Buff); "The Great Sioux Uprising" 1953 (Stephen Cook); "The Vanquished" 1953 (Roger Hale); "Destry" 1954 (Decker); "Drums Across the River" 1954 (Frank Walker); "The Lone Ranger" 1956 (Reece Kilgore); "Showdown at Abilene" 1956 (Dave Mosely); "Gunfight at the O.K. Corral" 1957 (Ike Clanton); "Guns of the Timberland" 1960 (Clay Bell); "Town Tamer" 1965 (Lee Ring); "Johnny Reno" 1966 (Jess Yates); "Nevada Smith" 1966 (Jack Rudabaugh); "The Fastest Guitar Alive" 1967 (Charlie); "Return of the Gunfighter" TVM-1967 (Clay Sutton). ¶TV: *Tales of Wells Fargo*—"John Wesley Hardin" 9-30-57 (John Wesley Hardin), "The Gunfighter" 11-17-58 (John Wesley Hardin), "Mr. Mute" 11-4-61 (LaPorte); *Wagon Train*—"The Sally Potter Story" 4-9-58 (Joe Trumbull); *Zane Grey Theater*—"Threat of Violence" 5-23-58 (Sheriff Griff Evans), "The Law and the Gun" 6-4-59 (John Welker); *Texas John Slaughter*—"Killers from Kansas" 1-9-59 (Mr. Barko); *The Rifleman*—"The Wrong Man" 3-31-59 (Jay Jefferson), "Skull" 1-1-62 (Holt Coyle); *The Law of the Plainsman*—"Full Circle" 10-8-59 (Sheriff Max Chafee); *Laramie*—"Night of the Quiet Man" 12-22-59 (John McCambridge), "Rimrock" 3-21-61 (Sheriff Grant McClintock), "The Lawless Seven" 12-26-61 (Calvin Hawks), "The Turn of the Wheel" 4-3-62 (Frank Mannus), "Beyond Justice" 11-27-62 (Leland Emory); *The Deputy*—"The Deadly Breed" 9-24-60 (Aces Thompson); *Rawhide*—"Incident of the Challenge" 10-14-60 (Major Victor Darius), "The Blue Sky" 12-8-61 (Dan Madox), "Incident of the Dowry Dundee" 1-23-64

(Richard Whiting); *The Tall Man*—"Hard Justice" 3-25-61 (Vince Obey); *Bonanza*—"The Guilty" 2-25-62 (Lem Partridge), "Something Hurt, Something Wild" 9-11-66 (Jed Ferguson); *Death Valley Days*—"Graydon's Charge" 1-12-64 (Maj. Ben Roberts); *Gunsmoke*—"The Kite" 2-29-64 (Ed Polk); *A Man Called Shenandoah*—"A Long Way Home" 1-31-66 (Sheriff); *Daniel Boone*—"Delo Jones" 3-2-67 (Lehman Henderson), "A Tall Tale of Prater Beasely" 1-16-69 (Montgomery); *Cimarron Strip*—"The Deputy" 12-21-67 (Tate).

Betti, Laura (1934-). Films: "Man Called Sledge" 1971-Ital./U.S. (Sister).

Betts, Jane (-4/24/76). TV: *Wild Wild West*—"The Night of the Samurai" 10-13-67 (Madame Moustache).

Betz, Carl (1921-1/18/78). Films: "City of Badmen" 1953 (Phil Ryan); "Powder River" 1953 (Loney Hogan); "The Daughters of Joshua Cabe Return" TVM-1975 (Will). ¶TV: *Gunsmoke*—"Gone Straight" 2-9-57 (Nate Timble).

Betz, Mathew (1881-1/26/38). Films: "The Flame of the Yukon" 1926 (Black Jack Hovey); "The Shepherd of the Hills" 1928 (Wash Gibbs); "The Fighting Marshal" 1931 (Red Larkin); "Broadway to Cheyenne" 1932 (Joe Carter); "Gold" 1932; "The Western Code" 1932 (Warden); "Silent Men" 1933 (Carl Lawler); "Via Pony Express" 1933; "The Whirlwind" 1933 (Sheriff Tate Hurley); "Trails of the Wild" 1935 (Hunt); "The Law Commands" 1937 (Fargo).

Beutel, Jack. *see* Buetel, Jack.

Bevan, Billy (1887-11/26/57). Films: "God's Country and the Woman" 1937 (Plug Hat); "The Girl of the Golden West" 1938 (Nick); "Let Freedom Ring" 1939 (Cockney).

Bevans, Clem (1879-8/11/63). Films: "The Phantom Rider" 1936-serial; "Rhythm on the Range" 1936 (Gila Bend); "Dodge City" 1939 (Charlie, the Barber); "The Oklahoma Kid" 1939 (Postman); "Stand Up and Fight" 1939 (Bum); "Go West" 1940 (Official); "Twenty Mule Team" 1940 (Chuckawalla); "Wyoming" 1940 (Pa McKinley); "The Parson of Panamint" 1941 (Crabapple Jones); "Tombstone, the Town Too Tough to Die" 1942 (Tadpole); "The Kansan" 1943 (Bridge Tender); "The Woman of the Town" 1943 (Buffalo Burns); "Tall in the Saddle" 1944; "Yankee Fakir" 1947 (Shaggy Hartley); "Loaded Pistols" 1948 (Jim

Hedge); "The Paleface" 1948 (Hank Billings); "Relentless" 1948 (Dad); "Big Jack" 1949 (Saltlick Joe); "Deputy Marshal" 1949 (Doc Vinson); "Rim of the Canyon" 1949 (Loco John); "Streets of Laredo" 1949 (Pop Lint); "Gold Raiders" 1951 (Doc Mason); "Man in the Saddle" 1951 (Pay Lankershim); "Silver City Bonanza" 1951 (Townsman); "Captive of Billy the Kid" 1952 (Skeeter Davis); "Hangman's Knot" 1952 (Plunkett); "The Stranger Wore a Gun" 1953 (Jim Martin); "The Boy from Oklahoma" 1954 (Pop Pruty); "Cattle Queen of Montana" 1954 (Tom McCord); "The Kentuckian" 1955 (Pilot); "Ten Wanted Men" 1955 (Tod Grinnel); "The Twinkle in God's Eye" 1955; "Davy Crockett and the River Pirates" 1956 (Cap'n Cobb). ¶TV: *Walt Disney Presents*—"Davy Crockett"—Regular 1954-55 (Captain Cobb); *The Adventures of Rin Tin Tin*—"Higgins' Last Stand" 1-4-57 (Kid Hooker); *Gunsmoke*—"Overland Express" 5-31-58 (Fly); *Maverick*—"Two Beggars on Horseback" 1-18-59 (Old Man); *Wagon Train*—"The Annie Griffith Story" 2-25-59 (Old Man); *Bonanza*—"The Many Faces of Gideon Flinch" 11-5-61; *Frontier Circus*—"Journey from Hannibal" 11-16-61 (McPhee).

Bevil, Leake. TV: *Bat Masterson*—"Marked Deck" 3-11-59 (Bartender); *Maverick*—"A Tale of Three Cities" 10-18-59 (Pete); *Wanted—Dead or Alive*—"The Showdown" 10-26-60; *Rawhide*—"The Little Fishes" 11-24-61.

Bey, Turhan (1920-). Films: "Frisco Sal" 1945 (Dude).

Beyer, Charles (1895-11/28/53). Films: "The Man Who Paid" 1922 (Guy Thornton); "A Horseman of the Plains" 1928 (J. Rutherford Gates); "Red Riders of Canada" 1928 (Sgt. Brian Scott); "Romance of the Rio Grande" 1929 (Dick Rivers).

Beyers, Clara. Films: "Salomy Jane" 1914 (Mrs. Heath); "The Lily of Poverty Flat" 1915 (Dolores).

Beymer, Richard (1939-). TV: *Sky King*—"Man Hunt" 9-23-51 (Joe Beldon); *The Virginian*—"You Take the High Road" 2-17-65 (Mark Shannon), "Show Me a Hero" 11-17-65 (Frank Colter); *Death Valley Days*—"Bread on the Desert" 3-2-68 (Zeb).

Bianchi, Eleonara. Films: "One Hundred Thousand Dollars for Ringo" 1966-Ital./Span.; "If One Is Born a Swine" 1972-Ital./Span.

Bibber, Otto. Films: "The Ridin' Demon" 1929 (Sheriff).

Biberman, Abner (1909-6/20/77). Films: "King of the Mounties" 1942-serial (Admiral Yamata); "Salome, Where She Danced" 1945 (Dr. Ling); "Winchester '73" 1950 (Latigo Means); "Viva Zapata!" 1952 (Captain). ¶TV: *Hec Ramsey*—"Hangman's Wages" 10-29-72 (Nathan Shotness).

Bice, Robert (1913-1/8/68). Films: "Fighting Valley" 1943 (Paul Jackson); "The Red Stallion" 1947 (Ho-Na); "The Sea of Grass" 1947 (Cowboy); "Bandit King of Texas" 1949 (Gus); "Susanna Pass" 1949 (Bob Oliver); "Bells of Coronado" 1950 (Jim); "The James Brothers of Missouri" 1950-serial (Frank James/Bob Carroll); "Under Mexicali Stars" 1950 (Deputy); "Al Jennings of Oklahoma" 1951 (Pete Kincaid); "Gunplay" 1951 (Sam); "Cripple Creek" 1952 (James Sullivan); "Desert Pursuit" 1952; "Hiawatha" 1952 (Wabeek); "Horizons West" 1952 (Righteous Citizen); "Junction City" 1952 (Bleaker); "Night Stage to Galveston" 1952 (Capt. Yancey); "Bandits of the West" 1953 (Dutch Clyburn); "The Marksman" 1953; "The Moonlighter" 1953; "On Top of Old Smoky" 1953 (Kirby); "Star of Texas" 1953 (Al Slade); "The Far Country" 1955 (Miner); "The Gun That Won the West" 1955 (Chief Red Cloud); "The Violent Men" 1955; "Good Day for a Hanging" 1958 (Griswold); "Winchester '73" TVM-1967. ¶TV: *The Lone Ranger*—"Rifles and Renegades" 5-4-50, "Backtrail" 1-25-51, "Outlaw's Trail" 10-21-54; *The Cisco Kid*—"Phony Heiress" 7-21-51, "Ghost Story" 9-1-51, "Water Well Oil" 10-13-51, "The Runaway Kid" 6-21-52; *Wild Bill Hickok*—"The Border City Election" 9-18-51, "Border City" 11-13-51, "Ambush" 1-13-53; *The Gene Autry Show*—"Blazeaway" 2-22-52, "Six Gun Romeo" 3-16-52, "Dynamite" 12-24-55; *The Roy Rogers Show*—"The Brothers O'Dell" 11-20-55 (Hal O'Dell), "Three Masked Men" 12-18-55 (Ward Harris), "Ambush" 1-15-56, "Paleface Justice" 11-18-56, "Fighting Sire" 12-16-56, "Junior Outlaw" 2-10-67, "High Stakes" 2-24-57, "Accessory to Crime" 3-3-57 (Mr. Williams), "Johnny Rover" 6-9-57 (Grabbit); *Tales of the Texas Rangers*—"The Black Eyes of Texas" 12-31-55 (Matt Haney), "The Hobo" 1-28-56 (Morton Kelley); *The Adventures of Rin Tin Tin*—"Fort Adventure" 11-30-56 (Flaming Arrow); *Have Gun Will Travel*—"The Englishman" 12-7-57; *Sergeant Preston of the Yukon*—"Lost River Roundup" 12-12-57 (Traggart); *Tales of Wells Fargo*—"Laredo" 12-23-57 (Morley), "The Counterfeiters" 12-8-58 (Hank); *Tombstone Territory*—"Johnny Ringo's Last Ride" 2-19-58 (Judge Reese); *Fury*—"Black Gold" 2-28-59 (Bob Lacy); *The Texan*—"The Gunfighter" 6-8-59 (Sheriff Glen Cutler); *Wanted—Dead or Alive*—"Montana Kid" 9-5-59; *The Rifleman*—"The Coward" 12-22-59, "Deadly Image" 2-26-62 (Len Richards); *Wagon Train*—"The Ruth Marshall Story" 12-30-59, "Swamp Devil" 4-4-62 (Bear Claw); *Wichita Town*—"The Legend of Tom Horn" 3-30-60 (Bill Mace); *Rawhide*—"Incident of the New Start" 3-3-61, "Judgment at Hondo Seco" 10-20-61; *Gunslinger*—"Road of the Dead" 3-30-61 (Sheriff); *Wyatt Earp*—"Requiem for Old Man Clanton" 5-30-61 (J.B. Ayers); *Gunsmoke*—"Ash" 2-16-63 (Driver), "Legends Don't Sleep" 10-12-63 (Filler), "The Bassops" 2-22-64 (Wilson), "Scot-Free" 5-9-64; *Wild Wild West*—"The Night of the Howling Light" 12-17-65 (Captain); *Death Valley Days*—"Shanghai Kelly's Birthday Party" 10-7-67 (Longden).

Bickford, Charles (1891-11/9/67). Films: "Hell's Heroes" 1930 (Bob Sangster); "River's End" 1930 (John Keith/Sgt. Derry Conniston); "The Squaw Man" 1931 (Cash Hawkins); "The Plainsman" 1936 (John Latimer); "Rose of the Rancho" 1936 (Joe Kincaid); "High, Wide and Handsome" 1937 (Red Scanlon); "Thunder Trail" 1937 (Lee Tate); "Stand Up and Fight" 1939 (Arnold); "Queen of the Yukon" 1940 (Ace Rincon); "Riders of Death Valley" 1941-serial (Wolf Reade); "Duel in the Sun" 1946 (Sam Pierce); "Four Faces West" 1948 (Pat Garrett); "Branded" 1951 (Mr. Lavery); "The Last Posse" 1953 (Sampson Drune); "The Big Country" 1958 (Major Henry Terrill); "The Unforgiven" 1960 (Zeb Rawlins); "A Big Hand for the Little Lady" 1966 (Benson Tropp). ¶TV: *Wagon Train*—"The Daniel Barrister Story" 4-16-58 (Ralph Barrister); *The Virginian*—"The Devil's Children" 12-5-62 (Tucker McCallum), Regular 1966-67 (John Grainger).

Biehn, Michael (1957-). Films: "Tombstone" 1993 (Johnny Ringo).

Bien, Lorenz (Lawrence Bien). Films: "Requiem for a Bounty Hunter" 1970-Ital. (Sabata).

Bieri, Ramon (1929-). Films: "The Honkers" 1972 (Jack Ferguson); "True Grit" TVM-1978 (Sheriff); "The Frisco Kid" 1979 (Mr. Jones); "Bret Maverick" TVM-1981 (Mr. Crow). ¶TV: *Gunsmoke*—"Railroad" 11-25-68 (Forbes), "The Prisoner" 3-17-69 (Jarvis), "Phoenix" 9-20-71 (John Sontag), "Alias Festus Haggen" 3-6-72 (Doyle), "Spratt" 10-2-72 (Musgrove), "A Town in Chains" 9-16-74 (Big Thickett); *Lancer*—"A Person Unknown" 11-25-69 (Nevill); *Daniel Boone*—"A Matter of Vengeance" 2-26-70 (Hanker); *Bonanza*—"The Desperado" 2-7-71 (Solomon), "The Marriage of Theodora Duffy" 1-9-73 (Jonas Holt); *Alias Smith and Jones*—"The Fifth Victim" 3-25-71 (Sheriff Moody), "The Clementine Incident" 10-7-72 (Ted Thompson); *Nichols*—3-7-72 (Cutler); *Kung Fu*—"The Salamander" 12-6-73 (John Bates); *How the West Was Won*—"L'Affaire Riel" 3-5-79 (General Sheridan); *Bret Maverick*—Regular 1981-82 (Mr. Crow).

Big Moon. Films: "The Call of the Tribe" 1914; "Kidnapped by Indians" 1914; "The Navajo Blanket" 1914.

Big Tree, Chief John (1875-1/21/60). Films: "The Cactus Blossom" 1915; "The Iron Horse" 1924 (Cheyenne Chief); "The Red Rider" 1925 (Indian Chief); "The Desert's Toll" 1926 (Red Eagle); "The Frontier Trail" 1926 (Chief Gray Wolf); "Ranson's Folly" 1926 (Chief Standing Bear); "The Frontiersman" 1927 (Grey Eagle); "The Outlaw Breaker" 1927; "Painted Ponies" 1927; "Winners of the Wilderness" 1927 (Pontiac); "Spoilers of the West" 1928 (Red Cloud); "Wyoming" 1928 (Indian); "The Overland Telegraph" 1929 (Medicine Man); "Sioux Blood" 1929 (Crazy Wolf); "Fighting Caravans" 1931 (Indian at Opening Scene); "Red Fork Range" 1931 (Chief Barking Fox); "The Golden West" 1932; "The Last of the Mohicans" 1932-serial; "King of the Arena" 1933; "Wheels of Destiny" 1934; "The Singing Vagabond" 1935 (White Eagle); "Custer's Last Stand" 1936-serial (Medicine Man); "Hills of Old Wyoming" 1937 (Chief Big John Tree); "The Painted Stallion" 1937-serial (Indian Chief); "The Girl of the Golden West" 1938 (Indian Chief); "Destry Rides Again" 1939 (Indian); "Drums Along the Mohawk" 1939 (Blue Back); "Stagecoach" 1939 (Indian Scout); "Susannah of the Mounties" 1939 (Chief); "Brigham Young—Frontiersman" 1940 (Big Elk); "Hudson Bay" 1941 (Chief); "Western Union" 1941 (Chief Spotted Horse); "She Wore a Yellow Ribbon" 1949 (Pony That Walks); "The Devil's Doorway" 1950 (Thundercloud).

Bigelow, Susan. Films: "Wild and Wooly" TVM-1978 (Liz Hannah).

Bighead, Jack. Films: "Ten Who Dared" 1960 (Ashtishkel); "The Last Challenge" 1967. ¶TV: *The Alaskans*—"Heart of Gold" 5-1-60 (Joe); *Wagon Train*—"The Kitty Pryer Story" 11-18-63, "The Miss Mary Lee McIntosh Story" 2-28-65 (Stinking Bear); *Bonanza*—"Love Me Not" 3-1-64 (Chief), "The Far, Far Better Thing" 1-10-65, "Ride the Wind" 1-16-66 & 1-23-66 (Bear Dance); *Laredo*—"That's Noway, Thataway" 1-20-66.

Biheller, Bob. Films: "Young Fury" 1965 (Biff). ¶TV: *Gunsmoke*—"Doctor's Wife" 10-24-64 (Jared Boake); *Bonanza*—"Between Heaven and Earth" 11-15-64, "Napoleon's Children" 4-16-67 (Napoleon); *Here Come the Brides*—Regular 1968-70 (Corky); *Lancer*—"The Escape" 12-31-68 (Hardy).

Bikel, Theodore (1924-). Films: "Testimony of Two Men" TVM-1977 (Peter Heger). ¶TV: *Hotel De Paree*—"Sundance Returns" 10-2-59; *Wagon Train*—"The Dr. Denker Story" 1-31-62 (Dr. Denker); *Rawhide*—"Canliss" 10-30-64; *Gunsmoke*—"Song for Dying" 2-13-65 (Martin Kellums).

Bilbao, Fernando. Films: "Finger on the Trigger" 1965-Span./Ital./U.S. (Mayer); "Apocalypse Joe" 1970-Ital./Span.; "Fasthand" 1972-Ital./Span.

Bilbrook, Lydia (1888-1/4/90). Films: "Mexican Spitfire Out West" 1940 (Lada Ada Epping).

Bill, Jr., Buffalo (Jay Wilsey) (1896-10/25/61). Films: "A Streak of Luck" 1925 (Billy Burton); "Bringin' Home the Bacon" 1924; "Fast and Fearless" 1924 (Lightning Bill Lewis); "Hard Hittin' Hamilton" 1924 (Bill Hamilton); "Rarin' to Go" 1924 (Bill Dillon); "Thundering Romance" 1924 (Lightning Bill); "The Desert Demon" 1925 (Bill Davis); "Double Action Daniels" 1925 (Double Action Daniels); "Full Speed" 1925; "On the Go" 1925 (Bill Drake); "Quicker'n Lightnin'" 1925 (Quicker'n Lightnin'); "Saddle Cyclone" 1925 (Bill Demming); "Bad Man's Bluff" 1926 (Zane Castleton); "The Bonanza Buckaroo" 1926 (Bill Merritt); "Comin an' Going" 1926 (Bill Martin); "Deuce High" 1926 (Ted Crawford); "Rawhide" 1926 (Rawhide Rawlson); "Speedy Spurs" 1926 (Bill Clark); "Trumpin' Trouble" 1926 (Bill Lawson); "The Galloping Gobs" 1927 (Bill Corbitt); "The Interferin' Gent" 1927 (Bill Stannard); "The

Obligin' Buckaroo" 1927; "Pals in Peril" 1927 (Bill Gordon); "The Ridin' Rowdy" 1927 (Bill Gibson); "Roarin' Broncs" 1927 (Bill Morris); "The Ballyhoo Buster" 1928 (Bob Warner); "The Valley of Hunted Men" 1928 (Tom Mallory); "Bar L Ranch" 1930 (Bob Tyler); "Beyond the Rio Grande" 1930 (Bill); "The Cheyenne Kid" 1930; "South of Sonora" 1930 (Bill Tracy); "Way Out West" 1930 (Hank); "Westward Bound" 1930 (Bob Lansing); "Pueblo Terror" 1931 (William Sommers); "Trails of the Golden West" 1931; "Riders of the Golden Gulch" 1932 (Bill Edwards); "The Texan" 1932 (William Lloyd Rusk); "Deadwood Pass" 1933 (Deputy Sheriff); "Fighting Cowboy" 1933 (Bill Carson); "Terror Trail" 1933 (Prisoner); "The Lawless Frontier" 1934; "Lightning Bill" 1934 (Lightning Bill); "'Neath the Arizona Skies" 1934 (Jim Moore); "Pals of the Prairie" 1934-short; "Rawhide Romance" 1934 (Bill "Buck" Cartwright, Jr.); "Riding Speed" 1934 (Steve Funney); "Wheels of Destiny" 1934 (Buffalo Bill, Jr.); "Five Bad Men" 1935 (Bad Man); "The Phantom Empire" 1935-serial; "Powdersmoke Range" 1935 (Tex Malcolm); "Rainbow Valley" 1935 (Austin "Butch" Galt); "The Roaring West" 1935-serial; "Texas Terror" 1935 (Chief Black Eagle); "Trails of Adventure" 1935; "The Whirlwind Rider" 1935; "Avenging Waters" 1936 (Ranch Hand); "Heroes of the Range" 1936; "Forlorn River" 1937 (Pete Hunter); "Law of the Ranger" 1937; "Ranger Courage" 1937; "The Rangers Step In" 1937 (Ranger Captain Thomas); "Reckless Ranger" 1937; "Way Out West" 1937 (Man in Audience); "Blue Montana Skies" 1939; "Texas Stampede" 1939; "Pioneers of the Frontier" 1940 (Durango); "The Lone Rider Crosses the Rio" 1941 (Bart); "The Lone Rider in Ghost Town" 1941.

Bill, Cheyenne. Films: "West of Paradise" 1929; "Rainbow Range" 1929; "Thundering Thompson" 1929 (Thompson).

Bill, Montana. *see* Church, Frederick.

Bill, Jr., Pawnee. *see* Wells, Ted.

Bill, Tony (1940-). Films: "Flap" 1970 (Eleven Snowflake). ¶TV: *The Loner*—"An Echo of Bugles" 9-18-65 (Jody Merriman); *The Virginian*—"Chaff in the Wind" 1-26-66 (Clipper Ellis); *Bonanza*—"The Oath" 11-20-66 (Charlie Two); *The Road West*—"The Predators" 1-23-67 (Andy Wilkins).

Billings, Elmo (1913-2/6/64). Films: "Tumbling River" 1927 (Kit Mason).

Billings, Gail. TV: *Wild Wild West*—"The Night of the Doomsday Formula" 10-4-68 (Verna Scott), "The Night of the Janus" 2-15-69 (Myra Bates); *Bonanza*—"The Trouble with Amy" 1-25-70 (Mary Ann).

Billings, George (1870-4/15/34). Films: "Hands Up!" 1926 (Abraham Lincoln); "Gallant Defender" 1935 (Jimmy McGrail).

Billings, Ted (1880-7/5/47). Films: "North of the Rio Grande" 1937; "The Trigger Trio" 1937; "Stagecoach" 1939.

Billingsley, Barbara (1922-). Films: "The Valiant Hombre" 1948 (Linda Mason); "Inside Straight" 1951 (Miss Meadson).

Billingsley, Jennifer (1942-). TV: *Gunsmoke*—"My Sisters' Keeper" 11-2-63 (Leah Shuler); *Wagon Train*—"The Betsy Blee Smith Story" 3-28-65 (Eloise/Betsy Blee); *The Rounders*—9-6-66 (Bonnie); *Cimarron Strip*—"Knife in the Darkness" 1-25-68 (Josie).

Billington, Francelia (1895-11/24/34). Films: "Hearts and Hoofs" 1913; "The Pride of Angry Bear" 1913; "Snap Judgment" 1917 (Marah); "Desert Love" 1920 (Barbara Remington); "The Terror" 1920 (Phyllis Harland); "The Ranger and the Law" 1921 (Ann Hobbs); "Blazing Arrows" 1922 (Martha Randolph); "Blue Blazes" 1922 (Mary Lee); "Lone Hand Texas" 1924; "Tex" 1926; "A Rough Shod Fighter" 1928; "The Mounted Stranger" 1930 (Mrs. Coy).

Bilyeu, Chick. TV: *The Texan*—"The Sheriff of Boot Hill" 6-1-59 (Sam Elser), "The Dishonest Posse" 10-5-59 (Marshal).

Bindley, Sarah. Films: "The Heart of a Texan" 1922 (Ma Jackson); "West of the Pecos" 1922 (Mrs. Osborne).

Bindon, John (1943-). Films: "Man in the Wilderness" 1971-U.S./Span. (Coulter).

Bing, Herman (1889-1/9/47). Films: "Call of the Wild" 1935 (Sam); "Rose Marie" 1936 (Mr. Danielle).

Bingham, Joseph. Films: "Ranson's Folly" 1915 (Rev. John Spaulding).

Bingham, Stanley J. (1880-1/9/62). Films: "Three Word Brand" 1921 (George Barton); "When Romance Rides" 1922 (Dick Sears); "Call of the Mate" 1924.

Binney, Faire (1900-8/28/57).

Films: "The Girl from Porcupine" 1922 (Hope Dugan).

Binns, Edward (1916-12/4/90). Films: "Curse of the Undead" 1959 (Sheriff); "Heller in Pink Tights" 1960 (Sheriff McClain); "The Plainsman" 1966 (Lattimer); "Lovin' Molly" 1974 (Mr. Fry). ¶TV: *Gunsmoke*—"Jesse" 10-19-57 (Bill Stapp); *Zane Grey Theater*—"Wire" 1-31-58 (Abel McHugh), "The Atoner" 4-6-61 (Sam Tompkins); *The Rifleman*—"The Apprentice Sheriff" 12-9-58 (Thompson); *The Outlaws*—"Shorty" 11-3-60 (Sam Decker); *Wagon Train*—"The Earl Packer Story" 1-4-61 (Sheriff Bill Strode), "The Jud Steele Story" 5-2-62 (Jud Steele), "The Santiago Quesada Story" 3-30-64 (Major Starbuck); *The Deputy*—"The Lonely Road" 2-18-61 (Shad Billings); *Stoney Burke*—"Sidewinder" 11-12-62 (Joe Gullion); *The Dakotas*—"Return to Drydock" 1-7-63 (Arlie Gibbs); *Death Valley Days*—"Diamond Field Jack" 10-27-63 (James Hawley); *The Virginian*—"A Gallows for Sam Horn" 12-2-64 (John Briscoe), "Ring of Silence" 10-27-65 (McCormick), "Sue Ann" 1-11-67 (Pa MacRae); *Daniel Boone*—"Doll of Sorrow" 4-22-65 (Seth Jennings); *A Man Called Shenandoah*—"The Fort" 9-27-65 (Major Morrison); *The Loner*—"The Trial in Paradise" 1-22-66 (Manet); *Laredo*—"The Small Chance Ghost" 3-3-67 (Durgom); *Wild Wild West*—"The Night of the Pistoleros" 2-21-69 (Col. Roper); *Bonanza*—"It's a Small World" 1-4-70 (John Flint); *The Men from Shiloh*—"The Price of the Hanging" 11-11-70 (Dr. Kinkaid).

Birch, Paul (1912-5/24/69). Films: "Ride Clear of Diablo" 1953 (Sheriff Kenyon); "Cattle Queen of Montana" 1954 (Col. Carrington); "Silver Lode" 1954 (Reverend Field); "Apache Woman" 1955 (Sheriff); "Five Guns West" 1955 (J.C. Haggard); "Man Without a Star" 1955 (Mark Tolliver); "Fastest Gun Alive" 1956 (Sheriff Bill Toledo); "The White Squaw" 1956 (Thad Arnold); "Gun for a Coward" 1957 (Andy Niven); "Joe Dakota" 1957 (Frank Weaver); "Gunman's Walk" 1958 (Bob Selkirk); "Wild Heritage" 1958 (Jake Breslin); "Gunmen from Laredo" 1959 (Matt Crawford); "Two Rode Together" 1961 (Edward Purcell); "The Man Who Shot Liberty Valance" 1962 (Mayor Winder); "The Raiders" 1964 (Paul King); "Welcome to Hard Times" 1967 (Mr. Fee). ¶TV: *The Lone Ranger*—"Tumblerock Law" 2-26-53, "The School Story" 1-20-55; *The Adventures of Rin Tin Tin*—"Rin Tin Tin Meets Mister

President" 10-21-55; *Broken Arrow*—"Apache Dowry" 1-15-57 (Col. Scott); *Cheyenne*—"The Broken Pledge" 6-4-57; *Trackdown*—"Like Father" 11-1-57; *The Restless Gun*—"General Gilford's Widow" 11-11-57 (General), "The Torn Flag" 5-5-58 (Mayor Wheeler); *Gunsmoke*—"Never Pester Chester" 11-16-57 (Boss), "Coventry" 3-17-62 (Jessie Ott); *Sugarfoot*—"The Stallion Trail" 12-24-57 (Emmett Clark); *Have Gun Will Travel*—"The Hanging of Roy Carter" 10-4-58 (Warden Bullock), "The Chase" 4-11-59 (Sheriff Scanlon), "Marshal of Sweetwater" 11-24-62 (Jenkins); *Zane Grey Theater*—"The Lonely Gun" 10-22-59 (Sheriff), "A Gun for Willie" 10-6-60 (Sheriff); *Bonanza*—"The Diedeshiemer Story" 10-31-59 (Tregalis), "Gift of Water" 2-11-62 (Mr. Kent), "A Dublin Lad" 1-2-66 (Porter); *Riverboat*—"Face of Courage" 12-27-59 (Sergeant Major Carmody); *Wagon Train*—"The Lita Foladaire Story" 1-6-60, "The Colter Craven Story" 11-23-60 (Sam Grant), "Path of the Serpent" 2-8-61, "The Lonnie Fallon Story" 2-7-62 (Henry Weeker), "The Gus Morgan Story" 9-30-63 (Sam); *Black Saddle*—"Mr. Simpson" 1-22-60 (President Grant); *Death Valley Days*—"Hang 'Em High" 2-14-60 (Mike Walsh), "Sponge Full of Vinegar" 3-14-62 (Sheriff Lick), "The Red Ghost of Eagle Creek" 5-30-64 (Jim Davidson); *Walt Disney Presents*—"Elfego Baca: Gus Tomlin Is Dead" 3-25-60 (Sheriff Jim Wilson); *The Alaskans*—"Heart of Gold" 5-1-60 (Dan Byers); *The Texan*—"Twenty-Four Hours to Live" 9-5-60 (Sheriff Benson); *Two Faces West*—"The Avengers" 1-16-61; *Maverick*—"Last Stop: Olivion" 2-12-61 (Sheriff Miller); *Bronco*—"The Buckbrier Trail" 2-20-61 (Marshal Kilgore); *Laramie*—"Bitter Glory" 5-2-61 (Major Stanton), "Justice in a Hurry" 3-20-62; *The Tall Man*—"The Leopard's Spots" 11-11-61 (Conway); *Tales of Wells Fargo*—"Who Lives by the Gun" 3-24-62 (Sheriff Maxon); *Empire*—"Long Past, Long Remembered" 10-23-62 (Sam Fowler); *Wide Country*—"Don't Cry for Johnny Devlin" 1-24-63 (Grady); *Temple Houston*—"Jubilee" 11-14-63 (Matt Clendennon); *Great Adventure*—"The Pathfinder" 3-6-64 (Webster); *Destry*—"Go Away, Little Sheba" 3-27-64 (Sam Hannibal); *The Virginian*—"Big Image ... Little Man" 10-28-64 (Ben Carter), "Six Graves at Cripple Creek" 1-27-65 (John Carver), "Morgan Starr" 2-9-66 (Mack Lewis); *A Man Called Shenandoah*—"The Clown" 4-18-66 (Farrell).

Bird, Billie (1908-). Films: "Dallas" 1950 (School Teacher). ¶TV: *Gunsmoke*—"The Hanging of Newly O'Brien" 11-26-73 (Old Woman).

Bird, Violet. Films: "The Cyclone Cowboy" 1927 (Norma); "The Scrappin' Fool" 1927.

Birk, Raye. TV: *Adventures of Brisco County, Jr.*—"High Treason" 5-13-94 & 5-20-94 (Capt. Phipps).

Birman, Len (1932-). Films: "Draw" CTVM-1984 (Ephraim). ¶TV: *Cowboy in Africa*—"The Quiet Death" 2-19-68 (Dr. Lawson); *Young Dan'l Boone*—"The Trail Blazer" 9-12-77 (Duval).

Birney, David (1939-). Films: "Testimony of Two Men" TVM-1977 (Jonathan Ferrier).

Biro, Barney. TV: *Wagon Train*—"The Elizabeth McQueeney Story" 10-28-59 (Phil).

Bishop, Jenifer (1941-). Films: "The Female Bunch" 1971 (Grace); "Jessi's Girls" 1976 (Rachel).

Bishop, Joey (1918-). Films: "Sergents 3" 1962 (Sgt. Maj. Roger Boswell); "Texas Across the River" 1966 (Kronk).

Bishop, John G. Films: "Last of the Mohicans" TVM-1977; "California Gold Rush" TVM-1981. ¶TV: *The Life and Times of Grizzly Adams*—"Unwelcome Neighbor" 3-2-77 (Robbie Cartman), 10-12-77 (Robbie Cartman), 12-21-77 (Robbie Cartman), 3-22-78 (Robbie Cartman).

Bishop, Julie (Jacqueline Wells, Diane Duval) (1917-). Films: "Heroes of the West" 1932-serial (Ann Blaine); "Clancy of the Mounted" 1933-serial (Ann Louise); "Square Shooter" 1935 (Sally Wayne); "The Kansas Terrors" 1939 (Maria); "The Ranger and the Lady" 1940 (Jane Tabor); "Young Bill Hickok" 1940 (Louise Mason); "Back in the Saddle" 1941 (Taffy); "Wild Bill Hickok Rides" 1942 (Violet); "Last of the Redmen" 1947 (Cora Munro); "Deputy Marshal" 1949 (Claire Benton); "Westward the Women" 1951 (Laurie Smith); "The Big Land" 1957 (Kate Johnson).

Bishop, Larry (1948-). TV: *Kung Fu*—"Chains" 3-8-73 (Major Trapnell).

Bishop, Wes. Films: "Blue" 1968 (Settler); "Hot Spur" 1968. ¶TV: *Bonanza*—"Gideon the Good" 10-18-70 (Hicks); *The High Chaparral*—"It Takes a Smart Man" 10-23-70.

Bishop, William (1918-10/3/59). Films: "Adventures in Silverado"

1948 (Driver); "Black Eagle" 1948 (Jason Bond); "Coroner Creek" 1948 (Leach Conover); "Thunderhoof" 1948 (the Kid); "The Untamed Breed" 1948 (Larch Keegan); "The Walking Hills" 1949 (Shep); "The Texas Rangers" 1951 (Sam Bass); "Cripple Creek" 1952 (Silver Kirby); "The Raiders" 1952 (Marshal Bill Henderson); "Gun Belt" 1953 (Ike Clinton); "The Redhead from Wyoming" 1953 (Jim Averell); "Overland Pacific" 1954 (Del Stewart); "Top Gun" 1955 (Canby Judd); "Wyoming Renegades" 1955 (Sundance Kid); "The White Squaw" 1956 (Bob Garth); "The Phantom Stagecoach" 1957 (Glen Hayden); "The Oregon Trail" 1959 (Capt. George Wayne). ¶TV: *The Rifleman*—"Outlaw's Inheritance" 6-16-59 (Dave Stafford); *Riverboat*—"Payment in Full" 9-13-59 (Monte).

Bisoglio, Val (1926-). Films: "The Frisco Kid" 1979 (Chief Gray Cloud). ¶TV: *Bonanza*—"The Real People of Muddy Creek" 10-6-68 (Cliff Harper).

Bissell, Whit (1909-). Films: "Wyoming Mail" 1950 (Sam Wallace); "The Great Missouri Raid" 1951 (Bob Ford); "Red Mountain" 1951 (Miles); "Devil's Canyon" 1953 (Virgil); "Three Hours to Kill" 1954 (Deke); "At Gunpoint" 1955 (Clark); "Dakota Incident" 1956 (Mark Chester); "Man from Del Rio" 1956 (Breezy Morgan); "The Proud Ones" 1956 (Mr. Bolton); "Gunfight at the O.K. Corral" 1957 (John P. Clum); "The Tall Stranger" 1957 (Judson); "No Name on the Bullet" 1959 (Thad Pierce); "Warlock" 1959 (Mr. Petrix); "The Magnificent Seven" 1960 (Chamlee); "Hud" 1963 (Burris); "Advance to the Rear" 1964 (Capt. Queeg); "The Hallelujah Trail" 1965 (Hobbs); "Five Card Stud" 1968 (Dr. Cooper); "The Incredible Rocky Mountain Race" TVM-1977 (Simon Hollaway); "Last of the Mohicans" TVM-1977 (General Webb); "Donner Pass: The Road to Survival" TVM-1978 (Uncle Billy Graves); "The Night Rider" TVM-1979. ¶TV: *The Lone Ranger*—"A Broken Match" 12-2-54, "False Accusations" 4-21-55; *Sheriff of Cochise*—"Vapor Lock" 3-15-57; *The Restless Gun*—"The Shooting of Jett King" 10-28-57; *Have Gun Will Travel*—"No Visitors" 11-30-57 (Mr. Jonas), "The Silver Queen" 5-3-58 (Vance Crawford), "The Burning Tree" 2-9-63 (Fairchild); *Jim Bowie*—"Mexican Adventure" 12-20-57 (Joel Poinsette); *The Californians*—"Pipeline" 4-22-58 (Dr. Haley); *Trackdown*—"Killer Take All" 9-5-58 (Pen-

dleton); *Lawman*—"The Oath" 10-26-58 (Thornton Eggles), "The Threat" 4-30-61 (Edgar Chase), "The Substitute" 10-22-61 (Al Skinner), "The Doctor" 5-6-62 (Alexander Burrell); *Wagon Train*—"The Millie Davis Story" 11-26-58 (Albert Sykes), "The Jane Hawkins Story" 11-30-60, "The Mary Beckett Story" 5-9-62 (Frank Lane), "The Ben Engel Story" 3-16-64 (McCloud), "The John Gillman Story" 10-4-64 (Moore); *Zorro*—"The Flaming Arrow" 12-18-58 (Del Amo); *Wyatt Earp*—"The Muleskinner" 1-27-59 (Lige Fuller); *The Texan*—"Caballero" 4-13-59 (Shep Crawford); *The Rifleman*—"The Patsy" 9-29-59 (Sam Barrows), "The Fourflusher" 5-3-60 (Gabe Fenway), "The Hangman" 5-31-60 (Volney Adams), "Long Gun from Tucson" 12-11-61 (Henry Waller); *Zane Grey Theater*—"The Ox" 11-3-60 (Major McConnell); *Maverick*—"Kiz" 12-4-60 (Clement Samuels); *Cheyenne*—"Outcast of Cripple Creek" 2-29-60 (Myron Ackelroyd); *Rawhide*—"Incident of the One Hundred Amulets" 5-6-60 (Doc Taggert); *Johnny Ringo*—"Killer, Choose a Card" 6-9-60 (Sheriff Arson); *Klondike*—"Saints and Stickups" 10-31-60 (Josiah Harless); *Walt Disney Presents*—"Daniel Boone: ... And Chase the Buffalo" 12-11-60 (Governor Tryon); *The Deputy*—"Enemy of the Town" 5-6-61 (Will Culp); *Stagecoach West*—"Blind Man's Bluff" 5-16-61 (Harmony); *Tales of Wells Fargo*—"The Gold Witch" 5-5-62 (Charlie); *Bonanza*—"The Long Night" 5-6-62 (Neighbor); *The Dakotas*—"One Day in Vermillion" 4-8-63 (Owen Teed); *The Virginian*—"The Final Hour" 5-1-63, "The Long Quest" 4-8-64 (Andrew Cass), "Return a Stranger" 11-18-64 (Whit Parson); *Daniel Boone*—"The Devil's Four" 3-4-65; *The Loner*—"An Echo of Bugles" 9-18-65 (Nichols); *A Man Called Shenandoah*—"The Debt" 10-18-65 (Henry Claymoor); *Laredo*—"Limit of the Law Larkin" 1-27-66 (Burke); *Time Tunnel*—Regular 1966-67 (Gen. Heywood Kirk); *Iron Horse*—"Wild Track" 12-16-67 (McDougall); *Barbary Coast*—"Mary Had More Than a Little" 1-2-76 (Minister).

Bisset, Jacqueline (1944-). Films: "The Life and Times of Judge Roy Bean" 1972 (Rose Bean).

Bixby, Bill (1935-11/21/93). Films: "Ride Beyond Vengeance" 1966 (Johnsy Boy Hood); "The Apple Dumpling Gang" 1975 (Russell Donavan); "The Barbara Coast" TVM-1975 (Philippe Despard); "The Invasion of Johnson County" TVM-

1976 (Sam Lowell). ¶TV: *Iron Horse*—"Appointment with an Epitaph" 2-13-67 (Dan Gilmore); *The Oregon Trail*—"The Scarlet Ribbon" 1977.

Black, Buck. Films: "Crossed Trail" 1924 (Tom Dawson, age 8); "The Bad Lands" 1925 (Freckles); "Durand of the Bad Lands" 1925 (Jimmie); "Rough Going" 1925 (Mickey); "Born to Battle" 1926 (Tuffy); "A Regular Scout" 1926 (Budd Monroe); "Senor Daredevil" 1926 (Pat Muldoon); "Hills of Peril" 1927 (Grimes' Boy).

Black, Clint (1962-). Films: "Maverick" 1994 (Sweet-Faced Gambler).

Black, Karen (1942-). Films: "A Gunfight" 1971 (Jenny Simms); "Mr. Horn" TVM-1979 (Ernestina Crawford). ¶TV: *The Big Valley*—"The Day of Grace" 4-17-67; *Iron Horse*—"The Prisoners" 12-30-67 (Patricia Dunne).

Black, Maurice (1891-1/18/38). Films: "West of the Pecos" 1934 (Shorty); "The Californian" 1937 (Pancho); "Under Strange Flags" 1937 (Pancho Villa).

Black, William W. Films: "The Hell Cat" 1918 (Pancha's Father); "High Pockets" 1919 (Jim Shute).

Black Hawk (1888-8/78). Films: "Painted Ponies" 1927; "The Miracle Rider" 1935-serial (Chief Two Hawks); "Range Warfare" 1935.

Blackburn, Julia. Films: "The Ramrodder" 1969 (Lucy).

Blackburn, Ward. TV: *The Lone Ranger*—"Billie the Great" 3-30-50, "Bullets for Ballots" 5-11-50, "Thieves' Money" 11-2-50, "Behind the Law" 2-1-51.

Blackman, Honor (1926-). Films: "Shalako" 1968-Brit./Fr. (Lady Julia Daggett); "Something Big" 1971 (Mary Anna Morgan).

Blackman, Joan (1938-). Films: "Good Day for a Hanging" 1958 (Laurie Cutler). ¶TV: *Bonanza*—"The Return" 5-2-65 (Clara Dorn); *Gunsmoke*—"Sanctuary" 2-26-66 (Phyllis Bowman).

Blackman, Lonie. TV: *Sugarfoot*—"The Canary Kid" 11-11-59 (Mary); *Man from Blackhawk*—"The Savage" 1-15-60 (Mrs. Goodhill); *Bat Masterson*—"Welcome to Paradise" 5-5-60 (Elsie Snow).

Blackmer, Sidney (1895-10/5/73). Films: "The Bad Man" 1930 (Morgan Pell); "Woman Hungry" 1931 (Geoffrey Brand); "Heart of the West" 1937 (Big John Trumbull); "Law of the Pampas" 1939 (Ralph

Merritt); "Down Mexico Way" 1941 (Gibson); "In Old Oklahoma" 1943 (Teddy Roosevelt); "Buffalo Bill" 1944 (President Theodore Roosevelt); "Duel in the Sun" 1946 (the Lover); "The San Francisco Story" 1952 (Andrew Cain). ¶TV: *The Californians*—"The Coward" 1-7-58 (Hector Jones); *Jim Bowie*—"Ursula" 2-14-58 (Don Juan de Veramendi), "Apache Silver" 2-21-58 (Don Juan de Veramendi), "Horse Thief" 3-21-58 (Don Juan de Veramendi); *Zane Grey Theater*—"The Sharpshooter" 3-7-58 (Judge Hanovan); *The Rifleman*—"The Sharpshooter" 9-30-58 (Judge Havanan), "The Safe Guard" 11-18-58 (Judge Hannavan), "The Photographer" 1-27-59 (Judge); *The Texan*—"The Edge of the Cliff" 10-27-58 (Orin McKnight); *Wanted—Dead or Alive*—"Rope Law" 1-3-59 (Judge Cooper); *Bonanza*—"The Dream Riders" 5-20-61 (Major Cayley), "The Late Ben Cartwright" 3-3-61 (Sam Endicott); *Daniel Boone*—"The Jasser Ledbedder Story" 2-2-67 (Jasper Ledbedder).

Blackwell, Carlyle (1884-6/17/55). Films: "The Apache Renegade" 1912; "Days of '49" 1912; "The Indian Uprising at Santa Fe" 1912; "The Peril of the Cliffs" 1912; "Red Wing and the Paleface" 1912; "The Suffragette Sheriff" 1912; "The Tragedy of Big Eagle Mine" 1912; "The Water Right War" 1912; "The Attack at Rocky Pass" 1913; "The Cheyenne Massacre" 1913; "The Fight at Grizzly Gulch" 1913; "The Invaders" 1913; "The Last Blockhouse" 1913; "The Skeleton in the Closet" 1913; "The Crimson Dove" 1917 (Brand Cameron); "The Price of Pride" 1917 (Jeffrey Black); "The Third Woman" 1920 (Luke Halliday).

Blackwell, Irene. Films: "Blind Hearts" 1921 (Mrs. Thomas).

Blackwell, William. Films: "Indian Paint" 1965 (Sutako). ¶TV: *Walt Disney Presents*—"Davy Crockett"—Regular 1954-55 (Major Norton).

Blain, Lucita. Films: "Five Bold Women" 1960 (Maria the Knife).

Blaine, James (-3/18/67). Films: "Rhythm on the Range" 1936 (Conductor); "Flaming Frontier" 1938-serial (Bart Eaton); "Oklahoma Frontier" 1939 (George Frazier); "The Oregon Trail" 1939-serial (Sam Morgan); "Man from Montreal" 1940; "Man from Montana" 1941 (Dunham); "Riders of Death Valley" 1941-serial (Joseph Kirby); "Fighting Bill Fargo" 1942 (Cash Scanlon).

Blaine, Martin. TV: *Gun-*

smoke—"The Violators" 10-17-64; *Wild Wild West*—"The Night of the Tartar" 2-3-67 (Millar Boyer); *Bonanza*—"The Stronghold" 5-26-68 (Moore).

Blaine, Ruby. Films: "Gun-Hand Garrison" 1927; "Lightning Lariats" 1927 (Cynthia Storne); "Ridin' Luck" 1927; "The Terror of Bar X" 1927 (Dorothy Hunter); "Wild Born" 1927.

Blair, Betsy (1923-). Films: "The Halliday Brand" 1957 (Martha).

Blair, Henry. Films: "Saginaw Trail" 1953 (Phillip Brissac). ¶TV: *Wild Bill Hickok*—"The Boy and the Bandit" 3-25-52.

Blair, Janet (1921-). TV: *Destry*—"Stormy Is a Lady" 3-6-64 (Bessie Hawkins).

Blair, Joan. Films: "Sons of Adventure" 1948 (Glenda).

Blair, June (1936-). Films: "Lone Texan" 1959 (Florrie Stuart); "Warlock" 1959 (Dance Hall Girl). ¶TV: *Bat Masterson*—"Dead Men Don't Pay Debts" 11-19-59, "Death by Decree" 12-22-60 (Constance Whitney); *The Texan*—"Town Divided" 3-21-60 (Ellen Warren).

Blair, Nicky (1929-). Films: "The Second Time Around" 1961 (Mr. Stone). ¶TV: *Tales of the Texas Rangers*—"Key Witness" 9-29-57 (Anton Tucek); *Wagon Train*—"The Marie Dupree Story" 3-19-58 (Joe); *Wild Wild West*—"The Night of the Death-Maker" 2-23-68, "The Night of the Janus" 2-15-69 (Thompson).

Blair, Patricia (1938-). TV: *The Rifleman*—Regular 1962-63 (Lou Mallory); *The Virginian*—"The Evil That Men Do" 10-16-63 (Rita Marlow); *Bonanza*—"The Lila Conrad Story" 1-5-64 (Lila Conrad); *Temple Houston*—"Thy Name Is Woman" 1-9-64 (Leslie Hale); *Daniel Boone*—Regular 1964-70 (Rebecca Boone).

Blair, Reno. see Browne, Reno.

Blair, Robert. Films: "Rocky Mountain Rangers" 1940 (Sgt. Bush); "The Trail Blazers" 1940 (Fowler); "Underground Rustlers" 1941 (Ford); "Jesse James Rides Again" 1947-serial (Bartender); "Last Frontier Uprising" 1947 (Texan).

Blair, W.J. Films: "Yodelin' Kid from Pine Ridge" 1937 (Tennessee Rambler).

Blaisdell, Charles (1874-5/10/30). Films: "The Mainspring" 1917 (J. J. O'Rourke).

Blake, A.D. (1877-11/5/66). Films: "The Charmed Arrow" 1914; "A Knight of the Range" 1916 (Nick).

Blake, Amanda (1931-8/16/89). Films: "Stars in My Crown" 1950 (Faith Radmore Samuels); "Cattle Town" 1952 (Marian); "Gunsmoke: Return to Dodge" TVM-1987 (Kitty Russell). ¶TV: *Gunsmoke*—Regular 1955-75 (Kitty Russell); *The Quest*—"Day of Outrage" 10-27-76 (Miss Sally).

Blake, Geoffrey. Films: "The Tracker" TVM-1988 (Miller); "Young Guns" 1988 (J. McCloskey). ¶TV: *Adventures of Brisco County, Jr.*—"Iron Horses" 11-19-93 (Flybaker).

Blake, Gladys. Films: "The Cisco Kid and the Lady" 1939; "Lady from Cheyenne" 1941 (Chorus Girl); "Rockin' in the Rockies" 1945 (Betty); "Under Western Skies" 1945 (Lulu).

Blake, Jean. TV: *Colt .45*—"Chain of Command" 4-5-60 (Honora); *Bat Masterson*—"High Card Loses" 11-10-60 (Mildred); *Sugarfoot*—"Man from Medora" 11-21-60 (Millie Larson).

Blake, Larry J. (1914-5/25/82). Films: "High Noon" 1952 (Gillis); "Devil's Canyon" 1953 (Hysterical Prisoner); "Badlands of Montana" 1957 (1st Outlaw); "The Rare Breed" 1966 (Auctioneer); "Hang 'Em High" 1968. ¶TV: *The Lone Ranger*—"Outlaw's Revenge" 10-5-50, "Paid in Full" 12-28-50, "Mr. Trouble" 3-8-51, "Special Edition" 9-25-52; *Wagon Train*—"The Riley Gratton Story" 12-4-57, "The Juan Ortega Story" 10-8-58 (Booley Herbert), "The Martha Barham Story" 11-4-59 (Chief White Cloud), "The Eli Bancroft Story" 11-11-63; *Broken Arrow*—"Massacre" 1-28-58 (Capt. Allison); *Sergeant Preston of the Yukon*—"Boy Alone" 2-20-58 (Studs Corey); *The Restless Gun*—"Pressing Engagement" 2-24-58 (Cattle Auctioneer); *Wyatt Earp*—"Plague Carrier" 12-9-58 (Trader); *Yancy Derringer*—"The Wayward Warrior" 4-16-59 (Jailer), "A State of Crisis" 4-30-59; *Have Gun Will Travel*—"The Return of Roy Carter" 5-2-59 (Chaplain April); *Rawhide*—"Incident in No Man's Land" 6-12-59; *Gunsmoke*—"Box O'Rocks" 12-5-59 (Jeb Crooder), "The Promoter" 4-25-64, "Help Me, Kitty" 11-7-64 (Passenger); *Sugarfoot*—"The Highbinder" 1-19-60 (Policeman); *Lawman*—"The Go-Between" 9-25-60 (Jennings), "The Juror" 9-24-61 (Parker); *The Virginian*—"The Man from the Sea" 12-26-62 (Fight Manager), "The Return of Golden Tom" 3-9-66 (Keel), "Jacob Was a Plain Man" 10-12-66 (Barker); *Klondike*—"River of Gold" 10-24-60 (Jason

Firth); *Daniel Boone*—"The Sisters O'Hannrahan" 12-3-64 (Auctioneer); *The Big Valley*—"Hazard" 3-9-66 (Clerk), "Boy into Man" 1-16-67 (Man); *Kung Fu*—"Superstition" 4-5-73 (Bartender), "The Garments of Rage" 11-8-74 (Foreman).

Blake, Madge (1899-2/19/69). Films: "The Iron Mistress" 1952 (Mrs. Cuny); "Sergents 3" 1962 (Mrs. Parent). ¶TV: *The Restless Gun*—"The Gold Buckle" 12-30-57 (Emily Davis).

Blake, Marie. *see* Rock, Blossom.

Blake, Mary. Films: "Code of the Range" 1937 (Janet Parker).

Blake, Oliver. Films: "The Paleface" 1948 (Westerner); "Colorado Territory" 1949 (Station Agent); "Fancy Pants" 1950 (Mr. Andrews); "Son of Paleface" 1952 (Telegrapher); "Hell's Outpost" 1954 (Hotel Clerk). ¶TV: *Maverick*—"Relic of Fort Tejon" 11-3-57 (Brimmer); *The Adventures of Rin Tin Tin*—"Wind-Wagon Mc-Clanahan" 4-4-58 (Seth Pillijohn), "Pillajohn's Progress" 3-6-59 (Seth Pillijohn).

Blake, Pamela (Adele Pearce). Films: "Utah Trail" 1938 (Sally Jeffers); "Wyoming Outlaw" 1939 (Irene Parker); "The Omaha Trail" 1942 (Julie Santley); "Son of God's Country" 1948 (Cathy Thornton); "Ghost of Zorro" 1949-serial (Rita White); "Border Rangers" 1950 (Ellen Reed); "The Daltons' Women" 1950; "Gunfire" 1950 (Cynthy); "Waco" 1952 (Kathy Clark). ¶TV: *The Cisco Kid*—"Big Switch" 2-10-51, "Railroad Land Rush" 3-17-51, "Renegade Son" 4-7-51; *The Range Rider*—"The Secret of Superstition Peak" 2-23-52, "The Holy Terror" 3-22-52.

Blake, Robert "Bobby" (1933-). Films: "Cheyenne Wildcat" 1944; "Marshal of Reno" 1944 (Little Beaver); "The San Antonio Kid" 1944 (Little Beaver); "Sheriff of Las Vegas" 1944; "Tucson Raiders" 1944 (Little Beaver); "Vigilantes of Dodge City" 1944 (Little Beaver); "Colorado Pioneers" 1945; "Lone Texas Ranger" 1945 (Little Beaver); "Dakota" 1945 (Little Boy); "Great Stagecoach Robbery" 1945; "Marshal of Laredo" 1945 (Little Beaver); "Phantom of the Plains" 1945 (Little Beaver); "Wagon Wheels Westward" 1945 (Little Beaver); "California Gold Rush" 1946 (Little Beaver); "Conquest of Cheyenne" 1946 (Little Beaver); "Home on the Range" 1946 (Cub Garth); "In Old Sacramento" 1946 (Newsboy); "Out California Way" 1946 (Danny McCoy); "Santa Fe Uprising" 1946 (Little

Beaver); "Sheriff of Redwood Valley" 1946; "Stagecoach to Denver" 1946 (Little Beaver); "Sun Valley Cyclone" 1946; "Homesteaders of Paradise Valley" 1947; "The Last Round-Up" 1947 (Mike); "The Marshal of Cripple Creek" 1947 (Little Beaver); "Oregon Trail Scouts" 1947 (Little Beaver); "Rustlers of Devil's Canyon" 1947 (Little Beaver); "Vigilantes of Boomtown" 1947 (Little Beaver); "The Treasure of the Sierra Madre" 1948 (Mexican Boy); "Apache War Smoke" 1952 (Luis); "Three Violent People" 1956 (Rafael); "Tell Them Willie Boy Is Here" 1969 (Willie Boy). ¶TV: *The Cisco Kid*—"Smuggled Silver" 6-14-52, "The Haunted Stage Stop" 3-7-53; *The Roy Rogers Show*—"Paleface Justice" 11-18-56; *Broken Arrow*—"Bear Trap" 4-29-58 (Viklai); *The Restless Gun*—"Thunder Valley" 10-13-58 (Lupe Sandoval); *The Californians*—"The Long Night" 12-23-58 (Cass); *Black Saddle*—"Client: Robinson" 2-21-59 (Wayne Robinson); *Zane Grey Theater*—"Heritage" 4-2-59 (Michael); *The Rebel*—"He's Only a Boy" 2-28-60 (Virgil); *Have Gun Will Travel*—"The Fatalist" 9-10-60 (Smollet), "The Shooting of Jesse May" 10-20-60 (Jessie Turnbow), "A Place for Abel Hix" 10-6-62 (Lauro); *Bat Masterson*—"No Amnesty for Death" 3-30-61 (Bill MacWilliams); *Wagon Train*—"The Joe Muharich Story" 4-19-61 (Johnny Kamen); *Laramie*—"Wolf Cub" 11-21-61 (Wolf Cub); *Rawhide*—"The Winter Soldier" 3-12-65 (Hap Johnson), "Hostage for Hanging" 10-19-65 (Max Gufler); *Death Valley Days*—"The Kid from Hell's Kitchen" 11-12-66 (Billy the Kid).

Blake, Tom. Films: "The Girl from Porcupine" 1922 (Dugan).

Blake, Whitney. TV: *Circus Boy*—"The Knife Thrower" 2-17-57 (Lola); *Zane Grey Theater*—"The Promise" 11-8-57 (Ellie), "Shadow of a Dead Man" 4-11-58 (Jessie Wheeler); *Cheyenne*—"Hired Gun" 12-17-57 (Lilli Bridgeman), "Riot at Arroyo Soco" 2-1-60 (Beth Tobin); *Maverick*—"The Burning Sky" 2-23-58 (Letty French), "The Day They Hanged Bret Maverick" 9-21-58 (Molly Clifford); *Gunsmoke*—"Wind" 3-21-59 (Dolly Varden), "A Game of Death ... An Act of Love" 11-5-73 & 11-12-73 (Lavinia Sanderson); *Rawhide*—"Incident at the Curious Street" 4-10-59 (Angie Miller), "Incident of the Murder Steer" 5-13-60 (Callie Carter); *The Restless Gun*—"One on the House" 4-20-59 (Ellen); Tales of Wells Fargo—"Doc Holliday" 5-4-59 (Amy); *The Texan*—"Cattle Drive" 9-

28-59, "Border Incident" 12-7-59; *The Deputy*—"Proof of Guilt" 10-24-59 (Ellen Hart); *Pony Express*—"The Good Samaritan" 11-11-59 (Lorrie); *Riverboat*—"The Blowup" 1-17-60 (Martha Crane); *Overland Trail*—"High Bridge" 2-28-60 (Kate); *Bronco*—"The Mustangers" 10-17-60 (Laurel Shelton), "Yankee Tornado" 3-13-61 (Julie); *Branded*—"Nice Day for a Hanging" 2-6-66 (Nan Richards); *The Legend of Jesse James*—"South Wind" 2-14-66 (Ina Stevens); *Laredo*—"One Too Many Voices" 11-18-66 (Sabrina Lane); *The Virginian*—"Bitter Harvest" 3-15-67 (Marie Adams).

Blakely, Gene (1921-11/23/87). Films: "September Gun" TVM-1983 (Merchant). ¶TV: *Wide Country*—"The Girl from Nob Hill" 3-8-63 (Hartshorn).

Blakeley, James. Films: "The Gay Desperado" 1936 (Bill Shay).

Blakeney, Olive (1894-10/21/-59). Films: "Billy the Kid" 1941 (Mrs. Patterson); "Dakota" 1945 (Mrs. Stowe). ¶TV: *Gunsmoke*—"Sky" 2-14-59 (Ma Toret).

Blanc, Erika (1946-). Films: "Colorado Charlie" 1965-Ital./Span.; "Deguello" 1966-Ital.; "He Who Shoots First" 1966-Ital.; "The Greatest Robbery in the West" 1968-Ital.; "Shoot, Gringo ... Shoot!" 1968-Ital./Fr.; "Blood at Sundown" 1969-Ital./Span.; "Shotgun" 1969-Ital. (Jo Anne); "Dig Your Grave, Friend ... Sabata's Coming" 1970-Ital./Span./Fr.; "I Am Sartana, Trade Your Guns for a Coffin" 1972-Ital.; "Thunder Over El Paso" 1972-Ital./Span.; "Stranger and the Gunfighter" 1973-Ital./Span./Hong Kong.

Blanch, Jewel. Films: "Against a Crooked Sky" 1975 (Charlotte Sutter). ¶TV: *Bonanza*—"Face of Fear" 11-14-71 (Neta).

Blanchard, Jackie. TV: *Tales of Wells Fargo*—"The Feud" 10-14-57; *Rough Riders*—"The Holdout" 6-25-59 (Laura).

Blanchard, Mari (1932-5/10/70). Films: "Overland Telegraph" 1951 (Stella); "Black Horse Canyon" 1954 (Aldia Spain); "Destry" 1954 (Brandy); "Rails into Laramie" 1954 (Lou Carter); "The Return of Jack Slade" 1955 (Texas Rose); "Stagecoach to Fury" 1956 (Barbara Duval); "McClintock" 1963 (Camille). ¶TV: *The Texan*—"Caballero" 4-13-59 (Catherine Crawford); *Rawhide*—"Incident of the Stalking Death" 11-13-59 (Margarita Colinas), "Incident of the Big Blowout" 2-10-61 (Laura

Carter); *Sugarfoot*—"Apollo with a Gun" 12-8-59 (Adah Isaacs Menken); *Tales of Wells Fargo*—"The Governor's Visit" 1-18-60 (Kitty); *Laramie*—"Rope of Steel" 2-16-60 (Sally); *Bronco*—"Montana Passage" 4-5-60 (Lola Dalzel); *Klondike*—Regular 1960-61 (Kathy O'Hara); *Gunslinger*—"Road of the Dead" 3-30-61 (Contessa); *The Virginian*—"Doctor Pat" 3-1-67 (Marie Coulter).

Blanchard, Moody. TV: *Bat Masterson*—"License to Cheat" 2-4-59 (Red); *Rawhide*—"Incident of the Haunted Hills" 11-6-59 (Crane).

Blanchard, Susan. Films: "The New Maverick" TVM-1978 (Nell McGarahan). TV: *Young Maverick*—Regular 1979-80 (Nell McGarahan).

Blancke, Kate (1860-6/24/42). Films: "The Trail of the Shadow" 1917 (Mrs. Hilliard).

Blanco, Eumenio. Films: "Sunset of Power" 1936 (Andreas); "Escape from Red Rock" 1958 (Mayor).

Blanco, Hugo. Films: "Texas, Adios" 1966-Ital./Span.; "The Ugly Ones" 1966-Ital./Span.; ; "Blood at Sundown" 1967-Span./Ital.; "Django Does Not Forgive" 1967-Ital./Span.; "Up the MacGregors!" 1967-Ital./Span. (David MacGregor); ; "One After Another" 1968-Span./Ital.; "Sartana Does Not Forgive" 1968-Span./Ital.; "Valley of the Dancing Widows" 1974-Span./Ger.

Blanco, Tomas (1910-). Films: "Billy the Kid" 1962-Span.; "Shoot to Kill" 1963-Span.; "Charge of the Seventh Cavalry" 1964-Ital./Span./Fr.; "Heroes of the West" 1964-Span./Ital.; "For a Few Dollars More" 1965-Ital./Ger./Span.; "Secret of Captain O'Hara" 1965-Span.; "The Man Who Killed Billy the Kid" 1967-Span./Ital.; "Fifteen Scaffolds for the Killer" 1968-Ital./Span.

Blandick, Clara (1881-4/15/62). Films: "Drums Along the Mohawk" 1939 (Mrs. Borst); "Northwest Mounted Police" 1940 (Mrs. Burns); "Frontier Gal" 1945 (Abigail).

Blane, Sally (1910-). Films: "Shootin' Irons" 1927 (Lucy Blake); "A Horseman of the Plains" 1928 (Dawn O'Day); "King Cowboy" 1928 (Polly Randall); "The Vanishing Pioneer" 1928 (June Shelby); "Outlawed" 1929 (Anne); "Heritage of the Desert" 1932 (Judy); "Local Bad Man" 1932 (Marion Meade); "Wild Horse Mesa" 1932 (Sandy Melberne); "Fighting Mad" 1939 (Ann Fenwick).

Blatchford, Edward. Films: "Son of the Morning Star" TVM-

1991 (Lt. Cooke). ¶TV: *Adventures of Brisco County, Jr.*—"Brisco for the Defense" 10-22-93 (Dr. Matthew Carter).

Bleifer, John (1901-1/24/92). Films: "The Crimson Trail" 1935 (Loco); "Sutter's Gold" 1936; "Frontier Marshal" 1939 (Man); "Mark of Zorro" 1940 (Pedro); "Northwest Outpost" 1947 (Groom). ¶TV: *Rawhide*—"Incident of the Judas Trap" 6-5-59; *Death Valley Days*—"One Man Tank" 3-29-60 (Dutch Charley Koehn).

Bletcher, William "Billy" (1894-1/5/79). Films: "Billy Jim" 1922 (Jimmy); "The Dude Cowboy" 1926 (Shorty O'Day); "One Hour of Love" 1927 (Half Pint Walker); "The Cowboy Kid" 1928 (Deputy); "Daredevil's Reward" 1928 (Slim); "Branded Men" 1931 (Half-A-Rod); "The Texas Ranger" 1931 (Tubby); "The Boiling Point" 1932 (Stubby); "Desert Gold" 1935; "God's Country and the Man" 1937 (Sandy Briggs); "High, Wide and Handsome" 1937 (Shorty); "California Frontier" 1938 (Bellhop); "The Lone Ranger" 1938-serial (Voice of Lone Ranger); "Mexicali Kid" 1938 (Stage Driver); "Destry Rides Again" 1939 (Pianist); "The Lone Ranger Rides Again" 1939-serial (Voice of Lone Ranger); "Zorro's Fighting Legion" 1939-serial (Voice of Don del Oro); "Buck Benny Rides Again" 1940 (Last Porter); "Melody Ranch" 1940; "Boss of Rawhide" 1944 (Jed Jones). ¶TV: *The Lone Ranger*—"Gold Train" 3-16-50.

Blevins, Eleanor. Films: "The Broken Parole" 1913; "The End of the Circle" 1913; "Love and the Law" 1913; "A Mixup on the Plains" 1913; "The Moving Picture Cowboy" 1914.

Blinn, Benjamin F. (1872-4/28/41). Films: "Danger" 1923 (Mark Baxter); "Quicker'n Lightnin'" 1925 (John Harlow).

Blinn, Genevieve (1876-7/20/56). Films: "The Rainbow Trail" 1918 (Ruth); "True Blue" 1918 (Lady Somerfield); "Last of the Duanes" 1919 (Mrs. Lee); "Sundown Slim" 1920 (Mrs. Fernando).

Blinn, Holbrook (1872-6/24/28). Films: "The Bad Man" 1923 (Pancho Lopez); "Zander the Great" 1925 (Juan Fernandez).

Bliss, John. Films: "Vengeance" 1964 (Deputy Sam); "The Scavengers" 1969 (the Captain).

Bliss, Lela (1896-5/15/80). Films: "Gas House Kids Go West" 1947 (Mrs. Crowley). ¶TV: *Wild Bill*

Hickok—"Money Shines" 6-2-53; *Wagon Train*—"The Honorable Don Charlie Story" 1-22-58 (Aunt Molly); *Maverick*—"Diamond in the Rough" 1-26-58 (Mrs. Shelbourne).

Bliss, Sally. Films: "Swing in the Saddle" 1944; "Rustlers of the Badlands" 1945. ¶TV: *The Rebel*—"Decision at Sweetwater" 4-23-61 (Mrs. Bishop); *Wagon Train*—"The Annie Duggan Story" 3-13-63 (Martha Leeds).

Blocker, Dan (1928-5/13/72). Films: "Something for a Lonely Man" TVM-1968 (John Killibrew); "The Cockeyed Cowboys of Calico County" 1970 (Charley). ¶TV: *Gunsmoke*—"Alarm at Pleasant Valley" 8-25-56 (Lieutenant), "Thoroughbreds" 10-18-58 (Keller); *Cheyenne*—"Land Beyond the Law" 1-15-57 (Pete); *Sheriff of Cochise*—"Grandfather Grandson" 2-11-57 (Bartender); *Sergeant Preston of the Yukon*—"Underground Ambush" 4-25-57 (Mule Conklin); *Tales of Wells Fargo*—"Renegade Raiders" 5-20-57 (Joe Purdy); *Colt .45*—"A Time to Die" 10-25-57 (Will); *The Restless Gun*—"Jody" 11-4-57 (Ike Burnett), "The Child" 12-23-57 (El Burto), "Mercyday" 10-6-58 "Take Me Home" 12-29-58 (Olaf Burland), "The Way Back" 7-13-59 (Olaf Burland); *Zane Grey Theater*—"Man Unforgiving" 1-3-58 (Matt); *Wagon Train*—"The Dora Gray Story" 1-29-58; *Have Gun Will Travel*—"Gun Shy" 3-29-58; *Decision*—"The Virginian" 7-6-58 (Salem); *Jefferson Drum*—"Stagecoach Episode" 10-10-58 (Craig); *Maverick*—"The Jail at Junction Flats" 11-9-58 (Hognose Hughes); *The Rifleman*—"The Sister" 11-25-58 (Pete); *The Rebel*—"Johnny Yuma" 10-4-59 (Pierce); *Bonanza*—Regular 1959-72 (Hoss Cartwright).

Blocker, Dirk (1957-). Films: "Bridger" TVM-1976 (Joe Meek); "Desperado" TVM-1987 (Grady); "Bonanza: The Return" TVM-1993 (Finster); "Bonanza: Under Attack" TVM-1995 (Finster).

Blodgett, Michael (1942-). Films: "40 Guns to Apache Pass" 1967 (Mike); "There Was a Crooked Man" 1970 (Coy Cavendish). ¶TV: *Daniel Boone*—"The Williamsburg Cannon" 1-12-67 & 1-19-67 (Sam Linn); *Bonanza*—"False Witness" 10-22-67 (Billy Slader); *Barbary Coast*—"The Day Cable Was Hanged" 12-26-75 (Whiting).

Blondell, Gloria (-3/25/86). TV: *Wanted—Dead or Alive*—"The Looters" 10-12-60 (Lucy).

Blondell, Joan (1906-12/25/79).

Films: "Advance to the Rear" 1964 (Jenny); "Ride Beyond Vengeance" 1966 (Mrs. Lavener); "Waterhole No. 3" 1967 (Lavinia); "Winchester '73" TVM-1967 (Larouge); "Support Your Local Gunfighter" 1971 (Jenny). ¶TV: *Death Valley Days*—"The Train and Lucy Tutaine" 3-13-63 (Lucy Tutaine); *The Virginian*—"To Make This Place Remember" 9-25-63 (Rosanna Dobie); *Wagon Train*—"The Bleeker Story" 12-9-63 (Ma Bleeker); *Bonanza*—"The Pressure Game" 5-10-64 (Aunt Lil); *The Guns of Will Sonnett*—"Sunday in Paradise" 12-15-67 (Miss Lottie); *Here Comes the Brides*—Regular 1968-70 (Lottie Hatfield).

Blondell, Simone. Films: "Shadow of Sartana … Shadow of Your Death" 1968-Ital.; "Four Came to Kill Sartana" 1969-Ital.; "Django and Sartana Are Coming … It's the End" 1970-Ital.; "His Name Was Sam Walbash, But They Call Him Amen" 1971-Ital.; "Man Called Django" 1971-Ital.; "One Damend Day at Dawn … Django Meets Sartana" 1971-Ital.; "Stranger That Kneels Beside the Shadow of a Corpse" 1971-Ital.; "Showdown for a Badman" 1972-Ital.; "Anything for a Friend" 1973-Ital.

Bloom, Claire (1931-). Films: "The Outrage" 1964 (Wife).

Bloom, Fred. "Man of Courage" 1922 (Morgan Deane).

Bloom, John. Films: "Hard Trail" 1969. ¶TV: *Paradise*—Regular 1988-91 (Tiny).

Bloom, Verna (1939-). Films: "The Hired Hand" 1971 (Hannah Collings); "High Plains Drifter" 1973 (Sarah Belding). ¶TV: *Bonanza*—"The Fence" 4-27-69 (Ellen); *Dr. Quinn, Medicine Woman*—Pilot 1-1-93 (Michaela's Mother).

Blore, Eric (1887-3/1/59). Films: "Fancy Pants" 1950 (Sir Wimbley).

Blossom, Roberts (1924-). Films: "The Quick and the Dead" 1995 (Doc Wallace).

Blossom, Rose. Films: "The Gentle Cyclone" 1926 (June Prowitt); "Whispering Smith Rides" 1927-serial; "Laddie Be Good" 1928 (Ruth Jones).

Blu, Susan. Films: "The Wild Wild West Revisited" TVM-1979 (Gabrielle).

Blue, Ben (1901-3/7/75). Films: "High, Wide and Handsome" 1937 (Zeke).

Blue, Monte (1890-2/18/63). Films: "Hands Up!" 1917 (Dan Tracy); "The Man from Painted Post" 1917 (Slim Carter); "Wild and Woolly" 1917; "M'Liss" 1918 (Mexican Joe); "The Only Road" 1918 (Pedro Lupo); "The Red, Red Heart" 1918 (Billy Porter); "The Squaw Man" 1918 (Happy); "In Mizzoura" 1919 (Sam Fowler); "Rustling a Bride" 1919 (Nick McCredie); "Told in the Hills" 1919 (Kalitan); "The Brute" 1927 (Easy Going Martin Sondes); "Tiger Rose" 1929 (Devlin); "The Last Round-Up" 1934 (Jack Kells); "The Thundering Herd" 1934 (Joe Billings); "Wagon Wheels" 1934 (Murdock); "Nevada" 1935 (Clem Dillon); "Trails of the Wild" 1935 (Doyle); "Wanderer of the Wasteland" 1935 (Guerd Larey); "Desert Gold" 1936 (Chetley Kasedon); "The Lawless Nineties" 1936 (Outlaw); "Ride, Ranger, Ride" 1936 (Tavibo/ Duval); "Song of the Gringo" 1936 (Sheriff); "Treachery Rides the Range" 1936 (Col. Drummond); "Born to the West" 1937 (Hammond); "The Outcasts of Poker Flat" 1937 (Indian Jim); "Rootin' Tootin' Rhythm" 1937 (Joe Stafford); "Thunder Trail" 1937 (Jeff Graves); "The Great Adventures of Wild Bill Hickok" 1938 (Cameron); "The Mysterious Rider" 1938 (Cap Folsom); "Days of Jesse James" 1939 (Fields); "Dodge City" 1939 (Barlow, the Indian Agent); "Frontier Pony Express" 1939 (Cherokee); "Union Pacific" 1939 (Indian); "Geronimo" 1940 (Interpreter); "Northwest Mounted Police" 1940 (Indian); "Texas Rangers Ride Again" 1940 (Slide Along); "Young Bill Hickok" 1940 (Marshal Evans); "Arkansas Judge" 1941 (Mr. Johnson); "Bad Man of Deadwood" 1941 (Sheriff); "King of the Texas Rangers" 1941-serial (Captain Tom King, Sr.); "Riders of Death Valley" 1941-serial (Rance Davis); "Sunset in Wyoming" 1941; "The Great Man's Lady" 1942 (Man at Hoyt City); "North to the Klondike" 1942 (Burke); "San Antonio" 1945 (Cleve Andrews); "The Bells of San Fernando" 1947 (Governor); "Cheyenne" 1947 (Timberline); "Silver River" 1948 (Buck Chevigee); "Two Guys from Texas" 1948 (Pete Nash); "Ranger of Cherokee Strip" 1949 (Chief Hunter); "South of St. Louis" 1949 (Capt. Jeffrey); "The Younger Brothers" 1949 (Joe); "Dallas" 1950 (Sheriff); "The Iroquois Trail" 1950 (Sagamore); "Montana" 1950 (Charlie Penrose); "Gold Raiders" 1951 (John Sawyer); "Snake River Desperadoes" 1951 (Jim Haverly); "Three Desperate Men" 1951 (Pete Coleman); "Warpath" 1951 (1st Emigrant); "Hangman's Knot" 1952 (Maxwell); "Rose of Cimarron" 1952 (Lone Eagle); "The Last Posse" 1953 (Kane); "Ride, Vaquero!" 1953 (Bartender); "Apache" 1954 (Geronimo). ¶TV: *The Lone Ranger*—"The Tenderfeet" 11-10-49, "Crime in Time" 10-19-50, "Letter of the Law" 1-4-51, "Through the Wall" 10-9-52, "The Condemned Man" 12-11-52; *Wild Bill Hickok*—"Indian Bureau Story" 7-31-51, "The Avenging Gunman" 7-29-52; *Annie Oakley*—"Flint and Steel" 10-14-56 (Tom Wheeler); *The Adventures of Rin Tin Tin*—"The Warrior's Promise" 1-25-57 (Maco), "Major Mockingbird" 1-30-59 (Buffalo Horn), "The Luck of O'Hara" 4-3-59 (Red Raven); *Wyatt Earp*—"Warpath" 10-22-57 (Brave Bull); *Tales of Wells Fargo*—"The Kid" 11-18-57 (Howie Taylor); *Wagon Train*—"The Clara Beauchamp Story" 12-11-57 (Indian Chief); *Rawhide*—"Incident at Tinker's Dam" 2-5-60 (Wanakawa).

Blue Cloud. Films: "The Santa Fe Trail" 1930 (Eagle Feather).

Blue Eagle, Chief (Lloyd Keith) (1904-5/15/58). Films: "Gunman's Walk" 1958 (Black Horse).

Blum, Sam (1889-5/30/45). Films: "Galloping Jinx" 1925; "The Winning of Barbara Worth" 1926 (Blanton); "Rose of the Rancho" 1936 (Tecolaro, the Master of Ceremonies); "Nevada" 1944 (Bartender); "West of the Pecos" 1945 (Gambler).

Blye, Margaret (1939-). Films: "Hombre" 1967 (Doris); "Waterhole No. 3" 1967 (Billee Copperud). ¶TV: *Gunsmoke*—"Journey for Three" 6-6-64 (Girl), "Winner Take All" 2-20-65 (Karen); *The Virginian*—"The Laramie Road" 12-8-65 (Velvet Rose).

Blystone, Stanley (1894-7/16/56). Films: "The Circus Ace" 1927 (Boss Canvass Man); "The Fighting Legion" 1930 (Burl Edwards); "Parade of the West" 1930 (Dude); "The Man from Death Valley" 1931 (Sheriff Jefferies); "Sundown Trail" 1931 (Joe Currier); "Galloping Thru" 1932; "The Golden West" 1932; "Honor of the Mounted" 1932; "Crossfire" 1933 (Krueger); "The Fighting Parson" 1933 (Bart McTague); "Lucky Larrigan" 1933; "Man of Action" 1933 (Masters); "Code of the Mounted" 1935 (Constable); "Fighting Pioneers" 1935 (Hadley); "Gallant Defender" 1935; "Ivory-Handled Gun" 1935 (Squint Barlow); "Justice of the Range" 1935 (Sheriff Joe Burns); "The Phantom Empire" 1935-serial; "Rainbow's End" 1935 (Butch); "The Revenge Rider" 1935

(Saunders); "Saddle Aces" 1935; "Trails End" 1935 (Randall); "End of the Trail" 1936 (Bartender); "The Riding Avenger" 1936 (Mort Ringer); "The Three Mesquiteers" 1936; "Vigilantes Are Coming" 1936-serial (Kramer); "Boots and Saddles" 1937 (Sergeant); "Galloping Dynamite" 1937 (Sam Jenkins); "Goofs and Saddles" 1937-short (Longhorn Pete); "Headin' East" 1937 (Bert Lohman); "California Frontier" 1938 (Ted Graham); "Red River Range" 1938 (Randall); "The Stranger from Arizona" 1938 (Haskell); "Allegheny Uprising" 1939 (Frontiersman); "Crashing Thru" 1939 (La Monte); "Drifting Westward" 1939 (Carga); "The Lone Ranger Rides Again" 1939-serial (Murdock); "Three Texas Steers" 1939 (Rankin); "Trigger Pals" 1939 (Steve); "Pony Post" 1940 (Griff Atkins); "The Tulsa Kid" 1940 (Sam Ellis); "Back in the Saddle" 1941; "King of the Texas Rangers" 1941-serial (A.J. Lynch); "Sunset in Wyoming" 1941; "West of Cimarron" 1941; "In Old California" 1942; "The Navajo Kid" 1945 (Matt Crandall); "King of the Forest Rangers" 1946-serial (Harry Lynch); "Moon Over Montana" 1946; "Six Gun Man" 1946 (Lon Kelly); "Out West" 1947-short (Colonel); "Eyes of Texas" 1948 (Sheriff); "Loaded Pistols" 1948; "The Paleface" 1948 (Onlooker); "Station West" 1948 (Bouncer); "Deputy Marshal" 1949 (Leo Hanald); "El Dorado Pass" 1949 (Barlow); "Ghost of Zorro" 1949-serial (Dan Foster); "Powder River Rustlers" 1949 (Rancher); "Range Land" 1949 (Mosley); "Ride, Ryder, Ride" 1949 (Sheriff); "Rustlers" 1949 (Cook); "Desperadoes of the West" 1950-serial (Storekeeper); "Six Gun Mesa" 1950; "Santa Fe" 1951; "Silver Canyon" 1951; "The Lawless Breed" 1952 (Card Player); "Road Agent" 1952 (Barton); "Jack McCall, Desperado" 1953 (Judge); "A Perilous Journey" 1953 (Ad Lib); "Pals and Gals" 1954-short (Colonel); "A Lawless Street" 1955; "Pardners" 1956 (Townsman). ¶TV: *The Roy Rogers Show*—"The Hermit's Secret" 5-1-52, "Blind Justice" 12-14-52, "The Mingo Kid" 4-26-53 (Titus Clay); *The Lone Ranger*—"El Toro" 5-7-53.

Blyth, Ann (1928-). Films: "Red Canyon" 1949 (Lucy Bostel); "Rose Marie" 1954 (Rose Marie Lemaitre). ¶TV: *Wagon Train*—"The Jenny Tannen Story" 6-24-59 (Phoebe Tannen/Jenny Tannen), "The Martha Barham Story" 11-4-59 (Martha Barham), "The Clementine Jones Story" 10-25-61 (Clementine Jones),

"The Eve Newhope Story" 12-5-62 (Eve Newhope), "The Fort Pierce Story" 9-23-63 (Nancy Winters).

Blythe, Betty (1893-4/7/72). Films: "Nomads of the North" 1920 (Nanette Roland); "Western Courage" 1935 (Mrs. Hanley); "Honky Tonk" 1941 (Mrs. Wilson); "Dawn on the Great Divide" 1942 (Elmira Corkle); "Bar 20" 1943 (Mrs. Stevens); "Madonna of the Desert" 1948 (Mrs. Brown); "The Lonesome Trail" 1955.

Boardman, Eleanor (1898-12/12/91). Films: "The Great Meadow" 1931 (Diony Hall); "The Squaw Man" 1931 (Lady Diana Kerhill).

Boardman, Nan. Films: "Mrs. Mike" 1949 (Georgette Beauclaire). ¶TV: *Jim Bowie*—"Ursula" 2-14-58 (Dona Josefa).

Boardman, True (1882-9/28/18). Films: "The Rose of Old St. Augustine" 1911; "An Outlaw's Sacrifice" 1912; "Broncho Billy's Gun-Play" 1913; "The End of the Circle" 1913; "The Naming of the Rawhide Queen" 1913; "The Rustler's Step-Daughter" 1913; "The Tenderfoot Sheriff" 1913; "Broncho Billy and the Sheriff" 1914; "The Calling of Jim Barton" 1914; "The Cast of the Die" 1914; "A Gambler's Way" 1914; "Single-Handed" 1914; "Broncho Billy's Sentence" 1915; "The Man in Irons" 1915; "The Pitfall" 1915 (Clive).

Boardman, Virginia True (Virginia Eames) (1889-6/10/71). Films: "The Light of Western Stars" 1918 (Bonita); "Pioneer Trails" 1923 (Mrs. Salter); "Three Jumps Ahead" 1923 (Mrs. Darrell); "The Red Rider" 1925 (Polly Fleming); "Brand of the Outlaws" 1936 (Mrs. Matlock); "The Fugitive Sheriff" 1936 (Mrs. Roberts).

Boaz, Charles. Films: "The Saga of Hemp Brown" 1958 (Alf Smedley). ¶TV: *MacKenzie's Raiders*—Regular 1958-59; *Bat Masterson*—"Marked Deck" 3-11-59 (Taggert).

Boccardo, Delia (1948-). Films: "Death Walks in Laredo" 1966-Ital./Span.

Bochner, Hart (1956-). Films: "Mad at the Moon" 1992 (Miller Brown); "Children of the Dust" TVM-1995 (Shelby Hornbeck).

Bochner, Lloyd (1924-). Films: "Scalplock" TVM-1966 (John Pendennis); "Stranger on the Run" TVM-1967 (Mr. Gorman); "Ulzana's Raid" 1972 (Capt. Gates). ¶TV: *Hudson's Bay*—"The Executioner" 5-3-58 (Bigod); *The Legend of Jesse*

James—"The Dead Man's Hand" 9-20-65 (Charles Jennings); *The Virginian*—"Ah Sing vs. Wyoming" 10-25-67 (Luke Evers); *Branded*—"$10,000 for Durango" 11-28-65 (Frank Ross); *A Man Called Shenandoah*—"The Reward" 11-29-65 (Murray); *Wild Wild West*—"The Night of the Puppeteer" 2-25-66 (Zachariah Skull); *Daniel Boone*—"The Scalp Hunter" 3-17-66 (Roger Morgan), "The Secret Code" 12-14-67 (Maksoana), "The Imposter" 1-18-68 (Colonel Chalmers), "The Landlords" 3-5-70 (Churchill James); *Death Valley Days*—"The Jolly Roger and Wells Fargo" 2-4-67 (Robert Lewis Stevenson); *Bonanza*—"The Prince" 4-2-67 (Peters); *The Big Valley*—"The Time After Midnight" 10-2-67 (Joshua Cunningham); *Custer*—"Desperate Mission" 11-8-67 (James Stanhope); *The Men from Shiloh*—"The Town Killer" 3-10-71 (Wilks); *Hec Ramsey*—"The Green Feather Mystery" 12-17-72 (Myles Wingate); *Gunsmoke*—"The Iron Blood of Courage" 2-18-74 (Colie Burdette); *Barbary Coast*—"Jesse Who?" 9-22-75 (Ezra Hubbard).

Bodalo, Jose (1916-7/24/85). Films: "Django" 1966-Ital./Span.; "Ringo's Big Night" 1966-Ital./Span.; "Thompson 1880" 1966-Ital./Ger.; "Train for Durango" 1967-Ital./Span. (Heraclio); "Dollars for a Fast Gun" 1968-Ital./Span. (Adam Martin); "One After Another" 1968-Span./Ital.; "Red Blood, Yellow Gold" 1968-Ital./Span. (El Primero); "Dead Are Countless" 1969-Ital./Span.; "Companeros" 1970-Ital./Span./Ger.; "Captain Apache" 1971-Brit.-Ital./Span. (General).

Boehm, Karl (1928-). TV: *The Virginian*—"The Golden Door" 3-13-63 (Karl Rilke).

Bogarde, Dirk (1921-). Films: "The Singer Not the Song" 1961-Brit. (Anacleto).

Bogart, Humphrey (1899-1/14/57). Films: "A Holy Terror" 1931 (Steve Nash); "The Oklahoma Kid" 1939 (Whip McCord); "Virginia City" 1940 (John Murrell); "The Treasure of the Sierra Madre" 1948 (Fred C. Dobbs).

Bogart, William. Films: "Kill Johnny Ringo" 1966-Ital.; "One Against One ... No Mercy" 1968-Span./Ital. (Grayson); "Rattler Kid" 1968-Ital./Span.; "Night of the Serpent" 1969-Ital.; "Sartana Kills Them All" 1970-Ital./Span.; "They Call Him Veritas" 1972-Ital./Span. (William James); "Carambola" 1974-Ital. (Howard).

Bogert, William (1936-). TV:

Centennial—Regular 1978-79 (William Bellamy).

Bohm, Marquard. Films: "Deadlock" 1970-Ital./Ger./Isr. (the Kid); "Chetan, Indian Boy" 1972-Ger.

Bohn, Merritt (1905-12/11/78). Films: "Nevada Smith" 1966 (River Boat Pilot). ¶TV: *Maverick*—"A Flock of Trouble" 2-14-60 (Big Coley); *Sugarfoot*—"Fernando" 2-16-60 (Dan Fargo); *Colt .45*—"Martial Law" 5-17-60 (Mayor Tullow).

Bohnen, Roman (1894-2/24/49). Films: "California" 1946 (Col. Stuart).

Boice, Helen. Films: "Abilene Town" 1946 (Big Annie).

Bokar, Hal. Films: "The Legend of Earl Durand" 1974. ¶TV: *The Virginian*—"Throw a Long Rope" 10-3-62, "Blaze of Glory" 12-29-65 (Kelly), "The Challenge" 10-19-66 (Hank Logan); *Gunsmoke*—"Like Old Times" 1-21-74 (Clay).

Boland, Eddie (1883-2/3/35). Films: "Hard-Boiled" 1926 (2nd Crook); "Wings of Adventure" 1930 (Viva); "Range Warfare" 1935; "Hit the Saddle" 1937 (Pete); "Riders of the Whistling Skull" 1937.

Boland, Mary (1880-6/23/65). Films: "Ruggles of Red Gap" 1935 (Effie Floud).

Bolder, Cal. Films: "Heller in Pink Tights" 1960 (Goober); "Jesse James Meets Frankenstein's Daughter" 1966 (Hank Tracy/Igor). ¶TV: *Bonanza*—"The Ape" 12-17-60 (Arnie Gurne), "The Fighters" 4-24-66 (Charlie); *The Outlaws*—"Sam Bass" 5-4-61 (Barnes); *Gunsmoke*—"The Summons" 4-21-62 (Dawkins); *Destry*—"Blood Brother-in-Law" 4-17-64 (Perk Motley); *Daniel Boone*—"Goliath" 9-29-66 (Alex, the Assassin); *Cimarron Strip*—"Knife in the Darkness" 1-25-68.

Bolder, Robert (1859-12/10/37). Films: "The Silent Call" 1921 (James Houston).

Bolding, Bonnie. TV: *Cheyenne*—"Incident at Indian Springs" 9-24-57 (Mrs. Ellis); *Have Gun Will Travel*—"Duel at Florence" 10-11-58 (Belle Hooper).

Boles, Jim (1914-5/26/77). Films: "Naked in the Sun" 1957; "A Big Hand for the Little Lady" 1966 (Pete); "Waterhole No. 3" 1967 (Cpl. Blyth); "Wild Women" TVM-1970; "Skin Game" 1971 (Auction Clerk); "The Apple Dumpling Gang" 1975 (Easy Archie). ¶TV: *Have Gun Will Travel*—"The Poker Friend" 11-12-60 (Billy); *The Tall Man*—"Full Payment" 9-9-61 (Holly Cameron);

Cheyenne—"Day's Pay" 10-30-61 (Dalton); *Bronco*—"Then the Mountains" 4-30-62 (Hawley); *The Virginian*—"A Killer in Town" 10-9-63 (Goren), "Blaze of Glory" 12-29-65 (Wirtz), "The Good-Hearted Badman" 2-7-68 (Farmer); *Bonanza*—"The Dark Past" 5-3-64 (Pete), "The Conquistadors" 10-1-67 (Aldrich); *The Big Valley*—"The Murdered Party" 11-1-65, "The Fallen Hawk" 3-2-66 (Storekeeper), "Ladykiller" 10-67-67; *A Man Called Shenandoah*—"The Bell" 12-20-65 (Clay); Dundee and the Culhane—10-25-67 (Murtagh); *The Guns of Will Sonnett*—"Find a Sonnett, Kill a Sonnett" 12-8-67 (Preacher), "Where There's Hope" 12-20-68; *Gunsmoke*—"Pike" 3-1-71 & 3-8-71 (Sutro), "The Sodbusters" 11-20-72 (Kestin); *Kung Fu*—"Cry of the Night Beast" 10-19-74 (Mooney).

Boles, John (1895-2/27/69). Films: "The Shepherd of the Hills" 1928 (Young Matt); "The Water Hole" 1928 (Bert Durland); "Song of the West" 1930 (Stanton); "Rose of the Rancho" 1936 (Jim Kearney).

Boley, May (1882-1/6/63). Films: "The Wagon Show" 1928 (the Strong Woman); "Fighting Caravans" 1931 (Jane); "Cowboy from Brooklyn" 1938 (Mrs. Krinkenheim).

Bolger, Ray (1904-1/15/87). Films: "The Harvey Girls" 1946 (Chris Maule).

Bolling, Tiffany (1946-). TV: *Bonanza*—"Five Candles" 3-2-69 (Callie); *The Life and Times of Grizzly Adams*—3-29-78 (Kate).

Bonaduce, Danny (1959-). Films: "Baker's Hawk" 1976 (Robertson).

Bonanova, Fortunio (1893-4/2/69). Films: "Mark of Zorro" 1940 (Sentry); "Bad Men of Tombstone" 1949 (Mingo); "Conquest of Cochise" 1953 (Mexican Minister); "The Saga of Hemp Brown" 1958 (Serge Bolanos, the Medicine Man); "Thunder in the Sun" 1959 (Fernando Christophe).

Bonar, Ivan (1924-12/8/88). TV: *Have Gun Will Travel*—"Penelope" 12-8-62; *Bonanza*—"Forever" 9-12-72 (Minister), "The Bucket Dog" 12-19-72 (Minister); *Father Murphy*—"Outrageous Fortune" 11-9-82 (Collier).

Bond, David (1915-2/16/89). Films: "Gun Fever" 1958 (Man). ¶TV: *Bonanza*—"The Love Child" 11-8-70 (Doctor); *Kung Fu*—"Barbary House" 2-15-75 (Henry, the Butler), "Flight to Orion" 2-22-75 (Henry,

the Butler), "The Brothers Cain" 3-1-75 (Henry, the Butler), "Full Circle" 3-15-75 (Henry, the Butler).

Bond, Johnny (and His Red River Valley Boys) (1915-6/12/78). Films: "Saga of Death Valley" 1939; "Stick to Your Guns" 1941 (Skinny); "Twilight on the Trail" 1941; "Heart of the Rio Grande" 1942 (Jimmy Wakely Trio); "Little Joe, the Wrangler" 1942; "Old Chisholm Trail" 1942; "Arizona Trail" 1943; "Cowboy Commandos" 1943 (Slim); "Frontier Fury" 1943; "Frontier Law" 1943; "The Lone Star Trail" 1943; "Robin Hood of the Range" 1943; "Tenting Tonight on the Old Camp Ground" 1943; "Marshal of Gunsmoke" 1944; "Oklahoma Raiders" 1944; "Riding West" 1944; "Song of the Range" 1944; "Springtime in Texas" 1945; "Song of the Wasteland" 1947; "Swing the Western Way" 1947.

Bond, Lillian (1910-1/18/91). Films: "Sagebrush Politics" 1930; "Rider of the Plains" 1931 (Betty); "The Squaw Man" 1931 (Babs); "The Westerner" 1940 (Lily Langtry); "The Big Trees" 1952. ¶TV: *The Californians*—"The Alice Pritchard Case" 2-4-58 (Alice Pritchard).

Bond, Raymond (1885-2/13/72). Films: "Lightning Guns" 1950 (Jud Norton); "Return of the Frontiersman" 1950 (Dr. Martin); "Ticket to Tomahawk" 1950 (Station Master).

Bond, Rudy (1914-3/29/82). Films: "The Hard Man" 1957 (John Rodman). ¶TV: *Empire*—"The Convention" 5-14-63 (Sam Callison).

Bond, Tommy (1927-). Films: "Out West with the Peppers" 1940 (Joey Pepper); "Gas House Kids Go West" 1947 (Chimp).

Bond, Ward (1903-11/5/60). Films: "The Big Trail" 1930 (Sid Bascom); "Hello Trouble" 1932 (Kennedy); "White Eagle" 1932 (Bart); "The Sundown Rider" 1933 (Gabe Powers); "Unknown Valley" 1933 (Elder Snead); "The Fighting Code" 1934 (Krull); "The Fighting Ranger" 1934 (Dave); "Frontier Marshal" 1934 (Ben Murchison); "The Crimson Trail" 1935 (Luke Long); "Fighting Shadows" 1935 (Brad Harrison); "Justice of the Range" 1935 (Bob Brennan); "Western Courage" 1935 (LaCrosse); "Avenging Waters" 1936 (Marv Slater); "The Cattle Thief" 1936 (Ranse); "White Fang" 1936 (Thief Robbin Hall); "Park Avenue Lodger" 1937 (Paul Sanger); "Gun Law" 1938 (Pecos); "The Law West of Tombstone" 1938 (Mulligan P. Martinez); "The Cisco Kid and the Lady" 1939 (Walton); "Dodge City" 1939

(Bud Taylor); "Drums Along the Mohawk" 1939 (Adam Hartmann); "Frontier Marshal" 1939 (Town Marshal); "The Oklahoma Kid" 1939 (Wes Handley); "The Return of the Cisco Kid" 1939 (Tough); "Trouble in Sundown" 1939 (Dusty); "Buck Benny Rides Again" 1940 (1st Outlaw); "Kit Carson" 1940 (Ape); "Santa Fe Trail" 1940 (Townley); "Virginia City" 1940 (Sgt. Sam McDaniel); "The Shepherd of the Hills" 1941 (Wash Gibbs); "Sin Town" 1942 (Rock Delaney); "Wild Bill Hickok Rides" 1942 (Sheriff Edmunds); "Tall in the Saddle" 1944 (Judge Garvey); "Dakota" 1945 (Jim Bender); "Canyon Passage" 1946 (Honey Bragg); "My Darling Clementine" 1946 (Morgan Earp); "Unconquered" 1947 (John Fraser); "Fort Apache" 1948 (Sgt. Maj. Michael O'Rourke); "The Three Godfathers" 1948 (Perley "Buck" Sweet); "Singing Guns" 1950 (Sheriff Jim Caradac); "Wagonmaster" 1950 (Elder Wiggs); "The Great Missouri Raid" 1951 (Major Trowbridge); "Only the Valiant" 1951 (Cpl. Timothy Gilchrist); "Hellgate" 1952 (Lt. Tod Vorhees); "Blowing Wind" 1953 (Dutch); "Hondo" 1953 (Buffalo); "The Moonlighter" 1953 (Cole); "Gypsy Colt" 1954 (Frank MacWade); "Johnny Guitar" 1954 (John McIvers); "A Man Alone" 1955 (Sheriff Gil Corrigan); "Dakota Incident" 1956 (Sen. Blakely); "Pillars of the Sky" 1956 (Dr. Joseph Holden); "The Searchers" 1956 (Capt. Rev. Samuel Clayton); "The Halliday Brand" 1957 (Big Dan); "Alias Jesse James" 1959 (Major Seth Adams); "Rio Bravo" 1959 (Pat Wheeler). ¶TV: *Wagon Train*—Regular 1957-65 (Major Seth Adams).

Bondhill, Gertrude (1880-9/15/60). Films: "Miss Arizona" 1919 (Miss Arizona Farnley).

Bondi, Beulah (1892-1/11/81). Films: "The Shepherd of the Hills" 1941 (Aunt Mollie Matthews); "The Baron of Arizona" 1950 (Lona Morales); "The Furies" 1950 (Mrs. Anaheim); "Lone Star" 1952 (Minniver Bryan); "Track of the Cat" 1954 (Ma Bridges). ¶TV: *Zane Grey Theater*—"Black Is for Grief" 4-12-57 (Ma Anderson); *Wagon Train*—"The Prairie Story" 2-1-61 (Grandma); *Dirty Sally*—3-8-74 (Louisa Badger).

Bonet, Nai (1940-). Films: "The Soul of Nigger Charley" 1973 (Anita).

Boniface, Isabel. Films: "True Grit" 1969 (Mrs. Bagby).

Boniface, Symona (1894-9/2/50). Films: "In Early Arizona" 1938;

"The Man from Colorado" 1948 (Matron).

Bonn, Frank A. (1873-3/4/44). Films: "Ben Blair" 1916 (John Rankin).

Bonn, Walter (1889-9/8/53). Films: "The Girl of the Golden West" 1938 (Lieutenant Johnson).

Bonne, Shirley (1934-). TV: *Bonanza*—"Justice" 1-8-67 (Sally).

Bonnell, Lee (1919-5/12/86). Films: "Land of the Open Range" 1942 (Stuart).

Bonner, Frank (1942-). Films: "No Man's Land" TVM-1984 (Deputy Thad Prouty).

Bonner, Joe (1882-4/13/59). Films: "The Man Who Waited" 1922 (Manuel Sanchez); "Western Grit" 1924 (Mickey).

Bonner, Marjorie (1905-9/28/88). Films: "Riding Romance" 1926; "The Four-Footed Ranger" 1928 (Katy Pearl Lee); "Made-to-Order Hero" 1928 (Margery Murray); "The Trail of Courage" 1928 (Ruth Tobin); "Dangerous Days" 1929; "A Rider of the Sierras" 1929.

Bonner, Priscilla. Films: "Honest Hutch" 1920 (Ellen); "Bob Hampton of Placer" 1921 (Schoolteacher); "A Desperate Adventure" 1924; "Three Bad Men" 1926 (Millie Stanley); "Melody Ranch" 1940.

Bonner, William. Films: "The Female Bunch" 1971.

Bonney, Gail (1904-12/7/84). Films: "Cat Ballou" 1965 (Mabel Bentley). ¶TV: *Sky King*—"The Haunted Castle" 4-13-52 (Mrs. Barrett); *Wagon Train*—"The Jonas Murdock Story" 4-13-60, "The Clay Shelby Story" 12-6-64 (Mrs. Mahoney), "The Chottsie Gubenheimer Story" 1-10-65 (Mrs. Wilson); *Tate*—"Voices of the Town" 7-6-60 (Maudeen); *Bonanza*—"Day of Reckoning" 10-22-60, "Bullet for a Bride" 2-16-64; *Lawman*—"Hassayampa" 2-12-61 (Woman), "The Barber" 2-25-62 (Mrs. Wilson); *Rawhide*—"The Pitchwagon" 3-2-62; *Gunsmoke*—"The Ditch" 10-27-62 (Mrs. Hawkins), "Patricia" 1-22-73 (Mrs. Peary); *The Dakotas*—"Requiem at Dancer's Hill" 2-18-63 (Amy Jackson); *Pistols 'n' Petticoats*—"A Crooked Line" 9-17-66 (Mrs. Sanders); *The Road West*—"Pariah" 12-5-66 (Mrs. Stone); *The Big Valley*—"The Disappearance" 11-6-67 (Housekeeper); *The Virginian*—"The Gentle Tamers" 1-24-68 (Lady).

Bonomo, Joe (1902-3/28/78). Films: "The College Cowboy" 1924; "The Riddle Rider" 1924-serial;

"Wolves of the North" 1924-serial; "Flaming Frontier" 1926 (Rain in the Face); "The Golden Stallion" 1927-serial; "Courtin' Wildcats" 1929 (Gorilla); "Phantom of the North" 1929 (Pierre Blanc); "Battling with Buffalo Bill" 1931-serial; "The Phantom of the West" 1931-serial (Keno); "The Sign of the Wolf" 1931-serial (Bud); "The Vanishing Legion" 1931-serial (Stuffy); "The Last Frontier" 1932-serial (Blackie).

Bonos, Gigi. Films: "Shoot, Gringo ... Shoot!" 1968-Ital./Fr.; "For a Book of Dollars" 1973-Ital./Span.

Bonsall, Brian. TV: *Young Riders*—"Old Scores" 2-16-91 (Jereym).

Bon Tempi, Nick. TV: *Wanted—Dead or Alive*—"Hero in the Dust" 2-1-61 (Harry Weaver).

Bon Tempi, Paul. TV: *Wanted—Dead or Alive*—"Hero in the Dust" 2-1-61 (Pete Weaver).

Bonuglia, Maurizio. Films: "The Reward's Yours, the Man's Mine" 1970-Ital.; "Brothers Blue" 1973-Ital./Fr.

Booke, Sorrell (1926-2/11/94). TV: *Wild Wild West*—"The Night of the Egyptian Queen" 11-15-68 (Heisel); *Gunsmoke*—"Milligan" 11-6-72 (Gerald Pandy); *Alias Smith and Jones*—"The Strange Fate of Conrad Meyer Zulick" 12-2-72 (Zulick); *Kung Fu*—"A Dream Within a Dream" 1-17-74 (Sheriff Hodges).

Boomer, Linwood (1955-). TV: *Little House on the Prairie*—Regular 1977-82 (Adam Kendall).

Boon, Robert. TV: *The Alaskans*—"The Abominable Snowman" 12-13-59; *Rawhide*—"Incident of the Music Maker" 5-20-60 (Ernest Zwahlen), "The Immigrants" 3-16-62 (Siegfried); *Tate*—"Before Sunup" 8-17-60 (Otto); *The Virginian*—"Man of the People" 12-23-64 (Hans Jungman); *Laredo*—"A Medal for Reese" 12-30-65 (Paul).

Boone, Brendon. Films: "The Hanged Man" TVM-1974 (Billy Irons). ¶TV: *The Virginian*—"An Echo of Thunder" 10-5-66 (Griff); *Rawhide*—"Duel at Daybreak" 11-16-65 (Roman Bedford); *Bonanza*—"The Last Mission" 5-8-66 (Lowell); *Gunsmoke*—"Hawk" 10-20-69 (Hawk).

Boone, Peter. TV: *Have Gun Will Travel*—"The Puppeteer" 12-24-60, "Genesis" 9-15-62 (Smoke), "The Fifth Bullet" 9-29-62 (Johnny Bartlett).

Boone, Randy (1942-). TV: *Wagon Train*—"The David Garner Story" 5-8-63 (David Garner), "The Robert Harrison Clarke Story" 10-14-

63 (Jamie), "The Eli Bancroft Story" 11-11-63 (Noah Bancroft); *The Virginian*—Regular 1963-66 (Randy Garth); *Bonanza*—"Ballad of the Ponderosa" 11-13-66 (Colter Preston); *Hondo*—"Hondo and the Eagle Claw" 9-8-67 (Sean), "Hondo and the War Cry" 9-15-67 (Sean); *Cimarron Strip*—Regular 1967-68 (Francis Wilde); *Gunsmoke*—"The Busters" 3-10-75 (Hub Miller); *Kung Fu*—"Ambush" 4-5-75 (Spiff).

Boone, Richard (1917-1/10/81). Films: "Kangaroo" 1952 (Gamble); "Return of the Texan" 1952 (Rod); "Way of a Gaucho" 1952 (Salinas); "City of Badmen" 1953 (John Ringo); "The Siege at Red River" 1954 (Brett Manning); "Man Without a Star" 1955 (Steve Miles); "Robbers' Roost" 1955 (Hays); "Ten Wanted Men" 1955 (Wick Campbell); "Star in the Dust" 1956 (Sam Hall); "The Tall T" 1957 (Usher); "The Alamo" 1960 (Gen. Sam Houston); "A Thunder of Drums" 1961 (Capt. Stephen Maddocks); "Rio Conchos" 1964 (Lassiter); "Hombre" 1967 (Grimes); "Madron" 1970-U.S./Israel (Madron); "Big Jake" 1971 (John Fain); "Hec Ramsey" TVM-1972 (Hec Ramsey); "Against a Crooked Sky" 1975 (Russian); "God's Gun" 1976-Ital./Israel; "The Shootist" 1976 (Sweeney). ¶TV: *Frontier*—"Salt War" 4-22-56 (Everett Brayer); *Have Gun Will Travel*—Regular 1957-63 (Paladin); *Cimarron Strip*—"The Roarer" 11-2-67 (Sgt. Bill Disher); *Hec Ramsey*—Regular 1972-74 (Hec Ramsey).

Booth, Adrian (Lorna Gray) (1924-). Films: "Red River Range" 1938 (Jane Mason); "Pest from the West" 1939-short; "The Stranger from Texas" 1939 (Joan Browning); "Bullets for Rustlers" 1940 (Ann Houston); "Deadwood Dick" 1940-serial (Ann Butler); "Rockin' Through the Rockies" 1940-short (Flossie); "Ridin' Down the Canyon" 1942 (Barbara Joyce); "Dakota" 1945 (Entertainer); "Home on the Range" 1946 (Bonnie Garth); "The Man from Rainbow Valley" 1946 (Kay North); "Out California Way" 1946 (Gloria McCoy); "Along the Oregon Trail" 1947 (Sally Dunn); "Last Frontier Uprising" 1947 (Mary Lou Gardner); "Under Colorado Skies" 1947 (Julia); "California Firebrand" 1948 (Joyce Mason); "The Gallant Legion" 1948 (Connie Faulkner); "The Plunderers" 1948 (Julie McCabe); "Brimstone" 1949 (Molly Bannister); "The Last Bandit" 1949 (Kate Foley); "Rock Island Trail" 1950 (Aleeta); "The Savage Horde" 1950 (Livvy Weston); "Oh! Susanna" 1951 (Lia Wilson).

Booth, Edwina (1909-5/18/91). Films: "The Vanishing Legion" 1931-serial (Caroline Hall); "The Last of the Mohicans" 1932-serial.

Booth, Elmer (1882-1/16/55). Films: "In the North Woods" 1921.

Booth, James (1930-). Films: "Macho Callahan" 1970 (King Harry Wheeler); "Zorro, the Gay Blade" 1981 (Velasquez); "Gunsmoke: To the Last Man" TVM-1991 (Preacher). ¶TV: *Wild Wild West*—"The Night of the Wolf" 3-31-67 (Stagedriver); *Bonanza*—"Second Sight" 1-9-72 (Jess).

Booth, Karin (1923-). Films: "The Cariboo Trail" 1950 (Frances); "Cripple Creek" 1952 (Julie Hanson); "Seminole Uprising" 1955 (Susan Hannah); "Top Gun" 1955 (Laura); "Badman's Country" 1958 (Lorna).

Booth, Nesdon (1918-3/25/64). Films: "Cattle Empire" 1958 (Barkeep); "Escape from Red Rock" 1958 (Pete Archer); "Rio Bravo" 1959 (Clark); "Gun Street" 1961; "One-Eyed Jacks" 1961 (Townsman). ¶TV: *Tales of Wells Fargo*—"Alder Gulch" 4-8-57 (Walter Bassett), "Defiant at the Gate" 11-25-61 (Colonel Biscayne); *The Restless Gun*—"The Shooting of Jett King" 10-28-57 (Mack Hawkins); *Maverick*—"Mano Nera" 10-23-60 (Hotel Detective), "The Money Machine" 4-8-62 (Hal Smythe); *The Texan*—"The Nomad" 4-18-60 (Kurt); *Bonanza*—"Sam Hill" 6-3-61 (Hotel Clerk); *Gunsmoke*—"Call Me Dodie" 9-22-62 (Bartender); *Wide Country*—"Journey Down a Dusty Road" 10-4-62 (Clyde Grainger); *Redigo*—"The Blooded Bull" 10-1-63; *Destry*—"Blood Brother-in-Law" 4-17-64 (Turner).

Booth, Robert. Films: "Davy Crockett, King of the Wild Frontier" 1955 (2nd Congressman); "Natchez Trace" 1960 (Clanton).

Boothe, Powers (1949-). Films: "Tombstone" 1993 (Curly Bill).

Borden, Cope. Films: "Texas Jack" 1935 (Skinny).

Borden, Eddie (1888-7/1/55). Films: "Rough Romance" 1930 (Laramie); "Rose of the Rancho" 1936 (Barfly); "Way Out West" 1937 (Man in Audience); "Twenty Mule Team" 1940; "Frontier Gal" 1945 (Man at Table); "Saginaw Trail" 1953 (Jules Brissac).

Borden, Eugene (1897-7/21/72). Films: "Mark of Zorro" 1940 (Officer of the Day); "Hudson Bay" 1941 (Sentry); "Dakota" 1945 (Italian); "Silver Canyon" 1951 (Gus Papalardo); "The Big Sky" 1952; "The Iron Mistress" 1952 (Cocquelon); "Jubilee Trail" 1954 (Kimball, the Detective); "The Far Country" 1955 (Doc Vallon).

Borden, Lynn (1935-). TV: *Centennial*—Regular 1978-79 (Vesta Volkema).

Borden, Olive (1907-10/1/47). Films: "My Own Pal" 1926 (Alice Deering); "Three Bad Men" 1926 (Lee Carlton); "The Yankee Senor" 1926 (Manuelita).

Borden, Renee (1908-9/8/92). Films: "Canyon Hawks" 1930 (Mildred Manning); "Ridin' Law" 1930 (Carmencita); "Fighting Hero" 1934 (Conchita Alvarez); "Kid Courageous" 1935 (Teresa); "Western Justice" 1935 (Beatrice Brent).

Bordine, Mabel. Films: "Beyond the Law" 1918 (Eugenia Moore).

Borelli, Carla. TV: *Wild Wild West*—"The Night of Montezuma's Hordes" 10-27-67 (Sun Goddess).

Borg, Sven Hugo (1896-2/19/81). Films: "Death Rides the Range" 1940 (Baron Strakoff); "Buzzy and the Phantom Pinto" 1941; "Santa Fe" 1951 (Swede Swanstrom).

Borg, Veda Ann (1915-8/16/73). Films: "The Law Comes to Texas" 1939 (Dora Lewis); "Melody Ranch" 1940 (Receptionist); "Arkansas Judge" 1941 (Hettie Huston); "Honky Tonk" 1941 (Pearl); "Marked Trails" 1944 (Blanche); "The Kangaroo Kid" 1950 (Stella Grey); "Rider from Tucson" 1950 (Gypsy); "A Perilous Journey" 1953 (Sadie); "Bitter Creek" 1954 (Whitey); "Frontier Gambler" 1956; "The Naked Gun" 1956; "Thunder in the Sun" 1959 (Marie); "The Alamo" 1960 (Blind Nell). ¶TV: *Wild Bill Hickok*—"The Sheriff Was a Redhead" 7-15-52; *The Restless Gun*—"Jenny" 10-21-57 (Jenny), "More Than Kin" 5-26-58 (Maggie), "Mercyday" 10-6-58 (Rollie); *Sugarfoot*—"The Dead Hills" 3-4-58 (Flo McGuire); *The Californians*—"Bella Union" 1-20-59 (Molly Wallis); *Rough Riders*—"Lesson in Violence" 3-26-59 (Confetti Kate); *Bonanza*—"The Fugitive" 2-4-61 (Beulah).

Borgato, Agostino (1871-3/14/39). Films: "Romance of the Rio Grande" 1929 (Vincente).

Borgese, Sal. Films: "The Greatest Robbery in the West" 1968-Ital.; "I Am Sartana, Your Angel of Death" 1969-Ital./Fr.; "Adios, Sabata" 1970-Ital./Span. (September); "The Bounty Hunters" 1970-Ital.; "It Can Be Done … Amigo" 1971-Ital./Fr./

Span.; "Man Called Invincible" 1973-Ital. (Tricky Dick); "Patience Has a Limit, We Don't" 1974-Span./Ital. (Duke); "Three Supermen of the West" 1974-Ital./Span.

Borgnine, Ernest (1917-). Films: "The Stranger Wore a Gun" 1953 (Bull Slager); "The Bounty Hunter" 1954 (Rachin); "Johnny Guitar" 1954 (Bart Lonergan); "Vera Cruz" 1954 (Donnegan); "Bad Day at Black Rock" 1955 (Coley Trimble); "The Last Command" 1955 (Mike Radin); "Run for Cover" 1955 (Morgan); "Jubal" 1956 (Sheb Horgan); "The Badlanders" 1958 (John McBain); "Chuka" 1967 (Sgt. Otto Hansbach); "The Wild Bunch" 1969 (Dutch Engstrom); "A Bullet for Sandoval" 1970-Ital./Span. (Don Pedro Sandoval); "Hannie Calder" 1971-Brit./Span./Fr. (Emme Clemens); "Sam Hill: Who Killed the Mysterious Mr. Foster?" TVM-1971 (Deputy Sam Hill); "The Trackers" TVM-1971 (Sam Paxton); "The Revengers" 1972-U.S./Mex. (Hoop); "Manhunt" 1984-Ital. ¶TV: *Zane Grey Theater*—"Black Creek Encounter" 3-8-57 (Jim Morrison), "A Gun for Willie" 10-6-60 (Willie); *Wagon Train*—"The Willy Moran Story" 9-18-57 (Willy Moran), "Around the Horn" 10-1-58 (Willie Morgan), "The Estaban Zamora Story" 10-21-59 (Estaban Zamora), "The Earl Packer Story" 1-4-61 (Earl Packer), "The Indian Girl Story" 4-18-65; *Laramie*—"Circle of Fire" 9-22-59 (Major Prescott), "Ride the Wild Wind" 10-11-60 (Boone Caudle).

Borio, Josephine. Films: "The Branded Sombrero" 1928 (Rosa); "Tyrant of Red Gulch" 1928 (Mitza).

Borland, Barlowe (1877-8/31/48). Films: "Forlorn River" 1937 (Cashier); "Thunder Trail" 1937 (Jim Morgan); "Gun Packer" 1938 (Prof. Angel).

Borman, Edward W. Films: "Blaze Away" 1922 (Tuck Marin); "When Law Comes to Hades" 1923; "Between Dangers" 1927.

Borrego, Jesse. Films: "Tecumseh: The Last Warrior" TVM-1995 (Tecumseh).

Borzage, Dan (1897-6/17/75). Films: "The Westerner" 1940 (Joe Yates); "My Darling Clementine" 1946 (Accordian Player); "The Searchers" 1956 (Accordionist at Funeral); "The Horse Soldiers" 1959; "Two Rode Together" 1961; "The Man Who Shot Liberty Valance" 1962 (Townsman); "McClintock" 1963 (Loafer); "Cheyenne Autumn" 1964 (Trooper).

Borzage, Frank (1893-6/19/62). Films: "Days of '49" 1913; "A Hopi Legend" 1913; "The Mystery of Yellow Aster Mine" 1913; "Desert Gold" 1914 (John Carson); "The Panther" 1914; "The Cactus Blossom" 1915; "Secret of Lost River" 1915; "Immediate Lee" 1916 (Immediate Lee); "The Land O' Lizards" 1916 (the Stranger).

Boschero, Dominique. Films: "Train for Durango" 1967-Ital./Span. (Helen); "And the Crows Will Dig Your Grave" 1971-Ital./Span.

Bose, Miguel. Films: "California" 1976-Ital./Span.; "Macho Killers" 1977-Ital. (Sheriff).

Bosic, Andrea (1919-). Films: "Arizona Colt" 1965-Ital./Fr./Span. (Pedro); "Fort Yuma Gold" 1966-Ital./Fr./Span.; "Kill or Be Killed" 1966-Ital.; "Day of Anger" 1967-Ital./Ger. (Murray Abel); "Days of Violence" 1967-Ital.; "Killer Caliber .32" 1967-Ital.; "Two Pistols and a Coward" 1967-Ital.; "Two Sides of the Dollar" 1967-Fr./Ital.; "Death Knows No Time" 1968-Span./Ital.; "Fifteen Scaffolds for the Killer" 1968-Ital./Span.; "I Want Him Dead" 1968-Ital./Span. (Malleck); "Heads You Die ... Tails I Kill You" 1971-Ital.

Bosier, Roy. Films: "Up the MacGregors!" 1967-Ital./Span. (Apache); "Duck, You Sucker!" 1971-Ital. (Landowner).

Bosley, Tom (1927-). Films: "The Bang Bang Kid" 1968-U.S./Span./Ital. (Merriweather Newberry); "Testimony of Two Men" TVM-1977 (Dr. Louis Hedler). ¶TV: *Bonanza*—"The Last Vote" 10-20-68 (Titus Simpson), "A Lawman's Lot Is Not a Happy One" 10-5-69 (Hiram Peabody); *The Virginian*—"Crime Wave at Buffalo Spring" 1-29-69 (Nat Trumbull).

Boss, Yale (1899-11/16/77). Films: "The Story of the Indian Lodge" 1911; "How the Boys Fought the Indians" 1912; "A Tale of Old Tucson" 1914.

Bosson, Barbara (1939-). TV: *Alias Smith and Jones*—"The Ten Days That Shook Kid Curry" 11-4-72 (Mrs. Schwedes).

Bostock, Evelyn (1917-11/28/44). Films: "Cowboy Millionaire" 1935 (Pamela Barclay).

Bosworth, Hobart (1867-12/30/43). Films: "In the Bad Lands" 1909; "On the Border" 1909; "On the Little Big Horn or Cuser's Last Stand" 1909; "The Pine Ridge Feud" 1909; "The Stampede" 1909; "The Tenderfoot" 1909; "Across the Plains" 1910;

"Davy Crockett" 1910; "The Chief's Daughter" 1911; "The Convert of San Clemente" 1911; "Evangeline" 1911; "A Frontier Girl's Courage" 1911; "George Warrington's Escape" 1911; "In the Days of Gold" 1911 (Dick Harding); "In the Shadow of the Pines" 1911; "The Indian Vestal" 1911; "It Happened in the West" 1911; "John Oakhurst—Gambler" 1911; "Kit Carson's Wooing" 1911; "Little Injin" 1911; "McKee Rankin's '49" 1911; "One of Nature's Noblemen" 1911; "Range Pals" 1911; "A Sacrifice to Civilization" 1911; "The Schoolmaster of Mariposa" 1911; "Sheriff of Tuolumne" 1911; "The White Medicine Man" 1911; "A Child of the Wilderness" 1912; "A Crucial Test" 1912; "Darkfeather's Strategy" 1912; "The End of the Romance" 1912; "The Hand of Fate" 1912; "A Message to Kearney" 1912; "The Price He Paid" 1912; "A Reconstructed Rebel" 1912; "The Shrinking Rawhide" 1912; "Tenderfoot Bob's Resignation" 1912; "The Trade Gun Bullet" 1912; "The Beaded Buckskin Bag" 1913; "Buck Richard's Bride" 1913; "Pierre of the North" 1913; "The Rancher's Failing" 1913; "Buckshot John" 1915 (Buckshot John Moran); "Colorado" 1915 (Thomas Doyle); "Fatherhood" 1915 (Lon); "Two Men of Sandy Bar" 1916 (John Oakhurst); "The Yaqui" 1916 (Tambor); "The Border Legion" 1918 (Jack Kells); "Blind Hearts" 1921 (Lars Larson); "Sundown" 1924 (John Brent); "The Golden Strain" 1925 (Major Milton Mulford); "Zander the Great" 1925 (the Sheriff); "The Last of the Mohicans" 1932-serial; "Wildcat Trooper" 1936 (Dr. Martin); "King of the Sierras" 1938 (Uncle Hank); "Rollin' Plains" 1938 (Gospel Moody); "They Died with Their Boots On" 1941 (Clergyman); "Sin Town" 1942 (Humiston).

Boteler, Wade (1891-5/7/43). Films: "Lahoma" 1920 (Henry Gledware); "Blind Hearts" 1921 (John Thomas); "Ridin' Wild" 1922 (Art Jordan); "While Satan Sleeps" 1922 (Red Barton); "The Phantom Horseman" 1924 (Jefferson Williams); "The Whipping Boss" 1924 (the Whipping Bond); "The Painted Desert" 1931; "Come on, Danger!" 1932 (Tex); "End of the Trail" 1932 (Sergeant O'Brien); "Unknown Valley" 1933 (Elder Crossett); "The Westerner" 1934 (Ed Ross); "Call of the Wild" 1935 (1st Miner in Dawson); "Melody Trail" 1935 (Timothy Thomas); "Wells Fargo" 1937 (Captain); "Billy the Kid Returns" 1938 (Garrett); "Days of Jesse James" 1939 (Dr. Samuels); "The Oklahoma Kid"

1939 (Sheriff Abe Collins); "Southward Ho!" 1939 (Colonel Denbigh); "Gaucho Serenade" 1940 (Rancher); "The Man from Dakota" 1940 (General); "My Little Chickadee" 1940 (Leading Citizen); "Three Faces West" 1940 (Harris); "Under Texas Skies" 1940 (Sheriff Brooke); "Young Buffalo Bill" 1940 (Col. Joe Calhoun); "The Kid from Kansas" 1941 (Russell); "The Singing Hill" 1941; "Jackass Mail" 1942 (Doctor); "Ride 'Em, Cowboy" 1942 (Rodeo Manager); "Riding High" 1943 (Mailman).

Botiller, Richard "Dick". Films: "Gun Law" 1933; "Fighting Hero" 1934 (Dick); "The Man Trailer" 1934; "The Prescott Kid" 1934 (Isadoro); "Thunder Over Texas" 1934; "Arizona Bad Man" 1935 (Pedro Gonzalez); "Cheyenne Tornado" 1935 (Felipe Farley); "Circle of Death" 1935 (Mexican Joe); "Five Bad Men" 1935; "Gallant Defender" 1935; "Gun Play" 1935 (General Torado); "Gunsmoke on the Guadalupe" 1935; "Justice of the Range" 1935; "Lightning Triggers" 1935 (Juan); "The Outlaw Deputy" 1935; "Range Warfare" 1935; "Riding Wild" 1935 (Joaquin Ortega); "Wagon Trail" 1935; "Wild Mustang" 1935; "Comin' Round the Mountain" 1936; "Gun Smoke" 1936 (Felipe); "Lightning Bill Carson" 1936; "The Mysterious Avenger" 1936; "Ramona" 1936 (Servant); "Rio Grande Ranger" 1936; "The Traitor" 1936 (Remos); "Treachery Rides the Range" 1936 (Antelope Boy); "West of Nevada" 1936 (Bald Eagle); "The Californian" 1937 (Pablo); "The Devil's Saddle Legion" 1937 (Chocktaw); "Dodge City Trail" 1937 (Bill); "The Idaho Kid" 1937 (Gunman); "The Old Wyoming Trail" 1937 (Cattle Rustler); "One Man Justice" 1937 (Pinto); "Two-Fisted Sheriff" 1937; "Colorado Trail" 1938 (Henchman); "Gold Is Where You Find It" 1938 (Ramon); "Pioneer Trail" 1938 (Pedro); "South of Arizona" 1938 (Latigo); "Stagecoach Days" 1938; "West of Santa Fe" 1938 (Foley); "The Fighting Gringo" 1939 (Jose); "The Man from Sundown" 1939 (Rio Mason); "Mexicali Rose" 1939 (Manuel); "North of the Yukon" 1939 (Barton); "Overland with Kit Carson" 1939-serial (Natchez); "South of the Border" 1939 (Pablo); "The Stranger from Texas" 1939 (Rankin); "Texas Stampede" 1939 (Amos); "Union Pacific" 1939 (Indian); "Wyoming" 1940 (Rusty); "The Masked Rider" 1941 (Pedro); "North from the Lone Star" 1941; "The Pinto Kid"

1941 (Cheyenne); "The Son of Davy Crockett" 1941; "Wyoming Wildcat" 1941; "Bad Men of the Hills" 1942 (Brant); "Wild Bill Hickok Rides" 1942 (Sager); "Hail to the Rangers" 1943; "The Vigilantes Ride" 1944 (Rogan); "The Yellow Rose of Texas" 1944 (Indian Pete); "Renegades of the Rio Grande" 1945 (Clem); "Return of the Durango Kid" 1945.

Bottoms, John (1939-). Films: "Doc" 1971 (Virgil Earp).

Bottoms, Joseph (1954-). Films: "The Long Riders" 1980 (Mortician); "I Married Wyatt Earp" TVM-1983 (Driver); "Gunsmoke: To the Last Man" TVM-1991 (Tommy Graham). ¶TV: *Young Riders*—"The Road Not Taken" 6-11-92 (Floyd Dobbins).

Bottoms, Sam (1956-). Films: "Zandy's Bride" 1974 (Mel Allan); "The Outlaw Josey Wales" 1976 (Jamie); "Bronco Billy" 1980 (Leonard).

Bouchet, Barbara (1943-). TV: *The Virginian*—"The Fortress" 12-27-67 (Francoise).

Bouchey, Willis (1900-9/28/77). Films: "Gun Belt" 1953 (Endicott); "Battle of Rogue River" 1954 (Major Wallich); "Drum Beat" 1954 (Gen. Gilliam); "The Spoilers" 1955 (Jonathan Struve); "The Violent Men" 1955 (Sheriff Martin Kenner); "Johnny Concho" 1956 (Sheriff Henderson); "Pillars of the Sky" 1956 (Col. Edson Stedlow); "Last of the Badmen" 1957 (Marshal Parker); "The Last Stagecoach West" 1957; "The Sheepman" 1958 (Mr. Payton); "The Horse Soldiers" 1959 (Col. Phil Secord); "No Name on the Bullet" 1959 (Sheriff); "Sergeant Rutledge" 1960 (Col. Otis Fosgate); "Five Guns to Tombstone" 1961; "Two Rode Together" 1961 (Mr. Harry J. Wringle); "How the West Was Won" 1962 (Surgeon); "The Man Who Shot Liberty Valance" 1962 (Jason Tulley); "Return of the Gunfighter" TVM-1967 (Judge Ellis); "Support Your Local Sheriff" 1969 (Thomas Devery); "Dirty Dingus Magee" 1970 (Ira Teasdale); "Support Your Local Gunfighter" 1971 (McLaglen). ¶TV: *Stories of the Century*—"Last Stagecoach West" 1954; *Zane Grey Theater*—"The Unrelenting Sky" 10-26-56 (Paul Travers), "Dangerous Orders" 2-8-57 (Mott), "Decision at Wilson's Creek" 5-17-57 (Gen. Price), "A Man to Look Up To" 11-29-57 (Case); *Broken Arrow*—"Fathers and Sons" 4-2-57 (Jeremy Chambers); *The Adventures of Rin Tin Tin*—"The Gentle Kingdom" 6-7-57 (Cunningham); *Have Gun Will Travel*—"A

Matter of Ethics" 10-12-57; *The Californians*—"Panic on Montgomery Street" 1-14-58 (Seth Woods); *Buckskin*—"Cash Robertson" 8-7-58 (Cash Robertson); *Tales of Wells Fargo*—"The Golden Owl" 9-29-58 (Sam Bankroft), "Man of Another Breed" 12-2-61 (Frank Dane); *Wanted—Dead or Alive*—"Drop to Drink" 12-27-58 (Inspector Bascom), "Amos Carter" 5-9-59 (Doc Kirk), "Vendetta" 4-9-60 (Colonel Bradley); *Lawman*—"The Journey" 4-26-59 (Jabez Bentham); *Colt .45*—"Amnesty" 5-24-59 (Governor Wallace); *Bat Masterson*—"The Conspiracy" 6-17-59 & 6-24-59 (Marshal); *Bonanza*—"A Rose for Lotta" 9-12-59 (George Garvey), "The Last Haircut" 2-3-63; *Cheyenne*—"Riot at Arroyo Soco" 2-1-60; *The Deputy*—"Lawman's Blood" 2-6-60 (Dr. Landy); *Wagon Train*—"The Colter Craven Story" 11-23-60; *Bronco*—"Ride the Whirlwind" 1-15-62 (Judge Fowler); *Laramie*—"The Dynamiters" 3-6-62, "The Fortune Hunter" 10-9-62; *Wide Country*—"Our Ernie Kills People" 11-1-62 (Judge Spencer); *The Dakotas*—"Incident at Rapid City" 3-4-63 (Colonel Fitch); *The Virginian*—"A Distant Fury" 3-20-63 (Glen Hubbard); *Stoney Burke*—"The Journey" 5-20-63 (Bowen); *F Troop*—"The Phantom Major" 9-28-65 (Colonel Saunders); *Gunsmoke*—"The Hostage" 12-4-65 (Sheriff Amos Hockley), "The Victim" 1-1-68 (Jim Stark); *Pistols 'n' Petticoats*—10-15-66 (Doctor); *Daniel Boone*—"A Tall Tale of Prater Beasely" 1-16-69.

Boudwin, Jimsy. Films: "The Scrappin' Kid" 1926 (Mike Brent); "The Unknown Cavalier" 1926 (Billy Gaunt).

Boulton, Betty. Films: "The Mollycoddle" 1920 (Molly Warren).

Bourke, Fan (1886-3/9/59). Films: "Beating Back" 1914.

Bourne, Peter. Films: "North to Alaska" 1960 (Olaf). TV: *Rawhide*—"The Lost Herd" 10-16-64 (Gustauf).

Bourneuf, Philip (1908-3/23/79). TV: *Gunsmoke*—"Legal Revenge" 11-17-56 (George Bassett), "Wild West" 2-15-58 (Mr. Kelly); *Wagon Train*—"Swamp Devil" 4-4-62 (Joshua), "The Emmett Lawton Story" 3-6-63 (Chad Kramer); *The Big Valley*—"The Martyr" 10-17-66 (Judge Adam Cross); *Pistols 'n' Petticoats*—2-11-67 (Clif Ledbetter); *Hec Ramsey*—"The Mystery of the Yellow Rose" 1-28-73 (Lawyer).

Boutell, Genee. Films: "Fighting Cowboy" 1933 (Lizabeth Horton); "Lightning Range" 1934; "Rawhide Romance" 1934 (Patricia Whitney); "The Whirlwind Rider" 1935.

Bouton, Betty. Films: "A Man's Fight" 1919 (Avis Dale); "Not a Drum Was Heard" 1924 (Jean Ross).

Bow, Clara (1905-9/27/65). Films: "The Best Bad Man" 1925 (Peggy Swain); "The Scarlet West" 1925 (Miriam).

Bow, Michael. Films: "The Bravos" TVM-1972 (Sergeant Boyd). ¶TV: *The Men from Shiloh*—"Lady at the Bar" 11-4-70 (Clyde Willis), "Nan Allen" 1-6-71 (Andy).

Bowakow, Deschingis. Films: "Chetan, Indian Boy" 1972-Ger. (Chetan).

Bowdon, Doris (1915-). Films: "Drums Along the Mohawk" 1939 (Mary Reall).

Bowe, Rosemarie. Films: "The Peacemaker" 1956 (Ann Davis).

Bowen, Harry. Films: "Ghost Valley" 1932 (Marty); "The Saddle Buster" 1932 (Calgary); "Rainbow Ranch" 1933 (Masher on Train); "Annie Oakley" 1935 (Father); "Crashing Broadway" 1935 (Fred Storm); "Heir to Trouble" 1935 (Hank); "Ruggles of Red Gap" 1935 (Photographer).

Bowen, Roger (1932-). TV: *Dirty Sally*—"The Old Soldier" 1-25-74 (Colonel Lockwood).

Bower, Antoinette (1932-). TV: *Hudson's Bay*—"The Accounting" 3-1-58 (Dorcas Cobb), "Montgomery Velvet" 3-15-58 (Joanna Balfour), "Civilization" 4-12-58 (Drussilla); *Have Gun Will Travel*—"The Piano" 11-11-61 (Sybil); *Wagon Train*—"The Bruce Saybrook Story" 11-22-61 (Diana Saybrook); *Stoney Burke*—"Point of Entry" 3-4-63 (Erna Bremen); *The Travels of Jaimie McPheeters*—"The Day of the Homeless" 12-8-63 (Nellie), "The Day of the Tin Trumpet" 2-2-64 (Nellie); *Great Adventure*—"The Special Courage of Captain Pratt" 2-14-64 (Anna Pratt); *Wild Wild West*—"The Night of the Sudden Death" 10-8-65 (Janet Coburn); *A Man Called Shenandoah*—"Aces and Kings" 3-28-66 (Lila Morgan); *Iron Horse*—"Town Full of Fear" 12-5-66 (Angie Bemis); *Cowboy in Africa*—"The New World" 9-11-67 (Bibi Graf), "The Lions" 3-25-68 (Ellen Cromwell); *The Big Valley*—"Deathtown" 10-28-68 (Alicia Akers); *Bonanza*—"Little Girl Lost" 11-3-68 (Martha Dorcas); *Lancer*—"The Black Angel" 10-21-69 (Angeline).

Bower, Tom. Films: "The Ballad of Gregorio Cortez" 1983 (Boone Choate); "Desperado: The Outlaw Wars" TVM-1989 (Dobbs).

Bowers, John (1899-11/17/36). Films: "The Silent Call" 1921 (Clark Moran); "The Sky Pilot" 1921 (the Sky Pilot); "Code of the Wilderness" 1924 (Rex Randerson); "When a Man's a Man" 1924 (Lawrence "Patches" Knight); "Whispering Smith" 1926 (McCloud); "Mounted Fury" 1931 (Jim Leyton).

Bowker, Aldrich (1875-3/21/47). Films: "Romance of the Rio Grande" 1941 (Padre Martinez).

Bowman, Lee (1914-12/25/79). "Wyoming" 1940 (Sgt. Connolly).

Bowman, Ralph. *see* Archer, John.

Bowman, Rudy (1890-10/29/72). Films: "Southward Ho!" 1939; "Cheyenne Wildcat" 1944; "West of Alamo" 1946; "Roaring Westward" 1949; "She Wore a Yellow Ribbon" 1949 (Pvt. John Smith/Gen. Rome Clay).

Boxleitner, Bruce (1950-). Films: "The Macahans" TVM-1976 (Seth Macahan); "The Gambler" TVM-1980 (Billy Montana); "Wild Times" TVM-1980 (Vern Tyree); "The Gambler, Part II—The Adventure Continues" TVM-1983 (Billy Montana); "I Married Wyatt Earp" TVM-1983 (Wyatt Earp); "Down the Long Hill" TVM-1987 (Collins); "The Gambler, Part III—The Legend Continues" TVM-1987 (Billy Montana); "The Gambler V: Playing for Keeps" TVM-1994 (Billy Montana); "Gunsmoke: One Man's Justice" TVM-1994 (Davis Healey); "Wyatt Earp: Return to Tombstone" TVM-1994 (Sheriff). ¶TV: *Gunsmoke*—"The Sharecroppers" 3-31-75 (Toby Hogue); *How the West Was Won*—Regular 1977-79 (Luke Macahan).

Boyce, George (1899-2/14/77). Films: "Ten Wanted Men" 1955.

Boyd, Betty (1908-9/16/71). Films: "Under a Texas Moon" 1930 (Girl of the Pool); "Gun Law" 1933 (Nita Hammond).

Boyd, Bill "Cowboy Rambler" (1910-12/7/77). Films: "Along the Sundown Trail" 1942; "Prairie Pals" 1942 (Bill); "Raiders of the West" 1942; "Rolling Down the Great Divide" 1942 (Bill Boyd); "Texas Man Hunt" 1942 (Bill Boyd).

Boyd, Rick. Films: "Cjamango" 1967-Ital.; "Face to Face" 1967-Ital.; "Run Man, Run" 1967-Ital./Fr.; "Django Kills Softly" 1968-Ital.; "The Greatest Robbery in the West" 1968-Ital.; "I Want Him Dead" 1968-Ital./Span.; "Payment in Blood" 1968-Ital.; "The Ruthless Four" 1968-Ital./Ger.; "A Sky Full of Stars for a Roof" 1968-Ital.; "I Am Sartana, Your Angel of Death" 1969-Ital./Fr.; "Django Challenges Sartana" 1970-Ital.; "Roy Colt and Winchester Jack" 1970-Ital.; "Gold of the Heroes" 1971-Ital./Fr.; "Have a Good Funeral, My Friend ... Sartana Will Pay" 1971-Ital.; "Heads You Die ... Tails I Kill You" 1971-Ital. (Duke Kranz); "His Name Was King" 1971-Ital.; "Vendetta at Dawn" 1971-Ital.; "I Am Sartana, Trade Your Guns for a Coffin" 1972-Ital.; "Jesse and Lester, Two Brothers in a Place Called Trinity" 1972-Ital.; "Shoot Joe, and Shoot Again" 1972-Ital.; "Anything for a Friend" 1973-Ital.; "Fighting Fists of Shanghai Joe" 1973-Ital.; "Halleluja to Vera Cruz" 1973-Ital.; "Here We Go Again, Eh Providence?" 1973-Ital./Fr./Span.; "Apache Woman" 1975-Ital.

Boyd, Stephen (1928-6/2/77). Films: "The Bravados" 1958 (Bill Zachary); "Shalako" 1968-Brit./Fr. (Bosky Fulton); "Hannie Calder" 1971-Brit./Span./Fr. (the Preacher); "The Man Called Noon" 1973-Brit./Span./Ital. (Rimes); "Those Dirty Dogs!" 1973-U.S./Ital./Span. (Chadwell); "Montana Trap" 1976-Ger. (Bill Addison).

Boyd, William (1895-9/12/72). Films: "The Last Frontier" 1926 (Tom Kirby); "Jim the Conqueror" 1927 (Jim Burgess); "The Painted Desert" 1931 (Bill Holbrook); "Men of America" 1933 (Jim Parker); "Hopalong Cassidy" 1935 (Bill "Hopalong" Cassidy); "Bar 20 Rides Again" 1936 (Hopalong Cassidy); "Call of the Prairie" 1936 (Hopalong Cassidy); "The Eagle's Brood" 1936 (Hopalong Cassidy); "Hopalong Cassidy Returns" 1936 (Hopalong Cassidy); "Three on the Trail" 1936 (Hopalong Cassidy); "Trail Dust" 1936 (Hopalong Cassidy); "Borderland" 1937 (Hopalong Cassidy); "Heart of the West" 1937 (Hopalong Cassidy); "Hills of Old Wyoming" 1937 (Hopalong Cassidy); "Hopalong Rides Again" 1937 (Hopalong Cassidy); "North of the Rio Grande" 1937 (Hopalong Cassidy); "Rustler's Valley" 1937 (Hopalong Cassidy); "Texas Trail" 1937 (Hopalong Cassidy); "Bar 20 Justice" 1938 (Hopalong Cassidy); "Cassidy of Bar 20" 1938 (Hopalong Cassidy); "The Frontiersman" 1938 (Hopalong Cassidy); "Heart of Arizona" 1938 (Hopalong Cassidy); "In Old Mexico" 1938 (Hopalong Cassidy); "Partners of the Plains" 1938 (Hopalong Cassidy); "Pride of the West" 1938 (Hopalong Cassidy); "Sunset Trail" 1938 (Hopalong Cassidy); "Law of the Pampas" 1939 (Hopalong Cassidy); "Range War" 1939 (Hopalong Cassidy); "Renegade Trail" 1939 (Hopalong Cassidy); "Silver on the Sage" 1939 (Hopalong Cassidy); "Hidden Gold" 1940 (Hopalong Cassidy); "Santa Fe Marshal" 1940 (Hopalong Cassidy); "The Showdown" 1940 (Hopalong Cassidy); "Stagecoach War" 1940 (Hopalong Cassidy); "Three Men from Texas" 1940 (Hopalong Cassidy); "Border Vigilantes" 1941 (Hopalong Cassidy); "Doomed Caravan" 1941 (Hopalong Cassidy); "In Old Colorado" 1941 (Hopalong Cassidy); "Outlaws of the Desert" 1941 (Hopalong Cassidy); "Pirates on Horseback" 1941 (Hopalong Cassidy); "Riders of the Timberline" 1941 (Hopalong Cassidy); "Secrets of the Wastelands" 1941 (Hopalong Cassidy); "Stick to Your Guns" 1941 (Hopalong Cassidy); "Twilight on the Trail" 1941 (Hopalong Cassidy); "Wide Open Town" 1941 (Hopalong Cassidy); "Undercover Man" 1942 (Hopalong Cassidy); "Bar 20" 1943 (Hopalong Cassidy); "Border Patrol" 1943 (Hopalong Cassidy); "Colt Comrades" 1943 (Hopalong Cassidy); "False Colors" 1943 (Hopalong Cassidy); "Hoppy Serves a Writ" 1943 (Hopalong Cassidy); "The Leather Burners" 1943 (Hopalong Cassidy); "Lost Canyon" 1943 (Hopalong Cassidy); "Riders of the Deadline" 1943 (Hopalong Cassidy); "Forty Thieves" 1944 (Hopalong Cassidy); "Lumberjack" 1944 (Hopalong Cassidy); "Mystery Man" 1944 (Hopalong Cassidy); "Texas Masquerade" 1944 (Hopalong Cassidy); "The Devil's Playground" 1946 (Hopalong Cassidy); "Fool's Gold" 1946 (Hopalong Cassidy); "Dangerous Venture" 1947 (Hopalong Cassidy); "Hoppy's Holiday" 1947 (Hopalong Cassidy); "The Marauders" 1947 (Hopalong Cassidy); "Unexpected Guest" 1947 (Hopalong Cassidy); "Borrowed Trouble" 1948 (Hopalong Cassidy); "The Dead Don't Dream" 1948 (Hopalong Cassidy); "False Paradise" 1948 (Hopalong Cassidy); "Silent Conflict" 1948 (Hopalong Cassidy); "Sinister Journey" 1948 (Hopalong Cassidy); "Strange Gamble" 1948 (Hopalong Cassidy). ¶TV: *Hopalong Cassidy*—Regular 1952 (Hopalong Cassidy).

Boyd, William "Stage" (1890-3/20/35). Films: "The Spoilers" 1930 (Alec McNamara); "The Storm" 1930 (Burr Winton); "Gun Smoke" 1931 (Kedge Darvis).

Boydston, Dan. Films: "Showdown" 1973 (Rawls).

Boyett, William. Films: "Sam Whiskey" 1969. ¶TV: *The Cisco Kid*—"The Gramophone" 9-20-52, "Indian Uprising" 11-8-52; *Death Valley Days*—"Eleven Thousand Miners Can't Be Wrong" 9-13-54, "The Luck of the Irish" 4-21-57, "A General Without Cause" 4-12-61 (Miles Owens); *Tales of the Texas Rangers*—"Ransom Flight" 8-27-55 (Wade Crowell), "Home in San Antone" 10-22-55 (Jan Krinlin), "Jail Bird" 10-29-55 (Ron Hackett), "Last Days of Boot Hill" 2-11-56 (Ludeen), "Riders of the Lone Star" 12-1-57 (Terry Ford); *Sergeant Preston of the Yukon*—"Go Fever" 3-29-56 (Constable Malloy); *Wagon Train*—"The John Cameron Story" 10-2-57 (Tacker Brother); *Maverick*—"The Third Rider" 1-5-58 (Collins); *Tombstone Territory*—"Fight for a Fugitive" 6-4-58 (Howie Dickerson); *Northwest Passage*—"The Red Coat" 9-21-58 (Deke); *Have Gun Will Travel*—"Fragile" 10-31-59 (Rancher); *Zane Grey Theater*—"Death in a Wood" 12-17-59 (Union Trooper); *Gunslinger*—"The Diehards" 4-20-61 (Roy Jessup); *Laramie*—"Among the Missing" 9-25-62, "The Wedding Party" 1-29-63 (Pike); *Gunsmoke*—"Gilt Guilt" 4-24-65 (Jake); *How the West Was Won*—Episode Five 3-12-78 (Dr. Dupree); *Young Maverick*—"A Fistful of Oats" 12-5-79.

Boyland, Mary (1913-2/18/84). Films: "Heartland" 1980 (Ma Gills).

Boyle, Irene. Films: "Heart of the Sunset" 1918 (Paloma).

Boyle, Jack (1916-11/30/69). TV: *Rawhide*—"The Long Count" 1-5-62 (Barber).

Boyle, Peter (1936-). Films: "Kid Blue" 1973 (Preacher Bob).

Boyle, Ray. TV: *Death Valley Days*—"Yaller" 1-27-54; *Gunsmoke*—"Word of Honor" 10-1-55 (Jeff Worth).

Boyle, Wally. Films: "The Paleface" 1948 (Hotel Clerk); "Son of Paleface" 1952 (Perkins).

Boyne, Hazel "Sunny" (1883-8/27/66). Films: "Son of Paleface" 1952 (Old Lady).

Bozlino, Paolo. Films: "Desperado" 1972-Span./Ital.

Bozzuffi, Marcel (1929-2/2/88). Films: "Chino" 1973-Ital./Span./Fr. (Maral).

Bracey, Clara T. (1847-2/22/41). Films: "The Gambler of the West" 1914.

Bracey, Sidney (1877-8/5/42). Films: "The Long Trail" 1917 (Paul Graham); "Ruggles of Red Gap" 1923 (Sam Henshaw); "A Man Four-Square" 1926 (Homer Webb); "Sioux Blood" 1929 (Cheyenne Jones); "The Avenger" 1931 (Windy); "Sutter's Gold" 1936 (Smythe); "Wild West Days" 1937-serial.

Bracken, Eddie (1920-). TV: *Rawhide*—"Incident of the Clown" 3-29-63 (Morris G. Stevens), "Incident of the Pied Piper" 2-6-64 (Edgar Allan Smithers).

Bradbury, Jr., Bob. Films: "Davy Crockett at the Fall of the Alamo" 1926 (Pinky Smith); "Sitting Bull at the Spirit Lake Massacre" 1927 (Bob Keefe).

Bradbury, Jr., James (1894-6/21/36). Films: "Fear-Bound" 1925 (Luke Tumble); "The Circus Ace" 1927 (Gus Peabody); "Tide of Empire" 1929 (Bejabbers); "The Glorious Trail" 1928 (Bill Keller); "Cheyenne" 1929 (Slim); "In Old Arizona" 1929 (Soldier); "Smilin' Guns" 1929 (Barber); "Last of the Duanes" 1930 (Euchre); "Cisco Kid" 1931 (Dixon); "Between Fighting Men" 1932 (Higgie).

Bradbury, Kitty. Films: "Code of the Wilderness" 1924 (Aunt Martha).

Bradbury, Lane. TV: *Gunsmoke*—"Outlaw's Woman" 12-11-65 (Allie Sommers), "Muley" 1-21-67 (Lucy), "Hill Girl" 1-29-68 (Merry Florene), "Uncle Finney" 10-14-68 (Merry Florene), "The Gold Mine" 1-27-69 (Merry Florene), "The Still" 11-10-69 (Merry Florene); *Iron Horse*—"Volcano Wagon" 1-16-67 (Rachel Sparrow); *Kung Fu*—"An Eye for an Eye" 1-25-73 (Annie Buchanan).

Bradbury, Robert. Films: "Cavanaugh of the Forest Rangers" 1918 (Sam Gregg).

Bradbury, Ronald (1886-11/24/49). Films: "Colorado" 1915 (Col. Kincaid).

Bradbury, William. Films: "Tennessee's Pardner" 1916 (Bill Kent).

Braddock, Martin. TV: *Death Valley Days*—"Shadow on the Window" 2-23-60 (Billy).

Braddock, Mickey. see Dolenz, Mickey.

Bradford, James. Films: "The Shepherd of the Hills" 1964 (Sheriff).

Bradford, John. Films: "The Old Corral" 1936 (Mike Scarlotti).

Bradford, Lane (1923-6/7/73). Films: "Frontier Crusader" 1940; "The Lone Rider in Ghost Town" 1941; "Valley of Vanishing Men" 1942-serial; "The Fighting Buckaroo" 1943; "Thundering Trails" 1943;

"Marshal of Laredo" 1945; "Overland Riders" 1946; "Shadows on the Range" 1946; "Silver Range" 1946; "Terrors on Horseback" 1946; "Ghost Town Renegades" 1947 (Wace); "Pioneer Justice" 1947 (Joe); "Prairie Raiders" 1947; "Return of the Lash" 1947 (Dave); "Riders of the Lone Star" 1947; "Shadow Valley" 1947 (Bob); "Swing the Western Way" 1947; "The Adventures of Frank and Jesse James" 1948-serial (Bill); "Black Hills" 1948 (Cooper); "Check Your Guns" 1948 (Slim); "Dead Man's Gold" 1948 (Ross Evans); "Frontier Agent" 1948; "The Hawk of Powder River" 1948 (Cooper); "Sundown in Santa Fe" 1948; "Tornado Range" 1948 (Thorne); "Bandit King of Texas" 1949 (Cal Barker); "Death Valley Gunfighter" 1949 (Snake Richards); "The Far Frontier" 1949 (Butch); "Law of the Golden West" 1949 (Belden); "Outcasts of the Trail" 1949; "Prince of the Plains" 1949 (Keller); "Ranger of Cherokee Strip" 1949; "Roll, Thunder, Roll" 1949 (Wolf); "San Antone Ambush" 1949 (Al); "Sheriff of Wichita" 1949; "Silver Butte" 1949-short; "South of Rio" 1949 (Tex); "Western Renegades" 1949; "The Wyoming Bandit" 1949 (Buck); "The Arizona Cowboy" 1950 (Applegate); "Bells of Coronado" 1950 (Jenks); "Code of the Silver Sage" 1950 (Curt Watson); "Cowboy and the Prizefighter" 1950; "The Fighting Redhead" 1950 (Windy); "Frisco Tornado" 1950 (Mike); "Hills of Oklahoma" 1950 (Webb); "The James Brothers of Missouri" 1950-serial (Monk Tucker); "The Missourians" 1950 (Stash); "The Old Frontier" 1950 (Spud); "Texas Dynamo" 1950; "Don Daredevil Rides Again" 1951-serial (Webber); "The Lady from Texas" 1951; "Lawless Cowboys" 1951 (Ace Malloy); "The Longhorn" 1951 (Purdy); "Oklahoma Justice" 1951; "Stage to Blue River" 1951 (Reardon); "Stagecoach Driver" 1951; "Texas Lawmen" 1951 (Mason); "Wanted Dead or Alive" 1951; "Whistling Hills" 1951 (Cassidy); "Dead Man's Trail" 1952; "Desert Passage" 1952 (Langdon); "Desperadoes' Outpost" 1952 (Mike); "Fort Osage" 1952 (Rawlins); "The Gunman" 1952; "Kansas Territory" 1952 (Fred Jethro); "The Lusty Men" 1952 (Jim-Bob Tyler); "The Man from Black Hills" 1952 (Sheriff Moran); "Night Raiders" 1952 (Talbot); "The Raiders" 1952 (Pete Robbins); "Rose of Cimarron" 1952; "Target" 1952 (Garrett); "Texas City" 1952 (Hank); "Waco" 1952 (Wallace); "The Great Sioux Uprising" 1953 (Lee); "Ride Clear of Diablo" 1953 (Harry); "Savage Frontier" 1953 (Tulsa Tom); "Son of Belle Star" 1953 (Beacher); "Drums Across the River" 1954 (Ralph Costa); "The Forty-Niners" 1954 (William Norris); "Man with the Steel Whip" 1954-serial (Tosco); "The Spoilers" 1955 (Sourdough); "The Rawhide Years" 1956 (Pirate); "Showdown at Abilene" 1956 (Loop); "Apache Warrior" 1957 (Sgt. Gaunt); "Gun Glory" 1957 (Ugly); "The Phantom Stagecoach" 1957 (Langton); "Shoot-Out at Medicine Bend" 1957; "The Lone Ranger and the Lost City of Gold" 1958 (Wilson); "Toughest Gun in Tombstone" 1958 (Bill); "The Gun Hawk" 1963 (Joe Sully); "A Distant Trumpet" 1964 (Maj. Miller); "Shenandoah" 1965 (Tinkham); "Journey to Shiloh" 1968 (Case Pettibone). ¶TV: *The Lone Ranger*—"Legion of Old Timers" 10-6-49, "Greed for Gold", 1-19-50, "White Man's Magic" 7-13-50, "Crime in Time" 10-19-50, "Desert Adventure" 11-30-50, "The Outcast" 1-18-51, "The Hooded Men" 2-22-51, "Jeb's Gold Mine" 10-16-52, "Stage for Mademoiselle" 3-12-53, "The Deserter" 4-23-53, "Message to Fort Apache" 9-23-54, "Stage to Tishomingo" 10-28-54, "The Cross of Santo Domingo" 10-11-56, "Christmas Story" 12-20-56, "Mission for Tonto" 5-2-57; *Judge Roy Bean*—"Sunburnt Gold" 10-1-55 (Big Ben Foster), "The Fugitive" 12-1-55 (Barr), "Letty Leaves Home" 12-1-55 (Trigo); *The Roy Rogers Show*—"The Mayor of Ghost Town" 11-30-52, "The Milliner from Medicine Hat" 10-11-53; *The Cisco Kid*—"Gold Strike" 3-14-53, "The Hospital" 5-16-53, "Man with the Reputation" 3-27-54, "Kilts and Sombreros" 5-1-54; *The Gene Autry Show*—"Bandidos" 9-1-53, "Guns Below the Border" 11-5-55; *Annie Oakley*—"Annie and the Silver Ace" 2-27-54; *Death Valley Days*—"Sequoia" 12-6-54, "The Blonde King" 3-24-59 (James Savage), "The Kid from Hell's Kitchen" 11-12-66 (Murphy), "A Simple Question of Justice" 11-22-69, "Talk to Me, Charley" 12-20-69; *The Adventures of Rin Tin Tin*—"The Dead Man's Gold" 4-22-55 (Pecos), "The Iron Horse" 10-28-55 (Barrows), "The Invaders" 12-14-56 (Chief Tubac), "Stagecoach Sally" 4-19-57 (Bullets); *Wyatt Earp*—"The Killer" 10-25-55, "The Vultures" 3-19-57 (Dave Ritchie), "Indian Wife" 12-10-57 (Two Moon), "Frontier Surgeon" 1-19-60 (Swanee), "Johnny Behind the Deuce" 10-11-60 (Schneider); *Tales of the Texas Rangers*—"Blazing Across the Pecos" 12-3-55 (Asa Brockway), "The Rough, Tough West" 12-10-55 (Big Jack); *Sergeant Preston of the Yukon*—"Skagway Secret" 2-16-56 (Big Ike Bancroft), "Rebellion in the North" 7-12-56 (Jason Bowhead), "King of Herschel Island" 10-25-56 (Jason Bowhead), "The Jailbreaker" 11-21-57 (Bart Larson); *Cheyenne*—"The Mustang Trail" 11-20-56 (Brock), "The Mutton Puncher" 10-22-57 (Mudcat); *Jim Bowie*—"Monsieur Francois" 12-28-56 (Regan); *26 Men*—"Border Incident" 11-5-57, "Destination Nowhere" 11-12-57, "Chain Gang" 5-6-58, "Scorpion" 4-21-59; *Tales of Wells Fargo*—"Man in the Box" 11-11-57 (Frank Benson), "Ride with the Killer" 12-2-57 (Merle Workman), Fort Massacre 2-2-59 (Sgt. Condon), "Mr. Mute" 11-4-61 (Hull); *The Restless Gun*—"The Coward" 1-6-57 (Howie), "Aunt Emma" 4-14-58 (Jesse Drake), "Hiram Grover's Strike" 5-12-58 (Thad), "Code for a Killer" 4-27-59 (Ben Webster); *Broken Arrow*—"Kingdom of Terror" 1-14-58 (Duke), "Iron Maiden" 3-18-58 (Hooker Jim), "Old Enemy" 5-6-58; *Sugarfoot*—"The Dead Hills" 3-4-58 (Chris Andrews); *Wagon Train*—"The Bernal Sierra Story" 3-12-58 (Hughie), "The Candy O'Hara Story" 12-7-60, "The Terry Morrell Story" 4-25-62 (Zeb Landrus), "The Story of Cain" 12-16-63, "The Last Circle Up" 4-27-64, "Herman" 2-14-65 (Biggers), "The Jarbo Pierce Story" 5-2-65 (Binnes); *Fury*—"Robber's Roost" 3-22-58 (Clancy), "Man-Killer" 10-31-59; *Frontier Doctor*—"San Francisco Story" 10-4-58; *Jefferson Drum*—"Stagecoach Episode" 10-10-58 (Hank); *Maverick*—"Holiday at Hollow Rock" 12-28-58 (Matt Hendricks), "The Saga of Waco Williams" 2-15-59 (Jack Regan), "The Iron Hand" 2-21-60 (Red), "Last Wire from Stop Gap" 10-16-60 (Beldon), "The Bold Fenian Men" 12-18-60 (Major Sergeant Hogjaw Hanson); *Zane Grey Theater*—"Day of the Killing" 1-8-59 (Clem Dobie), "Hang the Heart High" 1-15-59 (Ben Barrett); *Rough Riders*—"An Eye for an Eye" 1-15-59 (Arnold); *Gunsmoke*—"Jayhawkers" 1-31-59 (Jay), "Moo Moo Raid" 2-13-60 (Tush), "The Peace Officer" 10-15-60 (Clegg Rawlins), "Quint Asper Comes Home" 9-29-62 (Bob), "Abe Blocker" 11-24-62 (Till Gant), "Caleb" 3-28-64 (Lige Follet), "Chicken" 12-5-64, "The Gunrunners" 2-5-68 (Reese), "Exodus 21:22" 3-24-69 (Bradford), "New Doctor in Town" 10-11-71 (Dump Hart),

"Lijah" 11-8-71 (Dump Hart), "The Wedding" 3-13-72 (Joe Eggers); *The Texan*—"The Eyes of Captain Wylie" 2-23-59 (Spike Taylor), "Traildust" 10-19-59, "Killer's Road" 4-25-60 (Jed Burdette), "Mission to Monteray" 6-13-60; *Have Gun Will Travel*—"The Long Hunt" 3-7-59 (Frank Tanner); *Black Saddle*—"Client: Northrup" 3-14-59 (Cobb); *Bonanza*—"Enter Mark Twain" 10-10-59, "The Mission" 9-17-60 (Buck), "The Rescue" 2-25-61, "A Hot Day for a Hanging" 10-14-62, "Little Man—Ten Feet Tall" 5-26-63 (Tod), "Patchwork Man" 5-23-65 (Stimler), "Ballad of the Ponderosa" 11-13-66 (Charlie), "The Greedy Ones" 5-14-67, "In Defense of Honor" 4-28-68 (Jud), "The Last Vote" 10-20-68 (Tim), "The Night Virginia City Died" 9-13-70 (Ira), "The Trouble with Trouble" 10-25-70 (Jack Clanton), "Shadow of a Hero" 2-21-71 (Willis), "The Grand Swing" 9-19-71 (Jake Rasko); *Colt .45*—"The Devil's Godson" 10-18-59 (Pete Jessup); *Rawhide*—"Incident at the Buffalo Smokehouse" 10-30-59, "Incident of the Champagne Bottles" 3-18-60 (Matt Holden), "Incident on the Road Back" 2-24-61, "Inside Man" 11-3-61 (Baines), "The House of the Hunter" 4-20-62 (George Ash); *The Deputy*—"The Orphans" 12-26-59; *The Law of the Plainsman*—"Calculated Risk" 12-31-59 (Newt), "The Imposter" 2-4-60; *Hotel De Paree*—"Vengeance for Sundance" 4-8-60 (Sheriff); *Bat Masterson*—"Masterson's Arcadia Club" 4-28-60 (Rod Bradbury); *Johnny Ringo*—"Cave-In" 6-30-60 (Kincaid); *Tate*—"Comanche Scalps" 8-10-60 (William Easey); *Lawman*—"The Go-Between" 9-25-60 (Link Barker); *The Rifleman*—"Woman from Hog Ridge" 10-4-60 (Martin); *The Tall Man*—"Counterfeit Law" 11-19-60 (Coleridge); *Klondike*—"Queen of the Klondike" 1-23-61 (Tromp); *Laramie*—"The Runt" 2-20-62, "The Day of the Savage" 3-13-62 (Captain Claybourne), "Lost Allegiance" 10-30-62 (Ross Banister), "Time of the Traitor" 12-11-62 (Manton); *The Dakotas*—"Walk Through the Badlands" 3-18-63 (Sgt. Abel Round); *Daniel Boone*—"The Price of Friendship" 2-18-65 (Sam), "First in War, First in Peace" 10-13-66 (John Beachum); *Laredo*—"Rendezvous at Arillo" 10-7-65, "Which Way Did They Go?" 11-18-65, "The Treasure of San Diablo" 2-17-66 (Ben Slick), "Road to San Remo" 11-25-66; *The Loner*—"One of the Wounded" 10-16-65 (Gibbons); *Branded*—"Barbed Wire" 2-13-66 (Jack Kil-

gore); *A Man Called Shenandoah*—"Run and Hide" 2-14-66 (Arch); *The Road West*—"The Predators" 1-23-67 (Clute); *Rango*—"Shootout at Mesa Flats" 4-7-67 (Cole Colton); *The High Chaparral*—"Best Man for the Job" 9-24-67 (Gilcher), "The Covey" 10-18-68 (Roark); *Iron Horse*—"Five Days to Washtiba" 10-7-67; *Cimarron Strip*—"The Last Wolf" 12-14-67 (Brom); *Alias Smith and Jones*—"The Day the Amnesty Came Through" 11-25-72 (Ellen Anderson).

Bradford, Marshall (1896-1/11/71). Films: "Western Renegades" 1949 (Paul Gordon); "Colorado Ambush" 1951 (B. Williams); "The Longhorn" 1951 (Doctor); "Night Riders of Montana" 1951 (Sam Foster); "Hellgate" 1952 (Doctor Pelham); "Yukon Vengeance" 1954; "Strange Lady in Town" 1955 (Sheriff); "Shoot-Out at Medicine Bend" 1957; "Terror at Black Falls" 1962. ¶TV: *The Lone Ranger*—"Outlaw Town" 1-12-50, "Behind the Law" 2-1-51; *The Cisco Kid*—"Gun Totin' Papa" 5-24-52, "Bandaged Badman" 10-11-52; *Wyatt Earp*—"Mr. Earp Becomes a Marshal" 9-6-55 (Sheriff Whitney), "The Perfidy of Shotgun Gibbs" 10-13-59; *Maverick*—"Stampede" 11-17-57 (Marshal Hunt); *The Restless Gun*—"The Crisis at Easter Creek" 4-7-58 (Rev. Broome); *Temple Houston*—"Seventy Times Seven" 12-5-63 (Judge).

Bradford, Richard (1935-). Films: "The Missouri Breaks" 1976 (Pete Marker); "Goin' South" 1978 (Sheriff Kyle); "Sunset" 1988 (Capt. Blackworth). ¶TV: *Gunsmoke*—"Sanctuary" 2-26-66 (Paul Wiley); *Preview Tonight*—"Roaring Camp" 9-4-66 (Marshal Walker); *The High Chaparral*—"It Takes a Smart Man" 10-23-70 (Tulsa Red).

Bradford, Virginia. Films: "A Six Shootin' Romance" 1926 (Muriel Travis); "The One Man Dog" 1929 (Babette).

Bradley, Bart. Films: "Domino Kid" 1957 (Pepe Garcias). ¶TV: *Wild Bill Hickok*—"Treasure Trail" 12-30-52; *Have Gun Will Travel*—"The Statue of San Sebastian" 6-14-58; *The Texan*—"A Race for Life" 3-16-59 (Cris Hampton); *Rawhide*—"Incident of the Haunted Hills" 11-6-59 (Indian Boy); *The Alaskans*—"Million Dollar Kid" 1-3-60 (Kat); *Wagon Train*—"The Patience Miller Story" 1-11-61.

Bradley, Bea. TV: *Laredo*—"Limit of the Law Larkin" 1-27-66 (Adam Macallam); *Daniel Boone*—"Goliath" 9-29-66 (Susan Smith).

Bradley, Christopher. Films:

"Gunsmoke: The Long Ride" TVM-1993 (Will); "Gunsmoke: One Man's Justice" TVM-1994 (Josh).

Bradley, Donna. Films: "Hard Trail" 1969 (Sue).

Bradley, Grace. Films: "Rose of the Rancho" 1936 (Flossie); "Roaring Timber" 1937 (Kay MacKinley).

Bradley, Harry C. (1869-10/18/47) Films: "The Lone Cowboy" 1934 (1st Station Agent); "Rhythm on the Range" 1936 (Minister); "The Kid from Texas" 1939 (Appleby).

Bradley, Lee. Films: "She Wore a Yellow Ribbon" 1949 (Interpreter); "The Gun Hawk" 1963 (Pancho).

Bradley, Leslie. Films: "Kiss of Fire" 1955 (Vega); "Westward Ho the Wagons" 1956 (Spencer Armitage); "Frontier Gun" 1958 (Rev. Jacob Hall); "The Sad Horse" 1959 (Jonas); "Young Jesse James" 1960. ¶TV: *Colt .45*—"Rebellion" 12-20-57 (Col. Jack Killian); *The Restless Gun*—"Dragon for a Day" 9-29-58 (Rev. Fletcher), "Mme. Brimstone" 5-4-59 (Cedric Mayberry); *Tales of the Texas Rangers*—"Texas Flyer" 11-28-58 (Thomas Wiggins); *Wyatt Earp*—"Silver Dollar" 2-2-60; *Wanted—Dead or Alive*—"The Partners" 2-6-60.

Bradley, Stuart. TV: *Jim Bowie*—"Choctaw Honor" 1-3-58 (Whiskey Jack); *Tales of Wells Fargo*—"Deadwood" 4-7-58 (Stevens); *Lawman*—"The Brand Release" 1-25-59 (Chad William); *Maverick*—"Yellow River" 2-8-59 (Asher); *The Restless Gun*—"Lady by Law" 5-11-59 (King Warren); *Hotel De Paree*—"Sundance and the Marshal of Water's End" 3-18-60 (Wes); *Have Gun Will Travel*—"Full Circle" 5-14-60 (Roy Cabell); *Wyatt Earp*—"The Confidence Man" 5-17-60 (Carl Duval); *Bat Masterson*—"Barbary Castle" 6-30-60 (Tracy Crow); *Gunsmoke*—"The Worm" 10-29-60 (Archer); *Rawhide*—"Incident at Poco Tiempo" 12-9-60 (Payton); *The Tall Man*—"The Frame" 4-21-62 (Wrangler); *The Dakotas*—"Mutiny at Fort Mercy" 1-21-63 (Taylor); *Empire*—"No Small Wars" 2-5-63 (Norman Dierker); *The Virginian*—"A Bride for Lars" 4-15-64 (Harkness); *Death Valley Days*—"After the O.K. Corral" 5-2-64 (Curley Bill); *Lancer*—"The Prodigal" 11-12-68, "Lifeline" 5-19-70.

Bradley, Truman (1905-7/28/74). Films: "Northwest Passage" 1940 (Capt. Ogden); "Last of the Duanes" 1941 (Capt. Laramie); "Lone Star Ranger" 1942 (Phil Lawson).

Bradshaw, Terry (1948-). TV: *Adventures of Brisco County, Jr.*—

"High Treason" 5-13-94 & 5-20-94 (Col. March).

Brady, Alice (1892-10/28/39). Films: "The Lure of Woman" 1915.

Brady, Arizona. Films: "Tempest Cody Turns the Table" 1919; "To the Tune of Bullets" 1919.

Brady, Buff. Films: "Rodeo King and the Senorita" 1951 (Pablo Morales); "The Big Country" 1958 (Dude); "Bullet for a Badman" 1964; "The Rare Breed" 1966 (Stunts); "Last Ride of the Dalton Gang" TVM-1979 (Buffalo Bill). ¶TV: *The Roy Rogers Show*—"Haunted Mine of Paradise Valley" 5-18-52; *Zane Grey Theater*—"The Lariat" 11-2-56 (Roper); *Have Gun Will Travel*—"Juliet" 1-31-59; *Bat Masterson*—"Law of the Land" 10-6-60 (Guard); *The Legend of Jesse James*—"Three Men from Now" 9-13-65 (Leek); *F Troop*—"Corporal Agarn's Farewell to the Troops" 10-5-65 (Stagecoach Driver); *The Loner*—"The Burden of the Badge" 3-5-66 (Ed); *Laredo*—"The Short, Happy Fatherhood of Reese Bennett" 1-27-67; *Cimarron Strip*—"The Battleground" 9-28-67.

Brady, Edward J. (1888-3/31/42). Films: "A Hopi Legend" 1913; "A Child of the Prairie" 1915; "Ma's Girls" 1915; "The Outlaw's Bride" 1915; "Pals in Blue" 1915; "Sagebrush Tom" 1915; "The Stagecoach Driver and the Girl" 1915; "The Learnin' of Jim Benton" 1917 (Harvey Knowles); "Wild Sumac" 1917 (John Lewis); "Beyond the Shadows" 1918 (Horace DuBois); "Deuce Duncan" 1918 (John); "Faith Endurin'" 1918 (Edward Carne); "The Gun Woman" 1918 (the Bostonian); "Wild Life" 1918 (Steve Barton); "The Rough Diamond" 1921 (Pedro Sachet); "The Silent Call" 1921 (Jimmy the Dude); "Over the Border" 1922 (Inspector Jules); "The Siren Call" 1922 (Edward Brent); "The Eternal Struggle" 1923 (Jean Cardeau); "To the Last Man" 1923 (Daggs); "A Child of the Prairie" 1925 (Slippery Jim Watson); "The Thundering Herd" 1925 (Pruitt); "Whispering Canyon" 1926 (Gonzales); "Hoof Marks" 1927 (Rawhide Smith); "Code of the Scarlet" 1928 (Paddy Halloran); "The Virginian" 1929 (Greasy); "The Texan" 1930 (Henry); "The Conquering Horde" 1931 (Splint Goggin); "Desert Vengeance" 1931 (Beaver); "The Nevada Buckaroo" 1931 (Slade); "Oklahoma Jim" 1931 (Cash Riley); "The Squaw Man" 1931 (McSorley); "The Texas Ranger" 1931 (Nevady); "The Deadline" 1932 (Left); "Forbidden Trail" 1932 (Snod-

grass); "Law of the West" 1932 (Lee Morgan); "South of Sante Fe" 1932 (Jack Stone); "Without Honor" 1932 (Lopez Venero); "Galloping Romeo" 1933 (Mat Kent); "The Lone Avenger" 1933 (Nip); "The Ranger's Code" 1933 (Bert); "The Sundown Rider" 1933; "Under the Tonto Rim" 1933 (Sheriff); "Rose of the Rancho" 1936 (Bystander); "It Happened Out West" 1937; "Riders of the Dawn" 1937; "Wells Fargo" 1937 (Prospector); "Border Wolves" 1938; "The Great Adventures of Wild Bill Hickok" 1938; "The Mysterious Rider" 1938 (Jake); "The Texans" 1938 (Union Soldier); "Thunder in the Desert" 1938 (Reno); "The Arizona Wildcat" 1939 (Miner); "Mesquite Buckaroo" 1939 (Hank); "North of the Yukon" 1939 (Moreau); "The Oklahoma Kid" 1939 (Jury Foreman); "Saga of Death Valley" 1939; "Southward Ho!" 1939 (Mears); "Stagecoach" 1939 (Saloon Keeper); "Union Pacific" 1939 (Irish Paddy); "Adventures of Red Ryder" 1940-serial (Ed Madison); "Prairie Law" 1940; "Shooting High" 1940 (Mort Carson); "Twenty Mule Team" 1940 (Barfly); "Wagon Train" 1940 (Sam Bates); "When the Daltons Rode" 1940 (Deputy); "Fugitive Valley" 1941 (Doctor); "Wyoming Wildcat" 1941; "In Old California" 1942; "Valley of the Sun" 1942 (Man on Street); "The Outlaw" 1943 (Deputy).

Brady, Pat (1914-2/27/72). Films: "Outlaws of the Prairie" 1937; "The Colorado Kid" 1938 (Pat); "Law of the Plains" 1938 (Pat); "Rio Grande" 1938 (Pat); "South of Arizona" 1938 (Pat); "West of Cheyenne" 1938 (Pat); "The Man from Sundown" 1939 (Pat); "Western Caravans" 1939; "The Durango Kid" 1940 (Pat); "Texas Stagecoach" 1940 (Pat); "Thundering Frontier" 1940 (Pat); "Two-Fisted Rangers" 1940 (Pat); "West of Abilene" 1940; "Outlaws of the Panhandle" 1941; "The Pinto Kid" 1941; "Red River Valley" 1941; "Call of the Canyon" 1942; "Man from Cheyenne" 1942; "Romance on the Range" 1942; "Sunset on the Desert" 1942; "Man from Music Mountain" 1943 (Pat); "Silver Spurs" 1943; "Song of Texas" 1943; "Along the Navajo Trail" 1945; "Down Dakota Way" 1949 (Sparrow Biffle); "The Golden Stallion" 1949 (Sparrow Biffle); "Bells of Coronado" 1950 (Sparrow Biffle); "Trigger, Jr." 1950 (Biffle); "Twilight in the Sierras" 1950 (Sparrow Biffle); "South of Caliente" 1951 (Pat). ¶TV: *The Roy Rogers Show*—Regular 1951-57 (Pat Brady).

Brady, Scott (1924-4/16/85). Films: "Kansas Raiders" 1950 (Bill Anderson); "Bronco Buster" 1952 (Bart Eaton); "Montana Belle" 1952 (Bob Dalton); "Untamed Frontier" 1952 (Glenn Denbow); "A Perilous Journey" 1953 (Shard Benton); "Johnny Guitar" 1954 (Dancin' Kid); "The Law vs. Billy the Kid" 1954 (Billy the Kid); "The Vanishing American" 1955 (Blandy); "The Maverick Queen" 1956 (Sundance); "Mohawk" 1956 (Jonathan Adams); "The Restless Breed" 1957 (Mitch Baker); "The Storm Rider" 1957 (Jones); "Ambush at Cimarron Pass" 1958 (Sgt. Matt Blake); "Blood Arrow" 1958 (Dan Kree); "Stage to Thunder Rock" 1964 (Sam Swope); "Black Spurs" 1965 (Tanner); "Fort Utah" 1967 (Dajin); "Red Tomahawk" 1967 (Ep Wyatt); "Arizona Bushwhackers" 1968 (Tom Rile); "Cain's Way" 1969 (Capt. Cain); "Five Blood Graves" 1969 (Jim Wade); "Last Ride of the Dalton Gang" TVM-1979 (Poker Player). ¶TV: *Zane Grey Theater*—"A Man on the Run" 6-21-57 (Jeff Duane); *Shotgun Slade*—Regular 1959-60 (Shotgun Slade); *The Virginian*—"The Storm Gate" 11-13-68 (Hudson); *Gunsmoke*—"Danny" 10-13-69 (Heenan), "Horse Fever" 12-18-72 (Ed Wells), "Lynch Town" 11-19-73 (John King); *Lancer*—"The Experiment" 2-17-70 (Bowman); *The High Chaparral*—"Wind" 10-9-70 (Fraley); *The Men from Shiloh*—"The Animal" 1-20-71 (Dolby); *Dirty Sally*—"Right of Way" 1-11-74 (Kelly).

Brady, Tete. Films: "Flying Lariats" 1931 (Kate Weston); "Riders of the Cactus" 1931 (Pearl).

Braeden, Eric (Hans Gudegast) (1937-). Films: "100 Rifles" 1969. ¶TV: *The Virginian*—"No Drums, No Trumpets" 4-6-66 (Augustin); *Gunsmoke*—"The Convict" 2-1-71 (Carl Jaekel), "The Bullet" 11-29-71, 12-6-71 & 12-13-71 (Jack Sinclair), "The Iron Blood of Courage" 2-18-74 (William Talley); *Bearcats!*—"Dos Gringos" 9-30-71 (Colonel Reinert); *Barbary Coast*—"Crazy Cats" 9-15-75 (Bristol); *How the West Was Won*—Episode Ten 4-30-78 (Francis Britten), Episode Twelve 5-14-78 (Francis Britten).

Braidwood, Frank. Films: "Tempest Cody Backs the Trust" 1919; "Tempest Cody, Kidnapper" 1919; "Hearts Up" 1920 (Gordon Swayne); "West Is West" 1920 (Billy Armstrong); "The Man Who Waited" 1922 (Frank Magee).

Bralver, Bob. TV: *Kung Fu*—"Sun and Cloud Shadow" 2-22-73

(Miner), "Chians" 3-8-73 (Guard), "Alethea" 3-15-73 (Crowder).

Bramley, Flora (1909-6/23/94). Films: "The Dude Cowboy" 1926 (Doris Wrigmint).

Bramley, Raymond. Films: "Broken Arrow" 1950 (Col. Bernall).

Bramley, William (1928-). Films: "Gunpoint" 1966 (Hoag). ¶TV: *Gunsmoke*—"Half Straight" 2-17-62 (Hank Browder), "Collie's Free" 10-20-62, "My Father's Guitar" 2-21-66 (Jed Woodard), "The Goldtakers" 9-24-66 (Jake Struck), "The Favor" 3-11-67 (Adam Haley), "The Pillagers" 11-6-67 (Turner), "The Miracle Man" 12-2-68 (Miller), "Exodus 21:22" 3-24-69 (Cane), "Lynott" 11-1-71 (Anderson), "Whelan's Men" 2-5-73 (Loomis); *The Tall Man*—"The Runaway Groom" 4-28-62 (Bart Tugwell); *Bonanza*—"The Long Night" 5-6-62 (Townsend), "For a Young Lady" 12-27-70 (Gifford Owen), "The Initiation" 9-26-72 (Moeller); *Laramie*—"Among the Missing" 9-25-62; *The Dakotas*—"Mutiny at Fort Mercy" 1-21-63 (Jellicoe); *Wide Country*—"The Care and Handling of Tigers" 4-25-63 (Mike Knudsen); *Empire*—"The Convention" 5-14-63 (Marty Albee); *The Virginian*—"To Make This Place Remember" 9-25-63 (Charlie Tressider), "Timberland" 3-10-65 (John Ferguson), "Vengeance Trail" 1-4-67 (Del Hobart), "The Handy Man" 3-6-68 (Arnold Bowden); *Temple Houston*—"Jubilee" 11-14-63 (Ford Conley), "Do Unto Others, Then Gallop" 3-19-64 (Gus Finney); *Destry*—"Red Brady's Kid" 4-24-64 (Red Brady); *Death Valley Days*—"The Battle of San Francisco Bay" 4-11-65 (McCartney); *Iron Horse*—"A Dozen Ways to Kill a Man" 12-19-66 (Ferris), "Death Has Two Faces" 12-23-67 (Sheriff Stevenson); *Laredo*—"The Seventh Day" 1-6-67 (Luke Bergstrom); *The Road West*—"The Eighty-Seven Dollar Bride" 4-3-67; *Cimarron Strip*—"Journey to a Hanging" 9-7-67 (Whiskey Jack), "The Assassin" 1-11-68 (Fargo Jones); *The Outcasts*—"They Shall Rise Up" 1-6-69 (Stretter); *Nichols*—"Deer Crossing" 10-21-71; *Barbary Coast*—"Funny Money" 9-8-75 (Hatch).

Brammall, John. Films: "The Gambler of the West" 1914 (Richard Kent, Jr.); "Six Feet Four" 1919 (Kid Bedloe).

Brana, Francisco "Frank". Films: "Massacre at Fort Grant" 1963-Span.; "Two Gunmen" 1964-Span./Ital.; "Murieta" 1965-Span./ U.S.; "Secret of Captain O'Hara" 1965-Span.; "Savage Gringo" 1966-Ital.; "Django Does Not Forgive" 1967-Ital./Span.; "Django Kill" 1967-Ital./Span.; "Face to Face" 1967-Ital.; "Let Them Rest" 1967-Ital./Ger.; "Ringo, the Lone Rider" 1967-Ital./ Span.; "Awkward Hands" 1968-Span./Ital.; "Cowards Don't Pray" 1968-Ital./Span.; "Fifteen Scaffolds for the Killer" 1968-Ital./Span.; "I Want Him Dead" 1968-Ital./Span.; "Rattler Kid" 1968-Ital./Span.; "The Boldest Job in the West" 1969-Ital.; "Dead Are Countless" 1969-Ital./ Span.; "Death on High Mountain" 1969-Ital./Span.; "And the Crows Will Dig Your Grave" 1971-Ital./ Span.; "Light the Fuse ... Sartana Is Coming" 1971-Ital./Fr.; "Dallas" 1972-Span./Ital. (Johnny Black); "Fasthand" 1972-Ital./Span.; "God in Heaven ... Arizona on Earth" 1972-Span./Ital.; "In the Name of the Father, the Son and the Colt" 1972-Fr./Ital.; "Kill the Poker Player" 1972-Ital./Span. (Burton); "Prey of Vultures" 1973-Span./Ital.; "If You Shoot ... You Live!" 1974-Span.; "Three Supermen of the West" 1974-Ital./Span.

Brand, George. Films: "Frontier Gun" 1958 (Judge Ard Becker); "Texas Lady" 1955.

Brand, Jolene (1935-). TV: *Zorro*—Regular 1958-59 (Anna Maria); *Death Valley Days*—"Indian Emily" 12-8-59 (Indian Girl); *Maverick*—"A Technical Error" 11-26-61 (Penelope); *Cheyenne*—"Legacy of the Lost" 12-4-61 (Lorna Abbott); *Bronco*—"A Town That Lived and Died" 4-9-62 (Emily).

Brand, Mike. Films: "Texas Tornado" 1932 (Wolf Cassidy).

Brand, Neville (1921-4/16/92). Films: "Only the Valiant" 1951 (Sgt. Ben Murdock); "Red Mountain" 1951 (Dixon); "The Charge at Feather River" 1953 (Morgan); "Gun Fury" 1953 (Brazos); "The Man from the Alamo" 1953 (Dawes); "The Lone Gun" 1954 (Tray Moran); "The Return of Jack Slade" 1955 (Harry Sutton); "Fury at Gunsight Pass" 1956 (Dirk Hogan); "Gun Brothers" 1956 (Jubal); "Love Me Tender" 1956 (Mike Gavin); "Mohawk" 1956 (Rokhawah); "Raw Edge" 1956 (Tarp Penny); "The Three Outlaws" 1956; "The Lonely Man" 1957 (King Fisher); "The Tin Star" 1957 (Bart Bogardus); "Badman's Country" 1958 (Butch Cassidy); "The Last Sunset" 1961 (Frank Hobbs); "The Desperados" 1969 (Sheriff Kilpatrick); "Lock, Stock and Barrel" TVM-1971 (Sergeant Markey); "Cahill, United States Marshal" 1973 (Lightfoot); "Deadly Trackers" 1973 (Choo Choo); "Hitched" TVM-1973 (Banjo Reilly); "The Barbara Coast" TVM-1975 (Florrie Roscoe); "The Quest" TVM-1976 (Shea). ¶TV: *Screen Director's Playhouse*—"Arroyo" 10-26-55 (Bart Wheeler); *The Texan*—"Law of the Gun" 9-29-58 (Kyle Richards); *Zane Grey Theater*—"Trouble at Tres Cruces" 3-26-59 (Nick Karafus); *Rawhide*—"Incident of the Devil and His Due" 1-22-60 (Gaff), "Incident of the Red Wind" 9-26-63 (Lou Bowdark); *Bonanza*—"The Last Viking" 11-12-60 (Gunnar Borgstrom), "The Luck of Pepper Shannon" 11-22-70 (Pepper Shannon), "The Rattlesnake Brigade" 12-5-71 (Doyle); *Death Valley Days*—"Preacher with a Past" 4-11-62 (Hardin); *Wagon Train*—"The Jed Whitmore Story" 1-13-64 (Jed Whitmore), "The Zebedee Titus Story" 4-20-64 (Zebedee Titus); *Destry*—"The Solid Gold Girl" 2-14-64 (Johnny Washburn); *The Virginian*—"We've Lost a Train" 4-21-65 (Reese); *Laredo*—Regular 1965-67 (Reese Bennett); *Gunsmoke*—"Kioga" 10-23-65 (Jayce McCaw); *Daniel Boone*—"Tanner" 10-5-67 (Tanner); *The Men from Shiloh*—"Gun Quest" 10-21-70 (the Sheriff); *Alias Smith and Jones*—"Shootout at Diablo Station" 12-2-71 (Chuck Gorman), "Which Way to the O.K. Corral?" 2-10-72 (Sam Bacon).

Brandauer, Klaus Maria (1944-). Films: "White Fang" 1991 (Alex Larson).

Branden, Michael. Films: "Robin Hood of Texas" 1947 (Jim Preston); "The Gunfighter" 1950 (Johnny).

Brander, Leslie. TV: *Wild Wild West*—"The Night of the Dancing Death" 11-5-65 (Princess Gina Carlotta).

Brandes, Alaine. Films: "The Lone Rider in Ghost Town" 1941 (Helen).

Brando, Jocelyn (1919-). Films: "Ten Wanted Men" 1955 (Corinne Michaels). ¶TV: *Wagon Train*—"The Sally Potter Story" 4-9-58 (Millie Bennett), "The Will Santee Story" 5-3-61 (Agnes McDermott), "The Kitty Allbright Story" 10-4-61 (Lettie), "The Mary Beckett Story" 5-9-62 (Martha Lane), "The Martin Gatsby Story" 10-10-62 (Grace Lefton), "The Michael McGoo Story" 3-20-63 (Adam Meyers), "The Sam Pulaski Story" 11-4-63 (Mom Pulaski); *Buckskin*—"Mail-Order Groom" 4-20-59 (Lucy Corkle); *Riverboat*—"The

Night of the Faceless Men" 3-28-60 (Mrs. Pauley), "The Water of Gorgeous Springs" 11-7-60 (Charity Jennings); *Laramie*—"Cemetery Road" 4-12-60 (Julia Hassen), "Man from Kansas" 1-10-61 (Sarah Willoughby); *The Tall Man*—"The Legend and the Gun" 4-1-61 (Martha); *Tales of Wells Fargo*—"Treasure Coach" 10-14-61 (Frances Cobb); *Frontier Circus*—"The Hunter and the Hunted" 11-2-61 (Phyllis Jordan); *The Virginian*—"To Make This Place Remember" 9-25-63 (Leora Tressider), "The Welcoming Town" 3-22-67 (Ida Martin), "Last Grave at Socorro Creek" 1-22-69 (Mrs. Owens).

Brando, Marlon (1924-). Films: "Viva Zapata!" 1952 (Emiliano Zapata); "One-Eyed Jacks" 1961 (Rio); "The Appaloosa" 1966 (Matt Fletcher); "The Missouri Breaks" 1976 (Lee Clayton).

Brandon, Beverly. Films: "Distant Drums" 1951 (Mme. Duprez).

Brandon, Bob. Films: "Stallion Canyon" 1949 (Johnny Adams).

Brandon, Henry (1910-2/15/90). Films: "Wells Fargo" 1937 (Larry); "The Marshal of Mesa City" 1939 (Duke Allison); "The Ranger and the Lady" 1940 (General LaRue); "Under Texas Skies" 1940 (Blackton); "Bad Man of Deadwood" 1941 (Carver); "The Shepherd of the Hills" 1941 (Bald Knobber); "Hurricane Smith" 1942 (Sam Carson); "Northwest Outpost" 1947 (Chinese Junk Captain); "Old Los Angeles" 1948 (Larry Stockton); "The Paleface" 1948 (Wapato, the Medicine Man); "Cattle Drive" 1951 (Jim Currie); "Wagons West" 1952 (Clay Cook); "Pony Express" 1953 (Cooper); "War Arrow" 1953 (Maygro); "Vera Cruz" 1954 (Danette); "Bandido" 1956 (Gunther); "Comanche" 1956 (Black Cloud); "The Searchers" 1956 (Chief Scar); "Hell's Crossroads" 1957 (Jesse James); "Two Rode Together" 1961 (Chief Quanah Parker); "Kino, the Padre on Horseback" 1977; "Little House on the Prairie: Look Back to Yesterday" TVM-1983 (Otis Wagner). ¶TV: *Stories of the Century*—"Nate Champion" 11-4-55; *Broken Arrow*—"Passage Deferred" 10-30-56 (Judd Buckley); *Jim Bowie*—"Epitaph for an Indian" 9-6-57 (Quint Oxley); *The Restless Gun*—"The New Sheriff" 11-18-57 (Tracer Givens); *Wagon Train*—"The Charles Avery Story" 12-13-57 (Running Horse), "The Swift Cloud Story" 4-8-59 (Fire Cloud), "The Martha Barham Story" 11-4-59 (Black Panther), "The St. Nicholas Story" 12-23-59, "The Dr. Swift

Cloud Story" 5-25-60 (Chief Fire Cloud), "The Patience Miller Story" 1-11-61 (Dark Eagle); *Have Gun Will Travel*—"The Yuma Treasure" 12-14-57 (Chief Gerada), "Treasure Trail" 1-24-59 (Craig Wilson); *Decision*—"The Tall Man" 7-27-58 (Frank Dawson); *The Texan*—"The Man Hater" 6-15-59 (Crowley); *Lawman*—"The Last Man" 11-1-59 (Joshua Henry), "To Capture the West" 2-7-60 (Tall Horse); *The Deputy*—"The Big Four" 11-14-59 (Johnny Ringo); *Zane Grey Theater*—"The Ghost" 12-31-59 (Whit Ransome); *The Rebel*—"Gold Seeker" 1-17-60 (Running Wolf); *Bronco*—"Legacy of Twisted Creed" 4-19-60 (Yellow Moon); *Gunsmoke*—"The Deserter" 6-4-60 (Major), "Stolen Horses" 4-8-61 (Chief Quick Knife); *Maverick*—"A Bullet for the Teacher" 10-30-60 (Rand Storm); *Gunslinger*—"The Death of Yellow Singer" 5-11-61 (Two Bows); *Whispering Smith*—"The Mortal Coil" 7-24-61 (Claude Denton/Rex Denton); *Branded*—"Fill No Glass for Me" 11-7-65 & 11-14-65; *Daniel Boone*—"The Deserter" 1-20-66 (Lije Moody); *Laredo*—"Miracle at Massacre Mission" 3-3-66 (Quahada).

Brandon, Jane Alice. Films: "The Daughters of Joshua Cabe Return" TVM-1975 (Jenny Finch).

Brandon, Michael (1945-). Films: "Scott Free" TVM-1976 (Tony Scott).

Brands, X (1927-). Films: "The Naked Gun" 1956; "Escort West" 1959 (Tago); "Gunmen from Laredo" 1959 (Delgados); "Oklahoma Territory" 1960 (Running Cloud); "Santee" 1973; "Bridger" TVM-1976 (Crow Chief). ¶TV: *Judge Roy Bean*—"The Judge of Pecos Valley" 9-10-55 (Dan Wiler), "The Horse Thief" 10-1-55 (Hackett), "The Wedding of Old Sam" 10-1-55 (Stage Driver), "The Runaway" 10-15-55 (Dallas), "Slightly Prodigal" 10-15-55 (Jim Brown), "Black Jack" 11-1-55 (Rev. Peter Cable), "Connie Comes to Town" 12-1-55 (Daniels), "The Fugitive" 12-1-55 (Hickey), "Letty Leaves Home" 12-1-55 (Klondike), "Vinegarone" 12-1-55 (Buck), "Gunman's Bargain" 1-1-56 (Tyler), "The Hidden Truth" 1-1-56 (Grover), "The Judge's Dilemma" 1-1-56 (Danning), "Outlaw's Son" 1-1-56 (Ben Logan), "The Reformer" 1-1-56 (Jonas); *Annie Oakley*—"Annie and the First Phone" 7-22-56 (Randy), "Indian Justice" 7-29-56 (Tenanda); *The Adventures of Rin Tin Tin*—"Return of Rin Tin Tin" 10-26-56 (Angry Fox), "The In-

vaders" 12-14-56 (Cochise), "Brave Bow" 4-18-58 (Brave Bow); *Tales of the Texas Rangers*—"Whirlwind Raiders" 10-13-57 (Johnnie Tyce); *Sergeant Preston of the Yukon*—"Lost River Roundup" 12-12-57 (Metka Joe); *Broken Arrow*—"Duel" 3-18-58 (Nicaro); *Yancy Derringer*—Regular 1958-59 (Pahoo Ka-Ta-Wah); *Maverick*—"Alias Bart Maverick" 10-5-58 (Sioux Indian); *Northwest Passage*—"Trial by Fire" 3-6-59 (Indian); *Rawhide*—"Incident at Sulphur Creek" 3-11-60, "Incident of the Music Maker" 5-20-60, "Incident in the Middle of Nowhere" 4-7-61 (Indian), "Incident of the Clown" 3-29-63 (Comanche Brave); *Tales of Wells Fargo*—"The Trading Post" 4-11-60 (Spotted Tail); *Bat Masterson*—"Masterson's Arcadia Club" 4-28-60 (Jeb Mitchell); *Wagon Train*—"The River Crossing" 12-14-60 (Indian Scout), "The Sam Darland Story" 12-26-62 (Tulo); *The Tall Man*—"Rovin' Gambler" 3-18-61 (Rudabaugh); *Wyatt Earp*—"Wyatt Takes the Primrose Path" 3-28-61; *The Rifleman*—"The Clarence Bibbs Story" 4-4-61 (Longden); *Cheyenne*—"Massacre at Gunsight Pass" 5-1-61 (Powder Face); *Laramie*—"The Day of the Savage" 3-13-62; *Bonanza*—"The Far, Far Better Thing" 1-10-65 (Sharp Tongue); *Branded*—"One Way Out" 4-18-65; *Laredo*—"Yahoo" 9-30-65 (Blue Dog), "Jinx" 12-2-65 (Randoe); *Gunsmoke*—"Judge Calvin Strom" 12-18-65, "The Gunrunners" 2-5-68 (Singleton), "Hawk" 10-20-69 (Renegade Indian), "Snow Train" 10-19-70 & 10-26-70 (Chief Red Willow), "A Game of Death … An Act of Love" 11-5-73 & 11-12-73 (1st Renegade), "The Squaw" 1-6-75 (Chief); *Shane*—"High Road in Viator" 11-12-66 (Young Brave); *Daniel Boone*—"The Enchanted Gun" 11-17-66 (Tall Deer); *The Monroes*—"Ghosts of Paradox" 3-15-67; *The High Chaparral*—"The High Chaparral" 9-10-67 (Nock-Ay-Del), "The Assassins" 1-7-68 (Nock-Ay-Dell), "Pale Warrior" 12-11-70 (Fenah); *Hondo*—"Hondo and the Death Drive" 12-1-67 (Coro); *Here Come the Brides*—"The Deadly Trade" 4-16-69; *Bearcats!*—"Blood Knot" 11-4-71 (Mantano); *Alias Smith and Jones*—"The Biggest Game in the West" 2-3-72, "McGuffin" 12-9-72.

Brandt, Charles (1864-6/9/24). Films: "Nanette of the Wilds" 1916 (Joe Gauntier).

Brandt, Hank. TV: *Wagon Train*—"The Jim Bridger Story" 5-10-61 (Gray Beddoe), "The Trace McCloud Story" 3-2-64; *Tales of Wells Fargo*—"New Orleans Trackdown"

12-23-61 (Roger Montclair); *The Big Valley*—"The Velvet Trap" 11-7-66; *The Monroes*—"Gold Fever" 12-14-66 (Langdon); *Gunsmoke*—"Blood Money" 1-22-68 (Hank), "Exodus 21:22" 3-24-69, "Morgan" 3-2-70 (Clint), "The Cage" 3-23-70 (Luke Stewart), "Island in the Desert" 12-2-74 & 12-9-74 (Sheriff John Lipon); *Daniel Boone*—"Fort New Madrid" 2-15-68 (Zeb Brand).

Bransh, Marion (1939-). Films: "The McMasters" 1970 (Mrs. Watson). ¶TV: *Gunsmoke*—"Reunion '78" 3-3-56 (Belle Archer).

Branson, Ricky. TV: *Tales of Wells Fargo*—"Tanoa" 10-28-61 (Wahneehee); *Bonanza*—"The Deserter" 10-21-62.

Brantley, Nell. Films: "Saddle Cyclone" 1925 (Alice Roland); "White Thunder" 1925 (Alice Norris).

Brasselle, Keefe (1923-7/7/81). Films: "Three Young Texans" 1954 (Tony Ballew).

Braswell, Charles (1925-5/17/74). TV: *Sergeant Preston of the Yukon*—"Love and Honor" 5-3-56 (Constable Wayne), "Mark of Crime" 7-10-58 (Constable Drake).

Bratt, Benjamin. Films: "James A. Michener's Texas" TVM-1995 (Benito Garza).

Bratton, Marla. Films: "The Lone Rider" 1934; "The Way of the West" 1934 (Firey Parker); "West of the Law" 1934-short; "Timber Terrors" 1935 (Mildred Barton).

Brauer, Bill. Films: "The Vigilante" 1947-serial; "Tex Granger" 1948-serial. ¶TV: *Zane Grey Theater*—"The Long Shadow" 1-19-61.

Brauer, Tiny. Films: "The Outlaws Is Coming!" 1965 (Bartender).

Braun, Judith. Films: "Horizons West" 1952 (Sally). ¶TV: *Jefferson Drum*—"The Keeney Gang" 10-3-58 (Franny); *Wanted—Dead or Alive*—"Reunion for Revenge" 1-24-59 (Jane Burns); *Trackdown*—"The Eyes of Jerry Kelson" 4-22-59.

Bravo, Carlos "Charly". Films: "The Boldest Job in the West" 1969-Ital.; "100 Rifles" 1969 (Lopez); "El Condor" 1970 (Bandit); "Captain Apache" 1971-Brit./Span. (Sanchez); "The Man Called Noon" 1973-Brit./Span./Ital. (Lang); "China 9, Liberty 37" 1978-Ital./Span./U.S.; "White Apache" 1984-Ital./Span.; "Scalps" 1986-Ital./Ger.

Bravo, Danny. Films: "For the Love of Mike" 1960 (Michael). ¶TV:

Wagon Train—"The Adam MacKenzie Story" 3-27-63 (Felipe Perez); *The Travels of Jaimie McPheeters*—"The Day of the Pawnees" 12-22-63 & 12-29-63 (Kiwa).

Bray, Robert (1917-3/7/83). Films: "Sunset Pass" 1946 (Bank Clerk); "Wild Horse Mesa" 1947 (Tex); ; "The Arizona Ranger" 1948 (Jasper); "Blood on the Moon" 1948 (Bart Daniels); "Gun Smugglers" 1948 (Dodge); "Guns of Hate" 1948 (Rocky); "Indian Agent" 1948 (Nichols); "Return of the Badmen" 1948 (John Younger); "Western Heritage" 1948 (Pike); "Brothers in the Saddle" 1949; "Rustlers" 1949 (Hank); "Stagecoach Kid" 1949 (Clint); "The Great Missouri Raid" 1951 (Charlie Pitts); "Law of the Badlands" 1951 (Benson); "Overland Telegraph" 1951 (Steve); "Warpath" 1951 (Oldtimer); "Fargo" 1952; "The Gunman" 1952; "The Lusty Men" 1952 (Fritz); "The Man from Black Hills" 1952 (Ed Roper); "The Maverick" 1952 (Corporal Johnson); "The Marshal's Daughter" 1953 (Anderson); "Seminole" 1953 (Capt. Sibley); "Vigilante Terror" 1953. ¶TV: *Wild Bill Hickok*—"Masquerade at Moccasin Flats" 9-2-52; *The Lone Ranger*—"Jeb's Gold Mine" 10-16-52, "The Perfect Crime" 7-30-53, "Outlaw's Trail" 10-21-54, "Two from Juan Ringo" 12-23-54, "False Accusations" 4-21-55; *Wyatt Earp*—"The Killer" 10-25-55; *You Are There*—"The Gunfight at the O.K. Corral" 11-6-55; *Frontier*—"The Hanging at Thunder Butte Creek" 3-11-56; *Cheyenne*—"Noose at Noon" 6-3-58 (Duke Rhein); *Maverick*—"The Spanish Dancer" 12-14-58 (John Wilson); *Man from Blackhawk*—"The Trouble with Tolliver" 10-16-59 (Marcus Clagg); *Sugarfoot*—"Outlaw Island" 11-24-59 (Gill); *Wichita Town*—"The Devil's Choice" 12-23-59 (Rev. Nichols); *Hotel De Paree*—"Sundance and the Man in Room Seven" 2-12-60 (Willard Polk); *Riverboat*—"Three Graves" 3-14-60 (Tom Byson); *Laramie*—"The Protectors" 3-22-60 (Sam Willard), "The Dynamiters" 3-6-62 (Jim Tenney), "The Dispossessed" 2-19-63 (Luke); *Overland Trail*—"Fire in the Hole" 4-17-60 (Matt Peak); *Tales of Wells Fargo*—"Dead Man's Street" 4-18-60 (Alec Ferguson), "The Wayfarers" 5-19-62 (Henry Maxon); *Stagecoach West*—Regular 1960-61 (Simon Kane); *Gunsmoke*—"Shona" 2-9-63 (Gib); *Temple Houston*—"The Siege at Thayer's Bluff" 11-7-63 (Hal Kester).

Brazzi, Rossano (1916-12/24/94). Films: "The Girl of the Golden

West" 1942-Ital.; "Drummer of Vengeance" 1974-Brit./Ital.

Breakston, George (1920-5/21/73). Films: "Jesse James" 1939 (Farmer's Boy).

Breamer, Sylvia (1903-6/7/43). Films: "The Cold Deck" 1917 (Rose Larkin); "Doubling for Romeo" 1922 (Lulu); "Wolf Law" 1922; "The Girl of the Golden West" 1923 (the Girl).

Brecher, Egon (1880-8/12/46). Films: "To the Last Man" 1933 (Mark Hayden).

Breck, Peter (1929-). Films: "The Wild and the Innocent" 1959 (Chip Miller); "The Glory Guys" 1965 (Hodges). ¶TV: *Sheriff of Cochise*—"The Farmers" 9-21-56 (Doyle Ranker); *Zane Grey Theater*—"Sundown at Bitter Creek" 2-14-58 (Sundance Kid), "The Doctor Keeps a Promise" 3-21-58 (Marshal), "Day of the Killing" 1-8-59 (Roy Bancroft); *Tombstone Territory*—"The Lady Gambler" 5-28-58 (Sam Dixon); *Gunsmoke*—"The Patsy" 9-20-58 (Fly Hoyt), "The Odyssey of Jubal Tanner" 5-18-63 (Jubal Tanner); *Have Gun Will Travel*—"The Protege" 10-18-58 (Kurt Sprague); *Wagon Train*—"The Tobias Jones Story" 10-22-58 (Alf Meadows); *The Restless Gun*—"Take Me Home" 12-1-58 (Brett Dixon), "The Way Back" 7-13-59; *Black Saddle*—Regular 1959 (Clay Culhane); *Sugarfoot*—"Man from Medora" 11-21-60 (Theodore Roosevelt); *Maverick*—"Destination Devil's Flat" 12-25-60 (Dan Trevor), "Triple Indemnity" 3-19-61 (Doc Holliday), "A Technical Error" 11-26-61 (Doc Holliday), "The Maverick Report" 3-4-62 (Doc Holliday), "Marshal Maverick" 3-11-62 (Doc Holliday), "One of Our Trains Is Missing" 4-22-62 (Doc Holliday); *Bronco*—"Yankee Tornado" 3-13-61 (Theodore Roosevelt); *Lawman*—"Trapped" 9-17-61 (Hale Connors), "Jailbreak" 6-10-62 (Pete Bole); *Cheyenne*—"Legacy of the Lost" 12-4-61 (James), "Indian Gold" 10-29-62 (Matt Kilgore), "Dark Decision" 11-5-62 (Tony Chance); *Bonanza*—"The Cheating Game" 2-9-64 (Ward Bannister); *The Virginian*—"Rope of Lies" 3-25-64 (Jess Carver); *Branded*—"The Mission" 3-14-65, 3-21-65 & 3-28-65 (Crispo); *The Big Valley*—Regular 1965-69 (Nick Barkley); *The Men from Shiloh*—"Hannah" 12-30-70 (Lafe); *Alias Smith and Jones*—"The Great Shell Game" 2-18-71 (Charles Morgan); *Cliffhangers*—"The Secret Empire" 1979 (Keller).

Breeding, Richard. Films:

"Count Your Bullets" 1972 (Fat Man).

Breen, John (-8/72). TV: *Gunsmoke*—"Nitro!" 4-8-67 & 4-15-67 (Waiter).

Breen, Joseph. TV: *Wild Bill Hickok*—"The Gatling Gun" 5-5-53; *Gunsmoke*—"The Constable" 5-30-59 (Mike), "Miss Kitty" 10-14-61 (Driver), "Quaker Girl" 12-10-66 (George); *Have Gun Will Travel*—"The Unforgiven" 11-7-59; *The Rebel*—"Lady of Quality" 6-5-60 (Logan); *Bonanza*—"Mirror of a Man" 3-31-63 (Sol), "Twilight Town" 10-13-63, "No Less a Man" 3-15-64; *Rawhide*—"The Race" 9-25-64 (Jim Traynor).

Breese, Edmund (1871-4/6/36). Films: "The Shooting of Dan Mc-Grew" 1915 (Jim Maxwell); "The Spell of the Yukon" 1916 (Jim Carson); "Rough Waters" 1930 (Capt. Thomas); "The Painted Desert" 1931 (Judge Mathews); "The Golden West" 1932 (Sam Lynch); "Fighting with Kit Carson" 1933-serial.

Breeze, Michelle. TV: *Gunsmoke*—"South Wind" 11-27-65 (Bar Girl), "Nitro!" 4-8-67 & 4-15-67 (Saloon Girl), "Mannon" 1-20-69 (Chris), "A Quiet Day in Dodge" 1-29-73 (Sadie).

Brega, Mario. Films: "Buffalo Bill, Hero of the Far West" 1964-Ital./Ger./Fr. (Donaldson); "For a Few Dollars More" 1965-Ital./Ger./Span. (Indio's Gang Member); "The Good, the Bad, and the Ugly" 1966-Ital.; "The Ugly Ones" 1966-Ital./Span.; "Death Rides a Horse" 1967-Ital. (One-Eye); "A Minute to Pray, a Second to Die" 1967-Ital. (Kraut); "Great Silence" 1968-Ital./Fr.; "The Greatest Robbery in the West" 1968-Ital.; "Finders Killers" 1969-Ital. (Parker); "No Room to Die" 1969-Ital.; "The Reward's Yours, the Man's Mine" 1970-Ital.

Brehm, Richard J. Films: "Colt .45" 1950; "...And Now Miguel" 1966 (Bonafacio).

Brell, Sam. *see* Sambrell, Aldo.

Breman, Lennie (1914-3/21/86). TV: *Death Valley Days*—"The Little Trooper" 12-15-59.

Bremer, Sylvia. Films: "The Narrow Trail" 1918 (Betty Werdin).

Brendel, El (1890-4/9/64). Films: "Up or Down?" 1917 (Boy); "Man of the Forest" 1926 (Horace Pipp); "Arizona Bound" 1927 (Oley "Smoke" Oleson); "The Big Trail" 1930 (Gussie); "The Last Trail" 1933 (Newt Olsen); "God's Country and the Woman" 1937 (Ole Oleson); "Pis-

tol Packin' Nitwits" 1945-short. ¶TV: *Cowboy G-Men*—"Ghost Town Mystery" 4-4-53, "Sidewinder" 5-2-53; *Destry*—"Deputy for a Day" 4-3-64 (Olaf Olsen).

Brenlin, George. Films: "Cimarron" 1960 (Hoss). ¶TV: *Gunsmoke*—"Jesse" 10-19-57 (Jesse Pruett); *Wanted—Dead or Alive*—"Ransom for a Nun" 10-18-58 (Leu Kidder); *Trackdown*—"Tenner Smith" 10-24-58 (Del Taylor), "The Gang" 2-25-59 (Guthrie); *The Californians*—"Dangerous Journey" 11-25-58 (Dan Carmichael); *The Rifleman*—"The Blowout" 10-13-59; *The Deputy*—"The Hard Decision" 1-28-61 (Jimmie Burke); *Two Faces West*—"The Coward" 6-26-61; *Rawhide*—"Incident at the Trail's End" 1-11-63 (Frank Slade); *The Virginian*—"The Small Parade" 2-20-63 (Lembeck), "Johnny Moon" 10-11-67 (Sammyjay); *Bonanza*—"The Saga of Whizzer McGee" 4-28-63 (Whizzer McGee).

Brennan, Andy. Films: "San Antone" 1953 (Ike); "The Far Country" 1955 (Man); "Shoot Out at Big Sag" 1962.

Brennan, Claire (1934-11/27/77). TV: *Gunsmoke*—"Disciple" 4-1-74 (Sissy).

Brennan, John. TV: *Bordertown*—Regular 1989 (Corporal Clive Bennett).

Brennan, John E. (1865-12/27/40). Films: "The Tenderfoot's Luck" 1913; "The Medicine Show at Stone Gulch" 1914; "The Battle of Running Bull" 1915.

Brennan, Ruth. Films: "Blood on the Moon" 1948; "California Passage" 1950 (Stella); "Oh! Susanna" 1951 (Young Wife); "Hell's Outpost" 1954.

Brennan, Walter (1894-9/21/74). Films: "The Ridin' Rowdy" 1927 (Raye Hampton); "Tearin' into Trouble" 1927 (Billy Martin); "The Ballyhoo Buster" 1928; "The Lariat Kid" 1929 (Pat O'Shea); "The Long, Long Trail" 1929 (Skinny Rawlins); "Smilin' Guns" 1929 (Ranch Foreman); "Cornered" 1932 (Bailiff); "Fighting for Justice" 1932 (Zeke); "Hello Trouble" 1932; "Law and Order" 1932 (Lanky Smith); "Texas Cyclone" 1932 (Lew Collins); "Two-Fisted Law" 1932 (Deputy Sheriff Bendix); "The Fourth Horseman" 1933; "Man of Action" 1933 (Sommers); "Rustlers' Roundup" 1933; "Silent Men" 1933 (Coyote Cotter); "The Prescott Kid" 1934 (Stage Driver); "Law Beyond the Range" 1935 (Abner); "Northern Frontier" 1935

(Cook); "The Three Godfathers" 1936 (Gus/Sam Barstow); "Wild and Woolly" 1937 (Gramp Flynn); "Cowboy and the Lady" 1938 (Sugar); "The Texans" 1938 (Chuckawalla, the Foreman); "Northwest Passage" 1940 (Hunk Marriner); "The Westerner" 1940 (Judge Roy Bean); "Dakota" 1945 (Capt. Bounce); "My Darling Clementine" 1946 (Old Man Clanton); "Blood on the Moon" 1948 (Kris Barden); "Red River" 1948 (Groot Nadine); "Brimstone" 1949 (Pop Courteen); "Curtain Call at Cactus Creek" 1950 (Rimrock); "The Showdown" 1950 (Capt. MacKellar); "Singing Guns" 1950 (Dr. Jonathan Mark); "Surrender" 1950 (William Howard); "Ticket to Tomahawk" 1950 (Terence Sweeney); "Along the Great Divide" 1951 (Pop Keith); "Best of the Badmen" 1951 (Doc Butcher); "Return of the Texan" 1952 (Firth Crockett); "Drums Across the River" 1954 (Sam Brannon); "Four Guns to the Border" 1954 (Simon Bhumer); "At Gunpoint" 1955 (Doc Lacy); "Bad Day at Black Rock" 1955 (Doc Velie); "The Far Country" 1955 (Ben); "The Proud Ones" 1956 (Jake, the Jailer); "Rio Bravo" 1959 (Stumpy); "How the West Was Won" 1962 (Col. Hawkins); "Shoot Out at Big Sag" 1962 (Preacher Hawker); "The Over-the-Hill Gang" TVM-1969 (Nash Crawford); "Support Your Local Sheriff" 1969 (Pa Danby); "The Over-the-Hill Gang Rides Again" TVM-1970 (Nash Crawford); "The Young Country" TVM-1970 (Sheriff Matt Fenley); "Smoke in the Wind" 1975 (H.B. Kingman). ¶TV: *Zane Grey Theater*—"Vengeance Canyon" 11-30-56 (Joe), "Ride a Lonely Trail" 11-2-57 (Sheriff Larson); *The Guns of Will Sonnett*—Regular 1967-69 (Will Sonnett); *Alias Smith and Jones*—"The Day They Hanged Kid Curry" 9-16-71 (Silky O'Sullivan), "Twenty-One Days to Tenstrike" 1-6-72 (Gantry), "Don't Get Mad, Get Even" 2-17-72.

Brennan, Jr., Walter. TV: *Have Gun Will Travel*—"Show of Force" 11-9-57.

Brennon, Hazel. Films: "In Mizzoura" 1919 (Emily Radburn).

Brent, Eve (1930-). Films: "Raiders of the South" 1947; "Forty Guns" 1957 (Louvenia Spangler); "The Sad Horse" 1959 (Sheila); "The White Buffalo" 1977 (Frieda). ¶TV: *Sugarfoot*—"Misfire" 12-10-57 (Mercy Preston); *26 Men*—"Profane Masquerade" 3-10-59; *Bat Masterson*—"Deadline" 4-8-59 (Lorna Adams).

Brent, Evelyn (Betty Riggs)

(1899-6/4/75). Films: "The Shooting of Dan McGrew" 1915 (Nell at Age 12); "The Spell of the Yukon" 1916 (Dorothy Temple); "The Desert Outlaw" 1924 (May Halloway); "The Plunderer" 1924 (the Lily); "The Silver Horde" 1930 (Cherry Malotte); "Home on the Range" 1935 (Georgie Haley); "Hopalong Cassidy Returns" 1936 (Lil Halliday); "Song of the Trail" 1936 (Myra); "Sudden Bill Dorn" 1937 (Diana Villegas); "The Law West of Tombstone" 1938 (Clara Martinez); "Wide Open Town" 1941 (Belle Langtry); "Westward Ho" 1942 (Mrs. Healey); "Robin Hood of Monterey" 1947. ¶TV: *Wagon Train*—"The Lita Foladaire Story" 1-6-60.

Brent, George (1904-5/26/79). Films: "Fair Warning" 1931 (Les Haines); "Lightning Warrior" 1931-serial (Alan Scott); "God's Country and the Woman" 1937 (Steve Russett); "Gold Is Where You Find It" 1938 (Jared Whitney); "Silver Queen" 1942 (James Kincaid); "Red Canyon" 1949 (Mathew Boatel); "Montana Belle" 1952 (Tom Bradfield). ¶TV: *El Coyote Rides*—Pilot 1958 (Colonel Bart Edwards); *Rawhide*—"Incident at Chubasco" 4-3-59 (Jefferson Devereaux).

Brent, Linda. Films: "Below the Border" 1942 (Rosita); "Ride 'Em, Cowboy" 1942 (Sunbeam); "In Old Oklahoma" 1943; "Death Valley Rangers" 1944 (Lorna); "The Laramie Trail" 1944. ¶TV: *Death Valley Days*—"The Hoodoo Mine" 4-7-56 (Lupin); *Sergeant Preston of the Yukon*—"Remember the Maine" 4-26-56 (Rita Mendoza).

Brent, Lynton. Films: "Texas Bad Man" 1932 (Billy the Kid); "Mystery Mountain" 1934-serial (Matthews); "The Old Corral" 1936 (Dunn); "Git Along, Little Dogies" 1937 (Wilkin's Henchman); "The Mystery of the Hooded Horseman" 1937; "Tex Rides with the Boy Scouts" 1937 (Pete); "Frontier Town" 1938 (Grayson); "Rollin' Plains" 1938 (Lope); "Utah Trail" 1938 (Cheyenne); "Days of Jesse James" 1939; "Yes, We Have No Bonanza" 1939-short (Pete); "Adventures of Red Ryder" 1940-serial (Len Clark); "Pioneers of the Frontier" 1940; "Bad Man of Deadwood" 1941; "Forbidden Trails" 1941 (Bill); "The Gunman from Bodie" 1941; "The Pioneers" 1941 (Jingo); "Red River Valley" 1941; "Border Roundup" 1942; "The Lone Rider in Cheyenne" 1942; "Overland to Deadwood" 1942; "Raiders of the West" 1942; "The Rangers Take Over" 1942 (Block Nelson); "Riders of the West" 1942; "Sheriff of Sage Valley" 1942; "South of Santa Fe" 1942; "Trail Riders" 1942 (Jeff); "West of the Law" 1942; "Calling Wild Bill Elliott" 1943; "Six Gun Gospel" 1943; "The Stranger from Pecos" 1943; "Tenting Tonight on the Old Camp Ground" 1943 (Sheriff); "The Texas Kid" 1943 (Jess); "Two Fisted Justice" 1943; "Cowboy and the Senorita" 1944; "Marked Trails" 1944 (Tex); "Partners of the Trail" 1944 (Lem); "Raiders of the Border" 1944 (Davis); "Range Law" 1944; "Valley of Vengeance" 1944 (Carr); "West of the Rio Grande" 1944; "Frontier Feud" 1945; "The Lost Trail" 1945 (Hall); "Drifting Along" 1946 (Joe); "Gentleman from Texas" 1946; "The Haunted Mine" 1946; "Haunted Trails" 1949; "Riders in the Sky" 1949; "Beyond the Purple Hills" 1950.

Brent, Romney (1902-9/24/76). TV: *Zorro*—"Zorro Rides to the Mission" 10-24-57 (Padre Felipe); *Jim Bowie*—"Man on the Street" 5-16-58 (Bernard De Marigny).

Brent, Roy. Films: "Adventures of Red Ryder" 1940-serial (Joe); "One Man's Law" 1940; "Deep in the Heart of Texas" 1942 (Franklin); "Outlaws of Pine Ridge" 1942; "Arizona Trail" 1943; "Blazing Guns" 1943 (Jim Wade); "Carson City Cyclone" 1943; "Cattle Stampede" 1943 Slater); "The Man from Thunder River" 1943; "Raiders of Red Gap" 1943 (Butch); "Raiders of San Joaquin" 1943 (McQuarry); "The Drifter" 1944 (Sam); "Gunsmoke Mesa" 1944 (Deputy Mace Page); "Marshal of Gunsmoke" 1944; "Westward Bound" 1944 (Will); "Zorro's Black Whip" 1944-serial (Attacker #1/Wagner); "Bad Men of the Border" 1945; "Code of the Lawless" 1945 (Sam); "His Brother's Ghost" 1945 (Yaeger); "Trail to Vengeance" 1945 (Sanders); "Ambush Trail" 1946; "Lightning Raiders" 1946 (Phillips); "Outlaw of the Plains" 1946; "Rustler's Roundup" 1946 (Chuck); "Six Gun Man" 1946 (Slim Peters); "Wild Beauty" 1946 (Gus). ¶TV: *The Roy Rogers Show*—"The Knockout" 12-28-52 (Sheriff Jim Wiley), "The Silver Fox Hunt" 4-19-53.

Brent, Timothy (Giancarlo Prete). Films: "Sting of the West" 1972-Ital.; "Three Musketeers of the West" 1972-Ital. (Darth, Jr.).

Brereton, Tyrone (1894-4/25/39). Films: "The Canyon of Adventure" 1928 (Luis Villegas); "Cimarron" 1931 (Dabney Venable).

Breslin, Patricia. TV: *Mave-rick*—"Yellow River" 2-8-59 (Abigail Allen); *Hotel De Paree*—"Sundance and the Fallen Sparrow" 5-27-60 (Ellie); *Tate*—"The Return of Jessica Jackson" 9-14-60 (Jessica Jackson); *The Outlaws*—"Ballad for a Badman" 10-6-60 (Julie Kittrick); *The Rifleman*—"Flowers by the Door" 1-10-61 (Cora Seevers); *The Rebel*—"Miz Purdy" 4-2-61 (Elizabeth Purdy); *Tales of Wells Fargo*—"A Killing in Calico" 12-16-61 (Theresa Coburn); *Bonanza*—"The Miracle Worker" 5-20-62 (Susan Blanchard); *Stoney Burke*—"Point of Honor" 10-22-62 (Lee Anne Hewitt); *The Virginian*—"The Long Quest" 4-8-64 (Mary Ann Martin).

Brett, Jeremy (1935-9/12/95). TV: *Young Dan'l Boone*—"The Trail Blazer" 9-12-77 (Langford).

Brewer, Betty. Films: "Rangers of Fortune" 1940 (Mary Elizabeth "Squib" Clayborn); "The Round Up" 1941 (Mary); "Wild Bill Hickok Rides" 1942 (Janey Nolan).

Brewer, Teresa (1931-). Films: "Those Redheads from Seattle" 1953 (Pat Edmonds).

Brewster, Carol. Films: "The Maverick Queen" 1956 (Girl). ¶TV: *Gunsmoke*—"Dry Road to Nowhere" 4-3-65 (Kate Moreland); *Death Valley Days*—"The Fighting Sky Pilot" 4-25-65; *The Legend of Jesse James*—"The Raiders" 10-18-65 (Stella); *Branded*—"A Proud Town" 12-19-65 (Grace Stoddard); *Laredo*—"Miracle at Massacre Mission" 3-3-66.

Brewster, Diane (1931-11/12/91). Films: "Black Patch" 1957 (Helen Danner); "The Oklahoman" 1957 (Eliza); "Quantrill's Raiders" 1958 (Sue Walters); "King of the Wild Stallions" 1959 (Martha). ¶TV: *Cheyenne*—"The Traveler" 1-3-56 (Mary), "The Dark Rider" 9-11-56 (Samantha Crawford), "The Mustang Trail" 11-20-56 (Victoria), "Dark Decision" 11-5-62 (Constance Mason); *Death Valley Days*—"Faro Bill's Layout" 10-7-56 (Grace Fallon), "The $25,000 Wager" 2-7-65 (Flora); *Zane Grey Theater*—"Time of Decision" 1-18-57 (Nancy Tapper), "A Man to Look Up To" 11-29-57 (Mrs. Lester); *Tales of Wells Fargo*—"Rio Grande" 6-3-57 (Lillian Barkley), "Dr. Alice" 2-23-58 (Dr. Alice MacCauley); *Maverick*—"According to Hoyle" 10-6-57 (Samantha Crawford), "The Savage Hills" 2-9-58 (Samantha Crawford), "The Seventh Hand" 3-2-58 (Samantha Crawford), "Shady Deal at Sunny Acres" 11-23-58 (Samantha Crawford); *Wagon Train*—"The Honorable Don Charlie Story" 1-22-58 (Julie

Wharton), "The Lita Foladaire Story" 1-6-60 (Lita Foladaire), "The Echo Pass Story" 1-3-65 (Bea); *The Restless Gun*—"The Whip" 3-31-58 (Helen Bricker); *Tombstone Territory*—"The Lady Gambler" 5-28-58 (Julie Dixon); *Trackdown*—"Outlaw's Wife" 9-12-58 (Abigail Duke); *Cimarron City*—"Runaway Train" 1-31-59 (Lisa Caldwell); *Frontier Doctor*—"Law of the Badlands" 2-28-59; *Wanted—Dead or Alive*—"Double Fee" 3-21-59 (Amy Winter); *Bat Masterson*—"The Conspiracy" 6-17-59 & 6-24-59 (Lynn Harrison); *The Rifleman*—"Jealous Man" 3-26-62 (Fay Owens); *The Dakotas*—"Fargo" 2-25-63 (Jody); *Empire*—"The Convention" 5-14-63 (Caroline).

Brian, David (1914-7/15/93). Films: "Fort Worth" 1951 (Blair Lunsford); "Inside Straight" 1951 (Rip MacCool); "Springfield Rifle" 1952 (Austin McCool); "Ambush at Tomahawk Gap" 1953 (Egan); "A Perilous Journey" 1953 (Monty Breed); "Dawn at Socorro" 1954 (Dick Braden); "Timberjack" 1955 (Croft Brunner); "The First Traveling Saleslady" 1956 (James Carter); "Fury at Gunsight Pass" 1956 (Whitey Turner); "The White Squaw" 1956 (Sigrod Swanson); "How the West Was Won" 1962 (Attorney); "The Rare Breed" 1966 (Charles Ellsworth). ¶TV: *Rawhide*—"Incident at Jacob's Well" 10-16-59 (Jacob Calvin), "Incident of the Painted Lady" 5-12-61 (Thad Clemens); *Laramie*—"Protective Custody" 1-15-63 (Walt Douglas); *The Dakotas*—"Fargo" 2-25-63 (Fargo); *Death Valley Days*—"The Peacemaker" 11-3-63; *Daniel Boone*—"The Choosing" 10-29-64 (Major Russell Horton); *Laredo*—"Three's Company" 10-14-65 (Theo Henderson); *Branded*—"Call to Glory" 2-27-66, 3-6-66 & 3-13-66 (Gregory Hazin); *Iron Horse*—"No Wedding Bells for Tony" 11-7-66 (Charlie Farrow); *Hondo*—"Hondo and the Ghost of Ed Dow" 11-24-67 (Ben Dow); *Cimarron Strip*—"The Greeners" 3-7-68 (Turnbull); *Gunsmoke*—"Lobo" 12-16-68 (Branch Nelson), "McCabe" 11-30-70 (Clay White), "Thirty a Month a Found" 10-7-74 (Tait Cavanaugh); *Hec Ramsey*—"The Mystery of the Yellow Rose" 1-28-73 (Henry T. Madden).

Brian, Mary (1908-). Films: "The Enchanted Hill" 1926 (Hallie Purdy); "Under the Tonto Rim" 1928 (Lucy Watson); "The Virginian" 1929 (Molly Stark Wood); "The Light of the Western Stars" 1930 (Ruth Hammond); "Gun

Smoke" 1931 (Sue Vancey); "Calaboose" 1943.

Brice, Betty (1896-2/15/35). Films: "Who Knows?" 1918 (Jerry Weaver); "The Sagebrusher" 1920 (Annie Squires).

Brice, Pierre. Films: "Treasure of Silver Lake" 1963-Fr./Ger./Yugo. (Winnetou); "Among Vultures" 1964-Ger./Ital./Fr./Yugo. (Winnetou); "Apache Gold" 1965-Ger. (Winnetou); "The Desperado Trail" 1965-Ger./Yugo. (Winnetou); "Flmaing Frontier" 1965-Ger./Yugo. (Winnetou); "Rampage at Apache Wells" 1965-Ger./Yugo. (Winnetou); "Half Breed" 1966-Ger./Yugo./Ital. (Winnetou); "Last of the Renegades" 1966-Fr./Ital./Ger./Yugo. (Winnetou); "A Place Called Glory" 1966-Span./Ger. (Reece); "Thunder at the Border" 1967-Ger./Yugo. (Winnetou); "Old Shatterhand" 1968-Ger./Yugo./Fr./Ital. (Winnetou); "Winnetou and Shatterhand in the Valley of Death" 1968-Ger./Yugo./Ital. (Chief Winnetou).

Brickell, Beth (1941-). Films: "Posse" 1975 (Mrs. Ross). ¶TV: *Bonanza*—"Emily" 3-23-69 (Emily McPahil), "A Single Pilgrim" 1-3-71 (Dilsey Brennan); *The Men from Shiloh*—"Last of the Comancheros" 12-9-70 (Sally); *Alias Smith and Jones*—"The Wrong Train to Brimstone" 2-4-71 (Sara Blaine); *Gunsmoke*—"The Widow and the Rogue" 10-29-73 (Martha Cunningham); *Nakia*—"The Quarry" 9-28-74 (Ellie); *The Oregon Trail*—"Return from Death" 1977.

Bridge, Alan (1891-12/27/57). Films: "God's Country and the Man" 1931 (Livermore); "Rider of the Plains" 1931 (Gaynes); "The Ridin' Fool" 1931 (Nikkos); "Broadway to Cheyenne" 1932 (Dutch); "The Devil Horse" 1932-serial; "The Forty-Niners" 1932 (O'Hara); "Galloping Thru" 1932; "A Man's Land" 1932 (Steve); "South of Sante Fe" 1932 (Drunken Member of Stone's Gang); "Spirit of the West" 1932 (Tom Fallon); "Wyoming Whirlwind" 1932; "The Cheyenne Kid" 1933 (Denver Ed); "Cowboy Counsellor" 1933 (Sheriff Matt Verity); "Drum Taps" 1933 (Lariat); "The Fighting Texans" 1933 (Gus Durkin); "Fighting with Kit Carson" 1933-serial; "The Lone Avenger" 1933 (Burl Adams); "Son of the Border" 1933 (Henchey); "Sunset Pass" 1933 (Tom); "The Trail Drive" 1933; "When a Man Rides Alone" 1933 (Montana Slade); "The Fiddlin' Buckaroo" 1934; "Honor of the Range" 1934; "Mystery Moun-

tain" 1934-serial (Henderson); "The Thundering Herd" 1934 (Catlee); "Border Brigands" 1935; "Gallant Defender" 1935 (Salty Smith); "Melody Trail" 1935 (Matt Kirby); "The New Frontier" 1935 (Kit); "North of Arizona" 1935 (George Tully); "Outlaw Rule" 1935 (Bat Lindstrom); "Silent Valley" 1935 (Frank Harley); "Valley of Wanted Men" 1935; "Call of the Prairie" 1936 (Sam Porter); "Fast Bullets" 1936 (Travis); "The Lawless Nineties" 1936 (Steele); "The Three Mesquiteers" 1936 (Olin); "Trail Dust" 1936 (Babson); "Borderland" 1937 (Dandy Morgan); "Dodge City Trail" 1937 (Dawson); "One Man Justice" 1937 (Red Grindy); "Springtime in the Rockies" 1937 (Briggs); "Two-Fisted Sheriff" 1937; "Two Gun Law" 1937 (Kipp Faulkner); "Westbound Mail" 1937 (Bull Feeney); "Western Gold" 1937 (Holman); "Wild West Days" 1937-serial (Steve); "Call of the Rockies" 1938 (Weston); "Colorado Trail" 1938 (Mark Sheldon); "Flaming Frontier" 1938-serial; "The Great Adventures of Wild Bill Hickok" 1938 (Blackie); "Gunsmoke Trail" 1938 (Sheriff); "Law of the Plains" 1938 (Card Player); "Partners of the Plains" 1938 (Scar Lewis); "Two-Gun Justice" 1938 (Sheriff Tate); "Blue Montana Skies" 1939 (Marshall); "The Man from Sundown" 1939 (Slick Larson); "Oklahoma Frontier" 1939; "The Oklahoma Kid" 1939 (Settler); "The Stranger from Texas" 1939 (Jeff Browning); "Blazing Six Shooters" 1940 (Bert Kargin); "The Dark Command" 1940 (Bandit Leader); "My Little Chickadee" 1940 (Barfly); "Pioneers of the Frontier" 1940 (Marshal Larsen); "Santa Fe Trail" 1940 (Man); "West of Abilene" 1940; "West of Carson City" 1940 (Foreman of the Jury); "Honky Tonk" 1941 (Man in Meeting House); "The Kid's Last Ride" 1941 (Harmon); "Lady from Cheyenne" 1941 (Mr. Matthews); "Law of the Range" 1941 (Squint Jamison); "The Lone Rider Rides On" 1941; "Rawhide Rangers" 1941 (Rawlings); "Bad Men of the Hills" 1942 (Sheriff Arnold); "Bells of Capistrano" 1942 (Jake); "Fighting Bill Fargo" 1942 (Houston); "The Man from Thunder River" 1943; "Tenting Tonight on the Old Camp Ground" 1943 (Pete); "Blazing the Western Trail" 1945; "Both Barrels Blazing" 1945; "Cowboy Blues" 1946; "My Pal Trigger" 1946 (Wallace); "Singin' in the Corn" 1946 (Honest John Richards); "The Virginian" 1946 (Sheriff); "Last Days of Boot Hill" 1947 (Forrest Brent); "Robin

Hood of Texas" 1947 (Sheriff); "Fury at Furnace Creek" 1948 (Lawyer); "The Paleface" 1948 (Horseman); "Quick on the Trigger" 1948 (Judge Kormac); "Silver River" 1948 (Sam Slade); "Trail of the Yukon" 1949; "California Passage" 1950 (Conover); "In Old Amarillo" 1951; "Oh! Susanna" 1951 (Jake Ledbetter); "Barbed Wire" 1952; "The Last Musketeer" 1952 (Lem Shaver); "Iron Mountain Trail" 1953 (Marshall); "Hell's Outpost" 1954; "Jubilee Trail" 1954 (Mr. Turner). ¶TV: *Wild Bill Hickok*—"Jingles Becomes a Baby Sitter" 4-15-52; *The Gene Autry Show*—"Cold Decked" 9-15-53, "Santa Fe Raiders" 7-6-54.

Bridge, Loie (1889-3/9/74). Films: "Single-Handed Sanders" 1932; "Wyoming Whirlwind" 1932; "Rodeo Rhythm" 1942 (Aunt Tilly); "Riders in the Sky" 1949 (Widow Cathart); "Riders of the Whistling Pines" 1949 (Loie Weaver); "Wild Women" TVM-1970.

Bridges, Beau (1942-). Films: "Lovin' Molly" 1974 (Johnny). ¶TV: *Zane Grey Theater*—"Image of a Drawn Sword" 5-11-61; *Wagon Train*—"The John Bernard Story" 11-21-62 (Larry Gill); *Rawhide*—"Incident at Paradise" 10-24-63 (Billy Johanson); *The Loner*—"The Mourners for Johnny Sharp" 2-5-66 & 2-12-66 (Johnny Sharp); *Branded*—"Nice Day for a Hanging" 2-6-66 (Lon Allison); *Gunsmoke*—"My Father's Guitar" 2-21-66 (Jason); *Bonanza*—"Justice" 1-8-67 (Horace); *Cimarron Strip*—"The Legend of Jud Starr" 9-14-67 (Billy Joe Snow).

Bridges, Corey. TV: *The Loner*—"Incident in the Middle of Nowhere" 2-19-66 (Wendy).

Bridges, Jeff (1950-). Films: "Bad Company" 1972 (Jake Rumsey); "Hearts of the West" 1975 (Lewis Tater); "Rancho Deluxe" 1975 (Jack McKee); "Heaven's Gate" 1980 (John H. Bridges). ¶TV: *The Loner*—"The Ordeal of Bud Windom" 12-25-65 (Bud Windom).

Bridges, Jim. TV: *MacKenzie's Raiders*—Regular 1958-59.

Bridges, John (1888-7/11/73). Films: "The Law Rides Again" 1943 (Jess); "Wild Horse Stampede" 1943 (Col. Black); "Death Valley Rangers" 1944 (Cal); "Outlaw Trail" 1944 (Ed Knowles); "Sonora Stagecoach" 1944 (Pop Carson); "Westward Bound" 1944 (Ira Phillips); "The Lost Trail" 1945 (Dr. Brown); "Wild West" 1946 (Constable); "White Stallion" 1947 (Sheriff); "Prairie Outlaws" 1948.

Bridges, Lloyd (1913-). Films: "The Medico of Painted Springs" 1941; "The Royal Mounted Patrol" 1941 (Hap Andrews); "The Son of Davy Crockett" 1941; "North of the Rockies" 1942; "Pardon My Gun" 1942 (White); "Riders of the Northland" 1942 (Alex); "Shut My Big Mouth" 1942 (Skinny); "West of Tombstone" 1942; "Hail to the Rangers" 1943 (Dave Kerlin); "Saddle Leather Law" 1944; "Abilene Town" 1946 (Henry Dreiser); "Canyon Passage" 1946 (Johnny Steele); "Ramrod" 1947 (Red Cates); "Unconquered" 1947 (Lt. Hutchins); "Calamity Jane and Sam Bass" 1949 (Joel Collins); "Red Canyon" 1949 (Virgil Cordt); "Colt .45" 1950 (Paul Donovan); "Little Big Horn" 1951 (Capt. Phillips Donlin); "High Noon" 1952 (Harvey Pell); "Last of the Comanches" 1952 (Jim Starbuck); "City of Badmen" 1953 (Gar Stanton); "The Tall Texan" 1953 (Ben Trask); "Apache Woman" 1955 (Rex Moffet); "Wichita" 1955 (Gyp); "The Rainmaker" 1956 (Noah Curry); "Ride Out for Revenge" 1957 (Capt. George); "The Silent Gun" TVM-1969 (Brad Clinton); "Running Wild" 1973. ¶TV: *Studio One*—"The Silent Gun" 2-6-56; *Zane Grey Theater*—"Time of Decision" 1-18-57 (Evan Tapper), "Wire" 1-31-58 (Sam Fraser), "Ransom" 11-17-60 (Dundee), "Image of a Drawn Sword" 5-11-61 (Lt. Sam Kenyon); *Great Adventure*—"Wild Bill Hickok—the Legend and the Man" 1-3-64 (Wild Bill Hickok); *The Loner*—Regular 1965-66 (William Colton); *How the West Was Won*—Episode One 2-12-78 (Orville Gant), Episode Two 2-19-78 (Orville Gant), Episode Three 2-26-78 (Orville Gant), Episode Four 3-5-78 (Orville Gant).

Bridges, Rand. Films: "Young Pioneers' Christmas" TVM-1976 (Pike). ¶TV: *Gunsmoke*—"The Widow-Maker" 10-8-73 (Deak Towler); *Black Bart*—Pilot 4-4-75 (Porter).

Bridou, Lucienne. Films: "Black Jack" 1968-Ital.; "This Man Can't Die" 1968-Ital. (Susy Benson).

Briggs, Charlie (1933-2/6/85). Films: "How the West Was Won" 1962 (Barker); "A Time for Killing" 1967 (Sgt. Kettlinger). ¶TV: *The Restless Gun*—"Bonner's Squaw" 11-3-58 (Meacham); *Lawman*—"9:05 to North Platte" 12-6-59 (Logan Jute), "The Trojan Horse" 12-31-61 (Falk), "The Youngest" 4-22-62 (Darrel Martin); *The Deputy*—"The Hidden Motive" 1-30-60 (Bill Dawson); *Shotgun Slade*—"The Swindle" 3-8-60;

The Law of the Plainsman—"Stella" 3-31-60 (Bob Erby); *The Rifleman*—"The Jailbird" 5-10-60, "Short Rope for a Tall Man" 3-28-61; *Laramie*—".45 Calibre" 11-15-60 (Charley Wilkes); *Cheyenne*—"Savage Breed" 12-19-60 (Bart Hanson), "The Durango Brothers" 9-24-62 (Obed Durango); *Zane Grey Theater*—"Blood Red" 1-29-61 (Roustabout); *The Outlaws*—"The Brothers" 5-11-61 (Maury Kelly); *Wagon Train*—"The Jenna Douglas Story" 11-1-61 (Ed Linders), "The Trace McCloud Story" 3-2-64 (Joe Weaver); *Bonanza*—"The Law Maker" 3-11-62 (Charlie Fitch); *Tales of Wells Fargo*—"Don't Wake a Tiger" 5-12-62 (Andy Stone); *The Virginian*—"Throw a Long Rope" 10-3-62 (Soapy), "Fifty Days to Moose Jaw" 12-12-62 (Hard Pan); *Gunsmoke*—"Panacea Sykes" 4-13-63 (Stage Driver), "Easy Come" 10-26-63 (Riley); *Daniel Boone*—"A Short Walk to Salem" 11-19-64 (Hiram Girty); *Death Valley Days*—"The Rider" 12-4-65; *The Big Valley*—"The Martyr" 10-17-66; *Laredo*—"Road to San Remo" 11-25-66; *The Guns of Will Sonnett*—"Guilt" 11-29-68 (Lyle Merceen); *Lancer*—"Goodbye, Lizzie" 4-28-70 (Thede); *Alias Smith and Jones*—"Return to Devil's Hole" 2-25-71.

Briggs, Donald (1911-2/3/86). Films: "Sutter's Gold" 1936; "Cowboy from Brooklyn" 1938 (Star Reporter). ¶TV: *Gunsmoke*—"Hammerhead" 12-26-64 (Deggers); *Wild Wild West*—"The Night of the Fatal Trap" 12-24-65 (Cantrell); *Bonanza*—"Erin" 1-26-69 (Clint Murray); *Lancer*—"Angel Day and Her Sunshine Girls" 2-25-69 (Marshal).

Briggs, Harlan (1880-1/26/52). Films: "Frontier Marshal" 1939 (Editor); "My Little Chickadee" 1940 (Hotel Clerk); "The Vanishing Virginian" 1941 (Mr. Rogard); "Canyon Passage" 1946 (Dr. Balance); "My Pal Trigger" 1946 (Dr. Bentley); "Vigilantes of Boomtown" 1947 (Judge); "Fury at Furnace Creek" 1948 (Prosecutor). TV: *The Lone Ranger*—"Drink of Water" 10-26-50.

Briggs, Jack. Films: "New Mexico" 1951 (Pvt. Lindley). ¶TV: *The Lone Ranger*—"Danger Ahead" 10-12-50, "Thieves' Money" 11-2-50.

Briggs, Matt (1883-6/10/62). Films: "The Ox-Bow Incident" 1943 (Judge Daniel Tyler); "Buffalo Bill" 1944 (Gen. Blazier).

Bright, Mildred (1892-9/27/67). Films: "Partners of the Sunset" 1922 (Violet Moreland).

Bright, Richard (1937-). Films: "Pat Garrett and Billy the Kid" 1973

(Holly); "Rancho Deluxe" 1975 (Burt).

Briles, Charles. TV: *The Big Valley*—Regular 1965-66 (Eugene Barkley); *Bonanza*—"The Medal" 10-26-69 (Del), "Kingdom of Fear" 4-4-71 (Billy).

Brill, Charles (1938-). TV: *Broken Arrow*—"Duel" 3-18-58 (Pina); *Wanted—Dead or Alive*—"Journey for Josh" 10-5-60.

Brill, Patti (1923-1/18/63). Films: "Girl Rush" 1944 (Claire); "Nevada" 1944.

Brimley, Wilford (1934-). Films: "Lawman" 1971 (Marc Corman); "The Oregon Trail" TVM-1976 (Ludlow); "The Electric Horseman" 1979 (Farmer); "The Wild Wild West Revisited" TVM-1979 (President Grover Cleveland); "Rodeo Girl" TVM-1980 (Bingo Gibbs); "Blood River" TVM-1994 (Culler); "The Good Old Boys" TVM-1995 (C.C. Tarpley). ¶TV: *Kung Fu*—"One Step to Darkness" 1-25-75 (Blacksmith); *The Oregon Trail*—"Hard Ride Home"/"The Last Game" 9-21-77; *How the West Was Won*—"Hillary" 2-26-79 (Sheriff Daniels).

Brinckerhoff, Burt (1936-). TV: *Tales of Wells Fargo*—"Chauncey" 3-17-62 (Chuck Evans); *Laramie*—"The Sunday Shoot" 11-13-62 (Hobey Carson); *The Virginian*—"The Devil's Children" 12-5-62 (Dan Flood); *Gunsmoke*—"Run, Sheep, Run" 1-9-65 (Tom Stocker); *Rawhide*—"The Testing Post" 11-30-65 (Karl Denner).

Brindel, Eugene. Films: "Davy Crockett, King of the Wild Frontier" 1955 (Billy). ¶TV: *Walt Disney Presents*—"Davy Crockett"—Regular 1954-55 (Billy Crockett).

Brinegar, Paul (1917-3/27/95). Films: "Dawn at Socorro" 1954 (Desk Clerk); "Copper Sky" 1957 (Charlie Martin); "Cattle Empire" 1958 (Tom Jeffrey); "Charro!" 1969 (Opie Keetch); "High Plains Drifter" 1973 (Lutie Naylor); "The Wild Women of Chastity Gulch" TVM-1982 (Bodie); "The Gambler Returns: The Luck of the Draw" TVM-1991 (Cookie); "Maverick" 1994 (Stage Driver); "Wyatt Earp: Return to Tombstone" TVM-1994 (Spooner). ¶TV: *The Lone Ranger*—"Rendezvous at Whipsaw" 11-11-54; *Tales of the Texas Rangers*—"The Hobo" 1-28-56 (Hobo); *Wyatt Earp*—Regular 1956-58 (Mayor Jim "Dog" Kelley); *Cheyenne*—"Lone Gun" 12-4-56 (Slim Mantell); *Tales of Wells Fargo*—"Rene-

gade Raiders" 5-20-57 (Shorty Tannin); *The Texan*—"The Ringer" 2-16-59; *Trackdown*—"The Protector" 4-1-59 (Zack Armstead); *Rawhide*—Regular 1959-66 (Wishbone); *Death Valley Days*—"The Solid Gold Cavity" 10-1-66, "The Lady and the Sourdough" 10-8-66 (Rupert Johnson); *Bonanza*—"A Bride for Buford" 1-15-67 (Rev); *Iron Horse*—"The Execution" 3-13-67 (Waco Hobson); *Daniel Boone*—"Take the Southbound Stage" 4-6-67 (Gurney); *The Guns of Will Sonnett*—"A Fool and His Money" 3-8-68 (Charlie Moss); *Lancer*—Regular 1968-70 (Jelly Hoskins); *Barbary Coast*—"The Ballad of Redwing Jail" 9-29-75 (Jesse); *The Life and Times of Grizzly Adams*—11-9-77 (Trapper John); *Adventures of Brisco County, Jr.*—Pilot 8-27-93 (Frances Kilbride), "Brisco in Jalisco" 9-17-93 (Frances Kilbride).

Brinker, Kate. Films: "Desert Guns" 1936 (Cherry Millett).

Brinkley, John. TV: *Zane Grey Theater*—"A Gun Is for Killing" 10-18-57 (Rich Watson); *The Rebel*—"A Grave for Johnny Yuma" 5-1-60 (Sprague); *The Westerner*—"Going Home" 12-16-60.

Brinkley, Ritch. Films: "Wild Horses" TVM-1985 (Wedge Smithfield); "Houston: The Legend of Texas" TVM-1986 (Senator Buckner).

Brinley, Charles (1880-2/17/46). Films: "The Red Ace" 1917-serial; "The Double Hold-Up" 1919; "Down But Not Out" 1919; "The Lone Hand" 1919; "Tempest Cody Flirts with Death" 1919; "Tempest Cody Hits the Trail" 1919; "Tempest Cody Rides Wild" 1919; "A Son of the North" 1920; "Under Northern Lights" 1920 (Louis LaRocque); "The Beautiful Gambler" 1921 (Jim Devlin); "Cyclone Smith's Vow" 1921; "If Only Jim" 1921 (Parky); "Hills of Missing Men" 1922 (Bandini); "In the Days of Daniel Boone" 1923-serial; "Days of '49" 1924-serial; "Riders of the Plains" 1924-serial; "The Western Wallop" 1924 (Sheriff Malloy); "The Fighting Smile" 1925; "Hidden Loot" 1925 (Jordan); "Idaho" 1925-serial; "The Mystery Box" 1925-serial; "The White Outlaw" 1925 (Sheriff); "Desert Valley" 1926 (Sheriff); "Beau Bandit" 1930 (Slim); "Covered Wagon Trails" 1930 (Sheriff Brunton); "The Dawn Trail" 1930 (Nestor); "Treason" 1933 (Scout Johnson); "Spirit of the West" 1932 (Ramon); "The Dude Bandit" 1933; "The Fighting Code" 1934 (Betts); "The Prescott Kid" 1934 (Manuel);

"The Red Rider" 1934-serial; "The Westerner" 1934 (Posse Member); "The Crimson Trail" 1935 (Tom); "Fighting Shadows" 1935 (Lakue); "Lawless Range" 1935; "The Outlaw Deputy" 1935 (Draige); "The Revenge Rider" 1935 (Townsman); "Square Shooter" 1935; "Westward Ho" 1935; "End of the Trail" 1936; "Dodge City Trail" 1937 (Steve's Gang Member); "The Old Wyoming Trail" 1937; "Outlaws of the Prairie" 1937 (1st Guard); "Two-Fisted Sheriff" 1937 (Blake); "Yodelin' Kid from Pine Ridge" 1937; "Spoilers of the Range" 1939; "Texas Stampede" 1939; "The Thundering West" 1939 (Coach Driver); "Western Caravans" 1939.

Brissac, Virginia (1905-79). Films: "The Three Godfathers" 1936 (Mrs. McLane); "The Bad Man of Brimstone" 1937 (Mrs. Grant); "The Cisco Kid and the Lady" 1939 (Seamstress); "Destry Rides Again" 1939 (Sophie Claggett); "Jesse James" 1939 (Farmer's Wife); "Wagons Westward" 1940 (Angela Cook); "Bad Men of Missouri" 1941 (Mrs. Hathaway); "They Died with Their Boots On" 1941 (Woman); "The Daltons Ride Again" 1945 (Mrs. Walters); "Renegades" 1946 (Sarah Dembrow); "Pursued" 1947 (Woman at Wedding); "Old Los Angeles" 1948 (Senora Del Rey); "The Untamed Breed" 1948 (Mrs. Jones); "The Doolins of Oklahoma" 1949 (Mrs. Burton); "The Last Bandit" 1949 (Kate's Mother); "Bugles in the Afternoon" 1952 (Mrs. Carson); "Woman of the North Country" 1952 (Mrs. Dawson).

Britt, Elton (1912-6/23/72). Films: "Laramie" 1949 (Sergeant).

Brittany, Morgan (Suzanne Cupito) (1951-). Films: "Stage to Thunder Rock" 1964 (Sandy Swope); "The Wild Women of Chastity Gulch" TVM-1982 (Lanie); "Riders of the Storm" 1955 (Rita). ¶TV: *Rawhide*—"Incident of the Hostages" 4-19-63 (Winter Night); *Gunsmoke*—"Daddy Went Away" 5-11-63 (Jessica Damon); *Daniel Boone*—"The Family Fluellen" 10-15-64 (Naomi Fluellen); *Branded*—"Kellie" 4-24-66 (Kellie).

Britton, Barbara (1921-1/17/80). Films: "Secrets of the Wastelands" 1941 (Jennifer Kendall); "The Virginian" 1946 (Molly Wood); "The Gunfighters" 1947 (Bess Banner); "Albuquerque" 1948 (Letty Tyler); "Loaded Pistols" 1948 (Mary Evans); "The Untamed Breed" 1948 (Cherry Lucas); "I Shot Jesse James" 1949 (Cynthy Waters); "Bandit Queen" 1950 (Lola); "The Raiders" 1952

(Elizabeth Ainsworth); "Ride the Man Down" 1952 (Lottie Priest); "The Spoilers" 1955 (Helen Chester).

Britton, Pamela (1923-6/17/74). TV: *Gunslinger*—"Golden Circle" 4-13-61 (Peggy Morgan).

Brittone, Mozelle (1912-5/18/53). Films: "The Fighting Ranger" 1934 (Rose).

Broadhurst, Kent (1940-). Films: "The Gambler Returns: The Luck of the Draw" TVM-1991 (Sailor Johnson).

Broadus, Roger. TV: *Tales of the Texas Rangers*—"The Rough, Tough West" 12-10-55 (Buzz); *Fury*—"Joey and the Little League" 10-13-56 (Tom Wright).

Brocco, Peter (1903-12/27/92). Films: "Gunmen of Abilene" 1950 (Henry Turner); "Drums in the Deep South" 1951 (Union Corporal); "Cripple Creek" 1952 (Cashier); "Black Patch" 1957 (Harper); "Alias Smith and Jones" TVM-1971 (Pincus); "A Time for Dying" 1971 (Ed); "Butch and Sundance: The Early Days" 1979 (Old Robber). ¶TV: *Sheriff of Cochise*—"Vapor Lock" 3-15-57; *Have Gun Will Travel*—"A Matter of Ethics" 10-12-57, "Cream of the Jest" 5-5-62; *Zorro*—"Zorro Fights His Father" 2-6-58; *The Law of the Plainsman*—"Rabbit's Fang" 3-24-60 (Schuyler); *The Big Valley*—"The Secret" 1-27-69 (Judge), "Lightfoot" 2-17-69; *Overland Trail*—"First Stage to Denver" 5-1-60 (Courtney); *Alias Smith and Jones*—"The Posse That Wouldn't Quit" 10-14-71 (Judge).

Brochard, Martine (1946-). Films: "Man Called Blade" 1977-Ital.

Brock, Stanley (1931-). Films: "No Man's Land" TVM-1984 (Wilmot).

Brockwell, Gladys (1894-7/2/29). Films: "A Man and His Mate" 1915 (Betty); "On the Night Stage" 1915 (Saloon Girl); "The End of the Trail" 1916 (Adrienne Cabot); "One Touch of Sin" 1917 (Mary Livingston); "Chasing Rainbows" 1919 (Sadie); "The Rose of Nome" 1920 (Rose Donnay); "The Sage Hen" 1921 (Jane Croft); "The Reckless Sex" 1925 (Mrs. Garcia); "The Splendid Road" 1925 (Satan's Sister); "The Last Frontier" 1926 (Cynthia Jaggers).

Brodel, Mary. Films: "Down the Wyoming Trail" 1939 (Candy Parker).

Broderick, Helen (1891-9/25/59). Films: "Stand Up and Fight" 1939 (Amanda Griffith).

Broderick, James (1930-11/1/82). TV: *Gunsmoke*—"My Sisters' Keeper" 11-2-63 (Pete Sievers), "Doctor's Wife" 10-24-64 (Dr. Wesley May).

Brodhead, James E. (1932-). Films: "The Apple Dumpling Gang" 1975 (the Mouthpiece).

Brodie, Don (1899-). Films: "Man from Montreal" 1940 (Pete); "Hell's Outpost" 1954; "The Proud Ones" 1956 (Hotel Clerk); "The Comancheros" 1961; "Little Big Man" 1971 (Stage Passenger); "Hot Lead and Cold Feet" 1978.

Brodie, Kevin. Films: "Showdown" 1963 (Buster); "The Night of the Grizzly" 1966 (Charlie Cole). ¶TV: *Wyatt Earp*—"A Papa for Butch and Ginger" 5-9-61 (Butch).

Brodie, Steve (1919-1/9/92). Films: "Badman's Territory" 1946 (Bob Dalton); "Sunset Pass" 1946 (Slagle); "Code of the West" 1947 (Saunders); "Thunder Mountain" 1947 (Chick Jorth); "Trail Street" 1947 (Logan Maury); "The Arizona Ranger" 1948 (Quirt); "Guns of Hate" 1948 (Morgan); "Return of the Badmen" 1948 (Cole Younger); "Station West" 1948 (Stallman); "Brothers in the Saddle" 1949 (Steve Taylor); "Massacre River" 1949 (Burke Kimber); "Rustlers" 1949 (Wheeler); "Tough Assignment" 1949 (Morgan); "Winchester '73" 1950 (Wesley); "Only the Valiant" 1951 (Trooper Onstot); "The Charge at Feather River" 1953 (Ryan); "The Far Country" 1955 (Ives); "Gun Duel in Durango" 1957 (Dunston); "Sierra Baron" 1958 (Rufus Bynum); "Bullet for Billy the Kid" 1963. ¶TV: *Wild Bill Hickok*—"A Close Shave for the Marshal" 4-29-52; *The Lone Ranger*—"Tumblerock Law" 2-26-53, "The Old Cowboy" 6-25-53; *Stories of the Century*—"Harry Tracy" 7-29-55; *Trackdown*—"Matter of Justice" 10-17-58 (John Quince); *Wanted—Dead or Alive*—"Miracle at Pot Hole" 10-25-58 (Chester Miller/Penfold Crane), "Call Your Shot" 2-7-59 (Jed Miller), "Montana Kid" 9-5-59 (Johnny Deuce); *Rough Riders*—"A Matter of Instinct" 2-19-59 (Jason); *Wyatt Earp*—Regular 1959-61 (Sheriff John Behan); *Rawhide*—"Incident of the Wanted Painter" 1-29-60 (Marshal Coogan), "Incident of the Dogfaces" 11-9-62 (Cpl. Dan Healy), "Incident at Two Graves" 11-7-63 (Sloan); *Pony Express*—"Vendetta" 2-3-60; *The Alaskans*—"Peril at Caribou Crossing" 2-28-60 (Purvis); *Colt .45*—"Absent Without Leave" 4-19-60; *The Deputy*—"Palace of Chance"

5-21-60 (Fisher); *Stagecoach West*—"The Saga of Jeremy Boone" 11-29-60 (Deuce Stone), "The Guardian Angels" 6-6-61 (Casey Dunlap); *Tales of Wells Fargo*—"Fraud" 3-13-61 (Mayor Walt Lawson); *Maverick*—"The Devil's Necklace" 4-16-61 & 4-23-61 (Captain Score); *Cheyenne*—"Winchester Quarantine" 9-25-61 (Steve Maclay), "Man Alone" 10-15-62 (Buck Brown); *Gunsmoke*—"Old Yellow Boots" 10-7-61 (Welch), "No Tomorrow" 1-3-72 (Garth Brantley); *Bronco*—"The Equalizer" 12-18-61 (Butch Cassidy); *Laramie*—"The Confederate Express" 1-30-62 (Clay Kerrigan); *The Dakotas*—"Walk Through the Badlands" 3-18-63 (Capt. William Bowder Casey); *Bonanza*—"Any Friend of Walter's" 3-24-63 (Macie), "Walter and the Outlaws" 5-24-64 (Macie), "Trouble Town" 3-17-68 (Deputy Horn); *The Virginian*—"Run Away Home" 4-24-63 (Sheriff Martin); *A Man Called Shenandoah*—"Aces and Kings" 3-28-66 (Gilbert Bentten); *How the West Was Won*—"The Forgotten" 3-19-79.

Brody, Ann (1884-7/16/44). Films: "Red Love" 1925 (Mrs. LaVerne); "Wolf Song" 1929 (Duenna).

Brody, Marvin. TV: *Daniel Boone*—"The Reunion" 3-11-65 (Tom Bradley), "Crisis by Fire" 1-27-66 (Tupper), "Run a Crooked Mile" 10-20-66 (Cross); *The Virginian*—"The Return of Golden Tom" 3-9-66 (Potter), "Outcast" 10-26-66 (Horace); *Wild Wild West*—"The Night of the Undead" 2-2-68 (Harold).

Broeker, Ken. Films: "Fighting Cowboy" 1933 (Sheriff); "Lightning Range" 1934 (Sheriff); "Rawhide Romance" 1934 (Sheriff).

Brogan, Ron. TV: *Zane Grey Theater*—"A Man to Look Up To" 11-29-57 (Dickson); *Rawhide*—"Gold Fever" 5-4-62; *The Guns of Will Sonnett*—"A Difference of Opinion" 11-15-68.

Brokaw, Charles (1898-10/23/75). Films: "The Luck of Roaring Camp" 1937 (Dan Oakhurst).

Brolin, James (1942-). Films: "Westworld" 1973 (John Blane); "Cowboy" TVM-1983 (Ward McNally); "Bad Jim" 1990 (B.D.); "Gunsmoke: The Long Ride" TVM-1993 (John Parsley). ¶TV: *The Monroes*—"Incident at Hanging Tree" 10-12-66 (Dalton Wales), "Silent Night, Deathly Night" 11-23-66 (Dalton Wales), "Range War" 12-21-66 (Dalton Wales), "Mark of Death" 1-4-67 (Dalton Wales); *The Virginian*—"Crime Wave at Buffalo Spring" 1-29-69 (Ned).

Brolin, Josh. TV: *Young Riders*— Regular 1990-92 (Jimmy Hickok).

Bromberg, J. Edward (1903-12/6/51). Films: "Fair Warning" 1937 (Matthew Jericho); "Jesse James" 1939 (George Runyon); "Mark of Zorro" 1940 (Don Luis Quintero); "The Return of Frank James" 1940 (Runyon); "Hurricane Smith" 1942 (Eggs Bonelli); "Salome, Where She Danced" 1945 (Prof. Max); "I Shot Jesse James" 1949 (Kane).

Bromfield, John (1922-). Films: "The Furies" 1950 (Clay Jeffords); "The Cimarron Kid" 1951 (Tulsa Jack); "The Black Dakotas" 1954 (Mike Daugherty); "Frontier Gambler" 1956; "Quincannon, Frontier Scout" 1956 (Lt. Burke). ¶TV: *Frontier*—"The Suspects" 11-6-55; *Sheriff of Cochise*—Regular 1956-58 (Frank Morgan); *U.S. Marshal*—Regular 1958-60 (Marshal Frank Morgan).

Bromfield, Valri. TV: *Best of the West*—Regular 1981-82 (Laney Gibbs).

Bromilow, Peter (1933-10/16/94). TV: *Cowboy in Africa*—"Kifaru! Kifaru!" 9-18-67 (Tom Fordyce); *Daniel Boone*—"The King's Shilling" 10-19-67 (Colonel Holland), "The Printing Press" 10-23-69 (Captain Thurlow).

Bromley, Sheila (1911-). Films: "Death Goes North" 1939 (Elsie Barlow); "Silver Lode" 1954 (Townswoman); "A Day of Fury" 1956 (Marie); "The Lawless Eighties" 1958; "Young Jesse James" 1960 (Mrs. Samuels). ¶TV: *The Adventures of Rin Tin Tin*—"The Big Top" 2-3-56 (Maggie); *Maverick*—"Passage to Fort Doom" 3-8-59 (Mrs. Stanton); *Rawhide*—"Incident of the Devil and His Due" 1-22-60 (Mrs. Burton), "Incident of the Deserter" 4-29-60 (Mrs. Spencer), "The Gentleman's Gentleman" 12-15-61 (Lydia), "Incident of Decision" 12-28-62 (Mrs. Calvin), "Incident of the Married Widow" 3-1-63 (Thelma); *Lawman*—"The Man from New York" 3-19-61 (Winnie); *The Big Valley*—"Guilty" 10-30-67 (Mrs. Haley).

Broneau, Helen. Films: "The Desert Hawk" 1924 (Mercedes Nicholls); "Western Yesterdays" 1924 (Juanita).

Bronson, Betty (1907-10/19/71). Films: "The Golden Princess" 1925 (Betty Kent); "Open Range" 1927 (Lucy Blake); "Yodelin' Kid from Pine Ridge" 1937 (Milly Baynum).

Bronson, Charles (Charles Buchinsky) (1922-). Films: "Apache" 1954 (Hondo); "Drum Beat" 1954

(Capt. Jack); "Riding Shotgun" 1954 (Pinto); "Vera Cruz" 1954 (Pittsburgh); "Jubal" 1956 (Reb Haislipp); "Run of the Arrow" 1957 (Blue Buffalo); "Showdown at Boot Hill" 1958 (Marshal Luke Welsh); "The Magnificent Seven" 1960 (O'Reilly); "A Thunder of Drums" 1961 (Trooper Hanna); "Four for Texas" 1964 (Matson); "Guns of Diablo" 1964 (Linc Murdock); "Guns for San Sebastian" 1967-U.S./Fr./Mex./Ital. (Tecio); "Once Upon a Time in the West" 1968-Ital. (Harmonica Man); "Villa Rides" 1968 (Fierro); "Red Sun" 1971-Fr./Ital./Span. (Link); "Chato's Land" 1972 (Pardon Chato); "Chino" 1973-Ital./Span./Fr. (Chino Valdez); "Breakheart Pass" 1976 (John Deakin); "From Noon to Three" 1976 (Graham Dorsey); "The White Buffalo" 1977 (Wild Bill Hickok/James Otis); "Death Hunt" 1981 (Albert Johnson). ¶TV: *The Roy Rogers Show*—"The Knockout" 12-28-52 (Bil Conley); *Luke and the Tenderfoot*—Pilot 8-6-55 & 8-13-55 (John Wesley Hardin); *Gunsmoke*—"The Killer" 5-26-56 (Crego), "Uncle Oliver" 5-25-57, "The Lost Rifle" 11-1-58 (Ben Tiple); *Have Gun Will Travel*—"The Outlaw" 9-21-57 (Manfred Holt), "The Gentleman" 9-27-58 (Chris Sorenson), "A Proof of Love" 10-14-61 (Henry Grey), "Ben Jalisco" 11-18-61 (Ben Jalisco), "Brotherhood" 1-5-63 (Jim Redrock); *Colt .45*—"Young Gun" 12-13-57 (Danny Gordon); *Sheriff of Cochise*—"Apache Kid" 12-20-57; *Sugarfoot*—"Man Wanted" 2-18-58 (Sandy Randall), "The Bullet and the Cross" 5-27-58 (Cliff Raven); *Tales of Wells Fargo*—"Butch Cassidy" 10-13-58 (Butch Cassidy); *Yancy Derringer*—"Hell and High Water" 2-19-59 (Rogue Donovan); *Laramie*—"Street of Hate" 3-1-60 (Frank Buckley), "Run of the Hunted" 4-4-61 (Cory Lake); *Riverboat*—"Zigzag" 12-26-60 (Crowley); *Empire*—Regular 1963 (Paul Moreno); *The Travels of Jaimie McPheeters*—Regular 1963-64 (Linc Murdock); *Bonanza*—"The Underdog" 12-13-64 (Harry Starr); *The Big Valley*—"Earthquake!" 11-10-65 (Tate); *The Virginian*—"Nobility of Kings" 11-10-65 (Ben Justin), "Reckoning" 9-13-67 (Harge Talbot); *Rawhide*—"Duel at Daybreak" 11-16-65 (Del Lingman); *The Legend of Jesse James*—"The Chase" 3-7-66 (Cheyney).

Bronson, Lillian (1902-). Films: "Dakota Lil" 1950 (Sheriff's Wife); "Passage West" 1951 (Mom Brennan); "Rose of Cimarron" 1952 (Emmy Anders); "The Over-the-Hill Gang

Rides Again" TVM-1970 (Mrs. Murphy). ¶TV: *Wild Bill Hickok*—"Halley's Comet" 2-17-53; *The Adventures of Rin Tin Tin*—"Sorrowful Joe's Policy" 3-21-58 (Azalian Huntington); *The Restless Gun*—"The Battle of Tower Rock" 4-28-58 (Bessie Madden); *Wagon Train*—"The Juan Ortega Story" 10-8-58 (Alicia Thornton), "The Grover Allen Story" 2-3-64 (Phoebe); *Wanted—Dead or Alive*—"Ransom for a Nun" 10-18-58 (Mother Superior); *Trackdown*—"The Feud" 2-11-59 (Maude Turley); *The Rifleman*—"The Legacy" 12-8-59, "The Baby Sitter" 12-15-59; *Have Gun Will Travel*—"The Lady on the Wall" 2-20-60 (Miss Felton), "The Search" 6-18-60 (Mrs. Kilner), "The Uneasy Grave" 6-3-61 (Mrs. Johnson); *Tales of Wells Fargo*—"Bitter Vengeance" 6-12-61 (Sarah Martin); *Rawhide*—"The Sendoff" 10-6-61 (Mrs. Lefever); *Frontier Circus*—"Mr. Grady Regrets" 1-25-62 (Dorothy Barker); *Cheyenne*—"One Way Ticket" 2-19-62 (Mrs. Frazier); *The Virginian*—"Stopover in a Western Town" 11-27-63 (Aunt Grace); *The Guns of Will Sonnett*—"Where There's Hope" 12-20-68; *Nichols*—"The One Eyed Mule's Time Has Come" 11-23-71.

Bronston, Jack. Films: "Fighting Cowboy" 1933; "Lightning Range" 1934 (Deputy Sheriff).

Bronte, James. TV: *Sergeant Preston of the Yukon*—"Boy Alone" 2-20-58 (Jonathan Steele); *Wyatt Earp*—"Juveniles—1878" 3-10-58 (Cook); *The Californians*—"Second Trial" 5-6-58 (Joe Ortega).

Brook, Allen. Films: "Cattle Raiders" 1938 (Steve Reynolds).

Brook, Claudio (1927-). Films: "Fury in Paradise" 1955-U.S./Mex.; "Daniel Boone, Trail Blazer" 1957 (James Boone); "The Wonderful Country" 1959 (Ruelle); "The Last Rebel" 1961-Mex.; "Viva Maria" 1965-Fr./Ital. (Rodolfo); "Jory" 1972 (Ethan); "The Return of a Man Called Horse" 1976 (Chemin d'Fer); "Eagle's Wing" 1979-Brit./Span. (Sanchez).

Brook, Doris. Films: "The Lone Bandit" 1934 (Bess Mitchell); "Border Guns" 1935 (Senorita Camrillo); "Defying the Law" 1935 (Doris Lane); "The Phantom Cowboy" 1935 (Ruth Rogers); "Wilderness Mail" 1935 (Lita Landau).

Brooke, Hillary (1916-). Films: "The Lone Rider in Frontier Fury" 1941; "The Lone Rider Rides On" 1941; "Skipalong Rosenbloom" 1951 (Square Deal Sal). ¶TV: *Yancy Der-*

ringer—"The Louisiana Dude" 2-26-59 (Julia Bulette); *Lawman*—"The Ring" 5-24-59 (Claire Adams).

Brooke, Ralph (1920-12/4/63). Films: "The Charge at Feather River" 1953 (Wilhelm).

Brooke, Walter (1915-8/20/86). Films: "They Died with Their Boots On" 1941 (Rosser); "Lawman" 1971 (Luther Harris); "The Cowboys" 1972; "One Little Indian" 1973. ¶TV: *Trackdown*—"The Unwanted" 5-13-59 (Doc Walter); *Gunsmoke*—"Cheyennes" 6-13-59 (Captain Nichols); *Cheyenne*—"Cross Purpose" 10-9-61 (Edward De Vier); *Bronco*—"Moment of Doubt" 4-2-62 (Hammond Craig); *The Virginian*—"The Man Who Couldn't Die" 1-30-63 (Lt. Paul Keller); *Empire*—"No Small Wars" 2-5-63 (Dr. Sidney Morgan); *Death Valley Days*—"The Westside of Heaven" 3-28-64 (Floyd Manning), "Tribute to the Dog" 12-27-64 (Collins), "Dry Water Sailors" 3-12-66 (Jason Howard), "The Biggest Little Post Office in the World" 2-7-70 (Hull); *Bonanza*—"A Dime's Worth of Glory" 11-1-64 (Tobias Finch), "Stage Door Johnnies" 7-28-68 (Fillmore), "The Big Jackpot" 1-18-70 (Atworth Perry), "The Luck of Pepper Shannon" 11-22-70 (Corry); *Wild Wild West*—"The Night of the Legion of Death" 11-24-67 (Prosecutor), "The Night of the Egyptian Queen" 11-15-68 (Finley); *The Big Valley*—"Shadow of a Giant" 1-29-68 (Steigler); *The High Chaparral*—"The Champion of the Western World" 2-4-68 (Carney), "The Last Hundred Miles" 1-24-69 (Robert Morris); *The Outcasts*—"My Name Is Jemal" 11-18-68 (Trask); *Lancer*—"Juniper's Camp" 3-11-69 (James Harper); *Bearcats!*—11-25-71 (Fairfield); *Alias Smith and Jones*—"McGuffin" 12-9-72 (Chief Agent); *The Cowboys*—"The Accused" 3-13-74 (Reager); *Big Hawaii*—"Graduation Eve" 10-26-77 (Giles Webber).

Brooker, Tom (1886-1/29/29). Films: "Wanderer of the West" 1927; "Gun Law" 1929 (Surveyor).

Brookes, Jacqueline (1930-). Films: "Rodeo Girl" TVM-1980 (Charlene, Sammy's Mother).

Brookfield, Fred. Films: "The Cowboys" 1972 (Ruslter); "Ulzana's Raid" 1972. ¶TV: *Hec Ramsey*—"A Hard Road to Vengeance" 11-25-73 (Redsmith).

Brooks, Barry. Films: "The Stranger Wore a Gun" 1953; "A Lawless Street" 1955. ¶TV: *Tales of the Texas Rangers*—"Tornado" 11-5-55 (Lieutenant), "Last Days of Boot Hill" 2-11-56 (Ketner); *Maverick*—"The Wrecker" 12-1-57 (Clerk); *Have Gun Will Travel*—"A Sense of Justice" 11-1-58, "The Trial" 6-11-60; *The Law of the Plainsman*—"The Dude" 12-3-59; *Laramie*—"The Runaway" 1-23-62, "The Sunday Shoot" 11-13-62, "Double Eagles" 11-20-62; *The Virginian*—"The Executioners" 9-19-62 (Gravedigger); *Rawhide*—"The Race" 9-25-64 (Bartender).

Brooks, Charlene. TV: *Gunsmoke*—"Tape Day for Kitty" 3-24-56 (Blossom); *Bonanza*—"The Rival" 4-15-61.

Brooks, Clarence. Films: "Two Gun Man from Harlem" 1938 (John Barker); "The Bronze Buckaroo" 1939 (Gus); "Harlem Rides the Range" 1939 (Bradley).

Brooks, Foster (1912-). Films: "The Villain" 1979 (Bank Clerk); "The Giant of Thunder Mountain" 1991. ¶TV: *Gunsmoke*—"Quint Asper Comes Home" 9-29-62 (Ed), "The Gun" 11-19-70 (Sporting Gentleman #1); *Laredo*—"One Too Many Voices" 11-18-66; *Bonanza*—"Another Windmill to Go" 9-14-69 (Judge), "The Law and Billy Burgess" 2-15-70 (Judge Rogers); *Daniel Boone*—"Bringing Up Josh" 4-16-70.

Brooks, Geraldine (1925-6/19/77). Films: "The Younger Brothers" 1949 (Mary Hathaway). ¶TV: *Have Gun Will Travel*—"Love and a Bad Woman" 3-26-60 (Tamsen Sommers); *Bonanza*—"Elizabeth, My Love" 5-27-61 (Elizabeth), "To Bloom for Thee" 10-16-66 (Carol Attley); *The Virginian*—"Duel at Shiloh" 1-2-63 (Georgia Price), "Silver Image" 9-25-68 (Della Price); *Stoney Burke*—"Death Rides a Pale Horse" 1-14-63 (Linda Carson); *The Dick Powell Show*—"Colossus" 3-12-63 (Ruth Corbett); *Laramie*—"The Stranger" 3-23-63 (Lorena Carver); *Daniel Boone*—"The First Stone" 1-28-65 (Esther Craig); *A Man Called Shenandoah*—"A Long Way Home" 1-31-66 (Angie Brewster); *Gunsmoke*—"Killer at Large" 2-5-66 (Esther Harris); *The High Chaparral*—"The Pride of Revenge" 11-19-67 (Fay Layton); *Kung Fu*—"Nine Lives" 2-15-73 (Widow Thackaberry).

Brooks, Hildy. Films: "The Night Rider" TVM-1979 (Marie Hollister).

Brooks, Jan. TV: *Wanted—Dead or Alive*—"Die by the Gun" 12-6-58, "Detour" 3-1-61 (Jane Fairweather), "Dead Reckoning" 3-22-61 (Barbara Decker); *Gunsmoke*—"Panacea Sykes" 4-13-63 (Ethel).

Brooks, Jean (Jeanne Kelly) (1921-11/25/63). Films: "Son of Roaring Dan" 1940 (Eris Brooks); "Man from Montana" 1941 (Linda); "Riders of Death Valley" 1941-serial (Mary Morgan); "Boot Hill Bandits" 1942 (May Meadows); "Fighting Bill Fargo" 1942 (Linda).

Brooks, Jess Lee (1894-12/13/44). Films: "Two Gun Man from Harlem" 1938 (Sheriff); "Santa Fe Trail" 1940 (Doorman).

Brooks, Joe. Films: "Tall Man Riding" 1955; "Advance to the Rear" 1964 (Bannerman). ¶TV: *Rawhide*—"The Bosses' Daughter" 2-2-62 (Clerk), "The Pitchwagon" 3-2-62, "The Hostage Child" 3-9-62, "Abilene" 5-18-62; *F Troop*—Regular 1965-67 (Vanderbilt).

Brooks, Lloyd. Films: "Senor Jim" 1936 (Kent Hollis).

Brooks, Louise (1900-8/8/85). Films: "Empty Saddles" 1937 (Boots Boone); "Overland Stage Raiders" 1938 (Beth Hoyt).

Brooks, Lucius. Films: "The Bronze Buckaroo" 1939 (Dusty); "Harlem Rides the Range" 1939 (Dusty).

Brooks, Martin E. (1925-). TV: *The Loner*—"Pick Me Another Time to Die" 2-26-66 (Chris Meegan); *Gunsmoke*—"The Lure" 2-25-67 (Young); *Wild Wild West*—"The Night of the Hangman" 10-20-67 (Prof. Poore); *Barbary Coast*—"Sauce for the Goose" 10-20-75 (Adam Conway).

Brooks, Mel (1926-). Films: "Blazing Saddles" 1974 (Governor Lepetomane/Indian Chief).

Brooks, Norma. Films: "Blazing the Overland Trail" 1956-serial (Lola Martin). ¶TV: *Judge Roy Bean*—"Four Ladies from Laredo" 7-1-56 (Mary).

Brooks, Peter. Films: "Hud" 1963 (George). ¶TV: *Gunsmoke*—"Gilt Guilt" 4-24-65 (Sully Rice); *Cimarron Strip*—"The Roarer" 11-2-67.

Brooks, Phyllis (1914-8/1/95). Films: "Silver Spurs" 1943 (Mary Hardigan).

Brooks, Ralph (1920-12/4/63). Films: "Jubilee Trail" 1954 (Bartender).

Brooks, Rand (1918-). Films: "Northwest Passage" 1940 (Eben Towne); "Cowboy Serenade" 1942; "The Sombrero Kid" 1942 (Phillip Martin); "Valley of Hunted Men" 1942; "The Devil's Playground" 1946 (Luck Jenkins); "Fool's Gold" 1946

(Lucky Jenkins); "Dangerous Venture" 1947 (Lucky Jenkins); "Hoppy's Holiday" 1947 (Lucky Jenkins); "The Marauders" 1947 (Lucky Jenkins); "Unexpected Guest" 1947 (Lucky Jenkins); "Borrowed Trouble" 1948 (Lucky Jenkins); "The Dead Don't Dream" 1948 (Lucky Jenkins); "False Paradise" 1948 (Lucky Jenkins); "Silent Conflict" 1948 (Lucky Jenkins); "Sinister Journey" 1948 (Lucky Jenkins); "Strange Gamble" 1948 (Lucky Jenkins); "Sundown in Santa Fe" 1948; "The Wyoming Bandit" 1949 (Jim Howard); "The Vanishing Westerner" 1950 (Tim); "The Cimarron Kid" 1951 (Emmett Dalton); "Heart of the Rockies" 1951 (Corley); "Yukon Manhunt" 1951; "The Gunman" 1952; "The Man from Black Hills" 1952 (Jimmy Fallon); "The Maverick" 1952 (Trooper Barham); "Montana Incident" 1952; "Waco" 1952 (Al); "Born to the Saddle" 1953; "Comanche Station" 1960 (Station Man); "Stagecoach to Dancer's Rock" 1962 (Quint Rucker); "Requiem for a Gunfighter" 1965 (Gentry). ¶TV: *The Lone Ranger*—"The Tenderfeet" 11-10-49, "Jim Tyler's Luck" 2-16-50, "Treason at Dry Creek" 12-4-52, "The Deserter" 4-23-53, "Enfield Rifle" 1-13-55, "The Wooden Rifle" 9-23-56, "Hot Spell in Panamint" 11-22-56; *The Gene Autry Show*—"Gun Powder Range" 10-29-50, "The Breakup" 11-5-50, "Twisted Trails" 11-12-50; *Wild Bill Hickok*—"Behind Southern Lines" 6-26-51, "Mexican Gun Running Story" 1-8-52, "Wrestling Story" 4-8-52, "The Avenging Gunman" 7-29-52, "The Gorilla of Owl Hoot Mesa" 9-23-52; *The Roy Rogers Show*—"Jailbreak" 12-30-51 (Tom Lee), "The Desert Fugitive" 2-24-52 (Bill Harris), "Carnival Killer" 6-8-52, "The Scavenger" 11-27-55 (Thorpe), "Treasure of Paradise Valley" 12-11-55; *The Cisco Kid*—"The Photo Studio" 7-5-52; *Sky King*—"Money Has Wings" 8-31-52 (Weldon); *The Adventures of Rin Tin Tin*—Regular 1954-59 (Corporal Boone); *Tales of the Texas Rangers*—"Prairie Raiders" 11-12-55 (Steve Bradford); *Circus Boy*—"Daring Young Man" 12-30-56 (Cal Jones); *Tales of Wells Fargo*—"John Wesley Hardin" 9-30-57; *Sergeant Preston of the Yukon*—"Ghost Mine" 11-14-57 (Don Andrews); *Maverick*—"Stampede" 11-17-57 (Jack Blair), "The Rivals" 1-25-59 (Second); *Tombstone Territory*—"Postmarked for Death" 2-12-58 (Ed); *Jefferson Drum*—"Band of Iron" 10-23-58 (Ray Comstock); *Wyatt Earp*—"How to Be a Sheriff" 3-24-59 (Del Mathey); *Bat Masterson*—"Pi-

geon and Hawk" 1-21-60 (Willard Wynant); *Zane Grey Theater*—"Desert Flight" 10-13-60 (Wilson); *Gunsmoke*—"Melinda Miles" 6-3-61 (Rand), "Quint's Indian" 3-2-63 (Grissom); *Bonanza*—"Four Sisters from Boston" 10-30-66 (Cowboy).

Brooks, Ted. Films: "Hair-Trigger Burk" 1917; "Straight Shooting" 1917 (Tom Sims); "A Gun Fightin' Gentleman" 1919 (the Youngster); "Marked Men" 1919 (Tony Garcia); "The Rider of the Law" 1919 (the Kid); "Runnin' Straight" 1920; "Sundown Slim" 1920 (Billy Corliss); "West Is West" 1920 (Kirby); "The Black Sheep" 1921 (Al Carson).

Broome, Ray. Films: "The Thundering Trail" 1951 (Bartender); "The Vanishing Outpost" 1951 (Detective's Assistant).

Brophy, Edward S. (1895-5/30/60). Films: "Renegade Girl" 1946; "Two Rode Together" 1961. ¶TV: *Circus Boy*—"Hortense the Hippo" 6-2-57 (Jethroe Ames).

Brophy, Kevin. Films: "The Long Riders" 1980 (John Younger).

Brophy, Sallie. TV: *Frontier*—"The Founding of Omaha, Nebraska" 10-30-55, "The Long Road to Tucson" 12-2-55; *Wagon Train*—"The Les Rand Story" 10-16-57; *Buckskin*—Regular 1958-59 (Annie O'Connell); *Great Adventure*—"The Outlaw and the Nun" 12-6-63 (Mrs. Pierce).

Brothers, Dr. Joyce (1928-). Films: "More Wild Wild West" TVM-1980 (Bystander).

Brough, Candi. Films: "More Wild Wild West" TVM-1980 (Daphne). ¶TV: *Outlaws*—"Orleans" 1-17-87 (Tawny).

Brough, Randi. Films: "More Wild Wild West" TVM-1980 (Yvonne). ¶TV: *Outlaws*—"Orleans" 1-17-87 (Teri).

Brower, Robert (1850-12/8/34). Films: "The Maiden of the Pie-Faced Indians" 1911; "The Gay Defender" 1927 (Ferdinand Murietta); "The Last Trail" 1927 (Pete); "The Silver Bullet" 1935.

Brower, Tom (1878-7/19/37). Films: "Crossfire" 1933 (Charles Rudolph); "Rio Rattler" 1935; "The Singing Vagabond" 1935 (Old Scout); "The Lawless Nineties" 1936 (Marshall); "Treachery Rides the Range" 1936 (Marshal); "The California Mail" 1937 (Sam Harrison); "Cherokee Strip" 1937 (George Walton); "Empty Holsters" 1937 (Dad Brent); "Land Beyond the Law" 1937 (Douglas, Sr.).

Brown, Barry (1951-6/25/78). Films: "Bad Company" 1972 (Drew Dixon); "The Bravos" TVM-1972 (Garrett Chase); "The Great Northfield, Minnesota Raid" 1972 (Henry Wheeler); "Testimony of Two Men" TVM-1977 (Howard Best). ¶TV: *Gunsmoke*—"The Witness" 11-23-70 (Jared Sprague).

Brown, Betty. Films: "Hell's Oasis" 1920 (Mary Hardy); "Davy Crockett at the Fall of the Alamo" 1926 (Myra Winkler).

Brown, Blair (1948-). Films: "The Oregon Trail" TVM-1976 (Jessica Thorpe); "Charlie Cobb: Nice Night for a Hanging" TVM-1977 (Charity).

Brown, Calvin. TV: *Wild Wild West*—"The Night of the Burning Diamond" 4-8-66 (Clive); *The Virginian*—"The Gauntlet" 2-8-67 (Gus); *The Big Valley*—"Forty Rifles" 9-22-65 (Lillard).

Brown, Charles D. (1887-11/25/48). Films: "Santa Fe Trail" 1940 (Maj. Sumner); "A Lady Takes a Chance" 1943 (Dr. Humbolt).

Brown, Dwier. Films: "Desperado: Avalanche at Devil's Rider" TVM-1988 (Jim Buckner).

Brown, Edward. Films: "Colorado" 1915 (Old Morgan); "Pay Me!" 1917 (Martin); "The Counterfeit Trail" 1919.

Brown, Everett (1902-10/14/53). Films: "The Texans" 1938 (Man with Watches); "Stand Up and Fight" 1939 (Big Black Man).

Brown, Ewing. Films: "Son of the Renegade" 1953 (Wild Bil Hickock); "Frontier Gambler" 1956. ¶TV: *The Gene Autry Show*—"Ghost Mountain" 7-28-53, "Dry Gulch at Devil's Elbow" 9-8-53.

Brown, George Stanford (1943-). TV: *Here Come the Brides*—"A Bride for Obie Brown" 1-9-70 (Obie Brown).

Brown, Harry (1891-1/8/66). Films: "Wanderer of the Wasteland" 1945 (Papa Rafferty); "The Lawless Breed" 1946; "Massacre River" 1949 (Piano Player); "City of Badmen" 1953.

Brown, Helen (1916-9/9/74). Films: "The Three Godfathers" 1936 (Mrs. George Marshall); "Out West with the Peppers" 1940 (Alice Anderson); "Al Jennings of Oklahoma" 1951 (Mrs. Salter); "Shane" 1953 (Mrs. Lewis); "The Missouri Traveler" 1958 (Hattie Neely). ¶TV: *Death Valley Days*—"Black Bart" 11-8-54; *Fury*—"The Boy Scout Story" 2-11-56 (Mrs. Camfield); *Annie Oakley*—"Flint and

Steel" 10-14-56 (Mrs. Wheeler); *The Roy Rogers Show*—"High Stakes" 2-24-57; *Colt .45*—"The Peacemaker" 10-18-57 (Sister Howard); *Wagon Train*—"The Ruttledge Munroe Story" 5-21-58 (Mrs. Mitchell); *Bonanza*—"Inger, My Love" 4-15-62.

Brown, James (1920-4/11/92). Films: "The Fabulous Texan" 1947 (Shep Clayton); "The Gallant Legion" 1948 (Tom Bauner); "Brimstone" 1949 (Bud Courteen); "The Younger Brothers" 1949 (Bob Younger); "Montana" 1950 (Tex Coyne); "The Man Behind the Gun" 1952; "Springfield Rifle" 1952 (Pvt. Ferguson); "The Charge at Feather River" 1953 (Connors); "Thunder Over the Plains" 1953 (Conrad); "The Woman They Almost Lynched" 1953 (Frank James); "Five Guns to Tombstone" 1961 (Billy Wade); "Gun Fight" 1961 (Wayne Santley); "Gun Street" 1961 (Sheriff Morton); "Black Spurs" 1965 (Sheriff Nemo); "Town Tamer" 1965 (Davis); "Adios Amigo" 1975. ¶TV: *The Lone Ranger*—"Desperado at Large" 10-2-52; *The Adventures of Rin Tin Tin*—Regular 1954-59 (Lieutenant Ripley "Rip" Masters); *Laramie*—"Strange Company" 6-6-61 (Lon MacRae); *The Virginian*—"West" 11-20-62 (Lucky), "The Money Cage" 3-6-63; *Gunsmoke*—"Quint's Indian" 3-2-63 (Feeney); *Barbary Coast*—"An Iron-Clad Plan" 10-31-75 (Stroud).

Brown, James Bowen. TV: *The Virginian*—"The Brazos Kid" 10-21-64 (Sebastian), "Linda" 11-30-66 (Mark Fallon); *Daniel Boone*—"Not in Our Stars" 12-31-64 (Sergeant Quincy); *The Rounders*—Regular 1966-67 (Luke).

Brown, Jerry. Films: "The Lone Ranger" 1938-serial (Trooper); "Man with the Steel Whip" 1954-serial (Harker); "The Great Bank Robbery" 1969 (Driver); "Oklahoma Crude" 1973 (Rucker). ¶TV: *The Restless Gun*—"The Gold Buckle" 12-30-57 (Stage Driver); *Gunsmoke*—"The Wreckers" 9-11-67 (Shotgun Rider), "The Lost" 9-13-71 (Stage Driver); *Cimarron Strip*—"The Battleground" 9-28-67, "Nobody" 12-7-67.

Brown, Jim (1936-). Films: "Rio Conchos" 1964 (Sgt. Ben Franklyn); "100 Rifles" 1969 (Lyedecker); "El Condor" 1970 (Luke); "Powderkeg" TVM-1971; "Take a Hard Ride" 1974-Ital./Brit./Ger. (Pike); "Kid Vengeance" 1976-Ital./U.S./Israel.

Brown, Joe. Films: "The Oklahoma Woman" 1956; "The Rainmaker" 1956 (Townsman); "Hostile Guns" 1967 (Bunco). ¶TV: *The Rifleman*—"The Mescalero Curse" 4-18-61; *Tales of Wells Fargo*—"Jeremiah" 11-11-61 (Martin); *The Outlaws*—"Walk Tall" 11-16-61 (Banty); *Destry*—"Big Deal at Little River" 3-20-64 (Henry); *Nichols*—"Gulley vs. Hansen" 10-7-71 (Minister).

Brown, Joe E. (1892-7/6/73) Films: "In Old Arizona" 1929 (Bartender); "Song of the West" 1930 (Hasty); "Rodeo Dough" 1940-short; "Shut My Big Mouth" 1942 (Wellington Holmes).

Brown, Johnny Mack (1904-11/14/74). Films: "The Bugle Call" 1927; "Billy the Kid" 1930 (Billy); "Montana Moon" 1930 (Larry); "The Great Meadow" 1931 (Berk Jarvis); "Lasca of the Rio Grande" 1931 (Miles Kincaid); "The Vanishing Frontier" 1932 (Kirby Tornell); "Fighting with Kit Carson" 1933-serial (Kit Carson); "Between Men" 1935 (Johnny Wellington); "Branded a Coward" 1935 (Johnny Hume); "The Courageous Avenger" 1935 (Kirk Baxter); "Rustlers of Red Dog" 1935-serial (Jack Woods); "The Crooked Trail" 1936 (Jim Blake); "Everyman's Law" 1936 (the Dog Town Kid); "Rogue of the Range" 1936 (Dan Doran); "Undercover Man" 1936 (Steve McLain); "Valley of the Lawless" 1936 (Bruce Reynolds); "Bar Z Bad Men" 1937 (Jim Waters); "Boothill Brigade" 1937 (Lon Cardigan); "Born to the West" 1937 (Tom Fillmore); "Desert Phantom" 1937 (Billy Donovan); "The Gambling Terror" 1937 (Jeff Hayes); "Guns in the Dark" 1937 (Johnny Darrel); "Lawless Land" 1937 (Jeff Hayden); "A Lawman Is Born" 1937 (Tom Mitchell); "Trail of Vengeance" 1937 (Duke Ramsey/Kenneth Early); "Wells Fargo" 1937 (Talbot Carter); "Wild West Days" 1937-serial (Kentucky Wade); "Flaming Frontier" 1938-serial (Tex Houston); "Chip of the Flying U" 1939 (Chip Bennett); "Desperate Trails" 1939 (Steve Hayden); "Oklahoma Frontier" 1939 (Jeff McLeod); "The Oregon Trail" 1939-serial (Jeff Scott); "Bad Man from Red Butte" 1940 (Gil Brady/Buck Halliday); "Law and Order" 1940 (Bill Ralston); "Pony Post" 1940 (Cal Sheridan); "Ragtime Cowboy Joe" 1940 (Steve Logan); "Riders of Pasco Basin" 1940 (Leo Jameson); "Son of Roaring Dan" 1940 (Jim Reardon); "West of Carson City" 1940 (Jim Bannister); "Arizona Cyclone" 1941 (Tom); "Boss of Bullion City" 1941 (Tom Bryant); "Bury Me Not on the Lone Prairie" 1941; "Law of the Range" 1941 (Steve); "Man from Montana" 1941 (Bob Dawson); "The Masked Rider" 1941 (Larry); "Rawhide Rangers" 1941 (Brand); "Fighting Bill Fargo" 1942 (Bill Fargo); "Boss of Hangtown Mesa" 1942 (Steve Collins); "Deep in the Heart of Texas" 1942 (Jim Mallory); "Little Joe, the Wrangler" 1942 (Neal Wallace); "Old Chisholm Trail" 1942 (Dusty Gardner); "Ride 'Em, Cowboy" 1942 (Alabam); "The Silver Bullet" 1942; "Stagecoach Buckaroo" 1942 (Steve); "Cheyenne Roundup" 1943 (Gils Brandon/Buck Brandon); "The Ghost Rider" 1943; "The Lone Star Trail" 1943 (Blaze Barker); "Outlaws of Stampede Pass" 1943; "Raiders of San Joaquin" 1943 (Rocky Morgan); "Six Gun Gospel" 1943; "The Stranger from Pecos" 1943 (Nevada); "Tenting Tonight on the Old Camp Ground" 1943 (Wade Benson); "The Texas Kid" 1943 (Nevada)"Ghost Guns" 1944; "Land of the Outlaws" 1944; "Law Men" 1944 (Nevada); "Law of the Valley" 1944; "Partners of the Trail" 1944 (Nevada); "Raiders of the Border" 1944 (Nevada); "Range Law" 1944 (Nevada); "West of the Rio Grande" 1944; "Flame of the West" 1945 (John Poore); "Frontier Feud" 1945 (Nevada); "Gun Smoke" 1945; "The Lost Trail" 1945 (Nevada); "The Navajo Trail" 1945; "Stranger from Santa Fe" 1945; "Border Bandits" 1946 (Nevada); "Drifting Along" 1946 (Steve); "Gentleman from Texas" 1946; "The Haunted Mine" 1946; "Shadows on the Range" 1946; "Silver Range" 1946; "Trigger Fingers" 1946; "Under Arizona Skies" 1946; "Code of the Saddle" 1947; "Flashing Guns" 1947 (Johnny); "Gun Talk" 1947 (Johnny McVey); "Land of the Lawless" 1947; "Law Comes to Gunsight" 1947; "Prairie Express" 1947 (Johnny Hudson); "Raiders of the South" 1947; "Trailing Danger" 1947; "Valley of Fear" 1947; "Back Trail" 1948 (Johnny); "Crossed Trails" 1948 (Johnny); "The Fighting Ranger" 1948; "Frontier Agent" 1948 (Nevada Jack McKensie); "Gunning for Justice" 1948; "Overland Trails" 1948; "The Sheriff of Medicine Bow" 1948; "Triggerman" 1948; "Hidden Danger" 1949 (Johnny); "Law of the West" 1949 (Johnny Mack); "Range Justice" 1949 (Johnny); "Stampede" 1949 (Sheriff Ball); "Trail's End" 1949 (Johnny); "West of El Dorado" 1949 (Johnny); "Western Renegades" 1949 (Johnny); "Law of the Panhandle" 1950 (Johnny Mack); "Outlaw Gold" 1950 (Dave Willis); "Over the Border" 1950 (Johnny Mack); "Short Grass"

1950 (Keown); "Six Gun Mesa" 1950; "West of Wyoming" 1950 (Johnny); "Blazing Bullets" 1951; "Colorado Ambush" 1951 (Johnny); "Man from Sonora" 1951; "Montana Desperado" 1951 (Dave Borden); "Oklahoma Justice" 1951; "Texas Lawmen" 1951 (Johnny); "Whistling Hills" 1951 (Johnny); "Canyon Ambush" 1952; "Dead Man's Trail" 1952; "The Man from Black Hills" 1952 (Johnny); "Texas City" 1952 (Johnny); "The Marshal's Daughter" 1953; "The Bounty Killer" 1965 (Sheriff Green); "Requiem for a Gunfighter" 1965 (Enkoff); "Apache Uprising" 1966 (Sheriff Benn Hall). ¶TV: *Tales of Wells Fargo*—"Scapegoat" 5-5-58 (Sheriff Eaton).

Brown, Julia. Films: "The Galloping Ace" 1924 (Louise Williams).

Brown, Lee. TV: *Stoney Burke*—"Point of Honor" 10-22-62 (the Trooper); *Gunsmoke*—"Double Entry" 1-2-65 (Pete Elder), "Slocum" 10-21-68 (1st Cowboy).

Brown, Jr., Les. TV: *Gunsmoke*—"Judge Calvin Strom" 12-18-65 (Mark Strom).

Brown, Lew (1925-). Films: "The Gambler" TVM-1980 (Johnson). ¶TV: *Gunsmoke*—"Alarm at Pleasant Valley" 8-25-56 (Sam Fraser), "Print Asper" 5-23-59 (Will Asper), "Kangaroo" 10-10-59 (Jim Bride), "The Ex-Urbanites" 4-9-60 (Nate), "Unloaded Gun" 1-14-61 (Red Lime), "Kitty Shot" 2-11-61, "Hard Virtue" 5-6-61 (Andy Coe), "Chester's Indian" 5-12-62 (Frank Dill), "The New Society" 5-22-65 (Eli Wall), "Old Friend" 2-4-67 (Fred), "Ladies from St. Louis" 3-25-67 (Outlaw), "The Wreckers" 9-11-67 (Ben Paisley), "Cattle Barons" 9-18-67 (Frank Holtz), "McCabe" 11-30-70 (Weaver), "The Predators" 1-31-72 (Smith), "Milligan" 11-6-72 (Reeves), "Cowtown Hustler" 3-11-74 (Beeton); *Maverick*—"Maverick and Juliet" 1-17-60 (Jeb Carteret); *Two Faces West*—"Performance Under Fire" 1-30-61 (Bray); *Rawhide*—"Incident of the Running Man" 5-5-61, "The Violent Land" 3-5-65 (Gorman); *Have Gun Will Travel*—"Invasion" 4-28-62 (Michael Mahoney); *The Virginian*—"Throw a Long Rope" 10-3-62 (Garretson), "Duel at Shiloh" 1-2-63 (Dowdy), "The Golden Door" 3-13-63, "The Challenge" 10-19-66 (Deputy Ellis), "Jed" 1-10-68 (Clint Timmins), "The Orchard" 10-2-68 (Gummery); *Laramie*—"Bad Blood" 12-4-62; *Empire*—"Where the Hawk Is Wheeling" 1-29-63 (Cord); *Bonanza*—"The

Cheating Game" 2-9-64, "Stallion" 11-14-72 (Seth); *Death Valley Days*—"The $25,000 Wager" 2-7-65 (David Neal), "An Organ for Brother Brigham" 7-16-66 (Cory Jones), "Old Stape" 10-18-69, "The Taming of Trudy Bell" 12-6-69 (Danny); *F Troop*—"How to Be F Troop Without Really Trying" 9-15-66 (Lt. Mark Harrison); *Cimarron Strip*—"The Legend of Jud Starr" 9-14-67, "The Assassin" 1-11-68; *Wild Wild West*—"The Night Dr. Loveless Died" 9-29-67 (Guard); *The Men from Shiloh*—"Jenny" 9-30-70 (Alfie); *The High Chaparral*—"The Badge" 12-18-70 (Parsons); *Alias Smith and Jones*—"Escape from Wickenberg" 1-28-71 (Frank Johnson).

Brown, Milton (1896-3/29/48). Films: "Pride of the Range" 1910; "The Claim Jumper" 1913; "A Frontier Wife" 1913; "An Indian's Gratitude" 1913; "An Indian's Honor" 1913; "The Call of the North" 1914 (Me-en-gan); "The Desire of the Moth" 1917 (Matt Lisner); "Straight Shooting" 1917 (Black-Eyed Pete); "King's Creek Law" 1923 (Saul Jameson); "Ruggles of Red Gap" 1923 (Senator Pettingill); "Points West" 1929 (Parson); "The Mounted Stranger" 1930 (Pop Ainslee); "Local Bad Man" 1932 (Horsetail).

Brown, Mina. TV: *Lawman*—"The Prodigal Mother" 12-17-61 (Ella McCallan).

Brown, Mitch. TV: *The Cowboys*—Regular 1974 (Hardy).

Brown, Morgan (1884-1/4/61). Films: "The Taming of the West" 1925 (Terrence Weaver); "The Galloping Gobs" 1927 (Chub Barnes); "Range Courage" 1927 (Sheriff); "Jesse James" 1939; "Riding Shotgun" 1954.

Brown, Naaman. TV: *Yancy Derringer*—"V As in Voodoo" 5-14-59 (Dr. Yaya).

Brown, Peter (1935-). TV: *Colt .45*—"The Peacemaker" 10-18-57 (Dave); *Cheyenne*—"Top Hand" 12-31-57 (Clay), "Renegades" 2-11-58 (Jed Wayne), "Ghost of Cimarron" 3-25-58 (Billy Younger), "Pocketful of Stars" 11-12-62 (Ross Andrews); *Sugarfoot*—"Hideout" 4-1-58 (Davey), "The Trial of the Canary Kid" 9-15-59 (Johnny McKay); *Lawman*—Regular 1958-62 (Deputy Johnnie McKay); *Maverick*—"Point Blank" 9-29-57 (Chris Semple), "Stage West" 10-27-57 (Rip Fallon), "Hadley's Hunters" 9-25-60 (Deputy Johnny McKay); *Wagon Train*—"The Adam MacKenzie Story" 3-27-63 (Benedict O'Brien), "The Geneva Balfour Story" 1-20-64 (Aaron Balfour),

"Those Who Stay Behind" 11-8-64 (Ben Campbell); *Redigo*—"The Blooded Bull" 10-1-63 (Johnny Porter); *The Virginian*—"Return a Stranger" 11-18-64 (Craig Ryan), "We've Lost a Train" 4-21-65 (Chad), "A Small Taste of Justice" 12-20-67 (Tom Colnan); *Laredo*—Regular 1965-67 (Chad Cooper), "A Prince of a Ranger" 12-9-66 (Prince Lazlo).

Brown, Phil (1916-). Films: "Pierre of the Plains" 1942 (Val Denton); "Land Raiders" 1969-U.S./Span. (Mayfield); "Valdez Is Coming" 1971 (Malson). ¶TV: *Bonanza*—"The Night Virginia City Died" 9-13-70 (Tucker).

Brown, Ralph. Films: "The Hunting Party" 1971-Brit./Ital./Span. (Sheriff); "Valdez Is Coming" 1971 (Beaudry).

Brown, Raymond (1880-7/30/39). Films: "The Westerner" 1934 (Banker); "Moonlight on the Prairie" 1935 (Lafe Burns); "Comin' Round the Mountain" 1936 (Caldwell); "Black Aces" 1937 (Henry Kline); "High, Wide and Handsome" 1937 (P.T. Barnum); "Gold Is Where You Find It" 1938 (Rancher).

Brown, Reb (1948-). TV: *Centennial*—Regular 1978-79 (Jim Bridger).

Brown, Robert (1927-). TV: *Wagon Train*—"The Albert Farnsworth Story" 10-12-60 (Tim O'-Toole); *Bonanza*—"Blessed Are They" 4-22-62 (Reverend); *The Dick Powell Show*—"Colossus" 3-12-63 (John Reardon); *Shane*—"The Other Image" 10-29-66 (Warren Eliot); *Here Comes the Brides*—Regular 1968-70 (Jason Bolt).

Brown, Roger Aaron. Films: "Outlaws" TVM-1986 (Lt. Jack Kirkum); "Tall Tales: The Unbelievable Adventures of Pecos Bill" 1995 (John Henry).

Brown, Sedley (1856-9/18/28). Films: "The Mediator" 1916 (Channel Smith); "One Touch of Sin" 1917 (Old Livingston); "The Joyous Troublemaker" 1920 (1st Miner).

Brown, Stanley. Films: "Colorado Trail" 1938; "Rio Grande" 1938; "Outpost of the Mounties" 1939 (Larry Daniels); "Overland with Kit Carson" 1939-serial; "Riders of the Black River" 1939 (Terry Holden); "The Taming of the West" 1939 (Slim); "Blazing Six Shooters" 1940 (Cassidy); "The Man from Tumbleweeds" 1940 (Slash); "Pioneers of the Frontier" 1940 (Dave); "Texas Stagecoach" 1940 (Workman); "Hands Across the Rockies" 1941; "Outlaws of the Panhandle" 1941 (Neil Vaughn); "Thunder Over the Prairie" 1941 (Roy Mandan); "Wildcat of Tucson" 1941 (Dave); "The Devil's Trail" 1942; "Lawless Plainsmen" 1942 (Tascosa); "Riding Through Nevada" 1942; "Vengeance of the West" 1942; "The Fighting Buckaroo" 1943 (Don McBride); "Frontier Fury" 1943 (Gray Bear); "Law of the Northwest" 1943 (Neal Clayton); "Robin Hood of the Range" 1943 (Santana); "The Vigilantes Ride" 1944 (Rod Saunders).

Brown, Susan. TV: *Death Valley Days*—"A Wrangler's Last Ride" 4-8-67 (Nancy), "The Lone Grave" 10-28-67 (Susan), "Talk to Me, Charley" 12-20-69; *The Outcasts*—"Act of Faith" 2-10-69 (Ann Willard).

Brown, Tim. TV: *Gunsmoke*—"Cheyennes" 6-13-59 (Major); *Wild Wild West*—"Night of the Bubbling Death" 9-8-67 (Clint Cartweel).

Brown, Tom. Films: "Arizona Sweepstakes" 1926 (Detective); "Out West with the Hardys" 1938 (Aldrich Brown).

Brown, Tom (1913-6/3/90). Films: "I Killed Wild Bill Hickok" 1956 (Wild Bill Hickok); "The Naked Gun" 1956; "The Quiet Gun" 1957 (Reilly, the Saloonkeeper); "Cutter's Trail" TVM-1970 (Orville Mason); "Silverado" 1985 (Augie). ¶TV: *The Lone Ranger*—"Homer with a High Hat" 12-16-54, "Trouble at Tylerville" 12-13-56, "Outlaws in Grease Paint" 6-6-57; *Gunsmoke*—Regular 1955-75 (Ed O'Connor); *Wyatt Earp*—"It's a Wise Calf" 1-17-56, "The Manly Art" 1-21-58 (Burroughs); *Circus Boy*—"The Tumbling Clown" 5-5-57 (Ned Bailey); *Jim Bowie*—"A Night in Tennessee" 4-25-58 (Jeff Purky); *MacKenzie's Raiders*—"The Lost Raider" 10-22-58; *Have Gun Will Travel*—"Something to Live For" 12-20-58 (Bob Pelley); *Sugarfoot*—"The Twister" 4-14-59 (Sheriff Rayle); *The Rifleman*—"Skull" 1-1-62 (Sheriff); *Cimarron Strip*—"The Deputy" 12-21-67 (Sheriff Phillips), "The Greeners" 3-7-68.

Brown, Vanessa (1928-). Films: "Big Jack" 1949 (Patricia Mahoney); "The Fighter" 1952 (Kathy). ¶TV: *Wagon Train*—"The Sally Potter Story" 4-9-58 (Sally Potter).

Brown, W.H. Films: "M'Liss" 1918 (Sheriff Sandy Waddles).

Brown, Wally (1904-11/13/61). Films: "Girl Rush" 1944 (Jerry Miles); "The Wild Dakotas" 1956; "The Left-Handed Gun" 1958 (Moon); "Westbound" 1959

(Stubby). ¶TV: *Death Valley Days*—"A Piano Goes West" 1-6-59; *Cimarron City*—"Burn the Town Down" 1-24-59 (Jed Frame); *Maverick*—"A Fellow's Brother" 11-22-59 (Enoch); *Laramie*—"Bare Knuckles" 12-8-59 (Brad Hovey); *Johnny Ringo*—"The Liars" 2-4-60 (Marshal Spencer); *Wanted—Dead or Alive*—"Baa-Baa" 1-4-61 (Bartender); *The Tall Man*—"The Liberty Belle" 9-16-61 (Ethan); *Bonanza*—"The Burma Rarity" 10-22-61 (Henry Morgan); *Wagon Train*—"The Malachi Hobart Story" 1-24-62 (George Gresham).

Brown, Walter (1927-). Films: "Shalako" 1968-Brit./Fr. (Peter Wells).

Brown, William. Films: "A Yankee from the West" 1915 (Jan Hagnerg); "In Mizzoura" 1919 (Bill Sarber).

Browne, Cicely. Films: "Fort Ti" 1953 (Bess Chesney).

Browne, Kathie (1939-). TV: *Gunsmoke*—"Cows and Cribs" 12-7-57 (Mrs. Thorpe); *Man from Blackhawk*—"Drawing Account" 2-12-60 (Patricia Cash); *Tombstone Territory*—2-19-60 (Gay Monahan); *Two Faces West*—"Prognosis: Death" 10-24-60 (Laurie Parks); *Wagon Train*—"The Jane Hawkins Story" 11-30-60, "The Fort Pierce Story" 9-23-63 (Beth); *Bonanza*—"Tax Collector" 2-18-61 (Ellen), "The Tall Stranger" 1-7-62 (Margie Owens), "The Waiting Game" 12-8-63 (Laura Dayton), "The Cheating Game" 2-9-64 (Laura Dayton), "The Pressure Game" 5-10-64 (Laura Dayton), "Triangle" 5-17-64 (Laura Dayton); *Rawhide*—"Incident of the Phantom Burglar" 4-14-61 (Mary Donahoe), "Incent of the Wager on Payday" 6-16-61, "Judgment at Hondo Seco" 10-20-61 (Lily); *Whispering Smith*—"The Devil's Share" 5-22-61 (Ilsa Dunker); *Lawman*—"Heritage of Hate" 3-18-62 (Laurie); *Tales of Wells Fargo*—"Who Lives by the Gun" 3-24-62 (Peggy); *Frontier Circus*—"Incident at Pawnee Gun" 9-6-62 (Mauvereen); *Have Gun Will Travel*—"Taylor's Woman" 9-22-62 (Lydia), "Marshal of Sweetwater" 11-24-62 (Marie); *Laramie*—"Beyond Justice" 11-27-62 (Phyllis Wynn), "The Betrayers" 1-22-63 (Lottie); *The Slowest Gun in the West* 7-29-63 (Lulu Belle); *Redigo*—"Little Angel Blue Eyes" 10-29-63 (Angel Carr); *The Virginian*—"Brother Thaddeus" 10-30-63 (Floss Delaney); *Temple Houston*—"Fracas at Kiowa Flats" 12-12-63 (Meredith Nothing); *Branded*—"Call to Glory" 2-27-66, 3-6-66 & 3-13-66 (Jennie Galvin); *Bronco*—"The Harrigan" 12-25-61 (Heather); *Wild*

West—"The Night of the Human Trigger" 12-3-65 (Faith Cadwallader), "The Night of the Colonel's Ghost" 3-10-67 (Jennifer Caine); *Laredo*—"The Sweet Gang" 11-4-66 (Billie Lou); *Hondo*—Regular 1967 (Angie Dow); *The Big Valley*—"Deathtown" 10-28-68 (Sally).

Browne, Lucille (1907-5/10/76). Films: "Last of the Duanes" 1930 (Ruth Garrett); "Battling with Buffalo Bill" 1931-serial (Miss Archer); "The Last of the Mohicans" 1932-serial; "The Texan" 1932 (Mary Lou); "King of the Arena" 1933 (Mary Hiller); "Brand of Hate" 1934 (Margie Orkin); "The Law of the Wild" 1934-serial (Alice); "Rainbow Valley" 1935 (Eleanor); "Texas Terror" 1935 (Beth Matthews); "Tumbling Tumbleweeds" 1935 (Jerry); "Western Frontier" 1935 (Mary Harper); "The Crooked Trail" 1936 (Helen Carter); "Cheyenne Rides Again" 1937 (Sally Lane); "Fighting Playboy" 1937 (Connie).

Browne, Peggy. Films: "McGuire of the Mounted" 1923 (Mrs. Cordwell).

Browne, Ralph. Films: "Son of a Gunfighter" 1966-U.S./Span. (Sheriff); "The Spikes Gang" 1974 (Posse Leader).

Browne, Reno (Reno Blair) (1921-5/15/91). Films: "Gentleman from Texas" 1946; "Under Arizona Skies" 1946; "Law Comes to Gunsight" 1947; "Raiders of the South" 1947; "Frontier Agent" 1948; "Across the Rio Grande" 1949 (Sally Blaine); "Haunted Trails" 1949 (Marie Martel); "Range Land" 1949 (Doris); "Riders of the Dusk" 1949 (Nora); "Shadows of the West" 1949 (Ginny); "West of El Dorado" 1949 (Mary); "Fence Riders" 1950; "Gunslingers" 1950 (Libby).

Browne, Roscoe Lee (1925-). Films: "The Cowboys" 1972 (Jebediah Nightlinger). ¶TV: *The Outcasts*—"Gideon" 2-24-69 (Gideon); *Bonanza*—"He Was Only Seven" 3-5-72 (Joshua).

Brownell, Eddie. Films: "Code of the Northwest" 1926 (Clay Hamilton).

Brownell, Louise. Films: "Oh, Johnny!" 1918 (Mrs. Van Pelt Butler).

Browning, Jill. Films: "Utah" 1945 (Babe).

Browning, Susan. TV: *Wild Wild West*—"The Night of the Druid's Blood" 3-25-66 (Nurse); *Iron Horse*—"No Wedding Bells for Tony" 11-7-66 (Laura Farrow).

Brownlee, Frank (1874-2/10/

48). Films: "The Half Breed" 1916 (Winslow Wynn); "Wild Sumac" 1917 (Lupine); "Riders of the Dawn" 1920 (Glidden); "Fools of Fortune" 1922 (Ike Harper); "Romance Land" 1923 (Scrub Hazen); "The Desert Flower" 1925 (Mike Dyer); "The Ridin' Streak" 1925 (J.S. Dokes); "Ridin' Through" 1925; "Lightning Warrior" 1931-serial (McDonald); "The Vanishing Legion" 1931-serial (Bishop); "Tombstone Canyon" 1932 (Alf Sykes); "Terror Trail" 1933 (Sheriff Judell); "Desert Trail" 1935; "Trail of the Vigilantes" 1940 (Doctor); "The Apache Kid" 1941; "A Missouri Outlaw" 1941 (Jensen); "Riders of Death Valley" 1941-serial (Slim); "Arizona Terrors" 1942 (Henry Adams); "Jesse James, Jr." 1942; "Man from Cheyenne" 1942; "Shadows on the Sage" 1942; "The Sombrero Kid" 1942 (Barnett); "Stagecoach Buckaroo" 1942; "Dead Man's Gulch" 1943.

Broyles, Robert (1933-). TV: *Bonanza*—"The Cheating Game" 2-9-64; *The High Chaparral*—"The Badge" 12-18-70.

Brubaker, Robert (1916-). Films: "Pardners" 1956 (Businessman); "Apache Rifles" 1964 (Sgt. Cobb); "40 Guns to Apache Pass" 1967 (Sgt. Walker); "The Soul of Nigger Charley" 1973 (Aben). ¶TV: *Broken Arrow*—"Quarantine" 4-9-57 (Capt. Farrell); *Gunsmoke*—"How to Kill a Woman" 11-30-57 (Jim Buck), "Stage Holdup" 10-25-58 (Jim Buck), "Marshal Proudfoot" 1-10-59 (Jim Buck), "Kitty's Rebellion" 2-7-59 (Jim Buck), "Renegade White" 4-11-59 (Jim Buck), "The Choice" 5-9-59 (Jim Buck), "Johnny Red" 10-3-59 (Jim Buck), "Colleen So Green" 4-2-60 (Jim Buck), "Shooting Stopover" 10-8-60 (Jim Buck), "Old Faces" 3-18-61 (Jim Buck), "Perce" 9-30-61 (Jim Buck), "Catawomper" 2-10-62 (Lieutenant), "The Trappers" 11-3-62 (Jim Buck), "Deadman's Law" 1-8-68 (Wrangler), "The Long Night" 2-17-69 (Henry Wade), "Hawk" 10-20-69 (Dave Clifford), "The Pack Rat" 1-12-70 (Jake Hawkins), "Susan Was Evil" 12-3-73 (Glenn Murphy), "Like Old Times" 1-21-74 (Bartender), "The Foundling" 2-11-74 (Bartender), "Disciple" 4-1-74 (Bartender), "The Wiving" 10-14-74 (Floyd), "The Colonel" 12-16-74 (Floyd), "The First of Ignorance" 1-27-75 (Floyd); *Tombstone Territory*—"Postmarked for Death" 2-12-58 (Ben Burnett); *Tales of Wells Fargo*—"The Manuscript" 9-15-58 (Al Jones); *U.S. Marshal*—Regular 1958-60 (Deputy Blake); *Rough Riders*—"Breakout" 10-9-58 (Sergeant Baker); *Wanted—Dead or Alive*—"Twelve Hours to Crazy Horse" 11-21-59; *Bonanza*—"The Avenger" 3-19-60, "Blessed Are They" 4-22-62, "Ride the Wind" 1-16-66 & 1-23-66 (DeVere), "The Pursued" 10-2-66 & 10-9-66 (Menken), "A Woman in the House" 2-19-67 (Lassiter), "Judgment at Olympus" 10-8-67 (Sheriff Henning), "The Stronghold" 5-26-68 (Sheriff); *The Texan*—"Presentation Gun" 4-4-60 (Sheriff Jim Calvin); *The Rebel*—"The Captive of Tremblor" 4-10-60 (Dr. Sam Bates); *Man from Blackhawk*—"Trail by Combat" 5-27-60 (Claflin Pryor); *The Deputy*—"The Shackled Town" 2-11-61 (Pecos Smith); *Two Faces West*—"The Vials" 5-29-61; *Cheyenne*—"Dark Decision" 11-5-62 (Matt Silvers); *Wide Country*—"Step Over the Sky" 1-10-63 (Sam Wagoner); *The Virginian*—"Say Goodbye to All That" 1-23-63 (Trent), "Rich Man, Poor Man" 3-11-70 (Reardon); *Daniel Boone*—"River Passage" 12-15-66 (Talbot); *Kung Fu*—"A Small Beheading" 9-21-74 (Murphy).

Brubaker, Tony. Films: "Buck and the Preacher" 1972 (Headman); "A Cry in the Wilderness" TVM-1974 (Doctor); "Desperado" TVM-1987; "Posse" 1993 (Stunts).

Bruce, Belle (-6/15/60). Films: "God's Outlaw" 1919 (Edith).

Bruce, Clifford (1885-8/27/19). Films: "The Perils of Pauline" 1914-serial; "The Siren" 1917 (Derrick McClade); "The Winding Trail" 1918 (Zachary Wando).

Bruce, David (1914-5/3/76). Films: "Pony Express Days" 1940-short; "River's End" 1940 (Balt); "Santa Fe Trail" 1940 (Phil Sheridan); "Salome, Where She Danced" 1945 (Cleve); "Young Daniel Boone" 1950 (Daniel Boone); "Masterson of Kansas" 1954 (Clay Bennett). ¶TV: *The Lone Ranger*—"Buried Treasure" 3-2-50, "Banker's Choice" 11-23-50; *The Cisco Kid*—"Haven for Heavies" 5-19-51, "Phony Sheriff" 6-16-51, "Uncle Disinherits Niece" 7-14-51; *Wild Bill Hickok*—"Yellow Haired Kid" 8-28-51.

Bruce, Ed. Films: "Bret Maverick" TVM-1981 (Tom Guthrie); "The Last Days of Frank and Jesse James" TVM-1986 (Major Edwards); "Down the Long Hill" TVM-1987 (Bregman). ¶TV: *Bret Maverick*—Regular 1981-82 (Tom Guthrie).

Bruce, Eve (1939-). Films: "Tickle Me" 1965 (Pat).

Bruce, Gary. Films: "Fugitive from Sonora" 1937 (Tom Lawrence).

Bruce, Kate (1858-4/2/46). Films: "The Greaser's Gauntlet" 1908; "The Mountaineer's Honor" 1909; "The Broken Doll" 1910; "The Fugitive" 1910; "The Gold Seekers" 1910; "A Knot in the Plot" 1910; "Ramona" 1910; "A Romance of the Western Hills" 1910; "The Twisted Trails" 1910; "Two Brothers" 1910; "Fighting Blood" 1911; "Heredity" 1912; "The Battle at Elderbrush Gulch" 1913; "Just Gold" 1913; "A Misunderstood Boy" 1913; "The Yaqui Cur" 1913; "Madame Bo-Peep" 1917 (Aunt Sophie); "Scarlet Days" 1919 (Aunt).

Bruce, Nigel (1895-10/8/53). Films: "Hudson Bay" 1941 (Prince Rupert).

Bruce, Paul (1917-5/2/71). Films: "Billy Jack" 1971 (Councilman).

Bruce, Virginia (1910-2/24/82). Films: "The Bad Man of Brimstone" 1938 (Loretta Douglas); "Let Freedom Ring" 1939 (Maggie Adams).

Bruck, Bella (1912-4/5/82). TV: *Maverick*—"A State of Siege" 1-1-61 (Mamacita); *F Troop*—"The Phantom Major" 9-28-65 (Old Squaw); *Death Valley Days*—"The Other Side of the Mountain" 4-13-68 (Maudie).

Bruck, Karl (1906-8/21/87). Films: "Paint Your Wagon" 1969 (Schermerhorn).

Brueck, Betty. Films: "Jesse James' Women" 1954 (Cattle Kate Kennedy).

Bruggeman, George (1904-6/9/67). Films: "Rio Bravo" 1959 (Clem).

Brugger, Monika. Films: "Winchester Does Not Forgive" 1968-Ital.; "Wanted Johnny Texas" 1971-Ital. (Lucia Cancido).

Brummell, Beau. Films: "Three Bullets for a Long Gun" 1970-Ger./S.Afr. (Major Snap).

Brundage, Mathilde (1871-5/6/39). Films: "Blinky" 1923 (Mrs. Islip); "Oh, You Tony!" 1924 (Senator's Wife); "Westbound" 1924 (Aunt Abigail); "Border Intrigue" 1925 (Mrs. Lassen); "Comin an' Going" 1926 (Mrs. Brown); "The Denver Dude" 1927 (Mrs. Phipps); "Silver Comes Through" 1927 (Mrs. Bryce-Collins).

Brundin, Bo (1937-). TV: *Centennial*—Regular 1978-79 (Magnes Volkema).

Bruneau, Helen. Films: "Scar Hanan" 1925 (Julia Creighton).

Brunette, Fritzi (1890-9/28/43). Films: "When California Was Wild" 1915; "The Jaguar's Claws" 1917

(Beth Thomas); "Jacques of the Silver North" 1919 (Memory Baird); "The Coast of Opportunity" 1920 (Janet Ashley); "Sure Fire" 1921 (Elinor Parker); "Bells of San Juan" 1922 (Dorothy Page); "The Crusader" 1922 (Alice); "While Satan Sleeps" 1922 (Salome Deming); "The Footlight Ranger" 1923 (Janet Ainslee); "Rustlers of Red Dog" 1935-serial; "Way Out West" 1937 (Woman in Audience); "Wells Fargo" 1937 (Pioneer Woman); "Stagecoach" 1939.

Brunetti, Argentina. Films: "California" 1946 (Elvira); "Broken Arrow" 1950 (Nalikadeya); "Apache War Smoke" 1952 (Madre); "The Fighter" 1952 (Maria); "Rose of Cimarron" 1952; "San Antone" 1953 (Mexican Woman); "The Far Horizons" 1955 (Old Crone); "The Tall Men" 1955 (Maria); "Three Violent People" 1956 (Maria); "Duel at Apache Wells" 1957 (Tia Maria); "Showdown at Boot Hill" 1958 (Mrs. Bonaventure); "Stage to Thunder Rock" 1964 (Sarita); 'The Appaloosa" 1966 (Yaqui Woman). ¶TV: *Jim Bowie*—"Spanish Intrigue" 2-8-57 (Tai Rosa); *Bonanza*—"Dark Star" 4-23-60; *Rawhide*—"Incident of the One Hundred Amulets" 5-6-60 (Rosa Patines); *The Deputy*—"The Fatal Urge" 10-15-60 (Evita); *Wanted—Dead or Alive*—"Surprise Witness" 11-2-60 (Juanita); *Wagon Train—The Chalice* 5-24-61 (Lisa Canaveri); *The Rifleman*—"Guilty Conscience" 4-2-62 (Mrs. Ramirez); *Gunsmoke*—"Gold Mine" 12-25-65 (Louise Danby); *The High Chaparral*—"A Time to Laugh, a Time to Cry" 9-26-69 (Duena).

Bruno, Frank (-6/20/45). Films: "Treachery Rides the Range" 1936 (Little Big Fox); "King of the Texas Rangers" 1941-serial (Cole).

Bruns, Philip (1931-). TV: *Wild Wild West*—"The Night of the Circus of Death" 11-3-67 (Abner Lennox); *Here Come the Brides*—"A Hard Card to Play" 10-23-68 (Lorenzo); *The Outcasts*—"How Tall Is Blood?" 5-5-69 (Marshal Gandy); *Barbary Coast*—"Sharks Eat Sharks" 11-21-75 (Larkin); *How the West Was Won*—"L'Affaire Riel" 3-5-79 (Doc Tivers).

Brunton, William (1883-2/19/65). Films: "The Conversion of Smiling Tom" 1915; "Medicine Bend" 1916 (Tony Wickwire); "The Lost Express" 1917-serial; "The Railroad Raiders" 1917; "As the Sun Went Down" 1919 (Albert Atherton).

Bryan, Arthur Q. (1899-11/30/59). Films: "Hell's Outpost" 1954 (Harry Bogue).

Bryan, Jack (1908-9/15/64). TV: *Maverick*—"The White Widow" 1-24-60 (John Brinks).

Bryant, Bob. TV: *Wagon Train*—"The Major Adams Story" 4-23-58 & 4-30-58 (Soldier); *Klondike*—"Klondike Fever" 10-10-60 (Big Jack Rollins).

Bryant, Buel. Films: "Outlaws of the Prairie" 1937; "West of Santa Fe" 1938 (Henchman); "Spoilers of the Range" 1939 (Foley); "The Stranger from Texas" 1939 (Quirk); "Zorro's Fighting Legion" 1939-serial (Renaldo); "The Man from Tumbleweeds" 1940 (Ranger); "The Return of Wild Bill" 1940 (Mike); "Texas Renegades" 1940 (Murphy); "Two-Fisted Rangers" 1940 (Henchman); "Sierra Sue" 1941.

Bryant, Fletcher. TV: *Gunsmoke*—"Fandango" 2-11-67 (Ben Tyson), "Morgan" 3-2-70 (Hawkins); *Cimarron Strip*—"The Beast That Walks Like a Man" 11-30-67.

Bryant, Howard. Films: "Lost Ranch" 1937 (Happy); "Orphan of the Pecos" 1937 (Pete).

Bryant, Jan. Films: "Shadows on the Range" 1946; "Silver Range" 1946; "Flashing Guns" 1947 (Ann); "Cowboy Cavalier" 1948; "Crashing Thru" 1949. ¶TV: *The Cisco Kid*—"Sky Sign" 12-6-52, "Marriage by Mail" 1-3-53.

Bryant, Jane. Films: "Cherokee Strip" 1937 (Janie Walton).

Bryant, John (1917-7/13/89). Films: "Deadwood '76" 1965 (Hubert). ¶TV: *The Lone Ranger*—"Best Laid Plans" 12-25-52, "The Sheriff's Wife" 8-18-55; *Jim Bowie*—"Natchez Trace" 10-19-56 (Samuel Cummings); *Sergeant Preston of the Yukon*—"The Diamond Collar" 1-30-58 (Alex Keith); *Schlitz Playhouse of the Stars*—"Way of the West" 6-6-58 (Harry Ryan); *Laramie*—"Man of God" 12-1-59 (Family Man); *The Virginian*—Regular 1963-68 (Dr. Spaulding); *Wagon Train*—"The Michael Malone Story" 1-6-64; *The Monroes*—"Ordeal by Hope" 10-19-66 (Doctor).

Bryant, Joshua (1940-). TV: *Cimarron Strip*—"The Assassin" 1-11-68; *Here Come the Brides*—"The Last Winter" 3-27-70 (Eben); *Bret Maverick*—"Dateline: Sweetwater" 1-12-82 (Busted Bill Farley).

Bryant, Joyce. Films: "Across the Plains" 1939 (Mary Masters); "Fighting Renegade" 1939 (Marian Wills); "Trigger Fingers" 1939 (Margaret); "Trigger Smith" 1939 (Jean); "The Sagebrush Family Trails West" 1940 (Nellis Sawyer).

Bryant, Nana (1888-12/24/55). Films: "Out West with the Hardys" 1938 (Dora Northcote); "The Virginian" 1946 (Mrs. Wood); "Eyes of Texas" 1948 (Hattie Wates); "Only the Valiant" 1951 (Mrs. Drumm); "The Outcast" 1954 (Mrs. Banner).

Bryant, Theona. Films: "The Miracle of the Hills" 1959 (Alison Wingate). ¶TV: *Maverick*—"Black Fire" 3-16-58 (Cousin Hope); *Cheyenne*—"Noose at Noon" 6-3-58 (Mary); *The Texan*—"A Quart of Law" 1-12-59 (Marcia); *Johnny Ringo*—"The Derelict" 5-26-60 (Lisa); *Death Valley Days*—"Way Station" 5-2-62 (Cynthia Waterfield); *Wide Country*—"Good Old Uncle Walt" 12-13-62 (Doris).

Bryant, William (1924-). Films: "Battle of Rogue River" 1954 (Corporal); "Badman's Country" 1958; "The Missouri Traveler" 1958 (Henry Craig); "Ride Beyond Vengeance" 1966 (Bartender); "Heaven with a Gun" 1969 (Bart Patterson); "Chisum" 1970 (Jeff); "Macho Callahan" 1970; "The Animals" 1971 (Sheriff Martin Lord); "Black Noon" TVM-1971 (Jacob); "Powderkeg" TVM-1971 (Major Bull Buckner); "Wild Rovers" 1971 (Hereford); "Deadly Trackers" 1973; "The Hanged Man" TVM-1974 (Dr. Nye); "The Legend of the Golden Gun" TVM-1979 (William Ford). ¶TV: *Wild Bill Hickok*—"Mountain Men" 2-3-53, "Clem's Reformation" 7-7-53; *Wyatt Earp*—"The Gambler" 10-18-55, "The Almost Dead Cowhand" 10-23-56 (Chalk Benson), "The Schoolteacher" 3-11-58 (Ed Watkins); *The Adventures of Rin Tin Tin*—"The Missing Heir" 1-13-56 (Stephen); *Frontier*—"The Ballad of Pretty Polly" 4-1-56 (Logan); *Gunsmoke*—"The Bureaucrat" 3-16-57 (Charlie Frost), "The Constable" 5-30-59 (1st Cowboy), "False Front" 12-22-62 (Joe), "Once a Haggen" 2-1-64, "Quaker Girl" 12-10-66 (Deputy Marshal Kester), "Chato" 9-14-70 (Sheriff Cooter), "Alias Festus Haggen" 3-6-72 (Prosecutor Bennett), "The Iron Man" 10-21-74 (Sheriff); *Tales of the Texas Rangers*—"Double Reward" 12-15-57 (Pete Diamond); *Frontier Doctor*—"Double Boomerang" 11-1-58; *Maverick*—"Prey of the Cat" 12-7-58 (Chase); *Sugarfoot*—"Outlaw Island" 11-24-59 (Chris Van Ralt); *The Rifleman*—"Shivaree" 2-3-59, "Gunfire" 1-15-62 (Karl Hollis), "The Assailants" 11-12-62 (Trooper Coley); *Laramie*—"The Star Trail" 10-13-59 (Curly), "Ladies Day" 10-3-61, "Double Eagles" 11-20-62, "The Marshals" 4-30-63 (Reb Carlton); *Hotel De*

Paree—"The Man Who Believed in Law" 11-27-59 (Duke); *Have Gun Will Travel*—"Charley Red Dog" 12-12-59; *Man from Blackhawk*—"The Biggest Legend" 1-1-60 (Dawson); *The Rebel*—"Glory" 1-24-60 (Don), "You Steal My Eyes" 3-20-60 (Hump), "Johnny Yuma at Appomattox" 9-18-60 (Gen. Ulysses S. Grant), "The Waiting" 10-9-60 (Sheriff Stroud), "Vindication" 12-4-60 (Sam Boley), "The Ballad of Danny Brown" 4-9-61 (Danny Brown); *The Outlaws*—"Rape of Red Sky" 10-27-60 (Jack Roos); *Two Faces West*—"The Trespasser" 1-2-61; *Empire*—"End of an Image" 1-15-63 (Fred Rainey); *Death Valley Days*—"The Vintage Years" 1-30-63 (Meadows); *The Virginian*—"Man of Violence" 12-25-63 (Paul Judson); *Temple Houston*—"Sam's Boy" 1-23-64 (Cy Morgan); *Rawhide*—"The Race" 9-25-64 (Lockwood); *Branded*—"The Mission" 3-14-65, 3-21-65 & 3-28-65 (President Ulysses S. Grant), "The Golden Fleece" 1-2-66 (Ulysses S. Grant), "A Destiny Which Made Us Brothers" 1-23-66 (General Grant), "Call to Glory" 2-27-66, 3-6-66 & 3-13-66 (President Grant), "The Assassins" 3-27-66 & 4-3-66 (President Grant); *The Monroes*—"Court Martial" 11-16-66 (Lance Corporal Gardner); *Hondo*—Regular 1967 (Col Crook); *Bonanza*—"The Sure Thing" 11-12-67 (Harper), "The Stronghold" 5-26-68 (Jackson), "The Company of Forgotten Men" 2-2-69 (Beau), "Riot!" 10-3-72 (Governor); *The Guns of Will Sonnett*—"Stopover in a Troubled Town" 2-2-68; *Lancer*—"Jelly" 11-19-68, "The Last Train for Charlie Poe" 11-26-68 (Sheriff Gabe), "The Black McGloins" 1-21-69 (Sheriff Gabe), "Zee" 9-30-69 (Sheriff Gabe); *Wild Wild West*—"The Night of the Plague" 4-4-69 (Duncan Lansing); *Alias Smith and Jones*—"Jailbreak at Junction City" 9-30-71; *Barbary Coast*—"An Iron-Clad Plan" 10-31-75; *How the West Was Won*—"The Enemy" 2-5-79 (Colonel Worth); *The Chisholms*—"Chains" 3-8-80 (O'Herlihy); *Bret Maverick*—"Dateline: Sweetwater" 1-12-82 (John Davis); *Father Murphy*—"The Newlyweds" 9-28-82 (Sheriff).

Bryar, Claudia (1918-). Films: "Bad Company" 1972 (Mrs. Clum); "Pat Garrett and Billy the Kid" 1973 (Mrs. Horrell). ¶TV: *Wyatt Earp*—"Juveniles—1878" 3-10-58; *Buckskin*—"Tree of Death" 8-21-58 (Sara Taliaferro); *Maverick*—"The Jail at Junction Flats" 11-9-58 (Mrs. Pyne); *Wagon Train*—"The Mary Ellen

Thomas Story" 12-24-58 (Mrs. Mayhew), "The Marie Brant Story" 1-20-60 (Mrs. Taylor), "The River Crossing" 12-14-60, "The Janet Hale Story" 5-31-61 (Ada), "The Hiram Winthrop Story" 6-6-62 (Mary Carter); *Bonanza*—"The Spanish Grant" 2-6-60, "Rain from Heaven" 10-6-63 (Mrs. Weems), "Justice Deferred" 12-17-67 (Mrs. Scott), "He Was Only Seven" 3-5-72 (Martha); *Death Valley Days*—"The Stranger" 3-15-60 (Mary); *Wanted—Dead or Alive*—"The Cure" 9-28-60 (Emily Kendrick); *Lawman*—"The Trial" 5-7-61 (Clara); *Stoney Burke*—"Fight Night" 10-8-62 (Mrs. Miller); *The Virginian*—"The Small Parade" 2-20-63; *Laredo*—"A Very Small Assignment" 3-17-66 (Mrs. Cook); *The Big Valley*—"Night in a Small Town" 10-9-67; *The Guns of Will Sonnett*—"Meeting at Devil's Fork" 10-27-67 (Mrs. Stevens); *Alias Smith and Jones*—"The Girl in Boxcar Number Three" 2-11-71 (Minerva Lambert); *Gunsmoke*—"Homecoming" 1-8-73 (Nell Bronson).

Bryar, Paul (1910-). Films: "Sin Town" 1942 (Grady); "Robin Hood of Texas" 1947 (Ace Foley); "Call of the Klondike" 1950 (Fred Foley); "Callaway Went Thataway" 1951 (Gaffer); "Cavalry Scout" 1951; "The Far Country" 1955 (Sheriff); "Gunman's Walk" 1958 (Bartender); "How the West Was Won" 1962 (Auctioneer's Assistant); "The Quick Gun" 1964 (Mitchell); "Butch Cassidy and the Sundance Kid" 1969 (Card Player). ¶TV: *The Lone Ranger*—"The Red Mark" 9-3-53; *Jim Bowie*—"Broomstick Wedding" 10-12-56 (Papa Leprie); *Tales of Wells Fargo*—"The Bounty" 4-15-57 (George Curtis), "Death Raffle" 10-21-61 (Sam); *The Californians*—"The PO 8" 12-31-57 (Hamish Glourie); *Maverick*—"Mano Nera" 10-23-60 (Officer Noonan); *The Tall Man*—"Tiger Eye" 12-17-60 (Bartender); *Death Valley Days*—"White Gold" 2-15-61 (Charles "Doughy" Lucas); *Bonanza*—"The Hayburner" 2-17-63 (Horse Trader); *Laredo*—"Leave It to Dixie" 12-30-66; *The High Chaparral*—"The Terrorist" 12-17-67 (Sgt. Tousseau); *Gunsmoke*—"The Prisoner" 3-17-69 (Sheriff); *Kung Fu*—"Blood Brother" 1-18-73 (Pop Fuller).

Brynner, Yul (1920-10/10/85). Films: "The Magnificent Seven" 1960 (Chris); "Invitation to a Gunfighter" 1964 (Jules Gaspard D'Estaing); "Return of the Seven" 1966-Span. (Chris); "Villa Rides" 1968 (Pancho Villa); "Adios, Sabata" 1970-Ital./Span. (Sabata); "The Bounty Hunt-

ers" 1970-Ital.; "Catlow" 1971-Span. (Catlow); "Westworld" 1973 (Gunslinger).

Bryson, Winifred (1893-8/20/87). Films: "Suzanna" 1922 (Dolores).

Buccella, Maria Grazia (1940-). Films: "Villa Rides" 1968 (Fina Gonzalez); "Trinity Sees Red" 1971-Ital./Span.

Buchanan, Buck (1941-7/16/92). Films: "The Man from Button Willow" 1965 (Voice). ¶TV: *Iron Horse*—"T Is for Traitor" 12-2-66 (Hub).

Buchanan, Edgar (1903-4/4/79). Films: "Arizona" 1940 (Judge Bogardus); "When the Daltons Rode" 1940 (Man at Livery Stable); "Texas" 1941 (Doc Thorpe); "Tombstone, the Town Too Tough to Die" 1942 (Curly Bill Brocius); "The Desperadoes" 1943 (Willie MacLeod); "Buffalo Bill" 1944 (Sgt. Chips); "Abilene Town" 1946 (Bravo Trimble); "Renegades" 1946 (Krik Dembrow); "The Sea of Grass" 1947 (Jeff); "Adventures in Silverado" 1948; "Coroner Creek" 1948 (Sheriff O'Hea); "The Man from Colorado" 1948 (Doc Merriam); "The Untamed Breed" 1948 (John Rambeau); "Lust for Gold" 1949 (Wiser); "Red Canyon" 1949 (Jonah Johnson); "The Walking Hills" 1949 (Old Willy); "The Devil's Doorway" 1950 (Zeke Carmody); "Cave of Outlaws" 1951 (Dobbs); "The Great Missouri Raid" 1951 (Dr. Samuels); "Rawhide" 1951 (Sam Todd); "Silver City" 1951 (Dutch Surrency); "The Big Trees" 1952 (Yukon Burns); "Flaming Feather" 1952 (Sgt. O'Rourke); "Toughest Man in Arizona" 1952 (Jim Hadlock); "Wild Stallion" 1952 (Wintergreen); "Shane" 1953 (Lewis); "Dawn at Socorro" 1954 (Sheriff Cauthen); "Destry" 1954 (Mayor Hiram Sellers); "The Lonesome Trail" 1955; "Rage at Dawn" 1955 (Judge Hawkins); "The Silver Star" 1955 (Bill Dowdy); "Wichita" 1955 (Doc Black); "Day of the Bad Man" 1958 (Sam Wyckoff); "The Sheepman" 1958 (Milt Masters); "Four Fast Guns" 1959 (Dipper); "King of the Wild Stallions" 1959 (Idaho); "Cimarron" 1960 (Neal Hefner); "The Comancheros" 1961 (Judge Bean); "Ride the High Country" 1962 (Judge Tolliver); "McClintock" 1963 (Bunny Dull); "The Man from Button Willow" 1965 (Voice of Sorry); "The Rounders" 1965 (Vince Moore); "Gunpoint" 1966 (Bull); "Welcome to Hard Times" 1967 (Brown); "Something for a Lonely Man"

TVM-1968 (Old Man Wolenski); "The Over-the-Hill Gang" TVM-1969 (Jason Finch); "The Over-the-Hill Gang Rides Again" TVM-1970 (Jason Fitch); "Yuma" TVM-1971 (Mules McNeil). ¶TV: *Hopalong Cassidy*—Regular 1952 (Red Connors); *Luke and the Tenderfoot*—Pilot 8-6-55 & 8-13-55 (Luke Herkimer); *Judge Roy Bean*—Regular 1955-56 (Judge Roy Bean); *Tales of Wells Fargo*—"The Auction" 10-28-57 (Dawson), "The Prisoner" 2-17-58 (Bob Dawson), "The Manuscript" 9-15-58 (Bob Dawson), "Bob Dawson" 4-20-59 (Bob Dawson), "Doc Dawson" 9-19-60 (Doc Dawson), "The Repentant Outlaw" 5-29-61 (Doc Dawson); *Wagon Train*—"The John Darro Story" 11-6-57 (the Tramp), "The Jane Hawkins Story" 11-30-60 (Ben Mattox); *Jim Bowie*—"Deaf Smith" 2-7-58 (Ringtail); *The Restless Gun*—"Aunt Emma" 4-14-58 (Ethan Greenfield), "The Gold Star" 5-19-58 (Sheriff Gabe Starns); *The Californians*—"The Golden Bride" 5-20-58 (Dutch), "One Ton of Peppercorns" 5-12-59 (Major); *26 Men*—"Cross and Double Cross" 10-28-58; *Cimarron City*—"Kid on a Calico Horse" 11-22-58 (Shanty); *Maverick*—"Island in the Swamp" 11-30-58 (Daddy Forge), "Duel at Sundown" 2-1-59 (Jed Christiansen), "Easy Mark" 11-15-59 (Colonel Hambledon), "Hadley's Hunters" 9-25-60 (Sheriff Horace Hadley), "The Cactus Switch" 1-15-61 (Red Daniels); *The Rifleman*—"The Pet" 1-6-59 (Doc Burrage), "The Second Witness" 3-3-59 (Doc Burrage), "The Trade" 3-10-59 (Doc Burrage), "The Deadly Wait" 3-24-59 (Doc Burrage), "The Angry Man" 4-28-59 (Doc Burrage), "The Long Goodbye" 11-27-61 (Grandpa Fogarty); *Lawman*—"The Captives" 1-11-59 (Jess Miller), "The Senator" 5-17-59; *Wanted—Dead or Alive*—"Railroaded" 3-14-59 (Pop Michaels), "Amos Carter" 5-9-59 (Chester Blake); *Trackdown*—"The Trick" 4-15-59 (Tully Saxon); *The Deputy*—"Man of Peace" 12-19-59 (Isbel); *Laramie*—"Saddle and Spur" 3-29-60 (Calico), "Men of Defiance" 4-19-60 (Doc Collier), "Stolen Tribute" 1-31-61 (Tully Casper), "The Long Road Back" 10-23-62 (Cletus McBain); *Bronco*—"Winter Kill" 5-31-60 (Pop Owens); *Bat Masterson*—"Debt of Honor" 9-29-60 (Cactus Charlie); *Stagecoach West*—"Red Sand" 11-22-60 (Lum Jensen); *The Outlaws*—"Starfall" 11-24-60 & 12-1-60 (Nulty); *Bonanza*—"The Trail Gang" 11-26-60 (Hallelujah Hicks), "Sam Hill" 6-3-61 (John Henry Hill);

Riverboat—"Duel on the River" 12-12-60 (Wingate); *Klondike*—"The Golden Burro" 1-16-61 (Sam Perkins); *The Tall Man*—"The Judas Palm" 10-21-61 (Archie Keogh); *Gunsmoke*—"Old Dan" 1-27-62 (Dan Witter), "Old York" 5-4-63 (Dan York); *Stoney Burke*—"Fight Night" 10-8-62 (Dawes); *Have Gun Will Travel*—"Man in an Hourglass" 12-1-62 (Cardiff); *Wide Country*—"Good Old Uncle Walt" 12-13-62 (Uncle Walt Guthrie); *The Men from Shiloh*—"The Legacy of Spencer Flats" 1-27-71 (Birdwell).

Buchanan, West. Films: "The Long Riders" 1980 (McCorkindale).

Buchholz, Horst (1933-). Films: "The Magnificent Seven" 1960 (Chico). ¶TV: *How the West Was Won*—Episode One 2-12-78 (Sergei), Episode Two 2-19-78 (Sergei).

Buchinsky, Charles. see Bronson, Charles.

Buck, Connie. Films: "Gun Fight" 1961 (Coheela). ¶TV: *Rough Riders*—"Killers at Chocktaw Valley" 12-4-58 (Girl); *Northwest Passage*—"Trial by Fire" 3-6-59 (Tehura); *Gunsmoke*—"Cheyennes" 6-13-59 (Daughter), "Saludos" 10-31-59 (Sochi); *Rawhide*—"Incident of the Day of the Dead" 9-18-59, "Incident on the Road to Yesterday" 11-18-60, "Incident at Superstition Prairie" 12-2-60; *Black Saddle*—"Apache Trail" 11-20-59 (Maria); *Bat Masterson*—"Come Out Fighting" 4-7-60 (Lolita).

Buckland, Veda (1882-5/20/41). Films: "The Texan" 1930 (Mary, the Nurse).

Buckler, Hugh (1870-10/36). Films: "The Last of the Mohicans" 1936 (Col. Munro).

Buckley, Betty (1947-). Films: "Wyatt Earp" 1994 (Virginia Earp).

Buckley, Kay. Films: "Raiders of Tomahawk Creek" 1950 (Janet Clayton); "Stage to Tucson" 1950 (Kate Crocker).

Buckley, William. Films: "Just Pals" 1920 (Harvey Cahill); "Under Northern Lights" 1920 (Douglas MacLeod); "Bar Nothin'" 1921 (Harold Lynne); "Big Town Round-Up" 1921 (Rodney Curtis); "Colorado Pluck" 1921 (Reggie Featherstone); "The Bearcat" 1922 (Archer Aitken); "Sky High" 1922 (Victor Castle); "The Rattler" 1925 (Cecil Aubrey).

Bucko, Ralph "Buck" (1892-8/6/62). Films: "Code of the West" 1929; "Arizona Terror" 1931; "Branded Men" 1931; "The Two Gun Man" 1931; "Guns for Hire" 1932; "Texas Gun Fighter" 1932; "Whistlin'

Dan" 1932; "King of the Arena" 1933; "The Lone Avenger" 1933; "Strawberry Roan" 1933 (Cowboy); "The Trail Drive" 1933; "The Fiddlin' Buckaroo" 1934; "Gun Justice" 1934; "Honor of the Range" 1934; "Smoking Guns" 1934; "Bulldog Courage" 1935; "Gunsmoke on the Guadalupe" 1935; "Square Shooter" 1935; "Western Courage" 1935; "Avenging Waters" 1936; "Everyman's Law" 1936 (Henchman); "The Fugitive Sheriff" 1936; "Gun Smoke" 1936; "Dodge City Trail" 1937 (Dawson's Gang Member); "The Painted Stallion" 1937-serial; "Rollin' Plains" 1938; "Gaucho Serenade" 1940; "Melody Ranch" 1940; "Back in the Saddle" 1941; "Along the Sundown Trail" 1942; "Bar 20" 1943; "Bordertown Gunfighters" 1943; "Daredevils of the West" 1943-serial (Citizen #7/Gulch Heavy #2); "Devil Riders" 1944; "The Cherokee Flash" 1945; "Sunset Pass" 1946 (Posse Man); "Bells of San Angelo" 1947; "Son of Zorro" 1947-serial; "The Adventures of Frank and Jesse James" 1948-Serial (Davin); "Desperadoes of the West" 1950-serial (Rock Heavy); "The James Brothers of Missouri" 1950-serial; "The Man from Black Hills" 1952.

Bucko, Roy (1893-8/6/54). Films: "Arizona Terror" 1931; "Branded Men" 1931; "The Two Gun Man" 1931; "Guns for Hire" 1932; "One-Man Law" 1932; "Texas Gun Fighter" 1932; "Whistlin' Dan" 1932; "Young Blood" 1932 (Blackie); "The Lone Avenger" 1933; "Strawberry Roan" 1933 (Cowboy); "The Trail Drive" 1933; "Brand of Hate" 1934; "The Fiddlin' Buckaroo" 1934; "Gun Justice" 1934; "Honor of the Range" 1934; "Smoking Guns" 1934; "Wheels of Destiny" 1934; "Gunsmoke on the Guadalupe" 1935; "Heir to Trouble" 1935; "Square Shooter" 1935; "Western Courage" 1935; "The Fugitive Sheriff" 1936; "Gun Smoke" 1936; "The Mysterious Avenger" 1936 (Rustler); "Arizona Gunfighter" 1937; "Dodge City Trail" 1937 (Dawson's Gang Member); "The Gambling Terror" 1937; "The Painted Stallion" 1937-serial; "Rollin' Plains" 1938; "Along the Sundown Trail" 1942; "Riders of the Deadline" 1943; "Wolves of the Range" 1943; "Devil Riders" 1944; "Gun to Gun" 1944-short; "The Cherokee Flash" 1945; "Rio Grande Raiders" 1946; "Sunset Pass" 1946 (Posse Man); "Son of Zorro" 1947-serial; "The Adventures of Frank and Jesse James" 1948-serial (Citizen #2); "Dangers of the Canadian Mounted" 1948-serial; "Ghost of Zorro" 1949-serial (Townsman #2); "Dallas" 1950 (Prisoner); "Don Daredevil Rides Again" 1951-serial (Barnett); "The Man from Black Hills" 1952.

Budinger, Jean. Films: "Ride, Ryder, Ride" 1949 (Marge).

Buetel, Jack (Jack Beutel) (1917-6/27/89). Films: "The Outlaw" 1943 (Billy the Kid); "Best of the Badmen" 1951 (Bob Younger); "The Half-Breed" 1952 (Charlie Wolf); "Rose of Cimarron" 1952 (Marshal Hollister); "Jesse James' Women" 1954 (Frank James); "Mustang" 1959 (Gabe). ¶TV: *Judge Roy Bean*—Regular 1955-56 (Jeff Taggert); *26 Men*—"The Bells of St. Thomas" 5-13-58; *Wagon Train*—"The Andrew Hale Story" 6-3-59 (Joe Hamplar), "The Prairie Story" 2-1-61 (Jack); *Maverick*—"Easy Mark" 11-15-59 (Phillips).

Buehler, William. Films: "Crossed Trail" 1924 (J.M. Anders).

Buffington, Sam (1932-5/15/60). Films: "The Light in the Forest" 1958 (George Owens); "The Rawhide Trail" 1958 (James Willard); "They Came to Cordura" 1959 (Correspondent). ¶TV: *Maverick*—"The Quick and the Dead" 12-8-57 (Ponca), "The Seventh Hand" 3-2-58 (Logan), "The Thirty-Ninth Star" 11-16-58 (Bigelow), "Yellow River" 2-8-59 (Prof. von Schulenberg), "A Fellow's Brother" 11-22-59 (Burgess); *Tombstone Territory*—"The Epitaph" 2-26-58 (Monte Davis), "Outlaw's Bugle" 8-6-58 (Monte Davis); *Wanted—Dead or Alive*—"The Favor" 11-15-58 (Fred), "Eight Cent Record" 12-20-58, "Six-Up to Bannack" 1-10-59 (Abb Crawford); *Sugarfoot*—"Yampa Crossing" 12-9-58 (Henry Dixon); *Black Saddle*—"Client: Jessup" 4-18-59 (Noah Bailey), "The Freebooters" 10-2-59; *Gunsmoke*—"Buffalo Hunter" 5-2-59 (Cook); *Rough Riders*—"Reluctant Hostage" 6-18-59 (Ephraim Hoggs); *Man from Blackhawk*—"Execution Day" 3-4-60 (Josiah Cartwright); *Whispering Smith*—Regular 1961 (Chief John Richards).

Bujold, Genevieve (1942-). Films: "Another Man, Another Chance" 1977-Fr. (Jeanne Leroy).

Buka, Donald (1921-). Films: "New Mexico" 1951 (Pvt. Van Vechton). ¶TV: *Lawman*—"The Encounter" 1-18-59 (Cole Hawkins), "The Breakup" 11-8-59 (Harry Jensen); *Colt .45*—"The Man Who Loved Lincoln" 5-3-59 (David Belasco); *The Law of the Plainsman*—"Desperate Decision" 11-12-59 (Roy); *The Rebel*—"Decision at Sweetwater" 4-23-61 (Jess Galt); *Whispering Smith*—"The Trademark" 8-14-61

(Fred Gavin); *The High Chaparral*—"Alliance" 12-12-69 (Major Ramsey).

Bulifant, Joyce (1937-). TV: *The Tall Man*—"The Four Queens" 3-24-62 (Fifi); *Wide Country*—"A Guy for Clementine" 9-27-62 (Clemmie); *Gunsmoke*—"Uncle Sunday" 12-15-62 (Ellie); *Empire*—"The Tiger Inside" 2-12-63 (Betty Wormser); "Roar from the Mountain" 1-8-64 (Nancy Mayhew); *Wagon Train*—"The Michael Malone Story" 1-6-64 (Juli Holland); *Destry*—"Go Away, Little Sheba" 3-27-64 (Sheba Hannibal); *Lancer*—"Angel Day and Her Sunshine Girls" 2-25-69 (Cassie); *Bonanza*—"Return Engagement" 3-1-70 (Bonnie).

Bull, Charles Edward (1881-9/9/71). Films: "The Iron Horse" 1924 (Abraham Lincoln).

Bull, Richard (1924-). Films: "Hour of the Gun" 1967 (Thomas Fitch); "The Stalking Moon" 1969 (Doctor); "Lawman" 1971 (Dusaine); "Ulzana's Raid" 1972 (Ginsford); "High Plains Drifter" 1973 (Asa Goodwin); "Little House on the Prairie: Look Back to Yesterday" TVM-1983 (Nels Oleson); "Little House: The Last Farewell" TVM-1984 (Nels Oleson); "Little House: Bless All the Dear Children" TVM-1984 (Nels Oleson). ¶TV: *The Virginian*—"The Executioners" 9-19-62 (Doctor), "Throw a Long Rope" 10-3-62 (Doc Spence); *Destry*—"The Infernal Triangle" 5-1-64 (Bartender); *Iron Horse*—"Joy Unconfined" 9-12-66 (Spender); *Bonanza*—"To Stop a War" 10-19-69 (Jess Hill), "The Twenty-Sixth Grave" 10-31-72 (Goodman); *Here Come the Brides*—"The Legend of Big Foot" 11-14-69 (Carver); *Death Valley Days*—"Amos and the Black Bull" 2-28-70, "The Contract" 3-14-70; *Gunsmoke*—"The Sodbusters" 11-20-72 (Deems); *Nichols*—Regular 1971-72 (Judge Thatcher); *Little House on the Prairie*—Regular 1974-82 (Nels Oleson); *Paradise*—"The Last Warrior" 2-23-89 (Judge Hollister).

Bullock, Boris (William Barrymore) (1900-4/23/79). Films: "Don X" 1925 (Perez Blake); "The Range Terror" 1925 (Bud Allen); "Lawless Trails" 1926 (Frisco Mays); "Prince of the Saddle" 1926; "Border Cavalier" 1927 (Victor Harding); "Across the Plains" 1928 (Walla Walla Slim); "The Thrill Chaser" 1928; "Where the West Begins" 1928; "Fighting Cowboy" 1933 (Red); "Lightning Range" 1934 (Boob); "Rawhide Romance" 1934 (Red Conry); "Rawhide

Terror" 1934 (Black Brent); "The Whirlwind Rider" 1935.

Bullock, Elias. Films: "The Santa Fe Trail" 1923-serial; "Horse Sense" 1924 (Nat Culver); "In the West" 1924.

Bulnes, Quintin. Films: "Dalton That Got Away" 1960; "Jory" 1972 (Walker).

Bumatai, Ray. TV: *Adventures of Brisco County, Jr.*—"The Orb Scholar" 9-3-93 (Frenchie Bearpaux), "Ned Zed" 3-13-94 (French Bearpaux).

Bunce, Alan (1903-4/27/65). TV: *Stoney Burke*—"Fight Night" 10-8-62 (Willard).

Bundy, Brooke (1947-). Films: "Firecreek" 1968 (Leah). ¶TV: *Wagon Train*—"The Bleeker Story" 12-9-63 (Bessie); *Gunsmoke*—"The Magician" 12-21-63 (Alice Dark), "Sweet Billy, Singer of Songs" 1-15-66 (Orabelle Beal); *The Virginian*—"The Secret of Brynmar Hall" 4-1-64 (Jenny), "The Mark of a Man" 4-20-66 (Susan McDevitt); *Rawhide*—"The Winter Soldier" 3-12-65 (Ellie Kurtz); *Bonanza*—"The Debt" 9-12-65 (Annie Kane), "Judgment at Olympus" 10-8-67 (Mary Elizabeth); *The Big Valley*—"The Stallion" 1-30-67 (Andrea); *Cowboy in Africa*—"The Hesitant Hero" 12-18-67 (Ellen); *Daniel Boone*—"Be Thankful for the Fickleness of Women" 9-19-68 (Sarah Wadsworth); *Lancer*—"The Wedding" 1-7-69 (Jenny), "Cut the Wolf Loose" 11-4-69 (Laura Thompson); *Father Murphy*—"The First Miracle" 4-4-82 & 4-11-82 (Madeline).

Bunn, Earl. Films: "End of the Trail" 1936 (Peg Leg); "King of the Royal Mounted" 1940-serial (Joe); "King of the Texas Rangers" 1941-serial (Dirigible Heavy #2); "King of the Mounties" 1942-serial (Joe); "Daredevils of the West" 1943-serial (Citizen #3); "Canadian Mounties vs. Atomic Invaders" 1953-serial.

Bunny, George (1870-4/16/52). Films: "If Only Jim" 1921 (Uncle Johnny); "Breed of the Sunsets" 1928 (Don Alvaro); "Laddie Be Good" 1928 (Pierpoint Jones); "Wild Horse" 1931 (Colonel Ben Hall).

Bunny, John (1863-4/26/15). Films: "Kitty and the Cowboys" 1911.

Buntrock, Bobby. TV: *Wagon Train*—"The Ella Lindstrom Story" 2-4-59 (Bo); *The Virginian*—"The Masquerade" 10-18-67 (Tim Messinger).

Buono, Victor (1938-1/1/82). Films: "Four for Texas" 1964 (Harvey Burden); "Boot Hill" 1969-Ital.; "The Wrath of God" 1972 (Jennings); "More Wild Wild West" TVM-1980 (Dr. Henry Messenger). ¶TV: *The Rebel*—"Blind Marriage" 4-17-60 (Young), "The Earl of Durango" 6-12-60 (Ralph Babcock); *Wild Wild West*—"The Night of the Inferno" 9-17-65 (Wing Fat/Juan Manola), "The Night of the Eccentrics" 9-16-66 (Count Carlos Manzeppi), "The Night of the Feathered Fury" 1-13-67 (Count Carlos Manzeppi); *Daniel Boone*—"The Ballad of Sidewinder and Cherokee" 9-14-67 (Quaife).

Bupp, June. Films: "Border Vengeance" 1935 (June Griswold).

Bupp, Sonny (1928-). Films: "Renegade Trail" 1939 (Joey Joyce); "Three Faces West" 1940 (Billy Welles).

Bupp, Tommy. Films: "The Man from Hell" 1934 (Timmy McCarroll); "Rawhide Terror" 1934 (Tommie Brent); "Arizona Bad Man" 1935 (Dave Dunstan); "Roarin' Guns" 1936 (Buddy); "Roarin' Lead" 1936 (Bobby); "Arizona Days" 1937 (Billy); "Cherokee Strip" 1937 (Barty Walton); "High, Wide and Handsome" 1937 (Boy); "Hittin' the Trail" 1937 (Billy Reed); "Tex Rides with the Boy Scouts" 1937 (Buzzy Willis).

Burchett, Kevin. TV: *Gunsmoke*—"Parson Comes to Town" 4-30-66 (Boy), "Mirage" 1-11-71 (Adam); *The High Chaparral*—"For the Love of Carlos" 4-4-69 (Ted); *Bonanza*—"Speak No Evil" 4-20-69 (Coley); *Death Valley Days*—"The Tenderfoot" 11-15-69 (Billy), "The Visitor" 12-27-69.

Burdell, Marion. Films: "Under the Tonto Rim" 1933 (Mabel Turner).

Burdick, Rose. Films: "Ten Scars Make a Man" 1924-serial.

Burgess, Betty. Films: "Adventures of the Masked Phantom" 1939 (Carol Davis).

Burgess, Dorothy (1907-8/20/61). Films: "In Old Arizona" 1929 (Tonia Maria); "Lasca of the Rio Grande" 1931 (Lasca); "Rusty Rides Alone" 1933 (Mona Quillan); "Lone Star Ranger" 1942 (Trixie).

Burgess, Helen (1918-4/7/37). Films: "The Plainsman" 1936 (Louisa Cody).

Burgos, Jose. Films: "The Valley of Gwangi" 1969 (Dwarf).

Burk, Jim. Films: "Pony Express" 1953; "The Big Country" 1958 (Cracker); "Geronimo" 1962 (Cavalryman); "The Hallelujah Trail" 1965 (Elks-Runner); "The Way West" 1967 (Cattleman); "Big Jake" 1971 (Trooper); "One More Train to Rob"

1971 (Skinner); "The Cowboys" 1972; "The Life and Times of Judge Roy Bean" 1972 (Bart Jackson); "Oklahoma Crude" 1973 (Moody); "Belle Starr" TVM-1980 (Fuller). ¶TV: *Tales of Wells Fargo*—"Two Cartridges" 9-16-57 (Billy Knapp); *Wagon Train*—"The Jessie Cowan Story" 1-8-58 (Ansel Deale), "The Greenhorn Story" 10-7-59; *Wanted—Dead or Alive*—"The Bounty" 9-20-58 (Sheriff Tatum), "Call Your Shot" 2-7-59, "Chain Gang" 12-12-59; *Trackdown*—"Gift Horse" 4-29-59 (Levi); *Stagecoach West*—Regular 1960-61 (Zeke Bonner); *Lancer*—"Lifeline" 5-19-70.

Burke, Billie (1885-5/14/70). Films: "Gloria's Romance" 1916-serial; "Sergeant Rutledge" 1960 (Mrs. Cordelia Fosgate).

Burke, Caroline (1913-12/5/64). Films: "The Mysterious Rider" 1942.

Burke, Delta (1956-). Films: "Where the Hell's That Gold?!!!" TVM-1988 (Germany) ¶TV: *The Chisholms*—Regular 1980 (Bonnie Sue Chisholm).

Burke, Eldon. Films: "Breakheart Pass" 1976 (Ferguson).

Burke, J. Frank (1867-1/23/18). Films: "The Bargain" 1914 (Sheriff Bud Walsh); "The Dawn Maker" 1916 (Walter McRae); "The Square Deal Man" 1917 (Colonel Ransome); "Hell's Hinges" 1919 (Zeb Taylor).

Burke, James (1886-5/28/68). Films: "To the Last Man" 1933 (Sheriff); "Call of the Wild" 1935 (Ole); "Ruggles of Red Gap" 1935 (Jeff Tuttle); "Rhythm on the Range" 1936 (Wabash); "High, Wide and Handsome" 1937 (Stackpole); "The Cisco Kid and the Lady" 1939 (Pop Saunders); "Dodge City" 1939 (Cattle Auctioneer); "Buck Benny Rides Again" 1940 (Taxi Driver); "Riding High" 1943 (Pete Brown); "California" 1946 (Pokey); "The Virginian" 1946 (Andy Jones); "The Timber Trail" 1948 (Jed Baker); "Copper Canyon" 1950 (Jeb Bassett); "The Last Outpost" 1951 (Gregory); "Raton Pass" 1951 (Hank); "Denver and Rio Grande" 1952 (Sheriff Masters); "Lone Star" 1952 (Luther Kilgore); "Arrowhead" 1953; "Alias Jesse James" 1959 (Charlie).

Burke, Joseph (1884-12/17/42). Films: "The Royal Rider" 1929 (King's Tutor).

Burke, Kathleen (1914-4/9/80). Films: "Sunset Pass" 1933 (Jane Preston); "Nevada" 1935 (Hettie Ide); "Rocky Mountain Mystery" 1935 (Flora).

Burke, Marie (1894-1988). Films: "The Gray Towers Mystery" 1919 (Mrs. Bigby).

Burke, Orrin (1872-1/14/46). Films: "The Phantom Rider" 1936-serial.

Burke, Patrick Sullivan. Films: "The Castaway Cowboy" 1974. ¶TV: *Bonanza*—"Abner Willoughby's Return" 12-21-69 (Stokes).

Burke, Paul (1926-). Films: "Wild and Wooly" TVM-1978 (Tobias Singleton). ¶TV: *The Lone Ranger*—"Showdown at Sand Creek" 5-26-55; *Tales of Wells Fargo*—"The Killer" 12-1-58 (Bud Crawford); *Hotel De Paree*—"Sundance and the Long Trek" 4-22-60 (Frisbee); *Black Saddle*—"End of the Line" 5-6-60 (Cole Castleberry); *Death Valley Days*—"Cap'n Pegleg" 5-17-60; *Wanted—Dead or Alive*—"The Trial" 9-21-60 (Daniel Trenner); *Wagon Train*—"Path of the Serpent" 2-8-61; *Great Adventure*—"The Special Courage of Captain Pratt" 2-14-64 (Capt. Richard Pratt).

Burke, Robert. Films: "Tombstone" 1993 (Frank McLaury).

Burke, Ron. Films: "Welcome to Hard Times" 1967 (Young Miner). TV: *Laredo*—"Lazyfoot, Where Are You?" 9-16-65; *The Virginian*—"Nora" 12-11-68 (Private Henry).

Burke, Tom (-3/25/41). Films: "Wells Fargo" 1937; "Union Pacific" 1939 (Laborer).

Burke, Walter (1909-8/4/84). Films: "How the West Was Won" 1962 (Gambler); "The Plainsman" 1966 (Abe Ireland); "Stranger on the Run" TVM-1967; "Support Your Local Sheriff" 1969 (Fred Johnson); "The Over-the-Hill Gang Rides Again" TVM-1970 (Stableman); "Support Your Local Gunfighter" 1971 (Morris). ¶TV: *Gunsmoke*—"Wind" 3-21-59 (Bystander), "Hinka Do" 1-30-60 (Herman Bleeker), "Coventry" 3-17-62 (Jed Hager), "Extradition" 12-7-63 & 12-14-63 (Willie), "Circus Trick" 2-6-64 (Elko), "Roots of Fear" 12-15-69 (George Acton); *Black Saddle*—"Client: Neal Adams" 5-9-59 (Tim), "Client: Brand" 5-16-59 (Tom), "The Freebooters" 10-2-59; *Tales of Wells Fargo*—"The Little Man" 5-18-59 (Marty); *Have Gun Will Travel*—"The Fifth Man" 5-30-59 (Mr. Abbott), "Shadow of a Man" 1-28-61; *Zane Grey Theater*—"Confession" 10-15-59 (Gus Henessy); *The Alaskans*—"The Blizzard" 10-18-59 (Jenks), "Kangaroo Court" 5-8-60 (Sid Queed), "The Devil Made Five" 6-19-60

(Jenks); *The Law of the Plainsman*— "The Gibbet" 11-26-59; *Man from Blackhawk*—"Death Is the Best Policy" 12-18-59 (Tyce), "The Harpoon Story" 5-6-60 (Tom Abbot); *Rawhide*—"Incident of the Deserter" 4-29-60; *Lawman*—"Samson the Great" 11-20-60 (Jimmy Fresco); *Klondike*—"Bathhouse Justice" 12-26-60 (Sam Bronson); *Two Faces West*—"The Drought" 1-9-61; *Bonanza*—"Bank Run" 1-28-61 (Tim O'Brien), "Destiny's Child" 1-30-66 (Jesse), "The Twenty-Sixth Grave" 10-31-72 (Campbell); *The Outlaws*—"Sam Bass" 5-4-61 (Murphy); *Wide Country*—"Good Old Uncle Walt" 12-13-62 (Mayhew); *Empire*—"Where the Hawk Is Wheeling" 1-29-63 (Micah); *Temple Houston*—"Toll the Bell Slowly" 10-17-63 (Potts); *Death Valley Days*—"The Law of the Round Tent" 4-11-64, "The Hero of Apache Pass" 1-14-67 (Gopher Green); *Branded*—"A Taste of Poison" 5-2-65 (Luke); *The Legend of Jesse James*—"A Burying for Rosey" 5-9-66 (Smiley Jaspers); *The Big Valley*—"The Iron Box" 11-28-66 (Young Billy), "The Disappearance" 11-6-67 (George Gates), "Fall of a Hero" 2-5-68 (T.J. Dyce), "Point and Counterpoint" 5-19-69 (Ned Stokely); *Laredo*—"A Question of Guilt" 3-10-67 (Jake Taggert); *Rango*—"You Can't Scalp a Bald Indian" 4-28-67 (Brooks); *Wild Wild West*—"The Night of the Cut Throats" 11-17-67 (John P. Cassidy); *The Guns of Will Sonnett*—"A Fool and His Money" 3-8-68, "The Trap" 10-4-68 (Gideon Stark), "The Straw Man" 11-8-68 (Ollie); *Daniel Boone*—"Benvenuto … Who?" 10-9-69; *The Virginian*—"The Gift" 3-18-70 (Billy Neal); *Nichols*—"The One Eyed Mule's Time Has Come" 11-23-71 (Hartford); *The Life and Times of Grizzly Adams*—3-15-78 (McGinty).

Burkhart, Monte (-8/76). Films: "Flaming Star" 1960 (Ben Ford); "Gun Fight" 1961 (Hannah). ¶TV: *Whispering Smith*—"Swift Justice" 9-11-61 (Nat Prine).

Burkley, Dennis. Films: "The Call of the Wild" TVM-1976 (Stoney); "Four Eyes and Six-Guns" TVM-1992 (Luke Doom). ¶TV: *The Texas Wheelers*—7-24-75 (Bud); *Young Maverick*—"Half-Past Noon" 1-30-80 (Julius Higgins); *Outlaws*—"Primer" 1-10-87.

Burlinson, Tom. Films: "The Man from Snowy River" 1982-Australia (Jim Craig).

Burnett, Carol (1936-). TV: *Calamity Jane*—11-12-63 (Calamity Jane).

Burnett, Don. TV: *Northwest Passage*—Regular 1958-59 (Ensign Langdon Towne); *Stagecoach West*— "The Remounts" 3-14-61 (Hutch); *Bonanza*—"The Horse Breaker" 11-26-61 (Gordie).

Burnette, Lester "Smiley" (1911-2/16/67). Films: "In Old Santa Fe" 1934 (Smiley Burnette); "Mystery Mountain" 1934-serial; "Melody Trail" 1935 (Frog Millhouse); "The Phantom Empire" 1935-serial (Oscar); "Sagebrush Troubador" 1935 (Frog Millhouse); "The Singing Vagabond" 1935 (Frog); "Tumbling Tumbleweeds" 1935 (Smiley); "The Border Patrolman" 1936 (Chuck Owens); "Comin' Round the Mountain" 1936 (Frog Millhouse); "Guns and Guitars" 1936 (Smiley Burnette); "Oh, Susanna!" 1936 (Frog Millhouse); "The Old Corral" 1936 (Frog Millhouse); "Red River Valley" 1936 (Frog Millhouse); "Ride, Ranger, Ride" 1936 (Frog Jones); "The Singing Cowboy" 1936 (Frog Millhouse); "The Big Show" 1937 (Frog Millhouse); "Boots and Saddles" 1937 (Frog Millhouse); "Git Along, Little Dogies" 1937 (Frog Millhouse); "Public Cowboy No. 1" 1937 (Frog Millhouse); "Rootin' Tootin' Rhythm" 1937 (Frog Millhouse/Black Jim); "Round-Up Time in Texas" 1937 (Frog Millhouse); "Springtime in the Rockies" 1937 (Frog Millhouse); "Yodelin' Kid from Pine Ridge" 1937 (Frog Millhouse); "Billy the Kid Returns" 1938 (Frog Millhouse); "Gold Mine in the Sky" 1938 (Frog Millhouse); "Man from Music Mountain" 1938 (Frog Millhouse); "The Old Barn Dancer" 1938 (Frog Millhouse); "Prairie Moon" 1938 (Smiley Burnette); "Rhythm of the Saddle" 1938 (Frog Millhouse); "Under Western Stars" 1938 (Frog Milhouse); "Western Jamboree" 1938 (Frog Millhouse); "Blue Montana Skies" 1939 (Frog Millhouse); "Colorado Sunset" 1939 (Frog Millhouse); "Home on the Prairie" 1939 (Smiley Burnette); "In Old Monterey" 1939 (Frog Millhouse); "Mexicali Rose" 1939 (Frog Millhouse); "Mountain Rhythm" 1939 (Frog Millhouse); "Rovin' Tumbleweeds" 1939 (Frog Millhouse); "South of the Border" 1939 (Frog Millhouse); "Carolina Moon" 1940 (Frog Millhouse); "Gaucho Serenade" 1940 (Frog Millhouse); "Rancho Grande" 1940 (Frog Millhouse); "Ride, Tenderfoot, Ride" 1940 (Frog Millhouse); "Back in the Saddle" 1941 (Frog Millhouse); "Down Mexico Way" 1941 (Frog Millhouse); "Ridin' on a Rainbow" 1941 (Frog Millhouse); "Sierra Sue"

1941 (Frog Millhouse); "The Singing Hill" 1941; "Sunset in Wyoming" 1941 (Frog Millhouse); "Under Fiesta Stars" 1941; "Bells of Capistrano" 1942 (Frog Millhouse); "Call of the Canyon" 1942 (Frog Millhouse); "Cowboy Serenade" 1942 (Frog Millhouse); "Heart of the Golden West" 1942 (Smiley); "Heart of the Rio Grande" 1942 (Frog Millhouse); "Home in Wyomin'" 1942 (Frog Millhouse); "Stardust on the Sage" 1942 (Frog Millhouse); "Beyond the Last Frontier" 1943 (Frog Milhouse); "Idaho" 1943 (Frog Millhouse); "King of the Cowboys" 1943 (Frog Millhouse); "Raiders of Sunset Pass" 1943 (Frog Millhouse); "Silver Spurs" 1943 (Frog Millhouse); "Beneath Western Skies" 1944 (Frog Millhouse); "Bordertown Trail" 1944; "Call of the Rockies" 1944; "Code of the Prairie" 1944 (Frog Millhouse); "Firebrands of Arizona" 1944 (Beefsteak Discoe/Frog Millhouse); "The Laramie Trail" 1944; "Pride of the Plains" 1944 (Fred Millhouse); "The Desert Horseman" 1946 (Smiley Butterbeam); "The Fighting Frontiersman" 1946; "Galloping Thunder" 1946; "Gunning for Vengeance" 1946; "Heading West" 1946; "Landrush" 1946 (Smiley Burnette); "Roaring Rangers" 1946; "Terror Trail" 1946; "Two-Fisted Ranger" 1946; "Last Days of Boot Hill" 1947 (Smiley Burnette); "Law of the Canyon" 1947; "The Lone Hand Texan" 1947 (Smiley); "My Pal Ringeye" 1947-short; "Prairie Raiders" 1947; "Riders of the Lone Star" 1947; "South of the Chisholm Trail" 1947; "The Stranger from Ponca City" 1947; "West of Dodge City" 1947; "Blazing Across the Pecos" 1948; "Buckaroo from Powder River" 1948 (Smiley Burnette); "Phantom Valley" 1948 (Smiley); "Quick on the Trigger" 1948 (Smiley); "Six-Gun Law" 1948 (Smiley Burnette); "Trail to Laredo" 1948; "West of Sonora" 1948 (Smiley Burnette); "Whirlwind Raiders" 1948 (Smiley Burnette); "The Blazing Trail" 1949 (Smiley); "Challenge of the Range" 1949 (Smiley Burnette); "Desert Vigilante" 1949 (Smiley); "El Dorado Pass" 1949 (Smiley Burnette); "Laramie" 1949 (Smiley Burnette); "Renegades of the Sage" 1949 (Smiley); "South of Death Valley" 1949 (Smiley); "Across the Badlands" 1950 (Smiley Burnette); "Frontier Outpost" 1950 (Smiley Burnette); "Horsemen of the Sierras" 1950 (Smiley Burnette); "Lightning Guns" 1950 (Smiley Burnette); "Outcast of Black Mesa" 1950 (Smiley); "Raiders of Tomahawk Creek" 1950

(Smiley); "Streets of Ghost Town" 1950 (Smiley); "Texas Dynamo" 1950 (Smiley Burnette); "Trail of the Rustlers" 1950; "Bandits of El Dorado" 1951 (Smiley Burnette); "Bonanza Town" 1951 (Smniley Burnette); "Cyclone Fury" 1951 (Smiley); "Fort Savage Raiders" 1951 (Smiley); "The Kid from Amarillo" 1951 (Smiley Burnette); "Pecos River" 1951 (Smiley); "Prairie Roundup" 1951 (Smiley Burnette); "Ridin' the Outlaw Trail" 1951 (Smiley); "Snake River Desperadoes" 1951 (Smiley Burnette); "Whirlwind" 1951 (Smiley); "The Hawk of Wild River" 1952 (Smiley Burnette); "Junction City" 1952 (Smiley Burnette); "The Kid from Broken Gun" 1952 (Smiley Burnette); "Laramie Mountains" 1952 (Smiley Burnette); "The Rough, Tough West" 1952 (Smiley); "Smoke Canyon" 1952 (Smiley Burnette); "Goldtown Ghost Raiders" 1953 (Smiley Burnette); "Last of the Pony Riders" 1953 (Smiley Burnette); "On Top of Old Smoky" 1953 (Smiley Burnette); "Pack Train" 1953 (Smiley Burnette); "Saginaw Trail" 1953 (Smiley); "Winning of the West" 1953 (Smiley).

Burney, Hal (1900-11/11/33). Films: "A Man's Land" 1932 (Jake).

Burnham, Beatrice. Films: "Ramona" 1916; "Jack and Jill" 1917 (Doria Cabrillo); "Cyclone Smith's Partner" 1919; "Bullet Proof" 1920 (Jackie Boone); "Hitchin's Posts" 1920 (Barbara Bereton) "Get Your Man" 1921 (Leonore De Marney); "The One-Man Trail" 1921; "Tracks" 1922 (Elicia); "Trooper O'Neil" 1922 (Marie); "Kindled Courage" 1923 (Betty Paxton); "Western Luck" 1924 (Betty Gray); "Riders of the Purple Sage" 1925 (Millie Erne).

Burnham, Frances. Films: "As the Sun Went Down" 1919 (Mabel Morton).

Burnham, Louise. Films: "Lahoma" 1920 (Lahoma Gledware).

Burnham, Terry. TV: *Wagon Train*—"The Ella Lindstrom Story" 2-4-59 (Margareta), "The Jess MacAbbee Story" 11-25-59 (Mary Belle), "The Patience Miller Story" 1-11-61 (Prudence), "The Melanie Craig Story" 2-17-64; *Tales of Wells Fargo*—"The Branding Iron" 2-23-59 (Josie).

Burns, Bart (1918-). Films: "There Was a Crooked Man" 1970; "Scott Free" TVM-1976. ¶TV: *Zane Grey Theater*—"Decision at Wilson's Creek" 5-17-57 (Lt. Hobson); *Man from Blackhawk*—"Execution Day" 3-4-60 (Kelly); *The Rebel*—"Lady of Quality" 6-5-60 (Packer); *Wanted—*

Dead or Alive—"Epitaph" 2-8-61 (Deputy Walt Sommers); *Gunsmoke*—"Shona" 2-9-63; *Laredo*—"The Land Grabbers" 12-9-65 (Burt Sparr), "One Too Many Voices" 11-18-66; *The Loner*—"A Little Stroll to the End of the Line" 1-15-66 (Chisholm); *Daniel Boone*—"The Homecoming" 4-9-70; *Kung Fu*—"The Passion of Chen Yi" 2-28-74 (Prison Guard).

Burns, Bob "Bazooka" (1890-2/2/56). Films: "The Phantom Empire" 1935-serial; "The Courageous Avenger" 1935; "The Singing Vagabond" 1935 (Buffalo); "Guns and Guitars" 1936 (Jenkins); "Rhythm on the Range" 1936 (Buck Burns); "Git Along, Little Dogies" 1937; "Hit the Saddle" 1937 (Rancher); "Public Cowboy No. 1" 1937; "Wells Fargo" 1937 (Hank York); "New Frontier" 1939 (Fiddler); "Rovin' Tumbleweeds" 1939; "Prairie Schooners" 1940 (Jim Gibbs); "Call of the Canyon" 1942; "Belle of the Yukon" 1944 (Sam Slade); "Saddle Pals" 1947; "Twilight on the Rio Grande" 1947.

Burns, Edmund J. (1892-4/2/80). Films: "Up or Down?" 1917 (Ranch Foreman); "Wild and Woolly" 1917; "Headin' South" 1918; "The Trail of the Hold-Up Man" 1919; "Fighting Pals" 1920; "Blazing the Way" 1920; "The Lone Ranger" 1920; "Outlawed" 1921 (Sophy Robbin); "The Showdown" 1921; "Blaze Away" 1922 (Bill Lang); "The Freshie" 1922 (Ranch Foreman); "Lights of the Desert" 1922 (Andrew Reed); "Forty-Horse Hawkins" 1924 (Sheriff); "Fightin' Odds" 1925 (Sheriff Lane); "The Knockout Kid" 1925 (Ranch Foreman); "O.U. West" 1925 (Luke Crawley); "Two-Fisted Jones" 1925 (Sheriff); "Forlorn River" 1926 (Ben Ide); "Law and Lawless" 1932; "Rainbow Trail" 1932 (Cowboy); "Rusty Rides Alone" 1933; "When a Man Rides Alone" 1933; "The Westerner" 1934 (Cowboy); "Outlaws of Stampede Pass" 1943.

Burns, Emma. Films: "The Fighting Stranger" 1921 (Mrs. Ayre).

Burns, Forest. Films: "Zorro Rides Again" 1937-serial (Raider #7); "The Lone Ranger" 1938-serial (Trooper); "The Lone Ranger Rides Again" 1939-serial (Posseman #7); "Two-Fisted Rangers" 1940 (Henchman); "King of the Texas Rangers" 1941-serial (Gate Guard); "Santa Fe Uprising" 1946; "Sioux City Sue" 1946; "Desperadoes of the West" 1950-serial (Tom); "The James Brothers of Missouri" 1950-serial; "Rio Grande Patrol" 1950.

Burns, Fred (1878-7/18/55). Films: "The Spirit of the Range" 1912; "During the Round-Up" 1913; "An Indian's Loyalty" 1913; "Polly at the Ranch" 1913; "Sierra Jim's Reformation" 1914; "Jordan Is a Hard Road" 1915; "The Martyrs of the Alamo" 1915 (Capt. Dickinson); "The Good Bad Man" 1916 (the Sheriff); "Ben Blair" 1916 (Tom Blair); "Mountain Blood" 1916; "The Fighting Trail" 1917-serial; "Sunlight's Last Raid" 1917 (Bill Warned); "Vengeance and the Woman" 1917-serial; "Ruth of the Rockies" 1920-serial; "Shadows of Conscience" 1921 (Sheriff Bowers); "Cyclone Jones" 1923 (Jack Thompson); "The Breed of the Border" 1924 (Deputy Leverie); "The Western Wallop" 1924 (Marshal Malloy); "The Demon Rider" 1925 (Jim Lane); "O.U. West" 1925 (Jazebel Crawley); "Triple Action" 1925 (Chief of Rangers); "The Haunted Range" 1926 (Charlie Titus); "The Outlaw Express" 1926 (Borax Jones); "The Unknown Cavalier" 1926 (Sheriff); "Wild to Go" 1926 (Simon Purdy); "Without Orders" 1926 (Uncle Jody Miller); "The Galloping Gobs" 1927 (Sheriff); "The Overland Stage" 1927 (Butterfield); "The California Mail" 1929 (John Harrison); "The Virginian" 1929 (Ranch Hand); "The Cheyenne Kid" 1930; "Fighting Thru" 1930 (Sheriff); "Headin' North" 1930 (U.S Marshal); "The Land of Missing Men" 1930; "Men Without Law" 1930 (Sheriff Jim); "Mountain Justice" 1930 (Sandy McTavish); "The Mounted Stranger" 1930 (Steve Gary); "Oklahoma Cyclone" 1930; "Parade of the West" 1930 (Copeland); "Shadow Ranch" 1930; "Arizona Terror" 1931 (Sheriff); "Border Law" 1931; "Branded" 1931 (2nd Sheriff); "Near the Trail's End" 1931; "Sunrise Trail" 1931 (Sheriff); "The Devil Horse" 1932-serial; "Flaming Guns" 1932 (Sheriff); "Freighters of Destiny" 1932 (Sheriff); "Heritage of the Desert" 1932; "The Last Frontier" 1932-serial; "Law and Lawless" 1932 (Blane); "One-Man Law" 1932; "Partners" 1932 (Sheriff); "Ride Him, Cowboy" 1932; "The Saddle Buster" 1932 (Dan Hurn); "Texas Tornado" 1932 (Sheriff); "The Dude Bandit" 1933 (Sheriff); "The Fourth Horseman" 1933; "Trailing North" 1933 (Jim Powers); "War on the Range" 1933; "Brand of Hate" 1934; "Honor of the Range" 1934; "The Prescott Kid" 1934; "The Red Rider" 1934-serial; "Wheels of Destiny" 1934; "Border Vengeance" 1935 (Sheriff); "Law of the 45's" 1935 (Sheriff); "Lawless Range"

1935; "Westward Ho" 1935; "The Fugitive Sheriff" 1936; "Oh, Susanna!" 1936; "Too Much Beef" 1936 (Judge); "Vigilantes Are Coming" 1936-serial (Rancher); "The California Mail" 1937 (Ferguson); "Gunsmoke Ranch" 1937; "The Law Commands" 1937; "North of the Rio Grande" 1937; "The Old Wyoming Trail" 1937; "Outlaws of the Prairie" 1937 (Hank); "Springtime in the Rockies" 1937 (Harris); "Trailing Trouble" 1937 (Sheriff Jake Jones); "The Trigger Trio" 1937; "Two-Fisted Sheriff" 1937 (Stagecoach Guard); "Billy the Kid Returns" 1938; "Call of the Rockies" 1938 (Murdock); "In Old Mexico" 1938; "The Lone Ranger" 1938-serial (Holt); "Overland Stage Raiders" 1938; "The Painted Desert" 1938 (Miner); "Pioneer Trail" 1938; "Prairie Moon" 1938; "Rio Grande" 1938 (Jackson); "Sunset Trail" 1938; "Under Western Stars" 1938; "The Arizona Kid" 1939 (Melton); "Colorado Sunset" 1939; "Days of Jesse James" 1939 (Sheriff); "Frontier Pony Express" 1939; "In Old Monterey" 1939; "The Lone Ranger Rides Again" 1939-serial (Long); "Rovin' Tumbleweeds" 1939; "Saga of Death Valley" 1939; "Southward Ho!" 1939; "The Thundering West" 1939 (Coach Driver); "Wall Street Cowboy" 1939; "Adventures of Red Ryder" 1940-serial (Jackson); "The Border Legion" 1940; "Colorado" 1940 (Sheriff Harkins); "Gaucho Serenade" 1940; "Ghost Valley Raiders" 1940; "Ride, Tenderfoot, Ride" 1940; "Texas Stagecoach" 1940; "Thundering Frontier" 1940 (Hank Loomis); "Young Bill Hickok" 1940; "Bad Man of Deadwood" 1941; "Down Mexico Way" 1941; "In Old Cheyenne" 1941; "Jesse James at Bay" 1941; "Nevada City" 1941; "Rawhide Rangers" 1941; "Ridin' the Cherokee Trail" 1941 (Wyatt); "Roaring Frontiers" 1941; "The Singing Hill" 1941; "Sunset in Wyoming" 1941; "Wyoming Wildcat" 1941; "Heart of the Golden West" 1942; "Man from Cheyenne" 1942; "Sons of the Pioneers" 1942 (Rancher); "Stardust on the Sage" 1942; "Sunset on the Desert" 1942 (Prentiss); "Sunset Serenade" 1942; "Raiders of Sunset Pass" 1943 (Deaf Cowhand); "Silver Spurs" 1943; "Marshal of Reno" 1944; "In Old Sacramento" 1946; "Rio Grande Raiders" 1946.

Burns, Harry (1885-7/9/48). Films: "God's Country and the Woman" 1937 (2nd Man at Boundary); "Northwest Mounted Police" 1940 (the Crow).

Burns, Mrs. Harry (Helen Lockwood) (-4/27/46). Films: "The Fighting Guide" 1922 (Mrs. Carmody).

Burns, Hazel. Films: "One Man Justice" 1937 (Bronco-Riding Cowgirl).

Burns, J.P. TV: *The Big Valley*—"Young Marauders" 10-6-65 (Minister), "The River Monarch" 4-6-66 (Anson Gregory), "The Velvet Trap" 11-7-66, "Wagonload of Dreams" 1-2-67, "Rimfire" 2-19-68 (Land Salesman), "Danger Road" 4-21-69.

Burns, Jim (-7/16/75). Films: "O.U. West" 1925 (Sep Crawley).

Burns, Marion (1907-12/22/93). Films: "Oklahoma Jim" 1931 (Betty Rankin); "The Golden West" 1932 (Helen Sheppard); "Dawn Rider" 1935 (Alice); "Paradise Canyon" 1935 (Linda Carter).

Burns, Michael (1947-). Films: "The Raiders" 1964 (Jimmy McElroy); "40 Guns to Apache Pass" 1967 (Doug); "Stranger on the Run" TVM-1967 (Matt Johnson); "Journey to Shiloh" 1968 (Eubie Bell); "Santee" 1973 (Jody). ¶TV: *Wrangler*—"The Affair with Browning's Woman" 8-25-60 (Clary Browning); *Wagon Train*—"The Allison Justis Story" 10-19-60 (Billy Justis), "The Jeremy Dow Story" 12-28-60 (Bruce Millikan), "The Odyssey of Flint McCullough" 2-15-61 (Homer), "The Mark Miner Story" 11-15-61 (Matthew Miner), "The Dr. Denker Story" 1-31-62 (Billy Latham), Regular 1963-65 (Barnaby West), "The Silver Lady" 4-25-65 (Morgan Earp); *Tales of Wells Fargo*—"Frightened Witness" 12-26-60 (Billy Matson); *The Tall Man*—"Ransom of a Town" 5-6-61 (Danny); *A Man Called Shenandoah*—"Incident at Dry Creek" 11-15-65; *The Virginian*—"Long Ride to Wind River" 1-19-66 (Noah MacIntosh), "The Challenge" 10-19-66 (Bobby Crayton), "Long Journey Home" 12-14-66 (Jim Boyer, Jr.), "Seth" 3-20-68 (Seth), "The Bugler" 11-19-69 (Toby Hamilton); *Bonanza*—"The Trouble with Jamie" 3-20-66 (Jamie), "Napoleon's Children" 4-16-67 (Donny); *The Legend of Jesse James*—"A Field of Wild Flowers" 4-25-66 (Billy Dawson); *The Big Valley*—"A Day of Terror" 12-12-66 (Lon), "Run of the Savage" 3-11-68 (Danny); *The Road West*—"Eleven Miles to Eden" 3-13-67 (Harry Jr.); *Dundee and the Culhane*—10-25-67 (Nugget Hughes); *Daniel Boone*—"The Spanish Horse" 11-23-67 (Cal Trevor); *Gunsmoke*—"Nowhere to Run" 1-15-68 (Dale Stonecipher), "The Hide Cutters" 9-30-68 (Arlie Joe), "The Thieves" 3-9-70 (Eric Tabray); *Cowboy in Africa*—"First to Capture" 1-29-68 (Dan Crose); *The Outcasts*—"The Bounty Children" 12-23-68 (Randy); *The Men from Shiloh*—"Tate, Ramrod" 2-24-71 (Will Benson).

Burns, Neal (1891-10/3/69). Films: "Gun Law" 1938.

Burns, Paul E. (1881-5/17/67). Films: "The Mollycoddle" 1920 (Samuel Levinski); "The Cisco Kid and the Lady" 1939 (Jake); "Jesse James" 1939 (Hank); "The Return of the Cisco Kid" 1939 (Hotel Clerk); "Shooting High" 1940 (Hank); "Belle Starr" 1941 (Sergeant); "Last of the Duanes" 1941 (Horseshoe Player); "Men of the Timberland" 1941; "Western Union" 1941; "Wild Bill Hickok Rides" 1942; "The Ox-Bow Incident" 1943 (Winder); "Barbary Coast Gent" 1944 (Tim Shea); "Along Came Jones" 1945 (Small Man); "Dakota" 1945 (Swede); "Royal Mounted Rides Again" 1945-serial (Bucket); "My Pal Trigger" 1946 (Walling); "Renegades" 1946 (Alkali Kid); "Saddle Pals" 1947; "Smoky River Serenade" 1947; "Unconquered" 1947 (Dan McCoy); "Adventures in Silverado" 1948; "Black Eagle" 1948 (Hank Daniels); "Madonna of the Desert" 1948 (Hank Davenport); "The Paleface" 1948 (Justice of the Peace); "Relentless" 1948 (Len Briggs); "Lust for Gold" 1949 (Bill Bates); "Frenchie" 1950 (Rednose); "Montana" 1950 (Tecumseh Burke); "Sunset in the West" 1950 (Blink Adams); "Hot Lead" 1951 (Duke); "Santa Fe" 1951 (Uncle Dick Wootton); "Silver City" 1951 (Paxton); "Vengeance Valley" 1951 (Dr. Irwin); "Warpath" 1951 (Bum); "Flaming Feather" 1952; "The Lusty Men" 1952 (Waite); "Son of Paleface" 1952 (Ebenezer Hawkins); "Three Hours to Kill" 1954 (Albert, the Drunk); "Lay That Rifle Down" 1955 (Mr. Gribble); "Fury at Gunsight Pass" 1956 (Squint); "Love Me Tender" 1956 (Jethro); "The Proud Ones" 1956 (Billy Smith, the Town Drunk); "Gunman's Walk" 1958 (Cook); "Once Upon a Horse" 1958 (Bruno de Gruen); "Face of a Fugitive" 1959 (Jake); "Guns of the Timberland" 1960 (Bill Burroughs); "Stage to Thunder Rock" 1964. ¶TV: *Fury*—"The Feud" 1-5-57 (Caleb Burns); *Colt .45*—"Small Man" 11-15-57 (Hawkins); *Stripe Playhouse*—"Ballad to Die By" 7-31-59; *Laramie*—"The Replacement" 3-27-62; *Wagon Train*—"The Grover Allen Story" 2-3-64 (Fred Elkins).

Burns, Robert "Bob" (1884-3/14/57). Films: "The Spirit of the Range" 1912; "The Captain of the Gray Horse Troop" 1917 (Cal Streeter); "The Counterfeit Trail" 1919; "Blind Chance" 1920; "Kaintuck's Ward" 1920; "A Sagebrush Gentleman" 1920; "When the Cougar Called" 1920; "A Woman's Wits" 1921; "Thorobred" 1922 (Ben Grey); "The Riding Fool" 1924; "Desperate Odds" 1925; "The Outlaw's Daughter" 1925 (Sheriff); "Reckless Courage" 1925 (the Law); "Where the Worst Begins" 1925; "The Cherokee Kid" 1927 (Sheriff); "Just Travelin'" 1927; "The Long Loop on the Pecos" 1927; "Skedaddle Gold" 1927 (Sheriff); "Two-Gun of the Tumbleweed" 1927; "The Apache Raider" 1928; "The Bronc Stomper" 1928 (Rodeo Manager); "Riding for Fame" 1928; "A Son of the Desert" 1928 (Steve Kinard); "Thunder Riders" 1928 (Sheriff); "The Dawn Trail" 1930 (Settler); "Border Law" 1931; "Hard Hombre" 1931; "The Boiling Point" 1932; "Law and Lawless" 1932; "South of Sante Fe" 1932; "Texas Gun Fighter" 1932; "Tombstone Canyon" 1932 (Sheriff); "Gun Law" 1933; "King of the Arena" 1933; "Sagebrush Trail" 1933 (Sheriff Parker); "When a Man Rides Alone" 1933 (Sheriff Ed Brady); "Brand of Hate" 1934; "Wheels of Destiny" 1934; "Circle of Death" 1935 (Storekeeper); "Fighting Pioneers" 1935; "Paradise Canyon" 1935; "Thunderbolt" 1935; "The Fugitive Sheriff" 1936; "The Lonely Trail" 1936 (Rancher); "Pinto Rustlers" 1936; "Song of the Gringo" 1936; "Treachery Rides the Range" 1936 (Nevins); "Galloping Dynamite" 1937 (Sheriff); "Ghost Town Gold" 1937; "Guns of the Pecos" 1937 (Bob Jordan); "Outlaws of the Prairie" 1937; "Prairie Thunder" 1937; "Ranger Courage" 1937; "The Trigger Trio" 1937; "Yodelin' Kid from Pine Ridge" 1937; "Border G-Man" 1938 (Sheriff Clemens); "Cattle Raiders" 1938; "Gun Law" 1938; "Knight of the Plains" 1938; "Land of Fighting Men" 1938 (Sheriff); "The Painted Desert" 1938 (Miner); "Western Trails" 1938 (Dad Mason); "Arizona Legion" 1939 (Tucson Jones); "Feud of the Range" 1939 (Dad Wilson); "Mountain Rhythm" 1939; "Timber Stampede" 1939 (Sheriff Lyman); "Trouble in Sundown" 1939; "Adventures of Red Ryder" 1940-Serial (Jones); "Bullet Code" 1940 (Sheriff Ware); "Molly Cures a Cowboy" 1940-short; "My Little Chickadee" 1940 (Barfly Dandy); "Pioneers of the West" 1940;

"Ride, Tenderfoot, Ride" 1940; "Three Men from Texas" 1940; "Triple Justice" 1940 (Patterson); "Back in the Saddle" 1941; "Prairie Pals" 1942 (Deputy); "Riding the Wind" 1942; "False Colors" 1943; "Saddles and Sagebrush" 1943; "Cheyenne Wildcat" 1944; "Firebrands of Arizona" 1944 (Stage Driver); "Lumberjack" 1944 (Justice); "Mojave Firebrand" 1944; "Mystery Man" 1944 (Tom Hanlon); "Outlaws of Santa Fe" 1944; "Rustlers of Devil's Canyon" 1947; "The Wild Frontier" 1947; "Redwood Forest Trail" 1950 (Wescott); "Twilight in the Sierras" 1950; "Rough Riders of Durango" 1951.

Burns, Ronnie (1935-). TV: *The Deputy*—"Lawman's Blood" 2-6-60 (Morgan Burch).

Burns, Timothy. TV: *Gunsmoke*—"The Thieves" 3-9-70 (Billy Clarke), "Murdoch" 2-8-71 (Braly).

Burns, Vinnie. Films: "A Western Governor's Humanity" 1915; "Wild Honey" 1918 (Trixianita).

Burr, Donald (1907-2/27/79). TV: *Annie Get Your Gun* 11-27-57 (Charles Davenport).

Burr, Eugene (1884-6/7/40). Films: "The Pretender" 1918 (Otheloe Actwell).

Burr, Lonnie. TV: *The Range Rider*—"The Holy Terror" 3-22-52; *The Roy Rogers Show*—"The Minister's Son" 3-23-52.

Burr, Raymond (1917-9/12/93). Films: "Code of the West" 1947 (Carter); "Station West" 1948 (Mark Bristow); "New Mexico" 1951 (Pvt. Anderson); "Horizons West" 1952 (Cord Hardin); "Passion" 1954 (Capt. Rodriguez); "Thunder Pass" 1954; "Count Three and Pray" 1955 (Yancey Huggins); "A Man Alone" 1955 (Stanley); "The Brass Legend" 1956 (Tris Hatten); "Great Day in the Morning" 1956 (Jumbo Means); "Secret of Treasure Mountain" 1956 (Cash Larsen). ¶TV: *20th Century Fox Hour*—"The Ox-Bow Incident" 11-2-55 (Maj. Tetley); *Centennial*—Regular 1978-79 (Herman Bockweiss).

Burrell, George (1849-4/20/33). Films: "Crimson Gold" 1923 (Jake Higgins).

Burrell, Jan (1930-). Films: "The Culpepper Cattle Company" 1972 (Mrs. Mockridge). ¶TV: *Have Gun Will Travel*—"The Gold Toad" 11-21-59; *The Outcasts*—"The Heady Wine" 12-2-68 (Carrie); *Bonanza*—"Rock-a-Bye, Hoss" 10-10-71 (Clara); *Gunsmoke*—"The Hanging of Newly O'Brien" 11-26-73 (Anna).

Burress, William (1867-10/30/48). Films: "The End of the Trail" 1916 (Father Le Jeune); "The Man from Bitter Roots" 1916 (Toy); "The Rainbow Trail" 1918 (Waggoner); "The Girl Who Ran Wild" 1922 (Johnny Cake).

Burroughs, Clark "Buddy" (1883-2/4/37). Films: "Branded" 1931 (Tex); "Cow Town" 1950 (Duke Kirby).

Burrows, Bob. Films: "Colt .45" 1950; "Cattle Queen of Montana" 1954; "Jubilee Trail" 1954 (Velasco Rider). ¶TV: *Gunsmoke*—"A Matter of Honor" 11-17-69 (Ranch Hand), "Stark" 9-28-70 (Charlie), "Jenny" 12-28-70 (Driver).

Burrud, Billy (1925-7/11/90). Films: "The Cowboy and the Kid" 1936 (Jimmy Thomas); "Fair Warning" 1937 (Malcolm Berkhardt).

Burson, Polly. Films: "Night Passage" 1957 (Rosa). ¶TV: *The High Chaparral*—"Follow Your Heart" 10-4-68 (Bess), "Tornado Frances" 10-11-68 (Woman #2).

Burson, Wayne. Films: "The Phantom Rider" 1946-serial (Deputy); "Ridin' Down the Trail" 1947; "Song of the Drifter" 1948; "Desperadoes of the West" 1950-serial; "Wild Horse Ambush" 1952; "Cattle Queen of Montana" 1954. ¶TV: *Bat Masterson*—"Bear Bait" 11-12-58 (U.S. Marshal).

Burstyn, Ellen (Ellen McRae) (1932-). Films: "Silence of the North" 1981 (Olive Fredrickson). ¶TV: *Cheyenne*—"Day's Pay" 10-30-61 (Emmy Mae); *Gunsmoke*—"Wagon Girls" 4-7-62 (Polly), "Waste" 9-27-71 & 10-4-71 (Amy Waters); *Laramie*—"No Place to Run" 2-5-63; *Iron Horse*—Regular 1966-67 (Julie Parsons).

Burstyn, Neil (-1978). TV: *Dundee and the Culhane*—9-13-67 (Raoul Montoya).

Burt, Benny (1900-5/27/80). Films: "Hawaiian Buckaroo" 1938 (Mike).

Burt, Charlene. Films: "Beyond the Rio Grande" 1930 (Betty Burke).

Burt, Frederick (1876-10/2/43). Films: "The Cisco Kid" 1931 (Sheriff Tex Ransom).

Burt, Nellie (-11/3/86). Films: "The Great Northfield, Minnesota Raid" 1972 (Doll Woman). ¶TV: *Wagon Train*—"The Heather Mahoney Story" 6-13-62 (Mother O'Hara), "The Michael Malone Story" 1-6-64 (Nora); *Wide Country*—"Journey Down a Dusty Road" 10-4-62 (Gram Perry); *Empire*—"End of an

Image" 1-15-63 (Margaret Rainey); *Gunsmoke*—"Panacea Sykes" 4-13-63 (Panacea Sykes); *Lancer*—"Welcome to Genesis" 11-18-69.

Burt, William P. (1873-2/23/55) Films: "Rogue of the Rio Grande" 1930 (Trango Dancer); "Trouble Busters" 1933 (Dan Allen).

Burtis, James P. (1893-7/24/39). Films: "Texas Bad Man" 1932 (Pat Reilly); "Desert Gold" 1935 (Sleeping Passenger); "Stormy" 1935 (Greasy); "Arizona Mahoney" 1936 (Terry); "The Arizona Raiders" 1936 (1st Sheriff); "Ghost Patrol" 1936 (Henry Brownlee); "Wells Fargo" 1937 (Portly Gent); "The Texans" 1938 (Swenson).

Burton, Bill. Films: "Ulzana's Raid" 1972; "Bite the Bullet" 1975; "Posse" 1975 (McCanless); "The Long Riders" 1980.

Burton, Charlotte (1882-3/28/42). Films: "Quicksands" 1913; "Woman's Honor" 1913; "Lone Star" 1916 (Helen Mattes).

Burton, Clarence (1882-12/2/33). Films: "Snap Judgment" 1917 (Steve Bradley); "Fame and Fortune" 1918 (Sheriff of Palo); "Last of the Duanes" 1919 (Bland); "Six Feet Four" 1919 (Cole Dalton); "The Crimson Challenge" 1922 (Black Bart); "Salome Jane" 1923 (Baldwin); "The Mine with the Iron Door" 1924 (Sheriff).

Burton, Frederick (1871-10/23/57). Films: "Arizona" 1918 (Col. Benham); "Ruggles of Red Gap" 1918 (Cousin Egbert Floud); "The Man She Brought Back" 1922 (Bruce Webster); "The Big Trail" 1930 (Pa Bascom); "Cisco Kid" 1931; "Freighters of Destiny" 1932 (John Macey); "Silver on the Sage" 1939 (Tom Hamilton); "Brigham Young—Frontiersman" 1940 (Mr. Webb); "Go West" 1940 (Johnson); "The Man from Dakota" 1940 (Campbellite Leader); "Silver Queen" 1942 (Dr. Hartley); "Hands Across the Border" 1943 (Col. Ames).

Burton, George (1900-12/8/75). Films: "Idaho" 1925-serial; "Wild West" 1925-serial; "The Painted Desert" 1931; "Rainbow Trail" 1932 (Elliott); "Smoke Lightning" 1933 (Jordan); "In Old Santa Fe" 1934 (Red); "Law Beyond the Range" 1935 (Tex); "The Miracle Rider" 1935-serial; "Ruggles of Red Gap" 1935 (Buck Squires); "Tumbling Tumbleweeds" 1935 (Sheriff); "The Mysterious Avenger" 1936 (Ranger); "Come on Cowboys" 1937; "Dodge City Trail" 1937 (Steve's Gang Member);

"Wells Fargo" 1937; "The Lone Ranger Rides Again" 1939-serial (Ed Powers); "Riders of Pasco Basin" 1940 (Rancher).

Burton, Hal. TV: *Bonanza*—"Top Hand" 1-17-71 (Smokey), "The Marriage of Theodora Duffy" 1-9-73 (Read), "The Hunter" 1-16-73 (Man).

Burton, John (1853-3/25/20). Films: "The World Apart" 1917 (Roland Holt); "M'Liss" 1918 (Parson Bean).

Burton, Julian. Films: "Man or Gun" 1958 (Billy Corley). ¶TV: *Tales of Wells Fargo*—"Frightened Witness" 12-26-60 (Shattuck); *Two Faces West*—"The Witness" 1-23-61; *Rawhide*—"The Child Woman" 3-23-62 (Herrick); *Here Come the Brides*—"Break the Bank of Tacoma" 1-16-70 (Big George).

Burton, Laurie. Films: "Tickle Me" 1965 (Janet). ¶TV: *Wild Wild West*—"The Night of the Running Death" 12-15-67 (Alice).

Burton, Lee (Guido Lollobrigida) (1929-). Films: "He Who Shoots First" 1966-Ital.; "Kill Johnny Ringo" 1966-Ital.; "One Hundred Thousand Dollars for Ringo" 1966-Ital./Span.; "Man: His Pride and His Vengeance" 1967-Ital./Ger. (Juan); "Cemetery Without Crosses" 1968-Ital./Fr.; "Get the Coffin Ready" 1968-Ital.; "A Long Ride from Hell" 1968-Ital. (Sheriff); "Vengeance" 1968-Ital./Ger.; "And God Said to Cain" 1969-Ital.; "Beast" 1970-Ital.; "Roy Colt and Winchester Jack" 1970-Ital.; "Red Sun" 1971-Fr./Ital./Span.; "Vendetta at Dawn" 1971-Ital.; "Brothers Blue" 1973-Ital./Fr.; "Those Dirty Dogs!" 1973-U.S./Ital./Span.; "Drummer of Vengeance" 1974-Brit./Ital.

Burton, Martin (1905-8/4/76). Films: "Caught" 1931 (Curly Braydon).

Burton, Norman (1923-). TV: *Gunsmoke*—"The Reward" 11-6-65 (Ed).

Burton, Robert (1895-9/29/62). Films: "The Little Buckaroo" 1928 (Sheriff Al Durking); "Sky Full of Moon" 1952 (Customer); "Broken Lance" 1954 (Mac Andrews); "The Siege at Red River" 1954 (Sheriff); "Taza, Son of Cochise" 1954 (Gen. Crook); "Count Three and Pray" 1955 (Bishop); "Lay That Rifle Down" 1955 (Professor); "The Road to Denver" 1955 (Kraft); "The Brass Legend" 1956 (Gipson); "Jubal" 1956 (Dr. Grant); "Reprisal!" 1956 (Jeb Cantrell); "Domino Kid" 1957 (Sher-

iff Travers); "The Hard Man" 1957 (Sim Hacker); "The Hired Gun" 1957 (Nathan Conroy); "The Tall T" 1957 (Tenvoorde); "Man or Gun" 1958 (Burt Burton); "Seven Ways from Sundown" 1960 (Eavens). ¶TV: *The Adventures of Rin Tin Tin*—"The Education of Corporal Rusty" 11-19-54 (Mr. Bailey), "Rin Tin Tin and the Printer's Devil" 4-15-55; *Frontier*—"The Ten Days of John Leslie" 1-22-56 (Sheriff); *Zane Grey Theater*—"A Quiet Sunda in San Ardo" 11-23-56 (Mayor); *The Lone Ranger*—"The Twisted Track" 11-29-56, "Christmas Story" 12-20-56, "Mission for Tonto" 5-2-57; *Broken Arrow*—"Legacy of a Hero" 2-26-57 (Peterson), "Rebellion" 3-5-57 (Peterson); *Tales of Wells Fargo*—"The Thin Rope" 3-18-57 (Doctor), "The Kinfolk" 9-26-60 (Amos); *Gunsmoke*—"What the Whiskey Drummer Heard" 4-27-57 (Sheriff Tom Smith); *Trackdown*—"The Weddding" 2-14-58 (Sheriff Jeb Dobbs); *The Californians*—"The Marshal" 3-11-58 (Harrigan), "Mutineers from Hell" 9-30-58 (Capt. Eben Stone), "Crimps' Meat" 1-27-59 (John Gaines); *Decision*—"The Virginian" 7-6-58 (Judge Henry); *The Texan*—"The Man with the Solid Gold Star" 10-6-58, "No Place to Stop" 4-27-59 (Noah Whipple); *Wanted—Dead or Alive*—"Call Your Shot" 2-7-59 (Gregg Fenton); *Wagon Train*—"The Cappy Darrin Story" 11-11-59; *Man from Blackhawk*—"A Matter of Conscience" 12-11-59 (Dr. Stockwell); *Fury*—"Trottin' Horse" 2-6-60 (Norden); *The Deputy*—"Spoken in Silence" 4-29-61 (Mike Rogers); *Maverick*—"Dade City Dodge" 9-18-61 (Judge Kincaid); *The Rifleman*—"The Princess" 1-8-62 (Doc Burrage); *Bonanza*—"The Beginning" 11-25-62 (Lewis).

Burton, Robert. Films: "Massacre at Fort Holman" 1972-Ital./Fr./Span./Ger. (Donald MacIvers); "The Daughters of Joshua Cabe Return" TVM-1975 (Claver).

Burton, Sam (1889-7/16/46). Films: "Cheyenne Wildcat" 1944.

Burton, Wendell (1947-). TV: *Kung Fu*—"A Praying Mantis Kills" 3-22-73 (Martin Crossman).

Busch, Mae (1891-4/19/46). Films: "The Lone Ranger" 1920; "Pardon My Nerve!" 1922 (Marie); "Frivolous Sal" 1925 (Sal); "Rider of Death Valley" 1932 (Tillie, the Dance Hall Girl); "Without Honor" 1932 (Mary Ryan).

Busey, Gary (1944-). Films: "Dirty Little Billy" 1972 (Basil

Crabtree); "The Magnificent Seven Ride" 1972 (Hank Allan); "Barbarosa" 1982 (Karl); "My Heroes Have Always Been Cowboys" 1991 (Clint Hornby). ¶TV: *The High Chaparral*—"The Badge" 12-18-70; *Bonanza*—"The Hidden Enemy" 11-28-72 (Henry Johnson); *Kung Fu*—"The Ancient Warrior" 5-3-73 (Josh); *The Texas Wheelers*—Regular 1974-75 (Truckie Wheeler); *Gunsmoke*—"The Busters" 3-10-75 (Harve Daley).

Bush, Anita (-2/16/74). Films: "The Crimson Skull" 1921.

Bush, Billy Green (1935-). Films: "Monte Walsh" 1970 (Powder Kent); "The Culpepper Cattle Company" 1972 (Frank Culpepper); "Mackintosh & T.J." 1975 (Luke); "The Call of the Wild" TVM-1976 (Redsweater); "The Invasion of Johnson County" TVM-1976 (Frank Canton); "Tom Horn" 1980 (Joe Belle); "Conagher" TVM-1991. ¶TV: *Bonanza*—"Long Way to Ogden" 2-22-70 (Spanier); *Alias Smith and Jones*—"The Legacy of Charlie O'Rourke" 4-22-71 (Charlie); *Gunsmoke*—"The Hanging of Newly O'Brien" 11-26-73 (Kermit); *Dirty Sally*—2-1-74 (Otis); *Barbary Coast*—"The Dawson Marker" 1-9-76 (Dawson); *The Oregon Trail*—"Hannah's Girls" 10-26-77 (Niles Sharpe).

Bush, Grand L. Films: "Outlaws" TVM-1986 (Luther). ¶TV: *Outlaws*—"Hymn" 1-31-87 (Ross).

Bush, James. Films: "Wild Horse Mesa" 1932 (Bent Weymer); "Battle of Greed" 1934 (Mark Twain); "The Arizonian" 1935 (Orin Tallant); "O'Malley of the Mounted" 1936 (Bud Hyland); "The Glory Trail" 1937 (David Kirby); "Outlaws of the Orient" 1937 (Johnny Eaton); "West of Cimarron" 1941; "Idaho" 1943; "King of the Cowboys" 1943 (Dave Mason); "The Man from Colorado" 1948 (Dickson); "Massacre River" 1949 (Eddie); "Saddle Legion" 1951 (Gabe); "Sundown Jim" 1942 (Ring Barr). ¶TV: *Wild Bill Hickok*—"Lost Indian Mine" 12-11-51.

Bush, Nora. Films: "Valley of Vengeance" 1944 (Ma Carson).

Bush, Owen (1921-). Films: "The Man Who Loved Cat Dancing" 1973 (Conductor). ¶TV: *Wanted—Dead or Alive*—"The Most Beautiful Woman" 1-23-60 (Hose); *Maverick*—"Bolt from the Blue" 11-27-60 (Benson January); *Bonanza*—"Bank Run" 1-28-61, "The Many Faces of Gideon Flinch" 11-5-61, "Alias Joe Cartwright" 1-26-64 (Dugan), "The Meredith Smith" 10-31-65 (Ira),

"Four Sisters from Boston" 10-30-66 (Billings), "The Twenty-Sixth Grave" 10-31-72 (Station Agent); *Shane*—Regular 1966 (Ben); *Iron Horse*—"A Dozen Ways to Kill a Man" 12-19-66 (Sam); *The Big Valley*—"The Disappearance" 11-6-67 (Dr. Riley); *The Guns of Will Sonnett*—"Message at Noon" 10-13-67, "The Warriors" 3-1-68, "Reunion" 9-27-68; *Gunsmoke*—"A Noose for Dobie Price" 3-4-68 (Jackson Narramore), "A Game of Death … An Act of Love" 11-5-73 & 11-12-73 (Bailiff); *Adventures of Brisco County, Jr.*—"Socrates' Sister" 9-24-93 (Farmer).

Bush, Pauline (1886-11/1/69). Films: "The Call of the Open Range" 1911; "Cattle, Gold and Oil" 1911; "The Poisoned Flame" 1911; "The Sheepman's Daughter" 1911; "The Sheriff's Sisters" 1911; "The Smoke of the Forty-Five" 1911; "The Stranger at Coyote" 1911; "The Trail of the Eucalyptus" 1911; "The Agitator" 1912; "A Bad Investment" 1912; "The Brand" 1912; "The Coward" 1912; "Driftwood" 1912; "The Eastern Girl" 1912; "For the Good of Her Men" 1912; "From the Four Hundred to the Herd" 1912; "God's Unfortunate" 1912; "The Intrusion of Compoc" 1912; "The Jealous Rage" 1912; "The Land Baron of San Tee" 1912; "The Land of Death" 1912; "Maiden and Men" 1912; "Nell of the Pampas" 1912; "The New Cowpuncher" 1912; "Objections Overruled" 1912; "The Outlaw Cowboy" 1912; "The Pensioner" 1912; "The Power of Love" 1912; "The Promise" 1912; "The Ranchman's Marathon" 1912; "Reformation of Sierra Smith" 1912; "The Relentless Law" 1912; "The Reward of Valor" 1912; "The Thief's Wife" 1912; "The Thread of Life" 1912; "Under False Pretenses" 1912; "Where Broadway Meets the Mountain" 1912; "The Angel of the Canyons" 1913; "Bloodhounds of the North" 1913; "An Eastern Flower" 1913; "The Mystery of Yellow Aster Mine" 1913; "Women Left Alone" 1913; "The Honor of the Mounted" 1914; "The Tragedy of Whispering Creek" 1914; "The Unlawful Trade" 1914; "The Desert Breed" 1915; "The Accusing Evidence" 1916.

Bushman, Francis X. (1883-8/23/66). Films: "At the End of the Trail" 1912; "Ambushed" 1914; "Their Compact" 1917 (James Van Dyke Moore); "God's Outlaw" 1919 (Andrew Craig); "Silver Queen" 1942 (Creditor); "Apache Country" 1952 (Cdr. Latham).

Bushman, Jr., Francis X. (Ralph

Bushman) (1903-4/16/78). Films: "The Scarlet Arrow" 1928-serial; "The Dude Wrangler" 1930 (Canby); "Way Out West" 1930 (Steve); "Cyclone Kid" 1931 (Steve Andrews); "Human Targets" 1932 (Bart Travis); "The Last Frontier" 1932-serial (Jeff Maillad); "Caryl of the Mountains" 1936 (Sergeant Brad Sheridan); "Let Freedom Ring" 1939 (Gagan's Henchman); "Honky Tonk" 1941 (Dealer).

Bushman, Lenore. Films: "Red River Range" 1938 (Evelyn Maxwell).

Bushman, Ralph. *see* Bushman, Jr., Francis X.

Buskirk, Mrs. Hattie (1867-1/12/42). Films: "The Huron Converts" 1915; "The Race War" 1915; "The Tenderfoot" 1917 (Mrs. Rucker); "Cavanaugh of the Forest Rangers" 1918 (Mrs. Redfield); "Fighting for Gold" 1919 (Lady Farquar).

Bussey, C.H. Films: "Forty-Five Calibre Echo" 1932; "The Man from New Mexico" 1932 (Bud).

Bussey, Fargo. Films: "Hell Fire Austin" 1932 (Henchman); "Ghost Patrol" 1936 (Bill); "Lucky Terror" 1936 (Skeeter).

Bussieres, Raymond (1907-4/29/82). Films: "Return of Halleluja" 1972-Ital./Ger.

Buster, John L. "Budd" (George Selk) (1891-12/22/65). Films: "Battle of Greed" 1934; "Terror of the Plains" 1934 (Townsman); "Between Men" 1935 (Virginia Townsman); "Circle of Death" 1935; "Cyclone Ranger" 1935 (Clem Rankin); "The Laramie Kid" 1935 (Henchman); "Lawless Borders" 1935; "Law of the 45's" 1935 (Station Agent); "North of Arizona" 1935 (Grey Wolf); "The Pecos Kid" 1935 (Deputy); "The Reckless Buckaroo" 1935; "Six Gun Justice" 1935; Texas Jack" 1935 (Chief Kickapoo); "The Texas Rambler" 1935; "The Vanishing Riders" 1935 (Hiram McDuff); "Western Frontier" 1935; "Western Racketeers" 1935; "Wild Mustang" 1935; "Wolf Riders" 1935; "Blazing Justice" 1936 (Ed Peterson); "Brand of the Outlaws" 1936; "Cavalcade of the West" 1936 (Stage Passenger/Indian); "Cavalry" 1936 (Jake, the Wagon Boss); "Custer's Last Stand" 1936-serial (Major Ware); "Desert Guns" 1936 (Carroll); "Desert Justice" 1936; "Gun Grit" 1936 (Henchman); "The Law Rides" 1936; "Riddle Ranch" 1936 (Antonio); "The Riding Avenger" 1936 (Bud); "Song of the Gringo" 1936; "Toll of the Desert" 1936; "Arizona Gunfighter" 1937; "Arizona Days" 1937

(Sheriff Ed Higginbotham); "Bar Z Bad Men" 1937 (Sheriff); "Border Phantom" 1937; "Doomed at Sundown" 1937; "Drums of Destiny" 1937 (Kentucky); "Fighting Texan" 1937 (Old Timer); "Galloping Dynamite" 1937 (Barber); "Gun Lords of Stirrup Basin" 1937 (Sheriff); "The Gun Ranger" 1937 (Carl Beeman); "Guns in the Dark" 1937; "Headin' for the Rio Grande" 1937 (Senator Black); "Hit the Saddle" 1937 (Drunk); "The Law Commands" 1937 (Kentuck); "A Lawman Is Born" 1937; "Left-Handed Law" 1937; "Old Louisiana" 1937 (Kentucky); "Raw Timber" 1937 (Kentuck); "Roaring Six Guns" 1937 (Wildcat); "Roll Along, Cowboy" 1937 (Shorty); "Sing, Cowboy, Sing" 1937 (Marshal Pinker); "The Trusted Outlaw" 1937 (Adler); "Trail of Vengeance" 1937 (Town Citizen); "Under Strange Flags" 1937 (Tequilla); "Wild Horse Round-Up" 1937 (Mopey); "Code of the Rangers" 1938 (Mine Agent); "Colorado Kid" 1938 (Ab Hendry); "Desert Patrol" 1938 (Hezi Watts); "Durango Valley Raiders" 1938; "The Feud Maker" 1938 (Cowlick Conners); "Heroes of the Alamo" 1938; "Knight of the Plains" 1938; "Man's Country" 1938; "Panamint's Bad Man" 1938; "Paroled to Die" 1938 (Spike Travers); "The Singing Outlaw" 1938; "Songs and Bullets" 1938 (Zeke); "The Stranger from Arizona" 1938 (Trickett); "Thunder in the Desert" 1938 (Oscar); "Where the West Begins" 1938 (Sheriff Judson); "Whirlwind Horseman" 1938 (Cherokee Jake); "Chip of the Flying U" 1939; "Colorado Sunset" 1939; "Feud of the Range" 1939 (Happy); "Fighting Renegade" 1939 (Old Dobie); "Frontier Scout" 1939 (Mr. Jones); "The Law Comes to Texas" 1939; "Lone Star Pioneers" 1939 (Crittenden); "The Oregon Trail" 1939-serial; "Straight Shooter" 1939 (Sheriff Long); "Wyoming Outlaw" 1939; "Zorro's Fighting Legion" 1939-serial (Juan); "Adventures of Red Ryder" 1940-serial (Johnson); "Billy the Kid Outlawed" 1940; "Covered Wagon Trails" 1940 (Manny); "The Dark Command" 1940; "King of the Royal Mounted" 1940-serial (Vinegar Smith); "Murder on the Yukon" 1940 (Jim Smithers); "Pinto Canyon" 1940 (Bill Kellar); "Rocky Mountain Rangers" 1940; "West of Pinto Basin" 1940 (Jones); "Billy the Kid Wanted" 1941 (Storekeeper); "Billy the Kid's Fighting Pals" 1941 (Mason); "Gangs of Sonora" 1941 (Jed Pickins); "Jesse James at Bay" 1941; "The Lone Rider in Frontier Fury" 1941; "The Lone

Rider in Ghost Town" 1941 (Moosehide); "Sierra Sue" 1941 (Greg Travis); "The Texas Marshal" 1941 (Henderson); "Thunder Over the Prairie" 1941 (Judge Merryweather); "Tonto Basin Outlaws" 1941 (Stage Driver); "West of Cimarron" 1941; "Billy the Kid Trapped" 1942 (Montana); "Billy the Kid's Smoking Guns" 1942; "Boot Hill Bandits" 1942 (Mayor); "The Cyclone Kid" 1942; "Deep in the Heart of Texas" 1942; "Down Rio Grande Way" 1942 (Kearney); "Heart of the Rio Grande" 1942; "Law and Order" 1942; "The Lone Star Vigilantes" 1942 (Col. Monroe); "Old Chisholm Trail" 1942 (Hank); "Outlaws of Boulder Pass" 1942; "Overland Stagecoach" 1942; "Rock River Renegades" 1942; "Sunset Serenade" 1942; "Texas to Bataan" 1942 (Ted); "Thunder River Feud" 1942 (Sheriff); "Valley of Hunted Men" 1942; "West of Tombstone" 1942 (Wheeler); "Westward Ho" 1942 (Coffee); "The Blocked Trail" 1943; "Bullets and Saddles" 1943; "Cattle Stampede" 1943 (Jensen); "Cheyenne Roundup" 1943 (Bonanza); "Cowboy Commandos" 1943 (Werner); "Daredevils of the West" 1943-serial (Jim Brady); "Fugitive of the Plains" 1943; "Hail to the Rangers" 1943; "The Haunted Ranch" 1943; "Raiders of San Joaquin" 1943 (Deputy); "Raiders of Sunset Pass" 1943 (Nevada Jones); "Santa Fe Scouts" 1943 (Wid Neighton); "Thundering Trails" 1943; "Wolves of the Range" 1943 (Foster); "Beneath Western Skies" 1944; "Brand of the Devil" 1944; "Dead or Alive" 1944; "Firebrands of Arizona" 1944 (Printer); "Frontier Outlaws" 1944 (Clerk); "Guns of the Law" 1944; "Hidden Valley Outlaws" 1944; "Oath of Vengeance" 1944; "Outlaw Roundup" 1944; "The Pinto Bandit" 1944; "Pride of the Plains" 1944; "Riders of the Santa Fe" 1944 (Otis Wade); "Saddle Leather Law" 1944; "Thundering Gun Slingers" 1944 (Sheriff); "Trail of Terror" 1944 (Monte); "Trigger Trail" 1944 (Tug Catlett); "Valley of Vengeance" 1944; "Wild Horse Phantom" 1944; "Along the Navajo Trail" 1945; "Border Badmen" 1945 (Evans); "Code of the Lawless" 1945 (Rufe); "Fighting Bill Carson" 1945; "Frontier Fugitives" 1945; "Lone Texas Ranger" 1945; "The Navajo Kid" 1945 (Pinky); "Salome, Where She Danced" 1945 (Desert Rat); "Springtime in Texas" 1945; "Texas Panhandle" 1945; "Ambush Trail" 1946 (Jim Ugley); "California Gold Rush" 1946; "Galloping Thunder" 1946; "Gentlemen with Guns" 1946 (Sheriff); "Home on the

Range" 1946 (Sheriff Cutler); "Outlaw of the Plains" 1946; "Prairie Badmen" 1946 (Don Lattimer); "Rustler's Roundup" 1946 (Gunsmith); "Sheriff of Redwood Valley" 1946; "Six Gun Man" 1946 (Joe Turner); "Song of the Sierras" 1946; "Terror Trail" 1946; "Terrors on Horseback" 1946 (Sheriff Bartlett); "West of Alamo" 1946 (Shotgun); "Cheyenne Takes Over" 1947 (Bostwick); "Rainbow Over the Rockies" 1947; "Shadow Valley" 1947 (Grimes); "Valley of Fear" 1947; "Vigilantes of Boomtown" 1947 (Goff); "The Wild Frontier" 1947 (Sam Wheeler); "Check Your Guns" 1948; "Loaded Pistols" 1948; "Quick on the Trigger" 1948; "Six-Gun Law" 1948 (Bank Clerk Duffy); "The Westward Trail" 1948 (Benson); "City of Badmen" 1953 (Old Timer); "City of Badmen" 1953 (Old Timer); "Riding Shotgun" 1954; "Gun Fever" 1958 (Farmer); "Guns of the Timberland" 1960 (Amos Stearnes). ¶TV: *The Gene Autry Show*—"Outlaw Warning" 10-2-54; *Sergeant Preston of the Yukon*—"Limping King" 9-13-56 (Tom Elders); *Gunsmoke*—Regular 1956-65 (Moss Grimmick); *A Man Called Shenandoah*—"Care of General Delivery" 5-9-66 (Pierson).

Butkus, Dick (1942-). Films: "Cipolla Colt" 1975-Ital./Ger.

Butler, Betty. Films: "Fighting Cowboy" 1933 (Duke's Girl); "Lightning Range" 1934 (Eastern Girl).

Butler, Charles E. Films: "Battling Buddy" 1924 (Sam White).

Butler, Cindy. Films: "Grayeagle" 1977 (Ida Colter).

Butler, David (1895-6/15/79). Films: "Nugget Nell" 1919 (Big-Hearted Jim); "The Sky Pilot" 1921 (Bill Hendricks); "The Gold Hunters" 1925 (Roderick Drew); "Tracked in the Snow Country" 1925 (Terry Moulton); "Girl in the Rain" 1927.

Butler, Dean (1956-). Films: "Little House on the Prairie: Look Back to Yesterday" TVM-1983 (Almanzo Wilder); "Little House: The Last Farewell" TVM-1984 (Almanzo Wilder); "Little House: Bless All the Dear Children" TVM-1984 (Almanzo Wilder). ¶TV: *Little House on the Prairie*—Regular 1979-82 (Almanzo Wilder); *Little House: A New Beginning*—Regular 1982-83 (Almanzo Wilder).

Butler, Frank (1890-6/10/67). Films: "Call of the Wild" 1923 (Hal); "The King of the Wild Horses" 1924; "The Fighting Buckaroo" 1926 (Percy M. Wellington).

Butler, Fred (1867-2/22/29). Films: "Red Blood and Blue" 1925 (Jim Lane).

Butler, Jimmy (1921-2/18/45). Films: "Battle of Greed" 1934 (Danny Storm); "When a Man's a Man" 1935 (Newsboy); "Wells Fargo" 1937 (Nick, Jr.).

Butler, John (1884-10/9/67). Films: "Frontier Marshal" 1939 (Harassed Man); "The Man from Dakota" 1940 (Voss); "Silent Conflict" 1948 (Clerk); "Sinister Journey" 1948; "Branded" 1951 (Spig). ¶TV: *The Lone Ranger*—"Gold Fever" 4-13-50, "Crime in Time" 10-19-50.

Butler, Lois. Films: "High Lonesome" 1950 (Meagan Davis).

Butler, Roy (1895-7/28/73). Films: "The Return of Daniel Boone" 1941; "Sierra Sue" 1941; "Home in Wyomin'" 1942; "Old Chisholm Trail" 1942 (Larry); "The Fighting Buckaroo" 1943 (Sheriff); "Frontier Law" 1943 (Sheriff); "Wagon Tracks West" 1943; "West of Texas" 1943 (Sheriff); "Gun Smoke" 1945; "Lonesome Trail" 1945; "Renegades of the Rio Grande" 1945 (Sheriff); "Saddle Serenade" 1945; "Springtime in Texas" 1945; "Gun Talk" 1947 (Bartender); "Land of the Lawless" 1947; "Trail Street" 1947 (Farmer); "Overland Trails" 1948; "Calamity Jane and Sam Bass" 1949; "Deputy Marshal" 1949 (Weed Toler); "Stallion Canyon" 1949 (Breezy, the Sheriff); "Bandit Queen" 1950 (Guard); "Fast on the Draw" 1950; "Indian Territory" 1950; "King of the Bullwhip" 1950; "Colorado Ambush" 1951; "Gene Autry and the Mounties" 1951; "Santa Fe" 1951; "Texans Never Cry" 1951 (Sheriff Weems); "Vengeance Valley" 1951 (Man); "The Black Lash" 1952 (Mayor); "The Frontier Phantom" 1952; "Night Raiders" 1952 (Merchant).

Butler, William J. (1860-1/27/27). Films: "The Honor of the Family" 1909; "The Last Drop of Water" 1911; "Fate's Interception" 1912; "In the Aisles of the Wild" 1912; "Man's Lust for Gold" 1912; "A Tale of the Wilderness" 1912; "The Gambler of the West" 1914 (Tom Grey).

Butrick, Merritt (1959-3/17/89). Films: "Stagecoach" TVM-1986 (Lieutenant Blanchard).

Butt, W. Lawson (1883-1/14/56). Films: "The Danger Trail" 1917 (Jean Croisset); "The Goddess of Lost Lake" 1918 (Mark Hamilton); "Sting of the Lash" 1921 (Rhodes).

Butterfield, Herb (1896-5/2/57). TV: *Frontier*—"Ferdinand Meyer's Army" 12-18-55.

Butterworth, Charles (1896-6/14/46). Films: "Let Freedom Ring" 1939 (the Mackerel).

Butterworth, Ernest (1876-4/22/50). Films: "Arizona" 1918; "Selfish Yates" 1918 (Hotfoot); "The Knickerbocker Buckaroo" 1919; "The Deadwood Coach" 1924; "The Desert's Price" 1925 (Phil).

Butterworth, Joe. Films: "North of Nevada" 1924 (Red O'Shay); "Born to the West" 1926 (Bate as a Child); "Arizona Bound" 1927 (Tommy Winslow).

Buttons, Red (1919-). Films: "Stagecoach" 1966 (Mr. Peacock). ¶TV: *Death Valley Days*—"The Million Dollar Pants" 4-19-60 (Levi Strauss); *Frontier Circus*—"Never Won Fair Lady" 4-12-62 (Earl Youngblood).

Buttram, Pat (1917-1/8/94). Films: "The Strawberry Roan" 1948 (Hank); "Riders in the Sky" 1949 (Chuckwalla Jones); "Beyond the Purple Hills" 1950 (Mike Rawley); "The Blazing Sun" 1950 (Mike); "Indian Territory" 1950 (Shadrach Jones); "Mule Train" 1950 (Smokey Argyle); "Gene Autry and the Mounties" 1951 (Scatt Russell); "Hills of Utah" 1951 (Dusty Cosgrove); "Silver Canyon" 1951 (Cougar Claggett); "Texans Never Cry" 1951 (Pecos Bates); "Valley of Fire" 1951 (Breezie Larrabee); "Apache Country" 1952 (Pat Buttram); "Barbed Wire" 1952 (Buckeye Buttram); "Blue Canadian Rockies" 1952 (Rawhide); "Night Stage to Galveston" 1952 (Pat); "The Old West" 1952 (Panhandle Gibbs); "Wagon Team" 1952 (Pat Buttram); "Evil Roy Slade" TVM-1972 (Narrator); "The Gatling Gun" 1972 (Tin Pot); "The Sacketts" TVM-1979 (Tuthill); "Back to the Future, Part III" 1990 (Saloon Old Timer). ¶TV: *The Gene Autry Show*—Regular 1950-55 (Pat Buttram); *Pistols 'n' Petticoats*—"A Crooked Line" 9-17-66 (Pa Turner), 2-11-67 (Jake Turner); *Wild Wild West*—"The Night of the Camera" 11-29-68 (Bosley Cranston); *Alias Smith and Jones*—"Bad Night in Big Butte" 3-2-72; *Father Murphy*—"John Michael Murphy, R.I.P." 12-7-82.

Butts, Billy. Films: "Lone Hand Saunders" 1926 (Buddy); "The Tough Guy" 1926 (Buddy Hardy); "The Two-Gun Man" 1926 (Billy Stickley); "The Land Beyond the Law" 1927 (Pat O'Hara); "The Last Outlaw" 1927 (Chick); "The Black Ace" 1928; "Taking a Chance" 1928 (Little Billy); "Wild West Romance" 1928; "The Lone Star Ranger" 1930 (Bud Jones); "Scarlet River" 1933 (Buck Blake).

Buy, Darryl. Films: "The Badge of Marshal Brennan" 1957 (George).

Buyeff, Lillian. TV: *Tate*—"The Return of Jessica Jackson" 9-14-60 (Mrs. Rubidoux); *Riverboat*—"The Two Faces of Grey Holden" 10-3-60 (Mrs. Tourette).

Buzzanca, Lando (1937-). Films: "For a Few Dollars Less" 1966-Ital. (Bill); "Ringo and Gringo Against All" 1966-Ital./Span.

Buzzi, Ruth (1936-). Films: "The Apple Dumpling Gang Rides Again" 1979 (Tough Kate); "The Villain" 1979 (Damsel in Distress). ¶TV: *Gun Shy*—4-12-83.

Byer, Charles. *see* Beyer, Charles.

Byington, Spring (1893-9/7/71). Films: "Arkansas Judge" 1941 (Mary Shoemaker); "The Vanishing Virginian" 1941 (Rosa Yancey); "The Devil's Doorway" 1950 (Mrs. Masters). ¶TV: *Laramie*—Regular 1961-63 (Daisy Cooper).

Byles, Bobby (1931-8/26/69). TV: *Death Valley Days*—"Lady of the Plains" 7-23-66 (Hampton Tilwell III), "Out of the Valley of Death" 5-25-68 (the Rev. Mr. Parker); *Bonanza*—"A Real Nice, Friendly Little Town" 11-27-66 (Skinny); *The Guns of Will Sonnett*—"Jim Sonnett's Lady" 2-21-69 (Telegrapher).

Byrd, Beau. Films: "Girl of the Timber Claims" 1917 (Cora Abbott).

Byrd, Ralph (1909-8/18/52). Films: "Border Caballero" 1936 (Tex Weaver); "A Tenderfoot Goes West" 1937 (Steve); "The Trigger Trio" 1937 (Larry Smith); "Mark of Zorro" 1940 (Student/Officer); "Northwest Mounted Police" 1940 (Constable Ackroyd); "The Vigilante" 1947-serial (Greg Sanders/the Vigilante); "Thunder in the Pines" 1948 (Boomer Benson); "The Redhead and the Cowboy" 1951 (Capt. Andrews).

Byrne, Gabriel. Films: "Buffalo Girls" TVM-1995 (Teddy Blue); "Dead Man" 1995 (Charlie Dickinson).

Byrnes, Edd (1933-). Films: "Yellowstone Kelly" 1959 (Anse Harper); "Any Gun Can Play" 1968-Ital./Span. (Clayton); "Payment in Blood" 1968-Ital. (Stuart); "Red Blood, Yellow Gold" 1968-Ital./Span. (Chattanooga Jim); "The Silent Gun" TVM-1969 (Joe Henning). ¶TV: *Cheyenne*—"The Brand" 4-9-57 (Clay Rafferty), "The Last Comanchero" 1-14-58 (Benji Danton); *Maverick*—"Ghost Riders" 10-13-57 (the Kid),

"Stage West" 10-27-57 (Wes Fallon), "Hadley's Hunters" 9-25-60 (Black-smith); *Colt .45*—"Golden Gun" 2-28-58 (Frank Wilson, Jr.); *Sugar-foot*—"Ring of Sand" 9-16-58 (Borden); *Lawman*—"The Deputy" 10-5-58 (Hawks Brother), "The Mad Bunch" 10-2-60 (Joe Knox); *The Men from Shiloh*—"The Animal" 1-20-71 (Alex Newell); *Alias Smith and Jones*—"The Ten Days That Shook Kid Curry" 11-4-72 (Willard Riley).

Byrnes, Maureen (1944-). Films: "Goin' South" 1978 (Mrs. Warren).

Byron, A.S. (1877-2/6/64). Films: "The Arizona Wildcat" 1939 (Miner); "The Return of Frank James" 1940 (Engineer).

Byron, Carol. TV: *Wagon Train*—"The Jess MacAbbee Story" 11-25-59 (Lilly Belle); *Rawhide*—"Incident of the Woman Trap" 1-26-62 (Maggie); *Wide Country*—"The Girl from Nob Hill" 3-8-63 (Jane); *Gunsmoke*—"Lover Boy" 10-5-63 (Terry); *Temple Houston*—"The Law and Big Annie" 1-16-64 (Marian Carter), "A Slight Case of Larceny" 2-13-64 (Marian Carter); *The Virginian*—"We've Lost a Train" 4-21-65.

Byron, Jack. Films: "Taking a Chance" 1928 (Pete); "Under the Tonto Rim" 1928 (Middleton); "The Santa Fe Trail" 1930 (Webber); "Clearing the Range" 1931 (Tom Vache); "Hard Hombre" 1931; "The Devil Horse" 1932-serial; "Gold" 1932; "The Outcasts of Poker Flat" 1952 (Miner).

Byron, Jean (1925-). Films: "Johnny Concho" 1956 (Pearl Lang). ¶TV: *The Adventures of Rin Tin Tin*—"The Poor Little Rich Boy" 10-7-55 (Irene Larrimore); *Fury*—"The Choice" 2-4-56 (Cynthia Landon); *My Friend Flicka*—"Big Red" 6-22-56 (Barbara Schuyler); *Cheyenne*—"The Broken Pledge" 6-4-57 (Fay Kirby), "Blind Spot 9-21-59 (Ruth), "Road to Three Graves" 10-31-60 (Alice Norris), "The Idol" 1-29-62 (Deborah Morse); *Jefferson Drum*—"A Very Deadly Game" 5-30-58 (Angela); *Laramie*—"Fall into Darkness" 4-17-62 (Norma Frances), "Bad Blood" 12-4-62 (Annie Whitaker).

Byron, John. Films: "Fighting Jack" 1926 (Jose Cortez); "The Gay Caballero" 1940 (Bandit).

Byron, Keith. TV: *Death Valley Days*—"Birth of a Boom" 2-3-58 (Tasker Oddie); *Lawman*—"The Huntress" 5-3-59.

Byron, Marion (1912-7/5/85). "The Bad Man" 1930 (Angela

Hardy); "Song of the West" 1930 (Penny); "Breed of the Border" 1933 (Sonia Bedford).

Byron, Melinda. TV: *The Lone Ranger*—"Journey to San Carlos" 5-9-57; *The Adventures of Rin Tin Tin*—"The General's Daughter" 9-19-58 (April Lawrence).

Byron, Nina. Films: "Truthful Tulliver" 1917 (Daisy Burton); "Johnny, Get Your Gun" 1919 (Janet Burnham).

Byron, Walter (1899-3/2/72). Films: "Crashing Thru" 1939 (Mc-Clusky); "Death Goes North" 1939 (Albert Norton); "Frontier Scout" 1939 (Adams).

Caan, James (1939-). Films: "The Glory Guys" 1965 (Dugan); "El Dorado" 1967 (Alan Bourdillon "Mississippi" Traherne); "Journey to Shiloh" 1968 (Buck Burnett); "Another Man, Another Chance" 1977-Fr. (David Williams); "Comes a Horseman" 1978 (Frank). ¶TV: *Wide Country*—"A Cry from the Mountain" 1-17-63 (Buddie Simpson); *Death Valley Days*—"Shadow of Violence" 5-5-63 (Bob), "Deadly Decision" 10-13-63 (Jim McKinney); *Wagon Train*—"The Echo Pass Story" 1-3-65 (Paul).

Cabal, Robert. Films: "The Man Behind the Gun" 1952 (Joaquin Murietta). ¶TV: *The Cisco Kid*—"Face of Death" 2-16-52, "Lost City of the Incas" 3-29-52; *Annie Oakley*—"Annie and the First Phone" 7-22-56 (Red Pony), "Indian Justice" 7-29-56 (Red Pony); *Sergeant Preston of the Yukon*—"Pack Ice Justice" 9-27-56 (Waboo), "King of Herschel Island" 10-25-56 (Tukalik); *Broken Arrow*—"Doctor" 2-12-57; *The Californians*—"Skeleton in the Closet" 4-8-58 (Pico); *Wyatt Earp*—"Apache Gold" 3-7-61 (Nulah); *Stagecoach West*—"The Orphans" 5-30-61 (Jaime Toreno); *Rawhide*—Regular 1962-65 (Hey Soos); *The Big Valley*—"Winner Lose All" 10-27-65 (Luis).

Cabanne, W. Christy (1880-10/15/50). Films: "Black Sheep" 1912; "Goddess of Sagebrush Gulch" 1912; "Heredity" 1912; "Under Burning Skies" 1912; "A Misunderstood Boy" 1913; "The Yaqui Cur" 1913.

Cabot, Bruce (1904-5/3/72). Films: "Scarlet River" 1933 (Himself); "The Last of the Mohicans" 1936 (Magua); "Robin Hood of El Dorado" 1936 (Bill Warren); "The Bad Man of Brimstone" 1938 (Blackjack McCreedy); "Dodge City" 1939 (Jeff Surrett); "Pierre of the Plains" 1942 (Jap Durkin), "Silver Queen" 1942 (Gerald Forsythe); "Wild Bill

Hickok Rides" 1942 (Wild Bill Hickok); "Smoky" 1946 (Frank); "Angel and the Badman" 1947 (Laredo Stevens); "The Gunfighters" 1947 (Bard Macky); "The Gallant Legion" 1948 (Beau Laroux); "Fancy Pants" 1950 (Cart Belknap); "Rock Island Trail" 1950 (Kirby Morrow); "Best of the Badmen" 1951 (Cole Younger); "Lost in Alaska" 1952 (Jake Stillman); "The Sheriff of Fractured Jaw" 1958-Brit. (Jack); "The Comancheros" 1961 (Maj. Henry); "McClintock" 1963 (Ben Sage); "Law of the Lawless" 1964 (Joe Rile); "Black Spurs" 1965 (Henderson); "Cat Ballou" 1965 (Sheriff Maledon); "Town Tamer" 1965 (Riley Condor); "The War Wagon" 1967 (Frank Pierce); "The Undefeated" 1969 (Jeff Newby); "Chisum" 1970 (Sheriff Brady); "Big Jake" 1971 (Sam Sharpnose). ¶TV: *The Slowest Gun in the West* 7-29-63 (Nick Nolan); *Bob Hope Chrysler Theatre*—"Have Girls—Will Travel" 10-16-64 (Sheriff); *Bonanza*—"A Dime's Worth of Glory" 11-1-64 (Sheriff Reed Laramore); *Daniel Boone*—"The Devil's Four" 3-4-65 (Simon Bullard).

Cabot, Ceil. TV: *The Guns of Will Sonnett*—"The Secret of Hangtown Mine" 12-22-67 (Dressmaker); *Here Come the Brides*—"A Man's Errand" 3-19-69; *Daniel Boone*—"Readin', Ritin', and Revolt" 3-12-70.

Cabot, Sebastian (1918-8/23/77). Films: "Westward Ho the Wagons" 1956 (Bissonette); "Black Patch" 1957 (Frenchy De Vere); "Dragoon Wells Massacre" 1957 (Jonah); "Terror in a Texas Town" 1958 (Ed McNeil). ¶TV: *Gunsmoke*—"The Queue" 12-3-55 (Ed Bailey), "The Photographer" 4-6-57 (Prof. Jacoby); *Cheyenne*—"Border Affair" 11-5-57 (General Dubeauchaie); *Zorro*—"A Fair Trial" 12-5-57 (Judge Vasca); *Hotel De Paree*—"A Fool and His Gold" 11-13-59; *Bonanza*—"The Spanish Grant" 2-6-60 (Don Antonio Luga); *Pony Express*—"The Story of Julesburg" 3-9-60 (Jules Renni).

Cabot, Susan (1927-12/10/86). Films: "Tomahawk" 1951 (Monahseetah); "The Battle at Apache Pass" 1952 (Nono); "The Duel at Silver Creek" 1952 (Dusty Fargo); "Gunsmoke" 1953 (Rita Saxon); "Ride Clear of Diablo" 1953 (Laurie); "Fort Massacre" 1958 (Piute Girl). ¶TV: *Have Gun Will Travel*—"The High Graders" 1-18-58 (Angela De Marco), "Commanche" 5-16-59 (Becky Carver).

Cadiente, David. Films: "The Professionals" 1966. ¶TV: *Daniel*

Boone—"Tekawitha McLeod" 10-1-64 (Talequah).

Cady, Frank (1915-). Films: "Way Out West" 1937 (Man in Audience); "The Indian Fighter" 1955 (Trader Joe); "The Tin Star" 1957 (Abe Pickett); "The Missouri Traveler" 1958 (Willie Poole); "Zandy's Bride" 1974 (Pa Allan); "Hearts of the West" 1975 (Pa Tater). ¶TV: *Broken Arrow*—"Devil's Eye" 11-12-57 (Parker); *Maverick*—"Rope of Cards" 1-19-58 (Hamelin); *Wagon Train*—"The Bill Tawnee Story" 2-12-58 (George Barry), "The Lily Legend Story" 2-13-63 (Fitch), "The Sam Spicer Story" 10-28-63 (Hiram); *Trackdown*—"The Wedding" 2-14-58 (Bob Tail); *The Alaskans*—"The Last Bullet" 3-27-60 (Bradshaw); *Klondike*—"Swoger's Mules" 11-21-60 (Lester); *Rawhide*—"Incident of the Big Blowout" 2-10-61; *The Virginian*—"The Exiles" 1-9-63 (Harding); *Gunsmoke*—"Aunt Thede" 12-19-64 (Webb Norton).

Caesar, Harry (1928-). Films: "Barbarosa" 1982 (Sims).

Caffarel, Jose. Films: "The Bang Bang Kid" 1968-U.S./Span./Ital. (Mayor Skaggel).

Cagney, James (1899-3/30/86). Films: "The Oklahoma Kid" 1939 (Jim Kincaid), "Run for Cover" 1955 (Mat Dow); "Tribute to a Badman" 1956 (Jeremy Rudock).

Cagney, Jeanne (1919-12/7/84). Films: "Kentucky Rifle" 1956; "Town Tamer" 1965 (Mary). ¶TV: *Wild Bill Hickok*—"Trapper's Story" 3-18-52.

Cahill, Barry (1921-). Films: "Hang 'Em High" 1968. ¶TV: *Have Gun Will Travel*—"The Outlaw" 9-21-57, "The Bride" 10-19-57 (Guard), "The Yuma Treasure" 12-14-57, "A Sense of Justice" 11-1-58, "The Night the Town Died" 2-6-60 (Aaron Bell), "The Princess and the Gunfighter" 1-21-61 (Cosnik), "The Hanging of Aaron Gibbs" 11-4-61 (Perrell); *Bonanza*—"House Divided" 1-16-60, "Crucible" 4-8-62 (Jim Gann); *Gunsmoke*—"Minnie" 4-15-61 (Pete), "Jenny" 10-13-62 (Chuck), "Shadler" 1-15-73 (Walters); *Tales of Wells Fargo*—"Lady Trouble" 4-24-61 (Stu Redmond); *Laramie*—"Bad Blood" 12-4-62; *The Legend of Jesse James*—"Dark Side of the Moon" 4-18-66 (Henry Shepard); *Here Come the Brides*—"Here Come the Brides" 9-25-68, "And Jason Makes Five" 10-9-68 (McGee); *Nichols*—"Zachariah" 1-11-72 (Logan); *Alias Smith and Jones*—"Witness to a Lynching" 12-16-72 (Marshal Guthrie); *Bret Maverick*—"Dateline: Sweetwater" 1-12-82 (Moran).

Cahill, Drew. Films: "Canadian Mounties vs. Atomic Invaders" 1953-serial (Mills).

Caillou, Alan (1914-). Films: "The Rare Breed" 1966 (Taylor). ¶TV: *Maverick*—"Passage to Fort Doom" 3-8-59 (Fergus MacKenzie); *The Californians*—"A Hundred Barrels" 4-21-59 (Captain); *Sugarfoot*—"MacBrewster the Bold" 10-13-59 (Wee Rabbie MacBrewster); *Have Gun Will Travel*—"Fragile" 10-31-59 (Roy Cooney); *Bronco*—"Death of an Outlaw" 3-8-60 (John Tunstall); *Cheyenne*—"Duel at Judas Basin" 1-30-61 (Ian Stewart); *Bonanza*—"The War Comes to Washoe" 11-4-62 (Craigsmuir), "The Big Jackpot" 1-18-70 (Hare); *Death Valley Days*—"The Debt" 2-20-63 (Remy Nadeau); *Daniel Boone*—"Fort West Point" 3-23-67, "They Who Will They Hang from the Yardarm if Willy Gets Away?" (Sergeant McIntosh) 2-8-68, "The Printing Press" 10-23-69 (Sergeant Ridley), "Perilous Passage" 1-15-70; *The High Chaparral*—"The Forge of Hate" 11-13-70 (Hanrahan).

Cain, Ace. Films: "The Cyclone Ranger" 1935 (Outlaw); "Danger Trails" 1935 (Dad Pan); "The Irish Gringo" 1935; "The Law of the 45's" 1935; "Rio Rattler" 1935 (Sam); "Six Gun Justice" 1935; "The Texas Rambler" 1935; "The Vanishing Riders" 1935 (Kaintuck); "Toll of the Desert" 1936.

Cain, Guy. TV: *Rawhide*—"The Blue Sky" 12-8-61, "Twenty-Five Santa Clauses" 12-22-61 (McOann), "The Reunion" 4-6-62 (Sergeant Manning), "The Devil and the Deep Blue" 5-11-62.

Cain, Robert (1887-4/27/54). Films: "In Mizzoura" 1919 (Robert Travers); "Shod with Fire" 1920 (Ned Lytton).

Caine, Georgia (1876-4/4/64). Films: "Dodge City" 1939 (Mrs. Irving); "Santa Fe Trail" 1940 (Officer's Wife); "Ridin' on a Rainbow" 1941 (Maria Bartlett).

Caine, Howard (1928-12/28/93). Films: "Alvarez Kelly" 1966 (McIntyre). ¶TV: *Lawman*—"War path" 2-8-59 (Newt Whitaker); *Gunsmoke*—"Big Tom" 1-9-60 (Brady); *Two Faces West*—"The Vials" 5-29-61; *The Travels of Jaimie McPheeters*—"The Day of the Pawnees" 12-22-63 & 12-29-63 (Afraid-of-His-Horse); *Rawhide*—"Corporal Dasovik" 12-4-64 (Mumford); *Rango*—"Gunfight at the K.O. Saloon" 2-3-67 (Gaylor Ashton); *The Outcasts*—"Gideon" 2-24-69 (Sam Barnes); *The High Chaparral*—"Friends and Partners" 1-16-70 (Sanchez); *Bret Maverick*—"The Ballad of Bret Maverick" 2-16-82 (Tertius Openshaw).

Cairns, Sally (1920-2/9/65). Films: "Covered Wagon Trails" 1940 (Carol Bradford); "King of the Stallions" 1942.

Caits, Joe (1889-3/9/57). Films: "Hollywood Cowboy" 1937 (G. Gadsby Holmes); "Bullets and Ballads" 1940.

Calamie, Gloria. TV: *Wild Wild West*—"The Night of the Juggernaut" 10-11-68 (Lonnie Millard).

Calbert, Vera. Films: "Crashing Broadway" 1933 (Mrs. Pinkham).

Calder, King (1900-6/28/64). TV: *Have Gun Will Travel*—"The Prize Fight Story" 4-5-58 (Sheriff), "First, Catch a Tiger" 9-12-59 (Drogan); *Tales of Wells Fargo*—"A Matter of Honor" 11-3-58 (Fenton Hurley), "Threat of Death" 4-25-60 (Holly Crail); *Bronco*—"The Baron of Broken Lance" 1-13-59 (Matt Ryker); *Wanted—Dead or Alive*—"Competition" 1-31-59; *Trackdown*—"Back to Crawford" 9-9-59 (Sherif Jed); *Man from Blackhawk*—"Logan's Policy" 10-9-59 (Tom Roman); *Bat Masterson*—"The Pied Piper of Dodge City" 1-7-60 (Mayor Webber), "Farmer with a Badge" 5-18-61 (Dinny Cave); *Tate*—"Stopover" 6-15-60 (Ben Tracy); *Lawman*—"Fast Trip to Cheyenne" 6-19-60 (Frank Saunders), "The Squatters" 1-29-61 (Ad Prentice), "The Prodigal Mother" 12-17-61 (Dave McCallan); *Johnny Ringo*—"Killer, Choose a Card" 6-9-60 (Jim Miller); *Rawhide*—"Incident on the Road to Yesterday" 11-18-60 (John Slocum), "Incident at the Trail's End" 1-11-63 (Doctor); *The Rifleman*—"Assault" 3-21-61 (King Croxton); *Zane Grey Theater*—"Man from Everywhere" 4-13-61 (Sheriff Jed Morgan); *Stagecoach West*—"The Dead Don't Cry" 5-2-61 (Marshal); *The Deputy*—"The Legend of Dixie" 5-20-61 (Hoak); *The Virginian*—"The Money Cage" 3-6-63.

Caldwell, Betty. Films: "Fangs of Destiny" 1927 (Rose Shelby); "Prince of the Plains" 1927; "Wanderer of the West" 1927; "The Drifting Kid" 1928; "The Girl-Shy Cowboy" 1928 (Gladys Ward); "Greased Lightning" 1928 (Diana Standish).

Caldwell, Virginia. Films: "The U.P. Trail" 1920 (Ruby Cortez).

Calhern, Louis (1895-5/12/56). Films: "The Arizonian" 1935 (Jake Mannen); "Annie Get Your Gun"

1950 (Buffalo Bill); "The Devil's Doorway" 1950 (Verne Coolan).

Calhoun, Alice (1904-6/3/66). Films: "Pioneer Trails" 1923 (Rose Miller); "Code of the Wilderness" 1924 (Ruth Harkness); "The Everlasting Whisper" 1925; "The Power of the Weak" 1926 (Myra); "Bride of the Desert" 1929 (Joanna Benton).

Calhoun, Cathleen. Films: "Calibre 45" 1924; "Western Feuds" 1924 (Bonita); "Don Dare Devil" 1925 (Ynez Remado); "Under Fire" 1926.

Calhoun, Jean. Films: "The Feud" 1919 (Ray Saunders); "Two Kinds of Women" 1922 (Marcia Langworthy).

Calhoun, Rory (1922-). Films: "Massacre River" 1949 (Phil Acton); "Return of the Frontiersman" 1950 (Larrabee); "Rogue River" 1950 (Ownie Rogers); "Ticket to Tomahawk" 1950 (Dakota); "Way of a Gaucho" 1952 (Martin); "Powder River" 1953 (Chino Bullock); "The Silver Whip" 1953 (Sheriff Tom Davisson); "A Bullet Is Waiting" 1954 (Ed Stone); "Dawn at Socorro" 1954 (Brett Wade); "Four Guns to the Border" 1954 (Ray Cully); "River of No Return" 1954 (Harry Weston); "The Yellow Tomahawk" 1954 (Adam); "The Spoilers" 1955 (Alex McNamara); "The Treasure of Pancho Villa" 1955 (Tom Bryan); "Raw Edge" 1956 (Tex Kirby); "Red Sundown" 1956 (Alec Longmire); "Domino Kid" 1957 (Domino); "The Hired Gun" 1957 (Gil McCord); "Ride Out for Revenge" 1957 (Tate); "Utah Blaine" 1957 (Utah Blaine); "Apache Territory" 1958 (Logan Cates); "The Saga of Hemp Brown" 1958 (Hemp Brown); "The Gun Hawk" 1963 (Blaine Madden); "Black Spurs" 1965 (Santee); "Finger on the Trigger" 1965-Span./Ital./U.S. (Larry Winton); "Young Fury" 1965 (Clint McCoy); "Apache Uprising" 1966 (Jim Walker); "Kino, the Padre on Horseback" 1977; "Bad Jim" 1990 (Sam Harper). ¶TV: *Zane Grey Theater*—"Muletown Gold Strike" 12-21-56; *Telephone Time*—"Trail Blazer" 4-1-58 (Charles Goodnight); *The Texan*—Regular 1958-60 (Bill Longley); *Wagon Train*—"The Artie Matthewson Story" 11-8-61 (Artie Matthewson), "The Jarbo Pierce Story" 5-2-65 (Jarbo Pierce); *Western Star Theater*—Host 1963; *Death Valley Days*—"Measure of a Man" 11-17-63 (Burt Mossman), "The Water Bringer" 4-23-66 (William Richardson); *Bonanza*—"Thanks for Everything, Friend" 10-11-64 (Tom Wil-

son); *The Virginian*—"A Father for Toby" 11-4-64 (Jim Shea); *Gunsmoke*—"Honey Pot" 5-15-65 (Ben Stack); *Rawhide*—"The Testing Post" 11-30-65 (Captain Masters); *Custer*—"Blazing Arrows" 11-29-67 (Zebediah Jackson); *Lancer*—"The Rivals" 5-5-70 (Buck Addison); *Alias Smith and Jones*—"The Night of the Red Dog" 11-4-71 (Jason Holloway); *Hec Ramsey*—"The Green Feather Mystery" 12-17-72 (Jim Patton).

Calisti, Calisto. Films: "The Big Gundown" 1966-Ital. (Miller).

Call, Anthony (1940-). TV: *The Dakotas*—"Trial at Grand Forks" 3-25-63 (Lou Warren); *Temple Houston*—"The Twisted Rope" 9-19-63 (Chevenix Brother); *Bonanza*—"The Dilemma" 9-19-65 (Billy); *Gunsmoke*—"Muley" 1-21-67 (Pell); *The Virginian*—"The Gentle Tamers" 1-24-68 (Val Tussey), "Home to Methuselah" 11-26-69 (Jase Dubbins).

Call, Ed. Films: "Wild Women" TVM-1970 ¶TV: *Gunsmoke*—"The Town Tamers" 1-28-74 (Farmer).

Call, John (1907-4/3/73). Films: "Indian Uprising" 1951 (Sgt. Clancy); "Hangman's Knot" 1952 (Egan Walsh).

Call, Ken. Films: "Cattle Annie and Little Britches" 1981 (George Weightman); "Silverado" 1985 (Deputy Block); "Sunset" 1988 (Cowboy Fred); "Bonanza: Under Attack" TVM-1995 (Mears).

Call, R.D. Films: "Young Guns II" 1990 (D.A. Rynerson). TV: *Paradise*—"Devil's Escort" 1-13-90 (Fletcher).

Callahan, Bobby (1896-5/15/38). Films: "Battle of Greed" 1934 (Jockey Brown); "Horses' Collars" 1935-short (Drunk).

Callahan, Cordelia. Films: "Cupid, the Cowpuncher" 1920 (Mrs. Bergin); "Doubling for Romeo" 1922 (Maggie).

Callahan, Foxy. Films: "The Irish Gringo" 1935; "Black Market Rustlers" 1943; "Bordertown Gunfighters" 1943.

Callahan, James (1930-). Films: "A Man Called Gannon" 1969 (Bo); "Little House on the Prairie: Look Back to Yesterday" TVM-1983 (Dr. Houser). ¶TV: *The Californians*—"The Fur Story" 5-5-59 (James McFadden); *Two Faces West*—"Prognosis: Death" 10-24-60; *Have Gun Will Travel*—"Don't Shoot the Piano Player" 3-10-62 (Albert); *Stoney Burke*—"Spin a Golden Web" 11-26-62 (Bert); *Empire*—"A House in Order" 3-5-63 (Redford).

Callahan, Margaret. Films: "The Last Outlaw" 1936 (Sally Mason).

Callahan, Pepe. Films: "MacKenna's Gold" 1969 (Laguna); "Wild Women" TVM-1970 (Lt. Santos); "Joe Kidd" 1972 (Naco); "The Apple Dumpling Gang" 1975 (Clemons); "Go West, Young Girl" TVM-1978 (Librado). ¶TV: *The Westerner*—"Ghost of a Chance" 12-2-60; *The Virginian*—"Ring of Silence" 10-27-65 (Manuelo); *The Big Valley*—"Teacher of Outlaws" 2-2-66 (Julio Gallego); *Wild Wild West*—"The Night of the Headless Woman" 1-5-68 (Jon), "The Night of the Spanish Curse" 1-3-69 (Officer Rojas); *Bonanza*—"Salute to Yesterday" 9-29-68 (Rojo); *The Guns of Will Sonnett*—"The Hero" 12-29-67; *Death Valley Days*—"The King of Uvalde Road" 4-25-70; *Gunsmoke*—"The Noonday Devil" 12-7-70 (John Hike), "The Bullet" 11-29-71, 12-6-71 & 12-13-71 (Secos).

Callam, Alex. Films: "Thundering Frontier" 1940 (Square Deal Scottie); "The Cyclone Kid" 1942 (Big Jim Johnson); "The Phantom Plainsmen" 1942 (Kurt Redman).

Callan, Michael (1935-). Films: "They Came to Cordura" 1959 (Pvt. Andrew Hetherington); "Cat Ballou" 1965 (Clay Boone); "The Magnificent Seven Ride" 1972 (Noah Forbes); "Donner Pass: The Road to Survival" TVM-1978 (William Eddy).

Callaway, Bill. Films: "The Great Northfield, Minnesota Raid" 1972 (Calliopist). ¶TV: *Gunsmoke*—"The Thieves" 3-9-70 (Charles "Shuffles" Jones).

Callaway, Cheryl. TV: *Tales of the Texas Rangers*—"West of Sonora" 9-17-55 (Penny Clinton); *Buckskin*—"The Outlaw's Boy" 7-17-58 (Cissie).

Callaway, Thomas. Films: "The Alamo: 13 Days to Glory" TVM-1987 (Col. James Fannin); "Young Guns" 1988 (Texas Joe Grant).

Calleia, Joseph (1897-10/31/75). Films: "The Bad Man of Brimstone" 1938 (Portuguese Ben); "My Little Chickadee" 1940 (Jeff Badger, the Masked Bandit); "Wyoming" 1940 (John Buckley); "Four Faces West" 1948 (Monte Marquez); "The Palomino" 1950 (Miguel Gonzales); "Branded" 1951; "The Iron Mistress" 1952 (Juan Moreno); "The Treasure of Pancho Villa" 1955 (Pablo Morales); "The Light in the Forest" 1958 (Chief Cuyloga); "The Alamo" 1960 (Juan Sequin). ¶TV: *Have Gun Will*

Travel—"In an Evil Time" 9-13-58 (Sheriff Truett); *Zorro*—"The Sergeant Sees Red" 5-14-59 (Padre Simeon).

Callejo, Cecilia. Films: "Outlaw Express" 1938 (Lorita Ricardo); "Renegade Ranger" 1938 (Tonia Capillo); "The Cisco Kid Returns" 1945 (Rosita).

Calloway, Kirk (1960-). Films: "The Soul of Nigger Charley" 1973 (Marcellus).

Calo, Carla. Films: "The Tramplers" 1965-Ital. (Mrs. Temple Cordeen).

Calomee, Gloria. TV: *Gunsmoke*—"The Sisters" 12-29-69 (Sister Charles).

Caltabiano, Alfio (Al Northon, Alf Thunder). Films: "Ballad of a Gunman" 1967-Ital./Ger. (El Bedoja); "Man Called Amen" 1972-Ital. (Reverend Smith); "They Still Call Me Amen" 1972-Ital. (Smith); "California" 1976-Ital./Span.

Calvert, E.H. (1873-10/5/41). Films: "The Virginian" 1929 (Judge Henry); "The Border Legion" 1930 (Judge Savin); "A Man from Wyoming" 1930 (Maj. Gen. Hunter); "The Conquerors" 1932 (Doctor); "Wild Horse Mesa" 1932 (Sheriff); "The Mysterious Rider" 1933 (Sheriff Matt Arnold); "Western Courage" 1935 (Colonel Austin); "The Oregon Trail" 1936 (Jim Ridgley); "The Glory Trail" 1937 (Col. Strong); "Union Pacific" 1939 (Major).

Calvert, John. Films: "Return of the Durango Kid" 1945; "Lawless Empire" 1946 (Blaze Howard); "Gold Fever" 1952 (John Bonar).

Calvert, Vane. Films: "Rainbow Ranch" 1933 (Martha Randall); "Kid Courageous" 1935; "Smokey Smith" 1935; "Western Justice" 1935 (Aunt Emma); "Ambush Valley" 1936 (Ma Potter); "Feud of the Trail" 1938.

Calvet, Corinne (1926-). Films: "Powder River" 1953 (Frenchie); "The Far Country" 1955 (Renee); "Plunderers of Painted Flats" 1959 (Kathie); "Apache Uprising" 1966 (Janice MacKenzie).

Calvin, Henry (1918-10/6/75). Films: "The Broken Star" 1956 (Thornton Wills). ¶TV: *Zorro*—Regular 1957-59 (Sergeant Garcia).

Calvo, Armando. Films: "Sign of Zorro" 1964-Ital./Span.; "Coffin for the Sheriff" 1965-Ital./Span.; "Ringo's Big Night" 1966-Ital./Span.; "Django Does Not Forgive" 1967-Ital./Span.; "Ringo, the Lone Rider" 1967-Ital./Span.; "All Out" 1968-Ital./Span.; "Ringo: Face of Revenge"

1968-Ital./Span. (Fidel); "Two Crosses at Danger Pass" 1968-Ital./Span.; "Killer Goodbye" 1969-Ital./Span.; "I Am Sartana, Trade Your Guns for a Coffin" 1972-Ital.

Calvo, Jose "Pepe" (1917-). Films: "Terrible Sheriff" 1963-Span./Ital.; "A Fistful of Dollars" 1964-Ital./Ger./Span. (Silvanito); "In a Colt's Shadow" 1965-Ital./Span. (Duke Buchanan); "Man from Oklahoma" 1965-Ital./Span./Ger.; "For One Thousand Dollars Per Day" 1966-Ital./Span. (Carranza); "Fort Yuma Gold" 1966-Ital./Fr./Span. (Golden 44); "Blood at Sundown" 1967-Span./Ital. (Lopez); "Day of Anger" 1967-Ital./Ger. (Blind Bill); "Stranger in Paso Bravo" 1968-Ital.; "Twice a Judas" 1968-Span./Ital.; "Dead Men Ride" 1970-Ital./Span. (Pedro); "Dust in the Sun" 1971-Fr.

Calvo, Pepe. *see* Calvo, Jose.

Camardiel, Roberto. Films: "Jaguar" 1964-Span.; "Arizona Colt" 1965-Ital./Fr./Span. (Whisky); "Adios Gringo" 1965-Ital./Fr./Span. (Dr. Barfield); "For a Few Dollars More" 1965-Ital./Ger./Span.; "Left Handed Johnny West" 1965-Span./Ital.; "Murieta" 1965-Span./U.S. (Three Fingers); "Adios Hombre" 1966-Ital./Span.; "The Big Gundown" 1966-Ital. (Jellicol); "Jesse James' Kid" 1966-Span./Ital. (Stitch); "Relentless Four" 1966-Span./Ital.; "Django Kill" 1967-Ital./Span. (Zorro); "Train for Durango" 1967-Ital./Span. (Lobo); "Up the MacGregors!" 1967-Ital./Span. (Donovan); "Between God, the Devil and a Winchester" 1968-Ital./Span.; "Dollars for a Fast Gun" 1968-Ital./Span.; "Machine Gun Killers" 1968-Ital./Span.; "Challenge of the Mackennas" 1969-Ital./Span.; "Quinta: Fighting Proud" 1969-Ital./Span.; "Arizona" 1970-Ital./Span. (Double Whiskey); "Heads You Die ... Tails I Kill You" 1971-Ital. (General Ramirez); "God in Heaven ... Arizona on Earth" 1972-Span./Ital.; "Return of Halleluja" 1972-Ital./Ger.; "Tequila" 1974-Ital./Span. (Fuzzy).

Camargo, Ana. Films: "Ramona" 1936 (Dancer); "Valley of the Lawless" 1936 (Dancer); "Lawless Land" 1937 (Lolita); "Desperate Trails" 1939 (Rosita); "Gun to Gun" 1944-short; "Twilight on the Rio Grande" 1947; "Desert Fury" 1947 (Rosa).

Camaso, Claudio. Films: "10,000 Dollars Blood Money" 1966-Ital. (Manuel Cortes); "For One Hundred Thousand Dollars Per Killing" 1967-Ital.; "John the Bas-

tard" 1967-Ital. (Francisco); "Vengeance" 1968-Ital./Ger.

Cambridge, Edmund. Films: "Evil Roy Slade" TVM-1972 (Smith).

Camden, Joan. Films: "Gunfight at the O.K. Corral" 1957 (Betty Earp); "Strange Lady in Town" 1955 (Norah Muldoon). ¶TV: *Broken Arrow*—"The Missionaries" 1-29-57 (Amanda); *Black Saddle*—"Client: Starkey" 2-7-59 (June Starker); *Sugarfoot*—"The Giant Killer" 3-3-59 (Molly); *Riverboat*—"Fort Epitaph" 3-7-60 (Barbara Daniels); *The Outlaws*—"The Cutups" 10-26-61 (Jill).

Cameron, Gene (-11/16/28). Films: "Chain Lightning" 1927 (Binghamwell Stokes Hurlbert).

Cameron, Jeff. Films: "The Greatest Robbery in the West" 1968-Ital.; "Shadow of Sartana ... Shadow of Your Death" 1968-Ital. (Sartana); "Today It's Me ... Tomorrow You!" 1968-Ital.; "Four Came to Kill Sartana" 1969-Ital. (Link); "Evan Django Has His Price" 1971-Ital./Span. (Django); "Fistful of Death" 1971-Ital.; "Bounty Hunter In Trinity" 1972-Ital. (Alan Boyd); "God Is My Colt .45" 1972-Ital. (Captain Mike Jackson); "Paid in Blood" 1972-Ital. (Tom Carter); "Showdown for a Badman" 1972-Ital.

Cameron, Joanna (1954-). TV: *Daniel Boone*—"A Bearskin for Jamie Blue" 11-27-69.

Cameron, Kirk (1970-). Films: "Bret Maverick" TVM-1981 (Boy).

Cameron, Michael. Films: "The Soul of Nigger Charley" 1973 (Sgt. Foss). ¶TV: *Kung Fu*—"Nine Lives" 2-15-73 (George Skowrin).

Cameron, Rod (1912-12/21/83). Films: "Northwest Mounted Police" 1940 (Cpl. Underhill); "Rangers of Fortune" 1940 (Shelby Henchman); "The Parson of Panamint" 1941; "The Kansan" 1943 (Kelso); "Riding High" 1943 (Sam Welch); "Boss of Boomtown" 1944 (Steve); "The Old Texas Trail" 1944 (Jim); "Riders of the Santa Fe" 1944 (Matt Conway); "Trigger Trail" 1944 (Clint Farrel); "Beyond the Pecos" 1945; "Frontier Gal" 1945 (Johnny Hart); "Renegades of the Rio Grande" 1945 (Buck Emerson); "Salome, Where She Danced" 1945 (Jim); "Belle Starr's Daughter" 1947 (Bob "Bittercreek" Yauntis); "Pirates of Monterey" 1947 (Phillip Kent); "Panhandle" 1948 (John Sands); "The Plunderers" 1948 (John Druin); "River Lady" 1948 (Dan Corrigan); "Brimstone" 1949 (Johnny Tremaine); "Stampede" 1949 (Mike); "Dakota Lil" 1950 (Harve

Lopan); "Short Grass" 1950 (Steve); "Stage to Tucson" 1950 (Grif Holbrook); "Cavalry Scout" 1951 (Kirby Frye); "Oh! Susanna" 1951 (Capt. Calhoun); "Fort Osage" 1952 (Tom Clay); "Ride the Man Down" 1952 (Will Ballard); "Wagons West" 1952 (Jeff Curtis); "Woman of the North Country" 1952 (Kyle Ramlo); "San Antone" 1953 (Carl Miller); "Hell's Outpost" 1954 (Tully Gibbs); "Southwest Passage" 1954 (Edward Beale); "Santa Fe Passage" 1955 (Jess Griswold); "Yaqui Drums" 1956; "The Gun Hawk" 1963 (Sheriff Corey); "Bullets Don't Argue" 1964-Ital./Ger./Span. (Sheriff Johnston); "The Bounty Killer" 1965 (Johnny Liam); "Bullets and the Flesh" 1965-Ital./Fr./Span. (Masters); "Requiem for a Gunfighter" 1965 (Dave McCloud); "Thunder at the Border" 1967-Ger./Yugo. (Old Firehand); "Jessi's Girls" 1976 (Rufe). ¶TV: Laramie—"General Delivery" 11-3-59, "Drifter's Gold" 11-29-60 (Tom Bedloe), "Men in Shadows" 5-30-61 (Howard Gallery), "The Last Journey" 10-31-61 (John Cole), "Lost Allegiance" 10-30-62 (Christy), "Broken Honor" 4-9-63 (Roy Halloran); Tales of Wells Fargo—"Assignment in Gloribee" 1-27-62 (Nathan Chance); Bob Hope Chrysler Theatre—"Have Girls—Will Travel" 10-16-64 (Tiny); Bonanza—"Ride the Wind" 1-16-66 & 1-23-66 (Curtis Wade); Branded—"Barbed Wire" 2-13-66 (Holland Thorp); Iron Horse—"Pride at the Bottom of the Barrel" 10-10-66 (Major Rogers); Hondo—"Hondo and the sudden Town" 11-17-67 (Martin Blaine); The Men from Shiloh—"Gun Quest" 10-21-70 (Dunn); Bearcats!—"Conqueror's Gold" 10-28-71 (Warden Price); Alias Smith and Jones—"The Biggest Game in the West" 2-3-72 (Sheriff Grimly), "High Lonesome Country" 9-23-72 (Luke Billings).

Cameron, Rudolph (1894-2/17/58). Films: "Song of the West" 1930 (Lt. Singleton).

Camfield, Bill. Films: "The Outlaws Is Coming!" 1965 (Wyatt Earp).

Camhi, Patricia. TV: Zorro—Regular 1990-91 (Victoria).

Camp, Hamilton (1934-). Films: "The Cockeyed Cowboys of Calico County" 1970 (Mr. Fowler). ¶TV: Bonanza—"The Clarion" 2-9-69 (Dobbs), "What Are Pardners For?" 4-12-70 (Calvin).

Camp, Helen Page. Films: "The New Maverick" TVM-1978 (Flora Crupper). ¶TV: Here Come the Brides—"A Hard Card to Play" 10-23-68 (Lucy Dale); Wild Wild West—"The Night of the Gruesome Games" 10-25-68 (Charity Witherly); Gunsmoke—"A Quiet Day in Dodge" 1-29-73 (Mrs. Ballou), "The Widow and the Rogue" 10-29-73 (Woman).

Camp, Robin. Films: "Mrs. Mike" 1949 (Tommy Howard).

Campana, Nina (1897-6/21/50). Films: "Sunset of Power" 1936 (Rosita); "It Happened Out West" 1937 (Maria); "Rootin' Tootin' Rhythm" 1937 (Ynez); "Call of the Yukon" 1938 (Knudka); "Outlaw Express" 1938 (Lupe); "Arizona" 1940 (Teresa); "Twilight on the Rio Grande" 1947.

Campanella, Frank (1919-). Films: "High Noon, Part II: The Return of Will Kane" TVM-1980 (Dr. Losey). ¶TV: Wild Wild West—"The Night of the Sedgewick Curse" 10-18-68 (Fingers); The Virginian—"Journey to Scathelock" 12-10-69 (Sheriff); Hec Ramsey—"The Detroit Connection" 12-30-73 (Gus).

Campanella, Joseph (1927-). Films: "Kino, the Padre on Horseback" 1977. ¶TV: The Virginian—"Siege" 12-18-63 (Pedro Lopez), "The Long Quest" 4-8-64 (Corbett), "Ride the Misadventure" 11-6-68 (Walker); Shane—"Killer in the Valley" 10-15-66 (Barney Lucas); The Big Valley—"The Martyr" 10-17-66 (Francisco), "Turn of a Card" 3-20-67 (Spider Martinson); The Road West—"Power of Fear" 12-26-66 (Tom Burrus); Wild Wild West—"The Night of the Wolf" 3-31-67 (Talamantes); Gunsmoke—"The Hide Cutters" 9-30-68 (Amos McKee), "Milligan" 11-6-72 (Jack Norcross); Lancer—"Devil's Blessing" 4-22-69 (Douglas Blessing); Alias Smith and Jones—"The Fifth Victim" 3-25-71 (Jake Carlson); Barbary Coast—"Sauce for the Goose" 10-20-75 (Austin Benedict); Paradise—"The Gates of Paradise" 1-6-90 (Horseman).

Campbell, Alexander (-12/25/70). Films: "Rails into Laramie" 1954 (Higby); "Texas Lady" 1955 (Judge Herzog). ¶TV: Jefferson Drum—"Simon Pitt" 12-11-58 (Judge); The Californians—"Wolf's Head" 2-24-59 (Judge Henshaw); Maverick—"Cruise of the Cynthia B" 1-10-60 (Abner Morton), "The Town That Wasn't Thrree" 10-2-60 (Horatio Cromwell); Bonanza—"The Fear Merchants" 1-30-60.

Campbell, Bob. Films: "Five Guns West" 1955 (John Candy).

Campbell, Bruce. TV: The Adventures of Brisco County, Jr.—Regular 1993-94 (Brisco County, Jr.).

Campbell, Charles L. Films: "The Chisholms" TVM-1979 (Judge Wilson). ¶TV: The Chisholms—Regular 1979 (Judge Wilson).

Campbell, Colin (1883-3/25/66). Films: "Salome, Where She Danced" 1945 (Mate).

Campbell, Flo (1911-11/6/78). Films: "Overland with Kit Carson" 1939-serial.

Campbell, Glen (1937-). Films: "True Grit" 1969 (La Boeuf).

Campbell, Kate. Films: "Ghost City" 1932 (Ruby Blane); "Ghost Valley" 1932 (Miss Trumpet); "Come on Tarzan" 1933 (Aunt Martha).

Campbell, Lois Jane. Films: "Cimarron" 1931 (Felice, Jr.).

Campbell, Margaret (1873-6/27/39). Films: "The Lady from Hell" 1926 (Lady Darnely).

Campbell, Margaret. Films: "Gunslinger" 1956 (Felicity Polk).

Campbell, Newton. Films: "Daring Chances" 1924 (Bill); "Western Grit" 1924 (Jim Grayson).

Campbell, Patrick (1924-). Films: "The Culpepper Cattle Company" 1972 (Br. Ephraim).

Campbell, Paul. Films: "Last Days of Boot Hill" 1947 (Frank Rayburn); "Smoky River Serenade" 1947; "The Stranger from Ponca City" 1947; "Blazing Across the Pecos" 1948; "Buckaroo from Powder River" 1948 (Clint Ryland); "Six-Gun Law" 1948 (Jim Wallace); "Desert Vigilante" 1949 (Bob Gill); "Across the Badlands" 1950 (Pete); "Frontier Outpost" 1950 (Capt. Tanner); "Vigilante Hideout" 1950 (Ralph Barrows); "Merry Mavericks" 1951-short (Duke); "Pecos River" 1951 (Sniff); "Prairie Roundup" 1951 (Poke Joe). ¶TV: The Gene Autry Show—"The Breakup" 11-5-50, "Twisted Trails" 11-12-50; The Lone Ranger—"Mr. Trouble" 3-8-51; My Friend Flicka—"Act of Loyalty" 12-8-55, "Refuge for the Night" 4-20-56 (Criminal).

Campbell, Peggy. Films: "When a Man Sees Red" 1934 (Mary Lawrence); "Big Calibre" 1935 (June Bowers); "Stone of Silver Creek" 1935 (Nancy Raymond).

Campbell, Rob. Films: "Unforgiven" 1992 (Davey Buntin). ¶TV: Ned Blessing: The Story of My Life and Times—Regular 1993 (Roby Borgers).

Campbell, Virginia. Films: "Unconquered" 1947 (Mrs. John Fraser).

Campbell, William (1926-).

Films: "Escape from Fort Bravo" 1953 (Cabot Young); "Man Without a Star" 1955 (Jeff Jimson); "Backlash" 1956 (Johnny Cool); "Love Me Tender" 1956 (Brett Reno); "Money, Women and Guns" 1958 (Clint Gunston); "The Sheriff of Fractured Jaw" 1958-Brit. (Keno); "Natchez Trace" 1960 (Virgil Stewart). ¶TV: *Tales of Wells Fargo*—"Threat of Death" 4-25-60 (Crail); *Stagecoach West*—"Never Walk Alone" 4-18-61 (Cole Eldridge); *Gunsmoke*—"Old Dan" 1-27-62 (Luke Petch), "Judge Calvin Strom" 12-18-65, "The Squaw" 1-6-75 (Striker); *Wild Wild West*—"The Night of the Freebooters" 4-1-66 (Sgt. Bender); *Dundee and the Culhane*—"The Widow's Weeds Brief" 11-29-67 (Hobbs); *Bonanza*—"The Late Ben Cartwright" 3-3-68 (White); *Hec Ramsey*—"Scar Tissue" 3-10-74 (Vince Alexander).

Campeau, Frank (1864-11/5/43). Films: "Jordan Is a Hard Road" 1915 (Bill Minden); "The Heart of Texas Ryan" 1917 (Dice McAllister); "The Man from Painted Post" 1917 (Bull Madden); "A Modern Musketeer" 1917 (Indian Guide); "Headin' South" 1918 (Spanish Joe); "The Knickerbocker Buckaroo" 1919 (Crooked Sheriff); "The Killer" 1921 (Henry Hooper); "The Crimson Challenge" 1922 (Buck Courtney); "Just Tony" 1922 (Lew Herey); "The Yosemite Trail" 1922 (Jerry Smallbones); "Quicksands" 1923 (Ring Member); "The Spider and the Rose" 1923 (Don Fernando); "Three Who Paid" 1923 (Edward Sanderson); "To the Last Man" 1923 (Blue); "North of Hudson Bay" 1924 (Cameron McDonald); "Not a Drum Was Heard" 1924 (Banker Rand); "The Man from Red Gulch" 1925 (Falloner); "The Saddle Hawk" 1925 (Buck Brent); "The Frontier Trail" 1926 (Shad Donlin); "No Man's Gold" 1926 (Frank Healy); "Three Bad Men" 1926 (Spade Allen); "In Old Arizona" 1929 (Cowpuncher); "Points West" 1929 (McQuade); "Last of the Duanes" 1930 (Luke Stevens); "Captain Thunder" 1931 (Hank Riley); "Fighting Caravans" 1931 (Jeff Mofitt); "Lasca of the Rio Grande" 1931 (Jehosaphat Smith); "White Eagle" 1932 (Gray Wolf); "Smoky" 1933 (Jeff Nicks); "Call of the Wild" 1935 (Sourdough on Street); "Hopalong Cassidy" 1935 (Frisco); "The Border Patrolman" 1936; "Everyman's Law" 1936 (Thinker Gibbs); "Robin Hood of El Dorado" 1936 (Steve); "Black Aces" 1937 (Ike Bowlaigs); "Empty Saddles" 1937 (Kit Kress); "Border Wolves" 1938 (Tom Dawson); "King of the

Sierras" 1938 (Jim); "The Painted Trail" 1938 (Marshal G. Masters).

Campo, Wally (1923-). Films: "Warlock" 1959 (Barber). ¶TV: *Bat Masterson*—"Terror on the Trinity" 3-9-61 (Mickey).

Campos, Rafael (1936-7/9/85). Films: "The Light in the Forest" 1958 (Half Arrow); "Tonka" 1958 (Strong Bear); "Savage Sam" 1963 (Young Warrior); "The Appaloosa" 1966 (Paco); "Oklahoma Crude" 1973 (Jimmy); "The Hanged Man" TVM-1974 (Father Alvaro); "The Return of Josey Wales" 1987 (Chato). ¶TV: *Wagon Train*—"The Swift Cloud Story" 4-8-59 (Swift Cloud), "The Dr. Swift Cloud Story" 5-25-60 (Dr. Swift Cloud); *The Restless Gun*—"Ride with the Devil" 5-18-59 (Carlos Perez); *Have Gun Will Travel*—"Pancho" 10-24-59 (Doroteo), "A Miracle for St. Francis" 11-17-62 (Paco); *Wanted—Dead or Alive*—"Desert Seed" 11-14-59 (Pachito); *Death Valley Days*—"Goodbye Five Hundred Pesos" 3-8-60; *Sugarfoot*—"Shepherd with a Gun" 2-6-61 (Pablo); *The Outlaws*—"The Little Colonel" 5-18-61 (Valdez); *Laramie*—"The Barefoot Kid" 1-9-62 (Juan De La O); *Temple Houston*—"Find Angel Chavez" 9-26-63 (Angel Chavez); *Gunsmoke*—"Ten Little Indians" 10-9-65 (Miguel Samando), "The Mission" 10-8-66 (Young Soldier); *Branded*—"The Ghost of Murrieta" 3-20-66 (Luis); *The Big Valley*—"Four Days to Furnace Hill" 12-4-67; *Hondo*—"Hondo and the Rebel Hat" 12-29-67 (Hernandez); *Centennial*—Regular 1978-79 (Nacho Gomez).

Campos, Victor (1936-). Films: "The Master Gunfighter" 1975 (Maltese). ¶TV: *The High Chaparral*—"A Time to Laugh, a Time to Cry" 9-26-69 (Taniente); *Bonanza*—"Decision at Los Robles" 3-22-70 (Gunman #1); *Lancer*—"Goodbye, Lizzie" 4-28-70 (Julio).

Camron, Rocky. see Alsace, Gene.

Canada, Roy. Films: "Gold Raiders" 1951 (Slim); "Son of the Renegade" 1953 (the Gun Slinger); "The Lawless Rider" 1954 (Andy); "I Killed Wild Bill Hickok" 1956 (Nato).

Canalejas, Jose. Films: "Secret of Captain O'Hara" 1965-Span.; "God Forgives—I Don't" 1966-Ital./Span.; "The Hellbenders" 1966-U.S./Ital./Span.; "The Man Who Killed Billy the Kid" 1967-Span./Ital.; "A Minute to Pray, a Second to Die" 1967-Ital. (Seminole); "The Mercenary" 1968-Ital./Span. (Pablo);

"The Man Called Noon" 1973-Brit./Span./Ital. (Cherry); "If You Shoot ... You Live!" 1974-Span.

Canary, David (1938-). Films: "Hombre" 1967 (Lamar Dean); "Posse" 1975 (Pensteman). ¶TV: *Gunsmoke*—"Nitro!" 4-8-67 & 4-15-67 (George McClaney); *Dundee and the Culhane*—"The Dead Man's Brief" 10-4-67 (Charlie Montana); *Cimarron Strip*—"Knife in the Darkness" 1-25-68 (Tal St. James); *Bonanza*—Regular 1968-70, 72-73 (Candy Canaday); *Bearcats!*—"Hostages" 10-14-71 (Joe Bascom); *Alias Smith and Jones*—"Everything Else You Can Steal" 12-16-71 (Sheriff Coffin), "The Strange Fate of Conrad Meyer Zulick" 12-2-72 (Doc Donovan); *Kung Fu*—"The Elixir" 12-20-73 (Frank Grogan).

Candelli, Stelio. Films: "The Last Tomahawk" 1965-Ger./Ital./Span.; "Apocalypse Joe" 1970-Ital./Span.; "Man Called Django" 1971-Ital. (Carranza); "Trinity and Sartana Are Coming" 1972-Ital.

Candido, Candy. Films: "Cowboy from Brooklyn" 1938 (Spec); "Plunderers of Painted Flats" 1959 (Bartender).

Candy, John (1950-3/4/94). Films: "Wagons East!" 1994 (James Harlow).

Cane, Charles (1899-11/30/73). Films: "Bells of Capistrano" 1942 (Tex); "Adventures in Silverado" 1948; "Calamity Jane and Sam Bass" 1949 (J. Wells); "Belle Le Grand" 1951 (Cal); "Lone Star" 1952 (Mayhew); "A Perilous Journey" 1953 (Miner); "A Day of Fury" 1956 (Duggen); "Gun Battle at Monterey" 1957 (Mundy); "The Gambler Wore a Gun" 1961 (Kelly Barnum). ¶TV: *My Friend Flicka*—"The Wild Horse" 11-18-55; *Pony Express*—"Payoff" 4-13-60 (Trimble).

Canfield, William (1860-2/14/25). Films: "A Knight of the Range" 1916 (Gentleman Dick).

Cannon, Dyan (1937-). TV: *Bat Masterson*—"Lady Luck" 11-5-59 (Mary Lowery), "The Price of Paradise" 1-19-61 (Jean Jansen); *Zane Grey Theater*—"Shadows" 11-5-59 (Annie); *Wanted—Dead or Alive*—"Vanishing Act" 12-26-59 (Nicole); *Two Faces West*—"Sheriff of the Town" 10-31-60; *Stoney Burke*—"Death Rides a Pale Horse" 1-14-63 (Flatbush); *Gunsmoke*—"Aunt Thede" 12-19-64 (Ivy Norton).

Cannon, J.D. (1922-) Films: "Heaven with a Gun" 1969 (Mace); "Lawman" 1971 (Hurd Price); "Sam

Hill: Who Killed the Mysterious Mr. Foster?" TVM-1971; "Testimony of Two Men" TVM-1977 (Kenton Campion). ¶TV: *Wagon Train*—"The Abel Weatherly Story" 1-2-63 (Abel Weatherly); *Stoney Burke*—"The Weapons Man" 4-8-63 (Mark Vickers); *Rawhide*—"Piney" 10-9-64 (Jack Rose), "The Book" 1-8-65 (Austin Ware); *Gunsmoke*—"Big Man, Big Target" 11-28-64 (Pike Beechum), "MacGraw" 12-8-69 (Jake MacGraw); *Profiles in Courage*—"Sam Houston" 12-13-64 (Sam Houston); *Wild Wild West*—"Night of the Deadly Bed" 9-24-65 (Gen. Florey); *A Man Called Shenandoah*—"End of a Legend" 2-7-66 (Jason Brewster); *Shane*—"The Day the Wolf Laughed" 11-19-66 (Reno); *The Guns of Will Sonnett*—"Find a Sonnett, Kill a Sonnett" 12-8-67 (Pat Bridges); *Cimarron Strip*—"The Deputy" 12-21-67 (Bo Woodard); *Iron Horse*—"Dry Run to Glory" 1-6-68 (Victor Lamphier); *Lancer*—"Blood Rock" 10-1-68 (Morgan Price); *Bonanza*—"The Fence" 4-27-69 (Colonel Hudson); *The Men from Shiloh*—"Hannah" 12-30-70 (Roy); *Alias Smith and Jones*—"The Wrong Train to Brimstone" 2-4-71 (Harry Briscoe), "The Legacy of Charlie O'Rourke" 4-22-71 (Harry Briscoe), "The Reformation of Harry Briscoe" 11-11-71 (Harry Briscoe), "The Man Who Corrupted Hadleyburg" 1-27-72 (Harry Briscoe), "Bad Night in Big Butte" 3-2-72 (Harry Briscoe), "The Long Chase" 9-16-72 (Harry Briscoe); *Hallmark Hall of Fame*—"The Court-Martial of General George Armstrong Carter" 12-1-77 (General Sherman).

Cannon, Kathy (1953-). Films: "Fools' Parade" 1971 (Chanty); "High Noon, Part II: The Return of Will Kane" TVM-1980 (Amy Kane). ¶TV: *Bearcats!*—11-18-71 (Amy Latimer); *Gunsmoke*—"Susan Was Evil" 12-3-73 (Susan); *Father Murphy*—Regular 1981-82 (Mae Woodward).

Cannon, Peter. Films: "Ride in the Whirlwind" 1966 (Hagerman).

Cannon, Pomeroy "Doc" (1870-9/16/28). Films: "The Good Bad Man" 1916 (Bob Emmons); "The Parson of Panamint" 1916 (Chuckawalla Bill).

Cannon, Raymond (1892-6/7/77). Films: "Nugget Nell" 1919 (the City Chap); "Penny of Top Hill Trail" 1921 (Joe Gary); "His Back Against the Wall" 1922 (Jimmy Boyle).

Canova, Judy (1916-8/5/83). Films: "Meet Roy Rogers" 1941-short; "Singin' in the Corn" 1946 (Judy McCoy); "Oklahoma Annie" 1952 (Judy, Queen of the Cowgirls);

"Untamed Heiress" 1954 (Judy); "Carolina Cannonball" 1955 (Judy); "Lay That Rifle Down" 1955 (Judy). ¶TV: *Pistols 'n' Petticoats*—1-7-67 (Daisy Frogg), 2-11-67 (Sadie).

Canova, Tweeny. Films: "Untamed Heiress" 1954 (Tweeny); "Lay That Rifle Down" 1955 (Tweeny).

Canow, Fred. *see* Cassanova, Fernando.

Cansino, Carmela. Films: "Down Mexico Way" 1941; "The Masked Rider" 1941 (Carmencita); "Ride 'Em, Cowboy" 1942 (1st Indian Girl).

Cansino, Rita. *see* Hayworth, Rita.

Cansino, Vernon. Films: "Madonna of the Desert" 1948 (Enrico).

Cantafora, Antonio (Michael Coby) (1943-). Films: "And God Said to Cain" 1969-Ital.; "Black Killer" 1971-Ital./Ger.; "The Dirty Outlaws" 1971-Ital.; "Bounty Hunter In Trinity" 1972-Ital.; "Carambola" 1974-Ital. (Coby); "Carambola's Philosophy: In the Right Pocket" 1975-Ital. (Coby).

Cantlon, Wanda. Films: "The Kid from Gower Gulch" 1949; "Red Rock Outlaw" 1950.

Canty, Marietta (1906-7/9/86). Films: "Silver Queen" 1942 (Ruby); "The Spoilers" 1942 (Idabelle); "The Sea of Grass" 1947 (Rachael); "Belle Le Grand" 1951 (Daisy).

Canutt, Edward "Tap". Films: "The Stranger Wore a Gun" 1953; "The Lawless Rider" 1954 (Young Marshal); "The Cowboys" 1972 (Rustler). ¶TV: *26 Men*—"Tumbleweed Ranger" 6-2-59; *The Monroes*—"Ride with Terror" 9-21-66 (Pinkie).

Canutt, Joe. Films: "The Far Horizons" 1955. ¶TV: *The Adventures of Rin Tin Tin*—"The Indian Hater" 1-11-57 (Brave); *Daniel Boone*—"The Courtship of Jericho Jones" 4-19-65 (Pushmataha); *The Monroes*—"Ride with Terror" 9-21-66 (Ugly).

Canutt, Yakima (1895-5/24/86). Films: "The Girl Who Dared" 1920 (Bob Purdy); "The Heart of a Texan" 1922 (Link); "The Forbidden Range" 1923 (Buck Madison); "Branded a Bandit" 1924 (Jess Dean); "Days of '49" 1924-serial; "The Desert Hawk" 1924 (Handy Man); "Ridin' Mad" 1924 (Steve Carlson); "Sell 'Em Cowboy" 1924 (Luke Strong); "Branded a Thief" 1925; "The Cactus Cure" 1925 (Bud Osborne, the Foreman); "The Human Tornado" 1925 (Jim Marlow); "Ridin' Comet" 1925 (Slim Ranthers); "Ro-

mance and Rustlers" 1925 (Bud Kane); "Scar Hanan" 1925 (Scar Hanan); "The Strange Rider" 1925; "A Two-Fisted Sheriff" 1925 (Jerry O'Connell); "White Thunder" 1925 (Chick Richards); "Wolves of the Road" 1925; "Desert Greed" 1926; "The Devil Horse" 1926 (Dave Garson); "The Fighting Stallion" 1926; "Hellhounds of the Plains" 1926; "The Iron Rider" 1926 (Yak Halliday); "The Vanishing West" 1928-serial; "Bad Man's Money" 1929; "Captain Cowboy" 1929; "Riders of the Storm" 1929; "The Three Outcasts" 1929 (Dick Marsh); "A Texan's Honor" 1929; "Bar L Ranch" 1930 (Steve); "Canyon Hawks" 1930 (Jack Benson); "The Cheyenne Kid" 1930; "Firebrand Jordan" 1930 (Red Carson); "The Lonesome Tail" 1930 (Two Gun); "Ridin' Law" 1930 (Buck Lambert); "Westward Bound" 1930 (Jim); "Battling with Buffalo Bill" 1931-serial (Jack Brady); "Hurricane Horseman" 1931 (Sheriff Jones); "Lightning Warrior" 1931-serial; "Pueblo Terror" 1931 (Ballan); "Two-Fisted Justice" 1931 (Perkins); "The Vanishing Legion" 1931-serial (Cowboy); "Battling Buckaroo" 1932 (Sheriff Hank Jones); "The Cheyenne Cyclone" 1932 (Ed Brady); "The Devil Horse" 1932-serial; "Guns for Hire" 1932; "The Last Frontier" 1932-serial (Wild Bill Hickok); "The Last of the Mohicans" 1932-serial; "Law and Lawless" 1932 (Tex Barnes); "Riders of the Golden Gulch" 1932 (Yac); "The Texan" 1932; "Texas Tornado" 1932 (Jackson); "Wyoming Whirlwind" 1932; "The Fighting Texans" 1933 (Hank); "Riders of Destiny" 1933; "Sagebrush Trail" 1933 (Ed Walsh); "Scarlet River" 1933 (Yak); "The Telegraph Trail" 1933 (High Wolf); "Via Pony Express" 1933; "Blue Steel" 1934 (Danti, the Polka Dot Bandit); "Carrying the Mail" 1934-short; "Desert Man" 1934; "Fighting Through" 1934 (Big Jack Thorpe); "The Lawless Frontier" 1934 (Joe); "The Lucky Texan" 1934 (Cole); "The Man from Hell" 1934 (Yak); "The Man from Utah" 1934 (Cheyenne Kent); "'Neath the Arizona Skies" 1934 (Sam Black); "Pals of the West" 1934-short; "Randy Rides Alone" 1934 (Spike); "The Star Packer" 1934 (Yak); "West of the Divide" 1934 (Hank); "Branded a Coward" 1935; "Circle of Death" 1935 (Yak); "Cyclone of the Saddle" 1935 (Snake); "Dawn Rider" 1935 (Barkeep); "Lawless Range" 1935 (Joe Burns); "Outlaw Rule" 1935 (Blaze Tremaine); "Pals of the Range" 1935 (Brown);

"Paradise Canyon" 1935 (Curly Joe Gale); "Rough Riding Ranger" 1935 (Draw); "Texas Terror" 1935; "Westward Ho" 1935 (Red); "King of the Pecos" 1936 (Pete Smith); "The Lonely Trail" 1936 (Horell); "The Oregon Trail" 1936 (Tom Richards); "Roarin' Lead" 1936 (Canary); "Vigilantes Are Coming" 1936-serial (Barsam); "Wildcat Trooper" 1936 (the Raven); "Winds of the Wasteland" 1936 (Smoky); "Come on Cowboys" 1937; "Ghost Town Gold" 1937 (Buck); "Gunsmoke Ranch" 1937 (Spider); "Heart of the Rockies" 1937 (Enoch); "Hit the Saddle" 1937 (Buck); "The Painted Stallion" 1937-serial (Tom); "Prairie Thunder" 1937 (High Wolf); "Range Defenders" 1937 (Hodge); "Riders of the Dawn" 1937; "Riders of the Rockies" 1937 (Sgt. Beef); "Riders of the Whistling Skull" 1937 (Otah); "Trouble in Texas" 1937 (Squint Harmer); "Zorro Rides Again" 1937-serial; "The Lone Ranger" 1938-serial (Trooper); "Overland Stage Raiders" 1938 (Bus Driver); "Santa Fe Stampede" 1938; "Cowboys from Texas" 1939 (Dawson); "The Kansas Terrors" 1939 (Sergeant); "The Night Riders" 1939; "Stagecoach" 1939 (Cavalry Scout); "Wyoming Outlaw" 1939 (Ed Sims); "Zorro's Fighting Legion" 1939-serial (Soldier #1); "The Carson City Kid" 1940; "The Dark Command" 1940 (Townsman); "Deadwood Dick" 1940-serial; "Frontier Vengeance" 1940 (Zack); "Ghost Valley Raiders" 1940 (Marty Owens); "Oklahoma Renegades" 1940; "Pioneers of the West" 1940 (Nolan); "The Ranger and the Lady" 1940 (McNair); "Under Texas Skies" 1940 (Talbot); "Bad Man of Deadwood" 1941; "Gauchos of El Dorado" 1941 (Snakes); "Kansas Cyclone" 1941; "Nevada City" 1941; "Prairie Pioneers" 1941 (Morrison); "White Eagle" 1941-serial; "Shadows on the Sage" 1942 (Red); "Calling Wild Bill Elliott" 1943; "In Old Oklahoma" 1943; "King of the Cowboys" 1943 (Henchman); "Santa Fe Scouts" 1943; "Song of Texas" 1943; "Hidden Valley Outlaws" 1944; "Pride of the Plains" 1944 (Bowman); "Rocky Mountain" 1950 (Ryan); "The Showdown" 1950 (Davis).

Capers, Virginia (1925-). Films: "The Ride to Hangman's Tree" 1967 (Teressa Moreno); "Big Jake" 1971 (Delilah); "Support Your Local Gunfighter" 1971 (Maid). ¶TV: *Have Gun Will Travel*—"Odds for a Big Red" 10-7-61 (Ada); *Daniel Boone*—"Onatha" 11-3-66 (Elsie).

Capitani, Remo. Films: "Ace High" 1967-Ital./Span. (Cangaceiro);

"They Call Me Trinity" 1970-Ital. (Mezcal).

Capps, Henry. Films: "The Sackets" TVM-1979. ¶TV: *Branded*—"McCord's Way" 1-30-66 (Joe Latigo).

Capri, Anna (1944-). TV: *Cheyenne*—"Trouble Street" 10-2-61; *Bronco*—"A Town That Lived and Died" 4-9-62 (Girl); *Branded*—"Romany Roundup 12-5-65 & 12-12-65 (Robin Shields); *Laredo*—"The Land Slickers" 10-14-66 (Sally Fletcher); *The Monroes*—"Ghosts of Paradox" 3-15-67 (Polly Deaver); *Wild Wild West*—"The Night of the Hangman" 10-20-67 (Abigail); *Iron Horse*—"Steel Chain to a Music Box" 11-18-67 (Angie); *The Guns of Will Sonnett*—"Stopover in a Troubled Town" 2-2-68 (Laurie).

Capshaw, Kate (1953-). Films: "The Quick and the Dead" CTVM-1987 (Susanna McKaskel); "My Heroes Have Always Been Cowboys" 1991.

Capucine (1933-3/17/90). Films: "North to Alaska" 1960 (Michelle "Angel"); "Red Sun" 1971-Fr./Ital./Span. (Pepita).

Caravajal, Tony. Films: "Ten Days to Tulara" 1958 (Francisco).

Carbone, Anthony (1927-). TV: *Bonanza*—"The Campaneros" 4-19-64 (Vicente); *Cimarron Strip*—"The Hunted" 10-5-67; *The Big Valley*—"A Stranger Everywhere" 12-9-68 (Vega); *The High Chaparral*—"A Way of Justice" 12-13-68 (Mitch).

Card, Bob. Films: "Riders of the Rio" 1931 (Travis); "The Prescott Kid" 1934; "The Outlaw Deputy" 1935; "The Phantom Empire" 1935-serial; "Ridin' the Cherokee Trail" 1941; "Stick to Your Guns" 1941 (Frenchy).

Card, Kathryn (1893-3/1/64). Films: "Good Day for a Hanging" 1958 (Molly Cain). ¶TV: *The Lone Ranger*—"The Quiet Highwayman" 1-27-55; *Broken Arrow*—"The Captive" 10-23-56 (Abigail); *Jefferson Drum*—"A Very Deadly Game" 5-30-58 (Evie Barnes); *The Texan*—"The Troubled Town" 10-13-58 (Ma Kestler), "The Marshal of Yellow Jacket" 3-2-59 (Kate Mulvaney); *Zane Grey Theater*—"The Vaunted" 11-27-58 (Grandma Matson); *Wagon Train*—"The Christine Elliot Story" 3-23-60 (Abigail); *Rawhide*—"Incident of the Last Chance" 6-10-60 (Enda Gillespie), "Incident of the Captive" 12-16-60, "The Gentleman's Gentleman" 12-15-61 (Emily Osgood); *The Virginian*—"Vengeance Is the Spur" 2-27-63.

Card, Ken. Films: "Brand of Hate" 1934; "The Mystery of the Hooded Horseman" 1937; "Rhythm Wranglers" 1937-short; "Border G-Man" 1938; "A Buckaroo Broadcast" 1938-short; "Gun Law" 1938; "The Painted Desert" 1938; "Prairie Papas" 1938-short; "Renegade Ranger" 1938; "A Western Welcome" 1938-short; "Where the West Begins" 1938; "Bandits and Ballads" 1939-short; "Cupid Rides the Range" 1939-short; "Ranch House Romeo" 1939-short; "Sagebrush Serenade" 1939-short; "Trouble in Sundown" 1939; "Bar Buckaroos" 1940-short; "Molly Cures a Cowboy" 1940-short; "California or Bust" 1941-short; "The Musical Bandit" 1941-short; "Prairie Spooners" 1941-short; "Redskins and Redheads" 1941-short; "Cactus Capers" 1942-short; "Keep Shooting" 1942-short; "Range Rhythm" 1942-short.

Cardenas, Elsa (1935-). Films: "Giant" 1956 (Juana); "Dalton That Got Away" 1960; "For the Love of Mike" 1960 (Mrs. Eagle); "Taggart" 1964 (Consuela Stark); "The Wild Bunch" 1969 (Elsa). ¶TV: *Have Gun Will Travel*—"Tiger" 11-28-59 (Lahri).

Cardi, Pat (1952-). Films: "...And Now Miguel" 1966 (Miguel). ¶TV: *Temple Houston*—"Billy Hart" 11-28-63 (Billy Hart); *Gunsmoke*—"Twenty Miles from Dodge" 4-10-65 (Josh Starkey), "South Wind" 11-27-65 (Homer Bonney), "Old Friend" 2-4-67 (Tod); *Branded*—"A Proud Town" 12-19-65 (Mike).

Cardinal, Tantoo. Films: "Gunsmoke: Return to Dodge" TVM-1987 (Little Doe); "Dances with Wolves" 1990 (Black Shawl); "Black Robe" 1991-Can./Australia (Chomina's Wife); "Silent Tongue" 1993 (Silent Tongue); "Tecumseh: The Last Warrior" TVM-1995 (Turtle Mother). ¶TV: *Dr. Quinn, Medicine Woman*—"Heroes" 5-1-93 (Snowbird), "The Race" 9-25-93 (Snowbird), "Sanctuary" 10-2-93 (Snowbird), "The Offering" 1-8-94 (Snowbird).

Cardinale, Claudia (1939-). Films: "The Professionals" 1966 (Maria Grant); "Once Upon a Time in the West" 1968-Ital. (Jill McBain); "The Legend of Frenchie King" 1971-Fr./Ital./Span./Brit. (Maria).

Cardona, Annette. TV: *The High Chaparral*—"Follow Your Heart" 10-4-68 (Jill); *Gunsmoke*—"The Noonday Devil" 12-7-70 (Rita); *Bonanza*—"Customs of the Country" 2-6-72 (Carmen).

Cardos, John (1928-). Films:

"Deadwood '76" 1965; "Five Blood Graves" 1969 (Joe Lightfoot/Satago); "The Female Bunch" 1971 (Mexican Farmer). ¶TV: *The Monroes*—"Ghosts of Paradox" 3-15-67; *The High Chaparral*—"The Terrorist" 12-17-67 (3rd Bandit); *Daniel Boone*—"The Far Side of Fury" 3-7-68, "The Dandy" 10-10-68 (Longknife).

Cardwell, James (1921-2/4/54). Films: "Canyon Passage" 1946 (Gray Bartlett); "Robin Hood of Texas" 1947 (Duke Mantel); "Down Dakota Way" 1949 (Saunders); "San Antone Ambush" 1949 (Clint Wheeler); "The Arizona Cowboy" 1950 (Hugh Davenport).

Caress, William. Films: "Black Jack" 1927 (1st Deputy); "Chain Lightning" 1927 (Tom Yeats); "Hello Cheyenne" 1928 (Bus Driver).

Carew, Arthur (1894-4/23/37). Films: "Rio Grande" 1920 (Don Jose Alvarado); "Bar Nothin'" 1921 (Stinson).

Carew, Ora (1893-10/26/55). Films: "The Martyrs of the Alamo" 1915 (Mrs. Dickinson); "Go West, Young Man" 1918 (Rosa Crimmins); "The Terror of the Range" 1919-serial; "Big Town Round-Up" 1921 (Alice Beaumont); "Cold Fury" 1925.

Carewe, Edwin (1883-1/22/40). Films: "Down the Rio Grande" 1913; "The Mexican Spy" 1913.

Carey, Buck. Films: "The Denver Dude" 1927 (Red Quincy); "Man from Hell's Edges" 1932.

Carey, Ed. Films: "Rawhide Terror" 1934; "Arizona Trails" 1935; "Lightnin' Crandall" 1937.

Carey, Harry (1878-9/21/47). Films: "A Cry for Help" 1912; "Heredity" 1912; "In the Aisles of the Wild" 1912; "My Hero" 1912; "Three Friends" 1912; "The Abandoned Well" 1913; "The Battle at Elderbrush Gulch" 1913; "The Broken Ways" 1913; "The Brothers" 1913; "A Chance Deception" 1913; "The Ranchero's Revenge" 1913; "The Sheriff's Baby" 1913; "The Stolen Treaty" 1913; "Two Men of the Desert" 1913; "The Battle of Frenchman's Run" 1915; "The Gambler's I.O.U." 1915; "The Heart of a Bandit" 1915; "Judge Not, or the Woman of Mona Diggings" 1915 (Miles Rand); "Just Jim" 1915 (Jim); "The Sheriff's Dilemma" 1915; "The Bad Man of Cheyenne" 1916 (Cheyenne Harry); "The Committee on Credentials" 1916; "The Conspiracy" 1916; "The Devil's Own" 1916; "For the Love a Girl" 1916; "Guilty" 1916; "A Knight of the Range" 1916 (Cheyenne Harry); "Love's Lariat" 1916 (Sky High); "The Night Riders" 1916; "The Passing of Hell's Crown" 1916; "The Three Godfathers" 1916 (Bob Sangster); "The Almost Good Man" 1917; "Blood Money" 1917; "Bucking Broadway" 1917 (Cheyenne Harry); "Cheyenne's Pal" 1917 (Cheyenne Harry); "The Drifter" 1917; "The Fighting Gringo" 1917 (William "Red" Saunders); "A 45 Calibre Mystery" 1917; "Goin' Straight" 1917; "The Golden Bullet" 1917; "Hair-Trigger Burk" 1917; "The Honor of an Outlaw" 1917; "A Marked Man" 1917 (Cheyenne Harry); "The Outlaw and the Lady" 1917; "The Secret Man" 1917 (Cheyenne Harry); "Six-Shooter Justice" 1917; "The Soul Herder" 1917 (Cheyenne Harry); "Straight Shooting" 1917 (Cheyenne Harry); "Sure Shot Morgan" 1917; "The Texas Sphinx" 1917; "The Wrong Man" 1917; "Hell Bent" 1918 (Cheyenne Harry); "The Phantom Riders" 1918 (Cheyenne Harry); "The Scarlet Drop" 1918 (Kaintuck Ridge); "Thieves' Gold" 1918 (Cheyenne Harry); "Three Mounted Men" 1918 (Cheyenne Harry); "Wild Women" 1918 (Cheyenne Harry); "A Woman's Fool" 1918 (Lin McLean); "The Ace of the Saddle" 1919 (Cheyenne Harry Henderson); "Bare Fists" 1919 (Cheyenne Harry); "A Fight for Love" 1919 (Cheyenne Harry); "A Gun Fightin' Gentleman" 1919 (Cheyenne Harry); "Marked Men" 1919 (Harry); "The Outcasts of Poker Flat" 1919 (Square Shootin' Harry Lanyon/John Oakhurst); "The Rider of the Law" 1919 (Jim Kyneton); "Riders of Vengeance" 1919 (Cheyenne Harry); "Roped" 1919 (Cheyenne Harry); "Blue Streak McCoy" 1920 (Job McCoy); "Bullet Proof" 1920 (Pierre Winton); "Hearts Up" 1920 (David Brent); "Human Stuff" 1920 (Jim Pierce); "Overland Red" 1920 (Overland Red); "Sundown Slim" 1920 (Sundown Slim); "West Is West" 1920 (Dick Rainboldt); "Desperate Trails" 1921 (Bart Carson); "The Fox" 1921 (Ol' Santa Fe); "The Freeze-Out" 1921 (Ohio); "If Only Jim" 1921 (Jim Golden); "The Wallop" 1921 (John Wesley Pringle); "Good Men and True" 1922 (J. Wesley Pringle); "The Kick Back" 1922 (White Horse Harry); "Man to Man" 1922 (Steve Packard); "Canyon of the Fools" 1923 (Bob); "Crashin' Thru" 1923 (Blake); "Desert Driven" 1923 (Bob Grant); "The Miracle Baby" 1923 (Neil Allison); "The Lightning Rider" 1924 (Philip Morgan); "The Night Hawk" 1924 (the Hawk); "Tiger Thompson" 1924 (Tiger Thompson); "The Bad Lands" 1925 (Patrick Angus O'-Toole); "Beyond the Border" 1925 (Bob Smith); "The Flaming Forties" 1925 (Bill Jones); "The Man from Red Gulch" 1925 (Sandy); "The Prairie Pirate" 1925 (Brian Delaney); "Soft Shoes" 1925 (Pat Halahan); "Silent Sanderson" 1925 (Joe Parsons/ Silent Sanderson); "The Texas Trail" 1925 (Peter Grainger); "Driftin' Thru" 1926 (Dan Brown); "The Frontier Trail" 1926 (Jim Cardigan); "Satan Town" 1926 (Bill Scott); "The Seventh Bandit" 1926 (David Scanlon); "Border Patrol" 1928 (Bill Storm); "Burning Brides" 1928 (Jim Whitely/Bob Whitely); "The Trail of '98" 1929 (Jack Locasto); "Cavalier of the West" 1931 (Captain John Allister); "The Vanishing Legion" 1931-serial (Cardigan); "Border Devils" 1932 (Jim Gray); "The Devil Horse" 1932-serial (Norton Roberts); "The Last of the Mohicans" 1932-serial; "Law and Order" 1932 (Ed Brant); "The Night Rider" 1932 (John Brown); "Without Honor" 1932 (Pete Marlan); "Man of the Forest" 1933 (Jim Gaynor); "Sunset Pass" 1933 (John Hesbitt); "The Thundering Herd" 1934 (Clark Sprague); "The Last of the Clintons" 1935 (Trigger Carson); "Powdersmoke Range" 1935 (Tucson Smith); "Rustlers' Paradise" 1935 (Cheyenne Kincaid); "Wagon Trail" 1935 (Sheriff Hartley); "Wild Mustang" 1935 (Joe "Mustang" Norton); "Ghost Town" 1936 (Cheyenne Harry Morgan); "The Last Outlaw" 1936 (Dean Payton); "Sutter's Gold" 1936 (Kit Carson); "Aces Wild" 1937 (Cheyenne Harry); "Border Cafe" 1937 (Tex Stevens); "The Law West of Tombstone" 1938 (Bonanza Bill Barker); "The Shepherd of the Hills" 1941 (Daniel Howitt, the Shepherd); "The Spoilers" 1942 (Al Dextry); "Duel in the Sun" 1946 (Lem Smoot); "Angel and the Badman" 1947 (Wistful McClintock); "The Sea of Grass" 1947 (Doc Reid); "Red River" 1948 (Mr. Millville).

Carey, Jr., Harry (1921-). Films: "Pursued" 1947 (Prentice McComber); "Blood on the Moon" 1948; "Red River" 1948 (Dan Latimer); "The Three Godfathers" 1948 (William "the Abilene Kid" Kearney); "She Wore a Yellow Ribbon" 1949 (Lt. Ross Pennell); "Copper Canyon" 1950 (Lt. Ord); "Rio Grande" 1950 (Trooper Daniel "Sandy" Boone); "Wagonmaster" 1950 (Sandy Owens); "Warpath" 1951 (Capt. Gregson); "San Antone" 1953 (Dobe); "The Outcast" 1954 (Bert); "Silver Lode" 1954 (Johnson); "The

Great Locomotive Chase" 1956 (William Bensinger); "The Searchers" 1956 (Brad Jorgensen); "Seventh Cavalry" 1956 (Cpl. Morrison); "Gun the Man Down" 1957 (Deputy Lee); "From Hell to Texas" 1958 (Trueblood); "Escort West" 1959 (Travis); "Rio Bravo" 1959 (Harold); "Noose for a Gunman" 1960 (Jim Ferguson); "Two Rode Together" 1961 (Ortho Clegg); "Cheyenne Autumn" 1964 (Trooper Smith); "The Raiders" 1964 (Jellicoe); "Taggart" 1964 (Lt. Hudson); "Shenandoah" 1965 (Jenkins); "Alvarez Kelly" 1966 (Cpl. Peterson); "Billy the Kid vs. Dracula" 1966 (Ben); "The Rare Breed" 1966 (Ed Mabry); "The Way West" 1967 (McBee); "Ballad of Josie" 1968 (Mooney); "Bandolero!" 1968 (Cort Hyjack); "Death of a Gunfighter" 1969 (Rev. Rork); "The Undefeated" 1969 (Webster); "Dirty Dingus Magee" 1970 (Stuart); "Big Jake" 1971 (Pop Dawson); "One More Train to Rob" 1971 (Red); "Something Big" 1971 (Joe Pickens); "Cahill, United States Marshal" 1973 (Hank); "A Man from the East" 1974-Ital./Fr. (Holy Joe); "Take a Hard Ride" 1974-Ital./Brit./Ger. (Dumper); "Trinity Is Still My Name" 1974-Ital. (Father); "Kate Bliss and the Ticker Tape Kid" TVM-1978 (Deputy Luke); "The Long Riders" 1980 (George Arthur); "Wild Times" TVM-1980 (Fitz Bragg); "The Shadow Riders" TVM-1982 (Pa Traven); "Once Upon a Texas Train" TVM-1988; "Bad Jim" 1990 (C.J. Lee); "Back to the Future, Part III" 1990 (Saloon Old Timer); "Tombstone" 1993 (Marshal Fred White); "Wyatt Earp: Return to Tombstone" TVM-1994 (Digger). ¶TV: *Broken Arrow*—"Blood Brothers" 5-13-58 (Captain Ward); *Have Gun Will Travel*—"The Gentleman" 9-27-58 (Bud), "The Road to Wickenberg" 10-25-58 (Sheriff Jack Goodfellow), "The Posse" 10-3-59 (the Sheriff), "The Misguided Father" 2-27-60 (Sheriff Stander), "The Marshal's Boy" 11-26-60 (Gulley), "The Legacy" 12-10-60, "The Tax Gatherer" 2-11-61 (Jesse Turner), "The Revenger" 9-30-61 (Sheriff Conlon), "The Jonah" 5-26-62 (Ben Murdock), "Taylor's Woman" 9-22-62 (Thad Taylor), "Sweet Lady of the Moon" 3-9-63 (Ben Murdock), "Face of a Shadow" 4-20-63 (Earl Tibner), "The Sanctuary" 6-22-63 (Jonas Quincy); *Texas John Slaughter*—Regular 1958-61 (Ben Jenkins); *Wagon Train*—"Chuck Wooster, Wagonmaster" 5-20-59 (Wilkins), "The George B. Hanrahan Story" 3-28-62 (Tim

Hogan), "The Molly Kincaid Story" 9-16-63 (Hankins); *Gunsmoke*—"Kangaroo" 9-26-59 (Charlie Deesha), "Bad Sheriff" 1-7-61 (Deputy Turloe), "Quint Asper, Comes Home" 9-29-62 (Jim Grant), "Abe Blocker" 11-24-62 (Jake), "The Quest for Asa Janin" 6-1-63 (Colridge), "Bank Baby" 3-20-65 (Jim Fisher), "Baker's Dozen" 12-25-67 (Will Roniger), "Waco" 12-9-68 (Nathan Cade), "The Lost" 9-13-71 (Will Roniger), "The Bullet" 11-29-71, 12-6-71 & 12-13-71 (Kelliher), "Trail of Bloodshed" 3-4-74 (Amos Brodie); *Rawhide*—"Incident of the Shambling Men" 10-9-59 (Tanner), "Deserter's Patrol" 2-9-62 (Walsh); *Tombstone Territory*—3-4-60 (Vern Fawcett); *The Rifleman*—"The Deserter" 3-15-60 (Lt. Paul Rolfe), "The Journey Back" 10-30-61; *Hotel De Paree*—"Sundance and the Long Trek" 4-22-60 (Masters); *Overland Trail*—"Sour Annie" 5-8-60 (Storekeeper); *Bonanza*—"The Mission" 9-17-60 (Corporal Burton), "The Flannel-Mouth Gun" 1-31-65 (Shelton), "Judgment at Red Creek" 2-26-67 (Mapes); *The Tall Man*—"One of One Thousand" 12-31-60 (Dusty); *Laramie*—"The Debt" 4-18-61 (Harry Markle), "The Barefoot Kid" 1-9-62 (Dan Emery), "Lost Allegiance" 10-30-62 (Whitey Banister), "Time of the Traitor" 12-11-62 (Hobey); *Tales of Wells Fargo*—"Gunman's Revenge" 5-22-61 (Pete Carter); *Whispering Smith*—"Safety Value" 6-5-61 (Sergeant Stringer); *Lawman*—"Cort" 4-29-62 (Mitch Evers); *Frontier Circus*—"The Race" 5-3-62 (Anderson); Stoney Burke—"Tigress by the Tail" 5-6-63 (Jack Rollins); *Redigo*—"Man in a Blackout" 11-5-63 (Harry); *Branded*—"The Vindicator" 1-31-65 (Lt. John Pritchett); *The Legend of Jesse James*—"The Celebrity" 12-6-65 (Ellie's Father); *The Rounders*—9-6-66 (MacKenzie); *Cimarron Strip*—"Sound of a Drum" 2-1-68; *The Outcasts*—"The Thin Edge" 2-17-69 (Sheriff); *The Men from Shiloh*—"Follow the Leader" 12-2-70 (Thad).

Carey, Leonard (1887-9/11/77). Films: "Rose Marie" 1936 (Louis). ¶TV: *Circus Boy*—"Counterfeit Clown" 4-7-57 (Judson).

Carey, Macdonald (1913-3/21/94). Films: "Streets of Laredo" 1949 (Lorn Reming); "Comanche Territory" 1950 (James Bowie); "Copper Canyon" 1950 (Lane Travis); "Cave of Outlaws" 1951 (Pete Carver); "The Great Missouri Raid" 1951 (Jesse James); "Hannah Lee" 1953 (Bus Crow); "Stranger at My Door" 1956 (Hollis Jarret); "Man or Gun" 1958

(Maybe Smith). ¶TV: *Zane Grey Theater*—"License to Kill" 2-7-58 (Sheriff Tom Baker); *Wagon Train*—"The Bill Tawnee Story" 2-12-58 (Bill Tawnee); *Rawhide*—"Incident of the Golden Calf" 3-13-59 (Brother Bent); *Daniel Boone*—"A Place of 1000 Spirits" 2-4-65 (Lt. Henry Pitcairn); *Branded*—"The Mission" 3-14-65, 3-21-65 & 3-28-65 (Senator Lansing).

Carey, Mary Jane. Films: "Border Vengeance" 1935 (Sally Griswold); "The Lusty Men" 1952 (Girl).

Carey, Michelle (1943-). Films: "El Dorado" 1967 (Joey MacDonald); "Dirty Dingus Magee" 1970 (Anna); "The Animals" 1971 (Alice McAndrew); "Scandalous John" 1971 (Amanda McCanless); "The Legend of the Golden Gun" TVM-1979 (Maggie Oakley). ¶TV: *Wild Wild West*—"The Night of the Feathered Fury" 1-13-67 (Gerda), "The Night of the Winged Terror" 1-17-68 & 1-24-68 (Laurette); *Alias Smith and Jones*—"A Fistful of Diamonds" 3-4-71 (Betsy Samison); *Gunsmoke*—"Tara" 1-17-72 (Tara Hutson); *Dirty Sally*—"Right of Way" 1-11-74 (Dolly).

Carey, Olive (1896-3/13/88). Films: "Face to Face" 1952 ("The Bride Comes to Yellow Sky" segment—the Saloon Keeper); "Pillars of the Sky" 1956 (Mrs. Anne Avery); "The Searchers" 1956 (Mrs. Jorgensen); "Gunfight at the O.K. Corral" 1957 (Mrs. Clanton); "Night Passage" 1957 (Miss Vittles); "Run of the Arrow" 1957 (Mrs. O'Meara); "The Alamo" 1960 (Mrs. Dennison); "Two Rode Together" 1961 (Abby Frazer); "Billy the Kid vs. Dracula" 1966 (Dr. Henrietta Hull). ¶TV: *Tales of Wells Fargo*—"Jesse James" 7-1-57 (Maw Samuel); *The Restless Gun*—"Duel at Lockwood" 9-23-57 (Grandmother), "The Peddler" 6-9-58 (Osa Carpenter); *Wagon Train*—"The Jessie Cowan Story" 1-8-58 (Aunt Dorcas); *The Rifleman*—"Shivaree" 2-3-59; *Cimarron City*—"The Evil One" 4-4-59 (Widow Means); *Tombstone Territory*—"Trail's End" 4-10-59 (Frieda Thompson); *The Law of the Plainsman*—"The Innocents" 12-10-59; *Laramie*—"Deadly Is the Night" 11-7-61 (Ma Tolliver); *Have Gun Will Travel*—"Lazarus" 1-20-62 (Old Woman); *Lawman*—"The Youngest" 4-22-62 (Ma Martin).

Carey, Philip (1925-). Films: "Cattle Town" 1952 (Ben Curran); "The Man Behind the Gun" 1952 (Capt. Roy Giles); "Springfield Rifle" 1952 (Capt. Tennick); "Calamity

Jane" 1953 (Lt. Gilmartin); "Gun Fury" 1953 (Frank Slayton); "The Nebraskan" 1953 (Wade Harper); "Massacre Canyon" 1954 (Lt. Richard Faraday); "The Outlaw Stallion" 1954 (Doc Woodrow); "They Rode West" 1954 (Capt. Peter Blake); "Count Three and Pray" 1955 (Albert Loomis); "Wyoming Renegades" 1955 (Brady Sutton); "Return to Warbow" 1958 (Clay Hollister); "Tonka" 1958 (Capt. Miles Keogh); "The Great Sioux Massacre" 1965 (Col. Custer); "Town Tamer" 1965 (Slim Akins). ¶TV: *Zane Grey Theater*—"One Must Die" 1-12-61 (John Baylor); *Stagecoach West*—"The Root of Evil" 2-28-61 (Major Ralph Barnes); *The Rifleman*—"Death Trap" 5-9-61 (Dr. Simon Battle); *Tales of Wells Fargo*—"The Dodger" 10-7-61 (Jay Squire); *Lawman*—"Change of Venue" 2-11-62 (Barron Shaw); *Cheyenne*—"One Way Ticket" 2-19-62 (Cole Younger), "Johnny Brassbuttons" 12-3-62 (Marshal Frank Nolan);*Bronco*—"Until Kingdom Come" 3-26-62; *The Virginian*—"Siege" 12-18-63 (Duke Logan), "We've Lost a Train" 4-21-65 (Captain Parmalee); *Laredo*—Regular 1965-67 (Captain Parmalee); *Daniel Boone*—"The Necklace" 3-9-67 (Gordon Lang); *Custer*—"Massacre" 10-4-67 (Benton Conant); *Cimarron Strip*—"Knife in the Darkness" 1-25-68 (Kallman); *Gunsmoke*—"Trafton" 10-25-71 (Bannion).

Carey, Timothy (1925-5/11/94). Films: "Hellgate" 1952 (Wyand); "The Last Wagon" 1956 (Cole Harper); "The Naked Gun" 1956; "One-Eyed Jacks" 1961 (Howard Tetley); "The Second Time Around" 1961 (Bonner); "Rio Conchos" 1964 (Barman); "A Time for Killing" 1967 (Billy Cat); "Waterhole No. 3" 1967 (Hilb). ¶TV: *Gunsmoke*—"The Gentleman" 6-7-58 (Tiller Evans), "Quaker Girl" 12-10-66 (Charles "Buster" Rilla); *Rawhide*—"The Book" 1-8-65 (Carl Hatcher), "Encounter at Boot Hill" 9-14-65 (Deputy Walker); *The Big Valley*—"Teacher of Outlaws" 2-2-66 (Preacher); *Cowboy in Africa*—"The Red Hand of Michael O'Neill" 2-5-68 (Mike O'Neill); *Cimarron Strip*—"Big Jessie" 2-8-68 (Lobo); *Daniel Boone*—"The Blackbirder" 10-3-68 (Lute Purdy); *The Virginian*—"Home to Methuselah" 11-26-69 (Zach Ontro); *Kung Fu*—"Ambush" 4-5-75 (Bix Courtney).

Cargo, David (1929-). Films: "The Good Guys and the Bad Guys" 1969 (Newspaperman).

Carle, Naida. Films "Wild Bill Hickok" 1923 (Fanny Kate).

Carle, Richard (1871-6/28/41). Films: "Zander the Great" 1925 (Mr. Pepper); "The Last Round-Up" 1934 (Judge Savin); "Home on the Range" 1935 (James Butts); "Moonlight on the Prairie" 1935 (Col. Gowdy); "Nevada" 1935 (Judge Franklindge); "The Arizona Raiders" 1936 (Boswell Abernathy); "Arizona Mahoney" 1936 (Sheriff); "Drift Fence" 1936 (Sheriff Bingham); "The Texas Rangers" 1936 (Casper Johnson).

Carleton, Claire (1913-12/11/79). Films: "Frontier Gal" 1945 (Gracie); "Gun Town" 1946 (Belle Townley); "That Texas Jamboree" 1946; "Bad Men of Tombstone" 1949 (Nellie); "Satan's Cradle" 1949; "The Fighter" 1952 (Sheila); "Ride the Man Down" 1952 (Amelia); "Jubilee Trail" 1954 (Estelle, the Madame); "Fort Massacre" 1958 (Adele); "The Miracle of the Hills" 1959 (Sally). ¶TV: *The Gene Autry Show*—"Outlaw of Blue Mesa" 9-7-54; *Wyatt Earp*—"The Killer" 10-25-55, "Kill the Editor" 12-16-58 (Sally Bascom); *The Lone Ranger*—"The Letter Bride" 11-15-56; *Maverick*—"Lonesome Reunion" 9-28-58 (Flora); *Wanted–Dead or Alive*—"Miracle at Pot Hole" 10-25-58; *Rawhide*—"Incident of the Day of the Dead" 9-18-59; *Wagon Train*—"Trial for Murder" 4-27-60 & 5-4-60, "The Shad Bennington Story" 6-22-60 (Mrs. Teale), "The Cathy Eckhardt Story" 11-9-60 (Woman), "The Christopher Hale Story" 3-15-61 (Mrs. Hennessey), "The Chottsie Gubenheimer Story" 1-10-65 (Mrs. Mortimer); *The Tall Man*—"Ladies of the Town" 5-20-61 (Mrs. Tatum); *Laredo*—"That's Noway, Thataway" 1-20-66.

Carleton, George (1885-9/23/50). Films: "Jackass Mail" 1942 (Pastor); "Riding High" 1943 (Dad Castle); "Marshal of Laredo" 1945; "Sioux City Sue" 1946; "The Last Round-Up" 1947; "Night Time in Nevada" 1948 (Jason Howley); "Calamity Jane and Sam Bass" 1949 (Mr. Sherman); "Prince of the Plains" 1949 (Sam Phillips).

Carleton, William P. (1873-4/6/47). Films: "Gloria's Romance" 1916-serial; "The Border Patrolman" 1936 (Jeremiah Huntley).

Carlin, Jean. Films: "The Caravan Trail" 1946 (Paula Bristol); "Ghost of Hidden Valley" 1946 (Kaye); "Six Gun Man" 1946 (Laura Barton); "Song of the Sierras" 1946; "Wild West" 1946 (Mollie); "Prairie Outlaws" 1948.

Carlin, Lynn (1930-). Films: "Wild Rovers" 1971 (Sada Billings). ¶TV: *Gunsmoke*—"Milligan" 11-6-72 (Janet Milligan).

Carlisle, David. Films: "Apache Warrior" 1957 (Cavalry Leader). ¶TV: *Wyatt Earp*—"The Too Perfect Crime" 12-6-60 (Gibbens); *The Legend of Jesse James*—"Three Men from Now" 9-13-65 (Peters).

Carlisle, James. Films: "Adventures of Red Ryder" 1940-serial (Board Member); "Saddle Pals" 1947; "Dangers of the Canadian Mounted" 1948-serial (Martin Addison).

Carlisle, Mary. Films: "Rovin' Tumbleweeds" 1939 (Mary).

Carlisle, Richard. Films: "When a Man's a Man" 1935 (Dean Baldwin).

Carlos, Don. Films: "Gun Fury" 1953; "A Lawless Street" 1955 (Juan Tobrez); "Wyoming Renegades" 1955 (Bob Meeks); "The Professionals" 1966 (Bandit). ¶TV: *The Rebel*—"Deathwatch" 10-23-60 (Torres).

Carlson, Charles. TV: *The Outlaws*—"The Daltons Must Die" 1-26-61 & 2-2-61 (Grat Dalton); *Wagon Train*—"The Saul Bevins Story" 4-12-61 (Lloyd), "The Kate Crawley Story" 1-27-64 (Jessup Harmon); *Stoney Burke*—"Child of Luxury" 10-15-62 (Roger Chase).

Carlson, Erika. Films: "The Great Scout and Cathouse Thursday" 1976 (Monday).

Carlson, June. Films: "Queen of the Yukon" 1940 (Helen Martin); "The Hawk of Powder River" 1948 (Carole); "Jeep-Herders" 1949.

Carlson, Karen (1945-). Films: "Wild Horses" TVM-1985 (Ann Cooper). ¶TV: *Here Come the Brides*—"Here Come the Brides" 9-25-68, "Lovers and Wanderers" 11-6-68, "After a Dream Comes Mourning" 1-1-69, "Wives for Wakando" 1-22-69 (Mary Ellen); *Death Valley Days*—"The Mezcla Man" 1-3-70, "The Visitor" 12-27-69, "Pioneer Pluck" 4-4-70 (Annabelle); *Bonanza*—"The Marriage of Theodora Duffy" 1-9-73 (Duffy); *Centennial*—Regular 1978-79 (Lisette Mercy).

Carlson, Richard (1912-11/24/77). Films: "Seminole" 1953 (Maj. Harlan Degan); "The Last Command" 1955 (William Travis); "Kid Rodelo" 1966-U.S./Span. (Link); "The Valley of Gwangi" 1969 (Champ Connors). ¶TV: *MacKenzie's Raiders*—Regular 1958-59 (Colonel Ranald Mackenzie); *Riverboat*—"The Faithless" 11-22-59 (Paul Drake); *Wagon Train*—"The Cassie Vance

Story" 12-23-63 (Adam), "The Clay Shelby Story" 12-6-64 (Lieutenant Burns); *The Virginian*—"Smile of a Dragon" 2-26-64 (Sheriff Marden), "Farewell to Honesty" 3-24-65 (Major Ralph Forrester); *Rawhide*—"Brush War at Buford" 11-23-65 (Major Buford); *Bonanza*—"The Thirteenth Man" 1-21-68 (Arch Hollenbeck); *Lancer*—"Welcome to Genesis" 11-18-69 (Judah Abbott).

Carlson, Steve (1943-). Films: "The Brothers O'Toole" 1973. ¶TV: *The Virginian*—"Nobody Said Hello" 1-5-66 (Davis Pritikin), "Trail to Ashley Mountain" 11-2-66 (Willy Parker), "Bitter Autumn" 11-1-67 (Will), "The Decision" 3-13-68 (Deputy Frank North); *Wild Wild West*—"The Night of the Tycoons" 3-28-69 (Lionel Bronston); *Gunsmoke*—"The Cage" 3-23-70 (Roy Stewart).

Carlton, Ken. Films: "The Marauders" 1955 (Thumbo).

Carlyle, Aileen. Films: "The Dude Wrangler" 1930 (Dude Guest); "Return of the Texan" 1952 (Cordy Spiller).

Carlyle, David. Films: "Cherokee Strip" 1937 (Tom Valley).

Carlyle, Francis (1868-9/15/16). Films: "Arena" 1913 (Colonel Bonham); "The Perils of Pauline" 1914-serial.

Carlyle, Jack. Films: "The Girl Who Dared" 1920 (Joe Knowles); "Lahoma" 1920 (Kansas Kimball); "The Smoke Signal" 1920; "A Tough Tenderfoot" 1920; "North of the Rio Grande" 1922 (Brideman); "Desert Driven" 1923 (Warden); "Billy the Kid" 1930 (Brewer); "Ghost City" 1932 (Henchman); "Law of the North" 1932; "Mason of the Mounted" 1932 (Luke Kirby); "The Phantom Empire" 1935-serial; "The Mysterious Avenger" 1936 (Captain Ranger).

Carlyle, John. TV: *Northwest Passage*—"Dead Reckoning" 1-16-59; *The Dakotas*—"A Nice Girl from Goliah" 5-13-63 (Beau Kellog).

Carlyle, Pat. Films: "The Irish Gringo" 1935 (Don O'Brien).

Carlyle, Richard (1879-6/12/42). Films: "Shootin' Irons" 1927 (Jim Blake); "Taking a Chance" 1928 (Dan Carson); "In Old California" 1929 (Arturo); "Girl of the Golden West" 1930 (Jim Larkins); "Mountain Justice" 1930 (Judge Keets); "Quick Trigger Lee" 1931 (John "Dad" Saunders); "The Saddle Buster" 1932 (Bible Jude).

Carlyle, Richard. Films: "The

Iron Mistress" 1952 (Rezin Bowie). TV: *26 Men*—"Long Trail Home" 2-10-59, "Ricochet" 2-24-59; *The Texan*—"Reunion" 5-4-59 (Lacey Winans), "Mission to Monteray" 6-13-60 (Clay Beaumont); *Wanted—Dead or Alive*—"Breakout" 9-26-59 (Mr. Phipps), "Monday Morning" 3-8-61 (Charlie Glover); *Death Valley Days*—"The Million Dollar Pants" 4-19-60 (Patrick Mahoney); *The Alaskans*—"The Silent Land" 5-15-60 (Fleming); *The Tall Man*—"Trial by Hanging" 11-4-61 (Swade Hiney); *Rawhide*—"Incident of Judgment Day" 2-8-63 (Sam Jordan); *Great Adventure*—"The Outlaw and the Nun" 12-6-63 (Mr. Pierce); *Gunsmoke*—"One Killer on Ice" 1-23-65 (Rowdy); *A Man Called Shenandoah*—"The Verdict" 11-1-65 (Parks).

Carmel, Roger C. (1929-11/11/86). Films: "Alvarez Kelly" 1966 (Capt. Angus Ferguson). TV: *The High Chaparral*—"The New Lion of Sonora" 2-19-71 (Casados).

Carmen, Jean (1913-8/26/93). Films: "Born to Battle" 1935; "Arizona Gunfighter" 1937 (Beth Lorimer); "Gunsmoke Ranch" 1937 (Marion Warren); "The Painted Stallion" 1937-serial (the Rider); "Crashing Thru" 1939 (Ann Chambers); "In Old Montana" 1939 (June Allison); "Smoky Trails" 1939 (Marie); "Yes, We Have No Bonanza" 1939-short (Saloon Girl); "The Three Outlaws" 1956; "War Drums" 1957 (Yellow Moon).

Carmen, Jewel. Films: "The Half Breed" 1916 (Nellie); "Lawless Love" 1918 (LaBelle Geraldine).

Carmichael, Hoagy (1899-12/27/81). Films: "Canyon Passage" 1946 (Linnet); "Timberjack" 1955 (Jingles). ¶TV: *Laramie*—Regular 1959-60 (Jonesy).

Carmichael, Patsy. Films: "Heroes of the Saddle" 1940 (Annie).

Carnahan, Suzanne. *see* Peters, Susan.

Carne, Judy (1939-). TV: *Bonanza*—"A Question of Strength" 10-27-63 (Sister Mary Kathleen); *Gunsmoke*—"Sweet Billy, Singer of Songs" 1-15-66 (Pearl); *The Big Valley*—"Explosion!" 11-20-67 & 11-27-67 (Bridget Wells); *Alias Smith and Jones*—"The Root of It All" 4-1-71 (Leslie O'Hara).

Carnell, Cliff (1932-9-5-93). Films: "The White Buffalo" 1977 (Johnny Varner). ¶TV: *The Adventures of Rin Tin Tin*—"Boone's Wedding Day" 11-18-55, "The Last Chance" 12-16-55.

Carnell, Suzi. TV: *Wagon Train*—"The Odyssey of Flint McCullough" 2-15-61 (Kathie); *Have Gun Will Travel*—"Everyman" 3-25-61 (Juney Mincus), "The Gospel Singer" 10-21-61 (Melissa Griffin); *Cheyenne*—"The Brahma Bull" 12-11-61 (Lucy); *Empire*—"Seven Days on Rough Street" 2-26-63 (Twyla).

Carnera, Primo (1906-6/29/67). TV: *Sheriff of Cochise*—"Human Bomb" 10-12-56.

Carney, Alan (1911-5/2/73). Films: "Girl Rush" 1944 (Mike Strager); "North to Alaska" 1960 (Bartender with Hat); "The Comancheros" 1961; "The Adventures of Bullwhip Griffin" 1967 (Joe Turner); "Wild Rovers" 1971 (Palace Bartender). ¶TV: *Have Gun Will Travel*—"The Five Books of Owen Deaver" 4-26-58, "The Mark of Cain" 1-13-62 (Teague); *The Tall Man*—"The Liberty Belle" 9-16-61 (Wino); *Daniel Boone*—"Take the Southbound Stage" 4-6-67 (Stagecoach Driver).

Carney, Art (1918-). TV: *The Men from Shiloh*—"With Love, Bullets, and Valentines" 10-7-70 (Skeet).

Carney, Augustus. Films: "Alkali Bests Broncho Billy" 1912 (Alkali Kid); "Love on Tough Luck Ranch" 1912; "At the Lariat's End" 1913; "The Last Card" 1915; "The Martyrs of the Alamo" 1915 (Old Soldier); "Blue Blood and Red" 1916.

Carney, Marion. Films: "Driftin' River" 1946 (Mitzi); "Daughter of the West" 1949 (Okeema).

Carney, Thom. TV: *Wild Bill Hickok*—"Treasure Trail" 12-30-52; *Gunsmoke*—"Word of Honor" 10-1-55 (Jack); *Sergeant Preston of the Yukon*—"Dog Race" 1-19-56 (Buck Adams), "Rebellion in the North" 7-12-56 (Bone), "Turnabout" 8-22-56 (Ernie Stevens); *Wyatt Earp*—"The Arizona Lottery" 2-16-60 (Holbrook); *Bat Masterson*—"End of the Line" 1-26-61 (Captain Scott); *The Rifleman*—"Lou Mallory" 10-15-62 (Moss); *The Legend of Jesse James*—"A Real Tough Town" 1-24-66 (Meyers).

Carnovsky, Morris (1898-9/1/92). Films: "Western Pacific Agent" 1950.

Carol, Ann. Films: "The Ghost Rider" 1935 (Linda Bullard).

Carol, Sue (1909-2/4/82). Films: "The Lone Star Ranger" 1930 (Mary Aldridge).

Caron, Leslie (1931-). Films: "Madron" 1970-U.S./Israel (Sister Mary).

Caron, Patricia. Films: "Idaho Red" 1929 (Mary Regan); "The Singing Cowboy" 1936 (Miss Kane).

Caron, Rene. TV: *Tomahawk*—Regular 1957-58 (Medard).

Carpenter, Carlton (1926-). Films: "Vengeance Valley" 1951 (Hewie); "Sky Full of Moon" 1952 (Harley Williams). ¶TV: *Luke and the Tenderfoot*—Pilot 8-6-55 & 8-13-55 (Pete Queen); *Cimarron City*—"A Legacy for Ossie Harper" 1-10-59 (Ossie Harper); *Trackdown*—"The Eyes of Jerry Kelson" 4-22-59 (Jerry Kelso); *The Rifleman*—"The Coward" 12-22-59 (George Collins).

Carpenter, Deborah. Films: "Where the Hell's That Gold?!!!" TVM-1988 (Pearl).

Carpenter, Florence. Films: "The World Apart" 1917 (Rose de Braisy); "The Testing Block" 1920 (Rosita); "Belle of Alaska" 1922 (Chicago Belle).

Carpenter, Francis. Films: "The Patriot" 1916 (Billy Allen); "True Blue" 1918 (Bob as a Child); "The Lone Star Ranger" 1923 (Laramie's Son).

Carpenter, Frank "Red". Films: "The Lawless Rider" 1954 (Big Red); "Outlaw Treasure" 1955; "I Killed Wild Bill Hickok" 1956 (Ring Pardo).

Carpenter, H.C. Films: "The Border Raiders" 1918; "The Devil's Trail" 1919.

Carpenter, Hank. Films: "Rollin' Plains" 1938 (Hank Tomlin).

Carpenter, Horace B. (1875-5/21/45). Films: "The Call of the North" 1914 (Rand); "The Virginian" 1914 (Spanish Kid); "The Cost of Hatred" 1917 (Ramon); "The Jaguar's Claws" 1917; "Nan of Music Mountain" 1917 (McAlpin); "The Terror of the Range" 1919-serial; "King's Creek Law" 1923 (the Sheriff); "Headin' Through" 1924 (Pop Hilder); "The Silent Stranger" 1924 (Sam Hull); "Travelin' Fast" 1924 (Sheriff Ted Clark); "The Texas Terror" 1926; "The Arizona Kid" 1929 (Jack Grant); "Bride of the Desert" 1929 (Sheriff); "False Feathers" 1929; "Riders of the Rio Grande" 1929 (Dan Steelman); "West of the Rockies" 1929 (Hair-Trigger Strong); "South of Sonora" 1930; "Partners of the Trail" 1931 (Skeets Briggs); "Pueblo Terror" 1931 (Sheriff); "Riders of the Rio" 1931 (Sheriff); "Trails of the Golden West" 1931; "Wild West Whoopee" 1931; "The Galloping Kid" 1932; "Riders of the Desert" 1932 (Capt. Jim Reynolds); "Breed of the Border" 1933; "The Dude Bandit" 1933; "The Fighting Parson" 1933; "King of the Arena" 1933; "Gun Law" 1933; "The Lone Avenger" 1933; "Outlaw Justice" 1933; "The Phantom Thunderbolt" 1933; "Riders of Destiny" 1933; "Gun Justice" 1934; "In Old Santa Fe" 1934 (Ranch Hand); "The Pecos Dandy" 1934; "Range Riders" 1934; "Smoking Guns" 1934; "West of the Divide" 1934; "Between Men" 1935 (Dobson); "Desert Mesa" 1935 (Ed Calder); "The Irish Gringo" 1935; "Lawless Riders" 1935; "The Man from Guntown" 1935 (Gillespie); "Paradise Canyon" 1935; "Smokey Smith" 1935; "Sunset Range" 1935; "Western Frontier" 1935; "Cavalry" 1936; "The Fugitive Sheriff" 1936; "King of the Pecos" 1936; "The Last of the Warrens" 1936; "The Lawless Nineties" 1936; "The Lonely Trail" 1936; "Lucky Terror" 1936 (Coroner); "Oh, Susannah!" 1936; "Rogue of the Range" 1936 (Blacksmith Lem); "The Unknown Ranger" 1936; "Arizona Gunfighter" 1937; "Bar Z Bad Men" 1937; "The Big Show" 1937; "Border Phantom" 1937; "Doomed at Sundown" 1937 (Lew Sprague); "Git Along, Little Dogies" 1937; "Gun Lords of Stirrup Basin" 1937; "The Gun Ranger" 1937; "Gunsmoke Ranch" 1937 (Larkin); "The Law Commands" 1937; "North of the Rio Grande" 1937; "The Painted Stallion" 1937-serial (Old Timer); "Range Defenders" 1937 (Pete); "Ranger Courage" 1937; "The Red Rope" 1937; "Rustler's Valley" 1937 (Party Guest); "Trail of Vengeance" 1937 (Rancher); "Trailing Trouble" 1937; "Where Trails Divide" 1937; "Cattle Raiders" 1938; "Colorado Kid" 1938; "Flaming Frontier" 1938-serial; "Man from Music Mountain" 1938; "Panamint's Bad Man" 1938; "Paroled to Die" 1938; "Phantom Ranger" 1938; "Pride of the West" 1938; "Santa Fe Stampede" 1938; "Starlight Over Texas" 1938; "The Stranger from Arizona" 1938; "Sunset Trail" 1938; "Utah Trail" 1938; "Come on, Rangers" 1939; "Dodge City" 1939; "The Lone Ranger Rides Again" 1939-serial (Townman #1); "Rovin' Tumbleweeds" 1939; "Saga of Death Valley" 1939; "Spoilers of the Range" 1939; "Trigger Smith" 1939; "One Man's Law" 1940; "The Trail Blazers" 1940; "Bad Man of Deadwood" 1941; "Billy the Kid's Roundup" 1941; "Gauchos of El Dorado" 1941; "The Lone Rider in Frontier Fury" 1941; "Thunder Over the Prairie" 1941; "White Eagle" 1941-serial; "Wrangler's Roost" 1941; "Arizona Roundup" 1942; "Billy the Kid Trapped" 1942; "Heart of the Golden West" 1942; "In Old California" 1942; "Outlaws of Pine Ridge" 1942; "Rolling Down the Great Divide" 1942 (Townsman); "Shadows on the Sage" 1942; "Texas Justice" 1942; "Westward Ho" 1942; "Where Trails End" 1942; "Carson City Cyclone" 1943; "Silver City Raiders" 1943; "Cheyenne Wildcat" 1944; "Code of the Prairie" 1944 (Jim, the Townsman); "Marshal of Reno" 1944; "Range Law" 1944; "Sheriff of Sundown" 1944; "Silver City Kid" 1944; "Sonora Stagecoach" 1944; "Vigilantes of Dodge City" 1944; "Zorro's Black Whip" 1944-serial (Citizen #5); "Bandits of the Badlands" 1945; "Colorado Pioneers" 1945; "Corpus Christi Bandits" 1945; "Flame of the West" 1945; "Gangster's Den" 1945 (Barfly); "Great Stagecoach Robbery" 1945; "Lone Texas Ranger" 1945.

Carpenter, John (John Forbes). Films: "The Navajo Trail" 1945; "Northwest Trail" 1945; "Santa Fe Saddlemates" 1945; "Song of Old Wyoming" 1945 (Buck); "Trail of Kit Carson" 1945; "The El Paso Kid" 1946; "Song of the Wasteland" 1947; "The Stranger from Ponca City" 1947; "Relentless" 1948 (Posse Man); "Red Canyon" 1949 (Man); "Border Outlaws" 1950 (Keller); "The Fighting Stallion" 1950 (Chuck); "Badman's Gold" 1951 (Johnny), "Cattle Queen" 1951 (Tucson Kid); "Law and Order" 1953; "Son of the Renegade" 1953 (Red River Johnny); "The Lawless Rider" 1954 (Rod Tatum); "Outlaw Treasure" 1955; "I Killed Wild Bill Hickok" 1956 (Johnny Rebel); "Red Sundown" 1956 (Zellman); "Tomboy and the Champ" 1961 (Fred Anderson). ¶TV: *Wild Bill Hickok*—"Masked Riders" 10-30-51; *Judge Roy Bean*—"The Runaway" 10-15-55 (Bentril), "Slightly Prodigal" 10-30-55 (Sully), "Black Jack" 11-1-55 (Sam Ketchum), "Citizen Romeo" 12-1-55 (Bolger), "Murder in Langtry" 12-1-55 (Ted Sloan), "Vinegarone" 12-1-55 (Garth Davis); *Sergeant Preston of the Yukon*—"Totem Treasure" 3-1-57 (Burrows); *26 Men*—"Parrish Gang" 4-1-58; *The Rifleman*—"Nora" 5-24-60.

Carpenter, Virginia. Films: "Outlaws of the Rio Grande" 1941 (Rita); "Rollin' Home to Texas" 1941 (Mary); "Ghost Town Law" 1942 (Josie Hall); "The Lone Star Vigilantes" 1942 (Shary Monroe).

Carper, Larry. Films: "Distant Drums" 1951 (Chief Oscala).

Carr, Betty Ann (1947-). Films:

"The Deerslayer" TVM-1978 (Wa-Wa-Te). ¶TV: *Nakia*—"The Dream" 11-23-74 (Paulette); *The Life and Times of Grizzly Adams*—4-6-77 (Sumi).

Carr, Darleen (1950-). Films: "Death of a Gunfighter" 1969 (Hilda Jorgenson); "Law of the Land" TVM-1976 (Selina Jensen); "Bret Maverick" TVM-1981 (Mary Lou Springer). ¶TV: *The Virginian*—"Family Man" 10-15-69 (Anna); *Alias Smith and Jones*—"McGuffin" 12-9-72 (Kate); *The Oregon Trail*—Regular 1977 (Margaret Devlin); *Bret Maverick*—Regular 1981-82 (Mary Lou "M.L." Springer).

Carr, Darwin. Films: "Britton of the Seventh" 1916 (Lt. Tony Britton).

Carr, Estelle. Films: "Passage West" 1951 (Minna Karns).

Carr, Harry. Films: "Ridin' Down the Trail" 1947; "Rustlers of Devil's Canyon" 1947 (Tad).

Carr, Jack (1899-2/2/68). Films: "Bullwhip" 1958 (Trimble); "Seven Guns to Mesa" 1958 (Sam Denton); "Toughest Gun in Tombstone" 1958 (Telegraph Operator); "The Purple Hills" 1961 (A.J. Beaumont). ¶TV: *The Texan*—"Johnny Tuvo" 5-30-60; *Bonanza*—"The Auld Sod" 2-4-62.

Carr, June. Films: "Son of Billy the Kid" 1949 (Betty Raines).

Carr, Karen. Films: "The Life and Times of Judge Roy Bean" 1972 (Mrs. Grubb).

Carr, Lorena. Films: "Riders of the Rio" 1931 (Doris Hart).

Carr, Marian. Films: "The Fighting Marshal" 1931 (Aunt Emily).

Carr, Marion. Films: "Northern Patrol" 1953 (Quebec Kid); "Ghost Town" 1956 (Barbara Leighton).

Carr, Mary Kennevan (1874-6/24/73). Films: "The Sign Invisible" 1918 (Mrs. Winston); "Calibre 38" 1919 (Rosemary); "The Mine with the Iron Door" 1924 (Mother Burton); "The Gold Hunters" 1925 (Mary Mcallister); "Jesse James" 1927 (Mrs. Zerelda Samuels); "The Utah Kid" 1930 (Aunt Ada); "The Fighting Marshal" 1931; "The Fighting Fool" 1932; "Forbidden Trail" 1932 (Mrs. Middleton); "Gun Law" 1933 (Mother Andrews); "West of Rainbow's End" 1938 (Mrs. Carter); "Oregon Trail" 1945 (Granny Layton); "Friendly Persuasion" 1956 (Emma, the Quaker Woman).

Carr, Michael. Films: "Hills of Oklahoma" 1950 (Tommy); "Apache Warrior" 1957 (Apache); "He Rides Tall" 1964 (Lefty); "Convict Stage" 1965; "Fort Courageous" 1965; "War Party" 1965; "Powderkeg" TVM-1971; "The Barbary Coast" TVM-1975. ¶TV: *Wild Bill Hickok*—"Good Indian" 8-4-53; *The Adventures of Rin Tin Tin*—"O'Hara Gets Busted" 5-6-55 (Chief Broken Knife), "Rusty's Remedy" 2-28-58 (Brave), "Spanish Gold" 3-7-58 (Carlos); *Wyatt Earp*—"Warpath" 10-22-57 (Young Wolf), "Three" 5-13-58 (Young Wolf), "Four" 5-27-58 (Young Wolf), "Horse Race" 3-3-59 (Little Elk), "The Fugitive" 11-17-59 (Manuel Vasquez); *Maverick*—"Alias Bart Maverick" 10-5-58 (Sioux Indian #3); *Have Gun Will Travel*—"The Solid Gold Patrol" 12-13-58 (Courier); *Colt .45*—"The Magic Box" 4-19-59 (White Wolf); *Gunsmoke*—"Root Down" 10-6-62 (Cowboy); *Rango*—"Rango the Outlaw" 1-13-67 (Corporal Medwin), "What's a Nice Girl Like You Doing Holding Up a Place Like This?" 2-17-67 (Corporal Atkins); *The Guns of Will Sonnett*—"Of Lasting Summers and Jim Sonnett" 10-6-67 (Deputy); *Alias Smith and Jones*—"The Girl in Boxcar Number Three" 2-11-71 (Briggs), "Never Trust an Honest Man" 4-15-71 (Hank).

Carr, Nat (1886-7/6/44). Films: "The Man from Arizona" 1932 (Moe Ginsberg); "Red Blood of Courage" 1935 (Meyer); "Heart of the North" 1938 (Clerk); "Dodge City" 1939 (Crocker).

Carr, Paul (1934-). Films: "Posse from Hell" 1961 (Jack Wiley); "The Wild Women of Chastity Gulch" TVM-1982 (Captain). ¶TV: *Have Gun Will Travel*—"Young Gun" 11-8-58 (Jeff Calvert); *The Rifleman*—"Shivaree" 2-3-59 (Derek Hanaway), "The Woman" 5-5-59 (Garth Healey), "Letter of the Law" 12-1-59, "Smoke Screen" 4-5-60 (Doug Carter); *Trackdown*—"Stranger in Town" 3-25-59 (Joshua); *Wanted—Dead or Alive*—"The Conquerers" 5-2-59 (Arnold Wilson); *Zane Grey Theater*—"The Law and the Gun" 6-4-59 (Danny Crago), "Shadows" 11-5-59 (Branch Neeley); *Man from Blackhawk*—"The New Semaria Story" 10-23-59; *Black Saddle*—"The Deal" 12-4-59 (Joey); *Wichita Town*—"The Avengers" 2-3-60 (Jud); *Johnny Ringo*—"Border Town" 3-17-60 (Al Parker); *Pony Express*—"Payoff" 4-13-60 (Gunner Jackford); *Bonanza*—"Death at Dawn" 4-30-60 (McNeil); *Wrangler*—"A Time for Hanging" 8-11-60 (Billy John); *Rawhide*—"Incident at the Top of the World" 1-27-61 (Jason Adams), "Incident of the Wolvers" 11-16-62 (Luther Cannon), "Incident at Dead Horse" 4-16-64 & 4-23-64 (Mark Hammerklein); *The Tall Man*—"Big Sam's Boy" 3-4-61 (Lonnie); *Gunsmoke*—"The Squaw" 11-11-61 (Cully), "Gold Mine" 12-25-65 (Jud Gibbijohn); *The Outlaws*—"Walk Tall" 11-16-61 (Jan Batory); *Laramie*—"Time of the Traitor" 12-11-62 (Steve Prescott), "The Violent Ones" 3-5-63 (Bill Blayne); *The Virginian*—"The Golden Door" 3-13-63 (Kane), "A Distant Fury" 3-20-63, "Sue Ann" 1-11-67 (Joe), "To Bear Witness" 11-29-67 (Pete Varig); *The Travels of Jaimie McPheeters*—"The Day of the 12 Candles" 2-23-64 (Ross Oliver); *A Man Called Shenandoah*—"The Debt" 10-18-65 (Billy Claymoor); *Cimarron Strip*—"The Beast That Walks Like a Man" 11-30-67; *Lancer*—"Chase a Wild Horse" 10-8-68; *Alias Smith and Jones*—"Something to Get Hung About" 10-21-71.

Carr, Stephen. Films: "North of '36" 1924 (Cinquo Centavos); "The Thundering Herd" 1925 (Ory Tracks).

Carr, Stephen. Films: "Colorado Ranger" 1950 (Regan); "Crooked River" 1950 (Butch); "Fast on the Draw" 1950; "Hostile Country" 1950 (Curt); "Marshal of Heldorado" 1950 (Razor); "Outlaws of Texas" 1950 (Sheriff); "West of the Brazos" 1950 (Rusty).

Carr, Tom (-8/18/46). Films: "The Wild Bull's Lair" 1925 (Henry Harbison); "Men Without Law" 1930 (Tom Healy); "Range Defenders" 1937 (the Kid).

Carr, William (1867-2/13/37). Films: "The Taking of Rattlesnake Bill" 1913.

Carradine, Bruce. TV: *Kung Fu*—"Empty Pages of a Dead Book" 1-10-74 (Sheriff), "One Step to Darkness" 1-25-75 (Captain Starbuck).

Carradine, Calista. Films: "Kung Fu: The Movie" TVM-1986 (Bridget).

Carradine, David (1945-). Films: "Taggart" 1964 (Cal Dodge); "The Good Guys and the Bad Guys" 1969 (Waco); "Heaven with a Gun" 1969 (Coke Beck); "Young Billy Young" 1969 (Jessie Boone); "Macho Callahan" 1970 (Col. David Mountford); "The McMasters" 1970 (White Feather); "Kung Fu" TVM-1972 (Kwai Chang Caine); "Mr. Horn" TVM-1979 (Tom Horn); "High Noon, Part II: The Return of Will Kane" TVM-1980 (Ben Irons); "The Long Riders" 1980 (Cole Younger);

"Kung Fu: The Movie" TVM-1986 (Kwai Chang Caine); "The Gambler Returns: The Luck of the Draw" TVM-1991 (Kwai-Chang Caine). ¶TV: *The Virginian*—"The Intruders" 3-4-64 (the Utah Kid); Shane—Regular 1966 (Shane); *Cimarron Strip*—"The Hunted" 10-5-67 (Gene Gauge); *Gunsmoke*—"Lavery" 2-22-71 (Clint); *Kung Fu*—Regular 1972-75 (Kwai Chang Caine); *Young Riders*—"Ghosts" 9-28-90 ("the Buzzard Eater")

Carradine, John (John Peter Richmond) (1906-11/27/88). Films: "To the Last Man" 1933 (Pete Garon); "Daniel Boone" 1936 (Simon Girty); "Ramona" 1936 (Jim Farrar); "White Fang" 1936 (Beauty Smith); "Drums Along the Mohawk" 1939 (Caldwell); "Frontier Marshal" 1939 (Ben Carter); "Jesse James" 1939 (Bob Ford); "Stagecoach" 1939 (Hatfield); "Brigham Young—Frontiersman" 1940 (Porter Rockwell); "The Return of Frank James" 1940 (Bob Ford); "Western Union" 1941 (Doc Murdoch); "Northwest Rangers" 1942 (Martin Caswell); "Silver Spurs" 1943 (Lucky Miller); "Alaska" 1944; "Barbary Coast Gent" 1944 (Duke Cleat); "Johnny Guitar" 1954 (Old Tom); "Thunder Pass" 1954; "The Kentuckian" 1955 (Fletcher); "Stranger on Horseback" 1955 (Col. Streeter); "Hidden Guns" 1956 (Snipe Harding); "The True Story of Jesse James" 1957 (Rev. Jethro Bailey); "The Proud Rebel" 1958 (Travelling Salesman); "Showdown at Boot Hill" 1958 (Doc Weber); "The Oregon Trail" 1959 (Zachariah Garrison); "The Man Who Shot Liberty Valance" 1962 (Maj. Cassius Starbuckle); "Cheyenne Autumn" 1964 (Maj. Jeff Blair); "Billy the Kid vs. Dracula" 1966 (Dracula); "Cain's Way" 1969 (Preacher Sims); "Five Blood Graves" 1969 (Boone Hawkins); "The Good Guys and the Bad Guys" 1969 (Ticker); "The McMasters" 1970 (Preacher); "The Gatling Gun" 1972 (Rev. Harper); "The Shootist" 1976 (Beckum); "The White Buffalo" 1977 (Amos Briggs). ¶TV: *Wild Bill Hickok*—"The Gorilla of Owl Hoot Mesa" 9-23-52; *Gunsmoke*—"The Reed Survives" 12-31-55 (Ephraim Hunt), "Target" 9-5-59 (Mr. Kadar); *My Friend Flicka*—"The Cameraman" 2-24-56; *Cheyenne*—"Decision at Gunsight" 4-23-57 (Delos Gerrard); *Wagon Train*—"The Dora Gray Story" 1-29-58 (Doc), "The Colter Craven Story" 11-23-60 (Park Cleatus), "The Eli Bancroft Story" 11-11-63 (Mason); *The Restless Gun*—"More Than Kin" 5-26-58 (Archibald Plunkette); *Have*

Gun Will Travel—"The Statue of San Sebastian" 6-14-58 (Father Bartolome); *Sugarfoot*—"Devil to Pay" 12-23-58 (Mathew McDavitt); *Cimarron City*—"Child of Fear" 1-17-59 (Jared Tucker); *The Rifleman*—"The Photographer" 1-27-59 (Abel Goss), "The Mind Reader" 6-30-59 (James Barrow McBride); *Rough Riders*—"The End of Nowhere" 2-12-59 (Alexander Sugrue); *Bat Masterson*—"The Tumbleweed Wagon" 3-25-59 (Vince Morgan); *Wyatt Earp*—"The Fugitive" 11-17-59 (Don Ignacio Vasquez); *Wanted—Dead or Alive*—"Tolliver Bender" 2-13-60 (Amos McKenna); *The Rebel*—"Johnny Yuma" 10-4-59 (Dodson), "The Bequest" 9-25-60 (Elmer Dodson); *Overland Trail*—"The Reckoning" 5-29-60 (Nash); *Maverick*—"Red Dog" 3-5-61 (Judge Reest); *Bonanza*—"Springtime" 10-1-61 (Jebediah), "Dead Wrong" 12-7-69 (Dillard); *Death Valley Days*—"Miracle at Boot Hill" 1-24-62 (the Stranger); *Lawman*—"The Actor" 5-27-62 (Hendon); *Laredo*—"Sound of Terror" 4-7-66 (Prof. Smythe); *Branded*—"The Mission" 3-14-65, 3-21-65 & 3-28-65 (Gen. Joshua McCord), "The Assassins" 3-27-66 & 4-3-66 (Gen. Joshua McCord), "Kellie" 4-24-66 (Gen. Joshua McCord); *The Legend of Jesse James*—"As Far as the Sea" 3-21-66 (Noah); *Hondo*—"Hondo and the Judas" 11-3-67 (Doc Zeeber); *Daniel Boone*—"The Witness" 1-25-68 (Zack Pike); *The Big Valley*—"Town of No Exit" 4-7-69 (Brown); *Johnny Ringo*—"The Rain Man" 11-26-69 (the Rain Man); *Kung Fu*—"Dark Angel" 11-11-72 (Serenity Johnson), "The Nature of Evil" 3-21-74 (Serendipity Johnson), "Ambush" 4-5-75 (Serendipity Johnson); *The Cowboys*—2-27-74 (Oscar Schmidt).

Carradine, Keith (1950-). Films: "A Gunfight" 1971 (Cowboy); "McCabe and Mrs. Miller" 1971 (Cowboy); "Kung Fu" TVM-1972 (Middle Caine); "The Godchild" TVM-1974 (Lieutenant Louis); "The Long Riders" 1980 (Jim Younger). ¶TV: *Bonanza*—"Bushwacked" 10-3-71 (Ern).

Carradine, Robert (1954-). Films: "The Cowboys" 1972 (Slim Honeycutt); "The Long Riders" 1980 (Bob Younger). ¶TV: *Bonanza*—"A Home for Jamie" 12-19-71 (Phinney McLean); *Kung Fu*—"Dark Angel" 11-11-72 (Sunny Jim); *The Cowboys*—Regular 1974 (Slim).

Carrasco, Ada. Films: "The Bravados" 1958 (Mrs. Parral); "Two Mules for Sister Sara" 1970 (Juan's Mother).

Carraway, Robert. Films: "Soldier Blue" 1970 (Lt. John McNair). TV: *Pistols 'n' Petticoats*—12-24-66 (the Rev. Mr. Smith).

Carre, Bartlett A. (1897-4/26/71). Films: "Flying Hoofs" 1925 (Henry Moody); "Battling Buckaroo" 1932; "Guns for Hire" 1932; "The Reckless Rider" 1932; "Texas Tornado" 1932 (Slim); "Fighting Cowboy" 1933 (Pete Quimby); "Lightning Range" 1934 (Jim); "Outlaws' Highway" 1934 (Unger); "Rawhide Romance" 1934 (Hank); "Border Vengeance" 1935; "Cheyenne Tornado" 1935; "Circle of Death" 1935; "Five Bad Men" 1935 (Lige Jenkins); "Western Courage" 1935; "Gun Smoke" 1936; "Raw Timber" 1937.

Carrera, Barbara (1944-). Films: "The Master Gunfighter" 1975 (Eula). ¶TV: *Centennial*—Regular 1978-79 (Clay Basket).

Carricart, Robert (1917-). Films: "Blood on the Arrow" 1964 (Kai-La); "Guns of Diablo" 1964 (Mendez); "Apache Uprising" 1966 (Chico Lopez); "Villa Rides" 1968 (Don Luis Gonzalez); "Land Raiders" 1969-U.S./Span. (Rojas); "The Mark of Zorro" TVM-1974 (Dock Worker); "Donner Pass: The Road to Survival" TVM-1978. ¶TV: *Wanted—Dead or Alive*—"The Favor" 11-15-58; *Yancy Derringer*—"Fire on the Frontier" 4-2-59 (Thaddeus Stevens); *Tales of Wells Fargo*—"Wanted: Jim Hardie" 12-21-59 (Pedro), "Leading Citizen" 11-14-60 (Coley Davis); *Wichita Town*—"Brothers of the Knife" 2-10-60 (Micelli); *Johnny Ringo*—"Lobo Lawman" 6-23-60 (Gonzales); *Wrangler*—"Encounter at Elephant Butte" 9-15-60 (Laredo); *Cheyenne*—"Two Trails to Santa Fe" 10-28-60; *Zane Grey Theater*—"The Last Bugle" 11-24-60 (Patino); *Have Gun Will Travel*—"A Quiet Night in Town" 1-7-61 & 1-14-61 (Joselito Kincaid), "Duke of Texas" 4-22-61 (Pablo Mendez), "A Knight to Remember" 12-9-61 (Dirty Dog); *The Outlaws*—"The Sooner" 4-27-61 (Moretti); *Bonanza*—"The Deserter" 10-21-62, "A Stranger Passed This Way" 3-3-63 (Don Escobar); *The Travels of Jaimie McPheeters*—"The Day of the Reckoning" 3-15-64 (Mendez); *Branded*—"Survival" 1-24-65; *Death Valley Days*—"A Bell for Volcano" 1-24-65 (Gomez); *The Big Valley*—"Joaquin" 9-11-67 (Benito Flores); *The High Chaparral*—"The Firing Wall" 12-31-67 (Undertaker).

Carrick, Gene. Films: "Gun Town" 1946 (Davey Sawyer).

Carrie, Steve. Films: "Good Men and Bad" 1923 (Steve Kinnard).

Carrier, Albert (1919-). Films: "Major Dundee" 1965 (Capt. Jacques Tremaine). ¶TV: *Maverick*—"Island in the Swamp" 11-30-58 (Phillipe Theirot); *Northwest Passage*—"The Secret of the Cliff" 1-9-59 (Gen. Marquis de Montcalm); *Death Valley Days*—"A Town Is Born" 1-20-59 (Captain Molet); *Sugarfoot*—"Man from Medora" 11-21-60 (Count Raoul Beauchamp); *Daniel Boone*—"The Ben Franklin Encounter" 3-18-65 (M. Charles Penet), "Perilous Journey" 12-16-65 (Marquis De Lafayette).

Carrigan, Tom J. (1886-10/2/41). Films: "Told in Colorado" 1911; "Western Hearts" 1911 (Sam Long); "Why the Sheriff Is a Bachelor" 1911; "Salome Jane" 1923 (Rufe Waters).

Carrillo, Leo (1888-9/10/61). Films: "Lasca of the Rio Grande" 1931 (Jose Santa Cruz); "The Broken Wing" 1932 (Capt. Innocencio); "The Gay Desperado" 1936 (Pablo Braganza); "The Barrier" 1937 (Poleon Doret); "Arizona Wildcat" 1938 (Manuel Hernandez); "The Girl of the Golden West" 1938 (Mosquito); "The Girl and the Gambler" 1939 (El Rayo); "Twenty Mule Team" 1940 (Piute Pete); "Wyoming" 1940 (Pete Marillo); "The Kid from Kansas" 1941 (Pancho); "Riders of Death Valley" 1941-serial (Pancho); "Road Agent" 1941 (Pancho); "American Empire" 1942 (Dominique Beauchard); "Men of Texas" 1942 (Sam Sawyer); "Sin Town" 1942 (Angelo Colina); "Frontier Badman" 1943 (Chinito); "Moonlight and Cactus" 1944 (Pasualito); "Under Western Skies" 1945 (King Randall); "The Valiant Hombre" 1948 (Pancho); "The Daring Caballero" 1949 (Pancho); "The Gay Amigo" 1949 (Pancho); "Satan's Cradle" 1949 (Pancho); "The Girl from San Lorenzo" 1950 (Pancho); "Pancho Villa Returns" 1950-Mex. (Pancho Villa). ¶TV: *The Cisco Kid*—Regular 1951-55 (Pancho).

Carrington, Jack. Films: "Zorro's Fighting Legion" 1939-serial (Antonio Gomez).

Carrol, Regina (1943-11/4/92). Films: "The Female Bunch" 1971 (Waitress); "Jessi's Girls" 1976 (Claire).

Carroll, Alma. Films: "Pardon My Gun" 1942 (Dodie Cameron); "A Tornado in the Saddle" 1942; "Silver City Raiders" 1943 (Dolores Alvarez); "Wyoming Hurricane" 1944.

Carroll, Ann. Films: "The Road to Denver" 1955 (Miss Honeywell). TV: *Wild Bill Hickok*—"School Teacher Story" 1-15-52, "Marriage Feud of Ponca City" 5-13-52; *Death Valley Days*—"City of Widows" 12-21-60 (Mrs. Gibbs); *Empire*—"65 Miles Is a Long, Long Way" 4-23-63 (Helen).

Carroll, Brandon. Films: "Ride in the Whirlwind" 1966 (Sheriff). TV: *Bob Hope Chrysler Theatre*—"Massacre at Fort Phil Kearny" 10-26-66 (Sentry Hanify); *Gunsmoke*—"Exodus 21:22" 3-24-69 (Lloyd).

Carroll, Dee (1926-4/28/80). Films: "War Arrow" 1953 (Hysterical Woman); "A Day of Fury" 1956 (Miss Timmons); "Shoot-Out at Medicine Bend" 1957; "Five Bold Women" 1960 (Crazy Hannah). ¶TV: *Trackdown*—"Easton, Texas" 10-25-57 (Larissa); *Lawman*—"The Substitute" 10-22-61 (Trilby Johnson); *Bonanza*—"Journey Remembered" 11-11-63 (Rachel), "The Pursued" 10-2-66 & 10-9-66 (Mrs. Blaisdale); *Wagon Train*—"The Fenton Canaby Story" 12-30-63 (Elizabeth); *Daniel Boone*—"The Gun" 2-3-66 (Sarah Goodal); *The Virginian*—"The Return of Golden Tom" 3-9-66 (Sarah Tedler), "Requiem for a Country Doctor" 1-25-67 (Sarah Miller), "The Barren Ground" 12-6-67 (Rena Cameron); *The Big Valley*—"Alias Nellie Handley" 2-24-69 (Meely); *Gunsmoke*—"Sam McTavish, M.D." 10-5-70 (Ellen), "The Lost" 9-13-71 (Mrs. Grayson); *Hec Ramsey*—"Dead Heat" 2-3-74 (Mary).

Carroll, Diahann (1935-). TV: *Lonesome Dove*—Pilot 10-2-94, 10-9-94 & 10-16-94 (Ida Grayson).

Carroll, Jack "Jidge". Films: "Shooting High" 1940 (Gabby Cross); "Forty Guns" 1957 (Barney Cashman).

Carroll, Janice (1932-). Films: "Shane" 1953 (Susan Lewis).

Carroll, John (1907-4/24/79). Films: "Hi Gaucho!" 1936 (Lucio); "Zorro Rides Again" 1937-serial (James Vega/Zorro); "Rose of the Rio Grande" 1938 (El Gato/Don Ramon de Paralta); "Wolf Call" 1939 (Michael Vance); "Go West" 1940 (Terry Turner); "Pierre of the Plains" 1942 (Pierre); "The Fabulous Texan" 1947 (John Wesley Barker); "Wyoming" 1947 (Glenn Forrester); "Old Los Angeles" 1948 (Johnny Morrell); "Surrender" 1950 (Gregg Delaney); "Belle Le Grand" 1951 (John Kilton); "Decision at Sundown" 1957 (Tate Kimbrough); "Plunderers of Painted Flats" 1959 (Clint Jones). ¶TV: *Hondo*—"Hondo and the War Hawks" 10-20-67 (Buckeye Jack Smith).

Carroll, Laurie. TV: *Maverick*—"Hostage!" 11-10-57 (Yvette Devereaux); *Zorro*—"The Secret of the Sierra" 3-13-58 (Marya); *Tales of Wells Fargo*—"The Gun" 4-14-58 (Laurie Borkman); *Broken Arrow*—"Turncoat" 4-15-58 (Kodaysay); *Death Valley Days*—"The Big Rendezvous" 4-15-58, "A Bullet for the Captain" 1-13-59, "Hang 'Em High" 2-14-60 (Sharon); *The Adventures of Rin Tin Tin*—"Brave Bow" 4-18-58 (Small Flower); *Tales of the Texas Rangers*—"Kickback" 12-12-58 (Janet Carr).

Carroll, Leo G. (1892-10/16/72). TV: *Cheyenne*—"Rendezvous at Red Rock" 2-21-56.

Carroll, Lucia. Films: "Santa Fe Trail" 1940; "Wild Bill Hickok Rides" 1942 (Flora).

Carroll, Madeleine (1906-10/2/87). Films: "Northwest Mounted Police" 1940 (April Logan).

Carroll, Mary. Films: "The Secret of Convict Lake" 1951 (Millie Gower). ¶TV: *Rawhide*—"The Captain's Wife" 1-12-62 (Laundress).

Carroll, Nancy (1906-8/6/65). Films: "Riders of the Purple Sage" 1918 (Fay Larkin); "The Water Hole" 1928 (Judith Endicott).

Carroll, Pat (1927-). Films: "The Brothers O'Toole" 1973. ¶TV: *Nakia*—"A Matter of Choice" 12-7-74 (Belle Jones).

Carroll, Peggy (1915-3/3/81). Films: "A Lady Takes a Chance" 1943 (Jitterbug).

Carroll, Taylor. Films: "The Sawdust Trail" 1924 (Lafe Webster).

Carroll, Victoria. Films: "The Fastest Guitar Alive" 1967 (Margie).

Carroll, Virginia (1910-86). Films: "A Tenderfoot Goes West" 1937 (Ann Keith); "Oklahoma Terror" 1939 (Helen); "The Masked Rider" 1941 (Margerita); "The Phantom Cowboy" 1941 (Elanita); "Prairie Gunsmoke" 1942; "Raiders of the West" 1942; "The Last Round-Up" 1947; "Frontier Agent" 1948; "Overland Trails" 1948; "Triggerman" 1948; "Bad Men of Tombstone" 1949 (Mrs. Stover); "Crashing Thru" 1949; "Riders of the Whistling Pines" 1949; "The Blazing Sun" 1950. ¶TV: *The Roy Rogers Show*—"The Desert Fugitive" 2-24-52, "Hard Luck Story" 10-31-54 (Helen Graham), "Uncle Steve's Finish" 2-3-55 (Helen Everett), "Quick Draw" 3-20-55 (Julia Hanley), "His Weight in Wildcats" 11-11-56; *Wild Bill Hickok*—"Cry Wolf" 10-7-52.

Carroll, William A. (1876-1/26/28). Films: "John Ermine of the Yellowstone" 1917 (Crooked Bear); "A Woman's Fool" 1918 (Lusk); "North of '36" 1924 (Sanchez); "The Wanderer of the Wasteland" 1924 (Merryvale); "Born to the West" 1926 (Nell's Father).

Carrott, Ric. TV: *Dirty Sally*—"My Fair Laddie" 3-29-74 (Ortho).

Carruthers, Ben (1935-9/27/83). TV: *Gunsmoke*—"The Cast" 12-6-58 (Rufe Tucker).

Carruthers, Bruce (1901-1/1/54). Films: "Heart of the North" 1938 (Pedeault); "Gene Autry and the Mounties" 1951.

Carry, Jack. Films: "The Hawk of Wild River" 1952 (Pete); "Gun Belt" 1953 (Mort); "The Man from Laramie" 1955 (Mule Driver).

Carry, Julius. TV: *The Adventures of Brisco County, Jr.*—Regular 1993-94 (Lord Bowler).

Carson, Fred. Films: "The Charge at Feather River" 1953 (Chief Thunder Hawk); "Son of the Renegade" 1953 (Big Fred); "Requiem for a Gunfighter" 1965. TV: *Tales of Wells Fargo*—"The Hijackers" 6-17-57 (Jack); *The Virginian*—"The Brothers" 9-15-65 (Cut Hand), "The Gauntlet" 2-8-67 (Walvis); *Branded*—"The Richest Man in Boot Hill" 10-31-65 (Scotty); *Daniel Boone*—"Gun-Barrel Highway" 2-24-66 (Tall Bear); *Laredo*—"A Taste of Money" 4-28-66; *Wild Wild West*—"The Night of the Bottomless Pit" 11-4-66 (Le Cochon).

Carson, Jack (1910-1/2/63). Films: "Circle of Death" 1935 (Jerry Carr); "Destry Rides Again" 1939 (Jack Tyndall); "The Kid from Texas" 1939 (Stanley Brown); "Two Guys from Texas" 1948 (Danny Foster); "Red Garters" 1954 (Jason Carberry). TV: *Screen Director's Playhouse*—"Arroyo" 10-26-55 (Lamar Kendall); *Bonanza*—"Mr. Henry Comstock" 11-7-59 (Henry T.P. Comstock); *Zane Grey Theater*—"Sundown Smith" 3-24-60 (Sundown Smith).

Carson, Jean (1925-). TV: *Death Valley Days*—"Perilous Cargo" 6-23-57 (Della Allison); *Wagon Train*—"The Riley Gratton Story" 12-4-57 (Dance Hall Girl), "The Annie MacGregor Story" 2-5-58 (Annie MacGregor); *Sugarfoot*—"Small War at Custer Junction" 1-7-58 (Lilly); *Stoney Burke*—"Bandwagon" 12-17-62 (Merle).

Carson, John. Films: "The Black Lash" 1952 (Cord); "Thunder Over the Plains" 1953; "Saskatchewan" 1954 (Cook).

Carson, Kit (1909-2/11/78). Films: "Cowboy Courage" 1925 (Bud Austin); "His Greatest Battle" 1925; "Ridin' Wild" 1925 (Jim Warren); "Pony Express Rider" 1926; "Twin Six O'Brien" 1926; "Walloping Kid" 1926 (the Walloping Kid); "In Old Monterey" 1939; "The Outcasts of Poker Flat" 1952 (Man); "City of Badmen" 1953 (Deputy); "Fangs of the Arctic" 1953. TV: *Tales of Wells Fargo*—"Two Cartridges" 9-16-57 (Jake), "Deadwood" 4-7-58 (Morgan), "Day of Judgment" 9-5-60 (Man), "Reward for Gaine" 1-20-62 (Guard), "Who Lives by the Gun" 3-24-62 (Man).

Carson, May. Films: "The Fighting Ranger" 1922 (Ruth).

Carson, Robert "Bob" (1910-6/2/79). Films: "Ambush Trail" 1946 (Ed Blane); "The Fighting Stallion" 1950 (Tom Adams); "Indian Territory" 1950 (Capt. Wallace); "Mule Train" 1950 (Bill Cummings); "Advance to the Rear" 1964 (Col. Holbert). TV: *The Lone Ranger*—"The Man Who Came Back" 1-5-50, "Behind the Law" 2-1-51, "Treason at Dry Creek" 12-4-52, "The Empty Strongbox" 1-8-53, "Stage to Tishomingo" 10-28-54; *Sergeant Preston of the Yukon*—"Remember the Maine" 4-26-56 (Pete Calhoun), "Scourge of the Wilderness" 1-11-57 (Don Grady); *Maverick*—"According to Hoyle" 10-6-57 (Kittredge), "Lonesome Reunion" 9-28-58 (Masher), "The Thirty-Ninth Star" 11-16-58 (Dixon), "The Rivals" 1-25-59 (Hotel Manager), "Guatemala City" 1-31-60 (Clerk); *Wyatt Earp*—"The General's Lady" 1-14-58 (Colonel Bentine), "Juveniles—1878" 3-10-58, "The Convict's Revenge" 4-4-61; *Zane Grey Theater*—"Legacy of a Legend" 11-6-58 (Roger Fleming); *The Texan*—"The Duchess of Denver" 1-5-59 (Wittaker); *Rawhide*—"Incident of the Misplaced Indians" 5-1-59 (Captain Brandon); *Bonanza*—"Enter Mark Twain" 10-10-59, "A Hot Day for a Hanging" 10-14-62, "A Dublin Lad" 1-2-66 (Jury Foreman); *Tales of Wells Fargo*—"Dealer's Choice" 5-2-60 (Ward); *A Man Called Shenandoah*—"The Verdict" 11-1-65 (Judge); *Laredo*—"Miracle at Massacre Mission" 3-3-66 (Sheriff); *The Virginian*—"High Stakes" 11-16-66 (Elias Duke); *The High Chaparral*—"Bad Day for a Thirst" 2-18-68 (Allison).

Carson, Sunset (1927-5/1/90). Films: "Bordertown Trail" 1944; "Call of the Rockies" 1944; "Code of the Prairie" 1944 (Sunset Carson);

"Firebrands of Arizona" 1944 (Sunset Carson); "Bandits of the Badlands" 1945; "Bells of Rosarita" 1945; "The Cherokee Flash" 1945; "Oregon Trail" 1945 (Sunset); "Rough Riders of Cheyenne" 1945; "Santa Fe Saddlemates" 1945; "Sheriff of Cimarron" 1945 (Sunset Carson); "Alias Billy the Kid" 1946 (Sunset Carson); "Days of Buffalo Bill" 1946; "The El Paso Kid" 1946 (Sunset); "Red River Renegades" 1946; "Rio Grande Raiders" 1946; "Deadline" 1948; "Fighting Mustang" 1948; "Sunset Carson Rides Again" 1948; "Battling Marshal" 1950.

Carson, Ted. Films: "The Border Wolf" 1929; "Man of Daring" 1929; "The Red Coat's Code" 1929; "The Red Rider" 1929; "The Badge of Bravery" 1930; "Crimson Courage" 1930; "Crooked Trails" 1930; "Law in the Saddle" 1930; "The Lightning Rider" 1930; "The Man Hunter" 1930; "The Redcoat's Romance" 1930; "Trail of the Pack" 1930; "Wolf's Fangs" 1930.

Carson, Willie May. Films: "Big Stakes" 1922 (Mary); "Hellounds of the West" 1922 (Camille Daggett).

Carsten, Peter (1929-). Films: "My Name Is Pecos" 1966-Ital. (Joe Kline); "And God Said to Cain" 1969-Ital.; "Miss Dynamite" 1972-Ital./Fr.

Carter, Alice. Films: "Young Guns" 1988 (Yen Sun).

Carter, Ann. Films: "The Flyin' Cowboys" 1928 (Alice Gordon); "Last of the Duanes" 1941 (Cannon's Daughter).

Carter, Ben (1911-12/11/46). Films: "Ride on, Vaquero" 1941 (Watchman); "The Harvey Girls" 1946 (John Henry).

Carter, Betty. Films: "Captain Cowboy" 1929; "Fighters of the Saddle" 1929 (Patty Wayne); "The White Outlaw" 1929 (Mary Wagner).

Carter, Beverly (1941-6/8/92). TV: *Bonanza*—"He Was Only Seven" 3-5-72 (Alice).

Carter, Calvert (1859-8/29/32). Films: "Wild and Woolly" 1917 (Hotelkeeper); "Six Feet Four" 1919 (Poke Drury); "The Fighting Shepherdess" 1920 (Mayor).

Carter, Cathy. Films: "King of the Bandits" 1947 (Connie).

Carter, Conlan. Films: "Something for a Lonely Man" TVM-1968. TV: *The Westerner*—"Brown" 10-21-60 (Meed); *Gunsmoke*—"The Badge" 11-12-60 (Augie), "Harper's Blood" 10-21-61 (Jeff Cooley), "No Hands" 2-8-64 (Ben Ginnis), "The Hide

Cutters" 9-30-68 (Bodiddly), "The Twisted Heritage" 1-6-69 (Logan Dagget); *Zane Grey Theater*—"Ambush" 1-5-61 (McKenzie); *The Outlaws*—"The Brathwaite Brothers" 11-9-61 (Perry Brathwaite); *Rawhide*—"Deserter's Patrol" 2-9-62 (Baines); *The Rifleman*—"Lou Mallory" 10-15-62 (Haslam), "Which Way'd They Go?" 4-1-63 (Haslam Jackman); *The Virginian*—"The Judgment" 1-16-63 (Lennie Carewe), "Death Wait" 1-15-69 (Jory Kincaid); *Wide Country*—"The Quest for Jacob Blaufus" 3-7-63 (Tex Bannerman); *Destry*—"The Infernal Triangle" 5-1-64 (Al); *Bonanza*—"The Hostage" 9-27-64 (Tip), "Blood Tie" 2-18-68 (Clay); *Wild Wild West*—"The Night of the Assassin" 9-22-67 (Halverson); *The Big Valley*—"Hell Hath No Fury" 11-18-68 (Wilt), "The Battle of Mineral Springs" 3-24-69 (Elmer); *Death Valley Days*—"The Wizard of Aberdeen" 1-17-70 (Frank Baum); *Alias Smith and Jones*—"The Girl in Boxcar Number Three" 2-11-71 (Breon).

Carter, Dick. Films: "Let Him Buck" 1924; "Reckless Riding Bill" 1924; "Ranger Bill" 1925; "Battlin' Bill" 1927; "Blind Man's Bluff" 1927; "The Golden Trail" 1927; "Pioneers of the West" 1927; "Law Beyond the Range" 1935 (Ed Carter); "West of Carson City" 1940 (Townsman).

Carter, Dixie (1939-). Films: "The Gambler V: Playing for Keeps" TVM-1994 (Lily Langtry). ¶TV: *Bret Maverick*—"Hallie" 2-9-82 (Hallie McCulloch).

Carter, Frank (-5/9/20). Films: "The Curse of the Great Southwest" 1913.

Carter, Frank. Films: "Gunfight at the O.K. Corral" 1957 (Hotel Clerk); "Last Train from Gun Hill" 1959 (Cowboy on Train).

Carter, Harper. Films: "Gunplay" 1951 (Chip); "Pistol Harvest" 1951 (Johnny).

Carter, Harry. Films: "The Mistress of Deadwood Basin" 1914; "Judge Not, or the Woman of Mona Diggings" 1915 (Lee Kirk); "The Beckoning Trail" 1916 (Placer Murray); "Three Mounted Men" 1918 (Warden's Son); "Sure Fire" 1921 (Rufus Coulter); "Wolf Law" 1922; "Dead Game" 1923 (Jenks); "The Steel Trail" 1923-serial; "Trails of Adventure" 1935.

Carter, Harry. Films: "Smoky" 1946 (Bud); "Fury at Furnace Creek" 1948 (Clerk); "Yellow Sky" 1948 (Lieutenant); "Broken Arrow" 1950 (Miner); "Ticket to Tomahawk" 1950

(Charley); "Two Flags West" 1950 (Lt. Reynolds); "The Secret of Convict Lake" 1951 (Rudy); "The Outcasts of Poker Flat" 1952 (Townsman); "City of Badmen" 1953 (Jack); "Powder River" 1953 (Bo Curry); "The Silver Whip" 1953 (Tex Rafferty); "Broken Lance" 1954 (Prison Guard); "The Proud Ones" 1956 (Jouseman); "One Foot in Hell" 1960 (Mark Dobbs). ¶TV: *Laramie*—"The Barefoot Kid" 1-9-62; *The Virginian*—"The Money Cage" 3-6-63 (Station Master); *Great Adventure*—"The Pathfinder" 3-6-64 (Simpson).

Carter, Helena (1923-). Films: "River Lady" 1948 (Stephanie); "Fort Worth" 1951 (Amy Brooks); "Bugles in the Afternoon" 1952 (Josephine Russell); "The Pathfinder" 1952 (Welcome Alison).

Carter, Jack (1922-). TV: *The Road West*—"Never Chase a Rainbow" 3-6-67 (Tally); *Wild Wild West*—"The Night of the Janus" 2-15-69 (Alan Thorpe).

Carter, Janis (1917-7/31/94). Films: "Santa Fe" 1951 (Judith Chandler); "The Half-Breed" 1952 (Helen).

Carter, Jimmy. Films: "The Jayhawkers" 1959 (Paul); "Shenandoah" 1965 (Rider). ¶TV: *The Alaskans*—"Partners" 3-13-60 (Jimmy Hendricks); *Whispering Smith*—"The Jodie Tyler Story" 8-21-61 (Tim Tyler); *The Rifleman*—"Gun Shy" 12-10-62.

Carter, John (1927-). Films: "Monte Walsh" 1970 (Farmer); "Joe Kidd" 1972 (Judge). ¶TV: *Gunsmoke*—"Ladies from St. Louis" 3-25-67 (Doyle), "Shadler" 1-15-73 (Father Walsh); *The Big Valley*—"Showdown in Limbo" 3-27-67; *Cimarron Strip*—"The Assassin" 1-11-68; *Bonanza*—"The Survivors" 11-10-68 (Wayne Pursell); *Death Valley Days*—"The Lady Doctor" 10-11-69; *Sara*—4-2-76 (Henchard).

Carter, Julie. Films: "Song of the Saddle" 1936 (Woman in Coach); "Stagecoach War" 1940 (Shirley Chapman).

Carter, June. see Cash, June Carter.

Carter, Mrs. Leslie (1862-11/12/37). Films: "Rocky Mountain Mystery" 1935 (Mrs. Borg).

Carter, Louise (1875-11/10/57). Films: "Rose of the Rancho" 1936 (Guadalupe).

Carter, Lynda (1951-). TV: *Hawyeke*—Regular 1994- (Elizabeth Shields).

Carter, Mel. TV: *The Rifle-*

man—"End of a Young Gun" 10-14-58, "The Safe Guard" 11-18-58 (Walkerman), "The Challenge" 4-7-59, "The Woman" 5-5-59 (Jed Healey), "The Journey Back" 10-30-61, "Outlaw Shoes" 4-30-62 (Jeems), "Lou Mallory" 10-15-62 (Bo), "Death Never Rides Alone" 10-29-62; *Wanted—Dead or Alive*—"The Kovack Affair" 3-28-59 (Hotel Clerk).

Carter, Michael Patrick. TV: *Paradise*—Regular 1988-91 (George Cord).

Carter, Mitch. Films: "Last Ride of the Dalton Gang" TVM-1979 (Gunfighter). ¶TV: *Alias Smith and Jones*—"The McCreedy Bust—Going, Going Gone" 1-13-72 (Luke); *How the West Was Won*—"The Scavengers" 3-12-79 (Beard).

Carter, Monte (1886-11/14/50). Films: "Fighting Shadows" 1935 (Trapper).

Carter, Peter (Paolo Magalotti). Films: "Rojo" 1966-Ital./Span. (Sheriff); "Taste for Killing" 1966-Ital./Span.; "Up the MacGregors!" 1967-Ital./Span. (Kenneth MacGregor); "Hate Thy Neighbor" 1969-Ital.; "Wanted Sabata" 1970-Ital.; "I Am Sartana, Trade Your Guns for a Coffin" 1972-Ital.; "Death Is Sweet from the Soldier of God" 1972-Ital.; "Animal Called Man" 1973-Ital.

Carter, Red. see Stander, Lionel.

Carter, Sally. TV: *Laramie*—"The Runt" 2-20-62; *The New Land*—"The Word Is: Persistence" 9-14-74.

Carter, Ted. see Pazzafini, Nello.

Carter, Tom. Films: "The Clean-Up Man" 1928 (Sheriff); "The Phantom Rider" 1936-serial; "The Return of Daniel Boone" 1941 (Wagner); "Gentleman from Texas" 1946.

Cartldge, Bill. Films: "The Red Stallion" 1947 (Johnny Stevens).

Cartwright, Lynn. Films: "Black Patch" 1957 (Kitty). ¶TV: *Maverick*—"A Bullet for the Teacher" 10-30-60 (Anne Shepard).

Cartwright, Veronica (1949-). Films: "Goin' South" 1978 (Hermine). ¶TV: *Daniel Boone*—Regular 1964-70 (Jemima Boone); *Death Valley Days*—"A Simple Question of Justice" 11-22-69.

Caruso, Anthony (1913-). Films: "Northwest Mounted Police" 1940 (Half Breed at Riel's Headquarters); "Pals of the Golden West" 1951 (Jim Bradford); "Desert Pursuit" 1952 (Hassan); "The Iron Mistress" 1952 (Bloody Jack Sturdevant); "The Man Behind the Gun" 1952 (Vic

Sutro); "The Boy from Oklahoma" 1954 (Barney Turlock); "Cattle Queen of Montana" 1954 (Nachakos); "Drum Beat" 1954 (Manok); "Passion" 1954 (Sgt. Munox); "Saskatchewan" 1954 (Spotted Eagle); "Santa Fe Passage" 1955 (Chavez); "Tennessee's Partner" 1955 (Turner); "Walk the Proud Land" 1956 (Disalin); "The Big Land" 1957 (Brog); "Joe Dakota" 1957 (Marcus Vizzini); "The Oklahoman" 1957 (Jim Hawk); "The Badlanders" 1958 (Comanche); "Fort Massacre" 1958 (Pawnee); "The Lawless Eighties" 1958; "The Wonderful Country" 1959 (Ludwig "Chico" Turner); "Flap" 1970 (Silver Dollar); "Desperate Mission" TVM-1971 (Don Miguel Ruiz); "The Legend of Earl Durand" 1974; "Kino, the Padre on Horseback" 1977. ¶TV: *The Lone Ranger*—"The Tell-Tale Bullet" 4-14-55; *Stories of the Century*—"Tiburcio Vasquez" 6-24-55; *Fury*—"Joey and the Gypsies" 11-26-55 (Josef); *20th Century Fox Hour*—"Broken Arrow" 5-2-56 (Geronimo); *Circus Boy*—"The Great Gambino" 10-7-56 (Gambino), "The Great Gambino's Son" 3-10-57 (Gambino); *Broken Arrow*—"The Challenge" 2-5-57 (Chato); *Have Gun Will Travel*—"Winchester Quarantine" 10-5-57, "The Long Hunt" 3-7-59 (Jose), "Return to Fort Benjamin" 1-30-60 (the Indian), "The Revenger" 9-30-61 (Solomon); *Gunsmoke*—"Born to Hang" 11-2-57 (Pate), "Shooting Stopover" 10-8-60 (Bud Gurney), "Indian Ford" 12-2-61 (Lone Eagle), "Cody's Code" 1-20-62 (Cody Durham), "Ash" 2-16-63 (Ash Farior), "The Quest for Asa Janin" 6-1-63 (Macklin), "Father Love" 3-14-64 (Simms), "The Warden" 5-16-64 (Bull Foot), "Ring of Darkness" 12-1-69 (Gulley), "Murdoch" 2-8-71 (Townsend), "Lynott" 11-1-71 (Talley), "Sarah" 10-16-72 (Pappy Quinn), "A Family of Killers" 1-14-74 (Elton Sutterfield), "Larkin" 1-20-75 (Lon Toomes); *The Restless Gun*—"The Child" 12-23-57 (Padre Basilio); *Tombstone Territory*—"Mexican Bandito" 1-29-58 (Augustine Ramirez); *Zorro*—"Agent of the Eagle" 2-20-58 (Juan Ortega), "Zorro Springs a Trap" 2-27-58 (Juan Ortega), "The Unmasking of Zorro" 3-6-58 (Juan Ortega); *Wanted—Dead or Alive*—"Miracle at Pot Hole" 10-25-58, "Littlest Giant" 4-25-59 (Matt); *Death Valley Days*—"The Gunsmith" 12-23-58 (Frank Leslie), "The Invaders" 3-17-59 (Cabrio), "Amos and the Black Bull" 2-28-70 (Amos); *Sugarfoot*—"The Extra Hand" 1-20-59 (Vic Latour); *Buckskin*—"Annie's Old Beau"

4-13-59 (George Bradley); *Bonanza*—"The Paiute War" 10-3-59 (Chief Winnemucca), "Day of Reckoning" 10-22-60 (Lagos), "The Deserter" 10-21-62 (Keokuk), "The Saga of Squaw Charlie" 12-27-64 (Charlie); *Tales of Wells Fargo*—"Tom Horn" 10-26-59 (Broken Hand); *Wagon Train*—"The Vittorio Bottecelli Story" 12-16-59 (Josef), "The Traitor" 12-13-61 (Muerte); *Laramie*—"Night of the Quiet Man" 12-22-59 (Kurt Lang), "The Turn of the Wheel" 4-3-62 (Marty); *Wichita Town*—"Brothers of the Knife" 2-10-60 (Zitto Vizzini); *Maverick*—"The Iron Hand" 2-21-60 (Joe Vermillion), "Mano Nera" 10-23-60 (Lieutenant Joe Petrino); *The Texan*—"Showdown" 2-29-60; *Riverboat*—"The Long Trail" 4-4-60 (Chief White Bull); *Rawhide*—"Incident of the Dancing Death" 4-8-60 (Cullen), "The Reunion" 4-6-62 (Gray Hawk), "Prairie Fire" 3-19-65 (Milt Dexter); *Wyatt Earp*—"The Truth About Old Man Clanton" 9-27-60 (Don Sebastian); *Walt Disney Presents*—"Daniel Boone" 1960-61 (Chief Blackfish); *The Deputy*—"The Truly Yours" 4-9-60 (Fife); *Gunslinger*—"Appointment in Cascabel" 2-23-61 (Manuel Garcia); *Great Adventure*—"The Death of Sitting Bull"/ "Massacre at Wounded Knee" 10-4-63 & 10-11-63 (Sitting Bull); *The Travels of Jaimie McPheeters*—"The Day of the Dark Deeds" 3-8-64 (Lone Eagle); *The Virginian*—"The Inchoworm's Got No Wings at All" 2-2-66 (Pa Tait); *The Road West*—"This Dry and Thirsty Land" 10-10-66 (Amos Brubaker); *Wild Wild West*—"The Night of the Green Terror" 11-18-66 (Bright Star), "The Night Dr. Loveless Died" 9-29-67 (Deuce), "The Night of the Kraken" 11-1-68 (Jose Aguila); *Rango*—"You Can't Scalp a Bald Indian" 4-28-67 (Angry Bear); *The High Chaparral*—"Mark of the Turtle" 12-10-67 (El Lobo), "The Covey" 10-18-68 (El Lobo), "The Glory Soldiers" 1-31-69 (El Lobo); *The Guns of Will Sonnett*—"The Warriors" 3-1-68; *Lancer*—"The High Riders" 9-24-68 (Toledano); *The Men from Shiloh*—"Last of the Comancheros" 12-9-70 (Keller); *Dirty Sally*—"Wimmen's Rights" 3-15-74 (Paretti); *Nakia*—"The Fire Dancer" 12-28-74 (John Manygoats).

Caruth, Burr (1865-6/2/53). Films: "The Cowboy and the Kid" 1936 (Judge Talbot); "Ghost Town Gold" 1937 (Mayor Thornton); "Gunsmoke Ranch" 1937 (Warren); "Red River Range" 1938 (Pop Mason); "Under Western Stars" 1938 (Larkin); "Come on, Rangers" 1939;

"New Frontier" 1939 (Doc Hall); "Konga, the Wild Stallion" 1940 (Breckenridge); "Rocky Mountain Rangers" 1940 (John); "The Phantom Cowboy" 1941 (Motley); "Ridin' on a Rainbow" 1941 (Eben Carter); "Calling Wild Bill Elliott" 1943.

Carvajal, Tony. Films: "The Treasure of Pancho Villa" 1955 (Farolito).

Carver, Louise (1869-1/18/56). Films: "The Breed of the Border" 1924 (Ma Malone); "The Big Trail" 1930 (Gussie's Mother-in-Law); "Riders of the Desert" 1932 (Buck Lawlor).

Carver, Lynne (1909-8/12/55). Films: "In Old California" 1942; "Man from Cheyenne" 1942 (Marian); "Sunset on the Desert" 1942 (Ann); "Law of the Valley" 1944; "Flame of the West" 1945 (Compton); "Drifting Along" 1946 (Pat McBride); "Crossed Trails" 1948 (Maggie).

Carver, Mary (1924-). TV: *Gunsmoke*—"Chester's Mail Order Bride" 7-14-56 (Ann Smithwright), "Letter of the Law" 10-11-58 (Sarah Teek), "Unwanted Deputy" 3-5-60 (Maise), "Daddy Went Away" 5-11-63 (Lucy Damon); *Black Saddle*—"Client: Dawes" 1-31-59 (Ruth Dawes).

Carver, Randell. Films: "The Daughters of Joshua Cabe Return" TVM-1975 (Jim Finch); "The New Daughters of Joshua Cabe" TVM-1976 (Billy Linaker).

Carver, Tina (1924-2/18/82). TV: *Colt .45*—"Last Chance" 12-6-57 (Kate Grant); *Wichita Town*—"Death Watch" 12-16-59 (Millie Davis).

Cary, Christopher (1934-). Films: "The White Buffalo" 1977 (Short Man). ¶TV: *Wild Wild West*—"The Night of the Poisonous Posey" 10-28-66 (Snakes Tolliver), "The Night of the Winged Terror" 1-17-68 & 1-24-68 (Tycho); *The Road West*—"Shaman" 11-14-66 (Willie Lom); *The Big Valley*—"The Great Safe Robbery" 11-21-66 (Shorty); *The High Chaparral*—"A Quiet Day in Tucson" 10-1-67 (Fergus MacLeish), "For What We Are About to Receive" 11-29-68 (Fergus McLeish).

Casados, Eloy (1949-). Films: "The Legend of Walks Far Woman" TVM-1982; "The Alamo: 13 Days to Glory" TVM-1987 (Gregorio).

Casaravilla, Carlos. Films: "A Place Called Glory" 1966-Span./Ger.; "Return of the Seven" 1966-Span.; "The Man Who Killed Billy the Kid" 1967-Span./Ital.

Casares, Anna. Films: "Two Gangsters in the Wild West" 1965-Ital./Span.; "Up the MacGregors!" 1967-Ital./Span. (Dolly).

Casas, Antonio (1910-2/14/82). Films: "Minnesota Clay" 1964-Ital./Fr./Span. (Jonathan); "Ride and Kill" 1964-Ital./Span. (Steve Donnelly); "Four Dollars for Vengeance" 1965-Span./Ital.; "A Pistol for Ringo" 1965-Ital./Span. (Major Clyde); "The Big Gundown" 1966-Ital. (Dance); "The Good, the Bad, and the Ugly" 1966-Ital.; "The Return of Ringo" 1966-Ital./Span.; "Son of a Gunfighter" 1966-U.S./Span. (Pecos); "The Texican" 1966-U.S./Span. (Frank Brady); "Awkward Hands" 1968-Span./Ital.; "Twenty Thousand Dollars for Seven" 1968-Ital.; "Alive or Preferably Dead" 1969-Span./Ital.; "Three Supermen of the West" 1974-Ital./Span.

Case, Allen (1935-8/25/86). TV: *Sugarfoot*—"Brink of Fear" 6-30-58 (Deputy); *Bronco*—"The Besieged" 9-23-58 (Stu Baggot); *The Rifleman*—"Young Englishman" 12-16-58 (Jeremy); *Have Gun Will Travel*—"Juliet" 1-31-59 (Ted Pike), "Alaska" 4-18-59 (Ralph Morton); *Gunsmoke*—"Sky" 2-14-59 (Billy Daunt), "The Promoter" 4-25-64 (Lieutenant Gibbins), "The Good People" 10-15-66 (Gabe Rucker); *Wagon Train*—"The Jasper Cato Story" 3-4-59; *Lawman*—"Riding Shotgun" 4-19-59 (Larry Delong); *Colt .45*—"The Man Who Loved Lincoln" 5-3-59; *The Deputy*—Regular 1959-61 (Deputy Clay McCord); *The Virginian*—"West" 11-20-62 (Sheriff Blade); *The Legend of Jesse James*—Regular 1965-66 (Frank James); *Time Tunnel*—"Billy the Kid" 2-10-67 (Sheriff Pat Garrett).

Case, Cathy. TV: *The Texan*—"Letter of the Law" 3-23-59 (Julia); *Zane Grey Theater*—"The Ghost" 12-31-59 (Maria Ransome).

Case, Helen. Films: "The Return of Thunder Cloud's Spirit" 1913; "Old California" 1914; "The Cowboy and the Lady" 1915 (Margaret Primrose).

Case, Kathleen. "Junction City" 1952 (Penny); "Last of the Pony Riders" 1953 (Katie McEen). ¶TV: *Death Valley Days*—"The Gambler and the Lady" 7-7-57 (Ruth Stewart); *The Deputy*—"Three Brothers" 12-10-60 (Martha Towers).

Casey, Bernie (1939-). Films: "Guns of the Magnificent Seven" 1969 (Cassie).

Casey, Jack (1888-8/30/56). Films: "The Saddle King" 1929 (Sam Winters); "Ghost Patrol" 1936 (Mac); "The Lone Ranger" 1938-serial (Trooper); "Renegades of the Rio Grande" 1945 (Hank).

Casey, Lawrence (1941-). TV: *Gunsmoke*—"The Well" 11-19-66 (Jim Libby); *Bonanza*—"The Running Man" 3-30-69 (Jess Parker); *Barbary Coast*—"The Ballad of Redwing Jail" 9-29-75 (Sam Hatfield).

Casey, Sue (1926-). Films: "Paint Your Wagon" 1969 (Sarah Woodling). ¶TV: *Gunsmoke*—"The Hunger" 11-17-62 (Martha), "The Bad One" 1-26-63 (Saloon Girl).

Casey, Taggert. Films: "The Lonely Man" 1957; "Heller in Pink Tights" 1960 (1st Gunslinger). ¶TV: *The Lone Ranger*—"Trigger Finger 4-7-55; *Bonanza*—"Inger, My Love" 4-15-62.

Cash, John Carter. Films: "Stagecoach" TVM-1986 (Billy Pickett).

Cash, Johnny (1932-). Films: "A Gunfight" 1971 (Abe Cross); "The Last Days of Frank and Jesse James" TVM-1986 (Frank James); "Stagecoach" TVM-1986 (Marshal Curley Wilcox); "Davy Crockett: Rainbow in the Thunder" TVM-1988 (Older Davy Crockett). ¶TV: *The Rebel*—"The Death of Gray" 1-3-60 (Pratt); *The Deputy*—"The Deathly Quiet" 5-27-61 (Bo Braddock); *Dr. Quinn, Medicine Women*—"Law of the Land" 1-16-93 (Kid Cole), "Saving Souls" 11-13-93 (Kid Cole).

Cash, June Carter (1929-). Films: "The Last Days of Frank and Jesse James" TVM-1986 (Mother James); "Stagecoach" TVM-1986 (Mrs. Pickett). ¶TV: *Jim Bowie*—"The Pearls of Talimeco" 11-8-57, "Country Girl" 12-13-57 (Rachel); *Dr. Quinn, Medicine Woman*—"Saving Souls" 11-13-93 (Sister Ruth).

Cason, Chuck. TV: *The Cisco Kid*—"Quiet Sunday Morning" 12-5-53; *Maverick*—"Seed of Deception" 4-13-58 (Henchman), "Holiday at Hollow Rock" 12-28-58 (Pete); *The Rebel*—"Jerkwater" 1-22-61 (Smith).

Cason, John L. "Bob" (1918-7/7/61). Films: "The Apache Kid" 1941; "Riders of the Badlands" 1941; "Bad Men of the Hills" 1942; "Down Rio Grande Way" 1942; "Raiders of the Range" 1942; "Raiders of the West" 1942; "Shadows on the Sage" 1942; "Westward Ho" 1942; "Death Valley Rangers" 1944; "Ghost Guns" 1944; "Land of the Outlaws" 1944; "Sonora Stagecoach" 1944; "Spook Town" 1944; "The Vigilantes Ride" 1944 (Henchman); "Wild Horse Phantom" 1944; "Fighting Bill Carson" 1945; "Flame of the West" 1945; "Gangster's Den" 1945 (Burke); "Gun Smoke" 1945; "His Brother's Ghost" 1945 (Jarrett); "Shadows of Death" 1945; "Stagecoach Outlaws" 1945 (Joe); "Ghost of Hidden Valley" 1946 (Sweeney); "Outlaw of the Plains" 1946; "Overland Riders" 1946; "Prairie Badmen" 1946 (Steve); "The Last Round-Up" 1947 (Carter); "The Lone Hand Texan" 1947 (First Outlaw); "Prairie Raiders" 1947; "Dead Man's Gold" 1948 (Matt Conway); "Mark of the Lash" 1948; "Relentless" 1948 (Posse Man); "Six-Gun Law" 1948 (Ben); "Sunset Carson Rides Again" 1948; "The Big Sombrero" 1949 (Stacy); "The Blazing Trail" 1949 (Colton); "Challenge of the Range" 1949 (Spud Henley); "Laramie" 1949; "Range Land" 1949 (Rocky); "Red Desert" 1949 (Horn); "Rimfire" 1949 (Blazer); "Son of a Badman" 1949 (Bart); "Tough Assignment" 1949 (Joe); "Colorado Ranger" 1950 (Loco Joe); "Crooked River" 1950 (Kent); "Desperadoes of the West" 1950-serial (Casey); "Fast on the Draw" 1950 (Tex); "Hostile Country" 1950 (Ed); "Marshal of Heldorado" 1950 (Jake); "Punchy Cowpunchers" 1950-short (Black Jeff); "Redwood Forest Trail" 1950 (Curley); "Rustlers on Horseback" 1950 (Murray); "Streets of Ghost Town" 1950 (John Wicks); "West of the Brazos" 1950 (Cyclone); "Don Daredevil Rides Again" 1951-serial (Hagen); "Fort Savage Raiders" 1951 (Jug); "Prairie Roundup" 1951 (Drag Barton); "The Thundering Trail" 1951 (Conway); "Black Hills Ambush" 1952 (Jake); "The Hawk of Wild River" 1952 (Duke); "The Kid from Broken Gun" 1952 (Chuck); "Son of Geronimo" 1952-serial; "Wagon Team" 1952 (Sim); "Gun Fury" 1953 (Westy); "Red River Shore" 1953 (Joe); "Savage Frontier" 1953 (Buck Madsen); "Cattle Queen of Montana" 1954; "Count Three and Pray" 1955 (Charlie Vancouver); "Wyoming Renegades" 1955 (O.C. Hanks); "Jubal" 1956 (Cowboy); "The Storm Rider" 1957 (Jasper); "Snowfire" 1958 (Buff Stoner); "Cimarron" 1960 (Suggs). ¶TV: *The Lone Ranger*—"War Horse" 10-20-49, "Gold Train" 3-16-50, "Desert Adventure" 11-30-50, "Bad Medicine" 12-7-50, "Mrs. Banker" 3-26-53, "Ex-Marshal" 9-16-54, "Two from Juan Ringo" 12-23-54, "The Tell-Tale Bullet" 4-14-55; *The Gene Autry Show*—"Doublecross Valley" 9-10-50, "The Posse" 9-17-50, "The Devil's

Brand" 9-24-50, "Double Barrelled Vengeance" 4-21-51, "Law Comes to Scorpion" 10-22-55, "Feuding Friends" 11-26-55; *The Adventures of Kit Carson*—"Fury at Red Gulch" 10-27-51 (Trig); *The Cisco Kid*—"Carrier Pigeon" 11-3-51, "Jewelry Hold-Up" 12-15-51, "Big Steal" 4-12-52, "The Fugitive" 11-1-52, "Rodeo" 12-27-52, "Steel Plow" 1-31-53, "Pot of Gold" 4-25-53; *Sky King*—"Showdown" 1-27-52 (Fred Clay), "Rodeo Decathalon" 4-27-52 (Bull Harrison); *The Roy Rogers Show*—"Money to Burn" 6-28-53, "Gun Trouble" 11-22-53 (Colt Egger), "The Young Defenders" 10-3-54 (Luke Connors), "The Last of the Larrabee Kid" 10-17-54 (Ray Scott), "Hard Luck Story" 10-31-54 (Ben Pierson), "Boys' Day in Paradise Valley" 11-7-54, "Empty Saddles" 3-10-56 (Lou Conroy), "His Weight in Wildcats" 11-11-56, "Deadlock at Dark Canyon" 1-6-57; *The Adventures of Rin Tin Tin*—"The Education of Corporal Rusty" 11-19-54 (Maddick); *Tales of the Texas Rangers*—"The Rough, Tough West" 12-10-55 (Fulton); *Judge Roy Bean*—"The Elopers" 4-11-56 (Beeman), "Spirit of the Law" 4-11-56 (Jason Hart), "Deliver the Body" 6-1-56 (Blade), "Terror Rides the Trail" 6-1-56 (Dave), "Luck O' the Irish" 7-1-56 (Ed Jacobs); *Fury*—"Nature's Engineers" 2-2-57 (Brad); *Wyatt Earp*—"Wyatt Meets Doc Holliday" 4-23-57 (Mike Roarke); *Tales of Wells Fargo*—"Stage West" 1-13-58 (Brady); *The Restless Gun*—"The Manhunters" 6-2-58 (Todd Cotterman); *Jefferson Drum*—"Stagecoach Episode" 10-10-58 (Driver); *Man from Blackhawk*—"Logan's Policy" 10-9-59 (Poke); *Wanted—Dead or Alive*—"Vanishing Act" 12-26-59; *Maverick*—"Last Wire from Stop Gap" 10-16-60 (Clay); *Rawhide*—"Incident at Poco Tiempo" 12-9-60; *Sugarfoot*—"Angel" 3-6-61 (Chad); *Wagon Train*—"The Duke Shannon Story" 4-26-61 (Jeff).

Casper, Robert. Films: "Honky Tonk" TVM-1974 (Dr. Goodwin); "Scott Free" TVM-1976; "Little House on the Prairie: Look Back to Yesterday" TVM-1983 (Sherwood Montague); "Little House: The Last Farewell" TVM-1984 (Sherwood Montague); "Little House: Bless All the Dear Children" TVM-1984 (Sherwood Montague). ¶TV: *Maverick*—"Bundle from Britain" 9-18-60 (Freddie Bugnor).

Cass, Dave (1942-). Films: "Shenandoah" 1965 (Ray); "Dirty Dingus Magee" 1970 (Trooper); "Hot Lead and Cold Feet" 1978 (Jack); "The Apple Dumpling Gang Rides

Again" 1979; "The Gambler" TVM-1980 (Winters); "More Wild Wild West" TVM-1980 (Brother); "Desperado" TVM-1987; "Down the Long Hill" TVM-1987 (Mr. Andy); "Rio Diablo" TVM-1993 (Winslow); "The Gambler V: Playing for Keeps" TVM-1994 (Sheriff Boone). ¶TV: *Hondo*—"Hondo and the Death Drive" 12-1-67 (Harper); *Here Come the Brides*—"Land Grant" 11-21-69; *The High Chaparral*—"Sangre" 2-26-71 (Corporal); *Bonanza*—"Frenzy" 1-30-72 (Deputy), "One Ace Too Many" 4-2-72 (Deputy Coghlan); *Royce*—Pilot 5-21-76 (Dent); *Young Maverick*—"Clancy" 11-28-79.

Cass, Maurice (1884-6/9/54). Films: "Whispering Smith Speaks" 1935 (C. Luddington Colfax); "Sunset Trail" 1938 (E. Prescott Furbush); "Saddle Pals" 1947.

Cass County Boys (Fred S. Martin, Bert Dodson & Jerry Scoggins). Films: "Sioux City Sue" 1946; "Last Days of Boot Hill" 1947; "Robin Hood of Texas" 1947; "Saddle Pals" 1947; "Trail to San Antone" 1947; "Twilight on the Rio Grande" 1947; "Buckaroo from Powder River" 1948; "Trail to Laredo" 1948; "Tucson" 1949; "Apache Country" 1952; "Blue Canadian Rockies" 1952; "On Top of Old Smoky" 1953. ¶TV: *The Gene Autry Show*—"Gold Dust Charlie" 7-30-50, "Battle Axe" 8-31-54, "The Portrait of White Cloud" 10-15-55, "Ghost Ranch" 11-12-55, "Go West, Young Lady" 11-19-55, "Saddle Up" 12-3-55, "Ride, Rancheros" 12-10-55, "The Rangerette" 12-17-55, "Dynamite" 12-24-55.

Cassady, William. Films: "The Pecos Pistol" 1949-short. ¶TV: *Wyatt Earp*—"Dull Knife Strikes for Freedom" 5-7-57 (Corporal Jordan), "The Schoolteacher" 3-11-58 (Dr. McCarty), "Plague Carrier" 12-9-58 (Doc McCarthy), "The Reformation of Doc Holliday" 12-30-58 (Doc McCarthy), "She Almost Married Wyatt" 2-24-59, "One Murder—Fifty Suspects" 3-17-59, "Doc Fabrique's Greatest Case" 4-7-59 (Dr. McCarty), "The Actress" 4-14-59 (Dr. McCarty), "Love and Shotgun Gibbs" 4-21-59; *Sergeant Preston of the Yukon*—"Gold Rush Patrol" 1-16-58 (Jim); *Wild Wild West*—"The Night of the Sudden Death" 10-8-65 (Sterling).

Cassanova, Fernando (Fred Canow). Films: "Shots Ring Out!" 1965-Ital./Span. (Sheriff Poll).

Cassavetes, John (1929-2/3/89). Films: "Saddle the Wind" 1958 (Tony Sinclair). ¶TV: *Rawhide*—"Incident

Near Gloomy River" 3-17-61 (Cal Fletcher); *The Legend of Jesse James*—"The Quest" 11-1-65 (Blackie Dolan); *The Virginian*—"Long Ride to Wind River" 1-19-66 (Jonah MacIntosh).

Cassell, Malcolm. TV: *The Rebel*—"School Days" 11-15-59; *The Rifleman*—"The Spoiler" 2-16-60 (Joey Merrick).

Cassell, Seymour (1935-). Films: "The Mountain Men" 1980 (LaBont); "White Fang" 1991 (Skunker). ¶TV: *Laredo*—"I See By Your Outfit" 9-23-65 (Jud); *Cimarron Strip*—"The Battleground" 9-28-67.

Cassell, Sid (1897-1/17/60). *Sergeant Preston of the Yukon*—"Rebellion in the North" 7-12-56 (Kule); *Jim Bowie*—"Counterfeit Dixie" 9-27-57 (Capt. Ponet); *Fury*—"Private Eyes" 1-9-60 (Duleto).

Cassell, Wally. Films: "Bad Bascomb" 1946 (Curley); "Ramrod" 1947 (Virg Lee); "Little Big Horn" 1951 (Pvt. Danny Zecca); "Oh! Susanna" 1951 (Trooper Muro); "Law and Order" 1953 (the Durango Kid); "Timberjack" 1955 (Veazie). ¶TV: *Gunsmoke*—"Hack Prine" 5-12-56 (Oley); *Rawhide*—"Incident at Poco Tiempo" 12-9-60.

Cassenelli, Dolores (1893-4/26/84). Films: "Jamestown" 1923 (Pocahontas).

Cassidy, David (1950-). TV: *Bonanza*—"The Law and Billy Burgess" 2-15-70 (Billy Burgess).

Cassidy, Edward (1893-1/19/68). Films: "Bulldog Courage" 1935; "The Courageous Avenger" 1935 (Carson); "No Man's Range" 1935; "The Pecos Kid" 1935 (Dr. Evans); "The Reckless Buckaroo" 1935; "Ambush Valley" 1936 (Nester); "Brand of the Outlaws" 1936 (Sheriff); "Cavalry" 1936 (Bart Haines); "The Crooked Trail" 1936 (Grimby); "Everyman's Law" 1936 (Homesteader); "Feud of the West" 1936 (Greg Walters); "Ghost Town" 1936 (Sheriff Blair); "Gun Grit" 1936 (Tim Hess); "Hair-Trigger Casey" 1936 (Karney); "Law and Lead" 1936; "Men of the Plains" 1936 (J.J. Gray); "The Riding Avenger" 1936; "Rio Grande Ranger" 1936; "Rio Grande Romance" 1936 (Jailer Lewis); "Roarin' Guns" 1936; "Santa Fe Bound" 1936 (Logan); "Sundown Saunders" 1936 (Ben Taggart); "Toll of the Desert" 1936 (Doc Streeter); "Undercover Man" 1936 (Slim); "Valley of the Lawless" 1936; "Vengeance of Rannah" 1936 (Sam Barlow); "Wildcat Saunders" 1936 (Lawson); "Winds of the Wasteland" 1936

(Dodge); "Aces Wild" 1937 (Blacksmith); "Arizona Days" 1937; "Boothill Brigade" 1937 (John Porter); "Boots of Destiny" 1937 (Jack Harmon); "Borderland" 1937; "Come On, Cowboys" 1937 (Tom Rigby); "Cheyenne Rides Again" 1937 (Dave Gleason); "Fighting Texan" 1937 (Pete Hadley); "Hit the Saddle" 1937 (Sheriff Miller); "Hittin' the Trail" 1937 (Sheriff Grey); "The Idaho Kid" 1937; "Lawless Land" 1937 (Sheriff Jim); "Moonlight on the Range" 1937; "The Red Rope" 1937 (Logan); "The Roaming Cowboy" 1937; "Roaring Six Guns" 1937 (Commissioner); "Santa Fe Rides" 1937; "The Silver Trail" 1937 (Frank Sheridan); "Tex Rides with the Boy Scouts" 1937 (Sheriff Crane); "Trailing Trouble" 1937; "Border Wolves" 1938 (Jailer); "Cassidy of Bar 20" 1938 (Sheriff Hawley); "Flaming Frontier" 1938-serial; "Frontier Town" 1938 (Sheriff Welsh); "In Early Arizona" 1938 (Tom Weldon); "Man from Music Mountain" 1938 (William Brady); "Mexicali Kid" 1938 (Sheriff); "Outlaw Express" 1938 (Officer); "The Painted Trail" 1938 (Evans); "Panamint's Bad Man" 1938; "The Purple Vigilantes" 1938 (Sheriff Dyer); "Rawhide" 1938 (Fuller); "Red River Range" 1938; "Rollin' Plains" 1938 (Sheriff Tomlin); "Starlight Over Texas" 1938 (Capt. Brooks); "Utah Trail" 1938 (Sheriff Clayton); "Where the Buffalo Roam" 1938 (Hodge); "Wild Horse Canyon" 1938 (Tom Hall); "The Arizona Kid" 1939; "Colorado Sunset" 1939; "Cowboys from Texas" 1939 (Jed Taylor); "Desperate Trails" 1939 (Marshal Cort); "Frontiers of '49" 1939; "Mountain Rhythm" 1939 (Sheriff); "Rovin' Tumbleweeds" 1939; "Silver on the Sage" 1939 (Pierce); "Trigger Smith" 1939; "Adventures of Red Ryder" 1940-serial (Ira Withers); "Colorado" 1940; "Deadwood Dick" 1940-serial (Drew); "Gaucho Serenade" 1940; "Knights of the Range" 1940; "Ragtime Cowboy Joe" 1940 (Sheriff); "Riders of Pasco Basin" 1940 (Sheriff Ed Marlow); "Texas Renegades" 1940; "Winners of the West" 1940-serial; "Bury Me Not on the Lone Prairie" 1941; "King of the Texas Rangers" 1941-serial (Sedley); "Rawhide Rangers" 1941 (Martin); "Ridin' on a Rainbow" 1941; "Ridin' the Cherokee Trail" 1941; "Robbers of the Range" 1941 (Sheriff); "Wide Open Town" 1941 (Brad Jackson); "Wyoming Wildcat" 1941; "Arizona Roundup" 1942; "The Phantom Plainsmen" 1942 (Sheriff); "Pirates of the Prairie" 1942; "Silver Queen"

1942 (Colonel); "The Sombrero Kid" 1942; "Stardust on the Sage" 1942; "Sunset on the Desert" 1942; "The Avenging Rider" 1943 (Sheriff Lewis); "Bullets and Saddles" 1943; "Carson City Cyclone" 1943; "Cattle Stampede" 1943 (Sam Dawson); "Cowboy in the Clouds" 1943; "Daredevils of the West" 1943-serial (Russell); "The Man from Thunder River" 1943; "Raiders of Red Gap" 1943 (Roberts); "Sagebrush Law" 1943; "Santa Fe Scouts" 1943; "Thundering Trails" 1943; "Wolves of the Range" 1943 (Brady); "Boss of Rawhide" 1944 (Henry Colby); "Brand of the Devil" 1944; "Devil Riders" 1944 (Doc); "Fuzzy Settles Down" 1944; "Frontier Outlaws" 1944 (Sheriff); "Hidden Valley Outlaws" 1944; "The Pinto Bandit" 1944; "Rustlers' Hideout" 1944 (Sheriff); "Saddle Leather Law" 1944; "Spook Town" 1944; "Swing, Cowboy, Swing" 1944; "Trigger Law" 1944; "Tucson Raiders" 1944; "Valley of Vengeance" 1944; "Wells Fargo Days" 1944-short; "The Whispering Skull" 1944; "Along the Navajo Trail" 1945 (Sheriff Clem Wagner); "Bells of Rosarita" 1945; "Colorado Pioneers" 1945; "Corpus Christi Bandits" 1945 (Dan Adams); "The Daltons Ride Again" 1945 (Sproules); "Enemy of the Law" 1945; "Gangster's Den" 1945 (Sheriff); "Marked for Murder" 1945; "The Navajo Kid" 1945 (Sheriff Roy Landon); "The Navajo Trail" 1945; "Sheriff of Cimarron" 1945 (Sheriff Sam Tucker); "Stagecoach Outlaws" 1945 (Jed); "Sunset in El Dorado" 1945 (U.S. Marshal); "Three in the Saddle" 1945; "Utah" 1945; "Alias Billy the Kid" 1946 (Sheriff); "Ambush Trail" 1946 (Marshall Dowes); "Days of Buffalo Bill" 1946; "The El Paso Kid" 1946; "Prairie Badmen" 1946 (Doc Latimer); "Roaring Rangers" 1946; "Roll on, Texas Moon" 1946 (Tom Prescott); "Stagecoach to Denver" 1946 (Felton); "Sun Valley Cyclone" 1946; "Trigger Fingers" 1946; "Border Feud" 1947 (Sheriff Steele); "Buffalo Bill Rides Again" 1947 (Sheriff); "The Fabulous Texan" 1947; "Homesteaders of Paradise Valley" 1947; "Jesse James Rides Again" 1947-serial (Grant); "Oregon Trail Scouts" 1947 (Bliss); "Son of Zorro" 1947-serial (Sheriff Moody); "Valley of Fear" 1947; "The Bold Frontiersman" 1948 (Morton Harris); "Desperadoes of Dodge City" 1948 (Jim); "Roughshod" 1949 (Sheriff); "Fence Riders" 1950; "The Savage Horde" 1950; "Trail of Robin Hood" 1950 (Sheriff Duffy); "Train to Tombstone" 1950

(Conductor); "Blazing Bullets" 1951; "Buckaroo Sheriff of Texas" 1951 (Clint); "Oklahoma Justice" 1951; "Black Hills Ambush" 1952 (Sheriff); "Desperadoes' Outpost" 1952 (Deputy Marshal); "Night Raiders" 1952 (Banker); "Waco" 1952; "The First Traveling Saleslady" 1956 (Theodore Roosevelt). ¶TV: *The Lone Ranger*—"War Horse" 10-20-49; *Wild Bill Hickok*—"Marriage Feud of Ponca City" 5-13-52; *Circus Boy*—"General Pete" 4-28-57 (Col. Theodore Roosevelt).

Cassidy, Jack (1927-12/12/76). Films: "The Cockeyed Cowboys of Calico County" 1970 (Roger Hand). ¶TV: *Gunsmoke*—"The Gentleman" 6-7-58 (Marcus France); *Wagon Train*—"The Nancy Palmer Story" 3-8-61 (Dan Palmer); *Maverick*—"The Art Lovers" 10-1-61 (Roger Cushman); *Bronco*—"The Harrigan" 12-25-61 (Edward Miller), "One Evening in Abilene" 3-19-62 (Marshal Bill Hickok); *Wide Country*—"The Judas Goat" 2-21-63 (Jerry Manning); *Alias Smith and Jones*—"How to Rob a Bank in One Hard Lesson" 9-23-71 (Harry Wagoner); *Bonanza*—"Cassie" 10-24-71 (Kevin).

Cassidy, James F. Films: "Santa Fe Stampede" 1938 (Newton).

Cassidy, Maureen. TV: *The Cisco Kid*—"The Tumblers" 11-28-53; *Sergeant Preston of the Yukon*—"Cinderella of the Yukon" 3-22-56 (Jill Atwater); *Jim Bowie*—"The Cave" 5-9-58 (Amy).

Cassidy, Shaun (1958-). Films: "Once Upon a Texas Train" TVM-1988 (Cotton).

Cassidy, Ted (1933-1/16/79). Films: "Butch Cassidy and the Sundance Kid" 1969 (Harvey Logan); "MacKenna's Gold" 1969 (Hachita). ¶TV: *Laredo*—"The Small Chance Ghost" 3-3-67 (Monte); *Daniel Boone*—"The Scrimshaw Ivory Chart" 1-4-68 (Gentle Sam); *Bonanza*—"Decision at Los Robles" 3-22-70 (Garth).

Castel, Lou (1943-). Films: "A Bullet for the General" 1966-Ital. (Bill Tate); "My Name Is Pecos" 1966-Ital.; "Let Them Rest" 1967-Ital./Ger. (Requiescant); "Matalo!" 1971-Ital./Span. (Ray Matalo).

Castelli, Bertrand. Films: "Thunder in the Sun" 1959 (Edmond Duquette).

Castellano, Giuseppe. Films: "Death Rides a Horse" 1967-Ital. (Sheriff); "The Dirty Outlaws" 1971-Ital.

Castelnuovo, Nino (1937-).

Films: "The Reward" 1965 (Luis); "Massacre Time" 1966-Ital./Span./Ger. (Jason); "The Five Man Army" 1969-Ital. (Luis Dominguez).

Castenada, Movita. *see* Movita.

Castiglioni, Iphigenie (1901-7/30/63). Films: "Valerie" 1957 (Mrs. Horvat); "The Comancheros" 1961 (Josefina). ¶TV: *Jim Bowie*—"Man on the Street" 5-16-58 (Anna De Marigny); *Zane Grey Theater*—"Proud Woman" 10-25-57 (Maria Delgado); *Have Gun Will Travel*—"Lazarus" 1-20-62 (Pina).

Castile, Lynn (1898-4/8/75). Films: "Marshal of Amarillo" 1948 (Matilda).

Castillo, Gloria (1933-). Films: "The Vanishing American" 1955 (Yashi). ¶TV: *Gunsmoke*—"Professor Lute Bone" 1-7-56 (Mrs. Ringle); *Zorro*—"The Runaways" 1-8-59 (Buena).

Castle, Anita. Films: "West of Sonora" 1948 (Penelope Clinton); "Junction City" 1952 (Penelope Clinton).

Castle, Dolores. Films: "West to Glory" 1947 (Marta). ¶TV: *The Cisco Kid*—"Romany Caravan" 11-17-51, "Buried Treasure" 12-29-51.

Castle, Don (1917-5/26/66). Films: "Out West with the Hardys" 1938 (Dennis Hunt); "Northwest Passage" 1940 (Richard Towne); "Tombstone, the Town Too Tough to Die" 1942 (Johnny Duane); "Madonna of the Desert" 1948 (Joe Salinas); "Stampede" 1949 (Tim); "The Big Land" 1957 (Draper); "Gunfight at the O.K. Corral" 1957 (Drunken Cowboy).

Castle, Jack. Films: "The Terror of Bar X" 1927 (Reginald Brooks).

Castle, John (1942-). Films: "Eagle's Wing" 1979-Brit./Span. (the Priest).

Castle, Lillian (1865-4/24/59). Films: "Lightning Triggers" 1935 (Minerva).

Castle, Mary (1931-). Films: "Prairie Roundup" 1951 (Toni Eaton); "Texans Never Cry" 1951 (Rita Bagley); "When the Redskins Rode" 1951 (Elizabeth Leeds); "The Lawless Breed" 1952 (Jane Brown); "Gunsmoke" 1953 (Cora DuFrayne); "Yaqui Drums" 1956; "The Last Stagecoach West" 1957 (Louise McCord). ¶TV: *Stories of the Century*—"Last Stagecoach West" 1954 (Louise McCord), Regular 1955 (Frankie Adams); *Cheyenne*—"Test of Courage" 1-29-57 (Alice Wilson); *Frontier Doctor*—"The Big Gamblers" 3-7-59.

Castle, Peggie (1926-8/11/71). Films: "Wagons West" 1952 (Ann Wilkins); "Cow Country" 1953 (Melba Sykes); "Son of Belle Star" 1953 (Clara Wren); "Jesse James' Women" 1954 (Waco Gans); "Overland Pacific" 1954 (Ann Dennison); "The Yellow Tomahawk" 1954 (Katherine); "Tall Man Riding" 1955 (Reva, the Saloon Singer); "The Oklahoma Woman" 1956 (Marie "Oklahoma" Saunders); "Quincannon, Frontier Scout" 1956 (Maylene Mason); "Two-Gun Lady" 1956 (Kate Masters); "Hell's Crossroads" 1957 (Paula Collins). ¶TV: *Cheyenne*—"Fury at Rio Hondo" 4-17-56 (Mississippi), "The Spanish Grant" 5-7-57 (Amy Gordon); *Zane Grey Theater*—"A Quiet Sunda in San Ardo" 11-23-56 (Charity); *Gunsmoke*—"Chester's Murder" 3-30-57 (Nita Tucker); *The Restless Gun*—"Hornitas Town" 2-10-58 (Amity Hobbs), "Lady by Law" 5-11-59 (Fern Foster); *The Texan*—"The First Notch" 10-20-58 (Charlotta Rivera); *Lawman*—Regular 1959-62 (Lily Merrill); *The Virginian*—"Morgan Starr" 2-9-66 (Melissa).

Castleton, Barbara (1896-1981). Films: "The Branding Iron" 1920 (Joan Carver).

Castro, Raul Medza. Films: "El Condor" 1970 (Indian).

Caswell, Nancy. Films: "The Two-Fisted Lover" 1920; "Horses' Collars" 1935-short (Girl); "Custer's Last Stand" 1936-serial (Barbara Trent).

Catching, Bill (1926-). Films: "The Man from Laramie" 1955 (Mule Driver); "Ride Beyond Vengeance" 1966 (Drunk); "Heaven with a Gun" 1969 (Willy); "The Hanged Man" TVM-1974. ¶TV: *The Roy Rogers Show*—"Peril from the Past" 4-13-52, "Empty Saddles" 3-10-56, "Tossup" 12-2-56, "High Stakes" 2-24-57, "Accessory to Crime" 3-3-57; *The Cisco Kid*—"Pancho and the Wolf Dog" 9-13-52, "Freedom of the Press" 9-27-52, "Faded General" 10-25-52, "The Racoon Story" 11-15-52, "Cisco Meets the Gorilla" 12-13-52, "Rodeo" 12-27-52, "Double Deal" 1-17-53, "Horseless Carriage" 1-24-53, "Steel Plow" 1-31-53, "Stevens Gang and Telegraph" 1-2-54; *Wild Bill Hickok*—"Meteor Mesa" 6-16-53; *Death Valley Days*—"The Loggerheads" 12-16-56; *Zane Grey Theater*—"Village of Fear" 3-1-57, "The Freighter" 1-17-58 (Newt Murdock), "The Accuser" 10-30-58, "Man Alone" 3-5-59; *Tales of Wells Fargo*—"The Reward" 4-21-58 (Chorlis), "Portrait of Teresa" 2-10-

62 (Cowhand); *Jefferson Drum*—"Bad Day for a Tinhorn" 5-16-58 (Dealer); *Wyatt Earp*—"The Peacemaker" 9-23-58 (Hoodlum); *Bat Masterson*—"Cheyenne Club" 12-17-58 (Kansas), "Deadly Diamonds" 2-11-60; *Wanted—Dead or Alive*—"Secret Ballot" 2-14-59, "Jason" 1-30-60 (Townsend); *The Rifleman*—"The Second Witness" 3-3-59; *Gunsmoke*—"Kangaroo" 9-26-59 (Joe), "Hammerhead" 12-26-64 (Stomp), "Coreyville" 10-6-69 (Guard #2), "The Pack Rat" 1-12-70 (Trapp), "Trafton" 10-25-71 (Brant); *The Law of the Plainsman*—"Desperate Decision" 11-12-59 (Potter); *Wichita Town*—"Biggest Man in Town" 12-30-59 (Ab Singleton); *Bonanza*—"The Avenger" 3-19-60, "The Tin Badge" 12-17-61 (Bankey), "The Scapegoat" 10-25-64 (Pitts); *Laramie*—"The Wedding Party" 1-29-63; *Wild Wild West*—"Night of the Deadly Bed" 9-24-65 (Angelo), "The Night of the Raven" 9-30-66 (Man); *Branded*—"Cowards Die Many Times" 4-17-66 (Deke); *The Big Valley*—"Lightfoot" 2-17-69; *Kung Fu*—"This Valley of Terror" 9-28-74 (Frank).

Catching, J.P. TV: *Wild Bill Hickok*—"Old Cowboys Never Die" 12-16-52; *Bonanza*—"The Law Maker" 3-11-62.

Catenacci, Luciano. Films: "The Big and the Bad" 1971-Ital./Fr./Span.; "It Can be Done ... Amigo" 1971-Ital./Fr./Span.; "Here We Go Again, Eh Providence?" 1973-Ital./Fr./Span.

Catlett, Walter (1889-11/14/60). Films: "Bad Men of Missouri" 1941 (Mr. Pettibone); "Heart of the Golden West" 1942 (Col. Silas Popen); "Wild Bill Hickok Rides" 1942 (Sylvester Twigg); "Davy Crockett and the River Pirates" 1956 (Col. Plug); "Friendly Persuasion" 1956 (Professor Quigley).

Catron, Jack. TV: *Whispering Smith*—"Poet and Peasant Case" 8-28-61 (Carruthers); *The Guns of Will Sonnett*—"The Natural Way" 9-29-67.

Catron, Jerry. Films: "Hostile Guns" 1967. ¶TV: *Bat Masterson*—"A Lesson in Violence" 2-23-61 (John Grant).

Cattani, Rico (1928-). TV: *Wild Wild West*—"The Night of the Camera" 11-29-68 (Butler); *The High Chaparral*—"To Stand for Something More" 10-24-69 (Felipe).

Cattrall, Kim (1956-). Films: "The Night Rider" TVM-1979 (Regina Kenton); "Miracle in the

Wilderness" TVM-1991 (Dora Adams). ¶TV: *How the West Was Won*—"The Slavers" 4-23-79 (Dolores).

Caulfield, Joan (1922-6/28/91). Films: "Cattle King" 1963 (Sharleen); "Red Tomahawk" 1967 (Dakota Lil); "Buckskin" 1968 (Nora Johnson); "Pony Express Rider" 1976 (Charlotte). ¶TV: *Cheyenne*—"Showdown at Oxbend" 12-17-62 (Darcy Clay); *The High Chaparral*—"The High Chaparral" 9-10-67 (Annalee).

Cavalier, Nita. Films: "The Dead Line" 1926 (Alice Wilson); "The Stolen Ranch" 1926 (June Marston); "Twin Triggers" 1926 (Gwen); "Tearin' into Trouble" 1927 (Maisie).

Cavan, Allan (1880-1/19/41). Films: "The Primal Law" 1921 (Mat Lane); "The New Frontier" 1935 (Minister); "End of the Trail" 1936; "Rebellion" 1936 (President Zachary Taylor); "The Unknown Ranger" 1936; "Code of the Range" 1937 (Calamity Parker); "Empty Holsters" 1937 (Warden); "Hit the Saddle" 1937 (Judge); "Old Louisiana" 1937 (President Thomas Jefferson); "The Lone Ranger" 1938-serial (Brennan); "Blue Montana Skies" 1939; "Come on, Rangers" 1939; "In Old Montana" 1939 (Sheriff).

Cavan, Jess. Films: "Ramona" 1928 (Band Leader); "The Desert Rider" 1929 (Black Bailey); "Fighting Shadows" 1935 (Hawkins); "The Frontiersman" 1938 (Townsman); "In Early Arizona" 1938; "Allegheny Uprising" 1939 (Colonial Farmer); "Saga of Death Valley" 1939; "Sheriff of Tombstone" 1941; "Outlaws of Pine Ridge" 1942; "Fighting Valley" 1943; "In Old Oklahoma" 1943; "Firebrands of Arizona" 1944 (Townsman); "Mojave Firebrand" 1944; "Colorado Pioneers" 1945; "The Topeka Terror" 1945; "California Gold Rush" 1946; "Days of Buffalo Bill" 1946.

Cavanagh, Paul (1895-3/15/64). Films: "The Storm" 1930 (Dave Stewart); "The Squaw Man" 1931 (Henry, Kearl of Kerhill); "Reno" 1939 (John Banton); "The Iroquois Trail" 1950 (Col. Thorne); "The Law vs. Billy the Kid" 1954 (John H. Tunstall). ¶TV: *Sergeant Preston of the Yukon*—"The Skull in the Stone" 11-7-57 (Philip Northrup); *Northwest Passage*—"The Assassin" 11-16-58 (Col. George Clayton); *Have Gun Will Travel*—"The Gladiators" 3-19-60 (Everett Windrom).

Cavanaugh, Hobart (1887-4/27/50). Films: "Cowboy from Brooklyn" 1938 (Mr. Jordan); "Reno" 1939 (Abe Compass); "Santa Fe Trail" 1940 (Barber Doyle); "Shooting High" 1940 (Clem Perkie); "Stage to Chino" 1940 (J. Horatius Boggs); "Jackass Mail" 1942 (Gospel Jones); "Land of the Open Range" 1942 (Pinky Gardner); "The Kansan" 1943 (Mayor Josh Hudkins).

Cavanaugh, James (1912-9/30/81). Films: "Vengeance" 1964 (Uncle Ben).

Cavanaugh, Michael. Films: "Belle Starr" TVM-1980 (Jesse James). ¶TV: *Dr. Quinn, Medicine Woman*—"Bad Water" 2-6-93 (Clay Harding).

Cavanaugh, William H. Films: "Anona's Baptism" 1912; "The Sheriff's Brother" 1912; "The Sign Invisible" 1918 (Chin Loo); "Calibre 38" 1919 (Sure Shot Jessup); "Red Love" 1925 (Sheriff LaVerne).

Cavell, Mark (1938-). Films: "The Man from the Alamo" 1953 (Carlos); "Young Fury" 1965 (Pancho). ¶TV: *Cheyenne*—"Devil's Canyon" 11-19-57 (Manuel); *Daniel Boone*—"The Scalp Hunter" 3-17-66 (Luca); *Pistols 'n' Petticoats*—Regular 1966-67 (Gray Hawk); *Gunsmoke*—"Muley" 1-21-67 (Arky).

Cavender, Glen (1884-2/9/62). Films: "The Primal Law" 1921 (Ruis); "Straight from the Shoulder" 1921 (Pete); "Iron to Gold" 1922 (Sloan); "The Nevada Buckaroo" 1931 (Hank); "Moonlight on the Prairie" 1935 (1st Cowboy); "Heart of the North" 1938 (Trapper); "River's End" 1940 (Bartender).

Cavens, Al. Films: "The First Traveling Saleslady" 1956 (Man). ¶TV: *Have Gun Will Travel*—"Duke of Texas" 4-22-61 (Jailet).

Cavens, Fred (1882-4/30/62). Films: "Breed of the Border" 1933 (Mike Cavins). ¶TV: *Sergeant Preston of the Yukon*—"Revenge" 10-4-56 (Pierre La Fitte).

Cavett, Dick (1936-). TV: *Alias Smith and Jones*—"Twenty-One Days to Tenstrike" 1-6-72 (Sheriff).

Ceccarelli, Pietro. Films: "Three Silver Dollars" 1968-Ital.; "Pistol Packin' Preacher" 1972-Ital./Fr. (Garvey); "They Call Him Veritas" 1972-Ital./Span.

Cecconi, Aldo. Films: "Colt Is the Law" 1965-Ital./Span.; "The Tramplers" 1965-Ital. (Jim Hennessy); "Dynamite Joe" 1966-Ital./Span.; "If You Want to Live ... Shoot!" 1967-Ital./Span.

Cecil, Edward (1888-12/13/40). Films: "The Captain of the Gray Horse Troop" 1917; "The Love Gambler" 1922 (Cameo Colby); "Wolves of the North" 1924-serial; "Hidden Loot" 1925 (Dick Jones); "The Stolen Ranch" 1926 (Silas Marston); "The Desert of the Lost" 1927; "Hoof Marks" 1927 (Harold Cole); "Saddle Mates" 1928 (George Lemmer); "Secret Menace" 1931; "The Ferocious Pal" 1934 (Sykes); "His Fighting Blood" 1935; "The Cattle Thief" 1936 (Doc Brawley); "Riders of the Frontier" 1939 (Doctor); "Deadwood Dick" 1940-serial; "The Man from Tumbleweeds" 1940 (Butler); "White Eagle" 1941-serial.

Cecil, Nora (1879-1954). Films: "The Deadwood Coach" 1924 (Matilda Shields); "Chip of the Flying U" 1926 (Dr. Cecil Grantham); "Born to Battle" 1927 (Ma Cowan); "The Silent Rider" 1927 (Mrs. Randall); "The Cavalier" 1928 (the Aunt); "A Trick of Hearts" 1928; "Stagecoach" 1939 (Dr. Boone's Housekeeper); "Union Pacific" 1939; "The Sea of Grass" 1947 (Mrs. Ryan).

Cedar, Jon. Films: "Death Hunt" 1981 (Hawkins). ¶TV: *The Quest*—"The Freight Train Rescue" 12-29-76 (Sawyer).

Cedar, Larry. Films: "Calamity Jane" TVM-1984 (Rev. Sipes).

Celi, Adolfo (1922-2/19/86). Films: "Death Sentence" 1967-Ital.; "Yankee" 1967-Ital./Span. (Cobra)

Celli, Teresa. TV: *Hudson's Bay*—"Sally MacGregor" 2-15-58 (Sally MacGregor).

Cerra, Saturnino. Films: "Seven Guns for the MacGregors" 1965-Ital./Span. (Johnny MacGregor); "The Ugly Ones" 1966-Ital./Span.; "Up the MacGregors!" 1967-Ital./Span. (Johnny MacGregor).

Cervera, Jr., Jorge. Films: "The Mark of Zorro" TVM-1974 (Sergeant Gonzales); "Wanted: The Sundance Woman" TVM-1976 (Major Vasquez); "The Gambler Returns: The Luck of the Draw" TVM-1991 (Colonel Volcar); "Rio Diablo" TVM-1993 (Bartender). ¶TV: *Bonanza*—"Customs of the Country" 2-6-72 (Rafael).

Cesana, Renzo (1907-11/8/70). Films: "Mark of the Renegade" 1951 (Father Juan); "California Conquest" 1952 (Fray Lindos).

Cestie, Renato. Films: "They Still Call Me Amen" 1972-Ital.; "The Big and the Bad" 1971-Ital./Fr./Span.; "It Can Be Done ... Amigo" 1971-Ital./Fr./Span.; "Red Coat" 1975-Ital.

Chadwick, Cyril. Films: "The

Heart Buster" 1924 (Edward Gordon); "The Iron Horse" 1924 (Jesson); "The Best Bad Man" 1925 (Frank Dunlap).

Chadwick, Helen (1897-9/4/40). Films: "The Challenge" 1916 (Alberta Bradley); "Go Get 'Em Garringer" 1919 (Wilma Wharton); "Cupid, the Cowpuncher" 1920 (Macie Sewell); "Quicksands" 1923 (the Girl); "The Border Legion" 1924 (Joan Randle); "Hard-Boiled" 1926 (Marjorie Gregg).

Chadwick, Maurine. Films: "Trail of Hate" 1922 (Carmencita).

Chadwick, Robert. TV: *The Rifleman*—"The Indian" 2-17-59 (Eskimimzin); *Rawhide*—"Incident at Tinker's Dam" 2-5-60.

Chailee, Joseph S. (1851-12/17/24). Films: "The Spell of the Yukon" 1916 (Rusty).

Challee, William (1904-3/18/89). Films: "The Sea of Grass" 1947 (Deputy Sheriff); "The Big Trees" 1952; "Man Without a Star" 1955; "The Desperados Are in Town" 1956 (Tom Kesh); "Noose for a Gunman" 1960 (Gorse); "The Plunderers" 1960 (1st Citizen); "Billy the Kid vs. Dracula" 1966; "Zachariah" 1971 (the Old Man); "The Great Northfield, Minnesota Raid" 1972 (Old Timer). ¶TV: *The Lone Ranger*—"Buried Treasure" 3-2-50, "Son of Adoption" 3-19-53, "Wanted … the Lone Ranger" 5-5-55, "The Wooden Rifle" 9-23-56, "Hot Spell in Panamint" 11-22-56; *Sheriff of Cochise*—"Fire on Chiricahua Mountains" 11-2-56 (Callahan); *Wyatt Earp*—"Sweet Revenge" 1-28-58 (Dundee); *Jim Bowie*—"The Lion's Cub" 3-14-58 (Mark); *The Texan*—"No Tears for the Dead" 12-8-58 (Roy Tovers), "A Time of the Year" 12-22-58; Lawman—"The Hardcase" 1-31-60 (Nat Denning); *Maverick*—"The Misfortune Teller" 3-6-60 (Bartender); *G.E. Theater*—"Aftermath" 4-17-60; *Tate*—"Before Sunup" 8-17-60 (Old Man); *Klondike*—"Swoger's Mules" 11-21-60 (Henry Swoger); *Have Gun Will Travel*—"A Quiet Night in Town" 1-7-61 & 1-14-61; *Laramie*—"The Accusers" 11-14-61 (Charlie); *Gunsmoke*—"The Gallows" 3-3-62 (Jake Feist), "Cleavus" 2-15-71 (Baylock); *The Virginian*—"The Brazen Bell" 10-17-62; *Wagon Train*—"The Molly Kincaid Story" 9-16-63 (Stage Driver), "The Geneva Balfour Story" 1-20-64; *Bonanza*—"The Emperor Norton" 2-27-66 (Mark Twain), "The Younger Brothers' Younger Brother" 3-12-72 (Pa Younger), "Forever" 9-12-72 (Jake), "The Initiation" 9-26-72 (Stable-

man); *Iron Horse*—"T Is for Traitor" 12-2-67 (Jake Benson).

Challenger, Percy (1858-7/23/32). Films: "Ashes of Hope" 1917 (Flat Foot); "The Medicine Man" 1917 (Seth Hopkins); "Wild Sumac" 1917 (Deacon Bricketts); "The Fly God" 1918 (Shorty Stokes); "The Law's Outlaw" 1918 (Clarence Bartley); "Little Red Decides" 1918 (Little Doe); "The Pretender" 1918 (Rev. Harold Upright); "Old Dynamite" 1921; "Sting of the Lash" 1921 (Rorke); "The Galloping Kid" 1922 (Zek Hawkins); "Smiling Jim" 1922 (Judd Briggs); "Tracked to Earth" 1922 (Zed White); "Singled-Handed" 1923 (Prof. Weighoff); "Cyclone Bob" 1926 (Malcomb Mallory).

Chalmers, Thomas (1884-6/11/66). Films: "The Outrage" 1964 (Judge).

Chamberlain, Richard (1935-). Films: "A Thunder of Drums" 1961 (Lt. Porter); "Dream West" TVM-1986 (John Charles Fremont). ¶TV: *Gunsmoke*—"The Bobsy Twins" 5-21-60 (Pete); *The Deputy*—"The Edge of Doubt" 3-4-61 (Jerry Kirk); *Whispering Smith*—"Stain of Justice" 6-12-61 (Chris Harrington); *Centennial*—Regular 1978-79 (Alexander King).

Chamberlin, Howland (1911-9/1/84). Films: "Surrender" 1950 (Manager); "High Noon" 1952 (Hotel Clerk); "Barbarosa" 1982 (Emil).

Chamberlin, Ray (1886-12/2/57). Films: "The Great Divide" 1915 (Pedro); "The Sign Invisible" 1918 (Pierre).

Chambers, Phil (-1/16/93). Films: "Tumbleweed" 1953 (Trapper Ross); "The Bounty Hunter" 1954 (Ed); "Overland Pacific" 1954 (Weeks); "Ricochet Romance" 1954 (Mr. Daniels); "Rage at Dawn" 1955; "Run for Cover" 1955; "Backlash" 1956 (Dobbs); "A Day of Fury" 1956 (Burson); "Drango" 1957 (Luke); "Good Day for a Hanging" 1958 (Avery); "Six Black Horses" 1962 (Undertaker). ¶TV: *Wyatt Earp*—"Mr. Earp Becomes a Marshal" 9-6-55; *My Friend Flicka*—"Blind Faith" 10-7-55, "A Case of Honor" 10-14-55 (Dr. Harrow), "Against All Odds" 4-27-56; *Wagon Train*—"The Beauty Jamison Story" 12-17-58 (Luke Carter); *Bat Masterson*—"Marked Deck" 3-11-59 (Sheriff); *The Law of the Plainsman*—"Toll Road" 12-24-59 (Dan Dawson); *Man from Blackhawk*—"The Legacy" 12-25-59 (Sheriff Brawley); *Have Gun Will Travel*—"Jenny" 1-23-60 (Matlock); *Wichita Town*—"The Hanging Judge" 3-9-60

(Tully); *The Tall Man*—"Larceny and Young Ladies" 11-12-60 (Man); *Gunsmoke*—"Distant Drummer" 11-19-60 (Hugo), "The Avenger" 11-27-72 (Shotgun), "The Angry Land" 2-3-75 (Farmer); *Tales of Wells Fargo*—"Return to Yesterday" 1-13-62 (Clerk), "The Traveler" 2-24-62 (Clerk), "Chauncey" 3-17-62 (Ben Whipple); *Bonanza*—"Knight Errant" 11-18-62 (Dick Thompson), "The Colonel" 1-6-63, "Rich Man, Poor Man" 5-12-63, "She Walks in Beauty" 9-22-63, "Rain from Heaven" 10-6-63, "Pink Cloud Comes from Old Cathay" 4-12-64, "Old Sheba" 11-22-64 (Anderson), "The Search" 2-14-65, "The Return" 5-2-65 (Hubbell), "Found Child" 10-24-65 (Store Owner), "To Bloom for Thee" 10-16-66 (Storeman), "Ponderosa Explosion" 1-1-67 (Storekeeper), "The Greedy Ones" 5-14-67, "The Company of Forgotten Men" 2-2-69 (Webster); *Stoney Burke*—"King of the Hill" 1-21-63 (Doctor); *Wild Wild West*—"The Night of the Inferno" 9-17-65 (Train Captain); *The Loner*—"A Question of Guilt" 1-29-66 (Bartender); *Daniel Boone*—"Grizzly" 10-6-66 (Jed Weston); *Time Tunnel*—"Billy the Kid" 2-10-67 (Marshal); *The Big Valley*—"Brother Love" 2-20-67, "The Lady from Mesa" 4-3-67; *The Guns of Will Sonnett*—"End of the Rope" 1-12-68, "Time Is the Rider" 1-10-69; *Death Valley Days*—"Talk to Me, Charley" 12-20-69.

Chambers, Steve. Films: "The Long Riders" 1980; "Maverick" 1994 (Unshaven Man). ¶TV: *Kung Fu*—"The Third Man" 4-26-73 (Deputy), "The Chalice" 10-11-73 (Kunkel), "The Spirit Helper" 11-8-73 (Comanchero).

Chambers, Wheaton (1888-1/31/58). Films: "Adventures of Red Ryder" 1940-serial (Boswell); "Geronimo" 1940 (John A. Rawlins); "Prairie Pioneers" 1941; "Outlaws of Pine Ridge" 1942; "Beyond the Last Frontier" 1943 (Doc Jessup); "Black Hills Express" 1943; "Bordertown Gunfighters" 1943; "Girl Rush" 1944 (Dealer); "Nevada" 1944 (Dr. Darien); "Tall in the Saddle" 1944 (Ab Jenkins); "Marshal of Laredo" 1945; "The El Paso Kid" 1946 (Dr. Hamlin); "King of the Forest Rangers" 1946-serial (Ronald Spencer); "South of Monterey" 1946; "Stagecoach to Denver" 1946 (Braydon); "Trail to Mexico" 1946; "Gun Talk" 1947 (Herkimer Stone); "On the Old Spanish Trail" 1947 (Silas MacIntyre); "The Sea of Grass" 1947 (Dean); "Son of Zorro" 1947-serial (Caleb Baldwin); "The Wild Frontier" 1947

(Doc Hardy); "Song of the Drifter" 1948; "Deputy Marshal" 1949 (Harley Masters); "The Baron of Arizona" 1950 (Brother Gregory); "The Lawless Breed" 1952 (Doc); "Wagons West" 1952 (Sam Wilkins); "The Peacemaker" 1956 (Doc Runyan); "The Oklahoman" 1957 (Lounger). ¶TV: *The Lone Ranger*—"The Renegades" 11-3-49; *The Roy Rogers Show*—"The Set-Up" 1-20-52, "Doc Stevens' Traveling Store" 7-25-54 (Robert Ott).

Chambliss, Woodrow (1915- 1/8/81). Films: "The Wild Country" 1971 (Dakota); "Count Your Bullets" 1972 (Prospector). ¶TV: *Gunsmoke*— "Never Pester Chester" 11-16-57 (Shiloh), "Malachi" 11-13-65 (Knowles), "Sweet Billy, Singer of Songs" 1-15-66 (Waiter), "Sanctuary" 2-26-66 (Porter), "The Goldtakers" 9-24-66 (Garvey), "The Lure" 2-25- 67 (Swiger), Regular 1966-75 (Mr. Lathrop, the Storekeeper); *Have Gun Will Travel*—"The Colonel and the Lady" 11-23-57; *Bat Masterson*—"Six Feet of Gold" 2-25-60 (O'Malley); *Cimarron Strip*—"The Beast That Walks Like a Man" 11-30-67; *Dirty Sally*—3-22-74 (Doc Carter); *How the West Was Won*—Episode One 2-12-78 (Mr. Greevy).

Champion, Marge (Marjorie Bell) (1923-). Films: "Honor of the West" 1939 (Diane Allen); "The Cockeyed Cowboys of Calico County" 1970 (Mrs. Bester).

Chan, Michael Paul. Films: "Kung Fu: The Movie" TVM-1986; "Maverick" 1994 (Riverboat Poker Players).

Chance, Larry. Films: "The Battles of Chief Pontiac" 1952 (Hawkbill); "River of No Return" 1954; "War Drums" 1957 (Ponce); "Fort Bowie" 1958 (Victorio); "Fort Massacre" 1958 (Moving Cloud). ¶TV: *Sky King*—"Mickey's Birthday" 8-10- 52 (Brewer); *Wild Bill Hickok*—"Cry Wolf" 10-7-52, "Return of Chief Red Hawk" 2-10-53, "Jingles Wins a Friend" 4-28-53, "Money Shines" 6- 2-53; *Sergeant Preston of the Yukon*— "Golden Gift" 6-14-56 (Gabe); *The Adventures of Rin Tin Tin*—"The Lieutenant's Lesson" 2-8-57, "Rusty's Opportunity" 10-17-58 (Apache Jack), "Ol' Betsy" 1-16-59 (Medicine Man); *Tales of the Texas Rangers*— "Double Reward" 12-15-57 (Crewes); *Northwest Passage*—"The Gunsmith" 9-28-58 (Chief Black Wolf), "Surprise Attack" 10-5-58 (Chief Black Wolf); *Wichita Town*—"Seed of Hate" 1-27-60 (Indian); *The Texan*— "The Nomad" 4-18-60; *Bronco*—

"Legacy of Twisted Creed" 4-19-60 (Many Trees); *Bonanza*—"The Savage" 12-3-60 (Haddon); *The Rifleman*—"The Mescalero Curse" 4-18- 61 (Lobo); *Rawhide*—"The Lost Tribe" 10-27-61 (Two Eagles); *Maverick*—"Three Queens Full" 11-12-61 (Henry); *Tales of Wells Fargo*—"Moneyrun" 1-6-62 (Lucera); *The Tall Man*—"St. Louis Woman" 1-20-62 (Charlie Awatche); *The Outlaws*—"A Bit of Glory" 2-1-62 (Spangler); *Daniel Boone*—"The Choosing" 10- 29-64 (Indian Chief), "The Matchmaker" 10-27-66 (Lone Runner); *Laredo*—"Oh Careless Love" 12-23- 66 (Many Horses); *The Virginian*— "The Girl in the Shadows" 3-26-69 (Frank Lynch).

Chandler, Chick (1905-9/30/ 88). Films: "Red Love" 1925 (Tom Livingston); "Home in Wyomin'" 1942 (Hack Hackett); "Curtain Call at Cactus Creek" 1950 (Ralph); "Untamed Heiress" 1954 (Eddie Taylor); "The Naked Gun" 1956. ¶TV: *The Lone Ranger*—"Message to Fort Apache" 9-23-54, "Tenderfoot" 11- 25-54, "Homer with a High Hat" 12- 16-54; *Frontier Circus*—"The Balloon Girl" 1-11-62 (Luke Turlock); *Maverick*—"The Troubled Heir" 4-1-62 (Oliver "Slippery" Perkins); *Death Valley Days*—"Measure of a Man" 11- 17-63; *Daniel Boone*—"Dan'l Boone Shot a B'ar" 9-15-66 (Higgens); *Bonanza*—"Ponderosa Explosion" 1-1-67 (Nate), "My Friend, My Enemy" 1- 12-69 (Judge Butler), "Speak No Evil" 4-20-69 (Judge Butler), "A Darker Shadow" 11-23-69 (Dr. Mills), "Thorton's Account" 11-1-70 (Doctor), "Face of Fear" 11-14-71 (Garroway).

Chandler, Eddie (1894-3/23/ 48). Films: "Young Whirlwind" 1928 (Johnson); "Desert Trail" 1935 (Kansas Charlie); "Square Shooter" 1935 (Kelly); "Wild Brian Kent" 1936 (Jed); "God's Country and the Woman" 1937 (Logger); "Cowboy from Brooklyn" 1938 (Brakeman); "Gold Is Where You Find It" 1938 (Deputy); "The Kid from Texas" 1939 (Captain Babcock); "Buck Benny Rides Again" 1940 (1st Cowhand); "Santa Fe Trail" 1940 (Guard).

Chandler, George (1902-6/10/ 85). Films: "A Mixup on the Plains" 1913; "A Clean Sweep" 1928; "A Fighting Tenderfoot" 1928; "Saps and Saddles" 1928; "Speed and Spurs" 1928; "A Tenderfoot Hero" 1928; "A Close Call" 1929; "A Daring Dude" 1929; "The Go Get 'Em Kid" 1929; The Lone Rider" 1929; "Red Romance" 1929; "Riding for Life" 1929;

"A Tenderfoot Terror" 1929; "The Thrill Hunter" 1929; "Two-Gun Morgan" 1929; "The Virginian" 1929 (Ranch Hand); "The Light of the Western Stars" 1930 (Slig Whalen); "Wide Open Spaces" 1932-short; "Fair Warning" 1937 (Hotel Clerk); "God's Country and the Woman" 1937 (Flunky); "Jesse James" 1939 (Roy); "Arizona" 1940 (Haley); "Melody Ranch" 1940 (Cab Driver); "The Return of Frank James" 1940 (Boy); "Shooting High" 1940 (Charles Pritchard); "Trail of the Vigilantes" 1940 (Railroad Station Attendant); "Western Union" 1941 (Herb); "The Great Man's Lady" 1942 (Forbes); "In Old Oklahoma" 1943; "The Ox-Bow Incident" 1943 (Jimmy Cairnes); "Buffalo Bill" 1944 (Trooper Clancy); "Tall in the Saddle" 1944; "The Man from Oklahoma" 1945; "The Michigan Kid" 1947; "Saddle Pals" 1947 (Dippy); "The Vigilantes Return" 1947; "The Paleface" 1948 (Patient); "Sons of Adventure" 1948 (Billy Wilkes); "Kansas Raiders" 1950 (Willie); "Singing Guns" 1950 (Smitty); "Across the Wide Missouri" 1951 (Gowie); "Westward the Women" 1951; "Rails into Laramie" 1954 (Grimes); "Apache Ambush" 1955 (Chandler); "Gunsight Ridge" 1957 (Gus Withers); "Law of the Lawless" 1964 (Hotel Clerk); "Apache Uprising" 1966 (Jace Asher); "Buckskin" 1968 (Storekeeper); "One More Train to Rob" 1971 (Conductor); "The Apple Dumpling Gang Rides Again" 1979. ¶TV: *Wild Bill Hickok*—"Return of Chief Red Hawk" 2-10-53; *Wyatt Earp*—"The Desperate Half-Hour" 2-28-56 (McVey); *Circus Boy*—"Corky and the Circus Doctor" 10-21-56 (Henry Crump); *Fury*—"Joey and the Stranger" 12-1-56 (Sprague); *Tales of Wells Fargo*—"Renegade Raiders" 5- 20-57 (Mr. Billings), "The Dowry" 7-10-61 (Captain Billy); *Wagon Train*—"The Cassie Tanner Story" 6- 4-58 (Clee McMasters), "The Sacramento Story" 6-25-58 (Clee McMasters); *The Deputy*—"The Edge of Doubt" 3-4-61 (George Lake); *Rawhide*—"Incident of the Wild Deuces" 12-12-63 (Reverend Lincoln); *Laredo*—"The Callico Kid" 1-6-66 (Sam Lowell); *Bonanza*—"The Greedy Ones" 5-14-67 (Gus); *Alias Smith and Jones*—"The Fifth Victim" 3-25-71; *Gunsmoke*—"Waste" 9-27-71 & 10-4- 71.

Chandler, Helen (1909-4/30/ 65). Films: "Rough Romance" 1930 (Marna Reynolds).

Chandler, James (1922-6/15/ 88). Films: "Heaven with a Gun"

1969 (Doc Foster). ¶TV: *The Rifleman*—"The Mind Reader" 6-30-59, "The Silent Knife" 12-20-60; *Wanted—Dead or Alive*—"Man on Horseback" 12-5-59; *The Rebel*—"Fair Game" 3-27-60 (Farnum), "The Legacy" 11-13-60 (Sheriff Ricker); *Laramie*—"Queen of Diamonds" 9-20-60 (Rancher); *Maverick*—"Last Wire from Stop Gap" 10-16-60 (Ryan); *The Outlaws*—"The Sooner" 4-27-61 (Reverend); *Empire*—"The Fire Dancer" 11-13-62 (Phil Curtis); *Branded*—"The Greatest Coward on Earth" 11-21-65 (Charlie Stark); *Hondo*—"The Ghost of Ed Dow" 11-24-67 (Matt), "Hondo and the Gladiators" 12-15-67 (Sheriff); *Cimarron Strip*—"The Judgment" 1-4-68; *Gunsmoke*—"The Convict" 2-1-71 (Warden), "The Wedding" 3-13-72 (Reverend Keller), "The Gang" 12-11-72 (Governor Martinson), "The Widow-Maker" 10-8-73 (Preacher), "The Town Tamers" 1-28-74 (Preacher); *Bonanza*—"The Law and Billy Burgess" 2-15-70 (Osgood), "Blind Hunch" 11-21-71 (McKey), "The Initiation" 9-26-72 (George Adams).

Chandler, Janet (1915-3/16/94). Films: "The Golden West" 1932 (Betty Summers); "Cowboy Holiday" 1934 (Ruth Hopkins); "Cyclone of the Saddle" 1935 (Sue); "Rough Riding Ranger" 1935 (Dorothy White).

Chandler, Jeff (1918-6/17/61). Films: "Broken Arrow" 1950 (Cochise); "Two Flags West" 1950 (Kenniston); "The Battle at Apache Pass" 1952 (Cochise); "The Great Sioux Uprising" 1953 (Jonathan Westgate); "War Arrow" 1953 (Maj. Howell Brady); "Taza, Son of Cochise" 1954 (Cochise); "The Spoilers" 1955 (Roy Glennister); "Pillars of the Sky" 1956 (1st Sgt. Emmett Bell); "Drango" 1957 (Drango); "Man in the Shadow" 1957 (Sheriff Ben Sadler); "The Jayhawkers" 1959 (Luke Darcy); "Thunder in the Sun" 1959 (Lon Bennett); "The Plunderers" 1960 (Sam Christy).

Chandler, John Davis (1937-). Films: "Ride the High Country" 1962 (Jimmy Hammond); "Major Dundee" 1965 (Jimmy Lee Benteen); "Return of the Gunfighter" TVM-1967 (Sundance); "The Good Guys and the Bad Guys" 1969 (Deuce); "Barquero" 1970 (Fair); "Shoot Out" 1971 (Skeeter); "Pat Garrett and Billy the Kid" 1973 (Norris); "Shadow of Chikara" 1978 (Rafe); "Triumphs of a Man Called Horse" 1984 (Mason). ¶TV: *The Rifleman*—"The Executioner" 5-7-62 (Brooks); *The Virginian*—"The Brazen Bell" 10-17-62

(Dog); *Empire*—"Seven Days on Rough Street" 2-26-63 (Arlen); *The Travels of Jaimie McPheeters*—"The Day of the First Trail" 9-22-63 (Dick McBride), "The Day of the Picnic" 2-16-64 (Dick McBride); *A Man Called Shenandoah*—"Survival" 9-20-65 (Cassidy); *The High Chaparral*—"The Doctor from Dodge" 10-29-67 (Kid Curry); *Gunsmoke*—"Shadler" 1-15-73 (Rogers), "Cowtown Hustler" 3-11-74 (Willie Tomsen).

Chandler, Lane (1899-9/14/72). Films: "Open Range" 1927 (Tex Smith); "Beyond the Law" 1930 (Jack-Knife); "Firebrand Jordan" 1930 (Firebrand Jordan); "Rough Waters" 1930 (Cal Morton); "Under Texas Skies" 1930 (Martin); "Hurricane Horseman" 1931 (Gun Smith); "Riders of the Rio" 1931 (Bob Lane); "Battling Buckaroo" 1932 (Blackjack/Driftin' Slim Stanley); "The Cheyenne Cyclone" 1932 (Bob Carlton); "The Devil Horse" 1932-serial; "Guns for Hire" 1932 (Ken Wayne "Flip" Larue); "Lawless Valley" 1932 (Bob Rand); "The Reckless Rider" 1932; "Texas Tornado" 1932 (Tex Robbins); "Wyoming Whirlwind" 1932 (Keene Wallace/Wolf); "Fighting with Kit Carson" 1933-serial; "Sagebrush Trail" 1933 (Bob Jones); "Trouble Busters" 1933 (Jim Perkins); "Via Pony Express" 1933 (Buck Carson); "War on the Range" 1933; "The Lone Bandit" 1934 (Lane Cartwright); "The Outlaw Tamer" 1934 (Tex Broderick); "North of Arizona" 1935 (Ray Keeler); "Rio Rattler" 1935; "Law and Lead" 1936 (Ned Hyland); "The Lawless Nineties" 1936 (Bridger); "The Plainsman" 1936; "Red River Valley" 1936; "Stormy Trails" 1936 (Dunn); "Winds of the Wasteland" 1936 (Larry Adams); "The Idaho Kid" 1937 (Jess Peters); "Law of the Ranger" 1937 (Col Williams); "Reckless Ranger" 1937; "Wells Fargo" 1937 (Wells Fargo Messenger); "Zorro Rides Again" 1937-serial (Malloy); "Heart of Arizona" 1938 (Trimmer Windler); "Heroes of the Alamo" 1938 (Davy Crockett); "Heart of the North" 1938 (Pilot); "Land of Fighting Men" 1938 (Cliff); "The Lone Ranger" 1938-serial (Dick Forrest); "Two-Gun Justice" 1938 (Butch); "Come on, Rangers" 1939 (Ken Rogers); "The Law Comes to Texas" 1939; "Man of Conquest" 1939 (Bonham); "North of the Yukon" 1939 (Cpl. Atkins); "Oklahoma Frontier" 1939 (Sergeant); "The Oregon Trail" 1939-serial; "Outpost of the Mounties" 1939 (Cooper); "Saga of Death Valley"

1939; "Southward Ho!" 1939 (Crawford); "The Taming of the West" 1939 (Turkey); "Union Pacific" 1939 (Conductor); "Deadwood Dick" 1940-serial (Wild Bill Hickok); "Man from Montreal" 1940 (Constable Rankin); "My Little Chickadee" 1940 (Porter); "Northwest Mounted Police" 1940 (Constable Fyffe); "Pioneers of the West" 1940 (Steve Carson); "Pony Post" 1940 (Fairweather); "Santa Fe Trail" 1940 (Adjutant); "Virginia City" 1940 (Soldier Clerk); "Last of the Duanes" 1941 (Henchman); "The Round Up" 1941; "Six Gun Gold" 1941 (Brad Bardigan); "They Died with Their Boots On" 1941 (Sentry); "Sundown Jim" 1942 (Nat Oldroyd); "Valley of Vanishing Men" 1942-serial; "In Old Oklahoma" 1943 (Man on Train); "Law of the Saddle" 1943 (Steve Kinney); "Riding High" 1943 (Cowboy); "Tenting Tonight on the Old Camp Ground" 1943 (Duke Merrick); "Wild Horse Rustlers" 1943 (Smokey Beckman/Hans Beckman); "Oklahoma Raiders" 1944; "Riders of the Santa Fe" 1944 (Sheriff Earl Duncan); "Rustlers' Hideout" 1944 (Hammond); "Silver City Kid" 1944; "Trigger Law" 1944; "Trigger Trail" 1944 (Slade); "Along Came Jones" 1945 (Boone); "San Antonio" 1945 (Cowboy); "California" 1946 (Man); "Duel in the Sun" 1946 (U.S. Cavalry Captain); "Gunning for Vengeance" 1946; "Terror Trail" 1946; "Two-Fisted Ranger" 1946; "Pursued" 1947 (Callum); "Unconquered" 1947; "The Vigilantes Return" 1947 (Messenger); "Northwest Stampede" 1948 (Scrivner); "The Paleface" 1948 (Tough-Looking Galoot); "Red River" 1948 (Colonel); "Return of the Badmen" 1948 (Ed, the Posse Leader); "Riders of the Whistling Pines" 1949; "Montana" 1950 (Jake Overby); "Outcast of Black Mesa" 1950 (Ted Thorp); "Along the Great Divide" 1951 (Sheriff); "Cattle Queen" 1951 (Marshal); "Prairie Roundup" 1951 (Red Dawson); "Santa Fe" 1951; "The Hawk of Wild River" 1952 (George, the Storekeeper); "The Lion and the Horse" 1952 (the Sheriff); "The Lusty Men" 1952 (Announcer); "Rancho Notorious" 1952 (Sheriff Hardy); "The San Francisco Story" 1952 (Morton); "The Charge at Feather River" 1953 (Poinsett); "Take Me to Town" 1953 (Mike); "Thunder Over the Plains" 1953 (Faraday); "Border River" 1954 (Anderson); "Silver Lode" 1954 (Man at Fire); "The Indian Fighter" 1955 (Head Settler); "Shotgun" 1955 (Fletcher); "Tall Man Riding" 1955

(Hap Sutton, the Ordway Foreman); "The First Traveling Saleslady" 1956 (Rancher); "The Lone Ranger" 1956 (Whitebeard); "The Storm Rider" 1957 (Doctor); "Quantrill's Raiders" 1958 (Sheriff); "Noose for a Gunman" 1960 (Ed Folsey); "Requiem for a Gunfighter" 1965 (Bryan Comer). ¶TV: *The Lone Ranger*—"The Renegades" 11-3-49, "Man of the House" 1-26-50, "The Black Widow" 8-24-50, "The Squire" 11-9-50; *The Cisco Kid*—"Lynching Story" 4-28-51, "Confession for Money" 5-26-51, "Pancho Hostage" 6-23-51, "Doorway to Nowhere" 9-26-53; *The Gene Autry Show*—"Thunder Out West" 7-14-53, "Bandidos" 9-1-53; *Wild Bill Hickok*—"Good Indian" 8-4-53; *Cheyenne*—"Deadline" 2-26-57 (Sheriff Morley), "The Frightened Town" 3-20-61 (Joe Cooper); *Wyatt Earp*—"They Hired Some Guns" 2-26-57 (Dan Woodruff), "The Truth About Rawhide Geraghty" 2-17-59 (Brooks); *Maverick*—"The War of the Silver Kings" 9-22-57 (Lawson), "The Marquesa" 1-3-60 (Sheriff), "The Iron Hand" 2-21-60 (Marshal Rickter), "The Town That Wasn't There" 10-2-60 (Sheriff Crane), "The Cactus Switch" 1-15-61 (Sheriff Bill Wright); *The Californians*—"The Regulators" 11-5-57 (Purdy); *The Restless Gun*—"Imposter for a Day" 2-17-58 (Sheriff Croft); *Sugarfoot*—"Short Range" 5-13-58 (Sheriff Harkness), "Brink of Fear" 6-30-58 (Marshal); *Have Gun Will Travel*—"The Naked Gun" 12-19-59 (Lance), "The Twins" 5-21-60 (Sheriff), "Ben Jalisco" 11-18-61 (John Tay); *Gunsmoke*—"Bad Sheriff" 1-7-61 (Sam), "Indian Ford" 12-2-61 (Trumbull), "The Trappers" 11-3-62 (Luke), "Chicken" 12-5-64, "The Whispering Tree" 11-12-66 (Guard); *Wagon Train*—"The Pearlie Garnet Story" 2-24-64 (Sheriff).

Chandler, Linda. TV: *Wild Wild West*—"The Night of Miguelito's Revenge" 12-13-68 (Lynn Carstairs).

Chandler, Patricia. TV: *The Big Valley*—"Plunder at Hawk's Grove" 3-13-67 (Indian Girl); *Alias Smith and Jones*—"The Night of the Red Dog" 11-4-71 (Secretary).

Chandler, Robert (1860-3/17/50). Films: "Their Compact" 1917 (Pop Anderson); "Go West, Young Man" 1918 (Crimmins); "The Vigilantes" 1918; "The Last Straw" 1920 (Alf Cole); "Hurricane Horseman" 1926 (Parson Pettigrew); "Hawk of the Hills" 1927-serial (Clyde Selby); "Quick Triggers" 1928 (Jake Landis).

Chandler, Tanis. TV: *The Cisco Kid*—"Dog Story" 5-12-51, "The Old Bum" 6-9-51, "Water Rights" 7-7-51.

Chandler, Warren. Films: "The Gray Towers Mystery" 1919 (Tom Makinnon).

Chanel, Helen. Films: "Two Gangsters in the Wild West" 1965-Ital./Span.; "Cjamango" 1967-Ital. (Perla); "Two R-R-Ringos from Texas" 1967-Ital.

Chanel, Lorraine. Films: "The Revengers" 1972-U.S./Mex. (Mrs. Benedict); "Nevada Smith" TVM-1975 (Belva).

Chaney, Bill. Films: "The Lawless Rider" 1954 (Bill); "I Killed Wild Bill Hickok" 1956 (Tex).

Chaney, Creighton. see Chaney, Jr., Lon.

Chaney, Lon (1883-8/26/30). Films: "Bloodhounds of the North" 1913; "The Honor of the Mounted" 1914; "A Ranch Romance" 1914; "The Tragedy of Whispering Creek" 1914 (the Greaser); "The Unlawful Trade" 1914; "The Desert Breed" 1915; "The Accusing Evidence" 1916 (Waught Mohr); "The Empty Gun" 1917; "Pay Me!" 1917 (Joe Lawson); "The Grand Passion" 1918 (Paul Argos); "Riddle Gawne" 1918 (Hame Bozzam); "A Man's Country" 1919 (Three Card Duncan); "Nomads of the North" 1920 (Raoul Challoner).

Chaney, Jr., Lon (Creighton Chaney) (1905-7/12/73). Films: "The Last Frontier" 1932-serial (Tom Kirby); "Scarlet River" 1933 (Jeff Todd); "Son of the Border" 1933 (Jack Breen); "The Old Corral" 1936 (Garland); "The Singing Cowboy" 1936 (Martin); "Cheyenne Rides Again" 1937 (Girard); "Wild and Woolly" 1937 (Dutch); "Frontier Marshal" 1939 (Pringle); "Jesse James" 1939 (Outlaw); "Union Pacific" 1939 (Dollarhide); "Northwest Mounted Police" 1940 (Shorty); "Badlands of Dakota" 1941 (Jack McCall); "Billy the Kid" 1941 (Spike Hudson); "Riders of Death Valley" 1941-serial (Butch); "North to the Klondike" 1942 (Nate Carson); "Overland Mail" 1942-serial (Jim Lane); "Frontier Badman" 1943 (Chango); "The Daltons Ride Again" 1945 (Grat Dalton); "Albuquerque" 1948 (Steve Murkill); "Inside Straight" 1951 (Shocker); "Only the Valiant" 1951 (Trooper Kebussyan); "High Noon" 1952 (Martin Howe); "The Battles of Chief Pontiac" 1952 (Chief Pontiac); "The Bushwackers" 1952 (Mr. Taylor); "Springfield Rifle" 1952 (Elm); "The Boy from Okla-homa" 1954 (Crazy Charlie); "Passion" 1954 (Castro); "The Indian Fighter" 1955 (Chivington); "The Silver Star" 1955 (John W. Harmon); "Pardners" 1956 (Whitey); "Daniel Boone, Trail Blazer" 1957 (Blackfish); "Money, Women and Guns" 1958 (Art Birdwell); "Law of the Lawless" 1964 (Tiny); "Stage to Thunder Rock" 1964 (Henry Parker); "Black Spurs" 1965 (Kile); "Town Tamer" 1965 (Mayor Leach); "Young Fury" 1965 (Bartender); "Apache Uprising" 1966 (Charlie Russell); "Johnny Reno" 1966 (Sheriff Hodges); "Welcome to Hard Times" 1967 (Avery); "Buckskin" 1968 (Sheriff Tangely); "The Female Bunch" 1971 (Monty). ¶TV: *Hawkeye and the Last of the Mohicans*—Regular 1957 (Mohican); *Tombstone Territory*—"The Black Marshal from Deadwood" 9-3-58 (Marshal Dagett); *Rough Riders*—"An Eye for an Eye" 1-15-59 (Ben Hawkins); *Rawhide*—"Incident at the Edge of Madness" 2-6-59 (Lt. Jesse Childress), "Incident at Spider Rock" 1-18-63 (Rock); *Have Gun Will Travel*—"The Scorched Feather" 2-14-59 (William Ceilbleau), "Cage at McNaab" 2-16-63 (O'Connor); *The Texan*—"No Love Wasted" 3-9-59 (Wylie); *Wanted—Dead or Alive*—"The Hostage" 10-10-59 (Sheriff Paulson); *Johnny Ringo*—"The Raffertys" 3-3-60 (Ben Rafferty); *Bat Masterson*—"Bat Trap" 10-13-60 (Rance Fletcher); *Wagon Train*—"The Jose Morales Story" 10-19-60 (Louis Roque), "The Chalice" 5-24-61 (Carstairs); *Stagecoach West*—"Not in Our Stars" 2-7-61 (Ben Wait); *Klondike*—"The Hostages" 2-13-61 (Ben Maclin); *Zane Grey Theater*—"A Warm Day in Heaven" 3-23-61 (Michael Peters); *The Deputy*—"Brother in Arms" 4-15-61 (Tom Arnold); *The Rifleman*—"Gunfire" 1-15-62 (Charlie Gordon); *Lawman*—"The Tarnished Badge" 1-28-62 (Jess Bridges); *Empire*—"Hidden Asset" 3-26-63 (Bart Howe); *Pistols 'n' Petticoats*—Regular 1966-67 (Chief Eagle Shadow).

Chang, Jane. TV: *Have Gun Will Travel*—"The Haunted Trees" 6-13-59 (Birdie); *Frontier Circus*—"The Patriarch of Purgatory" 11-30-61 (Shan Lu).

Chang, W.T. TV: *Have Gun Will Travel*—"The Monster of Moon Ridge" 2-28-59; *The Alaskans*—"The Silent Land" 5-15-60 (Sityak).

Channing, Carol (1921-). Films: "The First Traveling Saleslady" 1956 (Molly Wade).

Channing, Ruth. Films: "Outlawed Guns" 1935 (Ruth Ellsworth).

Chao, Rosalind. TV: *Kung Fu*—"The Tide" 2-1-73 (Dancer); *How the West Was Won*—"China Girl" 4-16-79 (Li Sin).

Chapin, Billy (1943-). Films: "Tension at Table Rock" 1956 (Jody). ¶TV: *My Friend Flicka*—"The Silver Saddle" 12-16-55; *Fury*—"The Test" 3-3-56 (Lewis Baxter), "The Rocketeers" 12-5-59 (Vic Rockwell); *Zane Grey Theater*—"Black Creek Encounter" 3-8-57 (Billy Morrison); *The Californians*—"The Marshal" 3-11-58 (Joey).

Chapin, Jack. Films: "Union Pacific" 1939 (Fireman); "Northwest Mounted Police" 1940 (Bugler); "King of the Texas Rangers" 1941-serial (Stub Latner).

Chapin, Michael. Films: "Song of Arizona" 1946 (Cyclops); "Under California Stars" 1948 (Ted Conover); "Arizona Manhunt" 1951 (Red); "Buckaroo Sheriff of Texas" 1951 (Red White); "The Dakota Kid" 1951 (Red); "Wells Fargo Gunmaster" 1951 (Tommy Hines); "Springfield Rifle" 1952 (Jamie); "Wagons West" 1952 (Ben Wilkins); "Wild Horse Ambush" 1952 (Red). ¶TV: *The Lone Ranger*—"The Star Witness" 8-17-50.

Chaplain, Jack. TV: *The Rebel*—"The Last Drink" 2-26-61 (Eddie); *The Deputy*—"The Example" 3-25-61 (Jeb Barton); *The Outlaws*—"Sam Bass" 5-4-61 (Sam Bass); *Laramie*—"The Runaway" 1-23-62 (Bill Watkins), "The Violent Ones" 3-5-63; *Wagon Train*—"The Jeff Hartfield Story" 2-14-62 (Jeff Hartfield); *Bonanza*—"The Long Night" 5-6-62 (Billy McCord), "Five Sundowns to Sunup" 12-5-65 (Harry Lassiter); *Gunsmoke*—"Abelia" 11-18-68 (Deeter Ward).

Chaplin, Charles (1889-12/25/77). Films: "His Regeneration" 1915.

Chaplin, Jr., Charles (1925-3/20/68). Films: "Fangs of the Wild" 1954 (Roger). ¶TV: *Wild Bill Hickok*—"Ambush" 1-13-53.

Chaplin, Geraldine (1944-). Films: "Yankee Dudler" 1973-Ger./Span. (Kate Elder); "Buffalo Bill and the Indians, or Sitting Bull's History Lesson" 1976 (Annie Oakley).

Chaplin, Sydney (1926-). Films: "Pillars of the Sky" 1956 (Timothy, the Indian Scout); "Quantez" 1957 (Gato); "Death Knows No Time" 1968-Span./Ital.; "One Against One … No Mercy" 1968-Span./Ital.; "Sartana" 1968-Ital./Ger.

Chapman, Audrey. Films: "The Black Sheep" 1921 (Molly Morran);

"When Romance Rides" 1922 (Lucy's Chum).

Chapman, Edythe (1863-10/15/48). Films: "A Modern Musketeer" 1917 (Mrs. Thacker); "On the Level" 1917 (Joe Blanchard's Mother); "The Knickerbocker Buckaroo" 1919 (Mercedes' Mother); "North of the Rio Grande" 1922 (Belle Hannon); "The Shepherd of the Hills" 1928 (Aunt Mollie).

Chapman, Eric. Films: "Finger on the Trigger" 1965-Span./Ital./U.S. (McKay); "The Christmas Kid" 1966-Span./Ital. (Percy Martin).

Chapman, Freddie. Films: "Buffalo Bill" 1944 (Boy); "Sheriff of Las Vegas" 1944; "Colorado Pioneers" 1945; "Corpus Christi Bandits" 1945 (Stinky); "Great Stagecoach Robbery" 1945; "Trail of Kit Carson" 1945; "California Gold Rush" 1946.

Chapman, Janet. Films: "Heart of the North" 1938 (Judy Montgomery).

Chapman, Judith. TV: *Outlaws*—"Independents" 3-21-87 (Jo).

Chapman, Leigh. Films: "Law of the Lawless" 1964; "The Professionals" 1966 (Lady). ¶TV: *Iron Horse*—"Broken Gun" 10-17-66 (Crystal Cochran).

Chapman, Lonny (1920-). Films: "The Dangerous Days of Kiowa Jones" TVM-1966 (Roy); "Hour of the Gun" 1967 (Turkey Creek Johnson); "The Stalking Moon" 1969 (Purdue); "The Cowboys" 1972 (Preacher). ¶TV: *The Rifleman*—"Long Trek" 1-17-61 (Stanley), "And the Devil Makes Five" 2-11-63 (Scully Potter); *The Outlaws*—"The Brathwaite Brothers" 11-9-61 (Silas Brathwaite); *Wide Country*—"To Cindy, with Love" 2-28-63 (Chuck Martin); *Gunsmoke*—"Tell Chester" 4-20-63 (Wade Stringer), "Outlaw's Woman" 12-11-65 (Dove Bailey), "Parson Comes to Town" 4-30-66 (Sipes); *Laredo*—"The Heroes of San Gill" 12-23-65 (Julius); *The Virginian*—"Chaff in the Wind" 1-26-66 (Clemmet Ellis), "Without Mercy" 2-15-67 (Donovan Young), "Last Grave at Socorro Creek" 1-22-69 (Carl Luther), "The Long Ride Home" 9-17-69 (Burr); *The Loner*—"The Burden of the Badge" 3-5-66 (Chad Mitchell); *Bonanza*—"The Genius" 4-3-66 (Will Smith), "The Weary Willies" 9-27-70 (Colter); *The Road West*—"Lone Woman" 11-7-66 (Sergeant); *The Big Valley*—"Plunder at Hawk's Grove" 3-13-67 (Cody Grell), "The Buffalo Man" 12-25-67 (Dobbs); *Death Valley Days*—"Major

Horace Bell" 5-20-67 (Buzzer); *The Guns of Will Sonnett*—"Message at Noon" 10-13-67 (Sheriff Tom Landry), "A Difference of Opinion" 11-15-68 (O'Brian); *Iron Horse*—"Grapes of Grass Valley" 10-21-67 (Ike Bridger); *Dundee and the Culhane*—"The 3:10 to a Lynching Brief" 11-8-67 (Henry Taylor); *The Outcasts*—"Gideon" 2-24-69 (Cecil); *The Oregon Trail*—"The Waterhole" 9-28-77 (Coe Webster).

Chapman, Marguerite (1916-). "Coroner Creek" 1948 (Kate Hardison); "Relentless" 1948 (Luella Purdy); "Kansas Raiders" 1950 (Katre Clarke). ¶TV: *Rawhide*—"Incident with an Executioner" 1-23-59 (Madge); *Laramie*—"The Mark of the Maneaters" 3-14-61 (Val Faro).

Charbonneau, Patricia. Films: "Desperado: Badlands Justice" TVM-1989 (Emily Harris).

Charisse, Cyd (1923-). Films: "The Harvey Girls" 1946 (Deborah); "The Kissing Bandit" 1948 (Dancer); "Mark of the Renegade" 1951 (Manuella); "The Wild North" 1952 (Indian Girl).

Charles, John (1835-11/7/21). Films: "A Texas Steer" 1915 (Captain Farleigh Bright).

Charles, Lewis (1916-11/9/79). TV: *Sergeant Preston of the Yukon*—"Cinderella of the Yukon" 3-22-56 (Art Mapes), "Incident at Gordon Landing" 7-26-56 (Pete); *Wyatt Earp*—"The Hanging Judge" 12-18-56 (Five Spot Finley); *Jim Bowie*—"Spanish Intrigue" 2-8-57 (Don Carlos Miro); *Wanted—Dead or Alive*—"Shawnee Bill" 10-4-58 (Galt), "One Mother Too Many" 12-7-60 (Malcolm), "Epitaph" 2-8-61 (Hoyt Larson); *Man Without a Gun*—"Indian Fury" 2-7-59; *The Rifleman*—"The Indian" 2-17-59 (Slade), "One Went to Denver" 3-17-59, "Skull" 1-1-62 (Pascal); *Man from Blackhawk*—"Gold Is Where You Find It" 6-24-60 (Joe Smith); *Bonanza*—"The Dark Past" 5-3-64 (Wetzell); *The Loner*—"Pick Me Another Time to Die" 2-26-66 (Pete); *The Big Valley*—"Into the Widow's Web" 3-23-66 (Cully Tedrow).

Charleson, Harry. Films: "With Hoops of Steel" 1919 (Marguerite Delarue).

Charleson, Leslie (1945-). TV: *Wild Wild West*—"The Night of Fire and Brimstone" 11-22-68 (Dooley Sloan); *Kung Fu*—"One Step to Darkness" 1-25-75 (Amy).

Charleson, Mary (1893-12/3/61). Films: "The Spirit of the Range"

1912; "When California Was Young" 1912; "The Country That God Forgot" 1916 (Helen Brant); "Human Stuff" 1920 (Lee Tyndal).

Charlita. Films: "Brimstone" 1949 (Chiquita); "South of Caliente" 1951 (Rosina); "Rancho Notorious" 1952 (Mexican Girl in Bar); "Toughest Man in Arizona" 1952 (Senorita); "Ride, Vaquero!" 1953 (Singer); "Massacre Canyon" 1954 (Gita); "The Naked Dawn" 1955 (Tita); "Billy the Kid vs. Dracula" 1966 (Nana); "El Dorado" 1967. ¶TV: *The Adventures of Rin Tin Tin*—"The Invaders" 12-14-56 (Dolores Estaban); *Cheyenne*—"Deadline" 2-26-57 (Maria); *Gunslinger*—"Appointment in Cascabel" 2-23-61 (Soledad).

Charlot, Andre (1882–5/20/56). Films: "Annie Get Your Gun" 1950 (President Loubet of France).

Charney, Kim. Films: "At Gunpoint" 1955 (Eddie Ferguson); "The Guns of Fort Petticoat" 1957 (Bax); "Man from God's Country" 1958 (Stony Warren); "Quantrill's Raiders" 1958 (Joel); "How the West Was Won" 1962 (Samn Prescott). ¶TV: *Tales of the Texas Rangers*—"Shorty Sees the Light" 9-10-55, "Return of the Rough Riders" 11-26-55 (Buddy), "Panhandle" 9-22-57 (Link Webb); *Zane Grey Theater*—"Back Trail" 2-1-57 (Timmy Fallon); *Wagon Train*—"The John Darro Story" 11-6-57 (the Son); *Cheyenne*—"The Long Search" 4-22-58 (Kenny Carver); *The Rifleman*—"The Angry Man" 4-28-59 (Carey MacDonald); *Lawman*—"The Second Son" 11-27-60 (Charlie May).

Charny, Suzanne (1940-). TV: *Barbary Coast*—"Sharks Eat Sharks" 11-21-75 (Conchita).

Charters, Spencer (1875–1/25/43). Films: "Whispering Smith Speaks" 1935 (Cal Stone); "The Mine with the Iron Door" 1936 (Thad Hill); "The Bad Man of Brimstone" 1937 (Rufus Odlum); "Wells Fargo" 1937 (Jethrow); "Forbidden Valley" 1938 (Dr. Scudd); "The Texans" 1938 (Chairman); "Dodge City" 1939 (Clergyman); "Drums Along the Mohawk" 1939 (Fisk the Innkeeper); "Jesse James" 1939 (Preacher); "The Kid from Texas" 1939 (Deputy); "The Oklahoma Kid" 1939 (Homesteader); "Lucky Cisco Kid" 1940 (Hotel Guest); "Santa Fe Trail" 1940 (Conductor); "Three Faces West" 1940 (Dr. Nunk Atterbury); "Virginia City" 1940 (Bartender); "Lady from Cheyenne" 1941 (Mr. McGuinness); "The Singing Hill" 1941; "They Died with Their Boots On" 1941 (Clergy-

man); "Silver Queen" 1942 (Doc Stonebraker).

Chartoff, Melanie. Films: "The Gambler, Part III—The Legend Continues" TVM-1987 (Deborah).

Chartrand, Lois. Films: "The Great Missouri Raid" 1951 (Mary Bauer).

Chase, Alden. *see* Chase, Stephen.

Chase, Barrie (1934-). TV: *Have Gun Will Travel*—"A Sense of Justice" 11-1-58 (Julia Grayson); *Bonanza*—"The Ballerina" 1-24-65 (Kellie Conrad).

Chase, Charley (Charles Parrott) (1893–6/20/46). Films: "The King of the Wild Horses" 1924 (Boyd Fielding); "The Tabasco Kid" 1932-short; "Teacher's Pest" 1939-short.

Chase, Chevy (1944-). Films: "Three Amigos" 1986 (Dusty Bottoms).

Chase, Clarence (1900–6/5/64). Films: "The Man from Colorado" 1948 (Charlie Trumbull).

Chase, Colin (1886–4/24/37). Films: "The Parson of Panamint" 1916 (Chappie Ellerton); "Ace High" 1918 (Baptiste Dupre); "Bucking the Barrier" 1923 (Frank Farfax); "Snowdrift" 1923 (Murdo McFarlane); "The Iron Horse" 1924 (Tony); "The Loser Wins" 1925; "The Ropin' Venus" 1925; "The Lone Star Ranger" 1930 (Tom Laramie); "Cyclone Ranger" 1935 (Sheriff Luke Saunders); "Ridin' Thru" 1935 (Henchman); "The Texas Rambler" 1935; "The Unconquered Bandit" 1935; "The Vanishing Riders" 1935 (Cuke); "Feud of the Trail" 1938.

Chase, Dorothy. Films: "Ace of Cactus Range" 1924 (Cleora).

Chase, Eric. TV: *Here Comes the Brides*—Regular 1969-70 (Christopher Pruitt); *Gunsmoke*—"The Gun" 11-19-70 (Joseph).

Chase, Frank. Films: "Winchester '73" 1950 (Cavalryman); "Bend of the River" 1952 (Wasco); "Seminole" 1953 (Trooper); "Saskatchewan" 1954 (Keller); "Man Without a Star" 1955 (Little Waco); "Backlash" 1956 (Cassidy); "Walk the Proud Land" 1956 (Stone); "Night Passage" 1957 (Trinidad); "The Rawhide Trail" 1958 (Corporal); "Ride a Crooked Trail" 1958 (Ben, the Deputy). ¶TV: *Bonanza*—"The Artist" 10-7-62.

Chase, George (1890–7/29/18). Films: "The Gun Woman" 1918 (Vulture).

Chase, Guy "Alden". *see* Chase, Stephen.

Chase, Howard. Films: "Man from Music Mountain" 1938 (Abbott); "The Lone Ranger Rides Again" 1939-serial (Martin Gibson).

Chase, Stephen (Alden Chase, Guy Chase) (-1982). Films: "The Prescott Kid" 1934 (Ed Walton); "Cowboy Millionaire" 1935 (Hadley Thornton); "Rogue of the Range" 1936 (Lars Branscomb); "Heart of Arizona" 1938 (Dan Ringo); "Six-Gun Trail" 1938; "Under Western Stars" 1938 (Tom Andrews); "Code of the Cactus" 1939 (James); "Frontier Scout" 1939 (Bennett); "Gun Code" 1940 (James M. Bradley); "Riders on Black Mountain" 1940 (Emmett); "Billy the Kid's Range War" 1941 (Dave); "The Lone Rider Crosses the Rio" 1941 (Hatfield); "The Lone Rider in Ghost Town" 1941 (Sinclair); "The Daring Caballero" 1949 (Brady); "Frisco Tornado" 1950 (Jim Crall); "Belle Le Grand" 1951 (Montgomery Crane); "Cavalry Scout" 1951 (Col. Drumm); "Hiawatha" 1952 (Lakku); "Horizons West" 1952 (Borden); "The Lawless Breed" 1952 (Judge); "Old Oklahoma Plains" 1952 (Maj. Gen. Parker); "El Paso Stampede" 1953 (Mason Ransey); "The Great Sioux Uprising" 1953 (Maj. McKay); "Jubilee Trail" 1954 (Mr. Forbes); "Rails into Laramie" 1954 (Gen. Auger); "The Glory Guys" 1965 (Gen. Hoffman). ¶TV: *The Lone Ranger*—"Pardon for Curley" 6-22-50, "Dead Man's Chest" 9-28-50, "The Outcast" 1-18-51, "Jeb's Gold Mine" 10-16-52, "Sinner by Proxy" 3-5-53, "Embezzler's Harvest" 4-30-53; *The Cisco Kid*—"Boomerang" 1-20-51, "Medicine Man Story" 8-25-51, "Black Lightning" 10-6-51; *The Roy Rogers Show*—"The Desert Fugitive" 2-24-52, "The Minister's Son" 3-23-52; *Death Valley Days*—"The Mystery of Suicide Gulch" 4-1-58 (Ed Pratt), "The Girl Who Walked with a Giant" 4-22-58 (Sam Houston), "Eruption at Volcano" 2-24-59 (Coleman), "Deadline at Austin" 2-8-61; *Gunsmoke*—"Young Love" 1-3-59 (Enoch Miller); *Buckskin*—"The Greatest Man in History" 1-5-59 (Mayor); *The Rifleman*—"The Sheridan Story" 1-13-59 (Medical Colonel Stroud); *Bronco*—"Prairie Skipper" 5-5-59 (Tom Barclay); *Colt .45*—"The Rival Gun" 10-25-59 (Gen. Nelson Miles); *Tales of Wells Fargo*—"Escort to Santa Fe" 12-19-60 (Marshal Chaffee); *Maverick*—"The Art Lovers" 10-1-61 (Taber Scott); *Bonanza*—"The Tin Badge" 12-17-61.

Chasen, Dave (1899–6/16/73).

Films: "Arizona Mahoney" 1936 (Filt Smith).

Chastain, Don (1935-). TV: *Colt .45*—"Trial by Rope" 5-3-60 (Gerald Wiley); *Calamity Jane* 11-12-63 (Lt. Danny Gilmartin); *The Big Valley*—"Image of Yesterday" 1-9-67 (Horn), "Turn of a Card" 3-20-67, "Four Days to Furnace Hill" 12-4-67 (Stacey), "They Called Her Delilah" 9-30-68 (Worth Parker), "Hunter's Moon" 12-30-68 (Tony Semper); *Gunsmoke*—"The Miracle Man" 12-2-68 (Bob Sullivan); *The Chisholms*—2-23-80 (Zeke).

Chatterton, Joseph. Films: "The Galloping Devil" 1920 (the Kid).

Chatterton, Tom (1881-8/17/52). Films: "His Hour of Manhood" 1914; "Jim Cameron's Wife" 1914; "Shorty Escapes Marriage" 1914 (Tom Crowne); "The Operator at Big Sandy" 1915; "Satan McAllister's Heir" 1915; "According to St. John" 1916 (Sheriff Dick); "Boss Rider of Gun Creek" 1936 (Sheriff Blaine); "Sandflow" 1937 (Sheriff): "Sudden Bill Dorn" 1937 (Stock Morgan); "Under Western Stars" 1938 (Congressman Edward H. Marlowe); "Arizona Legion" 1939 (Commissioner Teagle); "Dodge City" 1939 (Passenger); "The Oklahoma Kid" 1939 (Homesteader); "Ranch House Romeo" 1939-short; "Rovin' Tumbleweeds" 1939; "Covered Wagon Days" 1940 (Maj. Norton); "Pony Post" 1940 (Major Goodwin); "Son of Roaring Dan" 1940 (Stuart Manning); "The Trail Blazers" 1940 (Major R.C. Kelton); "Desert Bandit" 1941 (Capt. Banning); "Outlaws of the Cherokee Trail" 1941; "Overland Mail" 1942-serial (Tom Gilbert); "Raiders of the Range" 1942 (Doc Higgins); "Santa Fe Scouts" 1943 (Neil Morgan); "Cheyenne Wildcat" 1944; "Code of the Prairie" 1944 (Bat Matson); "Marshal of Reno" 1944; "Tucson Raiders" 1944; "Zorro's Black Whip" 1944-serial (Merchant); "Colorado Pioneers" 1945; "Lone Texas Ranger" 1945; "Marshal of Laredo" 1945; "Wagon Wheels Westward" 1945; "Alias Billy the Kid" 1946 (Ed Pearson); "Conquest of Cheyenne" 1946; "Heading West" 1946; "Home on the Range" 1946 (Grizzly Garth); "Lawless Empire" 1946 (Sam Enders); "Sheriff of Redwood Valley" 1946; "Stagecoach to Denver" 1946 (Doc Kimball); "Jesse James Rides Again" 1947-serial (Mark Tobin); "Carson City Raiders" 1948 (John Davis); "Marshal of Amarillo" 1948 (James Underwood); "Outlaw Brand" 1948; "Gun Law Justice" 1949.

Chatton, Sydney (1918-10/6/66). Films: "Once Upon a Horse" 1958 (Engineer).

Chautard, Emile (1881-4/24/34). Films: "The Flaming Forest" 1926 (Andre Audemard); "Whispering Sage" 1927 (Jose Arastrade); "A Man from Wyoming" 1930 (French Mayor); "The California Trail" 1933 (Don Marco Ramirez).

Chauvin, Lilyan (1931-). Films: "North to Alaska" 1960 (Jenny Lamont); "Walk Like a Dragon" 1960 (Mme. Lile Raide); "Tickle Me" 1965 (Ronnie); "Machismo—40 Graves for 40 Guns" 1970 (Kate). ¶TV: *Jim Bowie*—"The Swordsman" 12-14-56 (Liane Trudeau); *The Californians*—"The Man from Paris" 2-11-58 (Suzy); *Maverick*—"High Card Hangs" 10-19-58 (Sydney Sue Shipley); *Daniel Boone*—"When a King Is a Pawn" 12-22-66; *The Outcasts*—"How Tall Is Blood?" 5-5-69 (Silent Woman).

Chaves, Richard. Films: "The Gambler, Part III—The Legend Continues" TVM-1987 (Iron Dog).

Chavez, Jose. Films: "The Beast of Hollow Mountain" 1956 (Manuel); "The Professionals" 1966 (Revolutionary); "Two Mules for Sister Sara" 1970 (Horacio); "The Culpepper Cattle Company" 1972 (Cantina Bartender). ¶TV: *Gunsmoke*—"Zavala" 10-7-68 (Jurato).

Chaykin, Maury. Films: "Death Hunt" 1981 (Clarence); "Dances with Wolves" 1990 (Maj. Fambrough); "Sommersby" 1993 (Lawyer Dawson).

Cheatham, Jack (1894-3/30/71). Films: "Racketeer Round-Up" 1934; "His Fighting Blood" 1935.

Checchi, Andrea (1916-3/31/74). Films: "A Bullet for the General" 1966-Ital. (Don Felipe).

Checco, Al (1925-). Films: "Skin Game" 1971 (Room Clerk). ¶TV: *The Big Valley*—"Town of No Exit" 4-7-69 (Desk Clerk); *Bonanza*—"The Big Jackpot" 1-18-70 (Hornsby), "Rock-a-Bye, Hoss" 10-10-71 (Rufus); *Kung Fu*—"Barbary House" 2-15-75 (Referee), "Flight to Orion" 2-22-75 (Referee), "The Brothers Cain" 3-1-75 (Referee), "Full Circle" 3-15-75 (Referee).

Chefe, Jack (1894-12/1/75). TV: *Maverick*—"Diamond in the Rough" 1-26-58 (Butler).

Chen, Tina (1945-). TV: *Kung Fu*—"The Tide" 2-1-73 (Su Yen Lu).

Chenault, Lawrence. Films: "The Crimson Skull" 1921; "Symbol of the Unconquered" 1921.

Cherokose, Eddie. Films: "Gold Mine in the Sky" 1938 (Kuzak); "Zorro's Fighting Legion" 1939-serial (Pedro); "Sierra Sue" 1941.

Cheron, Andre (1880-1/26/52). Films: "Rose of the Golden West" 1927 (Russian Prince); "God's Country and the Woman" 1937 (Mon. Gagnon); "Out West with the Peppers" 1940 (Frenchman).

Cherrington, Mary. Films: "Empty Saddles" 1937 (Mrs. Mills).

Cherrington, Ruth. Films: "Riding for Fame" 1928 (Miss Hemingway); "Empty Saddles" 1937 (Mrs. Hilton); "The Sea of Grass" 1947 (Bit).

Cherryman, Rex (1898-8/10/28). Films: "The Sunshine Trail" 1923 (Willis Duckworth).

Chesebro, George (1888-5/28/59). Films: "Humanizing Mr. Winsby" 1916; "The Land Just Over Yonder" 1916 (William King); "Broadway, Arizona" 1917 (John Keyes); "Wild Sumac" 1917 (Jacques Fontaine); "The Girl of Hell's Agony" 1918; "Hands Up" 1918-serial; "The She Wolf" 1919 (the Stranger); "Rustlers' Ranch" 1926 (Bud Harvey); "The Secret Outlaw" 1928; "Speed and Spurs" 1928; "The Range of Fear" 1929; "The Kid from Arizona" 1931; "The Sheriff's Secret" 1931; "Wild West Whoopee" 1931; "Fighting Champ" 1932 (Nifty Harmon); "Forty-Five Calibre Echo" 1932; "Mark of the Spur" 1932 (John Beckett); "Tex Takes a Holiday" 1932 (Sheriff); "Tombstone Canyon" 1932 (Henchman); "Crashing Broadway" 1933 (Stubbs); "Lariats and Sixshooters" 1933; "Lucky Larrigan" 1933; "Border Guns" 1934 (Captain Silina); "The Border Menace" 1934 (Chuck Adams); "Boss Cowboy" 1934 (Jack Kearns); "The Cactus Kid" 1934; "Fighting Hero" 1934 (Deputy); "The Fighting Trooper" 1934 (Renee); "In Old Santa Fe" 1934; "The Law of the Wild" 1934-serial (Parks); "Mystery Mountain" 1934-serial; "Mystery Ranch" 1934 (Kern); "Nevada Cyclone" 1934; "Potluck Pards" 1934; "Rawhide Mail" 1934 (Porky); "Ridin' Gent" 1934-short; "Born to Battle" 1935; "The Cowboy and the Bandit" 1935; "Coyote Trails" 1935 (Jim); "Cyclone of the Saddle" 1935 (Cherokee Carter); "Danger Trails" 1935; "Defying the Law" 1935 (Frank Saunders); "Fighting Caballero" 1935 (Devil Jackson); "Gallant Defender" 1935 (Joe Swale); "The Laramie Kid" 1935 (Ed Larkin); "Law Beyond the Range" 1935 (Cowboy); "The Man from Guntown"

1935 (Barnes); "The Miracle Rider" 1935-serial; "North of Arizona" 1935 (Dick Smith); "Pals of the Range" 1935 (Zed); "The Phantom Cowboy" 1935 (Buck Huston); "Rough Riding Ranger" 1935 (Bald); "Silent Valley" 1935; "The Silver Bullet" 1935 (Slim Walker); "Skull and Crown" 1935; "Tracy Rides" 1935; "Tumbling Tumbleweeds" 1935 (Connors); "The Unconquered Bandit" 1935; "Western Racketeers" 1935 (Fargo Roberts); "Wild Mustang" 1935; "Wolf Riders" 1935 (Al Pearce); "Caryl of the Mountains" 1936 (Constable O'Brien); "Code of the Range" 1936 (Post); "Custer's Last Stand" 1936-serial (Lieutenant Roberts); "The Lawless Nineties" 1936 (Green); "Lucky Terror" 1936 (Jim Thorton); "The Mysterious Avenger" 1936 (Foley); "Pinto Rustlers" 1936 (Spud); "Red River Valley" 1936 (Butt); "Roamin' Wild" 1936 (Tip); "Roarin' Lead" 1936 (Captain Gardner); "Toll of the Desert" 1936 (One Eye); "Trail Dust" 1936 (Saunders); "The Traitor" 1936 (Lynch Leader); "Vengeance of Rannah" 1936; "The Big Show" 1937; "Borderland" 1937 (Tom Parker); "Code of the Range" 1937; "The Devil's Saddle Legion" 1937 (Frayne); "Dodge City Trail" 1937 (Town Spy); "Empty Holsters" 1937 (Cutter Smith); "Hills of Old Wyoming" 1937 (Peterson); "The Old Wyoming Trail" 1937 (Hank Barstow); "Outlaws of the Prairie" 1937 (Citizen); "Prairie Thunder" 1937 (Matson); "The Roaming Cowboy" 1937; "Springtime in the Rockies" 1937 (Morgan); "Two-Fisted Sheriff" 1937 (Prosecutor Ed); "Two Gun Law" 1937 (Blair); "Westbound Mail" 1937 (Slim); "Call of the Rockies" 1938 (Monk); "Cattle Raiders" 1938 (Brand); "The Colorado Trail" 1938 (Hadely); "The Great Adventures of Wild Bill Hickok" 1938 (Metaxa); "Law of the Plains" 1938 (Bartender); "Lawless Valley" 1938; "Mexicali Kid" 1938 (Joe); "Outlaws of Sonora" 1938 (Slim); "The Purple Vigilantes" 1938 (Eggers); "Rio Grande" 1938 (Kruger); "Santa Fe Stampede" 1938; "Starlight Over Texas" 1938 (Ashley Hill); "West of Cheyenne" 1938 (Gorman); "Dodge City" 1939; "The Man from Sundown" 1939 (Taylor); "New Frontier" 1939; "Oklahoma Frontier" 1939; "Range War" 1939; "Riders of the Black River" 1939 (Ranch Hand); "Rough Riders' Round-Up" 1939 (Mosby); "Smoky Trails" 1939; "Song of the Buckaroo" 1939; "Southward Ho!" 1939; "The Stranger from Texas" 1939 (Barker); "Wall Street Cowboy" 1939; "West-

ern Caravans" 1939 (Mac); "Billy the Kid Outlawed" 1940 (Tex); "The Cheyenne Kid" 1940 (Davis); "Covered Wagon Trails" 1940 (Carter); "Frontier Crusader" 1940 (Trail Boss); "Gun Code" 1940 (Bart); "The Kid from Santa Fe" 1940 (Kent); "Land of the Six Guns" 1940 (Taylor); "Lightning Strikes West" 1940 (Sheriff); "Melody Ranch" 1940; "Pinto Canyon" 1940 (Pete Childers); "Pioneer Days" 1940 (Roper); "Pioneers of the Frontier" 1940 (Appleby); "Pioneers of the West" 1940; "Riders from Nowhere" 1940 (Bart); "Riders on Black Mountain" 1940 (Bart); "Texas Stagecoach" 1940; "Thundering Frontier" 1940 (Dirk); "West of Pinto Basin" 1940 (Lane); "Wild Horse Range" 1940 (Ed Baker); "Wild Horse Valley" 1940 (Raymer); "Young Buffalo Bill" 1940; "Billy the Kid's Fighting Pals" 1941 (Sheriff); "Billy the Kid's Range War" 1941; "Hands Across the Rockies" 1941; "King of Dodge City" 1941; "Law of the Wolf" 1941; "The Lone Rider Ambushed" 1941 (Pete); "The Lone Rider in Ghost Town" 1941 (Jed); "The Medico of Painted Springs" 1941 (Joe); "Outlaws of the Rio Grande" 1941; "Pals of the Pecos" 1941; "The Pioneers" 1941 (Wilson); "Roaring Frontiers" 1941; "Saddle Mountain Roundup" 1941 (Blackie); "Trail of the Silver Spurs" 1941 (Wilson); "White Eagle" 1941-serial; "Wildcat of Tucson" 1941; "Wrangler's Roost" 1941 (Miller); "Billy the Kid Trapped" 1942; "Boot Hill Bandits" 1942 (Stover); "Jesse James, Jr." 1942; "The Lone Rider in Cheyenne" 1942; "The Lone Star Vigilantes" 1942; "Perils of the Royal Mounted" 1942-serial (Gaspard); "Rolling Down the Great Divide" 1942 (Henchman); "Thunder River Feud" 1942 (Taggart); "Valley of Vanishing Men" 1942-serial (Taggert); "Black Market Rustlers" 1943 (Slade); "Cowboy Commandos" 1943; "Raiders of Red Gap" 1943 (Sheriff); "The Renegade" 1943; "Two Fisted Justice" 1943 (Decker); "Arizona Whirlwind" 1944 (Ace); "Blazing Frontier" 1944 (Slade); "Boss of Rawhide" 1944 (Joe Gordon); "Death Rides the Plains" 1944 (Trent); "Death Valley Rangers" 1944 (Red); "Devil Riders" 1944 (Curley); "The Drifter" 1944 (Blackie); "Marshal of Gunsmoke" 1944; "Thundering Gun Slingers" 1944 (Dave); "Colorado Pioneers" 1945; "Gangster's Den" 1945 (Dent); "Marshal of Laredo" 1945; "Outlaws of the Rockies" 1945 (Bill Jason); "Rough Ridin' Justice" 1945 (Lacey); "Salome, Where She Danced" 1945

(Miner); "Santa Fe Saddlemates" 1945; "Sheriff of Cimarron" 1945 (Ed Martin, the Mine Operator); "Stagecoach Outlaws" 1945; "Texas Panhandle" 1945; "Trail of Kit Carson" 1945; "Wagon Wheels Westward" 1945; "The Caravan Trail" 1946; "Days of Buffalo Bill" 1946; "The Fighting Frontiersman" 1946; "Gentlemen with Guns" 1946 (Slade); "Gunning for Vengeance" 1946; "Landrush" 1946 (Bil); "Lawless Empire" 1946 (Lenny); "Overland Riders" 1946; "The Phantom Rider" 1946-serial (Dalton); "Rainbow Over Texas" 1946; "Singin' in the Corn" 1946 (Texas); "Stagecoach to Denver" 1946 (Blackie); "Sun Valley Cyclone" 1946; "Terror Trail" 1946; "Terrors on Horseback" 1946; "That Texas Jamboree" 1946; "Two-Fisted Ranger" 1946; "Cheyenne Takes Over" 1947 (Dawson); "The Fighting Vigilantes" 1947 (Price Taylor); "Homesteaders of Paradise Valley" 1947; "Jesse James Rides Again" 1947-serial (Gus Simmons); "Law of the Canyon" 1947; "The Lone Hand Texan" 1947 (Scanlon); "Out West" 1947-short (Quirt); "Over the Santa Fe Trail" 1947; "Return of the Lash" 1947 (Kirby); "Riders of the Lone Star" 1947; "Shadow Valley" 1947 (Gunnison); "Son of Zorro" 1947-serial (Tom); "Song of the Wasteland" 1947; "South of the Chisholm Trail" 1947; "Stage to Mesa City" 1947 (Padgett); "The Vigilante" 1947-serial (Walt); "Vigilantes of Boomtown" 1947 (Dink); "West of Dodge City" 1947; "Wyoming" 1947 (Wolff); "The Adventures of Frank and Jesse James" 1948-serial (Jim, the Station Agent); "Black Hills" 1948 (Allen); "Check Your Guns" 1948 (Farrell); "Frontier Revenge" 1948 (Col. Winston); "Fury at Furnace Creek" 1948 (Card Player); "The Gallant Legion" 1948; "Six-Gun Law" 1948 (Bret Wallace); "Tornado Range" 1948 (Lance); "Trail to Laredo" 1948; "West of Sonora" 1948 (Sheriff Jeff Clinton); "Challenge of the Range" 1949 (Lon Collins); "Death Valley Gunfighter" 1949 (Sam); "Desert Vigilante" 1949 (Martin); "Ghost of Zorro" 1949-serial (Jason); "The Last Bandit" 1949; "Lust for Gold" 1949 (Man); "Renegades of the Sage" 1949 (Worker); "Roll, Thunder, Roll" 1949 (Garson); "Trail's End" 1949 (Stuart); "Crooked River" 1950 (Dad Ellison); "Desperadoes of the West" 1950-serial (Becker); "Fast on the Draw" 1950; "Frisco Tornado" 1950 (Gun Guard); "Gunmen of Abilene" 1950 (Martin); "Gunslingers" 1950 (Jeff Nugent); "Horsemen of the Sierras" 1950

(Ellory Webster); "Hostile Country" 1950 (Oliver); "Lightning Guns" 1950 (Blake); "Marshal of Heldorado" 1950 (Stanton); "Punchy Cowpunchers" 1950-short (Jeff); "Salt Lake Raiders" 1950 (Stage Driver); "The Savage Horde" 1950; "Streets of Ghost Town" 1950 (Bill Donner); "Texas Dynamo" 1950 (Kroger); "Trail of Robin Hood" 1950; "West of the Brazos" 1950 (Deputy); "Cyclone Fury" 1951 (Bret Fuller); "The Kid from Amarillo" 1951 (El Loco); "Night Riders of Montana" 1951 (Jamison); "Snake River Desperadoes" 1951 (Josh Haverly); "The Thundering Trail" 1951 (Jones); "The Frontier Phantom" 1952; "Junction City" 1952 (Sheriff Jeff Clinton); "Last of the Comanches" 1952 (Pete); "Montana Belle" 1952 (Deputy); "Montana Territory" 1952 (Weasel); "Winning of the West" 1953 (Boone); "Pals and Gals" 1954-short (Quirt). ¶TV: The Lone Ranger— "Enter the Lone Ranger" 9-15-49 (Dr. Drummond), "The Lone Ranger Fights On" 9-22-49 (Dr. Drummond), "The Lone Ranger's Triumph" 9-29-49 (Dr. Drummond), "Behind the Law" 2-1-51.

Cheshire, Harry V. (1892-6/16/68). Films: "Sioux City Sue" 1946; "The Fabulous Texan" 1947; "Springtime in the Sierras" 1947 (Capt. Foster); "Adventures of Gallant Bess" 1948 (Doctor Gray); "Black Eagle" 1948 (the General); "Smoky Mountain Melody" 1948 (Dr. Moffett); "Brimstone" 1949 (Calvin Willis); "Fighting Man of the Plains" 1949 (Lanyard); "Riders of the Whistling Pines" 1949 (Dr. Daniel Chadwick); "The Arizona Cowboy" 1950 (David Carson); "Thunder in God's Country" 1951 (Mayor Larkin); "Escape from Fort Bravo" 1953 (Chaplain); "The First Traveling Saleslady" 1956 (Judge Benson); "The Restless Breed" 1957 (Mayor Johnson). ¶TV: The Gene Autry Show—"Hot Lead" 11-26-50, "Killer Horse" 12-10-50; The Lone Ranger—"Word of Honor" 11-27-52; Buffalo Bill, Jr.—Regular 1955-56 (Judge Ben Wiley); Maverick—"Rope of Cards" 1-19-58 (Judge), "The Resurrection of Joe November" 2-28-60 (Brother Ambrose); Lawman— "The Prisoner" 10-12-58 (Judge Trager), "Lady in Question" 12-21-58 (Judge Trager), "Hassayampa" 2-12-61 (Judge Trager), "Detweiler's Kid" 2-26-61 (Judge Trager), "The Hold-Out" 2-18-62 (Judge Trager), "The Man Behind the News" 5-13-62 (Judge Trager); Tales of the Texas Rangers—"Desert Fury" 11-20-58 (Joe Chaney); The Texan—

"The Accuser" 6-6-60 (Doc McKenzie).

Chesis, Eileen. TV: Bonanza— "Gallagher Sons" 12-9-62 (Will Gallagher), "Rain from Heaven" 10-6-63 (Mary Beth Weems); Destry— "Stormy Is a Lady" 3-6-64 (Stormy).

Chester, Alma (1871-1/22/53). Films: "Sundown Trail" 1931 (Ma Stoddard); "When a Man Rides Alone" 1933 (Aggie Simpson); "Cowboy Holiday" 1934; "The Dude Ranger" 1934 (Martha); "The Old Wyoming Trail" 1937 (Mrs. Rance).

Chester, Colby (1941-). TV: Alias Smith and Jones—"Smiler with a Gun" 10-7-71 (Young Cowboy).

Chester, Virginia (1896-7/28/27). Films: "Yaqui Girl" 1911; "Big Rock's Last Stand" 1912; "The Massacre of Santa Fe Trail" 1912; "A Red Man's Love" 1912.

Chester, William. Films: "The Girl Who Wouldn't Quit" 1918 (Joe Morgan).

Cheung, George Kee. TV: How the West Was Won—"China Girl" 4-16-79 (the Jobber).

Cheung, Louie. Films: "The Branding Iron" 1920 (Wen Ho).

Chevret, Lita. Films: "Sandflow" 1937 (Rose Porter); "My Little Chickadee" 1940 (Indian Squaw).

Chew, Sam (1942-). Films: "Skin Game" 1971 (Courtney).

Chiang, George. TV: Kung Fu— "Besieged: Death on Cold Mountain" 11-15-74 (Shun Low's Sentry), "Besieged: Cannon at the Gate" 11-22-74 (Shun Low's Sentry).

Chiantoni, Renato (1906-). Films: "Arizona Colt" 1965-Ital./Fr./Span.

Chiari, Walter (1924-12/20/91). Films: "Terrible Sheriff" 1963-Span./Ital. (Bill); "Heroes of the West" 1964-Span./Ital. (Mike); "Twins from Texas" 1964-Ital./Span.

Chichester, Emily. Films: "God's Outlaw" 1919 (Lonesome Lizzie); "Nugget Nell" 1919 (the Ingenue).

Childers, Cleo. Films: "The Three Buckaroos" 1922 (Flores).

Childers, Ethel. Films: "Flashing Steeds" 1925 (Lady Rathburne).

Childers, Naomi (1892-5/8/64). Films: "The Sea of Grass" 1947 (Woman).

Childs, Ray. Films: "Beyond All Odds" 1926 (Casino Joe); "Born to Battle" 1926 (Moxley); "The Masquerade Bandit" 1926 (Spike); "The Cherokee Kid" 1927 (Joe Gault);

"Lure of the West" 1928; "The Trail of the Horse Thieves" 1929 (Rustler).

Chiles, Linden (1933-). Films: "Incident at Phantom Hill" 1966 (Dr. Hanneford); "Texas Across the River" 1966 (Yellow Knife). ¶TV: Rawhide— "Incident at Rojo Canyon" 9-30-60; Gunsmoke—"With a Smile" 3-30-63 (Pat Cain); The Virginian—"Big Image … Little Man" 10-28-64 (Paul Leland), "The Return of Golden Tom" 3-9-66 (Ira Lom), "An Echo of Thunder" 10-5-66 (Ben Fancher), "The Deadly Past" 9-20-67 (Chris Williams); Lancer—"The Fix-It Man" 2-11-69 (Kirby).

Ching, William (1912-7/1/89). Films: "The Michigan Kid" 1947; "The Wistful Widow of Wagon Gap" 1947 (Jim Simpson); "The Showdown" 1950 (Mike Shattay); "Surrender" 1950 (Johnny Hale); "Belle Le Grand" 1951 (Bill Shanks); "Oh! Susanna" 1951 (Cpl. Donlin); "The Moonlighter" 1953 (Tom Anderson); "Tall Man Riding" 1955 (Rex Willard); "Escort West" 1959 (Capt. Poole). ¶TV: Wild Bill Hickok—"The Music Teacher" 12-2-52; Jim Bowie— "The Bounty Hunter" 5-17-57 (Roark Purdom); The Californians— "Murietta" 5-27-58 (Pete Jordan).

Chisholm, Jack. Films: "Northern Frontier" 1935 (Durkin).

Chissell, Noble "Kid" (1905-11/8/87). Films: "Song of Arizona" 1946 (Jim); "Grand Canyon" 1949 (2nd Thug); "Machismo—40 Graves for 40 Guns" 1970 (Doc Peters).

Chittel, Christopher (1948-). Films: "They Call Him Cemetery" 1971-Ital./Span. (John McIntire).

Choate, Tim. Films: "The Gambler Returns: The Luck of the Draw" TVM-1991 (Bad Boy Jon Wilson); "Gunsmoke: The Long Ride" TVM-1993 (Sheriff Bert Meriweather). ¶TV: Paradise—"The News from St. Louis" 10-27-88 (Jack).

Chong, Peter. Films: "Tribute to a Badman" 1956 (Cooky) ¶TV: Bonanza—"The Truckee Strip" 11-21-59, "The Fear Merchants" 1-30-60.

Chong, Rae Dawn (1961-). TV: Lonesome Dove—"Firebrand" 2-5-95 (May).

Chorre, Gertrude (1885-9/3/72). Films: "The Sea of Grass" 1947 (Indian Nurse).

Chorre, Sunni. Films: "Ramona" 1936 (Indian); "Flaming Frontier" 1938-serial; "Buck Benny Rides Again" 1940 (Indian); "Ride, Ranger, Ride" 1936; "Union Pacific" 1939 (Indian Brave); "Red Canyon" 1949 (Indian).

Chow, David (1930-). Films: "Kung Fu" TVM-1972 (Little Monk). ¶TV: *Kung Fu*—"The Tong" 11-15-73 (Third Highbinder).

Chrisman, Ethelyn. Films: "Bad Man Bobbs" 1915; "The Desert Calls Its Own" 1916; "Trilby's Love Disaster" 1916.

Chrisman, Pat. Films: "The Man from the East" 1914; "Athletic Ambitions" 1915; "The Auction Sale of Run-Down Ranch" 1915; "Bad Man Bobbs" 1915; "The Chef at Circle G" 1915; "The Child, the Dog, and the Villain" 1915; "Forked Trails" 1915; "The Foreman of the Bar-Z Ranch" 1915; "Harold's Bad Man" 1915; "The Impersonation of Tom" 1915; "A Lucky Deal" 1915; "The Outlaw's Bride" 1915; "The Race for a Gold Mine" 1915; "The Taking of Mustang Pete" 1915; "The Tenderfoot's Triumph" 1915; "The Canby Hill Outlaws" 1916; "A Close Call" 1916; "A Corner in Water" 1916; "The Cowpuncher's Peril" 1916; "Crooked Trails" 1916; "The Desert Calls Its Own" 1916; "An Eventful Evening" 1916; "Legal Advice" 1916; "Making Good" 1916; "The Man Within" 1916; "A Mistake in Rustlers" 1916; "Mistakes Will Happen" 1916; "A Mix-Up in Movies" 1916; "The Pony Express Rider" 1916; "The Raiders" 1916; "The Sheriff's Duty" 1916; "Starring in Western Stuff" 1916; "Taking a Chance" 1916; "The Taming of Groucho Bill" 1916; "When Cupid Slipped" 1916; "Hearts and Saddles" 1917; "The Luck That Jealousy Brought" 1917; "A Soft Tenderfoot" 1917; "Ace High" 1918 (Louis Cartier); "Six-Shooter Andy" 1918 (Ned Skinner); "Western Blood" 1918 (Juan); "The Coming of the Law" 1919 (Yuma Ed); "Rough-Riding Romance" 1919 (Curley); "Slim Higgins" 1919; "The Wilderness Trail" 1919 (Indian); "The Daredevil" 1920 (Mexican Villain); "The Texan" 1920 (Bat); "The Untamed" 1920 (Kilduff); "A Ridin' Romeo" 1921 (Highblow, the Indian); "Catch My Smoke" 1922 (Joe Bloss); "Sky High" 1922 (Pasquale); "Up and Going" 1922 (Sandy McNabb); "Romance Land" 1923 (White Eagle); "Oh, You Tony!" 1924 (the Chief).

Christensen, Wes. Films: "Stampede" 1949 (Slim); "Domino Kid" 1957 (Dobbs).

Christi, Frank (1930-7/9/82). TV: *Lancer*—"Dream of Falcons" 4-7-70 (Bodyguard).

Christian, Claudia. Films: "Houston: The Legend of Texas" TVM-1986 (Eliza Allen). ¶TV: *Outlaws*—"Madrid" 2-7-87 (Elena Conlon).

Christian, Helen. Films: "Zorro Rides Again" 1937-serial (Joyce Andrews).

Christian, Michael (1947-). Films: "The Great Gundown" 1977 (Darwood).

Christians, Rudolph (1869-2/7/21). Films: "Human Stuff" 1920 (Washboard Pierce).

Christie, Audrey (1928-12/20/89). Films: "Ballad of Josie" 1968 (Annabelle Pettijohn).

Christie, Ivan (1888-5/9/49). Films: "Man of the Forest" 1926 (Snake Anson); "The Mysterious Rider" 1927 (Tom Saunders).

Christie, Julie (1940-). Films: "McCabe and Mrs. Miller" 1971 (Constance Miller).

Christie, Shannon. TV: *Alias Smith and Jones*—"The Night of the Red Dog" 11-4-71 (Florence); *Bonanza*—"Shanklin" 2-13-72 (Mary Elizabeth).

Christine, Virginia (1917-). Films: "The Old Texas Trail" 1944 (Queenie Leone); "Raiders of Ghost City" 1944-serial (Trina Dessard); "Phantom of the Plains" 1945; "The Scarlet Horseman" 1946-serial (Carla); "High Noon" 1952 (Mrs. Simpson); "The Woman They Almost Lynched" 1953 (Jenny); "Flaming Star" 1960 (Mrs. Phillips); "Cattle King" 1963 (Ruth Winters); "Four for Texas" 1964; "Billy the Kid vs. Dracula" 1966 (Eva Oster). ¶TV: *Jim Bowie*—"The Squatter" 9-14-56 (Katrina Gottschalk); *Trackdown*—"Alpine, Texas" 11-15-57 (Millie), "The Reward" 1-3-58 (Millie), "Matter of Justice" 10-17-58 (Mrs. Doan); *Gunsmoke*—"Fingered" 11-23-57 (Lila), "Bank Baby" 3-20-65 (Bess Clum); *The Restless Gun*—"Strange Family in Town" 1-20-58 (Amy Durant); *Zane Grey Theater*—"The Scaffold" 10-9-58 (Mrs. Hart); *Buckskin*—"Miss Pringle" 10-16-58 (Emily); *Wyatt Earp*—"Plague Carrier" 12-9-58 (Martha Evans); *Wanted—Dead or Alive*—"Rope Law" 1-3-59 (Bessie Logan), "The Matchmaker" 9-19-59 (Harriet); *The Rifleman*—"The Spiked Rifle" 11-24-59, "The Long Goodbye" 11-27-61 (Mrs. Dalrymple); *Man from Blackhawk*—"Death Is the Best Policy" 12-18-59 (Mary Schuler); *Rawhide*—"Incident of the One Hundred Amulets" 5-6-60, "Incident of the Blackstorms" 5-26-61 (Ada Covey); *Wagon Train*—"The Prairie Story" 2-1-61 (Clara), "The Will Santee Story" 5-3-61 (Amanda Santee), "The Martin Gatsby Story" 10-10-62 (Elaine Gatsby), "The Blane Wessels Story" 4-17-63 (Minna), "The Katy Piper Story" 4-11-65 (Mrs. Reed); *Maverick*—"Last Stop: Olivion" 2-12-61 (Verna Lyme); *The Deputy*—"Tension Point" 4-8-61 (Molly); *Tales of Wells Fargo*—Regular 1961-62 (Ovie); *Stoney Burke*—"A Matter of Pride" 11-5-62 (Flora Hill); *Bonanza*—"Song in the Dark" 1-13-63 (Mary), "The Saga of Squaw Charlie" 12-27-64 (Martha); *The Big Valley*—"Young Marauders" 10-6-65 (Margaret Coleman); *The Virginian*—"The Awakening" 10-13-65 (Mrs. Claypool), "A Small Taste of Justice" 12-20-67 (Margaret Conlan); *Laredo*—"Sound of Terror" 4-7-66 (Agnes Halsey); *A Man Called Shenandoah*—"Macauley's Cure" 5-16-66 (Fran Macauley); *Daniel Boone*—"Thirty Pieces of Silver" 3-28-68 (Marta), "Noblesse Oblige" 3-26-70; *Lancer*—"Child of Rock and Sunlight" 4-1-69 (Hannah Sickles).

Christmas, Eric (1916-). Films: "Monte Walsh" 1970 (Col. Wilson). ¶TV: *Bonanza*—"Dead Wrong" 12-7-69 (Bobby Dann); *The Men from Shiloh*—"Nan Allen" 1-6-71 (Parker), "The Regimental Line" 3-3-71 (Parker).

Christopher, Jordan (1940-). Films: "Return of the Seven" 1966-Span. (Manuel).

Christopher, Kay. Films: "South of Rio" 1949 (Carol Waterman); "Code of the Silver Sage" 1950 (Ann Gately). ¶TV: *The Marshal of Gunsight Pass* 1950.

Christopher, Robert. Films: "The Three Outlaws" 1956. ¶TV: *Sergeant Preston of the Yukon*—"All Is Not Gold" 5-10-56 (Ray Keane); *Bonanza*—"The Gift" 4-1-61, "Broken Ballad" 10-29-61 (Cahill), "Black Friday" 1-22-67 (Clerk); *The Virginian*—"Say Goodbye to All That" 1-23-63 (Rick).

Christopher, William (1932-). TV: *Nichols*—"Peanuts and Crackerjacks" 11-4-71, "The Unholy Alliance" 1-18-72.

Christy, Ann (1905-11/14/87). Films: "The Water Hole" 1928 (Dolores); "The Lariat Kid" 1929 (Mary Lou).

Christy, Dorothy. Films: "The Phantom Empire" 1935-serial (Queen Tika); "Rough Riders' Round-Up" 1939 (Blondie); "Sierra Sue" 1941 (Verebel); "Cowboy and the Senorita" 1944 (Lulubelle); "Dakota" 1945 (Nora); "Silver River" 1948 (Woman).

Christy, Ivan (1888-5/9/49). Films: "The Sheriff's Story" 1915; "Salt of the Earth" 1917 (Pyrites Kincaid); "Nevada" 1927 (Crawthorne); "Rose of the Rancho" 1936 (Bystander).

Christy, Jan. Films: "Hoppy Serves a Writ" 1943 (Jean Hollister).

Christy, Ken (1895-7/23/62). Films: "Bells of Capistrano" 1942; "Blackjack Ketchum, Desperado" 1956 (Sheriff Mach); "Fury at Showdown" 1957 (Mr. Phelps); "Outlaw's Son" 1957 (Mac Butler); "Utah Blaine" 1957 (Joe Neal). ¶TV: *Wild Bill Hickok*—"Kangaroo Kapers" 3-10-53; *Tales of the Texas Rangers*—"Singing on the Trail" 12-24-55 (Wendy Norton); *Death Valley Days*—"The Hangman Waits" 1-2-56; *Wyatt Earp*—"The Desperate Half-Hour" 2-28-56 (Gentry); *Broken Arrow*—"Ghost Face" 3-12-57 (Tabor), "Apache Child" 10-15-57 (Clyde Tabor); *Maverick*—"Rope of Cards" 1-19-58 (Sheriff); *Wagon Train*—"The Honorable Don Charlie Story" 1-22-58 (Storekeeper); *Tales of Wells Fargo*—"Bill Longley" 2-10-58 (Milt Jones); *Bat Masterson*—"Election Day" 1-14-59 (Morgan); *Laramie*—"Men in Shadows" 5-30-61 (Banks).

Christy, Lillian E. Films: "The Peril of the Cliffs" 1912; "The Post Telegrapher" 1912; "Red Wing and the Paleface" 1912; "A Rose of Old Mexico" 1913.

Church, Frederick. (Montana Bill). Films: "Broncho Billy's Heart" 1912; "The Dead Man's Claim" 1912; "An Indian's Friendship" 1912; "A Moonshiner's Heart" 1912; "The Smuggler's Daughter" 1912; "Their Promise" 1912; "Western Hearts" 1912; "At the Lariat's End" 1913; "Bonnie of the Hills" 1913; "The Broken Parole" 1913; "Broncho Billy's Brother" 1913; "Broncho Billy's Capture" 1913; "Broncho Billy's Reason" 1913; "The End of the Circle" 1913; "The Kid Sheriff" 1913; "Love and the Law" 1913; "The Struggle" 1913; "The Cast of the Die" 1914; "The Girl from Texas" 1914; "The Hills of Peace" 1914; "The Night on the Road" 1914; "What Came to Bar Q" 1914; "The Long Chance" 1915 (Oliver Corblay); "The End of the Rainbow" 1916 (Ferdinand Stocker); "Number 10, Westbound" 1917; "Squaring It" 1917; "All for Gold" 1918; "The Human Tiger" 1918; "Shootin' Mad" 1918 (Bull Martin); "Red Blood and Yellow" 1919; "The Son of a Gun" 1919 (Buck Saunders); "The Man from New York" 1923 (Bob Tarrant); "Prince of the Saddle"

1926; "Two Fisted Buckaroo" 1926; "The Lone Rider" 1927; "Riders of Vengeance" 1928; "Secrets of the Range" 1928; "Trails of Treachery" 1928; "The Vanishing West" 1928-serial; "The Unknown Rider" 1929; "Western Methods" 1929; "Lure of the Mine" 1929 (Allan Roscoe); "The Apache Kid's Escape" 1930; "Rough and Ready" 1930; "South of Sonora" 1930; "Flying Lariats" 1931 (Tex Johnson); "Riders of the Cactus" 1931 (Jim Venner); "The Riding Kid" 1931 (Sam Eldridge); "Wild West Whoopee" 1931; "Border Guns" 1935 (Buck Morgan); "Defying the Law" 1935 (Ace Lane); "Devil's Canyon" 1935; "Desert Guns" 1936 (Jennings).

Church, Thomas Haden. Films: "Tombstone" 1993 (Billy Clanton).

Churchill, Berton (1876-10/10/40). Films: "Tongues of Flame" 1924 (Boland); "The Big Stampede" 1932 (Gov. Lew Wallace); "The Mysterious Rider" 1933 (Mark King); "Frontier Marshal" 1934 (Hiram Melton); "Wild and Woolly" 1937 (Edward Ralston); "Cowboy and the Lady" 1938 (Henderson); "Stagecoach" 1939 (Henry Gatewood); "Twenty Mule Team" 1940 (Jackass Brown).

Churchill, Marguerite (1910-). Films: "The Big Trail" 1930 (Ruth Cameron); "Riders of the Purple Sage" 1931 (Jane Withersteen).

Churchill, Sarah (1914-9/24/82). TV: *Hallmark Hall of Fame*—"The Lonely Path" 11-8-53.

Cianfriglia, Giovanni (Ken Wood). Films: "The Tramplers" 1965-Ital.; "Five Giants from Texas" 1966-Ital./Span.; "If You Want to Live ... Shoot!" 1967-Ital./Span. (Johnny); "Kill Them All and Come Back Alone" 1967-Ital./Span. (Kid); "Killer Kid" 1967-Ital.; "Two Pistols and a Coward" 1967-Ital.; "Bury Them Deep" 1968-Ital. (Johnny Gunn); "No Graves on Boot Hill" 1968-Ital. (Reno); "Challenge of the Mackennas" 1969-Ital./Span.; "Blindman" 1971-Ital.; "Sometimes Life Is Hard, Right Providence?" 1972-Ital./Fr./Ger.; "Thunder Over El Paso" 1972-Ital./Span.; "Gunmen and the Holy Ghost" 1973-Ital.; "Keoma" 1975-Ital./Span.

Ciannelli, Eduardo (1887-10/8/69). Films: "California" 1946 (Padre); "Boot Hill" 1969-Ital.; "MacKenna's Gold" 1969 (Prairie Dog). ¶TV: *Have Gun Will Travel*—"Bitter Wine" 2-15-58 (Renato Donatello), "Gold and Brimstone" 6-20-59 (Willis Baird); *Wagon Train*—"The Clara Duncan Story" 4-22-59 (Sylvio Sori-

ano); *The Tall Man*—"Ransom of a Town" 5-6-61 (Padre); *The Virginian*—"No Drums, No Trumpets" 4-6-66.

Cichy, Martin (1892-4/26/62). Films: "Taking a Chance" 1928 (Luke); "Code of the West" 1929; "Riders of the Rio Grande" 1929 (Snakey Smiley); "Covered Wagon Trails" 1930 (Brag Vogel); "O'Malley Rides Alone" 1930.

Cilento, Diane (1933-). Films: "Hombre" 1967 (Jessie).

Cimarosa, Tano. Films: "Death on High Mountain" 1969-Ital./Span.; "Man Called Amen" 1972-Ital.; "They Still Call Me Amen" 1972-Ital.

Cioffi, Charles (1935-). TV: *Bonanza*—"Shanklin" 2-13-72 (Shanklin).

Cirillo, Michael A. (1903-8/29/68). Films: "Son of Paleface" 1952 (Micky, the Bartender).

Cisar, George (-6/13/79). Films: "The Buckskin Lady" 1957 (Cranston); "Billy the Kid vs. Dracula" 1966 (Joe Blake). ¶TV: *Wild Bill Hickok*—"Jingles Gets the Bird" 3-24-53; *Broken Arrow*—"Hired Killer" 3-4-58 (Holmes); *Tales of the Texas Rangers*—"Jace and Clay" 12-5-58 (Sheriff); *Have Gun Will Travel*—"Maggie O'Bannion" 4-4-59 (Matt Perk), "The Waiting Room" 2-24-62 (Marshal); *Colt .45*—"Queen of Dixie" 10-4-59; *The Alaskans*—"The Devil Made Five" 6-19-60 (Merchant); *Laramie*—"The Confederate Express" 1-30-62; *The Virginian*—"The Big Deal" 10-10-62 (George).

Claire, Edith. TV: *The Rebel*—"Panic" 11-1-59 (Mrs. Dobbs), "Dark Secret" 11-22-59 (Mrs. Simmons).

Clair, Ethlyne. Films: "A Hero on Horseback" 1927; "Painted Ponies" 1927 (Pony Blenning); "Guardians of the Wild" 1928 (Madge Warren); "Riding for Fame" 1928 (Kitty Barton); "The Vanishing Rider" 1928-serial; "Gun Law" 1929 (Nancy); "The Pride of Pawnee" 1929 (Madge Wilson); "Queen of the Northwoods" 1929-serial; "Wild Blood" 1929 (Mary Ellis).

Clair, Jany. Films: "The Road to Fort Alamo" 1966-Fr./Ital. (Janet).

Claire, Gertrude (1852-4/28/28). Films: "A True Westerner" 1911; "The Ruse" 1915; "The Apostle of Vengeance" 1916; "The Aryan" 1916 (Steve's Mother); "Lieutenant Danny, U.S.A." 1916 (Ysobel's Mother); "Golden Rule Kate" 1917; "The Silent Man" 1917 (Mrs. Hardy); "Blue Blazes Rawden" 1918 (Mrs. Hilgard); "The Fox" 1921 (Mrs.

Farwell); "The Crusader" 1922 (Mrs. Brent); "Ridin' Wild" 1922 (Mrs. Henderson); "Double Dealing" 1923 (Mother Slowbell); "Tumbleweeds" 1925 (Old Woman); "Out of the West" 1926 (Grannie Hanley).

Claire, Ted. Films: "Songs and Saddles" 1938 (Mark Bowers).

Clancy, Ellen. Films: "Prairie Thunder" 1937 (Joan Temple).

Clancy, Tom (1923-11/7/90). TV: *Father Murphy*—"A Horse from Heaven" 11-24-81 (Mitchell).

Clanton, Ralph (1914-86). TV: *Circus Boy*—"The Judge's Boy" 12-5-57 (Judge Bradley Sheldon); *Man from Blackhawk*—"Station Six" 11-13-59 (Williamson); *Have Gun Will Travel*—"The Lady on the Wall" 2-20-60 (Armand Boucher).

Clapham, Leonard. *see* London, Tom.

Clarges, Verner (1848-8/11/11). Films: "The Honor of the Family" 1909; "The Thread of Destiny" 1910.

Clark, Andrew (1903-11/16/60). Films: "How the Boys Fought the Indians" 1912; "Andy and the Redskins" 1914.

Clark, Betty Ross (1880-2/1/47). Films: "The Fox" 1921 (Annette Fraser).

Clark, Bill. Films: "Terror Trail" 1946; "Young Fury" 1965. ¶TV: *Bonanza*—"The Rival" 4-15-61, "The Quality of Mercy" 11-17-63 (John Dagliesh), "No Less a Man" 3-15-64, "Return to Honor" 3-22-64 (Jenner), "The Hostage" 9-27-64 (Jim), "The Underdog" 12-13-64 (Warren), "Once a Doctor" 2-28-65, "The Return" 5-2-65, "The Jonah" 5-9-65 (Will), "The Brass Box" 9-26-65 (Jim), "Ride the Wind" 1-16-66 & 1-23-66 (Wilson), "The Pursued" 10-2-66 & 10-9-66 (Dave), "Showdown at Tahoe" 11-19-67 (Tucker), "The Burning Sky" 1-28-68, "Top Hand" 1-17-71 (Jimpson), "New Man" 10-10-72 (Man), "The Marriage of Theodora Duffy" 1-9-73 (Bates).

Clark, Bobby. Films: "Thunder Trail" 1937 (Cowboy); "Overland with Kit Carson" 1939-serial (Andy); "Trigger Smith" 1939 (Buck); "The Sagebrush Family Trails West" 1940 (Bobby Sawyer); "Rim of the Canyon" 1949; "Sons of New Mexico" 1949; "Beyond the Purple Hills" 1950; "Silver Canyon" 1951; "Barbed Wire" 1952; "The Old West" 1952; "Man with the Steel Whip" 1954-serial (Mac); "Rebel in Town" 1956 (Petey Willoughby); "Gun Duel in Durango" 1957 (Robbie); "The Red, White and Black" 1970 (Kayitah);

"The Female Bunch" 1971. ¶TV: *Tales of the Texas Rangers*—"The Black Eyes of Texas" 12-31-55 (Jimmy); *Tales of Wells Fargo*—"Stage to Nowhere" 6-24-57; *Casey Jones*—Regular 1957-58 (Casey Jones, Jr.); *Northwest Passage*—"The Hostage" 11-2-58 (Jean Louis); *Wanted—Dead or Alive*—"The Kovack Affair" 3-28-59 (Shoeshine Boy); *Gunsmoke*—"The Wreckers" 9-11-67 (Stage Attendant), "Zavala" 10-7-68 (Colton), "9:12 to Dodge" 11-11-68 (Barstow), "Murdoch" 2-8-71 (Gatlin), "Disciple" 4-1-74 (Junior), "The Wiving" 10-14-74 (Cowboy #2); *Cimarron Strip*—"Whitey" 10-19-67; *Lancer*—"Chase a Wild Horse" 10-8-68; *Kung Fu*—"This Valley of Terror" 9-28-74 (Father).

Clark, Brian Patrick. TV: *Paradise*—"Shadow of a Doubt" 3-3-90 (Louis Petrie).

Clark, Candy (1949-). Films: "Rodeo Girl" TVM-1980 (J.R. Patterson).

Clark, Carrie Ward. Films: "True Blue" 1918 (Buck's Wife).

Clark, Cliff (1893-2/8/53). Films: "Santa Fe Trail" 1940 (Instructor); "Wagon Train" 1940 (Matt Gardner/Carl Anderson); "Western Union" 1941; "Wild Bill Hickok Rides" 1942 (Vic Kersey); "Barbary Coast Gent" 1944 (Jack Coda); "Adventures of Gallant Bess" 1948 (Sheriff); "False Paradise" 1948; "Fort Apache" 1948 (Stage Driver); "Fighting Man of the Plains" 1949 (Travers); "Powder River Rustlers" 1949 (Lucius Statton); "The Cariboo Trail" 1950 (Assayer); "Desperadoes of the West" 1950-serial (Colonel Arnold); "Vigilante Hideout" 1950 (Howard Sanders); "Cavalry Scout" 1951 (Col. Deering); "Desert of Lost Men" 1951 (Carl Landers); "Overland Telegraph" 1951 (Muldoon); "Saddle Legion" 1951 (Warren); "Silver City" 1951 (Bartender); "Sugarfoot" 1951; "Warpath" 1951 (Bartender); "The Big Sky" 1952; "Cripple Creek" 1952 (Winfield Hatton); "High Noon" 1952 (Weaver).

Clark, Dane (1915-). Films: "Barricade" 1950 (Bob Peters); "Fort Defiance" 1951 (Johnny Tallon); "Thunder Pass" 1954; "Massacre" 1956 (Ramon); "Outlaw's Son" 1957 (Nate Blaine); "The McMasters" 1970 (Spencer). ¶TV: *Wagon Train*—"The John Wilbot Story" 6-11-58 (John Wilbot); *Rawhide*—"Incident of the Night Visitor" 11-4-60 (Jeff Brkley); *The Men from Shiloh*—"The Mysterious Mr. Tate" 10-14-70 (Barton Ellis).

Clark, Davison (1881-11/4/72). Films: "The Plainsman" 1936 (James Speed); "Western Jamboree" 1938; "Oklahoma Terror" 1939 (Cartwright); "Geronimo" 1940 (2nd Politician); "Northwest Mounted Police" 1940 (Surgeon Roberts); "The Return of Frank James" 1940 (Officer); "Three Men from Texas" 1940 (Thompson); "Virginia City" 1940; "Belle Starr" 1941; "Prairie Pioneers" 1941 (Carlos Montoya); "Six Gun Gold" 1941 (Robinson); "Come on, Danger!" 1942 (Blake); "Down Rio Grande Way" 1942 (Col. Baldridge); "Riding Through Nevada" 1942; "Valley of Vanishing Men" 1942-serial; "The Avenging Rider" 1943 (Grayson); "Cowboy in the Clouds" 1943 (Amos Fowler); "Death Valley Manhunt" 1943 (Tex Benson); "Fighting Frontier" 1943 (Judge Halverson); "Hail to the Rangers" 1943 (Maj. Montgomery); "Law of the Northwest" 1943 (Tom Clayton); "Trigger Trail" 1944 (Silas Farrel); "Two-Fisted Ranger" 1946; "The Sea of Grass" 1947 (Cattleman); "Unconquered" 1947 (Mr. Carroll); "Four Faces West" 1948 (Burnett); "Lone Star" 1952 (Senator).

Clark, Dick (1929-). TV: *Stoney Burke*—"Kincaid" 4-22-63 (Sgt. Andy Kincaid); *Branded*—"The Greatest Coward on Earth" 11-21-65 (J.A.).

Clark, Dorothy Love. Films: "The Yaqui" 1916 (Lucia); "Who Knows?" 1918 (Dawn Weaver).

Clark, Dort (1917-3/30/89). Films: "Fools' Parade" 1971 (Enoch Purdy); "Skin Game" 1971 (Pennypacker). ¶TV: *Empire*—"Between Friday and Monday" 5-7-63 (Panhandler); *Redigo*—"Man in a Blackout" 11-5-63 (Doc); *Wild Wild West*—"The Night of the Circus of Death" 11-3-67 (Col. Housley), "The Night of Miguelito's Revenge" 12-13-68; *Daniel Boone*—"The Value of a King" 11-9-67 (Meecham); *Nichols*—"About Jesse James" 2-15-72 (Sheriff).

Clark, Edward (1879-11/18/54). Films: "Ticket to Tomahawk" 1950 (Jet); "Branded" 1951 (Dad Travis); "Cattle Queen" 1951 (Doc Hodges); "Thundering Caravans" 1952 (Tom); "El Paso Stampede" 1953 (Josh Bailey); "Topeka" 1953; "Hell's Outpost" 1954. ¶TV: *Wild Bill Hickok*—"Widow Muldane" 8-14-51, "Outlaw Flats" 10-9-51; *Hopalong Cassidy*—"The Last Laugh" 1-19-52; *The Cisco Kid*—"The Kid Brother" 2-9-52, "Dutchman's Flat" 3-15-52, "Commodore Goes West" 7-12-52, "Gold, Death and Dynamite" 2-13-54; *The*

Gene Autry Show—"Stage to San Dimas" 10-8-55.

Clark, Ellen. TV: *Gunsmoke*—"Brother Whelp" 11-7-59 (Tassy); *Have Gun Will Travel*—"Jenny" 1-23-60 (Jenny Lake); *Stagecoach West*—"Three Wise Men" 12-20-60 (Susan Crawford).

Clark, Frank M (1857–4/10/45). Films: "The Cowboy's Adopted Child" 1911; "Evangeline" 1911; "A Frontier Girl's Courage" 1911; "Heart of John Barlow" 1911; "How Algy Captured a Wild Man" 1911; "It Happened in the West" 1911; "Little Injin" 1911; "The Night Herder" 1911; "On Seperate Paths" 1911; "Range Pals" 1911; "A Broken Spur" 1912; "A Child of the Wilderness" 1912; "The Old Stage Coach" 1912; "In the Long Ago" 1913; "A Wild Ride" 1913; "Chip of the Flying U" 1914; "The Going of the White Swan" 1914; "In Defiance of the Law" 1914; "The Spoilers" 1914 (Dextry); "When the Cook Fell Ill" 1914; "When the West Was Young" 1914;"The Man from Painted Post" 1917 (Toby Madden); "The Light of Western Stars" 1918 (Bill Stillwell); "Western Blood" 1918 (Col. Stephens); "Fighting for Gold" 1919 (Sheriff); "The Wilderness Trail" 1919 (Angus Fitzpatrick); "Firebrand Trevison" 1920 (Judge Lindman); "The Untamed" 1920 (Sheriff Morris); "Hands Off" 1921 (Capt. Jim Ellison); "Two Kinds of Women" 1922 (Dr. Tripp); "The Lone Star Ranger" 1923 (Laramie); "Border Blackbirds" 1927; "Land of the Lawless" 1927 (Simpson); "Wanderer of the West" 1927; "The Boss of Rustler's Roost" 1928 (Jud Porter); "The Bronc Stomper" 1928 (James Hollister); "The Four-Footed Ranger" 1928 (Handsome Thomas); "Cowboy Pluck" 1929; "Outlawed" 1929 (Seth); "Roaring Ranch" 1930 (Tom Marlin); "Spurs" 1930 (Charles Bradley); "The Border Menace" 1934 (Harris); "The Phantom Cowboy" 1935 (Sheriff Nelson); "Western Racketeers" 1935 (Steve Harding); "The Whirlwind Rider" 1935.

Clark, Fred (1914-12/5/68). Films: "Fury at Furnace Creek" 1948 (Bird); "Two Guys from Texas" 1948 (Dr. Straeger); "The Younger Brothers" 1949 (Ryckman); "The Eagle and the Hawk" 1950 (Basil Danzeeger); "Return of the Frontiersman" 1950 (Ryan). ¶TV: *Wagon Train*—"The Martin Gatsby Story" 10-10-62 (Martin Gatsby); *Laredo*—"The Land Grabbers" 12-9-65 (Commissioner Smoot); *F Troop*—"The Day THey Shot Agarn" 2-16-67 (Major Hewitt);

Bonanza—"A Girl Named George" 1-14-68 (Judge Neely).

Clark, Gordon. Films: "Zorro's Fighting Legion" 1939-serial (Miguel Torres); "The Bells of San Fernando" 1947 (Enrico); "The Last Gunfighter" 1961-Can. ¶TV: *The Cisco Kid*—"Lodestone" 4-26-52, "Gun Totin' Papa" 5-24-52; *Wyatt Earp*—"The Vultures" 3-19-57 (Henry Brown).

Clark, Harvey (1886-7/19/38). Films: "The Land O' Lizards" 1916 (Ward Curtis); "Snap Judgment" 1917 (Franklin R. Manning); "Six Feet Four" 1919 (Two-Hand Billy Comstock); "This Hero Stuff" 1919 (Jonathan Pillsbury); "The Man Who Won" 1923 (Sunny Oaks); "The Arizona Romeo" 1925 (the Sheriff); "The Cowboy and the Countess" 1926 (Edwin Irving Mansfield); "The Flying Horseman" 1926 (Happy Joe); "The Frontier Trail" 1926 (Sgt. O'Shea); "Rose of the Golden West" 1927 (Thomas Larkin); "The Rainbow" 1929 (Baldy); "Boss Rider of Gun Creek" 1936 (Pop Greer); "The Singing Cowboy" 1936 (Henry Blake); "The Three Godfathers" 1936 (Marcus Treen); "Boss of Lonely Valley" 1937 (Jim Lynch); "Empty Saddles" 1937 (Swap Boone); "Law for Tombstone" 1937 (Doc Holliday); "Partners of the Plains" 1938 (Baldy).

Clark, Jack (1877-4/12/47). Films: "Home on the Range" 1935 (Sheriff); "Wells Fargo" 1937 (William Fargo).

Clark, Janet (1922-7/12/87). Films: "The Great Bank Robbery" 1969 (Lady).

Clark, John. Films: "Django Does Not Forgive" 1967-Ital./Span. (Django); "Land Raiders" 1969-U.S./Span. (Ace); "El Condor" 1970 (Prison Guard Captain).

Clark, Judy. Films: "South of Santa Fe" 1942 (Judy); "Western Whoopee" 1948-short; "Desperadoes of the West" 1950-serial (Sally Arnold).

Clark, Ken (1932-). Films: "The Last Wagon" 1956 (Sergeant); "Love Me Tender" 1956 (Kelso); "The Proud Ones" 1956 (Pike); "The Road to Fort Alamo" 1966-Fr./Ital. (Arizona Bill); "Savage Gringo" 1966-Ital. (Nebraska); "Man Called Sledge" 1971-Ital./U.S. (Floyd). ¶TV: *Death Valley Days*—"Yankee Pirate" 2-24-58 (Joseph Chapman); *Colt .45*—"The Saga of Sam Bass" 5-17-59 (Bass's Cohort); *Sugarfoot*—"Apollo with a Gun" 12-8-59 (Benecia Boy Heenan).

Clark, Marlene. TV: *Bonanza*—

"The Desperado" 2-7-71 (Liza Walters).

Clark, Matt (1936-). Films: "Will Penny" 1968 (Romulus); "Macho Callahan" 1970 (Jailer); "Monte Walsh" 1970 (Rufus Brady); "The Cowboys" 1972 (Smiley); "The Culpepper Cattle Company" 1972 (Pete; "The Great Northfield, Minnesota Raid" 1972 (Bob Younger); "Jeremiah Johnson" 1972 (Qualen); "The Life and Times of Judge Roy Bean" 1972 (Nick the Grub); "Pat Garrett and Billy the Kid" 1973 (Deputy J.W. Bell); "This Was the West That Was" TVM-1974 (Buffalo Bill Cody); "Hearts of the West" 1975 (Jackson); "Kid Vengeance" 1976-Ital./U.S./Israel; "The Outlaw Josey Wales" 1976 (Kelly); "Lacy and the Mississippi Queen" TVM-1978 (Reynolds); "Last Ride of the Dalton Gang" TVM-1979 (Bitter Creek); "The Legend of the Lone Ranger" 1981 (Sheriff Wiatt); "The Gambler, Part III—The Legend Continues" TVM-1987 (Sgt. Grinder); "The Quick and the Dead" CTVM-1987 (Doc Shabitt); "Back to the Future, Part III" 1990 (Bartender). ¶TV: *Dundee and the Culhane*—9-27-67 (Smith); *Death Valley Days*—"The Informer Who Cried" 11-11-67 (Montana Joe); *Bonanza*—"The Witness" 9-21-69 (Fantan); *Kung Fu*—"The Elixir" 12-20-73 (Niebo).

Clark, Oliver (1939-). Films: "Another Man, Another Chance" 1977-Fr. (Evans).

Clark, Paul (1927-5/20/60). TV: *Have Gun Will Travel*—"Tiger" 11-28-59 (Pahndu); *The Deputy*—"Last Gunfight" 4-30-60 (David Crawford).

Clark, Roy. Films: "The Little Indian Martyr" 1912; "A Little Hero" 1913; "The Noisy Six" 1913; "A Woman's Fool" 1918 (Billy).

Clark, Roydon. Films: "Colt .45" 1950; "Ride the Man Down" 1952 (Jim Young); "Badlands of Montana" 1957 (Posseman); "Escape from Red Rock" 1958; "The Great Bank Robbery" 1969 (Commandant); "Desperado" TVM-1987. ¶TV: *Maverick*—"Holiday at Hollow Rock" 12-28-58 (Chuck); *Bonanza*—"Heritage of Anger" 9-19-72 (Bartlett).

Clark, Russ. Films: "White Fang" 1936; "Wild and Woolly" 1937 (Cowboy); "Last of the Duanes" 1941 (Ranger Guard); "California" 1946 (Man); "Pursued" 1947.

Clark, Steve (1891-6/29/54). Films: "Silent Men" 1933 (Parker);

"The Man Trailer" 1934 (Dave Bishop); "Mystery Mountain" 1934-serial; "The Prescott Kid" 1934 (Crocker); "The Westerner" 1934 (Henchman); "Alias John Law" 1935 (Simi); "Danger Trails" 1935 (Hopkins); "Fighting Shadows" 1935 (Woodsman); "The Laramie Kid" 1935 (Sheriff); "Law Beyond the Range" 1935 (Townsman); "Lightning Triggers" 1935; "No Man's Range" 1935 (Ed Brady); "North of Arizona" 1935 (Bartender Steve); "The Revenge Rider" 1935 (Murphy); "The Rider of the Law" 1935; "Square Shooter" 1935 (Pete); "Texas Jack" 1935; "Caryl of the Mountains" 1936 (Captain Edwards); "Cavalcade of the West" 1936 (John Know); "Comin' Round the Mountain" 1936; "Gun Smoke" 1936; "The Last of the Warrens" 1936 (Spike); "The Lawless Nineties" 1936; "Song of the Saddle" 1936 (Man in Coach); "Too Much Beef" 1936 (Prosecutor); "Valley of the Lawless" 1936; "West of Nevada" 1936 (Milt Haldain); "Arizona Gunfighter" 1937 (Sheriff); "Boothill Brigade" 1937 (Holbrook); "Courage of the West" 1937; "The Gambling Terror" 1937 (McClure); "Gun Lords of Stirrup Basin" 1937 (Hammond); "Guns in the Dark" 1937 (Paul Small); "A Lawman Is Born" 1937 (Sam Brownlee); "Moonlight on the Range" 1937; "The Old Wyoming Trail" 1937 (Deputy Sheriff); "One Man Justice" 1937 (Henchman); "Outlaws of the Prairie" 1937 (Cobb); "Riders of the Dawn" 1937; "Ridin' the Lone Trail" 1937 (Sheriff Carson); "Romance of the Rockies" 1937 (Trigger); "The Silver Trail" 1937 (Tom); "Trail of Vengeance" 1937 (Bill); "Two-Fisted Sheriff" 1937 (Red); "Western Gold" 1937; "Where Trails Divide" 1937 (Wheezer); "Cattle Raiders" 1938 (Hank); "The Colorado Trail" 1938 (Owen); "Desert Patrol" 1938 (Captain); "Durango Valley Raiders" 1938 (Boone Cordner); "The Feud Maker" 1938 (Mark); "Heroes of the Alamo" 1938 (Frank Hunter); "Knight of the Plains" 1938 (Sheriff); "Paroled to Die" 1938 (Sheriff Blackman); "The Rangers' Roundup" 1938; "South of Arizona" 1938; "Thunder in the Desert" 1938 (Andrews); "West of Cheyenne" 1938 (Gambler); "West of Santa Fe" 1938 (Dunn); "Dodge City" 1939; "The Thundering West" 1939 (Steve); "Westbound Stage" 1939 (Butch); "Western Caravans" 1939 (Mac); "Beyond the Sacramento" 1940 (Curly); "Billy the Kid Outlawed" 1940 (Shorty); "The Durango Kid" 1940 (Bixby); "The Kid from Santa Fe" 1940 (Herman); "Land of the Six Guns" 1940 (Frank Stone); "Phantom Rancher" 1940 (Burton); "Pinto Canyon" 1940 (Hardy Kellar); "Roll, Wagons, Roll" 1940 (Trigger); "Wild Horse Range" 1940 (Sheriff); "Billy the Kid in Santa Fe" 1941 (Allen); "Billy the Kid's Range War" 1941; "The Driftin' Kid" 1941; "Hands Across the Rockies" 1941; "King of Dodge City" 1941; "Law of the Wolf" 1941; "The Lone Rider Ambushed" 1941; "The Lone Rider Crosses the Rio" 1941; "The Lone Rider in Ghost Town" 1941; "The Lone Rider Rides On" 1941; "The Medico of Painted Springs" 1941 (Ellis); "North from the Lone Star" 1941; "Outlaws of the Panhandle" 1941 (Lon Hewitt); "The Pinto Kid" 1941; "The Return of Daniel Boone" 1941; "Saddle Mountain Roundup" 1941 (Henderson); "The Son of Davy Crockett" 1941 (Curly); "Trail of the Silver Spurs" 1941; "Tumbledown Ranch in Arizona" 1941 (Shorty); "Underground Rustlers" 1941 (Jake); "White Eagle" 1941-serial; "Arizona Roundup" 1942; "Along the Sundown Trail" 1942; "Arizona Stagecoach" 1942; "Boot Hill Bandits" 1942 (Sheriff); "Dawn on the Great Divide" 1942; "The Devil's Trail" 1942; "Down Rio Grande Way" 1942; "The Lone Star Vigilantes" 1942; "Outlaws of Boulder Pass" 1942; "Prairie Gunsmoke" 1942; "Rock River Renegades" 1942; "Texas Justice" 1942; "Texas to Bataan" 1942 (Conroy); "Texas Trouble Shooters" 1942 (Ames); "Thunder River Feud" 1942 (Shorty); "Trail Riders" 1942 (Marshal Hammond); "Vengeance of the West" 1942; "Where Trails End" 1942; "Black Market Rustlers" 1943 (Prescott); "Bullets and Saddles" 1943; "Cattle Stampede" 1943 (Turner); "Cowboy Commandos" 1943 (Bartlett); "The Haunted Ranch" 1943; "Land of Hunted Men" 1943; "The Stranger from Pecos" 1943 (Clem); "Cheyenne Wildcat" 1944; "Cowboy from Lonesome River" 1944; "Death Valley Rangers" 1944; "Ghost Guns" 1944; "Land of the Outlaws" 1944; "Law Men" 1944 (Wilson); "Law of the Valley" 1944; "Marked Trails" 1944 (Harry Stevens); "Partners of the Trail" 1944 (Cobly); "Range Law" 1944 (Pop McGee); "Riding West" 1944 (Alexander Morton); "Saddle Leather Law" 1944; "Song of the Range" 1944 (Sheriff Duncan); "Valley of Vengeance" 1944 (Happy); "West of the Rio Grande" 1944; "Blazing the Western Trail" 1945; "Flame of the West" 1945 (Hendricks); "Frontier Feud" 1945 (Bill Corey); "Gangster's Den" 1945 (Bartender); "Gun Smoke" 1945; "The Lost Trail" 1945 (Mason); "Outlaws of the Rockies" 1945 (Potter); "Return of the Durango Kid" 1945; "Rough Ridin' Justice" 1945 (Gray); "Rustlers of the Badlands" 1945; "Song of Old Wyoming" 1945 (Bank Clerk); "Stagecoach Outlaws" 1945 (Sheriff); "Strange from Santa Fe" 1945; "Alias Billy the Kid" 1946; "Border Bandits" 1946 (Doc Bowles); "Drifting Along" 1946 (Lou Woods); "Gentleman from Texas" 1946; "Prairie Badmen" 1946 (Sheriff); "Rustler's Roundup" 1946 (Cal Dixon); "Shadows on the Range" 1946; "Six Gun Man" 1946 (Sheriff Jennings); "Terrors on Horseback" 1946 (Cliff Adams); "Three Troubledoers" 1946-short (Townsman); "Thunder Town" 1946 (Sheriff Matt Warner); "Trigger Fingers" 1946; "Under Arizona Skies" 1946; "Cheyenne Takes Over" 1947 (Sheriff); "The Fighting Vigilantes" 1947 (Frank Jackson); "Flashing Guns" 1947 (Cannon); "Ghost Town Renegades" 1947 (Trent); "Land of the Lawless" 1947; "The Last Round-Up" 1947; "Over the Santa Fe Trail" 1947; "Prairie Express" 1947 (Jarrett); "Prairie Raiders" 1947; "Range Beyond the Blue" 1947 (Sheriff); "Six Gun Serenade" 1947; "Stage to Mesa City" 1947 (Watson); "West of Dodge City" 1947; "The Adventures of Frank and Jesse James" 1948-serial (Sheriff Barton); "Courtin' Trouble" 1948 (Reed); "Cowboy Cavalier" 1948; "Crossed Trails" 1948 (Blake); "The Fighting Ranger" 1948; "The Hawk of Powder River" 1948 (Bill); "Oklahoma Blues" 1948 (Sheriff Oldring); "Range Renegades" 1948; "The Rangers Ride" 1948; "Song of the Drifter" 1948; "Sundown Riders" 1948 (Mr. Fraser); "Tornado Range" 1948 (Pop); "Under California Stars" 1948 (Sheriff); "Bandit King of Texas" 1949 (Tom Samson); "Ghost of Zorro" 1949-serial (Jonathan R. White); "Gun Runner" 1949 (Sheriff Harris); "Haunted Trails" 1949 (Foreman Lou); "Hidden Danger" 1949 (Russell); "Jeep-Herders" 1949; "The Last Bandit" 1949; "Law of the West" 1949 (Lane); "Lawless Code" 1949; "Navajo Trail Raiders" 1949 (Larkin); "Range Land" 1949 (Ben Allen); "Ride, Ryder, Ride" 1949; "Stampede" 1949 (Dawson); "Western Renegades" 1949 (Dusty); "Cactus Caravan" 1950-short; "Cowboy and the Prizefighter" 1950; "Desperadoes of the West" 1950-serial (Freight Agent); "Gunmen of Abilene" 1950

(Wells); "Gunslingers" 1950 (Lou Cramer); "Outlaw Gold" 1950; "Six Gun Mesa" 1950; "West of Wyoming" 1950 (Dalton); "Abilene Trail" 1951 (Old Man Dawson); "Along the Great Divide" 1951 (Witness); "The Longhorn" 1951 (Rancher); "Montana Desperado" 1951 (Sheriff); "Silver Canyon" 1951 (Dr. Seddon); "Stage to Blue River" 1951 (Clark); "Night Raiders" 1952 (Davis); "Night Stage to Galveston" 1952 (Old Ranger); "Cow Country" 1953 (Skeeter). ¶TV: *The Lone Ranger*—"The Man with Two Faces" 2-23-50, "Billie the Great" 3-30-50, "Death Trap" 4-20-50, "Spanish Gold" 6-1-50, "Eye for an Eye" 6-29-50, "Outlaw's Revenge" 10-5-50, "Desperado at Large" 10-2-52; *The Cisco Kid*—"Newspaper Crusade" 5-5-51, "Freight Line Feud" 6-2-51, "Performance Bond" 6-30-51, "Jewelry Store Fence" 8-11-51, "Water Toll" 9-22-51, "Chinese Gold" 10-18-52, "Sky Sign" 12-6-52, "Marriage by Mail" 1-3-53, "Man with the Reputation" 3-27-54; *The Roy Rogers Show*—"Jailbreak" 12-30-51; *The Gene Autry Show*—"The Western Way" 2-1-52, "Hot Lead and Old Lace" 2-15-52 (Pete Munroe); *The Range Rider*—"Outlaw Masquerade" 12-27-52, "The Grance Fleece" 4-4-53; *Death Valley Days*—"Halfway Girl" 11-22-54; *Annie Oakley*—"Annie and the Bicycle Riders" 7-8-56 (Terry King).

Clark, Susan (1940-). Films: "Something for a Lonely Man" TVM-1968 (Mary Duren); "Tell Them Willie Boy Is Here" 1969 (Liz Arnold); "Skin Game" 1971 (Ginger); "Valdez Is Coming" 1971 (Gay Erin); "Showdown" 1973 (Kate Jarvis); "The Apple Dumpling Gang" 1975 (Magnolia Dusty Clydesdale). ¶TV: *The Virginian*—"Melanie" 2-22-67 (Melanie Kohler).

Clark, Trilby. Films: "The Bad Lands" 1925 (Mary Owen); "The Prairie Pirate" 1925 (Teresa Esteban); "Silent Sanderson" 1925 (Judith Benson); "Triple Action" 1925 (Doris Clayton); "Satan Town" 1926 (Sheila Jerome); "The Seventh Bandit" 1926 (Ann Drath); "99 Wounds" 1931 (Carmencita Esteban).

Clark, Wallis (1889-2/14/61). Films: "Forbidden Trail" 1932 (Karger); "My Pal, the King" 1932 (Dr. Lorenz); "Massacre" 1934 (Cochran); "Allegheny Uprising" 1939 (McGlashan); "Tombstone, the Town Too Tough to Die" 1942 (Ed Schieffelin); "San Antonio" 1945 (Tip Brice).

Clarke, Angela (1909-). Films: "Mrs. Mike" 1949 (Sarah Carpenter);

"The Gunfighter" 1950 (Mac's Wife); "The Savage" 1952 (Pehangi). ¶TV: *Bonanza*—"The Jonah" 5-9-65 (Teresa), "It's a Small World" 1-4-70 (Mrs. Marshall); *Gunsmoke*—"Quint Asper Comes Home" 9-29-62 (Topsanah), "The Far Places" 4-6-63 (Carrie Newcomb), "Trip West" 5-2-64 (Mrs. Crabbe); *Death Valley Days*—"The Trouble with Taxes" 4-18-65 (Rosie Winters), "The Firebrand" 4-30-66 (Theresa Pico); *The Virginian*—"The Inchoworm's Got No Wings at All" 2-2-66 (Ma Tait); *Daniel Boone*—"The Allegiances" 9-22-66 (Wanona); *Dundee and the Culhane*—9-13-67 (Maria); *The High Chaparral*—"A Joyful Noise" 3-24-68 (Sister Luke); *Alias Smith and Jones*—"Stagecoach Seven" 3-11-71.

Clarke, Gage (1900-10/23/64). Films: "Fury at Showdown" 1957 (Chad Deasey); "Valerie" 1957 (Lawyer Griggs). ¶TV: *Gunsmoke*—"Cow Doctor" 9-8-56 (Hinkle), "Brush at Elkador" 9-15-56 (Hinkle), "Sins of the Father" 1-19-57 (Dobie), "Chester's Murder" 3-30-57 (Jim Dobie), "Kitty Lost" 12-21-57 (Dobie), "Belle's Bck" 5-14-60 (Dobie), "The Worm" 10-29-60 (Judge), "Potshot" 3-11-61 (Botkin), "All That" 10-28-61, "Reprisal" 3-10-62, "The Dealer" 4-14-62 (Johnny Cole), "The Dreamers" 4-28-62; *Maverick*—"A Rage for Vengeance" 1-12-58 (Bradshaw), "GunShy" 1-11-59 (Kenneth P. Badger), "Cruise of the Cynthia B" 1-10-60 (Montgomery Teague), "Greenbacks Unlimited" 3-13-60 (Foursquare Foley), "Maverick at Law" 2-26-61 (Myron Emerson), "Dade City Dodge" 9-18-61 (Harper), "One of Our Trains Is Missing" 4-22-62 (Montague Sprague); *Have Gun Will Travel*—"The Prize Fight Story" 4-5-58 (Jack Webber); *Bronco*—"Game at the Beacon Club" 9-22-59 (Blythe); *The Tall Man*—"Quarantine" 3-17-62 (Bob Kelso); *Laramie*—"The Fatal Step" 10-24-61 (Tad Kimball), "The Confederate Express" 1-30-62 (Firth), "Naked Steel" 1-1-63 (Jenks); *Destry*—"The Nicest Girl in Gomorrah" 3-13-64 (Minister); *Hondo*—Regular 1967 (Captain Richards).

Clarke, Gary (1936-). TV: *Sky King*—"Rodeo Decathalon" 4-27-52 (Stoney Harrison); *Tales of Wells Fargo*—"Death Raffle" 10-21-61 (Dave Hewitt), "Don't Wake a Tiger" 5-12-62 (Davie Sawyer); *Wagon Train*—"The Lonnie Fallon Story" 2-7-62 (Lonnie Fallon); *The Virginian*—Regular 1962-64 (Steve); *Young Riders*—"Old Scores" 2-16-91 (P.J. Curtis), "Between Rock Creek and a Hard Place" 10-25-91 (Colonel Sawyer).

Clarke, John. Films: "Gun Street" 1961 (Sam Freed); "The Tall Women" 1966-Austria/Ital./Span. (Col. Howard); "Shalako" 1968-Brit./Fr. (Hockett); "The Desperados" 1969 (Bandit); "Cannon for Cordoba" 1970 (Major Wall). ¶TV: *Gunsmoke*—"Brother Whelp" 11-7-59 (Tom), "Panacea Sykes" 4-13-63 (Young Man); *The Law of the Plainsman*—"Jeb's Daughter" 4-14-60; *Death Valley Days*—"The Great Lounsberry Scoop" 7-5-60, "After the O.K. Corral" 5-2-64 (Virgil Earp), "Raid on the San Francisco Mint" 5-23-65 (Dory), "The Fastest Nun in the West" 4-9-66 (Fred Gilmer), "Lottie's Legacy" 11-23-68.

Clarke, Lilly. Films: "Tongues of Flame" 1918 (Nellie Wynn).

Clarke, Lydia (1923-). Films: "Will Penny" 1968 (Mrs. Fraker).

Clarke, Mae (1916-4/29/92). Films: "Wild Brian Kent" 1936 (Betty Prentice); "Outlaws of the Orient" 1937 (Joan Manning); "Gun Runner" 1949 (Kate); "Annie Get Your Gun" 1950 (Mrs. Adams); "Callaway Went Thataway" 1951 (Mother); "Horizons West" 1952 (Mrs. Tarleton); "Wichita" 1955 (Mrs. McCoy); "The Desperados Are in Town" 1956 (Jane Kesh); "Mohawk" 1956 (Minikah); "A Big Hand for the Little Lady" 1966 (Mrs. Craig). ¶TV: *Broken Arrow*—"Attack on Fort Grant" 5-21-57 (Louise); *The Texan*—"Desert Passage" 12-1-58 (Ruth Clifford); *Wyatt Earp*—"Bat Jumps the Reservation" 2-10-59 (Sally Roweday); *F Troop*—"A Gift from the Chief" 11-23-65 (Woman).

Clarke, Paul. TV: *Maverick*—The Ghost Soldiers" 11-8-59 (Chief Running Horse); *The Rebel*—"The Crime" 2-7-60 (Solado).

Clarke, Redfield (-10/23/28). Films: "Pardners" 1917.

Clarke, Robert. Films: "Wanderer of the Wasteland" 1945 (Jay Collinshaw); "Sunset Pass" 1946 (Ash); "Code of the West" 1947 (Harry); "Thunder Mountain" 1947 (Lee Jorth); "Under the Tonto Rim" 1947 (Hooker); "Return of the Badmen" 1948 (Dave); "Riders of the Range" 1950 (Harry); "Pistol Harvest" 1951 (Jack); "Captain John Smith and Pocahontas" 1953 (Rolfe); "Outlaw Queen" 1957. ¶TV: *The Cisco Kid*—"Cisco Meets the Gorilla" 12-13-52, "The Powder Trail" 2-14-53; *Wild Bill Hickok*—"Sheriff of Buckeye" 6-30-53; *Wagon Train*—"The Clara Duncan Story" 4-22-59 (Claude Soriano); *Cheyenne*—"Savage Breed" 12-19-60 (Phil Kenton).

Clarke, Wescott B. (1886-1/26/59). Films: "North of the Rio Grande" 1922 (Clendenning).

Clarkson, Patricia. Films: "Four Eyes and Six-Guns" TVM-1992 (Lucy Laughton).

Clary, Charles (1873-3/24/31). Films: "Dad's Girls" 1911; "The Rose of Old St. Augustine" 1911; "The Totem Mark" 1911; "Wheels of Justice" 1911; "The Law of the North" 1912; "Sons of the Northwoods" 1912; "The Fifty Man" 1914; "Big Jim's Heart" 1915; "Tennessee's Pardner" 1916 (Romaine); "True Blue" 1918 (Gilbert Brockhurst); "Last of the Duanes" 1919 (Cheseldine); "The Lone Star Ranger" 1919 (Cyrus Longstreth/Cheseldine); "Sunset Jones" 1921 (Sunset Jones); "Two Kinds of Women" 1922 (Bayne Trevor); "Satan Town" 1926 (John Jerome); "Land of the Lawless" 1927 (Steve Dorman); "The Big Hop" 1928 (June's Father); "Lucky Larkin" 1930 (Colonel Lee).

Clary, Robert (1926-). TV: The High Chaparral—"The Last Hundred Miles" 1-24-69 (Lucien Charot).

Clauser, Al (and the Oklahoma Outlaws). Films: "Rootin' Tootin' Rhythm" 1937.

Clauson, Bill. Films: "The Wistful Widow of Wagon Gap" 1947 (Matt Hawkins).

Clavell, Aurora. Films: "Major Dundee" 1965 (Melinche); "The Wild Bunch" 1969 (Aurora); "Soldier Blue" 1970 (Indian Woman); "The Wrath of God" 1972 (Senora Moreno); "Pat Garrett and Billy the Kid" 1973 (Ida Garrett).

Clavering, Eric (1901-). Films: "Undercover Men" 1935. ¶TV: Hudson's Bay—"Batiste LeGrande" 3-8-58 (Sequoia), "Warrant's Depot" 3-29-58 (Fly Fly), "Fort Caribou" 4-19-58 (Kimbrough).

Claxton, William F. Films: "The Kill-Joy" 1917 (Sure Shot Mike).

Clay, Juanin. Films: "The Legend of the Lone Ranger" 1981 (Amy Striker). ¶TV: Father Murphy—"False Blesing" 2-9-82.

Clayton, Arthur. Films: "Outlaws of Red River" 1927 (Sam Hardwick).

Clayton, Edward. Films: "The Call of the Canyon" 1923 (Tenney Jones); "The Judgement Book" 1935.

Clayton, Ethel (1884-6/11/66). Films: "The Great Divide" 1915 (Ruth Jordan); "The Bar C Mystery" 1926-serial (Mrs. Lane); "Secrets" 1933 (Audrey Carlton); "Wells Fargo" 1937; "Geronimo" 1940.

Clayton, Gilbert (1860-3/1/50). Films: "Mark of Zorro" 1920; "Across the Divide" 1921 (Newton).

Clayton, Jan (1918-8/28/83). Films: "The Showdown" 1940 (Sue Willard); "Six Gun Gold" 1941 (Penny Blanchard); "The Wolf Hunters" 1949 (Greta). ¶TV: The Deputy—"Lady with a Mission" 3-5-60 (Agatha Stone); Tales of Wells Fargo—"The Bride and the Bandit" 12-12-60 (Ellen Stevens); Wagon Train—"The Prairie Story" 2-1-61 (Charity Kirby), "The Jed Whitmore Story" 1-13-64 (Jean Lewis), "Thye Isaiah Quickfox Story" 1-31-65; The Tall Man—"St. Louis Woman" 1-20-62 (Janet Harper); Gunsmoke—"Bently" 4-11-64 (Clara Wright), "Gilt Guilt" 4-24-65 (Mary Rice); Death Valley Days—"One Fast Injun" 3-4-67 (Margaret); Nakia—"The Sand Trap" 10-5-74 (Rudy).

Clayton, Jane. Films: "In Old Mexico" 1938 (Anita Gonzales); "Sunset Trail" 1938 (Dorrie Marsh); "The Llano Kid" 1939 (Lupita).

Clayton, Marguerite (1894-12/20/68). Films: "A Mexican's Gratitude" 1909; "The Ranchmen's Feud" 1910; "The Sheriff's Sacrifice" 1910 (Wilma Allerton); "The Sheriff" 1911; "Broncho Billy's Love Affair" 1912; "Belle of the Siskiyou" 1913; "Bonnie of the Hills" 1913; "Borrowed Identity" 1913; "Broncho Billy's Conscience" 1913; "Broncho Billy's Oath" 1913; "Broncho Billy's Squareness" 1913; "A Cowboy Samaritan" 1913; "The Doctor's Duty" 1913; "The Greed for Gold" 1913; "The Kid Sheriff" 1913; "Love and the Law" 1913; "The Struggle" 1913; "Three Gamblers" 1913; "Why Broncho Billy Left Bear County" 1913; "Broncho Billy a Friend in Need" 1914; "Broncho Billy and the Greaser" 1914; "Broncho Billy and the Settler's Daughter" 1914; "Broncho Billy and the Sheriff" 1914; "Broncho Billy's Favorite" 1914; "Broncho Billy Puts One Over" 1914; "Broncho Billy's Decision" 1914; "Broncho Billy's Leap" 1914; "The Hills of Peace" 1914; "The Warning" 1914; "Andy of the Royal Mounted" 1915; "The Bachelor's Baby" 1915; "The Bachelor's Burglar" 1915; "Broncho Billy and the Claim Jumpers" 1915; "Broncho Billy and the Land Grabber" 1915; "Broncho Billy and the Lumber King" 1915; "Broncho Billy and the Posse" 1915; "Broncho Billy Begins Life Anew" 1915; "Broncho Billy Evens Matters" 1915; "Broncho Billy Misled" 1915; "Broncho Billy Sheepman" 1915; "Broncho Billy Steps in" 1915; "Broncho Billy Well Repaid" 1915; "Broncho Billy's Cowardly Brother" 1915; "Broncho Billy's Marriage" 1915; "Broncho Billy's Parents" 1915; "Broncho Billy's Protege" 1915; "Broncho Billy's Surrender" 1915; "Broncho Billy's Teachings" 1915; "Broncho Billy's Word of Honor" 1915; "A Christmas Revenge" 1915; "The Convict's Threat" 1915; "The Face at the Curtain" 1915; "Her Return" 1915; "His Regeneration" 1915; "His Wife's Secret" 1915; "Ingomar of the Hills" 1915; "The Little Prospector" 1915; "The Other Girl" 1915; "The Revenue Agent" 1915; "An Unexpected Romance" 1915; "Canyon of the Fools" 1923 (May); "Desert Driven" 1923 (Mary); "Men in the Raw" 1923 (Eunice Hollis); "Circus Cowboy" 1924 (Norma Wallace); "Flashing Spurs" 1924 (Ruth Holden/Rema Holden); "Tiger Thompson" 1924 (Ethel Brannon); "Ridin' Through" 1925; "The Power of the Weak" 1926; "Sky High Coral" 1926 (Shasta Hayden).

Clayworth, June. TV: Wagon Train—"The Tobias Jones Story" 10-22-58 (Martha Folson).

Cleary, Leo (1895-4/11/55). Films: "Bells of Coronado" 1950 (Dr. Frank Harding); "Desert of Lost Men" 1951 (Dr. Stephens).

Cleaves, Robert (1928-). Films: "Flap" 1970 (Gus Kirk).

Cleese, John (1939-). Films: "Silverado" 1985 (Sheriff Langston); "An American Tail: Fievel Goes West" 1991 (voice of Cat R. Waul).

Cleethorpe, George. Films: "The Son of a Gun" 1919.

Clegg, Cy. Films: "The Painted Desert" 1931; "Rainbow Trail" 1932 (Cowboy).

Clem, Jimmy. Films: "Winterhawk" 1975 (Littlesmith); "The Winds of Autumn" 1976; "Grayeagle" 1977 (Abe Stoud).

Clemens, Zeke. Films: "Code of the Rangers" 1938 (the Dixie Yodeler).

Clemenson, Christian. Films: "Independence" TVM-1987 (Isaiah Creed). ¶TV: The Adventures of Brisco County, Jr.—Regular 1993-94 (Socrates Poole).

Clement, Clay (1888-10/20/56). Films: "Allegheny Uprising" 1939 (John Smith).

Clement, Dora. Films: "Under Western Stars" 1938 (Mrs. Marlowe).

Clemento, Steve (Steve Clemente) (1885-5/7/50). Films: "The Secret Man" 1917 (Pedro); "The

Scarlet Drop" 1918 (Buck); "The Arizona Catclaw" 1919 (Zapatti); "Lightning Bryce" 1919-serial; "The Girl Who Dared" 1920 (Pedro Ramez); "Cyclone Bliss" 1921 (Pedro); "The Double O" 1921 (Cholo Pete); "Outlawed" 1921 (Frank Kayner); "Sure Fire" 1921 (Gomez); "Two-Fisted Jefferson" 1922; "The Forbidden Trail" 1923 (Mose); "Crashin' Thru" 1924 (Pedro); "Fast and Fearless" 1924 (Gonzalez); "The Rainbow Trail" 1925 (Nas To Bega); "Chip of the Flying U" 1926 (Indian); "Davy Crockett at the Fall of the Alamo" 1926 (Mose); "Riding Romance" 1926; "Lightning Warrior" 1931-serial; "Guns for Hire" 1932; "Clancy of the Mounted" 1933-serial; "King of the Arena" 1933; "The Fighting Ranger" 1934; "Fighting Through" 1934 (Steve); "Five Bad Men" 1935 (Rodriguez); "Vigilantes Are Coming" 1936-serial (Pedro); "White Fang" 1936 (Indian); "Hills of Old Wyoming" 1937 (Lone Eagle); "It Happened Out West" 1937 (Pedro); "Stagecoach" 1939; "Valley of the Sun" 1942 (Knife Thrower).

Clements, Curly (and His Rodeo Rangers). Films: "Six-Gun Law" 1948.

Clements, Dudley (1889-11/4/47). Films: "The Outcasts of Poker Flat" 1937 (Wilkes).

Clements, Marjorie. Films: "Dead or Alive" 1944; "The Old Texas Trail" 1944 (Mary).

Clements, Roy (1877-7/15/48). Films: "The Naming of the Rawhide Queen" 1913; "Broncho Billy's Teachings" 1915; "The Devil Horse" 1926 (Major Morrow).

Clements, Stanley (1926-10/16/81). Films: "Fort Yuma" 1955; "Last of the Desperadoes" 1955 (Bert); "Robbers' Roost" 1955 (Chuck); "Hot Lead and Cold Feet" 1978. ¶TV: *The Lone Ranger*—"Ex-Marshal" 9-16-54; *Death Valley Days*—"Reno" 10-10-55; *Fury*—"Fury Runs to Win" 3-10-56 (Billy Drew); *The Adventures of Rin Tin Tin*—"Rin Tin Tin and the Rainmaker" 3-30-56 (Jock); *Tales of the Texas Rangers*—"Quarter Horse" 10-6-57 (Roby Wade); *Broken Arrow*—"The Outlaw" 6-10-58 (Mingo); *U.S. Marshal*—"The Fence" 11-29-58; *Tales of Wells Fargo*—"Showdown Trail" 1-5-59 (Ed Dooley); *Wyatt Earp*—"The Nugget and the Epitaph" 10-6-59, "Terror in the Desert" 1-24-61 (Dugan); *Rawhide*—"Incident at Red River Station" 1-15-60 (Lon Paris), "Incident at Rojo Canyon" 9-30-60 (Sergeant Willis); *Gunsmoke*—"The Tragedian" 1-23-60

(Brad), "The Mark of Cain" 2-3-69 (McInnery), "The Gun" 11-19-70 (Ed Jacobi), "Arizona Midnight" 1-1-73 (Red); *Wanted—Dead or Alive*—"The Long Search" 3-15-61; *Gunslinger*—"The Recruit" 3-23-61 (Corporal Sebastian); *Wagon Train*—"The Myra Marshall Story" 10-21-63; *Daniel Boone*—"Run a Crooked Mile" 10-20-66 (Timbo); *Iron Horse*—"The Golden Web" 3-27-67 (Harris); *Cimarron Strip*—"The Last Wolf" 12-14-67 (the Kiowa Kid).

Clennon, David. Films: "Tecumseh: The Last Warrior" TVM-1995 (William Henry Harrison).

Clerk, Clive. TV: *The Virginian*—"One Spring Like Long Ago" 3-2-66 (Tonka); *The High Chaparral*—"The Stallion" 9-20-68 (Chatto).

Cleveland, George (1883-7/15/57). Films: "Blue Steel" 1934 (Hank); "The Man from Utah" 1934 (Sheriff); "The Star Packer" 1934 (Old Jake, the Cook); "North of Nome" 1936; "Phantom Patrol" 1936 (Insp. McCloud); "The Plainsman" 1936 (Van Ellyn's Assistant); "Rio Grande Romance" 1936 (Sheriff Williams); "Ghost Town Riders" 1938 (Judge Stillwell); "The Lone Ranger" 1938-serial (George Blanchard); "Outlaws of Sonora" 1938; "Rose of the Rio Grande" 1938 (Pedro); "Home on the Prairie" 1939 (Jim Wheeler); "Overland Mail" 1939 (Porter); "The Phantom Stage" 1939 (Grizzly); "Wolf Call" 1939 (Dr. MacTavish); "Blazing Six Shooters" 1940 (Mark Rawlins); "Konga, the Wild Stallion" 1940 (Tabor); "One Man's Law" 1940 (Judge Wingate); "Pioneers of the West" 1940 (Dr. Bailey); "Queen of the Yukon" 1940 (Grub); "West of Abilene" 1940 (Bill Burnside); "Nevada City" 1941; "Sunset in Wyoming" 1941; "Wide Open Town" 1941; "Klondike Kate" 1942 (Judge Crossit); "The Spoilers" 1942 (Banty); "Valley of the Sun" 1942 (Bill Yard); "Man from Music Mountain" 1943 (Sheriff Joe Darcey); "The Woman of the Town" 1943 (Judge Blackburn); "Alaska" 1944; "The Yellow Rose of Tesas" 1944 (Capt. Joe); "Dakota" 1945 (Mr. Plummer); "Senorita from the West" 1945; "Wild Beauty" 1946 (Barney); "The Wistful Widow of Wagon Gap" 1947 (Judge Benbow); "Albuquerque" 1948 (John Armin); "Fury at Furnace Creek" 1948 (Judge); "The Plunderers" 1948 (Sam Borden); "Home in San Antone" 1949; "Rimfire" 1949 (Judge Gardner); "Trigger, Jr." 1950 (Col. Harkrider); "Fort Defiance" 1951 (Uncle Charlie Tallon); "Carson

City" 1952 (Henry Dodson); "Cripple Creek" 1952 (Hardrock Hanson); "Flaming Feather" 1952 (Doc Fallon); "San Antone" 1953 (Col. Allerby); "The Outlaw's Daughter" 1954 (Lem); "Rails into Laramie" 1954; "Untamed Heiress" 1954 (Andrew "Cactus" Clayton). ¶TV: *Wild Bill Hickok*—"Grandpa and Genie" 5-20-52; *Maverick*—"Bolt from the Blue" 11-27-60.

Clexx, Harvey. TV: *Bat Masterson*—"Double Trouble in Trinidad" 1-7-59 (Hotel Clerk), "The Last of the Night Raidrs" 11-24-60 (Stableman); *The Deputy*—"The World Against Me" 11-26-60 (Amos).

Cliff, John (1918-). Films: "Beyond the Purple Hills" 1950 (Dave Miller); "Best of the Badmen" 1951 (John Younger); "Law of the Badlands" 1951 (Madigan); "Back to God's Country" 1953 (Joe); "Devil's Canyon" 1953 (Bud Gorman); "Jesse James Versus the Daltons" 1954 (Grat Dalton); "The Law vs. Billy the Kid" 1954 (Carl Trumble); "River of No Return" 1954; "The Siege at Red River" 1954 (Sgt. Jenkins); "The Man from Bitter Ridge" 1955 (Wolf Landers); "Gunsmoke in Tucson" 1958 (Cass); "The Legend of Tom Dooley" 1959 (Lieutenant); "Oklahoma Territory" 1960 (Larkin). ¶TV: *The Lone Ranger*—"Pardon for Curley" 6-22-50, "The Whimsical Bandit" 8-31-50, "Two Gold Lockets" 2-15-51, "Triple Cross" 5-21-53, "Hot Spell in Panamint" 11-22-56; *My Friend Flicka*—"Cavalry Horse" 10-28-55; *The Adventures of Rin Tin Tin*—"The Burial Ground" 12-30-55 (Chuck Davis), "The Hunted" 12-6-57; *Frontier*—"Mother of the Brave" 1-15-56 (John Horn); *Fury*—"Stolen Fury" 1-28-56 (Slim); *20th Century Fox Hour*—"Gun in His Hand" 4-4-56 (Jackson); *Jim Bowie*—"Bayou Tontine" 2-15-57 (Hamil); *Wyatt Earp*—"The Nice Ones Always Die First" 4-2-57 (Jack Wagner), "The Underdog" 4-22-58 (Dick Jackson); *Cheyenne*—"Incident at Indian Springs" 9-24-57 (Ed Curran), "The Brahma Bull" 12-11-61 (Walt Hawker); *Maverick*—"Ghost Riders" 10-13-57 (Deputy), "The Day They Hanged Bret Maverick" 9-21-58 (Cliff Sharpe), "The Thirty-Ninth Star" 11-16-58 (1st Thug), "Two Beggars on Horseback" 1-18-59 (Sundown), "Flood's Folly" 2-19-61 (Elkins); *Colt .45*—"Final Payment" 11-22-57 (Cade Bluestone), "Blood Money" 1-17-58 (Roper); *Trackdown*—"The Toll Road" 1-31-58 (Sheriff); *Broken Arrow*—"Backlash" 5-27-58 (Zena); *Decision*—"The Tall Man" 7-27-58 (Hinshaw); *Wanted—*

Dead or Alive—"The Martin Poster" 9-6-58, "Eight Cent Record" 12-20-58 (Sheriff Howard Klate), "Drop to Drink" 12-27-58 (Dixon), "The Last Retreat" 1-11-61 (Tom Jenks); *The Texan*—"A Tree for Planting" 11-10-58 (Ty Beamer); *Northwest Passage*—"The Ambush" 2-6-59 (Thomas Harper); *Bat Masterson*—"Incident in Leadville" 3-18-59 (Jess Santola); *The Tall Man*—"Larceny and Young Ladies" 11-12-60 (Don); *Lawman*—"The Man from New York" 3-19-61 (Dawson); *Two Faces West*—"The Decision" 4-10-61; *Whispering Smith*—"Stakeout" 5-29-61 (Garrity); *Laramie*—"The Mountain Men" 10-17-61; *Tales of Wells Fargo*—"Trackback" 12-30-61 (Chuck Devers); *Temple Houston*—"The Siege at Thayer's Bluff" 11-7-63 (Joe Joyce); *Laredo*—"Yahoo" 9-30-65; *A Man Called Shenandoah*—"Muted Fifes, Muffled Drums" 2-28-66 (Jim Scully), "Requiem for the Second" 5-2-66 (Jim Scully); *The Rounders*—10-18-66 (Foreman); *Rango*—"Rango the Outlaw" 1-13-67 (Crandal); *Custer*—"Under Fire" 11-15-67 (Charley Miller); *The Guns of Will Sonnett*—"Stopover in a Troubled Town" 2-2-68; *The Virginian*—"Image of an Outlaw" 10-23-68 (Bounty Hunter); *Kung Fu*—"The Soul Is the Warrior" 2-8-73 (1st Townsman).

Cliffe, H. Cooper (1862-5/1/39). Films: "Gold and the Woman" 1916 (Col. Ernest Dent).

Clifford, Frances. Films: "Tombstone, the Town Too Tough to Die" 1942 (Ruth Grant).

Clifford, Gordon. Films: "West of Mojave" 1925; "Queen of Spades" 1925; "Sheep Trail" 1926; "The Wildcat" 1929; "Paradise Canyon" 1935 (Mike).

Clifford, Jack (1880-11/10/56). Films: "Caught" 1931 (Drunk); "Sunrise Trail" 1931 (Kansas); "Gold" 1932; "Local Bad Man" 1932 (Lafe McKee); "South of Sante Fe" 1932; "Tombstone Canyon" 1932 (Sheriff); "Gallant Defender" 1935 (Sheriff); "The Man from Guntown" 1935 (Sheriff); "The Revenge Rider" 1935 (Ludlow); "Drift Fence" 1936 (Rodeo Announcer); "King of the Pecos" 1936 (Ash); "High, Wide and Handsome" 1937 (Wash Miller); "One Man Justice" 1937 (Sheriff Ben Adams); "Wild West Days" 1937-serial; "Cattle Raiders" 1938 (Judge); "Colorado Trail" 1938 (Judge Bennett); "Union Pacific" 1939 (Bartender); "Beyond the Sacramento" 1940 (Sheriff); "Murder on the Yukon" 1940 (Whispering Smith);

"Ragtime Cowboy Joe" 1940 (Hank Clayton); "Sky Bandits" 1940 (Whispering Smith); "When the Daltons Rode" 1940 (Deputy); "Yukon Flight" 1940 (Whispering Smith); "Arizona Cyclone" 1941; "The Bandit Trail" 1941 (Kurt Halliday); "Riders of Death Valley" 1941-serial; "Overland Mail" 1942-serial; "The Old Texas Trail" 1944 (Sheriff); "Trail to Gunsight" 1944 (Bar-6 Cowboy); "Rockin' in the Rockies" 1945 (Sheriff Zeke); "Salome, Where She Danced" 1945 (Messenger); "Senorita from the West" 1945; "Canyon Passage" 1946 (Miner); "Dangers of the Canadian Mounted" 1948-serial (Marshal). ¶TV: *The Lone Ranger*—"Enter the Lone Ranger" 9-15-49 (Jerry), "The Lone Ranger Fights On" 9-22-49 (Jerry), "The Lone Ranger's Triumph" 9-29-49 (Jerry).

Clifford, Ruth. Films: "The Desire of the Moth" 1917 (Stella Vorhis); "The Savage" 1917 (Marie Louise); "Hands Down" 1918 (Hilda Stuyvesant); "Hungry Eyes" 1918 (Mary Jane Appleton); "The Red, Red Heart" 1918 (Rhoda Tuttle); "Hell's Hole" 1923 (Dorothy Owens); "Don Mike" 1927 (Mary Kelsey); "Along the Rio Grande" 1941 (Paula); "Wagonmaster" 1950 (Fleuretty Phyffe); "The Searchers" 1956 (Deranged Woman at Fort); "Two Rode Together" 1961 (Woman). ¶TV: *Fireside Theater*—"Man of the Comstock" 11-3-53 (Mrs. Kinkaid).

Clifford, William (1887-12/23/41). Films: "The Mission Waif" 1911; "A Spanish Love Song" 1911; "The Squatter's Child" 1912; "The Thespian Bandit" 1912; "The Battle of Bull Run" 1913; "The Green Shadow" 1913; "The Law of the Range" 1914; "The Trail Breakers" 1914; "The Vagabond Soldier" 1914; "Custer's Last Scout" 1915; "The Hidden Law" 1916 (John Carlton); "Pay Me!" 1917 (Hal Curtis); "Under Handicap" 1917 (Roger Hapgood); "Beyond the Smoke" 1929.

Clift, Faith. Films: "Captain Apache" 1971-Brit./Span. (Abigail).

Clift, Montgomery (1920-7/23/66). Films: "Red River" 1948 (Matthew Garth); "The Misfits" 1961 (Perce Howland).

Clifton, Dorinda. Films: "The Marauders" 1947 (Susan).

Clifton, George. TV: *The Outcasts*—"The Thin Edge" 2-17-69 (Watson); *Here Come the Brides*—"The Soldier" 10-10-69.

Clifton, Herbert (1884-9/26/47). Films: "Ride, Tenderfoot, Ride" 1940 (Butler).

Cline, Robert E. (1896-11/30/46). Films: "Border Intrigue" 1925 (Bull Harding).

Cline, Rusty. Films: "Rollin' Home to Texas" 1941; "Bad Men of Thunder Gap" 1943 (Cal Shrum's Rhythm Rangers); "Swing, Cowboy, Swing" 1944; "Trouble at Melody Mesa" 1944.

Clisbee, Edward (1878-7/24/36). Films: "The Big Horn Massacre" 1913; "The Pitfall" 1915; "The Secret of Lost Valley" 1917.

Clive, Henry (1883-12/12/60). Films: "Frontier Marshal" 1939 (Gambler).

Clive, Iris. Films: "Lonesome Trail" 1945; "Renegades of the Rio Grande" 1945 (Maria); "Song of the Sierras" 1946; "West of Alamo" 1946 (Jane Morgan).

Cliver, Al (Pier Luigi Conti). Films: "Apache Woman" 1975-Ital. (Tommy).

Cloninger, Ralph (1888-6/17/62). Films: "The Man Who Won" 1923 (Scipio).

Clooney, George. TV: *Hot Prospects*—Pilot 7-31-89 (Ben Braddock).

Clooney, Rosemary (1928-). Films: "Red Garters" 1954 (Calaveras Kate).

Close, Glenn (1947-). Films: "Orphan Train" TVM-1979 (Jessica).

Close, John (-12/18/64). Films: "Fangs of the Arctic" 1953; "The Storm Rider" 1957 (Forrest). ¶TV: *The Lone Ranger*—"Special Edition" 9-25-52; *The Gene Autry Show*—"The Portrait of White Cloud" 10-15-55, "Go West, Young Lady" 11-19-55; *Wyatt Earp*—"Justice" 12-25-56 (Miller), "The Truth About Rawhide Geraghty" 2-17-59 (Denman); *The Adventures of Rin Tin Tin*—"O'Hara's Gold" 3-1-57; *Sergeant Preston of the Yukon*—"Mark of Crime" 7-10-58 (Dobbs); *Tombstone Territory*—"The Black Marshal from Deadwood" 9-3-58 (Kenley); *Bat Masterson*—"Cheyenne Club" 12-17-58 (Homesteader), "Dead Man's Claim" 5-4-61 (Jenkins); *Gunsmoke*—"The Coward" 3-7-59 (Pete), "Moo Moo Raid" 2-13-60 (Joe), "The Peace Officer" 10-15-60 (Lighter); *Hotel De Paree*—"Sundance and the Kid from Nowhere" 1-15-60 (Simpson); *Have Gun Will Travel*—"The Fatalist" 9-10-60; *Bonanza*—"Elizabeth, My Love" 5-27-61 (Bell); *Rawhide*—"A Woman's Place" 3-30-62.

Clugston, Robert. Films: "The Siren" 1917 (Burt Hall).

Clute, Chester (1891-4/5/56).

Films: "Dodge City" 1939 (Coggins); "The Spoilers" 1942 (Montrose); "Valley of the Sun" 1942 (Secretary); "The Desperadoes" 1943 (Rollo); "Canyon Passage" 1946 (Proprietor); "Singing Spurs" 1948; "Square Dance Jubilee" 1949 (Yes-Man); "Colorado Sundown" 1952 (Lawyer Davis). ¶TV: *The Cisco Kid*—"Black Lightning" 10-6-51.

Clute, Sidney (1916-10/2/85). Films: "Sam Whiskey" 1969. ¶TV: *Gunsmoke*—"Young Man with a Gun" 10-20-56 (Spencer); *Wanted—Dead or Alive*—"Shawnee Bill" 10-4-58; *Wagon Train*—"The Myra Marshall Story" 10-21-63, "The Zebedee Titus Story" 4-20-64 (Major Hanley); *Laredo*—"Three's Company" 10-14-65; *Iron Horse*—"Wild Track" 12-16-67 (Keller); *The Big Valley*—"Run of the Savage" 3-11-68; *Daniel Boone*—"The Homecoming" 4-9-70, "Israel and Love" 5-7-70; *The Men from Shiloh*—"Hannah" 12-30-70 (Jenkins); *Alias Smith and Jones*—"The Posse That Wouldn't Quit" 10-14-71 (Prosecutor Clark).

Clutesi, George (-2/27/88). Films: "Nakia" TVM-1974 (Naiche); "The Legend of Walks Far Woman" TVM-1982 (Old Grandfather).

Clyde, Andy (1892-5/18/67). Films: "The Cow-Catcher's Daughter" 1931-short; "Annie Oakley" 1935 (MacIvor); "Yellow Dust" 1936 (Silas "Solitaire" Carter); "The Barrier" 1937 (No Creek Lee); "Bad Lands" 1939 (Cliff); "Cherokee Strip" 1940 (Tex Crawford); "Three Men from Texas" 1940 (California Carlson); "Border Vigilantes" 1941 (California Carlson); "Doomed Caravan" 1941 (California Jack); "In Old Colorado" 1941 (California Carlson); "Outlaws of the Desert" 1941 (California Carlson); "Pirates on Horseback" 1941 (California Carlson); "Riders of the Timberline" 1941 (California Carlson); "Secrets of the Wastelands" 1941 (California Carlson); "Stick to Your Guns" 1941 (California Carlson); "Twilight on the Trail" 1941 (California Carlson); "Wide Open Town" 1941 (California Jack); "Undercover Man" 1942 (California Carlson); "Bar 20" 1943 (California Carlson); "Border Patrol" 1943 (California Carlson); "Colt Comrades" 1943 (California Carlson); "False Colors" 1943 (California Carlson); "Hoppy Serves a Writ" 1943 (California Carlson); "The Leather Burners" 1943 (California Carlson); "Lost Canyon" 1943 (California Carlson); "Riders of the Deadline" 1943 (California Carlson); "Forty Thieves" 1944 (California

Carlson); "Lumberjack" 1944 (California Carlson); "Mystery Man" 1944 (California Carlson); "Texas Masquerade" 1944 (California); "Song of the Prairie" 1945; "The Devil's Playground" 1946 (California Carlson); "Fool's Gold" 1946 (California Carlson); "Plainsman and the Lady" 1946 (Dringo); "That Texas Jamboree" 1946; "Throw a Saddle on a Star" 1946; "Dangerous Venture" 1947 (California Carlson); "Hoppy's Holiday" 1947 (California Carlson); "The Marauders" 1947 (California Carlson); "Unexpected Guest" 1947 (California Carlson); "Borrowed Trouble" 1948 (California Carlson); "The Dead Don't Dream" 1948 (California Carlson); "False Paradise" 1948 (California Carlson); "Silent Conflict" 1948 (California Carlson); "Sinister Journey" 1948 (California Carlson); "Strange Gamble" 1948 (California Carlson); "Sundown Riders" 1948 (Sundown Rider); "Crashing Thru" 1949; "Haunted Trails" 1949 (Trigger Winks); "Range Land" 1949 (Winks); "Riders of the Dusk" 1949 (Winks); "Shadows of the West" 1949 (Winks); "Arizona Territory" 1950 (Luke); "Cherokee Uprising" 1950 (Jake); "Fence Riders" 1950; "Gunslingers" 1950 (Winks); "Outlaws of Texas" 1950 (Hungry); "Silver Raiders" 1950 (Quincy); "Abilene Trail" 1951 (Sagebrush); "Carolina Cannonball" 1955 (Grandpa Canova); "The Road to Denver" 1955 (Whipsaw). ¶TV: *The Adventures of Rin Tin Tin*—"The Star Witness" 12-9-55, "Homer the Great" 4-20-56 (Homer Tubbs), "Along Came Tubbs" 5-24-57 (Homer Tubbs), "Tomahawk Tubbs" 2-7-58 (Homer Tubbs); *Fury*—"Fury Runs to Win" 3-10-56 (Mike McClory), "Black Gold" 2-28-59 (Fred Farnum); *Circus Boy*—"The Fabulous Colonel Jack" 9-30-56 (Colonel Jack), "The Return of Colonel Jack" 2-10-57 (Colonel Jack), "Colonel Jack's Brother" 5-19-57 (Colonel Jack/Jonathan Bixby); *Tales of the Texas Rangers*—"Hardrock's Dilemma" 11-3-57, "Double Reward" 12-15-57; *Jefferson Drum*—"The Keeney Gang" 10-3-58 (Hepburn); *The Texan*—"The Troubled Town" 10-13-58 (Wild Jack Hastings), "Quarantine" 2-8-60, "Buried Treasure" 2-15-60 (Andy Miles), "Captive Crew" 2-22-60 (Andy Miles); *Wagon Train*—"The Jennifer Churchill Story" 10-15-58 (Fred); *Gunsmoke*—"Snakebite" 12-20-58 (Poney Thompson), "Durham Bull" 3-31-62 (Grandpa Henry Squires); *Buckskin*—"A Well of Gold" 3-16-59 (Shore); *Colt .45*—"Queen of Dixie" 10-4-59 (Scatterbrain Gibbs),

"Yellow Terror" 11-15-59 (Captain Gibbs); *The Restless Gun*—"A Very Special Investigation" 6-15-59 (Aldrick Newton); *Man from Blackhawk*—"The Man Who Wanted Everything" 6-3-60 (Perkins); *The Tall Man*—"Larceny and Young Ladies" 11-12-60 (Pa McBean), "McBean Rides Again" 12-10-60 (Pa McBean), "The Reluctant Bridegroom" 2-18-61 (Pa McBean), "Millionaire McBean" 4-15-61 (Pa McBean), "Substitute Sheriff" 1-6-62 (Pa McBean); *Wyatt Earp*—"Billy Buckett, Incorporated" 1-3-61 (Billy Buckett).

Clyde, David (1855-5/17/45). Films: "Rose Marie" 1936 (Doorman); "Union Pacific" 1939 (Irishman); "The Great Man's Lady" 1942 (Bartender).

Clyde, Jeremy (1945-). TV: *Laredo*—"That's Noway, Thataway" 1-20-66 (Dudley Leicester).

Clyde, June (1909-). Films: "Branded Men" 1931 (Dale Winters).

Coates, Franklin B. Films: "Jesse James Under the Black Flag" 1921 (Franklin B. Coates).

Coates, Phyllis (1927-). Films: "Outlaws of Texas" 1950 (Anne); "Canyon Raiders" 1951; "The Longhorn" 1951 (Gail); "Man from Sonora" 1951; "Nevada Badmen" 1951; "Oklahoma Justice" 1951; "So You Want to Be a Cowboy" 1951-short; "Stage to Blue River" 1951 (Joyce); "Canyon Ambush" 1952; "Fargo" 1952; "The Gunman" 1952; "The Maverick" 1952 (Della Watson); "Scorching Fury" 1952; "Wyoming Roundup" 1952 (Terry); "El Paso Stampede" 1953 (Alice Clark); "Marshal of Cedar Rock" 1953 (Martha Clark); "Topeka" 1953 (Marian Harrison); "Gunfighters of the Northwest" 1954-serial (Rita); "Blood Arrow" 1958 (Bess); "Cattle Empire" 1958 (Janice Hamilton). ¶TV: *The Cisco Kid*—"Haven for Heavies" 5-19-51, "Phony Sheriff" 6-16-51, "Uncle Disinherits Niece" 7-14-51; *The Lone Ranger*—"Stage to Estacado" 7-23-53, "The Perfect Crime" 7-30-53, "The Woman in the White Mask" 5-12-55; *Frontier*—"King of the Dakotas" 11-13-55 & 11-20-55; *Gunsmoke*—"Wild West" 2-15-58 (Hattie Kelly), "Homecoming" 5-23-64 (Edna Lowell); *Tales of Wells Fargo*—"Alias Jim Hardie" 3-10-58 (Pat Denton), "Bitter Vengeance" 6-12-61 (Ruby Martin); *Black Saddle*—"Client: Dawes" 1-31-59 (Maggie); *Rawhide*—"Incident of the Judas Trap" 6-5-59 (Nora Sage), "The Little Fishes" 11-24-61 (Elizabeth Gwynn); *Gunslinger*—

"Johnny Sergeant" 5-4-61 (Teresa Perez); *The Virginian*—"Smile of a Dragon" 2-26-64 (Mrs. Marden); *Death Valley Days*—"The Left Hand Is Damned" 11-1-64.

Coats, Tommy (1901-6/6/54). Films: "Tumbling Tumbleweeds" 1935 (Henchman); "Under the Pampas Moon" 1935 (Cesar's Gaucho); "Oh, Susannah!" 1936; "Vigilantes Are Coming" 1936-serial (Rancher); "Dodge City Trail" 1937 (Steve's Gang Member); "Fugitive from Sonora" 1937 (Ed); "Thunder Trail" 1937 (Cowboy); "Cattle Raiders" 1938 (Posse Man); "Overland Stage Raiders" 1938; "The Lone Ranger Rides Again" 1939-serial (Raider #1); "Wyoming Outlaw" 1939; "Geronimo" 1940 (Corporal Coot); "King of the Royal Mounted" 1940-serial (Mike); "The Apache Kid" 1941; "King of the Texas Rangers" 1941-serial (Rancho Heavy #1); "Jesse James, Jr." 1942; "King of the Mounties" 1942-serial (Mike); "Along Came Jones" 1945 (Coach Passenger); "The Desert Horseman" 1946 (Buddy); "Heading West" 1946; "The Phantom Rider" 1946-serial (Tim); "Sioux City Sue" 1946; "Terror Trail" 1946; "Jesse James Rides Again" 1947-serial (Saloon Patron); "Prairie Raiders" 1947; "Son of Zorro" 1947-serial; "Grand Canyon Trail" 1948 (Bannister); "San Antone Ambush" 1949 (Joe); "The James Brothers of Missouri" 1950-serial (Knox/Townsman #3).

Cobb, Edmund F. (1892-8/15/74). Films: "Across the Border" 1914; "Bringing in the Law" 1914; "The Cave on Thunder Cloud" 1915; "The Desert Scorpion" 1920 (the Sheepherder); "Out of the Depths" 1921; "At Devil's Gorge" 1923 (Paul Clayton); "Battling Bates" 1923 (Fred Porter); "Face to Face" 1923; "The Law Rustlers" 1923 (Harry Hartley); "The Miracle Baby" 1923 (Jim Starke); "No Tenderfoot" 1923; "Playing It Wild" 1923 (Chris Gideon); "Riders of the Range" 1923 (Martin Lethbridge); "The Sting of the Scorpion" 1923; "Between Fires" 1924; "Blasted Hopes" 1924 (Nathan Wagner); "Border Raid" 1924; "Days of '49" 1924-serial (Cal Coleman); "Cupid's Rustler" 1924 (Jim); "Midnight Shadows" 1924; "Range Blood" 1924; "A Rodeo Mixup" 1924 (William Saunder); "Western Feuds" 1924 (Ed Jones); "Western Yesterdays" 1924 (Deputy Jim Blake); "The Bashful Whirlwind" 1925; "A Battle of Wits" 1925; "The Burning Trail" 1925 (Tommy Corliss); "A Close Call" 1925; "One Glorious Scrap"

1925; "The Pronto Kid" 1925; "Queen of the Roundup" 1925; "The Raid" 1925; "Range Law" 1925; "The Road from Latigo" 1925; "The Ropin' Venus" 1925; "The Rustlers of Boulder Canyon" 1925; "The Storm King" 1925; "The Top Hand" 1925; "Tricked" 1925; "The Wild West Wallop" 1925; "The Emergency Man" 1926; "Fighting with Buffalo Bill" 1926-serial (Buffalo Bill); "Four Square Steve" 1926; "The Galloping Cowboy" 1926 (Jack Perry); "Hearts of the West" 1926; "Looking for Trouble" 1926 (Phil Curtis); "The Love Deputy" 1926; "Pep of the Lazy J" 1926; "Rustler by Proxy" 1926; "The Rustler's Secret" 1926; "The Saddle Tramp" 1926; "The Scrappin' Kid" 1926 (Cliff Barrowes); "The Show Cowpuncher" 1926; "The Terror" 1926 (Jim Hatley); "The Tin Bronc" 1926; "The Trail of Trickery" 1926; "The Winged Rider" 1926; "The Courage of Collins" 1927; "The Cowboy Chaperone" 1927; "An Exciting Day" 1927; "Fangs of Destiny" 1927 (Jerry Matthews); "Galloping Justice" 1927; "General Custer at the Little Big Horn" 1927 (Captain Page); "Little Big Horn" 1927 (Capt. Page); "The Man Tamer" 1927; "The Menace of the Mounted" 1927; "Pawns and Queens" 1927; "The Red Warning" 1927; "The Roaring Gulch" 1927; "The Silent Partner" 1927; "The Two Fister" 1927; "Wolf's Trail" 1927 (Capt. Tom Grant); "The Boundary Battle" 1928; "Buckskin Days" 1928; "Call of the Heart" 1928 (Jerry Wilson); "The Fightin' Redhead" 1928 (Ton Reynolds); "The Fighting Forester" 1928; "The Four-Footed Ranger" 1928 (Jack Dunne); "Riders of the Woods" 1928; "The Scrappin' Ranger" 1928; "Young Whirlwind" 1928 (Jack); "Beyond the Smoke" 1929; "The Boy and the Bad Man" 1929; "The Claim Jumpers" 1929; "The Danger Line" 1929; "Dangerous Days" 1929; "Dodging Danger" 1929; "In Line of Duty" 1929; "Just in Time" 1929; "Orphan of the Wagaon Trails" 1929; "Perilous Paths" 1929; "A Rider of the Sierras" 1929; "Beyond the Rio Grande" 1930 (Dick); "Breed of the West" 1930 (Sam Hardy); "The Indians Are Coming" 1930-serial (Bill Williams); "Arizona Terror" 1931 (Henchman); "Battling with Buffalo Bill" 1931-serial; "Branded Men" 1931; "Hell's Valley" 1931 (Manuel Valdez); "Law of the Rio Grande" 1931 (the Blanco Kid); "The Sign of the Wolf" 1931-serial (Chief Kuva); "Wild Horse" 1931 (Gil Baker); "Between Fighting Men" 1932; "Cornered" 1932 (Ranch

Hand); "Daring Danger" 1932 (Dusang's Brother); "Dynamite Ranch" 1932; "Heroes of the West" 1932-serial (Bart Eaton); "Human Targets" 1932 (Duke Remsden); "McKenna of the Mounted" 1932; "Rider of Death Valley" 1932 (Citizen); "Riders of the Golden Gulch" 1932 (Bart Smith); "Clancy of the Mounted" 1933-serial (Constable McIntosh); "Come on Tarzan" 1933; "Deadwood Pass" 1933 (Miteaway Thomas); "The Fourth Horseman" 1933 (Slim); "Gordon of Ghost City" 1933-serial (Scotty); "Gun Law" 1933; "Rusty Rides Alone" 1933; "The Law of the Wild" 1934-serial (Jim Luger); "Mystery Mountain" 1934-serial (the Rattler); "The Prescott Kid" 1934 (Buck); "Racketeer Round-Up" 1934; "Rawhide Terror" 1934 (Sheriff); "The Red Rider" 1934-serial (Johnny Snow); "Smoking Guns" 1934; "The Westerner" 1934 (Joe Allen); "Arizona Bad Man" 1935 (Sunny Carnes); "Bulldog Courage" 1935 (Jepson); "Cheyenne Tornado" 1935 (Pete Lang); "Danger Trails" 1935 (Hank); "Gallant Defender" 1935; "Lightning Triggers" 1935 (Blackie); "The Miracle Rider" 1935-serial; "Riding Wild" 1935 (Jones); "The Roaring West" 1935-serial; "Rustlers of Red Dog" 1935-serial (Buck); "Rustlers' Paradise" 1935 (Rance Kimball/El Diablo); "The Singing Vagabond" 1935; "Stormy" 1935 (Brakeman); "Tracy Rides" 1935 (Ned Hampton); "Avenging Waters" 1936; "The Fugitive Sheriff" 1936 (Wally); "Lightning Bill Carson" 1936 (Sam Bates); "The Mysterious Avenger" 1936 (Telegraph Operator); "Ride 'Em Cowboy" 1936; "Sundown Saunders" 1936; "The Traitor" 1936 (Joe); "The California Mail" 1937 (Roy Banton); "Cherokee Strip" 1937 (Link Carter); "Code of the Range" 1937 (Ed Randall); "Empty Holsters" 1937 (Cal Hardin); "Land Beyond the Law" 1937 (Mason); "One Man Justice" 1937 (Tex Wiley); "Outlaws of the Prairie" 1937 (Jed Stevens); "Smoke Tree Range" 1937 (Sandy); "Springtime in the Rockies" 1937 (Sheriff); "Two-Fisted Sheriff" 1937 (Deputy); "Two Gun Law" 1937 (Catlin); "Wild Horse Rodeo" 1937 (Hank); "Zorro Rides Again" 1937-serial (Larkin); "Call of the Rockies" 1938 (Barlow); "Cattle Raiders" 1938 (Burke); "Colorado Trail" 1938 (Cameron); "Gold Is Where You Find It" 1938 (Miner); "The Great Adventures of Wild Bill Hickok" 1938; "I'm from the City" 1938 (Red); "Law of the Plains" 1938 (Slagle); "The Lone Ranger" 1938-serial (Rance); "South of Arizona" 1938 (Dorn); "West of

Cheyenne" 1938 (Dirkin); "West of Santa Fe" 1938 (Barlow); "Blue Montana Skies" 1939 (Brennan); "The Law Comes to Texas" 1939; "The Man from Sundown" 1939 (Roper); "North of the Yukon" 1939 (Cpl. Hawley); "Outpost of the Mounties" 1939 (Burke); "Riders of the Black River" 1939 (Colt Foster); "Spoilers of the Range" 1939 (Kendall); "The Stranger from Texas" 1939 (Carver); "Texas Stampede" 1939 (Hobbs); "The Thundering West" 1939 (Dagger); "Western Caravans" 1939 (Tex); "Zorro's Fighting Legion" 1939-serial (Gonzales); "Blazing Six Shooters" 1940 (Sheriff); "The Dark Command" 1940 (Juror); "Deadwood Dick" 1940-serial; "Melody Ranch" 1940; "One Man's Law" 1940 (Red Mathews); "Pioneers of the Frontier" 1940 (Ed Carter); "Pony Post" 1940 (George Barber); "Prairie Schooners" 1940 (Rusty); "Santa Fe Trail" 1940 (Guard); "Texas Terrors" 1940; "Trail of the Vigilantes" 1940 (Rider); "West of Carson City" 1940 (Sleepy); "Winners of the West" 1940-serial (Maddox); "Across the Sierras" 1941; "Back in the Saddle" 1941 (Williams); "Gauchos of El Dorado" 1941; "Hands Across the Rockies" 1941; "King of Dodge City" 1941; "Man from Montana" 1941 (Dakota); "The Medico of Painted Springs" 1941 (Sheriff); "North from the Lone Star" 1941 (Dusty Daggett); "Prairie Stranger" 1941 (Dr. Westridge); "Riders of Death Valley" 1941-serial; "The Return of Daniel Boone" 1941 (Henderson); "Riders of the Badlands" 1941; "The Son of Davy Crockett" 1941 (Lance); "Texas" 1941 (Blaire); "Tonto Basin Outlaws" 1941 (Stark); "White Eagle" 1941-serial; "Wildcat of Tucson" 1941 (Seth); "Wyoming Wildcat" 1941; "The Cyclone Kid" 1942; "Deep in the Heart of Texas" 1942 (Mathews); "The Devil's Trail" 1942; "Down Rio Grande Way" 1942 (Stoner); "Heart of the Rio Grande" 1942; "The Lone Prairie" 1942; "The Lone Star Vigilantes" 1942 (Charlie Cobb); "Old Chisholm Trail" 1942 (Joe Rankin); "Riding Through Nevada" 1942; "Shut My Big Mouth" 1942 (Stage Agent); "Stardust on the Sage" 1942; "Vengeance of the West" 1942; "Westward Ho" 1942; "California Joe" 1943 (Dave); "Daredevils of the West" 1943-serial (Ed); "Frontier Fury" 1943 (Tracy Meade); "The Ghost Rider" 1943; "Hail to the Rangers" 1943; "The Man from Thunder River" 1943; "Outlaws of Stampede Pass" 1943; "Saddles and Sagebrush" 1943; "Sagebrush Law" 1943; "Silver City Raiders" 1943

(Ringo); "Six Gun Gospel" 1943; "The Stranger from Pecos" 1943 (Burt); "The Texas Kid" 1943 (Scully); "Call of the Rockies" 1944; "Cyclone Prairie Rangers" 1944; "Law Men" 1944 (Slade); "Law of the Valley" 1944; "Marshal of Reno" 1944; "The Old Texas Trail" 1944 (Joe Dardner); "Outlaws of Santa Fe" 1944 (Marshal Billings); "Raiders of Ghost City" 1944-serial; "Raiders of the Border" 1944 (McGee); "Song of the Range" 1944 (Gang Leader); "West of the Rio Grande" 1944; "Bad Men of the Border" 1945; "Blazing the Western Trail" 1945; "The Cherokee Flash" 1945; "Code of the Lawless" 1945 (Nelson); "Frontier Feud" 1945 (Moran); "The Man from Oklahoma" 1945 (Ferguson); "The Navajo Trail" 1945; "Renegades of the Rio Grande" 1945 (Karl Holbrook); "Rough Ridin' Justice" 1945 (Harns); "Salome, Where She Danced" 1945 (Stage Driver); "Santa Fe Saddlemates" 1945; "Sunset in El Dorado" 1945; "Days of Buffalo Bill" 1946; "The El Paso Kid" 1946 (Sheriff Frank Stone); "Galloping Thunder" 1946; "Red River Renegades" 1946; "Renegade Girl" 1946; "Rio Grande Raiders" 1946; "Roaring Rangers" 1946; "Rustler's Roundup" 1946 (Vic Todd); "Santa Fe Uprising" 1946; "The Scarlet Horseman" 1946-serial (Kyle); "Song of Arizona" 1946 (Sheriff); "Stagecoach to Denver" 1946 (Duke); "Sun Valley Cyclone" 1946; "Two-Fisted Ranger" 1946; "Buffalo Bill Rides Again" 1947 (Morgan); "Flashing Guns" 1947 (Sheriff); "Jesse James Rides Again" 1947-serial (Wilkie); "Land of the Lawless" 1947; "Last Frontier Uprising" 1947 (Sheriff Hanlon); "Law of the Canyon" 1947; "The Michigan Kid" 1947 (Joe); "Oregon Trail Scouts" 1947 (Jack); "Riders of the Lone Star" 1947; "Robin Hood of Texas" 1947; "Son of Zorro" 1947-serial (Stockton); "The Vigilante" 1947-serial (Miller); "The Wistful Widow of Wagon Gap" 1947 (Lem); "The Bold Frontiersman" 1948 (Pete); "Carson City Raiders" 1948 (Sheriff); "Fury at Furnace Creek" 1948 (Court Clerk); "River Lady" 1948 (Rider); "The Daring Caballero" 1949 (Marshal Scott); "The Far Frontier" 1949 (Sheriff); "Gun Law Justice" 1949; "Hidden Danger" 1949 (Sheriff); "Lust for Gold" 1949 (Man); "Red Canyon" 1949 (Man); "San Antone Ambush" 1949 (Marshal Kennedy); "Sheriff of Wichita" 1949 (James); "The Wyoming Bandit" 1949 (Deputy Marshal); "The Arizona Cowboy" 1950 (Sheriff Fuller); "Bells of Coro-

nado" 1950 (Rafferty); "Comanche Territory" 1950 (Ed); "Desperadoes of the West" 1950-serial (Bowers); "Frisco Tornado" 1950 (Stage Driver); "The Girl from San Lorenzo" 1950 (Wooly); "Hills of Oklahoma" 1950 (Johnson); "The James Brothers of Missouri" 1950-serial (Sheriff); "Ready to Ride" 1950-short; "The Vanishing Westerner" 1950 (Morton); "Winchester '73" 1950 (Target Watcher); "Montana Desperado" 1951 (Jim Berry); "Blazing Bullets" 1951; "Carson City" 1952; "Canadian Mounties vs. Atomic Invaders" 1953-serial (Mr. Warner); "The Redhead from Wyoming" 1953 (Sprague); "Broken Lance" 1954 (Court Clerk); "Man with the Steel Whip" 1954-serial (Lee); "River of No Return" 1954 (Barber); "Lay That Rifle Down" 1955 (Sheriff Cushing); "The Violent Men" 1955 (Anchor Rider); "Hidden Guns" 1956 (Ben Williams); "The Oklahoma Woman" 1956; "The Bounty Killer" 1965 (Townsman); "Requiem for a Gunfighter" 1965; "Johnny Reno" 1966 (Townsman). ¶TV: *The Lone Ranger*—"A Matter of Courage" 4-26-50, "Million Dollar Wallpaper" 9-14-50, "The Squire" 11-9-50, "The Outcast" 1-18-51, "Stage for Mademoiselle" 3-12-53; *The Cisco Kid*—"Boomerang" 1-20-51; "Chain Lightning" 3-3-51, "Vigilante Story" 10-20-51, "The Census Taker" 6-7-52, "Double Deal" 1-17-53, "Fool's Gold" 5-9-53, "Pancho's Niece" 9-5-53; *Wild Bill Hickok*—"The Boy and the Bandit" 3-25-52; *The Gene Autry Show*—"Outlaw Stage" 7-21-53, "Border Justice" 8-18-53; *Sergeant Preston of the Yukon*—"Crime at Wounded Moose" 1-12-56 (Judd Sparks), "The Coward" 4-12-56 (Editor Hewitt); *Circus Boy*—"Little Vagabond" 6-23-57 (Sheriff Thompson); *Tombstone Territory*—"Postmarked for Death" 2-12-58 (Clem Hawley); *Bat Masterson*—"Mr. Fourpaws" 2-18-60.

Cobb, Jerry. *see* Cobos, German.

Cobb, Julie. TV: *Gunsmoke*—"Lynch Town" 11-19-73 (Minnie Nolen), "The Colonel" 12-16-74 (Anne); *Dirty Sally*—4-12-74 (Melinda); *The Quest*—"Incident at Drucker's Tavern" 1976.

Cobb, Lee J. (Lee Colt) (1911-2/11/76). Films: "North of the Rio Grande" 1937 (Goodwin); "Rustler's Valley" 1937 (Cal Howard); "Buckskin Frontier" 1943 (Jeptha Marr); "The Fighter" 1952 (Durango); "The Tall Texan" 1953 (Capt. Theodore Bess); "The Road to Denver" 1955

(Jim Donovan); "Man of the West" 1958 (Dock Tobin); "How the West Was Won" 1962 (Lou Ramsey); "MacKenna's Gold" 1969 (the Editor); "Macho Callahan" 1970 (Duffy); "Lawman" 1971 (Vincent Bronson); "The Man Who Loved Cat Dancing" 1973 (Lapchance). ¶TV: *Zane Grey Theater*—"Death Watch" 11-9-56 (Capt. Andrew Watling), "Legacy of a Legend" 11-6-58 (Drifter); *The Virginian*—Regular 1962-66 (Judge Henry Garth); *Gunsmoke*—"The Colonel" 12-16-74 (Josiah).

Cobos, German (Jerry Cobb). Films: "Massacre at Fort Grant" 1963-Span. (Captain Jackson); "Secret of Captain O'Hara" 1965-Span. (Captain Richard O'Hara); "Black Tigress" 1967-Ital.; "Blood Calls to Blood" 1968-Ital.; "Wanted" 1968-Ital./Fr.; "Quinta: Fighting Proud" 1969-Ital./Span.; "Reverend Colt" 1970-Ital./Span.

Coburn, Buck. Films: "Gun Smoke" 1936 (Steve Branning).

Coburn, Charles (1852-11/23/45). Films: "Three Faces West" 1940 (Dr. Karl Braun); "Green Grass of Wyoming" 1948 (Beaver).

Coburn, Gladys. Films: "The Primitive Call" 1917 (Betty Malcolm); "Out of the Snows" 1920 (Ruth Hardy).

Coburn, James (1928-). Films: "Face of a Fugitive" 1959 (Purdy); "Ride Lonesome" 1959 (Wid); "The Magnificent Seven" 1960 (Britt); "The Man from Galveston" 1964 (Boyd Palmer); "Major Dundee" 1965 (Samuel Potts); "Waterhole No. 3" 1967 (Lewton Cole); "Duck, You Sucker!" 1971-Ital. (Sean Mallory); "The Honkers" 1972 (Lew Lathrop); "Massacre at Fort Holman" 1972-Ital./Fr./Span./Ger. (Colonel Pembroke); "Pat Garrett and Billy the Kid" 1973 (Pat Garrett); "Bite the Bullet" 1975 (Luke Matthews); "The Last Hard Men" 1976 (Zach Provo); "Draw" CTVM-1984 (Sam Starret); "Young Guns II" 1990 (John Chisum); "Maverick" 1994 (Commodore Duvall); "The Avenging Angel" TVM-1995. ¶TV: *Tales of Wells Fargo*—"Butch Cassidy" 10-13-58 (Idaho), "The Wayfarers" 5-19-62 (Ben Crider); *Wagon Train*—"The Millie Davis Story" 11-26-58 (Ike); *The Rifleman*—"Young Englishman" 12-16-58 (Wrangler), "The High Country" 12-18-61 (Ambrose); *The Restless Gun*—"Take Me Home" 12-29-58 (Tom Quinn), "The Pawn" 4-6-59 (Vestry), "The Way Back" 7-13-59 (Tom Quinn); *Wanted—Dead or*

Alive—"Reunion for Revenge" 1-24-59 (Turner), "The Kovack Affair" 3-28-59 (Jesse Holloway), "The Trial" 9-21-60 (Howard Catlett); *Bronco*—"Payroll of the Dead" 1-27-59 (Adam Coverly), "Shadow of Jesse James" 1-12-60 (Jesse James); *Zane Grey Theater*—"A Thread of Respect" 2-12-59 (Jess Newton), "Desert Flight" 10-13-60 (Doyle); *Trackdown*—"Hard Lines" 3-11-59 (Joker Wells); *Black Saddle*—"Client: Steele" 3-21-59 (Niles); *The Californians*—"One Ton of Peppercorns" 5-12-59 (Anthony Wayne), "Act of Fait" 5-26-59 (Anthony Wayne); *Rough Riders*—"Deadfall" 5-21-59 (Judson); *Bat Masterson*—"The Black Pearls" 7-1-59 (Polk Otis), "Six Feet of Gold" 2-25-60 (Leo Talley); *Johnny Ringo*—"The Arrival" 10-1-59; *Tombstone Territory*—10-16-59 (Gunfighter); *Bonanza*—"The Truckee Strip" 11-21-59 (Pete Jessup), "The Dark Gate" 3-4-61 (Ross Marquett), "The Long Night" 5-6-62 (Trace); *Walt Disney Presents*—"Elfego Baca: Mustang Men, Mustang Maid" 11-20-59 (Jack Carter); *Wyatt Earp*—"The Noble Outlaws" 11-24-59 (Buckskin Frank Leslie), "The Clantons' Family Row" 12-8-59; *Have Gun Will Travel*—"One Came Back" 12-26-59 (Jack Harvey), "The Gladiators" 3-19-60 (Bill Sledge); *The Texan*—"Friend of the Family" 1-4-60 (Cal Gruder); *Wichita Town*—"Afternoon in Town" 2-17-60 (Wally); *The Deputy*—"The Truly Yours" 4-9-60 (Coffer); *Tate*—"Home Town" 6-8-60 (Jory); *Klondike*—Regular 1960-61 (Jeff Durain); *Death Valley Days*—"Pamela's Oxen" 9-28-60; *Lawman*—"The Showdown" 1-10-60 (Blake Carr), "The Catcher" 12-4-60 (Lank Bailey); *Stagecoach West*—"Come Home Again" 1-10-61 (Sam Murdock); *The Tall Man*—"The Best Policy" 1-28-61 (John Miller); *The Outlaws*—"Culley" 2-16-61 (Culley Scott); *Laramie*—"The Mark of the Maneaters" 3-14-61 (Gil Spanner); *Cheyenne*—"Trouble Street" 10-2-61 (Deputy Kell); *Rawhide*—"The Hostage Child" 3-9-62 (Colonel Briscoe); *Stoney Burke*—"The Test" 5-13-63 (Jamison); *Temple Houston*—"The Man from Galveston" 1963 (Boyd Palmer).

Coburn, Margaret. Films: "The Girl-Shy Cowboy" 1928 (Eva Adams).

Coburn, Wallace C. Films: "The Sunset Princess" 1918 (Buck Dawson).

Coby, Fred (1916-9/27/70). Films: "Don Ricardo Returns" 1946; "The Scarlet Horseman" 1946-serial

(Toga); "The Prairie" 1947 (Abner Bush); "The Man from Colorado" 1948 (Veteran); "Horizons West" 1952 (Irate Citizen); "Devil's Canyon" 1953 (Cole Gorman); "Fury at Gunsight Pass" 1956 (Spencer). ¶TV: *The Lone Ranger*—"Triple Cross" 5-21-53, "A Broken Match" 12-2-54; *The Roy Rogers Show*—"The Showdown" 5-22-55 (Stake Morris), "Ranch War" 10-23-55 (Huck Kent); *Fury*—"The Claim Jumpers" 4-5-58 (David); *Wyatt Earp*—"Behan's Double Game" 3-29-60 (Pony Deal); *Laramie*—"The Long Riders" 10-25-60 (Charley Graig), "The Mountain Men" 10-17-61, "The Accusers" 11-14-61, "Beyond Justice" 11-27-62 (Ed Rigby), "The Betrayers" 1-22-63; *Gunsmoke*—"The Search" 9-15-62 (Horn), "Prairie Wolfer" 1-18-64 (Charlie), "Thursday's Child" 3-6-65 (Clint Marston), "Harvest" 3-26-66 (Marty), "The Whispering Tree" 11-12-66 (Station Attendant), "The Moonstone" 12-17-66 (Rankin), "The Lure" 2-25-67 (Driver), "Cattle Barons" 9-18-67 (Tooley), "9:12 to Dodge" 11-11-68 (Mokey), "Lobo" 12-16-68 (Wes Flood), "The Badge" 2-2-70 (Sloan), "The Noonday Devil" 12-7-70 (Doctor); *The Virginian*— "Run Away Home" 4-24-63 (Axel Swenson); *Wagon Train*—"The Sam Spicer Story" 10-28-63 (Kirk); *Cimarron Strip*—"Whitey" 10-19-67 (Ramey), "The Assassin" 1-11-68.

Coby, Michael. *see* Cantafora, Antonio.

Coca, Imogene (1909-). TV: *Ruggles of Red Gap* 2-3-57 (Effie Floud).

Coch, Jr., Edward. Films: "Horizons West" 1952 (Juan); "The Pathfinder" 1952 (Uncas); "Riding Shotgun" 1954; "Riding with Buffalo Bill" 1954-serial (Jose Perez); "Seminole Uprising" 1955 (Marsh); "Blazing the Overland Trail" 1956-serial (Carl); "Perils of the Wilderness" 1956-serial. ¶TV: *Tales of Wells Fargo*—"The Sooners" 3-3-58 (Darby); *The Rebel*—"Don Gringo" 11-20-60 (Padre).

Cochran, Steve (1917-6/15/65). Films: "Dallas" 1950 (Brant Marlow); "Raton Pass" 1951 (Cy Van Cleave); "The Lion and the Horse" 1952 (Ben Kirby); "Back to God's Country" 1953 (Paul Blake); "Shark River" 1953 (Dan Webley); "Quantrill's Raiders" 1958 (Capt. Alan Westcott); "The Deadly Companions" 1961 (Billy). ¶TV: *Zane Grey Theater*—"Debt of Gratitude" 4-18-58 (Marshal Cam Tolby); *The Virginian*—"West" 11-20-62 (Jamie Dobbs);

Stoney Burke—"Death Rides a Pale Horse" 1-14-63 (Mal Torrance); *Death Valley Days*—"The Westside of Heaven" 3-28-64 (Father Patrick Manogue); *Bonanza*—"The Trap" 3-28-65 (Burk Shannon/Booth Shannon).

Cockrell, Gary. TV: *Wagon Train*—"The Hollister John Garrison Story" 2-6-63 (Stevenson Drake).

Codee, Ann (1890-5/18/61). Films: "Under the Pampas Moon" 1935 (Mme. LaMarr); "Hi Gaucho!" 1936 (Dona Vincenta del Campo). ¶TV: *Jim Bowie*—"The Ghost of Jean Battoo" 11-2-56 (Madame Landi).

Cody, Albert (1885-3/30/66). Films: "Two-Gun Betty" 1919 (Mushy).

Cody, Sr., Bill (1891-1/24/48). Films: "Border Justice" 1925 (Joseph Welland); "Cold Nerve" 1925; "Dangerous Odds" 1925; "The Fighting Sheriff" 1925 (Larry O'Donnell); "The Fighting Smile" 1925 (Bud Brant); "Love on the Rio Grande" 1925; "Moccasins" 1925 (Tom Williams); "Riders of Mystery" 1925 (Bob Merriwell); "The Galloping Cowboy" 1926 (Bill Crane); "King of the Saddle" 1926 (Bill); "The Arizona Whirlwind" 1927 (Bill Farley); "Born to Battle" 1927 (Billy Cowan); "Gold from Weepah" 1927 (Bill Carson); "Laddie Be Good" 1928 (Bill Cody); "Under Texas Skies" 1930 (Agent); "Dugan of the Badlands" 1931 (Bill Dugan); "The Montana Kid" 1931 (Bill Denton); "Oklahoma Jim" 1931 (Oklahoma Jim Kirby); "Ghost City" 1932 (Bill Temple); "Land of Wanted Men" 1932 (Silent); "Law of the North" 1932 (Bill Roberts); "Mason of the Mounted" 1932 (Bill Mason); "Texas Pioneers" 1932 (Captain Bill Clyde); "Border Guns" 1934 (Bill Harris); "The Border Menace" 1934 (Bill "the Shadow" Williams); "Frontier Days" 1934 (Bill Maywood/the Pinto Kid); "Cyclone Ranger" 1935 (the Pecos Kid); "Lawless Borders" 1935; "The Reckless Buckaroo" 1935; "The Texas Rambler" 1935 (Tom Manning/the Rambler); "The Vanishing Riders" 1935 (Bill Jones); "Western Racketeers" 1935 (Bill Bowers); "Blazing Justice" 1936 (Ray Healy); "Outlaws of the Range" 1936 (Steve Hopper); "The Fighting Gringo" 1939 (Sheriff Warren); "Stagecoach" 1939 (Cowboy); "Blood on the Moon" 1948.

Cody, Jr., Bill. Films: "Border Guns" 1934; "Frontier Days" 1934 (Bart Wilson); "The Reckless Buckaroo" 1935; "Six Gun Justice" 1935; "The Vanishing Riders" 1935 (Tim); "Outlaws of the Range" 1936 (Jimmy Wilson); "Romance of the Rockies" 1937 (Jimmy Allan); "The Girl of the Golden West" 1938 (Gringo); "Desperate Trails" 1939 (Little Bill); "Destry Rides Again" 1939 (Small Boy); "The Oregon Trail" 1939-serial (Jimmie Clark); "Bad Man from Red Butte" 1940 (Skip Todhunter); "Two-Fisted Rangers" 1940 (Silver); "Raiders of the West" 1942.

Cody, Eric. Films: "Fort Utah" 1967 (Shirt); "Hostile Guns" 1967 (Alfie); "Arizona Bushwhackers" 1968 (Bushwacker).

Cody, Harry (1896-10/22/56). Films: "Mark of the Lash" 1948; "The Vanquished" 1953. ¶TV: *The Cisco Kid*—"The Tumblers" 11-28-53; *Death Valley Days*—"Jimmy Dayton's Treasure" 3-10-54, "Jimmy Dayton's Treasure" 3-24-57; *Tales of the Texas Rangers*—"The Atomic Trail" 11-19-55 (Miles Miller).

Cody, Iron Eyes (1915-). Films: "Fighting Caravans" 1931 (Indian After Firewater); "99 Wounds" 1931 (Running Bear); "Oklahoma Jim" 1931 (War Eagle); "Rainbow Trail" 1932 (Indian); "Rider of Death Valley" 1932; "Texas Pioneers" 1932 (Little Eagle); "Whistlin' Dan" 1932; "Fighting with Kit Carson" 1933-serial; "King of the Arena" 1933; "Custer's Last Stand" 1936-serial; "The Phantom Rider" 1936-serial; "Ride, Ranger, Ride" 1936; "Toll of the Desert" 1936; "Treachery Rides the Range" 1936; "Old Louisiana" 1937; "Prairie Thunder" 1937; "Riders of the Whistling Skull" 1937 (Indian); "Wild West Days" 1937-serial; "Flaming Frontier" 1938-serial; "The Lone Ranger" 1938-serial (White Feather); "Crashing Thru" 1939 (Indian Joe); "The Oregon Trail" 1939-serial; "Overland with Kit Carson" 1939-serial; "Union Pacific" 1939 (Indian Brave); "Kit Carson" 1940 (Indian); "Pony Post" 1940; "Young Bill Hickok" 1940; "Young Buffalo Bill" 1940; "King of the Texas Rangers" 1941-serial (Carlos); "Outlaws of the Cherokee Trail" 1941; "Saddlemates" 1941 (Black Eagle); "King of the Stallions" 1942; "Perils of the Royal Mounted" 1942-serial; "Valley of the Sun" 1942 (Indian); "Black Arrow" 1944-serial; "Plainsman and the Lady" 1946; "Under Nevada Skies" 1946; "Bowery Buckaroos" 1947 (Indian Joe); "The Last Round-Up" 1947; "Unconquered" 1947; "The Gallant Legion" 1948; "Indian Agent" 1948 (Wovoka); "The Paleface" 1948 (Chief Iron Eyes); "The Cowboy and the Indians" 1949; "Massacre River" 1949 (Chief Yellowstone); "Broken Arrow" 1950 (Teese); "California Passage" 1950 (Indian); "Cherokee Uprising" 1950 (Longknife); "North of the Great Divide" 1950; "Fort Defiance" 1951 (Brave Bear); "Red Mountain" 1951 (Indian); "Apache Country" 1952; "Fort Osage" 1952 (Old Indian); "Lost in Alaska" 1952 (Nanook); "Montana Belle" 1952 (Cherokee); "Night Raiders" 1952 (Cherokee); "Son of Paleface" 1952 (Indian Chief); "Sitting Bull" 1954 (Chief Crazy Horse); "White Feather" 1955 (Indian Chief); "Westward Ho the Wagons" 1956 (Many Stars); "The Wild Dakotas" 1956; "Gun for a Coward" 1957 (Chief); "Gun Fever" 1958 (1st Indian Chief); "Heller in Pink Tights" 1960 (Indian); "The Great Sioux Massacre" 1965 (Crazy Horse); "The Fastest Guitar Alive" 1967 (1st Indian); "Something for a Lonely Man" TVM-1968; "The Cockeyed Cowboys of Calico County" 1970 (Crazy Foot); "El Condor" 1970 (Santana); "A Man Called Horse" 1970 (Medicine Man, Son Vow Ritual); "The Quest" TVM-1976 (Old Indian); "Grayeagle" 1977 (Standing Bear). ¶TV: *The Cisco Kid*—"The Gramophone" 9-20-52, "Indian Uprising" 11-8-52; *Wild Bill Hickok*—"Buckshot Comes Home" 11-25-52, "Bold Raven Rodeo" 4-7-53; *Sergeant Preston of the Yukon*—"Totem Treasure" 3-1-56 (Mulak), "Trouble at Hogback" 7-19-56 (White Eagle); *Wyatt Earp*—"Wyatt and the Captain" 1-15-57 (Indian); *Disneyland*—"The Saga of Andy Burnett"—Regular 1957-58 (Mad Wolf); *The Restless Gun*—"Pressing Engagement" 2-24-58 (George Washington Smith); *The Adventures of Rin Tin Tin*—"Miracle of the Mission" 12-12-58 (Long Buffalo), "Pillajohn's Progress" 3-6-59; *Maverick*—"Gun-Shy" 1-11-59 (Indian); *Rawhide*—"Incident of the Thirteenth Man" 10-23-59, "Incident at Ten Trees" 1-2-64 (Medicine Man); *The Tall Man*—"McBean Rides Again" 12-10-60 (Apache); *Zane Grey Theater*—"Blood Red" 1-29-61 (Nemana); *The Rebel*—"The Burying of Sammy Hart" 3-5-61 (Sammy Hart); *The Virginian*—"The Intruders" 3-4-64 (Black Feather); *Branded*—"One Way Out" 4-18-65; *Hondo*—"Hondo and the Singing Wire" 9-22-67 (Chief); *Bonanza*—"The Burning Sky" 1-28-68; *Gunsmoke*—"O'Quillian" 10-28-68 (Indian); *How the West Was Won*—Episode Five 3-12-78 (Medicine Man).

Cody, J.W. Films: "Oklahoma Jim" 1931; "The Lone Ranger" 1938-serial (Running Elk); "Overland with

Kit Carson" 1939-serial; "Wagon Tracks West" 1943; "The Last Round-Up" 1947; "Where the North Begins" 1947; "Broken Arrow" 1950 (Pionsenay); "Bullwhip" 1958 (Indian Chief). ¶TV: *Sergeant Preston of the Yukon*—"Totem Treasure" 3-1-56 (Titchik).

Cody, Kathleen. TV: *Gunsmoke*—"Women for Sale" 9-10-73 & 9-17-73 (Cynthia), "To Ride a Yellow Horse" 3-18-74 (Anna May), "Larkin" 1-20-75 (Melissa Cass); *Dirty Sally*—4-19-74 (Samantha); *Barbary Coast*—"Funny Money" 9-8-75 (Leslie Buddwing).

Cody, Lewis J. (1887-5/31/34). Films: "As the Sun Went Down" 1919 (Faro Bill); "The Valley of Silent Men" 1922 (Cpl. James Kent); "Three Rogues" 1931 (Ace Beaudry).

Cody, William F. "Buffalo Bill" (1846-1/10/17). Films: "The Adventures of Buffalo Bill" 1914.

Coe, Barry (1934-). Films: "Love Me Tender" 1956 (Davis); "The Bravados" 1958 (Tom); "One Foot in Hell" 1960 (Stu Christian); "The Naked Man" 1987-Mex. (Moe). ¶TV: *Bonanza*—"The First Born" 9-23-62 (Clay Stafford).

Coe, David Allan (1939-). Films: "The Last Days of Frank and Jesse James" TVM-1986 (Whiskeyhead Ryan); "Stagecoach" TVM-1986 (Luke Plummer).

Coe, Peter (1918-6/9/93). Films: "Rocky Mountain" 1950 (Pierre Duchesne); "Hellgate" 1952 (Jumper Hall); "Arrowhead" 1953 (Spanish); "Passion" 1954 (Colfre); "Shotgun" 1955 (Apache); "Smoke Signal" 1955 (Ute Prisoner). ¶TV: *The Cisco Kid*—"Romany Caravan" 11-17-51, "Buried Treasure" 12-29-51, "Not Guilty" 12-20-52, "Horseless Carriage" 1-24-53; *The Adventures of Rin Tin Tin*—"Attack on Fort Apache" 4-13-56 (Culebra), "Forward Ho" 9-7-56 (Culebra), "O'Hara Gets Amnesia" 5-17-57 (Stone Cub); *Broken Arrow*—"Black Moment" 10-29-57 (Moreno); *Have Gun Will Travel*—"Show of Force" 11-9-57 (Carlos Valdez), "Heritage of Anger" 6-6-59 (Garcia); *Tales of Wells Fargo*—"A Matter of Honor" 11-3-58 (Eagle Wing); *Wagon Train*—"The Tent City Story" 12-10-58 (White Eagle); *Zane Grey Theater*—"The Last Raid" 2-26-59 (Manuel); *Bonanza*—"The Paiute War" 10-3-59; *Wyatt Earp*—"Wyatt Takes the Primrose Path" 3-28-61; *Daniel Boone*—"My Brother's Keeper" 10-8-64 (the Chieftain), "A Rope for Mingo" 12-2-65 (Cherokee Brave); *The Virginian*—"Men with Guns" 1-12-66 (Adrian).

Coe, Vivian. *see* Austin, Vivian.

Coffer, Jack (1939-2/18/67). Films: "The Way West" 1967 (Cattleman). ¶TV: *Laredo*—"I See By Your Outfit" 9-23-65, "Rendezvous at Arillo" 10-7-65.

Coffey, Clark. Films: "The Santa Fe Trail" 1923-serial; "Cupid's Rustler" 1924 (Sheriff); "Days of '49" 1924-serial; "Western Yesterdays" 1924 (Clarence); "The Man from Nowhere" 1930 (Sheriff Blake).

Coffin, Frederic. Films: "Lonesome Dove" TVM-1989 (Big Zwey); "James A. Michener's Texas" TVM-1995 (Zave).

Coffin, Tristram (1909-3/20/90). Films: "Oklahoma Terror" 1939 (Mason); "Overland Mail" 1939 (Polini); "Arizona Frontier" 1940 (Lt. James); "Cowboy from Sundown" 1940; "Queen of the Yukon" 1940 (Carson); "Rhythm of the Rio Grande" 1940 (Banister); "West of Pinto Basin" 1940 (Harvey); "Arizona Bound" 1941; "Forbidden Trails" 1941 (Nelson); "King of Dodge City" 1941; "Roaring Frontiers" 1941; "Tonto Basin Outlaws" 1941 (Miller); "Bells of Capistrano" 1942 (Jed Johnson); "Cowboy Serenade" 1942; "Dawn on the Great Divide" 1942 (Rand); "The Devil's Trail" 1942; "Prairie Gunsmoke" 1942; "A Tornado in the Saddle" 1942; "The Vigilantes Ride" 1944 (Anse Rankin); "Wyoming Hurricane" 1944; "The Gay Cavalier" 1946; "Gentleman from Texas" 1946; "Rio Grande Raiders" 1946; "Sioux City Sue" 1946; "Under Arizona Skies" 1946; "Under Nevada Skies" 1946 (Dan Adams); "The Fabulous Texan" 1947; "Jesse James Rides Again" 1947-serial (James Clark); "Land of the Lawless" 1947; "Swing the Western Way" 1947; "Trail to San Antone" 1947 (Cal Young); "Valley of Fear" 1947; "Where the North Begins" 1947; "California Firebrand" 1948 (Jim Requa/Jud Babbit); "Desperadoes of Dodge City" 1948 (Ace Durant); "Crashing Thru" 1949; "Desert Vigilante" 1949 (Thomas Hadley); "Lawless Code" 1949; "Range Justice" 1949 (Dutton); "Riders of the Dusk" 1949 (Hall); "The Baron of Arizona" 1950 (McCleary); "Cactus Caravan" 1950-short; "The Old Frontier" 1950 (John Wagner); "Short Grass" 1950 (John Devore); "Buckaroo Sheriff of Texas" 1951 (Jim Tuland); "Northwest Territory" 1951 (Kinkaid); "Rodeo King and the Senorita" 1951 (Jack Foster); "The Kid from Broken Gun" 1952 (Martin Donohugh); "Smoky Canyon" 1952 (Buckley); "Hannah Lee" 1953 (Paul-

son); "Law and Order" 1953 (Parker); "The First Traveling Saleslady" 1956 (Day Hotel Clerk); "The Maverick Queen" 1956 (Card Player); "The Last Stagecoach West" 1957; "Kino, the Padre on Horseback" 1977. ¶TV: *The Lone Ranger*—"Enter the Lone Ranger" 9-15-49 (Dan Reid), "The Lone Ranger Fights On" 9-22-49 (Dan Reid), "The Lone Ranger's Triumph" 9-29-49 (Dan Reid), "Mission Bells" 9-21-50, "The Avenger" 1-10-57; *The Cisco Kid*—"Dog Story" 5-12-51, "The Old Bum" 6-9-51, "Water Rights" 7-7-51, "Hidden Valley Pirates" 10-27-51, "Quarter Horse" 12-8-51, "Not Guilty" 12-20-52, "Horseless Carriage" 1-24-53, "Witness" 12-19-53, "New York's Priest 1-9-54; *Wild Bill Hickok*—"Homer Atchison" 9-11-51, "Outlaw Flats" 10-9-51, "Civilian Clothes Story" 12-18-51, "Indians and the Delegates" 7-8-52, "Boy and the Hound Dog" 10-14-52, "The Outlaw's Portrait" 11-18-52, "Halley's Comet" 2-17-53; *Judge Roy Bean*—"The Judge of Pecos Valley" 9-10-55 (Sam Dillon), "The Horse Thief" 10-1-55 (Doyle, "The Wedding of Old Sam" 10-1-55 (Sam Haskins), "Border Raiders" 7-1-56 (Kenyon), "The Cross-Draw Kid" 7-1-56 (Jim Sabine), "The Refugee" 7-1-56 (Vargas); *Wyatt Earp*—"Trail's End for a Cowboy" 12-6-55 (Foster), "Wyatt and the Captain" 1-15-57; *West Point*—"Dragoon Patrol" 5-10-57; *26 Men*—Regular 1958-59 (Captain Tom Rynning); *Colt .45*—"The Cause" 2-28-60 (Col. Willis Murdock); *Bat Masterson*—"Three Bullets for Bat" 3-24-60 (Marshal Roy Dunning); *The Alaskans*—"Calico" 5-22-60 (Wheaton); *Sugarfoot*—"A Noose for Nora" 10-24-60 (Fenell); *Maverick*—"Kiz" 12-4-60 (Dr. Pittman); *Bronco*—"Yankee Tornado" 3-13-61 (George Mayfield); *Wagon Train*—"The Joe Muharich Story" 4-19-61 (Mr. Whittaker); *Bonanza*—"Mirror of a Man" 3-31-63 (Ralph Austin); *The Legend of Jesse James*—"The Quest" 11-1-65 (Whicher); *Death Valley Days*—"Hugh Glass Meets the Bear" 6-11-66 (Major Henry), "The Hat That Huldah Wore" 6-25-66 (George Bennett), "Sense of Justice" 12-10-66, "The Duke of Tombstone" 1-10-70, "Clum's Constabulary" 4-11-70.

Coffin, Winifred "Winnie" (1911-12/18/86). TV: *Bonanza*—"The Spotlight" 5-16-65 (Mrs. Brown), "The Meredith Smith" 10-31-65 (Widow Smith); *Death Valley Days*—"The Resurrection of Deadwood Dick" 10-22-66 (Bessie Brenner); *The High Chaparral*—"Tornado Frances"

10-11-68 (Woman #1); *Lancer*—"The Lorelei" 1-27-70 (Gus Guthrie).

Coghlan, Frank "Junior" (1916-). Films: "The Last Frontier" 1926 (Buddy); "River's End" 1930 (Mickey); "The Last of the Mohicans" 1932-serial; "Drum Taps" 1933 (Eric Cartwright).

Coghlan, Phyllis (-1980). TV: *Gunsmoke*—"Baker's Dozen" 12-25-67 (Old Lady).

Cogley, Nick (1869-5/20/36). Films: "The Convert of San Clemente" 1911; "On Seperate Paths" 1911; "The End of the Romance" 1912; "The Epidemic in Paradise Gulch" 1912; "The Peacemaker" 1912; "The Sergeant's Boy" 1912; "The Shrinking Rawhide" 1912; "Tenderfoot Bob's Resignation" 1912; "Honest Hutch" 1920 (Hiram Joy); "Hey! Hey! Cowboy" 1927 (Julius Decker); "Crossfire" 1933 (Doc Stiles); "Treason" 1933.

Cohen, Emma (1946-). Films: "The Legend of Frenchie King" 1971-Fr./Ital./Span./Brit. (Sister); "Cut-Throats Nine" 1973-Span./Ital.; "Cipolla Colt" 1975-Ital./Ger.

Cohen, Sammy (1902-5/30/81). Films: "The Phantom of the Range" 1936; "Rip Roarin' Buckaroo" 1936 (Frozen Face Cohen).

Cohoon, Patti. TV: *Here Comes the Brides*—Regular 1969-70 (Molly Pruitt); *Gunsmoke*—"Trafton" 10-25-71 (Maria Farrell), "P.S. Murry Christmas" 12-27-71 (Mary), "The River" 9-11-72 & 9-18-72 (Hanna Kinkaid), "Milligan" 11-6-72 (Wendy Milligan), "The Iron Blood of Courage" 2-18-74 (Ronilou Talley); *Dirty Sally*—1-18-74 (Millie).

Coit, Stephen. Films: "Honky Tonk" TVM-1974. ¶TV: *Maverick*—"The Jeweled Gun" 11-24-57 (George Seevers), "The Saga of Waco Williams" 2-15-59 (Charlie), "Last Wire from Stop Gap" 10-16-60 (Deevers), "A Technical Error" 11-26-61 (Mr. Craft); *Have Gun Will Travel*—"In an Evil Time" 9-13-58 (John Dunham); *Bronco*—"Hero of the Town" 6-2-59 (Tod Biggs); *The Virginian*—"A Small Taste of Justice" 12-20-67; *Bonanza*—"Anatomy of a Lynching" 10-12-69 (Lassen), "A Deck of Aces" 1-31-71 (Mel Waters), "A Place to Hide" 3-19-72 (Plummer).

Colbert, Claudette (1907-). Films: "Drums Along the Mohawk" 1939 (Lana Borst Martin); "Texas Lady" 1955 (Prudence Webb). ¶TV: *Zane Grey Theater*—"Blood in the Dust" 10-11-57 (Lucy Horncuff), "So

Young the Savage Land" 11-20-60 (Beth Brayden).

Colbert, Robert (1931-). TV: *Bronco*—"Night Train to Denver" 12-29-59, "Montana Passage" 4-5-60 (Lieutenant O'Neil), "End of a Rope" 6-14-60 (Pete Andrews), "The Last Letter" 3-5-62 (Quill); *The Alaskans*—"The Challenge" 1-24-60 (Phil), "White Vengeance" 6-5-60 (Shawn); *Sugarfoot*—"Blackwater Swamp" 3-1-60 (Ben Crain), "A Noose for Nora" 10-24-60 (Clark Henderson); *Colt .45*—"Strange Encounter" 4-26-60 (Bill Mannix), "Attack" 5-24-60 (Clay), "Showdown at Goldtown" 6-14-60 (Johnny Moore); *Maverick*—"Hadley's Hunters" 9-25-60 (Cherokee Dan Evans), Regular 1961-62 (Brent Maverick); *Cheyenne*—"Two Trails to Santa Fe" 10-28-60 (Howie Burch); *Lawman*—"The Locket" 1-7-62 (Breen); *Wagon Train*—"The Cole Crawford Story" 4-11-62 (Blake Dorty), "The Blane Wessels Story" 4-17-63 (Blane Wessels); *Tales of Wells Fargo*—"The Angry Sky" 4-21-62 (Rossi); *The Virginian*—"Impasse" 11-14-62 (Miles Kroeger), "Return a Stranger" 11-18-64 (Joe Barker); *Death Valley Days*—"Grotto of Death" 3-24-63 (Yank Van Duzen), "A Bargain Is for Keeping 2-28-65, "The Duke of Tombstone" 1-10-70; *Laramie*—"The Road to Helena" 5-21-63 (Ross); *Temple Houston*—"Thunder Gap" 11-21-63 (Tom Bannister); *Bonanza*—"The Meredith Smith" 10-31-65 (Ace); *Time Tunnel*—Regular 1966-67 (Doug Phillips); *Alias Smith and Jones*—"Twenty-One Days to Tenstrike" 1-6-72 (Bud).

Colbin, Rod. Films: "Little House: The Last Farewell" TVM-1984 (Mr. Davis).

Colby, Barbara (1940-7/4/75). TV: *Kung Fu*—"The Nature of Evil" 3-21-74 (Josie); *Gunsmoke*—"The Iron Man" 10-21-74 (Kathy Carter).

Colby, Charles. Films: "In the Days of Buffalo Bill" 1922-serial (William H. Seward); "Ace of Cactus Range" 1924 (Sheriff Buck Summers); "Ace of Action" 1926 (Farber); "The Buckaroo Kid" 1926; "Galloping Jinx" 1925; "Thundering Through" 1925 (Blaze Burroughs); "Speedy Spurs" 1926 (City Father); "Put 'Em Up" 1928 (Bobby Flynn).

Colby, Marion. Films: "Singing Spurs" 1948; "Son of Billy the Kid" 1949 (Norma); "Webb Pierce and His Wanderin' Boys" 1955-short.

Colcord, Mabel (1872-6/6/52). Films: "Smoke Tree Range" 1937 (Ma Kelly); "Sudden Bill Dorn" 1937

(Maggie); "Cowboy and the Lady" 1938 (Old Woman); "The Mysterious Rider" 1938 (Woman); "Out West with the Hardys" 1938 (Mrs. Foster).

Cole, Albert. Films: "The Female Bunch" 1971 (Barkeep).

Cole, Dennis (1943-). Films: "The Comancheros" 1961; "Powderkeg" TVM-1971 (Johnny Reach); "The Barbara Coast" TVM-1975 (Cash Conover). ¶TV: *Lancer*—"Juniper's Camp" 3-11-69 (Bobby Cooper); *Bearcats!*—Regular 1971 (Johnny Reach); *The Quest*—"The Captive" 9-22-76 (Stormer).

Cole, Frederick (1901-9/20/64). Films: "Daring Days" 1925 (Henry Sheldon); "Two-Fisted Jones" 1925 (Paul Jones).

Cole, Gary. Films: "Son of the Morning Star" TVM-1991 (George Armstrong Custer).

Cole, John. TV: *G.E. Theater*—"Aftermath" 4-17-60; *Rawhide*—"Incident in the Garden of Eden" 6-17-60 (Indian), "Incident at El Toro" 4-9-64 (Bailey); *Bonanza*—"The Horse Breaker" 11-26-61 (Gunnar)

Cole, Michael (1945-). Films: "Chuka" 1967 (Pvt. Spivey). ¶TV: *Gunsmoke*—"Snap Decision" 9-17-66 (Kipp).

Cole, Mildred. Films: "Marshal of Amarillo" 1948 (Marjorie Underwood).

Cole, Nat "King" (1919-2/15/65). Films: "Cat Ballou" 1965 (Singer).

Cole, Slim. Films: "Smashing Barriers" 1919-serial; "Where Is This West?" 1923 (Wild Honey); "Ridin' Pretty" 1925 (Big Bill); "Prowlers of the Night" 1926 (Al Parsons); "The Last Frontier" 1932-serial (Happy); "Texas Bad Man" 1932 (Cal Thurston).

Cole, Tommy. Films: "Westward Ho the Wagons" 1956 (Jim Stephen).

Colee, Forrest R. (1893-2/10/62). Films: "Colt .45" 1950.

Coleman, Charles (1885-3/8/51). Films: "The Vagabond Trail" 1924 (Aces); "Mexican Spitfire Out West" 1940 (Ponsby); "The Westerner" 1940 (Langtry's Manager); "Grand Canyon Trail" 1948 (J. Malcolm Vanderpool); "The Blazing Sun" 1950.

Coleman, Claudia (1889-8/17/38). Films: "Son of the Border" 1933 (Sadie); "The Country Beyond" 1936 (Mrs. Rawlings).

Coleman, Dabney (1932-).

Films: "The Scalphunters" 1968 (Jed); "Bite the Bullet" 1975 (Gebhardt). ¶TV: *Dundee and the Culhane*—10-18-67 (Sheriff Wren); *Iron Horse*—"Death Has Two Faces" 12-23-67 (Archer); *Bonanza*—"Queen High" 12-1-68 (Ivar Peterson), "A Darker Shadow" 11-23-69 (Clyde).

Coleman, Don (1893-12/16/85). Films: "Border Blackbirds" 1927; "The Devil's Twin" 1927 (Bud Kemper); "The Apache Raider" 1928 (Dal Cartwright); "The Black Ace" 1928 (Dan Stockton); "The Boss of Rustler's Roost" 1928 (Smiler Cavanaugh); "The Bronc Stomper" 1928 (Richard Thurston); "45 Calibre War" 1929 (Reed Lathrop); "Billy the Kid" 1930.

Coleman, Frank. Films: "Sin Town" 1942 (Man); "Valley of the Sun" 1942 (Man on Street).

Coleman, Majel. Films: "Soft Shoes" 1925 (Mabel Packer); "West of Broadway" 1926 (Muriel Styles); "Romance of the Rio Grande" 1929 (Dorry Wayne).

Coleman, Pat. Films: "Hellgate" 1952 (Hunchy). ¶TV: *Sergeant Preston of the Yukon*—"Lost Patrol" 10-18-56 (Little Moose).

Coleman, Robert. Films: "The Fabulous Texan" 1947. ¶TV: *The Virginian*—"No Tears for Savannah" 10-2-63 (Gordon Madden).

Coleman, Ruth. Films: "Headin' East" 1937 (Helen Calhoun).

Coles, Mildred. Films: "Santa Fe Trail" 1940 (Girl); "Back Trail" 1948 (Helen); "Desperadoes of Dodge City" 1948 (Gloria Lamoreaux); "Oklahoma Badlands" 1948 (Leslie Rawlins); "Song of the Drifter" 1948.

Coley, Thomas (1914-5/23/89). TV: *Gunsmoke*—"Gun for Chester" 9-21-57 (Asa Ledbetter), "Groat's Grudge" 1-2-60 (Tom Haskett); *Death Valley Days*—"The White Healer" 11-30-60 (Captain MacGruder).

Colicos, John (1928-). Films: "War Drums" 1957 (Chino); "The Wrath of God" 1972 (Col. Santilla). ¶TV: *The High Chaparral*—"The Journal of Death" 1-9-70 (Matt Kendel); *Gunsmoke*—"Hard Labor" 2-24-75 (Judge Flood).

Collentine, Barbara. TV: *Tombstone Territory*—"Reward for a Gunslinger" 10-23-57 (Lucy Masters); *Nichols*—"The Siege" 9-23-71, "Zachariah" 1-11-72.

Colley, Don Pedro (1938-). Films: "The Legend of Nigger Charley" 1972 (Joshua). ¶TV: *The Virgin-*

ian—"The Gentle Tamers" 1-24-68 (Ira Diller); *Cimarron Strip*—"Without Honor" 2-29-68; *Daniel Boone*—"The Far Side of Fury" 3-7-68 (Gideon), "The Blackbirder" 10-3-68 (Gideon), "Big, Black and Out There" 11-14-68 (Gideon), "To Slay a Giant" 1-9-69 (Gideon); *Here Come the Brides*—"Stand Off" 11-27-68 (Ox); *Wild Wild West*—"The Night of Miguelito's Revenge" 12-13-68 (Abby Carter); *Nichols*—"Ketcham Power" 11-11-71 (Joe Cramme).

Collier, Don (1928-). Films: "Seven Ways from Sundown" 1960 (Duncan); "Incident at Phantom Hill" 1966 (Drum); "El Dorado" 1967 (Deputy Joe Braddock); "The War Wagon" 1967 (Shack); "Five Card Stud" 1968 (Rowan); "The Undefeated" 1969 (Goodyear); "Flap" 1970 (Mike Lyons); "Kate Bliss and the Ticker Tape Kid" TVM-1978 (Tim); "Last Ride of the Dalton Gang" TVM-1979 (Frank Dalton); "Mr. Horn" TVM-1979 (Mr. Nickel); "The Sacketts" TVM-1979; "September Gun" TVM-1983 (Sheriff Mills); "Once Upon a Texas Train" TVM-1988; "El Diablo" CTVM-1990 (Jake); "Gunsmoke: To the Last Man" TVM-1991 (Sheriff); "Gunsmoke: One Man's Justice" TVM-1994 (Sheriff); "Bonanza: Under Attack" TVM-1995 (U.S. Marshal). ¶TV: *Bonanza*—"The Mission" 9-17-60 (Sergeant), "The Good Samaritan" 12-23-62 (Wade Tyree), "The Flannel-Mouth Gun" 1-31-65 (Tatum), "Credit for a Kill" 10-23-66 (Sheriff Fenton), "Saddle Stiff" 1-16-72 (Paul Walker); *The Outlaws*—Regular 1960-62 (Deputy Will Moreman); *Wide Country*—"Our Ernie Kills People" 11-1-62 (Van Anda); *Death Valley Days*—"Loss of Faith" 1-2-63 (Sheriff Gabriel), "The Man Who Died Twice" 12-22-63 (Jack Slade), "There Was Another Dalton Brother" 6-6-65 (Frank Dalton), "One Fast Injun" 3-4-67 (Josiah Wilbarger); *Temple Houston*—"The Dark Madonna" 12-26-63 (Seth Warrener); *The Virginian*—"The Girl from Yesterday" 11-11-64 (Marshal Cass); *Wagon Train*—"The Silver Lady" 4-25-65 (Wyatt Earp); *Branded*—"Romany Roundup 12-5-65 & 12-12-65 (Jud Foley); *Hondo*—"Hondo and the War Cry" 9-15-67 (Drover); *The High Chaparral*—Regular 1967-71 (Sam Butler); *Gunsmoke*—"The Foundling" 2-11-74 (Eli Baines); *Sara*—3-5-76 (Karl); *How the West Was Won*—Episode One 2-12-78 (Captain Poynton); *Young Riders*—Regular 1991-92 (Tompkins).

Collier, Johnnie. TV: *The Rest-*

less Gun—"A Trial for Jenny May" 5-25-59 (Bruce); *Wanted—Dead or Alive*—"The Healing Woman" 9-12-59 (Carey Summers); *The Rifleman*—"Smoke Screen" 4-5-60; *Maverick*—"Maverick and Juliet" 1-17-60 (Jody Montgomery)

Collier, Lois (1919-). Films: "Gauchos of El Dorado" 1941 (Ellen); "Outlaws of the Cherokee Trail" 1941; "West of Cimarron" 1941; "The Phantom Plainsmen" 1942 (Judy Barrett); "Raiders of the Range" 1942 (Jean Travers); "Westward Ho" 1942 (Anna Henderson); "Santa Fe Scouts" 1943 (Claire Robbins); "Wild Beauty" 1946 (Linda Gibson). ¶TV: *Cheyenne*—"West of the River" 3-20-56 (Ruth McKeever).

Collier, Marian. Films: "The Last Challenge" 1967 (Sadie). ¶TV: *Have Gun Will Travel*—"The Gentleman" 9-27-58 (Fifi); *Wanted—Dead or Alive*—"Littlest Giant" 4-25-59; *Laramie*—"Midnight Rebellion" 4-5-60 (Jeanette Durand).

Collier, Richard (1919-). Films: "North to Alaska" 1960 (Skinny Sourdough); "The Cheyenne Social Club" 1970 (Nathan Potter); "Blazing Saddles" 1974 (Dr. Sam Johnson). ¶TV: *Maverick*—"Ghost Riders" 10-13-57 (Barfly); *Broken Arrow*—"War Trail" 4-8-58 (Webb); *The Alaskans*—"The Devil Made Five" 6-19-60 (Piano Player); *Bonanza*—"Elizabeth, My Love" 5-27-61 (Otto); *Rawhide*—"Abilene" 5-18-62 (Dooley); *Temple Houston*—"The Town That Trespassed" 3-26-64 (Mr. Huckabee); *Laredo*—"Jinx" 12-2-65 (Jones); *The Big Valley*—"The Velvet Trap" 11-7-66; *Kung Fu*—"A Praying Mantis Kills" 3-22-73 (Grissom).

Collier, Jr., William "Buster" (1902-2/6/87). Films: "The Bugle Call" 1916 (Billy); "The Girl from Porcupine" 1922 (Jim McTavish); "The Mine with the Iron Door" 1924 (Chico); "The Reckless Sex" 1925 (Juan); "Tide of Empire" 1929 (Romauldo).

Collins, Alan (Luciano Pignozzi). Films: "Cowards Don't Pray" 1968-Ital./Span.; "And God Said to Cain" 1969-Ital.; "Sabata" 1969-Ital. (False Father Brown); "Dead Men Ride" 1970-Ital./Span.; "Sartana in the Valley of Death" 1970-Ital.

Collins, Cora Sue (1927-). Films: "The Mysterious Rider" 1933 (Jo-Jo).

Collins, Denver John. Films: "Doc" 1971 (the Kid).

Collins, Eddie (1884-9/2/40). Films: "Drums Along the Mohawk"

1939 (Christian Reall); "The Return of Frank James" 1940 (Station Agent at Eldora).

Collins, G. Pat (1895-8/5/59). Films: "West of the Pecos" 1934 (Sam Sawtell); "Robin Hood of El Dorado" 1936 (Doc); "They Died with Their Boots On" 1941 (Corporal); "The Wild North" 1952 (Bartender); "Yaqui Drums" 1956. ¶TV: *Wild Bill Hickok*—"Blake's Kid" 12-23-52.

Collins, Gary (1938-). TV: *Iron Horse*—Regular 1966-68 (Dave Tarrant); *The Virginian*—"Incident at Diablo Crossing" 3-12-69 (Jace Adams); *The Quest*—"Welcome to America, Jade Snow" 11-24-76.

Collins, Gene. Films: "I Shot Jesse James" 1949 (Young Man who Tries to Kill Bob Ford); "The Miracle of the Hills" 1959 (Silas Jones); "Doc" 1971 (Hotel Clerk). ¶TV: *Rawhide*—"Incident of the Calico Gun" 4-24-59 (Kid).

Collins, Jack (1918-). Films: "Last Ride of the Dalton Gang" TVM-1979 (Poker Player). ¶TV: *Bonanza*—"A Ride in the Sun" 5-11-69 (Bishop), "Meena" 11-16-69 (Banker), "The Horse Traders" 4-5-70 (Banker), "A Matter of Faith" 9-20-70 (Mayor Corey), "A Deck of Aces" 1-31-71 (Ned Blaine), "The Iron Butterfly" 11-28-71 (Mayor), "One Ace Too Many" 4-2-72 (Mayor Harlow); *Gunsmoke*—"P.S. Murry Christmas" 12-27-71 (Edgecomb); *Dirty Sally*—2-22-74 (Drummer).

Collins, Joan (1933-). Films: "The Bravados" 1958 (Josefa Velarde); "The Wild Women of Chastity Gulch" TVM-1982 (Annie McCulloch). ¶TV: *The Virginian*—"The Lady from Wichita" 9-27-67 (Lorna Marshall).

Collins, Kathleen. Films: "Cyclone Jones" 1923 (Sylvia Billings); "Black Cyclone" 1925 (Jane Logan); "Daniel Boone Thru the Wilderness" 1926; "Satan Town" 1926 (Sue); "The Unknown Cavalier" 1926 (Ruth Gaunt); "The Devil's Saddle" 1927 (Jane Grey); "The Overland Stage" 1927 (Barbara Marshall); "Somewhere in Sonora" 1927 (Mary Burton); "Border Patrol" 1928 (Beverly Dix); "Burning Brides" 1928 (Ellen Wilkins); "The Two Outlaws" 1928 (Mary Ransome); "The Valley of Hunted Men" 1928 (Betty Phillips); "Grit Wins" 1929 (Nan Pickens); "The Ridin' Demon" 1929 (Marie); "Border Devils" 1932 (Marcia Brandon).

Collins, Lisa. TV: *Adventures of Brisco County, Jr.*—"Stagecoach" 4-1-94 (Emma Steed).

Collins, Jr., Monte (1898-6/1/51). Films: "The Old Fool" 1923 (Pop Hardy); "All Around the Frying Pan" 1925 (Mike Selby); "Cold Nerve" 1925; "The Desert Flower" 1925 (Mr. McQuade); "That Man Jack!" 1925 (Joe Leland); "Tumbleweeds" 1925 (Hicks); "The Cowboy and the Countess" 1926 (Slim); "Arizona Wildcat" 1927 (Low Jack Wilkins); "The Great Adventures of Wild Bill Hickok" 1938 (Danny); "Hollywood Roundup" 1938 (Freddie Foster); "Buck Benny Rides Again" 1940 (Bellboy); "Cactus Makes Perfect" 1942-short (Monte Collins).

Collins, Pat. Films: "Indian Territory" 1950 (Jim Colton); "A Lawless Street" 1955; "Ten Wanted Men" 1955 (Bartender).

Collins, Ray (1890-7/11/65). Films: "Barbary Coast Gent" 1944 (Johnny Adair); "Badman's Territory" 1946 (Col. Farewell); "Boy's Ranch" 1946 (Davis Banton); "The Red Stallion" 1947 (Barton); "The Man from Colorado" 1948 (Big Ed Carter); "Red Stallion in the Rockies" 1949 (Matthew Simpson); "Vengeance Valley" 1951 (Arch Strobie); "Column South" 1953 (Brig. Gen. Storey); "Rose Marie" 1954 (Inspector Appleby); "Texas Lady" 1955 (Ralston). ¶TV: *20th Century Fox Hour*—"Gun in His Hand" 4-4-56 (Callicott); *Zane Grey Theater*—"The Long Road Home" 10-19-56 (Evan Gracie).

Collins, Roberta (1946-). TV: *Here Come the Brides*—"Another Game in Town" 2-6-70.

Collins, Russell (1897-11/14/65). Films: "The Walking Hills" 1949 (Bibbs); "Bad Day at Black Rock" 1955 (Mr. Hastings); "Canyon Crossroads" 1955 (Dr. Rand); "The Last Frontier" 1955 (Capt. Clark). ¶TV: *The Rifleman*—"Eight Hours to Die" 11-4-58 (Mr. Denton), "The Apprentice Sheriff" 12-9-58; *Have Gun Will Travel*—"Crowbait" 11-19-60 (Crowbait); *The Tall Man*—"Big Sam's Boy" 3-4-61 (Sam Masters), "A Tombstone for Billy" 12-16-61 (Abner Brown); *Wagon Train*—"The Tiburcio Mendez Story" 3-22-61 (Joaquin Delgado), "The Nancy Davis Story" 5-16-62 (Doc Shaw); *Bonanza*—"The Secret" 5-6-61 (John Hardner); *A Man Called Shenandoah*—"The Accused" 1-3-66 (Clerk).

Collison, Frank. TV: *Dr. Quinn, Medicine Woman*—Regular 1993- (Horace).

Collyer, June (1907-3/16/68). Films: "A Man from Wyoming" 1930 (Patricia Hunter); "Dude Ranch" 1931 (Susan Meadows).

Colman, Booth (1923-). Films: "The Big Sky" 1952 (Pascal); "Scandalous John" 1971 (Gov. Murray). ¶TV: *Jim Bowie*—"An Adventure with Audubon" 9-21-56 (Lantanac), "Trapline" 10-5-56 (Brissac), "Jim Bowie and His Slave" 11-30-56 (Jacques); *Broken Arrow*—"The Conspirators" 12-18-56 (Wilkins), "Warrant for Arrest" 2-11-58 (Spruance); *The Californians*—"The Fugitive" 4-28-59 (Ralph Keel); *Zorro*—"An Affair of Honor" 5-7-59; *The Rifleman*—"The High Country" 12-18-61 (Jeremiah); *Death Valley Days*—"The $275,000 Sack of Flour" 11-7-62 (Dr. Fred Shelton); *Have Gun Will Travel*—"Marshal of Sweetwater" 11-24-62 (Tyler); *Gunsmoke*—"The Bad One" 1-26-63 (Gant Parker), "Alias Festus Haggen" 3-6-72 (Rand); *Bonanza*—"Look to the Stars" 3-18-62, "A Man to Admire" 12-6-64 (Flint Durfee), "The Pursued" 10-2-66 & 10-9-66 (Parson Parley); *Daniel Boone*—"Cain's Birthday" 4-1-65 & 4-8-65 (Private Slimpsey), "The Williamsburg Cannon" 1-12-67 & 1-19-67 (Governor Patrick Henry); *Wild Wild West*—"The Night of the Dancing Death" 11-5-65 (Ambassador Xavier Perkins); *Alias Smith and Jones*—"Return to Devil's Hole" 2-25-71, "The Day They Hanged Kid Curry" 9-16-71; *Kung Fu*—"The Squaw Man" 11-1-73 (Sentinel); *Barbary Coast*—"The Day Cable Was Hanged" 12-26-75 (Dr. Mattwick).

Colman, Ronald (1891-5/19/58). Films: "The Winning of Barbara Worth" 1926 (Willard Holmes).

Colmans, Edward (1908-5/25/77). Films: "California Conquest" 1952 (Junipero); "The Iron Mistress" 1952 (Don Juan de Veramendi); "The Man Behind the Gun" 1952; "Conquest of Cochise" 1953 (Don Francisco de Cordova); "Jubilee Trail" 1954 (Orosco Guest); "The Badge of Marshal Brennan" 1957 (Governor). ¶TV: *The Cisco Kid*—"Thunderhead" 4-5-52, "Bell of Santa Margarite" 4-19-52; *Tales of the Texas Rangers*—"Bandits of El Dorado" 2-18-56 (Vargus); *The Adventures of Rin Tin Tin*—"Rin Tin Tin and the Rainmaker" 3-30-56 (Don Chaves); *Jim Bowie*—"Bayou Tontine" 2-15-57 (Emile Broussard); *Zane Grey Theater*—"Proud Woman" 10-25-57 (Esteban); *Boots and Saddles*—"The Treasure" 12-12-57 (Willis Rodney); *Death Valley Days*—"Yankee Pirate" 2-24-58, "By the Book" 5-4-68 (Don Julio); *Walt Disney Presents*—"Elfego Baca: Elfego Baca, Attorney at Law" 2-6-59 (Fernando Bernal); *Have Gun Will Travel*—"Pancho" 10-24-59

(Don Luis); *Riverboat*—"Tampico Raid" 1-3-60 (Justin Marchand); *Maverick*—"Mano Nera" 10-23-60 (Alberto); *Gunslinger*—"The Death of Yellow Singer" 5-11-61 (Don Galarzo); *Wagon Train*—"The Chalice" 5-24-61 (Padre), "The Captain Dan Brady Story" 9-27-61 (Brown); *Rawhide*—"The Sendoff" 10-6-61 (Padre); *Temple Houston*—"Last Full Moon" 2-27-64 (Two Suns); *Time Tunnel*—"The Alamo" 12-9-66; *The Big Valley*—"Explosion!" 11-20-67 & 11-27-67; *Hondo*—"Hondo and the Hanging Town" 12-8-67 (Father Vorona); *Wild Wild West*—"The Night of the Spanish Curse" 1-3-69 (Juan); *The High Chaparral*—"A Good, Sound Profit" 10-30-70 (Sanchez); *Gunsmoke*—"Survival" 1-10-72 (Cuero).

Colon, Alex (1941-1/6/95). TV: *Centennial*—Regular 1978-79 (Truinfador Marquez).

Colon, Miriam (1935-). Films: "One-Eyed Jacks" 1961 (Red Head); "The Appaloosa" 1966 (Ana); "Desperate Mission" TVM-1971 (Claudina). ¶TV: *Tales of Wells Fargo*—"Desert Showdown" 9-14-59 (Rita); *Wanted—Dead or Alive*—"Desert Seed" 11-14-59 (Mrs. Gomez); *Bronco*—"Death of an Outlaw" 3-8-60 (Abrana); *The Deputy*—"The Truly Yours" 4-9-60 (Cita); *Overland Trail*—"Escort Detail" 5-22-60 (Akoka); *Gunsmoke*—"He Learned About Women" 2-24-62 (Kisla), "Shona" 2-9-63 (Shona), "Zavala" 10-7-68 (Amelita Avila), "Charlie Noon" 11-3-69 (Indian Woman), "Chato" 9-14-70 (Mora), "The River" 9-11-72 & 9-18-72 (Paulette Duvalier), "The Iron Blood of Courage" 2-18-74 (Mignon Anderson); *The Tall Man*—"Property of the Crown" 2-24-62 (Angelita Sanchez); *Have Gun Will Travel*—"Caravan" 2-23-63 (Punya); *Laramie*—"The Unvanquished" 3-12-63; *Great Adventure*—"The Death of Sitting Bull"/"Massacre at Wounded Knee" 10-4-63 & 10-11-63 (Sarah Crow); *The Legend of Jesse James*—"The Empty Town" 1-3-66 (Theresa); *The Virginian*—"Reckoning" 9-13-67 (Eva Talbot); *The High Chaparral*—"Follow Your Heart" 10-4-68 (Trinidad); *Bonanza*—"To Stop a War" 10-19-69 (Anita).

Colosimo, Clara. Films: "For a Book of Dollars" 1973-Ital./Span.

Colt, Dennys. Films: "Shadow of Sartana … Shadow of Your Death" 1968-Ital. (Baby Face); "Four Came to Kill Sartana" 1969-Ital.; "Once Upon a Time in the Wild, Wild West" 1969-Ital. (Joe); "Fistful of

Death" 1971-Ital.; "His Name Was Sam Walbash, But They Call Him Amen" 1971-Ital.; "One Damned Day at Dawn … Django Meets Sartana" 1971-Ital. (Sanchez); "Reach You Bastard!" 1971-Ital.; "Stranger That Kneels Beside the Shadow of a Corpse" 1971-Ital.; "Showdown for a Badman" 1972-Ital.; "Anything for a Friend" 1973-Ital.

Colter, Jessi. Films: "Stagecoach" TVM-1986 (Martha).

Colti, Anthony. TV: *Bonanza*—"Long Way to Ogden" 2-22-70 (Ollie), "The Imposters" 12-13-70 (Randy), "Bushwacked" 10-3-71 (Orv).

Columbo, Russ (1908-9/2/34). Films: "Wolf Song" 1929 (Ambrosia Guiterrez); "The Texan" 1930 (Singing Cowboy at Campfire).

Colvig, Vance D. "Pinto" (1892-10/3/67). Films: "The Man from Button Willow" 1965 (Voice).

Colvin, Jack. Films: "Monte Walsh" 1970 (Card Cheat); "Jeremiah Johnson" 1972 (Lt. Mulvey); "The Life and Times of Judge Roy Bean" 1972 (Pimp); "Rooster Cogburn" 1975 (Red).

Colvin, William (1876-8/10/30). Films: "The Ranger" 1918 (Carl Werner); "My Own Pal" 1926 (Jud McIntire).

Colwell, Goldie. Films: "Cactus Jake, Heart-Breaker" 1914; "Jimmy Hayes and Muriel" 1914; "The Man from the East" 1914; "The Mexican" 1914; "A Militant School Ma'am" 1914; "The Ranger's Romance" 1914; "The Real Thin in Cowboys" 1914 (Elsie Mitchell); "The Rival Stage Lines" 1914 (Elsie); "Saved by a Watch" 1914; "The Scapegoat" 1914 (Nell); "The Sheriff's Reward" 1914; "The Telltale Knife" 1914; "The Way of the Redman" 1914; "Why the Sheriff Is a Bachelor" 1914; "Bill Haywood, Producer" 1915; "Cactus Jim's Shopgirl" 1915; "Forked Trails" 1915; "Harold's Bad Man" 1915; "Ma's Girls" 1915; "Roping a Bride" 1915; "Sagebrush Tom" 1915; "The Stagecoach Driver and the Girl" 1915; "In the Days of Daring" 1916; "The Yaqui" 1916 (Modesta); "The Heart of Texas Ryan" 1917 (Marion Smith); "Code of the Yukon" 1918 (Goldie); "Slim Higgins" 1919.

Comar, Richard. TV: *Bordertown*—Regular 1989 (Marshal Jack Craddock).

Combs, Gary. Films: "The Life and Times of Judge Roy Bean" 1972 (Outlaw); "Belle Starr" TVM-1980 (Frank James). ¶TV: *Gunsmoke*—"Murdoch" 2-8-71 (Fairchild).

Comer, Anjanette (1942-). Films: "The Appaloosa" 1966 (Trini); "Guns for San Sebastian" 1967-U.S./Fr./Mex./Ital. (Kinita). ¶TV: *Gunsmoke*—"Carter Caper" 11-16-63 (Cara Miles); *Bonanza*—"Love Me Not" 3-1-64 (Joan); *Barbary Coast*—"The Day Cable Was Hanged" 12-26-75 (Mary Louise).

Comerate, Sheridan. Films: "3:10 to Yuma" 1957 (Bob Moons).

Comi, Paul (1932-). Films: "Warlock" 1959 (Friendly). ¶TV: *Tombstone Territory*—"Pick Up the Gun" 5-14-58 (Frank McLowery); *Lawman*—"The Go-Between" 9-25-60 (Cole Reese); *Two Faces West*—"Sheriff of the Town" 10-31-60 (Sheriff Johnny Evans); *Wagon Train*—"The Captain Dan Brady Story" 9-27-61 (John Grey Cloud); *The Tall Man*—"Fool's Play" 12-2-61 (Pollitt); *Stoney Burke*—"The Scavenger" 11-12-62 (Frank Foley); *The Virginian*—"A Time Remembered" 12-11-63 (Elliott Powers), "All Nice and Legal" 11-25-64 (Brad Carter), "Two Men Named Laredo" 1-6-65 (Brad Carter), "The Gentle Tamers" 1-24-68 (Warden Keane); *Rawhide*—"A Man Called Mushy" 10-23-64 (Yo Yo), "Damon's Road" 11-13-64 & 11-20-64 (Yo Yo); *The Big Valley*—"The Fallen Hawk" 3-2-66 (Pursey), "Legend of a General" 9-19-66 & 9-26-66 (Sergeant), "Court Martial" 3-6-67; *Wild Wild West*—"The Night of the Two-Legged Buffalo" 3-11-66 (Vittorie Pellegrini), "The Night of the Ready-Made Corpse" 11-25-66 (Pellargo #2), "The Night of the Circus of Death" 11-3-67 (Bert Farnsworth); *Time Tunnel*—"Massacre" 10-28-66 (Capt. Benteen).

Comingore, Dorothy (Linda Winters) (1913-12/30/71). Films: "North of the Yukon" 1939 (Jean Duncan); "Pioneers of the Frontier" 1940 (Joan Darcey); "Rockin' Through the Rockies" 1940-short (Daisy).

Comiskey, Pat. Films: "Gun Battle at Monterey" 1957 (Frank). ¶TV: *Maverick*—"Stampede" 11-17-57 (Battling Krueger); *Sugarfoot*—"Fernando" 2-16-60 (Big Jim Fitzgibbons).

Como, Rosella (1939-12/20/86). Films: "The Tall Women" 1966-Austria/Ital./Span. (Katy).

Comont, Mathilde (1886-6/21/38). Films: "The Enchanted Hill" 1926 (Conchita); "Ramona" 1928 (Marda); "The Lash" 1930 (Concha); "Hard Hombre" 1931 (Senora Romero); "Robin Hood of El Dorado" 1936 (Senorita Martinez); "God's

Country and the Woman" 1937 (Mary).

Compson, Betty (1897-4/18/74). Films: "The Border Raiders" 1918; "The Devil's Trail" 1919 (Julie Delisle); "The Prodigal Liar" 1919 (Hope Deering); "The Terror of the Range" 1919-serial; "Over the Border" 1922 (Jen Galbraith); "The Pony Express" 1925 (Molly Jones); "The Spoilers" 1930 (Cherry Malotte); "God's Country and the Man" 1937 (Roxy Moore); "Two-Gun Justice" 1938 (Kate); "Cowboys from Texas" 1939 (Belle Starkey).

Compson, John R. (1868-3/15/13). Films: "The Maiden of the Pie-Faced Indians" 1911.

Compton, Forrest (1925-). TV: *Fury*—"The Rocketeers" 12-5-59.

Compton, John. Films: "Cheyenne" 1947 (Limpy Bill); "Jesse James Rides Again" 1947-serial (Steve Lane); "Oh! Susanna" 1951 (Lt. Cutler); "Friendly Persuasion" 1956 (Rebel Lieutenant); "Thunder Over Arizona" 1956. ¶TV: *The Cisco Kid*—"Quick on the Trigger" 2-6-54; *Sergeant Preston of the Yukon*—"Escape to the North" 1-9-58 (Rick Farley); *Gunsmoke*—"Kitty Caught" 1-18-58 (Blain); *Jim Bowie*—"The Cave" 5-9-58 (Sam); *Fury*—"The Pulling Contest" 1-3-59, "Packy, the Lion Tamer" 1-2-60 (Chris Lambert).

Compton, Joyce (1907-). Films: "Border Cavalier" 1927 (Madge Lawton); "Three Rogues" 1931 (Ace's Girl); "Fighting for Justice" 1932 (Amy Tracey); "Rustlers of Red Dog" 1935-serial (Mary Lee); "Valley of the Lawless" 1936 (Joan Jenkins); "Reno" 1939 (Bonnie); "Silver Spurs" 1943 (Mildred "Millie" Love); "Grand Canyon" 1949 (Mabel); "The Persuader" 1957. ¶TV: *Jim Bowie*—"Pirate on Horseback" 1-17-58 (Mme. Madeline).

Comstock, Clark (1862-5/24/34). Films: "The Eagle's Nest" 1915 (Sheriff Haggard); "The Double Hold-Up" 1919; "The Jaws of Justice" 1919; "The Westerners" 1919 (Lone Wolf); "A Broadway Cowboy" 1920 (Sheriff Sims); "The Ranger and the Law" 1921 (Red Hobbs); "Singing River" 1921 (John Thornton); "Blazing Arrows" 1922 (Gray Eagle); "Hellounds of the West" 1922 (Clayt Stacy); "In the Days of Buffalo Bill" 1922-serial (Thomas C. Durant); "Perils of the Yukon" 1922-serial; "Huntin' Trouble" 1924; "Ride for Your Life" 1924 (Tim Murphy); "Riders of the Plains" 1924-serial; "The Sunset Trail" 1924 (Constable Hicks); "Wolves of the North" 1924-

serial; "The Bashful Whirlwind" 1925; "The Calgary Stampede" 1925 (Jean LaFarge); "The Red Rider" 1925 (Indian Chief); "The Buckaroo Kid" 1926; "The Fighting Peacemaker" 1926 (Marshal); "Looking for Trouble" 1926 (Jim Helliler); "The Man in the Saddle" 1926 (Pete); "Wild Horse Stampede" 1926 (Cross Hayden); "The Arizona Whirlwind" 1927; "Hey! Hey! Cowboy" 1927 (Joe Billings); "Rough and Ready" 1927 (John Stone); "Silver Valley" 1927 (Wash Taylor); "Whispering Smith Rides" 1927-serial; "The Boundary Battle" 1928; "The Scarlet Arrow" 1928-serial; "Tracked" 1928 (Nathan Butterfield); "The Man from Nowhere" 1930 (Pat McCloud); "The Oklahoma Sheriff" 1930.

Conant, Bill. Films: "The Three Buckaroos" 1922 (Aramor); "The Arizona Kid" 1929 (Sheriff Morton).

Conde, Rita (1918-). Films: "Barquero" 1970 (Layeta).

Condon, David. *see* Gorcey, David.

Conforti, Gino (1932-). Films: "Hawmps!" 1976 (Hi Jolly); "More Wild Wild West" TVM-1980 (Georges, the French Ambassador). ¶TV: *The Outcasts*—"The Outcasts" 9-23-68 (Bandit); *The High Chaparral*—"To Stand for Something More" 10-24-69 (Raul); *The Life and Times of Grizzly Adams*—9-28-77.

Congdon, James (1929-). Films: "The Left-Handed Gun" 1958 (Charlie Boudre).

Conklin, Charles "Heinie" (1880-7/30/59). Films: "Clash of the Wolves" 1925 (Alkali Bill); "Hard-Boiled" 1926 (Bill Grimes); "Night Cry" 1926 (Tony); "Drums of the Desert" 1927 (Hi-Lo); "A Horseman of the Plains" 1928 (Showshoe); "A Trick of Hearts" 1928 (the Crook); "Tiger Rose" 1929 (Gus); "Law of the North" 1932; "Trailing the Killer" 1932 (Windy); "Riders of Destiny" 1933 (Stage Driver); "Ruggles of Red Gap" 1935 (Waiter); "Rhythm on the Range" 1936 (Driver); "White Fang" 1936 (Man with Magic Lantern); "Frontier Marshal" 1939 (Man); "Trail of the Vigilantes" 1940 (Bartender); "The Westerner" 1940 (Man at Window); "Pistol Packin' Nitwits" 1945-short; "Out West" 1947-short (Bartender); "Loaded Pistols" 1948; "Smoky Mountain Melody" 1948; "Pals and Gals" 1954-short (Henchman).

Conklin, Chester (1888-10/11/71). Films: "The Under-Sheriff" 1914; "Wild West Love" 1914; "North

of Nevada" 1924 (Lem Williams); "Stairs of Sand" 1929 (Tim); "Sunset Pass" 1929 (Windy); "The Virginian" 1929 (Uncle Hughes); "Call of the Prairie" 1936 (Sandy McQueen); "Forlorn River" 1937 (Sheriff Grundy); "Sing, Cowboy, Sing" 1937; "Chip of the Flying U" 1939; "Henry Goes Arizona" 1939 (Barney Eastland); "Sagebrush Serenade" 1939-short; "Teacher's Pest" 1939-short; "Adventures of Red Ryder" 1940-serial (Judge #1); "In Old California" 1942; "Sons of the Pioneers" 1942 (Old Timer); "Valley of the Sun" 1942 (Man on Street); "Phony Express" 1943-short (Mr. Higgins); "Singin' in the Corn" 1946 (Austin Driver); "Jesse James Rides Again" 1947-serial (Roy); "Song of the Wasteland" 1947; "Springtime in the Sierras" 1947 (Old Timer); "The Golden Stallion" 1949 (Old Man); "Fancy Pants" 1950 (Guest); "Son of Paleface" 1952 (Townsman); "Apache Woman" 1955 (Mooney); "A Big Hand for the Little Lady" 1966 (Old Man in Saloon).

Conklin, Russ. Films: "Unconquered" 1947 (Wamaultee); "The Pathfinder" 1952 (Togamak); "Son of Paleface" 1952 (Indian); "The Wild North" 1952 (Indian); "Seminole Uprising" 1955 (High Cloud). ¶TV: *The Lone Ranger*—"Rifles and Renegades" 5-4-50, "Trouble for Tonto" 7-20-50; *Sergeant Preston of the Yukon*—"Scourge of the Wilderness" 1-11-57 (Taranga); *The Adventures of Rin Tin Tin*—"The General's Daughter" 9-19-58; *Hotel De Paree*—"A Rope Is for Hanging" 11-6-59 (Sam); *Rawhide*—"Incident at Tinker's Dam" 2-5-60.

Conklin, William (1872-3/21/35). Films: "Arizona" 1913 (Captain Hodgeman); "Pierre of the Plains" 1914 (Durkin); "Golden Rule Kate" 1917 (Reverend McGregor); "North of '53" 1917 (Andrew Bush); "Flare-Up Sal" 1918 (Dandy Dave Hammond); "Blind Hearts" 1921 (James Curdy); "Iron to Gold" 1922 (George Conklin); "Up and Going" 1922 (Basil DuBois); "The Lone Star Ranger" 1923 (Major Longstreth/Cheseldine); "Three Who Paid" 1923 (Jude Cartright); "Rose of the Golden West" 1927 (Commander Sloat)."Outlaws of Red River" 1927 (Capt. Dunning); "Tumbling River" 1927 (Jim Barton).

Conlan, Frank (1874-8/24/55). Films: "Fear-Bound" 1925 (Cooky); "Billy the Kid" 1941 (Judge Blake); "My Darling Clementine" 1946 (Piano Player); "Rachel and the

Stranger" 1948 (Jabez); "Winchester '73" 1950 (Clerk).

Conley, Darlene (1934-). TV: *Gunsmoke*—"Gentry's Law" 10-12-70 (Leelah Case).

Conley, Joe. TV: *Jim Bowie*—"The Ghost of Jean Battoo" 11-2-56 (Raimo); *Wanted—Dead or Alive*—"The Empty Cell" 10-17-59; *Gunsmoke*—"Help Me, Kitty" 11-7-64 (Carl).

Conlon, James (1884-5/7/62). Films: "Rose Marie" 1936 (Joe, the Piano Player); "My Little Chickadee" 1940 (Squawk Mulligan, the Bartender); "Ridin' on a Rainbow" 1941 (Frisco).

Connell, Jim. TV: *Wild Wild West*—"The Night of the Freebooters" 4-1-66 (Richard Henry); *Bonanza*—"Dead Wrong" 12-7-69 (Hotel Manager).

Connelly, Bobby (1909-7/5/22). Films: "Britton of the Seventh" 1916 (Bobby).

Connelly, Christopher (1943-12/7/88). Films: "Hawmps!" 1976 (Uriah Tibbs); "Charlie Cobb: Nice Night for a Hanging" TVM-1977 (Waco); "The Incredible Rocky Mountain Race" TVM-1977 (Mark Twain); "Django Strikes Again" 1987-Ital./Span./Ger. (Orlowsky). ¶TV: *Gunsmoke*—"The Warden" 5-16-64 (Trainey); "Kitty's Love Affair" 10-22-73 (Sheb Deems); *Daniel Boone*—"A Bearskin for Jamie Blue" 11-27-69 (Jamie Blue); *Bonanza*—"The Lady and the Mark" 2-1-70 (Chris Keller); *The Quest*—"The Captive" 9-22-76 (Callender); *Walt Disney Presents*—"Kit Carson and the Mountain Men" 1-9-77 & 1-16-77 (Kit Carson).

Connelly, Edward (1855-11/21/28). Films: "The Conflict" 1921 (John Remalie); "Winners of the Wilderness" 1927 (General Contrecoeur); "The Desert Rider" 1929 (Padre Quintada).

Connelly, Erwin (1873-2/12/31). Films: "The Winning of Barbara Worth" 1926 (Pat); "Fair Warning" 1931 (Morgan).

Connelly, Jack. Films: "The End of the Rainbow" 1916 (Sheriff Connelly); "True Blue" 1918 (Earl's Secretary); "The One Way Trail" 1920 (Jack Hanlon); "Shod with Fire" 1920 (Tommy Clary); "Ghost City" 1921 (Dick Carroll); "The Wolverine" 1921 (Ward Warren); "The Mysterious Witness" 1923 (Ed Carney).

Connelly, Sheila (Kelly Ryan). Films: "The Outlaw's Daughter" 1954 (Kate).

Conner, Betty. TV: *Gunsmoke*—"Help Me, Kitty" 11-7-64 (Hope Farmer); *Rawhide*—"The Calf Women" 4-30-65 (Betsy Teall).

Connery, Sean (1930-). Films: "Shalako" 1968-Brit./Fr. (Shalako).

Connolly, Mattie. Films: "The Ranger" 1918 (Belle Werner).

Connor, Allen. Films: "The Three Mesquiteers" 1936 (Milt); "Gunsmoke Ranch" 1937 (Reggie); "Union Pacific" 1939 (Card Player).

Connor, Edric (1915-10/16/68). Films: "Four for Texas" 1964 (Prince George).

Connor, Philip. Films: "The Westerner" 1940 (John Yancy).

Connor, Velma (1905-7/19/87). Films: "Rustler by Proxy" 1926; "The Scrappin' Kid" 1926 (Betty Brent); "The Terror" 1926 (Molly Morton).

Connor, Whitfield (1916-7/16/88). Films: "City of Badmen" 1953 (Jim London).

Connors, Buck. *see* Connors, George "Buck."

Connors, Chuck (1924-11/20/92). Films: "The Hired Gun" 1957 (Judd Farrow); "Old Yeller" 1957 (Burn Sanderson); "Tomahawk Trail" 1957 (Sgt. Wade McCoy); "The Big Country" 1958 (Buck Hannassey); "Geronimo" 1962 (Geronimo); "Ride Beyond Vengeance" 1966 (Jonas Trapp); "Kill Them All and Come Back Alone" 1967-Ital./Span. (Clyde Link); "Deserter" 1970-U.S./Ital./Yugo. (Chaplain); "Support Your Local Gunfighter" 1971 (Swifty Morgan); "Pancho Villa" 1975-Span.; "Banjo Hackett: Roamin' Free" TVM-1976 (Sam Ivory); "Standing Tall" TVM-1978 (Major Hartline); "The Capture of Grizzly Adams" TVM-1982 (Frank Briggs); "Once Upon a Texas Train" TVM-1988 (Nash); "The Gambler Returns: The Luck of the Draw" TVM-1991 (the Rifleman). ¶TV: *Frontier*—"Assassin" 3-4-56 (Thorpe Henderson); *Gunsmoke*—"The Preacher" 6-16-56 (Sam Keeler); *Wagon Train*—"The Charles Avery Story" 12-13-57 (Sumpter); *The Restless Gun*—"Silver Threads" 12-16-57 (Toby Yeager); *Tales of Wells Fargo*—"The Thin Rope" 3-18-57 (Button Smith), "Sam Bass" 6-10-57 (Sam Bass); *Zane Grey Theater*—"The Sharpshooter" 3-7-58 (Lucas McCain); *Jim Bowie*—"Horse Thief" 3-21-58 (Cephas K. Ham), "Jim Bowie, Apache" 3-28-58 (Cephas K. Ham); *The Rifleman*—Regular 1958-63 (Lucas McCain), "Deadly Image" 2-26-62 (Earl Bantry); *Western Hour*—Host 1963; *Branded*—Regular 1965-66 (Jason McCord); *Cowboy in*

Africa—Regular 1967-68 (Jim Sinclair); *The Men from Shiloh*—"The Animal" 1-20-71 (Gustaveson); *Best of the West*—"Frog Gets Lucky" 1-7-82; *Paradise*—"A Matter of Honor" 4-8-89 & 4-15-89 (Gideon McKay), "A Gathering of Guns" 2-17-90 (Gideon McKay).

Connors, George "Buck". Films: "The Code of the Mounted" 1916; "The Fast Mail" 1918; "The Phantom Riders" 1918 (Pebble Grant); "Quick Triggers" 1918; "The Black Horse Bandit" 1919; "The Canyon Mystery" 1919; "Action" 1921 (Pat Casey); "Duke of Chimney Butte" 1921 (Taters); "Outlawed" 1921 (Bud Knowles); "Giants of the Open" 1922; "Tracked to Earth" 1922 (Shorty Fuller); "The Black Trail" 1924 (Shorty); "Biff Bang Buddy" 1924 (Dad Norton); "Fighting Fury" 1924 (Shorty); "Hidden Loot" 1925 (Buck); "The Red Rider" 1925 (Tom Fleming); "Ridin' Thunder" 1925 (Bill Croft); "The Saddle Tramp" 1926; "The Yellow Back" 1926 (John Pendleton); "The Broncho Buster" 1927 (Sourdough Jones); "The Fighting Three" 1927 (Marshal Skinner); "Hands Off" 1927 (Stills Manners); "Jaws of Steel" 1927 (Alkali Joe); "The Mojave Kid" 1927 (Silent); "On Special Duty" 1927; "Open Range" 1927 (Sheriff Daley); "Shooting Straight" 1927 (John Hale); "The Slingshot Kid" 1927 (Clem Windloss); "Straight Shootin'" 1927 (John Hale); "The Crimson Canyon" 1928 (Dad Packard); "The Fearless Rider" 1928 (Jeff Lane); "The Phantom Flyer" 1928 (John Crandall); "The Go Get 'Em Kid" 1929 (Grit Wins" 1929 (Ted Pickens); "Perilous Paths" 1929; "Red Romance" 1929; "The Thrill Hunter" 1929'; "The Dawn Trail" 1930 (Jim Anderson); "Hell's Heroes" 1930 (Parson Jones); "Trails of Danger" 1920 (John Martin); "Desert Vengeance" 1931 (Parson); "Headin' for Trouble" 1931 (John Courtney); "Riders of the Golden Gulch" 1932 (Sheriff); "The Last Round-Up" 1934 (Old Man Tracy); "The Thundering Herd" 1934 (Buffalo Hunter); "Alias John Law" 1935 (Bootch McCrumb); "Gallant Defender" 1935; "Moonlight on the Prairie" 1935 (Bearded Mann); "No Man's Range" 1935 (Fuzz); "The Law Rides" 1936 (Whitney); "White Fang" 1936 (Stubby); "South of Arizona" 1938 (Doctor); "West of Santa Fe" 1938 (Hardpan); "The Westerner" 1940 (Abraham Wilson).

Connors, Joan. Films: "The Gun Hawk" 1963 (Roan's Woman). ¶TV: *Tombstone Territory*—12-4-59

(Karen Thomas); *Bonanza*—"The Gentleman from New Orleans" 2-2-64.

Connors, Kathleen. Films: "Ace High" 1918 (Annette Dupre); "Mr. Logan, U.S.A." 1918.

Connors, Michael "Touch" (1925–). Films: "Five Guns West" 1955 (Hale Clinton); "The Twinkle in God's Eye" 1955 (Lou); "The Oklahoma Woman" 1956 (Sheriff); "Flesh and the Spur" 1957 (Stacy); "Dalton That Got Away" 1960; "Stagecoach" 1966 (Hatfield). ¶TV: *Frontier*—"Tomas and the Widow" 10-2-55; *Wyatt Earp*—"The Big Baby Contest" 11-22-55 (Pat Smith); *Jim Bowie*—"Broomstick Wedding" 10-12-56 (Rafe Bradford); *Gunsmoke*—"The Mistake" 11-24-56 (Jim Bostick); *Maverick*—"Point Blank" 9-29-57 (Ralph Jordan), "Naked Gallows" 12-15-57 (Sheriff Fillmore); *Have Gun Will Travel*—"The Bride" 10-19-57 (Johnny); *Wagon Train*—"The Dora Gray Story" 1-29-58; *Cheyenne*—"Dead to Rights" 5-20-58 (Roy Simmons); *The Texan*—"The Edge of the Cliff" 10-27-58; *Cimarron City*—"Hired Hand" 11-15-58 (Bill Vatcher); *Jefferson Drum*—"Simon Pitt" 12-11-58 (Simon Pitt); *Lawman*—"Lady in Question" 12-21-58 (Hal Daniels); *Rough Riders*—"Wilderness Trace" 1-29-59 (Randall Garrett); *The Californians*—"The Bell Tolls" 5-19-59 (Charles Cora); *Redigo*—"Shadow of the Cougar" 11-26-63 (Jack Marston).

Conrad, Charles. TV: *Sergeant Preston of the Yukon*—"Border Action" 12-27-56 (Clint Hyde), "Out of the Night" 11-28-57 (John Corwin); *Gunsmoke*—"Chester's Murder" 3-30-57 (Man), "Gunfighter, R.I.P." 10-22-66 (Paul Douglas); *The Rifleman*—"The Spiked Rifle" 11-24-59.

Conrad, Eddie (1891-4/27/41). Films: "In Old Monterey" 1939 (Proprietor); "Man from Montreal" 1940 (Marcel Bircheaux).

Conrad, Francis. Films: "Ruggles of Red Gap" 1918 (Mrs. Belknap Jackson); "Sundown Slim" 1920 (Eleanor Loring).

Conrad, Michael (1925-11/22/83). Films: "Bandit Queen" 1950 (Capt. Gray); "Monte Walsh" 1970 (Dally Johnson); "Cattle Annie and Little Britches" 1981 (Engineer). ¶TV: *Philco Television Playhouse*—"The Death of Billy the Kid" 7-24-55 (Charles Boudre); *Bronco*—"School for Cowards" 4-21-59 (Hurd Elliott); *Wagon Train*—"The Sandra Cummings Story" 12-2-63 (Luke); *Gunsmoke*—"Hung High" 11-14-64 (Dick

Corwin), "The Raid" 1-22-66 & 1-29-66 (Cash McLean); *Rawhide*—"Prairie Fire" 3-19-65 (Jerry Munson); *Daniel Boone*—"My Name Is Rawls" 10-7-65 (Sharben); *Laredo*—"No Bugles, One Drum" 2-24-66 (Willie G. Tinney); *Bonanza*—"The Fighters" 4-24-66 (Hank Kelly); *Cowboy in Africa*—"African Rodeo" 1-15-68 & 1-22-68 (Jorge); *The Outcasts*—"The Man from Bennington" 12-16-68 (Sergeant McCracker); *The Virginian*—"The Stranger" 4-9-69 (Sam Marish), "Nightmare" 1-21-70 (John); *Alias Smith and Jones*—"Bushwack!" 10-21-72 (Mike McCloskey); *How the West Was Won*—Episode Eight 4-16-78 (Marshal Russell), Episode Ten 4-30-78 (Marshal Russell), Episode Twelve 5-14-78 (Marshal Russell), Episode Thirteen 5-21-78 (Marshal Russell).

Conrad, Mikel (1919-9/11/82). Films: "Border Feud" 1947 (Elmore); "Check Your Guns" 1948 (Ace); "The Man from Colorado" 1948 (Morris); "Phantom Valley" 1948 (Crag Parker).

Conrad, Paul. Films: "Return of the Durango Kid" 1945; "Blazing Across the Pecos" 1948.

Conrad, Robert (1935–). Films: "The Wild Wild West Revisited" TVM-1979 (James T. West); "More Wild Wild West" TVM-1980 (James T. West); "Samurai Cowboy" 1993 (Gabe McBride). ¶TV: *Maverick*—"Yellow River" 2-8-59 (Davie Barrows); *Lawman*—"Battle Scar" 3-22-59 (Catterton); *Colt .45*—"Amnesty" 5-24-59 (Billy the Kid); *Temple Houston*—"The Town That Trespassed" 3-26-64 (Martin Purcell); *Wild Wild West*—Regular 1965-69 (James West); *Centennial*—Regular 1978-79 (Pasquinel).

Conrad, William (1923-2/11/93). Films: "Four Faces West" 1948 (Sheriff Egan); "Lone Star" 1952 (Mizzette); "The Cowboy" 1954 (Narrator); "Johnny Concho" 1956 (Tallman); "The Ride Back" 1957 (Hamish); "The Macahans" TVM-1976 (Narrator). ¶TV: *Bat Masterson*—"Stampede at Tent City" 10-29-58 (Clark Benson), "Terror on the Trinity" 3-9-61 (Dick MacIntyre); *Rough Riders*—"The Governor" 11-6-58 (Wade Hacker); *Have Gun Will Travel*—"The Man Who Struck Moonshine" 3-24-62 (Moses Kadish), "Genesis" 9-15-62 (Norge); *The High Chaparral*—"Spokes" 9-25-70 (China Pierce).

Conried, Hans (1917-1/5/82). Films: "A Lady Takes a Chance" 1943 (Gregg); "New Mexico" 1951 (Lin-

coln); "Davy Crockett, King of the Wild Frontier" 1955 (Thimbelrig); "The Brothers O'Toole" 1973. ¶TV: *Walt Disney Presents*—"Davy Crockett"—Regular 1954-55 (Thimbelrig); *Maverick*—"Black Fire" 3-16-58 (Homer Eakins); *Jim Bowie*—"Patron of the Arts" 4-11-58 (Cecil Algernon Justus); *The Californians*—"The Painless Extractionist" 12-9-58 (Painless Pepper); *Have Gun Will Travel*—"A Knight to Remember" 12-9-61 (Don Esteban Caloca); *Daniel Boone*—"Orlando, the Prophet" 2-29-68 (Orlando).

Conroy, Frank (1890-2/24/64). Films: "Frontier Marshal" 1934 (Oscar Reid); "Call of the Wild" 1935 (John Blake); "Wells Fargo" 1937 (Ward, the Banker); "The Ox-Bow Incident" 1943 (Maj. Tetley).

Conroy, Thom (1911-11/16/71). Films: "Man with the Gun" 1955 (Bill Emory).

Considine, John (1937–). Films: "Buffalo Bill and the Indians, or Sitting Bull's History Lesson" 1976 (Frank Butler). ¶TV: *Death Valley Days*—"Treasure of Elk Creek Canyon" 12-13-61, "Clum's Constabulary" 4-11-70.

Considine, Tim (1940–). TV: *The Adventures of Rin Tin Tin*—"Rin Tin Tin and the Flaming Forest" 10-29-54 (Sydney Rogers), "The Flaming Forest" 12-7-56 (Sydney Rogers); *Zane Grey Theater*—"Trail Incident" 1-29-59 (Peter Owens); *Cheyenne*—"Reprieve" 10-5-59 (Billy McQueen); *Johnny Ringo*—"Bound Boy" 12-31-59 (Jamie); *Bonanza* "The Reluctant Rebel" 11-21-65 (Billy Penn); *Gunsmoke*—"Snow Train" 10-19-70 & 10-26-70 (Scott); *Legend*—"The Gospel According to Legend" 6-12-95 (Taggert).

Constantine, Michael (1927–). Films: "Wanted: The Sundance Woman" TVM-1976 (Dave Riley). ¶TV: *The Dakotas*—"Trouble at French Creek" 1-28-63 (Marshak); *Gunsmoke*—"Old York" 5-4-63 (Jim Baca), "The Gunrunners" 2-5-68 (Noah Meek), "Buffalo Man" 11-4-68; *Death Valley Days*—"Paid in Full" 1-3-65 (John Chisum), "The Fastest Nun in the West" 4-9-66 (George Burnet); *The Virginian*—"The Dream of Stavros Karas" 12-1-65 (Stavros Karas), "The Death Wagon" 1-3-68 (Private Essex Kanin), "A Touch of Hands" 12-3-69 (Mr. Halstead); *The Road West*—"To Light a Candle" 11-28-66 (Jacob Adams); *Dundee and the Culhane*—"The Turn the Other Cheek Brief" 9-6-67; *Iron Horse*—"Consignment, Betsy the Boiler" 9-23-67 (Sam McGinty).

Conte, John (1915-). TV: *Bonanza*—"The Return" 5-2-65 (Paul Dorn).

Conte, Maria Pia. Films: "Dynamite Jim" 1966-Span./Ital.; "Five Dollars for Ringo" 1968-Ital./Span.; "Twenty Paces to Death" 1970-Ital./Span. (Clare); "God in Heaven ... Arizona on Earth" 1972-Span./Ital.

Conte, Richard (1914-4/15/75). Films: "Big Jack" 1949 (Dr. Alexander Meade); "The Fighter" 1952 (Filipe Rivera); "The Raiders" 1952 (Jan Morrell); "They Came to Cordura" 1959 (Cpl. Milo Trubee); "Death Sentence" 1967-Ital. ¶TV: *Frontier Circus*—"Naomi Champagne" 3-29-62 (Dan Diego).

Conte, Steve. Films: "Gunfire" 1950 (Riley); "Cattle Queen" 1951 (Mac); "Goldtown Ghost Raiders" 1953 (Blackwell). ¶TV: *The Gene Autry Show*—"Trouble at Silver Creek" 3-9-52, "Trail of the Witch" 3-30-52, "Outlaw Stage" 7-21-53, "Border Justice" 8-18-53, "Stage to San Dimas" 10-8-55, "Guns Below the Border" 11-5-55; *The Adventures of Rin Tin Tin*—"The Blushing Brides" 3-18-55; *Death Valley Days*—"I Am Joaquin" 3-28-55, "The Calico Dog" 12-2-57 (Narrer Frost); *Cheyenne*—"The Argonauts" 11-1-55 (Acuna); *Fury*—"Ghost Town" 12-31-55 (Speed); *My Friend Flicka*—"Wind from Heaven" 2-3-56; *Broken Arrow*—"Hermano" 11-20-56 (Chee), "Ghost Face" 3-12-57 (Chee), "Backlash" 5-27-58 (Teesay); *26 Men*—"Incident at Yuma" 11-19-57, "Dead Man in Tucson" 12-3-57; *The Texan*—"The Peddler" 1-26-59; *The Rifleman*—"The Lariat" 3-29-60 (Doyle Blake).

Conterno, Norma. Films: "Cyclone Buddy" 1924 (Doris Martin).

Conti, Audrey. TV: *Wild Bill Hickok*—"The Iron Major" 4-21-53; *Death Valley Days*—"The Baron of Arizona" 2-25-56, "Train of Events" 5-19-57, "Jerkline Jitters" 1-6-58 (Enid).

Conti, Pier Luigi. *see* Cliver, Al.

Conti, Tom (1942-). Films: "The Quick and the Dead" CTVM-1987 (Duncan McKaskel).

Contreras, Luis. Films: "The Long Riders" 1980; "Barbarosa" 1982 (Angel); "Straight to Hell" 1987-Brit. (Sal); "Sunset" 1988 (Jail Inmate); "El Diablo" CTVM-1990 (Pestoso); "Rio Diablo" TVM-1993 (Almenzar). ¶TV: *Adventures of Brisco County, Jr.*—"Bounty Hunter's Convention" 1-7-94 (El Gato).

Contreras, Roberto. Films: "The Beast of Hollow Mountain"

1956 (Carlos); "Ride a Violent Mile" 1957 (Abruzo); "Gold of the Seven Saints" 1961 (Armendarez); "California" 1963 (Lt. Sanchez); "The Professionals" 1966 (Bandit); "Barbarosa" 1982 (Cantina Owner). ¶TV: *Maverick*—"The Third Rider" 1-5-58 (Jose), "Plunder of Paradise" 3-9-58 (Alfredo); *Have Gun Will Travel*—"Heritage of Anger" 6-6-59 (Bartender), "Duke of Texas" 4-22-61; *Rough Riders*—"Ransom of Rita Renee" 6-11-59; *Wyatt Earp*—"The Paymaster" 12-1-59 (Garcia); *Rawhide*—"Incident at Spanish Rock" 12-18-59; *The Westerner*—"Ghost of a Chance" 12-2-60; *Wanted—Dead or Alive*—"El Gato" 2-22-61 (Jiminez); *Zane Grey Theater*—"Storm Over Eden" 5-4-61 (Estrada); *The Rifleman*—"The Vaqueros" 10-2-61 (Angelo); *Tales of Wells Fargo*—"Portrait of Teresa" 2-10-62 (Antonia); *Laredo*—"I See By Your Outfit" 9-23-65 (Lopez), "Scourge of San Rosa" 1-20-67; *The Big Valley*—"Day of the Comet" 12-26-66 (Rafael Ruiz); *The High Chaparral*—Regular 1967-71 (Pedro); *The Cowboys*—"The Accused" 3-13-74 (Julio); *Kung Fu*—"A Lamb to the Slaughter" 1-11-75 (Regas).

Converse, Frank (1938-). Films: "Hour of the Gun" 1967 (Virgil Earp). ¶TV: *Alias Smith and Jones*—"Bushwack!' 10-21-72 (Cress Truett).

Converse, Peggy. Films: "Drum Beat" 1954 (Mrs. Grant); "They Rode West" 1954 (Mrs. Walters); "Day of the Bad Man" 1958 (Mrs. Quary).

Conversi, Spartaco (Spean Convery). Films: "Adios Hombre" 1966-Ital./Span.; "The Big Gundown" 1966-Ital. (Mitchell); "A Bullet for the General" 1966-Ital. (Cirillo); "Seven Guns for Timothy" 1966-Span./Ital.; "Three Graves for a Winchester" 1966-Ital.; "Death at Owell Rock" 1967-Ital.; "Two Sides of the Dollar" 1967-Fr./Ital.; "All Out" 1968-Ital./Span.; "Django Kills Softly" 1968-Ital.; "Get the Coffin Ready" 1968-Ital.; "I'll Sell My Skin Dearly" 1968-Ital.; "A Long Ride from Hell" 1968-Ital.; "Once Upon a Time in the West" 1968-Ital.; "Twenty Thousand Dollars for Seven" 1968-Ital.; "Paths of War" 1969-Ital.; "Quintana: Dead or Alive" 1969-Ital./Span.; "Sabata" 1969-Ital. (Slim); "Shango" 1969-Ital.; "Fighters from Ave Maria" 1970-Ital./Ger.; "If One Is Born a Swine" 1972-Ital./Span. (Pops); "And They Smelled the Strange, Exciting, Dangerous Scent of Dollars" 1973-Ital.

Convery, Spean. *see* Conversi, Spartaco.

Conville, Robert (1881-2/28/50). Films: "Nanette of the Wilds" 1916 (Constable Jevne); "Laughing Bill Hyde" 1918 (Denny Slevin); "Cotton and Cattle" 1921 (Buck Garrett); "A Cowboy Ace" 1921 (Snake Bullard); "Flowing Gold" 1921; "Out of the Clouds" 1921; "The Range Pirate" 1921; "Rustlers of the Night" 1921; "The Trail to Red Dog" 1921.

Convy, Bert (1934-7/15/91). Films: "Gunman's Walk" 1958 (Paul Chouard).

Conway, Bert (1915-). Films: "The Man from Texas" 1947 (Bob Jackson); "The Spikes Gang" 1974 (Teller); "Rancho Deluxe" 1975 (Wilbur Fargo).

Conway, Curt (1915-4/11/74). Films: "Hud" 1963 (Truman Peters); "Invitation to a Gunfighter" 1964 (McKeever); "Macho Callahan" 1970 (Judge). ¶TV: *Bonanza*—"To Own the World" 4-18-65 (Harry Towers), "The Twenty-Sixth Grave" 10-31-72 (Caldwell); *The Loner*—"The Trial in Paradise" 1-22-66 (Dichter); *The Big Valley*—"The River Monarch" 4-6-66 (Cyrus); *Alias Smith and Jones*—"Journey from San Juan" 4-8-71.

Conway, Gary (1936-). Films: "Young Guns of Texas" 1963 (Tyler Duane) ¶TV: *Sky King*—"Man Hunt" 9-23-51 (Jack Beal); *Colt .45*—"Absent Without Leave" 4-19-60 (Lt. Charles Williams); *Maverick*—"Thunder from the North" 11-13-60 (Orderly); *Daniel Boone*—"Fort New Madrid" 2-15-68 (Billy Carver).

Conway, Jack (1887-10/11/52). Films: "Her Indian Mother" 1910; "The Indian Scout's Revenge" 1910; "Arizona Bill" 1911; "The Chief's Daughter" 1911; "The Indian Vestal" 1911; "John Oakhurst—Gambler" 1911; "Sheriff of Tuolumne" 1911; "Across the Sierras" 1912; "The Bugler of Battery B" 1912; "Her Indian Hero" 1912; "The Love Trail" 1912; "Mary of the Mines" 1912; "The Post Telegrapher" 1912; "The Sheriff's Round-Up" 1912; "The Squatter's Child" 1912; "The Thespian Bandit" 1912; "Brought to Bay" 1913; "The Claim Jumper" 1913; "The Tell Tale Hat Band" 1913; "The Killer" 1921 (William Sanborn).

Conway, Joseph. TV: *Zorro*—"Welcome to Monterey" 10-9-58, "Zorro Rides Alone" 10-16-58 (Palomares), "Horse of Another Color" 10-23-58 (Palomares), "The Senorita Makes a Choice" 10-30-58 (Palomares), "Rendezvous at Sundown" 11-

6-58 (Paolomares); *The Tall Man*—"Sidekick" 12-23-61 (Jose).

Conway, Kevin (1942-). Films: "The Quick and the Dead" 1995 (Eugene Dred).

Conway, Lita. Films: "King of the Royal Mounted" 1940-serial (Linda Merritt); "Trailing Double Trouble" 1940 (Marian Horner); "Saddle Mountain Roundup" 1941 (Nancy).

Conway, Melora. Films: "Vengeance" 1964 (Jean Harmon). TV: *Bronco*—"End of a Rope" 6-14-60 (Melissa Brierly); *Empire*—"End of an Image" 1-15-63 (Ruthie Mathis); *Bonanza*—"The Prime of Life" 12-29-63 (Martha).

Conway, Morgan (1900-11/16/81). Films: "Bells of Capistrano" 1942 (Shag Johnson); "Canyon City" 1943 (Craig Morgan); "Badman's Territory" 1946 (Bill Hampton).

Conway, Pat (-4/24/81). Films: "Geronimo" 1962 (Maynard). ¶TV: *Gunsmoke*—"Obie Tater" 10-15-55 (Quade), "Kitty Caught" 1-18-58 (Billy Gunter), "How to Kill a Friend" 11-22-58 (Toque Marlan), "Shadler" 1-15-73 (Varnum); *Tombstone Territory*—Regular 1957-60 (Sheriff Clay Hollister); *The Texan*—"The Troubled Town" 10-13-58 (Mike Kaler); *Laramie*—"The Killer Legend" 12-12-61 (Tom Wade); *Empire*—"Season of Growth" 2-19-63 (Dan Bishop); *Rawhide*—"Moment in the Sun" 1-29-65 (Reed McCuller); *Branded*—"The Bounty" 2-21-65 (Johnny Dolan); *Bonanza*—"The Lonely Runner" 10-10-65 (Pete), "The Gentle Ones" 10-29-67 (Frank Cole), "Salute to Yesterday" 9-29-68 (Captain Harris); *The Loner*—"Mantrap" 1-8-66 (Ballinger); *Iron Horse*—"Big Deal" 12-12-66 (Brill); *Hondo*—"Hondo and the Singing Wire" 9-22-67 (Rendell).

Conway, Robert. Films: "The Cowboy and the Blonde" 1941 (Don Courtney).

Conway, Russell (1913-78). Films: "Calamity Jane and Sam Bass" 1949 (Baggage Man); "Tomahawk" 1951 (Maj. Horton); "Fort Osage" 1952; "The Outcasts of Poker Flat" 1952 (Vigilante); "Tall Man Riding" 1955 (Jim Feathergill, the U.S. Marshal); "Love Me Tender" 1956 (Ed Galt); "Fort Dobbs" 1958 (Sheriff); "Guns of Diablo" 1964 (Dr. McPheeters). ¶TV: *The Lone Ranger*—"Sheep Thieves" 2-9-50, "Sinner by Proxy" 3-5-53, "Son of Adoption" 3-19-53, "The Bounty Hunter" 5-19-55; *The Cisco Kid*—"Cisco Meets the

Gorilla" 12-13-52, "The Powder Trail" 2-14-53; *Fury*—"Joey Goes Hunting" 11-5-55 (Red Cummings), "A Present for Packy" 1-30-60 (Gregory); *Zane Grey Theater*—"No Man Living" 1-11-57 (Andy Barrow); *Have Gun Will Travel*—"Show of Force" 11-9-57; *Maverick*—"A Rage for Vengeance" 1-12-58 (Sheriff); *Cheyenne*—"Ghost of Cimarron" 3-25-58 (Marshal Short); *Wanted—Dead or Alive*—"The Fourth Headstone" 11-1-58 (Sheriff Pete Link), "The Tyrant" 10-31-59; *U.S. Marshal*—"The Fence" 11-29-58; *Trackdown*—"McCallin's Daughter" 1-2-59 (Bart McCallin); *Rawhide*—"Incident of the Town in Terror" 3-6-59 (Josh Miller), "Incident of the Running Man" 5-5-61, "Deserter's Patrol" 2-9-62 (Colonel Hiller); *Bronco*—"The Silent Witness" 3-10-59 (Willis Turner); *Tombstone Territory*—"Warrant for Death" 5-8-59; *Rough Riders*—"The Highgraders" 5-28-59 (Tom Wooley); *Tales of Wells Fargo*—"Long Odds" 12-14-59 (Dangler), "Long Odds" 6-27-60 (Dangler); *Hotel De Paree*—"Sundance and the Blood Money" 1-1-60 (Coble); *The Texan*—"Borrowed Time" 3-7-60 (Bob Jason); *Bonanza*—"Tax Collector" 2-18-61 (Dave Hart), "False Witness" 10-22-67 (Judge Wheeler), "The Passing of a King" 10-13-68 (Ballenger); *Lawman*—"The Threat" 4-30-61 (Herm Villiers); *Wagon Train*—"The Maud Frazer Story" 10-11-61 (Isaac Frazer); *The Tall Man*—"St. Louis Woman" 1-20-62 (Tom Davis); *The Dakotas*—"Incident at Rapid City" 3-4-63 (Sheriff Landauer); *The Virginian*—"Run Away Home" 4-24-63 (Walter Moody), "Ryker" 9-16-64, "The Dream of Stavros Karas" 12-1-65 (Charley), "Bitter Harvest" 3-15-67 (Tom Hadley); *Temple Houston*—"Billy Hart" 11-28-63 (Henry Hart); *Branded*—"Elsie Brown" 2-14-65 (Sheriff Pollard); *The Loner*—"The Homecoming of Lemuel Stove" 11-20-65 (Sheriff Stimpson); *Daniel Boone*—"Seminole Territory" 1-13-66 (Tom Mayberry), "Flag of Truce" 11-21-68 (Secretary of War); *The Monroes*—"The Intruders" 9-7-66 (Albert Monroe).

Conway, Tim (1933-). Films: "The Apple Dumpling Gang" 1975 (Amos); "The Apple Dumpling Gang Rides Again" 1979 (Amos). ¶TV: *Rango*—Regular 1967 (Rango).

Conway, Tom (1904-4/22/67). Films: "The Bad Man" 1941 (Morgan Pell). ¶TV: *Cheyenne*—"The Conspirators" 10-8-57 (George Willis); *Rawhide*—"Incident of the Tumbleweed Wagon" 1-9-59 (Sinclair Win-

nington); *Have Gun Will Travel*—"The Revenger" 9-30-61.

Conwell, Carolyn (1933-). Films: "The Magnificent Seven Ride" 1972 (Martha). ¶TV: *The Big Valley*—"Brother Love" 2-20-67, "Run of the Savage" 3-11-68 (Mrs. Wiggins); *The Monroes*—"Teach the Tigers to Purr" 3-8-67.

Coogan, Gene (-1/21/72). Films: "The Girl of the Golden West" 1938 (Manuel); "Gun Glory" 1957 (Farmer); "Gun Fight" 1961 (Bole).

Coogan, Jackie (1914-3/1/84). Films: "The Bugle Call" 1927 (Billy Randolph); "Home on the Range" 1935 (Jack Hatfield); "Skipalong Rosenbloom" 1951 (Buck James); "Outlaw Women" 1952 (Piute Bill); "The Proud Ones" 1956 (Man on Make); "The Shakiest Gun in the West" 1968 (Matthew Basch); "Cahill, United States Marshal" 1973 (Charlie Smith). ¶TV: *Cowboy G-Men*—Regular 1952-53 (Stoney Crockett); *The Outlaws*—"Rape of Red Sky" 10-27-60 (Corbett), "The Sisters" 2-15-62 (Ed Durant); *Klondike*—"Halliday's Club" 12-19-60 (First Mate); *Wild Wild West*—"The Night of the Cut Throats" 11-17-67 (Sheriff Koster), "The Night of the Winged Terror" 1-17-68 & 1-24-68 (Mayor Pudney); *Alias Smith and Jones*—"Dreadful Sorry, Clementine" 11-18-71, "Which Way to the O.K. Corral?" 2-10-72 (Clifford), "McGuffin" 12-9-72 (Passenger Agent); *Dirty Sally*—"The Hanging of Cyrus Pike" 4-5-74 (Sheriff); *Gunsmoke*—"The Guns of Cibola Blanca" 9-23-74 & 9-30-74 (Sheriff Stoudenaire).

Coogan, Richard. Films: "Three Hours to Kill" 1954 (Niles Hendricks). ¶TV: *The Californians*—Regular 1958-59 (Marshal Matthew Wayne); *Wichita Town*—"The Devil's Choice" 12-23-59 (Rev. Nichols); *Bronco*—"Shadow of Jesse James" 1-12-60 (Cole Younger); *Sugarfoot*—"Wolf Pack 2-2-60 (Mallory); *Cheyenne*—"Alibi for a Scalped Man" 3-7-60 (Sheriff Charley Emmett); *Maverick*—"Thunder from the North" 11-13-60 (Hank Lawson); *Stagecoach West*—"A Time to Run" 11-15-60 (Major St. Clair); *Laramie*—"No Second Chance" 12-6-60 (Sheriff Lon Matthews), "Riders of the Night" 3-7-61 (Doc Kingsly), "Widow in White" 6-13-61 (Sheriff), "The Barefoot Kid" 1-9-62 (Sheriff Cutter), "The Replacement" 3-27-62 (Paul Halleck), "No Place to Run" 2-5-63; *Bonanza*—"The Rescue" 2-25-61 (Jake Moss); *Gunsmoke*—"Lover Boy" 10-5-63 (Luke).

Cook, Clyde (1891-8/13/84). Films: "The Winning of Barbara Worth" 1926 (Tex); "The Brute" 1927 (Oklahoma Red); "White Gold" 1927 (Homer); "The Dude Wrangler" 1930 (Pinkey Fripp); "Wings of Adventure" 1930 (Skeets Smith).

Cook, Donald (1901-10/1/61). Films: "The Conquerors" 1932 (Warren Lennon).

Cook, Donald. Films: "Vengeance" 1964 (Billy Todd). ¶TV: *Wanted—Dead or Alive*—"Angels of Vengeance" 4-18-59 (Boy).

Cook, Edwin. Films: "Vengeance" 1964 (Clay). ¶TV: *Branded*—"$10,000 for Durango" 11-28-65 (Tiny Bradford).

Cook, Jr., Elisha (1902-5/18/95). Films: "Shane" 1953 (Torrey); "Thunder Over the Plains" 1953 (Standish); "Drum Beat" 1954 (Crackel); "The Outlaw's Daughter" 1954 (Tulas); "The Indian Fighter" 1955 (Briggs); "Timberjack" 1955 (Punky); "The Lonely Man" 1957 (Willie); "Day of the Outlaw" 1959 (Larry); "One-Eyed Jacks" 1961 (Bank Teller); "Blood on the Arrow" 1964 (Tex); "Welcome to Hard Times" 1967 (Hanson); "The Great Bank Robbery" 1969 (Jeb); "El Condor" 1970 (Old Convict); "The Great Northfield, Minnesota Raid" 1972 (Bunker); "Pat Garrett and Billy the Kid" 1973 (Cody); "Winterhawk" 1975 (Rev. Will Finley); "Tom Horn" 1980 (Stable Hand). ¶TV: *Wild Bill Hickok*—"Boy and the Hound Dog" 10-14-52; *Schlitz Playhouse of the Stars*—"Flowers for Jenny" 8-3-56 (Joe Heron); *Wyatt Earp*—"The Equalizer" 4-16-57 (Guns McCallum); *Sheriff of Cochise*—"The Safe Man" 4-26-57; *Trackdown*—"The Trail" 2-28-58 (Clint Serle); *Gunsmoke*—"Matt for Murder" 9-13-58 (Henchman), "Odd Man Out" 11-21-59 (Cyrus Tucker), "Hung High" 11-14-64 (George), "Breckinrdige" 3-13-65 (Jocko); *Bat Masterson*—"Double Showdown" 10-8-58 (Pete Sheeley), "No Funeral for Thorn" 10-22-59 (Thorn Loomis); *Rawhide*—"Incident of a Burst of Evil" 6-26-59 (Bain), "Incident in the Middle of Nowhere" 4-7-61 (Joel Turner), "Piney" 10-9-64 (Jim); *Johnny Ringo*—"Dead Wait" 11-19-59 (Maxie Dolan); *Tombstone Territory*—1-8-60 (Adam Kirby); *Wagon Train*—"The Tracy Sadler Story" 3-9-60 (Cadge Waldo), "The Nancy Palmer Story" 3-8-61 (Lem Salters), "The Ben Engel Story" 3-16-64; *The Rebel*—"The Bequest" 9-25-60 (Jeremy Hake); *Laramie*—"The Tumbleweed Wagon" 5-9-

61; *The Deputy*—"Brand of Honesty" 6-10-61 (Miller); *The Outlaws*—"The Dark Sunrise of Griff Kincaid" 1-4-62 (Cully); *The Dakotas*—"A Nice Girl from Goliah" 5-13-63 (Brinkman); *Temple Houston*—"Gallows in Galilee" 10-31-63 (John Alvorsen); *Destry*—"Law and Order Day" 2-28-64 (Leech); *Wild Wild West*—"The Night of the Double-Edged Knife" 11-12-65 (Mike McGreavy), "The Night of the Bars of Hell" 3-4-66 (Gideon McCoy); *Bonanza*—"A Dollar's Worth of Trouble" 5-15-66 (John Walker), "The Weary Willies" 9-27-70 (Marcus); *The Road West*—"Shaman" 11-14-66 (Wild Man); *The Monroes*—"To Break a Colt" 1-11-67 (Jed); *Cimarron Strip*—"The Battle of Blood Stone" 12-10-67.

Cook, Fred (1941-). Films: "True Grit" TVM-1978 (Chaka).

Cook, Glen. Films: "The Saddle King" 1929 (Dr. Harvey Baine).

Cook, Jimmy Lee. TV: *The Rebel*—"Grant of Land" 5-22-60 (Moody); *The Westerner*—Regular 1960; *Rawhide*—"Incident Before Black Pass" 5-19-61; *The Virginian*—"Impasse" 11-14-62 (Fred), "Nobility of Kings" 11-10-65 (Jimmy), "Beyond the Border" 11-24-65 (Bartender), "A Bald-Faced Boy" 4-13-66 (Blacksmith).

Cook, Joe (1890-5/16/59). Films: "Arizona Mahoney" 1936 (Arizona Mahoney).

Cook, John. Films: "Thieves' Gold" 1918 (Uncle Larkin); "What Am I Bid?" 1919 (John Yarnell).

Cook, Lucius (1891-6/2/52). Films: "Lone Star" 1952.

Cook, Mary Lou. Films: "Ride 'Em, Cowboy" 1942 (Dotty Davis).

Cook, Perry. TV: *Have Gun Will Travel*—"The Solid Gold Patrol" 12-13-58, "Incident at Borasca Bend" 3-21-59 (Sugie), "The Posse" 10-3-59 (Dobie O'Brien), "The Search" 6-18-60 (Mosley), "Out at the Old Ball Park" 10-1-60 (Sheriff Fix), "The Road" 5-27-61 (Sibley), "Odds for a Big Red" 10-7-61, "Alive" 3-17-62; *The Rebel*—"Angry Town" 1-10-60 (Leach), "Night on a Rainbow" 5-29-60 (Roy Cale); *Bat Masterson*—"A Picture of Death" 1-14-60 (Casey); *The Law of the Plainsman*—"Trojan Horse" 5-5-60; *Gunsmoke*—"Speak Me Fair" 5-7-60 (Gunner); *Zane Grey Theater*—"So Young the Savage Land" 11-20-60 (Henry Sloan); *The Virginian*—"Duel at Shiloh" 1-2-63; *The Guns of Will Sonnett*—"The Guns of Will Sonnett" 9-8-67; *Cimarron Strip*—"The Last Wolf" 12-14-67 (Polter).

Cook, Rowena. Films: "Kit Carson" 1940 (Alice Terry).

Cook, Tommy. Films: "Adventures of Red Ryder" 1940-serial (Little Beaver); "Wanderer of the Wasteland" 1945 (Chito as a Boy); "Song of Arizona" 1946 (Chip); "Daughter of the West" 1949 (Ponca); "The Battle at Apache Pass" 1952 (Little Elk); "Thunder Pass" 1954; "Canyon Crossroads" 1955 (Mickey Rivers); "Mohawk" 1956 (Keoga); "Night Passage" 1957 (Howdy Sladen). ¶TV: *Wild Bill Hickok*—"The Maverick" 8-19-52; *Wyatt Earp*—"Trail's End for a Cowboy" 12-6-55 (Brad Collins), "One" 4-15-58 (Will Dade), "Two" 4-29-58 (Will Dade), "Three" 5-13-58 (Will Dade), "Horse Race" 3-3-59 (Hal Walters); *20th Century Fox Hour*—"Broken Arrow" 5-2-56 (Machogee); *Zane Grey Theater*—"A Thread of Respect" 2-12-59 (Link Harris); *Have Gun Will Travel*—"One Came Back" 12-26-59 (Clay Harvey); *The Rifleman*—"Sheer Terror" 10-16-61 (Andy Carr).

Cooke, John J. (1876-10/2/21). Films: "Just Pals" 1920 (Constable).

Cookie, Johnnie. Films: "A Gun Fightin' Gentleman" 1919 (Old Sheriff).

Cookson, Peter (1913-1/6/90). Films: "The Scarlet Horseman" 1946-serial (Kirk Norris).

Cooley, Charles (1903-11/15/60). Films: "The Paleface" 1948 (Mr. X); "Fancy Pants" 1950 (Man); "Son of Paleface" 1952 (Charley).

Cooley, Hal (1895-3/20/71). Films: "Bull's Eye" 1918-serial.

Cooley, Marjorie. Films: "West of Abilene" 1940 (Judith Burnside).

Cooley, Spade (1910-11/23/69). Films: "Redskins and Redheads" 1941-short; "Cactus Capers" 1942-short; "Home in Wyomin'" 1942; "The Singing Sheriff" 1944; "Outlaws of the Rockies" 1945; "Rockin' in the Rockies" 1945; "Senorita from the West" 1945; "Spade Cooley, King of Western Swing" 1945-short; "Texas Panhandle" 1945; "Tumbleweed Tempos" 1946-short; "The Kid from Gower Gulch" 1949; "Spade Cooley and His Orchestra" 1949-short; "Square Dance Jubilee" 1949 (Spade); "Border Outlaws" 1950 (Spade Cooley); "The Silver Bandit" 1950.

Cooley, Willard. Films: "The Wanderer of the Wasteland" 1924 (Camp Doctor); "The Enchanted Hill" 1926 (Curley MacMahon); "Man of the Forest" 1926 (Deputy Sheriff).

Coolidge, Philip (1908-5/23/
67). TV: *Gunsmoke*—"Grass" 11-29-
58 (Harry Pope), "Old Dan" 1-27-62
(Lem Petch), "One Killer on Ice" 1-
23-65 (Owney Dales); *Have Gun
Will Travel*—"The Sons of Aaron
Murdock" 5-9-59 (Aaron Murdock),
"Lazarus" 1-20-62 (Dr. Avatar); *Tales
of Wells Fargo*—"End of a Legend" 11-
23-59 (Old John).

Coolidge, Rita (1945-). Films:
"Pat Garrett and Billy the Kid" 1973
(Maria).

Cooney, Denis. TV: *Iron
Horse*—"Dry Run to Glory" 1-6-68
(Billy Joe Scofield); *The Virginian*—
"The Substitute" 12-5-69 (Josh
Gates); *Here Come the Brides*—
"Lorenzo Bush" 12-19-69 (Wesley).

Coons, Johnny (1917-7/6/75).
Films: "Tell Them Willie Boy Is
Here" 1969 (Clerk). ¶TV: *Wide
Country*—"Straightjacket for an In-
dian" 10-25-62 (Tourist).

Coontz, Bill (1916-4/7/78).
Films: "The Lawless Rider" 1954
(Red Rooks); "Hidden Guns" 1956;
"Raiders of Old California" 1957;
"Lone Texan" 1959 (Indian); "Buffalo
Gun" 1961. ¶TV: *Wild Bill Hickok*—
"Medicine Show" 12-25-51, "Ol'
Pardner Rides Again" 9-16-52; *Wyatt
Earp*—"Earp Ain't Even Wearing
Guns" 2-3-59 (Lafe Harin).

Cooper, Ashley (1882-1/3/52).
Films: "Shadows of Conscience" 1921
(Judson Craft); "The Son of the
Wolf" 1922 (Ben Harrington); "Des-
ert Driven" 1923 (Kendall).

Cooper, Ben (1930-). Films: "A
Perilous Journey" 1953 (Sam Austin);
"The Woman They Almost Lynched"
1953 (Jesse James); "Hell's Outpost"
1954 (Alec Bacchione); "Johnny Guitar" 1954 (Turkey Ralston); "The
Outcast" 1954 (the Kid); "The Last
Command" 1955 (Jeb Lacey); "Rebel
in Town" 1956 (Gray Mason); "Duel
at Apache Wells" 1957 (Johnny Shattuck); "Outlaw's Son" 1957 (Jeff
Blaine); "Gunfight at Comanche
Creek" 1964 (Carter); "The Raiders"
1964 (Tom King); "Arizona Raiders"
1965 (Willie Martin); "Waco" 1966
(Scotty Moore); "The Fastest Guitar
Alive" 1967 (Rink); "Red Tomahawk"
1967 (Lt. Drake); "One More Train
to Rob" 1971 (1st Deputy); "Support
Your Local Gunfighter" 1971 (Colorado). ¶TV: *Zane Grey Theater*—
"Vengeance Canyon" 11-30-56 (Clint
Harding), "Miss Jenny" 1-7-60 (Darryl Thompson), "The Sunrise Gun"
5-19-60 (Sam Duskin, Jr.), "Desert
Flight" 10-13-60 (Sandy); *Wagon
Train*—"The Steve Campden Story"
5-13-59, "The Tom Tuckett Story" 3-

2-60 (Tom Tuckett); *Tales of Wells
Fargo*—"Home Town" 11-16-59 (Matthew Land); *Wichita Town*—"Passage
to the Enemy" 12-2-59 (Tom Warren); *Johnny Ringo*—"The Reno
Brothers" 2-25-60 (Mike Reno); *Bonanza*—"Showdown" 9-10-60 (Sam
Kirby), "The Horse Breaker" 11-26-61
(Johnny Lightly); *Best of the Post*—
"Command" 10-6-60 (Lieutenant
Flint Cohill); *Stagecoach West*—"The
Saga of Jeremy Boone" 11-29-60 (Je-
remy Boone); *The Westerner*—"Hand
on the Gun" 12-23-60; *The Rifle-
man*—"Face of Yesterday" 1-31-61 (Si-
mon Lee); *Gunsmoke*—"Apprentice
Doc" 12-9-61 (Pitt), "Breckinridge"
3-13-65 (Breck Taylor), "Two Tall
Men" 5-8-65 (Breck Taylor); *Lara-
mie*—"The Runt" 2-20-62 (Sandy
Catlin), "Gun Duel" 12-25-62
(Johnny Hartley); *Rawhide*—"The
Photographer" 12-11-64 (Clell);
Death Valley Days—"Biscuits and
Billy the Kid" 11-1-69 (Billy the Kid);
The Men from Shiloh—"With Love,
Bullets, and Valentines" 10-7-70
(Jason); *Kung Fu*—"The Centoph" 4-
4-74 & 4-11-74 (Captain Good-
night).

Cooper, Bigelow. Films: "A Tale
of Old Tucson" 1914; "The Law of the
Yukon" 1920 (Dr. Meredith).

Cooper, Charles. Films: "Gun
Fight" 1961 (Cole Fender). ¶TV: *Colt
.45*—"Rare Specimen" 2-7-58 (Jed
Dailey), "Breakthrough" 3-27-60;
Sugarfoot—"A Wreath for Charity
Lloyd" 3-18-58 (Wesley Jerome);
Gunsmoke—"Chester's Hanging" 5-
17-58 (Jim Cando), "Young Love" 1-
3-59 (Jim Box); *The Rifleman*—"End
of a Young Gun" 10-14-58, "The
Stand-In" 10-23-61 (Rudy Croft),
"Honest Abe" 11-20-61 (Matt Yorty),
"I Take This Woman" 11-5-62 (Lar-
sen); *Tales of Wells Fargo*—"The De-
serter" 11-24-58 (Lt. Rath), "The Lat
Mayor Brown" 3-7-60 (Sonny);
Wanted—Dead or Alive—"Rawhide
Breed" 12-13-58 (Frank Kreager); *The
Restless Gun*—"The Painted Beauty"
1-5-59 (Boyd Lively), "Dead Man's
Hand" 3-16-59 (Hode Emory); *The
Texan*—"A Quart of Law" 1-12-59
(Walt Carlin), "Twenty-Four Hours
to Live" 9-5-60 (Steve Murrow);
Wagon Train—"The Flint McCul-
lough Story" 1-14-59 (Lt. Quincy
Abbot); *Trackdown*—"The Feud" 2-
11-59 (Matthew Turley); *Bronco*—
"Borrowed Glory" 2-24-59 (Frank
Stover), "Montana Passage" 4-5-60
(Wild Bill Hickok); *Lawman*—"The
Visitor" 3-15-59 (Jack Rollins); *Mav-
erick*—"Burial Ground of the Gods"
3-30-59 (Phil Stanton), "Passage to
Fort Doom" 3-8-59 (Claude Rogan),

"Trooper Maverick" 11-29-59 (Captain Berger); *Bonanza*—"The Diedeshiemer Story" 10-31-59 (Gil Fenton);
The Deputy—"Backfire" 1-2-60 (Con
Marlowe); *Johnny Ringo*—"The Raffertys" 3-3-60 (Slim Pardee); *Riverboat*—"Fort Epitaph" 3-7-60 (Major
Daniels); *Death Valley Days*—"Diamond Jim Brady" 6-2-63 (Buchanan), "The $25,000 Wager" 2-7-
65 (MacCrellish), "The Firebrand"
4-30-66 (Gillespie); *Father Murphy*—
Regular 1981-82 (Sheriff).

Cooper, Chris. Films: "Lonesome Dove" TVM-1989 (July Johnson); "Return to Lonesome Dove"
TVM-1993 (July Johnson).

Cooper, Clancy (1907-6/14/75).
Films: "Riding Through Nevada"
1942; "West of Tombstone" 1942
(Dave Shurlock); "Dead Man's
Gulch" 1943 (Walt Bledsoe); "Deer-
slayer" 1943 (Mr. Barlow); "Frontier
Fury" 1943 (Dan Bentley); "Cyclone
Prairie Rangers" 1944; "Riding West"
1944 (Blackburn); "Sundown Valley"
1944 (Hodge Miller); "The Man
from Texas" 1947 (Jim Walsh); "Da-
kota Lil" 1950 (Bartender); "Distant
Drums" 1951 (Sgt. Shane); "The Man
Behind the Gun" 1952 (Kansas Col-
lins); "The Wild North" 1952
(Sloan); "The Silver Whip" 1953
(Bert Foley); "The True Story of Jesse
James" 1957 (Sheriff Yoe); "The Sher-
iff of Fractured Jaw" 1958-Brit. (R.
Barber). ¶TV: *The Adventures of Rin
Tin Tin*—"The Poor Little Rich Boy"
10-7-55 (Matt Parish), "The Indian
Hater" 1-11-57 (Josh Deering), "The
Lieutenant's Lesson" 2-8-57 (Sgt.
Walker); *Broken Arrow*—"Quaran-
tine" 4-9-57 (Harrison); *Gunsmoke*—
"The Man Who Would Be Marshal"
6-15-57 (Bozeman); *Buckskin*—"A
Man from the Mountains" 10-30-58
(Judge); *Rough Riders*—"End of the
Track" 3-5-59 (Major Hanson); *The
Rifleman*—"The Raid" 6-9-59;
Wanted—Dead or Alive—"Montana
Kid" 9-5-59; *Lawman*—"Lily" 10-4-
59 (Timmo McQueen), "The Prodi-
gal" 11-22-59 (Timmo McQueen),
"The Stranger" 1-17-60 (Timmo Mc-
Queen); *Wyatt Earp*—"The Paymas-
ter" 12-1-59 (Clancy), "The Big Fight
at Total Wreck" 1-12-60 (Jock Welsh),
"Roscoe Turns Detective" 5-3-60
(Skinner Malone), "The Good Mule
and the Bad Mule" 3-14-61 (Morgan);
The Law of the Plainsman—"The In-
nocents" 12-10-59 (Connie); *Maver-
ick*—"Bundle from Britain" 9-18-60
(McGee); *The Deputy*—"Second Cousin to the Czar" 12-24-60 (Hawkins);
Wagon Train—"Weight of Command" 1-25-61; *Rawhide*—"The
Pitchwagon" 3-2-62 (Logan); *The

Tall Man—"The Long Way Home" 3-31-62 (Sheriff Lorney); *The Virginian*—"The Mountain of the Sun" 4-17-63; *Wild Wild West*—"The Night of the Howling Light" 12-17-65 (Trowbridge); *The Guns of Will Sonnett*—"The Straw Man" 11-8-68.

Cooper, Dee. Films: "Saddle Serenade" 1945; "Silver Range" 1946; "Trail to Mexico" 1946; "Cheyenne Takes Over" 1947 (Johnson); "Ghost Town Renegades" 1947; "Pioneer Justice" 1947 (Criler); "Raiders of the South" 1947; "Return of the Lash" 1947 (Hank); "Stage to Mesa City" 1947; "Trailing Danger" 1947; "Check Your Guns" 1948 (Rider #2); "Gunning for Justice" 1948; "Triggerman" 1948; "Brand of Fear" 1949; "Crashing Thru" 1949; "Outlaw Country" 1949 (Jeff Thomas); "Range Land" 1949 (Pete); "Riders of the Dusk" 1949 (Tom); "Shadows of the West" 1949 (Joe); "Western Renegades" 1949 (Cook); "Belle Starr" TVM-1980 (Morris). ¶TV: *Pistols 'n' Petticoats*—11-12-66 (Ern).

Cooper, Dulcie (1904-9/3/81). Films: "Do and Dare" 1922 (Mary Lee).

Cooper, Edna Mae (1901-6/27/86). Films: "Rimrock Jones" 1918 (Hazel Hardesty); "Beauty and the Bad Man" 1925 (Mayme).

Cooper, Gary (1901-5/13/61). Films: "The Winning of Barbara Worth" 1926 (Abe Lee); "Arizona Bound" 1927 (Dave Saulter); "The Last Outlaw" 1927 (Buddy Hale); "Nevada" 1927 (Nevada); "The Virginian" 1929 (the Virginian); "Wolf Song" 1929 (Sam Lash); "A Man from Wyoming" 1930 (Jim Baker); "The Spoilers" 1930 (Roy Glenister); "The Texan" 1930 (Enrique Quico, the Llano Kid); "Fighting Caravans" 1931 (Clint Belmet); "The Plainsman" 1936 (Wild Bill Hickok); "Cowboy and the Lady" 1938 (Stretch); "Northwest Mounted Police" 1940 (Dusty Rivers); "The Westerner" 1940 (Cole Hardin); "Along Came Jones" 1945 (Melody Jones); "Unconquered" 1947 (Capt. Christopher Holden); "Dallas" 1950 (Blayde "Reb" Hollister); "Distant Drums" 1951 (Capt. Quincy Wyatt); "High Noon" 1952 (Will Kane); "Springfield Rifle" 1952 (Maj. Lex Kearney); "Blowing Wind" 1953 (Jeff); "Garden of Evil" 1954 (Hooker); "Vera Cruz" 1954 (Benjamin Trane); "Friendly Persuasion" 1956 (Jess Birdwell); "Man of the West" 1958 (Link Jones); "Alias Jesse James" 1959 (Himself); "The Hanging Tree" 1959

(Doc Joe Frail); "They Came to Cordura" 1959 (Maj. Thomas Thorn).

Cooper, George (1892-12/9/43). Films: "The Outlaw" 1913; "The Tragedy of Whispering Creek" 1914; "The Unlawful Trade" 1914; "The Battle of Frenchman's Run" 1915; "From Out of the Big Snows" 1915 (Jean LaSalle); "The Fox" 1921 (K.C. Kid); "Suzanna" 1922 (Miguel); "Quicksands" 1923 (Matt Patterson); "The Great Divide" 1925 (Shorty); "The Trail of '98" 1929 (Samuel Foote, the Worm); "Girl of the Golden West" 1930 (Trinidad Joe); "Under a Texas Moon" 1930 (Philipe); "Forbidden Trail" 1932 (Happy); "The Man from Arizona" 1932 (Mrs. Sutton); "Wide Open Spaces" 1932-short; "West of the Pecos" 1934 (Wes); "The Phantom Rider" 1936-serial (Spooky); "Ride 'Em Cowboy" 1936 (Chuck Morse); "Riders of the Dawn" 1937 (Grizzly); "West of Rainbow's End" 1938 (Happy); "Stand Up and Fight" 1939.

Cooper, George. Films: "Blood on the Moon" 1948 (Fred Borden); "Roughshod" 1949 (Jim Clayton). ¶TV: *The Gene Autry Show*—"The Raiders" 4-14-51 (Buckeye).

Cooper, Georgia (1882-9/3/68). Films: "The Man from Thunder River" 1943.

Cooper, Gladys (1888-11/17/71). Films: "Headin' North" 1922 (Madge Mullins).

Cooper, Inez. Films: "'Neath Canadian Skies" 1946; "North of the Border" 1946; "Riding the California Trail" 1947; "Border Treasure" 1950 (Anita).

Cooper, Jack. Films: "Rodeo Rhythm" 1942 (Joe Stegge).

Cooper, Jackie (1922-). Films: "The Lone Cowboy" 1934 (Scooter O'Neal); "The Return of Frank James" 1940 (Clem/Tom Grayson); "Men of Texas" 1942 (Robert Houston Smith). ¶TV: *Hec Ramsey*—"Dead Heat" 2-3-74 (Barney Tolliver).

Cooper, Jeanne (1928-). Films: "The Man from the Alamo" 1953 (Kate Lamar); "The Redhead from Wyoming" 1953 (Myra); "Shadows of Tombstone" 1953 (Marge); "The Glory Guys" 1965 (Mrs. McCabe); "There Was a Crooked Man" 1970 (Prostitute). ¶TV: *Death Valley Days*—"Sixth Sense" 6-9-54, "I Am Joaquin" 3-28-55; *Tales of Wells Fargo*—"Belle Starr" 9-9-57 (Belle Starr), "Clay Allison" 6-15-59 (Duchess); *Maverick*—"Naked Gallows" 12-15-57 (Virginia Cory),

"Flood's Folly" 2-19-61 (Martha Flood); *Cheyenne*—"Top Hand" 12-31-57 (Marie Conover), "A Man Called Ragan" 4-23-62 (Mati Stevens), "The Quick and the Deadly" 10-22-62; *Zane Grey Theater*—"Sundown at Bitter Creek" 2-14-58 (Lucy); *Jefferson Drum*—"Wheel of Fortune" 6-27-58 (Duane); *Bronco*—"School for Cowards" 4-21-59 (Martha Reynolds), "Shadow of Jesse James" 1-12-60 (Belle Starr); *Wanted—Dead or Alive*—"Man on Horseback" 12-5-59 (Myra); *Man from Blackhawk*—"Death at Noon" 1-8-60 (Liza); *Sugarfoot*—"The Captive Locomotive" 6-7-60 (Rachel Barnes); *The Tall Man*—"The Reversed Blade" 2-4-61 (Elmira Webster); *Rawhide*—"Incident on the Road Back" 2-24-61 (Clara Wilson), "Incident at Crooked Hat" 2-1-63 (Kate Merrill); *Wagon Train*—"The Traitor" 12-13-61 (Madge Upton), "The Donna Fuller Story" 12-19-62 (Donna Fuller), "The Kitty Pryer Story" 11-18-63 (Martha Harpe), "The Whipping" 3-23-64 (Molly Garland), "The Story of Hector Heatherington" 12-20-64 (Harriet Heatherington); *Bonanza*—"The Good Samaritan" 12-23-62 (Abigail Hinton), "She Walks in Beauty" 9-22-63 (Emilia); *Have Gun Will Travel*—"The Treasure" 12-29-62 (Edna Hardin); *The Dakotas*—"Mutiny at Fort Mercy" 1-21-63 (Rebecca Ridgeway); *Stoney Burke*—"Webb of Fear" 2-18-63 (Loren Schuyler); *Gunsmoke*—"Ex-Con" 11-30-63 (Lily Pitts); *The Virginian*—"The Fortunes of J. Jimerson Jones" 1-15-64 (Julia Montgomery); *Branded*—"Elsie Brown" 2-14-65 (Elsie Brown); *A Man Called Shenandoah*—"Survival" 9-20-65 (Bess); *The Big Valley*—"Boots with My Father's Name" 9-29-65 (Martha), "Tunnel of Gold" 4-20-66 (Elaine Jason); *The Loner*—"The Lonely Calico Queen" 10-2-65 (Marge); *Daniel Boone*—"Crisis by Fire" 1-27-66 (Amy Barr), "The Young Ones" 2-23-67 (Addie Ogilvie); *The Monroes*—"Ride with Terror" 9-21-66 (Mae Duvall); *Laredo*—"The Small Chance Ghost" 3-3-67 (Kay Comstock); *Cimarron Strip*—"Knife in the Darkness" 1-25-68 (Pony Jane); *Lancer*—"The Heart of Pony Alice" 12-17-68 (Florida).

Cooper, Jeff. Films: "Duel at Diablo" 1966 (Casey). ¶TV: *The Virginian*—"All Nice and Legal" 11-25-64 (Matt Potter).

Cooper, Ken. Films: "Beau Bandit" 1930 (Cowhand); "The Devil Horse" 1932-serial; "Stormy" 1935 (Cowboy); "The Arizona Raiders" 1936 (Cowboy); "Comin' Round the

Mountain" 1936 (Slim); "Custer's Last Stand" 1936-serial (Spike); "Guns and Guitars" 1936 (Deputy Clark); "Red River Valley" 1936 (Long); "The Singing Cowboy" 1936 (Bill); "Vigilantes Are Coming" 1936-serial (Rancher); "Riders of the Whistling Skull" 1937; "Round-Up Time in Texas" 1937 (Tex Autry); "The Lone Ranger" 1938-serial (Trooper); "Cowboy Serenade" 1942; "Home in Wyomin'" 1942; "Jesse James, Jr." 1942; "Sons of the Pioneers" 1942; "Cow Town" 1950; "Desperadoes of the West" 1950-serial (Ed).

Cooper, Maxine. TV: *Maverick*—"Relic of Fort Tejon" 11-3-57 (Donna Selly); *Wanted—Dead or Alive*—"The Inheritance" 4-30-60 (Constance Howard).

Cooper, Melville (1896-3/29/73). TV: *The Californians*—"Truce of the Tree" 12-17-57 (Lord Charlie).

Cooper, Miriam (1892-4/12/76). Films: "The Bugler of Battery B" 1912; "The Pony Express Girl" 1912; "The Water Right War" 1912; "The Gunman" 1914; "The Horse Wrangler" 1914; "Evangeline" 1919 (Evangeline).

Cooper, Philip. Films" "Under the Pampas Moon" 1935 (Little Jose).

Cooper, Rosemary. Films: "The Phantom Bullet" 1926 (Dolores).

Cooper, Stan. Films: "Great Treasure Hunt" 1967-Ital./Span. (Deam); "More Dollars for the MacGregors" 1970-Ital./Span. (Ross Stewart); "You're Jinxed, Friend, You Just Met Sacramento" 1970-Ital./Span.; "Go Away! Trinity Has Arrived in Eldorado" 1972-Ital.

Cooper, Tamara. TV: *Broken Arrow*—"The Trial" 1-22-57 (Julie); *Black Bart*—Pilot 4-4-75 (Mrs. Swenson); *Big Bend Country*—Pilot 8-27-81 (Plantation Woman).

Cooper, Ted. Films: "Arizona Manhunt" 1951 (Charlie); "Wild Horse Ambush" 1952 (Spy).

Cooper, Tex (1877-3/29/51). Films: "The Outlaw Deputy" 1935; "Rustlers of Red Dog" 1935-serial; "Tumbling Tumbleweeds" 1935; "The Fugitive Sheriff" 1936; "The Old Wyoming Trail" 1937; "Reckless Ranger" 1937; "Riders of the Dawn" 1937; "Two-Fisted Sheriff" 1937; "Two Gun Law" 1937; "Valley of Terror" 1937; "Heroes of the Alamo" 1938; "The Lone Ranger" 1938-serial (Rancher); "Under Western Stars" 1938; "West of Cheyenne" 1938; "The Man from Sundown" 1939; "The Oklahoma Kid" 1939 (Old

Man in Bar); "Spoilers of the Range" 1939 (Old Timer); "Cherokee Strip" 1940; "The Dark Command" 1940; "Melody Ranch" 1940; "Take Me Back to Oklahoma" 1940; "Across the Sierras" 1941; "Wagons Westward" 1940; "Beyond the Sacremento" 1941; "Billy the Kid's Roundup" 1941; "Hands Across the Rockies" 1941; "The Lone Rider in Frontier Fury" 1941; "North from the Lone Star" 1941; "The Return of Daniel Boone" 1941; "Tumbledown Ranch in Arizona" 1941; "Underground Rustlers" 1941; "Wrangler's Roost" 1941; "Overland Stagecoach" 1942; "A Tornado in the Saddle" 1942; "Black Market Rustlers" 1943; "Cattle Stampede" 1943; "Daredevils of the West" 1943-serial; "Frontier Law" 1943; "Outlaws of Stampede Pass" 1943; "The Ox-Bow Incident" 1943 (Posse); "Alaska" 1944; "Boss of Boomtown" 1944; "Pistol Packin' Nitwits" 1945-short; "Prairie Rustlers" 1945; "Sunset in El Dorado" 1945; "Gun Town" 1946; "The Phantom Rider" 1946-serial; "Romance of the West" 1946; "Quick on the Trigger" 1948.

Cooper, William. Films: "The Danger Trail" 1917 (Jackpine).

Coote, Robert (1909-11/25/82). Films: "Bad Lands" 1939 (Eaton); "Rangle River" 1939-Australia (Reginald Mannister). ¶TV: *Rawhide*— "Incident in the Garden of Eden" 6-17-60 (Sir Richard Ashley).

Copas, Cowboy (1914-3/5/63). Films: "Square Dance Jubilee" 1949.

Cope, Kenneth (1931-). Films: "The Desperados" 1969 (Carlin).

Copeland, Nick (1895-8/17/40). Films: "The Cowboy Star" 1936; "Song of the Saddle" 1936 (Immigrant); "Treachery Rides the Range" 1936.

Copley, Terri. Films: "The Gambler Returns: The Luck of the Draw" TVM-1991 (Daisy McKee).

Coppin, Doug. Films: "Prairie Raiders" 1947; "Buckaroo from Powder River" 1948 (Tommy Ryaldn).

Corazzari, Bruno. Films: "For One Hundred Thousand Dollars Per Killing" 1967-Ital.; "Belle Starr Story" 1968-Ital.; "Cost of Dying" 1968-Ital./Fr.; "A Long Ride from Hell" 1968-Ital.; "The Mercenary" 1968-Ital./Span. (Studs); "Roy Colt and Winchester Jack" 1970-Ital.; "Light the Fuse ... Sartana Is Coming" 1971-Ital./Fr.; "Man Called Sledge" 1971-Ital./U.S. (Bice); "Vendetta at Dawn" 1971-Ital.; "Four Horsemen of the Apocalpyse" 1975-Ital.

Corbett, Ben (1892-5/19/61). Films: "Lightning Bryce" 1919-serial; "Tempest Cody Hits the Trail" 1919; "Tempest Cody Rides Wild" 1919; "The Man with the Punch" 1920; "The Trail of the Hound" 1920; "Under Northern Lights" 1920 (Burke); "The Black Sheep" 1921 (Pete Miller); "The Cactus Kid" 1921; "The Cowpuncher's Comeback" 1921; "Who Was That Man?" 1921; "The Heart of a Texan" 1922 (Commanche Horse); "Lure of Gold" 1922 (Latigo Bob); "Rangeland" 1922 (Chuck Quigley); "South of the Northern Lights" 1922 (Chick Rawlins); "West of the Pecos" 1922 (Wolf Bradley); "Don Quickshot of the Rio Grande" 1923 (Henchman); "The Red Warning" 1923 (Bud Osman); "The Man from Wyoming" 1924 (Red); "The Phantom Horseman" 1924 (Benny); "The Riddle Rider" 1924-serial; "Brakin' Loose" 1925; "The Circus Cyclone" 1925 (Referee); "Daring Days" 1925 (Ambrose Carson); "Just Cowboys" 1925; "The Outlaw's Daughter" 1925 (Bill); "The Sagebrush Lady" 1925 (Doyle's Foreman); "Shootin' Wild" 1925; "Too Many Bucks" 1925; "Barely Reasonable" 1926; "The Big Game" 1926; "Desperate Dan" 1926; "Fade Away Foster" 1926; "The Hen Punchers of Piperock" 1926; "The Hero of Piperock" 1926; "Let Loose" 1926; "A Man's Size Pet" 1926; "One Wild Time" 1926; "Piperock Goes Wild" 1926; "The Rescue" 1926; "When East Meets West" 1926; "Without Orders" 1926 (Squinty Moore); "Border Cavalier" 1927 (Bennie); "Cows Is Cows" 1927; "Flaming Snow" 1927; "The Man from Hardpan" 1927 (Jack Burton); "One Glorious Scrap" 1927 (Benny); "The Piperock Blaze" 1927; "The Pride of Peacock" 1927; "The Rest Cure" 1927; "Somewhere in Sonora" 1927 (Sockeye Kelly); "A Strange Inheritance" 1927; "Tied Up" 1927; "Too Much Progress for Piperock" 1927; "When Oscar Went Wild" 1927; "Arizona Cyclone" 1928 (Benny); "The Black Ace" 1928; "The Boss of Rustler's Roost" 1928 (Tip Reardon); "The Bronc Stomper" 1928 (Yea Bo Smith); "The Fearless Rider" 1928 (Two-Spot Tommy); "Made-to-Order Hero" 1928 (Babbling Ben); "The Mystery Rider" 1928-serial; "Put 'Em Up" 1928 (Tradin' Sam); "Quick Triggers" 1928 (Benny); "45 Calibre War" 1929 (Toad Hunter); "The Royal Rider" 1929 (Wild West Show Member); "Bar L Ranch" 1930 (Barney McCool); "Beau Bandit" 1930 (Cowhand); "The Lonesome Tail" 1930

(Sweetheart); "Men Without Law" 1930; "Ridin' Law" 1930; "Romance of the West" 1930 (Buck); "Shadow Ranch" 1930; "Westward Bound" 1930 (Ben); "Branded" 1931; "Cavalier of the West" 1931 (Sergeant Regan); "Riders of the Rio" 1931 (One Shot); "Shotgun Pass" 1931; "West of Cheyenne" 1931 (Banty); "Wild West Whoopee" 1931; "Forty-Five Calibre Echo" 1932; "Guns for Hire" 1932; "Hell Fire Austin" 1932; "Partners" 1932 (Shorty); "The Reckless Rider" 1932; "Ride Him, Cowboy" 1932; "The Saddle Buster" 1932 (Shorty); "Tex Takes a Holiday" 1932 (Joe); "Texas Tornado" 1932 (Shorty Walker); "Come on Tarzan" 1933 (Shorty); "Girl Trouble" 1933; "Gun Law" 1933; "Strawberry Roan" 1933 (Slim); "The Trail Drive" 1933; "Trouble Busters" 1933 (Windy Wallace); "Arizona Nights" 1934; "The Border Menace" 1934 (Dragon); "Fighting Through" 1934 (Ben); "Gun Justice" 1934; "Honor of the Range" 1934; "The Last Round-Up" 1934 (2nd Miner); "The Lone Bandit" 1934 (Benny Broderick); "Nevada Cyclone" 1934; "The Outlaw Tamer" 1934 (Bud McClure); "Pals of the Prairie" 1934-short; "Potluck Pards" 1934; "Rainbow Riders" 1934; "Ridin' Gent" 1934-short; "Smoking Guns" 1934; "Thunder Over Texas" 1934; "West on Parade" 1934; "Arizona Bad Man" 1935 (Cowboy); "Border Vengeance" 1935 (Bud Benson); "Born to Battle" 1935; "Circle of Death" 1935 (Dan Quinn); "The Cowboy and the Bandit" 1935; "Coyote Trails" 1935 (Windy); "Gunsmoke on the Guadalupe" 1935; "Ivory-Handled Gun" 1935 (Steve); "Moonlight on the Prairie" 1935; "Pals of the Range" 1935; "Ridin' Thru" 1935 (Barney); "Rustlers of Red Dog" 1935-serial; "The Silent Code" 1935 (Breen); "The Unconquered Bandit" 1935; "Western Racketeers" 1935 (Jack Price); "The Whirlwind Rider" 1935; "For the Service" 1936 (Ben); "Gun Smoke" 1936 (Shorty); "Sunset of Power" 1936 (Red); "Black Aces" 1937; "Blazing Sixes" 1937 (Slim); "Cherokee Strip" 1937; "The Devil's Saddle Legion" 1937; "Empty Holsters" 1937; "Empty Saddles" 1937 (Vegas); "Hopalong Rides Again" 1937; "It Happened Out West" 1937 (Dizzy); "Sandflow" 1937; "Texas Trail" 1937 (Orderly); "Way Out West" 1937 (Man in Audience); "Gold Mine in the Sky" 1938 (Spud Grogan); "Heroes of the Alamo" 1938; "Lawless Valley" 1938; "Lightning Carson Rides Again" 1938; "The Mysterious Rider" 1938; "The Overland Express" 1938; "Six-Gun Trail" 1938; "Six Shootin' Sheriff" 1938 (Red); "Songs and Saddles" 1938 (Sparks); "Code of the Cactus" 1939 (Magpie); "Come on, Rangers" 1939; "The Fighting Gringo" 1939 (Shorty); "Fighting Renegade" 1939 (Magpie); "Outlaw's Paradise" 1939 (Magpie); "Racketeers of the Range" 1939 (Dutch); "Straight Shooter" 1939 (Magpie); "Texas Wildcats" 1939 (Magpie); "Timber Stampede" 1939 (Phony Witness); "Trigger Fingers" 1939 (Magpie); "Arizona Gangbusters" 1940; "Prairie Law" 1940; "In Old Cheyenne" 1941; "Bad Men of the Hills" 1942; "Ghost Town Law" 1942 (Red Larkin); "Pirates of the Prairie" 1942; "Hoppy Serves a Writ" 1943 (Card Player); "Saddles and Sagebrush" 1943; "Sagebrush Law" 1943; "Wagon Tracks West" 1943; "Marked Trails" 1944 (Blackie); "Partners of the Trail" 1944 (Duke); "Range Law" 1944 (Joe); "Enemy of the Law" 1945; "Fool's Gold" 1946 (Sergeant); "Blood on the Moon" 1948; "The Man from Colorado" 1948 (Deputy); "Silver River" 1948 (Henchman); "Haunted Trails" 1949 (Townsman); "Cody of the Pony Express" 1950-serial (Eric); "Colt .45" 1950; "Dallas" 1950 (Bystander); "Montana Desperado" 1951; "Springfield Rifle" 1952 (Sergeant Major); "The Charge at Feather River" 1953 (Carver).

Corbett, Glenn (1929-1/16/93). Films: "Shenandoah" 1965 (Jacob Anderson); "Chisum" 1970 (Pat Garrett); "Big Jake" 1971 (O'Brien); "Law of the Land" TVM-1976 (Andy Hill). ¶TV: *Gunsmoke*—"Chicken" 12-5-64 (Dan Collins), "Phoenix" 9-20-71 (Phoenix), "A Family of Killers" 1-14-74 (Hargraves); *The Virginian*—"The Awakening" 10-13-65 (David Henderson); *Bonanza*—"Mighty Is the Word" 11-7-65 (Rev. Paul Watson), "Winter Kill" 3-28-71 (Howie); *The Legend of Jesse James*—"The Hunted and the Hunters" 4-11-66 (Luke Canby); *The Road West*—Regular 1966-67 (Chance Reynolds); *Alias Smith and Jones*—"Twenty-One Days to Tenstrike" 1-6-72 (Ralph), "Bushwack!' 10-21-72 (Marty Alcott).

Corbett, Gretchen (1947-). TV: *Gunsmoke*—"A Town in Chains" 9-16-74 (Arlene); *Barbary Coast*—"Arson and Old Lace" 11-14-75 (Lily Colt).

Corbett, James J. (1867-2/18/33). Films: "The Man from the Golden West" 1913 (Gentleman Jim).

Corbett, Louis J. Films: "The Tioga Kid" 1948 (Sam).

Corbin, Barry (1940-). Films: "The Ballad of Gregorio Cortez" 1983 (Abernethy); "Lonesome Dove" TVM-1989 (Roscoe Brown); "Conagher" TVM-1991.

Corbin, Virginia Lee (1910-6/5/42). Films: "Ace High" 1918 (Annette Dupre as a Child); "Six-Shooter Andy" 1918; "Hands Up!" 1926 (the Other Girl); "Shotgun Pass" 1931 (Sally Seagrue).

Corby, Ellen (1913-). Films: "In Old Sacramento" 1946; "The Gunfighter" 1950 (Mrs. Devlin); "The Big Trees" 1952 (Mrs. Blackburn); "Shane" 1953 (Mrs. Torrey); "The Vanquished" 1953 (Mrs. Barbour); "The Woman They Almost Lynched" 1953 (1st Woman); "Untamed Heiress" 1954 (Mrs. Flanny); "Stagecoach to Fury" 1956 (Sarah); "Night Passage" 1957 (Mrs. Feeney); "Four for Texas" 1964; "The Night of the Grizzly" 1966 (Hazel Squires); "Support Your Local Gunfighter" 1971 (Abigail). ¶TV: *The Roy Rogers Show*—"Head for Cover" 10-21-56 (Amity Bailey); *Wyatt Earp*—"Shootin' Woman" 1-1-57 (Mrs. McGill); *The Adventures of Rin Tin Tin*—"Stagecoach Sally" 4-19-57 (Sally Benton); *Jim Bowie*—"A Fortune for Madame" 10-18-57 (Adorine); *The Restless Gun*—"The Suffragette" 3-24-58 (Emma Birch), "A Trial for Jenny May" 5-25-59 (Ruth Purcell); *Decision*—"The Tall Man" 7-27-58 (Granny Dawson); *Trackdown*—Regular 1958-59 (Henrietta Porter); *The Texan*—"The Lord Will Provide" 12-29-58 (Katy Clayton); *Wagon Train*—"The Greenhorn Story" 10-7-59 (Aunt Em), "Wagons Ho!" 9-28-60; *Bonanza*—"The Gunmen" 1-23-60 (Lorna Doone), "The Hayburner" 2-17-63 (Cora); *The Rifleman*—"The Spoiler" 2-16-60 (Mrs. Avery), "The High Country" 12-18-61 (Mrs. Morgan); *The Rebel*—"To See the Elephant" 10-16-60 (Carrie Blyden); *Tales of Wells Fargo*—"The Bride and the Bandit" 12-12-60 (Kate Wiggam); *The Tall Man*—"The Reluctant Bridegroom" 2-18-61 (Hannah Blossom); *Cheyenne*—"The Durango Brothers" 9-24-62 (Hortense Durango); *Destry*—"Blood Brother-in-Law" 4-17-64 (Granny Jellico); *The Virginian*—"All Nice and Legal" 11-25-64 (Mrs. Clancy); *Daniel Boone*—"The Hostages" 1-7-65 (Hilda Brock); *Laredo*—"The Sweet Gang" 11-4-66 (Ma Sweet); *Rango*—"You Can't Scalp a Bald Indian" 4-28-67 (Ma Brooks); *The Big Valley*—"A Noose Is Waiting" 11-13-67; *The High Chaparral*—"Tornado Frances" 10-11-68 (Mrs. Dilts); *The Guns of Will Sonnett*—"Pariah" 10-18-68 (Molly Cobb);

Lancer—"Zee" 9-30-69 (Widow Hargis).

Corcoran, Billy. TV: *Bonanza*—"No Less a Man" 3-15-64; *Daniel Boone*—"The Ordeal of Israel Boone" 9-21-67 (2nd Boy), "Pride of a Man" 6-2-68 (Tommy), "Readin', Ritin', and Revolt" 3-12-70 (Joe).

Corcoran, Brian. TV: *Texas John Slaughter*—Regular 1958-61 (Willie Slaughter); *Walt Disney Presents*—"Daniel Boone: ...And Chase the Buffalo" 12-11-60 (Israel Boone).

Corcoran, Donna (1943-). Films: "Gypsy Colt" 1954 (Meg Mac-Wade).

Corcoran, Kelly (1958-). TV: *The Road West*—Regular 1966-67 (Kip Pride); *The Big Valley*—"The Secret" 1-27-69 (David Howard).

Corcoran, Kevin (1949-). Films: "Old Yeller" 1957 (Arliss Coates); "Savage Sam" 1963 (Arliss Coates); "Blue" 1968. ¶TV: *Walt Disney Presents*—"Daniel Boone" 1960-61 (James); *Wagon Train*—"The Cassie Vance Story" 12-23-63 (Davie).

Corcoran, Noreen (1943-). TV: *Circus Boy*—"The Cub Reporter" 4-21-57 (Jill); *Gunsmoke*—"Owney Tupper Had a Daughter" 4-4-64 (Ellen); *The Big Valley*—"The Brawlers" 12-15-65 (Sharon).

Cord, Alex (1931-). Films: "Stagecoach" 1966 (Ringo); "A Minute to Pray, a Second to Die" 1967-Ital. (Clay McCord); "Grayeagle" 1977 (Grayeagle). ¶TV: *Branded*—"Survival" 1-24-65 (Jed Colbee); *Gunsmoke*—"The Sodbusters" 11-20-72 (Pete Brown); *The Quest*—"The Buffalo Hunters" 9-29-76 (McWhorley); *Hunter's Moon*—Pilot 12-1-79 (the Captain).

Cord, Bill. TV: *Cheyenne*—"Prisoner of Moon Mesa" 11-16-59 (Wes Lassiter); *Wyatt Earp*—"The Confidence Man" 5-17-60 (Billy Costane); *Pony Express*—Regular 1960-61 (Tom Clyde).

Cord, Robert. Films: "Breed of the Border" 1933 (Spud); "Across the Plains" 1939 (Buff).

Corday, Mara (1932-). Films: "Dawn at Socorro" 1954 (Lotty Diamond); "Drums Across the River" 1954 (Sue); "The Man from Bitter Ridge" 1955 (Holly Kenton); "Man Without a Star" 1955 (Moccasin Mary); "A Day of Fury" 1956 (Sharman Fulton); "The Naked Gun" 1956; "Raw Edge" 1956 (Paca); "The Quiet Gun" 1957 (Irene, the Indian Girl). ¶TV: *The Adventures of Kit Carson*—"Fury at Red Gulch" 10-27-51 (Lola La Vada); *The Restless Gun*—

"Shadow of a Gunfighter" 1-12-59 (Della); *Tales of Wells Fargo*—"The Train Robbery" 10-12-59 (Ruby); *Man from Blackhawk*—"Contraband Cargo" 12-4-59 (Annabel); *Wanted—Dead or Alive*—"Death, Divided by Three" 4-23-60 (Lucinda Lorenz); *Laramie*—"A Sound of Bells" 12-27-60 (Rose).

Corday, Paula. *see* Corday, Rita.

Corday, Rita (Paula Corday) (1924-11/23/92). Films: "Girl Rush" 1944 (Troupe Member); "West of the Pecos" 1945 (Suzanne, the French Maid).

Corday, Sandra. Films: "The Trigger Trio" 1937 (Anne Evans).

Cordell, Cathleen. TV: *Wagon Train*—"The Michael McGoo Story" 3-20-63 (Mrs. Lawson).

Cordell, Frank (1898-10/25/77). Films: "Robbers' Roost" 1933 (Horseman); "The Westerner" 1934 (Bucking Horse Rider); "Under the Pampas Moon" 1935 (Bazan's Gaucho); "Arizona Mahoney" 1936 (Player); "The Texas Rangers" 1936 (Ranger Ditson); "Thunder Trail" 1937 (Cowboy); "Geronimo" 1940 (Sergeant Cord); "The Westerner" 1940 (Man); "Along Came Jones" 1945 Coach Guard); "Duel in the Sun" 1946 (Frank); "High Lonesome" 1950 (Frank); "The Sundowners" 1950 (Strake); "Silver City" 1951 (Townsman); "Son of Paleface" 1952 (Dade); "Arrowhead" 1953; "The Man from Laramie" 1955 (Mule Driver); "Run for Cover" 1955; "Pardners" 1956 (Townsman); "The Tin Star" 1957 (Posse Member); "Heller in Pink Tights" 1960 (Theodore).

Corden, Henry (1920-). Films: "Hiawatha" 1952 (Ottobang); "Viva Zapata!" 1952 (Senior Officer); "The Wild North" 1952 (Clerk). ¶TV: *The Restless Gun*—"The Crisis at Easter Creek" 4-7-58 (Mike Morgan), "No Way to Kill" 11-24-58 (Will Gerrard); *Gunsmoke*—"The Gentleman" 6-7-58 (Butler); *Tales of Wells Fargo*—"Wild Cargo" 1-19-59 (Renner); *Have Gun Will Travel*—"An International Affair" 4-2-60 (Prince Alexi); *Tate*—"The Return of Jessica Jackson" 9-14-60 (Rubidoux); *Bonanza*—"Tax Collector" 2-18-61; *Wagon Train*—"The Clementine Jones Story" 10-25-61 (Frank); *Maverick*—"The Money Machine" 4-8-62 (Professor Raynard); *Wide Country*—"Yanqui, Go Home!" 4-4-63 (Herrero); *Rawhide*—"El Hombre Bravo" 5-14-65 (General Velasquez); *Daniel Boone*—"First in War, First in Peace" 10-13-66 (Peter Mornay).

Cordero, Maria-Elena. Films: "Nakia" TVM-1974 (Diane Little Eagle). ¶TV: *Kung Fu*—"The Brujo" 10-25-73 (Maria); *The Quest*—"Seventy-Two Hours" 11-3-76 (Sweet Woman).

Cordic, Regis J. Films: "Law of the Land" TVM-1976; "Testimony of Two Men" TVM-1977; "Standing Tall" TVM-1978 (Hodges). ¶TV: *Gunsmoke*—"Bohannan" 9-25-72 (Reverend), "The Avenger" 11-27-72 (Sheriff Crane), "Jessie" 2-19-73 (Marshal Halstead), "Island in the Desert" 12-2-74 & 12-9-74 (Sheriff Grimes); *Kung Fu*—"Alethea" 3-15-73 (Prosecutor Stoddard); *Young Maverick*—"Makin' Tracks" 1-9-80.

Cording, Harry (1891-9/1/54). Films: "Black Jack" 1927 (Haskins); "Daredevil's Reward" 1928 (Outlaw); "Rough Romance" 1930 (Chick Carson); "The Conquering Horde" 1931 (Butch Daggett); "Fighting for Justice" 1932 (Bull Barnard); "Texas Cyclone" 1932 (Jake Farwell); "To the Last Man" 1933 (Harry Malone); "Daniel Boone" 1936 (Joe Burch); "Sutter's Gold" 1936 (Lars); "Fugitive from Sonora" 1937 (Iron Joe Martin); "Heart of the North" 1938 (Miner); "The Painted Desert" 1938 (Burke); "Arizona Legion" 1939 (Whiskey Joe); "Destry Rides Again" 1939; "The Marshal of Mesa City" 1939 (Bat Cardigan); "North of the Yukon" 1939 (MacGregor); "Outpost of the Mounties" 1939 (McGregor); "Racketeers of the Range" 1939; "Stand Up and Fight" 1939 (Blacksmith); "The Dark Command" 1940 (Killer); "Santa Fe Trail" 1940 (Man); "Stage to Chino" 1940 (Pete Branagan); "Texas Stagecoach" 1940 (Clancy); "Trail of the Vigilantes" 1940 (Phil); "Virginia City" 1940 (Scarecrow); "When the Daltons Rode" 1940 (Sam Fleeson); "Bury Me Not on the Lone Prairie" 1941; "Rawhide Rangers" 1941 (Blackie); "Riders of the Badlands" 1941 (Higgins); "Overland Mail" 1942-serial (Sam Gregg); "The Man from the Rio Grande" 1943 (John King); "San Antonio" 1945 (Hawker); "Fool's Gold" 1946 (Duke); "Renegade Girl" 1946; "Dangerous Venture" 1947 (Morgan); "The Marauders" 1947; "Trail of the Mounties" 1947 (Hawkins); "Dangers of the Canadian Mounted" 1948-serial (Track Heavy #2); "Bad Men of Tombstone" 1949; "Al Jennings of Oklahoma" 1951 (Mike Bridges); "Santa Fe" 1951 (Moore Legrande); "The Big Trees" 1952 (Cleve Gregg); "Brave Warrior" 1952 (Shayne Macgregor); "Cripple Creek" 1952 (Hibbs); "Night Stage to Galveston" 1952 (Ted Driscoll). ¶TV: *The Lone Ranger*—"Sheep Thieves" 2-9-50; *Wild Bill Hickok*—"Chain of Events" 6-24-52.

Cordova, Fred. Films: "Boots of Destiny" 1937 (Frederico); "Ride 'Em, Cowgirl" 1939 (Philbin); "The Masked Rider" 1941 (Pablo); "North to the Klondike" 1942; "Pirates of Monterey" 1947 (Sentry); "Robin Hood of Monterey" 1947.

Cordova, Linda. Films: "The Long Rope" 1961 (Mexican Waitress); "Hombre" 1967 (Mrs. Delgado). ¶TV: *Wanted—Dead or Alive*—"El Gato" 2-22-61 (Maria); *Have Gun Will Travel*—"A Place for Abel Hix" 10-6-62 (Saloon Girl).

Cordova, Margarita. Films: "One-Eyed Jacks" 1961 (Nika, the Flamenco Dancer); "Guns of Diablo" 1964 (Florrie); "Bridger" TVM-1976 (Shoshone Woman). ¶TV: *Zane Grey Theater*—"Hang the Heart High" 1-15-59 (Serafina); *The Outlaws*—"Sam Bass" 5-4-61 (Marisa); *Tales of Wells Fargo*—"Jeremiah" 11-11-61 (Serafina); *Cheyenne*—"The Wedding Rings" 1-8-62 (Alita); *Laredo*—"The Heroes of San Gill" 12-23-65 (Girl Vendor); *Branded*—"The Assassins" 3-27-66 & 4-3-66 (Socorro); *The Big Valley*—"Joaquin" 9-11-67 (Elena Santos), "The Other Face of Justice" 3-31-69 (Rose); *Gunsmoke*—"A Man Called Smith" 10-27-69 (Saloon Girl), "The Judas Gun" 1-19-70 (Bargirl); *The High Chaparral*—"Only the Bad Come to Sonora" 10-2-70 (Constanza).

Cordova, Pancho (1916-). Films: "Two Mules for Sister Sara" 1970 (Juan's Father); "The Wrath of God" 1972 (Tacho).

Core, Virginia. TV: *Jim Bowie*—"Gone to Texas" 5-24-57 (Josefa); *Wyatt Earp*—"The Schoolteacher" 3-11-58 (Maria).

Corey, Eugene. Films: "The Law of the Great Northwest" 1918 (Charles Morin).

Corey, James "Jim" (1883-1/10/56). Films: "Cheyenne's Pal" 1917; "Cyclone Smith's Partner" 1919; "The Broncho Kid" 1920; "The Champion Liar" 1920; "Cinders" 1920; "Double Danger" 1920; "Fight It Out" 1920; "The Fightin' Terror" 1920; "A Gamblin' Fool" 1920; "The Grinning Granger" 1920; "'In Wrong' Wright" 1920; "The Man with the Punch" 1920; "Marryin' Marion" 1920; "One Law for All" 1920; "A Pair of Twins" 1920; "Ransom" 1920; "The Shootin' Kid" 1920; "The Smilin' Kid" 1920; "Some Shooter" 1920; "Superstition"

1920; "Tipped Off" 1920; "The Trail of the Hound" 1920; "The Two-Fisted Lover" 1920; "Wolf Tracks" 1920; "The Alarm" 1921; "Action" 1921 (Sam Waters); "Both Barrels" 1921; "The Danger Man" 1921; "The Driftin' Kid" 1921; "Fighting Blood" 1921; "The Grip of the Law" 1921; "In the Nick of Time" 1921; "The Midnight Raiders" 1921; "Out O' Luck" 1921; "The Outlaw" 1921; "Red Courage" 1921 (Steve Carrol); "The Rim of the Desert" 1921; "The Saddle King" 1921; "Stand Up and Fight" 1921; "Sweet Revenge" 1921; "The Valley of the Rogues" 1921; "Winners of the West" 1921-serial (Squire Blair); "Headin' West" 1922 (Red Malone); "In the Days of Buffalo Bill" 1922-serial (Qunatral); "Jaws of Steel" 1922; "Timberland Treachery" 1922; "Unmasked" 1922; "The Oregon Trail" 1923-serial; "Shootin' em Up" 1923; "The Border Legion" 1924 (Pearch); "The Dangerous Coward" 1924 (the Weazel); "Headin' Through" 1924 (Lige Gilson); "Payable on Demand" 1924 (Slim Miller); "The Perfect Alibi" 1924 (Lon Elwell); "Riding Double" 1924; "Western Vengeance" 1924 (Santag); "The Burning Trail" 1925 (Black Loring); "The Calgary Stampede" 1925 (Fred Burgess); "The Circus Cyclone" 1925 (Greasey); "Double Fisted" 1925; "Blind Trail" 1926 (Al Leitz); "Hair Trigger Baxter" 1926 (Jim Dodds); "The Iron Rider" 1926 (Larbun); "Red Hot Leather" 1926 (Red Hussey); "The Shoot 'Em Up Kid" 1926; "Hey! Hey! Cowboy" 1927 (Blake); "Open Range" 1927 (Red); "Courtin' Wildcats" 1929 (Fugitive); "Points West" 1929 (Steve); "Fighting Thru" 1930; "The Mounted Stranger" 1930 (White-Eye); "Alias the Bad Man" 1931; "Arizona Terror" 1931 (Posse Member); "The Range Feud" 1931; "Red Fork Range" 1931 (Apache Joe); "The Two Gun Man" 1931; "Cornered" 1932; "Haunted Gold" 1932; "Hell Fire Austin" 1932; "One-Man Law" 1932; "Come on Tarzan" 1933; "The Fourth Horseman" 1933; "Gordon of Ghost City" 1933-serial (Jeff); "The Man from Monterey" 1933; "Outlaw Justice" 1933; "Somewhere in Sonora" 1933; "Terror Trail" 1933 (Henry); "The Fighting Code" 1934; "The Fighting Ranger" 1934; "In Old Santa Fe" 1934 (Deputy); "The Last Round-Up" 1934 (1st Outlaw); "Rainbow Riders" 1934; "The Red Rider" 1934-serial; "Smoking Guns" 1934; "Between Men" 1935 (Brawler); "Heir to Trouble" 1935; "No Man's Range" 1935; "The Outlaw Deputy" 1935; "Rustlers of Red Dog"

1935-serial; "Sunset Range" 1935; "Comin' Round the Mountain" 1936; "Everyman's Law" 1936 (Homesteader); "Guns and Guitars" 1936 (Henchman); "The Phantom Rider" 1936-serial; "Rio Grande Ranger" 1936; "Wildcat Saunders" 1936; "Boothill Brigade" 1937 (Healy); "Come on Cowboys" 1937; "Gun Lords of Stirrup Basin" 1937 (Mart); "Guns in the Dark" 1937 (Jim Badger); "Law of the Ranger" 1937; "Left-Handed Law" 1937; "Mystery Range" 1937 (Morgan's Man); "Outlaws of the Prairie" 1937 (Outlaw); "Prairie Thunder" 1937; "Ranger Courage" 1937; "Reckless Ranger" 1937; "Riders of the Dawn" 1937; "Romance of the Rockies" 1937; "Round-Up Time in Texas" 1937 (Bill); "Springtime in the Rockies" 1937; "Trail of Vengeance" 1937 (Henchman Joe); "Yodelin' Kid from Pine Ridge" 1937; "Billy the Kid Returns" 1938; "Brothers of the West" 1938; "Feud of the Trail" 1938; "Flaming Frontier" 1938-serial; "The Frontiersman" 1938 (Bar 20 Cowboy); "Gold Min in the Sky" 1938 (Chet); "Heroes of the Alamo" 1938 (Hank Hunter); "Outlaws of Sonora" 1938; "Partners of the Plains" 1938; "Santa Fe Stampede" 1938; "Six Shootin' Sheriff" 1938; "Sunset Trail" 1938; "Whirlwind Horseman" 1938; "In Old Monterey" 1939; "Silver on the Sage" 1939 (Martin); "Southward Ho!" 1939; "Trigger Smith" 1939; "Deadwood Dick" 1940-serial; "Gaucho Serenade" 1940; "Melody Ranch" 1940; "One Man's Law" 1940; "The Return of Wild Bill" 1940 (Henchman); "Three Men from Texas" 1940; "The Westerner" 1940 (Lee Webb); "Bury Me Not on the Lone Prairie" 1941; "Desert Bandit" 1941; "In Old Cheyenne" 1941 (Outlaw); "Law of the Range" 1941; "The Medico of Painted Springs" 1941; "Prairie Stranger" 1941 (Undertaker); "Robin Hood of the Pecos" 1941; "The Shepherd of the Hills" 1941 (Bald Knobber); "Six Gun Gold" 1941 (Chuck); "Tonto Basin Outlaws" 1941; "Wrangler's Roost" 1941; "Down Rio Grande Way" 1942; "Jesse James, Jr." 1942; "Stagecoach Buckaroo" 1942; "The Haunted Ranch" 1943.

Corey, Jeff (1914-). Films: "North to the Klondike" 1942 (Man); "My Friend Flicka" 1943 (Tim Murphy); "California" 1946 (Man); "Hoppy's Holiday" 1947 (Jed); "Ramrod" 1947 (Bice); "Unconquered" 1947; "Roughshod" 1949 (Jed Graham); "The Nevadan" 1950 (Bart); "The Outriders" 1950 (Keeley); "Rock Island Trail" 1950 (Abe

Lincoln); "Singing Guns" 1950 (Richards); "New Mexico" 1951 (Coyote); "Only the Valiant" 1951 (Joe Harmony); "Rawhide" 1951 (Luke Davis); "Red Mountain" 1951 (Skee); "Butch Cassidy and the Sundance Kid" 1969 (Sheriff Bledsoe); "True Grit" 1969 (Tom Chaney); "Catlow" 1971-Span. (Merridew); "Little Big Man" 1971 (Wild Bill Hickok); "Shoot Out" 1971 (Trooper); "The Gun and the Pulpit" TVM-1974 (Head of Posse); "Banjo Hackett: Roamin' Free" TVM-1976 (Judge Janeway); "Testimony of Two Men" TVM-1977; "Butch and Sundance: The Early Days" 1979 (Ray Bledsoe). ¶TV: *Rawhide*—"Encounter at Boot Hill" 9-14-65 (Morgan Kane); *Wild Wild West*—"The Night of a Thousand Eyes" 10-22-65 (Captain Coffin), "The Night of the Underground Terror" 1-19-68 (Col. Tacitus Mosely/Douglas Craig); *Bonanza*—"The Bridegroom" 12-4-66 (Tuck Dowling), "A Single Pilgrim" 1-3-71 (Frank Brennan); *Iron Horse*—"Gallows for Bill Pardew" 9-30-67 (the Judge); *Gunsmoke*—"The Night Riders" 2-24-69 (Judge Proctor); *Alias Smith and Jones*—"The Day the Amnesty Came Through" 11-25-72 (Gov. George W. Baxter).

Corey, Sr., Milton (1879-10/23/51). Films: "The Great Missouri Raid" 1950; "Rawhide" 1951 (Dr. Tucker).

Corey, Wendell (1914-11/9/68). Films: "Desert Fury" 1947 (Johnny Ryan); "The Furies" 1950 (Rip Darrow); "The Great Missouri Raid" 1951 (Frank James); "The Wild North" 1952 (Constable Pedley); "The Rainmaker" 1956 (File); "The Light in the Forest" 1958 (Wilse Owens); "Alias Jesse James" 1959 (Jesse James); "Blood on the Arrow" 1964 (Clint Mailer); "Waco" 1966 (Preacher Sam Stone); "Red Tomahawk" 1967 (Elkins); "Buckskin" 1968 (Rep. Marlow). ¶TV: *Zane Grey Theater*—"A Quiet Sunda in San Ardo" 11-23-56 (Clay Burnett), "Killer Instinct" 3-17-60 (Marshal Bigger), "The Man from Yesterday" 12-22-60 (Mapes); *Branded*—"The Mission" 3-14-65, 3-21-65 & 3-28-65 (Major Whitcomb); *The Road West*—"Piece of Tin" 10-31-66 (Tilman Ash); *The Guns of Will Sonnett*—"The Natural Way" 9-29-67 (Sheriff Morg Braham); *Wild Wild West*—"The Night of the Death-Maker" 2-23-68 (Cullen Dane), "The Night of Miguelito's Revenge" 12-13-68 (Cyrus Barlow).

Corey, Will. TV: *Have Gun Will Travel*—"The Knight" 6-2-62 (Carl Frome); *Gunsmoke*—"Quint's Indian" 3-2-63 (Stope).

Corlett, Irene. TV: *Wagon Train*—"The Nels Stack Story" 10-23-57, "The Emily Rossiter Story" 10-30-57 (Mrs. Hathaway), "The John Darro Story" 11-6-57.

Corley, Pat. Films: "Poker Alice" TVM-1987 (McCarthy).

Cornell, Ann. Films: "Gold Fever" 1952 (Rusty). ¶TV: *Sergeant Preston of the Yukon*—"The Diamond Collar" 1-30-58 (Anita Varden).

Cornell, Lillian. Films: "Buck Benny Rides Again" 1940 (Peggy).

Corner, Sally (1894-3/5/59). Films: "Two Flags West" 1950 (Mrs. Magowan). ¶TV: *Gunsmoke*—"Professor Lute Bone" 1-7-56 (Mrs. Stooler).

Cornthwaite, Robert (1917-). Films: "Mark of the Renegade" 1951 (Innkeeper); "Stranger on Horseback" 1955 (Arnold Hammer); "Day of the Outlaw" 1959 (Tommy); "The Ride to Hangman's Tree" 1967 (T.L. Harper); "Waterhole No. 3" 1967 (George, the Hotel Clerk); "Journey Through Rosebud" 1972 (Hearing Officer). ¶TV: *Jim Bowie*—"An Adventure with Audubon" 9-21-56 (John James Audubon), "The Beggar of New Orleans" 1-11-57 (John James Audubon), "Bayou Tontine" 2-15-57 (John James Audubon); *Broken Arrow*—"Return from the Shadows" 12-4-56 (Lt. Haskell); *Zane Grey Theater*—"Dangerous Orders" 2-8-57 (Wade), "Mission to Marathon" 5-14-59 (John Scobie); *Gunsmoke*—"Mavis McCloud" 10-26-57 (Lou Staley), "Cleavus" 2-15-71 (Clerk); *The Californians*—"Man from Boston" 11-12-57 (Dr. Henry Jameson), "The Man from Paris" 2-11-58 (Charles Girard), "A Girl Named Sam" 10-14-58 (Brother Evans); *Trackdown*—"Right of Way" 1-17-58 (Jerome Ballard), "The Schoolteacher" 11-7-58 (Jim Martin); *Yancy Derringer*—"Collector's Item" 3-26-59 (Mathew Brady); *Rawhide*—"Incident of the Thirteenth Man" 10-23-59 (Ronald Smith), "The Long Count" 1-5-62 (Martin Gedwell), "Incident at Zebulon" 3-5-64 (Laughton Wallace); *Tales of Wells Fargo*—"The Journey" 1-25-60 (Dodd), "Remember the Yazoo" 4-14-62 (Anthony Boaz); *The Rifleman*—"The Deserter" 3-15-60 (Major Damler); *Maverick*—"Last Wire from Stop Gap" 10-16-60 (Wembly), "Family Pride" 1-8-61 (Honest John Cruppen); *Lawman*—"The Grubstake" 4-16-61 (Edward Coughill); *Wagon Train*—"The Mark

Miner Story" 11-15-61 (Reverend Norris), "The Orly French Story" 12-12-62 (Dr. Wilson), "The Fenton Canaby Story" 12-30-63 (Byron Lowe); *Laramie*—"Naked Steel" 1-1-63 (Heron); *Destry*—"Stormy Is a Lady" 3-6-64 (Anthony Payne); *The Virginian*—"It Takes a Big Man" 10-23-63 (Minister); *Laredo*—"Pride of the Rangers" 12-16-65 (Wilson Jones), "A Taste of Money" 4-28-66 (Filmore Wills); *The Big Valley*—"A Time to Kill" 1-19-66 (Luther Kirby), "The Lady from Mesa" 4-3-67; *Death Valley Days*—"Canary Harris vs. the Almighty" 2-26-66 (the Rev. Mr. Farr); *Lancer*—"The Last Train for Charlie Poe" 11-26-68 (Homer Ord); *Daniel Boone*—"The Return of Sidewinder" 12-12-68 (Sir Ives Wallace), "The Landlords" 3-5-70 (Sir Ives); *The High Chaparral*—"No Irish Need Apply" 1-17-69 (Belding); *Bonanza*—"What Are Pardners For?" 4-12-70 (Blake); *Kung Fu*—"The Passion of Chen Yi" 2-28-74 (Bank Teller); *Barbary Coast*—"Mary Had More Than a Little" 1-2-76 (Reverend Wilcox).

Cornwall, Anne (1897-3/2/80). Films: "Forty-Horse Hawkins" 1924 (Mary Darling); "The Rainbow Trail" 1925 (Fay Larkin); "Flaming Frontier" 1926 (Betty Stanwood); "Under Western Skies" 1926; "Triple Justice" 1940.

Cornwallis, Mary. Films: "The Phantom Flyer" 1928 (Julia Hart).

Corra, Teodoro. Films: "Django the Bastard" 1969-Ital./Span.; "Heads or Tails" 1969-Ital./Span.; "Roy Colt and Winchester Jack" 1970-Ital. (Reverendo); "Mallory Must Not Die" 1971-Ital.

Corrado, Gino (1895-12/23/82). Films: "The Desert Flower" 1925 (Jose Lee); "The Dead Line" 1926 (Juan Alvarez); "The Rainbow" 1929 (Slug); "Senor Americano" 1929 (Ramirez); "Song of the Cabellero" 1930 (Don Jose); "The Man from Death Valley" 1931 (Ortego); "Paradise Canyon" 1935 (Rurale Captain); "The Oregon Trail" 1936 (Forrenza, the Californian Leader); "Rebellion" 1936 (Pablo); "Rose of the Rio Grande" 1938 (Castro); "Pest from the West" 1939-short; "The Return of the Cisco Kid" 1939 (Waiter); "Mark of Zorro" 1940 (Caballero); "Sunset in El Dorado" 1945.

Correll, Mady. Films: "Old Chisholm Trail" 1942 (Belle Turner); "Texas Masquerade" 1944 (Virginia Curtis).

Corri, Adrienne (1930-). Films: "Dynamite Jack" 1963-Fr.; "Africa-Texas Style!" 1967-U.S./Brit. (Fay Carter).

Corrigan, D'Arcy (1870-12/25/45). Films: "Double Action Daniels" 1925 (Richard Booth); "Law and Order" 1932 (Parker Brother); "Ramona" 1936 (Jeff); "Wells Fargo" 1937 (Preacher).

Corrigan, Emmett (1867-10/29/32). Films: "The Golden West" 1932 (Colonel Horace Summers).

Corrigan, James (1875-2/28/29). Films: "The Sky Pilot" 1921 (Honorable Ashley); "The Man from Wyoming" 1924 (Governor of Wyoming); "Durand of the Bad Lands" 1925 (Joe Gore).

Corrigan, Lloyd (1900-11/5/69). Films: "The Return of Frank James" 1940 (Randolph Stone); "The Great Man's Lady" 1942 (Mr. Cadwallader); "North to the Klondike" 1942 (Dr. Curtis); "The Lights of Old Santa Fe" 1944 (Marty Malzely); "Song of Nevada" 1944 (Prof. Jeremiah Hanley); "Home in San Antone" 1949; "New Mexico" 1951 (Judge Wilcox); "Sierra Passage" 1951 (Thad King); "Son of Paleface" 1952 (Doc Lovejoy); "Hidden Guns" 1956 (Judge Wallis). ¶TV: *Screen Director's Playhouse*—"Arroyo" 10-26-55 (Hank); *Wyatt Earp*—"The Buntline Special" 12-20-55 (Ned Buntline), "Command Performance" 2-19-57 (Ned Buntline), "Mr. Buntline's Vacation" 11-19-57 (Ned Buntline), "King of the Frontier" 11-11-58 (Ned Buntline), "The Noble Outlaws" 11-24-59 (Ned Buntline), "Woman of Tucson" 11-15-60 (Ned Buntline); *Jim Bowie*—"Charivari" 11-15-57 (Jean Martel); *The Restless Gun*—"The New Sheriff" 11-18-57 (Doc Corss), "The Battle of Tower Rock" 4-28-58 (Kermit Taylor), "The Lady and the Gun" 1-19-59 (Jesse Alden); *Trackdown*—"The Threat" 3-4-59; *Wanted—Dead or Alive*—"Eight Cent Record" 12-20-58 (Ben); *Tombstone Territory*—"Marked for Murder" 3-20-59 (Whit Purcell); *Riverboat*—"Race to Cincinnati" 10-4-59 (John Jenkins); *Death Valley Days*—"Money to Burn" 2-2-60, "Sponge Full of Vinegar" 3-14-62 (Dorsey); *Gunslinger*—"The Diehards" 4-20-61 (Doctor Bennet); *Rawhide*—"Incident of the Running Man" 5-5-61 (Simon Baines); *Have Gun Will Travel*—"One, Two Three" 2-17-62 (Carl Wellsley); *Maverick*—"The Maverick Report" 3-4-62 (Senator Porter); *The Travels of Jaimie McPheeters*—"The Day of the Flying Dutchman" 12-1-63 (Capt. Rembrandt Van Creel); *Gunsmoke*—"The Magician" 12-21-63 (Jeremiah Dark); *Bonanza*—"The Pure Truth" 3-8-64 (Simmons), "A Good Night's Rest" 4-11-65.

Corrigan, Ray "Crash" (Ray Bernard) (1907-8/10/76). Films: "The Singing Vagabond" 1935 (Private Hobbs); "Roarin' Lead" 1936 (Tucson Smith); "The Three Mesquiteers" 1936 (Tucson Smith); "Vigilantes Are Coming" 1936-serial (Captain John Charles Fremont); "Come on Cowboys" 1937 (Tucson Smith); "Ghost Town Gold" 1937 (Tucson Smith); "Gunsmoke Ranch" 1937 (Tucson Smith); "Heart of the Rockies" 1937 (Tucson Smith); "Hit the Saddle" 1937 (Tucson Smith); "The Painted Stallion" 1937-serial (Clark Stewart); "Range Defenders" 1937 (Tucson Smith); "Riders of the Whistling Skull" 1937 (Tucson Smith); "The Trigger Trio" 1937 (Tucson Smith); "Wild Horse Rodeo" 1937 (Tucson Smith); "Call the Mesquiteers" 1938 (Tucson Smith); "Heroes of the Hills" 1938 (Tucson Smith); "Outlaws of Sonora" 1938 (Tucson Smith); "Overland Stage Raiders" 1938 (Tucson Smith); "Pals of the Saddle" 1938 (Tucson Smith); "The Purple Vigilantes" 1938 (Tucson Smith); "Red River Range" 1938 (Tucson Smith); "Riders of the Black Hills" 1938 (Tucson Smith); "Santa Fe Stampede" 1938 (Tucson Smith); "New Frontier" 1939 (Tucson Smith); "The Night Riders" 1939 (Tucson Smith); "Three Texas Steers" 1939 (Tucson Smith); "Wyoming Outlaw" 1939 (Tucson Smith); "The Range Busters" 1940 (Crash); "Trailing Double Trouble" 1940 (Crash); "West of Pinto Basin" 1940 (Crash); "Fugitive Valley" 1941 (Crash); "Saddle Mountain Roundup" 1941 (Crash); "Tonto Basin Outlaws" 1941 (Crash); "Trail of the Silver Spurs" 1941 (Crash); "Tumbledown Ranch in Arizona" 1941 (Crash); "Underground Rustlers" 1941 (Crash); "Wrangler's Roost" 1941 (Crash); "Arizona Stagecoach" 1942 (Crash); "Boot Hill Bandits" 1942 (Crash); "Rock River Renegades" 1942 (Tucson Smith); "Texas Trouble Shooters" 1942 (Crash); "Thunder River Feud" 1942 (Crash); "Black Market Rustlers" 1943 (Crash); "Bullets and Saddles" 1943; "Cowboy Commandos" 1943 (Crash); "Renegade Girl" 1946; "Trail of Robin Hood" 1950; "Apache Ambush" 1955 (Mark Calvin); "Domino Kid" 1957 (Buck).

Corsaro, Franco. Films: "Western Trails" 1938 (Indian Joe); "Mark of Zorro" 1940 (Orderly). ¶TV: *Broken Arrow*—"Aztec Treasure" 2-25-58 (Arista).

Corsaut, Anita (1933-11/6/95). TV: *Black Saddle*—"Client: Peter Warren" 10-30-59 (Mary Warren);

Johnny Ringo—"Black Harvest" 4-7-60 (Lettie Frome); *Zane Grey Theater*—"Ransom" 11-17-60 (Amy); *Death Valley Days*—"Suzie" 10-24-62, "Paid in Full" 1-3-65 (Kathy McLennan), "The Red Shawl" 2-5-66 (Emma Donaldson), "Dry Water Sailors" 3-12-66 (Sarah Howard); *Bonanza*—"The Way of Aaron" 3-10-63 (Rebecca Kaufmann); *Gunsmoke*—"Twenty Miles from Dodge" 4-10-65 (Eleanor Starkey), "Ladies from St. Louis" 3-25-67 (Sister Ellen).

Corsentino, Frank. TV: *Gunsmoke*—"Phoenix" 9-20-71 (Fraker), "A Family of Killers" 1-14-74 (Jacob).

Cort, William (1940-9/23/93). Films: "A Big Hand for the Little Lady" 1966 (Arthur); "The Wackiest Wagon Train in the West" 1976 (Andy). ¶TV: *Branded*—"Very Few Heroes" 4-11-65 (Alan Winters); *Dusty's Trail*—Regular 1973 (Andy).

Cortese, Joe. Films: "Jessi's Girls" 1976 (Baldry).

Cortese, Valentina (1925-). Films: "The Girl of the Golden West" 1942-Ital.

Cortez, Armand (1880-11/19/48). Films: "Galloping Hoofs" 1924-serial.

Cortez, Lita. Films: "Rebellion" 1936 (Marquita); "Three on the Trail" 1936 (Conchita); "Arizona Gangbusters" 1940 (Lola).

Cortez, Ricardo (1899-4/28/77). Films: "The Call of the Canyon" 1923 (Larry Morrison); "The Pony Express" 1925 (Jack Weston); "Montana Moon" 1930 (Jeff); "The Californian" 1937 (Ramon Escobar); "Romance of the Rio Grande" 1941 (Ricardo). ¶TV: *Bonanza*—"El Toro Grande" 1-2-60 (Don Xavier).

Corthell, Herbert (1875-1/23/47). Films: "The Lone Cowboy" 1934 (Cowboy Cook); "Rollin' Westward" 1939 (Lawson).

Cory, Robert (1883-11/9/55). Films: "Hudson Bay" 1941 (Orderly).

Cory, Steve. TV: *Bonanza*—"Pride of a Man" 6-6-68 (Billy); *Death Valley Days*—"Amos and the Black Bull" 2-28-70.

Cosby, Bill (1938-). Films: "Man and Boy" 1971 (Caleb Revers).

Cosby, Ronnie. Films: "Moonlight on the Prairie" 1935; "Wells Fargo" 1937 (Ramsay, Jr.).

Cosgrave, Luke (1862-6/28/49). Films: "The Border Legion" 1924 (Bill Randle); "Durand of the Bad Lands" 1925 (Kingdom Come Knapp); "The Squaw Man" 1931 (Shanks).

Cosgrove, Douglas. Films: "Winds of the Wasteland" 1936 (Cal Drake).

Cosnack, Barney. Films: "Trail of Terror" 1935 (Wrestler Dizzy Dugan).

Cossar, John (1865-4/28/35). Films: "The Feud" 1919 (Horace Summers); "Doubling for Romeo" 1922 (Foster); "The Steel Trail" 1923-serial.

Costello, Anthony (1941-8/15/83). Films: "Blue" 1968 (Jess Parker); "Will Penny" 1968 (Bigfoot). ¶TV: *Temple Houston*—"Miss Katherina" 4-2-64 (Lieutenant Greeley); *Death Valley Days*—"Peter the Hunter" 2-14-65, "The Four Dollar Law Suit" 4-16-66, "Crullers at Sundown!" 5-21-66 (Sam Davis); *Bonanza*—"Justice" 1-8-67 (Cliff); *Daniel Boone*—"The Terrible Tarbots" 12-11-69 (Shadrach); *Gunsmoke*—"Luke" 11-2-70 (Austin Keep), "Lavery" 2-22-71 (Keith Lavery).

Costello, Don (1901-10/24/45). Films: "Ride on, Vaquero" 1941 (Redge); "Sundown Jim" 1942 (Dobe Hyde); "Mystery Man" 1944 (Bud Trilling); "Texas Masquerade" 1944 (Ace Maxson); "Along Came Jones" 1945 (Gledhill); "Great Stagecoach Robbery" 1945; "Marshal of Laredo" 1945.

Costello, Elvis (1954-). Films: "Straight to Hell" 1987-Brit. (Hives, the Butler).

Costello, Helen (1903-1/26/57). Films: "Ranger of the Big Pines" 1925 (Virginia Weatherford); "Broncho Twister" 1927 (Paulita Brady).

Costello, Lou (1906-3/3/59). Films: "Ride 'Em, Cowboy" 1942 (Willoughby); "The Wistful Widow of Wagon Gap" 1947 (Chester Wooley); "Lost in Alaska" 1952 (George Bell). ¶TV: *Wagon Train*—"The Tobias Jones Story" 10-22-58 (Tobias Jones).

Costello, Mariclare. TV: *Sara*—Regular 1976 (Julia Bailey).

Costello, Maurice (1877-10/29/50). Films: "The Wagon Show" 1928 (Colonel Beldan); "Rovin' Tumbleweeds" 1939.

Costello, Ward. Films: "Law of the Land" TVM-1976 (E.J. Barnes).

Costello, William (1898-10/9/71). Films: "Border Romance" 1930 (Lieutenant of Rurales); "Heroes of the Alamo" 1938 (General Los); "Death Rides the Range" 1940 (Dr. Flotow).

Coster, Nicholas (1934-). Films: "The Outcast" 1954 (Asa Polsen); "The Electric Horseman" 1979 (Fitzgerald). ¶TV: *Hallmark Hall of Fame*—"The Court-Martial of General George Armstrong Carter" 12-1-77 (General Sheridan).

Costner, Kevin (1955-). Films: "Silverado" 1985 (Jake); "Dances with Wolves" 1990 (Lt. Dunbar); "Wyatt Earp" 1994 (Wyatt Earp).

Cothell, Herbert. Films: "Renfrew of the Royal Mounted" 1937 (James Bronson).

Cotner, Carl (1916-11/14/86). Films: "Melody Ranch" 1940.

Cotsworth, Staats (1908-4/9/79). TV: *Schlitz Playhouse of the Stars*—"Way of the West" 6-6-58 (Colonel Taylor); *Bonanza*—"The Twenty-Sixth Grave" 10-31-72 (Judge Hale).

Cott, Jonathan. Films: "Lone Star" 1952 (Ben McCulloch); "Sky Full of Moon" 1952 (Balladeer).

Cotten, Joseph (1904-2/6/94). Films: "Duel in the Sun" 1946 (Jesse McCanles); "Two Flags West" 1950 (Col. Clay Tucker); "Untamed Frontier" 1952 (Kirk Denbow); "The Halliday Brand" 1957 (Daniel); "The Great Sioux Massacre" 1965 (Maj. Reno); "The Tramplers" 1965-Ital. (Temple Cordeen); "The Hellbenders" 1966-U.S./Ital./Span. (Jonas); "White Comanche" 1967-Ital./Span./U.S.; "Cutter's Trail" TVM-1970 (General Spalding); "Heaven's Gate" 1980 (the Reverend Doctor). ¶TV: *Zane Grey Theater*—"Man Unforgiving" 1-3-58 (Ben Harper); *Wagon Train*—"The Captain Dan Brady Story" 9-27-61 (Capt. Dan Brady), "The John Augustus Story" 10-17-62 (John Augustus); *Cimarron Strip*—"The Search" 11-9-67 (Dr. Tio); *The Virginian*—"A Time of Terror" 2-11-70 (Judge Will McMasters); *The Men from Shiloh*—"Gun Quest" 10-21-70 (Judge Hobbs).

Cotter, Catherine. Films: "The Texas Rambler" 1935 (Billie Conroy); "Under the Pampas Moon" 1935 (Maid); "Outlaws of the Range" 1936 (Betty Wilson); "Pinto Rustlers" 1936 (Ann Walton); "Sundown Saunders" 1936 (Bess Preston).

Cotton, Carolina. Films: "Outlaws of the Rockies" 1945; "Song of the Prairie" 1945; "Texas Panhandle" 1945; "Cowboy Blues" 1946; "Singing on the Trail" 1946; "That Texas Jamboree" 1946; "Smoky River Serenade" 1947; "Smoky Mountain Melody" 1948 (Parky Darkin); "Stallion Canyon" 1949 (Ellen); "Hoedown" 1950 (Carolina Cotton); "Apache Country" 1952 (Carolina Cotton); "Blue Canadian Rockies" 1952 (Carolina Cotton); "The Rough, Tough West" 1952 (Carolina).

Cotton, Harry. Films: "Seven Guns for the MacGregors" 1965-Ital./Span. (Harold MacGregor).

Cotton, Lucy (1891-12/12/48). Films: "The Fugitive" 1910.

Cottrell, William. Films: "Captain John Smith and Pocahontas" 1953 (Macklin).

Couch, Chuck. TV: *Tombstone Territory*—1-15-60 (Marshal); *Have Gun Will Travel*—"Dream Girl" 2-10-62 (Saddlemaker), "Bandit" 5-12-62 (Earl).

Coughlin, Kevin (1946-1/19/76). Films: "Duel at Diablo" 1966 (Norton). ¶TV: *The Virginian*—"The Crooked Pat" 2-21-68 (Kiley Cheever), "Last Grave at Socorro Creek" 1-22-69 (Dan Burden); *Bonanza*—"Pride of a Man" 6-6-68 (Willie McNab); *Gunsmoke*—"The Mark of Cain" 2-3-69 (Tom), "Coreyville" 10-6-69 (Billy Joe Corey), "The Gun" 11-19-70 (Randy Gogan), "The Golden Land" 3-5-73 (Calvin), "Hard Labor" 2-24-75 (Elton Prine).

Coulouris, George (1903-4/25/89). Films: "California" 1946 (Pharoah Coffin). ¶TV: *Dundee and the Culhane*—"The 3:10 to a Lynching Brief" 11-8-67 (Jeremiah Scrubbs).

Coulouris, Keith. Films: "Dead Man's Revenge" TVM-1994 (Bodeen).

Coulson, Roy (1890-5/10/44). Films: "If Only Jim" 1921 (Henry); "Don Q, Son of Zorro" 1925 (Admirer); "The Flaming Forest" 1926 (Francois).

Counts, Eleanor. Films: "Border Buckaroos" 1943 (Marge Leonard).

Court, Hazel (1926-). TV: *Bonanza*—"The Last Trophy" 3-26-60 (Lady Dunsford); *Stagecoach West*—"Finn McColl" 1-24-61 (Mrs. Allison); *Rawhide*—"Incident of the Dowry Dundee" 1-23-64 (Kathleen Dundee); *Wild Wild West*—"The Night of the Flying Pie Plate" 10-21-66 (Elizabeth Carter); *Iron Horse*—"Big Deal" 12-12-66 (Elizabeth Conner).

Courtland, Jerome (1926-). Films: "The Man from Colorado" 1948 (Johnny Howard); "The Walking Hills" 1949 (Johnny); "The Palomino" 1950 (Steve Norris); "Santa Fe" 1951 (Terry Canfield); "The Texas Rangers" 1951 (Danny Bonner); "Cripple Creek" 1952 (Larry Galland); "Tonka" 1958 (Lt. Henry

Nowlan); "Black Spurs" 1965 (Sam Grubbs). ¶TV: *The Adventures of Rin Tin Tin*—"The Lieutenant's Lesson" 2-8-57 (Lt. Cliff Walker); *Disneyland*—"The Saga of Andy Burnett"—Regular 1957-58 (Andy Burnett); *The Rifleman*—"The Brother-in-Law" 10-28-58 (Johnny Gibbs); *The Virginian*—"A Slight Case of Charity" 2-10-65 (Byron Prescot); *Death Valley Days*—"The Race at Cherry Creek" 3-7-65.

Courtleigh, Stephen (1913-12/15/67). Films: "Yellowneck" 1955 (the Colonel); "North to Alaska" 1960 (Duggan). ¶TV: *Lawman*—"The Oath" 10-26-58 (Doc Brewer); *Bonanza*—"Denver McKee" 10-15-60 (Harley); *Rawhide*—"Incident of the Slavemaster" 11-11-60; *Sugarfoot*—"Toothy Thompson" 1-16-61 (Sheriff Ben Caldwell); *Tales of Wells Fargo*—"A Quiet Little Town" 6-5-61 (Judd Sellers); *Daniel Boone*—"Ken-Tuck-E" 9-24-64 (George Washington).

Courtney, Charles "Chuck". Films: "Born to the Saddle" 1953; "Two Guns and a Badge" 1954 (Val Moore); "At Gunpoint" 1955 (Horseman); "Friendly Persuasion" 1956 (Reb Courier); "Billy the Kid vs. Dracula" 1966 (Billy the Kid); "El Dorado" 1967 (Jared MacDonald); "Rio Lobo" 1970 (Whitey's Henchman); "The Cowboys" 1972 (Rustler); "Santee" 1973. ¶TV: *The Lone Ranger*—"Sheep Thieves" 2-9-50 (Dan Reid), "The Whimsical Bandit" 8-31-50 (Dan Reid), "The Deserter" 4-23-53 (Dan Reid), "El Toro" 5-7-53 (Dan Reid), "Dan Reid's Fight for Life" 11-18-54 (Dan Reid), "The Quiet Highwayman" 1-27-55 (Dan Reid), "Code of the Pioneers" 2-17-55 (Dan Reid), "Sunstroke Mesa" 3-17-55 (Dan Reid), "Trigger Finger 4-7-55 (Dan Reid), "Gold Freight" 4-28-55 (Dan Reid), "The Woman in the White Mask" 5-12-55 (Dan Reid); *Wild Bill Hickok*—"Chain of Events" 6-24-52, "Angel of Cedar Mountain" 7-28-53; *Tales of the Texas Rangers*—"Buckaroo from Powder River" 2-4-56 (Tommy); *Tales of Wells Fargo*—"Hoss Tamer" 1-20-58 (Tim Farland); *Jefferson Drum*—"Law and Order" 5-9-58 (Jimmy); *The Adventures of Rin Tin Tin*—"Deadman's Valley" 11-7-58 (Pvt. Jimmy Jersey), "The Epidemic" 11-21-58 (Hal); *Lawman*—"Bloodline" 11-30-58 (Mark Saint); *Zane Grey Theater*—"A Thread of Respect" 2-12-59 (Til Crow); *26 Men*—"The Unwanted" 3-31-59; *Laramie*—"The Replacement" 3-27-62 (Knute Duncan), "The Wedding Party" 1-29-63; *Wagon Train*—"The Michael Malone Story" 1-6-64, "The

Alice Whitetree Story" 11-1-64 (Tom Vincent); *Laredo*—"A Matter of Policy" 11-11-65 (Pete), "No Bugles, One Drum" 2-24-66; *The Legend of Jesse James*—"A Field of Wild Flowers" 4-25-66 (Trooper Thorn); *Wild Wild West*—"The Night of the Death Masks" 1-26-68 (Soldier); *The Virginian*—"The Decision" 3-13-68 (Carmody).

Courtright, William (1848-3/6/33). Films: "The Sunshine Trail" 1923 (Mystery Man); "The Heart Buster" 1924 (Justice of the Peace); "All Around the Frying Pan" 1925 (All Around Austin); "Hands Across the Border" 1926 (Grimes); "Lone Hand Saunders" 1926 (Dr. Bandy); "A Regular Scout" 1926 (Luke Baxteer); "The Tough Guy" 1926 (Minister); "The Two-Gun Man" 1926 (Dad Stickley); "Arizona Nights" 1927 (Bill Barrow); "Don Mike" 1927 (Gomez); "Jesse James" 1927 (Parson Bill); "Silver Comes Through" 1927 (Zeke, the Ranchowner); "The Pioneer Scout" 1928 (Old Bill); "The Sunset Legion" 1928 (Old Bill).

Cousins, Kay. TV: *Wagon Train*—"The Daniel Barrister Story" 4-16-58 (Mrs. Miller); *The Rifleman*—"The Boarding House" 2-24-59.

Covington, Bruce. Films: "The Flying Horseman" 1926 (Col. Savary); "Under a Texas Moon" 1930 (Don Roberto).

Cowan, Jerome (1897-1/24/72). Films: "The Fighting Parson" 1933; "Melody Ranch" 1940 (Tommy Summerville); "Girl from Alaska" 1942 (Ravenhill); "Silver Spurs" 1943 (Jerry Johnson); "Dallas" 1950 (Matt Coulter). ¶TV: *Bat Masterson*—"The Conspiracy" 6-17-59 & 6-24-59 (Jasper Salt), "Flume to the Mother Lode" 1-28-60 (Ben Wilson); *Rawhide*—"Incident of the Thirteenth Man" 10-23-59 (Judge Gerald T. Crenshaw); *The Alaskans*—"Winter Song" 11-22-59 (Horatio Styles); *U.S. Marshal*—"Paper Bullets" 12-5-59 (Brock); *Hotel De Paree*—"Sundance and the Hero of Bloody Blue Creek" 3-11-60 (Colonel Parrington); *The Outlaws*—"Ballad for a Badman" 10-6-60 (Lafe Dabney), "A Bit of Glory" 2-1-62 (MacNeil); *Klondike*—"Bathhouse Justice" 12-26-60 (Judge Bickle); *Wide Country*—"What Are Friends For?" 10-18-62 (Ben Stanton); *Destry*—"Law and Order Day" 2-28-64 (Grubbs); *Bonanza*—"The Saga of Muley Jones" 3-29-64 (Thornbridge); *Daniel Boone*—"Goliath" 9-29-66 (Jeremiah Loomis); *Alias Smith and Jones*—"The Root of It All" 4-1-71.

Cowan, Karla. Films: "Riders of the Rio" 1931 (Kieta); "The Galloping Kid" 1932 (Mary Parker); "Arizona Cyclone" 1934.

Cowell, Jack. Films: "Alias John Law" 1935 (Lawyer); "Bulldog Courage" 1935 (Pete Brennan); "Kid Courageous" 1935; "Western Justice" 1935 (Brent); "Men of the Plains" 1936 (Lucky Gordon); "Rio Grande Romance" 1936 (Police Officer); "Too Much Beef" 1936 (George Thompson).

Cowen, Ashley. Films: "Whispering Smith" 1948; "Jeep-Herders" 1949. ¶TV: *The Californians*—"Shanghai Queen" 6-3-58 (Alfie); *Wyatt Earp*—"The Bounty Killer" 9-30-58 (Bill Hicks), "Doc Fabrique's Greatest Case" 4-7-59; *The Restless Gun*—"Peligroso" 12-15-58 (Craig); *Stagecoach West*—"By the Deep Six" 12-27-60 (Liverpool Jack); *Wagon Train*—"The Duncan McIvor Story" 3-9-64; *Bonanza*—"Once a Doctor" 2-28-65 (Thomas Crippin).

Cowl, Darry. *see* Darry-Cowl.

Cowl, George (1878-4/4/42). Films: "The Crimson Dove" 1917 (Dr. Stewart); "The Adventurer" 1928 (Esteban de Silva).

Cowl, Richard S. Films: "Deadwood '76" 1965 (Preacher Smith). ¶TV: *Wrangler*—"The Affair with Browning's Woman" 8-25-60 (Vince Carter).

Cowles, Jules (1878-5/22/43). Films: "Tangled Trails" 1921 (the Stranger); "The Love Bandit" 1924; "The Ace of Clubs" 1926 (Jake McGill); "Man Rustlin'" 1926 (Jim Tucker); "Terror Mountain" 1928 (Jed Burke); "Secret Menace" 1931; "Heroes of the West" 1932-serial (Missouri); "Renegades of the West" 1932; "Crossfire" 1933 ((Judge Whitney T. Wilson); "The Fighting Parson" 1933 (Marshal J.A. Darby); "Law Beyond the Range" 1935 (Lockjaw); "Wanderer of the Wasteland" 1935 (2nd Man); "Rose of the Rancho" 1936 (Vigilante); "The Bad Man of Brimstone" 1937 (Saddlenose Sawtelle).

Cowling, Bruce (-8/22/86). Films: "Ambush" 1950 (Tom Conovan); "The Devil's Doorway" 1950 (Lt. Grimes); "The Painted Hills" 1951 (Lin Taylor); "Westward the Women" 1951 (Cat); "The Battle at Apache Pass" 1952 (Neil Baylor); "Gun Belt" 1953 (Virgil Earp); "Masterson of Kansas" 1954 (Wyatt Earp). ¶TV: *The Lone Ranger*—"The Frightened Woman" 9-30-54, "Uncle Ed" 3-3-55, "False Accusations" 4-21-55;

The Adventures of Rin Tin Tin—"The Third Rider" 3-16-56 (Cole), "Rin Tin Tin and the Second Chance" 6-1-56 (Clint Cole); *Cheyenne*—"Deadline" 2-26-57 (Garth); *Have Gun Will Travel*—"Hey Boy's Revenge" 4-12-58; *Zane Grey Theater*—"Threat of Violence" 5-23-58 (Verg Cheney); *Northwest Passage*—"The Vulture" 12-28-58 (Sir Martin Stanley); *The Texan*—"The Eyes of Captain Wylie" 2-23-59 (Hank Rogers).

Cowper, William (1853-6/13/18). Films: "A Yellow Streak" 1915 (Tobias Rader).

Cox, Brian (1946-). Films: "Iron Will" 1994 (Angus McTeague).

Cox, Buddy. Films: "Courage of the West" 1937 (Jackie Saunders); "Reckless Ranger" 1937 (Jimmie Allen); "The Roaming Cowboy" 1937 (Buddy Barry); "Pioneers of the Frontier" 1940 (Tommy).

Cox, Ronny (1938-). Films: "The Girl Called Hatter Fox" TVM-1977 (Dr. Teague Summer). ¶TV: *Bonanza*—"New Man" 10-10-72 (Lucas); *The Life and Times of Grizzly Adams*—"Unwelcome Neighbor" 3-2-77 (Jacob Cartman).

Cox, Victor. Films: "Reckless Ranger" 1937; "Springtime in the Rockies" 1937; "In Old Monterey" 1939; "Zorro's Fighting Legion" 1939-serial (Gun Heavy); "Adventures of Red Ryder" 1940-serial; "Back in the Saddle" 1941; "The Lost Trail" 1945; "Pistol Packin' Nitwits" 1945-short; "Jesse James Rides Again" 1947-serial; "The Adventures of Frank and Jesse James" 1948-serial (Dick); "Beyond the Purple Hills" 1950; "Cow Town" 1950; "Barbed Wire" 1952. ¶TV: *The Cisco Kid*—"Lynching Story" 4-28-51, "Confession for Money" 5-26-51, "Pancho Hostage" 6-23-51.

Cox, Virginia. Films: "Brothers in the Saddle" 1949 (Nancy Austin).

Cox, Wally (1924-2/15/73). Films: "The Cockeyed Cowboys of Calico County" 1970 (Mr. Bester); "The Young Country" TVM-1970 (Aaron Grimes/Ira Greebe). ¶TV: *Wagon Train*—"The Vincent Eaglewood Story" 4-15-59 (Vincent Eaglewood), "The Sam Elder Story" 1-18-61 (Ben Allen); *Bonanza*—"The Gold Detector" 12-24-67 (McNulty), "The Last Vote" 10-20-68 (Phineas Burke); *Alias Smith and Jones*—"The Man Who Corrupted Hadleyburg" 1-27-72 (Mark Tapscott).

Coxen, Edward (1884-11/21/54). Films: "The Girl Bandit's Hoodoo" 1912; "The End of Black Bart" 1913; "The Ghost of the Hacienda" 1913; "A Rose of Old Mexico" 1913; "A Spartan Girl of the West" 1913; "Taming a Cowboy" 1913; "Her Fighting Chance" 1914; "Jim" 1914; "The Silent Way" 1914; "The Castle Ranch" 1915; "Reformation" 1915; "The Senor's Silver Buckle" 1915; "The Water Carrier of San Juan" 1915; "Carmen of the Klondike" 1918 (Cameron Stewart); "Go West, Young Man" 1918 (Dandy Jim); "Desert Gold" 1919 (Captain George Thorn); "Desperate Trails" 1921 (Walter A. Walker); "No Man's Woman" 1921 (the Man); "Nine Points of the Law" 1922 (Bruce McLeod); "The Stranger of the Hills" 1922; "Flashing Spurs" 1924 (Steve Clammert); "Singer Jim McKee" 1924 (Hamlin Glass, Jr.); "Cold Nerve" 1925; "Galloping Fury" 1927 (James Gordon); "The Spoilers" 1930 (Lawyer); "The Trail Drive" 1933; "Gun Justice" 1934 (Lance); "Smoking Guns" 1934 (Bob Masters); "Wheels of Destiny" 1934 (Dad); "Five Bad Men" 1935 (Sim Bartlett); "The Ghost Rider" 1935 (Dad Burns); "The Silent Code" 1935 (Nathan); "Code of the Range" 1937 (Angus Mcleod); "Riders of the Dawn" 1937; "Thunder Trail" 1937 (Martin); "Cattle Raiders" 1938 (Doc Connors); "South of Arizona" 1938 (Jed); "West of Rainbow's End" 1938 (Joel Carter); "Down the Wyoming Trail" 1939 (Old Whiskers); "Texas Stampede" 1939 (Seth); "Pioneers of the Frontier" 1940 (Hardrock).

Coy, Charles. Films: "Gun Fight" 1961 (Sheriff).

Coy, Walter (1906-12/11/74). Films: "Barricade" 1950 (Benson); "Colt .45" 1950 (Carl); "Saddle Tramp" 1950 (Giles Starkey); "Under Mexicali Stars" 1950 (Giles Starkey); "The Lusty Men" 1952 (Buster Burgess); "Pillars of the Sky" 1956 (Maj. Donahue); "The Searchers" 1956 (Aaron Edwards); "The Young Guns" 1956 (Peyton); "The Gunfight at Dodge City" 1959 (Ben); "Gunmen from Laredo" 1959 (Ben); "Warlock" 1959 (Deputy Thompson); "Five-Guns to Tombstone" 1961 (Ike Garvey). ¶TV: *The Lone Ranger*—"Enfield Rifle" 1-13-55; *Wyatt Earp*—"Wichita Is Civilized" 8-18-56, "Dodge Is Civilized" 4-28-59 (Ben Thompson), "The Doctor" 10-4-60 (Henry Mason); *Zane Grey Theater*—"Badge of Honor" 5-3-57 (Jim Shane), "This Man Must Die" 1-24-58 (Sheriff Baker), "Utopia, Wyoming" 6-6-58 (Hank Cluny); *Tales of Wells Fargo*—"Stage to Nowhere" 6-24-57, "Hoss Tamer" 1-20-58 (Dude Randell); *The Restless Gun*—"Duel at Lockwood" 9-23-57 (Sheriff), "The Dead Ringer" 2-16-59 (Nick Dawson); *Wagon Train*—"The Mary Halstead Story" 11-20-57 (Tracy), "The Santiago Quesada Story" 3-30-64 (Meachum), "Those Who Stay Behind" 11-8-64 (Ord Whaley); *Cheyenne*—"Town of Fear" 12-3-57 (Sheriff Sam Townley), "Savage Breed" 12-19-60 (George Naylor); *Bronco*—"The Turning Point" 10-21-58 (Sheriff Walters), "Backfire" 4-7-59 (Victor Leggett); *Cimarron City*—"Kid on a Calico Horse" 11-22-58 (Ed Brayder); *Trackdown*—"Every Man a Witness" 12-26-58 (Sheriff Freemont); *Have Gun Will Travel*—"The Monster of Moon Ridge" 2-28-59; *Lawman*—"Battle Scar" 3-22-59 (Col. French); *Yancy Derringer*—"A State of Crisis" 4-30-59 (Slade Donovan); *Wanted—Dead or Alive*—"Breakout" 9-26-59; *Bonanza*—"The Paiute War" 10-3-59, Thunderhead Swindle" 4-29-61 (Frank Furnas), "Twilight Town" 10-13-63; *Rough Riders*—"Hired Gun" 4-23-59 (Sunday); *Rawhide*—"Incident of the Thirteenth Man" 10-23-59 (Ott), "Incident of the Running Man" 5-5-61 (Lem Trager); *Man from Blackhawk*—"The Savage" 1-15-60 (Capt. John Goodhill); *Maverick*—"Maverick and Juliet" 1-17-60 (Preacher); *Hotel De Paree*—"Hard Luck for Sundance" 2-19-60 (Meachum); *The Texan*—"Town Divided" 3-21-60 (Doc Nelson); *Laramie*—"Saddle and Spur" 3-29-60 (Bishop); *Overland Trail*—"Vigilantes of Montana" 4-3-60 (Sheriff Plummer); *Bat Masterson*—"Blood on the Money" 6-23-60 (Andrew Strathmere); *Two Faces West*—"Sheriff of the Town" 10-31-60 (Cauter); *The Big Valley*—"Hide the Children" 12-19-66 (Sheriff), "Lightfoot" 2-17-69 (District Attorney); *The Virginian*—"Doctor Pat" 3-1-67, "Jed" 1-10-68 (Tom Tallman), "Last Grave at Socorro Creek" 1-22-69 (Bartender); *Laredo*—"Like One of the Family" 3-24-67; *Daniel Boone*—"A Matter of Blood" 12-28-67 (Tribal Elder), "How to Become a Goddess" 4-30-70; *The Outcasts*—"Take Your Lover in the Ring" 10-28-68 (Sheriff Patton).

Coyle, Walter (1888-8/3/48). Films: "The Sheriff's Story" 1915.

Coyote, Peter (1942-). Films: "Timerider" 1983 (Porter Reese); "Buffalo Girls" TVM-1995 (Bufalo Bill Cody).

Cozine, Arthur. Films: "The Danger Trail" 1917 (Francois Thoreau).

Crabbe, Larry "Buster" (1908-

4/23/83). Films: "Man of the Forest" 1933 (Yegg); "To the Last Man" 1933 (Bill Hayden); "The Thundering Herd" 1934 (Bill Hatch); "Nevada" 1935 (Nevada); "Wanderer of the Wasteland" 1935 (Big Ben); "The Arizona Raiders" 1936 (Laramie Nelson); "Arizona Mahoney" 1936 (Kirby Talbott); "Desert Gold" 1936 (Moya); "Drift Fence" 1936 (Slinger Dunn); "Forlorn River" 1937 (Nevada); "Colorado Sunset" 1939 (Dave Haines); "Billy the Kid Wanted" 1941 (Billy the Kid); "Billy the Kid's Roundup" 1941 (Billy the Kid); "Billy the Kid Trapped" 1942 (Billy the Kid); "Billy the Kid's Smoking Guns" 1942 (Billy the Kid); "The Mysterious Rider" 1942 (Billy the Kid); "Sheriff of Sage Valley" 1942 (Billy the Kid/Kansas Ed); "Cattle Stampede" 1943 (Billy the Kid); "Fugitive of the Plains" 1943 (Billy Carson); "The Renegade" 1943; "Western Cyclone" 1943 (Billy the Kid); "Blazing Frontier" 1944 (Billy the Kid); "Devil Riders" 1944 (Billy Carson); "The Drifter" 1944 (Billy Carson/Drifter Davis); "Frontier Outlaws" 1944 (Billy Carson); "Fuzzy Settles Down" 1944 (Billy Carson); "Oath of Vengeance" 1944 (Billy Carson); "Rustlers' Hideout" 1944 (Billy Carson); "Thundering Gun Slingers" 1944 (Billy Carson); "Valley of Vengeance" 1944 (Billy Carson); "Wild Horse Phantom" 1944 (Billy Carson); "Border Badmen" 1945 (Billy Carson); "Fighting Bill Carson" 1945 (Bill Carson); "Gangster's Den" 1945 (Billy Carson); "His Brother's Ghost" 1945 (Billy "the Kid" Carson); "Prairie Rustlers" 1945 (Billy Carson); "Shadows of Death" 1945 (Billy Carson); "Stagecoach Outlaws" 1945 (Billy Carson); "Gentlemen with Guns" 1946 (Billy Carson); "Ghost of Hidden Valley" 1946 (Billy Carson); "Lightning Raiders" 1946 (Billy Carson); "Outlaw of the Plains" 1946; "Overland Riders" 1946 (Billy Carson); "Prairie Badmen" 1946 (Billy Carson); "Terrors on Horseback" 1946 (Billy Carson); "Gun Brothers" 1956 (Chad); "Badman's Country" 1958 (Wyatt Earp); "The Lawless Eighties" 1958; "Gunfighters of Abilene" 1960 (Kip); "Arizona Raiders" 1965 (Capt. Andrews); "The Bounty Killer" 1965 (Mike Clayman).

Craft, Robert. Films: "The White Rider" 1920 (Jackson Grade).

Craig, Alec (1885-6/25/45). Films: "Border Cafe" 1937.

Craig, Carolyn (-12/11/70). Films: "Giant" 1956 (Lacey Lynnton); "Fury at Showdown" 1957

(Ginny Clay); "Gunsight Ridge" 1957 (Girl); "Apache Territory" 1958 (Junie Hatchett). ¶TV: *The Californians*—"The Search for Lucy Manning" 10-22-57, "Dangerous Journey" 11-25-58 (Lorna); *Tales of Wells Fargo*—"The Inscrutable Man" 12-9-57 (Glory Harper), "The Stage Line" 10-5-59 (Ann); *Wyatt Earp*—"County Seat War" 4-8-58 (Edna Granger), "Truth About Gunfighting" 11-18-58 (Janey Travis), "Johnny Behind the Deuce" 10-11-60 (Marcia); *The Rifleman*—"End of a Young Gun" 10-14-58; *Northwest Passage*—"The Deserter" 2-27-59 (Betty Jason); *Overland Trail*—"West of Boston" 2-21-60 (Priscilla Cabot); *The Deputy*—"The Dream" 2-4-61 (Selene Hammer); *Laramie*—"The Fortune Hunter" 10-9-62 (Kitty McAllen).

Craig, Catherine. Films: "Hellhounds of the West" 1922 (Virginia Stacy); "Albuquerque" 1948 (Celia Wallace); "El Paso" 1949 (Mrs. John Elkins).

Craig, Gordon. Films: "The Man from Nevada" 1929 (Wiggles Watkins).

Craig, Hal. Films: "God's Country and the Woman" 1937 (Motorcycle Cop); "Wells Fargo" 1937 (Southerner); "Dodge City" 1939; "Union Pacific" 1939 (Cassidy).

Craig, James (1912-6/28/85). Films: "Born to the West" 1937 (Brady); "Thunder Trail" 1937 (Bob Ames); "Pride of the West" 1938 (Nixon); "Overland with Kit Carson" 1939-serial (Tennessee); "The Taming of the West" 1939 (Handy); "Konga, the Wild Stallion" 1940 (Ed); "Two-Fisted Rangers" 1940 (Frisco Kid); "Winners of the West" 1940-serial (Jim Jackson); "Northwest Rangers" 1942 (Frank "Blackie" Marshall); "The Omaha Trail" 1942 (Pat Crandall); "Valley of the Sun" 1942 (Jonathan Ware); "Gentle Annie" 1944 (Lloyd Richland); "Boy's Ranch" 1946 (Dan Walker); "The Man from Texas" 1947 (El Paso Kid); "Northwest Stampede" 1948 (Dan Bennett); "Drums in the Deep South" 1951 (Clay); "Fort Vengeance" 1953 (Dick); "Massacre" 1956 (Ezparza); "Naked in the Sun" 1957; "The Persuader" 1957 (Bick Justin); "Shoot-Out at Medicine Bend" 1957 (Clark); "Man or Gun" 1958 (Pinch Corley); "Four Fast Guns" 1959 (Sabin); "Fort Utah" 1967 (Bo Greer); "Hostile Guns" 1967 (Ned Cooper); "Arizona Bushwhackers" 1968 (Ike Clanton). ¶TV: *The Westerner*—Pilot 11-53 (Sheriff); *Annie Oakley*—"Dude's Decision" 2-10-57 (Penny

Granger); *Broken Arrow*—"Johnny Flagstaff" 3-19-57 (Johnny Flagstaff); *Have Gun Will Travel*—"Birds of a Feather" 3-8-58 (Ralph Coe); *Death Valley Days*—"The Man Everyone Hated" 4-12-60 (General Edward F. Beale); *Tales of Wells Fargo*—"Vignette of a Sinner" 6-2-62 (Sheriff); *Daniel Boone*—"The Renegade" 9-28-67; *Custer*—"War Lance and Saber" 10-11-67.

Craig, John. Films: "The Gambler Wore a Gun" 1961 (Rebe Larkin). ¶TV: *Tales of Wells Fargo*—"Captain Scoville" 1-9-61 (Murdock); *The Rifleman*—"Which Way'd They Go?" 4-1-63 (Bo Jackman); *Rawhide*—"Incident at El Crucero" 10-10-63 (Charles Cornelius); *Wagon Train*—"The Melanie Craig Story" 2-17-64 (Prentiss).

Craig, Michael (1928-). Films: "A Town Called Hell" 1971-Span./Brit. (Paco).

Craig, Neil. Films: "Crashin' Thru" 1923 (Garcia); "Wells Fargo" 1937.

Craig, Nell (1891-1/5/65). Films: "Cimarron" 1931 (Arminta Greenwood); "Come on, Danger!" 1932.

Craig, Yvonne (1941-). Films: "The Young Land" 1959 (Elena de la Madrid); "Advance to the Rear" 1964 (Ora). ¶TV: *Tales of Wells Fargo*—"The Remittance Man" 4-3-61 (Libby Gillette); *Laramie*—"The Long Road Back" 10-23-62 (Ginny Malone); *Wide Country*—"The Bravest Man in the World" 12-6-62 (Anita Callahan); *Wagon Train*—"The Link Cheney Story" 4-13-64 (Ellie Riggs); *The Big Valley*—"The Invaders" 12-29-65 (Allie Kay); *Wild Wild West*—"The Night of the Grand Emir" 1-28-66 (Ecstasy La Joie).

Crain, Earl. Films: "The Orphan" 1920 (Bucknel); "Steelheart" 1921 (Dick Colter).

Crain, Jeanne (1925-). Films: "City of Badmen" 1953 (Linda Culligan); "Man Without a Star" 1955 (Reed Bowman); "Fastest Gun Alive" 1956 (Dora Temple); "Guns of the Timberland" 1960 (Laura Riley). ¶TV: *Riverboat*—"Escape to Memphis" 10-25-59 (Laura Sutton).

Cramer, Marc (1910-88). Films: "Adventures of Don Coyote" 1947 (Dave).

Cramer, Richard "Dick" (1889-8/9/60). Films: "The Painted Desert" 1931; "The Pocatello Kid" 1931 (Pete Larkin); "Forty-Five Calibre Echo" 1932; "Lawless Valley" 1932 (Bull Lemoyne); "Rider of Death Valley"

1932; "The Fourth Horseman" 1933 (Thad); "The Law of the Wild" 1934-serial (Nolan); "Rawhide Mail" 1934 (Hal Drummond); "The Red Rider" 1934-serial (Joe Portos); "Defying the Law" 1935 (Buck Morgan); "The Judgement Book" 1935 (Ross Rankin); "The Phantom Cowboy" 1935 (Hank Morgan); "Trail of Terror" 1935 (Muggs); "Western Racketeers" 1935 (Coroner); "End of the Trail" 1936 (Bartender); "Frontier Justice" 1936 (Gilbert Ware); "O'Malley of the Mounted" 1936 (Butch); "The Phantom of the Range" 1936; "Pinto Rustlers" 1936; "Rip Roarin' Buckaroo" 1936; "Riddle Ranch" 1936 (Jim Riddle); "Ridin' On" 1936; "Rio Grande Romance" 1936 (Police Officer); "Robin Hood of El Dorado" 1936 (Bartender); "Santa Fe Bound" 1936 (Stanton); "Sutter's Gold" 1936; "The Three Godfathers" 1936 (Prospector); "Courage of the West" 1937 (Murphy); "Guns in the Dark" 1937; "Lightnin' Crandall" 1937; "North of the Rio Grande" 1937; "The Rangers Step In" 1937; "The Red Rope" 1937; "The Roaming Cowboy" 1937 (Dan Morgan); "Trail of Vengeance" 1937 (Rancher Joe); "The Trusted Outlaw" 1937 (Rogan); "Two-Fisted Sheriff" 1937 (Taggert); "Wells Fargo" 1937 (Miner); "Where Trails Divide" 1937 (Ike); "Heroes of the Alamo" 1938; "Knight of the Plains" 1938 (Clem Peterson); "The Painted Trail" 1938; "Phantom Ranger" 1938 (Barton); "The Rangers' Roundup" 1938 (Burton, the Express Manager); "Rolling Caravans" 1938; "Six Shootin' Sheriff" 1938; "Songs and Bullets" 1938 (Henchman); "Thunder in the Desert" 1938 (Tramp); "Dodge City" 1939 (Clerk); "Feud of the Range" 1939 (Tom Gray); "In Old Montana" 1939 (Sheepman); "Arizona Frontier" 1940 (Graham); "Legion of the Lawless" 1940; "Northwest Passage" 1940 (Sheriff Packer); "Pioneer Days" 1940 (Bartender); "Trailing Double Trouble" 1940; "West of Pinto Basin" 1940; "Billy the Kid's Roundup" 1941; "Underground Rustlers" 1941; "White Eagle" 1941-serial; "Arizona Stagecoach" 1942; "Billy the Kid Trapped" 1942; "Boot Hill Bandits" 1942 (Hawkins); "Pirates of the Prairie" 1942; "Rock River Renegades" 1942; "Texas Trouble Shooters" 1942 (Bartender); "Thunder River Feud" 1942; "Trail Riders" 1942; "Beyond the Last Frontier" 1943; "Two Fisted Justice" 1943; "Song of Old Wyoming" 1945 (Hodges); "Border Feud" 1947; "Law of the Lash" 1947 (Bartender); "Wild Country" 1947 (Guard); "Santa Fe" 1951.

Cramer, Susanne (1937-1/7/69). TV: *The Dakotas*—"Trial at Grand Forks" 3-25-63 (Maria Hoenig); *Temple Houston*—"Seventy Times Seven" 12-5-63 (Helmi Bergen); *Bonanza*—"Dead and Gone" 4-4-65 (Hilda); *The Guns of Will Sonnett*—"One Angry Juror" 3-7-69 (Christine).

Crampton, Howard (1865-6/15/22). Films: "The Devil's Trail" 1919; "With Hoops of Steel" 1919 (Pierre Delarue); "Nan of the North" 1922-serial.

Crandall, Edward "Eddie" (1904-5/9/68). Films: "The Badge of Marshal Brennan" 1957 (Pepe Joe); "Buffalo Gun" 1961.

Crandall, Suzi. Films: "Mark of the Lash" 1948; "Station West" 1948 (Girl). ¶TV: *Wichita Town*—"The Hanging Judge" 3-9-60 (Mark Parker).

Crandall, Will. TV: *Wild Bill Hickok*—"The Maverick" 8-19-52; *Annie Oakley*—"Annie Finds Strange Treasure" 3-6-54; *The Gene Autry Show*—"Saddle Up" 12-3-55, "Ride, Rancheros" 12-10-55, "The Rangerette" 12-17-55.

Crane, Erle. Films: "Drag Harlan" 1920 (Storm Rogers).

Crane, Frank Hall (1873-9/1/48). Films: "The Man from Nevada" 1929 (Wobbles Watkins); "Mason of the Mounted" 1932; "Mystery Ranch" 1934 (Percy Jenkins); "'Neath the Arizona Skies" 1934 (Express Agent).

Crane, James (1889-6/3/68). Films: "Dude Ranch" 1931 (Blaze Denton).

Crane, Norma (1931-9/28/73). TV: *Zane Grey Theater*—"Black Creek Encounter" 3-8-57 (Kelly); *Have Gun Will Travel*—"Ella West" 1-4-58 (Ella West), "The Taffeta Mayor" 1-10-59 (Lucky Kellawan), "Episode in Laredo" 9-19-59 (Eileen Tuttle), "The Cure" 5-20-61 Martha Jane Conroy); *Gunsmoke*—"The Bear" 2-28-59 (Tilda), "Perce" 9-30-61 (Ida); *Riverboat*—"Rive Champion" 10-10-60 (Saran Prentice); *The Deputy*—"The Return of Widow Brown" 4-22-61 (Amelia Brown); *The Big Valley*—"Last Stage to Salt Flats" 12-5-66 (Emilie); *The Guns of Will Sonnett*—"Jim Sonnett's Lady" 2-21-69 (Angela Drake).

Crane, Ogden (1873-5/14/40). Films: "The End of the Trail" 1916 (Jacues Fauve); "The Parson of Panamint" 1916 (Absalom Randall); "The Light of Western Stars" 1918 (Nels); "Her Five-Foot Higness" 1920 (Wesley Saunders).

Crane, Richard (1918-3/9/69). Films: "The Phantom Plainsmen" 1942 (Tad); "Riders of the Deadline" 1943 (Tim Mason); "Man in the Saddle" 1951 (Juke Virk); "The Iron Mistress" 1952; "Leadville Gunslinger" 1952 (Jim Blanchard); "Thundering Caravans" 1952 (Dan Reed); "Winning of the West" 1953 (Jack Austin); "The Woman They Almost Lynched" 1953 (Lieutenant); "Thirteen Fighting Men" 1960 (Loomis). ¶TV: *The Lone Ranger*—"One Jump Ahead" 12-14-50, "Frame for Two" 10-23-52, "Tumblerock Law" 2-26-53, "Prisoner in Jeopardy" 8-20-53, "The Breaking Point" 1-24-57, "Ghost Town Fury" 3-28-57; *My Friend Flicka*—"The Night Rider" 1-20-56; *Maverick*—"The Long Hunt" 10-20-57 (Jedd Ferris); *Sugarfoot*—"Quicksilver" 11-26-57; *Trackdown*—"The Farrand Story" 1-10-58 (Jeff Krail), "Outlaw's Wife" 9-12-58 (Lem Duke); *Tales of Wells Fargo*—"Deadwood" 4-7-58 (Billy Reno), "The Last Stand" 4-13-59 (Jackman); *26 Men*—"Manhunt" 12-16-58, "Trial at Verde River" 4-14-59; *Death Valley Days*—"Half a Loaf" 5-5-59 (Monte); *Wagon Train*—"The Lita Foladaire Story" 1-6-60 (Clay Foladaire), "Weight of Command" 1-25-61 (Dan Foster), "The Lizabeth Ann Calhoun Story" 12-6-61 (Lon Harper); *Wanted—Dead or Alive*—"Black Belt" 3-19-60 (Paul Cameron); *Stagecoach West*—"The Unwanted" 10-25-60 (Johnny Kelly); *Wyatt Earp*—"Terror in the Desert" 1-24-61 (Tom Grover); *Whispering Smith*—"Three for One" 7-3-61 (Lucas); *The Virginian*—"Farewell to Honesty" 3-24-65 (Paul Denning); *Iron Horse*—"Sister Death" 4-3-67 (Sands).

Crane, Stephen (1916-2/5/85). Films: "Black Hills" 1948.

Crane, Susan. TV: *Sugarfoot*—"Wolf Pack 2-2-60 (Julie Beaumont); *The Alaskans*—"The Devil Made Five" 6-19-60 (Mary Simon); *Wanted—Dead or Alive*—"To the Victor" 11-9-60 (Alice Adams); *Cheyenne*—"The Greater Glory" 5-15-61 (Mary Wiley); *The Tall Man*—"The Female Artillery" 9-30-61 (Martha); *Death Valley Days*—"The Hold-Up Proof Safe" 10-4-61 (Katie).

Crane, Ward (1891-7/21/28). Films: "Flaming Frontier" 1926 (Sam Belden).

Cranford, Jean. Films: "Feud of the Range" 1939 (Helen Wilson).

Cranshaw, Joseph Patrick (1919-). Films: "Bandolero!" 1968 (Bank Clerk). ¶TV: *Best of the West*—"The Prisoner" 9-17-81 (Bob), 9-24-81 (Bob).

Cravat, Nick (1911-1/29/94). Films: "Davy Crockett, King of the Wild Frontier" 1955 (Bustedluck); "Cat Ballou" 1965 (Ad-Lib); "The Way West" 1967 (Calvelli); "The Scalphunters" 1968 (Ramon); "Valdez Is Coming" 1971 (Gang Member); "Ulzana's Raid" 1972. ¶TV: *Walt Disney Presents*—"Davy Crockett"—Regular 1954-55 (Bustedluck); *The Outcasts*—"The Glory Wagon" 2-3-69 (Miner).

Craven, James. Films: "Tumbledown Ranch in Arizona" 1941 (Slocum); "White Eagle" 1941-serial (Darnell); "Little Joe, the Wrangler" 1942 (Lloyd Chapin); "Days of Buffalo Bill" 1946; "Sheriff of Redwood Valley" 1946; "Desperadoes of Dodge City" 1948 (Cal Sutton); "Strange Gamble" 1948; "Wells Fargo Gunmaster" 1951 (Henry Mills); "The Old West" 1952 (Daniels). ¶TV: *The Gene Autry Show*—"Frontier Guard" 10-13-51, "Killer's Trail" 10-27-51, "Outlaw Escape" 12-1-51 (Brad Bidwell), "The Return of Maverick Dan" 12-15-51.

Craven, John (1916-11/24/95). Films: "Friendly Persuasion" 1956 (Leader). ¶TV: *Wyatt Earp*—"One of Jesse's Gang" 3-13-56 (Harry Dolan); *Sergeant Preston of the Yukon*—"Scourge of the Wilderness" 1-11-57 (Al Stone); *Rawhide*—"Incident Below the Brazos" 5-15-59; *Wanted—Dead or Alive*—"Criss Cross" 11-16-60 (Zach Dawson); *Whispering Smith*—"The Hemp Reeger Case" 7-17-61 (Bolling); *The Big Valley*—"Earthquake!" 11-10-65 (Doctor).

Cravy, George. Films: "West of the Rio Grande" 1921 (Tom Sadler).

Crawford, Andrew (1917-). TV: *Masterpiece Theatre*—"The Last of the Mohicans" 1972 (Colonel Munro).

Crawford, Bobby. Films: "Duel at Diablo" 1966 (Swenson). ¶TV: *The Rifleman*—"Eight Hours to Die" 11-4-58 (Boy), "The Gaucho" 12-30-58, "The Second Witness" 3-3-59; *Laramie*—Regular 1959-63 (Andy Sherman); *Gunsmoke*—"The Brothers" 3-12-66 (Billy).

Crawford, Broderick (1910-4/26/86). Films: "Texas Rangers Ride Again" 1940 (Mace Townsley); "Trail of the Vigilantes" 1940 (Swanee); "When the Daltons Rode" 1940 (Bob Dalton); "Badlands of Dakota" 1941 (Bob Holliday); "Men of Texas" 1942 (Henry Clay Jackson); "North to the Klondike" 1942 (John Thorn); "Sin Town" 1942 (Dude McNair); "Bad Men of Tombstone" 1949 (Morgan); "Lone Star" 1952 (Thomas Craven); "Fastest Gun Alive" 1956 (Vinnie

Harold); "Mutiny at Fort Sharp" 1966-Ital. (Colonel Lennox); "The Texican" 1966-U.S./Span. (Luke Starr); "Red Tomahawk" 1967 (Columbus Smith). ¶TV: *Rough Riders*—"The Plot to Assassinate President Johnson" 2-5-59 (William Quantrill); *Destry*—"The Solid Gold Girl" 2-14-64 (Oakley); *Rawhide*—"Incident at Dead Horse" 4-16-64 & 4-23-64 (Jud Hammerklein); *Cimarron Strip*—"The Blue Moon Train" 2-15-68 (Joe Lehigh); *Bat Masterson*—"Two Graves for Swan Valley" 10-15-58 (Ben Thompson); *The Virginian*—"A Killer in Town" 10-9-63 (George Wolfe); *Alias Smith and Jones*—"The Man Who Broke the Bank at Red Gap" 1-20-72 (Powers).

Crawford, Diana. TV: *Have Gun Will Travel*—"The Return of Roy Carter" 5-2-59 (Margie); *Bat Masterson*—"Wanted—Alive Please" 5-26-60 (Renee); *Maverick*—"Bundle from Britain" 9-18-60 (Molly); *Wanted—Dead or Alive*—"To the Victor" 11-9-60.

Crawford, Earl. Films: "Arizona" 1940 (Joe Briggs); "The Navajo Trail" 1945.

Crawford, Edward (1962-). TV: *Bonanza*—"He Was Only Seven" 3-5-72 (Jonah).

Crawford, Florence. Films: "The Deputy's Chance That Won" 1915; "The Scarlet West" 1925 (Mrs. Harper).

Crawford, Joan (1906-5/10/77). Films: "Winners of the Wilderness" 1927 (Renee Contracouer); "The Law of the Range" 1928 (Betty Dallas); "Montana Moon" 1930 (Joan Prescott); "Old Oklahoma Plains" 1952 (Chuck Ramsey); "Johnny Guitar" 1954 (Vienna). ¶TV: *Zane Grey Theater*—"Rebel Ranger" 12-3-59 (Stella Faring), "One Must Die" 1-12-61 (Sarah/Melanie).

Crawford, John (1926-). Films: "The Adventures of Frank and Jesse James" 1948-serial (Amos Ramsey); "Dangers of the Canadian Mounted" 1948-serial (Danton); "Sons of Adventure" 1948 (Norton); "Ghost of Zorro" 1949-serial (Mulvaney); "The James Brothers of Missouri" 1950-serial (Carson); "Northwest Territory" 1951 (LeBeau); "Raton Pass" 1951 (Sam); "Son of Geronimo" 1952-serial (Ace); "Conquest of Cochise" 1953 (Bill Lawson); "Marshal of Cedar Rock" 1953 (Chris Peters); "Rebel City" 1953 (Spencer); "Star of Texas" 1953 (Ranger Stockton); "Battle of Rogue River" 1954 (Capt. Richard Hillman); "Duel at Diablo" 1966 (Clay Dean); "Return of the

Gunfighter" TVM-1967 (Butch Cassidy); "J.W. Coop" 1971 (Rancher); "The Macahans" TVM-1976 (Hale Crowley); "The Apple Dumpling Gang Rides Again" 1979 (Sheriff). ¶TV: *Wild Bill Hickok*—"Outlaw Flats" 10-9-51, "Hands Across the Border" 7-22-52, "Spurs for Johnny" 5-26-63; *The Roy Rogers Show*—"The Outlaw's Girl" 2-17-52, "Outlaws' Town" 3-1-52; *The Cisco Kid*—"The Iron Mask" 1-10-53; *The Lone Ranger*—"Trader Boggs" 1-15-53, "The Cross of Santo Domingo" 10-11-56.; *The Adventures of Rin Tin Tin*—"Rin Tin Tin and the Second Chance" 6-1-56 (Johnny Thor); *Circus Boy*—"The Masked Marvel" 12-9-56 (Matt); *Trackdown*—"The Boy" 3-28-58 (Eric Paine), "The Deal" 4-25-58 (Eric Paine); *Gunsmoke*—"Kangaroo" 10-10-59 (Hod), "The Summons" 4-21-62 (Loy Bishop), "Shona" 2-9-63 (Torbert), "Honey Pot" 5-15-65 (Hal Biggs), "The Miracle Man" 12-2-68 (Drunk), "Johnny Cross" 12-23-68 (Yates), "Ring of Darkness" 12-1-69 (Pinto), "The War Priest" 1-5-70 (Amos Strange), "The Convict" 2-1-71 (Norman Wilson), "The Bullet" 11-29-71, 12-6-71 & 12-13-71 (Blanchard), "The Boy and the Sinner" 10-1-73 (Hugh Eaton), "A Town in Chains" 9-16-74 (Mueller); *Wagon Train*—"The Will Santee Story" 5-3-61 (the Stranger); *Daniel Boone*—"The Christmas Story" 12-23-65 (Jeremy), "Crisis by Fire" 1-27-66 (Tolliver), "Requiem for Craw Green" 12-1-66 (Press Boker); *Time Tunnel*—"Billy the Kid" 2-10-67 (Deputy John Poe); *Hondo*—"Hondo and the Judas" 11-3-67 (Gar Harker); *Wild Wild West*—"The Night of Fire and Brimstone" 11-22-68 (Prof. Philip Colchrist); *The Big Valley*—"Hunter's Moon" 12-30-68 (Gandy), "The Other Face of Justice" 3-31-69 (Billy Norris); *The Guns of Will Sonnett*—"The Man Who Killed James Sonnett" 3-21-69 (Charlie); *The Virginian*—"Nightmare" 1-21-70 (Stephanie White); *Bonanza*—"The Trouble with Amy" 1-25-70 (Barton Roberts); *Nichols*—"Wings of an Angel" 2-8-72 (Sergeant Kessler).

Crawford, Johnny (1949-). Films: "Indian Paint" 1965 (Nishko); "El Dorado" 1967 (Luke MacDonald); "The Gambler, Part II—The Adventure Continues" TVM-1983 (Masket); "The Gambler Returns: The Luck of the Draw" TVM-1991 (Mark McCain). ¶TV: *Zane Grey Theater*—"Man Unforgiving" 1-3-58 (Billy Prescott), "The Sharpshooter" 3-7-58 (Mark McCain); *Wagon Train*—"The Sally Potter Story" 4-9-

58 (Jimmy Bennett); *The Restless Gun*—"Gratitude" 6-16-58; *The Rifleman*—Regular 1958-63 (Mark McCain); *Tales of Wells Fargo*—"The Dealer" 12-29-58 (Tommy Peel); *Branded*—"Coward Step Aside" 3-7-65 (Clay Holden); *Rawhide*—"Crossing at White Feather" 12-7-65 (Aaron Bolt); *Lancer*—"The Prodigal" 11-12-68 (Jeff Dane); *Paradise*—"A Gather of Guns" 9-10-89 (Doug McKay), "A Gathering of Guns" 2-17-90 (Doug McKay)

Crawford, Katherine (1944-). TV: *The Virginian*—"Say Goodbye to All That" 1-23-63 (Alice Lawford), "A Bride for Lars" 4-15-64 (Anna Swenson); *Wagon Train*—"The Ben Engel Story" 3-16-64 (Evvie Diel); *Destry*—"Big Deal at Little River" 3-20-64 (Melinda Carter); *Here Come the Brides*—"His Sister's Keeper" 12-12-69 (Julie); *The Men from Shiloh*—"The Animal" 1-20-71 (Karen).

Crawford, Kathryn (1908-12/7/80). Films: "Riding for Life" 1929; "Senor Americano" 1929 (Carmelita); "Two-Gun Morgan" 1929; "The Concentratin' Kid" 1930 (Betty Lou Vaughn); "Mountain Justice" 1930 (Coral Harland).

Crawford, Pete. Films: "West of the Rockies" 1929 (Sheriff).

Crawford, Jr., Robert. Films: Indian Paint" 1965 (Wacopi). ¶TV: *Zorro*—"The Well of death" 5-29-58; *Cheyenne*—"Blind Spot" 9-21-59 (Gerald); *The Californians*—"Act of Faith" 5-26-59 (James Dobbs), "Storm Center" 11-20-61 (Frank Garcia); *Zane Grey Theater*—"Cry Hope! Cry Hate!" 10-20-60 (Boy); *Rawhide*—"Incident of the Blackstorms" 5-26-61 (Danny Blackstorm).

Crawford, Sr., Robert. Films: "Son of Roaring Dan" 1940 (Slim); "Indian Paint" 1965 (Motopi).

Crayne, Dani. Films: "A Day of Fury" 1956 (Claire); "Shoot-Out at Medicine Bend" 1957 (Nell). ¶TV: *Cheyenne*—"The Iron Trail" 1-1-57 (Mary Ellen).

Creach, Everett. Films: "The Way West" 1967 (Cattleman); "The Great Bank Robbery" 1969; "Tell Them Willie Boy Is Here" 1969 (Fake Indian); "Big Jake" 1971 (Walt Devries). ¶TV: *Kung Fu*—"The Spirit Helper" 11-8-73 (Comanchero).

Creatore, Victor. TV: *The Virginian*—"Jed" 1-10-68 (Texas).

Creed, Roger. Films: "Ghost of Zorro" 1949-serial (Mike); "Tall Man Riding" 1955; "Gunfight at the O.K. Corral" 1957 (Deputy/Killer/Towns-

man); "Jesse James Meets Frankenstein's Daughter" 1966.

Cregar, Laird (1913-12/9/44). Films: "Hudson Bay" 1941 (Gooseberry).

Crehan, Joseph (1886-4/15/66). Films: "Trailin' West" 1936 (Col. Douglas); "Cherokee Strip" 1937 (Army Officer); "God's Country and the Woman" 1937 (Jordan); "Guns of the Pecos" 1937 (Capt. Norris); "Outlaws of the Orient" 1937 (Snyder); "Billy the Kid Returns" 1938 (Conway); "Dodge City" 1939 (Hammond); "Union Pacific" 1939 (Gen. U.S. Grant); "Colorado" 1940; "Gaucho Serenade" 1940 (Edward Martin); "Geronimo" 1940 (U.S. President Grant); "Santa Fe Trail" 1940 (Officer); "Texas Rangers Ride Again" 1940 (Johnson); "Nevada City" 1941; "Texas" 1941 (Dusty King); "They Died with Their Boots On" 1941 (President Grant); "Men of Texas" 1942 (Crittenden); "Wild Bill Hickok Rides" 1942 (Ray Trent); "Hands Across the Border" 1943 (Jeff Adams); "The Woman of the Town" 1943; "Royal Mounted Rides Again" 1945-serial (Sergeant Nelson); "Bad Bascomb" 1946 (Governor Ames); "Plainsman and the Lady" 1946 (Postmaster General); "The Sea of Grass" 1947 (Sen. Graw); "Adventures in Silverado" 1948; "The Gallant Legion" 1948; "Night Time in Nevada" 1948 (Casey); "Silver River" 1948 (President Grant); "Sundown in Santa Fe" 1948; "Bad Men of Tombstone" 1949; "Red Desert" 1949 (President U.S. Grant); "The Arizona Cowboy" 1950 (Col. Jefferson). ¶TV: *The Lone Ranger*—"Rustler's Hideout" 10-13-49, "Never Say Die" 4-6-50, "Sunstroke Mesa" 3-17-55; *Bat Masterson*—"The Prescott Campaign" 2-2-61 (Thomas Bolland).

Creley, Jack. Films: "The Canadians" 1961-Brit.

Crenna, Richard (1927-). Films: "Deserter" 1970-U.S./Ital./Yugo. (Major Brown); "Catlow" 1971-Span. (Cowan); "The Man Called Noon" 1973-Brit./Span./Ital. (Noon); "Honky Tonk" TVM-1974 (Candy Johnson); "Shootout in a One-Dog Town" TVM-1974 (Zack Wells); "Breakheart Pass" 1976 (Richard Fairchild); "Montana" TVM-1990 (Hoyce Guthrie). ¶TV: *Cheyenne*—"Hard Bargain" 5-21-57 (Curley Galway); *The Deputy*—"A Time to Sow" 4-23-60 (Andy Willis); *Centennial*—Regular 1978-79 (Col. Frank Skimmerhorn).

Cress, Duane. TV: *Death Valley Days*—"The Washington Elm" 3-31-

57; *Tales of Wells Fargo*—"Wanted: Jim Hardie" 12-21-59 (Greg); *Bonanza*—"El Toro Grande" 1-2-60; *The Deputy*—"Judas Town" 12-31-60 (Touhy).

Cressman, Babe. Films: "Durand of the Bad Lands" 1917 (May Bond).

Cressoy, Pierre (Peter Cross). Films: "Adios Gringo" 1965-Ital./Fr./Span. (Clayton Ranchester); "Seven Guns for the MacGregors" 1965-Ital./Span.; "Navajo Joe" 1966-Ital./Span. (Lynne).

Crest, Patricia. TV: *Maverick*—"The Maverick Report" 3-4-62 (Molly Malone); *Bronco*—"The Last Letter" 3-5-62 (Della Harte).

Crews, Laura Hope (1880-11/13/42). Films: "Reno" 1939 (Mrs. Gardner).

Crider, Dorothy (1918-7/3/80). Films: "The Guns of Fort Petticoat" 1957 (Jane Gibbons). ¶TV: *The Roy Rogers Show*—"The Treasure of Howling Dog Canyon" 1-27-52 (Mama Briggs); *Tales of the Texas Rangers*—"Jail Bird" 10-29-55 (Sally Hackett).

Crigler, Tharon. TV: *Wagon Train*—"The Gabe Carswell Story" 1-15-58, "The John Wilbot Story" 6-11-58 (Henrietta Broxton); *Buckskin*—"The Trial of Chrissy Miller" 7-31-58 (Chrissy Miller).

Crimmins, Dan (1863-7/11/45). Films: "Johnny, Get Your Gun" 1919 (Pollitt); "Straight from the Shoulder" 1921 (Hotel Owner); "Desert Driven" 1923 (Brown).

Crinley, Myrtis. Films: "Greased Lightning" 1928 (Annie Murphy); "The Phantom Flyer" 1928 (Isabella Pipp).

Crinley, William A. (-1/1/27). Films: "The Dawn Road" 1915; "Just Jim" 1915; "Big Town Round-Up" 1921 (Tim Johnson).

Crino, Isa (1930-4/6/76). TV: *Daniel Boone*—"Four-Leaf Clover" 3-25-65 (Mrs. Wilson).

Cripps, Kernan (1886-8/12/53). Films: "Northern Frontier" 1935 (Mike); "Stone of Silver Creek" 1935 (Ben); "Wilderness Mail" 1935 (Inspector Logan); "The Cowboy and the Kid" 1936 (Jim Thomas); "Silver Spurs" 1936 (Sheriff); "Hit the Saddle" 1937 (Bartender); "Gaucho Serenade" 1940; "Mexican Spitfire Out West" 1940 (Cop); "The Return of Frank James" 1940 (Deputy); "When the Daltons Rode" 1940 (Freight Agent); "Sin Town" 1942 (Man); "Six Gun Gospel" 1943; "Girl Rush" 1944 (Bartender).

Crisa, Erno (1924-4/4/68). Films: "Pecos Cleans Up" 1967-Ital.

Crisp, Donald (1880-5/25/74). Films: "In the Days of '49" 1911; "The Sheriff's Baby" 1913; "Two Men of the Desert" 1913; "The Mountain Rat" 1914 (Steve); "The Love Route" 1915 (Henry Marshall); "Don Q, Son of Zorro" 1925 (Don Sebastian); "The Oklahoma Kid" 1939 (Judge Hardwick); "Ramrod" 1947 (Sheriff Jim Crew); "Whispering Smith" 1948 (Barney Rebstock); "The Man from Laramie" 1955 (Alec Waggoman); "Drango" 1957 (Allen); "Saddle the Wind" 1958 (Mr. Deneen).

Cristal, Linda (1935-). Films: "Comanche" 1956 (Margarita); "The Fiend Who Walked the West" 1958 (Ellen Hardy); "The Alamo" 1960 (Flaca); "Two Rode Together" 1961 (Elena de la Madriaga). ¶TV: *Rawhide*—"Incidcent of a Burst of Evil" 6-26-59 (Louise); *Iron Horse*—"The Passenger" 3-6-67 (Angela Teran); *The High Chaparral*—Regular 1967-71 (Victoria); *Bonanza*—"Warbonnet" 12-26-71 (Teresa).

Cristal, Perla (1937-). Films: "Seven Guns for the MacGregors" 1965-Ital./Span. (Perla); "Two Thousand Dollars for Coyote" 1965-Span.; "The Christmas Kid" 1966-Span./Ital. (Marie Lefleur); "The Tall Women" 1966-Austria/Ital./Span. (Perla); "White Comanche" 1967-Ital./Span./U.S. (White Fawn); "Dust in the Sun" 1971-Fr.

Cristofer, Michael (1945-). TV: *Gunsmoke*—"The Guns of Cibola Blanca" 9-23-74 & 9-30-74 (Ben).

Criswell, Floyd (1899-12/28/74). Films: "The Border Sheriff" 1926 (Frenchie).

Crittenden, Dwight (1878-2/17/38). Films: "Bob Hampton of Placer" 1921 (Gen. Custer); "Pioneer Trails" 1923 (Rodney Miller).

Crittenden, James. Films: "Last Ride of the Dalton Gang" TVM-1979 (Hugh McElhennie); "Rio Diablo" TVM-1993 (Hopper). ¶TV: *Paradise*—Regular 1988-90 (Charlie).

Crittendon, T.D. (1878-2/17/38). Films: "The Fighting Gringo" 1917 (Belknap); "All for Gold" 1918.

Croccolo, Carlo (1927-). Films: "Sheriff Was a Lady" 1965-Ger.

Crockett, Charles (1872-6/12/34). Films: "The Millionaire Cowboy" 1924 (Granville Truce); "Sundown" 1924 (Joe Patton); "The Vanishing American" 1925 (Amos Halliday); "Arizona Bound" 1927 (John Winslow).

Crockett, Dick (1915-1/25/79).

Crockett, Luther "Lute" (1890-4/6/52). Films: "The Wolf Hunters" 1949 (Cameron); "Colt .45" 1950 (Judge Tucker); "I Killed Geronimo" 1950; "Rider from Tucson" 1950 (Sheriff); "Bonanza Town" 1951 (Judge Anthony Dilon). ¶TV: *The Lone Ranger*—"Trouble Waters" 3-9-50; *The Cisco Kid*—"Counterfeit Money" 1-27-51, "Oil Land" 2-24-51, "Cattle Quarantine" 3-31-51, "False Marriage" 4-14-51, "Wedding Blackmail" 4-21-51.

Cromer, Dean. Films: "Hannah Lee" 1953 (Beven); "The Forty-Niners" 1954 (Sloane). ¶TV: *Wanted-Dead or Alive*—"The Corner" 2-21-59.

Cromwell, James. Films: "Dream West" TVM-1986 (Major General Hunter). ¶TV: *Barbary Coast*—"The Ballad of Redwing Jail" 9-29-75 (Roy); *Born to the Wind* 1982 (Fish Belly); *Wildside*—4-18-85 (Buffalo Bill); *Young Riders*—"The Peacemakers" 1-19-91 (Jacob); *Hawkeye*—"The Visit" 5-24-95 (Jonathan Longworth).

Cronyn, Hume (1911-). Films: "There Was a Crooked Man" 1970 (Dudley Whinner).

Crosby, Bing (1903-10/14/77). Films: "Rhythm on the Range" 1936 (Jeff Larrabee); "Son of Paleface" 1952 (Cameo); "Alias Jesse James" 1959 (Himself); "Stagecoach" 1966 (Doc Josiah Boone).

Crosby, Bob (1913-3/9/93). Films: "Trouble in Texas" 1937; "The Singing Sheriff" 1944 (Bob Richards).

Crosby, Denise. TV: *Adventures of Brisco County, Jr.*—"No Man's Land" 9-10-93 (Sheriff Jenny Taylor).

Crosby, Dennis (1934-5/4/91). Films: "Sergents 3" 1962 (Pvt. Page).

Crosby, Gary (1938-8/24/95). TV: *Hondo*—"Hondo and the Hanging Town" 12-8-67 (Tim Bixby).

Crosby, Gene. Films: "The Better Man Wins" 1922 (Grace Parker); "West vs. East" 1922 (Mrs. De Wyle Jenkins); "The Lone Wagon" 1923; "Smilin' On" 1923; "Let Him Buck" 1924; "Battlin' Bill" 1927; "Pioneers of the West" 1927.

Crosby, Harry. TV: *Riding for the Pony Express*—Pilot 9-3-80 (Albie Foreman).

Crosby, Lindsay (1938-12/11/89). Films: "Sergents 3" 1962 (Pvt. Wills); "Santee" 1973.

Crosby, Mary (1959-). Films: "Stagecoach" TVM-1986 (Lucy Mallory). ¶TV: *Paradise*—"The Search for K.C. Cavanaugh" 4-5-91 (K.C. Cavanaugh).

Crosby, Phillip (1934-). Films: "Sergents 3" 1962 (Cpl. Ellis).

Crosby, Wade (1905-10/1/75). Films: "Arizona" 1940 (Longstreet); "Wagon Train" 1940 (O'Follard); "They Died with Their Boots On" 1941 (Bartender); "In Old California" 1942; "The Sundown Kid" 1942 (Vince Ganley); "In Old Oklahoma" 1943; "The Woman of the Town" 1943 (Crockett); "Gentle Annie" 1944 (Brakeman); "Bandits of the Badlands" 1945; "Rough Riders of Cheyenne" 1945; "In Old Sacramento" 1946; "Along the Oregon Trail" 1947 (Tom); "The Wistful Widow of Wagon Gap" 1947 (Squint); "The Paleface" 1948 (Web); "The Timber Trail" 1948 (Walt); "Under California Stars" 1948 (Lye McFarland); "Streets of Laredo" 1949 (Bartender); "Valley of Fire" 1951; "Old Overland Trail" 1953 (Draftsman); "J.W. Coop" 1971 (Billy Sol Gibbs); "Westworld" 1973 (Bartender). ¶TV: *The Gene Autry Show*—"Doublecross Valley" 9-10-50; *Wild Bill Hickok*—"Silver Stage Holdup" 10-16-51.

Cross, Alexander. Films: "Texas Trail" 1937 (Black Jack Carson).

Cross, David. TV: *Wild Bill Hickok*—"Ambush" 1-13-53; *26 Men*—"Run No More" 12-9-58, "Showdown" 2-3-59.

Cross, Dennis (1925-). Films: "The Brass Legend" 1956 (Carl Barlow); "Naked in the Sun" 1957; "Bounty Man" TVM-1972 (Rufus). ¶TV: *Gunsmoke*—"Yorky" 2-18-56 (Tom), "Brush at Elkador" 9-15-56 (Bartender); "Cheyennes" 6-13-59 (Jim), "Doc Judge" 2-6-60 (Bob), "The Far Places" 4-6-63 (Colley), "Carter Caper" 11-16-63 (Bud), "The New Society" 5-22-65, "Rope Fever" 12-4-67 (Zeb Butler), "The Reprisal" 2-10-69 (Jinks); *Have Gun Will Travel*—"The Hanging Cross" 12-21-57, "Hey Boy's Revenge" 4-12-58; *Wanted—Dead or Alive*—"The Bounty" 9-20-58 (Charley Two Hawks); *Jefferson Drum*—"Showdown" 9-26-58 (Gideon Easton); *Zane Grey Theater*—"Sundown at Bitter Creek" 2-14-58 (Darnell), "Trail Incident" 1-29-59 (Sam Duncan); *The Rifleman*—"The Safe Guard" 11-18-58 (Witeherly), "The Gaucho" 12-

30-58, "The Hero" 2-2-60 (Dorn), "The Vision" 3-22-60 (Fance Degnan), "The Quiet Fear" 1-22-62; *Rawhide*—"Incident at the Curious Street" 4-10-59 (Waldo Lucas), "The Patsy" 9-29-59 (Lafe Oberly), "Incident of the Wanted Painter" 1-29-60 (Clements), "Incident Before Black Pass" 5-19-61 (Satanga), "The Captain's Wife" 1-12-62 (Tonkin), "Incident at Two Graves" 11-7-63 (Navajo Chief); *Black Saddle*—"Client: Vardon" 5-30-59 (Walt), "The Indian Tree" 2-19-60 (Bradford); *Trackdown*—"Blind Alley" 9-16-59 (Stokes); *Wichita Town*—"Second Chance" 3-16-60 (Fred Keever); *Hotel De Paree*—"Sundance and the Black Widow" 4-1-60 (Tanning); *The Deputy*—"Palace of Chance" 5-21-60 (George Reed); *Tales of Wells Fargo*—"Man for the Job" 5-30-60 (Lambert); *Two Faces West*—"The $10,000 Reward" 4-17-61; *Death Valley Days*—"Treasure of Elk Creek Canyon" 12-13-61, "The Captain Dick Mine" 11-27-65, "The Rider" 12-4-65; *Branded*—"Coward Step Aside" 3-7-65; *The Big Valley*—"Palms of Glory" 9-15-65 (Hoke), "Teacher of Outlaws" 2-2-66 (Bates), "The Fallen Hawk" 3-2-66 (Keel), "Last Stage to Salt Flats" 12-5-66; *The Legend of Jesse James*—"The Pursuers" 10-11-65 (Meager); *Daniel Boone*—"Gun-Barrel Highway" 2-24-66 (Chief Red Hand); *Iron Horse*—"Town Full of Fear" 12-5-66 (Jim Vail); *Bonanza*—"A Woman in the House" 2-19-67 (Monk); *Cimarron Strip*—"The Hunted" 10-5-67 (Aaron); *The Guns of Will Sonnett*—"The Hero" 12-29-67, "Pariah" 10-18-68 (Torrey), "Join the Army" 1-3-69 (Charlie), "Robber's Roost" 1-17-69; *The Outcasts*—"The Town That Wouldn't" 3-31-69 (Tark).

Cross, Jimmy (1907-6/14/81). TV: *Gunsmoke*—"Overland Express" 5-31-58 (Hank), "The Hostage" 12-4-65 (Arly Phillips).

Cross, Peter. *see* Cressoy, Pierre.

Crosse, Rupert (1928-3/5/73). Films: "Ride in the Whirlwind" 1966 (Indian Joe); "Waterhole No. 3" 1967 (Prince). ¶TV: *Rawhide*—"Incident of the Buffalo Soldier" 1-1-61; *Have Gun Will Travel*—"The Hanging of Aaron Gibbs" 11-4-61 (Aaron Gibbs); *Cowboy in Africa*—"Incident at Derati Wells" 9-25-67 (Jama); *Bonanza*—"The Power of Life and Death" 10-11-70 (Davis).

Crossley, Syd (1885-11/60). Films: "The Cowboy Kid" 1928 (Sheriff).

Crosson, Robert. TV: *Zane Grey*

Theater—"Back Trail" 2-1-57 (Hugh Beckworth); *Schlitz Playhouse of the Stars*—"The Restless Gun" 3-29-57 (Al); *The Lone Ranger*—"The Prince of Buffalo Gap" 4-4-57; *Laramie*—"The Tumbleweed Wagon" 5-9-61 (Morgan Warner).

Crothers, Joel (1941-11/6/85). TV: *Zane Grey Theater*—"Lone Woman" 10-8-59 (David Butler); *Death Valley Days*—"3-7-77" 12-14-60 (Jim Badger); *Have Gun Will Travel*—"The Road" 5-27-61 (John).

Crothers, Scatman (1910-11/26/86). Films: "The Shootist" 1976 (Moses); "Bronco Billy" 1980 (Doc Lynch). ¶TV: *Bonanza*—"The Smiler" 9-24-61 (Judd).

Crowe, Eleanor. Films: "The End of the Trail" 1916 (La Petite Adrienne).

Crowe, Russell. Films: "The Quick and the Dead" 1995 (Cort).

Crowell, Josephine (-7/27/32). Films: "The Mountain Rat" 1914 (Mrs. Williams); "A Man and His Mate" 1915; "A Yankee from the West" 1915 (Mrs. Stuvic); "Lights of the Desert" 1922 (Ma Curtis); "Son of the Plains" 1931 (Saloon Girl).

Crowell, William. Films: "The Glory Trail" 1937 (Wainwright); "Dodge City" 1939.

Crowley, Kathleen (1930-). Films: "The Silver Whip" 1953 (Kathy); "Ten Wanted Men" 1955 (Marva Gibbons); "Westward Ho the Wagons" 1956 (Laura Thompson); "The Phantom Stagecoach" 1957 (Fran Maroon); "The Quiet Gun" 1957 (Teresa, the Rancher's Wife); "Curse of the Undead" 1959 (Dolores Carter); "Showdown" 1963 (Estelle). ¶TV: *The Westerner*—Pilot 11-53; *The Lone Ranger*—"Homer with a High Hat" 12-16-54; *Maverick*—"The Jeweled Gun" 11-24-57 (Daisy Harris), "Maverick Springs" 12-6-59 (Melanie Blake), "The Misfortune Teller" 3-6-60 (Melanie Blake), "A Bullet for the Teacher" 10-30-60 (Flo Baker), "Kiz" 12-4-60 (Kiz Bouchet), "Dade City Dodge" 9-18-61 (Marla), "The Troubled Heir" 4-1-62 (Marla), "One of Our Trains Is Missing" 4-22-62 (Modesty Blaine); *Cheyenne*—"Town of Fear" 12-3-57 (Marilee Curtis); *Colt .45*—"Decoy" 1-31-58 (Elena); *Wagon Train*—"The Mark Hanford Story" 2-26-58 (Ann Jamison); *The Restless Gun*—"The Woman from Sacramento" 3-3-58 (Mary Blackwell); *Tombstone Territory*—"Guilt of a Town" 3-19-58 (Wyn Simmons); *Rough Riders*—"Blood Feud" 11-13-58 (Tess Pearce); *Bronco*—"The Long

Ride Back" 11-18-58 (Redemption McNally), "Destinies West" 2-26-62 (Belle Siddons); *Yancy Derringer*—"Marble Fingers" 12-18-58 (Desiree); *Cimarron City*—"McGowan's Debt" 12-27-58 (Claire Norris); *Bat Masterson*—"Incident in Leadville" 3-18-59 (Jo Hart), "Murder Can Be Dangerous" 11-3-60 (Marri Brewster); *Rawhide*—"Incident Below the Brazos" 5-15-59 (Millie Wade); *Tales of Wells Fargo*—"The Jackass" 9-28-59, "Royal Maroon" 4-28-62 (Royal Maroon); *Laramie*—"Street of Hate" 3-1-60 (Laurie Allen); *Bonanza*—"San Francisco Holiday" 4-2-60 (Kathleen), "Five into the Wind" 4-21-63 (Lory Hayden), "Stage Door Johnnies" 7-27-68 (Miss Denise); *The Deputy*—"The Fatal Urge" 10-15-60 (Martha Jackson); *Redigo*—"Shadow of the Cougar" 11-26-63 (Laura); *The Virginian*—"Farewell to Honesty" 3-24-65 (Jennifer); *Branded*—"Judge Not" 9-12-65 (Laura Rock); *The High Chaparral*—"Once, on a Day in Spring" 2-14-69 (Countess Maria).

Crowley, Matt. TV: *Philco Television Playhouse*—"The Death of Billy the Kid" 7-24-55 (Gov. Lew Wallace); *Our American Heritage*—"Destiny West" 1-24-60 (McDuffie).

Crowley, Patricia (1929-). Films: "Red Garters" 1954 (Susana Martinez De La Cruz); "Walk the Proud Land" 1956 (Mary Dennison). ¶TV: *Maverick*—"The Rivals" 1-25-59 (Lydia Linley), "Betrayal" 3-22-59 (Ann Saunders), "A Tale of Three Cities" 10-18-59 (Stephanie Malone); *Wanted—Dead or Alive*—"Competition" 1-31-59 (Helen Martin); *Bronco*—"Game at the Beacon Club" 9-22-59 (Amanda Stover); *Cheyenne*—"Trial by Conscience" 10-26-59 (Jenny Girard); *Riverboat*—"Tampico Raid" 1-3-60 (Joan Marchand); *Tales of Wells Fargo*—"Treasure Coach" 10-14-61 (Lydia); *Rawhide*—"Incident of the Mountain Man" 1-25-63 (Sara Green); *Bonanza*—"The Actress" 2-24-63 (Julia Grant); *The Virginian*—"The Hell Wind" 2-14-68 (Mrs. Van Owen); *Alias Smith and Jones*—"Miracle at Santa Marta" 12-30-71 (Meg Parker).

Cruickshanks, Reid. Films: "High Plains Drifter" 1973 (Gunsmith); "Donner Pass: The Road to Survival" TVM-1978. ¶TV: *Gunsmoke*—"The Avenger" 11-27-72 (Denton).

Cruise, Tom (1962-). Films: "Far and Away" 1992 (Joseph Donelly).

Cruz, Brandon (1962-). TV: *Gunsmoke*—"The Drummer" 10-9-72

(Jimmy Morgan); *Kung Fu*—"King of the Mountain" 10-14-72 (Peter Gideon).

Cruz, Mara (1941-). Films: "Seven for Pancho Villa" 1966-Span.; "The Tall Women" 1966-Austria/Ital./Span. (Blanche); "Two Crosses at Danger Pass" 1968-Ital./Span.

Cruze, James (1894-8/3/42). Films: "Nan of Music Mountain" 1917 (Gale Morgan); "On the Level" 1917 (Ozmun); "Johnny, Get Your Gun" 1919 (Duke of Bullconia).

Crystal, Billy (1947-). Films: "City Slickers" 1991; "City Slickers II: The Legend of Curly's Gold" 1994 (Mitch Robbins).

Cudney, Roger. Films: "Nevada Smith" TVM-1975 (Perkins); "Cattle Annie and Little Britches" 1981 (Capps); "Triumphs of a Man Called Horse" 1984 (Durand); "The Cisco Kid" CTVM-1994 (Alcott). ¶TV: *The Men from Shiloh*—"Flight from Memory" 2-17-71 (Cowboy).

Cullen, Brett. Films: "The Gambler V: Playing for Keeps" TVM-1994 (the Sundance Kid); "Wyatt Earp" 1994 (Saddle Tramp). ¶TV: *The Chisholms*—Regular 1980 (Gideon Chisholm); *Young Riders*—Regular 1990-92 (Marshal Sam Cain).

Cullen, William Kirby. Films: "The Macahans" TVM-1976 (Jeb Macahan). ¶TV: *How the West Was Won*—Regular 1977-79 (Jed Macahan).

Cullington, Margaret (1891-7/18/25). Films: "Little Red Decides" 1918 (Miss Hanley); "Three Gold Coins" 1920 (Maria Bimble); "Wolves of the Border" 1923; "That Wild West" 1924.

Cullison, Webster (1880-7/7/38). Films: "The Silent Signal" 1912; "Down the Rio Grande" 1913.

Culliton, Patrick. TV: *The Big Valley*—"Judgement in Heaven" 12-22-65 (Corey).

Cullum, John (1930-). TV: *The Outcasts*—"And Then There Was One" 3-3-69 (Pale Hands).

Cully, Zara (1892-2/28/78). TV: *Cowboy in Africa*—"Lake Sinclair" 11-13-67 (Jacob's Mother).

Culp, Robert (1930-). Films: "The Raiders" 1964 (James Butler "Wild Bill" Hickok); "Hannie Calder" 1971-Brit./Span./Fr. (Thomas Luther Price); "The Castaway Cowboy" 1974 (Bryson); "The Great Scout and Cathouse Thursday" 1976 (Jack Colby). ¶TV: *Zane Grey Theater*—"Badge of Honor" 5-3-57 (Hoby Gilman),

"Calico Bait" 3-31-60 (Sam Applegate), "Morning Incident" 12-29-60 (Shad Hudson); *Trackdown*—Regular 1957-59 (Hoby Gilman); *The Rifleman*—"The Hero" 2-2-60 (Colly Vane), "The Man from Salinas" 2-12-62 (Dave Foley); *Tate*—"The Bounty Hunter" 6-22-60 (Tom Sandee); *Johnny Ringo*—"Cave-In" 6-30-60 (Clay Horn); *The Outlaws*—"Thirty a Month" 9-29-60 (Sam Yadkin); *The Westerner*—"Line Camp" 12-9-60; *Rawhide*—"Incident at the Top of the World" 1-27-61 (Craig Kern); *Bonanza*—"Broken Ballad" 10-29-61 (Ed Payson); *Death Valley Days*—"Alias James Stuart" 11-1-61 (Thomas Burdue/James Stuart); *Wagon Train*—"The Baylor Crowfoot Story" 3-21-62 (Baylor Crofoot); *The Virginian*—"The Black Stallion" 9-30-64 (Charlie); *Gunsmoke*—"Hung High" 11-14-64 (Joe Costa); *Dr. Quinn, Medicine Woman*—"Great American Medicine Show" 2-13-93 (Doc Eli); *Lonesome Dove*—Pilot 10-2-94, 10-9-94 & 10-16-94 (Farnsworth).

Culver, Howard B. (1918-8/5/84). Films: "The Black Whip" 1956 (Dr. Gillette); "Cattle Empire" 1958 (Preacher). ¶TV: *Gunsmoke*—Regular 1955-75 (Howie Uzzel, the Hotel Clerk); *Zane Grey Theater*—"Checkmate" 4-30-59, "The Sunday Man" 2-25-60; *The Men from Shiloh*—"The Price of the Hanging" 11-11-70 (Gunsmith).

Cumbuka, Ji-Tu. TV: *Daniel Boone*—"Run for the Money" 2-19-70 (Lucas Hunter); *Kung Fu*—"Barbary House" 2-15-75 (Omar), "Flight to Orion" 2-22-75 (Omar), "The Brothers Cain" 3-1-75 (Omar), "Full Circle" 3-15-75 (Omar); *Young Dan'l Boone*—Regular 1977 (Hawk).

Cummings, Billy. Films: "Colorado Pioneers" 1945; "Oregon Trail Scouts" 1947 (Barking Squirrel).

Cummings, George (1880-3/11/46). Films: "The Light of Western Stars" 1918 (Nick Steele); "The Whipping Boss" 1924 (Brady).

Cummings, Irving (1888-4/18/59). Films: "The Round Up" 1920 (Dick Lane); "Cameron of the Royal Mounted" 1922; "The Man from Hell's River" 1922 (Pierre de Barre).

Cummings, Richard (1858-12/25/38). Films: "Two from Texas" 1920; "Red Courage" 1921 (Judge Fay); "Wolf Law" 1922; "The Galloping Cowboy" 1926 (the Sheriff).

Cummings, Robert (1910-12/1/90). Films: "Arizona Mahoney" 1936 (Phil Randall); "Desert Gold" 1936 (Fordyce Mortimer); "Wells Fargo"

1937 (Trimball); "The Texans" 1938 (Capt. Alan Sanford); "Heaven Only Knows" 1947 (Mike); "Stagecoach" 1966 (Mr. Gatewood). ¶TV: *Zane Grey Theater*—"The Last Bugle" 11-24-60 (Gatewood); *Here Come the Brides*—"The She-Bear" 1-30-70 (Jack Crosse).

Cummings, Susan. Films: "Secret of Treasure Mountain" 1956 (Tawana); "Tomahawk Trail" 1957 (Ellen Carter); "Utah Blaine" 1957 (Angie Kinyon); "Man from God's Country" 1958 (Mary Jo Ellis). ¶TV: *Union Pacific*—Regular 1958-59 (Georgia); *Bat Masterson*—"Dynamite Blows Two Ways" 10-22-58 (Valorie Mitchell), "Death and Taxes" 11-26-59 (Lili Napoleon), "Last Stop to Austin" 12-1-60 (Rona Glyn); *Rough Riders*—"Ransom of Rita Renee" 6-11-59 (Rita Renee); *Man from Blackhawk*—"The Biggest Legend" 1-1-60 (Glory Vestal); *Overland Trail*—"Fire in the Hole" 4-17-60 (Nitro Nell); *Johnny Ringo*—"The Stranger" 5-19-60 (Lil Blanchard); *Riverboat*—"End of a Dream" 9-19-60 (Tekia Kronen); *Gunsmoke*—"The Peace Officer" 10-15-60 (Stella); *Wyatt Earp*—"Miss Sadie" 12-20-60 (Sadie Hunter); *Laramie*—"Rimrock" 3-21-61 (Holly Matthews); *Cheyenne*—"Winchester Quarantine" 9-25-61 (Helen Ransom).

Cummins, Gregory Scott. TV: *Paradise*—"Bad Blood" 2-1-91 (Sisk); *Ned Blessing: The Story of My Life and Times*—"Return to Plum Creek" 8-18-93 (Leola).

Cummins, Peggy (1925-). Films: "Green Grass of Wyoming" 1948 (Carey Greenway).

Cunard, Grace (1893-1/19/67). Films: "Custer's Last Fight" 1912; "His Squaw" 1912; "An Indian Legend" 1912; "The White Vaquero" 1912; "The Battle of Bull Run" 1913; "The Black Masks" 1913; "The Tell Tale Hat Band" 1913; "Texas Kelly at Bay" 1913; "Wynona's Vengeance" 1913; "The Ghost of Smiling Jim" 1914; "The Return of the Twins' Double" 1914; "The Curse of the Desert" 1915; "Three Bad Men and a Girl" 1915; "The Bandit's Wager" 1916; "The Dumb Bandit" 1916; "The Unexpected" 1916; "Hell's Crater" 1918 (Cherry Maurice); "Fighting with Buffalo Bill" 1926-serial; "The Denver Dude" 1927 (Mrs. Bird); "The Return of the Riddle Rider" 1927-serial; "Heroes of the West" 1932-serial; "The Fourth Horseman" 1933 (Mrs. Elmer Brown); "Rustlers of Red Dog" 1935-serial; "Great Stagecoach Robbery" 1945.

Cuneo, Lester (1888-11/1/25). Films: "Between Love and the Law" 1912; "The Brand Blotter" 1912; "Buck's Romance" 1912; "The Cattle Rustlers" 1912; "A Cowboy's Mother" 1912; "The Dynamiters" 1912; "An Equine Hero" 1912; "Jim's Vindication" 1912; "The Ranger and His Horse" 1912; "Roped In" 1912; "A Rough Ride with Nitroglycerine" 1912; "So-Jun-Wah and the Tribal Law" 1912; "The Whiskey Runners" 1912; "Why Jim Reformed" 1912; "The Bank's Messenger" 1913; "Bill's Birthday Present" 1913; "Buster's Little Game" 1913; "The Capture of Bad Brown" 1913; "The Cattle Thief's Escape" 1913; "A Child of the Prairies" 1913; "The Cowboy Editor" 1913; "Cupid in the Cow Camp" 1913; "The Deputy's Sweetheart" 1913; "Dishwash Dick's Counterfeit" 1913 (Dick Mason); "The Escape of Jim Dolan" 1913; "The Galloping Romeo" 1913; "His Father's Deputy" 1913; "How Betty Made Good" 1913; "How It Happened" 1913; "Juggling with Fate" 1913; "The Life Timer" 1913; "Made a Coward" 1913; "The Marshal's Capture" 1913; "A Mixup on the Plains" 1913; "Mother Love vs. Gold" 1913; "Physical Culture on the Quarter Circle V Bar" 1913; "The Range Law" 1913; "The Rejected Lover's Luck" 1913 (Ben); "Religion and Gun Practice" 1913; "Sallie's Sure Shot" 1913; "The Schoolmarm's Shooting Match" 1913; "The Sheriff and the Rustler" 1913; "The Sheriff of Yawapai County" 1913; "The Silver Grindstone" 1913; "The Stolen Moccasins" 1913; "Taming a Tenderfoot" 1913 (Willie Clever); "That Mail Order Suit" 1913 (Steve); "A Friend in Need" 1914; "The Moving Picture Cowboy" 1914; "The Hidden Children" 1917 (Lt. Boyd); "The Hidden Spring" 1917 (Bill Wheeler); "The Promise" 1917 (Buck Moncrossen); "Under Handicap" 1917 (Brayley); "Desert Love" 1920 (the Whelp); "Lone Hand Wilson" 1920 (Lone Hand Wilson); "The Terror" 1920 (Con Norton); "The Devil's Ghost" 1921; "Pat O' the Range" 1921; "The Ranger and the Law" 1921 (Dick Dawson); "Blazing Arrows" 1922 (John Strong/Sky Fire); "Blue Blazes" 1922 (Jerry Connors); "The Masked Avenger" 1922 (Austin Patterson); "Silver Spurs" 1922; "The Eagle's Feather" 1923 (Jeff Carey); "Fighting Jim Grant" 1923; "The Vengeance of Pierre" 1923; "Lone Hand Texas" 1924; "The Ridin' Fool" 1924; "Western Grit" 1924 (Walt Powers); "Hearts of the West" 1925; "Range Vultures" 1925 (the Ranger); "Two Fisted Thompson" 1925; "Western Promise" 1925.

Cunningham, Bob. Films: "Shalako" 1968-Brit./Fr. (Luther); "Dust in the Sun" 1971-Fr. ¶TV: *Jim Bowie*—"Convoy Gold" 2-1-57 (Capt. Gregory); *Wyatt Earp*—"Old Jake" 4-9-57 (Soldier).

Cunningham, Cecil (1888-4/17/59). Films: "Cowboy Serenade" 1942; "In Old Oklahoma" 1943 (Mrs. Ames).

Cunningham, Frank. Films: "Natchez Trace" 1960 (Nobby Simpkins).

Cunningham, Joe (1890-4/3/43). Films: "Dudes Are Pretty People" 1942 (Joe).

Cunningham, Owen. TV: *Wagon Train*—"A Man Called Horse" 3-26-58 (Lorimer); *Have Gun Will Travel*—"The Gladiators" 3-19-60.

Cunningham, Robert. Films: "Shark River" 1953 (Curtis Parker); "Badlands of Montana" 1957 (Paul). ¶TV: *Sergeant Preston of the Yukon*—"The Devil's Roost" 4-11-57 (Borneo).

Cunningham, Sarah (1917-3/24/86). Films: "The Cowboys" 1972 (Annie Andersen); "Belle Starr" TVM-1980 (Mrs. Chandler).

Cuny, Alain (1908-5/16/94). Films: "Don't Touch White Women!" 1974-Ital. (Sitting Bull).

Cupito, Suzanne. *see* Brittany, Morgan.

Curley, Leo (1878-4/11/60). Films: "City of Badmen" 1953 (Harry Wade). ¶TV: *Sergeant Preston of the Yukon*—"All Is Not Gold" 5-10-56 (Emil Dillon), "Fantastic Creatures" 11-1-56 (Hank).

Curley, Pauline. Films: "Santa Fe Max" 1912; "A Case of Law" 1917; "Hands Off" 1921 (Ramona Wadley); "Judge Her Not" 1921 (May Harper); "The Prairie Mystery" 1922; "Cowboy Courage" 1925 (Ruth Dawson); "His Greatest Battle" 1925; "Ridin' Wild" 1925 (Betty Blake); "Pony Express Rider" 1926; "Twin Six O'Brien" 1926; "Walloping Kid" 1926; "West of the Rainbow's End" 1926 (Daisy Kent); "Code of the Range" 1927; "Thunderbolt's Tracks" 1927 (Alice Hayden).

Curran, Dandy. Films: "Blood on the Arrow" 1964 (Tim).

Curran, Lynette. Films: "Bullseye!" 1986-Australia (Dora McKensie).

Curran, Pamela. TV: *Laramie*—"The Perfect Gift" 1-2-62, "The Dynamiters" 3-6-62, "Double Eagles" 11-20-62; *Branded*—"The Greatest Coward on Earth" 11-21-65 (Princess Salome).

Curran, Thomas (1880-1/24/41). Films: "Ghost City" 1932; "Cowboy Millionaire" 1935 (Hotel Clerk); "Wells Fargo" 1937.

Currie, Louise. Films: "Billy the Kid Outlawed" 1940 (Molly Fitzgerald); "Billy the Kid's Gun Justice" 1940 (Ann Roberts); "Dude Cowboy" 1941 (Gail Sargent); "The Pinto Kid" 1941 (Betty Ainsley); "Stardust on the Sage" 1942 (Nancy Drew); "Forty Thieves" 1944 (Katherine Reynolds); "Gun Town" 1946 (Buckskin Jane Sawyer); "Wild West" 1946 (Florabelle); "Prairie Outlaws" 1948.

Currie, Sondra. Films: "Rio Lobo" 1970; "Jessi's Girls" 1976 (Jessica Hartwell).

Currier, Frank (1857-4/22/28). Films: "The Trail of the Shadow" 1917 (Mr. Mason); "The Heart Buster" 1924 (John Hillyer); "California" 1927 (Don Carlos del Rey); "Winners of the Wilderness" 1927 (Governor de Vandreuil); "Riders of the Dark" 1928 (Old Man Redding).

Curry, Mason (1909-4/1/80). TV: *My Friend Flicka*—"The Golden Promise" 1-6-56; *Sergeant Preston of the Yukon*—"Crime at Wounded Moose" 1-12-56 (Struth), "Totem Treasure" 3-1-56 (Dr. Haywood); *Gunsmoke*—"Reunion '78" 3-3-56 (Marty), "The Roundup" 9-29-56 (Jake); *Maverick*—"Diamond in the Rough" 1-26-58 (2nd Teller); *Have Gun Will Travel*—"The Silver Queen" 5-3-58; *The Californians*—"Second Trial" 5-6-58 (Terrence Buchanan); *Rawhide*—"Incident at Jacob's Well" 10-16-59 (Jason Henry), "Grandma's Money" 2-23-62 (Liveryman); *The Guns of Will Sonnett*—"The Straw Man" 11-8-68.

Curtis, Alan (1909-2/1/53). Films: "The Daltons Ride Again" 1945 (Emmett Dalton); "Frisco Sal" 1945 (Ric); "Renegade Girl" 1946; "Apache Chief" 1949 (Young Eagle).

Curtis, Barry. Films: "3:10 to Yuma" 1957 (Mathew); "The Missouri Traveler" 1958 (Jimmy Price). ¶TV: *The Adventures of Champion*—Regular 1955-56 (Ricky North); *Sergeant Preston of the Yukon*—"Border Action" 12-27-56 (Billy Walker); *Annie Oakley*—"The Dutch Gunmaker" 2-17-57 (Billy Nelson); *Desilu Playhouse*—"Six Guns for Donegan" 10-16-59 (Orville's Son).

Curtis, Billy (1909-11/9/88). Films: "The Terror of Tiny Town" 1938 (Buck Lawson, the Hero);

"Three Texas Steers" 1939 (Hercules); "High Plains Drifter" 1973 (Mordecai). ¶TV: *The Lone Ranger*—"Code of the Pioneers" 2-17-55; *Man from Blackhawk*—"Destination Death" 3-11-60 (Colonel Petite); *Bonanza*—"Hoss and the Leprechauns" 12-22-63; *Gunsmoke*—"Arizona Midnight" 1-1-73 (Arizona).

Curtis, Bob. Films: "Deadline" 1948; "Fighting Mustang" 1948; "Sunset Carson Rides Again" 1948; "Across the Rio Grande" 1949 (Lewis); "Brand of Fear" 1949; "Gun Law Justice" 1949; "Lawless Code" 1949; "Battling Marshal" 1950.

Curtis, Carolyn. Films: "Mesquite Buckaroo" 1939 (Betty Bond).

Curtis, Craig. Films: "A Time for Killing" 1967 (Bagnef); "The Great Northfield, Minnesota Raid" 1972 (Chadwell). ¶TV: *The Outlaws*—"The Little Colonel" 5-18-61 (Ben); *Bonanza*—"Gallagher Sons" 12-9-62 (Tully), "The Reluctant Rebel" 11-21-65 (Sport); *Stoney Burke*—"Kincaid" 4-22-63 (Tommy); *Gunsmoke*—"Deadman's Law" 1-8-68 (Sonny).

Curtis, Dick (1902-1/3/52). Films: "Code of the Mounted" 1935 (Snakey); "Northern Frontier" 1935 (Pete); "Trails of the Wild" 1935 (Roper); "Western Courage" 1935; "Western Frontier" 1935; "Wilderness Mail" 1935 (Jacques); "The Crooked Trail" 1936 (Henchman); "Ghost Patrol" 1936 (Charlie); "The Lion's Den" 1936 (Slim); "Phantom Patrol" 1936 (Josef); "The Traitor" 1936 (Morgan); "Wildcat Trooper" 1936 (Henri); "Bar Z Bad Men" 1937 (Brent); "Boothill Brigade" 1937 (Bull Berke); "The Gambling Terror" 1937 (Dirk); "Guns in the Dark" 1937 (Brace Stevens); "A Lawman Is Born" 1937 (Lefty Doogan); "Moonlight on the Range" 1937; "The Old Wyoming Trail" 1937 (Ed Slade); "One Man Justice" 1937 (Hank Skinner); "The Singing Buckaroo" 1937; "Outlaws of the Prairie" 1937 (Dragg); "Trail of Vengeance" 1937 (Cartwright); "Two Gun Law" 1937 (Len Edwards); "Valley of Terror" 1937 (Buck Mason); "Wild Horse Round-Up" 1937 (Bill); "Call of the Rockies" 1938 (Matt Clark); "Cattle Raiders" 1938; "Colorado Trail" 1938 (Slash Driscoll); "Law of the Plains" 1938 (Jim Fletcher); "Rawhide" 1938 (Butch); "Rio Grande" 1938 (Ed Barker); "South of Arizona" 1938 (Ed Martin); "West of Cheyenne" 1938 (Link Murdock); "West of Santa Fe" 1938 (Matt Taylor); "Outpost of the Mounties" 1939 (Wade Beaumont);

"Overland with Kit Carson" 1939-serial (Drake); "Riders of the Black River" 1939 (Blaze Carewe); "Spoilers of the Range" 1939 (Lobo Savage); "The Stranger from Texas" 1939 (Bat Springer); "The Taming of the West" 1939 (Rawhide); "The Thundering West" 1939 (Wolf); "Western Caravans" 1939 (Mort Kohler); "Yes, We Have No Bonanza" 1939-short (Jack); "Blazing Six Shooters" 1940 (Lash Bender); "Bullets for Rustlers" 1940 (Strang); "Pioneers of the Frontier" 1940 (Matt Brawley); "Ragtime Cowboy Joe" 1940 (Bo Gillman); "Texas Stagecoach" 1940 (Shoshone Larsen); "Three Men from Texas" 1940 (Gardner); "Two-Fisted Rangers" 1940 (Dick Hogan); "Wyoming" 1940 (Corky); "Arizona Cyclone" 1941 (Quirt); "Across the Sierras" 1941 (Mitch); "Billy the Kid" 1941 (Kirby Claxton); "The Round Up" 1941 (Ed Crandall); "In Old California" 1942; "Jackass Mail" 1942 (Jim Swade); "Pardon My Gun" 1942 (Clint); "Shut My Big Mouth" 1942 (Joe); "Tombstone, the Town Too Tough to Die" 1942 (Frank McLowery); "Vengeance of the West" 1942; "Westward Ho" 1942 (Rick West); "Cowboy in the Clouds" 1943; "Riders of the Northwest Mounted" 1943; "Cowboy Canteen" 1944; "Spook Town" 1944; "Pistol Packin' Nitwits" 1945-short; "Song of the Prairie" 1945; "Wagon Wheels Westward" 1945; "Abilene Town" 1946 (Ryker); "California Gold Rush" 1946; "The Lawless Breed" 1946; "Renegade Girl" 1946; "Santa Fe Uprising" 1946; "Song of Arizona" 1946 (Bart); "Three Troubledoers" 1946-short (Badlands Blackie); "Wild Beauty" 1946 (John Andrews); "Wyoming" 1947 (Ed Lassiter); "The Dalton Gang" 1949; "Navajo Trail Raiders" 1949 (Brad); "Sheriff of Wichita" 1949; "Covered Wagon Raid" 1950 (Grif); "Roar of the Iron Horse" 1950-serial (Campo); "The Vanishing Westerner" 1950 (Bartender); "Merry Mavericks" 1951-short (Pitts); "Rawhide" 1951 (Hawley); "Whirlwind" 1951 (Lon Kramer); "Rose of Cimarron" 1952 (Clem Dawley). ¶TV: *The Lone Ranger*—"Man of the House" 1-26-50, "A Matter of Courage" 4-26-50, "Bad Medicine" 12-7-50; *The Gene Autry Show*—"The Sheriff of Santa Rosa" 12-24-50, "T.N.T." 12-31-50, "Frame for Trouble" 11-3-51, "Revenge Trail" 11-17-51; *Wild Bill Hickok*—"The Lady Mayor" 7-10-51; *Annie Oakley*—"Desperate Men" 2-24-57 (Rush Harper).

Curtis, Dick. Films: "Support

Your Local Gunfighter" 1971 (Bud Barton).

Curtis, Donald (1915-). Films: "Northwest Mounted Police" 1940; "Take Me Back to Oklahoma" 1940 (Snapper); "Texas Rangers Ride Again" 1940 (Ranger Stafford); "Hands Across the Rockies" 1941; "The Royal Mounted Patrol" 1941 (Frenchy Duvalle); "The Son of Davy Crockett" 1941 (Jack Ringe); "Thunder Over the Prairie" 1941 (Taylor); "Code of the Outlaw" 1942; "Tombstone, the Town Too Tough to Die" 1942 (Phineas Clanton); "A Tornado in the Saddle" 1942; "Law of the Northwest" 1943 (Frank Mason); "Bad Bascomb" 1946 (John Felton); "Stampede" 1949 (Stanton); "Seventh Cavalry" 1956 (Lt. Bob Fitch); "Night Passage" 1957 (Jubilee). ¶TV: *The Cisco Kid*—"Canyon City Kit" 3-1-52; *Stories of the Century*—"Johnny Ringo" 5-13-55; *Annie Oakley*—"Western Privateer" 9-30-56 (Lee Tobey); *Wyatt Earp*—"A Quiet Day in Dodge City" 10-9-56 (Jensen).

Curtis, Jack (1880-3/16/56). Films: "In the Sunset Country" 1915; "The Valley of Regeneration" 1915; "The End of the Rainbow" 1916 (Thursday Simpson); "Two Men of Sandy Bar" 1916 (Pritchard); "The Yaqui" 1916 (Martinez); "Broadway, Arizona" 1917 (Jack Boggs); "The Firefly of Tough Luck" 1917 (Happy Jack Clarke); "The Greater Law" 1917 (Laberge); "Until They Get Me" 1917 (Kirby); "Up or Down? 1917 (Texas Jack); "Little Red Decides" 1918 (Tom Gilroy); "Wolves of the Border" 1918; "The Coming of the Law" 1919 (Judge Graney); "Hell Roarin' Reform" 1919 (Baxter); "Treat 'Em Rough" 1919 (John Stafford); "Desert Love" 1920 (the Wolf); "The Big Punch" 1921 (Jed); "Steelheart" 1921 (Butch Dorgan); "His Back Against the Wall" 1922 (Lew Shaler); "The Long Chance" 1922 (Borax O'Rourke); "Two Kinds of Women" 1922 (Chris Quinnion); "Western Speed" 1922 (Spunk Lemm); "Canyon of the Fools" 1923 (Maricopia); "Dangerous Trails" 1923 (Wang); "Quicksands" 1923 (Ring Member); "Soft Boiled" 1923 (Ranch Foreman); "The Spoilers" 1923 (Bill Nolan); "Fighter's Paradise" 1924; "Baree, Son of Kazan" 1925 (Bush McTaggart); "The Texas Streak" 1926 (Jiggs Cassidy); "Jaws of Steel" 1927 (Thomas Grant Taylor); "The Dawn Trail" 1930 (Hank); "Under a Texas Moon" 1930 (Buck Johnson); "The Deadline" 1932 (Shores); "The Prescott Kid" 1934 (Bartender); "Lawless Range" 1935 (Marshal); "Square

Shooter" 1935 (Bartender); "West-ward Ho" 1935 (Walt Ballard); "White Fang" 1936 (Posse Member); "Wells Fargo" 1937; "Rustler's Roundup" 1946 (Wrangler).

Curtis, John. Films: "Trail Riders" 1942 (Tiny); "Two Fisted Justice" 1943.

Curtis, Ken (1916-4/28/91). Films: "Rhythm Round-Up" 1945; "Song of the Prairie" 1945; "Cowboy Blues" 1946; "Lone Star Moonlight" 1946; "Singing on the Trail" 1946; "That Texas Jamboree" 1946; "Throw a Saddle on a Star" 1946; "My Pal Ringeye" 1947-short; "Over the Santa Fe Trail" 1947; "Call of the Forest" 1949; "Riders of the Pony Express" 1949; "Stallion Canyon" 1949 (Curt Benson); "Rio Grande" 1950 (Regimental Singer); "Don Daredevil Rides Again" 1951-serial (Lee Hadley/Don Daredevil); "The Searchers" 1956 (Charlie McCorry); "The Missouri Traveler" 1958 (Fred Mueller); "Escort West" 1959 (Burch); "The Horse Soldiers" 1959 (Wilkie); "The Young Land" 1959 (Lee Hearn); "The Alamo" 1960 (Capt. Almeron Dickinson); "Two Rode Together" 1961 (Greely Clegg); "How the West Was Won" 1962 (Ben, the Union Corporal); "Cheyenne Autumn" 1964 (Homer); "Pony Express Rider" 1976 (Jed); "California Gold Rush" TVM-1981 (Kentucke); "Once Upon a Texas Train" TVM-1988 (Kelly); "Conagher" TVM-1991. ¶TV: *Gunsmoke*—"Jayhawkers" 1-31-59 (Phil Jacks), "Change of Heart" 4-25-59 (Brisco Cass), "The Ex-Urbanites" 4-9-60 (Jesse), "Speak Me Fair" 5-7-60 (Scout), "Us Haggens" 12-8-62 (Fergus Hagen), "Lover Boy" 10-5-63 (Kyle Kelly), Regular 1964-75 (Festus Haggen), "Alias Festus Haggen" 3-6-72 (Frank Eaton); *Have Gun Will Travel*—"The Posse" 10-3-59 (Curley), "The Naked Gun" 12-19-59 (Monk), "Love's Young Dream" 9-17-60 (Monk), "Soledad Crossing" 6-10-61 (Tom Strickland), "Pandora's Box" 5-19-62 (Laski); *Wagon Train*—"The Horace Best Story" 10-5-60 (Pappy Lightfoot), "The Colter Craven Story" 11-23-60; *Rawhide*—"Incident of the Lost Idol" 4-28-61 (Vic Slade); *Death Valley Days*—"Graydon's Charge" 1-12-64 (Graydon); *The Life and Times of Grizzly Adams*—"Once Upon a Starry Night" 12-19-78 (Uncle Ned); *How the West Was Won*—"Hillary" 2-26-79 (Orville Gant).

Curtis, Tony (1925-). Films: "Sierra" 1950 (Brent Coulter); "Winchester '73" 1950 (Doan); "The Rawhide Years" 1956 (Ben Mathews).

Curtis, Willa Pearl (1896-12/19/70). TV: *Wide Country*—"To Cindy, with Love" 2-28-63 (Maid); *Wagon Train*—"Those Who Stay Behind" 11-8-64 (Clemsie).

Curtwright, Jorja (1909-5/11/85). Films: "Heaven Only Knows" 1947 (Drusilla). ¶TV: *Gunsmoke*—"Unmarked Grave" 8-18-56 (Cara); *Sheriff of Cochise*—"Triangle" 2-22-57 (Mrs. Sheldon); *Zane Grey Theater*—"Threat of Violence" 5-23-58 (Felicia Cheney); *Bonanza*—"The Genius" 4-3-66 (Lydia Evans); *Iron Horse*—"Banner with a Strange Device" 2-6-67 (Jessica Clayborne).

Curwood, Bob. Films: "The Battling Buckaroo" 1927; "Dangerous Double" 1927; "Ridin' Wild" 1927; "The Scrappin' Fool" 1927; "Boss of the Rancho" 1928; "The Brand of Courage" 1928; "The Death's Head" 1928; "Framed" 1928; "The Getaway Kid" 1928; "The Gold Claim" 1928; "Hidden Money" 1928; "The Looters" 1928; "The Payroll Roundup" 1928; "A Romeo of the Range" 1928; "The Secret Outlaw" 1928; "Speed and Spurs" 1928; "The Valiant Rider" 1928; "Cowboy Pluck" 1929; "Days of Daring" 1929; "The Lone Rider" 1929; "Playing False" 1929; "The Range of Fear" 1929; "The Range Wolf" 1929; "Ridin' Leather" 1929.

Cusack, Cyril (1910-10/7/93). Films: "The Secret of Convict Lake" 1951 (Limey).

Cusanelli, Peter (1898-4/10/54). Films: "Dakota" 1945 (Italian).

Custer, Bob (Raymond Glenn) (1898-12/27/74). Films: "Flashing Spurs" 1924 (Sergeant Stuart); "Trigger Finger" 1924 (Sgt. Steele); "The Bloodhound" 1925 (Belleau/Sgt. Bill McKenna); "Galloping Vengeance" 1925 (Tom Hardy); "A Man of Nerve" 1925 (Hackamore Henderson); "No Man's Law" 1925 (Dave Carson); "The Range Terror" 1925 (Speed Meredith); "The Ridin' Streak" 1925 (Bill Pendleton); "The Texas Bearcat" 1925 (Dave Sethman); "That Man Jack!" 1925 (Jack Burton); "Beyond the Rockies" 1926 (Con Benteen); "The Border Whirlwind" 1926 (Tom Blake, Jr.); "The Dead Line" 1926 (Sonora Slim); "The Devil's Gulch" 1926 (Ace Remsen/Deuce Remsen); "The Dude Cowboy" 1926 (Bob Ralston); "The Fighting Boob" 1926 (El Tigre); "Hair Trigger Baxter" 1926 (Baxter Brant); "Man Rustlin'" 1926 (Buck Hayden); "The Texas Terror" 1926 (Texas Cooper); "The Valley of Bravery" 1926 (Steve Tucker); "Bulldog Pluck"

1927 (Bob Hardwick); "Cactus Trails" 1927 (Ross Fenton); "The Fighting Hombre" 1927 (Bob Camp); "Galloping Thunder" 1927 (Kincaid Currier); "The Terror of Bar X" 1927 (Bob Willis); "Arizona Days" 1928 (Chuck Drexel); "Headin' Westward" 1928 (Oklahoma Adams); "Law of the Mounted" 1928; "Manhattan Cowboy" 1928; "On the Divide" 1928 (Jim Carson); "The Silent Trail" 1928; "West of Santa Fe" 1928 (Jack); "Code of the West" 1929 (Jack Hartley); "The Fighting Terror" 1929; "The Oklahoma Kid" 1929 (the Kid); "Riders of the Rio Grande" 1929 (Jack Beresford); "Covered Wagon Trails" 1930 (Smoke Sanderson); "O'Malley Rides Alone" 1930 (Sgt. O'Malley); "Parting of the Trails" 1930 (Rambler Raymond); "Under Texas Skies" 1930 (Rankin); "Headin' for Trouble" 1931 (Cyclone Crosby); "Law of the Rio Grande" 1931 (Jim "the Cub" Norris); "Quick Trigger Lee" 1931 (Phil "Quick Trigger" Lee); "Riders of the North" 1931 (Sergeant Ned Stone); "Son of the Plains" 1931 (Bob Brent); "Mark of the Spur" 1932 (the Kid); "Scarlet Brand" 1932 (Bud Bryson); "The Law of the Wild" 1934-serial (Sheldon); "Ambush Valley" 1936 (Bruce Manning); "Vengeance of Rannah" 1936 (Ted Saunders); "Santa Fe Rides" 1937.

Cutell, Lou (1930-). Films: "Little Big Man" 1971 (Deacon); "Mr. Horn" TVM-1979. ¶TV: *Wild Wild West*—"The Night of the Pelican" 12-27-68 (Major Frederick Prey).

Cutler, Bill. TV: *Rawhide*—"Incident at the Top of the World" 1-27-61 (Thompkins), "Incident of the New Start" 3-3-61, "Incident of the Phantom Burglar" 4-14-61.

Cutler, Vic. Films: "Canyon Passage" 1946 (Vane Blazier); "The Man from Texas" 1947 (Charles Jackson).

Cutter, Frank. Films: "The Web of the Law" 1923 (Squint Castile).

Cutter, Lise. Films: "Desperado" TVM-1987 (Nora Malloy); "Desperado: Avalanche at Devil's Rider" TVM-1988 (Nora); "Desperado: The Outlaw Wars" TVM-1989 (Nora).

Cutting, Richard (1912-3/7/72). Films: "City of Badmen" 1953 (Mr. Davis); "The Great Jesse James Raid" 1953 (Sam Wells); "War Paint" 1953 (Kirby); "Drum Beat" 1954 (Meek); "The Law vs. Billy the Kid" 1954 (Pete Maxwell); "Taza, Son of Cochise" 1954 (Cy Hagen); "The Gun That Won the West" 1955

(Edwin M. Stanton); "Seminole Uprising" 1955 (Col. Robert E. Lee); "Shotgun" 1955 (Holly); "Showdown at Abilene" 1956 (Nelson); "War Drums" 1957 (Judge Bolton); "Ride a Crooked Trail" 1958 (Mr. Curtis); "The Horse Soldiers" 1959 (Gen. Sherman); "Gunfighters of Abilene" 1960 (Hendricks); "The Raiders" 1964 (Jack Goodnight); "The Ride to Hangman's Tree" 1967 (Ed Mason). ¶TV: *Maverick*—"Naked Gallows" 12-15-57 (Cardoza), "The Town That Wasn't There" 10-2-60 (Ralph Hobbs); *Wagon Train*—"The Dan Hogan Story" 5-14-58 (Dr. Quade), "The Mary Ellen Thomas Story" 12-24-58 (Ben Mayhew), "The St. Nicholas Story" 12-23-59, "The Candy O'Hara Story" 12-7-60, "The Janet Hale Story" 5-31-61 (Josh), "Swamp Devil" 4-4-62 (Mr. Harris), "The Caroline Casteel Story" 9-26-62 (Adam Stryker), "The Trace McCloud Story" 3-2-64, "Little Girl Lost" 12-13-64 (Dixon); *Jefferson Drum*—"The Lawless" 7-18-58 (Bash); *Buckskin*—"The Bullnappers" 11-6-58 (Ed Foley), "The Better Mouse Trap" 5-25-59 (Ed Foley); *The Restless Gun*—"The Dead Ringer" 2-16-59 (Pid); *Death Valley Days*—"Old Blue" 4-7-59 (Wilkes); *Sugarfoot*—"The Avengers" 5-12-59 (Deputy); *Bonanza*—"Mr. Henry Comstock" 11-7-59 (Old Virginny); *Wichita Town*—"Paid in Full" 3-23-60 (Roy Higgins); *The Alaskans*—"Calico" 5-22-60 (Jud); *The Deputy*—"Meet Sergeant Tasker" 10-1-60 (Gus); *The Dakotas*—"Reformation at Big Nose Butte" 4-1-63 (Cavalry Officer); *The Legend of Jesse James*—"The Quest" 11-1-65 (Woodson James), "The Last Stand of Captain Hammel" 4-4-66; *A Man Called Shenandoah*—"Macauley's Cure" 5-16-66 (Townsman).

Cutts, Patricia (1927-9/6/74). TV: *Yancy Derringer*—"Hell and High Water" 2-19-59 (Lady Charity).

Cypher, Jon (1932-). Films: "Valdez Is Coming" 1971 (Frank Tanner). ¶TV: *Bonanza*—"A Place to Hide" 3-19-72 (Ransom).

Cyphers, Charles (1939-). Films: "Little House on the Prairie: Look Back to Yesterday" TVM-1983 (Zack Taylor).

Dade, Frances (1908-1/21/68). Films: "Range Law" 1931 (Ruth Warren); "The Phantom Thunderbolt" 1933.

Dae, Frank (1882-8/29/59). Films: "The Daltons Ride Again" 1945 (Judge); "Panhandle" 1948 (Regan); "Surrender" 1950 (Elderly Gentleman).

Dagmar, Florence. Films: "The Call of the North" 1914 (Elodie); "Chimmie Fadden Out West" 1915 (Betty Van Cortlandt).

Daheim, John. Films: "Wildcat of Tucson" 1941; "Son of Zorro" 1947-serial (Van); "Ghost of Zorro" 1949-serial (Black); "Desperadoes of the West" 1950-serial (Bill Murdock); "Colorado Sundown" 1952 (Dusty Hurley); "Wild Horse Ambush" 1952 (Turk); "Wings of the Hawk" 1953 (Capt. Rivera); "Shenandoah" 1965 (Osborne); "Duel at Diablo" 1966 (Stableman).

Dahl, Alice. Films: "Deadwood Pass" 1933 (Betty Rawlins); "The Whirlwind" 1933 (Mollie Curtis); "Coyote Trails" 1935 (Helen Baker); "Horses' Collars" 1935-short (Girl).

Dahl, Arlene (1924-). Films: "Ambush" 1950 (Ann Duverall); "The Outriders" 1950 (Jen Gort); "Inside Straight" 1951 (Lily Douvane); "Land Raiders" 1969-U.S./Span. (Martha Carden). ¶TV: *Riverboat*—"That Taylor Affair" 9-26-60 (Lucy Belle).

Daighton, Marga. Films: "Stagecoach" 1939 (Mrs. Pickett).

Dailey, Dan (1915-10/16/78). Films: "Ticket to Tomahawk" 1950 (Johnny Behind-the-Deuces); "The Daughters of Joshua Cabe Return" TVM-1975 (Joshua Cabe); "Testimony of Two Men" TVM-1977 (Father McGuire).

Dalbert, Suzanne (1927-12/31/70). Films: "Trail of the Yukon" 1949 (Marie).

Dalbes, Alberto. Films: "Billy the Kid" 1962-Span.; "100 Rifles" 1969 (Padre Francisco); "Cut-Throats Nine" 1973-Span./Ital.

D'Albrook, Sidney (1886-5/30/48). Films: "Heart of the Wilds" 1918 (Grey Cloud); "The Fighting Guide" 1922 (Grant Knowles); "Over the Border" 1922 (Snow Devil); "West of Chicago" 1922 (English Kid); "Bucking the Barrier" 1923 (Tyson); "Call of the Wild" 1923 (Charles); "The King of the Wild Horses" 1924; "Boots of Destiny" 1937 (Sheriff); "Wells Fargo" 1937 (Townsman); "Stand Up and Fight" 1939; "Union Pacific" 1939; "The Sea of Grass" 1947 (Man).

Dale, Arvon. Films: "King of the Mounties" 1942-serial (Craig); "Dangers of the Canadian Mounted" 1948-serial (Roy Watson).

Dale, E.L. Films: "Outlaws of the Prairie" 1937 (Village Doctor); "West of Santa Fe" 1938 (Doctor); "Spoilers of the Range" 1939 (Doctor).

Dale, Esther (1886-7/23/61). Films: "Smoky" 1946 (Gram); "Surrender" 1950 (Aunt May); "The Oklahoman" 1957 (Mrs. Fitzgerald); "North to Alaska" 1960 (Woman at Picnic). ¶TV: *Maverick*—"According to Hoyle" 10-6-57 (Ma Braus); *Wagon Train*—"The Julia Gage Story" 12-18-57 (Grandma).

Dale, James. Films: "The Adventures of Frank and Jesse James" 1948-serial (J.B. Nichols); "Dangers of the Canadian Mounted" 1948-serial (Andy Knight); "Sons of Adventure" 1948 (Whitey).

Dale, Jim (1935-). Films: "Hot Lead and Cold Feet" 1978 (Eli/Wild Billy/Jasper Bloodshy).

Dale, Virginia (1917-10/3/94). Films: "Shadows of the West" 1921 (Lucy Norton); "The Kid from Texas" 1939 (Okay Kinney); "Buck Benny Rides Again" 1940 (Virginia); "The Singing Hill" 1941. ¶TV: *Annie Oakley*—"Flint and Steel" 10-14-56 (Ma Wiggins); *Wyatt Earp*—"Fortitude" 11-26-57 (Gene).

Daley, Cass (1915-3/22/75). Films: "Riding High" 1943 (Tess Connors); "Red Garters" 1954 (Minnie Redwing).

Daley, Jack (1882-8/28/67). Films: "Born to the West" 1937 (Gambler); "Thunder Trail" 1937 (Bartender); "Queen of the Yukon" 1940 (Captain); "Arizona Bound" 1941; "Down Texas Way" 1942 (John Dodge); "West of the Law" 1942; "The Ghost Rider" 1943; "Six Gun Gospel" 1943.

Daley, Jeff. Films: "Outlaw's Son" 1957 (Ridley). ¶TV: *Tales of Wells Fargo*—"The Sooners" 3-3-58 (Ken Hunter); *The Restless Gun*—"Take Me Home" 12-1-58 (Marsh Lomer), "The Painted Beauty" 1-5-59 (Watkins), "The Englishman" 6-8-59 (Ralston), "The Way Back" 7-13-59; *Wagon Train*—"The Old Man Charvanaugh Story" 2-18-59 (Tucknis Charvanaugh); *Wanted—Dead or Alive*—"Bad Gun" 10-24-59 (Tobin); *The Rifleman*—"Eddie's Daughter" 11-3-59.

Daley, Ray. TV: *Maverick*—"You Can't Beat the Percentage" 10-4-59 (Brazos); *Bonanza*—"Blood on the Land" 2-13-60 (Billy), "Broken Ballad" 10-29-61 (Billy Buckley); *Colt .45*—"Martial Law" 5-17-60 (Sgt. Jim Perris); *The Tall Man*—"A Bounty for Billy" 10-15-60 (Jack Harper); *Frontier Circus*—"The Good Fight" 4-19-62 (Luke Sanders); *Death Valley Days*—"Girl with a Gun" 6-6-62 (Outlaw).

D'Algy, Helen. Films: "The Cowboy and the Countess" 1926 (Countess Justina).

Dalio, Marcel (1900-11/20/83). TV: *Maverick*—"Game of Chance" 1-4-59 (Baron Dulot); *Death Valley Days*—"The Battle of Mokelumne Hill" 3-1-60 (Victor Rosseau).

Dallesandro, Joe (1948). Films: "Lonesome Cowboys" 1968; "Sunset" 1988 (Cutch Kieffer).

Dallimore, Maurice (1912-2/20/73). Films: "North to Alaska" 1960 (Bartender). ¶TV: *The Rifleman*—"Hostages to Fortune" 2-4-63 (Bullock).

Dalroy, Harry "Rube" (1879-3/8/54). Films: "Valley of the Lawless" 1936 (Townsman); "Sing, Cowboy, Sing" 1937; "Code of the Cactus" 1939; "A Tornado in the Saddle" 1942.

Dalton, Abby (1935-). Films: "Cole Younger, Gunfighter" 1958 (Lucy); "The Plainsman" 1966 (Calamity Jane). ¶TV: *Schlitz Playhouse of the Stars*—"Way of the West" 6-6-58 (Belle Starr); *Have Gun Will Travel*—"Young Gun" 11-8-58 (Meg Wellman); *Jefferson Drum*—"Thicker Than Water" 11-27-58 (Eloise Barton); *Sugarfoot*—"The Desperadoes" 1-6-59 (Elizabeth Bingham); *Maverick*—"Duel at Sundown" 2-1-59 (Carrie Christiansen); *Rawhide*—"Incident West of Lano" 2-27-59 (Ruth Haley).

Dalton, Audrey (1934-). Films: "Drum Beat" 1954 (Nancy Meek); "Lone Texan" 1959 (Susan Harvey); "The Bounty Killer" 1965 (Carole). ¶TV: *Wagon Train*—"The John Wilbot Story" 6-11-58 (Harriet Field), "The Liam Fitzmorgan Story" 10-28-58 (Laura Grady), "The Jose Maria Moran Story" 5-27-59 (Mary Naughton), "The Roger Bigelow Story" 12-21-60 (Nancy Bigelow), "The Trace McCloud Story" 3-2-64 (Lola), "The Brian Conlin Story" 10-25-64 (Dana Bannon); *Bat Masterson*—"The Treasure of Worry Hill" 12-3-58 (Abigail Feather), "To the Manner Born" 10-1-59 (Abby Chancellor), "The Fourth Man" 4-27-61 (Cally Armitage); *Walt Disney Presents*—"Elfego Baca: The Griswold Murder" 2-20-59 (Mrs. Cunningham); *Whispering Smith*—"Cross Cut" 7-31-61 (April); *Bonanza*—"The Lady from Baltimore" 1-14-62 (Melinda Banning); *Gunsmoke*—"The Renegades" 1-12-63 (Lavinia Pate); *Death Valley Days*—"The Lion of Idaho" 3-6-63 (Mary O'Connell); *Wide Country*—"The Lucky Punch" 4-18-63 (Nancy Kidwell); *The Dakotas*—"A Nice Girl

from Goliah" 5-13-63 (Ronnie Kane); *Temple Houston*—"Billy Hart" 11-28-63 (Amy Hart); *The Big Valley*—"Earthquake!" 11-10-65 (Ann Snyder), "Hazard" 3-9-66 (Amy); *Laredo*—"The Land Grabbers" 12-9-65 (Alice Coverly); *Wild Wild West*—"The Night of the Golden Cobra" 9-23-66 (Veda).

Dalton, Dorothy (1893-4/12/72). Films: "Pierre of the Plains" 1914 (Jen Galbraith); "The Disciple" 1915 (Mary Houston); "The Flame of the Yukon" 1917 (Ethel Evans); "Flare-Up Sal" 1918 (Flare-up Sal); "The Lady of Red Butte" 1919 (Faro Fan); "The Crimson Challenge" 1922 (Tharon Last); "The Siren Call" 1922 (Charlotte Woods).

Dalton, Emmett (1937-7/13/37). Films: "Beyond the Law" 1918 (Bob Dalton).

Dalton, Lezlie. Films: "The New Daughters of Joshua Cabe" TVM-1976 (Mae).

Dalton, Timothy (1944-). TV: *Centennial*—Regular 1978-79 (Oliver Secombe).

Daltry, Roger (1944-). Films: "Lightning Jack" 1994-Australia (John T. Coles).

Daly, Arnold. TV: *Sergeant Preston of the Yukon*—"Justice at Goneaway Creek" 2-9-56 (Father Le Clerc), "Littlest Rookie" 10-11-56 (Constable); *Bat Masterson*—"Flume to the Mother Lode" 1-28-60 (Spencer).

Daly, Emmett. Films: "Trail Dust" 1936 (George).

Daly, Hazel. Films: "The Chef at Circle G" 1915; "The Impersonation of Tom" 1915; "The Tenderfoot's Triumph" 1915; "Shooting Up the Movies" 1916.

Daly, Jack (1914-6/2/68). Films: "Badman's Gold" 1951 (Professor); "Law and Order" 1953 (Allie Marshall). ¶TV: *Death Valley Days*—"Riggs and Riggs" 4-25-55; *The Gene Autry Show*—"Stage to San Dimas" 10-8-57, "The Portrait of White Cloud" 10-15-55, "Go West, Young Lady" 11-19-55; *Circus Boy*—"The Remarkable Ricardo" 1-20-57 (Mr. Baily).

Daly, James (1918-7/2/78). Films: "The Five Man Army" 1969-Ital. (Augustus); "Four Rode Out" 1969-Ital./Span./U.S. ¶TV: *Our American Heritage*—"Destiny West" 1-24-60 (Kit Carson); *The Road West*—"The Gunfighter" 9-26-66 (Andy Benteen); *The Virginian*—"Nightmare at Fort Killman" 3-8-67 (Sergeant Trapp), "Silver Image" 9-

25-68 (Dan Sheppard); *Gunsmoke*—"The Favor" 3-11-67 (John Crowley); *Custer*—"Accused" 9-13-67 (John Rudford).

Daly, Marcella. Films: "West of Chicago" 1922 (Patricia Daly); "The Arizona Romeo" 1925 (Mary); "Arizona Wildcat" 1927 (Helen Van Acker).

Daly, Robert. Films: "Pardon My Nerve!" 1922 (Henry Dale); "Three Who Paid" 1923 (Sam Lowrie).

Daly, Tom. Films: "Frontier Gun" 1958 (Cowhand); "The Miracle of the Hills" 1959 (Mike); "The Firebrand" 1962.

Daly, William Robert. Films: "Action" 1921 (J. Plimsoll); "Ride for Your Life" 1924 (Dan Donnegan).

Dalya, Jacqueline (1919-). Films: "The Gay Caballero" 1940 (Carmelita); "Viva Cisco Kid" 1940 (Helena); "The Treasure of the Sierra Madre" 1948 (Flashy Girl).

D'Amico, Rita. TV: *Laredo*—"Which Way Did They Go?" 11-18-65; *Wild Wild West*—"The Night of the Big Blast" 10-7-66 (Carmen); *Iron Horse*—"Sister Death" 4-3-67 (Gypsy).

Damita, Lily (1907-3/21/94). Films: "Fighting Caravans" 1931 (Felice).

Damler, John. Films: "The Charge at Feather River" 1953 (Dabney); "Rose Marie" 1954 (Orderly); "The Marauders" 1955 (Cooper); "Gun Battle at Monterey" 1957; "Last of the Badmen" 1957 (Elkins); "Ambush at Cimarron Pass" 1958 (Private Zach); "Gun Fight" 1961 (Hank); "How the West Was Won" 1962 (Lawyer); "Sam Whiskey" 1969 (Hank). ¶TV: *The Cisco Kid*—"Smuggled Silver" 6-14-52, "Outlaw's Gallery" 11-22-52; *Wild Bill Hickok*—"Masquerade at Moccasin Flats" 9-2-52, "Buckshot Comes Home" 11-25-52, "Ghost Town Lady" 1-27-53, "The Gatling Gun" 5-5-53; *The Lone Ranger*—"Frame for Two" 10-23-52, "Right to Vote" 2-12-53, "Death in the Forest" 6-4-53, "Uncle Ed" 3-3-55; *Death Valley Days*—"I Am Joaquin" 3-28-55; *Sergeant Preston of the Yukon*—"Relief Train" 2-23-56 (Brand); *Wanted—Dead or Alive*—"The Corner" 2-21-59, "Payoff at Pinto" 5-21-60; *Wagon Train*—"The Martha Barham Story" 11-4-59 (Orderly); *Tales of Wells Fargo*—"Run for the River" 11-7-60 (Fred Haig); *Stagecoach West*—"Red Sand" 11-22-60 (Doc), "Songs My Mother Told Me" 2-21-61 (Marshal); *The Tall Man*—

"Big Sam's Boy" 3-4-61 (Clegg); *Have Gun Will Travel*—"Trial at Tablerock" 12-15-62; *The Loner*—"Widow on the Evening Stage" 10-30-65 (Stableman); *A Man Called Shenandoah*—"End of a Legend" 2-7-66 (Bartender).

Damon, Cathryn (1930-5/4/87). TV: *Calamity Jane* 11-12-63 (Adelaide Adams).

Damon, Les (1909-7/20/62). TV: *Have Gun Will Travel*—"Shootout at Hogtooth" 11-10-62 (Tillbury).

Damon, Mark (1935-). Films: "Johnny Yuma" 1966-Ital. (Johnny Yuma); "Ringo and His Golden Pistol" 1966-Ital. (Ringo); "Death at Owell Rock" 1967-Ital. (Lawrence); "Great Treasure Hunt" 1967-Ital./Span. (Kansas Lee); "Let Them Rest" 1967-Ital./Ger.; "Train for Durango" 1967-Ital./Span. (Luca); "All Out" 1968-Ital./Span.; "Cry for Revenge" 1968-Ital./Span. (Johnny); "Pistol Packin' Preacher" 1972-Ital./Fr. (Slim); "They Call Him Veritas" 1972-Ital./Span. (Veritas). ¶TV: *Tales of Wells Fargo*—"A Matter of Honor" 11-3-58 (Running Horse); *Zorro*—"The Iron Box" 1-15-59 (Eugenio); *Walt Disney Presents: Zorro*—"The Postponed Wedding" 1-1-61 (Migel Serrano).

Damon, Matt. Films: "Geronimo: An American Legend" 1993 (Lt. Britton Davis).

Damone, Vic (1928-). TV: *The Rebel*—"The Proxy" 4-16-61 (Wilkerson).

Dan, Judy. Films: "Stagecoach to Dancer's Rock" 1962 (Loi Yan Wu). ¶TV: *The Cisco Kid*—"Chinese Gold" 10-18-52; *The Lone Ranger*—"The Letter Bride" 11-15-56; *Sugarfoot*—"The Highbinder" 1-19-60 (Ah Yung).

Dana, Bill (1924-). TV: *Zorro and Son*—Regular 1983 (Bernardo).

Dana, Frederick. Films: "Don Desperado" 1927 (Nathan Jessup); "Hawk of the Hills" 1927-serial (Larry); "The Long Loop on the Pecos" 1927 (Arnold); "Two-Gun of the Tumbleweed" 1927 (Brunelle); "The Apache Raider" 1928 (Bit Ward); "The Bronc Stomper" 1928 (Ranger R.M. Thompson); "The Wagon Master" 1929 (Bill Hollister).

Dana, Leora (1923-12/13/83). Films: "3:10 to Yuma" 1957 (Alice Evans); "Wild Rovers" 1971 (Nell Buckman). ¶TV: *Zane Grey Theater*—"King of the Valley" 11-26-59 (Anne Coleman); *Stoney Burke*—"King of the Hill" 1-21-63 (Ellen Mundorf).

Dana, Mark. Films: "Thunder Over the Plains" 1953 (Lt. Williams). ¶TV: *Wyatt Earp*—"The Frontier Theatre" 2-7-56 (Robert Barlow), "Hung Jury" 10-29-57 (Dan Bolton), "Kill the Editor" 12-16-58 (Cal McDavid), "The Paymaster" 12-1-59 (Major Fletcher); *Death Valley Days*—"Escape" 4-21-56 (Harry Neilson), "The Gambler and the Lady" 7-7-57; *The Restless Gun*—"Friend in Need" 1-13-58 (George Willis); *Have Gun Will Travel*—"Lady on the Stagecoach" 1-17-59 (Wilbur Grayson); *The Texan*—"The Governor's Lady" 3-14-60 (John Maddox); *Laramie*—"Strange Company" 6-6-61 (Bracket), "The Fugitives" 2-12-63 (Doan).

Dana, Muriel Frances. Films: "The Sunshine Trail" 1923 (Algernon Aloysius Fitzmaurice Bangs).

Dana, Viola (1897-7/3/87). Films: "Flower of No Man's Land" 1916 (Echo); "The Only Road" 1918 (Nita); "The Winding Trail" 1918 (Audrey Graham).

Dandridge, Ruby (1900-10/17/87). Films: "Home in Oklahoma" 1946 (Devoria Lassiter).

Dane, Bruce. Films: "Riders of the Sage" 1939 (Rusty); "Smoky Trails" 1939 (Cooksy); "Wagon Train" 1940 (McKenzie).

Dane, Karl (1886-4/15/34). Films: "The Everlasting Whisper" 1925; "War Paint" 1926 (Petersen); "The Trail of '98" 1929 (Lars Petersen); "Billy the Kid" 1930 (Swenson); "Montana Moon" 1930 (Hank).

Dane, Lawrence (1937-). Films: "Black Fox" TVM-1995; ¶TV: *The Virginian*—"The Decision" 3-13-68 (Tasker), "The Wind of Outrage" 10-16-68 (Jacques), "Journey to Scathelock" 12-10-69 (Frenchman); *Bonanza*—"Sweet Annie Laurie" 1-5-69 (Rogers); *Lancer*—"The Wedding" 1-7-69.

Dane, Peter. TV: *Tales of the Texas Rangers*—"Ransom Flight" 8-27-55 (Jim Warren); *Death Valley Days*—"Miracle of the Sea Gulls" 12-19-55.

Dane, Robert. Films: "Seminole" 1953 (Trader Taft).

Dangcil, Linda (1941-). Films: "Jubilee Trail" 1954 (Rosita); "Escape from Red Rock" 1958 (Elena Chavez); "El Dorado" 1967. ¶TV: *Maverick*—"Guatemala City" 1-31-60 (Angelita); *The Tall Man*—"The Shawl" 10-1-60 (Rosita); *The Rifleman*—"Baranca" 11-1-60; *Stagecoach West*—"The Orphans" 5-30-61 (Angela Toreno); *Tales of Wells Fargo*—"Reward for Gaine" 1-20-62

(Feather); *Temple Houston*—"Find Angel Chavez" 9-26-63 (Maria); *Branded*—"The Ghost of Murrieta" 3-20-66 (Rosita); *Hondo*—"Hondo and the Rebel Hat" 12-29-67 (Mrs. Hernandez); *Here Come the Brides*—"Marriage Chinese Style" 4-9-69 (Toy Quan).

D'Angelo, Beverly (1952-). Films: "Lightning Jack" 1994-Australia (Lana).

Daniel, Bill (1912-5/15/62). Films: "The Alamo" 1960 (Col. Neill).

Daniel, Paul. Films: "Apache Uprising" 1966 (Old Antone); "Johnny Reno" 1966 (Chief Little Bear).

Daniell, Henry (1894-10/31/63). Films: "The Comancheros" 1961 (Gireaux). ¶TV: *The Californians*—"Strange Quarantine" 12-10-57 (Dr. Rodman), "Gold-Tooth Charlie" 3-10-59, "The Bell Tolls" 5-19-59 (James King); *Maverick*—"Pappy" 9-13-59 (Rene St. Cloud); *Wagon Train*—"Trial for Murder" 4-27-60 & 5-4-60 (Sir Alexander Drew).

Daniels, Ann. TV: *The Californians*—"Halfway House" 12-2-58; *Wyatt Earp*—"She Almost Married Wyatt" 2-24-59 (Cathy Prentice).

Daniels, Bebe (1901-3/16/71). Films: "North of the Rio Grande" 1922 (Val Hannon); "Heritage of the Desert" 1924 (Mescal).

Daniels, Bette. Films: "San Antone Ambush" 1949 (Sally Wheeler).

Daniels, Hank (1919-12/21/73). Films: "In Old Sacramento" 1946 (Sam Chase).

Daniels, Harold (1903-12/27/71). Films: "Hi Gaucho!" 1936; "Trail Dust" 1936 (Lewis); "Doomed at Sundown" 1937 (Dante Sprague); "Hollywood Cowboy" 1937 (Hotel Clerk); "Oklahoma Renegades" 1940 (Orv Liscomb); "Ride 'Em, Cowboy" 1942 (Reporter).

Daniels, Jerry. TV: *The Outcasts*—"Alligator King" 1-20-69 (Cat Dancing); *The High Chaparral*—"Surtee" 2-28-69.

Daniels, John. TV: *The Loner*—"The Burden of the Badge" 3-5-66 (Jimmy); *The Big Valley*—"Rimfire" 2-19-68 (Daniel Barrett); *The Virginian*—"The Land Dreamer" 2-26-69 (William McKinley).

Daniels, Lisa (1933-). Films: "The Gambler from Natchez" 1954 (Yvette Rivage).

Daniels, Mark. Films: "The Vanishing Virginian" 1941 (Jack Holden); "The Last Round-Up" 1947 (Matt Mason).

Daniels, Thelma. Films: "The Amazing Vagabond" 1929 (Alice Dunning).

Daniels, Viora. Films: "The Cowboy and the Lady" 1922 (Molly X); "Bulldog Pluck" 1927 (Jess Haviland).

Daniels, William (1927-). TV: *Barbary Coast*—"Irish Coffee" 10-13-75 (Boyle); *Hallmark Hall of Fame*—"The Court-Martial of General George Armstrong Carter" 12-1-77 (Major Reno).

Danner, Blythe (1945-). Films: "Lovin' Molly" 1974 (Molly); "Sidekicks" TVM-1974 (Prudy Jenkins); "Hearts of the West" 1975 (Miss Trout). ¶TV: *Hallmark Hall of Fame*—"The Court-Martial of General George Armstrong Carter" 12-1-77 (Elizabeth Custer).

Danning, Sybil (1951-). Films: "God's Gun" 1976-Ital./Israel

Dano, Royal (1922-5/15/94). Films: "Bend of the River" 1952 (Long Tom); "Johnny Guitar" 1954 (Corey); "The Far Country" 1955 (Luke); "Tension at Table Rock" 1956 (Jameson); "Tribute to a Badman" 1956 (Abe); "Man in the Shadow" 1957 (Aiken Clay); "Trooper Hook" 1957 (Trude); "Man of the West" 1958 (Trout); "Saddle the Wind" 1958 (Clay Ellison); "Three Thousand Hills" 1959 (Carmichael); "Cimarron" 1960 (Ike Howes); "Posse from Hell" 1961 (Uncle Billy Caldwell); "Savage Sam" 1963 (Pack Underwood); "The Dangerous Days of Kiowa Jones" TVM-1966 (Otto); "Gunpoint" 1966 (Ode); "The Last Challenge" 1967 (Pretty Horse); "Welcome to Hard Times" 1967 (John Baer); "Day of the Evil Gun" 1968 (Dr. Prather); "Death of a Gunfighter" 1969 (Arch Brandt); "The Undefeated" 1969 (Major Sanders); "Machismo—40 Graves for 40 Guns" 1970 (Zach); "Run, Simon, Run" TVM-1970 (Sheriff Tackaberry); "Skin Game" 1971 (John Brown); "The Culpepper Cattle Company" 1972 (Rustler); "The Great Northfield, Minnesota Raid" 1972 (Gustavson); "Cahill, United States Marshal" 1973 (MacDonald); "The Outlaw Josey Wales" 1976 (Ted Spot); "Donner Pass: The Road to Survival" TVM-1978 (Wutter); "Last Ride of the Dalton Gang" TVM-1979 (Pa Dalton); "Red Headed Stranger" 1987 (Larn Claver); "Once Upon a Texas Train" TVM-1988 (Nitro). ¶TV: *Gunsmoke*—"Obie Tater" 10-15-55 (Obie Tater), "The Preacher" 6-16-56 (Seth Tandy), "Now That April's There" 3-21-64 (Bender),

"Crooked Mile" 10-3-64 (Praylie), "Deputy Festus" 1-16-65 (Lambert), "Sweet Billy, Singer of Songs" 1-15-66 (Lambert), "Vengeance" 10-2-67 & 10-9-67 (Rory Luken), "Hard Luck Henry" 10-23-67 (Jefferson Dooley), "Stryker" 9-29-69 (Jessup), "The Thieves" 3-9-70 (Gideon Hale), "Captain Sligo" 1-4-71 (Watney), "The Lost" 9-13-71 (Henry Mather); *20th Century Fox Hour*—"Gun in His Hand" 4-4-56 (Jed Martin); *Cavalry Patrol*—Pilot 1956 (Chattez); *The Restless Gun*—"Cheyenne Express" 12-2-57 (Wilbur English); *The Rifleman*—"The Sheridan Story" 1-13-59 (Frank Blandon), "A Matter of Faith" 5-19-59 (Jonas Epps), "A Case of Identity" 1-19-60 (Aaron Wingate), "Honest Abe" 11-20-61 (Able Lincoln), "Day of Reckoning" 4-9-62 (Reverend Jamison); *Wagon Train*—"The Kate Parker Story" 5-6-59 (Boone Calder), "The Robert Harrison Clarke Story" 10-14-63 (Bouchette); *Wanted—Dead or Alive*—"The Matchmaker" 9-19-59 (Charlie Wright); *Hotel De Paree*—"Vein of Ore" 10-16-59 (Sam Crail); *The Rebel*—"Yellow Hair" 10-18-59 (Man), "The Proxy" 4-16-61 (Crowe); *Tales of Wells Fargo*—"Cole Younger" 1-4-60 (Cole Younger), "Don't Wake a Tiger" 5-12-62 (Robert Mapes); *Johnny Ringo*—"Black Harvest" 4-7-60 (Lucas Frome); *Tate*—"Home Town" 6-8-60 (Morty Taw); *Gunslinger*—"Border Incident" 2-9-61 (El Senor); *Have Gun Will Travel*—"The Fatal Flaw" 2-25-61 (Curley Ashburne); *Zane Grey Theater*—"Image of a Drawn Sword" 5-11-61 (Will); *Frontier Circus*—"The Patriarch of Purgatory" 11-30-61 (Jethro); *Bonanza*—"Gift of Water" 2-11-62 (Ganther), "The Reluctant Rebel" 11-21-65 (Hank Penn), "A Man Without Land" 4-9-67 (Matt Jeffers); *The Virginian*—"The Brazen Bell" 10-17-62 (Molder), "Say Goodbye to All That" 1-23-63 (Faraway MacPhail), "Ring of Silence" 10-27-65 (Daniels), "A Bald-Faced Boy" 4-13-66 (Uncle Del); *Rawhide*—"Incident at Quivira" 12-14-62 (Monty Fox), "Incident at Ten Trees" 1-2-64 (Jeb Newton), "The Lost Herd" 10-16-64 (Teisner), "Texas Fever" 2-5-65 (Sam Wentworth); *The Dakotas*—"Terror at Heart River" 4-15-63 (Walter Wyman); *Temple Houston*—"Toll the Bell Slowly" 10-17-63 (Sheriff Smiley); *The Travels of Jaimie McPheeters*—"The Day of the Haunted Trail" 1-26-64 (James Weston); *Death Valley Days*—"The Trouble with Taxes" 4-18-65 (Aaron Winters), "Traveling Trees" 11-13-65, "The Other Side of

the Mountain" 4-13-68 (Winters), "A Simple Question of Justice" 11-22-69, "The Visitor" 12-27-69 (Hannibal), "The Mezcla Man" 1-3-70; *The Legend of Jesse James*—"Jail Break" 11-15-65 (Jailer); *The Big Valley*—"The Death Merchant" 2-23-66 (Ezra Craddock), "Hide the Children" 12-19-66 (Veterinarian), "Ladykiller" 10-16-67 (Jesse Bleeck), "Joshua Watson" 1-20-69 (Rufus Morton); *Daniel Boone*—"Cibola" 3-31-66 (Matty Brenner), "The Inheritance" 10-26-67 (John Maddox); *Iron Horse*—"A Dozen Ways to Kill a Man" 12-19-66 (Ross), "Welcome for the General" 1-2-67 (Captain Hugh Sinclair); *Pistols 'n' Petticoats*—2-4-67 (Virgil); *Cimarron Strip*—"Broken Wing" 9-21-67, "The Beast That Walks Like a Man" 11-30-67 (Walking Man); *The Guns of Will Sonnett*—"A Son for a Son" 10-20-67 (Vance Murdock), "The Trap" 10-4-68 (Arvis Peebles); *Hondo*—"Hondo and the Mad Dog" 10-27-67 (Liebel); *Cowboy in Africa*—"The Lions" 3-25-68 (Steven Cromwell); *The Outcasts*—"The Heroes" 11-11-68 (Walt Madsen); *Alias Smith and Jones*—"The Girl in Boxcar Number Three" 2-11-71 (John Lambert); *Kung Fu*—"Nine Lives" 2-15-73 (Henry Skowrin); *The Quest*—"The Captive" 9-22-76; *How the West Was Won*—Episode One 2-6-77 (Elam Hanks), Episode Two 2-7-77 (Elam Hanks).

Danova, Cesare (1926-3/19/92). TV: *The Rifleman*—"Duel of Honor" 11-11-58 (Count Di Montova), "Baranca" 11-1-60 (Baranca), "The Guest" 3-11-63 (Mario Arsatti); *Tales of Wells Fargo*—"Vasquez" 5-16-60 (Vasquez); *Zane Grey Theater*—"The Release" 4-17-61 (Lee Duval); *The Outlaws*—"The Sooner" 4-27-61 (Grigor Zacod); *Stoney Burke*—"Point of Entry" 3-4-63 (Lieutenant Escalon); *Bonanza*—"Woman of Fire" 1-17-65 (Don Luis); *Daniel Boone*—"Cain's Birthday" 4-1-65 & 4-8-65 (Colonel Michelet), "When a King Is a Pawn" 12-22-66.

Danson, Ted (1947-). Films: "Cowboy" TVM-1983 (Dale Weeks).

Dante, Michael (1931-). Films: "Fort Dobbs" 1958 (Billings); "Westbound" 1959 (Rod Miller); "Apache Rifles" 1964 (Red Hawk); "Arizona Raiders" 1965 (Brady); "Winterhawk" 1975 (Chief Winterhawk). ¶TV: *Maverick*—"Stage West" 10-27-57 (Sam Harris), "The Third Rider" 1-5-58 (Turk Mason), "Betrayal" 3-22-59 (Outlaw); *Colt .45*—"The Three Thousand Dollar Bullet" 11-1-57 (Davey Bryant), "The Deserters" 3-28-58 (Ab Saunders); *Cheyenne*—

"Hired Gun" 12-17-57 (Whitey); *Sugarfoot*—"The Dead Hills" 3-4-58 (Mike Wilson); *Tales of the Texas Rangers*—"Edge of Danger" 10-23-58 (Alfredo); *Lawman*—"The Captives" 1-11-59 (Jack McCall); *The Adventures of Rin Tin Tin*—"The Matador" 2-6-59 (Ramon Estrada); *Death Valley Days*—"Olvera" 10-13-59; *The Texan*—"Stampede" 11-2-59 (Stan Chambers), "Showdown at Abilene" 11-9-59 (Steve Chambers), "The Reluctant Bridegroom" 11-16-59 (Steve Chambers), "Trouble on the Trail" 11-23-59 (Steve Chambers); *Bonanza*—"The Brass Box" 9-26-65 (Miguel); *Custer*—Regular 1967 (Crazy Horse); *The Big Valley*—"Deathtown" 10-28-68 (Francisco).

Dantine, Helmut (1918-5/2/82). TV: *Sugarfoot*—"The Royal Raiders" 3-17-59 (Major Horst Von Hoffstadt).

Danton, Ray (1931-2/11/92). Films: "Chief Crazy Horse" 1955 (Little Big Man); "The Spoilers" 1955 (Bronco Blackie); "Yellowstone Kelly" 1959 (Sayapi); "Pursuit" 1975. ¶TV: *Sugarfoot*—"Bunch Quitter" 10-29-57, "The Wild Bunch" 9-29-57 (Duke McGann); *Trackdown*—"Like Father" 11-1-57; *Wagon Train*—"The Monte Britton Story" 6-18-58 (Monte Britton), "The Molly Kincaid Story" 9-16-63 (Kincaid), "The Stark Bluff Story" 4-6-64 (Zeb Stark); *Bronco*—"Quest of the Thirty Dead" 10-7-58 (Bill Magrider), "The Buckbrier Trail" 2-20-61 (Deputy Larkin); *Yancy Derringer*—"An Ace Called Spade" 10-30-58 (Spade Stuart); *Bat Masterson*—"The Romany Knives" 7-22-59 (Tonio); *The Alaskans*—Regular 1959-60 (Nifty Cronin); *Lawman*—"Lily" 10-4-59 (Len Farrell), "Yawkey" 10-23-60 (Yawkey); *Colt .45*—"Bounty List" 5-31-60 (Kane); *Cheyenne*—"Savage Breed" 12-19-60 (Al Lestrade); *Maverick*—"A State of Siege" 1-1-61 (Don Felipe); *Laramie*—"The Fortune Hunter" 10-9-62 (Vince Jackson); *The Virginian*—"Riff-Raff" 11-7-62 (Lt. Drexel Hamilton); *Wide Country*—"The Bravest Man in the World" 12-6-62 (Warren Price); *Empire*—"The Four Thumbs Story" 1-8-63 (Four Thumbs); *Redigo*—"The Thin Line" 12-3-63 (Jeff Burton); *Temple Houston*—"The Case for William Gotch" 2-6-64 (Martin Royale); *Death Valley Days*—"The Wooing of Perilous Pauline" 2-22-64 (Jere Fryer); *The Big Valley*—"The Devil's Masquerade" 3-4-68 (Reed Clayton); *Nichols*—"Deer Crossing" 10-21-71 (Juan); *Nakia*—"No Place to Hide" 10-19-74 (Rodale).

D'Antonio, Carmen. Films: "Destry Rides Again" 1939; "Cheyenne Autumn" 1964 (Pawnee Woman). ¶TV: *Daniel Boone*—"The Returning" 1-14-65 (Cherokee Woman); *Wagon Train*—"The Stark Bluff Story" 4-6-64 (Olgala).

Dapo, Ronnie. TV: *Wagon Train*—"The Greenhorn Story" 10-7-59; *Cheyenne*—"One Way Ticket" 2-19-62 (Roy Barrington).

D'Arbanville, Patti (1951-). Films: "Rancho Deluxe" 1975 (Betty Fargo).

Darby, Ken (1909-1/24/92). Films: "Renegade Trail" 1939 (Rider).

Darby, Kim (1947-). Films: "True Grit" 1969 (Mattie Ross); "This Was the West That Was" TVM-1974 (Calamity Jane); "The Capture of Grizzly Adams" TVM-1982 (Kate Brady). ¶TV: *Wagon Train*—"The Story of Hector Heatherington" 12-20-64 (Heather Heatherington); *Gunsmoke*—"The Lure" 2-25-67 (Carrie Neely), "Vengeance" 10-2-67 & 10-9-67 (Angel); *The Road West*—"Fair Ladies of France" 2-27-67 (Sister Marie Aimee); *Bonanza*—"The Sure Thing" 11-12-67 (Trudy Loughlin).

Darcel, Denise (1925-). Films: "Thunder in the Pines" 1948 (Yvette); "Westward the Women" 1951 (Fifi Danon); "Vera Cruz" 1954 (Countess Marie Duvarre).

D'Arcy, Alexander (1908-). TV: *Daniel Boone*—"Cibola" 3-31-66 (1st Soldier).

Darcy, Ann. Films: "The Man from Hell" 1934 (Nancy Campbell); "Rustlers of Red Dog" 1935-serial.

D'Arcy, Camille (1879-9/26/16). Films: "The Cave on Thunder Cloud" 1915.

D'Arcy, Roy (1894-11/15/69). Films: "Winners of the Wilderness" 1927 (Captain Dumas); "Beyond the Sierras" 1928 (Owens); "Riders of the Dark" 1928 (Eagan); "Broadway to Cheyenne" 1932 (Jess); "The Gay Buckaroo" 1932 (Dave Dumont); "The Man from Hell" 1934; "Outlawed Guns" 1935 (Jack Keeler); "Under Strange Flags" 1937 (Morales).

Darcy, Sheila. Films: "Wells Fargo" 1937 (Lola Montez); "South of the Border" 1939 (Rosita); "Union Pacific" 1939 (Rose); "Zorro's Fighting Legion" 1939-serial (Volita); "Tumbledown Ranch in Arizona" 1941 (Dorothy); "Tomahawk" 1951 (Woman).

Darden, Severn (1929-5/26/95). Films: "The Hired Hand" 1971 (McVey); "Dirty Little Billy" 1972 (Big Jim); "Orphan Train" TVM-1979 (Barrington); "Wanda Nevada" 1979 (Merlin Bitterstix). ¶TV: *Daniel Boone*—"The Valley of the Sun" 11-28-68 (Sir Hubert Spencer); *Alias Smith and Jones*—"Never Trust an Honest Man" 4-15-71 (Oscar/Allen); *Barbary Coast*—"An Iron-Clad Plan" 10-31-75 (Bekhim); *Bonanza*—"The Rattlesnake Brigade" 12-5-71 (Price); *The Quest*—"Day of Outrage" 10-27-76 (Circuit Preacher); *Young Maverick*—"Hearts O'Gold" 12-12-79.

Dare, Dorris (1899-8/16/27). Films: "Fightin' Odds" 1925 (Helen Morrison).

Dare, Frances. Films: "The Cowboy Musketeer" 1925 (Leila Gordon).

Dare, Helena (-8/3/72). Films: "Cody of the Pony Express" 1950-serial (Emma); "Buffalo Bill in Tomahawk Territory" 1952.

Darien, Frank (1876-10/20/55). Films: "Cimarron" 1931 (Mr. Bixby); "Undercover Man" 1936 (Dizzy Slocum); "Fair Warning" 1937 (Hotel Doctor); "Cassidy of Bar 20" 1938 (Pappy); "Western Jamboree" 1938 (Dad Haskell); "Stand Up and Fight" 1939 (Daniels); "Arizona" 1940 (Joe); "Viva Cisco Kid" 1940 (Express Man); "Arkansas Judge" 1941 (Henry Marden); "King of the Texas Rangers" 1941-serial (Pop Evans); "Under Fiesta Stars" 1941; "Hurricane Smith" 1942 (Pop Wessell); "Jackass Mail" 1942 (Postmaster); "The Outlaw" 1943 (Shorty); "Gentle Annie" 1944 (Jake); "Tall in the Saddle" 1944; "Bad Bascomb" 1946 (Elder McCabe); "The Sea of Grass" 1947 (Minister).

Darin, Bobby (1936-12/20/73). Films: "Heller in Pink Tights" 1960 (Servant); "Gunfight in Abilene" 1967 (Cal Wayne). ¶TV: *Schlitz Playhouse of the Stars*—"Way of the West" 6-6-58 (Joe); *Wagon Train*—"The John Gillman Story" 10-4-64 (John Gillman).

Daris, James. TV: *Bonanza*—"Trouble Town" 3-17-68 (Short); *Daniel Boone*—"The Bait" 11-7-68 (Matt); *Nichols*—"Eddie Joe" 1-4-72 (Curtiss).

Dark, Christopher (1926-10/8/71). Films: "Johnny Concho" 1956 (Walker); "The Halliday Brand" 1957 (Jivaro); "Day of the Bad Man" 1958 (Rudy Hayes); "Wild Heritage" 1958 (Brazos); "How the West Was Won" 1962 (Poker Player); "Scandalous John" 1971 (Card Dealer). ¶TV: *The Lone Ranger*—"Texas Draw" 11-5-54

(Dr. William Hubbard); *Frontier*— "The Well" 4-8-56 (Stacy), "Patrol" 4-29-56 (Walker); *Broken Arrow*— "Return from the Shadows" 12-4-56 (Jose), "The Challenge" 2-5-57 (Toweega); *Colt .45*—"Decoy" 1-31-58 (Don Ramon); *Tombstone Territory*—"Sermons and Six Guns" 12-25-57 (Tuttle); *Trackdown*—"The Young Gun" 2-7-58 (Dover); *Texas John Slaughter*—"Killers from Kansas" 1-9-59 (Reed); *The Texan*—"Outpost" 1-19-59 (Jack Arno), "Reunion" 5-4-59 (Trevor Jackson); *Northwest Passage*— "The Killers" 3-13-59 (Philip Clark); *Have Gun Will Travel*—"Death of a Gunfighter" 3-14-59 (Juan Morrita), "Cage at McNaab" 2-16-63 (Brian Larson); *Wanted—Dead or Alive*— "Double Fee" 3-21-59 (Henry Gaspard); *Man Without a Gun*—"Reward" 4-11-59 (Steve Bell); *Bonanza*—"A Rose for Lotta" 9-12-59 (Langford Poole), "The Fear Merchants" 1-30-60 (Jesse Tibbs), "Calamity Over the Comstock" 11-3-63 (Doc Holliday), "Showdown at Tahoe" 11-19-67 (Testy); *The Rifleman*—"Bloodlines" 10-6-59; *The Deputy*—"Powder Keg" 10-10-59 (Hawk); *Laramie*—"The Lawbreakers" 10-20-59 (Rickert), "Strange Company" 6-6-61 (N'Codee); *U.S. Marshal*—"Honeymoon" 12-26-59 (Johnny Lowell); *The Law of the Plainsman*—"Rabbit's Fang" 3-24-60 (Macklin); *Death Valley Days*—"Human Sacrifice" 5-31-60 (Washaki); *Stagecoach West*—"The Butcher" 3-28-61 (Abrham Fontaine); *Frontier Circus*—"Never Won Fair Lady" 4-12-62 (Manfredi); *Gunsmoke*—"The Ditch" 10-27-62 (Lafe Crider); *The Virginian*—"The Accomplice" 12-19-62, "Brother Thaddeus" 10-30-63 (Benny Caboose); *Rawhide*—"Incident of the Comanchero" 3-22-63 (Sam Barnes), "The Photographer" 12-11-64 (Jordan), "Escape to Doom" 10-12-65 (Quadero); *The Legend of Jesse James*—"Reunion" 1-10-66 (Swain); *Laredo*—"Miracle at Massacre Mission" 3-3-66 (Frank Ford); *Daniel Boone*—"Forty Rifles" 3-10-66 (Kashita); *Time Tunnel*—"Massacre" 10-28-66 (Crazy Horse); *Iron Horse*— "Death by Triangulation" 3-20-67 (Curry); *The High Chaparral*—"Surtee" 2-28-69 (Chato), "The Lost Ones" 11-21-69 (Ramadan); *The Men from Shiloh*—"Jenny" 9-30-70.

Dark Cloud, Beulah (-1/2/46). Films: "Desert Gold" 1919 (Papago Indian Mother); "The Crimson Challenge" 1922 (Anita).

Dark Cloud, John (-1918). Films: "The Song of the Wildwood Flute" 1910; "The Squaw's Love" 1911;

"A Tale of the Wilderness" 1912; "An Indian's Loyalty" 1913; "Sierra Jim's Reformation" 1914; "The Ceremonial Turquoise" 1915; "The Huron Converts" 1915; "The Indian Trapper's Vindication" 1915; "John Ermine of the Yellowstone" 1917 (Fire Bear); "What Am I Bid?" 1919 (Dark Cloud).

Dark Cloud, William. Films: "The Boundary Line" 1915; "Naked Fists" 1918.

Darkfeather, Princess Mona (1882-9/3/77). Films: "A Forest Romance" 1911; "The Night Herder" 1911; "At Old Fort Dearborn" 1912 (Singing Bird); "Big Rock's Last Stand" 1912; "Black Foot's Conspiracy" 1912; "A Crucial Test" 1912; "Darkfeather's Strategy" 1912; "The End of the Romance" 1912; "The Hand of Fate" 1912; "The Massacre of Santa Fe Trail" 1912; "A Red Man's Love" 1912; "Trapper Bill, King of the Scouts" 1912; "When Uncle Sam Is Young" 1912; "A White Indian" 1912; "Darkfeather's Sacrifice" 1913; "A Forest Romance" 1913; "An Indian Maid's Strategy" 1913; "Juanita" 1913; "The Love of Men" 1913; "The Oath of Conchita" 1913; "The Return of Thunder Cloud's Spirit" 1913; "The Spring in the Desert" 1913; "At the End of the Rope" 1914; "The Bottled Spider" 1914; "Brought to Justice" 1914; "The Call of the Tribe" 1914; "The Coming of Lone Wolf" 1914; "Defying the Chief" 1914; "Dream of the Wild" 1914; "The Fate of a Squaw" 1914; "The Fight of Deadwood Trail" 1914; "The Fuse of Death" 1914; "The Gambler's Reformation" 1914; "Grey Eagle's Last Stand" 1914; "His Indian Nemesis" 1914; "The Indian Agent" 1914; "The Indian Suffragettes" 1914; "Kidnapped by Indians" 1914; "Lame Dog's Treachery" 1914; "The Legend of the Amulet" 1914; "The Medicine Man's Vengeance" 1914; "The Moonshiners" 1914; "The Navajo Blanket" 1914; "The New Medicine Man" 1914; "The Paleface Brave" 1914; "Priest or Medicine Man?" 1914; "The Redskins and the Renegades" 1914; "The Squaw's Revenge" 1914; "The Tigers of the Hills" 1914; "The Vanishing Tribe" 1914; "The Vengeance of Winona" 1914; "The War Bonnet" 1914; "The Miser of Monterey" 1915; "The Western Border" 1915; "The Circle of Death" 1916; "None So Blind" 1916; "The Seeds of Jealousy" 1916; "The Hidden Danger" 1917; "The Red Goddess" 1917.

Darling, Ida (1875-6/5/36). Films: "Davy Crockett" 1916.

Darling, Romere. Films: "The

Cowboy and the Indians" 1949; "Mrs. Mike" 1949 (Mrs. Henderson).

Darling, Sally. Films: "Guns for Hire" 1932; "Five Bad Men" 1935 (Janet Bartlett).

Darmond, Grace (1898-10/8/63). Films: "A Texas Steer" 1915 (Bossy Brander); "The Beautiful Gambler" 1921 (Molly Hanlon); "Where the Worst Begins" 1925 (Annice Van Dorn).

Darnell, Linda (1921-4/10/65). Films: "Brigham Young—Frontiersman" 1940 (Zina Webb); "Mark of Zorro" 1940 (Lolita Quintero); "Buffalo Bill" 1944 (Dawn Starlight); "My Darling Clementine" 1946 (Chihauhua); "Two Flags West" 1950 (Elena Kenniston); "Dakota Incident" 1956 (Amy Clarke); "Black Spurs" 1965 (Sadie). ¶TV: *Wagon Train*—"The Dora Gray Story" 1-29-58 (Dora Gray), "The Sacramento Story" 6-25-58 (Dora Gray); *Cimarron City*—"Kid on a Calico Horse" 11-22-58 (Mary Clinton).

D'Arpe, Gustave (Gus Harper). Films: "Johnny Yuma" 1966-Ital. (Henchman).

Darr, Vondell. Films: "Border Vengeance" 1925 (Bimps Jackson); "The Pony Express" 1925 (Baby).

Darrell, Steve (1905-8/14/70). Films: "They Died with Their Boots On" 1941 (Officer); "Gentlemen with Guns" 1946 (McAllister); "Heldorado" 1946 (Mitch); "Lightning Raiders" 1946 (Hayden); "Roll on, Texas Moon" 1946 (Joe Cummings); "Terrors on Horseback" 1946 (Jim Austin); "On the Old Spanish Trail" 1947 (Al); "Prairie Express" 1947; "Riders of the Lone Star" 1947; "Trailing Danger" 1947; "Under Colorado Skies" 1947 (Clip); "Valley of Fear" 1947; "The Adventures of Frank and Jesse James" 1948-serial (Frank James/Bob Carroll); "Carson City Raiders" 1948 (Tom Drew); "Mark of the Lash" 1948; "Night Time in Nevada" 1948 (1st Tramp); "Overland Trails" 1948; "Partners of the Sunset" 1948; "Son of God's Country" 1948 (Bigelow); "The Timber Trail" 1948 (Sheriff); "West of Sonora" 1948 (Black Murphy); "The Blazing Trail" 1949 (Sam Brady); "Challenge of the Range" 1949 (Cal Matson); "Crashing Thru" 1949; "El Dorado Pass" 1949 (Page); "Ghost of Zorro" 1949-serial (Marshal Ben Simpson); "Outcasts of the Trail" 1949 (Sheriff Wilson); "Riders in the Sky" 1949 (Ralph Lawson); "The Arizona Cowboy" 1950 (Sheriff Mason); "The Blazing Sun" 1950 (Sheriff Phillips); "Cow Town" 1950 (Chet

Hilliard); "Frontier Outpost" 1950 (Forsythe); "Under Mexicali Stars" 1950 (Sheriff Meadows); "Winchester '73" 1950 (Masterson); "Along the Great Divide" 1951 (Prosecutor); "Pecos River" 1951 (Whip Rockland); "Rough Riders of Durango" 1951 (John Blake); "Junction City" 1952 (Black Murphy); "Thunder Over the Plains" 1953 (McAvoy); "The Law vs. Billy the Kid" 1954 (Tom Watkins); "The Tall Men" 1955 (Colonel); "Treasure of Ruby Hills" 1955 (Hull); "The Proud Ones" 1956 (Trail Boss); "Red Sundown" 1956 (Bert Flynn); "Joe Dakota" 1957 (Sam Cook); "Utah Blaine" 1957 (Lud Fuller); "Three Thousand Hills" 1959 (McLean). ¶TV: *The Gene Autry Show*—"Gold Dust Charlie" 7-30-50, "The Doodle Bug" 8-13-50; *The Range Rider*—"Buckskin" 9-27-52; *The Lone Ranger*—"Hidden Fortune" 6-18-53; *My Friend Flicka*—"The Golden Promise" 1-6-56; *Cheyenne*—"Rendezvous at Red Rock" 2-21-56 (Grayson), "Town of Fear" 12-3-57 (Jed Curtis), "Renegades" 2-11-58 (Little Elk); *Zane Grey Theater*—"Until the Man Dies" 1-25-57 (Jess Kipple), "The Tall Shadow" 11-20-58 (Dan Hardaway); *Broken Arrow*—"The Bounty Hunters" 11-26-57 (Don Diego), "Escape" 2-18-58 (Ottola); *Colt .45*—"The Gypsies" 12-27-57 (Marshal Terry Wilson); *26 Men*—"Dead or Alive" 3-17-59; *Wanted—Dead or Alive*—"The Conquerors" 5-2-59, "Bad Gun" 10-24-59 (Simmons), "Vanishing Act" 12-26-59 (Sheriff Toole); *Wyatt Earp*—"Arizona Comes to Dodge" 5-26-59 (Old Man Clanton); *The Rifleman*—"Obituary" 10-20-59, "Dead Cold Cash" 11-22-60 (Eli Benson); *Lawman*—"The Last Man" 11-1-59 (Chief Torn Cloud); *Laramie*—"Ride or Die" 3-8-60 (Sheriff), "The Tumbleweed Wagon" 5-9-61 (Joe Warner); *Bat Masterson*—"Wanted—Alive Please" 5-26-60 (Alec Hudson); *Wagon Train*—"The Shad Bennington Story" 6-22-60 (Robertson), "The Jose Morales Story" 10-19-60 (Dr. Stern), "The Malachi Hobart Story" 1-24-62 (Roy Standish); *The Tall Man*—"Larceny and Young Ladies" 11-12-60 (Hank Sims); *The Deputy*—"The Lesson" 1-14-61 (Jenkins); *Tales of Wells Fargo*—"The Dodger" 10-7-61 (Sheriff), "Trackback" 12-30-61 (Sheriff), "Return to Yesterday" 1-13-62 (Sheriff), "Assignment in Gloribee" 1-27-62 (Sheriff), "End of a Minor God" 4-7-62 (Sheriff); *Gunsmoke*—"The Storm" 9-25-65 (Judge); *The Loner*—"Pick Me Another Time to Die" 2-

26-66 (Sheriff Walter Cantrell); *Daniel Boone*—"The Fallow Land" 4-13-67 (Nefromo).

Darren, James (1936-). Films: "Gunman's Walk" 1958 (Davy Hackett). ¶TV: *Time Tunnel*—Regular 1966-67 (Tony Newman).

Darrin, Diana (1933-). Films: "Blood Arrow" 1958 (Lennie); "The Broken Land" 1962 (Waitress). ¶TV: *Tales of the Texas Rangers*—"Riders of the Lone Star" 12-1-57 (Sandra Clark); *The Law of the Plainsman*—"Trojan Horse" 5-5-60; *Bonanza*—"The Wooing of Abigail Jones" 3-4-62 (Margie).

Darro, Frankie (1918-12/25/76). Films: "The Cowboy Musketeer" 1925 (Billy); "Let's Go Gallagher" 1925 (Little Joey); "The Wyoming Wildcat" 1925 (Barney Finn); "The Arizona Streak" 1926 (Mike); "Born to Battle" 1926 (Birdie); "The Cowboy Cop" 1926 (Frankie); "The Masquerade Bandit" 1926 (Tim Marble); "Out of the West" 1926 (Frankie); "Red Hot Hoofs" 1926 (Frankie Buckley); "Tom and His Pals" 1926 (Frankie Smith); "Wild to Go" 1926 (Frankie Blake); "Cyclone of the Range" 1927 (Frankie Butler); "The Desert Pirate" 1927 (Jimmy Rand); "The Flying U Ranch" 1927 (Chip, Jr.); "Lightning Lariats" 1927 (Alexis, King of Roxenburg); "Tom's Gang" 1927 (Spuds); "Phantom of the Range" 1928 (Spuds O'Brien); "Terror Mountain" 1928 (Buddy Roberts); "The Texas Tornado" 1928 (Bud Martin); "Tyrant of Red Gulch" 1928 (Tip); "When the Law Rides" 1928 (Frankie Ross); "Gun Law" 1929 (Buster Brown); "Idaho Red" 1929 (Tadpole); "The Pride of Pawnee" 1929 (Jerry Wilson); "The Trail of the Horse Thieves" 1929 (Buddy); "Lightning Warrior" 1931-serial (Jimmy Carter); "The Vanishing Legion" 1931-serial (Jimmie Williams); "The Cheyenne Cyclone" 1932; "The Devil Horse" 1932-serial (the Wild Boy); "The Phantom Empire" 1935-serial (Frankie); "Valley of Wanted Men" 1935 (Slivvers Sanderson); "The Great Adventures of Wild Bill Hickok" 1938 (Jerry); "Sons of New Mexico" 1949 (Gig Jackson); "Wyoming Mail" 1950 (Rufe); "Across the Wide Missouri" 1951 (Cadet); "Westward the Women" 1951; "The Lawless Rider" 1954 (Jim Bascom). ¶TV: *Wild Bill Hickok*—"The Slocum Family" 12-4-51; *Judge Roy Bean*—"The Cross-Draw Kid" 7-1-56 (Hugh Lonagan), "The Refugee" 7-1-56 (Cass); *Bat Masterson*—"Garrison Finish" 12-10-59 (Snapper Garrison).

Darrow, Henry (1933-). Films: "Maverick" 1994 (Riverboat Poker Player). ¶TV: *Iron Horse*—"Cougar Man" 10-24-66 (Cougar Man); *Gunsmoke*—"The Hanging" 12-31-66 (Oro), "Ladies from St. Louis" 3-25-67 (Ross Sigurra); *Wild Wild West*—"The Night of the Tottering Tontine" 1-6-67 (Maurice); *Bonanza*—"Amigo" 2-12-67 (Amigo); *Daniel Boone*—"Take the Southbound Stage" 4-6-67 (Gideon); *The High Chaparral*—Regular 1967-71 (Manolito); *Bearcats!*—12-23-71 (Raoul Esteban); *Kung Fu*—"The Brujo" 10-25-73 (Don Fierro); *Sara*—3-19-76 (Angelo); *Centennial*—Regular 1978-79 (Alvarez); *Born to the Wind* 1982 (Lost Robe); *Zorro and Son*—Regular 1983 (Don Diego de la Vega/Zorro).

Darrow, John (1907-2/24/80). Films: "Avalanche" 1928 (Verde); "Square Shooter" 1935 (Johnny Lloyd).

Darry-Cowl. Films: "Magnificent Brutes of the West" 1965-Ital./Span./Fr. (Jackson); "Don't Touch White Women!" 1974-Ital. (Archibald).

Darvas, Lili (1902-7/22/74). Films: "Cimarron" 1960 (Felicia Venable).

Darvi, Andrea. TV: *Bonanza*—"The Deserter" 10-21-62; *Death Valley Days*—"Kingdom for a Horse" 12-1-63 (Becky); *Gunsmoke*—"Owney Tupper Had a Daughter" 4-4-64 (Amity Tupper).

Darwell, Jane (1880-8/13/67). Films: "Rose of the Rancho" 1914 (Senora Castro-Kenton); "Fighting Caravans" 1931 (Pioneer Woman); "Ramona" 1936 (Aunt Ri Hyar); "White Fang" 1936 (Maud Mahoney); "Jesse James" 1939 (Mrs. Samuels); "Brigham Young—Frontiersman" 1940 (Eliza Kent); "Men of Texas" 1942 (Mrs. Scott); "The Ox-Bow Incident" 1943 (Ma Grier); "My Darling Clementine" 1946 (Kate); "The Red Stallion" 1947 (Mrs. Curtis); "The Three Godfathers" 1948 (Miss Florie); "Red Canyon" 1949 (Aunt Jane); "Redwood Forest Trail" 1950 (Hattie Hickory); "Surrender" 1950 (Mrs. Hale); "Wagonmaster" 1950 (Sister Ledeyard). ¶TV: *The Adventures of Rin Tin Tin*—"Rin Tin Tin Meet's O'Hara's Mother" 2-17-56 (O'Hara's Mother); *My Friend Flicka*—"Mister Goblin" 3-23-56; *Circus Boy*—"Big Top Angel" 1-27-57 (Mamie LaRue); *Maverick*—"Black Fire" 3-16-58 (Mrs. Knowles); *Buckskin*—"Mr. Rush's Secretary" 1-19-59 (Mrs. Hale); *Wagon Train*—"The Vivian Carter Story" 3-11-59, "The

Andrew Hale Story" 6-3-59 (Mrs. Anderson), "The Artie Matthewson Story" 11-8-61 (Angie Matthewson).

Das Bolas, Xan. Films: "Gunmen of the Rio Grande" 1964-Fr./Ital./Span.; "Jaguar" 1964-Span.; "Clint the Stranger" 1968-Ital./Span./Ger.

da Silva, Howard (1909-2/16/86). Films: "Bad Men of Missouri" 1941 (Greg Bilson); "The Omaha Trail" 1942 (Ben Santley); "Wild Bill Hickok Rides" 1942 (Ringo); "Unconquered" 1947 (Martin Garth); "Wyoming Mail" 1950 (Cavanaugh); "The Outrage" 1964 (Prospector); "Nevada Smith" 1966 (Warden). ¶TV: *The Loner*—"To Hang a Dead Man" 3-12-66 (Merrick); *Kung Fu*—"The Hoots" 12-13-73 (Otto Schultz).

Daugherty, Jack (1895-5/16/38). Films: "Forgettin' the Law" 1923; "Lonesome Luck" 1923; "True Gold" 1923; "The Lone Round-Up" 1924; "The Fighting Ranger" 1925-serial; "The Meddler" 1925 (Jesse Danfield); "Arizona Bound" 1927 (Buck Hanna); "Gypsy of the North" 1928 (Chappie Evans); "The Vanishing West" 1928-serial.

Daughton, James (1950-). Films: "The Revengers" 1972-U.S./Mex. (Morgan).

Davalos, Ellen. TV: *Gunsmoke*—"The Jackals" 2-12-68 (Wife); *Bonanza*—"The Deserter" 3-16-69 (Nanata).

Davalos, Elyssa. Films: "Wild and Wooly" TVM-1978 (Shiloh); "The Apple Dumpling Gang Rides Again" 1979 (Millie). ¶TV: *How the West Was Won*—Episode One 2-12-78 (Hillary Gant), Episode Two 2-19-78 (Hillary Gant), Episode Three 2-26-78 (Hillary Gant), "Hillary" 2-26-79 (Hillary Gant).

Davalos, Richard (1930-). Films: "Death Hunt" 1981 (Beeler). ¶TV: *Bonanza*—"The Trail Gang" 11-26-60 (Johnny Logan); *Laramie*—"The Last Journey" 10-31-61 (Danny Hode); *How the West Was Won*—"The Slavers" 4-23-79 (Captain Olini).

Davenport, Alice (1853-6/24/36). Films: "The Love Trail" 1912; "Wild West Love" 1914; "Little Red Decides" 1918 (Widow Bolton); "The Dude Wrangler" 1930 (Dude Guest).

Davenport, Blanche (-10/17/21). Films: "The Crimson Dove" 1917 (Mrs. Lundy).

Davenport, Doris (1915-6/18/80). Films: "The Westerner" 1940 (Jane-Ellen Mathews).

Davenport, Dorothy (Mrs. Wallace Reid) (1896-10/12/77). Films: "A Mohawk's Way" 1910; "Her Indian Hero" 1912; "A Hopi Legend" 1913; "Pierre of the North" 1913; "A Yoke of Gold" 1916 (Carmen); "The Squaw Man's Song" 1917 (Lady Effington); "The Masked Avenger" 1922 (Valerie Putnam).

Davenport, Harry (1866-8/9/49). Films: "Wells Fargo" 1937 (Ingalls, the Banker); "Cowboy and the Lady" 1938 (Uncle Hannibal Smith); "Gold Is Where You Find It" 1938 (Dr. Parsons); "Hurricane Smith" 1942 (Robert Ingersoll Reed); "The Ox-Bow Incident" 1943 (Harry Davies); "The Fabulous Texan" 1947 (Reverend Barker); "The Man from Texas" 1947 (Pop Hickey).

Davenport, Havis (1933-7/23/75). TV: *Jim Bowie*—"Natchez Trace" 10-19-56 (Lucy Anne Pope).

Davenport, Milla (1871-5/17/36). Films: "In Mizzoura" 1919 (Mrs. Vernon); "Wild West" 1925-serial; "The Man Who Waited" 1922 (Madre Sanchez); "Hey! Hey! Cowboy" 1927 (Aunt Jane); "The Danger Rider" 1928 (Housekeeper).

Davenport, Ned. Films: "The Lawless Breed" 1952 (Blunt); "Montana Belle" 1952 (Bank Clerk).

Davenport, Nigel (1928-). Films: "Charley One-Eye" 1973-Brit. (Bounty Hunter).

Davi, Jana. Films: "Fort Bowie" 1958 (Chenzana); "Gun Fever" 1958 (Tanan); "The Rawhide Trail" 1958 (Keetah); "Gunmen from Laredo" 1959 (Rosita).

Davi, Robert (1953-). Films: "The Legend of the Golden Gun" TVM-1979 (William Quantrill).

David, Brad. TV: *Gunsmoke*—"The Judas Gun" 1-19-70 (Teddy).

David, Clifford (1932-). Films: "Invitation to a Gunfighter" 1964 (Crane Adams). ¶TV: *The Big Valley*—"Point and Counterpoint" 5-19-69 (Ritch Stokely); *Nichols*—"Ketcham Power" 11-11-71 (Billings).

David, Keith. Films: "The Quick and the Dead" 1995 (Sgt. Cantrell).

David, Thayer (1927-7/17/78). Films: "Little Big Man" 1971 (Rev. Silas Pendrake); "Hearts of the West" 1975 (Bank Manager); "The Duchess and the Dirtwater Fox" 1976 (Widdicombe). ¶TV: *Wild Wild West*—"The Night of the Samurai" 10-13-67 (Hannibal Egloff), "The Night of the Spanish Curse" 1-3-69 (Cortez).

Davidson, Clifford. Films: "Ace of Cactus Range" 1924 (Bull Davidson); "Code of the Wilderness" 1924 (Jim Picket); "A Two-Fisted Sheriff" 1925 (Stranger).

Davidson, James (1942-). Films: "A Time for Killing" 1967 (Little Jo). ¶TV: *Wagon Train*—"The Bonnie Brooke Story" 2-21-65 (Don Brooke); *Bonanza*—"Five Sundowns to Sunup" 12-5-65 (Carver Lassiter), "Black Friday" 1-22-67 (Cole Berry), "The Stronghold" 5-26-68 (Due O'Brien); *Cimarron Strip*—"Without Honor" 2-29-68; *Daniel Boone*—"Be Thankful for the Fickleness of Women" 9-19-68 (Bart Cooley); *The Outcasts*—"And Then There Was One" 3-3-69 (Kid Kiem); *Here Come the Brides*—"Candy and the Kid" 2-13-70 (Holiday).

Davidson, John (1886-1/15/68). Films: "King of the Royal Mounted" 1940-serial (Dr. Sheton).

Davidson, John (1941-). TV: *Daniel Boone*—"A Touch of Charity" 2-27-69 (Jimmy McGill), "Perilous Passage" 1-15-70 (Sam Weaver).

Davidson, Lawford. Films: "The Golden Strain" 1925 (Major Gaynes); "Tony Runs Wild" 1926 (Slade); "Blood Will Tell" 1928 (Jim Cowen); "Daredevil's Reward" 1928 (Foster); "The Overland Telegraph" 1929 (Briggs).

Davidson, Max (1875-9/4/50). Films: "Daring Danger" 1932 (Toby); "Roamin' Wild" 1936 (Alone); "Rogue of the Range" 1936 (Salesman); "Union Pacific" 1939 (Card Player).

Davidson, Wayne. TV: *Wild Bill Hickok*—"Angel of Cedar Mountain" 7-28-53; *Man from Blackhawk*—"Death at Noon" 1-8-60 (Telegrapher).

Davidson, William B. (1888-9/28/47). Films: "A Yellow Streak" 1915 (Jack Rader); "American Maid" 1917 (David Starr); "The Valley of Doubt" 1920 (Macey); "Salome Jane" 1923 (the Gambler); "Hearts and Spurs" 1925 (Victor Dufresne); "The Last Trail" 1927 (Morley); "A Man from Wyoming" 1930 (Major); "The Silver Horde" 1930 (Thomas Hilliard); "Massacre" 1934 (Senator Beale); "Cowboy from Brooklyn" 1938 (Mr. Alvey); "The Texans" 1938 (Mr. Jessup, the Railroad Man); "My Little Chickadee" 1940 (Sheriff); "Lady from Cheyenne" 1941 (Dunbar); "Calaboose" 1943; "Song of Nevada" 1944 (Worthington); "In Old Sacramento" 1946; "My Darling Clementine" 1946 (Oriental Saloon Owner); "Plainsman and the Lady" 1946 (Mr. Russell).

Davies, Howard (1879-12/30/47). Films: "Davy Crockett" 1916 (Oscar Crampton); "The Parson of Panamint" 1916 (Bud Deming); "The Hidden Children" 1917 (Gen. Sullivan); "It's a Bear" 1919 (William Cogney); "The White Man's Courage" 1919 (Hugh Hankins); "The Return of the Riddle Rider" 1927-serial; "The Two Fister" 1927; "A Romeo of the Range" 1928; "The White Outlaw" 1929 (Colonel Holbrook).

Davies, James. Films: "Streets of Laredo" 1949 (Ranger); "The Furies" 1950 (Cowhand); "Pony Express" 1953 (Cassidy); "Gunfight at the O.K. Corral" 1957 (Card Player).

Davies, Marion (1897-9/22/61). Films: "Zander the Great" 1925 (Mamie Smith).

Davies, Richard. Films: "Road Agent" 1941 (Martin).

Davila, Luis (Louis Dawson) (1927-). Films: "Man from Canyon City" 1965-Span./Ital.; "Dynamite Jim" 1966-Span./Ital. (Dynamite Jim); "Man with the Golden Pistol" 1966-Span./Ital. (Slater); "Three from Colorado" 1967-Span.; "Death on High Mountain" 1969-Ital./Span. (Mark Harrison); "Matalo!" 1971-Ital./Span.; "Pancho Villa" 1975-Span.

DaVinci, Elena. Films: "Badlands of Montana" 1957 (1st Girl); "Escape from Red Rock" 1958 (Antonia Chavez); "Lone Texan" 1959 (Woman Passenger).

Davion, Alex (1929-). Films: "Charley One-Eye" 1973-Brit. (Tony). ¶TV: *Death Valley Days*— "The Grand Duke" 11-10-59 (Duke Alexis), "Loophole" 4-5-61 (Mitchell); *Have Gun Will Travel*—"Ransom" 6-4-60 (Edward); *Custer*— "Sabres in the Sun" 9-6-67 (Capt. Marcus Reno).

Davis, Allan (1913-12/11/43). Films: "The Barrier" 1937 (Sgt. Tobin); "Gold Is Where You Find It" 1938 (Clerk).

Davis, Ann B. (1926-). TV: *Wagon Train*—"The Countess Baranof Story" 5-11-60 (Mrs. Foster).

Davis, Art (Larry Mason) (1902-11/16/87). Films: "Sagebrush Troubador" 1935; "Guns and Guitars" 1936; "Rootin' Tootin' Rhythm" 1937; "Springtime in the Rockies" 1937; "The Trigger Trio" 1937; "In Early Arizona" 1938 (Art); "Pioneer Trail" 1938; "The Adventures of the Masked Phantom" 1939 (Tooney); "Code of the Cactus" 1939; "Six-Gun Rhythm" 1939 (Mike); "The Texas Marshal" 1941; "Along the Sundown Trail" 1942; "Prairie Pals" 1942 (Art); "Raiders of the West" 1942; "Rolling Down the Great Divide" 1942 (Art Davis); "Texas Man Hunt" 1942 (Art Davis).

Davis, Bette (1908-10/16/89). TV: *Wagon Train*—"The Ella Lindstrom Story" 2-4-59 (Ella Lindstrom), "The Elizabeth McQueeney Story" 10-28-59 (Elizabeth McQueeney), "The Bettina May Story" 12-20-61 (Bettina May); *The Virginian*—"The Accomplice" 12-19-62 (Delia Miller); *Gunsmoke*—"The Jailor" 10-1-66 (Etta Stone).

Davis, Bob (1910-9/22/71). TV: *Cimarron Strip*—"Nobody" 12-7-67.

Davis, Boyd (1885-1/25/63). Films: "Ride 'Em, Cowboy" 1942 (Doctor); "Born to the Saddle" 1953.

Davis, Brent. TV: *Wild Wild West*—"The Night of the Kraken" 11-1-68 (Lt. Dave Bartlett).

Davis, Charles. TV: *Death Valley Days*—"The Man Everyone Hated" 4-12-60 (Alf); *Have Gun Will Travel*—"The Campaign of Billy Banjo" 5-28-60 (Jansen); *Rawhide*—"Incident in the Garden of Eden" 6-17-60 (Higgins); *Maverick*—"Diamond Flush" 2-5-61 (Hotel Clerk); *Wild Wild West*—"The Night of the Casual Killer" 10-15-65 (Tennyson), "The Night of the Double-Edged Knife" 11-12-65 (Tennyson), "The Night of the Fatal Trap" 12-24-65 (Tennyson); *Alias Smith and Jones*—"The Man Who Murdered Himself" 3-18-71 (Kevin Finney).

Davis, Chet. Films: "Django and Sartana Are Coming ... It's the End" 1970-Ital. (Django); "Stranger That Kneels Beside the Shadow of a Corpse" 1971-Ital. (Blonde); "Death Played the Flute" 1972-Ital./Span.

Davis, Chick. Films: "Cyclone of the Saddle" 1935 (High Hawk); "Custer's Last Stand" 1936-serial (Rain-in-the-Face); "Starlight Over Texas" 1938.

Davis, Dix. Films: "The Singing Cowgirl" 1939 (Billy Harkins).

Davis, Don S. Films: "The Gambler Returns: The Luck of the Draw" TVM-1991 (Rodeo Announcer); "Black Fox" TVM-1995.

Davis, Edwards (1871-5/16/36). Films: "Hook and Ladder" 1924 (Big Tom O'Rourke); "The Splendid Road" 1925 (Banker John Grey).

Davis, Elaine. TV: *Death Valley Days*—"Yankee Confederate" 10-26-60 (Belle); *Tales of Wells Fargo*—"The Border Renegade" 1-2-61 (Carolyn Robbins).

Davis, Gail (1925-). Films: "Brand of Fear" 1949; "Death Valley Gunfighter" 1949 (Trudy Clark); "The Far Frontier" 1949 (Susan Hathaway); "Frontier Marshal" 1949 (Janet Adams); "Law of the Golden West" 1949 (Ann Calvert); "Sons of New Mexico" 1949 (Eileen MacDonald); "South of Death Valley" 1949 (Molly Tavish); "Cow Town" 1950 (Ginger Kirby); "Indian Territory" 1950 (Melody Colton); "Six Gun Mesa" 1950; "Trail of the Rustlers" 1950; "West of Wyoming" 1950 (Jennifer); "Overland Telegraph" 1951 (Terry); "Silver Canyon" 1951 (Dell Middler); "Texans Never Cry" 1951 (Nancy Carter); "Valley of Fire" 1951 (Laurie); "Whirlwind" 1951 (Elaine Lassiter); "Yukon Manhunt" 1951; "Blue Canadian Rockies" 1952 (Sandy Higbee); "The Old West" 1952 (Arlie Williams); "Wagon Team" 1952 (Connie Weldon); "Goldtown Ghost Raiders" 1953 (Cathy Wheeler); "On Top of Old Smoky" 1953 (Jen Larrabee); "Pack Train" 1953 (Jennifer Coleman); "Winning of the West" 1953 (Ann Randolph); "Alias Jesse James" 1959 (Annie Oakley). ¶TV: *The Lone Ranger*—"Buried Treasure" 3-2-50, "Spanish Gold" 6-1-50; *The Gene Autry Show*—"Blackwater Valley Feud" 9-3-50, "Doublecross Valley" 9-10-50, "The Devil's Brand" 9-24-50, "Gun Powder Range" 10-29-50, "Fight at Peaceful Mesa" 11-19-50, "Frame for Trouble" 11-3-51, "Revenge Trail" 11-17-51, "Outlaw Escape" 12-1-51, "Galloping Hoofs" 12-22-51, "Heir to the Lazy L" 12-29-51, "Melody Mesa" 1-4-52, "Horse Sense" 1-11-52, "Steel Ribbon" 9-22-53 (Billie Davis), "Ransom Cross" 10-6-53, "Civil War at Deadwood" 9-14-54; *The Cisco Kid*—"Convict Story" 2-17-51, "The Will" 3-24-51, "False Marriage" 4-14-51, "Wedding Blackmail" 4-21-51, "Talking Dog" 2-23-52, "Big Steal" 4-12-52; *The Range Rider*—"Outlaw's Double" 9-23-51, "Greed Rides the Range" 5-31-52; *Death Valley Days*—"Land of the Free" 2-11-53; *Annie Oakley*—Regular 1954-57 (Annie Oakley).

Davis, George (1889-4/19/65). Films: "The Wagon Show" 1928 (Hank); "Men of the North" 1930 (Cpl. Smith). ¶TV: *The Cisco Kid*—"Medicine Man Story" 8-25-51, "Black Lightning" 10-6-51; *Wyatt Earp*—"Old Jake" 4-9-57 (Sgt. McCafferty).

Davis, Hal (1910-1/4/60). Films: "The Bandit's Son" 1927 (Matt Bolton).

Davis, Harry (1911-). Films: "Waterhole No. 3" 1967 (Ben Agajanian); "A Man Called Gannon" 1969 (Harry). ¶TV: *Gunsmoke*—"The Pretender" 11-20-65 (Daniels), "The Gold Mine" 1-27-69 (Shorty).

Davis, J. Gunnis (1874-3/23/37). Films: "The Lucky Horseshoe" 1925 (Valet to Denman); "Headin' North" 1930 (Smith).

Davis, Jack. Films: "The Sea of Grass" 1947 (Foreman); "Silver River" 1948 (Judge Advocate).

Davis, Jeff (1884-4/5/68). TV: *Have Gun Will Travel*—"Cream of the Jest" 5-5-62 (Blessington).

Davis, Jim (1915-4/26/81). Films: "The Fabulous Texan" 1947 (Sam Bass); "Brimstone" 1949 (Mick Courteen); "Hellfire" 1949 (Gyp Stoner); "Red Stallion in the Rockies" 1949 (Dave Ryder); "California Passage" 1950 (Linc Corey); "The Cariboo Trail" 1950 (Miller); "The Savage Horde" 1950 (Lt. Mike Baker); "The Showdown" 1950 (Cochran); "Cavalry Scout" 1951 (Lt. Spaulding); "Little Big Horn" 1951 (Cpl. Doan Moylan); "Oh! Susanna" 1951 (Ira Jordan); "Silver Canyon" 1951 (Wade McQuarrie); "Three Desperate Men" 1951 (Fred Denton); "The Big Sky" 1952 (Streak); "Ride the Man Down" 1952 (Red Courteen); "Rose of Cimarron" 1952 (Willie Whitewater); "Woman of the North Country" 1952 (Steve Powell); "The Woman They Almost Lynched" 1953 (Cole Younger); "Hell's Outpost" 1954 (Sam Horne); "Jubilee Trail" 1954 (Silky); "The Outcast" 1954 (Maj. Cosgrave); "The Outlaw's Daughter" 1954 (Dan); "The Last Command" 1955 (Evans); "Last of the Desperadoes" 1955 (John W. Poe); "Timberjack" 1955 (Poole); "The Vanishing American" 1955 (Glendon); "Frontier Gambler" 1956; "The Maverick Queen" 1956 (Stranger); "The Wild Dakotas" 1956; "Apache Warrior" 1957 (Ben); "The Badge of Marshal Brennan" 1957 (Jeff Harlan, the Stranger); "Duel at Apache Wells" 1957 (Dean Cannary); "The Last Stagecoach West" 1957 (Bill Cameron); "The Quiet Gun" 1957 (Ralph, the Rancher); "Raiders of Old California" 1957; "The Restless Breed" 1957 (Rev. Simmons); "Flaming Frontier" 1958-Can. (Col. Hugh Carver); "Toughest Gun in Tombstone" 1958 (Johnny Ringo); "Wolf Dog" 1958-Can. (Jim Hughes); "Alias Jesse James" 1959 (Frank James); "Noose for a Gunman" 1960 (Case Britton); "Frontier Uprising" 1961 (Jim Stockton); "The Gambler Wore a Gun" 1961 (Case Silverthorn); "Jesse James Meets Frankenstein's Daughter" 1966 (Marshal McFee); "El Dorado" 1967 (Jason's Foreman); "Fort Utah" 1967 (Scarecrow); "Five Blood Graves" 1969 (Clay Bates); "Monte Walsh" 1970 (Cal Brennan); "Rio Lobo" 1970 (Riley); "Big Jake" 1971 (Lynching Party Leader); "The Trackers" TVM-1971 (Sheriff Naylor); "Bad Company" 1972 (Marshal); "The Honkers" 1972 (Mel Potter); "One Little Indian" 1973; "Law of the Land" TVM-1976 (Sheriff Pat Lambrose); "Comes a Horseman" 1978 (Julie Blocker). ¶TV: *Stories of the Century*—Regular 1955 (Matt Clark); *Cavalcade Theatre*—"The Texas Rangers" 9-27-55 (J.L. Armstrong); *DuPont Theater*—"The Texas Ranger" 4-9-57 (Jim Armstrong); *Tales of Wells Fargo*—"Two Cartridges" 9-16-57 (Al Porter), "The Lobo" 5-8-61 (Sam Horne), "Don't Wake a Tiger" 5-12-62 (Jonus Sawyer); *26 Men*—"The Bells of St. Thomas" 5-13-58; *Yancy Derringer*—"Two Tickets to Promontory" 6-4-59 (Bullet Pike); *Laramie*—"Trail Drive" 1-12-60 (Hake Ballard), "Shadow of the Past" 10-16-62 (Ben McKittrick), "The Dispossessed" 2-19-63, "Trapped" 5-14-63 (Genoway); *The Tall Man*—"Forty-Dollar Boots" 9-17-60 (Bob Orringer), "The Lonely Star" 10-8-60 (Bob Orringer); *Wagon Train*—"The Candy O'Hara Story" 12-7-60 (Gabe Henry), "The Eve Newhope Story" 12-5-62 (Dan Ryan), "The Melanie Craig Story" 2-17-64 (Rudd); *Bonanza*—"The Gift" 4-1-61 (Sam Wolfe), "Lothario Larkin" 4-25-65 (Johnny), "The Arrival of Eddie" 5-19-68 (Sam Butler); *The Outlaws*—"The Brothers" 5-11-61 (Steed); *Gunsmoke*—"The Imposter" 5-13-61 (Rob Curtin), "The Raid" 1-22-66 & 1-29-66 (Clell Williams), "Treasure of John Walking Fox" 4-16-66 (Gainer), "The Mission" 10-8-66 (Jim Basset), "The Gunrunners" 2-5-68 (Jubal Gray), "Zavala" 10-7-68 (Ben Rawlins), "Railroad" 11-25-68 (Wes Cameron), "McCabe" 11-30-70 (Sheriff Shackwood), "Murdoch" 2-8-71 (Amos Carver), "Jessie" 2-19-73 (Dave Carpenter), "The Town Tamers" 1-28-74 (Luke Rumbaugh); *Gunslinger*—"The New Savannah Story" 5-18-61 (Jeb Crane); *Rawhide*—"The Greedy Town" 2-16-62 (Sam Jason), "The Pursuit" 11-9-65 (Sheriff); *Stoney Burke*—"Cousin Eunice" 12-24-62 (Shep Winters); *Have Gun Will Travel*—"The Treasure" 12-29-62 (Long); *Death Valley Days*—"Loss of Faith" 1-2-63 (Joe Phy), "Three Minutes to Eternity" 1-26-64 (Grat Dalton), "After the O.K. Corral" 5-2-64 (Wyatt Earp), "Big John and the Rainmaker" 12-6-64 (Big John), "Brute Angel" 10-15-66 (Pony Cragin), "The Man Who Wouldn't Die" 4-29-67 (Luke), "By the Book" 5-4-68 (Manly); *Branded*—"One Way Out" 4-18-65 (Malachi Murdock), "Salute the Soldier Briefly" 10-24-65 (Wheeler). "The Assassins" 3-27-66 & 4-3-66 (Swaney); *Laredo*—"The Golden Trail" 11-4-65 (Sheriff Wess Cottrell); *Time Tunnel*—"The Alamo" 12-9-66 (Col. Bowie); *Daniel Boone*—"River Passage" 12-15-66 (Carpenter), "The Ordeal of Israel Boone" 9-21-67 (Sam Ralston), "A Pinch of Salt" 5-1-69, "The Road to Freedom" 10-2-69 (Rafe Carson); *Hondo*—"Hondo and the War Cry" 9-15-67 (Krantz), "Hondo and the War Hawks" 10-20-67 (Krantz); *Cimarron Strip*—"The Search" 11-9-67 (Clo Vardeman); *The Guns of Will Sonnett*—"The Warriors" 3-1-68 (Sheriff Hawks); *The Virginian*—"The Heritage" 10-30-68 (Mc Kinley); *The High Chaparral*—"New Hostess in Town" 3-20-70 (Robbins); *The Men from Shiloh*—"The Politician" 1-13-71 (Roper); *Kung Fu*—"The Soul Is the Warrior" 2-8-73 (Walker), "The Well" 9-27-73 (Sheriff Grogan); *The Cowboys*—Regular 1974 (Marshal Bill Winter); *The Quest*—"Prairie Woman" 11-10-76 (Marshal Pullman).

Davis, Jimmy (and His Rainbow Ramblers). Films: "Riding Through Nevada" 1942; "Frontier Fury" 1943; "Cyclone Prairie Rangers" 1944.

Davis, Johnnie. Films: "Cowboy from Brooklyn" 1938 (Jeff Hardy).

Davis, Karl (1906-5/30/79). Films: "The Road to Denver" 1955 (Hunsaker); "Timberjack" 1955 (Red Bush); "Apache Warrior" 1957 (Bounty Man); "Man or Gun" 1958 (Swede). ¶TV: *The Cisco Kid*—"Robber Crow" 11-24-51, "Spanish Dagger" 1-5-52; *Wild Bill Hickok*—"Wrestling Story" 4-8-52; *Bronco*—"The Silent Witness" 3-10-59 (Marcus Traxel); *Lawman*—"The Gang" 3-29-59 (Hayes).

Davis, Lindy. TV: *The Loner*—"The House Rules at Mrs. Wayne's" 11-6-65 (Jamie Wayne); *Daniel Boone*—"The Printing Press" 10-23-69.

Davis, Lisa. Films: "The Dalton Girls" 1957 (Rose Dalton). ¶TV: *Northwest Passage*—"The Gunsmith" 9-28-58 (Elizabeth Browne).

Davis, Margaret. Films: "Honeymoon Ranch" 1920 (Ruth Lawhorn); "The Throwback" 1935 (Muriel as a Girl).

Davis, Marguerite. Films: "West of the Rio Grande" 1921 (Wanda).

Davis, Michael (1936-). Films: "Ballad of a Gunfighter" 1964 (Miguelito). ¶TV: *Zane Grey Theater*—"The Last Raid" 2-26-59 (Panchito); *Lawman*—"Fugitive" 4-2-61 (Joey Cormack); *Rawhide*—"Incident at Rio Salado" 9-29-61, "Incident of the Hostages" 4-19-63; *Empire*—"Arrow in the Sky" 4-9-63 (Bobby); *Bonanza*—"Little Man—Ten Feet Tall" 5-26-63 (Mario Biancci); *Redigo*—"Boy from Rio Bravo" 10-8-63 (Carlos); *Gunsmoke*—"South Wind" 11-27-65 (Coy Print); *The Big Valley*—"Legend of a General" 9-19-66 & 9-26-66 (Pepe).

Davis, Mildred ((1900-8/18/69). Films: "Fighting Mad" 1917 (Lily Sawyer).

Davis, Morgan (1890-9/2/41). Films: "The Cowboy and the Flapper" 1924 (Deputy Jack Harrison); "On the Go" 1925 (Sheriff); "Border Blackbirds" 1927; "Don Desperado" 1927 (Joe Jessup).

Davis, Nancy (Nancy Reagan) (1921-). TV: *Zane Grey Theater*—"The Long Shadow" 1-19-61 (Amy Lawson); *The Tall Man*—"Shadow of the Past" 10-7-61 (Sarah Wiley); *Wagon Train*—"The Sam Darland Story" 12-26-62 (Mrs. Baxter).

Davis, Neil. Films: "The McMasters" 1970 (Sylvester).

Davis, Nita. Films: "The Awakening" 1915; "A Life at Stake" 1915; "Under Azure Skies" 1915; "Curlew Corliss" 1916.

Davis, Ossie (1921-). Films: "The Scalphunters" 1968 (Joseph Winfield Lee); "Sam Whiskey" 1969 (Jedidiah Hooker). ¶TV: *Bonanza*—"The Wish" 3-9-69 (Sam Davis).

Davis, Jr., Owen (1907-5/21/49). Films: "The Luck of Roaring Camp" 1937 (Davy); "Henry Goes Arizona" 1939 (Danny Regan).

Davis, Phyllis (1940-). Films: "The Wild Women of Chastity Gulch" TVM-1982 (Sugar Harris). TV: *Wild Wild West*—"The Night of the Grand Emir" 1-28-66 (2nd Girl), "The Night of the Assassin" 9-22-67 (Lt. Ramirez).

Davis, Robert O. (1910-9/22/71). Films: "King of the Texas Rangers" 1941-serial (His Excellency); "The Phantom Plainsmen" 1942 (Col. Eric Hartwig); "Riders of the Northland" 1942 (Nazi Agent).

Davis, Roger (1939-). Films: "The Young Country" TVM-1970 (Stephen Foster Moody); "This Was the West That Was" TVM-1974 (Narrator) ¶TV: *Redigo*—Regular 1963 (Mike); *Bonanza*—"Ballad of the Ponderosa" 11-13-66 (Harold Stanley), "Top Hand" 1-17-71 (Bert Yates); *The Big Valley*—"The Haunted Gun" 2-6-67 (Walt Tompkins); *Alias Smith and Jones*—"Smiler with a Gun" 10-7-71 (Danny Bilson), Regular 1972-73 (Hannibal Heyes/Joshua Smith).

Davis, Rufe (1908-12/13/74). Films: "Lone Star Raiders" 1940 (Lullaby Joslin); "The Trail Blazers" 1940 (Lullaby Joslin); "Under Texas Skies" 1940 (Lullaby Joslin); "Gangs of Sonora" 1941 (Lullaby Joslin); "Gauchos of El Dorado" 1941 (Lullaby Joslin); "Outlaws of the Cherokee Trail" 1941 (Lullaby Joslin); "Pals of the Pecos" 1941 (Lullaby Joslin); "Prairie Pioneers" 1941 (Lullaby Joslin); "Saddlemates" 1941 (Lullaby Joslin); "West of Cimarron" 1941; "West of the Rockies" 1941-short; "Code of the Outlaw" 1942; "The Phantom Plainsmen" 1942 (Lullaby Joslin); "Raiders of the Range" 1942 (Lullaby Joslin); "Westward Ho" 1942 (Lullaby Joslin); "The Strawberry Roan" 1948 (Chuck). ¶TV: *The Lone Ranger*—"Pete and Pedro" 10-27-49.

Davis, Jr., Sammy (1925-5/16/90). Films: "Sergents 3" 1962 (Jonah Williams); "The Trackers" TVM-1971 (Zeke Smith). ¶TV: *Zane Grey Theater*—"Mission" 11-12-59 (Corporal Smith); *Lawman*—"Blue Boss and Willie Shay" 3-12-61 (Willie Shay); *Frontier Circus*—"Coals of Fire" 1-4-62 (Cata); *The Rifleman*—"Two Ounces of Tin" 2-19-62 (Tip Corey), "The Most Amazing Man" 11-26-62 (Wade Randall); *Wild Wild West*—"The Night of the Flying Pie Plate" 10-21-66 (Jeremiah).

Davis, Shirley. Films: "Prince of the Plains" 1949 (Julie Phillipos).

Davis, Tim. Films: "Riders of the Dawn" 1937; "Tex Rides with the Boy Scouts" 1937 (Tommie Kent).

Davis, Tony. Films: "Guns of the Magnificent Seven" 1969 (Emiliano Zapata). ¶TV: *Iron Horse*—"The Red Tornado" 2-20-67 (Red Feather); *Gunsmoke*—"Wonder" 12-18-67 (Wonder), "The Noonday Devil" 12-7-70 (Indian Boy); *Lancer*—"Jelly" 11-19-68, "The Man Without a Gun" 3-25-69; *Daniel Boone*—"Readin', Ritin', and Revolt" 3-12-70 (Little Hawk).

Davis, Vance (1938-). Films: "Cahill, United States Marshal" 1973 (Negro).

Davis, Walt (-1983). Films: "The Cheyenne Social Club" 1970 (Bannister Gang Member); "The Legend of the Golden Gun" TVM-1979 (Soldier). ¶TV: *Alias Smith and Jones*—"The Root of It All" 4-1-71, "Which Way to the O.K. Corral?" 2-10-72, "High Lonesome Country" 9-23-72 (Clyde).

Davis, William "Wee Willie". Films: "Wildfire" 1945 (Moose Harris); "Fool's Gold" 1946 (Blackie); "Son of Paleface" 1952 (Blacksmith). ¶TV: *The Cisco Kid*—"Hidden Valley Pirates" 10-27-51.

Davison, Bruce (1948-). Films: "Ulzana's Raid" 1972 (Lt. Garnett DeBuin). ¶TV: *Hec Ramsey*—"The Mystery of Chalk Hill" 2-18-73 (Josh Hollister).

Davison, Davey. Films: "War Party" 1965 (Sarah). ¶TV: *Rawhide*—"Gold Fever" 5-4-62 (Meg Brewer), "The Violent Land" 3-5-65 (Fanah); *Empire*—"Season of Growth" 2-19-63 (Judy Hollister); *Bonanza*—"Twilight Town" 10-13-63 (Louise Corman), "False Witness" 10-22-67 (Valerie Townsend); *Gunsmoke*—"Run, Sheep, Run" 1-9-65 (Mary Stocker); *The Virginian*—"Letter of the Law" 12-22-65 (Joan Westley).

Daw, Evelyn (1912-11/29/70). Films: "Panamint's Bad Man" 1938 (Joan DeLysa); "Pals of the Silver Sage" 1940.

Daw, Marjorie (1902-3/18/79). Films: "The Jaguar's Claws" 1917 (Nancy Jordan); "A Modern Musketeer" 1917 (Dorothy Moran); "Arizona" 1918 (Bonita); "Headin' South" 1918; "The Sunset Princess" 1918 (Beauty); "The Knickerbocker Buckaroo" 1919 (Mercedes); "The Great Redeemer" 1920 (the Girl); "Bob Hampton of Placer" 1921 (the Kid); "The Lone Hand" 1922 (Jane Sheridan); "The Long Chance" 1922 (Kate Corbaly/Dana Corbaly); "The Sagebrush Trail" 1922; "The Call of the Canyon" 1923 (Flo Hutter); "Notch Number One" 1924; "Fear-Bound" 1925 (Falfi Tumble); "Outlaws of Red River" 1927 (Mary Torrence); "Spoilers of the West" 1928 (the Girl).

Dawber, Pam (1951-). Films: "Wild Horses" TVM-1985 (Daryl Reese).

Dawn, Consuelo. Films: "The Ambuscade" 1928; "Two Gun Caballero" 1931.

Dawn, Isabelle (1904-6/29/66). TV: *Wild Bill Hickok*—"The Kid from Red Butte" 8-26-52.

Dawn, Katherine. Films: "Lure of the Yukon" 1924 (Ruth Baird).

Dawn, Sugar. Films: "The Golden Trail" 1940; "Pals of the Silver Sage" 1940 (Sugar); "Dynamite

Canyon" 1941 (Sugar Grey); "Lone Star Law Men" 1941 (Sugar); "Riding the Sunset Trail" 1941 (Sugar Dawn); "Wanderers of the West" 1941 (Sugar Lee); "Arizona Roundup" 1942.

Dawson, Anthony (Antonio Margheriti). Films: "Death Rides a Horse" 1967-Ital. (Manina); "A Sky Full of Stars for a Roof" 1968-Ital.; "Deadlock" 1970-Ital./Ger./Isr. (Sunshine); "Red Sun" 1971-Fr./Ital./Span.

Dawson, Doris (1896-11/14/50). Films: "Arizona Wildcat" 1927 (Marie); "Gold from Weepah" 1927 (Elsie Blaine).

Dawson, Frank (1870-11/11/53). Films: "Rhythm on the Range" 1936 (Butler).

Dawson, Hal K. (1896-2/17/87). Films: "Wells Fargo" 1937 (Correspondent); "Riding High" 1943 (Master of Ceremonies); "Dallas" 1950 (Drummer); "The Yellow Mountain" 1954 (Sam Torrence); "A Lawless Street" 1955; "The Tin Star" 1957 (Andy Miller); "Cattle Empire" 1958 (George Jeffrey); "Face of a Fugitive" 1959 (Stableman). ¶TV: *The Gene Autry Show*—"Killer Horse" 12-10-50 (Blowfly Jones); *The Cisco Kid*—"Lodestone" 4-26-52, "Gun Totin' Papa" 5-24-52; *The Lone Ranger*—"Special Edition" 9-25-52; *Sergeant Preston of the Yukon*—"Vindication of Yukon" 7-5-56 (Gus); *Broken Arrow*—"The Trial" 1-22-57 (Carter); *The Restless Gun*—"General Gilford's Widow" 11-11-57 (Dan Traylor); *Fury*—"The Horse Nobody Wanted" 2-15-58 (Sam); *Wrangler*—"Encounter at Elephant Butte" 9-15-60 (Rancher); *Klondike*—"The Unexpected Candidate" 11-7-60 (Aaron); *Wanted—Dead or Alive*—"To the Victor" 11-9-60; *The Rifleman*—"Six Years and a Day" 1-3-61; *Lawman*—"The Squatters" 1-29-61 (Storekeeper); *Wyatt Earp*—"Old Slanders Never Die" 1-31-61 (Barber); *The Deputy*—"Spoken in Silence" 4-29-61 (Sam); *The Tall Man*—"The Liberty Belle" 9-16-61 (Clerk), "The Hunt" 1-27-62 (Clerk), "The Frame" 4-21-62 (Hotel Clerk); *Laramie*—"The Runaway" 1-23-62, "Shadow of the Past" 10-16-62.

Dawson, Louis. *see* Davila, Luis.

Dawson, Maurine. TV: *Maverick*—"The Art Lovers" 10-1-61 (Anne Sutton); *The Rifleman*—"Quiet Night, Deadly Night" 10-22-62 (Molly Carpenter); *A Man Called Shenandoah*—"Requiem for the Second" 5-2-66 (Ellen).

Day, Alice (1905-). Films: "Gold" 1932 (Marian); "Two-Fisted Law" 1932 (Betty Owen).

Day, Dennis (1917-6/22/88). Films: "Buck Benny Rides Again" 1940 (Dennis). ¶TV: *Death Valley Days*—"Way Station" 5-2-62 (Jason).

Day, Doris. Films: "Saga of Death Valley" 1939 (Ann Meredith).

Day, Doris (1925-). Films: "Calamity Jane" 1953 (Calamity Jane); "Ballad of Josie" 1968 (Josie Minick).

Day, Joel. Films: "Red Courage" 1921 (Chuckwalla Bill); "In the Days of Buffalo Bill" 1922-serial (Abraham Lincoln).

Day, John. Films: "Saddle Pals" 1947; "Jeep-Herders" 1949; "City of Badmen" 1953 (James Corbett); "The Man from the Alamo" 1953 (Cavish); "Seminole" 1953 (Scott); "Star in the Dust" 1956 (Jiggs Larribee); "Night Passage" 1957 (Latigo); "The Badlanders" 1958 (Lee); "Westbound" 1959 (Russ); "Advance to the Rear" 1964 (Loafer); "Tell Them Willie Boy Is Here" 1969 (Sam Wood). ¶TV: *The Lone Ranger*—"Sheep Thieves" 2-9-50, "Eye for an Eye" 6-29-50, "Paid in Full" 12-28-50; *Colt .45*—"A Time to Die" 10-25-57 (Burke); *Riverboat*—"The Blowup" 1-17-60 (Sailor); *Rawhide*—"The Long Count" 1-5-62 (Brant); *Wagon Train*—"The Nels Stack Story" 10-23-57, "The Amos Gibbon Story" 4-20-60; *Whispering Smith*—"Death at Even Money" 7-10-61; *The Virginian*—"Duel at Shiloh" 1-2-63; *Laramie*—"The Renegade Brand" 2-26-63; *Nichols*—"Away the Rolling River" 12-7-71.

Day, Laraine (Laraine Johnson, Lorraine Hayes) (1920-). Films: "Doomed at Sundown" 1937 (Jane Williams); "Border G-Man" 1938 (Betty Holden); "Arizona Legion" 1939 (Letty Meade); "The Bad Man" 1941 (Lucia Pell); "The Law Commands" 1937 (Mary Lee Johnson); "The Painted Desert" 1938 (Carol Banning). ¶TV: *Wagon Train*—"The Cassie Vance Story" 12-23-63 (Cassie Vance).

Day George, Lynda (1944-). Films: "Chisum" 1970 (Sue McSween); "The Barbara Coast" TVM-1975 (Clo Du Bois). ¶TV: *The Virginian*—"The Welcoming Town" 3-22-67 (Judy); *Cowboy in Africa*—"What's an Elephant Mother to Do?" 10-2-67 (Liz Carter); *Bonanza*—"The Stronghold" 5-26-68 (Lisa); *Lancer*—"The Escape" 12-31-68 (Sarah Cassidy); *Here Come the Brides*—"Two Women" 4-3-70 (Valerie); *Kung Fu*—"In Uncertain Bondage" 2-7-74 (Dora Burnham).

Day, Marceline. Films: "Renegade Holmes, M.D." 1925; "The Splendid Road" 1925 (Lilian Grey); "The Taming of the West" 1925 (Beryl); "The White Outlaw" 1925 (Mary Gale); "Looking for Trouble" 1926 (Tulip Hellier); "Western Pluck" 1926 (Clare Dyer); "Red Clay" 1927 (Agnes Burr); "The Pocatello Kid" 1931 (Mary); "Broadway to Cheyenne" 1932 (Ruth Carter); "The Fighting Fool" 1932 (Judith); "The Fighting Parson" 1933 (Susan); "The Telegraph Trail" 1933 (Alice Ellis); "Via Pony Express" 1933 (Betty Castelar).

Day, Shanon (1896-2/24/77). Films: "Captain Fly-By-Night" 1922 (Senorita Anita); "His Back Against the Wall" 1922 (Dorothy Petwell); "North of the Rio Grande" 1922 (Lola Sanchez); "Silent Pal" 1925 (Marjorie Winters); "The Vanishing American" 1925 (Gekin Yashi).

Day-Lewis, Daniel (1958-). Films: "The Last of the Mohicans" 1992 (Hawkeye).

Daye, Harold T. TV: *Death Valley Days*—"Head of the House" 4-7-57; *Wagon Train*—"The Ella Lindstrom Story" 2-4-59 (Stig).

Dayton, Howard (1927-). TV: *The Californians*—"Strange Quarantine" 12-10-57 (Soldier); *Wanted—Dead or Alive*—"The Favor" 11-15-58; *Have Gun Will Travel*—"Full Circle" 5-14-60; *Rawhide*—"Incident of Judgment Day" 2-8-63 (Cal Mason).

Dayton, June (1923-6/13/94). TV: *Gunsmoke*—"Laughing Gass" 3-29-58 (Mrs. Stafford), "Bently" 4-11-64 (Emily Calvin), "Jonah Hutchison" 11-21-64 (Phoebe Hutchison), "The Witness" 11-23-70 (Martha Sprague); *Zane Grey Theater*—"Medal for Valor" 12-25-58 (Kate Manning); *Death Valley Days*—"The Devil's Due" 1-26-60 (Rose), "The Wind at Your Back" 12-7-60 (Sister Mary), "The Battle of San Francisco Bay" 4-11-65 (Virginia Farragut), "The Solid Gold Pie" 11-29-69; *Wanted—Dead or Alive*—"The Showdown" 10-26-60 (Gloria Haywood); *Hondo*—"Hondo and the Ghost of Ed Dow" 11-24-67 (Wilma Hendrix); *Lancer*—"Foley" 10-15-68, "The Gifts" 10-28-69 (Mrs. Moran); *The New Land*—"The Word Is: Growth" 9-21-74.

Deacon, Richard (1923-8/8/84). Films: "Lay That Rifle Down" 1955 (Glover Speckleton); "The Proud Ones" 1956 (Barber); "Decision at Sundown" 1957 (Zaron); "North to Alaska" 1960 (Angus, the Desk Clerk); "The Raiders" 1964 (Commissioner Mailer). ¶TV: *Gunsmoke*—

"Pucket's New Year" 1-5-57 (Botkin); *Tales of Wells Fargo*—"The Gambler" 9-8-58 (Sam Potter); *Zorro*—"Senor China Boy" 6-25-59 (Padre Ignacio); *Maverick*—"The Cats of Paradise" 10-11-59 (Floyd Gimbel); *Bonanza*—"San Francisco Holiday" 4-2-60 (Captain Shark); *The Rifleman*—"The Hangman" 5-31-60 (Colonel Sims); *Rango*—"What's a Nice Girl Like You Doing Holding Up a Place Like This?" 2-17-67 (Pennypacker).

Deadrick, Vince. Films: "The Apple Dumpling Gang Rides Again" 1979. ¶TV: *Wanted—Dead or Alive*—"The Voice of Silence" 2-15-61 (Ken Brice), "Barney's Bounty" 3-29-61 (Sy Benton); *The Big Valley*—"The Secret" 1-27-69 (Foley), "Alias Nellie Handley" 2-24-69 (Guard); *Gunsmoke*—"The War Priest" 1-5-70 (1st Trooper).

De Alba, Aurora. Films: "Rattler Kid" 1968-Ital./Span.; "Raise Your Hands, Dead Man ... You're Under Arrest" 1971-Ital./Span.

de Alcaniz, Luana. Films: "Frontiers of '49" 1939 (Dolores de Cervantes).

Dean, Eddie (1908-). Films: "Western Jamboree" 1938; "Law of the Pampas" 1939 (Curly); "The Llano Kid" 1939; "The Lone Ranger Rides Again" 1939-serial (Cooper); "Range War" 1939; "Renegade Trail" 1939; "The Golden Trail" 1940 (Injun); "Hidden Gold" 1940 (Logan); "Knights of the Range" 1940; "The Light of Western Stars" 1940 (Nels); "Oklahoma Renegades" 1940 (Jack); "Santa Fe Marshal" 1940 (Marshal); "The Showdown" 1940 (Sheriff); "Stagecoach War" 1940 (Tom); "Down Mexico Way" 1941; "Gauchos of El Dorado" 1941; "Kansas Cyclone" 1941; "Pals of the Pecos" 1941; "Rollin' Home to Texas" 1941 (Sheriff); "Sierra Sue" 1941 (Jerry Willis); "Trail of the Silver Spurs" 1941 (Stoner); "Arizona Stagecoach" 1942; "Fighting Bill Fargo" 1942; "The Lone Rider and the Bandit" 1942; "Raiders of the West" 1942; "Stagecoach Express" 1942; "King of the Cowboys" 1943 (Tex); "Song of Old Wyoming" 1945 (Eddie Reed); "Wildfire" 1945 (Johnny Deal); "The Caravan Trail" 1946 (Eddie Dean); "Colorado Serenade" 1946 (Eddie); "Driftin' River" 1946 (Eddie); "Romance of the West" 1946 (Eddie Dean); "Stars Over Texas" 1946 (Eddie Dean); "Tumbleweed Trail" 1946 (Eddie); "Wild West" 1946 (Eddie Dean); "My Pal Ringeye" 1947-short; "Range Beyond the Blue" 1947 (Eddie Dean); "Shadow Valley" 1947

(Eddie); "West to Glory" 1947 (Eddie Dean); "White Stallion" 1947 (Eddie Dean); "Wild Country" 1947 (Eddie Dean); "Black Hills" 1948 (Eddie); "Check Your Guns" 1948 (Eddie Dean); "The Hawk of Powder River" 1948 (Eddie); "Prairie Outlaws" 1948; "The Tioga Kid" 1948 (Eddie/the Tioga Kid); "Tornado Range" 1948 (Eddie); "The Westward Trail" 1948 (Eddie); "Night Rider" 1962-short. ¶TV: *The Marshal of Gunsight Pass* 1950 (Marshal).

Dean, Fabian (1930-1/15/71). Films: "The Ride to Hangman's Tree" 1967 (Indian). ¶TV: *Laredo*—"Coup de Grace" 10-7-66 (Jean Lebec); *The High Chaparral*—"Trail to Nevermore" 10-31-69 (Wilse).

Dean, Isabelle (1918-). TV: *Cheyenne*—"Ghost of Cimarron" 3-25-58 (Powder Kate).

Dean, Jack (1875-6/23/50). Films: "Tennessee's Pardner" 1916 (Jack Hunter); "On the Level" 1917 (Pete Sontag).

Dean, James (1931-9/30/55). Films: "Giant" 1956 (Jett Rink). ¶TV: *You Are There*—"The Capture of Jesse James" 2-18-53 (Jesse James).

Dean, Jeanne (1925-8/20/93). Films: "Sundown in Santa Fe" 1948. ¶TV: *The Cisco Kid*—"Stolen Bonds" 7-28-51, "Protective Association" 9-8-51, "Horseless Carriage" 1-24-53; *Wild Bill Hickok*—"Savvy, the Smart Little Dog" 2-19-52; *The Roy Rogers Show*—"Carnival Killer" 6-8-52; *26 Men*—"Death in the Dragoons" 2-17-59.

Dean, Jimmy (1928-). TV: *Daniel Boone*—"Delo Jones" 3-2-67 (Delo Jones), Regular 1967-69 (Josh Clements).

Dean, Julia (1878-10/17/52). Films: "Judge Not, or the Woman of Mona Diggings" 1915 (Molly Hanlon).

Dean, Mae (-9/1/37). Films: "Riders of the Range" 1923 (Neil Barclay).

Dean, Margia. Films: "Grand Canyon" 1949 (Script Girl); "I Shot Jesse James" 1949 (Saloon Singer); "Red Desert" 1949 (Hazel Carter); "Rimfire" 1949 (Lolita); "Bandit Queen" 1950 (Carol Grayson); "The Baron of Arizona" 1950 (Marquesa); "The Return of Jesse James" 1950; "Western Pacific Agent" 1950; "Fangs of the Wild" 1954 (Linda); "Last of the Desperadoes" 1955 (Sarita); "The Lonesome Trail" 1955; "Frontier Gambler" 1956; "Stagecoach to Fury" 1956 (Ruth); "Badlands of Montana" 1957 (Emily); "Ambush at Cimarron

Pass" 1958 (Theresa); "Villa!" 1958 (Julie North).

Dean, Max. Films: "Adios Gringo" 1965-Ital./Fr./Span. (Avery Ranchester); "Blood for a Silver Dollar" 1965-Ital./Fr.; "Seven Guns for the MacGregors" 1965-Ital./Span.; "My Name Is Pecos" 1966-Ital.; "Killer Caliber .32" 1967-Ital.; "Two Pistols and a Coward" 1967-Ital.

Dean, Priscilla (1901-12/27/87). Films: "The Conflict" 1921 (Dorcas Remalie); "West of Broadway" 1926 (Freddy Hayden); "Klondike" 1932 (Miss Porter).

Dean, Quentin (1947-). Films: "Will Penny" 1968 (Jennie). ¶TV: *The Virginian*—"The Saddle Warmer" 9-18-68 (Saranora); *Lancer*—"A Person Unknown" 11-25-69 (Lucrece); *The Big Valley*—"Journey into Violence" 12-18-67 (Bettina); *The High Chaparral*—"Feather of an Eagle" 2-7-69 (Sarah).

Dean, Rick. Films: "Cheyenne Warrior" 1994 (Kearney). ¶TV: *Paradise*—"A Gather of Guns" 9-10-89 (Captain Kaye); *Adventures of Brisco County, Jr.*—Pilot 8-27-93 (Lookout).

de Anda, Miguel. Films: "Guns of Diablo" 1964 (Bryce). ¶TV: *Have Gun Will Travel*—"The Fatal Flaw" 2-25-61 (Salazar); *Gunsmoke*—"He Learned About Women" 2-24-62 (Pepe), "The Ditch" 10-27-62 (Boss); *Rawhide*—"Incident of Decision" 12-28-62 (Pedro); *The Big Valley*—"Palms of Glory" 9-15-65 (Ciego), "Hazard" 3-9-66 (Ciego); *The Legend of Jesse James*—"The Empty Town" 1-3-66 (Jose); *Rango*—"In a Little Mexican Town" 4-14-67 (El Diablo); *The High Chaparral*—"The High Chaparral" 9-10-67, "Young Blood" 10-8-67, "Our Lady of Guadalupe" 12-20-68, "To Stand for Something More" 10-24-69 (Guard); *Bonanza*—"The Conquistadors" 10-1-67 (Quail), "The Gold Detector" 12-24-67 (Corrales), "Customs of the Country" 2-6-72 (Blacksmith).

Deane, Dorris (1901-3/24/74). Films: "The Half-Breed" 1922 (Nanette).

Deane, Hazel. Films: "Butterfly Range" 1922; "South of the Northern Lights" 1922 (Jane Wilson); "The Secret of the Pueblo" 1923 (Ruth Bryson); "The Devil's Gulch" 1926 (Merrill Waverly); "Fighting Jack" 1926 (Betty Bingham).

Deane, Shirley (1913-83). Films: "Prairie Moon" 1938 (Peggy).

Deane, Sidney. Films: "The Call of the North" 1914 (MacTavish); "Rose of the Rancho" 1914 (Senor

Espinoza); "The Virginian" 1914 (Uncle Hughey); "The Girl of the Golden West" 1915 (Sid Duck); "The Last of the Mohicans" 1920 (General Webb).

De Angelis, Remo. Films: "The Mercenary" 1968-Ital./Span. (Hudo).

Deans, Herbert (1908-10/8/67). Films: "The Man Behind the Gun" 1952. ¶TV: *My Friend Flicka*—"The Little Visitor" 12-30-55 (Norris).

Dearden, Robin. TV: *Outlaws*—"Pursued" 3-7-87 (Elektra).

Dearholt, Ashton (1894-4/27/42). Films: "Film Tempo" 1915; "Man-Afraid-of-His-Wardrobe" 1915; "This Is the Life" 1915; "Lone Star" 1916 (Jefferson Mattes); "Snap Judgment" 1917 (Tom West); "The Sheriff of Sun-Dog" 1922 (Pete Kane); "At Devil's Gorge" 1923 (Stranger in Town); "The Law Rustlers" 1923 (Eph Sillman); "The Sting of the Scorpion" 1923; "Cupid's Rustler" 1924 (Harry); "The Cowboy Prince" 1924; "Lash of the Whip" 1924 (Pinto Pete); "A Rodeo Mixup" 1924 (the Bum); "Western Feuds" 1924 (Joe); "Western Yesterdays" 1924 (Pinto Pete); "Baited Trap" 1926 (Red Killifer); "West of the Law" 1926 (Frank Armstrong).

Dearing, Edgar (1893-8/17/74). Films: "A Man from Wyoming" 1930 (Sergeant); "End of the Trail" 1936; "Rose Marie" 1936 (Mounted Policeman); "Rose of the Rancho" 1936 (Stranger); "Border G-Man" 1938 (Smoky Joslin); "Buck Benny Rides Again" 1940 (Police Officer); "Go West" 1940 (Ticket Seller); "When the Daltons Rode" 1940 (Sheriff); "Wyoming" 1940 (Officer); "Don't Fence Me In" 1945 (Chief of Police); "Unconquered" 1947 (Soldier at Gilded Beaver); "The Paleface" 1948 (Sheriff); "Fancy Pants" 1950 (Mr. Jones); "Lightning Guns" 1950 (Capt. Dan Saunders); "Raiders of Tomahawk Creek" 1950 (Randolph Dike); "Pecos River" 1951 (Ol' Henry); "Ridin' the Outlaw Trail" 1951 (Pop Willard); "Santa Fe" 1951; "Silver Canyon" 1951 (Col. Middler); "The Kid from Broken Gun" 1952 (Judge Halloway). ¶TV: *The Gene Autry Show*—"The Breakup" 11-5-50, "Prize Winner" 7-27-54; *Sergeant Preston of the Yukon*—"Dog Race" 1-19-56 (Hank Weber), "Follow the Leader" 3-15-56 (Brady), "Border Action" 12-27-56 (El Walker); *Annie Oakley*—"The Saga of Clement O'-Toole" 11-4-56 (Jonathan Meriwether); *The Roy Rogers Show*—"Portrait of Murder" 3-17-57; *Wagon Train*—"A Man Called Horse" 3-26-

58; *The Rifleman*—"Shivaree" 2-3-59; *Tales of Wells Fargo*—"Bitter Vengeance" 6-12-61 (Jake Snyder); *The Tall Man*—"Three for All" 3-10-62 (Farmer).

Deas, Justin. Films: "Montana" TVM-1990 (Clyde Guthrie).

Deaver, Nancy. Films: "The Law of the Yukon" 1920 (Goldie); "The Mohican's Daughter" 1922 (Jees Uck); "Shootin' em Up" 1923; "Gold Digger Jones" 1924; "The Circus Cyclone" 1925 (Doraldina); "The Trail Rider" 1925 (Sally McCoy).

DeBenning, Burr. TV: *Lawman*—"Marked Man" 1-22-61 (Ross Darby); *Maverick*—"The Forbidden City" 3-26-61 (Dave Taylor); *Iron Horse*—"Explosion at Waycrossing" 11-21-66 (Curly Webb); *Custer*—"Breakout" 11-1-67 (Uvalde); *Cimarron Strip*—"The Judgment" 1-4-68 (Emmet Lloyd); *The Outcasts*—"The Outcasts" 9-23-68 (Lieutenant); *The Virginian*—"The Storm Gate" 11-13-68 (Jason Crowder), "Journey to Scathelock" 12-10-69 (Orrey); *Lancer*—"Warburton's Edge" 2-4-69 (Isham); *Bonanza*—"Is There Any Man Here?" 2-8-70 (Tuttle Ames); *Daniel Boone*—"Before the Tall Man" 2-12-70 (Tom Lincoln); *Nakia*—"The Quarry" 9-28-74 (Frank); *Barbary Coast*—"Sauce for the Goose" 10-20-75 (Harry Darcy); *Father Murphy*—Regular 1981-82 (Mr. Garrett).

DeBenning, Jeff (1920-). Films: "Five Guns to Tombstone" 1961. ¶TV: *Tombstone Territory*—"Fight for a Fugitive" 6-4-58 (Dan Kirby), "Trail's End" 4-10-59 (Marshal Clifford); *Bat Masterson*—"Dynamite Blows Two Ways" 10-22-58 (Horton); *Wanted—Dead or Alive*—"Estrelita" 10-3-59; *Wyatt Earp*—"Wyatt's Bitterest Enemy" 6-7-60 (Dodie Jones); *The Tall Man*—"Where Is Sylvia?" 9-23-61 (Marshal); *Bonanza*—"The Auld Sod" 2-4-62 (Higgins); *Gunsmoke*—"He Learned About Women" 2-24-62 (Red); *Cheyenne*—"The Bad Penny" 3-12-62 (Sheriff Lyons); *Here Come the Brides*—"Marriage Chinese Style" 4-9-69.

de Beranger, Andre. *see* Beranger, Geroge.

de Blas, Manuel. Films: "A Bullet for Sandoval" 1970-Ital./Span. (Jose); "The White, the Yellow, and the Black" 1974-Ital./Span./Fr.

DeBord, Sharon (1939-). Films: "The Cheyenne Social Club" 1970 (Sara Jean).

De Briac, Jean (1891-10/18/70). Films: "Over the Border" 1922

(Pretty Pierre); "Under the Pampas Moon" 1935 (Stenographer); "Buck Benny Rides Again" 1940 (Head Waiter). ¶TV: *The Lone Ranger*—"War Horse" 10-20-49.

DeBroux, Lee. Films: "Tell Them Willie Boy Is Here" 1969 (Meathead); "Wild Rovers" 1971 (Leaky); "Female Artillery" TVM-1973 (Squat); "Hawmps!" 1976 (Fitzgerald); "The Invasion of Johnson County" TVM-1976 (Richard Allen); "Standing Tall" TVM-1978 (Bob Workett); "True Grit" TVM-1978 (Skorby); "The Sacketts" TVM-1979 (Simpson); "Dream West" TVM-1986 (Provost); "Longarm" TVM-1988 (Garrett); "Geronimo: An American Legend" 1993 (City Marshal Hawkins). ¶TV: *Gunsmoke*—"A Hat" 10-16-67 (Cowpuncher), "Blood Money" 1-22-68 (Stu), "9:12 to Dodge" 11-11-68 (Tim), "Waco" 12-9-68 (Fuller), "The Innocent" 11-24-69 (Zeal Yewker), "The Hiders" 1-13-75 (Quincannon); *The Guns of Will Sonnett*—"The Trap" 10-4-68; *Bonanza*—"Decision at Los Robles" 3-22-70 (Gunman #2), "Warbonnet" 12-26-71 (Elias); *Alias Smith and Jones*—"Return to Devil's Hole" 2-25-71; *The Quest*—"The Buffalo Hunters" 9-29-76 (Colton); *How the West Was Won*—"The Scavengers" 3-12-79 (Larch); *Outlaws*—"Pursued" 3-7-87 (Mark); *Paradise*—"Ghost Dance" 11-24-88 (Christmas).

de Brulier, Nigel (1878-1/30/48). Films: "Ramona" 1916 (Felipe Moreno); "Life in the Raw" 1933 (McTavish); "Life in the Raw" 1933; "Robin Hood of El Dorado" 1936 (Padre); "The Californian" 1937 (Don Francisco Escobar); "Zorro Rides Again" 1937-serial (Manuel Vega); "Viva Cisco Kid" 1940 (Moses).

De Camp, Rosemary (1913-). Films: "The Treasure of Lost Canyon" 1952 (Samuella Brown); "Many Rivers to Cross" 1955 (Lucy Hamilton). ¶TV: *Rawhide*—"Incident Near Gloomy River" 3-17-61 (Ma Fletcher), "The House of the Hunter" 4-20-62 (Mrs. Armstrong); *Death Valley Days*—"Canary Harris vs. the Almighty" 2-26-66 (Canary Harris), "Mrs. Romney and the Outlaws" 4-2-66 (Caroline Romney); *Here Come the Brides*—"The Crimpers" 3-5-69 (Mrs. Fletcher).

De Camp, Valerie. TV: *Death Valley Days*—"Lady with a Past" 12-28-68 (Betty), "The Taming of Trudy Bell" 12-6-69 (Trudy Bell).

DeCarl, Nancy. TV: *The Restless Gun*—"A Trial for Jenny May" 5-25-59 (Betty Sue).

De Carlo, Yvonne (1924-). Films: "Deerslayer" 1943 (Wah-Teh); "Frontier Gal" 1945 (Lorena Dumont); "Salome, Where She Danced" 1945 (Salome); "Black Bart" 1948 (Lola Montez); "River Lady" 1948 (Sequin); "Calamity Jane and Sam Bass" 1949 (Calamity Jane); "Silver City" 1951 (Candace Surrency); "Tomahawk" 1951 (Julie Madden); "The San Francisco Story" 1952 (Adelaide McCall); "Border River" 1954 (Carmelita Caris); "Passion" 1954 (Rosa Melo/Tonya Melo); "Shotgun" 1955 (Abby); "Raw Edge" 1956 (Hannah Montgomery); "McClintock" 1963 (Louise Warren); "Law of the Lawless" 1964 (Ellie Irish); "Hostile Guns" 1967 (Laura Mannon); "Arizona Bushwhackers" 1968 (Jill Wyler); "The Mark of Zorro" TVM-1974 (Isabella Vega). ¶TV: *Bonanza*—"A Rose for Lotta" 9-12-59 (Lotta Crabtree); *Death Valley Days*—"The Lady Was an M.D." 1-11-61 (Dr. Clare Reed); *The Virginian*—"A Time Remembered" 12-11-63 (Elena), "Crime Wave at Buffalo Spring" 1-29-69 (Mme. Imogene); *Custer*—"The Raiders" 12-27-67 (Vanessa Ravenhill).

Decker, Tony. TV: *The Texas Wheelers*—Regular 1974-75 (T.J. Wheeler).

de Cordoba, Pedro (1881-9/17/50). Films: "Ramona" 1936 (Father Salvierderra); "Rose of the Rancho" 1936 (Gomez); "Heart of the North" 1938 (Father Claverly); "Law of the Pampas" 1939 (Jose Valdez); "Man of Conquest" 1939 (Oolooteko); "Range War" 1939 (Padre Jose); "Mark of Zorro" 1940 (Don Miguel); "Romance of the Rio Grande" 1941 (Don Fernando de Vega); "Shut My Big Mouth" 1942 (Don Carlos Montoya); "Gun to Gun" 1944-short; "In Old New Mexico" 1945 (Padre); "San Antonio" 1945 (Ricardo Torreon); "Robin Hood of Monterey" 1947; "The Daring Caballero" 1949 (Padre); "Daughter of the West" 1949 (Indian Chief); "Comanche Territory" 1950 (Quisima); "When the Redskins Rode" 1951 (Chief Shiniss); "Thunder in the Sun" 1959 (Gabrielle's Dance Partner). ¶TV: *The Lone Ranger*—"Sheep Thieves" 2-9-50.

de Cordova, Leander (1878-9/19/69). Films: "Quick Trigger Lee" 1931 (Jeremy Wales); "Zorro's Fighting Legion" 1939-serial (Felipe); "The Laramie Trail" 1944; "Tough Assignment" 1949 (Mr. Schultz); "The Mysterious Desperado" 1949 (Padre).

DeCorsia, Ted (1904-4/11/73).

Films: "The Outriders" 1950 (Bye); "New Mexico" 1951 (Acuma, the Indian Chief); "Vengeance Valley" 1951 (Herb Backett); "The Savage" 1952 (Iron Breast); "Ride, Vaquero!" 1953 (Sheriff Parker); "Man with the Gun" 1955 (Rex Stang); "Mohawk" 1956 (Indian Chief Kowanen); "Showdown at Abilene" 1956 (Dan Claudius); "Gun Battle at Monterey" 1957 (Reno); "Gunfight at the O.K. Corral" 1957 (Shanghai Pierce); "The Lawless Eighties" 1958; "Noose for a Gunman" 1960 (Cantrell); "Oklahoma Territory" 1960 (Buffalo Horn); "Blood on the Arrow" 1964 (Jud); "The Quick Gun" 1964 (Spangler); "Nevada Smith" 1966 (Hudson, the Bartender); "Five Card Stud" 1968 (Eldon Bates). ¶TV: *The Lone Ranger*—"Gold Freight" 4-28-55; *Frontier*—"The Return of Jubal Dolan" 8-26-56 (Jim Teech), "The Hostage" 9-9-56; *Broken Arrow*—"The Mail Riders" 9-25-56 (Cartwright), "Battle at Apache Pass" 10-2-56 (Cartwright); *Maverick*—"According to Hoyle" 10-6-57 (Joe Riggs), "Diamond Flush" 2-5-61 (Amos Parker), "The Money Machine" 4-8-62 (Cannonball Clyde Bassett); *Tales of Wells Fargo*—"The Feud" 10-14-57; *Jim Bowie*—"The Pearls of Talimeco" 11-8-57 (Cow Chief); *The Californians*—"Man from Boston" 11-12-57 (Jake Reeves); *Have Gun Will Travel*—"The Englishman" 12-7-57; *The Restless Gun*—"Thicker Than Water" 12-9-57 (Cal Jason); *Trackdown*—"The Trail" 2-28-58 (Lt. Bailey), "Guilt" 12-19-58 (George Caldwell); *Zorro*—"Quintana Makes a Choice" 4-24-58, "Zorro Lights a Fuse" 5-1-58; *26 Men*—"Manhunt" 12-16-58, "False Witness" 12-30-58; *Tales of the Texas Rangers*—"Ambush" 12-26-58 (Drum Hartnell); *Sugarfoot*—"Hideout" 4-1-58 (Chief Big Bear), "Wolf" 6-9-59 (Lee Stapes); *MacKenzie's Raiders*—"Scalphunters" 12-3-58; *Jefferson Drum*—"Simon Pitt" 12-11-58 (Jim); *Lawman*—"Short Straw" 12-14-58 (Jess Crowthers), "The Senator" 5-17-59 (Barrett), "Blind Hate" 5-14-61 (Lem Pastor); *The Rifleman*—"Young Englishman" 12-16-58 (Waggoner); *Zane Grey Theater*—"Trouble at Tres Cruces" 3-26-59; *Frontier Doctor*—"Gringo Pete" 5-2-59; *Rough Riders*—"Forty-Five Calibre Law" 5-14-59 (Kyle Heber); *Bat Masterson*—"The Conspiracy" 6-17-59 & 6-24-59 (Bartender), "Death by the Half Dozen" 2-4-60 (Hank Griswell); *Wanted—Dead or Alive*—"Chain Gang" 12-12-59 (George Winters), "The Medicine Man" 11-23-60

(Arthur Barchester); *Laramie*—"The Protectors" 3-22-60 (Greer), "Siege at Jubilee" 10-10-61 (Witmore); *Rawhide*—"Incident of the Stargazer" 4-1-60, "Incident of the Lost Idol" 4-28-61 (Sheriff), "The Devil and the Deep Blue" 5-11-62 (Ben Wade), "Incident of the Portrait" 10-5-62 (Sheriff), "Incident of the Clown" 3-29-63 (Lame Bear), "Incident of the Peyote Cup" 5-14-64 (Chief Pala); *The Deputy*—"Two-way Deal" 3-11-61 (Slade Blatner); *Gunsmoke*—"He Learned About Women" 2-24-62 (Garvy), "By Line" 4-9-66 (Merle Benlan); *Wide Country*—"Our Ernie Kills People" 11-1-62 (Henry McMath), "Speckle Bird" 1-31-63 (Sheriff); *Stoney Burke*—"King of the Hill" 1-21-63 (Burlington), "Webb of Fear" 2-18-63 (Sheriff Bixton); *The Dakotas*—"Fargo" 2-25-63 (Winters); *The Slowest Gun in the West* 7-29-63 (Black Bart); *Daniel Boone*—"Cain's Birthday" 4-1-65 & 4-8-65 (Chief Talawa), "Hannah Comes Home" 12-25-69 (Chief Ankara); *Death Valley Days*—"Crullers at Sundown!" 5-21-66 (Jim Jennet); *Rango*—"Rango the Outlaw" 1-13-67 (Butch Durham); *Wild Wild West*—"The Night of the Spanish Curse" 1-3-69 (Elder), "The Night of the Sabatini Death" 2-2-69 (Johnny Sabatini/Capt. Aylmer Nolan); *The Guns of Will Sonnett*—"Trail's End" 1-31-69 (Sheriff); *The Outcasts*—"The Long Ride" 4-28-69 (Sheriff); *The High Chaparral*—"The Forge of Hate" 11-13-70 (Dull Knife).

Dee, Frances (1907-). Films: "Caught" 1931 (Kate Winslow); "Wells Fargo" 1937 (Justine Pryer); "Four Faces West" 1948 (Fay Hollister); "Gypsy Colt" 1954 (Em MacWade).

Dee, George (1901-8/24/74). TV: *Maverick*—"Island in the Swamp" 11-30-58 (Andre).

Dee, Ruby (1924-). Films: "Buck and the Preacher" 1972 (Ruth).

Dee, Sandra (1942-). Films: "The Wild and the Innocent" 1959 (Rosalie Stocker); "The Daughters of Joshua Cabe" TVM-1972 (Ada).

Deem, Miles. see Fidani, Demofilo.

Deebank, Felix. TV: *Bronco*—"Manitoba Manhunt" 4-3-61 (Cpl. Sandy Scott).

Deel, Sandra (1929-). Films: "Junior Bonner" 1972 (Nurse Arlis).

Deeley, Ben (1878-9/23/24). Films: "Kazan" 1921 (Jim Thorpe).

Deemer, Ed. Films: "Joe Kidd" 1972 (Bartender). ¶TV: *The Virgin-*

ian—"The Inchoworm's Got No Wings at All" 2-2-66 (Evans).

Deer, Alma. Films: "Fighting Jim Grant" 1923; "Lone Hand Texas" 1924; "Western Grit" 1924 (Alma Grayson).

DeFoe, Annette (1889-8/7/60). Films: "The Red Stain" 1916; "Fame and Fortune" 1918 (Mattie Carson); "Lone Hand Wilson" 1920 (Lolita Hansen).

DeFore, Don (1917-12/22/93). Films: "Ramrod" 1947 (Bill Schell). ¶TV: *The Men from Shiloh*—"The West vs. Colonel MacKenzie" 9-16-70 (Evans).

DeForest, Patsey. Films: "The Square Shooter" 1920 (Barbara Hampton); "Sunset Sprague" 1920 (Rose Loring).

DeFreest, Babe. Films: "Outlawed Guns" 1935; "The Painted Stallion" 1937-serial; "Daredevils of the West" 1943-serial; "Zorro's Black Whip" 1944-serial.

DeGore, Janet. TV: *Sugarfoot*—"Blue Bonnet Stray" 4-26-60 (Mary Kirk); *Branded*—"Survival" 1-24-65 (Sally Colbee); *Bonanza*—"Tommy" 12-18-66 (Allie Miller).

De Grasse, Joseph (1873-5/25/40). Films: "The Cowboy Kid" 1928 (John Grover); "The Dawn Rider" 1935 (Henchman).

de Grasse, Sam (1875-11/29/53). Films: "Blue Peter's Escape" 1914; "The Gunman" 1914; "A Man and His Mate" 1915 (Choo); "The Martyrs of the Alamo" 1915 (Silent Smith); "The Good Bad Man" 1916 (Bud Fraser); "The Half Breed" 1916 (Sheriff Dunn); "Anything Once" 1917 (Sir Mortimer Beggs); "The Empty Gun" 1917; "Madame Bo-Peep" 1917 (Jose Alvarez); "Wild and Woolly" 1917 (Steve Shelby); "Six-Shooter Andy" 1918 (Tom Slade); "Smashing Through" 1918 (Earl Foster); "Winner Takes All" 1918 (Mark Thorne); "A Woman's Fool" 1918; "The Spoilers" 1923 (Judge Stillman); "Tiger Rose" 1923 (Dr. Cusick).

de Grey, Sidney (1886-6/30/41). Films: "Mark of Zorro" 1920 (Don Pulido Alejandao); "The Half-Breed" 1922 (Leon Pardeau); "The Love Brand" 1923; "The Oregon Trail" 1923-serial; "Singled-Handed" 1923 (Rancher); "The King of the Wild Horses" 1924 (John Fielding); "Brand of Cowardice" 1925; "Steele of the Royal Mounted" 1925 (Col. Becker); "The Gay Buckaroo" 1932 (Uncle Abner).

De Haven, Jr., Carter (1910-

3/1/79). TV: *The Law of the Plainsman*—"The Innocents" 12-10-59.

DeHaven, Gloria (1925-). Films: "Banjo Hackett: Roamin' Free" TVM-1976 (Lady Jane Gray). ¶TV: *The Rifleman*—"Eddie's Daughter" 11-3-59 (Lil Halstead); *Johnny Ringo*—"Love Affair" 12-17-59 (Rosemary Blake); *Wagon Train*—"The Allison Justis Story" 10-19-60 (Allison Justis); *Gunsmoke*—"Like Old Times" 1-21-74 (Carrie Louise Thompson); *Nakia*—Regular 1974 (Deputy Irene James).

de Havilland, Olivia (1916-). Films: "Gold Is Where You Find It" 1938 (Serena Ferris); "Dodge City" 1939 (Abbie Irving); "Santa Fe Trail" 1940 (Kit Carson Halliday); "They Died with Their Boots On" 1941 (Elizabeth Bacon Custer); "The Proud Rebel" 1958 (Linnett Moore).

Dehner, John (1915-2/4/92). Films: "Out California Way" 1946 (Rod Mason); "Vigilantes of Boomtown" 1947 (Bob Fitzsimmons); "Riders of the Pony Express" 1949; "Dynamite Pass" 1950 (Thurber); "Horsemen of the Sierras" 1950 (Duke Webster); "Texas Dynamo" 1950 (Stanton); "Al Jennings of Oklahoma" 1951 (Tom Marsden); "Bandits of El Dorado" 1951 (Charles Bruton); "Fort Savage Raiders" 1951 (Capt. Michael Craydon); "Hot Lead" 1951 (Turk Thorne); "The Texas Rangers" 1951 (John Wesley Hardin); "When the Redskins Rode" 1951 (John Delmont); "California Conquest" 1952 (Fredo Brios); "Cripple Creek" 1952 (Emil Cabeau); "Desert Passage" 1952 (Bronson); "Junction City" 1952 (Emmett Sanderson); "Gun Belt" 1953 (Matt Ringo); "Powder River" 1953 (Harvey Logan); "Apache" 1954 (Weddle); "The Cowboy" 1954 (Narrator); "Southwest Passage" 1954 (Matt Carol); "The Man from Bitter Ridge" 1955 (Ranse Jackman); "Tall Man Riding" 1955 (Lawyer Ames Luddington); "Top Gun" 1955 (Quentin); "A Day of Fury" 1956 (Preacher Jason); "Fastest Gun Alive" 1956 (Taylor Swope); "Tension at Table Rock" 1956 (Hampton); "The Iron Sheriff" 1957 (Roger Pollock); "Revolt at Fort Laramie" 1957 (Maj. Seth Bradner); "Trooper Hook" 1957 (Fred Sutliff); "Apache Territory" 1958 (Grant Kimbrough); "The Left-Handed Gun" 1958 (Pat Garrett); "Man of the West" 1958 (Claude); "Cast a Long Shadow" 1959 (Chip Donohue); "The Canadians" 1961-Brit. (Frank Boone); "The Hallelujah Trail" 1965 (Narrator); "Win-

chester '73" TVM-1967 (High-Spade Johnny); "Something for a Lonely Man" TVM-1968 (Sam Batt); "The Cheyenne Social Club" 1970 (Clay Carroll); "Dirty Dingus Magee" 1970 (General); "Support Your Local Gunfighter" 1971 (Col. Ames); "Honky Tonk" TVM-1974 (Brazos); "Guardian of the Wilderness" 1976 (John Muir); "The New Daughters of Joshua Cabe" TVM-1976 (Warden Mannering); "California Gold Rush" TVM-1981 (Captain John Sutter). ¶TV: *Stories of the Century*—"Henry Plummer" 7-15-55; *Gunsmoke*—"Hot Spell" 9-17-55 (Cope Borden), "Tap Day for Kitty" 3-24-56 (Nip Dullers), "Daddy-O' 6-1-57 (Wayne Russell), "Crackup" 9-14-57 (Nate Springer), "Bottleman" 3-22-58 (Tom Cassidy), "The Badge" 11-12-60 (Rack), "The Squaw" 11-11-61 (Hardy Tate), "Root Down" 10-6-62 (Luke Dutton), "Ash" 2-16-63 (Ben Galt), "Caleb" 3-28-64 (Caleb Marr), "The Pariah" 4-17-65 (Paolo Scanzano), "Deadman's Law" 1-8-68 (Sam Wall); *Frontier*—"The Texicans" 1-8-56 (Yancy), "Georgia Gold" 6-10-56 (John Masterson); *Zane Grey Theater*—"Decision at Wilson's Creek" 5-17-57 (Jim Randolph), "Gift from a Gunman" 12-13-57 (Col. Overton), "Legacy of a Legend" 11-6-58 (Marshal Harvey), "So Young the Savage Land" 11-20-60 (Jim Brayden); *Cheyenne*—"The Broken Pledge" 6-4-57 (Naxel); *Wagon Train*—"The Emily Rossiter Story" 10-30-57 (Ned Rossiter), "The Annie Griffith Story" 2-25-59 (Cleve Colter); *Have Gun Will Travel*—"High Wire" 11-2-57 (Ben Marquette); *Zorro*—"The Fall of Monastario" 1-2-58 (Viceroy); *The Restless Gun*—"The Coward" 1-6-59 (Noah Temple), "Quiet City" 2-3-58 (Sheriff Heck Partridge), "The Hill of Death" 6-22-59 (Aaron Dixon); *Cimarron City*—"Twelve Guns" 11-1-58 (Will Buckley); *Maverick*—"Shady Deal at Sunny Acres" 11-23-58 (John Bates), "Greenbacks Unlimited" 3-13-60 (Big Ed Murphy), "The Devil's Necklace" 4-16-61 & 4-23-61 (Luther Cannonbaugh), "Marshal Maverick" 3-11-62 (Archie Walker); *Bronco*—"Payroll of the Dead" 1-27-59 (Otis Dameyer); *Black Saddle*—"Client: Robinson" 2-21-59 (Aaron Robinson), "A Case of Slow" 4-15-60 (Park Forrest); *Wanted—Dead or Alive*—"Angels of Vengeance" 4-18-59 (Abraham Saxon), "The Conquerers" 5-2-59 (Grant Mandeville), "Twelve Hours to Crazy Horse" 11-21-59 (Sheriff Hayes); *The Rifleman*—"The Money Gun" 5-12-59 (Tom King), "The Blowout" 10-13-59 (Al Walker),

"The Baby Sitter" 12-15-59 (Bartell), "The Prisoner" 3-14-61 (Major Aaron King); *Tales of Wells Fargo*—"Young Jim Hardie" 9-7-59 (High Willy Crane), "Day of Judgment" 9-5-60 (Cather), "Jeff Davis' Treasure" 12-5-60 (Wade Cather), "A Quiet Little Town" 6-5-61 (Wade Cather); *Bat Masterson*—"Wanted—Dead" 10-15-59 (Sheriff), "The Prescott Campaign" 2-2-61 (Marshal Ben Holt); *The Alaskans*—"The Blizzard" 10-18-59 (Cornish), "Big Deal" 11-8-59 (Soapy Smith), "Remember the Main" 12-20-59 (Soapy Smith), "The Devil Made Five" 6-19-60 (Cornish); *Wichita Town*—"Death Watch" 12-16-59 (Lou Loury); *The Law of the Plainsman*—"Clear Title" 12-17-59 (Walter Shannon); *The Texan*—"Friend of the Family" 1-4-60 (Major Randolph); *Laramie*—"Company Man" 2-9-60 (Jack Slade); *Rawhide*—"Incident at Sulphur Creek" 3-11-60 (Arvid Lacey), "Incident of the New Start" 3-3-61 (Jubal Wade), "Incident of the Four Horsemen" 10-26-62 (Gus Marsdon), "Incident of Judgment Day" 2-8-63 (Capt. Francis Cabot), "Incident of the Swindler" 2-20-64 (Straw Coleman); *The Westerner*—Regular 1960 (Burgundy Smith); *Bonanza*—"The Mission" 9-17-60 (Captain Pender), "The Gentleman from New Orleans" 2-2-64 (Jean Lafitte); *The Rebel*—"The Scalp Hunter" 12-11-60 (Uncle John Sims), "Jerkwater" 1-22-61 (John Sims); *Stagecoach West*—"Image of a Man" 1-31-61 (Henchard), "The Root of Evil" 2-28-61, "The Butcher" 3-28-61 (Sam Carlin); *Lawman*—"The Long Gun" 3-4-62 (Ben Wyatt); *Empire*—"Echo of a Man" 12-11-62 (Dan Tabor); *Stoney Burke*—"King of the Hill" 1-21-63 (Zack Mundorf); *The Virginian*—"Echo from Another Day" 3-27-63 (George Bleeck), "To Make This Place Remember" 9-25-63 (Frank Sturgis), Regular 1965-66 (Starr), "Halfway Back from Hell" 10-1-69 (Marshal Teague); *Temple Houston*—"Enough Rope" 12-19-63 (Benedict Williams), "The Gun That Swept the West" 3-5-64 (Jed Dobbs); *Branded*—"One Way Out" 4-18-65 (Joshua Murdock); *Wild Wild West*—"The Night of the Casual Killer" 10-15-65 (John Maxwell Avery), "The Night of the Steel Assassin" 1-7-66 (Iron Man Torres); *F Troop*—"Honest Injun" 11-30-65 (Prof. Cornelius Clyde); *A Man Called Shenandoah*—"The Young Outlaw" 12-27-65 (Moberly); *The Big Valley*—"The Invaders" 12-29-65 (Daddy Cade); *The Road West*—"Power of Fear" 12-26-66 (Dr. Kruger); *The Monroes*—"Gun Bound" 1-25-67 (Pete Lamson); *The Outcasts*—"Take Your Lover in the Ring" 10-28-68 (Colonel Romulus); *The High Chaparral*—"Surtee" 2-28-69 (Surtee), "The Legacy" 11-28-69 (Gar Burnett); *Barbary Coast*—"The Day Cable Was Hanged" 12-26-75 (General Barton); *How the West Was Won*—Episode One 2-6-77 (Bishop Benjamin), Episode Two 2-7-77 (Bishop Benjamin); *Big Hawaii*—Regular 1977 (Barrett Fears); *Young Maverick*—Regular 1979-80 (Marshal Edge Troy).

Dekker, Albert (1904-5/5/68). Films: "Rangers of Fortune" 1940 (George Bird); "Honky Tonk" 1941 (Brazos Hearn); "In Old California" 1942 (Britt Dawson); "Buckskin Frontier" 1943 (Gideon Skene); "In Old Oklahoma" 1943 (Jim "Hunk" Gardner); "The Kansan" 1943 (Steve Barat); "The Woman of the Town" 1943 (Bat Masterson); "Salome, Where She Danced" 1945 (Von Bohlen); "California" 1946 (Mr. Pike); "The Fabulous Texan" 1947 (Gibson Hart); "Wyoming" 1947 (Lassiter); "Fury at Furnace Creek" 1948 (Leverett); "The Furies" 1950 (Reynolds); "The Kid from Texas" 1950 (Alexander Kain); "Three Thousand Hills" 1959 (Conrad); "The Wonderful Country" 1959 (Capt. Rucker); "The Wild Bunch" 1969 (Pat Marrigan). ¶TV: *Rawhide*—"Josh" 1-15-65 (Josh), "Crossing at White Feather" 12-7-65 (Jonas Bolt); *Bonanza*—"The Bottle Fighter" 5-12-68 (Barney Sturgess).

De Kova, Frank (1910-10/15/81). Films: "The Big Sky" 1952 (Moleface); "Pony Soldier" 1952 (Gustin); "Viva Zapata!" 1952 (Col. Guajarado); "Arrowhead" 1953 (Chief Chattez); "Drum Beat" 1954 (Modoc Jim); "Passion" 1954 (Martinez); "They Rode West" 1954 (Isatai); "The Man from Laramie" 1955 (Padre); "Strange Lady in Town" 1955 (Anse Hatlo); "The Lone Ranger" 1956 (Red Hawk); "Pillars of the Sky" 1956 (Zachariah); "Reprisal!" 1956 (Charlie Washackle); "The White Squaw" 1956 (Yellow Elk); "Ride Out for Revenge" 1957 (Yellow Wolf); "Run of the Arrow" 1957 (Red Cloud); "Apache Territory" 1958 (Lugo); "Cowboy" 1958 (Alcide); "Day of the Outlaw" 1959 (Denver); "The Jayhawkers" 1959 (Evans); "The Wild Country" 1971 (Two Dog). ¶TV: *Gunsmoke*—"Greater Love" 12-1-56 (Tobeel), "Kick Me" 1-26-57 (Tobeel), "The Last Fling" 3-23-57 (Mulligan Rives), "Gunsmuggler" 9-27-58 (Tobeel), "Target" 9-5-59 (Gypsy Chief); *The Adventures of Rin Tin Tin*—"Major Swanson's Choice" 5-31-57 (Culebra), "Return to Fort Apache" 9-20-57 (Okoma); *Wagon Train*—"The Emily Rossiter Story" 10-30-57, "The Gabe Carswell Story" 1-15-58, "The Rodney Lawrence Story" 6-10-59 (Ocheo), "The Tom Tuckett Story" 3-2-60, "Clyde" 12-27-61 (Arapahoe Chief), "The George B. Hanrahan Story" 3-28-62 (Running Bear), "Thye Isaiah Quickfox Story" 1-31-65 (Isaiah Quickfox); *Cheyenne*—"Wagon Tongue North" 4-8-58, "The Rebellion" 10-12-59 (Juarez), "Cross Purpose" 10-9-61 (Spotted Bull), "Pocketful of Stars" 11-12-62 (Red Knife); *The Restless Gun*—"Dragon for a Day" 9-29-58 (Lupo Lazaro); *The Californians*—"The Painless Extractionist" 12-9-58 (Up-A-Mug); *Buckskin*—"Coup Stick" 2-2-59 (Potato Man); *The Rifleman*—"The Indian" 2-17-59 (Old Chief), "Meeting at Midnight" 5-17-60 (Carl Miller); *Black Saddle*—"Client: Martinez" 3-7-59 (Rubio Calderon); *Laramie*—"Circle of Fire" 9-22-59 (Yellow Knife), "Wolf Cub" 11-21-61 (Chief Red Wolf), "The Unvanquished" 3-12-63 (Tah-sa); *The Deputy*—"Back to Glory" 9-26-59 (the Killer); *The Alaskans*—Regular 1959-60 (Fantan); *Rawhide*—"Incident at Spanish Rock" 12-18-59 (Villegro), "Incident of the Boomerang" 3-24-61 (Chief Tawyawp); *Tales of Wells Fargo*—"Red Ransom" 2-8-60 (Joe Black); *Hotel De Paree*—"Sundance and the Hero of Bloody Blue Creek" 3-11-60 (Indian); *Lawman*—"Cornered" 12-11-60 (Jed Barker); *The Rebel*—"Shriek of Silence" 3-19-61 (Sturgis); *The Tall Man*—"The Cloudbusters" 4-29-61 (Mike Gray Eagle); *Gunslinger*—"The New Savannah Story" 5-18-61 (Don Ignacio Alesandro); *Maverick*—"A Technical Error" 11-26-61 (Blackjack Carney); *Frontier Circus*—"The Shaggy Kings" 12-7-61 (Karl Maynard); *The Outlaws*—"Charge!" 3-22-62 (Chief White Tongue); *The Dakotas*—"A Nice Girl from Goliah" 5-13-63 (Matt Kellog); *The Travels of Jaimie McPheeters*—"The Day of the 12 Candles" 2-23-64 (Arapaho Chief); *Daniel Boone*—"The Sound of Wings" 11-12-64 (Chief Talakum), "Four-Leaf Clover" 3-25-65 (Saugus); *F Troop*—Regular 1965-67 (Wild Eagle); *The High Chaparral*—"A Way of Justice" 12-13-68 (Aguirre); *Death Valley Days*—"The Lady Doctor" 10-11-69.

DeKoven, Roger (1906-1/28/88). TV: *The High Chaparral*—"The Fillibusteros" 10-22-67 (Rodolfo).

de la Cruz, Joe (1892-12/14/61). Films: "The Night Rider" 1920; "The

Bearcat" 1922 (One Eye); "The Santa Fe Trail" 1923-serial; "Western Yesterdays" 1924 (Rude Reverence); "Call of the West" 1930 (Mexicali); "Hell's Heroes" 1930 (Jose); "The Battling Buckaroo" 1932; "Hidden Valley" 1932 (Henchman); "Law and Lawless" 1932; "Trailing the Killer" 1932 (Pedro); "The Cactus Kid" 1934 (Cheyenne); "The Prescott Kid" 1934 (Antonio); "Lawless Borders" 1935; "The Unconquered Bandit" 1935; "Ramona" 1936 (Servant); "Sunset of Power" 1936 (Indian Joe); "Vigilantes Are Coming" 1936-serial (Peon Slave); "Frontiers of '49" 1939 (Romero); "Oklahoma Frontier" 1939 (Cheyenne); "Zorro's Fighting Legion" 1939-serial (Bridge Heavy); "Adventures of Red Ryder" 1940-serial (Apache Kid); "The Tulsa Kid" 1940; "The Westerner" 1940 (Mex).

De Lacy, Phillipe (1917-). Films: "The Royal Rider" 1929 (King Michael XI).

De La Mothe, Leon (1880-6/12/43). Films: "The Desert Hawk" 1924 (Sheriff Jackson); "Cyclone Bob" 1926 (Bert Rodgers); "Desperate Chance" 1926; "Road Agent" 1926; "The Painted Trail" 1928 (Bluff Gunter); "The Trail Riders" 1928; "Trailin' Back" 1928.

De La Motte, Marguerite (1902-3/10/50). Films: "A Sage Brush Hamlet" 1919 (Dora Lawrence); "Arizona" 1918 (Lena); "Mark of Zorro" 1920 (Lolita); "The Sagebrusher" 1920 (Mary Warren); "The U.P. Trail" 1920 (Alice Lee); "Fools of Fortune" 1922 (Marion DePuyster); "The Last Frontier" 1926 (Beth); "Shadow Ranch" 1930 (Ruth); "Overland Mail" 1942-serial.

de Lancie, John. Films: "Testimony of Two Men" TVM-1977 (Jerome Eaton); "Houston: The Legend of Texas" TVM-1986 (John Van Fossen). ¶TV: *Young Riders*—"Good Night Sweet Charlotte" 1-4-92 (Lyle Wicks); *Legend*—Regular 1995 (Prof. Janos Bartok).

Delaney, Charles (1892-8/31/59). Films: "Satan Town" 1926 (Frisco Bob); "The Adventurer" 1928 (Barney O'Malley); "The Lonesome Trail" 1930 (Judd Rascomb); "The Fighting Trooper" 1934 (Blackie); "Trails of the Wild" 1935 (Brent); "Secret Valley" 1937; "Kansas Raiders" 1950 (Pell); "The Half-Breed" 1952 (Sergeant); "Winning of the West" 1953 (Jules Brent); "The Bounty Hunter" 1954; "Running Target" 1956 (Barker).

Delaney, Leo (1885-2/4/20).

Films: "The Auction Sale of Run-Down Ranch" 1915.

Delaney, Pat. TV: *Here Comes the Brides*—"A Crying Need" 10-2-68; *The Big Valley*—"Flight from San Miguel" 4-28-69 (Sarah Mendez).

Delano, Lee. TV: *Branded*—"I Killed Jason McCord" 10-3-65.

Delano, Michael (1940-). Films: "Catlow" 1971-Span. (Rio).

de Lanti, Stella. Films: "Don Q, Son of Zorro" 1925 (the Queen).

Delany, Dana (1957-). Films: "Tombstone" 1993 (Josephine).

De La Riva, Miguel. Films: "Colt Is the Law" 1965-Ital./Span.; "Joe Dexter" 1965-Span./Ital.; "Django Does Not Forgive" 1967-Ital./Span.; "Sartana Does Not Forgive" 1968-Span./Ital.; "Adios Cjamango" 1969-Ital./Span.

Delcambre, Alfred. Films: "Wagon Wheels" 1934 (Ebe); "Home on the Range" 1935 (Lem); "Wanderer of the Wasteland" 1935 (Deputy Hines).

Del Castillo, Miguel. Films: "Charge of the Seventh Cavalry" 1964-Ital./Span./Fr.; "Heroes of the West" 1964-Span./Ital.; "Twins from Texas" 1964-Ital./Span.; "Coffin for the Sheriff" 1965-Ital./Span.; "Kid Rodelo" 1966-U.S./Span. (Chavas); "Ringo and Gringo Against All" 1966-Ital./Span.; "Ringo, the Lone Rider" 1967-Ital./Span.; "All Out" 1968-Ital./Span.; "Cowards Don't Pray" 1968-Ital./Span.; "Death Knows No Time" 1968-Span./Ital.; "One Against One ... No Mercy" 1968-Span./Ital.; "Rattler Kid" 1968-Ital./Span.; "Two Crosses at Danger Pass" 1968-Ital./Span.; "Killer Goodbye" 1969-Ital./Span. (Sam Bradshaw); "Matalo!" 1971-Ital./Span.

Del Conte, Ken (1941-). TV: *Daniel Boone*—9-23-65 (Deerfoot); *Death Valley Days*—"The Man Who Didn't Want Gold" 3-25-67 (Redmond); *Bonanza*—"Napoleon's Children" 4-16-67 (Sampson).

Delegall, Bob (1945-). TV: *Bonanza*—"Riot!" 10-3-72 (Willie Noon).

DeLeon, Raoul (1905-1/6/72). TV: *Have Gun Will Travel*—"Saturday Night" 10-8-60 (Francisco); *Sugarfoot*—"Shepherd with a Gun" 2-6-61 (Joachin); *Cheyenne*—"The Wedding Rings" 1-8-62 (Don Ignacio).

Delevanti, Cyril (1887-12/13/75). Films: "The Daltons Ride Again" 1945 (Jennings); "Ride Out for Revenge" 1957 (Preacher);

"Trooper Hook" 1957 (Junius); "Macho Callahan" 1970. ¶TV: *Gunsmoke*—"No Handcuffs" 1-21-56 (Turnkey), "The Mistake" 11-24-56 (Driver), "Laughing Gas" 3-29-58 (Old Man), "Love Thy Neighbor" 1-28-61 (Sy Tewksbury), "Double Entry" 1-2-65 (Jake), "Killer at Large" 2-5-66 (Granpa Harris); *The Adventures of Rin Tin Tin*—"Tomahawk Tubbs" 2-7-58 (Chief Nana); *Jefferson Drum*—Regular 1958-59 (Lucius Coin); *Have Gun Will Travel*—"Charley Red Dog" 12-12-59, "The Pledge" 1-16-60; *The Tall Man*—5-26-62 (Summers); *Wagon Train*—"The Heather Mahoney Story" 6-13-62 (Jamison); *The Virginian*—"The Money Cage" 3-6-63, "Execution at Triste" 12-13-67 (Stonecutter); *Daniel Boone*—10-14-65 (Nitashanta).

Delfino, Frank. TV: *Bonanza*—"Hoss and the Leprechauns" 12-22-63 (Timothy); *Wild Wild West*—"The Night of the Glowing Corpse" 10-29-65 (Barker).

DelGado, Louis. Films: "The Young Country" TVM-1970; "The Castaway Cowboy" 1974; "The New Maverick" TVM-1978; "Bret Maverick" TVM-1981 (Shifty). ¶TV: *Maverick*—"A Rage for Vengeance" 1-12-58 (Gunman).

Delgado, Roger (1918-6/17/73). Films: "The Singer Not the Song" 1961-Brit. (De Cortinez).

De Linsky, Victor (1883-5/9/51). Films: "Union Pacific" 1939 (Card Player).

DeLisle, Chris. Films: "Wild and Wooly" TVM-1978 (Lacey Sommers).

Dell, Claudia (1910-9/5/77). Films: "Destry Rides Again" 1932 (Sally Dangerfield); "Trails End" 1935 (Janet Moorehead); "Ghost Patrol" 1936 (Natalie Brent); "Boots of Destiny" 1937 (Alice Wilson).

Dell, Gabriel (1919-7/3/88). Films: "Bowery Buckaroos" 1947 (Gabe). ¶TV: *Nakia*—"No Place to Hide" 10-19-74 (Archie).

Dell, Myrna (1923). Films: "Raiders of Red Gap" 1943 (Jane); "Arizona Whirlwind" 1944 (Ruth Hampton); "Guns of Hate" 1948 (Dixie); "Lust for Gold" 1949 (Lucille); "Roughshod" 1949 (Helen); "The Furies" 1950 (Dallas Hart); "The Bushwackers" 1952 (Norah Taylor); "Last of the Desperadoes" 1955 (Clara); "The Naked Hills" 1956 (Aggie). ¶TV: *Jim Bowie*—"The Lottery" 4-19-57 (Helen Harris); *Maverick*—"The Seventh Hand" 3-2-

58 (Anita); *The Texan*—"Rough Track to Payday" 12-28-59 (Miss Delly).

Dell'Acqua, Alberto (Robert Widmark, Albert Waterman, Cole Kitosh). Films: "Seven Guns for the MacGregors" 1965-Ital./Span. (Dick MacGregor); "Texas, Adios" 1966-Ital./Span. (Jim); "The Avengers" 1966-Ital.; "Kill Them All and Come Back Alone" 1967-Ital./Span. (Blade); "Up the MacGregors!" 1967-Ital./Span. (Dick MacGregor); "Man: His Pride and His Vengeance" 1967-Ital./Ger. (Lt. Garzas); "Killer Caliber .32" 1967-Ital. (Averell); "Vengeance" 1968-Ital./Ger.; "Boot Hill" 1969-Ital.; "Fighters from Ave Maria" 1970-Ital./Ger. (Serrano); "Calibre .38" 1971-Ital.; "Have a God Funeral, My Friend … Sartana Will Pay" 1971-Ital.; "Trinity and Sartana Are Coming" 1972-Ital. (Sartana); "Son of Zorro" 1973-Ital./Span.

Dells, Dorothy. TV: *Have Gun Will Travel*—"The Gold Toad" 11-21-59, "Fight at Adobe Wells" 3-12-60, "The Campaign of Billy Banjo" 5-28-60, "One, Two Three" 2-17-62, "The Jonah" 5-26-62 (Mary Murdock), "The Fifth Bullet" 9-29-62 (Emmy Bartlett), "Sweet Lady of the Moon" 3-9-63 (Mary Murdock); *Rawhide*—"Incident of the Woman Trap" 1-26-62 (Jane); *Laredo*—"Lazyfoot, Where Are You?" 9-16-65 (Saloon Girl).

Delmar, Thomas. Films: "Their Compact" 1917 (Pay Dirt Thompson); "A Broadway Cowboy" 1920 (Sheriff Pat McCann); "Across the Divide" 1921 (Dago); "The Bad Man" 1923 (Capt. Blake); "The Girl of the Golden West" 1923 (Handsome Harry); "The Rainbow Trail" 1925 (Venters); "The Wyoming Wildcat" 1925 (Cyclops).

Delon, Alain (1935-). Films: "Texas Across the River" 1966 (Don Andrea Baldasar); "Red Sun" 1971-Fr./Ital./Span. (Gauche); "Zorro" 1974-Ital./Fr. (Diego/Miguel Eorrieta).

DeLongis, Anthony. TV: *Hawkeye*—"Amnesty" 2-9-95 (Jack Munch).

del Pozo, Angel (1934-). Films: "Fort Yuma Gold" 1966-Ital./Fr./Span. (Lefevre); "A Place Called Glory" 1966-Span./Ger. (Josh); "Savage Pampas" 1966-U.S./Span./Arg. (Lt. Del Rio); "The Man Called Noon" 1973-Brit./Span./Ital. (Janish); "Pancho Villa" 1975-Span.

del Rey, Pilar. Films: "The Kid from Texas" 1950 (Margarita); "Black Horse Canyon" 1954 (Juanita); "Jubilee Trail" 1954 (Carmelita Velasco);

"The Siege at Red River" 1954 (Lukoa); "Giant" 1956 (Mrs. Obregon); "…And Now Miguel" 1966 (Tomasita). ¶TV: *Have Gun Will Travel*—"The Return of the Lady" 2-21-59 (Maria); *Daniel Boone*—"Flag of Truce" 11-21-68 (Moranta); *Wild Wild West*—"The Night of the Plague" 4-4-69 (Mexican Matron); *The High Chaparral*—"Fiesta" 11-20-70.

Del Rio, Dolores (1905-4/11/83). Films: "Ramona" 1928 (Ramona); "The Trail of '98" 1929 (Berna); "The Man from Dakota" 1940 (Jenny); "Flaming Star" 1960 (Neddy Burton); "Cheyenne Autumn" 1964 (Spanish Woman). ¶TV: *Branded*—"The Ghost of Murrieta" 3-20-66 (Antonia Molinera).

De Luca, Lorealla (Hally Hammond) (1940-). Films: "A Pistol for Ringo" 1965-Ital./Span. (Ruby); "The Return of Ringo" 1966-Ital./Span.

De Luca, Pupo. Films: "Trinity Is Still My Name" 1974-Ital. (Padre).

DeLuise, Dom (1933-). Films: "Evil Roy Slade" TVM-1972 (Logan Delp); "Blazing Saddles" 1974 (Buddy Bizarre); "An American Tail: Fievel Goes West" 1991 (voice of Tiger).

De Luna, Alvaro. Films: "The Christmas Kid" 1966-Span./Ital. (Burt Froelich); "The Hellbenders" 1966-U.S./Ital./Span.; "Navajo Joe" 1966-Ital./Span. (Sancho Ramirez); "The Mercenary" 1968-Ital./Span. (Ramon).

Del Val, Jean (1892-3/13/75). Films: "Hudson Bay" 1941 (Captain); "Outlaws of the Desert" 1941 (Faran El Kalar); "Triple Justice" 1940 (Don Solas); "The Iron Mistress" 1952 (St. Sylvain). ¶TV: *Maverick*— "Hostage!" 11-10-57 (Anton Riviage); *Bonanza*—"Marie, My Love" 2-10-63.

Del Vando, Amapola (1909-2/25/88). Films: "Along the Navajo Trail" 1945; "Conquest of Cochise" 1953 (Senora de Cordova); "Cowboy" 1958 (Aunt).

DeMain, Gordon (G.D. Woods) (1897-3/5/54). Films: "Headin' North" 1930 (Foreman); "God's Country and the Man" 1931; "The Montana Kid" 1931 (Sheriff Barclay); "Oklahoma Jim" 1931; "Rider of the Plains" 1931 (Sheriff); "The Ridin' Fool" 1931 (Sheriff Anderson); "Son of the Plains" 1931 (Sheriff); "Two-Fisted Justice" 1931 (Huston); "Broadway to Cheyenne" 1932; "The Forty-Niners" 1932 (Jed Hawkins); "Galloping Thru" 1932;

"Honor of the Mounted" 1932; "Single-Handed Sanders" 1932; "The Western Code" 1932 (Sheriff Purdy); "Cowboy Counsellor" 1933 (State's Attorney); "Crashing Broadway" 1933 (Sheriff Jenks); "The Dude Bandit" 1933 (Dad Mason); "The Fighting Texans" 1933 (Julian Nash); "The Fugitive" 1933 (Nicholson); "Lucky Larrigan" 1933; "Rainbow Ranch" 1933 (Sheriff); "The Cactus Kid" 1934; "The Fighting Trooper" 1934; "The Lawless Frontier" 1934 (Miller); "The Lucky Texan" 1934 (Sheriff Miller); "The Painted Stallion" 1937-serial (Governor); "King of the Stallions" 1942; "Overland to Deadwood" 1942; "Thundering Hoofs" 1942 (Underwood); "West of Tombstone" 1942 (Wilfred Barnet).

DeMarc, Bert. Films: "Fighting Fury" 1924 (Crooked-Nose Evans); "Hidden Loot" 1925 (Manning); "Ridin' Thunder" 1925 (Art Osgood); "The Border Sheriff" 1926 (Joe Martinez); "Wild Horse Stampede" 1926 (Henchman); "Rough and Ready" 1927 (Bill Blake).

Demarest, William (1892-12/28/83). Films: "Ride on, Vaquero" 1941 (Barney); "Along Came Jones" 1945 (George Fury); "Whispering Smith" 1948 (Bill Dansing); "Escape from Fort Bravo" 1953 (Campbell); "The Yellow Mountain" 1954 (Jackpot Wray); "The Far Horizons" 1955 (Sergeant Gass); "The Rawhide Years" 1956 (Brand Comfort). ¶TV: *The Rebel*—"The Hope Chest" 12-25-60 (Ulysses Bowman); *Tales of Wells Fargo*—Regular 1961-62 (Jeb); *Bonanza*—"The Hayburner" 2-17-63 (Enos), "Old Sheba" 11-22-64 (Tweedy).

DeMario, Donna. Films: "Apache Rose" 1947 (Rosa Vega); "Robin Hood of Monterey" 1947.

De Marney, Terence (1909-5/26/71). TV: *The Adventures of Rin Tin Tin*—"The Lost Puppy" 11-9-56 (Willie Markham); *Maverick*—"The Jeweled Gun" 11-24-57 (Snopes), "Diamond in the Rough" 1-26-58 (Murphy), "Game of Chance" 1-4-59 (Auctioneer), "Arizona Black Maria" 10-9-60 (Fingers Louie), "Mr. Muldoon's Partner" 4-15-62 (Terrance E. Rafferty); *Wagon Train*—"The Liam Fitzmorgan Story" 10-28-58 (Carney), "The Hunter Malloy Story" 1-21-59 (Whitey Burke), "The Albert Farnsworth Story" 10-12-60 (Mike O'Toole); *Johnny Ringo*—Regular 1959-60 (Case Thomas); *Bonanza*—"Mr. Henry Comstock" 11-7-59 (Pat O'Reilly); *Have Gun Will Travel*—"The Black Handkerchief" 11-14-59

(Fitzgerald), "Tiger" 11-28-59, "Saturday Night" 10-8-60 (Kip).

de Mendoza, Alberto. Films: "Awkward Hands" 1968-Span./Ital. (the Whip); "A Bullet for Sandoval" 1970-Ital./Span. (Lucky Boy); "Forgotten Pistolero" 1970-Ital./Span.

Demetrio, Anna (1900-11/8/59). Films: "Arizona Mahoney" 1936 (Indian Woman); "In Old Mexico" 1938 (Elena); "The Texans" 1938 (Rosita Rodriguez); "Law of the Pampas" 1939 (Dolores Rameriez); "The Llano Kid" 1939 (Fat Maria); "Young Buffalo Bill" 1940 (Elena); "Bandit Queen" 1950 (Maria). ¶TV: *The Cisco Kid*—"Bates Story" 9-29-51.

DeMetz, Danielle. Films: "Sign of Zorro" 1964-Ital./Span. ¶TV: *Have Gun Will Travel*—"Les Girls" 9-26-59 (Annette).

DeMille, Cecil B. (1881-1/21/59). Films: "Son of Paleface" 1952 (Cameo).

DeMille, Katherine (1911-4/27/95). Films: "Call of the Wild" 1935 (Marie); "Drift Fence" 1936 (Molly Dunn); "Ramona" 1936 (Margarita); "The Californian" 1937 (Chata); "In Old Caliente" 1939 (Rita); "Unconquered" 1947 (Hannah); "Man from Del Rio" 1956 (Woman).

DeMillie, William C. (1878-3/8/55). Films: "Rose of the Rancho" 1914.

Demongeot, Mylene (1936-). Films: "The Singer Not the Song" 1961-Brit. (Locha).

de More, Harry C. Films: "The Plow Woman" 1917 (Andy MacTavish); "A Prisoner for Life" 1919; "The Brand of Courage" 1921; "Old Dynamite" 1921.

Demourelle, Jr., Vic. Films: "The Man from Texas" 1939 (Jeff Hall); "Mexicali Rose" 1939 (Hollister).

Dempster, Carol (1901-2/1/91). Films: "Scarlet Days" 1919 (Lady Fair).

DeMunn, Jeffrey. Films: " I Married Wyatt Earp" TVM-1983 (Doc Holliday).

Demyan, Lincoln (1925-10/6/91). TV: *The Rifleman*—"The Lonesome Ride" 5-2-61 (Kelly Banner); *The Outlaws*—"The Connie Masters Story" 10-12-61 (Cass Andrews); *Bonanza*—"The Cheating Game" 2-9-64, "The Dilemma" 9-19-65 (Hicks), "The Deserter" 3-16-69 (Trooper), "The Arrival of Eddie" 5-19-68 (Amos); *Gunsmoke*—"The Storm" 9-25-65 (Cowboy); *Branded*—"Kellie" 4-24-66; *Cimarron*

Strip—"The Judgment" 1-4-68; *The Big Valley*—"They Called Her Delilah" 9-30-68 (Townsman), "The Battle of Mineral Springs" 3-24-69; *The Men from Shiloh*—"The Price of the Hanging" 11-11-70 (Gannon); *Kung Fu*—"The Garments of Rage" 11-8-74 (Stanley).

D'Enery, Guy. Films: "Zorro's Fighting Legion" 1939-serial (Don Francisco); "Covered Wagon Days" 1940 (Diego); "Mark of Zorro" 1940 (Don Jose); "The Masked Rider" 1941 (Don Sebastian); "Prairie Pioneers" 1941 (Don Miguel).

Deneuve, Catherine (1943-). Films: "Don't Touch White Women!" 1974-Ital. (Marie-Helene).

Dengate, Dennis. Films: "Hang 'Em High" 1968.

Dengel, Jake (1933-11/14/94). Films: "The Tracker" TVM-1988; "Four Eyes and Six-Guns" TVM-1992 (Kid O'Banion).

Dennehy, Brian (1938-). Films: "Butch and Sundance: The Early Days" 1979 (O.C. Hanks); "Silverado" 1985 (Cobb). ¶TV: *Shelley Duvall's Tall Tales*—"Wild Bill Hickok" 9-85 (Wild Bill Hickok).

Denning, Richard (1914-). Films: "The Texans" 1938 (Cpl. Parker); "Union Pacific" 1939 (Reporter); "Geronimo" 1940 (Lt. Larned); "Northwest Mounted Police" 1940 (Constable Thornton); "Hangman's Knot" 1952 (Lee Kemper); "Battle of Rogue River" 1954 (Stacey Wyatt); "The Gun That Won the West" 1955 (Jack Gaines); "The Oklahoma Woman" 1956 (Steve Ward); "The Buckskin Lady" 1957 (Dr. Bruce Merritt). ¶TV: *Cheyenne*—"The Black Hawk War" 1-24-56 (Capt. Quinlan).

Dennis, Eddie. Films: "Rainbow Rangers" 1924 (Anteater Jake).

Dennis, Fred. Films: "Doc" 1971 (Johnny Ringo).

Dennis, John (1920-7/30/73). Films: "The Return of Jack Slade" 1955 (Kid Stanley); "Tickle Me" 1965 (Adolph the Chef). ¶TV: *Sergeant Preston of the Yukon*—"Father of the Crime" 4-19-56 (Hank Manners); *The Restless Gun*—"Remember the Dead" 11-17-58 (Jed Baldwin); *Maverick*—"Betrayal" 3-22-59 (Pete); *The Deputy*—"Dark Reward" 3-26-60 (Hawkins), "The Hard Decision" 1-28-61 (John); *Tales of Wells Fargo*—"The Repentant Outlaw" 5-29-61 (Red); *Wagon Train*—"The Kitty Pryer Story" 11-18-63; *The Legend of Jesse James*—"The Judas Boot" 11-8-65 (Brad Curtis); *The Outcasts*—"The

Town That Wouldn't" 3-31-69 (Binns); *Kung Fu*—"The Soldier" 11-29-73 (Sgt. Dismore).

Dennis, Nick (1904-11/14/80). "Four for Texas" 1964 (Angel); "The Iron Mistress" 1952 Nex Coupe); "Gunpoint" 1966 (Nicos); "The Good Guys and the Bad Guys" 1969 (Engineer). ¶TV: *Jim Bowie*—"Counterfeit Dixie" 9-27-57 (Pierre Lamond); *Have Gun Will Travel*—"Helen of Abajinian" 12-28-57; *The Rebel*—"The Earl of Durango" 6-12-60 (Durango), "The Hunted" 11-6-60 (Trapper), "The Liberators" 1-1-61 (Greco); *Lawman*—"The Mad Bunch" 10-2-60 (Skitter); *Death Valley Days*—"The Unshakable Man" 5-9-62 (Pietro Ferragano).

Dennison, Eva. Films: "The Squaw Man" 1931 (Lady Phoebe Kerhill).

Dennison, Jo Carroll. Films: "Beyond the Purple Hills" 1950 (Mollie Rayburn). ¶TV: *Wild Bill Hickok*—"Ex-Convict Story" 11-20-51.

Denny, Malcolm. Films: "Drug Store Cowboy" 1925 (Wilton).

Denny, Reginald (1891-6/16/67). Films: "Jaws of Steel" 1922; "Never Let Go" 1922; "Plain Grit" 1922; "The Iroquois Trail" 1950 (Capt. Brownell); "Fort Vengeance" 1953 (Maj. Trevett); "Cat Ballou" 1965 (Sir Harry Percival).

Denny, Susan (1934-). Films: "The Sheriff of Fractured Jaw" 1958-Brit. (Cora).

DeNormand, George (1904-12/23/76). Films: "Melody Trail" 1935 (Pete); "The Painted Stallion" 1937-serial (Oldham); "The Kid from Texas" 1939 (Sailor); "The Lone Ranger Rides Again" 1939-serial (Posseman #8); "King of the Royal Mounted" 1940-serial (Kent); "Stardust on the Sage" 1942; "West of the Law" 1942; "The Ghost Rider" 1943; "Law of the Valley" 1944; "Nevada" 1944 (Bartender); "The Gay Amigo" 1949 (Corporal); "Satan's Cradle" 1949 (Idaho); "Fence Riders" 1950; "Gunslingers" 1950 (Pete); "Law of the Panhandle" 1950; "Outlaw Gold" 1950 (Whitey); "Outlaws of Texas" 1950 (Bilson); "Over the Border" 1950 (Tucker); "Silver Raiders" 1950 (Clark); "Six Gun Mesa" 1950; "Blazing Bullets" 1951; "Colorado Ambush" 1951; "Man from Sonora" 1951; "Oklahoma Justice" 1951; "Stagecoach Driver" 1951; "Canyon Ambush" 1952; "Canadian Mounties vs. Atomic Invaders" 1953-serial (Ed Peters). ¶TV: *The Cisco Kid*—

"Boomerang" 1-20-51, "Counterfeit Money" 1-27-51, "Cattle Rustling" 2-3-51, "Medicine Flats" 3-10-51, "Railroad Land Rush" 3-17-51, "The Will" 3-24-51; *The Roy Rogers Show*—"Tossup" 12-2-56 (Jed Coolin).

Dent, Vernon (1900-11/5/63). Films: "Daring Danger" 1932 (Pee Wee); "The Riding Tornado" 1932 (Hefty); "Texas Cyclone" 1932 (Hefty); "The Fugitive Sheriff" 1936; "Back to the Woods" 1937-Short (Governor); "Outlaws of the Prairie" 1937 (Bearded Man); "Teacher's Pest" 1939-short; "Yes, We Have No Bonanza" 1939-short (Sheriff); "Cactus Makes Perfect" 1942-short (Red); "Pistol Packin' Nitwits" 1945-short; "Rockin' in the Rockies" 1945 (Stanton); "Cowboy Blues" 1946; "The Harvey Girls" 1946 (Engineer); "Lone Star Moonlight" 1946; "Renegades" 1946 (Daleb Smart); "Out West" 1947-short (Doctor); "The Sea of Grass" 1947 (Conductor); "Bonanza Town" 1951 (Whiskers); "Pals and Gals" 1954-short (Doctor);

Denton, Crahan (1914-12/4/66). Films: "Hud" 1963 (Jesse). ¶TV: *Tate*—"The Reckoning" 8-24-60 (Abel King); *Have Gun Will Travel*—"The Puppeteer" 12-24-60 (Jack Burnaby), "The Trap" 3-3-62 (Marshal Jim Buell), "The Jonah" 5-26-62 (Carl Soddenberg), "Sweet Lady of the Moon" 3-9-63 (Carl Soddenberg); *Bonanza*—"The Secret" 5-6-61 (Jake Parson); *Gunsmoke*—"Apprentice Doc" 12-9-61 (Clint), "Blind Man's Bluff" 2-23-63 (Frank Walker), "The Magician" 12-21-63 (Wells); *The Virginian*—"Run Away Home" 4-24-63 (John Lewis); *Temple Houston*—"Letter of the Law" 10-3-63 (Judge Brandon); *The Travels of Jaimie McPheeters*—"The Day of the Wizard" 1-12-64 (Col. Ewen Pollux).

Denver, Bob (1935-). Films: "The Wackiest Wagon Train in the West" 1976 (Dusty). ¶TV: *Dusty's Trail*—Regular 1973 (Dusty).

De Palma, Walter. Films: "Hollywood Cowboy" 1937 (Rolfe Metzger); "Rhythm of the Saddle" 1938 (Leach).

De Paul, David. Films: "The Sad Horse" 1959 (Sam); "Walk Tall" 1960 (Buffalo Horn).

Depp, Harry (1886-3/31/57). Films: "Pals of the Saddle" 1938 (Hotel Clerk); "The Return of the Cisco Kid" 1939; "Danger Ahead" 1940 (James); "Heart of the Rio Grande" 1942; "In Old New Mexico" 1945 (Printer).

Depp, Johnny (1963-). Films: "Dead Man" 1995 (William Blake).

Derek, John (1926-). Films: "Ambush at Tomahawk Gap" 1953 (Kid); "The Last Posse" 1953 (Jed Clayton); "The Outcast" 1954 (Jet Cosgrave); "Run for Cover" 1955 (Davey Bishop); "Fury at Showdown" 1957 (Brock Mitchell). ¶TV: *Zane Grey Theater*—"They Were Four" 3-15-57 (Andy Todd), "Storm Over Eden" 5-4-61 (Chet Loring); *Frontier Circus*—Regular 1961-62 (Ben Travis).

De Rita, Joe (1909-7/3/93). Films: "The Bravados" 1958 (Simms); "The Outlaws Is Coming!" 1965 (Curley Joe).

Dern, Bruce (1936-). Films: "The War Wagon" 1967 (Hammond); "Waterhole No. 3" 1967 (Deputy); "Hang 'Em High" 1968 (Miller); "Will Penny" 1968 (Rafe Quint); "Support Your Local Sheriff" 1969 (Joe Danby); "Sam Hill: Who Killed the Mysterious Mr. Foster?" TVM-1971 (Doyle Pickett); "The Cowboys" 1972 (Long Hair); "Posse" 1975 (Jack Strawhorn); "Harry Tracy—Desperado" 1982 (Harry Tracy); "Into the Badlands" TVM-1991 (Barston); "Dead Man's Revenge" TVM-1994 (Payton McCay). ¶TV: *Stoney Burke*—Regular 1962-63 (E.J. Stocker); *Wagon Train*—"The Eli Bancroft Story" 11-11-63 (Seth Bancroft), "Those Who Stay Behind" 11-8-64 (Jud Fisher), "The Indian Girl Story" 4-18-65; *The Virginian*—"First to Thine Own Self" 2-12-64 (Pell), "The Payment" 12-16-64 (Lee Darrow), "A Little Learning…" 9-29-65 (Bert Kramer); *Rawhide*—"Walk into Terror" 10-5-65 (Ed Rankin); *Laredo*—"Rendezvous at Arillo" 10-7-65 (Durkee); *Gunsmoke*—"Ten Little Indians" 10-9-65 (Doyle Phleger), "South Wind" 11-27-65 (Judd Print), "The Jailor" 10-1-66 (Lou Stone), "The Long Night" 2-17-69 (Guerin); *A Man Called Shenandoah*—"The Verdict" 11-1-65 (Bobby Ballantine); *Branded*—"The Wolfers" 1-9-66 (Les); *The Big Valley*—"Under a Dark Sea" 2-9-66 (Follet), "By Force and Violence" 3-30-66 (Harry Dixon), "Lost Treasure" 9-12-66 (Clovis), "Four Days to Furnace Hill" 12-4-67 (Gabe Skeets), "The Prize" 12-16-68 (John Weaver); *The Loner*—"To Hang a Dead Man" 3-12-66 (Merrick); *Bonanza*—"The Trackers" 1-7-68 (Cully Maco), "The Gold Mine" 3-8-70 (Bayliss); *Lancer*—"Julie" 10-29-68 (Lucas), "A Person Unknown" 11-25-69 (Tom Nevill); *The High Chaparral*—"Only the Bad Come to Sonora" 10-2-70 (Wade).

De Rosa, Franco (1944-). Films: "Ringo and His Golden Pistol" 1966-Ital. (Juanito Perez); "Yankee" 1967-Ital./Span.

DeRosas, Enrique (1888-1/20/48). Films: "Hi Gaucho!" 1936 (Miguel); "Sandflow" 1937 (Joaquin).

De Rosselli, Rex (1876-7/21/41). Films: "The Brand Blotter" 1912; "Buck's Romance" 1912; "The Cattle Rustlers" 1912; "The Cowboy's Best Girl" 1912; "A Cowboy's Mother" 1912; "The Dynamiters" 1912; "An Equine Hero" 1912; "The Horseshoe" 1912; "Jim's Vindication" 1912; "The Ranger and His Horse" 1912; "A Rough Ride with Nitroglycerine" 1912; "So-Jun-Wah and the Tribal Law" 1912; "Two Men and a Girl" 1912; "Why Jim Reformed" 1912; "Buster's Little Game" 1913; "The Capture of Bad Brown" 1913; "The Cattle Thief's Escape" 1913; "The Deputy's Sweetheart" 1913; "Dishwash Dick's Counterfeit" 1913 (Dishwash Dick); "The Escape of Jim Dolan" 1913; "The Galloping Romeo" 1913; "His Father's Deputy" 1913; "How Betty Made Good" 1913; "Howlin' Jones" 1913; "Juggling with Fate" 1913; "Physical Culture on the Quarter Circle V Bar" 1913; "The Rejected Lover's Luck" 1913 (John); "Religion and Gun Practice" 1913; "Saved from a Vigilantes" 1913; "The Schoolmarm's Shooting Match" 1913; "The Sheriff and the Rustler" 1913; "The Sheriff of Yawapai County" 1913; "The Silver Grindstone" 1913; "The Trail Breakers" 1914; "The Ghost Wagon" 1915 (Jeff); "The Superior Claim" 1915; "The Timber Wolf" 1916; "The Fighting Gringo" 1917 (Ramon Orinez); "The Secret Peril" 1919; "Lazy Lightning" 1926 (William Harvey).

de Rouen, Reed (1921-). Films: "The Sheriff of Fractured Jaw" 1958-Brit. (Clayborn).

Derr, Richard (1917-5/8/92). TV: *Walt Disney Presents*—"Gallegher" 1965-67 (Dwyer).

De Rue, Baby Carmen (1908-9/28/86). Films: "The Squaw Man" 1914 (Hal).

DeRuiz, Nick. Films: "The Half-Breed" 1922 (Juan Del Rey); "The Night Hawk" 1924 (Manuel Valdez); "Call of the West" 1930 (Frijoles); "Wings of Adventure" 1930 (Manuel); "Robin Hood of El Dorado" 1936 (Mexican Peon); "White Fang" 1936 (Posse Member).

De Sade, Ana. Films: "The Return of a Man Called Horse" 1976 (Moonstar); "Triumphs of a Man Called Horse" 1984 (Redwing).

De Sales, Francis (1912-9/25/88). Films: "Apache Territory" 1958 (Sgt. Sheehan); "Return to Warbow" 1958 (Sheriff); "Face of a Fugitive" 1959 (Allison). ¶TV: *Sergeant Preston of the Yukon*—"Trapped" 2-2-56 (Milt Strang), "One Good Turn" 3-8-56 (Ben Barlow), "Incident at Gordon Landing" 7-26-56 (Harry), "Revenge" 10-4-56 (Carl Stack); *Colt .45*—"Sign in the Sand" 1-3-58; *Maverick*—"The Seventh Hand" 3-2-58 (Mr. Gilling), "The People's Friend" 2-7-60 (Mayor Culpepper); *Tales of Wells Fargo*—"Faster Gun" 10-6-58; *Jefferson Drum*—"$50 for a Dead Man" 11-13-58 (Bass Williard); *Sugarfoot*—"The Hunted" 11-25-58 (Major Sterling), "Outlaw Island" 11-24-59 (Warren); *Wanted—Dead or Alive*—"Sheriff of Red Rock" 11-29-58; *Wyatt Earp*—"The Judas Goat" 3-31-59, "Love and Shotgun Gibbs" 4-21-59, "The Scout" 3-1-60 (Smith); *The Deputy*—"The Chain of Action" 5-7-60 (Porter), "The Deadly Breed" 9-24-60 (Mattson); *Man from Blackhawk*—"Gold Is Where You Find It" 6-24-60 (Sheriff); *Wagon Train*—"The Jim Bridger Story" 5-10-61 (Mark); *Laramie*—"The Jailbreakers" 12-19-61, "War Hero" 10-2-62; *The Virginian*—"It Tolls for Thee" 11-21-62, "The Exiles" 1-9-63, "A Distant Fury" 3-20-63 (Dave McCoy); *Bonanza*—"The Beginning" 11-25-62, "The Arrival of Eddie" 5-19-68 (Major); *Great Adventure*—"The Testing of Sam Houston" 1-31-64 (Speaker of the House); *Wild Wild West*—"The Night of the Skulls" 12-16-66 (Charleston).

De Santis, Joe (1909-8/30/89). Films: "The Last Hunt" 1956 (Ed Black); "Tension at Table Rock" 1956 (Burrows); "Buchanan Rides Alone" 1958 (Esteban Gomez); "…And Now Miguel" 1966 (Padre de Chavez); "The Professionals" 1966 (Ortega); "Blue" 1968 (Carlos); "God Will Forgive My Pistol" 1969-Ital.; "Powderkeg" TVM-1971. ¶TV: *Gunsmoke*—"Home Surgery" 10-8-55 (Hawtree), "Gone Straight" 2-9-57 (Gunter), "The Jackals" 2-12-68 (Sheriff Handlin), "Lyle's Kid" 9-23-68 (Hoxy); *Tales of Wells Fargo*—"Rio Grande" 6-3-57 (Garrett); *Zane Grey Theater*—"The Deserters" 10-4-57 (Balam); *Have Gun Will Travel*—"The Bostonian" 2-1-58 (Clint Bryant); *Tombstone Territory*—"Legacy of Death" 6-11-58 (Commandante Nexor); *Wanted—Dead or Alive*—"Dead End" 9-27-58 (Luis Portilla); *Rawhide*—"Incident at Alabaster Plain" 1-16-59 (Justice Cardin), "Incident of the Blue Fire" 12-

11-59 (Jed Bates), "Incident of the Captive" 12-16-60 (Ellis Crowley); *Sugarfoot*—"The Royal Raiders" 3-17-59 (Gen Carlos Jose Perez); *Cheyenne*—"The Rebellion" 10-12-59 (Manuel), "Road to Three Graves" 10-31-60 (Manuel Loza); *Man from Blackhawk*—"Vendetta for the Lovelorn" 11-20-59 (Fidelio Pirozzi); *The Law of the Plainsman*—"The Rawhiders" 1-28-60 (Mr. Cooper); *Maverick*—"A State of Siege" 1-1-61 (Don Manuel); *Riverboat*—"Chicota Landing" 12-5-60 (Juan Cortilla); *Bonanza*—"The Rival" 4-15-61, "Look to the Stars" 3-18-62 (Samuel Michelson), "Second Chance" 9-17-67 (Dawson), "Decision at Los Robles" 3-22-70 (Father Xavier); *The Tall Man*—"Death or Taxes" 5-27-61 (Waco); *The Virginian*—"The Mountain of the Sun" 4-17-63 (General Rodello), "Ring of Silence" 10-27-65 (Juan Pablo); *Great Adventure*—"The Pathfinder" 3-6-64 (General Vallejo); *Wagon Train*—"The Last Circle Up" 4-27-64 (Samuel Morse); *Daniel Boone*—"The Prophet" 1-21-65 (Jogossassee); *Branded*—"The Test" 2-7-65 (Indian Chief); *Laredo*—"The Would-Be Gentleman of Laredo" 4-14-66; *The Road West*—"A War for the Gravediggers" 4-10-67 (Octaviano); *Lancer*—"The Escape" 12-31-68 (Doc Hildenbrand); *The High Chaparral*—"A Good, Sound Profit" 10-30-70 (Ruiz); *Sara*—3-19-76 (Vittori).

Descher, Sandy. TV: *Tales of the Texas Rangers*—"Prairie Raiders" 11-12-55 (Vicky Bradford); *My Friend Flicka*—"Old Danny" 3-2-56 (Betty Jepson); *Wagon Train*—"Around the Horn" 10-1-58 (Pat Cobb).

DeShannon, Jackie (1944-). TV: *Wild Wild West*—"The Night of the Janus" 2-15-69 (Torry Elder); *The Virginian*—"A King's Ransom" 2-25-70 (Mag).

DeShon, Nancy. Films: "Silent Valley" 1935 (Helen Jones); "Tombstone Terror" 1935 (Blond Flapper); "Trail of Terror" 1935 (June O'Day); "Wolf Riders" 1935 (Peggy).

De Silva, Aura. Films: "Sutter's Gold" 1936 (Senora Alvarado).

DeSilva, Fred (1885-2/16/29). Films: "The Fighting Guide" 1922 (Indian Bill); "Durand of the Bad Lands" 1925 (Pete Garson); "Idaho" 1925-serial; "The Rainbow Trail" 1925 (Shadd); "The Bar C Mystery" 1926-serial (Grisp); "Buffalo Bill on the U.P. Trail" 1926 (Bill Henry).

DeSimone, Bonnie. Films: "Rodeo King and the Senorita" 1951 (Juanita Morales).

Desmond, Mary Jo. Films: "The Last Frontier" 1932-serial (Aggie Kirby).

Desmond, William (1878-11/3/49). Films: "The Dawn Maker" 1916 (Bruce Smithson); "Lieutenant Danny, U.S.A." 1916 (Lt. Danny Ward); "Fighting Back" 1917 (the Weakling); "Beyond the Shadows" 1918 (Jean DuBois); "Closin' In" 1918 (Jack Brandon); "Deuce Duncan" 1918 (Deuce Duncan); "The Pretender" 1918 (Bob Baldwin); "Wild Life" 1918 (Chick Ward); "Bare-Fisted Gallagher" 1919 (Gallagher); "The Blue Bandanna" 1919 (Jerry Jerome); "The Mints of Hell" 1919 (Dan Burke); "The Prodigal Liar" 1919 (Percival Montgomery Edwards); "A Sage Brush Hamlet" 1919 (Larry Lang); "A Broadway Cowboy" 1920 (Burke Randolph); "Fightin' Mad" 1921 (Bud McGraw); "Perils of the Yukon" 1922-serial; "McGuire of the Mounted" 1923 (Bob McGuire); "Shadows of the North" 1923 (Ben "Wolf" Darby); "The Measure of a Man" 1924 (John Fairmeadow); "The Riddle Rider" 1924-serial; "The Sunset Trail" 1924 (Happy Hobo); "Ace of Spades" 1925-serial; "Blood and Steel" 1925 (Gordon Steele); "The Burning Trail" 1925 (Smiling Bill Flannigan); "The Meddler" 1925 (Richard Gilmore); "Ridin' Pretty" 1925 (Sky Parker); "Ridin' Through" 1925 (O'Day); "Strings of Steel" 1926-serial; "Red Clay" 1927 (Chief John Nisheto); "The Return of the Riddle Rider" 1927-serial; "The Mystery Rider" 1928-serial (Winthrop Lane); "The Vanishing Rider" 1928-serial; "Battling with Buffalo Bill" 1931-serial (John Mills); "Lightning Warrior" 1931-serial; "Oklahoma Jim" 1931 (Lacey); "The Phantom of the West" 1931-serial (Martin Blain); "The Vanishing Legion" 1931-serial (Sheriff of Milesburg); "Heroes of the West" 1932-serial (John Blaine); "The Last Frontier" 1932-serial (Custer); "Clancy of the Mounted" 1933-serial (Dave Moran); "Fargo Express" 1933 (Sheriff); "Gordon of Ghost City" 1933-serial (John); "Rustlers' Roundup" 1933 (Sheriff Holden); "Strawberry Roan" 1933 (Colonel Brownlee); "Border Guns" 1934 (Tulsa Pete); "Frontier Days" 1934; "Rawhide Terror" 1934 (Tom Blake); "The Red Rider" 1934-serial (Sheriff); "The Way of the West" 1934 (Cash Horton); "Born to Battle" 1935; "Courage of the North" 1935; "The Cowboy and the Bandit" 1935 (Sheriff); "Cyclone of the Saddle" 1935 (Wagon Master); "Defying the Law" 1935 (Jim Kenmore); "Devil's

Canyon" 1935; "Five Bad Men" 1935 (Mattoon); "The Ghost Rider" 1935 (Guard); "Gunfire" 1935; "Nevada" 1935 (Wilson); "The Phantom Cowboy" 1935; "Powdersmoke Range" 1935 (Happy Hopkins); "The Roaring West" 1935-serial (Jim Parker); "Rough Riding Ranger" 1935 (Major Wright); "Rustlers of Red Dog" 1935-serial (Ira Dale); "Timber Terrors" 1935 (Bob Parker, the Timber Terror); "Cavalry" 1936 (Major); "Custer's Last Stand" 1936-serial (Wagon Boss); "Song of the Gringo" 1936 (Court Clerk); "Song of the Saddle" 1936 (Tim); "Treachery Rides the Range" 1936 (Driver); "Vigilantes Are Coming" 1936-serial (Anderson); "Arizona Days" 1937 (Stranger); "Headin' for the Rio Grande" 1937 (Mack); "Winners of the West" 1940-serial (Brine); "Young Bill Hickok" 1940; "Bury Me Not on the Lone Prairie" 1941; "Down Rio Grande Way" 1942; "Raiders of the West" 1942; "The Silver Bullet" 1942; "Cheyenne Roundup" 1943; "The Lone Star Trail" 1943 (Bartender); "Marshal of Gunsmoke" 1944; "Oklahoma Raiders" 1944; "The Old Texas Trail" 1944; "Tall in the Saddle" 1944; "Beyond the Pecos" 1945; "Frontier Gal" 1945 (Man in Saloon).

Desny, Ivan (1922-). Films: "Guns for San Sebastian" 1967-U.S./ Fr./Mex./Ital. (Col. Calleja).

DeStefani, Joseph (1879-10/26/ 40). Films: "Bar 20 Justice" 1938 (Perkins); "Rancho Grande" 1940 (Jose); "Sky Bandits" 1940 (Professor Lewis).

Deste, Luli (1909-7/7/51). Films: "Outlaws of the Desert" 1941 (Marie Karitza).

Deuel, Geoffrey. Films: "Chisum" 1970 (Billy the Kid). ¶TV: *The High Chaparral*—"The Assassins" 1-7-68 (Kelso); *Nakia*—"The Driver" 11-2-74 (Brennon).

Deuel, Peter (1940-12/31/71). Films: "Cannon for Cordoba" 1970 (Andy Rice); "The Young Country" TVM-1970 (Honest John Smith); "Alias Smith and Jones" TVM-1971 (Hannibal Hayes/Joshua Smith). ¶TV: *The Virginian*—"The Good-Hearted Badman" 2-7-68 (Jim Dewey), "The Price of Love" 2-12-69 (Denny Todd); *Alias Smith and Jones*—Regular 1971 (Hannibal Heyes/Joshua Smith).

Deus, Beny. Films: "Gunmen of the Rio Grande" 1964-Fr./Ital./Span.; "Heroes of the West" 1964-Span./ Ital.; "Jaguar" 1964-Span.; "Finger on the Trigger" 1965-Span./Ital./U.S. (O'Brien); "Woman for Ringo" 1966-

Ital./Span.; "Magnificent Texan" 1967-Ital./Span.; "Clint the Stranger" 1968-Ital./Span./Ger.

de Valdez, Carlos (1894-10/30/ 39). Films: "The Prescott Kid" 1934 (Don Rafael Ortega); "Bold Caballero" 1936 (Alcalde); "Drums of Destiny" 1937 (Don Salvador Dominguez); "Old Louisiana" 1937 (Governor Don Jose Gonzales); "The Llano Kid" 1939 (Don Pedro).

Devane, William (1939-). Films: "McCabe and Mrs. Miller" 1971 (the Lawyer). ¶TV: *Gunsmoke*—"Kimbro" 2-12-73 (Moss Stratton).

De Vargas, Valentin. Films: "The Firebrand" 1962 (Joaquin Murieta); "Powderkeg" TVM-1971. ¶TV: *Colt .45*—"The Mirage" 1-10-58 (Carlos Hernandez); *Broken Arrow*—"Manhunt" 6-3-58 (Miguel); *The Tall Man*—"The Woman in Black" 5-12-62 (Ramon); *Great Adventure*—"The Special Courage of Captain Pratt" 2-14-64; *Rawhide*—"The Book" 1-8-65 (Ernie); *Bonanza*—"Woman of Fire" 1-17-65; *Death Valley Days*—"Death in the Desert" 5-9-65 (Nick Avote), "Biscuits and Billy the Kid" 11-1-69, "Amos and the Black Bull" 2-28-70; *Daniel Boone*—"The Christmas Story" 12-23-65 (Oneha); *Gunsmoke*—"Old Friend" 2-4-67 (Cheeno), "The Devil's Outpost" 9-22-69 (Pacos); *Wild Wild West*—"The Night of the Winged Terror" 1-17-68 & 1-24-68 (Col. Cheveros); *The High Chaparral*—"An Anger Greather Than Mine" 9-18-70 (Rodrigo), "The New Lion of Sonora" 2-19-71 (Rodrigo); *Kung Fu*—"Barbary House" 2-15-75 (Mendoza), "Flight to Orion" 2-22-75 (Mendoza), "The Brothers Cain" 3-1-75 (Mendoza), "Full Circle" 3-15-75 (Mendoza).

Devaull, William P. (1871-6/4/ 45). Films: "With Hoops of Steel" 1919 (Jim Harlin); "In the Days of Buffalo Bill" 1922-serial (Edward M. Stanton); "Kentucky Days" 1923 (Scipio).

De Vega, Jose (1934-4/8/90). TV: *Death Valley Days*—"Showdown at Kamaaina Flats" 7-4-62; *Wagon Train*—"The Wagon Train Mutiny" 9-19-62 (Renaldo); *Bonanza*—"To Kill a Buffalo" 1-9-66 (Tatu); *Branded*—"The Ghost of Murrieta" 3-20-66 (Juan Molinera); *Wild Wild West*—"The Night of the Golden Cobra" 9-23-66 (John Mountaintop); *The High Chaparral*—"Bad Day for a Thirst" 2-18-68 (Sourdough).

Deverall, Helen. Films: "Boss of Hangtown Mesa" 1942 (Betty Wilkins); "The Blocked Trail" 1943.

De Vere, Harry (1870-10/10/ 23). Films: "Davy Crockett" 1916 (James Vaughn); "The End of the Trail" 1916 (John Robinson); "The Man from Bitter Roots" 1916 (Ogden Crane); "The Highway of Hope" 1917 (Philip Garst); "True Blue" 1918 (Buck); "Last of the Duanes" 1919 (Buck's Uncle); "The Love Call" 1919 (Bill Slade); "The Joyous Troublemaker" 1920 (Richard Stanton); "The Orphan" 1920 (Joe Sneed); "Penny of Top Hill Trail" 1921 (Louis Kingdon); "Ruth of the Range" 1923-serial.

Devereaux, Shawn. Films: "Fandango" 1970 (Mona DeLyse).

Devi, Kamala. "Geronimo" 1962 (Teela). ¶TV: *Branded*—"The Mission" 3-14-65, 3-21-65 & 3-28-65 (Laurette Lansing), "The Assassins" 3-27-66 & 4-3-66 (Laurette Ashley); *Cowboy in Africa*—"To Build a Beginning" 12-11-67 (M'Koru).

Devine, Andy (1905-2/18/77). Films: "Destry Rides Again" 1932; "Law and Order" 1932 (Johnny Kinsman); "Stagecoach" 1939 (Buck Rickabaugh, the Stagecoach Driver); "Buck Benny Rides Again" 1940 (Andy); "Geronimo" 1940 (Sneezer); "Man from Montreal" 1940 (Constable Bones Blair); "Trail of the Vigilantes" 1940 (Meadows); "When the Daltons Rode" 1940 (Ozark); "Badlands of Dakota" 1941 (Spearfish); "The Kid from Kansas" 1941 (Andy); "Men of the Timberland" 1941; "Road Agent" 1941 (Andy); "North to the Klondike" 1942 (Klondike); "Sin Town" 1942 (Judge Eustace Vale); "Frontier Badman" 1943 (Slim); "Frisco Sal" 1945 (Bunny); "Frontier Gal" 1945 (Big Ben); "Canyon Passage" 1946 (Ben Dance); "Bells of San Angelo" 1947 (Cookie); "The Fabulous Texan" 1947 (Elihu); "The Michigan Kid" 1947 (Buster); "On the Old Spanish Trail" 1947 (Cookie Bullfincher); "Springtime in the Sierras" 1947 (Cookie Bullfincher); "The Vigilantes Return" 1947 (Andy); "Eyes of Texas" 1948 (Cookie Bullfincher); "The Gallant Legion" 1948 (Windy Hornblower); "The Gay Ranchero" 1948 (Cookie Bullfincher); "Grand Canyon Trail" 1948 (Cookie Bullfincher); "Night Time in Nevada" 1948 (Cookie Bullfincher); "Old Los Angeles" 1948 (Sam Bowie); "Under California Stars" 1948 (Cookie Bullfincher); "The Far Frontier" 1949 (Judge Cookie Bullflacher); "The Last Bandit" 1949 (Casey Brown); "New Mexico" 1951 (Sgt. Garrity); "Slaughter Trail" 1951 (Sgt. McIntosh); "Montana Belle" 1952 (Pete Bivins);

"Thunder Pass" 1954; "Two Rode Together" 1961 (Sgt. Darius P. Posey); "How the West Was Won" 1962 (Cpl. Peterson); "The Man Who Shot Liberty Valance" 1962 (Link Appleyard); "Ballad of Josie" 1968 (Judge Tatum); "The Over-the-Hill Gang" TVM-1969 (Judge Amos Polk); "Ride a Northbound Horse" 1969; "The Over-the-Hill Gang Rides Again" TVM-1970 (Amos Polk). ¶TV: *Wild Bill Hickok*—Regular 1951-53 (Jingles B. Jones); *Wagon Train*—"The Jess MacAbbee Story" 11-25-59 (Jess MacAbbee); *The Rounders*—11-29-66 (Honest John Denton), 12-20-66 (Honest John Denton); *The Virginian*—"Yesterday's Timepiece" 1-18-67 (Amos Tyke); *Bonanza*—"A Girl Named George" 1-14-68 (Roscoe); *Gunsmoke*—"Stryker" 9-29-69 (Jed Whitlow); *The Men from Shiloh*—"The Animal" 1-20-71 (Dr. Houseman); *Alias Smith and Jones*—"The Man Who Corrupted Hadleyburg" 1-27-72 (Sheriff Pintell).

Devine, Ted. Films: "Canyon Passage" 1946 (Asa Dance).

DeVito, Danny (1944-). Films: "Goin' South" 1978 (Hog).

Devlin, Don. Films: "Three Violent People" 1956 (Juan). ¶TV: *The Adventures of Rin Tin Tin*—"The Epidemic" 11-21-58 (Dae), "The Ming Vase" 3-13-59; *Tombstone Territory*—12-25-59 (Seth).

Devlin, Joe (1899-10/1/73). Films: "The Oklahoma Kid" 1939 (Keely); "They Died with Their Boots On" 1941 (Bartender); "Blood on the Moon" 1948; "Bitter Creek" 1954 (Pat Cleary); "Silver Lode" 1954 (Walt Little); "Tennessee's Partner" 1955 (Prendergast). ¶TV: *Wanted—Dead or Alive*—"Baa-Baa" 1-4-61; *Gunsmoke*—"Catawomper" 2-10-62 (Jester), "Reprisal" 3-10-62 (Dan Binny).

deVol, Gordon (1946-). TV: *Here Come the Brides*—"Stand Off" 11-27-68, "Next Week, East Lynne" 10-17-69; *The Big Valley*—"The Profit and the Lost" 12-2-68 (Ned).

Devon, Laura (1940-). TV: *Wide Country*—"My Candle Burns at Both Ends" 12-20-62 (Valerie Moore); *Stoney Burke*—"Forget Me More" 3-25-63 (Stacy Morgan); *Rawhide*—"Canliss" 10-30-64 (Augusta Canliss); *The Big Valley*—"The Velvet Trap" 11-7-66 (Sabrina).

Devon, Richard (1931-). Films: "Scorching Fury" 1952; "Badman's

Country" 1958 (Harvey Logan); "Money, Women and Guns" 1958 (Setting Sun); "Gunfighters of Abilene" 1960 (Ruger); "The Comancheros" 1961 (Estevan); "Cattle King" 1963 (Vince Bodine). ¶TV: *The Adventures of Rin Tin Tin*—"The Bugle Call" 9-9-55 (Chief Sasabi) "Sorrowful Joe" 9-21-56 (Kessala); *Zane Grey Theater*—"Badge of Honor" 5-3-57 (Army Hendricks), "License to Kill" 2-7-58 (Walker); *Wyatt Earp*—"The Time for All Good Men" 6-4-57 (Rance Purcell), "The Reformation of Doc Holliday" 12-30-58 (Dan Leving); *Sergeant Preston of the Yukon*—"The Rebel Yell" 10-10-57 (Wolfe Trahern); *Tales of Wells Fargo*—"Dr. Alice" 2-23-58 (Mr. Bolton); *Trackdown*—"The Brothers" 5-16-58 (Fenn Dooley), "A Stone for Benny French" 10-3-58 (Morgan), "Blind Alley" 9-16-59 (Rufus Cole); *Wanted—Dead or Alive*—"The Giveaway Gun" 10-11-58, "Eager Man" 2-28-59 (Gar Foley), "Montana Kid" 9-5-59 (Freighter); *Yancy Derringer*—"Collector's Item" 3-26-59 (Jody Barker), "Duel at the Oaks" 4-9-59 (Jody Barker), "The Quiet Firecracker" 5-21-59 (Jody Barker); *Rough Riders*—"Paradise Gap" 4-16-59 (Sam Blackwell); *The Rifleman*—"Brood Brothers" 5-26-59 (Jethroe), "The Spiked Rifle" 11-24-59, "The Grasshopper" 3-1-60 (Walt Ryerson), "Miss Milly" 11-15-60 (Jack Adams), "The Silent Knife" 12-20-60 (Ben Macowan), "The Stand-In" 10-23-61 (Gus Potter), "The Most Amazing Man" 11-26-62 (Lovett); *The Law of the Plainsman*—"Prairie Incident" 10-1-59, "Stella" 3-31-60 (Cy Erby); *Johnny Ringo*—"The Hunters" 10-29-59 (Jess Meade); *Colt .45*—"Yellow Terror" 11-15-59 (Ed Pike); *Riverboat*—"Landlubbers" 1-10-60 (Barney); *The Texan*—"The Taming of Rio Nada" 1-11-60 (Tim Craven), "Sixgun Street" 1-18-60 (Tim Craven), "The Terrified Town" 1-25-60 (Tim Craven); *The Rebel*—"The Crime" 2-7-60 (Collmer); *Hotel De Paree*—"Sundance and the Greenhorn Trader" 2-26-60 (Pemmican Joe); *Bonanza*—"The Avenger" 3-19-60, "The Trail Gang" 11-26-60, "The Scapegoat" 10-25-64 (Weaver), "A Bride for Buford" 1-15-67 (Blackie); *Laramie*—"Saddle and Spur" 3-29-60 (Trask), "Gun Duel" 12-25-62 (Del Shamley); *Sugarfoot*—"Vinegaroom" 3-29-60 (Steve Wyatt); *Overland Trail*—"Sour Annie" 5-8-60 (Deal); *The Tall Man*—"The Parson" 10-29-60 (John Lesley); *Stagecoach West*—"A Fork in the Road" 11-1-60 (Ohio), "Songs My Mother Told Me" 2-21-61

(Dan Murchison), "The Remounts" 3-14-61 (Hody), "The Renegades" 6-20-61 (Ed Bush); *Death Valley Days*—"Preacher with a Past" 4-11-62 (Deke); *Rawhide*—"Incident of the Buryin' Man" 1-4-63 (Cole Striker); *Wagon Train*—"The Emmett Lawton Story" 3-6-63 (Perk Lopely); *Gunsmoke*—"The Quest for Asa Janin" 6-1-63 (Asa Janin), "Ex-Con" 11-30-63 (Pitts); *The Virginian*—"Brother Thaddeus" 10-30-63 (Arthur Faber), "Long Ride to Wind River" 1-19-66 (Beamer), "No Drums, No Trumpets" 4-6-66 (Ed Beal); *Destry*—"Big Deal at Little River" 3-20-64 (Benson); *Daniel Boone*—"The Choosing" 10-29-64 (Tice Fowler), "Seminole Territory" 1-13-66 (Hotalla), "The Loser's Racer" 11-10-66 (Stokes), "The Plague That Came to Ford's Run" 10-31-68 (Archer), "The Traitor" 10-30-69 (Many Lives); *A Man Called Shenandoah*—"The Onslaught" 9-23-65 (Lloyd Fitts); *The Big Valley*—"Boots with My Father's Name" 9-29-65 (Phelps), "A Stranger Everywhere" 12-9-68 (Link); *Laredo*—"Jinx" 12-2-65 (Max Fander), "No Bugles, One Drum" 2-24-66 (Max Vander); *Iron Horse*—"Shadow Run" 1-30-67 (DeWitt); *The High Chaparral*—"A Quiet Day in Tucson" 10-1-67 (Kansas); *The Guns of Will Sonnett*—"End of the Rope" 1-12-68 (Crawford); *Lancer*—"Warburton's Edge" 2-4-69 (Sexton Joe).

Devore, Dorothy (1899-9/10/76). Films: "The Prairie Wife" 1925 (Chaddie Green); "Senor Daredevil" 1926 (Sally Blake).

De Vries, George. Films: "Gavilan" 1968.

de Vries, Hans. Films: "Shalako" 1968-Brit./Fr. (Adjutant).

Devry, Elaine (1935-). Films: "The Cheyenne Social Club" 1970 (Pauline). ¶TV: *Bonanza*—"The Search" 2-14-65 (Valerie).

Dew, Eddie (1909-4/6/72). Films: "Wagon Train" 1940 (O'Connor); "Cyclone on Horseback" 1941; "King of the Texas Rangers" 1941-serial (Thomas); "Sunset in Wyoming" 1941; "Pirates of the Prairie" 1942; "Riding the Wind" 1942 (Henry Dodge); "Shadows on the Sage" 1942; "Beyond the Last Frontier" 1943 (John Paul Revere); "Fighting Frontier" 1943 (Walton); "Raiders of Sunset Pass" 1943 (John Paul Revere); "Red River Robin Hood" 1943; "Six Gun Gospel" 1943; "Lucky Cowboy" 1944-short; "The Old Texas Trail" 1944 (Dave); "Riders of the Santa Fe" 1944 (Larry Anderson); "Trail to Gunsight" 1944 (Dan Creede); "Trigger Trail" 1944 (Bob Reynolds); "Beyond the Pecos" 1945; "Renegades of the Rio Grande" 1945 (Cal Benedict).

Dewey, Elmer (1884-10/28/54). Films: "Bring Him In" 1921 (Baptiste); "The Escape" 1926 (Silas Peele).

Dewey, Jane. Films: "Wells Fargo" 1937 (Lucy Dorsett Trimball).

Dewhurst, Colleen (1926-8/22/91). Films: "The Cowboys" 1972 (Kate). ¶TV: *The Virginian*—"The Executioners" 9-19-62 (Celia Ames); *The Big Valley*—"A Day of Terror" 12-12-66 (Annie).

De Wilde, Brandon (1942-7/6/72). Films: "Shane" 1953 (Joey); "Night Passage" 1957 (Joey Adams); "The Missouri Traveler" 1958 (Brian Turner); "Hud" 1963 (Lon Bannon); "Deserter" 1970-U.S./Ital./Yugo. (Ferguson). ¶TV: *Wagon Train*—"The Danny Benedict Story" 12-2-59 (Danny Benedict), "The Mark Miner Story" 11-15-61 (Mark Miner); *The Virginian*—"Fifty Days to Moose Jaw" 12-12-62 (Mike Flynn), "The Orchard" 10-2-68 (Walt Bradbury); *The Men from Shiloh*—"Gun Quest" 10-21-70 (Rem Garvey).

de Wit, Jacqueline. Films: "Moonlight and Cactus" 1944 (Elsie); "Wild Beauty" 1946 (Sissy); "Lay That Rifle Down" 1955 (Aunt Sarah). ¶TV: *Man Without a Gun*—"The Quiet Strangers" 1-24-59; *Wagon Train*—"The Colonel Harris Story" 1-13-60.

de Witt, Alan (1924-6/2/76). TV: *Laredo*—"The Land Slickers" 10-14-66 (Fred Wiggins).

De Witt, Elizabeth. Films: "The Cowboy King" 1922 (Mrs. Stacey).

DeWitt, Fay (1933-). Films: "The Shakiest Gun in the West" 1968 (Violet).

DeWolfe, Billy (1907-3/5/74). TV: *Rango*—"Requiem for a Ranger" 2-24-67 (Cribs).

Dexter, Alan (1918-12/19/83). Films: "City of Badmen" 1953 (Flint); "Paint Your Wagon" 1969 (Parson). ¶TV: *Gunsmoke*—"The Big Con" 5-3-58 (Hook), "Legends Don't Sleep" 10-12-63 (Grosset); *Zane Grey Theater*—"Mission to Marathon" 5-14-59 (Reese Miner), "Shadows" 11-5-59 (Wes Torrington); *Colt .45*—"The Devil's Godson" 10-18-59 (Sheriff Ken Ryan); *Laramie*—"Duel at Alta Mesa" 2-23-60 (Lorn Gallagher); *Have Gun Will Travel*—"Ambush" 4-23-60 (Devereaux); *The Virginian*—"The Small Parade" 2-20-63.

Dexter, Anthony (1919-). Films: "Captain John Smith and Pocahontas" 1953 (Capt. John Smith); "The Parson and the Outlaw" 1957 (Billy the Kid). ¶TV: *26 Men*—"The Last Rebellion" 11-4-58; *Rawhide*—"Incident at Tinker's Dam" 2-5-60 (Chief), "Incident of the Blackstorms" 5-26-61 (Tom Lindomar); *Bat Masterson*—"The Big Gamble" 6-16-60 (Allesandro); *The High Chaparral*—"Sudden Country" 11-5-67.

Dexter, Brad (1922-). Films: "The Oklahoman" 1957 (Cass Dobie); "Last Train from Gun Hill" 1959 (Beer); "The Magnificent Seven" 1960 (Harry Luck); "Thirteen Fighting Men" 1960 (Maj. Boyd); "Invitation to a Gunfighter" 1964 (Kenarsie); "Jory" 1972 (Jack). ¶TV: *Have Gun Will Travel*—"The Hanging Cross" 12-21-57, "Deliver the Body" 5-24-58 (Jud Pelk); *Wagon Train*—"The Sally Potter Story" 4-9-58 (Billings); *Jefferson Drum*—"The Keeney Gang" 10-3-58 (Scott Keeney); *Zane Grey Theater*—"The Tall Shadow" 11-20-58 (Cleland Ames); *Cimarron City*—"Return of the Dead" 2-14-59 (Sam Masters); *Yancy Derringer*—"V As in Voodoo" 5-14-59 (Charles Hammond); *Colt .45*—"Yellow Terror" 11-15-59 (John Barker); *Bronco*—"Night Train to Denver" 12-29-59 (Al Simon); *Man from Blackhawk*—"The Biggest Legend" 1-1-60 (Jim Hayes); *Bat Masterson*—"Cattle and Cane" 3-3-60 (Dallas Agate); *Wanted—Dead or Alive*—"Prison Trail" 5-14-60 (the Stranger); *Tales of Wells Fargo*—"Stage from Yuma" 3-20-61 (Bud Pierce); *Death Valley Days*—"A Gun Is Not a Gentleman" 4-14-63 (Terry).

Dexter, John. Films: "Buffalo Bill Rides Again" 1947 (Tom Russell).

Dexter, Elliott (1870-6/23/41). Films: "A Romance of the Redwoods" 1917 (Black Brown); "The Squaw Man" 1918 (Jim Wynnegate); "A Daughter of the Wolf" 1919 (Robert Draly).

Dexter, Rosemarie (1945-). Films: "For a Few Dollars More" 1965-Ital./Ger./Span. (Colonel's Sister); "Big Ripoff" 1967-Span./Ital.; "The Dirty Outlaws" 1971-Ital. (Katy).

Dexter, Sharon. Films: "Buffalo Bill in Tomahawk Territory" 1952 (Janet).

Dey, Susan (1952-). TV: *The Quest*—"The Captive" 9-22-76 (Charlotte).

DeYoung, Cliff (1945-). TV: *Centennial*—Regular 1978-79 (John Skimmerhorn); *Hunter's Moon*—Pilot 12-1-79 (Fayette Randall).

Dhiegh, Khigh (1910-10/25/91).

TV: *Wild Wild West*—"The Night of the Samurai" 10-13-67 (Baron Saiga), "The Night of the Pelican" 12-27-68 (Din Chang); *Kung Fu*—"Alethea" 3-15-73 (Shang Tzu), "The Spirit Helper" 11-8-73 (Chung), "Besieged: Death on Cold Mountain" 11-15-74 (Sing Lu Chan), "Besieged: Cannon at the Gate" 11-22-74 (Sing Lu Chan).

D'Hondt, Danica. TV: *Wild Wild West*—"Night of the Deadly Bed" 9-24-65 (Roxanne).

Diamond, Bobby. Films: "The Silver Whip" 1953 (Jody); "The Silent Gun" TVM-1969. ¶TV: *Fury*—Regular 1955-60 (Joey Newton); *Wagon Train*—"The Dick Jarvis Story" 5-18-60 (Joe Henshaw), "The Melanie Craig Story" 2-17-64; *Empire*—"Arrow in the Sky" 4-9-63 (Arturo).

Diamond, Don (1924-). Films: "Raiders of Old California" 1957. ¶TV: *The Lone Ranger*—"Pete and Pedro" 10-27-49; *The Adventures of Kit Carson*—Regular 1951-55 (El Toro); *Circus Boy*—"The Amazing Mr. Sinbad" 10-14-56 (Ben Ali), "Alex the Great" 10-10-57 (Zarno); *Wyatt Earp*—"Justice" 12-25-56 (Stevens), "Wyatt Meets Doc Holliday" 4-23-57 (John Shanessy), "The Paymaster" 12-1-59 (Moore); *Zane Grey Theater*—"Village of Fear" 3-1-57 (Jones), "The Accuser" 10-30-58, "Interrogation" 10-1-59 (Cota); *Zorro*—Regular 1957-59 (Corporal Reyes); *Rawhide*—"Incident of the Broken Word" 1-20-61; *Empire*—"The Four Thumbs Story" 1-8-63 (Arturo); *Redigo*—"The Blooded Bull" 10-1-63 (Arturo), "Prince Among Men" 10-15-63 (Arturo), "Man in a Blackout" 11-5-63 (Arturo), "The Hunters" 12-31-63 (Trooper); *Wild Wild West*—"Night of the Deadly Bed" 9-24-65 (Bartender); *F Troop*—Regular 1965-67 (Crazy Cat); *The Big Valley*—"Tunnel of Gold" 4-20-66 (Border), "Flight from San Miguel" 4-28-69 (1st Federale); *The Guns of Will Sonnett*—"A Grave for James Sonnett" 9-22-67 (Drago); *The High Chaparral*—"To Stand for Something More" 10-24-69 (Miguel).

Diamond, Jack. TV: *The Lone Ranger*—"The Woman in the White Mask" 5-12-55; *Schlitz Playhouse of the Stars*—"The Bitter Land" 4-13-56 (Tip Case); *Gunsmoke*—"Young Man with a Gun" 10-20-56 (Peyt Kertcher); *Wyatt Earp*—"Juveniles 1878" 3-10-58 (Alf Horton); *The Adventures of Rin Tin Tin*—"Royal Recruit" 2-20-59 (Prince Michael).

Di Aquino, John. TV: *Wild-*

side—Regular 1985 (Varges De La Cosa).

Diaz, Rudy (1918-). Films: "Bandolero!" 1968 (Angel); "Mac-Kenna's Gold" 1969 (Besh); "The Undefeated" 1969 (Sanchez); "Flap" 1970 (Larry Standing Elk); "One Little Indian" 1973; "The Macahans" TVM-1976 (Chief Bear Dance); "Donner Pass: The Road to Survival" TVM-1978; "Windwalker" 1980 (Crow Eyes). ¶TV: *Bonanza*—"Salute to Yesterday" 9-29-68 (Rio); *Alias Smith and Jones*—"The McCreedy Bush" 1-21-71, "Miracle at Santa Marta" 12-30-71, "The McCreedy Feud" 9-30-72; *Kung Fu*—"A Dream Within a Dream" 1-17-74 (Toluca); *Barbary Coast*—"Arson and Old Lace" 11-14-75; *Born to the Wind* 1982 (Red Leggins).

Dibbs, Kem. Films: "Riding Shotgun" 1954 (Ben); "The Twinkle in God's Eye" 1955 (Johnny); "Daniel Boone, Trail Blazer" 1957 (Girty); "How the West Was Won" 1962 (Blacksmith). ¶TV: *Wild Bill Hickok*—"The Music Teacher" 12-2-52; *Wyatt Earp*—"Mr. Earp Meets a Lady" 9-13-55, "Bill Thompson Gives In" 9-22-55, "The Time for All Good Men" 6-4-57 (Mannen Clements), "A Papa for Butch and Ginger" 5-9-61; *Jim Bowie*—"The Birth of the Blade" 9-7-56 (Gypsy Joe), "Jim Bowie Comes Home" 10-26-56 (Curley Lambert), "The Ghost of Jean Battoo" 11-2-56 (Curley Lambert), "Thieves' Market" 3-29-57 (Eddie Harper); *Broken Arrow*—"Hermano" 11-20-56 (Sanchi); *Tales of Wells Fargo*—"Shotgun Messenger" 5-6-57 (Ed), "The Cleanup" 1-26-59 (Laredo); *Maverick*—"Relic of Fort Tejon" 11-3-57 (Connors), "Yellow River" 2-8-59 (Mills), "Maverick at Law" 2-26-61 (McGaffy), "The Maverick Report" 3-4-62 (Ames); *The Californians*—"The Barber's Boy" 11-19-57 (Steve Hazard); *Trackdown*—"The Weddding" 2-14-58 (Murray Venner); *Telephone Time*—"Trail Blazer" 4-1-58 (Simp Walker); *Decision*—"The Tall Man" 7-27-58 (Bill Dawson); *Wanted—Dead or Alive*—"Fatal Memory" 9-13-58 (Bounty Man); *Zorro*—"Zorro Rides Alone" 10-16-58 (Lucas); *The Texan*—"The Widow of Paradise" 11-24-58 (Cully Crawford), "A Race for Life" 3-16-59, "No Way Out" 9-14-59 (Troy Ferris), "Quarantine" 2-8-60 (Matt Horton), "Captive Crew" 2-22-60 (Matt Horton); *Rawhide*—"Incident of the Town in Terror" 3-6-59 (Yaeger); *Bonanza*—"The Julia Bulette Story" 10-17-59 (Sheriff Olins); *Man from Blackhawk*—"The Lady in Yellow" 6-

17-60 (Mike); *Laramie*—"License to Kill" 11-22-60 (Tibbs), "The Marshals" 4-30-63.

DiCaprio, Leonardo. Films: "The Quick and the Dead" 1995 (Kid).

DiCenzo, George (1940-). Films: "The Frisco Kid" 1979 (Darryl Diggs); "Cowboy" TVM-1983 (Davis Bentlow). ¶TV: *Gunsmoke*—"Susan Was Evil" 12-3-73 (Newt), "The First of Ignorance" 1-27-75 (Herman Bruce); *Kung Fu*—"The Predators" 10-5-74 (Jess); *How the West Was Won*—"Luke" 4-2-79 (Tomaz); *Paradise*—"A Bullet Through the Heart" 2-15-91 (Ned Wick).

Dick, Douglas (1920-). Films: "The Iron Mistress" 1952 (Narcisse de Bornay); "The Gambler from Natchez" 1954 (Claude St. Germaine); "The Oklahoman" 1957 (Mel Dobie); "Flaming Star" 1960 (Will Howard); "North to Alaska" 1960 (Lieutenant). ¶TV: *Wyatt Earp*—"Shoot to Kill" 10-8-57 (Dave McAlester), "The Schoolteacher" 3-11-58 (Billy Hanley); *Bronco*—"Freeze-Out" 12-30-58 (James Jones); *Bonanza*—"Alias Joe Cartwright" 1-26-64 (Captain Merced).

Dickerson, Dudley (1906-9/23/68). Films: "Prairie Chickens" 1943.

Dickinson, Angie (1936-). Films: "Man with the Gun" 1955 (Kitty); "The Return of Jack Slade" 1955 (Polly Logan); "Tennessee's Partner" 1955 (Girl); "The Black Whip" 1956 (Sally); "Hidden Guns" 1956 (Becky Carter); "Tension at Table Rock" 1956 (Cathy); "Gun the Man Down" 1957 (Janice); "Run of the Arrow" 1957 (Voice of Yellow Moccasin); "Shoot-Out at Medicine Bend" 1957 (Priscilla); "Rio Bravo" 1959 (Feathers); "The Last Challenge" 1967 (Lisa Denton); "Sam Whiskey" 1969 (Laura Breckinridge); "Young Billy Young" 1969 (Lily Beloit); "Death Hunt" 1981 (Vanessa); "Once Upon a Texas Train" TVM-1988 (Maggie). ¶TV: *Death Valley Days*—"Sequoia" 12-6-54; *Wyatt Earp*—"One of Jesse's Gang" 3-13-56 (Ann); *Broken Arrow*—"The Conspirators" 12-18-56 (Terry Weaver); *Gunsmoke*—"Sins of the Father" 1-19-57 (Rose Daggit); *Cheyenne*—"War Party" 2-12-57; *Have Gun Will Travel*—"A Matter of Ethics" 10-12-57; *The Restless Gun*—"Imposter for a Day" 2-17-58 (Evelyn Niemack); *Tombstone Territory*—"Geronimo" 3-5-58 (Dolores); *Colt .45*—"The Deserters" 3-28-58 (Laura Meadows); *Northwest Passage*—"The Bound Women" 10-12-58 (Rose Carver);

Wagon Train—"The Clara Duncan Story" 4-22-59 (Clara Duncan); *The Virginian*—"Ride to Delphi" 9-21-66 (Annie Carlson); *Hec Ramsey*—"The Detroit Connection" 12-30-73 (Sarah Detweiler).

Dickinson, Dick. Films: "The Fighting Marshal" 1931 (Bill Ainsley); "Lightning Warrior" 1931-serial; "The Phantom of the West" 1931-serial (Stewart); "The Vanishing Legion" 1931-serial (Rawlins); "Broadway to Cheyenne" 1932 (Gangster); "The Devil Horse" 1932-serial; "Hidden Valley" 1932 (Henchman); "Law of the West" 1932 (Buck); "Man from Hell's Edges" 1932 (Drake Brother); "Mason of the Mounted" 1932; "Texas Buddies" 1932 (Burns); "Vanishing Men" 1932; "The Fugitive" 1933 (Cook); "Galloping Romeo" 1933; "The Ranger's Code" 1933 (Henchman); "Trailing North" 1933 (Slash); "West of the Divide" 1934 (Joe); "Desert Trail" 1935; "Trail Dust" 1936 (Waggoner); "Black Bandit" 1938 (Evans); "Honor of the West" 1939 (Luke Grimes); "Silver on the Sage" 1939; "Lightning Strikes West" 1940 (Mack); "The Lost Trail" 1945 (Ed); "Pirates of Monterey" 1947 (Jailer); "The Far Country" 1955 (Miner).

Dickinson, Dorothea (1893-9/25/95). Films: "Headin' North" 1922 (Frances Wilson).

Dickinson, Homer (1890-6/6/59). Films: "Son of Paleface" 1952 (Townsman).

Dickson, Gloria (1916-4/10/45). Films: "Heart of the North" 1938 (Joyce McMillan).

Diehl, Jim. Films: "The Fighting Frontiersman" 1946; "The Lone Hand Texan" 1947 (Strawboss); "Over the Santa Fe Trail" 1947; "South of the Chisholm Trail" 1947; "The Stranger from Ponca City" 1947; "The Rangers Ride" 1948; "Tex Granger" 1948-serial (Conroy); "The Hawk of Wild River" 1952 (Al Travis). ¶TV: *The Cisco Kid*—"Stolen Bonds" 7-28-51, "Protective Association" 9-8-51; *The Roy Rogers Show*—"The Ride of the Ranchers" 4-20-52, "Go for Your Gun" 11-23-52, "The Mayor of Ghost Town" 11-30-52, "The Milliner from Medicine Hat" 10-11-53, "The Hijackers" 10-24-54; *The Lone Ranger*—"Gold Freight" 4-28-55.

Diehl, John. Films: "Buffalo Girls" TVM-1995 (General Custer).

Dierkes, John (1908-1/8/75). Films: "Silver City" 1951 (Arnie); "The Moonlighter" 1953 (Sheriff

Daws); "A Perilous Journey" 1953 (First Mate); "Shane" 1953 (Morgan); "The Vanquished" 1953 (Gen. Morris); "The Desperado" 1954 (Sgt. Rafferty); "Hell's Outpost" 1954; "Passion" 1954 (Escobar); "Silver Lode" 1954 (Blacksmith); "The Vanishing American" 1955 (Friel); "Jubal" 1956 (Carson); "The Buckskin Lady" 1957 (Swanson); "Duel at Apache Wells" 1957 (Bill Sowers); "The Halliday Brand" 1957; "Valerie" 1957; "Blood Arrow" 1958 (Ez); "The Left-Handed Gun" 1958 (McSween); "The Rawhide Trail" 1958; "The Hanging Tree" 1959 (Society Red); "The Oregon Trail" 1959 (Gabe Hastings); "The Alamo" 1960 (Jocko Robertson); "The Comancheros" 1961 (Bill); "One-Eyed Jacks" 1961 (Barber); "Oklahoma Crude" 1973 (Farmer). ¶TV: *Death Valley Days*—"Sego Lilies" 1-14-53 (Erastus); *The Adventures of Rin Tin Tin*—"The Guilty One" 3-25-55; *Gunsmoke*—"The Roundup" 9-29-56 (Sam Rydell), "Gone Straight" 2-9-57 (Ace), "My Brother's Keeper" 11-15-71 (Indian), "A Child Between" 12-24-73 (Dahoma); *Wagon Train*—"The Les Rand Story" 10-16-57; *The Restless Gun*—"The Suffragette" 3-24-58 (Sheriff John Dratton); *Wanted—Dead or Alive*—"Miracle at Pot Hole" 10-25-58 (Charlie); *The Rifleman*—"Duel of Honor" 11-11-58 (Nels Svenson), "The Sister" 11-25-58 (Blacksmith Nels); *Bonanza*—"Mr. Henry Comstock" 11-7-59 (Pat McLaughlin); *Rawhide*—"Incident at Quivira" 12-14-62 (Private); *The Slowest Gun in the West* 7-29-63 (Wild Bill).

Dierkop, Charles (1936-). Films: "Butch Cassidy and the Sundance Kid" 1969 (Flat Nose Curry); "Alias Smith and Jones" TVM-1971 (Shields); "Lock, Stock and Barrel" TVM-1971 (Corporal Fowler); "Female Artillery" TVM-1973 (Sam); "The Deerslayer" TVM-1978 (Hurry Harry March). ¶TV: *Gunsmoke*—"My Father's Guitar" 2-21-66 (Dan), "The Newcomers" 12-3-66 (Silvee), "The Deadly Innocent" 12-17-73 (Barnett); *Custer*—"Desperate Mission" 11-8-67 (Matt Ryker); *Cimarron Strip*—"The Judgment" 1-4-68; *Lancer*—"Blood Rock" 10-1-68, "Devil's Blessing" 4-22-69 (Bleaker), "The Experiment" 2-17-70; *The Outcasts*—"My Name Is Jemal" 11-18-68 (Jeeter); *Daniel Boone*—"The Return of Sidewinder" 12-12-68 (Dumas), "A Bearskin for Jamie Blue" 11-27-69; *Bonanza*—"The Fence" 4-27-69 (Sawyer), "A Deck of Aces" 1-31-71 (Nicholson), "New Man" 10-10-72 (Shorty); *The High Chaparral*—

"Friends and Partners" 1-16-70 (Slim); *Nichols*—"The Dirty Half Dozen Run Amuck" 10-28-71 (Nose); *Alias Smith and Jones*—"Everything Else You Can Steal" 12-16-71, "The Day the Amnesty Came Through" 11-25-72 (Clayton Crewes); *Kung Fu*—"The Chalice" 10-11-73 (Traphagen).

Dietrich, Marlene (1904-5/6/92). Films: "Destry Rides Again" 1939 (Frenchy); "The Spoilers" 1942 (Cherry Malotte); "Rancho Notorious" 1952 (Altar Keane).

Diffring, Anton (1918-5/20/89). Films: "Montana Trap" 1976-Ger. (Lieutenant Slade).

Digges, Dudley (1879-10/24/47). Films: "Massacre" 1934 (Elihu P. Quissenberry).

Dill, J. Webster. Films: "The One Way Trail" 1920 (Poleon); "Hands Off" 1921 (the Terrible Swede).

Dill, Jack. Films: "Follow the Girl" 1917 (Olaf); "Fame and Fortune" 1918 (Ben Davis); "Mr. Logan, U.S.A." 1918; "The Coming of the Law" 1919 (Ace); "West Is West" 1920 (Denjy); "The Big Hop" 1928 (Mechanic).

Dill, Max (1878-11/21/49). Films: "Three Pals" 1916 (Mike).

Dillard, Art (1907-3/30/60). Films: "Courageous Avenger" 1935; "Coyote Trails" 1935; "No Man's Range" 1935; "Rainbow Valley" 1935; "Red Blood of Courage" 1935 (Henchman); "The Rider of the Law" 1935; "Tracy Rides" 1935 (Outlaws); "Cavalcade of the West" 1936; "Code of the Range" 1936 (Posse); "Everyman's Law" 1936 (Saloon Man); "The Fugitive Sheriff" 1936; "Ghost Patrol" 1936 (Shorty); "The Last of the Warrens" 1936; "The Law Rides" 1936; "The Riding Avenger" 1936; "Roarin' Guns" 1936; "Rogue of the Range" 1936 (Artie, the Henchman); "The Traitor" 1936 (Roadblock Man); "Bar Z Bad Men" 1937; "Fugitive from Sonora" 1937; "The Gambling Terror" 1937; "The Old Wyoming Trail" 1937; "Outlaws of the Prairie" 1937 (Outlaw); "Range Defenders" 1937; "Two-Fisted Sheriff" 1937 (Slim); "Wild Horse Rodeo" 1937 (Bud); "Yodelin' Kid from Pine Ridge" 1937; "Billy the Kid Returns" 1938; "Gold Mine in the Sky" 1938; "Gunsmoke Trail" 1938; "The Lone Ranger" 1938-serial (Gunman #2); "Outlaws of Sonora" 1938; "Pals of the Saddle" 1938; "Riders of the Black Hills" 1938; "The Lone Ranger Rides Again" 1939-serial (Stage Guard); "Saga of Death Valley" 1939;

"Adventures of Red Ryder" 1940-serial (Stage Heavy); "The Border Legion" 1940; "The Carson City Kid" 1940; "Oklahoma Renegades" 1940; "Pioneers of the West" 1940; "The Ranger and the Lady" 1940; "The Tulsa Kid" 1940; "Billy the Kid's Fighting Pals" 1941; "The Phantom Cowboy" 1941; "The Pioneers" 1941; "Sheriff of Tombstone" 1941; "Sierra Sue" 1941; "Wyoming Wildcat" 1941; "Along the Sundown Trail" 1942; "Heart of the Golden West" 1942; "Man from Cheyenne" 1942; "North of the Rockies" 1942; "Prairie Pals" 1942 (Barfly); "Ridin' Down the Canyon" 1942; "Beyond the Last Frontier" 1943; "The Blocked Trail" 1943; "Daredevils of the West" 1943-serial (Indian); "Days of Old Cheyenne" 1943; "Mojave Firebrand" 1944; "The Phantom Rider" 1946-serial (Attacker #2); "Santa Fe Uprising" 1946; "Son of Zorro" 1947-serial (Deputy #1); "The Wild Frontier" 1947; "The Adventures of Frank and Jesse James" 1948-serial (Citizen #3); "Renegades of Sonora" 1948; "Ghost of Zorro" 1949-serial (Townsman #3); "Desperadoes of the West" 1950-serial (Ben); "The James Brothers of Missouri" 1950-serial (Blears/Townsman #1); "Vigilante Hideout" 1950 (Pete); "Don Daredevil Rides Again" 1951-serial (Attacker #1); "Leadville Gunslinger" 1952 (Sentry); "Man with the Steel Whip" 1954-serial (Barn Heavy #1). ¶TV: *The Gene Autry Show*—"Gray Dude" 12-3-50, "The Peace Maker" 12-17-50; "Ghost Town Raiders" 10-6-51, "Silver Dollars" 10-20-51; *The Roy Rogers Show*—"The Outlaw's Girl" 2-17-52, "Outlaws' Town" 3-1-52; *Wild Bill Hickok*—"The Kid from Red Butte" 8-26-52.

Dillard, Bert (1909-6/19/60). Films: "Dawn Rider" 1935 (Buck); "Rainbow Valley" 1935 (Spike); "Smokey Smith" 1935; "Texas Terror" 1935 (Red); "Code of the Range" 1936 (Posse); "The Mysterious Avenger" 1936 (Rustler); "Outlaws of the Prairie" 1937 (Outlaw); "The Colorado Trail" 1938 (Henchman); "The Lone Ranger Rides Again" 1939-serial (Raider #5); "Zorro's Fighting Legion" 1939-serial (Jaimo); "Billy the Kid Trapped" 1942; "Billy the Kid's Smoking Guns" 1942; "Devil Riders" 1944; "The Navajo Kid" 1945; "Ghost of Hidden Valley" 1946; "Three Desperate Men" 1951 (Hangman).

Dillaway, Donald (1904-11/18/82). Films: "Cimarron" 1931 (Cim); "Frontier Pony Express" 1939 (Brett Langhorne); "Gunmen of Abilene"

1950 (Bill Harper). ¶TV: *Maverick*—"Naked Gallows" 12-15-57 (Ben); *Wagon Train*—"The Dan Hogan Story" 5-14-58, "Weight of Command" 1-25-61 (Prudence), "The Odyssey of Flint McCullough" 2-15-61 (Cassie); *Wyatt Earp*—"Frontier Woman" 11-25-58 (Mr. Hildreth); *Bonanza*—"Twilight Town" 10-13-63; *The Big Valley*—"Legend of a General" 9-19-66 & 9-26-66 (Harlow Perkins); *Gunsmoke*—"Baker's Dozen" 12-25-67 (Mary).

Dillman, Bradford (1930-). Films: "The Plainsman" 1966 (Lt. Stiles); "The Legend of Walks Far Woman" TVM-1982 (Stinger). ¶TV: *The Virginian*—"Echo from Another Day" 3-27-63 (Sam Harder); *Shane*—"The Great Invasion" 12-17-66 & 12-24-66 (Major Hackett); *Wagon Train*—"The Kitty Pryer Story" 11-18-63 (Myles Brisbane); *The Big Valley*—"Day of the Comet" 12-26-66 (Eric Mercer), "A Noose Is Waiting" 11-13-67 (Dr. James Beldon); *Wild Wild West*—"The Night of the Cut Throats" 11-17-67 (Mike Trayne); *The Men from Shiloh*—"The Legacy of Spencer Flats" 1-27-71 (Slaughter); *Bonanza*—"Face of Fear" 11-14-71 (Bannon), *Alias Smith and Jones*—"The McCreedy Bust — Going, Going Gone" 1-13-72 (McCreedy); *How the West Was Won*—"The Forgotten" 3-19-79 (Col. Roland Craig).

Dillon, Brendan. Films: "Young Pioneers" TVM-1976 (Doyle); "Young Pioneers' Christmas" TVM-1976 (Doyle) ¶TV: *The Virginian*—"Woman from White Ting" 9-26-62, "The Big Deal" 10-10-62 (Mr. Bemis), "It Tolls for Thee" 11-21-62, "The Man Who Couldn't Die" 1-30-63 (Mr. Bemis), "The Thirty Days of Gavin Heath" 1-22-64 (Oliphant), "Man of the People" 12-23-64 (James Dolan); *Bonanza*—"My Brother's Keeper" 4-7-63 (Emmet); *Wide Country*—"The Care and Handling of Tigers" 4-25-63 (Coppy Donovan); *The Dakotas*—"Feud at Snake River" 4-29-63 (Alf Hinds); *The Big Valley*—"Heritage" 10-20-65 (Tim Hanrihan).

Dillon, Dickie. Films: "Sheriff of Las Vegas" 1944; "Corpus Christi Bandits" 1945 (Brush); "Great Stagecoach Robbery" 1945; "Sheriff of Cimarron" 1945 (Little Boy); "Trail of Kit Carson" 1945; "California Gold Rush" 1946.

Dillon, Edward (1880-7/11/33). Films: "The Kentuckian" 1908; "The Stage Rustler" 1908; "The Tavern-Keeper's Daughter" 1908; "The Fugitive" 1910; "The Massacre" 1912;

"The Broken Ways" 1913; "An Indian's Loyalty" 1913; "Fatty and Minnie He-Haw" 1915; "The Golden West" 1932 (Pat).

Dillon, Forrest. Films: "Days of Jesse James" 1939; "Allegheny Uprising" 1939 (Jim's Man); "The Man from Sundown" 1939 (Kirk); "Spoilers of the Range" 1939 (Red); "The Ox-Bow Incident" 1943 (Mark).

Dillon, Jack (1866-12/29/37). Films: "The Tenderfoot's Money" 1913; "The Martyrs of the Alamo" 1915 (Col. Travis); "A Case of Law" 1917; "The Law of the Yukon" 1920; "Without Compromise" 1922 (Jackson); "Double Dealing" 1923 (Jobson's Assistant); "Cisco Kid" 1931 (Bouse).

Dillon, John Webb (1877-12/20/49). Films: "Three Friends" 1912; "The Primitive Call" 1917 (Bart Jennings); "The Mohican's Daughter" 1922 (Halfbreed); "Rip Roarin' Roberts" 1924 (Sam Morgan); "Tiger Thompson" 1924 (Jim Morley); "The Vanishing American" 1925 (Naylor); "The Seventh Bandit" 1926 (Jim Gresham); "In Old Arizona" 1929 (2nd Soldier); "Diamond Trail" 1933 (Mac).

Dillon, Melinda (1939-). TV: *Bonanza*—"A Lawman's Lot Is Not a Happy One" 10-5-69 (Cissie Summers); *Sara*—4-2-76 (Lily).

Dillon, Thomas (1895-9/14/62). Films: "Duel in the Sun" 1946 (Engineer); "The Oklahoma Woman" 1956; "North to Alaska" 1960 (Barber). ¶TV: *Tales of the Texas Rangers*—"Whirlwind Raiders" 10-13-57 (Harry); *The Californians*—"The First Gold Brick" 1-6-59 (Trent); *Whispering Smith*—"Three for One" 7-3-61 (Thad).

Dills, William (1878-3/25/32). Films: "The Golden Trail" 1920 (the Dean); "Headin' North" 1922 (Hank Wilson); "The Fighting Romeo" 1925 (Gerald Mertagh).

Dilson, John H. (1891-6/1/44). Films: "The Westerner" 1934 (Sen. Lockhart); "Arizona Legion" 1939; "Racketeers of the Range" 1939 (Benson); "Stand Up and Fight" 1939 (Auctioneer); "Trouble in Sundown" 1939 (Cameron); "Adventures of Red Ryder" 1940-serial (Hale); "Beyond the Sacramento" 1940; "Danger Ahead" 1940 (Hatch); "The Dark Command" 1940; "King of the Royal Mounted" 1940-serial (Dr. Wall); "Konga, the Wild Stallion" 1940 (Judge); "Legion of the Lawless" 1940 (Morgan); "Pioneers of the West" 1940 (Morgan); "Stage to Chino" 1940;

"Thundering Frontier" 1940 (Carter Filmore); "Across the Sierras" 1941; "Cyclone on Horseback" 1941; "The Musical Bandit" 1941-short; "Sunset in Wyoming" 1941; "Buffalo Bill" 1944 (President Hayes); "The Yellow Rose of Texas" 1944.

Di Milo, Tony. Films: "Hang 'Em High" 1968.

Dinehart, Alan (1889-7/17/44). Films: "The Country Beyond" 1936 (Ray Jennings); "King of the Royal Mounted" 1936 (Becker).

Dinehart, III, Alan. Films: "Copper Canyon" 1950 (Youngest Bassett Boy). ¶TV: *Wyatt Earp*—Regular 1955-59 (Bat Masterson); *Judge Roy Bean*—"Outlaw's Son" 1-1-56 (Clint Donovan).

Dinehart, Mason Alan. TV: *Sky King*—"Frog Man" 6-29-52 (Jimmy); *The Lone Ranger*—"The Tell-Tale Bullet" 4-14-55; *The Texan*—"The Duchess of Denver" 1-5-59 (Chet Dawson), "The Taming of Rio Nada" 1-11-60 (Brazos Kid), "Sixgun Street" 1-18-60 (Brazos Kid), "The Terrified Town" 1-25-60 (Brazos Kid); *26 Men*—"The Unwanted" 3-31-59; *Death Valley Days*—"Half a Loaf" 5-5-59 (Greg).

Dingle, Charles (1887-1/19/56). Films: "Duel in the Sun" 1946 (Sheriff Hardy); "Big Jack" 1949 (Mathias Taylor).

Dion, Hector. Films: "Fighting Mad" 1917 (Clean-Up West); "The Wolf and His Mate" 1917 (Snaky Burns).

Di Reda, Joe. Films: "The True Story of Jesse James" 1957 (Bill Ryan); "Lock, Stock and Barrel" TVM-1971 (Kane). ¶TV: *Zane Grey Theater*—"Decision at Wilson's Creek" 5-17-57 (Sgt. Jasper); *The Texan*—"Private Account" 4-6-59 (Johnny Hinshaw); *Colt .45*—"The Reckoning" 10-11-59 (Hicks); *The Alaskans*—"Starvation Stampede" 11-1-59 (Dick Gray); *Man from Blackhawk*—"The Legacy" 12-25-59 (Rupe June); *Wanted—Dead or Alive*—"Prison Trail" 5-14-60 (Joe Kelly); *Bonanza*—"The Dark Gate" 3-4-61; *Gunsmoke*—"Reprisal" 3-10-62 (Blake), "The Sodbusters" 11-20-72 (Navin); *The Dakotas*—"Sanctuary at Crystal Springs" 5-6-63 (Clarence Barton); *Rawhide*—"Duel at Daybreak" 11-16-65.

Dirkson, Douglas. Films: "Dirty Little Billy" 1972 (Orville). ¶TV: *Nichols*—3-7-72; *Bonanza*—"Ambush at Rio Lobo" 10-24-72 (Gabe); *Kung Fu*—"The Soldier" 11-29-73 (Hamel); *Gunsmoke*—"Matt Dillon Must Die!"

9-9-74 (Abel); *How the West Was Won*—"The Enemy" 2-5-79 (Tally); *Young Maverick*—"Hearts O'Gold" 12-12-79.

Divine (Harris Glenn Milstead) (1944-3/7/88). Films: "Lust in the Dust" 1985 (Rosie Velez).

Divoff, Andrew. Films: "Oblivion" 1994 (Redeye). ¶TV: *Adventures of Brisco County, Jr.*—"Pirates" 10-8-93 (Blackbeard Lacutt).

Dix, Billy (1911-3/22/73). Films: "Silver Range" 1946; "Song of the Sierras" 1946; "Trail to Mexico" 1946; "West of Alamo" 1946; "Raiders of the South" 1947; "Rainbow Over the Rockies" 1947; "Frontier Revenge" 1948 (Sheriff Morgan); "Six-Gun Law" 1948 (Crowly); "The Kid from Gower Gulch" 1949; "Desperadoes of the West" 1950-serial (Townsman #2); "The Silver Bandit" 1950; "Buckaroo Sheriff of Texas" 1951; "Callaway Went Thataway" 1951 (Cowboy); "The Lion and the Horse" 1952 (Clint Adams); "Rose Marie" 1954 (Mess Waiter); "Tribute to a Badman" 1956 (Cowboy); "The Wild Dakotas" 1956; "The Lonely Man" 1957. ¶TV: *Laramie*—"Drifter's Gold" 11-29-60 (Ben).

Dix, Dorothy (1892-1/70). Films: "A Fighting Tenderfoot" 1928; "The Nevada Buckaroo" 1931 (Joan); "Drum Taps" 1933 (Eileen Carey); "The Gold Ghost" 1934-short; "Wheels of Destiny" 1934 (Mary); "Guns and Guitars" 1936 (Marjorie Miller); "Sunset of Power" 1936 (Ruth Brannum).

Dix, Richard (1894-9/20/49). Films: "The Call of the Canyon" 1923 (Glen Kilbourne); "Quicksands" 1923 (1st Lieutenant); "To the Last Man" 1923 (Jean Isbel); "The Vanishing American" 1925 (Nophaie); "The Gay Defender" 1927 (Joaquin Murietta); "Redskin" 1929 (Wing Foot); "Cimarron" 1931 (Yancey Cravat); "The Conquerors" 1932 (Roger Standish/Roger Lennox); "West of the Pecos" 1934 (Pecos Smith); "The Arizonian" 1935 (Clay Tallant); "Yellow Dust" 1936 (Bob Culpepper); "Man of Conquest" 1939 (Sam Houston); "Reno" 1939 (Bill Shear); "Cherokee Strip" 1940 (Dave Morrell); "Badlands of Dakota" 1941 (Wild Bill Hickok); "The Round Up" 1941 (Steve); "American Empire" 1942 (Dan Taylor); "Tombstone, the Town Too Tough to Die" 1942 (Wyatt Earp); "Buckskin Frontier" 1943 (Stephen Bent); "The Kansan" 1943 (John Bonniwell).

Dix, Robert (1935-). Films: "Forty Guns" 1957 (Chico Bonnell);

"Lone Texan" 1959 (Carpetbagger); "Thirteen Fighting Men" 1960 (Lt. Wilcox); "Young Jesse James" 1960 (Frank James); "Deadwood '76" 1965 (Wild Bill Hickok); "Cain's Way" 1969 (the Gang Chief); "Five Blood Graves" 1969 (Ben Thompson); "The Red, White and Black" 1970 (Walking Horse). ¶TV: *Death Valley Days*—"Sailor on a Horse" 1-27-59; *Frontier Doctor*—"Superstition Mountain" 5-9-59; *The Rifleman*—"The Raid" 6-9-59; *Gunsmoke*—"Long, Long Trail" 11-4-61 (Jamie), "Indian Ford" 12-2-62 (Spotted Wolf); *Rawhide*—"Deserter's Patrol" 2-9-62 (Kano).

Dixon, Denver (Victor Adamson) (1901-11/9/72). Films: "The Lone Rider" 1922 (Lone Rider/Hobo); "The Fighting Ranger" 1934; "Lightning Range" 1934; "Range Riders" 1934; "Riding Speed" 1934; "Arizona Trails" 1935; "Desert Mesa" 1935; "The Ghost Rider" 1935; "Ambush Valley" 1936 (Nester); "Guns and Guitars" 1936; "Danger Valley" 1937; "Way Out West" 1937 (Man in Audience); "Heroes of the Alamo" 1938; "Man's Country" 1938; "Mexicali Kid" 1938; "The Old Barn Dance" 1938; "Starlight Over Texas" 1938; "Utah Trail" 1938; "Where the Buffalo Roam" 1938 (Henchman); "Feud of the Range" 1939; "Trigger Smith" 1939; "The Golden Trail" 1940; "Ridin' the Trail" 1940; "Tonto Basin Outlaws" 1941; "Pardon My Gun" 1942; "Cowboy Commandos" 1943; "The Lone Star Trail" 1943 (Townsman); "San Antonio" 1945 (Barfly); "Moon Over Montana" 1946; "Unconquered" 1947 (Citizen); "Brand of Fear" 1949; "Riders in the Sky" 1949; "Roaring Westward" 1949; "Five Blood Graves" 1969 (Rawhide).

Dixon, Donna (1957-). Films: "No Man's Land" TVM-1984 (Sarah Wilder).

Dixon, Glenn (1917-). Films: "The Dalton Girls" 1957 (Mr. Slidell, the Mortician). ¶TV: *Shotgun Slade*—"The Deadly Key" 5-17-60 (Rance); *Rawhide*—"Incident of the Running Man" 5-5-61; *Alias Smith and Jones*—"Never Trust an Honest Man" 4-15-71 (Butler).

Dixon, Ivan (1931-). TV: *Have Gun Will Travel*—"Long Way Home" 2-4-61 (Isham Spruce); *Laramie*—"Among the Missing" 9-25-62 (Jamie Davis); *Stoney Burke*—"The Test" 5-13-63 (Dr. Manning); *Great Adventure*—"The Special Courage of Captain Pratt" 2-14-64 (Sergeant Willis).

Dixon, Joan (1931-2/20/92). Films: "Gunplay" 1951 (Terry); "Hot

Lead" 1951 (Gail Martin); "Law of the Badlands" 1951 (Velvet); "Pistol Harvest" 1951 (Felice); "Desert Passage" 1952 (Emily).

Dixon, Lee (1914-1/8/53). Films: "Angel and the Badman" 1947 (Randy McCall).

Dizon, Jesse. TV: *Kung Fu*—"The Raiders" 1-24-74 (Quoy), "Forbidden Kingdom" 1-18-75 (Potter's Apprentice).

Dobbins, Bennie (1932-2/5/88). Films: "Ride Lonesome" 1959 (Outlaw); "Barquero" 1970 (Encow); "Wild Rovers" 1971 (Sheepman); "The Life and Times of Judge Roy Bean" 1972 (Outlaw); "The Duchess and the Dirtwater Fox" 1976 (Bloodworth Gang Member); "The Mountain Men" 1980; "The Legend of the Lone Ranger" 1981 (Lopez). ¶TV: *Nichols*—"Where Did Everybody Go?" 11-30-71 (Ben); *Gunsmoke*—"Yankton" 2-7-72 (Cowboy #2); *Kung Fu*—"A Dream Within a Dream" 1-17-74 (Todd).

Dobbins, Earl (1911-2/9/49). Films: "Three Rogues" 1931 (Teamster); "Lone Texas Ranger" 1945.

Dobkin, Lawrence (1920-). Films: "Frenchie" 1950; "Kiss of Fire" 1955 (Padre Domingo); "The Badge of Marshal Brennan" 1957 (Chickamon); "Raiders of Old California" 1957; "Wild Heritage" 1958 (Josh Burrage); "Geronimo" 1962 (Gen. Crook); "Johnny Yuma" 1966-Ital. (L.J. Carradine). ¶TV: *Gunsmoke*—"How to Die for Nothing" 6-23-56 (Jacklin), "Bloody Hands" 2-16-57 (Jack Brand), "Don Mateo" 10-22-60 (Esteban Garcia); *Have Gun Will Travel*—"The Great Mojave Chase" 9-28-57 (Billy Jo Kane), "Love and a Bad Woman" 3-26-60 (Haskel Sommers), "Penelope" 12-8-62 (Col. Oliver Lacey); *Jim Bowie*—"The Alligator" 12-6-57 (Capt. Ponet), "Pirate on Horseback" 1-17-58 (Police Captain); *Trackdown*—"Look for the Woman" 12-6-57 (Lee Caldwell), "The Boy" 3-28-58 (Joel Paine), "The End of the World" 5-9-58 (Walter Trump); *Wagon Train*—"The Bije Wilcox Story" 11-19-58 (Medicine Mark); *The Rifleman*—"The Gaucho" 12-30-58 (Juan), "The Sheridan Story" 1-13-59 (Gen. Phil Sheridan), "Knight Errant" 11-13-61 (Don Chimera del Laredo), "The Day a Town Slept" 4-16-62 (Ben Judson); *Lawman*—"Conclave" 6-14-59 (Buck Walsh); *Riverboat*—"Strange Request" 12-13-59 (David Fields); *Wanted—Dead or Alive*—"Vanishing Act" 12-26-59 (Bartolo); *The Law of the Plainsman*—"The Imposter" 2-4-

60 (Hempner); *Bronco*—"The Human Equation" 3-22-60 (Colonel Arthur); *Klondike*—"The Man Who Owned Skagway" 1-30-61 (Chilkoot Sam); *Rawhide*—"The Prairie Elephant" 11-17-61 (Pascal), "The Diehard" 4-9-65 (Colonel Reed); *Empire*—"Duet for Eight Wheels" 4-30-63 (Dr. Karr); *Destry*—"Ride to Rio Verde" 4-10-64 (Molder); *The Big Valley*—"Hunter's Moon" 12-30-68 (Ben Dawes); *Bret Maverick*—"Anything for a Friend" 12-15-81 (Mondragon).

Dobson, James (1920-12/6/87). Films: "Friendly Persuasion" 1956 (Rebel Soldier); "The Storm Rider" 1957 (Cooper); "The Tall Stranger" 1957 (Dud); "The Undefeated" 1969 (Jamison). ¶TV: *Sky King*—"Bullet Bait" 8-3-52 (Joe Halliday); *Sergeant Preston of the Yukon*—"Father of the Crime" 4-19-56 (Jim Manners); *Sheriff of Cochise*—"Grandfather Grandson" 2-11-57 (Ernie); *Gunsmoke*—"Blood Money" 9-28-57 (Joe Harpe); *Boots and Saddles*—"The Marquis of Donnybrook" 12-26-57 (Hatfield), "The Last Word" 1-23-58, "The Cook" 3-13-58 (Pvt. Hatfield); *Wagon Train*—"The Bernal Sierra Story" 3-12-58 (Art); *Wanted—Dead or Alive*—"The Corner" 2-21-59 (Boone Morgan); *The Outlaws*—"Ballad for a Badman" 10-6-60 (Seth Craven); *Daniel Boone*—"Tanner" 10-5-67 (Jenkins).

Dobson, Kevin (1943-). Films: "Orphan Train" TVM-1979.

Dockson, Evelyn (1888-5/20/52). Films: "Come on, Danger!" 1942 (Aunt Fanny).

Dodd, Claire (1909-11/23/73). Films: "The Broken Wing" 1932 (Cecilia Cross); "Massacre" 1934 (Norma).

Dodd, Jimmie (1910-11/10/64). Films: "Law and Order" 1940 (Jimmy); "Shadows on the Sage" 1942 (Lullaby Joslin); "Valley of Hunted Men" 1942 (Lullaby Joslin); "The Blocked Trail" 1943; "Riders of the Rio Grande" 1943 (Lullaby Joslin); "Santa Fe Scouts" 1943 (Lullaby Joslin); "Thundering Trails" 1943; "Twilight on the Prairie" 1944; "Western Whoopee" 1948-short; "Singing Guns" 1950 (Stage Guard); "Al Jennings of Oklahoma" 1951 (Buck Botkin); "The Lusty Men" 1952 (Red Logan).

Dodd, Molly (1925-3/26/81). TV: *The Rifleman*—"The Jailbird" 5-10-60.

Dodd, Rev. Neal (1879-5/26/66). Films: "Santa Fe Trail" 1940 (Minister).

Dodds, Larry. Films: "Susannah of the Mounties" 1939 (Churchill); "The Ox-Bow Incident" 1943 (Posse).

Dodge, Anna (1867-5/4/45). Films: "It Happened in the West" 1911; "Little Injin" 1911; "On Seperate Paths" 1911; "Range Pals" 1911; "The Regeneration of the Apache Kid" 1911; "Told in the Sierras" 1911; "The White Medicine Man" 1911; "The Peacemaker" 1912; "Tenderfoot Bob's Resignation" 1912; "The Redemption of Railroad Jack" 1913; "The Timber Wolf" 1916; "The Devil Dodger" 1917 (Mrs. Ricketts); "Until They Get Me" 1917 (Mrs. Draper).

Dodson, Bert (1915-10/2/84). Films: "Riders of the Whistling Pines" 1949 (Bert); "Indian Territory" 1950; "Wagon Team" 1952 (Bert Cass); "On Top of Old Smoky" 1953 (Bert Cass).

Dodson, Jack (1931-9/16/94). Films: "Pat Garrett and Billy the Kid" 1973 (Llewellyn Howland). ¶TV: *The Virginian*—"The Inchoworm's Got No Wings at All" 2-2-66 (Henry Brodie); *The Road West*—"A Mighty Hunter Before the Lord" 1-30-67 (Jack Hanson).

Dodsworth, John (1910-9/11/64). TV: *Maverick*—"The Savage Hills" 2-9-58 (Clayton Palmer).

Doherty, Charla (1947-5/29/88). TV: *Wagon Train*—"The Hide Hunters" 9-27-64 (Samantha); *Branded*—"Coward Step Aside" 3-7-65 (Karin); *The Guns of Will Sonnett*—"The Natural Way" 9-29-67.

Doherty, Shannon (1971-). Films: "Little House on the Prairie: Look Back to Yesterday" TVM-1983 (Jenny Wilder); "Little House: The Last Farewell" TVM-1984 (Jenny Wilder); "Little House: Bless All the Dear Children" TVM-1984 (Jenny Wilder); "Outlaws" TVM-1986 (Andrea Halifax). ¶TV: *Father Murphy*—"By the Bear That Bit Me" 12-1-81 & 12-8-81 (Dru); *Little House: A New Beginning*—Regular 1982-83 (Jenny).

Dolan, John (1930-3/9/74). TV: *The Big Valley*—"The Lady from Mesa" 4-3-67; *Gunsmoke*—"Uncle Finney" 10-14-68 (Frank); *Here the Brides*—"The Firemaker" 1-15-69 (Marshall).

Dolan, Rudy. TV: *The Westerner*—"Brown" 10-21-60, "The Courting of Libby" 11-11-60, "Going Home" 12-16-60; *Zane Grey Theater*—"The Ox" 11-3-60; *Gunsmoke*—"Old York" 5-4-63 (Harry).

Dolan, Trent. TV: *Maverick*—"Thunder from the North" 11-13-60 (Lieutenant); *Bronco*—"Ordeal at Dead Tree" 1-2-61 (Roy Anders).

Doleman, Guy (1923-). Films: "The Kangaroo Kid" 1950 (Sgt. Jim Penrose); "Kangaroo" 1952 (Pleader). ¶TV: *Whiplash*—"The Wreckers" 8-5-61, "Dark Runs the Sea" 9-2-61, "Act of Courage" 10-7-61.

Dolenz, George (1908-2/8/63). Films: "Royal Mounted Rides Again" 1945-serial (French); "Wings of the Hawk" 1953 (Col. Guiz). ¶TV: *The Restless Gun*—"The Outlander" 4-21-58 (Count Von Gilsa); *Cimarron City*—"The Town Is a Prisoner" 3-28-59 (Col. Gutterez); *The Rebel*—"The Uncourageous" 5-7-61 (Juan Amontillo); *The Deputy*—"Brand of Honesty" 6-10-61 (Ramon Ortega); *Tales of Wells Fargo*—"Moneyrun" 1-6-62 (Rafael De Lopa); *Bonanza*—"Marie, My Love" 2-10-63 (D'Arcy).

Dolenz, Mickey (Mickey Braddock) (1945-). TV: *Circus Boy*—Regular 1956-58 (Corky); *Zane Grey Theater*—"The Vaunted" 11-27-58 (Ted Matson).

Dollaghan, Patrick. Films: "Gunsmoke: The Long Ride" TVM-1993 (Monaghan). ¶TV: *Outlaws*—"Potboiler" 2-28-87; *Paradise*—"Devil's Escort" 1-13-90 (Ted Ramsey).

Dollarhyde, Ross (1922-9/8/77). Films: "The Honkers" 1972 (Travis). ¶TV: *Cimarron Strip*—"The Battleground" 9-28-67.

Domasin, Larry (1956-). Films: "The Rare Breed" 1966 (Alberto); "Ride Beyond Vengeance" 1966 (Mexican Boy). ¶TV: *Daniel Boone*—"The Peace Tree" 11-11-65 (Montutha); *The Big Valley*—"Target" 10-31-66.

Dombre, Barbara (1950-1/3/73). Films: "Heaven with a Gun" 1969 (Townsperson).

Domergue, Faith (1925-). Films: "The Duel at Silver Creek" 1952 (Opal Lacey); "The Great Sioux Uprising" 1953 (Joan Britton); "Santa Fe Passage" 1955 (Aurelie St. Clair); "Escort West" 1959 (Martha Drury); "California" 1963 (Carlotta Torres). ¶TV: *The Rifleman*—"The Marshal" 10-21-58 (Lloyd Carpenter), "Death Trap" 5-9-61 (Spicer); *Sugarfoot*—"The Vultures" 4-28-59 (Isabel Starkey); *Cheyenne*—"The Rebellion" 10-12-59 (Maria Rivera); *Colt .45*—"Breakthrough" 3-27-60 (Suzanne Tremaine); *Bronco*—"La Rubia" 5-17-60 (Catalina); *The Tall Man*—"Rovin' Gambler" 3-18-61 (Kate Elder); *Tales of Wells Fargo*—"The Jealous Man" 4-10-61 (Kitty Thorpe); *Bonanza*—"The Lonely House" 10-15-61 (Lee Bolden), "The Campaneros" 4-19-64 (Carla); *Have Gun Will Travel*—"Beau Beste" 10-13-62 (Ria), "The Black Bull" 4-13-63 (Elena Ybarra).

Dominiguez, Beatrice (1897-2/27/21). Films: "The Sundown Trail" 1919 (Mexican Girl); "The Moon Riders" 1920-serial.

Dominguez, Joe (1894-4/11/70). Films: "The White Horseman" 1921-serial; "The Broken Wing" 1932 (Captain); "Mason of the Mounted" 1932 (Riveras); "Riders of the Desert" 1932 (Gomez); "The Whirlwind" 1933; "Under the Pampas Moon" 1935 (Newsboy); "The Texas Rangers" 1936 (Ranger); "The Painted Stallion" 1937-serial; "The Girl of the Golden West" 1938 (Felipe); "Out West with the Hardys" 1938 (Jose); "Outlaw Express" 1938; "Mexicali Rose" 1939; "Gaucho Serenade" 1940; "Geronimo" 1940 (Pedro); "Outlaws of the Rio Grande" 1941 (Castro); "Undercover Man" 1942 (Caballero); "The Kissing Bandit" 1948 (Francisco); "The Big Sombrero" 1949; "Streets of Laredo" 1949 (Francisco); "Bandit Queen" 1950 (Morales); "Dallas" 1950 (Carlos); "The Furies" 1950 (Wagon Driver); "Ride, Vaquero!" 1953 (Vicente); "Son of Belle Star" 1953 (Pablo); "Gypsy Colt" 1954 (Tony); "Jubilee Trail" 1954 (Ernest); "The Broken Star" 1956 (Nachez); "The Ride Back" 1957 (Luis); "Man of the West" 1958 (Mexican Man); "One-Eyed Jacks" 1961 (Corral Keeper). ¶TV: *Cheyenne*—"Standoff" 5-6-58 (the Mayor); *Laramie*—"The Run to Rumavaca" 11-10-59 (Old Mexican); *The Rebel*—"The Hunted" 11-6-60 (Garcia); *Wyatt Earp*—"Requiem for Old Man Clanton" 5-30-61 (Roca); *The Guns of Will Sonnett*—"Robber's Roost" 1-17-69.

Dominici, Arturo. Films: "Zorro, Rider of Vengeance" 1971-Span./Ital.

Donahue, Elinor (1937-). TV: *Man from Blackhawk*—"The Man Who Wanted Everything" 6-3-60 (Laura White); *Have Gun Will Travel*—"The Burning Tree" 2-9-63 (Letty May); *Redigo*—"Hostage Hero Riding" 12-10-63 (Joanie-Mae Kilpatrick); *The Virginian*—"Siege" 12-18-63 (Carol); *A Man Called Shenandoah*—"Town on Fire" 11-8-65 (Julie Wade); *Dr. Quinn, Medicine Woman*—"Where the Heart Is" 11-20-93 (Rebecca).

Donahue, Patricia (1930-). Films: "The Fastest Guitar Alive" 1967 (Stella). ¶TV: *Death Valley Days*—"The Longest Beard in the

World" 7-7-56; *The Californians*—"Gentleman from Philadelphia" 3-4-58 (Junie); *Bat Masterson*—"Bear Bait" 11-12-58 (Joyce), "A Picture of Death" 1-14-60 (Bill Tuesday); *Tales of Wells Fargo*—"The Counterfeiters" 12-8-58 (Joyce Kendall); *Northwest Passage*—"The Vulture" 12-28-58 (Gwen); *Trackdown*—"False Witness" 4-8-59; *Zane Grey Theater*—"The Lonely Gun" 10-22-59 (Sally Esky); *Black Saddle*—"Means to an End" 1-29-60 (Fran Whitney); *U.S. Marshal*—"Death and Taxes" 2-13-60 (Barbara McLain); *Wyatt Earp*—"The Arizona Lottery" 2-16-60 (Clara); *The Law of the Plainsman*—"The Question of Courage" 2-25-60 (Edie Shaw); *Bonanza*—"The Hopefuls" 10-8-60 (Regina Darien); *The Tall Man*—"The Liberty Belle" 9-16-61 (Elena); *The Virginian*—"Dead Eye Dick" 11-9-66 (Livvy Underhill).

Donahue, Troy (1936-). Films: "Wild Heritage" 1958 (Jesse Bascomb); "A Distant Trumpet" 1964 (Lt. Matthew Hazard). ¶TV: *Rawhide*—"Incident at Alabaster Plain" 1-16-59 (Buzz Travis); *Wagon Train*—"The Hunter Malloy Story" 1-21-59 (Ted Garner); *Tales of Wells Fargo*—"The Rawhide Kid" 3-16-59 (Smith); *Bronco*—"Backfire" 4-7-59 (Roy Parrott), "The Devil's Spawn" 12-1-59 (Bart Donner); *Maverick*—"Pappy" 9-13-59 (Dan Jamison); *Sugarfoot*—"The Wild Bunch" 9-29-59 (Ken Savage); *Colt .45*—"The Hothead" 11-1-59 (Jim Gibson); *The Alaskans*—"Heart of Gold" 5-1-60 (Ted Andrews); *Lawman*—"The Payment" 5-8-60 (David Manning); *The Virginian*—"Fox, Hound, and the Widow McCloud" 4-2-69 (Bracken).

Donald, Dorothy. Films: "The Riding Fool" 1924; "Desperate Odds" 1925; "Fangs of Fate" 1925 (Azalia Bolton); "Flashing Steeds" 1925 (Helen Randall); "Eyes of the Desert" 1926; "Just Travelin'" 1927.

Donaldson, Arthur (1869-9/28/55). Films: "The Mystery of Pine Creek Camp" 1913; "The Danger Trail" 1917 (Pierre Thoreau).

Donath, Ludwig (1900-9/29/67). Films: "Renegades" 1946 (Jackorski). ¶TV: *Bonanza*—"The Way of Aaron" 3-10-63 (Aaron Kaufmann); *Branded*—"A Proud Town" 12-19-65 (Julius Perrin).

Donde, Manuel. Films: "The Treasure of the Sierra Madre" 1948 (El Jefe); "Garden of Evil" 1954 (Waiter); "The Last Frontier" 1955 (Red Cloud).

Donlan, James (1889-6/7/38).

Films: "Beau Bandit" 1930 (Buck); "The Painted Desert" 1931.

Donlevy, Brian (1899-4/5/72). Films: "Allegheny Uprising" 1939 (Callendar); "Destry Rides Again" 1939 (Kent); "Jesse James" 1939 (Barshee); "Union Pacific" 1939 (Sid Campeau); "Brigham Young—Frontiersman" 1940 (Angus Duncan); "When the Daltons Rode" 1940 (Grat Dalton); "Billy the Kid" 1941 (Jim Sherwood); "The Great Man's Lady" 1942 (Steele Edwards); "Canyon Passage" 1946 (George Camrose); "The Virginian" 1946 (Trampas); "Heaven Only Knows" 1947 (Duke); "Kansas Raiders" 1950 (Quantrill); "Slaughter Trail" 1951 (Capt. Dempster); "Ride the Man Down" 1952 (Bide Marriner); "The Woman They Almost Lynched" 1953 (William Quantrill); "Cowboy" 1958 (Doc Bender); "Escape from Red Rock" 1958 (Bronc Grierson); "Waco" 1966 (Ace Ross); "Hostile Guns" 1967 (Marshal Willett); "Arizona Bushwhackers" 1968 (Major Smith). ¶TV: *The Texan*—"The Man Behind the Star" 2-9-59 (Sheriff Gleason), "Traildust" 10-19-59 (Sam Gallup); *Rawhide*—"Incident of the Power and the Plow" 2-13-59 (Jed Reston); *Wagon Train*—"The Jasper Cato Story" 3-4-59 (Joseph Cato); *Hotel De Paree*—"Juggernaut" 10-9-59; *Zane Grey Theater*—"The Sunday Man" 2-25-60 (Fred Childress).

Donlon, Dolores. TV: *The Texan*—"The Duchess of Denver" 1-5-59 (Gay Brewster); *The Californians*—"The Fur Story" 5-5-59 (Peggy); *Maverick*—"A Cure for Johnny Rain" 12-20-59 (Millie Reid), "Maverick at Law" 2-26-61 (Clover Moore); *Have Gun Will Travel*—"The Gladiators" 3-19-60 (Allison Windrom), "A Knight to Remember" 12-9-61 (Dulcinea Caloca); *Sugarfoot*—"Blue Bonnet Stray" 4-26-60 (Vera); *Overland Trail*—"The Baron Comes Back" 5-15-60 (Trudy).

Donnell, Jeff (1921-4/11/88). Films: "Cowboy Canteen" 1944; "Song of the Prairie" 1945; "Cowboy Blues" 1946; "Singing on the Trail" 1946; "That Texas Jamboree" 1946; "Throw a Saddle on a Star" 1946; "My Pal Ringeye" 1947-short; "Outcasts of the Trail" 1949 (Lavinia White); "Roughshod" 1949 (Elaine); "Stagecoach Kid" 1949 (Jessie); "Hoedown" 1950 (Vera Wright); "Redwood Forest Trail" 1950 (Julie Westcott); "Massacre Canyon" 1954 (Cora); "The Guns of Fort Petticoat" 1957 (Mary Wheeler). ¶TV: *Daniel Boone*—"A Tall Tale of Prater Beasely"

1-16-69 (Varna); *Overland Trail*—"The Most Dangerous Gentleman" 6-5-60 (Jennifer Dean).

Donnelly, Dorothy (1881-1/3/28). Films: "The Sealed Valley" 1915.

Donnelly, Jim (1865-4/13/37). Films: "The Border Menace" 1934 (Milete).

Donnelly, Ruth (1896-11/17/82). Films: "Rainbow Trail" 1932 (Abigail); "Roaring Timber" 1937 (Aunt Mary MacKinley); "My Little Chickadee" 1940 (Aunt Lou); "The Round Up" 1941 (Polly); "In Old Sacramento" 1946 (Zebby Booker); "The Fabulous Texan" 1947 (Utopia Mills); "The Secret of Convict Lake" 1951 (Mary); "A Lawless Street" 1955 (Molly Higgins); "The Spoilers" 1955 (Duchess).

Donnelly, Tim (1946-). TV: *The Virginian*—"Day of the Scorpion" 9-22-65 (Tippy); *The Legend of Jesse James*—"A Real Tough Town" 1-24-66 (Sonny Walters).

Donner, Robert (1931-). Films: "El Dorado" 1967 (Milt); "The Undefeated" 1969 (Judd Mailer); "Chisum" 1970 (Morton); "The Intruders" TVM-1970; "Rio Lobo" 1970 (Whiter Carter); "Fools' Parade" 1971 (Willis Hubbard); "One More Train to Rob" 1971 (Sheriff Adams); "Something Big" 1971 (Angel Moon); "High Plains Drifter" 1973 (Preacher); "The Man Who Loved Cat Dancing" 1973 (Dub); "Santee" 1973; "Mrs. Sundance" TVM-1974 (Ben Lant); "Nakia" TVM-1974 (Fincher); "Take a Hard Ride" 1974-Ital./Brit./Ger. (Skave); "Bite the Bullet" 1975 (Reporter); "The Last Hard Men" 1976 (Lee Roy Tucker); "Young Pioneers" TVM-1976 (Mr. Peters); "Young Pioneers' Christmas" TVM-1976 (Mr. Peters); "Standing Tall" TVM-1978 (Sheriff Brumfield). ¶TV: *Rawhide*—"Incident of the Running Man" 5-5-61 (Toland), "Judgment at Hondo Seco" 10-20-61, "Incident of the Travellin' Man" 10-17-63 (Billy Harger); *Daniel Boone*—"The Scalp Hunter" 3-17-66 (Coot), "Take the Southbound Stage" 4-6-67 (Pike); *Laredo*—"A Question of Guilt" 3-10-67; *The Guns of Will Sonnett*—"Look for the Hound Dog" 1-26-68 (Parkin), "Guilt" 11-29-68 (Arch Merceen); *Gunsmoke*—"A Noose for Dobie Price" 3-4-68 (Gil Boylan), "The Hiders" 1-13-75 (Belnap); *The Virginian*—"Ride the Misadventure" 11-6-68 (Matt Dooley); *The Big Valley*—"Town of No Exit" 4-7-69 (Pete); *Bonanza*—"Meena" 11-16-69 (Owen), "The Horse Traders" 4-5-70 (Owen); *The High Chap-*

arral—"The Reluctant Deputy" 3-6-70 (Pelletier), "A Matter of Vengeance" 11-27-70 (Wiley); *Alias Smith and Jones*—"Never Trust an Honest Man" 4-15-71 (Preacher), "The Bounty Hunter" 12-9-71 (Nate), "The Day the Amnesty Came Through" 11-25-72 (Charlie Taylor); *Kung Fu*—"The Tide" 2-1-73 (Houlton); *The Quest*—"Incident at Drucker's Tavern" 1976; *Sara*—3-26-76 (Stevens); *The Young Pioneers*—Regular 1978 (Mr. Peters); *Legend*—Regular 1995 (Mayor Chamberlain Brown).

Donno, Eddy. Films: "Kid Blue" 1973 (Huey). ¶TV: *Daniel Boone*—"A Pinch of Salt" 5-1-69.

Donohue, Jill (1939-). TV: *The Virginian*—"Doctor Pat" 3-1-67 (Dr. Pat O'Neill), "Ah Sing vs. Wyoming" 10-25-67 (Lucy Evers), "With Help from Ulysses" 1-17-68 (Barbara).

Donovan, Bill. Films: "The Masked Avenger" 1922 (Sheriff Dan Dustin); "The Breed of the Border" 1924 (Pablo, the Bandit); "O.U. West" 1925 (Ranch Foreman); "Ridin' Comet" 1925 (Max Underly).

Donovan, Jack. Films: "Hoof Marks" 1927 (Cal Wagner); "The Bullet Mark" 1928; "Outlaws' Highway" 1934 (Gordon Matthews).

Donovan, King (1919-6/30/87). Films: "The Man from Texas" 1947 (Sam); "Little Big Horn" 1951 (Pvt. James Corbo); "The Redhead and the Cowboy" 1951 (Munroe); "Tumbleweed" 1953 (Wrangler); "Broken Lance" 1954 (Clerk); "The Iron Sheriff" 1957 (Leveret, the Telegrapher); "Cowboy" 1958 (Joe Capper); "The Hanging Tree" 1959 (Wonder). ¶TV: *Wild Bill Hickok*—"The Iron Major" 4-21-53, "Jingles Wins a Friend" 4-28-53; *Frontier*—"Paper Gunman" 9-25-55 (Joe Thornton); *Jim Bowie*—"Convoy Gold" 2-1-57 (Pierre Lamont); *Tales of Wells Fargo*—"The Feud" 10-14-57; *Trackdown*—"The Boy" 3-28-58 (Dean Burke), "The Set Up" 9-26-58 (Lane Sawyer); *Wagon Train*—"The Sally Potter Story" 4-9-58 (Henry Bennett); *Bat Masterson*—"Double Showdown" 10-8-58 (Shorty Keenan); *Wanted—Dead or Alive*—"Bad Gun" 10-24-59 (Sheridan Appleby); *Hotel De Paree*—"The Man Who Believed in Law" 11-27-59 (Ralph), "Bounty for Sundance" 4-29-60 (Jess); *Maverick*—"Maverick Springs" 12-6-59 (Mark Dawson); *Bonanza*—"The Gunmen" 1-23-60; *Shotgun Slade*—"Backtrack" 7-26-60 (Baxter); *The Tall Man*—"Garrett and the Kid" 9-10-60 (Spieler); *Rawhide*—"Incident of the Buryin' Man" 1-4-63

(Poke Tolliver); *The Big Valley*—"Into the Widow's Web" 3-23-66 (Ambrose).

Donovan, Mike (1878-11/11/60). Films: "Wells Fargo" 1937 (Miner); "Stage to Chino" 1940; "The Sea of Grass" 1947 (Nestor); "Dallas" 1950 (Citizen).

Donovan, Warde (1916-4/16/88). Films: "Hot Lead and Cold Feet" 1978. ¶TV: *Wyatt Earp*—"The Convict's Revenge" 4-4-61 (Jed Lorimer).

Doohan, James (1920-). Films: "Scalplock" TVM-1966; "Man in the Wilderness" 1971-U.S./Span. (Benoit). ¶TV: *Bonanza*—"Gift of Water" 2-11-62 (Bill Collins), "The Legacy" 12-15-63; *Gunsmoke*—"Quint Asper Comes Home" 9-29-62 (Davit); *The Virginian*—"The Man Who Couldn't Die" 1-30-63 (George Mitchell); *Empire*—"A House in Order" 3-5-63 (Doctor); *Laredo*—"I See By Your Outfit" 9-23-65 (Mike Pripton); *A Man Called Shenandoah*—"Care of General Delivery" 5-9-66 (Cousin Howard); *Daniel Boone*—"The Cache" 12-4-69, "Perilous Passage" 1-15-70.

Dooley, Billy (1893-8/4/38). Films: "Call of the Yukon" 1938 (Watchman).

Do'Qui, Robert (1934-). Films: "The Red, White and Black" 1970 (Trooper Eli Brown); "Buffalo Bill and the Indians, or Sitting Bull's History Lesson" 1976 (Wrangler). ¶TV: *Cowboy in Africa*—"The Quiet Death" 2-19-68 (Rendula); *The Guns of Will Sonnett*—"The Trap" 10-4-68 (Walter); *The High Chaparral*—"The Buffalo Soldiers" 11-22-68 (Larrabee); *Gunsmoke*—"The Mark of Cain" 2-3-69 (Sadler), "The Good Samaritans" 3-10-69 (Benji); *Centennial*—Regular 1978-79 (Nate Person III); *Hunter's Moon*—Pilot 12-1-79 (Isham Hart).

Dor, Karin (1936-). Films: "Treasure of Silver Lake" 1963-Fr./Ger./Yugo. (Ellen Patterson); "The Last Tomahawk" 1965-Ger./Ital./Span. (Cora Monroe); "Last of the Renegades" 1966-Fr./Ital./Ger./Yugo. (Ribanna); "Winnetou and Shatterhand in the Valley of Death" 1968-Ger./Yugo./Ital.

Doran, Ann (1913-). Films: "Rio Grande" 1938 (Jean Andrews); "The Kid from Kansas" 1941 (Smitty); "Calamity Jane and Sam Bass" 1949 (Mrs. Egan); "The Painted Hills" 1951 (Martha Blake); "Tomahawk" 1951 (Mrs. Carrington); "Rodeo" 1952; "Shoot-Out at Medicine Bend" 1957; "Day of the Bad Man" 1958 (Mrs. Mordigan); "The

Rawhide Trail" 1958 (Mrs. Cartwright); "Cast a Long Shadow" 1959 (Ma Calvert); "Warlock" 1959 (Mrs. Richardson); "There Was a Crooked Man" 1970; "The Hired Hand" 1971 (Mrs. Sorenson); "The Macahans" TVM-1976 (Grandma Macahan); "Peter Lundy and the Medicine Hat Stallion" TVM-1977 (Grandma Lundy). ¶TV: *The Roy Rogers Show*—"Peril from the Past" 4-13-52; *The Lone Ranger*—"Treason at Dry Creek" 12-4-52, "Hidden Fortune" 6-18-53; *The Gene Autry Show*—"Johnny Jackaroo" 7-13-54 (Lynne Moore), "The Carnival Comes West" 8-24-54; *My Friend Flicka*—"Old Danny" 3-2-56 (Martha Jepson); *Broken Arrow*—"Legacy of a Hero" 2-26-57 (Mrs. Randolph); *Frontier Doctor*—"Drifting Sands" 3-28-59; *Colt .45*—"The Saga of Sam Bass" 5-17-59 (Liz Sawyer), "Impasse" 1-31-60 (Mrs. Staley); *Wagon Train*—"The Ricky and Laura Bell Story" 2-24-60 (Aunt Lizzie); *Rawhide*—"Incident of the Challenge" 10-14-60 (Millie Darius); *The Virginian*—"Run Away Home" 4-24-63 (Minerva Lewis), "The Fortunes of J. Jimerson Jones" 1-15-64 (Maggie Hyeth), "Portrait of a Widow" 12-9-64 (Reba), "The Lady from Wichita" 9-27-67 (Mrs. Graves); *The Legend of Jesse James*—Regular 1965-66 (Mrs. James); *Bonanza*—"Ballad of the Ponderosa" 11-13-66 (Lisa Stanley), "The Real People of Muddy Creek" 10-6-68 (Mrs. Walker); *The Guns of Will Sonnett*—"And He Shall Lead the Children" 1-19-68 (Margaret); *Alias Smith and Jones*—"Witness to a Lynching" 12-16-72 (Mrs. Simpson); *Father Murphy*—"The Horse" 3-21-82 (Abby).

Doran, Johnny (1962-). TV: *Nakia*—"Pete" 12-21-74 (Pete).

Doran, Mary. Films: "Ridin' for Justice" 1932 (Mary Slyde); "Sunset Range" 1935 (Bonnie Shay); "The Border Patrolman" 1936 (Myra).

Dore, Anne. Films: "Son of Paleface" 1952 (She-Devil). ¶TV: *Bat Masterson*—"Sharpshooter" 2-11-59 (Jezebel); *Laredo*—"Pride of the Rangers" 12-16-65.

Dorety, Charles (1898-4/2/57). Films: "Beneath Western Skies" 1944 (Spike).

Dorian, Angela. *see* Vetri, Victoria.

Dorian, Charles (1893-10/21/42). Films: "Lone Larry" 1917; "The Red Haired Cupid" 1918; "Cyclone Smith Plays Trumps" 1919; "Blind Chance" 1920; "Kaintuck's Ward" 1920; "When the Cougar Called" 1920.

Dorin, Phoebe (1940-). TV: *Wild Wild West*—"The Night the Wizard Shook the Earth" 10-1-65 (Antoinette), "The Night That Terror Stalked the Town" 11-19-65 (Antoinette), "The Night of the Whirring Death" 2-18-66 (Antoinette), "The Night of the Murderous Spring" 4-15-66 (Antoinette), "The Night of the Raven" 9-30-66 (Antoinette), "The Night of the Green Terror" 11-18-66 (Antoinette).

Dorn, Dolores (1935-). Films: "The Bounty Hunter" 1954 (Julie Spencer).

Dorn, Philip (1902-5/9/75). Films: "The Fighting Kentuckian" 1949 (Colonel George Geraud).

Dorr, Dorothy. Films: "Quicker'n Lightnin'" 1925 (Helen Harlow).

Dorr, Lester (1893-8/25/80). Films: "Riders of the Purple Sage" 1931 (Judkins); "Phantom Patrol" 1936; "Ride 'Em Cowboy" 1936; "Hollywood Cowboy" 1937 (Joe Garvey); "Way Out West" 1937 (Cowboy); "Wells Fargo" 1937; "Hollywood Roundup" 1938 (Louis Lawson); "In Early Arizona" 1938; "The Cisco Kid and the Lady" 1939 (Telegraph Operator); "Ride 'Em, Cowgirl" 1939; "Danger Ahead" 1940 (Lefty); "Mexican Spitfire Out West" 1940 (Harry); "The Return of Frank James" 1940 (Reporter); "Pursued" 1947; "Robin Hood of Texas" 1947; "Silver River" 1948 (Taylor); "Covered Wagon Raid" 1950 (Pete); "Night Riders of Montana" 1951 (Drummer); "The First Traveling Saleslady" 1956 (Salesman). ¶TV: *Wyatt Earp*—"Caught by a Whisker" 10-7-58 (Clerk), "The Confidence Man" 5-17-60; *Wanted—Dead or Alive*—"The Kovack Affair" 3-28-59 (Telegraph Operator).

Dorrell, Don. Films: "The Gambler Wore a Gun" 1961 (Jud Donovan). ¶TV: *Pony Express*—Regular 1960-61 (Donovan); *Walt Disney Presents*—"Daniel Boone: ... And Chase the Buffalo" 12-11-60 (John Stewart).

Dors, Diana (1931-5/4/84). Films: "Hannie Calder" 1971-Brit./Span./Fr. (Madame).

D'Orsay, Fifi (1908-12/2/83). TV: *Bonanza*—"Calamity Over the Comstock" 11-3-63 (Babette).

D'Orsay, Lawrence (1853-9/13/31). Films: "Ruggles of Red Gap" 1918 (Hon. George Vane-Bassingwell).

D'Orsi, Umberto (1921-8/31/76). Films: "Death Walks in Laredo" 1966-Ital./Span.; "Two Sons of Ringo" 1966-Ital.; "Return of Halleluja" 1972-Ital./Ger.; "Man Called Invincible" 1973-Ital.; "Dick Luft in Sacramento" 1974-Ital.

Dossett, Chappell (1883-12/19/61). Films: "The Cowboy and the Countess" 1926 (Alexis Verlaine).

Dotson, Ernie. Films: "Outlaw's Son" 1957 (Ben Jorgenson). ¶TV: *Fury*—"Joey's Father" 12-3-55, "Bike Road-eo" 12-14-57 (Carl Page).

Doucet, Catherine (1875-6/24/58). Films: "The Dude Goes West" 1948 (Grandma Crockett).

Doucette, John (1921-8/16/94). Films: "Station West" 1948 (Bartender); "Border Treasure" 1950 (Bat); "Broken Arrow" 1950 (Mule Driver); "The Iroquois Trail" 1950 (Sam Girty); "Sierra" 1950 (Jed Coulter); "Winchester '73" 1950 (Roan Daley); "Bandits of El Dorado" 1951 (Tucker); "Cavalry Scout" 1951 (Varney); "The Texas Rangers" 1951 (Butch Cassidy); "Thunder in God's Country" 1951 (Slack Breedon); "Yukon Manhunt" 1951; "Bugles in the Afternoon" 1952 (Bill); "Desert Pursuit" 1952 (Kafan); "High Noon" 1952 (Trumbull); "Rancho Notorious" 1952 (Whitey); "The San Francisco Story" 1952 (Slade); "Toughest Man in Arizona" 1952; "The Treasure of Lost Canyon" 1952 (Gyppo); "Ambush at Tomahawk Gap" 1953 (Bartender); "City of Badmen" 1953 (Cinch); "Goldtown Ghost Raiders" 1953 (Bailey); "War Paint" 1953 (Charnofsky); "Destry" 1954 (Cowhand); "The Forty-Niners" 1954 (Ernie Walker); "River of No Return" 1954 (Spectator in Black Nugget); "The Far Country" 1955 (Miner); "Dakota Incident" 1956 (Rick Largo); "Fastest Gun Alive" 1956 (Ben Buddy); "Ghost Town" 1956 (Doc Clawson); "The Maverick Queen" 1956 (Loudmouth); "Quincannon, Frontier Scout" 1956 (Sgt. Calvin); "Thunder Over Arizona" 1956; "Gunfire at Indian Gap" 1957 (Leder); "Last of the Badmen" 1957 (Johnson); "The Lonely Man" 1957 (Sundown Whipple); "The Phantom Stagecoach" 1957 (Harry Farrow); "The True Story of Jesse James" 1957 (Hillstrom); "The Lawless Eighties" 1958; "The Sons of Katie Elder" 1965 (Undertaker Hyselman); "Nevada Smith" 1966 (Uncle Ben McCanles); "The Fastest Guitar Alive" 1967 (Sheriff Max Cooper); "Winchester '73" TVM-1967; "Journey to Shiloh" 1968 (Gen. Braxton Bragg); "True Grit" 1969 (Sheriff); "Big Jake" 1971 (Buck Dugan); "One More Train to Rob" 1971 (Sheriff Monte); "One

Little Indian" 1973 (Sgt. Waller); "Donner Pass: The Road to Survival" TVM-1978 (George Donner). ¶TV: *The Lone Ranger*—"Gold Fever" 4-13-50, "Sheriff of Gunstock" 7-27-50, "Thieves' Money" 11-2-50, "The Hooded Men" 2-22-51, "The Fugitive" 9-9-54, "Rendezvous at Whipsaw" 11-11-54, "The School Story" 1-20-55; *The Gene Autry Show*—"The Posse" 9-17-50, "The Devil's Brand" 9-24-50, "Bullets and Bows" 3-2-52, "The Sheriff Is a Lady" 3-23-52, "Ghost Mountain" 7-28-53, "Dry Gulch at Devil's Elbow" 9-8-53; *Wild Bill Hickok*—"Ghost Town Story" 8-21-51; *The Range Rider*—"Bullets and Badmen" 3-29-52; *The Roy Rogers Show*—"Peril from the Past" 4-13-52, "Shoot to Kill" 4-27-52, "Outlaw's Return" 9-28-52 (Carl Adams), "Huntin' for Trouble" 10-5-52 (Oley Wolf), "Backfire" 10-10-54 (Hook Carter), "Strangers" 12-5-54 (Gil Wiley); *The Cisco Kid*—"Pancho and the Wolf Dog" 9-13-52, "Faded General" 10-25-52; *My Friend Flicka*—"Rogue Stallion" 11-25-55, "Black Dust" 1-13-56 (Andy Benson); *Sheriff of Cochise*—"Closed for Repairs" 11-30-56 (Vince Walker), "Approach with Caution" 4-19-57 (Barber); *Tales of Wells Fargo*—"Alder Gulch" 4-8-57 (Boone Helm), "The Renegade" 5-12-58 (Shorty), "The Train Robbery" 10-12-59 (Matt), "Reward for Gaine" 1-20-62 (Sergeant Gaine); *Gunsmoke*—"Liar from Blackhawk" 6-22-57; *Cheyenne*—"Town of Fear" 12-3-57 (Bill Jenkins); *The Californians*—"Little Lost Man" 12-3-57 (Martin Loomis); *Trackdown*—"The Reward" 1-3-58 (Joe Garth); *Zorro*—"Slaves of the Eagle" 1-23-58; *Have Gun Will Travel*—"The O'Hare Story" 3-1-58 (Joe Marsh), "Lady on the Stagecoach" 1-17-59; *Tombstone Territory*—"Geronimo" 3-5-58 (Geronimo), "Surrender at Sunglow" 5-15-59 (Logan), 5-13-60 (Parsons); *Broken Arrow*—"War Trail" 4-8-58 (Cagle); *Rough Riders*—"The Murderous Sutton Gang" 10-2-58 (Wes Sutton); *Lawman*—"The Prisoner" 10-12-58 (Dick Sellers), "The Chef" 3-1-59 (Harry Dorn); *Wyatt Earp*—"Little Brother" 12-23-58 (Smiley Dunlap); *U.S. Marshal*—"Inside Job" 1-3-59; *Colt .45*—"Dead Aim" 4-12-59 (Lou Gore); *The Texan*—"South of the Border" 5-18-59 (Sheriff Ben Carter); *Union Pacific*—"To the Death" 6-13-59; *Bat Masterson*—"Buffalo Kills" 7-29-59 (Luke Simes), "A Grave Situation" 5-12-60 (Carstairs); *Wagon Train*—"The Jim Bridger Story" 5-10-61 (General Jameson), "The Orly French Story"

12-12-62 (Marshal Jason Hartman), "The Michael McGoo Story" 3-20-63 (Michael McGoo), "The Fort Pierce Story" 9-23-63 (Colonel Lathrop), "The Ben Engel Story" 3-16-64 (Ben Engel), "Little Girl Lost" 12-13-64 (Boone Gillis), "The Chottsie Gubenheimer Story" 1-10-65 (Chandler Ames), "Thye Isaiah Quickfox Story" 1-31-65 (Burt Enders); *Rawhide*—"Incident of the Dogfaces" 11-9-62 (Private Vasily Kandinsky), "Josh" 1-15-65 (Pine); *The Virginian*—"Six Graves at Cripple Creek" 1-27-65 (Sheriff Goodbody), "The Awakening" 10-13-65 (Calder), "Requiem for a Country Doctor" 1-25-67 (Lumberfield), "The Stranger" 4-9-69 (Arthur Willis); *The Loner*—"The Mourners for Johnny Sharp" 2-5-66 & 2-12-66 (Benneke); *Bonanza*—"Knight Errant" 11-18-62 (Walter Prescott), The Rev. Evan Morgan), "The Price of Salt" 2-4-68 (Cash Talbot); *Laramie*—"Naked Steel" 1-1-63 (Sheriff Tate); *Wide Country*—"The Man Who Ran Away" 2-7-63 (Palmer); *Wild Wild West*—"The Night of the Flaming Ghost" 2-4-66 (John Obediah Brown), "The Night of the Surreal McCoy" 3-3-67 (Axel Morgan); *The Monroes*—"The Intruders" 9-7-66 (Buttermore); *Pistols 'n' Petticoats*—2-25-67 (Curt Morton); *The Big Valley*—"The Devil's Masquerade" 3-4-68 (Jim North); *Kung Fu*—"The Soul Is the Warrior" 2-8-73 (Ed Rankin); *How the West Was Won*—"The Slavers" 4-23-79 (Sheriff Boland).

Dougherty, Jack (1895-5/16/ 38). Films: "The Burning Trail" 1925 (John Corliss); "Yodelin' Kid from Pine Ridge" 1937 (Jeff Galloway).

Douglas, Burt. Films: "The Law and Jake Wade" 1958 (Lieutenant). ¶TV: *Gunsmoke*—"Robber and Bridegroom" 12-13-58 (Jack Fitch), "Bad Seed" 2-4-61 (Gar Kline), "Melinda Miles" 6-3-61 (Tom Potter), "Help Me, Kitty" 11-7-64 (Ed); *Northwest Passage*—"The Deserter" 2-27-59 (Tom Jason); *Lawman*—"The Return" 5-10-59, "Girl from Grantsville" 4-10-60 (Jeff Hacker); *Bronco*—"Red Water North" 6-16-59 (Rolf); *Zane Grey Theater*—"Calico Bait" 3-31-60 (Davey Morse); *Black Saddle*—"The Return" 4-8-60 (Jamie Scott); *Wanted—Dead or Alive*—"The Choice" 12-14-60 (Stacy Lenz); *Bonanza*—"The Rescue" 2-25-61 (Jack Tatum), "The Dream Riders" 5-20-61 (Bill Kingsley); *Rawhide*—"Incident of the New Start" 3-3-61 (Webb Church), "Judgment at Hondo Seco" 10-20-61 (Brad Lyons), "The Empty Sleeve" 4-2-65 (Tom Cowan); *Em-*

pire—"Burnout" 3-19-63 (Jack Pitman); *Death Valley Days*—"Dry Water Sailors" 3-12-66 (Charlie Pancoast); *The Monroes*—"Court Martial" 11-16-66 (Sgt. Mark Ryan); *The Virginian*—"Execution at Triste" 12-13-67 (Burt).

Douglas, Byron (1865-4/21/35). Films: "That Devil Quemado" 1925 (John Thatcher); "Two-Fisted Jones" 1925 (John Wilbur, Sr.); "Red Clay" 1927 (Senator Burr); "Born to the Saddle" 1929 (John Pearson).

Douglas, Chet. Films: "Two Rode Together" 1961 (Ward Corbey); "Requiem for a Gunfighter" 1965 (Larry Young).

Douglas, Damon. Films: "From Noon to Three" 1976 (Boy). ¶TV: *Gunsmoke*—"The Hiders" 1-13-75 (Billy).

Douglas, Diana (1923-). Films: "The Indian Fighter" 1955 (Susan Rogers); "Another Man, Another Chance" 1977-Fr. (Mary's Mother). ¶TV: *Kung Fu*—"The Tong" 11-15-73 (Sister Richardson); *The Cowboys*—Regular 1974 (Kate Andersen).

Douglas, Don (1905-12/31/45). Films: "Headin' East" 1937 (Eric Ward); "Law of the Texan" 1938 (Hackett); "Jesse James" 1939 (Infantry Captain); "Deadwood Dick" 1940-serial (Deadwood Dick); "Tall in the Saddle" 1944 (Mr. Haroldday).

Douglas, Don. TV: *Bat Masterson*—"High Card Loses" 11-10-60 (Bank Manager); *Branded*—"Price of a Name" 5-23-65 (Banker).

Douglas, Earl. Films: "Fighting Caballero" 1935 (Pedro); "Wild Horse Canyon" 1938 (Valdesto); "Crashing Thru" 1939 (Slant Eyes); "Down the Wyoming Trail" 1939 (Silent Smith); "Riders of the Sage" 1939 (Hank Halsey); "Trigger Pals" 1939 (Jake); "Danger Ahead" 1940 (Eggface); "Murder on the Yukon" 1940 (Steve); "Rhythm of the Rio Grande" 1940 (Blackie); "Yukon Flight" 1940 (Smokey Joe); "The Gunman from Bodie" 1941; "Riding the Sunset Trail" 1941 (Drifter Smith).

Douglas, George. Films: "Out West with the Hardys" 1938 (Mr. Carter); "Pals of the Saddle" 1938 (Paul Hartman); "The Adventures of the Masked Phantom" 1939 (Murdock); "The Kansas Terrors" 1939 (Commandante); "The Night Riders" 1939 (Pierce Talbot/Don Luis De Serrano); "Covered Wagon Days" 1940 (Ransome); "Lone Star Raiders" 1940 (Henry Martin); "The Tulsa Kid" 1940 (Dick Saunders); "Home in Wyomin'" 1942 (Crowley); "Riders of the Santa Fe" 1944 (Tom Benner); "Showdown at Boot Hill" 1958 (Charles Maynor). ¶TV: *The Roy Rogers Show*—"Flying Bullets" 6-15-52 (Roger Wilson), "Loaded Guns" 4-15-53 (Martin Kelsey); *Gunsmoke*—"Wind" 3-21-59 (Man); *Have Gun Will Travel*—"Fragile" 10-31-59; *The Deputy*—"Passage to New Orleans" 11-19-60 (Captain).

Douglas, J. Ian. Films: "Fort Bowie" 1958 (Maj. Wharton).

Douglas, James. Films: "A Thunder of Drums" 1961 (Lt. Gresham). ¶TV: *Wyatt Earp*—"Doc Fabrique's Greatest Case" 4-7-59.

Douglas, Jennifer. TV: *Wild Wild West*—"The Night of the Cossacks" 3-21-69 (Princess Lina); *Bonanza*—"The Running Man" 3-30-69 (Barbara Parker); *Lancer*—"The Kid" 10-7-69 (Dorrie).

Douglas, Jerry (1936-). TV: *Empire*—"Seven Days on Rough Street" 2-26-63 (Le Roy); *Gunsmoke*—"Seven Hours to Dawn" 9-18-65 (Clark); *Bonanza*—"False Witness" 10-22-67 (Jeremiah); *The Quest*—"Welcome to America, Jade Snow" 11-24-76.

Douglas, Kirk (1916-). Films: "Along the Great Divide" 1951 (U.S. Marshal Len Merrick); "The Big Sky" 1952 (Deakins); "The Big Trees" 1952 (John Fallon); "The Indian Fighter" 1955 (Johnny Hawks); "Man Without a Star" 1955 (Dempsey Rae); "Gunfight at the O.K. Corral" 1957 (John H. "Doc" Holiday); "Last Train from Gun Hill" 1959 (Matt Morgan); "The Last Sunset" 1961 (Brendan O'Malley); "Lonely Are the Brave" 1962 (Jack Burns); "The War Wagon" 1967 (Lomax); "The Way West" 1967 (Sen. William J. Tadlock); "There Was a Crooked Man" 1970 (Paris Pitman, Jr.); "A Gunfight" 1971 (Will Tenneray); "Posse" 1975 (Marshal Howard Nightingale); "The Villain" 1979 (Cactus Jack); "The Man from Snowy River" 1982-Australia (Harrison/Spur); "Draw" CTVM-1984 (Handsome Harry H. Holland).

Douglas, Linda (Mary Jo Tarola). Films: "Target" 1952 (Marshal Terry); "Trail Guide" 1952 (Peg).

Douglas, Marian. Films: "The Shepherd of the Hills" 1928 (Maggie); "The Upland Rider" 1928 (Sally Graham); "The Wagon Show" 1928 (Sally Beldan); "Sioux Blood" 1929 (Barbara Ingram).

Douglas, Melvyn (1901-8/4/81). Films: "The Broken Wing" 1932 (Phil Marvin); "Annie Oakley" 1935 (Jeff Hogarth); "The Sea of Grass"

1947 (Brice Chamberlain); "Hud" 1963 (Homer Bannon); "Advance to the Rear" 1964 (Col. Claude Brackenby). ¶TV: *Frontier Justice*—Host 1959.

Douglas, Milton (1906-9/5/70). Films: "Horses' Collars" 1935-short (Waiter).

Douglas, Paul (1907-9/11/59). TV: *Zane Grey Theater*—"Day of the Killing" 1-8-59 (Jonas Sutton).

Douglas, Robert (1909-). Films: "Barricade" 1950 (Aubry Milburn); "Saskatchewan" 1954 (Inspector Benton). ¶TV: *Maverick*—"Bundle from Britain" 9-18-60 (Herbert); *Centennial*—Regular 1978-79 (Claude Richards).

Douglas, Warren. Films: "Law of the Badlands" 1945-short; "Northwest Territory" 1951 (Morgan); "Fangs of the Arctic" 1953; "Dragoon Wells Massacre" 1957 (Jud). ¶TV: *The Lone Ranger*—"Letter of the Law" 1-4-51; *Cheyenne*—"The Durango Brothers" 9-24-62 (Ronald Gardner).

Dourif, Brad (1951-). Films: "Desperado: The Outlaw Wars" TVM-1989 (Camillus Fly); "Grim Prairie Tales" 1990 (Farley).

Dove, Billie (1900-). Films: "The Lone Star Ranger" 1923 (Helen Longstreth); "Soft Boiled" 1923 (the Girl); "The Thrill Chaser" 1923; "The Wanderer of the Wasteland" 1924 (Ruth Virey); "The Light of Western Stars" 1925 (Madeline Hammond); "The Lucky Horseshoe" 1925 (Eleanor Hunt); "Wild Horse Mesa" 1925 (Sue Melerne).

Dove Eye (-7/13/69). Films: "The Arrow Maiden" 1915; "The Boundary Line" 1915.

Dover, Nancy. Films: "The Fighting Parson" 1930-short; "Cimarron" 1931 (Donna Cravat).

Dover, Robert Foster. Films: "Broken Arrow" 1950 (Machogee); "Indian Uprising" 1951 (Tubai).

Dowd, Mel (1933-). TV: *Jim Bowie*—"The Bounty Hunter" 5-17-57 (Nun).

Dowdell, Robert. Films: "Macho Callahan" 1970 (Blind Man). ¶TV: *Stoney Burke*—Regular 1962-63 (Cody Bristol).

Dowlan, William (1882-11/6/47). Films: "The Tragedy of Whispering Creek" 1914; "The Unlawful Trade" 1914; "The Desert Breed" 1915.

Dowling, Doris (1921-). Films: "Running Target" 1956 (Smitty). ¶TV: *Cheyenne*—"The Outlander" 12-13-55 (Cora Culver); *Have Gun*

Will Travel—"The Haunted Trees" 6-13-59 (Sara Howard); *Tales of Wells Fargo*—"Day of Judgment" 9-5-60 (Verna); *The Tall Man*—"The Long Way Home" 3-31-62 (Maisie Turner); *Bonanza*—"Twilight Town" 10-13-63 (Katy).

Dowling, Joseph J. (1848-7/10/28). Films: "The Man from Oregon" 1915; "The Apostle of Vengeance" 1916 (Tom McCoy); "The Deserter" 1916 (Colonel Taylor); "The Gunfighter" 1916 (Ace High Larkins); "The Square Deal Man" 1917 (Two Spots); "Carmen of the Klondike" 1918 (Salcratus Joe); "The Ghost of the Rancho" 1918 (Jeffrey's Grandfather); "The Goddess of Lost Lake" 1918 (Marshal Thorne); "A Man in the Open" 1919 (James Brown); "A Man's Country" 1919 (Marshal Leland); "The Midnight Stage" 1919 (Twisted Tuttle); "The White Man's Courage" 1919 (William Roberts); "With Hoops of Steel" 1919 (Col. Whittaker); "Riders of the Dawn" 1920 (Tom Anderson); "The U.P. Trail" 1920 (Place Hough); "Fightin' Mad" 1921 (James McGraw); "The Girl Who Ran Wild" 1922 (Calaveras John); "The Half-Breed" 1922 (Judge Huntington); "The Trail of the Axe" 1922 (Dr. Somers); "The Spider and the Rose" 1923 (the Governor); "Tiger Rose" 1923 (Father Thibault); "The Golden Princess" 1925 (Padre); "The Two-Gun Man" 1926 (Dad Randall).

Downey, John. Films: "Last of the Pony Riders" 1953 (Tom McEwen).

Downing, Barry. Films: "Between Men" 1935 (Johnny as a Boy); "Cavalcade of the West" 1936 (Ace as a Boy); "Phantom Gold" 1938 (Buddy Wright).

Downing, Joseph (1903-10/16/75). Films: "Belle Starr" 1941 (Jim Cole). ¶TV: *Sergeant Preston of the Yukon*—"Cinderella of the Yukon" 3-22-56 (Bert Trask), "Fancy Dan" 4-5-56 (Alec Dawar).

Downing, Maryan. Films: "Desert Justice" 1936 (Ellen Hansen).

Downing, Rex. Films: "Branded a Coward" 1935; "Black Bandit" 1938 (Young Don).

Downing, Walter (1874-12/21/37). Films: "Code of the Range" 1936 (Doctor); "One Man Justice" 1937 (Doc Willat); "Two-Fisted Sheriff" 1937 (Doc Pierce).

Downs, Cathy (1924-12/8/78). Films: "My Darling Clementine" 1946 (Clementine); "Panhandle" 1948 (Dusty Stewart); "Massacre

River" 1949 (Kitty Reid); "Short Grass" 1950 (Sharon); "The Sundowners" 1950 (Mrs. Boyce); "Bandits of the West" 1953 (Joanne Collier); "Kentucky Rifle" 1956; "The Oklahoma Woman" 1956 (Susan Grant). ¶TV: *The Lone Ranger*—"Best Laid Plans" 12-25-52; *Tombstone Territory*—"Triangle of Death" 5-7-58 (Patricia Camden), "Surrender at Sunglow" 5-15-59 (Anna); *Bat Masterson*—"Marked Deck" 3-11-59 (Amelia Roberts), "Incident at Fort Bowie" 4-31-60 (Julie Giles); *Rawhide*—"Incident Before Black Pass" 5-19-61 (Jenny Stone).

Downs, Frederick (1916–). TV: *Death Valley Days*—"Storm Over Truckee" 11-15-61 (Mr. Woolf); *Empire*—"Ballard Number One" 10-2-62 (Harry Phelps), "Season of Growth" 2-19-63 (Denton); *Gunsmoke*—"The Good People" 10-15-66 (Judge Evers), "Saturday Night" 1-7-67 (Storekeeper); *Bonanza*—"False Witness" 10-22-67 (Haskell); *Lancer*—"Julie" 10-29-68 (Liveryman); *Alias Smith and Jones*—"The Fifth Victim" 3-25-71 (Judge Peters), "The Man Who Corrupted Hadleyburg" 1-27-72 (Prosecutor), "The Ten Days That Shook Kid Curry" 11-4-72 (Judge).

Downs, Hugh (1921–). TV: *Riverboat*—"The Night of the Faceless Men" 3-28-60 (Dan Flynn).

Downs, Johnny (1913-6/13/94). Films: "The Arizona Raiders" 1936 (Lonesome Alonzo Mulhall); "Twilight on the Prairie" 1944; "Square Dance Jubilee" 1949; "Hills of Oklahoma" 1950 (Square Dance Caller); "Column South" 1953 (Lt. Posick).

Downs, Rex (1885-2/3/75). Films: "Kidnapped by Indians" 1914; "North of '53" 1917 (Joe Brooks); "Cavanaugh of the Forest Rangers" 1918 (Joe Gregg).

Downs, Watson (1879-5/26/69). Films: "Jesse James Rides Again" 1947-serial (Farmer #2); "Law and Order" 1953 (Doctor); "The Oklahoman" 1957 (Farmer). ¶TV: *The Cisco Kid*—"Face of Death" 2-16-52.

Doyle, David (1925–). Films: "Wild and Wooly" TVM-1978 (Teddy Roosevelt).

Doyle, Maxine (1915-5/8/73). Films: "Rio Grande Romance" 1936 (Joan Williams); "Come on Cowboys" 1937 (Ellen Rand); "Round-Up Time in Texas" 1937 (Gwen Barclay); "Overland Mail Robbery" 1943; "Raiders of Sunset Pass" 1943 (Sally Meehan); "San Fernando Valley" 1944.

Doyle, Patsy (1910-9/22/75). Films: "Stagecoach" 1939.

Doyle, Regina (1907-9/30/31). Films: "The Lone Prairie" 1926; "A Clean Sweep" 1928; "Saps and Saddles" 1928; "Beyond the Smoke" 1929; "The Danger Line" 1929; "A Daring Dude" 1929; "Just in Time" 1929; "Perilous Paths" 1929; "Red Romance" 1929; "Ridin' Leather" 1929.

Doyle, Robert. TV: *Gunsmoke*—"Root Down" 10-6-62 (Grudie Dutton); *Stoney Burke*—"Cat's Eyes" 2-11-63 (Doyle Yates); *The Legend of Jesse James*—"Dark Side of the Moon" 4-18-66 (Beau Tamblyn); *Bonanza*—"A Real Nice, Friendly Little Town" 11-27-66 (Jeb Rikeman), "He Was Only Seven" 3-5-72 (Clem); *Custer*—"Dangerous Prey" 12-6-67 (Lieutenant Lamey); *Lancer*—"The Lawman" 10-22-68 (Al Evans), "Blind Man's Bluff" 9-23-69 (Harrison Meek); *Nakia*—"The Driver" 11-2-74 (Paul).

Doyle, Ron (1938–). TV: *Death Valley Days*—"A Calamity Called Jane" 2-11-67 (Joe Makroff).

Dozier, William (1908-4/23/91). Films: "Kino, the Padre on Horseback" 1977.

Drago, Billy. Films: "The Chisholms" TVM-1979; "Windwalker" 1980 (Crow Scout); "Pale Rider" 1985 (Deputy Mather). ¶TV: *The Chisholms*—4-16-79 (Teetonkah); *Adventures of Brisco County, Jr.*—Pilot 8-27-93 (John Bly), "The Orb Scholar" 9-3-93 (John Bly), "Senior Spirit" 10-15-93 (John Bly), "Crystal Hawks" 11-12-93 (John Bly), "Fountain of Youth" 1-14-94 (John Bly), "Bye Bly" 2-18-94 (John Bly).

Drake, Betsy (1923–). TV: *Wanted—Dead or Alive*—"The Spur" 1-17-59 (Lucy Fremont).

Drake, Charles (1914-9/10/94). Films: "Comanche Territory" 1950 (Stacey Howard); "Winchester '73" 1950 (Steve Miller); "The Treasure of Lost Canyon" 1952 (Jim Anderson); "Gunsmoke" 1953 (Johnny Lake); "The Lone Hand" 1953 (George Hadley); "War Arrow" 1953 (Sgt. Luke Schermerhorn); "Four Guns to the Border" 1954 (Sheriff Jim Flannery); "Walk the Proud Land" 1956 (Tom Sweeney); "No Name on the Bullet" 1959 (Dr. Luke Canfield); "Showdown" 1963 (Bert Pickett). ¶TV: *The Lone Ranger*—"The Man with Two Faces" 2-23-50, "Outlaw's Trail" 10-21-54, "Showdown at Sand Creek" 5-26-55; *20th Century Fox Hour*—"Gun in His Hand" 4-4-56 (Macauley); *Wagon Train*—"The Charles Maury Story" 5-7-58 (Charles Maury), "The Sam Livingston Story" 6-15-60 (Sam Liv-

ingston), "The Caroline Casteel Story" 9-26-62 (Frank Casteel), "The Hollister John Garrison Story" 2-6-63 (John Hollister), "The Myra Marshall Story" 10-21-63 (Verne), "The Link Cheney Story" 4-13-64 (Link Cheney); *Laramie*—"Ride into Darkness" 10-18-60 (Matt Jessup), "The Accusers" 11-14-61 (Allen Winter); *Destry*—"Red Brady's Kid" 4-24-64 (Sheriff Connell); *F Troop*—"Is This Fort Really Necessary?" 4-6-67 (Maj. Terrence McConnell); *Daniel Boone*—"Heroes Welcome" 2-22-68 (Simon Jarvis), "The Plague That Came to Ford's Run" 10-31-68 (Andy Wharton); *The Virginian*—"A Woman of Stone" 12-17-69 (Milo Cantrell); *The Men from Shiloh*—"Jenny" 9-30-70 (Jeremy).

Drake, Christian. TV: *Wyatt Earp*—"The Almost Dead Cowhand" 10-23-56 (Thad Milburn), "Bad Woman" 12-31-57 (Lance Morfit), "Caught by a Whisker" 10-7-58 (Clint Dunbar); *Tales of Wells Fargo*—"Jesse James" 7-1-57 (Charlie Ford); *Have Gun Will Travel*—"Three Bells to Perdido" 9-14-57.

Drake, Claudia. Films: "Border Patrol" 1943 (Inez); "False Colors" 1943 (Faith Lawton); "Gentleman from Texas" 1946; "The Lawless Breed" 1946; "Lone Star Moonlight" 1946; "Renegade Girl" 1946; "Indian Agent" 1948 (Turquoise); "The Cowboy and the Indians" 1949 (Lucky Broken Arm); "Northern Patrol" 1953 (Oweena). ¶TV: *The Cisco Kid*—"Medicine Man Story" 8-25-51; *Wagon Train*—"The Sarah Drummond Story" 4-2-58 (the Squaw).

Drake, Dona (1920-1989). Films: "The Doolins of Oklahoma" 1949 (Cattle Annie); "Down Laredo Way" 1953 (Narita); "Son of Belle Star" 1953 (Dolores).

Drake, Douglass (1919-1/19/51). Films: "Law of the Northwest" 1943 (Paul Darcy); "Robin Hood of the Range" 1943 (Ned Harding).

Drake, James. TV: *The Texan*—"The Easterner" 12-15-58 (Buck), "Quarantine" 2-8-60, "Borrowed Time" 3-7-60 (Matt Stacey), "Lady Tenderfoot" 5-9-60; *Wanted—Dead or Alive*—"Epitaph" 2-8-61; *Gunsmoke*—"Prairie Wolfer" 1-18-64 (Dude); *Branded*—"$10,000 for Durango" 11-28-65 (Deputy).

Drake, Ken (1921-1/30/87). TV: *Gunsmoke*—"Jealousy" 7-6-57 (Cowboy), "Hard Luck Henry" 10-23-67 (Sheriff), "O'Quillian" 10-28-68 (Parker); *Tombstone Territory*—"Reward for a Gunslinger" 10-23-57 (Frank Masters); *Bat Masterson*—

"The Treasure of Worry Hill" 12-3-58 (Burdette), "Murder Can Be Dangerous" 11-3-60 (Secret), "Episode in Eden" 3-16-61 (Ron Daigle); *The Law of the Plainsman*—"The Question of Courage" 2-25-60 (Bill Downs); *Wyatt Earp*—"Casey and the Clowns" 2-21-61 (Tim Murdock); *The Outlaws*—"The Bitter Swede" 1-18-62 (Ken Horses); *Empire*—"Down There, the World" 3-12-63 (Ludwell); *Bonanza*—"Rich Man, Poor Man" 5-12-63, "The Saga of Muley Jones" 3-29-64 (Brave Pony), "Black Friday" 1-22-67 (Charlie), "The Price of Salt" 2-4-68 (Jackson), "Queen High" 12-1-68 (Sam Jacks), "The Wish" 3-9-69 (Leatham); *Great Adventure*—"The Testing of Sam Houston" 1-31-64 (Miller); *Destry*—"Law and Order Day" 2-28-64 (Deputy); *The Loner*—"The Kingdom of McComb" 10-9-65 (Townsend, Sr.); *The Big Valley*—"Teacher of Outlaws" 2-2-66 (Dr. Briggs), "Day of the Comet" 12-26-66 (Dr. Merar); *Wild Wild West*—"The Night of the Cadre" 3-24-67 (Dr. Frim), "The Night of the Gruesome Games" 10-25-68 (Gen. Crocker); *The High Chaparral*—"A Hanging Offense" 11-12-67 (Lieutenant Colonel), "The Hostage" 3-5-71 (Marshal); *Cimarron Strip*—"Big Jessie" 2-8-68.

Drake, Pauline (1912-). Films: "Under Fiesta Stars" 1941. ¶TV: *Wyatt Earp*—"The Cyclone" 5-12-59.

Drake, Peggy. Films: "King of the Mounties" 1942-serial (Carol Brent).

Drake, Steve (1923-12/19/48). Films: "Pioneer Justice" 1947 (Al Walters); "Black Hills" 1948 (Larry); "The Gallant Legion" 1948 (Dispatch Rider); "The Westward Trail" 1948 (Tim).

Drake, Tom (1919-8/11/82). Films: "Money, Women and Guns" 1958 (Jess Ryerson); "Warlock" 1959 (Abe McQuown); "Johnny Reno" 1966 (Joe Connors); "Red Tomahawk" 1967 (Bill Kane). ¶TV: *Wanted—Dead or Alive*—"Ricochet" 11-22-58 (Victor Kincaid), "The Showdown" 10-26-60 (Johnny Haywood); *Cimarron City*—"Return of the Dead" 2-14-59 (Steve); *Lawman*—"The Hunch" 10-11-59 (Frank Judson), "The Kids" 2-21-60 (Uncle Lou Evans), "Dilemma" 10-30-60 (Dr. Sam Burbage); *Riverboat*—"Face of Courage" 12-27-59 (Homer Atkins); *Wagon Train*—"The Lita Foladaire Story" 1-6-60 (Dr. Cannon); *The Alaskans*—"Black Sand" 2-14-60 (Dan Weber); *Laramie*—"Duel at Alta Mesa" 2-23-60 (Tom Mannering);

Rawhide—"Incident of the Dust Flower" 3-4-60 (Henry Fisher); *Wichita Town*—"Second Chance" 3-16-60 (Rafe McCloud); *Zane Grey Theater*—"Stagecoach to Yuma" 5-5-60 (Dave Harmon); *Stagecoach West*—"The Storm" 12-13-60 (Selby Moss); *The Rebel*—"Berserk" 12-18-60 (Sheriff Matt Dunsen), "The Last Drink" 2-26-61 (Dawes); *Cheyenne*—"Trouble Street" 10-2-61; *The Dakotas*—"Walk Through the Badlands" 3-18-63 (Cpl. Steven Agard); *Branded*—"Very Few Heroes" 4-11-65 (Jordan Payne), "Judge Not" 9-12-65 (Major Tom Rock); *Bonanza*—"Five Sundowns to Sunup" 12-5-65 (Kirt); *Wild Wild West*—"The Night of the Bottomless Pit" 11-4-66 (Vincent Reed); *The Road West*—"Pariah" 12-5-66 (Oliver); *Gunsmoke*—"Ring of Darkness" 12-1-69 (Ben Hurley); *Hec Ramsey*—"Scar Tissue" 3-10-74.

Drake, Virgil (1896-2/12/46). Films: "Renegades of the Rio Grande" 1945 (Villager).

Drayton, Noel (1913-12/7/81). TV: *Northwest Passage*—"Stab in the Back" 2-20-59 (Oliver Leyton); *Bat Masterson*—"The Tumbleweed Wagon" 3-25-59 (Guitarist); *Great Adventure*—"The Pathfinder" 3-6-64 (Buchanan).

Dreier, Alex (1916-). TV: *Cowboy in Africa*—"First to Capture" 1-29-68 (Philip Martin).

Dresden, Curley. Films: "The Lawless Nineties" 1936; "The Old Wyoming Trail" 1937 (Outlaw); "Outlaws of the Prairie" 1937; "The Painted Stallion" 1937-serial (Harris); "Range Defenders" 1937 (Brown); "Roaring Six Guns" 1937 (Slug); "Rootin' Tootin' Rhythm" 1937; "Rough Ridin' Rhythm" 1937 (Soapy); "Call the Mesquiteers" 1938; "Cattle Raiders" 1938 (Rustler); "The Colorado Trail" 1938 (Henchman); "Gun Packer" 1938; "Heroes of the Alamo" 1938; "Heroes of the Hills" 1938; "The Lone Ranger" 1938-serial (Trooper); "Outlaws of Sonora" 1938; "Overland Stage Raiders" 1938; "Pals of the Saddle" 1938; "Panamint's Bad Man" 1938; "Rhythm of the Saddle" 1938; "Rolling Caravans" 1938; "Santa Fe Stampede" 1938; "Two-Gun Justice" 1938; "Under Western Stars" 1938; "The Adventures of the Masked Phantom" 1939 (Outlaw); "In Old Monterey" 1939; "The Kansas Terrors" 1939; "Mountain Rhythm" 1939; "New Frontier" 1939; "South of the Border" 1939; "Southward Ho!" 1939; "Wyoming Outlaw" 1939; "Zorro's Fighting Legion" 1939-serial (Tomas); "Arizona Gang-

busters" 1940; "Adventures of Red Ryder" 1940-serial (Judd); "Billy the Kid in Texas" 1940; "The Carson City Kid" 1940; "Ghost Valley Raiders" 1940 (Rawhide); "King of the Royal Mounted" 1940-serial (Kelly); "Melody Ranch" 1940; "One Man's Law" 1940; "Ride, Tenderfoot, Ride" 1940; "The Trail Blazers" 1940; "Under Texas Skies" 1940 (Jackson); "Bad Man of Deadwood" 1941; "Back in the Saddle" 1941; "Billy the Kid in Santa Fe" 1941 (Outlaw); "Billy the Kid Wanted" 1941; "Billy the Kid's Fighting Pals" 1941 (Burke); "Billy the Kid's Roundup" 1941; "Border Vigilantes" 1941; "Desert Bandit" 1941; "Gangs of Sonora" 1941; "Hands Across the Rockies" 1941; "In Old Colorado" 1941; "Jesse James at Bay" 1941; "The Lone Rider Crosses the Rio" 1941; "The Lone Rider in Frontier Fury" 1941; "The Lone Rider in Ghost Town" 1941; "The Lone Rider Rides On" 1941; "A Missouri Outlaw" 1941; "Prairie Pioneers" 1941; "The Son of Davy Crockett" 1941; "Two-Gun Sheriff" 1941; "Under Fiesta Stars" 1941; "Wyoming Wildcat" 1941; "Along the Sundown Trail" 1942; "Arizona Terrors" 1942; "Billy the Kid Trapped" 1942; "Border Roundup" 1942; "The Lone Rider and the Bandit" 1942; "Prairie Pals" 1942 (Henchman); "Raiders of the West" 1942; "Rolling Down the Great Divide" 1942; "Shadows on the Sage" 1942; "Sheriff of Sage Valley" 1942; "The Sombrero Kid" 1942; "Texas Justice" 1942; "Westward Ho" 1942; "Beyond the Last Frontier" 1943 (Ranger); "Black Hills Express" 1943; "Carson City Cyclone" 1943 (Tom Barton); "Death Valley Manhunt" 1943; "Hands Across the Border" 1943; "In Old Oklahoma" 1943; "The Kid Rides Again" 1943; "Law of the Saddle" 1943 (Joe); "The Man from Thunder River" 1943; "Santa Fe Scouts" 1943; "Wagon Tracks West" 1943; "Death Valley Rangers" 1944; "The Last Horseman" 1944; "Westward Bound" 1944 (Monte).

Dressler, Lieux. TV: *Gunsmoke*—"Waste" 9-27-71 & 10-4-71 (Victoria), "Alias Festus Haggen" 3-6-72 (Susie), "Women for Sale" 9-10-73 & 9-17-73 (Liz).

Dresser, Louise (1880-4/24/65). Films: "Ruggles of Red Gap" 1923 (Mrs. Effie Floud); "Salome Jane" 1923 (Mrs. Pete); "Caught" 1931 (Calamity Jane).

Drew, Ann (1891-2/6/74). Films: "Love and Law" 1915; "Riders of the Range" 1923 (Mary Smithson); "Red Raiders" 1927 (Jane Logan).

Drew, Donna. Films: "'49-'17" 1917 (Lady Ann Bobbett); "The Ghost Girl" 1919.

Drew, Donna. Films: "The Return of Jack Slade" 1955 (Laughing Sam). ¶TV: *Wild Bill Hickok*—"Marvins' Mix-Up" 5-19-53; *Death Valley Days*—"California's First Ice Man" 1-14-56 (Laura); *Bronco*—"The Prince of Darkness" 11-6-61 (Enid Taylor).

Drew, Ellen (1915-). Films: "Buck Benny Rides Again" 1940 (Joan Cameron); "Geronimo" 1940 (Alice Hamilton); "Texas Rangers Ride Again" 1940 (Ellen "Slats" Dangerfield); "The Parson of Panamint" 1941 (Mary Mallory); "The Man from Colorado" 1948 (Caroline Emmett); "The Baron of Arizona" 1950 (Sofia Peralta-Reaves); "Davy Crockett, Indian Scout" 1950 (Frances); "Stars in My Crown" 1950 (Harriet Gray); "The Great Missouri Raid" 1951 (Bee Moore); "Man in the Saddle" 1951 (Nan Melotte); "Outlaw's Son" 1957 (Ruth Sewall).

Drew, Lillian. Films: "Man from Music Mountain" 1938 (Mrs. Chris).

Drew, Lowell (1882-10/14/42). Films: "Wells Fargo" 1937 (Townsman); "Gun Packer" 1938 (Dad Adams); "The Lone Star Vigilantes" 1942 (Peabody).

Drew, Paula. "The Vigilantes Return" 1947 (Louise Holden).

Drew, Philip Yale (1880-7/2/40). Films: "The Root of Evil" 1919; "His Pal's Gal" 1920; "The Hobo of Pizen City" 1920; "The Hold-Up Man" 1920; "The Law of the Border" 1920; "Tex of the Timberlands" 1920 (Young Buffalo).

Drew, Roland (1901-3/16/88). Films: "Ramona" 1928 (Felipe).

Drew, S. Rankin (1892-5/19/18). Films: "O'Garry of the Royal Mounted" 1915.

Drexel, Nancy (1910-11/19/89). Films: "Breed of the Sunsets" 1928 (the Spanish Girl); "Law of the West" 1932 (Sally Tracy); "Man from Hell's Edges" 1932 (Betty Williams); "Mason of the Mounted" 1932 (Marion Kirby); "Partners" 1932 (Jean Morgan); "Texas Buddies" 1932 (June Collins).

Drexel, Steve. Films: "Badman's Country" 1958; "The Red, White and Black" 1970 (Capt. Carpenter). ¶TV: *Colt .45*—"Appointment in Agoura" 6-7-60.

Dreyfuss, Richard (1947-). TV: *The Big Valley*—"Boy into Man" 1-16-67 (Lud Akely); *Gunsmoke*—"The Golden Land" 3-5-73 (Gearshon).

Drier, Moosie (1964-). TV:

Royce—Pilot 5-21-76 (Stephen Mabry).

Driggers, Don (1893-11/19/72). Films: "Pirates of Monterey" 1947 (Thug).

Driscoll, Bobby (1937-3/3/68). Films: "The Big Bonanza" 1944 (Spud Kilton); "Melody Time" 1948. ¶TV: *Zane Grey Theater*—"Death Watch" 11-9-56 (Trumpeter Jones).

Driscoll, Robert Miller (1928-83). TV: *Rawhide*—"Incident of Fear in the Streets" 5-8-59 (Wilt Mason), "Incident of the Captive" 12-16-60 (Billy Chance); *Trackdown*—"Blind Alley" 9-16-59 (Mike Driscoll); *The Travels of Jaimie McPheeters*—"The Day of the Picnic" 2-16-64 (Billy Slocum); *Wild Wild West*—"The Night of the Big Blast" 10-7-66 (Lyle Peters); *Daniel Boone*—"Fort West Point" 3-23-67 (Robey).

Driscoll, Tex (1889-6/1/70). Films: "The Virginian" 1914 (Shorty); "The Girl of the Golden West" 1915 (Nick the Bartender); "The Plainsman" 1936; "Way Out West" 1937 (Bearded Miner); "Stagecoach" 1939; "The Ox-Bow Incident" 1943 (Posse); "Giant" 1956 (Clay Hodgins, Sr.).

Drivas, Robert (1938-6/29/86). TV: *Wild Wild West*—"The Night of the Burning Diamond" 4-8-66 (Midas Morgan); *Bonanza*—"Blood Tie" 2-18-68 (Tracy Blaine).

Driver, Ada Belle (1874-10/12/52). Films: "The Fighting Terror" 1929; "The Last Roundup" 1929; "Mark of the Spur" 1932 (Mrs. Beckett); "The Cowboy and the Bandit" 1935 (Mother Alexander Barton).

Drouet, Mike (1870-8/17/14). Films: "The Gambler of the West" 1914 (Mike Clancy).

Dru, Joanne (1923-). Films: "Red River" 1948 (Tess Millay); "She Wore a Yellow Ribbon" 1949 (Olivia Dandridge); "Wagonmaster" 1950 (Denver); "Vengeance Valley" 1951 (Jen Strobie); "Return of the Texan" 1952 (Ann Marshall); "Hannah Lee" 1953 (Hallie); "The Siege at Red River" 1954 (Nora Curtis); "Southwest Passage" 1954 (Lilly); "Drango" 1957 (Kate); "The Light in the Forest" 1958 (Milly Elders); "The Wild and the Innocent" 1959 (Marcy Howard). ¶TV: *Wagon Train*—"The Nels Stack Story" 10-23-57 (Laura Collins).

Drum, James (1918-11/28/76). TV: *Redigo*—"The Thin Line" 12-3-63 (Deputy Sheriff); *The Loner*—"Hunt the Man Down" 12-11-65 (Merv).

Drumier, Jack (1869-4/22/29). Films: "The Girl from Porcupine" 1922 (Bill Higgins).

Drummond, Jane. Films: "The Fargo Kid" 1940 (Jennie Winters).

Drury, James (1934-). Films: "The Last Wagon" 1956 (Lt. Kelly); "Love Me Tender" 1956 (Ray Reno); "Good Day for a Hanging" 1958 (Paul Ridgely); "Ten Who Dared" 1960 (Walter Powell); "Ride the High Country" 1962 (Billy Hammond); "Alias Smith and Jones" TVM-1971 (Sheriff Lom Trevors); "The Devil and Miss Sarah" TVM-1971 (Gil Turner); "The Gambler Returns: The Luck of the Draw" TVM-1991 (the Virginian). ¶TV: *Gunsmoke*—"The Reed Survives" 12-31-55 (Booth Rider), "Change of Heart" 4-25-59 (Jerry Cass), "Johnny Red" 10-3-59 (Johnny Red), "Old Faces" 3-18-61 (Tom Cook); *Zane Grey Theater*—"Wire" 1-31-58 (Jess McHugh), "Welcome Home a Stranger" 1-15-59 (Roy); *Broken Arrow*—"Power" 4-22-58 (Tanzay); *Decision*—"The Virginian" 7-6-58 (the Virginian); *The Texan*—"The Troubled Town" 10-13-58 (Johnny Kaler); *Bronco*—"Freeze-Out" 12-30-58 (John Smith); *Rawhide*—"Incident with an Executioner" 1-23-59 (Kenley), "Incident of the Boomerang" 3-24-61 (Johnny Adler), "Incident of the Night on the Town" 6-2-61 (Rance); *Have Gun Will Travel*—"The Man Who Lost" 2-7-59 (Tony DeVries); *Trackdown*—"Stranger in Town" 3-25-59 (John Ward); *Lawman*—"The Gang" 3-29-59 (Clay); *Black Saddle*—"Client: Neal Adams" 5-9-59 (Neal Adams); *Cheyenne*—"The Imposter" 11-2-59 (Bill); *Death Valley Days*—"Ten Feet of Nothing" 1-5-60 (Joe Plato); *The Rebel*—"Fair Game" 3-27-60 (Burt Pace), "Vindication" 12-4-60 (Capt. Paul Travers); *Wagon Train*—"The Bleymier Story" 11-16-60 (Justin Clairborne), "The Cole Crawford Story" 4-11-62 (Cole Crawford); *Stagecoach West*—"Blind Man's Bluff" 5-16-61 (Stace); *The Virginian*—Regular 1962-70 (the Virginian); *The Men from Shiloh*—Regular 1970-71 (the Virginian); *Alias Smith and Jones*—"The Long Chase" 9-16-72 (Sheriff Tankersley); *Adventures of Brisco County, Jr.*—Pilot 8-27-93 (Ethan Emerson), "Ned Zed" 3-13-94 (Ethan Emerson).

Drysdale, Don (1936-7/3/93). TV: *Lawman*—"The Hardcase" 1-31-60 (Roy Grant); *The Rifleman*—"Skull" 1-1-62; *Cowboy in Africa*—"Search and Destroy" 3-4-68 (Fairchild).

Duane, Jack. see Padjan, Jack

Dubbins, Don (1929-8/17/91). Films: "Tribute to a Badman" 1956 (Steve Miller); "Gunfight in Abilene" 1967 (Scrague); "Run, Simon, Run" TVM-1970 (Freddy Tom). ¶TV: *Sugarfoot*—"The Mountain" 3-31-59 (Vic Bradley), "The Twister" 4-14-59 (Sid Garvin); *Rawhide*—"Incident of the Dog Days" 4-17-59 (Johnny Camber); *Gunsmoke*—"Kitty's Injury" 9-19-59 (Lutie Judson), "Milly" 11-25-61 (Potts), "Marry Me" 12-23-61 (Orkey Cathcart), "Prairie Wolfer" 1-18-64 (Rolly Wendt); *Wichita Town*—"Biggest Man in Town" 12-30-59 (Petey McGlasson); *The Alaskans*—"The Challenge" 1-24-60 (Grant); *Johnny Ringo*—"Uncertain Vengeance" 3-10-60 (Harley Krale); *The Law of the Plainsman*—"Rabbit's Fang" 3-24-60 (Mite Rankin); *Wanted—Dead or Alive*—"The Parish" 3-26-60 (Randy Holleran); *Bonanza*—"Bitter Water" 4-9-60 (Tod McKaren); *The Rifleman*—"The Martinet" 11-8-60 (Ben Barry); *Zane Grey Theater*—"Ambush" 1-5-61 (Lt. William Homeyer); *Stagecoach West*—"The Outcasts" 3-7-61 (Ken Rawlins); *Great Adventure*—"The Pathfinder" 3-6-64 (Jason Chiles); *The Virginian*—"The Horse Fighter" 12-15-65 (Albie); *The Road West*—"Long Journey to Leavenworth" 10-17-66 (Wesley); *The Big Valley*—"Hell Hath No Fury" 11-18-68 (Grady); *The Guns of Will Sonnett*—"The Marriage" 3-14-69 (Burt Damon); *The New Land*—"The Word Is: Mortal" 10-5-74; *Kung Fu*—"Superstition" 4-5-73 (Meador).

DuBois, Diane. Films: "Dakota Incident" 1956 (Giselle). ¶TV: *Zane Grey Theater*—"Picture of Sal" 1-28-60 (Yvette); *Death Valley Days*—"The Battle of Mokelumne Hill" 3-1-60 (Monique).

Du Bois, Lucille. Films: "Four Hearts" 1922 (Betty Davis).

Dubov, Paul (1918-9/20/79). Films: "North to the Klondike" 1942; "High Noon" 1952 (Scott); "Apache Woman" 1955 (Ben); "Forty Guns" 1957 (Judge Macey). ¶TV: *Gunsmoke*—"The Preacher" 6-16-56 (Humbert), "Cain" 3-9-57 (Pritchard); *Wyatt Earp*—"The Wicked Widow" 5-21-57 (Tobe Larson), "Caught by a Whisker" 10-7-58 (Matt Dunbar); *Broken Arrow*—"Iron Maiden" 3-25-58 (Kaytowa), "Old Enemy" 5-6-58 (Kaytowa); *The Restless Gun*—"The Painted Beauty" 1-5-59 (Hopper); *Bat Masterson*—"Sharpshooter" 2-11-59 (Danny Dowling), "Jeopardy at Jackson Hole" 6-1-61

(Tom Fulton); *Cheyenne*—"The Rebellion" 10-12-59 (Captain Andre); *Zorro*—"The Fortune Teller" 6-18-59 (Gustavo); *Wanted—Dead or Alive*—"Mental Lapse" 1-2-60 (Blade Tomson); *The Deputy*—"Queen Bea" 2-20-60 (Fletcher); *Bonanza*—"The Courtship" 1-7-61 (Dealer), "The Long Night" 5-6-62.

DuBrey, Claire (1893-8/1/93). Films: "The Almost Good Man" 1917; "Anything Once" 1917 (Senorita Dolores); "The Drifter" 1917; "The Fighting Gringo" 1917 (May Smith); "Follow the Girl" 1917 (Donna); "A 45 Calibre Mystery" 1917; "Hair-Trigger Burk" 1917; "Pay Me!" 1917 (Nita); "Six-Shooter Justice" 1917; "Sure Shot Morgan" 1917; "The Human Target" 1918; "Prisoner of the Pines" 1918 (Louise); "The Devil's Trail" 1919 (Dubec's Wife); "The Ghost Girl" 1919; "A Man in the Open" 1919 (Polly); "That Girl Montana" 1921 (Lottie); "Ramona" 1936 (Marda); "Jesse James" 1939 (Mrs. Ford); "South of the Border" 1939 (Duenna); "Brigham Young—Frontiersman" 1940 (Emma Smith); "Bells of Capistrano" 1942 (Ma McCracken); "The Lights of Old Santa Fe" 1944 (Rosie McGerk); "Dakota" 1945 (Wahtonka); "Don Ricardo Returns" 1946; "The Bells of San Fernando" 1947 (Manta); "Unconquered" 1947; "Frontier Gun" 1958 (Bess Loveman); "Escort West" 1959 (Mrs. Fenniman). ¶TV: *Broken Arrow*—"Ghost Face" 3-12-57 (Tesal Bestinay); *Tales of Wells Fargo*—"The Newspaper" 3-24-58 (Effie Sutton); *The Californians*—"The Fugitive" 4-28-59 (Mrs. Dupres).

Du Count, George (1898-2/7/60). Films: "The Gay Desperado" 1936 (Salvador); "White Fang" 1936 (Francois).

Du Crow, Tote (1858-12/12/27). Films: "The Fighting Gringo" 1917 (Enrique); "Rimrock Jones" 1918 (Juan Soto); "Mark of Zorro" 1920 (Bernardo); "The Moon Riders" 1920-serial; "One He Man" 1920; "The Rattler's Hiss" 1920; "Man of the Forest" 1921 (Lone Wolf); "Border Justice" 1925 (Lone Star); "Don Q, Son of Zorro" 1925 (Bernardo); "The Prairie Pirate" 1925 (Jose); "The Saddle Hawk" 1925 (Vasquez); "Spook Ranch" 1925 (Navarro).

Dudgeon, Elspeth (1871-12/11/55). Films: "Yankee Fakir" 1947 (Scrubwoman); "Lust for Gold" 1949 (Mrs. Bannister).

Dudley, Charles. Films: "Boots and Saddles" 1916 (Walter Harris); "The Secret of Black Mountain" 1917

(Ed Stanley); "The Yellow Bullet" 1917 (Perkins); "Petticoats and Politics" 1918 (Sheriff Joe Roberts); "Whatever the Cost" 1918 (Uncle Dud); "Steelheart" 1921 (Old Tom Shelley); "Where Men Are Men" 1921 (Monty Green); "The Fighting Guide" 1922 (John MacDonald); "When Danger Smiles" 1922 (Jim Barker).

Dudley, Florence. Films: "Rogue of the Rio Grande" 1930 (Big Bertha).

Dudley, Robert (1869-11/12/55). Films: "Springtime in the Rockies" 1937; "When the Daltons Rode" 1940 (Juror Pete Norris); "Singin' in the Corn" 1946 (Gramp McCoy).

Duel, Peter. see Deuel, Peter.

Dufau, C.R. (1879-2/20/57). Films: "The Land of Missing Men" 1930 (Senor Madero).

Duff, Howard (1917-7/8/90). Films: "Calamity Jane and Sam Bass" 1949 (Sam Bass); "Red Canyon" 1949 (Lin Sloan/Cordt); "The Lady from Texas" 1951 (Dan Mason); "The Yellow Mountain" 1954 (Pete Menlo); "Blackjack Ketchum, Desperado" 1956 (Blackjack Ketchum); "The Broken Star" 1956 (Frank Smead); "Sierra Stranger" 1957 (Jess Collins); "The Wild Women of Chastity Gulch" TVM-1982 (Colonel Samuel Isaacs). ¶TV: *Bonanza*—"Enter Mark Twain" 10-10-59 (Samuel Langhorn Clemens); *The Virginian*—"A Distant Fury" 3-20-63 (Ed Frazer); *The Men from Shiloh*—"The Town Killer" 3-10-71 (Stuart Masters); *Alias Smith and Jones*—"Shootout at Diablo Station" 12-2-71 (George Fendler); *Kung Fu*—"A Dream Within a Dream" 1-17-74 (Noah Fleck), "This Valley of Terror" 9-28-74 (Jenkins); *The Quest*—"Dynasty of Evil" 1976; *Young Maverick*—"Dead Man's Hand" 12-26-79 & 1-2-80 (Herman Rusk).

Duff-Griffin, William (1940-11/13/94). Films: "Four Eyes and Six-Guns" TVM-1992 (Mr. Laughton).

Duffield, Harry S. (-10/31/21). Films: "Rio Grande" 1920 (Father O'Brien).

Duffin, Shay. Films: "The White Buffalo" 1977 (Tim Brady); "The Frisco Kid" 1979 (O'Leary).

Duffy, Jack (1882-7/23/39). Films: "Texas Terror" 1935; "Trails End" 1935 (Deke); "Wild Brian Kent" 1936 (Old Timer).

Duffy, Patrick (1949-). Films: "James A. Michener's Texas" TVM-1995 (Stephen F. Austin).

Dufour, Val (1927-). TV: *Gunsmoke*—"Reward for Matt" 1-28-56

(Day Barrett), "Reunion '78" 3-3-56 (Jerry Shand), "Gentleman's Disagreement" 4-30-60 (Ed Beaudry), "A Man a Day" 12-30-61 (Cooner); *Jim Bowie*—"Land Jumpers" 11-16-56 (Armand Duprez), "Spanish Intrigue" 2-8-57 (Don Jose Litri); *Sheriff of Cochise*—"Triangle" 2-22-57 (Jack Saunders); *Zane Grey Theater*—"Ride a Lonely Trail" 11-2-57 (Horse Daley); *Trackdown*—"The Reward" 1-3-58 (Mort Williams); *Rawhide*—"Incident of the Tumbleweed Wagon" 1-9-59 (Luke Storm); *Hotel De Paree*—"Sundance Goes to Kill" 1-22-60 (Heslop).

Dugan, Alberta. Films: "Senor Jim" 1936 (Carole Cartier).

Dugan, Michael. Films: "The Three Godfathers" 1948 (Posse Member); "Range Land" 1949 (Guard); "She Wore a Yellow Ribbon" 1949 (Sgt. Hochbauer); "Escape from Fort Bravo" 1953 (Sims); "The Marauders" 1955 (Sal); "Fastest Gun Alive" 1956 (Clement Farley); "Gun Glory" 1957 (Farmer).

Dugan, Tom (1889-3/6/55). Films: "The Phantom of the West" 1931-serial (Oscar); "The Vanishing Legion" 1931-serial (Warren); "Woman Hungry" 1931 (Sam Beeman); "Wide Open Spaces" 1932-short; "Virginia City" 1940 (Spieler); "Trail of Kit Carson" 1945.

Dugay, Yvette. Films: "The Cimarron Kid" 1951 (Rose of Cimarron); "Hiawatha" 1952 (Minnehaha); "Cattle Queen of Montana" 1954 (Starfire); "Domino Kid" 1957 (Rosita). ¶TV: *Jim Bowie*—"Broomstick Wedding" 10-12-56 (Annette Leprie); *Circus Boy*—"Little Vagabond" 6-23-57 (Maria Gaetano); *Maverick*—"Prey of the Cat" 12-7-58 (Raquel Morales); *Zorro*—"The Flaming Arrow" 12-18-58 (Milana); *Bronco*—"School for Cowards" 4-21-59; *Frontier Doctor*—"The Counterfeiters" 6-13-59; *Cheyenne*—"Gold, Glory and Custer—Prelude" 1-4-60 (Lone Woman), "Gold, Glory and Custer—Requiem" 1-11-60 (Lone Woman).

Duggan, Andrew (1923-5/15/88). Films: "Decision at Sundown" 1957 (Sheriff Swede Hanson); "Domino Kid" 1957 (Wade Harrington); "The Bravados" 1958 (Padre); "Return to Warbow" 1958 (Murray Fallam); "Westbound" 1959 (Clay Putnam); "The Glory Guys" 1965 (Gen. McCabe); "Skin Game" 1971 (Calloway). ¶TV: *Cheyenne*—"The Bounty Killer" 10-23-56 (Marshal Moxon), "Land Beyond the Law" 1-15-57 (Major Ellwood), "The Angry Sky" 6-17-58 (Granger Ward), "The

Frightened Town" 3-20-61 (Marshal Ben Delaney), "Satonka" 10-1-62 (Mark Kendall), "Showdown at Oxbend" 12-17-62 (Ed Foster); *Gunsmoke*—"How to Cure a Friend" 11-10-56 (Nick Search), "Cheap Labor" 5-4-57 (Fos Capper), "Gilt Guilt" 4-24-65 (John Crail); *Schlitz Playhouse of the Stars*—"The Restless Gun" 3-29-57 (Red Dawson); *Wagon Train*—"The Willy Moran Story" 9-18-57 (Brady); *Disneyland*—"The Saga of Andy Burnett"—Regular 1957-58 (Jack Kelly); *Colt .45*—"The Peacemaker" 10-18-57 (Jim Rexford); *Tombstone Territory*—"The Epitaph" 2-26-58 (Kirk Stevens), "Outlaw's Bugle" 8-6-58 (Kirk Stevens); *Jefferson Drum*—"The Cheater" 5-23-58 (Charles McGowan); *Decision*—"The Virginian" 7-6-58 (Stocker); *Lawman*—"Marked Man" 1-22-61 (Tod Larson), "Sunday" 4-15-62 (Frank Boone); *Maverick*—"The Ice Man" 1-29-61 (Cal Powers), "The Money Machine" 4-8-62 (Big Ed Murphy); *The Dakotas*—"Red Sky Over Bismarck" 1-14-63 (Colonel Withers); *The Travels of Jaimie McPheeters*—"The Day of the Golden Fleece" 10-6-63 (Morgan); *Bonanza*—"The Lila Conrad Story" 1-5-64 (Judge Knowlton); *Great Adventure*—"Kentucky's Bloody Ground"/"The Siege of Boonesborough" 4-3-64 & 4-10-64 (Colonel Callaway); *The Big Valley*—"Forty Rifles" 9-22-65 (Wallant), "The Haunted Gun" 2-6-67 (Senator Jud Robson); *F Troop*—"The New I.G." 2-8-66 (Major Winchester); *A Man Called Shenandoah*—"Run and Hide" 2-14-66 (Harley Kern); *The Virginian*—"A Bald-Faced Boy" 4-13-66 (Jim Claiborne); *Cimarron Strip*—"The Battleground" 9-28-67 (Major Ben Covington), "The Roarer" 11-2-67 (Major Ben Covington), "Without Honor" 2-29-68 (Major Ben Covington); *Lancer*—Regular 1968-70 (Murdoch Lancer); *Kung Fu*—"The Tide" 2-1-73 (Sheriff Boggs); *Barbary Coast*—"The Ballad of Redwing Jail" 9-29-75 (Sheriff Hyde).

Duggan, Bob. TV: *Rawhide*—"Incident of the Music Maker" 5-20-60; *Gunsmoke*—"The Wreckers" 9-11-67 (Man).

Duggan, Jan (1881-3/10/77). Films: "Wagon Wheels" 1934 (Abby Masters); "Drift Fence" 1936 (Carrie Bingham); "My Little Chickadee" 1940 (Woman); "Dudes Are Pretty People" 1942 (Radio Girl).

Duggan, Tom (1916-). Films: "Born Reckless" 1959 (Wilson).

Duke, John. TV: *Circus Boy*—"Alex the Great" 10-10-57 (Alex Con-

rad); *The Adventures of Rin Tin Tin*—"Top Gun" 1-24-58 (Toby Caution); *Have Gun Will Travel*—"The Hanging of Roy Carter" 10-4-58 (Keno Smith); *U.S. Marshal*—"Mass Escape" 2-7-59; *Bat Masterson*—"The Court Martial of Major Mars" 1-12-61 (Magnus); *Gunsmoke*—"Jenny" 10-13-62 (Al Flack); *Empire*—"Where the Hawk Is Wheeling" 1-29-63 (Leo Heller).

Duke, Patty (1946-). Films: "September Gun" TVM-1983 (Sister Dulcina). ¶TV: *Wide Country*—"To Cindy, with Love" 2-28-63 (Cindy Hopkins); *The Virginian*—"Sue Ann" 1-11-67 (Sue Ann MacRae).

Dukes, David (1945-). Films: "Go West, Young Girl" TVM-1978 (Reverend Crane). ¶TV: *How the West Was Won*—"L'Affaire Riel" 3-5-79 (Louis Riel).

Dullaghan, John. TV: *Gunsmoke*—"Trafton" 10-25-71 (Priest).

Dullea, Keir (1936-). Films: "Mail Order Bride" 1964 (Lee Carey); "Welcome to Blood City" 1977-Brit./Can. (Lewis); "The Legend of the Golden Gun" TVM-1979 (General Custer). ¶TV: *Empire*—"Stopover on the Way to the Moon" 1-1-63 (Skip Wade); *Bonanza*—"Elegy for a Hangman" 1-20-63 (Bob Jolley).

Dulo, Jane (1918-5/22/94). TV: *The Tall Man*—"The Impatient Brides" 2-3-62 (Emma); *Gunsmoke*—"Champion of the World" 12-24-66 (Cora Argyle); *Daniel Boone*—"Noblesse Oblige" 3-26-70.

Dumas, Jean. Films: "The Prairie Pirate" 1925 (Ruth Delaney); "99 Wounds" 1931 (Rose Purdue).

Dumas, Wade. Films: "Harlem Rides the Range" 1939 (Sheriff).

Dumbrille, Douglas (1890-4/2/74). Films: "Rustlers' Roundup" 1933 (Bill Brett); "Smoke Lightning" 1933 (Sam Edson); "Massacre" 1934 (Chairman); "End of the Trail" 1936 (Bill Mason); "The Mysterious Rider" 1938 (Pecos Bill/Ben Wade); "Rovin' Tumbleweeds" 1939 (Holloway); "Virginia City" 1940 (Maj. Drewery); "The Round Up" 1941 (Capt. Lane); "King of the Mounties" 1942-serial (Gil Harper); "Ride 'Em, Cowboy" 1942 (Jake Rainwater); "False Colors" 1943 (Mark Foster); "Forty Thieves" 1944 (Tad Hammond); "Lumberjack" 1944 (Keeper); "The Daltons Ride Again" 1945 (Sheriff); "Flame of the West" 1945 (Nightlander); "Under Nevada Skies" 1946 (Arthur Courtney); "The Fabulous Texan" 1947 (Luke Roland); "Last of the Wild Horses" 1948

(Charlie Cooper); "Riders of the Whistling Pines" 1949 (Henry Mitchell); "The Kangaroo Kid" 1950 (Vincent Moller); "The Savage Horde" 1950 (Col. Price); "Apache War Smoke" 1952 (Major Dekker); "Sky Full of Moon" 1952 (Rodeo Official); "Son of Paleface" 1952 (Sheriff McIntyre); "Captain John Smith and Pocahontas" 1953 (Powhatan); "The Lawless Rider" 1954 (Marshal Brady); "Davy Crockett and the River Pirates" 1956 (Saloon Owner). ¶TV: *The Californians*—"The Marshal" 3-11-58 (John W. Geary), "Murietta" 5-27-58 (Mayor Geary); *Laramie*—"Duel at Alta Mesa" 2-23-60 (T.J. Patterson); *Bat Masterson*—"Wanted—Alive Please" 5-26-60 (Taylor Millard).

Dumke, Ralph (1899-1/4/64). Films: "The San Francisco Story" 1952 (Winfield Holbert); "Hannah Lee" 1953 (Alesworth); "Massacre Canyon" 1954 (Parson Canfield); "Rails into Laramie" 1954 (Mayor Brown); "They Rode West" 1954 (Dr. Gibson). ¶TV: *Ford Theater*—"Sudden Silence" 10-10-56 (Mayor); *The Texan*—"Letter of the Law" 3-23-59 (Doc Fry); *Rawhide*—"Incident of the Night on the Town" 6-2-61 (Judge Aikens).

Dumont, Margaret (1889-3/6/65). Films: "Sunset in El Dorado" 1945 (Aunt Dolly).

Duna, Steffi (1913-4/22/92). Films: "Hi Gaucho!" 1936 (Inez del Campo); "The Girl and the Gambler" 1939 (Dolores "the Dove" Romero); "Law of the Pampas" 1939 (Chiquita); "River's End" 1940 (Cheeta).

Dunaev, Nick. Films: "Lightnin' Smith Returns" 1931 (Mexican Pete); "The Riding Kid" 1931 (Pedro).

Dunaway, Faye (1941-). Films: "Doc" 1971 (Kate Elder); "Little Big Man" 1971 (Mrs. Pendrake); "Oklahoma Crude" 1973 (Lena Doyle).

Dunbar, Bill. Films: "The Apple Dumpling Gang" 1975 (Fast Eddie).

Dunbar, David (1893-11/7/53). Films: "Leatherstocking" 1924-serial; "North of '36" 1924 (Dell Williams); "Trail Dust" 1924; "The Bloodhound" 1925 (Rambo); "The Cowboy Musketeer" 1925 (Tony Vaquerrelli); "Galloping Vengeance" 1925 (Duke Granby); "A Man of Nerve" 1925 (Rangey Greer); "Ridin' the Wind" 1925 (Black Hart Gangleader); "Beyond the Rockies" 1926 (Cottle); "The Galloping Cowboy" 1926 (Pedro); "The Arizona Whirlwind" 1927 (Bert Hawley); "The Boy

Rider" 1927 (Bill Hargus); "The Broncho Buster" 1927 (Curtis Harris); "The Fighting Hombre" 1927 (Goldstud Hopkins); "Gold from Weepah" 1927; "The Boundary Battle" 1928; "Plunging Hoofs" 1928 (Squint Jones); "Dallas" 1950 (Prisoner).

Dunbar, Dorothy (1902-10/30/92). Films: "The Flaming Crisis" 1924 (Tex Miller); "The Masquerade Bandit" 1926 (Molly Marble); "Red Hot Hoofs" 1926 (Frances Morris); "Lightning Lariats" 1927 (Janet Holbrooke).

Dunbar, Helen (1868-8/28/33). Films: "The Squaw Man" 1918 (Dowager Countess); "Fighting Through" 1919 (Mrs. Warren); "God's Outlaw" 1919 (Mrs. Heatherly); "Man of Courage" 1922 (Mrs. Deane); "The Call of the Canyon" 1923 (Aunt Mary); "The Reckless Sex" 1925.

Dunbar, Olive. TV: *Laredo*—"Enemies and Brother" 2-17-67, "A Question of Guilt" 3-10-67; *The Big Valley*—"A Passage of Saints" 3-10-69 (Eliza Grant).

Dunbar, Robert N. (1858-1/16/43). Films: "Broadway, Arizona" 1917 (Doctor); "Fighting for Gold" 1919 (Lord Farquar).

Duncan, Angus (1936-). TV: *Wichita Town*—"The Long Night" 1-20-60 (Boy); *Alias Smith and Jones*—"Jailbreak at Junction City" 9-30-71; *Gunsmoke*—"The Avenger" 11-27-72 (Jay Wrecken).

Duncan, Archie (1914-7/24/79). TV: *The Alaskans*—"Contest at Gold Bottom" 11-15-59 (Jake Bee); *Johnny Ringo*—"The Cat" 12-3-59 (Keating); *Colt .45*—"Breakthrough" 3-27-60 (Jeff Kincaid); *Lawman*—"The Wolfer" 1-24-60 (Pike Reese); *Black Saddle*—"End of the Line" 5-6-60 (Pat Cudahy).

Duncan, Arletta. Films: "Fighting Champ" 1932 (Jean Mullins); "The Gallant Fool" 1933 (Alecia Rousselet).

Duncan, Bob (1904-3/13/67). Films: "The Cisco Kid Returns" 1945; "Flame of the West" 1945; "Flaming Bullets" 1945; "Northwest Trail" 1945; "Saddle Serenade" 1945; "Colorado Serenade" 1946 (Ringo); "The Caravan Trail" 1946 (Killer); "Moon Over Montana" 1946; "The Phantom Rider" 1946-serial (Indian Guard); "Tumbleweed Trail" 1946 (Brad Barton); "Wild West" 1946 (Rockey); "Border Feud" 1947 (Barton); "Range Beyond the Blue" 1947 (Lash Taggart); "Prairie Outlaws" 1948; "The Westward Trail" 1948

(Larson); "Outlaw Country" 1949 (Fighting Deputy); "Son of Billy the Kid" 1949 (Yantis); "The Fighting Redhead" 1950 (Sheriff); "Law of the Panhandle" 1950 (Evans); "New Mexico" 1951 (Cpl. Mack); "The Marshal's Daughter" 1953 (Trigger Gans); "The Parson and the Outlaw" 1957.

Duncan, Bud (1883-11/25/60). Films: "Ham Among the Redskins" 1915; "Riders of the Rio" 1931 (Peddler).

Duncan, Charles. Films: "All Man" 1916 (John Sherman Blake).

Duncan, Craig. Films: "How the West Was Won" 1962 (James Marshall). ¶TV: *Sky King*—"Man Hunt" 9-23-51 (Deputy Burke); *My Friend Flicka*—"A Case of Honor" 10-14-55 (Marshal), "The Little Secret" 12-2-55 (Marshal), "Refuge for the Night" 4-20-56; *The Roy Rogers Show*—"Money Is Dangerous" 1-29-56, "Horse Crazy" 2-26-56; *Sergeant Preston of the Yukon*—"Justice at Goneaway Creek" 2-9-56 (Doc); *Tales of Wells Fargo*—"Chips" 11-4-57, "Stage West" 1-13-58 (Colton), "Home Town" 11-16-59 (Biler); *Wyatt Earp*—"The Kansas Lily" 2-11-58 (Nate); *Gunsmoke*—"Joke's on Us" 3-15-58 (Jim Duval), "The Cook" 12-17-60 (Joe); *Wagon Train*—"The Major Adams Story" 4-23-58 & 4-30-58 (Thompson), "The Myra Marshall Story" 10-21-63; *The Restless Gun*—"The Gold Star" 5-19-58 (Wingo Jenner); *Rough Riders*—"Breakout" 10-9-58, "The Holdout" 6-25-59; *The Adventures of Rin Tin Tin*—"The Best Policy" 12-5-58 (Lemmon); *Wanted—Dead or Alive*—"Eager Man" 2-28-59; *Have Gun Will Travel*—"The Return of Roy Carter" 5-2-59, "The Cure" 5-20-61 (Bartender); *Johnny Ringo*—"Black Harvest" 4-7-60 (Vern Seager); *Bat Masterson*—"Stage to Nowhere" 4-14-60 (Casey), "Dead Man's Claim" 5-4-61 (Clay Adams); *Maverick*—"Hadley's Hunters" 9-25-60 (Wesley), "The Town That Wasn't Threre" 10-2-60 (Jake Moody), "The Forbidden City" 3-26-61 (Val Joyce); *The Tall Man*—"One of One Thousand" 12-31-60 (Bartender), "The Judas Palm" 10-21-61 (Wilson); *Cheyenne*—"The Idol" 1-29-62 (Dave Kirby); *Bonanza*—"She Walks in Beauty" 9-22-63, "The Waiting Game" 12-8-63 (Driver); *Great Adventure*—"The Pathfinder" 3-6-64 (Sergeant Brown).

Duncan, Henry "Slim". Films: "The Blazing Trail" 1949; "Frontier Outpost" 1950 (Musician); "Texas Dynamo" 1950; "Bonanza Town"

1951; "Desperadoes' Outpost" 1952 (Army Sergeant); "South Pacific Trail" 1952; "Firecreek" 1968 (Fyte).

Duncan, Johnny. Films: "Call of the Canyon" 1942; "Trail to San Antone" 1947 (Ted Malloy).

Duncan, Julie. Films: "Texas Terrors" 1940 (Jane Bennett); "Fugitive Valley" 1941 (Ann); "Wyoming Wildcat" 1941; "Along the Sundown Trail" 1942; "Overland Stagecoach" 1942; "Texas Man Hunt" 1942 (Carol Price); "Texas Trouble Shooters" 1942 (Judy Wilson); "Bullets and Saddles" 1943; "Cowboy in the Clouds" 1943 (Dorris Bishop); "The Haunted Ranch" 1943.

Duncan, Kenne (Kenneth) (1902-2/5/72). Films: "Undercover Men" 1935; "Fugitive from Sonora" 1937 (Cole); "Colorado Kid" 1938 (Sims Leathers); "Six-Gun Trail" 1938; "Flaming Lead" 1939 (Larry); "Frontier Scout" 1939 (Davis); "The Man from Texas" 1939 (Speed Dennison); "North of the Yukon" 1939 (Meeker); "Trigger Fingers" 1939 (Johnson); "Westbound Stage" 1939 (Captain Jim); "Arizona Gangbusters" 1940 (Dan Kirk); "Billy the Kid Outlawed" 1940 (David Hendricks); "Billy the Kid's Gun Justice" 1940 (Bragg); "The Cheyenne Kid" 1940 (Chet Adams); "Covered Wagon Trails" 1940 (Blaine); "Deadwood Dick" 1940-serial; "Frontier Crusader" 1940 (Mesa Kid); "The Kid from Santa Fe" 1940 (Joe Lavida); "Land of the Six Guns" 1940 (Max); "Murder on the Yukon" 1940 (Tom); "Pinto Canyon" 1940 (Fred Jones); "Roll, Wagons, Roll" 1940 (Clay); "The Sagebrush Family Trails West" 1940 (Bart Wallace); "Sky Bandits" 1940; "Texas Renegades" 1940 (Bill Willis); "Trailing Double Trouble" 1940 (Bob Horner); "Billy the Kid in Santa Fe" 1941 (Scott); "Billy the Kid's Roundup" 1941; "Dynamite Canyon" 1941 (Rod); "King of the Texas Rangers" 1941-serial (Nick); "A Missouri Outlaw" 1941 (Chandler); "Outlaws of the Rio Grande" 1941 (Brett); "Riding the Sunset Trail" 1941 (Jay Lynch); "White Eagle" 1941-serial; "Billy the Kid Trapped" 1942; "Code of the Outlaw" 1942; "Law and Order" 1942 (Dungan); "The Lone Rider and the Bandit" 1942; "The Lone Rider in Cheyenne" 1942; "Outlaws of Boulder Pass" 1942; "Raiders of the West" 1942; "The Sombrero Kid" 1942; "The Sundown Kid" 1942 (Tex Bronner); "Texas Man Hunt" 1942; "Texas to Bataan" 1942 (Capt. Anders); "Trail Riders" 1942 (Hammond, Jr.); "Val-

ley of Hunted Men" 1942; "Westward Ho" 1942; "The Avenging Rider" 1943 (Blackie); "Blazing Guns" 1943; "Border Buckaroos" 1943 (Tom Bancroft); "Canyon City" 1943; "Cheyenne Roundup" 1943; "Daredevils of the West" 1943-serial (George Hooker); "Days of Old Cheyenne" 1943 (Pete); "Hands Across the Border" 1943; "In Old Oklahoma" 1943; "The Kid Rides Again" 1943; "The Man from the Rio Grande" 1943 (Chick Benton); "Overland Mail Robbery" 1943; "Raiders of Sunset Pass" 1943 (Tex Coburn); "Red River Robin Hood" 1943; "Santa Fe Scouts" 1943; "Wagon Tracks West" 1943; "Wild Horse Stampede" 1943; "Wolves of the Range" 1943 (Adams); "Beneath Western Skies" 1944 (Rod Barrow); "Cheyenne Wildcat" 1944; "Hidden Valley Outlaws" 1944; "The Laramie Trail" 1944; "Marshal of Reno" 1944; "Mojave Firebrand" 1944; "Outlaws of Santa Fe" 1944 (Chuck); "Pride of the Plains" 1944 (Snyder); "Sheriff of Las Vegas" 1944; "Sheriff of Sundown" 1944 (Albert Wilkes); "Song of Nevada" 1944; "Stagecoach to Monterey" 1944; "Trail of Terror" 1944 (Sam); "Tucson Raiders" 1944; "Vigilantes of Dodge City" 1944; "Bells of Rosarita" 1945; "Corpus Christi Bandits" 1945 (Spade); "Oregon Trail" 1945 (Johnny Slade); "Rough Riders of Cheyenne" 1945; "Santa Fe Saddlemates" 1945; "Trail of Kit Carson" 1945; "Wagon Wheels Westward" 1945; "California Gold Rush" 1946; "Conquest of Cheyenne" 1946; "Home on the Range" 1946 (Slim Wallace); "The Man from Rainbow Valley" 1946 (Lafe); "My Pal Trigger" 1946 (Croupier); "The Phantom Rider" 1946-serial (Ben Brady); "Rainbow Over Texas" 1946 (Pete McAvoy); "Red River Renegades" 1946; "Rio Grande Raiders" 1946; "Roll on, Texas Moon" 1946 (Brunnigan); "Santa Fe Uprising" 1946; "Sheriff of Redwood Valley" 1946; "Sioux City Sue" 1946; "Sun Valley Cyclone" 1946; "Code of the Saddle" 1947; "Echo Ranch" 1948-short; "Hidden Valley Days" 1948-short; "Powder River Gunfire" 1948-short; "Sundown in Santa Fe" 1948; "Across the Rio Grande" 1949 (Bardet); "Crashing Thru" 1949; "Deputy Marshal" 1949 (Kyle Freeling); "Gun Runner" 1949 (Nebraska); "Hidden Danger" 1949 (Benda); "Law of the West" 1949 (Stevens); "Lawless Code" 1949; "Range Justice" 1949 (Kirk); "Range Land" 1949 (Sheriff); "Riders in the Sky" 1949 (Travis); "Roaring Westward" 1949 (Morgan);

"Shadows of the West" 1949; "Sons of New Mexico" 1949 (Ed); "Stampede" 1949 (Steve); "West of El Dorado" 1949 (Steve); "The Blazing Sun" 1950 (Al Bartlett); "Code of the Silver Sage" 1950 (Dick Cantwell); "Davy Crockett, Indian Scout" 1950 (Sgt. Gordon); "Indian Territory" 1950; "Mule Train" 1950 (Latigo); "Surrender" 1950 (Rider); "Badman's Gold" 1951 (Rance); "Hills of Utah" 1951 (Ingo Hubbard); "Nevada Badmen" 1951; "Oklahoma Justice" 1951; "Silver Canyon" 1951; "Whirlwind" 1951 (Slim); "The Frontier Phantom" 1952; "On Top of Old Smoky" 1953 (McQuaid); "Pack Train" 1953 (Ross McLain); "The Lawless Rider" 1954 (Freno Frost); "Flesh and the Spur" 1957 (Tarner); "Outlaw Queen" 1957; "Revolt at Fort Laramie" 1957 (Capt. Foley); "Natchez Trace" 1960 (William Murrell). ¶TV: *The Lone Ranger*—"Greed for Gold" 1-19-50, "Death Trap" 4-20-50, "Trader Boggs" 1-15-53; *The Gene Autry Show*—"Six Shooter Sweepstakes" 10-1-50, "Lost Chance" 10-15-55, "Hot Lead" 11-26-50, "Killer Horse" 12-10-50, "Cold Decked" 9-15-53, "Santa Fe Raiders" 7-6-54, "Battle Axe" 8-31-54, "Boots and Ballots" 9-25-54, "Ride, Rancheros" 12-10-55, "The Rangerette" 12-17-55; *The Cisco Kid*—"Dog Story" 5-12-51, "The Old Bum" 6-9-51, "Water Rights" 7-7-51; *Wild Bill Hickok*—"Widow Muldane" 8-14-51, "Lumber Camp Story" 3-11-52, "Sagebrush Manhunt" 11-11-52, "Great Obstacle Race" 3-3-53; *My Friend Flicka*—"Refuge for the Night" 4-20-56; *Circus Boy*—"The Amazing Mr. Sinbad" 10-14-56 (Barlow); *Annie Oakley*—"The Saga of Clement O'Toole" 11-4-56 (Rick); *Sergeant Preston of the Yukon*—"Border Action" 12-27-56 (Ram Stevens); *Tombstone Territory*—"Fight for a Fugitive" 6-4-58 (Bartender); *Rawhide*—"Incident of the Sharpshooter" 2-26-60.

Duncan, Kenneth. *see* Duncan, Kenne.

Duncan, Mary (1895-5/9/93). Films: "Romance of the Rio Grande" 1929 (Carlotta).

Duncan, Pamela. Films: "Lawless Cowboys" 1951 (Nora Clayton); "Whistling Hills" 1951 (Cora); "Seven Men from Now" 1956 (Senorita); "Gun Battle at Monterey" 1957 (Maria). ¶TV: *Wild Bill Hickok*—"Papa Antinelli" 11-27-51, "The Doctor Story" 7-1-52 (Mrs. Johnson); *The Roy Rogers Show*—"The Outlaws of Paradise Valley" 11-8-53, "The Lady Killer" 9-12-54; *The Adventures of Rin Tin Tin*—"Rusty Volunteers" 9-30-55

(Maria Curtis); *Wyatt Earp*—"The War of the Colonels" 4-10-56 (Mary Ellen Frentress), "One Murder—Fifty Suspects" 3-17-59 (Janey Logan); *Tales of Wells Fargo*—"The Silver Bullets" 7-8-57 (Lydia Kennelly); *Maverick*—"Stampede" 11-17-57 (Coral Stacey); *Tombstone Territory*—"Guns of Silver" 11-27-57 (Beth Williams), "Gun Hostage" 5-1-59 (Amy Hendricks); *Death Valley Days*—"Yankee Pirate" 2-24-58 (Lupe Ortega), "RX—Slow Death" 4-28-59 (Princess Nadja), "The Devil's Due" 1-26-60 (Sadie); *Jim Bowie*—"The Puma" 5-23-58 (Florita); *Rawhide*—"Incident of the Shambling Men" 10-9-59; *Bat Masterson*—"Lady Luck" 11-5-59 (Rachel Lowery); *Laramie*—"Duel at Alta Mesa" 2-23-60 (Dolly); *Colt .45*—"Trial by Rope" 5-3-60 (Dora Lacey), "The Trespasser" 6-21-60 (Belle O'Tara); *Whispering Smith*—"Three for One" 7-3-61 (Helen); *The Tall Man*—"An Hour to Die" 2-17-62 (Angela).

Duncan, Rosetta (1896-12/4/59). TV: *Wild Bill Hickok*—"Angel of Cedar Mountain" 7-28-53.

Duncan, Sandy (1946-). TV: *Bonanza*—"An Earthquake Called Callahan" 4-11-71 (Angeline).

Duncan, Slim. *see* Duncan, Henry "Slim".

Duncan, Taylor (1877-7/23/57). Films: "Ranson's Folly" 1926 (Captain Carr).

Duncan, Ted. Films: "In Mizzoura" 1919 (Clarke); "Strings of Steel" 1926-serial.

Duncan, Tommy (1910-7/24/67). Films: "South of Death Valley" 1949.

Duncan, William (1880-2/8/61). Films: "The Bully of Bingo Gulch" 1911 (Easy Thompson); "Romance of the Rio Grande" 1911; "The Telltale Knife" 1911; "Told in Colorado" 1911; "Western Hearts" 1911; "Why the Sheriff Is a Bachelor" 1911; "Between Love and the Law" 1912; "The Brand Blotter" 1912; "Buck's Romance" 1912; "The Cattle Rustlers" 1912; "The Cowboy's Best Girl" 1912; "A Cowboy's Mother" 1912; "Driftwood" 1912; "The Dynamiters" 1912; "An Equine Hero" 1912; "The Horseshoe" 1912; "Jim's Vindication" 1912; "The Law of the North" 1912; "The Ranger and His Horse" 1912; "A Rough Ride with Nitroglycerine" 1912; "The Scapegoat" 1912; "So-Jun-Wah and the Tribal Law" 1912; "Two Men and a Girl" 1912; "The Whiskey Runners" 1912; "Why Jim Reformed" 1912; "An Apache's Gratitude" 1913; "The Bank's Messenger" 1913; "Bill's

Birthday Present" 1913; "Buster's Little Game" 1913 (Buster Holmes); "The Capture of Bad Brown" 1913; "The Cattle Thief's Escape" 1913 (Rev. John Morrison); "The Cowboy Editor" 1913; "The Deputy's Sweetheart" 1913; "The Galloping Romeo" 1913; "The Good Indian" 1913; "His Father's Deputy" 1913; "How It Happened" 1913; "Howlin' Jones" 1913 (Howland Jones); "The Life Timer" 1913; "Made a Coward" 1913; "The Marshal's Capture" 1913; "A Mixup on the Plains" 1913; "Mother Love vs. Gold" 1913 (Dick Mackey); "Physical Culture on the Quarter Circle V Bar" 1913; "The Range Law" 1913; "Sallie's Sure Shot" 1913; "Saved from a Vigilantes" 1913 (Bud Lee); "The Schoolmarm's Shooting Match" 1913 (Bill Swift); "The Sheriff of Yawapai County" 1913; "The Shotgun Man and the Stage Driver" 1913; "The Silver Grindstone" 1913 (Stratton); "The Stolen Moccasins" 1913; "The Taming of Texas Pete" 1913 (Texas Pete); "Two Sacks of Potatoes" 1913; "Anne of the Mines" 1914; "A Friend in Need" 1914 (Jimmy Donovan); "The Horse Thief" 1914; "The Navajo Ring" 1914; "The Servant Question Out West" 1914; "Wards Claim" 1914; "A Child of the North" 1915; "Love and Law" 1915; "The Man from the Desert" 1915; "Dead Shot Baker" 1917 (Dead Shot Baker); "The Fighting Trail" 1917-serial; "The Tenderfoot" 1917 (Tenderfoot Jim); "Vengeance and the Woman" 1917-serial; "A Fight for Millions" 1918-serial; "Smashing Barriers" 1919-serial; "Steelheart" 1921 (Frank Worthing); "Where Men Are Men" 1921 (Vic Foster); "The Fighting Guide" 1922 (Ned Lightning); "When Danger Smiles" 1922 (Ray Chapman); "Playing It Wild" 1923 (Jerry Hoskins); "The Steel Trail" 1923-serial; "Wolves of the North" 1924-serial; "Range Law" 1931; "Nevada" 1935 (Ben Ide); "Three on the Trail" 1936 (Buck Peters); "Forlorn River" 1937 (Blaine); "Hopalong Rides Again" 1937 (Buck Peters); "Thunder Trail" 1937 (John Ames); "The Frontiersman" 1938 (Buck Peters); "Law of the Pampas" 1939 (Buck Peters); "Texas Rangers Ride Again" 1940 (Capt. Inglis).

Dundee, Jimmie (1901-11/20/53). Films: "Frontier Marshal" 1939 (Bully); "The Kid from Texas" 1939 (Sailor); "Lucky Cisco Kid" 1940 (Stagecoach Passenger); "Northwest Mounted Police" 1940 (Constable Grove); "Whispering Smith" 1948; "Fancy Pants" 1950 (Henchman). ¶TV: *The Lone Ranger*—"Six Gun

Legacy" 11-24-49, "Trouble for Tonto" 7-20-50.

Dunham, Maudie (1902-10/3/82). Films: "The Night Rider" 1920 (Diana Marbolt).

Dunham, Phil (1885-9/5/72). Films: "The Fighting Parson" 1933 (George Larkin); "The Fugitive" 1933 (Cook); "Rainbow Ranch" 1933 (Wilbur Hall); "The Pecos Kid" 1935; "Powdersmoke Range" 1935; "Wild Mustang" 1935; "Cavalcade of the West" 1936 (Clemens); "Ghost Town" 1936 (Abe Rankin); "Gun Grit" 1936 (Looey); "Hair-Trigger Casey" 1936 (Abner); "Romance Rides the Range" 1936 (Doctor); "Aces Wild" 1937 (Anson); "The Idaho Kid" 1937 (Tumblebug); "Trailing Trouble" 1937 (Nester); "Westbound Stage" 1939 (Attorney Wells); "West of Pinto Basin" 1940 (Summers); "Code of the Outlaw" 1942; "Swing, Cowboy, Swing" 1944.

Dunhill, Steve. Films: "Duel in the Sun" 1946 (Jake); "Outlaw Country" 1949 (Turk); "Dallas" 1950 (Dink); "Rocky Mountain" 1950 (Ash); "Buckaroo Sheriff of Texas" 1951. ¶TV: *The Lone Ranger*—"Trigger Finger 4-7-55; *Wyatt Earp*—"Call Me Your Honor" 9-17-57.

Dunigan, Tim. Films: "Davy Crockett: Rainbow in the Thunder" TVM-1988 (Davy Crockett).

Dunkinson, Harry (1876-3/14/36). Films: "Follow the Girl" 1917 (Hong Foo); "Selfish Yates" 1918 (the Oklahoma Hog); "Chasing Rainbows" 1919 (Jerry); "The Coming of the Law" 1919 (Sheriff); "The Daredevil" 1920 (Ranch Owner); "Forbidden Trails" 1920 (Henry Parsons); "Prairie Trails" 1920 (Ike Stork); "Big Town Round-Up" 1921 (Luther Beaumont); "Duke of Chimney Butte" 1921 (Jedlick); "The Last Trail" 1921 (Kenworth Samson); "The Primal Law" 1921 (Carson); "A Ridin' Romeo" 1921 (King Brentwood); "Trailin'" 1921 (Sandy Ferguson); "The Fast Mail" 1922 (Harry Joyce); "Soft Boiled" 1923 (Storekeeper); "The Sting of the Scorpion" 1923; "Lash of the Whip" 1924 (Servant); "The Desert's Price" 1925 (Sheriff); "Silver Valley" 1927 (Mike McCool); "The Ferocious Pal" 1934; "Nevada" 1935 (Card Player).

Dunlap, Al (-11/25/88). TV: *The Legend of Jesse James*—"A Real Tough Town" 1-24-66 (Taylor).

Dunlap, Jack. Films: "Little House: Bless All the Dear Children" TVM-1984 (Sheriff); "Poker Alice" TVM-1987.

Dunlap, Pamela. TV: *Here Come the Brides*—"The Log Jam" 1-8-69 (Abigail); *The High Chaparral*—"The Legacy" 11-28-69 (Trece); *Gunsmoke*—"Ring of Darkness" 12-1-69 (Susan Hurley), "Snow Train" 10-19-70 & 10-26-70 (Ada Coleman).

Dunlap, Robert. TV: *Cheyenne*—"The Frightened Town" 3-20-61 (Mark); *Death Valley Days*—"The Other Cheek" 11-16-68 (Sam Smith).

Dunn, Bobby (1891-3/24/37). Films: "The Upland Rider" 1928 (Shorty); "Captain Cowboy" 1929; "Code of the West" 1929; "'Neath Western Skies" 1929 (Percival Givens); "Riders of the Storm" 1929; "The Royal Rider" 1929 (Wild West Show Member); "The Wagon Master" 1929 (Buckeye Peter); "Breed of the West" 1930 (Shorty); "Call of the Desert" 1930; "Canyon Hawks" 1930 (Shorty); "The Canyon of Missing Men" 1930 (Gimpy Lamb); "Parade of the West" 1930 (Shorty); "Parting of the Trails" 1930 (Restless Roberts); "Trails of Danger" 1930 (Shorty); "Hell's Valley" 1931 (Shorty); "Wheels of Destiny" 1934; "Way Out West" 1937 (Man in Audience).

Dunn, Eddie (1896-5/5/51). Films: "The Fighting Parson" 1930-short; "Headin' North" 1930 (Announcer); "The Land of Missing Men" 1930 (Sheriff Bower); "Riders of the North" 1931 (Tim McGuire); "Sunrise Trail" 1931 (Rand); "South of Sante Fe" 1932 (Lankey); "Annie Oakley" 1935 (Wrangler); "Powdersmoke Range" 1935 (Elliott); "Rose of the Rancho" 1936 (Waiter); "Wells Fargo" 1937 (Stagecoach Driver); "The Cisco Kid and the Lady" 1939 (Jailer); "Frontier Marshal" 1939 (Card Player); "Henry Goes Arizona" 1939 (Slim Pickens); "Let Freedom Ring" 1939 (Curly); "Mexican Spitfire Out West" 1940 (Skinner); "Billy the Kid" 1941 (Pat Shanahan); "Ride 'Em, Cowboy" 1942 (2nd Detective); "Frontier Gal" 1945 (Bailiff); "Salome, Where She Danced" 1945 (Lineman); "Canyon Passage" 1946 (Mormon); "I Shot Jesse James" 1949 (Bartender); "Buckaroo Sheriff of Texas" 1951. ¶TV: *The Lone Ranger*—"Man Without a Gun" 6-15-50.

Dunn, Emma (1875-12/14/66). Films: "The Texan" 1930 (Senora Ibarra); "Cowboy and the Lady" 1938 (Ma Hawkins); "Cowboy from Brooklyn" 1938 (Ma Hardy); "The Llano Kid" 1939 (Donna Teresa).

Dunn, George. Films: "Joe Dakota" 1957 (Jim Baldwin); "Stranger on the Run" TVM-1967. ¶TV: *Jim Bowie*—"A Night in Tennessee" 4-25-58 (Davey Crockett); *Cimarron City*—"The Beast of Cimarron" 11-29-58 (Jesse Williams), "Cimarron Holiday" 12-20-58 (Jesse Williams), "Burn the Town Down" 1-24-59 (Jesse Williams); *The Alaskans*—"Contest at Gold Bottom" 11-15-59 (Stampede Pete); *Bonanza*—"The Many Faces of Gideon Flinch" 11-5-61, "The Desperado" 2-7-71 (Andy); *The Virginian*—"Woman from White Ting" 9-26-62 (Biggs); *Lawman*—"The Long Gun" 3-4-62 (Ed Love); *Wagon Train*—"The Fenton Canaby Story" 12-30-63.

Dunn, Harvey (1894-2/21/68). Films: "Vengeance Valley" 1951 (Dealer); "I Killed Wild Bill Hickok" 1956 (Doc Reid). ¶TV: *The Cisco Kid*—"Smuggled Silver" 6-14-52; *Tales of the Texas Rangers*—"Carnival Criss-Cross" 9-3-55 (Haskins); *The Deputy*—"Passage to New Orleans" 11-19-60 (Sleepy Man).

Dunn, James (1901-9/1/67). TV: *Wagon Train*—"The Rex Montana Story" 5-28-58 (Clyde Winslow); *Walt Disney Presents*—"Elfego Baca" Regular 1958-60 (J. Henry Newman); *Wanted—Dead or Alive*—"Call Your Shot" 2-7-59 (Gabe Henshaw); *Rawhide*—"Incident at Red River Station" 1-15-60 (Dr. Solomon Flood); *Stagecoach West*—"The Arsonist" 2-14-61 (Jethrow Burke); *Bonanza*—"The Auld Sod" 2-4-62 (Danny Lynch); *Great Adventure*—"The Death of Sitting Bull"/"Massacre at Wounded Knee" 10-4-63 & 10-11-63 (Agent McLean); *The Virginian*—"Man of the People" 12-23-64 (Matthew J. Cosgrove); *Branded*—"The First Kill" 4-4-65 (Sam Manning); *Dundee and the Culhane*—11-15-67 (Milo).

Dunn, Josephine (1906-4/83). Films: "Between Fighting Men" 1932 (Goldie).

Dunn, Liam (1917-4/11/76). Films: "The Great Northfield, Minnesota Raid" 1972 (Drummer); "Blazing Saddles" 1974 (Reverend Johnson); "A Cry in the Wilderness" TVM-1974 (Hainie). ¶TV: *Bonanza*—"Six Black Horses" 11-26-67 (Father O'Brien); *Alias Smith and Jones*—"The Girl in Boxcar Number Three" 2-11-71; *Gunsmoke*—"No Tomorrow" 1-3-72 (Eli Bruder); *Nichols*—"The Unholy Alliance" 1-18-72.

Dunn, Mary. Films: "Riders of the Golden Gulch" 1932 (Mary Parker).

Dunn, Michael (1934-4/29/73). TV: *Wild Wild West*—"The Night the Wizard Shook the Earth" 10-1-65 (Dr. Miguelito Loveless), "The Night That Terror Stalked the Town" 11-19-65 (Dr. Miguelito Loveless), "The Night of the Whirring Death" 2-18-66 (Dr. Miguelito Loveless), "The Night of the Murderous Spring" 4-15-66 (Dr. Miguelito Loveless), "The Night of the Raven" 9-30-66 (Dr. Miguelito Loveless), "The Night of the Green Terror" 11-18-66 (Dr. Miguelito Loveless), "The Night of the Surreal McCoy" 3-3-67 (Dr. Miguelito Loveless), "The Night of the Bogus Bandits" 4-7-67 (Dr. Miguelito Loveless), "The Night Dr. Loveless Died" 9-29-67 (Dr. Miguelito Loveless/Werner Leibknicht), "The Night of Miguelito's Revenge" 12-13-68 (Dr. Miguelito Loveless); *The Monroes*—"Ghosts of Paradox" 3-15-67 (Nemo); *Bonanza*—"It's a Small World" 1-4-70 (George Marshall).

Dunn, Paul. Films: "Trail Street" 1947 (Boy); "The Wistful Widow of Wagon Gap" 1947 (Lincoln Hawkins).

Dunn, Peter (1922-4/14/90). TV: *Wagon Train*—"The Beauty Jamison Story" 12-17-58 (Rancher); *Cimarron City*—"Cimarron Holiday" 12-20-58 (Dody Hamer), "Burn the Town Down" 1-24-59 (Dody Hamer); *Tales of Wells Fargo*—Fort Massacre 2-2-59 (Billy Welch); *Gunsmoke*—"Hammerhead" 12-26-64 (Squatty Reynolds); *Branded*—"$10,000 for Durango" 11-28-65 (Taylor); *Laredo*—"A Medal for Reese" 12-30-65 (Pierre); *Hondo*—"Hondo and the Apache Trail" 12-22-67 (Pete).

Dunn, Ralph (1902-2/19/68). Films: "Billy the Kid Returns" 1938; "Desperate Trails" 1939 (Lon); "The Lone Ranger Rides Again" 1939-serial (Bart Dolan); "The Return of the Cisco Kid" 1939 (Guard); "Brigham Young—Frontiersman" 1940 (Jury Foreman); "Son of Roaring Dan" 1940 (Deputy); "Trail of the Vigilantes" 1940 (Deputy Sheriff); "Lady from Cheyenne" 1941 (Cork's Henchman); "Western Union" 1941 (Man); "Trial by Trigger" 1944-short; "Along Came Jones" 1945 (Cotton); "The Treasure of the Sierra Madre" 1948 (Flophouse Man); "Singing Guns" 1950 (Traveler); "Surrender" 1950 (Jailer).

Dunn, William. Films: "Beyond the Law" 1918 (Grat Dalton); "Vanishing Hoofs" 1926 (Jack Slade); "Painted Ponies" 1927 (Pinto Pete).

Dunne, Dominique (1960-11/4/82). Films: "The Shadow Riders" TVM-1982 (Sissy Traven).

Dunne, Elizabeth (1889-11/12/54). Films: "Surrender" 1950 (Elderly Woman).

Dunne, Irene (1904-9/4/90). Films: "Cimarron" 1931 (Sabra Cravat); "High, Wide and Handsome" 1937 (Sally Watterson). ¶TV: *Frontier Circus*—"Dr. Sam" 10-26-61 (Dr. Sam).

Dunne, Stephen (1918-8/27/77). Films: "Law of the Barbary Coast" 1949 (Phil Morton); "The Big Sombrero" 1949 (James Garland).

Dunning, Don. Films: "Silver City" 1951 (Townsman); "Flaming Feather" 1952; "Son of Paleface" 1952 (Wally); "Three Violent People" 1956 (Carpetbagger).

Dunning, George. Films: "Greased Lightning" 1928 (Mickey Murphy).

Dunnock, Mildred (1901-7/5/91). Films: "Viva Zapata!" 1952 (Senora Espejo); "Love Me Tender" 1956 (the Mother).

DuPea, Tatzumbia (1849-2/28/70). Films: "Buffalo Bill" 1944 (Old Indian Woman).

Dupree, V.C. TV: *Paradise*—"Childhood's End" 12-29-88 (Bobby).

DuPuis, Art (1901-4/8/52). Films: "The Last of the Mohicans" 1936 (DeLevis); "The Arizona Wildcat" 1939 (Deputy); "Mark of Zorro" 1940 (Soldier); "Stage to Chino" 1940; "The Bandit Trail" 1941. ¶TV: *The Cisco Kid*—"Counterfeit Money" 1-27-51, "Convict Story" 2-17-51, "The Will" 3-24-51, "Cattle Quarantine" 3-31-51.

Duran, Edna. Films: "Drifting Westward" 1939 (Wanda Careta).

Duran, Larry. Films: "One-Eyed Jacks" 1961 (Modesto); "The Hallelujah Trail" 1965 (2nd Brother-in-Law). ¶TV: *Gunsmoke*—"Sarah" 10-16-72 (Vesco).

Durand, David. Films: "Son of the Border" 1933 (Frankie Breen); "Wells Fargo" 1937 (Trimball); "The Tulsa Kid" 1940 (Bob Wallace).

Durant, Don. TV: *Sergeant Preston of the Yukon*—"Phantom of Phoenixville" 1-26-56 (Jack Flynn), "Limping King" 9-13-56 (Jack Elders), "The Black Ace" 1-3-57 (Sam Tanner); *Wagon Train*—"The John Darro Story" 11-6-57 (Lucas), "The Cliff Grundy Story" 12-25-57, "The Kitty Pryer Story" 11-18-63 (Victor Harpe); *Maverick*—"Hostage!" 11-10-57 (Jody Collins); *Trackdown*—"Killer Take All" 9-5-58 (Bobby Carlyle), "Quiet Night in Porter" 9-23-59 (Frank Dooley); *Zane Grey Theater*—"The Tall Shadow" 11-20-58 (Vern Mitchell), "Man Alone" 3-5-59 (Johnny Ringo); *Wanted—Dead or Alive*—"The Spur" 1-17-59 (Vic Warsaw); *Johnny Ringo*—Regular 1959-60 (Johnny Ringo); *Laramie*—Regular 1960-63 (Gandy); *The Virginian*—"Riff-Raff" 11-7-62 (Captain Langhorne); *Wide Country*—"Yanqui, Go Home!" 4-4-63 (Bonhamn).

Durant, Marjorie. Films: "Friendly Persuasion" 1956 (Widow Hudspeth's Daughter); "The Great Northfield, Minnesota Raid" 1972 (Maybelle).

Durante, Jimmy (1893-1/28/80). Films: "Melody Ranch" 1940 (Cornelius J. Courtney).

Du Rey, Peter (1903-4/6/43). Films: "Union Pacific" 1939 (Reporter).

Durfee, Minta (1890-9/9/75). Films: "The Under-Sheriff" 1914; "Fatty and Minnie He-Haw" 1915; "Rollin' Home to Texas" 1941.

Durham, Louis (1852-10/16/37). Films: "A Law Unto Himself" 1916 (Bill Holden); "One Shot Ross" 1917 (Shorty); "Closin' In" 1918 (Jules LaRoche); "The Law of the Great Northwest" 1918 (Mont Brennan); "The Law's Outlaw" 1918 (Ramon); "Wolves of the Border" 1918.

Durkin, James (1879-3/12/34). Films: "The Conquering Horde" 1931 (Mr. Corely); "Gun Smoke" 1931 (J.K. Horton); "South of the Rio Grande" 1932 (Ruiz).

Durkin, Junior (1915-5/4/35). Films: "The Santa Fe Trail" 1930 (Old Timer).

Durning, Charles (1923-). Films: "Breakheart Pass" 1976 (Frank O'Brien); "The Gambler, Part III—The Legend Continues" TVM-1987. ¶TV: *The High Chaparral*—"The Reluctant Deputy" 3-6-70 (Hewitt).

Durock, Dick. Films: "Silverado" 1985 (Bar Fighter).

Durran, John. *The Rifleman*—"The Challenge" 4-7-59 (Dave Pardee), "Bloodlines" 10-6-59; *Rawhide*—"Incident of the Music Maker" 5-20-60 (Willy Zwahlen); *Cheyenne*—"Day's Pay" 10-30-61 (Phil McCracken).

Durren, John. Films: "The Girl Called Hatter Fox" TVM-1977 (Claude); "Mr. Horn" TVM-1979 (Marshal Joe LeFlors).

Duryea, Dan (1907-6/7/68). Films: "Along Came Jones" 1945 (Monte Jarrad); "Black Bart" 1948 (Charles E. Boles); "River Lady" 1948 (Beauvais); "Winchester '73" 1950 (Waco Johnny Dean, the Kansas Kid); "Al Jennings of Oklahoma" 1951 (Al Jennings); "Ride Clear of Diablo" 1953 (Whitey Kincade); "Rails into Laramie" 1954 (Jim Shanessy); "Silver Lode" 1954 (Ned McCarthy); "The Marauders" 1955 (Mr. Avery); "Night Passage" 1957 (Whitey Harbin); "Six Black Horses" 1962 (Frank Jesse); "He Rides Tall" 1964 (Bart Thorne); "Taggart" 1964 (Jason); "The Bounty Killer" 1965 (Willie Duggan); "The Hills Run Red" 1966-Ital. (Getz); "Incident at Phantom Hill" 1966 (Joe Barlow); "Stranger on the Run" TVM-1967 (O.W. Hotchkiss); "Winchester '73" TVM-1967 (Bart McAdam). ¶TV: *Wagon Train*—"The Cliff Grundy Story" 12-25-57 (Cliff Grundy), "The Sacramento Story" 6-25-58 (Cliff Grundy), "The Last Man" 2-11-59 (the Stranger), "The Joshua Gilliam Story" 3-30-60 (Joshua Gilliam), "The Bleymier Story" 11-16-60 (Samuel Bleymier), "The Wagon Train Mutiny" 9-19-62 (Amos), "The Race Town Story" 10-11-64 (Sam Rice); *Zane Grey Theater*—"This Man Must Die" 1-24-58 (Kirk Joiner), "Knight of the Sun" 3-9-61 (Henry Jacob Hanley); *Cimarron City*—"Terror Town" 10-18-58 (Roy Bodinger); *Rawhide*—"Incident with an Executioner" 1-23-59 (Jardin), "Incident of the Wolvers" 11-16-62 (Cannon), "Incident of the Prophecy" 11-21-63 (Brother William); *Texas John Slaughter*—"Showdown at Sandoval" 1-23-59 (Dan Trask); *Laramie*—"Stage Stop" 9-15-59 (Bud Carlin), "The Long Riders" 10-25-60 (Luke Gregg), "The Mountain Men" 10-17-61 (Ben Sanford); *Riverboat*—"The Wichita Arrows" 2-29-60 (Brad Turner), "Fort Epitaph" 3-7-60 (Brad Turner); *Bonanza*—"Badge Without Honor" 9-24-60 (Gerald Eskith), "Logan's Treasure" 10-18-64 (Sam Logan); *Frontier Circus*—"The Shaggy Kings" 12-7-61 (Tiber); *Tales of Wells Fargo*—"Winter Storm" 3-3-62 (Marshal Blake); *Wide Country*—"Tears on a Painted Face" 11-29-62 (Willie Xeno); *Daniel Boone*—"The Sound of Fear" 2-11-65 (Simon Perigore); *The Loner*—"A Little Stroll to the End of the Line" 1-15-66 (Matthew Reynolds); *The Virginian*—"The Challenge" 10-19-66 (Ben Crayton); *The Monroes*—"Gold Fever" 12-14-66 (T.J. Elderbush).

Duryea, George. *see* Keene, Tom.

Duryea, Peter (1939-). Films: "Taggart" 1964 (Rusty Bob Blazer); "The Bounty Killer" 1965 (Youth). ¶TV: *Daniel Boone*—"The Sound of Fear" 2-11-65 (Andrew Perigore); *The Virginian*—"Jacob Was a Plain Man" 10-12-66 (Nicky).

Dusay, Marj (1936-). TV: *Wild Wild West*—"The Night of the Turncoat" 12-1-67 (Crystal Fair), "The Night of the Kraken" 11-1-68 (Dolores Hammond); *Cimarron Strip*—"The Deputy" 12-21-67 (Zena); *Bonanza*—"Commitment at Angelus" 4-7-68 (Stephanie), "A Ride in the Sun" 5-11-69 (April Horn); *Daniel Boone*—"Benvenuto ... Who?" 10-9-69 (Eugenie); *Alias Smith and Jones*—"Never Trust an Honest Man" 4-15-71 (Christine McNiece); *Bret Maverick*—Regular 1981-82 (Kate Hanrahan).

Dusenberry, Ann (1952-). TV: *Paradise*—"Treasure" 5-6-89 (Lorna).

Duval, Diane. see Bishop, Julie.

Duval, Georgette. TV: *The Californians*—"Mr. Valejo" 1-28-58 (Yolande); *Tales of Wells Fargo*—"Portrait of Teresa" 2-10-62 (Teresa).

DuVal, Juan (1899-4/1/54). Films: "The California Trail" 1933 (Jose); "Renfrew on the Great White Trail" 1938 (Pierre); "Rhythm of the Rio Grande" 1940 (Rego); "Trail to Mexico" 1946; "The Palomino" 1950 (Manuel). ¶TV: *The Lone Ranger*—"A Matter of Courage" 4-26-50.

Duval, Leon. Films: "Clancy of the Mounted" 1933-serial (Pierre LaRue).

Duvall, Robert (1931-). Films: "True Grit" 1969 (Ned Pepper); "Lawman" 1971 (Vernon Adams); "The Great Northfield, Minnesota Raid" 1972 (Jesse James); "Joe Kidd" 1972 (Frank Harlan); "Lonesome Dove" TVM-1989 (Gus McCrae); "Geronimo: An American Legend" 1993 (Al Sieber). ¶TV: *The Virginian*—"The Golden Door" 3-13-63 (Johnny Grimes); *Stoney Burke*—"Joby" 3-18-63 (Joby Pierce); *Shane*—"Poor Tom's A-Cold" 11-5-66 (Tom Gary); *Cimarron Strip*—"The Roarer" 11-2-67 (Joe Wyman); *Wild Wild West*—"The Night of the Falcon" 11-10-67 (Dr. Horace Humphries/the Falcon).

Duvall, Shelley (1949-). Films: "McCabe and Mrs. Miller" 1971 (Ida Coyle); "Buffalo Bill and the Indians, or Sitting Bull's History Lesson" 1976 (Mrs. Cleveland).

Dvorak, Ann (1912-12/10/79). Films: "Massacre" 1934 (Lydia); "Flame of the Barbary Coast" 1945 (Flaxen Terry); "Abilene Town" 1946 (Rita); "The Return of Jesse James" 1950 (Sue Younger); "The Secret of Convict Lake" 1951 (Rachel).

Dwan, Dorothy. Films: "The Breed of the Border" 1924 (Ethel Slocum); "The Dangerous Dude" 1925 (Janet Jordan); "Call of the Klondike" 1926 (Violet Kenney); "The Canyon of Light" 1926; "The Great K & A Train Robbery" 1926 (Madge Cullen); "The Land Beyond the Law" 1927 (Ginger O'Hara); "Silver Valley" 1927 (Sheila Blaine); "Tumbling River" 1927 (Edna Barton); "Riders of the Dark" 1928 (Molly Graham); "The California Mail" 1929 (Molly Butler); "The Drifter" 1929 (Ruth Martin); "The Fighting Legion" 1930 (Molly Williams).

Dwire, Earl (1884-1/16/40). Films: "The Kingfisher's Roost" 1922 (Dave Butler, the Grocer); "Alias the Bad Man" 1931; "Dugan of the Badlands" 1931 (Lang); "Oklahoma Jim" 1931 (Sergeant); "Broadway to Cheyenne" 1932 (Rancher); "Law of the West" 1932 (Butch); "Man from Hell's Edges" 1932 (Morgan); "Mason of the Mounted" 1932 (Dwire); "Riders of the Desert" 1932; "Son of Oklahoma" 1932 (Brent); "Texas Buddies" 1932; "The Fugitive" 1933 (Spike); "Galloping Romeo" 1933 (Pete Manning); "Riders of Destiny" 1933 (Skip Morman); "Sagebrush Trail" 1933 (Blind Pete); "Blue Steel" 1934 (Henchman); "The Dude Ranger" 1934; "The Lawless Frontier" 1934 (Zanti); "The Lucky Texan" 1934 (Banker Williams); "The Man from Utah" 1934 (Rodeo Announcer); "'Neath the Arizona Skies" 1934 (Tom); "Randy Rides Alone" 1934 (Sheriff); "The Star Packer" 1934 (Mason); "The Trail Beyond" 1934 (Benoit); "West of the Divide" 1934 (Red); "Alias John Law" 1935 (the Kootney Kid); "Between Men" 1935 (Trent); "Big Calibre" 1935 (Sheriff); "Born to Battle" 1935; "The Courageous Avenger" 1935 (Prisoner); "The Dawn Rider" 1935 (Expressman); "Fighting Pioneers" 1935 (Sgt. Luke); "Justice of the Range" 1935; "The Last of the Clintons" 1935 (Luke Todd); "Lawless Range" 1935 (Emmett); "The New Frontier" 1935; "No Man's Range" 1935; "Paradise Canyon" 1935; "The Pecos Kid" 1935 (Jose); "The Rider of the Law" 1935; "Saddle Aces" 1935; "Smokey Smith" 1935; "Tombstone Terror" 1935 (Regan); "The Unconquered Bandit" 1935; "Wagon Trail" 1935 (Bob Collins); "Western Justice" 1935 (Doctor); "Westward Ho" 1935; "Wolf Riders" 1935 (Red Wolf); "Caryl of the Mountains" 1936 (Inspector Bradshaw); "Cavalcade of the West" 1936 (Chrisman); "Cavalry" 1936; "Desert Justice" 1936; "The Crooked Trail" 1936; "Ghost Town" 1936 (Dan McCall); "Gun Grit" 1936 (Joe Hess); "The Kid Ranger" 1936 (Brent); "King of the Pecos" 1936; "Law and Lead" 1936 (Hawley); "Oh, Susanna!" 1936; "Pinto Rustlers" 1936 (Bud Walton); "Red River Valley" 1936; "Ridin' On" 1936 (Buck O'Neill); "Roamin' Wild" 1936 (Jim Madison); "Santa Fe Bound" 1936 (Tobbets); "Song of the Gringo" 1936; "Stormy Trails" 1936 (Stephen Varick); "Sundown Saunders" 1936 (Sheriff Baker); "Toll of the Desert" 1936 (Dad Carson); "Wildcat Saunders" 1936; "Arizona Days" 1937 (Joe Workman); "Danger Valley" 1937 (Old Timer); "Doomed at Sundown" 1937 (Butch Brawley); "Empty Holsters" 1937 (Doctor); "Galloping Dynamite" 1937 (Pop); "The Gambling Terror" 1937 (Bradley); "Git Along, Little Dogies" 1937; "The Gun Ranger" 1937 (Bud Cooper); "Headin' for the Rio Grande" 1937 (Rand); "Hittin' the Trail" 1937 (Clark); "The Idaho Kid" 1937 (Clint Hollister); "Lightnin' Crandall" 1937 (Parson Durkin); "The Mystery of the Hooded Horseman" 1937 (Sheriff Walker); "Riders of the Dawn" 1937 (Two-Gun Gardner); "Riders of the Rockies" 1937 (Jeffries); "Romance of the Rockies" 1937 (Joe); "Stars Over Arizona" 1937 (Sidewinder); "Trouble in Texas" 1937 (Barker); "The Trusted Outlaw" 1937 (Swain); "Gold Mine in the Sky" 1938; "The Great Adventures of Wild Bill Hickok" 1938; "Man from Music Mountain" 1938 (Martin); "The Mysterious Rider" 1938 (Sheriff Burley); "The Old Barn Dancer" 1938 (Clem); "Outlaws of Sonora" 1938; "The Purple Vigilantes" 1938 (David Ross); "Six Shootin' Sheriff" 1938 (Bill Holman); "Two-Gun Justice" 1938 (Old Timer); "Under Western Stars" 1938 (Mayor Biggs); "The Arizona Kid" 1939 (Dr. Radford); "Dodge City" 1939; "Timber Stampede" 1939 (Henry Clay Baylor); "Trouble in Sundown" 1939.

Dwyer, Ethel (1899-9/2/85). Films: "Cotton and Cattle" 1921 (Ethel Carson); "A Cowboy Ace" 1921 (Ethel Filson).

Dwyer, Ruth (1898-3/2/78). Films: "Broadway or Bust" 1924 (Virginia Redding); "The Covered Trail" 1924; "The Gambling Fool" 1925 (Mary Hartford).

Dyas, David (1895-11/5/29). Films: "The Timber Wolf" 1925 (Babe Deveril).

Dye, Florence. Films: "Buck's Romance" 1912; "The Scapegoat" 1912; "So-Jun-Wah and the Tribal Law" 1912; "Buster's Little Game" 1913; "The Capture of Bad Brown"

1913; "A Child of the Prairies" 1913; "The Cowboy Editor" 1913; "The Galloping Romeo" 1913; "Howlin' Jones" 1913; "The Law and the Outlaw" 1913; "The Life Timer" 1913; "A Mixup on the Plains" 1913; "Mother Love vs. Gold" 1913; "The Shotgun Man and the Stage Driver" 1913; "The Silver Grindstone" 1913; "Taming a Tenderfoot" 1913; "A Friend in Need" 1914; "The Tenderfoot" 1917 (Ellen of the East).

Dyer, Bob (1900-11/19/65). Films: "Sunset Pass" 1946 (Posse Man).

Dyer, William J. (1881-12/23/33). Films: "Anything Once" 1917 (Jethro Quail); "Lone Larry" 1917; "The Law of the Great Northwest" 1918 (Hal Sinclair); "Paying His Debt" 1918 (Joe); "The Four-Bit Man" 1919; "The Love Call" 1919 (Mate Allen); "Cupid's Brand" 1921 (Slade Crosby); "Cyclone Bliss" 1921 (Slim); "Fightin' Mad" 1921 (Obadiah Brennan); "The Sheriff of Hope Eternal" 1921 (Judge Clayton); "The Silent Call" 1921 (Ash Brent); "The Cowboy King" 1922 (Bart Hadley); "The Crow's Nest" 1922 (Timberline); "Gun Shy" 1922 (Bill Williams); "Quicksands" 1923 (Ring Member); "Wild Bill Hickok" 1923 (Colonel Horatio Higginbotham); "Wolves of the Border" 1923; "Marry in Haste" 1924 (Champion); "The Measure of a Man" 1924 (Billy the Beast); "Singer Jim McKee" 1924 (Hamlin Glass); "Trigger Finger" 1924 (Sheriff Mackhart); "The Fighting Strain" 1926; "Lone Hand Saunders" 1926 (Sheriff); "Looking for Trouble" 1926 (Sheriff Tom Plump); "The Man in the Saddle" 1926 (Sheriff); "The Desert of the Lost" 1927 (Steve Wolfe); "The Fighting Three" 1927 (Timothy); "Gun Gospel" 1927 (Sheriff); "Hands Off" 1927 (Judge Emory); "Spurs and Saddles" 1927 (Bud Bailey); "Desperate Courage" 1928 (Brannon Brother); "Thunder Riders" 1928 (Lon Seeright); "Overland Bound" 1929 (Boss Wheeler); "Code of Honor" 1930; "Honor of the Mounted" 1932; "Texas Buddies" 1932 (Sheriff); "Sagebrush Trail" 1933; "Gun Justice" 1934 (Red Hogan).

Dylan, Bob (1941-). Films: "Pat Garrett and Billy the Kid" 1973 (Alias).

Dynarski, Gene (1933-). TV: *The Big Valley*—"The Guilt of Matt Bentell" 12-8-65 (Pollick); *Bonanza*—"Silence at Stillwater" 9-28-69 (Hostler), "One Ace Too Many" 4-2-72 (Wheeler); *Kung Fu*—"Ambush" 4-5-75 (Fred).

Dyneley, Peter (1921-8/19/77). Films: "Chato's Land" 1972 (Ezra).

Dysart, Richard (1929-). Films: "Pale Rider" 1985 (Coy LaHood); "Back to the Future, Part III" 1990 (Barbed Wire Salesman). ¶TV: *Sara*—2-27-76 (Noonan); *Hallmark Hall of Fame*—"The Court-Martial of General George Armstrong Carter" 12-1-77 (President Grant).

Dzundza, George (1945-). TV: *Kung Fu*—"Night of the Owls, Day of the Doves" 2-14-74; *Young Maverick*—"Dead Man's Hand" 12-26-79 & 1-2-80 (Cal Spahn).

Eagle Eye (William Ens) (1877-1/17/27). Films: "An Indian's Loyalty" 1913; "Sierra Jim's Reformation" 1914; "The Arrow Maiden" 1915; "Big Jim's Heart" 1915; "The Ceremonial Turquoise" 1915; "The Lamb" 1915; "Neola, the Sioux" 1915; "The Outlaw's Revenge" 1916 (the Outlaw's Servant); "Untamed" 1918 (Pedro); "The Son of the Wolf" 1922 (Shaman); "Lure of the Yukon" 1924 (Black Otter).

Eagle Wing, Chief. Films: "The Navajo Blanket" 1914; "Ranson's Folly" 1926 (Indian Pete).

Eagles, James (1907-12/15/59). Films: "To the Last Man" 1933 (Ely Bruce); "Massacre" 1934 (Adam); "Rocky Mountain Mystery" 1935 (John Borg); "Sunset Range" 1935 (Eddie Shea); "Heroes of the Hills" 1938 (the Kid); "The Painted Trail" 1938 (Sammy).

Eagleshirt, William. Films: "Custer's Last Fight" 1912; "His Squaw" 1912; "The Indian Massacre" 1912; "The Invaders" 1912; "War on the Plains" 1912; "Last of the Line" 1914.

Eames, Virginia. *see* Boardman, Virginia True.

Earl, Elizabeth. Films: "River's End" 1940 (Linda Conniston).

Earlcott, Gladys (-5/18/39). Films: "The Red Woman" 1917 (Chica).

Earle, Dorothy (1892-7/5/57). Films: "Pioneers of the West" 1927.

Earle, Edward (1882-12/15/72). Films: "Ranson's Folly" 1915 (Lt. Ranson); "The Law of the Yukon" 1920 (Morgan Kleath); "The Splendid Road" 1925 (Dr. Bidwell); "The Wind" 1928 (Beverly); "The Revenge Rider" 1935 (Kramer); "Phantom of the Desert" 1930 (Dan Denton); "Mystery Mountain" 1934-serial (Blayden); "Wells Fargo" 1937 (Padden); "Code of the Rangers" 1938 (Price); "Phantom Ranger" 1938 (J.P. Matthews); "Riders of the Black

Hills" 1938 (Steward); "The Dark Command" 1940; "Border Vigilantes" 1941 (Banker Stevens); "Bordertown Gunfighters" 1943 (Daniel Forrester); "California Joe" 1943 (Col. Burgess); "King of the Cowboys" 1943 (Manufacturer); "In Old New Mexico" 1945; "The Harvey Girls" 1946 (Jed Adams); "River Lady" 1948 (Executive); "Annie Get Your Gun" 1950 (Footman); "The Texas Rangers" 1951 (Banker Lowden); "Hangman's Knot" 1952; "The Lawless Breed" 1952 (Henry Johnson); "The Stranger Wore a Gun" 1953 (Jeb); "Three Hours to Kill" 1954 (Rancher). ¶TV: *The Deputy*—"Marked for Bounty" 4-2-60 (Judge Jenson); *The Texan*—"The Nomad" 4-18-60.

Earle, Frank. Films: "The Devil's Tower" 1928 (Tom Murdock); "Lightnin' Shot" 1928.

Earle, Marilee. Films: "Terror in a Texas Town" 1958 (Monsy).

Early, Pearl (1879-6/17/60). Films: "In Old California" 1942; "In Old Oklahoma" 1943; "Springtime in Texas" 1945.

Eason, B. Reeves "Breezy" (1886-6/9/56). Films: "The Purple Hills" 1915; "Blue Streak McCoy" 1920 (Albert Marlowe); "The Danger Rider" 1928 (Tucson Joe).

Eason, Jr., Breezy (1913-10/24/21). Films: "The Kid and the Cowboy" 1919; "The Lone Ranger" 1920; "The Prospector's Vengeance" 1920; "The Texas Kid" 1920; "The Fox" 1921 (Pard); "Sure Fire" 1921 (Sonny).

Eason, Lorraine. Films: "The Border Rider" 1924; "Ridin' Mad" 1924 (Marion Putman); "The Grey Devil" 1926; "The Boy Rider" 1927 (Sally Parker).

East, Carlos. Films: "Blue" 1968 (Xavier).

East, Jeff (1958-). Films: "Dream West" TVM-1986 (Tim Donovan). ¶TV: *How the West Was Won*—"The Rustler" 1-22-79 (Orly).

East, Stewart. Films: "The Mountain Men" 1980. ¶TV: *Have Gun Will Travel*—"Incident at Borasca Bend" 3-21-59, "Commanche" 5-16-59, "The Unforgiven" 11-7-59, "The Gold Toad" 11-21-59, "One Came Back" 12-26-59, "The Campaign of Billy Banjo" 5-28-60 (Miner), "The Poker Friend" 11-12-60, "The Tax Gatherer" 2-11-61 (Morton), "Broken Image" 4-29-61, "The Race" 10-28-61, "The Hanging of Aaron Gibbs" 11-4-61 (Mullaney), "The Brothers" 11-25-61 (Rider), "The Walking Years" 3-2-63 (Bartender).

Eastham, Richard (1918-). TV: *Tombstone Territory*—Regular 1957-60 (Harris Claibourne); *Zane Grey Theater*—"Never Too Late" 2-4-60 (Jim Amber); *Bat Masterson*—"A Lesson in Violence" 2-23-61 (Orin Dilts); *Bonanza*—"Dark Enough to See the Stars" 3-12-67 (Tom Yardley), "The Marriage of Theodora Duffy" 1-9-73 (Stanton); *Cowboy in Africa*—"The Hesitant Hero" 12-18-67 (Whittaker).

Eastman, Elaine. Films: "The Fighting Romeo" 1925 (Helen McMasters).

Eastman, George (Luigi Montefiori). Films: "Django, Last Killer" 1967-Ital. (Ramon); "Poker with Pistols" 1967-Ital. (Lucas); "Belle Starr Story" 1968-Ital.; "Django Kills Softly" 1968-Ital. (Django); "Get the Coffin Ready" 1968-Ital.; "Hate Thy Neighbor" 1969-Ital. (Gary Stevens); "Ben and Charlie" 1970-Ital. (Charlie Logan); "Chuck Moll" 1970-Ital.; "Bastard, Go and Kill" 1971-Ital.; "Vendetta at Dawn" 1971-Ital. (Dr. George Benton); "Three Musketeers of the West" 1972-Ital.

Eastman, Janet. Films: "Bill Brennan's Claim" 1917; "Double Suspicion" 1917; "The Honor of Men" 1917; "The Raid" 1917; "Right-of-Way Casey" 1917; "Squaring It" 1917; "Beating the Limited" 1918; "Captive Bride" 1919; "The Four Gun Bandit" 1919; "The Gun Runners" 1919.

Easton, Jane. Films: "Son of Paleface" 1952 (Clara); "City of Badmen" 1953 (Singer in Saloon); "Bitter Creek" 1954 (Oak's Girl).

Easton, Jr., Jack. TV: *Bonanza*—"The Guilty" 2-25-62; *The Virginian*—"To Make This Place Remember" 9-25-63 (Ben Sturgis); *Wagon Train*—"The Sandra Cummings Story" 12-2-63 (Jefferson Smith).

Easton, Robert (1930-). Films: "Drums in the Deep South" 1951 (Jerry); "The First Traveling Saleslady" 1956 (Young Cowboy); "The Incredible Rocky Mountain Race" TVM-1977; "Last of the Mohicans" TVM-1977 (David Gamut). TV: *Annie Oakley*—Semi-Regular 1954-57; *Gunsmoke*—"Magnus" 12-24-55 (Magnus Goode); *Ford Theater*—"Sudden Silence" 10-10-56; *Johnny Ringo*—"Coffin Sam" 6-16-60 (Billy); *The Adventures of Rin Tin Tin*—"The Cloudbusters" 10-31-58 (Swapper Sam Scott); *Wagon Train*—"The Clara Duncan Story" 4-22-59 (Cowhand); *Rawhide*—"Incident at Rojo Canyon" 9-30-60 (Bugler); *Wanted—Dead or Alive*—"Baa-Baa" 1-4-61 (Jeff); *Death Valley Days*—"There Was Another

Dalton Brother" 6-6-65 (Moore); *Pistols 'n' Petticoats*—12-31-66 (Will Dill); *Alias Smith and Jones*—"The Bounty Hunter" 12-9-71.

Easton, Sheena (1959-). TV: *Adventures of Brisco County, Jr.*—"Crystal Hawks" 11-12-93 (Crystal Hawks).

Eastwood, Clint (1930-). Films: "The First Traveling Saleslady" 1956 (Jack Rice); "Star in the Dust" 1956; "Ambush at Cimarron Pass" 1958 (Keith Williams); "A Fistful of Dollars" 1964-Ital./Ger./Span. (the Man with No Name); "For a Few Dollars More" 1965-Ital./Ger./Span. (the Man with No Name); "The Good, the Bad, and the Ugly" 1966-Ital. (Joe); "Hang 'Em High" 1968 (Jed Cooper); "Paint Your Wagon" 1969 (Pardner); "Two Mules for Sister Sara" 1970 (Hogan); "Joe Kidd" 1972 (Joe Kidd); "High Plains Drifter" 1973 (the Stranger); "The Outlaw Josey Wales" 1976 (Josey Wales); "Bronco Billy" 1980 (Bronco Billy); "Pale Rider" 1985 (Preacher); "Unforgiven" 1992 (Bill Munny). TV: *Death Valley Days*—"The Last Letter" 1-13-57 (John Lucas); *Maverick*—"Duel at Sundown" 2-1-59 (Red Hardigan); *Rawhide*—Regular 1959-66 (Rowdy Yates).

Eaton, Evelyn (1924-6/17/64). Films: "The Utah Kid" 1944; "Adventures of Gallant Bess" 1948 (Billie).

Eaton, Marjorie (1900-4/25/86). TV: *The Lone Ranger*—"Never Say Die" 4-6-50.

Eberg, Victor. Films: "Desperate Mission" TVM-1971; "The Wrath of God" 1972 (Delgado). TV: *Gunsmoke*—"Sergeant Holly" 12-14-70 (Luke Pinero).

Eberhardt, Norma. TV: *Wild Bill Hickok*—"Civilian Clothes Story" 12-18-51.

Eberts, John. Films: "Dan Morgan's Way" 1914; "Man of Courage" 1922 (Johnny Rivers); "Cornered" 1932 (Half-Breed); "Under the Pampas Moon" 1935 (Cesar's Gauchos).

Ebsen, Buddy (1908-). Films: "The Girl of the Golden West" 1938 (Alabama); "The Kid from Texas" 1939 (Snifty); "Under Mexicali Stars" 1950 (Homer Oglethorpe); "Rodeo King and the Senorita" 1951 (Muscles Benton); "Silver City Bonanza" 1951 (Gabriel Horne); "Thunder in God's Country" 1951 (Happy Hooper); "Utah Wagon Train" 1951 (Snooper Trent); "Red Garters" 1954 (Ginger Pete); "Davy Crockett, King of the Wild Frontier" 1955 (George Rus-

sell); "Davy Crockett and the River Pirates" 1956 (George Russell); "Mail Order Bride" 1964 (Will Lane); "The Daughters of Joshua Cabe" TVM-1972 (Joshua Cabe). TV: *Walt Disney Presents*—"Davy Crockett"—Regular 1954-55 (George Russell); *Northwest Passage*—Regular 1958-59 (Sergeant Hunk Marriner); *Maverick*—"The Cats of Paradise" 10-11-59 (Sheriff Scratch Mannon), "The Maverick Line" 10-20-60 (Rumsey Plum), "Last Stop: Olivion" 2-12-61 (Nero Lyme); *Black Saddle*—"The Apprentice" 3-11-60 (Gurney Rhodes); *Rawhide*—"Incident of the Stargazer" 4-1-60 (Will Kinch), "The Pitchwagon" 3-2-62 (George Simpson); *Johnny Ringo*—"The Killing Bug" 4-18-60 (Sample); *Tales of Wells Fargo*—"Dead Man's Street" 4-18-60, "To Kill a Town" 3-21-62 (Lou Reese); *Bronco*—"Apache Treasure" 11-7-60 (Sergeant Cass); *Riverboat*—"The Water of Gorgeous Springs" 11-7-60 (Niles Cox); *Gunsmoke*—"Old Fool" 12-24-60 (Hannibal Bass), "All That" 10-28-61 (Print Quimby), "Drago" 11-22-71 (Drago); *Gunslinger*—"Golden Circle" 4-13-61 (Jed Spangler); *Have Gun Will Travel*—"El Paso Stage" 4-15-61 (Elmo Crane), "The Brothers" 11-25-61 (Bram Holden); *Bonanza*—"Saddle Stiff" 1-16-72 (Cactus Murphy); *Alias Smith and Jones*—"What's in It for Mia?" 2-24-72 (George Austin), "High Lonesome Country" 9-23-72 (Phil Archer).

Eburne, Maude (1875-10/8/60). Films: "Robbers' Roost" 1933 (Aunt Ellen); "Ruggles of Red Gap" 1935 (Ma Pettingill); "Hollywood Cowboy" 1937 (Violet Butler); "Riders of the Black Hills" 1938 (Mrs. Peg Garth); "Mountain Rhythm" 1939 (Ma Hutchins); "The Border Legion" 1940 (Hurricane Hattie); "Colorado" 1940 (Etta Mae); "The Man from Oklahoma" 1945 (Grandma Lane); "The Plunderers" 1948 (Old Dame).

Eby, Earl (1903-1/24/74). Films: "The Singing Cowboy" 1936 (Herbert Trenton).

Eby-Rock, Helyn (1896-7/20/79). Films: "Callaway Went Thataway" 1951 (Phone Operator).

Eccles, Amy. Films: "Little Big Man" 1971 (Sunshine); "Ulzana's Raid" 1972 (McIntosh's Indian Woman). TV: *Kung Fu*—"Sun and Cloud Shadow" 2-22-73 (Cloud Shadow).

Eccles, Teddy (1957-). Films: "The Honkers" 1972 (Bob Lathrop). TV: *Wide Country*—"The Care and Handling of Tigers" 4-25-63 (David

Garner); *Great Adventure*—"Kentucky's Bloody Ground"/"The Siege of Boonesborough" 4-3-64 & 4-10-64 (James Boone); *The Big Valley*—"Price of Victory" 2-13-67; *Daniel Boone*—"The Ordeal of Israel Boone" 9-21-67 (1st Boy), "The Patriot" 12-5-68 (Hal Gist), "Hannah Comes Home" 12-25-69 (Jason); *The Guns of Will Sonnett*—"The Marriage" 3-14-69 (Clay Damon); *Lancer*—"Welcome to Genesis" 11-18-69 (Billy).

Eckemyr, Agneta. Films: "Blindman" 1971-Ital. (Pilar).

Eckert, John. Films: "The Texans" 1938 (Cowboy); "Stagecoach" 1939.

Eckhardt, Oliver (1873-9/15/52). Films: "The Last Trail" 1927 (Carrol); "The Cavalier" 1928 (the Padre); "The Lone Star Ranger" 1930 (Lem Parker); "The Cowboy and the Kid" 1936 (Dr. Wilson); "Empty Saddles" 1937 (Mr. Hilton); "Wells Fargo" 1937 (Townsman).

Eddy, Bonnie Kay. Films: "Winchester '73" 1950 (Betty Jameson).

Eddy, Duane (1938-). Films: "A Thunder of Drums" 1961 (Trooper Eddy); "The Wild Westerners" 1962 (Deputy Marshal Clint Fallon). ¶TV: *Have Gun Will Travel*—"The Education of Sara Jane" 9-23-61 (Carter Whitney), "Be Not Forgetful to Strangers" 12-22-62 (Young Cowboy); *Gunsmoke*—"Kate Heller" 9-28-63.

Eddy, Helen Jerome (1897-1/27/90). Films: "Winner Takes All" 1918 (Frances Landcrafe); "The Great Meadow" 1931 (Sally Tolliver).

Eddy, Nelson (1901-3/6/67). Films: "Rose Marie" 1936 (Sgt. Bruce); "The Girl of the Golden West" 1938 (Ramerez/Lieutenant Johnson); "Let Freedom Ring" 1939 (Steve Logan); "Northwest Outpost" 1947 (Capt. James Laurence).

Edelman, Herb (1933-). Films: "Hearts of the West" 1975 (Polo). ¶TV: *Bob Hope Chrysler Theatre*—"The Reason Nobody Hardly Ever Seen a Fat Outlaw in the Old West Is as Follows: 3-8-67 (Seth Swine).

Eden, Barbara (1936-). Films: "Flaming Star" 1960 (Roslyn Pierce). ¶TV: *Gunsmoke*—"Romeo" 11-9-57 (Judy Pierce); *Rawhide*—"Incident at Confidence Creek" 11-28-63 (Crystal Simpson), "Damon's Road" 11-13-64 & 11-20-64 (Goldie); *The Virginian*—"The Brazos Kid" 10-21-64 (Samantha Fry).

Eden, Chana. TV: *The Rifleman*—"The Gaucho" 12-30-58

(Nita); *Bat Masterson*—"The Romany Knives" 7-22-59 (Leda); *Bonanza*—"The Last Hunt" 12-19-59 (Shoshoni Girl); *Wanted—Dead or Alive*—"Triple Vise" 2-27-60 (Juanita); *The Alaskans*—"Sign of the Kodiak" 5-29-60 (Zeena); *Have Gun Will Travel*—"A Proof of Love" 10-14-61 (Callie).

Edeson, Robert (1868-3/24/31). Films: "The Colonel's Peril" 1912; "The Hidden Trail" 1912; "The Call of the North" 1914 (Graehme/Ned Stewart); "Where the Trail Divides" 1914 (How Lander); "The Girl I Left Behind Me" 1915 (Lieutenant Hawkesworth); "On the Night Stage" 1915 (Alexander Austin, the Sky Pilot); "The Spoilers" 1923 (Joe Dextry); "To the Last Man" 1923 (Gaston Isbel); "Blood and Steel" 1925 (W.L. Grimshaw); "Braveheart" 1925 (Hobart Nelson); "The Prairie Pirate" 1925 (Don Esteban); "The Scarlet West" 1925 (Gen. Kennard); "Whispering Smith" 1926 (J.S. Bucks); "Romance of the Rio Grande" 1929 (Don Fernando); "The Lash" 1930 (Mariano Delfino); "Pardon My Gun" 1930 (Pa Martin).

Edgington, Lyn. TV: *Rawhide*—"Clash at Broken Bluff" 11-2-65 (Sue Henley); *Gunsmoke*—"Prime of Life" 5-7-66 (Wilma); *Bonanza*—"Four Sisters from Boston" 10-30-66 (Gabrielle).

Edler, Charles (1877-3/29/42). Films: "One Touch of Sin" 1917 (Red); "The Heart of Wetona" 1919 (Comanche Jack).

Edmiston, Walker. Films: "Stagecoach" 1966 (Wells Fargo Agent); "The Silent Gun" TVM-1969; "The Oregon Trail" TVM-1976 (George Cutter). ¶TV: *Maverick*—"Gun-Shy" 1-11-59 (Clyde Diefendorfer); *Have Gun Will Travel*—"Soledad Crossing" 6-10-61; *The Virginian*—"Legend for a Lawman" 3-3-65 (Jimmy Tench); *The Big Valley*—"Forty Rifles" 9-22-65 (Spock), "The Madas Man" 4-13-66 (Titus), "Price of Victory" 2-13-67, "Point and Counterpoint" 5-19-69 (Henry Banner); *Wild Wild West*—"The Night of the Fatal Trap" 12-24-65 (Charlie), "The Night of the Colonel's Ghost" 3-10-67 (Sheriff), "The Night of the Turncoat" 12-1-67 (Preacher); *Daniel Boone*—"The Accused" 3-24-66 (Grover Matthews); *Pistols 'n' Petticoats*—"A Crooked Line" 9-17-66 (Ernie Turner); *The Rounders*—Regular 1966-67 (Regan); *Gunsmoke*—"Celia" 2-23-70 (Burnett), "The Tycoon" 1-25-71 (Henry Folsom), "A Quiet Day in Dodge" 1-29-73 (Ludlow), "The Widow and the Rogue"

10-29-73 (Station Manager); *Bonanza*—"Cassie" 10-24-71 (Auctioneer); *Paradise*—"The Bounty" 1-11-91 (Doc Thomas).

Edmonson, William (1903-5/28/79). TV: *Man from Blackhawk*—"El Patron" 2-5-60 (Garcia); *Bonanza*—"Crucible" 4-8-62.

Edmunds, William (1896-1981). Films: "Geronimo" 1940 (Scout); "Mark of Zorro" 1940 (Peon Selling Cocks); "Deerslayer" 1943 (Huron Sub-Chief); "The Big Sombrero" 1949 (Luis Alvarado).

Edmundson, Al (1896-5/11/54). Films: "The Ghost Wagon" 1915 (Old Fleming).

Edwards, Aaron. Films: "The Firefly of Tough Luck" 1917 (Silent Dan); "The Medicine Man" 1917 (Joe Malone); "Wolf Lowry" 1917 (Buck Fanning); "Boss of the Lazy Y" 1918 (Neal Taggart); "The Fly God" 1918 (Jimmy Hit-the-Bottle); "The Red Haired Cupid" 1918.

Edwards, Alan (1900-5/8/54). Films: "Life in the Raw" 1933 (Colonel Nicholai Petroff); "Frontier Marshal" 1934 (Doc Warren); "South of the Border" 1939 (Saunders); "Salome, Where She Danced" 1945 (Bret Harte).

Edwards, Anthony (1963-). Films: "El Diablo" CTVM-1990 (Billy Ray Smith).

Edwards, Bill (1918-). Films: "The Virginian" 1946 (Sam Bennett); "Home in San Antone" 1949; "Trail of the Yukon" 1949 (Jim Blaine); "Border Outlaws" 1950 (Mike Hoskins); "The Fighting Stallion" 1950 (Lon Evans). ¶TV: *Bonanza*—"Death at Dawn" 4-30-60, "The Secret" 5-6-61, "A Woman Lost" 3-17-63, "Ride the Wind" 1-16-66 & 1-23-66 (Hoffman); *Big Hawaii*—"Gandy" 9-21-77.

Edwards, Blake (1922-). Films: "Marshal of Reno" 1944; "Panhandle" 1948 (Floyd Schofield).

Edwards, Bruce. Films: "West of the Pecos" 1945 (Clyde Morgan); "Powder River Rustlers" 1949 (Bob Manning); "The Denver Kid" 1948; "Fort Dodge Stampede" 1951 (Jeff Bryan); "Lawless Cowboys" 1951 (Bob Rank); "Oklahoma Justice" 1951; "Montana Incident" 1952. ¶TV: *Wild Bill Hickok*—"Ex-Convict Story" 11-20-51, "The Boy and the Bandit" 3-25-52; *The Lone Ranger*—"The Devil's Bog" 2-5-53.

Edwards, Cliff "Ukelele Ike" (1895-7/17/71). Films: "Montana Moon" 1930 (Froggy); "Way Out West" 1930 (Trilby); "The Bad Man of Brimstone" 1938 (Buzz Mc-

Creedy); "The Girl of the Golden West" 1938 (Minstrel Joe); "The Royal Rodeo" 1939-short; "Cliff Edwards and His Buckaroos" 1941-short; "Prairie Stranger" 1941 (Bones); "Riders of the Badlands" 1941 (Bones Malloy); "Thunder Over the Prairie" 1941 (Bones Malloy); "American Empire" 1942 (Runty); "Bad Men of the Hills" 1942 (Harmony Haines); "Bandit Ranger" 1942; "Lawless Plainsmen" 1942 (Harmony Stubbs); "Overland to Deadwood" 1942; "Pirates of the Prairie" 1942; "Riders of the Northland" 1942 (Harmony Bumpas); "Sundown Jim" 1942 (Stable Proprietor); "West of Tombstone" 1942 (Harmony Haines); "The Avenging Rider" 1943 (Ike); "Fighting Frontier" 1943 (Ike); "Red River Robin Hood" 1943; "Sagebrush Law" 1943; "The Man from Button Willow" 1965 (Voice). ¶TV: *Bat Masterson*—"The Death of Bat Masterson" 5-20-59 (A.J. Mulcaney).

Edwards, Edgar. Films: "Death Goes North" 1939 (Ken Strange); "Winners of the West" 1940-serial.

Edwards, Elaine (1930-). Films: "Old Oklahoma Plains" 1952 (Terry Ramsey). ¶TV: *The Lone Ranger*—"The Sheriff's Wife" 8-18-55; *Colt .45*—"Split Second" 3-14-58 (Alice), "The Gandy Dancers" 5-10-60 (Dr. Wallen); *Tales of Wells Fargo*—"The Golden Owl" 9-29-58 (Mary Farnum); *The Texan*—"The Invisible Noose" 5-16-60 (Lois Bentley).

Edwards, Ella. TV: *Wild Wild West*—"The Night of the Pelican" 12-27-68 (Amy Stafford).

Edwards, Gerald B. TV: *Cowboy in Africa*—Regular 1967-68 (Samson).

Edwards, Guy (1935-5/2/86). TV: *Cowboy in Africa*—"The Lions" 3-25-68.

Edwards, Jack Gordon (1867-12/31/25). Films: "Forty-Horse Hawkins" 1924 (Johnny).

Edwards, James (1912-1/4/70). Films: "Seven Angry Men" 1955 (Green). ¶TV: *Zane Grey Theater*—"Mission" 11-12-59 (Sergeant Morgan); *Texas John Slaughter*—"Kentucky Gunslick" 2-26-60 (Batt); *Death Valley Days*—"The Other White Man" 11-15-64 (Scipio Gaines); *Cowboy in Africa*—"A Man of Value" 2-26-68 (Shendi Suakiri); *The Outcasts*—"My Name Is Jemal" 11-18-68 (Taggert); *The Virginian*—"The Mustangers" 12-4-68 (Ben Harper).

Edwards, Jennifer. Films: "Sunset" 1988 (Victoria Alperin). ¶TV: *Death Valley Days*—"The Wizard of Aberdeen" 1-17-70.

Edwards, Kaye. Films: "Trouble Busters" 1933 (Mary Ann Perkins).

Edwards, Mark (1942-). Films: "The Boldest Job in the West" 1969-Ital. (Michigan).

Edwards, Neeley (1883-7/10/65). Films: "Sutter's Gold" 1936; "Sin Town" 1942 (Gambler). ¶TV: *The Texan*—"Rough Track to Payday" 12-28-59.

Edwards, Penny (1919-). Films: "Two Guys from Texas" 1948 (Maggie Reed); "Tucson" 1949 (Laurie Sherman); "North of the Great Divide" 1950 (Ann Keith); "Sunset in the West" 1950 (Dixie Osborne); "Trail of Robin Hood" 1950 (Toby Aldridge); "Heart of the Rockies" 1951 (June); "In Old Amarillo" 1951 (Madge Adams); "Spoilers of the Plains" 1951 (Frankie Manning); "Utah Wagon Train" 1951 (Nancy Bonner); "Captive of Billy the Kid" 1952 (Nancy McCreary); "Pony Soldier" 1952 (Emerald Neeley); "Powder River" 1953 (Debbie); "The Dalton Girls" 1957 (Columbine Dalton); "Ride a Violent Mile" 1957 (Susan). ¶TV: *Cheyenne*—"Johnny Bravo" 5-15-56 (Molly Crowley); *Tales of Wells Fargo*—"Chips" 11-4-57, "The Tired Gun" 3-30-59 (Pearl), "Frightened Witness" 12-26-60 (Jen Matson); *The Restless Gun*—"Thicker Than Water" 12-9-57 (Amy Neilsen); *26 Men*—"Cattle Embargo" 3-4-58, "Sundown Decision" 3-25-58; *Death Valley Days*—"Two-Gun Nan" 3-10-58 (Nan), "Miracle at Boot Hill" 1-24-62 (Ella Woods); *The Californians*—"The Painless Extractionist" 12-9-58 (Little Sheba); *Rough Riders*—"A Matter of Instinct" 2-19-59 (Ellen Fletcher); *Cimarron City*—"The Town Is a Prisoner" 3-28-59 (Saloon Girl); *Wyatt Earp*—"The Judas Goat" 3-31-59 (Joan Deming); *Wagon Train*—"The Steele Family" 6-17-59 (Hope); *The Alaskans*—"The Challenge" 1-24-60 (Nancy Trenton).

Edwards, Sam (1918-). Films: "Scandalous John" 1971 (Bald Head); "The Incredible Rocky Mountain Race" TVM-1977 (Milford Petrie). ¶TV: *Zane Grey Theater*—"Blood Red" 1-29-61 (Roustabout); *Gunsmoke*—"Chester's Hanging" 5-17-58 (Lee Binders), "The Typsum Hills Feud" 12-27-58 (Ben Cade), "The Pretender" 11-20-65 (Albert), "The Devil's Outpost" 9-22-69 (Telegrapher), "MacGraw" 12-8-69 (Barfly), "Eleven Dollars" 10-30-72, "Tarnished Badge" 11-11-74 (Travis);

Wanted—Dead or Alive—"The Corner" 2-21-59; *Have Gun Will Travel*—"Shot by Request" 10-10-59; *Laramie*—"Man of God" 12-1-59 (Captain); *Black Saddle*—"The Penalty" 4-22-60 (Brimsey); *The Texan*—"The Mountain Man" 5-23-60; *Klondike*—"Klondike Fever" 10-10-60 (Little Billie Leith); *Wagon Train*—"The Nancy Davis Story" 5-16-62 (Hody), "The Davey Baxter Story" 1-9-63 (Mr. Forbes), "The Cassie Vance Story" 12-23-63; *Wide Country*—"Journey Down a Dusty Road" 10-4-62 (Paul Perry); *Temple Houston*—"Seventy Times Seven" 12-5-63 (Bartender); *The Virginian*—"Lost Yesterday" 2-3-65 (Clerk); *Laredo*—"Yahoo" 9-30-65 (Sammy); *The Road West*—"Long Journey to Leavenworth" 10-17-66 (Clerk); *Wild Wild West*—"The Night of the Death Masks" 1-26-68 (Station Master); *The Guns of Will Sonnett*—"Time Is the Rider" 1-10-69; *Bearcats!*—"Hostages" 10-14-71 (Charlie Doyle).

Edwards, Sarah (1883-1/7/65). Films: "Ruggles of Red Gap" 1935 (Mrs. Myron Carey); "Gold Is Where You Find It" 1938 (Guest); "Lucky Cisco Kid" 1940 (Spinster); "Sunset in Wyoming" 1941; "Dudes Are Pretty People" 1942 (Miss Priddle); "Calaboose" 1943; "Song of Arizona" 1946 (Dolly Finnocin); "California Firebrand" 1948 (Granny Mason); "Carson City" 1952.

Edwards, Saundra. TV: *Maverick*—"Burial Ground of the Gods" 3-30-59 (Lottie), "Holiday at Hollow Rock" 12-28-58 (Nora Taylor); *Sugarfoot*—"The Canary Kid" 11-11-59 (Prudence), "The Return of the Canary Kid" 2-3-59 (Prudence); *Cheyenne*—"Alibi for a Scalped Man" 3-7-60 (Jane Emmett); *The Alaskans*—"The Ballad of Whitehorse" 6-12-60 (Molly).

Edwards, Snitz (1862-5/1/37). Films: "Mark of Zorro" 1920; "The Huntress" 1923.

Edwards, Thornton. Films: "Lieutenant Danny, U.S.A." 1916 (Don Mario Ventura); "Fighting Back" 1917 (Tony); "The Learnin' of Jim Benton" 1917 (Sid Harvey); "The Gun Woman" 1918 (Vulture); "Lucky Cisco Kid" 1940 (Ranch Foreman); "Three Men from Texas" 1940 (Pico Serrano); "Down Mexico Way" 1941 (Capt. Rodriguez); "The Lone Rider Crosses the Rio" 1941 (Torres); "Outlaws of the Rio Grande" 1941 (Alvarado); "Silver Stallion" 1941 (Tronco); "Drifting Along" 1946 (Pedro); "Robin Hood of Monterey" 1947; "Haunted Trails" 1949

(Blacksmith); "Riders of the Dusk" 1949.

Edwards, Vince (1928-). Films: "Hiawatha" 1952 (Hiawatha); "The Hired Gun" 1957 (Kell Beldon); "Ride Out for Revenge" 1957 (Little Wolf); "The Desperados" 1969 (David Galt). ¶TV: *Laramie*—"The Protectors" 3-22-60 (Gil Craig); *The Deputy*—"The Choice" 6-25-60 (Dory Matson).

Edwards, Walter (1870-4/12/20). Films: "A Double Reward" 1912; "The Sheriff of Stony Butte" 1912; "The Vengeance of Fate" 1912; "The Land of Dead Things" 1913; "The Panther" 1914; "The Gun Fighter" 1915; "A Midas of the Desert" 1915; "Satan McAllister's Heir" 1915.

Effee, William. Films: "Code of the Yukon" 1918 (Father Paul).

Efron, Marshall (1938-). Films: "Doc" 1971 (Mexican Bartender).

Egan, Gladys. Films: "The Vaquero's Vow" 1908; "The Broken Doll" 1910; "Unexpected Help" 1910; "In the North Woods" 1921.

Egan, Richard (1923-6/17/87). Films: "Kansas Raiders" 1950 (1st Lieutenant); "Wyoming Mail" 1950 (Beale); "Cripple Creek" 1952 (Strap Galland); "Love Me Tender" 1956 (Vance); "Tension at Table Rock" 1956 (Wes Tancred); "Three Thousand Hills" 1959 (Jehu); "Shootout in a One-Dog Town" TVM-1974 (Petry); "Kino, the Padre on Horseback" 1977; "The Sweet Creek County War" 1979 (Judd Firman). ¶TV: *Empire*—Regular 1962-63 (Jim Redigo); *Redigo*—Regular 1963 (Jim Redigo); *Bob Hope Chrysler Theatre*—"Massacre at Fort Phil Kearny" 10-26-66 (Colonel Carrington); *The Quest*—"The Captive" 9-22-76 (Captain Wilson).

Eggar, Samantha (1939-). Films: "Welcome to Blood City" 1977-Brit./Can. (Katherine); "Davy Crockett: Rainbow in the Thunder" TVM-1988 (Older Ory Palmer). ¶TV: *Outlaws*—"Hymn" 1-31-87 (Sister Rachel).

Eggenton, Joseph (1870-6/3/46). Films: "Rangers of Fortune" 1940 (Tom Bagby); "The Bandit Trail" 1941 (Andrew Grant); "Down Rio Grande Way" 1942 (Judge Henderson); "Fighting Bill Fargo" 1942 (Judge); "Saddle Leather Law" 1944.

Eichhorn, Lisa (1952-). Films: "Grim Prairie Tales" 1990 (Maureen).

Eikenberry, Jill (1947-). Films: "Butch and Sundance: The Early Days" 1979 (Mary); "Orphan Train" TVM-1979 (Emma Symns).

Eilbacher, Bobby. Films: "The Hanged Man" TVM-1974 (Benjamin Gault). ¶TV: *The Men from Shiloh*—"The West vs. Colonel MacKenzie" 9-16-70 (Petey); *Gunsmoke*—"Captain Sligo" 1-4-71 (Tim Burney).

Eilbacher, Cynthia "Cindy" (1957-). Films: "Donner Pass: The Road to Survival" TVM-1978 (Mary Graves). ¶TV: *Laredo*—"Rendezvous at Arillo" 10-7-65 (Dolly Sue); *Cowboy in Africa*—"Search for Survival" 10-9-67 (Carol); *The Guns of Will Sonnett*—"Where There's Hope" 12-20-68 (Hope); *Alias Smith and Jones*—"The Posse That Wouldn't Quit" 10-14-71 (Beth Jordan); *Bonanza*—"Rock-a-Bye, Hoss" 10-10-71 (Cathie); *Big Hawaii*—"The Trouble with Tina" 1977.

Eilbacher, Lisa (1959-). TV: *Alias Smith and Jones*—"The Posse That Wouldn't Quit" 10-14-71 (Bridget Jordan); *Bonanza*—"First Love" 12-26-72 (Eloise); *Gunsmoke*—"Kimbro" 2-12-73 (Melody), "The Sharecroppers" 3-31-75 (Lailee Pugh); *The Texas Wheelers*—Regular 1974-75 (Sally).

Eiler, Barbara. TV: *Cheyenne*—"The Last Train West" 5-29-56 (Ruth Maller); *Jim Bowie*—"An Adventure with Audubon" 9-21-56 (Mrs. Audobon); *Zane Grey Theater*—"Muletown Gold Strike" 12-21-56; *Tales of Wells Fargo*—"Stage to Nowhere" 6-24-57; *Wanted—Dead or Alive*—"Ricochet" 11-22-58; *Trackdown*—"Mc-Callin's Daughter" 1-2-59 (Janet McCallin), "The Vote" 5-6-59; *Wagon Train*—"The Steele Family" 6-17-59 (Faith), "The Sam Livingston Story" 6-15-60 (Abigail), "The Hobie Redman Story" 1-17-62 (Ruth Carlson); *The Rifleman*—"The Tinhorn" 3-12-62 (Mary); *The Virginian*—"Vengeance Trail" 1-4-67 (Fredrika King).

Eilers, Sally (1908-1/5/78). Films: "The Long, Long Trail" 1929 (June); "Roaring Ranch" 1930 (June Marlin); "Trigger Tricks" 1930 (Betty Dawley); "Clearing the Range" 1931 (Mary Lou Moran); "A Holy Terror" 1931 (Jerry Foster); "Coroner Creek" 1948 (Della Harms); "Stage to Tucson" 1950 (Annie Benson).

Eiman, Johnny. TV: *Have Gun Will Travel*—"Episode in Laredo" 9-19-59 (Boy), "Broken Image" 4-29-61 (Larry Decker); *The Rebel*—"Dark Secret" 11-22-59 (Ike); *Wagon Train*—"The Marie Brant Story" 1-20-60 (Billy).

Einer, Robert. Films: "Don Daredevil Rides Again" 1951-serial (Gary Taylor). ¶TV: *Broken Arrow*—

"Warrant for Arrest" 2-11-58 (Toweekga).

Eisenmann, Ike (1962-). Films: "Banjo Hackett: Roamin' Free" TVM-1976 (Jubal Winner). ¶TV: *Gunsmoke*—"Eleven Dollars" 10-30-72 (Clay), "Patricia" 1-22-73 (Johnny), "The Town Tamers" 1-28-74 (Caleb); *Kung Fu*—"The Stone" 4-12-73 (Todd Lovitt); *Walt Disney Presents*—"Kit Carson and the Mountain Men" 1-9-77 & 1-16-77 (Randy Benton).

Eisenmann, Robin G. TV: *Young Maverick*—"Half-Past Noon" 1-30-80.

Eisley, Anthony (1925-). TV: *Tales of the Texas Rangers*—"Kickback" 12-12-58 (Jack Carr); *Wild Wild West*—"The Night of the Eccentrics" 9-16-66 (Deadeye), "The Night of the Janus" 2-15-69 (Warren Blessing); *Lancer*—"The Lorelei" 1-27-70 (Jess Barton); *Outlaws*—"Jackpot" 4-4-87 (Griswell).

Eissa, Mickey. Films: "Outlaws of the Desert" 1941 (Salim); "Riders of the Timberline" 1941 (Larry); "Stick to Your Guns" 1941 (Ed).

Eitner, Don. TV: *Bat Masterson*—"A Personal Matter" 1-28-59 (Stage Driver); *The Legend of Jesse James*—"A Real Tough Town" 1-24-66 (O'Rourke); *The High Chaparral*—"A Hanging Offense" 11-12-67 (Captian Purdy).

Ekberg, Anita (1931-). Films: "Take Me to Town" 1953 (Dancehall Girl); "Valerie" 1957 (Valerie); "Four for Texas" 1964 (Elya Carlson); "Deadly Trackers" 1972-Ital.

Elam, Jack (1916-). Films: "Trailin' West" 1949; "High Lonesome" 1950 (Smiling Man); "The Sundowners" 1950 (Boyce); "Ticket to Tomahawk" 1950 (Fargo); "Rawhide" 1951 (Tevis); "The Battle at Apache Pass" 1952 (Mescal Jack); "The Bushwackers" 1952 (Cree); "High Noon" 1952 (Charlie); "Montana Territory" 1952 (Gimp); "Rancho Notorious" 1952 (Geary); "Gun Belt" 1953 (Kolloway); "The Moonlighter" 1953 (Strawboss); "Ride Clear of Diablo" 1953 (Tim); "Ride, Vaquero!" 1953 (Barton); "Cattle Queen of Montana" 1954 (Yost); "Jubilee Trail" 1954 (Sergeant); "Vera Cruz" 1954 (Tex); "The Far Country" 1955 (Newberry); "The Man from Laramie" 1955 (Chris Boldt); "Man Without a Star" 1955 (Drifter); "Wichita" 1955 (Al); "Jubal" 1956 (McCoy); "Pardners" 1956 (Pete); "Thunder Over Arizona" 1956; "Dragoon Wells Massacre" 1957 (Tioga);

"Gunfight at the O.K. Corral" 1957 (Tom McLowery); "Night Passage" 1957 (Shotgun); "The Comancheros" 1961 (Horseface); "The Last Sunset" 1961 (Ed Hobbs); "Four for Texas" 1964 (Dobie); "The Night of the Grizzly" 1966 (Hank); "The Rare Breed" 1966 (Deke Simons); "The Last Challenge" 1967 (Ernest Scarned); "The Way West" 1967 (Weatherby); "Firecreek" 1968 (Norman); "Once Upon a Time in the West" 1968-Ital. (Knuckles); "Sartana Does Not Forgive" 1968-Span./Ital.; "The Over-the-Hill Gang" TVM-1969 (Sheriff Clyde Barnes); "Ride a Northbound Horse" 1969; "Support Your Local Sheriff" 1969 (Jake); "The Cockeyed Cowboys of Calico County" 1970 (Kittrick); "Dirty Dingus Magee" 1970 (John Wesley Hardin); "Rio Lobo" 1970 (Phillips); "Hannie Calder" 1971-Brit./Span./Fr. (Frank Clemens); "The Last Rebel" 1971-Ital./U.S./Span. (Matt Graves); "Support Your Local Gunfighter" 1971 (Jug May); "The Wild Country" 1971 (Thompson); "The Daughters of Joshua Cabe" TVM-1972 (Bitterroot); "A Knife for the Ladies" 1973 (Jarrod); "Pat Garrett and Billy the Kid" 1973 (Alamosa Bill); "Shootout in a One-Dog Town" TVM-1974 (Handy); "Sidekicks" TVM-1974 (Boss); "Hawmps!" 1976 (Bad Jack Cutter); "The New Daughters of Joshua Cabe" TVM-1976 (Bitterroot); "Pony Express Rider" 1976 (Crazy); "The Winds of Autumn" 1976; "Grayeagle" 1977 (Trapper Willis); "Hot Lead and Cold Feet" 1978 (Rattlesnake); "Lacy and the Mississippi Queen" TVM-1978 (Willie Red Fire); "The Apple Dumpling Gang Rides Again" 1979 (Big Mac); "The Sacketts" TVM-1979 (Ira Bigelow); "The Villain" 1979 (Avery Simpson); "Down the Long Hill" TVM-1987 (Squires); "Once Upon a Texas Train" TVM-1988 (Jack); "Where the Hell's That Gold?!!!" TVM-1988 (Boone); "The Giant of Thunder Mountain" 1991 (Hezekiah Crow); "Bonanza: The Return" TVM-1993 (Buckshot); "Bonanza: Under Attack" TVM-1995 (Buckshot). ¶TV: *The Lone Ranger*—"Outlaw's Trail" 10-21-54, "The Sheriff's Wife" 8-18-55; *Stories of the Century*—"Black Jack Ketchum" 8-26-55; *Frontier*—"Ferdinand Meyer's Army" 12-18-55 (Father Matias); *Zane Grey Theater*—"Dangerous Orders" 2-8-57 (Hock Ellis), "Miss Jenny" 1-7-60 Little Jimmy Lehigh), "Deception" 4-14-60 (Cass), "Ambush" 1-5-61 (Dirk Ryan); *Tales of Wells Fargo*—"The Hijackers" 6-17-57 (Chris); *The Restless*

Gun—"Trail to Sunset" 9-30-57 (Link Jerrod), "Hornitas Town" 2-10-58 (Tony Molinor); *Wagon Train*—"The John Cameron Story" 10-2-57; *Bronco*—"The Besieged" 9-23-58 (Dooley); *Lawman*—"The Deputy" 10-5-58 (Hawks Brother), "The Senator" 5-17-59 (Spence), "Thirty Minutes" 3-20-60 (Jake Wilson), "The Four" 10-1-61 (Herm Forrest), "Clootey Hutter" 3-11-62 (Paul Henry); *The Rifleman*—"Duel of Honor" 11-11-58 (Sim Groder), "Tension" 10-27-59, "Shotgun Man" 4-12-60, "Knight Errant" 11-13-61 (Gates), "The Shattered Idol" 12-4-61 (Russell); *The Texan*—"The Easterner" 12-15-58 (Tug Swann), "South of the Border" 5-18-59 (Luke Watson), "Lady Tenderfoot" 5-9-60 (Dud Parsons); *Gunsmoke*—"Jayhawkers" 1-31-59 (Dolph Quince), "Saludos" 10-31-59 (Clem Steed), "Where'd They Go?" 3-12-60 (Clint Dodie), "Love Thy Neighbor" 1-28-61 (Ben Scooper), "Homecoming" 5-23-64 (Hector Lowell), "Help Me, Kitty" 11-7-64 (Specter), "Clayton Thaddeus Greenwood" 10-2-65 (Sam Band), "Malachi" 11-13-65 (Del Ordman), "My Father, My Son" 4-23-66 (Jim Barrett), "The First People" 2-19-61 (William Prange), "The Sisters" 12-29-69 (Pack Landers), "Murdoch" 2-8-71 (Marshal Lucas Murdoch), "P.S. Murry Christmas" 12-27-71 (Titus Spangler), "The River" 9-11-72 & 9-18-72 (Pierre Audobon); *Tombstone Territory*—"Day of the Amnesty" 4-3-59 (Wally Jobe); *Have Gun Will Travel*—"Hunt the Man Down" 4-25-59 (Joe Gage), "One, Two Three" 2-17-62 (Arnold Shoffner); *Desilu Playhouse*—"Six Guns for Donegan" 10-16-59 (Clinton); *Stagecoach West*—"A Fork in the Road" 11-1-60 (Clell); *Bonanza*—"The Spitfire" 1-14-61 (Dodie), "A Bride for Buford" 1-15-67 (Buford Buckalew), "Honest John" 12-20-70 (Honest John); *Sugarfoot*—"Toothy Thompson" 1-16-61 (Toothy Thompson), "Angel" 3-6-61 (Toothy Thompson); *Klondike*—"Queen of the Klondike" 1-23-61 (Elip Roper); *Gunslinger*—"The Hostage Fort" 2-16-61 (Clint Gannet); *Death Valley Days*—"A General Without Cause" 4-12-61 (Juan Cortina); *The Rebel*—"Helping Hand" 4-30-61 (Uncle Luce); *Cheyenne*—"Massacre at Gunsight Pass" 5-1-61 (Nicholas Potosi), "A Man Called Ragan" 4-23-62 (J.D. Smith), "The Durango Brothers" 9-24-62 (Calhoun Durango); *Laramie*—"The Tumbleweed Wagon" 5-9-61 (Charley Fox), "Gun Duel" 12-25-62; *The Outlaws*—"The Outlaw Marshals" 12-14-61 (Diamond);

Rawhide—"The Pitchwagon" 3-2-62 (Turkey Creek Jack Johnson); *Temple Houston*—Regular 1963-64 (George Taggart); *The Slowest Gun in the West* 7-29-63 (Ike Dalton); *The Dakotas*—Regular 1963 (Deputy J.D. Smith); *Daniel Boone*—"The Sound of Fear" 2-11-65 (Dr. Miller Petch); *The Legend of Jesse James*—"Three Men from Now" 9-13-65 (The Deacon); *F Troop*—"Dirge for the Scourge" 10-19-65 (Sam Urp); *The Guns of Will Sonnett*—"A Son for a Son" 10-20-67 (Sheriff); *Wild Wild West*—"The Night of Montezuma's Hordes" 10-27-67 (Zack Slade); *Hondo*—"Hondo and the Rebel Hat" 12-29-67 (Diablo); *Cimarron Strip*—"Big Jessie" 2-8-68 (Moon); *The High Chaparral*—"North to Tucson" 11-8-68 (Macklin); *The Outcasts*—"The Glory Wagon" 2-3-69 (Blacknere); *Lancer*—"Zee" 9-30-69 (Tom Mangrum); *The Virginian*—"Rich Man, Poor Man" 3-11-70 (Harve Yost); *Nichols*—"About Jesse James" 2-15-72 (Baxter); *Alias Smith and Jones*—"Bad Night in Big Butte" 3-2-72 (Boot Coby); *Kung Fu*—"The Squaw Man" 11-1-73 (Marcus Taylor); *The Texas Wheelers*—Regular 1974-75 (Zack Wheeler); *How the West Was Won*—Episode Three 2-14-77 (Cully); *The Life and Times of Grizzly Adams*—3-1-78; *Father Murphy*—"By the Bear That Bit Me" 12-1-81 & 12-8-81 (Eli McQuade); *Paradise*—"A Gather of Guns" 9-10-89 (Skragg); *Lonesome Dove*—"High Lonesome" 2-12-95 (Curtis).

Elan, Joan. TV: *Maverick*—"The Belcastle Brand" 10-12-58 (Ellen), "The Iron Hand" 2-21-60 (Ursula Innerscourt); *Bat Masterson*—"Man of Action" 4-22-59 (Deborah Jenkins); *Rawhide*—"Incident in the Garden of Eden" 6-17-60; *Stagecoach West*—"By the Deep Six" 12-27-60 (Molly Moriarty); *Have Gun Will Travel*—"The Hunt" 2-3-62 (Vanessa Stuart).

Elcar, Dana (1927-). Films: "Soldier Blue" 1970 (Capt. Battles); "A Gunfight" 1971 (Marv Green); "The Bravos" TVM-1972 (Captain Detroville); "The Great Northfield, Minnesota Raid" 1972 (Allen); "Law of the Land" TVM-1976 (Rev. Mr. Endicott). ¶TV: *Bonanza*—"Speak No Evil" 4-20-69 (Caleb Melton), "The Twenty-Sixth Grave" 10-31-72 (Merrick); *Gunsmoke*—"Snow Train" 10-19-70 & 10-26-70 (Pennigrath); *Alias Smith and Jones*—"Stagecoach Seven" 3-11-71 (Benjamin T. Bowers), "Only Three to a Bed" 1-13-73 (Sam Haney); *Kung Fu*—"Nine Lives" 2-15-73 (Tod Pritiken), "The Assassin" 10-4-73 (Noah Jones); *Centennial*—Regular 1978-79 (Judge Hart).

Elder, Ann (1942-). TV: *Death Valley Days*—"Dry Water Sailors" 3-12-66 (Annette Morrow), "Crullers at Sundown!" 5-21-66 (Ellen Fuller); *Wild Wild West*—"The Night of the Druid's Blood" 3-25-66 (Lilith/Astarte Waterford).

Elder, Mary. Films: "The Winged Horseman" 1929 (Joby Hobson).

Elder, Ray. Films: "Land of the Outlaws" 1944; "Song of Old Wyoming" 1945 (Slim); "Strange from Santa Fe" 1945; "South of the Chisholm Trail" 1947.

Eldredge, George. Films: "Buzzy Rides the Range" 1940 (Fred Ames); "Northwest Passage" 1940 (McMullen); "Take Me Back to Oklahoma" 1940; "Roaring Frontiers" 1941; "They Died with Their Boots On" 1941 (Capt. Riley); "Silver Queen" 1942 (Admirer); "Frontier Badman" 1943 (Cattle Buyer); "Frontier Law" 1943 (Slinger); "The Lone Star Trail" 1943 (Doug Ransom); "Raiders of San Joaquin" 1943 (Gus Sloan); "Tenting Tonight on the Old Camp Ground" 1943; "Outlaw Trail" 1944 (Carl Beldon); "Raiders of Ghost City" 1944-serial; "Song of the Range" 1944; "Sonora Stagecoach" 1944 (Larry Payne); "Trigger Law" 1944; "Trigger Trail" 1944 (Rance Hudson); "Frontier Gal" 1945 (Henchman); "Royal Mounted Rides Again" 1945-serial (Grail); "Rustlers of the Badlands" 1945; "The Devil's Playground" 1946 (U.S. Marshal); "False Paradise" 1948; "Oklahoma Raiders" 1944 (James Prescott); "The Old Texas Trail" 1944 (Sparks Diamond); "Quick on the Trigger" 1948 (Alfred Murdock); "Coyote Canyon" 1949-short; "Roar of the Iron Horse" 1950-serial (Karl Ulrich/the Baron); "Sierra Passage" 1951 (Sheriff); "Brave Warrior" 1952 (Barney Demming); "California Conquest" 1952 (Capt. John C. Fremont); "The Duel at Silver Creek" 1952 (Jim Ryan); "Springfield Rifle" 1952 (Judge Advocate); "The Man from the Alamo" 1953; "Man with the Steel Whip" 1954-serial (Clem Stokes); "Overland Pacific" 1954 (Broden). ¶TV: *The Cisco Kid*—"Hidden Valley Pirates" 10-27-51, "Quarter Horse" 12-8-51; *Wild Bill Hickok*—"Border City" 11-13-51, "The Steam Wagon" 5-12-53; *The Roy Rogers Show*—"The Brothers O'Dell" 11-20-55, "The Morse Mixup" 3-24-56 (Charley Morse); *Wyatt Earp*—"Trail's End for a Cowboy" 12-6-55 (Santel); *My Friend Flicka*—"The Phantom Herd" 12-23-55; *Sergeant Preston of the Yukon*—

"Relief Train" 2-23-56 (Jim Brady), "Escape to the North" 1-9-58 (Bill O'Day); *Jim Bowie*—"The Squatter" 9-14-56 (Doctor); *The Adventures of Rin Tin Tin*—"The Frame-Up" 3-15-57, "The Accusation" 2-13-59 (Col. Stanton); *Circus Boy*—"The Dancing Bear" 11-14-57 (Sheriff); *Wagon Train*—"The Ruttledge Munroe Story" 5-21-58 (Mr. Mitchell); *Rough Riders*—"The Counterfeiters" 12-11-58 (Col. Pritchard); *The Restless Gun*—"The Dead Ringer" 2-16-59 (Burt Newcomb); *Bat Masterson*—"Brunette Bombshell" 4-1-59 (Monroe Fowler), "Dagger Dance" 4-20-61 (Colonel Downey); *Wanted—Dead or Alive*—"The Inheritance" 4-30-60; *Gunsmoke*—"About Chester" 2-25-61 (Ed Cluney); *Laramie*—"The Runt" 2-20-62.

Eldredge, John (1904-9/23/61). Films: "Fair Warning" 1937 (Dr. Galt); "Son of Roaring Dan" 1940 (Thorndyke); "Bad Men of the Hills" 1942; "Song of Nevada" 1944 (Rollo Bingham); "Bad Men of the Border" 1945; "Whispering Smith" 1948 (George McCloud); "Square Dance Jubilee" 1949 (Stratton); "Stampede" 1949 (Cox); "Rustlers on Horseback" 1950 (George Parradine); "The First Traveling Saleslady" 1956 (Greavy); "Five Guns to Tombstone" 1961. ¶TV: *The Lone Ranger*—"Outlaw Town" 1-12-50, "The Black Hat" 5-18-50, "One Jump Ahead" 12-14-50; *Wild Bill Hickok*—"Lost Indian Mine" 12-11-51, "Stolen Church Funds" 9-9-52, "Ambush" 1-13-53; *Death Valley Days*—"Little Washington" 9-9-53; *Zane Grey Theater*—"Dangerous Orders" 2-8-57 (Col. Phelps); *Tales of Wells Fargo*—"The Silver Bullets" 7-8-57 (Roy Fulton); *Wanted—Dead or Alive*—"The Conquerers" 5-2-59 (Matthew Wilson), "The Looters" 10-12-60; *Bonanza*—"Feet of Clay" 4-16-60.

Eldridge, Charles (1854-10/29/22). Films: "Hearts and Spurs" 1925 (Sheriff).

Elg, Taina (1930-). TV: *Northwest Passage*—"The Secret of the Cliff" 1-9-59 (Audrey Bonay); *Wagon Train*—"The Countess Baranof Story" 5-11-60 (Countess Olga Baranof).

Elhardt, Kaye. Films: "Wild Women" TVM-1970. ¶TV: *Tombstone Territory*—"The Rebels' Last Charge" 1-15-58, 3-11-60 (Craig Rice); *Yancy Derringer*—"Outlaw at Liberty" 5-7-59 (Sally Snow); *Maverick*—"Pappy" 9-13-59 (Josephine St. Cloud); *Colt .45*—"Yellow Terror" 11-15-59 (Lucie); *Wagon Train*—"The

Luke Grant Story" 6-1-60 (Sue); *Bat Masterson*—"Blood on the Money" 6-23-60 (Eva Rogers); *Bronco*—"Cousin from Atlanta" 10-16-61 (Gail Summers).

Elias, Hector (1936-). Films: "The Master Gunfighter" 1975 (Juan); "Wanted: The Sundance Woman" TVM-1976 (Fierro); "More Wild Wild West" TVM-1980 (Spanish Ambassador); "Three Amigos" 1986 (Pedro).

Elias, Louie. Films: "Tickle Me" 1965 (Jerry, the Groom); "Posse" 1975 (Rains); "The Apple Dumpling Gang Rides Again" 1979; "Gunsmoke: Return to Dodge" TVM-1987 (Bubba). ¶TV: *Gunsmoke*—"Alias Festus Haggen" 3-6-72 (Cowboy), "Kitty's Love Affair" 10-22-73 (Zeke).

Elias, Mike (1940-). Films: "The Apple Dumpling Gang Rides Again" 1979; "Children of the Dust" TVM-1995 (Reporter).

Elic, Josip (1921-). Films: "Dirty Little Billy" 1972 (Jawbone).

Eliot, Kathleen. Films: "Paroled to Die" 1938 (Joan Blackman); "West of Rainbow's End" 1938 (Joan Carter).

Eliscu, Fernanda (1880-9/27/68). Films: "Unconquered" 1947; "Viva Zapata!" 1952 (Fuentes' Wife).

Elizondo, Hector (1936-). Films: "Valdez Is Coming" 1971 (Mexican Rider); "Pocket Money" 1972 (Juan); "Wanted: The Sundance Woman" TVM-1976 (Pancho Villa). ¶TV: *Bret Maverick*—"The Hidalgo Thing" 5-4-82 (Gomez).

Elizondo, Joaquin. Films: "Twilight on the Rio Grande" 1947; "Streets of Laredo" 1949 (Mexican).

Ellenstein, Robert (1923-). Films: "3:10 to Yuma" 1957 (Ernie Collins). ¶TV: *Gunsmoke*—"Prairie Happy" 7-7-56 (Tewksbury); *The Californians*—"The PO 8" 12-31-57 (Collie Andrews); *Bonanza*—"The Code" 2-13-66 (Fitts); *Jim Bowie*—"A Grave for Jim Bowie" 2-28-58 (Johnny Appleseed); *Wanted—Dead or Alive*—"The Spur" 1-17-59 (Mr. Sims); *The Rifleman*—"The Photographer" 1-27-59 (Orderly); *Rawhide*—"Incident of the Roman Candles" 7-10-59 (Stan Brodie); *Man from Blackhawk*—"The Man Who Stole Happiness" 10-30-59 (Matthew Larkin); *Riverboat*—"That Taylor Affair" 9-26-60 (Sheriff Stone); *Tales of Wells Fargo*—"The Wayfarers" 5-19-62 (Augustus Parmalee); *Wild Wild West*—"The Night of the Flaming Ghost" 2-4-66 (Luis Vasquez), "The Night Dr.

Loveless Died" 9-29-67 (Arthur Tickle), "The Night of the Gruesome Games" 10-25-68 (Dr. Theobald Raker), "The Night of the Winged Terror" 1-17-68 & 1-24-68 (Dr. Occularis II); *The Big Valley*—"The Haunted Gun" 2-6-67 (Salazar), "Top of the Stairs" 1-6-69 (Dr. Amos Pearce); *The Virginian*—"Ah Sing vs. Wyoming" 10-25-67 (Milo Temple); *Death Valley Days*—"A Saint of Travellers" 2-14-70.

Ellerbe, Harry (1901-12/3/92). TV: *Rawhide*—"Incident of the Sharpshooter" 2-26-60, "Incident of the Challenge" 10-14-60, "Grandma's Money" 2-23-62 (Asa Simms); *Riverboat*—"Three Graves" 3-14-60 (Harrison); *Gunslinger*—"Johnny Sergeant" 5-4-61 (Clay); *Wild Wild West*—"The Night of the Eccentrics" 9-16-66 (Col. Armstrong).

Ellingford, William (1863-5/20/36). Films: "Fighting Back" 1917 (James Newton); "The Learnin' of Jim Benton" 1917; "One Shot Ross" 1917 (Mr. Sheridan); "Boss of the Lazy Y" 1918 (Dane Toban); "Cactus Crandall" 1918 (Helen's Father); "Deuce Duncan" 1918 (Brant); "Keith of the Border" 1918 (Gen. Waite); "The Law's Outlaw" 1918 (Pop Atwood); "Paying His Debt" 1918 (Simon Christy); "Two-Gun Betty" 1919 (Billy Yeaman); "The Cyclones" 1920 (Silas Sturgis); "Two Moons" 1920 (Timberline Todd); "Hands Off" 1927 (Sheriff Daws).

Ellingwood, Elmer (1907-10/13/71). Films: "Pursued" 1947 (Callum).

Elliot, Biff (1923-). Films: "The True Story of Jesse James" 1957 (Jim Younger). ¶TV: *The Law of the Plainsman*—"Amnesty" 4-7-60 (Mike Williams); *Laramie*—"The Lawless Seven" 12-26-61 (Eliot); *Bonanza*—"The Initiation" 9-26-72 (Harley Lewis).

Elliot, Laura. Films: "Silver City" 1951 (Josephine); "Denver and Rio Grande" 1952 (Linda Prescott). ¶TV: *The Lone Ranger*—"Trigger Finger 4-7-55; *Frontier*—"Tomas and the Widow" 10-2-55.

Elliott, Alice. Films: "The Sleeping Lion" 1919 (Carlotta); "The Sundown Trail" 1919 (the Girl).

Elliott, Cecil. Films: "Surrender" 1950 (Mrs. Schultz); "The Marshal's Daughter" 1953 (Miss Tiddlefod; "The Miracle of the Hills" 1959 (Miss Willowbird). ¶TV: *Maverick*—"The Judas Mask" 11-2-58 (Seamstrett).

Elliott, Dick (1886-12/22/61). Films: "The Outcasts of Poker Flat"

1937 (Stumpy Carter); "A Buckaroo Broadcast" 1938-short; "Man from Music Mountain" 1938 (Power Company Executive); "Riders of the Black Hills" 1938 (Speaker in Movie); "Under Western Stars" 1938 (Congressman William P. Scully); "Frontier Marshal" 1939 (Mine Owner); "Melody Ranch" 1940 (Sheriff); "One Man's Law" 1940 (Pendergrast); "Young Bill Hickok" 1940; "Sunset in Wyoming" 1941; "The Outlaw" 1943 (Salesman); "Rainbow Over Texas" 1946 (Capt. Monroe); "That Texas Jamboree" 1946; "The Dude Goes West" 1948 (Whiskey Drummer); "The Paleface" 1948 (Mayor); "Singing Spurs" 1948; "Trail of the Yukon" 1949 (Sullivan); "Across the Badlands" 1950 (Rufus Downey); "Rock Island Trail" 1950 (Conductor); "The Silver Bandit" 1950; "Surrender" 1950 (Sen. Clowe); "Western Pacific Agent" 1950; "Fort Defiance" 1951 (Kincaid); "High Noon" 1952 (Kibbee); "Montana Belle" 1952 (Banker Jeptha Rideout); "Rancho Notorious" 1952 (Storyteller). ¶TV: *Wild Bill Hickok*—"A Joke on Sir Antony" 4-1-52; *The Lone Ranger*—"Right to Vote" 2-12-53, "The School Story" 1-20-55; *Tales of the Texas Rangers*—"Uranium Pete" 10-1-55 (Pete Cooper), "Both Barrels Blazing" 10-20-57 (Tiny Morris); *Schlitz Playhouse of the Stars*—"Flowers for Jenny" 8-3-56 (Judge Ricker); *The Adventures of Rin Tin Tin*—"Pritikin's Predicament" 2-21-58 (Cornelius); *The Restless Gun*—"The Gold Star" 5-19-58 (Mayor Hancock); *Rawhide*—"Incident of the Thirteenth Man" 10-23-59 (McTavish), "Incident of the Last Chance" 6-10-60 (Sam Davis), "Incident on the Road Back" 2-24-61; *The Rifleman*—"Day of the Hunter" 1-5-60; *Laramie*—"A Grave for Cully Brown" 2-13-62.

Elliott, Edythe. Films: "The Medico of Painted Springs" 1941 (Maw Blaine); "Bullets for Bandits" 1942; "Valley of Hunted Men" 1942 (Mrs. Schiller); "Cowboy Canteen" 1944 (Mrs. Bradley); "Santa Fe Uprising" 1946; "The Fabulous Texan" 1947; "Homesteaders of Paradise Valley" 1947.

Elliott, Frank (1880-7/70). Films: "Ruggles of Red Gap" 1923 (Honorable George); "The Gold Hunters" 1925 (Hugh Beresford); "The Lady from Hell" 1926 (Sir Hugh Stafford).

Elliott, Gordon. *see* Elliott, William "Wild Bill".

Elliott, John (1876-12/12/56). Films: "The Eagle's Feather" 1923

(Parson Winger); "The Spoilers" 1923 (Bill Wheaton); "Outlaw Love" 1926; "The Conquering Horde" 1931 (Capt. Wilkins); "Dugan of the Badlands" 1931 (Sheriff Manning); "God's Country and the Man" 1931; "The Montana Kid" 1931 (John Burke); "Oklahoma Jim" 1931 (Agent); "Secret Menace" 1931; "Two-Fisted Justice" 1931 (Cameron); "Broadway to Cheyenne" 1932 (Martin Kildare); "Cornered" 1932; "Galloping Thru" 1932; "Hidden Valley" 1932 (Judge); "The Man from Arizona" 1932; "Riders of the Desert" 1932 (Houston); "Single-Handed Sanders" 1932; "South of Sante Fe" 1932 (Thornton); "Texas Pioneers" 1932 (Colonel Thomas); "Vanishing Men" 1932; "Breed of the Border" 1933 (Judge Stafford); "The Gallant Fool" 1933 (Chris McDonald); "Lucky Larrigan" 1933; "Big Calibre" 1935 (Bowers); "Bulldog Courage" 1935 (Judge); "Danger Trails" 1935 (George Wilson/Pecos); "Fighting Pioneers" 1935 (Major Denton); "Kid Courageous" 1935; "Lawless Borders" 1935; "Rainbow's End" 1935 (Adam Ware); "The Rider of the Law" 1935; "Saddle Aces" 1935; "Skull and Crown" 1935 (John Morton); "Sunset Range" 1935 (Dan Caswell); "Tombstone Terror" 1935 (Mr. Dixon); "Trails of the Wild" 1935 (Mason); "Trigger Tom" 1935 (Nord Jergenson); "The Unconquered Bandit" 1935; "Wagon Trail" 1935; "Ambush Valley" 1936; "Avenging Waters" 1936 (Charles Mortimer); "Frontier Justice" 1936 (Ben Livesay); "The Fugitive Sheriff" 1936 (Judge Roberts); "Men of the Plains" 1936 (Dad Baxter); "The Phantom of the Range" 1936; "Rip Roarin' Buckaroo" 1936 (Colonel Hayden); "Ridin' On" 1936 (Jess Roarke); "Rio Grande Ranger" 1936 (Allen); "Roamin' Wild" 1936 (Reed); "Roarin' Guns" 1936 (Bob Morgan); "Toll of the Desert" 1936 (Gangster); "Trail Dust" 1936 (John Clark); "Vengeance of Rannah" 1936 (Doc Adams); "Dodge City Trail" 1937 (Banker); "Headin' East" 1937 (M.H. Benson); "Heart of the West" 1937; "Orphan of the Pecos" 1937; "Santa Fe Rides" 1937; "Smoke Tree Range" 1937 (Jim Cary); "Cassidy of Bar 20" 1938 (Tom Dillon); "Frontier Town" 1938; "Heart of Arizona" 1938 (Buck Peters); "Santa Fe Stampede" 1938; "Songs and Saddles" 1938 (John Lawton); "Fighting Renegade" 1939 (Prospector); "Jesse James" 1939 (Judge Mathews); "Mesquite Buckaroo" 1939 (Hawks); "Trigger Fingers" 1939 (Bolton); "Covered Wagon

Trails" 1940 (Beaumont); "Death Rides the Range" 1940 (Hiram Crabtree); "Gun Code" 1940 (Parson Hammond); "Lone Star Raiders" 1940 (Cameron); "Lightning Strikes West" 1940 (Doctor); "Phantom Rancher" 1940 (Markham); "The Tulsa Kid" 1940 (Perkins); "Young Bill Hickok" 1940; "The Apache Kid" 1941 (Judge Taylor); "Billy the Kid's Roundup" 1941; "The Kid's Last Ride" 1941 (Disher); "The Lone Rider in Frontier Fury" 1941; "Saddle Mountain Roundup" 1941 (Magpie Harper); "The Texas Marshal" 1941 (Gorham); "Tumbledown Ranch in Arizona" 1941; "Underground Rustlers" 1941; "Border Roundup" 1942; "Come on, Danger!" 1942 (Saunders); "Land of the Open Range" 1942 (Dad Cook); "Overland Stagecoach" 1942; "Perils of the Royal Mounted" 1942-serial (Blake); "Pirates of the Prairie" 1942; "Raiders of the West" 1942; "Rock River Renegades" 1942; "Rolling Down the Great Divide" 1942 (Lem); "Cattle Stampede" 1943 (Doctor); "Fighting Valley" 1943 (Frank Burke); "Law of the Saddle" 1943 (Dan Kirby); "Raiders of San Joaquin" 1943 (Morgan); "Sagebrush Law" 1943; "Tenting Tonight on the Old Camp Ground" 1943 (Talbot); "Two Fisted Justice" 1943 (Hodgins); "Death Rides the Plains" 1944 (Marshall); "Fuzzy Settles Down" 1944; "Oklahoma Raiders" 1944 (Judge Masters); "Wild Horse Phantom" 1944; "Frontier Gunlaw" 1946; "Moon Over Montana" 1946; "The Fighting Vigilantes" 1947 (Old Man); "Law of the Lash" 1947 (Dad Hilton); "Smoky Mountain Melody" 1948; "The Arizona Cowboy" 1950 (Ace Allen); "Perils of the Wilderness" 1956-serial (Homer Lynch).

Elliott, Maxine (1868-3/5/40). Films: "When the West Was Young" 1913.

Elliott, Robert (1879-11/15/51). Films: "Men of the North" 1930 (Sgt. Mooney); "Captain Thunder" 1931 (Pete Morgan); "White Eagle" 1932 (Capt. Blake); "White Eagle" 1941-serial; "The Devil's Playground" 1946 (Judge Morton).

Elliott, Ross (1917-). Films: "Cody of the Pony Express" 1950-serial (Irv); "Dynamite Pass" 1950 (Stryker); "Desert of Lost Men" 1951 (Dr. Jim Haynes); "Hot Lead" 1951 (Dave Collins); "Tumbleweed" 1953 (Seth); "Massacre Canyon" 1954 (George Davis); "Carolina Cannonball" 1955 (Don Mack); "Day of the Evil Gun" 1968 (Rev. Yearby); "The

Trackers" TVM-1971 (Captain). ¶TV: *The Lone Ranger*—"Word of Honor" 11-27-52, "Sinner by Proxy" 3-5-53; *Fury*—"The Choice" 2-4-56 (Richard Landon); *Broken Arrow*—"Battle at Apache Pass" 10-2-56 (Capt. Carstairs); *Jim Bowie*—"Trapline" 10-5-56 (Jacques), "Natchez Trace" 10-19-56 (Hawk); *Cheyenne*—"The Mustang Trail" 11-20-56 (Sam Wilson), "Alibi for a Scalped Man" 3-7-60 (Reed Kingsley), "Winchester Quarantine" 9-25-61 (Ernie Ransom); *Zane Grey Theater*—"Village of Fear" 3-1-57 (Donnelly), "The Accuser" 10-30-58; *Trackdown*—"Look for the Woman" 12-6-57 (Bill Judson), "Trapped" 10-10-58 (Brett Hudson); *Wanted—Dead or Alive*—"Ricochet" 11-22-58 (Dr. Matt Connors), "The Last Retreat" 1-11-61 (Jim Lawton); *The Texan*—"The Lord Will Provide" 12-29-58 (Rev. Kilgore); *Rawhide*—"Incident of the Dog Days" 4-17-59 (Carl Myers), "Incident of the Broken Word" 1-20-61 (Hunneker), "The Greedy Town" 2-16-62 (Bix Thompson); *Wyatt Earp*—Regular 1959 (Virgil Earp); *Death Valley Days*—"The Reluctant Gun" 10-27-59 (Temple); *Gunsmoke*—"Groat's Grudge" 1-2-60 (Lee Grayson), "The Lady Killer" 4-23-60 (Grant Lucas), "Tarnished Badge" 11-11-74 (Conway); *Pony Express*—"The Theft" 1-20-60 (Callen); *Maverick*—"The White Widow" 1-24-60 (Mayor Cosgrove); *The Rebel*—"Land" 2-21-60 (Dr. Mac), "Explosion" 11-27-60 (Sheriff); *Colt .45*—"Chain of Command" 4-5-60 (Major Parker); *Laramie*—"Three Roads West" 10-4-60 (Jack Adams), "Widow in White" 6-13-61 (Collins), "Handful of Fire" 12-5-61; *Stagecoach West*—"By the Deep Six" 12-27-60 (Frank Walker); *Sugarfoot*—"Trouble at Sand Springs" 4-17-61 (Jeff Hackett); *Bonanza*—"Thunderhead Swindle" 4-29-61 (Watkins), "The Trouble with Jamie" 3-20-66 (Mathew); *The Rifleman*—"Gunfire" 1-15-62 (Ben Johnson); *Wagon Train*—"The Jeff Hartfield Story" 2-14-62 (Mr. Adams); *The Dakotas*—"Trial at Grand Forks" 3-25-63 (Roger Carlson); *A Man Called Shenandoah*—"Requiem for the Second" 5-2-66 (Sheriff); *The Virginian*—Regular 1966-70 (Sheriff Abbott); *Pistols 'n' Petticoats*—2-25-67 (Link Lawson); *Wild Wild West*—"The Night of the Avaricious Actuary" 12-6-68 (Gen. Caswell); *The Men from Shiloh*—"Follow the Leader" 12-2-70 (Sheriff); *Kung Fu*—"An Eye for an Eye" 1-25-73 (Captain Burns).

Elliott, Sam (1944-). Films:

"Butch Cassidy and the Sundance Kid" 1969 (Card Player); "Molly and Lawless John" 1972 (Johnny Lawler); "I Will Fight No More Forever" TVM-1975 (Captain Wood); "The Sacketts" TVM-1979 (Tell Sackett); "Wild Times" TVM-1980 (Hugh Cardiff); "The Shadow Riders" TVM-1982 (Dal Traven); "Houston: The Legend of Texas" TVM-1986 (Sam Houston); "The Quick and the Dead" CTVM-1987 (Vallian); "Conagher" TVM-1991 (Conn Conagher); "Tombstone" 1993 (Virgil Earp); "Buffalo Girls" TVM-1995 (Wild Bill Hickok); "The Desperate Trail" TVM-1995 (Marshal Bill Speaks). ¶TV: *The Guns of Will Sonnett*—"Join the Army" 1-3-69; *Lancer*—"Death Bait" 1-14-69, "The Great Humbug" 3-4-69 (Canopus), "Blue Skies for Willie Sharpe" 1-13-70 (Cowboy); *Gunsmoke*—"The Wedding" 3-13-72 (Cory Soames).

Elliott, Scott. Films: "King of the Forest Rangers" 1946-serial (Andrews/Bryan/Merkle); "Law of the Golden West" 1949 (Wayne Calvert). ¶TV: *The Lone Ranger*—"Message to Fort Apache" 9-23-54.

Elliott, Stephen (1918-). Films: "Three Hours to Kill" 1954 (Ben East); "Canyon Crossroads" 1955 (Larson); "The Invasion of Johnson County" TVM-1976 (Colonel Van Horn). ¶TV: *Hallmark Hall of Fame*—"The Court-Martial of General George Armstrong Carter" 12-1-77 (Maj. Gen. Schofield); *How the West Was Won*—Episode Twelve 5-14-78 (Zachary Knight), Episode Thirteen 5-21-78 (Zachary Knight).

Elliott, William "Wild Bill" (Gordon Elliott) (1904-11/26/65). Films: "Arizona Wildcat" 1927 (Roy Schyler); "The Great Divide" 1929 (Ruth's Friend); "Cowboy Holiday" 1934; "Moonlight on the Prairie" 1935 (Jeff Holt); "Romance of the West" 1935-short; "Trailin' West" 1936 (Jefferson Duane); "Boots and Saddles" 1937 (Jim Neale); "Guns of the Pecos" 1937 (Wellman); "Roll Along, Cowboy" 1937 (Odie Fenton); "The Great Adventures of Wild Bill Hickok" 1938 (U.S. Marshal Wild Bill Hickok); "In Early Arizona" 1938 (Whit Gordon); "Frontiers of '49" 1939 (John Freeman); "The Law Comes to Texas" 1939 (John Haynes); "Lone Star Pioneers" 1939 (Pat Barrett/Bob Cantrell); "Overland with Kit Carson" 1939-serial (Kit Carson); "The Taming of the West" 1939 (Wild Bill Saunders); "The Man from Tumbleweeds" 1940 (Wild Bill Saunders); "Pioneers of the

Frontier" 1940 (Wild Bill Saunders); "Prairie Schooners" 1940 (Wild Bill Hickok); "The Return of Wild Bill" 1940 (Wild Bill Saunders); "Across the Sierras" 1941 (Wild Bill Hickok); "Beyond the Sacremento" 1941 (Wild Bill Hickok); "Hands Across the Rockies" 1941; "King of Dodge City" 1941 (Wild Bill Hickok); "Meet Roy Rogers" 1941-short; "North from the Lone Star" 1941 (Wild Bill Hickok); "The Return of Daniel Boone" 1941 (Dan Boone); "Roaring Frontiers" 1941; "The Son of Davy Crockett" 1941 (Dave Crockett); "Wildcat of Tucson" 1941 (Wild Bill Hickok); "Bullets for Bandits" 1942; "The Devil's Trail" 1942; "The Lone Star Vigilantes" 1942 (Wild Bill Hickok); "North of the Rockies" 1942; "Prairie Gunsmoke" 1942; "Valley of Vanishing Men" 1942-serial (Bill Tolliver); "Vengeance of the West" 1942; "Bordertown Gunfighters" 1943 (Wild Bill Elliott); "Calling Wild Bill Elliott" 1943 (Bill Elliott); "Death Valley Manhunt" 1943 (Wild Bill); "The Man from Thunder River" 1943; "Overland Mail Robbery" 1943 (Wild Bill); "Wagon Tracks West" 1943 (Wild Bill Elliott); "Cheyenne Wildcat" 1944; "Hidden Valley Outlaws" 1944; "Marshal of Reno" 1944 (Red Ryder); "Mojave Firebrand" 1944; "The San Antonio Kid" 1944 (Red Ryder); "Sheriff of Las Vegas" 1944; "Tucson Raiders" 1944 (Red Ryder); "Vigilantes of Dodge City" 1944 (Red Ryder); "Bells of Rosarita" 1945; "Colorado Pioneers" 1945; "Great Stagecoach Robbery" 1945; "Lone Texas Ranger" 1945 (Red Ryder); "Marshal of Laredo" 1945 (Red Ryder); "Phantom of the Plains" 1945 (Red Ryder); "Wagon Wheels Westward" 1945 (Red Ryder); "California Gold Rush" 1946; "Conquest of Cheyenne" 1946 (Red Ryder); "In Old Sacramento" 1946 (Johnny Barrett); "Plainsman and the Lady" 1946 (Sam Cotten); "Sheriff of Redwood Valley" 1946; "Sun Valley Cyclone" 1946; "The Fabulous Texan" 1947 (Jim McWade); "Wyoming" 1947 (Charles Alderson); "The Gallant Legion" 1948 (Gary Conway); "Old Los Angeles" 1948 (Bill Stockton); "Hellfire" 1949 (Zeb Smith); "The Last Bandit" 1949 (Frank Norris/ Frank Plummer); "The Savage Horde" 1950 (Ringo); "The Showdown" 1950 (Shadrach Jones); "The Longhorn" 1951 (Jim Kirk); "Fargo" 1952; "Kansas Territory" 1952 (Joe Daniels); "The Maverick" 1952 (Lt. Devlin); "Waco" 1952 (Matt Boone); "The Homesteaders" 1953 (Mace Corbin); "Rebel City" 1953 (Frank Graham); "Topeka" 1953 (Jim Levering); "Vigilante Terror" 1953; "Bitter Creek" 1954 (Clay Tyndall); "The Forty-Niners" 1954 (Sam Nelson).

Ellis, Arden. Films: "The Canyon of Missing Men" 1930 (Peg Slagel).

Ellis, Bobby. Films: "El Paso" 1949 (Jack Elkins).

Ellis, Diane (1909-12/16/30). Films: "Chain Lightning" 1927 (Glory Jackson).

Ellis, Edward (1871-7/26/52). Films: "Wanderer of the Wasteland" 1935 (Dismukes); "The Texas Rangers" 1936 (Maj. Bailey); "Man of Conquest" 1939 (Andrew Jackson); "West of Abilene" 1940; "The Omaha Trail" 1942 (Mr. Vane).

Ellis, Frank (1897-2/24/69). Films: "King's Creek Law" 1923 (James Lawton); "The Desert Demon" 1925 (Jim Slade); "The Fighting Sheriff" 1925 (Jeff Bains); "Tearin' Loose" 1925 (the Law); "Ace of Action" 1926; "The Lost Trail" 1926; "The Outlaw Express" 1926 (Scott); "Speedy Spurs" 1926 (Mr. Wells); "The Texas Terror" 1926; "Vanishing Hoofs" 1926 (Jack Warren); "Without Orders" 1926 (Taylor Beal); "Code of the Cow Country" 1927 (Tallas); "Law of the Mounted" 1928; "The Valley of Hunted Men" 1928; "Breed of the West" 1930; "The Cheyenne Kid" 1930; "Shadow Ranch" 1930; "Trails of Danger" 1930 (Butch Coleson); "The Avenger" 1931; "99 Wounds" 1931 (Moreland); "Quick Trigger Lee" 1931 (Pete); "The Range Feud" 1931; "Three Rogues" 1931 (Deputy); "The Big Stampede" 1932; "The Boiling Point" 1932; "Law of the West" 1932 (Deputy); "The Sunset Trail" 1932; "Texas Gun Fighter" 1932; "Whistlin' Dan" 1932; "The Cowboy Counsellor" 1933; "The Dude Bandit" 1933; "Fighting with Kit Carson" 1933-serial; "Outlaw Justice" 1933; "The Phantom Thunderbolt" 1933; "The Telegraph Trail" 1933; "The Trail Drive" 1933; "Treason" 1933 (2nd Lieutenant); "Unknown Valley" 1933; "Cowboy Holiday" 1934; "The Fiddlin' Buckaroo" 1934; "The Fighting Code" 1934; "The Fighting Ranger" 1934; "Gun Justice" 1934; "In Old Santa Fe" 1934 (Deputy); "Mystery Mountain" 1934-serial; "The Red Rider" 1934-serial; "Big Boy Rides Again" 1935 (Gunner); "Bulldog Courage" 1935; "Desert Trail" 1935; "Gallant Defender" 1935; "Justice of the Range" 1935; "Lawless Range" 1935; "Lawless Riders" 1935 (Twister); "The Phantom Empire" 1935-serial; "Powdersmoke Range" 1935; "Rainbow Valley" 1935; "Silent Valley" 1935; "North of Arizona" 1935 (Joe Borga); "Rio Rattler" 1935 (Tonto); "Square Shooter" 1935 (Cowboy); "Thunderbolt" 1935; "The Unconquered Bandit" 1935; "Western Frontier" 1935; "Westward Ho" 1935; "Wolf Riders" 1935 (Jennings); "Aces and Eights" 1936; "Comin' Round the Mountain" 1936; "End of the Trail" 1936 (Mason's Man); "The Fugitive Sheriff" 1936; "The Lion's Den" 1936 (Bar Patron); "Lightning Bill Carson" 1936 (Henchman); "The Phantom Rider" 1936-serial; "Rio Grande Ranger" 1936; "Roamin' Wild" 1936; "Roarin' Guns" 1936; "The Texas Rangers" 1936 (Ranger); "Too Much Beef" 1936; "The Traitor" 1936 (Ranger); "Treachery Rides the Range" 1936; "Vigilantes Are Coming" 1936-serial (Rancher); "Blazing Sixes" 1937; "Boothill Brigade" 1937 (Brown); "Borderland" 1937; "The Gambling Terror" 1937 (Blackie); "Git Along, Little Dogies" 1937; "Gun Lords of Stirrup Basin" 1937 (Horner); "Guns in the Dark" 1937; "Hopalong Rides Again" 1937 (Rider); "The Old Wyoming Trail" 1937 (Cattle Rustler); "One Man Justice" 1937 (Henchman); "Outlaws of the Prairie" 1937; "Phantom of Santa Fe" 1937; "Prairie Thunder" 1937; "Public Cowboy No. 1" 1937; "Range Defenders" 1937 (Henchman); "Riders of the Whistling Skull" 1937 (Coggins); "Roll Along, Cowboy" 1937; "Romance of the Rockies" 1937; "Springtime in the Rockies" 1937; "Trail of Vengeance" 1937 (Red Cassidy); "Two-Fisted Sheriff" 1937 (Gargan); "Wild West Days" 1937-serial; "Zorro Rides Again" 1937-serial; "Border Wolves" 1938 (McCone); "California Frontier" 1938; "Call the Mesquiteers" 1938; "Cattle Raiders" 1938 (Rustler); "Flaming Frontier" 1938-serial; "Ghost Town Riders" 1938; "Heroes of the Alamo" 1938; "The Last Stand" 1938; "Law of the Plains" 1938 (Turner); "The Lone Ranger" 1938-serial (Gunman #4); "Panamint's Bad Man" 1938; "Phantom Ranger" 1938; "Sunset Trail" 1938; "West of Cheyenne" 1938 (Kells); "Western Jamboree" 1938; "Chip of the Flying U" 1939; "Desperate Trails" 1939; "Frontiers of '49" 1939; "In Old Monterey" 1939; "The Law Comes to Texas" 1939; "The Lone Ranger Rides Again" 1939-serial (Joe Parker); "Lone Star Pioneers" 1939; "The Man from Sundown" 1939; "The Marshal of Mesa City" 1939 (Slim Walker); "New Frontier"

1939 (Man at Dance); "The Oregon Trail" 1939-serial; "Ride 'Em, Cowgirl" 1939 (Sheriff Larson); "Rough Riders' Round-Up" 1939; "Rovin' Tumbleweeds" 1939; "Six-Gun Rhythm" 1939; "Southward Ho!" 1939; "Sundown on the Prairie" 1939 (Chuck); "Texas Wildcats" 1939 (Al); "Westbound Stage" 1939 (Spider); "Zorro's Fighting Legion" 1939-serial; "Arizona Gangbusters" 1940; "Covered Wagon Trails" 1940; "Frontier Crusader" 1940; "Law and Order" 1940 (Townsman); "My Little Chickadee" 1940 (Townsman); "Prairie Law" 1940; "Roll, Wagons, Roll" 1940 (Doc); "Stage to Chino" 1940; "Young Bill Hickok" 1940; "Arizona Cyclone" 1941; "Back in the Saddle" 1941; "The Bandit Trail" 1941 (Al); "Billy the Kid in Santa Fe" 1941 (Hank Baxter); "Billy the Kid Wanted" 1941 (Bart); "Boss of Bullion City" 1941 (Deputy); "Bury Me Not on the Lone Prairie" 1941; "The Kid's Last Ride" 1941 (Wash); "The Lone Rider Crosses the Rio" 1941 (Fred); "The Lone Rider Fights Back" 1941; "The Lone Rider in Frontier Fury" 1941; "The Lone Rider in Ghost Town" 1941; "The Lone Rider Rides On" 1941; "Man from Montana" 1941 (Decker); "Outlaws of the Rio Grande" 1941; "Pals of the Pecos" 1941; "The Phantom Cowboy" 1941; "The Pinto Kid" 1941; "Prairie Pioneers" 1941; "Rawhide Rangers" 1941; "Sheriff of Tombstone" 1941; "The Son of Davy Crockett" 1941; "Stick to Your Guns" 1941; "The Texas Marshal" 1941; "Trail of the Silver Spurs" 1941; "Tumbledown Ranch in Arizona" 1941; "Twilight on the Trail" 1941; "Wrangler's Roost" 1941 (Brady); "Wyoming Wildcat" 1941; "Along the Sundown Trail" 1942; "Arizona Stagecoach" 1942; "Bandit Ranger" 1942; "Billy the Kid's Smoking Guns" 1942; "Border Roundup" 1942; "Deep in the Heart of Texas" 1942; "In Old California" 1942; "Land of the Open Range" 1942 (Dode); "The Mysterious Rider" 1942; "Outlaws of Boulder Pass" 1942; "Prairie Pals" 1942; "Raiders of the West" 1942; "Rock River Renegades" 1942; "Sons of the Pioneers" 1942; "Stagecoach Buckaroo" 1942; "Stardust on the Sage" 1942; "Texas Justice" 1942; "Texas Man Hunt" 1942 (Hank Smith); "Texas to Bataan" 1942 (Richards); "Texas Trouble Shooters" 1942 (Duke); "Thundering Hoofs" 1942 (Carver); "Trail Riders" 1942; "Undercover Man" 1942; "Black Hills Express" 1943; "Black Market Rustlers" 1943 (Kyper); "Blazing Guns" 1943; "Carson City

Cyclone" 1943; "Cattle Stampede" 1943 (Elkins); "Cowboy Commandos" 1943; "Law of the Saddle" 1943 (Vic); "Overland Mail Robbery" 1943; "Raiders of Red Gap" 1943 (Jed); "Two Fisted Justice" 1943 (Harve); "Wagon Tracks West" 1943; "Western Cyclone" 1943; "Wild Horse Rustlers" 1943 (Jake); "Arizona Whirlwind" 1944 (Lefty); "Blazing Frontier" 1944 (Biff); "Cheyenne Wildcat" 1944; "Code of the Prairie" 1944 (Outlaw in Officer); "Death Rides the Plains" 1944; "Devil Riders" 1944; "Firebrands of Arizona" 1944 (Outlaw); "Frontier Outlaws" 1944; "Mojave Firebrand" 1944; "Oath of Vengeance" 1944; "Oklahoma Raiders" 1944; "Outlaw Roundup" 1944; "Outlaw Trail" 1944; "Sonora Stagecoach" 1944; "Swing, Cowboy, Swing" 1944; "Trail of Terror" 1944 (Joe); "Westward Bound" 1944 (Judd); "Wild Horse Phantom" 1944; "Corpus Christi Bandits" 1945; "Enemy of the Law" 1945 (Red); "Frontier Fugitives" 1945; "Gun Smoke" 1945; "Shadows of Death" 1945; "Sunset in El Dorado" 1945; "Three in the Saddle" 1945; "Wagon Wheels Westward" 1945; "Wildfire" 1945; "Ambush Trail" 1946 (Frank Gwen); "California Gold Rush" 1946; "The Fighting Frontiersman" 1946; "Gentlemen with Guns" 1946 (Cassidy); "Overland Riders" 1946; "Prairie Badmen" 1946 (Thompson); "Santa Fe Uprising" 1946; "Terrors on Horseback" 1946; "Tumbleweed Trail" 1946; "Border Feud" 1947; "Out West" 1947-short (Jake); "Return of the Lash" 1947; "Son of Zorro" 1947-serial; "Stage to Mesa City" 1947 (Stocker); "The Vigilante" 1947-serial; "The Adventures of Frank and Jesse James" 1948-serial (Citizen #1); "Deadline" 1948; "The Valiant Hombre" 1948; "The Westward Trail" 1948 (Taggart); "Ghost of Zorro" 1949-serial (Townsman #4); "Law of the West" 1949; "Beyond the Purple Hills" 1950; "Cody of the Pony Express" 1950-serial (Durk); "Indian Territory" 1950; "Roar of the Iron Horse" 1950-serial (Bat); "Whistling Hills" 1951; "Canyon Ambush" 1952; "The Frontier Phantom" 1952; "Junction City" 1952; "Montana Belle" 1952 (Kibitzer); "The Old West" 1952; "Pack Train" 1953; "The Stranger Wore a Gun" 1953; "Pals and Gals" 1954-short (Jake); "Silver Lode" 1954 (Searcher).

Ellis, Herb. Films: "Hang 'Em High" 1968 (Swede). ¶TV: *Frontier*—"Patrol" 4-29-56; *Sheriff of Cochise*—"Fire on Chiricahua Mountains" 11-

2-56 (Prisoner #2); *Riverboat*—"The Two Faces of Grey Holden" 10-3-60 (Papite).

Ellis, Juney (1905–). Films: "Count Three and Pray" 1955 (Lilly Mae); "Giant" 1956 (Essie Lou Hodgins); "Jubal" 1956 (Charity Hoktor); "The Last Wagon" 1956 (Mrs. Clinton); "Joe Dakota" 1957 (Ethel Cook); "Valerie" 1957 (Nurse Linsey); "The Legend of Tom Dooley" 1959 (1st Old Maid). ¶TV: *Wagon Train*—"The Riley Gratton Story" 12-4-57, "The Tent City Story" 12-10-58 (Sally Jo Jeffers), "The Bleymier Story" 11-16-60 (Mrs. Cowan), "The Jed Polke Story" 3-1-61, "The Kate Crawley Story" 1-27-64 (Emma); *The Restless Gun*—"Dragon for a Day" 9-29-58 (Elisabeth Fletcher); *The Big Valley*—"The Invaders" 12-29-65 (Bessie); *Laredo*—"A Very Small Assignment" 3-17-66 (Mrs. Bates); *Daniel Boone*—"Grizzly" 10-6-66 (Mrs. Stubbs).

Ellis, Mary Joe (1900–). Films: "Gunfire" 1935 (Jane McGregor).

Ellis, Mirko. Films: "Buffalo Bill, Hero of the Far West" 1964-Ital./Ger./Fr. (Yellow Hand); "Arizona Colt" 1965-Ital./Fr./Span. (Sheriff); "For One Thousand Dollars Per Day" 1966-Ital./Span. (Wayne Clark); "Rojo" 1966-Ital./Span.; "Bad Kids of the West" 1967-Ital.; "Django, Last Killer" 1967-Ital.; "Hate for Hate" 1967-Ital. (Moxon); "Killer Caliber .32" 1967-Ital.; "Man and a Colt" 1967-Span./Ital.; "Canadian Wilderness" 1969-Span./Ital.; "Kill Django ... Kill First" 1971-Ital.; "Don't Turn the Other Cheek" 1974-Ital./Ger./Span.; "Tequila" 1974-Ital./Span.

Ellis, Paul. Films: "Fighting Caballero" 1935 (Manuel); "California Frontier" 1938 (Friar Miguel Cantova); "Heroes of the Alamo" 1938 (General Castrilian).

Ellis, Robert (1892-12/29/74). Films: "Whispering Canyon" 1926 (Bob Cameron); "Desert Vengeance" 1931; "The Fighting Sheriff" 1931 (Flash Holloway); "Mounted Fury" 1931 (Paul Marsh); "Daring Danger" 1932 (Hugo Dusang); "Broadway to Cheyenne" 1932 (Butch Owens); "Come on, Danger!" 1932 (Frank Sanderson); "The Deadline" 1932 (Ira Coleman/Clink Durand); "The Fighting Fool" 1932 (Crip Mason); "A Man's Land" 1932 (John Thomas); "One-Man Law" 1932 (Jonathan P. Streeter); "White Eagle" 1932 (Gregory); "The Thrill Hunter" 1933 (Blake); "Treason" 1933 (Colonel Jedcott); "Pillars of the Sky" 1956

(Albie). ¶TV: *Sheriff of Cochise*—"Approach with Caution" 4-19-57 (Jaekel); *Wyatt Earp*—"Wyatt and the Captain" 1-15-57 (Pvt. Crenshaw); *Death Valley Days*—"Wheelbarrow Johnny" 2-10-59 (Ben).

Ellison, James (1910-12/23/93). Films: "Hopalong Cassidy" 1935 (Johnny Nelson); "Bar 20 Rides Again" 1936 (Johnny Nelson); "Call of the Prairie" 1936 (Johnny Nelson); "The Eagle's Brood" 1936 (Johnny Nelson); "The Plainsman" 1936 (Buffalo Bill Cody); "Three on the Trail" 1936 (Johnny Nelson); "Trail Dust" 1936 (Johnny Nelson); "The Barrier" 1937 (Lt. Burrell); "Borderland" 1937 (Johnny Nelson); "Heart of the West" 1937 (Johnny Nelson); "Last of the Wild Horses" 1948 (Duke Barnum); "Colorado Ranger" 1950 (Shamrock); "Crooked River" 1950 (Shamrock); "Fast on the Draw" 1950 (Shamrock); "Hostile Country" 1950 (Shamrock); "I Killed Geronimo" 1950 (Capt. Jeff Packard); "Marshal of Heldorado" 1950 (Shamrock); "The Texan Meets Calamity Jane" 1950 (Gordon Hastings); "West of the Brazos" 1950 (Shamrock); "Oklahoma Justice" 1951; "Texas Lawmen" 1951 (Sheriff Todd); "Whistling Hills" 1951 (Dave Holland); "Dead Man's Trail" 1952; "The Man from Black Hills" 1952 (Jim Fallon); "Texas City" 1952 (Jim Kirby).

Ellison, Trudy. TV: *Bat Masterson*—"Ledger of Guilt" 4-6-61 (Honey Evans); *Bonanza*—"To Kill a Buffalo" 1-9-66 (Julie).

Ellsler, Effie (1855-10/9/42). Films: "Drift Fence" 1936 (Grandma Dunn).

Ellsworth, Stephen (1908-9/10/85). Films: "Wild Heritage" 1958 (Bolivar Bascomb). ¶TV: *Gunsmoke*—"Kitty Lost" 12-21-57 (Pence); *Maverick*—"Diamond in the Rough" 1-26-58 (2nd Millionaire); *Sugarfoot*—"Short Range" 5-13-58 (Salem Turner); *Rawhide*—"Incident of the Silent Web" 6-3-60; *Bat Masterson*—"The Court Martial of Major Mars" 1-12-61 (Amos Rapp); *Lawman*—"The Squatters" 1-29-61 (Doctor); *Death Valley Days*—"South of Horror Flats" 2-1-61 (Burt Britton); *The Tall Man*—"Ransom of a Town" 5-6-61 (Harkins).

Elmer, William (1870-2/24/45). Films: "Rose of the Rancho" 1914 (Half Breed); "The Squaw Man" 1914 (Cash Hawkins); "The Virginian" 1914 (Trampas); "The Girl of the Golden West" 1915 (Ashby); "The Sunset Trail" 1917 (Price Lovell); "Playing the Game" 1918 (Hodges);

"Wolves of the Rail" 1918 (Pablo Triles); "Forbidden Trails" 1920 (Davis); "Prairie Trails" 1920 (Rod Blake); "Big Town Round-Up" 1921 (Jerry Casey); "Iron to Gold" 1922 (Bat Piper); "Two Kinds of Women" 1922 (Poker Face); "The Whipping Boss" 1924 (Spike).

Elsom, Isobel (1893-1/12/81). Films: "The Guns of Fort Petticoat" 1957 (Mrs. Ogden); "The Second Time Around" 1961 (Mrs. Rogers).

Elson, Donald. Films: "Day of the Outlaw" 1959 (Vic). ¶TV: *The Rifleman*—"The Coward" 12-22-59, "Outlaw Shoes" 4-30-62 (Liveryman); *Tales of Wells Fargo*—"Chauncey" 3-17-62 (J.C. Clegg); *Bonanza*—"The Roper" 4-5-64, "The Pursued" 10-2-66 & 10-9-66 (Lang), "The Running Man" 3-30-69 (Clerk); *Gunsmoke*—"Patricia" 1-22-73 (Brown), "The Hanging of Newly O'Brien" 11-26-73 (Farmer Buey).

Elston, Robert (1932-12/10/87). TV: *Death Valley Days*—"Learnin' at Dirty Devil" 11-2-60 (Ralph Edmunds).

Elton, Edmund (1871-1/4/62). Films: "Konga, the Wild Stallion" 1940 (Governor); "The Return of Frank James" 1940 (Jury Foreman); "Back in the Saddle" 1941 (Judge Bent).

Elvidge, June (1893-5/1/65). Films: "The Crimson Dove" 1917 (Adrienne Durant); "The Price of Pride" 1917 (Nan Westland); "The Red Woman" 1917 (Dora Wendell); "The Law of the Yukon" 1920 (Mrs. Meredith).

Ely, Ron (1938-). Films: "The Fiend Who Walked the West" 1958 (Dyer); "The Night of the Grizzly" 1966 (Td Curry); "Halleluja and Sartana Strikes Again" 1972-Ger./Ital. (Halleluja). ¶TV: *Wyatt Earp*—"The Posse" 5-10-60 (Arleigh Smith); *Hawyeke*—"Out of the Past" 11-9-94.

Emerson, Allen. TV: *Gunsmoke*—"Cheap Labor" 5-4-57 (Joe), "Gunfighter, R.I.P." 10-22-66 (Burt); *Laredo*—"The Bitter Yen of General Ti" 2-3-67; *Bonanza*—"Gideon the Good" 10-18-70 (Pike Rogers); *Alias Smith and Jones*—"Jailbreak at Junction City" 9-30-71; *Kung Fu*—"Barbary House" 2-15-75 (Bartender), "Flight to Orion" 2-22-75 (Bartender), "The Brothers Cain" 3-1-75 (Bartender), "Full Circle" 3-15-75 (Bartender).

Emerson, Faye (1917-3/9/83). Films: "Bad Men of Missouri" 1941 (Martha Adams); "Wild Bill Hickok Rides" 1942 (Peg).

Emerson, Hope (1897-4/25/60). Films: "Copper Canyon" 1950 (Ma Tarbet); "Belle Le Grand" 1951 (Emma McGee); "Westward the Women" 1951 (Patience Hawley); "A Perilous Journey" 1953 (Olivia Schuyler); "The Guns of Fort Petticoat" 1957 (Hannah Lacey). ¶TV: *20th Century Fox Hour*—"The Ox-Bow Incident" 11-2-55 (Woman); *Death Valley Days*—"Big Liz" 5-26-57.

Emery, Gilbert (1875-10/26/45). Films: "River's End" 1940 (Justice); "King of the Mounties" 1942-serial (Commissioner Morrison).

Emery, John (1905-11/16/64). Films: "Dakota Lil" 1950 (Vincent); "Frenchie" 1950 (Clyde Gorman); "A Lawless Street" 1955 (Cody Clark). ¶TV: *Have Gun Will Travel*—"The Fifth Man" 5-30-59 (Merle Corvin); *Wagon Train*—"The Heather Mahoney Story" 6-13-62 (Harry Breckenridge).

Emery, Katherine (1907-2/7/80). Films: "Hiawatha" 1952 (Nokomis); "Untamed Frontier" 1952 (Camilla Denbow).

Emery, Matt. TV: *Bonanza*—"The Sure Thing" 11-12-67 (Official); *Gunsmoke*—"Prairie Wolfers" 11-13-67 (Trail Boss), "The Long Night" 2-17-69 (Keever), "Captain Sligo" 1-4-71 (Trail Boss); *Lancer*—"Glory" 12-10-68.

Emhardt, Robert (1916-12/29/94). Films: "The Iron Mistress" 1952 (Gen. Cuny); "3:10 to Yuma" 1957 (Mr. Butterfield); "The Badlanders" 1958 (Sample); "Hostile Guns" 1967 (R.C. Crawford); "Lawman" 1971 (Hersham); "Lock, Stock and Barrel" TVM-1971 (Sam Hartwig). ¶TV: *Riverboat*—"The Boy from Pittsburgh" 11-29-59 (Jeb Carter), "Duel on the River" 12-12-60 (Brian Cloud); *Wagon Train*—"The St. Nicholas Story" 12-23-59 (Papa Kling), "The Bonnie Brooke Story" 2-21-65 (Roger Crowell); *Gunsmoke*—"Thick 'n' Thin" 12-26-59 (Brace McCoy), "9:12 to Dodge" 11-11-68 (Conductor); *Overland Trail*—"The Most Dangerous Gentleman" 6-5-60 (Jonathan Edwards); *Wrangler*—"Encounter at Elephant Butte" 9-15-60 (Crane); *Have Gun Will Travel*—"A Quiet Night in Town" 1-7-61 & 1-14-61 (Renny), "Silent Death" 3-31-62 (Hodges), "The Debutante" 1-19-63 (Amos Powers); *Laramie*—"The Lost Dutchman" 2-14-61 (Senator Lake); *The Tall Man*—"Trial by Fury" 4-14-62 (Judge Oliver Cromwell); *Stoney Burke*—"A Matter of Percentage" 1-28-63 (Sam Marigold);

Bonanza—"A Stranger Passed This Way" 3-3-63 (Klass), "The Last Vote" 10-20-68 (Judge Clampton), "A Lawman's Lot Is Not a Happy One" 10-5-69 (Paul Forbes); *Temple Houston*—"The Guardian" 1-2-64 (Owen Judd); *Great Adventure*—"The Testing of Sam Houston" 1-31-64 (Stanbery); *The Loner*—"A Little Stroll to the End of the Line" 1-15-66 (Preacher Wheatley); *Wild Wild West*—"The Night of the Two-Legged Buffalo" 3-11-66 (Claude Duchamps), "The Night of the Tottering Tontine" 1-6-67 (Grevely); *Iron Horse*—"Appointment with an Epitaph" 2-13-67 (Alexander Fremont); *Daniel Boone*—"The Spanish Horse" 11-23-67 (Squire Breen); *Kung Fu*—"Blood Brother" 1-18-73 (Postmaster); *The New Land*—"The Word Is: Mortal" 10-5-74.

Emmanuel, Takis (1933-). Films: "Cannon for Cordoba" 1970.

Emmett, Fern (1896-9/3/46). Films: "Bar L Ranch" 1930; "The Land of Missing Men" 1930 (Martha Evans); "Ridin' Law" 1930; "Romance of the West" 1930 (Landlady); "Westward Bound" 1930 (Emma); "Rider of the Plains" 1931 (Miss Whipple); "The Ridin' Fool" 1931 (Miss Scully); "West of Cheyenne" 1931; "The Forty-Niners" 1932 (Widow Spriggs); "The Lone Avenger" 1933; "Riders of Destiny" 1933 (Farm Woman); "The Trail Drive" 1933 (Aunt Marthe); "Loser's End" 1934 (Molly O'Hara); "Terror of the Plains" 1934 (Rose); "Wagon Wheels" 1934 (Settler); "West on Parade" 1934; "Gunfire" 1935 (Aunt Lydia); "Heir to Trouble" 1935 (Amanda); "Melody Trail" 1935 (Nell); "Rainbow Valley" 1935; "The Silver Bullet" 1935; "Texas Terror" 1935 (Aunt Martha Hubbard); "The Oregon Trail" 1936 (Minnie, the Old Maid); "Come on Cowboys" 1937; "Riders of the Whistling Skull" 1937 (Henrietta McCoy); "Wells Fargo" 1937 (Mrs. Jenkins); "Overland Stage Raiders" 1938 (Ma Hawkins); "Desperate Trails" 1939 (Mrs. Plunkett); "Frontier Marshal" 1939 (Hotel Maid); "Saga of Death Valley" 1939; "Rangers of Fortune" 1940 (Mrs. Ellis); "Triple Justice" 1940; "Jesse James at Bay" 1941; "The Shepherd of the Hills" 1941 (Mrs. Palestrom); "Six Gun Gold" 1941 (Jenny Blanchard); "The Great Man's Lady" 1942 (Secretary to City Editor); "Shut My Big Mouth" 1942 (Maggie); "The Sundown Kid" 1942 (Mrs. Peabody); "Valley of the Sun" 1942 (Spinster); "Frontier Badman" 1943 (Millner); "The Daltons Ride Again" 1945 (Miss Crain).

Emmett, Michael. Films: "Gun the Man Down" 1957 (Billy Deal). ¶TV: *Wyatt Earp*—"The Englishman" 2-21-56, "Big Brother Virgil" 3-25-58 (Larry Herrick), "Remittance Man" 11-4-58 (Jonathan Milton), "The Arizona Lottery" 2-16-60 (Hennings); *Gunsmoke*—"Poor Pearl" 12-22-56 (Webb Thorne); *Boots and Saddles*—"The Treasure" 12-12-57 (Cpl. Davis); *Death Valley Days*—"A Bullet for the Captain" 1-13-59 (Capt. Owen Manners), "The Talking Wire" 4-21-59 (Steve Warren).

Emmich, Cliff (1936-). TV: *Bret Maverick*—"The Ballad of Bret Maverick" 2-16-82 (Titus Openshaw).

Emory, Maud. Films: "Liberty" 1916-serial; "The Greater Law" 1917 (Anne Malone); "The Purple Riders" 1921-serial.

Emory, Richard (1918-3/4/94). Films: "Bandit King of Texas" 1949 (Jim Baldwin); "South of Death Valley" 1949 (Tommy Tavish); "Code of the Silver Sage" 1950 (Lt. John Case); "Gene Autry and the Mounties" 1951 (Terry Dillon); "Lawless Cowboys" 1951 (Jeff); "Little Big Horn" 1951 (Pvt. Mitch Shovels); "Captive of Billy the Kid" 1952 (Sam); "Hellgate" 1952 (Dan Mott); "Wyoming Roundup" 1952 (Jack Craven); "Perils of the Wilderness" 1956-serial (Sergeant Gray). ¶TV: *The Cisco Kid*—"Lynching Story" 4-28-51, "Confession for Money" 5-26-51, "Pancho Hostage" 6-23-51; *The Roy Rogers Show*—"Dead Men's Hills" 3-15-52, "Ride in the Death Wagon" 4-6-52; *The Gene Autry Show*—"Steel Ribbon" 9-22-53; *Sergeant Preston of the Yukon*—"The Black Ace" 1-3-57 (Constable Drake); *Circus Boy*—"Corky's Big Parade" 3-24-57 (John Ashcroft); *The Adventures of Rin Tin Tin*—"The Outcast of Fort Apache" 12-10-54 (Lt. Sharp); *Rough Riders*—"An Eye for an Eye" 1-15-59 (Steve Johnston); *Bat Masterson*—"Marked Deck" 3-11-59 (William Roberts).

Encinas, Lalo (1886-5/5/59). Films: "Snowdrift" 1923 (Joe Pete); "Call of the Wild" 1935 (Kali); "Rose of the Rancho" 1936 (Overseer).

Endfield, Frances. Films: "The Secret of Convict Lake" 1951 (Tess).

Endoso, Kenny. Films: "The Great Bank Robbery" 1969 (Chinese Laundryman). ¶TV: *Daniel Boone*—"The Dandy" 10-10-68; *Kung Fu*—"The Tide" 2-1-73 (2nd Henchman).

Enfield, Hugh. *see* Reynolds, Craig.

Engel, Roy (1913-12/29/80).

Films: "Rogue River" 1950 (Ed Colby); "The Naked Dawn" 1955 (Guntz); "Frontier Gambler" 1956; "Three Violent People" 1956 (Carpetbagger); "Tribute to a Badman" 1956 (2nd Buyer); "The Storm Rider" 1957 (Bonnard); "When the Legends Die" 1972 (Sam Turner). ¶TV: *The Cisco Kid*—"New Evidence" 9-19-53; *My Friend Flicka*—"Rebels in Hiding" 3-30-56 (Mr. Forbes); *Gunsmoke*—"Prairie Happy" 7-7-56 (Citizen), "The Cover-Up" 1-12-57 (Hoffer), "Wind" 3-21-59 (Jed Garvey), "Don Mateo" 10-22-60 (Grimes), "The Do-Badder" 1-6-62, "The Raid" 1-22-66 & 1-29-66 (Sheriff), "Snow Train" 10-19-70 & 10-26-70 (Tibbett), "Eleven Dollars" 10-30-72 (Hider); *Sheriff of Cochise*—"Wyatt Earp" 6-7-57 (Deputy Dave); *Trackdown*—"The Mistake" 4-18-58 (Jeff); *Wagon Train*—"The John Wilbot Story" 6-11-58 (Broxton), "The Countess Baranof Story" 5-11-60; *Tales of Wells Fargo*—"The Manuscript" 9-15-58 (Sheriff Anderson); *Maverick*—"Island in the Swamp" 11-30-58 (Sampson), "Greenbacks Unlimited" 3-13-60 (Marshal Ratcliffe); *Have Gun Will Travel*—"The Ballad of Oscar Wilde" 12-6-58 (Matson), "Everyman" 3-25-61 (Sheriff), "The Gospel Singer" 10-21-61 (Barber), "Squatter's Rights" 12-23-61 (Bartender); *Death Valley Days*—"Sailor on a Horse" 1-27-59, "The Gentle Sword" 11-9-60, "Big John and the Rainmaker" 12-6-64 (Nate Freed), "The Red Shawl" 2-5-66 (Nate Donaldson), "Dry Water Sailors" 3-12-66 (Captain Morrow), "Tracy's Triumph" 10-4-69, "The Mezcla Man" 1-3-70"The Visitor" 12-27-69; *The Restless Gun*—"The Dead Ringer" 2-16-59 (Sheriff Willard), "One on the House" 4-20-59 (Sheriff); *Bat Masterson*—"Battle of the Pass" 2-25-59 (Maloney); *Tombstone Territory*—"Marked for Murder" 3-20-59 (Martin Ramsey); *Sugarfoot*—"The Vultures" 4-28-59 (Sgt. Jacey); *Black Saddle*—"Client: Reynolds" 5-23-59 (Amos Pryor); *Bonanza*—"The Julia Bulette Story" 10-17-59, "Day of Reckoning" 10-22-60, "Vengeance" 2-11-61 (Doc Tolliver), "The Dark Gate" 3-4-61, "The Secret" 5-5-61, "The Law Maker" 3-11-62, "The Dowry" 4-29-62 (Doctor), "Knight Errant" 11-18-62 (Doctor), "The Good Samaritan" 12-23-62 (Doctor), "Elegy for a Hangman" 1-20-63, "The Boss" 5-19-63, "The Prime of Life" 12-29-63, "The Campaneros" 4-19-64 (Doc), "Anatomy of a Lynching" 10-12-69 (Clyde Quinn), "It's a Small World" 1-4-70 (Dr. Martin),

"Is There Any Man Here?" 2-8-70 (Dr. Thomas); *Colt .45*—"Impasse" 1-31-60 (Marshal Ben Staley); *Wanted—Dead or Alive*—"Dead Reckoning" 3-22-61 (Sheriff Art Hampton); *Wyatt Earp*—"Hiding Behind a Star" 5-23-61 (Zack Herrick); *Rawhide*—"Incident of the Lost Woman" 11-2-62 (Whit Stokes), "Incident of the Married Widow" 3-1-63 (Mr. Amy); *Stoney Burke*—"The Wanderer" 12-3-62 (Farley); *The Virginian*—"Duel at Shiloh" 1-2-63 (Loomis), "Say Goodbye to All That" 1-23-63 (Wilkins), "A Distant Fury" 3-20-63, Regular 1963-67 (Barney Wingate); *Wild Wild West*—"The Night of the Steel Assassin" 1-7-66 (President Grant), "The Night of the Colonel's Ghost" 3-10-67 (President Grant), "The Night of the Arrow" 12-29-67 (President Grant), "The Night of the Death-Maker" 2-23-68 (President Grant), "The Night of the Big Blackmail" 9-27-68 (President Grant), "The Night of the Winged Terror" 1-17-68 & 1-24-68 (President Grant); *Pistols 'n' Petticoats*—12-3-66 (Wyatt Earp); *Lancer*—"The Prodigal" 11-12-68; *The Guns of Will Sonnett*—"Joby" 11-1-68; *Here Come the Brides*—"Hosanna's Way" 10-31-69.

England, Hal (1932-). Films: "Hang 'Em High" 1968. ¶TV: *F Troop*—"El Diablo" 1-18-66 (Lt. George Anderson), "Our Brave in F Troop" 3-30-67 (Lieutenant Goodbody); *Here Come the Brides*—"Loggerheads" 3-26-69 (Barnabus).

England, Sue (1931-). Films: "Hell's Outpost" 1954. ¶TV: *The Lone Ranger*—"Eye for an Eye" 6-29-50; *The Cisco Kid*—"Quick on the Trigger" 2-6-54; *Broken Arrow*—"Indian Agent" 10-9-56 (Sonseeahray), "Conquistador" 10-8-57; *Laramie*—"Ride or Die" 3-8-60 (Deborah Farnum), "Widow in White" 6-13-61 (Sheila Dawson), "The Runt" 2-20-62 (Marcy Catlin); *Daniel Boone*—"The Christmas Story" 12-23-65 (Nanteen); *Cowboy in Africa*—"The Kasubi Death" 4-1-68 (Claudia Rolf).

Engle, Billy (1889-11/28/66). Films: "Red Hot Leather" 1926 (Dinkey Hook); "The Western Whirlwind" 1927 (Beans Baker); "The Nevada Buckaroo" 1931 (Elmer); "Ridin' for Justice" 1932 (Sam); "The Lone Star Trail" 1943 (Stage Passenger); "Along Came Jones" 1945 (Wagon Driver); "Frontier Gal" 1945 (Barfly); "The Wistful Widow of Wagon Gap" 1947 (Undertaker's Halper); "The Paleface" 1948 (Pioneer).

Engle, Paul. Films: "The Persuader" 1957 (Paul Bonham); "Gunsmoke in Tucson" 1958 (Young Chip). ¶TV: *Tales of the Texas Rangers*—"The Atomic Trail" 11-19-55 (Terry Marlowe); *The Lone Ranger*—"The Wooden Rifle" 9-23-56, "Code of Honor" 2-14-57; *Sergeant Preston of the Yukon*—"Littlest Rookie" 10-11-56 (Danny Lawson); *Cheyenne*—"The Law Man" 11-6-56 (Buddy); *Zane Grey Theater*—"A Gun Is for Killing" 10-18-57 (Bobby Andrews); *Tales of Wells Fargo*—"The Witness" 12-30-57 (Billy Burns), "Scapegoat" 5-5-58 (Len Spears); *Colt .45*—"Long Odds" 4-11-58 (Billy); *Gunsmoke*—"Wild West" 2-15-58 (Yorky Kelly), "The Lost Rifle" 11-1-58 (Andy Spangler); *Trackdown*—"The Unwanted" 5-13-59 (Jeremiah); *Wanted—Dead or Alive*—"The Healing Woman" 9-12-59 (Ted Bridges); *The Deputy*—"Like Father" 10-17-59 (Ted); *Fury*—"Gaucho" 2-20-60; *Stagecoach West*—"High Lonesome" 10-4-60 (Tom Osgood, Jr.).

English, Marla (1930-). Films: "Flesh and the Spur" 1957 (Willow).

Englund, Robert (1947-). TV: *Legend*—"The Gospel According to Legend" 6-12-95 (Mordecai).

Engstrom, Jean. TV: *Rawhide*—"Incident of the Lost Idol" 4-28-61 (Mrs. Manson).

Engstrom, Jena. TV: *Gunslinger*—"The Hostage Fort" 2-16-61 (Mrs. Barnes); *Have Gun Will Travel*—"The Fatal Flaw" 2-25-61 (Cassandra), "The Gold Bar" 3-18-61 (Woman), "The Education of Sara Jane" 9-23-61 (Sarah Jane Darrow), "Alive" 3-17-62 (Maya), "A Place for Abel Hix" 10-6-62 (Mrs. Hix); *Rawhide*—"Incident of the Lost Idol" 4-28-61 (Laurie Manson), "The Child Woman" 3-23-62 (Posie Mushgrove), "Incident of the Four Horsemen" 10-26-62 (Amy Gault); *Bonanza*—"Springtime" 10-1-61 (Ann), "The Deadly Ones" 12-2-62 (Molly); *The Tall Man*—"An Item for Auction" 10-14-61 (Susan); *The Outlaws*—"Night Riders" 11-2-61 (Louise); *Death Valley Days*—"Storm Over Truckee" 11-15-61 (Maggie Woolf), "Brute Angel" 10-15-66 (Esther McBain); *Gunsmoke*—"Milly" 11-25-61 (Milly Glover), "Chester's Indian" 5-12-62 (Callie Dill); *Laramie*—"The Lawless Seven" 12-26-61 (Ginny Hawks), "The Sunday Shoot" 11-13-62 (Nancy); *Frontier Circus*—"Mighty Like Rogues" 4-5-62 (Bety Ross Jokes); *Stoney Burke*—"A Matter of Pride" 11-5-62 (Meryle Hill); *Empire*—"65 Miles Is a Long, Long Way"

4-23-63 (Mrs. Sangster); *The Travels of Jaimie McPheeters*—"The Day of Leaving" 9-15-63 (Jenny); *Wagon Train*—"The Santiago Quesada Story" 3-30-64 (Kim Case); *The Virginian*—"The Black Stallion" 9-30-64 (Jody).

Enriquez, Rene (1933-3/23/90). Films: "Dream West" TVM-1986 (General Castro). ¶TV: *Centennial*—Regular 1978-79 (Manolo Marquez).

Ensign, Michael. Films: "Dream West" TVM-1986 (Preuss). ¶TV: *Paradise*—Regular 1989-91 (Axelrod).

Enseadt, Howard (1906-12/13/28). Films: "The Ace of the Saddle" 1919 (Child); "Bare Fists" 1919 (Bud).

Entwistle, Harold (1865-4/1/44). Films: "Salomy Jane" 1914 (Larabee).

Epper, Gary. Films: "The Cowboys" 1972. ¶TV: *Kung Fu*—"The Elixir" 12-20-73 (Billy); *Paradise*—"Vengeance" 3-16-89 (Matt).

Epper, John Anthony (1906-12/3/92). Films: "Three Thousand Hills" 1959 (Swede); "The Scalphunters" 1968 (Scalphunter). ¶TV: *Daniel Boone*—"The Patriot" 12-5-68 (Charley Pete).

Epper, Tony (1938-). Films: "The Scalphunters" 1968 (Scalphunter); "Valdez Is Coming" 1971 (Bodyguard); "Ulzana's Raid" 1972; "More Wild Wild West" TVM-1980 (Brother); "Gunsmoke: Return to Dodge" TVM-1987 (Farnum); "Lonesome Dove" TVM-1989; "The Good Old Boys" TVM-1995. ¶TV: *Daniel Boone*—"The Value of a King" 11-9-67; *Cimarron Strip*—"Nobody" 12-7-67; *Hondo*—"Hondo and the Apache Trail" 12-22-67 (Running Bear); *The High Chaparral*—"Auld Lang Syne" 4-10-70; *Kung Fu*—"A Dream Within a Dream" 1-17-74 (Dirk), "Barbary House" 2-15-75 (1st Bounty Hunter), "Flight to Orion" 2-22-75 (1st Bounty Hunter), "The Brothers Cain" 3-1-75 (1st Bounty Hunter), "Full Circle" 3-15-75 (1st Bounty Hunter); *Paradise*—"Childhood's End" 12-29-88 (Bouncer), "A Proper Stranger" 11-11-89 (Federal Marshal Burnette).

Epperson, Don (1938-3/17/73). Films: "Big Jake" 1971 (Saloon Bully); "The Female Bunch" 1971 (Singer).

Erdman, Richard (1925-). Films: "The San Francisco Story" 1952 (Shorty); "The Rawhide Trail" 1958 (Rupe Pardee); "Saddle the Wind" 1958 (Dallas Hansen); "The Brothers O'Toole" 1973.

Erdway, Ben. Films: "Sin Town" 1942 (Dr. Prendergast).

Eric, Martin. Films: "Baker's Hawk" 1976 (Wattle). ¶TV: *Overland Trail*—"Daughter of the Sioux" 3-20-60 (Indian Agent); *Lawman*—"Yawkey" 10-23-60 (Man); *The Virginian*—"The Big Deal" 10-10-62 (Bartender); *Laramie*—"Protective Custody" 1-15-63.

Erickson, Bob (1898-1/21/41). Films: "Riders of the Rio Grande" 1929 (Pinto Quantrell); "Beau Bandit" 1930 (Cowhand).

Erickson, Glen. *see* Erickson, Leif.

Erickson, Knute (1871-1/1/46). Films: "The Conflict" 1921 (Hannibal Ginger); "The Spoilers" 1930 (Capt. Stevens); "The Deadline" 1932 (Otto).

Erickson, Lee. Films: "The Kentuckian" 1955 (Luke). ¶TV: *Frontier*—"A Stillness in Wyhoming" 10-16-55; *Wyatt Earp*—"Rich Man's Son" 12-13-55 (Buddy Grimes); *Jim Bowie*—"The Intruder" 4-26-57; *Fury*—"Joey's Jalopy" 4-4-59, "The Skin Divers" 2-27-60 (Bud Kane); *Great Adventure*—"The Outlaw and the Nun" 12-6-63 (Abel Parrish).

Erickson, Leif (Glen Erickson) (1911-1/29/86). Films: "Nevada" 1935 (Bill Ide); "Wanderer of the Wasteland" 1935 (Lawrence); "Desert Gold" 1936 (Glenn Kasedon); "Drift Fence" 1936 (Curley Prentiss); "Dallas" 1950 (Martin Weatherby); "The Showdown" 1950 (Big Mart); "The Cimarron Kid" 1951 (Marshall Sutton); "Born to the Saddle" 1953; "A Perilous Journey" 1953 (Richards); "Fastest Gun Alive" 1956 (Lou Glover); "Star in the Dust" 1956 (George Ballard); "Once Upon a Horse" 1958 (Granville Dix); "Shoot Out at Big Sag" 1962 (Sam Barbee); "Man and Boy" 1971 (Sheriff Mossman); "The Daughters of Joshua Cabe" TVM-1972 (Amos Wetherall); "Winterhawk" 1975 (Elkhorn Guthrie); "Wild Times" TVM-1980 (John Tyree). ¶TV: *Zane Grey Theater*—"The Sharpshooter" 3-7-58 (Jim Lewis), "The Sunday Man" 2-25-60 (Cash Wilson); *The Rifleman*—"The Sharpshooter" 9-30-58 (Jim Lewis); *Hotel De Paree*—"The High Cost of Justice" 10-23-59; *Rawhide*—"Incident at the Buffalo Smokehouse" 10-30-59 (Jeremiah Walsh), "Incident Near Gloomy River" 3-17-61 (Frank Travis); *Bonanza*—"The Rescue" 2-25-61 (Josh Tatum), "All Ye His Saints" 12-19-65 (Caine); *The Rebel*—"Helping Hand" 4-30-61 (Dave); *Wagon Train*—"The Eli Bancroft Story" 11-11-63 (Eli Bancroft); *The Travels of Jaimie McPheeters*—"The

Day of the Toll Takers" 1-5-64 (Sugar Bob Devlin); *The Virginian*—"The Drifter" 1-29-64 (Miles Peterson), "Return a Stranger" 11-18-64 (Charley Ryan), "Blaze of Glory" 12-29-65 (Bill King); *Daniel Boone*—"The Aaron Burr Story" 10-28-65 (Aaron Burr), "River Passage" 12-15-66 (Bill Sedley); *A Man Called Shenandoah*—"Incident at Dry Creek" 11-15-65 (Sheriff Dan Grier); *Branded*—"Barbed Wire" 2-13-66 (Roy Beckwith); *Gunsmoke*—"Saturday Night" 1-7-67 (Virgil Powell); *The High Chaparral*—Regular 1967-71 (John Cannon); *The Quest*—"The Last of the Mountain Men" 1976; *Hunter's Moon*—Pilot 12-1-79 (George Randall).

Ericson, Devon. Films: "Testimony of Two Men" TVM-1977 (Priscilla "Prissy" Madden Witherby); "The Awakening Land" TVM-1978 (Huldah as an Adult); "The Mystic Warrior" TVM-1984 (Heyatawin); "Houston: The Legend of Texas" TVM-1986 (Tiana Rogers). ¶TV: *Young Dan'l Boone*—Regular 1977 (Rebecca Bryant); *The Busters*—Pilot 5-28-78 (Marti Hamilton); *The Chisholms*—Regular 1980 (Betsy O'Neil).

Ericson, John (1927-). Films: "Bad Day at Black Rock" 1955 (Pete Wirth); "The Return of Jack Slade" 1955 (Jack Slade); "Forty Guns" 1957 (Brockie Drummond); "Day of the Bad Man" 1958 (Sheriff Barney Wiley); "Oregon Passage" 1958 (Lt. Niles Ord); "Seven for Pancho Villa" 1966-Span.; "Heads or Tails" 1969-Ital./Span. (Will Hunter); "Bounty Man" TVM-1972 (Billy Riddle). ¶TV: *Zane Grey Theater*—"Stage to Tucson" 11-16-56 (Will Ruxton), "License to Kill" 2-7-58 (Lane Baker), "The Tall Shadow" 11-20-58 (Linc Hardaway), "Trail Incident" 1-29-59 (Andy McCall); *The Restless Gun*—"The Hand Is Quicker" 3-17-58 (Henry Wilson), "Four Lives" 4-13-59 (Bud Rainey); *Wagon Train*—"The Dick Richardson Story" 12-31-58 (Dick Richardson); *Rawhide*—"Incident at Chubasco" 4-3-59 (Tom Bryan), "Incident Near Gloomy River" 3-17-61 (Dan Fletcher); *Bonanza*—"Breed of Violence" 11-5-60 (Vince Dagen), "Journey to Terror" 2-5-67 (Wade); *Gunsmoke*—"The Twisted Heritage" 1-6-69 (Blaine Copperton); *The Men from Shiloh*—"The Politician" 1-13-71 (Jack Bonham); *Barbary Coast*—"Guns for a Queen" 10-6-75 (McCord); *Hunter's Moon*—Pilot 12-1-79 (Kels Johansen).

Erlanger, Frank. Films: "The

Girl Angle" 1917 (Village Storekeeper); "The Yellow Bullet" 1917 (Pedro).

Ermey, R. Lee. Films: "Sommersby" 1993 (Dick Mead). ¶TV: *Adventures of Brisco County, Jr.*—Pilot 8-27-93 (Brisco County, Sr.).

Ernest, George. Films: "Destry Rides Again" 1932 (Willie); "The Deadline" 1932 (Jimmy Evans); "The Plainsman" 1936 (Urchin); "Song of the Saddle" 1936 (Frank Wilson); "Stardust on the Sage" 1942 (Curly).

Errol, Leon (1881-10/12/51). Films: "Mexican Spitfire Out West" 1940 (Uncle Mat Lindsay/Lord Basil Epping); "Twilight on the Prairie" 1944; "Under Western Skies" 1945 (Willie); "Cactus Cut-Up" 1949-short.

Erskine, Marilyn. Films: "Westward the Women" 1951 (Jean Johnson). ¶TV: *Zane Grey Theater*—"Man Alone" 3-5-59 (Laura Thomas); *Wichita Town*—"Ruby Dawes" 1-6-60 (Ruby Dawes); *The Virginian*—"Shadows of the Past" 2-24-65 (Rita); *Laredo*—"Hey Diddle Diddle" 2-24-67 (Milly Beamish).

Erway, Ben (1892-2/6/81). Films: "Rimfire" 1949 (Deputy Sheriff Wilson). ¶TV: *Bonanza*—"The First Born" 9-23-62.

Erwin, Roy (1925-6/18/58). TV: *Wild Bill Hickok*—"Jingles on Jail Road" 7-14-53; *The Adventures of Rin Tin Tin*—"The Babe in the Woods" 2-11-55, "The Silent Witness" 3-29-57 (Fred Carter), "Sorrowful Joe's Policy" 3-21-58; *Judge Roy Bean*—"Judge Declares a Holiday" 11-1-55 (Mickey Lant); *Maverick*—"The Day They Hanged Bret Maverick" 9-21-58 (Claude).

Erwin, Stuart (1902-12/21/67). Films: "Dude Ranch" 1931 (Chester Carr); "Under the Tonto Rim" 1933 (Tonto Duley); "When the Daltons Rode" 1940 (Ben Dalton); "Heaven Only Knows" 1947 (Sheriff); "For the Love of Mike" 1960 (Dr. Mills). ¶TV: *Gunsmoke*—"Killer at Large" 2-5-66 (Doc Brown); *Bonanza*—"Three Brides for Hoss" 2-20-66 (Jester); *The Virginian*—"Yesterday's Timepiece" 1-18-67 (Williams); *The Big Valley*—"Explosion!" 11-20-67 & 11-27-67 (Clem Carter).

Erwin, William "Bill" (1914-). Films: "Man from Del Rio" 1956 (Roy Higgens); "Gun Fever" 1958 (Bartender); "Terror at Black Falls" 1962. ¶TV: *Zane Grey Theater*—"Time of Decision" 1-18-57 (Sam Townley), "The Ox" 11-3-60, "A Warm Day in Heaven" 3-23-61 (Clay

Davis); *Gunsmoke*—"Romeo" 11-9-57 (Preacher), "The Squaw" 11-11-61 (Rev. Tucker), "Bently" 4-11-64 (Ned Wright), "A Hat" 10-16-67 (Townsman), "The First People" 2-19-61 (Captain), "Slocum" 10-21-68 (Judge), "Coreyville" 10-6-69 (Juror), "Hackett" 3-16-70 (Businessman), "Alias Festus Haggen" 3-6-72 (Bailiff), "Bohannan" 9-25-72 (Greeves), "Shadler" 1-15-73 (Mr. Jonas); *Trackdown*—"The Toll Road" 1-31-58 (Dawson); *The Rifleman*—"The Pet" 1-6-59 (Joe Flecker); *Wagon Train*—"The Hunter Malloy Story" 1-21-59 (Clegg), "The Barnaby West Story" 6-5-63 (Barnaby West); *Tales of Wells Fargo*—"The Town That Wouldn't Talk" 2-9-59 (Justin Peevy); *Bat Masterson*—"Lottery of Death" 5-13-59 (Teller); *Black Saddle*—"Client: Brand" 5-16-59 (Kelly); *The Texan*—"The Dishonest Posse" 10-5-59 (Les Cosby), "The Invisible Noose" 5-16-60 (Sheriff Rand); *Desilu Playhouse*—"Six Guns for Donegan" 10-16-59; *The Law of the Plainsman*—"The Gibbet" 11-26-59; *Rawhide*—"Incident of the New Start" 3-3-61; *Maverick*—"The Forbidden City" 3-26-61 (Hotel Clerk); *The Dakotas*—"Sanctuary at Crystal Springs" 5-6-63 (Doctor); *Wild Wild West*—"The Night of the Legion of Death" 11-24-67 (Jury Foreman); *The Guns of Will Sonnett*—"Of Lasting Summers and Jim Sonnett" 10-6-67; *Here Come the Brides*—"Democracy in Action" 2-5-69, "The Last Winter" 3-27-70.

Escalante, Henry "Blackie". Films: "The Three Outlaws" 1956; "Monte Walsh" 1970.

Escandon, Gilbert. Films: "Pocket Money" 1972 (Rustler); "Ulzana's Raid" 1972. ¶TV: *Gunsmoke*—"Women for Sale" 9-10-73 & 9-17-73; *Kung Fu*—"The Brujo" 10-25-73 (Miguel).

Esformes, Nate (1932-). Films: "Female Artillery" TVM-1973 (Johnny). ¶TV: *Wild Wild West*—"The Night of the Assassin" 9-22-67 (Perico Mendoza); *The Virginian*—"Execution at Triste" 12-13-67; *The Big Valley*—"Flight from San Miguel" 4-28-69 (Ramon); *The High Chaparral*—"An Anger Greather Than Mine" 9-18-70 (Francisco); *Kung Fu*—"Empty Pages of a Dead Book" 1-10-74 (Judge Alonzo); *Barbary Coast*—"Guns for a Queen" 10-6-75 (Morales).

Eskow, Jerry. TV: *Sergeant Preston of the Yukon*—"One Good Turn" 3-8-56 (Buck Eagan); *The Adventures of Rin Tin Tin*—"Boone's Commission" 3-22-57 (Brave), "Corporal Carson" 5-3-57 (Yellow Horse).

Esmelton, Fred (1872-10/23/33). Films: "The Gay Defender" 1927 (Commissioner Ainsworth).

Esmond, Carl (1905-). Films: "Thunder in the Sun" 1959 (Andre Dauphin). ¶TV: *Cheyenne*—"Fury at Rio Hondo" 4-17-56 (Col. Picard); *The Deputy*—"Second Cousin to the Czar" 12-24-60 (Duke Dmitri); *Maverick*—"Diamond Flush" 2-5-61 (Comte de Lisle); *The Travels of Jaimie McPheeters*—"The Day of the Pretenders" 3-1-64 (Baron Pyrrhos); *The Big Valley*—"Explosion!" 11-20-67 & 11-27-67 (Marquis de Lacaise).

Espinosa, Jose Angel (Ferrusquilla). Films: "Fury in Paradise" 1955-U.S./Mex.; "Bandido" 1956; "Villa!" 1958 (Posado); "Viva Maria" 1965-Fr./Ital. (El Presidente); "Rio Lobo" 1970; "Two Mules for Sister Sara" 1970; "Something Big" 1971 (Emilio Estevez).

Essler, Fred (1896-1/17/73). Films: "The First Traveling Saleslady" 1956 (Schlessinger). ¶TV: *Maverick*—"Game of Chance" 1-4-59 (German Jeweler).

Estabrook, Howard (1884-7/16/78). Films: "M'Liss" 1915 (John Gray).

Estelita. Films: "Jesse James Meets Frankenstein's Daughter" 1966 (Juanita). ¶TV: *Laredo*—"Three's Company" 10-14-65 (Carla).

Estevez, Emilio (1962-). Films: "Young Guns" 1988 (William H. Bonney); "Young Guns II" 1990 (William H. Bonney).

Estrada, Erik (1948-). TV: *The Quest*—"The Longest Drive" 12-1-76 & 12-8-76 (Santos).

Estrella, Esther. Films: "The Light of Western Stars" 1940 (Bonita); "Three Men from Texas" 1940 (Paquita Serrano); "Down Mexico Way" 1941; "Prairie Pioneers" 1941 (Dolores Ortega); "Prairie Pals" 1942 (Betty); "Undercover Man" 1942 (Dolores Gonzales).

Ethier, Alphonse (1875-1/4/43). Films: "The Last of the Mohicans" 1911; "Oh, Johnny!" 1918 (John Bryson); "Rough and Ready" 1918 (Jack Belmont); "Sandy Burke of the U-Bar-U" 1919 (Jim Diggs); "Gold and the Girl" 1925 (Sam Donald); "In Old Arizona" 1929 (Sheriff); "Smoke Bellew" 1929 (Harry Sprague); "The Big Trail" 1930 (Marshal); "The Storm" 1930 (Jacques Fachard); "Fair Warning" 1931 (Mr. Cumberland); "Law and Order" 1932 (Fin Elder); "Men of America" 1933 (Indian Tom); "Boss Rider of Gun Creek" 1936 (Dr. Northrup); "Sunset Trail" 1938 (Superintendent).

Ethridge, Ella. Films: "The Plunderers" 1960 (Mrs. Phelps). ¶TV: *Wild Bill Hickok*—"Masquerade at Moccasin Flats" 9-2-52; *Death Valley Days*—"Sego Lillies" 1-14-53 (Sarah), "Riggs and Riggs" 4-25-55; *Wide Country*—"Who Killed Edde Gannon?" 10-11-62 (Mrs. Gannon).

Etienne, Roger. TV: *Jim Bowie*—"The Select Females" 11-23-56 (Emile Dusard); *Bonanza*—"Ride the Wind" 1-16-66 & 1-23-66 (Fontaine).

Eustrel, Anthony (1904-7/2/79). Films: "Captain John Smith and Pocahontas" 1953 (King James). ¶TV: *Jim Bowie*—"Convoy Gold" 2-1-57 (M. Remy), "A Fortune for Madame" 10-18-57 (Samuel Jebb); *Broken Arrow*—"The Archaeologist" 4-30-57 (Regis); *Maverick*—"The Iron Hand" 2-21-60 (Major Innerscourt).

Evans, Charles. Films: "The Prairie" 1947 (Ishmael Bush); "Twilight on the Rio Grande" 1947 (Henry Blackstone); "The Cowboy and the Indians" 1949 (Broken Army); "Across the Badlands" 1950 (Gregory Banion); "Colt .45" 1950 (Redrock Sheriff); "The Furies" 1950 (Old Anaheim); "Stage to Tucson" 1950 (John Butterfield); "The Kid from Amarillo" 1951 (Jason Summerville); "The Last Outpost" 1951 (Chief Grey Cloud); "Santa Fe" 1951; "Bugles in the Afternoon" 1952 (Gen. Terry); "Desperadoes' Outpost" 1952 (Maj. Seley); "A Perilous Journey" 1953 (Minister); "The Vanquished" 1953 (Gen. Hildebrandt); "Battle of Rogue River" 1954 (Matt Parish); "The Rawhide Years" 1956 (Col. Swope). ¶TV: *The Lone Ranger*—"Treason at Dry Creek" 12-4-52; *My Friend Flicka*—"Cavalry Horse" 10-28-55; *Wyatt Earp*—"Vengeance Trail" 2-12-57 (Jake Antrim), "Earp Ain't Even Wearing Guns" 2-3-59 (Major Landreth); *The Adventures of Rin Tin Tin*—"Major Mockingbird" 1-30-59 (Gen. Van Buren).

Evans, Dale (1912-). Films: "In Old Oklahoma" 1943 (Cuddles Walker); "Cowboy and the Senorita" 1944 (Ysobel Martinez); "The Lights of Old Santa Fe" 1944 (Marjorie Brooks); "San Fernando Valley" 1944 (Dale Kenyon); "Song of Nevada" 1944 (Joan Barrabee); "The Yellow Rose of Tesas" 1944 (Betty Weston); "Along the Navajo Trail" 1945 (Lorry Alastair); "Bells of Rosarita" 1945 (Sue Farnum); "Don't Fence Me In" 1945 (Toni Ames); "The Man from Oklahoma" 1945 (Peggy Lane); "Sunset in El Dorado" 1945 (Lucille

Wiley); "Utah" 1945 (Dorothy Bryant); "Heldorado" 1946 (Carol Randall); "Home in Oklahoma" 1946 (Connie Edwards); "My Pal Trigger" 1946 (Susan); "Out California Way" 1946; "Rainbow Over Texas" 1946 (Jackie Dalrymple); "Roll on, Texas Moon" 1946 (Jill Delaney); "Song of Arizona" 1946 (Clare Summers); "Under Nevada Skies" 1946 (Helen Williams); "Bells of San Angelo" 1947 (Lee Madison); "Apache Rose" 1947 (Billie Colby); "Down Dakota Way" 1949 (Ruth Shaw); "The Golden Stallion" 1949 (Stormy Billings); "Susanna Pass" 1949 (Kay "Doc" Parker); "Bells of Coronado" 1950 (Pam Reynolds); "Trigger, Jr." 1950 (Kay Harkrider); "Twilight in the Sierras" 1950 (Pat Callahan); "Pals of the Golden West" 1951 (Cathy Marsh); "South of Caliente" 1951 (Doris Stewart). ¶TV: *The Roy Rogers Show*—Regular 1951-57 (Dale Evans).

Evans, Douglas (1904-3/25/68). Films: "Public Cowboy No. 1" 1937; "King of the Royal Mounted" 1940-serial (Sergeant); "Dangerous Venture" 1947 (Dr. Atwood); "Flashing Guns" 1947 (Longden); "Gun Talk" 1947 (Rod Jackson); "California Firebrand" 1948 (Lance Dawson); "Cowboy Cavalier" 1948; "Crossed Trails" 1948 (Hudson); "The Golden Stallion" 1949 (Jeff Middleton); "Powder River Rustlers" 1949 (Devereaux); "Trail's End" 1949 (Porter); "The Arizona Cowboy" 1950 (Radio Announcer); "North of the Great Divide" 1950 (Sgt. Douglas); "Rustlers on Horseback" 1950 (Jordan); "South Pacific Trail" 1952 (Rodney Brewster); "City of Badmen" 1953 (William Brady). ¶TV: *The Cisco Kid*—"Cattle Rustling" 2-3-51, "Medicine Flats" 3-10-51; *The Roy Rogers Show*—"Jailbreak" 12-30-51, "The Minister's Son" 3-23-52; *Wild Bill Hickok*—"Prairie Flats Land Swindle" 5-6-52; *The Lone Ranger*—"Through the Wall" 10-9-52, "Stage for Mademoiselle" 3-12-53; *The Range Rider*—"Hidden Gold" 10-25-52; *Wyatt Earp*—"The Pinkertons" 3-20-56, "Remittance Man" 11-4-58 (George Cantwell); *My Friend Flicka*—"The Recluse" 5-25-56; *Sheriff of Cochise*—"Triangle" 2-22-57 (Mr. Landry).

Evans, Evan (1936-). TV: *Gunsmoke*—"Harper's Blood" 10-21-61 (Jenny); *Wagon Train*—"The Hollister John Garrison Story" 2-6-63 (Melody Drake); *The Virginian*—"Strangers at Sundown" 4-3-63 (Phyllis Carter); *Death Valley Days*—"Thar She Blows" 10-6-63; *Redigo*—"Man in a Blackout" 11-5-63 (Hope).

Evans, Frank (1889-1951). Films: "High Pockets" 1919 (Bull Bellows).

Evans, Gene (1922-). Films: "Under Colorado Skies" 1947 (Red); "Dallas" 1950 (Drunk); "Wyoming Mail" 1950 (Shep); "Sugarfoot" 1951 (Billings); "Wyoming Renegades" 1955 (Butch Cassidy); "The Bravados" 1958 (Butler); "Money, Women and Guns" 1958 (Sheriff Crowley); "The Hangman" 1959 (Big Murph); "Gold of the Seven Saints" 1961 (McCracken); "Apache Uprising" 1966 (Jess Cooney); "Nevada Smith" 1966 (Sam Sand); "Waco" 1966 (Deputy Sheriff O'Neill); "The War Wagon" 1967 (Hoag); "Support Your Local Sheriff" 1969 (Tom Danby); "The Ballad of Cable Hogue" 1970 (Clete); "The Intruders" TVM-1970 (Cole Younger); "There Was a Crooked Man" 1970 (Col. Wolff); "Support Your Local Gunfighter" 1971 (Butcher); "Bounty Man" TVM-1972 (Tom Brady); "A Knife for the Ladies" 1973 (Hooker); "Pat Garrett and Billy the Kid" 1973 (Mr. Horrell); "Shootout in a One-Dog Town" TVM-1974 (Gabe); "Sidekicks" TVM-1974 (Sam); "The Macahans" TVM-1976 (Dutton); "Kate Bliss and the Ticker Tape Kid" TVM-1978 (Fred Williker); "The Sacketts" TVM-1979 (Benson Bigelow); "Wild Times" TVM-1980 (Celetus Hatch); "California Gold Rush" TVM-1981 (Sam Brannan); "The Shadow Riders" TVM-1982 (Holiday Hammond); "The Alamo: 13 Days to Glory" TVM-1987 (McGregory); "Once Upon a Texas Train" TVM-1988 (Fargo). ¶TV: *The Lone Ranger*—"Devil's Pass" 5-25-50, "The Star Witness" 8-17-50, "Behind the Law" 2-1-51; *My Friend Flicka*—Regular 1955-56 (Rob McLaughlin); *The Restless Gun*—"The Coward" 1-6-58 (Will Fetter); *Wagon Train*—"The Sarah Drummond Story" 4-2-58 (Jeb Drummond), "The Duncan McIvor Story" 3-9-64 (Sgt. Jake Orly); *Yancy Derringer*—"The Saga of Lonesome Jackson" 11-27-58 (Jackson); *Rawhide*—"Incident at the Buffalo Smokehouse" 10-30-59 (Wes Thomas), "Incident on the Road Back" 2-24-61 (Sheriff Tom Wilson), "Incident of the Prodigal Son" 10-19-62 (Sam Hargis), "Incident at El Crucero" 10-10-63 (Gus Cornelius), "Incident at Gila Flats" 1-30-64 (Sergeant Pike), "Moment in the Sun" 1-29-65 (Marshal Royal Shaw); *Johnny Ringo*—"Die Twice" 1-21-60 (Boone Hackett); *Bonanza*—"The Fear Merchants" 1-30-60 (Andrew Fulmer), "Journey Remembered" 11-

63 (Lucas), "The Trouble with Trouble" 10-25-70 (Montana Perkins); *Wichita Town*—"The Frontiersman" 3-2-60 (Otis Stockett); *Riverboat*—"The Quota" 11-28-60 (Sgt. Dan Phillips); *The Outlaws*—"The Quiet Killer" 12-29-60 (Tom Doan); *Gunslinger*—"The Recruit" 3-23-61 (Sergeant Croft); *The Virginian*—"The Accomplice" 12-9-62 (Luke Donaldson), "Trail to Ashley Mountain" 11-2-66 (Blanchard); *Gunsmoke*—"Extradition" 12-7-63 & 12-14-63 (Charlie Hacker), "A Hat" 10-16-67 (Clint Sorils), "The First People" 2-19-61 (Thomas Evans), "Snow Train" 10-19-70 & 10-26-70 (Billy), "Phoenix" 9-20-71 (Jesse Hume), "Tatum" 11-13-72 (Bodie Tatum), "The Iron Blood of Courage" 2-18-74 (Shaw Anderson), "Thirty a Month a Found" 10-7-74 (Will Parmalee); *Temple Houston*—"Find Angel Chavez" 9-26-63 (Sam Clanton); *Death Valley Days*—"Sixty-Seven Miles of Gold" 2-2-64 (Winfield Stratton); *Daniel Boone*—"The First Stone" 1-28-65 (Joshua Craig), "The Man" 10-16-69 (Stark); *Branded*—"The Bounty" 2-21-65 (Matthew Paxton); *Iron Horse*—"Pride at the Bottom of the Barrel" 10-10-66 (Sergeant Stoddard); *Cimarron Strip*—"The Battle of Blood Stone" 10-12-67 (Wildcat Gallagher); *The Legend of Jesse James*—"Vendetta" 10-25-67 (Jake Burnett); *Custer*—"Breakout" 11-1-67 (Deedricks); *Here Come the Brides*—"Two Worlds" 2-20-70 (Jacob); *The Men from Shiloh*—"With Love, Bullets, and Valentines" 10-7-70 (Harv Plimpton); *Nichols*—"Deer Crossing" 10-21-71 (Durand); *Alias Smith and Jones*—"The Man Who Corrupted Hadleyburg" 1-27-72 (Phillips); *Dirty Sally*—"The Old Soldier" 1-25-74 (Sam Concannon).

Evans, Herbert (1882-2/10/52). Films: "The Squaw Man" 1931 (Conductor); "Secrets" 1933 (Lord Hurley); "Susannah of the Mounties" 1939 (Doctor).

Evans, Jack (1893-3/14/50). Films: "Border Law" 1931; "Cornered" 1932; "Fighting Cowboy" 1933 (Buck); "The Law of the Wild" 1934-serial; "Lightning Range" 1934 (Jack Knife); "Rawhide Mail" 1934; "Rawhide Romance" 1934 (Butch); "Wheels of Destiny" 1934; "Born to Battle" 1935; "Cheyenne Tornado" 1935; "Coyote Trails" 1935; "The Dawn Rider" 1935 (Man at Bar); "Law Beyond the Range" 1935 (Cowboy); "Law of the 45's" 1935 (Henchman); "The Pecos Kid" 1935 (Townsman); "Rio Rattler" 1935; "Rough Riding Ranger" 1935; "The Silver

Bullet" 1935; "Skull and Crown" 1935; "Square Shooter" 1935; "Tracy Rides" 1935 (Outlaw); "Aces and Eights" 1936; "Border Caballero" 1936; "Cavalcade of the West" 1936 (Outlaw); "Everyman's Law" 1936 (Saloon Bit); "Fast Bullets" 1936; "Frontier Justice" 1936 (Henchman); "Guns and Guitars" 1936; "Lightning Bill Carson" 1936; "The Lion's Den" 1936 (Henchman); "The Mysterious Avenger" 1936 (Rustler); "Ridin' On" 1936; "The Riding Avenger" 1936 (Henchman); "Roarin' Guns" 1936; "Romance Rides the Range" 1936 (Buck); "Valley of the Lawless" 1936 (Spectator); "The Fighting Deputy" 1937 (Shorty); "The Idaho Kid" 1937; "Left-Handed Law" 1937; "Moonlight on the Range" 1937; "Range Defenders" 1937; "Ranger Courage" 1937; "The Roaming Cowboy" 1937; "Sing, Cowboy, Sing" 1937; "Two-Fisted Sheriff" 1937; "Valley of Terror" 1937; "Yodelin' Kid from Pine Ridge" 1937; "Border Wolves" 1938; "Heroes of the Alamo" 1938; "Six Shootin' Sheriff" 1938; "Riders from Nowhere" 1940; "A Tornado in the Saddle" 1942; "Frontier Revenge" 1948 (Man in Saloon).

Evans, Jacqueline (1915-6/22/89). Films: "Daniel Boone, Trail Blazer" 1957 (Rebecca Boone); "The Bravados" 1958; "The Singer Not the Song" 1961-Brit. (Dona Marian). ¶TV: *Daniel Boone*—"The High Cumberland" 4-14-66 & 4-21-66 (Martha).

Evans, Joan (1934-). Films: "Column South" 1953 (March Whitlock); "The Outcast" 1954 (Judy Polsen); "No Name on the Bullet" 1959 (Ann). ¶TV: *Cheyenne*—"The Angry Sky" 6-17-58 (Lilac); *Wagon Train*—"The Duke LeMay Story" 4-29-59 (Sarah); *Zorro*—"Invitation to Death" 5-21-59 (Leonar), "The Captain Regrets" 5-28-59 (Leonar), "Masquerade for Murder" 6-4-59 (Leonar), "Long Live the Governor" 6-11-59 (Leonar); *The Rebel*—"The Waiting" 10-9-60 (Cassie); *The Outlaws*—"The Daltons Must Die" 1-26-61 & 2-2-61 (Molly Moore); *Tales of Wells Fargo*—"Stage from Yuma" 3-20-61 (Kathy Davidson); *The Tall Man*—"The Female Artillery" 9-30-61 (Lou Belle Martin); *Laramie*—"The Killer Legend" 12-12-61 (Julie Wade).

Evans, Linda (1943-). Films: "Female Artillery" TVM-1973 (Charlotte Paxton); "Nakia" TVM-1974 (Samantha Lowell); "Standing Tall" TVM-1978 (Jill Shasta); "Tom Horn" 1980 (Glendolene Kimmel); "The

Gambler, Part II—The Adventure Continues" TVM-1983 (Kate Muldoon); "The Gambler Returns: The Luck of the Draw" TVM-1991 (Kate Muldoon). ¶TV: *Wagon Train*—"Herman" 2-14-65 (Martha Temple); *The Big Valley*—Regular 1965-69 (Audra Barkley).

Evans, Maurice (1901-3/12/89). TV: *Daniel Boone*—"Beaumarchais" 10-12-67 (Pierre Augustin Caron de Beaumarchais); *The Big Valley*—"Danger Road" 4-21-69 (Edward Hewitt).

Evans, Michael. Films: "The Plainsman" 1966 (Estrick). ¶TV: *Laredo*—"Any Way the Wind Blows" 10-28-66 (Edmond Tolliver); *Pistols 'n' Petticoats*—3-4-67 (Col. Randolph Rodney).

Evans, Muriel. Films: "The New Frontier" 1935 (Hanna Lewis); "The Roaring West" 1935-serial (Mary Parker); "The Throwback" 1935 (Muriel Fergus); "Boss Rider of Gun Creek" 1936 (Starr Landerson); "Call of the Prairie" 1936 (Linda Mc-Henry); "King of the Pecos" 1936 (Belle Jackson); "Silver Spurs" 1936 (Janet Allison); "Three on the Trail" 1936 (Mary Stevens); "Boss of Lonely Valley" 1937 (Retta Lowrey); "Law for Tombstone" 1937 (Nellie Gray); "Rustler's Valley" 1937 (Agnes Glenn); "Smoke Tree Range" 1937 (Nan Page); "Westbound Stage" 1939 (Jean Hale); "Roll, Wagons, Roll" 1940 (Ruth).

Evans, Nancy (1910-7/29/63). Films: "The Desperados Are in Town" 1956 (Mrs. Rutherford); "The Peacemaker" 1956 (Miss Smith).

Evans, Rex (1903-4/3/69). Films: "Out West with the Peppers" 1940 (Martin).

Evans, Richard (1935-). Films: "Macho Callahan" 1970 (Mulvey); "Dirty Little Billy" 1972 (Goldie Evans); "Honky Tonk" TVM-1974. ¶TV: *Tales of Wells Fargo*—"White Indian" 9-22-58 (Boy); *Wagon Train*—"The Bije Wilcox Story" 11-19-58 (1st Son); *The Rebel*—"The Scavengers" 11-8-59 (Ezel), "In Memory of a Son" 5-8-60 (Tony); *Bronco*—"The Masquerade" 1-26-60 (Tim Willis); *Gunsmoke*—"Moo Moo Raid" 2-13-60 (Pete), "The Storm" 9-25-65 (Ab Benteen), "Death Watch" 1-8-66 (Austin Boyle), "The Prodigal" 9-25-67 (William Cole); *The Alaskans*—"A Barrel of Gold" 4-3-60 (Roy Stevenson); *The Rifleman*—"Sins of the Father" 4-19-60 (Shep Coleman), "A Young Man's Fancy" 2-5-62 (Bruce Henry); *Lawman*—"The Town Boys" 9-18-60 (Pete Goff),

"Sunday" 4-15-62 (Billy Deal); *Laramie*—"Two for the Gallows" 4-11-61 (Len); *Cheyenne*—"The Young Fugitives" 10-23-61 (Gilby); *Stoney Burke*—"Image of Glory" 2-4-63 (Jess Hagen); *Empire*—"The Tiger Inside" 2-12-63 (Monte Clifford); *Temple Houston*—"The Twisted Rope" 9-19-63 (Chevenix Brother); *Redigo*—"The Blooded Bull" 10-1-63 (David Porter); *Bonanza*—"The Other Son" 10-3-65 (Ellis Watson), "Dark Enough to See the Stars" 3-12-67 (Billy), "What Are Pardners For?" 4-12-70 (John); *Shane*—"An Echo of Anger" 10-1-66 (J.D.); *Iron Horse*—"Town Full of Fear" 12-5-66 (Will Bemis); *The Big Valley*—"Shadow of a Giant" 1-29-68 (Seth Campbell, Jr.); *The High Chaparral*—"The Hair Hunter" 3-10-68 (Chad Stoner); *The Guns of Will Sonnett*—"Home Free" 11-22-68 (Ben Harper); *Lancer*—"Zee" 9-30-69 (Olin); *How the West Was Won*—"The Slavers" 4-23-79 (Druey).

Evans, Robert (1930-). Films: "The Fiend Who Walked the West" 1958 (Felix Griffin).

Evans, Roy (1930-). TV: *Sheriff of Cochise*—"Approach with Caution" 4-19-57 (Deputy Carson).

Evans, Terrence. Films: "Pale Rider" 1985 (Jake Henderson); "Dream West" TVM-1986 (Farmer); "The Gambler, Part III—The Legend Continues" TVM-1987. ¶TV: *Paradise*—"The Traveler" 2-2-89 (Richie Rolleri).

Evanson, Edith (-11/29/80). Films: "Rawhide" 1951 (Mrs. Hickman); "The Redhead and the Cowboy" 1951 (Mrs. Barrett); "Shane" 1953 (Mrs. Shipstead); "The Stranger Wore a Gun" 1953; "The Silver Star" 1955 (Mrs. Dowdy); "Drango" 1957 (Mrs. Blackford); "The Quiet Gun" 1957 (Mrs. Merric). ¶TV: *Wagon Train*—"The Bill Tawnee Story" 2-12-58 (Mrs. Kirk), "The Larry Hanify Story" 1-27-60, "The Candy O'Hara Story" 12-7-60; *The Restless Gun*—"Pressing Engagement" 2-24-58 (Aunt Minnie Rockwood), "Jebediah Bonner" 9-22-58 (Mrs. Ludlow), "The Sweet Sisters" 3-23-59 (Elizabeth Sweet); *Wyatt Earp*—"The Truth About Rawhide Geraghty" 2-17-59 (Mrs. Geraghty); *Colt .45*—"Night of Decision" 6-28-59 (Ma Thorpe); *Tales of Wells Fargo*—"Moment of Glory" 5-1-61 (Grandma Bridger); *Gunsmoke*—"Father Love" 3-14-64 (Nell).

Evelyn, Judith (1913-5/7/67). Films: "Giant" 1956 (Mrs. Horace Lynnton). ¶TV: *Tales of Wells Fargo*—"Double Reverse" 10-19-59 (Ann

Rawlins), "Who Lives by the Gun" 3-24-62 (Emily Callan).

Everett, Chad (1937-). Films: "The Last Challenge" 1967 (Lot McGuire); "Return of the Gunfighter" TVM-1967 (Lee Sutton). ¶TV: *Bronco*—"Apache Treasure" 11-7-60 (Lieutenant Finley), "Ride the Whirlwind" 1-15-62 (Johnny); *Maverick*—"The Devil's Necklace" 4-16-61 & 4-23-61 (Lieutenant Gregg); *Lawman*—"The Son" 10-8-61 (Cole Herod); *Cheyenne*—"A Man Called Ragan" 4-23-62 (Del Stark); *The Dakotas*—Regular 1963 (Deputy Del Stark); *Redigo*—"Papa-San" 11-12-63 (Chick); *Branded*—"The First Kill" 4-4-65 (Adam Manning/Tad Manning); *Centennial*—Regular 1978-79 (Capt. Maxwell Mercy).

Evers, Ann (-6/4/87). Films: "Wells Fargo" 1937; "Frontier Town" 1938 (Gail Hawthorne); "Riders of the Black Hills" 1938 (Joyce Garth).

Evers, Jason (1922-). Films: "A Man Called Gannon" 1969 (Mills). ¶TV: *Wrangler*—Regular 1960 (Pitcairn); *Cheyenne*—"Road to Three Graves" 10-31-60 (Carl Tower), "Retaliation" 11-13-61 (Clark); *Bonanza*—"The Duke" 3-11-61 (Lambert), "Journey to Terro" 2-5-67 (Tom); *Branded*—"The Test" 2-7-65 (Father Durant); *The Rebel*—"Miz Purdy" 4-2-61 (George Tess); *Laramie*—"The Debt" 4-18-61 (Hanson), "The Mountain Men" 10-17-61 (Carl Sanford), "Trial by Fire" 4-10-62 (Hank); *Lawman*—"Blind Hate" 5-14-61 (Shag Warner); *Gunsmoke*—"Reprisal" 3-10-62 (Ben Harden), "Collie's Free" 10-20-62 (Collie Patten), "Innocence" 12-14-62 (Charlie Ross); *Tales of Wells Fargo*—"Remember the Yazoo" 4-14-62 (Tom Kelly); *Frontier Circus*—"The Good Fight" 4-19-62 (Judd Halleck); *Death Valley Days*—"Birthright" 5-30-65 (Dan Hardy); *The Big Valley*—"The Odyssey of Jubal Tanner" 10-13-65 (Colter), "Deathnown" 10-28-68 (George Akers); *The Virginian*—"An Echo of Thunder" 10-5-66 (Sheriff Lundee); *The Road West*—"The Insider" 2-13-67 (Divvy Peters); *The Guns of Will Sonnett*—Regular 1967-69 (Jim Sonnett); *Wild Wild West*—"The Night of the Running Death" 12-15-67 (Christopher Kohner), "The Night of the Kraken" 11-1-68 (Commander Beach); *Hec Ramsey*—"Scar Tissue" 3-10-74 (Peter Jonas).

Evers, King. Films: "The Half-Breed" 1922 (Dick Kennion).

Everson, Corey. TV: *Adventures of Brisco County, Jr.*—"No Man's Land" 9-10-93 (Katrina Schwenke), "Iron Horses" 11-19-93 (Katrina Schwenke).

Everton, Paul (1869-2/26/48). Films: "Gun Law" 1938 (Mayor Blaine); "The Law Comes to Texas" 1939 (Governor); "Stand Up and Fight" 1939 (Allan); "Union Pacific" 1939 (Rev. Dr. Tadd); "Prairie Law" 1940 (Judge Curry); "Triple Justice" 1940 (Tatum).

Ewell, Tom (1909-9/12/94). Films: "Desert Bandit" 1941 (Ordway); "Lost in Alaska" 1952 (Nugget Joe McDermott). ¶TV: *Wagon Train*—"The Story of Hector Heatherington" 12-20-64 (Hector Heatherington); *The Men from Shiloh*—"With Love, Bullets, and Valentines" 10-7-70 (Hoy Valentine); *Alias Smith and Jones*—"The Root of It All" 4-1-71 (Deputy Treadwell); *Best of the West*—Regular 1981-82 (Doc Jerome Kullens).

Ewing, Diana. Films: "A Knife for the Ladies" 1973 (Jenny). TV: *The Big Valley*—"Town of No Exit" 4-7-69 (Maggie); *Gunsmoke*—"MacGraw" 12-8-69 (Ella Horton); *Lancer*—"Splinter Group" 3-3-70 (Sarah).

Ewing, Roger (1942-). Films: "Smith" 1969 (Donald Maxwell). TV: *Gunsmoke*—"Song for Dying" 2-13-65 (Ben Lukens), Regular 1965-67 (Thad Greenwood); *Rawhide*—"The Calf Women" 4-30-65 (Billy Wallace).

Eyer, Richard (1945-). Films: "Canyon River" 1956 (Chuck Hale); "Friendly Persuasion" 1956 (Little Jess); "Fort Dobbs" 1958 (Chad Gray). ¶TV: *The Roy Rogers Show*—"Huntin' for Trouble" 10-5-52 (Bobby Sharon); *Wagon Train*—"The Vincent Eaglewood Story" 4-15-59 (Elwood Hennepin), "The Marie Brant Story" 1-20-60 (Matthew); *Rawhide*—"Incident of the Roman Candles" 7-10-59 (Davey Colby); *Wanted—Dead or Alive*—"Montana Kid" 9-5-59 (the Montana Kid); *Gunsmoke*—"The Boots" 11-14-59 (Tommy); *Man from Blackhawk*—"The Montreal Story" 5-13-60 (Davey); *Stagecoach West*—Regular 1960-61 (Davey Kane); *Stoney Burke*—"The Test" 5-13-63 (Davey).

Eythe, William (1918-1/26/57). Films: "The Ox-Bow Incident" 1943 (Gerald Tetley).

Eyton, Bessie. Films: "The Chief's Daughter" 1911; "In the Shadow of the Pines" 1911; "McKee Rankin's '49" 1911; "Sheriff of Tuolumne" 1911; "The End of the Romance" 1912; "The God of Gold" 1912; "John Colter's Escape" 1912; "The Last of Her Tribe" 1912; "The Legend of the Lost Arrow" 1912; "Opitsah" 1912; "The Peacemaker" 1912; "The Shrinking Rawhide" 1912; "In the Long Ago" 1913; "The Noisy Six" 1913; "The Prisoner of Cabanas" 1913; "Vengeance Is Mine" 1913; "A Wild Ride" 1913; "Chip of the Flying U" 1914; "Etienne of the Glad Heart" 1914; "The Fifty Man" 1914; "In Defiance of the Law" 1914; "In the Days of the Thundering Herd" 1914 (Sally Madison); "Me an' Bill" 1914; "Shotgun Jones" 1914; "The Spoilers" 1914 (Helen Chester); "The Test" 1914; "When the West Was Young" 1914; "The Wilderness Mail" 1914; "An Arizona Wooing" 1915; "The Golden Spurs" 1915; "The Regeneration of Jim Halsey" 1916; "Twisted Trails" 1916; "The Heart of Texas Ryan" 1917 (Texas Ryan).

Fabares, Shelley (1944-). TV: *Annie Oakley*—Semi-Regular 1954-57 (Trudy); *Daniel Boone*—"A Touch of Charity" 2-27-69 (Charity Brown); *Lancer*—"Juniper's Camp" 3-11-69 (Melissa Harper).

Fabian (Fabian Forte) (1942-). Films: "North to Alaska" 1960 (Billy Pratt). ¶TV: *The Virginian*—"Say Goodbye to All That" 1-23-63 (Martin Belden), "Two Men Named Laredo" 1-6-65 (Eddie Laredo), "Outcast" 10-26-66 (Charley Ryan); *Wagon Train*—"The Molly Kincaid Story" 9-16-63 (Rome Wolfson); *Daniel Boone*—"The First Beau" 12-9-65 (David Ellis).

Fabian, Francoise (1932-). Films: "Drop Them Or I'll Shoot" 1969-Fr./Ger./Span.

Fabiani, Joel. Films: "The New Daughters of Joshua Cabe" TVM-1976 (Matt Cobley).

Fabray, Nanette (1920-). Films: "The Cockeyed Cowboys of Calico County" 1970 (Sadie). ¶TV: *Laramie*—"Glory Road" 9-22-59.

Fabregas, Manolo. Films: "Two Mules for Sister Sara" 1970 (Col. Beltran).

Fabrizi, Valeria. Films: "Ringo and His Golden Pistol" 1966-Ital.; "Four Gunmen of the Holy Trinity" 1971-Ital.

Fadden, Tom (1895-4/14/80). Films: "Destry Rides Again" 1939 (Lem Claggett); (Trooper); "The Man from Dakota" 1940 (Driver); "Winners of the West" 1940-serial (Tex Houston); "The Shepherd of the Hills" 1941 (Jim Lane); "Lone Star Ranger" 1942 (Sam); "Sundown Jim" 1942 (Stage Coach Driver); "Frontier Badman" 1943 (Thompson); "A Lady

Takes a Chance" 1943 (Mullen); "Royal Mounted Rides Again" 1945-serial (Lode MacKenzie); "Trail to Vengeance" 1945 (Horace Glumm); "Cheyenne" 1947 (Charlie); "Pursued" 1947; "The Dude Goes West" 1948 (J.J. Jines); "Bad Men of Tombstone" 1949 "Dallas" 1950 (Mountaineer); "Singing Guns" 1950 (Express Agent); "Drums in the Deep South" 1951 (Purdy); "Vengeance Valley" 1951 (Obie Rune); "The Lawless Breed" 1952 (Chick Noonan); "Kansas Pacific" 1953 (Gustavson); "The Tall Men" 1955 (Stable Owner); "The Second Time Around" 1961 (Feed Store Owner); "Dirty Dingus Magee" 1970. ¶TV: *20th Century Fox Hour*—"Broken Arrow" 5-2-56 (Duffield); *Broken Arrow*—Regular 1956-58 (Duffield), "Blood Brothers" 5-13-58 (Duffield); *Cimarron City*—"I, the People" 10-11-58 (Silas Perry); *Maverick*—"Royal Four-Flush" 9-20-59 (Silvan); *The Texan*—"The Taming of Rio Nada" 1-11-60 (Ezekiel Waters), "Sixgun Street" 1-18-60 (Ezekiel Waters), "The Terrified Town" 1-25-60 (Ezekiel Waters); *Rawhide*—"Incident of the Stargazer" 4-1-60; *Riverboat*—"Zigzag" 12-26-60 (Lear); *Laramie*—"The Fatal Step" 10-24-61; *The Tall Man*—"The Impatient Brides" 2-3-62 (Jud); *The Slowest Gun in the West* 7-29-63 (Jed Slocum); *The Legend of Jesse James*—"Put Me in Touch with Jesse" 9-27-65 (the Conductor); *The Big Valley*—"The Invaders" 12-29-65 (Cleek); *Laredo*—"Limit of the Law Larkin" 1-27-66 (Fish Simpson); *Bonanza*—"Check Rein" 12-3-67 (Cowboy); *Daniel Boone*—"Be Thankful for the Fickleness of Women" 9-19-68 (Sam Cooley); *The Guns of Will Sonnett*—"A Difference of Opinion" 11-15-68; *Lancer*—"The Heart of Pony Alice" 12-17-68 (Ollice Hummer); *Gunsmoke*—"Sam McTavish, M.D." 10-5-70 (Harley).

Fafara, Tiger. TV: *My Friend Flicka*—"Mister Goblin" 3-23-56, "The Recluse" 5-25-56; *The Adventures of Rin Tin Tin*—"Witch of the Woods" 9-14-56 (Alfred), "Rodeo Clown" 11-8-57; *Wyatt Earp*—"The Good and Perfect Gift" 12-3-57 (Benny Burkett).

Fahey, Jeff. Films: "Silverado" 1985 (Tyree); "Wyatt Earp" 1994 (Ike Clanton).

Fahey, Myrna (1939-5/6/73). Films: "Face of a Fugitive" 1959 (Janet). ¶TV: *Zorro*—"Shadow of Doubt" 1-9-58 (Maria Crespo), "Garcia Stands Accused" 1-16-58 (Maria Crespo), "Slaves of the Eagle" 1-23-58 (Maria Crespo), "The Man with

the Whip" 5-8-58 (Maria), "The Cross of the Andes" 5-15-58 (Maria); *Gunsmoke*—"Innocent Broad" 4-26-58 (Linda Bell); *Maverick*—"Duel at Sundown" 2-1-59 (Susie), "A Flock of Trouble" 2-14-60 (Dee Cooper), "Mano Nera" 10-23-60 (Carla Marchese); *Colt .45*—"The Escape" 4-5-59 (Sue); *Overland Trail*—"Vigilantes of Montana" 4-3-60 (Harriet Plummer); *The Alaskans*—"Calico" 5-22-60 (Calico); *Bonanza*—"Breed of Violence" 11-5-60 (Dolly Kincaid); *Wagon Train*—"The Jane Hawkins Story" 11-30-60 (Jane Hawkins), "The Melanie Craig Story" 2-17-64 (Melanie Craig); *Laramie*—"Lost Allegiance" 10-30-62 (Sharon Helford); *Daniel Boone*—"The Price of Friendship" 2-18-65 (Sara); *Laredo*—"Three's Company" 10-14-65 (Emily Henderson); *Rango*—"The Not So Great Train Robbery" 3-17-67 (Kit Clanton).

Fahrney, Milton (1871-3/27/41). Films: "Not Guilty for Runnin'" 1924 (Tod Randall); "Yankee Speed" 1924 (Jose T. Vegas); "Chasing Trouble" 1926 (Sheriff).

Fain, Matty. Films: "Boss of Lonely Valley" 1937; "Left-Handed Law" 1937 (One-Shot Brady).

Fair, Elinor (1903-4/26/57). Films: "The End of the Game" 1919 (Mona); "The Able-Minded Lady" 1922 (Daphne Meadows); "Big Stakes" 1922 (Senorita Mercedes Aloyez); "The Eagle's Feather" 1923 (Martha); "The Mysterious Witness" 1923 (Ruth Garland); "Gold and the Girl" 1925 (Ann Conald); "The Timber Wolf" 1925 (Reenee Brooks); "Jim the Conqueror" 1927 (Polly Graydon); "Sin Town" 1929 (Mary Barton); "Forty-Five Calibre Echo" 1932; "The Night Rider" 1932 (Barbara Rogers).

Fair, Jody. Films: *Bonanza*—"The Gunmen" 1-23-60; *Riverboat*—"Trunk Full of Dreams" 10-31-60 (Birdie Belle); *Wide Country*—"Don't Cry for Johnny Devlin" 1-24-63 (Maureen).

Fairbanks, Douglas (1883-12/12/39). Films: "The Lamb" 1915 (Gerlad); "The Good Bad Man" 1916 (Passin' Through); "The Half Breed" 1916 (Lo Dorman); "The Man from Painted Post" 1917 (Fancy Jim Sherwood); "A Modern Musketeer" 1917 (Ned Thacker); "Wild and Woolly" 1917 (Jeff HIllington); "Arizona" 1918 (Lt. Denton); "Headin' South" 1918 (Headin' South); "The Knickerbocker Buckaroo" 1919 (Teddy Drake); "Mark of Zorro" 1920 (Zorro/Don Diego Vega); "The Mol-

lycoddle" 1920 (Richard Marshall); "Don Q, Son of Zorro" 1925 (Don Cesar de Vega/Zorro).

Fairbanks, Jr., Douglas (1909-). Films: "Wild Horse Mesa" 1925 (Chess Weymer); "A Texas Steer" 1927 (Farleigh Bright).

Fairbanks, William (1894-4/1/45). Films: "Broadway Buckaroo" 1921; "Montana Bill" 1921; "A Western Adventurer" 1921; "The Clean Up" 1922; "Hell's Borer" 1922; "Peaceful Peters" 1922 (Peaceful Peters); "The Sheriff of Sun-Dog" 1922 (Silent Davidson); "A Western Demon" 1922 (Ned Underwood); "The Devil's Dooryard" 1923 (Paul Stevens); "The Law Rustlers" 1923 (Phil Stanley); "Spawn of the Desert" 1923 (Duke Steele); "Sun Dog Trails" 1923; "Border Women" 1924 (Big Boy Merritt); "Call of the Mate" 1924; "The Cowboy and the Flapper" 1924 (Dan Patterson); "Do It Now" 1924; "Down by the Rio Grande" 1924; "Her Man" 1924; "The Man from God's Country" 1924 (Bill Holliday); "Marry in Haste" 1924 (Wayne Sturgis); "That Wild West" 1924; "Fighting Bill" 1927; "Spoilers of the West" 1928 (the Girl's Brother); "The Vanishing West" 1928-serial; "Wyoming" 1928 (Buffalo Bill).

Fairchild, Margaret. Films: "Ulzana's Raid" 1972 (Mrs. Ginsford). ¶TV: *Kung Fu*—"The Soldier" 11-29-73 (Catherine Piper).

Fairchild, Morgan (1950-). Films: "Red Headed Stranger" 1987 (Raysha Shay). ¶TV: *Young Maverick*—"Makin' Tracks" 1-9-80 (Selene).

Faire, Helen Brown. Films: "Burning the Wind" 1928 (Maria Valdes).

Faire, Virginia Browne (1904-6/30/80). Films: "Big Stakes" 1920; "The Forest Runners" 1920; "The Girl and the Law" 1920; "Masked" 1920; "Ransom" 1920; "Runnin' Straight" 1920; "A Son of the North" 1920; "The Timber Wolf" 1920; "Under Northern Lights" 1920 (Suzanne Foucharde); "When the Devil Laughed" 1920; "Fightin' Mad" 1921 (Peggy Hughes); "Shadows of the North" 1923 (Beatrice Neilson); "The Lightning Rider" 1924 (Patricia Alvarez); "Romance Ranch" 1924 (Carmen Hendley); "The Calgary Stampede" 1925 (Marie LaFarge); "Chip of the Flying U" 1926 (Dr. Della Whitmore); "Desert Valley" 1926 (Mildred Dean); "Wings of the Storm" 1926 (Anita Baker); "The Wolf Hunters" 1926; "The Devil's Masterpiece" 1927; "Gun Gospel"

1927 (Mary Carrol); "Tracked by the Police" 1927 (Marcella Bradley); "The Canyon of Adventure" 1928 (Dolores Castanares); "Danger Patrol" 1928 (Celeste Gambier); "Untamed Justice" 1929 (Louise Hill); "Breed of the West" 1930 (Betty Sterner); "The Lonesome Tail" 1930 (Martha); "Trails of Danger" 1930 (Mary Martin); "Alias the Bad Man" 1931 (Mary Warner); "Hell's Valley" 1931 (Rosita Fernando); "Secret Menace" 1931; "The Sign of the Wolf" 1931-serial (Ruth Farnum); "Tex Takes a Holiday" 1932 (Dolores); "Rainbow Riders" 1934; "West of the Divide" 1934 (Fay Winters); "Tracy Rides" 1935 (Molly Hampton).

Fairfax, James (1897-5/8/61). Films: "Mrs. Mike" 1949 (Danny Hawkins); "The Battles of Chief Pontiac" 1952 (Sentry). ¶TV: *Jim Bowie*—"Monsieur Francois" 12-28-56 (Farley), "The Quarantine" 10-11-57 (Three Fingers Jacques); *Tales of Wells Fargo*—"The Pickpocket" 4-28-58 (Homer Pittman); *Wagon Train*—"The Albert Farnsworth Story" 10-12-60 (Jeremy Oakes).

Faison, Frankie. Films: "Sommersby" 1993 (Joseph).

Faith, Dolores. TV: *Have Gun Will Travel*—"Caravan" 2-23-63 (Skiri).

Fajardo, Eduardo (1918-). Films: "Charge of the Seventh Cavalry" 1964-Ital./Span./Fr.; "Coffin for the Sheriff" 1965-Ital./Span. (Russell); "Adios Hombre" 1966-Ital./Span.; "Django" 1966-Ital./Span.; "Ringo's Big Night" 1966-Ital./Span. (Mayor Joseph Findley); "Time of Vultures" 1967-Ital. (Don Jaime); "All Out" 1968-Ital./Span.; "Death Knows No Time" 1968-Span./Ital.; "The Mercenary" 1968-Ital./Span. (Alfonso Garcia); "One Against One ... No Mercy" 1968-Span./Ital.; "Pistol for a Hundred Coffins" 1968-Ital./Span.; "Ringo: Face of Revenge" 1968-Ital./Span. (Davy); "Stranger in Paso Bravo" 1968-Ital.; "Gentleman Killer" 1969-Span./Ital.; "Killer Goodbye" 1969-Ital./Span.; "The Magnificent Bandits" 1969-Ital./Span. (Colonel Branco); "Shango" 1969-Ital. (the Major); "Apocalypse Joe" 1970-Ital./Span.; "Companeros" 1970-Ital./Span./Ger.; "Dead Men Ride" 1970-Ital./Span. (Redfield); "Sabata the Killer" 1970-Ital./Span. (Garfield); "Bad Man's River" 1971-Span./Ital./Fr. (Duarte); "Sting of the West" 1972-Ital.; "Three Musketeers of the West" 1972-Ital.; "Bandera Bandits" 1973-Ital./Span./Ger.; "What Am I Doing in the Middle of the Revolution?" 1973-Ital.; "Don't Turn the Other Cheek" 1974-Ital./Ger./Span.; "Tequila" 1974-Ital./Span. (Zenfield).

Falana, Lola (1942-). Films: "Black Tigress" 1967-Ital.

Falk, Peter (1927-). TV: *Have Gun Will Travel*—"The Poker Friend" 11-12-60 (Waller); *Wagon Train*—"The Gus Morgan Story" 9-30-63 (Gus Morgan).

Falkenberg, Jinx (1919-). Films: "The Lone Ranger Rides Again" 1939-serial (Sue Dolan); "Song of the Buckaroo" 1939 (Evelyn).

Falkenberg, Kort. TV: *Dr. Quinn, Medicine Woman*—"A Cowboy's Lullaby" 2-20-93 (Eddy); *Adventures of Brisco County, Jr.*—"Senior Spirit" 10-15-93 (Old Man).

Fallon, Charles (1875-3/12/36). Films: "Ruggles of Red Gap" 1935 (Waiter in Paris Cafe).

Fancher, III, Hampton. TV: *Have Gun Will Travel*—"In an Evil Time" 9-13-58 (Brother), "The Unforgiven" 11-7-59 (Beauregard Crommer), "The Misguided Father" 2-27-60 (Keith Loring); *Black Saddle*—"Client: Meade" 1-17-59 (Orv Tibbett), "Client: Nelson" 5-2-59 (Deputy Simms); *The Rebel*—"Misfits" 11-29-59 (Bull); *Tate*—"Quiet After the Storm" 9-7-60 (Coley); *The Outlaws*—"Shorty" 11-3-60 (Mike Duane); *Gunsmoke*—"Old Fool" 12-24-60 (Dunc), "The Hunger" 11-17-62 (Clem Dorf), "Bank Baby" 3-20-65 (Milton Clum); *Cheyenne*—"Incident at Dawson Flats" 1-9-61 (Jasper Dawson); *Maverick*—"Last Stop: Olivion" 2-12-61 (Tate McKenna); *Lawman*—"Conditional Surrender" 5-28-61 (Lester Beason); *The Rifleman*—"The Decision" 11-6-61 (Corey Hazlett); *Rawhide*—"Incident of the Lost Woman" 11-2-62 (Billy Hobson), "Incident at Dead Horse" 4-16-64 & 4-23-64 (Jake Hammerklein); *Temple Houston*—"The Third Bullet" 10-24-63 (Jim Stocker); *Bonanza*—"A Dollar's Worth of Trouble" 5-15-66 (Craig Bonner); *The Road West*—"Piece of Tin" 10-31-66 (Gray Yeater); *The Monroes*—"Silent Night, Deathly Night" 11-23-66; *Daniel Boone*—"Fort West Point" 3-23-67 (Tad Arlen), "The Desperate Raid" 11-16-67 (Lieutenant Roland).

Fanning, Frank (1879-3/1/34). Films: "Thundering Hoofs" 1942 (Adams).

Fantasia, Franco. Films: "Three Swords of Zorro" 1963-Ital./Span.; "A Long Ride from Hell" 1968-Ital. (Roy); "Wrath of God" 1968-Ital./Span.; "Adios Cjamango" 1969-Ital./Span.; "Blood at Sundown" 1969-Ital./Span.; "Canadian Wilderness" 1969-Span./Ital.; "Hate Thy Neighbor" 1969-Ital.; "Adios, Sabata" 1970-Ital./Span. (Ocano); "The Bounty Hunters" 1970-Ital.; "I Am Sartana, Trade Your Guns for a Coffin" 1972-Ital.; "Son of Zorro" 1973-Ital./Span.; "Carambola" 1974-Ital.

Fantoni, Sergio (1930-). Films: "Bad Man's River" 1971-Span./Ital./Fr. (Fierro).

Farah, Jameel. *see* Farr, Jamie.

Farber, Arlene. TV: *Kung Fu*—"Night of the Owls, Day of the Doves" 2-14-74 (Faye).

Farentino, James (1938-). Films: "The Ride to Hangman's Tree" 1967 (Matt Stone). ¶TV: *Laredo*—"I See By Your Outfit" 9-23-65 (Paco Vargas); *The Road West*—"Reap the Whirlwind" 1-9-66 (Emmett Bethel); *The Virginian*—"The Wolves Up Front, the Jackals Behind" 3-23-66 (Frank Colby); *The Men from Shiloh*—"The Best Man" 9-23-70 (Pick Lexington).

Fargas, Frank. Films: "Django, Last Killer" 1967-Ital.; "Shadow of Sartana ... Shadow of Your Death" 1968-Ital. (Benny).

Farina, Dennis. Films: "Bonanza: Under Attack" TVM-1995 (Charley Siringo).

Farley, Albert. Films: "Kill or Be Killed" 1966-Ital.; "Dollar of Fire" 1967-Ital./Span. (Mayor Baker); "Seven Pistols for a Gringo" 1967-Ital./Span. (Torrence); "Five Dollars for Ringo" 1968-Ital./Span.; "Fighters from Ave Maria" 1970-Ital./Ger.; "Twenty Paces to Death" 1970-Ital./Span. (Kellaway); "White Apache" 1984-Ital./Span. (Redeath); "Scalps" 1986-Ital./Ger.

Farley, Dorothea "Dot" (1881-5/2/71). Films: "The Peril of the Plains" 1912; "The Lust of the Red Man" 1914; "The Toll of the War-Path" 1914; "The First Law of Nature" 1915; "The Mask of Lopez" 1923; "Border Intrigue" 1925 (Tough's Sister); "The Overland Stage" 1927 (Aunt Viney); "Code of the Scarlet" 1928 (Widow Malone); "Arizona Mahoney" 1936 (Woman at Circus); "Lawless Valley" 1938 (Anna Marsh); "Lawless Valley" 1938 (Anna); "The Stranger from Arizona" 1938 (Martha); "San Fernando Valley" 1944 (Hattie O'Toole).

Farley, James (1882-10/12/47). Films: "The Highway of Hope" 1917 (Missouri Joe); "Desert Law" 1918

(Deputy); "Nugget Nell" 1919 (1st Badman); "Rustling a Bride" 1919 (Sheridan); "The Challenge of the Law" 1920 (Pere DuBarre); "Bar Nothin'" 1921 (Bill Harliss); "The One-Man Trail" 1921; "Travelin' On" 1922 (Dandy Dan McGee); "When Danger Smiles" 1922 (Jacob Holnar); "Wild Bill Hickok" 1923 (Jack Mc-Queen); "A Son of His Father" 1925 (Indian Pete); "Courtin' Wildcats" 1929 (Doctor); "Lucky Larkin" 1930 (Martin Brierson); "Fighting Caravans" 1931 (Amos); "Three Rogues" 1931 (Marshal Dunn); "The Deadline" 1932 (Cassiday); "Texas Cyclone" 1932 (Webb Oliver); "Westward Ho" 1935 (Lafe Gordon); "Song of the Saddle" 1936 (Tom Coburn); "The California Mail" 1937 (Dan); "The Californian" 1937 (Sheriff Stanton); "Flaming Frontier" 1938-serial; "Gold Is Where You Find It" 1938 (Miner); "Union Pacific" 1939 (Irish Paddy); "Santa Fe Trail" 1940; "Sky Bandits" 1940 (Inspector Warner); "Trail of the Vigilantes" 1940 (Rancher); "Virginia City" 1940 (Southerner); "The Bandit Trail" 1941; "Rawhide Rangers" 1941 (Banker); "Riders of Death Valley" 1941-serial (Graham); "The Silver Bullet" 1942; "Frontier Law" 1943 (Bates); "Gentle Annie" 1944 (Conductor); "Marshal of Gunsmoke" 1944; "In Old New Mexico" 1945.

Farley, Morgan (1898-10/11/88). Films: "A Man from Wyoming" 1930 (Lt. Lee); "Barricade" 1950 (the Judge); "The Lady from Texas" 1951 (Lawyer Haddon); "High Noon" 1952 (Minister); "The Wild North" 1952 (Father Simon); "Orphan Train" TVM-1979 (McGarrity). ¶TV: *The Big Valley*—"Legend of a General" 9-19-66 & 9-26-66 (Morelos); *Wild Wild West*—"The Night of the Golden Cobra" 9-23-66 (Muhjaj, the Snake Charmer).

Farley, Patricia. Films: "Sunset Pass" 1933 (Grace); "Under the Tonto Rim" 1933 (Sally Mumford).

Farmer, Frances (1914-8/1/70). Films: "Rhythm on the Range" 1936 (Doris Halliday); "Badlands of Dakota" 1941 (Calamity Jane).

Farmer, Mimsy (1945-). TV: *Laredo*—"The Callico Kid" 1-6-66 (Lorrie Thatcher), "A Prince of a Ranger" 12-9-66 (Antonia).

Farmer, Richard. Films: "I Shot Billy the Kid" 1950 (McSween).

Farmer, Virginia (1898-5/19/88). Films: "Gauchos of El Dorado" 1941; "Surrender" 1950 (Mrs. Brown).

Farnon, Shannon. Films: "Against a Crooked Sky" 1975. ¶TV: *Bonanza*—"Justice Deferred" 12-17-67 (Eleanor); *Lancer*—"Jelly Hoskins' American Dream" 11-11-69.

Farnsworth, Richard (1920-). Films: "Duel at Diablo" 1966 (1st Wagon Driver); "Texas Across the River" 1966 (Medicine Man); "Monte Walsh" 1970 (Cowboy); "The Cowboys" 1972; "The Life and Times of Judge Roy Bean" 1972 (Outlaw); "Pocket Money" 1972; "Ulzana's Raid" 1972; "The Soul of Nigger Charley" 1973 (Walker); "The Duchess and the Dirtwater Fox" 1976; "Another Man, Another Chance" 1977-Fr. (Stagecoach Driver); "Comes a Horseman" 1978 (Dodger); "Tom Horn" 1980 (John Coble); "The Legend of the Lone Ranger" 1981 (Wild Bill Hickok); "The Grey Fox" 1983-Can. (Bill Miner); "Wild Horses" TVM-1985 (Chuck Reese); "Desperado: The Outlaw Wars" TVM-1989 (Sheriff Campbell). ¶TV: *Wild Bill Hickok*—"Jingles on Jail Road" 7-14-53; *Wanted—Dead or Alive*—"The Partners" 2-6-60, "To the Victor" 11-9-60; *The Big Valley*—"Image of Yesterday" 1-9-67; *Cimarron Strip*—"The Battleground" 9-28-67; *The High Chaparral*—"The Long Shadow" 1-2-70; *Bonanza*—"Top Hand" 1-17-71 (Sourdough), "Saddle Stiff" 1-16-72 (Tate), "He Was Only Seven" 3-5-72 (Troy); *The Cherokee Trail*—Pilot 11-28-81 (Ridge Fenton).

Farnum, Dustin (1874-7/3/29). Films: "The Squaw Man" 1914 (Corporal James Wynnegate); "The Virginian" 1914 (the Virginian); "Captain Courtesy" 1915 (Leonardo Davis); "Ben Blair" 1916 (Ben Blair); "Davy Crockett" 1916 (Davy Crockett); "The Parson of Panamint" 1916 (Philo Pharo); "Durand of the Bad Lands" 1917 (Dick Durand); "North of '53" 1917 (Roaring Bill Wagstaff); "The Light of Western Stars" 1918 (Gene Stewart); "A Man in the Open" 1919 (Sailor Jesse); "A Man's Fight" 1919 (Roger Carr); "The Primal Law" 1921 (Brian Wayne); "Iron to Gold" 1922 (Tom Curtis); "The Trail of the Axe" 1922 (Dave Malkern); "While Justice Waits" 1922 (Dan Hunt); "The Yosemite Trail" 1922 (Jim Thorpe); "Bucking the Barrier" 1923 (Kit Carew); "The Buster" 1923 (Bill Coryell); "The Grail" 1923 (Chic Shelby); "Kentucky Days" 1923 (Don Buckner); "The Man Who Won" 1923 (Wild Bill); "Three Who Paid" 1923 (Riley Sinclair); "Flaming Frontier" 1926 (General Custer).

Farnum, Franklyn (1876-7/4/61). Films: "Anything Once" 1917 (Theodore Crosby); "The Man Who Took a Chance" 1917 (Monty Gray); "The Fighting Grin" 1918 (Billy Kennedy); "Go Get 'Em Garringer" 1919 (Dixie Garringer); "The Galloping Devil" 1920 (Andy Green); "The Uphill Climb" 1920; "Vanishing Trails" 1920-serial; "Vengeance and the Girl" 1920 (Jim Westagard, Jr.); "Wolves of the Border" 1923; "The Fighting Stranger" 1921 (Australia Joe); "Hunger of the Blood" 1921 (Maslun); "The Last Chance" 1921 (Rance Sparr); "The Struggle" 1921 (Dick Storm); "The White Masks" 1921 (Jack Bray); "Angel Citizens" 1922 (Frank Bartlett); "Cross Roads" 1922 (the Hero); "The Firebrand" 1922 (Bill Holt); "The Gold Grabbers" 1922; "Gun Shy" 1922 (James Brown); "Smiling Jim" 1922 (Smiling Jim/Frank Harmon); "So This Is Arizona" 1922 (Norman Russell); "Texas" 1922; "Trail's End" 1922 (Wilder Armstrong); "When East Comes West" 1922 (Jones); "It Happened Out West" 1923; "Baffled" 1924; "Courage" 1924; "Calibre 45" 1924 (Yaqui Dan); "Crossed Trail" 1924 (Tom Dawson); "A Desperate Adventure" 1924; "A Two Fisted Tenderfoot" 1924; "Western Vengeance" 1924 (Jack Caldwell); "The Bandit Tamer" 1925; "Border Intrigue" 1925 (Tom Lassen); "Double-Barreled Justice" 1925; "Drug Store Cowboy" 1925 (Marmaduke Grandon); "The Gambling Fool" 1925 (Jack Stanford); "Rough Going" 1925 (Franklyn Farnum); "Two Gun Sap" 1925; "Beyond the Law" 1930 (Lieutenant); "Beyond the Rio Grande" 1930 (Joe Kemp); "Battling with Buffalo Bill" 1931-serial; "Hell's Valley" 1931 (Carlos Valdez); "99 Wounds" 1931 (Reese); "Oklahoma Jim" 1931 (Army Captain); "Three Rogues" 1931 (Nelson); "Human Targets" 1932 (Sheriff); "Mark of the Spur" 1932 (Sheriff Ludlow); "The Reckless Rider" 1932; "Texas Bad Man" 1932 (Slim); "Arizona Cyclone" 1934; "Border Guns" 1934 (Fred Palmer); "Carrying the Mail" 1934-short; "Desert Man" 1934; "Frontier Days" 1934 (Wilson); "Honor of the Range" 1934 (Saloonkeeper); "The Lone Rider" 1934; "Pals of the West" 1934-short; "West of the Law" 1934-short; "West on Parade" 1934; "The Cowboy and the Bandit" 1935 (Dealer); "Desert Mesa" 1935 (Jones); "Fighting Caballero" 1935; "The Ghost Rider" 1935 (Jim Bullard); "Hopalong Cassidy" 1935 (Doc Riley); "Powdersmoke Range" 1935; "The Silver

Bullet" 1935 (Marshal Mullane); "Custer's Last Stand" 1936-serial (Major Reno); "Frontier Justice" 1936 (Attorney George Clark Lessin); "Lightning Bill Carson" 1936 (Townsman); "The Plainsman" 1936; "Three on the Trail" 1936; "Ranger Courage" 1937; "Romance of the Rockies" 1937 (Stone); "In Early Arizona" 1938 (Spike); "Rolling Caravans" 1938; "Stagecoach" 1939 (Deputy); "Deadwood Dick" 1940-serial; "Belle Starr" 1941 (Barfly); "Lone Star Law Men" 1941; "Silver Queen" 1942 (Creditor); "Stardust on the Sage" 1942; "Cheyenne Wildcat" 1944; "Saddle Leather Law" 1944; "The Fabulous Texan" 1947; "Silver River" 1948 (Officer); "Colt .45" 1950; "Montana Belle" 1952 (Man in Audience); "The Stranger Wore a Gun" 1953; "Ten Wanted Men" 1955.

Farnum, Geraldine. Films: "The Man from Oklahoma" 1945; "Son of Paleface" 1952 (Cigarette Girl).

Farnum, William (1876-6/5/53). Films: "The Crisis" 1912; "The Spoilers" 1914 (Roy Glennister); "The Plunderer" 1915 (Bill Matthews); "The End of the Trail" 1916 (Jules Le Clerq); "Fighting Blood" 1916 (Lem Hardy); "The Man from Bitter Roots" 1916 (Bruce Burt); "Riders of the Purple Sage" 1918 (Lassiter); "Rough and Ready" 1918 (Bill Stratton); "True Blue" 1918 (Bob McKeefer); "Last of the Duanes" 1919 (Buck Duane); "The Lone Star Ranger" 1919 (Steele); "Drag Harlan" 1920 (Drag Harlan); "The Joyous Troublemaker" 1920 (William Steele); "The Orphan" 1920 (the Orphan); "Moonshine Valley" 1922 (Ned Connors); "Without Compromise" 1922 (Dick Leighton); "Brass Commandments" 1923 (Stephen "Flash" Lanning); "The Gunfighter" 1923 (Billy Buell); "The Painted Desert" 1931 (Cash Holbrook); "Flaming Guns" 1932 (Henry Ramsey); "Wide Open Spaces" 1932-short; "Fighting with Kit Carson" 1933-serial; "Brand of Hate" 1934 (Joe Orkin); "Between Men" 1935 (Wellington Rand); "The Irish Gringo" 1935 (Pop Wiley); "Powdersmoke Range" 1935 (Banker Orchan); "Custer's Last Stand" 1936-serial (Fitzpatrick); "The Eagle's Brood" 1936 (El Toro); "The Kid Ranger" 1936 (Bill Mason); "Vigilantes Are Coming" 1936-serial (Father Jose); "Git Along, Little Dogies" 1937 (Maxwell); "The Lone Ranger" 1938-serial (Father McKim); "Santa Fe Stampede" 1938 (Dave Carson); "Shine on Harvest Moon" 1938 (Milt Brower); "Colorado Sunset" 1939

(Sheriff); "Mexicali Rose" 1939 (Padre Dominic); "Rovin' Tumbleweeds" 1939 (Senator Nolan); "South of the Border" 1939 (Padre); "Adventures of Red Ryder" 1940-serial (Colonel Tom Ryder); "Kit Carson" 1940 (Don Miguel Murphy); "Gangs of Sonora" 1941 (Ward Beecham); "Last of the Duanes" 1941 (Maj. McNeil); "American Empire" 1942 (Louisiana Judge); "Boss of Hangtown Mesa" 1942 (Judge Ezra Binns); "Deep in the Heart of Texas" 1942 (Col. Mallory); "Lone Star Ranger" 1942 (Maj. McNeil); "Men of Texas" 1942 (Gen. Sam Houston); "The Silver Bullet" 1942; "The Spoilers" 1942 (Wheaton); "Frontier Badman" 1943 (Courtwright); "Wildfire" 1945 (Judge Polson); "God's Country" 1946; "Daughter of the West" 1949 (Father Vallejo); "Trail of Robin Hood" 1950; "Lone Star" 1952 (Sen. Tom Crockett).

Farr, Felicia (1932-). Films: "The First Texan" 1956 (Katherine); "Jubal" 1956 (Naomi Hoktor); "The Last Wagon" 1956 (Jenny); "Reprisal!" 1956 (Catherine Cantrell); "3:10 to Yuma" 1957 (Emmy); "Hell Bent for Leather" 1960 (Janet). ¶TV: *Zane Grey Theater*—"Wayfarers" 1-21-60 (Cassie); *Wagon Train*—"The Eleanor Culhane Story" 5-17-61 (Eleanor Culhane); *Bonanza*—"Marie, My Love" 2-10-63 (Marie).

Farr, Hugh (Sons of the Pioneers) (1904-3/1/80). Films: "Gallant Defender" 1935; "The Mysterious Avenger" 1936; "Rhythm on the Range" 1936; "Song of the Saddle" 1936; "The Big Show" 1937; "The California Mail" 1937; "The Old Wyoming Trail" 1937; "Outlaws of the Prairie" 1937; "Law of the Plains" 1938 (Hugh); "South of Arizona" 1938; "Western Caravans" 1939; "Rio Grande" 1950 (Regimental Singer).

Farr, Jamie (Jameel Farah) (1934-). Films: "Three Violent People" 1956 (Pedro); "Ride Beyond Vengeance" 1966 (Pete). ¶TV: *The Rebel*—"Two Weeks" 3-26-61 (Pooch); *Laredo*—"That's Noway, Thataway" 1-20-66; *Hondo*—"Hondo and the Hanging Town" 12-8-67 (John-Choo), "Hondo and the Gladiators" 12-15-67 (Smithers).

Farr, Karl (Sons of the Pioneers) (1909-9/20/61). Films: "Gallant Defender" 1935; "The Mysterious Avenger" 1936; "Rhythm on the Range" 1936; "Song of the Saddle" 1936; "The Big Show" 1937; "The California Mail" 1937; "The Old Wyoming Trail" 1937; "Outlaws of the Prairie" 1937; "Law of the Plains" 1938

(Karl); "South of Arizona" 1938; "Western Caravans" 1939; "Rio Grande" 1950 (Regimental Singer).

Farr, Lee. Films: "Lone Texan" 1959 (Riff); "Gunfighters of Abilene" 1960 (Jud). ¶TV: *The Rifleman*—"Home Ranch" 10-7-58 (Sam Montgomery), "A Friend in Need" 12-25-61 (Carl Avery); *Lawman*—"The Brand Release" 1-25-59 (Ben Greene); *Trackdown*—"Bad Judgment" 1-28-59 (Charley Wagner), "Toss Up" 5-20-59; *Wanted—Dead or Alive*—"Competition" 1-31-59 (Jarrett); *The Restless Gun*—"The Red Blood of Courage" 2-2-59 (Jack Wilse); *Have Gun Will Travel*—"The Chase" 4-11-59 (Paul Martin); *Wyatt Earp*—"Johnny Ringo's Girl" 12-13-60; *Laramie*—"Lost Allegiance" 10-30-62 (Lon); *Bonanza*—"The Deadly Ones" 12-2-62 (Sims), "The Running Man" 3-30-69 (Torrance); *Lancer*—"The Kid" 10-7-69 (Lucky).

Farr, Lynn. Films: "West of Sonora" 1948 (Dickson); "Whirlwind Raiders" 1948 (Slim); "Riders of the Whistling Pines" 1949; "Rim of the Canyon" 1949; "Callaway Went Thataway" 1951 (Cowboy).

Farrar, Geraldine (1882-3/11/67). Films: "The Hell Cat" 1918 (Pancha O'Brien).

Farrar, Stanley (1911-4/5/74). Films: "Badlands of Montana" 1957 (Rayburn); "Face of a Fugitive" 1959 (Eakins). ¶TV: *The Lone Ranger*—"Man of the House" 1-26-50; *The Restless Gun*—"The Outlander" 4-21-58 (the Vespers); *Maverick*—"The Rivals" 1-25-59 (Doctor), "The Art Lovers" 10-1-61 (Leighton Borg); *Bat Masterson*—"The Elusive Baguette" 6-2-60 (Mr. Stacy).

Farrell, Brioni. TV: *Bonanza*—"Big Shadow on the Land" 4-17-66 (Regina Rossi), "The Deed and the Dilemma" 3-26-67 (Regina Rossi), "The Sound of Drums" 11-17-68 (Regina); *Wild Wild West*—"The Night of the Braine" 2-17-67 (Voulee); *Daniel Boone*—"The Fleeing Nuns" 10-24-68 (Louise); *Death Valley Days*—"Lady with a Past" 12-28-68 (Sue); *Lancer*—"The Wedding" 1-7-69 (Laurie); *Bearcats!*—12-23-71 (Sally).

Farrell, Charles (1901-5/6/90). Films: "Clash of the Wolves" 1925 (Dave Weston).

Farrell, Charles (1905-8/27/88). Films: "The Sheriff of Fractured Jaw" 1958-Brit. (Bartender).

Farrell, Glenda (1904-5/1/71). Films: "Klondike Kate" 1942 (Molly); "Apache War Smoke" 1952 (Fanny

Webson). ¶TV: *Cimarron City*—"A Respectable Girl" 12-6-58 (Maggie Atkins); *Wagon Train*—"The Jess MacAbbee Story" 11-25-59 (Belle MacAbbee); *Frontier Circus*—"Mighty Like Rogues" 4-5-62 (Ma Jukes); *Rawhide*—"Incident at Farragut Pass" 10-31-63 (Elizabeth Farragut); *Bonanza*—"The Pure Truth" 3-8-64 (Looney).

Farrell, Howard. Films: "Her Slight Mistake" 1915; "Shooting Up the Movies" 1916; "Tom's Sacrifice" 1916; "Tom's Strategy" 1916.

Farrell, John (1885-7/8/53). Films: "Desert Fury" 1947 (Drunk in Jail).

Farrell, Mike (1939-). TV: *Bonanza*—"The Hidden Enemy" 11-28-72 (Dr. Will Agar); *The New Land*—"The Word Is: Persistence" 9-14-74.

Farrell, Sharon (1946-). Films: "Last Ride of the Dalton Gang" TVM-1979 (Flo Quick). ¶TV: *Wagon Train*—"The Orly French Story" 12-12-62 (Judy), "The Pearlie Garnet Story" 2-24-64 (Pearlie Garnet); *Empire*—"Stopover on the Way to the Moon" 1-1-63 (Lisa); *Gunsmoke*—"With a Smile" 3-30-63 (Lottie Foy), "Quint's Trail" 11-9-63 (Belle Neff), "Trip West" 5-2-64 (Annie Gilroy); *Death Valley Days*—"The Holy Terror" 12-8-63 (Cora Franklin); *Rawhide*—"Hostage for Hanging" 10-19-65 (Billie Lou Gufler); *Iron Horse*—"The Pembrooke Blood" 1-9-67 (Carrie); *The Virginian*—"Execution at Triste" 12-13-67 (Mavis Williams); *Wild Wild West*—"The Night of the Amnesiac" 2-9-68 (Cloris Colter).

Farrell, Tommy (1921-). Films: "Gunfire" 1950 (Lerner); "Outlaws of Texas" 1950 (Jeff); "Abilene Trail" 1951 (Ed Dawson); "Colorado Ambush" 1951 (Terry Williams); "Night Raiders" 1952 (Jim Dugan); "Son of Geronimo" 1952-serial (Frank Baker); "Wyoming Roundup" 1952 (Bob Burke); "Gunfighters of the Northwest" 1954-serial (Arch Perry). ¶TV: *The Adventures of Rin Tin Tin*—"The Lost Patrol" 12-2-55 (Carpenter), Regular 1957-59 (Cpl. Thad Carson); *Maverick*—"The Long Hunt" 10-20-57 (Lefty Dolan); *Cheyenne*—"The Long Search" 4-22-58 (Charlie Carver); *Gunsmoke*—"Carmen" 5-24-58 (Private Atwood); *Wanted—Dead or Alive*—"The Corner" 2-21-59; *Rawhide*—"Incident at Farragut Pass" 10-31-63 (Mr. Buzby).

Farrington, Adele (1867-12/19/36). Films: "Buck Parvin and the Movies" 1915; "This Is the Life" 1915; "The Mollycoddle" 1920 (Mrs. Warren); "Rio Grande" 1920 (Alice Lopez); "The Bachelor Daddy" 1922 (Mrs. McVae).

Farrington, Betty (1885-12/22/67). Films: "Home in Wyomin'" 1942; "Stardust on the Sage" 1942 (Mrs. Haskins). ¶TV: *Sergeant Preston of the Yukon*—"Go Fever" 3-29-56 (Ma Greenwood).

Farrington, Frank (1874-5/27/24). Films: "Beating Back" 1914.

Farrow, David. TV: *The Virginian*—"With Help from Ulysses" 1-17-68 (Harkness); *Daniel Boone*—"Flag of Truce" 11-21-68 (Sentry); *The High Chaparral*—"Time of Your Life" 9-19-69 (Frank).

Faulk, John Henry (1913-4/9/90). Films: "Lovin' Molly" 1974 (Mr. Grinsom).

Faulkner, David. TV: *Wagon Train*—"The Don Alvarado Story" 6-21-61 (Rudolfo), "The Captain Dan Brady Story" 9-27-61 (Murray).

Faulkner, Edward (1932-). Films: "McClintock" 1963 (Young Ben Sage); "Shenandoah" 1965 (Union Sergeant); "Tickle Me" 1965 (Brad Bentley); "The Shakiest Gun in the West" 1968 (Huggins); "The Undefeated" 1969 (Anderson); "Chisum" 1970 (Dolan); "The Intruders" TVM-1970; "Rio Lobo" 1970 (Lt. Harris); "Scandalous John" 1971 (Hillary); "Something Big" 1971 (Capt. Tyler). ¶TV: *Have Gun Will Travel*—"The Road to Wickenberg" 10-25-58 (Jim Goodfellow), "Incident at Borasca Bend" 3-21-59, "The Black Handkerchief" 11-14-59, "Love and a Bad Woman" 3-26-60 (Gunslinger), "Black Sheep" 4-30-60 (Marshal), "Soledad Crossing" 6-10-61 (Bud McPhater), "The Hanging of Aaron Gibbs" 11-4-61 (Harden), "The Brothers" 11-25-61, "The Hunt" 2-3-62 (Lieutenant Brager), "Be Not Forgetful to Strangers" 12-22-62 (Ben); *Gunsmoke*—"The F.U." 3-14-59 (2nd Cowboy), "Unwanted Deputy" 3-5-60 (Harry), "Drago" 11-22-71 (Trask), "The Avenger" 11-27-72 (Barkley), *Rawhide*—"Incident of Fear in the Streets" 5-8-59 (Brett Mason), "Incident of the Shambling Men" 10-9-59, "The Long Shakedown" 10-13-61 (Lobey), "Deserter's Patrol" 2-9-62 (Rutledge), "Incident of the Four Horsemen" 10-26-62 (Carl Gault), "Incident of the Gallows Tree" 2-22-63 (Cryder), "Incident at Gila Flats" 1-30-64; *Hotel De Paree*—"Vengeance for Sundance" 4-8-60 (Deputy); *Bonanza*—"The Friendship" 11-12-61 (Bob Stevens), "No Less a Man "3-15-64, "Credit for a Kill" 10-23-66 (Casey); *Laramie*—"The Violent

Ones" 3-5-63; *The Virginian*—"Siege" 12-18-63 (Gambler), "Dark Destiny" 4-29-64 (Striker), "You Take the High Road" 2-17-65 (Bert), "The Showdown" 4-14-65 (Tom Landers), "Day of the Scorpion" 9-22-65 (Proctor), "Nobility of Kings" 11-10-65 (Blaylock), "Morgan Starr" 2-9-66 (Procter), "Jacob Was a Plain Man" 10-12-66 (Packer), "Death Wait" 1-15-69 (Matt Clayton); *Destry*—"Destry Had a Little Lamb" 2-21-64 (Foggy); *The Loner*—"The Lonely Calico Queen" 10-2-65 (Bounty Hunter); *The Monroes*—"Ordeal by Hope" 10-19-66 (Ferris); *Laredo*—"The Other Cheek" 2-10-67 (Ed Garmes); *Cimarron Strip*—"The Assassin" 1-11-68; *The Outcasts*—"The Candidates" 1-27-69 (Willis); *The Men from Shiloh*—"With Love, Bullets, and Valentines" 10-7-70 (Leroy Plimpton); *Bearcats!*—11-11-71 (Mills); *Nichols*—"Zachariah" 1-11-72 (Randall).

Faulkner, Ralph (1892-1/28/87). Films: "Zorro's Fighting Legion" 1939-serial (Rodriguez). ¶TV: *Maverick*—"Escape to Tampico" 10-26-58 (Herr Ziegler).

Faust, Louis R. Films: "King of the Wild Horses" 1947; "The Plunderers" 1948 (Sentry); "Hellfire" 1949 (Red Stoner); "The Last Bandit" 1949 (Hank Morse).

Faust, Martin J. (1886-7/20/43). Films: "A Yellow Streak" 1915 (Outlaw); "The Blue Streak" 1917 (Half-and-Half); "Chain Lightning" 1927 (Bannack); "Hello Cheyenne" 1928 (Jeff Bardeen); "Heir to Trouble" 1935 (Ike); "Ramona" 1936 (Luigi); "Wells Fargo" 1937; "Henry Goes Arizona" 1939 (Jake); "Union Pacific" 1939 (Engineer); "Zorro's Fighting Legion" 1939-serial (Mabesa); "Buck Benny Rides Again" 1940 (Cowhand); "West of Carson City" 1940; "Saddlemates" 1941 (Thunder Bird); "They Died with Their Boots On" 1941 (Officer).

Faversham, William (1868-4/7/40). Films: "Arizona Days" 1937 (Prof. McGill); "The Singing Buckaroo" 1937.

Fawcett, Charles. Films: "The Last Rebel" 1961-Mex. (Capt. Harry Love); "Savage Pampas" 1966-U.S./Span./Arg. (El Gato); "Old Shatterhand" 1968-Ger./Yugo./Fr./Ital. (General Taylor). ¶TV: *Rough Riders*—"Blood Feud" 11-13-58 (Hays Maddox).

Fawcett, Farrah (1946-). Films: "Substitute Wife" TVM-1994 (Pearl); "Children of the Dust" TVM-1995 (Nora).

Fawcett, George (1860-6/6/39). Films: "The Country That God Forgot" 1916 (Cal Hearn); "The Heart of Texas Ryan" 1917 (Col. William Ryan); "Scarlet Days" 1919 (Sheriff); "Salome Jane" 1923 (Yuba Bill); "Nine and Three-Fifths Seconds" 1925 (Jasper Raymond); "Flaming Frontier" 1926 (Senator Stanwood); "Man of the Forest" 1926 (Nancy's Uncle); "Under Western Skies" 1926; "The Great Divide" 1929 (MacGregor); "Tide of Empire" 1929 (Don Jose).

Fawcett, Jimmy (1905-6/9/42). Films: "Zorro's Fighting Legion" 1939-serial (Jose); "Adventures of Red Ryder" 1940-serial (Bartender #1); "King of the Royal Mounted" 1940-serial (Smelter Heavy #2); "King of the Texas Rangers" 1941-serial (Truck Heavy #2); "King of the Mounties" 1942-serial (Smelter Heavy #2).

Fawcett, William (1894-1/25/74). Films: "The Rainbow Trail" 1918 (Lassiter/Shefford); "Public Cowboy No. 1" 1937 (Sheriff Matt Doniphon); "Driftin' River" 1946 (Tennessee); "Stars Over Texas" 1946 (Judge Smith); "Tumbleweed Trail" 1946 (Judge Town); "Ghost Town Renegades" 1947 (Watson); "Pioneer Justice" 1947 (Uncle Bob); "Wild Country" 1947 (Spindle); "Black Hills" 1948 (Tuttle); "Check Your Guns" 1948 (Judge Hammond); "Tex Granger" 1948-serial; "The Tioga Kid" 1948 (Tennessee); "Ride, Ryder, Ride" 1949 (Judge); "Roll, Thunder, Roll" 1949 (Josh Culvert); "Cody of the Pony Express" 1950-serial (Ezra Graham); "Roar of the Iron Horse" 1950-serial (Rocky); "Cattle Queen" 1951 (Alkali); "Hills of Utah" 1951 (Washoe); "The Longhorn" 1951 (Bartender); "Stage to Blue River" 1951 (Perkins); "Valley of Fire" 1951; "Barbed Wire" 1952 (Uncle John Copeland); "Kansas Territory" 1952 (Weatherbee); "The Lion and the Horse" 1952 (Pappy Cole); "Montana Incident" 1952; "Oklahoma Annie" 1952 (Painter); "Springfield Rifle" 1952 (Cpl. Ramsey); "Canadian Mounties vs. Atomic Invaders" 1953-serial (Murphy); "The Homesteaders" 1953 (Hector); "The Marksman" 1953; "Star of Texas" 1953 (Soapy); "The Law vs. Billy the Kid" 1954 (Parsons); "Riding with Buffalo Bill" 1954-serial (Rocky Ford); "The Yellow Mountain" 1954 (Old Prospector); "Lay That Rifle Down" 1955 (Wurpie); "Seminole Uprising" 1955 (Cubby Crouch, Scout); "Tall Man Riding" 1955 (Andy, the Saloon Handyman); "Canyon River" 1956 (Jergens); "Dakota Incident" 1956 (Mathew Barnes); "The First Traveling Saleslady" 1956 (Oldtimer); "The Proud Ones" 1956 (Driver); "Gun Glory" 1957 (Martin); "The Storm Rider" 1957 (Cruikshank); "Good Day for a Hanging" 1958 (Farmer); "The Quick Gun" 1964 (Mike); "Jesse James Meets Frankenstein's Daughter" 1966 (Jensen, the Pharmacist); "Hostile Guns" 1967 (Jensen). ¶TV: *Wild Bill Hickok*—"The Dog Collar Story" 7-17-51, "Hands Across the Border" 7-22-52, "Ol' Pardner Rides Again" 9-16-52; *The Gene Autry Show*—"Ghost Town Raiders" 10-6-51, "Silver Dollars" 10-20-51, "The Kid Comes West" 12-8-51, "Rocky River Feud" 1-18-52, "Thunder Out West" 7-14-53, "Bandidos" 9-1-53, "Cold Decked" 9-15-53, "Johnny Jackaroo" 7-13-54, "The Hold-Up" 12-14-52, "Talking Guns" 8-10-54 (Grandpa Decker), "The Hoodoo Canyon" 8-17-54, "The Carnival Comes West" 8-24-54, "Civil War at Deadwood" 9-14-54; *The Adventures of Kit Carson*—"Fury at Red Gulch" 10-27-51 (Tom Phillips); *The Roy Rogers Show*—"The Train Robbery" 2-3-52, "The Unwilling Outlaw" 3-8-52, "Ghost Gulch" 3-30-52, "The Feud" 11-16-52, "Go for Your Gun" 11-23-52, "The Long Chance" 5-24-53, "Hidden Treasure" 12-19-54 (Lade Turner); *The Range Rider*—"Feud at Friendship City" 3-1-52, "Last of the Pony Express" 11-1-52; *The Cisco Kid*—"The Census Taker" 6-7-52, "Outlaw's Gallery" 11-22-52, "Horseless Carriage" 1-24-53, "The Tumblers" 11-28-53, "He Couldn't Quit" 4-24-54, "Magician of Jamesville" 5-22-54; *The Lone Ranger*—"Mrs. Banker" 3-26-53, "Blind Witness" 5-30-57; *Annie Oakley*—"The Tomboy" 7-17-54 (Tom Jennings); *The Adventures of Rin Tin Tin*—"Rin Tin Tin and the Ancient Mariner" 12-17-54, "Higgins Rides Again" 11-11-55 (George Higgins), "Higgins' Last Stand" 1-4-57 (George Higgins), "The Courtship of Marshal Higgins" 9-27-57 (Marshal Higgins); *Fury*—Regular 1955-60 (Pete); *Zane Grey Theater*—"The Necessary Breed" 2-15-57 (Petey); *Circus Boy*—"Man from Cimarron" 3-3-57 (Cimarron Kid); *Have Gun Will Travel*—"The Great Mojave Chase" 9-28-57; *The Restless Gun*—"The New Sheriff" 11-18-57 (Tom), "Aunt Emma" 4-14-58 (Doctor); *Sergeant Preston of the Yukon*—"The Criminal Collie" 2-27-58 (Skagway Bill); *Maverick*—"Gun-Shy" 1-11-59 (Rube), "Poker Face" 1-7-62 (Stallion); *Lawman*—"Warpath" 2-8-59 (Billy Bright), "The Return of Owny O'Reilly" 10-16-60 (Jenkins), "The Catalog Woman" 11-5-61 (John), "Mountain Man" 3-25-62 (Barber); *Wanted—Dead or Alive*—"Littlest Giant" 4-25-59, "The Monsters" 1-16-60 (Prospector); *26 Men*—"Cave-In" 5-12-59; *Sugarfoot*—"Wolf" 6-9-59 (Juf Wilkes); *Rawhide*—"Incident of the Day of the Dead" 9-18-59, "Incident of the Swindler" 2-20-64; *Gunsmoke*—"Box O'Rocks" 12-5-59 (Packy Rountree), "Ash" 2-16-63 (Hawkins), "Carter Caper" 11-16-63 (Turner), "Jonah Hutchison" 11-21-64 (Lefferts), "Twenty Miles from Dodge" 4-10-65 (Bert Fraley), "A Man Called Smith" 10-27-69 (Prospector), "The Judas Gun" 1-19-70 (Liveryman), "The Noose" 9-21-70 (Nebs); *Laramie*—"Death Wind" 2-2-60 (Ben), "License to Kill" 11-22-60 (Ben), "The Replacement" 3-27-62, "The Sunday Shoot" 11-13-62, "Time of the Traitor" 12-11-62 (Josh); *Bat Masterson*—"Six Feet of Gold" 2-25-60 (Sheriff); *The Law of the Plainsman*—"Stella" 3-31-60 (Shep Collins); *G.E. Theater*—"Aftermath" 4-17-60; *The Texan*—"The Nomad" 4-18-60; *Bonanza*—"Denver McKee" 10-15-60 (Pete), "Pink Cloud Comes from Old Cathay" 4-12-64, "Check Rein" 12-3-67 (Asa), "The Night Virginia City Died" 9-13-70 (Whiskey Smith); *The Deputy*—"Lady for a Hanging" 12-3-60 (Jipsom); *Riverboat*—"Zigzag" 12-26-60 (Pinty Walters); *The Rifleman*—"The Lost Treasure of Canyon Town" 2-28-61 (Mr. Newman), "Suspicion" 1-14-63 (Pyrite Rand); *Cheyenne*—"The Frightened Town" 3-20-61 (Luke), "Winchester Quarantine" 9-25-61 (Uncle Rufe); *The Outlaws*—"The Outlaw Marshals" 12-14-61 (1st Man); *Tales of Wells Fargo*—"Portrait of Teresa" 2-10-62 (Stage Driver); *Bronco*—"The Immovable Object" 4-16-62 (Tom Christopher); *Wagon Train*—"The Frank Carter Story" 5-23-62 (Tapper), "The John Bernard Story" 11-21-62 (Budgen), "The Abel Weatherly Story" 1-2-63 (Drifter), "The Whipping" 3-23-64 (Finley); *The Virginian*—"The Small Parade" 2-20-63, "Return a Stranger" 11-18-64 (Sam Elberry), "High Stakes" 11-16-66 (Hostler), "The Gentle Tamers" 1-24-68 (Telegrapher), "Seth" 3-20-68 (Stationmaster), "Stopover" 1-8-69 (Clem); *The Dakotas*—"Incident at Rapid City" 3-4-63 (Prospector); *Temple Houston*—"Sam's Boy" 1-23-64 (Billy Rogers); *Destry*—"The Solid Gold Girl" 2-14-64 (Rancher); *Daniel Boone*—"A Short Walk to Salem" 11-19-64 (Ben Pickens); *The Big Valley*—"Earthquake!" 11-10-65 (Jeb), "Image of Yesterday" 1-9-67; *Wild Wild*

West—"The Night of the Murderous Spring" 4-15-66 (Man); *The Road West*—"Power of Fear" 12-26-66 (Douty); *Pistols 'n' Petticoats*—1-28-67 (Old Timer); *The Guns of Will Sonnett*—"The Hero" 12-29-67, Robber's Roost" 1-17-69; *Death Valley Days*—"The Biggest Little Post Office in the World" 2-7-70; *The Men from Shiloh*—"Last of the Comancheros" 12-9-70 (Hostler).

Fax, Jesslyn (1893-2/16/75). Films: "Shoot-Out at Medicine Bend" 1957; "Four for Texas" 1964 (Widow). ¶TV: *Gunsmoke*—"Cotter's Girl" 1-19-63 (Proprietress); *Cimarron Strip*—"Big Jessie" 2-8-68.

Fay, Dorothy. Films: "Law of the Texan" 1938 (Helen Clifford); "Law of the Texan" 1938 (Helen); "Prairie Justice" 1938 (Anita Benson); "The Stranger from Arizona" 1938 (Ann); "Frontier Scout" 1939; "Rollin' Westward" 1939 (Betty Lawson); "Song of the Buckaroo" 1939 (Anna); "Sundown on the Prairie" 1939 (Ruth Graham); "Trigger Pals" 1939 (Doris Allen); "Rainbow Over the Range" 1940 (Mary Manners); "North from the Lone Star" 1941 (Madge Wilson); "White Eagle" 1941-serial (Janet).

Fay, Frank (1897-9/25/61). Films: "Under a Texas Moon" 1930 (Don Carlos).

Fay, Gaby. *see* Holden, Fay.

Faye, Herbie (1899-6/28/80). TV: *Rango*—"Rango the Outlaw" 1-13-67 (Storekeeper), "If You Can't Take It with You, Don't Go" 4-21-67 (Storekeeper).

Faye, Joey (1910-). Films: "North to Alaska" 1960 (Sourdough).

Faye, Julia (1896-4/6/66). Films: "As in the Days of Old" 1915; "The Squaw Man" 1918 (Lady Faye); "The Squaw Man" 1931 (Mrs. Chichester Jones); "Union Pacific" 1939 (Mame); "Northwest Mounted Police" 1940 (Wapiskau); "California" 1946 (Wagon Woman); "Unconquered" 1947 (Widow Swivens); "Copper Canyon" 1950 (Proprietor's Wife).

Faylen, Frank (1907-8/2/85). Films: "Cherokee Strip" 1937 (Joe Brady); "Headin' East" 1937 (Joe); "Reno" 1939 (Hezzy Briggs); "Prairie Chickens" 1943; "California" 1946 (Whitey); "Blood on the Moon" 1948 (Jake Pindalest); "Whispering Smith" 1948 (Whitey DuSang); "Copper Canyon" 1950 (Mullins); "The Eagle and the Hawk" 1950 (Buck Hyatt); "The Nevadan" 1950 (Jeff); "Passage West" 1951 (Curly); "Hangman's

Knot" 1952 (Cass Browne); "The Lusty Men" 1952 (Al Dawson); "The Lone Gun" 1954 (Fairweather); "Red Garters" 1954 (Billy Buckett); "Seventh Cavalry" 1956 (Kruger); "Gunfight at the O.K. Corral" 1957 (Cotton Wilson); "North to Alaska" 1960 (Arnie). ¶TV: *Maverick*—"The Third Rider" 1-5-58 (Red Harrison); *Wanted—Dead or Alive*—"The Giveaway Gun" 10-11-58 (Sheriff Earl Tipton); *Rough Riders*—"The Wagon Raiders" 4-6-59 (Daniel Eddiman); *Zane Grey Theater*—"The Sunrise Gun" 5-19-60 (Doc Alvarez).

Fazenda, Louise (1889-4/17/62). Films: "The Romance of the Utah Pioneers" 1913; "The Old Fool" 1923 (Dolores Murphy); "The Spider and the Rose" 1923 (Doctor); "The Spoilers" 1923 (Tilly Nelson); "A Texas Steer" 1927 (Mrs. Ma Brander); "Gun Smoke" 1931 (Hampsey Dell).

Fealy, Maude (1883-11/9/71). Films: "Union Pacific" 1939.

Fearnley, Jane. Films: "The Widow's Claim" 1912; "The Blindness of Courage" 1913.

Featherstone, Eddie (Eddie Fetherston) (1896-6/12/65). Films: "The Ridin' Fool" 1931 (Bud Warren); "End of the Trail" 1936 (Orderly); "Union Pacific" 1939 (Reporter); "Deadwood Dick" 1940-serial; "Sky Bandits" 1940 (Buzz Murphy); "White Eagle" 1941-serial; "The Man from Colorado" 1948 (Jones); "Pecos River" 1951 (Mr. Grey). ¶TV: *Tales of the Texas Rangers*—"The Steel Trap" 11-13-58 (Fred Mortenson).

Fehmiu, Bekim (1936-). Films: "Deserter" 1970-U.S./Ital./Yugo. (Capt. Kaleb).

Fein, Bernie. TV: *The Alaskans*—"Heart of Gold" 5-1-60 (Tom); *Man from Blackhawk*—"Remember Me Not" 9-9-60 (Renard); *Lawman*—"Chantay" 11-13-60 (Great Bear); *The Tall Man*—"The Runaway Groom" 4-28-62 (Sam).

Feinberg, Ronald. TV: *Here Come the Brides*—"The Deadly Trade" 4-16-69, "Lorenzo Bush" 12-19-69 (Lorenzo Bush), "Two Worlds" 2-20-70 (Haynie), "Apache Trust" 11-7-69 (Griswold); *Kung Fu*—"Sun and Cloud Shadow" 2-22-73 (Ezekiel).

Feinstein, Alan (1941-). Films: "Joe Panther" 1976 (Rocky).

Feld, Fritz (1900-11/19/93). Films: "Shut My Big Mouth" 1942 (Robert Oglethorpe); "Riding Shotgun" 1954 (Fritz); "Four for Texas" 1964 (Maitre d'). ¶TV: *Wild Wild*

West—"The Night of the Avaricious Actuary" 12-6-68 (Chef).

Feldary, Eric (1912-2/25/68). Films: "Salome, Where She Danced" 1945 (Uhlan Sergeant).

Feldman, Corey (1971-). Films: "Maverick" 1994 (Bank Robber).

Feliciani, Mario (1918-). Films: "Shadow of Zorro" 1963-Span./Ital.; "Sign of Coyote" 1964-Ital./Span.

Feliciano, Jose (1945-). TV: *Kung Fu*—"Battle Hymn" 2-8-75 (Jonno Marcada).

Felix, Art. Films: "Desert Guns" 1936 (Norton); "The Lion's Den" 1936 (Henchman); "Riddle Ranch" 1936 (Pedro); "Ridin' On" 1936; "Lightnin' Crandall" 1937; "Zorro Rides Again" 1937-serial (Raider #8); "The Lone Ranger" 1938-serial (Trooper); "The Lone Ranger Rides Again" 1939-serial (Cave Heavy #4); "Six-Gun Rhythm" 1939; "Riders of the Deadline" 1943; "Law of the Badlands" 1951.

Fell, Norman (1924-). Films: "Guardian of the Wilderness" 1976. ¶TV: *Wild Wild West*—"The Night of the Whirring Death" 2-18-66 (Jeremiah Ratch); *A Man Called Shenandoah*—"Muted Fifes, Muffled Drums" 2-28-66 (Capt. Arnold Dudley); *The Life and Times of Grizzly Adams*—"The Redemption of Ben" 3-23-77 (Morgan).

Felleghi, Tom. Films: "Arizona Colt" 1965-Ital./Fr./Span.; "Man from Oklahoma" 1965-Ital./Span./Ger. (Jacobs); "The Big Gundown" 1966-Ital. (Chet); "Cisco" 1966-Ital. (Deputy); "Massacre Time" 1966-Ital./Span./Ger.; "Ringo's Big Night" 1966-Ital./Span. (John Crowe); "Black Tigress" 1967-Ital.; "If You Want to Live … Shoot!" 1967-Ital./Span.; "Two Pistols and a Coward" 1967-Ital.; "Two Sides of the Dollar" 1967-Fr./Ital.; "His Name Was King" 1971-Ital.; "Deaf Smith and Johnny Ears" 1972-Ital.; "Born to Kill" 1967-Ital.; "Machine Gun Killers" 1968-Ital./Span.; "California" 1976-Ital./Span.

Fellowes, Rockliffe (1885-1/30/50). Films: "The Spoilers" 1923 (Matthews); "The Border Legion" 1924 (Kells); "The Golden Princess" 1925 (Tom Romaine); "Renegades of the West" 1932 (Curly Bogard); "Rusty Rides Alone" 1933 (Bart Quillan).

Fellows, Edith (1923-). Films: "Law and Lawless" 1932 (Betty Kelly); "Rider of Death Valley" 1932 (Betty Joyce); "Out West with the Peppers" 1940 (Polly Pepper); "Heart of the Rio Grande" 1942 (Connie Lane); "Stardust on the Sage" 1942 (Judy Drew). ¶TV: *Father Murphy*— "The Robber" 12-14-82 (Louise Walker).

Felton, Verna (1890-12/14/66). Films: "Northwest Passage" 1940 (Mrs. Towne); "The Gunfighter" 1950 (Mrs. Pennyfeather); "New Mexico" 1951 (Mrs. Fenway); "The Oklahoman" 1957 (Mrs. Waynebrook); "Guns of the Timberland" 1960 (Aunt Sarah); "The Man from Button Willow" 1965 (Voice).

Fenady, Albert J. TV: *The Rebel*—"Johnny Yuma at Appomattox" 9-18-60 (Gen. Philip Sheridan); *Branded*—"A Destiny Which Made Us Brothers" 1-23-66 (General Sherman).

Fenech, Edwige (1948-). Films: "Heads or Tails" 1969-Ital./Span.

Fennec, Sylvie. Films: "Drop Them or I'll Shoot" 1969-Fr./Ger./Span.

Fennelly, Parker (1892-1/22/88). TV: *Have Gun Will Travel*—"Three Sons" 5-10-58 (Rupe Bosworth), "The Calf" 10-15-60 (Abraham Lee).

Fenner, Walter (1882-11/7/47). Films: "Mountain Rhythm" 1939 (Cavanaugh).

Fenton, Frank (1906-7/24/57). Films: "Buffalo Bill" 1944 (Murdo Carvell); "Adventures of Don Coyote" 1947 (Big Foot); "Relentless" 1948 (Jim Rupple); "Renegades of Sonora" 1948; "The Doolins of Oklahoma" 1949 (Red Buck); "The Golden Stallion" 1949 (Sheriff); "Ranger of Cherokee Strip" 1949 (Randolph McKinnon); "Rustlers" 1949 (Carew); "Rogue River" 1950 (Joe Dandridge); "Streets of Ghost Town" 1950 (Bart Selby); "Trigger, Jr." 1950 (Sheriff Pettigrew); "Wyoming Mail" 1950 (Gilson); "Prairie Roundup" 1951 (Buck Prescott); "Silver City" 1951 (Creede); "Texans Never Cry" 1951 (Capt. Weldon); "Fury at Gunsight Pass" 1956 (Sheriff Meeker); "The Naked Hills" 1956 (Harold); "Gun the Man Down" 1957. ¶TV: *The Lone Ranger*—"Gold Train" 3-16-50, "Treason at Dry Creek" 12-4-52, "The Red Mark" 9-3-53; *Wild Bill Hickok*—"Rustling Stallion" 3-4-52, "The Rainmaker" 4-14-53; *Tales of the Texas Rangers*— "Bandits of El Dorado" 2-18-56 (Bruton); *Sergeant Preston of the Yukon*—"Trouble at Hogback" 7-19-56 (Conway); *Annie Oakley*—"Annie and the First Phone" 7-22-56 (Tut Emerson), "Indian Justice" 7-29-56 (Sam King); "The Saga of Clement

O'Toole" 11-4-56 (Bragan); *Sheriff of Cochise*—"The Kidnaper" 1-18-57 (Ed Craft); *The Adventures of Rin Tin Tin*—"Sorrowful Joe Returns" 2-1-57 (Sheriff); *Wyatt Earp*—"Young Guns" 3-26-57 (Ed Beatty).

Fenton, Mark (1870-7/29/25). Films: "John Ermine of the Yellowstone" 1917 (Colonel Searles); "The Man Who Took a Chance" 1917 (Richard Lanning); "The Dead Shot" 1918; "The Girl Who Wouldn't Quit" 1918 (Joshua Siddons); "A Fight for Love" 1919 (Angus McDougal); "Rosalind at Red Gate" 1919; "The Fightin' Terror" 1920; "Hitchin' Posts" 1920; "The Wallop" 1921 (Maj. Vorhis); "Headin' West" 1922 (Judge Dean); "The Passing of Wolf MacLean" 1924; "Brand of Cowardice" 1925; "Double Fisted" 1925.

Fenwick, Harry (1880-12/24/32). Films: "Come on Cowboys!" 1924 (Wallace Rampart); "Buffalo Bill on the U.P. Trail" 1926 (Dr. Roy Webb).

Fenwick, Jean. TV: *Sheriff of Cochise*—"Triangle" 2-22-57 (Mrs. Talbot); *Gunsmoke*—"Doc's Reward" 12-14-57 (2nd Lady).

Ferdin, Pamelyn (1959-). TV: *Branded*—"A Proud Town" 12-19-65 (Abigail); *The Legend of Jesse James*—"A Burying for Rosey" 5-9-66 (Rosey Bryant); *Gunsmoke*—"The Money Store" 12-30-68 (Annie Jarvis); *The High Chaparral*—"No Bugles, No Women" 3-14-69 (Jennie), "For the Love of Carlos" 4-4-69 (Charity).

Ferguson, Al (1888-12/4/71). Films: "A Life at Stake" 1915; "Lone Star" 1916 (Jim Harper); "Where the West Begins" 1919 (Blackthorn Kennedy); "Smiling Jim" 1922 (Sheriff Thomas); "The Timber Queen" 1922-serial; "The Range Patrol" 1923; "The Fighting Romeo" 1925 (Dave Mathews); "Baited Trap" 1926 (Robert Barton); "Hi-Jacking Rustlers" 1926; "West of the Law" 1926 (Surly Dorgan); "The Wolf Hunters" 1926; "Fangs of Destiny" 1927 (Thomas Shields); "The Range Riders" 1927 (Sundown Sykes); "Shooting Straight" 1927 (Sheriff); "Straight Shootin'" 1927 (Stephen Clemens); "Western Courage" 1927; "A Clean Sweep" 1928; "Guardians of the Wild" 1928 (Mark Haman); "The Little Buckaroo" 1928 (Luke Matthews); "The Scarlet Arrow" 1928-serial; "Terror Mountain" 1928 (Luke Thorne); "Grit Wins" 1929 (Logan); "Hoofbeats of Vengeance" 1929 (Jud Regan); "The Man from Nevada" 1929 (Luke Baldridge); "Law of the Plains" 1929; "Outlawed" 1929 (Sher-

iff); "The Saddle King" 1929 (Mort Landreau); "The Smiling Terror" 1929 (Hanks Sims); "Thundering Thompson" 1929; "The Vagabond Cub" 1929 (James Sykes); "The Wagon Master" 1929 (Jacques Frazalle); "Near the Rainbow's End" 1930 (Buck Rankin); "The Mystery Trooper" 1931-serial; "The One Way Trail" 1931 (Coldeye Carnell); "Red Fork Range" 1931 (Black Bard); "Pueblo Terror" 1931 (Al); "The Sign of the Wolf" 1931-serial (Winslow); "Two Gun Caballero" 1931; "Clancy of the Mounted" 1933-serial; "Arizona Nights" 1934; "Desert Trail" 1935 (Pete); "Gallant Defender" 1935; "The Red Rider" 1934-serial (Madden); "The Laramie Kid" 1935 (Jim Morley); "Roamin' Wild" 1936 (Clark); "North of the Rio Grande" 1937 (Plunkett); "Round-Up Time in Texas" 1937; "Rustler's Valley" 1937 (Joe); "Wells Fargo" 1937 (Southerner); "In Early Arizona" 1938; "Come on, Rangers" 1939; "Frontiers of '49" 1939 (Red); "Stand Up and Fight" 1939 (Teamster); "Billy the Kid's Gun Justice" 1940 (Cobb Allen); "Deadwood Dick" 1940-serial; "My Little Chickadee" 1940 (Train Passenger); "The Bandit Trail" 1941; "Saddle Mountain Roundup" 1941; "White Eagle" 1941-serial; "Jackass Mail" 1942 (Miner); "Shut My Big Mouth" 1942 (Pursuer); "Texas to Bataan" 1942 (Tuillax); "Valley of the Sun" 1942 (Man on Street); "Law of the Saddle" 1943 (Bart); "Death Valley Rangers" 1944 (Ross); "Devil Riders" 1944; "Outlaw Trail" 1944; "Riders of the Santa Fe" 1944 (Bartender); "Rustlers' Hideout" 1944 (Steve); "Sonora Stagecoach" 1944 (Red); "Westward Bound" 1944 (Henchman); "Beyond the Pecos" 1945; "Northwest Trail" 1945; "Salome, Where She Danced" 1945 (Deputy); "Wildfire" 1945 (Steve Kane); "God's Country" 1946; "Lightning Raiders" 1946 (Lorrin); "Overland Riders" 1946; "Wild West" 1946 (Kansas); "The Fabulous Texan" 1947; "Son of Zorro" 1947-serial (Lawton/Raider #1); "Unconquered" 1947; "White Stallion" 1947 (Red); "Blood on the Moon" 1948; "Fighting Mustang" 1948; "Prairie Outlaws" 1948; "Dallas" 1950 (Citizen); "The James Brothers of Missouri" 1950-serial (Heavy #1); "Along the Great Divide" 1951 (Bailiff); "Vengeance Valley" 1951 (Man); "Son of Paleface" 1952 (Man); "Rose Marie" 1954 (Woodsman); "Blazing the Overland Trail" 1956-serial; "Perils of the Wilderness" 1956-serial (Mike).

Ferguson, Casson (1894-2/12/

29). Films: "The Only Road" 1918 (Bob Armstrong); "Unclaimed Goods" 1918 (Cocopah Kid); "The Ghost Girl" 1919; "Johnny, Get Your Gun" 1919 (Bert Whitney); "Partners Three" 1919 (Arthur Gould); "Over the Border" 1922 (Val Galbraith).

Ferguson, Elsie (1883-11/15/61). Films: "Heart of the Wilds" 1918 (Jen Galbraith).

Ferguson, Frank (1899-9/12/78). Films: "They Died with Their Boots On" 1941 (Grant's Secretary); "Canyon Passage" 1946 (Minister); "The Fabulous Texan" 1947; "Fort Apache" 1948 (Reporter); "Rachel and the Stranger" 1948 (Mr. Green); "Frenchie" 1950 (Jim Dobbs); "The Furies" 1950 (Dr. Grieve); "Under Mexicali Stars" 1950 (Goldie); "Santa Fe" 1951 (Marshal Bat Masterson); "Thunder in God's Country" 1951 (Bates); "Warpath" 1951 (Marshal); "Bend of the River" 1952; "Oklahoma Annie" 1952 (Eldridge Haskell); "Rancho Notorious" 1952 (Preacher); "Rodeo" 1952 (Harry Cartwright); "Wagons West" 1952 (Cyrus Cook); "Hannah Lee" 1953 (Britton); "The Lone Hand" 1953 (Mr. Dunn); "The Marksman" 1953; "Powder River" 1953 (Johnny Slaughter); "Star of Texas" 1953 (Marshal Bullock); "Texas Bad Man" 1953 (Gil); "The Woman They Almost Lynched" 1953 (Bartender); "Drum Beat" 1954 (Mr. Dyar); "Johnny Guitar" 1954 (Marshal Williams); "The Outcast" 1954 (Chad Polsen); "At Gunpoint" 1955 (Henderson); "A Lawless Street" 1955 (Abe Deland); "The Violent Men" 1955 (Mahoney); "Gun Duel in Durango" 1957 (Sheriff Howard); "The Iron Sheriff" 1957 (Holloway); "The Phantom Stagecoach" 1957 (Joe Patterson); "Cole Younger, Gunfighter" 1958 (Wittrock); "The Lawless Eighties" 1958; "The Light in the Forest" 1958 (Harry Butler); "Man of the West" 1958 (Marshal); "Terror in a Texas Town" 1958 (Holmes); "The Quick Gun" 1964 (Dan Evans); "The Great Sioux Massacre" 1965 (Gen. Terry); "The Macahans" TVM-1976 (Grandpa Macahan). ¶TV: *The Lone Ranger*—"Enfield Rifle" 1-13-55; *My Friend Flicka*—Regular 1955-56 (Gus); *Zane Grey Theater*—"The Three Graves" 1-4-57 (T.J. Barnett), "Legacy of a Legend" 11-6-58 (Paul Parker), "Let the Man Die" 12-18-58 (Tom Menken); *Tales of Wells Fargo*—"John Wesley Hardin" 9-30-57 (Sheriff Ed Tige), "Toll Road" 3-23-59 (Huckaby), "Defiant at the Gate" 11-25-61 (Deacon), "Royal Maroon" 4-28-62 (Sedge); *Trackdown*—"Law in

Lampasas" 10-11-57 (Judge Tolliver), "Terror" 2-4-59 (Adam Turner); *Colt .45*—"Rare Specimen" 2-7-58 (Tood), "Law West of the Pecos" 6-7-59 (Judge Roy Bean); *Maverick*—"Seed of Deception" 4-13-58 (Sheriff McPeter), "High Card Hangs" 10-19-58 (Genessee Jones), "Easy Mark" 11-15-59 (Conductor), "Destination Devil's Flat" 12-25-60 (Deacon Curt Eaker), "Three Queens Full" 11-12-61 (Sheriff Mattson), "The Troubled Heir" 4-1-62 (Sheriff Luther Hawkins); *Tales of the Texas Rangers*—"Deadfall" 11-6-58 (Dembrow); *The Restless Gun*—"Remember the Dead" 11-17-58 (Sheriff Cullen); *Bronco*—"Trail to Taos" 12-2-58 (Parson), "Ordeal at Dead Tree" 1-2-61 (Marshal Bob Harrod); *The Texan*—"A Race for Life" 3-16-59 (Dobie), "Quarantine" 2-8-60 (Thomas Laurie), "Buried Treasure" 2-15-60 (Mac); *Sugarfoot*—"Wolf" 6-9-59 (Doc Spooner), "Vinegaroom" 3-29-60 (Judge Bean); *Laramie*—"Circle of Fire" 9-22-59 (Abner Crable); *Wichita Town*—"The Night the Cowboys Roared" 9-30-59 (Eric Holbein); *The Alaskans*—"Cheating Cheaters" 10-11-59 (Brother Bowers), "Heart of Gold" 5-1-60 (Brother Barlow); *Bat Masterson*—"The Inner Circle" 12-31-59 (Old Billy North), "Bat Trap" 10-13-60 (Dick Pearch); *Bonanza*—"The Fear Merchants" 1-30-60, "The Long Night" 5-6-62, "Ponderosa Matador" 1-12-64 (Jigger), "Lothario Larkin" 4-25-65 (Abner); *Cheyenne*—"Riot at Arroyo Soco" 2-1-60; *The Rifleman*—"The Hero" 2-2-60 (Sam Bedford); *Overland Trail*—"Daughter of the Sioux" 3-20-60 (Jason Coolidge); *The Deputy*—"A Time to Sow" 4-23-60 (Tim McCullough), "Blood Brother-in-Law" 4-17-64 (Doc Finley); *Lawman*—"The Mad Bunch" 10-2-60 (Uncle Ben), "The Grubstake" 4-16-61 (Rainbow Jack), "A Friend o the Family" 1-14-62 (Joe Henry), "Jailbreak" 6-10-62 (Howard Callaghan); *The Westerner*—"The Old Man" 11-25-60; *Klondike*—"Taste of Danger" 12-5-60; *Stagecoach West*—"The Butcher" 3-28-61 (Sheriff Doolin); *Wyatt Earp*—"Wyatt Earp's Baby" 4-25-61 (Sheriff Lydell); *Have Gun Will Travel*—"Bear Bait" 5-13-61 (Kincaid); *The Tall Man*—"The Great Western" 6-3-61 (Lew Wallace); *Wagon Train*—"The Ah Chong Story" 6-14-61 (Sheriff), "Charlie Wooster—Outlaw" 2-20-63 (Sheriff), "The Ben Engel Story" 3-16-64; *Wide Country*—"The Man Who Ran Away" 2-7-63 (Hackett); *The Virginian*—"If You Have Tears" 2-13-63 (Dunson); *Temple Houston*—Regular 1963-64 (Judge

Ben Gurney); *Gunsmoke*—"Big Man, Big Target" 11-28-64; *Alias Smith and Jones*—"Bad Night in Big Butte" 3-2-72; *Kung Fu*—"The Centoph" 4-4-74 & 4-11-74 (Bissell).

Ferguson, Helen (1901-3/14/77). Films: "The Challenge of the Law" 1920 (Madeline DuBarre); "Getting Some" 1920; "Just Pals" 1920 (Mary Bruce); "Shod with Fire" 1920 (Anny Lytton); "The Call of the North" 1921 (Elodie Albret); "The Freeze-Out" 1921 (Zoe Whipple); "Straight from the Shoulder" 1921 (Maggie, the Waitress); "To a Finish" 1921 (Doris Lane); "The Crusader" 1922 (Mary); "Rough Shod" 1922 (Betty Lawson); "Double Dealing" 1923 (the Slavey); "Nine and Three-Fifths Seconds" 1925 (Mary Bowser); "The Scarlet West" 1925 (Nestina); "Spook Ranch" 1925 (Elvira); "Wild West" 1925-serial; "Jaws of Steel" 1927 (Mary Warren); "In Old California" 1929 (Dolores Radanell).

Ferguson, William J. (1845-5/4/30). Films: "The Yosemite Trail" 1922 (Peter Blunt).

Fern, Fritzi (1901-9/10/32). Films: "The Last Frontier" 1932-serial.

Fernandel (1903-2/26/71). Films: "Dynamite Jack" 1963-Fr. (Dynamite Jack/Antoine).

Fernandez, Abel. Films: "Rose Marie" 1954 (Indian Warrior); "Fort Yuma" 1955 (Mangas); "Many Rivers to Cross" 1955; "The Last Wagon" 1956 (Apache Medicine Man); "Apache Uprising" 1966 (Young Apache). ¶TV: *The Adventures of Rin Tin Tin*—"Rin Tin Tin and the Christmas Story" 12-23-55 (Tsa-Fah), "Attack on Fort Apache" 4-13-56 (Oye-tza), "Rinty Finds a Bone" 4-27-56, "Rusty's Remedy" 2-28-58 (Panjito); *Gunsmoke*—"Indian White" 10-27-56 (Little Wolf), "Buffalo Man" 1-11-58 (Indian), "Johnny Red" 10-3-59 (Nate); *Zane Grey Theater*—"Death Watch" 11-9-56 (Indian), "The Last Raid" 2-26-59 (Cota); *Jim Bowie*—"Osceola" 1-18-57 (Osceola); *Disneyland*—"The Saga of Andy Burnett"—Regular 1957-58 (Kiasax); *Have Gun Will Travel*—"The Englishman" 12-7-57; *Wagon Train*—"The Charles Avery Story" 12-13-57 (Choya), "The Kitty Angel Story" 1-7-59 (Indian Brave); *U.S. Marshal*—"Mass Escape" 2-7-59; *The Restless Gun*—"Ricochet" 3-9-59; *The Texan*—"Caballero" 4-13-59 (Juan); *Bonanza*—"Mr. Henry Comstock" 11-7-59 (Lean Knife); *The Travels of Jaimie McPheeters*—"The Day of the Haunted Trail" 1-26-64 (Joseph);

Daniel Boone—"Cain's Birthday" 4-1-65 & 4-8-65 (Little Turtle), "Empire of the Lost" 9-16-65 (White Feather), "The Peace Tree" 11-11-65 (Tafend), "The Jasser Ledbedder Story" 2-2-67 (Warrior), "The Flaming Rocks" 2-1-68, "The Grand Alliance" 11-13-69; *Iron Horse*—"War Cloud" 10-31-66 (War Cloud); *Hondo*—"Hondo and the War Cry" 9-15-67 (Indian).

Fernandez, Emilio (1904-8/6/86). Films: "The Land of Missing Men" 1930 (Lopez); "Oklahoma Cyclone" 1930 (Panchez Gomez); "The Western Code" 1932 (Half-Breed); "The Reward" 1965 (Sargento Lopez); "The Appaloosa" 1966 (Lazaro); "Return of the Seven" 1966-Span. (Lorca); "The War Wagon" 1967 (Calito); "The Wild Bunch" 1969 (Mapache); "Pat Garrett and Billy the Kid" 1973 (Paco). ¶TV: *Kung Fu*—"The Brujo" 10-25-73 (Carlos).

Fernandez, Felix (1899-7/5/66). Films: "The Savage Guns" 1961-U.S./Span. (Paco); "Three Swords of Zorro" 1963-Ital./Span.

Fernandez, Jaime. Films: "Massacre" 1956 (Juan Pedro); "A Bullet for the General" 1966-Ital. (Gen. Elias); "Guns for San Sebastian" 1967-U.S./Fr./Mex./Ital. (Golden Lance).

Ferr, Johnnie. Films: "The Terror of Tiny Town" 1938 (Diamond Dolly).

Ferrady, Lisa. Films: "California Conquest" 1952 (Helena de Gagarine); "Rancho Notorious" 1952 (Maxine); "The Kentuckian" 1955 (Woman Gambler).

Ferrante, Joseph. Films: "The Rare Breed" 1966 (Esteban). ¶TV: *Gunsmoke*—"He Learned About Women" 2-24-62 (Juan); *Cimarron Strip*—"The Battleground" 9-28-67; *Lancer*—"The Man Without a Gun" 3-25-69.

Ferrara, James. Films: "Tombstone, the Town Too Tough to Die" 1942 (Billy Clanton).

Ferrare, Christina (1950-). Films: "J.W. Coop" 1971 (Bean).

Ferrell, Conchata (1943-). Films: "The Girl Called Hatter Fox" TVM-1977 (Nurse Rhinehart); "Heartland" 1980 (Elinore); "Samurai Cowboy" 1993.

Ferrell, Ray. Films: "The Plunderers" 1960 (Billy Miller). ¶TV: *My Friend Flicka*—"The Foundlings" 6-1-56 (Sandy); *Fury*—"The Baby Sitters" 2-8-58 (Mark); *Zane Grey Theater*—"Utopia, Wyoming" 6-6-58 (Chris Cannon), "Sundown Smith" 3-24-60 (Bobby Bromley); *The*

Texan—"Jail for the Innocents" 11-3-58 (Peter Swenson).

Ferrer, Mel (1917-). Films: "Rancho Notorious" 1952 (French Fairmont); "Dream West" TVM-1986 (Judge Elkins). ¶TV: *Zane Grey Theater*—"The Ghost" 12-31-59 (Marshal Monty Elstrode); *How the West Was Won*—Episode Two 2-12-78 (Hale Burton), Episode Two 2-19-78 (Hale Burton).

Ferris, Michael. TV: *Death Valley Days*—"Lola Montez" 12-20-54, "The Crystal Gazer" 4-11-55; *Have Gun Will Travel*—"Ambush" 4-23-60 (Blandings).

Ferrone, Dan (1937-). Films: "Welcome to Hard Times" 1967 (Bert Albany). ¶TV: *The Big Valley*—"Down Shadow Street" 1-23-67 (Buddy Tyrone); *Gunsmoke*—"Nowhere to Run" 1-15-68 (Honker), "The Gunrunners" 2-5-68 (Tahohon), "The Good Samaritans" 3-10-69 (Jeb), "A Matter of Honor" 11-17-69 (Otis Fletcher), "The Bullet" 11-29-71, 12-6-71 & 12-13-71 (Harper), "Women for Sale" 9-10-73 & 9-17-73 (Dan Ross); *Cimarron Strip*—"The Greeners" 3-7-68 (Will Arlyn); *Bonanza*—"Don't Cry, My Son" 10-31-71 (Eli Johnson), "The Sound of Loneliness" 12-5-72 (Mr. Holcombe); *How the West Was Won*—Episode One 2-6-77 (Micah Sloane).

Ferrusquilla. *see* Espinosa, Jose Angel.

Ferzetti, Gabriele (1925-). Films: "Once Upon a Time in the West" 1968-Ital. (Morton).

Fetchit, Stepin' (1902-11/19/85). Films: "Wild Horse" 1931 (Stepin); "Bend of the River" 1952 (Adam).

Fetherston, Eddie. *see* Featherstone, Eddie.

Feuer, Debra. Films: "Lacy and the Mississippi Queen" TVM-1978 (Queenie); "Desperado: The Outlaw Wars" TVM-1989 (Maggie).

Feusier, Norman (1885-12/27/45). Films: "Diamond Trail" 1933 (Harry Jones); "Border Vengeance" 1935 (Old Man Benson).

Fickett, Mary. TV: *Have Gun Will Travel*—"The Vigil" 9-16-61 (Adella Forsyth); *Lancer*—"The Last Train for Charlie Poe" 11-26-68 (Mollie Poe), "The Rivals" 5-5-70 (Aggie); *Bonanza*—"Erin" 1-26-69 (Erin O'Donnell); *Daniel Boone*—"Hannah Comes Home" 12-25-69 (Hannah).

Fidani, Demofilo (Miles Deem). Films: "Shadow of Sartana ... Shadow of Your Death" 1968-Ital.

Fieberling, Hal. *see* Baylor, Hal.

Fiedler, John (1925-). Films: "Guns of Diablo" 1964 (Ives); "Ballad of Josie" 1968 (Simpson); "The Great Bank Robbery" 1969 (Brother Dismas); "True Grit" 1969 (Lawyer J. Noble Daggett); "Hitched" TVM-1973 (Henry). ¶TV: *Have Gun Will Travel*—"The Gold Bar" 3-18-61 (Turner); *The Outlaws*—"No More Horses" 3-1-62 (Ludlow Pratt); *The Tall Man*—"A Time to Run" 4-7-62 (Abner Moody); *Bonanza*—"Rich Man, Poor Man" 5-12-63 (Claude Miller); *The Travels of Jaimie McPheeters*—"The Day of the Reckoning" 3-15-64 (Ives); *Destry*—"Deputy for a Day" 4-3-64 (Bill Simpson); *Gunsmoke*—"Hammerhead" 12-26-64 (Fitch Tallman), "A Quiet Day in Dodge" 1-29-73 (Mr. Ballou); *Death Valley Days*—"The Great Diamond Mines" 3-9-68 (Slack); *Dirty Sally*—"The Hanging of Cyrus Pike" 4-5-74 (Al Fromley); *Father Murphy*—"Outrageous Fortune" 11-9-82 (Nathan Alley).

Field, Betty (1913-9/13/73). Films: "The Shepherd of the Hills" 1941 (Sammy Lane).

Field, Charlotte. Films: "The Mysterious Rider" 1938 (Collie Wade); "Pride of the West" 1938 (Mary Martin).

Field, Chelsea. Films: "James A. Michener's Texas" TVM-1995 (Mattie Quimper).

Field, Cliff. TV: *Death Valley Days*—"I Am Joaquin" 3-28-55; *Wichita Town*—"Bought" 1-13-60 (Gregg); *Wanted—Dead or Alive*—"The Monsters" 1-16-60.

Field, Elinor. Films: "The Purple Riders" 1921-serial; "Blinky" 1923 (Priscilla Islip); "Don Quickshot of the Rio Grande" 1923 (Tulip Hellier); "The Red Warning" 1923 (Louise Ainslee); "Singled-Handed" 1923 (Ruth Randolph); "Stolen Gold" 1923; "Western Skies" 1923; "Peace for a Gunfighter" 1967.

Field, George (1878-3/9/25). Films: "Spike Shannon's Last Fight" 1911; "The Girl and the Sheriff" 1912; "The Sheriff's Round-Up" 1912; "Young Wild West Leading a Raid" 1912; "The Ghost of the Hacienda" 1913; "Hearts and Horses" 1913; "A Spartan Girl of the West" 1913; "Calamity Anne's Love Affair" 1914; "Jim" 1914; "The Silent Way" 1914; "The Senor's Silver Buckle" 1915; "Truth or Fiction" 1915; "The Water Carrier of San Juan" 1915; "Deuce Duncan" 1918 (Pedro Estavan); "The Light of Western Stars" 1918 (Don Carlos); "Riddle Gawne" 1918 (Nigger Paisley); "The End of the Game"

1919 (Four-Ace Baker); "The Fighting Line" 1919; "The Gray Wolf's Ghost" 1919 (Miguel); "The Kid and the Cowboy" 1919; "A Sage Brush Hamlet" 1919 (Pedro); "The White Man's Courage" 1919 (Juan Lopez); "Hair-Trigger Stuff" 1920; "Held Up for the Makin's" 1920; "The Moon Riders" 1920-serial; "The Prospector's Vengeance" 1920; "The Rattler's Hiss" 1920; "The Crimson Challenge" 1922 (Wylackie); "North of the Rio Grande" 1922 (Paul Perez); "Trigger Finger" 1924 (Dr. Deering).

Field, Gladys (-9/2/20). Films: "A Pal's Oath" 1911; "The Stage Driver's Daughter" 1911.

Field, Helen. Films: "Desperate Trails" 1921 (Carrie); "Up and Going" 1922 (Jacquette McNab).

Field, Karin. Films: "Return of Shanghai Joe" 1974-Ger./Ital.

Field, Logan. TV: *Wagon Train*—"The Flint McCullough Story" 1-14-59 (Hayes); *Tales of Wells Fargo*—"Return of Doc Bell" 11-30-59 (Baker), "The Kinfolk" 9-26-60; *Bonanza*—"Feet of Clay" 4-16-60 (Vance Allen); *Man from Blackhawk*—"Gold Is Where You Find It" 6-24-60 (Tony Wilson); *Rawhide*—"Gold Fever" 5-4-62 (Les); *Wild Wild West*—"The Night of the Arrow" 12-29-67 (Sergeant).

Field, Margaret. Films: "The Paleface" 1948 (Guest); "The Dakota Kid" 1951 (Mark Lewis); "Yukon Manhunt" 1951; "The Raiders" 1952 (Mary Morrell). TV: *The Lone Ranger*—"Greed for Gold" 1-19-50; *The Range Rider*—"Convict at Large" 10-4-52, "Marshal from Madero" 1-24-53; *The Gene Autry Show*—"Sharpshooter" 8-3-54, "Outlaw of Blue Mesa" 9-7-54.

Field, Mary (1905-). Films: "Cowboy from Brooklyn" 1938 (Myrtle Semple); "The Fighting Gringo" 1939 (Sandra Courtney); "Legion of the Lawless" 1940 (Mrs. Barton); "Legion of the Lawless" 1940; "The Trail Blazers" 1940 (Alice Chapman); "A Lady Takes a Chance" 1943 (Florrie Bendix); "Passage West" 1951 (Miss Swingate); "Four Guns to the Border" 1954 (Mrs. Pritchard); "The Missouri Traveler" 1958 (Nelda Hamilton); "Ride a Crooked Trail" 1958 (Mrs. Curtis); "Seven Ways from Sundown" 1960 (Ma Kerrington). TV: *Death Valley Days*—"Man on the Run" 2-10-58; *Gunsmoke*—"Til Death Do Us" 1-16-60 (Minerva Cobb), "Coventry" 3-17-62 (Clara Ott); *Wagon Train*—"The Horace Best Story" 10-5-60.

Field, Sally (1946-). Films: "The Way West" 1967 (Mercy McBee); "Hitched" TVM-1973 (Roselle Bridgeman); "Bridger" TVM-1976 (Jennifer Melford). TV: *Alias Smith and Jones*—"Dreadful Sorry, Clementine" 11-18-71 (Clementine Hale), "The Clementine Incident" 10-7-72 (Clementine Hale).

Field, Virginia (1917-1/2/92). Films: "The Cisco Kid and the Lady" 1939 (Billie Graham); "Hudson Bay" 1941 (Nell Gwynn). TV: *The Rebel*—"The Actress" 2-5-61 (Lotta Langley); *Tales of Wells Fargo*—"Kelly's Clover Girls" 12-9-61 (Kelly Green); *Iron Horse*—"No Wedding Bells for Tony" 11-7-66 (Madge).

Fielding, Edward (1879-1/10/45). Films: "Belle of the Yukon" 1944 (C.V. Atterbury).

Fielding, Margaret (1895-11/25/74). Films: "Kentucky Days" 1923 (Elizabeth Clayborne).

Fielding, Romaine (1882-12/16/27). Films: "Chief White Eagle" 1912; "The Cringer" 1912; "The Forest Ranger" 1912; "His Western Way" 1912; "An Indian's Gratitude" 1912; "The Salted Mine" 1912; "A Soldier's Furlough" 1912; "An Adventure on the Mexican Border" 1913; "Hiawanda's Cross" 1913; "The Eagle's Nest" 1915 (Robert Blasedon); "A Western Governor's Humanity" 1915; "The Valley of Lost Hope" 1915 (John Royce); "A Woman's Man" 1920 (Larry Moore)"Gun Gospel" 1927 (Richard Carroll); "Rose of the Golden West" 1927 (Secretary); "The Shepherd of the Hills" 1928 (Old Matt).

Fields, Darlene. Films: "Gunsight Ridge" 1957 (Rosa). TV: *Circus Boy*—"Counterfeit Clown" 4-7-57 (Doris); *Tales of the Texas Rangers*—"Double Reward" 12-15-57; *Tales of Wells Fargo*—"Stage West" 1-13-58 (Ellen Lamson); *Wagon Train*—"The Amos Gibbon Story" 4-20-60; *Cheyenne*—"Two Trails to Santa Fe" 10-28-60 (Belle).

Fields, Izack. Films: "The Red, White and Black" 1970 (1st Sgt. Roberson). TV: *Cowboy in Africa*—"Search for Survival" 10-9-67 (Kanya); *Daniel Boone*—"The Value of a King" 11-9-67; *The High Chaparral*—"The Buffalo Soldiers" 11-22-68 (Higgins).

Fields, Stanley (1880-4/23/41). Films: "The Border Legion" 1930 (Hack Gulden); "A Holy Terror" 1931 (Butch Morgan); "Riders of the Purple Sage" 1931 (Oldring); "Destry Rides Again" 1932 (Sheriff Wendell);

"Rocky Rhodes" 1934 (Harp Haverty); "The Gay Desperado" 1936 (Butch); "The Mine with the Iron Door" 1936 (Dempsey); "O'Malley of the Mounted" 1936 (Red Jagger); "Roll Along, Cowboy" 1937 (Barry Barker); "Way Out West" 1937 (Sheriff); "Wells Fargo" 1937 (Abe); "Wild and Woolly" 1937; "The Painted Desert" 1938 (Placer Bill); "Panamint's Bad Man" 1938 (Black Jack Deevers); "Viva Cisco Kid" 1940 (Ross); "Wyoming" 1940 (Curley); "Lady from Cheyenne" 1941 (Stover).

Fields, W.C. (1879-12/25/46). Films: "My Little Chickadee" 1940 (Cuthbert J. Twillie).

Fiermonte, Enzo (1908-). Films: "A Minute to Pray, a Second to Die" 1967-Ital. (Dr. Chase); "The Greatest Robbery in the West" 1968-Ital.; "A Long Ride from Hell" 1968-Ital.; "They Call Him Veritas" 1972-Ital./Span.; "Trinity Is Still My Name" 1974-Ital.

Fierro, Paul. Films: "Red River" 1948 (Fernandez); "River Lady" 1948 (Man on Deck); "Callaway Went Thataway" 1951 (Mexican Bartender); "Passage West" 1951 (Ramon); "The Fighter" 1952 (Fierro); "Waco" 1952 (Lou Garcia); "A Perilous Journey" 1953 (Pepe); "Ride, Vaquero!" 1953 (Valero); "San Antone" 1953 (Bandit Leader); "Wings of the Hawk" 1953 (Carlos); "Dig That Uranium" 1956 (Indian); "Raw Edge" 1956 (Bull, the Bartender); "Stagecoach to Fury" 1956 (Pedro); "Yaqui Drums" 1956; "War Drums" 1957 (Fiero); "Oregon Passage" 1958 (Nato). TV: *The Roy Rogers Show*—"Peril from the Past" 4-13-52; *The Lone Ranger*—"Treason at Dry Creek" 12-4-52; *The Cisco Kid*—"Choctaw Justice" 12-26-53; *The Adventures of Rin Tin Tin*—"Return of the Chief" 9-28-56 (Lopez); *Cheyenne*—"The Mustang Trail" 11-20-56 (Manuel); *Jim Bowie*—"Deaf Smith" 2-7-58 (Pedro); *Maverick*—"Trail West to Fury" 2-16-58 (Miguel), "The Judas Mask" 11-2-58 (Manuel); *Wyatt Earp*—"Dig a Grave for Ben Thompson" 5-20-58 (Valdez), "The Case of Senor Huerto" 2-9-60 (Cortez); *Sugarfoot*—"Outlaw Island" 11-24-59 (Miguel); *Bat Masterson*—"Blood on the Money" 6-23-60 (Hidalgo), "High Card Loses" 11-10-60 (Jose Tomas Reilly); *Bronco*—"Rendezvous with a Miracle" 2-12-62 (Lobo); *Tales of Wells Fargo*—"The Wayfarers" 5-19-62 (Bandit); *Empire*—"Down There, the World" 3-12-63 (Bob Lopez); *Lancer*—"The High Riders" 9-24-68 (Cipriano); *The High Chaparral*—

"New Hostess in Town" 3-20-70 (Domingo), "Only the Bad Come to Sonora" 10-2-70.

Figueroa, Laura (1948-). TV: *Gunsmoke*—"The Cage" 3-23-70 (Maria).

Filauri, Antonio (1889-1/18/64). Films: "King of the Bandits" 1947 (Padre); "The Big Sombrero" 1949 (Pablo).

Fillmore, Clyde (1874-12/19/46). Films: "The Sundown Trail" 1919 (Velvet); "Sting of the Lash" 1921 (Joel Gant); "Bad Bascomb" 1946 (Governor Clark).

Filmer, Robert W. Films: "The El Paso Kid" 1946 (Gil Santos); "The Fighting Frontiersman" 1946; "Cheyenne" 1947 (Gambler); "Phantom Valley" 1948 (Bob Reynolds); "Challenge of the Range" 1949 (Grat Largo); "Viva Zapata!" 1952 (Captain). ¶TV: *The Gene Autry Show*—"Gray Dude" 12-3-50, "The Peace Maker" 12-17-50; *Wild Bill Hickok*—"A Close Shave for the Marshal" 4-29-52, "Old Cowboys Never Die" 12-16-52.

Filpi, Carmen. TV: *Adventures of Brisco County, Jr.*—"Brisco for the Defense" 10-22-93 (Titus Miller).

Filson, Al (1857-11/14/25). Films: "A Yankee from the West" 1915 (Whitney Mills); "Hands Down" 1918 (Jack Dedlow).

Fimple, Dennis. Films: "Alias Smith and Jones" TVM-1971 (Kyle); "Sam Hill: Who Killed the Mysterious Mr. Foster?" TVM-1971; "The Culpepper Cattle Company" 1972 (Wounded Man in Bar); "Honky Tonk" TVM-1974; "The Apple Dumpling Gang" 1975 (Rudy Hooks); "Mackintosh & T.J." 1975 (Schuster); "Winterhawk" 1975 (Scobie); "Young Pioneers" TVM-1976 (Man in Land Officer); "Last Ride of the Dalton Gang" TVM-1979 (Blackface); "Goin' South" 1978; "Shadow of Chikara" 1978 (Posey); "The Wild Women of Chastity Gulch" TVM-1982 (Lamont); "Once Upon a Texas Train" TVM-1988; "My Heroes Have Always Been Cowboys" 1991; "Maverick" 1995 (Stuttering). ¶TV: *Here Come the Brides*—"The Crimpers" 3-5-69; *Alias Smith and Jones*—"Return to Devil's Hole" 2-25-71 (Kyle), "The Man Who Murdered Himself" 3-18-71 (Kyle), "The Day They Hanged Kid Curry" 9-16-71 (Kyle), "The Man Who Broke the Bank at Red Gap" 1-20-72 (Kyle), "The Biggest Game in the West" 2-3-72 (Kyle), "The McCreedy Feud" 9-30-72 (Kyle); *Kung Fu*—"Cross-ties" 2-21-

74 (Riley); *Adventures of Brisco County, Jr.*—"Iron Horses" 11-19-93 (Gully Barton).

Finch, Flora (1869-1/4/40). Films: "Some Duel" 1915; "Rose of the Golden West" 1927 (Senora Comba); "Way Out West" 1937 (Maw, the Miner's Wife).

Finch, Peter (1916-1/14/77). Films: "Robbery Under Arms" 1958-Brit. (Capt. Starlight).

Findlay, Ruth (1904-7/13/49). Films: "The Last of the Clintons" 1935; "The Pecos Kid" 1935 (Mary Evans); "Ghost Town" 1936 (Billie Blair); "Heroes of the Alamo" 1938 (Anne Dickinson).

Fine, Bud (1894-2/9/66). Films: "The Texas Ranger" 1931 (Breed); "Drift Fence" 1936 (Sam Haverly); "The Gay Desperado" 1936; "The Return of Frank James" 1940 (Deputy); "Three Troubledoors" 1946-short (Townsman); "The Sea of Grass" 1947 (Brakeman); "Santa Fe" 1951.

Fine, Larry (1911-1/24/75). Films: "Horses' Collars" 1935-short; "Whoops, I'm an Indian" 1936-short (Larry); "Back to the Woods" 1937-short (Larry); "Goofs and Saddles" 1937-short (Larry); "Yes, We Have No Bonanza" 1939-short (Larry); "Rockin' Through the Rockies" 1940-short (Larry); "Cactus Makes Perfect" 1942-short; "Phony Express" 1943-short (Larry); "Rockin' in the Rockies" 1945 (Larry); "Three Troubledoors" 1946-short (Larry); "Out West" 1947-short (Larry); "Punchy Cowpunchers" 1950-short (Larry); "Gold Raiders" 1951 (Larry); "Merry Mavericks" 1951-short (Larry); "Pals and Gals" 1954-short (Larry); "Shot in the Frontier" 1954-short (Larry); "The Outlaws Is Coming!" 1965 (Larry).

Fine, Travis. TV: *Young Riders*—Regular 1990-92 (Ike McSwain).

Fineschi, Lorenzo. Films: "His Name Was King" 1971-Ital.; "Man Called Sledge" 1971-Ital./U.S. (Toby); "Deaf Smith and Johnny Ears" 1972-Ital.; "Magnificent West" 1972-Ital. (Lefty); "On the Third Day Arrive the Crow" 1972-Ital./Span. (Tornado).

Finlayson, James (1887-10/9/53). Films: "No Man's Law" 1927 (Jack Belcher); "Way Out West" 1937 (Mickey Finn); "Grand Canyon Trail" 1948 (Sheriff).

Finley, Evelyn (1916-4/7/89). Films: "Arizona Frontier" 1940 (Honey Lane); "Dynamite Canyon" 1941 (Midge Reed); "Trail Riders" 1942 (Mary); "Black Market Rustlers" 1943 (Linda); "Cowboy Com-

mandos" 1943 (Joan); "Ghost Guns" 1944; "Valley of Vengeance" 1944 (Helen); "Prairie Rustlers" 1945 (Helen); "Gunning for Justice" 1948; "The Sheriff of Medicine Bow" 1948; "Sundown Riders" 1948 (Donna Fraser). ¶TV: *The Roy Rogers Show*—"The Hermit's Secret" 5-1-52 (Ruby Barton).

Finley, Larry. Films: "The Man Who Shot Liberty Valance" 1962 (Bar X Man); "The Cowboys" 1972 (Jake); "The Culpepper Cattle Company" 1972 (Mr. Slater); "The Man Who Loved Cat Dancing" 1973 (Bartender). ¶TV: *Bonanza*—"The Imposters" 12-13-70 (Petey); *Gunsmoke*—"Captain Sligo" 1-4-71 (Bartender), "Jessie" 2-19-73 (Barkeep); *Kung Fu*—"King of the Mountain" 10-14-72 (Blacksmith).

Finley, Ned (-9/27/20). Films: "O'Garry of the Royal Mounted" 1915; "West Wind" 1915; "Britton of the Seventh" 1916 (Gen. Custer); "The Blue Streak" 1917 (Sheriff).

Finn, Mickey. Films: "Pardners" 1956 (Red); "The Tin Star" 1957 (McCall); "One-Eyed Jacks" 1961 (Blacksmith); "Sergents 3" 1962 (Morton); "Incident at Phantom Hill" 1966 (2nd Hunter). ¶TV: *Tales of the Texas Rangers*—"Key Witness" 9-29-57 (Hunk); *Tales of Wells Fargo*—"End of the Trail" 10-20-58 (Ben Costa); *Have Gun Will Travel*—"The Road to Wickenberg" 10-25-58 (Ed Goodfellow), "Tiger" 11-28-59; *Wagon Train*—"The Old Man Charvanaugh Story" 2-18-59 (Sump Charvanaugh), "The Amos Gibbon Story" 4-20-60, "The Myra Marshall Story" 10-21-63, "The Hide Hunters" 9-27-64 (Barbu), "The Jarbo Pierce Story" 5-2-65 (Edgar); *The Law of the Plainsman*—"The Imposter" 2-4-60 (Curley); *The Rebel*—"Fair Game" 3-27-60 (Stage Driver); *Maverick*—"The Bold Fenian Men" 12-18-60 (Mike O'Connell); *Bonanza*—"Bank Run" 1-28-61; *The Rifleman*—"The Lost Treasure of Canyon Town" 2-28-61 (James Newman); *Bat Masterson*—"The Fourth Man" 4-27-61 (Hunk Bass); *Rawhide*—"Incent of the Wager on Payday" 6-16-61; *Laredo*—"Anybody Here Seen Billy?" 10-21-65 (Heath), "A Matter of Policy" 11-11-65 (Pat Brannigan).

Finn, Sam (1893-12/14/58). Films: "The Furies" 1950 (Dealer).

Finnegan, Joe. Films: "Young Fury" 1965; "Duel at Diablo" 1966 (2nd Wagon Driver); "The Legend of the Lone Ranger" 1981 (Westlake).

Finnerty, Warren (1934-12/22/74). Films: "Kid Blue" 1973 (Wills).

¶TV: *The Outcasts*—"The Outcasts" 9-23-68 (Henderson); *Bonanza*—"Kingdom of Fear" 4-4-71 (2nd Gunman).

Fiorentino, Linda. Films: "The Desperate Trail" TVM-1995 (Sarah O'Rourke).

Firestone, Eddie (1920-). Films: "The Brass Legend" 1956 (Shorty); "The Great Locomotive Chase" 1956 (Robert Buffum); "The Law and Jake Wade" 1958 (Burke); "Scalplock" TVM-1966; "A Man Called Gannon" 1969 (Maz); "Standing Tall" TVM-1978 (Strickland). ¶TV: *Black Saddle*—"Client: Braun" 4-4-59 (Lucas Braun), "The Killer" 1-1-60 (Willis House); *Bonanza*—"Tax Collector" 2-18-61 (Jock Henry), "A Good Night's Rest" 4-11-65 (Potts), "Five Candles" 3-2-69 (Banty); *Tales of Wells Fargo*—"Winter Storm" 3-3-62 (Kelly); *Death Valley Days*—"Miracle at Whiskey Gulch" 5-16-62 (Jim), "Old Stape" 10-18-69, "The Great Pinto Bean Gold Hunt" 12-13-69; *Temple Houston*—"Jubilee" 11-14-63 (Tobe Gillard); *The Legend of Jesse James*—"The Pursuers" 10-11-65 (Caleb Bentley); *Rawhide*—"The Testing Post" 11-30-65 (Smitty); *Gunsmoke*—"The Brothers" 3-12-66 (Carl Wilkins), "Nitro!" 4-8-67 & 4-15-67 (Red Bailey), "The Hide Cutters" 9-30-68 (Weevil), "Lobo" 12-16-68 (Riney), "Snow Train" 10-19-70 & 10-26-70 (Hap), "The Bullet" 11-29-71, 12-6-71 & 12-13-71 (Orey), "Tarnished Badge" 11-11-74 (Hotel Clerk); *Dundee and the Culhane*—9-27-67 (Shorty); *The Big Valley*—"Explosion!" 11-20-67 & 11-27-67 (Toby); *Cimarron Strip*—"The Last Wolf" 12-14-67 (Crawford); *The High Chaparral*—"No Irish Need Apply" 1-17-69 (Scanlon); *The Guns of Will Sonnett*—"The Trial" 2-28-69 (Coley Flynn); *Wild Wild West*—"The Night of the Plague" 4-4-69 (Stills); *Here Come the Brides*—"Hosanna's Way" 10-31-69 (Trapper); *Kung Fu*—"The Squaw Man" 11-1-73 (1st Man); *How the West Was Won*—Episode One 2-6-77 (Louie).

Fischer, Bruce M. (1936-). Films: "Doc" 1971 (Billy Clanton); "Man in the Wilderness" 1971-U.S./Span. (Wiser); "A Town Called Hell" 1971-Span./Brit. (Miguel); "The Man Called Noon" 1973-Brit./Span./Ital. (Ranch Hand); "Baker's Hawk" 1976 (Blacksmith); "The Sacketts" TVM-1979; "The Gambler" TVM-1980 (Tabor); "Grim Prairie Tales" 1990 (Colochez). ¶TV: *Gunsmoke*—"The Angry Land" 2-3-75 (Man); *The Quest*—"The Freight Train Rescue"

12-29-76 (Dooley); *How the West Was Won*—Episode One 2-12-78 (Booster); *Young Maverick*—"Have I Got a Girl for You" 1-16-80; *Best of the West*—11-5-81 (Hickerson); *Father Murphy*—"John Michael Murphy, R.I.P." 12-7-82 (Big Jake).

Fischer, Corey. Films: "McCabe and Mrs. Miller" 1971 (Mr. Elliott). ¶TV: *Daniel Boone*—"The Jasser Ledbedder Story" 2-2-67 (Freddie Ledbedder).

Fischer, Margarita (1886-3/11/75). Films: "The Parson and the Medicine Man" 1912; "Tribal Law" 1912; "Put Up Your Hands" 1919 (Olive Barton); "The Gamesters" 1920 (Rose).

Fisher, Edna. Films: "Broncho Billy's Christmas Dinner" 1911; "A Frontier Doctor" 1911; "The Deputy and the Girl" 1912; "The Sheepman's Escape" 1912; "The Tenderfoot Foreman" 1912.

Fisher, Frances. Films: "Unforgiven" 1992 (Strawberry Alice). ¶TV: *Young Riders*—"A House Divided" 9-28-91 (Clara Turner).

Fisher, George (1894-8/13/60). Films: "The Darkening Trail" 1915 (Jack Sturgess); "The Roughneck" 1915; "The Promise" 1917 (St. Ledger); "The Texas Kid" 1920; "Colorado Pluck" 1921 (Philip Meredith); "Sure Fire" 1921 (Burt Rawlings); "The Trail of the Axe" 1922 (Jim Malkern).

Fisher, Larry (1891-12/6/37). Films: "The Golden Strain" 1925 (Captain Powell); "Breed of the Sunsets" 1928 (Hank Scully).

Fisher, LeRoy "Shug" (1907-). Films: "The Last Round-Up" 1947 (Marvin); "Riders of the Pony Express" 1949; "Stallion Canyon" 1949 (Red); "Rio Grande" 1950 (Regimental Singer); "Border Fence" 1951; "Sergeant Rutledge" 1960 (Mr. Owens); "The Man Who Shot Liberty Valance" 1962 (Kaintuck, the Drunk); "Cheyenne Autumn" 1964 (Trail Boss); "Shenandoah" 1965 (Confederate Soldier); "Cutter's Trail" TVM-1970 (Tuttle); "Guns of a Stranger" 1973; "The Castaway Cowboy" 1974 (Captain Cary); "The Apple Dumpling Gang Rides Again" 1979; "The Sacketts" TVM-1979. ¶TV: *Have Gun Will Travel*—"The Revenger" 9-30-61 (Altman), "The Fifth Bullet" 9-29-62, "Brotherhood" 1-5-63 (Kroll); *Gunsmoke*—"The Summons" 4-21-62 (Telegrapher), "The Dreamers" 4-28-62, "Chester's Indian" 5-12-62 (Obie), "No Hands" 2-8-64 (Barkeep), "Kitty Cornered"

4-18-64 (Harry Obie), "Deputy Festus" 1-16-65 (Emery), "The Storm" 9-25-65 (Hank Cooters), "Sweet Billy, Singer of Songs" 1-15-66 (Emery), "The Good People" 10-15-66 (Silas Shute), "Fandango" 2-11-67 (Chongra), "A Noose for Dobie Price" 3-4-68 (Dobie Price), "Railroad" 11-25-68 (Jim Graham), "Johnny Cross" 12-23-68 (Franks), "The Still" 11-10-69 (Uncle Titus), "Gentry's Law" 10-12-70 (Orly Grimes), "The Tycoon" 1-25-71 (Titus), "Waste" 9-27-71 & 10-4-71 (Jed Rascoe), "A Quiet Day in Dodge" 1-29-73 (Dobie Crimps), "The Guns of Cibola Blanca" 9-23-74 & 9-30-74 (Mule Skinner); *Temple Houston*—"The Siege at Thayer's Bluff" 11-7-63 (Augie Wren); *The Virginian*—"Legend for a Lawman" 3-3-65 (Pony Bill Steele), "An Echo of Thunder" 10-5-66 (Telegrapher); *Daniel Boone*—"Cain's Birthday" 4-1-65 & 4-8-65 (Jake Tench), 9-23-65 (Blacksmith); *The Legend of Jesse James*—"The Celebrity" 12-6-65 (Barber); *Laredo*—"The Land Grabbers" 12-9-65, "A Double Shot of Nepenthe" 9-30-66 (Prospector), "The Small Chance Ghost" 3-3-67 (Old Charlie); *Wild Wild West*—"The Night of the Poisonous Posey" 10-28-66 (Sheriff Blayne Cord), "The Night of the Cut Throats" 11-17-67 (Jeremiah); *The Monroes*—"Lost in the Wilderness" 11-30-66 (Zeph); *Cimarron Strip*—"Journey to a Hanging" 9-7-67 (Smitty), "The Greeners" 3-7-68 (Pinky); *Bonanza*—"Stage Door Johnnies" 7-28-68 (Driver), "El Jefe" 11-15-70 (Toler); *The Men from Shiloh*—"The Animal" 1-20-71 (Tinker).

Fisher, Millicent (1896-1/1/79). Films: "Fighting Through" 1919 (Maryland Warren); "Billy Jim" 1922 (Marsha Dunforth); "Man of Courage" 1922 (Dorothy Deane).

Fiske, Richard (1915-8/44). Films: "The Purple Vigilantes" 1938 (Drake); "The Man from Sundown" 1939 (Tom Kellogg); "Overland with Kit Carson" 1939-serial (David Brent); "Pest from the West" 1939-short; "Teacher's Pest" 1939-short; "The Man from Tumbleweeds" 1940 (Dixon); "Pioneers of the Frontier" 1940 (Bart); "Prairie Schooners" 1940 (Adams); "Texas Stagecoach" 1940 (Workman); "Across the Sierras" 1941 (Larry); "The Medico of Painted Springs" 1941 (Kentucky Lane); "North from the Lone Star" 1941 (Clint Wilson); "Outlaws of the Panhandle" 1941 (Britt); "The Son of Davy Crockett" 1941 (Jesse Gordon); "Perils of the Royal Mounted" 1942-serial (Brady); "Valley of the Sun" 1942 (Lieutenant).

Fiske, Robert (1889-9/12/44). Films: "Battle of Greed" 1934 (Hammond); "The Cowboy Star" 1936 (Director); "Song of the Gringo" 1936; "Raw Timber" 1937 (Bart Williams); "Drums of Destiny" 1937 (Holston); "The Law Commands" 1937 (John Abbott); "The Law Commands" 1937 (Abbott); "Old Louisiana" 1937 (Luke Gilmore); "Roaring Six Guns" 1937 (Jake Harmon); "Cassidy of Bar 20" 1938 (Clay Allison); "Colorado Trail" 1938 (Deacon Webster); "The Great Adventures of Wild Bill Hickok" 1938; "South of Arizona" 1938 (Martin Kenyon); "Sunset Trail" 1938 (Monte Keller); "West of Santa Fe" 1938 (Frank Parker); "The Man from Sundown" 1939 (Capt. Prescott); "North of the Yukon" 1939 (Mart Duncan); "Overland with Kit Carson" 1939-serial; "Racketeers of the Range" 1939 (Whitlock); "The Stranger from Texas" 1939 (Ned Browning); "The Taming of the West" 1939 (Blake); "The Thundering West" 1939 (Harper, the Barkeep); "Timber Stampede" 1939 (Matt Chaflin); "Carolina Moon" 1940 (Barrett); "Colorado" 1940; "Deadwood Dick" 1940-serial (Ashton); "Konga, the Wild Stallion" 1940 (Steve Calhoun); "Law and Order" 1940 (Deal); "Texas Terrors" 1940 (Barker); "The Apache Kid" 1941 (Joe Walker); "Along the Rio Grande" 1941 (Doc Randall); "Valley of Vanishing Men" 1942-serial; "Vengeance of the West" 1942; "Dead Man's Gulch" 1943; "The Texas Kid" 1943 (Naylor).

Fiske, Warren. Films: "Daredevils of the West" 1943-serial (Indian); "Colt .45" 1950; "Silver City" 1951 (Townsman); "Son of Paleface" 1952 (Trav.).

Fitch, Louise. Films: "Starbird and Sweet William" 1975. ¶TV: *Bonanza*—"Five Candles" 3-2-69 (Mrs. Connor).

Fite, Bob (and His Six Saddle Tramps). Films: "The Phantom Rider" 1936-serial; "Roll Along, Cowboy" 1937.

Fitzgerald, Barry (1888-1/4/61). Films: "California" 1946 (Michael Fabian); "Silver City" 1951 (R.R. Jarboe).

Fitzgerald, Cissy (1874-5/5/41). Films: "Arizona Wildcat" 1927 (Mother Schyler).

Fitzharis, Ed (1890-10/12/74). Films: "Four Hearts" 1922 (Jim Hawkins).

Fitzgerald, Ella (1918-). Films: "Ride 'Em, Cowboy" 1942 (Ruby).

Fitzpatrick, John. Films: "Last Ride of the Dalton Gang" TVM-1979 (Texas Jack Broadwell).

Fitzroy, Emily (1861-3/3/54). Films: "Galloping Jinx" 1925; "Zander the Great" 1925 (the Matron); "Hard-Boiled" 1926 (Abigail Gregg); "Bold Caballero" 1936 (Duenna); "The Frontiersman" 1938 (Miss Snook).

Fitzroy, Louis (1870-1/26/47). Films: "Captured Alive" 1918; "Wolves of the Range" 1918; "The Four Gun Bandit" 1919; "Two Moons" 1920 (Uncle Alf); "On the Go" 1925 (Mr. Evans).

Fix, Paul (1902-10/14/83). Films: "The Avenger" 1931; "The Fighting Sheriff" 1931 (Jack Cameron); "South of the Rio Grande" 1932 (Juan); "Fargo Express" 1933 (Morton Clark); "Gun Law" 1933 (Tony Andrews); "Somewhere in Sonora" 1933 (Bart Leadly); "Rocky Rhodes" 1934 (Joe Hilton); "The Westerner" 1934 (Henchman); "Bulldog Courage" 1935 (Bailey); "The Crimson Trail" 1935 (Paul); "Desert Trail" 1935 (Jim); "His Fighting Blood" 1935; "Sunset Range" 1935; "The Throwback" 1935 (Spike Travis); "Valley of Wanted Men" 1935 (Mike Masters); "Bar 20 Rides Again" 1936 (Gila); "The Eagle's Brood" 1936 (Steve); "Phantom Patrol" 1936 (Jojo Regan); "Border Cafe" 1937 (Dolson); "Western Gold" 1937; "Gun Law" 1938; "The Girl and the Gambler" 1939 (Charlie); "Heritage of the Desert" 1939 (Chick Chancer); "Wall Street Cowboy" 1939; "The Fargo Kid" 1940 (Deuce Mallory); "Trail of the Vigilantes" 1940 (Lefty); "Triple Justice" 1940 (Cleary); "Down Mexico Way" 1941 (Davis); "A Missouri Outlaw" 1941 (Mark Roberts); "South of Santa Fe" 1942 (Joe); "In Old Oklahoma" 1943 (the Cherokee Kid); "Tall in the Saddle" 1944 (Bob Clews); "Dakota" 1945 (Carp); "Flame of the Barbary Coast" 1945 (Calico Jim); "The Plunderers" 1948 (Calico); "Red River" 1948 (Teeler Yacy); "The Fighting Kentuckian" 1949 (Beau Merritt); "Fighting Man of the Plains" 1949 (Yancey); "Hellfire" 1949 (Dusty Stoner); "She Wore a Yellow Ribbon" 1949 (Gunrunner); "California Passage" 1950 (Whalen); "Surrender" 1950 (Williams); "The Great Missouri Raid" 1951 (Sgt. Brill); "Warpath" 1951 (Pvt. Fiore); "Denver and Rio Grande" 1952 (Engineer Monyhan); "Ride the Man Down" 1952 (Ray Cavanaugh); "Devil's Canyon" 1953 (Gatling Guard); "Hondo" 1953

(Major Sherry); "Star of Texas" 1953 (Luke Andrews); "Johnny Guitar" 1954 (Eddie); "Giant" 1956 (Dr. Horace Lynnton); "Stagecoach to Fury" 1956 (Tim O'Connors); "Star in the Dust" 1956 (Mike MacNamara); "Man in the Shadow" 1957 (Herb Parker); "Night Passage" 1957 (Mr. Feeney); "Mail Order Bride" 1964 (Jess Linley); "The Outrage" 1964 (Indian); "Shenandoah" 1965 (Dr. Tom Witherspoon); "The Sons of Katie Elder" 1965 (Sheriff Billy Wilson); "An Eye for an Eye" 1966 (Quince); "Incident at Phantom Hill" 1966 (Gen. Hood); "Nevada Smith" 1966 (Sheriff Bonnell); "Ride Beyond Vengeance" 1966 (Hanley); "El Dorado" 1967 (Doc Miller); "Welcome to Hard Times" 1967 (Maj. Munn); "Winchester '73" TVM-1967 (Ben McAdam); "Ballad of Josie" 1968 (Alpheus Minick); "Day of the Evil Gun" 1968 (Sheriff); "The Undefeated" 1969 (Gen. Joe Masters); "Dirty Dingus Magee" 1970 (Chief Crazy Blanket); "Shoot Out" 1971 (Brakeman); "Cahill, United States Marshal" 1973 (Old Man); "Pat Garrett and Billy the Kid" 1973 (Pete Maxwell); "Grayeagle" 1977 (Running Wolf); "Wanda Nevada" 1979 (Texas Curly). ¶TV: *The Lone Ranger*—"Million Dollar Wallpaper" 9-14-50; *Gunsmoke*—"Cholera" 12-29-56 (McCready), "The Other Half" 5-30-64 (Sam Bartell), "Clayton Thaddeus Greenwood" 10-2-65 (Greenwood, Sr.), "Fandango" 2-11-67 (Doc Lacey), "Vengeance" 10-2-67 & 10-9-67 (Sloan); *The Restless Gun*—"Jody" 11-4-57 (Old Man Burnett); *Wagon Train*—"The Mark Hanford Story" 2-26-58 (Jake), "The Amos Billings Story" 3-14-62 (Amos Billings), "The Brian Conlin Story" 10-25-64 (Sean Bannon); *Colt .45*—"Golden Gun" 2-28-58 (Frank Wilson, Sr.); *Sugarfoot*—"Hideout" 4-1-58 (Bandit); *The Rifleman*—Regular 1958-63 (Marshal Micha Torrance); *The Texan*—"A Tree for Planting" 11-10-58 (Bert Gorman); *Bronco*—"The Long Ride Back" 11-18-58 (Mr. McNally); *Tales of Wells Fargo*—"The Killer" 12-1-58 (Senator Claymore); *Northwest Passage*—"Vengeance Trail" 12-21-58 (Joe Waters); *Zane Grey Theater*—"Medal for Valor" 12-25-58 (Rufus Stewart), "Cry Hope! Cry Hate!" 10-20-60 (Burkett); *Lawman*—"Riding Shotgun" 4-19-59 (Pop Marrady); *Rawhide*—"Incident of the Thirteenth Man" 10-23-59 (Ellis Williams); *The Law of the Plainsman*—"Toll Road" 12-24-59; *Riverboat*—"That Taylor Affair" 9-26-60 (Zachary Taylor);

Have Gun Will Travel—"The Burning Tree" 2-9-63 (Sheriff); *The Travels of Jaimie McPheeters*—"The Day of the Picnic" 2-16-64 (Sheriff); *A Man Called Shenandoah*—"Plunder" 3-7-66 (Sam Winters); *The Big Valley*—"The Murdered Party" 11-17-65 (Greene), "The Stallion" 1-30-67 (Brahma), "Top of the Stairs" 1-6-69 (Ben Abbott); *Daniel Boone*—"The Allegiances" 9-22-66 (Quonab), "Three Score and Ten" 2-6-69 (Chief Great Bear); *Wild Wild West*—"The Night of the Green Terror" 11-18-66 (Old Chief), "The Night of the Hangman" 10-20-67 (Judge Blake); *The Virginian*—"The Modoc Kid" 2-1-67 (Dr. Hinton); *Death Valley Days*—"One Fast Injun" 3-4-67 (Doc); *The Guns of Will Sonnett*—"The Guns of Will Sonnett" 9-8-67 (Olenhausen), "Pariah" 10-18-68 (Buck Cobb); *The High Chaparral*—"A Hanging Offense" 11-12-67 (Cochise), "The Peacemaker" 3-3-68 (Cochise); *Bonanza*—"The Gold Detector" 12-24-67 (Barney), "For a Young Lady" 12-27-70 (Buford Sturgis); *The Outcasts*—"The Thin Edge" 2-17-69 (Old Man); *Here Come the Brides*—"The Legend of Big Foot" 11-14-69 (Caleb); *The Men from Shiloh*—"Lady at the Bar" 11-4-70 (Boyle); *Alias Smith and Jones*—"The Day They Hanged Kid Curry" 9-16-71, "The Night of the Red Dog" 11-4-71 (Clarence), "Only Three to a Bed" 1-13-73 (Bronc); *How the West Was Won*—Episode Two 2-7-77 (Portagee), Episode Three 2-14-77 (Portagee).

Flaherty, Harper. TV: *Laredo*—"Which Way Did They Go?" 11-18-65; *The Virginian*—"The Decision" 3-13-68 (Harper), "Seth" 3-20-68 (Harper), "Silver Image" 9-25-68, "Storm Over Shiloh" 3-19-69 (Harper), "Fox, Hound, and the Widow McCloud" 4-2-69 (Harper), "The Sins of the Father" 3-4-70 (Harper); *Lancer*—"Foley" 10-15-68.

Flaherty, Pat (1903-12/2/70). Films: "End of the Trail" 1936 (Bouncer); "Dodge City" 1939; "Man from Montreal" 1940 (Tom); "Angel and the Badman" 1947 (Baker Brother); "The Treasure of the Sierra Madre" 1948 (Customer).

Flanagan, Bud. see O'Keefe, Dennis.

Flanagan, Fionnuala (1941-). Films: "The Godchild" TVM-1974 (Virginia); "Mad at the Moon" 1992 (Mrs. Hill). ¶TV: *Bonanza*—"Heritage of Anger" 9-19-72 (Elizabeth); *Gunsmoke*—"The Drummer" 10-9-72 (Sarah Morgan); *Hec Ramsey*—"Only

Birds and Fools" 4-7-74 (Nellie); *How the West Was Won*—Regular 1977-79 (Molly Culhan); *Dr. Quinn, Medicine Woman*—"The Circus" 1-15-94 (Heart); *Legend*—"Legend on His President's Secret Serice" 5-2-95 (Julia Grant).

Flanders, Ed (1934-2/22/95). TV: *Cimarron Strip*—"The Roarer" 11-2-67 (Arliss Blynn); *Daniel Boone*—"The Traitor" 10-30-69 (Colonel Lackland); *Bearcats!*—"Hostages" 10-14-71 (Ben Tillman); *Nichols*—"Flight of the Century" 2-22-72 (Flanders); *Kung Fu*—"The Salamander" 12-6-73 (Alonzo Davis).

Flannery, Susan (1943-). TV: *Death Valley Days*—"Birthright" 5-30-65 (Jenny Hardy).

Flato, Richard. Films: "Texans Never Cry" 1951 (Carlos Corbal).

Flavin, James (1906-4/23/76). Films: "McKenna of the Mounted" 1932 (Corporal Randall McKenna); "Brand of Hate" 1934; "Lightning Carson Rides Again" 1938 (Bill's Aide); "The Cisco Kid and the Lady" 1939 (Sergeant); "Jesse James" 1939 (Cavalry Captain); "Union Pacific" 1939 (Paddy); "Lucky Cisco Kid" 1940 (Ranch Foreman); "Northwest Mounted Police" 1940 (Mountie); "Belle Starr" 1941 (Sergeant); "Texas" 1941 (Announcer); "Western Union" 1941 (Man); "Ride 'Em, Cowboy" 1942 (Railroad Detective); "Riding High" 1943; "San Antonio" 1945 (Cattleman); "Desert Fury" 1947 (Pat Johnson); "Robin Hood of Texas" 1947 (Capt. Danforth); "Fury at Furnace Creek" 1948 (Judge Advocate); "The Plunderers" 1948 (Sergeant Major); "Dakota Lil" 1950 (Chief); "The Savage Horde" 1950; "Oh! Susanna" 1951 (Capt. Worth); "Star of Texas" 1953 (Captain of Rangers); "Massacre Canyon" 1954 (Col. Joseph Tarant); "Untamed Heiress" 1954 (Cop); "Apache Ambush" 1955 (Col. Marshall); "Night Passage" 1957 (Tim Riley); "The Restless Breed" 1957 (Secret Service Chief); "Cheyenne Autumn" 1964 (Sergeant of the Guard). ¶TV: *The Lone Ranger*—"Billie the Great" 3-30-50; *Broken Arrow*—"Hired Killer" 3-4-58 (Sheriff); *Buckskin*—"The Bullnappers" 11-6-58 (Caleb Quinn); *The Rifleman*—"The Lariat" 3-29-60; *Laramie*—"Naked Steel" 1-1-63; *Walt Disney Presents*—"Gallegher" 1965-67 (Lieutenant Flynn).

Fleer, Harry (-10/14/94). Films: "The Gun Hawk" 1963. ¶TV: *Wyatt Earp*—"Command Performance" 2-19-57 (Horner), "Wyatt Earp Rides Shotgun" 2-18-58 (Tom Russell),

"King of the Frontier" 11-11-58 (Gormley); *The Restless Gun*—"Cheyenne Express" 12-2-57 (Floyd Winters), "Friend in Need" 1-13-58 (Clyde Hemper), "Dragon for a Day" 9-29-58 (El Alecran); *Tombstone Territory*—"Shoot Out at Dark" 1-8-58 (Hank); *Tales of Wells Fargo*—"The Cleanup" 1-26-59 (Matt Carson); *Bat Masterson*—"Sharpshooter" 2-11-59 (Darby Cole), "Jeopardy at Jackson Hole" 6-1-61 (Harvey Field); *The Texan*—"The Telegraph Story" 10-26-59 (Gil Sommers), "End of Track" 12-21-59, "Killer's Road" 4-25-60 (Marshal Ray Gibbons); *Have Gun Will Travel*—"The Day of the Bad Men" 1-9-60 (Bart Reynolds); *The Deputy*—"The Legend of Dixie" 5-20-61 (Mace); *Laramie*—"The Accusers" 11-14-61; *Rawhide*—"The Bosses' Daughter" 2-2-62 (Art Durgin); *Branded*—"Coward Step Aside" 3-7-65 (Adams).

Fleischmann, Harry (1899-11/28/43). Films: "One Man Justice" 1937 (Joe Craig); "Let Freedom Ring" 1939 (Gagan's Henchman); "Rangers of Fortune" 1940 (Whitey); "Jackass Mail" 1942 (Carp).

Fleming, Alice (1882-12/6/52). Films: "Overland Mail Robbery" 1943 (Mrs. Patterson); "Cheyenne Wildcat" 1944; "Marshal of Reno" 1944 (the Duchess); "The San Antonio Kid" 1944; "Sheriff of Las Vegas" 1944; "Tucson Raiders" 1944 (Duchess); "Vigilantes of Dodge City" 1944; "Great Stagecoach Robbery" 1945; "Lone Texas Ranger" 1945; "Marshal of Laredo" 1945 (the Duchess); "Phantom of the Plains" 1945; "Wagon Wheels Westward" 1945; "California Gold Rush" 1946; "Conquest of Cheyenne" 1946 (the Duchess); "Sheriff of Redwood Valley" 1946; "Sun Valley Cyclone" 1946.

Fleming, Arthur. TV: *The Californians*—Regular 1958-59 (Jeremy Pitt).

Fleming, Ethel. Films: "The Pretender" 1918 (Dolly Longstreet); "The Silent Rider" 1918 (Jean Carson); "Untamed" 1918 (Ruth Allen).

Fleming, Eric (1926-9/28/66). Films: "Curse of the Undead" 1959 (Preacher Dan). ¶TV: *Rawhide*—Regular 1959-65 (Gil Favor); *Bonanza*—"Peace Officer" 2-6-66 (Wes Dunn), "The Pursued" 10-2-66 & 10-9-66 (Heber Clawson).

Fleming, Rhonda (1923-). Films: "In Old Oklahoma" 1943; "Abilene Town" 1946 (Sherry Balder); "The Eagle and the Hawk" 1950 (Madeline Danzeeger); "The Last Outpost" 1951 (Julie McCloud);

"The Redhead and the Cowboy" 1951 (Candace Bronson); "Pony Express" 1953 (Evelyn); "Those Redheads from Seattle" 1953 (Kathie Edmonds); "Tennessee's Partner" 1955 (Elizabeth "Duchess" Farnham); "Gunfight at the O.K. Corral" 1957 (Laura Denbow); "Gun Glory" 1957 (Jo); "Bullwhip" 1958 (Cheyenne); "Alias Jesse James" 1959 (the Duchess). ¶TV: *Wagon Train*—"The Jennifer Churchill Story" 10-15-58 (Jennifer Churchill), "The Patience Miller Story" 1-11-61 (Patience Miller), "The Sandra Cummings Story" 12-2-63 (Sandra Cummings); *Death Valley Days*—"Loss of Faith" 1-2-63 (Kitty Bolton); *Bob Hope Chrysler Theatre*—"Have Girls—Will Travel" 10-16-64 (Purity); *The Virginian*—"We've Lost a Train" 4-21-65 (Carmelita); *Kung Fu*—"Ambush" 4-5-75 (Jennie Malone).

Fleming, Robert "Bob" (1878-10/4/33). Films: "The Love Mask" 1916 (Jim); "Six-Shooter Andy" 1918 (Whiskey Bill); "Nugget Nell" 1919 (2nd Badman); "Daring Danger" 1922 (Bull Weaver); "Fighting Streak" 1922 (Chick Heath); "Biff Bang Buddy" 1924 (Shane McCune); "The Fighting Sap" 1924 (Sheriff); "Saddle Cyclone" 1925 (Regan); "Davy Crockett at the Fall of the Alamo" 1926 (Colonel Bowie); "Hurricane Horseman" 1926 (Sheriff); "Riding for Life" 1926; "Trumpin' Trouble" 1926 (John Lawson); "Gun Gospel" 1927 (Dad Walker); "The Love of Paquita" 1927; "The Mojave Kid" 1927 (Big Olaf); "The Bantam Cowboy" 1928 (Jason Todd); "The Fightin' Redhead" 1928 (Bob Anderson); "King Cowboy" 1928 (Jim Randall); "The Riding Renegade" 1928 (Ed Stacey); "The Dawn Trail" 1930 (Henchman); "The Lone Star Ranger" 1930 (2nd Deputy); "Desert Vengeance" 1931 (Winnipeg); "Texas Gun Fighter" 1932 (Clayton).

Fleming, Susan. Films: "The Range Feud" 1931 (Judy Walton); "Heritage of the Desert" 1932; "God's Country and the Woman" 1937 (Grace Moran).

Fletcher, Bill (1922-). Films: "Hour of the Gun" 1967 (Jimmy Ryan); "Five Card Stud" 1968 (Joe Hurley); "Alias Smith and Jones" TVM-1971 (Kane). ¶TV: *Shane*—"The Wild Geese" 9-24-66 (Wynn Truscott), "The Big Fifty" 12-10-66 (Lee Maddox); *Bonanza*—"Old Charlie" 11-6-66 (Sam), "The Unseen Wound" 1-29-67 (Tollar), "False Witness" 10-22-67 (Doug); *Laredo*—"One Too Many Voices" 11-18-66;

The Virginian—"Linda" 11-30-66 (Whitey Luder); *Daniel Boone*—"Fort West Point" 3-23-67 (Major John Andre); *Cimarron Strip*—"The Hunted" 10-5-67 (Harlin); *Wild Wild West*—"The Night of the Iron Fist" 12-8-67 (Joe Stark); *The High Chaparral*—"Our Lady of Guadalupe" 12-20-68 (Gillis); *The Men from Shiloh*—"The Town Killer" 3-10-71 (Greer); *Alias Smith and Jones*—"Never Trust an Honest Man" 4-15-71 (Logan), "Shootout at Diablo Station" 12-2-71, "Which Way to the O.K. Corral?" 2-10-72 (Doc Holliday), "The Ten Days That Shook Kid Curry" 11-4-72 (Doc Holliday); *Kung Fu*—"A Praying Mantis Kills" 3-22-73 (Fox), "A Lamb to the Slaughter" 1-11-75 (Father); *The Quest*—"The Captive" 9-22-76; *How the West Was Won*—"China Girl" 4-16-79 (Boatswain).

Fletcher, Jack (1921-). Films: "True Grit" TVM-1978 (Clerk).

Fletcher, Lester (1928-). TV: *Wild Wild West*—"The Night of the Diva" 3-7-69 (Karl Crenshaw).

Fletcher, Louise (1934-). TV: *Bat Masterson*—"Cheyenne Club" 12-17-58 (Sarah Pou); *Yancy Derringer*—"Old Dixie" 12-25-58 (Miss Nellie); *Lawman*—"The Encounter" 1-18-59 (Betty Horgan); *Maverick*—"The Saga of Waco Williams" 2-15-59 (Kathy Bent); *Wagon Train*—"The Andrew Hale Story" 6-3-59 (Martha English), "The Tom Tuckett Story" 3-2-60 (Elizabeth); *The Restless Gun*—"The Englishman" 6-8-59 (Archibald Jared III); *Sugarfoot*—"Funeral at Forty Mile" 5-24-60 (Julie Frazer); *Tate*—"The Bounty Hunter" 6-22-60 (Roberta McConnell); *Wyatt Earp*—"The Law Must Be Fair" 5-2-61 (Aithra McLowery).

Fletcher, Tex (1908-3/18/87). Films: "Six-Gun Rhythm" 1939 (Tex Fletcher).

Flicker, Ted. Films: "The Legend of the Lone Ranger" 1981 (Buffalo Bill Cody).

Flint, Sam (1882-10/24/80). Films: "Lawless Range" 1935; "The New Frontier" 1935 (Milt Dawson); "The Lawless Nineties" 1936 (Pierce); "The Lonely Trail" 1936 (Governor); "Red River Valley" 1936 (George Baxter); "Winds of the Wasteland" 1936 (Dr. William Forsythe); "Roaring Six Guns" 1937 (Ringold); "The Last Stand" 1938 (Calhoun); "The Singing Hill" 1941; "Under Fiesta Stars" 1941; "South of Santa Fe" 1942 (Prentiss); "False Colors" 1943 (Judge Stevens); "The Kansan" 1943; "Outlaws of Stampede Pass" 1943; "The Stranger from Pecos" 1943 (Ward);

"Thundering Trails" 1943; "Boss of Boomtown" 1944 (Cornwall); "The Lights of Old Santa Fe" 1944 (the Sheriff); "Silver City Kid" 1944; "Song of the Range" 1944 (McDonald); "Along the Navajo Trail" 1945 (Breck Alastair); "The Man from Oklahoma" 1945 (Mayor); "Lone Star Moonlight" 1946; "My Pal Trigger" 1946 (Sheriff); "Singing on the Trail" 1946; "Sioux City Sue" 1946; "Swing the Western Way" 1947; "The Wild Frontier" 1947 (Steve Lawson); "The Adventures of Frank and Jesse James" 1948-serial (Paul Thatcher); "Four Faces West" 1948 (Storekeeper); "Phantom Valley" 1948 (Jim Durant); "Smoky Mountain Melody" 1948; "The Strawberry Roan" 1948 (Dr. Nelson); "The Gay Amigo" 1949 (Paulsen); "Home in San Antone" 1949; "The Blazing Sun" 1950; "Cherokee Uprising" 1950 (Judge); "Kansas Raiders" 1950 (Bank President); "The Return of Jesse James" 1950; "Rock Island Trail" 1950 (Mayor); "Fort Savage Raiders" 1951 (Col. Markham); "Man from Sonora" 1951; "Northwest Territory" 1951 (Kellog, the Prospector); "Snake River Desperadoes" 1951 (Jason Fox); "The Hawk of Wild River" 1952 (Clark Mahoney); "The Lusty Men" 1952 (Doctor); "Road Agent" 1952 (George Drew); "Yukon Gold" 1952; "Cow Country" 1953 (Maitland); "The Moonlighter" 1953 (Mr. Mott); "The Vanquished" 1953 (Connors); "The Outlaw's Daughter" 1954 (Doctor); "Shoot-Out at Medicine Bend" 1957. ¶TV: *The Gene Autry Show*—"Gold Dust Charlie" 7-30-50, "Double Switch" 8-27-50, "Gray Dude" 12-3-50, "The Peace Maker" 12-17-50, "Ghost Town Raiders" 10-6-51; *Wild Bill Hickok*—"Tax Collecting Story" 8-7-51, "Blacksmith Story" 1-1-52, "Prairie Flats Land Swindle" 5-6-52, "The Kid from Red Butte" 8-26-52, "Stolen Church Funds" 9-9-52, "Ambush" 1-13-53, "Blind Alley" 2-24-53, "Meteor Mesa" 6-16-53; *Sky King*—"Fish Out of Water" 12-9-51; *The Cisco Kid*—"Extradition Papers" 9-12-53, "Son of a Gunman" 10-10-53; *Annie Oakley*—"Annie Finds Strange Treasure" 3-6-54; *The Roy Rogers Show*—"The Land Swindle" 3-14-54 (Will Colton); *Wyatt Earp*—"Rich Man's Son" 12-13-55, "The Pinkertons" 3-20-56, "The Almost Dead Cowhand" 10-23-56 (Ruger), "The Imitation Jesse James" 2-4-58 (Limestone Parker), "Caught by a Whisker" 10-7-58, "Doc Fabrique's Greatest Case" 4-7-59 (Dad Lenhart), "Wyatt's Decision" 9-22-59, "The Nugget and the Epitaph"

10-6-59, "Let's Hang Curly Bill" 1-26-60 (Fred White), "The Toughest Judge in Arizona" 5-24-60 (Spouter), "Miss Sadie" 12-20-60, "Casey and the Clowns" 2-21-61; *The Adventures of Rin Tin Tin*—"Homer the Great" 4-20-56 (Larson); *Zane Grey Theater*—"A Quiet Sunda in San Ardo" 11-23-56 (Jason O'Neill); *Gunsmoke*—"Death Watch" 1-8-66 (Jake).

Flippen, Jay C. (1898-2/3/71). Films: "Two Flags West" 1950 (Sgt. Terrance Duffy); "Winchester '73" 1950 (Sgt. Wilkes); "The Lady from Texas" 1951 (Sheriff); "Bend of the River" 1952 (Jeremy Baile); "Woman of the North Country" 1952 (Axel Nordlund); "Devil's Canyon" 1953 (Capt. Wells); "The Far Country" 1955 (Rube); "Man Without a Star" 1955 (Strap Davis); "Oklahoma!" 1955 (Skidmore); "King and Four Queens" 1956 (Bartender); "Seventh Cavalry" 1956 (Sgt. Bates); "The Deerslayer" 1957 (Old Tom Hutter); "The Halliday Brand" 1957 (Chad Burris); "Night Passage" 1957 (Ben Kimball); "The Restless Breed" 1957 (Marshal Steve Evans); "Run of the Arrow" 1957 (Walking Coyote); "Escape from Red Rock" 1958 (John Costaine); "From Hell to Texas" 1958 (Jake Leffertfinger); "The Plunderers" 1960 (Sheriff McCauley); "How the West Was Won" 1962 (Huggins); "Cat Ballou" 1965 (Sheriff Cardigan); "Firecreek" 1968 (Mr. Pittman); "Sam Hill: Who Killed the Mysterious Mr. Foster?" TVM-1971. ¶TV: *Wanted—Dead or Alive*—"Miracle at Pot Hole" 10-25-58 (Shute Wilson); *Rawhide*—"Incident of the Widowed Dove" 1-30-59 (Marshal Lindstrom), "Incident at Hourglass" 3-12-64 (Sergeant Shaler), "Josh" 1-15-65 (Bigger); *Johnny Ringo*—"Four Came Quietly" 1-28-60 (Gabe Jethro); *Stagecoach West*—"Not in Our Stars" 2-7-61 (Aaron Sutter); *Bonanza*—"The Prime of Life" 12-29-63 (Barney Fuller); *Gunsmoke*—"Owney Tupper Had a Daughter" 4-4-64 (Owney Tupper); *The Virginian*—"The Wolves Up Front, the Jackals Behind" 3-23-66 (Pa Golby), "The Barren Ground" 12-6-67 (Asa Keogh), "Stopover" 1-8-69 (the Judge); *A Man Called Shenandoah*—"The Imposter" 4-4-66 (Andrew O'Rourke); *The Rounders*—12-6-66 (Kenny Fahrbush); *The Road West*—"Charade of Justice" 3-27-67 (Judge Platt); *Here Come the Brides*—"The She-Bear" 1-30-70 (Pryor).

Flippin, Lucy Lee (1943-). Films: "Goin' South" 1978 (Mrs. Haber). ¶TV: *Little House on the Prairie*—Regular 1979-82 (Eliza Jane Wilder).

Flori, Agata (Agatha Flory). Films: "Seven Guns for the MacGregors" 1965-Ital./Span. (Rosita Carson); "Up the MacGregors!" 1967-Ital./Span. (Rosita Carson); "I Came, I Saw, I Shot" 1968-Ital./Span.; "Nephews of Zorro" 1969-Ital. (Carmencita); "Heads You Die … Tails I Kill You" 1971-Ital. (Anna Lee); "Return of Halleluja" 1972-Ital./Ger. (Fleurette).

Flory, Med. Films: "Gun Street" 1961 (Willie Driscoll); "The Night of the Grizzly" 1966 (Duke Squires); "Wild and Wooly" TVM-1978 (Burgie). ¶TV: *Lawman*—"The Catcher" 12-4-60 (Catcher), "Whiphand" 4-23-61 (Jed Pennyman), "Mountain Man" 3-25-62 (Lex Buckman); *Maverick*—"Dodge City or Bust" 12-11-60 (Deputy Nevers), "Marshal Maverick" 3-11-62 (Wyatt Earp); *Bonanza*—"The Dark Gate" 3-4-61 (Monk), "The Saga of Whizzer McGee" 4-28-63 (Otis), "The Grand Swing" 9-19-71 (Clint); *Bronco*—"Then the Mountains" 4-30-62 (Pelham); *The Dakotas*—"One Day in Vermillion" 4-8-63 (Captain Driscoll); *Rawhide*—"Incident of the Death Dancer" 12-5-63 (Billy Barton), "Incident at Gila Flats" 1-30-64; *Destry*—"Go Away, Little Sheba" 3-27-64 (Bret Hartley); *The Virginian*—"The Payment" 12-16-64 (Sardo), "The Return of Golden Tom" 3-9-66 (Ingram); *Daniel Boone*—"A Rope for Mingo" 12-2-65 (Luke), "Orlando, the Prophet" 2-29-68, "The Far Side of Fury" 3-7-68 (Dobbs), "The Bait" 11-7-68 (Jubal), "Love and Equity" 3-13-69 (Bingen), "The Landlords" 3-5-70 (Bingen), "How to Become a Goddess" 4-30-70 (Bingen); *F Troop*—"The Loco Brothers" 12-29-66 (Loco Brothers); *The Monroes*—"Wild Bull" 2-15-67; *Cimarron Strip*—"The Roarer" 11-2-67; *Gunsmoke*—"Sergeant Holly" 12-14-70 (Corporal Steckey), "A Town in Chains" 9-16-74 (Sheriff Van Berkle); *Alias Smith and Jones*—"Journey from San Juan" 4-8-71; *Nichols*—"Peanuts and Crackerjacks" 11-4-71 (Cyrus); *How the West Was Won*—Episode One 2-6-77 (Sheriff Rose); *Young Maverick*—"A Fistful of Oats" 12-5-79.

Flower, Amber. TV: *Gunsmoke*—"The Bounty Hunter" 10-30-65 (Amy Jensen); *A Man Called Shenandoah*—"The Clown" 4-18-66 (Little Girl).

Flower, Danny. TV: *Bonanza*—"Square Deal Sam" 11-8-64 (Danny); *Death Valley Days*—"Tribute to the Dog" 12-27-64 (Andy Cody).

Flower, George "Buck". Films: "Across the Great Divide" 1976 (Indian Chief); "The Giant of Thunder Mountain" 1991. ¶TV: *Paradise*—"A Gather of Guns" 9-10-89 (Dr. Jeffries); *Adventures of Brisco County, Jr.*—"Socrates' Sister" 9-24-93 (49'er).

Flowers, Bess (1900-7/28/84). Films: "Hands Across the Border" 1926 (Ysabel Castro); "Lone Hand Saunders" 1926 (Alice Mills); "The Scarlet Arrow" 1928-serial.

Fluellen, Joel (1910-2/2/90). Films: "The Moonlighter" 1953; "Sitting Bull" 1954 (Sam); "Friendly Persuasion" 1956 (Enoch); "He Rides Tall" 1964 (Dr. Sam); "Skin Game" 1971 (Abram); "Thomasine and Bushrod" 1974 (Nathaniel). ¶TV: *Jim Bowie*—"Jim Bowie and His Slave" 11-30-56 (Joseph); *Wild Wild West*—"The Night of the Sudden Death" 10-8-65 (Chief Vonoma); *Death Valley Days*—"No Place for a Lady" 1-8-66 (Arthur); *Laredo*—"Above the Law" 1-13-66; *Iron Horse*—"The Dynamite Driver" 9-19-66 (Studge), "Dry Run to Glory" 1-6-68 (Miguel); *Cimarron Strip*—"Broken Wing" 9-21-67, "The Hunted" 10-5-67 (Bartender); *The Big Valley*—"Rimfire" 2-19-68 (Butler); *Daniel Boone*—"The Grand Alliance" 11-13-69 (Joselito).

Flynn, Charles. Films: "Call of the Canyon" 1942; "Valley of Hunted Men" 1942; "The Secret of Convict Lake" 1951 (Steve Gower).

Flynn, Elinor (1910-7/4/38). Films: "A Close Call" 1929; "The Go Get 'Em Kid" 1929

Flynn, Emmett (1892-6/4/37). Films: "Big Jim's Heart" 1915; "Blazing Guns" 1943.

Flynn, Errol (1909-10/14/59). Films: "Dodge City" 1939 (Wade Hatton); "Santa Fe Trail" 1940 (Jeb Stuart); "Virginia City" 1940 (Kerry Bradford); "They Died with Their Boots On" 1941 (George Armstrong Custer); "San Antonio" 1945 (Clay Hardin); "Silver River" 1948 (Capt. Mike McComb); "Montana" 1950 (Morgan Lane); "Rocky Mountain" 1950 (Lafe Barstow).

Flynn, Gertrude (1914-). Films: "Invitation to a Gunfighter" 1964 (Widow Guthrie). ¶TV: *Maverick*—"The Brasada Spur" 2-22-59 (Dorrit MacGregor), "The Forbidden City" 3-26-61 (Nettie Moss), "The Art Lovers" 10-1-61 (Rheba Sutton); *Gunsmoke*—"Box O'Rocks" 12-5-59 (Mrs. Blouze), "By Line" 4-9-66 (Essie Benlan), "Rope Fever" 12-4-67

(Woman); *Have Gun Will Travel*—"The Piano" 11-11-61 (Mona); *Outlaws*—"Madrid" 2-7-87 (Liz Wade).

Flynn, Joe (1924-7/19/74). TV: *The Restless Gun*—"Remember the Dead" 11-17-58 (Bert Rosett); *Gunsmoke*—"The F.U." 3-14-59 (Onie Becker), "The Hunger" 11-17-62 (Drummer); *Wagon Train*—"The Horace Best Story" 10-5-60 (Edwin Crook); *Laredo*—"Walk Softly" 3-31-67; *Alias Smith and Jones*—"The Night of the Red Dog" 11-4-71 (Ralph Marsden).

Flynn, Maurice "Lefty" (1893-3/4/59). Films: "The Last Trail" 1921 (the Stranger); "Rough Shod" 1922 (Satan Latimer); "Hell's Hole" 1923 (Dell Hawkins); "Salome Jane" 1923 (the Man); "The Breed of the Border" 1924 (Circus Lacey); "The Millionaire Cowboy" 1924 (Charles Christopher "Gallop" Meredyth, Jr.); "The No-Gun Man" 1925 (Robert Jerome Vincent); "O.U. West" 1925 (O.U. West); "The Golden Stallion" 1927-serial.

Flynn, Sean (1941-70). Films: "Sign of Zorro" 1964-Ital./Span. (Don Ramon/Zorro); "Seven Guns for Timothy" 1966-Span./Ital.; "Woman for Ringo" 1966-Ital./Span. (Luke)

Foch, Nina (1924-). Films: "Wagon Wheels West" 1943-short; "Four Guns to the Border" 1954 (Maggie Flannery); "Female Artillery" TVM-1973 (Amelia Craig). TV: *Wagon Train*—"The Clara Beauchamp Story" 12-11-57 (Clara Beauchamp); *Rawhide*—"Incident of the Judas Trap" 6-5-59 (Madrina Wilcox); *The Virginian*—"Vengeance Is the Spur" 2-27-63 (Carol Frances); *A Man Called Shenandoah*—"Marlee" 3-14-66 (Marlee Cole); *Wild Wild West*—"The Night of the Cossacks" 3-21-69 (Duchess Sophia); *Gunsmoke*—"Coreyville" 10-6-69 (Agatha Corey).

Foley, Brian (1946-). TV: *Gunsmoke*—"Captain Sligo" 1-4-71 (Cowboy).

Foley, Red (1910-9/19/68). Films: "The Pioneers" 1941 (Red).

Folkerson, Robert J. (1919-3/23/76). Films: "Shut My Big Mouth" 1942 (Boy); "Run for Cover" 1955. TV: *Wagon Train*—"The Christine Elliot Story" 3-23-60; *Cimarron Strip*—"The Battleground" 9-28-67, "Whitey" 10-19-67, "Sound of a Drum" 2-1-68.

Fonda, Henry (1905-8/12/82). Films: "Drums Along the Mohawk" 1939 (Gilbert Martin); "Jesse James" 1939 (Frank James); "The Return of Frank James" 1940 (Frank James/Ben Woodson); "The Ox-Bow Incident" 1943 (Gil Carter); "My Darling Clementine" 1946 (Wyatt Earp); "Fort Apache" 1948 (Lt. Col. Owen Thursday); "The Tin Star" 1957 (Morg Hickman); "Warlock" 1959 (Clay Blaisdell); "How the West Was Won" 1962 (Jethro Stuart); "The Rounders" 1965 (Howdy Lewis); "A Big Hand for the Little Lady" 1966 (Meredith); "Stranger on the Run" TVM-1967 (Ben Chamberlin); "Welcome to Hard Times" 1967 (Will Blue); "Firecreek" 1968 (Larkin); "Once Upon a Time in the West" 1968-Ital. (Frank); "The Cheyenne Social Club" 1970 (Harley Sullivan); "There Was a Crooked Man" 1970 (Woodward Lopeman); "My Name Is Nobody" 1973-Ital. (Jack Beauregard); "Wanda Nevada" 1979 (Alonzo). TV: *The Deputy*—Regular 1959-61 (Chief Marshal Simon Fry).

Fonda, Jane (1937-). Films: "Cat Ballou" 1965 (Cat Ballou); "Comes a Horseman" 1978 (Ella); "The Electric Horseman" 1979 (Hallie Martin); "Old Gringo" 1989 (Harriet Winslow).

Fonda, Peter (1940-). Films: "The Hired Hand" 1971 (Harry Collings); "Wanda Nevada" 1979 (Beaudray Demerille). TV: *Wagon Train*—"The Orly French Story" 12-12-62 (Orly French).

Fong, Benson (1916-8/1/87). Films: "Walk Like a Dragon" 1960 (Wu); "Kung Fu" TVM-1972 (Han Fei); "Kung Fu: The Movie" TVM-1986 (Old One). TV: *Death Valley Days*—"Sam Kee and Uncle Sam" 11-3-59 (Sam Kee); *Have Gun Will Travel*—"The Hatchet Man" 3-5-60 (Joe Tsin); *Bonanza*—"Pink Cloud Comes from Old Cathay" 4-12-64 (Na Shan); *Wild Wild West*—"The Night the Dragon Screamed" 1-14-66 (Mo Ti); *Dundee and the Culhane*—9-13-67; *Kung Fu*—"Blood Brother" 1-18-73 (Soong), "The Brujo" 10-25-73 (Sorcerer Liu), "The Vanishing Image" 12-20-74 (Li Yu).

Fong, Brian (1948-). TV: *Kung Fu*—"Besieged: Death on Cold Mountain" 11-15-74 (Cho Dak), "Besieged: Cannon at the Gate" 11-22-74 (Cho Dak).

Fong, Frances (1927-). TV: *Tombstone Territory*—"Tong War" 2-5-58 (Mei Lon); *Lawman*—"The Intruders" 12-7-58 (May Ling); *Kung Fu*—"A Small Beheading" 9-21-74 (Woman), "One Step to Darkness" 1-25-75 (Nurse).

Fong, Harold. TV: *My Friend Flicka*—"Rough and Ready" 3-9-56; *Have Gun Will Travel*—"Hey Boy's Revenge" 4-12-58; *Tales of Wells Fargo*—"The Golden Owl" 9-29-58 (Wong); *Wagon Train*—"Around the Horn" 10-1-58 (Wong); *Wide Country*—"The Bravest Man in the World" 12-6-62 (Archie); *The Virginian*—"A Bald-Faced Boy" 4-13-66 (Chinese Cook).

Fontaine, Jacqueline. Films: "The Daltons' Women" 1950; "Skipalong Rosenbloom" 1951 (Caroline); "Outlaw Women" 1952 (Ellen Larabee).

Fontaine, Joan (1917-). Films: "Man of Conquest" 1939 (Eliza Allen). TV: *Wagon Train*—"The Naomi Kaylor Story" 1-30-63 (Naomi Kaylor).

Foo, Lee Tung (1875-5/1/66). Films: "Stand Up and Fight" 1939 (Chinese Cook); "Secrets of the Wastelands" 1941 (Doy Kee); "Strange Gamble" 1948; "Annie Get Your Gun" 1950 (Waiter); "The Cariboo Trail" 1950 (Ling); "Short Grass" 1950 (Lin); "Badlands of Montana" 1957 (Ling). TV: *The Lone Ranger*—"Damsels in Distress" 6-8-50.

Foote, Courtenay (-3/4/25). Films: "Buckshot John" 1915 (Jake Gilmore); "Captain Courtesy" 1915 (George Granville).

Foote, Dick. Films: "Wild Horse Mesa" 1947 (Rusty); "Bad Men of Tombstone" 1949 (Jery); "Streets of Laredo" 1949 (Pipes); "Young Daniel Boone" 1950 (Lt. Perkins); "Saddle Legion" 1951 (Sandy). TV: *Wyatt Earp*—"The Trail to Tombstone" 9-8-59 (Carney).

Foran, Dick (1910-8/10/79). Films: "Moonlight on the Prairie" 1935 (Ace Andrews); "Song of the Saddle" 1936 (Frank Wilson, Jr.); "Trailin' West" 1936 (Lt. Red Colton); "Treachery Rides the Range" 1936 (Capt. Red Tyler); "Blazing Sixes" 1937 (Red Barton); "The California Mail" 1937 (Bill Harkins); "Cherokee Strip" 1937 (Dick Hudson); "The Devil's Saddle Legion" 1937 (Tal Holladay); "Empty Holsters" 1937 (Clay Brent); "Guns of the Pecos" 1937 (Steve Ainslee); "Land Beyond the Law" 1937 (Chip Douglas); "Prairie Thunder" 1937 (Rod Farrell); "Cowboy from Brooklyn" 1938 (Sam Thorne); "Heart of the North" 1938 (Sgt. Alan Baker); "My Little Chickadee" 1940 (Wayne Carter, Editor); "Rangers of Fortune" 1940 (Johnny Cash); "Winners of the West" 1940-serial (Jeff Ramsay); "The Kid from Kansas" 1941 (Kansas); "Riders of Death Valley" 1941-serial (Jim Benton); "Road Agent" 1941 (Duke Masters); "Ride 'Em, Cowboy" 1942 (Robert "Bronco Bob" Mitchell); "Fort Apache" 1948 (Sgt. Quincannon); "Deputy Marshal" 1949 (Joel Benton); "El Paso" 1949 (Sheriff La Farge); "Al Jennings of Oklahoma" 1951 (Frank Jennings); "Treasure of Ruby Hills" 1955 (Doran); "Sierra Stranger" 1957 (Bert Gaines); "Taggart" 1964 (Stark). ¶TV: *Wild Bill Hickok*—"Old Cowboys Never Die" 12-16-52; *Stage 7*—"Billy and the Bride" 5-8-55 (Archie Peters); *Sheriff of Cochise*—"The Kidnaper" 1-18-57 (Buck); *Colt .45*—"Final Payment" 11-22-57 (Tuck Degan); *Circus Boy*—"The Return of Buffalo Bill" 12-12-57 (Buffalo Bill); *Maverick*—"The Third Rider" 1-5-58 (Sheriff Edwards); *Have Gun Will Travel*—"Young Gun" 11-8-58 (Roy Calvert); *Yancy Derringer*—"Two of a Kind" 1-1-59 (Holligan); *Wanted—Dead or Alive*—"The Spur" 1-17-59 (Sheriff Wilkes), "The Choice" 12-14-60 (Frank Koster); *Laramie*—"A Sound of Bells" 12-27-60 (Tom), "Bitter Glory" 5-2-61 (Billy Jacobs), "The Killer Legend" 12-12-61 (Milt Lane), "Double Eagles" 11-20-62 (Joe Farley); *The Deputy*—"The Dream" 2-4-61 (Clint Hammer); *Lawman*—"The Wanted Man" 4-8-62 (Frank Jesse); *Death Valley Days*—"The Breaking Point" 6-13-62 (Ferguson), "Pioneer Doctor" 1-23-63, "The Holy Terror" 12-8-63 (Bill Franklin), "Kate Melville and the Law" 6-20-65 (Will Melville); *Cheyenne*—"Wanted for the Murder of Cheyenne Bodie" 12-10-62 (Sheriff Bigelow); *The Dakotas*—"Requiem at Dancer's Hill" 2-18-63 (Matt Kendrick); *Gunsmoke*—"With a Smile" 3-30-63 (Sheriff Ben Carver); *The Virginian*—"A Man Called Kane" 5-6-64 (Duggan), "Requiem for a Country Doctor" 1-25-67 (Mayor), "Reckoning" 9-13-67 (Frank Devereaux), "Big Tiny" 12-18-68 (Adam Burnsdie); *Rawhide*—"The Testing Post" 11-30-65 (Taggart); *Daniel Boone*—"Dan'l Boone Shot a B'ar" 9-15-66 (Jeremiah); *Bonanza*—"Mark of Guilt" 12-15-68 (Giltner).

Forbes, Colette. Films: "Blind Hearts" 1921 (Hilda Larson); "Three Word Brand" 1921 (Jean).

Forbes, John. see Carpenter, John.

Forbes, Ralph (1896-3/31/51). Films: "The Trail of '98" 1929 (Larry); "Daniel Boone" 1936 (Stephen Marlowe).

Forbes, Scott (1921-). Films:

"Rocky Mountain" 1950 (Lt. Rickey); "Raton Pass" 1951 (Prentice). ¶TV: *Frontier*—"Paper Gunman" 9-25-55, "The Shame of a Nation" 10-23-55, "The Big Dry" 3-18-56 (Ben Hart), "Salt War" 4-22-56 (Howard); *Jim Bowie*—Regular 1956-58 (Jim Bowie); *Zane Grey Theater*—"Man Alone" 3-5-59 (Evans), "Rebel Ranger" 12-3-59 (Cass Taggart); *Black Saddle*—"Client: Steele" 3-21-59 (Bill Steele); *Trackdown*—"Toss Up" 5-20-59 (Paul Wallace).

Force, Charles (1876-6/9/47). Films: "The Square Shooter" 1920 (Bull); "Cupid's Brand" 1921 (Bull Devlin); "The Lone Rider" 1922 (Big Harrison).

Ford, Constance (1929-2/26/93). Films: "The Last Hunt" 1956 (Peg); "The Iron Sheriff" 1957 (Claire); "Shoot Out at Big Sag" 1962 (Goldie Bartholomew). ¶TV: *Zane Grey Theater*—"The Lariat" 11-2-56 (Laura Lovett); *Gunsmoke*—"Poor Pearl" 12-22-56 (Pearl Bender), "Wagon Girls" 4-7-62 (Florida); *Trackdown*—"Self-Defense" 11-22-57 (Polly Webster); *Have Gun Will Travel*—"The Bostonian" 2-1-58 (Gloria Prince); *Bat Masterson*—"Lottery of Death" 5-13-59 (Gwen Parsons), "Stage to Nowhere" 4-14-60 (Ivy Dickson); *Tombstone Territory*—2-26-60 (Lily Murdock); *The Law of the Plainsman*—"Rabbit's Fang" 3-24-60 (Jessie); *Wanted—Dead or Alive*—"The Last Retreat" 1-11-61 (Sarah Lawton); *The Outlaws*—"The Waiting Game" 1-19-61 (Hannah Wolk); *The Deputy*—"The Lonely Road" 2-18-61 (Meg Billings); *Frontier Circus*—"Naomi Champagne" 3-29-62 (Naomi Champagne); *Rawhide*—"Incident of the Buryin' Man" 1-4-63 (Georgia); *The Dakotas*—"Red Sky Over Bismarck" 1-14-63 (Deborah James); *Temple Houston*—"The Dark Madonna" 12-26-63 (Lily Lamont); *Shane*—"The Great Invasion" 12-17-66 & 12-24-66 (Jenny).

Ford, Dorothy. Films: "The Three Godfathers" 1948 (Ruby Latham); "A Perilous Journey" 1953 (Rose, the Singer); "Gun Brothers" 1956 (Molly); "Pardners" 1956 (Amanda).

Ford, Eugenia. Films: "Ma's Girls" 1915; "The Outlaw's Bride" 1915; "Pals in Blue" 1915.

Ford, Francis (1882-9/5/53). Films: "Billy's Sister" 1910; "Branding a Thief" 1910; "Cyclone Pete's Matrimony" 1910; "In the Mission Shadows" 1910; "In the Tall Grass Country" 1910; "Old Norris' Gal" 1910; "Out for Mischief" 1910; "Pals"

1910; "A Plucky American Girl" 1910; "The Return of Ta-Wa-Wa" 1910; "A Texas Joke" 1910; "Uncle Jim" 1910; "At the Gringo Mine" 1911; "Bessie's Ride" 1911; "Billy and His Pal" 1911; "The Call of the Wilderness" 1911; "Changing Cooks" 1911; "The Crimson Scars" 1911; "The Great Heart of the West" 1911; "The Immortal Alamo" 1911; "In the Hot Lands" 1911; "Jack Mason's Last Deed" 1911; "The Mission Father" 1911; "My Prairie Flower" 1911; "The Owner of the L.L. Ranch" 1911; "Red Cloud's Secret" 1911; "The Reformation of Jack Robbins" 1911; "Sir Percy and the Punchers" 1911; "The Snake in the Grass" 1911; "A Spanish Love Song" 1911; "Tony, the Greaser" 1911; "The Warrant for Red Rube" 1911; "Army Surgeon" 1912; "The Bugle Call" 1912; "The Burning Brand" 1912; "The Crisis" 1912; "Custer's Last Fight" 1912; "The Deserter" 1912; "A Double Reward" 1912; "The Empty Water Keg" 1912; "Falsely Accused" 1912; "Finding the Last Chance Mine" 1912; "The Ghost of Sulfur Mountain" 1912; "The Governor's Clemency" 1912; "His Partner's Share" 1912; "His Squaw" 1912; "An Indian Legend" 1912; "The Indian Massacre" 1912; "The Invaders" 1912; "The Laugh on Dad" 1912; "The Law of the West" 1912; "Linked by Fate" 1912; "Making Good" 1912; "Mellita's Rose" 1912; "The Outcast" 1912; "The Post Telegrapher" 1912; "The Ranger's Girls" 1912; "The Reformed Outlaw" 1912; "Seven Bars of Gold" 1912; "Smiling Bob" 1912; "A String of Beads" 1912; "Troubles of the XL Outfit" 1912; "War on the Plains" 1912; "The White Vaquero" 1912; "The Black Masks" 1913; "An Indian's Gratitude" 1913; "The Tell Tale Hat Band" 1913; "Texas Kelly at Bay" 1913; "Wynona's Vengeance" 1913; "The Ghost of Smiling Jim" 1914; "The Return of the Twins' Double" 1914; "The Curse of the Desert" 1915; "Three Bad Men and a Girl" 1915; "The Bandit's Wager" 1916; "The Dumb Bandit" 1916; "The Powder Trail" 1916; "The Unexpected" 1916; "John Ermine of the Yellowstone" 1917 (John Ermine); "Flower of the Range" 1920; "The Man from Nowhere" 1920 (Drunkard); "Action" 1921 (Soda Water Manning); "The Stampede" 1921 (Robert Wagner); "Thunderbolt Jack" 1921; "Another Man's Boots" 1922 (the Stranger); "So This Is Arizona" 1922 (Ned Kendall); "Three Jumps Ahead" 1923 (Virgil); "In the Days of the Covered Wagon" 1924; "Lash of the Whip" 1924 (Hurricane Smith); "The Measure of a

Man" 1924 (Pale Peter); "A Rodeo Mixup" 1924 (Uncle); "Western Feuds" 1924 (J.P. Hartley); "Western Yesterdays" 1924 (Twitchie); "The Red Rider" 1925 (Brown Bear); "Ridin' Thunder" 1925 (Frank Douglas); "A Roaring Adventure" 1925 (Col. Burns/Bennett Hardy); "Scar Hanan" 1925 (Jury Foreman); "The Sign of the Cactus" 1925 (Panhandle George); "Soft Shoes" 1925 (Quig Mundy); "The Taming of the West" 1925 (Frosty Miller); "The Devil's Saddle" 1927 (Pete Hepburn); "Men of Daring" 1927 (Black Roger); "One Glorious Scrap" 1927 (Ralph Curtis); "The Branded Sombrero" 1928 (Link Jarvis); "The Four-Footed Ranger" 1928 (Brom Hockley); "The Lariat Kid" 1929 (Cal Gregg); "The Indians Are Coming" 1930-serial (Tom Woods/George Woods); "The Mounted Stranger" 1930 (Spider Coy); "Song of the Cabellero" 1930 (Don Pedro Madera); "Sons of the Saddle" 1930 (Red Slade); "Battling with Buffalo Bill" 1931-serial (Jim Rodney); "Destry Rides Again" 1932 (Judd Ogden); "Heroes of the West" 1932-serial (Captain Donovan); "Rider of Death Valley" 1932 (Gabe Dillon); "Clancy of the Mounted" 1933-serial (Inspector Cabot); "Gordon of Ghost City" 1933-serial (Jim Carmody); "Life in the Raw" 1933 (Myles); "Life in the Raw" 1933; "The Man from Monterey" 1933 (Don Pablo Gonzales); "Secrets" 1933; "Smoky" 1933; "Gun Justice" 1934 (Denver); "The Thundering Herd" 1934; "The Arizonian" 1935 (Mayor Ed Comstock); "The Plainsman" 1936 (Veteran); "The Girl of the Golden West" 1938 (Miner); "The Texans" 1938 (Uncle Dud); "Bad Lands" 1939 (Garth); "Drums Along the Mohawk" 1939 (Joe Boleo); "Stagecoach" 1939 (Billy Pickett); "Geronimo" 1940 (Scout); "Lucky Cisco Kid" 1940 (Court Clerk); "The Man from Dakota" 1940 (Horseman); "Viva Cisco Kid" 1940 (Proprietor); "Last of the Duanes" 1941 (Luke Stevens); "Romance of the Rio Grande" 1941 (Stage Driver); "They Died with Their Boots On" 1941 (Veteran); "Western Union" 1941 (Stagecoach Driver); "King of the Mounties" 1942-serial (Zeke Collins); "Outlaws of Pine Ridge" 1942 (Bartender); "The Desperadoes" 1943 (Hank); "The Ox-Bow Incident" 1943 (Old Man); "San Antonio" 1945 (Old Cowboy Greeting Coach); "Wildfire" 1945 (Ezra Mills); "My Darling Clementine" 1946 (Town Drunk); "Renegades" 1946 (Eph); "Bandits of Dark Canyon"

1947 (Horse Trader); "Unconquered" 1947; "Eyes of Texas" 1948 (Thaddeus Cameron); "Fort Apache" 1948 (Fen, the Stagecoach Guard); "The Plunderers" 1948 (Barnaby); "The Three Godfathers" 1948 (Drunk Oldtimer at Bar); "The Timber Trail" 1948 (Ralph Baker); "The Far Frontier" 1949 (Alf Sharper); "Frontier Marshal" 1949 (Ed Garnett); "San Antone Ambush" 1949 (Maj. Farnsworth); "She Wore a Yellow Ribbon" 1949 (Barman); "Wagonmaster" 1950 (Mr. Peachtree); "The Lawless Breed" 1952 (Old Timer); "Toughest Man in Arizona" 1952 (Hanchette); "The Marshal's Daughter" 1953 (Gramps). ¶TV: *The Lone Ranger*—"Gold Fever" 4-13-50; *The Gene Autry Show*—"The Posse" 9-17-50, "The Devil's Brand" 9-24-50; *Rough Riders*—"The Rifle" 5-7-59 (Poker Kate Jones).

Ford, Frederick. Films: "Revolt at Fort Laramie" 1957; "Tomahawk Trail" 1957 (Pvt. Macy). ¶TV: *Death Valley Days*—"Lady Engineer" 5-5-57; *Have Gun Will Travel*—"The Bostonian" 2-1-58 (Cowboy).

Ford, Fritz. TV: *The Rifleman*—"The Safe Guard" 11-18-58 (Townsman), "The Apprentice Sheriff" 12-9-58, "The Sheridan Story" 1-13-59 (Lieutenant), "The Angry Man" 4-28-59; *Hondo*—"Hondo and the Judas" 11-3-67 (Charlie Ford).

Ford, Glenn (1916-). Films: "Go West, Young Lady" 1941 (Tex Miller); "Texas" 1941 (Tod Ramsey); "The Desperadoes" 1943 (Cheyenne Rogers); "The Man from Colorado" 1948 (Col. Owen Devereaux); "Lust for Gold" 1949 (Jacob Walz); "The Redhead and the Cowboy" 1951 (Gil Kyle); "The Secret of Convict Lake" 1951 (Canfield); "The Man from the Alamo" 1953 (John Stoud); "The Americano" 1955 (Sam Dent); "The Violent Men" 1955 (John Parrish); "Fastest Gun Alive" 1956 (George Temple); "Jubal" 1956 (Jubal Troop); "3:10 to Yuma" 1957 (Ben Wade); "Cowboy" 1958 (Tom Reece); "The Sheepman" 1958 (Jason Sweet); "Cimarron" 1960 (Yancey Cravet); "Advance to the Rear" 1964 (Capt. Jared Heath); "The Rounders" 1965 (Ben Jones); "The Last Challenge" 1967 (Marshal Dan Blaine); "A Time for Killing" 1967 (Major Charles Wolcott); "Day of the Evil Gun" 1968 (Warfield); "Heaven with a Gun" 1969 (Jim Killian); "Smith" 1969 (Smith); "Santee" 1973 (Santee); "The Sacketts" TVM-1979 (Tom Sunday).

Ford, Harrison (1894-12/2/57). Films: "On the Level" 1917 (Joe Blanchard); "The Sunset Trail" 1917

(Kirke Levington); "Unclaimed Goods" 1918 (Danny Donegan); "Zander the Great" 1925 (Dan Murchison).

Ford, Harrison (1942-). Films: "A Time for Killing" 1967 (Lt. Shafer); "Journey to Shiloh" 1968 (Willie Bill Bearden); "The Intruders" TVM-1970; "The Frisco Kid" 1979 (Tommy). ¶TV: *The Virginian*—"The Modoc Kid" 2-1-67 (Cullen Tindall); *Gunsmoke*—"The Sodbusters" 11-20-72 (Print Underwood), "Whelan's Men" 2-5-73 (Hobey); *Kung Fu*—"Cross-ties" 2-21-74 (Harrison).

Ford, John (1895-8/31/73). Films: "Three Bad Men and a Girl" 1915; "The Bandit's Wager" 1916; "The Scrapper" 1917; "The Tornado" 1917; "The Trail of Hate" 1917 (Lt. Jack Brewer).

Ford, Montgomery. see Halsey, Brett.

Ford, Paul (1901-4/12/76). Films: "Lust for Gold" 1949 (Sheriff Lynn Early); "The Kid from Texas" 1950 (Copeland); "The Missouri Traveler" 1958 (Finas Daugherty); "A Big Hand for the Little Lady" 1966 (Ballinger). ¶TV: *The Outlaws*—"Outrage at Pawnee Bend" 4-6-61 (Captain Griggs).

Ford, Ross (1923-6/22/88). Films: "Silver River" 1948 (Soldier); "Law of the Barbary Coast" 1949 (Wayne Adams); "Frisco Tornado" 1950 (Paul Weston); "Rough Riders of Durango" 1951 (Sheriff Walters); "Blue Canadian Rockies" 1952 (Tod Markley). ¶TV: *The Lone Ranger*—"The Tenderfeet" 11-10-49, "Spanish Gold" 6-1-50, "The Silent Voice" 1-11-51; *The Gene Autry Show*—"Ghost Mountain" 7-28-53, "Dry Gulch at Devil's Elbow" 9-8-53; *Gunsmoke*—"Spring Team" 12-15-56 (Dane Shaw); *Rawhide*—"Incident at Sulphur Creek" 3-11-60 (Brad Lacey).

Ford, Ruth (1915-). Films: "Roaring Frontiers" 1941; "The Devil's Trail" 1942.

Ford, Col. Starrett. Films: "The Lone Cowboy" 1934 (Mr. Carmichael).

Ford, Steven (1956-). Films: "Cattle Annie and Little Britches" 1981 (Deputy Marshal).

Ford, Tennessee Ernie (1919-10/17/91). Films: "Man in the Saddle" 1951; "Corral Cuties" 1954-short.

Ford, Wallace (1898-6/11/66). Films: "Belle Starr's Daughter" 1947 (Bailey); "The Man from Texas" 1947 (Jed); "Coroner Creek" 1948 (Andy

West); "Red Stallion in the Rockies" 1949 (Talky Carson); "Dakota Lil" 1950 (Carter); "The Furies" 1950 (Scotty Hyslip); "Warpath" 1951 (Pvt Potts); "The Great Jesse James Raid" 1953 (Elias Hobbs); "The Nebraskan" 1953 (McBride); "The Boy from Oklahoma" 1954 (Wally Higgins); "Destry" 1954 (Doc Curtis); "A Lawless Street" 1955 (Dr. Amos Wynn); "The Man from Laramie" 1955 (Charley O'Leary); "The Spoilers" 1955 (Flapjack Simms); "Wichita" 1955 (Whiteside); "The First Texan" 1956 (Delaney); "Johnny Concho" 1956 (Albert Dark); "The Maverick Queen" 1956 (Jamie); "The Rainmaker" 1956 (Sheriff Thomas); "Stagecoach to Fury" 1956 (Lester Farrell); "Thunder Over Arizona" 1956; "Warlock" 1959 (Judge Holloway). ¶TV: *20th Century Fox Hour*—"The Ox-Bow Incident" 11-2-55 (Derelict); *Trackdown*—"A Stone for Benny French" 10-3-58 (Eli Zach); *The Deputy*—Regular 1959-60 (Marshal Herk Lamson); *Tales of Wells Fargo*—"Dead Man's Street" 4-18-60 (Murphy); *Klondike*—"88 Keys to Trouble" 11-14-60 (Temperance Pete); *Wide Country*—"Journey Down a Dusty Road" 10-4-62 (Dad Perry); *The Travels of Jaimie McPheeters*—"The Day of the Tin Trumpet" 2-2-64 (Buffalo Pete).

Forde, Eugenia (1879-9/5/40). Films: "Across the Sierras" 1912; "Her Indian Hero" 1912; "A Frontier Mystery" 1913; "A Frontier Providence" 1913; "A Frontier Mystery" 1913; "A Frontier Providence" 1913; "Jim's Atonement" 1913; "Across the Desert" 1915; "The Conversion of Smiling Tom" 1915; "The Girl and the Mail Bag" 1915; "The Girl of Gold Gulch" 1916; "Going West to Make Good" 1916; "The Golden Thought" 1916; "Cupid's Round Up" 1918 (the Red Bird); "Tempest Cody Hits the Trail" 1919; "A Ridin' Romeo" 1921 (Queenie Farrell).

Forde, Victoria (1897-7/24/64). Films: "At Rolling Forks" 1912; "Her Indian Hero" 1912; "The Love Trail" 1912; "The Renegade" 1912; "Young Wild West Leading a Raid" 1912; "The Battle of Bull Run" 1913; "The Yaqui Cur" 1913; "Athletic Ambitions" 1915; "The Auction Sale of Run-Down Ranch" 1915; "The Brave Deserve the Fair" 1915; "How Weary Went Wooing" 1915; "Never Again" 1915; "On the Eagle Trail" 1915; "The Race for a Gold Mine" 1915; "The Range Girl and the Cowboy" 1915; "The Stagecoach Guard" 1915; "An Angelic Attitude" 1916; "Along the Border" 1916; "A Bear of a Story"

1916; "The Canby Hill Outlaws" 1916; "A Close Call" 1916; "A Corner in Water" 1916; "The Country That God Forgot" 1916 (Ruth Randall); "The Cowpuncher's Peril" 1916; "Crooked Trails" 1916; "The Desert Calls Its Own" 1916; "An Eventful Evening" 1916; "Legal Advice" 1916; "Local Color" 1916; "Making Good" 1916; "The Man Within" 1916; "A Mistake in Rustlers" 1916; "Mistakes Will Happen" 1916; "The Passing of Pete" 1916; "The Pony Express Rider" 1916; "The Raiders" 1916; "Roping a Sweetheart" 1916; "The Sheriff's Blunder" 1916; "Shooting Up the Movies" 1916; "Starring in Western Stuff" 1916; "Taking a Chance" 1916; "The Taming of Groucho Bill" 1916; "Tom's Sacrifice" 1916; "Tom's Strategy" 1916; "Too Many Chefs" 1916; "Trilby's Love Disaster" 1916; "A Western Masquerade" 1916; "When Cupid Slipped" 1916; "Hearts and Saddles" 1917; "A Soft Tenderfoot" 1917; "Tom and Jerry Mix" 1917; "Western Blood" 1918 (Roberta Stephens).

Fordyce, John (1950-). Films: "They Call Him Cemetery" 1971-Ital./Span. (George McIntire).

Foreman, Ruth (1913-11/22/88). Films: "Shark River" 1953 (Mrs. Daugherty).

Forest, Dennis. TV: *Adventures of Brisco County, Jr.*—"No Man's Land" 9-10-93 (Will Swill), "Mail Order Brides" 12-10-93 (Will Swill).

Forest, Michael (1929-). Films: "The Glory Guys" 1965 (Marshal Cushman); "100 Rifles" 1969 (Humara); "The Silent Gun" TVM-1969; "Requiem for a Bounty Hunter" 1970-Ital.; "The Last Rebel" 1971-Ital./U.S./Span. (Cowboy Pool Hustler); "Death Played the Flute" 1972-Ital./Span. (Ryan); "Desperado" 1972-Span./Ital. ¶TV: *Wild Bill Hickok*—"Daughter of Casey O'-Grady" 7-21-53; *Death Valley Days*—"One in a Hundred" 12-23-53 (Larry Brooks); *Tombstone Territory*—"Apache Vendetta" 12-11-57 (Floyd Rank); *The Adventures of Rin Tin Tin*—"Rusty's Remedy" 2-28-58 (Brave); *Zorro*—"Horse of Another Color" 10-23-58 (Anastacio Malarin); *Have Gun Will Travel*—"The Road to Wickenberg" 10-25-58 (Peter Keystone); *Zane Grey Theater*—"Trail Incident" 1-29-59 (Joe Sampson); *26 Men*—"The Hasbeen" 3-24-59; *The Texan*—"Blood Money" 4-20-59; *The Rifleman*—"The Raid" 6-9-59 (Chaqua); *Bronco*—"Red Water North" 6-16-59; *Bat Masterson*—"The Desert Ship" 7-15-59 (Les

Wilkins), "Stage to Nowhere" 4-14-60 (Noah Gannon); *Maverick*—"Pappy" 9-13-59 (Jean Paul St. Cloud), "The Devil's Necklace" 4-16-61 & 4-23-61 (Bob Tallhorse); *Bonanza*—"The Paiute War" 10-3-59 (Young Winnemucca), "A Good Night's Rest" 4-11-65 (Schirmer), "Sense of Duty" 9-24-67 (Wabuska); *The Alaskans*—Regular 1960 (Pierre Duran); *The Westerner*—"The Old Man" 11-25-60; *The Tall Man*—"Ransom of a Town" 5-6-61 (Ledall); *Wagon Train*—"The Don Alvarado Story" 6-21-61 (Julio), "The Jeff Hartfield Story" 2-14-62 (Dallas); *Cheyenne*—"Cross Purpose" 10-9-61 (Capt. Robert Holman); *Frontier Circus*—"Mr. Grady Regrets" 1-25-62 (Roy Clatter); *Tales of Wells Fargo*—"Incident at Crossbow" 2-3-62 (Duke Tolliver); *Laramie*—"The High Country" 2-6-62 (Dev Bardeen), "The Runt" 2-20-62 (Lew Catlin), "The Dispossessed" 2-19-63 (Cobey), "The Sometime Gambler" 3-19-63 (Wilkerson); *Gunsmoke*—"The Cousin" 2-2-63 (Chance Hopper), "Innocence" 12-12-64 (Bob Sullins), "The Lady" 3-27-65 (Ray Pate); *The Virginian*—"The Drifter" 1-29-64 (Hugh Stager), "Portrait of a Widow" 12-9-64 (MacGregor), "Beyond the Border" 11-24-65 (Zach Wheeler); *Rawhide*—"The Violent Land" 3-5-65 (Yuma); *Branded*—"Yellow for Courage" 2-20-66 (Newt Woolery); *Laredo*—"Hey Diddle Diddle" 2-24-67 (Miguel); *Daniel Boone*—"The Fallow Land" 4-13-67 (Canuda); *Here Come the Brides*—"A Kiss Just for You" 1-29-69 (Gallagher), "The Eyes of London Bob" 11-28-69 (Donegan).

Forman, Carol. Films: "Code of the West" 1947 (Milly); "Gunsmoke" 1947; "Under the Tonto Rim" 1947 (Juanita); "Brothers in the Saddle" 1949 (Flora Trigby). ¶TV: *The Cisco Kid*—"Lynching Story" 4-28-51, "Confession for Money" 5-26-51, "Pancho Hostage" 6-23-51.

Forman, Joey (1919-12/9/82). Films: "The Twinkle in God's Eye" 1955 (Ted).

Forman, Tom (1893-11/7/26). Films: "Chimmie Fadden Out West" 1915 (Antoine); "The Cost of Hatred" 1917 (Ned Amory); "The Jaguar's Claws" 1917 (Harry Knowles); "Told in the Hills" 1919 (Charles Stuart); "The Round Up" 1920 (Jack Payson); "Saps and Saddles" 1928; "Speed and Spurs" 1928; "The Canyon of Missing Men" 1930 (Juan Sepulveda); "The Cheyenne Kid" 1930; "The Man from Nowhere" 1930 (Hank Jordan); "Sagebrush Politics" 1930; "Forbidden Trail" 1932 (Ranch Foreman); "The Man Trailer" 1934; "The Westerner" 1934 (Henchman); "Pals of the Range" 1935 (Uncle); "Blazing Sixes" 1937 (Buck); "The Californian" 1937 (Boylan); "It Happened Out West" 1937 (Cal); "Law for Tombstone" 1937; "Rawhide" 1938 (Rudy); "West of Carson City" 1940 (Pony Express Rider).

Formes, Karl (1841-11/18/39). Films: "The Struggle" 1921 (Dr. Beer); "Trooper O'Neil" 1922 (Jules Lestrange).

Forrest, Allan (1889-7/25/41). Films: "Lights of the Desert" 1922 (Clay Truxall); "The Great Divide" 1925 (Dr. Winthrop Newbury); "The Phantom Bullet" 1926 (Dan Barton); "Riding for Fame" 1928 (Donald Morgan); "The Wild West Show" 1928 (Alexander); "The Winged Horseman" 1929 (Curly Davis).

Forrest, Ann. Films: "The Rainbow Trail" 1918 (Fay Larkin); "Ridin' Pretty" 1925 (Maize).

Forrest, Frederic (1946-). Films: "When the Legends Die" 1972 (Tom Black Bull); "The Missouri Breaks" 1976 (Cary); "Calamity Jane" TVM-1984 (Wild Bill Hickok); "Lonesome Dove" TVM-1989 (Blue Duck). ¶TV: *Young Riders*—"'Til Death Do Us Part" 7-22-92 (Erbach).

Forrest, Lottie Pickford. see Pickford, Lottie.

Forrest, Sally (1928-). Films: "Vengeance Valley" 1951 (Lily Fasken). ¶TV: *Rawhide*—"Incident of the Widowed Dove" 1-30-59 (Clovis Lindstrom), "Incident of the Swindler" 2-20-64 (Loreen).

Forrest, Steve (William Andrews) (1924-). Films: "Last of the Comanches" 1952 (Lt. Floyd); "Flaming Star" 1960 (Clint Burton); "Heller in Pink Tights" 1960 (Clint Mabry); "The Second Time Around" 1961 (Dan Jones); "The Wild Country" 1971 (Jim Tanner); "The Hanged Man" TVM-1974 (James Devlin); "Wanted: The Sundance Woman" TVM-1976 (Charlie Siringo); "Last of the Mohicans" TVM-1977 (Hawkeye); "Testimony of Two Men" TVM-1977 (Martin Eaton); "The Deerslayer" TVM-1978 (Hawkeye); "Gunsmoke: Return to Dodge" TVM-1987 (Will Mannon). ¶TV: *Desilu Playhouse*—"Ballad for a Badman" 1-26-59 (Chris Hody); *Zane Grey Theater*—"Setup" 3-3-60 (Mike Bagley); *The Outlaws*—"Thirty a Month" 9-29-60 (Rance Hollister);

Wide Country—"The Royce Bennett Story" 9-20-62 (Royce Bennett); *Death Valley Days*—"The Lion of Idaho" 3-6-63 (William E. Borah), "See the Elephant and Hear the Owl" 5-9-64; *The Virginian*—"The Money Cage" 3-6-63 (Will Martin); *Cimarron Strip*—"Broken Wing" 9-21-67 (Wiley Harpe), "Sound of a Drum" 2-1-68 (Sgt. Clay Tyce); *Bonanza*—"Desperate Passage" 11-5-67 (Josh Tanner), "To Top a War" 10-19-69 (Dan Logan); *Gunsmoke*—"Mannon" 1-20-69 (Will Mannon), "Morgan" 3-2-70 (Cole Morgan), "The Avenger" 11-27-72 (Cord Wreccken), "The Widow-Maker" 10-8-73 (Scott Coltrane); *The High Chaparral*—"The Guns of Johnny Rondo" 2-6-70 (Johnny Rondo); *Nichols*—"Away the Rolling River" 12-7-71 (Sam Yeager); *Alias Smith and Jones*—"Twenty-One Days to Tenstrike" 1-6-72 (Jake); *Hec Ramsey*—"Hangman's Wages" 10-29-72 (Wess Durham).

Forrest, William (1902-1/26/89). Films: "They Died with Their Boots On" 1941 (Adjutant); "Bells of Capistrano" 1942; "Fort Apache" 1948 (Reporter); "Trail of the Yukon" 1949 (Dawson); "The Younger Brothers" 1949 (Hendricks); "Fort Dodge Stampede" 1951 (Hutchinson); "Spoilers of the Plains" 1951 (Dr. J.D. Manning); "Winning of the West" 1953 (John Randolph); "Rage at Dawn" 1955 (Amos Peterson); "The First Traveling Saleslady" 1956 (Supreme Court Justice); "Pardners" 1956 (Hocker); "Toughest Gun in Tombstone" 1958 (Governor); "The Horse Soldiers" 1959 (Gen. Steve Hurburt); "One-Eyed Jacks" 1961 (Banker); "Billy the Kid vs. Dracula" 1966 (James Underhill). ¶TV: *The Lone Ranger*—"Tenderfoot" 11-25-54; *The Adventures of Rin Tin Tin*—"Rusty Resigns from the Army" 2-25-55, "The Silent Battle" 10-5-56 (Major Swanson), "The Warrior's Promise" 1-25-57 (Major Swanson), "Sorrowful Joe Returns" 2-1-57 (Major Swanson), "Corporal Carson" 5-3-57 (Maj. Swanson); *Maverick*—"A Rage for Vengeance" 1-12-58 (Laramie Banker); *Bronco*—"Shadow of Jesse James" 1-12-60 (Marshal Joe Shelby).

Forrester, Fred (1872-10/14/52). Films: "The Tenderfoot" 1917 (Exhorting Evangelist).

Forrester, Kay. Films: "Blazing Guns" 1943 (Betty); "San Fernando Valley" 1944; "Song of the Range" 1944 (Dale Harding).

Forster, Robert (1941-). Films: "The Stalking Moon" 1969 (Nick Tana); "Journey Through Rosebud"

1972 (Frank); "Standing Tall" TVM-1978 (Luke Shasta). ¶TV: *Nakia*—Regular 1974 (Deputy Nakia Parker); *Royce*—Pilot 5-21-76 (Royce).

Forsyte, Stephen. Films: "In a Colt's Shadow" 1965-Ital./Span. (Steve Blane); "Death at Owell Rock" 1967-Ital. (Harry Boyd); "Blood Calls to Blood" 1968-Ital. (Angela).

Forsyth, Rosemary (1944-). Films: "Texas Across the River" 1966 (Phoebe Ann Taylor); "Shenandoah" 1965 (Jannie Anderson). ¶TV: *Kung Fu*—"A Small Beheading" 9-21-74 (Ellie Crowell); *Barbary Coast*—"Jesse Who?" 9-22-75 (Lauralee Bell).

Forsythe, John (1918-). Films: "Escape from Fort Bravo" 1953 (Capt. John Marsh). ¶TV: *Zane Grey Theater*—"Decision at Wilson's Creek" 5-17-57 (Lt. David Marr); *Schlitz Playhouse of the Stars*—"Way of the West" 6-6-58 (Dr. John Carter).

Forte, Fabian. see Fabian.

Forte, Joe (1896-2/22/67). Films: "Pals of the Saddle" 1938 (Judge Hastings); "King of the Texas Rangers" 1941-serial (Professor Nelson); "Riders in the Sky" 1949 (Willard Agnew); "Rodeo King and the Senorita" 1951 (Dr. Teal); "Fury at Gunsight Pass" 1956 (Andrew Ferguson); "Gunfight at the O.K. Corral" 1957 (Card Player); "Return to Warbow" 1958 (Doc Appleby); "Law of the Lawless" 1964. ¶TV: *The Cisco Kid*—"Hypnotist Murder" 11-10-51, "Ghost Town Story" 12-22-51, "Quicksilver Murder" 1-12-52; *Tales of Wells Fargo*—"Defiant at the Gate" 11-25-61 (Justice of the Peace).

Fortier, Herbert (1867-2/16/9). Films: "The Western Wallop" 1924 (Jim Stillwell); "Ridgeway of Montana" 1924 (Simon Hanley).

Fortier, Robert. Films: "McCabe and Mrs. Miller" 1971 (Town Drunk). ¶TV: *Colt .45*—"Mantrap" 2-14-58 (Tom Simons); *Have Gun Will Travel*—"The Monster of Moon Ridge" 2-28-59; *The Outlaws*—"Walk Tall" 11-16-61 (Fin Spruce); *Bonanza*—"The Tin Badge" 12-17-61 (Higgler); *Gunsmoke*—"False Front" 12-22-62 (Ray Costa), "The Promoter" 4-25-64 (Sergeant Clyde).

Foss, Darrell (1892-9/15/62). Films: "The Firefly of Tough Luck" 1917 (Bert Wilcox); "The Square Deal Man" 1917 (Pedro); "Closin' In" 1918 (Burt Calhoun).

Foster, Alan (1905-11/15/85). Films: "Wells Fargo" 1937 (Confederate Captain); "Saddle Serenade" 1945. ¶TV: *Wild Bill Hickok*—"Papa Antinelli" 11-27-51.

Foster, Bill. Films: "The Okla-homan" 1957 (Dobie Henchman); "Smoke in the Wind" 1975 (Stapp). ¶TV: *Wagon Train*—"The Cappy Darrin Story" 11-11-59; *Rango*—"My Teepee Runneth Over" 3-10-67 (Brave); *The Guns of Will Sonnett*— "Meeting at Devil's Fork" 10-27-67 (Pev Williams), "Trail's End" 1-31-69 (Ketugh); *Lawman*—"The Return of Owny O'Reilly" 10-16-60 (Ed Wrangle).

Foster, Buddy (1957-). Films: "Black Noon" TVM-1971 (Ethan). ¶TV: *Hondo*—Regular 1967 (Johnny Dow); *Alias Smith and Jones*— "Bushwack!' 10-21-72.

Foster, Dianne. Films: "Three Hours to Kill" 1954 (Chris Plumber); "The Kentuckian" 1955 (Hannah); "The Violent Men" 1955 (Judith Wilkison); "Night Passage" 1957 (Charlotte Drew). ¶TV: *Riverboat*— "Path of an Eagle" 2-1-60 (Marian Templeton); *Tales of Wells Fargo*— "Black Trail" 3-14-60 (Elaine), "Return to Yesterday" 1-13-62 (Ella Congreve); *Overland Trail*—"Lawyer in Petticoats" 3-27-60 (Helen Jackson); *Wagon Train*—"Trial for Murder" 4-27-60 & 5-4-60 (Leslie Ivers); *Bonanza*—"The Mill" 10-1-60 (Joyce Edwards); *The Deputy*—"The Jason Harris Story" 10-8-60 (Laurie Harris); *The Outlaws*—"The Fortune Stone" 12-15-60 (Ann Dineen), "Roly" 11-23-61 (Lainie); *Have Gun Will Travel*—"Shadow of a Man" 1-28-61 (Marion Sutter); *Laramie*— "Bitter Glory" 5-2-61 (Ellie Jacobs); *Gunsmoke*—"Reprisal" 3-10-62 (Cornelia Conrad); *The Big Valley*— "Caesar's Wife" 10-3-66; *Wild Wild West*—"The Night of the Lord of Limbo" 12-30-66 (Amanda Vautrain).

Foster, Donald (1889-12/22/69). Films: "The Horse Soldiers" 1959 (Dr. Marvin). ¶TV: *Bonanza*— "The Stranger" 2-27-60 (Alfred Gibbons), "The Dark Gate" 3-4-61.

Foster, Edward. TV: *Wild Bill Hickok*—"The Iron Major" 4-21-53, "Jingles Wins a Friend" 4-28-53; *Sergeant Preston of the Yukon*—"Trapped" 2-2-56 (Pierre Bourget), "The Rookie" 9-20-56 (Francois Valle), "Fantastic Creatures" 11-1-56 (Lefty), "Boy Alone" 2-20-58 (Bart); *The Deputy*—"The X Game" 5-28-60; *Rawhide*—"The Pitchwagon" 3-2-62 (Hugo Fuller), "Incident of the Reluctant Bridegroom" 11-30-62 (Waiter).

Foster, Helen (1906-12/25/82). Films: "The Bandit's Baby" 1925 (Esther Lacy); "On the Go" 1925

(Nell Hall); "Reckless Courage" 1925 (Doris Bayne); "The Courage of Collins" 1927; "Hands Off" 1927 (Myra Perkins); "The Outlaw Dog" 1927 (Helen Meadows); "Harvest of Hate" 1929 (Margie Smith); "Hoof-beats of Vengeance" 1929 (Mary Martin); "The Boiling Point" 1932 (Laura Kirk); "Ghost City" 1932 (Laura Martin); "The Saddle Buster" 1932 (Sunny Hurn); "Young Blood" 1932 (Gail Winters); "Lucky Larri-gan" 1933 (Virginia Bailey); "The Westerner" 1940 (Janice).

Foster, J. Morris (1882-4/24/66). Films: "The Secret Man" 1917 (Henry Beaufort); "The Fighting Grin" 1918 (Harold De Vanderveer); "Overland Red" 1920; "Sundown Slim" 1920 (Jack Corliss); "The Blue Fox" 1921; "Nan of the North" 1922-serial; "Men in the Raw" 1923 (Phil Hollis).

Foster, Jodie (1962-). Films: "One Little Indian" 1973 (Martha); "Sommersby" 1993 (Laurel); "Maverick" 1994 (Annabelle Bransford). ¶TV: *Gunsmoke*—"Roots of Fear" 12-15-69 (Susan Sadler), "P.S. Murry Christmas" 12-27-71 (Patricia), "The Predators" 1-31-72 (Marienne); *Daniel Boone*—"Bringing Up Josh" 4-16-70 (Rachel); *Bonanza*—"A Place to Hide" 3-19-72 (Bluebird); *Kung Fu*— "Alethea" 3-15-73 (Alethea Ingram).

Foster, Linda (1944-). Films: "Young Fury" 1965 (Sally Miller). ¶TV: *Bonanza*—"Thanks for Every-thing, Friend" 10-11-64 (Sue), "Dark Enough to See the Stars" 3-12-67 (Jennifer); *Gunsmoke*—"Hammer-head" 12-26-64 (Carrie Ponder); *F Troop*—"Will the Real Captain Try to Stand Up" 5-10-66 (Cindy Charles); *Rango*—"Diamonds Look Better Around Your Neck Than a Rope" 3-3-67 (Cris Harper).

Foster, May (1893-1/6/51). Films: "Two Moons" 1920 (Red Agnew's Wife); "A Knight of the West" 1921 (Mother McKitrick); "The Frontiersman" 1927 (Mandy).

Foster, Meg (1948-). Films: "Oblivion" 1994 (Stell Barr). ¶TV: *Here Come the Brides*—"Two Worlds" 2-20-70 (Callie); *Bonanza*—"The Silent Killers" 2-28-71 (Evangeline Woodtree).

Foster, Preston (1900-7/14/70). Films: "The Arizonian" 1935 (Tex Randolph); "Annie Oakley" 1935 (Toby Walker); "The Outcasts of Poker Flat" 1937 (John Oakhurst); "Geronimo" 1940 (Capt. Bill Starrett); "Northwest Mounted Police" 1940 (Sgt. Jim Brett); "The Round Up" 1941 (Greg); "American Empire"

1942 (Paxton Bryce); "My Friend Flicka" 1943 (Rob McLaughlin); "The Harvey Girls" 1946 (Judge Sam Purvis); "King of the Wild Horses" 1947; "Ramrod" 1947 (Frank Ivey); "Thunderhoof" 1948 (Scotty Mason); "I Shot Jesse James" 1949 (John Kelley); "Three Desperate Men" 1951 (Tom Denton); "Tomahawk" 1951 (Col. Carrington); "Montana Territory" 1952 (Sheriff Plummer); "Law and Order" 1953 (Kurt Durling); "The Marshal's Daughter" 1953; "Advance to the Rear" 1964 (Gen. Bateman); "The Man from Galveston" 1964 (Judge Homer Black). ¶TV: *The Outlaws*—"Return to New March" 6-22-61 (Major Ramsur); *Gunslinger*—Regular 1961 (Captain Zachary Wingate); *Temple Houston*— "The Man from Galveston" 1963 (Judge Homer Black).

Foster, Ronald. Films: "The Storm Rider" 1957 (Burns); "Cattle Empire" 1958 (Stitch). ¶TV: *Wagon Train*—"The John Cameron Story" 10-2-57, "The Julia Gage Story" 12-18-57; *Death Valley Days*—"Rough and Ready" 12-23-57 (Siles Begg); *Rough Riders*—"The Scavengers" 1-8-59 (Jeff Lee); *Rawhide*—"Incident in No Man's Land" 6-12-59, "Incident at the Top of the World" 1-27-61 (Bill Rudd), "Incident at Zebulon" 3-5-64 (Johnny Larkin); *Wyatt Earp*—"The Arizona Lottery" 2-16-60 (Johnny-Behind-the-Deuce); *Bat Masterson*— "Six Feet of Gold" 2-25-60 (Toby Dawson), "Jeopardy at Jackson Hole" 6-1-61 (Sheriff Simpson); *Colt .45*— "Bounty List" 5-31-60 (Tommy Potts); *Gunsmoke*—"Bless Me Till I Die" 4-22-61 (Cole Treadwell), "Nina's Revenge" 12-16-61 (Jim Garza); *Tales of Wells Fargo*—"Royal Maroon" 4-28-62 (Ken Logan); *Laramie*—"The Wedding Party" 1-29-63 (Lee Taylor); *The Virginian*—"The Money Cage" 3-6-63 (Charley Dorsey); *Bonanza*—"Invention of a Gunfighter" 9-20-64 (Al Mooney), "Peace Officer" 2-6-66 (Dave Morissey), "Something Hurt, Something Wild" 9-11-66 (Stark), "Sense of Duty" 9-24-67 (Steve); *The High Chaparral*— "The Peacemaker" 3-3-68 (Lt. Corey).

Foster, Susanna (1924-). Films: "Frisco Sal" 1945 (Sally).

Foster, William. Films: "Plunderers of Painted Flats" 1959 (Bill); "Old Rex" 1961; "Shoot Out at Big Sag" 1962. ¶TV: *Wyatt Earp*—"The Nugget and the Epitaph" 10-6-59, "The Court vs. Doc Holliday" 4-26-60, "Wyatt Takes the Primrose Path" 3-28-61; *The Rebel*—"Vicious Circle"

10-25-59 (Sim); *Rawhide*—"Incident of the Running Iron" 3-10-61.

Foulger, Byron (1900-4/4/70). Films: "The Luck of Roaring Camp" 1937 (Kentuck); "Union Pacific" 1939 (Andrew Whipple); "Arizona" 1940 (Pete Kitchen); "Heroes of the Saddle" 1940 (Melloney); "Dude Cowboy" 1941 (Mr. Adams); "Ridin' on a Rainbow" 1941 (Matt Evans); "Hoppy Serves a Writ" 1943 (Storekeeper Danvers); "In Old Oklahoma" 1943 (Wilkins); "The Kansan" 1943; "Silver Spurs" 1943 (Justice of the Peace); "Girl Rush" 1944 (Oscar); "Swing in the Saddle" 1944; "Plainsman and the Lady" 1946 (Simmons); "Adventures of Don Coyote" 1947 (Felton); "The Bells of San Fernando" 1947 (Garcia); "The Michigan Kid" 1947 (Mr. Porter); "Unconquered" 1947 (Townsman); "The Kissing Bandit" 1948 (Grandee); "Relentless" 1948 (Assayer); "The Dalton Gang" 1949 (Amos Boling); "I Shot Jesse James" 1949 (Room Clerk); "Red Desert" 1949 (Sparky Johnson); "Satan's Cradle" 1949 (Henry Lane); "Streets of Laredo" 1949 (Artist); "The Girl from San Lorenzo" 1950 (Cal); "The Return of Jesse James" 1950 (Bakin); "Salt Lake Raiders" 1950 (John Sutton); "Best of the Badmen" 1951; "Apache Country" 1952 (Bartlett); "Cripple Creek" 1952 (Hawkins); "Bandits of the West" 1953 (Eric Strikler); "The Moonlighter" 1953; "A Perilous Journey" 1953 (Mr. Martin, the Desk Clerk); "Cattle Queen of Montana" 1954 (Land Office Employee); "Silver Lode" 1954 (Prescott, the Banker); "At Gunpoint" 1955 (Larry, the Teller); "The Spoilers" 1955 (Montrose); "The Desperados Are in Town" 1956 (Jim Day); "The Buckskin Lady" 1957 (Latham); "Gun Battle at Monterey" 1957 (Carson); "Sierra Stranger" 1957 (Claim Clerk); "King of the Wild Stallions" 1959 (Orcutt); "Guns of Diablo" 1964 (Hickey); "The Cockeyed Cowboys of Calico County" 1970 (Reu Marshall); "There Was a Crooked Man" 1970. ¶TV: *The Lone Ranger*—"Trouble Waters" 3-9-50, "Trouble for Tonto" 7-20-50, "Tumblerock Law" 2-26-53, "Blind Witness" 5-30-57; *The Cisco Kid*—"Boomerang" 1-20-51; *Wild Bill Hickok*—"The Dog Collar Story" 7-17-51, "A Close Shave for the Marshal" 4-29-52, "Missing Diamonds" 3-17-53, "Sheriff of Buckeye" 6-30-53; *The Gene Autry Show*—"The Golden Chariot" 10-29-55; *Judge Roy Bean*—"The Defense Rests" 6-1-56 (Judge Parks); *The Roy Rogers Show*—"Head for Cover" 10-21-56

(Ezra); *The Adventures of Rin Tin Tin*—"O'Hara's Gold" 3-1-57, "The Failure" 5-8-59 (Pineas Crabtree); *Maverick*—"The Seventh Hand" 3-2-58 (Hotel Clerk), "Lonesome Reunion" 9-28-58 (Clerk); *Bonanza*—"The Newcomers" 9-26-59 (Justin Flannery), "The Jury" 12-30-62, "King of the Mountain" 2-23-64 (Parson); *Wagon Train*—"The Greenhorn Story" 10-7-59 (Humphrey Pumphret), "The Geneva Balfour Story" 1-20-64, "The Grover Allen Story" 2-3-64 (Mr. Duskin); *Rawhide*—"Incident of the Druid's Curse" 1-8-60 (Dr. Lismore), "Incident at Confidence Creek" 11-28-63 (Farmer); *Tales of Wells Fargo*—"A Killing in Calico" 12-16-61 (Telegraph Clerk); *Have Gun Will Travel*—"The Waiting Room" 2-24-62 (Undertaker); *Gunsmoke*—"The Hunger" 11-17-62 (Dooley), "The Hanging" 12-31-66 (Ollie); *Laredo*—"A Taste of Money" 4-28-66 (Martingale), "The Land Slickers" 10-14-66 (Leslie Weems); *Daniel Boone*—"The Williamsburg Cannon" 1-12-67 & 1-19-67 (Thomas Goodleaf); *The Guns of Will Sonnett*—"A Son for a Son" 10-20-67; *Wild Wild West*—"The Night of the Juggernaut" 10-11-68 (County Clerk).

Foulk, Robert (1908-2/25/89). Films: "The San Francisco Story" 1952 (Thompson); "Apache Ambush" 1955 (Red Jennings); "The Far Country" 1955 (Kingman); "Strange Lady in Town" 1955 (Joe); "Backlash" 1956 (Sheriff Olson); "The Rawhide Years" 1956 (Mate); "Last of the Badmen" 1957 (Taylor); "Sierra Stranger" 1957 (Tom Simmons); "The Tall Stranger" 1957 (Pagones); "Day of the Bad Man" 1958 (Silas Mordigan); "The Left-Handed Gun" 1958 (Brady); "Quantrill's Raiders" 1958 (Hager); "Cast a Long Shadow" 1959 (Rigdon); "Skin Game" 1971 (Sheriff); "Testimony of Two Men" TVM-1977. ¶TV: *Sheriff of Cochise*—"The Relatives" 3-8-57 (Hank); *Tales of Wells Fargo*—"John Wesley Hardin" 9-30-57 (Sam Adams), "Gunman's Revenge" 5-22-61 (Sheriff Nolan); *Tombstone Territory*—"Gunslinger from Galeville" 10-16-57 (Curly Bill); *Trackdown*—"Easton, Texas" 10-25-57 (Dan Cutler); *26 Men*—"Montezuma's Cave" 3-18-58; *The Texan*—"Desert Passage" 12-1-58, "Dangerous Ground" 12-14-59, "Town Divided" 3-21-60; *Wanted—Dead or Alive*—"Eight Cent Record" 12-20-58; *Wichita Town*—"Day of Battle" 1-18-59 (Kingston), "Compadre" 11-25-59 (Joe Kingston); *Texas John Slaughter*—"Showdown at Sandoval"

1-23-59 (Pitts); *The Rifleman*—"The Second Witness" 3-3-59, "Three-Legged Terror" 4-21-59, "The Raid" 6-9-59 (Johannson), "Outlaw's Inheritance" 6-16-59 (Toomey), "The Lost Treasure of Canyon Town" 2-28-61 (Herbert Newman); *The Restless Gun*—"The Pawn" 4-6-59; *The Rebel*—"The Vagrants" 12-20-59 (Sheriff); *The Lone Ranger*—"Delayed Action" 11-6-52, "The Deserter" 4-23-53, "Stage to Tishomingo" 10-28-54, "Sawtelle Saga's End" 3-24-55; *Gunsmoke*—"Night Incident" 10-29-55 (Hinton), "Death Watch" 1-8-66 (Fields); *My Friend Flicka*—"The Little Secret" 12-2-55 (Crain); *Jim Bowie*—"The Birth of the Blade" 9-7-56 (Yancy); *Fury*—"Joey and the Little League" 10-13-56 (Mr. Wright), "Black Gold" 2-28-59 (Mart); *Circus Boy*—"The Good Samaritans" 12-23-56 (Ben Farmer); *Broken Arrow*—"Doctor" 2-12-57 (Hank Woodley); *Maverick*—"Point Blank" 9-29-57 (Moose), "A Fellow's Brother" 11-22-59 (Sheriff), "The Forbidden City" 3-26-61 (Sheriff Shadley); *Cheyenne*—"Devil's Canyon" 11-19-57 (Garth), "The Beholden" 2-27-61 (Jake Scott), "Pocketful of Stars" 11-12-62 (Tom Fanshaw); *Colt .45*—"The Deserters" 3-28-58 (Fur Trader), "The Pirate" 5-31-59 (Bosun Boggs), "Martial Law" 5-17-60 (Marshal Hacker); *Jefferson Drum*—"Wheel of Fortune" 6-27-58 (Jake); *Northwest Passage*—"The Ambush" 2-6-59; *Man from Blackhawk*—"The Ghost of Lafitte" 2-26-60 (Hoag Lafitte); *Bonanza*—"The Stranger" 2-27-60 (Sheriff), "The Smiler" 9-24-61 (Deputy), "The Many Faces of Gideon Flinch" 11-5-61, "The Gamble" 4-1-62, "Blessed Are They" 4-22-62, "Any Friend of Walter's" 3-24-63, "The Spotlight" 5-16-65, "Big Shadow on the Land" 4-17-66 (Seth), "A Dollar's Worth of Trouble" 5-15-66 (Seth), "Ballad of the Ponderosa" 11-13-66 (Sheriff), "A Real Nice, Friendly Little Town" 11-27-66 (Deputy), "Clarissa" 4-30-67 (Peterson), "The Burning Sky" 1-28-68; *Bat Masterson*—"Welcome to Paradise" 5-5-60 (Judge Pete Perkins); *The Deputy*—"The Deathly Quiet" 5-27-61 (Colonel Belknap); *The Tall Man*—"Time of Foreshadowing" 11-25-61 (Gimp); *Temple Houston*—"Toll the Bell Slowly" 10-17-63 (O'Garrick); *Daniel Boone*—"Tekawitha McLeod" 10-1-64 (Sledy Clayburn); *A Man Called Shenandoah*—"The Onslaught" 9-23-65 (Milt); *Laredo*—"One Too Many Voices" 11-18-66; *The Guns of Will Sonnett*—"Sunday in Paradise" 12-15-67 (Luke Landry), "The Trap" 10-4-68; *Cimarron Strip*—

"The Blue Moon Train" 2-15-68; *The Big Valley*—"The Long Ride" 11-25-68; *Lancer*—"The Wedding" 1-7-69; *Here Come the Brides*—"The Last Winter" 3-27-70 (Phelps); *Kung Fu*—"The Soul Is the Warrior" 2-8-73 (Moss); *The Cowboys*—"A Matter of Honor" 3-20-74 (O.J. Prouty); *Barbary Coast*—"Funny Money" 9-8-75.

Fowkes, Conrad. Films: "Lovin' Molly" 1974 (Eddie).

Fowler, Art (1902-4/4/53). Films: "Tonto Basin Outlaws" 1941 (Brown); "Arizona Trail" 1943 (Curley); "Black Market Rustlers" 1943 (Specialty Act); "Frontier Law" 1943 (Dirk); "West of Texas" 1943 (Clem); "Land of the Outlaws" 1944; "Law Men" 1944 (Gus); "The Old Texas Trail" 1944; "Range Law" 1944 (Swede Larson); "West of the Rio Grande" 1944.

Fowler, Brenda (1883-10/27/42). Films: "Ruggles of Red Gap" 1935 (Judy Ballard); "Stagecoach" 1939 (Mrs. Gatewood).

Fowler, Jean. Films: "Under Western Stars" 1938 (Mrs. Wilson).

Fowler, John C. "Jack" (1869-6/27/52). Films: "Reckless Courage" 1925 (Jasper Bayne); "The Power of the Weak" 1926; "Ranson's Folly" 1926 (Colonel Patten); "The Fighting Legion" 1930 (John Blake); "Fighting Thru" 1930; "Union Pacific" 1939 (Official).

Fowley, Douglas V. (1911-). Films: "Wild and Woolly" 1937 (Blackie Morgan); "Arizona Wildcat" 1938 (Rufe Calloway); "Dodge City" 1939 (Munger); "Henry Goes Arizona" 1939 (Ricky Dole); "Cherokee Strip" 1940 (Alf Barrett); "Twenty Mule Team" 1940 (Stag Roper); "Wagons Westward" 1940 (Bill Marsden); "The Parson of Panamint" 1941 (Chappie Ellerton); "Secrets of the Wastelands" 1941 (Salters); "Sunset on the Desert" 1942 (McCall); "Bar 20" 1943 (Slash); "Colt Comrades" 1943 (Joe Brass); "The Kansan" 1943 (Ben Nash); "Lost Canyon" 1943 (Jeff Burton); "Riding High" 1943 (Brown); "Along the Navajo Trail" 1945 (J. Richard Bentley); "Don't Fence Me In" 1945 (Gordon); "Drifting Along" 1946 (Jack Dailey); "'Neath Canadian Skies" 1946; "North of the Border" 1946; "Ridin' Down the Trail" 1947; "The Sea of Grass" 1947 (Joe Horton); "Wild Country" 1947 (Clark Varney); "Yankee Fakir" 1947 (Yankee Davis); "Black Bart" 1948 (Sheriff Mix); "Coroner Creek" 1948 (Stew Shallis); "The Denver Kid" 1948; "The Dude Goes West" 1948 (Beetie); "Gun Smugglers" 1948 (Steve); "Renegades of Sonora" 1948; "Bad Men of Tombstone" 1949; "Massacre River" 1949 (Simms); "Renegades of the Sage" 1949 (Sloper); "Satan's Cradle" 1949 (Steve Gentry); "Susanna Pass" 1949 (Del Roberts); "Hoedown" 1950 (Buttons); "Rider from Tucson" 1950 (Rankin); "Rio Grande Patrol" 1950 (Bragg); "Stage to Tucson" 1950 (Ira Prentiss); "Across the Wide Missouri" 1951 (Tin Cup Owens); "Callaway Went Thataway" 1951 (Gaffer); "South of Caliente" 1951 (Dave Norris); "Horizons West" 1952 (Tompkins); "The Man Behind the Gun" 1952 (Buckley); "Kansas Pacific" 1953 (Janus); "Red River Shore" 1953 (Case Lockwood); "The Lone Gun" 1954 (Charlie); "Untamed Heiress" 1954 (Pal); "The Lonesome Trail" 1955; "Texas Lady" 1955 (Clay Ballard); "Bandido" 1956 (McGee); "The Broken Star" 1956 (Hiram Charleton); "Man from Del Rio" 1956 (Doc Adams); "The Badge of Marshal Brennan" 1957 (Marshal Matt Brennan); "Raiders of Old California" 1957; "Three Thousand Hills" 1959 (Whitney); "Buffalo Gun" 1961 (Sheriff); "Guns of Diablo" 1964 (Knudson); "The Good Guys and the Bad Guys" 1969 (Grundy); "From Noon to Three" 1976 (Buck Bowers); "The Oregon Trail" TVM-1976 (Eli Thorpe); "The White Buffalo" 1977 (Amos Bixby). ¶TV: *Wild Bill Hickok*—"Wrestling Story" 4-8-52, "Boy and the Hound Dog" 10-14-52; *Wyatt Earp*—Regular 1955-56 (Doc Fabrique), 1957-61 (Doc Holliday), "One Murder—Fifty Suspects" 3-17-59 (Grandpa Logan), "The Judge" 4-19-60 (Judge Amos Waggoner); *The Adventures of Rin Tin Tin*—"The Big Top" 2-3-56 (Dingle), "Rusty's Opportunity" 10-17-58 (Benedict Benson); *Cheyenne*—"Rendezvous at Red Rock" 2-21-56 (Pritchard); *Jefferson Drum*—"Wheel of Fortune" 6-27-58 (Wooley); *Trackdown*—"The Set Up" 9-26-58 (Carlson); *The Texan*—"A Race for Life" 3-16-59 (Mar Anderson); *Pony Express*—"Showdown at Thirty Mile Ridge" 12-30-59; *Death Valley Days*—"Cap'n Pegleg" 5-17-60 (Quirt), "By the Book" 5-4-68 (Arcane); *Wanted—Dead or Alive*—"Tolliver Bender" 2-13-60 (Tolliver Bender); *Temple Houston*—"Sam's Boy" 1-23-64 (Doc Webb); *The Travels of Jaimie McPheeters*—"The Day of the Reckoning" 3-15-64 (Knudson); *The Virginian*—"Hideout" 1-13-65 (Sorrowful), "Show Me a Hero" 11-17-65 (Sheriff Tolliver); *Bonanza*—"The Ballerina" 1-24-65 (Ned Conrad); *Laredo*—"A Question of Discipline" 10-28-65 (Jerky Collins); *Daniel Boone*—"The Search" 3-3-66 (Rufus C. Hoops); *A Man Called Shenandoah*—"The Death of Matthew Eldridge" 3-21-66 (Gil Harden); *Pistols 'n' Petticoats*—Regular 1966-67 (Andrew "Grandpa" Hanks); *Iron Horse*—"T Is for Traitor" 12-2-67 (Dusty); *Dundee and the Culhane*—"The Dead Man's Brief" 10-4-67 (Judge); *The Guns of Will Sonnett*—"Time Is the Rider" 1-10-69 (Hi Lowe); *Gunsmoke*—"A Quiet Day in Dodge" 1-29-73 (Buck Doolin); *Kung Fu*—"The Assassin" 10-4-73 (Trapper); *Barbary Coast*—"The Dawson Marker" 1-9-76 (Stumpy); *The Quest*—"The Last of the Mountain Men" 1976; *Father Murphy*—"Graduation" 1-5-82 (Amos Perry).

Fox, Bernard (1927-). TV: *F Troop*—"The Phantom Major" 9-28-65 (Major Bentley-Royce); *Wild Wild West*—"The Night of the Winged Terror" 1-17-68 & 1-24-68 (Dr. Occularis-Jones); *Here Come the Brides*—"The Wealthiest Man in Seattle" 10-3-69 (Father Ned); *Daniel Boone*—"A Bearskin for Jamie Blue" 11-27-69 (Carruthers); *Dirty Sally*—"Right of Way" 1-11-74 (Horton); *Barbary Coast*—"Sharks Eat Sharks" 11-21-75 (Irish Murphy); *Gun Shy*—3-15-83 (Sir Charles).

Fox, Colin. Films: "Silence of the North" 1981 (Arthur Herriott).

Fox, Elsa. Films: "The Land Just Over Yonder" 1916 (Mrs. McAlpin).

Fox, Fred (1884-12/1/49). Films: "Buffalo Bill Rides Again" 1947 (Mr. Howard).

Fox, Jimmy (1891-6/16/74). Films: "Cheyenne Rides Again" 1937 (Dopey Andrews); "Cowboy from Brooklyn" 1938 (Photographer); "Stardust on the Sage" 1942.

Fox, Jr., John. Films: "Do It Now" 1924; "The Passing of Wolf MacLean" 1924; "When a Man's a Man" 1924 (Little Billy).

Fox, John J. TV: *Pistols 'n' Petticoats*—12-17-66 (Bartender); *The Big Valley*—"Night in a Small Town" 10-9-67, "Bounty on a Barkley" 2-26-68, "Point and Counterpoint" 5-19-69 (Jury Foreman); *Death Valley Days*—"The Taming of Trudy Bell" 12-6-69; *The High Chaparral*—"A Matter of Vengeance" 11-27-70 (Bartender); *Bonanza*—"Forever" 9-12-72 (Jack); *Dirty Sally*—2-15-74 (Broyles).

Fox, Johnny. Films: "The Covered Wagon" 1923 (Jed Wingate); "The Bar C Mystery" 1926-serial (Tommy).

Fox, Lucy. Films: "Teeth" 1924

(Paula Grayson); "The Arizona Romeo" 1925 (Sylvia Wayne); "The Trail Rider" 1925 (Fanny Goodnight).

Fox, Michael (1921-). Films: "Riding with Buffalo Bill" 1954-serial (King Carney). ¶TV: *Tombstone Territory*—"Desert Survival" 12-4-57 (Warren); *Wanted—Dead or Alive*—"Reunion for Revenge" 1-24-59; *Trackdown*—"The Gang" 2-25-59 (Blake Yedor), "The Threat" 3-4-59, "Gift Horse" 4-29-59 (Blake Yedor); *The Rifleman*—"The Trade" 3-10-59, "Letter of the Law" 12-1-59, "Nora" 5-24-60 (Joe Hanna), "The Hangman" 5-31-60 (Joe Hagna), "Miss Milly" 11-15-60; *Johnny Ringo*—"Soft Cargo" 5-5-60 (Logan); *The Virginian*—"The Brazen Bell" 10-17-62; *Empire*—"Long Past, Long Remembered" 10-23-62 (Chester Atkins); *Gunsmoke*—"Carter Caper" 11-16-63 (Waiter), "Wishbone" 2-19-66 (Buffalo Hunter), "Hard Luck Henry" 10-23-67 (Jed Walsh); *The Big Valley*—"Forty Rifles" 9-22-65, "Point and Counterpoint" 5-19-69 (Jonathan Williams); *Laredo*—"The Seventh Day" 1-6-67 (Bartender); *Wild Wild West*—"The Night of the Death-Maker" 2-23-68 (Gillespie).

Fox, Michael J. (1961-). Films: "Back to the Future, Part III" 1990 (Marty McFly/Seamus McFly).

Fox, Spencer. Films: "Shark River" 1953 (Johnny Daugherty).

Foxe, Earle (1888-12/10/73). Films: "The Love Mask" 1916 (Silver Spurs); "The Man She Brought Back" 1922 (John Ramsey); "Oh, You Tony!" 1924 (Jim Overton); "Destry Rides Again" 1932 (Brent); "My Darling Clementine" 1946 (Gambler).

Foxworth, Robert (1941-). Films: "Mrs. Sundance" TVM-1974 (Jack Maddox); "The Return of Desperado" TVM-1988 (Marcus Dryden). ¶TV: *Kung Fu*—"Empty Pages of a Dead Book" 1-10-74 (Clyde McNelly); *Hec Ramsey*—"Only Birds and Fools" 4-7-74 (Jonas Goodwin).

Foy, Charles (1898-8/22/84). Films: "The Woman of the Town" 1943 (Eddie Foy, Sr.).

Foy, Jr., Eddie (1905-7/15/83). Films: "Frontier Marshal" 1939 (Eddie Foy); "Texas Rangers Ride Again" 1940 (Mandolin).

Foy, III, Eddie. Films: "Outlaw's Son" 1957 (Tod Wentworth).

Foy, Mary (1904-12/13/87). Films: "The Lariat Kid" 1929 (Aunt Bella); "A Man from Wyoming" 1930 (Inspector); "Thunder Trail" 1937 (Woman).

Frakes, Jonathan. Films:

"Dream West" TVM-1986 (Lieutenant Gillespie).

Frame, Park (1888-6/1/43). Films: "Flashing Spurs" 1924 (Bill Carbee).

Framer, Samuel. Films: "God's Outlaw" 1919 (Rufus Sanborn).

Francen, Victor (1888-11/18/77). Films: "San Antonio" 1945 (Legare).

Franchi, Franco (1922-12/92). Films: "For a Fist in the Eye" 1965-Ital./Span.; "Two Gangsters in the Wild West" 1965-Ital./Span. (Franco); "Two Sergeants of General Custer" 1965-Ital./Span.; "Two Sons of Ringo" 1966-Ital.; "The Handsome, the Ugly, and the Stupid" 1967-Ital.; "Two R-R-Ringos from Texas" 1967-Ital.; "Ciccio Forgives, I Don't" 1968-Ital.; "Grandsons of Zorro" 1968-Ital. (Franco); "Nephews of Zorro" 1969-Ital. (Franco); "Paths of War" 1969-Ital.; "Two Sons of Trinity" 1972-Ital.

Franciosa, Tony (1928-). Films: "Rio Conchos" 1964 (Rodriguez); "A Man Called Gannon" 1969 (Gannon); "This Was the West That Was" TVM-1974 (J.W. McCanles); "Stagecoach" TVM-1986 (Henry Gatewood). ¶TV: *The Virginian*—"The Shiloh Years" 1-28-70 (Kordick); *The Men from Shiloh*—"Follow the Leader" 12-2-70 (Ritter).

Francis, Alec B. (1867-7/6/34). Films: "All Man" 1916 (John Maynard); "North of the Rio Grande" 1922 (Father Hillaire); "The Spider and the Rose" 1923 (Good Padre); "Do It Now" 1924; "The Reckless Sex" 1925 (Emanuel Garcia); "Where the Worst Begins" 1925 (August Van Dorn); "Three Bad Men" 1926 (Rev. Calvin Benson); "The Yankee Senor" 1926 (Don Fernando); "The Shepherd of the Hills" 1928 (David Howitt, the Shepherd).

Francis, Anne (1930-). Films: "Bad Day at Black Rock" 1955 (Liz Wirth); "The Hired Gun" 1957 (Ellen Beldon); "More Dead Than Alive" 1968 (Monica Alton); "The Intruders" TVM-1970 (Leora Garrison); "Wild Women" TVM-1970 (Jean Marshek); "Pancho Villa" 1975-Span.; "Banjo Hackett: Roamin' Free" TVM-1976 (Flora Dobbs). ¶TV: *Rawhide*—"Incident of the Shambling Men" 10-9-59 (Rose Wittman); *Temple Houston*—"Ten Rounds for Baby" 1-30-64 (Kate Fitzpatrick); *Death Valley Days*—"The Last Stagecoach Robbery" 3-21-64 (Pearl Hart); *The Virginian*—"All Nice and Legal" 11-25-64 (Victoria Greenly); *Walt Disney Presents*—"Gallegher" 1965-67 (Adele Jones); *The Men from Shiloh*—

"Gun Quest" 10-21-70 (Myra); *Gunsmoke*—"Sarah" 10-16-72 (Sarah); *Kung Fu*—"Night of the Owls, Day of the Doves" 2-14-74 (Ida Quinlan).

Francis, Coleman (1919-1/15/73). TV: *Sergeant Preston of the Yukon*—"Relief Train" 2-23-56 (Powers), "The Assassins" 6-7-56 (Martin), "Border Action" 12-27-56 (Matt Lance), "Mark of Crime" 7-10-58 (Jonathan Dewey).

Francis, Connie (1938-). Films: "The Sheriff of Fractured Jaw" 1958-Brit. (Voice).

Francis, Ivor (1918-10/22/86). Films: "The Wackiest Wagon Train in the West" 1976 (Carter Brookhaven). ¶TV: *Here Come the Brides*—"The Fetching of Jenny" 12-5-69; *Bonanza*—"Dead Wrong" 12-7-69 (Banker); *Dusty's Trail*—Regular 1973 (Carson Brookhaven); *The Quest*—"Portrait of a Gunfighter" 12-22-76 (Neilson).

Francis, Jon. Films: "Will Penny" 1968 (Horace Greeley Allen).

Francis, Kay (1899-8/26/68). Films: "When the Daltons Rode" 1940 (Julie King).

Francis, Martha. Films: "The Scarlet West" 1925 (Harriett Kinnard).

Francis, Missy. TV: *Little House on the Prairie*—Regular 1981-82 (Cassandra).

Francis, Noel (1911-10/30/59). Films: "Rough Romance" 1930 (Flossie); "My Pal, the King" 1932 (Princess Elsa); "Stone of Silver Creek" 1935 (Lola); "Left-Handed Law" 1937 (Betty Golden); "Sudden Bill Dorn" 1937 (Lorna Kent).

Francis, Olin (1892-6/30/52). Films: "A Knight of the West" 1921 (Jack "Zip" Garvin); "Fightin' Devil" 1922; "The Powerful Eye" 1924; "Rarin' to Go" 1924 (Hawk Morton); "Walloping Wallace" 1924 (Sheriff); "Let's Go Gallagher" 1925 (Black Carter); "Call of the Klondike" 1926 (Dolan); "Born to Battle" 1927 (Zack Barstow); "The Flying U Ranch" 1927 (Dunk Whitaker); "Pioneers of the West" 1927; "Battling Buckaroo" 1932 (Bull); "Forty-Five Calibre Echo" 1932; "Tex Takes a Holiday" 1932; "The Lone Avenger" 1933; "Lariats and Sixshooters" 1933; "Lightning Range" 1934 (Black Pete); "Lightning Range" 1934; "Circle of Death" 1935 (Deputy Sheriff); "The Irish Gringo" 1935; "Lightning Triggers" 1935 (Deputy Sheriff); "End of the Trail" 1936 (Deputy); "O'Malley of the Mounted" 1936 (Andy); "The Phantom Rider" 1936-serial; "Rose of the Rancho" 1936 (Bouncer); "Rough Ridin' Rhythm" 1937 (Jake Horne); "Knight of the Plains" 1938; "Overland Stage Raiders" 1938 (Jake); "Pals of the Saddle" 1938; "Red River Range" 1938 (Kenton); "Two-Gun Justice" 1938 (Blackie); "The Night Riders" 1939; "Overland with Kit Carson" 1939-serial (Pierre); "Riders of the Black River" 1939 (Whit Kane); "Riders of the Frontier" 1939 (Sam); "Beyond the Sacramento" 1940 (Jimson); "The Man from Tumbleweeds" 1940 (Ranger); "Take Me Back to Oklahoma" 1940 (Mule Bates); "Rollin' Home to Texas" 1941.

Francis, Robert. Films: "They Rode West" 1954 (Dr. Allen Seward).

Francisco, Betty (1900-11/25/50). Films: "A Broadway Cowboy" 1920 (Betty Jordan); "Riding with Death" 1921 (Anita Calhoun); "Double Dealing" 1923 (Stella Fern); "The Old Fool" 1923 (Mary Manners); "Mystery Ranch" 1932 (Appetite Mae).

Francisco, Evelyn. Films: "O.U. West" 1925 (Sally Walker); "King of the Herd" 1927.

Franciscus, James (1934-7/8/91). Films: "The Valley of Gwangi" 1969 (Tuck Kirby). TV: *Have Gun Will Travel*—"The Manhunter" 6-7-58 (Tom Nelson); *Tales of Wells Fargo*—"The Stage Line" 10-5-59 (Joe Braddock); *Desilu Playhouse*—"Six Guns for Donegan" 10-16-59 (Clay Darrow); *The Rifleman*—"The Legacy" 12-8-59 (Phillip Simmons); *Death Valley Days*—"Lady of the Press" 12-29-59; *Wagon Train*—"The Benjamin Burns Story" 2-17-60 (John Colter); *Black Saddle*—"The Penalty" 4-22-60 (Quinn Jackson); *Rawhide*—"Incident of the Murder Steer" 5-13-60 (Andy Nye); *The Deputy*—"Mother and Son" 10-29-60 (William Stanhope).

Francks, Don (1932-). TV: *Wild Wild West*—"The Night of the Grand Emir" 1-28-66 (T. Wiggett Jones); *The Virginian*—"The Land Dreamer" 2-26-69 (Jack/Caleb); *Lancer*—"Little Darling of the Sierras" 12-30-69 (Noah Fletcher).

Francks, Lili. Films: "McCabe and Mrs. Miller" 1971 (Mrs. Washington).

Franco, Abel. Films: "Three Amigos" 1986 (Papa Sanchez). ¶TV: *Gunslinger*—"Road of the Dead" 3-30-61 (Tomas); *Daniel Boone*—"Bitter Mission" 3-30-67; *The High Chaparral*—"The Fillibusteros" 10-22-67 (Mayor).

Franey, William "Billy" (1885-

12/9/40). Films: "A Knight of the West" 1921 (Mana Palover); "A Western Demon" 1922 (the Cook); "Border Women" 1924 (McGilligan); "The Dangerous Dude" 1925; "Kit Carson Over the Great Divide" 1925 (Oswald Bliffing); "Code of the Northwest" 1926 (Posty McShanigan); "The Dead Line" 1926 (Extra Long); "Moran of the Mounted" 1926 (Mooch Mullens); "Senor Daredevil" 1926 (the Cook); "Aflame in the Sky" 1927 (Cookie); "King of the Herd" 1927; "The Canyon of Adventure" 1928 (Buzzard Koke); "The Glorious Trail" 1928 (Jimmy Bacon); "Under the Tonto Rim" 1928 (One Punch); "Cheyenne" 1929 (Judge Boggs); "The Royal Rider" 1929 (Wild West Show Member); "The Sheriff's Secret" 1931; "White Renegade" 1931; "Freighters of Destiny" 1932 (Ready); "Ghost Valley" 1932 (Scrubby Watson); "Partners" 1932 (Carry-All Roach); "Renegades of the West" 1932 (Barfly); "Somewhere in Sonora" 1933 (Shorty); "War on the Range" 1933; "The Fiddlin' Buckaroo" 1934 (Postmaster); "The Star Packer" 1934 (Pete, the Town Bum); "Five Bad Men" 1935 (Billy); "Western Racketeers" 1935 (Old Timer); "Stage to Chino" 1940; "Triple Justice" 1940.

Frank, Ben (1934-9/11/90). Films: "Jessi's Girls" 1976 (Frank Brock). ¶TV: *Kung Fu*—"Chains" 3-8-73 (Turnkey).

Frank, Burt. Films: "In the Days of Buffalo Bill" 1922-serial (General Hancock).

Frank, Charles. Films: "Go West, Young Girl" TVM-1978 (Captain Anson); "The New Maverick" TVM-1978 (Ben Maverick); "The Chisholms" TVM-1979 (Lester Hackett). ¶TV: *The Chisholms*—Regular 1979 (Lester Hackett); *Young Maverick*—Regular 1979-80 (Ben Maverick); *Paradise*—"Long Lost Lawson" 5-20-89 (Pierce), "A Gather of Guns" 9-10-89 (Pierce Lawson).

Frank, Christian J. (1890-12/10/67). Films: "Out of the Silent North" 1922 (Pete Bellew); "The Love Bandit" 1924; "Black Cyclone" 1925 (Joe Pangle); "Forlorn River" 1926 (Les Setter); "Arizona Bound" 1927 (Texas Frank); "Nevada" 1927 (Sheriff of Winthrop); "The Cavalier" 1928 (Pierre Gaston); "Sunset Pass" 1929 (Chuck); "Under Montana Skies" 1930 (Frank Blake); "Hard Hombre" 1931 (Sheriff); "My Pal, the King" 1932 (Etzel); "Sunset Pass" 1933 (Buck).

Frank, Horst (1929-). Films:

"Pirates of the Mississippi" 1963-Ger./Ital./Fr.; "Black Eagle of Santa Fe" 1964-Ger./Ital./Fr.; "Bullets Don't Argue" 1964-Ital./Ger./Span. (Ike Clanton); "Massacre at Marble City" 1964-Ger./Ital./Fr. (Dan McCormick); "Johnny Hamlet" 1966-Ital. (Claude); "Get the Coffin Ready" 1968-Ital. (David); "The Moment to Kill" 1968-Ital./Ger.; "Hate Thy Neighbor" 1969-Ital. (Chris Malone); "Big Showdown" 1972-Ital./Fr. (Newland); "Carambola" 1974-Ital.

Frank, Jerry. Films: "Boots and Saddles" 1937; "The Trigger Trio" 1937; "Zorro Rides Again" 1937-serial (Duncan); "Heroes of the Hills" 1938 (Slim); "The Lone Ranger" 1938-serial (Trooper); "Santa Fe Stampede" 1938; "The Kid from Texas" 1939 (1st Cowboy); "Zorro's Fighting Legion" 1939-serial (Throne Guard); "Fort Bowie" 1958 (Lt. Maywood); "Seven Guns to Mesa" 1958 (Grandall).

Frank, John (1888-2/15/61). Films: "Rodeo Rhythm" 1942 (Grandpa Twitchell).

Frank, Sterling. Films: "Rebel in Town" 1956 (Cain Mason).

Franke, Chris. Films: "Winds of the Wasteland" 1936 (Grahme).

Frankel, Fanchon (1874-8/12/37). Films: "Desperate Courage" 1928 (Brannon Brother).

Franken, Steve (1933-). Films: "Westworld" 1973 (Technician); "The Missouri Breaks" 1976 (Lonesome Kid). ¶TV: *Wild Wild West*—"The Night of the Bottomless Pit" 11-4-66 (Le Fou); *The Big Valley*—"Hell Hath No Fury" 11-18-68 (Bank Teller).

Frankenberg, Julius. Films: "Humanizing Mr. Winsby" 1916; "The Land Just Over Yonder" 1916 (Hassayampa Jim Titus).

Frankham, David (1926-). Films: "Ten Who Dared" 1960 (Frank Goodman). ¶TV: *Death Valley Days*—"Ship of No Return" 4-28-57; *Maverick*—"Royal Four-Flush" 9-20-59 (Captain Rory Fitzgerald); *Tales of Wells Fargo*—"The Remittance Man" 4-3-61 (Noel Briggs).

Franklin, Camille. TV: *Death Valley Days*—"Bill Bottle's Birthday" 5-19-56, "The Loggerheads" 12-16-56; *Wyatt Earp*—"The Almost Dead Cowhand" 10-23-56 (Ginger).

Franklin, Carl (1930-). Films: "The Legend of the Golden Gun" TVM-1979 (Joshua "Book" Brown).

Franklin, Cherie. Films: "Dirty Little Billy" 1972 (Greta Schmidt).

Franklin, Don. TV: *Young Riders*—Regular 1990-92 (Noah Dixon).

Franklin, Irene (1876-6/16/41). Films: "Land Beyond the Law" 1937 (Cattle Kate).

Franklin, Martha (1876-4/19/29). Films: "Don Q, Son of Zorro" 1925 (the Duenna); "Points West" 1929 (the Mother).

Franklin, Pamela (1949-). TV: *Bonanza*—"First Love" 12-26-72 (Kelly Edwards).

Franklin, Rupert (1862-1/14/39). Films: "The Prairie Wife" 1925 (Rufus Green).

Franklin, Sidney (1870-3/18/31). Films: "The Sleeping Lion" 1919 (Carlotta's Father); "The Texas Trail" 1925 (Ike Collander); "The Fighting Failure" 1926.

Franklin, Wendell Phillips. Films: "The Silent Rider" 1927 (Tommy).

Frankovich, Mike (1910-1/1/92). Films: "Son of Zorro" 1947-serial (Auctioneer).

Franz, Arthur (1920-). Films: "Red Stallion in the Rockies" 1949 (Thad Avery); "Running Target" 1956 (Scott); "Alvarez Kelly" 1966 (Captain Towers). ¶TV: *The Lone Ranger*—"Finders Keepers" 12-8-49; *Zane Grey Theater*—"Man of Fear" 3-14-58 (Lee Brand); *Wanted—Dead or Alive*—"The Most Beautiful Woman" 1-23-60 (John Garth); *Rawhide*—"Incident of the Wanted Painter" 1-29-60 (Charles Fredericks), "Incident at Sugar Creek" 11-23-62 (Sheriff Harris); *The Alaskans*—"The Silent Land" 5-15-60 (Dr. Jim Manning); *Gunsmoke*—"Cherry Red" 6-11-60 (Red Larned); *Death Valley Days*—"The Young Gun" 1-4-61 (Matt Warner), "Justice at Jackson Creek" 2-28-62 (Payne P. Prim); *Tales of Wells Fargo*—"Portrait of Teresa" 2-10-62 (Mel Akins); *Bonanza*—"The Law Maker" 3-11-62 (Asa Moran), "Marie, My Love" 2-10-63 (Marius); *Wagon Train*—"The Jud Steele Story" 5-2-62 (Nathan Forge), "The Annie Duggan Story" 3-13-63 (Dan Highet); *The Virginian*—"No Tears for Savannah" 10-2-63 (Fitz Warren); *Custer*—"Massacre" 10-4-67 (Grey Fox/Bledsoe); *The Outcasts*—"My Name Is Jemal" 11-18-68 (Anse Farnum); *Lancer*—"Devil's Blessing" 4-22-69 (Sheriff Platt); *The Quest*—"Portrait of a Gunfighter" 12-22-76 (Charles Minter).

Franz, Eduard (1902-2/10/83). Films: "Broken Lance" 1954 (Two Moons); "The Indian Fighter" 1955 (Red Cloud); "The Last Command" 1955 (Lorenzo de Quesada); "White

Feather" 1955 (Chief Broken Hand); "The Burning Hills" 1956 (Jacob Lantz); "Day of the Bad Man" 1958 (Andrew Owens); "The Last of the Fast Guns" 1958 (Padre Jose). ¶TV: *Gunsmoke*—"Indian Scout" 3-31-56 (Amos Cartwright), "In Performance of Duty" 11-18-74 (Judge Kendall); *Wagon Train*—"The Les Rand Story" 10-16-57, "The Hiram Winthrop Story" 6-6-62 (Hiram Winthrop); *The Restless Gun*—"The Peddler" 6-9-58 (David Marcus); *Zorro*—"Welcome to Monterey" 10-9-58 (Gregorio Verdugo), "Zorro Rides Alone" 10-16-58 (Gregorio Verdugo), "Horse of Another Color" 10-23-58 (Gregorio Verdugo), "The Senorita Makes a Choice" 10-30-58 (Gregorio Verdugo), "Rendezvous at Sundown" 11-6-58 (Gregorio Verdugo); *Cimarron City*—"The Evil One" 4-4-59 (Prof. King); *Wanted—Dead or Alive*—"Angels of Vengeance" 4-18-59 (Isaac Rankin), "A House Divided" 2-20-60; *The Deputy*—"Focus of Doom" 11-7-59 (Wilk); *Have Gun Will Travel*—"Duke of Texas" 4-22-61 (Ludwig); *Death Valley Days*—"Abel Duncan's Dying Wish" 2-21-62 (Rabbi); *Rawhide*—"A Woman's Place" 3-30-62 (Mayor Arnold Opel); *Stoney Burke*—"Child of Luxury" 10-15-62 (Terry Meade); *Wide Country*—"Whose Hand at My Throat?" 2-14-63 (Dr. Carl Lukins); *The Virginian*—"One Spring Like Long Ago" 3-2-66 (Two Hawks); *A Man Called Shenandoah*—"Macauley's Cure" 5-16-66 (Dr. Joshua Macauley).

Franz, Joseph J. (1883-9/9/70). Films: "The Girl from Texas" 1914; "The Gun Men of Plumas" 1914; "The Law at Silver Camp" 1915; "The Pretender" 1918 (Percival Longstreet); "The End of the Game" 1919 (Hotel Clerk); "The Mints of Hell" 1919 (Sgt. Blake).

Franzen, Nell. Films: "Film Tempo" 1915; "In the Sunset Country" 1915; "The Trail of the Serpent" 1915; "Sagebrush Gospel" 1924 (Mrs. Harper).

Fraser, Elisabeth (1920-). Films: "Hills of Oklahoma" 1950 (Sharon Forbes); "Callaway Went Thataway" 1951 (Marie); "The Way West" 1967 (Mrs. Fairman); "Ballad of Josie" 1968 (Widow Renfrew). ¶TV: *Telephone Time*—"Sam Houston's Decision" 12-10-57 (Mrs. Dickenson); *Wagon Train*—"The St. Nicholas Story" 12-23-59 (Mama Kling), "The Eli Bancroft Story" 11-11-63, "The John Gillman Story" 10-4-64 (Mrs. Gorman); *Rawhide*—

"Clash at Broken Bluff" 11-2-65 (Belle Connelly); *Gunsmoke*—"Which Doctor" 3-19-66 (Daisy Lou).

Fraser, Harry (1889-4/8/74). Films: "Westbound" 1924.

Fraser, Phyllis. Films: "Winds of the Wasteland" 1936 (Barbara Forsythe).

Fraser, Robert. Films: "Silver Spurs" 1936 (Art Holden); "Phantom Ranger" 1938 (MacGregor); "Renfrew on the Great White Trail" 1938 (Andrew Larkin); "Whirlwind Horseman" 1938; "Six-Gun Rhythm" 1939 (Lem Baker).

Fraser, Sally (1927-). TV: *The Cisco Kid*—"The Two Wheeler" 11-21-53; *Annie Oakley*—"The Saga of Clement O'Toole" 11-4-56 (Susan Meriwether); *The Gene Autry Show*—"Ghost Ranch" 11-12-55 (Torrey Palmer), "Dynamite" 12-24-55; *Cheyenne*—"The Trap" 12-18-56 (Virginia); *Broken Arrow*—"Legacy of a Hero" 2-26-57 (Faith), "Rebellion" 3-5-57 (Faith); *Wyatt Earp*—"Bat Jumps the Reservation" 2-10-59 (Cora Watrous); *The Texan*—"No Place to Stop" 4-27-59 (Laura Whipple), "Cowards Don't Die" 11-30-59 (Martha).

Frasher, Jim. Films: "Redwood Forest Trail" 1950 (Wyomin'); "Gene Autry and the Mounties" 1951 (Jack Duval). ¶TV: *The Gene Autry Show*—"Head for Texas" 7-23-50, "Silver Arrow" 8-6-50 (Randy Edwards), "Hot Lead" 11-26-50.

Frawley, James (1937-). TV: *Gunsmoke*—"Help Me, Kitty" 11-7-64 (Furnas); *A Man Called Shenandoah*—"Special Talent for Killing" 12-6-65 (Luther Hayes).

Frawley, William (1887-3/3/66). Films: "High, Wide and Handsome" 1937 (Mac); "Flame of the Barbary Coast" 1945 (Smooth Wylie); "The Virginian" 1946 (Honey Wiggen); "Home in San Antone" 1949; "Rancho Notorious" 1952 (Baldy Gunder).

Frazee, Jane (1918-9/6/85). Films: "The Big Bonanza" 1944 (Chiquita McSweeney); "Cowboy Canteen" 1944 (Connie Gray); "Swing in the Saddle" 1944; "On the Old Spanish Trail" 1947 (Candy Martin); "Springtime in the Sierras" 1947 (Taffy Baker); "The Gay Ranchero" 1948 (Betty Richard); "Grand Canyon Trail" 1948 (Carol Martin); "Last of the Wild Horses" 1948 (Jane Cooper); "Under California Stars" 1948 (Caroline Maynard). ¶TV: *The Lone Ranger*—"White Man's Magic"

7-13-50; *The Gene Autry Show—*"Ruthless Renegade" 2-8-52.

Frazer, Alex (1900-7/30/58). Films: "The Cowboy and the Indians" 1949 (Fred Bradley); "Fancy Pants" 1950 (Stagehand);"Hannah Lee" 1953 (Old Man).

Frazer, Dan (1921-). TV: *The Outlaws—*"The Quiet Killer" 12-29-60 (Sam Childers); *The Road West—*"The Agreement" 4-24-67 (Sheriff Lyle Saunders).

Frazer, Robert (1891-8/17/44). Films: "The Squatter" 1914; "Partners of the Sunset" 1922 (David Brooks); "The Mine with the Iron Door" 1924 (Natachee); "When a Man's a Man" 1924 (Phil Acton); "The Golden Strain" 1925 (Sergeant); "The Scarlet West" 1925 (Cardelanche); "The Splendid Road" 1925 (Stanton Halliday); "Desert Gold" 1926 (Dick Gale); "Lightning" 1927 (Lee Stewart); "One Hour of Love" 1927 (James Warren); "The Silent Hero" 1927 (Bud Taylor); "Sioux Blood" 1929 (Lone Eagle); "Beyond the Law" 1930 (Dan Wright); "The Mystery Trooper" 1931-serial; "Two Gun Caballero" 1931; "Fighting for Justice" 1932 (Raney); "Rainbow Trail" 1932 (Lone Eagle); "The Saddle Buster" 1932 (Rance); "The Fighting Parson" 1933 (Reverend Joseph Doolittle); "The Fighting Trooper" 1934 (Jim Hatfield); "The Trail Beyond" 1934 (Jules LaRocque); "The Miracle Rider" 1935-serial (Chief Black Wing); "Trails of the Wild" 1935 (Stacy); "Black Aces" 1937 (Homer Truesdale); "Left-Handed Law" 1937 (Tom Willis); "Crashing Thru" 1939 (Dr. Smith); "Riders of the Frontier" 1939; "One Man's Law" 1940 (Russell Fletcher); "Bad Man of Deadwood" 1941; "Gangs of Sonora" 1941 (Sam Tredwell); "The Gunman from Bodie" 1941; "Law of the Wolf" 1941; "Pals of the Pecos" 1941 (Stevens); "Code of the Outlaw" 1942; "Dawn on the Great Divide" 1942 (Judge Corkle): "Daredevils of the West" 1943-serial (Martin Dexter); "Dead Man's Gulch" 1943; "The Stranger from Pecos" 1943 (Burstow); "Wagon Tracks West" 1943 (Robert Warren); "Forty Thieves" 1944 (Judge Reynolds); "Law Men" 1944 (Bradford); "Partners of the Trail" 1944 (Edwards).

Freadenthall, Anthony. Films: "Battlin' Buckaroo" 1924 (Tiny Summers).·

Freberg, Stan (1926-). Films: "Callaway Went Thataway" 1951 (Marvin).

Frederic, Norman. Films: "Utah Blaine" 1957 (Davis); "Gun Fever"

1958 (Whitman); "The Light in the Forest" 1958 (Niskitoon); "The Lone Ranger and the Lost City of Gold" 1958 (Dr. James Rolfe). ¶TV: *The Adventures of Rin Tin Tin—*"The White Buffalo" 10-14-55 (Komawi), "Boone's Wedding Day" 11-18-55 (Cherokee Kid), "The Last Chance" 12-16-55, "Return of the Chief" 9-28-56 (Komawi), "Major Swanson's Choice" 5-31-57 (Komawi); *Cheyenne—*"Quicksand" 4-3-56 (Chief Yellow Knife), "The Broken Pledge" 6-4-57 (Little Chief), "The Long Search" 4-22-58 (Char); *Circus Boy—*"The Little Gypsy" 12-2-56 (Jano); *Maverick—*"The Jeweled Gun" 11-24-57 (Mitchell).

Frederici, Blanche (1878-12/24/33). Films: "Billy the Kid" 1930 (Mrs. McSween); "Last of the Duanes" 1930 (Mrs. Duane); "Woman Hungry" 1931 (Mrs. Temple); "Man of the Forest" 1933 (Mrs. Forney); "Secrets" 1933 (Mrs. Marlowe); "The Thundering Herd" 1934 (Mrs. Jane Jett).

Frederick, John (1916-). Films: "Once Upon a Time in the West" 1968-Ital. (Member of Frank's Gang); "Duck, You Sucker!" 1971-Ital. (American).

Frederick, Lynn (1954-4/27/94). Films: "Four Horsemen of the Apocalpyse" 1975-Ital. (Lisa); "Red Coat" 1975-Ital.

Frederick, Pauline (1884-9/19/38). Films: "Nanette of the Wilds" 1916 (Nanette Gauntier); "Sting of the Lash" 1921 (Dorothy Keith); "Two Kinds of Women" 1922 (Judith Sanford); "Ramona" 1936 (Senora Moreno).

Frederick, William (1861-3/2/31). Films: "Heart of the Sunset" 1918 (Blaze Jones).

Fredericks, Charles (1920-5/14/70). Films: "Thunder Pass" 1954; "Treasure of Ruby Hills" 1955 (Payne); "Hell Canyon Outlaws" 1957. ¶TV: *Wild Bill Hickok—*"The Kid from Red Butte" 8-26-52, "Old Cowboys Never Die" 12-16-52; *Wyatt Earp—*"Clay Allison" 9-25-56 (Pete Albright), "The Reformation of Jim Kelley" 10-30-56 (Pete Albright), "Justice" 12-25-56 (Pete Albright), "The Gatling Gun" 10-21-58 (Col. Dunphy), "Behan Shows His Hand" 10-27-59, "The Ring of Death" 11-3-59 (Dan Priddy); *Sergeant Preston of the Yukon—*"Fantastic Creatures" 11-1-56 (Jack Steadman); *Broken Arrow—*"The Assassin" 4-23-57 (Dilson), "The Duel" 3-18-58 (McQueen); *Colt .45—*"Small Man" 11-15-57 (Larkin), "Don't Tell Joe" 6-14-59

(Ollie Blaine), "The Gandy Dancers" 5-10-60 (Marshal Ed Springer); *Cheyenne—*"The Gamble" 1-28-58 (Dutch Teagle); *Maverick—*"Trail West to Fury" 2-16-58 (Jesse Hayden), "High Card Hangs" 10-19-58 (Joe Hayes), "Cruise of the Cynthia B" 1-10-60 (Jefferson Cantrell), "The Maverick Line" 10-20-60 (Shotgun Shanks), "Bolt from the Blue" 11-27-60 (Stark), "The Money Machine" 4-8-62 (Marshal Hedgkins); *Bronco—*"The Long Ride Back" 11-18-58 (Crane), "Stage to the Sky" 4-24-61 (Mike); *Gunsmoke—*"Grass" 11-29-58 (Earl Brant), "Marshal Proudfoot" 1-10-59 (Jack Pargo), "Fawn" 4-4-59 (Band), "The Deserter" 6-4-60 (Sergeant Strate), "False Front" 12-22-62 (Senator McGovern), "Coreyville" 10-6-69 (Clel Wilson); *Jefferson Drum—*"Prison Hill" 12-4-58 (Warden Johns); *The Rifleman—*"The Boarding House" 2-24-59; *Bat Masterson—*"Brunette Bombshell" 4-1-59 (Marty), "Last Stop to Austin" 12-1-60 (Sheriff Ankers); *Rough Riders—*"The Promise" 4-2-59; *Yancy Derringer—*"Fire on the Frontier" 4-2-59 (Jack Dingo); *The Deputy—*"The Big Four" 11-14-59 (Ike Clanton); *Man from Blackhawk—*"The Legacy" 12-25-59 (Will Traymore); *Johnny Ringo—*"The Reno Brothers" 2-25-60 (Brinker); *Rawhide—*"Incident of the Arana Sacar" 4-22-60, "Incident in the Middle of Nowhere" 4-7-61 (Banning); *Sugarfoot—*"Blue Bonnet Stray" 4-26-60 (Bartender), "Angel" 3-6-61 (Big Ed); *The Alaskans—*"The Devil Made Five" 6-19-60 (Marks); *Lawman—*"The Go-Between" 9-25-60 (Kelly); *Klondike—*"88 Keys to Trouble" 11-14-60 (Corky); *Zane Grey Theater—*"Ambush" 1-5-61 (Confederate Captain); *Gunslinger—*"The Zone" 3-2-61 (Jake Forsythe); *The Outlaws—*"The Connie Masters Story" 10-12-61 (Ned Bell); *The Tall Man—*"An Item for Auction" 10-14-61 (Frank Engle); *Bonanza—*"Inger, My Love" 4-15-62; *Laramie—*"The Fugitives" 2-12-63; *The Virginian—*"Ride a Dark Trail" 9-18-63 (Fitch); *Death Valley Days—*"The Trouble with Taxes" 4-18-65 (Sheriff); *Branded—*"Price of a Name" 5-23-65.

Fredericks, Dean. Films: "Savage Sam" 1963 (Comanche Chief). ¶TV: *The Deputy—*"Silent Gun" 1-23-60 (Pete Clemson); *Laramie—*"Street of Hate" 3-1-60 (Chad Morgan); *Walt Disney Presents—*"Daniel Boone" 1960-61 (Crowfeather); *Bronco—*"Seminole War Pipe" 12-12-60 (Greywolf); *Rawhide—*"The Greedy Town" 2-16-62 (Jed Harvey); *The Rifleman—*"Squeeze Play" 12-3-

62 (Phil Carver), "Requiem at Mission Springs" 3-4-63 (Rance); *The Virginian*—"The Final Hour" 5-1-63 (Jan Wolski).

Freed, Bert (1919-8/2/94). Films: "Red Mountain" 1951 (Randall); "Invitation to a Gunfighter" 1964 (Sheriff); "Nevada Smith" 1966 (Quince); "Hang 'Em High" 1968 (Schmidt the Hangman); "There Was a Crooked Man" 1970 (Skinner); "Billy Jack" 1971 (Posner). ¶TV: *Sheriff of Cochise*—"The Dude" 10-4-57 (Gallardo); *Gunsmoke*—"The F.U." 3-14-59 (Al Clovis), "The Bounty Hunter" 10-30-65 (Chris Thornton); *The Rifleman*—"The Money Gun" 5-12-59 (Jackford), "Short Rope for a Tall Man" 3-28-61 (Ben Crown); *Riverboat*—"The Faithless" 11-22-59 (Kester); *The Law of the Plainsman*—"Toll Road" 12-24-59 (Benson); *Bonanza*—"The Last Trophy" 3-26-60 (Simon Betcher), "The Late Ben Cartwright" 3-3-68 (Broome); *Wide Country*—"The Judas Goat" 2-21-63 (Gov. Leroy Martin); *The Dakotas*—"Incident at Rapid City" 3-4-63 (Lloyd Mitchell); *The Virginian*—"The Final Hour" 5-1-63 (Milo Henderson), "Execution at Triste" 12-13-67, "A Small Taste of Justice" 12-20-67 (Jason Ainsworth); *The Loner*—"Hunt the Man Down" 12-11-65 (Sheriff Ross); *The Big Valley*—"Hazard" 3-9-66 (Judge Ben Coulter), "Caesar's Wife" 10-3-66 (Henry Marvin), "The Day of Grace" 4-17-67, "The Profit and the Lost" 12-2-68 (Rance Kendell); *A Man Called Shenandoah*—"Aces and Kings" 3-28-66 (Sheriff Wade); *Shane*—Regular 1966 (Rufe Ryker); *Iron Horse*—"The Pembrooke Blood" 1-9-67 (Breed Pembrooke); *The Guns of Will Sonnett*—"And He Shall Lead the Children" 1-19-68 (Frank); *The High Chaparral*—"A Fella Named Kilroy" 3-7-69 (Telford Burris); *Lancer*—"The Kid" 10-7-69 (Toby Jencks); *The Men from Shiloh*—"The Regimental Line" 3-3-71 (Colonel Harmon).

Freeman, Anthony. Films: "Ballad of a Gunman" 1967-Ital./Ger.; "The Stranger Returns" 1967-U.S./Ital./Ger./Span.; "Two Crosses at Danger Pass" 1968-Ital./Span.; "Holy Water Joe" 1971-Ital.; "Death Played the Flute" 1972-Ital./Span.

Freeman, Arny (1908-). TV: *Have Gun Will Travel*—"The Piano" 11-11-61 (Freddie).

Freeman, Howard (1899-12/11/67). Films: "Abilene Town" 1946 (Ed Balder); "California" 1946 (Sen. Creel).

Freeman, Joan (1942-). Films: "Pistol Harvest" 1951 (Little Felice); "The Rounders" 1965 (Meg Moore); "The Fastest Guitar Alive" 1967 (Sue). ¶TV: *Wyatt Earp*—"The Frontier Theatre" 2-7-56 (Jeannie); *Gunsmoke*—"Phoebe Strunk" 11-10-62 (Annie Shields); *The Virginian*—"The Devil's Children" 12-5-62 (Tabby McCallum), "Stopover in a Western Town" 11-27-63 (Caroline Witman), "Timberland" 3-10-65 (Katy), "Blaze of Glory" 12-29-65 (Judy King); *The Dakotas*—"Trouble at French Creek" 1-28-63 (Gilla Marshak); *Laramie*—"Trapped" 5-14-63 (Nina Richards); *Wagon Train*—"Alias Bill Hawks" 5-15-63 (Karen Wells); *The Travels of Jaimie McPheeters*—"The Day of the 12 Candles" 2-23-64 (Sarah Oliver); *Bonanza*—"The Trap" 3-28-65 (Hallie Shannon), "Night of Reckoning" 10-15-67 (Kelly); *The Loner*—"The Vespers" 9-25-65.

Freeman, Kathleen (1920-). Films: "A Perilous Journey" 1953 (Leah); "The Far Country" 1955 (Grits); "Pawnee" 1957 (Mrs. Carter); "The Missouri Traveler" 1958 (Serena Poole); "North to Alaska" 1960 (Lena Nordquist); "Mail Order Bride" 1964 (Sister Sue); "The Rounders" 1965 (Agatha Moore); "Death of a Gunfighter" 1969 (Mary Elizabeth); "The Good Guys and the Bad Guys" 1969 (Mrs. Stone); "Support Your Local Sheriff" 1969 (Mrs. Danvers); "The Ballad of Cable Hogue" 1970 (Mrs. Jensen); "Support Your Local Gunfighter" 1971 (Mrs. Perkins); "Hitched" TVM-1973 (Rainbow McLeod); "The Daughters of Joshua Cabe Return" TVM-1975 (Essie); "Last Ride of the Dalton Gang" TVM-1979 (Ma Dalton). ¶TV: *Buckskin*—"The Gold Watch" 8-28-58 (Myrtle), "Tell Me, Leonardo" 9-25-58 (Martha), "The Venus Adjourner" 3-30-59 (Myrtha); *Wagon Train*—"The Kitty Angel Story" 1-7-59 (Salrey Hogg), "The Kitty Allbright Story" 10-4-61 (Lolly), "The Geneva Balfour Story" 1-20-64; *Lawman*—"The Substitute" 10-22-61 (Mavis Martingale); *Rawhide*—"The Greedy Town" 2-16-62 (Mrs. Beamish); *Laramie*—"Justice in a Hurry" 3-20-62 (Edna Holtzhoff); *Laredo*—"Scourge of San Rosa" 1-20-67 (Mio); *Bonanza*—"Maestro Hoss" 5-7-67 (Miss Hibbs), "Long Way to Ogden" 2-22-70 (Ma Brinker); *Daniel Boone*—"The Fleeing Nuns" 10-24-68 (Berthe); *The High Chaparral*—"A Way of Justice" 12-13-68 (Maude); *Lancer*—"Legacy" 12-9-69.

Freeman, Mona (1926-). Films: "Streets of Laredo" 1949 (Rannie

Carter); "Copper Canyon" 1950 (Caroline Desmond); "Branded" 1951 (Ruth Lavery); "The Lady from Texas" 1951 (Bonnie Lee); "The Road to Denver" 1955 (Elizabeth Sutton); "Dragoon Wells Massacre" 1957 (Ann Bradley). ¶TV: *Zane Grey Theater*—"Stage to Tucson" 11-16-56 (Sandy Neal); *Wagon Train*—"The Monte Britton Story" 6-18-58; *Wanted—Dead or Alive*—"The Fourth Headstone" 11-1-58 (Jackie Harris), "Breakout" 9-26-59 (Margaret Dunn); *Maverick*—"The Cats of Paradise" 10-11-59 (Modesty Blaine), "Cruise of the Cynthia B" 1-10-60 (Modesty Blaine); *Riverboat*—"The Boy from Pittsburgh" 11-29-59 (Louise Rutherford); *Johnny Ringo*—"Mrs. Ringo" 2-11-60 (Mrs. Ringo); *The Tall Man*—"Petticoat Crusade" 11-18-61 (Amy Dodds); *Branded*—"McCord's Way" 1-30-66 (Dora Kendal).

Freeman, Morgan (1937-). Films: "Unforgiven" 1992 (Ned Logan).

Frees, Paul (1920-11/1/86). Films: "The Big Sky" 1952 (MacMasters); "The Outlaws Is Coming!" 1965 (Narrator). ¶TV: *Jim Bowie*—"German George" 2-22-57 (Etienne).

Fremont, Al (1860-6/16/30). Films: "Drag Harlan" 1920 (Laskar); "The Orphan" 1920 (Martin); "The Square Shooter" 1920 (Sam Curtis); "The Big Punch" 1921 (Jed's Friend); "Trailin'" 1921 (Lawlor); "Fighting Streak" 1922 (Jasper Lanning); "For Big Stakes" 1922 (Sheriff Blaisdell); "Brass Commandments" 1923 (Bill Perrin); "Not a Drum Was Heard" 1924 (Sheriff).

French, Charles K. (1860-8/2/52). Films: "Davy Crockett in Hearts United" 1909; "A True Indian's Heart" 1909; "A Prisoner of the Mohicans" 1911; "Army Surgeon" 1912; "The Colonel's Peril" 1912; "The Colonel's Ward" 1912; "Custer's Last Fight" 1912; "His Punishment" 1912; "The Law of the West" 1912; "The Prospector's Daughter" 1912; "The Sheriff of Stony Butte" 1912; "The Vengeance of Fate" 1912; "The Invaders" 1913; "The Disciple" 1915 (Birdshot Bivens); "His Partner's Sacrifice" 1915; "The Aryan" 1916 (Ivory Wells); "The Patriot" 1916 (Col. Bracken); "The Son of His Father" 1917 (James Carbhoy); "The Law of the North" 1918 (Michel de Montcalm); "The Tiger Man" 1918 (Sheriff Sandy Martin); "Jubilo" 1919 (Jim Hardy); "The Mints of Hell" 1919 (Old Man Chaudiare); "The Sheriff's Son" 1919 (Hal Rutherford);

"Six Feet Four" 1919 (Henry Pollard); "This Hero Stuff" 1919 (Samuel Barnes); "The Daredevil" 1920 (Ralph Spencer); "Desert Love" 1920 (Jack Remington); "Prairie Trails" 1920 (Stephen McWhorter); "The Square Shooter" 1920 (Zeke Hampton); "The Terror" 1920 (Sheriff Jim Canby); "The Texan" 1920 (Wolf River Mayor); "The Untamed" 1920 (Tex Calder); "Hands Off" 1921 (Clint Wadley); "The Last Trail" 1921 (Sheriff Nelson); "The Night Horsemen" 1921 (Marshal); "The Bearcat" 1922 (Sheriff Bill Garfield); "West of Chicago" 1922 (Judson Malone); "The Yosemite Trail" 1922 (Sheriff); "Blinky" 1923 (Major Kileen); "Hell's Hole" 1923 (Sheriff); "Man's Size" 1923 (Angus McRae); "The Ramblin' Kid" 1923 (Joshua Heck); "Oh, You Tony!" 1924 (Blakely); "The Sawdust Trail" 1924 (Square Deal McKenzie); "Let 'Er Buck" 1925 (Col. Jeff McCall); "The Saddle Hawk" 1925 (Jim Newall); "The Texas Trail" 1925 (Ring 'Em Foster); "Flaming Frontier" 1926 (Senator Hargess); "Hands Up!" 1926 (Brigham Young); "Lazy Lightning" 1926 (Dr. Hull); "Under Western Skies" 1926; "War Paint" 1926 (Maj. Hopkins); "Good as Gold" 1927 (Sheriff John Gray); "The Meddlin' Stranger" 1927 (Mr. Crawford); "Ride 'Em High" 1927 (Bill Demming); "The Big Hop" 1928 (Buck's Father); "The Cowboy Cavalier" 1928; "The Flying Buckaroo" 1928 (Banker Brown); "Riding for Fame" 1928 (Dad Barton); "King of the Rodeo" 1929 (Chip, Sr.); "Overland Bound" 1929 (Underwood); "The Spoilers" 1930 (Man in Bar); "Caught" 1931 (Bradford); "Destry Rides Again" 1932 (Jury Foreman); "Crossfire" 1933 (Jonathan Wheeler); "Man of Action" 1933 (Dr. James Duncan); "Via Pony Express" 1933; "War on the Range" 1933 (the Rancher); "Arizona Nights" 1934; "Brand of Hate" 1934; "The Man from Hell" 1934 (Sandy); "Pals of the Prairie" 1934-short; "The Red Rider" 1934-serial (Roberto Maxwell); "Ridin' Gent" 1934-short; "When a Man Sees Red" 1934 (Padre); "Big Boy Rides Again" 1935 (John Duncan); "The Crimson Trail" 1935 (Frank Carter); "Gun Play" 1935 (Old John Holt); "No Man's Range" 1935 (Oliver); "The Phantom Empire" 1935-serial (Mal); "Rustlers of Red Dog" 1935-serial (Tom Lee); "The Throwback" 1935 (Ted Smalley); "Tracy Rides" 1935 (John Hampton); "Trail of Terror" 1935 (Sheriff Baxter); "Western Courage" 1935 (Henry Hanley); "Desert

Guns" 1936 (Colonel Nelson); "The Last of the Warrens" 1936 (Bruce Warren); "The Phantom Rider" 1936-serial; "Courage of the West" 1937 (Secretary Stanton); "Headin' for the Rio Grande" 1937 (Pop Hart); "Where Trails Divide" 1937 (Deacon); "Chip of the Flying U" 1939; "Rovin' Tumbleweeds" 1939.

French, Georgia. Films: "The Wolf and His Mate" 1917 (Rose Nolan).

French, George (1883-6/9/61). Films: "Red Hot Leather" 1926 (Dr. Robert Marsh); "Grinning Guns" 1927 (Amos Felden); "One Glorious Scrap" 1927 (Ezra Kramer); "Arizona Cyclone" 1928 (John Cosgrave); "Silver Spurs" 1936 (Station Agent).

French, Hugh (1910-11/2/76). Films: "Fancy Pants" 1950 (George Van Basingwell).

French, Leslie (1899-). Films: "The Singer Not the Song" 1961-Brit. (Father Gomez).

French, Richard. Films: "Valley of Hunted Men" 1942 (Toller).

French, Ted (-7/3/78). Films: "Saddle Leather Law" 1944; "West of Alamo" 1946; "Law of the Lash" 1947 (Smitty); "Range Beyond the Blue" 1947 (Sneezer); "Ridin' Down the Trail" 1947; "West to Glory" 1947; "The Hawk of Powder River" 1948 (Heavy); "Bad Men of Tombstone" 1949; "Roaring Westward" 1949 (Burns). ¶TV: *Gunsmoke*—"Prime of Life" 5-7-66 (Barkeep), "Mail Drop" 1-28-67 (Drover), "Stryker" 9-29-69 (Dish).

French, Valerie (1932-11/3/90). Films: "Jubal" 1956 (Mae Horgan); "Secret of Treasure Mountain" 1956 (Audrey Lancaster); "Decision at Sundown" 1957 (Ruby James); "The Hard Man" 1957 (Fern Martin); "Shalako" 1968-Brit./Fr. (Elena Clarke). ¶TV: *Trackdown*—"Like Father" 11-1-57; *Have Gun Will Travel*—"Chapagne Safari" 12-5-59 (Charity), "Ransom" 6-4-60 (Secura); *The Alaskans*—"Odd Man Hangs" 4-17-60 (Marie Forbes).

French, Victor (1935-6/15/89). Films: "Charro!" 1969 (Vince); "Death of a Gunfighter" 1969 (Phil Miller); "Cutter's Trail" TVM-1970 (Alex Bowen); "Flap" 1970 (Rafferty); "Rio Lobo" 1970 (Ketcham); "There Was a Crooked Man" 1970 (Whisky); "Wild Rovers" 1971 (Sheriff); "Chato's Land" 1972 (Martin Hall); "Little House on the Prairie" TVM-1974 (Edwards); "Little House on the Prairie: Look Back to Yesterday"

TVM-1983 (Isaiah Edwards); "Little House: Bless All the Dear Children" TVM-1984 (Isaiah Edwards). ¶TV: *Two Faces West*—"The Noose" 5-15-61; *Bonanza*—"Gallagher Sons" 12-9-62, "The Burning Sky" 1-28-63 (Aaron), "Meena" 11-16-69 (Jesse), "The Horse Traders" 4-5-70 (Jesse), "An Earthquake Called Callahan" 4-11-71 (Tom Callahan); *The Virginian*—"The Accomplice" 12-19-62; *The Dakotas*—"Fargo" 2-25-63 (Larrimore); *Temple Houston*—"Letter of the Law" 10-3-63 (Willie Harrod); *Wild Wild West*—"The Night of a Thousand Eyes" 10-22-65 (Arnold); *Gunsmoke*—"Wishbone" 2-19-66 (Travers), "Prime of Life" 5-7-66 (Joe Smith), "Saturday Night" 1-7-67 (C.K. Ross), "Vengeance" 10-2-67 & 10-9-67 (Eben Luken), "Major Glory" 10-30-67 (Sergeant Spear), "Hill Girl" 1-29-68 (Roland Daniel), "Uncle Finney" 10-14-68 (Roland Daniel), "O'Quillian" 10-28-68 (Clay Tynan), "Waco" 12-9-68 (Waco Thompson), "Kitowa!" 2-16-70 (Ed Vail), "Trafton" 10-25-71 (Trafton), "Phoebe" 2-21-72 (Jed Fraser), "The Drummer" 10-9-72 (Daniel Shay), "The Golden Land" 3-5-73 (Ruxton), "Matt's Love Story" 9-24-73 (Les Dean), "Tarnished Badge" 11-11-74 (Sheriff Bo Harker), "The Sharecroppers" 3-31-75 (Dibble Pugh); *Death Valley Days*—"Hugh Glass Meets the Bear" 6-11-66 (Louis Baptiste); *F Troop*—"The Day THey Shot Agarn" 2-16-67 (Matt Delaney); *Iron Horse*—"Decision at Sundown" 2-27-67 (Cleary); *Daniel Boone*—"The Ballad of Sidewinder and Cherokee" 9-14-67 (Blue Belly Sangster), "Love and Equity" 3-13-69 (Ess), "The Landlords" 3-5-70 (Ess), "How to Become a Goddess" 4-30-70 (Ess); *Cimarron Strip*—"Till the End of the Night" 11-16-67 (Rafe Coleman); *Lancer*—"The Measure of a Man" 4-8-69 (Travis Caudle); *Kung Fu*—"The Ancient Warrior" 5-3-73 (Sheriff Pool); *Sara*—4-23-76 (Achille); *Little House on the Prairie*—Regular 1974-77 (Isaiah Edwards); *Riding for the Pony Express*—Pilot 9-3-80 (Irving G. Peacock); *The Cherokee Trail*—Pilot 11-28-81 (Scant Luther); *Little House: A New Beginning*—Regular 1982-83 (Isaiah Edwards).

Fresco, David. TV: *Wyatt Earp*—"Terror in the Desert" 1-24-61 (Moody); *The Legend of Jesse James*—"A Real Tough Town" 1-24-66 (Toby); *Wild Wild West*—"The Night of the Undead" 2-2-68 (Grizzly); *Gunsmoke*—"The Prisoner" 3-17-69 (Barber); *The Big Valley*—"Point and Counterpoint" 5-19-69 (Bartender).

Fresson, Bernard (1931-). Films: "The Call of the Wild" TVM-1976 (Francois).

Frey, Arno (1900-6/26/61). Films: "Arizona Gangbusters" 1940 (Schmidt); "Texas Man Hunt" 1942 (Otto Reuther); "Valley of Hunted Men" 1942 (Von Breckner); "Valley of Vanishing Men" 1942-serial (Carl Engler).

Frey, Barbara. Films: "Stranger in Sacramento" 1964-Ital. (Liza); "Let Them Rest" 1967-Ital./Ger.

Frey, Leonard (1938-8/24/88). Films: "Testimony of Two Men" TVM-1977 (David Paxton). ¶TV: *Best of the West*—Regular 1981-82 (Parker Tillman).

Friebus, Florida (1909-5/27/88). TV: *Gunsmoke*—"The Boy and the Sinner" 10-1-73 (Mrs. Travis).

Friedkin, Joel (1885-9/19/54). Films: "Outlaws of the Cherokee Trail" 1941; "Bad Men of the Hills" 1942 (Judge Malotte); "The Cyclone Kid" 1942 (Judge Phillips); "The Devil's Trail" 1942; "Pardon My Gun" 1942; "Raiders of the Range" 1942; "The Sombrero Kid" 1942 (Uriah Martin); "Frontier Fury" 1943 (Doc Hewes); "Phony Express" 1943-short (Doc Abdul); "Sundown Valley" 1944 (Joe Calloway); "California Gold Rush" 1946; "Saddle Pals" 1947; "Unexpected Guest" 1947 (Phineas Phipps); "False Paradise" 1948; "Phantom Valley" 1948 (Sam Littlejohn); "Strange Gamble" 1948; "Dakota Lil" 1950; "Lightning Guns" 1950 (Crawley).

Friedman, David. Films: "Little House on the Prairie: Look Back to Yesterday" TVM-1983 (Jason Carter); "Little House: The Last Farewell" TVM-1984 (Jason Carter); "Little House: Bless All the Dear Children" TVM-1984 (Jason Carter). ¶TV: *Little House: A New Beginning*—Regular 1982-83 (Jason Carter).

Friel, Francis. Films: "Chasing Trouble" 1926 (Sal Karney).

Fries, Otto (1887-9/15/38). Films: "Broncho Twister" 1927 (Sheriff); "Land of the Lawless" 1927 (Deputy Sheriff).

Fries, Ted. Films: "Redwood Forest Trail" 1950 (Hawk).

Friganza, Trixie (1870-2/27/55). Films: "Wanderer of the Wasteland" 1935 (Big Jo).

Frisco, Joe (1890-2/16/58). Films: "Western Jamboree" 1938

(Joseph Frisco); "Ride, Tenderfoot, Ride" 1940 (Haberdasher).

Fritchie, Barbara. Films: "The Last Round-Up" 1934 (Joan Randall); "Thunder Mountain" 1935 (Sydney Blair); "Wild Mustang" 1935 (Jill).

Fritts, Donnie. Films: "Pat Garrett and Billy the Kid" 1973 (Beaver).

Fritz, Stanley. Films: "The Ruse of the Rattlesnake" 1921 (Squint Smiley).

Frizzell, Lou (1920-6/17/79). Films: "The Stalking Moon" 1969 (Stationmaster); "Tell Them Willie Boy Is Here" 1969 (Station Agent); "Lawman" 1971 (Cobden). ¶TV: *Daniel Boone*—"Faith's Way" 4-4-68; *The Outcasts*—"The Heady Wine" 12-2-68 (Dr. Traynor); *Bonanza*—"Mark of Guilt" 12-15-68 (Jackson), "The Lady and the Mark" 2-1-70 (Charley), Regular 1970-72 (Dusty Rhodes); *The High Chaparral*—"The Brothers Cannon" 10-3-69 (Jeff Patterson), "A Piece of Land" 10-10-69 (Jeff Patterson); *Nichols*—"Eddie Joe" 1-4-72 (Warden); *The New Land*—Regular 1974 (Murdock); *Centennial*—Regular 1978-79 (Mr. Norris).

Frome, Milton (1910-3/21/89). Films: "Ride 'Em, Cowgirl" 1939 (Oliver Shea); "Pardners" 1956 (Hawkins, the Butler); "The Lonely Man" 1957; "Evil Roy Slade" TVM-1972 (Foss, the Telegrapher). ¶TV: *Bat Masterson*—"Bear Bait" 11-12-58 (Sheriff Clark); *Tales of the Texas Rangers*—"Texas Flyer" 11-28-58 (Barlow); *Tales of Wells Fargo*—"The Counterfeiters" 12-8-58 (Mel Carter); *The Texan*—"The Lord Will Provide" 12-29-58 (Judge Hawks); *Wagon Train*—"The Flint McCullough Story" 1-14-59 (Tom Yates), "The Kitty Pryer Story" 11-18-63; *Riverboat*—"That Taylor Affair" 9-26-60 (Governor DeWitt); *Klondike*—"Bathhouse Justice" 12-26-60 (Dan Ryker); *Gunslinger*—"Golden Circle" 4-13-61 (Bartender); *Rawhide*—"The Long Count" 1-5-62; *The Dakotas*—"Requiem at Dancer's Hill" 2-18-63 (Sam Johnson); *The Big Valley*—"Point and Counterpoint" 5-19-69 (Dr. Covey); *Alias Smith and Jones*—"Smiler with a Gun" 10-7-71.

Frommer, Ben (1913-5/5/92). TV: *Sergeant Preston of the Yukon*—"The Skull in the Stone" 11-7-57 (Atoga).

Froner, Barry. TV: *The Cisco Kid*—"Kilts and Sombreros" 5-1-54; *My Friend Flicka*—"The Recluse" 5-25-56; *Fury*—"The Strong Man" 2-16-57 (Will Coulter); *The Adventures*

of Rin Tin Tin—"Rusty Gets Busted" 2-22-57 (Georgie).

Frost, Alice. TV: *Hotel De Paree*—"The Man Who Believed in Law" 11-27-59 (Mollie); *The Tall Man*—"Full Payment" 9-9-61 (Hortense); *Wagon Train*—"The Dick Pederson Story" 1-10-62 (Mrs. Cutler), "The Caroline Casteel Story" 9-26-62 (Abigail Stryker); *Bonanza*—"A Passion for Justice" 9-29-63, "Enter Thomas Bowers" 4-26-64; *The Virginian*—"A Little Learning..." 9-29-65 (Mrs. Kobey); *Gunsmoke*—"I Thee Wed" 4-16-69 (Hester Lackett).

Frost, Sadie. Films: "The Cisco Kid" CTVM-1994 (Dominique).

Frost, Terry (1906-3/1/93). Films: "The Bandit Trail" 1941; "Cyclone on Horseback" 1941; "Gauchos of El Dorado" 1941; "Law of the Range" 1941; "California Joe" 1943 (Melbourne Tommy Atkinson); "Rustlers' Hideout" 1944 (Jack Crockett); "Trail to Gunsight" 1944 (Bar-6 Cowboy); "Frontier Feud" 1945; "Border Bandits" 1946; "The Caravan Trail" 1946 (Bart Barton); "Drifting Along" 1946 (Gus); "Gentleman from Texas" 1946; "The Haunted Mine" 1946; "Moon Over Montana" 1946; "Shadows on the Range" 1946; "Silver Range" 1946; "South of Monterey" 1946; "Trail to Mexico" 1946; "Wild West" 1946 (Drake Dawson); "Apache Rose" 1947 (Sheriff Jim Mason); "Ghost Town Renegades" 1947 (Flint); "Pioneer Justice" 1947; "Stage to Mesa City" 1947 (Ed); "Trail of the Mounties" 1947 (Gumdrop); "The Vigilante" 1947-serial; "Black Hills" 1948 (Kirby); "Check Your Guns" 1948 (Sloane); "Dead Man's Gold" 1948 (Joe Quirt); "The Hawk of Powder River" 1948 (Mitchell); "Oklahoma Badlands" 1948 (Sheriff Heyman); "Prairie Outlaws" 1948; "Tex Granger" 1948-serial (Adams); "The Tioga Kid" 1948 (Ranger Captain); "Tornado Range" 1948 (Thayer); "Lawless Code" 1949; "The Pecos Pistol" 1949-short; "Son of Billy the Kid" 1949 (Cy Schaeffer); "West of El Dorado" 1949 (Stone); "Western Renegades" 1949 (Carl); "The Baron of Arizona" 1950 (Morelle); "The Daltons' Women" 1950; "Fence Riders" 1950; "Outlaws of Texas" 1950 (Jordan); "Silver Canyon" 1951 (Irving Wyatt); "Stage to Blue River" 1951 (Yarrow); "Texas Lawmen" 1951; "Valley of Fire" 1951 (Grady McKean); "Barbed Wire" 1952 (Perry); "Dead Man's Trail" 1952; "Fargo" 1952; "The Gunman" 1952; "Kansas Territory" 1952 (Stark); "The Man

Behind the Gun" 1952; "The Maverick" 1952 (Trooper Westman); "Montana Incident" 1952; "Night Raiders" 1952 (Lorch); "Texas City" 1952 (Crag); "Waco" 1952 (Richards); "The Stranger Wore a Gun" 1953; "Winning of the West" 1953; "Gunfighters of the Northwest" 1954-serial (Wildfoot); "The Spoilers" 1955 (Deputy); "Ten Wanted Men" 1955; "Perils of the Wilderness" 1956-serial (Baptiste); "Utah Blaine" 1957 (Gavin); "Buchanan Rides Alone" 1958; "The Wild Westerners" 1962 (Ashley Cartwright). ¶TV: *Wild Bill Hickok*—"Indian Bureau Story" 7-31-51, "Prairie Flats Land Swindle" 5-6-52, "Chain of Events" 6-24-52, "The Hideout" 1-20-53, "Great Obstacle Race" 3-3-53, "Jingles Wins a Friend" 4-28-53; *The Cisco Kid*—"Foreign Agent" 8-18-51, "Bates Story" 9-29-51, "The Kidnapped Cameraman" 10-24-53, "The Two Wheeler" 11-21-53, "Witness" 12-19-53, "New York's Priest 1-9-54, "Roundup" 4-17-54; *The Gene Autry Show*—"Heir to the Lazy L" 12-29-51, "Horse Sense" 1-11-52, "The Old Prospector" 8-4-53, "Gypsy Woman" 8-25-53, "Cold Decked" 9-15-53, "Steel Ribbon" 9-22-53, "Ransom Cross" 10-6-53, "Santa Fe Raiders" 7-6-54, "Battle Axe" 8-31-54, "Boots and Ballots" 9-25-54, "The Portrait of White Cloud" 10-15-55, "Go West, Young Lady" 11-19-55; *The Roy Rogers Show*—"Jailbreak" 12-30-51, "The Desert Fugitive" 2-24-52, "The Minister's Son" 3-23-52, "Blind Justice" 12-14-52, "The Mingo Kid" 4-26-53 (the Mingo Kid), "Pat's Inheritance" 11-11-53 (Bill Henderson), "Bullets and a Burro" 11-15-53, "The Deputy Sheriff" 2-7-54, "End of the Trail" 1-27-57 (Hank Hickman), "Junior Outlaw" 2-10-57; *The Lone Ranger*—"The Perfect Crime" 7-30-53, "Homer with a High Hat" 12-16-54; *Annie Oakley*—"Sharpshooting Annie" 6-12-54; "Annie and the Leprechauns" 9-2-56 (Henchman), "Flint and Steel" 10-14-56 (Butler); *Sergeant Preston of the Yukon*—"Phantom of Phoenixville" 1-26-56 (Lars Ulvik), "The Assassins" 6-7-56 (Roland), "Pack Ice Justice" 9-27-56 (Hank Mullen); *Schlitz Playhouse of the Stars*—"The Bitter Land" 4-13-56 (Joe Case); *My Friend Flicka*—"Big Red" 6-22-56 (Shorty); *Wyatt Earp*—"The Hanging Judge" 12-18-56 (Mr. Benton), "Truth About Gunfighting" 11-18-58; *The Adventures of Rin Tin Tin*—"Racing Rails" 12-28-56 (John Anders), "Stagecoach Sally" 4-19-57 (Cole); *Zane Grey Theater*—"The Three Graves" 1-4-57 (Blaze Moy-

lan); *Tales of Wells Fargo*—"The Hijackers" 6-17-57 (Frank Jeffers), "Alias Jim Hardie" 3-10-58 (Bill Manton), "The Last Stand" 4-13-59 (Tate), "The Bride and the Bandit" 12-12-60 (Stage Driver); *Maverick*—"Comstock Conspiracy" 12-29-57 (Sheriff), "The Iron Hand" 2-21-60 (Purdy); *The Restless Gun*—"The Gold Buckle" 12-30-57 (Doc); *Broken Arrow*—"Shadow of Cochise" 2-4-58 (Dave); *Trackdown*—"The Governor" 5-23-58 (James Wilton); *Wanted—Dead or Alive*—"Ransom for a Nun" 10-18-58 (Harry Wilson); *26 Men*—"Run No More" 12-9-58; *Bat Masterson*—"Death by the Half Dozen" 2-4-60 (Tom Kearns); *Cheyenne*—"Duel at Judas Basin" 1-30-61 (Sheriff Hoag); *Rawhide*—"Incident of the Running Man" 5-5-61; *Gunsmoke*—"The Wrong Man" 10-29-66 (Stage Driver).

Fry, Stephen. TV: *Ned Blessing: The Story of My Life and Times*—"Oscar" 9-8-93 (Oscar Wilde).

Frye, Dwight (1899-11/7/43). Films: "The Western Code" 1932 (Dick Lumas); "Sky Bandits" 1940.

Frye, Gilbert. Films: "Sons of Adventure" 1948 (Sam Hodges). ¶TV: *Sky King*—"The Neckerchief" 9-16-51; *Wild Bill Hickok*—"Meteor Mesa" 6-16-53; *Sergeant Preston of the Yukon*—"Out of the Night" 11-28-57 (Jerry Hall); *Wagon Train*—"The Bernal Sierra Story" 3-12-58; *The High Chaparral*—"The Terrorist" 12-17-67 (Soldier).

Frye, Virgil. Films: "Lucky Johnny: Born in America" 1973-Ital./ Mex.; "The Missouri Breaks" 1976 (Woody). ¶TV: *Bonanza*—"Another Windmill to Go" 9-14-69 (Andy); *Young Dan'l Boone*—"The Game" 10-10-77 (Leonard Harker); *Bret Maverick*—"Welcome to Sweetwater" 12-8-81 (Luke).

Fuchs, Leo (1910-12/31/94). Films: "The Frisco Kid" 1979 (Chief Rabbi). ¶TV: *Wagon Train*—"The Levy-McGowan Story" 11-14-62 (Simon Levy).

Fuchsberger, Joachim (1927-). Films: "The Last Tomahawk" 1965-Ger./Ital./Span.; "Who Killed Johnny R.?" 1966-Ital./Span.

Fudge, Alan (1944-). Films: "The Invasion of Johnson County" TVM-1976 (Teschmacher). ¶TV: *Gunsmoke*—"No Tomorrow" 1-3-72 (Bailiff); *Kung Fu*—"The Gunman" 1-3-74 (Bob Gardner); *The Quest*—"The Freight Train Rescue" 12-29-76 (Ira Butler); *Young Maverick*—"Dead

Man's Hand" 12-26-79 & 1-2-80 (Amos Layton).

Fuji. TV: *Have Gun Will Travel*—"The Hatchet Man" 3-5-60 (Sing Chuck), "Coming of the Tiger" 4-14-62 (Samurai); *Wild Wild West*—"The Night of the Camera" 11-29-68 (Mandarin).

Fujikawa, Jerry (1912-4/30/83). TV: *Wild Wild West*—"The Night of the Samurai" 10-13-67 (Prince Shinosuke); *Kung Fu*-"The Elixir" 12-20-73 (Poor Man), "Forbidden Kingdom" 1-18-75 (Potter).

Fujioka, John. TV: *Kung Fu*—"My Brother, My Executioner" 10-12-74 (Huang Chu), "The Devil's Champion" 11-29-74 (Hsiang), "Barbary House" 2-15-75 (Cook), "Flight to Orion" 2-22-75 (Cook), "The Brothers Cain" 3-1-75 (Cook), "Full Circle" 3-15-75 (Cook), "The Thief of Chendo" 3-29-75 (Shen Ming Tien); *How the West Was Won*—"China Girl" 4-16-79 (Song).

Fuller, Barbara. Films: "Rock Island Trail" 1950 (Annabelle); "The Savage Horde" 1950 (Louise Cole); "City of Badmen" 1953. ¶TV: *Trackdown*—"The Bounty Hunter" 3-7-58 (Mrs. Phillips); *Daniel Boone*—"Noblesse Oblige" 3-26-70.

Fuller, Clem (1909-5/24/61). Films: "Twilight on the Trail" 1941 (Stage Driver); "Sunset Pass" 1946 (Posse Man); "Gun Runner" 1949 (Tex); "Shadows of the West" 1949 (Ed Mayberry); "High Lonesome" 1950 (Dixie); "The Sundowners" 1950 (Turkey); "Cave of Outlaws" 1951 (Whitey); "The Great Sioux Uprising" 1953 (Jake); "Gunsmoke" 1953 (Two Dot); "Riding Shotgun" 1954. ¶TV: *Maverick*—"Seed of Deception" 4-13-58 (Stage Driver); *Gunsmoke*—"Robber and Bridegroom" 12-13-58 (Joe), "Kangaroo" 10-10-59 (Clem), "Brother Whelp" 11-7-59 (Clem), "Odd Man Out" 11-21-59 (Clem), "False Witness" 12-12-59 (Clem), "Tag, You're It" 12-19-59 (Clem), "Moo Moo Raid" 2-13-60 (Clem); *Rawhide*—"Incident of the Golden Calf" 3-13-59, "Incident of the Stargazer" 4-1-60.

Fuller, Haidee. Films: "The Squaw Man" 1914 (Lady Mabel Wynnegate).

Fuller, Lance (1928-). Films: "War Arrow" 1953 (Trooper); "Cattle Queen of Montana" 1954 (Colorados); "Taza, Son of Cochise" 1954 (Lt. Willis); "Apache Woman" 1955 (Armand); "Frontier Woman" 1956; "Kentucky Rifle" 1956; "Secret of Treasure Mountain" 1956 (Juan

Alvarado); "Day of the Outlaw" 1959 (Pace). ¶TV: *The Rifleman*—"The Sister" 11-25-58; *Maverick*—"Island in the Swamp" 11-30-58 (Oliver Offord), "The Cats of Paradise" 10-11-59 (Faro Jack Norcross); *Bat Masterson*—"Double Trouble in Trinidad" 1-7-59 (Mornsby), "A Grave Situation" 5-12-60 (Powers), "The Price of Paradise" 1-19-61 (Walker Hayes); *Colt .45*—"The Pirate" 5-31-59 (Orin Mason); *Lawman*—"Parphyrias Lover" 11-19-61 (Galt Stevens).

Fuller, Mary (1888-12/9/73). Films: "The House of Cards" 1909; "The Luck of Roaring Camp" 1910; "Ononko's Vow" 1910; "The Daisy Cowboy" 1911; "The Story of the Indian Lodge" 1911; "A Cowboy's Stratagem" 1912; "The Girl and the Outlaw" 1913; "Joyce of the North Woods" 1913; "When East Met West in Boston" 1914; "The Long Trail" 1917 (Louise Graham).

Fuller, Robert (1934-). Films: "Incident at Phantom Hill" 1966 (Matt Martin); "Return of the Seven" 1966-Span. (Vin); "The Gatling Gun" 1972 (Sneed); "Mustang Country" 1976 (Griff); "Donner Pass: The Road to Survival" TVM-1978 (James Reed); "Bonanza: The Next Generation" TVM-1988 (Charley Poke); "Maverick" 1994 (Riverboat Poker Player). ¶TV: *The Californians*—"Pipeline" 4-22-58; *Buckskin*—"The Trial of Chrissy Miller" 7-31-58 (Hargis); *The Adventures of Rin Tin Tin*—"The Epidemic" 11-21-58 (Stan); *The Restless Gun*—"Peligroso" 12-15-58 (Bud Bardeen), "Shadow of a Gunfighter" 1-12-59 (Jim Winfield); *Wagon Train*—"The Ella Lindstrom Story" 2-4-59 (Fitzpatrick), "The Kate Parker Story" 5-6-59 (Chris Finley), "The Widow O'Rourke Story" 10-7-63 (O'Rourke), Regular 1963-65 (Cooper); *Cimarron City*—"Blind Is the Killer" 2-21-59; *Wyatt Earp*—"The Judas Goat" 3-31-59 (Hank Drew); *Lawman*—"The Friend" 6-28-59 (Buck Harmon); *Laramie*—Regular 1959-63 (Jess Harper); *Bob Hope Chrysler Theatre*—"Massacre at Fort Phil Kearny" 10-26-66 (Captain Fetterman); *The Monroes*—"Court Martial" 11-16-66 (Captain Stone); *The Virginian*—"The Welcoming Town" 3-22-67 (Clint Richards); *The Big Valley*—"A Flock of Trouble" 9-25-67 (Carl Wheeler); *The Men from Shiloh*—"Flight from Memory" 2-17-71 (Carl Ellis); *Hec Ramsey*—"The Mystery of Chalk Hill" 2-18-73 (Dixie); *Paradise*—"Home Again" 9-16-89 (Sam Clanton), "Out of Ashes" 1-4-91 (Marshal Blake); *Adventures of Brisco County, Jr.*—Pilot 8-27-93

(Kenyon Drummond), "Brisco in Jalisco" 9-17-93 (Kenyon Drummond).

Fulton, James F. Films: "The Kill-Joy" 1917 (Shoot-Em Up Bob); "Ruggles of Red Gap" 1918 (Jeff Tuttle); "Beyond the Trail" 1926 (Buck, the Ranchhand).

Fulton, Joan. *see* Shawlee, Joan.

Fulton, Lou. Films: "The Old Corral" 1936 (Elmer); "Gunsmoke Ranch" 1937 (Oscar); "The Painted Stallion" 1937-serial (Elmer); "Arizona Gangbusters" 1940 (Lanky); "Frontier Crusader" 1940 (Lank Lent); "Gun Code" 1940 (Curly).

Fulton, Rad. Films: "Hell Bent for Leather" 1960 (Moon); "The Last Sunset" 1961 (Julesurg Kid). ¶TV: *Laramie*—"Company Man" 2-9-60 (Johnny Leach).

Funai, Helen. ¶TV: *Wild Wild West*—"The Night of the Samurai" 10-13-67 (Japanese Maiden); *Bonanza*—"Rock-a-Bye, Hoss" 10-10-71 (Lem Toy).

Fung, Willie (1896-4/16/45). Films: "Chip of the Flying U" 1926 (Chinese Cook); "The Two-Gun Man" 1926 (Quong); "The Yellow Back" 1926 (Chinese); "The Virginian" 1929 (Hong the Cook); "Gun Smoke" 1931 (John, the Chinese Cook); "The Thrill Hunter" 1933 (Wung Lo); "Gunfire" 1935 (Loo Fat); "Hopalong Cassidy" 1935 (Salem, the Cook); "Rocky Mountain Mystery" 1935 (Ling Yat); "Ruggles of Red Gap" 1935 (Chinese Servant); "Call of the Prairie" 1936 (Wong); "Come on Cowboys" 1937 (Charlie); "Git Along, Little Dogies" 1937 (Sing Low); "The Red Rope" 1937; "Secret Valley" 1937 (Tobasco); "The Trigger Trio" 1937 (Chong); "Wells Fargo" 1937 (Wang); "Border Wolves" 1938 (Ling Wong); "Pride of the West" 1938 (Sing Loo); "Buck Benny Rides Again" 1940 (Chinese Cook); "Viva Cisco Kid" 1940 (Wang); "Saddle Mountain Roundup" 1941 (Fan Way); "North to the Klondike" 1942 (Waterlily); "The Spoilers" 1942 (Jailed Chinaman).

Funicello, Annette (1942-). TV: *Walt Disney Presents*—"Elfego Baca: Elfego Baca, Attorney at Law" 2-6-59 (Chuchita Bernal); *Zorro*—"The Missing Father" 2-26-59 (Senorita Anita Cecilia Cabrillo), "Please Believe Me" 3-5-59 (Senorita Anita Cecilia Cabrillo), "The Brooch" 3-12-59 (Senorita Anita Cecilia Cabrillo); *Walt Disney Presents: Zorro*—"The Postponed Wedding" 1-1-61 (Constancia De La Torre); *Wagon Train*—

"The Sam Pulaski Story" 11-4-63 (Rose Pulaski); *Hondo*—"Hondo and the Apache Trail" 12-22-67 (Anne).

Funk, Terry. TV: *Wildside*—Regular 1985 (Prometheus Jones); *Adventures of Brisco County, Jr.*—Pilot 8-27-93 (Defendant).

Furey, Barney (1888-1/18/38). Films: "The Gambler's I.O.U." 1915; "D'Arcy of the Northwest Mounted" 1916; "The Golden Thought" 1916; "True Blue" 1918 (Pedro); "Western Blood" 1918 (Wallace Payton); "The Man Trackers" 1921 (Jules); "Four Hearts" 1922 (Gordon Ferris); "Headin' North" 1922 (the Boob); "The Sunshine Trail" 1923 (Man Crook); "The Loser's End" 1924 (Simmie Busch); "Riding Double" 1924; "Ranchers and Rascals" 1925 (Williams); "The Trouble Buster" 1925 (Robert Willis); "Out of the West" 1926 (Scout); "Red Hot Hoofs" 1926 (Al Skelly); "The Flying U Ranch" 1927 (Pink); "The Sonora Kid" 1927 (Doc Knight); "Splitting the Breeze" 1927 (Rev. Otis Briggs); "Tom's Gang" 1927 (Ray Foster); "King Cowboy" 1928 (Shorty Sims); "Red Riders of Canada" 1928 (Nicholas); "Tyrant of Red Gulch" 1928 (Anton); "When the Law Rides" 1928 (the Little Man); "The Big Diamond Robbery" 1929 (Barney McGill); "The Drifter" 1929 (Happy Hogan); "Gun Law" 1929 (Cy Brown); "Idaho Red" 1929 (Dave Lucas); "'Neath Western Skies" 1929 (Lem Johnson); "Outlawed" 1929 (Sagebrush); "The Pride of Pawnee" 1929 (Scotty Wilson); "The Trail of the Horse Thieves" 1929 (the Eagle); "Beau Bandit" 1930 (Cowhand); "When a Man Rides Alone" 1933 (Deputy Sheriff); "Fighting Caballero" 1935 (Sheriff); "Nevada" 1935 (Card Game Bystander); "Powdersmoke Range" 1935; "The Silent Code" 1935 (Peter Barkley); "Thunderbolt" 1935 (Krause); "Custer's Last Stand" 1936-serial (Sergeant Peters); "The Law Rides" 1936 (Pete); "The Law Rides" 1936; "Wells Fargo" 1937 (Bandit).

Furlong, John. Films: "More Wild Wild West" TVM-1980 (Bavarian Ambassador); "The Alamo: 13 Days to Glory" TVM-1987; "Once Upon a Texas Train" TVM-1988; "Conagher" TVM-1991; "Wyatt Earp" 1994 (Clem Hafford); "The Desperate Trail" TVM-1995. ¶TV: *The High Chaparral*—"Bad Day for a Thirst" 2-18-68 (Halliday); *Legend*—Pilot 4-18-95 (Governor Dennehy).

Furlong, Kevin. Films: "The Gambler Returns: The Luck of the

Draw" TVM-1991 (Johnny Loughlin).

Furman, Rose. Films: "Guns for San Sebastian" 1967-U.S./Fr./Mex./Ital. (Agueda); "Two Mules for Sister Sara" 1970.

Furness, Betty (1916-4/2/94). Films: "Renegades of the West" 1932 (Mary Fawcett); "Crossfire" 1933 (Patricia Plummer); "Scarlet River" 1933 (Babe Jewel); "Fair Warning" 1937 (Kay Farnham).

Furstenberg, Ira von (1940-). Films: "Deaf Smith and Johnny Ears" 1972-Ital. (Hester).

Furth, George (1932-). Films: "Butch Cassidy and the Sundance Kid" 1969 (Woodcock); "Sam Hill: Who Killed the Mysterious Mr. Foster?" TVM-1971; "Blazing Saddles" 1974 (Van Johnson); "Charlie Cobb: Nice Night for a Hanging" TVM-1977 (Conroy). ¶TV: *The Road West*—"This Dry and Thirsty Land" 10-10-66 (Virgil Slaughter); *F Troop*—"Survival of the Fittest" 12-15-66 (Captain Blair); *Laredo*—"Walk Softly" 3-31-67; *Bonanza*—"Another Windmill to Go" 9-14-69 (Horace Keylot); *Dr. Quinn, Medicine Woman*—"The Visitor" 1-9-93 (Jedediah Bancroft), "The First Circle" 3-26-94 (Jedediah Bancroft).

Fury, Ed. Films: "Raw Edge" 1956 (Whitey).

Fury, Men. *see* Meniconi, Furio.

Fux, Herbert. Films: "Beyond the Law" 1968-Ital.; "Bandera Bandits" 1973-Ital./Span./Ger.; "Trinity Plus the Clown and a Guitar" 1975-Ital./Austria/Fr.

Gabel, Martin (1912-5/22/86). Films: "There Was a Crooked Man" 1970 (Warden Le Goff). ¶TV: *Have Gun Will Travel*—"The Fatalist" 9-10-60 (Nathan Shotness), "A Drop of Blood" 12-2-61 (Nathan Shotness).

Gabel, Scilla (1937-). Films: "Djurado" 1966-Ital./Span. (Barbara); "Bastard, Go and Kill" 1971-Ital.

Gable, Clark (1901-11/16/60). Films: "The Painted Desert" 1931 (Rance Brett); "Call of the Wild" 1935 (Jack Thornton); "Honky Tonk" 1941 (Candy Johnson); "Across the Wide Missouri" 1951 (Flint Mitchell); "Lone Star" 1952 (Devereaux Burke); "The Tall Men" 1955 (Ben Allison); "King and Four Queens" 1956 (Dan Kehoe); "The Misfits" 1961 (Gay Langland).

Gable, Jack. *see* Perrin, Jack.

Gable, John Clark. Films: "Bad Jim" 1990 (John T. Coleman).

Gabo, Louise. Films: "Mystery Ranch" 1934 (Mrs. Henderson).

Gabor, Zsa Zsa (1919-). TV: *F Troop*—"Play, Gypsy, Play" 3-1-66 (Marika); *The Rounders*—10-11-66 (Ilona Hobson); *Bonanza*—"Maestro Hoss" 5-7-67 (Mme. Morova).

Gabourie, Fred. Films: "Yukon Vengeance" 1954; "Yaqui Drums" 1956. ¶TV: *Wild Bill Hickok*—"Ol' Pardner Rides Again" 9-16-52, "Kangaroo Kapers" 3-10-53.

Gabriel, John (1931-). Films: "Stagecoach" 1966 (Capt. Mallory); "El Dorado" 1967 (Pedro). ¶TV: *The Big Valley*—"Hide the Children" 12-19-66 (Ion).

Gabriel, Lynn. Films: "Heart of the West" 1937 (Sally Jordan).

Gaddi, Carlo. Films: "Duel in the Eclipse" 1967-Span.; "For One Hundred Thousand Dollars Per Killing" 1967-Ital.; "Pecos Cleans Up" 1967-Ital.; "Beyond the Law" 1968-Ital.; "Death Rides Alone" 1968-Ital./Span.; "To Hell and Back" 1968-Ital./Span.; "Django the Bastard" 1969-Ital./Span.; "God in Heaven ... Arizona on Earth" 1972-Span./Ital.; "I Am Sartana, Trade Your Guns for a Coffin" 1972-Ital.; "Kill the Poker Player" 1972-Ital./Span.; "My Horse, My Gun, Your Widow" 1972-Ital./Span.

Gadson, Jacqueline. Films: "The Man Who Won" 1923 (Jessie); "The Flaming Forties" 1925 (Sally); "Ridin' the Wind" 1925 (May Lacy).

Gage, Ben (1915-4/28/78). TV: *Maverick*—"Gun-Shy" 1-11-59 (Marshal Mort Dooley), "A Tale of Three Cities" 10-18-59 (Sheriff Hardy), "The Misfortune Teller" 3-6-60 (Sheriff Lem Watson), "A Technical Error" 11-26-61 (Sheriff); *Destry*—"Law and Order Day" 2-28-64 (Sheriff); *F Troop*—"Reunion for O'Rourke" 3-8-66 (Mike O'Hanlon), *Bonanza*—"The Oath" 11-20-66 (Sheriff Calvin), "Sense of Duty" 9-24-67 (Deputy).

Gagnon, Erminie. Films: "The Man Who Paid" 1922 (Lizette).

Gahan, Oscar. Films: "Border Guns" 1935; "Cheyenne Tornado" 1935; "Defying the Law" 1935; "Gallant Defender" 1935; "Lawless Riders" 1935; "The Man from Guntown" 1935; "North of Arizona" 1935 (Fiddler); "The Phantom Cowboy" 1935; "Texas Jack" 1935 (Nip); "Tumbling Tumbleweeds" 1935; "The Vanishing Riders" 1935; "Western Frontier" 1935; "Ambush Valley" 1936 (Diggs); "Arizona Mahoney" 1936 (Chinese Man); "Border Caballero" 1936;

"Cavalcade of the West" 1936; "The Fugitive Sheriff" 1936; "Gun Grit" 1936 (Don); "Lightning Bill Carson" 1936 (Townsman); "The Lonely Trail" 1936; "Rogue of the Range" 1936 (Stage Guard); "The Singing Cowboy" 1936 (Tom); "The Traitor" 1936 (Outlaw in Cantina); "The Unknown Ranger" 1936; "Vengeance of Rannah" 1936 (Nolan); "Arizona Gunfighter" 1937; "Bar Z Bad Men" 1937; "Cheyenne Rides Again" 1937; "Courage of the West" 1937 (George Wilkins); "Danger Valley" 1937; "Galloping Dynamite" 1937; "The Gambling Terror" 1937; "Git Along, Little Dogies" 1937; "Guns in the Dark" 1937; "A Lawman Is Born" 1937; "Moonlight on the Range" 1937; "The Mystery of the Hooded Horseman" 1937 (Bartender); "The Red Rope" 1937; "Riders of the Dawn" 1937; "The Roaming Cowboy" 1937 (Tom); "Santa Fe Rides" 1937; "The Silver Trail" 1937 (Curt); "Sing, Cowboy, Sing" 1937; "The Singing Buckaroo" 1937; "Springtime in the Rockies" 1937; "The Trusted Outlaw" 1937; "Where Trails Divide" 1937; "Yodelin' Kid from Pine Ridge" 1937; "Billy the Kid Returns" 1938; "Ghost Town Riders" 1938; "Gunsmoke Trail" 1938; "Heroes of the Alamo" 1938; "In Early Arizona" 1938; "Rollin' Plains" 1938 (Telegraph Clerk); "Rolling Caravans" 1938; "Utah Trail" 1938; "Western Trails" 1938; "Whirlwind Horseman" 1938; "The Man from Sundown" 1939; "New Frontier" 1939 (Musician); "The Carson City Kid" 1940; "Billy the Kid Trapped" 1942.

Gaige, Russell (Bruce Hamilton) (1894-10/17/74). Films: "The Vanquished" 1953 (Rev. Babcock). ¶TV: *The Lone Ranger*—"Spanish Gold" 6-1-50.

Gaines, Mel. Films: "Flesh and the Spur" 1957 (Blackie); "Man or Gun" 1958 (Diego). ¶TV: *Wanted—Dead or Alive*—"The Spur" 1-17-59; *Gunsmoke*—"The Wrong Man" 10-29-66 (Squeak).

Gaines, Richard (1904-7/20/75). Films: "Unconquered" 1947 (Col. George Washington); "Drum Beat" 1954 (Dr. Thomas). ¶TV: *TV Reader's Digest*—"Cochise—Greatest of All the Apaches" 1-30-56; *The Law of the Plainsman*—"Passenger to Mescalero" 10-29-59 (J. Roberts Pauley).

Gainey, M.C. Films: "El Diablo" CTVM-1990 (Bebe); "Geronimo: An American Legend" 1993 (Unafraid Miner). ¶TV: *Adventures of Brisco County, Jr.*—Pilot 8-27-93

(Big Smith), "Crystal Hawks" 11-12-93 (Big Smith).

Gains, Courtney. Films: "Lust in the Dust" 1985 (Red Dick Barker). ¶TV: *Legend*—"Knee-High Noon" 5-23-95.

Gajoni, Cristina (1941-). Films: "Magnificent Three" 1963-Span./Ital.; "Cisco" 1966-Ital.

Galante, James. TV: *Bonanza*—"Denver McKee" 10-15-60; *The Rifleman*—"Outlaw Shoes" 4-30-62 (Handyman); *Empire*—"Breakout" 4-16-63 (Hank); *Rawhide*—"Incident of the Woman Trap" 1-26-62, "The Greedy Town" 2-16-62 (Handyman), "The Immigrants" 3-16-62 (Hans); *Wild Wild West*—"The Night of the Watery Death" 11-11-66 (Naval Officer); *Hondo*—"Hondo and the Hanging Town" 12-8-67 (Deputy).

Galbo, Cristina (1950-). Films: "Fury of Johnny Kid" 1967-Span./Ital.; "Twice a Judas" 1968-Span./Ital.

Gale, David (-9/91). TV: *Paradise*—"Stray Bullet" 12-8-88 (Doc Garrison).

Gale, Eddra (1921-). Films: "A Man Called Gannon" 1969 (Louisa); "Desperate Mission" TVM-1971. ¶TV: *The High Chaparral*—"The New Lion of Sonora" 2-19-71 (Lola).

Gale, Joan. Films: "The Last of the Mohicans" 1932-serial; "The Miracle Rider" 1935-serial (Ruth); "Outlawed Guns" 1935 (Marj. Ellsworth).

Gale, June. Films: "Rainbow's End" 1935 (Ann Ware); "Swifty" 1935 (Helen McNeil); "Heroes of the Range" 1936 (Joan Peters); "The Riding Avenger" 1936 (Jessie McCoy).

Gale, Lillian (1885-4/2/72). Films: "Ten Scars Make a Man" 1924-serial; "Walloping Wallace" 1924 (Ma Fagin); "Way of a Man" 1924-serial; "Idaho" 1925-serial.

Gale, Roberta. Films: "Mystery Ranch" 1934 (Mary Henderson); "Terror of the Plains" 1934 (Bess); "Alias John Law" 1935 (Jean); "No Man's Range" 1935 (Helen Green).

Galento, Mario. Films: "Frontier Woman" 1956; "Natchez Trace" 1960 (Turner).

Galik, Denise. TV: *The Oregon Trail*—"Hannah's Girls" 10-26-77 (Libby Owens).

Galindo, Jose Hector. Films: "Smoky" 1966 (Manuel). ¶TV: *Daniel Boone*—"Cibola" 3-31-66 (Antonio).

Galindo, Nacho (1908-7/23/73). Films: "The Gay Cavalier" 1946; "Twilight on the Rio Grande" 1947 (Torres); "Relentless" 1948 (Peon);

"South of St. Louis" 1949 (Manuel); "Dakota Lil" 1950; "Montana" 1950 (Pedro); "The Showdown" 1950 (Gonzales); "Surrender" 1950 (Grigo); "Flaming Feather" 1952; "Lone Star" 1952 (Vincente); "The Woman They Almost Lynched" 1953 (John Pablo); "Border River" 1954 (Lopez); "Broken Lance" 1954 (Cook); "Gypsy Colt" 1954 (Pancho); "Jubilee Trail" 1954 (Rico, the Bartender); "The Outcast" 1954 (Curly); "Thunder Over Arizona" 1956; "Buchanan Rides Alone" 1958 (Nacho); "Saddle the Wind" 1958; "Born Reckless" 1959 (Papa Gomez); "One-Eyed Jacks" 1961 (Mexican Townsman); "El Dorado" 1967 (Mexican Saloonkeeper). ¶TV: *The Lone Ranger*—"Dan Reid's Fight for Life" 11-18-54 (Pancho); *Maverick*—"Plunder of Paradise" 3-9-58 (Chucho Morales), "Escape to Tampico" 10-26-58 (Carlos), "Guatemala City" 1-31-60 (Spanish Driver); *Jim Bowie*—"The Puma" 5-23-58 (Puma); *The Restless Gun*—"Mme. Brimstone" 5-4-59; *Man from Blackhawk*—"The Sons of Don Antonio" 4-22-60 (Pablo); *Wanted—Dead or Alive*—"To the Victor" 11-9-60; *The Deputy*—"Two-way Deal" 3-11-61 (Sancho); *Wild Wild West*—"The Night of the Deadly Bubble" 2-24-67 (Pepe); *Gunsmoke*—"Zavala" 10-7-68 (Rojas).

Gallagher, Don. Films: "Code of the Fearless" 1939 (Pete Howard); "Outlaw's Paradise" 1939 (Mort); "West of Carson City" 1940.

Gallagher, Glen B. (1908-3/31/60). Films: "Fool's Gold" 1946 (Lieutenant Anderson); "Callaway Went Thataway" 1951 (Salesman).

Gallagher, Mel. Films: "When the Legends Die" 1972 (Cowboy). ¶TV: *Gunsmoke*—"Double Entry" 1-2-65 (Yuma Joe); *Laredo*—"The Last of the Caesars—Absolutely" 12-2-66; *The Guns of Will Sonnett*—"Jim Sonnett's Lady" 2-21-69 (Duke); *The High Chaparral*—"The Guns of Johnny Rondo" 2-6-70 (Jason).

Gallagher, Ray (1885-3/6/53). Films: "An Obstinate Sheriff" 1915; "The Trail of '98" 1929; "Border Devils" 1932 (Neil Denham); "The Lone Bandit" 1934 (Bob Mitchell); "The Judgement Book" 1935 (Duffy Miller); "Desert Guns" 1936 (Walker); "Riddle Ranch" 1936 (Deputy Sheriff); "Song of the Trail" 1936 (Blore).

Gallagher, Skeets (1890-5/22/55). Films: "The Conquerors" 1932 (Benson).

Gallagher, Toy. Films: "Action Galore" 1925 (Betty McLean).

Gallardo, Silvana. Films: "Windwalker" 1980 (Little Feather). ¶TV: *How the West Was Won*—Episode One 2-12-78 (Shewelah); *Born to the Wind* 1982 (Digger Woman).

Gallaudet, John (1903-83). Films: "Wagons Westward" 1940 (Blackie); "Road Agent" 1941 (Steve); "Outcasts of the Trail" 1949 (Tom "Ivory" White). ¶TV: *The Californians*—"The Alice Pritchard Case" 2-4-58 (Pritchard); *Bat Masterson*—"Garrison Finish" 12-10-59 (Colonel Pierce); *Wyatt Earp*—"Wells Fargo Calling Marshal Earp" 12-29-59 (Thacker), "Frontier Surgeon" 1-19-60 (John Thacker); *Lancer*—"The Gifts" 10-28-69 (Lloyd Bush).

Gallego, Gina. Films: "Lust in the Dust" 1985 (Ninfa). ¶TV: *Zorro and Son*—4-20-83.

Gallendo, Silvana. TV: *Centennial*—Regular 1978-79 (Seraina Marques).

Galli, Ida. see Stewart, Evelyn.

Galli, Rosina. Films: "The Oklahoma Kid" 1939 (Manuelita); "Gauchos of El Dorado" 1941 (Isabella).

Gallian, Ketti (1913-12/72). Films: "Under the Pampas Moon" 1935 (Yvonne LaMarr).

Gallo, Lew. TV: *Gunsmoke*—"The Lost Rifle" 11-1-58 (Joe Spangler), "Brother Whelp" 11-7-59 (Sted Rutger), "Wishbone" 2-19-66 (Spellman), "The Favor" 3-11-67 (Kelly Bates); *Lawman*—"Warpath" 2-8-59 (Weed); *Zane Grey Theater*—"Heritage" 4-2-59 (Sergeant); *Fury*—"The Forty" 12-12-59 (Alf Thorson); *Death Valley Days*—"Ten Feet of Nothing" 1-5-60 (Dude); *Hotel De Paree*—"Hard Luck for Sundance" 2-19-60 (Bud Turnbull); *Rawhide*—"Incident at Poco Tiempo" 12-9-60 (Colley), "The Long Shakedown" 10-13-61 (Haskell); *The Deputy*—"Three Brothers" 12-10-60 (Frank Bennett); *The Tall Man*—"Big Sam's Boy" 3-4-61 (Jarrico); *Gunslinger*—"Rampage" 3-16-61 (Pete Jenks); *Tales of Wells Fargo*—"The Repentant Outlaw" 5-29-61 (Maxey), "Return to Yesterday" 1-13-62 (Harry); *The Dakotas*—"Mutiny at Fort Mercy" 1-21-63 (Sergeant Smythe); *The Virginian*—"Run Quiet" 11-13-63 (Vince); *The Big Valley*—"Hazard" 3-9-66 (Matt); *Iron Horse*—"Appointment with an Epitaph" 2-13-67 (Frank Mason).

Gallotti, Dada. Films: "Johnny Yuma" 1966-Ital.; "Three Silver Dollars" 1968-Ital.; "Once Upon a Time in the Wild, Wild West" 1969-Ital.; "Deadly Trackers" 1972-Ital.; "Prey of Vultures" 1973-Span./Ital.

Galloway, Don (1937-). Films: "The Rare Breed" 1966 (Jamie Bowen); "Gunfight in Abilene" 1967 (Ward Kent); "The Ride to Hangman's Tree" 1967 (Nevada Jones); "Rough Night in Jericho" 1967 (Jace). ¶TV: *The Virginian*—"The Final Hour" 5-1-63 (Jack Henderson), "The Challenge" 10-19-66 (Jim Tyson); *Wagon Train*—"The Silver Lady" 4-25-65 (Virgil Earp); *The Life and Times of Grizzly Adams*—"Adams' Ark" 3-16-77 (Allan Pinkerton).

Galloway, Michael. TV: *Broken Arrow*—"Transfer" 6-24-58 (Sergeant); *Maverick*—"The Strange Journey of Jenny Hill" 3-29-59 (Jim Hedges); *The Texan*—"Badlands" 5-11-59 (Frank Kincaid).

Galvan, Pedro. Films: "Sierra Baron" 1958 (Judson Jeffers); "Two Mules for Sister Sara" 1970.

Galvez, Fernando. Films: "The Ranger and the Law" 1921 (Bootlegger); "Galloping Thunder" 1927 (Lash M'Graw); "Hard Hombre" 1931 (Juan).

Gam, Rita (1928-). Films: "Mohawk" 1956 (Onida); "Sierra Baron" 1958 (Felicia Delmonte); "Shoot Out" 1971 (Emma).

Gamble, Fred (Fred Gambold) (1868-2/17/39). Films: "Bullet Proof" 1920 (Father Jacques); "The Firebrand" 1922 (Judd Acker); "The Virginian" 1923 (Fat Drummer); "Tumbleweeds" 1925 (Hotel Proprietor); "Born to Battle" 1926 (Morgan); "Chasing Trouble" 1926 (Bartender); "Painted Post" 1928 (Theatrical Manager); "Laddie Be Good" 1928 (Henry Cody).

Gamble, Jim. Films: "The Lone Fighter" 1923 (Patrick Schayer).

Gamble, Warburton (1883-8/27/45). Films: "The Law of the Yukon" 1920 (Medford Delaney).

Gamboa, Elias (1895-12/9/59). Films: "Two-Gun Troubador" 1939; "Ridin' the Trail" 1940; "Down Mexico Way" 1941; "Under Fiesta Stars" 1941.

Gambold, Fred. *see* Gamble, Fred.

Gammon, James (1940-). Films: "Journey to Shiloh" 1968 (Tellis Teager); "The Intruders" TVM-1970; "Macho Callahan" 1970 (Cowboy); "A Man Called Horse" 1970 (Ed); "The Sacketts" TVM-1979 (Wes Bigelow); "The Ballad of Gregorio Cortez" 1983 (Sheriff Fly); "Silverado" 1985 (Dawson); "Conagher" TVM-1991; "Wyatt Earp" 1994 (Mr. Sutherland). ¶TV: *Wild Wild West*—"The Night of the Freebooters" 4-1-

66 (Egan); *Gunsmoke*—"My Father, My Son" 4-23-66 (Arnie Jeffords), "Susan Was Evil" 12-3-73 (Dudley); *The Monroes*—"Night of the Wolf" 9-14-66 (Stennis); *The Road West*—"The Gunfighter" 9-26-66 (Pete Fowler), "The Agreement" 4-24-67 (Deputy Virgil Bramley); *Bonanza*—"A Man Without Land" 4-9-67 (Harry Jeffers); *The Virginian*—"A Small Taste of Justice" 12-20-67 (Cal Mason); *Lancer*—"Chase a Wild Horse" 10-8-68 (Wes), "Blind Man's Bluff" 9-23-69 (Clint Meek); *The High Chaparral*—"Only the Bad Come to Sonora" 10-2-70 (Lafe); *Kung Fu*—"The Nature of Evil" 3-21-74 (Jake); *Young Riders*—"The Blood of Others" 10-12-91 (Elias Mills).

Gampu, Ken. TV: *Cowboy in Africa*—"The Time of the Predator" 11-6-67 (Mulanda); *Daniel Boone*—"The Value of a King" 11-9-67 (Kamba).

Gan, Chester (1909-6/30/59). Films: "Fighting Through" 1934 (Wong); "The Red Rider" 1934-serial; "Moonlight on the Prairie" 1935 (Chinese Cook); "Stormy" 1935 (Chinaman); "Wanderer of the Wasteland" 1935 (Ling); "Arizona Mahoney" 1936 (Chinese Man); "The Country Beyond" 1936 (Chinese Cook); "Drift Fence" 1936 (Clarence); "Wells Fargo" 1937 (Chinese Workman); "Mexicali Kid" 1938 (McCarty); "Westbound Stage" 1939 (Chinese Man); "The Carson City Kid" 1940 (Wong); "My Little Chickadee" 1940 (Chinaman); "Pals of the Silver Sage" 1940 (Ling); "Rawhide Rangers" 1941 (Sin Lo).

Gantvoort, Carl (1883-9/28/35). Films: "Man of the Forest" 1921 (Milt Dale); "The Mysterious Rider" 1921 (Wilson Moore); "When Romance Rides" 1922 (Lin Slone).

Ganzer, Gerry. Films: "Powder River Rustlers" 1949 (Louise Manning).

Ganzhorn, Jack (1881-9/19/56). Films: "Thorobred" 1922 (Blackie Wells); "The Iron Horse" 1924 (Thomas Durant); "Fightin' Odds" 1925 (Dave Ormsby); "Hawk of the Hills" 1927-serial (Henry Selby); "The Apache Raider" 1928 (Breed Artwell); "The Valley of Hunted Men" 1928 (French Durant).

Garas, Kaz (1940-). TV: *Gunsmoke*—"Exocus 21:22" 3-24-69 (Keith); *The Virginian*—"Train of Darkness" 2-4-70 (Buster Floyd); *The High Chaparral*—"Sangre" 2-26-71 (Lieutenant Allen); *Barbary Coast*—"Mary Had More Than a Little" 1-2-76 (Butch).

Garber, Terri. Films: "No Man's Land" TVM-1984 (Brianne Wilder).

Garbo, James. Films: "The Soul of Nigger Charley" 1973 (Collins).

Garcia, Allan (1887-9/4/38). "The Cowboy's Adopted Child" 1911; "How Algy Captured a Wild Man" 1911; "The Regeneration of the Apache Kid" 1911; "Told in the Sierras" 1911; "The Bandit's Mask" 1912; "The Epidemic in Paradise Gulch" 1912; "The Little Indian Martyr" 1912; "The Vow of Ysobel" 1912; "Pierre of the North" 1913; "Her Atonement" 1915 (John De Forrest); "The Law at Silver Camp" 1915; "Sunlight's Last Raid" 1917 (Pedro); "Baree, Son of Kazan" 1918 (Bush McTaggart); "The Counterfeit Trail" 1919; "Six Feet Four" 1919 (Ben Broderick); "The Golden Trail" 1920 (Jean, the Half-Breed); "Skyfire" 1920 (Pierre Piquet); "The Three Buckaroos" 1922 (Card Ritchie); "Morgan's Last Raid" 1929 (Morgan); "The Cisco Kid" 1931; "The Gay Caballero" 1932; "South of Sante Fe" 1932 (Captain Felipe Menendez Anunciado Gunzales Rodriguez); "The California Trail" 1933 (Sergeant); "Under the Tonto Rim" 1933 (Police Chief); "The Gay Desperado" 1936 (Police Captain); "In Old Mexico" 1938 (Don Carlos Gonazles).

Garcia, David. Films: "Blue Canadian Rockies" 1952 (Indian Boy); "Warlock" 1959 (Pony Benner). ¶TV: *Wagon Train*—"The Jeremy Dow Story" 12-28-60 (Brave), "The Tiburcio Mendez Story" 3-22-61 (Providencio Gomez).

Garcia, Harry (1904-11/3/70). Films: "The Palomino" 1950 (Johnny); "Border Fence" 1951.

Garcia, Joe. Films: "West of Santa Fe" 1938 (Henchman); "Where the West Begins" 1938 (Miller); "Overland Mail" 1939 (Buck); "Overland with Kit Carson" 1939-serial; "Bullets and Saddles" 1943; "The San Antonio Kid" 1944; "Three Troubledoers" 1946-short (Waiter).

Garcia, Joe "Running Fox." Films: "The Chisholms" TVM-1979 (Howahkan). ¶TV: *The Chisholms*—Regular 1979-80 (Howahkan).

Garcia, Juan. Films: "Blowing Wind" 1953 (El Gavilan); "Vera Cruz" 1954 (Pedro); "The Tall Men" 1955 (Luis); "The Bravados" 1958; "Ten Days to Tulara" 1958 (Piranha); "The Undefeated" 1969 (Col. Gomez); "Desperate Mission" TVM-1971; "Something Big" 1971 (Juan Garcia).

Garcia, Sancho. Films: "Savage

Pampas" 1966-U.S./Span./Arg. (Carlos); "Sheriff Won't Shoot" 1967-Ital./Fr./Brit.; "Guns of the Magnificent Seven" 1969 (Miguel).

Garcia, Stella. Films: "Joe Kidd" 1972 (Helen Sanchez). ¶TV: *Laredo*—"Scourge of San Rosa" 1-20-67 (Marguerita); *Gunsmoke*—"Survival" 1-10-72 (Chona).

Garcia, Tito. Films: "Finger on the Trigger" 1965-Span./Ital./U.S. (Zubarri); "God Forgives—I Don't" 1966-Ital./Span.; "Seven Guns for Timothy" 1966-Span./Ital.; "The Ugly Ones" 1966-Ital./Span.; "Up the MacGregors!" 1967-Ital./Span. (Miguelito); "All Out" 1968-Ital./Span.; "The Mercenary" 1968-Ital./Span. (Vigilante); "I Came, I Saw, I Shot" 1968-Ital./Span.; "A Town Called Hell" 1971-Span./Brit. (Malombre); "With Friends, Nothing Is Easy" 1971-Span./Ital.

Gardenhire, Raleigh. Films: "Showdown" 1973 (Deputy Joe Williams).

Gardenia, Vincent (1922-12/9/92). TV: *The Big Valley*—"Palms of Glory" 9-15-65 (John Sample), "Image of Yesterday" 1-9-67 (Briggs); *Gunsmoke*—"Noose of Gold" 3-4-67 (Charles Shepherd).

Gardiner, Reginald (1903-7/7/80). Films: "Fury at Furnace Creek" 1948 (Capt. Walsh). ¶TV: *Laramie*—"The Marshals" 4-30-63 (Patches).

Gardner, Ava (1922-1/25/90). Films: "Lone Star" 1952 (Martha Ronda); "Ride, Vaquero!" 1953 (Cordelia Cameron); "The Life and Times of Judge Roy Bean" 1972 (Lily Langtry).

Gardner, Buster. Films: "Eyes of the Forest" 1923 (Sheriff); "Three Jumps Ahead" 1923 (Brutus); "The Deadwood Coach" 1924 (Bill Howland); "The Best Bad Man" 1925 (Hank Smith); "The Circus Ace" 1927 (Sheriff); "Tumbling River" 1927 (Cory); "Crashing Through" 1928 (Slim).

Gardner, Dolores. Films: "Triple Action" 1925 (Donna Mendez); "The Desperate Game" 1926 (Marguerite Grayson).

Gardner, Don (1932-9/21/58). TV: *The Cisco Kid*—"Mr. X" 4-10-54; *Gunsmoke*—"Professor Lute Bone" 1-7-56 (Mr. Ringle); *Tombstone Territory*—"Strange Vengeance" 4-9-58 (Cliff Beaumont).

Gardner, Helen (1884-11/20/68). Films: "The Girl and the Sheriff" 1911; "Yellow Bird" 1912.

Gardner, Hunter (1899-1/16/

52). TV: *The Cisco Kid*—"Quicksilver Murder" 1-12-52.

Gardner, Jack (1876-12/29/29). Films: "The Land of Long Shadows" 1917 (Joe Mauchin); "Men of the Desert" 1917 (Jack); "Open Places" 1917 (Constable Calhoun); "The Range Boss" 1917 (Rex Randerson); "Wild Bill Hickok" 1923 (Bat Masterson); "Wells Fargo" 1937 (Clerk).

Gardner, Jack (1900-2/13/77). TV: *Death Valley Days*—"The Baron of Arizona" 2-25-56; *Zane Grey Theater*—"Badge of Honor" 5-3-57 (Tim Dougherty).

Gardner, Richard (1915-7/1/72). TV: *Riverboat*—"Jessie Quinn" 12-6-59 (Perry Quinn); *Lawman*—"The Four" 10-1-61 (Frank).

Garfield, Allen (1939-). TV: *Bonanza*—"The Iron Butterfly" 11-28-71 (Charlie); *Gunsmoke*—"The First of Ignorance" 1-27-75 (Henry Decory).

Garfield, Jr., John. *see* Garfield, John David.

Garfield, John David (John Garfield, Jr.) (1943-). Films: "MacKenna's Gold" 1969 (Adams' Boy); "Where the Hell's That Gold?!!!" TVM-1988 (Young Fargo Man); "Gunsmoke: The Long Ride" TVM-1993 (Skinner). ¶TV: *Shane*—"The Hant" 9-17-66 (Young Man).

Gargan, Edward (1902-2/19/64). Films: "High, Wide and Handsome" 1937 (Foreman); "The Texans" 1938 (Sgt. Grady); "Buck Benny Rides Again" 1940 (Policeman); "Go West" 1940 (Ticket Seller); "Northwest Passage" 1940 (Capt. Butterfield); "In Old Oklahoma" 1943 (Kelsey, the Waiter); "Prairie Chickens" 1943; "San Fernando Valley" 1944 (Keno); "Saddle Pals" 1947 (Jailer); "Adventures of Gallant Bess" 1948 (Deputy); "The Dude Goes West" 1948 (Conductor).

Gargan, Jack (1900-9/30/58). Films: "West of the Pecos" 1945 (Croupier) ¶TV: *Maverick*—"The Long Hunt" 10-20-57 (Player #2).

Gargan, William (1905-2/16/79). Films: "The Rawhide Years" 1956 (Marshal Sommers).

Gargano, Omero. Films: "Winchester Does Not Forgive" 1968-Ital.; "Ringo, It's Massacre Time" 1970-Ital.; "Deadly Trackers" 1972-Ital.

Gargiullo, Giorgio. Films: "Day of Anger" 1967-Ital./Ger.; "Death Rides Alone" 1968-Ital./Span.; "Hole in the Forehead" 1968-Ital./Span.

Garina, Tamara. Films: "A Man Called Horse" 1970 (Elk Woman).

Garko, Gianni "John" (Gary Hudson). Films: "10,000 Dollars Blood Money" 1966-Ital. (Django); "For One Hundred Thousand Dollars Per Killing" 1967-Ital.; "Cowards Don't Pray" 1968-Ital./Span. (Brian); "Sartana" 1968-Ital./Ger. (Sartana); "Blood at Sundown" 1969-Ital./Span.; "I Am Sartana, Your Angel of Death" 1969-Ital./Fr. (Sartana); "His Name Was Holy Ghost" 1970-Ital./Span. (Holy Ghost); "Sartana Kills Them All" 1970-Ital./Span. (Sartana); "Bad Man's River" 1971-Span./Ital./Fr. (Pace); "Forewarned, Half-Killed ... The Word of the Holy Ghost" 1971-Ital./Span. (the Holy Ghost); "Have a God Funeral, My Friend ... Sartana Will Pay" 1971-Ital. (Sartana); "Light the Fuse ... Sartana Is Coming" 1971-Ital./Fr. (Sartana); "They Call Him Cemetery" 1971-Ital./Span. (the Stranger); "Price of Death" 1972-Ital. (Silver); "Those Dirty Dogs!" 1973-U.S./Ital./Span. (Korano).

Garland, Beverly (1926-). Films: "Bitter Creek" 1954 (Gail Bonner); "The Desperado" 1954 (Lauren Bannerman); "Gunslinger" 1956 (Rose Hood); "Badlands of Montana" 1957 (Susan); "Two Guns and a Badge" 1954 (Gail Sterling); "The Saga of Hemp Brown" 1958 (Mona Langley); "Cutter's Trail" TVM-1970 (Maggie). ¶TV: *Frontier*—"Cattle Drive to Casper" 11-27-55; *Zane Grey Theater*—"Courage Is a Gun" 12-14-56 (Ellen), "Hanging Fever" 3-12-59 (Margaret Walston), "A Small Town That Died" 3-10-60 (Ruth Clarke), "Jericho" 5-18-61 (Amy Schroeder); *Walt Disney Presents*—"Elfego Baca" 1958-60 (Suzanna); *Texas John Slaughter*—"Killers from Kansas" 1-9-59 (Mrs. Barko); *Yancy Derringer*—"The Fair Freebooter" 1-15-59 (Coco LaSalle), "The Wayward Warrior" 4-16-59 (Coco LaSalle); *Rawhide*—"Incident of the Roman Candles" 7-10-59 (Jennie Colby), "Incident at Sugar Creek" 11-23-62 (Marcia), "Incident of the Gallows Tree" 2-22-63 (Della Locke); *Trackdown*—"Hard Lines" 3-11-59 (Dora Crow); *Man from Blackhawk*—"Logan's Policy" 10-9-59 (Sarah Marshall); *Riverboat*—"Three Graves" 3-14-60 (Nora James); *Laramie*—"Saddle and Spur" 3-29-60 (Terry Blake); *Tales of Wells Fargo*—"Pearl Hart" 5-9-60 (Pearl Hart); *Wanted—Dead or Alive*—"Prison Trail" 5-14-60 (Sally Lind); *Stagecoach West*—"The Storm" 12-13-60 (Sherry Hilton); *The Dakotas*—"The Chooser of the Slain" 4-22-63 (Katherine Channing); *Gunsmoke*—"The Odyssey of Jubal

Tanner" 5-18-63 (Leah Brunson), "The Victim" 1-1-68 (Lee Stark), "Time of the Jackals" 1-13-69 (Leona), "The Badge" 2-2-70 (Claire Hollis); *Walt Disney Presents*—"Gallegher" 1965-67 (Laurie Carlson); *Laredo*—"Lazyfoot, Where Are You?" 9-16-65 (Aggie); *A Man Called Shenandoah*—"The Onslaught" 9-23-65 (Kate); *The Loner*—"Incident in the Middle of Nowhere" 2-19-66 (Colores); *Pistols 'n' Petticoats*—11-5-66 (Ross Guttley); *Wild Wild West*—"The Night of the Cut Throats" 11-17-67 (Sally Yarnell), "The Night of Bleak Island" 3-14-69 (Celia Rydell); *Lancer*—"Devil's Blessing" 4-22-69 (Clara Dunbar); *Kung Fu*—"Battle Hymn" 2-8-75 (Theresa Hobart); *How the West Was Won*—"The Slavers" 4-23-79 (Hanna).

Garland, Judy (1922-6/22/69). Films: "The Harvey Girls" 1946 (Susan Bradley).

Garland, Richard (1927-5/24/69). Films: "The Cimarron Kid" 1951 (Jim Moore); "The Battle at Apache Pass" 1952 (Culver); "The Lawless Breed" 1952 (Joe Clements); "Untamed Frontier" 1952 (Charlie Fentress); "Column South" 1953 (Lt. Fry); "Dawn at Socorro" 1954 (Tom Ferris); "Jesse James Versus the Daltons" 1954 (Gilkie); "The Man from Bitter Ridge" 1955 (Jace Gordon); "Rage at Dawn" 1955 (Bill Reno); "Friendly Persuasion" 1956 (Bushwhacker); "Thirteen Fighting Men" 1960 (Prescott). ¶TV: *Frontier*—"The Texicans" 1-8-56 (Jim Reed), "The Ballad of Pretty Polly" 4-1-56 (Tom); *Maverick*—"Point Blank" 9-29-57 (Wes Corwin), "The Judas Mask" 11-2-58 (Elliot Larkin); *Colt .45*—"The Three Thousand Dollar Bullet" 11-1-57 (Bill Hodges), "Split Second" 3-14-58 (Tack Bleeker), "Attack" 5-24-60 (Seth Johnson); *Wyatt Earp*—"Indian Wife" 12-10-57 (Dick Melaney), "The Gatling Gun" 10-21-58 (Chief Joseph); *Wagon Train*—"The Clara Beauchamp Story" 12-11-57 (Pearson); *Fury*—"The Baby Sitters" 2-8-58 (Dan); *Cheyenne*—"White Warrior" 3-11-58 (Lyle Bordon), "Standoff" 5-6-58 (Beloin), "Trial by Conscience" 10-26-59 (Quinn Lacy); *Sugarfoot*—"The Desperadoes" 1-6-59 (Col. Winslow), "Wolf Pack 2-2-60 (Martin Rain); *Rough Riders*—"The End of Nowhere" 2-12-59 (Kenyon Sprague); *26 Men*—"The Last Kill" 4-28-59, "Cave-In" 5-12-59; *Zorro*—"Finders Keepers" 7-2-59 (Senor Lopez); *Riverboat*—"Salvage Pirates" 1-31-60 (Jacques Tremaine); *Walt Disney Presents*—"Elfego Baca: Gus Tomlin Is

Dead" 3-25-60 (Ben Palmer); *The Deputy*—"Dark Reward" 3-26-60 (Matt Ross); *Wanted—Dead or Alive*—"Death, Divided by Three" 4-23-60 (Jake Lorenz); *Lawman*—"Man on a Mountain" 6-12-60 (Ben Jaegers); *Zane Grey Theater*—"Morning Incident" 12-29-60 (Lucas); *Bronco*—"Manitoba Manhunt" 4-3-61 (Dana Powell); *The Virginian*—"Duel at Shiloh" 1-2-63, "The Final Hour" 5-1-63; *Temple Houston*—"Thunder Gap" 11-21-63 (Jess Newmark); *Daniel Boone*—"The Witness" 1-25-68.

Garner, Don. Films: "My Darling Clementine" 1946 (James Earp); "Two Flags West" 1950 (Ash Cooper); "Wild Stallion" 1952; "Law and Order" 1953 (Johnny Benton).

Garner, Jack. Films: "Wild Rovers" 1971 (Cap Swilling); "The New Maverick" TVM-1978 (Homer); "Bret Maverick" TVM-1981 (Jack); "No Man's Land" TVM-1984 (Sam Craypool); "Sunset" 1988 (Cowboy Henry). ¶TV: *Daniel Boone*—"Be Thankful for the Fickleness of Women" 9-19-68; *Lancer*—"The Lawman" 10-22-68 (Gibbs); *Gunsmoke*—"Morgan" 3-2-70 (Telegrapher), "The Gun" 11-19-70 (Kemble), "The Deadly Innocent" 12-17-73 (Pete); *Alias Smith and Jones*—"The Girl in Boxcar Number Three" 2-11-71 (Stacey).

Garner, James (1928-). Films: "Shoot-Out at Medicine Bend" 1957 (Maitland); "Alias Jesse James" 1959 (Bret Maverick); "Duel at Diablo" 1966 (Jess Remsberg); "Hour of the Gun" 1967 (Wyatt Earp); "Support Your Local Sheriff" 1969 (Jason McCullough); "Man Called Sledge" 1971-Ital./U.S. (Luther Sledge); "Skin Game" 1971 (Quncy Drew); "Support Your Local Gunfighter" 1971 (Latigo Smith); "One Little Indian" 1973 (Clint Keyes); "The Castaway Cowboy" 1974 (Lincoln Costain); "The New Maverick" TVM-1978 (Brett Maverick); "Bret Maverick" TVM-1981 (Bret Maverick); "Sunset" 1988 (Wyatt Earp); "Maverick" 1994 (Marshal Zane Cooper). ¶TV: *Cheyenne*—"Mountain Fortress" 9-20-55, "The Black Hawk War" 1-24-56 (Lt. Rogers), "The Last Train West" 5-29-56 (Rev. Brett Maller); *Zane Grey Theater*—"Stars Over Texas" 12-28-56 (Lt. Jim Collins); *Maverick*—Regular 1957-61 (Bret Maverick), "Pappy" 9-13-59 (Pappy Maverick); *Nichols*—Regular 1971-72 (Nichols); *Young Maverick*—"Clancy" 11-28-79 (Bret Maverick); *Bret Maverick*—Regular 1981-82 (Bret Maverick).

Garner, Paul "Mousie" (1909-).

TV: *Maverick*—"Guatemala City" 1-31-60 (Newsboy).

Garner, Peggy Ann (1931-10/16/84). TV: *Zane Grey Theater*—"Deception" 4-14-60 (Sarah); *Tate*—"Stopover" 6-15-60 (Julie); *Bonanza*—"The Rival" 4-15-61 (Cameo Johnson); *Have Gun Will Travel*—"Dream Girl" 2-10-62 (Ginger); *Rawhide*—"Incident at Spider Rock" 1-18-63.

Garnett, Gale (1946-). TV: *Tales of Wells Fargo*—"Winter Storm" 3-3-62 (Ruth); *Bonanza*—"The Deserter" 10-21-62 (Maria); *Have Gun Will Travel*—"The Debutante" 1-19-63 (Prudence Powers).

Garon, Pauline (1904-8/27/65). Films: "The Splendid Road" 1925 (Angel Allie); "Song of the Saddle" 1936.

Garr, Eddie (1900-9/3/56). TV: *Circus Boy*—"The Great Gambino" 10-7-56 (Doctor).

Garralaga, Martin (1895-6/12/81). Films: "The Gay Caballero" 1932 (Manuel); "Law of the 45's" 1935 (Sanchez); "Lawless Borders" 1935; "Under the Pampas Moon" 1935 (Court Clerk); "Song of the Gringo" 1936 (Don Esteban Del Valle); "Boots of Destiny" 1937 (Jose Vasco); "Riders of the Rockies" 1937 (Captain Mendoza); "Outlaw Express" 1938 (Don Ricardo); "Rose of the Rio Grande" 1938 (Luis); "Starlight Over Texas" 1938 (Capt. Gomez); "The Fighting Gringo" 1939 (Pedro); "Law of the Pampas" 1939 (Bolo Carrier); "Overland with Kit Carson" 1939-serial; "Legion of the Lawless" 1940; "Rangers of Fortune" 1940 (Mexican Officer); "Rhythm of the Rio Grande" 1940 (Pablo); "Stage to Chino" 1940 (Pedro); "Wagon Train" 1940; "The Son of Davy Crockett" 1941; "In Old California" 1942; "Undercover Man" 1942 (Cortez); "The Outlaw" 1943 (Waiter); "Black Arrow" 1944-serial (Pancho); "The Laramie Trail" 1944; "The Cisco Kid Returns" 1945 (Pancho); "In Old New Mexico" 1945 (Pancho); "South of the Rio Grande" 1945 (Pancho); "West of the Pecos" 1945 (Don Manuel); "Beauty and the Bandit" 1946; "Don Ricardo Returns" 1946; "The Gay Cavalier" 1946; "Plainsman and the Lady" 1946 (Alvarades); "South of Monterey" 1946; "The Virginian" 1946 (Spanish Ed); "Riding the California Trail" 1947; "Twilight on the Rio Grande" 1947 (Mucho Pesos); "Four Faces West" 1948 (Florencio); "Madonna of the Desert" 1948 (Papa Baravelli); "The Treasure of the Sierra Madre" 1948 (Railroad

Conductor); "The Big Sombrero" 1949 (Felipe Gonzales); "The Last Bandit" 1949 (Patrick Moreno); "Susanna Pass" 1949 (Carlos Mendoza); "Bandit Queen" 1950 (Father Antonio); "The Kid from Texas" 1950 (Morales); "The Outriders" 1950 (Father Demasco); "Branded" 1951 (Hernandez); "The Fighter" 1952 (Luis); "Law and Order" 1953 (Rancher); "San Antone" 1953 (Mexican); "Jubilee Trail" 1954 (Don Rafael Velasco); "The Law vs. Billy the Kid" 1954 (Miguel Bolanos); "A Man Alone" 1955 (Ortega); "Blackjack Ketchum, Desperado" 1956 (Jaime Brigo); "Gunsight Ridge" 1957 (Ramon); "Man in the Shadow" 1957 (Jesus Cisneros); "The Left-Handed Gun" 1958 (Saval); "Lonely Are the Brave" 1962 (Old Man). ¶TV: *Death Valley Days*—"The Saint's Portrait" 10-11-54 (Father Lopez); *The Lone Ranger*—"Tenderfoot" 11-25-54; *Circus Boy*—"The Little Gypsy" 12-2-56 (King Kolya); *Have Gun Will Travel*—"Three Bells to Perdido" 9-14-57; *The Restless Gun*—"Jody" 11-4-57 (Porfirio); *El Coyote Rides*—Pilot 1958 (Father Gomez); *Jim Bowie*—"The Puma" 5-23-58 (Don Sebastian Gomez); *The Texan*—"A Tree for Planting" 11-10-58 (Ramirez); *Rawhide*—"Incident of the Stalking Death" 11-13-59 (Pedrillo); *Sugarfoot*—"Outlaw Island" 11-24-59 (Pedro); *The Tall Man*—"Maria's Little Lamb" 2-25-61 (Miguel); *Gunsmoke*—"The Jackals" 2-12-68 (Older Padre); *The High Chaparral*—"The Glory Soldiers" 1-31-69, "Once, on a Day in Spring" 2-14-69 (Francisco), "The Lion Sleeps" 3-28-69.

Garrard, Don. Films: "Flaming Frontier" 1958-Can. (Sgt. Haggerty); "Wolf Dog" 1958-Can. (Trent).

Garrett, Andi. TV: *Wild Wild West*—"The Night of the Ready-Made Corpse" 11-25-66 (Barmaid).

Garrett, Don. Films: "Seminole" 1953 (Officer). ¶TV: *Wild Bill Hickok*—"The Music Teacher" 12-2-52; *The Adventures of Rin Tin Tin*—"Yo-o Rinty" 10-12-56 (Jordan).

Garrett, Gary. Films: "Code of the Saddle" 1947; "Flashing Guns" 1947 (Duke); "Land of the Lawless" 1947; "Law Comes to Gunsight" 1947; "Prairie Express" 1947 (Kent); "Song of the Wasteland" 1947; "Trailing Danger" 1947; "Valley of Fear" 1947. ¶TV: *The Cisco Kid*—"Carrier Pigeon" 11-3-51.

Garrett, Leif (1958-). Films: "God's Gun" 1976-Ital./Israel (Johnny); "Kid Vengeance" 1976-Ital./U.S./Israel; "Peter Lundy and the Medicine Hat Stallion" TVM-1977 (Peter Lundy). ¶TV: *Gunsmoke*—"The Sodbusters" 11-20-72 (John Callahan).

Garrett, Michael. Films: "The Brass Legend" 1956 (Charlie). ¶TV: *Wyatt Earp*—"The Pinkertons" 3-20-56; *Zane Grey Theater*—"The Lariat" 11-2-56 (Sheriff); *Maverick*—"Maverick and Juliet" 1-17-60 (Ty Carteret); *The Deputy*—"The Deathly Quiet" 5-27-61 (Con Hawkins).

Garrett, Sam. Films: "Flying Lariats" 1931 (Sam Dunbar); "Vigilantes Are Coming" 1936-serial (Rancher); "One Man Justice" 1937 (Deputy Sheriff); "Western Caravans" 1939 (Joe).

Garrick, Richard (1879-8/21/62). Films: "Green Grass of Wyoming" 1948 (Old Timer); "Viva Zapata!" 1952 (Old General); "Law and Order" 1953 (Judge Williams); "Powder River" 1953 (Ferry Master); "Riding Shotgun" 1954 (Walters). ¶TV: *My Friend Flicka*—"The Royal Carriage" 3-16-56.

Garrison, Sean (1937-). TV: *Cheyenne*—"The Empty Gun" 2-25-58 (Mike); *Colt .45*—"Circle of Fear" 3-7-58 (Chuck Dudley); *The Big Valley*—"Young Marauders" 10-6-65 (Lloyd Garner); *Gunsmoke*—"Sanctuary" 2-26-66 (Rev. Mr. John Porter); *Dundee and the Culhane*—Regular 1967 (the Culhane); *Alias Smith and Jones*—"The Fifth Victim" 3-25-71 (Harvey Bishop); *Cliffhangers*—"The Secret Empire" 1979 (Yannuck).

Garro, Joseph A. Films: "Under California Stars" 1948 (Joe); "Twilight in the Sierras" 1950 (Henchman).

Garrone, Riccardo. Films: "Two Sergeants of General Custer" 1965-Ital./Span.; "Deguello" 1966-Ital.; "If You Want to Live ... Shoot!" 1967-Ital./Span.; "The Bang Bang Kid" 1968-U.S./Span./Ital. (Killer Kissock); "Django the Bastard" 1969-Ital./Span.; "No Room to Die" 1969-Ital.; "Kill Django ... Kill First" 1971-Ital.; "Man Called Sledge" 1971-Ital./U.S.; "Return of Halleluja" 1972-Ital./Ger.; "Sting of the West" 1972-Ital.; "What Am I Doing in the Middle of the Revolution?" 1973-Ital.

Garroway, Dave (1913-7/21/82). TV: *Alias Smith and Jones*—"The Man Who Corrupted Hadleyburg" 1-27-72 (Judge Martin).

Garson, Greer (1908-). Films: "Strange Lady in Town" 1955 (Dr. Julia Winslow Garth). ¶TV: *The Men from Shiloh*—"Lady at the Bar" 11-4-70 (Frances Finch).

Garth, Michael. Films: "Good Day for a Hanging" 1958 (Pike). ¶TV: *Tales of the Texas Rangers*—"Tornado" 11-5-55 (Sergeant); *Death Valley Days*—"Wildcat's First Piano" 12-5-55 (Chuck Latham).

Garth, Otis (1901-12/21/55). Films: "The Law vs. Billy the Kid" 1954 (Gov. Wallace).

Garver, Kathy (1948-). TV: *The Travels of Jaimie McPheeters*—"The Day of the Pawnees" 12-22-63 & 12-29-63 (Pretty Walker); *Death Valley Days*—"Magic Locket" 5-16-65 (Dorita Duncan), "Lady of the Plains" 7-23-66 (Peggy Conway); *The Big Valley*—"The Royal Road" 3-3-69 (Laura Hayden).

Garvey, Robert. Films: "The Black Whip" 1956 (Red Leg); "Pardners" 1956 (Townsman).

Garwood, John (1927-). TV: *Great Adventure*—"The Pathfinder" 3-6-64 (Striker).

Garwood, Kelton. Films: "The Miracle of the Hills" 1959 (Seth Jones). ¶TV: *Hotel De Paree*—"A Rope Is for Hanging" 11-6-59 (Simp); *Have Gun Will Travel*—"Charley Red Dog" 12-12-59 (Joe Denver), "Never Help the Devil" 4-16-60 (Informer); *The Rebel*—"The Vagrants" 12-20-59 (Charlie); *Rawhide*—"Incident of the Stargazer" 4-1-60; *The Rifleman*—"Sins of the Father" 4-19-60; *Wagon Train*—"The Joe Muharich Story" 4-19-61 (Claude); *Two Faces West*—"Double Action" 5-8-61 (Ridge); *Gunsmoke*—"Colorado Sheriff" 6-17-61 (Sam Jones), "The Hunger" 11-17-62 (Fred), "Parson Comes to Town" 4-30-66 (Percy Crump); *Empire*—"Echo of a Man" 12-11-62 (Jennison); *Laredo*—"Which Way Did They Go?" 11-18-65; *Daniel Boone*—"The Prisoners" 2-10-66 (Rufus Hubbard); *The Big Valley*—"The Great Safe Robbery" 11-21-66 (Elwood Barnes).

Garwood, William (1884-12/28/50). Films: "Hearts and Hoofs" 1913; "Cameo of Yellowstone" 1914; "Redbird Wins" 1914; "A Ticket to Red Horse Gulch" 1914; "A Proxy Husband" 1919.

Gary, Lorraine (1935-). TV: *The Men from Shiloh*—"Hannah" 12-30-70 (Mrs. Nelson); *Hec Ramsey*—"The Green Feather Mystery" 12-17-72 (Bella Grant).

Gary, Paul. Films: "Gunfight at the O.K. Corral" 1957 (Killer). ¶TV: *Wyatt Earp*—"Shootin' Woman" 1-1-57 (Lacey), "The Trail to Tombstone" 9-8-59 (Slim); *Laramie*—"The Turn of the Wheel" 4-3-62 (Billy O'Neill).

Gassman, Vittorio (1922-).

Films: "What Am I Doing in the Middle of the Revolution?" 1973-Ital. (Don Albino).

Gastrock, Phil (1877-4/10/56). Films: "Desert Law" 1918 (Logan); "A Man's Country" 1919 (Connell); "Lone Hand Wilson" 1920 (Andy Walker); "The Ranger and the Law" 1921 (Apache Joe, the Weasel); "Blue Blazes" 1922 (Lawyer); "The Masked Avenger" 1922 (Ebenezer Jones).

Gates, Larry (1915-). Films: "Take Me to Town" 1953 (Ed Daggett); "One Foot in Hell" 1960 (Doc Selter); "Cattle King" 1963 (President Chester A. Arthur); "Hour of the Gun" 1967 (John P. Clum); "Death of a Gunfighter" 1969 (Mayor Chesteer Sayre). ¶TV: *Bonanza*—"The Hopefuls" 10-8-60 (Jacob Darien); *The Outlaws*—"The Waiting Game" 1-19-61 (Teel); *Stoney Burke*—"Bandwagon" 12-17-62 (Senator Lockridge); *Rawhide*—"Duel at Daybreak" 11-16-65 (Mason Woodruff); *Cimarron Strip*—"Broken Wing" 9-21-67 (Kilgallen); *The Outcasts*—"The Night Riders" 11-25-68 (General Carver).

Gates, Maxine (1917-7/27/90). Films: "Oklahoma Annie" 1952 (Tillie); "Giant" 1956 (Mrs. Sarge). ¶TV: *The Gene Autry Show*—"Ghost Ranch" 11-12-55; *Rawhide*—"The Prairie Elephant" 11-17-61.

Gates, Nancy (1926-). Films: "Nevada" 1944 (Hattie Ide); "Cheyenne Takes Over" 1947 (Foy); "Check Your Guns" 1948 (Cathy); "Roll, Thunder, Roll" 1949 (Carol Loomis); "Masterson of Kansas" 1954 (Amy Merrick); "Stranger on Horseback" 1955 (Caroline Webb); "The Brass Legend" 1956 (Linda); "The Rawhide Trail" 1958 (Marsha Collins); "The Gunfight at Dodge City" 1959 (Lily); "Comanche Station" 1960 (Mrs. Lowe). ¶TV: *Trackdown*—"Killer Take All" 9-5-58 (Ellen Hackett); *Wagon Train*—"The Millie Davis Story" 11-26-58 (Millie Davis), "The Shiloh Degnan Story" 11-7-62 (Mrs. Marriott), "The Grover Allen Story" 2-3-64 (Della); *Maverick*—"Burial Ground of the Gods" 3-30-59 (Laura Stanton), "Passage to Fort Doom" 3-8-59 (Mrs. Chapman); *Riverboat*—"Payment in Full" 9-13-59 (Sister Angela); *Laramie*—"Death Wind" 2-2-60 (Angela Cole); *Wichita Town*—"The Legend of Tom Horn" 3-30-60 (Laurie Carter); *Zane Grey Theater*—"Storm Over Eden" 5-4-61 (Ellen Gaynor); *Tales of Wells Fargo*—"Jeremiah" 11-11-61 (Amelia Cavendish); *Gunsmoke*—"The Prisoner" 5-19-62 (Sarah); *The Virginian*—

"Portrait of a Widow" 12-9-64; *Rawhide*—"Clash at Broken Bluff" 11-2-65 (Cassie Webster); *The Loner*—"The House Rules at Mrs. Wayne's" 11-6-65 (Mrs. Wayne); *Bonanza*—"Her Brother's Keeper" 3-6-66 (Claire Amory).

Gates, Rick (1947-). Films: "Hang 'Em High" 1968 (Ben). TV: *The High Chaparral*—"The Hostage" 3-5-71 (Cullen); *Gunsmoke*—"Drago" 11-22-71 (Gillis).

Gateson, Marjorie (1891-4/17/77). Films: "Arizona Mahoney" 1936 (Safrony Jones); "Geronimo" 1940 (Mrs. Steele); "Dudes Are Pretty People" 1942 (Aunt Elsie).

Gatlin, Jerry (1933-). Films: "The Hallelujah Trail" 1965 (1st Brother-in-Law); "The Sons of Katie Elder" 1965 (Amboy); "An Eye for an Eye" 1966 (Jonas); "Blue" 1968 (Wes Lambert); "Five Card Stud" 1968 (Stranger); "Big Jake" 1971 (Stubby); "Buck and the Preacher" 1972 (Deputy); "The Cowboys" 1972 (Howdy); "The Culpepper Cattle Company" 1972 (Wallop); "The Honkers" 1972 (Shorty); "The Legend of Nigger Charley" 1972 (Sheriff Rhinehart); "Ulzana's Raid" 1972; "The Train Robbers" 1973 (Sam Turner); "Bite the Bullet" 1975; "Nevada Smith" TVM-1975 (Brill); "Rooster Cogburn" 1975 (Nose); "The Duchess and the Dirtwater Fox" 1976 (Bloodworth Gang Member); "Cattle Annie and Little Britches" 1981 (Cop); "Cowboy" TVM-1983 (Stunts); "Triumphs of a Man Called Horse" 1984 (Winslow); "Bonanza: The Next Generation" TVM-1988. ¶TV: *Have Gun Will Travel*—"Bandit" 5-12-62, "Man in an Hourglass" 12-1-62; *Wide Country*—"The Bravest Man in the World" 12-6-62 (Vern); *Bonanza*—"Thorton's Account" 11-1-70 (Harvey), "Top Hand" 1-17-71 (Quincy), "The Marriage of Theodora Duffy" 1-9-73 (Barnes); *Gunsmoke*—"The River" 9-11-72 & 9-18-72 (Lapin), "The Widow-Maker" 10-8-73 (Buck Lennard), "The Iron Blood of Courage" 2-18-74 (Toey); *Father Murphy*—"The Horse" 3-21-82 (Rawlins).

Gatteys, Bennye. TV: *Tales of Wells Fargo*—"Death Raffle" 10-21-61 (Jessamie); *The Tall Man*—"The Leopard's Spots" 11-11-61 (Charity); *Stoney Burke*—"Five by Eight" 12-10-62 (Joyce Carrol); *Laramie*—"The Dispossessed" 2-19-63 (Ellen); *Gunsmoke*—"The Far Places" 4-6-63 (Millie Smith).

Gatzert, Nate (1890-9/1/59). Films: "Ranger Courage" 1937.

Gaunthier, Gene (1880-12/18/66). Films: "The Stage Rustler" 1908; "The Mystery of Pine Creek Camp" 1913; "Wolfe, or the Conquest of Quebec" 1914.

Gaut, Slim (1893-4/17/64). Films: "Square Dance Jubilee" 1949 (Secretary); "Silver City" 1951 (Storekeeper).

Gautier, Dick (1939-). TV: *Zorro and Son*—6-1-83 (El Excellente).

Gavin, James (1932-). Films: "Face of a Fugitive" 1959 (Stockton). ¶TV: *Cheyenne*—"The Bounty Killer" 10-23-56 (Sevier); *Zane Grey Theater*—"They Were Four" 3-15-57 (Dutch); *Tales of the Texas Rangers*—"Whirlwind Raiders" 10-13-57 (Capt. Cammack); *Fury*—"Robber's Roost" 3-22-58 (Fred); *Tales of Wells Fargo*—"Hide Jumpers" 1-27-58 (Billy Thompson); *Gunsmoke*—"Overland Express" 5-31-58 (Wells); *Rawhide*—"Incident of the Town in Terror" 3-6-59, "Incident at Sulphur Creek" 3-11-60, "Incident of the Slavemaster" 11-11-60, "Grandma's Money" 2-23-62 (Hank Higgins); *Have Gun Will Travel*—"Heritage of Anger" 6-6-59 (Avery); *Maverick*—"The Sheriff of Duck 'n' Shoot" 9-27-59 (Buck Danton), "Hadley's Hunters" 9-25-60 (Deputy Smith); *Two Faces West*—"Fallen Gun" 11-21-60; *The Rifleman*—"Six Years and a Day" 1-3-61 (Lee Marston); *Wagon Train*—"The Shiloh Degnan Story" 11-7-62 (McClellan); *The Virginian*—"Portrait of a Widow" 12-9-64 (Claude Boulanger); *The Big Valley*—"Young Marauders" 10-6-65 (Graff), "Wagonload of Dreams" 1-2-67 (Sheriff), "Boy into Man" 1-16-67 (Sheriff), "Down Shadow Street" 1-23-67 (Sheriff), "The Haunted Gun" 2-6-67 (Sheriff), "Plunder at Hawk's Grove" 3-13-67 (Sheriff), "The Lady from Mesa" 4-3-67; *A Man Called Shenandoah*—"The Verdict" 11-1-65 (Ferguson); *Cimarron Strip*—"The Search" 11-9-67 (Herald); *Wild Wild West*—"The Night of the Iron Fist" 12-8-67 (Sheriff); *The High Chaparral*—"The Last Hundred Miles" 1-24-69.

Gavin, John (1928-). Films: "Quantez" 1957 (Teach); "Cutter's Trail" TVM-1970 (Ben Cutter). ¶TV: *Destry*—Regular 1964 (Harrison Destry).

Gavric, Aleksandar. Films: "The Desperado Trail" 1965-Ger./Yugo. (Kid); "Flaming Frontier" 1965-Ger./Yugo.

Gay, Nancy. Films: "The Man from the Rio Grande" 1943 (Doris

King); "Overland Mail Robbery" 1943 (Lola Patterson); "Pride of the Plains" 1944 (Joan Bradford).

Gaye, Gregory (1900-8/23/93). Films: "The Man from Dakota" 1940 (Col. Borodin); "When the Redskins Rode" 1951 (St. Pierre). ¶TV: *Judge Roy Bean*—"Deliver the Body" 6-1-56 (Bradford), "Terror Rides the Trail" 6-1-56 (Doc Warren); *The Dakotas*—"Justice at Eagle's Nest" 3-11-63 (Anton Lang).

Gaye, Howard (-12/26/55). Films: "Arms and the Gringo" 1914.

Gaye, Lisa (1935-). Films: "Drums Across the River" 1954 (Jennie Marlowe). ¶TV: *Jim Bowie*—"Trapline" 10-5-56 (Jeanne), "Spanish Intrigue" 2-8-57 (Maira Miro); *Have Gun Will Travel*—"Helen of Abajinian" 12-28-57 (Helen Abajinian), "Gun Shy" 3-29-58 (Nancy); *Zorro*—"The Fall of Monastario" 1-2-58 (Viceroy's Daughter); *Tombstone Territory*—"The Tin Gunman" 4-16-58 (Lizette), "Grave Near Tombstone" 5-22-59 (Nancy); *Northwest Passage*—"The Gunsmith" 9-28-58 (Natula), "Surprise Attack" 10-5-58 (Natula); *The Californians*—"The Man Who Owned San Francisco" 12-30-58 (Donna Louise); *Black Saddle*—"Client: McQueen" 1-24-59 (Susan McQueen Kent); *Bat Masterson*—"Sharpshooter" 2-11-59 (Lori Dowling), "Buffalo Kill" 7-29-59 (Susan Carver), "The Fatal Garment" 5-25-61 (Elena); *Colt .45*—"Law West of the Pecos" 6-7-59 (June Webster); *Sugarfoot*—"The Trial of the Canary Kid" 9-15-59 (Mrs. Hoyt); *Pony Express*—"The Peace Offering" 11-18-59; *Cheyenne*—"Outcast of Cripple Creek" 2-29-60 (Jenny), "Counterfeit Gun" 10-10-60 (Francie Scott); *Death Valley Days*—"The Million Dollar Pants" 4-19-60 (Yvonne Benet), "A General Without a Cause" 4-12-61 (Dolores), "The Other White Man" 11-15-64 (Healing Woman), "The Captain Dick Mine" 11-27-65, "The Rider" 12-4-65, "The Gypsy" 1-21-67 (Gypsy), "The Other Side of the Mountain" 4-13-68 (Rosie), "Lottie's Legacy" 11-23-68, "Tracy's Triumph" 10-4-69 (Lisa); *Wanted—Dead or Alive*—"Journey for Josh" 10-5-60 (Susan); *Rawhide*—"Incident of the Slavemaster" 11-11-60 (Odette Laurier); *Maverick*—"A State of Siege" 1-1-61 (Soledad); *Wagon Train*—"The Tiburcio Mendez Story" 3-22-61 (Alma); *Tales of Wells Fargo*—"The Dowry" 7-10-61 (Michelle Bovarde), "Kelly's Clover Girls" 12-9-61 (Sunset); *Laramie*—"The Perfect Gift" 1-2-62 (Winona); *Bronco*—"One Evening

in Abilene" 3-19-62 (Donna Coe); *Wild Wild West*—"The Night of the Skulls" 12-16-66 (Lorelei), "The Night of the Falcon" 11-10-67 (Lana Benson).

Gayer, Echlin P. (1878-2/14/26). Films: "Sandy Burke of the U-Bar-U" 1919 (Hon. Cyril Harcourt Stammers).

Gayle, Monica. TV: *The Cowboys*—"A Matter of Honor" 3-20-74 (Laurinda Tatum).

Gaynes, George (1917-). TV: *Cheyenne*—"Vengeance Is Mine" 11-26-62 (Rod Delaplane); *Empire*—"The Four Thumbs Story" 1-8-63 (Johnson); *Bonanza*—"The Late Ben Cartwright" 3-3-68 (Purdy); *The Quest*—"Day of Outrage" 10-27-76 (Gorham).

Gaynor, Grace. TV: *Bonanza*—"The Ride" 1-21-62 (Mary Enders); *Wild Wild West*—"The Night of the Bogus Bandits" 4-7-67 (Pearling Hastings), "The Night of the Simian Terror" 2-16-68 (Naomi Buckley).

Gaynor, Janet (1907-9/14/84). Films: "Fade Away Foster" 1926; "Pep of the Lazy J" 1926.

Gaynor, Jock. TV: *Wichita Town*—"Ruby Dawes" 1-6-60 (Joe Malone); *Colt .45*—"Alibi" 4-12-60; *Wyatt Earp*—"Roscoe Turns Detective" 5-3-60 (Lieutenant Grang); *The Outlaws*—Regular 1960-62 (Deputy Heck Martin); *Tate*—"The Return of Jessica Jackson" 9-14-60 (Tayibo); *Cheyenne*—"Incident at Dawson Flats" 1-9-61 (Johnny McIntyre); *Rawhide*—"Incident of the Fish Out of the Water" 2-17-61 (Ogalia), "Deserter's Patrol" 2-9-62 (Ogalia); *Gunslinger*—"Johnny Sergeant" 5-4-61 (Johnny Sereant); *Laramie*—"The Unvanquished" 3-12-63 (Giamo); *Iron Horse*—"Pride at the Bottom of the Barrel" 10-10-66 (Cochero), "The Red Tornado" 2-20-67 (Cabot).

Gaynor, Mitzi (1931-). Films: "Three Young Texans" 1954 (Rusty Blair).

Gaze, Gwen. Films: "Bar 20 Justice" 1938 (Ann Dennis); "Partners of the Plains" 1938 (Lorna Drake); "West of Pinto Basin" 1940 (Joan Brown); "Underground Rustlers" 1941 (Irene); "Wrangler's Roost" 1941 (Molly); "Two Fisted Justice" 1943 (Joan).

Gazzaniga, Don (1930-). TV: *Wagon Train*—"The Nancy Davis Story" 5-16-62 (Jeb Martin); *Wild Wild West*—"The Night of the Sudden Death" 10-8-65 (Hotel Clerk); *Rango*—"If You Can't Take It with You, Don't Go" 4-21-67 (Ranger Morgan).

Gazzolo, Virgilio (1928-). Films: "Day of Anger" 1967-Ital./Ger.

Geary, Bud (Maine Geary) (1899-2/22/46). Films: "Four Hearts" 1922 (Bob Berkley); "The Smoking Trail" 1924; "The Arizona Romeo" 1925 (Richard Barr); "Song of the Saddle" 1936; "Zorro's Fighting Legion" 1939-serial (Dungeon Heavy); "Adventures of Red Ryder" 1940-serial (Pecos Bates); "King of the Royal Mounted" 1940-serial (Klondike); "Northwest Mounted Police" 1940 (Constable Herrick); "The Bandit Trail" 1941; "Gangs of Sonora" 1941; "Gauchos of El Dorado" 1941; "Outlaws of the Cherokee Trail" 1941; "West of Cimarron" 1941; "Bandit Ranger" 1942; "Cowboy Serenade" 1942; "Home in Wyomin'" 1942; "Overland to Deadwood" 1942; "The Phantom Plainsmen" 1942 (Outlaw); "Pirates of the Prairie" 1942; "Raiders of the Range" 1942; "The Sombrero Kid" 1942; "The Sundown Kid" 1942 (Nick Parker); "The Blocked Trail" 1943; "Bordertown Gunfighters" 1943 (Buck Newcombe); "Calling Wild Bill Elliott" 1943; "Canyon City" 1943; "Carson City Cyclone" 1943 (Walker); "Death Valley Manhunt" 1943 (Roberts); "In Old Oklahoma" 1943; "The Man from the Rio Grande" 1943; "The Man from Thunder River" 1943; "Overland Mail Robbery" 1943 (Slade); "Santa Fe Scouts" 1943; "Thundering Trails" 1943; "Beneath Western Skies" 1944 (Hank); "Cheyenne Wildcat" 1944; "Code of the Prairie" 1944 (Lem); "Cowboy from Lonesome River" 1944; "Firebrands of Arizona" 1944 (Slugs); "Hidden Valley Outlaws" 1944; "The Laramie Trail" 1944; "Marshal of Reno" 1944; "Mojave Firebrand" 1944; "Outlaws of Santa Fe" 1944 (Steve); "Pride of the Plains" 1944 (Gerard); "The San Antonio Kid" 1944; "Sheriff of Las Vegas" 1944; "Sheriff of Sundown" 1944 (Ward); "Silver City Kid" 1944; "Stagecoach to Monterey" 1944; "Tucson Raiders" 1944; "Vigilantes of Dodge City" 1944; "The Cherokee Flash" 1945; "Colorado Pioneers" 1945; "Great Stagecoach Robbery" 1945; "Lone Texas Ranger" 1945; "Marshal of Laredo" 1945; "Oregon Trail" 1945 (Fletch); "Phantom of the Plains" 1945; "Santa Fe Saddlemates" 1945; "The Topeka Terror" 1945 (Clyde Flint); "Trail of Kit Carson" 1945; "Wagon Wheels Westward" 1945; "Heading West" 1946; "King of the Forest Rangers" 1946-serial (Rance Barton); "Landrush" 1946 (Hawkins); "The Man from Rainbow

Valley" 1946 (Tracy); "Sheriff of Red-wood Valley" 1946; "Smoky" 1946 (Peters); "Thunder Town" 1946 (Chuck Wilson); "Under Arizona Skies" 1946; "Frisco Tornado" 1950.

Geary, Cynthia. Films: "8 Seconds" 1994 (Kellie Frost).

Geary, Maine. see Geary, Bud.

Gebhart, George (1879-5/2/19). Films: "The Girl and the Outlaw" 1908; "The Greaser's Gauntlet" 1908; "The Red Girl" 1908; "The Tavern-Keeper's Daughter" 1908; "Getting His Man" 1911; "The Sheriff's Brother" 1911; "At Rolling Forks" 1912; "Across the Sierras" 1912; "The Cactus Country Lawyer" 1912; "The Frame-Up" 1912; "Her Indian Hero" 1912; "The Love Trail" 1912; "The Penalty Paid" 1912; "A Redman's Loyalty" 1912; "A Redskin's Appeal" 1912; "The Renegade" 1912; "The Mexican's Defeat" 1913; "The Pioneer's Recompense" 1913; "The Outlaw Reforms" 1914 (Bill); "The Great Barrier" 1915; "Man of Courage" 1922 (El Cholo).

Geddes, Jack. Films: "Tough Assignment" 1949 (Rancher); "I Shot Billy the Kid" 1950 (Sheriff); "Marshal of Heldorado" 1950 (Customer).

Geer, Ellen (1941-). Films: "Kung Fu: The Movie" TVM-1986. ¶TV: *The New Land*—"The Word Is: Growth" 9-21-74.

Geer, Lenny (1913-1/9/89). Films: "Masterson of Kansas" 1954 (Lt. Post); "Robbers' Roost" 1955 (Sparrow); "The Great Locomotive Chase" 1956 (J.A. Wilson); "The Oklahoman" 1957 (Bushwacker); "The Tall Stranger" 1957 (Worker); "Shoot Out at Big Sag" 1962. ¶TV: *Wild Bill Hickok*—"Silver Stage Holdup" 10-16-51; *The Restless Gun*—"The Nowhere Kid" 10-20-58 (Jeb); *Bat Masterson*—"Cheyenne Club" 12-17-58 (Woody); *Wagon Train*—"The Last Man" 2-11-59 (Mr. Kenny), "The Duke Shannon Story" 4-26-61 (Clay), "The Pearlie Garnet Story" 2-24-64 (Cole); *The Rifleman*—"The Indian" 2-17-59; *Black Saddle*—"Client: Steele" 3-21-59 (Norton); *Wanted—Dead or Alive*—"Jason" 1-30-60; *Wyatt Earp*—"Woman of Tucson" 11-15-60, "Johnny Behan Falls in Love" 2-14-61 (Cowboy), "Wyatt's Brothers Join Up" 6-6-61 (Hoodlum); *The Westerner*—"Treasure" 11-18-60; *Tales of Wells Fargo*—"Jeff Davis' Treasure" 12-5-60 (Amos Birely), "Assignment in Gloribee" 1-27-62 (Jeelo Curran); *Laramie*—"Run of the Hunted" 4-4-61 (Crowley), "The Barefoot Kid" 1-9-62 (Blacksmith), "Bad Blood" 12-4-62, "The Wedding Party" 1-29-63;

The Tall Man—"Sidekick" 12-23-61 (Hondo); *Wide Country*—"The Royce Bennett Story" 9-20-62; *The Virginian*—"The Brazen Bell" 10-17-62, "Impasse" 11-14-62 (Spence); *Laredo*—"Rendezvous at Arillo" 10-7-65, "A Matter of Policy" 11-11-65, "Above the Law" 1-13-66, "A Double Shot of Nepenthe" 9-30-66 (Ward), "The Other Cheek" 2-10-67; *The Loner*—"Incident in the Middle of Nowhere" 2-19-66 (Lawman).

Geer, Will (1902-4/22/78). Films: "Lust for Gold" 1949 (Deputy Ray Covin); "Broken Arrow" 1950 (Ben Slade); "Comanche Territory" 1950 (Dan'l Seeger); "The Kid from Texas" 1950 (O'Fallon); "Winchester '73" 1950 (Wyatt Earp.); "Bandolero!" 1968 (Pop Chaney); "Sam Hill: Who Killed the Mysterious Mr. Foster?" TVM-1971 (Simon Anderson); "Jeremiah Johnson" 1972 (Bear Claw); "The Hanged Man" TVM-1974 (Nameless); "Honky Tonk" TVM-1974 (Judge Cotton). ¶TV: *Gunsmoke*—"Slocum" 10-21-68 (Slocum); *Here Come the Brides*—"A Dream That Glitters" 2-26-69 (Benjamin Pruitt); *Bonanza*—"The Running Man" 3-30-69 (Calvin Butler), "The Love Child" 11-8-69 (Zac), "A Home for Jamie" 12-19-71 (Callahan); *Daniel Boone*—"Target Boone" 11-20-69 (Adam Jarrett); *Alias Smith and Jones*—"Smiler with a Gun" 10-7-71 (Seth); *Kung Fu*—"The Ancient Warrior" 5-3-73 (Judge Marcus).

Geeson, Judy (1948-). Films: "Sam Hill: Who Killed the Mysterious Mr. Foster?" TVM-1971 (Jody Kenyon).

Gehrig, Lou (1903-6/2/41). Films: "Rawhide" 1938 (Lou Gehrig).

Gehring, Ted. Films: "40 Guns to Apache Pass" 1967 (Barrett); "The Intruders" TVM-1970; "Monte Walsh" 1970 (Skimpy Eagans); "Sam Hill: Who Killed the Mysterious Mr. Foster?" TVM-1971; "Wild Rovers" 1971 (Benson Sheriff); "Bad Company" 1972 (Zeb); "The Culpepper Cattle Company" 1972 (Tascosa Bartender); "Oklahoma Crude" 1973 (Wobbly); "Mackintosh & T.J." 1975; "The Invasion of Johnson County" TVM-1976; "The Apple Dumpling Gang Rides Again" 1979 (Frank Starrett); "The Legend of the Lone Ranger" 1981 (Stillwell). ¶TV: *The Big Valley*—"Night of the Wolf" 12-1-65 (Larsh); *Gunsmoke*—"Treasure of John Walking Fox" 4-16-66 (Holtz), "The Well" 11-19-66 (Boyd), "The Prodigal" 9-25-67 (Lemuel), "Rope Fever" 12-4-67 (Keno), "Jessie" 2-19-73 (Sheriff Bradley); *Daniel*

Boone—"The Desperate Raid" 11-16-67, "Perilous Passage" 1-15-70; *Hondo*—"Hondo and the Death Drive" 12-1-67 (Kemp); *Cimarron Strip*—"Nobody" 12-7-67 (Sutter); *Bonanza*—"The Trackers" 1-7-68, "Five Candles" 3-2-69 (Arch Tremayne), "Anatomy of a Lynching" 10-12-69 (Jim Fisher), "A Matter of Circumstance" 4-19-70 (Griffin), "The Power of Life and Death" 10-11-70 (Matt), "An Earthquake Called Callahan" 4-11-71 (Marshal), "The Grand Swing" 9-19-71 (Harlow), "The Younger Brothers' Younger Brother" 3-12-72 (Bart Younger); *The High Chaparral*—"Gold Is Where You Leave It" 1-21-68 (Shorty Bleeson), "Time of Your Life" 9-19-69 (Jed Fox), "The Hostage" 3-5-71 (Bodeen); *The Virginian*—"The Storm Gate" 11-13-68 (Edgar Wood); *Lancer*—"Yesterday's Vendetta" 1-28-69, "The Fix-It Man" 2-11-69; *Death Valley Days*—"Early Candle Lighten" 11-8-69, "The Solid Gold Pie" 11-29-69; *Nichols*—"Deer Crossing" 10-21-71; *Alias Smith and Jones*—"The McCreedy Bust — Going, Going Gone" 1-13-72 (Seth Griffin), "The Ten Days That Shook Kid Curry" 11-4-72 (Jorgensen); *Kung Fu*—"The Raiders" 1-24-74 (Sarnicky), "Barbary House" 2-15-75 (Fuller), "Flight to Orion" 2-22-75 (Fuller), "The Brothers Cain" 3-1-75 (Fuller), "Full Circle" 3-15-75 (Fuller); *The Cowboys*—"Requiem for a Lost Son" 5-8-74 (Eben Graff); *Little House on the Prairie*—Regular 1975-76 (Ebenezer Sprague); *The Quest*—"The Seminole Negro Indian Scouts" 1976; *The Oregon Trail*—"Trapper's Rendezvous" 10-12-77 (Tobias).

Geise, Sugar (1917-10/30/88). Films: "A Lady Takes a Chance" 1943 (Linda Belle); "Advance to the Rear" 1964 (Mamie).

Geldert, Clarence H. (1867-5/13/35). Films: "Jordan Is a Hard Road" 1915; "The Golden Fetter" 1917 (Flynn); "The Squaw Man's Song" 1917 (David Ladd); The Squaw Man" 1918 (Solicitor); "A Daughter of the Wolf" 1919 (Wolf Ainsworth); "Johnny, Get Your Gun" 1919 (Director); "North of '36" 1924 (Col. Griswold); "The Whipping Boss" 1924 (Jackknife Woodward); "The Bandit's Baby" 1925 (Sheriff); "The Flaming Forest" 1926 (Maj. Charles McVane); "Hands Across the Border" 1926 (Don Castro); "A One Man Game" 1927 (Jake Robbins); "The Overland Telegraph" 1929 (Maj. Hammond); "Sioux Blood" 1929 (Miles Ingram); "White Eagle" 1932 (Doctor); "The Lone Avenger" 1933

(Doctor); "Rusty Rides Alone" 1933 (Tom Martin); "The Telegraph Trail" 1933 (Cavalry Commander); "The Man Trailer" 1934 (Sheriff John Ryan); "The Westerner" 1934 (Doctor); "Border Vengeance" 1935 (Sam Griswold).

Gelin, Xavier. Films: "Judge Roy Bean" 1970-Fr. (Burke).

Gemma, Giuliano (Montgomery Wood) (1938-). Films: "Arizona Colt" 1965-Ital./Fr./Span. (Arizona Colt); "Adios Gringo" 1965-Ital./Fr./Span. (Brent Landers); "Blood for a Silver Dollar" 1965-Ital./Fr. (Gary O'Hara); "A Pistol for Ringo" 1965-Ital./Span. (Ringo); "Fort Yuma Gold" 1966-Ital./Fr./Span. (Gary Diamond); "The Return of Ringo" 1966-Ital./Span. (Ringo); "Day of Anger" 1967-Ital./Ger. (Scott Mary); "Long Days of Vengeance" 1967-Ital./Span. (Ted Barnett); "A Sky Full of Stars for a Roof" 1968-Ital. (Tim); "Wanted" 1968-Ital./Fr. (Sheriff Gary Ryan); "Alive or Preferably Dead" 1969-Span./Ital. (Monty); "The Price of Power" 1969-Ital./Span.; "Ben and Charlie" 1970-Ital. (Ben Bellow); "The White, Yellow, and the Black" 1974-Ital./Span./Fr. (White); "California" 1976-Ital./Span. (California); "Silver Saddle" 1978-Ital. (Roy Blood); "Tex and the Lord of the Deep" 1985-Ital. (Tex Willer).

Genero, Tony. TV: *Ned Blessing: The Story of My Life and Times*—"Return to Plum Creek" 8-18-93 (General Blanco), "A Ghost Story" 8-25-93 (General Blanco).

Genest, Emile (1922-). Films: "Nikki, Wild Dog of the North" 1961-U.S./Can. (Jacques Lebeau). ¶TV: *Laramie*—"Double Eagles" 11-20-62 (Duval); *Gunsmoke*—"Jeb" 5-25-63 (Chouteau), "Homecoming" 5-23-64; *The Virginian*—"Roar from the Mountain" 1-8-64 (Louis Dubois), "Harvest of Strangers" 2-16-66 (Brule); *Rawhide*—"The Race" 9-25-64 (Curt Mathison); *Daniel Boone*—"Lac Duquesne" 11-5-64 (Lac Duquesne); *Laredo*—"A Medal for Reese" 12-30-65 (Andre Bouchet); *The Road West*—"Road to Glory" 2-20-67 (Sewell Trask); *Iron Horse*—"Grapes of Grass Valley" 10-21-67 (Henri); *Walt Disney Presents*—"Kit Carson and the Mountain Men" 1-9-77 & 1-16-77 (Basil Lajeunesse).

Genge, Paul (1913-5/13/88). TV: *Zane Grey Theater*—"Trail to Nowhere" 10-2-58 (Carl Benson); *Desilu Playhouse*—"Six Guns for Donegan" 10-16-59 (Doctor); *Bonanza*—"The Hopefuls" 10-8-60, "A Dublin Lad" 1-2-66 (Judge); *Wild Wild West*—"The Night of the Bars of Hell" 3-4-66 (Kross).

Genn, Leo (1905-1/26/78). TV: *The Virginian*—"The Thirty Days of Gavin Heath" 1-22-64 (Gavin Heath).

Genovese, Mike. Films: "The Chisholms" TVM-1979.

Gentry, Beau. Films: "Hell Bent for Leather" 1960 (Stone).

Gentry, Race. Films: "The Lawless Breed" 1952 (Young John Hardin); "Black Horse Canyon" 1954 (Ti). ¶TV: *Circus Boy*—"The Swamp Man" 5-26-57 (Jean Giroux); *The Adventures of Rin Tin Tin*—"The Last Navajo" 10-18-57 (Grey Fox).

Gentry, Robert. Films: "Standing Tall" TVM-1978 (Tom Sparkman). ¶TV: *Gunsmoke*—"Larkin" 1-20-75 (Tucker).

George, Anthony (1925-). Films: "Gunfire at Indian Gap" 1957 (Juan Morales). ¶TV: *The Adventures of Rin Tin Tin*—"The Tin Soldier" 1-27-56 (Dark Cloud); *20th Century Fox Hour*—"Broken Arrow" 5-2-56 (Nahilzay); *Cheyenne*—"The Spanish Grant" 5-7-57 (Sancho Mendariz); *Zorro*—"Agent of the Eagle" 2-20-58, "The New Commandante" 3-20-58 (Peralta), "The Fox and the Coyote" 3-26-58 (Peralta); *Tombstone Territory*—"Legacy of Death" 6-11-58 (Santiago); *Sugarfoot*—"The Desperadoes" 1-6-59 (Padre John); *Death Valley Days*—"Perilous Refuge" 4-14-59 (Carlos Ortega); *Wagon Train*—"The Johnny Masters Story" 1-16-63 (Johnny Masters); *Wide Country*—"The Care and Handling of Tigers" 4-25-63 (Edward Garner).

George, Bill. Films: "Masked Raiders" 1949 (Luke). ¶TV: *The Cisco Kid*—"Vigilante Story" 10-20-51, "Quicksilver Murder" 1-12-52, "Gold Strike" 3-14-53, "The Hospital" 5-16-53; *The Gene Autry Show*—"Trail of the Witch" 3-30-52; *The Roy Rogers Show*—"Flying Bullets" 6-15-52, "Death Medicine" 9-7-52, "The Last of the Larrabee Kid" 10-17-54 (Jim Crosswick), "Violence in Paradise Valley" 11-2-55, "Accessory to Crime" 3-3-57; *Wild Bill Hickok*—"Stolen Church Funds" 9-9-52; *The Restless Gun*—"The Way Back" 7-13-59.

George, Christopher (1929-11/28/83). Films: "El Dorado" 1967 (Nelse McLeod); "Gavilan" 1968; "Chisum" 1970 (Dan Nodeen); "The Train Robbers" 1973 (Calhoun).

George, Chief Dan (1899-9/23/81). Films: "Smith" 1969 (Ol' Antoine); "Little Big Man" 1971 (Old Lodge Skins); "Dan Candy's Law" 1975-U.S./Can.; "The Outlaw Josey Wales" 1976 (Lone Watie); "Shadow of the Hawk" 1976 (Old Man Hawk). ¶TV: *The High Chaparral*—"Apache Trust" 11-7-69 (Chief Morales); *Bonanza*—"Warbonnet" 12-26-71 (Red Cloud); *Kung Fu*—"The Ancient Warrior" 5-3-73 (Ancient Warrior); *Centennial*—Regular 1978-79 (Old Sioux).

George, Gladys (1900-12/8/54). Films: "Lady from Cheyenne" 1941 (Elsie); "Silver City" 1951 (Mrs. Barber).

George, Goetz. Films: "Treasure of Silver Lake" 1963-Fr./Ger./Yugo. (Fred Engel); "Among Vultures" 1964-Ger./Ital./Fr./Yugo. (Martin Baumann); "Man Called Gringo" 1964-Ger./Span. (Mace Carson); "Half Breed" 1966-Ger./Yugo./Ital.

George, John (1898-8/25/68). Films: "Rose Marie" 1936 (Barfly); "The Devil's Playground" 1946 (Dwarf); "Son of Paleface" 1952 (Johnny).

George, Maude (1888-10/10/63). Films: "The Beckoning Trail" 1916 (Georgette Fallon); "Blue Blazes Rawden" 1918 (Babette Du Fresne); "The Midnight Stage" 1919 (Nita).

George, Sue. Films: "The Dalton Girls" 1957 (Marigold Dalton). ¶TV: *Cheyenne*—"The Brand" 4-9-57 (Kat); *Wyatt Earp*—"One-Man Army" 1-7-58 (Sally Davis); *Tales of Wells Fargo*—"The Newspaper" 3-24-58 (Sue Sayers); *Jefferson Drum*—"The Outlaw" 6-20-58 (Kate Sparks); *The Californians*—"A Girl Named Sam" 10-14-58 (Samantha Jackson); *Sugarfoot*—"The Hunted" 11-25-58 (Cynthia Comstock); *Overland Trail*—"First Stage to Denver" 5-1-60 (Calamity Jane); *The Tall Man*—"The Cloudbusters" 4-29-61 (Henrietta Russel); *Two Faces West*—"Music Box" 7-17-61.

George, Susan (1950-). Films: "Bandera Bandits" 1973-Ital./Span./Ger. (Sonny).

George, Victoria. Films: "El Dorado" 1967 (Jared's Wife); "The Last Rebel" 1971-Ital./U.S./Span. (Pearl).

Georgiade, Nick (1933-). Films: "Eye for an Eye" 1972-Ital./Span./Ital. ¶TV: *The Travels of Jaimie McPheeters*—"The Day of the Toll Takers" 1-5-64 (Cairo), "The Day of the Pretenders" 3-1-64 (Rob); *Hondo*—"Hondo and the Hanging Town" 12-8-67 (Bartender).

Geraghty, Carmelita (1901-7/7/66). Films: "Brand of Cowardice"

1925; "Cyclone Cavalier" 1925 (Rosita Gonzales); "The Last Trail" 1927 (Nita Carroll); "Fighting Thru" 1930 (Queenie); "Men Without Law" 1930 (Juanita); "Rogue of the Rio Grande" 1930 (Dolores); "The Texas Ranger" 1931 (Helen Clayton); "Phantom of Santa Fe" 1937 (Lola).

Gerard, Carl (1885-1/6/66). Films: "Wild Bill Hickok" 1923 (Clayton Hamilton).

Gerard, Gil (1940-). Films: "Ransom for Alice!" TVM-1977 (Clint Kirby).

Gerard, Hal. Films: "Snow Dog" 1950 (Antoine). ¶TV: *Wild Bill Hickok*—"Trapper's Story" 3-18-52, "Monster in the Lake" 8-12-52; *Wyatt Earp*—"The Hanging Judge" 12-18-56 (Eph Morgan), "Hung Jury" 10-29-57 (Jury Foreman); *Sergeant Preston of the Yukon*—"Storm the Pass" 10-24-57 (Bart Adams).

Geray, Steven (1898-12/26/73). Films: "The Gunfighters" 1947 (Jose); "El Paso" 1949 (Mexican Joe); "The Big Sky" 1952 (Jourdonnais); "Kiss of Fire" 1955 (Ship Captain); "Stagecoach to Fury" 1956 (Nichols); "Jesse James Meets Frankenstein's Daughter" 1966 (Rudolph Frankenstein). ¶TV: *Jim Bowie*—"The Squatter" 9-14-56 (Johann Gottschalk); *Zane Grey Theater*—"The Unrelenting Sky" 10-26-56 (Alex Rozky); *The Californians*—"The Barber's Boy" 11-19-57 (Max); *Bonanza*—"The Dowry" 4-29-62 (Alexander Dubois); *Wagon Train*—"The John Turnbull Story" 5-30-62 (Jacob Solomon); *The Travels of Jaimie McPheeters*—"The Day of the Pretenders" 3-1-64 (Anton Berg).

Gerber, Neva. Films: "The Water Right War" 1912; "Hell Bent" 1918 (Bess Thurston); "Three Mounted Men" 1918 (Lola Masters); "A Fight for Love" 1919 (Kate McDougal); "Roped" 1919 (Aileen); "The Santa Fe Trail" 1923-serial; "The Seventh Sheriff" 1923 (Mary Tweedy); "Days of '49" 1924-serial (Sierra Sutter); "In the West" 1924 (Florence Jackson); "Sagebrush Gospel" 1924 (Lucy Sanderson); "Western Fate" 1924; "The Whirlwind Ranger" 1924; "A Daughter of the Sioux" 1925 (Nanette); "Fort Frayne" 1925 (Helen Farrar); "The Mystery Box" 1925-serial; "Tonio, Son of the Sierras" 1925 (Evelyn Archer); "Vic Dyson Pays" 1925 (Neva); "Warrior Gap" 1925 (Elinor Folsom); "Baited Trap" 1926 (Helen Alder); "West of the Law" 1926 (Alice Armstrong); "The Mystery Brand" 1927; "The Range Riders" 1927 (Betty Grannan); "Riders of the West" 1927; "A Yellow

Streak" 1927; "The Old Code" 1928 (Lola); "The Saddle King" 1929 (Felice Landreau); "Thundering Thompson" 1929.

Gere, Richard (1949-). Films: "Sommersby" 1993 (Jack).

Gerner, Don. Films: "The Iroquois Trail" 1950 (Tom Cutler).

Gerrard, Charles (1887-). Films: "The Country That God Forgot" 1916 (Craig Wells); "The Heart of Texas Ryan" 1917 (Senator J. Murray Allison).

Gerritsen, Lisa (1957-). TV: *Gunsmoke*—"The Miracle Man" 12-2-68 (Nettie), "The Twisted Heritage" 1-6-69 (Tracey Copperton), "Sam McTavish, M.D." 10-5-70 (Christina), "Jenny" 12-28-70 (Jenny Pritchard); *Lancer*—"The Great Humbug" 3-4-69 (Vinny); *The Men from Shiloh*—"Hannah" 12-30-70 (Hannah Carson); *Bonanza*—"Cassie" 10-24-71 (Cassie).

Gerry, Alex. Films: "Panhandle" 1948 (McBride); "Covered Wagon Raid" 1950 (Harvey Grimes); "Rose of Cimarron" 1952 (Judge Kirby). ¶TV: *Circus Boy*—"The Dancing Bear" 11-14-57 (Karl Hofer); *Zane Grey Theater*—"Threat of Violence" 5-23-58 (James Ballinger); *Wagon Train*—"The Ella Lindstrom Story" 2-4-59 (Dr. Monroe); *Zorro*—"The Fortune Teller" 6-18-59; *The Law of the Plainsman*—"The Rawhiders" 1-28-60 (Judge Mason); *Walt Disney Presents*—"Daniel Boone: The Warrior's Path" 12-4-60 (Henderson), "Daniel Boone: ...And Chase the Buffalo" 12-11-60 (Henderson); *Wild Wild West*—"The Night of the Legion of Death" 11-24-67 (Judge).

Gerry, Toni. Films: "Oregon Passage" 1958 (Little Deer). ¶TV: *Wyatt Earp*—"Hang 'Em High" 3-12-57 (Alice Hendricks); *Colt .45*—"The Three Thousand Dollar Bullet" 11-1-57 (Amy Hodges); *Broken Arrow*—"Duel" 3-18-58 (Waa-nibbo); *Wanted—Dead or Alive*—"Eager Man" 2-28-59 (Anne Nelson).

Gerson, Betty Lou. Films: "The Miracle of the Hills" 1959 (Kate Peacock). ¶TV: *The Rifleman*—"The Hangman" 5-31-60; *Wanted—Dead or Alive*—"One Mother Too Many" 12-7-60 (Irene Morrison).

Gerstle, Frank (1915-2/23/70). Films: "The Proud Ones" 1956 (Tim, the Bartender); "Ambush at Cimarron Pass" 1958 (Sam Prescott); "The Quick Gun" 1964 (George Keely). ¶TV: *Death Valley Days*—"The Jackass Mail" 6-30-57, "Cockeyed Charlie Parkhurst" 3-25-58; *The Califor-*

nians—"The Avenger" 10-15-57; *Tales of Wells Fargo*—"The Renegade" 5-12-58 (John Curtis), "Moneyrun" 1-6-62 (Tim); *Jefferson Drum*—"The Lawless" 7-18-58 (Hardy); *Wagon Train*—"The Beauty Jamison Story" 12-17-58 (Chris Grimes), "The Jed Polke Story" 3-1-61 (Otto), "The Hiram Winthrop Story" 6-6-62 (Frank Carter); *Wyatt Earp*—"A Good Man" 1-6-59 (Ganly), "Wyatt's Decision" 9-22-59, "The Big Fight at Total Wreck" 1-12-60 (Dick Gird), "Shoot to Kill" 10-18-60; *U.S. Marshal*—"Honeymoon" 12-26-59 (Max); *Bat Masterson*—"Mr. Fourpaws" 2-18-60; *Colt .45*—"Attack" 5-24-60 (Ed Garrick); *Wanted—Dead or Alive*—"Baa-Baa" 1-4-61; *Rawhide*—"Incident of the Broken Word" 1-20-61; *Lawman*—"The Promoter" 2-19-61 (David Ferris); *Cheyenne*—"Cross Purpose" 10-9-61 (Hammond); *Bonanza*—"The Quest" 9-30-62 (Weber), "False Witness" 10-22-67 (Strand); *Laramie*—"No Place to Run" 2-5-63; *The Virginian*—"Dangerous Road" 3-17-65 (Clint Koski); *Branded*—"The Golden Fleece" 1-2-66; *The Loner*—"A Question of Guilt" 1-29-66 (Miner); *Lancer*—"Blind Man's Bluff" 9-23-69 (Lem Cable).

Gerwin, George (1902-1/9/79). Films: "Breed of the West" 1930 (Cook); "Red Fork Range" 1931 (Steve Alden); "Tex Takes a Holiday" 1932; "Tombstone Canyon" 1932 (Clem).

Gest, Inna. *see* Guest, Ina.

Gettinger, William. *see* Steele, William.

Getty, Balthazar. Films: "Young Guns II" 1990 (Tom O'Folliard); "My Heroes Have Always Been Cowboys" 1991 (Jud Meadows).

Getty, Estelle (1924-). Films: "No Man's Land" TVM-1984 (Euroi Muller).

Ghia, Dana (Ghia Arlen). Films: "Four Dollars for Vengeance" 1965-Span./Ital. (Mercedes); "Deguello" 1966-Ital.; "Big Ripoff" 1967-Span./Ital.; "Django, Last Killer" 1967-Ital.; "Wrath of God" 1968-Ital./Span.; "The Dirty Outlaws" 1971-Ital. (Lucy); "Trinity Is Still My Name" 1974-Ital.; "California" 1976-Ital./Span.

Ghidra, Anthony. Films: "Ballad of a Gunman" 1967-Ital./Ger. (Blackie); "Django, Last Killer" 1967-Ital. (Django); "Hole in the Forehead" 1968-Ital./Span. (John Blood); "May God Forgive You ... But I Won't" 1968-Ital.; "Time and Place for Killing" 1968-Ital.

Ghostley, Alice (1926-). TV: *Nichols*—Regular 1971-72 (Bertha).

Giacobini, Franco. Films: "The Mercenary" 1968-Ital./Span. (Pepote); "Bandera Bandits" 1973-Ital./Span./Ger.

Giallelis, Stathis (1943-). Films: "Blue" 1968 (Manuel).

Giambalvo, Louis. TV: *Adventures of Brisco County, Jr.*—"Wild Card" 4-8-94 (Enzio).

Gibbons, Ayllene. Films: "Cat Ballou" 1965 (Hedda); "Sam Whiskey" 1969 (Big Annie). ¶TV: *The Legend of Jesse James*—"The Pursuers" 10-11-65 (Maybelle).

Gibbons, Robert (1918-2/21/77). TV: *Have Gun Will Travel*—"The Silver Queen" 5-3-58, "Invasion" 4-28-62 (Official).

Gibson, Althea (1927-). Films: "The Horse Soldiers" 1959 (Lukey).

Gibson, Curley. Films: "End of the Trail" 1936; "Cattle Raiders" 1938 (Posse Man); "The Singing Outlaw" 1938; "Code of the Saddle" 1947; "Prairie Express" 1947 (Langford).

Gibson, Diana. Films: "The Phantom Rider" 1936-serial (Helen Moore).

Gibson, Don. Films: "Seminole" 1953 (Capt. Streller).

Gibson, Florence. Films: "A Sage Brush Hamlet" 1919 (Mother Dolan).

Gibson, Helen (1892-10/10/77). Films: "Border Watch Dogs" 1917; "Fighting Mad" 1917 (Mary Lambert); "The Ghost of Canyon Diablo" 1917; "The Girl of Gopher City" 1917; "The Perilous Leap" 1917; "The Branded Man" 1918; "Captured Alive" 1918; "Danger Ahead" 1918; "The Dead Shot" 1918; "The Fast Mail" 1918; "The Midnight Flyer" 1918; "The Payroll Express" 1918; "Play Straight or Fight" 1918; "The Robber" 1918; "The Silent Sentinel" 1918; "Under False Pretenses" 1918; "Wolves of the Range" 1918; "Ace High" 1919; "The Black Horse Bandit" 1919; "The Canyon Mystery" 1919; "Down But Not Out" 1919; "Gun Law" 1919; "The Rustlers" 1919; "The Secret Peril" 1919; "No Man's Woman" 1921 (the Girl); "The Wolverine" 1921 (Billy Louise); "Nine Points of the Law" 1922 (Cherie Du Bois); "Thorobred" 1922 (Helen); "The Vanishing West" 1928-serial; "Lightning Warrior" 1931-serial; "Human Targets" 1932 (Mrs. Dale); "Law and Lawless" 1932 (Molly); "King of the Arena" 1933; "The Way of the West" 1934; "Cyclone of the Saddle" 1935 (Ma); "Five Bad Men" 1935 (Mrs. Swift); "Custer's Last Stand" 1936-serial (Calamity Jane);

"Flaming Frontier" 1938-serial; "Stagecoach" 1939 (Dancing Girl); "The Oregon Trail" 1939-serial; "Crooked River" 1950 (Mother); "Fast on the Draw" 1950; "The Man Who Shot Liberty Valance" 1962.

Gibson, Henry (1935-). Films: "The Outlaws Is Coming!" 1965 (Charlie Horse); "Evil Roy Slade" TVM-1972 (Clifford Stool). ¶TV: *Laredo*—"Pride of the Rangers" 12-16-65 (Freddy Gruber); *F Troop*—"Wrongo Starr and the Lady in Black" 1-11-66 (Wrongo Starr), "The Return of Wrongo Starr" 12-8-66 (Wrongo Starr); *Barbary Coast*—"Sharks Eat Sharks" 11-21-75 (Dasher).

Gibson, Hoot (1892-8/23/62). Films: "Pride of the Range" 1910; "Cowboy Sports and Pastimes" 1913; "The Man from the East" 1914; "Shotgun Jones" 1914; "The Man from Texas" 1915; "The Ring of Destiny" 1915; "A Knight of the Range" 1916 (Bob Graham); "The Night Riders" 1916; "A 45 Calibre Mystery" 1917; "The Golden Bullet" 1917; "A Marked Man" 1917; "The Secret Man" 1917 (Chuck Fadden); "The Soul Herder" 1917; "Straight Shooting" 1917 (Danny Morgan); "Sure Shot Morgan" 1917; "The Texas Sphinx" 1917; "The Wrong Man" 1917; "The Branded Man" 1918; "Headin' South" 1918; "The Midnight Flyer" 1918; "Play Straight or Fight" 1918; "Ace High" 1919; "The Black Horse Bandit" 1919; "By Indian Post" 1919; "The Crow" 1919; "The Double Hold-Up" 1919; "The Face in the Watch" 1919; "The Fighting Brothers" 1919; "The Fighting Heart" 1919; "The Four-Bit Man" 1919; "Gun Law" 1919; "The Gun Packer" 1919; "His Buddy" 1919; "The Jack of Hearts" 1919; "The Lone Hand" 1919; "Riding Wild" 1919; "The Rustlers" 1919; "The Tell Tale Wire" 1919; "The Trail of the Hold-Up Man" 1919; "The Big Catch" 1920; "The Broncho Kid" 1920; "The Champion Liar" 1920; "Cinders" 1920; "Double Danger" 1920; "Fight It Out" 1920; "The Fightin' Terror" 1920; "A Gamblin' Fool" 1920; "The Grinning Granger" 1920; "Hair-Trigger Stuff" 1920; "Held Up for the Makin's" 1920; "'In Wrong' Wright" 1920; "The Jay Bird" 1920; "The Man with the Punch" 1920; "Marryin' Marion" 1920; "Masked" 1920; "One Law for All" 1920; "A Pair of Twins" 1920; "Ransom" 1920; "The Rattler's Hiss" 1920; "Roarin' Dan" 1920; "Runnin' Straight" 1920; "The Sheriff's Oath" 1920; "The Shootin' Fool" 1920; "The Shootin' Kid" 1920;

"The Smilin' Kid" 1920; "Some Shooter" 1920; "Superstition" 1920; "Teacher's Pet" 1920; "The Texas Kid" 1920; "Thieves' Clothes" 1920; "Tipped Off" 1920; "The Trail of the Hound" 1920; "The Two-Fisted Lover" 1920; "West Is Best" 1920; "Wolf Tracks" 1920; "Action" 1921 (Sandy Bourke); "Bandits Beware" 1921; "Beating the Game" 1921; "The Cactus Kid" 1921; "Crossed Clues" 1921; "Double Crossers" 1921; "The Driftin' Kid" 1921; "The Fire Eater" 1921 (Bob Corey); "Kickaroo" 1921; "The Man Who Woke Up" 1921; "The Movie Trail" 1921; "Out O' Luck" 1921; "Red Courage" 1921 (Pinto Peters); "Sure Fire" 1921 (Jeff Bransford); "Sweet Revenge" 1921; "Too-Tired Jones" 1921; "The Bearcat" 1922 (the Singin' Kid); "The Saddle King" 1921; "Who Was That Man?" 1921; "The Wild Wild West" 1921; "The Galloping Kid" 1922 (Simplex Cox); "Headin' West" 1922 (Bill Perkins); "The Loaded Door" 1922 (Bert Lyons); "The Lone Hand" 1922 (Laramie Lad); "Ridin' Wild" 1922 (Cyril Henderson); "Step on It!" 1922 (Vic Collins); "Trimmed" 1922 (Dale Garland); "Blinky" 1923 (Geoffrey Arbuthnot "Blinky" Islip); "Dead Game" 1923 (Katy Didd); "Double Dealing" 1923 (Ben Slowbell); "Kindled Courage" 1923 (Andy Walker); "Out of Luck" 1923 (Sam Perkins); "The Ramblin' Kid" 1923 (the Ramblin' Kid); "Shootin' for Love" 1923 (Duke Travis); "Singled-Handed" 1923 (Hector MacKnight); "The Thrill Chaser" 1923; "Broadway or Bust" 1924 (Dave Hollis); "Forty-Horse Hawkins" 1924 (Luke "Bud" Hawkins); "Hook and Ladder" 1924 (Ace Cooper); "Ride for Your Life" 1924 (Bud Watkins); "The Ridin' Kid from Powder River" 1924 (Bud Watkins); "The Sawdust Trail" 1924 (Clarence Elwood Butts); "The Calgary Stampede" 1925 (Dan Malloy); "The Hurricane Kid" 1925 (the Hurricane Kid); "Let 'Er Buck" 1925 (Bob Carson); "The Saddle Hawk" 1925 (Ben Johnson); "Spook Ranch" 1925 (Bill Bangs); "The Taming of the West" 1925 (John Carleton); "Arizona Sweepstakes" 1926 (Coot Cadigan); "The Buckaroo Kid" 1926 (Ed Harley); "Chip of the Flying U" 1926 (Chip Bennett); "Flaming Frontier" 1926 (Bob Langdon); "The Man in the Saddle" 1926 (Jeff Morgan, Jr.); "The Phantom Bullet" 1926 (Tom "Click" Farlane); "The Shoot 'Em Up Kid" 1926; "The Texas Streak" 1926 (Chad Pennington); "The Denver Dude" 1927 (Rodeo Randall); "Galloping Fury" 1927 (Billy Halen); "A

Hero on Horseback" 1927; "Hey! Hey! Cowboy" 1927 (Jimmie Roberts); "Painted Ponies" 1927 (Bucky Simms); "The Prairie King" 1927 (Andy Barden); "The Silent Rider" 1927 (Jerry Alton); "Burning the Wind" 1928 (Richard Gordon, Jr.); "Clearing the Trail" 1928 (Pete Watson); "The Danger Rider" 1928 (Hal Doyle); "The Flyin' Cowboys" 1928 (Bill Hammond); "The Rawhide Kid" 1928 (Dennis O'Hara); "Riding for Fame" 1928 (Scratch 'Em Hank Scott); "A Trick of Hearts" 1928 (Ben Tully); "The Wild West Show" 1928 (Rodeo Bill); "Courtin' Wildcats" 1929 (Clarence Butts); "King of the Rodeo" 1929 (Chip, the Montana Kid); "The Lariat Kid" 1929 (Tom Richards); "The Long, Long Trail" 1929 (the Ramblin' Kid); "Points West" 1929 (Cole Lawson, Jr.); "Smilin' Guns" 1929 (Jack Purvin); "The Winged Horseman" 1929 (Skyball Smith); "The Concentratin' Kid" 1930 (Concentratin' Kid); "The Mounted Stranger" 1930 (Pete Ainslee); "Roaring Ranch" 1930 (Jim Dailey); "Spurs" 1930 (Bob Merrill); "Trailin' Trouble" 1930 (Ed King); "Trigger Tricks" 1930 (Tim Brennan); "Clearing the Range" 1931 (Curt Fremont); "Hard Hombre" 1931 (William Penn "Peaceful" Patton); "Wild Horse" 1931 (Jim Wright); "The Boiling Point" 1932 (Jimmy Duncan); "The Gay Buckaroo" 1932 (Clint Hale); "Local Bad Man" 1932 (Jim Bonner); "A Man's Land" 1932 (Tex Mason); "Spirit of the West" 1932 (Johnny Ringo); "Cowboy Counsellor" 1933 (Dan Alton); "The Dude Bandit" 1933 (Ace Cooper/Tex); "The Fighting Parson" 1933 (Steve Hartly); "Wheels of Destiny" 1934; "Powdersmoke Range" 1935 (Stony Brooke); "Rainbow's End" 1935 (Neil Gibson, Jr.); "Sunset Range" 1935 (Reasoning Bates); "Swifty" 1935 (Swifty Wade); "Cavalcade of the West" 1936 (Clint Knox); "Feud of the West" 1936 (Whitey Revel); "Frontier Justice" 1936 (Brent Halston); "The Last Outlaw" 1936 (Chuck Wilson); "Lucky Terror" 1936 (Lucky Carson); "The Riding Avenger" 1936 (Buck Conners/the Morning Glory Kid); "The Painted Stallion" 1937-serial (Walter Jamison); "Blazing Guns" 1943 (Hoot); "The Law Rides Again" 1943 (Hoot); "Arizona Whirlwind" 1944 (Hoot Gibson); "Death Valley Rangers" 1944 (Hoot); "Marked Trails" 1944 (Parkford); "Outlaw Trail" 1944 (Hoot); "Sonora Stagecoach" 1944 (Hoot); "Trigger Law" 1944; "The Utah Kid" 1944; "Wild Horse Stam-pede" 1943 (Hoot); "Westward Bound" 1944 (Hoot); "The Marshal's Daughter" 1953 (Ben Dawson); "The Horse Soldiers" 1959 (Brown).

Gibson, Jim (1866-10/13/38). Films: "The Arizona Kid" 1930 (Stage Driver).

Gibson, John (-9/14/71). Films: "Return of the Lash" 1947 (Pete).

Gibson, Margaret. see Palmer, Patricia.

Gibson, Mel (1951-). Films: "Maverick" 1994 (Bret Maverick).

Gibson, Mimi (1948-). Films: "At Gunpoint" 1955 (Cynthia Clark); "Lay That Rifle Down" 1955 (Terry); "Rebel in Town" 1956 (Lisbeth Anstadt); "The Oklahoman" 1957 (Louise Brighton). ¶TV: *Rough Riders*—"The Wagon Raiders" 6-4-59 (Susan Eddiman); *The Rebel*—"The Captive of Tremblor" 4-10-60 (Tildy Gain); *The Tall Man*—"Dark Moment" 2-11-61 (Judy).

Gibson, Virginia. Films: "I Killed Wild Bill Hickok" 1956 (Ann James).

Gibson-Gowland, T.H. Films: "The Promise" 1917 (Stromberg); "Under Handicap" 1917 (Bat Truxton).

Gierasch, Stefan (1926-). Films: "Jeremiah Johnson" 1972 (Del Gue); "High Plains Drifter" 1973 (Mayor Jason Hobart); "This Was the West That Was" TVM-1974 (Carmedly); "Dream West" TVM-1986 (Trenor Park). ¶TV: *Empire*—"End of an Image" 1-15-63 (Jack Morgan); *Stoney Burke*—"Point of Entry" 3-4-63 (Graff Erlich); *Gunsmoke*—"Gunfighter, R.I.P." 10-22-66 (Mark Douglas); *Bonanza*—"The Witness" 9-21-69 (Orvil Winters), "The Iron Butterfly" 11-28-71 (Grady); *Nichols*—"The Siege" 9-23-71; *Kung Fu*—"The Centoph" 4-4-74 & 4-11-74 (McBurney/Kai Tong); *Big Bend Country*—Pilot 8-27-81 (Sam Purdy).

Gifford, Alan (1910-3/20/89). Films: "The Kangaroo Kid" 1950 (Steve Corbett); "The Legend of Nigger Charley" 1972 (Hill Carter). ¶TV: *Gunsmoke*—"Carmen" 5-24-58 (Mayor Harris).

Gifford, Frances (1920-1/22/94). Films: "Border Vigilantes" 1941 (Helen Forbes); "American Empire" 1942 (Abby Taylor).

Giftos, Elaine (1945-). TV: *Bonanza*—"The Trouble with Amy" 1-25-70 (Charity), "The Lady and the Mark" 2-1-70 (Charity McGill).

Gilbert, Billy (1894-9/23/71). Films: "The Tabasco Kid" 1932-short; "Sutter's Gold" 1936 (Gen. Ramos); "The Outcasts of Poker Flat" 1937 (Charley); "Destry Rides Again" 1939 (Loupgerou, the Bartender); "Meet Roy Rogers" 1941-short; "Valley of the Sun" 1942 (Justice of the Peace); "The Kissing Bandit" 1948 (General Torro). ¶TV: *El Coyote Rides*—Pilot 1958 (Manuel).

Gilbert, Ed (1931-). TV: *Wild Wild West*—"The Night of the Casual Killer" 10-15-65 (Tom Hendrix); *Here Come the Brides*—"Break the Bank of Tacoma" 1-16-70.

Gilbert, Eugenia. Films: "Man of the Forest" 1921 (Bessie Beasley); "The Half-Breed" 1922 (Marianne); "The Back Trail" 1924 (Ardis Andrews); "Beyond the Rockies" 1926 (Flossie); "Hair Trigger Baxter" 1926 (Rose Moss); "The Man from the West" 1926 (Iris Millar); "The Valley of Bravery" 1926 (Helen Coburn); "Wild to Go" 1926 (Marjorie Felton); "Border Blackbirds" 1927 Marion Kingsley); "Don Desperado" 1927 (Doris Jessup); "The Long Loop on the Pecos" 1927 (Rose Arnold); "The Man from Hardpan" 1927 (Elizabeth Warner); "The Apache Raider" 1928 (Dixie Stillwell); "The Boss of Rustler's Roost" 1928 (Fay Everman); "The Bronc Stomper" 1928 (Daisy Hollister); "The Danger Rider" 1928 (Mollie Dare); "Phantom City" 1928 (Sally Ann Drew); "Courtin' Wildcats" 1929 (Calamity Jane).

Gilbert, Florence. Films: "A Rodeo Mixup" 1924 (Edith Cummins); "A Guilty Cause" 1922; "Gun Shy" 1922 (Betty Benson); "Hills of Missing Men" 1922 (Hilma Allis); "The Sheriff of Sun-Dog" 1922 (Jean Martin); "Spawn of the Desert" 1923 (Nola "Luck" Sleed); "Cupid's Rustler" 1924 (the Girl); "Lash of the Whip" 1924 (Florence); "Western Feuds" 1924 (Sally Warner); "Western Yesterdays" 1924 (Rose Silver); "The Desert's Price" 1925 (Julia); "A Man Four-Square" 1926 (Bertie Roberts).

Gilbert, Helen. Films: "Death Valley" 1946; "God's Country" 1946. ¶TV: *Death Valley Days*—"The Man Who'd Bet on Anything" 2-11-56; *Wyatt Earp*—"The Lonesomest Man in the World" 11-27-56 (Sharlene); *Hawkeye and the Last of the Mohicans*—"False Faces" 10-23-57.

Gilbert, Jack. Films: "The Apostle of Vengeance" 1916 (Willie Hudson); "The Devil Dodger" 1917 (Roger Ingraham); "Golden Rule Kate" 1917; "Up or Down?" 1917 (Allen Corey).

Gilbert, Joanne. Films: "Red

Garters" 1954 (Sheila Winthrop); "Ride Out for Revenge" 1957 (Pretty Willow). ¶TV: *Zane Grey Theater*—"Utopia, Wyoming" 6-6-58 (Jennie Cannon); *Bronco*—"Trail to Taos" 12-2-58 (Mike Torrence).

Gilbert, Jody (1916-2/3/79). Films: "New Frontier" 1939 (Woman at Dance); "Hudson Bay" 1941 (Germain); "Ride 'Em, Cowboy" 1942 (Moonbeam); "Singing on the Trail" 1946; "Albuquerque" 1948 (Pearl); "The Paleface" 1948 (Woman in Bath House); "Hellfire" 1949 (Full Moon); "Gene Autry and the Mounties" 1951 (Squaw); "Blue Canadian Rockies" 1952 (Guest); "Butch Cassidy and the Sundance Kid" 1969 (Large Woman).

Gilbert, Joe (1903-5/26/59). Films: "Wells Fargo" 1937 (Practical Telegraph Operator); "Union Pacific" 1939 (Telegrapher).

Gilbert, John (1897-1/9/36). Films: "The Dawn of Understanding" 1918 (Ira Beasley); "Hell's Hinges" 1919 (Townsman); "The Love Gambler" 1922 (Dick Manners); "A California Romance" 1923 (Don Patricio Fernando); "Romance Ranch" 1924 (Carlos Brent).

Gilbert, Jonathan. Films: "Little House on the Prairie: Look Back to Yesterday" TVM-1983 (Willie Oleson). ¶TV: *Little House on the Prairie*—Regular 1975-82 (Willie Oleson).

Gilbert, Lauren (1911-). Films: "Westworld" 1973 (Supervisor) ¶TV: *Empire*—"Duet for Eight Wheels" 4-30-63 (Dr. Clymer).

Gilbert, Lou (1909-11/6/78). Films: "Viva Zapata!" 1952 (Pablo).

Gilbert, Melissa (1964-). Films: "Little House on the Prairie" TVM-1974 (Laura Ingalls); "Little House on the Prairie: Look Back to Yesterday" TVM-1983 (Laura Ingalls Wilder); "Little House: The Last Farewell" TVM-1984 (Laura Ingalls Wilder); "Little House: Bless All the Dear Children" TVM-1984 (Laura Ingalls Wilder). ¶TV: *Gunsmoke*—"Spratt" 10-2-72 (Spratt's Child); *Little House on the Prairie*—Regular 1974-82 (Laura Ingalls); *Little House: A New Beginning*—Regular 1982-83 (Laura Ingalls Wilder).

Gilbert, Mickey. Films: "Pocket Money" 1972 (Stunts); "Rooster Cogburn" 1975 (Gang Member); "The Apple Dumpling Gang Rides Again" 1979. ¶TV: *The Quest*—"The Buffalo Hunters" 9-29-76 (Frazer).

Gilbert, Nancy. TV: *The Gene Autry Show*—"The Rangerette" 12-17-55; *Buffalo Bill, Jr.*—Regular 1955-56 (Calamity).

Gilbert, Paul (1917-2/12/76). Films: "Cat Ballou" 1965 (Train Messenger). ¶TV: *The Deputy*—"The Challenger" 2-25-61 (Dillon).

Gilbert, Philip (1931-). Films: "The Singer Not the Song" 1961-Brit. (Phil Brown).

Gilbert, Robert L. "Bob". Films: "Song of the Sierras" 1946; "Rainbow Over the Rockies" 1947; "The Kid from Gower Gulch" 1949; "Red Rock Outlaw" 1950; "The Silver Bandit" 1950; "The Parson and the Outlaw" 1957.

Gilchrist, Connie (1901-3/3/85). Films: "Apache Trail" 1943 (Senora Martinez); "Bad Bascomb" 1946 (Annie Freemont); "Stars in My Crown" 1950 (Sarah Isbell); "Ticket to Tomahawk" 1950 (Mme. Adelaide); "The Half-Breed" 1952 (Ma Higgins); "The Far Country" 1955 (Hominy); "Tickle Me" 1965 (Hilda). ¶TV: *The Adventures of Rin Tin Tin*—"Mother O'Hara's Marriage" 10-25-57; *The Restless Gun*—"Aunt Emma" 4-14-58 (Aunt Emma); *Wagon Train*—"Trial for Murder" 4-27-60 & 5-4-60 (Molly Cassidy); *The Tall Man*—"The Great Western" 6-3-61 (Big Mamacita); *Daniel Boone*—"Cain's Birthday" 4-1-65 & 4-8-65 (Keziah Tench).

Gilden, Richard. Films: "The Black Whip" 1956 (Dewey); "Ride a Violent Mile" 1957 (Gomez); "Blood Arrow" 1958 (Little Otter). ¶TV: *Gunsmoke*—"The Hunter" 11-26-55 (Golden Calf), "Honor Before Justice" 3-5-66 (Little Walker); *Death Valley Days*—"The Hidden Treasure of Cucamonga" 12-2-56, "The Man Everyone Hated" 4-12-60 (Nahilo), "The Courtship of Carrie Huntington" 6-4-66 (Lieutenant), "The Hat That Huldah Wore" 6-25-66 (Ken Matson); *The Adventures of Rin Tin Tin*—"Escape to Danger" 9-26-58 (Leading Star); *Rawhide*—"Incident at Barker Springs" 2-20-59 (Lance Ford); *Iron Horse*—"Pride at the Bottom of the Barrel" 10-10-66 (Tepoca).

Giles, Sandra (1935-). Films: "Black Spurs" 1965 (Sadie's Girl). ¶TV: *Rawhide*—"Incident of the Wild Deuces" 12-12-63 (Ellie).

Gilfether, Daniel (1854-5/3/19). Films: "The Girl Angle" 1917 (Gambling House Proprietor).

Gilford, Gwynne (1946-). TV: *Gunsmoke*—"The Tycoon" 1-25-71 (Dora Lou).

Gilkyson, Terry. Films: "Slaughter Trail" 1951 (Singalong); "Star in the Dust" 1956 (the Music Man).

Gill, John Richard. Films: "Showdown" 1973 (Earl Cole).

Gill, Vince. Films: "Maverick" 1994 (Spectator).

Gilland, Gladys. Films: "The Fighting Strain" 1923 (Miss Canfield).

Gillard, Stuart (1946-). Films: "Draw" CTVM-1984 (Dr. West).

Gillespie, Gina. Films: "Face of a Fugitive" 1959 (Alice Bailey). ¶TV: *The Law of the Plainsman*—Regular 1959-60 (Tess Logan); *G.E. Theater*—"Aftermath" 4-17-60 (Young Girl); *Wagon Train*—"The Albert Farnsworth Story" 10-12-60 (Peggy O'-Toole); *Stagecoach West*—"By the Deep Six" 12-27-60 (Annie); *Tales of Wells Fargo*—"Prince Jim" 3-27-61 (Carol Butler), "A Fistful of Pride" 11-18-61 (Cindy Croydon); *The Outlaws*—"The Sisters" 2-15-62 (Bridget); *Laramie*—"Fall into Darkness" 4-17-62 (Kathy Frances); *The Travels of Jaimie McPheeters*—"The Day of the Picnic" 2-16-64 (Little Girl); *Laredo*—"The Deadliest Kid in the West" 3-31-66 (Kim Mabray).

Gillespie, Jennifer. TV: *Tales of Wells Fargo*—"Jeremiah" 11-11-61 (Karen); *Laramie*—"The Confederate Express" 1-30-62 (Tina).

Gillespie, Larrian. TV: *Tales of Wells Fargo*—"Gunman's Revenge" 5-22-61 (Kathie); *Bonanza*—"Gallagher Sons" 12-9-62 (Charlie Gallagher).

Gillespie, William. Films: "The Valley of Bravery" 1926 (Percy Winthrop).

Gillette, James. Films: "Desert Bandit" 1941 (Tim Martin); "Riders of the Purple Sage" 1941 (Venters).

Gillette, Ruth (1905-5/13/94). Films: "Frontier Marshal" 1934 (Queenie LaVerne); "The Return of the Cisco Kid" 1939 (Blonde).

Gilli, Luciana. Films: "Coffin for the Sheriff" 1965-Ital./Span.; "Death at Owell Rock" 1967-Ital.; "Pecos Cleans Up" 1967-Ital.

Gilliam, Burton (1938-). Films: "Blazing Saddles" 1974; "Hearts of the West" 1975 (Lester); "Another Man, Another Chance" 1977-Fr. (Sheriff Murphy); "Dream West" TVM-1986 (Martineau); "Back to the Future, Part III" 1990 (Colt Gun Salesman). ¶TV: *How the West Was Won*—Episode One 2-12-78 (Woodley); "The Gunfighter" 1-15-79 (Cory Nealson); *Young Maverick*—"Clancy" 11-28-79 (the Barbary Kid); *Best of the West*—10-1-81 (Ringo).

Gilliam, Stu (1943-). Films: "The Apple Dumpling Gang Rides Again" 1979.

Gilliland, Richard. Films: "The White Buffalo" 1977 (Cpl. Kileen).

Gillin, Hugh (1925-). Films: "Butch and Sundance: The Early Days" 1979 (Cyrus Antoon); "Back to the Future, Part III" 1990 (Mayor).

Gillingwater, Claude (1870-10/31/39). Films: "Tiger Rose" 1923 (Hector McCollins); "The Great Divide" 1929 (Winthrop Amesbury); "The Conquering Horde" 1931 (Jim Nabours); "Wide Open Spaces" 1932-short.

Gillis, Ann (1927-). Films: "The Singing Cowboy" 1936 (Lou Ann); "The Californian" 1937 (Rosalia as a Child); "Man from Music Mountain" 1943 (Penny Winters).

Gillis, William (1867-4/24/46). Films: "The Last Straw" 1920 (Two Bits); "Ruth of the Rockies" 1920-serial; "Riding with Death" 1921 (Capt. Jack Hughes); "Ridin' Pretty" 1925 (Gloom); "Sunset Range" 1935; "The Texas Rangers" 1936 (Ranger); "The Westerner" 1940 (Leon Beauregard).

Gills, Norbert (-2/21/20). Films: "Keith of the Border" 1918 (Black Bart); "The Law's Outlaw" 1918 (Ethan Ransford).

Gilman, Fred (1902-3/30/88). Films: "Law of the North" 1926; "Martin of the Mounted" 1926; "Pioneer Blood" 1926; "The Shoot 'Em Up Kid" 1926; "Barrymore Tommy" 1927; "Battling Justice" 1927; "Daze of the West" 1927; "The Dude Desperado" 1927; "The Fighting Texan" 1927; "Gun Justice" 1927; "The Haunted Homestead" 1927; "The Home Trail" 1927; "The Horse Trader" 1927; "The Law Rider" 1927; "The Lone Ranger" 1927; "The Lone Star" 1927; "On Special Duty" 1927; "The Ore Raiders" 1927; "The Peace Deputy" 1927; "The Phantom Outlaw" 1927; "The Plumed Rider" 1927; "A Ranger's Romance" 1927; "The Smiling Wolf" 1927; "The Square Shooter" 1927; "Tenderfoot Courage" 1927; "The Ambuscade" 1928; "The Card of Destiny" 1928; "Clearing the Trail" 1928 (Steve Watson); "Fighting Destiny" 1928; "The Gauge of Battle" 1928; "The Ranger Patrol" 1928; "An Unexpected Hero" 1928; "Wolves of the Range" 1928; "Wild Horse" 1931 (Wally); "A Man's Land" 1932; "Cowboy Counsellor" 1933 (Luke Avery); "The Dude Bandit" 1933 (Jim Saxon); "The Fighting Parson" 1933; "Rainbow's End" 1935; "Sunset Range" 1935 (Freddie); "The Sea of Grass" 1947 (Cattleman); "Annie Get Your Gun" 1950 (Rider).

Gilman, Sam (1915-). Films:

"One-Eyed Jacks" 1961 (Harvey); "Wild Rovers" 1971 (Hansen); "The Missouri Breaks" 1976 (Hank Rate). ¶TV: *Have Gun Will Travel*—"The Hanging Cross" 12-21-57, "Twenty-Four Hours to North Fork" 5-17-58 (Laird); *The Rifleman*—"Heller" 2-23-60; *Wyatt Earp*—"The Salvation of Emma Clanton" 4-5-60 (Gringo Hawkby); *Shane*—Regular 1966 (Grafton); *Gunsmoke*—"Snap Decision" 9-17-66 (Gilcher), "Noose of Gold" 3-4-67 (Jim Gunther), "Rope Fever" 12-4-67 (Bates); *The Legend of Jesse James*—"Vendetta" 10-25-67 (Granger); *The Guns of Will Sonnett*—"The Secret of Hangtown Mine" 12-22-67 (Sheriff); *The Big Valley*—"The Good Thieves" 1-1-68 (Marshal Moore).

Gilmore, Barney (1869-4/18/49). Films: "The Galloping Cowboy" 1926 (Prof. Pinkleby); "The Bandit's Son" 1927 (Amos Jordan).

Gilmore, Douglas (1903-7/26/50). Films: "Desert Vengeance" 1931 (Hugh).

Gilmore, Helen (1862-11/16/36). Films: "Good Men and True" 1922 (Mrs. Fite).

Gilmore, Lillian. Films: "The Fighting Texan" 1927; "The Mojave Kid" 1927 (Thelm Vaddez); "Shooting Straight" 1927 (Bess Hale); "Straight Shootin'" 1927 (Bess Hale); "The Boundary Battle" 1928; "Buckskin Days" 1928; "The Death's Head" 1928; "The Phantom Flyer" 1928 (Mary Crandall); "A Romeo of the Range" 1928; "Rawhide Mail" 1934 (Nora Hastings); "The Unconquered Bandit" 1935 (Helen Cleyburn); "Wolf Riders" 1935 (Mary Clark).

Gilmore, Lowell (1906-2/1/60). Films: "Lone Star" 1952 (Capt. Elliott); "Saskatchewan" 1954 (Banks); "Comanche" 1956 (Ward). ¶TV: *My Friend Flicka*—"The Little Visitor" 12-30-55 (Jim Williams); *The Californians*—"The Avenger" 10-15-57.

Gilmore, Virginia (1919-3/28/86). Films: "Western Union" 1941 (Sue Creighton); "Sundown Jim" 1942 (Tony Black).

Gilson, Tom (1934-10/6/62). TV: *Lawman*—"The Young Toughs" 4-12-59 (Boak Barnes), "The Go-Between" 9-25-60 (Charlie Dane), "The Squatters" 1-29-61 (Stape), "The Youngest" 4-22-62 (Sam Martin); *Rough Riders*—"Ransom of Rita Renee" 6-11-59 (Billy Paul); *Wanted—Dead or Alive*—"Desert Seed" 11-14-59, "The Looters" 10-12-60 (Frank); *Zane Grey Theater*—"Lonesome Road" 11-19-59 (Wes Cooper); *Wi-*

chita Town—"The Avengers" 2-3-60 (Kinard); *Cheyenne*—"Alibi for a Scalped Man" 3-7-60 (Deputy Babe Riker), "Day's Pay" 10-30-61 (Claude McCracken); *Shotgun Slade*—"Backtrack" 7-26-60 (Monty); *Bat Masterson*—"Dakota Showdown" 11-17-60 (Jocko Dakota); *Maverick*—"The Cactus Switch" 1-15-61 (Jimmy Daniels); *The Outlaws*—"No More Pencils—No More Books" 3-16-61 (Red McCool); *The Tall Man*—"The Legend and the Gun" 4-1-61 (Claude Baker), "Three for All" 3-10-62 (Dwig Killgore); *Tales of Wells Fargo*—"Bitter Vengeance" 6-12-61 (Joe Snyder), "Man of Another Breed" 12-2-61 (Buck Timmons); *The Rifleman*—"Outlaw Shoes" 4-30-62 (Frank Weiden).

Gim, H.W. (1908-3/15/73). Films: "McClintock" 1963 (Ching); "Paint Your Wagon" 1969 (Wong); "True Grit" 1969 (Chen Lee).

Gimpera, Teresa (1936-). Films: "Wanted" 1968-Ital./Fr.; "The Legend of Frenchie King" 1971-Fr./Ital./Span./Brit. (Caroline).

Ging, Jack (1931-). Films: "Hang 'Em High" 1968 (Marshal Hayes); "High Plains Drifter" 1973 (Morgan Allen). ¶TV: *Bat Masterson*—"Dead Men Don't Pay Debts" 11-19-59 (Clark Bassett), "Bat Trap" 10-13-60 (Billy Webb); *Black Saddle*—"Means to an End" 1-29-60 (Boyd Parsons); *Wyatt Earp*—"Johnny Behind the Deuce" 10-11-60 (Johnny O'Rourke); *The Deputy*—"Three Brothers" 12-10-60 (Jay Bennett); *Tales of Wells Fargo*—Regular 1961-62 (Beau McCloud); *Gunsmoke*—"Stage Stop" 11-26-66 (Simon Dobbs); *Shane*—"The Silent Gift" 11-26-66 (Kyle); *Bonanza*—"The Crime of Johnny Mule" 2-25-68 (Cleve Lowden); *The Men from Shiloh*—"The Animal" 1-20-71 (Owen).

Ginger, Johnny. Films: "The Outlaws Is Coming!" 1965 (Billy the Kid). ¶TV: *The Rifleman*—"Two Ounces of Tin" 2-19-62 (Ted).

Ginty, Robert (198-). TV: *Nakia*—"The Sand Trap" 10-5-74.

Giordana, Andrea (Chip Gorman). Films: "Massacre at Grand Canyon" 1963-Ital.; "Johnny Hamlet" 1966-Ital. (Johnny); "Big Ripoff" 1967-Span./Ital.; "Cost of Dying" 1968-Ital./Fr. (Skaif).

Giordana, Carlo. Films: "Hatred of God" 1967-Ital./Ger.; "Sartana in the Valley of Death" 1970-Ital.; "He Was Called the Holy Ghost" 1972-Ital.; "I Am Sartana, Trade Your Guns for a Coffin" 1972-Ital.

Giordano, Daniela (1948-). Films: "Find a Place to Die" 1968-Ital.; "Long Day of the Massacre" 1968-Ital.; "Challenge of the Mackennas" 1969-Ital./Span.; "The Five Man Army" 1969-Ital. (Maria); "Four Came to Kill Sartana" 1969-Ital.; "Four Gunmen of the Holy Trinity" 1971-Ital.; "Have a God Funeral, My Friend ... Sartana Will Pay" 1971-Ital. (Jasmine); "Hero Called Allegria" 1971-Ital.; "Go Away! Trinity Has Arrived in Eldorado" 1972-Ital.; "Trinity and Sartana Are Coming" 1972-Ital.

Giordano, Maria Angela. Films: "No Graves on Boot Hill" 1968-Ital.; "No Room to Die" 1969-Ital. (Fargo).

Giorgelli, Gabriella (1942-). Films: "Long Days of Vengeance" 1967-Ital./Span.; "Two Sides of the Dollar" 1967-Fr./Ital. (Jane); "Shango" 1969-Ital.; "Durango Is Coming, Pay or Die" 1972-Ital./Span.

Giornelli, Franco. Films: "Big Ripoff" 1967-Span./Ital.; "Execution" 1968-Ital./Fr.; "The Dirty Outlaws" 1971-Ital. (Asher).

Giraci, May. Films: "His Enemy, the Law" 1918 (Young Girl); "Man Above the Law" 1918 (Tonah); "Untamed" 1918 (Carmelita).

Girard, Joseph W. (1871-8/12/49). Films: "Shotgun Jones" 1914; "The Trail of the Upper Yukon" 1915; "'49-'17" 1917 (Judge Brand); "What Am I Bid?" 1919 (John McGibbon); "The Blue Fox" 1921; "Dead or Alive" 1921 (Sheriff Lamar); "Red Courage" 1921 (Joe Reedly); "The Sheriff of Hope Eternal" 1921 (Silk Lowry); "Nan of the North" 1922-serial; "Perils of the Yukon" 1922-serial; "Step on It!" 1922 (Lafe Brownell); "The Devil's Dooryard" 1923 (Snag Thorn); "Hearts of Oak" 1923; "The Law Rustlers" 1923 (Sol Vane); "Soft Boiled" 1923 (Ranch Owner); "The Sting of the Scorpion" 1923; "Three Jumps Ahead" 1923 (Annie's Father); "Where Is This West?" 1923 (Lawyer Browns); "The Night Hawk" 1924 (Sheriff Milton); "The Western Wallop" 1924 (Prison Warden); "Wolves of the North" 1924-serial; "The Fugitive" 1925 (Satan Saunders); "The Gambling Fool" 1925 (George Hartford); "Romance and Rustlers" 1925 (John Larrabee); "Vic Dyson Pays" 1925 (Dayton Keever); "The Dangerous Dub" 1926 (W.J. Cooper); "Driftin' Thru" 1926 (Sheriff); "Forlorn River" 1926 (Hart Blaine); "The Silent Hero" 1927 (John Stoddard); "Whispering Sage" 1927 (Hugh Ack-lin); "The Bullet Mark" 1928; "Hello Cheyenne" 1928 (Fremont Cody); "Courtin' Wildcats" 1929 (Mr. Butts); "King of the Rodeo" 1929 (Harlan); "Redskin" 1929 (Commissioner); "Girl of the Golden West" 1930 (Ashby); "Sons of the Saddle" 1930 (Martin Stavnow); "Desert Vengeance" 1931 (Captain Scott); "The Big Stampede" 1932 (Major Parker); "Renegades of the West" 1932 (James Dowling); "Texas Bad Man" 1932 (Captain Charley Carter); "Man of Action" 1933 (President Frank Caldwell); "Silent Men" 1933 (Two Block Burnett); "Via Pony Express" 1933; "The Whirlwind" 1933 (Pa Reynolds); "The Fiddlin' Buckaroo" 1934 (Harriman); "The Fighting Trooper" 1934 (Inspector O'Keefe); "Blazing Guns" 1935 (Sheriff Crabtree); "Branded a Coward" 1935; "His Fighting Blood" 1935; "Ivory-Handled Gun" 1935 (Pat Moore); "The Outlaw Deputy" 1935 (Rutledge); "Outlaw Rule" 1935 (Lance Peyton); "Outlawed Guns" 1935 (Rocky Ellsworth); "The Silent Code" 1935 (Inspector Manning); "Tonto Kid" 1935 (Rance Cartwright); "Tumbling Tumbleweeds" 1935; "Aces and Eights" 1936 (Don Hernandez); "Frontier Justice" 1936 (Samuel Halston); "Lightning Bill Carson" 1936 (John Mount); "The Oregon Trail" 1936 (Colonel Delmont); "Ride 'Em Cowboy" 1936 (Sam Parker); "The Mystery of the Hooded Horseman" 1937 (Dan Farley); "The Rangers Step In" 1937; "A Tenderfoot Goes West" 1937 (Groth); "Wild West Days" 1937-serial; "Whirlwind Horseman" 1938 (Jim Radford); "Crashing Thru" 1939 (Captain); "Frontier Scout" 1939; "Ride 'Em, Cowgirl" 1939 (Ruf Rickson); "Deadwood Dick" 1940-serial.

Girardot, Etienne (1856-11/10/39). Films: "Arizona Wildcat" 1938 (Judge White).

Giraud, Octavia (1890-6/3/58). Films: "The Oregon Trail" 1936 (Don Miguel); "Drifting Westward" 1939 (Manuel Careta); "Frontiers of '49" 1939 (Don Miguel).

Giraud, Wesley. Films: "The Gay Caballero" 1932; "One-Man Law" 1932; "War on the Range" 1933.

Girolami, Ennio (1934-). Films: "Bullets and the Flesh" 1965-Ital./Fr./Span.; "The Hellbenders" 1966-U.S./Ital./Span. (Commander of Fort Brent); "Two R-R-Ringos from Texas" 1967-Ital.; "Johnny Hamlet" 1966-Ital. (Ross); "Between God, the Devil and a Winchester" 1968-Ital./Span.; "Payment in Blood" 1968-Ital. (Chamaco).

Girotti, Mario. *see* Hill, Terence.

Giroux, Lee (1911-1/26/73). TV: *Circus Boy*—"The Magic Lantern" 11-7-57 (Sam Conway).

Gish, Annabeth. Films: "Wyatt Earp" 1994 (Unilla Sutherland).

Gish, Dorothy (1898-6/4/68). Films: "My Hero" 1912; "Just Gold" 1913; "Arms and the Gringo" 1914; "The Mountain Rat" 1914 (Nell); "Jordan Is a Hard Road" 1915 (Cora Findlay); "Nugget Nell" 1919 (Nugget Nell).

Gish, Lillian (1896-2/27/93). Films: "In the Aisles of the Wild" 1912; "The Battle at Elderbrush Gulch" 1913; "During the Round-Up" 1913; "An Indian's Loyalty" 1913; "Just Gold" 1913; "A Misunderstood Boy" 1913; "The Angel of Contention" 1914; "The Wind" 1928 (Letty); "Duel in the Sun" 1946 (Laura Belle McCanles); "The Unforgiven" 1960 (Mattilda Zachary).

Gist, Robert (1924-). TV: *Gunsmoke*—"The Queue" 12-3-55 (Rabb), "Wild West" 2-15-58 (Rourke), "Monopoly" 10-4-58 (Speegle); *Have Gun Will Travel*—"The Manhunter" 6-7-58 (Ben Tyler), "Shot by Request" 10-10-59 (Matt), "The Pledge" 1-16-60 (Brennan), "Fandango" 3-4-61 (Sheriff Ernie Backwater), "Invasion" 4-28-62 (Gavin O'Shea); *Decision*—"The Virginian" 7-6-58 (Dawes); *Black Saddle*—"Client: Dawes" 1-31-59 (Milo Dawes); *Rawhide*—"Incident of the Power and the Plow" 2-13-59 (Sheriff), "Incident on the Road to Yesterday" 11-18-60 (Ed Stockton), "Incident of the Woman Trap" 1-26-62 (Harleck); *Johnny Ringo*—"The Accused" 10-15-59 (Kincaid); *Zane Grey Theater*—"Setup" 3-3-60 (Casey Hydecker); *Death Valley Days*—"The Stranger" 3-15-60 (Aaron Taggert); *Hotel De Paree*—"Sundance and the Good-Luck Coat" 5-6-60 (Zack); *Pony Express*—"Trial by Fury" 5-10-60 (Slater); *Nichols*—"Gulley vs. Hansen" 10-7-71 (Gulley).

Gittelson, June. Films: "Horses' Collars" 1935-short (Girl); "The Old Wyoming Trail" 1937 (Stout Girl); "The Colorado Trail" 1938.

Giuffre, Aldo (1924-). Films: "Two Gangsters in the Wild West" 1965-Ital./Span.; "The Good, the Bad, and the Ugly" 1966-Ital.

Giuliano, Luigi (Jim Reed). Films: "Ruthless Colt of the Gringo" 1967-Ital./Span. (Sol Lester).

Givney, Kathryn (1897-3/16/78). Films: "Count Three and Pray" 1955 (Mrs. Decrais). ¶TV: *The Virginian*—"A Slight Case of Charity" 2-10-65 (Caroline Prescott); *Prudence and the Chief*—Pilot 8-26-70 (Letitia MacKenzie).

Givot, George (1903-6/7/84). Films: "The Leather Burners" 1943 (Sam Bucktoe).

Gladwin, Frances. Films: "Cattle Stampede" 1943 (Mary); "West of Texas" 1943 (Marie Moenette); "Wolves of the Range" 1943 (Ann); "Frontier Outlaws" 1944 (Pat); "Thundering Gun Slingers" 1944 (Bab Halliday); "Stagecoach Outlaws" 1945 (Linda).

Glass, Everett (1891-3/22/66). Films: "Two Flags West" 1950 (Rev. Simpkins); "Best of the Badmen" 1951; "Friendly Persuasion" 1956 (Elder); "The Quiet Gun" 1957 (Judge); "Gunman's Walk" 1958 (Rev. Arthur Stotheby). ¶TV: *The Cisco Kid*—"Thunderhead" 4-5-52, "Bell of Santa Margarite" 4-19-52; *Rawhide*—"Grandma's Money" 2-23-62 (Pop).

Glass, Gaston (1898-11/11/65). Films: "Cameron of the Royal Mounted" 1922 (Corporal Cameron); "I Am the Law" 1922 (Tom Fitzgerald); "The Spider and the Rose" 1923 (Don Marcello); "The Bad Lands" 1925 (Hal Owen); "The Scarlet West" 1925 (Captain Howard); "Call of the Klondike" 1926 (Norton Mitchell); "A Gentleman Preferred" 1928 (James Fargo); "Tiger Rose" 1929 (Pierre); "Untamed Justice" 1929 (Norman Bard); "Sutter's Gold" 1936 (Lt. Bacalenakoff).

Glass, Ned (1906-6/15/84). Films: "Pest from the West" 1939-short; "Prairie Schooners" 1940 (Skinny Hutch); "Beyond the Sacremento" 1941; "King of Dodge City" 1941; "Callaway Went Thataway" 1951 (Mailman); "The Yellow Tomahawk" 1954 (Willy); "A Big Hand for the Little Lady" 1966 (Owney Price). ¶TV: *Gunsmoke*—"The Bureaucrat" 3-16-57 (Husk), "The Photographer" 4-6-57 (Grubby), "Texas Cowboys" 4-5-58 (Sam Peeples), "Crowbait Bob" 3-26-60 (Elbin), "The Worm" 10-29-60 (Ritchie), "Dry Well" 1-11-64 (Ira Vickers), "Old Man" 10-10-64 (Old Man), "The Prisoner" 3-17-69 (Pink Simmons); *Have Gun Will Travel*—"Strange Vendetta" 10-26-57, "Show of Force" 11-9-57, "The Long Weekend" 4-8-61; *Jefferson Drum*—"Wheel of Fortune" 6-27-58 (Hitale); *Black Saddle*—"Client: Meade" 1-17-59 (Wheeler Boone); *Bonanza*—"A

Rose for Lotta" 9-12-59 (Coach Driver); *Wanted—Dead or Alive*—"The Monsters" 1-16-60 (Assay Clerk); *The Law of the Plainsman*—"The Comet" 1-21-60 (Potter); *Shotgun Slade*—"Charcoal Bullet" 8-16-60 (Eli); *Lancer*—"Cut the Wolf Loose" 11-4-69; *Here Come the Brides*—"The She-Bear" 1-30-70.

Glass, Seamon (1925-). Films: "Winterhawk" 1975 (Big Smith); "Mr. Horn" TVM-1979. ¶TV: *Gunsmoke*—"Whelan's Men" 2-5-73 (Acker); *Barbary Coast*—"Guns for a Queen" 10-6-75 (the Seaman).

Glass, Ursula (Wanda Vismara). Films: "Half Breed" 1966-Ger./Yugo./Ital. (Apanachi); "Halleluja and Sartana Strikes Again" 1972-Ger./Ital.

Glassmire, Gus (1879-7/23/46). Films: "Wells Fargo" 1937; "Union Pacific" 1939 (Governor Stafford).

Glaum, Louise (1900-11/25/70). Films: "The Quakeress" 1913; "The Panther" 1914; "The Conversion of Frosty Blake" 1915; "The Darkening Trail" 1915 (Fanny); "The Golden Trail" 1915; "Keno Bates—Liar" 1915; "The Renegade" 1915; "The Aryan" 1916 (Trixie); "The Return of Draw Egan" 1916 (Poppy); "Golden Rule Kate" 1917 (Mercedes Murphy); "The Goddess of Lost Lake" 1918 (Mary Thorne); "Staking His Life" 1918 (Bubbles); "Hell's Hinges" 1919 (Dolly).

Gleason, Ada (1888-2/6/71). Films: "Pals in Blue" 1915; "Ramona" 1916 (Ramona); "Snap Judgment" 1917 (Phoebe Lind); "True Blue" 1918 (Mary Brockhurst).

Gleason, James (1886-4/12/59). "The Dude Goes West" 1948 (Sam Briggs); "Star in the Dust" 1956 (Orval Jones); "Man in the Shadow" 1957 (Hank James); "Man or Gun" 1958 (Sheriff Jackson); "Money, Women and Guns" 1958 (Henry Devers); "Once Upon a Horse" 1958 (Postmaster). ¶TV: *Cheyenne*—"The Traveler" 1-3-56 (Pop Keith); *The Restless Gun*—"The Child" 12-23-57 (Padre Terrence).

Gleason, James. TV: *Young Riders*—"Jesse" 10-5-91 (McDermott); *Adventures of Brisco County, Jr.*—"Crystal Hawks" 11-12-93 (Marvin Lee).

Gleason, Lucille (1888-5/18/47). Films: "Rhythm on the Range" 1936 (Penelope Ryland); "Don't Fence Me In" 1945 (Mrs. Prentiss).

Gleason, Pat. Films: "Call the Mesquiteers" 1938 (Joe); "Saddle Serenade" 1945; "Deadline" 1948; "Sun-

set Carson Rides Again" 1948; "Battling Marshal" 1950; "Call of the Klondike" 1950 (Billy).

Gleason, Redmond. Films: "True Grit" TVM-1978 (Harrison); "Cattle Annie and Little Britches" 1981 (Red Buck).

Gleason, Regina. Films: "The Outlaw's Daughter" 1954 (Eastern Girl). ¶TV: *Death Valley Days*—"Little Papeete" 11-25-53, "The Rose of Rhyolite" 12-30-56; *Yancy Derringer*—"Fire on the Frontier" 4-2-59 (Margot Chatham); *Have Gun Will Travel*—"The Fatalist" 9-10-60 (Viola), "A Drop of Blood" 12-2-61 (Viola); *The Rifleman*—"Six Years and a Day" 1-3-61 (Sarah Marston); *Bonanza*—"Credit for a Kill" 10-23-66 (Martha Tanner); *Laredo*—"Hey Diddle Diddle" 2-24-67.

Gleason, Russell (1908-12/26/45). Films: "A Tenderfoot Goes West" 1937 (Pike); "Dudes Are Pretty People" 1942 (Brad).

Gleckler, Robert (1890-2/26/39). Films: "North of Nome" 1936 (Bruno); "The Bad Man of Brimstone" 1937 (Skunk Rogers); "Gun Law" 1938 (Flash Arnold); "Stand Up and Fight" 1939 (Sheriff Barney).

Glendon, J. Frank (1887-3/17/37). Films: "The Dawn of Understanding" 1918 (John Wynd); "Belle of Alaska" 1922 (Lucky Vail); "Tricks" 1925 (the New Foreman); "Border Romance" 1930 (Buck); "The Cheyenne Cyclone" 1932; "Law and Lawless" 1932; "The Reckless Rider" 1932; "Texas Tornado" 1932 (Three Star Henley); "Gun Law" 1933 (Nevada); "The Red Rider" 1934-serial; "Circle of Death" 1935 (Sheriff); "Justice of the Range" 1935; "The Phantom Empire" 1935-serial (Prof. Beetson); "Sagebrush Troubador" 1935 (John Martin); "Aces and Eights" 1936 (Harden); "Border Caballero" 1936 (Wiley Taggart); "King of the Pecos" 1936 (Brewster); "The Lion's Den" 1936 (Nate Welsh); "The Traitor" 1936 (Big George).

Glenn, Claire. Films: "Boots and Saddles" 1916 (Beth Ward).

Glenn, Goober. Films: "The Ramblin' Kid" 1923 (Parker); "Sunset Range" 1935.

Glenn, Louise. Films: "The Wild and the Innocent" 1959 (Dancehall Girl); "A Big Hand for the Little Lady" 1966 (Celie Drummond).

Glenn, Raymond. see Custer, Bob.

Glenn, Sr., Roy E. (1915-3/12/71). Films: "The Way West"

1967 (Saunders); "Hang 'Em High" 1968 (Guard); "Support Your Local Gunfighter" 1971 (Headwaiter). ¶TV: *Maverick*—"Hostage!" 11-10-57 (Straw Boss); *Zane Grey Theater*— "Mission" 11-12-59; *Rawhide*—"Incident of the Slavemaster" 11-11-60, "Incident of the Buffalo Soldier" 1-1-61 (Cpl. Boneface Jones), "The Greedy Town" 2-16-62 (Joshua); *Stoney Burke*—"The Scavenger" 11-12-62 (Tate); *Cimarron Strip*—"The Battle of Blood Stone" 10-12-67.

Glenn, Scott (1942-). Films: "Cattle Annie and Little Britches" 1981 (Bill Dalton); "Silverado" 1985 (Emmett); "My Heroes Have Always Been Cowboys" 1991 (H.D. Dalton); "Tall Tales: The Unbelievable Adventures of Pecos Bill" 1995 (J.P. Stiles).

Gless, Sharon (1943-). TV: *Centennial*—Regular 1978-79 (Sidney Andermann).

Glover, Bruce (1932-). Films: "Scandalous John" 1971 (Sludge); "Yuma" TVM-1971 (Sam King); "One Little Indian" 1973 (Schrader); "This Was the West That Was" TVM-1974; "Ghost Town" 1988 (Dealer). ¶TV: *The Guns of Will Sonnett*—"The Favor" 11-10-67, "Jim Sonnett's Lady" 2-21-69 (Sandy); *The Big Valley*— "Hunter's Moon" 12-30-68 (Bodkin); *Gunsmoke*—"Coreyville" 10-6-69 (Titus Wylie), "The Drummer" 10-9-72 (Enoch Brandt); *Bonanza*— "What Are Pardners For?" 4-12-70 (Scooter); *Bearcats!*—11-11-71 (Schiller).

Glover, Crispin (1964-). Films: "Dead Man" 1995 (the Fireman).

Glover, Danny (1947-). Films: "Silverado" 1985 (Mal); "Lonesome Dove" TVM-1989 (Joshua Deets).

Glover, Edmund (1914-11/24/78). Films: "Nevada" 1944 (Ed Nelson); "Shadows of the West" 1949 (Keefe). ¶TV: *Buckskin*—"The Knight Who Owned Buckskin" 3-2-59 (Leander Enderby); *Have Gun Will Travel*—"Charley Red Dog" 12-12-59.

Glover, John (1944-). Films: "The Mountain Men" 1980 (Nathan Wyeth); "El Diablo" CTVM-1990 (Preacher).

Glover, William (1927-). Films: "Dream West" TVM-1986 (Sir Roger Dunston). ¶TV: *Kung Fu*—"The Assassin" 10-4-73 (Andrew Swan).

Go, Hiromi. Films: "Samurai Cowboy" 1993 (Yutaka Sato).

Gobble, Hank (1923-5/19/61). Films: "The Deadly Companions" 1961 (Bartender). ¶TV: *The Westerner*—Regular 1960 (Digger).

Gobel, George (1920-2/24/91). TV: *Wagon Train*—"The Horace Best Story" 10-5-60 (Horace Best); *Death Valley Days*—"Thar She Blows" 10-6-63 (Baylor Thomas); *Daniel Boone*— "Four-Leaf Clover" 3-25-65 (Francis Clover); *F Troop*—"Go for Broke" 1-25-66 (Henry Terkel).

Goddard, John. Films: "The Storm Rider" 1957 (Rorick); "Gun Fever" 1958 (Lee). ¶TV: *Wild Bill Hickok*—"Kangaroo Kapers" 3-10-53; *Wyatt Earp*—"The General's Lady" 1-14-58; *Tales of Wells Fargo*—"The Gunfighter" 11-17-58 (Pete Rucker); *The Restless Gun*—"Shadow of a Gunfighter" 1-12-59 (Clay Lawson); *Cimarron City*—"Return of the Dead" 2-14-59 (Joe); *The Rifleman*—"One Went to Denver" 3-17-59 (Naylor), "Letter of the Law" 12-1-59; *Wagon Train*—"The Conchita Vasquez Story" 3-18-59 (Wes Arthur); *Daniel Boone*—"Be Thankful for the Fickleness of Women" 9-19-68 (Simon).

Goddard, Mark (1936-). TV: *The Rifleman*—"The Raid" 6-9-59, "Mark's Rifle" 11-19-62 (Marty Blair); *Johnny Ringo*—Regular 1959-60 (Cully); *The Rebel*—"To See the Elephant" 10-16-60 (Seldon Hollingsworth); *Zane Grey Theater*—"The Mormons" 12-15-60 (Tod Rowland); *The Virginian*—"The Secret of Brynmar Hall" 4-1-64 (Richard); *Gunsmoke*—"Journey for Three" 6-6-64 (Boyd Lambert).

Goddard, Paulette (1911-4/23/90). Films: "Northwest Mounted Police" 1940 (Louvette Corbeau); "Unconquered" 1947 (Abigail Martha "Abby" Hale).

Godet, Jacques. TV: *Tomahawk*—Regular 1957-58 (Pierre Radison).

Godfrey, Arthur (1904-3/16/83). Films: "Four for Texas" 1964. ¶TV: *Bob Hope Chrysler Theatre*— "The Reason Nobody Hardly Ever Seen a Fat Outlaw in the Old West Is as Follows:" 3-8-67 (Sheriff).

Godfrey, George. Films: "Riders of the Whistling Skull" 1937 (Prof. Fronc).

Godfrey, Renee (1920-5/2/64). TV: *Zane Grey Theater*—"Picture of Sal" 1-28-60 (Alicia); *Wagon Train*— "The Maud Frazer Story" 10-11-61 (Willa Mae), "The Barnaby West Story" 6-5-63 (Mrs. Palmer); *Frontier Circus*—"Mighty Like Rogues" 4-5-62 (Stella).

Going, Joanna. Films: "Wyatt Earp" 1994 (Josie Marcus); "Children of the Dust" TVM-1995 (Rachel).

Golan, Gila (1940-). Films:

"The Valley of Gwangi" 1969 (T.J. Breckenridge).

Gold, Missy (1970-). TV: *How the West Was Won*—"The Forgotten" 3-19-79 (Stacy Willow).

Gold, Tracey (1969-). TV: *Father Murphy*—"The Piano" 1-19-82 (Jenny).

Goldblum, Jeff (1952-). Films: "Silverado" 1985 (Slick).

Golden, Bob (1925-11/5/79). TV: *Gunsmoke* -"The Convict" 2-1-71 (Guard).

Golden, Mignonne. Films: "Hearts Up" 1920 (Lorelei Drew); "The Wallop" 1921 (Stella Vorhis); "Canyon of the Fools" 1923 (Aurelia).

Golden, Olive Fuller (1896-3/13/88). Films: "Just Jim" 1915; "The Committee on Credentials" 1916; "A Knight of the Range" 1916 (Bess Dawson); "Love's Lariat" 1916 (Goldie LaCroix); "The Night Riders" 1916; "The Passing of Hell's Crown" 1916; "The Vanishing Legion" 1931-serial.

Golden, Ruth Fuller (1901-8/15/31). Films: "Blue Streak McCoy" 1920 (Diana Hughes); "Human Stuff" 1920 (James' Sister).

Goldin, Pat (1902-4/24/71). Films: "King of the Bandits" 1947 (Pedro); "Jiggs and Maggie Out West" 1950 (Dugan). ¶TV: *The Rifleman*—"Gun Shy" 12-10-62 (Salesman).

Goldin, Sidney M. (1880-9/19/37). Films: "The Fightin' Comeback" 1927 (Sam Phillips).

Goldina, Marian (-11/14/79). Films: "Flaming Star" 1960 (Ph'Sha Knay).

Goldsworthy, J.H. (1884-7/10/58). Films: "A Yellow Streak" 1915 (Richard Marvin).

Golonka, Arlene (1938-). Films: "Welcome to Hard Times" 1967 (Mae); "Hang 'Em High" 1968 (Jennifer). ¶TV: *The Big Valley*—"Explosion!" 11-20-67 & 11-27-67 (Gail Miller).

Gombell, Minna (1892-4/14/73). Films: "Rainbow Trail" 1932 (Ruth); "Doomed Caravan" 1941 (Jane Travers); "Wyoming" 1947 (Queenie); "Return of the Badmen" 1948 (Emily); "The Last Bandit" 1949 (Winnie McPhail).

Gomez, Augie (1891-1/1/66). Films: "The California Trail" 1933 (Governor's Driver); "The Fourth Horseman" 1933; "Big Boy Rides Again" 1935; "The Arizona Raiders" 1936 (Cowboy); "The Painted Stallion" 1937-serial; "The Singing

Buckaroo" 1937; "Rollin' Plains" 1938 (Weevil); "Blue Montana Skies" 1939 (Blackfeather); "The Lone Ranger Rides Again" 1939-serial (Tonswman #4); "Rough Riders' Round-Up" 1939; "Zorro's Fighting Legion" 1939-serial (Cave Indian); "Adventures of Red Ryder" 1940-serial (Breed); "The Sagebrush Family Trails West" 1940 (Bart); "Arizona Bound" 1941; "Kansas Cyclone" 1941; "The Lone Rider in Ghost Town" 1941; "Along the Sundown Trail" 1942; "Billy the Kid Trapped" 1942; "Cowboy Commandos" 1943; "Daredevils of the West" 1943-serial (Indian #2/Indian Scalper); "The Haunted Ranch" 1943; "Zorro's Black Whip" 1944-serial (Citizen #2); "The Phantom Rider" 1946-serial (Indian Heavy); "The Adventures of Frank and Jesse James" 1948-serial (Hall); "The Gallant Legion" 1948; "Old Los Angeles" 1948 (Miguel); "Desperadoes of the West" 1950-serial. ¶TV: The Cisco Kid—"Thunderhead" 4-5-52, "Bell of Santa Margarite" 4-19-52; The Roy Rogers Show—"The Ride of the Ranchers" 4-20-52, "The Silver Fox Hunt" 4-19-53.

Gomez, Inez. Films: "Hell's Oasis" 1920 (Luna); "Cactus Trails" 1927 (Aunt Crater); "West of the Rockies" 1929 (Rosita); "The Dawn Trail" 1930 (Maria); "Under a Texas Moon" 1930 (Mother).

Gomez, Louis. TV: Tales of Wells Fargo—"Rio Grande" 6-3-57 (Pedro); Have Gun Will Travel—"The Bostonian" 2-1-58 (Jose); Maverick—"The Judas Mask" 11-2-58 (Juan); Wanted—Dead or Alive—"A House Divided" 2-20-60; Zane Grey Theater—"Calico Bait" 3-31-60 (Guitarist).

Gomez, Maria. Films: "The Professionals" 1966 (Chiquita); "Barquero" 1970 (Nola). ¶TV: The High Chaparral—"A Quiet Day in Tucson" 10-1-67 (Perlita), "The Champion of the Western World" 2-4-68 (Perlita), "For What We Are About to Receive" 11-29-68 (Perlita), "Stinky Flanagan" 2-21-69 (Perlita); Wild Wild West—"The Night of the Jack O'Diamonds" 10-6-67 (Isabel); Iron Horse—"Grapes of Grass Valley" 10-21-67 (Rosa); Hondo—"Hondo and the Commancheros" 11-10-67 (Teresa).

Gomez, Thomas (1905-6/18/71). Films: "Pony Soldier" 1952 (Natayo); "Frontier Badman" 1943 (Ballard); "The Daltons Ride Again" 1945 (McKenna); "Frisco Sal" 1945 (Dan); "The Eagle and the Hawk" 1950 (Gen. Liguaras); "The Furies"

1950 (El Tigre); "The Gambler from Natchez" 1954 (Capt. Barbee). ¶TV: The Texan—"The Man with the Solid Gold Star" 10-6-58 (Jake Romer); The Rifleman—"Stranger at Night" 6-2-59 (Artemus Quarles); Riverboat—"The Two Faces of Grey Holden" 10-3-60 (Mr. Tourette); The Virginian—"Beyond the Border" 11-24-65 (Fidencio); Laredo—"Oh Careless Love" 12-23-66 (Kicking Bear); Gunsmoke—"Survival" 1-10-72 (Agustin).

Gonzales, Indio. Films: "Dollar of Fire" 1967-Ital./Span.; "Five Dollars for Ringo" 1968-Ital./Span.; "Dig Your Grave, Friend ... Sabata's Coming" 1970-Ital./Span./Fr. (Miller); "And the Crows Will Dig Your Grave" 1971-Ital./Span.; "God in Heaven ... Arizona on Earth" 1972-Span./Ital.; "Shoot Joe, and Shoot Again" 1972-Ital.

Gonzales, Myrtle (1891-10/22/18). Films: "Anne of the Mines" 1914; "The Little Sheriff" 1914; "The Sea Gull" 1914; "Wards Claim" 1914; "A Child of the North" 1915; "The Legend of the Lone Tree" 1915; "The Man from the Desert" 1915; "The Sage Brush Girl" 1915; "The End of the Rainbow" 1916 (Ruth Bennett); "The Greater Law" 1917 (Barbara Hendeson).

Gonzalez, Felix. Films: "Sitting Bull" 1954 (Young Buffalo); "Villa!" 1958 (Don Octavio).

Gonzalez, Fidel. Films: "Johnny Yuma" 1966-Ital. (Sanchez); "10,000 Dollars Blood Money" 1966-Ital. (Mendoza); "Time and Place for Killing" 1968-Ital.

Gonzales Gonzales, Jose. Films: "The Three Outlaws" 1956; "Showdown at Boot Hill" 1958. ¶TV: Judge Roy Bean—"Family Ties" 10-1-55 (Juan Peralta), "Vinegarone" 12-1-55 (Juan Peralta), "The Katcina Doll" 1-1-56 (Juan); The Rebel—"Angry Town" 1-10-60 (Barber); Wagon Train—"The Jose Morales Story" 10-19-60 (Carlos); The Tall Man—"Rio Doloroso" 2-10-62 (Umberto).

Gonzalez-Gonzalez, Pedro (1925-). Films: "Wings of the Hawk" 1953 (Tomas); "Ricochet Romance" 1954 (Manuel Gonzales); "Strange Lady in Town" 1955 (Trooper Martinez-Martinez); "The Sheepman" 1958 (Angelo); "Rio Bravo" 1959 (Carlos); "The Young Land" 1959 (Santiago); "McLintock" 1963 (Carlos); "The Adventures of Bullwhip Griffin" 1967 (Bandido); "Hostile Guns" 1967 (Angel); "Chisum" 1970 (Mexican Ancher); "Support Your Local Gunfighter" 1971 (Ortiz); "Lust in the Dust" 1985 (Toothless Mexi-

can). ¶TV: The Cisco Kid—"Not Guilty" 12-20-52, "Horseless Carriage" 1-24-53; Tombstone Territory—"Mexican Bandito" 1-29-58 (Sancho); Frontier Doctor—"South of the Rio Grande" 4-18-59; The Texan—"Stampede" 11-2-59 (Pedro Vasquez), "Showdown at Abilene" 11-9-59 (Pedro Vasquez), "The Reluctant Bridegroom" 11-16-59 (Pedro Vasquez), "Trouble on the Trail" 11-23-59 (Pedro Vasquez), "Lady Tenderfoot" 5-9-60; Bonanza—"El Toro Grande" 1-2-60 (Valienta); Wanted—Dead or Alive—"Triple Vise" 2-27-60 (Tomas), "Baa-Baa" 1-4-61; Cheyenne—"The Wedding Rings" 1-8-62 (Pepe); Branded—"Fill No Glass for Me" 11-7-65 & 11-14-65 (Jose); Laredo—"The Treasure of San Diablo" 2-17-66 (Gonzales), "Scourge of San Rosa" 1-20-67 (Liveryman); The Big Valley—"Legend of a General" 9-19-66 & 9-26-66 (El Payaso); Rango—"In a Little Mexican Town" 4-14-67 (Drunk); Hondo—"Hondo and the Death Drive" 12-1-67 (Sancho); The High Chaparral—"The Firing Wall" 12-31-67 (Bartender), "Mi Casa, Su Casa" 2-20-70 (Pepe).

Goodall, Grace (1889-9/27/40). Films: "The Singing Vagabond" 1935 (Hortense); "Boss of Lonely Valley" 1937.

Goodboy, Joe. Films: "The Bugle Call" 1916 (Lame Bear); "The Dawn Maker" 1916 (Chief Trouble Thunder); "The Patriot" 1916 (Joe Goodboy); "The Primal Lure" 1916.

Gooding, Jr., Cuba. Films: "Lightning Jack" 1994-Australia (Ben Doyle).

Goodfellow, Joan (1950-). Films: "The Gun and the Pulpit" TVM-1974 (Dixie).

Goodrich, Edna (1883-5/26/71). Films: "American Maid" 1917 (Virginia Lee).

Goodwin, Aline. Films: "Warrior Gap" 1925 (Mrs. Hal Folsom); "Desert Gold" 1926 (Alarcon's Wife); "Riding for Life" 1926; "The Scarlet Arrow" 1928-serial; "Firebrand Jordan" 1930 (Joan Howe); "Pueblo Terror" 1931 (Martha).

Goodwin, Betty. Films: "The Empty Saddle" 1925 (Mary Manning); "One Shot Ranger" 1925; "Stampede Thunder" 1925; "West of Arizona" 1925.

Goodwin, Bill (1910-5/9/58). Films: "Riding High" 1943 (Chuck Stuart); "Heaven Only Knows" 1947 (Plumber).

Goodwin, Garry. Films: "Whirlwind" 1951 (Carl); "Captive of

Billy the Kid" 1952 (Pete); "Night Stage to Galveston" 1952.

Goodwin, Harold (1902-7/13/87). Films: "As in the Days of Old" 1915; "The Silent Man" 1917 (David Bryce); "Overland Red" 1920; "The Bearcat" 1922 (Peter May); "Man to Man" 1922 (Slim Barbee); "Tracked to Earth" 1922 (Dick Jones); "Trickery" 1922; "Kindled Courage" 1923 (Hugh Paxton); "The Ramblin' Kid" 1923 (Skinny Rawlins); "Riders of the Purple Sage" 1925 (Bern Venters); "Flaming Frontier" 1926 (Lawrence Stanwood); "Strawberry Roan" 1933 (Bart Hawkins); "The Lone Cowboy" 1934 (Hotel Clerk); "Smoking Guns" 1934 (Hank Stone); "Wagon Wheels" 1934 (Nancy's Butler); "Western Frontier" 1935 (Morgan); "Robin Hood of El Dorado" 1936 (Slocum); "The Cisco Kid and the Lady" 1939; "Jesse James" 1939 (Bill); "Susannah of the Mounties" 1939 (Union); "Union Pacific" 1939 (E.E. Calvin); "Ragtime Cowboy Joe" 1940 (Duncan); "Shooting High" 1940 (Gangster); "Texas Rangers Ride Again" 1940 (Comstock); "Viva Cisco Kid" 1940 (Hank Gunther); "Frontier Gal" 1945 (Bailiff); "The Scarlet Horseman" 1946-serial (Idaho); "The Bold Frontiersman" 1948 (Cowboy); "Carson City Raiders" 1948 (Starkey); "River Lady" 1948 (Larson); "Law of the Golden West" 1949 (Gibson); "The Wyoming Bandit" 1949 (Sheriff); "Desperadoes of the West" 1950-serial (Sheriff); "The Kid from Texas" 1950 (Matt Curtis); "The Vanishing Westerner" 1950 (Glumm the Undertaker); "The Redhead from Wyoming" 1953 (Henchman); "Night Passage" 1957 (Pick Gannon). ¶TV: *The Lone Ranger*—"Gold Fever" 4-13-50; *Gunsmoke*—"False Witness" 12-12-59 (Clerk), "Tag, You're It" 12-19-59 (Clerk), "Colleen So Green" 4-2-60 (Clerk); *Rawhide*—"Incident of the Sharpshooter" 2-26-60; *Wagon Train*—"The Whipping" 3-23-64 (Man); *Daniel Boone*—"My Name Is Rawls" 10-7-65 (Harper), "The Peace Tree" 11-11-65 (David), "Grizzly" 10-6-66 (Grover Hanks), "The Inheritance" 10-26-67 (Evans).

Goodwin, James (1929-80). Films: "The Young Guns" 1956 (Georgie). ¶TV: *Frontier*—"Mother of the Brave" 1-15-56; *Trackdown*—"A Stone for Benny French" 10-3-58 (Francis Zach); *Laredo*—"A Taste of Money" 4-28-66 (Fred Partens), "One Too Many Voices" 11-18-66 (Emerson Whitby, III); *Here Come the Brides*—"Land Grant" 11-21-69.

Goodwin, Laurel. Films: "Stage

to Thunder Rock" 1964 (Julie Parker); "The Glory Guys" 1965 (Beth). ¶TV: *The Virginian*—"A Gallows for Sam Horn" 12-2-64 (Peg Dineen).

Goodwin, Ruby (1903-5/31/61). TV: *Jim Bowie*—"The Cave" 5-9-58 (Rebekah); *The Texan*—"A Tree for Planting" 11-10-58 (Sarah).

Gora, Claudio (1913-). Films: "The Tramplers" 1965-Ital. (Fred Wickett); "The Hellbenders" 1966-U.S./Ital./Span. (Reverend Pierce); "John the Bastard" 1967-Ital.; "The Five Man Army" 1969-Ital. (Manuel Estaban).

Gorcey, Bernard (1888-9/11/55). Films: "Bowery Buckaroos" 1947 (Louie); "Dig That Uranium" 1956 (Louie).

Gorcey, David (David Condon) (1921-10/23/84). Films: "Prairie Moon" 1938 (Hector "Slick" Barton); "Bowery Buckaroos" 1947 (Chuck); "Dig That Uranium" 1956 (Chuck).

Gorcey, Leo (1915-6/2/69). Films: "Bowery Buckaroos" 1947 (Slip); "Dig That Uranium" 1956 (Slip).

Gordon, Bobby. Films: "The Measure of a Man" 1924 (Donald); "The Sign of the Cactus" 1925 (Jack as a Boy); "Lazy Lightning" 1926 (Dickie Rogers); "Law of the Wolf" 1941.

Gordon, Bruce. Films: "Bring Him In" 1921 (McKenna); "The Love Gambler" 1922 (Joe McClelland); "The Timber Queen" 1922-serial; "Kentucky Days" 1923 (Gordon Carter); "Ruth of the Range" 1923-serial; "Western Luck" 1924 (Leonard Pearson); "Brand of Cowardice" 1925; "The Dangerous Dude" 1925 (Harold Simpson); "Don X" 1925 (Frank Blair/Don X); "Gold and the Girl" 1925 (Bart Colton); "No Man's Law" 1925 (Monte Mallory); "Stampedin' Trouble" 1925; "The Vanishing American" 1925 (Rhur); "Ahead of the Law" 1926; "Beyond the Rockies" 1926 (Monte Lorin); "Born to the West" 1926 (Bate Fillmore); "Bucking the Truth" 1926 (Matt Holden); "The Dude Cowboy" 1926 (Carl Croth); "The Escape" 1926 (Howard Breen); "Lawless Trails" 1926 (Bud Clews); "Man of the Forest" 1926 (Jim Wilson); "Moran of the Mounted" 1926 (Carlson); "The Unknown Cavalier" 1926 (Bob Webb); "Blazing Days" 1927 (Dude Dutton); "Desert Dust" 1927 (Butch Rorke); "Hands Off" 1927 (Simeon Coe); "The Outlaw Dog" 1927 (Ed); "The Sonora Kid" 1927 (James Poindex-

ter); "Under the Tonto Rim" 1928 (Killer Higgins).

Gordon, Bruce (1916-). Films: "Curse of the Undead" 1959 (Buffer); "Rider on a Dead Horse" 1962 (Barney Senn); "Machismo—40 Graves for 40 Guns" 1970 (Burt); "Timerider" 1983 (Earl). ¶TV: *Have Gun Will Travel*—"The Bride" 10-19-57 (Louis Drydan), "Treasure Trail" 1-24-59 (Decker); *Tombstone Territory*—"Killer Without a Conscience" 11-20-57 (Jake Hoyt); *Gunsmoke*—"Kitty Caught" 1-18-58 (Jed Gunter), "Matt for Murder" 9-13-58 (Red Samples), "Distant Drummer" 11-19-60 (Sloat); *Trackdown*—"The Mistake" 4-18-58 (Steve Marriner); *Jefferson Drum*—"Bad Day for a Tinhorn" 5-16-58 (Juan Cavanaugh); *Northwest Passage*—"Break Out" 10-19-58 (Captain Hugo Marten); *U.S. Marshal*—"The Stool Pigeon" 12-6-58; *The Californians*—"Wolf's Head" 2-24-59 (Charles Savage); *Johnny Ringo*—"Cully" 10-8-59; *Bat Masterson*—"Shakedown at St. Joe" 10-29-59 (Jason Medford); *Riverboat*—"Forbidden Island" 1-24-60 (Garnett); *Tales of Wells Fargo*—"The Canyon" 2-1-60 (Garner), "Run for the River" 11-7-60 (Carl Orleans); *Laramie*—"Midnight Rebellion" 4-5-60 (Major Cantrell); *The Outlaws*—"Last Chance" 11-10-60 (Mercer), "The Cutups" 10-26-61 (Skinner), "Buck Breeson Rides Again" 1-25-62 (Fenn); *Stagecoach West*—"Life Sentence" 12-6-60 (Leo Calloway); *Sugarfoot*—"Welcome Enemy" 12-26-60 (Elias Stone); *Maverick*—"The Ice Man" 1-29-61 (Rath Lawson); *Death Valley Days*—"Loophole" 4-5-61 (Claypoole); *Bonanza*—"Mr. Henry Comstock" 11-7-59 (Winemucca), "Patchwork Man" 5-23-65 (Bronson), "A Matter of Faith" 9-20-70 (Scott); *Hotel De Paree*—"Sundance and Useless" 3-4-60 (Tom Reddiger).

Gordon, C. Henry (1883-12/3/40). Films: "The Gay Caballero" 1932 (Don Paco Morales); "Heritage of the Desert" 1939 (Henry Holderneys); "Man of Conquest" 1939 (Santa Ana); "The Return of the Cisco Kid" 1939 (Mexican Captain); "Kit Carson" 1940 (Gen. Castro).

Gordon, Clarke (1918-). Films: "Invitation to a Gunfighter" 1964 (Hickman); "The Way West" 1967 (Caleb Greenwood); "Journey to Shiloh" 1968 (Col. Mirabeau Cooney); "More Dead Than Alive" 1968 (Linus Carson). ¶TV: *Gunsmoke*—"Texas Cowboys" 4-5-58 (Gil Choate); *The Texan*—"A Tree for Planting" 11-10-58 (Brad Emory);

Rawhide—"Incident of the Haunted Hills" 11-6-59 (Henderson), "The Black Sheep" 11-10-61 (Jack Stone); *Empire*—"The Loner" 1-22-63 (Andy Owens); *Branded*—"A Taste of Poison" 5-2-65 (Howland); *Alias Smith and Jones*—"A Fistful of Diamonds" 3-4-71, "The Man Who Broke the Bank at Red Gap" 1-20-72 (Powers), "McGuffin" 12-9-72 (McGuffin); *Bonanza*—"Shanklin" 2-13-72 (Beasley); *The Texas Wheelers*—7-17-75 (Klate).

Gordon, Del. Films: "The Last of the Clintons" 1935 (Marty Todd); "Wild Mustang" 1935 (Reno Norton).

Gordon, Don (1926-). Films: "Revolt at Fort Laramie" 1957 (Jean Salignac); "Cannon for Cordoba" 1970 (Sgt. Jackson Harkness). ¶TV: *Sugarfoot*—"Brink of Fear" 6-30-58 (Robber); *Trackdown*—"Guilt" 12-19-58 (Hector); *Rough Riders*—"The Plot to Assassinate President Johnson" 2-5-59 (Jake); *Wanted—Dead or Alive*—"The Corner" 2-21-59 (Morley Teton), "A House Divided" 2-20-60; *The Deputy*—"The X Game" 5-28-60 (Queed); *Empire*—"Breakout" 4-16-63 (Quinn Serrato); *Shane*—"The Wild Geese" 9-24-66 (Johnny Wake); *Wild Wild West*—"The Night of the Cadre" 3-24-67 (Gen. Titus Trask).

Gordon, Edward (1886-11/10/38). Films: "The Dude Cowboy" 1926 (Count Duse); "Gun-Hand Garrison" 1927; "Ride 'Em, Cowgirl" 1939 (Grigg); "The Singing Cowgirl" 1939 (Trigger Wilkins); "Water Rustlers" 1939 (Sherman).

Gordon, Gavin (1901-4/7/83). Films: "The Silver Horde" 1930 (Fred Marsh); "The Great Meadow" 1931 (Evan Muir); "The Lone Cowboy" 1934 (Jim Weston); "The Lone Star Vigilantes" 1942 (Maj. Clark); "Pardners" 1956 (Businessman).

Gordon, Glen (1916-9/16/77). TV: *The Lone Ranger*—"A Broken Match" 12-2-54; *Rawhide*—"Incident with an Executioner" 1-23-59 (Stage Driver), "Incident at Red River Station" 1-15-60 (Guard), "Gold Fever" 5-4-62; *Bat Masterson*—"The Court Martial of Major Mars" 1-12-61 (Jake Sims).

Gordon, Grace. Films: "Lone Hand Wilson" 1920 (Madge Walker); "Three Bad Men" 1926 (Millie's Pal).

Gordon, Harold (1919-1/19/59). Films: "The Iron Mistress" 1952 (Andrew Marschalk); "Viva Zapata!" 1952 (Don Francisco Madero); "Yellowneck" 1955 (Cockney).

Gordon, Harris (1884-3/31/47).

Films: "Beyond the Law" 1918 (Young Emmett Dalton); "Out of the Silent North" 1922 (Reginald Stannard); "Romance and Rustlers" 1925 (George Wallace).

Gordon, Huntley (1897-12/7/56). Films: "Out of the Snows" 1920 (Sgt. Graham); "Secrets" 1933 (William Carlton); "The Great Divide" 1925 (Philip Jordan); "Gypsy of the North" 1928 (Steve Farrell); "Broadway to Cheyenne" 1932 (District Attorney); "Daniel Boone" 1936 (Sir John Randolph).

Gordon, James (1881-5/12/41). Films: "A Perilous Ride" 1911; "The Sheriff" 1911; "The Sheriff's Decision" 1911; "The Red Man's Burden" 1912; "The El Dorado Lode" 1913; "Jacques of the Silver North" 1919 (Don Baird); "The Last of the Mohicans" 1920 (Colonel Munro); "Sunset Jones" 1921 (David Rand); "Trailin'" 1921 (William Drew); "The Love Gambler" 1922 (Col. Angus McClelland); "The Grail" 1923 (James Trammel); "Man's Size" 1923 (Carl Morse); "The Iron Horse" 1924 (David Brandon, Sr.); "The Wanderer of the Wasteland" 1924 (Alex MacKay); "Beauty and the Bad Man" 1925 (Gold Hill Cassidy); "Tumbleweeds" 1925 (Hinman of the Box K Ranch); "The Buckaroo Kid" 1926 (Mulford); "The War Horse" 1927 (Gen. Evans).

Gordon, Julia Swayne (1879-5/28/33). Films: "The Dude Wrangler" 1930 (Dude Guest); "The Golden West" 1932 (Mrs. Summers).

Gordon, Leo. Films: "Pardners" 1917 (Alonzo Struthers).

Gordon, Leo V. (1922-). Films: "City of Badmen" 1953 (Russell); "Gun Fury" 1953 (Jess Burges); "Hondo" 1953 (Ed Lowe); "The Yellow Mountain" 1954 (Drake); "Man with the Gun" 1955 (Ed Pinchot); "Robbers' Roost" 1955 (Jeff); "Santa Fe Passage" 1955 (Tuss McLawery); "Seven Angry Men" 1955 (White); "Ten Wanted Men" 1955 (Frank Scavo); "Tennessee's Partner" 1955 (Sheriff); "Great Day in the Morning" 1956 (Zeff Masterson); "Johnny Concho" 1956 (Mason); "Red Sundown" 1956 (Rod Zellman); "Seventh Cavalry" 1956 (Vogel); "Black Patch" 1957 (Hank Danner); "Man in the Shadow" 1957 (Chet Huneker); "The Restless Breed" 1957 (Cherokee); "The Tall Stranger" 1957 (Stark); "Apache Territory" 1958 (Zimmerman); "Quantrill's Raiders" 1958 (William Quantrill); "Ride a Crooked Trail" 1958 (Sam Mason); "Escort West" 1959 (Vogel); "The

Jayhawkers" 1959 (Jake); "Noose for a Gunman" 1960 (Link Roy); "McClintock" 1963 (Jones); "The Night of the Grizzly" 1966 (Cass Dowdy); "Hostile Guns" 1967 (Hank Pleasant); "Buckskin" 1968 (Travis); "The Trackers" TVM-1971 (Higgins); "My Name Is Nobody" 1973-Ital. (Red); "The Barbara Coast" TVM-1975 (Chief Macdonald Keogh); "Maverick" 1995 (Poker Player). ¶TV: *Stories of the Century*—"The Doolin Gang" 8-12-55; *The Adventures of Rin Tin Tin*—"Wolf Cry" 10-22-65 (Charlie), "The White Buffalo" 10-14-55 (Garth), "The Third Rider" 3-16-56 (Pete Cregar); *Cheyenne*—"The Outlander" 12-13-55 (MacDonald), "Death Deals This Hand" 10-9-56 (Santell), "The Idol" 1-29-62 (Greg Kirby); *Frontier*—"Ferdinand Meyer's Army" 12-18-55 (Brandon), "The Big Dry" 3-18-56 (Pauk); *Gunsmoke*—"Hack Prine" 5-12-56 (Hank Prine), "No Chip" 12-3-60 (Hutch Dolan), "No Tomorrow" 1-3-72 (Hargis), "A Quiet Day in Dodge" 1-29-73 (Job Snelling), "The Town Tamers" 1-28-74 (Badger); *Circus Boy*—"Meet Circus Boy" 9-23-56 (Hank Miller); *Broken Arrow*—"The Raiders" 12-25-56 (Will Carr); *Tales of Wells Fargo*—"The Hasty Gun" 3-25-57 (Nick Breese), "Jeff Davis' Treasure" 12-5-60 (Adam Kemper), "Trackback" 12-30-61 (Frank Lambert); *Maverick*—"The War of the Silver Kings" 9-22-57 (Big Mike McComb), "According to Hoyle" 10-6-57 (Big Mike McComb), "Plunder of Paradise" 3-9-58 (Big Mike McComb), "Shady Deal at Sunny Acres" 11-23-58 (Big Mike McComb), "The Strange Journey of Jenny Hill" 3-29-59 (Big Mike McComb); *Have Gun Will Travel*—"Winchester Quarantine" 10-5-57, "The Fifth Man" 5-30-59 (Bert Talman), "Vernon Good" 12-31-60 (Harkness), "The Last Judgment" 3-11-61 (Moley); *Tombstone Territory*—"Guns of Silver" 11-27-57 (Pete Carter); *Rough Riders*—"The Imposters" 10-30-58 (Maj. Adams); *Tales of the Texas Rangers*—"Desert Fury" 11-20-58 (Joe Brock); *Bat Masterson*—"Dude's Folly" 11-26-58 (Joe Quinch), "Law of the Land" 10-6-60 (Red Eric Pederson); *26 Men*—"Run No More" 12-9-58, "Showdown" 2-3-59; *The Rifleman*—"The Angry Gun" 12-23-58 (Abe Jordan), "Which Way'd They Go?" 4-1-63 (Stack Wade); *Bonanza*—"The Sun Mountain Herd" 9-19-59 (Early Thorne), "The Deadly Ones" 12-2-62 (Forsythe), "Blood Tie" 2-18-68 (Fargo); *Bronco*—"The Soft Answer" 11-3-59 (Barnaby Spence), "Destinies

West" 2-26-62 (Nero Hollister); *Rawhide*—"Incident of the Valley in Shadow" 11-20-59 (Daggett), "The Lost Herd" 10-16-64 (Chris Jensen); *The Deputy*—"The Border Between" 3-12-60 (Evan Sloat); *The Law of the Plainsman*—"The Show-Off" 3-17-60 (Garth Rand); *Wyatt Earp*—"The Shooting Starts" 4-18-61 (Miggles Hannegan); *The Alaskans*—"Calico" 5-22-60 (Tracy); *The Outlaws*—"Rape of Red Sky" 10-27-60 (Hutch); *Lawman*—"Whiphand" 4-23-61 (Bull Nickerson); *Empire*—"The Tall Shadow" 11-20-62 (Jake); *The Virginian*—"West" 11-20-62 (Scratch), "The Hour of the Tiger" 12-30-64 (Lafferty); *Death Valley Days*—"The Debt" 2-20-63, "No Gun Behind His Badge" 3-28-66 (Bender); *Temple Houston*—"Toll the Bell Slowly" 10-17-63 (Charles Grimm); *Great Adventure*—"Wild Bill Hickok—the Legend and the Man" 1-3-64 (McCanles); *Laredo*—"Lazyfoot, Where Are You?" 9-16-65 (Moose), "The Land Slickers" 10-14-66 (Wayne Emerson); *Daniel Boone*—"A Rope for Mingo" 12-2-65 (Silas Morgan); *Pistols 'n' Petticoats* -11-12-66 (Cyrus Breech); *Rango*—"The Daring Holdup of the Deadwood Stage" 1-20-67 (Slade); *The High Chaparral*—"Gold Is Where You Leave It" 1-21-68 (Lije Driskill); *The Outcasts*—"The Town That Wouldn't" 3-31-69 (Mark Fenner); *The Men from Shiloh*—"Hannah" 12-30-70 (Bartender); *Alias Smith and Jones*—"Smiler with a Gun" 10-7-71.

Gordon, Marianne (1944-). Films: "The Gambler" TVM-1980 (Dallas); "The Gambler, Part II—The Adventure Continues" TVM-1983 (Dallas). ¶TV: *Laredo*—"Yahoo" 9-30-65 (Lady); *The Rounders*—9-6-66 (Lorene).

Gordon, Marjorie. Films: "Danger Trails" 1935 (Ruth Hopkins).

Gordon, Mary (1882-8/23/63). Films: "The Old Code" 1928 (Mary MacGregor); "Texas Cyclone" 1932 (Kate); "The Whirlwind" 1933; "The Man from Hell" 1934 (Mrs. Frank McCarroll); "One Man Justice" 1937 (Bridget); "Way Out West" 1937 (Cook); "Cowboy from Brooklyn" 1938 (Chambermaid); "The Marshal of Mesa City" 1939 (Ma Dudley); "Racketeers of the Range" 1939; "When the Daltons Rode" 1940 (Ma Dalton); "Singin' in the Corn" 1946 (Mrs. O'Rourke); "Fort Apache" 1948 (Woman in Stagecoach Station); "Deputy Marshal" 1949 (Mrs. Lance); "Haunted Trails" 1949 (Aunt Libby); "West of Wyoming" 1950 (Nora).

Gordon, Muriel. Films: "The Lone Avenger" 1933 (Ruth Winters).

Gordon, Olive. Films: "Border Devils" 1932 (Ethel Denham).

Gordon, Phyllis. Films: "The Hand of Fate" 1912; "A Message to Kearney" 1912; "Calamity Anne's Beauty" 1913; "The Vagabond Soldier" 1914.

Gordon, Richard (1893-9/20/56). Films: "Union Pacific" 1939 (Reporter); "In Old New Mexico" 1945 (Don Wills).

Gordon, Robert (1895-10/26/71). Films: "Blue Blazes Rawden" 1918 (Eric Hilgard); "The Mysterious Witness" 1923 (Johnny Brant); "The Wildcat" 1924.

Gordon, Roy (1884-7/23/72). Films: "Virginia City" 1940 (Maj. Gen. Taylor); "The Last Round-Up" 1947 (Smith); "Apache Chief" 1949 (Col. Martin); "The Cowboy and the Indians" 1949; "Riders in the Sky" 1949 (J.B. Balloway); "Riders of the Whistling Pines" 1949 (Hoagland); "Sons of New Mexico" 1949 (Maj. Hynes); "Indian Territory" 1950 (Maj. Farrell); "Mule Train" 1950 (John MacKnight); "Two Flags West" 1950 (Capt. Stanley); "Texans Never Cry" 1951 (Frank Bagley); "Lone Star" 1952 (Man); "Fangs of the Arctic" 1953; "The Vanquished" 1953 (Dr. Colfax); "Cattle Queen of Montana" 1954; "Silver Lode" 1954 (Dr. Elmwood); "The Gun That Won the West" 1955 (Col. Carrington); "Plunderers of Painted Flats" 1959 (Minister). ¶TV: *The Lone Ranger*—"The Man Who Came Back" 1-5-50; *The Gene Autry Show*—"The Lawless Press" 1-25-52, "Ruthless Renegade" 2-8-52; *The Adventures of Rin Tin Tin*—"The Frame-Up" 3-15-57 (Stanley Hale); *Death Valley Days*—"Gold Rush in Reverse" 10-21-57, "The Last Bad Man" 12-16-57; *Northwest Passage*—"The Deserter" 2-27-59 (William Jason).

Gordon, Russell. Films: "The Night Rider" 1920 (Jake Harnach); "Rounding Up the Law" 1922 (Branch Doughty).

Gordon, Susan. TV: *Gunsmoke*—"Little Girl" 4-1-61 (Charity Gill).

Gordon, William D. Films: "Powderkeg" TVM-1971. ¶TV: *Maverick*—"Escape to Tampico" 10-26-58 (Sam Garth), "Prey of the Cat" 12-7-58 (Fred Bender), "Two Tickets to Ten Strike" 3-15-59 (Eddie Burke); *The Law of the Plainsman*—"Prairie Incident" 10-1-59; *Riverboat*—"The Fight Back" 10-18-59 (Travis),

"Strange Request" 12-13-59 (Travis); *Rawhide*—"Incident of the Last Chance" 6-10-60 (Sid Gorman); *Laramie*—"A Grave for Cully Brown" 2-13-62; *The Virginian*—"West" 11-20-62 (Blench); *Alias Smith and Jones*—"What Happened at the XST?" 10-28-72.

Gore, Rosa (1867-2/4/41). Films: "The Man from Hardpan" 1927 (Sarah Lackey); "The Prairie King" 1927 (Aunt Hattie); "Hard Hombre" 1931 (Maw).

Gorman, Annette. TV: *Texas John Slaughter*—Regular 1958-61 (Addie).

Gorman, Charles (1865-1/25/28). Films: "The Call of the Wild" 1908; "Black Sheep" 1912; "The Chief's Blanket" 1912; "A Temporary Truce" 1912; "The Gambler of the West" 1914; "The Indian Trapper's Vindication" 1915; "The Primal Law" 1921 (Norton).

Gorman, Chip. *see* Giordana, Andrea.

Gorshin, Frank (1933-). Films: "The True Story of Jesse James" 1957 (Charley); "Warlock" 1959 (Billy Gannon); "Ride Beyond Vengeance" 1966 (Tod Wisdom). ¶TV: *Frontier Doctor*—"Shadows of Belle Starr" 1-3-59; *Empire*—"The Fire Dancer" 11-13-62 (Billy Roy Fix); *A Man Called Shenandoah*—"The Clown" 4-18-66 (Otto); *The High Chaparral*—"Stinky Flanagan" 2-21-69 (Stinky Flanagan); *The Men from Shiloh*—"Follow the Leader" 12-2-70 (Dutch).

Gorss, Saul (1908-9/10/66). Films: "Moonlight on the Prairie" 1935 (3rd Cowboy); "God's Country and the Woman" 1937 (Logger); "Heart of the North" 1938 (Anders); "They Died with Their Boots On" 1941 (Adjutant); "Dakota Lil" 1950; "Don Daredevil Rides Again" 1951-serial (Briggs); "Yaqui Drums" 1956; "Bullwhip" 1958 (Deputy Luke); "Warlock" 1959 (Bob Nicholson); "How the West Was Won" 1962 (Henchman); "Red Tomahawk" 1967 (Townsman). ¶TV: *The Deputy*—"Passage to New Orleans" 11-19-60 (Steward); *Laramie*—"The Long Road Back" 10-23-62 (Steeger); *The Loner*—"Escort for a Dead Man" 12-18-65 (Ferguson); *Branded*—"Headed for Doomsday" 4-10-66.

Gortner, Marjoe (1944-). Films: "The Gun and the Pulpit" TVM-1974 (Ernie Parsons). ¶TV: *Nakia*—"The Moving Target" 11-9-74 (Sonny Streeter).

Gosa, James. Films: "High Plains Drifter" 1973 (Tommy Morris). ¶TV: *Daniel Boone*—"The Renegade" 9-28-67, "A Bearskin for Jamie Blue" 11-27-69; *The Big Valley*—"Rimfire" 2-19-68 (Prospector), "Danger Road" 4-21-69.

Gossett, Jr., Louis (1936-). Films: "Skin Game" 1971 (Jason O'Rourke); "Sidekicks" TVM-1974 (Jason O'Rourke); "El Diablo" CTVM-1990 (Thomas Van Leek); "Return to Lonesome Dove" TVM-1993. ¶TV: *Cowboy in Africa*—"Fang and Claw" 10-30-67 (Fulah), "The Quiet Death" 2-19-68 (Hemera); *Bonanza*—"The Desperado" 2-7-71 (Buck Walters); *Alias Smith and Jones*—"The Bounty Hunter" 12-9-71 (Joe Sims); Black Bart—Pilot 4-4-75 (Sheriff Black Bart).

Gothie, Robert. TV: *Zane Grey Theater*—"A Man to Look Up To" 11-29-57 (Ben Mansen), "Man of Fear" 3-14-58, "Utopia, Wyoming" 6-6-58 (Blake Scott); *Trackdown*—"The Governor" 5-23-58 (Lance); *Wyatt Earp*—"My Enemy—John Behan" 5-31-60 (Will Morris); *The Virginian*—"All Nice and Legal" 11-25-64 (George Potter).

Goudal, Jetta (1898-1/4/85). Films: "White Gold" 1927 (Dolores Carson).

Goude, Ingrid (1937-). Films: "Once Upon a Horse" 1958 (Beulah); "Wild Heritage" 1958 (Hilda Jansen).

Gough, John (1897-6/30/68). Films: "Buck Parvin and the Movies" 1915; "This Is the Life" 1915; "Six Feet Four" 1919 (Jimmie Clayton); "Some Liar" 1919 (Locolke/Octogenarian Suitor); "Border Justice" 1925 (Phillip Gerard).

Gough, Lloyd (1907-7/23/84). Films: "Black Bart" 1948 (Sheriff Gordon); "River Lady" 1948 (Mike); "Rancho Notorious" 1952 (Kinch); "Tell Them Willie Boy Is Here" 1969 (Dexter). ¶TV: *The Loner*—"Widow on the Evening Stage" 10-30-65 (Harry Sullivan); *Gunsmoke*—"Treasure of John Walking Fox" 4-16-66 (Jacob Beamus); *Iron Horse*—"Diablo" 9-16-67 (Fitzpatrick); *Cimarron Strip*—"Sound of a Drum" 2-1-68 (Captain Bragg).

Gould, Graydon. TV: *The Big Valley*—"The Martyr" 10-17-66 (Russ Miller); *The High Chaparral*—"Follow Your Heart" 10-4-68 (Ed Lynch).

Gould, Harold (1923-). Films: "The Gambler" TVM-1980 (Arthur Stobridge); "The Gambler, Part II—The Adventure Continues" TVM-1983 (Arthur Stowbridge). ¶TV: *The Virginian*—"The Accomplice" 12-19-62, "Farewell to Honesty" 3-24-65

(John Harrison), "Day of the Scorpion" 9-22-65 (Lacey); *Empire*—"Stopover on the Way to the Moon" 1-1-63 (Judge); *Gunsmoke*—"Doctor's Wife" 10-24-64 (Hadley Boake), "The Guns of Cibola Blanca" 9-23-74 & 9-30-74 (Lucius Shindrow); *The Big Valley*—"Cage of Eagles" 4-24-67 (Major Wilson), "The Challenge" 3-18-68 (Judge William Daggett), "The Royal Road" 3-3-69 (Captain Crawford); *Wild Wild West*—"Night of the Bubbling Death" 9-8-67 (Victor Freemantle), "The Night of the Avaricious Actuary" 12-6-68 (Tebory Kovacks/John Taney); *Daniel Boone*—"The Imposter" 1-18-68 (Maj. John Richardson); *Lancer*—"The Last Train for Charlie Poe" 11-26-68 (Charlie Poe), "Dream of Falcons" 4-7-70 (Otto Mueller); *Here Come the Brides*—"Break the Bank of Tacoma" 1-16-70 (Cyrus Malone); *The High Chaparral*—"A Good, Sound Profit" 10-30-70 (Carlyle); *Dirty Sally*—4-12-74 (Lucius).

Gould, Sandra (1923-). TV: *Maverick*—"The Rivals" 1-25-59 (Lucy); *Wagon Train*—"The Donna Fuller Story" 12-19-62 (Edith).

Gould, William (-3/29/60). Films: "The Desert Outlaw" 1924 (Sheriff); "The Riddle Rider" 1924-serial; "The Phantom Thunderbolt" 1933 (Red Matthews); "The Trail Drive" 1933 (Honest John); "Gun Justice" 1934 (Jones); "Loser's End" 1934 (Bill Meeker); "Mystery Mountain" 1934-serial; "Smoking Guns" 1934 (Silas Stone); "Terror of the Plains" 1934 (Raymer/Butcher Wells); "Wheels of Destiny" 1934 (Deacon); "Big Boy Rides Again" 1935 (Bert Hartecker); "The Judgement Book" 1935 (Hank Osborne); "Rio Rattler" 1935 (Mason); "Swifty" 1935 (Cheevers); "Trigger Tom" 1935 (Mose Jeckyl); "The Unconquered Bandit" 1935; "Valley of Wanted Men" 1935; "Western Frontier" 1935; "Wolf Riders" 1935 (Butch Weldon); "Desert Guns" 1936 (Bagley); "Desert Justice" 1936; "Fast Bullets" 1936 (Drummond); "The Fugitive Sheriff" 1936; "Pinto Rustlers" 1936 (Inspector); "Sutter's Gold" 1936; "Wildcat Saunders" 1936 (Manager Joe Pitts); "Ranger Courage" 1937 (Harper); "Renfrew of the Royal Mounted" 1937 (Inspector Newcomb); "Wild Horse Rodeo" 1937 (Harkley); "The Purple Vigilantes" 1938 (Jenkins); "The Lone Ranger Rides Again" 1939-serial (Jed Scott); "Lightning Strikes West" 1940 (Marshal Jim Correy); "Ragtime Cowboy Joe" 1940 (Mansfield); "Riders of Pasco Basin" 1940 (Caleb Scott);

"When the Daltons Rode" 1940 (Deputy on Train); "Bad Men of Missouri" 1941 (Sheriff Brennan); "Man from Montana" 1941 (Thompson); "Texas" 1941 (Cattle Buyer); "The Spoilers" 1942 (Marshal Thompson); "Fighting Frontier" 1943 (Slocum); "San Antonio" 1945 (Wild Cowman); "Texas Panhandle" 1945; "Beauty and the Bandit" 1946; "Wild Horse Mesa" 1947 (Marshal Bradford); "Yellow Sky" 1948 (Banker); "Outcast of Black Mesa" 1950 (Walt Dorn); "Heart of the Rockies" 1951 (Warden Parker); "Law and Order" 1953 (Man). ¶TV: *The Lone Ranger*—"Buried Treasure" 3-2-50; *The Texan*—"No Love Wasted" 3-9-59.

Gould-Porter, Arthur E. (1905-1/2/87). TV: *Wild Wild West*—"The Night of the Grand Emir" 1-28-66 (George).

Goulet, Robert (1933-). TV: *The Big Valley*—"Brother Love" 2-20-67 (Brother Love).

Gover, Mildred (1903-9/11/47). Films: "The Dark Command" 1940 (Ellie, the Maid); "Santa Fe Trail" 1940 (Black).

Gowland, Gibson (1872-9/9/51). Films: "The Secret of Black Mountain" 1917 (Jack Rance); "The Fighting Shepherdess" 1920 (Bowers); "The Border Legion" 1924 (Gulden); "The Prairie Wife" 1925 (Ollie); "The Land Beyond the Law" 1927 (Silent Oklahoma Joe); "Land of Wanted Men" 1932 (Terry); "Without Honor" 1932 (Mike Donovan); "Northwest Passage" 1940 (MacPherson).

Gozier, Bernie (-10/2/79). Films: "Kiss of Fire" 1955. ¶TV: *Broken Arrow*—"Powder Keg" 2-19-57 (Miguel); *Wagon Train*—"A Man Called Horse" 3-26-58.

Gozlino, Paolo. Films: "Clint the Stranger" 1968-Ital./Span./Ger.; "One After Another" 1968-Span./Ital. (Jefferson); "To Hell and Back" 1968-Ital./Span.; "Vengeance" 1968-Ital./Ger. (Richie); "Django the Bastard" 1969-Ital./Span.; "Forewarned, Half-Killed ... The Word of the Holy Ghost" 1971-Ital./Span. (General Ruiz); "Heads You Die ... Tails I Kill You" 1971-Ital. (Fortune); "Thunder Over El Paso" 1972-Ital./Span.

Grace, Charity (1879-11/28/65). TV: *The Californians*—"Deadly Tintype" 3-31-59 (Hetty Kimball); *The Law of the Plainsman*—"The Comet" 1-21-60 (Mrs. Alymer); *Maverick*—"Triple Indemnity" 3-19-61 (Mrs. Parker).

Gradoli, Antonio (Anthony

Gradwell). Films: "Death on High Mountain" 1969-Ital./Span. (Braddock); "Sabata" 1969-Ital. (Fergusson); "Adios, Sabata" 1970-Ital./Span. (Major).

Gradwell, Anthony. see Gradoli, Antonio.

Grady, Don (1944-). TV: *The Restless Gun*—"No Way to Kill" 11-24-58 (Donny Maas), "Mme. Brimstone" 5-4-59 (Sylvester Cromwell III), "The Cavis Boy" 6-1-59 (Andy Cavis); *Buckskin*—"The Greatest Man in History" 1-5-59 (Mike Delany); *The Rifleman*—"The Patsy" 9-29-59 (Jeff Barrows), "Heller" 2-23-60 (David); *Wichita Town*—"Man on the Hill" 11-4-59 (Arnie Slocum); *Zane Grey Theater*—"Rebel Ranger" 12-3-59 (Ron Faring), "Death in a Wood" 12-17-59 (Zachary); *The Law of the Plainsman*—"Calculated Risk" 12-31-59 (Clint); *Wagon Train*—"The Christine Elliot Story" 3-23-60; *Have Gun Will Travel*—"The Calf" 10-15-60 (Lawson).

Graef, Neola. Films: "Fandango" 1970 (Joy).

Graeff, Jr., William. Films: "Rio Concho" 1968; "Monte Walsh" 1970 (Bartender).

Graff, Wilton (1903-1/13/69). Films: "Springfield Rifle" 1952 (Col. Sharpe). ¶TV: *My Friend Flicka*—"Blind Faith" 10-7-55; *Gunsmoke*—"20-20" 2-25-56 (Troy Carver); *Broken Arrow*—"Kingdom of Terror" 1-14-58 (Castellucci); *Jim Bowie*—"The Brothers" 4-4-58 (Joe Davis); *Tales of Wells Fargo*—"The Gambler" 9-8-58 (Roy Emmett), "New Orleans Trackdown" 12-23-61 (Manfred Montclair); *Wagon Train*— "The Last Man" 2-11-59 (Mr. Wentworth), "Weight of Command" 1-25-61 (Colonel); *The Restless Gun*—"The Cavis Boy" 6-1-59 (Bob Cavis); *Riverboat*—"Path of an Eagle" 2-1-60 (Henry Schofield); *Death Valley Days*—"Extra Guns" 11-23-60 (A.B. Webster); *The Virginian*—"The Judgment" 1-16-63.

Graham, Betty Jane. Films: "Rough Ridin' Justice" 1945 (Gail Trent).

Graham, Bobby. Films: "Gold Fever" 1952 (Cougar).

Graham, Charles (1897-10/9/43). Films: "On the High Card" 1921 (Pecos Bill/Don Antonio).

Graham, Fred (1918-10/10/79). Films: "Rose Marie" 1936 (Corporal); "Dodge City" 1939 (Al); "Santa Fe Marshal" 1940; "In Old Oklahoma" 1943; "The Lone Star Trail" 1943; "The Big Bonanza" 1944; "Buffalo Bill" 1944 (Editor); "Marshal of Reno" 1944; "Mojave Firebrand" 1944; "Outlaws of Santa Fe" 1944; "Silver City Kid" 1944; "Stagecoach to Monterey" 1944; "Tucson Raiders" 1944; "Zorro's Black Whip" 1944-serial (Black); "Bandits of the Badlands" 1945; "The Cherokee Flash" 1945; "Code of the Lawless" 1945; "Colorado Pioneers" 1945; "Dakota" 1945 (Bouncer); "Phantom of the Plains" 1945; "Santa Fe Saddlemates" 1945; "The Topeka Terror" 1945; "My Pal Trigger" 1946; "Out California Way" 1946 (Ace Carter); "The Phantom Rider" 1946-serial (Harry); "Buffalo Bill Rides Again" 1947 (Mr. Dawson); "Jesse James Rides Again" 1947-serial (Amos Hawks); "On the Old Spanish Trail" 1947 (Marco the Great); "The Sea of Grass" 1947 (Man); "Son of Zorro" 1947-serial (Quirt); "The Adventures of Frank and Jesse James" 1948-serial (Dirk #1); "The Bold Frontiersman" 1948 (Smokey); "Fort Apache" 1948 (Irish Recruit); "Son of God's Country" 1948 (Hagen); "The Timber Trail" 1948 (Frank); "The Fighting Kentuckian" 1949 (Carter Ward); "She Wore a Yellow Ribbon" 1949 (Hench); "Dallas" 1950 (Lou); "Heart of the Rockies" 1951 (Devery); "Overland Telegraph" 1951 (Joe); "The Big Sky" 1952; "Colorado Sundown" 1952 (Dan Hurley); "Old Oklahoma Plains" 1952 (Nat Cameron); "Rancho Notorious" 1952 (Ace Maguire); "The San Francisco Story" 1952 (Scud); "Canadian Mounties vs. Atomic Invaders" 1953-serial (Mills); "Escape from Fort Bravo" 1953 (Jones); "A Perilous Journey" 1953 (Whiskers, the Stowaway); "Backlash" 1956 (Ned McCloud); "The Last Hunt" 1956 (Bartender); "Seven Men from Now" 1956 (Henchman); "Badman's Country" 1958; "The Horse Soldiers" 1959 (Union Scout); "Rio Bravo" 1959 (2nd Burdette Man in Shootout); "North to Alaska" 1960 (Ole); "Seven Ways from Sundown" 1960 (Chief Waggoner); "Arizona Raiders" 1965 (Quantrill); "Pocket Money" 1972 (Herb). ¶TV: *The Lone Ranger*—"The Beeler Gang" 8-10-50; *The Roy Rogers Show*—"The Hermit's Secret" 5-1-52, "Haunted Mine of Paradise Valley" 5-18-52, "Flying Bullets" 6-15-52, "Death Medicine" 9-7-52, "Outlaw's Return" 9-28-52, "The Hijackers" 10-24-54, "Violence in Paradise Valley" 11-2-55; *Sergeant Preston of the Yukon*—"The Rebel Yell" 10-10-57 (Ed Latimer); *Broken Arrow*—"White Savage" 12-24-57 (Sergeant Dobbs), "Water Witch" 1-7-58 (Thug); *Wagon Train*—"The Cliff Grundy Story" 12-25-57; *The Restless Gun*—"The Gold Buckle" 12-30-57 (Sheriff Barclay); *Tales of Wells Fargo*—"Deadwood" 4-7-58 (Craig); *Maverick*—"The Spanish Dancer" 12-14-58 (1st Miner); *Rawhide*—"Incident of the Widowed Dove" 1-30-59, "Incident of the Fish Out of Water" 2-17-61, "The Black Sheep" 11-10-61; *The Texan*—"Caballero" 4-13-59 (Torrey Davis), "The Telegraph Story" 10-26-59; *The Law of the Plainsman*—"Amnesty" 4-7-60 (Joe Graham); *Laramie*—"A Grave for Cully Brown" 2-13-62; *Death Valley Days*—"The Lady and the Sourdough" 10-8-66 (Toomey).

Graham, Gerrit (1949-). TV: *Black Bart*—Pilot 4-4-75 (Curley).

Graham, Lyla. Films: "The Return of Jack Slade" 1955 (Abilene).

Graham, Malcolm (1897-1/59). Films: "Sandflow" 1937 (Parable).

Graham, Ronnie (1919-). Films: "Dirty Little Billy" 1972 (Charlie Niles).

Graham, Scott. TV: *Death Valley Days*—"The Fight San Francisco Never Forgot" 5-14-66 (Hans Eisman), "A Saint of Travellers" 2-14-70 (Forbes); *Bonanza*—"The Weary Willies" 9-27-70 (Trimble).

Graham, Tim. Films: "Cave of Outlaws" 1951 (Jones); "High Noon" 1952 (Sawyer); "Bullwhip" 1958 (Pete); "Gunfight at Comanche Creek" 1964. ¶TV: *The Lone Ranger*—"Man of the House" 1-26-50, "The Beeler Gang" 8-10-50; *Gunsmoke*—"Magnus" 12-24-55 (Cowboy), "Chester's Murder" 3-30-57 (Jonas); *Zane Grey Theater*—"A Quiet Sunda in San Ardo" 11-23-56 (Jess Robbins); *Tales of Wells Fargo*—"Alder Gulch" 4-8-57 (Store Proprietor); *Maverick*—"Ghost Riders" 10-13-57 (Hotel Clerk), "You Can't Beat the Percentage" 10-4-59 (Pop), "Full House" 10-25-59 (Willie Thimble), "A Flock of Trouble" 2-14-60 (Jensen), "Bolt from the Blue" 11-27-60 (Eben Blue); *The Restless Gun*—"Cheyenne Express" 12-2-57 (Hotel Clerk), "The Battle of Tower Rock" 4-28-58 (Harry Turner); *Sergeant Preston of the Yukon*—"The Generous Hobo" 1-2-58 (Charles Martin); *Wagon Train*—"The Dan Hogan Story" 5-14-58, "The Jud Steele Story" 5-2-62 (Sam Broderick), "The Gus Morgan Story" 9-30-63 (Walters), "The Michael Malone Story" 1-6-64; *Trackdown*—"The Brothers" 5-16-58 (Bartender); *Buckskin*—"The Venus Adjourner" 3-30-59 (Ted Edegardh); *Colt .45*—"Under False Pretenses" 1-10-60 (Ed Mills); *G.E.*

Theater—"Aftermath" 4-17-60; *The Alaskans*—"White Vengeance" 6-5-60 (Gil); *Cheyenne*—"The Frightened Town" 3-20-61 (Jeb Conroy); *Lawman*—"The Trial" 5-7-61 (Charlie), "Get Out of Town" 5-20-62 (Amos Hall); *Rawhide*—"The Gentleman's Gentleman" 12-15-61; *The Tall Man*—"Sidekick" 12-23-61 (Linus), "Enough Rope" 12-19-63 (Fred Jackson); *The Virginian*—"The Accomplice" 12-19-62, "Requiem for a Country Doctor" 1-25-67 (Clerk), "Silver Image" 9-25-68; *The Dakotas*—"Fargo" 2-25-63 (Johnny); *Redigo*—"Prince Among Men" 10-15-63 (Pop); *Daniel Boone*—"Not in Our Stars" 12-31-64 (Sparrow).

Grahame, Gloria (1929-10/5/81). Films: "Roughshod" 1949 (Mary); "Oklahoma!" 1955 (Ado Annie); "Ride Out for Revenge" 1957 (Amy Porter); "Ride Beyond Vengeance" 1966 (Bonnie Shelley); "Black Noon" TVM-1971 (Bethia). ¶TV: *Iron Horse*—"Appointment with an Epitaph" 2-13-67 (Rita Talbot); *Daniel Boone*—"Perilous Passage" 1-15-70 (Molly).

Grahame, Margot (1911-1/1/82). Films: "The Arizonian" 1935 (Kitty Rivers).

Grainger, Dorothy. Films: "The Woman of the Town" 1943 (Belle); "The Paleface" 1948 (Bath House Attendant); "The Desperados Are in Town" 1956 (Woman).

Granada, Maria. Films: "The Savage Guns" 1961-U.S./Span. (Juana); "The Big Gundown" 1966-Ital. (Rosita); "Son of a Gunfighter" 1966-U.S./Span. (Pilar).

Granby, Joseph (1885-9/22/65). Films: "Silver Butte" 1949-short; "Redwood Forest Trail" 1950 (Bart Bryant); "Viva Zapata!" 1952 (Gen. Fuentes). ¶TV: *The Cisco Kid*—"Phony Heiress" 7-21-51, "Ghost Story" 9-1-51, "Water Well Oil" 10-13-51; *Sergeant Preston of the Yukon*—"Rebellion in the North" 7-12-56 (Omiak).

Grandee, George (1903-8/1/85). Films: "Bustin' Thru" 1925 (Rudolph Romano); "The Meddler" 1925 (Secretary); "The Demon" 1926 (the Secretary); "The Man from the West" 1926; "Loco Luck" 1927; "Burning the Wind" 1928 (Manuel Valdes).

Grandin, Ethel (1894-9/28/88). Films: "Bar Z's New Cook" 1911; "Cowgirls' Pranks" 1911; "The Colonel's Peril" 1912; "The Colonel's Ward" 1912; "The Crisis" 1912; "The Deserter" 1912; "The Invaders" 1912; "The Law of the West" 1912; "The

Prospector's Daughter" 1912; "The Reckoning" 1912; "The Tenderfoot's Revenge" 1912; "The Vengeance of Fate" 1912; "Texas Kelly at Bay" 1913; "Wynona's Vengeance" 1913.

Grandon, Francis J. (1879-7/11/29). Films: "The Dancing Girl of Butte" 1909; "The Gold Seekers" 1910; "In Old California" 1910; "The Man" 1910; "Ramona" 1910; "Fighting Blood" 1911; "In the Days of '49" 1911; "The Indian Brothers" 1911; "The Last Drop of Water" 1911; "Was He a Coward?" 1911.

Granger, Dorothy (1911-1/4/95). Films: "The Fighting Fool" 1932 (Nina); "Blue Montana Skies" 1939 (Mrs. Potter); "When the Daltons Rode" 1940 (Nancy); "Honky Tonk" 1941 (Saloon Girl); "Lady from Cheyenne" 1941 (Myrtle); "North to the Klondike" 1942 (Mayme Cassidy); "Marshal of Laredo" 1945; "Sunset in El Dorado" 1945 (Maisie); "Under Western Skies" 1945 (Maybelle); "Dangers of the Canadian Mounted" 1948-serial (Skagway Kate); "Cactus Cut-Up" 1949-short. ¶TV: *Death Valley Days*—"California's First Schoolmarm" 11-4-57.

Granger, Farley (1925-). Films: "They Call Me Trinity" 1970-Ital. (Maj. Harriman); "The Man Called Noon" 1973-Brit./Span./Ital. (Judge Niland). ¶TV: *Wagon Train*—"The Charles Avery Story" 12-13-57 (Charles Avery); *Hondo*—"Hondo and the Apache Kid" 10-13-67 (Graham); *Nakia*—"A Matter of Choice" 12-7-74 (O'Hare).

Granger, Michael (1923-10/22/81). Films: "Hiawatha" 1952 (Ajawac); "Fort Vengeance" 1953 (Sitting Bull); "Battle of Rogue River" 1954 (Chief Mike); "Mohawk" 1956 (Priest); "Gunman's Walk" 1958 (Curley). ¶TV: *Tales of the Texas Rangers*—"Shorty Sees the Light" 9-10-55; *Gunsmoke*—"Helping Hand" 3-17-56 (Hander); *Broken Arrow*—"The Missionaries" 1-29-57 (Nantish); *Have Gun Will Travel*—"The Long Night" 11-16-57; *Rawhide*—"Incident of the Deserter" 4-29-60 (Yuber).

Granger, Stewart (1913-8/16/93). Films: "The Wild North" 1952 (Jules Vincent); "The Last Hunt" 1956 (Sandy McKenzie); "Gun Glory" 1957 (Tom Early); "North to Alaska" 1960 (George Pratt); "Among Vultures" 1964-Ger./Ital./Fr./Yugo. (Old Shurehand); "Flaming Frontier" 1965-Ger./Yugo. (Old Surehand); "Rampage at Apache Wells" 1965-Ger./Yugo. (Old Surehand). ¶TV: *The Men from Shiloh*—Regular 1970-71 (Colonel Alan MacKenzie).

Granstedt, Greta (1907-10/7/87). Films: "The Devil Horse" 1932-serial; "McKenna of the Mounted" 1932 (Shirley Kennedy); "Unconquered" 1947. ¶TV: *The Lone Ranger*—"Outlaw Town" 1-12-50, "Bad Medicine" 12-7-50, "Two Gold Lockets" 2-15-51, "Sinner by Proxy" 3-5-53.

Grant, Barra (1947-). TV: *Gunsmoke*—"The Widow-Maker" 10-8-73 (Teresa).

Grant, Cameron. Films: "The Silver Whip" 1953 (Charles Hatt).

Grant, Corrine. Films: "The Lady of the Dugout" 1918 (the Woman); "Whatever the Cost" 1918 (Belle).

Grant, Frances. Films: "Thunder Mountain" 1935 (Nugget); "Cavalry" 1936 (Betty Lee Harvey); "Oh, Susanna!" 1936 (Mary Ann Lee); "Red River Valley" 1936 (Mary Baxter); "The Traitor" 1936 (Mary Allen).

Grant, Gloria. TV: *Tales of the Texas Rangers*—"The Devil's Deputy" 1-7-56 (Ann Hartley), "Key Witness" 9-29-57 (Donna Tucek); *Circus Boy*—"The Fortune Teller" 6-9-57 (Alice Lilly).

Grant, Harvey. Films: "Take Me to Town" 1953 (Petey); "The Sons of Katie Elder" 1965 (Jeb). ¶TV: *The Adventures of Rin Tin Tin*—"The Poor Little Rich Boy" 10-7-55 (Whit Larrimore, Jr.); *Sergeant Preston of the Yukon*—"The Boy Nobody Wanted" 8-9-56 (Denny), "Blind Justice" 1-17-57 (Donny Andrews); *Circus Boy*—"The Little Fugitive" 11-11-56 (Robin); *Gunsmoke*—"Bloody Hands" 2-16-57 (Billy).

Grant, Katherine. Films: "Ridin' Thunder" 1925 (Jean Croft).

Grant, Kathryn (1933-). Films: "Reprisal!" 1956 (Taini); "The Guns of Fort Petticoat" 1957 (Ann Martin); "Gunman's Walk" 1958 (Clee Chouard).

Grant, Kirby (Robert Stanton) (1911-10/30/85). Films: "Lawless Valley" 1938; "Red River Range" 1938 (Tex Reilly); "The Wolf Hunters" 1949 (Rod); "Bullet Code" 1940 (Bud Matthews); "The Stranger from Pecos" 1943 (Tom); "Law Men" 1944 (Clyde Miller); "Bad Men of the Border" 1945; "Code of the Lawless" 1945 (Grant Carter); "Trail to Vengeance" 1945 (Jeff); "Gun Town" 1946 (Kip); "Gunman's Code" 1946; "The Lawless Breed" 1946; "Rustler's Roundup" 1946 (Bob Ryan); "Singing Spurs" 1948; "Song of Idaho" 1948 (King Russell); "Trail of the Yukon" 1949 (Bob McDonald); "Call of the Klondike" 1950 (Rod); "Indian Territory" 1950 (Lt. Randolph Mason); "Snow Dog" 1950 (Rod); "Northwest Territory" 1951 (Rod Webb); "Yukon Manhunt" 1951; "Yukon Gold" 1952; "Fangs of the Arctic" 1953; "Northern Patrol" 1953 (Cpl. Rod Webb); "Yukon Vengeance" 1954. ¶TV: *Sky King*—Regular 1951-53 (Schuyler J. "Sky" King).

Grant, Larry (1908-12/23/79). Films: "Man or Gun" 1958 (Rough).

Grant, Lawrence (1869-2/19/52). Films: "The Squaw Man" 1931 (Gen. Stafford).

Grant, Lee (1927-). Films: "There Was a Crooked Man" 1970 (Mrs. Bullard). ¶TV: *The Big Valley*—"The Lady from Mesa" 4-3-67 (Rosemary Williams).

Grant, Paul. TV: *The Restless Gun*—"Aunt Emma" 4-14-58 (Link Drake); *Shane*—"Killer in the Valley" 10-15-66 (Matthew Eberle).

Grant, Rodney A. Films: "Dances with Wolves" 1990 (Wind in His Hair); "Son of the Morning Star" TVM-1991 (Crazy Horse); "Geronimo: An American Legend" 1993 (Mangas); "Wagons East!" 1994 (Little Feather). ¶TV: *Hawkeye*—Regular 1994- (Chingachgook).

Grant, Shelby (1940-). TV: *Bonanza*—"The Last Haircut" 2-3-63; *The High Chaparral*—"Gold Is Where You Leave It" 1-21-68 (Dolly).

Grant, Stephen. Films: "Angel and the Badman" 1947 (Johnny Worth).

Grant, Wylie. Films: "Across the Plains" 1939 (Rawhide); "Jesse James" 1939 (Barshee's Cohort); "Zorro's Fighting Legion" 1939-serial (Martinez); "The Caravan Trail" 1946; "Driftin' River" 1946 (Sam).

Grantvoort, Carl. Films: "The Crusader" 1922 (Bob Josephson).

Granville, Bonita (1923-10/11/88). Films: "Song of the Saddle" 1936 (Little Jen); "Senorita from the West" 1945; "The Lone Ranger" 1956 (Welcome Kilgore).

Granville, Charlotte (1860-7/8/42). Films: "The Red Woman" 1917 (Dora's Mother); "Rose of the Rancho" 1936 (Dona Petrona).

Granville, Joan (-1/3/74). TV: *Sergeant Preston of the Yukon*—"Father of the Crime" 4-19-56 (Nancy Manners); *Rough Riders*—"End of the Track" 3-5-59 (Martha Healey); *Bat Masterson*—"Come Out Fighting" 4-7-60 (Belinda Muldoon); *Gunsmoke*—"Wishbone" 2-19-66 (Stage

Passenger), "Parson Comes to Town" 4-30-66 (Mother).

Granville, Louise (1895-12/22/68). Films: "The Scrapper" 1917; "The Trail of Hate" 1917 (Madge).

Grapewin, Charley (1875-2/2/56). Films: "Wild Horse Mesa" 1932 (Sam Bass); "The Bad Man of Brimstone" 1938 (Barney Lane); "The Girl of the Golden West" 1938 (Uncle Davy); "Stand Up and Fight" 1939 (Old Puff); "Texas Rangers Ride Again" 1940 (Ben Caldwalder); "They Died with Their Boots On" 1941 (California Joe); "The Gunfighters" 1947 (Inskip).

Grassby, Bertram (1880-12/7/53). Films: "The Coyote" 1915; "His Father's Rifle" 1915; "Liberty" 1916-serial; "Pioneer Trails" 1923 (Philip Blaney); "One Law for the Woman" 1924 (Bartlett).

Grassle, Karen (1944-). Films: "Little House on the Prairie" TVM-1974 (Caroline Ingalls); "Little House: The Last Farewell" TVM-1984; "Wyatt Earp" 1994 (Mrs. Sutherland). ¶TV: *Gunsmoke*—"The Wiving" 10-14-74 (Fran); *Little House on the Prairie*—Regular 1974-82 (Caroline Ingalls).

Gratz, Humphrey. Films: "Buffalo Bill and the Indians, or Sitting Bull's History Lesson" 1976 (Old Soldier).

Grauman, Sid (1879-3/5/50). Films: "Call of the Wild" 1935 (2nd Poker Player).

Gravage, Robert. Films: "The Rare Breed" 1966 (Cattle Guyer); "The Undefeated" 1969 (Joe Hicks); "Something Big" 1971 (Sam); "The Great Northfield, Minnesota Raid" 1972 (Farmer). ¶TV: *Gunsmoke*—"Catawomper" 2-10-62 (Wit), "The Gallows" 3-3-62 (Hangman), "Quint Asper Comes Home" 9-29-62 (Charlie), "The Bad One" 1-26-63 (Telegrapher), "Comanches Is Safe" 3-7-64, "The Intruders" 3-3-69 (Ennis); *Bonanza*—"A Lawman's Lot Is Not a Happy One" 10-5-69 (Barney); *Lancer*—"Chad" 1-20-70; *The Virginian*—"The Sins of the Father" 3-4-70 (Blacksmith).

Graver, Gary. Films: "Machismo—40 Graves for 40 Guns" 1970 (Tim Harris).

Gravers, Steve (1922-8/26/78). Films: "Hell Bent for Leather" 1960 (Grover). ¶TV: *Have Gun Will Travel*—"The Wager" 1-3-59 (Howard Gorman); *The Law of the Plainsman*—"Clear Title" 12-17-59; *Klondike*—"Taste of Danger" 12-5-60; *Rawhide*—"The Backshooter" 11-27-

64 (Fred Adams); *A Man Called Shenandoah*—"The Onslaught" 9-23-65 (Carl); *The Loner*—"One of the Wounded" 10-16-65 (Doc); *Death Valley Days*—"The Captain Dick Mine" 11-27-65; *Gunsmoke*—"Death Watch" 1-8-66 (Wales), "The Good People" 10-15-66 (Jed Bailey); *Bonanza*—"To Kill a Buffalo" 1-9-66 (Martinez); *The Virginian*—"Ride a Cock-Horse to Laramie Cross" 2-23-66 (Valera); *The Monroes*—"War Arrow" 11-2-66 (Hadley); *Here Come the Brides*—"Another Game in Town" 2-6-70 (Barney); *Alias Smith and Jones*—"The Legacy of Charlie O'Rourke" 4-22-71, "Miracle at Santa Marta" 12-30-71, "The Biggest Game in the West" 2-3-72, "The Ten Days That Shook Kid Curry" 11-4-72.

Graves, Gayla. TV: *Cheyenne*—"Two Trails to Santa Fe" 10-28-60 (Mary North); *Maverick*—"The Cactus Switch" 1-15-61 (Dottie Rand), "A Technical Error" 11-26-61 (Holly); *Rawhide*—"Grandma's Money" 2-23-62 (Melanie Agee).

Graves, Jessie (1879-3/4/49). Films: "The Sea of Grass" 1947 (Luke).

Graves, Peter (1925-). Films: "Rogue River" 1950 (Pete Dandridge); "Fort Defiance" 1951 (Ned Tallon); "War Paint" 1953 (Tolson); "The Yellow Tomahawk" 1954 (Sawyer); "Fort Yuma" 1955 (Lt. Ben Keegan); "Robbers' Roost" 1955 (Heesman); "Wichita" 1955 (Morgan Earp); "Canyon River" 1956 (Bob Andrews); "Texas Across the River" 1966 (Caapt. Stimpson); "Ballad of Josie" 1968 (Jason Meredith); "The Five Man Army" 1969-Ital. (Dutchman). ¶TV: *Fury*—Regular 1955-60 (Jim Newton); *Cimarron City*—"The Unaccepted" 2-28-59 (Jens); *Whiplash*—Regular 1961-62 (Chris Cobb); *The Virginian*—"A Matter of Destiny" 2-19-64 (Robert Gaynor); *Great Adventure*—"Kentucky's Bloody Ground"/"The Siege of Boonesborough" 4-3-64 & 4-10-64 (Daniel Boone); *Laredo*—"That's Noway, Thataway" 1-20-66 (Ben Conrad); *Branded*—"The Assassins" 3-27-66 & 4-3-66 (Senator Keith Ashley); *Daniel Boone*—"Run a Crooked Mile" 10-20-66 (Logan Harris).

Graves, Ralph (1900-2/18/77). Films: "Scarlet Days" 1919 (Randolph); "What Am I Bid?" 1919 (Ralph McGibbon); "The Long Chance" 1922 (Bob McGraw); "Three Texas Steers" 1939 (George Ward).

Graves, Robert (1888-8/19/54).

Films: "Ranger of the Big Pines" 1925 (Redfield); "Smilin' Guns" 1929 (Durkin); "Beyond the Law" 1930 (Stone).

Graves, Taylor. Films: "Crashin' Thru" 1924 (Freddy); "North of Nevada" 1924 (Reginald Ridgeway).

Gravey, Fernand (1904-11/2/70). Films: "Guns for San Sebastian" 1967-U.S./Fr./Mex./Ital. (Governor).

Gravina, Cesare (1858-1954). Films: "The Siren" 1917 (Rose's Father); "God's Country and the Law" 1922 ('Poleon); "The Circus Cyclone" 1925 (Pepe); "Don Dare Devil" 1925 (Esteban Salazar); "Burning the Wind" 1928 (Don Ramon Valdes); "The Trail of '98" 1929 (Berna's Grandfather).

Gray, Arnold. *see* Gregg, Arnold.

Gray, Beatrice. Films: "Trigger Law" 1944; "The Utah Kid" 1944; "Strange from Santa Fe" 1945; "Trail to Vengeance" 1945 (Alice). ¶TV: *The Gene Autry Show*—"The Star Toter" 8-20-50, "The Breakup" 11-5-50.

Gray, Billy (1938-). Films: "Bad Men of Tombstone" 1949; "Singing Guns" 1950 (Albert); "Gene Autry and the Mounties" 1951; "Sierra Passage" 1951 (Young Johnny Yorke); "The Outlaw Stallion" 1954 (Danny Saunders). ¶TV: *The Gene Autry Show*—"The Star Toter" 8-20-50, "Twisted Trails" 11-12-50; *Cheyenne*—"The Mutton Puncher" 10-22-57; *Stagecoach West*—"Dark Return" 10-18-60 (Frankie Niles); *The Deputy*—"Two-way Deal" 3-11-61 (Johnny Blatner); *Rawhide*—"Moment in the Sun" 1-29-65; *Custer*—"Desperate Mission" 11-8-67 (Billy Nixon).

Gray, Bonnie Jean. Films: "Flying Lariats" 1931 (Bonnie Starr).

Gray, Carole (1940-). Films: "Duel at Sundown" 1965-Fr./Ger. (Nancy).

Gray, Charles H. (1921-). Films: "The Black Whip" 1956 (Hainline); "Ride a Violent Mile" 1957 (Dory); "Trooper Hook" 1957; "Cattle Empire" 1958 (Tom Powis); "Charro!" 1969 (Mody); "Powderkeg" TVM-1971; "Wild Rovers" 1971 (Savage); "Junior Bonner" 1972 (Burt). ¶TV: *Gunsmoke*—"No Handcuffs" 1-21-56 (Sheriff), "The Guitar" 7-21-56 (Tyler), "Lynching Man" 11-15-58 (Bob Gringle), "Melinda Miles" 6-3-61 (Ray Tayloe), "May Blossoms" 2-15-64 (Lon); *Cavalry Patrol*—Pilot 1956 (Pvt. Reb Weeb); *Zane Grey Theater*—"The Deserters" 10-4-57 (Benson), "Hand on the Latch" 10-29-59 (Jared); *Have Gun Will*

Travel—"Duel at Florence" 10-11-58, "The Pledge" 1-16-60 (Cavalry Lieutenant); *Black Saddle*—"Client: McQueen" 1-24-59 (Josh Holt); *Rawhide*—"Incident of the Golden Calf" 3-13-59 (Flagg), "Incident of the Haunted Hills" 11-6-59 (Flagg); *The Texan*—"Blood Money" 4-20-59; *Yancy Derringer*—"Gone But Not Forgotten" 5-28-59 (Clay Wellman); *Riverboat*—"The Night of the Faceless Men" 3-28-60 (Joe Oliver); *Death Valley Days*—"White Gold" 2-15-61 (Cullen); *Gunslinger*—Regular 1961 (Pico McGuire); *Laredo*—"A Matter of Policy" 11-11-65 (Tom Davis); *The Road West*—"This Savage Land" 9-12-66 & 9-19-66 (Lieutenant Galloway); *Iron Horse*—"High Devil" 9-26-66 (Red Vitel); *The High Chaparral*—"The Champion of the Western World" 2-4-68 (Killian), "The Buffalo Soldiers" 11-22-68 (Lieutenant Beckert); *Alias Smith and Jones*—"The Posse That Wouldn't Quit" 10-14-71 (Jesse Jordan), "Bushwack!" 10-21-72 (Sheriff Wiggins); *Bonanza*—"Saddle Stiff" 1-16-72 (Cass Breckenridge).

Gray, Coleen (1922-). Films: "Fury at Furnace Creek" 1948 (Molly Baxter); "Red River" 1948 (Fen); "Apache Drums" 1951 (Sally); "The Vanquished" 1953 (Jane Colfax); "Arrow in the Dust" 1954 (Christella); "Tennessee's Partner" 1955 (Goldie Slater); "The Twinkle in God's Eye" 1955 (Laura); "The Black Whip" 1956 (Jeannie); "Frontier Gambler" 1956; "Star in the Dust" 1956 (Nellie Mason); "The Wild Dakotas" 1956; "Copper Sky" 1957 (Nora); "Town Tamer" 1965 (Carol Rosser). ¶TV: *Frontier*—"The Texicans" 1-8-56 (Ruth); *Tales of Wells Fargo*—"The Journey" 1-25-60 (Sandra); *Walt Disney Presents*—"Elfego Baca: Gus Tomlin Is Dead" 3-25-60 (Peggy Minters); *The Deputy*—"A Time to Sow" 4-23-60 (Lucy Willis); *Lawman*—"Mark of Cain" 3-26-61 (Rene Kennedy); *Maverick*—"Substitute Gun" 4-2-61 (Greta Blauvelt); *The Tall Man*—"The Woman" 10-28-61 (Edna); *Have Gun Will Travel*—"Ben Jalisco" 11-18-61 (Lucy Jalisco); *Rawhide*—"The Devil and the Deep Blue" 5-11-62 (Helen Wade); *Wide Country*—"A Devil in the Chute" 11-8-62 (Gypsy); *The Dakotas*—"Terror at Heart River" 4-15-63 (Mrs. Wyman); *Branded*—"Seward's Folly" 10-17-65 (Leslie Gregg); *The Virginian*—"Men with Guns" 1-12-66 (Pearl), "Requiem for a Country Doctor" 1-25-67 (Mrs. Marsh); *Bonanza*—"The Crime of Johnny Mule" 2-25-68 (Marcy).

Gray, Don (1901-7/24/66). Films: "Deadline" 1948; "Fighting Mustang" 1948; "Sunset Carson Rides Again" 1948; "Battling Marshal" 1950.

Gray, Dorothy (1922-5/9/76). Films: "Rose Marie" 1936 (Edith).

Gray, Gary (1936-). Films: "Gun Smugglers" 1948 (Danny); "Rachel and the Stranger" 1948 (Little Davey); "Return of the Badmen" 1948 (Johnny); "Whispering Smith" 1948 (Boy); "Masked Raiders" 1949 (Artie); "The Painted Hills" 1951 (Tommy Blake); "Rodeo" 1952 (Joey Cartwright); "Wild Heritage" 1958 (Hugh); "Terror at Black Falls" 1962. ¶TV: *Trackdown*—"The Feud" 2-11-59 (Luke Turley); *Wyatt Earp*—"The Buntline Special" 3-8-60 (Billy Clanton).

Gray, George (1894-9/8/67). Films: "Goofs and Saddles" 1937-short (Man).

Gray, Gilda (1899-12/22/59). Films: "Rose Marie" 1936 (Belle).

Gray, Gloria (1882-4/17/57). Films: "The Millionaire Cowboy" 1924 (Pauline Truce); "The No-Gun Man" 1925 (Carmen Harroway); "The Broncho Buster" 1927 (Barbara Furth); "On Special Duty" 1927; "Range Courage" 1927 (Betty Martin); "The Red Warning" 1927; "Put 'Em Up" 1928 (Helen Turner); "A Tenderfoot Hero" 1928; "Winged Hoofs" 1928; "Days of Daring" 1929; "Dodging Danger" 1929; "Western Pacific Agent" 1950.

Gray, Janine. TV: *Wild Wild West*—"The Night of a Thousand Eyes" 10-22-65 (Crystal); *The Loner*—"The Flight of the Arctic Tern" 10-23-65 (Terna).

Gray, Laurence (1898-2/2/70). Films: "The Rainbow" 1929 (Jim Forbes); "Timber War" 1935 (Larry Keane).

Gray, Linda (1940-). Films: "The Gambler, Part III—The Legend Continues" TVM-1987 (Mary Collins); "Bonanza: The Return" TVM-1993. ¶TV: *Big Hawaii*—"Pipeline" 10-12-77 (Annie Quinlan).

Gray, Lorna. *see* Booth, Adrian.

Gray, Margaret. Films: "Arizona Cyclone" 1928 (Kathleen Cosgrave); "The Bullet Mark" 1928.

Gray, Nadia. Films: "Sandy Burke of the U-Bar-U" 1919 (Dolly Morgan).

Gray, Nadia (1923-). Films: "Thunder at the Border" 1967-Ger./Yugo.

Gray, Roger (1887-1/20/59).

Films: "Everyman's Law" 1936 (the Lobo Kid); "Oh, Susanna!" 1936; "Rebellion" 1936 (Honneycutt); "Wild and Woolly" 1937 (Engineer); "Outpost of the Mounties" 1939 (Gaspar); "Buck Benny Rides Again" 1940 (Ranch Foreman); "The Durango Kid" 1940 (Jergens); "Out West with the Peppers" 1940 (Tom); "The Westerner" 1940 (Eph Stringer); "The Pinto Kid" 1941 (Dan Foster); "Pardon My Gun" 1942 (Sheriff).

Graybill, Joe (1887-8/3/13). Films: "The Fugitive" 1910; "The Heart of a Savage" 1911; "The Last Drop of Water" 1911.

Grayson, Donald. Films: "Dodge City Trail" 1937 (Slim Grayson); "The Old Wyoming Trail" 1937 (Sandy); "Outlaws of the Prairie" 1937 (Slim Grayson); "Call of the Rockies" 1938 (Slim Grayson); "Cattle Raiders" 1938 (Slim Grayson).

Grayson, Kathryn (1923-). Films: "The Vanishing Virginian" 1941 (Rebecca Yancey); "The Kissing Bandit" 1948 (Teresa).

Graziosi, Franco. Films: "Duck, You Sucker!" 1971-Ital. (Governor); "Deaf Smith and Johnny Ears" 1972-Ital. (Gen. Morton).

Grear, Geraine. see Barclay, Joan.

Greaves, Jr., Robert. Films: "Code of Honor" 1930 (Jed Harden); "Men of the North" 1930 (Priest).

Greaza, Walter (1897-6/1/73). Films: "New Mexico" 1951 (Col. McComb).

Green, Al (1889-9/4/60). Films: "Pride of the Range" 1910; "Pierre of the North" 1913.

Green, Austin. TV: *Jim Bowie*— "The Bound Girl" 5-10-57; *The Restless Gun*—"Quiet City" 2-3-58 (Abe Norton), "No Way to Kill" 11-24-58 (Doc Seton); *Tales of Wells Fargo*— "The Killing of Johnny Lash" 11-21-60 (Preacher).

Green, Dennis (1905-11/6/54). Films: "Northwest Passage" 1940 (Capt. Williams).

Green, Dorothy (1920-). Films: "Face of a Fugitive" 1959. ¶TV: *Wyatt Earp*—"The General's Lady" 1-14-58 (Mrs. George Armstrong Custer), "Cattle Thieves" 10-28-59 (Mrs. Morrison), "A Papa for Butch and Ginger" 5-9-61 (Amy Blyfield); *The Californians*—"The Duel" 2-18-58 (Hannah); *Sugarfoot*—"Price on His Head" 4-29-58 (Mother); *Wagon Train*—"The Old Man Charvanaugh Story" 2-18-59 (Helen Lerner), "The Clayton Tucker Story" 2-10-60 (Sab-

rina Tucker), "The Charley Shutup Story" 3-7-62 (Ethel Muskie); *Bonanza*—"Enter Mark Twain" 10-10-59 (Minaie), "The Way Station" 10-29-62 (Lucy), "Lothario Larkin" 4-25-65 (Laura); *Rawhide*—"Incident of the Stargazer" 4-1-60 (Marissa Turner), "Incident of the Fish Out of the Water" 2-17-61 (Eleanor Bradley), "The Bosses' Daughter" 2-2-62 (Eleanor Bradley); *Gunsmoke*—"Say Uncle" 10-1-60 (Nancy Nagle), "Lacey" 1-13-62 (Ellen Parcher), "Caleb" 3-28-64 (Julie); *Gunslinger*—"The New Savannah Story" 5-18-61 (Ella St. Clair); *Cheyenne*—"Storm Center" 11-20-61 (Lilly Mae); *Laramie*—"The Lawless Seven" 12-26-61 (Marian Hawks); *Wide Country*—"To Cindy, with Love" 2-28-63 (Mrs. Hopkins); *The Virginian*—"Farewell to Honesty" 3-24-65 (Laura Forrester), "Girl on the Glass Mountain" 12-28-66 (Mrs. Maguire); *Daniel Boone*—"The Flaming Rocks" 2-1-68 (Evelyn).

Green, Duke (-11/22/84). Films: "Hills of Peril" 1927 (Jake); "Call of the Wild" 1935 (Frank); "Robin Hood of El Dorado" 1936 (Guerrera); "The Lone Ranger" 1938-serial (Jailer); "Adventures of Red Ryder" 1940-serial (Janitor); "King of the Royal Mounted" 1940-serial; "Santa Fe Marshal" 1940; "King of the Texas Rangers" 1941-serial; "King of the Mounties" 1942-serial (Lookout/Ord/Spike #1); "Outlaws of Pine Ridge" 1942; "Daredevils of the West" 1943-serial (Dave/Henry/Attacker #1/Indian Rustler #4/Trail Heavy #2); "Zorro's Black Whip" 1944-serial (Evans/Brown); "Robin Hood of Texas" 1947; "The Adventures of Frank and Jesse James" 1948-serial (Carver); "The James Brothers of Missouri" 1950-serial (Brad/Cowl).

Green, Gilbert (1915-4/15/84). TV: *Gunsmoke*—"Durham Bull" 3-31-62 (Rudd); *Empire*—"Ballard Number One" 10-2-62 (Ed Jarvis); *The Virginian*—"The Judgment" 1-16-63 (Mercer), "Ah Sing vs. Wyoming" 10-25-67 (Sy Bailey); *Death Valley Days*—"Grotto of Death" 3-24-63 (Bennett), "The Westwide of Heaven" 3-28-64 (John McKay), "The Wild West's Biggest Train Holdup" 5-2-65 (Howell Hendricks), "Canary Harris vs. the Almighty" 2-26-66 (Jason Spoonover), "The Informer Who Cried" 11-11-67 (Starrett); *Rawhide*—"No Dogs or Drovers" 12-18-64 (Farnsworth); *Bonanza*—"Ride the Wind" 1-16-66 & 1-23-66 (Jensen); *The Big Valley*— "Danger Road" 4-21-69 (Jace Timmons).

Green, Harry (1892-5/31/58). Films: "The Light of the Western Stars" 1930 (Pie Pan Pultz); "The Spoilers" 1930 (Herman); "The Cisco Kid and the Lady" 1939 (Teasdale).

Green, Joseph. Films: "Roll, Thunder, Roll" 1949 (Pat); "The Baron of Arizona" 1950 (Gunther).

Green, Karen. TV: *The Adventures of Rin Tin Tin*—"Rin Tin Tin and the Apache Chief" 11-26-54 (Susan); *Fury*—"Girl Scout" 3-7-59 (Sally Ann Johnson); *Wagon Train*—"The Jess MacAbbee Story" 11-25-59 (Anna Belle), "The Cassie Vance Story" 12-23-63, "The Last Circle Up" 4-27-64 (Heather Browne); *Death Valley Days*—"The Gentle Sword" 11-9-60; *Stagecoach West*— "Not in Our Stars" 2-7-61 (Lucy Carr).

Green, Mitzi (1920-5/24/69). Films: "The Santa Fe Trail" 1930 (Emily); "Dude Ranch" 1931 (Alice Merridew); "Lost in Alaska" 1952 (Rosette).

Green, Nigel (1924-5/15/72). Films: "Africa—Texas Style!" 1967-U.S./Brit. (Karl Bekker).

Green, Seymour. TV: *Maverick*—"The Belcastle Brand" 10-12-58 (Albert); *Wild Wild West*—"The Night of the Bottomless Pit" 11-4-66 (Lime).

Green, William E. (1894-1/3/62) Films: "Lone Star" 1952 (Man). ¶TV: *The Lone Ranger*—"Danger Ahead" 10-12-50.

Greene, Angela (1923-2/9/78). Films: "Law of the Badlands" 1945-short; "King of the Bandits" 1947 (Alice Mason); "A Perilous Journey" 1953 (Mavis); "Shotgun" 1955 (Aletha); "Tickle Me" 1965 (Donna). ¶TV: *Wyatt Earp*—"The Frontier Theatre" 2-7-56 (Mrs. Harlow), "The Toughest Judge in Arizona" 5-24-60 (Alma Ross); *El Coyote Rides*—Pilot 1958 (Claire); *Wagon Train*—"Around the Horn" 10-1-58 (Belle), "The Lonnie Fallon Story" 2-7-62 (Laura); *Frontier Doctor*—"Danger Valley" 4-11-59; *Cheyenne*—"The Frightened Town" 3-20-61 (Harriet); *Lawman*—"The Unmasked" 6-17-62 (Marion Brockway).

Greene, Billy M. (1897-8/24/73). TV: *The Texan*—"A Quart of Law" 1-12-59 (Will Mathers), "Lady Tenderfoot" 5-9-60; *Maverick*—"The Sheriff of Duck 'n' Shoot" 9-27-59 (Herman), "The Goose-Drownder" 12-13-59 (Latimer); *Sugarfoot*— "Apollo with a Gun" 12-8-59 (Toby); *Bronco*—"Legacy of Twisted Creed" 4-19-60 (Washburne); *The Alaskans*—

"Calico" 5-22-60 (Nathaniel); *Bonanza*—"King of the Mountain" 2-23-64 (Storekeeper), "The Saga of Muley Jones" 3-29-64, "The Spotlight" 5-16-65, "A Real Nice, Friendly Little Town" 11-27-66 (Freddie).

Greene, Ellen. Films: "Wagons East!" 1994 (Belle).

Greene, Graham. Films: "Dances with Wolves" 1990 (Kicking Bird); "The Last of His Tribe" TVM-1994 (Ishi); "Maverick" 1994 (Joseph). ¶TV: *Lonesome Dove*—Pilot 10-2-94, 10-9-94 & 10-16-94 (Red Hawk).

Greene, Harrison (1884-9/28/45). Films: "The Westerner" 1934 (Announcer); "Guns and Guitars" 1936 (Dr. Schaefer); "The Lion's Den" 1936 (Auctioneer); "Senor Jim" 1936 (Boomer); "The Singing Cowboy" 1936 (Mayor); "Range Defenders" 1937 (Auctioneer); "New Frontier" 1939 (Bill Proctor); "Heroes of the Saddle" 1940; "The Trail Blazers" 1940; "Viva Cisco Kid" 1940 (Frank Snodgrass Benson); "Arkansas Judge" 1941 (Mr. Neill); "Bad Man of Deadwood" 1941; "Hands Across the Rockies" 1941; "King of Dodge City" 1941 (Stephen Kimball); "The Royal Mounted Patrol" 1941 (Office Manager); "The Son of Davy Crockett" 1941 (President U.S. Grant).

Greene, Jaclynne. Films: "The Stand at Apache River" 1953 (Ann Kenyon); "Stranger on Horseback" 1955 (Paula Morison). ¶TV: *Zane Grey Theater*—"Stage to Tucson" 11-16-56 (May Farrell); *Colt .45*—"Young Gun" 12-13-57 (Julie), "The Manbuster" 4-4-58 (Harriet Brenner), "Dead Aim" 4-12-59 (Millie).

Greene, James (1926-). Films: "Doc" 1971 (Frank McLowrey); "The Missouri Breaks" 1976 (Hellsgate Rancher). ¶TV: *Nichols*—"The Indian Giver" 9-30-71; *Adventures of Brisco County, Jr.*—"Pirates" 10-8-93 (Cartwright), "Deep in the Heart of Dixie" 11-5-93 (Cartwright), "Iron Horses" 11-12-93 (Cartwright).

Greene, Joseph J. Films: "Arizona Trail" 1943 (Doc Wallace); "The Old Texas Trail" 1944 (Jeff Talbot); "The Devil's Playground" 1946 (Sheriff); "Skipalong Rosenbloom" 1951; "Man in the Shadow" 1957 (Harry Youngquist). ¶TV: *Wild Bill Hickok*—"Ambush" 1-13-53; *Wanted—Dead or Alive*—"The Twain Shall Meet" 10-19-60.

Greene, Lorne (1915-9/11/87). Films: "The Hard Man" 1957 (Rice Martin); "The Last of the Fast Guns" 1958 (Michael O'Reilly); "Nevada Smith" TVM-1975 (Jonas Cord); "The Alamo: 13 Days to Glory" TVM-1987 (Sam Houston). ¶TV: *Wagon Train*—"The Vivian Carter Story" 3-11-59 (Christopher Webb); *Bronco*—"Prairie Skipper" 5-5-59 (Amos Carr); *Bonanza*—Regular 1959-73 (Ben Cartwright); *Cheyenne*—"Gold, Glory and Custer—Prelude" 1-4-60 (Colonel Bell), "Gold, Glory and Custer—Requiem" 1-11-60 (Colonel Bell).

Greene, Michael (1933-). Films: "Savage Red—Outlaw White" 1974; "The Great Gundown" 1977 (Preacher Gage); "The Mountain Men" 1980; "Gunsmoke: The Long Ride" TVM-1993 (Ike Berry). ¶TV: *Johnny Ringo*—"East Is East" 1-7-60 (Ferber); *Gunsmoke*—"Hinka Do" 1-30-60 (Cowboy), "The Goldtakers" 9-24-66 (Holcroft), "A Noose for Dobie Price" 3-4-68 (Corny Tate), "The Legend" 10-18-71 (Slim); *The Westerner*—"Jeff" 9-30-60, "The Courting of Libby" 11-11-60; *Wanted—Dead or Alive*—"Bounty on Josh" 1-25-61 (Sheriff Willis); *Cheyenne*—"A Man Called Ragan" 4-23-62 (Vance Porter); *The Rifleman*—"Outlaw Shoes" 4-30-62 (George Vale); *The Dakotas*—Regular 1963 (Deputy Vance Porter); *The Big Valley*—"The Invaders" 12-29-65 (Pinto Cade); *The Virginian*—"Girl on the Glass Mountain" 12-28-66 (Rail); *The Monroes*—"Gun Bound" 1-25-67 (Joel); *Laredo*—"The Short, Happy Fatherhood of Reese Bennett" 1-27-67 (Red Gully); *The Guns of Will Sonnett*—"Message at Noon" 10-13-67; *Bonanza*—"Stallion" 11-14-72 (Travis); *Kung Fu*—"Chains" 3-8-73 (Huntoon), "The Demon God" 12-13-74 (Aztec Priest).

Greene, Otis. TV: *Empire*—"No Small Wars" 2-5-63 (Don McKellar).

Greenleaf, Raymond (1892-10/29/63). Films: "Ticket to Tomahawk" 1950 (Mayor); "Al Jennings of Oklahoma" 1951 (Judge Jennings); "The Secret of Convict Lake" 1951 (Tom Fancher); "Horizons West" 1952 (Eli Dodson); "The Last Posse" 1953 (Albert Hagen); "Powder River" 1953 (Prudy); "Texas Lady" 1955; "The Violent Men" 1955 (Dr. Henry Crowell); "Three Violent People" 1956 (Carleton). ¶TV: *The Lone Ranger*—"Jeb's Gold Mine" 10-16-52, "Death in the Forest" 6-4-53; *Wagon Train*—"The Marie Dupree Story" 3-19-58 (Dupree), "Princess of a Lost Tribe" 11-2-60 (Joe); *Rawhide*—"Incident of the Sharpshooter" 2-26-60; *The Texan*—"Borrowed Time" 3-7-60 (Rev. Hibbs); *Wanted—Dead or*

Alive—"One Mother Too Many" 12-7-60 (Judge); *Laramie*—"The Fatal Step" 10-24-61; *Bonanza*—"The Gamble" 4-1-62 (Judge).

Greenstreet, Sydney (1879-1/18/54). Films: "They Died with Their Boots On" 1941 (Gen. Winfield Scott).

Greenway, Tom (1909-2/8/85). Films: "Deputy Marshal" 1949 (Bartenders); "Dakota Lil" 1950; "High Noon" 1952 (Ezra); "The Outcasts of Poker Flat" 1952 (Townsman); "Ride, Vaquero!" 1953 (Deputy); "Last of the Badmen" 1957 (Dallas); "The True Story of Jesse James" 1957 (Deputy Leo); "The Sheepman" 1958; "Three Thousand Hills" 1959 (Channault); "The Second Time Around" 1961 (Shack). ¶TV: *Gunsmoke*—"Chester's Murder" 3-30-57 (Ned Pickard), "Never Pester Chester" 11-16-57 (Treavitt), "The Lost Rifle" 11-1-58 (Will Gibbs), "The Cook" 12-17-60 (Gus); *West Point*—"Dragoon Patrol" 5-10-57; *Sheriff of Cochise*—"Copper Wire" 5-24-57; *Tombstone Territory*—"Geronimo" 3-5-58 (Kylie); *Wagon Train*—"The Dan Hogan Story" 5-14-58 (the Marshal); *Have Gun Will Travel*—"Death of a Gunfighter" 3-14-59 (John Sebrey); *Bonanza*—"Desert Justice" 2-20-60, "Feet of Clay" 4-16-60, "Gallagher Sons" 12-9-62 (Sheriff); *Bat Masterson*—"Dagger Dance" 4-20-61 (Ben Pick); *Rawhide*—"Incident of the Blackstorms" 5-26-61 (Hawthorne), "Judgment at Hondo Seco" 10-20-61; *Laramie*—"The Day of the Savage" 3-13-62; *Tales of Wells Fargo*—"Don't Wake a Tiger" 5-12-62 (Henry Sharp); *A Man Called Shenandoah*—"The Verdict" 11-1-65 (Marshal).

Greenwood, Bruce. Films: "Rio Diablo" TVM-1993 (Jarvis Walker).

Greenwood, Charlotte (1893-1/18/78). Films: "Oklahoma!" 1955 (Aunt Eller).

Greenwood, Monty. *see* Poli, Maurice.

Greenwood, Winnifred (1892-11/23/61). Films: "The End of Black Bart" 1913; "The Ghost of the Hacienda" 1913; "The Millionaire and the Squatter" 1913; "A Spartan Girl of the West" 1913; "Taming a Cowboy" 1913; "Her Fighting Chance" 1914; "Jim" 1914; "The Silent Way" 1914; "The Castle Ranch" 1915; "Reformation" 1915; "The Senor's Silver Buckle" 1915; "Truth or Fiction" 1915; "The Water Carrier of San Juan" 1915; "M'Liss" 1918 (Clara Parker); "To the Last Man" 1923 (Mrs. Guy); "The Flame of the Yukon" 1926 (Dolly).

Greer, Allen. Films: "Defying the Law" 1935; "Desert Mesa" 1935 (Bill Dobbs); "The Last of the Clintons" 1935; "The Phantom Cowboy" 1935; "The Reckless Buckaroo" 1935; "Rough Riding Ranger" 1935 (Lt. Rodriguez); "Rustlers' Paradise" 1935; "Saddle Aces" 1935; "The Silver Bullet" 1935; "The Texas Rambler" 1935; "Wagon Trail" 1935; "Custer's Last Stand" 1936-serial (Wild Bill Hickok); "Defying the Law" 1936; "Feud of the West" 1936; "The Riding Avenger" 1936; "Romance Rides the Range" 1936; "Arizona Gunfighter" 1937; "Galloping Dynamite" 1937 (Deputy Sheriff); "The Glory Trail" 1937 (Indian Joe).

Greer, Dabbs (1917-). Films: "Bitter Creek" 1954 (Sheriff); "The Desperado" 1954 (Jim Langley); "Rose Marie" 1954 (Committeeman); "Seven Angry Men" 1955 (Doctor); "Pawnee" 1957 (Brewster); "Day of the Outlaw" 1959 (Doc Langer); "Lone Texan" 1959 (Doc Jansen); "Showdown" 1963 (Express Man); "Shenandoah" 1965 (Abernathy); "The Cheyenne Social Club" 1970 (Willowby); "Little House on the Prairie: Look Back to Yesterday" TVM-1983 (Rev. Robert Alden); "Little House: The Last Farewell" TVM-1984 (Rev. Robert Alden); "Bonanza: The Next Generation" TVM-1988. ¶TV: *The Lone Ranger*—"Through the Wall" 10-9-52; *Gunsmoke*—Regular 1955-60 (Jonas Jones, the Storekeeper), "Marshal Proudfoot" 1-10-59 (Uncle Wesley), "Cowtown Hustler" 3-11-74 (Joe Bean); *Wyatt Earp*—"Mr. Earp Becomes a Marshal" 9-6-55; *Fury*—"My Horse Ajax" 3-9-57 (Sanders); *Trackdown*—"Easton, Texas" 10-25-57 (Station Agent); *Tombstone Territory*—"Ambush at Gila Gulch" 12-18-57 (Jim Edwards); *Wanted—Dead or Alive*—"The Martin Poster" 9-6-58 (Tom Wade), "Drop to Drink" 12-27-58 (Elder Boone), "Twelve Hours to Crazy Horse" 11-21-59 (Bartender); *The Restless Gun*—"Peligroso" 12-15-58 (Roy Stanton); *Black Saddle*—"Client: Banke" 4-11-59 (Denver Pollock); *Rough Riders*—"Paradise Gap" 4-16-59 (Sheriff Jenkins); *Zane Grey Theater*—"Checkmate" 4-30-59 (Sheriff Jim Roarke); *The Rifleman*—"Outlaw's Inheritance" 6-16-59, "Boomerang" 6-23-59 (Sam Elder), "Panic" 11-10-59 (Brett Conway), "The Jailbird" 5-10-60 (Farley), "The Promoter" 12-6-60 (Jack Tully), "The Wyoming Story" 2-7-61 & 2-14-61 (Finny), "The Stand-In" 10-23-61 (Bert Taylor); *Bat Masterson*—"Wanted—Dead" 10-15-59 (Will);

The Law of the Plainsman—"The Hostiles" 10-22-59; *Wichita Town*—"The Devil's Choice" 12-23-59 (John Matthews); *Death Valley Days*—"One Man Tank" 3-29-60 (Leo Harris); *Wagon Train*—"The Dr. Swift Cloud Story" 5-25-60, "The Wanda Snow Story" 1-17-65 (Hiram Snow); *Tales of Wells Fargo*—"The Bride and the Bandit" 12-12-60 (Ben Wilson); *Two Faces West*—"The Proud Man" 12-26-60 (Willie Medford); *Lawman*—"The Frame-Up" 1-15-61 (Les Courtney), "The Unmasked" 6-17-62 (Joe Brockway); *Rawhide*—"Incident of the Big Blowout" 2-10-61, "Incident of the Married Widow" 3-1-63 (Jedediah Haddlebird), "No Dogs or Drovers" 12-18-64 (Sheriff); *Bonanza*—"Broken Ballad" 10-29-61 (Will Cass), "Five into the Wind" 4-21-63, "A Christmas Story" 12-25-66 (Sam), "Judgment at Olympus" 10-8-67 (Dawes), "The Lady and the Mountain Lion" 2-23-69 (Doc Chukett), "What Are Pardners For?" 4-12-70 (Judge), "Terror at 2:00" 3-7-71 (Sam); *Have Gun Will Travel*—"Justice in Hell" 1-6-62 (Doc Halop); *Laramie*—"Justice in a Hurry" 3-20-62; *Empire*—"End of an Image" 1-15-63 (Joseph Williams); *Stoney Burke*—"Image of Glory" 2-4-63 (Doctor); *Temple Houston*—"Gallows in Galilee" 10-31-63 (Marshal Cloud); *Destry*—"Destry Had a Little Lamb" 2-21-64 (Dr. Forbes); *The Virginian*—"The Showdown" 4-14-65 (Doc), "Bitter Autumn" 11-1-67 (Harger); *Laredo*—"Road to San Remo" 11-25-66 (Ira); *Rango*—"Gunfight at the K.O. Saloon" 2-3-67 (Sheriff Simmons); *The Road West*—"Elizabeth's Odyssey" 5-1-67 (Thomas Grimmer); *Cimarron Strip*—"Nobody" 12-7-67 (Judge); *The Big Valley*—"Night of the Executioners" 12-11-67 (Matt Carson); *Wild Wild West*—"The Night of the Simian Terror" 2-16-68 (Senator Buckley), "The Night of Fire and Brimstone" 11-22-68 (Capt. Lyman Butler); *Lancer*—"The Kid" 10-7-69 (Sheriff); *Nichols*—"Sleight of Hand" 2-1-72 (Harrigan); *Little House on the Prairie*—Regular 1974-82 (Reverend Robert Alden).

Greer, Jane (1924-). Films: "Sunset Pass" 1946 (Helen); "Station West" 1948 (Charlie); "The Shadow Riders" TVM-1982 (Ma Traven). ¶TV: *Zane Grey Theater*—"A Gun for My Bride" 12-27-57 (Ellen Morrow), "The Vaunted" 11-27-58 (Ellie Matson), "Stagecoach to Yuma" 5-5-60 (Julie); *Stagecoach West*—"High Lonesome" 10-4-60 (Kathleen).

Gregg, Alan (1893-1965). Films:

"The Devil's Saddle Legion" 1937 (Jim Cudlow); "Rhythm of the Saddle" 1938; "Zorro's Fighting Legion" 1939-serial (Salvador); "King of the Royal Mounted" 1940-serial (Mills); "King of the Texas Rangers" 1941-serial (Carl).

Gregg, Arnold (Arnold Gray) (1899-5/3/36). Films: "The Line Runners" 1920; "The Power of the Weak" 1926 (the Man); "The Flame of the Yukon" 1926 (George Fowler); "West of Broadway" 1926 (Bruce Elwood); "The Slingshot Kid" 1927 (Foreman).

Gregg, Bradley. Films: "Lonesome Dove" TVM-1989 (Sean).

Gregg, Julie (1944-). TV: *Jefferson Drum*—"The Hanging of Joe Lavetti" 8-1-58 (Louise Hammond); *Bonanza*—"Mighty Is the Word" 11-7-65 (Dolly); *Iron Horse*—"The Execution" 3-13-67 (Nela Cromarty); *The Virginian*—"The Gift" 3-18-70 (Sally Anne); *Gunsmoke*—"The Convict" 2-1-71 (Beth Wilson).

Gregg, Virginia (1917-9/15/86). Films: "Fastest Gun Alive" 1956 (Rose Ribbs); "The Hanging Tree" 1959 (Edna Flaunce); "Shoot Out at Big Sag" 1962 (Sarah Hawker); "A Big Hand for the Little Lady" 1966 (Mrs. Drummond); "Heaven with a Gun" 1969 (Mrs. Patterson). ¶TV: *Colt .45*—"Gallows at Granite Gap" 11-8-57 (Martha Naylor); *Maverick*—"Day of Reckoning" 2-2-58 (Amy Hardie), "Pappy" 9-13-59 (Gilda Jamison), "The Ice Man" 1-29-61 (Abbey); *Tombstone Territory*—"Postmarked for Death" 2-12-58 (Ella Hawley); *Trackdown*—"The Wedding" 2-14-58 (Matilda Parsons); *Gunsmoke*—"Joke's on Us" 3-15-58 (Mrs. Tilman), "Minnie" 4-15-61 (Minnie Higgens), "The Imposter" 5-13-61 (Mrs. Curtin), "The Search" 9-15-62 (Ess Cutler), "Phoebe Strunk" 11-20-62 (Phoebe Strunk), "Sanctuary" 2-26-66 (Miss Howell), "The Twisted Heritage" 1-6-69 (Jessie Copperton); *Sugarfoot*—"Price on His Head" 4-29-58 (Girl), "Wolf" 6-9-59 (Belle Kellogg); *Have Gun Will Travel*—"A Sense of Justice" 11-1-58 (Widow Briggs), "A Sense of Justice" 11-1-58, "Don't Shoot the Piano Player" 3-10-62 (Nellie); *Wanted—Dead or Alive*—"Eight Cent Record" 12-20-58 (Hilda Stone), "The Healing Woman" 9-12-59 (Manda); *Rawhide*—"Incident of the Misplaced Indians" 5-1-59 (Clarissa Gray), "Incident of the Comanchero" 3-22-63 (Sister Margaret), "Incident of the Banker" 4-2-64 (Sarah); *Wichita Town*—"Man on the Hill" 11-4-59

(Mal Slocum); *Man from Black-hawk*—"The Last Days of Jessie Turnbull" 4-1-60 (Julie Turnbull); *Bronco*—"Winter Kill" 5-31-60 (Kate Crowley); *Klondike*—"Saints and Stickups" 10-31-60 (Harmony Harless); *The Deputy*—"Bitter Foot" 11-5-60 (Hester Macklin); *The Westerner*—"Going Home" 12-16-60; *The Rebel*—"Paperback Hero" 1-29-61 (Emily Stevens); *Bat Masterson*—"A Lesson in Violence" 2-23-61 (Nora Grant); *Zane Grey Theater*—"The Atoner" 4-6-61 (Sarah Tompkins); *Lawman*—"Clootey Hutter" 3-11-62 (Clootey Hutter); *Wide Country*—"Whose Hand at My Throat?" 2-14-63 (Alice Bearing); *Empire*—"A House in Order" 3-5-63 (Mrs. Austin); *Temple Houston*—"Jubilee" 11-14-63 (Elizabeth Clendennon); *Wagon Train*—"The Fenton Canaby Story" 12-30-63 (Grace Lowe), "The John Gillman Story" 10-4-64 (Miss Roberts); *The Virginian*—"The Secret of Brynmar Hall" 4-1-64, "Bitter Autumn" 11-1-67 (Hattie McLain), "Ride the Misadventure" 11-6-68 (Ma Daggert), "A Time of Terror" 2-11-70 (Mary McMasters); *Bonanza*—"Logan's Treasure" 10-18-64 (Angie); *The Legend of Jesse James*—"Three Men from Now" 9-13-65 (Mrs. Haynes); *The Big Valley*—"The Stallion" 1-30-67; *The Road West*—"The Agreement" 4-24-67 (Lavinia Bishop); *The Guns of Will Sonnett*—"A Son for a Son" 10-20-67 (Mrs. Murdock); *Daniel Boone*—"The Witness" 1-25-68 (Nettie Pike); *The Outcasts*—"Take Your Lover in the Ring" 10-28-68 (Odette); *The Big Valley*—"Point and Counterpoint" 11-19-69 (Sarah Clark); *Alias Smith and Jones*—"Which Way to the O.K. Corral?" 2-10-72; *Hec Ramsey*—"The Mystery of the Yellow Rose" 1-28-73 (Mrs. Lambert).

Gregg, Walter. Films: "Hour of the Gun" 1967 (Billy Clanton). ¶TV: *Dundee and the Culhane*—9-27-67 (Jesse Carson).

Gregory, Bob (1900-5/13/71). Films: "Dudes Are Pretty People" 1942.

Gregory, Ena (1905-7/3/65). Films: "A Western Romance" 1913; "The Devil's Dooryard" 1923 (Mary Jane Haley); "The Law Rustlers" 1923 (Glory Stillman); "The Calgary Stampede" 1925 (Trixie); "Cold Nerve" 1925; "The Desert Flower" 1925 (Fay Knight); "Red Hot Leather" 1926 (Ellen Rand); "Blazing Days" 1927 (Milly Morgan); "Grinning Guns" 1927 (Mary Felden); "Men of Daring" 1927 (Nancy

Owen); "The One-Man Trail" 1927; "Rough and Ready" 1927 (Beth Stone); "The Western Rover" 1927 (Millie Donlin).

Gregory, James (1911-). Films: "Gun Glory" 1957 (Grimsell); "A Distant Trumpet" 1964 (Gen. Quait); "The Sons of Katie Elder" 1965 (Morgan Hastings); "Shoot Out" 1971 (Sam Foley). ¶TV: *Laramie*—"Man of God" 12-1-59 (Father Elliot), "The Sometime Gambler" 3-19-63 (Richards); *Wagon Train*—"The Ricky and Laura Bell Story" 2-24-60 (Ricky Bell); *Frontier Circus*—"The Depths of Fear" 10-5-61 (Jacob Carno); *The Virginian*—"Fifty Days to Moose Jaw" 12-12-62 (Slim Jessup), "Without Mercy" 2-15-67 (Cal Young), "The Price of Love" 2-12-69 (Kimbro); *Empire*—"When the Gods Laugh" 12-18-62 (Theron Haskell); *Rawhide*—"Incident at Crooked Hat" 2-1-63 (Owen Spencer/Jack Jennings), "Incident of the Peyote Cup" 5-14-64 (Brothers), "Six Weeks to Bent Fork" 9-28-65 (Lash); *Bonanza*—"A Man to Admire" 12-6-64 (Whit Parker), "Second Chance" 9-17-67 (Mulvaney), "Company of Forgotten Men" 2-2-69 (Sgt. Mike Russell); *Gunsmoke*—"The New Society" 5-22-65 (John Scanlon), "Judge Calvin Strom" 12-18-65 (Judge Calvin Strom), "The Victim" 1-1-68 (Wes Martin); *Wild Wild West*—"The Night of the Inferno" 9-17-65 (President Ulysses S. Grant); *A Man Called Shenandoah*—"The Lost Diablo" 1-24-66 (Jake Roberts); *The Loner*—"A Question of Guilt" 1-29-66 (Major Crane); *F Troop*—"Lieutenant O'Rourke, Front and Center" 4-26-66 (Major Duncan), "Carpetbagging, Anyone?" 3-16-67 (Parker); *The Big Valley*—"Pursuit" 10-10-66 (Simon Carter), "Ambush" 9-18-67 (Simon Carter), "The Challenge" 3-18-68 (Senator Jim Bannard), "The Other Face of Justice" 3-31-69 (Harry Bodine); *Cimarron Strip*—"The Hunted" 10-5-67 (Buckman); *Cowboy in Africa*—"Fang and Claw" 10-30-67 (Blue Eyes); *Daniel Boone*—"The Value of a King" 11-9-67 (Captain Asa Webb); *The High Chaparral*—"The Hair Hunter" 3-10-68 (Jake Stoner); *The Outcasts*—"Three Ways to Die" 10-7-68 (Sheriff Giles); *Lancer*—"The Lawman" 10-22-68 (Marshal Joe Barker); *The Men from Shiloh*—"Last of the Comancheros" 12-9-70 (Sheriff).

Gregory, Mary. Films: "Trooper Hook" 1957. ¶TV: *Gunsmoke*—"Yorky" 2-18-56 (Mrs. Seldon); *Wagon Train*—"The Vincent Eaglewood Story" 4-15-59 (Mrs. Benadarsi),

"The Jeff Hartfield Story" 2-14-62 (Mrs. Adams); *Have Gun Will Travel*—"The Night the Town Died" 2-6-60 (Frieda Howard), "Alive" 3-17-62; *The Rebel*—"Unsurrendered Sword" 4-3-60 (Elvira).

Gregory, Mildred. Films: "The Valley of Lost Hope" 1915 (Dora Royce).

Gregory, Sebastian. Films: "Fandango" 1970 (Muck Mulligan).

Greig, Robert (1880-6/27/58). Films: "The Conquerors" 1932; "Robbers' Roost" 1933 (Tulliver); "Rose Marie" 1936 (Cafe Manager); "Drums Along the Mohawk" 1939 (Mr. Borst); "Hudson Bay" 1941 (Sir Robert).

Greigo, Sandra. Films: "The Chisholms" TVM-1979 (Kewedinok). ¶TV: *The Chisholms*—Regular 1979 (Kewedinok Chisholm); *Born to the Wind* 1982 (Red Stone).

Grey, Duane (Duane Thorsen) (1921-). Films: "Canadian Mounties vs. Atomic Invaders" 1953-serial; "Jack Slade" 1953; "Seminole" 1953 (Hendricks); "The Black Whip" 1956 (Deputy Floyd); "Cattle Empire" 1958 (Aruzza); "Charro!" 1969 (Gabe); "Powderkeg" TVM-1971. ¶TV: *Wild Bill Hickok*—"Clem's Reformation" 7-7-53; *The Adventures of Rin Tin Tin*—"Rusty Goes to Town" 11-25-55, "The Old Soldier" 4-12-57 (Shag); *Death Valley Days*—"Mr. Bigfoot" 3-24-56, "The Hoodoo Mine" 4-7-56 (Bill Snyder), "The Gold Mine on Main Street" 5-11-68; *Gunsmoke*—"The Guitar" 7-21-56 (Delmer), "The Way It Is" 12-1-62 (Rancher), "I Call Him Wonder" 3-23-63 (Keogh); *Zane Grey Theater*—"Man Alone" 3-5-59; *The Texan*—"South of the Border" 5-18-59; *Have Gun Will Travel*—"High Wire" 11-2-57, "The Haunted Trees" 6-13-59; *Sugarfoot*—"The Dead Hills" 3-4-58 (Art Beal); *Maverick*—"Two Beggars on Horseback" 1-18-59 (Howie Horwitz), "Two Tickets to Ten Strike" 3-15-59 (Sheriff); *Rawhide*—"Incident at the Edge of Madness" 2-6-59, "Incident of the Thirteenth Man" 10-23-59, "Incident at Sulphur Creek" 3-11-60, "Incident at Dragoon Crossing" 10-21-60 (Jose Becerra), "Incident of the Pied Piper" 2-6-64 (Frank Travis); *Man from Blackhawk*—"In His Steps" 5-20-60 (Bodyguard); *Gunslinger*—"Johnny Sergeant" 5-4-61 (Luke); *Empire*—"The Tall Shadow" 11-20-62 (Fred); *Wagon Train*—"The Melanie Craig Story" 2-17-64; *Branded*—"The Bounty" 2-21-65; *Iron Horse*—"The Man from New Chicago" 11-14-66, "Dealer's Choice" 12-9-67

(Bartender); *Bonanza*—"The Sure Thing" 11-12-67 (Townsman), "My Friend, My Enemy" 1-12-69, "The Deserter" 3-16-69 (Henderson), "Abner Willoughby's Return" 12-21-69 (Captain Price), "The Grand Swing" 9-19-71 (Sheriff Snell); *The Guns of Will Sonnett*—"A Difference of Opinion" 11-15-68, "Guilt" 11-29-68 (Bartender); *Lancer*—"Juniper's Camp" 3-11-69 (Bartender); *The High Chaparral*—"Time of Your Life" 9-19-69 (Matt); *Alias Smith and Jones*—"The McCreedy Bush" 1-21-71.

Grey, Fanny. Films: "With Friends, Nothing Is Easy" 1971-Span./Ital. (Nora); "None of the Three Were Called Trinity" 1974-Span.

Grey, Joel (1932-). Films: "Buffalo Bill and the Indians, or Sitting Bull's History Lesson" 1976 (Nate Salsbury). ¶TV: *Maverick*—"Full House" 10-25-59 (Billy the Kid); *Bronco*—"The Masquerade" 1-26-60 (Runt Bowles); *Lawman*—"The Salvation of Owny O'Reilly" 4-24-60 (Owny O'Reilly), "The Return of Owny O'Reilly" 10-16-60 (Owny O'Reilly), "Owny O'Reilly, Esq." 10-15-61 (Owny O'Reilly).

Grey, Nan (1918-7/25/93). Films: "Sutter's Gold" 1936 (Ann Eliza Sutter). ¶TV: *Rawhide*—"Incident on the Road to Yesterday" 11-18-60 (Carlie Stockton).

Grey, Olga (1898-4/25/73). Films: "When a Man Rides Alone" 1919 (Beatriz de Taos).

Grey, Robert Henry (1891-4/26/34). Films: "Boots and Saddles" 1916 (John James English); "Petticoats and Politics" 1918 (Leonard Blair); "The White Rider" 1920 (James Marsh); "Big Stakes" 1922 (El Capitan Montoya); "West vs. East" 1922 (Murray Brierson).

Grey, Shirley. Films: "Cornered" 1932 (Jane Herrick); "Get That Girl" 1932 (Ruth Dale); "One-Man Law" 1932 (Grace Duncan); "The Riding Tornado" 1932 (Patsy Olcott); "Texas Cyclone" 1932 (Helena Rawlins); "Treason" 1933 (Joan Randall).

Grey, Virginia (1917-). Films: "Secrets" 1933 (Audrey Carlton as a Child); "Secret Valley" 1937 (Jean Carlo); "Bells of Capistrano" 1942 (Jennifer Benton); "Idaho" 1943 (Terry); "Flame of the Barbary Coast" 1945 (Rita Dane); "Unconquered" 1947 (Diana); "Wyoming" 1947 (Lila Regan); "Slaughter Trail" 1951 (Lorabelle Larkin); "Three Desperate Men" 1951 (Laura Brock); "Desert

Pursuit" 1952 (Mary Smith); "The Fighting Lawman" 1953; "A Perilous Journey" 1953 (Abby); "The Forty-Niners" 1954 (Stella Walker); "The Last Command" 1955 (Mrs. Dickinson); "No Name on the Bullet" 1959 (Mrs. Frader). ¶TV: *Wagon Train*—"The Major Adams Story" 4-23-58 & 4-30-58 (Ranie), "The Kate Parker Story" 5-6-59 (Kate Parker), "The Beth Pearson Story" 2-22-61 (Beth Pearson); *Trackdown*—"Trapped" 10-10-58 (Laurie Tabor); *Yancy Derringer*—"V As in Voodoo" 5-14-59 (Emily Dubois); *Stagecoach West*—"Life Sentence" 12-6-60 (Clara); *Bonanza*—"The Artist" 10-7-62 (Ann Loring); *The Virginian*—"Nobody Said Hello" 1-5-66 (Laura Pritikin).

Gribbon, Edward (1890-9/29/65). Films: "Captain Fly-By-Night" 1922 (Cassara); "Double Dealing" 1923 (Alonzo B. Keene); "The Border Legion" 1924 (Blicky); "Code of the West" 1925 (Tuck Merry); "Desert Gold" 1926 (One Round Kelley); "Flaming Frontier" 1926 (Jonesy); "Under Western Skies" 1926; "Song of the West" 1930 (Sgt. Major); "The Cow-Catcher's Daughter" 1931-short; "Three Rogues" 1931 (Bronco Dawson); "Hidden Gold" 1933 (Benjamin B. "Bib Ben" Cooper); "Cyclone Ranger" 1935 (Duke); "The Man from Guntown" 1935; "The Outlaw Deputy" 1935 (Soapy); "Rio Rattler" 1935 (Soapy); "The Phantom Rider" 1936-serial (Sheriff Mark); "Renfrew on the Great White Trail" 1938 (Patsy); "Honky Tonk" 1941 (Pallbearer); "Canyon City" 1943.

Gribbon, Harry (1885-7/28/61). Films: "Tide of Empire" 1929 (O'Shea); "Ride Him, Cowboy" 1932 (Clout).

Grier, Pam (1949-). Films: "Posse" 1993 (Phoebe).

Grier, Roosevelt (1932-). Films: "Desperate Mission" TVM-1971 (Morgan). ¶TV: *Wild Wild West*—"The Night of the Undead" 2-2-68 (Tiny Joe); *Daniel Boone*—Regular 1969-70 (Gabe Cooper).

Grier, Russ. TV: *Laredo*—"The Land Slickers" 10-14-66 (Sheriff).

Gries, Jonathan. Films: "September Gun" TVM-1983 (Brian Brian); "Four Eyes and Six-Guns" TVM-1992 (Deputy Elmo). ¶TV: *Paradise*—"Dead Run" 10-7-89 (Emmet).

Griffeth, Simone. TV: *Bret Maverick*—"Faith, Hope and Clarity" 4-13-82 & 4-20-82 (Jasmine Dubois).

Griffies, Ethel (1878-9/9/75).

Films: "Billy the Kid" 1941 (Mrs. Hanky).

Griffin, Frank. Films: "Lightning Guns" 1950 (Jim Otis); "Fort Savage Raiders" 1951 (Reg Beck); "Bullwhip" 1958 (Keeler). ¶TV: *Death Valley Days*—"Reno" 10-10-55; *Zane Grey Theater*—"Ransom" 11-17-60.

Griffin, Merv (1925-). Films: "Cattle Town" 1952 (Joe); "The Boy from Oklahoma" 1954 (Steve).

Griffin, Robert E. (1902-12/19/60). Films: "Barricade" 1950 (Kirby); "Broken Arrow" 1950 (Lowrie); "Indian Uprising" 1951 (Can Avery); "Vengeance Valley" 1951 (Cal); "Montana Territory" 1952 (Yeager); "Conquest of Cochise" 1953 (Sam Maddock); "The Great Jesse James Raid" 1953 (Morgan); "The Black Dakotas" 1954 (Boggs); "The Law vs. Billy the Kid" 1954 (L.G. Murphy); "Shotgun" 1955 (Doctor); "The Brass Legend" 1956 (Dock Ward); "Fury at Showdown" 1957 (Sheriff Clay); "Gunsight Ridge" 1957 (Babcock); "Pawnee" 1957 (Doc); "The Bravados" 1958. ¶TV: *Hopalong Cassidy*—"Frontier Law" 6-21-52; *Fireside Theater*—"Man of the Comstock" 11-3-53 (El Dorado Johnny); *Death Valley Days*—"One in a Hundred" 12-23-53 (Lucas), "Fair Exchange" 11-24-59 (Major Bullock); *Tales of the Texas Rangers*—"West of Sonora" 9-17-55 (Black Murphy); *Zane Grey Theater*—"Vengeance Canyon" 11-30-56 (Killion), "The Mormons" 12-15-60 (Doc Kimball); *Gunsmoke*—"Wrong Man" 4-13-57 (Catlin), "False Witness" 12-12-59 (Judge); *Maverick*—"The War of the Silver Kings" 9-22-57 (Fennelly), "The Day They Hanged Bret Maverick" 9-21-58 (Mayor), "The Brasada Spur" 2-22-59 (Adam Sheppley), "The Cats of Paradise" 10-11-59 (Bartender); *The Adventures of Rin Tin Tin*—"The Last Navajo" 10-18-57 (Tom); *The Californians*—"The Lost Queue" 10-29-57; *Trackdown*—"The Governor" 5-23-58 (Sheriff Bill Welch); *Jefferson Drum*—"The Outlaw" 6-20-58 (Marshal); *Wanted Dead or Alive*—"Dead End" 9-27-58 (J. Noonan), "Angels of Vengeance" 4-18-59 (Eustace Branley); *The Texan*—"The Man Behind the Star" 2-9-59 (Ben Carter); *Northwest Passage*—"The Witch" 2-13-59 (Jacob Browning); *Black Saddle*—"Client: Braun" 4-4-59 (Tobe Slack); *Colt .45*—"The Escape" 4-5-59; *The Restless Gun*—"Four Lives" 4-13-59 (Cole Ramsey); *Rawhide*—"Incident of the Roman Candles" 7-10-59, "Incident of the Music Maker" 5-20-60;

Bonanza—"The Hanging Posse" 11-28-59, "The Avenger" 3-19-60 (Sheriff Hansen), "Vengeance" 2-11-61 (Sheriff); *Johnny Ringo*—"The Vindicator" 3-31-60 (Seth Martin); *Klondike*—"The Unexpected Candidate" 11-7-60 (Dave Barbour); *The Tall Man*—"A Gun Is for Killing" 1-14-61 (Mayor); *The Deputy*—"The Means and the End" 3-18-61 (Wiley).

Griffin, Stephanie. Films: "The Last Wagon" 1956 (Valinda). ¶TV: *Cheyenne*—"West of the River" 3-20-56 (Jennie McKeever).

Griffin, Todd. Films: "The Desperados Are in Town" 1956 (Ranger). ¶TV: *Maverick*—"Day of Reckoning" 2-2-58 (Jack Wade), "Holiday at Hollow Rock" 12-28-58 (Jesse Carson); *The Texan*—"Trouble on the Trail" 11-23-59, "Badman" 6-20-60 (Kurt Branden); *The Deputy*—"Lady with a Mission" 3-5-60 (Tinney); *Cheyenne*—"The Greater Glory" 5-15-61 (Rafe Donovan).

Griffith, Andy (1926-). Films: "The Second Time Around" 1961 (Pat Collins); "Hearts of the West" 1975 (Howard Pike); "Rustler's Rhapsody" 1985 (Col. Ticonderoga). ¶TV: *Centennial*—Regular 1978-79 (Prof. Lewis Venor); *Best of the West*—10-8-81.

Griffith, Billy. Films: "Jiggs and Maggie Out West" 1950 (Lawyer Blakely); "Hills of Utah" 1951. ¶TV: *The Cisco Kid*—"Lost City of the Incas" 3-29-52, "The Ventriloquist" 2-7-53.

Griffith, D.W. (1875-7/23/48). Films: "The Kentuckian" 1908; "The Stage Rustler" 1908.

Griffith, Ed (1938-). Films: "Scalplock" TVM-1966. ¶TV: *Bonanza*—"The Stalker" 11-2-69 (Jim Campbell).

Griffith, Frank. Films: "The Valley of Hunted Men" 1928 (Yucca Jake).

Griffith, Gordon (1907-10/12/58). Films: "Ben Blair" 1916 (Ben Blair); "Catch My Smoke" 1922 (Bub Jessup); "Gun Play" 1935 (Mark); "Western Frontier" 1935 (Steve); "Blazing Justice" 1936 (Max); "Outlaws of the Range" 1936 (Grant).

Griffith, Harry (1886-5/4/26). Films: "The Beckoning Trail" 1916 (Big Jim Helton); "Catch My Smoke" 1922 (Al Draper).

Griffith, Helen. Films: "Jesse James Rides Again" 1947-serial; "The James Brothers of Missouri" 1950-serial.

Griffith, James (1919-9/17/93). Films: "Daughter of the West" 1949 (Jed Morgan); "Fighting Man of the Plains" 1949 (Quantrell); "The Cariboo Trail" 1950 (Higgins); "Indian Territory" 1950 (the Apache Kid); "Al Jennings of Oklahoma" 1951 (Slim Harris); "Apache Drums" 1951 (Lt. Glidden); "The Great Missouri Raid" 1951 (Jack Ladd); "Kansas Pacific" 1953 (Farley); "The Black Dakotas" 1954 (Warren); "The Boy from Oklahoma" 1954 (Joe Downey); "Jesse James Versus the Daltons" 1954 (Bob Dalton); "The Law vs. Billy the Kid" 1954 (Pat Garrett); "Masterson of Kansas" 1954 (Doc Holliday); "Rails into Laramie" 1954 (Orrie Sommers); "At Gunpoint" 1955 (the Stranger); "Count Three and Pray" 1955 (Swallow); "The First Texan" 1956 (Crockett); "Rebel in Town" 1956 (Adam Russell); "Tribute to a Badman" 1956 (Barjack); "Domino Kid" 1957 (Sam Beal); "The Guns of Fort Petticoat" 1957 (Kipper); "Bullwhip" 1958 (Karp); "Frontier Gun" 1958 (Cash Skelton); "Man from God's Country" 1958 (Mark Faber); "Return to Warbow" 1958 (Frank Hollister); "Seven Guns to Mesa" 1958 (Clellan); "North to Alaska" 1960 (Salvationist); "How the West Was Won" 1962 (Gambler); "Advance to the Rear" 1964 (Hugo Zattig); "A Big Hand for the Little Lady" 1966 (Mr. Stribling); "Day of the Evil Gun" 1968 (Storekeeper); "Heaven with a Gun" 1969 (Abraham Murdock); "Seven Alone" 1974 (Billy). ¶TV: *The Lone Ranger*—"Death Trap" 4-20-50, "Mission Bells" 9-21-50, "Delayed Action" 11-6-52, "The Durango Kid" 4-16-53, "The Lost Challice" 2-10-55, "A Message from Abe" 2-7-57; *The Gene Autry Show*—"Gray Dude" 12-3-50 (Dude Devlin), "The Peace Maker" 12-17-50; *The Range Rider*—"Fatal Bullet" 11-25-51, "Fight Town" 12-16-51; *Death Valley Days*—"Solomon in All His Glory" 11-11-53; *Frontier*—"A Stillness in Wyoming" 10-16-55, "Patrol" 4-29-56 (Tad); *Gunsmoke*—"Kite's Reward" 11-12-55 (Joe Kite), "Twelfth Night" 12-28-57 (Joth Monger), "Milly" 11-25-61 (Tillman), "Quint's Indian" 3-2-53 (Bettis), "The Bassops" 2-22-64 (Harford), "The Gunrunners" 2-5-68 (Wade Lester); *Buffalo Bill, Jr.*—"Runaway Renegade" 3-31-56; *Cheyenne*—"Land Beyond the Law" 1-15-57 (Joe Epic), "The Frightened Town" 3-20-61 (Gorrell), "Showdown at Oxbend" 12-17-62 (Milt Krebs); *Zane Grey Theater*—"The Necessary Breed" 2-15-57 (Taggert); *Tales of Wells Fargo*—"Jesse James" 7-1-57 (Tom Rankins), "The Angry Sky" 4-21-62 (Roland Jensen); *Trackdown*—"Marple Brothers" 10-4-57, Regular 1958-59 (Aaron Adams); *U.S. Marshal*—Regular 1958-60 (Deputy Tom Ferguson); *Jefferson Drum*—"Return" 10-30-58 (Troy Bendick); *Wagon Train*—"The Sakae Ito Story" 12-3-58 (Sailor Blaine), "The Estaban Zamora Story" 10-21-59, "The Duke Shannon Story" 4-26-61 (Sterkel), "The Geneva Balfour Story" 1-20-64, "The Duncan McIvor Story" 3-9-64 (Garrett), "The Nancy Styles Story" 11-22-64 (Phineas); *Maverick*—"Duel at Sundown" 2-1-59 (John Wesley Hardin); *The Restless Gun*—"Dead Man's Hand" 3-16-59 (Dr. Hallop); *Buckskin*—"Act of Faith" 3-23-59 (Logan Maxwell); *The Deputy*—"The Deputy" 9-12-59 (Ballard); *The Texan*—"No Way Out" 9-14-59 (Morgan Lewis), "The Taming of Rio Nada" 1-11-60 (Shawn O'Rourke); *Wichita Town*—"Bullet for a Friend" 10-14-59 (Vic Parker); *Rawhide*—"Incident of the Devil and His Due" 1-22-60 (Maury), "Incident in the Middle of Nowhere" 4-7-61, "Incident of the Prophecy" 11-21-63 (Gurnery); *Two Faces West*—"The Return" 10-24-60; *Riverboat*—"The Quota" 11-28-60 (Cpl. Sam Giler); *Bonanza*—"Silent Thunder" 12-10-60 (Preacher), "The Burma Rarity" 10-22-61, "Judgment at Olympus" 10-8-67 (Deputy Gibbs); *Klondike*—"Swing Your Partner" 1-9-61 (Clag Botser); *The Outlaws*—"Culley" 2-16-61 (Lawyer Ephraim); *Laramie*—"Riders of the Night" 3-7-61 (Gabe), "Double Eagles" 11-20-62; *Stagecoach West*—"The Remounts" 3-14-61 (Cowboy); *The Tall Man*—"A Kind of Courage" 4-8-61 (Clint Latimer), "Trial by Fury" 4-14-62 (Jason Cutter); *Wyatt Earp*—"Hiding Behind a Star" 5-23-61 (Tim Connell); *Bronco*—"Trail of Hatred" 2-5-62 (Corporal Fonda); *Have Gun Will Travel*—"The Waiting Room" 2-24-62 (Dave Wilder), "The Savages" 3-16-63 (Spencer); *Lawman*—"Jailbreak" 6-10-62 (Heracles Snead); *Empire*—"A Place to Put a Life" 10-9-62 (Pete Stroud); *Great Adventure*—"Wild Bill Hickok—the Legend and the Man" 1-3-64 (Harry Young); *The Travels of Jaimie McPheeters*—"The Day of the Picnic" 2-16-64 (Bagsley), "The Day of the Pretenders" 3-1-64 (Snake); *Daniel Boone*—"Lac Duquesne" 11-5-64 (Feathers), 9-23-65 (Coll), "The Matchmaker" 10-27-66 (Coll), "The Necklace" 3-9-67 (Coll); *A Man Called Shenandoah*—"Obion—1866" 10-25-65 (Andrews), "Marlee" 3-14-66 (Smithy); *Laredo*—"Pride of the Rangers" 12-16-65; *The Big Valley*—"A Time to Kill" 1-19-66 (Clyde); *The Monroes*—"Court

Martial" 11-16-66 (Henri "Fox" Bonnard); *Iron Horse*—"Welcome for the General" 1-2-67 (Howley); *The Virginian*—"The Gentle Tamers" 1-24-68 (Kyle Spanner); *Lancer*—"The Heart of Pony Alice" 12-17-68 (Constable Becket), "Jelly Hoskins' American Dream" 11-11-69, "A Scarecrow at Hacket's" 12-16-69; *The Guns of Will Sonnett*—"Time Is the Rider" 1-10-69 (Major Cross); *Kung Fu*—"Dark Angel" 11-11-72 (Purdy); *Barbary Coast*—"The Day Cable Was Hanged" 12-26-75 (Eikel); *The Quest*—"The Buffalo Hunters" 9-29-76 (Donkin); *The Life and Times of Grizzly Adams*—11-2-77 (Watts).

Griffith, Julia. Films: "A One Man Game" 1927 (Mrs. Delacey); "Thunder Riders" 1928 (Cynthia Straight); "Lawless Range" 1935 (Maria Mason).

Griffith, Kay. Films: "Covered Wagon Days" 1940 (Maria).

Griffith, Melanie (1957-). Films: "Buffalo Girls" TVM-1995 (Dora).

Griffith, Raymond (1890-11/25/57). Films: "The Red Haired Cupid" 1918; "Hands Up!" 1926 (Confederate Spy). ¶TV: *Gunsmoke*—"The Search" 9-15-62 (Sam Cutler); *Death Valley Days*—"Early Candle Lighten" 11-8-69.

Griffith, William (1897-7/21/60). Films: "Whirlwind Horseman" 1938 (Happy Holmes); "Range Land" 1949 (Professor); "Pistol Harvest" 1951 (Prouty). ¶TV: *The Adventures of Rin Tin Tin*—"The Southern Colonel" 10-18-57 (Fred French).

Grimaldi, Gabriella. Films: "Johnny Hamlet" 1966-Ital. (Ophelia).

Grimes, Gary (1955-). Films: "The Culpepper Cattle Company" 1972 (Ben Mockridge); "Cahill, United States Marshal" 1973 (Danny Cahill); "The Spikes Gang" 1974 (Will Young). ¶TV: *Gunsmoke*—"Baker's Dozen" 12-25-67 (Bede).

Grimes, Tammy (1934-). TV: *The Virginian*—"The Exiles" 1-9-63 (Angela); *Destry*—"The Solid Gold Girl" 2-14-64 (Patience Dailey); *The Outcasts*—"Hung for a Lamb" 3-10-69 (Polly); *Young Riders*—"The Play's the Thing" 12-29-90 (Margaret).

Grimes, Tommy (1887-8/19/34). Films: "Headin' South" 1918; "The Secret of the Pueblo" 1923 (Pueblo Charlie); "Don Dare Devil" 1925 (Texas).

Grimm, Maria. Films: "Friendly Persuasion" TVM-1975 (Lily Truscott). ¶TV: *Bonanza*—"Customs of the Country" 2-6-72 (Leonora).

Grinnage, Jack (1931-). TV: *Wagon Train*—"The Ruttledge Munroe Story" 5-21-58 (Guard), "The John Bernard Story" 11-21-62 (Sampson), "The Geneva Balfour Story" 1-20-64; *The Restless Gun*—"Tomboy" 11-10-58 (Lonnie); *Gunsmoke*—"Doc Quits" 2-21-59 (Andy Wirth), "Distant Drummer" 11-19-60 (Raffie Bligh), "Brother Love" 12-31-60 (Gus), "Sanctuary" 2-26-66 (Gorman); *The Rifleman*—"The Legacy" 12-8-59 (Kirby Mitchell); *Rawhide*—"Incident of the Wolvers" 11-16-62 (Matt Cannon); *Stoney Burke*—"A Girl Named Amy" 4-29-63 (Joe); *Laredo*—"Above the Law" 1-13-66, "The Last of the Caesars—Absolutely" 12-2-66.

Grippe, Harry. Films: "The Great K & A Train Robbery" 1926 (DeLuxe Harry); "No Man's Gold" 1926 (Lefty Logan); "Tumbling River" 1927 (Titus); "Blood Will Tell" 1928 (Sandy).

Grippon, Eva. Films: "Clearing the Range" 1931 (Senora Conares).

Grisel, Louis R. (1848-11/19/28). Films: "The Crimson Dove" 1917 (Joseph Burbank).

Griswold, Claire. TV: *Wanted—Dead or Alive*—"Ransom for a Nun" 10-18-58 (Sister Grace); *Lawman*—"Conditional Surrender" 5-28-61 (Iona Beason); *Empire*—"Echo of a Man" 12-11-62 (Ellen Connors); *Bonanza*—"The Prince" 4-2-67 (Countess Elena).

Griswold, James (1882-10/4/35). Films: "The Virginian" 1914 (Stage Driver).

Grizzard, George (1928-). Films: "Comes a Horseman" 1978 (Neil Atkinson); "The Night Rider" TVM-1979 (Dan Kenton). ¶TV: *Rawhide*—"A Time for Waiting" 1-22-65 (Captain Ballinger).

Grodenchik, Max. Films: "The Gambler Returns: The Luck of the Draw" TVM-1991 (Bailiff).

Grodin, Charles (1935-). TV: *Shane*—"The Great Invasion" 12-17-66 & 12-24-66 (Jed); *Iron Horse*—"The Pembrooke Blood" 1-9-67 (Alex); *The Virginian*—"Reckoning" 9-13-67 (Arnie Doud); *The Guns of Will Sonnett*—"A Bell for Jeff Sonnett" 9-15-67 (Bells Pickering); *The Big Valley*—"The Good Thieves" 1-1-68 (Mark Dunigan).

Groom, Sam. TV: *Gunsmoke*—"No Tomorrow" 1-3-72 (Ben Justin), "A Child Between" 12-24-73 (Lew Harrod); *Sara*—3-26-76 (Harrington).

Gross, Robert. Films: "The

Marshal's Daughter" 1953 (Frenchie). ¶TV: *Branded*—"A Proud Town" 12-19-65 (Randy Stoddard).

Groves, Charles (1875-5/23/55). Films: "Out West with the Hardys" 1938 (Al).

Grubbs, Gary. Films: "Davy Crockett: Rainbow in the Thunder" TVM-1988 (George Russell). ¶TV: *Young Maverick*—"Have I Got a Girl for You" 1-16-80 (Kincaid); *Paradise*—"Treasure" 5-6-89 (Burt).

Gruber, Frank (1904-12/9/69). Films: "Town Tamer" 1965.

Gruning, Ilka (1876-11/11/64). Films: "Passage West" 1951 (Mama Ludwig).

Grunveld, Svea. TV: *Have Gun Will Travel*—"The Black Handkerchief" 11-14-59 (Michelle); *The Road West*—"Fair Ladies of France" 2-27-67 (Sister Marie Venard).

Guard, Kit (1894-7/18/61). Films: "Two-Fisted Justice" 1931 (Temple); "Fighting Champ" 1932 (Spike Sullivan); "The Cactus Kid" 1934 (Smiley); "Kid Courageous" 1935; "Code of the Rangers" 1938 (Red); "Gunsmoke Trail" 1938 (Clem); "Heroes of the Hills" 1938 (Mac); "In Early Arizona" 1938; "Where the West Begins" 1938 (Smiley); "El Diablo Rides" 1939; "Frontier Scout" 1939 (Slim); "Frontiers of '49" 1939; "Lone Star Pioneers" 1939; "The Man from Sundown" 1939; "Six-Gun Rhythm" 1939 (Slim); "The Carson City Kid" 1940; "Deadwood Dick" 1940-serial; "Jesse James at Bay" 1941; "White Eagle" 1941-serial; "Frontier Gal" 1945 (Man in Saloon); "South of the Chisholm Trail" 1947; "Trail Street" 1947 (Drunk); "Copper Canyon" 1950 (Storekeeper/Miner); "Fort Defiance" 1951 (Barfly); "The Bushwackers" 1952 (Oldster).

Guardino, Harry (1925-7/17/95). Films: "The Adventures of Bullwhip Griffin" 1967 (Sam Trimble). ¶TV: *Overland Trail*—"Perilous Passage" 2-7-60 (Johnny Caldwell); *The Virginian*—"The Horse Fighter" 12-15-65 (Sanders).

Gudegast, Hans. *see* Braeden, Eric.

Gudgeon, Bert (1889-10/22/48). Films: "The Blue Streak" 1917.

Guest, Christopher (1948-). Films: "The Long Riders" 1980 (Charlie Ford).

Guest, Ina (Inna Gest). Films: "The Golden Trail" 1940 (Chita); "Gun Code" 1940 (Betty Garrett); "Six Gun Gospel" 1943.

Guest, Nicholas. Films: "The Long Riders" 1980 (Bob Ford).

Guglielmi, Marco (1926-). Films: "Bandidos" 1967-Ital. (Billy Kane); "The Stranger Returns" 1967-U.S./Ital./Ger./Span. (the Preacher).

Guhl, George (1875-6/27/43). Films: "Wells Fargo" 1937 (Passenger); "Gold Mine in the Sky" 1938 (Cy Wheeler); "Dodge City" 1939 (Jason, the Marshal); "Union Pacific" 1939 (Irishman); "Buck Benny Rides Again" 1940 (Porter #5); "Twenty Mule Team" 1940 (Doorman); "When the Daltons Rode" 1940 (Deputy in Baggage Car); "Virginia City" 1940 (Bartender).

Guilbert, Nina. Films: "Cavalcade of the West" 1936 (Martha Knox); "Trigger Pals" 1939 (Aunt Minnie Archer); "The Sagebrush Family Trails West" 1940 (Minerva Sawyer); "Outlaws of the Desert" 1941 (Mrs. Jane Grant).

Guilfoyle, Jimmy (1892-11/13/64). Films: "Get That Girl" 1932. ¶TV: *The Lone Ranger*—"Bad Medicine" 12-7-50, "Behind the Law" 2-1-51.

Guilfoyle, Paul (1902-6/27/61). Films: "End of the Trail" 1936 (Captain Blake); "The Law West of Tombstone" 1938 (Bud McQuinn); "I'm from the City" 1938 (Willie); "Heritage of the Desert" 1939 (Snap Thornton); "Riders of Pasco Basin" 1940 (Evans); "The Scarlet Horseman" 1946-serial (Jim Bannion); "The Virginian" 1946 (Shorty); "Davy Crockett, Indian Scout" 1950 (Ben); "Apache" 1954 (Santos); "Chief Crazy Horse" 1955 (Worm). ¶TV: *Gunsmoke*—"Shooting Stopover" 10-8-60 (Reverend Beckett).

Guillaume, Robert (1928-). Films: "Children of the Dust" TVM-1995 (Mossburger).

Guinan, Texas (1895-11/5/33). Films: "The Stainless Barrier" 1917; "The Girl of Hell's Agony" 1918; "The Gun Woman" 1918 (the Tigress); "The Night Raider" 1918; "The Desert Vulture" 1919; "Letters of Fire" 1919; "Little Miss Deputy" 1919; "My Lady Robin Hood" 1919; "The She Wolf" 1919 (the She Wolf); "The Stampede" 1921 (Tex Henderson).

Guise, Thomas S. (-1930). Films: "The Bugle Call" 1916 (Sergeant Hogan); "Broadway, Arizona" 1917 (Old Producer); "Fighting Back" 1917 (Col. Hampton); "The Man from Funeral Range" 1918 (Col. Leighton); "The Midnight Stage" 1919 (Elias Lynch); "Wolf Law" 1922;

"Stepping Fast" 1923 (Quentin Durant).

Guizar, Tito. Films: "Under the Pampas Moon" 1935 (Cafe Singer); "The Llano Kid" 1939 (the Llano Kid); "On the Old Spanish Trail" 1947 (Ricco); "The Gay Ranchero" 1948 (Nicci Lopez).

Guizon, Richard (1928-). Films: "Hang 'Em High" 1968.

Gulager, Clu (1928-). Films: "...And Now Miguel" 1966 (Johnny); "Molly and Lawless John" 1972 (Deputy); "Charlie Cobb: Nice Night for a Hanging" TVM-1977 (Charlie Cobb); "The Gambler" TVM-1980 (Rufe Bennett); "My Heroes Have Always Been Cowboys" 1991. ¶TV: *Black Saddle*—"Client: Meade" 1-17-59 (Andy Meade); *Wanted—Dead or Alive*—"Crossroad" 4-11-59 (Collins); *Have Gun Will Travel*—"The Return of Roy Carter" 5-2-59 (Roy Carter); *Wagon Train*—"The Andrew Hale Story" 6-3-59 (Elliott Garrison), "The Stagecoach Story" 9-30-59 (Caleb Jamison), "The Clarence Mullins Story" 5-1-63 (Clarence Mulins), "The Sam Spicer Story" 10-28-63 (Sam Spicer), "The Ben Engel Story" 3-16-64 (Harry Diel); *The Deputy*—"Shadow of the Noose" 10-3-59 (the Drifter), "Trail of Darkness" 6-18-60 (Sanford); *Laramie*—"Fugitive Road" 10-6-59 (Gil Brady); *Riverboat*—"Jessie Quinn" 12-6-59 (Beau Chandler); *The Rebel*—"Paint a House with Scarlet" 5-15-60 (Virgil Taber); *The Tall Man*—Regular 1960-62 (William H. Bonney); *Whispering Smith*—"The Devil's Share" 5-22-61 (Jeff Whalen); *The Virginian*—"The Judgment" 1-16-63 (Jake Carewe), "Run Quiet" 11-13-63 (Judd), Regular 1964-68 (Deputy Ryker); *Bonanza*—"Stallion" 11-14-72 (Billy Brenner); *Kung Fu*—"Blood Brother" 1-18-73 (Sheriff Rutledge); *The Oregon Trail*—"The Army Deserter" 10-19-77 (Harris).

Gulliver, Dorothy (1908-). Films: "One Wild Time" 1926; "The Shoot 'Em Up Kid" 1926; "The Dude Desperado" 1927; "One Glorious Scrap" 1927 (Joan Curtis); "The Rambling Ranger" 1927 (Ruth Buxley); "Clearing the Trail" 1928 (Ellen); "The Wild West Show" 1928 (Ruth Henson); "The Fighting Marshal" 1931 (Alice Wheeler); "In Old Cheyenne" 1931 (Helen Sutter); "The Phantom of the West" 1931-serial (Mona Cortez); "The Last Frontier" 1932-serial (Betty Halliday); "Outlaw Justice" 1933; "The Pecos Dandy" 1934 (the Sweetheart); "Fighting Caballero" 1935 (Pat); "Custer's Last

Stand" 1936-serial (Red Fawn); "In Early Arizona" 1938 (Alice Weldon); "Under Montana Skies" 1930 (Mary); "Lone Star Pioneers" 1939 (Virginia Crittenden).

Gulpilil, David (1953-). Films: "Mad Dog Morgan" 1975-Australia (Billy).

Gunderson, Robert. TV: *Wyatt Earp*—"Get Shotgun Gibbs" 12-22-59 (Assassins); *Gunslinger*—"The Death of Yellow Singer" 5-11-61 (Mangus); *The Monroes*—"Ghosts of Paradox" 3-15-67.

Gunn, Bill (1930-4/5/89). TV: *Stoney Burke*—"The Mob Riders" 10-29-62 (Bud Sutter).

Gunn, Charles (1883-12/6/18). Films: "The Firefly of Tough Luck" 1917 (Danny Ward); "The Flame of the West" 1918; "The Midnight Stage" 1919 (Harvey James).

Gunn, Earl (1902-4/14/63). Films: "Wells Fargo" 1937; "Texas Renegades" 1940 (Lefty Higgins); "Billy the Kid" 1941 (Jessie Martin); "Secrets of the Wastelands" 1941 (Clanton); "North of the Rockies" 1942.

Gunn, Moses (1929-12/17/93). Films: "Wild Rovers" 1971 (Ben); "Law of the Land" TVM-1976 (Jacob). ¶TV: *Kung Fu*—"The Stone" 4-12-73 (Isaac Montolla); *The Cowboys*—Regular 1974 (Nightliner); *Father Murphy*—Regular 1981-82 (Moses Gage).

Gunnels, Chester. Films: "Shine on Harvest Moon" 1938 (Chet); "Come on, Rangers" 1939 (Smith).

Gur, Alizia (1942-). TV: *The Big Valley*—"Earthquake!" 11-10-65 (Naomi); *Daniel Boone*—"The Christmas Story" 12-23-65 (Tawha); *Wild Wild West*—"The Night of the Cossacks" 3-21-69 (Maria).

Gurie, Sigrid (1911-8/14/69). Films: "Three Faces West" 1940 (Leni Braun).

Gurwitch, Annabelle. Films: "Where the Hell's That Gold?!!!" TVM-1988 (Jesse).

Gustine, Paul (1893-7/16/74). Films: "Hills of Old Wyoming" 1937 (Daniels); "King of the Texas Rangers" 1941-serial (Army Observer); "Dangers of the Canadian Mounted" 1948-serial (Ken); "Desperadoes of the West" 1950-serial (Oil Forker).

Guth, Raymond. Films: "Monte Walsh" 1970 (Sunfish Perkins); "Bad Company" 1972 (Big Joe's Gang Member); "The Culpepper Cattle Company" 1972 (Cook); "The Call of the Wild" TVM-1976 (Will). ¶TV: *Wagon Train*—"The Riley Gratton Story" 12-4-57; *Gunsmoke*—"Fawn" 4-4-59 (Lu), "Ex-Con" 11-30-63 (Clabe); *Death Valley Days*—"Splinter Station" 10-19-60 (Mel), "The Solid Gold Pie" 11-29-69; *Gunslinger*—"The Hostage Fort" 2-16-61 (Floyd Braden); *Rawhide*—"Incident of the Painted Lady" 5-12-61 (Sheriff George Harms), "Incident of the Prophecy" 11-21-63 (Orville), "Incident at the Odyssey" 3-26-64; *Have Gun Will Travel*—"Beau Beste" 10-13-62 (Tate); *Bonanza*—"The Way Station" 10-29-62, "A Question of Strength" 10-27-63 (Toby), "The Prime of Life" 12-29-63, "The Pure Truth" 3-8-64, "Ride the Wind" 1-16-66 & 1-23-66 (Homer), "Four Sisters from Boston" 10-30-66 (Toothless), "A Woman in the House" 2-19-67 (Goliath), "My Friend, My Enemy" 1-12-69, "The Luck of Pepper Shannon" 11-22-70 (Jones), "The Grand Swing" 9-19-71 (Bill Cooper); *The Virginian*—"West" 11-20-62 (Klotz), "Requiem for a Country Doctor" 1-25-67 (Josh Miller); *The Rifleman*—"Incident at Line Shack Six" 1-7-63 (Charlie Breen); *Laramie*—"Vengeance" 1-8-63; *The High Chaparral*—"The Kinsman" 1-28-68 (Stableman); *Alias Smith and Jones*—"The Girl in Boxcar Number Three" 2-11-71 (Farmer).

Guthrie, Tani Phelps. *see* Phelps Guthrie, Tani.

Guy, Eula. Films: "The Woman of the Town" 1943 (Mrs. Brown); "Yankee Fakir" 1947 (Mrs. Tetley); "Yellow Sky" 1948 (Woman in Bank).

Guyton, George. Films: "Good Men and Bad" 1923 (Don Esteban Valdes).

Guzman, Jesus. Films: "Up the MacGregors!" 1967-Ital./Span. (the Priest); "Death on High Mountain" 1969-Ital./Span. (General Valiente); "The Magnificent Bandits" 1969-Ital./Span.

Gwinn, Bill. TV: *Wild Wild West*—"The Night of the Infernal Machine" 12-23-66 (Judge); *Death Valley Days*—"The Informer Who Cried" 11-11-67 (Dr. Evans), "The Duke of Tombstone" 1-10-70, "Clum's Constabulary" 4-11-70.

Gwynn, Dorothy. Films: "A Yellow Streak" 1915 (Virginia Dale).

Gwynne, Anne (1918-). Films: "Oklahoma Frontier" 1939 (Janet Rankin); "Bad Man from Red Butte" 1940 (Tibby Mason); "Man from Montreal" 1940 (Doris Blair); "Road Agent" 1941 (Patricia Leavitt); "Men

of Texas" 1942 (Jane Baxter Scott); "Ride 'Em, Cowboy" 1942 (Anne Shaw); "Sin Town" 1942 (Laura Kirby); "Frontier Badman" 1943 (Chris); "Panhandle" 1948 (June O'-Carroll); "The Blazing Sun" 1950 (Kitty); "Call of the Klondike" 1950 (Nancy); "King of the Bullwhip" 1950 (Jane Kerrigan). ¶TV: *Death Valley Days*—"Train of Events" 5-19-57; *Northwest Passage*—"The Ambush" 2-6-59 (Sheila Stark).

Gwynne, Michael C. (1942-). Films: "Butch and Sundance: The Early Days" 1979 (Mike Cassidy); "Harry Tracy—Desperado" 1982 (Dave Merrill); "Houston: The Legend of Texas" TVM-1986 (Mosley Baker); "Sunset" 1988 (Mooch).

Haade, William (1903-11/15/66). Films: "The Texans" 1938 (Sgt. Cahill); "Reno" 1939 (George Fields); "Union Pacific" 1939 (Dusky Clayton); "Bullet Code" 1940 (Scar Atwood); "Cherokee Strip" 1940 (Grimes); "Geronimo" 1940 (Cherrycow); "The Man from Dakota" 1940 (Union Soldier); "Northwest Mounted Police" 1940; "Stage to Chino" 1940 (Slim); "Desert Bandit" 1941 (Largo); "In Old Cheyenne" 1941 (Davidge); "Kansas Cyclone" 1941 (Sheriff Ed King); "Pirates on Horseback" 1941 (Bill Watson); "Robin Hood of the Pecos" 1941 (Capt. Morgan); "The Round Up" 1941 (Fran Battles); "The Shepherd of the Hills" 1941 (Bald Knobber); "Heart of the Golden West" 1942 (Cully Bronson); "Heart of the Rio Grande" 1942 (Hap Callahan); "Jackass Mail" 1942 (Red Gargan); "Man from Cheyenne" 1942 (Ed); "The Spoilers" 1942 (Deputy); "Daredevils of the West" 1943-serial (Barton Ward); "Days of Old Cheyenne" 1943 (Big Bill Harmon); "Song of Texas" 1943 (Fred Calvert); "Buffalo Bill" 1944 (Barber); "Sheriff of Las Vegas" 1944; "The Yellow Rose of Texas" 1944 (Buster); "Dakota" 1945 (Roughneck); "Phantom of the Plains" 1945; "In Old Sacramento" 1946; "My Pal Trigger" 1946 (Davis); "Unconquered" 1947; "Under Colorado Skies" 1947 (Marlowe); "Last of the Wild Horses" 1948 (Rocky Rockford); "The Wyoming Bandit" 1949 (Lonnegan); "The Old Frontier" 1950 (Pills Fowler); "Outcast of Black Mesa" 1950 (Dayton); "Priairie Pirates" 1950-short; "Buckaroo Sheriff of Texas" 1951 (Mark Branigan); "Oh! Susanna" 1951 (Trooper Riorty); "Rawhide" 1951 (Gil Scott); "Santa Fe" 1951; "Three Desperate Men" 1951 (Bill Devlin); "Carson City" 1952 (Hardrock Haggerty); "Rancho

Notorious" 1952 (Sheriff Bullock); "Red River Shore" 1953 (Link Howard); "Jubilee Trail" 1954 (Jake the Sailor); "Silver Lode" 1954 (Searcher); "Untamed Heiress" 1954 (Friend). ¶TV: *The Lone Ranger*—"The Beeler Gang" 8-10-50, "Outlaw's Revenge" 10-5-50; *The Gene Autry Show*—"Blackwater Valley Feud" 9-3-50, "Doublecross Valley" 9-10-50; *Wild Bill Hickok*—"Outlaw Flats" 10-9-51, "Silver Stage Holdup" 10-16-51, "Monster in the Lake" 8-12-52, "The Sheriff's Secret" 10-21-52, "Battle Line" 1-6-53, "The Rainmaker" 4-14-53; *The Range Rider*—"The Holy Terror" 3-22-52; *Tales of the Texas Rangers*—"The Shooting of Sam Bass" 10-15-55 (Underwood); *Sergeant Preston of the Yukon*—"Tobacco Smugglers" 11-29-56 (Rusty).

Haas, Hugo (1903-12/1/68). Films: "Dakota" 1945 (Marko Poli); "Northwest Outpost" 1947 (Prince Nickolai Balinin); "The Fighting Kentuckian" 1949 (General Paul DeMarchand). ¶TV: *Bonanza*—"Dark Star" 4-23-60 (Zurka).

Hack, Herman (1899-10/19/67). Films: "Border Law" 1931; "The One Way Trail" 1931; "Battling Buckaroo" 1932; "The Lone Avenger" 1933; "When a Man Rides Alone" 1933; "The Law of the Wild" 1934-serial; "The Lawless Frontier" 1934; "'Neath the Arizona Skies" 1934 (Henchman); "The Outlaw Tamer" 1934; "Randy Rides Alone" 1934; "Range Riders" 1934; "Rawhide Terror" 1934; "Terror of the Plains" 1934 (Henchman); "Arizona Trails" 1935; "Courageous Avenger" 1935; "The Dawn Rider" 1935 (Henchman); "Defying the Law" 1935; "Law of the 45's" 1935; "Lawless Range" 1935; "No Man's Range" 1935; "Paradise Canyon" 1935; "The Phantom Cowboy" 1935; "Rainbow Valley" 1935; "Rio Rattler" 1935; "Smokey Smith" 1935; "Tombstone Terror" 1935; "Tumbling Tumbleweeds" 1935; "The Unconquered Bandit" 1935; "Western Frontier" 1935; "Westward Ho" 1935; "The Whirlwind Rider" 1935; "Cavalcade of the West" 1936; "Everyman's Law" 1936 (Henchman); "The Last of the Warrens" 1936; "Lightning Bill Carson" 1936 (Henchman); "The Riding Avenger" 1936; "Rogue of the Range" 1936 (Prison Guard); "Sundown Saunders" 1936; "Toll of the Desert" 1936; "Vigilantes Are Coming" 1936-serial (Rancher); "The Gambling Terror" 1937; "Gun Lords of Stirrup Basin" 1937; "The Idaho Kid" 1937; "Law of the Ranger" 1937; "Moonlight on the Range" 1937; "North of the Rio Grande" 1937; "The Rangers

Step In" 1937; "Roll Along, Cowboy" 1937; "Sing, Cowboy, Sing" 1937; "Trail of Vengeance" 1937 (Rancher); "Valley of Terror" 1937; "Whistling Bullets" 1937; "Yodelin' Kid from Pine Ridge" 1937; "California Frontier" 1938; "Code of the Rangers" 1938; "Gun Law" 1938; "Heroes of the Alamo" 1938; "Phantom Ranger" 1938; "Renfrew on the Great White Trail" 1938; "The Singing Outlaw" 1938; "Utah Trail" 1938; "Western Trails" 1938; "The Lone Ranger Rides Again" 1939-serial (Posseman #1); "New Frontier" 1939 (Jim, the Construction Wagon Driver); "Silver on the Sage" 1939; "Western Caravans" 1939; "Billy the Kid in Texas" 1940; "Covered Wagon Days" 1940; "Frontier Crusader" 1940; "Melody Ranch" 1940; "Phantom Rancher" 1940; "Pioneers of the West" 1940; "The Ranger and the Lady" 1940; "Riders from Nowhere" 1940; "The Trail Blazers" 1940; "Back in the Saddle" 1941; "King of the Texas Rangers" 1941-serial (Raider #2); "The Lone Rider in Frontier Fury" 1941; "A Missouri Outlaw" 1941; "Sheriff of Tombstone" 1941; "The Singing Hill" 1941; "Sunset in Wyoming" 1941; "Wrangler's Roost" 1941; "Along the Sundown Trail" 1942; "Arizona Terrors" 1942; "Billy the Kid Trapped" 1942; "Overland to Deadwood" 1942; "The Phantom Plainsmen" 1942 (Townsman); "Calling Wild Bill Elliott" 1943; "The Leather Burners" 1943; "Lost Canyon" 1943; "Riders of the Deadline" 1943 (Tom); "Western Cyclone" 1943; "Beneath Western Skies" 1944; "Call of the Rockies" 1944; "Devil Riders" 1944; "Raiders of Ghost City" 1944-serial; "The San Antonio Kid" 1944; "Sheriff of Sundown" 1944; "Zorro's Black Whip" 1944-serial (Citizen #6); "Beyond the Pecos" 1945; "The Cherokee Flash" 1945; "Gangster's Den" 1945 (Mine Guard); "Prairie Rustlers" 1945; "Return of the Durango Kid" 1945; "Trail of Kit Carson" 1945; "California Gold Rush" 1946; "Roaring Rangers" 1946; "Two-Fisted Ranger" 1946; "Homesteaders of Paradise Valley" 1947; "Jesse James Rides Again" 1947-serial (Joe #2/Kaw); "The Marauders" 1947; "Son of Zorro" 1947-serial (Raider #3); "Under the Tonto Rim" 1947; "Carson City Raiders" 1948; "Son of God's Country" 1948; "The Valiant Hombre" 1948; "Gun Law Justice" 1949; "Powder River Rustlers" 1949; "Beyond the Purple Hills" 1950; "Cow Town" 1950; "The James Brothers of Missouri" 1950-serial; "Over the Border" 1950; "Desert of Lost Men" 1951; "Don Daredevil

Rides Again" 1951-serial (Townsman #8); "The Longhorn" 1951; "Pack Train" 1953; "Man with the Steel Whip" 1954-serial (Townsman #3). ¶TV: The Gene Autry Show—"Gypsy Woman" 8-25-53.

Hackathorne, George (1896-6/25/40). Films: "The Last of the Mohicans" 1920 (Captain Randolph); "When a Man's a Man" 1924 (Yapavai Joe); "Beyond the Law" 1930 (Monty); "The Lonesome Trail" 1930 (Oswald); "Riders of the North" 1931 (Canuck Joe); "Flaming Guns" 1932 (Hugh).

Hackett, Buddy (1924-). Films: "The Good Guys and the Bad Guys" 1969 (Townsman). ¶TV: The Rifleman—"Bloodlines" 10-6-59, "The Clarence Bibbs Story" 4-4-61 (Clarence Bibbs); The Big Valley—"Lost Treasure" 9-12-66 (Sawyer).

Hackett, Joan (1934-10/8/83). Films: "Will Penny" 1968 (Catherine Allen); "Support Your Local Sheriff" 1969 (Prudy Perkins); "The Young Country" TVM-1970 (Clementine Hale); "Mackintosh & T.J." 1975 (Maggie). ¶TV: Gunsmoke—"The Widow" 3-24-62 (Mady Arthur); Empire—"Between Friday and Monday" 5-7-63 (Dolores Lanza); Great Adventure—"The Outlaw and the Nun" 12-6-63 (Sister Blandina); Bonanza—"Woman of Fire" 1-17-65 (Margarita), "Second Sight" 1-9-72 (Judith); Alias Smith and Jones—"The Legacy of Charlie O'Rourke" 4-22-71 (Alilce Banion).

Hackett, John (1930-). Films: "Ride in the Whirlwind" 1966 (Sheriff's Aide). ¶TV: Wanted—Dead or Alive—"The Favor" 11-15-58, "Eager Man" 2-28-59 (Ted Nelson); Trackdown—"Stranger in Town" 3-25-59 (Joseph); Zane Grey Theater—"Heritage" 4-2-59 (Lieutenant); Wyatt Earp—"Roscoe Turns Detective" 5-3-60 (Whitey Jones).

Hackett, Karl (1893-10/24/48). Films: "Bulldog Courage" 1935 (Williams); "Cavalry" 1936 (Rance); "Law and Lead" 1936; "Lightning Bill Carson" 1936 (Stack Stone); "The Lion's Den" 1936 (Sheriff); "Roarin' Guns" 1936 (Evans); "Stormy Trails" 1936 (Durante); "The Traitor" 1936 (Ranger Captain); "Arizona Gunfighter" 1937 (Durkin); "Border Phantom" 1937 (Obed Young); "Borderland" 1937; "Desert Phantom" 1937 (Tom Jackson); "Fugitive from Sonora" 1937; "Gun Lords of Stirrup Basin" 1937 (Gabe Bowdre); "The Red Rope" 1937 (Grant Brade); "Rootin' Tootin' Rhythm" 1937; "Sing, Cowboy, Sing" 1937 (Kalmus);

"Tex Rides with the Boy Scouts" 1937 (Kemp); "Texas Trail" 1937 (Maj. McCready); "Trail of Vengeance" 1937 (Matt Pierson); "Whistling Bullets" 1937 (Dave Stone); "Colorado Kid" 1938 (Wolf Hines); "Durango Valley Raiders" 1938 (John McKay); "The Feud Maker" 1938 (Rand Lassiter); "Flaming Frontier" 1938-serial; "Frontier Town" 1938 (Nat Regan); "Lightning Carson Rides Again" 1938 (Mr. Grey); "Paroled to Die" 1938 (Harvey Meline); "Phantom Ranger" 1938 (Sharpe); "The Rangers' Roundup" 1938 (Hank); "Rollin' Plains" 1938 (Dan Barrow); "Six-Gun Trail" 1938; "Songs and Bullets" 1938 (Harry Skelton); "Songs and Saddles" 1938 (George Morrow); "Starlight Over Texas" 1938 (Kildare); "Utah Trail" 1938 (Hiram Slaughter); "Where the Buffalo Roam" 1938 (Don "Three-Fingers" Rogel); "Chip of the Flying U" 1939 (Hennessey); "Lure of the Wasteland" 1939 (Parker); "The Oregon Trail" 1939-serial; "Sundown on the Prairie" 1939 (Hendricks); "Billy the Kid Outlawed" 1940 (Sheriff Long); "Billy the Kid's Gun Justice" 1940 (Mr. Martin, the Lawyer); "Deadwood Dick" 1940-serial; "Frontier Crusader" 1940 (Barney Bronson); "The Man from Dakota" 1940 (Guard); "Man from Montreal" 1940 (McLennon); "Murder on the Yukon" 1940 (Hawks); "The Range Busters" 1940; "Take Me Back to Oklahoma" 1940 (Storm); "Yukon Flight" 1940 (Raymond); "Bad Man of Deadwood" 1941; "Billy the Kid in Santa Fe" 1941 (Davis); "Billy the Kid's Range War" 1941 (Williams); "Boss of Bullion City" 1941 (Tug); "Jesse James at Bay" 1941; "The Lone Rider in Frontier Fury" 1941; "The Lone Rider in Ghost Town" 1941; "The Lone Rider Rides On" 1941; "Man from Montana" 1941 (Trig); "A Missouri Outlaw" 1941; "Outlaws of the Cherokee Trail" 1941; "Outlaws of the Rio Grande" 1941 (Marlow); "The Pioneers" 1941 (Carson); "The Texas Marshal" 1941 (Moore); "Along the Sundown Trail" 1942; "Billy the Kid's Smoking Guns" 1942; "Come on, Danger!" 1942 (Ramsey); "In Old California" 1942; "Jesse James, Jr." 1942 (Sam Carson); "The Lone Rider in Cheyenne" 1942; "Outlaws of Boulder Pass" 1942; "Pirates of the Prairie" 1942; "Prairie Pals" 1942 (Sherff); "Rolling Down the Great Diide" 1942 (Pete); "Riding the Wind" 1942; "Sons of the Pioneers" 1942; "Texas Justice" 1942 (Stewart); "Texas Man Hunt" 1942 (Paul Clay); "Western Mail" 1942 (Rivers); "The

Avenging Rider" 1943 (Sheriff Allen); "Bordertown Gunfighters" 1943 (Frank Holden); "California Joe" 1943 (Ned Potter); "Fugitive of the Plains" 1943; "The Kid Rides Again" 1943; "Lost Canyon" 1943 (Haskell); "The Renegade" 1943; "Sagebrush Law" 1943; "Thundering Trails" 1943; "Western Cyclone" 1943 (Governor Arnold); "Wild Horse Rustlers" 1943 (Sheriff); "Wolves of the Range" 1943 (Corrigan); "Arizona Whirlwind" 1944 (Steve Lynch); "Brand of the Devil" 1944; "Code of the Prairie" 1944 (Deputy Sheriff); "Death Valley Rangers" 1944 (Charles W. Gifford); "Death Rides the Plains" 1944 (Simms); "Death Valley Rangers" 1944; "Mojave Firebrand" 1944; "Oath of Vengeance" 1944; "The Pinto Bandit" 1944; "Sonora Stagecoach" 1944 (Joe Kenton); "Thundering Gun Slingers" 1944 (Jeff Halliday); "Tucson Raiders" 1944; "Wells Fargo Days" 1944-short; "Westward Bound" 1944 (Henry Wagner); "Enemy of the Law" 1945; "Frontier Fugitives" 1945; "Gangster's Den" 1945 (Taylor); "His Brother's Ghost" 1945 (Doc Packard); "Prairie Rustlers" 1945 (Dan Foster); "Rustlers of the Badlands" 1945; "Shadows of Death" 1945; "Canyon Passage" 1946 (Miner); "Gentlemen with Guns" 1946 (Justice of the Peace); "Ghost of Hidden Valley" 1946 (Jed); "Gunman's Code" 1946; "The Lawless Breed" 1946; "Lightning Raiders" 1946 (Murray); "Outlaw of the Plains" 1946; "Terrors on Horseback" 1946 (Ed Sperling); "The Fabulous Texan" 1947; "The Michigan Kid" 1947 (Sam); "The Golden Stallion" 1949.

Hackett, Lillian (1899-2/28/73). Films: "Danger" 1923 (Nan Higgins); "No Tenderfoot" 1923.

Hackett, William. Films: "Trail of Hate" 1922 (Sheriff); "Ridin' Comet" 1925 (Doctor).

Hackman, Gene (1930-). Films: "The Hunting Party" 1971-Brit./Ital./Span. (Brandt Ruger); "Zandy's Bride" 1974 (Zandy Allan); "Bite the Bullet" 1975 (Sam Clayton); "Unforgiven" 1992 (Little Bill Daggett); "Geronimo: An American Legend" 1993 (Brig. Gen. George Crook); "Wyatt Earp" 1994 (Nicholas Earp); "The Quick and the Dead" 1995 (Herod). ¶TV: *Iron Horse*—"Leopards Try, But Leopard's Can't" 10-28-67 (Harry Wadsworth).

Hadden, Pauline. Films: "A Buckaroo Broadcast" 1938-short; "Arizona Gangbusters" 1940 (Sue Lambert); "Cowboy from Sundown" 1940 (Bec Davis); "Riders on Black Mountain" 1940 (Betty Harper).

Haddon, Laurence. TV: *Death Valley Days*—"The Hat That Huldah Wore" 6-25-66 (Phillips); *Here Come the Brides*—"The Legend of Big Foot" 11-14-69; *Paradise*—"See No Evil" 2-22-91 (Mr. Bass).

Haden, Sara (1899-9/15/81). Films: "The Barrier" 1937 (Alluna); "Out West with the Hardys" 1938 (Aunt Milly); "Bad Bascomb" 1946 (Tillie Lovejoy); "Rachel and the Stranger" 1948 (Mrs. Jackson); "Roughshod" 1949 (Ma Wyatt); "Rodeo" 1952 (Agatha Cartwright); "Wagons West" 1952 (Mrs. Cook); "The Outlaw's Daughter" 1954 (Mrs. Merril). ¶TV: *Wild Bill Hickok*—"The Slocum Family" 12-4-51; *Bonanza*—"The Jury" 12-30-62.

Hadley, Bert. Films: "The Cowboy and the Lady" 1915; "The Indian Trapper's Vindication" 1915; "The Operator of Black Rock" 1915; "Three Gold Coins" 1920 (J.M. Ballinger); "The Virginian" 1923 (Spanish Ed); "The Lightning Rider" 1924 (Manuel); "The Flying U Ranch" 1927 (Chip Bennett); "Little Big Horn" 1951 (Sgt. Maj. Peter Grierson).

Hadley, Nancy. Films: "Frontier Uprising" 1961 (Consuela). ¶TV: *Frontier*—"The Ballad of Pretty Polly" 4-1-56 (Polly); *Sheriff of Cochise*—"Grandfather Grandson" 2-11-57 (Alice); *Wyatt Earp*—"Woman Trouble" 12-17-57 (Jennie Brant), "The Confidence Man" 5-17-60 (Evie Marlowe); *Bat Masterson*—"Dude's Folly" 11-26-58 (Jan Larkin); *Jefferson Drum*—"Prison Hill" 12-4-58 (Ellie Drake); *Rough Riders*—"The Counterfeiters" 12-11-58 (Alice Thompson); *Have Gun Will Travel*—"Something to Live For" 12-20-58 (Lane Evans); *Rawhide*—"Incident West of Lano" 2-27-59 (Emily Haley), "Incident of the Day of the Dead" 9-18-59 (Ellen Hadley); *Pony Express*—"The Golden Circle" 2-24-60 (Belle Terry); *Sugarfoot*—"Shepherd with a Gun" 2-6-61 (Mattie Peel); *Bonanza*—"The Mountain Girl" 5-13-62 (Stephanie); *Empire*—"Burnout" 3-19-63 (Ruth Barton).

Hadley, Reed (1911-12/11/74). Films: "The Great Adventures of Wild Bill Hickok" 1938 (Blakely); "Zorro's Fighting Legion" 1939-serial (Don Diego Vega/Zorro); "Man from Montreal" 1940 (Ross Montgomery); "Road Agent" 1941 (Shayne); "Arizona Terrors" 1942 (Halliday/Don Pedro); "The Fabulous Texan" 1947 (Jessup); "The Man from Texas" 1947 (U.S. Marshal); "Last of the Wild Horses" 1948 (Riley); "Panhandle" 1948 (Matt Carson); "The Return of Wildfire" 1948 (Marty Quinn); "Grand Canyon" 1949 (Mitch Bennett); "I Shot Jesse James" 1949 (Jesse James); "Rimfire" 1949 (the Abilene Kid); "The Wyoming Bandit" 1949; "The Baron of Arizona" 1950 (Griff); "Dallas" 1950 (Wild Bill Hickok); "The Return of Jesse James" 1950 (Frank James); "Riders of the Range" 1950 (Burrows); "The Half-Breed" 1952 (Crawford); "Kansas Pacific" 1953 (Quantrill); "The Woman They Almost Lynched" 1953 (Bitterroot Bill Maris). ¶TV: *The Restless Gun*—"The Outlander" 4-21-58 (Col. Bromley), "A Very Special Investigation" 6-15-59 (Mayor); *Wagon Train*—"The Sacramento Story" 6-25-58 (Mort Galvin); *Bat Masterson*—"Dynamite Blows Two Ways" 10-22-58 (Raoul Cummings); *The Texan*—"The Sheriff of Boot Hill" 6-1-59 (Sheriff Ben Tildy), "The Taming of Rio Nada" 1-11-60 (Wild Jack Tobin), "Sixgun Street" 1-18-60 (Wild Jack Tobin), "The Terrified Town" 1-25-60 (Wild Jack Tobin); *Rawhide*—"Incident in No Man's Land" 6-12-59 (Clement); *The Deputy*—"The Shackled Town" 2-11-61 (Judge Denton); *Hondo*—"Hondo and the Death Drive" 12-1-67 (Slade).

Haefeli, Charles "Jockey" (1887-2/12/55). Films: "Rainbow Ranch" 1933 (Johnny); "Wells Fargo" 1937 (Gambler).

Haerter, Gerard. Films: "Two Sides of the Dollar" 1967-Fr./Ital. (Blackgrave); "Any Gun Can Play" 1968-Ital./Span. (Backman); "Machine Gun Killers" 1968-Ital./Span.; "Red Blood, Yellow Gold" 1968-Ital./Span. (Major Lloyd); "To Hell and Back" 1968-Ital./Span.; "Adios, Sabata" 1970-Ital./Span. (Skimmel); "The Bounty Hunters" 1970-Ital.

Hagar, Dorothy "Dot". Films: "His Enemy, the Law" 1918 (Jane Allen); "Wild Life" 1918 (Mae Gorcon); "The Westerners" 1919 (Bismarck Annie).

Hageman, Richard (1883-3/6/66). Films: "The Three Godfathers" 1948 (Saloon Pianist).

Hagen, Anna. TV: *Lonesome Dove*—"The Cattle Drive" 12-4-94 (Ma Laster).

Hagen, Jean (1923-8/29/77). Films: "Ambush" 1950 (Martha Conovan); "Arena" 1953 (Meg Hutchins). ¶TV: *Desilu Playhouse*—"Six Guns for Donegan" 10-16-59 (Mrs. Darrow), "The Hanging Judge" 12-4-59 (Nora Anderson); *Wagon Train*—

"The Marie Brant Story" 1-20-60 (Marie Brant), "The Sara Proctor Story" 2-27-63 (Sarah Proctor); *Stagecoach West*—"The Brass Lily" 1-17-61 (Lilly de Milo); *Zane Grey Theater*—"The Empty Shell" 3-30-61 (Anne Madden).

Hagen, Kevin (1928-). Films: "Gunsmoke in Tucson" 1958 (Clem Haney); "Rider on a Dead Horse" 1962 (Jake Fry); "The Man from Galveston" 1964 (John Dillard); "Rio Conchos" 1964 (Blondebeard); "Shenandoah" 1965 (Mule); "The Last Challenge" 1967 (Frank Garrison); "The Soul of Nigger Charley" 1973 (Col. Blanchard); "Little House on the Prairie: Look Back to Yesterday" TVM-1983 (Dr. Baker); "Bonanza: The Next Generation" TVM-1988. ¶TV: *Tales of Wells Fargo*—"Shotgun Messenger" 5-6-57 (Milt); *Wagon Train*—"The Nels Stack Story" 10-23-57 (Claymore), "The Annie MacGregor Story" 2-5-58 (Claymore); *Gunsmoke*—"Joke's on Us" 3-15-58 (Bill Jennings), "Love of a Good Woman" 1-24-59 (Coney Thorn), "Brother Love" 12-31-60 (Nate Cumbers), "Wagon Girls" 4-7-62 (Kelly Bowman), "The Odyssey of Jubal Tanner" 5-18-63, "No Hands" 2-8-64 (Emmett Ginnis), "The Victim" 1-1-68 (Judge Josh Pike); *Have Gun Will Travel*—"Three Sons" 5-10-58 (Half Brother), "The Gold Toad" 11-21-59, "A Quiet Night in Town" 1-7-61 & 1-14-61, "A Place for Abel Hix" 10-6-62 (Judd Bowman); *Yancy Derringer*—Regular 1958-59 (John Colton); *Laramie*—"The Run to Rumavaca" 11-10-59 (Josh Crystal), "Run of the Hunted" 4-4-61 (David), "The Killer Legend" 12-12-61 (Roy Bartell), "The Renegade Brand" 2-26-63; *The Deputy*—"Final Payment" 3-19-60 (Kemmer); *The Rifleman*—"The Prodigal" 4-26-60 (Billy St. John), "The Decision" 11-6-61 (Harry Devers); *Hotel De Paree*—"Sundance and the Fallen Sparrow" 5-27-60 (Orville); *The Outlaws*—"Assassin" 2-9-61 (McKinnon); *Bat Masterson*—"The Fourth Man" 4-27-61 (Ace Williams); *Cheyenne*—"The Brahma Bull" 12-11-61 (Moran); *Bonanza*—"Gabrielle" 12-24-61 (Everett), "Elegy for a Hangman" 1-20-63 (Hubie), "Journey Remembered" 11-11-63 (Simon), "Journey to Terror" 2-5-67 (King), "Showdown at Tahoe" 11-19-67 (Guy); *Rawhide*—"The Long Count" 1-5-62 (Jess Cain); *Lawman*—"The Vintage" 1-21-62 (Kulp), "Cort" 4-29-62 (Cort Evers); *Maverick*—"One of Our Trains Is Missing" 4-22-62 (Justin Radcliff); *Temple Houston*—"The Man from Galveston"

1963 (John Dillard); *The Virginian*—"Run Away Home" 4-24-63 (Oscar Swenson), "Seth" 3-20-68 (Judd Hadlock), "Stopover" 1-8-69 (Morgan); *Daniel Boone*—"The Prophet" 1-21-65 (John Dobson), "The Plague That Came to Ford's Run" 10-31-68 (Stokes), "A Very Small Rifle" 9-18-69 (Bart Wallace); *Branded*—"Mightier Than the Sword" 9-26-65 (Paul Mandell); *The Big Valley*—"Young Marauders" 10-6-65 (Coleman), "Last Stage to Salt Flats" 12-5-66 (Charlie), "Night in a Small Town" 10-9-67 (Amos Farrell), "Days of Wrath" 1-8-68 (Sheriff Fain), "The Long Ride" 11-25-68 (Barney), "The Twenty-five Graves of Midas" 2-3-69 (Zack); *A Man Called Shenandoah*—"The Reward" 11-29-65 (Pike); *The High Chaparral*—"Shadows on the Land" 10-15-67 (Tanner); *Wild Wild West*—"The Night of the Amnesiac" 2-9-68 (Silas Crotty); *Cimarron Strip*—"The Blue Moon Train" 2-15-68 (Dum Dum); *Lancer*—"The Prodigal" 11-12-68 (Packer); *The Guns of Will Sonnett*—"One Angry Juror" 3-7-69 (Kingman); *The Outcasts*—"Hung for a Lamb" 3-10-69 (Sheriff); *The Cowboys*—2-13-74 (Josh Redding); *Sara*—3-19-76 (Griffus); *Little House on the Prairie*—Regular 1974-82 (Doc Baker).

Hagen, Ross (1938-). TV: *The Virginian*—"The Return of Golden Tom" 3-9-66 (Stacy); *The Big Valley*—"A Day of Terror" 12-12-66 (Troy); *Shane*—"The Great Invasion" 12-17-66 & 12-24-66 (Floyd); *Gunsmoke*—"Muley" 1-21-67 (Kay Cee), "Slocum" 10-21-68 (Luke Riker), "Pike" 3-1-71 & 3-8-71 (Hicks); *The Road West*—"The Insider" 2-13-67; *Wild Wild West*—"The Night of the Iron Fist" 12-8-67 (Gabe Kelso); *The Guns of Will Sonnett*—"What's in a Name?" 1-5-68 (Doak); *The Outcasts*—"The Thin Edge" 2-17-69 (Clay); *Lancer*—"Juniper's Camp" 3-11-69 (Harmon Cooper), "The Lion and the Lamb" 2-3-70 (Clint); *Here Come the Brides*—"The Deadly Trade" 4-16-69 (Jobe), "The Road to the Cradle" 11-7-69 (Blackburn); *Kung Fu*—"Nine Lives" 2-15-73 (Herman Skowrin); *Bret Maverick*—"The Not So Magnificent Six" 3-2-82 (Farnsworth).

Hagerthy, Ron. Films: "The Charge at Feather River" 1953 (Johnny McKeever); "The Horse Soldiers" 1959 (Bugler); "Guns of Diablo" 1964 (Corey Macklin). ¶TV: *Sky King*—Regular 1951-53 (Clipper); *Tales of the Texas Rangers*—"The Devil's Deputy" 1-7-56 (Jim Hartley); *The Adventures of Rin Tin Tin*—"Homer the Great" 4-20-56 (Tom

Mack), "The Silent Witness" 3-29-57 (Cpl. Tim Crane); *Gunsmoke*—"Unmarked Grave" 8-18-56 (Rusty), "Ma Tennis" 2-2-58 (Andy Tennis); *Annie Oakley*—"The Waco Kid" 10-28-56 (Chuck Hutchins/the Waco Kid); *Sheriff of Cochise*—"The Promise" 11-22-57 (Wally Burke); *Wyatt Earp*—"The Manly Art" 1-21-58 (Bob Fitzsimmons); *The Texan*—"The First Notch" 10-20-58 (Neil Pearce), "Johnny Tuvo" 5-30-60 (Johnny Tuvo); *Have Gun Will Travel*—"A Score for Murder" 11-22-58 (Joe); *Jefferson Drum*—"Thicker Than Water" 11-27-58 (Will Barton); *Death Valley Days*—"Old Gabe" 12-16-58 (Felix); *Frontier Doctor*—"The Homesteaders" 4-4-59; *Rawhide*—"Incident of the Dry Drive" 5-22-59 (Jim Hode), "Incident at Cactus Wells" 10-12-62 (Danny Clayton); *Tombstone Territory*—10-16-59 (Jeff Harper); *Bonanza*—"The Hanging Posse" 11-28-59; *Wichita Town*—"Biggest Man in Town" 12-30-59 (Tod); *Man from Blackhawk*—"Drawing Acount" 2-12-60 (Oliver Jergens); *Zane Grey Theater*—"The Sunday Man" 2-25-60; *The Rifleman*—"The Deserter" 3-15-60 (Ben); *They Went Thataway*—Pilot 8-15-60 (Poison Pete); *Riverboat*—"The Quota" 11-28-60 (Phelan); *Two Faces West*—"The Trigger" 2-13-61; *Gunslinger*—"The Recruit" 3-23-61 (Trooper Gurney), "The New Savannah Story" 5-18-61 (Phil Nevis); *The Travels of Jaimie McPheeters*—"The Day of the Reckoning" 3-15-64 (Carey Macklin); *The High Chaparral*—"Best Man for the Job" 9-24-67 (Morgan).

Hagerty, Michael G. Films: "Rio Diablo" TVM-1993 (Dyke Holland).

Haggard, Merle (1937-). TV: *Centennial*—Regular 1978-79 (Cisco Calendar).

Haggerty, Dan (1942-). Films: "The Night of the Grizzly" 1966 (Sam Potts); "The Life and Times of Grizzly Adams" 1975 (James Capen "Grizzly" Adams); "Starbird and Sweet William" 1975; "The Adventures of Frontier Fremont" 1976 (Frontier Fremont); "The Incredible Rocky Mountain Race" TVM-1977 (Sheriff Benedict); "California Gold Rush" TVM-1981 (Jake Brown); "The Capture of Grizzly Adams" TVM-1982 (James "Grizzly" Adams); "Cheyenne Warrior" 1994 (Barkley). ¶TV: *Lawman*—"The Promise" 6-11-61 (Simm Bracque); *Maverick*—"Epitaph of a Gambler" 2-11-62 (Lucky Matt Elkins); *Daniel Boone*—"The Wolf Man" 1-26-67 (Jed Cudahy); *Rango*—

"In a Little Mexican Town" 4-14-67 (Sheriff); *The Life and Times of Grizzly Adams*—Regular 1977-78 (James "Grizzly" Adams).

Haggerty, Don (1914-8/19/88). Films: "The Dead Don't Dream" 1948 (Deputy); "False Paradise" 1948; "Gun Smugglers" 1948 (Sheriff Shurlsock); "Silent Conflict" 1948 (2nd Rancher); "Sinister Journey" 1948; "Canadian Pacific" 1949 (Cagle); "Rustlers" 1949 (Drake); "South of Rio" 1949 (Chuck Bowers); "Cowboy and the Prizefighter" 1950 (Steve); "Dynamite Pass" 1950 (Sheriff); "The Kid from Texas" 1950 (Morgan); "Storm Over Wyoming" 1950 (Marshal); "The Sundowners" 1950 (Elmer Gaul); "The Vanishing Westerner" 1950 (Art); "Vigilante Hideout" 1950 (Jim Benson); "Callaway Went Thataway" 1951 (Director); "Spoilers of the Plains" 1951 (Ben Rix); "Bronco Buster" 1952 (Dobie); "Denver and Rio Grande" 1952 (Bob Nelson); "Wild Stallion" 1952 (Sgt. Keach); "City of Badmen" 1953 (Thrailkill); "Hannah Lee" 1953 (Crashaw); "Jubilee Trail" 1954 (Detective); "The Phantom Stallion" 1954; "Texas Lady" 1955 (Sheriff Herndon); "Blood Arrow" 1958 (Gabe); "Cattle Empire" 1958 (Ralph Hamilton); "Day of the Bad Man" 1958 (Floyd); "The Gunfight at Dodge City" 1959 (Regan); "Seven Ways from Sundown" 1960 (Dorton); "The Great Sioux Massacre" 1965 (Sen. Blaine); "Skin Game" 1971 (Speaker). ¶TV: *The Lone Ranger*— "Six Gun Legacy" 11-24-49, "A Matter of Courage" 4-26-50, "Danger Ahead" 10-12-50, "Heritage of Treason" 2-3-55, "The Sheriff of Smoke Tree" 9-20-56, "The Banker's Son" 5-16-57; *Wild Bill Hickok*—"Cry Wolf" 10-7-52; *Wyatt Earp*—Regular 1955-56 (Marsh Murdock), "Santa Fe War" 12-2-58 (Dean Burns), "Requiem for Old Man Clanton" 5-30-61 (Mort Herrick); *The Adventures of Rin Tin Tin*—"Rusty Gets Busted" 2-22-57 (Col. Adams); *Tales of Wells Fargo*— "The Feud" 10-14-57, "Doc Dawson" 9-19-60 (Joe Haynes); *26 Men*—"The Recruit" 10-15-57, "The Glory Road" 10-7-58; *The Californians*—"The Alice Pritchard Case" 2-4-58 (David Douglas), "Cat's Paw" 3-3-59 (Dr. Kellog); *Sugarfoot*—"Mule Team" 6-10-58 (Vance Stanton), "The Highbinder" 1-19-60 (James Reilly), "Shepherd with a Gun" 2-6-61 (Simon Getty); *Rough Riders*—"The Electioners" 1-1-59 (Col. Donahue); *Have Gun Will Travel*—"Maggie O'Bannion" 4-4-59 (Cyrus); *Rawhide*—"Incident of Fear in the Streets"

5-8-59 (Mort Hendricks), "Incident of the Silent Web" 6-3-60 (Chaney), "Incident of the Night on the Town" 6-2-61 (Brewster), "Incident at Cactus Wells" 10-12-62 (Sheriff Brinkley), "Incident of the Married Widow" 3-1-63 (Abe), "Incident at Two Graves" 11-7-63 (Bartender); *Frontier Doctor*—"Superstition Mountain" 5-9-59; *Zorro*—"Masquerade for Murder" 6-4-59; *The Texan*—"Image of Guilt" 9-21-59, "The Accuser" 6-6-60 (Lew Taylor); *Bat Masterson*— "Lady Luck" 11-5-59; *Colt .45*—"Impasse" 1-31-60, "Alibi" 4-12-60; *Cheyenne*—"Riot at Arroyo Soco" 2-1-60, "The Young Fugitives" 10-23-61 (Sam), "The Bad Penny" 3-12-62 (Tod Kimball); *Riverboat*—"The Wichita Arrows" 2-29-60 (Albert Scott); *Stagecoach West*—"The Root of Evil" 2-28-61 (Capt. Jackson Lee); *Bronco*—"Yankee Tornado" 3-13-61; *Death Valley Days*—"A Bullet for the D.A." 11-22-61, "Hangtown Fry" 10-3-62 (Marshal), "The Hat That Won the West" 10-31-62 (Dan Willis), "Thar She Blows" 10-6-63, "The Peacemaker" 11-3-63 (McCarthy), "Honor the Name Dennis Driscoll" 10-25-64, "The Other White Man" 11-15-64, "Hero of Fort Halleck" 6-27-65 (Ham McCain), "The Fastest Nun in the West" 4-9-66 (Sheriff Wheeler), "The Resurrection of Deadwood Dick" 10-22-66 (Ev Morley), "The Hero of Apache Pass" 1-14-67 (Aaron), "Chicken Bill" 10-14-67 (Tabor), "Old Stape" 10-18-69, "The Great Pinto Bean Gold Hunt" 12-13-69 (Dan Purcell); *Frontier Circus*—"The Race" 5-3-62 (Marshal Walworth); *Bonanza*—"The Jury" 12-30-62 (Murdock), "The Lila Conrad Story" 1-5-64, "To Bloom for Thee" 1-16-66 (Demers), "Six Black Horses" 11-26-67 (O'Neill), "The Last Vote" 10-20-68 (Pete), "An Earthquake Called Callahan" 4-11-71 (Sheriff); *Gunsmoke*—"Legends Don't Sleep" 10-12-63 (Sheriff), "Quint's Trail" 11-9-63 (Clardy); *Redigo*—"The Crooked Circle" 10-22-63 (Roberts); *Destry*—"The Solid Gold Girl" 2-14-64 (Bartender); *The Legend of Jesse James*—"Jail Break" 11-15-65 (Steele); *The Guns of Will Sonnett*—"End of the Rope" 1-12-68 (Sheriff), "Chapter and Verse" 10-11-68.

Haggerty, H.B. (1925-). Films: "Paint Your Wagon" 1969 (Steve Bull). ¶TV: *Nichols*—"Flight of the Century" 2-22-72 (Gorman); *Zorro and Son*—6-1-83 (Butcher of Barcelona).

Hagin, John. Films: "Honeymoon Ranch" 1920 (John Lawhorn); "West of the Rio Grande" 1921 (Handy Adams).

Hagman, Larry (1931-). Films: "Sidekicks" TVM-1974 (Quince Drew). ¶TV: *Dupont Show of the Week*—"The Silver Burro" 11-3-63 (Phil O'Rourke).

Hagney, Frank (1884-6/25/73). Films: "The Mask of Lopez" 1923 (Steve Gore/Lopez); "The Breed of the Border" 1924 (Sheriff Wells); "The Dangerous Coward" 1924 (Wildcat Rea); "The Fighting Sap" 1924 (Nebraska Brent); "Galloping Gallagher" 1924 (Joseph Burke); "Lightning Romance" 1924 (Arizona Joe); "The Silent Stranger" 1924 (Dick Blackwell); "Braveheart" 1925 (Ki-Yote); "The Wild Bull's Lair" 1925 (Eagle Eye); "Lone Hand Saunders" 1926 (Buck); "The Two-Gun Man" 1926 (Bowie Bill); "The Frontiersman" 1927 (White Snake); "The Last Trail" 1927 (Ben Ligget); "The Glorious Trail" 1928 (Gus Lynch); "The Rawhide Kid" 1928 (J. Francis Jackson); "Fighting Caravans" 1931 (the Renegade); "The Phantom of the West" 1931-serial (Sheriff Ryan); "The Squaw Man" 1931 (Clark, the Deputy); "Ride Him, Cowboy" 1932 (the Hawk); "White Eagle" 1932; "Honor of the Range" 1934 (Boots); "Thunderbolt" 1935 (Blackie); "Western Frontier" 1935 (Link); "Gun Grit" 1936 (Henry Hess); "Heroes of the Range" 1936 (Lightnin' Smith); "Robin Hood of El Dorado" 1936 (Phil); "Valley of the Lawless" 1936 (Tiger Garlow); "Wildcat Trooper" 1936 (Jim Foster); "The Bad Man of Brimstone" 1937 (Horntoad); "Ghost Town Gold" 1937 (Wild Man Joe Kamatski); "Hollywood Cowboy" 1937 (Gillie); "Riders of the Dawn" 1937; "Wild Horse Round-Up" 1937 (Steve); "Timber Stampede" 1939 (Champ); "The Dark Command" 1940; "The Man from Dakota" 1940 (Guard); "Melody Ranch" 1940; "Northwest Passage" 1940 (Capt. Grant); "Rangers of Fortune" 1940; "The Lone Rider Ambushed" 1941 (Blackie Dawson); "The Lone Rider Crosses the Rio" 1941; "The Lone Rider Fights Back" 1941; "The Lone Rider in Ghost Town" 1941 (O'Shead); "The Lone Rider Rides On" 1941; "Boss of Hangtown Mesa" 1942; "In Old California" 1942; "Men of Texas" 1942; "Sin Town" 1942 (Bartender); "Texas Man Hunt" 1942 (Jensen); "Calling Wild Bill Elliott" 1943; "Law of the Saddle" 1943; "The Renegade" 1943; "Blazing Frontier" 1944 (Tragg); "Lucky Cowboy" 1944-short; "Along Came Jones" 1945 (Townsman); "The Sea of Grass" 1947 (Man); "Unconquered" 1947; "Where the North

Begins" 1947; "The Wistful Widow of Wagon Gap" 1947 (Barfly); "The Paleface" 1948 (Greg); "River Lady" 1948 (Sands); "Grand Canyon" 1949 (1st Thug); "Man in the Saddle" 1951 (Ned Bale); "Santa Fe" 1951; "Hangman's Knot" 1952; "The San Francisco Story" 1952 (Palmer); "A Perilous Journey" 1953 (Ad Lib); "The Stranger Wore a Gun" 1953; "Rose Marie" 1954 (Woodsman); "Three Hours to Kill" 1954 (Cass); "A Lawless Street" 1955 (Dingo Brion); "A Man Alone" 1955 (Dorfman); "Friendly Persuasion" 1956 Lemonade Vendor); "Gunfight at the O.K. Corral" 1957 (Bartender); "Last Train from Gun Hill" 1959 (Craig's Man); "McClintock" 1963 (Bartender). ¶TV: *Wild Bill Hickok*—"The Sheriff Was a Redhead" 7-15-52, "The Hideout" 1-20-53; *The Cisco Kid*—"Double Deal" 1-17-53, "Fool's Gold" 5-9-53; *The Lone Ranger*—"Uncle Ed" 3-3-55; *Tales of Wells Fargo*—"Special Delivery" 3-31-58 (Hostler); *The Westerner*—"School Days" 10-7-60 (Al); *Daniel Boone*—"Requiem for Craw Green" 12-1-66 (Settler), "The Jasper Ledbedder Story" 2-2-67 (Indian Chief).

Hagon, Garrick. Films: "The Last Gunfighter" 1961-Can.

Hahn, Gisela. Films: "They Call Me Trinity" 1970-Ital. (Sarah); "Don't Turn the Other Cheek" 1974-Ital./Ger./Span.

Hahn, Jess (1921-). Films: "Dynamite Jack" 1963-Fr.; "Bad Man's River" 1971-Span./Ital./Fr. (Odie); "Big Showdown" 1972-Ital./Fr.

Hahn, Paul (1921-8/4/88). TV: *Wild Bill Hickok*—"Runaway Wizard" 6-9-53; *The Cisco Kid*—"Man with the Reputation" 3-27-54; *Zane Grey Theater*—"The Fearful Courage" 10-12-56 (Neighbor); *Have Gun Will Travel*—"The Taffeta Mayor" 1-10-59; *Gunsmoke*—"The Bobsy Twins" 5-21-60 (Les).

Haid, Charles (1943-). TV: *Gunsmoke*—"Like Old Times" 1-21-74 (Lem Hargis); *Kung Fu*—"The Last Raid" 4-26-75 (Sheriff).

Haig, Sid (1939-). Films: "The Firebrand" 1962 (Diego); "Alias Smith and Jones" TVM-1971 (Outlaw). ¶TV: *Laredo*—"The Last of the Caesars—Absolutely" 12-2-66 (Brunning); *Iron Horse*—"Town Full of Fear" 12-5-66 (Vega); *Daniel Boone*—"The Scrimshaw Ivory Chart" 1-4-68 (Typhoon); *Gunsmoke*—"Time of the Jackals" 1-13-69 (Cawkins), "A Man Called Smith" 10-27-69 (Buffalo Hunter), "MacGraw" 12-8-69 (Eli Crawford); *Here Come the Brides*—

"Break the Bank of Tacoma" 1-16-70; *Alias Smith and Jones*—"Return to Devil's Hole" 2-25-71, "The Day They Hanged Kid Curry" 9-16-71; *Bret Maverick*—"The Eight Swords of Cyrus and Other Illusions of Grandeur" 3-23-83 (Sampson).

Haig, Tony. TV: *Fury*—"The Big Brothers" 12-26-59; *Zane Grey Theater*—"Miss Jenny" 1-7-60 (Alex); *Have Gun Will Travel*—"The Day of the Bad Men" 1-9-60 (Ted), "The Poker Friend" 11-12-60; *The Rebel*—"The Rattler" 3-13-60 (Davy); *The Rifleman*—"Hostages to Fortune" 2-4-63 (Percy); *Rawhide*—"Incident of the Hostages" 4-19-63 (Running Dog); *Gunsmoke*—"Twenty Miles from Dodge" 4-10-65 (Johnny), "The Raid" 1-22-66 & 1-29-66 (Boy), "Stage Stop" 11-26-66 (Wade Hansen).

Haines, Rhea (1895-3/12/64). Films: "Buckshot John" 1915 (Mrs. Hayden); "The Man from Painted Post" 1917 (Wah-na Madden); "Scarlet Days" 1919 (Spasm Sal).

Haines, William (1900-12/26/73). Films: "Way Out West" 1930 (Windy).

Hairston, Jester (1901-). Films: "Gypsy Colt" 1954 (Carl); "The Alamo" 1960 (Jethro). ¶TV: *Gunsmoke*—"Professor Lute Bone" 1-7-56 (Wellington); *Rawhide*—"Incident at the Edge of Madness" 2-6-59; *The Virginian*—"The Long Ride Home" 9-17-69 (Gar).

Haldeman, Tim. TV: *Kung Fu*—"Dark Angel" 11-11-72 (Man Moving Away), "Empty Pages of a Dead Book" 1-10-74 (Jason), "The Centoph" 4-4-74 & 4-11-74 (Shattrow), "Barbary House" 2-15-75 (1st Gunfighter), "Flight to Orion" 2-22-75 (1st Gunfighter), "The Brothers Cain" 3-1-75 (1st Gunfighter), "Full Circle" 3-15-75 (1st Gunfighter).

Hale, Alan (1892-1/22/50). Films: "Stronghart" 1914; "The Fox" 1921 (Rufus B. Coulter); "The Covered Wagon" 1923 (Sam Woodhull); "Quicksands" 1923 (Ferrago); "Code of the Wilderness" 1924 (Willard Masten); "The Country Beyond" 1936 (Jim Alison); "God's Country and the Woman" 1937 (Bjorn Skalka); "High, Wide and Handsome" 1937 (Walt Brennan); "Dodge City" 1939 (Rusty Hart); "Santa Fe Trail" 1940 (Barefoot Brody); "Virginia City" 1940 (Olaf "Moose" Swenson); "Cheyenne" 1947 (Fred Durkin); "Pursued" 1947 (Jake Dingle); "South of St. Louis" 1949 (Jake Evarts); "The Younger Brothers" 1949 (Sheriff Knudson); "Colt .45" 1950

(Sheriff Harris); "Stars in My Crown" 1950 (Jed Isbell).

Hale, Jr., Alan (1918-1/2/90). Films: "Riders in the Sky" 1949 (Marshal Riggs); "Rim of the Canyon" 1949 (Matt Kimbrough); "The Blazing Sun" 1950 (Ben Luber); "The Gunfighter" 1950 (1st Brother); "Short Grass" 1950 (Chris); "Sierra Passage" 1951 (Yance); "The Big Trees" 1952 (Tiny); "The Man Behind the Gun" 1952 (Olof); "Springfield Rifle" 1952 (Mizzell); "Captain John Smith and Pocahontas" 1953 (Fleming); "Destry" 1954 (Jack Larson); "The Law vs. Billy the Kid" 1954 (Bob Ollinger); "Silver Lode" 1954 (Kirk); "The Indian Fighter" 1955 (Will Crabtree); "A Man Alone" 1955 (Anderson); "Many Rivers to Cross" 1955 (Luke Radford); "Canyon River" 1956 (Lynch); "The Three Outlaws" 1956; "The True Story of Jesse James" 1957 (Cole Younger); "The Long Rope" 1961 (Sheriff John Millard); "Advance to the Rear" 1964 (Sgt. Beauregard Davis); "Bullet for a Badman" 1964 (Leach); "Hang 'Em High" 1968 (Stone); "There Was a Crooked Man" 1970 (Tobaccy). ¶TV: *The Gene Autry Show*—"Gold Dust Charlie" 7-30-50, "The Doodle Bug" 8-13-50, "Double Switch" 8-27-50, "The Breakup" 11-5-50, "Twisted Trails" 11-12-50, "Hot Lead" 11-26-50, "Killer Horse" 12-10-50, "Heir to the Lazy L" 12-29-51, "Horse Sense" 1-11-52; *Wild Bill Hickok*—"Johnny Deuce" 9-4-51, "Hepsibah" 11-6-51, "Hands Across the Border" 7-22-52; *Annie Oakley*—"Annie and the Silver Ace" 2-27-54; *Fury*—"Pirate Treasure" 3-31-56 (Long John); *Cheyenne*—"Hired Gun" 12-17-57 (Bridgeman), "Road to Three Graves" 10-31-60 (Tuk); *Casey Jones*—Regular 1958-59 (Casey Jones); *Northwest Passage*—"The Red Coat" 9-21-58 (Sam Beal); *Wanted—Dead or Alive*—"Shawnee Bill" 10-4-58 (Dan Poe); *The Texan*—"The Widow of Paradise" 11-24-58 (Jake Bricker), "Border Incident" 12-7-59 (Sculley), "Dangerous Ground" 12-14-59 (Sculley), "End of Track" 12-21-59 (Sculley), "Quarantine" 2-8-60 (Sculley), "Captive Crew" 2-22-60 (Sculley), "Captive Crew" 2-22-60 (Sculley), "Showdown" 2-29-60 (Sculley); *Bat Masterson*—"A Personal Matter" 1-28-59 (Bailey Harper); *The Restless Gun*—"Incident at Bluefield" 3-30-59 (Sheriff Clark); *Colt .45*—"The Saga of Sam Bass" 5-17-59 (Sam Bass); *Bronco*—"Bodyguard" 10-20-59 (Dan Flood), "A Sure Thing" 1-22-62 (Squire); *Bonanza*—"The Saga of Annie O'Toole" 10-24-59 (Swede

Lunberg); *Man from Blackhawk*—
"The Hundred Thousand Dollar Policy" 1-22-60 (Miles Mackenzie); *The Alaskans*—"Partners" 3-13-60 (Hap Johnson); *Walt Disney Presents*—"Elfego Baca: Gus Tomlin Is Dead" 3-25-60 (Bill Minters); *Wichita Town*—"Sidekicks" 4-6-60 (Wally); *The Deputy*—"The Standoff" 6-11-60 (Frank Engle); *Johnny Ringo*—"Coffin Sam" 6-16-60 (Coffin Sam Sabine); *Shotgun Slade*—"Lost Gold" 8-30-60; *Maverick*—"Arizona Black Maria" 10-9-60 (Capt. Jim Pattishal), "The Troubled Heir" 4-1-62 (Big Jim Watson); *The Outlaws*—"The Waiting Game" 1-19-61 (Blunden); *Zane Grey Theater*—"The Scar" 3-2-61 (Cal); *Gunsmoke*—"Minnie" 4-15-61 (Jake Higgens), "Champion of the World" 12-24-66 (Bull Bannock), "Horse Fever" 12-18-72 (Dave Chaney); *Whispering Smith*—"The Idol" 9-18-61 (Ole Brindessen); *Death Valley Days*—"Treasure of Elk Creek Canyon" 12-13-61; *Rawhide*—"Incident of the Woman Trap" 1-26-62 (Wagon Master); *Wagon Train*—"The Lonnie Fallon Story" 2-7-62 (Kirby); *Frontier Circus*—"The Inheritance" 3-15-62 (Lait); *Tales of Wells Fargo*—"The Gold Witch" 5-5-62 (Denning); *Wide Country*—"Good Old Uncle Walt" 12-13-62 (Tom Yort); *Laramie*—"Edge of Evil" 4-2-63 (Roger Canby); *Empire*—"The Convention" 5-14-63 (Fletcher); *Hondo*—"Hondo and the Death Drive" 12-1-67 (Cobb); *Wild Wild West*—"The Night of the Sabatini Death" 2-2-69 (Ned Brown); *The Virginian*—"The Bugler" 11-19-69 (Sergeant O'Rourke); *Here Come the Brides*—"The Fetching of Jenny" 12-5-69 (Luther); *Alias Smith and Jones*—"The Girl in Boxcar Number Three" 2-11-71 (Andrew J. Greer); *The Men from Shiloh*—"Tate, Ramrod" 2-24-71 (Sam Donner).

Hale, Barbara (1922-). Films: "West of the Pecos" 1945 (Rill Lambeth); "Last of the Comanches" 1952 (Julia Lanning); "The Lone Hand" 1953 (Sarah Jane Skaggs); "Seminole" 1953 (Revere Muldoon); "The Far Horizons" 1955 (Julia Hancock); "Seventh Cavalry" 1956 (Martha Kellogg); "The Oklahoman" 1957 (Anne Barnes); "Slim Carter" 1957 (Allie Hanneman); "Buckskin" 1968 (Sarah Cody); "The Red, White and Black" 1970 (Mrs. Grierson). ¶TV: *Custer*—"Death Hunt" 11-22-67 (Melinda Terry).

Hale, Barnaby (1927-11/5/64). Films: "Advance to the Rear" 1964 (Lieutenant).

Hale, Betsy. TV: *Tales of Wells*

Fargo—"The Lobo" 5-8-61 (Hi Walker); *Have Gun Will Travel*—"The Mark of Cain" 1-13-62 (Anne Marie); *Gunsmoke*—"The Kite" 2-29-64 (Letty Cassidy); *Wagon Train*—"The John Gillman Story" 10-4-64 (Abigail).

Hale, Bill. Films: "Gun Talk" 1947 (Joe); "Courtin' Trouble" 1948 (Stewart); "Frontier Agent" 1948; "Hidden Danger" 1949 (Sanderson); "Range Justice" 1949 (Bud); "Raiders of Tomahawk Creek" 1950 (Jeff); "Silver Canyon" 1951; "Hannah Lee" 1953 (1st Cowboy); "Battle of Rogue River" 1954 (Henry); "Massacre Canyon" 1954 (Lt. Farnum); "Apache Ambush" 1955 (Bob Jennings); "Giant" 1956 (Bartender); "Cattle Empire" 1958 (Grainger); "Snowfire" 1958 (Skip Stoner). ¶TV: *Wild Bill Hickok*—"Civilian Clothes Story" 12-18-51, "The Doctor Story" 7-1-52 (Curly), "Runaway Wizard" 6-9-53; *The Cisco Kid*—"Smuggled Silver" 6-14-52; *Tales of the Texas Rangers*—"Buckaroo from Powder River" 2-4-56 (Dave); *Gunsmoke*—"The Guitar" 7-21-56 (Tom); *The Adventures of Rin Tin Tin*—"The Courtship of Marshal Higgins" 9-27-57 (J.B. Tardash), "The Last Navajo" 10-18-57 (Matt), "Hostage of War Bonnet" 11-1-57 (Cole Hogarth), "Rodeo Clown" 11-8-57; *Sergeant Preston of the Yukon*—"Storm the Pass" 10-24-57 (Kurt Miller); *Wagon Train*—"A Man Called Horse" 3-26-58; *Rawhide*—"Incident of the Tumbleweed Wagon" 1-9-59, "Incident at Barker Springs" 2-20-59 (Marshal Tobin), "Incident at Poco Tiempo" 12-9-60; *Tales of Wells Fargo*—"The Diamond Dude" 2-27-61 (Neilsen); *The Deputy*—"Brother in Arms" 4-15-61 (Garth Cabot).

Hale, Chanin (1937-). Films: "Will Penny" 1968 (Girl). ¶TV: *The Legend of Jesse James*—"The Quest" 11-1-65 (Marie); *Hondo*—"Hondo and the Gladiators" 12-15-67 (Carrot Top); *Bonanza*—"Mrs. Wharton and the Lesser Breeds" 1-19-69 (Laura Mae), "The Trouble with Trouble" 10-25-70 (Lily); *Gunsmoke*—"Lavery" 2-22-71 (Verna), "Talbot" 2-26-73 (Sally).

Hale, Creighton (1882-8/9/65). Films: "The Mine with the Iron Door" 1924 (Dr. James Burton); "The Great Divide" 1929 (Edgar Blossom); "The Country Beyond" 1936 (Mountie); "Custer's Last Stand" 1936-serial (Hank); "Santa Fe Trail" 1940 (Telegraph Operator); "Montana" 1950 (Rancher); "Westbound" 1959 (Passenger).

Hale, Fiona. Films: "Shotgun"

1955 (Midge). ¶TV: *Gunsmoke*—"Doc Quits" 2-21-59 (Mrs. Crummley); *The Law of the Plainsman*—"Blood Trails" 11-5-59; *Zane Grey Theater*—"Morning Incident" 12-29-60 (Mrs. Pritchard).

Hale, Frona. Films: "The Black Sheep" 1921 (Mrs. Carson); "The Taming of the West" 1925 (Aunt Lodenna); "Fighting Jack" 1926 (Jack's Mother).

Hale, Georgia (1896-6/7/85). Films: "Man of the Forest" 1926 (Nancy Raynor); "Hills of Peril" 1927 (Ellen Wade); "Gypsy of the North" 1928 (Alice Culhane); "The Rawhide Kid" 1928 (Jessica Silverberg); "A Trick of Hearts" 1928 (the Girl); "Lightning Warrior" 1931-serial (Dianne).

Hale, Jean (1938-). Films: "Taggart" 1964 (Miriam Stark). ¶TV: *The Virginian*—"A Matter of Destiny" 2-19-64 (Janet); *Wild Wild West*—"The Night That Terror Stalked the Town" 11-19-65 (Marie Pincher); *The Loner*—"A Question of Guilt" 1-29-66 (Myra Bromley); *Wagon Train*—"The Stark Bluff Story" 4-6-64 (Suzy Durfee); *The Legend of Jesse James*—"Return to Lawrence" 1-31-66 (Elizabeth); *Bonanza*—"The Real People of Muddy Creek" 10-6-68 (Casey Collins); *The Men from Shiloh*—"The Politician" 1-13-71 (Eileen Terry).

Hale, Jonathan (1891-2/28/66). Films: "In Old Monterey" 1939 (Stevenson); "Stand Up and Fight" 1939 (Col. Webb); "Lone Star Ranger" 1942 (Judge Longstreth); "Dakota" 1945 (Col. Wordin); "The Vigilantes Return" 1947 (Judge Holden); "Silver River" 1948 (Maj. Spencer); "Stampede" 1949 (Varick); "Short Grass" 1950 (Bissel); "Rodeo King and the Senorita" 1951 (Dr. Sands); "Son of Paleface" 1952 (Governor); "Kansas Pacific" 1953 (Gen. Scott); "The Three Outlaws" 1956; "Four for Texas" 1964 (Renee). ¶TV: *The Cisco Kid*—"Cattle Rustling" 2-3-51, "Medicine Flats" 3-10-51; *Wild Bill Hickok*—"Behind Southern Lines" 6-26-51; *The Range Rider*—"The Grance Fleece" 4-4-53; *Fireside Theater*—"Man of the Comstock" 11-3-53 (John McKay); *Wyatt Earp*—"Remittance Man" 11-4-58 (Cookie).

Hale, Monte (1921-). Films: "The Big Bonanza" 1944 (Singer); "Bandits of the Badlands" 1945; "Colorado Pioneers" 1945; "Oregon Trail" 1945 (Cowboy); "Rough Riders of Cheyenne" 1945; "The Topeka Terror" 1945; "California Gold Rush" 1946; "Home on the Range" 1946 (Monte Hale); "The Man from Rainbow Valley" 1946 (Monte); "Out

California Way" 1946 (Monte); "The Phantom Rider" 1946-serial (Cass); "Sun Valley Cyclone" 1946; "Along the Oregon Trail" 1947 (Monte Hale); "Last Frontier Uprising" 1947 (Monte Hale); "Under Colorado Skies" 1947 (Monte Hale); "California Firebrand" 1948 (Monte Hale); "Son of God's Country" 1948 (Monte Hale); "The Timber Trail" 1948 (Monte Hale); "Law of the Golden West" 1949 (William F. Cody); "Outcasts of the Trail" 1949 (Pat Garrett); "Pioneer Marshal" 1949 (Ted Post); "Prince of the Plains" 1949 (Bat Masterson); "Ranger of Cherokee Strip" 1949 (Steve Howard); "San Antone Ambush" 1949 (Lt. Ross Kincaid); "South of Rio" 1949 (Jeff Lanning); "The Missourians" 1950 (Bill Blades); "The Old Frontier" 1950 (Barney Regan); "Trail of Robin Hood" 1950; "The Vanishing Westerner" 1950 (Chris Adams); "Yukon Vengeance" 1954; "Giant" 1956 (Bale Clinch). ¶TV: *Wild Bill Hickok*— "Runaway Wizard" 6-9-53; *Tales of Wells Fargo*—"The Deserter" 11-24-58 (Col. Meston); *Gunsmoke*—"Blue Horse" 6-6-59 (Sergeant), "Uncle Finney" 10-14-68 (Bank Teller).

Hale, Nancy. Films: "The White Squaw" 1956 (Kerry Arnold). ¶TV: *The Cisco Kid*—"Stolen River" 10-3-53; *Death Valley Days*—"Dear Teacher" 10-14-53, "The Kickapoo Run" 5-12-54, "The Capture" 4-14-57 (Mary Jane); *The Lone Ranger*— "Message to Fort Apache" 9-23-54, "Showdown at Sand Creek" 5-26-55; *Annie Oakley*—"Western Privateer" 9-30-56 (Kathleen Scott), "Desperate Men" 2-24-57 (Deborah Scott); *Cheyenne*—"The Black Hawk War" 1-24-56 (Ann Saunders), "Lone Gun" 12-4-56 (Susan); *Wyatt Earp*— "Wyatt's Love Affair" 10-2-56 (Sally Fabian), "Earp Ain't Even Wearing Guns" 2-3-59 (Amy Landreth); *Zane Grey Theater*—"A Man on the Run" 6-21-57 (Ray Longstreth).

Hale, Peter. TV: *Wild Wild West*—"The Night Dr. Loveless Died" 9-29-67 (Layden), "The Night of the Simian Terror" 2-16-68 (Layden), "The Night of the Juggernaut" 10-11-68 (Tom Harwell), "The Night of the Winged Terror" 1-17-68 & 1-24-68.

Hale, Richard (1893-5/18/81). Films: "Abilene Town" 1946 (Charlie Fair); "Badman's Territory" 1946 (Ben Wade); "Inside Straight" 1951 (Undertaker); "Springfield Rifle" 1952 (Gen. Henry W. Halleck); "San Antone" 1953 (Abraham Lincoln); "Passion" 1954 (Don Domingo); "Red Garters" 1954 (Dr. J. Pott Troy);

"Canyon Crossroads" 1955 (Joe Rivers); "Friendly Persuasion" 1956 (Elder Purdy); "Pillars of the Sky" 1956 (Isaiah); "Sergents 3" 1962 (White Eagle); "Scandalous John" 1971 (Old Indian). ¶TV: *Broken Arrow*—"The Archaeologist" 4-30-57 (Katena); *Wagon Train*—"The Willy Moran Story" 9-18-57 (Palmer), "The Ben Courtney Story" 1-28-59 (Rev. Butler), "The Cassie Vance Story" 12-23-63; *Trackdown*— "The Town" 12-13-57 (Dad McCready); *The Californians*—"The Alice Pritchard Case" 2-4-58 (Humboldt); *Jim Bowie*— "Apache Silver" 2-21-58 (Chief Xolic), "Horse Thief" 3-21-58 (Xolic); *The Texan*—"Letter of the Law" 3-23-59 (Judge Bradford); *Rawhide*—"Incident of the Misplaced Indians" 5-1-59 (Mr. Moon), "Incident of the Clown" 3-29-63 (Medicine Man), "Incident of the Peyote Cup" 5-14-64 (Munyo); *Riverboat*— "The Treasure of Hawk Hill" 2-8-60 (Arden Dexter); *Lawman*—"The Surface of Truth" 4-17-60 (Washita); *Bronco*—"Legacy of Twisted Creed" 4-19-60 (Long Shadow), "Apache Treasure" 11-7-60 (Chief Victorio); *Maverick*—"The Town That Wasn't Three" 10-2-60 (Wilbur Shanks), "Bolt from the Blue" 11-27-60 (Judge Hookstraten), "Poker Face" 1-7-62 (Dr. Robespierre Jones); *Gunsmoke*— "The First People" 2-19-61 (White Buffalo), "The War Priest" 1-5-70 (El Cuerno), "No Tomorrow" 1-3-72 (Old Luke), "Whelan's Men" 2-5-73 (Miner); *Tales of Wells Fargo*—"Bitter Vengeance" 6-12-61 (Ben Martin), "Tanoa" 10-28-61 (Pochalo); *Cheyenne*—"Legacy of the Lost" 12-4-61 (Red Cloud); *Wide Country*—"Memory of a Filly" 1-3-63 (Old Man Bilbo); *The Dakotas*—"Return to Drydock" 1-7-63 (Reverend Smith); *The Travels of Jaimie McPheeters*— "The Day of the Picnic" 2-16-64 (Hardy); *Destry*—"The Nicest Girl in Gomorrah" 3-13-64 (Pilgrim); *The Big Valley*—"Heritage" 10-20-65; *Bonanza*—"Ride the Wind" 1-16-66 & 1-23-66 (Winnemucca), "Journey to Terror" 2-5-67 (Neal), "Sense of Duty" 9-24-67 (Chief Winetka); *Iron Horse*—"Cougar Man" 10-24-66 (Man-Who-Talks), "Five Days to Washtiba" 10-7-67 (Chief Saul); *The Road West*—"Fair Ladies of France" 2-27-67 (Old Man); *Hondo*—"Hondo and the Gladiators" 12-15-67 (Jamarro); *Wild Wild West*—"The Night of the Sedgewick Curse" 10-18-68 (Philip Sedgewick); *The Guns of Will Sonnett*—"A Town in Terror" 2-7-69 & 2-14-69 (Yates); *Here Come the Brides*—"The Last Winter" 3-27-70

(Old Indian); *The Cowboys*—"The Indian Givers" 5-1-74 (Chief Tu-Chech-Oh).

Hale, Scott. TV: *Gunsmoke*— "My Father, My Son" 4-23-66 (Gunsmith), "Nitro!" 4-8-67 & 4-15-67 (Dying Man), "A Hat" 10-16-67 (Clem), "The Night Riders" 2-24-69 (Bernaby); *Cimarron Strip*—"The Legend of Jud Starr" 9-14-67.

Haley, Earl. Films: "The Cowboy Cop" 1926 (2nd Crook); "The Masquerade Bandit" 1926 (Tony); "Wild to Go" 1926 (Baldy).

Hall, Anthony (1934-1/28/88). TV: *The Tall Man*—"Apache Daughter" 12-30-61 (Tolano); *Death Valley Days*—"Bloodline" 1-9-63 (Prince Amir).

Hall, Anthony Michael (1968-). Films: "James A. Michener's Texas" TVM-1995 (Yancey).

Hall, Jr., Arch. Films: "Deadwood '76" 1965 (Billy May).

Hall, Sr., Arch "Archie" (William Watters) (1909-4/28/78). Films: "The Mysterious Rider" 1938 (Andrews); "Overland Stage Raiders" 1938 (Joe Waddell); "Rhythm of the Saddle" 1938 (Rusty); "The Sagebrush Family Trails West" 1940 (Jim Barton); "The Lone Rider in Ghost Town" 1941 (Roper); "Two-Gun Sheriff" 1941 (Dunn); "Texas Justice" 1942; "Border Badmen" 1945 (Gilian); "His Brother's Ghost" 1945 (Deputy Sheriff Bentley); "Deadwood '76" 1965 (Boone May).

Hall, Ben (1899-5/20/85). Films: "Satan Town" 1926 (Crippy Jack); "A Man from Wyoming" 1930 (Orderly); "Smoke Tree Range" 1937 (Pete); "Riders of the Black Hills" 1938 (Ethelbert); "Ridin' on a Rainbow" 1941; "My Darling Clementine" 1946 (Barber).

Hall, Bobby. Films: "The Animals" 1971 (Cat Norman); "The Honkers" 1972 (Davis); "Kid Blue" 1973 (Bartender). ¶TV: *Bat Masterson*—"Bear Bait" 11-12-58 (Roger), "Flume to the Mother Lode" 1-28-60 (Miller); *Have Gun Will Travel*—"The Taffeta Mayor" 1-10-59 (Ben Trask); *Tales of Wells Fargo*—"Return of Doc Bell" 11-30-59 (Garvey); *The Rifleman*—"Gun Shy" 12-10-62; *Branded*— "The Golden Fleece" 1-2-66; *Gunsmoke*—"MacGraw" 12-8-69 (Hamilton), "Whelan's Men" 2-5-73 (Musgrove), "The Hanging of Newly O'Brien" 11-26-73 (Adrian); *Here Come the Brides*—"Bolt of Kilmaren" 3-13-70; *Bonanza*—"The Rattlesnake Brigade" 12-5-71 (Goatman).

Hall, Claude. TV: *The Rifleman*—"Incident at Line Shack Six" 1-

7-63 (Jeb Croton); *Rawhide*—"The Race" 9-25-64 (Doctor); *Branded*—"Leap Upon Mountains…" 2-28-65 (Buckrum), "Salute the Soldier Briefly" 10-24-65 (Sample); *The Big Valley*—"The Invaders" 12-29-65 (Cooper); *Bonanza*—"Three Brides for Hoss" 2-20-66 (Ned); *Daniel Boone*—"Dan'l Boone Shot a B'ar" 9-15-66 (Wilse Mott); *Shane*—"The Hant" 9-17-66 (2nd Drover), "The Silent Gift" 11-26-66 (Claude); *Hondo*—"Hondo and the Superstition Massacre" 9-29-67 (Unwashed); *The Guns of Will Sonnett*—"Guilt" 11-29-68 (Harvey).

Hall, Donald (1878-7/25/48). Films: "From Out of the Big Snows" 1915 (Carl Brandon).

Hall, Edna (1886-7/17/45). Films: "Double Action Daniels" 1925 (Mother Rose Daniels).

Hall, Ella (1896-9/3/81). Films: "The Mistress of Deadwood Basin" 1914.

Hall, Ellen. Films: "Outlaws of Stampede Pass" 1943; "Brand of the Devil" 1944; "Call of the Rockies" 1944; "Lumberjack" 1944 (Julie); "Raiders of the Border" 1944 (Bonita); "Range Law" 1944 (Lucille Gray); "Thunder Town" 1946 (Betty Morgan); "Lawless Code" 1949. ¶TV: *The Cisco Kid*—"Newspaper Crusade" 5-5-51, "Freight Line Feud" 6-2-51, "Performance Bond" 6-30-51.

Hall, Genee. Films: "Santa Fe Stampede" 1938 (Julie Jane Carson).

Hall, Gertrude. Films: "The Last Chance" 1921 (Vivian Morrow).

Hall, Henry (1876-12/11/54). Films: "Young Blood" 1932; "Rainbow Ranch" 1933 (Judge); "Sagebrush Trail" 1933 (Dad Blake); "The Dude Ranger" 1934 (Sam Hepburn); "Fighting to Live" 1934; "Circle of Death" 1935 (J.F. Henry); "Desert Trail" 1935 (Banker); "Gunsmoke on the Guadalupe" 1935; "Lawless Range" 1935; "Outlaw Rule" 1935 (Link Bishop); "Paradise Canyon" 1935; "Trail of the Hawk" 1935; "Tumbling Tumbleweeds" 1935; "Westward Ho" 1935; "Gun Smoke" 1936 (George Culverson); "Rio Grande Ranger" 1936; "The Unknown Ranger" 1936; "Vigilantes Are Coming" 1936-serial (Senor Loring); "Rootin' Tootin' Rhythm" 1937; "Yodelin' Kid from Pine Ridge" 1937 (Sheriff Martin); "Chip of the Flying U" 1939 (Wilson); "Prairie Law" 1940 (Mr. Bramble); "Santa Fe Trail" 1940 (Abolitionist); "King of the Texas Rangers" 1941-serial (L.H. Bowen); "Pirates on Horseback" 1941

(Sheriff Blake); "Stick to Your Guns" 1941 (Winters); "Boss of Hangtown Mesa" 1942 (John Wilkins); "Stagecoach Buckaroo" 1942 (Denton); "Raiders of San Joaquin" 1943 (Bodine Carter); "The Return of the Rangers" 1943; "Riders of the Rio Grande" 1943; "West of Texas" 1943 (Bart Yaeger); "Dead or Alive" 1944; "Sonora Stagecoach" 1944 (Sheriff Hampton); "The Whispering Skull" 1944; "The Daltons Ride Again" 1945 (Marshal); "Enemy of the Law" 1945 (Sheriff); "Marked for Murder" 1945; "The Navajo Kid" 1945 (Dr. Cole); "Phantom of the Plains" 1945; "San Antonio" 1945 (Cattleman); "Lightning Raiders" 1946 (Wright); "Terrors on Horseback" 1946 (Doc Jons); "Ghost Town Renegades" 1947 (Jennings); "Pioneer Justice" 1947 (Sheriff); "Song of the Wasteland" 1947; "Wild Country" 1947 (Marshal Thayer); "Crossed Trails" 1948 (Stoddard); "Panhandle" 1948 (Wells); "Challenge of the Range" 1949 (Jim Barton).

Hall, Huntz (1920-). Films: "Bowery Buckaroos" 1947 (Sach); "Dig That Uranium" 1956 (Sach).

Hall, J. Albert (1884-4/18/20). Films: "The Girl I Left Behind Me" 1915.

Hall, John (1878-4/25/36). Films: "The Fighting Shepherdess" 1920 (Tetters); "The Fighting Texan" 1927; "The Wild West Show" 1928 (Sheriff).

Hall, Jon (Charles Locher) (1915-12/13/79). Films: "The Mysterious Avenger" 1936 (Lafe); "Winds of the Wasteland" 1936 (Jim, the Pony Express Rider); "Kit Carson" 1940 (Kit Carson); "Last of the Redmen" 1947 (Major Heyward); "The Michigan Kid" 1947 (the Michigan Kid); "The Vigilantes Return" 1947 (Johnnie Taggart); "Deputy Marshal" 1949 (Ed Garry); "When the Redskins Rode" 1951 (Prince Hannoc); "Brave Warrior" 1952 (Steve Ruddell).

Hall, Josephine. Films: "The Sign of the Wolf" 1931-serial (Pearl).

Hall, Lillian (1896-3/18/59). Films: "Getting Some" 1920; "The Last of the Mohicans" 1920 (Alice Munro).

Hall, Lois. Films: "Roaring Westward" 1949 (Susan); "Cherokee Uprising" 1950 (Mary Lou); "Frontier Outpost" 1950 (Alice Tanner); "Horsemen of the Sierras" 1950 (Patty McGregor); "Texas Dynamo" 1950 (Julia Beck); "Blazing Bullets" 1951; "Colorado Ambush" 1951 (Janet Williams); "Slaughter Trail"

1951 (Susan); "Night Raiders" 1952 (Laura Davis); "Texas City" 1952 (Lois); "Little House on the Prairie: Look Back to Yesterday" TVM-1983 (Secretary). ¶TV: *Wild Bill Hickok*—"The Dog Collar Story" 7-17-51; *The Cisco Kid*—"Vigilante Story" 10-20-51, "Sleeping Gas" 12-1-51, "Quicksilver Murder" 1-12-52; *The Lone Ranger*—"Embezzler's Harvest" 4-30-53.

Hall, Mark (1955-). Films: "Across the Great Divide" 1976 (Jason).

Hall, Michael. Films: "Black Hills Ambush" 1952 (Larry Stewart); "The Last Musketeer" 1952 (Johnny Becker).

Hall, Philip Baker (1934-). TV: *Riding for the Pony Express*—Pilot 9-3-80 (Mr. Durfee).

Hall, Porter (1888-10/6/53). Films: "The Plainsman" 1936 (Jack McCall); "Wells Fargo" 1937 (James Oliver); "Henry Goes Arizona" 1939 (Edward Walsh); "Arizona" 1940 (Lazarus Ward); "The Dark Command" 1940 (Angus McCloud); "Trail of the Vigilantes" 1940 (Sheriff Corley); "The Parson of Panamint" 1941 (Jonathan Randall); "The Desperadoes" 1943 (Stanley Clanton); "The Woman of the Town" 1943 (Dog Kelly); "Unconquered" 1947 (Leach); "The Half-Breed" 1952 (Kraemer); "Pony Express" 1953 (Bridger).

Hall, Robert. Films: "Custer of the West" 1967-U.S./Span. (Sgt. Buckley); "Shalako" 1968-Brit./Fr. (Johnson).

Hall, Ruth (1912-). Films: "Between Fighting Men" 1932 (Judy Winters); "Dynamite Ranch" 1932 (Doris Collins); "Flaming Guns" 1932 (Mary Ramsey); "Ride Him, Cowboy" 1932 (Ruth Gaunt); "The Man from Monterey" 1933 (Dolores Castanares); "Strawberry Roan" 1933 (Alice Edwards).

Hall, Sherry. Films: "The Three Godfathers" 1936 (Piano Player); "High, Wide and Handsome" 1937 (Piano Player); "Wells Fargo" 1937 (Clerk); "The Gentleman from Arizona" 1939 (Gimp); "Mexicali Rose" 1939; "The Return of Frank James" 1940 (Court Clerk); "Canyon Passage" 1946 (Clerk); "Girl Rush" 1944 (Monk).

Hall, Thurston (1883-2/20/58). Films: "Flare-Up Sal" 1918 (the Red Rider); "The Squaw Man" 1918 (Henry, Jim's Cousin); "The Valley of Doubt" 1920 (Jules); "Out West with the Hardys" 1938 (H.R. Bruxton);

"Dodge City" 1939 (Twitchell); "Jeepers Creepers" 1939 (M.K. Durant); "Virginia City" 1940 (Gen. Meade); "Call of the Canyon" 1942 (Grantley B. Johnson); "The Great Man's Lady" 1942 (Mr. Sempler); "Song of Nevada" 1944 (John Barrabee); "Song of the Prairie" 1945; "West of the Pecos" 1945 (Col. Lambeth); "Swing the Western Way" 1947; "Rim of the Canyon" 1949 (Big Tim Hanlon); "Square Dance Jubilee" 1949 (G.K.); "Stagecoach Kid" 1949 (Arnold); "Bandit Queen" 1950 (Governor); "Belle Le Grand" 1951 (Parkington); "Whirlwind" 1951 (Big Jim Lassiter); "Carson City" 1952 (Charles Crocker). ¶TV: *Hopalong Cassidy*—"The Jinx Wagon" 1-26-52; *Tales of the Texas Rangers*—"Quarter Horse" 10-6-57 (Col. Titus); *The Adventures of Rin Tin Tin*—"The Southern Colonel" 10-18-57 (Col. Ulysses X. Stonewell); *Maverick*—"The Savage Hills" 2-9-58 (Judge).

Hall, Virginia. Films: "Old Overland Trail" 1953 (Mary Peterson).

Hall, William "Bill". Films: "In Old Monterey" 1939 (Gilman); "California" 1946 (Man); "The Harvey Girls" 1946 (Big Joe); "Annie Get Your Gun" 1950 (Tall Man).

Hall, Winter (1878-2/10/47). Films: "A Romance of the Redwoods" 1917 (John Lawrence); "The Squaw Man" 1918 (Fletcher); "The Money Corral" 1919 (Gregory Collins); "The Third Woman" 1920 (Judson Halliday).

Hall, Zooey (1947-). TV: *Here Come the Brides*—"The Last Winter" 3-27-70 (Junior).

Hallahan, Charles. Films: "Pale Rider" 1985 (McGill). ¶TV: *Bret Maverick*—"Anything for a Friend" 12-15-81 (McShane).

Hallett, Al (1870-4/3/35). Films: "The Gold Hunters" 1925 (Mukoki); "The Haunted Range" 1926 (Executor).

Halligan, Tom. Films: "Trail Dust" 1936 (Skinny).

Halligan, William (1884-1/28/57). Films: "The Cowboy and the Blonde" 1941 (Franklyn); "Black Hills Express" 1943 (Harvey Dorman); "Riders of the Deadline" 1943 (Crandall).

Hallor, Edith (1896-5/21/71). Films: "Thou Shalt Not" 1914 (Jane Cooper).

Hallor, Ray (1900-4/16/44). Films: "Circus Cowboy" 1924 (Paul Bagley); "In Old California" 1929 (Pedro DeLeon); "Hidden Valley" 1932 (Jimmie).

Halloran, John. Films: "Badman's Territory" 1946 (Hank McGee); "Angel and the Badman" 1947 (Thomas Worth); "The Last Round-Up" 1947 (Taylor); "Albuquerque" 1948 (Matt Wayne); "Fighting Man of the Plains" 1949 (Harmer); "Wild Stallion" 1952 (Mr. Light); "Jack Slade" 1953; "The Vanquished" 1953; "Jubilee Trail" 1954 (Turner's Man); "The Far Country" 1955 (Bartender); "The Violent Men" 1955 (2nd Farmer); "Tribute to a Badman" 1956 (Cowboy); "The Deerslayer" 1957 (Old Warrior); "The Halliday Brand" 1957. ¶TV: *The Lone Ranger*—"Letter of the Law" 1-4-51; *The Gene Autry Show*—"Frame for Trouble" 11-3-51, "Revenge Trail" 11-17-51; *The Tall Man*—"The Leopard's Spots" 11-11-61 (Joshua).

Halloway, Carol. Films: "If Only Jim" 1921 (Miss Amay Dot Denniham); "The Rainbow Trail" 1925 (Jane); "Thunder Trail" 1937 (Woman).

Halls, Ethel May (1882-9/16/67). Films: "Heroes of the Saddle" 1940 (Miss Dobbs).

Hallyday, Johnny (1943-). Films: "Drop Them Or I'll Shoot" 1969-Fr./Ger./Span.

Halop, William "Billy" (1920-11/9/76). Films: "Challenge of the Range" 1949 (Reb Watson). ¶TV: *The Cisco Kid*—"Battle of Bad Rock" 10-4-52, "The Haunted Stage Stop" 3-7-53; *Wanted—Dead or Alive*—"Mental Lapse" 1-2-60; *Gunsmoke*—"My Father, My Son" 4-23-66 (Bartender), "The Returning" 2-18-67 (Barney), "Stranger in Town" 11-20-67.

Halpin, Luke (1948-). TV: *Annie Get Your Gun* 11-27-57 (Little Jake).

Halsey, Brett (Montgomery Ford) (1933-). Films: "Four Fast Guns" 1959 (Johnny Naco); "Kill Johnny Ringo" 1966-Ital. (Johnny Ringo); "Today It's Me ... Tomorrow You!" 1968-Ital. (Bill); "Twenty Thousand Dollars for Seven" 1968-Ital.; "Wrath of God" 1968-Ital./Span. (Mike); "Roy Colt and Winchester Jack" 1970-Ital. (Roy Colt). ¶TV: *Gunsmoke*—"Helping Hand" 3-17-56 (Steve Elser); *Jim Bowie*—"Bad Medicine" 4-18-58 (Dr. Gibson); *Bat Masterson*—"River Boat" 2-18-59 (Kyle); *Alias Smith and Jones*—"Return to Devil's Hole" 2-25-71 (Hamilton), "The Day the Amnesty Came Through" 11-25-72 (Ed Starr).

Halton, Charles (1876-4/16/59). Films: "Gold Is Where You Find It" 1938 (Turner); "Dodge City" 1939 (Surrett's Lawyer); "Jesse James" 1939 (Heywood); "Reno" 1939 (Welch); "Brigham Young—Frontiersman" 1940 (Prosecutor); "Twenty Mule Team" 1940 (Adams); "Virginia City" 1940 (Ralston); "The Westerner" 1940 (Mort Borrow); "In Old California" 1942 (Mr. Hayes); "The Spoilers" 1942 (Jonathan Struve); "Tombstone, the Town Too Tough to Die" 1942 (Dan Crane); "Singin' in the Corn" 1946 (Obediah Davis); "The Three Godfathers" 1948 (Mr. Latham); "The Daring Caballero" 1949 (Hodges); "The Moonlighter" 1953 (Clem Usquebaugh); "Friendly Persuasion" 1956 (Elder). ¶TV: *Lone Ranger*—"Heritage of Treason" 2-3-55; *Jim Bowie*—"The Close Shave" 1-10-58 (Joseph).

Hamblen, Stuart. Films: "The Arizona Kid" 1939 (McBride); "In Old Monterey" 1939 (Bugler); "The Sombrero Kid" 1942 (Smoke Denton); "Carson City Cyclone" 1943 (Frank Garrett); "King of the Cowboys" 1943 (Duke Wilson); "King of the Forest Rangers" 1946-serial (Professor Carver); "The Savage Horde" 1950 (Stuart).

Hamel, William R. (1906-3/8/58). Films: "Streets of Laredo" 1949 (Townsman); "Hellgate" 1952 (Lt. Col. Woods); "Pony Express" 1953; "The Black Whip" 1956 (Constable); "Copper Sky" 1957 (Trumble).

Hamer, Fred (1873-12/30/53). Films: "A Man and His Mate" 1915.

Hamill, Mark (1952-). TV: *The Texas Wheelers*—Regular 1974-75 (Doobie Wheeler).

Hamilton, Bernie (1928-). Films: "Stranger on the Run" TVM-1967 (Dickory). ¶TV: *The Virginian*—"Ride to Delphi" 9-21-66 (Ransome Kiley), "Incident at Diablo Crossing" 3-12-69; *Cimarron Strip*—"Heller" 1-18-68 (Ollie Whippet); *Hec Ramsey*—"The Mystery of Chalk Hill" 2-18-73 (Obie Watson).

Hamilton, Bruce. *see* Gaige, Russell.

Hamilton, Charles "Chuck". Films: "End of the Trail" 1936 (Deputy); "Two-Fisted Sheriff" 1937 (Tex); "Union Pacific" 1939 (Card Player); "Deadwood Dick" 1940-serial; "Konga, the Wild Stallion" 1940 (Workman); "Texas Rangers Ride Again" 1940 (Truck Driver); "The Medico of Painted Springs" 1941 (Pete); "The Son of Davy Crockett" 1941; "White Eagle" 1941-serial; "Badman's Territory" 1946; "The Last Round-Up" 1947; "Unconquered"

1947; "Santa Fe" 1951; "Pony Express" 1953 (Man). ¶TV: *Branded*—"Salute the Soldier Briefly" 10-24-65.

Hamilton, Donna. Films: "Gunmen of Abilene" 1950 (Mary Clark).

Hamilton, Dran (1928-). Films: "Dirty Little Billy" 1972 (Catherine McCarty); "Ulzana's Raid" 1972 (Mrs. Riordan). ¶TV: *Gunsmoke*—"The Foundling" 2-11-74 (Agnes Graham).

Hamilton, George (1939-). Films: "Lone Star" 1952 (Noah); "A Thunder of Drums" 1961 (Lt. Curtis McQuade); "Viva Maria" 1965-Fr./Ital. (Flores); "A Time for Killing" 1967 (Capt. Dorrit Bentley); "The Man Who Loved Cat Dancing" 1973 (Crocker); "Zorro, the Gay Blade" 1981 (Don Diego Vega/Bunny Wigglesworth); "Poker Alice" TVM-1987 (John). ¶TV: *The Adventures of Rin Tin Tin*—"The Misfit Marshal" 1-9-59 (Elwood Masterson); *Cimarron City*—"The Beauty and the Sorrow" 2-7-59 (Tom).

Hamilton, Hale (1880-5/19/42). Films: "Girl in the Rain" 1927.

Hamilton, John (1887-10/15/58). Films: "They Died with Their Boots On" 1941 (Colonel); "The Great Man's Lady" 1942 (Senator Grant); "Daredevils of the West" 1943-serial (Senator Garfield); "Sheriff of Las Vegas" 1944; "Zorro's Black Whip" 1944-serial (Banker Walsh); "Northwest Trail" 1945; "Badman's Territory" 1946 (Commissioner); "Home on the Range" 1946 (Statesman); "The Phantom Rider" 1946-serial (Senator Williams); "Bandits of Dark Canyon" 1947 (Ben Shaw); "The Fabulous Texan" 1947; "Raiders of the South" 1947; "The Sea of Grass" 1947 (Forrest Cochran); "Desperadoes of Dodge City" 1948 (Stockton); "The Gallant Legion" 1948; "Return of the Badmen" 1948 (Doc Peters); "Bandit King of Texas" 1949 (Marshal John Turner); "Canadian Pacific" 1949 (Pere Lacomb); "Fighting Man of the Plains" 1949 (Currier); "Law of the Golden West" 1949 (Isaac); "Pioneer Marshal" 1949 (Elliott); "Sheriff of Wichita" 1949 (Warden); "The Wyoming Bandit" 1949 (Head Marshal); "Annie Get Your Gun" 1950 (Ship's Captain); "Bells of Coronado" 1950 (Linden); "Davy Crockett, Indian Scout" 1950 (Col. Pollard); "The James Brothers of Missouri" 1950-serial (Lon Royer); "The Missourians" 1950 (McDowell); "Sugarfoot" 1951; "Target" 1952 (Bailey); "El Paso Stampede" 1953 (Rancher); "Iron Mountain Trail"

1953 (Circuit Judge); "Jack McCall, Desperado" 1953 (Col. Cornish); "Marshal of Cedar Rock" 1953 (Prison Warden); "Sitting Bull" 1954 (President U.S. Grant). ¶TV: *The Range Rider*—"Feud at Friendship City" 3-1-52; *The Cisco Kid*—"The Devil's Deputy" 5-10-52, "The Fire Engine" 5-31-52, "Fear" 6-28-52; *The Gene Autry Show*—"Steel Ribbon" 9-22-53 (Dan Parker), "Ransom Cross" 10-6-53; *Tales of the Texas Rangers*—"Carnival Criss-Cross" 9-3-55 (Sheriff Pruitt); *The Roy Rogers Show*—"Three Masked Men" 12-18-55.

Hamilton, John F. (1894-7/11/67). Films: "Allegheny Uprising" 1939 (Professor); "Men of Texas" 1942 (Dwight Douglass).

Hamilton, John "Big John" (1916-12/5/84). Films: "The Deadly Companions" 1961 (Gambler); "Two Rode Together" 1961 (Settler); "McClintock" 1963 (Fauntleroy); "Bandolero!" 1968 (Bank Clerk); "The Undefeated" 1969 (Mudlow). ¶TV: *Gunsmoke*—"Poor Pearl" 12-22-56 (Big John); *Bonanza*—"Calamity Over the Comstock" 11-3-63.

Hamilton, John. Films: "Django, Last Killer" 1967-Ital.; "Revenge for Revenge" 1968-Ital. (Chaliko); "Red Sun" 1971-Fr./Ital./Span.

Hamilton, Joseph (1898-2/20/65). Films: "Strange Lady in Town" 1955 (Mr. Harker); "The Plunderers" 1960 (Abilene); "Cat Ballou" 1965 (Frenchie). ¶TV: *Tales of the Texas Rangers*—"Blood Trail" 9-24-55 (Harry Baxter); *Tombstone Territory*—"Trail's End" 4-10-59; *Buckskin*—"Mary MacNamara" 5-18-59 (Lawyer Sims); *Have Gun Will Travel*—"The Pledge" 1-16-60 (Father); *Gunsmoke*—"Gentleman's Disagreement" 4-30-60 (Pete), "Harriet" 3-4-61 (James Horne), "Cale" 5-5-62 (Nick Archer), "The Glory and the Mud" 1-4-64 (Dan Binney); *Maverick*—"Substitute Gun" 4-2-61 (Stableman).

Hamilton, Judd. Films: "Talent for Loving" 1969-Brit./Span.

Hamilton, Judge. Films: "Branded a Bandit" 1924 (Grandaddy Jim); "Branded a Thief" 1925.

Hamilton, Kipp. Films: "The Unforgiven" 1960 (Georgia Rawlins). ¶TV: *The Texan*—"Border Incident" 12-7-59 (Steve), "Dangerous Ground" 12-14-59 (Steve), "End of Track" 12-21-59 (Steve), "Captive Crew" 2-22-60 (Steve), "Showdown" 2-29-60 (Steve); *Rawhide*—"Incident of the Dancing Death" 4-8-60 (Shezoe); *Wild Wild West*—"The Night of the

Glowing Corpse" 10-29-65 (Cluny Ormont); *The Virginian*—"The Fortress" 12-27-67 (Gloria).

Hamilton, Lloyd (1891-1/19/35). Films: "Ham Among the Redskins" 1915.

Hamilton, Lynn (1930-). Films: "Buck and the Preacher" 1972 (Sarah). ¶TV: *Gunsmoke*—"The Good Samaritans" 3-10-69 (Reba), "The Sisters" 12-29-69 (Mother Tabitha).

Hamilton, Mahlon (1883-6/20/60). Films: "The Red Woman" 1917 (Morton Deal); "That Girl Montana" 1921 (Dan Overton); "Idaho" 1925-serial; "Morganson's Finish" 1926 (Dan Morganson); "Code of Honor" 1930 (Jack Cardigan); "Boss Rider of Gun Creek" 1936 (Red Vale).

Hamilton, Margaret (1902-5/16/85). Films: "My Little Chickadee" 1940 (Mrs. Gideon); "The Ox-Bow Incident" 1943 (Mrs. Larch). ¶TV: *Laramie*—"Beyond Justice" 11-27-62; *Gunsmoke*—"A Quiet Day in Dodge" 1-29-73 (Edsel Pry).

Hamilton, Mark "Slim". Films: "Western Yesterdays" 1924 (Blackstone); "The Light of Western Stars" 1925 (Monty Price); "The Man from Red Gulch" 1925 (Frisbee); "The Rainbow Trail" 1925 (Beasley Willets); "Chip of the Flying U" 1926 (Slim); "The Devil's Gulch" 1926 (Sheriff); "Trumpin' Trouble" 1926 (Cal Libby); "Aflame in the Sky" 1927 (Slim); "Black Jack" 1927 (Slim); "The Sonora Kid" 1927 (Chuck Saunders); "Son of the Golden West" 1928 (Kane); "Smoke Bellew" 1929 (Shorty).

Hamilton, Mark (1922-5/12/87). Films: "Giant" 1956 (Guard); "The Great Locomotive Chase" 1956 (John Wollam); "Man from Del Rio" 1956 (George Dawson).

Hamilton, Murray (1925-9/1/86). TV: *Gunsmoke*—"Chester's Murder" 3-30-57 (Jake Buley), "Wild West" 2-15-58 (Cutter), "Land Deal" 11-8-58 (Calhoun); *Have Gun Will Travel*—"The Last Laugh" 1-25-58 (Ed McKay); *Bret Maverick*—"A Night at the Red Ox" 2-23-82 (Cobb).

Hamilton, Neil (1899-9/24/84). Films: "The Golden Princess" 1925 (Tennessee Hunter); "Desert Gold" 1926 (George Thorne); "King of the Texas Rangers" 1941-serial (John Barton). ¶TV: *Tales of Wells Fargo*—"White Indian" 9-22-58 (Niles Lawson); *Maverick*—"The Rivals" 1-25-59 (Brig. Gen. Archibald Vandergelt); *Zorro*—"Spark of Revenge" 2-19-59

(Don Hilario de la Guerra); *Colt .45*—"The Pirate" 5-31-59 (Captain Johnson); *Man from Blackhawk*—"The Lady in Yellow" 6-17-60 (Stapleton); *Frontier Circus*—"Naomi Champagne" 3-29-62 (Jason Glass).

Hamilton, Ray. TV: *Riverboat*—"Hang the Men High" 3-21-60 (Brad Phelan); *Bat Masterson*—"Run for Your Money" 3-2-61 (Terry Bowen).

Hamilton, Raye. Films: "Action Galore" 1925 (Ma Kruger); "The Masquerade Bandit" 1926 (Kate Mahoney).

Hamilton, Richard (1920-). Films: "Bret Maverick" TVM-1981 (Cy Whitaker); "Pale Rider" 1985 (Jed Blankenship); "Wild Horses" TVM-1985 (Blue Houston); "Dream West" TVM-1986 (General Murdoch). ¶TV: *Bret Maverick*—Regular 1981-82 (Cy Whitaker).

Hamilton, Shorty (1879-3/7/25). Films: "The Sergeant's Boy" 1912; "The Sergeant's Secret" 1913; "Shorty and the Fortune Teller" 1914 (Shorty); "Shorty Escapes Marriage" 1914 (Shorty); Shorty Turns Judge" 1914 (Shorty); "Shorty's Sacrifice" 1914 (Shorty); "Shorty's Strategy" 1914 (Shorty); "Shorty's Trip to Mexico" 1914 (Shorty); "On the Night Stage" 1915 (Cowboy); "Shorty's Ranch" 1915 (Shorty); "Shorty's Secret" 1915 (Shorty); "The Ranger" 1918 (Jim Slater); "The White Masks" 1921 (Battling Rush); "Angel Citizens" 1922 (Smoky Nivette); "Cross Roads" 1922 (Onate); "The Gold Grabbers" 1922; "So This Is Arizona" 1922 (Art Pulvers); "Trail's End" 1922 (Cahoots); "It Happened Out West" 1923; "Lone Hand Texas" 1924.

Hammack, Warren. TV: *The Virginian*—"Vengeance Trail" 1-4-67 (Joe Willard), "Without Mercy" 2-15-67 (Gil Blinns), "With Help from Ulysses" 1-17-68 (Kane), "Image of an Outlaw" 10-23-68 (Gunsmith); *Wild Wild West*—"The Night of the Falcon" 11-10-67 (Soldier).

Hammer, Alvin (1915-10/31/93). Films: "Dakota Lil" 1950.

Hammer, Ben (1925-). TV: *The Virginian*—"Vengeance Trail" 1-4-67 (Quincey King); *Bonanza*—"My Friend, My Enemy" 1-12-69 (Quinn); *Barbary Coast*—"Mary Had More Than a Little" 1-2-76 (Hendricks).

Hammond, Billy. Films: "Northwest Trail" 1945; "Riders of the Dawn" 1945; "Range Beyond the Blue" 1947 (Kyle); "West to Glory" 1947; "Ride, Ryder, Ride" 1949 (Pinto); "Shadows of the West" 1949

(Ranson); "Stallion Canyon" 1949 (Little Bear); "The Fighting Redhead" 1950 (Evans).

Hammond, C. Norman (1878-6/5/41). Films: "Wolves of the Rail" 1918 (David Cassidy).

Hammond, Hally. *see* De Luca, Lorella.

Hammond, Harriet. Films: "The Man from Red Gulch" 1925 (Betsey); "Soft Shoes" 1925 (Mrs. Bradley); "Driftin' Thru" 1926 (the Girl); "The Seventh Bandit" 1926 (Dr. Shirley Chalmette).

Hammond, Nicholas (1950-). Films: "Law of the Land" TVM-1976 (Brad Jensen). ¶TV: *Gunsmoke*—"Women for Sale" 9-10-73 & 9-17-73 (Britt), "Thirty a Month a Found" 10-7-74 (Doak); *Dirty Sally*—4-19-74 (John); *The Oregon Trail*—"The Army Deserter" 10-19-77.

Hampden, Walter (1879-6/11/55). Films: "Northwest Mounted Police" 1940 (Chief Big Bear); "They Died with Their Boots On" 1941 (Sen. Sharp); "Strange Lady in Town" 1955 (Father Gabriel Mendoza).

Hampton, Gladys. Films: "Tangled Trails" 1921 (Blanche Hall).

Hampton, Grayce (1876-12/20/63). Films: "Silver River" 1948 (Woman).

Hampton, James (1936-). Films: "Soldier Blue" 1970 (Pvt. Menzies); "Mackintosh & T.J." 1975 (Cotton); "Hawmps!" 1976 (Howard Clemmons). ¶TV: *Gunsmoke*—"Jeb" 5-25-63 (Jeb Willis), "Pa Hack's Brook" 12-28-63 (Jeb Willis), "Eliab's Aim" 2-27-65 (Eliab Haggen); *Death Valley Days*—"The Paper Dynasty" 2-29-64; *F Troop*—Regular 1965-67 (Dobbs); *Cimarron Strip*—"The Battle of Blood Stone" 10-12-67 (Sam); *The Guns of Will Sonnett*—"Look for the Hound Dog" 1-26-68; *Centennial*—Regular 1978-79 (Defense Attorney); *Paradise*—"Dust on the Wind" 4-28-90 (Graham).

Hampton, Margaret. Films: "The Arizona Whirlwind" 1927 (Helen Dykeman).

Hampton, Paul (1940-). Films: "More Dead Than Alive" 1968 (Billy Eager). ¶TV: *Nichols*—Regular 1971-72 (Johnson).

Hampton, Raye. Films: "Fighting Blood" 1921; "Rainbow Rangers" 1924 (Tilly); "Western Grit" 1924 (Minnie Smith); "On the Go" 1925 (Matilda Graves); "Quicker'n Lightnin'" 1925 (Squaw); "The Cyclone Cowboy" 1927 (Ma Tuttle); "The Galloping Gobs" 1927 (Fanny); "The

Obligin' Buckaroo" 1927; "Pals in Peril" 1927 (Mrs. Bassett).

Hampton, Ruth. Films: "Law and Order" 1953 (Maria); "Take Me to Town" 1953 (Dancehall Girl); "Ricochet Romance" 1954 (Angela Ann Mansfield).

Hamrick, Burwell (1906-9/21/70). Films: "John Ermine of the Yellowstone" 1917 (White Weasel).

Hancock, Elinor. Films: "A Desert Wooing" 1918 (Mrs. Bereton); "Out of Luck" 1923 (Aunt Edith Bristol).

Hanford, Raymond. Films: "The Beckoning Trail" 1916 (Dodd); "Desert Law" 1918 (Sheriff); "Thunder Trail" 1937 (Miner); "Wells Fargo" 1937 (Miner).

Hanin, Roger (1925-). Films: "The Revengers" 1972-U.S./Mex. (Quiberon).

Hankin, Larry (1937-). Films: "Evil Roy Slade" TVM-1972 (Snake). ¶TV: *Paradise*—"Childhood's End" 12-29-88.

Hanley, Bridget (1943-). TV: *Iron Horse*—"Sister Death" 4-3-67 (Bess); *Here Comes the Brides*—Regular 1968-70 (Candy Pruitt); *How the West Was Won*—Episode Three 2-14-77 (Sheila).

Hanlon, Bert (1895-1/1/72). Films: "The Golden West" 1932 (Dennis Epstein); "Park Avenue Lodger" 1937 (Nick).

Hanlon, Jackie. Films: "The Wagon Master" 1929 (Billie Hollister); "Parade of the West" 1930 (Billy Rand).

Hanlon, Tom (1907-9/29/70). Films: "Heroes of the Saddle" 1940; "Home in Wyomin'" 1942; "Ride 'Em, Cowboy" 1942 (Announcer). ¶TV: *Fury*—"Gymkhana" 1-23-60 (Announcer).

Hanmer, Don (1919-). TV: *The Tall Man*—"An Hour to Die" 2-17-62 (Ambrose Bier); *Death Valley Days*—"Diamond Field Jack" 10-27-63 (Jeff Gray); *The Virginian*—"The Thirty Days of Gavin Heath" 1-22-64 (Gentry), "The Captive" 9-28-66 (Roger Emory); *Gunsmoke*—"Gunfighter, R.I.P." 10-22-66 (Barber), "Railroad" 11-25-68 (Lindsey); *Cimarron Strip*—"Knife in the Darkness" 1-25-68; *Here Come the Brides*—"Two Worlds" 2-20-70 (Dr. Bryce); *Bonanza*—"The Trouble with Trouble" 10-25-70 (Fred); *Kung Fu*—"The Centoph" 4-4-74 & 4-11-74 (Sheriff Jaffe).

Hanna, Mark. Films: "Border Saddlemates" 1952 (Manero); "Southwest Passage" 1954 (Hi Jolly);

"Man Without a Star" 1955. ¶TV: *20th Century Fox Hour*—"Gun in His Hand" 4-4-56 (Matty).

Hanneford, Edwin "Poodles" (1891-1/9/67). Films: "Bells of Rosarita" 1945; "Northwest Trail" 1945; "San Antonio" 1945 (San Antonio Stage Driver); "Springfield Rifle" 1952 (Cpl. Hamel). ¶TV: *The Cisco Kid*—"Monkey Business" 1-26-52.

Hannon, Chick. Films: "Tumbling Tumbleweeds" 1935; "Danger Valley" 1937 (Old Timer); "The Fighting Deputy" 1937 (Henchman); "Guns in the Dark" 1937; "The Mystery of the Hooded Horseman" 1937 (Pete); "Reckless Ranger" 1937; "Riders of the Dawn" 1937; "Sing, Cowboy, Sing" 1937 (Henchman); "Stars Over Arizona" 1937 (Yucca Bill); "Trouble in Texas" 1937; "The Trusted Outlaw" 1937; "California Frontier" 1938; "Man's Country" 1938; "The Singing Outlaw" 1938; "Starlight Over Texas" 1938; "Utah Trail" 1938; "Come on, Rangers" 1939; "The Lone Ranger Rides Again" 1939-serial (Cave Heavy #5); "The Man from Texas" 1939; "The Oregon Trail" 1939-serial; "Trigger Smith" 1939; "Westbound Stage" 1939 (Chip); "Arizona Frontier" 1940 (Outlaw); "Adventures of Red Ryder" 1940-serial (Water Heavy #1); "The Border Legion" 1940; "The Carson City Kid" 1940; "Cowboy from Sundown" 1940 (Pete); "The Golden Trail" 1940; "Lightning Strikes West" 1940; "Melody Ranch" 1940; "The Ranger and the Lady" 1940; "Rhythm of the Rio Grande" 1940 (Pete); "Roll, Wagons, Roll" 1940 (Pioneer Rider); "Take Me Back to Oklahoma" 1940; "King of the Texas Rangers" 1941-serial (Raider #1); "The Pioneers" 1941 (Pete); "Robin Hood of the Pecos" 1941; "Tumbledown Ranch in Arizona" 1941; "White Eagle" 1941-serial; "Wrangler's Roost" 1941; "Man from Cheyenne" 1942; "The Sombrero Kid" 1942; "Where Trails End" 1942; "Wild Horse Stampede" 1943; "Bordertown Trail" 1944; "Land of the Outlaws" 1944; "Raiders of Ghost City" 1944-serial; "The Cherokee Flash" 1945; "Gun Smoke" 1945; "Code of the Saddle" 1947; "Six Gun Serenade" 1947; "Navajo Trail Raiders" 1949; "Desperadoes of the West" 1950-serial (Guard); "The James Brothers of Missouri" 1950-serial; "Vigilante Hideout" 1950; "Don Daredevil Rides Again" 1951-serial (Townsman #7); "Arrowhead" 1953.

Hanold, Marilyn. TV: *The Texan*—"The Widow of Paradise" 11-24-58 (Iris Crawford); *Have Gun Will Travel*—"Hunt the Man Down" 4-25-59.

Hansen, Earl. TV: *Wagon Train*—"The Tent City Story" 12-10-58 (Bartender); *The Deputy*—"The Deputy" 9-12-59 (Stubber); *Rawhide*—"Incident at Red River Station" 1-15-60; *Tales of Wells Fargo*—"Fraud" 3-13-61 (Marshal Saul Williams), "Kelly's Clover Girls" 12-9-61 (Benson); *Whispering Smith*—"The Blind Gun" 5-8-61 (Rex Avery); *Maverick*—"The Cats of Paradise" 10-11-59 (Mr. Wilkins); *The Tall Man*—"Sidekick" 12-23-61 (Sledge).

Hansen, Eleanor. Films: "Flaming Frontier" 1938-serial (Mary Grant).

Hansen, Janis (1940-). Films: "Cannon for Cordoba" 1970 (Girl). ¶TV: *Bonanza*—"The Reluctant Rebel" 11-21-65 (Millie); *Wild Wild West*—"The Night of the Puppeteer" 2-25-66 (Waitress); *The Rounders*—Regular 1966-67 (Sally); *The Big Valley*—"Run of the Cat" 10-21-68, "The Battle of Mineral Springs" 3-24-69 (Janie); *Death Valley Days*—"The World's Greatest Swimming Horse" 2-8-69 (Anne).

Hansen, Joachim (1930-). Films: "Black Eagle of Santa Fe" 1964-Ger./Ital./Fr.

Hansen, John (1951-). Films: "The Incredible Rocky Mountain Race" TVM-1977 (Bill Cody); "Donner Pass: The Road to Survival" TVM-1978; "California Gold Rush" TVM-1981.

Hansen, Juanita (1897-9/26/61). Films: "The Love Route" 1915 (Lilly Belle); "The Martyrs of the Alamo" 1915 (Old Soldier's Daughter); "The Mediator" 1916 (Maggie); "Breezy Jim" 1919 (Patricia Wentworth); "Rough-Riding Romance" 1919 (Princess); "The Phantom Foe" 1920-serial; "Girl from the West" 1923.

Hansen, Myrna (1934-). Films: "Man Without a Star" 1955 (Ted Cassidy).

Hansen, Peter (Peter Hanson) (1922-). Films: "Branded" 1951 (Tonio); "The Last Outpost" 1951 (Lt. Crosby); "Passage West" 1951 (Michael Karns); "The Savage" 1952 (Lt. Weston Hathersall); "Drum Beat" 1954 (Lt. Goodsall); "The Violent Men" 1955 (George Menefee); "Three Violent People" 1956 (Lt. Marr); "Apache Rifles" 1964. ¶TV: *The Lone Ranger*—"Homer with a High Hat" 12-16-54, "The Law Lady" 2-24-55, "Sawtelle Saga's End" 3-24-

55; *Jim Bowie*—"Jim Bowie Comes Home" 10-26-56 (Rezin Bowie), "Land Jumpers" 11-16-56 (Rezin Bowie), "Osceola" 1-18-57 (Rezin Bowie), "Rezin Bowie, Gambler" 3-22-57 (Rezin Bowie), "Curfew Cannon" 1-24-58 (Rezin Bowie); *Zane Grey Theater*—"Village of Fear" 3-1-57 (Holton), "The Accuser" 10-30-58; *The Restless Gun*—"Pressing Engagement" 2-24-58 (Quent Todd); *Tombstone Territory*—"Triangle of Death" 5-7-58 (George Camden); *Bat Masterson*—"Election Day" 1-14-59 (Teddy Wright); *Maverick*—"The Cactus Switch" 1-15-61 (Lawrence Deville); *Death Valley Days*—"Dead Man's Tale" 3-8-61 (Dr. Allen Camden), "Miracle at Boot Hill" 1-24-62 (Bill Groat); *How the West Was Won*—Episode One 2-6-77 (Major Drake), Episode Two 2-7-77 (Major Drake), Episode Three 2-14-77 (Major Drake), Episode One 2-12-78 (Major Drake).

Hansen, Vaida (-7/21/93). Films: "Cain's Way" 1969; "The Great Northfield, Minnesota Raid" 1972 (Nude Girl).

Hansen, William (1911-6/23/75). TV: *DuPont Show of the Week*—"Big Deal in Laredo" 10-7-62 (Dr. Scully); *Bonanza*—"Abner Willoughby's Return" 12-21-69 (Vinson).

Hanson, Arthur. Films: "They Came to Cordura" 1959 (Correspondent). ¶TV: *Broken Arrow*—"The Archaeologist" 4-30-57 (Morgan); *Telephone Time*—"Sam Houston's Decision" 12-10-57 (Mosely Baker); *The Big Valley*—"The Haunted Gun" 2-6-67 (Bartender), "The Royal Road" 3-3-69 (Reverend Hamilton); *Cimarron Strip*—"The Search" 11-9-67 (Andrews); *The Virginian*—"Rich Man, Poor Man" 3-11-70 (John).

Hanson, Lars (1887-4/8/65). Films: "The Wind" 1928 (Lige).

Hanson, Marcy. Films: "The Sacketts" TVM-1979 (Laura Pritts).

Hanson, Peter. see Hansen, Peter.

Hanson, Preston. TV: *Rough Riders*—"The Maccabites" 10-16-58 (Cliff); *Wyatt Earp*—"The Court vs. Doc Holliday" 4-26-60.

Happy, Don. Films: "Westbound" 1959. ¶TV: *Rawhide*—"Incident of the Dust Flower" 3-4-60; *Gunsmoke*—"Wishbone" 2-19-66 (Stage Driver), "A Hat" 10-16-67 (Storekeeper), "The Prisoner" 3-17-69 (Freighter), "Stryker" 9-29-69 (Cowboy #1).

Haran, Ronnie. TV: *Cheyenne*—"Sweet Sam" 10-8-62 (Mary DeLieu);

Death Valley Days—"Davy's Friend" 11-28-62; *Wide Country*—"Memory of a Filly" 1-3-63 (Cally Walker).

Harbaugh, Carl (1886-2/26/60). Films: "The Texans" 1938 (Union Soldier); "They Died with Their Boots On" 1941 (Sergeant); "Along the Great Divide" 1951 (Jerome); "Distant Drums" 1951 (M. Duprez); "The Far Country" 1955 (Sourdough); "The Tall Men" 1955 (Salesman).

Harden, Jack. Films: "Desperadoes of the West" 1950-serial (Ed Harper); "Don Daredevil Rides Again" 1951-serial (Jake Miller); "The Bushwackers" 1952 (Mr. Lloyd); "The Maverick Queen" 1956 (Logan).

Hardin, Eileen. Films: "The Westward Trail" 1948 (Mrs. Benson).

Hardin, Jerry. Films: "The Oregon Trail" TVM-1976 (Macklin); "Kate Bliss and the Ticker Tape Kid" TVM-1978 (Bud Dozier); "The Chisholms" TVM-1979 (Jonah Comyns); "Heartland" 1980 (Cattle Buyer). ¶TV: *Gunsmoke*—"The Foundling" 2-11-74 (Bob Ranger); *Sara*—2-13-76 (Frank Dixon), 2-20-76 (Frank Dixon); *The Chisholms*—Regular 1979 (Jonah Comyns); *Young Maverick*—"Half-Past Noon" 1-30-80 (Purnell Sims); *Father Murphy*—"The First Miracle" 4-4-82 & 4-11-82 (Ray Walker); *Paradise*—"The Gates of Paradise" 1-6-90 (Uncle Peter); *Dr. Quinn, Medicine Woman*—"The Race" 9-25-93 (Dr. Cassidy).

Hardin, Melora. Films: "Little House on the Prairie: Look Back to Yesterday" TVM-1983 (Michele Pierson).

Hardin, Ty (Ty Hungerford) (1930-). Films: "Last Train from Gun Hill" 1959 (Cowboy); "Man from the Cursed Valley" 1964-Ital./Span. (Johnny Walscott); "Savage Pampas" 1966-U.S./Span./Arg. (Carreras); "Custer of the West" 1967-U.S./Span. (Maj. Marcus Reno); "You're Jinxed, Friend, You Just Met Sacramento" 1970-Ital./Span. (Jack "Sacramento" Thompson); "Holy Water Joe" 1971-Ital. (Jeff Donovan); "The Last Rebel" 1971-Ital./U.S./Span. (Sheriff); "Vendetta at Dawn" 1971-Ital. (Jonathan); "Drummer of Vengeance" 1974-Brit./Ital.; "Bad Jim" 1990 (Tom Jefferd). ¶TV: *Bronco*—Regular 1958-62 (Bronco Layne); *Sugarfoot*—"The Trial of the Canary Kid" 9-15-59 (Bronco Layne), "Angel" 3-6-61 (Bronco Layne); *Maverick*—"Hadley's Hunters" 9-25-60 (Bronco Layne); *Cheyenne*—"Duel at Judas Basin" 1-30-61 (Bronco Layne);

The Quest—"Prairie Woman" 11-10-76 (Tom Kurd); *Hunter's Moon*—Pilot 12-1-79 (Marshal).

Harding, Ann (1902-9/1/81). Films: "Girl of the Golden West" 1930 (Minnie); "The Conquerors" 1932 (Caroline Ogden Standish).

Harding, Frank. TV: *The Texan*—"Desert Passage" 12-1-58; *Zane Grey Theater*—"Hang the Heart High" 1-15-59 (True Wessels); *Bat Masterson*—"Flume to the Mother Lode" 1-28-60 (Will).

Harding, John (1911-). TV: *Hawkeye and the Last of the Mohicans*—"La Salle's Treasure" 10-9-57; *Bonanza*—"The Search" 2-14-65 (Jason); *Wild Wild West*—"The Night of the Winged Terror" 1-17-68 & 1-24-68 (Thaddeus Toombs); *Nichols*—Regular 1971-72 (Salter).

Harding, Tex. Films: "Blazing the Western Trail" 1945; "Both Barrels Blazing" 1945; "Outlaws of the Rockies" 1945 (Tex Harding); "Return of the Durango Kid" 1945; "Rustlers of the Badlands" 1945; "Texas Panhandle" 1945; "Frontier Gunlaw" 1946; "Lawless Empire" 1946 (Rev. Tex Harding); "Desert Vigilante" 1949 (Jim Gill).

Hardt, Eloise (1927-). Films: "Escape from Fort Bravo" 1953 (Girl). ¶TV: *Death Valley Days*—"The Madstone" 1-18-61 (Ellen); *Lawman*—"The Doctor" 5-6-62 (Cissy Lawson); *The Loner*—"The Burden of the Badge" 3-5-66 (Martha Mitchell).

Hardt, Ludwig (-1947). Films: "Arizona" 1940 (Meyer).

Hardwicke, Sir Cedric (1893-8/6/64). Films: "Valley of the Sun" 1942 (Warrick).

Hardy, Oliver (1892-8/7/57). Films: "The Gentle Cyclone" 1926 (Sheriff Bill); "No Man's Law" 1927 (Sharkey Nye); "Way Out West" 1937 (Ollie); "The Fighting Kentuckian" 1949 (Willie Paine).

Hardy, Sam (1883-10/16/35). Films: "A Texas Steer" 1927 (Brassy Gall); "The Rainbow" 1929 (Derby Scanlon); "Song of the West" 1930 (Davolo); "Powdersmoke Range" 1935 (Mayor Big Steve Ogden).

Hardy, Sophie (1940-). Films: "The Desperado Trail" 1965-Ger./Yugo. (Ann).

Hare, Lumsden (1874-8/28/64). Films: "The Last of the Mohicans" 1936 (General Abercrombie); "Northwest Passage" 1940 (Gen. Amherst); "Hudson Bay" 1941; "Rose Marie" 1954 (Judge); "The Oregon Trail" 1959 (British Ambassador). ¶TV: *The Adventures of Rin Tin Tin*—"The Lost

Scotchman" 5-27-55 (Angus Mac-Tavish).

Hare, Marilyn. Films: "West of Texas" 1943 (Ellen Yeager).

Hare, Will (1919-). Films: "Butch and Sundance: The Early Days" 1979 (Conductor); "The Electric Horseman" 1979 (Gus); "Dream West" TVM-1986 (Dr. McClain); "Grim Prairie Tales" 1990 (Lee).

Harens, Dean (1921-). TV: *Gunsmoke*—"Laughing Gass" 3-29-58 (Stafford); *Have Gun Will Travel*—"Duel at Florence" 10-11-58 (Ernie Teller); *Northwest Passage*—"The Long Rifle" 11-23-58 (Judd Ramsey); *Bat Masterson*—"Cheyenne Club" 12-17-58 (Steven Haley), "The Canvas and the Cane" 12-17-59; *U.S. Marshal*—"Anything for a Friend" 10-17-59 (Carl Donahue); *Black Saddle*—"Change of Venue" 12-11-59 (Tom Brandon); *Riverboat*—"The Blowup" 1-17-60 (Simon); *Death Valley Days*—"A Woman's Rights" 5-10-60; *The Outlaws*—"A Bit of Glory" 2-1-62 (Lou Milroy); *The Travels of Jaimie McPheeters*—"The Day of the Giants" 11-3-63 (Simmons); *The Virginian*—"Felicity's Springs" 10-14-64 (the Reverend); *Bonanza*—"The Jonah" 5-9-65 (Poole), "Credit for a Kill" 10-23-66 (Morgan Tanner); *Iron Horse*—"Volcano Wagon" 1-16-67 (George); *Lancer*—"The Fix-It Man" 2-11-69.

Harewood, Dorian (1952-). TV: *Dr. Quinn, Medicine Woman*—"Buffalo Soldiers" 2-5-94 (Carver).

Harford, Betty. Films: "The Wild and the Innocent" 1959 (Mrs. Forbes). ¶TV: *Gunsmoke*—"Where'd They Go?" 3-12-60 (Medora); *The Big Valley*—"Last Train to the Fair" 4-27-66 (Grace Stullman).

Hargitay, Mariska. Films: "The Gambler V: Playing for Keeps" TVM-1994 (Etta Place).

Hargitay, Mickey (1926-). Films: "Stranger in Sacramento" 1964-Ital. (Mike Jordan); "Three Graves for a Winchester" 1966-Ital.; "Cjamango" 1967-Ital. (Don Pablo); "Sheriff Won't Shoot" 1967-Ital./Fr./Brit.; "Ringo, It's Massacre Time" 1970-Ital. ¶TV: *Wild Wild West*—"The Night of the Fugitives" 11-8-68 (Monk).

Hargrave, Ron. Films: "Jack Slade" 1953 (Ned Prentice). ¶TV: *You Are There*—"The End of the Dalton Gang" 5-12-57 (Bob Dalton); *Tales of the Texas Rangers*—"Whirlwind Raiders" 10-13-57 (Clint Weldon).

Harker, Charmienne. Films:

"Unconquered" 1947; "Son of Pale-face" 1952 (Bessie). ¶TV: *Death Valley Days*—"Nevada's Plymouth Rock" 3-10-56; *Sergeant Preston of the Yukon*—"Mad Wolf of Lost Canyon" 8-16-56 (Helen Townsend); *Colt .45*—"Long Odds" 4-11-58 (Mother); *Tales of Wells Fargo*—Fort Massacre" 2-2-59 (Mrs. Oliver).

Harkins, John (1933-). Films: "Dream West" TVM-1986 (Secretary of State George Bancroft).

Harlam, Macey (-6/17/23. Films: "Nanette of the Wilds" 1916 (Baptiste Flammant).

Harlan, Kenneth (1895-3/6/67). Films: "The Flame of the Yukon" 1917 (George Fowler); "Getting Some" 1920; "I Am the Law" 1922 (Robert Fitzgerald); "The Virginian" 1923 (the Virginian); "The Golden Strain" 1925 (Milt Mulford, Jr.); "Ranger of the Big Pines" 1925 (Ross Cavanaugh); "Under Montana Skies" 1930 (Clay Conning); "Wanderer of the Wasteland" 1935 (Bob); "Song of the Saddle" 1936 (Marshal); "Trail Dust" 1936 (Officer Bowman); "Blazing Sixes" 1937 (Major Taylor); "Gunsmoke Ranch" 1937 (Phineas Flagg); "Renfrew of the Royal Mounted" 1937 (Angel Carroll); "Law of the Texan" 1938 (Allen Spencer/El Coyote); "Pride of the West" 1938 (Caldwell); "Sunset Trail" 1938 (John Marsh); "Under Western Stars" 1938 (Richards); "Whirlwind Horseman" 1938 (John Harper); "The Oregon Trail" 1939-serial; "Range War" 1939 (Charles Higgins); "Prairie Schooners" 1940 (Dalton Stull); "Santa Fe Marshal" 1940 (Blake); "King of Dodge City" 1941 (Jeff Carruthers); "Wide Open Town" 1941 (Tom Wilson); "Bandit Ranger" 1942; "Deep in the Heart of Texas" 1942 (Sneed); "Fighting Bill Fargo" 1942 (Hackett); "The Sundown Kid" 1942; "Daredevils of the West" 1943-serial (Commissioner); "The Law Rides Again" 1943 (Hampton); "Wild Horse Stampede" 1943 (Borman); "Death Valley Rangers" 1944 (Kirk).

Harlan, Marion. Films: "Rough Going" 1925 (Patricia Burke); "The Gentle Cyclone" 1926; "A Man Four-Square" 1926 (Polly); "Tony Runs Wild" 1926 (Ethel Johnson).

Harlan, Otis (1864-1/20/40). Films: "Two Kinds of Women" 1922 (Major Langworthy); "Without Compromise" 1922 (Dr. Evans); "Pioneer Trails" 1923 (Easy Aaron Cropsey); "The Spider and the Rose" 1923 (the Secretary); "Code of the Wilderness" 1924 (Uncle Jephon);

"One Law for the Woman" 1924 (Judge Blake); "Nine and Three-Fifths Seconds" 1925 (Motherbund); "Three Bad Men" 1926 (Zack Leslie); "The Unknown Cavalier" 1926 (Judge Blowfly Jones); "Galloping Fury" 1927 (Pop Halen); "The Silent Rider" 1927 (Sourdough Jackson); "The Shepherd of the Hills" 1928 (By Thunder); "Mountain Justice" 1930 (Jud McTavish); "Parade of the West" 1930 (Prof. Clayton); "Partners" 1932 (Auctioneer); "Ride Him, Cowboy" 1932 (Judge Jones); "Rider of Death Valley" 1932 (Peck); "The Telegraph Trail" 1933 (Zeke Keller); "Western Frontier" 1935 (Cookie); "Western Gold" 1937 (Jake); "Outlaws of Sonora" 1938 (Newt); "The Texans" 1938 (Henry).

Harlan, Rosita. Films: "Arizona Wildcat" 1938 (Margarita).

Harland, Robert. TV: *The Law of the Plainsman*—Regular 1959-60 (Deputy Billy Jordan); *Zane Grey Theater*—"The Reckoning" 1-14-60 (Les), "Killer Instinct" 3-17-60 (Lee Phelps), "Knife of Hate" 12-8-60 (Jack Hoyt); *Stagecoach West*—"The Land Beyond" 10-11-60 (Lin Proctor); *The Outlaws*—"Shorty" 11-3-60 (Clem Decker); *Wagon Train*—"Path of the Serpent" 2-8-61 (Cpl. Clay Taylor); *Wyatt Earp*—"The Convict's Revenge" 4-4-61 (Phil Davies); *Paradise*—"The Holstered Gun" 11-3-88 (Jack Kelly).

Harley, Amanda. Films: "Sam Whiskey" 1969 (Mrs. Perkins). ¶TV: *The Big Valley*—"A Day of Terror" 12-12-66, "Journey into Violence" 12-18-67, "The Royal Road" 3-3-69 (Mrs. Owens).

Harley, Ed (1848-10/29/33). Films: "The Girl of the Golden West" 1915 (Old Minstrel).

Harlow, William. TV: *The Rebel*—"Johnny Yuma at Appomattox" 9-18-60 (Bud), "The Champ" 10-2-60 (Ace Linhart), "Run, Killer, Run" 10-30-60 (Jed Morgan), "The Hope Chest" 12-25-60 (Burke); *Branded*—"A Proud Town" 12-19-65.

Harmer, Lillian (1886-5/15/46). Films: "The Lone Cowboy" 1934 (Boardinghouse Keeper).

Harmon, John (-1982). Films: "Cowboy from Brooklyn" 1938 (Technician); "Union Pacific" 1939 (One Armed Reporter); "The Shepherd of the Hills" 1941 (Charlie, the Deputy); "Call of the Canyon" 1942 (the Pigeon); "Adventures of Gallant Bess" 1948 (Blake); "Horizons West" 1952 (Deputy Sheriff Johnson); "Jack Slade" 1953 (Hollis); "Bitter Creek"

1954 (A.Z. Platte); "Three Young Texans" 1954 (Thorpe); "The Man from Bitter Ridge" 1955 (Norman Roberts); "The Spoilers" 1955 (Kelly); "Canyon River" 1956 (Ben); "Three Violent People" 1956 (Massey); "Badman's Country" 1958; "Texas Across the River" 1966 (Gabe Hutchins); "The Honkers" 1972 (Sam Martin). ¶TV: *Wagon Train*—"The Willy Moran Story" 9-18-57 (Fabor), "The Cassie Vance Story" 12-23-63 (Jenkins); *Maverick*—"Point Blank" 9-29-57, "Hostage!" 11-10-57 (Ziggy), "The Jail at Junction Flats" 11-9-58 (Saloon Keeper), "Two Tickets to Ten Strike" 3-15-59 (Stranger), "A Bullet for the Teacher" 10-30-60 (Depot Agent); *Trackdown*—"The Weddding" 2-14-58 (Henry Bennett); *The Adventures of Rin Tin Tin*—"The Secret Weapon" 4-11-58 (Walt Mathers); *Tales of Wells Fargo*—"The Pickpocket" 4-28-58 (Desk Clerk), "The Last Stand" 4-13-59 (Long); *Jefferson Drum*—"A Matter of Murder" 7-11-58; *Wanted—Dead or Alive*—"The Giveaway Gun" 10-11-58, "Double Fee" 3-21-59, "Death, Divided by Three" 4-23-60 (Hotel Clerk); *The Rifleman*—"Duel of Honor" 11-11-58 (Hotel Clerk), "The Trade" 3-10-59, "One Went to Denver" 3-17-59, "The Mind Reader" 6-30-59, "Eddie's Daughter" 11-3-59 (Eddie Halstead), "The Spiked Rifle" 11-24-59, "The Legacy" 12-8-59, "The Visitors" 1-26-60, "Shotgun Man" 4-12-60 (Eddie), "The Shattered Idol" 12-4-61 (Eddie), "Long Gun from Tucson" 12-11-61 (Eddie), "The Day a Town Slept" 4-16-62 (Eddie); *Buckskin*—"Mr. Rush's Secretary" 1-19-59 (Mr. Mullum); *The Texan*—"Return to Friendly" 2-2-59 (Lobo Cooms), "Badman" 6-20-60 (Russ Hardin); *Bonanza*—"The Hanging Posse" 11-28-59, "Cut-Throat Junction" 3-18-61, "A Hot Day for a Hanging" 10-14-62, "The Last Haircut" 2-3-63 (Barber), "A Dime's Worth of Glory" 11-1-64 (Telegrapher), "Meena" 11-16-69 (Rider), "The Horse Traders" 4-5-70 (Rider); *Death Valley Days*—"One Man Tank" 3-29-60 (Mike Shannon); *Cheyenne*—"Two Trails to Santa Fe" 10-28-60 (Harris); *Rawhide*—"Incident Near the Promised Land" 2-3-61; *Gunsmoke*—"Potshot" 3-11-61, "Coventry" 3-17-62, "Gold Mine" 12-25-65 (Hotel Clerk); *The Tall Man*—"Ladies of the Town" 5-20-61 (Pinky); *Whispering Smith*—"The Quest" 6-26-61 (Jackie Rouge); *Laramie*—"The Replacement" 3-27-62; *Wide Country*—"Don't Cry for Johnny Devlin" 1-24-63 (Elmer);

Have Gun Will Travel—"Cage at Mc-Naab" 2-16-63 (Trowbridge); *The Virginian*—"The Money Cage" 3-6-63, "Ride a Cock-Horse to Laramie Cross" 2-23-66 (Bartender), "The Barren Ground" 12-6-67 (Dow); *Temple Houston*—"Enough Rope" 12-19-63 (Crane); *The Travels of Jaimie McPheeters*—"The Day of the Haunted Trail" 1-26-64 (Huddlestone), "The Day of the 12 Candles" 2-23-64 (Wagontrainer); *The Big Valley*—"Boots with My Father's Name" 9-29-65 (Storekeeper), "The Brawlers" 12-15-65 (Conductor), "The Great Safe Robbery" 11-21-66 (Conductor), "Boy into Man" 1-16-67, "Cage of Eagles" 4-24-67 (Telegrapher), "Guilty" 10-30-67 (Walt Tenner), "The Long Ride" 11-25-68; *Laredo*—"Meanwhile, Back at the Reservation" 2-10-66 (Sam Price), "Finnegan" 10-21-66 (Jonas Kale); *Wild Wild West*—"The Night of the Infernal Machine" 12-23-66 (Moody); *Rango*—"The Spy Who Was Out Cold" 2-10-67 (Stacey); *Lancer*—"Devil's Blessing" 4-22-69, "The Lion and the Lamb" 2-3-70; *The Cowboys*—"The Avenger" 3-6-74 (Nedrick); *Dirty Sally*—4-12-74 (Miller).

Harmon, Marie. Films: "Springtime in Texas" 1945; "The El Paso Kid" 1946 (Sally Stone); "Gunsmoke" 1947; "Night Time in Nevada" 1948 (Toni Bordon).

Harmon, Mark (1951-). Films: "Comes a Horseman" 1978 (Billy Joe Meynert), "Wyatt Earp" 1994 (Johnny Behan). ¶TV: *Centennial*—Regular 1978-79 (John McIntosh).

Harmon, Pat (1888-11/26/58). Films: "The Firebrand" 1922 (Hank Potter); "In the Days of Buffalo Bill" 1922-serial (Gaspard); "The Eternal Struggle" 1923 (Oily Kirby); "Ruth of the Range" 1923-serial; "The Back Trail" 1924 (Curry); "Ridgeway of Montana" 1924 (Pete Shagmire); "The Sawdust Trail" 1924 (Ranch Foreman); "The Lure of the Wild" 1925 (Mike Murdock); "The Cowboy Cop" 1926 (Dago Jack); "The Phantom Bullet" 1926 (Billy Haynes); "The Unknown Cavalier" 1926 (Bad Man); "Lightning" 1927 (Simon Legree); "Sunset Pass" 1929 (Clink Peeples); "Secret Menace" 1931; "Two Gun Caballero" 1931; "The Fourth Horseman" 1933; "Border Vengeance" 1935 (Tex "Slats" Pryor); "Devil's Canyon" 1935; "Five Bad Men" 1935 (Cafe Manager); "The Silent Code" 1935 (Carney); "Trails End" 1935 (Gimpy).

Harmonica Bill. Films: "Across the Badlands" 1950 (Harmonica Bill); "Pecos River" 1951.

Harmstorf, Raimund. Films: "Genius" 1975-Ital./Fr./Ger.; "California" 1976-Ital./Span. (Rupp Whittaker); "Manhunt" 1984-Ital.

Harolde, Ralf (1899-11/1/74). Films: "Bad Man of Deadwood" 1941 (Jake Marvel); "Ridin' on a Rainbow" 1941 (Binke); "Sin Town" 1942 (Kentucky Jones). ¶TV: *The Deputy*—"The Shackled Town" 2-11-61 (the Padre).

Harper, Gus. *see* D'Arpe, Gustave.

Harper, Jonathan. TV: *Gunsmoke*—Regular 1955-75 (Percy Crump); *Hondo* "Hondo and the Commancheros" 11-10-67 (Kyle).

Harper, Paul (1933-). Films: "The Wild Bunch" 1969; "Fandango" 1970 (Greaser); "J.W. Coop" 1971 (Warden Morgan); "Bounty Man" TVM-1972 (Hargus); "The Culpepper Cattle Company" 1972 (Trooper). ¶TV: *Bonanza*—"The Law and Billy Burgess" 2-15-70 (Sully); *Kung Fu*—"King of the Mountain" 10-14-72 (Amos), "Dark Angel" 11-11-72 (Davey Peartree), "Night of the Owls, Day of the Doves" 2-14-74 (Sam Wallace).

Harper, Ron (1935-). TV: *Tales of Wells Fargo*—"All That Glitters" 10-24-60 (Dan); *Laramie*—"Duel at Parkison Town" 12-13-60 (Lee Parkinson), "Edge of Evil" 4-2-63 (Steve Rhodes); *Wagon Train*—"The River Crossing" 12-14-60; *The Deputy*—"Duty Bound" 1-7-61 (Jay Elston); *The Tall Man*—"The Best Policy" 1-28-61 (Judge Danby); *The Big Valley*—"Top of the Stairs" 1-6-69 (Eric Abbott).

Harper, Tess (1950-). Films: "My Heroes Have Always Been Cowboys" 1991 (Cheryl Hornby).

Harr, Silver (1893-9/19/68). Films: "Cyclone Kid" 1931 (Sheriff); "The Law of the Wild" 1934-serial; "Arizona Bad Man" 1935; "Son of Zorro" 1947-serial; "Bullets and Saddles" 1943; "The Desperadoes" 1943; "Wild Horse Rustlers" 1943; "California Gold Rush" 1946; "Ghost of Hidden Valley" 1946 (Stage Guard); "Bells of San Angelo" 1947; "The Wild Frontier" 1947.

Harrell, James. Films: "Mackintosh & T.J." 1975; "The Chisholms" TVM-1979 (Doc Simpson). ¶TV: *The Chisholms*—Regular 1979 (Doc Simpson).

Harrell, Scotty. Films: "Little Joe, the Wrangler" 1942; "Old Chisholm Trail" 1942; "The Lone Star Trail" 1943; "Tenting Tonight on the Old Camp Ground" 1943.

Harrigan, William (1894-2/1/66). Films: "Desert Fury" 1947 (Judge Berle Lindquist).

Harrington, Kate (1903-11/23/78). Films: "Come on, Danger!" 1942 (Maggie); "Riding the Wind" 1942 (Martha).

Harrington, Pat (1901-65). Films: "Channing of the Northwest" 1922 (Sport McCool).

Harrington, Jr., Pat (1929-). TV: *F Troop*—"Spy, Counterspy, Counter Counterspy" 2-15-66 (Wise); *Here Come the Brides*—"Debt of Honor" 1-23-70 (Morgan).

Harrington, Vikki. TV: *Daniel Boone*—"The Ben Franklin Encounter" 3-18-65 (Mary Merivale); *Death Valley Days*—"The Fight San Francisco Never Forgot" 5-14-66 (Emily).

Harris, Arlene (1899-6/12/76). Films: "North to Alaska" 1960 (Queen Lil).

Harris, Berkeley. Films: "Bullet for a Badman" 1964 (Jeff); "Shenandoah" 1965 (Capt. Richards). ¶TV: *Wagon Train*—"The Fort Pierce Story" 9-23-63 (Sergeant Kincaid), "The Clay Shelby Story" 12-6-64 (Corporal Reece); *Gunsmoke*—"Owney Tupper Had a Daughter" 4-4-64 (Mal), "The Reward" 11-6-65 (Farmer); *The Virginian*—"The Laramie Road" 12-8-65 (Crouch); *A Man Called Shenandoah*—"Run and Hide" 2-14-66 (Tad Kern).

Harris, Bob (1930-). TV: *Bonanza*—"The Secret" 5-6-61 (Bill Parson), "The Ride" 1-21-62, "The Jury" 12-30-62.

Harris, Brad (1933-). Films: "Thirteen Fighting Men" 1960 (Pvt. Fowler); "Pirates of the Mississippi" 1963-Ger./Ital./Fr.; "Black Eagle of Santa Fe" 1964-Ger./Ital./Fr. (Cliff McPherson); "Massacre at Marble City" 1964-Ger./Ital./Fr. (Phil Stone); "Rattler Kid" 1968-Ital./Span. (Sheriff Bill Manors); "Wanted Sabata" 1970-Ital.; "Death Is Sweet from the Soldier of God" 1972-Ital.; "Durango Is Coming, Pay or Die" 1972-Ital./Span.

Harris, Buddy (1891-9/5/71). Films: "The Little Sheriff" 1914.

Harris, Eddie. Films: "Beyond the Rockies" 1926 (Sartwell); "Buffalo Bill on the U.P. Trail" 1926 (Mose); "The Fighting Strain" 1926; "King of the Herd" 1927.

Harris, Fox (1936-12/27/88). Films: "Straight to Hell" 1987-Brit. (Kim Blousson).

Harris, Jack W. TV: *Sergeant Preston of the Yukon*—"Blind Justice" 1-17-57 (Jack Daniels); *Circus Boy*—"The Lady and the Circus" 3-31-57 (Sam Gordon); *Tales of the Texas Rangers*—"Both Barrels Blazing" 10-20-57 (Mr. Tompkins); *Man from Blackhawk*—"Death at Noon" 1-8-60 (Sheriff).

Harris, Jo Ann. Films: "The Wild Wild West Revisited" TVM-1979 (Carmelita). ¶TV: *The High Chaparral*—"The Little Thieves" 12-26-69 (Annie); *The Men from Shiloh*—"Jenny" 9-30-70 (Mary Ann Travers), "Tate, Ramrod" 2-24-71 (Amanda Donner); *Nakia*—"The Sand Trap" 10-5-74 (Kitty).

Harris, Joe (1870-6/11/53). Films: "Hell Bent" 1918 (Beau Ross); "Three Mounted Men" 1918 (Buck Masters); "Bare Fists" 1919 (Boone Travis); "A Fight for Love" 1919 (Black Michael); "A Gun Fightin' Gentleman" 1919 (Seymour); "Marked Men" 1919 (Tom Gibbons); "The Outcasts of Poker Flat" 1919 (Ned Stratton); "The Rider of the Law" 1919 (Buck Soutar); "Riders of Vengeance" 1919 (Gale Thurman); "Bullet Proof" 1920 (Bandit); "Hitchin's Posts" 1920; "Human Stuff" 1920 (Ramero); "Overland Red" 1920 (Sago); "Sundown Slim" 1920 (Fernando); "West Is West" 1920 (Spencer); "The White Rider" 1920 (Sheriff); "Red Courage" 1921 (Blackie Holloway); "Sure Fire" 1921 (Romero); "The Wallop" 1921 (Barela); "The Freeze-Out" 1921 (Headlight Whipple); "The Bearcat" 1922 (Doc Henderson); "For Big Stakes" 1922 (Ramon Valdez); "The Loaded Door" 1922 (Stan Calvert); "Pardon My Nerve!" 1922 (Jack Harpe); "Canyon of the Fools" 1923 (Terazaz); "Crashin' Thru" 1923 (Morelos).

Harris, Jonathan (1914-). TV: *Zorro*—"The Mountain Man" 3-19-59 (Don Carlos Fernandez), "The Hound of the Sierras" 3-26-59 (Don Carlos Fernandez), "Manhunt" 4-2-59 (Don Carlos Fernandez); *The Outlaws*—"Outrage at Pawnee Bend" 4-6-61 (Sam Twyfford); *Bonanza*—"A Passion for Justice" 9-29-63 (Charles Dickens); *Lancer*—"The Black McGloins" 1-21-69 (Padraic McGloin).

Harris, Julie (1925-). TV: *Rawhide*—"The Calf Women" 4-30-65 (Emma Teall); *Laredo*—"Rendezvous at Arillo" 10-7-65 (Anna-Maye Davidson); *Daniel Boone*—"Faith's Way" 4-4-68 (Faith Griswald); *Bonanza*—"A Dream to Dream" 4-14-68 (Sarah Carter); *The*

Big Valley—"A Stranger Everywhere" 12-9-68 (Jennie Hall); *The Men from Shiloh*—"Wolf Track" 3-17-71 (Jenny).

Harris, Julius (1923-). TV: *Outlaws*—"Primer" 1-10-87.

Harris, Kay (1920-10/23/71). Films: "The Fighting Buckaroo" 1943 (Carol Comstock); "Robin Hood of the Range" 1943 (Julie Marlowe).

Harris, Lucretia. Films: "The Feud" 1919 (Nancy).

Harris, Marcia. Films: "The Girl from Porcupine" 1922 (Schoolteacher); "The Big Trail" 1930 (Mrs. Riggs).

Harris, Mercer. Films: "Death of a Gunfighter" 1969 (Will Oxley).

Harris, Michael. Films: "Flesh and the Spur" 1957 (Deputy Marshal). ¶TV: *The Rifleman*—"The Challenge" 4-7-59; *Maverick*—"You Can't Beat the Percentage" 10-4-59 (Charley); *Gunsmoke*—"Potshot" 3-11-61; *The Big Valley*—"Barbary Red" 2-16-66 (Deputy Sheriff), "The Death Merchant" 2-23-66 (Sheriff), "Into the Widow's Web" 3-23-66 (Deputy), "Caesar's Wife" 10-3-66; *Hondo*—"Hondo and the Mad Dog" 10-27-67 (Mills).

Harris, Mildred (1901-7/20/44). Films: "A Shadow of the Past" 1913; "The Wheels of Destiny" 1913; "The Indian Trapper's Vindication" 1915; "The Cold Deck" 1917 (Alice Leigh); "Golden Rule Kate" 1917; "When a Girl Loves" 1919 (Bess); "The Desert Hawk" 1924 (Marie Nicholls); "One Law for the Woman" 1924 (Polly Barnes); "Beyond the Border" 1925 (Molly Smith); "Frivolous Sal" 1925 (Chita); "The Wolf Hunters" 1926; "One Hour of Love" 1927 (Gwen).

Harris, Mitchell (1883-11/16/48). Films: "Fair Warning" 1931 (Jim Silent); "Freighters of Destiny" 1932 (Randolph Carter); "Ghost Valley" 1932 (Judge J. Drake).

Harris, Phil (1906-8/11/95). Films: "Buck Benny Rides Again" 1940 (Phil); "The Gatling Gun" 1972 (Boland). ¶TV: *F Troop*—"Where Were You at the Last Massacre?" 1-19-67 (Flaming Arrow).

Harris, Richard (1932-). Films: "Major Dundee" 1965 (Capt. Benjamin Tyreen); "A Man Called Horse" 1970 (Lord John Morgan); "Man in the Wilderness" 1971-U.S./Span. (Zachary Bass); "Deadly Trackers" 1973 (Kilpatrick); "The Return of a Man Called Horse" 1976 (John Morgan); "Triumphs of a Man Called Horse" 1984 (Man Called Horse);

"Unforgiven" 1992 (English Bob); "Silent Tongue" 1993 (Prescott Roe).

Harris, Robert H. (1909-11/30/81). Films: "Apache Uprising" 1966 (Hoyt Taylor); "The Dangerous Days of Kiowa Jones" TVM-1966 (Dobie); "The Great Northfield, Minnesota Raid" 1972 (Wilcox). ¶TV: *Gunsmoke*—"Cow Doctor" 9-8-56 (Ben Pitcher), "Kick Me" 1-26-57 (Fred Mysers); *Zane Grey Theater*—"The Freighter" 1-17-58 (Rufus Murdock); *Have Gun Will Travel*—"Birds of a Feather" 3-8-58 (John Sukey), "Ransom" 6-4-60 (Schermer); *Rough Riders*—"Breakout" 10-9-58 (Major Dawson); *Rawhide*—"Incident West of Lano" 2-27-59 (Joe Planey); *The Restless Gun*—"Ricochet" 3-9-59 (Matt Devlon); *Wanted—Dead or Alive*—"Double Fee" 3-21-59 (Mason); *The Rifleman*—"The Wrong Man" 3-31-59 (Curly Smith), "Tension" 10-27-59 (Ezra Martin); *Wichita Town*—"Out of the Past" 12-9-59 (Gus Ritter); *Man from Blackhawk*—"Destination Death" 3-11-60 (Baron von Danzig); *The Outlaws*—"The Dark Sunrise of Griff Kincaid" 1-4-62 (Veasy); *Bonanza*—"The Jacknife" 2-18-62 (Chad), "The Legacy" 12-15-63 (Dormann); *The Virginian*—"Stacey" 2-28-68 (Dr. Andrews); *Wild Wild West*—"The Night of Bleak Island" 3-14-69 (Steven Rydell).

Harris, Rosemary (1930-). Films: "The Chisholms" TVM-1979 (Minerva Chisholm). ¶TV: *The Chisholms*—Regular 1979-80 (Minerva Chisholm).

Harris, Roy. see Hill, Riley.

Harris, Major Sam (1877-10/22/69). Films: "Rose Marie" 1936 (Guest); "King of the Royal Mounted" 1940-serial (Harold Bolton); "Fancy Pants" 1950 (Umpire); "The Vanquished" 1953; "The Horse Soldiers" 1959 (Confederate Major); "Two Rode Together" 1961 (Post Doctor); "The Man Who Shot Liberty Valance" 1962; "Cheyenne Autumn" 1964 (Townsman).

Harris, Stacy B. (1918-3/13/73). Films: "The Great Sioux Uprising" 1953 (Uriah); "The Redhead from Wyoming" 1953 (Chet Jones); "The Brass Legend" 1956 (George Barlow); "Comanche" 1956 (Downey); "Good Day for a Hanging" 1958 (Coley); "Cast a Long Shadow" 1959 (Eph Brown); "The Great Sioux Massacre" 1965 (Mr. Turner). ¶TV: *Wyatt Earp*—"The Vultures" 3-19-57 (Sam Rolfe), Regular 1960-61 (Mayor John Clum); *Sheriff of Cochise*—"The Dude" 10-4-57 (Ralph Parker); *The*

Adventures of Rin Tin Tin—"Rodeo Clown" 11-8-57, "Rusty's Remedy" 2-28-58 (Thomas Ferguson); *The Restless Gun*—"The New Sheriff" 11-18-57 (Roy Cotten); *Trackdown*—"Self-Defense" 11-22-57 (Duke Kinkaid); *Zane Grey Theater*—"License to Kill" 2-7-58 (Doc Currie), "Shadows" 11-5-59 (Sheriff Hanscom), "Stagecoach to Yuma" 5-5-60 (Santee); *Buckskin*—"The Man Who Waited" 7-10-58 (Whit Lassiter); *Tales of the Texas Rangers*—"Midway Kewpie" 10-16-58 (Leo Nash); *Frontier Doctor*—"Mystery of the Black Stallion" 11-8-58; *The Texan*—"The Hemp Tree" 11-17-58 (Max Bowen), "Rough Track to Payday" 12-28-59 (Abel Crowder); *Wanted—Dead or Alive*—"Six-Up to Bannack" 1-10-59 (John Gillette); *Rawhide*—"Incident at Chubasco" 4-3-59, "The Sendoff" 10-6-61 (Sheriff); *Man Without a Gun*—"Reward" 4-11-59 (Mungo); *Have Gun Will Travel*—"First, Catch a Tiger" 9-12-59, "Black Sheep" 4-30-60 (McNab); *Black Saddle*—"The Long Rider" 10-16-59; *Bonanza*—"House Divided" 1-16-60 (Regis), "The Honor of Cochise" 10-8-61 (Colonel Wilcox), "Twilight Town" 10-13-63 (McDermott), "The Far, Far Better Thing" 1-10-65, "Five Sundowns to Sunup" 12-5-65 (Judge Simpson), "Anatomy of a Lynching" 10-12-69 (Teague); *Laramie*—"Death Wind" 2-2-60 (Teague), "The Track of the Jackal" 9-27-60 (Firth), "Double Eagles" 11-20-62; *The Rebel*—"Fair Game" 3-27-60 (Kramer); *Stagecoach West*—"The Outcasts" 3-7-61 (Mack Knowles); *Wagon Train*—"The Joe Muharich Story" 4-19-61 (Sheriff), "The Lonnie Fallon Story" 2-7-62 (Sheriff Francher), "The Bob Stuart Story" 9-30-64 (Sheriff); *The Outlaws*—"The Sooner" 4-27-61 (Larson); *The Virginian*—"If You Have Tears" 2-13-63 (Gambler); *Temple Houston*—"The Dark Madonna" 12-26-63 (Cliff Carteret); *Daniel Boone*—"Perilous Journey" 12-16-65 (Captain Grant); *Laredo*—"A Medal for Reese" 12-30-65 (DuBois); *Pistols 'n' Petticoats*—11-5-66 (Touch Wilson); *Custer*—"Blazing Arrows" 11-29-67 (John Glixton); *Gunsmoke*—"Captain Sligo" 1-4-71 (Leonard).

Harris, Steve. TV: *The Virginian*—"The Judgment" 1-16-63; *Bonanza*—"Bullet for a Bride" 2-16-64 (Lon Caldwell).

Harris, Theresa. Films: "Buck Benny Rides Again" 1940 (Josephine); "Santa Fe Trail" 1940 (Maid); "Al Jennings of Oklahoma" 1951 (Terese).

Harris, Viola (1928-). TV: *Rawhide*—"Incident of His Brother's Keeper" 3-31-61 (Mrs. Besson).

Harris, Wadsworth (1864-11/1/42). Films: "The Daisy Cowboy" 1911; "The Midnight Stage" 1919 (Joe Statler); "The Iron Rider" 1920 (Sheriff Donovan); "The Plainsman" 1936 (William Dennison).

Harrison, Carey (1890-3/25/57). Films: "Call of the Canyon" 1942; "Code of the Lawless" 1945 (Reb).

Harrison, Dan. Films: "Bullets and the Flesh" 1965-Ital./Fr./Span.; "Seven Pistols for a Gringo" 1967-Ital./Span. (Dan); "Belle Starr Story" 1968-Ital.; "Piluk, the Timid One" 1968-Ital.

Harrison, Gregory (1950-). TV: *Centennial*—Regular 1978-79 (Levi Zendt).

Harrison, Irma. Films: "The Yellowback" 1929 (Elsie Loisel).

Harrison, James (1908-11/9/77). Films: "Madame Bo-Peep" 1917 (Willie Cooper).

Harrison, James H. (1908-11/9/77). Films: "The Lawless Nineties" 1936 (Telegraph Operator); "Panhandle" 1948 (Harland); "Silent Conflict" 1948 (Speed Blaney); "Silver River" 1948 (Soldier); "Fighting Man of the Plains" 1949 (Slattery); "Law of the West" 1949 (Sheriff); "Stampede" 1949 (Roper); "Western Renegades" 1949 (Billy); "Annie Get Your Gun" 1950 (Mac); "Callaway Went Thataway" 1951 (Heavy); "Vengeance Valley" 1951 (Orv Esterly). ¶TV: *The Lone Ranger*—"Man Without a Gun" 6-15-50; *The Gene Autry Show*—"The Sheriff of Santa Rosa" 12-24-50, "T.N.T." 12-31-50; *The Cisco Kid*—"The Runaway Kid" 6-21-52.

Harrison, Jan. Films: "Fort Bowie" 1958 (Allison Garrett). ¶TV: *Sheriff of Cochise*—"The Farmers" 9-21-56 (Kathy Ranker); *Gunsmoke*—"The Patsy" 9-20-58 (Holly Fanshaw), "Robber and Bridegroom" 12-13-58 (Laura Church), "The Lady Killer" 4-23-60 (Mae Talmey), "Brother Love" 12-31-60 (Polly); *Tales of Wells Fargo*—"The Gunfighter" 11-17-58 (Jane Hardin); *Lawman*—"The Souvenir" 4-5-59 (Nan Brooks); *Bat Masterson*—"Bat Plays a Dead Man's Hand" 12-3-59 (Belle Sims), "Run for Your Money" 3-2-61 (Lori Adams); *Death Valley Days*—"Deadline at Austin" 2-8-61; *Rawhide*—"Incident of the New Start" 3-3-61 (Charity Wade); *Bonanza*—"The Gamble" 4-1-62.

Harrison, June (1926-3/10/74). Films: "Land of the Lawless" 1947; "Jiggs and Maggie Out West" 1950 (Nora).

Harrison, Kay. Films: "Under Northern Lights" 1920 (Na Fa Kowa).

Harrison, Lottie. Films: "Driftin' River" 1946 (Senora); "Romance of the West" 1946 (Miss Twitchell).

Harrison, Mark (1864-6/1/52). Films: "Circle Canyon" 1934.

Harrison, O.V. Films: "The Old Fool" 1923 (Larry Bellows).

Harrison, Richard. Films: "Gringo" 1963-Span./Ital. (Gringo Martinez); "Gunfight at High Noon" 1963-Span./Ital. (Jeff); "One Hundred Thousand Dollars for Ringo" 1966-Ital./Span. (Ringo); "Rojo" 1966-Ital./Span. (El Rojo); "Between God, the Devil and a Winchester" 1968-Ital./Span. (Pat Jordan); "One After Another" 1968-Span./Ital. (Sam); "Vengeance" 1968-Ital./Ger. (Joko); "Dig Your Grave, Friend ... Sabata's Coming" 1970-Ital./Span./Fr. (Steve McGowan); "Reverend Colt" 1970-Ital./Span. (Sheriff Donovan); "His Name Was King" 1971-Ital. (John "King" Marley); "Holy Water Joe" 1971-Ital. (Charlie); "Sheriff of Rock Spring" 1971-Ital.; "With Friends, Nothing Is Easy" 1971-Span./Ital. (Scott); "Deadly Trackers" 1972-Ital. (James Luke); "Jesse and Lester, Two Brothers in a Place Called Trinity" 1972-Ital. (Jesse); "Shoot Joe, and Shoot Again" 1972-Ital. (Joe Dakota).

Harron, Donald (1924-). TV: *The Texan*—"The Easterner" 12-15-58 (Julian Dowd).

Harron, John (1903-11/24/39). Films: "The Fox" 1921 (Dick Farwell); "Night Cry" 1926 (John Martin); "Prairie Thunder" 1937 (Lt. Adams); "Gold Is Where You Find It" 1938 (Man at Stock Exchange); "Heart of the North" 1938 (First Mate); "The Oklahoma Kid" 1939 (Secretary).

Harron, Robert "Bobby" (1893-9/6/20). Films: "Billy's Stratagem" 1911; "Fighting Blood" 1911; "The Last Drop of Water" 1911; "Fate's Interception" 1912; "Heredity" 1912; "Man's Lust for Gold" 1912; "The Massacre" 1912; "My Hero" 1912; "A Pueblo Legend" 1912; "A Temporary Truce" 1912; "The Battle at Elderbrush Gulch" 1913; "The Broken Ways" 1913; "A Misunderstood Boy" 1913; "The Sheriff's Baby" 1913; "The Yaqui Cur" 1913; "Deputy Sheriff's

Star" 1914; "Big Jim's Heart" 1915; "The Outlaw's Revenge" 1916 (the Lover).

Harrow, Kathryn. TV: *Gunsmoke*—"The Brothers" 3-12-66 (Ellen Crandall).

Harrower, Elizabeth (1918-). Films: "Thunder Pass" 1954; "The Wild Westerners" 1962 (Martha Bernard); "True Grit" 1969 (Mrs. Ross). ¶TV: *Wild Bill Hickok*—"Papa Antinelli" 11-27-51, "The Fortune Telling Story" 4-22-52, "Masquerade at Moccasin Flats" 9-2-52, "Bold Raven Rodeo" 4-7-53; *The Gene Autry Show*—"The Golden Chariot" 10-29-55; *Wyatt Earp*—"The Desperate Half-Hour" 2-28-56 (Mrs. McVey), "The Sharpshooter" 1-29-57 (Mrs. Hamble), "She Almost Married Wyatt" 2-24-59; *Tales of Wells Fargo*—"White Indian" 9-22-58 (Grace Lawson); *The Virginian*—"Legacy of Hate" 9-14-66 (Mrs. Grant); *Gunsmoke*—"Bohannan" 9-25-72 (Mrs. Simmons), "The Iron Blood of Courage" 2-18-74 (Mrs. O'Roarke), "To Ride a Yellow Horse" 3-18-74 (Mrs. O'Roarke).

Hart, Albert (1874-1/10/40). Films: "The Challenge of Chance" 1919 (Captain Burr); "Cotton and Cattle" 1921 (Bill Carson); "A Cowboy Ace" 1921 (Pete Filson); "Flowing Gold" 1921; "Out of the Clouds" 1921; "The Range Pirate" 1921; "Rustlers of the Night" 1921; "The Trail to Red Dog" 1921; "The White Masks" 1921 (Jim Dougherty); "Angel Citizens" 1922 (London Edwards); "Cross Roads" 1922 (the Yaqui); "Doubling for Romeo" 1922 (Big Alec); "The Girl Who Ran Wild" 1922; "The Gold Grabbers" 1922; "So This Is Arizona" 1922 (Buck Saunders); "Trail's End" 1922 (Stanley); "Kindled Courage" 1923 (Overland Pete); "Shadows of the North" 1923 (Hemingway); "Spawn of the Desert" 1923 (Sam Le Saint); "The Sunshine Trail" 1923 (Col. Duckworth); "The Pony Express" 1925 (Senator Glen); "Blind Trail" 1926 (William Skinner); "Forlorn River" 1926 (Sheriff Stroble); "The Outlaw Express" 1926 (Carl Larson); "The Devil's Twin" 1927 (Juriah Hodge); "The Long Loop on the Pecos" 1927 (Vining); "The Man from Hardpan" 1927 (Sheriff); "The Mysterious Rider" 1927 (Sheriff); "The Ridin' Rowdy" 1927 (Mose Gibson); "The Ballyhoo Buster" 1928 (Medicine Show Proprietor); "The Boss of Rustler's Roost" 1928 (Henry Everman); "45 Calibre War" 1929 (Rev. Mr. Simpson);

"Home on the Range" 1935 (Undertaker).

Hart, Bill. Films: "Duel at Diablo" 1966 (Cpl. Harrington); "The Apple Dumpling Gang Rides Again" 1979; "The Sacketts" TVM-1979; "The Gambler, Part II—The Adventure Continues" TVM-1983 (Daniels). ¶TV: *Stoney Burke*—Regular 1962-63 (Red); *Laredo*—"A Question of Discipline" 10-28-65; *Gunsmoke*—"Sanctuary" 2-26-66 (Wiley's Friend), "Hawk" 10-20-69 (Renegade #2), "Yankton" 2-7-72 (Cowboy #1), "A Child Between" 12-24-73 (2nd Hyde Cutter); *The Loner*—"The Burden of the Badge" 3-5-66 (Vic); *Best of the West*—10-8-81 (Dirty Jack).

Hart, Christina. Films: "The Daughters of Joshua Cabe Return" TVM-1975 (Charity). ¶TV: *The Texas Wheelers*—7-3-75.

Hart, Dolores (1938-). Films: "The Plunderers" 1960 (Ellie Walters). ¶TV: *The Virginian*—"The Mountain of the Sun" 4-17-63 (Cathy Maywood).

Hart, Dorothy (1923-). Films: "The Gunfighters" 1947 (Jane Banner); "Calamity Jane and Sam Bass" 1949 (Katherine Egan); "Raton Pass" 1951 (Lena Casamajor).

Hart, Eddie. Films: "Call the Mesquiteers" 1938 (Lefty); "Rhythm of the Saddle" 1938 (Alec); "Jackass Mail" 1942 (Miner).

Hart, Gordon (1884-12/27/73). Films: "Blazing Sixes" 1937 (Flank); "Cherokee Strip" 1937 (Judge Ben Parkinson); "The Devil's Saddle Legion" 1937 (John Ordley); "Empty Holsters" 1937; "Guns of the Pecos" 1937 (Maj. Burton); "Land Beyond the Law" 1937 (Maj. Adair); "Cassidy of Bar 20" 1938 (Judge (Belcher); "Man from Music Mountain" 1938; "Overland Stage Raiders" 1938 (Mullins); "Home on the Prairie" 1939 (H.R. Shelby); "Rovin' Tumbleweeds" 1939 (Fuller); "Riders of Pasco Basin" 1940 (Rancher); "Secrets of the Wastelands" 1941 (Prof. Birdsall).

Hart, John (1902-). Films: "Northwest Mounted Police" 1940 (Constable Norman); "The Vigilantes Return" 1947 (Henchman); "Cowboy and the Prizefighter" 1950 (Palmer); "The Fighting Redhead" 1950 (Faro); "Colorado Ambush" 1951; "The Longhorn" 1951 (Moresby); "Stage to Blue River" 1951 (Kingsley); "Stagecoach Driver" 1951; "Texas Lawmen" 1951; "Warpath" 1951 (Sgt. Plennert); "Kansas Territory" 1952 (Marshal); "Texas City" 1952

(1st Sergeant); "Noose for a Gunman" 1960 (Barker); "Santee" 1973; "The Legend of the Lone Ranger" 1981 (Lucas Striker). ¶TV: *The Lone Ranger*—"Rifles and Renegades" 5-4-50, "Sheriff of Gunstock" 7-27-50, Regular 1951 (the Lone Ranger); *Tales of the Texas Rangers*—"Double Edge" 10-8-55 (Sam Crane), "The Shooting of Sam Bass" 10-15-55 (Steve MacDonald); *Fury*—"The Miracle" 2-25-56 (Val Benton); *Hawkeye and the Last of the Mohicans*—Regular 1957 (Hawkeye); *The Adventures of Rin Tin Tin*—"Grandpappy's Love Affair" 11-14-58 (Sharps); *Bat Masterson*—"The Conspiracy" 6-17-59 & 6-24-59 (Wilson), "A Picture of Death" 1-14-60 (Jacobs); *Rawhide*—"Incident of the Thirteenth Man" 10-23-59, "Incident of the Sharpshooter" 2-26-60, "Incident of the Champagne Bottles" 3-18-60 (Murdoch), "Incident of the Challenge" 10-14-60, "Incident of the Broken Word" 1-20-61, "Incident of the New Start" 3-3-61, "The Sendoff" 10-6-61, "The Lost Tribe" 10-27-61 (Sheriff), "Twenty-Five Santa Clauses" 12-22-61 (Narbo), "The Captain's Wife" 1-12-62 (Narbo), "Deserter's Patrol" 2-9-62 (Narbo), "The Pitchwagon" 3-2-62, "The Child Woman" 3-23-62, "The Reunion" 4-6-62, "The House of the Hunter" 4-20-62, "The Devil and the Deep Blue" 5-11-62, "Abilene" 5-18-62 (Narbo); *Shotgun Slade*—"Marked Money" 12-15-59.

Hart, Louis (1917-4/25/72). Films: "Gun Smoke" 1945; "Strange from Santa Fe" 1945.

Hart, Maria. Films: "Border Outlaws" 1950 (Jill); "The Fighting Stallion" 1950 (Dude); "Cattle Queen" 1951 (Queenie Hart); "The Lusty Men" 1952 (Rosemary Maddox); "Outlaw Women" 1952 (Big Dora).

Hart, Mary. see Roberts, Lynne.

Hart, Neal (1879-4/2/49). Films: "The Committee on Credentials" 1916; "Liberty" 1916-serial; "Love's Lariat" 1916 (Skeeter); "The Night Riders" 1916; "The Passing of Hell's Crown" 1916; "Bill Brennan's Claim" 1917; "Double Suspicion" 1917; "The Getaway" 1917; "The Honor of Men" 1917; "The Man from Montana" 1917 (Duke Farley); "The Raid" 1917; "Right-of-Way Casey" 1917; "Squaring It" 1917; "Swede Hearts" 1917; "Beating the Limited" 1918; "The Husband Hunter" 1918; "Naked Fists" 1918; "Quick Triggers" 1918; "Roped and Tied" 1918; "Smashing Through" 1918 (Dave

Marco); "The Trail of No Return" 1918; "The Gun Runners" 1919; "Out of the West" 1919; "When the Desert Smiles" 1919; "Hell's Oasis" 1920 (Bob Spaulding); "Skyfire" 1920 (Barr Conroy); "The Testing Block" 1920 (Sierra Bill); "The Black Sheep" 1921 (Rex Carson); "Tangled Trails" 1921 (Cpl. Jack Borden); "Butterfly Range" 1922 (Steve Saunders); "The Heart of a Texan" 1922 (King Calhoun); "The Kingfisher's Roost" 1922 (Barr Messenger); "Lure of Gold" 1922 (Jack Austin); "Rangeland" 1922 (Ned Williams); "South of the Northern Lights" 1922 (Jack Hampton); "Table Top Ranch" 1922 (John Marvin); "West of the Pecos" 1922 (Jack Laramie); "Below the Rio Grande" 1923 (King Calhoun); "The Devil's Bowl" 1923 (Sam Ramsey); "The Fighting Strain" 1923 (Jack Barlow); "The Forbidden Range" 1923 (Jack Wilson); "Salty Saunders" 1923 (Salty Saunders); "The Secret of the Pueblo" 1923 (Bob Benson); "Lawless Men" 1924; "The Left-Hand Brand" 1924; "Tucker's Top Hand" 1924; "The Valley of Vanishing Men" 1924 (Dick Benton); "The Verdict of the Desert" 1925 (Jack Dawson); "The Scarlet Brand" 1927-serial; "Trigger Tricks" 1930 (Sheriff); "Wild Horse" 1931 (Hank Howard); "Guns for Hire" 1932; "Law and Order" 1932; "Law and Order" 1932; "The Reckless Rider" 1932; "The Dude Bandit" 1933 (Jack Hargan); "The Texas Rangers" 1936 (Ranger); "Danger Valley" 1937 (Doug McBride); "Empty Holsters" 1937 (Pete); "Renegade Ranger" 1938 (Sheriff Joe Rawlings); "The Arizona Wildcat" 1939; "Bordertown Gunfighters" 1943; "Bordertown Trail" 1944; "Corpus Christi Bandits" 1945; "California Gold Rush" 1946; "Saddle Pals" 1947; "Stampede" 1949.

Hart, Susan (1941-). TV: *Laramie*—"The Runt" 2-20-62; *Death Valley Days*—"Major Horace Bell" 5-20-67 (Rose); *Wild Wild West*—"The Night of the Fugitives" 11-8-68 (Rhoda).

Hart, William S. (1862-6/23/46). Films: "The Bargain" 1914 (Jim Stokes); "The Gringo" 1914; "His Hour of Manhood" 1914; "Jim Cameron's Wife" 1914; "The Passing of Two-Gun Hicks" 1914; "The Bad Buck of Santa Ynez" 1915; "Cash Parrish's Pal" 1915; "The Conversion of Frosty Blake" 1915; "The Darkening Trail" 1915 (Yukon Ed); "The Disciple" 1915 (Shootin' Iron Parson Jim Houston); "The Grudge" 1915; "In the Sage Brush Country" 1915; "Keno Bates—Liar" 1915; "A Knight of the Trails" 1915; "The Man from Nowhere" 1915; "Mr. Silent Haskins" 1915; "On the Night Stage" 1915 (Silent Texas Smith); "Pinto Ben" 1915; "The Roughneck" 1915; "The Ruse" 1915; "The Scourge of the Desert" 1915; "The Sheriff's Streak of Yellow" 1915; "The Taking of Luke McVane" 1915; "Tools of Providence" 1915; "The Aryan" 1916 (Steve Denton); "The Apostle of Vengeance" 1916 (David Hudson); "The Dawn Maker" 1916 (Joe Elk); "The Devil's Double" 1916 (Bowie Blake); "The Gunfighter" 1916 (Cliff "the Killer" Hudspeth); "The Patriot" 1916 (Bob Wiley); "The Primal Lure" 1916 (Angus McConnell); "The Return of Draw Egan" 1916 (Draw Egan); "The Cold Deck" 1917 (Level Leigh); "The Desert Man" 1917 (Jim Alton); "The Silent Man" 1917 (Silent Budd Marr); "The Square Deal Man" 1917 (Jack O'Diamonds); "Truthful Tulliver" 1917 (Truthful Tulliver); "Wolf Lowry" 1917 (Wolf Lowry); "Blue Blazes Rawden" 1918 (Rawden); "The Border Wireless" 1918 (Steve Ransom); "Branding Broadway" 1918 (Robert Sands); "The Narrow Trail" 1918 (Ice Harding); "Riddle Gawne" 1918 (Jefferson "Riddle" Gawne); "Selfish Yates" 1918 (Selfish Yates); "Staking His Life" 1918 (Bud Randall); "The Tiger Man" 1918 (Hawk Parsons); "Wolves of the Rail" 1918 (Buck Andrade); "Breed of Men" 1919 (Careless Carmody); "Hell's Hinges" 1919 (Blaze Tracey); "The Money Corral" 1919 (Lem Beason); "Square Deal Sanderson" 1919 (Square Deal Sanderson); "Wagon Tracks" 1919 (Buckskin Hamilton); "Sand!" 1920 (Dan Kurrie); "The Toll Gate" 1920 (Black Deering); "O'-Malley of the Mounted" 1921 (O'-Malley); "Three Word Brand" 1921 (Three Word Brand/Ben Trego); "White Oak" 1921 (Oak Miller); "Travelin' On" 1922 (J.B., the Stranger); "Wild Bill Hickok" 1923 (Wild Bill Hickok); "Singer Jim McKee" 1924 (Singer Jim McKee); "Tumbleweeds" 1925 (Don Carver).

Hart, Winifred. *see* Westover, Winifred.

Harte, Bette (1883-1/3/65). Films: "In the Bad Lands" 1909; "On the Border" 1909; "On the Little Big Horn or Cuser's Last Stand" 1909; "The Pine Ridge Feud" 1909; "The Stampede" 1909; "The Tenderfoot" 1909; "Across the Plains" 1910; "Pride of the Range" 1910; "A Frontier Girl's Courage" 1911; "George Warrington's Escape" 1911; "Heart of John Barlow" 1911; "How Algy Captured a Wild Man" 1911; "In the Days of Gold" 1911 (Juanita Lopez); "It Happened in the West" 1911; "Kit Carson's Wooing" 1911; "Range Pals" 1911; "The Regeneration of the Apache Kid" 1911; "Romance of the Rio Grande" 1911; "The Schoolmaster of Mariposa" 1911; "Told in the Sierras" 1911; "The White Medicine Man" 1911; "The Ace of Spades" 1912; "A Child of the Wilderness" 1912; "The Epidemic in Paradise Gulch" 1912; "A Reconstructed Rebel" 1912; "The Shrinking Rawhide" 1912; "The Vow of Ysobel" 1912; "The Escape of Jim Dolan" 1913; "The Noisy Six" 1913; "Me an' Bill" 1914; "Davy Crockett" 1916; "The Man from Bitter Roots" 1916.

Hartford, David (1873-10/30/32). Films: "Under the Black Flag" 1913; "Shootin' Mad" 1918 (John Cowan); "Rough Romance" 1930 (Dad Reynolds).

Hartford, Dee (1927-). TV: *Gunsmoke*—"Ash" 2-16-63 (Tillie).

Hartigan, Pat C. (1881-5/8/51). Films: "The Indian Maid's Warning" 1913; "Out of the Snows" 1920 (John Blakeman); "The King of the Wild Horses" 1924 (Wade Galvin); "Western Luck" 1924 (James Evart); "Clash of the Wolves" 1925 (Borax Horton); "Code of the West" 1925 (Cal Bloom); "The Thundering Herd" 1925 (Catlett); "Ranson's Folly" 1926 (Sgt. Clancy); "In Old Arizona" 1929 (Cowpuncher); "Union Pacific" 1939 (Irishman).

Hartleben, Jerry. Films: "3:10 to Yuma" 1957 (Mark); "King of the Wild Stallions" 1959 (Bucky). TV: *Tales of the Texas Rangers*—"Tornado" 11-5-55 (Boy).

Hartley, Charles (1852-10/13/30). Films: "The Crimson Dove" 1917 (Cameron's Servant).

Hartley, Mariette (1941-). Films: "Ride the High Country" 1962 (Elsa Knudsen); "Barquero" 1970 (Anna); "The Magnificent Seven Ride" 1972 (Arilla). TV: *Stoney Burke*—"Bandwagon" 12-17-62 (Laura); *Gunsmoke*—"Cotter's Girl" 1-19-63 (Clarey Cotter), "Big Man, Big Target" 11-28-64 (Ellie Merchant), "Phoenix" 9-20-71 (Kate Hume), "Spratt" 10-2-72 (Fiona Gideon), "The Iron Blood of Courage" 2-18-74 (Ellie Talley); *The Travels of Jaimie McPheeters*—"The Day of the Misfits" 12-15-63 (Hagar); *The Virginian*—"The Drifter" 1-29-64 (Maria Peterson), "Felicity's Springs" 10-14-64 (Kate Andrews); *Bonanza*—"Right Is the Fourth R" 3-7-65, "The Survivors" 11-10-68 (Alicia Pursell), "Is There Any Man Here?" 2-8-70

(Jennifer Carlis), "The Iron Butterfly" 11-28-71 (Lola); *Death Valley Days*—"The Red Shawl" 2-5-66 (Jessica Scott), "The Informer Who Cried" 11-11-67 (Sister Blandina), "Bread on the Desert" 3-2-68 (Cynthia), "Lady with a Past" 12-28-68 (Tiger Lil); *The Legend of Jesse James*—"A Burying for Rosey" 5-9-66 (Polly Dockery); *Cimarron Strip*—"Big Jessie" 2-8-68 (Jessie Cabot); *Daniel Boone*—"The Valley of the Sun" 11-28-68 (Millie Boyd), "An Angel Cried" 1-8-70 (Sister Cecilia); *The Quest*—"Shanklin" 10-13-76 (Vay); *The Oregon Trail*—"The Race" 1977.

Hartley, Ted (1930-). Films: "High Plains Drifter" 1973 (Lewis Belding); "The Wild Wild West Revisited" TVM-1979 (Russian Tsar).

Hartman, David (1935-). Films: "Ballad of Josie" 1968 (Fonse Pruitt). ¶TV: *The Virginian*—"The Masquerade" 10-18-67 (George Foster), Regular 1968-69 (David Sutton).

Hartman, Gretchen (1897-1/27/79). Films: "Do and Dare" 1922 (Zita); "While Justice Waits" 1922 (Mollie Adams).

Hartman, Paul (1904-10/2/73). TV: *The Outlaws*—"Ballad for a Badman" 10-6-60 (Winny); *Have Gun Will Travel*—"The Brothers" 11-25-61 (Possum Corbin); *The Tall Man*—"G.P." 5-19-62 (Marlowe); *The Legend of Jesse James*—"A Real Tough Town" 1-24-66 (Bellows).

Hartman, Ruth (1893-7/9/56). Films: "The American Insurrecto" 1911.

Harty, Patricia. TV: *Custer*—"Death Hunt" 11-22-67 (Mrs. Peverley); *The Men from Shiloh*—"The Price of the Hanging" 11-11-70 (Tracy); *Bonanza*—"Rock-a-Bye, Hoss" 10-10-71 (Cissy Porter)

Harvey, Clem. Films: "Johnny Guitar" 1954 (Posse); "One-Eyed Jacks" 1961 (Tim); "A Thunder of Drums" 1961 (Trooper Denton).

Harvey, Don C. (1911-4/24/63). Films: "Rimfire" 1949 (Rainbow Raymond); "Son of a Badman" 1949 (Sheriff Ragel); "Dynamite Pass" 1950 (Mizzouri); "The Fighting Stallion" 1950 (Cmdr. Patrick); "The Girl from San Lorenzo" 1950 (Kansas); "Gunmen of Abilene" 1950 (Todd); "Hoedown" 1950 (Sapper); "Trail of the Rustlers" 1950; "Don Daredevil Rides Again" 1951-serial (Townsman #3); "Merry Mavericks" 1951-short (Red Morgan); "Night Riders of Montana" 1951 (Janney); "Northwest Territory" 1951 (Barton);

"Prairie Roundup" 1951 (Hawk Edwards); "Texans Never Cry" 1951 (Blackie Knight); "The Old West" 1952 (Hod Evers); "Gunfighters of the Northwest" 1954-serial (Otis Green); "Apache Ambush" 1955 (Major McGuire); "The Far Country" 1955 (Tom Kane); "The Violent Men" 1955 (Jackson); "Wyoming Renegades" 1955 (Ben Kilpatrick); "Blackjack Ketchum, Desperado" 1956 (Mac Gill); "Blazing the Overland Trail" 1956-serial (Rance Devlin); "Dig That Uranium" 1956 (Tex); "Jubal" 1956 (Jim Tolliver); "Perils of the Wilderness" 1956-serial (Kruger); "Buchanan Rides Alone" 1958 (Lafe); "Gunmen from Laredo" 1959 (Dave Marlow); "The Wild Westerners" 1962 (Hanna). ¶TV: *The Gene Autry Show*—"The Poisoned Waterhole" 10-8-50, "The Black Rider" 10-22-50, "Hot Lead" 11-26-50 (Nat Ellis), "Killer Horse" 12-10-50, "Frame for Trouble" 11-3-51, "Revenge Trail" 11-17-51, "The Western Way" 2-1-52, "Hot Lead and Old Lace" 2-15-52, "Outlaw Stage" 7-21-53, "Border Justice" 8-18-53; *The Cisco Kid*—"Chain Lightning" 3-3-51; *Wild Bill Hickok*—"Mexican Rustlers Story" 10-23-51, "School Teacher Story" 1-15-52, "Ol' Pardner Rides Again" 9-16-52, "Buckshot Comes Home" 11-25-52, "Blind Alley" 2-24-53, "The Steam Wagon" 5-12-53; *The Roy Rogers Show*—"The Treasure of Howling Dog Canyon" 1-27-52 (John Briggs), "Ghost Town Gold" 5-25-52, "The Double Crosser" 6-1-52, "Carnival Killer" 6-8-52, "Born Fugitive" 11-29-53, "The Last of the Larrabee Kid" 10-17-54 (Cub Wiley), "Hard Luck Story" 10-31-54 (Link Hadley), "Boys' Day in Paradise Valley" 11-7-54 (William Miner), "Dead End Trail" 2-20-55 (Curt Carson), "Quick Draw" 3-20-55 (Marv Hanley), "The Ginger Horse" 3-27-55; *Annie Oakley*—"Annie Finds Strange Treasure" 3-6-54; *The Lone Ranger*—"The Frightened Woman" 9-30-54, "A Broken Match" 12-2-54, "Sunstroke Mesa" 3-17-55, "A Message from Abe" 2-7-57, "Clover in the Dust" 3-7-57; *Wyatt Earp*—"Mr. Earp Becomes a Marshal" 9-6-55, "The Englishman" 2-21-56, "The Mysterious Cowhand" 10-14-58 (Jumbo), "Shoot to Kill" 10-18-60; *My Friend Flicka*—"One Man's Horse" 9-30-55, "Lost River" 6-15-56; *Tales of the Texas Rangers*—"Return of the Rough Riders" 11-26-55 (Paxin); *Fury*—"Search for Joey" 2-18-56; *Death Valley Days*—"The Bear Flag" 10-21-56 (Ezekial Merritt), "California's Paul Revere" 3-17-57;

The Adventures of Rin Tin Tin—"Fort Adventure" 11-30-56 (Capt. Carlson); *Frontier Doctor*—"The Crooked Circle" 10-18-58; *Tales of Wells Fargo*—"End of the Trail" 10-20-58 (Fred Heston), "The Barefoot Banit" 1-30-61 (Al Wiley); *The Restless Gun*—"Tomboy" 11-10-58 (Jim Belknap), "Mme. Brimstone" 5-4-59; *Maverick*—"Holiday at Hollow Rock" 12-28-58 (Clyde), "Last Wire from Stop Gap" 10-16-60 (Sheriff), "The Maverick Report" 3-4-62 (Sheriff Bentley); *Rawhide*—"Incident of the Town in Terror" 3-6-59 (Joe Greevey); *Colt .45*—"The Confession" 4-26-59 (Sheriff Clinter); *Black Saddle*—"Blood Money" 12-18-59 (George Baker); *The Texan*—"End of Track" 12-21-59, "The Guilty and the Innocent" 3-28-60; *Tombstone Territory*—2-12-60 (Frank Fallon); *Sugarfoot*—"Vinegaroom" 3-29-60 (Doc); *Bonanza*—"The Spitfire" 1-14-61 (Jeb Hoad); *Two Faces West*—"The Trigger" 2-13-61; *Wagon Train*—"The Nellie Jefferson Story" 4-5-61 (the Marshal); *Gunslinger*—"Johnny Sergeant" 5-4-61 (Ben Rawlings); *The Tall Man*—"The Woman" 10-28-61 (Jeboriah Henry); *Laramie*—"Deadly Is the Night" 11-7-61 (Sheriff), "The High Country" 2-6-62 (Mather), "Lost Allegiance" 10-30-62 (Sheriff McKay), "Time of the Traitor" 12-11-62 (Colie), "The Last Battleground" 4-16-63; *The Virginian*—"The Exiles" 1-9-63, "Run Away Home" 4-24-63; *Empire*—"A House in Order" 3-5-63 (Caine).

Harvey, Forrester (1880-12/14/45). Films: "Mystery Ranch" 1932 (Artie Drower).

Harvey, Fred. Films: "Firebrand Jordan" 1930 (Judd Howe).

Harvey, Jr., Harry (-12/8/78). Films: "The Rangers Step In" 1937; "King of the Sierras" 1938 (Pete); "Two-Gun Troubador" 1939 (Billy Barton as a Boy); "The Lone Rider Rides On" 1941; "Silver City Bonanza" 1951 (Groggins); "Shotgun" 1955 (Davey). ¶TV: *The Roy Rogers Show*—"Flying Bullets" 6-15-52 (Hank Fisher), "Money to Burn" 6-28-53, "Gun Trouble" 11-22-53 (Jerry King), "Ranch War" 10-23-55 (John Wagner), "The Morse Mixup" 3-24-56 (Terry Hawkins), "Accessory to Crime" 3-3-57 (Johnny Williams); *Broken Arrow*—"Return from the Shadows" 12-4-56 (Judge), "The Arsenal" 11-5-57 (Len); *Tales of Wells Fargo*—"The Hijackers" 6-17-57 (Billy Thompson), "The Daltons" 5-25-59 (Emmett Dalton), "Stage from Yuma" 3-20-61 (Lew Walter); *The*

Adventures of Rin Tin Tin—"The Hunted" 12-6-57; *Wagon Train*—"The Cliff Grundy Story" 12-25-57; *Trackdown*—"Right of Way" 1-17-58 (Billy); *Tales of the Texas Rangers*—"Traitor's Gold" 10-2-58 (Jeff Thorpe); *Wyatt Earp*—"Doc Fabrique's Greatest Case" 4-7-59; *Tombstone Territory*—"Trail's End" 4-10-59 (Mark Thompson); *Wichita Town*—"Seed of Hate" 1-27-60 (Gil Larson); *The Tall Man*—"Counterfeit Law" 11-19-60 (Surveyor); *Laramie*—"Run of the Hunted" 4-4-61 (Tolan); *Daniel Boone*—"Run a Crooked Mile" 10-20-66 (Luther Michaels); *The Guns of Will Sonnett*—"One Angry Juror" 3-7-69.

Harvey, Sr., Harry (1901-11/27/85). Films: "The Oregon Trail" 1936 (Tim); "Ghost Town Gold" 1937; "King of the Sierras" 1938 (Tom); "Man from Music Mountain" 1938; "Man's Country" 1938 (Sergeant James); "The Painted Trail" 1938 (Reed); "Six Shootin' Sheriff" 1938 (Todd); "Code of the Fearless" 1939 (Old Timer); "In Old Montana" 1939 (Doc Flanders); "Lone Star Pioneers" 1939 (Eph Brown); "Rollin' Westward" 1939 (Watkins); "Two-Gun Troubador" 1939 (Elmer Potts); "Deadwood Dick" 1940-serial (Dave); "The Fargo Kid" 1940; "Pals of the Silver Sage" 1940; "Phantom Rancher" 1940 (Gopher); "Ridin' the Trail" 1940 (Fuzzy Jones); "Texas Renegades" 1940 (Noisy); "Wagon Train" 1940 (Thompson); "Bad Man of Deadwood" 1941; "Redskins and Redheads" 1941-short; "Robbers of the Range" 1941 (Brady); "Rollin' Home to Texas" 1941 (Lockwood); "Six Gun Gold" 1941 (Vander); "Bullets for Bandits" 1942; "Keep Shooting" 1942-short; "The Rangers Take Over" 1942 (Bill Summers); "The Return of the Rangers" 1943; "Black Arrow" 1944-serial; "Gangsters of the Frontier" 1944; "Spook Town" 1944; "Sunset Pass" 1946 (Doab); "Code of the West" 1947 (Stockton); "Thunder Mountain" 1947 (Sheriff Bagley); "Under the Tonto Rim" 1947 (Sheriff); "The Arizona Ranger" 1948 (Peyton); "The Paleface" 1948 (Justice of the Peace); "Calamity Jane and Sam Bass" 1949 (Station Agent); "Death Valley Gunfighter" 1949 (Vinson McKnight); "Stagecoach Kid" 1949 (Dabney); "Beyond the Purple Hills" 1950 (Sheriff Whiteside); "Cow Town" 1950 (Sheriff Steve Calhoun); "Hoedown" 1950 (Sheriff); "Rio Grande Patrol" 1950 (Station Master); "Arizona Manhunt" 1951 (Dr. Sawyer); "Hills of Utah" 1951 (Marshal Duffield); "Rodeo King and the Senorita" 1951 (Jed Bailey); "Whirlwind" 1951 (Sheriff Barlow); "Barbed Wire" 1952; "High Noon" 1952 (Coy); "The Outcasts of Poker Flat" 1952 (George Larabee); "Target" 1952 (Carson); "Wagon Team" 1952 (Doc Weldon); "Bandits of the West" 1953 (Judge Wolters); "Law and Order" 1953 (Land Agent); "The Marshal's Daughter" 1953 (Bartender); "Old Overland Trail" 1953 (Proprietor); "Tumbleweed" 1953 (Prospector); "Man with the Steel Whip" 1954-serial (Jim Kirkwood); "The Outlaw Stallion" 1954 (Mace); "Wyoming Renegades" 1955 (Medford); "Showdown at Abilene" 1956 (Ross Bigelow); "Man in the Shadow" 1957 (Dr. Creighton); "Shoot-Out at Medicine Bend" 1957 (King); "The Sheepman" 1958; "Cat Ballou" 1965 (Train Conductor); "Ride Beyond Vengeance" 1966 (Vogan). ¶TV: *The Lone Ranger*—"The Renegades" 11-3-49, "Pardon for Curley" 6-22-50, "Bad Medicine" 12-7-50, "Mr. Trouble" 3-8-51, "The Devil's Bog" 2-5-53, "Embezzler's Harvest" 4-30-53, "Message to Fort Apache" 9-23-54, "The Quiet Highwayman" 1-27-55, "False Accusations" 4-21-55; *The Gene Autry Show*—"Six Shooter Sweepstakes" 10-1-50, "Lost Chance" 10-15-55, "Galloping Hoofs" 12-22-51, "Melody Mesa" 1-4-52, "Rio Renegades" 9-29-53, "Outlaw Warning" 10-2-54, "Ghost Ranch" 11-12-55, "Dynamite" 12-24-55; *The Roy Rogers Show*—Regular 1951-57 (Sheriff Potter); *Wild Bill Hickok*—"A Close Shave for the Marshal" 4-29-52; *The Cisco Kid*—"The Runaway Kid" 6-21-52; *Wyatt Earp*—"The War of the Colonels" 4-10-56 (Mr. Bradus), "Wyatt and the Captain" 1-15-57 (Mr. Whittle); *Tales of Wells Fargo*—"Two Cartridges" 9-16-57 (McHale); *Maverick*—"The Long Hunt" 10-20-57 (Stagecoach Driver), "Rope of Cards" 1-19-58 (Store Owner), "Black Fire" 3-16-58 (Cousin Seeby), "Hadley's Hunters" 9-25-60 (Dad Brewster), "The Golden Fleecing" 10-8-61 (Captain Owens), "Epitaph of a Gambler" 2-11-62 (Wes Taylor); *Sugarfoot*—"A Wreath for Charity Lloyd" 3-18-58 (Sheriff); *The Texan*—"The Troubled Town" 10-13-58 (Bartender), "The Marshal of Yellow Jacket" 3-2-59 (Clyde Harbridge), "A Race for Life" 3-16-59, "Presentation Gun" 4-4-60; *Rawhide*—"Incident of the Widowed Dove" 1-30-59; *Colt .45*—"Alias Mr. Howard" 12-6-59 (Thompson); *The Rifleman*—"The Legacy" 12-8-59; *Wagon Train*—"The Christine Elliot Story" 3-23-60, "The Charlene Brenton Story" 6-8-60 (Sheriff), "The David Garner Story" 5-8-63 (Vern Orton), "The Zebedee Titus Story" 4-20-64 (Parsons); *Laramie*—"The Fatal Step" 10-24-61; *Lawman*—"The Actor" 5-27-62 (Dr. Wilson); *Branded*—"Survival" 1-24-65, "Judge Not" 9-12-65 (Stationmaster), "Yellow for Courage" 2-20-66 (Doc Shackley); *The Virginian*—"A Slight Case of Charity" 2-10-65 (Ira Corwin), "Ride a Cock-Horse to Laramie Cross" 2-23-66 (Horation), "The Barren Ground" 12-6-67 (Judge), "Silver Image" 9-25-68; *Laredo*—"Any Way the Wind Blows" 10-28-66 (Strother); *Cimarron Strip*—"Broken Wing" 9-21-67, "The Assassin" 1-11-68; *The Guns of Will Sonnett*—"First Love" 11-3-67 (Sheriff), "Pariah" 10-18-68; *Gunsmoke*—"The Pillagers" 11-6-67 (Eli), "Nowhere to Run" 1-15-68 (Storekeeper), "9:12 to Dodge" 11-11-68 (Dispatcher), "Sam McTavish, M.D." 10-5-70 (Johnson), "The Bullet" 11-29-71, 12-6-71 & 12-13-71 (Drummer); *Bonanza*—"A Girl Named George" 1-14-68 (Coroner), "The Imposters" 12-13-70 (Bixle), "Heritage of Anger" 9-19-72 (Sangster); *Lancer*—"The Wedding" 1-7-69, "The Man Without the Gun" 3-25-69 (Mayor Higgs); *Alias Smith and Jones*—"Twenty-One Days to Tenstrike" 1-6-72 (Telegrapher).

Harvey, Jack (1881-11/10/54). Films: "Headin' for Trouble" 1931 (Williams); "Pueblo Terror" 1931 (John Weston); "Riders of the Golden Gulch" 1932 (Dan Parker).

Harvey, Jean (1900-12/14/66). TV: *The Roy Rogers Show*—"Haunted Mine of Paradise Valley" 5-18-52, "Born Fugitive" 11-29-53; *Wyatt Earp*—"The Bounty Killer" 9-30-58 (Emma Rash); *The Restless Gun*—"Take Me Home" 12-1-58 (Mrs. Thomas), "The Way Back" 7-13-59; *Wagon Train*—"The Jenny Tannen Story" 6-24-59 (Mrs. Malvin).

Harvey, Laurence (1928-11/25/73). Films: "The Alamo" 1960 (Col. William Travis); "The Outrage" 1964 (Husband).

Harvey, Lew (1887-12/19/53). Films: "The Half-Breed" 1922 (the Snake); "Ranger of the Big Pines" 1925 (Joe Gregg); "A Horseman of the Plains" 1928 (Flash Egan); "The Country Beyond" 1936 (Pierre); "Robin Hood of El Dorado" 1936 (Bill Young); "The Oklahoma Kid" 1939 (Curley); "Go West" 1940 (Card Player); "Desert Fury" 1947 (Doorman); "Trail Street" 1947 (Heavy); "Return of the Badmen" 1948 (Arkansas Kid).

Harvey, Michael. Films: "Return of the Badmen" 1948 (Grat Dalton); "Duck, You Sucker!" 1971-Ital. (Yankee). ¶TV: *Death Valley Days*—"The Fastest Nun in the West" 4-9-66 (Ed Burnet).

Harvey, Orwin. TV: *Daniel Boone*—"Minnow for a Shark" 1-2-69 (2nd Sentry); *Nichols*—"The Unholy Alliance" 1-18-72 (Ray); *Kung Fu*—"The Stone" 4-12-73 (Floyd), "The Squaw Man" 11-1-73 (U.S. Marshal).

Harvey, Paul (1884-12/14/55). Films: "The Plainsman" 1936 (Chief Yellow Hand); "Rose of the Rancho" 1936 (Boss Martin); "Arizona" 1940 (Solomon Warner); "Ride on, Vaquero" 1941 (Colonel); "Heart of the Golden West" 1942 (James Barrabee); "Man from Music Mountain" 1943 (Arthur Davis); "Don't Fence Me In" 1945 (the Governor); "Heldorado" 1946 (W.W. Driscoll); "Wyoming" 1947 (Ludge Sheridan); "Ticket to Tomahawk" 1950 (Mr. Bishop); "Thunder in God's Country" 1951 (Carson Masterson); "Calamity Jane" 1953 (Henry Miller). ¶TV: *The Roy Rogers Show*—"The Brothers O'Dell" 11-20-55, "Three Masked Men" 12-18-55, "Ambush" 1-15-56, "Johnny Rover" 6-9-57 (Jackson Revere).

Harvey, Phil (1908-78). Films: "Wild Heritage" 1958 (Jud). ¶TV: *Gunsmoke*—"Fawn" 4-4-59 (Henry).

Harvey, Verna (1954-). Films: "Chato's Land" 1972 (Shelby Hooker).

Hasbrouck, Olive. Films: "The Little Savage" 1924; "Ridgeway of Montana" 1924 (Aline Hanley); "The Call of Courage" 1925 (June Hazleton); "Hidden Loot" 1925 (Anna Jones); "The Wild West Wallop" 1925; "The Border Sheriff" 1926 (Joan Belden); "A Regular Scout" 1926 (Olive Monroe); "The Ridin' Rascal" 1926 (Phyllis Sanderson); "Rustlers' Ranch" 1926 (Lois Shawn); "A Six Shootin' Romance" 1926 (Donaldeen Travis); "The Two-Gun Man" 1926 (Grace Stickley); "The Fighting Three" 1927 (Jeane D'Arcy); "The Interferin' Gent" 1927 (Ann Douglas); "The Obligin' Buckaroo" 1927; "Pals in Peril" 1927 (Mary Bassett); "Ride 'Em High" 1927 (Betty Allen); "The Ridin' Rowdy" 1927 (Patricia Farris); "Set Free" 1927 (Holly Farrell); "Tearin' into Trouble" 1927 (Ruth Martin); "White Pebbles" 1927 (Bess Allison); "The Cowboy Cavalier" 1928; "Desperate Courage" 1928 (Ann Halliday); "The Flyin' Cowboys" 1928 (Connie Lamont); "The Royal Rider" 1929 (Ruth Elliott).

Hashim, Edmund (1932-7/2/74). Films: "Ghost Town" 1956 (Dull Knife); "Quincannon, Frontier Scout" 1956 (Iron Wolf); "...And Now Miguel" 1966 (Eli). ¶TV: *The Adventures of Rin Tin Tin*—"Rusty Resigns from the Army" 2-25-55; *Brave Eagle*—"The Gentle Warrior" 1-25-56; *The Lone Ranger*—"White Hawk's Decision" 10-18-56, "Ghost Canyon" 12-27-56; *Tales of Wells Fargo*—"Belle Starr" 9-9-57 (Jim July), "Rifles for Red Hand" 5-15-61 (Wing); *Tales of the Texas Rangers*—"Warpath" 10-9-58 (Black Eagle); *Wagon Train*—"The Swift Cloud Story" 4-8-59 (Wamsutta); *Gunsmoke*—"The Brothers" 3-12-66 (Durgen), "The Hanging" 12-31-66 (Saline), "The Wreckers" 9-11-67 (Monk Wiley), "The Victim" 1-1-68 (Brock), "Time of the Jackals" 1-13-69 (Tim Jackson), "Charlie Noon" 11-3-69 (Lone Wolf); *Wild Wild West*—"The Night of Montezuma's Hordes" 10-27-67 (Col. Pedro Sanchez).

Haskell, Al (1886-1/6/69). Films: "Brand of Hate" 1934; "The Prescott Kid" 1934; "Gallant Defender" 1935; "Riding Wild" 1935; "Dodge City Trail" 1937 (Dawson's Gang Member); "North of the Rio Grande" 1937; "The Painted Stallion" 1937-serial; "Two-Fisted Sheriff" 1937; "Zorro Rides Again" 1937-serial; "Desperate Trails" 1939; "The Kansas Terrors" 1939; "The Man from Sundown" 1939; "Mexicali Rose" 1939; "Rough Riders' Round-Up" 1939; "Stage to Chino" 1940; "Texas Terrors" 1940; "Border Vigilantes" 1941; "Down Mexico Way" 1941; "The Masked Rider" 1941 (Jose); "Sheriff of Tombstone" 1941; "Wrangler's Roost" 1941; "Wyoming Wildcat" 1941; "The Lone Star Vigilantes" 1942; "Bordertown Gunfighters" 1943; "Western Cyclone" 1943; "Roaring Westward" 1949; "The Stranger Wore a Gun" 1953; "Vigilante Terror" 1953; "Silver Lode" 1954 (Deputy).

Haskell, Peter (1934-). Films: "The Legend of Earl Durand" 1974. ¶TV: *Death Valley Days*—"The Left Hand Is Damned" 11-1-64; *Rawhide*—"Encounter at Boot Hill" 9-14-65 (Jethroe Kane); *The Big Valley*—"The Fallen Hawk" 3-2-66 (Ward), "Bounty on a Barkley" 2-26-68 (Wheeler Johnson), "The Prize" 12-16-68 (Ben Rawlins); *Iron Horse*—10-14-67 (Joel Tanner); *Father Murphy*—"Outrageous Fortune" 11-9-82 (Alex Clark).

Haslett, Marilyn. Films: "Heroes of the Alamo" 1938 (Angelina Dickinson).

Hassall, Imogen (1942-11/16/80). Films: "El Condor" 1970 (Dolores); "Charley One-Eye" 1973-Brit. (Chris).

Hassett, Marilyn (1949-). Films: "Shadow of the Hawk" 1976 (Maureen).

Hasso, Signe (1910-). TV: *Bonanza*—"A Stranger Passed This Way" 3-3-63 (Christina); *The Road West*—"Fair Ladies of France" 2-27-67 (Mother Superior).

Hastings, Bob (1925-). TV: *Gunsmoke*—"The Squaw" 11-11-61 (Bill Craig), "Call Me Dodie" 9-22-62 (Whip); *The Tall Man*—"Substitute Sheriff" 1-6-62 (J. Simpson Chase).

Hastings, Henry (1879-2/21/63). Films: "Stand Up and Fight" 1939 (Old Black Man).

Hatch, Richard (1946-). TV: *Kung Fu*—"Sun and Cloud Shadow" 2-22-73 (Dave Binns); *Nakia*—"The Dream" 11-23-74 (Allen Bishop).

Hatch, William Riley (1865-9/6/25). Films: "Pierre of the Plains" 1914 (Peter Galbraith); "The Plunderer" 1915 (Bully Presby); "A Case of Law" 1917.

Hatfield, Hurd (1918-). Films: "The Left-Handed Gun" 1958 (Moultrie). ¶TV: *Wild Wild West*—"The Night of the Man-Eating House" 12-2-66 (Liston Day), "The Night of the Undead" 2-2-68 (Dr. Articulus); *Bonanza*—"A Place to Hide" 3-19-72 (Major Donahue).

Hathaway, Jean (1876-8/23/38). Films: "The Divorcee" 1917 (Mrs. Pelham-Wilson); "The Scrapper" 1917; "The Tornado" 1917.

Hathaway, Rhody (1869-2/18/44). Films: "Not a Drum Was Heard" 1924 (James Ross); "Riders of the Plains" 1924-serial; "A Daughter of the Sioux" 1925 (Maj. John Webb); "The Old Code" 1928 (Father Lefane)."Fighting Shadows" 1935 (Woodsman).

Hatswell, Donald (1898-6/29/76). Films: "Blinky" 1923 (Bertrand Van Dusen); "The Meddler" 1925 (Capt. Forsythe).

Hatton, Clare (1869-6/26/43). Films: "Dangerous Love" 1920; "The Desert Scorpion" 1920 (the Cattle King); "Riders of the Range" 1923 (Gregg Randall).

Hatton, Edward (1891-7/9/31). Films: "Last of the Duanes" 1919 (Stevens).

Hatton, Frances (1888-10/16/71). Films: "Straight from the Shoulder" 1921 (Mrs. Bill Higgins); "The Grail" 1923 (Mrs. Trammel).

Hatton, Raymond (1892-10/21/71). Films: "Chimmie Fadden Out West" 1915 (Larry Fadden); "The Girl of the Golden West" 1915 (Castro); "Tennessee's Pardner" 1916 (Gewilliker Hay); "Nan of Music Mountain" 1917 (Logan); "A Romance of the Redwoods" 1917 (Dick Roland); "The Squaw Man's Song" 1917 (Storekeeper); "Arizona" 1918 (Tony); "A Daughter of the Wolf" 1919 (Doc); "Johnny, Get Your Gun" 1919 (Milton C. Milton); "Doubling for Romeo" 1922 (Steve Woods); "His Back Against the Wall" 1922 (Jeremy Dice); "The Virginian" 1923 (Shorty); "The Mine with the Iron Door" 1924 (Bill Jansen); "Western Fate" 1924; "A Son of His Father" 1925 (Charlie Gray); "The Thundering Herd" 1925 (Jude Pilchuk); "Warrior Gap" 1925 (Hal Folsom); "A Western Engagement" 1925 (Dick Rawlins); "Born to the West" 1926 (Jim Fallon); "Forlorn River" 1926 (Arizona Pete); "In Broncho Land" 1926; "Western Courage" 1927; "Hell's Heroes" 1930 (Barbwire Gibbons); "Rogue of the Rio Grande" 1930 (Pedro); "The Silver Horde" 1930 (Fraser); "The Squaw Man" 1931 (Shorty); "The Vanishing Legion" 1931-serial (Dodger); "Woman Hungry" 1931 (Joao); "Cornered" 1932 (Deputy Sheriff Jackson); "Law and Order" 1932 (Deadwood); "The Vanishing Frontier" 1932 (Waco); "The Fourth Horseman" 1933 (Gabby); "Hidden Gold" 1933 (Horace "Spike" Weber); "Terror Trail" 1933 (Lucky Dawson); "Under the Tonto Rim" 1933 (Porky); "The Thundering Herd" 1934 (Jude Pilchuk); "Wagon Wheels" 1934 (Jim Burch); "Nevada" 1935 (Sheriff Frank); "Rustlers of Red Dog" 1935-serial (Laramie); "Wanderer of the Wasteland" 1935 (G. August Merryvale); "The Arizona Raiders" 1936 (Tracks Williams); "Desert Gold" 1936 (Doc Belding); "Vigilantes Are Coming" 1936-serial (Whipsaw); "The Devil's Saddle Legion" 1937; "The Bad Man of Brimstone" 1937 (Cal Turner); "Roaring Timber" 1937 (Tennessee); "The Texans" 1938 (Cal Tuttle); "Come on, Rangers" 1939 (Jeff); "Cowboys from Texas" 1939 (Rusty Joslin); "Frontier Pony Express" 1939 (Horseshoe); "The Kansas Terrors" 1939 (Rusty Joslin); "New Frontier" 1939 (Rusty Joslin); "Rough Riders' Round-Up" 1939 (Rusty Coburn); "Wall Street Cowboy" 1939 (Chuckwalla); "Wyoming Outlaw" 1939 (Rusty Joslin); "Covered Wagon Days" 1940 (Rusty Joslin); "Heroes of the Saddle" 1940 (Rusty Joslin); "Hi-Yo Silver" 1940; "Kit Carson" 1940 (Jim Bridger); "Oklahoma Renegades" 1940 (Rusty Joslin); "Pioneers of the West" 1940 (Rusty Joslin); "Rocky Mountain Rangers" 1940 (Rusty Joslin); "Arizona Bound" 1941; "Forbidden Trails" 1941 (Sandy); "The Gunman from Bodie" 1941; "Texas" 1941 (Judge); "White Eagle" 1941-serial (Grizzly); "Below the Border" 1942 (Sandy); "Dawn on the Great Divide" 1942 (Sandy Hokins); "Down Texas Way" 1942 (Sandy); "Ghost Town Law" 1942 (Sandy); "Girl from Alaska" 1942 (Shorty); "Riders of the West" 1942 (Sandy); "West of the Law" 1942; "The Ghost Rider" 1943; "Outlaws of Stampede Pass" 1943; "Prairie Chickens" 1943; "Six Gun Gospel" 1943; "The Stranger from Pecos" 1943 (Sandy); "The Texas Kid" 1943 (Sandy); "Ghost Guns" 1944; "Land of the Outlaws" 1944; "Law Men" 1944 (Sandy); "Law of the Valley" 1944; "Partners of the Trail" 1944 (Sandy); "Raiders of the Border" 1944 (Sandy); "Range Law" 1944 (Sandy); "Tall in the Saddle" 1944 (Zeke); "West of the Rio Grande" 1944; "Flame of the West" 1945 (Add); "Frontier Feud" 1945 (Sandy); "Gun Smoke" 1945; "The Lost Trail" 1945 (Sandy); "The Navajo Trail" 1945; "Northwest Trail" 1945; "Rhythm Round-Up" 1945; "Strange from Santa Fe" 1945; "Border Bandits" 1946 (Sandy); "Drifting Along" 1946 (Pawnee); "Gentleman from Texas" 1946; "The Haunted Mine" 1946; "Shadows on the Range" 1946; "Silver Range" 1946; "Trigger Fingers" 1946; "Under Arizona Skies" 1946; "Code of the Saddle" 1947; "Flashing Guns" 1947 (Shelby); "Gun Talk" 1947 (Lucky Danvers); "Land of the Lawless" 1947; "Law Comes to Gunsight" 1947; "Prairie Express" 1947 (Faro Jenkins); "Raiders of the South" 1947; "Trailing Danger" 1947; "Unconquered" 1947 (Venango Scout); "Valley of Fear" 1947; "Back Trail" 1948 (Casoose); "Crossed Trails" 1948 (Bodie); "The Fighting Ranger" 1948; "Frontier Agent" 1948 (Sandy Hopkins); "Gunning for Justice" 1948; "Overland Trails" 1948; "The Sheriff of Medicine Bow" 1948; "Triggerman" 1948; "Hidden Danger" 1949 (Banty); "Colorado Ranger" 1950 (Colonel); "Crooked River" 1950 (Colonel); "The Daltons' Women" 1950; "Fast on the Draw" 1950 (Colonel); "Hostile Country" 1950 (Colonel); "Marshal of Heldorado" 1950 (Colonel); "West of the Brazos" 1950 (Colonel); "Skipalong Rosenbloom" 1951; "Cow Country" 1953 (Smokey); "Thunder Pass" 1954; "Treasure of Ruby Hills" 1955 (Scotty); "The Twinkle in God's Eye" 1955 (Yahoo Man); "Dig That Uranium" 1956 (Mac); "Flesh and the Spur" 1957 (Windy); "Pawnee" 1957 (Obie Dilks); "The Quick Gun" 1964 (Elderly Man); "Requiem for a Gunfighter" 1965 (Hoops). ¶TV: *The Cisco Kid*—"Cattle Rustling" 2-3-51, "Medicine Flats" 3-10-51, "The Puppeteer" 1-19-52, "Canyon City Kit" 3-1-52, "Mining Madness" 4-11-53, "Three Suspects" 5-23-53; *The Gene Autry Show*—"The Raiders" 4-14-51, "Double Barrelled Vengeance" 4-21-51; *Wild Bill Hickok*—"Indian Bureau Story" 7-31-51, "The Slocum Family" 12-4-51, "Jingles Becomes a Baby Sitter" 4-15-52, "Ol' Pardner Rides Again" 9-16-52, "Golden Rainbow" 12-9-52, "Old Cowboys Never Die" 12-16-52, "Jingles Gets the Bird" 3-24-53; *The Roy Rogers Show*—"The Minister's Son" 3-23-52, "Bullets and a Burro" 11-15-53; *Annie Oakley*—"Annie and the Leprechauns" 9-2-56 (Tim Lafferty); *Circus Boy*—"The Amazing Mr. Sinbad" 10-14-56 (Sgt. Price); *Cheyenne*—"The Gamble" 1-28-58 (Mousey); *26 Men*—"Gun Hand" 2-25-58; *Death Valley Days*—"Auto Intoxication" 3-3-58; *Tales of the Texas Rangers*—"Warpath" 10-9-58 (Elihu Styles); *Bat Masterson*—"A Personal Matter" 1-28-59 (Adam Fairbanks); *Maverick*—"Burial Ground of the Gods" 3-30-59 (Stableman), "Royal Four-Flush" 9-20-59 (Harry), "The Marquesa" 1-3-60 (Charlie Plank); *Tombstone Territory*—"Gun Hostage" 5-1-59; *Gunsmoke*—"Moo Moo Raid" 2-13-60 (Onie); *Wanted—Dead or Alive*—"A House Divided" 2-20-60; *The Deputy*—"Marked for Bounty" 4-2-60 (Pete); *Have Gun Will Travel*—"Full Circle" 5-14-60 (Eph Trager), "The Trial" 6-11-60 (Bounty Hunter), "The Tax Gatherer" 2-11-61 (Mayor Trevor); *Klondike*—"The Man Who Owned Skagway" 1-30-61 (Miner); *The Tall Man*—"A Scheme of Hearts" 4-22-61 (Stage Driver).

Hatton, Richard "Dick" (1891-7/9/31). Films: "Fearless Dick" 1922; "Four Hearts" 1922 (Dick Reynolds); "Hellhounds of the West" 1922 (Dick Sinclair); "Blood Test" 1923; "The Golden Flame" 1923; "Playing Dobule" 1923; "Ridin' Thru" 1923; "The Seventh Sheriff" 1923 (Jack Rockwell); "Come on Cowboys!" 1924 (Jim Cartwright); "Horse Sense" 1924 (Robert Mayfield); "In the West" 1924 (Bill Frazer); "Sagebrush Gospel" 1924 (Judd Davis); "Sell 'Em Cowboy" 1924 (Frank Mathewson,

Jr.); "Two Fisted Justice" 1924 (Rance Raine); "Western Fate" 1924; "The Whirlwind Ranger" 1924; "The Cactus Cure" 1925 (Jimmy King); "My Pal" 1925; "Range Justice" 1925; "Ridin' Easy" 1925; "The Rip Snorter" 1925 (Dick Meadows); "Scar Hanan" 1925 (Shorty); "The Secret of Black Canyon" 1925 (Dick Halsey); "Warrior Gap" 1925 (Hal Folsom); "A Western Engagement" 1925 (Dick Rawlins); "Where Romance Rides" 1925 (Dick Manners); "A He-Man's Country" 1926; "In Broncho Land" 1926; "Roaring Bill Atwood" 1926; "Temporary Sheriff" 1926; "The Action Craver" 1927; "Saddle Jumpers" 1927; "Speeding Hoofs" 1927; "Western Courage" 1927; "The Boss of Rustler's Roost" 1928 (Bill Everman); "Romance of the West" 1930 (Parson); "The Vanishing Legion" 1931-serial (Dodger).

Hatton, Rondo (1894-2/2/46). Films: "The Ox-Bow Incident" 1943 (Hart).

Hauser, Wings. TV: *Young Riders*—"Lessons Learned" 7-9-92 (Randall).

Haver, Phyllis (1899-11/19/60). Films: "Singer Jim McKee" 1924 (Mary Holden); "The Golden Princess" 1925 (Kate Kent); "Hard-Boiled" 1926 (Justine Morton); "Three Bad Men" 1926 (Prairie Beauty).

Hawke, Ethan. Films: "White Fang" 1991 (Jack Conroy); "White Fang 2: Myth of the White Wolf" 1994 (Jack Conroy).

Hawkins, Georgia. Films: "The Light of Western Stars" 1940 (Helen); "Doomed Caravan" 1941 (Diana Westcott).

Hawkins, Jack (1910-7/18/73). Films: "Shalako" 1968-Brit./Fr. (Sir Charles Daggett).

Hawkins, Jimmy. Films: "Savage Frontier" 1953 (Davie); "The Woman They Almost Lynched" 1953 (Boy); "Count Three and Pray" 1955 (Corey). ¶TV: *Annie Oakley*—Regular 1954-57 (Tagg Oakley).

Hawks, Capt. Frank (1897-8/23/38). Films: "Klondike" 1932 (Donald Evans).

Hawley, Helen. Films: "Two-Gun Betty" 1919 (Florence Kennedy).

Hawley, Patrick. Films: "Paint Your Wagon" 1969 (Clendennon). ¶TV: *Wyatt Earp*—"The Posse" 5-10-60; *The Big Valley*—"The Invaders" 12-29-65 (Johnson); *Bonanza*—"The Fence" 4-27-69 (Stubbs).

Hawley, Wanda (Wanda Petit) (1895-3/18/63). Films: "The Border Wireless" 1918 (Elsa Miller); "Cupid's Round Up" 1918 (Helen Baldwin); "Told in the Hills" 1919 (Ann Belleau); "Brass Commandments" 1923 (Gloria Hallowell); "The Man Who Played Square" 1925 (Bertie); "Pueblo Terror" 1931 (Helen Weston); "Trails of the Golden West" 1931.

Hawn, Goldie (1945-). Films: "The Duchess and the Dirtwater Fox" 1976 (Amanda Quaid).

Haworth, Jill (1945-). TV: *Rawhide*—"Duel at Daybreak" 11-16-65 (Vicki Woodruff); *Bonanza*—"The Reluctant American" 2-14-71 (Gillian Harwood).

Haworth, Joe. Films: "Frontier Gal" 1945 (Henchman); "Royal Mounted Rides Again" 1945-serial (Bunker); "Salome, Where She Danced" 1945 (Henry); "Singing on the Trail" 1946; "The Outcasts of Poker Flat" 1952 (Gunman); "Gun Belt" 1953 (Hoke); "The Wonderful Country" 1959 (Stoker); "Five Guns to Tombstone" 1961 (Hoke); "Showdown" 1963 (Guard). ¶TV: *The Lone Ranger*—"Triple Cross" 5-21-53, "Texas Draw" 11-5-54 (Brazos); *Annie Oakley*—"The Tomboy" 7-17-54 (Vic); *My Friend Flicka*—"One Man's Horse" 9-30-55; *Fury*—"Tungsten Queen" 1-14-56 (Millard); *Sheriff of Cochise*—"Helldorado" 12-7-56 (Duke); *Tombstone Territory*—"Fight for a Fugitive" 6-4-58 (Vince Harper); *The Rifleman*—"End of a Young Gun" 10-14-58, "The Grasshopper" 3-1-60; *Johnny Ringo*—"Die Twice" 1-21-60 (Walt); *Gunsmoke*—"Unwanted Deputy" 3-5-60 (Charlie), "Old Dan" 1-27-62 (Gates), "The Wreckers" 9-11-67 (Townsman), "The Devil's Outpost" 9-22-69 (Cowboy), "No Tomorrow" 1-3-72 (Rider); *Wanted—Dead or Alive*—"Vendetta" 4-9-60; *Laramie*—"Bad Blood" 12-4-62; *Bonanza*—"Horse of a Different Hue" 9-18-66 (O'Leary); *Laredo*—"The Dance of the Laughing Death" 9-23-66; *Cimarron Strip*—"Nobody" 12-7-67 (Seth); *Alias Smith and Jones*—"Twenty-One Days to Tenstrike" 1-6-72 (Steve), "The Clementine Incident" 10-7-72.

Hayakawa, Sessue (1889-11/23/73). Films: "Last of the Line" 1914; "The Jaguar's Claws" 1917 (El Jaguar). ¶TV: *Wagon Train*—"The Sakae Ito Story" 12-3-58 (Sakae Ito).

Hayden, Harry (1882-7/24/55). Films: "God's Country and the Woman" 1937 (Barnes); "Wells Fargo" 1937 (Clerk); "The Cisco Kid and the Lady" 1939 (Sheriff); "Frontier Marshal" 1939 (Mayor Henderson); "Last of the Duanes" 1941 (Banker); "The Parson of Panamint" 1941 (Timothy Hadley); "Lone Star Ranger" 1942 (Sheriff); "Valley of the Sun" 1942 (Governor); "Barbary Coast Gent" 1944 (Elias Porter); "The Dude Goes West" 1948 (Horace Hotchkiss); "Silver River" 1948 (Schaefer, the Teller); "Bad Men of Tombstone" 1949; "The Last Posse" 1953 (Davis). ¶TV: *Wild Bill Hickok*—"The Sheriff's Secret" 10-21-52.

Hayden, Nora. TV: *Gunsmoke*—"Lacey" 1-13-62 (Bessie); *Bonanza*—"The Infernal Machine" 4-11-62 (Big Red).

Hayden, Russell (1912-6/10/81). Films: "Hills of Old Wyoming" 1937 (Lucky Jenkins); "Hopalong Rides Again" 1937 (Lucky Jenkins); "North of the Rio Grande" 1937 (Lucky Jenkins); "Rustler's Valley" 1937 (Lucky Jenkins); "Texas Trail" 1937 (Lucky Jenkins); "Bar 20 Justice" 1938 (Lucky Jenkins); "Cassidy of Bar 20" 1938 (Lucky Jenkins); "The Frontiersman" 1938 (Lucky); "Heart of Arizona" 1938 (Lucky Jenkins); "In Old Mexico" 1938 (Lucky Jenkins); "The Mysterious Rider" 1938 (Wils Moore); "Partners of the Plains" 1938 (Lucky Jenkins); "Pride of the West" 1938 (Lucky Jenkins); "Sunset Trail" 1938 (Lucky Jenkins); "Heritage of the Desert" 1939 (David Naab); "Law of the Pampas" 1939 (Lucky Jenkins); "Range War" 1939 (Lucky Jenkins); "Renegade Trail" 1939 (Lucky Jenkins); "Silver on the Sage" 1939 (Lucky Jenkins); "Hidden Gold" 1940 (Lucky Jenkins); "The Light of Western Stars" 1940 (Alfred Hammond); "Knights of the Range" 1940 (Renn Frayne); "Santa Fe Marshal" 1940 (Lucky Jenkins); "The Showdown" 1940 (Lucky Jenkins); "Stagecoach War" 1940 (Lucky Jenkins); "Three Men from Texas" 1940 (Lucky Jenkins); "Border Vigilantes" 1941 (Luck Jenkings); "Doomed Caravan" 1941 (Lucky Jenkins); "In Old Colorado" 1941 (Lucky Jenkins); "Pirates on Horseback" 1941 (Lucky Jenkins); "Riders of the Badlands" 1941 (Lucky Barton); "The Royal Mounted Patrol" 1941 (Lucky Lawrence); "Wide Open Town" 1941 (Lucky Jenkins); "Bad Men of the Hills" 1942 (Luck Shelton); "Down Rio Grande Way" 1942 (Lucky Haines); "Lawless Plainsmen" 1942 (Lucky Bannon); "The Lone Prairie" 1942; "Overland to Deadwood" 1942 (Lucky Laidlaw); "Riders of the Northland" 1942 (Lucky Laidlaw); "A Tornado in the Saddle" 1942; "West of Tombstone" 1942 (Lucky Barnet);

"Frontier Law" 1943 (Jim Warren); "Riders of the Northwest Mounted" 1943; "Saddles and Sagebrush" 1943; "Silver City Raiders" 1943 (Lucky Harlan); "The Last Horseman" 1944 (Lucky Rawlins); "Marshal of Gunsmoke" 1944 (Tom); "The Vigilantes Ride" 1944 (Lucky Saunders); "Wyoming Hurricane" 1944; "'Neath Canadian Skies" 1946; "North of the Border" 1946; "Trail of the Mounties" 1947 (Lucky Sanderson/Johnny); "Where the North Begins" 1947; "Albuquerque" 1948 (Ted Wallace); "Sons of Adventure" 1948 (Steve); "Apache Chief" 1949 (Black Wolf); "Deputy Marshal" 1949 (Bill Masters); "Colorado Ranger" 1950 (Lucky); "Crooked River" 1950 (Lucky); "Fast on the Draw" 1950 (Lucky); "Hostile Country" 1950 (Lucky); "Marshal of Heldorado" 1950 (Lucky); "West of the Brazos" 1950 (Lucky); "Texans Never Cry" 1951 (Steve Diamond); "Valley of Fire" 1951 (Steve Guiford). ¶TV: *The Marshal of Gunsight Pass*—Regular 1950 (Marshal); *The Gene Autry Show*—"The Peace Maker" 12-17-50; *Cowboy G-Men*—Regular 1952-53 (Pat Gallagher); *Judge Roy Bean*—Regular 1955-56 (Ranger Steve Allison).

Hayden, Sterling (1916-5/23/86). Films: "El Paso" 1949 (Burt Donner); "Denver and Rio Grande" 1952 (McCabe); "Flaming Feather" 1952 (Tex McCloud); "Hellgate" 1952 (Gil Hanley); "Kansas Pacific" 1953 (John Nelson); "Take Me to Town" 1953 (Will Hall); "Arrow in the Dust" 1954 (Bart Laish); "Johnny Guitar" 1954 (Johnny Guitar); "The Last Command" 1955 (James Bowie); "Shotgun" 1955 (Clay); "Timberjack" 1955 (Tim Chipman); "Top Gun" 1955 (Rick Martin); "Gun Battle at Monterey" 1957 (Turner); "Valerie" 1957 (John Garth); "Ten Days to Tulara" 1958 (Scotty); "Terror in a Texas Town" 1958 (George Hansen); "The Iron Sheriff" 1957 (Sheriff Sam Galt); "Cipolla Colt" 1975-Ital./Ger. ¶TV: *Zane Grey Theater*—"The Necessary Breed" 2-15-57 (Link); *Wagon Train*—"The Les Rand Story" 10-16-57 (Les Rand).

Haydn, Richard (1905-4/25/85). Films: "The Adventures of Bullwhip Griffin" 1967 (Quentin Bartlett). ¶TV: *Laredo*—"A Very Small Assignment" 3-17-66 (Jonathan Pringle); *Bonanza*—"The Lady and the Mountain Lion" 2-23-69 (Malcolm the Magnificent).

Haydon, Julie (1910-12/24/94). Films: "Come on, Danger!" 1932

(Joan Stanton); "The Conquerors" 1932 (Frances Standish); "Scarlet River" 1933 (Herself); "Son of the Border" 1933 (Doris).

Hayes, Adrienne. TV: *Bonanza*—"The Truckee Strip" 11-21-59; *Rawhide*—"Incident on the Road Back" 2-24-61 (Miss Winkle); *Death Valley Days*—"The Red Ghost of Eagle Creek" 5-30-64 (Amy); *Daniel Boone*—"Doll of Sorrow" 4-22-65 (Rising Star), "A Matter of Blood" 12-28-67 (Lawana).

Hayes, Allison (1930-2/27/77). Films: "Count Three and Pray" 1955 (Georgina Decrais); "Gunslinger" 1956 (Erica Page); "Mohawk" 1956 (Greta); "Wolf Dog" 1958-Can. (Ellen Hughes); "Tickle Me" 1965 (Mabel). ¶TV: *Death Valley Days*—"Lady Engineer" 5-5-57 (Mary Granger); *Tombstone Territory*—"A Bullet for an Editor" 11-13-57 (Carole Thayer), "Red Terror of Tombstone" 10-9-59, 10-30-59 (Elizabeth Blythe), 3-25-60 (Liz Dolthan); *Bat Masterson*—"Dude's Folly" 11-26-58 (Ellie Winters), "License to Cheat" 2-4-59 (Ellie Winters), "The Secret Is Death" 5-27-59 (Ellie Winters), "Deadly Diamonds" 2-11-60 (Ellie Winters), "The Reluctant Witness" 3-31-60 (Ellie Winters), "The Elusive Baguette" 6-2-60 (Ellie Winters), "Murder Can Be Dangerous" 11-3-60 (Ellie Winters); *Rough Riders*—"An Eye for an Eye" 1-15-59 (Ellen Johnston); *Rawhide*—"Incident at the Buffalo Smokehouse" 10-30-59 (Rose Morton); *The Alaskans*—"Starvation Stampede" 11-1-59 (Stella); *Iron Horse*—"Death by Triangulation" 3-20-67 (Dana); *Laramie*—"The Fatal Step" 10-24-61 (Francie).

Hayes, Annelle. Films: "Two Rode Together" 1961 (Belle Aragon). ¶TV: *Death Valley Days*—"Dangerous Crossing" 3-22-61 (Mrs. Norgate).

Hayes, Bernadine (1912-8/29/87). Films: "The Judgement Book" 1935 (Madge Williams); "Trigger Tom" 1935 (Dorothy Jergenson); "North of the Rio Grande" 1937 (Faro Annie); "Rustler's Valley" 1937; "Santa Fe Marshal" 1940 (Paula Bates). ¶TV: *Judge Roy Bean*—"Slightly Prodigal" 10-15-55 (Mrs. Brown), "Outlaw's Son" 1-1-56 (Mrs. Clemens), "The Reformer" 1-1-56 (Dolly Mason), "The Travelers" 1-1-56 (Mrs. Atkins).

Hayes, Billie (1924-). TV: *The Monroes*—"Manhunt" 3-1-67 (Mrs. Peabody).

Hayes, Charlie. TV: *Annie Oakley*—"Western Privateer" 9-30-56 (Eddie Sloane), "Desperate Men" 2-

24-57 (Sid Muncy); *Sergeant Preston of the Yukon*—"Ghost Mine" 11-14-57 (Slim); *Tales of Wells Fargo*—"The Town That Wouldn't Talk" 2-9-59 (Ed Cook).

Hayes, Chester. Films: "The Wonderful Country" 1959 (Rascon). ¶TV: *Wagon Train*—"The Stark Bluff Story" 4-6-64 (Vladimir); *A Man Called Shenandoah*—"The Clown" 4-18-66 (Man).

Hayes, Frank (1875-12/28/23). Films: "The Killer" 1921 (Windy Smith); "Man of the Forest" 1921 (Los Vegas); "The Mysterious Rider" 1921 (Smokey Joe Lem Billings); "When Romance Rides" 1922 (Dr. Binks); "Double Dealing" 1923 (the Sheriff).

Hayes, George "Gabby" (1885-2/9/69). Films: "Cavalier of the West" 1931 (Sheriff Bill Ryan); "God's Country and the Man" 1931 (Stingeree Kelly); "The Nevada Buckaroo" 1931 (Cherokee); "The Boiling Point" 1932 (George Duncan); "Border Devils" 1932 (Squint Sanders); "Broadway to Cheyenne" 1932; "Fighting Champ" 1932 (Pete); "Hidden Valley" 1932 (Henchman); "Klondike" 1932 (Tom Ross); "Man from Hell's Edges" 1932 (Shamrock); "The Night Rider" 1932 (Tourist); "Riders of the Desert" 1932 (Hashknife Brooks); "Texas Buddies" 1932 (Si Haller); "Wild Horse Mesa" 1932 (Slack); "Without Honor" 1932; "Breed of the Border" 1933 (Chuck Wiggins); "Crashing Broadway" 1933 (J. Talbot Thorndyke); "The Fighting Texans" 1933 (Old Man Martin); "The Fugitive" 1933 (Judge Childers); "The Gallant Fool" 1933 (Charles Denton); "Galloping Romeo" 1933 (Grizzly); "The Ranger's Code" 1933 (Baxter); "Riders of Destiny" 1933 (Dad Denton); "Trailing North" 1933 (Flash Ryan); "Blue Steel" 1934 (Sheriff Jake); "Brand of Hate" 1934; "In Old Santa Fe" 1934 (Cactus); "The Lawless Frontier" 1934 (Dusty); "The Lucky Texan" 1934 (Jake Benson); "The Man from Hell" 1934 (Col. Campbell); "The Man from Utah" 1934 (George Higgins); "'Neath the Arizona Skies" 1934 (Matt Downing); "The Outlaw Tamer" 1934 (Cactus Barnes); "Randy Rides Alone" 1934 (Matt the Mute/Marvin Black); "The Star Packer" 1934 (Matt Matlock/the Shadow); "West of the Divide" 1934 (Dusty Rhodes); "Hopalong Cassidy" 1935 (Uncle Ben); "Justice of the Range" 1935 (Pegleg Sanderson/John Coffin); "Rainbow Valley" 1935 (George Hale); "Smokey Smith" 1935

(Blaze); "Swifty" 1935 (Sheriff Dan Hughes); "Texas Terror" 1935 (Sheriff Ed Williams); "The Throwback" 1935 (Ford Cruze); "Thunder Mountain" 1935 (Foley); "Tombstone Terror" 1935 (Soupy Baxter); "Tumbling Tumbleweeds" 1935 (Dr. Parker); "Bar 20 Rides Again" 1936 (Windy Halliday); "Call of the Prairie" 1936 (Shanghai); "The Eagle's Brood" 1936 (Spike); "Hopalong Cassidy Returns" 1936 (Windy Halliday); "The Lawless Nineties" 1936 (Maj. Carter); "The Plainsman" 1936 (Breezy); "Silver Spurs" 1936 (Drag Harlan); "Song of the Trail" 1936 (Ben Hobson); "The Texas Rangers" 1936 (Judge); "Three on the Trail" 1936 (Windy); "Trail Dust" 1936 (Windy); "Valley of the Lawless" 1936 (Jenkins); "Borderland" 1937 (Windy); "Heart of the West" 1937 (Windy Halliday); "Hills of Old Wyoming" 1937 (Windy Halliday); "Hopalong Rides Again" 1937 (Windy Halliday); "North of the Rio Grande" 1937 (Windy); "Rustler's Valley" 1937 (Windy Halliday); "Texas Trail" 1937 (Windy Halliday); "Bar 20 Justice" 1938 (Windy Halliday); "The Frontiersman" 1938 (Windy); "Gold Is Where You Find It" 1938 (Enoch Howitt); "Heart of Arizona" 1938 (Windy Halliday); "In Old Mexico" 1938 (Windy Halliday); "Pride of the West" 1938 (Windy Halliday); "Sunset Trail" 1938 (Windy Halliday); "The Arizona Kid" 1939 (Gabby); "Days of Jesse James" 1939 (Gabby Whittaker); "In Old Caliente" 1939 (Gabby Whittaker); "In Old Monterey" 1939 (Gabby Whittaker); "Let Freedom Ring" 1939 (Pop Wilkie); "Man of Conquest" 1939 (Lannie Upchurch); "Renegade Trail" 1939 (Marshal Windy Halliday); "Saga of Death Valley" 1939 (Gabby); "Silver on the Sage" 1939 (Windy Halliday); "Southward Ho!" 1939 (Gabby Whittaker); "Wall Street Cowboy" 1939 (Gabby); "The Border Legion" 1940 (Honest John Whittaker); "The Carson City Kid" 1940 (Gabby Whittaker); "Colorado" 1940 (Gabby); "The Dark Command" 1940 (Doc Grunch); "Melody Ranch" 1940 (Pop Laramie); "The Ranger and the Lady" 1940 (Sgt. Gabby Whittaker); "Wagons Westward" 1940 (Hardtack); "Young Bill Hickok" 1940 (Gabby Whitaker); "Young Buffalo Bill" 1940 (Gabby); "Bad Man of Deadwood" 1941 (Prof. Blackstone); "In Old Cheyenne" 1941 (Arapahoe Brown); "Jesse James at Bay" 1941 (Sheriff); "Meet Roy Rogers" 1941-short; "Nevada City" 1941; "Red River Valley" 1941; "Robin Hood of the Pecos"

1941 (Gabby Hornaday); "Sheriff of Tombstone" 1941 (Gabby); "Heart of the Golden West" 1942 (Gabby); "Man from Cheyenne" 1942 (Gabby Whittaker); "Ridin' Down the Canyon" 1942 (Gabby); "Romance on the Range" 1942 (Gabby); "Sons of the Pioneers" 1942 (Gabby Whittaker); "South of Santa Fe" 1942 (Mayor Whittaker); "Sunset on the Desert" 1942 (Gabby Whittaker); "Sunset Serenade" 1942 (Gabby Whittaker); "Bordertown Gunfighters" 1943 (Gabby Whittaker); "Calling Wild Bill Elliott" 1943 (Gabby); "Death Valley Manhunt" 1943 (Gabby); "In Old Oklahoma" 1943 (Desprit Dan); "The Man from Thunder River" 1943; "Overland Mail Robbery" 1943 (Gabby); "Wagon Tracks West" 1943 (Gabby Whittaker); "The Big Bonanza" 1944 (Hap Selby); "Hidden Valley Outlaws" 1944; "The Lights of Old Santa Fe" 1944 (Gabby Whittaker); "Marshal of Reno" 1944; "Mojave Firebrand" 1944; "Tall in the Saddle" 1944 (Dave); "Tucson Raiders" 1944 (Gabby); "Along the Navajo Trail" 1945 (Gabby Whittaker); "Bells of Rosarita" 1945 (Gabby Whittaker); "Don't Fence Me In" 1945 (Gabby Whittaker); "The Man from Oklahoma" 1945 (Gabby Whittaker); "Sunset in El Dorado" 1945 (Gabby Whittaker); "Utah" 1945 (Gabby Whittaker); "Badman's Territory" 1946 (Coyote); "Heldorado" 1946 (Gabby Whittaker); "Home in Oklahoma" 1946 (Gabby Whittaker); "My Pal Trigger" 1946 (Gabby Kendrick); "Rainbow Over Texas" 1946 (Gabby Whittaker); "Roll on, Texas Moon" 1946 (Gabby Whittaker); "Song of Arizona" 1946 (Gaby Whittaker); "Under Nevada Skies" 1946 (Gabby Whittaker); "Trail Street" 1947 (Billy Jones/Brandyhead Jones); "Wyoming" 1947 (Windy); "Albuquerque" 1948 (Juke); "Return of the Badmen" 1948 (John Pettit); "The Untamed Breed" 1948 (Windy Lucas); "El Paso" 1949 (Pesky); "The Cariboo Trail" 1950 (Grizzly). ¶TV: The Gabby Hayes Show—Host 1950-54.

Hayes, Helen (1900-3/17/93). Films: "Riders of the Range" 1923 (Inez); "A Rodeo Mixup" 1924 (the Maid).

Hayes, Isaac (1942-). Films: "Posse" 1993 (Cable).

Hayes, Linda. Films: "Mexican Spitfire Out West" 1940 (Elizabeth); "Men of the Timberland" 1941; "Ridin' Down the Canyon" 1942 (Alice Blake); "Romance on the Range" 1942 (Joan Stuart); "South of Santa Fe" 1942 (Carol Stevens).

Hayes, Lorraine. see Day, Laraine.

Hayes, Margaret "Maggie" (1915-1/26/77). Films: "In Old Colorado" 1941 (Myra Woods); "Good Day for a Hanging" 1958 (Ruth Granger). ¶TV: Wyatt Earp—Regular 1955-56 (Dora Hand); Cheyenne—"The Trap" 12-18-56 (Iris); Zane Grey Theater—"No Man Living" 1-11-57 (Susan), "The Deserters" 10-4-57 (Rose); Trackdown—"The San Saba Incident" 10-18-57 (Abby Lincoln); Tombstone Territory—"Cave-In" 3-26-58 (Sally); Yancy Derringer—"The Saga of Lonesome Jackson" 11-27-58 (Ruby); Rawhide "Incident of the Night on the Town" 6-2-61 (Mrs. North); Bonanza—"The Countess" 11-19-61 (Linda Chadwick).

Hayes, Mary. Films: "Roaring Six Guns" 1937 (Beth); "Rough Ridin' Rhythm" 1937.

Hayes, Ronald. Films: "Face of a Fugitive" 1959 (Danny); "Gunmen from Laredo" 1959 (Walt Keefer); "Standing Tall" TVM-1978 (Elroy Bones). ¶TV: Maverick—"Seed of Deception" 4-13-58 (Max Evers), "Passage to Fort Doom" 3-8-59 (Joe); Bronco—"Trail to Taos" 12-2-58 (Pitt); The Texan—"The Ringer" 2-16-59, "Showdown" 2-29-60; Tombstone Territory—"Day of the Amnesty" 4-3-59 (Chuck Umber); Rawhide—"Incident of the Haunted Hills" 11-6-59 (Owens), "Incident of the Four Horsemen" 10-26-62 (Frank Louden); Wanted—Dead or Alive—"Reckless" 11-7-59; Bat Masterson—"The Pied Piper of Dodge City" 1-7-60 (Wyatt Earp), "The Reluctant Witness" 3-31-60 (Wyatt Earp), "The Rage of Princess Ann" 10-20-60 (Jeremy French), "The Fatal Garment" 5-25-61 (Wyatt Earp); Hotel De Paree—"Sundance Goes to Kill" 1-22-60 (Dave Carter); Gunsmoke—"Moo Moo Raid" 2-13-60 (Cary), "Harriet" 3-4-61 (Hoagler), "Old Faces" 3-18-61 (Milt Varden), "Jenny" 10-13-62 (Zel Meyers), "I Call Him Wonder" 3-23-63 (Jud Sorrell), "South Wind" 11-27-65 (Wade Bonney), "The Judas Gun" 1-19-70 (Boyd Avery), "Snow Train" 10-19-70 & 10-26-70 (Floyd Coleman); Bonanza—"Desert Justice" 2-20-60 (Hurd Cutler), "The Rescue" 2-25-61 (Johnny Reed), "Mirror of a Man" 3-31-63 (Jud Barnes/Rube Barnes), "The Bridegroom" 12-4-66 (Jared Wilson), "Night of Reckoning" 10-15-67 (Buckler), "Emily" 3-23-69 (Wade McPhail); Laramie—"Duel at Alta Mesa" 2-23-60 (Ray), "Shadow of the Past" 10-16-62 (Carl Keefer), "Protective Custody" 1-15-63

(Cass); *The Deputy*—"Marked for Bounty" 4-2-60 (Ralph Jenson); *Wichita Town*—"Sidekicks" 4-6-60 (Scotty); *Wagon Train*—"Trial for Murder" 4-27-60 & 5-4-60, "The Cathy Eckhardt Story" 11-9-60 (Whitey), "The Jed Polke Story" 3-1-61 (Ross), "The Bettina May Story" 12-20-61 (Gene), "The Story of Cain" 12-16-63 (John Cain), "The Duncan McIvor Story" 3-9-64 (Lt. Duncan McIvor); *Death Valley Days*—"Devil's Bar" 10-5-60 (Don Bartlett); *Tales of Wells Fargo*—"Run for the River" 11-7-60 (Ira Kyle); *The Rifleman*—"Six Years and a Day" 1-3-61; *Klondike*—"Sitka Madonna" 2-6-61 (Harold Enright); *Two Faces West*—"Music Box" 7-17-61; *Temple Houston*—"Billy Hart" 11-28-63 (Lambert); *The Virginian*—"Siege" 12-18-63 (Marshal Brett Cole); *Destry*—"Blood Brother-in-Law" 4-17-64 (Jethro Jellico); *Walt Disney Presents*—"Gallegher" 1965-67 (George Moran); *A Man Called Shenandoah*—"A Long Way Home" 1-31-66 (Jamie Brewster); *The Rounders*—Regular 1966-67 (Ben Jones); *The High Chaparral*—"Threshold of Courage" 3-31-68 (Stacey Carr), "A Fella Named Kilroy" 3-7-69 (Kilroy); *How the West Was Won*—"The Innocent" 2-12-79 (Sheriff Pinter).

Hayes, Ryan. TV: *The Westerner*—"The Old Man" 11-25-60; *Zane Grey Theater*—"The Black Wagon" 12-1-60 (Mead).

Hayes, Sam (1905-7/28/58). Films: "Cowboy from Brooklyn" 1938 (News Commentator).

Hayes, William (1887-7/13/37). Films: "Flashing Spurs" 1924 (Scarbee); "Ace of Action" 1926.

Haymer, Johnny (1920-11/18/89). TV: *Pistols 'n' Petticoats*—12-17-66 (Etienne LaVoissiere); *Wild Wild West*—"The Night of the Vipers" 1-12-68 (Aloyisius Moriarity); *Gunsmoke*—"9:12 to Dodge" 11-11-68 (Ned Stallcup).

Haymes, Dick (1919-3/28/80). TV: *Alias Smith and Jones*—"Smiler with a Gun" 10-7-71; *Hec Ramsey*—"Scar Tissue" 3-10-74 (Hamilton Hobbs).

Haynes, Dick (1911-11/25/80). Films: "Sidekicks" TVM-1974. ¶TV: *Frontier Circus*—"Incident at Pawnee Gun" 9-6-62 (Phillips); *The Rounders*—11-15-66 (Sheriff); *The High Chaparral*—"The Little Thieves" 12-26-69.

Haynes, Lloyd (1934-12/31/86). TV: *Lancer*—"Chase a Wild Horse" 10-8-68, "The Lawman" 10-22-68 (Frank).

Haynes, Roberta. Films: "The Fighter" 1952 (Nevis); "Gun Fury" 1953 (Estella Morales); "The Nebraskan" 1953 (Paris); "Valdez Is Coming" 1971 (Polly). ¶TV: *Black Saddle*—"Apache Trail" 11-20-59 (Chata).

Haynes, William. Films: "The Desert Outlaw" 1924 (Tom Halloway).

Haynie, Jim. Films: "Silverado" 1985 (Bradley); "Kung Fu: The Movie" TVM-1986. ¶TV: *Young Riders*—"The Talisman" 2-23-91 (Father Peter Reilly).

Hays, Barry. Films: "Heroes of the Hills" 1938 (Regan); "The Lone Ranger Rides Again" 1939-serial (Raider #3); "Zorro's Fighting Legion" 1939-serial (Soldier #3); "Adventures of Red Ryder" 1940-serial (Water Heavy #2); "Covered Wagon Days" 1940; "One Man's Law" 1940; "The Trail Blazers" 1940; "King of the Texas Rangers" 1941-serial (Dirigible Heavy #1).

Hays, Kathryn (1936-). Films: "Ride Beyond Vengeance" 1966 (Jessie); "Yuma" TVM-1971 (Julie Williams). ¶TV: *Wide Country*—"The Girl from Nob Hill" 3-8-63 (Lila Never); *Bonanza*—"The Wild One" 10-4-64 (Prudence); *The Virginian*—"A Slight Case of Charity" 2-10-65 (Charity); *Branded*—"Very Few Heroes" 4-11-65 (Christine Adams); *The Road West*—Regular 1966-67 (Elizabeth Pride); *The High Chaparral*—"Tornado Frances" 10-11-68 (Frances O'Toole); *Here Come the Brides*—"A Kiss Just for You" 1-29-69 (Dena); *Bearcats!*—12-23-71 (Milly).

Hays, Robert (1947-). Films: "Young Pioneers" TVM-1976 (Dan Grey); "Young Pioneers' Christmas" TVM-1976 (Dan Grey); "California Gold Rush" TVM-1981. ¶TV: *The Young Pioneers*—Regular 1978 (Dan Gray).

Haysbert, Dennis. Films: "Return to Lonesome Dove" TVM-1993 (Cherokee Jack Jackson).

Hayward, Brooke (1937-). TV: *Bonanza*—"The Storm" 1-28-62 (Laura White).

Hayward, Chuck. Films: "Desperadoes of the West" 1950-serial (Al); "The Fargo Phantom" 1950-short; "Wagonmaster" 1950 (Jackson); "Jubilee Trail" 1954 (Velasco Rider); "Man with the Steel Whip" 1954-serial (Barn Heavy #2); "The Searchers" 1956 (Stunts); "Forty Guns" 1957 (Charlie Savage); "Run of the Arrow" 1957 (Corporal); "The Big Country" 1958 (Rafe); "Escort

West" 1959 (Indian); "The Horse Soldiers" 1959 (Capt. Woodward); "Sergeant Rutledge" 1960 (Capt. Dickinson); "The Deadly Companions" 1961 (Card Sharp); "Two Rode Together" 1961; "The Man Who Shot Liberty Valance" 1962 (Henchman); "Five Card Stud" 1968 (O'Hara); "Rio Lobo" 1970; "Joe Kidd" 1972 (Eljay); "Rooster Cogburn" 1975 (Gang Member); "The Legend of the Lone Ranger" 1981 (Wald). ¶TV: *Zane Grey Theater*—"This Man Must Die" 1-24-58 (Posse Man), "Man of Fear" 3-14-58, "The Man from Yesterday" 12-22-60 (Farmer); *Gunsmoke*—"Lynching Man" 11-15-58 (Jake), "Jayhawkers" 1-31-59 (Studer), "Perce" 9-30-61 (Kemp), "Hammerhead" 12-26-64 (Cowhand); *Wichita Town*—"The Night the Cowboys Roared" 9-30-59 (Bridey); *Have Gun Will Travel*—"A Head of Hair" 9-24-60 (Chiyup); *Wanted—Dead or Alive*—"The Cure" 9-28-60, "The Choice" 12-14-60 (Bob Bradley), "Dead Reckoning" 3-22-61 (Burl Taggert); *Wagon Train*—"The Colter Craven Story" 11-23-60; *Maverick*—"Destination Devil's Flat" 12-25-60 (Guard); *Bonanza*—"New Man" 10-10-72 (Guard); *Kung Fu*—"The Stone" 4-12-73 (Sheriff), "The Well" 9-27-73 (Drifter).

Hayward, David. Films: "The Chisholms" TVM-1979 (Timothy Oates); "The Legend of the Lone Ranger" 1981 (Collins). ¶TV: *Bonanza*—"The Weary Willies" 9-27-70 (Hurley); *The Chisholms*—Regular 1979 (Timothy Oates); *The Cherokee Trail*—Pilot 11-28-81 (Temple Boone); *Paradise*—"The Return of Johnny Ryan" 12-2-89 (Guthrie).

Hayward, Jim (-7/12/81). Films: "Coyote Canyon" 1949-short; "Vengeance Valley" 1951 (Sheriff Con Alvis); "Pony Soldier" 1952 (Tim Neeley); "Arena" 1953 (Cal Jamison); "Devil's Canyon" 1953 (Man in Saloon); "Bitter Creek" 1954 (Dr. Prentiss); "Man Without a Star" 1955; "The First Traveling Saleslady" 1956 (Sam); "The Naked Gun" 1956; "The Naked Hills" 1956 (Counter Man); "The Storm Rider" 1957 (Emery); "Terror at Black Falls" 1962. ¶TV: *The Lone Ranger*—"Black Gold" 4-9-53, "El Toro" 5-7-53; *The Roy Rogers Show*—"Bad Company" 12-27-53 (Zeb Waller), "The Land Swindle" 3-14-54; *Fury*—"The Horse Coper" 10-29-55 (Sheriff), "Joey Goes Huting" 11-5-55 (Sheriff); *The Adventures of Rin Tin Tin*—"Rusty's Romance" 1-20-56 (Sam Russell); *Ford Theater*—"Sudden Silence" 10-10-56 (Deputy); *Circus Boy*—"Corky and the Circus

Doctor" 10-21-56 (Madden); *Tales of Wells Fargo*—"The Silver Bullets" 7-8-57 (Joe Kennelly); *Maverick*—"Stampede" 11-17-57 (Miner), "Maverick Springs" 12-6-59 (Bartender); *Wagon Train*—"The Riley Gratton Story" 12-4-57; *Northwest Passage*—"The Gunsmith" 9-28-58 (Jonas); *Wanted—Dead or Alive*—"Vanishing Act" 12-26-59, "The Twain Shall Meet" 10-19-60; *The Texan*—"Caballero" 4-13-59, "The Accuser" 6-6-60 (Clem Potter); *Bonanza*—"The Truckee Strip" 11-21-59, "Cut-Throat Junction" 3-18-61; *Man from Blackhawk*—"Execution Day" 3-4-60 (Carley Andrews); *Tate*—"Home Town" 6-8-60 (Carpenter); *Lawman*—"The Old War Horse" 10-9-60 (Man), "The Juror" 9-24-61 (Larkin); *Whispering Smith*—"Cross Cut" 7-31-61 (Gratch); *The Rifleman*—"The Tinhorn" 3-12-62; *The Virginian*—"The Mountain of the Sun" 4-17-63; *The Big Valley*—"The Haunted Gun" 2-6-67 (Blind Man).

Hayward, Lillian (1891-6/29/77). Films: "Heart of John Barlow" 1911; "In the Shadow of the Pines" 1911; "The God of Gold" 1912; "The Legend of the Lost Arrow" 1912; "Opitsah" 1912; "A Wild Ride" 1913; "The Wilderness Mail" 1914; "When California Was Wild" 1915; "The Hidden Children" 1917 (Mr. Rannock); "The Promise" 1917 (Mrs. Appleton).

Hayward, Louis (1909-2/21/85). Films: "The Christmas Kid" 1966-Span./Ital. (Mike Culligan); "Chuka" 1967 (Maj. Benson). ¶TV: *Riverboat*—"Payment in Full" 9-13-59 (Ash Cowan); *Rawhide*—"The Backshooter" 11-27-64 (John Tasker).

Hayward, Susan (1918-3/14/75). Films: "Canyon Passage" 1946 (Lucy Overmire); "Rawhide" 1951 (Vinnie Holt); "The Lusty Men" 1952 (Louise Merritt); "Garden of Evil" 1954 (Leah Fuller); "Thunder in the Sun" 1959 (Gabrielle Dauphin); "The Revengers" 1972-U.S./Mex. (Elizabeth).

Hayworth, Rita (Rita Cansino) (1918-5/14/87). Films: "Under the Pampas Moon" 1935 (Carmen); "Rebellion" 1936 (Paula Castillo); "Hit the Saddle" 1937 (Rita); "Old Louisiana" 1937 (Angela Gonzales); "Trouble in Texas" 1937 (Carmen Serrano); "Renegade Ranger" 1938 (Judith Alvarez); "They Came to Cordura" 1959 (Adelaide Geary); "The Wrath of God" 1972 (Senora De La Plata).

Hayworth, Vinton (1906-5/21/70). Films: "Mexican Spitfire Out West" 1940 (Brown). ¶TV: *Gun-smoke*—"Cooter" 5-19-56 (Sissle), "Blood Money" 9-28-57 (Harry Spener), "Trip West" 5-2-64 (Prof. Ramsay); *Zorro*—Regular 1958 (Magistrate Galindo); *Lawman*—"The Press" 11-29-59 (Oren Slauson), "The Lady Belle" 5-1-60 (Oren Slauson), "The Old War Horse" 10-9-60 (Oren Slauson), "Firehouse Lil" 1-8-61 (Oren Slauson), "Trapped" 9-17-61 (Oren Slauson), "The Catalog Woman" 11-5-61 (Oren Slauson), "A Friend o the Family" 1-14-62 (Oren Slauson), "The Barber" 2-25-62 (Oren Slauson), "Get Out of Town" 5-20-62 (Oren Slauson); *Laramie*—"Day of Vengeance" 1-19-60 (Joshua Meeker), "Man from Kansas" 1-10-61 (Carter Simpson), "Deadly Is the Night" 11-7-61 (Mr. Thomas), "Broken Honor" 4-9-63 (Art Potter); *Tales of Wells Fargo*—"Moneyrun" 1-6-62 (Travers); *The Dakotas*—"A Nice Girl from Goliah" 5-13-63 (Doc Holderman); *Laredo*—"Oh Careless Love" 12-23-66; *Pistols 'n' Petticoats*—2-25-67 (Doc Fenmore); *The Big Valley*—"The Good Thieves" 1-1-68 (Doc Landrum).

Haze, Jonathan (1935-). Films: "Apache Woman" 1955 (Tom Chandler); "Five Guns West" 1955 (Billy Candy); "Gunslinger" 1956 (Jack Hays); "The Oklahoma Woman" 1956. ¶TV: *Cimarron City*—"Terror Town" 10-18-58 (Jim Budinger).

Hazel, George. Films: "Circle Canyon" 1934 (Tom); "Lightning Bill" 1934 (Henchman); "The Unconquered Bandit" 1935.

Hazelton, Joseph (1853-10/8/36). Films: "The White Man's Courage" 1919 (Pedro); "Cyclone Smith's Vow" 1921; "If Only Jim" 1921 (Bill Bones); "In the Days of Buffalo Bill" 1922-serial (Gideon Wells).

Hazelton, Marie. Films: "The Plow Woman" 1917 (Ruth MacTavish).

Hazlett, William "Bill". *see* Many Treaties, Chief.

Headley, Josephine. Films: "The Desert Man" 1917 (Katy).

Headly, Glenne. Films: "Lonesome Dove" TVM-1989 (Elmira).

Headrick, Richard. Films: "The Testing Block" 1920 (Sonny); "The Toll Gate" 1920 (the Little Fellow); "The Spider and the Rose" 1923 (Don Marcello as a Child); "The Silent Stranger" 1924 (Laddie Warner).

Healey, Michael. TV: *Wyatt Earp*—"Shoot to Kill" 10-8-57 (Tom McAlester); *Colt .45*—"One Good Turn" 11-29-57 (Becker).

Healey, Myron (1922-). Films: "The Man from Colorado" 1948 (Powers); "Across the Rio Grande" 1949 (Kane); "Brand of Fear" 1949; "The Girl from Gunsight" 1949-short; "Gun Law Justice" 1949; "Haunted Trails" 1949 (Lasser); "Hidden Danger" 1949 (Carson); "Laramie" 1949 (Lt. Reed); "Lawless Code" 1949; "Pioneer Marshal" 1949 (Larry Forester); "Range Justice" 1949 (Dade); "Riders of the Dusk" 1949 (Sheriff); "South of Rio" 1949 (Travis); "Trail's End" 1949 (Drake); "Western Renegades" 1949 (Gus); "Fence Riders" 1950; "I Killed Geronimo" 1950 (Frank); "Law of the Panhandle" 1950 (Henry Faulkner); "Outlaw Gold" 1950 (Sonny Lang); "Over the Border" 1950 (Jeff Grant); "Roar of the Iron Horse" 1950-serial (Ace); "Salt Lake Raiders" 1950 (Fred Mason); "Short Grass" 1950 (Les); "Trail of the Rustlers" 1950; "West of Wyoming" 1950 (Brody); "Bonanza Town" 1951 (Krag Boseman); "Colorado Ambush" 1951 (Chet Murdock); "The Longhorn" 1951 (Andy); "Montana Desperado" 1951 (Ron Logan); "Night Riders of Montana" 1951 (Steve Bauer); "Silver City" 1951 (Bleek); "Slaughter Trail" 1951 (Heath); "The Texas Rangers" 1951 (Capt. June Peak); "Apache War Smoke" 1952 (Pike Curtis); "Desperadoes' Outpost" 1952 (Lt. Dan Boylan); "Fargo" 1952; "Fort Osage" 1952 (Martin); "The Kid from Broken Gun" 1952 (Sheriff); "The Maverick" 1952 (Sergeant Frick); "Montana Territory" 1952 (Bill Landers); "Rodeo" 1952 (Richard Durston); "The Fighting Lawman" 1953; "Kansas Pacific" 1953 (Morey); "The Moonlighter" 1953; "Saginaw Trail" 1953 (Miller Webb); "Son of Belle Star" 1953 (Sheriff); "Texas Bad Man" 1953 (Jackson); "Vigilante Terror" 1953; "Cattle Queen of Montana" 1954 (Hank); "Rails into Laramie" 1954 (Con Winton); "Silver Lode" 1954 (Rider); "Count Three and Pray" 1955 (Floyd Miller); "The Man from Bitter Ridge" 1955 (Clem Jackman); "Man Without a Star" 1955 (Mogollon); "Rage at Dawn" 1955 (John Reno); "Tennessee's Partner" 1955 (Reynolds); "Dig That Uranium" 1956 (Joe Hody); "Running Target" 1956 (Kaygo); "The White Squaw" 1956 (Eric Swanson); "The Young Guns" 1956 (Deputy Nix); "The Hard Man" 1957 (Ray Hendry); "Hell's Crossroads" 1957 (Cole Younger); "The Restless Breed" 1957 (Sheriff William); "Shoot-Out at Medicine Bend" 1957 (Sanders); "Apache Territory" 1958 (Webb);

"Cole Younger, Gunfighter" 1958 (Bennett Twins); "Escape from Red Rock" 1958 (Joe Skinner); "Quantrill's Raiders" 1958 (Jarrett); "The Gunfight at Dodge City" 1959 (Forbes); "Rio Bravo" 1959 (Burdette Henchman in Saloon); "Cavalry Command" 1963-U.S./Phil. (Lt. Worth); "He Rides Tall" 1964 (2nd Sheriff); "Journey to Shiloh" 1968 (Sheriff Briggs); "True Grit" 1969 (Deputy); "The Cheyenne Social Club" 1970 (Deuter); "Smoke in the Wind" 1975 (Mort). ¶TV: *The Lone Ranger*—"Dead Man's Chest" 9-28-50, "The Condemned Man" 12-11-52, "Gold Town" 10-7-54, "Journey to San Carlos" 5-9-57, "Blind Witness" 5-30-57; *The Cisco Kid*—"Postal Inspector" 8-4-51, "Kid Sister Trouble" 9-15-51, "Mad About Money" 3-22-52, "The Fugitive" 11-1-52, "Pot of Gold" 4-25-53; *The Gene Autry Show*—"Outlaw Escape" 12-1-51, "The Return of Maverick Dan" 12-15-51, "Bullets and Bows" 3-2-52, "The Sheriff Is a Lady" 3-23-52, "The Old Prospector" 8-4-53, "Gypsy Woman" 8-25-53, "Cold Decked" 9-15-53, "Rio Renegades" 9-29-53, "Santa Fe Raiders" 7-6-54, "Outlaw Warning" 10-2-54, "Stage to San Dimas" 10-8-55, "Law Comes to Scorpion" 10-22-55, "Guns Below the Border" 11-5-55, "Feuding Friends" 11-26-55; *The Range Rider*—"Feud at Friendship City" 3-1-52, "The Border City Affair" 4-26-52; *The Roy Rogers Show*—"Outlaw's Return" 9-28-52 (Gil Murray), "Huntin' for Trouble" 10-5-52 (Ken Pierce), "The Long Chance" 5-24-53, "Pat's Inheritance" 11-11-53 (Mack Johnson), "M Stands for Murder" 12-6-53, "The Secret of Indian Gap" 1-24-54 (Mace), "The Deputy Sheriff" 2-7-54 (Deputy Morgan), "The High-Graders of Paradise Valley" 2-28-54 (John Baldwin), "Uncle Steve's Finish" 2-3-55 (Steve Everett), "And Sudden Death" 10-9-55; *The Adventures of Rin Tin Tin*—"The Babe in the Woods" 2-11-55, "Rin Tin Tin Meets Shakespeare" 9-16-55, "Rin Tin Tin and the Rainmaker" 3-30-56 (Morrel); *Stories of the Century*—"The Dalton Gang" 5-20-55; *Cheyenne*—"Border Showdown" 11-22-55 (Thompson), "The Dark Rider" 9-11-56 (Lew Lattimer), "Devil's Canyon" 11-19-57 (Chip Claney), "The Return of Mr. Grimm" 2-13-61 (Wesley Mason), "The Frightened Town" 3-20-61 (Tully); *Tales of the Texas Rangers*—"Hail to the Rangers" 12-17-55 (Monte); *Judge Roy Bean*—"Checkmate" 1-1-56 (Reno), "The Eyes of Texas" 1-1-56 (Winters), "The

Katcina Doll" 1-1-56 (Hurley), "The Travelers" 1-1-56 (Gorman); *Wyatt Earp*—"Clay Allison" 9-25-56 (Clay Allison), Regular 1958-59 (Doc Holliday); *Annie Oakley*—"Dude's Decision" 2-10-57 (Link); *You Are There*—"The End of the Dalton Gang" 5-12-57 (Broadwell); *Jim Bowie*—"Hare and Tortoise" 11-22-57 (Brian Turner); *Tombstone Territory*—"Johnny Ringo's Last Ride" 2-19-58 (Johnny Ringo), "Whipsaw" 3-13-59 (Dempsey); *Colt .45*—"The Deserters" 3-28-58 (Fur Trader); *Maverick*—"Seed of Deception" 4-13-58 (Ross Aikens), "Trooper Maverick" 11-29-59 (Benedict), "The Golden Fleecing" 10-8-61 (Frank Mercer); *Sugarfoot*—"Short Range" 5-13-58 (Claude Miles), "MacBrewster the Bold" 10-13-59 (Ben Cadigan); *Wagon Train*—"The Rex Montana Story" 5-28-58 (Bill), "The Clara Duncan Story" 4-22-59 (Steve Wilson), "The Traitor" 12-13-61 (Sergeant Oakes), "The Levi Hale Story" 4-18-62 (Deputy), "The Tom O'Neal Story" 4-24-63 (Mr. O'Neal), "The Molly Kincaid Story" 9-16-63 (Doc Curley), "The Andrew Elliott Story" 2-10-64, "The Last Circle Up" 4-27-64; *Zane Grey Theater*—"Utopia, Wyoming" 6-6-58 (Cliff Merson), "Seed of Evil" 4-7-60 (Sam Brady); *Buckskin*—"The Trial of Chrissy Miller" 7-31-58 (Ed Miller); *26 Men*—"Judge Not" 11-25-58 (Branch Ford); *Tales of Wells Fargo*—"Showdown Trail" 1-5-59 (Pat Dooley), "The Bride and the Bandit" 12-12-60 (Tip Rollins); *Bronco*—"The Baron of Broken Lance" 1-13-59 (Mitch Krass), "Night Train to Denver" 12-29-59 (Matt Larker); *Rawhide*—"Incident at Alabaster Plain" 1-16-59 (Gun Guard), "Incident of the Calico Gun" 4-24-59 (Jeb), "Incident of the Big Blowout" 2-10-61 (Lou Calvert); *Cimarron City*—"Runaway Train" 1-31-59 (Clayton Buckley); *The Texan*—"Badlands" 5-11-59 (Sheriff), "The Governor's Lady" 3-14-60, "Johnny Tuvo" 5-30-60 (Galt Gaylor); *Bat Masterson*—"Lottery of Death" 5-13-59 (Jack Latigo), "To the Manner Born" 10-1-59 (Col. Marc James); *Zorro*—"The Captain Regrets" 5-28-59 (Don Gabriele Luna); *Riverboat*—"Path of an Eagle" 2-1-60 (Steven Barrows).*The Alaskans*—"Odd Man Hangs" 4-17-60 (Fred Simmons); *Laramie*—"Three Roads West" 10-4-60 (Frank Skinner), "Handful of Fire" 12-5-61, "The Dynamiters" 3-6-62, "Beyond Justice" 11-27-62, "The Unvanquished" 3-12-63; *The Deputy*—"The Jason Harris Story" 10-8-60 (Johnny Dustin); *Death Valley*

Days—"The Madstone" 1-18-61 (Big Matt Denby); *The Rebel*—"The Pit" 3-12-61 (McGowan); *Whispering Smith*—"Double Edge" 8-7-61 (Jim Conley); *The Outlaws*—"The Bitter Swede" 1-18-62 (Kirby), "Farewell Performance" 3-15-62 (Duke Jones); *Gunsmoke*—"The Summons" 4-21-62 (Moseley), "Quint Asper Comes Home" 9-29-62 (Mike); *The Virginian*—"The Final Hour" 5-1-63 (Martin Croft), "Siege" 12-18-63 (Yance Cooper), "You Take the High Road" 2-17-65 (Slauson), "Ride a Cock-Horse to Laramie Cross" 2-23-66 (Lomax), "A Bad Place to Die" 11-8-67 (Potts); *The Dakotas*—"Sanctuary at Crystal Springs" 5-6-63 (Sheriff); *Destry*—"Stormy Is a Lady" 3-6-64 (Sam Bender); *Bonanza*—"The Saga of Squaw Charlie" 12-27-64 (Buck), "The Wormwood Cup" 4-23-67 (Sam), "The Thirteenth Man" 1-21-68 (Johannsen), "The Price of Salt" 2-4-68 (Williams); *Laredo*—"Which Way Did They Go?" 11-18-65 (Bolt), "Above the Law" 1-13-66 (Frank Garrett), "The Dance of the Laughing Death" 9-23-66 (John Garth), "Split the Difference" 4-7-67 (Jake); *Daniel Boone*—"The First Beau" 12-9-65 (Mike Kravic), "Run a Crooked Mile" 10-20-66 (Lynch); *A Man Called Shenandoah*—"The Young Outlaw" 12-27-65 (Colt); *The Road West*—"The Insider" 2-13-67 (Big Foot); *The Guns of Will Sonnett*—"The Natural Way" 9-29-67, "A Difference of Opinion" 11-15-68 (Sheriff Flagg); *The High Chaparral*—"Shadows on the Land" 10-15-67 (Major Corbett), "A Man to Match the Land" 3-12-71; *Iron Horse*—"The Return of Hode Avery" 11-4-67 (Clay Hennings); *The Men from Shiloh*—"Jenny" 9-30-70; *Kung Fu*—"The Soldier" 11-29-73 (Capt. Malachy); *The Cowboys*—4-3-74 (Army Captain).

Heard, Charles MacDonald. Films: "Hidden Guns" 1956; "The Young Land" 1959. ¶TV: *The Roy Rogers Show*—"The Train Robbery" 2-3-52; *Death Valley Days*—"Two Bits" 5-5-56 (Col. Downey); *Bat Masterson*—"Trail Pirate" 12-31-58 (Vail); *The Rebel*—"The Threat" 2-12-61 (Gillette).

Hearn, Edward (Guy Edward Hearn) (1888-4/15/63). Films: "The Lost Express" 1917-serial; "Man from Tiajuana" 1917; "The Secret of Lost Valley" 1917; "Lawless Love" 1918 (Freddie Montgomery); "The Light of Western Stars" 1918 (Al Hammond); "Jacques of the Silver North" 1919 (Warren Sherman); "The Last of His People" 1919 (Reynard Lacey);

"The Coast of Opportunity" 1920 (Tommy DeBoer); "The Avenging Arrow" 1921-serial; "Beyond the Trail" 1921; "The Miracle Baby" 1923 (Hal Norton); "When a Man's a Man" 1924 (Stanford Manning); "Daring Days" 1925 (Catamount Carson); "The Outlaw's Daughter" 1925 (Jim King); "Jim Hood's Ghost" 1926; "The Desert Pirate" 1927 (Norton); "A Hero on Horseback" 1927; "Pals in Peril" 1927 (Blackie Burns); "Winners of the Wilderness" 1927 (George Washington); "The Big Hop" 1928 (Pilot); "The Fightin' Redhead" 1928 (Jim Dalton); "The Yellow Cameo" 1928-serial; "The One Man Dog" 1929 (Pierre); "The Spoilers" 1930 (Lieutenant); "The Avenger" 1931 (Captain Lake); "Clearing the Range" 1931 (Jim Fremont); "The Painted Desert" 1931 (Tex); "Son of the Plains" 1931 (Dan Farrell); "The Vanishing Legion" 1931-serial (Jed Williams); "The Cheyenne Cyclone" 1932; "The Last of the Mohicans" 1932-serial; "Local Bad Man" 1932 (Ben Murdock); "Rainbow Trail" 1932 (Jim Lassiter); "Texas Tornado" 1932 (Fanner Kirby); "Fighting with Kit Carson" 1933-serial; "Fighting Hero" 1934 (Bart Hawley); "Fighting Through" 1934 (Lenihan); "In Old Santa Fe" 1934 (Villain); "Mystery Mountain" 1934-serial (Lake); "Tumbling Tumbleweeds" 1935 (Craven); "Westward Ho" 1935; "Avenging Waters" 1936 (Jim); "Boss Rider of Gun Creek" 1936; "The Cattle Thief" 1936; "Code of the Range" 1935 (Wade); "The Miracle Rider" 1935-serial (Janes); "King of the Pecos" 1936 (Eli Jackson); "The Lawless Nineties" 1936; "The Mysterious Avenger" 1936; "Red River Valley" 1936 (Sheriff); "The Unknown Ranger" 1936; "The Big Show" 1937; "The Old Wyoming Trail" 1937 (Hammond); "Springtime in the Rockies" 1937 (Thorpe); "Westbound Mail" 1937 (Collins); "West of Santa Fe" 1938 (Crane); "Stand Up and Fight" 1939 (Joe); "Texas Stampede" 1939 (Owens); "Western Caravans" 1939 (Murdock); "Adventures of Red Ryder" 1940-serial (Lang); "Covered Wagon Days" 1940; "Covered Wagon Trails" 1940; "The Dark Command" 1940 (Juror); "Deadwood Dick" 1940-serial; "The Man from Dakota" 1940 (Captain); "My Little Chickadee" 1940 (Barfly); "Santa Fe Trail" 1940 (Guard); "White Eagle" 1941-serial; "Pistol Harvest" 1951 (Terry); "Sugarfoot" 1951; "The Man Behind the Gun" 1952; "Road Agent" 1952 (Sheriff); "Springfield Rifle" 1952

(Calhoun); "Conquest of Cochise" 1953 (General Gadsden); "Tall Man Riding" 1955.

Hearn, Sam (1889-10/28/64). Films: "Once Upon a Horse" 1958 (Justice of the Peace). ¶TV: *Wanted—Dead or Alive*—"Surprise Witness" 11-2-60.

Heath, Ariel. Films: "Black Hills Express" 1943 (Gale Southern); "A Lady Takes a Chance" 1943 (Flossie).

Heath, Dody (1928-). TV: *Colt .45*—"Calamity" 12-13-59 (Calamity Jane); *Lawman*—"The Hardcase" 1-31-60 (Beth Denning); *Overland Trail*—"Westbound Stage" 3-6-60 (Martha Cabel); *Riverboat*—"The Water of Gorgeous Springs" 11-7-60 (Lovie Jennings); *Stagecoach West*—"The Butcher" 3-28-61 (Linda Barton).

Heather, Jean. Films: "The Last Round-Up" 1947 (Carol); "Red Stallion in the Rockies" 1949 (Cindy Smith).

Heatherton, Joey (1944-). TV: *The Virginian*—"A Distant Fury" 3-20-63 (Gloria Blaine).

Heaton, Tom. Films: "Bandolero!" 1968 (Joe Chaney); "Monte Walsh" 1970 (Sugar Wyman); "Call of the Wild" TVM-1993. ¶TV: *Iron Horse*—"Gallows for Bill Pardew" 9-30-67 (Billy Pardew); *Death Valley Days*—"The Informer Who Cried" 11-11-67 (Billy the Kid).

Heazlitt, Eve. *see* McKenzie, Eva.

Hebert, H.J. *see* Herbert, Henry J.

Hecht, Jenny (1943-3/25/71). TV: *Wagon Train*—"The Mary Ellen Thomas Story" 12-24-58 (Sally Mayhew).

Hecht, Ted (1908-6/24/69). Films: "Riding the California Trail" 1947; "Apache Chief" 1949 (Pani); "Bad Men of Tombstone" 1949; "The Wolf Hunters" 1949 (Muskoka).

Heck, Stanton (1877-12/16/29). Films: "Firebrand Trevison" 1920 (Jefferson Corrigan); "Forbidden Trails" 1920 (William Carrington); "The Rose of Nome" 1920 (Bill Carnon); "The Bad Man" 1923 (Jasper Hardy); "The Lone Star Ranger" 1923 (Poggin); "Man's Size" 1923 (Bully West); "One Law for the Woman" 1924 (Brennan); "Silent Sanderson" 1925 (Silver Smith); "Soft Shoes" 1925 (Bradley); "Driftin' Thru" 1926 (Bull Dunn); "The Gentle Cyclone" 1926 (Wilkes Senior); "Rustlers' Ranch" 1926 (Bull Dozier); "The Branded Sombrero" 1928 (Honest John Hallett).

Heckart, Eileen (1919-). Films: "Heller in Pink Tights" 1960 (Lorna Hathaway); "Zandy's Bride" 1974 (Ma Allen). ¶TV: *Gunsmoke*—"The Lady" 3-27-65 (Hattie Silks), "The Innocent" 11-24-69 (Athena Royce).

Hector, Jay. TV: *Bonanza*—"The Sun Mountain Herd" 9-19-59 (Harold Harris); *Gunsmoke*—"Friend's Pay-Off" 9-3-60 (Boy).

Hector, Kim Kristofer. TV: *Rawhide*—"Incident at Red River Station" 1-15-60; *Laramie*—"A Sound of Bells" 12-27-60 (Neil Hunter); *Laredo*—"Rendezvous at Arillo" 10-7-65 (Wilbur); *The Road West*—"Power of Fear" 12-26-66 (Jamie).

Hedaya, Dan. Films: "Four Eyes and Six-Guns" TVM-1992 (Lester Doom); "Maverick" 1994 (Twitchy).

Hedison, David (1929-). Films: "The Gambler, Part II—The Adventure Continues" TVM-1983 (Garson).

Hedlund, Guy (1884-12/29/64). Films: "Last of the Redmen" 1947 (Gen. Munro).

Heffley, Wayne (1927-). TV: *Have Gun Will Travel*—"The Hanging Cross" 12-21-57, "Deliver the Body" 5-24-58 (Son); *Tombstone Territory*—"The Rebels' Last Charge" 1-15-58; *Rough Riders*—"Deadfall" 5-21-59; *Colt .45*—"Amnesty" 5-24-59 (Pat Garrett); *Wanted—Dead or Alive*—"The Partners" 2-6-60; *Hotel De Paree*—"Hard Luck for Sundance" 2-19-60, "Sundance and the Man in the Shadows" 4-15-60 (Jim); *The Virginian*—"It Tolls for Thee" 11-21-62; *Empire*—"Echo of a Man" 12-11-62 (Christy); *Gunsmoke*—"Old Comrade" 12-29-62 (Lem); *Bonanza*—"Home from the Sea" 5-1-66 (Andy), "The Twenty-Sixth Grave" 10-31-72 (Bert); *Wild Wild West*—"The Night of the Iron Fist" 12-8-67 (Deputy); *Lancer*—"The Fix-It Man" 2-11-69; *Nichols*—"The Siege" 9-23-71, "Peanuts and Crackerjacks" 11-4-71 (Major Duncan); *Kung Fu*—"The Soldier" 11-29-73 (Reede).

Heflin, Van (1910-7/23/71). Films: "The Outcasts of Poker Flat" 1937 (Rev. Samuel Woods); "Santa Fe Trail" 1940 (Rader); "Tomahawk" 1951 (Jim Bridger); "Shane" 1953 (Joe Starrett); "Wings of the Hawk" 1953 (Irish Gallagher); "Count Three and Pray" 1955 (Luke Fargo); "3:10 to Yuma" 1957 (Dan Evans); "Gunman's Walk" 1958 (Lee Hackett); "They Came to Cordura" 1959 (Sgt. John Chawk); "Stagecoach" 1966 (Curly); "The Ruthless Four" 1968-Ital./Ger. (Sam Cooper).

Heggie, O.P. (1876-2/7/36). Films: "The Bad Man" 1930 (Henry Taylor).

Heigh, Helen (1905-12/20/91). TV: *The Adventures of Rin Tin Tin*—"Pritikin's Predicament" 2-21-58 (Abigail), "The Failure" 5-8-59 (Emma Crabtree); *Wyatt Earp*—"Love and Shotgun Gibbs" 4-21-59 (Mrs. Denton).

Heim, Edward. Films: "The Lone Rider" 1922 (Jud Harrison); "Lightning Bill" 1926 (John R. Denton); "Gun-Hand Garrison" 1927; "Wild Born" 1927.

Heimel, Otto "Coco". Films: "Songs and Saddles" 1938 (Porky); "My Little Chickadee" 1940 (Coco).

Heitgert, Don. TV: *The Deputy*—"The Challenger" 2-25-61 (Dan), "The Means and the End" 3-18-61 (Hotel Clerk), "The Example" 3-25-61 (Dan); *Laramie*—"Wolf Cub" 11-21-61.

Held, Karl (1931-). TV: *The Rebel*—"The Found" 6-4-61 (Danny); *The Dakotas*—"Justice at Eagle's Nest" 3-11-63 (Emil Lang); *The Big Valley*—"The Murdered Party" 11-17-65.

Heller, Barbara (1931-). Films: "Lone Texan" 1959 (Amy Todd).

Heller, Gloria. Films: "Galloping Jinx" 1925 (Madge Walling).

Hellman, Les. TV: *Bat Masterson*—"A Noose Fits Anybody" 11-19-58 (Ray Clinton), "Mr. Fourpaws" 2-18-60, "Dakota Showdown" 11-17-60 (Gus Dakota), "The Fatal Garment" 5-25-61 (Outlaw); *Rawhide*—"Incident of the Running Man" 5-5-61; *Maverick*—"Epitaph of a Gambler" 2-11-62 (Whitey).

Hellstrom, Gunnar. TV: *Empire*—"Burnout" 3-19-63 (Chris Norden); *Gunsmoke*—"Deadman's Law" 1-8-66 (Eriksson).

Helm, Anne (1938-). TV: *Tales of Wells Fargo*—"The Killing of Johnny Lash" 11-21-60 (Nell); *Gunsmoke*—"Bad Seed" 2-4-61 (Trudy Trent), "One Killer on Ice" 1-23-65 (Helena Dales); *Rawhide*—"Incident Near Gloomy River" 3-17-61 (Flora Travis), "Inside Man" 11-3-61 (Sheila Brewster); *Gunslinger*—"The New Savannah Story" 5-18-61 (Ruth St. Clair); *Bronco*—"Cousin from Atlanta" 10-16-61 (Amanda Layne); *Wagon Train*—"The Dick Pederson Story" 1-10-62 (Janey Cutler), "Heather and Hamish" 4-10-63 (Heather), "The Story of Cain" 12-16-63 (Ruth); *Frontier Circus*—"Mr. Grady Regrets" 1-25-62 (Rosa Blanchard); *Death Valley Days*—"Girl with a Gun" 6-6-62 (Jenny); *Wide Coun-try*—"The Girl in the Sunshine Smile" 11-15-62 (Jenny Callan); *Laramie*—"Protective Custody" 1-15-63; *Empire*—"The Convention" 5-14-63 (Joanie); *Temple Houston*—"The Third Bullet" 10-24-63 (Francie); *The Virginian*—"Ryker" 9-16-64 (Jane Hale), "Journey to Scathelock" 12-10-69 (Karen); *Daniel Boone*—"The Courtship of Jericho Jones" 4-19-65 (Sumah); *The Big Valley*—"Heritage" 10-20-65 (Bridey), "The Devil's Masquerade" 3-4-68 (Nancy); *Bonanza*—"The Meredith Smith" 10-31-65 (Meredith Smith), "Pride of a Man" 6-2-68 (Abigail Pettigrew); *A Man Called Shenandoah*—"Muted Fifes, Muffled Drums" 2-28-66 (Christie Dudley).

Helm, Frances. Films: "Revolt at Fort Laramie" 1957 (Melissa Bradner). ¶TV: *The Deputy*—"Spoken in Silence" 4-29-61 (Laura Rogers); *Gunsmoke*—"All That" 10-28-61 (Clara Shanks).

Helm, Peter. TV: *Wagon Train*—"The Daniel Clay Story" 2-21-62 (Ethan Clay), "The Wagon Train Mutiny" 9-19-62 (Leland), "The Tom O'Neal Story" 4-24-63 (Tom O'Neal); *Tales of Wells Fargo*—"To Kill a Town" 3-21-62 (Jason Moore); *Stoney Burke*—"A Girl Named Amy" 4-29-63 (Todd); *Rawhide*—"Incident at Paradise" 10-24-63 (Grover); *Bonanza*—"Devil on Her Shoulder" 10-17-65 (Gwylem); *The Legend of Jesse James*—"The Cave" 2-7-66 (Zeb Hicks).

Helmond, Katherine (1934-). Films: "Wanted: The Sundance Woman" TVM-1976 (Mattie Riley). ¶TV: *Gunsmoke*—"Spratt" 10-2-72 (Ena Spratt).

Helmore, Tom (1904-9/12/95). TV: *Have Gun Will Travel*—"The Englishman" 12-7-57 (James Brunswick).

Helton, Jo. TV: *Gunsmoke*—"Tell Chester" 4-20-63 (Wendy Stringer).

Helton, Percy (1894-9/11/71). Films: "Lust for Gold" 1949 (Barber); "Copper Canyon" 1950 (Scamper); "Fancy Pants" 1950 (Maj. Fogarty); "Under Mexicali Stars" 1950 (Nap Wellington); "Ambush at Tomahawk Gap" 1953 (Marlowe); "Down Laredo Way" 1953 (Judge Sully); "Ride, Vaquero!" 1953 (Storekeeper); "Fury at Gunsight Pass" 1956 (Boggs); "The Phantom Stagecoach" 1957 (Mr. Wiggins); "Ride the High Country" 1962; "Four for Texas" 1964 (Ansel); "The Sons of Katie Elder" 1965 (Storekeeper Peevey); "Butch Cassidy and the Sundance Kid" 1969 (Sweet Face). ¶TV: *Death Valley Days*—"Lit-tle Oscar's Millions" 3-11-53, "The Hangman Waits" 1-2-56, "Big Liz" 5-26-57; *Stories of the Century*—"Last Stagecoach West" 1954 (Telegraph Operator); *Circus Boy*—"The Good Samaritans" 12-23-56 (Toomis Flager); *The Adventures of Rin Tin Tin*—"Higgins' Last Stand" 1-4-57 (Conductor), "Wind-Wagon Mc-Clanahan" 4-4-58 (Ichabod Pillijohn), "Pillajohn's Progress" 3-6-59 (Ichabod Pillijohn); *Maverick*—"Comstock Conspiracy" 12-29-57 (Mr. Vincent), "Bolt from the Blue" 11-27-60 (Bradley); *Jim Bowie*—"The Close Shave" 1-10-58 (Editor Asbury); *Bonanza*—"Enter Mark Twain" 10-10-59 (Blurry Jones), "The Hayburner" 2-17-63 (Lafe), "The Legacy" 12-15-63, "The Unseen Wound" 1-29-67 (Bleeker); *Man from Blackhawk*—"The Gypsy Story" 11-6-59 (Constable Critton); *Lawman*—"Shadow Witness" 11-15-59 (Oren); *Gunsmoke*—"Thick 'n' Thin" 12-26-59 (Otie Perkins), "The Summons" 4-21-62 (Old Duffer), "Trip West" 5-2-64 (Arbuckle), "The Raid" 1-22-66 & 1-29-66 (Mr. Early); *Wanted-Dead or Alive*—"Tolliver Bender" 2-13-60; *The Law of the Plainsman*—"Dangerous Barriers" 3-10-60; *The Texan*—"The Guilty and the Innocent" 3-28-60; *Colt .45*—"Martial Law" 5-17-60 (Wes Mason); *Sugarfoot*—"Angel" 3-6-61 (McTavish); *Rawhide*—"Incident of the Wager on Payday" 6-16-61 (Bartender); *Laramie*—"Siege at Jubilee" 10-10-61 (Frazer), "The Renegade Brand" 2-26-63; *The Dakotas*—"Crisis at High Banjo" 2-11-63 (Doctor); *Daniel Boone*—"Grizzly" 10-6-66 (Stubbs), "The Scrimshaw Ivory Chart" 1-4-68 (Jud); *Bob Hope Chrysler Theatre*—"The Reason Nobody Hardly Ever Seen a Fat Outlaw in the Old West Is as Follows:" 3-8-67 (Old Man); *Cimarron Strip*—"The Legend of Jud Starr" 9-14-67; *The Virginian*—"Execution at Triste" 12-13-67; *Wild Wild West*—"The Night of Miguelito's Revenge" 12-13-68 (Newspaper Salesman); *The Guns of Will Sonnett*—"Jim Sonnett's Lady" 2-21-69 (Bartender).

Heming, Violet (1895-7/4/81). Films: "The Danger Trail" 1917 (Meleese Thoreau).

Hemingway, Mariel (1961-). Films: "Sunset" 1988 (Cheryl King); "Into the Badlands" TVM-1991 (Alma Heusser).

Hemmings, David (1941-). Films: "Calamity Jane" TVM-1984 (Capt. James O'Neill); "Davy Crockett: Rainbow in the Thunder" TVM-1988 (Older Andrew Jackson).

Hemphill, Ray. TV: *Bonanza*—"The Hanging Posse" 11-28-59 (Buck), "The Mission" 9-17-60 (Johnson), "The Lonely House" 10-15-61, "King of the Mountain" 2-23-64, "Love Me Not" 3-1-64, "The Reluctant Rebel" 11-21-65 (Shale); *Gunsmoke*—"Hammerhead" 12-26-64 (Gambler).

Henabery, Joseph (1887-2/18/76). Films: "The Huron Converts" 1915; "The Race War" 1915.

Henderson, A.C. Films: "Arizona Gunfighter" 1937 (Governor Gray).

Henderson, Bill (1930-). Films: "City Slickers" 1991 (Ben Jessup); "Maverick" 1994 (Riverboat Poker Player).

Henderson, Chuck. TV: *Wagon Train*—"The Jenny Tannen Story" 6-24-59 (John Barclay); *The Texan*—"Traildust" 10-19-59 (Jim Hasty Fox).

Henderson, Dell (1883-12/2/56). Films: "Over Silent Paths" 1910; "The Tenderfoot's Triumph" 1910; "That Chink at Golden Gulch" 1910; "Unexpected Help" 1910; "Fighting Blood" 1911; "In the Days of '49" 1911; "The Last Drop of Water" 1911; "The Battle at Elderbrush Gulch" 1913; "The Lone Cowboy" 1934 (Mr. Burton); "Ruggles of Red Gap" 1935 (Sam); "The Texas Rangers" 1936 (Citizen); "High, Wide and Handsome" 1937 (Bank President); "Wells Fargo" 1937 (Customer); "Frontier Marshal" 1939 (Bella Union Cafe Proprietor).

Henderson, Douglas (1919-4/5/78). Films: "The Dalton Girls" 1957 (Bank Cashier). ¶TV: *Death Valley Days*—"To Big Charlie from Little Charlie" 1-3-55; *Sergeant Preston of the Yukon*—"Fancy Dan" 4-5-56 (Dirk), "Golden Gift" 6-14-56 (Purdy), "Girl from Vancouver" 6-28-56 (Smitty), "Return Visit" 11-22-56 (Harry Evans); *Rough Riders*—"Forty-Five Calibre Law" 5-14-59 (Doc Gorman); *The Virginian*—"Farewell to Honesty" 3-24-65 (Leonard Walters), "That Saunders Woman" 3-30-66 (Jenkins), "Stopover" 1-8-69 (Ben Cooper); *Bonanza*—"Five Sundowns to Sunup" 12-5-65 (the Rev. Mr. Holmes), "The Unseen Wound" 1-29-67 (Dr. Evens), "The Gentle Ones" 10-29-67 (Major Dawson); *Daniel Boone*—"The Loser's Race" 11-10-66 (Gerald Ainsley); *Wild Wild West*—"The Night of the Skulls" 12-16-66 (Col. Richmond), "The Night of the Falcon" 11-10-67 (Col. Richamond), "The Night of the Turncoat" 12-1-67 (Col. Richmond), "The Night of the

Underground Terror" 1-19-68 (Col. Richmond), "The Night of the Death Masks" 1-26-68 (Col. Richmond), "The Night of Miguelito's Revenge" 12-13-68 (Col. Richmond), "The Night of the Sabatini Death" 2-2-69 (Col. Richmond), "The Night of the Diva" 3-7-69 (Col. Richmond), "The Night of the Plague" 4-4-69 (Col Richmond).

Henderson, Jack (1878-1/1/57). Films: "The Mystery Box" 1925-serial; "Lightning Bill" 1926 (Edward G. Hookem); "Thunderbolt's Tracks" 1927 (Pop Hayden); "Taking a Chance" 1928 (Jake); "Tracked" 1928 (the Rustler); "Headin' North" 1930 (Drunk); "The Ridin' Fool" 1931 (Col. Butterfield); "Tall Man Riding" 1955; "Westbound" 1959.

Henderson, Kelo. Films: "Pyramid of the Sun God" 1965-Ger./Ital./Fr. ¶TV: *26 Men*—Regular 1958-59 (Ranger Clint Travis).

Henderson, Lars. Films: "Last Train from Gun Hill" 1959 (Petey Morgan). ¶TV: *The Restless Gun*—"Thicker Than Water" 12-9-57 (Ted Marlow); *Fury*—"An Old Indian Trick" 2-14-59 (Ronnawa).

Henderson, Marcia (1929-11/30/87). Films: "Back to God's Country" 1953 (Dolores Keith); "Canyon River" 1956 (Janet Hale); "The Naked Hills" 1956 (Julie); "Natchez Trace" 1960 (Ruth Henning). ¶TV: *Colt .45*—"Point of Honor" 3-21-58 (Dr. Lee Taylor); *Tales of Wells Fargo*—"The Reward" 4-21-58 (June); *Bat Masterson*—"Two Graves for Swan Valley" 10-15-58 (Molly Doyle), "The Inner Circle" 12-31-59 (Susan Stevens); *The Restless Gun*—"Peligroso" 12-15-58 (Lorry Bardeen); *Northwest Passage*—"The Fourth Brother" 1-30-59 (Joan Paget); *Wanted—Dead or Alive*—"The Empty Cell" 10-17-59; *The Deputy*—"Silent Gun" 1-23-60 (Marian Whelan).

Henderson, Ray. Films: "Circle of Death" 1935; "Danger Trails" 1935; "Lawless Range" 1935; "North of Arizona" 1935 (Barfly); "The Pecos Kid" 1935; "The Rider of the Law" 1935; "The Unconquered Bandit" 1935; "Westward Ho" 1935; "Border Caballero" 1936; "The Law Rides" 1936; "Lightning Bill Carson" 1936; "Santa Fe Bound" 1936 (Cowboy); "The Traitor" 1936 (Ranger); "The Unknown Ranger" 1936; "The Gambling Terror" 1937; "Law of the Ranger" 1937; "The Red Rope" 1937; "Trail of Vengeance" 1937 (Henchman); "The Trusted Outlaw" 1937; "Valley of Terror" 1937; "Panamint's

Bad Man" 1938; "Phantom Ranger" 1938; "Frontier Crusader" 1940; "Riders from Nowhere" 1940; "Billy the Kid's Fighting Pals" 1941; "Billy the Kid Trapped" 1942.

Henderson, Theodore (1888-7/20/62). Films: "Beyond All Odds" 1926 (Dan Mason); "The Mojave Kid" 1927 (Panamint Pete).

Hendrian, O.C. "Dutch" (1896-12/13/53). Films: "The Westerner" 1934 (Cowboy); "Nevada" 1935 (Cawthorne's Henchman); "The Texans" 1938 (Union Soldier); "Union Pacific" 1939 (Card Player).

Hendricks, Jr., Ben (1893-8/15/38). Films: "The Challenge" 1916; "The Old Fool" 1923 (Pete Harkins); "Against All Odds" 1924 (Jim Sawyer); "The Man Who Played Square" 1925 (Spangler); "The Fighting Buckaroo" 1926 (First Cook); "Satan Town" 1926 (Malamute); "The Great Divide" 1929 (Dutch Romero); "Girl of the Golden West" 1930 (Handsome Charlie); "His Fighting Blood" 1935; "Law Beyond the Range" 1935 (Sheriff Burke); "Law Beyond the Range" 1935; "Northern Frontier" 1935 (Sam Keene); "Red Blood of Courage" 1935 (Bart Slager); "North of Nome" 1936 (Grail); "The Oregon Trail" 1936 (Major Harris); "Roaring Timber" 1937 (Stumpy); "Wells Fargo" 1937 (Sailor).

Hendricks, Dudley (1870-2/3/42). Films: "His Back Against the Wall" 1922 (Dr. Farley); "The Scrappin' Kid" 1926 (Sheriff Bolton); "The Terror" 1926 (Pop Morton); "The Flying U Ranch" 1927 (Weary); "Grinning Guns" 1927 (Sheriff).

Hendricks, Jack (1973-2/26/49). Films: "Caryl of the Mountains" 1936 (Constable Gary); "Zorro Rides Again" 1937-serial (Raider #4); "The Lone Ranger" 1938-serial (Trooper); "Phantom Ranger" 1938; "Frontier Fugitives" 1945; "Saddle Serenade" 1945; "Code of the Saddle" 1947; "Prairie Express" 1947 (Blane); "Trailing Danger" 1947; ; "Six Gun Serenade" 1947; "Frontier Revenge" 1948 (Red); "Mark of the Lash" 1948; "Tornado Range" 1948; "Marshal of Heldorado" 1950 (Zero).

Hendricks, Noah E. "Shorty" (1889-3/4/73). Films: "Battling Buddy" 1924 (Fred Burrows); "Cyclone Buddy" 1924 (Shorty); "Galloping Gallagher" 1924 (Tub); "Walloping Wallace" 1924 (Shorty); "Double Action Daniels" 1925 (Davis); "Reckless Courage" 1925 (Shorty Baker); "Double Daring" 1926 (the Law); "The Land of Missing Men" 1930 (Texas); "Oklahoma Cyclone"

1930 (Shorty); "At the Ridge" 1931 (Alabam); "Trails of Adventure" 1935.

Hendrix, Wanda (1928-2/1/81). Films: "Saddle Tramp" 1950 (Della); "Sierra" 1950 (Riley Martin); "My Brother, the Outlaw" 1951 (Senorita Carmel Alvarado); "Montana Territory" 1952 (Clair Enoch); "The Last Posse" 1953 (Deborah Morley); "The Black Dakotas" 1954 (Ruth Lawrence); "Stage to Thunder Rock" 1964 (Mrs. Swope). ¶TV: *Wagon Train*—"The Charles Maury Story" 5-7-58 (Juliette Creston); *Bat Masterson*—"The Lady Plays Her Hand" 12-29-60 (Daphne Kaye); *The Deputy*—"The Lesson" 1-14-61 (Mary Willis).

Hendry, Ian (1931-12/24/84). TV: *Preview Tonight*—"Roaring Camp" 9-4-66 (Angus).

Hendry, Len (-2-18/81). Films: "Copper Canyon" 1950 (Bartender); "Pony Express" 1953 (Maldin); "Pardners" 1956 (Western Cowboy); "Gunfight at the O.K. Corral" 1957 (Cowboy); "The Fastest Guitar Alive" 1967 (Deputy). ¶TV: *Tombstone Territory*—"The Outcast" 4-23-58 (Marshal); *Rawhide*—"Incident of Fear in the Streets" 5-8-59, "Incident of the Dust Flower" 3-4-60, "Incident at Rojo Canyon" 9-30-60, "Incident of the Captive" 12-16-60, "Incident of the Big Blowout" 2-10-61, "Incident on the Road Back" 2-24-61, "Incident at Rio Salado" 9-29-61, "The Devil and the Deep Blue" 5-11-62 (Dr. Miller); *Bat Masterson*—"Lottery of Death" 5-13-59 (the Manager); *Gunsmoke*—"False Witness" 12-12-59 (Hank), "May Blossoms" 2-15-64 (Man); *Branded*—"A Destiny Which Made Us Brothers" 1-23-66; *Bonanza*—"False Witness" 10-22-67 (Jensen).

Henley, Don (1948-). Films: "Cry Blood, Apache" 1970 (Benji).

Henner, Marilu (1952-). Films: "Rustler's Rhapsody" 1985 (Miss Tracy).

Hennesey, Tom. Films: "The Comancheros" 1961 (Graile's Bodyguard); "Big Jake" 1971 (Saloon Brawler); "Squares" 1972. ¶TV: *26 Men*—"Cattle Embargo" 3-4-58; *Tales of Wells Fargo*—"The Barefoot Banit" 1-30-61 (Miller Sledge); *Gunsmoke*—"Cody's Code" 1-20-62 (Art), "The Summons" 4-21-62 (Bartender); *Have Gun Will Travel*—"Taylor's Woman" 9-22-62 (Clyde).

Hennessy, David (1852-3/24/26). Films: "The Man Who Paid" 1922 (McNeill).

Henning, Pat (1911-4/28/73). Films: "Shine on Harvest Moon" 1938 (Shag); "Ride 'Em, Cowgirl" 1939 (Lingstrom).

Henriksen, Lance (1939-). Films: "The Quick and the Dead" 1995 (Ace Hanlon); "Dead Man" 1995 (Cole Wilson).

Henry, Carol. Films: "The Stranger from Pecos" 1943; "Santa Fe Saddlemates" 1945; "Sheriff of Cimarron" 1945 (Townsman); "Gun Talk" 1947 (Burke); "Back Trail" 1948; "Courtin' Trouble" 1948 (Bartender); "Cowboy Cavalier" 1948; "Gunning for Justice" 1948; "The Rangers Ride" 1948; "The Sheriff of Medicine Bow" 1948; "Across the Rio Grande" 1949 (Gill); "Gun Law Justice" 1949; "Gun Runner" 1949 (Stacey); "Haunted Trails" 1949 (Outlaw); "Hidden Danger" 1949 (Trigger); "Range Land" 1949 (Joe); "Roll, Thunder, Roll" 1949 (Henchman); "Shadows of the West" 1949 (Lee); "Stampede" 1949 (Ben); "Trail's End" 1949 (Rocky); "Annie Get Your Gun" 1950 (Rider); "Arizona Territory" 1950 (Joe); "Gunslingers" 1950 (Steve); "Law of the Panhandle" 1950 (Ace Parker); "Outlaw Gold" 1950 (Joe); "Over the Border" 1950 (Stage Guard); "Winchester '73" 1950 (Dudeen); "The Longhorn" 1951 (Henchman); "Three Desperate Men" 1951 (Deputy Smith); "Canyon Ambush" 1952; "Night Raiders" 1952 (Blair); "The Deerslayer" 1957 (Stunts); "Shoot-Out at Medicine Bend" 1957; "The Hallelujah Trail" 1965 (A Company Sergeant). ¶TV: *The Cisco Kid*—"Big Switch" 2-10-51, "Railroad Land Rush" 3-17-51, "Renegade Son" 4-7-51; *Wild Bill Hickok*—"The Avenging Gunman" 7-29-52; *Sergeant Preston of the Yukon*—"Father of the Crime" 4-19-56 (Constable York), "Vindication of Yukon" 7-5-56 (Trask), "Tobacco Smugglers" 11-29-56 (Jake); *The Restless Gun*—"The Coward" 1-6-58 (Chavez); *Wagon Train*—"The Tent City Story" 12-10-58 (Vic Trainier); *Rough Riders*—"An Eye for an Eye" 1-15-59 (Sam); *Cimarron Strip*—"The Battleground" 9-28-67.

Henry, Charlotte (1915-4/11/80). Films: "God's Country and the Man" 1937 (Betty Briggs).

Henry, Emmaline (1930-10/8/79). ¶TV: *Bonanza*—"Abner Willoughby's Return" 12-21-69 (Widow Sprague).

Henry, Frank (1894-10/3/63). Films: "Hoppy's Holiday" 1947 (Bart); "Saddle Pals" 1947.

Henry, Gale (1893-6/17/72).

Films: "The Wild West Show" 1928 (Zella).

Henry, George. Films: "American Maid" 1917 (Senator Lee); "The Gray Towers Mystery" 1919 (Mr. Orchard).

Henry, Gloria. Films: "Adventures in Silverado" 1948; "The Strawberry Roan" 1948 (Connie Bailey); "Law of the Barbary Coast" 1949 (Julie Adams); "Riders in the Sky" 1949 (Ann Lawson); "Lightning Guns" 1950 (Susan Atkins); "Al Jennings of Oklahoma" 1951 (Alice Calhoun); "Rancho Notorious" 1952 (Beth); "Calamity Jane" TVM-1984 (Lady). ¶TV: *Tales of Wells Fargo*—"The Witness" 12-30-57 (Sharon Burns).

Henry, Hank (1906-3/31/81). Films: "Sergents 3" 1962 (Blacksmith).

Henry, John (1882-8/12/58). Films: "Yankee Speed" 1924 (Ramon Garcia).

Henry, Louise. Films: "End of the Trail" 1936 (Belle Parson).

Henry, Mike (1936-). Films: "More Dead Than Alive" 1968 (Luke Santee); "Rio Lobo" 1970 (Sheriff To Hendricks); "Adios Amigo" 1975. ¶TV: *Daniel Boone*—"Bringing Up Josh" 4-16-70.

Henry, Pat (1923-2/18/82). Films: "Tall Man Riding" 1955. ¶TV: *The Rifleman*—"The Most Amazing Man" 11-26-62 (Hardware Man).

Henry, Robert "Buzzy" (1931-9/30/71). Films: "Western Frontier" 1935 (Peewee Harper); "Rio Grande Ranger" 1936 (Buzzy Cullen); "The Unknown Ranger" 1936 (Buzzy); "Ranger Courage" 1937 (Buzzy); "Buzzy Rides the Range" 1940 (Buzzy Harding); "Buzzy and the Phantom Pinto" 1941; "Ridin' Down Canyon" 1942 (Bobbie Blake); "Calling Wild Bill Elliott" 1943 (Demi-John); "Trail to Gunsight" 1944 (Tim Wagner); "Trigger Trail" 1944 (Chip); "Wild Beauty" 1946 (Johnny); "Wild West" 1946 (Skinny); "King of the Wild Horses" 1947; "Last of the Redmen" 1947 (Davy); "Law of the Canyon" 1947; "Prairie Outlaws" 1948; "Tex Granger" 1948-serial (Tim); "Rocky Mountain" 1950 (Kip Waterson); "Heart of the Rockies" 1951 (Dave Braddock); "The Homesteaders" 1953 (Charlie); "Last of the Pony Riders" 1953 (Yank); "Hell's Outpost" 1954; "Jubilee Trail" 1954 (Velasco's Son); "Man with the Steel Whip" 1954-serial (Orco); "The Outcast" 1954 (Zeke Polsen); "The Indian Fighter" 1955 (Lt. Shaeffer);

"The Road to Denver" 1955 (Pete); "Jubal" 1956 (Tolliver Boy); "Cowboy" 1958 (Slim Barrett); "The Lawless Eighties" 1958; "The Sheepman" 1958 (Red); "Tonka" 1958 (Lt. Crittenden); "Face of a Fugitive" 1959 (Burton); "Shenandoah" 1965 (Rider); "El Dorado" 1967; "Waterhole No. 3" 1967 (Cowpoke). ¶TV: *Wild Bill Hickok*—"The Right of Way" 8-5-52, "Marvins' Mix-Up" 5-19-53; *Broken Arrow*—"The Broken Wire" 5-14-57; *Zane Grey Theater*—"Desert Flight" 10-13-60 (Deputy); *Lawman*—"Sunday" 4-15-62 (Young); *The Rounders*—9-6-66 (Shorty).

Henry, Thomas Browne (-6/30/80). Films: "Law and Order" 1953 (Dixon); "Sitting Bull" 1954 (Webber); "A Man Alone" 1955 (Maybanks); "The Violent Men" 1955 (Mr. Vail); "Quantrill's Raiders" 1958 (Griggs); "Showdown at Boot Hill" 1958 (Con Maynor); "Gunfight at Comanche Creek" 1964. ¶TV: *My Friend Flicka*—"The Old Champ" 5-4-56 (Throckmorton); *Zane Grey Theater*—"Dangerous Orders" 2-8-57 (Col. Radford); *Circus Boy*—"The Lady and the Circus" 3-31-57 (R. Gordon); *Tombstone Territory*—"Gunslinger from Galeville" 10-16-57 (J. Homer Radcliffe); "Killer Without a Conscience" 11-20-57 (J. Homer Radcliffe); *Maverick*—"The Wrecker" 12-1-57 (Auctioneer), "Passage to Fort Doom" 3-8-59 (Charles Stanton), "A Cure for Johnny Rain" 12-20-59 (Mayor Pembroke H. Hadley), "Kiz" 12-4-60 (Attorney Hanford), "The Forbidden City" 3-26-61 (McGuire); *Wagon Train*—"The Gabe Carswell Story" 1-15-58 (Yellow Bear); *Wanted—Dead or Alive*—"The Inheritance" 4-30-60 (Dr. Parks), "The Cure" 9-28-60; *Bonanza*—"The Blood Line" 12-31-60 (Jenkins); *Tales of Wells Fargo*—"A Show from Silver Lode" 3-6-61 (Henry Dobson); *Rawhide*—"Grandma's Money" 2-23-62 (Coctor); *The Daniel Boone*—"Empire of the Lost" 9-16-65 (Antawah), "The Enchanted Gun" 11-17-66 (Noheemo); *Big Valley*—"The Odyssey of Jubal Tanner" 10-13-65 (Chairman).

Henry, William "Bill" (1918-). Films: "Arizona Wildcat" 1938 (Donald Clark); "Cherokee Strip" 1940 (Tom Cross); "Geronimo" 1940 (Lt. John Steele, Jr.); "Stardust on the Sage" 1942 (Jeff Drew); "Calaboose" 1943; "Trail to San Antone" 1947 (Rick Malloy); "The Denver Kid" 1948; "Renegades of Sonora" 1948; "Death Valley Gunfighter" 1949 (Sheriff Keith Ames); "The Old Frontier" 1950 (Dr. Creighton); "Cana-

dian Mounties vs. Atomic Invaders" 1953-serial (Sergeant Don Roberts); "Thundering Caravans" 1952 (Bert Cranston); "Marshal of Cedar Rock" 1953 (Bill Anderson); "Savage Frontier" 1953 (Dan Longley); "Masterson of Kansas" 1954 (Charlie Fry); "The Three Outlaws" 1956; "Gunsmoke in Tucson" 1958 (Sheriff Blane); "The Lone Ranger and the Lost City of Gold" 1958 (Travers); "The Horse Soldiers" 1959 (Confederate Lieutenant); "The Alamo" 1960 (Dr. Sutherland); "Sergeant Rutledge" 1960 (Capt. Dwyer); "Two Rode Together" 1961; "How the West Was Won" 1962 (Staff Officer); "The Man Who Shot Liberty Valance" 1962; "Cheyenne Autumn" 1964 (Infantry Captain); "Taggart" 1964 (Army Sergeant); "El Dorado" 1967 (Sheriff Bill Moreland). ¶TV: *The Gene Autry Show*—"The Poisoned Waterhole" 10-8-50, "The Black Rider" 10-22-50, "Narrow Escape" 8-11-53; *The Cisco Kid*—"Newspaper Crusade" 5-5-51, "Freight Line Feud" 6-2-51, "Performance Bond" 6-30-51, "The Fire Engine" 5-31-52, "Fear" 6-28-52, "Bandaged Badman" 10-11-52, "The Black Terror" 11-29-52, "Double Deal" 1-17-53, "Fool's Gold" 5-9-53; *Hopalong Cassidy*—"Frontier Law" 6-21-52; *Wild Bill Hickok*—"Monster in the Lake" 8-12-52, "Marvins' Mix-Up" 5-19-53; *Judge Roy Bean*—"Sunburnt Gold" 10-1-55 (Jess Cutter), "The Fugitive" 12-1-55 (Dover), "Letty Leaves Home" 12-1-55 (Brady); *My Friend Flicka*—"Cavalry Horse" 10-28-55; *Wyatt Earp*—"It's a Wise Calf" 1-17-56, "Witness for the Defense" 1-22-57 (Riggs Miller), "Fortitude" 11-26-57 (Lon Ashby), "The Hole Up" 9-16-58; *Fury*—"Search for Joey" 2-18-56 (Dr. Walton), "The Baby Sitters" 2-8-58 (Al); *Annie Oakley*—"Western Privateer" 9-30-56 (John Boone), "Annie Rides the Navajo Trail" 11-18-56 (Stevens), "Desperate Men" 2-24-57 (Buck Kirby); *The Lone Ranger*—"The Twisted Track" 11-29-56, "Christmas Story" 12-20-56; *Zane Grey Theater*—"The Necessary Breed" 2-15-57 (Carter), "Badge of Honor" 5-3-57 (George Wallace), "The Sunrise Gun" 5-19-60 (Sheriff Moss); *Colt .45*—"Gallows at Granite Gap" 11-8-57 (Deputy Trask); *Sergeant Preston of the Yukon*—"Out of the Night" 11-28-57 (Reno); *Tales of the Texas Rangers*—"Riders of the Lone Star" 12-1-57 (Keno); *The Adventures of Rin Tin Tin*—"Boundary Busters" 12-20-57 (Bill Anderson), "The Epidemic" 11-21-58 (Charlie), "The Failure" 5-8-59; *Tales of Wells Fargo*—"The Wit-

ness" 12-30-57 (Frank Copeland), "A Quiet Little Town" 6-5-61 (Dave Prescott); *Trackdown*—"The Young Gun" 2-7-58 (Turley); *Broken Arrow*—"Manhunt" 6-3-58 (Lieutenant); *Buckskin*—"Cash Robertson" 8-7-58 (Corcoran), "Hunter's Moon" 9-11-58 (Corcoran); *Lawman*—"The Prisoner" 10-12-58 (Doug Sutherland); *Bat Masterson*—"Two Graves for Swan Valley" 10-15-58 (Griff), "A Noose Fits Anybody" 11-19-58 (Griff Hanley), "The Snare" 3-17-60 (Sheriff Brady); *Wagon Train*—"The Tent City Story" 12-10-58 (Joe Conway); *26 Men*—"Ranger Without a Badge" 1-27-59; *Tombstone Territory*—"Gun Hostage" 5-1-59 (Roy Hendricks); *Rough Riders*—"The Holdout" 6-25-59 (Joshua Claggett); *Rawhide*—"Incident of the Roman Candles" 7-10-59 (Sam Colby), "Incident at Quivira" 12-14-62 (Corporal), "Incident of the Gallows Tree" 2-22-63 (Corey), "Incident of the White Eyes" 5-3-63 (Stage Driver), "Incident at Farragut Pass" 10-31-63 (Bartender); *The Rebel*—"Ben White" 5-28-61 (Ab Jason); *Bonanza*—"Gallagher Sons" 12-9-62, "False Witness" 10-22-67 (Farrell); *Gunsmoke*—"Dry Well" 1-11-64 (Dave Yuma), "Hammerhead" 12-26-64 (Feeney), "Clayton Thaddeus Greenwood" 10-2-65 (Waiter); *Branded*—"The Richest Man in Boot Hill" 10-31-65 (Sheriff), "A Proud Town" 12-19-65 (Regan); *Wild Wild West*—"The Night of the Human Trigger" 12-3-65 (Sheriff); *The Loner*—"The Burden of the Badge" 3-5-66 (Ben); *Laredo*—"The Other Cheek" 2-10-67; *Lancer*—"Devil's Blessing" 4-22-69.

Hensley, Pamela (1950). Films: "There Was a Crooked Man" 1970 (Edwina).

Hentelhoff, Alex. TV: *Pistols 'n' Petticoats*—Regular 1966-67 (Little Bear); *Kung Fu*—"Alethea" 3-15-73 (Abner Tutt), "Cry of the Night Beast" 10-19-74 (Vern Dixon).

Hepburn, Audrey (1929-1/20/93). Films: "The Unforgiven" 1960 (Rachel Zachary).

Hepburn, Katharine (1907-). Films: "The Sea of Grass" 1947 (Lutie Cameron); "The Rainmaker" 1956 (Lizzie Curry); "Rooster Cogburn" 1975 (Eula Goodnight).

Herbert, Charles. Films: "Gun Glory" 1957 (Boy); "Gunfight at the O.K. Corral" 1957 (Tommy Earp). ¶TV: *Wichita Town*—"Second Chance" 3-16-60 (Jed McCloud); *Wagon Train*—"The Shad Bennington Story" 6-22-60 (Winfy), "The Jose Morales Story" 10-19-60 (Joseph

Oliver), "The Saul Bevins Story" 4-12-61 (Job), "The Davey Baxter Story" 1-9-63 (Wally), "The Antone Rose Story" 5-22-63 (Nico); *Klondike*—"Halliday's Club" 12-19-60 (Seth Bailey); *Rawhide*—"Incident at Sugar Creek" 11-23-62 (Jody).

Herbert, Henry J. (H.J. Hebert) (1879-4/18/56). Films: "The End of the Trail" 1916 (Wapau); "Fighting Blood" 1916 (Harry Blake); "The Hidden Children" 1917 (Mayaro); "Wild Honey" 1918 (Ed Southern); "Last of the Duanes" 1919 (Cal Bain); "Rose of the West" 1919 (Major Hilton); "The Cyclones" 1920 (Ferdinand Baird); "The Joyous Troublemaker" 1920 (Joe Embry); "The Orphan" 1920 (Tex Willard); "Sunset Sprague" 1920 (Mace Dennison); "Twins of Suffering Creek" 1920; "Blind Hearts" 1921 (James Bradley); "When Danger Smiles" 1922 (Francisco Caravalle); "The Range Terror" 1925 (Reagan); "The Enchanted Hill" 1926 (Bud Shannon); "Whispering Smith Rides" 1927-serial; "The Clean-Up Man" 1928 (the Hawk); "Laddie Be Good" 1928 (John Norton).

Herbert, Holmes (1882-12/26/56). Films: "Moonshine Valley" 1922 (Dr. Martin); "The Country Beyond" 1936 (Inspector Reed); "Wolf Call" 1939 (Winton); "Over the Santa Fe Trail" 1947; "The Iroquois Trail" 1950 (Gen. Johnson); "The Wild North" 1952 (Magistrate).

Herbert, Hugh (1887-3/13/52). Films: "Badlands of Dakota" 1941 (Rocky).

Herbert, Jack. Films: "The Squaw Man" 1918 (Nick); "A Daughter of the Wolf" 1919 (Jacques); "Told in the Hills" 1919 (Skulking Brave); "The Call of the North" 1921 (Louis Placide).

Herbert, Joseph (1887-10/7/60). Films: "Laughing Bill Hyde" 1918 (Joseph Wesley Slayforth).

Herbert, Percy (1925-12/6/92). Films: "Man in the Wilderness" 1971-U.S./Span. (Fogarty). ¶TV: *Cimarron Strip*—Regular 1967-68 (MacGregory).

Herbert, Pitt (1915-6/23/89). Films: "Hud" 1963 (Larker); "Captain Apache" 1971-Brit./Span. (Moon); "The Honkers" 1972 (Hat Store Proprietor). ¶TV: *Gunsmoke*—"20-20" 2-25-56 (Dealer), "The Constable" 5-30-59 (Green); *Sergeant Preston of the Yukon*—"Vindication of Yukon" 7-5-56 (Dr. McLeod); *Rawhide*—"Incident at Dangerfield Dip" 10-2-59 (Harry); *Man from Black-

hawk*—"El Patron" 2-5-60 (Curator); *Wagon Train*—"The Joshua Gilliam Story" 3-30-60 (Mr. Miller); *Wyatt Earp*—"The Confidence Man" 5-17-60 (Sam Dutton); *The Deputy*—"Mother and Son" 10-29-60 (Clerk); *Lawman*—"The Barber" 2-25-62 (Sylvester O'Toole); *The Virginian*—"The Devil's Children" 12-5-62 (Emmet Delaney), "Portrait of a Widow" 12-9-64 (Clerk), "Man of the People" 12-23-64 (Telegrapher), "Morgan Starr" 2-9-66 (Telegrapher), "The Gauntlet" 2-8-67 (Doctor); *Have Gun Will Travel*—"American Primitive" 2-2-63 (Slim); *Time Tunnel*—"Billy the Kid" 2-10-67 (McKinney); *Wild Wild West*—"The Night of the Deadly Blossom" 3-17-67 (Assistant Secret of State Levering Davis); *The Guns of Will Sonnett*—"First Love" 11-3-67 (Clerk); *The Big Valley*—"Deathtown" 10-28-68; *Bonanza*—"The Stalker" 11-2-69 (Postal Clerk), "The Initiation" 9-26-72 (Mr. Cropin); *The Men from Shiloh*—"Nan Allen" 1-6-71 (Finley).

Herbert, Tim (1915-6/20/86). TV: *Bonanza*—"Amigo" 2-12-67 (Mosquito).

Herbert, Tom (1888-4/3/46). Films: "Stars Over Arizona" 1937 (Doc); "Along Came Jones" 1945 (Card Player).

Herbst, Joseph. Films: "The Terror of Tiny Town" 1938 (the Sheriff).

Herd, Richard. TV: *Adventures of Brisco County, Jr.*—"Bye Bly" 2-18-94 (President Cleveland), "High Treason" 5-13-94 & 5-20-94 (President Cleveland); *Dr. Quinn, Medicine Woman*—"Where the Heart Is" 11-20-93 (Dr. John Hanson).

Herford, William (1853-12/27/34). Films: "The Man from Hell's River" 1922 (the Padre).

Herlin, Jacques. Films: "Adios Hombre" 1966-Ital./Span.; "Fort Yuma Gold" 1966-Ital./Fr./Span.; "Two Sides of the Dollar" 1967-Fr./Ital. (Mad Michael); "Yankee" 1967-Ital./Span.

Herman, Al (1886-7/2/67). Films: "Headin' East" 1937 (Maxie); "Hollywood Cowboy" 1937 (Stger); "Oklahoma Renegades" 1940 (Hank Blake).

Herman, Jimmy. Films: "Dances with Wolves" 1990 (Stone Calf); "Geronimo" TVM-1993 (Geronimo as an Old Man).

Hern, Pepe (1927-). Films: "Bandit Queen" 1950 (Raphael); "The Furies" 1950 (Felix Herrera); "Heart of the Rockies" 1951 (Rocky);

"Jubilee Trail" 1954 (Ranch Hand); "Stranger on the Run" TVM-1967; "Joe Kidd" 1972 (Priest). ¶TV: *My Friend Flicka*—"Rebels in Hiding" 3-30-56; *Broken Arrow*—"Passage Deferred" 10-30-56 (Tokumo), "Escape" 2-18-58 (Ruklai); *Rawhide*—"Incident at Spanish Rock" 12-18-59 (Frank Volero); *The Rifleman*—"The Vaqueros" 10-2-61 (Lazaro), "Waste" 10-1-62 & 10-8-62 (Sleeper); *Gunsmoke*—"Extradition" 12-7-63 & 12-14-63 (Miguel); *Bonanza*—"The Campaneros" 4-19-64 (Maximo), "El Jefe" 11-15-70 (Rojas); *The Big Valley*—"The Way to Kill a Killer" 11-24-65 (Vaquero), "The Death Merchant" 2-23-66 (Pedro), "Legend of a General" 9-19-66 & 9-26-66; *The High Chaparral*—"Mark of the Turtle" 12-10-67 (Teofilo).

Hernandez, Anna (1867-5/4/45). Films: "Leave It to Susan" 1919 (Ma Burbridge).

Hernandez, George (1863-12/31/22). Films: "The Cowboy's Adopted Child" 1911; "Heart of John Barlow" 1911; "The Rival Stage Lines" 1911; "Told in the Sierras" 1911; "The White Medicine Man" 1911; "A Broken Spur" 1912; "The Old Stage Coach" 1912; "The Peacemaker" 1912; "Tenderfoot Bob's Resignation" 1912; "The Beaded Buckskin Bag" 1913; "The Trail of Cards" 1913; "The End of the Rainbow" 1916 (Elihu Bennett); "Broadway, Arizona" 1917 (Uncle Isaac Horn); "The Greater Law" 1917 (Tully Winkle); "Up or Down?" 1917 (Mike); "The Daredevil" 1920 (Buchanan Atkinson); "The Third Woman" 1920 (James Riley); "Arabia" 1922 (Arthur Edward Terhune); "Billy Jim" 1922 (Dudley Dunforth); "Flaming Hearts" 1922.

Hernandez, Mrs. George (Anna Hernandez) (1867-5/4/45). Films: "Ride for Your Life" 1924 (Mrs. Donnegan).

Hernandez, Juano (1896-7/17/70). Films: "Stars in My Crown" 1950 (Uncle Famous Prill); "Sergeant Rutledge" 1960 (Sgt. Matthew Luke Skidmore).

Hernandez, Tom. TV: *Cheyenne*—"Fury at Rio Hondo" 4-17-56 (Roman Montalban); *Wanted—Dead or Alive*—"Witch Woman" 12-28-60; *The Virginian*—"Riff-Raff" 11-7-62; *Daniel Boone*—"The Grand Alliance" 11-13-69.

Herndon, Irene. Films: "Overland with Kit Carson" 1939-serial; "The Taming of the West" 1939 (Mary Jenkins); "Texas Stampede" 1939.

Herrera, Anthony. Films: "The Night Rider" TVM-1979 (Tru Sheridan).

Herrick, Frederick. Films: "Pistol Harvest" 1951 (Capt. Rand). ¶TV: Gunsmoke—"Matt Dillon Must Die!" 9-9-74 (Laban).

Herrick, Jack (1891-6/18/52). Films: "Walloping Kid" 1926 (Battling Lewis); "The Arizona Kid" 1930 (the Hoboken Hooker).

Herrick, Joseph (1889-4/16/66). Films: "White Fang" 1936 (Kobi).

Herrick, Samuel. Films: "The Tall Texan" 1953 (Sheriff Chadbourne).

Herrick, Virginia. Films: "I Killed Geronimo" 1950 (Julie); "Roar of the Iron Horse" 1950-serial (Carol Lane); "Silver Raiders" 1950 (Patricia); "Vigilante Hideout" 1950 (Marigae Sanders); "Montana Desperado" 1951 (Sally Wilson); "The Frontier Phantom" 1952. ¶TV: The Cisco Kid—"Hidden Valley Pirates" 10-27-51, "Quarter Horse" 12-8-51.

Herring, Aggie (1876-10/28/39). Films: "A Man in the Open" 1919; "A Man's Fight" 1919 (Mrs. Murphy); "The Sagebrusher" 1920 (Mrs. Jensen); "The Mysterious Rider" 1921 (Maria the Cook); "Nine Points of the Law" 1922 (Mrs. Prouty); "Pioneer Trails" 1923 (Laundry Lou); "The Frontier Trail" 1926 (Mrs. O'Shea); "Loco Luck" 1927 (Mrs. Vernon); "Billy the Kid" 1930 (Mrs. Hatfield); "Daniel Boone" 1936 (Mrs. Burch).

Herron, Robert "Bob". Films: "Gun Fury" 1953 (Curly Jordan); "Four Guns to the Border" 1954 (Evans); "Saskatchewan" 1954 (Brill); "The Far Horizons" 1955; "Oklahoma Crude" 1973 (Dulling). ¶TV: Wild Wild West—"Night of the Deadly Bed" 9-24-65 (Capt. Jackson), "The Night of the Bars of Hell" 3-4-66 (Borg); Laredo—"The Golden Trail" 11-4-65 (Hunk); Gunsmoke—"A Noose for Dobie Price" 3-4-68 (Jabez), "Captain Sligo" 1-4-71 (Vern); Kung Fu—"Dark Angel" 11-11-72 (2nd Tough).

Hersent, Philippe. Films: "If One Is Born a Swine … Kill Him" 1968-Ital. (Harrison); "Four Gunmen of the Holy Trinity" 1971-Ital.

Hershey, Barbara (1948-). Films: "Heaven with a Gun" 1969 (Leloopa); "The Last Hard Men" 1976 (Susan Burgade); "Return to Lonesome Dove" TVM-1993. ¶TV: The Monroes—Regular 1966-67 (Kathy Monroe); Daniel Boone—"The King's Shilling" 10-19-67

(Dinah Hubbard); The High Chaparral—"The Peacemaker" 3-3-68 (Moonfire); Kung Fu—"Besieged: Death on Cold Mountain" 11-15-74 (Nan Chi), "Besieged: Cannon at the Gate" 11-22-74 (Nan Chi).

Hersholt, Jean (1886-6/2/56). Films: "The Disciple" 1915 (Man in Crowd); "The Apostle of Vengeance" 1916; "Fighting for Love" 1917 (Ferdinand); "'49-'17" 1917 (Gentleman Jim Rayner); "The Greater Law" 1917 (Basil Pelly); "The Soul Herder" 1917; "Little Red Decides" 1918 (Sour Milk); "Hell's Hinges" 1919 (Townsman); "The Golden Trail" 1920 (Harry Teal); "Man of the Forest" 1921 (Lem Beasley); "When Romance Rides" 1922 (Joel Creech); "Quicksands" 1923 (Ring Member); "Don Q, Son of Zorro" 1925 (Don Fabrique); "Run for Cover" 1955 (Mr. Swenson).

Herter, Gerard. see Haerter, Gerard.

Hertford, Will. Films: "Saddle Cyclone" 1925 (Joshua Lowery).

Hervey, Irene (1916-). Films: "The Dude Ranger" 1934 (Anne Hepburn); "The Three Godfathers" 1936 (Molly); "Destry Rides Again" 1939 (Janice Tyndall). ¶TV: Circus Boy—"Farewell to the Circus" 1-6-57 (Martha Neilson); Wide Country—"Our Ernie Kills People" 11-1-62 (Dorothy Stannard).

Hervey, Jason. TV: Wildside—Regular 1985 (Zeke).

Herzberg, Elmer. Films: "The Texan Meets Calamity Jane" 1950 (Henry the Whistler).

Herzinger, Charles W. (164-2/18/53). Films: "The Plainsman" 1936 (William H. Seward); "Wells Fargo" 1937 (Wagon Train Driver).

Herzog, Fred (1869-5/2/28). Films: "Last of the Duanes" 1919 (Euchre); "The Lone Star Ranger" 1919 (Joe Laramie); "Forbidden Trails" 1920 (Larry Harlan).

Hess, David. Films: "Montana Trap" 1976-Ger.; "Jonathan of the Bears" 1994-Ital./Rus. (Maddock).

Hesseman, Howard (1940-). Films: "Kid Blue" 1973 (Confectionery Man).

Hester, Harvey (1897-3/28/67). Films: "The Great Locomotive Chase" 1956 (Jes McIntyre).

Heston, Charlton (1923-). Films: "The Savage" 1952 (Warbonnet/Jim Ahern); "Arrowhead" 1953 (Ed Bannon); "Pony Express" 1953 (Buffalo Bill Cody); "The Far Horizons" 1955 (Bill Clark); "Three Vio-

lent People" 1956 (Colt Saunders); "The Big Country" 1958 (Steve Leech); "Major Dundee" 1965 (Maj. Amos Charles Dundee); "Will Penny" 1968 (Will Penny); "The Last Hard Men" 1976 (Sam Burgade); "The Mountain Men" 1980 (Bill Tyler); "Proud Men" TVM-1987 (Charley MacLeod); "Tombstone" 1993 (Henry Hooker); "The Avenging Angel" TVM-1995 (Brigham Young); "James A. Michener's Texas" TVM-1995 (Narrator).

Hetrick, Jennifer. TV: Young Riders—"Good Night Sweet Charlotte" 1-4-92 (Charlotte Rowen).

Hewitt, Alan (1915-11/7/86). TV: Sugarfoot—"Return to Boot Hill" 3-15-60 (Henry Plummer); Maverick—"Triple Indemnity" 3-19-61 (George Parker), "One of Our Trains Is Missing" 4-22-62 (Amos Skinner); The Outlaws—"All in a Day's Work" 5-10-62 (Hatter Keenan); F Troop—"Scourge of the West" 9-14-65 (Colonel Malcolm); Wild Wild West—"The Night of the Colonel's Ghost" 3-10-67 (Pernell); Iron Horse—"Wild Track" 12-16-67 (Holt); Hec Ramsey—"The Green Feather Mystery" 12-17-72 (Samuels).

Hewlett, Bentley. Films: "Speed Wings" 1934 (Gregory); "Western Jamboree" 1938 (Randolph Kimball).

Hewston, Alfred (1880-9/6/47). Films: "The Web of the Law" 1923 (Jasper Leveen); "Cyclone Buddy" 1924 (Judd Martin); "Fightin' Odds" 1925 (Sam Winton); "Flashing Steeds" 1925 (Shorty); "Let's Go Gallagher" 1925 (Bendy Mulligan); "On the Go" 1925 (Snoopy O'Sullivan); "Tearin' Loose" 1925 (Dad Burns); "Warrior Gap" 1925 (Sgt. Casey); "The Wyoming Wildcat" 1925 (Dan Slade); "The Arizona Streak" 1926 (Smiling Morn); "Beyond All Odds" 1926 (Sheriff); "The Iron Rider" 1926 (Flash Clayton); "The Masquerade Bandit" 1926 (Pat); "Out of the West" 1926 (John O'Connor); "Splitting the Breeze" 1927 (Hank Robbins); "Lure of the West" 1928; "The Cowboy and the Outlaw" 1929 (Walter Driver); "The Man from Nevada" 1929 (Jim Watkins); "'Neath Western Skies" 1929 (James Garfield); "A Texas Cowboy" 1929; "West of the Rockies" 1929 (Tex); "Breezy Bill" 1930 (Henry Pennypincher); "Firebrand Jordan" 1930 (Ah Sing); "Near the Rainbow's End" 1930 (Tug Wilson).

Heyburn, Weldon (1904-5/18/51). Films: "The Gay Caballero" 1932 (Jito); "Git Along, Little Dogies" 1937 (Wilkins); "The Mysterious

Rider" 1938 (Jack Bellounds); "Northwest Mounted Police" 1940 (Constable Cameron); "The Trail Blazers" 1940 (Jeff Bradley); "In Old Colorado" 1941 (Burton); "The Round Up" 1941; "Stick to Your Guns" 1941; "They Died with Their Boots On" 1941 (Staff Officer); "Code of the Outlaw" 1942; "Rock River Renegades" 1942; "Blazing Guns" 1943; "Death Valley Manhunt" 1943 (Richard Quinn); "Overland Mail Robbery" 1943 (John Patterson); "Bordertown Trail" 1944; "Code of the Prairie" 1944 (Jess Thorpe); "Death Valley Rangers" 1944; "Westward Bound" 1944 (Albert Lane); "The Yellow Rose of Tesas" 1944 (Charlie Goss); "Frontier Gunlaw" 1946.

Heydt, Louis Jean (1905-1/29/ 60). Films: "Let Freedom Ring" 1939 (Ned Wilkie); "Reno" 1939 (Judge Howard); "Santa Fe Trail" 1940 (Farmer); "Bad Men of Tombstone" 1949 (Mr. Stover); "The Furies" 1950 (Bailey); "Al Jennings of Oklahoma" 1951 (John Jennings); "Drums in the Deep South" 1951 (Col. House); "The Great Missouri Raid" 1951 (Charles Ford); "Raton Pass" 1951 (Jim Ponzer); "Rawhide" 1951 (Fickert); "Warpath" 1951 (Herb Woodson); "The Old West" 1952 (Jeff Blecker); "The Vanquished" 1953 (Luke Taylor); "The Boy from Oklahoma" 1954 (Paul Evans); "Ten Wanted Men" 1955 (Tom Baines); "Stranger at My Door" 1956 (Sheriff John Tatum); "The Badge of Marshal Brennan" 1957 (Col. Donaphin); "Raiders of Old California" 1957. ¶TV: *My Friend Flicka*—"The Little Secret" 12-2-55 (Burton); *Fury*—"The Test" 3-3-56 (Mr. Baxter); *Wagon Train*—"The Bernal Sierra Story" 3-12-58 (Casey), "The Clayton Tucker Story" 2-10-60; *MacKenzie's Raiders*— Regular 1958-59; *Northwest Passage*— "Court Martial" 10-26-58 (Adam Pierce); *Maverick*—"A Tale of Three Cities" 10-18-59 (Jim Malone); *Man from Blackhawk*—"The Winthrop Woman" 11-27-59; *Rawhide*—"Incident of the Devil and His Due" 1-22-60 (Wilson); *Zane Grey Theater*— "Man in the Middle" 2-11-60 (Dan Mulvey); *Best of the Post*—"Command" 10-6-60 (Sergeant Utterbach).

Heyes, Herbert (1889-5/30/58). Films: "Heart of the Sunset" 1918 (Dave Law); "The Ranger of Pike's Peak" 1919; "Winning a Bride" 1919; "Ruth of the Rockies" 1920-serial; "Calling Wild Bill Elliott" 1943 (Governor Nichols); "Death Valley Manhunt" 1943 (Judge Jim Hobart); "Outlaws of Santa Fe" 1944 (Henry

Jackson); "Only the Valiant" 1951 (Col. Drumm); "The Far Horizons" 1955 (President Jefferson). ¶TV: *Sugarfoot*—"Deadlock" 2-4-58 (Calvin Williams).

Heyman, Barton (1937-). Films: "Valdez Is Coming" 1971 (El Segundo); "Dream West" TVM-1986 (Judge Advocate Lee). ¶TV: *Gunsmoke*—"Potshot" 3-11-61.

Heywood, Herbert (1881-9/15/ 64). Films: "Moonlight on the Prairie" 1935 (Pop Powell); "The Arizona Raiders" 1936 (Sheriff); "King of the Pecos" 1936 (Josh Billings); "White Fang" 1936 (Mac); "Wells Fargo" 1937 (Bartender); "The Return of the Cisco Kid" 1939 (Proprietor); "Susannah of the Mounties" 1939 (Hostler); "Konga, the Wild Stallion" 1940 (Sheriff); "Legion of the Lawless" 1940 (Doc Denton); "Legion of the Lawless" 1940 (Doc Denton); "They Died with Their Boots On" 1941 (Newsman); "Along Came Jones" 1945 (Townsman); "Smoky" 1946 (Livery Stable Proprietor); "Green Grass of Wyoming" 1948 (Storekeeper Johnson); "Ticket to Tomahawk" 1950 (Old Timer).

Hiatt, Ruth (1908-4/21/94). Films: "The Vigilantes" 1918; "Dynamite Ranch" 1932; "The Sunset Trail" 1932 (Molly); "Ridin' Thru" 1935 (Dolores Brooks).

Hice, Eddie. Films: "Young Fury" 1965; "The Soul of Nigger Charley" 1973 (Mexican). ¶TV: *The Texan*—"The Peddler" 1-26-59; *Gunsmoke*—"Blue Heaven" 9-26-64 (Duster), "Bad Lady from Brookline" 5-1-65 (Cowboy).

Hickey, Howard (1897-3/25/ 42). Films: "Gunfire" 1935 (Higgins); "The Lone Ranger Rides Again" 1939-serial (Raider #2).

Hickey, William (1928-). Films: "Invitation to a Gunfighter" 1964 (Jo-Jo); "Little Big Man" 1971 (Historian).

Hickland, Catherine. Films: "Ghost Town" 1988 (Kate).

Hickman, Charles H. (1876-9/19/38). Films: "Two Men of Sandy Bar" 1916 (Col. Starbottle); "The Yaqui" 1916 (Senor Estaban).

Hickman, Darryl (1931-). Films: "Jackass Mail" 1942 (Tommie Gargan); "Northwest Rangers" 1942 (Blackie as a Boy); "Boy's Ranch" 1946 (Hank); "Ricochet Romance" 1954 (Dave King); "Southwest Passage" 1954 (Jeb); "The Iron Sheriff" 1957 (Benjie Galt); "The Persuader" 1957 (Toby Bonham). ¶TV: *The Lone Ranger*—"Two Gold Lockets" 2-15-

51; *Wyatt Earp*—"Hang 'Em High" 3-12-57 (Dal Royal); *Wanted—Dead or Alive*—"Rope Law" 1-3-59 (Damon Ring, Jr.); *Gunsmoke*—"The Choice" 5-9-59 (Andy Hill), "Target" 9-5-59 (Danny Kadar); *Tales of Wells Fargo*— "The Bounty Hunter" 6-1-59 (Dan Francis); *Texas John Slaughter*—"The Robber Stallion" 12-4-59 (Ashley Carstairs), "Wild Horse Revenge" 12-11-59 (Ashley Carstairs), "Range War at Tombstone" 12-18-59 (Ashley Carstairs), "Kentucky Gunslick" 2-26-60 (Ashley Carstairs), "Geronimo's Revenge" 3-4-60 (Ashley Carstairs); *Rawhide*—"Incident of the Running Iron" 3-10-61 (Andy Miller), "The Reunion" 4-6-62 (Lt. Matthew Perry).

Hickman, Dwayne (1934-). Films: "Cat Ballou" 1965 (Jed). ¶TV: *The Lone Ranger*—"Two Gold Lockets" 2-15-51, "Sunstroke Mesa" 3-17-55; *Wagon Train*—"The Clay Shelby Story" 12-6-64 (Clay Shelby).

Hickman, George. Films: "Cowboy from Brooklyn" 1938 (Newsboy); "Buck Benny Rides Again" 1940 (Page Boy). ¶TV: *Rawhide*—"Incident at the Edge of Madness" 2-6-59, "Incident of the Sharpshooter" 2-26-60, "Incident of the Blackstorms" 5-26-61, "The Pitchwagon" 3-2-62, "The Devil and the Deep Blue" 5-11-62; *The Tall Man*—"Rovin' Gambler" 3-18-61 (Bartender).

Hickman, Howard (1880-12/31/ 49). Films: "The Man from Oregon" 1915 (Honest Jim Martin); "The Roughneck" 1915; "Fighting Shadows" 1935 (Insp. Rutledge); "Law Beyond the Range" 1935 (Captain Wood); "Wild Brian Kent" 1936; "Western Gold" 1937 (Thatcher); "The Kansas Terrors" 1939 (Governor General); "The Kid from Texas" 1939 (Doctor); "Trouble in Sundown" 1939 (Tex); "Bullet Code" 1940 (John Mathews); "The Dark Command" 1940; "The Man from Dakota" 1940 (Colonel); "Virginia City" 1940 (Gen. Page); "Belle Starr" 1941 (Col. Thornton); "Robbers of the Range" 1941 (Tremaine); "Bells of Capistrano" 1942; "Hurricane Smith" 1942 (Senator Bradley); "The Big Bonanza" 1944 (Abraham).

Hickman, Mark. Films: "The True Story of Jesse James" 1957 (Sam Wells); "Thirteen Fighting Men" 1960 (Sgt. Mason).

Hickman, William "Bill" (1920-2/24/86). TV: *Klondike*—"88 Keys to Trouble" 11-14-60 (Loader); *Bonanza*—"Rich Man, Poor Man" 5-12-63, "The Prince" 4-2-67 (Ketch);

Branded—"Very Few Heroes" 4-11-65 (Ensor).

Hickox, Harry (1915-6/3/94). TV: *Wild Bill Hickok*—"Spurs for Johnny" 5-26-63; *The Roy Rogers Show*—"Born Fugitive" 11-29-53, "Dead End Trail" 2-20-55 (Jeb Horton), "The Ginger Horse" 3-27-55; *The Adventures of Rin Tin Tin*—"Rin Tin Tin, Outlaw" 12-3-54 (John Carter), "Rusty's Romance" 1-20-56 (Tom Brace), "The Accusation" 2-13-59 (Paul Brinker); *Tales of the Texas Rangers*—"Blood Trail" 9-24-55 (Sheriff Fellows), "Hail to the Rangers" 12-17-55 (Jessup); *Circus Boy*—"Farewell to the Circus" 1-6-57 (Victor MacGregor); *The Rifleman*—"The Angry Gun" 12-23-58 (Stage Driver); *Wagon Train*—"The Johnny Masters Story" 1-16-63 (Captain Sanborn); *Bonanza*—"A Woman Lost" 3-17-63 (Dink), "Child" 9-22-68 (Mayor Brigham), "A Lawman's Lot Is Not a Happy One" 10-5-69 (Mr. Green), "The Trouble with Amy" 1-25-70 (Mr. Eads); *Laredo*—"Lazyfoot, Where Are You?" 9-16-65 (Sheriff), "The Callico Kid" 1-6-66 (Hotel Keeper); *The Virginian*—"High Stakes" 11-16-66 (Charley Kane), "The Masquerade" 10-18-67 (Bill Manders); *The High Chaparral*—"Tornado Frances" 10-11-68 (Sheriff); *Lancer*—"Jelly Hoskins' American Dream" 11-11-69; *Alias Smith and Jones*—"The Wrong Train to Brimstone" 2-4-71 (Strothers), "Jailbreak at Junction City" 9-30-71; *Hec Ramsey*—"A Hard Road to Vengeance" 11-25-73 (Uker).

Hicks, Chuck (1927-). Films: "Gunfire at Indian Gap" 1957 (Deputy); "Johnny Reno" 1966 (Bellows); "Wild Women" TVM-1970; "Something Big" 1971 (Cpl. James); "Bronco Billy" 1980 (Cowboy at Bar). ¶TV: *My Friend Flicka*—"The Medicine Man" 5-11-56; *The Rebel*—"The Champ" 10-2-60 (the Frontier Kid); *Rawhide*—"The Greedy Town" 2-16-62; *Cheyenne*—"The Durango Brothers" 9-24-62 (Young Man); *Branded*—"The Greatest Coward on Earth" 11-21-65 (Young Samson); *Iron Horse*—"Grapes of Grass Valley" 10-21-67 (Caleb); *Nichols*—"The Unholy Alliance" 1-18-72, "Wings of an Angel" 2-8-72 (Dutchman); *Alias Smith and Jones*—"McGuffin" 12-9-72; *Gunsmoke*—"Cowtown Hustler" 3-11-74 (Turner); *Kung Fu*—"Battle Hymn" 2-8-75 (Saxon).

Hicks, Hilly (1950-). TV: *The Buffalo Soldiers*—Pilot 5-26-79 (Willie).

Hicks, Maxine Elliott. Films:

"The Crimson Dove" 1917 (Minnie Zugg); "The Thundering Herd" 1925 (Sally Hudnall).

Hicks, Russell (1895-6/1/57). Films: "Rose Marie" 1936 (Commandant); "Dodge City Trail" 1937 (Kenyon Phillips); "It Happened Out West" 1937 (Cooley); "Secret Valley" 1937 (Austin Martin); "Union Pacific" 1939 (Sergeant); "The Return of Frank James" 1940 (Prosecutor); "Santa Fe Trail" 1940 (J. Boyce Russell); "Virginia City" 1940 (Armistead); "Arkansas Judge" 1941 (John Root); "The Parson of Panamint" 1941 (Prosecuting Attorney); "They Died with Their Boots On" 1941 (Colonel of the 1st Michigan); "Western Union" 1941 (Governor); "King of the Mounties" 1942-serial (Marshal Carleton); "Ride 'Em, Cowboy" 1942 (Announcer); "King of the Cowboys" 1943 (Governor Shuville); "The Woman of the Town" 1943 (Publisher); "Flame of the Barbary Coast" 1945 (Cyrus Danver); "Plainsman and the Lady" 1946 (Sen. Twin); "The Sea of Grass" 1947 (Maj. Harney); "Smoky River Serenade" 1947; "The Gallant Legion" 1948 (Sen. Beale); "The Plunderers" 1948 (Cavalry Colonel); "Silver River" 1948 (Edwards, the Architect); "Overland Telegraph" 1951 (Colonel); "The Maverick" 1952 (Major Hook); "Old Oklahoma Plains" 1952 (Col. Bigelow); "Seventh Cavalry" 1956 (Col. Kellogg). ¶TV: *The Cisco Kid*—"False Marriage" 4-14-51, "Wedding Blackmail" 4-21-51; *The Lone Ranger*—"The Condemned Man" 12-11-52.

Hiers, Walter (1893-2/27/33). Films: "Leave It to Susan" 1919 (Horace Peddingham).

Hiestand, John "Bud" (1906-2/5/87). Films: "King of the Mounties" 1942-serial (Lane); "Riding High" 1943 (Commentator).

Higby, Wilbur (1866-12/1/34). Films: "As in the Days of Old" 1915; "Mixed Blood" 1916 (Joe Nagle); "Girl of the Timber Claims" 1917 (Senator Hoyle); "The Medicine Man" 1917 (Doc Hamilton); "Until They Get Me" 1917 (Draper); "Wild Sumac" 1917 (Armand du Fere); "By Proxy" 1918 (the Cattle Buyer); "Keith of the Border" 1918 (Dr. Fairban); "Under False Pretenses" 1918; "Nugget Nell" 1919 (Nell's Uncle); "The Lone Hand" 1920 (Sheriff Hampton); "The Terror" 1920 (John D. Sutherland); "Do and Dare" 1922 (Col. Handy Lee); "The Flaming Forties" 1925 (the Sheriff); "The Border Whirlwind" 1926 (Tom Blake, Sr.).

Higgins, David (1858-6/30/36). Films: "Rough and Ready" 1918 (Matthew Durant).

Higgins, Joe (1914-). Films: "Geronimo" 1962 (Kincaide). ¶TV: *The Rifleman*—"Strange Town" 10-25-60 (Bartender), "The Wyoming Story" 2-7-61 & 2-14-61 (Rafe), "Short Rope for a Tall Man" 3-28-61 (Henry Schneider), "Stopover" 4-25-61 (Scotty), Regular 1961-63 (Nils Swenson); *Bonanza*—"The Last Haircut" 2-3-63; *The Big Valley*—"Winner Lose All" 10-27-65, "The Brawlers" 12-15-65 (Passenger), "Into the Widow's Web" 3-23-66 (Fats Mortensen), "Tunnel of Gold" 4-20-66 (Salesman), "The Great Safe Robbery" 11-21-66 (Railroad Detective), "Turn of a Card" 3-20-67, "Guilty" 10-30-67 (the Baker); *The Legend of Jesse James*—"The Quest" 11-1-65 (Bartender); *Gunsmoke*—"Fandango" 2-11-67 (Smithy), "The Devil's Outpost" 9-22-69 (George Miller); *The Guns of Will Sonnett*—"End of the Rope" 1-12-68, "Time Is the Rider" 1-10-69.

Higgins, Joel (1946-). TV: *Best of the West*—Regular 1981-82 (Sam Best).

Higgins, Michael (1922-). TV: *Gunsmoke*—"Two of a Kind" 3-16-63 (Tim Finnegan), "The Kite" 2-29-64 (Rod Cassidy); *The Virginian*—"Johnny Moon" 10-11-67 (Lawson).

Higgins, Rose. Films: "The Silent Code" 1935 (Indian Servant); "Ramrod" 1947 (Annie); "Unconquered" 1947.

Hightower, Brian "Slim". Films: "Three Rogues" 1931 (Teamster); "Thunder Trail" 1937 (Cowboy); "The Texans" 1938 (Cowboy); "Sunset Pass" 1946 (Robber); "Dakota Lil" 1950; "Fort Defiance" 1951 (Hankey); "Flaming Feather" 1952; "The Searchers" 1956 (Stunts); "The Man Who Shot Liberty Valance" 1962 (Shotgun).

Hightower, Red. Films: "Sudden Bill Dorn" 1937 (Bud Williams).

Hiken, Gerald (1927-). Films: "Invitation to a Gunfighter" 1964 (Gully). ¶TV: *Bonanza*—"Search in Limbo" 2-20-72 (Dr. Penner); *Wildside*—4-18-85 (Crool).

Hilbeck, Fernando (1933-). Films: "Terrible Sheriff" 1963-Span./ Ital.; "The Christmas Kid" 1966-Span./Ital. (Jud Walters); "Kid Rodelo" 1966-U.S./Span. (Perryman); "Son of a Gunfighter" 1966-U.S./ Span. (Joaquin); "The Tall Women" 1966-Austria/Ital./Span. (White Cloud); "The Man Called Noon" 1973-Brit./Span./Ital. (Ford).

Hildebrand, Rodney (1893-2/22/62). Films: "The Escape of Broncho Billy" 1915; "Stone of Silver Creek" 1935 (Graves); "The Lonely Trail" 1936 (Captain of Cavalry).

Hill, Al (1892-7/14/54). Films: "The Border Patrolman" 1936 (Frank Adams); "Call of the Prairie" 1936 (Slade); "Three on the Trail" 1936 (Kit Thorpe); "Hollywood Cowboy" 1937 (Camby); "Secret Valley" 1937; "Partners of the Plains" 1938 (Doc Galer); "Rawhide" 1938; "The Man from Tumbleweeds" 1940 (Honest John Webster); "San Antonio" 1945 (Hap Winters); "Fury at Furnace Creek" 1948 (Card Player); "The Paleface" 1948 (Pioneer); "River Lady" 1948 (Lumberjack); "Station West" 1948 (Croupier); "The Stranger Wore a Gun" 1953; "Silver Lode" 1954 (Townsman).

Hill, Arthur (1922-). Films: "Butch and Sundance: The Early Days" 1979 (Wyoming Governor). ¶TV: *Lancer*—"Warburton's Edge" 2-4-69 (Charles Warburton).

Hill, Ben (1894-11/30/69). Films: "Dangerous Trails" 1920; "The Unknown Ranger" 1920 (Chandler); "The Border Raiders" 1921; "On the High Card" 1921 (Ben Stiles).

Hill, Carol. TV: *Sergeant Preston of the Yukon*—"The Old Timer" 12-19-57 (Nancy Croydon); *Have Gun Will Travel*—"Heritage of Anger" 6-6-59 (Alice Avery).

Hill, Charles (1888-11/2/38). Films: "Rainbow's End" 1935 (Bert Kendall); "Lucky Terror" 1936 (Doc Haliday).

Hill, Craig. Films: "The Outcasts of Poker Flat" 1952 (Tom Dakin); "The Siege at Red River" 1954 (Lt. Braden); "Hands of a Gunman" 1965-Ital./Span. (Galen Stark); "Adios Hombre" 1966-Ital./Span. (Will Flarity); "Taste for Killing" 1966-Ital./Span. (Lanky Fellow); "Rick and John, Conquerors of the West" 1967-Ital. (Captain Stuart); "Bury Them Deep" 1968-Ital. (Clive Norton); "Fifteen Scaffolds for the Killer" 1968-Ital./Span. (Billy Mack); "I Want Him Dead" 1968-Ital./Span. (Clayton); "No Graves on Boot Hill" 1968-Ital. (Jerry); "And the Crows Will Dig Your Grave" 1971-Ital./Span.; "Go Away! Trinity Has Arrived in Eldorado" 1972-Ital.; "In the Name of the Father, the Son and the Colt" 1972-Fr./Ital (Sheriff Johnston); "My Horse, My Gun, Your Widow" 1972-Ital./Span. (Dr. Janos Saxon); "Animal Called Man" 1973-Ital.; "Gunmen and the Holy Ghost" 1973-Ital.; "Drummer of Vengeance"

1974-Brit./Ital. ¶TV: *My Friend Flicka*—"Lock, Stock and Barrel" 4-6-56 (Lieutenant Blake), "When Bugles Blow" 5-18-56; *Death Valley Days*—"Year of Destiny" 1-27-57, "Train of Events" 5-19-57; *Sugarfoot*—"Trouble at Sand Springs" 4-17-61 (Rance Benbow).

Hill, Doris (1905-). Films: "Tom and His Pals" 1926 (Mary Smith); "Avalanche" 1928 (Kitty Mains); "Code of Honor" 1930 (Doris Bradfield); "Song of the Caballero" 1930 (Anita); "Sons of the Saddle" 1930 (Ronnie Stavnow); "The Montana Kid" 1931 (Molly Moore); "The One Way Trail" 1931 (Helen Beck); "Battling Buckaroo" 1932 (Tonia Mendoza); "South of the Rio Grande" 1932 (Dolores); "Spirit of the West" 1932 (Dorothy Moore); "Texas Tornado" 1932 (Ruth O'Byrne); "Crashing Broadway" 1933 (Sally Sunshine); "Galloping Romeo" 1933 (Mary Kent); "The Ranger's Code" 1933 (Mary Clayton); "Trailing North" 1933 (Mitzi); "Via Pony Express" 1933; "Ridin' Gent" 1934-short.

Hill, Hallene (1876-1/6/66). Films: "Cat Ballou" 1965 (Honey Girl). ¶TV: *The Roy Rogers Show*—"The Set-Up" 1-20-52 (Granny Hobbs).

Hill, Howard (1899-2/4/75). Films: "The Singing Buckaroo" 1937; "San Antonio" 1945 (Cowboy).

Hill, Jack. *see* Keefe, Cornelius.

Hill, Josephine (1899-12/17/89). Films: "At the Point of the Gun" 1919; "The Double Hold-Up" 1919; "The Face in the Watch" 1919; "The Fighting Heart" 1919; "The Four-Bit Man" 1919; "The Jack of Hearts" 1919; "The Lone Hand" 1919; "The Jay Bird" 1920; "One He Man" 1920; "The Gun Game" 1920; "The Sheriff's Oath" 1920; "West Is Best" 1920; "Beauty and the Bandit" 1921; "The Call of Duty" 1921; "Fair Fighting" 1921; "The Fight Within" 1921; "The Honor of the Mounted" 1921; "The Man Trackers" 1921 (Molly Killbridge); "The Raiders of the North" 1921; "Roaring Waters" 1921; "The Bar Cross War" 1922; "Come and Get Me" 1922; "Deputized" 1922; "The Drifter" 1922; "Here's Your Man" 1922; "His Enemy's Friend" 1922; "His Own Law" 1922; "One Jump Ahead" 1922; "Rough Going" 1922; "Under Suspicion" 1922; "The Extra Seven" 1923; "Hyde and Zeke" 1923; "In Wrong Right" 1923; "King's Creek Law" 1923 (Milly Jameson); "The Lone Fighter" 1923 (Rose Trimball); "The Lone Horse-

man" 1923; "100% Nerve" 1923; "Partners Three" 1923; "Steel Shod Evidence" 1923; "Tom, Dick and Harry" 1923; "The Unsuspecting Stranger" 1923; "Warned in Advance" 1923; "Western Justice" 1923 (Grace); "When Fighting's Necessary" 1923; "Wings of the Storm" 1923; "Yellow Gold and Men" 1923; "Coyote Fangs" 1924 (Sylvia Dodge); "Headin' Through" 1924 (Rhoda Hilder); "Lightnin' Jack" 1924 (Mildred Manning); "The Loser's End" 1924 (Lois Kincaid); "Not Guilty for Runnin'" 1924 (Lou Coberly); "Payable on Demand" 1924 (Mona Selby); "Riding Double" 1924 (Elizabeth Walters); "Across the Deadline" 1925 (Shirley Revelle); "The Blood Bond" 1925 (Martha Hazard); "Border Vengeance" 1925; "Don X" 1925 (Gladys Paget); "Flash O'Lightning" 1925 (Edith Willett); "Luck and Sand" 1925 (Lois Wetzel); "The Shield of Silence" 1925 (Marjorie Stone); "Silent Sheldon" 1925 (Mary Watkins); "The Trouble Buster" 1925 (Helen Williams); "Win, Lose or Draw" 1925 (Heloise); "Winning a Woman" 1925; "Blind Trail" 1926 (Alice Bartlett); "The High Hand" 1926 (Edith Oaks); "Hi-Jacking Rustlers" 1926; "Lawless Trails" 1926 (Josephine Sturgess); "Without Orders" 1926 (Martha Wells); "Danger Ahead" 1927; "The Devil's Twin" 1927 (Alice Kemper); "Two-Gun of the Tumbleweed" 1927 (Nan Brunelle); "The Apache Kid's Escape" 1930; "The Kid from Arizona" 1931; "West of Cheyenne" 1931 (Bess); "Wild West Whoopee" 1931; "Potluck Pards" 1934.

Hill, Kathryn. Films: "The Yankee Senor" 1926 (Doris Mayne).

Hill, Lee. Films: "The Indian's Lament 1917; "The Good Loser" 1918 (Harry Littlejohn); "Wolves of the Range" 1918; "The Challenge of Chance" 1919 (Bob Edmunds); "Tapering Fingers" 1919.

Hill, Marianna (1941-). Films: "El Condor" 1970 (Claudine); "High Plains Drifter" 1973 (Callie Travers). ¶TV: *Tate*—"A Lethal Pride" 7-20-60 (Carmela Arriega); *The Tall Man*—"A Bounty for Billy" 10-15-60 (Rita), "And the Beast" 11-26-60 (Rita), "Billy's Baby" 12-24-60 (Rita), "The Last Resource" 3-11-61 (Rita), "The Judas Palm" 10-21-61 (Rita); *The Westerner*—"Dos Pinos" 11-4-60; *Two Faces West*—"The Witness" 1-23-61; *Gunsmoke*—"Pa Hack's Brood" 12-28-63 (Annie); *Bonanza*—"Ponderosa Matador" 1-12-64 (Dolores Tenino); *Death Valley Days*—"From the Earth, a Heritage" 12-13-64 (Tula); *Wild Wild West*—"The Night of the Bogus Bandits" 4-7-67 (Belladonna); *The High Chaparral*—"Bad Day for Bad Men" 10-17-69 (Juanita); *Daniel Boone*—"Before the Tall Man" 2-12-70 (Nancy Hanks); *Kung Fu*—"The Passion of Chen Yi" 2-28-74 (Louise Coblenz); *Nakia*—"The Sand Trap" 10-5-74 (Julia); *Big Hawaii*—"The Sugar War" 1977.

Hill, Maury (1923-). TV: *Tales of Wells Fargo*—"Black Trail" 3-14-60 (Davis).

Hill, Phyllis. TV: *Death Valley Days*—"The Stranger" 3-15-60 (Jessica); *The Road West*—"Pariah" 12-5-66 (Mrs. Oliver); *Bonanza*—"Napoleon's Children" 4-16-67 (Grace).

Hill, Ramsey (1891-2/3/76). Films: "Old Louisiana" 1937 (James Madison); "The Battles of Chief Pontiac" 1952 (Gen. Amherst); "The Iron Mistress" 1952 (Malot). TV: *Jim Bowie*—"The Return of the Alciblade" 12-21-56.

Hill, Riley (Roy Harris) (1914-). Films: "Oklahoma Frontier" 1939 (Trooper); "Law of the Range" 1941 (the Kid); "Men of the Timberland" 1941; "Rawhide Rangers" 1941 (Steve); "Arizona Stagecoach" 1942; "North to the Klondike" 1942 (Ben Sloan); "Overland Mail" 1942-serial; "Texas Trouble Shooters" 1942 (Bret Travis); "Ghost Guns" 1944; "Flame of the West" 1945 (Midland); "Gun Smoke" 1945; "The Lost Trail" 1945 (Ned Turner); "The Navajo Trail" 1945; "Sheriff of Cimarron" 1945 (Ted Carson); "Border Bandits" 1946 (Steve Halliday); "The Desert Horseman" 1946 (Eddie); "The Haunted Mine" 1946; "Trigger Fingers" 1946; "Under Arizona Skies" 1946; "Code of the Saddle" 1947; "Flashing Guns" 1947; "Frontier Agent" 1948; "Range Renegades" 1948; "The Rangers Ride" 1948; "Singing Spurs" 1948; "Across the Rio Grande" 1949 (Steven Blaine); "Law of the West" 1949 (Charley); "Lawless Code" 1949; "Range Justice" 1949 (Glenn Hadley); "Shadows of the West" 1949 (Bud); "Western Renegades" 1949 (Joe Gordon); "Fence Riders" 1950; "Gunslingers" 1950 (Tim Cramer); "Jiggs and Maggie Out West" 1950 (Bob Carter); "Law of the Panhandle" 1950 (Tom Stocker); "Short Grass" 1950 (Randee); "Silver Raiders" 1950 (Bill); "Six Gun Mesa" 1950; "Canyon Raiders" 1951; "Nevada Badmen" 1951; "Valley of Fire" 1951 (Colorado); "The Vanishing Outpost" 1951 (Walker); "The Lusty Men" 1952 (Hoag, the Ranch

Hand); "Night Stage to Galveston" 1952; "The Raiders" 1952 (Clark Leftus); "Target" 1952 (Foster); "Wagons West" 1952 (Gaylor Cook); "Buchanan Rides Alone" 1958; "Rio Bravo" 1959 (Messenger); "The Deadly Companions" 1961 (Gambler); "El Dorado" 1967; "The Trial of Billy Jack" 1974 (Posner); "Wanda Nevada" 1979. TV: *The Marshal of Gunsight Pass*—Regular 1950; *The Lone Ranger*—"Double Jeopardy" 9-7-50, "Backtrail" 1-25-51; *The Cisco Kid*—"Counterfeit Money" 1-27-51, "Convict Story" 2-17-51, "The Will" 3-24-51, "Cattle Quarantine" 3-31-51, "Hypnotist Murder" 11-10-51, "Ghost Town Story" 12-22-51; *Wild Bill Hickok*—"Johnny Deuce" 9-4-51, "Jingles Becomes a Baby Sitter" 4-15-52, "Heading for Trouble" 6-10-52; *The Gene Autry Show*—"Frontier Guard" 10-13-51, "Killer's Trail" 10-27-51, "Melody Mesa" 1-4-52; *The Roy Rogers Show*—"Jailbreak" 12-30-51, "Badman's Brother" 2-10-52 (Alabama Al), "The Desert Fugitive" 2-24-52, "The Minister's Son" 3-23-52, "Phantom Rustlers" 4-25-54 (Carson).

Hill, Robert (1886-3/18/66). Films: "Cheyenne Rides Again" 1937; "Little Joe, the Wrangler" 1942 (Hammond); "Wolves of the Range" 1943 (Judge Brandon); "Boss of Rawhide" 1944 (Capt. Wyatt); "Fuzzy Settles Down" 1944; "Trail of Terror" 1944 (Capt. Curtis).

Hill, Stephanie. Films: "Alvarez Kelly" 1966 (Mary Ann); "Scalplock" TVM-1966. TV: *Frontier Circus*—"The Good Fight" 4-19-62 (Evvy Sanders); *Iron Horse*—"Joy Unconfined" 9-12-66 (Lucy).

Hill, Steven (1924-). TV: *Rawhide*—"The Gray Rock Hotel" 5-21-65 (Marty Brown).

Hill, Terence (Mario Girotti) (1939-). Films: "Among Vultures" 1964-Ger./Ital./Fr./Yugo. (Baker); "Duel at Sundown" 1965-Fr./Ger. (Larry McGow); "Flaming Frontier" 1965-Ger./Yugo. (Toby); "Rampage at Apache Wells" 1965-Ger./Yugo. (Richard Forsythe); "God Forgives—I Don't" 1966-Ital./Span. (Cat Stevens); "Last of the Renegades" 1966-Fr./Ital./Ger./Yugo. (Lt. Merril); "Ace High" 1967-Ital./Span. (Cat Stevens); "Rita of the West" 1967-Ital. (Black Star); "Get the Coffin Ready" 1968-Ital. (Django); "Boot Hill" 1969-Ital. (Cat Stevens); "They Call Me Trinity" 1970-Ital. (Trinity); "Trinity Sees Red" 1971-Ital./Span. (Trinity); "My Name Is Nobody" 1973-Ital. (Nobody); "A Man from

the East" 1974-Ital./Fr. (Sir Thomas More); "Trinity Is Still My Name" 1974-Ital. (Trinity); "Genius" 1975-Ital./Fr./Ger. (Joe Thanks).

Hillaire, Marcel (1907-1/1/88). Films: "North to Alaska" 1960 (Butler, Jenny's Husband). TV: *Daniel Boone*—"The Fleeing Nuns" 10-24-68 (Pelletier); *Here Come the Brides*—"How Dry We Are" 3-6-70 (La Fond).

Hillerman, John (1932-). Films: "Lawman" 1971 (Totts); "High Plains Drifter" 1973 (Bootmaker); "Blazing Saddles" 1974 (Howard Johnson); "The Invasion of Johnson County" TVM-1976 (Major Walcott). TV: *Young Maverick*—"Makin' Tracks" 1-9-80 (McBurney).

Hilliard, Ernest (1890-9/3/47). Films: "Galloping Hoofs" 1924-serial; "The Fighting Failure" 1926; "The Frontier Trail" 1926 (Captain Blackwell); "The Silent Hero" 1927 (Wade Burton); "The Big Hop" 1928 (Ben Barnett); "The Big Diamond Robbery" 1929 (Rodney Stevens); "Boss Rider of Gun Creek" 1936 (Ed Randall).

Hilliard, Harry (1886-4/21/66). Films: "Gold and the Woman" 1916 (Lee Duskara).

Hilliard, Jack. Films: "The Pride of Pawnee" 1929 (George LaForte).

Hillias, Margaret "Peg" (-3/18/60). TV: *Gunsmoke*—"Cholera" 12-29-56 (Jenny); *The Californians*—"Man from Boston" 11-12-57 (Sarah Jameson), "The Inner Circle" 5-13-58 (Nellie); *Have Gun Will Travel*—"No Visitors" 11-30-57 (Mrs. Jonas); *Wagon Train*—"The Daniel Barrister Story" 4-16-58 (Jenny Barrister).

Hillie, Verna. Films: "Man of the Forest" 1933 (Alice Gaynor); "Under the Tonto Rim" 1933 (Nina Weston); "Mystery Mountain" 1934-serial (Jane Corwin); "The Star Packer" 1934 (Anita Matlock); "The Trail Beyond" 1934 (Felice Newsome).

Hills, Beverly (1939-). Films: "The Last Challenge" 1967 (Saloon Hostess). TV: *The High Chaparral*—"The Fillibusteros" 10-22-67 (Lily).

Hilton, George. Films: "Massacre Time" 1966-Ital./Span./Ger. (Jeff); "Two Sons of Ringo" 1966-Ital.; "Kitosch, the Man who Came from the North" 1967-Ital./Span. (Major Zachary Baker); "Poker with Pistols" 1967-Ital. (Ponson); "Time of Vultures" 1967-Ital. (Kitosch); "Any Gun Can Play" 1968-Ital./Span. (the Stranger); "Dead for a Dollar" 1968-Ital.; "The Greatest Robbery in the West" 1968-Ital. (David Faylord); "The Moment to Kill" 1968-Ital./ Ger. (Lord); "Red Blood, Yellow Gold" 1968-Ital./Span. (Frank the Preacher); "The Ruthless Four" 1968-Ital./Ger. (Manolo); "To Hell and Back" 1968-Ital./Span.; "A Bullet for Sandoval" 1970-Ital./Span. (Warner); "Heads You Die … Tails I Kill You" 1971-Ital. (Hallelujah); "I Am Sartana, Trade Your Guns for a Coffin" 1972-Ital. (Sartana); "Return of Halleluja" 1972-Ital./Ger. (Halleluja); "Man Called Invincible" 1973-Ital. (Tressette); "Dick Luft in Sacramento" 1974-Ital. (Dick Luft); "Trinity Plus the Clown and a Guitar" 1975-Ital./Austria/Fr.   (Trinity); "Who's Afraid of Zorro?" 1975-Ital./Span. (Zorro); "Macho Killers" 1977-Ital. (Duke).

Hilton, Robert. Films: "Cow Town" 1950 (Miller); "Indian Territory" 1950; "Mule Train" 1950 (Bancroft); "Gene Autry and the Mounties" 1951; "The Old West" 1952.

Hilton, Robyn (1949-). Films: "Blazing Saddles" 1974.

Hincks, Reginald. Films: "Secret Patrol" 1936 (Superintendent Barkley); "Stampede" 1936 (Sheriff Ed); "Fighting Playboy" 1937 (Bill); "Death Goes North" 1939 (Freddie).

Hinde, Madeline (1949-). Films: "Charley One-Eye" 1973-Brit. (Penelope).

Hindle, Art (1948-). TV: *Lonesome Dove*—3-5-95.

Hindman, Earl (1940-). Films: "Silverado" 1985 (J.T.).

Hinds, Samuel S. (1875-10/13/ 48). Films: "Massacre" 1934; "West of the Pecos" 1934 (Colonel Lambeth); "Law Beyond the Range" 1935 (Alexander); "Rhythm on the Range" 1936 (Robert Halliday); "Forbidden Valley" 1938 (Jeff Hazzard); "Destry Rides Again" 1939 (Judge Slade); "Trail of the Vigilantes" 1940 (George Preston); "Badlands of Dakota" 1941 (Uncle Wilbur); "Lady from Cheyenne" 1941 (Governor Howard); "Road Agent" 1941 (Sam Leavitt); "The Shepherd of the Hills" 1941 (Andy Beeler); "Ride 'Em, Cowboy" 1942 (Sam Shaw); "The Spoilers" 1942 (Judge Stillman); "The Singing Sheriff" 1944 (Seth); "Frisco Sal" 1945 (Doc).

Hindy, Joseph (1939-). TV: *Gunsmoke*—"The Golden Land" 3-5-73 (Laibel), "Matt Dillon Must Die!" 9-9-74 (Jacob).

Hines, Connie. TV: *Bronco*— "Game at the Beacon Club" 9-22-59 (Cynthy Harkness); *Shotgun Slade*—

"Backtrack" 7-26-60 (Katy); *Riverboat*—"Chicota Landing" 12-5-60 (Lucy Bridges); *Bonanza*—"The Witness" 9-21-69 (Hilda).

Hines, Harry (1889-5/3/67). Films: "City of Badmen" 1953 (Stewpot); "Last of the Pony Riders" 1953 (Bindlestiff); "Powder River" 1953 (Drunk); "Riding Shotgun" 1954; "Friendly Persuasion" 1956 (Barker). ¶TV: *The Restless Gun*—"Imposter for a Day" 2-17-58 (Willy Beebe), "The Manhunters" 6-2-58 (Sam Henneberry), "The Hill of Death" 6-22-59 (Edward); *Wagon Train*—"The Cassie Tanner Story" 6-4-58 (Obie Harper), "The Millie Davis Story" 11-26-58 (Hank); *Maverick*—"Yellow River" 2-8-59 (Pete Mulligan); *Cheyenne*—"Alibi for a Scalped Man" 3-7-60 (Stableman).

Hines, Johnny (1897-10/24/70). Films: "All Man" 1916 (Snap Higgins); "Eastward Ho!" 1919.

Hingle, Pat (1923-). Films: "Invitation to a Gunfighter" 1964 (Sam Brewster); "Nevada Smith" 1966 (Big Foot); "Hang 'Em High" 1968 (Judge Adam Fenton); "One Little Indian" 1973 (Capt. Stewart); "Running Wild" 1973; "Wild Times" TVM-1980 (Bob Halburton); "Gunsmoke: To the Last Man" TVM-1991 (Colonel Tucker); "Lightning Jack" 1994-Australia (Marshal Kurtz); "The Quick and the Dead" 1995 (Horace the Bartender). ¶TV: *Rawhide*—"The Book" 1-8-65 (Pop Starke); *Daniel Boone*—"The Returning" 1-14-65 (Will Carey); *The Loner*—"The Mourners for Johnny Sharp" 2-5-66 & 2-12-66 (Bob Pierson); *A Man Called Shenandoah*—"Plunder" 3-7-66 (Tenney); *Cimarron Strip*—"Broken Wing" 9-21-67 (Mike McQueen); *The High Chaparral*—"Threshold of Courage" 3-31-68 (Finley Carr); *Bonanza*—"Silence at Stillwater" 9-28-69 (Sheriff Austin); *Lancer*—"A Scarecrow at Hacket's" 12-16-69 (Absolem Weir); *Gunsmoke*—"New Doctor in Town" 10-11-71 (Dr. John Chapman), "The Legend" 10-18-71 (Dr. John Chapman), "Lynott" 11-1-71 (Dr. John Chapman), "Lijah" 11-8-71 (Dr. John Chapman), "My Brother's Keeper" 11-15-71 (Dr. John Chapman), "Drago" 11-22-71 (Dr. John Chapman); *Kung Fu*—"The Soul Is the Warrior" 2-8-73 (Sheriff Thoms); *Hec Ramsey*—"The Mystery of Chalk Hill" 2-18-73 (Charlie Hollister); *Barbary Coast*—"Funny Money" 9-8-75 (Emory Van Cleve).

Hinkle, Ed. Films: "The Treasure of Lost Canyon" 1952 (Miner). ¶TV: *The Gene Autry Show*—"The

Lawless Press" 1-25-52, "Ruthless Renegade" 2-8-52; *The Roy Rogers Show*—"The Feud" 11-16-52, "The Run-A-Round" 2-22-53 (Lee Gray).

Hinkle, Robert. Films: "The First Traveling Saleslady" 1956 (Pete); "The Oklahoman" 1957 (Ken, the Driver); "Old Rex" 1961; "Young Guns of Texas" 1963 (Sheriff Hubbard). ¶TV: *Gunsmoke*—"The Mistake" 11-24-56 (Rider), "Quint Asper Comes Home" 9-29-62 (Cowboy); *Annie Oakley*—"Dude's Decision" 2-10-57 (Reno); *Tales of Wells Fargo*—"Deadwood" 4-7-58 (Mac); *Frontier Circus*—"Stopover in Paradise" 2-22-62 (Dave).

Hinn, Michael. Films: "The Halliday Brand" 1957; "Gun Fever" 1958 (Stableman); "Valdez Is Coming" 1971 (Merchant). ¶TV: *Sky King*—"Bounty Hunters" 7-27-52 (Al Collier); *Gunsmoke*—"The Roundup" 9-29-56 (Zel Blatnick), "The Executioner" 2-2-57 (Morgan Curry), "Joke's on Us" 3-15-58 (Frank Tilman), "Lynching Man" 11-15-58 (Gil Mather), "Kangaroo" 9-26-59 (Wirth), "The Wake" 12-10-60 (Joe Brant); *Boots and Saddles*—Regular 1957-59 (Luke Cummings); *Zane Grey Theater*—"A Gun Is for Killing" 10-18-57 (Ebie Brenner), "Trail Incident" 1-29-59 (Loco Thompson), "Ransom" 11-17-60 (Scotsman), "The Last Bugle" 11-24-60 (Tom Horn), "The Mormons" 12-15-60 (Adam Lawson); *Have Gun Will Travel*— "The Hanging Cross" 12-21-57; *El Coyote Rides*—Pilot 1958 (Sheriff); *Broken Arrow*—"The Outlaw" 6-10-58 (Sheriff Lincoln); *Tales of Wells Fargo*—"The House I Enter" 3-2-59; *The Law of the Plainsman*—"Blood Trails" 11-5-59, "The Matriarch" 2-18-60 (Hodie Carver); *Johnny Ringo*—"Black Harvest" 4-7-60 (Haig Konopka), "The Killing Bug" 4-18-60 (Haig), "Coffin Sam" 6-16-60 (Haig), "Lobo Lawman" 6-23-60 (Haig); *The Tall Man*—"Tiger Eye" 12-17-60 (Forbes); *Bonanza*—"The Jury" 12-30-62, "A Matter of Faith" 9-20-70 (Garrison); *Rawhide*—"The Race" 9-25-64 (Clerk); *The Guns of Will Sonnett*—"Robber's Roost" 1-17-69.

Hinton, Darby. TV: *Daniel Boone*—Regular 1964-70 (Israel Boone); *The Big Valley*—"Boy into Man" 1-16-67.

Hinton, Ed (1928-10/12/58). Films: "Hellgate" 1952 (Ault); "Leadville Gunslinger" 1952 (Deputy Ned Smith); "The Lion and the Horse" 1952 (Al Richie); "River of No Return" 1954 (Gambler); "Seminole Uprising" 1955 (Capt. Phillip Dudley); "Walk the Proud Land" 1956 (Naylor); "The Dalton Girls" 1957 (Detective Hiram Parsh); "Shoot-Out at Medicine Bend" 1957; "Escape from Red Rock" 1958 (Tarrant); "Fort Bowie" 1958 (Gentleman); "Good Day for a Hanging" 1958 (Citizen). ¶TV: *The Lone Ranger*—"The Black Hat" 5-18-50, "Letter of the Law" 1-4-51, "Heritage of Treason" 2-3-55, "Uncle Ed" 3-3-55; *The Cisco Kid*—"The Lowest Bidder" 4-4-53, "Sundown's Gun" 4-18-53; *The Adventures of Rin Tin Tin*—"The Bounty Hunters" 5-13-55, "The Poor Little Rich Boy" 10-7-55 (Whitley Larrimore), "Circle of Fire" 5-11-56 (Seth Ramsey); *Tales of the Texas Rangers*—"The Rough, Tough West" 12-10-55 (Walker); *Sergeant Preston of the Yukon*—"Remember the Maine" 4-26-56 (Barry Jeffers), "The Rookie" 9-20-56 (Lefty Burke); *Circus Boy*—"The Return of Colonel Jack" 2-10-57 (Mike), "The Magic Lantern" 11-7-57 (Sheriff), "The Judge's Boy" 12-5-57 (Glenn Keyes); *The Roy Rogers Show*—"High Stakes" 2-24-57; *Wyatt Earp*—"The Manly Art" 1-21-58 (Moresby), "Frontier Woman" 11-25-58 (Snakey); *Tales of Wells Fargo*—"The Sooners" 3-3-58 (Colonel); *Rough Riders*—"Shadows of the Past" 11-27-58 (Capt. Alcorn).

Hinz, Michael. Films: "Return of Halleluja" 1972-Ital./Ger.

Hippe, Laura (-2/21/86). TV: *How the West Was Won*—Episode One 2-6-77 (Alice).

Hippe, Lewis (1880-7/19/52). Films: "The Mollycoddle" 1920 (First Mate); "The Taming of the West" 1925 (Perry Potter).

Hirson, Alice (1929-). Films: "Kate Bliss and the Ticker Tape Kid" TVM-1978 (Betty Dozier).

Hirt, Christianne. TV: *Lonesome Dove*—Regular 1994- (Hannah).

Hiser, Joe. Films: "Deadline" 1948; "Fighting Mustang" 1948; "Sunset Carson Rides Again" 1948; "The Kid from Gower Gulch" 1949; "Battling Marshal" 1950.

Hitchcock, Keith. *see* Kenneth, Keith.

Hitchcock, Walter (1872-6/23/17). Films: "The Girl I Left Behind Me" 1915 (Genera).

Hix, Don (1891-12/31/64). TV: *The Restless Gun*—"Incident at Bluefield" 3-30-59; *Frontier Circus*—"Stopover in Paradise" 2-22-62 (Perkins).

Ho, Linda (1939-). TV: *Wagon Train*—"The Widow O'Rourke"

Story" 10-7-63 (Ming Lu); *Wild Wild West*—"The Night of a Thousand Eyes" 10-22-65 (Oriana), "The Night of the Pelican" 12-27-68.

Hoag, Curley. Films: "Santa Fe Rides" 1937; "Bar Buckaroos" 1940-short; "Corralling a School Marm" 1940-short; "California or Bust" 1941-short; "Redskins and Redheads" 1941-short; "Keep Shooting" 1942-short.

Hoag, Judith. TV: *Young Riders*—"The Littlest Cowboy" 11-23-90 (Helen); *Adventures of Brisco County, Jr.*—"Socrates' Sister" 9-24-93 (Ephigenia Poole).

Hoag, Mitzi (1932-). TV: *Gunsmoke*—"Tell Chester" 4-20-63 (Polly Donahue), "Baker's Dozen" 12-25-67 (Clara Remick); *Bonanza*—"Three Brides for Hoss" 2-20-66 (Libby), "Stallion" 11-14-72 (Alice Brenner); *Here Comes the Brides*—Regular 1968-70 (Essie), "Absalom" 3-20-70 (Sister Agnes); *Alias Smith and Jones*—"Stagecoach Seven" 3-11-71 (Winifred Bowers); *Father Murphy*—"Stopover in a One-Way Horse Town" 10-26-82 (Mrs. Douglas).

Hoag, Robert. Films: "Rollin' Home to Texas" 1941; "Bad Men of Thunder Gap" 1943 (Cal Shrum's Rhythm Rangers); "Swing, Cowboy, Swing" 1944.

Hobart, Lyndon. Films: "Ridgeway of Montana" 1924 (Pierre Gendron).

Hobart, Rose (1906-). Films: "Canyon Passage" 1946 (Marita Lestrade). ¶TV: *Gunsmoke*—"A Noose for Dobie Price" 3-4-68 (Melanie Katcher).

Hobbes, Halliwell (1877-2/20/62). Films: "Canyon Passage" 1946 (Clenchfield).

Hobbie, Duke (1942-). Films: "Cat Ballou" 1965 (Homer); "Alvarez Kelly" 1966 (John Beaurider); "A Time for Killing" 1967 (Lt. Frist); "MacKenna's Gold" 1969 (Lieutenant). ¶TV: *Gunsmoke*—"Mr. Sam'l" 2-26-68 (Dave Akins).

Hobbs, Hayford. Films: "Bucking the Barrier" 1923 (Cyril Cavendish); "That Man Jack!" 1925 (Sammy Sills).

Hobbs, Peter (1918-). Films: "Belle Starr" TVM-1980 (Jenkins). ¶TV: *The Big Valley*—"Days of Wrath" 1-8-68 (Cliff Hyatt); *Bonanza*—"A Lonely Man" 1-2-72 (Judge Hill).

Hodge, Harold. Films: "Law for Tombstone" 1937; "Sandflow" 1937 (Rillito); "Sudden Bill Dorn" 1937 (Mike Bundy).

Hodges, Eddie (1947-). TV: *Bonanza*—"A Natural Wizard" 12-12-65 (Skeeter Dexter); *Gunsmoke*—"Mail Drop" 1-28-67 (Billy); *Cimarron Strip*—"Big Jessie" 2-8-68 (Bud Baylor).

Hodgins, Earle (1899-4/14/64). Films: "Cyclone Ranger" 1935 (Pancho Gonzales); "Moonlight on the Prairie" 1935 (Spieler); "Paradise Canyon" 1935 (Dr. Carter); "The Texas Rambler" 1935; "Aces and Eights" 1936 (Marshal); "Border Caballero" 1936 (Doc Shaw); "Guns and Guitars" 1936 (Professor Parker); "Oh, Susanna!" 1936 (Professor Daniels); "The Singing Cowboy" 1936 (Prof. Sandow); "Borderland" 1937 (Major Stafford); "Ghost Town Gold" 1937; "Headin' East" 1937 (Fred W. Calhoun); "Hills of Old Wyoming" 1937 (Thompson); "Law for Tombstone" 1937 (Jack Dunn/ Twin Gun Jack); "A Lawman Is Born" 1937 (Sheriff Lance); "Outlaws of the Prairie" 1937 (Neenah); "Range Defenders" 1937 (Sheriff Gray); "Roaring Six Guns" 1937 (Sundown); "Round-Up Time in Texas" 1937 (Barkey McCuskey); "Smoke Tree Range" 1937 (Sheriff Day); "Texas Trail" 1937; "Trail of Vengeance" 1937 (Buck Andrews); "Call the Mesquiteers" 1938 (Dr. Aurelius Irving); "Flaming Frontier" 1938-serial; "The Great Adventures of Wild Bill Hickok" 1938; "Heroes of the Alamo" 1938 (Stephen Austin); "The Last Stand" 1938 (Thorn Evans); "The Last Stand" 1938 (Thom); "Lawless Valley" 1938 (Sheriff Heck Hampton); "The Old Barn Dancer" 1938 (Terwilliger); "Partners of the Plains" 1938 (Sheriff); "Pride of the West" 1938 (Sheriff Tom Martin); "The Purple Vigilantes" 1938 (J.T. "Mack" McAllister); "The Rangers' Roundup" 1938 (Doc Aikman); "Under Western Stars" 1938 (Master of Ceremonies); "Dodge City" 1939 (Spieler); "Home on the Prairie" 1939 (Prof. Wentworth); "In Old Monterey" 1939; "Range War" 1939 (Deputy Sheriff); "Bad Man from Red Butte" 1940; "Law and Order" 1940 (Elder); "The Range Busters" 1940 (Uncle Rolf); "The Sagebrush Family Trails West" 1940 (Doc Sawyer); "Santa Fe Marshal" 1940 (Doc Bates); "Trail of the Vigilantes" 1940 (Medicine Man); "Under Texas Skies" 1940 (Smithers); "Boss of Bullion City" 1941 (Mike Calhoun); "Sierra Sue" 1941 (Brandywine); "Call of the Canyon" 1942; "Deep in the Heart of Texas" 1942; "Fighting Bill Fargo" 1942; "Old Chisholm Trail" 1942 (Chief Hopping Crow);

"Riding the Wind" 1942 (Burt MacLeod); "Shut My Big Mouth" 1942 (Stagecoach Guard); "Silver Queen" 1942 (Desk Clerk); "Undercover Man" 1942 (Sheriff Blackton); "Bar 20" 1943 (Tom); "The Avenging Rider" 1943 (Deputy); "The Blocked Trail" 1943; "Colt Comrades" 1943 (Wildcat Willy); "False Colors" 1943 (Lawyer Jay Grifin); "Frontier Badman" 1943 (Desk Clerk); "Frontier Law" 1943 (Coroner); "Hoppy Serves a Writ" 1943 (Jim Belnap, Clerk); "The Lone Star Trail" 1943 (Maj. Cyrus Jenkins); "The Man from the Rio Grande" 1943; "Raiders of San Joaquin" 1943; "Red River Robin Hood" 1943; "Riders of the Deadline" 1943 (Sourdough); "Tenting Tonight on the Old Camp Ground" 1943 (Judge Higgins); "Firebrands of Arizona" 1944 (Sheriff Hoag); "Hidden Valley Outlaws" 1944; "Lumberjack" 1944; "Riders of the Santa Fe" 1944 (Ed Milton); "The San Antonio Kid" 1944; "Bells of Rosarita" 1945 (Carnival Pitchman); "Oregon Trail" 1945 (Judge); "Phantom of the Plains" 1945; "The Topeka Terror" 1945 (Don Quixote); "Under Western Skies" 1945 (Mayfield); "The Devil's Playground" 1946 (Daniel); "Fool's Gold" 1946 (Sandler); "Gun Town" 1946 (Sheriff); "Rustler's Roundup" 1946 (Sheriff Finn Elder); "Hollywood Barn Dance" 1947 (Cartwright); "The Marauders" 1947 (Clerk); "Oregon Trail Scouts" 1947 (Judge); "The Sea of Grass" 1947 (Cowboy); "Unexpected Guest" 1947 (Joshua Coulter); "Vigilantes of Boomtown" 1947 (Governor); "Oklahoma Badlands" 1948 (Jonathan Walpole); "Old Los Angeles" 1948 (Horatius P. Gassoway); "The Paleface" 1948 (Clem); "Return of the Badmen" 1948 (Auctioneer); "Silent Conflict" 1948 (Doc Richards); "Sheriff of Wichita" 1949 (Jenkins); "Trailin' West" 1949; "Copper Canyon" 1950 (Miner); "The Savage Horde" 1950 (Buck Yallop); "Lone Star" 1952 (Windy Barton); "The Great Jesse James Raid" 1953 (Soapy Smith); "Thunder Over the Plains" 1953 (Auctioneer); "Bitter Creek" 1954 (Charles Hammond); "The Forty-Niners" 1954 (1st Hotel Clerk); "Fastest Gun Alive" 1956 (Medicine Man); "The First Traveling Saleslady" 1956 (Veterinarian); "Friendly Persuasion" 1956 (Shooting Gallery Operator); "The Oklahoman" 1957 (Sam, the Bartender); "The Missouri Traveler" 1958 (Old Sharecropper); "The Man Who Shot Liberty Valance" 1962 (Clue Dumfires). ¶TV: The Lone Ranger—"High Heels" 11-

17-49, "The Man with Two Faces" 2-23-50, "Pardon for Curley" 6-22-50, "Mr. Trouble" 3-8-51, "Gold Town" 10-7-54; The Cisco Kid—"Oil Land" 2-24-51, "Cattle Quarantine" 3-31-51, "False Marriage" 4-14-51, "Wedding Blackmail" 4-21-51, "Vigilante Story" 10-20-51, "Mad About Money" 3-22-52, "Cisco Plays the Ghost" 2-21-53, "A Six-Gun for No Pain" 2-28-53, "Harry the Heir" 3-28-53, "Pancho's Niece" 9-5-53, "Bounty Men" 1-30-54, "Magician of Jamesville" 5-22-54; Wild Bill Hickok—"Battle Line" 1-6-53, "The Rainmaker" 4-14-53, "Counterfeit Ghost" 8-11-53; The Roy Rogers Show—"Uncle Steve's Finish" 2-3-55; The Gene Autry Show—"Law Comes to Scorpion" 10-22-55; Judge Roy Bean—"Checkmate" 1-1-56 (Doc Bentley), "The Eyes of Texas" 1-1-56 (Dr. Retina), "The Travelers" 1-1-56 (Kerns), "Bad Medicine" 6-1-56 (Doc Malone), "The Defense Rests" 6-1-56 (Banker), "Lone Star Killer" 8-1-56 (Smithy); Gunsmoke—"Uncle Oliver" 5-25-57 (Oliver Stang), "Chesterland" 11-18-61 (Tubby), "Quint Asper Comes Home" 9-29-62 (Dobie), "Two of a Kind" 3-16-63 (Judge); Have Gun Will Travel—"The Great Mojave Chase" 9-28-57 (2nd Gunman), "Ella West" 1-4-58 (Tomahawk Carter), "The Silver Queen" 5-3-58 (Leadhead Kane), "Juliet" 1-31-59 (Jeremiah Pike), "The Search" 6-18-60 (Sheriff Plummer); Maverick—"Relic of Fort Tejon" 11-3-57 (Johnson), "A Rage for Vengeance" 1-12-58 (Charley), "Shady Deal at Sunny Acres" 11-23-58 (Plunkett); Sugarfoot—"Yampa Crossing" 12-9-58 (Old Man); The Rifleman—"The Money Gun" 5-12-59; Rawhide—"Incident of the Shambling Men" 10-9-59, "Incident at Red River Station" 1-15-60; The Law of the Plainsman—"The Dude" 12-3-59; Wichita Town—"The Devil's Choice" 12-23-59 (Professor); Wanted—Dead or Alive—"Angela" 1-9-60; Overland Trail—"West of Boston" 2-21-60 (Ed Flynn); The Westerner—"The Old Man" 11-25-60.

Hodgson, Leyland (1892-3/16/49). Films: "Susannah of the Mounties" 1939 (Randall); "Buck Benny Rides Again" 1940 (Waiter); "The Kid from Kansas" 1941 (York); "Under Nevada Skies" 1946 (Tom Craig).

Hodiak, John (1914-10/19/55). Films: "The Harvey Girls" 1946 (Ned Trent); "Desert Fury" 1947 (Eddie Bendix); "Ambush" 1950 (Capt. Ben Lorrison); "Across the Wide Missouri" 1951 (Brecan); "Ambush at Tomahawk Gap" 1953 (McCord);

"Conquest of Cochise" 1953 (Cochise).

Hoey, Dennis (1893-7/25/60). Films: "Roll on, Texas Moon" 1946 (Cole Gregory); "Bad Men of Tombstone" 1949 (Mr. Smith); "The Kid from Texas" 1950 (Maj. Harper).

Hoffman, Basil (1938-). Films: "Comes a Horseman" 1978 (George Bascomb); "The Electric Horseman" 1979 (Toland); "Outlaws" TVM-1986. ¶TV: Kung Fu—"Blood of the Dragon" 9-14-74 (Telegrapher).

Hoffman, Bern (1913-12/15/79). TV: Buckskin—"A Man from the Mountains" 10-30-58 (Matt Dowd); The Restless Gun—"Better Than a Cannon" 2-9-59 (Baron Wilhelm Augustus Von Ritter); Colt .45—"The Escape" 4-5-59; The Texan—"Cowards Don't Die" 11-30-59 (Marshal), "End of Track" 12-21-59, "The Taming of Rio Nada" 1-11-60 (Bull Brinkley); Riverboat—"Salvage Pirates" 1-31-60 (Savage); Wrangler—"Affair at the Trading Post" 8-18-60 (Tall Hat); The Deputy—"Tension Point" 4-8-61 (Club); Rawhide—"Incident of the Blackstorms" 5-26-61 (Vetch); Frontier Circus—"The Depths of Fear" 10-5-61 (Bannister); Empire—"Down There, the World" 3-12-63 (George Neimeyer); Bonanza—"A Woman Lost" 3-17-63 (Fisherman), "Little Man—Ten Feet Tall" 5-26-63 (Bartender), "Calamity Over the Comstock" 11-3-63 (Bartender), "The Gentleman from New Orleans" 2-2-64 (Bartender), "The Saga of Muley Jones" 3-29-64 (Bartender), "The Pressure Game" 5-10-64, "Invention of a Gunfighter" 9-20-64 (Bartender), "A Man to Admire" 12-6-64, "The Flapjack Contest" 1-3-65, "A Dublin Lad" 1-2-66 (Bartender), "The Lady and the Mountain Lion" 2-23-69 (Bartender), "A Deck of Aces" 1-31-71 (Bartender); Wagon Train—"The Jarbo Pierce Story" 5-2-65 (Marcus); Laredo—"Lazyfoot, Where Are You?" 9-16-65 (Town Drunk), "A Double Shot of Nepenthe" 9-30-66 (Turnkey); The Road West—"The Gunfighter" 9-26-66 (Blacksmith); The Big Valley—"Caesar's Wife" 10-3-66 (Bert Seeger); Death Valley Days—"The Resurrection of Deadwood Dick" 10-22-66 (Hal Bishop); Lancer—"Death Bait" 1-14-69; Dirty Sally—"Wimmen's Rights" 3-15-74 (Paretti's Bartender).

Hoffman, Dustin (1937-). Films: "Little Big Man" 1971 (Jack Crabb).

Hoffman, Gertrude W. (1898-6/3/55). Films: "Cassidy of Bar 20"

1938 (Ma Caffrey); "North of the Rockies" 1942; "Texas Trouble Shooters" 1942 (Granny); "California" 1946 (Old Woman).

Hoffman, Howard (1893-6/26/69). TV: *Wild Wild West*—"The Night of the Raven" 9-30-66 (War Eagle).

Hoffman, Max. Films: "Angel Citizens" 1922 (the Doctor).

Hoffman, Jr., Max (1902-3/31/45). Films: "The Devil's Saddle Legion" 1937 (Butch); "Rootin' Tootin' Rhythm" 1937 (the Apache Kind); "They Died with Their Boots On" 1941 (Orderly).

Hoffman, Otto (1879-6/23/44). Films: "The Sheriff's Son" 1919 (Jess Tighe); "Pardon My Nerve!" 1922 (Luke Tweezy); "Ridin' Wild" 1922 (Andrew McBride); "Trimmed" 1922 (Nebo Slayter); "Double Dealing" 1923 (Uriah Jobson); "Painted Ponies" 1927 (Jim); "The Avenger" 1931 (Black Kelly); "Cimarron" 1931 (Murch Rankin); "Haunted Gold" 1932 (Simon); "Hello Trouble" 1932 (Calvin Sharp); "The Cheyenne Kid" 1933 (Cal Winters); "Fighting Shadows" 1935 (Stalkey); "Lucky Cisco Kid" 1940 (Storekeeper Ed Stoke); "My Little Chickadee" 1940 (Pete the Printer); "Red River Robin Hood" 1943; "Sagebrush Law" 1943.

Hoffman, Robert W. (1939-). Films: "Joe Panther" 1976 (George Harper).

Hoffmann, Pato. Films: "Geronimo: An American Legend" 1993 (the Dreamer); "Cheyenne Warrior" 1994 (Hawk).

Hogan, Dick (1918-8/18/95). Films: "The Fargo Kid" 1940 (Young Prospector); "Mexican Spitfire Out West" 1940 (Bellhop); "Prairie Law" 1940 (Larry); "Rancho Grande" 1940 (Tom Dodge).

Hogan, Jack. Films: "Man from Del Rio" 1956 (Boy); "The Legend of Tom Dooley" 1959 (Charlie Grayson). ¶TV: *Broken Arrow*—"Aztec Treasure" 2-25-58 (Morro); *Rough Riders*—"The Nightbinders" 11-20-58 (Paul); *Have Gun Will Travel*—"The Ballad of Oscar Wilde" 12-6-58 (Chris Rook); *Tombstone Territory*—"Death Is to Write About" 5-29-59 (Dan Harlan); *The Rifleman*—"Stranger at Night" 6-2-59 (Carson), "The Man from Salinas" 2-12-62 (Rudy Gray); *Bat Masterson*—"To the Manner Born" 10-1-59 (Stuart), "Ledger of Guilt" 4-6-61 (Johnny Quinn); *Colt .45*—"Under False Pretenses" 1-10-60 (Cliff); *The Rebel*—"In Memory of a Son" 5-8-60 (Vic);

The Deputy—"Ma Mack" 7-9-60 (Abner); *Tate*—"The Gunfighters" 8-31-60 (Cromley); *Lawman*—"The Mad Bunch" 10-2-60 (Duke Janks), "The Juror" 9-24-61 (Cawley), "Clootey Hutter" 3-11-62 (Earl Henry); *Riverboat*—"Rive Champion" 10-10-60 (Fletcher); *The Tall Man*—"Hard Justice" 3-25-61 (Jim); *Bonanza*—"The Gift" 4-1-61 (Cash); *Cheyenne*—"Storm Center" 11-20-61 (Garson); *Custer*—"Accused" 9-13-67 (Sergeant Mason); *The Quest*—"The Freight Train Rescue" 12-29-76 (Billy McGraff); *The Oregon Trail*—"Return from Death" 1977; *Outlaws*—"Tintype" 1-3-87 (Sal Carve).

Hogan, Pat (1931-11/22/66). Films: "In Old Oklahoma" 1943; "Arrowhead" 1953 (Jim Eagle); "Back to God's Country" 1953 (Uppy); "Gun Fury" 1953; "The Nebraskan" 1953 (Yellow Knife); "Pony Express" 1953 (Yellow Hand); "Man with the Steel Whip" 1954-serial (Chief); "Overland Pacific" 1954 (Dark Thunder); "Chief Crazy Horse" 1955 (Dull Knife); "Davy Crockett, King of the Wild Frontier" 1955 (Chief Red Stick); "Kiss of Fire" 1955 (Pahvant); "The Last Frontier" 1955 (Mungo); "Smoke Signal" 1955 (Delche); "Pillars of the Sky" 1956 (Jacob); "Secret of Treasure Mountain" 1956 (Vahoe); "Seventh Cavalry" 1956 (Young Hawk); "Ten Who Dared" 1960 (Indian Chief); "Savage Sam" 1963 (Broken Nose); "Indian Paint" 1965 (Sutamakis). ¶TV: *Walt Disney Presents*—"Davy Crockett"—Regular 1954-55 (Red Stick); *Gunsmoke*—"Indian Scout" 3-31-56 (Buffalo Tongue); *Broken Arrow*—"The Challenge" 2-5-57 (Victorio); *Tales of Wells Fargo*—"Sam Bass" 6-10-57 (Murphy); *Northwest Passage*—"The Gunsmith" 9-28-58 (Rivas); *Texas John Slaughter*—Regular 1958-61 (Geronimo); *The Rifleman*—"The Raid" 6-9-59 (Artak); *Daniel Boone*—"The Returning" 1-14-65 (Hotekna).

Hogan, Paul. TV: *The Lone Ranger*—"Pardon for Curley" 6-22-50; *The Cisco Kid*—"Foreign Agent" 8-18-51, "Bates Story" 9-29-51.

Hogan, Paul (1940-). Films: "Lightning Jack" 1994-Australia (Lightning Jack Kane).

Hogan, Robert (1936-). Films: "Ransom for Alice!" TVM-1977 (Whitaker Halliday). ¶TV: *Cheyenne*—"The Bad Penny" 3-12-62 (Billy Hay); *Bronco*—"The Immovable Object" 4-16-62 (Captain Meadows); *Gunsmoke*—"Old Man" 10-10-64 (Danny Adams), "The Bullet" 11-29-71, 12-6-71 & 12-13-71 (Cap-

tain Darnell); *Bonanza*—"A Ride in the Sun" 5-11-69 (Tobias Horn); *Young Maverick*—"Hearts O'Gold" 12-12-79 (Billy Peachtree).

Hogan, Susan. Films: "White Fang" 1991 (Belinda).

Hohl, Arthur (1889-3/10/64). Films: "Massacre" 1934 (Dr. Turner); "The Bad Man of Brimstone" 1938 (Doc Laramie); "Twenty Mule Team" 1940 (Salters); "Ride on, Vaquero" 1941 (Sheriff); "Idaho" 1943 (Spike Madagan); "The Woman of the Town" 1943 (Robert Wright); "Salome, Where She Danced" 1945 (Bartender); "The Vigilantes Return" 1947 (Sheriff).

Hokanson, Mary Alan (1916-2/15/94). TV: *Cimarron City*—"I, the People" 10-11-58 (Martha Tillot).

Holbrook, Allen. Films: "Fighting Cowboy" 1933 (Duke Neill); "Boss Cowboy" 1934 (Ranch Hand); "Circle Canyon" 1934 (Vic Byrd); "Lightning Bill" 1934 (Pete); "Riding Speed" 1934 (Roberts); "Trails of Adventure" 1935.

Holbrook, David. Films: "The Legend of the Golden Gun" TVM-1979 (Outlaw).

Holbrook, Hal (1925-). Films: "The Awakening Land" TVM-1978 (Portius "the Solitary" Wheeler); "The Legend of the Golden Gun" TVM-1979 (Jim Hammer).

Holcomb, Kathryn. Films: "The Macahans" TVM-1976 (Laura Macahan). ¶TV: *How the West Was Won*—Regular 1977-79 (Laura Macahan).

Holcombe, Harry (1907-9/15/87). TV: *Death Valley Days*—"The White Healer" 11-30-60 (General Miles), "The $25,000 Wager" 2-7-65 (Gov. Leland Stanford), "The Courtship of Carrie Huntington" 6-4-66 (Father); *Cheyenne*—"Lone Patrol" 4-10-61 (Major Prewitt); *Wagon Train*—"The Heather Mahoney Story" 6-13-62 (Mr. Waterbury), "The Cassie Vance Story" 12-23-63; *Bonanza*—"Emily" 3-23-69 (Dr. Lewis), "A Ride in the Sun" 5-11-69 (Dr. Lewis), "The Stalker" 11-2-69 (Doctor), "A Matter of Circumstance" 4-19-70 (Doctor), "The Weary Willies" 9-27-70 (Doctor), "The Luck of Pepper Shannon" 11-22-70 (Dr. Harris), "For a Young Lady" 12-27-70 (Doctor), "The Silent Killers" 2-28-71 (Dr. Martin), "The Stillness Within" 3-14-71 (Doctor), "Cassie" 10-24-71 (Doc Martin), "He Was Only Seven" 3-5-72 (Dr. Martin), "One Ace Too Many" 4-2-72 (Dr. Martin), "The Hidden Enemy" 11-28-72 (Dr. Martin), "The

Sound of Loneliness" 12-5-72 (Dr. Martin).

Holcombe, Herbert (-10/15/70). Films: "Phantom Ranger" 1938 (Henchman); "Six Shootin' Sheriff" 1938 (Henchman).

Holden, Eddie. Films: "The Fighting Deputy" 1937 (Axel).

Holden, Fay (Gaby Fay) (1895-6/23/73). Films: "Guns of the Pecos" 1937 (Aunt Carrie); "Out West with the Hardys" 1938 (Mrs. Hardy); "Canyon Passage" 1946 (Mrs. Overmire); "Whispering Smith" 1948 (Emmy Dansing).

Holden, Gloria (1911-3/22/91). Films: "Dodge City" 1939 (Mrs. Cole); "Apache Trail" 1943 (Mrs. James V. Thorne).

Holden, Harry (1868-2/4/44). Films: "The Gay Defender" 1927 (Padre Sebastian); "Code of Honor" 1930.

Holden, Joyce (1950-). Films: "Bronco Buster" 1952 (Judy Bream).

Holden, Scott (1946-). Films: "Calibre .38" 1971-Ital. (Jerusalem Wade); "The Revengers" 1972-U.S./Mex. (Lieutenant).

Holden, William (1918-11/16/81). Films: "Arizona" 1940 (Peter Muncie); "Texas" 1941 (Dan Thomas); "The Man from Colorado" 1948 (Capt. Del Stewart); "Rachel and the Stranger" 1948 (Big Davey Harvey); "Streets of Laredo" 1949 (Jim Dawkins); "Escape from Fort Bravo" 1953 (Capt. Roper); "The Horse Soldiers" 1959 (Maj. Henry Kendall); "Alvarez Kelly" 1966 (Alvarez Kelly); "The Wild Bunch" 1969 (Pike Bishop); "Wild Rovers" 1971 (Ross Bodine); "The Revengers" 1972-U.S./Mex. (John Benedict).

Holding Thomas (1880-5/4/29). Films: "The Lady of Red Butte" 1919 (Webster Smith); "Ruggles of Red Gap" 1923 (Earl of Brinstead).

Holdren, Judd (1915-3/11/74). Films: "Coyote Canyon" 1949-short; "Gold Fever" 1952 (Jud Jerson). ¶TV: *The Lone Ranger*—"Special Edition" 9-25-52, "Best Laid Plans" 12-25-52, "The Durango Kid" 4-16-53, "Death in the Forest" 6-4-53; *Sergeant Preston of the Yukon*—"The Boy Nobody Wanted" 8-9-56 (Jack Darby); *Man from Blackhawk*—"The Hundred Thousand Dollar Policy" 1-22-60 (Tibbs).

Holdridge, Cheryl. TV: *The Rifleman*—"A Young Man's Fancy" 2-5-62 (Sally Walker); *Wagon Train*—"The Race Town Story" 10-11-64 (Annabelle).

Hole, Jonathan (1904-). Films: "The Over-the-Hill Gang Rides Again" TVM-1970 (Parson). ¶TV: *Have Gun Will Travel*—"The Great Mojave Chase" 9-28-57; *Jim Bowie*—"The Quarantine" 10-11-57 (Dr. Fry); *Wyatt Earp*—"Hung Jury" 10-29-57 (Heber Morse); *Maverick*—"A Rage for Vengeance" 1-12-58 (Desk Clerk), "Shady Deal at Sunny Acres" 11-23-58 (Desk Clerk), "Game of Chance" 1-4-59 (San Francisco Jeweler), "A Fellow's Brother" 11-22-59 (Marvin Dilbey), "Greenbacks Unlimited" 3-13-60 (Secretary); *Cheyenne*—"The Last Comanchero" 1-14-58 (Photographer); *Zane Grey Theater*—"Day of the Killing" 1-8-59 (Ned Watley); *Wanted—Dead or Alive*—"The Spur" 1-17-59; *Bat Masterson*—"Incident in Leadville" 3-18-59 (Mart); *Fury*—"The Fort" 12-12-59 (Ben Carr); *Trackdown*—"The Eyes of Jerry Kelson" 4-22-59 (Mike Kilroy); *Rawhide*—"Incident of the Stargazer" 4-1-60, "Incient of the Wager on Payday" 6-16-61, "Grandma's Money" 2-23-62 (Otis Eames), "Incident of the Rusty Shotgun" 1-9-64 (Drummer); *Bonanza*—"The Dream Riders" 5-20-61 (Hershell), "A Man to Admire" 12-6-64; *Wide Country*—"The Girl from Nob Hill" 3-8-63 (Clerk); *The Virginian*—"A Distant Fury" 3-20-63; *Temple Houston*—"Fracas at Kiowa Flats" 12-12-63 (T.T. Teague); *Laredo*—"Above the Law" 1-13-66 (Undertaker); *Rango*—"Shootout at Mesa Flats" 4-7-67 (Sweeper); *Wild Wild West*—"The Night Dr. Loveless Died" 9-29-67 (Mr. Wells), "The Night of the Simian Terror" 2-16-68 (Bank Manager); *The Guns of Will Sonnett*—"The Favor" 11-10-67, "Sunday in Paradise" 12-15-67 (Rob Quail); *The Big Valley*—"The Battle of Mineral Springs" 3-24-69; *Kung Fu*—"The Vanishing Image" 12-20-74 (Hobbs).

Holiday, Hope (1932-). Films: "The Rounders" 1965 (Sister). ¶TV: *Have Gun Will Travel*—"Odds for a Big Red" 10-7-61 (Big Red).

Holland, Anthony (1928-7/9/88). Films: "McCabe and Mrs. Miller" 1971 (Hollander); "The Grey Fox" 1983-Can. (Judge).

Holland, Bert (1923-3/8/80). TV: *The Lone Ranger*—"Two from Juan Ringo" 12-23-54; *Alias Smith and Jones*—"The Posse That Wouldn't Quit" 10-14-71.

Holland, Cecil (1887-6/29/73). Films: "The Girl of the Golden West" 1923 (Antonio).

Holland, Edna. Films: "The Prairie" 1947 (Esther Bush); "Son of

a Badman" 1949 (Mrs. Burley); "Ten Wanted Men" 1955. ¶TV: *The Lone Ranger*—"The Perfect Crime" 7-30-53; *Laramie*—"Shadow of the Past" 10-16-62.

Holland, Erik (1933-). Films: "The Glory Guys" 1965 (Gentry); "Tell Them Willie Boy Is Here" 1969 (Digger); "The Great Northfield, Minnesota Raid" 1972 (Sheriff); "Friendly Persuasion" TVM-1975 (Enoch); "Little House on the Prairie: Look Back to Yesterday" TVM-1983 (Gunnar Lindstrom). ¶TV: *Laredo*—"A Very Small Assignment" 3-17-66 (Harry); *Bonanza*—"Something Hurt, Something Wild" 9-11-66 (Cleve Ferguson); *The Outcasts*—"A Ride to Vengeance" 9-30-68 (Dobbs); *The Guns of Will Sonnett*—"One Angry Juror" 3-7-69 (Jon Anderson); *Alias Smith and Jones*—"The Legacy of Charlie O'Rourke" 4-22-71 (Kurt Schmitt); *Best of the West*—"Mail Order Bride" 1-28-82 (Olaf).

Holland, Gladys (1921-). Films: "Ulzana's Raid" 1972 (Mrs. Rukeyser).

Holland, Harold. Films: "The Man Trackers" 1921 (Inspector); "Call of the Klondike" 1926 (Downing).

Holland, John (1900-5/21/93). Films: "Pals of the Pecos" 1941 (Buckley); "Call of the Canyon" 1942 (Willy Hitchcock); "Sons of Adventure" 1948 (Paul Kenyon); "Law of the Golden West" 1949 (Quentin Morell); "Massacre River" 1949 (Roberts); "Rio Grande Patrol" 1950 (Fowler); "Rock Island Trail" 1950 (Maj. Porter); "Jubilee Trail" 1954 (Mr. Drake). ¶TV: *Broken Arrow*—"The Arsenal" 11-5-57 (Major Winters); *Death Valley Days*—"Fifty Years a Mystery" 11-11-57, "Pioneer Circus" 3-10-59 (Duke Jordan); *Buckskin*—"A Permanent Juliet" 10-23-58 (Harris); *Have Gun Will Travel*—"Shot by Request" 10-10-59 (Cortwright), "Silent Death" 3-31-62 (Courtney Burgess); *Cheyenne*—"Trial by Conscience" 10-26-59 (the Actor); *Maverick*—"Guatemala City" 1-31-60 (Tall Man), "Greenbacks Unlimited" 3-13-60 (Tamblyn), "Arizona Black Maria" 10-9-60 (Farnsworth McCoy); *F Troop*—"The Phantom Major" 9-28-65 (Colonel Willoughby).

Holland, Kristina (1944-). TV: *Here Come the Brides*—"A Jew Named Sullivan" 11-20-68 (Amanda).

Holland, Tina. TV: *Laredo*—"Miracle at Massacre Mission" 3-3-66 (Sister Joan of Arc); *Here Come the Brides*—"None to a Customer" 2-19-69 (Amanda).

Holland, Tom. TV: *The Cisco Kid*—"Hypnotist Murder" 11-10-51; *Tombstone Territory*—"The Youngest Gun" 1-1-58 (Dude Capper); *Gunsmoke*—"Buffalo Hunter" 5-2-59 (Alvin); *Temple Houston*—"Seventy Times Seven" 12-5-63 (Lee Bates).

Holliday, Fred (1936-). TV: *The Big Valley*—"The Murdered Party" 11-17-65 (Emmet).

Holliman, Earl (Anthony Earl Numkena) (1928-). Films: "Pony Soldier" 1952 (Comes Running); "Devil's Canyon" 1953 (Joe); "Broken Lance" 1954 (Denny Devereaux); "Strange Lady in Town" 1955 (Tomasito Diaz); "The Burning Hills" 1956 (Mort Bayliss); "Giant" 1956 (Bob Dace); "The Rainmaker" 1956 (Jim Curry); "Westward Ho the Wagons" 1956 (Little Thunder); "Gunfight at the O.K. Corral" 1957 (Charles Bassett); "Trooper Hook" 1957 (Jeff Bennett); "Last Train from Gun Hill" 1959 (Rick Belden); "The Sons of Katie Elder" 1965 (Matt Elder); "Alias Smith and Jones" TVM-1971 (Wheat); "Desperate Mission" TVM-1971 (Shad Clay); "Gunsmoke: Return to Dodge" TVM-1987 (Jake Flagg). ¶TV: *Wagon Train*—"A Man Called Horse" 3-26-58 (Little Hunter); *Hotel De Paree*—Regular 1959-60 (Sundance); *Alcoa Premiere*—"Second Chance" 3-13-62 (Mitch Guthrie); *Wide Country*—Regular 1962-63 (Mitch Guthrie); *Great Adventure*—"Teeth of the Lion" 1-17-64 (Will Cross); *Bonanza*—"The Flannel-Mouth Gun" 1-31-65 (Clegg); *The Virginian*—"Ring of Silence" 10-27-65 (Wiley); *Gunsmoke*—"A Man Called Smith" 10-27-69 (Will), "Hackett" 3-16-70 (Hackett), "Shadler" 1-15-73 (Boone Shadler); *Alias Smith and Jones*—"The Day They Hanged Kid Curry" 9-16-71 (Wheat).

Hollingsworth, Alfred (1874-6/20/26). Films: "The Gambler of the West" 1914 (Kansas Joe); "The Law's Outlaw" 1918 (Rodney Hicks); "Hell's Hinges" 1919 (Silk Miller); "Leave It to Susan" 1919 (Pa Burbridge); "A Man's Country" 1919 (Oliver Kemp); "The One Way Trail" 1920 (Thundering Ames); "The Bearcat" 1922 (John P. May); "Trimmed" 1922 (John Millard); "Marry in Haste" 1924 (Manager); "The Mystery Box" 1925-serial.

Hollister, Alice (1886-2/24/73). Films: "The Brand" 1914.

Hollister, Flora. Films: "The Coast of Opportunity" 1920 (Rosita); "Across the Divide" 1921 (White Flower); "The Fighting Stranger" 1921 (Madeline Ayre).

Holloway, Carol. Films: "Dead Shot Baker" 1917 (Evelyn Baldwin); "The Fighting Trail" 1917-serial; "The Tenderfoot" 1917 (Cynthia of the West); "Vengeance and the Woman" 1917-serial; "The Perils of Thunder Mountain" 1919-serial; "Dangerous Love" 1920 (the Woman); "Two Moons" 1920 (Hilma Ring); "Up and Going" 1922 (Marie Brandon); "Knights of the Timber" 1923; "The Ramblin' Kid" 1923 (Mrs. Ophelia Cobb); "The Cherokee Kid" 1927 (Rose); "Wells Fargo" 1937 (Townswoman).

Holloway, Mary Lou. Films: "The Stranger Wore a Gun" 1953; "The Bounty Hunter" 1954 (Mrs. Ed); "Riding Shotgun" 1954 (Cynthia Biggert).

Holloway, Sterling (1905-11/22/92). Films: "Avenging Waters" 1936; "Wildfire" 1945 (Alkali); "Death Valley" 1946; "Sioux City Sue" 1946 (Nelson "Nellie" Bly); "Robin Hood of Texas" 1947 (Droopy); "Saddle Pals" 1947 (Waldo T. Brooks, Jr.); "Trail to San Antone" 1947 (Droopy Stearns); "Twilight on the Rio Grande" 1947 (Pokie); "Kentucky Rifle" 1956. ¶TV: *The Adventures of Rin Tin Tin*—"Sorrowful Joe" 9-21-56 (Sorrowful Joe), "Sorrowful Joe Returns" 2-1-57 (Sorrowful Joe), "Sorrowful Joe's Policy" 3-21-58 (Sorrowful Joe); *Circus Boy*—"Elmer the Aeronaut" 1-13-57 (Elmer Purdy), "Elmer, Rainmaker" 9-19-57 (Elmer Purdy), "The Magic Lantern" 11-7-57 (Elmer Purdy); *Zane Grey Theater*—"Blood Red" 1-29-61 (Luther); *F Troop*—"Milton, the Kid" 12-1-66 (Sheriff Lawton).

Holly, Helen. Films: "White Oak" 1921 (Rose Miller).

Hollywood, Jimmy (1895-7/2/55). Films: "The Lone Ranger" 1938-serial (Guard).

Holm, Celeste (1919-). TV: *Zane Grey Theater*—"A Fugitive" 3-22-57 (Sarah Kimball).

Holman, Harry (1874-5/2/47). Films: "The Conquerors" 1932 (Stubby); "The Phantom Thunderbolt" 1933 (Judge Tobias Wingate); "Western Jamboree" 1938 (Doc Trimble); "Jesse James" 1939 (Engineer); "Shadows on the Sage" 1942 (Lippy); "The Silver Bullet" 1942; "Badman's Territory" 1946 (Hodge).

Holman, Rex (1935-). Films: "Thirteen Fighting Men" 1960 (Root); "Young Jesse James" 1960 (Zack); "The Quick Gun" 1964 (Rick Morrison); "The Outlaws Is Coming!" 1965 (Sunstroke Kid); "Bounty

Man" TVM-1972 (Driskill); "When the Legends Die" 1972 (Neil Swenson); "The Apple Dumpling Gang Rides Again" 1979; "The Legend of the Golden Gun" TVM-1979 (Sturges); "The Wild Women of Chastity Gulch" TVM-1982 (Lt. Pritchard). ¶TV: *Rawhide*—"Incident of the Wanted Painter" 1-29-60 (Harry), "The Gray Rock Hotel" 5-21-65 (Bill); *Hotel De Paree*—"Sundance and the Fallen Sparrow" 5-27-60 (Luther); *The Deputy*—"The Choice" 6-25-60 (Ben Sutton); *Gunsmoke*—"Small Water" 9-24-60 (Seth Pickett), "No Chip" 12-3-60 (Pete Mossman), "Comanches Is Safe" 3-7-64 (Malachi), "Malachi" 11-13-65 (Shobin), "The Whispering Tree" 11-12-66 (Garr), "The Wreckers" 9-11-67 (Frankie), "Zavala" 10-7-68 (Smitty), "The Long Night" 2-17-69 (Broker), "Ring of Darkness" 12-1-69 (Carr), "Luke" 11-2-70 (Moses Reedy), "Waste" 9-27-71 & 10-4-71 (Oakley), "Sarah" 10-16-72 (Ed), "The Town Tamers" 1-28-74 (Aikens), "The Guns of Cibola Blanca" 9-23-74 & 9-30-74 (Badger); *Two Faces West*—"The Hanging" 12-12-60; *The Tall Man*—"Tiger Eye" 12-17-60 (Purdy); *Wagon Train*—"The Earl Packer Story" 1-4-61 (Harry), "The Nancy Styles Story" 11-22-64 (Homer); *Laramie*—"Killer Without Cause" 1-24-61 (Ken Vail); *Lawman*—"The Inheritance" 3-5-61 (Owlie Pruitt); *Tales of Wells Fargo*—"Who Lives by the Gun" 3-24-62 (Tolly Sherman); *The Rifleman*—"The Wanted Man" 9-25-62 (Bob Sherman), "Death Never Rides Alone" 10-29-62 (Billie Graves); *Bonanza*—"The Last Haircut" 2-3-63 (Otie); *Have Gun Will Travel*—"Two Plus One" 4-6-63 (Blake); *The Virginian*—"The Drifter" 1-29-64 (Donovan), "No Drums, No Trumpets" 4-6-66 (Harmon); *Death Valley Days*—"Kate Melville and the Law" 6-20-65 (Amos Marsh), "The Fastest Nun in the West" 4-9-66 (Pete Collins); *Laredo*—"Which Way Did They Go?" 11-18-65, "The Legend of Midas Mantee" 9-16-66 (Greevy); *The Big Valley*—"Hazard" 3-9-66 (Will Hover), "Last Stage to Salt Flats" 12-5-66, "Ambush" 9-18-67, "A Stranger Everywhere" 12-9-68 (Croft), "Danger Road" 4-21-69; *The Legend of Jesse James*—"1863" 3-28-66 (Finn Davis); *The Road West*—"This Savage Land" 9-12-66 & 9-19-66, "The Insider" 2-13-67 (Indian); *Iron Horse*—"High Devil" 9-26-66 (Minstrel), "Six Hours to Sky High" 11-25-67; *The Monroes*—"The Hunter" 10-26-66 (Whit); *Cimarron Strip*—"Journey to a Hanging" 9-7-67; *The Guns of Will Sonnett*—"The Guns of Will Sonnett" 9-8-67, "Find a Sonnett, Kill a Sonnett" 12-8-67 (Truitt Reed), "Chapter and Verse" 10-11-68 (Wiley); *Daniel Boone*—"The Traitor" 11-2-67 (Penango), "The Return of Sidewinder" 12-12-68 (Davy Rock); *Cowboy in Africa*—"First to Capture" 1-29-68 (Matt Crose); *The High Chaparral*—"Threshold of Courage" 3-31-68 (Jube); *Lancer*—"Child of Rock and Sunlight" 4-1-69 (Luke Sickles), "The Buscaderos" 3-17-70 (Chapel); *The Outcasts*—"How Tall Is Blood?" 5-5-69 (Crail); *The Men from Shiloh*—"Experiment at New Life" 11-18-70 (Buck); *Bearcats!*—10-7-71 (Pauk); *Kung Fu*—"The Squaw Man" 11-1-73 (Canby).

Holmes, Dennis. TV: *The Restless Gun*—"Jebediah Bonner" 9-22-58 (Robby/Young Vint Bonner); *Wagon Train*—"The Dick Richardson Story" 12-31-58 (Dan Milford), "The Jed Polke Story" 3-1-61 (Cotton), "Those Who Stay Behind" 11-8-64 (Danny Blake); *Bonanza*—"The Gunmen" 1-23-60; *The Deputy*—"The Return of Widow Brown" 4-22-61 (Tommy); *Laramie*—Regular 1961-63 (Mike).

Holmes, Fred. Films: "The Gambling Fool" 1925 (Plump Parker); "A Streak of Luck" 1925 (Burton's Valet); "Lightning Lariats" 1927 (Henry Storne).

Holmes, George (1918-2/19/85). Films: "Back Trail" 1948.

Holmes, Gerda. Films: "Pierre of the North" 1914; "All Man" 1916 (Ethel Maynard).

Holmes, Gilbert "Pee Wee" (1894-8/17/36). Films: "Big Town Round-Up" 1921 (Pee Wee); "The Buster" 1923 (Light Laurie); "The Man Who Won" 1923 (Toby Jenks); "The Mask of Lopez" 1923 (Shorty); "Brakin' Loose" 1925; "Just Cowboys" 1925; "Shootin' Wild" 1925; "Too Many Bucks" 1925; "The Big Game" 1926; "Barely Reasonable" 1926; "The Border Sheriff" 1926 (Tater-Bug Gilbert); "Chip of the Flying U" 1926 (Shorty); "Desperate Dan" 1926; "Fade Away Foster" 1926; "The Hen Punchers of Piperock" 1926; "The Hero of Piperock" 1926; "Let Loose" 1926; "A Man's Size Pet" 1926; "One Wild Time" 1926; "The Phantom Bullet" 1926 (Short); "Piperock Goes Wild" 1926; "The Rescue" 1926; "When East Meets West" 1926; "Border Cavalier" 1927 (Pee Wee); "Cows Is Cows" 1927; "The Denver Dude" 1927 (Shorty Dan); "Galloping Fury" 1927 (Pee Wee); "One Glorious Scrap" 1927 (Pee Wee); "The

Piperock Blaze" 1927; "The Pride of Peacock" 1927; "The Rest Cure" 1927; "A Strange Inheritance" 1927; "Tied Up" 1927; "Too Much Progress for Piperock" 1927; "When Oscar Went Wild" 1927; "Arizona Cyclone" 1928 (Pee Wee); "Burning the Wind" 1928 (Peewee); "The Fearless Rider" 1928 (Hank Hook); "Made-to-Order Hero" 1928 (Bill Purtwee); "Put 'Em Up" 1928 (Shorty Mullins); "Quick Triggers" 1928 (Pee Wee); "Thunder Riders" 1928 (Rider); "The Trail Riders" 1928; "Sunset Pass" 1929 (Shorty); "Mountain Justice" 1930 (Rusty); "Sagebrush Politics" 1930; "Spurs" 1930 (Shorty); "Desert Vengeance" 1931 (Alabama); "Lightnin' Smith Returns" 1931 (Bandit); "Lightnin' Smith Returns" 1931; "Flaming Guns" 1932 (Gabe); "Man from Hell's Edges" 1932 (Half Pint); "Robbers' Roost" 1933 (Briggs); "Rustlers' Roundup" 1933 (Husky); "Western Racketeers" 1935 (Breed Morgan).

Holmes, Helen (1892-7/8/50). Films: "The Battle at Fort Laramie" 1913; "Brought to Bay" 1913; "The Identification" 1914; "The Oil Well Conspiracy" 1914; "A Desperate Leap" 1915; "The Girl and the Game" 1915-serial; "The Mettle of Jerry McGuire" 1915; "The Operator of Black Rock" 1915; "Lass of the Lumberland" 1916-serial; "The Manager of the B & A" 1916; "Medicine Bend" 1916 (Marion Sinclair); "Whispering Smith" 1916 (Marion Sinclair); "The Lost Express" 1917-serial; "A Crook's Romance" 1921; "Ghost City" 1921; "Hills of Missing Men" 1922 (Amy Allis); "The Lone Hand" 1922 (Margie Vanney); "The Riddle Rider" 1924-serial; "Fighting Fury" 1924 (June Sanford); "Forty-Horse Hawkins" 1924 (Sylvia Dean); "Blood and Steel" 1925 (Helen Grimshaw); "The Sign of the Cactus" 1925 (Belle Henderton); "The Californian" 1937 (Josephine); "Dude Cowboy" 1941 (Miss Carter).

Holmes, John Merrill "Jack" (1889-2/27/50). Films: "The Last Round-Up" 1934 (Bartender); "The Last Round-Up" 1934; "Queen of the Yukon" 1940 (Walker); "The Bandit Trail" 1941 (Sheriff Saunders); "Saddle Mountain Roundup" 1941 (Sheriff); "Tumbledown Ranch in Arizona" 1941 (Sheriff Nye); "Wrangler's Roost" 1941 (Collins); "Gauchos of El Dorado" 1941; "Land of the Open Range" 1942 (Sam Walton); "The Lone Rider in Cheyenne" 1942; "Along the Sundown Trail" 1942; "Prairie Pals" 1942 (Wainwright); "Riders of the West" 1942; "Rolling

Down the Great Divide" 1942 (Sheriff); "Texas Trouble Shooters" 1942 (Perry); "Thunder River Feud" 1942 (Pembroke); "Wolves of the Range" 1943.

Holmes, Lee. Films: "Hard Fists" 1927 (Jed Leach).

Holmes, Leon. Films: "A Man of Nerve" 1925 (Buddy Simms); "Union Pacific" 1939 (Vendor).

Holmes, Madeleine Taylor (-12/18/87). Films: "The Long Rope" 1961 (Senora Dona Vega); "MacKenna's Gold" 1969 (Old Apache Woman); "The Great Northfield, Minnesota Raid" 1972 (Old Granny Woman). ¶TV: *Rawhide*—"Incident of the Night Horse" 2-19-60; *Gunslinger*—"Road of the Dead" 3-30-61 (Aunt Serafina).

Holmes, Salty. Films: "Arizona Days" 1937 (Salty); "Saddle Leather Law" 1944.

Holmes, Stuart (1887-12/29/71). Films: "Thou Shalt Not" 1914 (Bob Cooper); "The Girl I Left Behind Me" 1915 (Lt. Parlow); "Steele of the Royal Mounted" 1925 (Buck Nome); "Beyond the Trail" 1926 (Archibald Van Jones); "The Cavalier" 1928 (Sgt. Juan Dinero); "My Pal, the King" 1932 (Baron Kluckstein); "Trailin' West" 1936 (Edwin H. Stanton); "Cowboy from Brooklyn" 1938 (Doorman); "The Oklahoma Kid" 1939 (President Cleveland); "River's End" 1940 (Foreman); "Copper Canyon" 1950 (Barber/Townsman); "The Horse Soldiers" 1959 (Train Passenger); "The Man Who Shot Liberty Valance" 1962.

Holmes, Taylor (1872-9/30/59). Films: "Ruggles of Red Gap" 1918 (Marmaduke Ruggles); "It's a Bear" 1919 (Orlando Winthrop); "One Hour of Love" 1927 (Joe Monahan); "The Plunderers" 1948 (Eben Martin); "Copper Canyon" 1950 (Theodosius Roberts); "Drums in the Deep South" 1951 (Albert Monroe); "Ride the Man Down" 1952 (Lowell Priest); "Woman of the North Country" 1952 (Dawson); "Hell's Outpost" 1954 (Timothy Byers); "The Outcast" 1954 (Andrew Devlin); "Untamed Heiress" 1954 (Walter Martin); "The Maverick Queen" 1956 (Pete Callaher). ¶TV: *Frontier Doctor*—"The Desperate Game" 11-29-58.

Holmes, Wendell (1915-4/26/62). Films: "Good Day for a Hanging" 1958 (Tallant Joslin). ¶TV: *The Californians*—"Death by Proxy" 3-18-58 (Krego); *Gunsmoke*—"Doc Quits" 2-21-59 (Dr. Bechtel); *Zorro*—"The Missing Father" 2-26-59, "Please

Believe Me" 3-5-59, "The Brooch" 3-12-59; *Rough Riders*—"Hired Gun" 4-23-59 (Sam Hanks); *Maverick*—"The Cats of Paradise" 10-11-59 (Mayor Uli Bemus), "Greenbacks Unlimited" 3-13-60 (Colonel Dutton); *Lawman*—"The Press" 11-29-59 (Cal Nibley); *The Texan*—"Dangerous Ground" 12-14-59, "Twenty-Four Hours to Live" 9-5-60 (Henry Morton); *Tales of Wells Fargo*—"The Governor's Visit" 1-18-60 (Governor); *Bonanza*—"Death at Dawn" 4-30-60 (Judge Scribner), "Badge Without Honor" 9-24-60 (Judge Rand); *Zane Grey Theater*—"Never Too Late" 2-4-60 (Cobson); *Overland Trail*—"First Stage to Denver" 5-1-60 (Mayor Filmore); *The Westerner*—"Mrs. Kennedy" 10-28-60.

Holmes, William. Films: "The Sea of Grass" 1947 (Gambler); "In Old Amarillo" 1951 (Martin); "Utah Wagon Train" 1951 (Millan).

Holmes, William J. (1877-12/1/46). Films: "Terror Trail" 1933 (Dr. Wilson).

Holt, Charlene (1938-). Films: "El Dorado" 1967 (Maudie).

Holt, George. Films: "When the West Was Young" 1913; "The Little Sheriff" 1914; "The Navajo Ring" 1914; "Wards Claim" 1914; "A Child of the North" 1915; "The Legend of the Lone Tree" 1915; "The Man from the Desert" 1915; "The Sage Brush Girl" 1915; "The Fighting Trail" 1917-serial; "Vengeance and the Woman" 1917-serial; "Dangerous Trails" 1920.

Holt, Hazel. Films: "The Fighting Sheriff" 1925 (Madge Blair).

Holt, Jack (1888-1/18/51). Films: "Salomy Jane" 1914; "The Desperado" 1916; "Liberty" 1916-serial; "The Cost of Hatred" 1917 (Huertez); "A Desert Wooing" 1918 (Barton Masters); "Headin' South" 1918; "The Squaw Man" 1918 (Cash Hawkins); "North of the Rio Grande" 1922 (Bob Haddington); "While Satan Sleeps" 1922 (Phil); "North of '36" 1924 (Don McMasters); "The Wanderer of the Wasteland" 1924 (Adam Larey); "The Light of Western Stars" 1925 (Gene Stewart); "The Thundering Herd" 1925 (Tom Doan); "Wild Horse Mesa" 1925 (Chane Weymer); "Born to the West" 1926 (Colorado Dare Rudd); "The Enchanted Hill" 1926 (Lee Purdy); "Forlorn River" 1926 (Nevada); "Man of the Forest" 1926 (Milt Dale); "The Mysterious Rider" 1927 (Hell Bent Wade); "Avalanche" 1928 (Jack Dunton); "The Vanishing Pioneer" 1928 (John Ballard/Anthony Ballard); "The Water Hole" 1928

(Philip Randolph); "Sunset Pass" 1929 (Jack Rock); "The Border Legion" 1930 (Jack Kells); "End of the Trail" 1936 (Dale Brittenham); "North of Nome" 1936 (John Raglan); "Outlaws of the Orient" 1937 (Chet Eaton); "Roaring Timber" 1937 (Jim Sherwood); "Northwest Rangers" 1942 (Duncan Frazier); "My Pal Trigger" 1946 (Brett Scoville); "Renegade Girl" 1946; "The Wild Frontier" 1947 (Charles "Saddles" Barton); "The Arizona Ranger" 1948 (Rawhide); "The Gallant Legion" 1948 (Captain Banner); "Loaded Pistols" 1948 (Dave Randall); "The Strawberry Roan" 1948 (Walt Bailey); "The Treasure of the Sierra Madre" 1948 (Flophouse Man); ; "Brimstone" 1949 (Marshal Walter Greenside); "The Last Bandit" 1949 (Mort Pemberton); "Red Desert" 1949 (Deacon Smith); "The Daltons' Women" 1950; "King of the Bullwhip" 1950 (James Kerrigan); "Return of the Frontiersman" 1950 (Sam Barrett); "Trail of Robin Hood" 1950 (Jack Holt); "Across the Wide Missouri" 1951 (Bear Ghost).

Holt, Jacqueline. Films: "Stick to Your Guns" 1941 (June Winters). ¶TV: *Tales of Wells Fargo*—"The Thin Rope" 3-18-57 (Girl), "The Hijackers" 6-17-57 (Jeannie Wilcox), "Bill Longley" 2-10-58 (Marge), "Home Town" 11-16-59 (Ella); *Shotgun Slade*—"Charcoal Bullet" 8-16-60 (Peggy).

Holt, Jennifer (1921-). Films: "Deep in the Heart of Texas" 1942 (Nan Taylor); "Little Joe, the Wrangler" 1942 (Janet Hammond); "Old Chisholm Trail" 1942 (Mary Lee); "The Silver Bullet" 1942; "Cheyenne Roundup" 1943 (Ellen Randall); "Frontier Law" 1943 (Lois Rogers); "The Lone Star Trail" 1943 (Joan Winters); "Raiders of San Joaquin" 1943 (Jane Carter); "Raiders of Sunset Pass" 1943 (Betty Mathews); "Tenting Tonight on the Old Camp Ground" 1943 (Kay Randolph); "Marshal of Gunsmoke" 1944 (Ellen); "Oklahoma Raiders" 1944 (Donna); "Outlaw Trail" 1944 (Alice Thornton); "Riders of the Santa Fe" 1944 (Carla/Paula Anderson); "Beyond the Pecos" 1945; "Gun Smoke" 1945; "The Lost Trail" 1945 (Jane Burns); "The Navajo Trail" 1945; "Renegades of the Rio Grande" 1945 (Dolores Salezar); "Song of Old Wyoming" 1945 (Vickey); "Under Western Skies" 1945 (Charity); "Moon Over Montana" 1946; "Trigger Fingers" 1946; "Buffalo Bill Rides Again" 1947 (Lale Harrington); "The Fighting Vigilantes" 1947 (Abby Jackson);

"Ghost Town Renegades" 1947 (Diane); "Over the Santa Fe Trail" 1947; "Pioneer Justice" 1947 (Betty); "Shadow Valley" 1947 (Mary Ann); "Stage to Mesa City" 1947 (Margie Watson); "Trail of the Mounties" 1947 (Kathie); "Where the North Begins" 1947; "The Hawk of Powder River" 1948 (Vivian); "Range Renegades" 1948; "The Tioga Kid" 1948 (Jenny); "Tornado Range" 1948 (Mary).

Holt, Patrick (1912-10/2/93). Films: "The Desperados" 1969 (Haller).

Holt, Tim (1919-2/1/73). Films: "The Vanishing Pioneer" 1928 (John Ballard at Age 7); "Gold Is Where You Find It" 1938 (Lanceford Ferris); "The Law West of Tombstone" 1938 (the Tonto Kid); "Renegade Ranger" 1938 (Larry Corwin); "The Girl and the Gambler" 1939 (Johnny Powell); "Stagecoach" 1939 (Lt. Blanchard); "The Fargo Kid" 1940 (the Fargo Kid); "Wagon Train" 1940 (Zack Sibley); "Along the Rio Grande" 1941 (Jeff); "The Bandit Trail" 1941 (Steve); "Cyclone on Horseback" 1941; "Dude Cowboy" 1941 (Terry); "Robbers of the Range" 1941 (Drummond); "Six Gun Gold" 1941 (Don Cardigan); "Bandit Ranger" 1942; "Come on, Danger!" 1942 (Johnny); "Land of the Open Range" 1942 (Dave); "Pirates of the Prairie" 1942; "Riding the Wind" 1942 (Clay Stewart); "Thundering Hoofs" 1942 (Bill); "The Avenging Rider" 1943 (Brit); "Fighting Frontier" 1943 (Kit); "Red River Robin Hood" 1943; "Sagebrush Law" 1943; "My Darling Clementine" 1946 (Virgil Earp); "Thunder Mountain" 1947 (Marvin Hayden); "Under the Tonto Rim" 1947 (Brad); "Wild Horse Mesa" 1947 (Dave Jordan); "The Arizona Ranger" 1948 (Bob Wade); "Gun Smugglers" 1948 (Tim Holt); "Guns of Hate" 1948 (Bob); "Indian Agent" 1948 (Dave); "The Treasure of the Sierra Madre" 1948 (Curtin); "Western Heritage" 1948 (Ross Daggett); "Brothers in the Saddle" 1949 (Tim Taylor); "Masked Raiders" 1949 (Tim); "The Mysterious Desperado" 1949 (Tim); "Rustlers" 1949 (Dick); "Stagecoach Kid" 1949 (Dave); "Border Treasure" 1950 (Ed Porter); "Dynamite Pass" 1950 (Ross); "Rider from Tucson" 1950 (Dave); "Riders of the Range" 1950 (Kansas); "Rio Grande Patrol" 1950 (Nebraska); "Storm Over Wyoming" 1950 (Dave); "Gunplay" 1951 (Tim); "Hot Lead" 1951 (Tim); "Law of the Badlands" 1951 (Dave); "Overland Telegraph" 1951 (Tim); "Pistol Harvest" 1951 (Tim); "Saddle Legion"

1951 (Dave Saunders); "Desert Passage" 1952 (Tim); "Road Agent" 1952 (Tim); "Target" 1952 (Tim); "Trail Guide" 1952 (Tim). ¶TV: *The Virginian*—"A Woman of Stone" 12-17-69 (Abe Landeen).

Holtz, George. Films: "Rawhide Terror" 1934; "The Outlaw Deputy" 1935 (Crentz).

Holtz, Tenen (1887-7/1/71). Films: "The Law of the Range" 1928 (Cohen); "The Trail of '98" 1929 (Mr. Bulkey); "Henry Goes Arizona" 1939 (Boris); "Let Freedom Ring" 1939 (Hunky).

Holtzman, Glen (1931-5/6/80). TV: *Bonanza*—"Blood on the Land" 2-13-60; *Wyatt Earp*—"The Court vs. Doc Holliday" 4-26-60 (Hoss).

Homans, Robert E. (1875-7/28/47). Films: "Wolves of the North" 1924-serial; "Border Justice" 1925 (Robert Maitland); "The Bandit Buster" 1926 (Romeo); "Fighting with Buffalo Bill" 1926-serial; "The Fightin' Comeback" 1927 (Sheriff Beasley); "The Galloping Gobs" 1927 (the Banker); "Pals in Peril" 1927 (Sheriff Kipp); "Range Courage" 1927 (Pop Gallagher); "Ride 'Em High" 1927 (Rufus Allen); "Burning the Wind" 1928 (Richard Gordon, Sr.); "The Concentratin' Kid" 1930 (C.C. Stile); "Spurs" 1930 (Pop Merrill); "Trigger Tricks" 1930 (Thomas Kingston); "Branded Men" 1931; "Clearing the Range" 1931 (Dad Moran); "Alias the Bad Man" 1931 (Mr. Warner); "Man from Hell's Edges" 1932 (Sheriff Williams); "Son of Oklahoma" 1932 (John Clayton); "Nevada" 1935 (Carver); "Stormy" 1935 (Conductor); "Ride, Ranger, Ride" 1936 (Col. Summerall); "Rose of the Rancho" 1936 (Passenger); "Forlorn River" 1937 (Jeff Winters); "Gold Is Where You Find It" 1938 (Grogan); "Gold Mine in the Sky" 1938 (Lucky Langham); "Heart of the North" 1938 (Captain Ashmun); "Dodge City" 1939 (Mail Clerk); "The Oklahoma Kid" 1939 (Bartender); "Stagecoach" 1939 (Lordsburg Editor); "Union Pacific" 1939; "Son of Roaring Dan" 1940 (Dan McPhail); "Virginia City" 1940 (Southerner); "West of Carson City" 1940 (Judge Harkins); "Red River Valley" 1941; "Sierra Sue" 1941 (Larabee); "In Old California" 1942 (Marshal); "The Sombrero Kid" 1942 (Tom Holden, Sr.); "The Spoilers" 1942 (Sea Captain); "Frontier Badman" 1943 (Sheriff); "The Man from the Rio Grande" 1943; "Buffalo Bill" 1944 (Muldoon, the Policeman); "Beyond the Pecos" 1945;

"Badman's Territory" 1946 (Trial Judge).

Homeier, G.V. "Skip" (1930-). Films: "Boy's Ranch" 1946 (Skippy); "The Gunfighter" 1950 (Hunt Bromley); "The Last Posse" 1953 (Art Romer); "Dawn at Socorro" 1954 (Buddy Ferris); "The Lone Gun" 1954 (Cass Downing); "At Gunpoint" 1955 (Bob Dennis); "The Road to Denver" 1955 (Sam Mayhew); "Ten Wanted Men" 1955 (Howie Stewart); "The Burning Hills" 1956 (Jack Sutton); "Dakota Incident" 1956 (Brank Banner); "Stranger at My Door" 1956 (Clay Anderson); "Thunder Over Arizona" 1956; "The Tall T" 1957 (Billy Jack); "Day of the Bad Man" 1958 (Howard Hayes); "Plunderers of Painted Flats" 1959 (Joe Martin); "Comanche Station" 1960 (Frank); "Showdown" 1963 (Caslon); "Bullet for a Badman" 1964 (Pink); "Starbird and Sweet William" 1975; "The Wild Wild West Revisited" TVM-1979 (Joseph). ¶TV: *Zane Grey Theater*—"Black Is for Grief" 4-12-57 (Cleve Roarke); *Jefferson Drum*—"The Post" 7-4-58 (Kading); *Walt Disney Presents*—"Elfego Baca" Regular 1958-60 (Ross Mantee); *Wanted—Dead or Alive*—"The Favor" 11-15-58 (Ted Jenks); *Lawman*—"The Bandit" 5-31-59 (Ches Ryan); *The Deputy*—"The Johnny Shanks Story" 10-31-59 (Johnny Shanks); *Wichita Town*—"Out of the Past" 12-9-59 (Murdock); *Rawhide*—"Incident of the Blue Fire" 12-11-59 (Lucky Markley), "The Long Shakedown" 10-13-61 (Jess Clayton), "Brush War at Buford" 11-23-65 (the Wichita Kid); *The Rifleman*—"The Spoiler" 2-16-60 (Brud Evans); *The Outlaws*—"Rape of Red Sky" 10-27-60 (Gabe Cutter); *Frontier Circus*—"The Race" 5-3-62 (Colonel Rastatt); *The Virginian*—"Strangers at Sundown" 4-3-63 (Jed Carter), "A Portrait of Marie Valonne" 11-6-63 (Sgt. Dan Bohannon), "The Brazos Kid" 10-21-64 (Joe Cleary), "The Price of Love" 2-12-69 (Callan); *Wagon Train*—"The Andrew Elliott Story" 2-10-64 (George); *Death Valley Days*—"The Quiet and the Fury" 4-25-64 (Doc Holliday), "The Fighting Sky Pilot" 4-25-65; *Branded*—"Coward Step Aside" 3-7-65 (Luke Garrett); *The Loner*—"The Mourners for Johnny Sharp" 2-5-66 & 2-12-66 (Philby); *Bonanza*—"Horse of a Different Hue" 9-18-66 (Jack Geller); *Shane*—"The Day the Wolf Laughed" 11-19-66 (Augie); *Iron Horse*—"A Dozen Ways to Kill a Man" 12-19-66 (Marshal Gault); *How the West Was Won*—"The Rustler" 1-22-79 (Miniter Boyle).

Hong, James (1928-). TV: *The Californians*—"Gold-Tooth Charlie" 3-10-59 (Charlie Wong); *The Adventures of Rin Tin Tin*—"The Ming Vase" 3-13-59 (Danny); *Zorro*—"Senor China Boy" 6-25-59 (Chinese Boy); *Bat Masterson*—"To the Manner Born" 10-1-59 (Ching Sun); *Sugarfoot*—"The Highbinder" 1-19-60 (the Hatchetman); *Bonanza*—"San Francisco Holiday" 4-2-60, "Badge Without Honor" 9-24-60 (Cousin); *Have Gun Will Travel*—"Coming of the Tiger" 4-14-62 (Priest); *Iron Horse*—"The Dynamite Driver" 9-19-66 (Chun Lee), "Sister Death" 4-3-67 (Ching Lee); *Kung Fu*—"The Tide" 2-1-73 (Old Man), "The Squaw Man" 11-1-73 (Lin), "The Passion of Chen Yi" 2-28-74 (Yam Tin), "Arrogant Dragons" 3-14-74 (Men Han), "A Small Beheading" 9-21-74 (Kwang Kyu), "This Valley of Terror" 9-28-74 (Madman), "The Garments of Rage" 11-8-74 (Han Tsung), "The Thief of Chendo" 3-29-75 (Chun Yen); *Outlaws*—"Primer" 1-10-87 (Mr. Luc); *Adventures of Brisco County, Jr.*—Pilot 8-27-93 (Le Pow), "Fountain of Youth" 1-14-94 (Lee Pow), "And Baby Makes Three" 4-22-94 (Lee Pow).

Hood, Foster. Films: "Comanche Station" 1960 (Comanche Lance Beaver); "The Professionals" 1966. ¶TV: *Laramie*—"Handful of Fire" 12-5-61 (Chief Chato); *Branded*—"The Wolfers" 1-9-66; *Pistols 'n' Petticoats*—11-12-66 (Floating Cloud).

Hooker, Buddy Joe. Films: "The Castaway Cowboy" 1974; "Take a Hard Ride" 1974-Ital./Brit./Ger. (Angel).

Hooker, Hugh. Films: "Texas Panhandle" 1945; "Fighting Mustang" 1948; "Bandit Queen" 1950 (Dawson); "The Texan Meets Calamity Jane" 1950 (Sam); "Gold Raiders" 1951 (Sandy).

Hooker, Ken. TV: *The Restless Gun*—"More Than Kin" 5-26-58 (Fred); *Wagon Train*—"The Allison Justis Story" 10-19-60 (Ira).

Hooker, Son (1939-10/14/74). Films: "J.W. Coop" 1971 (Motorcycle Cop).

Hooks, Robert (1937-). Films: "Posse" 1993 (King David).

Hoopes, Ralph. Films: "Riders of the Sage" 1939 (Buddy Martin); "Wild Horse Range" 1940 (Buddy Mitchell).

Hoops, Arthur (1870-9/16/16). Films: "The Spell of the Yukon" 1916 (Albert Temple).

Hoose, Fred (1868-3/12/52).

Films: "Rogue of the Range" 1936; "The Driftin' Kid" 1941; "Dynamite Canyon" 1941 (Col. Blake); "Lone Star Law Men" 1941 (James); "Riding the Sunset Trail" 1941 (Judge Little); "Silver Stallion" 1941 (Dad); "Wanderers of the West" 1941 (Saloonkeeper); "Arizona Roundup" 1942; "Where Trails End" 1942; "The Law Rides Again" 1943 (Hank); "Surrender" 1950 (Assistant Editor); "Oklahoma Annie" 1952 (Bookkeeper). ¶TV: Wild Bill Hickok—"The Border City Election" 9-18-51.

Hootkins, William. TV: Bret Maverick—"Horse of Yet Another Color" 1-5-82 (Theodore Roosevelt).

Hoover, Joseph. Films: "The Man Who Shot Liberty Valance" 1962 (Hasbrouck); "Black Spurs" 1965 (Swifty); "Stagecoach" 1966 (Lt. Blanchard). ¶TV: Empire—"Hidden Asset" 3-26-63 (Johnny Howe); Rawhide—"The Backshooter" 11-27-64 (Sam Jefferson); Gunsmoke—"The Brothers" 3-12-66 (Dave Crandall); Daniel Boone—"The Lost Colony" 12-8-66 (Chad Oliver); Kung Fu—"An Eye for an Eye" 1-25-73 (Sentry).

Hoover, Phil. Films: "Hard Trail" 1969; "Baker's Hawk" 1976 (Sled).

Hope, Bob (1903-). Films: "The Paleface" 1948 (Painless Peter Potter); "Fancy Pants" 1950 (Humphrey); "Son of Paleface" 1952 (Junior); "Alias Jesse James" 1959 (Milford Farnsworth). ¶TV: Bob Hope Chrysler Theatre—"Have Girls—Will Travel" 10-16-64 (Horatio Lovelace).

Hope, Faith. Films: "Good Men and Bad" 1923 (Rosalia); "A Son of the Desert" 1928 (Zuebida).

Hope, Gloria (1899-10/29/76). Films: "The Law of the North" 1918 (Virginia de Montcalm); "The Outcasts of Poker Flat" 1919 (Ruth Watson/Sophy); "The Rider of the Law" 1919 (Betty); "Prairie Trails" 1920 (Alice Endicott); "The Texan" 1920 (Alice Marcum); "The Third Woman" 1920 (Marcelle Riley); "That Devil Quemado" 1925 (Joanna Thatcher).

Hope, Jim (1891-7/27/75). TV: Maverick—"Ghost Riders" 10-13-57 (Player), "Trail West to Fury" 2-16-58 (Lieutenant).

Hopkins, Bo (1942-). Films: "The Wild Bunch" 1969 (Crazy Lee); "Macho Callahan" 1970 (Yancy); "Monte Walsh" 1970 (Jumpin' Joe Joslin); "The Culpepper Cattle Company" 1972 (Dixie Brick); "The Man Who Loved Cat Dancing" 1973 (Billy); "Posse" 1975 (Wesley); "The Invasion of Johnson County" TVM-

1976 (George Dunning); "Last Ride of the Dalton Gang" TVM-1979 (Bill Doolin); "Rodeo Girl" TVM-1980 (Wil Garrett); "Houston: The Legend of Texas" TVM-1986 (Colonel Sidney Sherman); "Down the Long Hill" TVM-1987 (Jud); "The Ballad of Little Jo" 1993 (Frank Badger); "Cheyenne Warrior" 1994 (Andrews); "Wyatt Earp: Return to Tombstone" TVM-1994 (Rattlesnake Reynolds); "Riders of the Storm" 1955 (Billy Van Owen). ¶TV: The Virginian—"Johnny Moon" 10-11-67 (Will); Gunsmoke—"Hard Luck Henry" 10-23-67 (Harper Haggen); Wild Wild West—"The Night of the Iron Fist" 12-8-67 (Zack Garrison); The Guns of Will Sonnett—"What's in a Name?" 1-5-68, "Guilt" 11-29-68 (Ben Merceen); Bonanza—"The Witness" 9-21-69 (Stretch); Nichols—"Sleight of Hand" 2-1-72 (Kansas); The Busters—Pilot 5-28-78 (Chad Kimbrough).

Hopkins, Bob (1918-10/5/62). TV: Wyatt Earp—"The General's Lady" 1-14-58 (Chris Hendon); Have Gun Will Travel—"The Unforgiven" 11-7-59, "Love and a Bad Woman" 3-26-60 (Dandy), "The Exiles" 1-27-62 (Crocker); Gunsmoke—"Hinka Do" 1-30-60 (Pete); The Deputy—"The Two Faces of Bob Claxton" 2-27-60 (Mike Claxton); The Texan—"Ruthless Woman" 4-11-60 (Ewell); Wagon Train—"The Amos Gibbon Story" 4-20-60 (Hank Morton); Rawhide—"Incident of the Last Chance" 6-10-60 (Denton); Bonanza—"The Abduction" 10-29-60, "Elizabeth, My Love" 5-27-61 (Mariner).

Hopkins, Clyde (1893-11/19/58). Films: "Girl of the Timber Claims" 1917 (Bob Mullen).

Hopkins, John. Films: "American Maid" 1917 (Sam Benson); "Wild Honey" 1918 (Joe Stacey); "A Gentleman Preferred" 1928 (Kent Carlington).

Hopkins, May. Films: "The Night Horsemen" 1921 (Kate Cumberland).

Hopkins, Miriam (1902-10/9/72). Films: "Virginia City" 1940 (Julia Hayne); "The Outcasts of Poker Flat" 1952 (Duchess).

Hopper, Dennis (1935-). Films: "Giant" 1956 (Jordan Benedict III); "Gunfight at the O.K. Corral" 1957 (Billy Clanton); "From Hell to Texas" 1958 (Tom Boyd); "The Young Land" 1959 (Hatfield Carnes); "The Sons of Katie Elder" 1965 (Dave Hastings); "Hang 'Em High" 1968 (the Prophet); "True Grit" 1969 (Moon); "Kid Blue" 1973 (Bickford Waner); "Mad Dog Morgan" 1975-Australia

(Dan Morgan); "Wild Times" TVM-1980 (Doc Holliday); "Straight to Hell" 1987-Brit. (I.G. Farben). ¶TV: Cheyenne—"The Traveler" 1-3-56, "Quicksand" 4-3-56 (the Utah Kid), "The Iron Trail" 1-1-57 (Abe Larson); Sugarfoot—"Brannigan's Boots" 9-17-57 (Billy the Kid); Zane Grey Theater—"The Sharpshooter" 3-7-58 (Vern), "The Sunrise Gun" 5-19-60 (Danny Sunrise); The Rifleman—"The Sharpshooter" 9-30-58 (Vernon Tippert), "Three-Legged Terror" 4-21-59 (Johnny Clover); The Dakotas—"Requiem at Dancer's Hill" 2-18-63 (Ross Kendrick); Wagon Train—"The Emmett Lawton Story" 3-6-63 (Emmett Lawson); Bonanza—"The Dark Past" 5-3-64 (Dev Farnum); Gunsmoke—"One Killer on Ice" 1-23-65 (Billy Kimbro); The Legend of Jesse James—"South Wind" 2-14-66 (Jud Salt); The Big Valley—"Plunder at Hawk's Grove" 3-13-67 (Leon Grell), "Night of the Executioners" 12-11-67 (Jimmy Sweetwater); The Guns of Will Sonnett—"Find a Sonnett, Kill a Sonnett" 12-8-67 (Vern Reed).

Hopper, De Wolfe. see Hopper, William.

Hopper, Hal (1912-11/2/70). TV: The Adventures of Rin Tin Tin—Regular 1955-57 (Cpl. Clark), "Higgins' Last Stand" 1-4-57 (Jimmy Kling), "Decision of Rin Tin Tin" 10-3-58 (Dana); Judge Roy Bean—"The Judge of Pecos Valley" 9-10-55 (Elliott), "Checkmate" 1-1-56 (Thompson), "The Eyes of Texas" 1-1-56 (Owens), "The Travelers" 1-1-56 (Brock), "The Defense Rests" 6-1-56 (Court Clerk), "Four Ladies from Laredo" 7-1-56 (Bartender), "The Refugee" 7-1-56 (Ben), "Lone Star Killer" 8-1-56 (Ranger); Circus Boy—"Elmer the Aeronaut" 1-13-57 (Baldy); Maverick—"The Quick and the Dead" 12-8-57 (Jim Elkins), "The Day They Hanged Bret Maverick" 9-21-58 (Stanley), "Alias Bart Maverick" 10-5-58 (Horace); Desilu Playhouse—"Six Guns for Donegan" 10-16-59.

Hopper, Hedda (1890-2/1/66). Films: "Zander the Great" 1925 (Mrs. Caldwell).

Hopper, Wesley. Films: "The Lone Ranger" 1938-serial (Trooper); "The Lone Ranger Rides Again" 1939-serial (Posseman #3); "Surrender" 1950 (Barney Gale).

Hopper, William (De Wolf Hopper) (1915-3/6/70). Films: "Santa Fe Trail" 1940 (Officer); "Virginia City" 1940 (Lieutenant); "They Died with Their Boots On" 1941

(Frazier); "Sitting Bull" 1954 (Wentworth); "Track of the Cat" 1954 (Arthur); "Robbers' Roost" 1955 (Robert Bell); "The First Texan" 1956 (Travis); "Slim Carter" 1957 (Joe Brewster). ¶TV: *Fury*—"The Hobo" 1-7-56 (Sam Wilson); *Gunsmoke*—"Robin Hood" 2-4-56 (John Henry Jordan), "Unmarked Grave" 8-18-56 (Tasker Sloane); *Schlitz Playhouse of the Stars*—"The Restless Gun" 3-29-57 (Dan Maler).

Hopson, Alfred. Films: "The Hired Hand" 1971 (Bartender). ¶TV: *Maverick*—"The Jeweled Gun" 11-24-57 (Carter); *Gunsmoke*—"Overland Express" 5-31-58 (Bill); *Wrangler*—"Encounter at Elephant Butte" 9-15-60 (Wilkins).

Hopton, Russell (1900-4/7/45). Films: "Law and Order" 1932 (Luther Johnson); "Northern Frontier" 1935 (Duke Milford); "Valley of Wanted Men" 1935 (Kelly Dillon); "The Last Outlaw" 1936 (Billings); "Rose of the Rancho" 1936 (Frisco); "Renegade Trail" 1939 (Smoky Joslin); "Nevada" 1944 (Henchman); "Tall in the Saddle" 1944; "West of the Pecos" 1945 (Jeff Stinger).

Horan, Charles (1882-1/11/28). Films: "The Blindness of Courage" 1913.

Horan, James W. (1908-5/4/67). Films: "The Far Country" 1955. ¶TV: *Maverick*—"Black Fire" 3-16-58 (Cousin Pliney), "Last Wire from Stop Gap" 10-16-60 (Kibitzer).

Horgan, Patrick (1929-). TV: *Pistols 'n' Petticoats*—10-8-66 (Sir Richard); *The High Chaparral*—"The Ghost of Chaparral" 9-17-67 (Anthony Grey); *Cimarron Strip*—"Knife in the Darkness" 1-25-68 (Tipton); *The Guns of Will Sonnett*—"Alone" 2-9-68 (Captain Darby); *Cowboy in Africa*—"A Man of Value" 2-26-68 (Sean Bassity); *Wild Wild West*—"The Night of the Diva" 3-7-69 (Max Crenshaw).

Horino, Tad. TV: *Kung Fu*—"Sun and Cloud Shadow" 2-22-73 (1st Elder), "The Tong" 11-15-73 (Li), "Blood of the Dragon" 9-14-74 (Cowled Head), "The Devil's Champion" 11-29-74 (Innkeeper), "The Demon God" 12-13-74 (Chemist), "The Thief of Chendo" 3-29-75 (Priest); *How the West Was Won*—"China Girl" 4-16-79 (Chang).

Hornbuckle, Benjamin. Films: "Davy Crockett, King of the Wild Frontier" 1955 (Henderson).

Horne, David (1898-3/15/70). Films: "The Sheriff of Fractured Jaw" 1958-Brit. (James).

Horne, Geoffrey (1933-). Films: "Magnificent Three" 1963-Span./Ital. ¶TV: *The Virginian*—"Harvest of Strangers" 2-16-66 (Regan); *The Road West*—"Long Journey to Leavenworth" 10-17-66 (Fred Collins); *Gunsmoke*—"A Game of Death ... An Act of Love" 11-5-73 & 11-12-73 (Lieutenant Briggs).

Horne, James (1881-6/29/42). Films: "The Invaders" 1913; "The Pitfall" 1915.

Horne, James. Films: "Back Trail" 1948 (Terry).

Horne, Lena (1917-). Films: "Death of a Gunfighter" 1969 (Claire Quintana).

Horne, Victoria (1920-). Films: "In Old Sacramento" 1946 (Ma Dodge); "The Scarlet Horseman" 1946-serial (Loma).

Horne, William (1869-12/15/42). Films: "Western Firebrands" 1921 (Richard Stanton).

Horse, Michael. Films: "The Legend of the Lone Ranger" 1981 (Tonto); "Buckeye and Blue" 1988; "Riders of the Storm" 1995 (Dirty Bob). ¶TV: *Paradise*—"The Burial Ground" 11-4-89 (Walking Water); *Hawkeye*—"Vengeance Is Mine" 2-23-95 (Gin-Daga).

Horsey, Martin (1946-). TV: *Daniel Boone*—"They Who Will They Hang from the Yardarm if Willy Gets Away?" 2-8-68 (Willy Crawford).

Horsley, David. Films: "Rough Riding Ranger" 1935 (Slim).

Horsley, Lee (1955-). Films: "The Wild Women of Chastity Gulch" TVM-1982 (Capt. John Cain). ¶TV: *Paradise*—Regular 1988-91 (Ethan Allen Cord); *Hawkeye*—Regular 1994- (Hawkeye).

Horton, Clara (1904-12/4/76). Films: "The Plow Woman" 1917 (Mary as a Child); "The Whirlwind Finish" 1918; "Action" 1921 (Molly Casey); "All Around the Frying Pan" 1925 (Jean Donovan); "Beyond the Trail" 1926 (Clarabelle Simpkins); "The Fightin' Comeback" 1927 (Goldie Lamont).

Horton, Clem. Films: "Code of the Range" 1936 (Gunman); "Fighting Texan" 1937; "One Man Justice" 1937 (Sam); "Two-Fisted Sheriff" 1937 (Barstow); "Cattle Raiders" 1938 (Slash); "The Colorado Trail" 1938 (Henchman); "Law of the Plains" 1938 (Cole); "West of Cheyenne" 1938 (Dawson); "West of Santa Fe" 1938 (Hager); "The Man from Sundown" 1939 (Bat); "Riders of the Black River" 1939; "Spoilers of the

Range" 1939 (Shorty); "The Thundering West" 1939 (Santos); "Beyond the Sacramento" 1940 (Barlow); "Two-Fisted Rangers" 1940 (Henchman).

Horton, Edward Everett (1886-9/29/70). Films: "Ruggles of Red Gap" 1923 (Ruggles). ¶TV: *F Troop*—Regular 1965-67 (Roaring Chicken).

Horton, Robert (1924-). Films: "Apache War Smoke" 1952 (Tom Herrera); "Pony Soldier" 1952 (Jess Calhoun); "Return of the Texan" 1952 (Dr. Harris); "Arena" 1953 (Jackie Roach); "The Dangerous Days of Kiowa Jones" TVM-1966 (Kiowa Jones). ¶TV: *The Lone Ranger*—"Tenderfoot" 11-25-54; *Wagon Train*—Regular 1957-60,61-62 (Flint Mccullough); *A Man Called Shenandoah*—Regular 1965-66 (Shenandoah).

Horvath, Charles (1921-7/23/78). Films: "Dallas" 1950 (Cowpuncher); "Bonanza Town" 1951 (Smoker); "Cave of Outlaws" 1951 (Job Delancey); "Don Daredevil Rides Again" 1951-serial (Davis); "Snake River Desperadoes" 1951 (Black Eagle); "The Man Behind the Gun" 1952; "Back to God's Country" 1953 (Nelson); "Thunder Over the Plains" 1953; "Border River" 1954 (Crowe); "Rails into Laramie" 1954 (Pike Murphy); "Taza, Son of Cochise" 1954 (Kocha); "Vera Cruz" 1954 (Reno); "Chief Crazy Horse" 1955 (Hardy); "Dakota Incident" 1956 (Indian Leader); "Pillars of the Sky" 1956 (Sgt. Dutch Williams); "Drango" 1957 (Ragan); "The Guns of Fort Petticoat" 1957 (Indian Chief); "Man in the Shadow" 1957 (Len Bookman); "Pawnee" 1957 (Crazy Fox); "Gunmen from Laredo" 1959 (Coloraas); "Posse from Hell" 1961 (Hash); "The Wild Westerners" 1962 (Moose); "California" 1963 (Manuel); "Showdown" 1963 (Hebron); "Advance to the Rear" 1964 (Jones); "Cat Ballou" 1965 (Hardcase); "War Party" 1965; "Johnny Reno" 1966 (Wooster); "Desperate Mission" TVM-1971 (Yuma). ¶TV: *The Lone Ranger*—"Desert Adventure" 11-30-50; *Cheyenne*—"The Law Man" 11-6-56 (Henley); *The Adventures of Rin Tin Tin*—"Boone's Commission" 3-22-57 (Black Cloud), "Return to Fort Apache" 9-20-57 (Brave); *Gunsmoke*—"The Photographer" 4-6-57 (Left Hand); *Broken Arrow*—"Attack on Fort Grant" 5-21-57 (Geronimo); *The Californians*—"Sorley Boy" 2-25-58 (Tully O'Neil); *Zane Grey Theater*—"Utopia, Wyoming" 6-6-58 (Sam Vincent); *Have

Gun Will Travel—"The Man Who Wouldn't Talk" 9-20-58 (Bull Swanson); *The Texan*—"The Man Hater" 6-15-59 (Sam), "The Telegraph Story" 10-26-59 (Chuck Rogers); *Zorro*—"Senor China Boy" 6-25-59 (Vinson); *Bonanza*—"The Truckee Strip" 11-21-59, "The Many Faces of Gideon Flinch" 11-5-61; *The Westerner*—"Jeff" 9-30-60 (Crow); *Lawman*—"Samson the Great" 11-20-60 (Pat Cassidy); *Wagon Train*—"The Christopher Hale Story" 3-15-61 (Muerto); *Laramie*—"Badge of Glory" 5-7-63; *Daniel Boone*—"The Devil's Four" 3-4-65 (Erik Strasser), "The Trek" 10-21-65 (Pike), "The High Cumberland" 4-14-66 & 4-21-66 (Luther Wills), "A Pinch of Salt" 5-1-69; *Branded*—"Mightier Than the Sword" 9-26-65 (Deke), "The Wolfers" 1-9-66 (Jud), "A Proud Town" 12-19-65; *Wild Wild West*—"The Night of the Glowing Corpse" 10-29-65 (Ironfoot), "The Night of the Gypsy Peril" 1-20-67 (Gombol); *Laredo*—"The Callico Kid" 1-6-66, "That's Noway, Thataway" 1-20-66, "The Last of the Caesars—Absolutely" 12-2-66; *The Big Valley*—"Last Train to the Fair" 4-27-66 (Ford); *Iron Horse*—"Grapes of Grass Valley" 10-21-67 (Sam); *The High Chaparral*—"The Firing Wall" 12-31-67 (Pedro's Cousin), "Shadow of the Wind" 1-10-69 (Burt Alvord); *Cimarron Strip*—"The Greeners" 3-7-68.

Hossein, Robert (1927-). Films: "Taste of Violence" 1961-Fr.; "Cemetery Without Crosses" 1968-Ital./Fr.; "Judge Roy Bean" 1970-Fr. (Judge Roy Bean).

Hotaling, Arthur (1872-7/13/38). Films: "Kit Carson Over the Great Divide" 1925 (Lt. John C. Fremont); "King of the Herd" 1927.

Hotchkis, Joan (1927-). TV: *Frontier*—"The Hunted" 5-13-56; *Iron Horse*—"Four Guns to Scalplock" 11-11-67 (Catharine); *The Outcasts*—"The Night Riders" 11-25-68 (Melissa).

Hoton, Russell. Films: "High, Wide and Handsome" 1937 (John Thompson).

Hotton, Donald (1931-). Films: "The Girl Called Hatter Fox" TVM-1977 (Dr. Levering).

Houck, Doris. Films: "Landrush" 1946 (Mary Parker); "Two-Fisted Ranger" 1946.

Houck, Jr., Joy. Films: "The Shepherd of the Hills" 1964 (Ollie Stewart); "Shadow of Chikara" 1978 (Half Moon O'Brien).

House, Billy (1890-9/23/61).

Films: "Trail Street" 1947 (Carmody); "Santa Fe" 1951 (Luke Plummer); "Silver City" 1951 (Malone); "Outlaw Women" 1952 (Barney); "The Naked Gun" 1956. ¶TV: *The Californians*—"Crimps' Meat" 1-27-59 (Papa Kelly).

House, Donald. Films: "Bury Me Not on the Lone Prairie" 1941; "The Ox-Bow Incident" 1943 (Posse); "Pardners" 1956 (Townsman). ¶TV: *Trackdown*—"Marple Brothers" 10-4-57.

House, Jack (1887-11/20/63). Films: "The Smoking Trail" 1924; "Fightin' Odds" 1925 (Flash Lamore).

House, Newton (1865-12/16/48). Films: "The Ridin 'Kid from Powder River" 1924 (Bud at Age 10); "The Buckaroo Kid" 1926; "Clearing the Trail" 1927; "The Racing Wizard" 1927; "The Red Warning" 1927; "The Riding Whirlwind" 1927; "Buckskin Days" 1928; "The Danger Trail" 1928; "The Fighting Kid" 1928; "The Ride for Help" 1928; "Riding Gold" 1928; "Ropin' Romance" 1928; "A Son of the Frontier" 1928; "The Untamed" 1928; "Winged Hoofs" 1928; "Girl of the Golden West" 1930 (Pony Express Rider); "Son of Zorro" 1947-serial (Haynes).

Houser, Jerry (1952-). Films: "Bad Company" 1972 (Arthur Simms).

Houser, Patrick. Films: "Outlaws" TVM-1986 (Billy Pike). ¶TV: *Outlaws*—Regular 1986-87 (Billy Pike).

Housman, Arthur (1890-4/7/42). Films: "The Colonel's Dauhter" 1915; "The Desert's Price" 1925 (Tom Martin); "Girl of the Golden West" 1930 (Sidney Dick); "Where the West Begins" 1938 (Beano); "Go West" 1940 (Drunk).

Houston, George (1900-11/12/44). Films: "Frontier Scout" 1939 (Wild Bill Hickok); "The Lone Rider Ambushed" 1941 (Tom Cameron/ Keno Harris); "The Lone Rider Crosses the Rio" 1941 (Tom Cameron); "The Lone Rider Fights Back" 1941 (Tom Cameron); "The Lone Rider in Frontier Fury" 1941 (Tom Cameron); "The Lone Rider in Ghost Town" 1941 (Tom Cameron); "The Lone Rider Rides On" 1941 (Tom Cameron); "Border Roundup" 1942; "The Lone Rider and the Bandit" 1942 (Tom Cameron); "The Lone Rider in Cheyenne" 1942 (Tom Cameron); "Outlaws of Boulder Pass" 1942; "Texas Justice" 1942 (Tom Cameron).

Houtchens, Pat. TV: *Bonanza*—

"The Reluctant American" 2-14-71 (Reverend Williams).

Hoven, Adrian (1924-4/28/81). Films: "Seven Hours of Gunfire" 1964-Span./Ital. (Wild Bill Hickok); "Jesse James' Kid" 1966-Span./Ital. (Sheriff Alan Davies).

Hovey, Ann. Films: "The Glory Trail" 1937 (Julie Morgan).

Hovey, Tim (1945-9/9/89). Films: "Slim Carter" 1957 (Leo Gallagher); "Money, Women and Guns" 1958 (Davey Kingman). ¶TV: *Cimarron City*—"Cimarron Holiday" 12-20-58 (Avery Wickham).

Hovis, Larry (1936-). Films: "The New Daughters of Joshua Cabe" TVM-1976 (Clel Tonkins).

Howard, Anne. Films: "Lawless Valley" 1932 (Minerva Huff); "Lawless Valley" 1932; "Crashing Broadway" 1933 (Mrs. Reilly); "The Fighting Texans" 1933 (Mrs. Whimple); "Lightning Range" 1934 (Hester); "Arizona Bad Man" 1935 (Dancer); "Tombstone Terror" 1935 (Nellie, the Dancer).

Howard, Boothe (1873-10/27/58). Films: "Texas Bad Man" 1932 (Phil); "Oh, Susanna!" 1936 (Wolf Benson); "Red River Valley" 1936 (Steve Howard); "Robin Hood of El Dorado" 1936 (Tabbard).

Howard, Breena. TV: *Stoney Burke*—"Cat's Eyes" 2-11-63 (Nurse); *The Loner*—"The Lonely Calico Queen" 10-2-65 (Suzanne).

Howard, Clint (1959-). Films: "An Eye for an Eye" 1966 (Jo-Hi); "The Wild Country" 1971 (Andrew Tanner); "Far and Away" 1992; "Cheyenne Warrior" 1994 (Otto Nielsen). ¶TV: *Bonanza*—"All Ye His Saints" 12-19-65 (Michael Thorpe); *The Virginian*—"Ride a Cock-Horse to Laramie Cross" 2-23-66 (Manuel), "Melanie" 2-22-67 (Tommy); *Laredo*—"Leave It to Dixie" 12-30-66 (Midge); *The Monroes*—"Teach the Tigers to Purr" 3-8-67 (Jody Hillman); *Lancer*—"Blue Skies for Willie Sharpe" 1-13-70 (Willie Sharpe); *Gunsmoke*—"Murdoch" 2-8-71 (Lonny); *The Men from Shiloh*—"Wolf Track" 3-17-71 (Will); *The Cowboys*—Regular 1974 (Steve).

Howard, Curly (Jerome Howard) (1906-1/19/52). Films: "Horses' Collars" 1935-short; "Whoops, I'm an Indian" 1936-short (Curly); "Back to the Woods" 1937-short (Curly); "Goofs and Saddles" 1937-short (Curly); "Yes, We Have No Bonanza" 1939-short (Curly); "Rockin' Through the Rockies" 1940-short (Curly); "Cactus Makes Perfect" 1942-short; "Phony

Express" 1943-short (Curly); "Rockin' in the Rockies" 1945 (Curly); "Three Troubledoers" 1946-short (Curly).

Howard, Edward M. (1910-9/16/46). Films: "Tucson Raiders" 1944; "Bad Men of the Border" 1945; "Both Barrels Blazing" 1945; "Code of the Lawless" 1945 (Bart Rogan); "Frontier Gal" 1945 (Henchman at Bar); "The Navajo Kid" 1945 (Bo Talley); "Rustlers of the Badlands" 1945; "Texas Panhandle" 1945; "Three in the Saddle" 1945; "The Scarlet Horseman" 1946-serial (Zero Quick); "Thunder Town" 1946 (Dunc Rankin).

Howard, Esther (1893-3/8/65). Films: "The Texans" 1938 (Madame); "Lady from Cheyenne" 1941 (Landlady); "Jackass Mail" 1942 (Dance Hall Girl); "Hellfire" 1949 (Birdie).

Howard, Frederick. Films: "Destry Rides Again" 1932 (Edward Clifton); "The Fourth Horseman" 1933 (Elmer Brown); "Great Stagecoach Robbery" 1945.

Howard, Gene. Films: "Code of the Fearless" 1939; "In Old Montana" 1939 (Jailer); "Two-Gun Troubador" 1939 (Pedro Yorba); "Ridin' the Trail" 1940.

Howard, Gertrude (1892-9/30/34). Films: "The Circus Cyclone" 1925 (Mrs. Jackson); "Forbidden Trail" 1932 (Negro Mammy); "The Fighting Code" 1934 (Martha).

Howard, Harold (1870-12/9/44). Films: "The Danger Trail" 1917 (MacDonald).

Howard, Helen (1903-3/14/27). Films: "The Line Runners" 1920; "When Romance Rides" 1922 (Lucy's Chum).

Howard, John (1913-2/19/95). Films: "The Man from Dakota" 1940 (Oliver Clark); "Texas Rangers Ride Again" 1940 (Jim Kingston); "The Fighting Kentuckian" 1949 (Blake Randolph); "Buck and the Preacher" 1972 (George). ¶TV: *TV Reader's Digest*—"Cochise—Greatest of All the Apaches" 1-30-56 (Cochise); *Lawman*—"The Showdown" 1-10-60 (Lance Creedy); *Wagon Train*—"The Colonel Harris Story" 1-13-60 (Colonel Harris); *Cheyenne*—"Home Is the Brave" 3-14-60 (John Thompson); *The Outlaws*—"The Bell" 3-9-61 (Parson); *Gunslinger*—"The Recruit" 3-23-61 (Marcus Tollman); *Bronco*—"The Prince of Darkness" 11-6-61 (Millar); *Rawhide*—"The Captain's Wife" 1-12-62 (James Carr); *The Legend of Jesse James*—"1863" 3-28-66 (Dr. Samuel).

Howard, Ken (1944-). TV: *Hallmark Hall of Fame*—"The Court-Martial of General George Armstrong Carter" 12-1-77 (Major Gardiner); *Bonanza*—"The Twenty-Sixth Grave" 10-31-72 (Samuel Clemens).

Howard, Laura. Films: "Blazing Arrows" 1922 (Mocking Bird).

Howard, Leslie (1893-6/1/43). Films: "Secrets" 1933 (John Carlton).

Howard, Mary (1923-12/13/89). Films: "Billy the Kid" 1941 (Edith Keating); "Riders of the Purple Sage" 1941 (Jane Withersteen).

Howard, Moe (1897-5/4/75). Films: "Horses' Collars" 1935-short; "Whoops, I'm an Indian" 1936-short (Moe); "Back to the Woods" 1937-short; "Goofs and Saddles" 1937-short (Moe); "Yes, We Have No Bonanza" 1939-short (Moe); "Rockin' Through the Rockies" 1940-short (Moe); "Cactus Makes Perfect" 1942-short; "Phony Express" 1943-short (Moe); "Rockin' in the Rockies" 1945 (Moe); "Three Troubledoers" 1946-short (Moe); "Out West" 1947-short (Moe); "Punchy Cowpunchers" 1950-short (Moe); "Gold Raiders" 1951 (Moe); "Merry Mavericks" 1951-short (Moe); "Pals and Gals" 1954-short (Moe); "Shot in the Frontier" 1954-short (Moe); "The Outlaws Is Coming!" 1965 (Moe).

Howard, Rance (1928-). Films: "Frontier Woman" 1956; "An Eye for an Eye" 1966 (Harry); "The Wild Country" 1971 (Cleve); "Far and Away" 1992. ¶TV: *Bat Masterson*—"Promised Land" 6-10-59 (Fletcher); *The Virginian*—"Ride a Cock-Horse to Laramie Cross" 2-23-66 (Luka); *The Monroes*—"The Intruders" 9-7-66, "Killer Cougar" 2-1-67, "Teach the Tigers to Purr" 3-8-67; *Lancer*—"Jelly" 11-19-68 (Willy), "The Measure of a Man" 4-8-69 (Turk Caudle); *Here Come the Brides*—"Two Worlds" 2-20-70 (Goff); *Gunsmoke*—"Jenny" 12-28-70 (Judge Franklin), "In Performance of Duty" 11-18-74 (Frank Benton); *Bonanza*—"Shanklin" 2-13-72 (Bogardus); *Nichols*—"About Jesse James" 2-15-72 (Deputy); *Kung Fu*—"The Hoots" 12-13-73 (Sheriff Byrd).

Howard, Richard. Films: "The Vanishing American" 1925 (Glendon); "Desert Gold" 1926 (Sergeant); "Cyclone of the Range" 1927 (Jake Darkin).

Howard, Ron (1954-). Films: "The Wild Country" 1971 (Virgil Tanner); "The Shootist" 1976 (Gillom Rogers). ¶TV: *Johnny Ringo*—"The Accused" 10-15-59; *The Big Valley*—"Night of the Wolf" 12-1-65

(Tommy); *The Monroes*—"Teach the Tigers to Purr" 3-8-67 (Timothy Prescott); *Gunsmoke*—"Charlie Noon" 11-3-69 (Jamie); *Bonanza*—"The Initiation" 9-26-72 (Ted Hoag).

Howard, Ronald (1918-). Films: "Drango" 1957 (Clay); "Africa—Texas Style!" 1967-U.S./Brit. (Hugo Copp); "The Hunting Party" 1971-Brit./Ital./Span. (Watt Nelson); "The Spikes Gang" 1974 (Les Richter); "Take a Hard Ride" 1974-Ital./Brit./Ger. (Halsey). ¶TV: *Cowboy in Africa*—Regular 1967-68 (Wing Commander Hayes).

Howard, Shemp (1900-11/22/55). Films: "Headin' East" 1937 (Windy); "Hollywood Roundup" 1938 (Oscar); "Moonlight and Cactus" 1944 (Punchy); "Out West" 1947-short (Shemp); "Punchy Cowpunchers" 1950-short (Shemp); "Gold Raiders" 1951 (Shemp); "Merry Mavericks" 1951-short (Shemp); "Pals and Gals" 1954-short (Shemp); "Shot in the Frontier" 1954-short (Shemp).

Howard, Sherman. TV: *Young Riders*—"Blood Money" 11-10-90 (Marshal Cole Lambert).

Howard, Susan (1943-). Films: "The Silent Gun" TVM-1969 (Louise Cole). ¶TV: *Iron Horse*—"Appointment with an Epitaph" 2-13-67 (Sara Collins), "The Return of Hode Avery" 11-4-67 (Bess Hennings); *Here Come the Brides*—"Wives for Wakando" 1-22-69 (Jane); *The Outcasts*—"The Candidates" 1-27-69 (Julie Mason); *The Virginian*—"Halfway Back from Hell" 10-1-69 (Rebecca Teague); *Bonanza*—"The Medal" 10-26-69 (Lori); *The Oregon Trail*—"The Gold Dust Queen" 1977; *The Busters*—Pilot 5-28-78 (Joanna Bailey).

Howard, Trevor (1916-1/7/88). Films: "Windwalker" 1980 (Windwalker).

Howard, Vince (1939-). TV: *Wild Wild West*—"The Night of the Cadre" 3-24-67 (Ralph Kleed), "The Night of the Doomsday Formula" 10-4-68 (Bartender).

Howard, Vincent (1869-11/2/46). Films: "The Indian Maid's Warning" 1913; "Sunlight's Last Raid" 1917 (Captain Sunlight); "Vengeance and the Woman" 1917-serial; "Breaking Through" 1921-serial; "The Purple Riders" 1921-serial.

Howard, Willie (1886-1/14/49). Films: "Rose of the Rancho" 1936 (Pancho Spiegelgass).

Howat, Clark (1917-). Films: "Billy Jack" 1971 (Sheriff Cole). ¶TV:

Death Valley Days—"The Mormon's Grindstone" 2-28-55 (Murphy), "The Hangman Waits" 1-2-56; *Tales of Wells Fargo*—"Special Delivery" 3-31-58 (Mace Kimball); *Tales of the Texas Rangers*—"The Steel Trap" 11-13-58 (Burt Wilson); *The Restless Gun*—"Multiply One Boy" 12-8-58 (Arthur); *Bat Masterson*—"River Boat" 2-18-59 (Murdock); *Wyatt Earp*—"The Posse" 5-10-60; *Wagon Train*—"The Jose Morales Story" 10-19-60 (Aaron Oliver).

Howden, Mike. TV: *Gunsmoke*—"Cattle Barons" 9-18-67 (Drovers), "The Hide Cutters" 9-30-68 (Colton); *Cimarron Strip*—"The Roarer" 11-2-67.

Howdy, Clyde (1920-10/3/69). TV: *Maverick*—"The Ice Man" 1-29-61 (Man at Glacier); *Cheyenne*—"Lone Patrol" 4-10-61 (Trooper Yawkey), "The Brahma Bull" 12-11-61 (Sam Varney); Cimarron Strip—"Nobody" 12-7-67 (Cooper); *Wide Country*—"My Candle Burns at Both Ends" 12-20-62 (Cowboy); *Laredo*—"Three's Company" 10-14-65, "Pride of the Rangers" 12-16-65); *F Troop*—"Wrongo Starr and the Lady in Black" 1-11-66 (Man); *Bonanza*—"Peace Officer" 2-6-66 (Deputy Bill Harris), "The Prince" 4-2-67 (Sgt. Bell), "The Conquistadors" 10-1-67 (Boke); *The Virginian*—"Legacy of Hate" 9-14-66 (Nash), "The Challenge" 10-19-66 (Marshal Coons), "With Help from Ulysses" 1-17-68 (Doc Naylor), "Fox, Hound, and the Widow McCloud" 4-2-69 (Livery Man); *Gunsmoke*—"The Good People" 10-15-66 (Henry Biggs), "Cattle Barons" 9-18-67 (Cowboy); *The Road West*—"Ashes and Tallow and One True Love" 10-24-66 (Davis); *The Rounders*—10-25-66 (Dave); *The Big Valley*—"Ladykiller" 10-16-67; *Death Valley Days*—"Son of Thunder" 10-25-69, "The Great Pinto Bean Gold Hunt" 12-13-69.

Howe, Jimmie. Films: "White Eagle" 1932 (Zachariah Kershaw).

Howe, Wally (1879-7/31/57). Films: "Lawless Range" 1935 (Hank Mason).

Howell, Arlene. TV: *Maverick*—"Alias Bart Maverick" 10-5-58 (Cindy Lou Brown), "Shady Deal at Sunny Acres" 11-23-58 (Cindy Lou Brown), "Island in the Swamp" 11-30-58 (Ladybird Forge), "Passage to Fort Doom" 3-8-59 (Cindy Lou Brown); *Bronco*—"Prairie Skipper" 5-5-59 (Miranda Carr).

Howell, Hoke (1929-). Films: "Shenandoah" 1965 (Crying Prisoner); "From Noon to Three" 1976 (Deke); "The Oregon Trail" TVM-1976 (Vaughn); "Geronimo: An American Legend" 1993 (Billy Pickett). ¶TV: *Bonanza*—"Big Shadow on the Land" 4-17-66 (Billy); *Gunsmoke*—"Mad Dog" 1-14-67 (Roan Watson); *Laredo*—"The Other Cheek" 2-10-67; *Here Comes the Brides*—Regular 1968-70 (Ben Jenkins); *Nichols*—"Ketcham Power" 11-11-71 (Ernie); *Kung Fu*—"The Last Raid" 4-26-75 (Lt. Varnum); *The Oregon Trail*—"Hard Ride Home"/ "The Last Game" 9-21-77 (Vaughn); *Outlaws*—"Pursued" 3-7-87 (Eddie); *Paradise*—"Bad Blood" 2-1-91 (Judge Sweeney).

Howell, Jean. Films: "Apache Woman" 1955 (Mrs. Chandler); "Hell's Crossroads" 1957 (Mrs. Jesse James). ¶TV: *Four Star Playhouse*—"Trail's End" 1-29-53; *The Roy Rogers Show*—"Bad Neighbors" 11-21-54 (Vinny Clark); *The Gene Autry Show*—"The Million Dollar Fiddle" 10-1-55, "The Golden Chariot" 10-29-55; *My Friend Flicka*—"Lock, Stock and Barrel" 4-6-56 (Becky Hoskins); *Broken Arrow*—"The Raiders" 12-25-56 (Mrs. Krohl), "Water Witch" 1-7-58 (Laurie); *Zane Grey Theater*—"Time of Decision" 1-18-57 (Mrs. Townley); *Wyatt Earp*—"Bat Masterson for Sheriff" 3-3-57 (Alma Drew), "Frontier Woman" 11-25-58 (Martha Hildreth); *Tales of Wells Fargo*—"The Bounty" 4-15-57 (Cora Williams); *Tombstone Territory*—"Revenge Town" 11-6-57 (Blanche Taylor); *Jim Bowie*—"Charivari" 11-15-57 (Ellen Hill); *The Adventures of Rin Tin Tin*—"Spanish Gold" 3-7-58 (Marina Contreres); *Wanted—Dead or Alive*—"The Bounty" 9-20-58 (Juanita Hernandez); *Trackdown*—"The Schoolteacher" 11-7-58 (Bess Martin), "Bad Judgment" 1-28-59 (Greta Wagner), "Toss Up" 5-20-59 (Naomi Wallace); *Death Valley Days*—"A Town Is Born" 1-20-59 (Ruth); *The Restless Gun*—"Code for a Killer" 4-27-59 (Nancy Sturges); *Gunsmoke*—"The Bobsy Twins" 5-21-60 (Lavinia); *Frontier Circus*—"Dr. Sam" 10-26-61 (Janet Jones); *The Guns of Will Sonnett*—"Where There's Hope" 12-20-68 (Maggie).

Howes, Reed (1900-8/6/64). Films: "Lightning Romance" 1924 (Jack Wade); "Cyclone Cavalier" 1925 (Ted Clayton); "The Dangerous Dude" 1925 (Bob Downs); "The Gentle Cyclone" 1926 (Marshall Junior); "Moran of the Mounted" 1926 (Moran); "Wings of the Storm" 1926 (Allen Gregory); "White Renegade" 1931; "Fighting with Kit Carson" 1933-serial; "The Trail Beyond" 1934 (Henchman); "Dawn Rider" 1935 (Ben); "Paradise Canyon" 1935 (Trigger); "Custer's Last Stand" 1936-serial (Tom "Keen" Blade); "Feud of the West" 1936 (Bart Hunter); "Zorro Rides Again" 1937-serial (Philip Andrews); "Ghost Town Riders" 1938 (Fred); "Lightning Carson Rides Again" 1938; "The Lone Ranger" 1938-serial (Brown); "West of Rainbow's End" 1938; "Fighting Renegade" 1939 (Sheriff); "Flaming Lead" 1939 (Tex); "Honor of the West" 1939 (Deputy Tom Morrison); "The Phantom Stage" 1939 (Denver); "Riders of the Sage" 1939 (Sam); "Six-Gun Rhythm" 1939 (Jim Davis); "South of the Border" 1939; "Straight Shooter" 1939 (Slade); "Texas Wildcats" 1939 (Ace); "Trigger Smith" 1939; "Westbound Stage" 1939 (Greer); "Zorro's Fighting Legion" 1939-serial (Soldier #2); "Adventures of Red Ryder" 1940-serial (Slade); "Billy the Kid Outlawed" 1940 (Whitey); "The Cheyenne Kid" 1940 (Jeff Baker); "Covered Wagon Days" 1940 (Stevens); "Frontier Crusader" 1940; "Heroes of the Saddle" 1940 (Wilson); "Lightning Strikes West" 1940 (Frank); "Phantom Rancher" 1940; "Roll, Wagons, Roll" 1940 (Coleman); "Texas Terrors" 1940 (Ed); "Virginia City" 1940 (Sergeant); "Back in the Saddle" 1941; "Down Mexico Way" 1941; "Fugitive Valley" 1941 (Brandon); "Kansas Cyclone" 1941; "The Lone Rider in Ghost Town" 1941 (Gordon); "Lone Star Law Men" 1941 (Ace); "Sunset in Wyoming" 1941; "Tonto Basin Outlaws" 1941 (Captain); "Along the Sundown Trail" 1942; "Dawn on the Great Divide" 1942; "Pirates of the Prairie" 1942; "Raiders of the West" 1942; "Border Buckaroos" 1943; "Carson City Cyclone" 1943; "Law of the Saddle" 1943 (Dave); "Raiders of Red Gap" 1943; "Red River Robin Hood" 1943; "Santa Fe Scouts" 1943; "Tenting Tonight on the Old Camp Ground" 1943 (Smokey); "Thundering Trails" 1943; "Wild Horse Stampede" 1943 (Tex); "Brand of the Devil" 1944; "Death Valley Rangers" 1944; "Dead or Alive" 1944; "Outlaw Roundup" 1944; "Saddle Leather Law" 1944; "Under Arizona Skies" 1946; "Loaded Pistols" 1948; "River Lady" 1948 (Logger); "The Untamed Breed" 1948 (Oklahoma); "Range Land" 1949 (Red); "The Walking Hills" 1949 (Young King); "Gunslingers" 1950 (Stoner); "The Savage Horde" 1950; "Silver Raiders" 1950 (George); "Stage to Tucson" 1950 (Eddie); "Santa Fe" 1951; "The Thundering Trail" 1951 (Schaeffer); "Hangman's Knot" 1952 (Hank Fletcher); "The Iron Mistress" 1952 (Player); "The Man Behind the Gun" 1952; "The Stranger Wore a Gun" 1953 (Harve Comis); "Three Hours to Kill" 1954 (Bit); "A Lawless Street" 1955; "Ten Wanted Men" 1955; "Blazing the Overland Trail" 1956-serial; "Seven Guns to Mesa" 1958 (Stage Driver); "Sierra Baron" 1958 (Sheriff); "Dalton That Got Away" 1960; "Gunfighters of Abilene" 1960 (Durwood). ¶TV: *The Gene Autry Show*—"Gray Dude" 12-3-50 (Sheriff Davis), "The Peace Maker" 12-17-50, "The Raiders" 4-14-51, "Ghost Town Raiders" 10-6-51, "Feuding Friends" 11-26-55; *The Cisco Kid*—"Stolen Bonds" 7-28-51, "Protective Association" 9-8-51, "Bandaged Badman" 10-1-52, "The Black Terror" 11-29-52; *Wild Bill Hickok*—"Silver Stage Holdup" 10-16-51, "The Fortune Telling Story" 4-22-52, "The Gorilla of Owl Hoot Mesa" 9-23-52; *The Adventures of Kit Carson*—"Fury at Red Gulch" 10-27-51 (Monte); *The Roy Rogers Show*—"The Train Robbery" 2-3-52, "Outlaws' Town" 3-1-52, "The Unwilling Outlaw" 3-8-52, "Ghost Gulch" 3-30-52, "Go for Your Gun" 11-23-52, "The Brothers O'Dell" 11-20-55, "Three Masked Men" 12-18-55 (Sheriff Blodgett), "Johnny Rover" 6-9-57; *Sergeant Preston of the Yukon*—"The Boy Nobody Wanted" 8-9-56 (Inspector); *Broken Arrow*—"Water Witch" 1-7-58 (Fred Hosper); *The Restless Gun*—"Quiet City" 2-3-58 (Pipe Clamper); *Buckskin*—"Cash Robertson" 8-7-58 (Lane); *The Californians*—"Hangtown" 11-18-58 (Elmer).

Howes, Sally Ann (1930-). Films: "Female Artillery" TVM-1973 (Sybil Townsend). ¶TV: *Prudence and the Chief*—Pilot 8-26-70 (Prudence MacKenzie); *The Men from Shiloh*—"Tate, Ramrod" 2-24-71 (Martha Clayton).

Howlin, Olin (1896-9/20/59). Films: "Zander the Great" 1925 (Elmer Lovejoy); "Wagon Wheels" 1934 (Bill O'Meary); "The Bad Man of Brimstone" 1937 (Jardge, the Stage Driver); "The Girl of the Golden West" 1938 (Trinidad Joe); "Days of Jesse James" 1939 (Under-Sheriff); "Henry Goes Arizona" 1939 (Ted Slocum); "Belle Starr" 1941 (Jasper Trench); "The Shepherd of the Hills" 1941 (Corky); "Home in Wyomin'" 1942 (Sunrise); "In Old California" 1942; "Ridin' Down the Canyon" 1942 (Jailer); "Twilight on the Prairie" 1944; "Dakota" 1945 (Devlin's Driver); "Santa Fe Saddlemates" 1945; "Senorita from the West" 1945;

"Sheriff of Cimarron" 1945 (Pinkly Snyder); "Angel and the Badman" 1947 (Bradley); "Apache Rose" 1947 (Alkali Elkins); "The Fabulous Texan" 1947; "The Wistful Widow of Wagon Gap" 1947 (Undertaker); "Wyoming" 1947 (Cowboy); "The Dude Goes West" 1948 (Finnegan); "Last of the Wild Horses" 1948 (Remedy Williams); "The Paleface" 1948 (Undertaker); "Smoky Mountain Melody" 1948; "Station West" 1948 (Cook); "Bad Men of Tombstone" 1949 (Proprietor); "Grand Canyon" 1949 (Windy); "The Nevadan" 1950 (Rusty); "Rock Island Trail" 1950 (Saloon Keeper); "Stage to Tucson" 1950 (Chantry); "Ticket to Tomahawk" 1950 (Conductor); "Santa Fe" 1951 (Dan Dugan); "The Storm Rider" 1957 (Collins). ¶TV: *Circus Boy*—"Meet Circus Boy" 9-23-56 (Swifty); *Jim Bowie*—"Up the Creek" 3-7-58 (Paw); *The Californians*—"The Fugitive" 4-28-59 (Martin Chandler).

Hoxie, Al (1901-4/6/82). Films: "Ruth of the Rockies" 1920-serial; "Days of '49" 1924-serial; "Tumbleweeds" 1925; "The Ace of Clubs" 1926 (Jack Horton); "Battling Kid" 1926; "Buried Gold" 1926; "The Fighting Ranger" 1926; "The Lost Trail" 1926; "Red Blood" 1926 (Buck Marsden); "Riding Romance" 1926; "Road Agent" 1926; "Son of a Gun" 1926; "Unseen Enemies" 1926; "Outlaw's Paradise" 1927; "The Range Raiders" 1927; "Rider of the Law" 1927; "Smoking Guns" 1927; "Battling Burke" 1928; "Blue Streak O'Neil" 1928 (O'Neil); "Deadshot Casey" 1928; "His Last Bullet" 1928; "Outlawed" 1928; "The Ranger's Oath" 1928; "Rip Roaring Logan" 1928; "The Rustler's End" 1928; "Throwing Lead" 1928; "Two Gun Murphy" 1928; "The White Outlaw" 1929 (Sheriff Ralston of Grant Pass); "The Fighting Cowboy" 1930; "Roaring Guns" 1930; "Carrying the Mail" 1934-short; "Desert Man" 1934; "Pals of the West" 1934-short.

Hoxie, Jack (Hart Hoxie) (1890-3/28/65). Films: "The Tragedy of Big Eagle Mine" 1912; "The Battle at Fort Laramie" 1913; "The Big Horn Massacre" 1913; "Brought to Bay" 1913; "The Holdup at Black Rock" 1913; "The Invaders" 1913; "The Conductor's Courtship" 1914; "The Identification" 1914; "Captain Courtesy" 1915 (Martinez); "Fatherhood" 1915; "The Operator of Black Rock" 1915; "The Three Godfathers" 1916 (Rusty Connors); "Jack and Jill" 1917 (Cactus Jim); "Man from Tiajuana" 1917; "Nan of Music Mountain" 1917 (San-

dusky); "The Secret of Lost Valley" 1917; "The Wolf and His Mate" 1917 (Donald Bayne/the Wolf); "Blue Blazes Rawden" 1918 (Joe La Barge); "Nobody's Wife" 1918 (Jack Darling); "Johnny, Get Your Gun" 1919 (Bill Burnham); "Lightning Bryce" 1919-serial; "Told in the Hills" 1919 (Henry Hardy); "The Man from Nowhere" 1920 (Clay Norton); "The Broken Spur" 1921 (Silent Joe Dayton/Jacques Durand); "Cupid's Brand" 1921 (Reese Wharton); "Cyclone Bliss" 1921 (Jack Bliss); "Dead or Alive" 1921 (Jack Stokes); "The Double O" 1921 (Happy Hanes); "Hills of Hate" 1921; "The Sheriff of Hope Eternal" 1921 (Drew Halliday); "Sparks of Flint" 1921; "Back Fire" 1922; "Barb Wire" 1922 (Jack Harding); "The Crow's Nest" 1922 (Esteban); "A Desert Bridegroom" 1922; "The Desert's Crucible" 1922 (Jack Hardy, Jr./Deerfoot); "The Marshal of Moneymint" 1922 (Jack Logan); "Riders of the Law" 1922; "Two-Fisted Jefferson" 1922; "The Desert Rider" 1923 (Jack Sutherland); "Don Quickshot of the Rio Grande" 1923 (Pep Pepper); "The Forbidden Trail" 1923 (Jack Merriwell); "Galloping Thru" 1923; "Men in the Raw" 1923 (Windy Watkins); "The Red Warning" 1923 (Philip Haver); "Where Is This West?" 1923 (John Harley); "Wolf Tracks" 1923 (John Hastings); "The Back Trail" 1924 (Jeff Prouty); "Daring Chances" 1924 (Jack Armstrong); "Fighting Fury" 1924 (Clay Hill); "The Galloping Ace" 1924 (Jim Jordon); "The Man from Wyoming" 1924 (Ned Bannister); "The Phantom Horseman" 1924 (Bob Winton); "Ridgeway of Montana" 1924 (Buck Ridgeway); "The Western Wallop" 1924 (Bart Tullison); "Bustin' Thru" 1925 (Jack Savage); "Don Dare Devil" 1925 (Jack Bannister); "Flying Hoofs" 1925 (Frank Moody); "Hidden Loot" 1925 (Cranne); "The Red Rider" 1925 (White Elk); "Ridin' Thunder" 1925 (Jack Douglas); "A Roaring Adventure" 1925 (Duffy Burns); "The Sign of the Cactus" 1925 (Jack Hayes); "Two-Fisted Jones" 1925 (Jack Wilbur); "The White Outlaw" 1925 (Jack Lupton); "The Border Sheriff" 1926 (Cultus Collins); "The Demon" 1926 (Dane Gordon); "The Fighting Peacemaker" 1926 (Peace River Parker); "The Last Frontier" 1926 (Buffalo Bill Cody); "Looking for Trouble" 1926 (Jack William Pepper); "Red Hot Leather" 1926 (Jack Lane); "A Six Shootin' Romance" 1926 (Lightning Jack); "Wild Horse Stampede" 1926 (Jack Tanner); "The Fighting Three" 1927 (Jack

Conway); "Grinning Guns" 1927 (Grinner Martin); "Men of Daring" 1927 (Jack Benton); "The Rambling Ranger" 1927 (Hank Kinney); "Rough and Ready" 1927 (Ned Raleigh); "The Western Whirlwind" 1927 (Jack Howard); "Gold" 1932 (Jack Tarrant); "Law and Lawless" 1932 (Montana) "Gun Law" 1933 (the Sonora Kid); "Outlaw Justice" 1933; "Trouble Busters" 1933 (Tex Blaine); "Via Pony Express" 1933 (Bud Carson).

Hoy, Robert (1927-). Films: "The Lawless Breed" 1952; "Four Guns to the Border" 1954 (Smitty); "Taza, Son of Cochise" 1954 (Lobo); "Raw Edge" 1956 (Five Crows); "Gun for a Coward" 1957 (Danny); "Tickle Me" 1965 (Henry, the Gardner); "Five Card Stud" 1968; "A Cry in the Wilderness" TVM-1974; "The Barbara Coast" TVM-1975 (Sergeant Hatch); "Bite the Bullet" 1975 (Lee Christie); "The Duchess and the Dirtwater Fox" 1976 (Bloodworth Gang Member); "Bronco Billy" 1980 (Cowboy at Bar); "The Legend of the Lone Ranger" 1981 (Perimutter); "The Gambler, Part II—The Adventure Continues" TVM-1983 (Juno); "Houston: The Legend of Texas" TVM-1986 (Colonel Burleson); "Desperado" TVM-1987; "Bonanza: The Next Generation" TVM-1988. ¶TV: *Zane Grey Theater*—"The Freighter" 1-17-58 (Red Murdock), "Desert Flight" 10-13-60 (Deputy); *Have Gun Will Travel*—"The Ballad of Oscar Wilde" 12-6-58; *Walt Disney Presents*—"Elfego Baca: Mustang Men, Mustang Maid" 11-20-59 (Sam Carter); *The Rifleman*—"Woman from Hog Ridge" 10-4-60 (Lester), "The Promoter" 12-6-60 (Dabbs); *The Tall Man*—"Maria's Little Lamb" 2-25-61 (Fidel); *Laramie*—"No Place to Run" 2-5-63; *Bonanza*—"The Actress" 2-24-63, "The Prisoners" 10-17-71 (Yancy); *Branded*—"Seward's Folly" 10-17-65 (Grimes); *Laredo*—"Anybody Here Seen Billy?" 10-21-65 (Donovan), "Scourge of San Rosa" 1-20-67 (Willie); *The Virginian*—"Legacy of Hate" 9-14-66 (Pete); *Shane*—"Killer in the Valley" 10-15-66 (Billy Cain); *The High Chaparral*—Regular 1967-71 (Joe); *The Guns of Will Sonnett*—"Message at Noon" 10-13-67, "Robber's Roost" 1-17-69; *Bearcats!*—"Blood Knot" 11-4-71 (Pete); *Kung Fu*—"King of the Mountain" 10-14-72 (Curry McCoy), "The Third Man" 4-26-73 (Norris); *The Cowboys*—"David Done It" 5-15-74 (Idaho Simms); *The Quest*—"The Buffalo Hunters" 9-29-76 (Dundee); *Father Murphy*—"Stopover in a One-

Way Horse Town" 10-26-82 (Turner); *Young Riders*—"Daisy" 2-2-91 (Mingus).

Hoyos, Sr., Rodolfo (1896-5/24/80). Films: "Raton Pass" 1951 (Ben); "The First Texan" 1956 (Cos); "The Three Outlaws" 1956; "Toughest Gun in Tombstone" 1958 (Col. Emilio); "California" 1963 (Padre Solder); "The Gun Hawk" 1963 (Miguel).

Hoyos, Jr., Rodolfo (1915-4/15/83). Films: "The Fighter" 1952 (Alvarado); "Gypsy Colt" 1954 (Rodolfo); "Jubilee Trail" 1954 (Spaniard); "The Americano" 1955 (Cristino); "Secret of Treasure Mountain" 1956 (Francisco Martinez); "Stagecoach to Fury" 1956 (Lorenzo Garcia); "Ten Days to Tulara" 1958 (Cesar); "Villa!" 1958 (Pancho Villa); "El Dorado" 1967; "Return of the Gunfighter" TVM-1967 (Luis Domingo). ¶TV: *The Cisco Kid*—"Thunderhead" 4-5-52, "Bell of Santa Margarite" 4-19-52; *The Adventures of Rin Tin Tin*—"The Bandit Kingdom" 4-8-55; *Jim Bowie*—"Gone to Texas" 5-24-57 (Capt. Sanchez), "Mexican Adventure" 12-20-57 (Gen. Santa Ana); *Tales of Wells Fargo*—"Laredo" 12-23-57 (Armand), "Vasquez" 5-16-60 (Chavez), "Moneyrun" 1-6-62 (Colonel Navarro); *Tombstone Territory*—"Skeleton Canyon Massacre" 4-2-58 (Don Jacinto Orosco); *The Rifleman*—"Home Ranch" 10-7-58 (Pablo), "The Prodigal" 4-26-60 (Luis); *Death Valley Days*—"Price of a Passport" 3-3-59 (Governor); *Zorro*—"Finders Keepers" 7-2-59 (Montez); *Zane Grey Theater*—"Interrogation" 10-1-59 (Gonzales), "The Last Bugle" 11-24-60 (Commandante); *The Texan*—"Border Incident" 12-7-59; *Maverick*—"The Marquesa" 1-3-60 (Miguel Ruiz); *Colt .45*—"The Cause" 2-28-60 (Martinez); *Johnny Ringo*—"Lobo Lawman" 6-23-60 (Garcia); *Bonanza*—"The Ape" 12-17-60 (Mexican), "The Campaneros" 4-19-64 (Luis), "Tommy" 12-18-66 (Police Chief), "The Conquistadors" 10-1-67 (Emiliano); *Wanted—Dead or Alive*—"Witch Woman" 12-28-60 (Don Emilio Flores); *Stagecoach West*—"The Butcher" 3-28-61 (Domingo); *Wyatt Earp*—"Requiem for Old Man Clanton" 5-30-61 (Don Pedro); *Laredo*—"The Heroes of San Gill" 12-23-65 (Maguilas); *Wild Wild West*—"The Night of the Fatal Trap" 12-24-65 (Police Chief); *Time Tunnel*—"The Alamo" 12-9-66 (Capt. Rodriguez); *Rango*—"In a Little Mexican Town" 4-14-67 (Gomez); *The Outcasts*—"Give Me Tomorrow" 4-21-69

(Emilio); *Gunsmoke*—"Chato" 9-14-70 (Juanito); *The High Chaparral*—"Fiesta" 11-20-70 (Bartender); *Kung Fu*—"The Brujo" 10-25-73 (Esteban).

Hoyt, Arthur (1874-1/4/53). Films: "The Man Who Took a Chance" 1917 (James); "Red Courage" 1921 (Nathan Hitch)l "Do It Now" 1924; "Sundown" 1924 (Henry Crawley); "When a Man's a Man" 1924 (Prof. Parkhill); "The Mysterious Rider" 1927 (King's Secretary); "A Texas Steer" 1927 (Knott Innit); "Dynamite Ranch" 1932 (Smithers); "Smoke Lightning" 1933 (Parson); "Cowboy and the Lady" 1938 (Valet).

Hoyt, Clegg (1911-10/6/67). Films: "The Restless Breed" 1957; "The True Story of Jesse James" 1957 (Tucker); "Gun Fever" 1958 (Kane); "Advance to the Rear" 1964 (Loafer). ¶TV: *Cheyenne*—"The Black Hawk War" 1-24-56 (Sgt. Beaugard); *Gunsmoke*—"Young Man with a Gun" 10-20-56 (Jack Rynning), "Indian White" 10-27-56 (Dutchholder), "Hung High" 11-14-64 (Stable); *Buckskin*—"Annie's Old Beau" 4-13-59 (Blackie); *Wanted—Dead or Alive*—"The Matchmaker" 9-19-59 (Ed); *Have Gun Will Travel*—"Tiger" 11-28-59, "The Long Weekend" 4-8-61; *The Law of the Plainsman*—"The Dude" 12-3-59 (Hungerford); *The Rifleman*—"The Horse Traders" 2-9-60 (Lester Chard); *Bonanza*—"The Hopefuls" 10-8-60, "Rich Man, Poor Man" 5-12-63, "A Passion for Justice" 9-29-63, "Hoss and the Leprechauns" 12-22-63 (Dorsel), "Old Sheba" 11-22-64 (Barney), "A Real Nice, Friendly Little Town" 11-27-66 (Sheriff); *The Outlaws*—"The Quiet Killer" 12-29-60 (Isham Dart); *The Tall Man*—5-26-62 (Bartender); *Empire*—"Seven Days on Rough Street" 2-26-63 (Beanie); *The Big Valley*—"The Murdered Party" 11-17-65.

Hoyt, John (1905-9/15/91). Films: "Inside Straight" 1951 (Flutey Johnson); "New Mexico" 1951 (Sgt. Harrison); "Mohawk" 1956 (Butler); "Sierra Stranger" 1957 (Sheriff); "Curse of the Undead" 1959 (Dr. Carter); "Duel at Diablo" 1966 (Chata); "Winchester '73" TVM-1967; "The Intruders" TVM-1970. ¶TV: *The Adventures of Rin Tin Tin*—"Meet Rin Tin Tin" 10-15-54 (Col. Barker); *The Lone Ranger*—"Two from Juan Ringo" 12-23-54; *Frontier*—"Assassin" 3-4-56 (Marshal); *Zane Grey Theater*—"You Only Run Once" 10-5-56 (Frank Hale), "The Hanging Tree" 2-22-57 (Frank Hale); *Jim Bowie*—"The Beggar of New Orleans" 1-11-57 (the Beggar);

Gunsmoke—"The Bureaucrat" 3-16-57 (Rex Propter), "No Chip" 12-3-60 (Jeff Mossman); *Lawman*—"The Intruders" 12-7-58 (Thomas Clemens), "The Judge" 5-15-60 (Judge Loren Grant); *Frontier Doctor*—"Trouble in Paradise Valley" 12-27-58; *Zorro*—"The Runaways" 1-8-59 (Yorba); *The Rifleman*—"Three-Legged Terror" 4-21-59 (Gus Fremont), "The Martinet" 11-8-60 (Capt. Josiah Perry); *Riverboat*—"About Roger Mowbray" 9-27-59 (Antoine Rigaud); *Laramie*—"General Delivery" 11-3-59 (Colonel Brandon), "The General Must Die" 11-17-59 (Col. Brandon), "The Last Battleground" 4-16-63 (Major John Ellis); *The Alaskans*—"The Challenge" 1-24-60 (Captain Ezra); *The Law of the Plainsman*—"The Imposter" 2-4-60 (Colonel Springer); *Have Gun Will Travel*—"The Ledge" 2-13-60 (Dr. Stark), "The Bird of Time" 10-20-62 (Stryker); *The Deputy*—"The X Game" 5-28-60 (Hap Allison); *Death Valley Days*—"Mission to the Mountains" 6-14-60; *Rawhide*—"Incident in the Garden of Eden" 6-17-60 (Harry Wilks); *The Outlaws*—"Starfall" 11-24-60 & 12-1-60 (Colonel Pringle); *Gunslinger*—"Golden Circle" 4-13-61 (Shubel Morgan); *Maverick*—"The Devil's Necklace" 4-16-61 & 4-23-61 (General Bassington), "The Art Lovers" 10-1-61 (George Cushman); *Bonanza*—"The Decision" 12-16-62 (Judge Grant), "Five Sundowns to Sunup" 12-5-65 (Major Sutcliffe); *The Virginian*—"The Golden Door" 3-13-63 (Judge Wickerson), "To Make This Place Remember" 9-25-63 (Judge Harper), "Ring of Silence" 10-27-65 (Marshal), "Ah Sing vs. Wyoming" 10-25-67 (Judge Manton); *The Dakotas*—"Sanctuary at Crystal Springs" 5-6-63 (the Governor); *Wagon Train*—"The Fenton Canaby Story" 12-30-63 (Clayton), "The Alice Whitetree Story" 11-1-64 (Reed); *Destry*—"Stormy Is a Lady" 3-6-64 (Archibald Tuttle); *The Loner*—"An Echo of Bugles" 9-18-65 (Colonel); *Laredo*—"Limit of the Law Larkin" 1-27-66 (Judge Josiah Larkin), "Coup de Grace" 10-7-66 (Juan Morales); *The Big Valley*—"Barbary Red" 2-16-66 (Captain Waterman), "Legend of a General" 9-19-66 & 9-26-66 (Don Alfredo); *Daniel Boone*—"The Fifth Man" 2-17-66 (Governor Patrick Henry), "First in War, First in Peace" 10-13-66 (Col. James Lamport); *Wild Wild West*—"The Night of the Puppeteer" 2-25-66 (Justice Vincent Chayne), "The Night of the Plague" 4-4-69 (Guild); *Pistols 'n' Petticoats*—10-29-66 (Simon); *The Road West*—"Power of Fear" 12-26-66 (Dr. Bayliss); *The Outcasts*—"Give Me Tomorrow" 4-21-69 (Justin Hawley).

Hoyt, Richard. Films: "Support Your Local Sheriff" 1969 (Gunfighter). ¶TV: *Daniel Boone*—"The Ballad of Sidewinder and Cherokee" 9-14-67 (Davy Rock).

Hsueh, Nancy (1941-82). Films: "Cheyenne Autumn" 1964 (Little Bird). ¶TV: *The Alaskans*—"The Silent Land" 5-15-60 (Anook); *Maverick*—"Poker Face" 1-7-62 (Rose Kwan); *Wild Wild West*—"The Night the Dragon Screamed" 1-14-66 (Tsu Hsi).

Hubbard, Elizabeth (1933-). TV: *The Virginian*—"You Can Lead a Horse to Water" 1-7-70 (Mary Charles Marshall).

Hubbard, John (1914-11/6/88). Films: "Cowboy and the Senorita" 1944 (Craig Allen); "The Cimarron Kid" 1951 (George Weber); "Horizons West" 1952 (Sam Hunter); "The Tall T" 1957 (Willard Mims); "Escort West" 1959 (Lt. Weeks); "Gunfight at Comanche Creek" 1964 (Marshal Shearer); "Duel at Diablo" 1966 (Major Novak); "Gunpoint" 1966 (Mayor Osborne). ¶TV: *Circus Boy*—"The Little Fugitive" 11-11-56 (Arthur); *Maverick*—"The War of the Silver Kings" 9-22-57 (Bixby), "Escape to Tampico" 10-26-58 (Paul Brooks), "Pappy" 9-13-59 (Bronze); *Colt .45*—"Long Odds" 4-11-58; *Wyatt Earp*—"The Frame-Up" 6-3-58 (Tim Maxwell); *Bronco*—"Four Guns and a Prayer" 11-4-58 (Aaron Lake); *Lawman*—"The Hoax" 12-20-59, "Get Out of Town" 5-20-62 (Sy); *Cheyenne*—"The Beholden" 2-27-61 (John Mercer); *Bonanza*—"The Roper" 4-5-64 (Doctor), "Invention of a Gunfighter" 9-20-64 (Doctor), "To Own the World" 4-18-65 (Carl Davis), "The Dilemma" 9-19-65 (Snell), "Justice Deferred" 12-17-67 (Eads); *Rawhide*—"A Man Called Mushy" 10-23-64 (Smitty); *The Virginian*—"Legend for a Lawman" 3-3-65 (Dr. Wagner); *Gunsmoke*—"Bad Lady from Brookline" 5-1-65 (LaFarge), "Kioga" 10-23-65 (Storekeeper); *Wild Wild West*—"The Night of the Samurai" 10-13-67 (Clive Finsbury).

Hubbard, Tom (1919-6/4/74). Films: "Swing, Cowboy, Swing" 1944; "Buffalo Bill in Tomahawk Territory" 1952 (Stokey); "Thunder Pass" 1954; "Hidden Guns" 1956 (Grandy); "Secret of Treasure Mountain" 1956 (Sam); "Hell Canyon Outlaws" 1957; "Raiders of Old California" 1957. ¶TV: *Wild Bill Hickok*—"The Doctor Story" 7-1-52 (Dr. Johnson), "Masquerade at Moccasin Flats" 9-2-52.

Huber, Harold (1910-9/29/59). Films: "The Gay Desperado" 1936 (Campo); "Outlaws of the Orient" 1937 (Ho-Fang); "Kit Carson" 1940 (Lopez); "Down Mexico Way" 1941 (Pancho Grande).

Hubley, Season (1951-). TV: *Kung Fu*—"Blood of the Dragon" 9-14-74 (Margit Kingsley McLean).

Hubley, Whip. Films: "Desperado: The Outlaw Wars" TVM-1989 (Cates).

Huckabee, Cooper. Films: "Little House on the Prairie: Look Back to Yesterday" TVM-1983 (Vance Reed). ¶TV: *The Quest*—"The Longest Drive" 12-1-76 & 12-8-76 (Jess).

Huddleston, David (1930-). Films: "Rio Lobo" 1970 (Dr. Jones); "Fools' Parade" 1971 (Homer Grindstaff); "Something Big" 1971 (Malachi Morton); "Bad Company" 1972 (Big Joe); "Billy Two Hats" 1973-Brit. (Copeland); "Blazing Saddles" 1974 (Olson Johnson); "The Gun and the Pulpit" TVM-1974 (Mr. Ross); "Breakheart Pass" 1976 (Dr. Molyneux); "The Oregon Trail" TVM-1976 (Painted Face Kelly); "Kate Bliss and the Ticker Tape Kid" TVM-1978 (Sheriff); "The Tracker" TVM-1988 (Marshal Crawford). ¶TV: *Gunsmoke*—"Lavery" 2-22-71 (Arno), "The Widow-Maker" 10-8-73 (Dad Goodpastor), "Disciple" 4-1-74 (Asa, the Bounty Hunter), "In Performance of Duty" 11-18-74 (Emmett); *Bonanza*—"Bushwacked" 10-3-71 (Doc Scully), "The Hidden Enemy" 11-28-72 (Myles Johnson); *Kung Fu*—"The Salamander" 12-6-73 (Nathaniel), "One Step to Darkness" 1-25-75 (Shelby Cross); *Dirty Sally*—4-19-74 (Slick); *Nakia*—"The Sand Trap" 10-5-74 (Horace); *How the West Was Won*—Episode Two 2-7-77 (Christy Judson).

Hudgins, Ken. TV: *Gunsmoke*—"Jenny" 10-13-62 (Pete); *Have Gun Will Travel*—"Two Plus One" 4-6-63 (Lou).

Hudis, Stephen. Films: "Sam Hill: Who Killed the Mysterious Mr. Foster?" TVM-1971 (Jethro); "The Cowboys" 1972 (Charlie Schwartz).

Hudkins, John "Bear". Films: "Westbound" 1959; "Tell Them Willie Boy Is Here" 1969 (3rd Man); "Monte Walsh" 1970 (Sonny Jacobs); "Oklahoma Crude" 1973 (Bloom). ¶TV: *Gunsmoke*—"A Noose for Dobie Price" 3-4-68 (Mick Smith).

Hudman, Wesley (1916-2/29/64). Films: "Satan's Cradle" 1949 (Peters); "The Girl from San Lorenzo" 1950 (Rusty); "I Killed Geronimo" 1950 (Red); "Indian Territory" 1950; "Fort Defiance" 1951 (1st Stranger); "Fort Dodge Stampede" 1951 (Butler); "Barbed Wire" 1952; "Black Hills Ambush" 1952 (Buck); "Leadville Gunslinger" 1952 (Driver); "Pack Train" 1953; "Battle of Rogue River" 1954 (Roy); "Masterson of Kansas" 1954 (Gage); "Blackjack Ketchum, Desperado" 1956 (Grat Barbey); "The Lonely Man" 1957. ¶TV: *The Gene Autry Show*—"The Star Toter" 8-20-50, "The Devil's Brand" 9-24-50, "Six Shooter Sweepstakes" 10-1-50, "The Poisoned Waterhole" 10-8-50, "Lost Chance" 10-15-55, "The Black Rider" 10-22-50, "Gun Powder Range" 10-29-50, "The Breakup" 11-5-50, "Twisted Trails" 11-12-50, "Fight at Peaceful Mesa" 11-19-50, "The Raiders" 4-14-51, "Battle Axe" 8-31-54; *The Cisco Kid*—"Face of Death" 2-16-52; *Wild Bill Hickok*—"Rustling Stallion" 3-4-52, "Masquerade at Moccasin Flats" 9-2-52; *Hopalong Cassidy*—"Death by Proxy" 6-14-52; *Death Valley Days*—"Death and Taxes" 1-17-55; *Fury*—"The Hobo" 1-7-56 (Watkins); *My Friend Flicka*—"Mister Goblin" 3-23-56; *Wyatt Earp*—"The Almost Dead Cowhand" 10-23-56.

Hudson, Gary. *see* Garko, John.

Hudson, John (1922-). Films: "The Cimarron Kid" 1951 (Dynamite Dick); "The Battle at Apache Pass" 1952 (Lt. George Bascom); "Silver Lode" 1954 (Michael "Mitch" Evans); "Fort Yuma" 1955 (Sgt. Jonas); "Many Rivers to Cross" 1955 (Hugh); "The Marauders" 1955 (Roy Rutherford); "Mohawk" 1956 (Capt. Langley); "Gunfight at the O.K. Corral" 1957 (Virgil Earp). ¶TV: *Gunsmoke*—"Once a Haggen" 2-1-64; *Cimarron Strip*—"The Battleground" 9-28-67.

Hudson, Larry (1920-1/8/61). Films: "Smoky Canyon" 1952 (Sheriff Bogart); "The Redhead from Wyoming" 1953 (Man); "Jubal" 1956 (Bayne). ¶TV: *Wild Bill Hickok*—"Homer Atchison" 9-11-51, "Medicine Show" 12-25-51; *The Roy Rogers Show*—"Dead Men's Hills" 3-15-52, "Ride in the Death Wagon" 4-6-52; *The Lone Ranger*—"The New Neighbor" 12-18-52; *The Gene Autry Show*—"Thunder Out West" 7-14-53, "Bandidos" 9-1-53; *Fury*—"The Hobo" 1-7-56 (Corky); *Sergeant Preston of the Yukon*—"Battle at Bradley's" 12-26-57 (Chet Bradley); *Wyatt Earp*—"Little Gray Home in the

West" 5-5-59 (Nosey); *Man from Blackhawk*—"Portrait of Cynthia" 1-29-60 (Aggie Temple); *Bat Masterson*—"Masterson's Arcadia Club" 4-28-60 (Clark Chisum).

Hudson, Rochelle (1914-1/17/72). Films: "Beyond the Rockies" 1932 (Betty Allen); "Scarlet River" 1933 (Herself); "The Country Beyond" 1936 (Jean Allison); "Konga, the Wild Stallion" 1940 (Judith Hadley). ¶TV: *Branded*—"The Mission" 3-14-65, 3-21-65 & 3-28-65 (Alice Whitcomb).

Hudson, Rock (1925-10/2/85). Films: "Winchester '73" 1950 (Young Bull); "Tomahawk" 1951 (Burt Hanna); "Bend of the River" 1952 (Trey Wilson); "Horizons West" 1952 (Neal Hammond); "The Lawless Breed" 1952 (John Wesley Hardin); "Back to God's Country" 1953 (Peter Keith); "Gun Fury" 1953 (Ben Warren); "Seminole" 1953 (Lt. Lance Caldwell); "Taza, Son of Cochise" 1954 (Taza); "Giant" 1956 (Bick Benedict); "The Last Sunset" 1961 (Dana Stribling); "The Undefeated" 1969 (Col. James Langdon); "Showdown" 1973 (Chuck Jarvis).

Hudson, William (William Woodson) (1925-4/5/74). Films: "More Dead Than Alive" 1968 (Warden). ¶TV: *Death Valley Days*—"Sixth Sense" 6-9-54, "The Man Who Was Never Licked" 6-2-57 (Elias Jackson Baldwin), "Wheel of Fortune" 1-20-58; *The Roy Rogers Show*—"Empty Saddles" 3-10-56; *The Restless Gun*—"The Painted Beauty" 1-5-59 (Stuart Woolsey); *Klondike*—"Sure Thing, Men" 11-28-60 (Professor); *Wanted—Dead or Alive*—"The Last Retreat" 1-11-61; *Have Gun Will Travel*—"One, Two, Three" 2-17-62, "Face of a Shadow" 4-20-63; *The Rifleman*—"Outlaw Shoes" 4-30-62 (Sheriff); *Empire*—"The Tiger Inside" 2-12-63 (Al Pope); *Redigo*—"Little Angel Blue Eyes" 10-29-63 (Grady Tipton); *F Troop*—"Our Hero—What's His Name" 1-4-66 (Secretary of War), "Spy, Counterspy, Counter Counterspy" 2-15-66 (Secretary of War).

Huerta, Cris. Films: "Massacre at Fort Grant" 1963-Span.; "Seven Hours of Gunfire" 1964-Span./Ital.; "Seven Guns for the MacGregors" 1965-Ital./Span. (Crawford); "Navajo Joe" 1966-Ital./Span. (El Gordo); "Relentless Four" 1966-Span./Ital.; "Bandidos" 1967-Ital.; "One Against One ... No Mercy" 1968-Span./Ital.; "A Sky Full of Stars for a Roof" 1968-Ital.; "Alive or Preferably Dead" 1969-Span./Ital.; "His Name Was Holy Ghost" 1970-Ital./Span.; "Rev-

erend Colt" 1970-Ital./Span.; "Sabata the Killer" 1970-Ital./Span.; "Sartana Kills Them All" 1970-Ital./Span.; "A Town Called Hell" 1971-Span./Brit. (Gonzales); "With Friends, Nothing Is Easy" 1971-Span./Ital.; "Let's Go and Kill Sartana" 1972-Ital./Span.; "My Colt, Not Yours" 1972-Span./Fr./Ital. (Jefferson); "My Horse, My Gun, Your Widow" 1972-Ital./Span. (Grasco); "Three Musketeers of the West" 1972-Ital.; "Man Called Invincible" 1973-Ital. (McPherson); "Dick Luft in Sacramento" 1974-Ital.; "None of the Three Were Called Trinity" 1974-Span. (Sheriff); "Three Supermen of the West" 1974-Ital./Span.; "Valley of the Dancing Widows" 1974-Span./Ger.

Huff, Jack. Films: "Zander the Great" 1925 (Zander).

Huff, Louise (1896-8/22/73). Films: "Jack and Jill" 1917 (Mary Dwyer).

Huffman, David (1944-2/27/85). Films: "Testimony of Two Men" TVM-1977 (Harald Ferrier). ¶TV: *Nakia*—"The Hostage" 10-12-74 (Earl).

Hughes, Barnard (1915-). Films: "Ransom for Alice!" TVM-1977 (Jess Halliday).

Hughes, Billy. Films: "Old Rex" 1961; "Geronimo" 1962 (Indian Scout). ¶TV: *Wagon Train*—"The Selena Hartnell Story" 10-18-61 (Matt), "The Eli Bancroft Story" 11-11-63, "The Melanie Craig Story" 2-17-64; *Gunsmoke*—"Milly" 11-25-61 (Joey Glover), "Us Haggens" 12-8-62 (Timmy); *The Rifleman*—"Long Gun from Tucson" 12-11-61 (Jeffrey Waller), "Day of Reckoning" 4-9-62 (Aaron), "The Sidewinder" 1-21-63 (Gridley Mau); *Laramie*—"The Fugitives" 2-12-63.

Hughes, Carol (1915-). Films: "Renfrew of the Royal Mounted" 1937 (Virginia Bronson); "Gold Mine in the Sky" 1938 (Cody Langam); "Man from Music Mountain" 1938 (Helen); "Under Western Stars" 1938 (Eleanor Fairbanks); "The Border Legion" 1940 (Alice Randall); "Under Fiesta Stars" 1941; "Home in Oklahoma" 1946 (Jan Holloway); "Stagecoach Kid" 1949 (Birdie).

Hughes, Charles A. "Tony" (1890-1968). Films: "The Frontiersman" 1938 (Mayor Judson Thorpe). ¶TV: *The Roy Rogers Show*—"Tossup" 12-2-56 (Ben Wheeling).

Hughes, Chris. Films: "Requiem for a Gunfighter" 1965 (Billy Parker).

Hughes, Gareth (1894-10/1/65).

Films: "The Sunset Trail" 1924 (Collie King).

Hughes, J. Anthony (1904-2/11/70). Films: "Call of the Yukon" 1938 (Bill); "The Cisco Kid and the Lady" 1939 (Drake); "Fighting Man of the Plains" 1949 (Kerrigan); "The Cariboo Trail" 1950 (Dr. Rhodes); "Tribute to a Badman" 1956 (1st Buyer); "Warlock" 1959 (Shaw). ¶TV: *Wild Bill Hickok*—"Monster in the Lake" 8-12-52, "Sagebrush Manhunt" 11-11-52; *Tales of the Texas Rangers*—"Panhandle" 9-22-57 (Pop Tatum); *The Restless Gun*—"Rink" 10-14-57; *Tales of Wells Fargo*—"Rifles for Red Hand" 5-15-61 (Pitt Simes).

Hughes, Kathleen (1928-). Films: "Dawn at Socorro" 1954 (Clare). ¶TV: *Hotel De Paree*—"The Only Wheel in Town" 11-20-59; *The Tall Man*—"A Scheme of Hearts" 4-22-61 (Nita Jardine).

Hughes, Kay. Films: "Ride, Ranger, Ride" 1936 (Dixie Summerall); "Robin Hood of El Dorado" 1936 (Louise); "The Three Mesquiteers" 1936 (Marian Brian); "Vigilantes Are Coming" 1936-serial (Doris Colton); "The Big Show" 1937 (Marion); "Ghost Town Gold" 1937 (Sabina); "Riders of the Badlands" 1941 (Cella); "Enemy of the Law" 1945 (Ruby Martin); "Fighting Bill Carson" 1945.

Hughes, Lloyd (1897-6/6/58). Films: "The Huntress" 1923 (Sam); "The Old Fool" 1923 (John Steele); "Heritage of the Desert" 1924; "The Whipping Boss" 1924 (Dick Forrest); "The Desert Flower" 1925 (Rance Conway).

Hughes, Mary Beth (1919-8/27/95). Films: "Lucky Cisco Kid" 1940 (Lola); "The Cowboy and the Blonde" 1941 (Crystal Wayne); "Ride on, Vaquero" 1941 (Sally); "The Ox-Bow Incident" 1943 (Rose Mapen); "Rockin' in the Rockies" 1945 (June McGuire); "Last of the Wild Horses" 1948 (Terry Williams); "The Return of Wildfire" 1948 (Judy Marlowe); "El Paso" 1949 (Stage Coach Nellie); "Grand Canyon" 1949 (Terry Lee); "Riders in the Sky" 1949 (Julie Stewart); "Rimfire" 1949 (Polly); "Square Dance Jubilee" 1949 (Barbara); "Passage West" 1951 (Nellie); "Dig That Uranium" 1956 (Jeanette); "Gun Battle at Monterey" 1957 (Cleo). ¶TV: *Colt .45*—"Rebellion" 12-20-57 (Clover Haig); *Buckskin*—"A Permanent Juliet" 10-23-58 (Diana); *Frontier Doctor*—"Great Stagecoach Robbery" 12-6-58; *The Adventures of Rin Tin Tin*—"Stagecoach to Phoenix" 1-23-59 (Lil Morris); *Wanted—Dead or Alive*—"Secret Ballot" 2-14-59 (Dolly King); *Rawhide*—"Incident in No Man's Land" 6-12-59 (Sarah), "Incident at Spider Rock" 1-18-63 (Lola).

Hughes, Morrie. Films: "The Mollycoddle" 1920 (Patrick O'Flannigan).

Hughes, Robin (1921-). Films: "Fancy Pants" 1950 (Cyril). ¶TV: *Wild Bill Hickok*—"Halley's Comet" 2-17-53; *Zorro*—"Shadow of Doubt" 1-9-58 (Rojas); *Sugarfoot*—"Mac-Brewster the Bold" 10-13-59 (Dougal MacBrewster); *The Loner*—"The Sheriff of Fetterman's Crossing" 11-13-65 (Carruthers).

Hughes, Roy (1894-1/12/28). Films: "The Bashful Whirlwind" 1925.

Hughes, Tony. *see* Hughes, J. Anthony.

Hughes, Whitey. Films: "Son of the Renegade" 1953 (the Long-Haired Kid); "Old Rex" 1961; "Night Rider" 1962-short. ¶TV: *Wild Wild West*—"The Night of the Burning Diamond" 4-8-66 (Rudd), "The Night of the Firebrand" 9-15-67, "The Night of the Iron Fist" 12-8-67 (George), "The Night of the Running Death" 12-15-67, "The Night of the Underground Terror" 1-19-68 (Private Steiner); *Gunsmoke*—"Horse Fever" 12-18-72 (Billy Banner).

Hugo, Laurence (1917-3/2/94). Films: "Three Hours to Kill" 1954 (Marty Lasswell).

Hugo, Mauritz (1909-6/16/74). Films: "Outlaws of Stampede Pass" 1943; "Marked Trails" 1944 (Slade); "The Utah Kid" 1944; "Blazing the Western Trail" 1945; "Both Barrels Blazing" 1945; "Rustler's Roundup" 1946 (Faro King); "Homesteaders of Paradise Valley" 1947; "Fury at Furnace Creek" 1948 (Defense Counsel); "Renegades of Sonora" 1948; "Death Valley Gunfighter" 1949 (Tony Richards); "Desperadoes of the West" 1950-serial (Hadley); "Frisco Tornado" 1950 (Brod); "Ticket to Tomahawk" 1950 (Dawson); "The Dakota Kid" 1951 (Squire Mason); "Gunplay" 1951 (Landry); "Pistol Harvest" 1951 (Norton); "Saddle Legion" 1951 (Kelso); "Blue Canadian Rockies" 1952 (Mitchell); "Captive of Billy the Kid" 1952 (Randy Brown); "Road Agent" 1952 (Milo Brand); "Trail Guide" 1952; "Yukon Gold" 1952; "Man with the Steel Whip" 1954-serial (Barnett); "The First Traveling Saleslady" 1956 (Buyer); "Gun Battle at Monterey" 1957 (Charley); "The Tall Stranger" 1957 (Purcell); "War Drums" 1957 (Clay Staub); "Seven Guns to Mesa" 1958 (Lt. Franklin); "The Gunfight at Dodge City" 1959 (Purley); "Thirteen Fighting Men" 1960 (Ives); "Stagecoach to Dancer's Rock" 1962 (Roy); "Alvarez Kelly" 1966 (Ely Harrison). ¶TV: *The Cisco Kid*—"Phony Heiress" 7-21-51, "Ghost Story" 9-1-51, "Water Well Oil" 10-13-51; *Sky King*—"Double Trouble" 2-24-52 (Redick); *Wild Bill Hickok*—"The Sheriff's Secret" 10-21-52, "Kangaroo Kapers" 3-10-53; *The Lone Ranger*—"The Woman from Omaha" 7-2-53, "A Message from Abe" 2-7-57; *Tales of the Texas Rangers*—"Blood Trail" 9-24-55 (Jim Ford); *Death Valley Days*—"Emperor Norton, 1st" 11-4-56 (Horace Cooper), "Half a Loaf" 5-5-59 (Murdock); *Wyatt Earp*—"The Man Who Rode with Custer" 1-8-57, "One-Man Army" 1-7-58 (Zinner); *Sergeant Preston of the Yukon*—"Old Ben's Gold" 10-3-57 (Duke Larson); *Tales of Wells Fargo*—"Stage West" 1-13-58 (Ivo); *The Restless Gun*—"Aunt Emma" 4-14-58 (Jed Baker); *Rough Riders*—"The Scavengers" 1-8-59 (Joe Naves); *Wanted—Dead or Alive*—"The Matchmaker" 9-19-59; *Bonanza*—"The Magnificent Adah" 11-14-59 (Hotel Manager); *Wagon Train*—"The Captain Dan Brady Story" 9-27-61 (Haines); *Destry*—"Big Deal at Little River" 3-20-64 (Hoyt); *The Virginian*—"A Man Called Kane" 5-6-64 (Ray Duval); *The Big Valley*—"A Passage of Saints" 3-10-69 (Mr. Clay).

Hugueny, Sharon. TV: *Colt .45*—"Attack" 5-24-60 (Running Deer); *Maverick*—"The Bold Fenian Men" 12-18-60 (Diedre Fogarty), "The Devil's Necklace" 4-16-61 & 4-23-61 (Tawney).

Hulett, Otto. Films: "Ambush at Tomahawk Gap" 1953 (Stranton); "Reprisal!" 1956 (Sheriff Jim Dixon).

Hulette, Gladys (1896-8/8/91). Films: "Hiawatha" 1909 (Minnehaha); "The Colonel's Daughter" 1915; "The Iron Horse" 1924 (Ruby); "The Ridin 'Kid from Powder River" 1924 (Miss).

Hull, Arthur Stuart (1878-2/28/51). Films: "Buck Benny Rides Again" 1940 (Sponsor).

Hull, Cynthia. Films: "Wild Women" TVM-1970 (Mit-O-Ne). ¶TV: *Here Comes the Brides*—Regular 1968-70 (Ann).

Hull, Henry (1890-3/8/77). Films: "Jesse James" 1939 (Major Rufus Cobb); "The Return of the Cisco Kid" 1939 (Colonel Jonathan Bixby); "Blazing Six Shooters" 1940 (Dan Kenyon); "The Return of Frank

James" 1940 (Maj. Rufus Cobb); "The Woman of the Town" 1943 (Inky Wilkinson); "Colorado Territory" 1949 (Winslow); "El Paso" 1949 (Judge Jeffers); "Rimfire" 1949 (Editor Greeley)."The Return of Jesse James" 1950 (Hank Younger); "The Treasure of Lost Canyon" 1952 (Lucius Cooke); "The Last Posse" 1953 (Stokely); "Thunder Over the Plains" 1953 (Lt. Col. Chandler); "Man with the Gun" 1955 (Marshal Sims); "Kentucky Rifle" 1956; "The Buckskin Lady" 1957 (Doc); "The Proud Rebel" 1958 (Judge Morley); "The Sheriff of Fractured Jaw" 1958-Brit. (Mayor Masters); "The Oregon Trail" 1959 (Seton). ¶TV: Trackdown— "Three Legged Fox" 12-5-58 (Moss); Wagon Train—"The Kitty Angel Story" 1-7-59 (Obediah Finch), "Trial for Murder" 4-27-60 & 5-4-60 (Mark Applewhite), "The Odyssey of Flint McCullough" 2-15-61 (Gideon); The Restless Gun—"The Last Grey Man" 2-23-59 (Jesse McKee), "Dead Man's Hand" 3-16-59 (Doc Kemmer), "One on the House" 4-20-59 (Matt Harper); U.S. Marshal—"The Tarnished Star" 11-21-59; Bonanza— "The Gunmen" 1-23-60 (B. Bannerman Brown), "The Mission" 9-17-60 (Charlie Trent); Zane Grey Theater— "A Small Town That Died" 3-10-60 (Hutch Wallace); Laramie—"Duel at Parkison Town" 12-13-60 (Ben Parkinson), "The Road to Helena" 5-21-63 (David Franklin); The Outlaws—"Culley" 2-16-61 (Jeb Woods); The Travels of Jaimie McPheeters— "The Day of the Misfits" 12-15-63 (Abel Menifee).

Hull, Josephine (1886-3/12/57). Films: "Ranchers and Rascals" 1925 (Helen Williams); "The Lady from Texas" 1951 (Miss Birdie).

Hull, Warren (1903-9/14/74). Films: "Crashing Thru" 1939 (Corn Kelly); "Ride, Tenderfoot, Ride" 1940 (Donald Gregory); "Wagons Westward" 1940 (Tom as a Boy); "Yukon Flight" 1940 (Bill Shipley).

Hulswit, Mart (1940-). Films: "Doc" 1971 (Rev. Foster).

Human, William. Films: "The Forfeit" 1919 (Bob Whitstone); "The Unbroken Promise" 1919 (Billy Corliss).

Humann, Helena Enize (1942-12/13/94). Films: "Lonesome Dove" TVM-1989 (Peaches).

Humbert, George (1881-5/8/63). Films: "The California Trail" 1933 (Mayor Don Alberto); "Yukon Flight" 1940 (Nick); "Boss of Bullion City" 1941 (Mario).

Hume, Douglas (1937-). Films: "The White Buffalo" 1977 (Aaron Pratt).

Humes, Buck. Films: "The Three Buckaroos" 1922 (Dartigan).

Humes, Fred (1901-). Films: "The Galloping Ace" 1924 (Fred); "Ride for Your Life" 1924 (the Cocopah Kid); "The Ridin' Kid from Powder River" 1924 (the Scorpion); "The Boundary Line" 1925; "The Gold Trap" 1925; "The Hurricane Kid" 1925 (Jed Hawks); "Let 'Er Buck" 1925 (Sheriff); "The Rider of the Pass" 1925; "The Rustlin' Kid" 1925; "The Saddle Hawk" 1925 (Draw Collins); "Taking Chances" 1925; "The Call of Hazard" 1926; "Coming Back" 1926; "The Frame-Up" 1926; "Grinning Fists" 1926; "The Man With a Scar" 1926; "Prowlers of the Night" 1926 (Jack Morton); "Quick on the Draw" 1926; "Rustler by Proxy" 1926; "The Stolen Ranch" 1926 (Breezy Hart); "Trapped" 1926; "Under Desert Skies" 1926; "The Yellow Back" 1926 (Andy Hubbard); "Blazing Days" 1927 (Smilin' Sam Perry); "Border Cavalier" 1927 (Larry Day); "The Broncho Buster" 1927 (Charlie Smith); "Hands Off" 1927 (Sandy Loom); "One Glorious Scrap" 1927 (Larry Day); "A One Man Game" 1927 (Fred Hunter); "Range Courage" 1927 (Lem Gallagher); "Arizona Cyclone" 1928 (Larry Day/Tom Day); "The Fearless Rider" 1928 (Larry Day); "Put 'Em Up" 1928 (Tom Evans); "Quick Triggers" 1928 (Larry Day); "Battling with Buffalo Bill" 1931-serial; "Clancy of the Mounted" 1933-serial; "The Cactus Kid" 1934 (Jimmie Kane); "Nevada Cyclone" 1934; "The Roaring West" 1935-serial; "Sunset Range" 1935.

Humes, Mary-Margaret. TV: Outlaws—"Primer" 1-10-87 (Laura); Legend—"Knee-High Noon" 5-23-95.

Hummell, Wilson. Films: "Youth Must Have Love" 1922 (Austin Hibbard); "Soft Boiled" 1923 (Reformer).

Humphrey, Harry (1873-4/1/47). Films: "Law and Order" 1940 (Cal Dixon); "Law and Order" 1940 (Dixon); "Along the Rio Grande" 1941 (Pop).

Humphrey, Orral (1880-8/12/29). Films: "Wild Life" 1918 (Red Kelley); "In Old California" 1929 (Ike Boone).

Humphrey, William (1875-10/4/42). Films: "The Gold Hunters" 1925 (John McAllister); "Aflame in the Sky" 1927 (Maj. Savage); "Cow-

boy Counsellor" 1933 (Judge); "The Plainsman" 1936 (Hugh McCulloch).

Hundar, Robert (Claudio Undari). Films: "Gunfight at High Noon" 1963-Span./Ital. (Chet); "Magnificent Three" 1963-Span./Ital.; "Shadow of Zorro" 1963-Span./Ital.; "Ride and Kill" 1964-Ital./Span.; "Seven Guns from Texas" 1964-Span./Ital. (Bob Carey); "Jesse James' Kid" 1966-Span./Ital. (Jesse James/Billy Smith); "Ramon the Mexican" 1966-Ital./Span. (Slim); "Relentless Four" 1966-Span./Ital. (Lobo); "Man and a Colt" 1967-Span./Ital. (Dallas); "Death Rides Alone" 1968-Ital./Span.; "Dollars for a Fast Gun" 1968-Ital./Span. (Lassiter); "Hole in the Forehead" 1968-Ital./Span. (Maguja) "Hour of Death" 1968-Span./Ital.; "Man Who Cried for Revenge" 1969-Ital./Span.; "Sabata" 1969-Ital. (Oswald); "Cut-Throats Nine" 1973-Span./Ital.; "Fighting Fists of Shanghai Joe" 1973-Ital.; "Too Much Gold for One Gringo" 1974-Ital./Span.; "Red Coat" 1975-Ital./Span.; "California" 1976-Ital./Span.

Hundley, Craig. TV: The Virginian—"A Little Learning…" 9-29-65 (Kenny Beesom), "Bitter Autumn" 11-1-67 (Johnny McLain); Gunsmoke—"Killer at Large" 2-5-66 (James Harris), "The Sisters" 12-29-69 (Toby); Lancer—"Jelly" 11-19-68, "Child of Rock and Sunlight" 4-1-69, "The Measure of a Man" 4-8-69 (Todd Wilson); Kung Fu—"The Last Raid" 4-26-75 (Jimmy).

Hungerford, Marguerite. Films: "Jesse James as the Outlaw" 1921; "Jesse James Under the Black Flag" 1921.

Hungerford, Ty. see Hardin, Ty.

Hunley, Gary. Films: "The Legend of Tom Dooley" 1959 (the Kid). ¶TV: Sky King—Regular 1951-53 (Mickey); Zane Grey Theater—"Village of Fear" 3-1-57; Sugarfoot— "Small Hostage" 5-26-59 (Chico); Wagon Train—"The Christine Elliot Story" 3-23-60.

Hunnicutt, Arthur (1911-9/27/79). Films: "Pardon My Gun" 1942 (Arkansas); "Riding Through Nevada" 1942; "Silver Queen" 1942 (Brett, the Editor); "The Fighting Buckaroo" 1943 (Arkansas); "Frontier Fury" 1943 (Arkansas Tuttle); "Hail to the Rangers" 1943 (Arkansas); "Law of the Northwest" 1943 (Arkansas); "Robin Hood of the Range" 1943 (Arkansas); "Riding West" 1944 (Prof. Arkansas Higgins); "Lust for Gold" 1949 (Ludi); "Broken Arrow" 1950 (Dutfield); "The Furies" 1950

(Cowhand); "Stars in My Crown" 1950 (Chloroform Wiggins); "Ticket to Tomahawk" 1950 (Sad Eyes); Two Flags West" 1950 (Sgt. Pickens); "Distant Drums" 1951 (Monk); "Passage West" 1951 (Pop Brennan); "Sugarfoot" 1951 (Fly-Up-the-Creek Jones); "The Big Sky" 1952 (Zeb); "The Lusty Men" 1952 (Booker Davis); "Devil's Canyon" 1953 (Frank Taggert); "The Last Command" 1955 (Davy Crockett); "The Tall T" 1957 (Ed Rintoon); "Born Reckless" 1959 (Cool Man); "Cat Ballou" 1965 (Butch Cassidy); "Apache Uprising" 1966 (Bill Gibson); "The Adventures of Bullwhip Griffin" 1967 (Referee); "El Dorado" 1967 (Bull Harris); "Shoot Out" 1971 (Homer Page); "The Trackers" TVM-1971 (Ben Vogel); "Bounty Man" TVM-1972 (Sheriff); "The Revengers" 1972-U.S./Mex. (Free State); "Mrs. Sundance" TVM-1974 (Walt Putney); "The Spikes Gang" 1974 (Kid White); "The Daughters of Joshua Cabe Return" TVM-1975 (Miner); "Winterhawk" 1975 (Trader Mc-Cluskey). ¶TV: Cheyenne—"Death Deals This Hand" 10-9-56 (Hoot Hollister); Sugarfoot—"Brannigan's Boots" 9-17-57 (Pop Purty); Walt Disney Presents—"Elfego Baca" Regular 1958-60 (Elias); Black Saddle—"Client: Tagger" 2-14-59 (Roy Tagger); Wanted—Dead or Alive—"Amos Carter" 5-9-59 (Ames Carter); Bonanza—"The Hanging Posse" 11-28-59 (Piute), "Any Friend of Walter's" 3-24-63 (Obie), "Walter and the Outlaws" 5-24-64 (Obie), "Dead Wrong" 12-7-69 (Salty Hubbard); Man from Blackhawk—"The Biggest Legend" 1-1-60 (Eb Clark); Overland Trail—"West of Boston" 2-21-60 (Reb Haslit); The Rifleman—"The Grasshopper" 3-1-60 (Nathaniel Cameron); The Westerner—"Treasure" 11-18-60; Laramie—"Cactus Lady" 2-21-61 (Ezra), "Wolf Cub" 11-21-61 (Earl Droody), "The Dispossessed" 2-19-63 (Sam Dillard); The Outlaws—"The Sisters" 2-15-62 (Luke); The Virginian—"Strangers at Sundown" 4-3-63 (Tom Croft); Great Adventure—"Kentucky's Bloody Ground"/"The Siege of Boonesborough" 4-3-64 & 4-10-64 Simon Kenton); Wagon Train—"The Jarbo Pierce Story" 5-2-65 (Deets); Laredo—"The Golden Trail" 11-4-65 (Old Timer); Daniel Boone—"Run a Crooked Mile" 10-20-66 (Gabe); Wild Wild West—"The Night of the Colonel's Ghost" 3-10-67 (Doc Gavin); The Outcasts—"And Then There Was One" 3-3-69; The Men from Shiloh—"Lady at the Bar" 11-4-70 (Drover); Gun-

smoke—"Cleavus" 2-15-71 (Uriah Spessard).

Hunnicutt, Gayle (1942-). Films: "Dream West" TVM-1986 (Maria Crittenden).

Hunt, Eleanor (-9/81). Films: "Blue Steel" 1934 (Betty Mason); "Northern Frontier" 1935 (Beth Braden).

Hunt, Governor George W.P. (1856-12/24/34). Films: "A Western Governor's Humanity" 1915.

Hunt, Helen. Films: "Wagon Wheels" 1934 (Mrs. Jed).

Hunt, Helen (1963-). Films: "Pioneer Woman" TVM-1973 (Sarah Sergeant); "Into the Badlands" TVM-1991 (Blossom).

Hunt, Irene. Films: "The Mountain Rat" 1914 (Harriet Copley); "On the Border" 1914; "The Ceremonial Turquoise" 1915; "The Outlaw's Revenge" 1916 (the Outlaw's Elder Sister); "His Enemy, the Law" 1918 (Sally Randolph/Sarah Catherwood); "The Big Punch" 1921 (Dance Hall Girl); "The Crimson Challenge" 1922 (Ellen Courtney); "The Gunfighter" 1923 (Alice Benchley).

Hunt, Jay (1857-11/18/32). Films: "Yankee Speed" 1924 (Don Verdugo); "The Gentle Cyclone" 1926 (Judge Summerfield); "A Man Four-Square" 1926 (Polly's Father); "My Own Pal" 1926 (Clown); "Three Bad Men" 1926 (Old Prospector); "The Overland Stage" 1927 (John Gregg); "In Old Cheyenne" 1931 (Frank Sutter); "The Cheyenne Cyclone" 1932.

Hunt, Jimmy. Films: "The Capture" 1950 (Mike); "Rock Island Trail" 1950 (Stinky); "Saddle Tramp" 1950; "The Lone Hand" 1953 (Joshua Hallock).

Hunt, Linda (1945-). Films: "Silverado" 1985 (Stella).

Hunt, Marsha (1917-). Films: "The Arizona Raiders" 1936 (Harriet Lindsay); "Desert Gold" 1936 (Jane Belding); "Born to the West" 1937 (Judy Worstall); "Thunder Trail" 1937 (Amy Morgan); "The Plunderers" 1960 (Kate Miller). ¶TV: Zane Grey Theater—"A Gun Is for Killing" 10-18-57 (Claire Andrews), "Let the Man Die" 12-18-58 (Julie Reynolds), "Checkmate" 4-30-59 (Dr. Sarah Martin), "The Man from Yesterday" 12-22-60 (Catha Duncan); Laramie—"Circle of Fire" 9-22-59 (Martha Chambers); Gunsmoke—"The Glory and the Mud" 1-4-64 (Sarah Carr).

Hunt, Will. TV: Paradise—Regular 1989-91 (Carl).

Hunt, William. TV: Sergeant Preston of the Yukon—"The Black Ace" 1-3-57 (Tom Tanner); Zorro—"The Fortune Teller" 6-18-59 (Prosecuting Attorney); Wagon Train—"The Jenny Tannen Story" 6-24-59 (Rollie Malvin); Have Gun Will Travel—"The Trial" 6-11-60; Gunsmoke—"Jeb" 5-25-63 (Codge).

Hunter, Buddy. Films: "The Mounted Stranger" 1930 (Pete as a Boy); "Spurs" 1930 (Buddy Hazlet); "The Sunset Trail" 1932 (Buddy).

Hunter, Henry (1906-). Films: "Forbidden Valley" 1938 (Bagley). ¶TV: Tales of Wells Fargo—"Doc Holliday" 5-4-59 (Conway); Maverick—"Guatemala City" 1-31-60 (U.S. Consul); Wagon Train—"The Shad Bennington Story" 6-22-60 (Dr. Stevens); The Tall Man—"Big Sam's Boy" 3-4-61 (Doc); Wide Country—"Speckle Bird" 1-31-63 (Doctor); The Virginian—"The Golden Door" 3-13-63, "Rope of Lies" 3-25-64 (Makely), "The Brothers" 9-15-65 (Defense Attorney); Wild Wild West—"The Night of the Sudden Death" 10-8-65 (Boone); Laredo—"The Bitter Yen of General Ti" 2-3-67; The Guns of Will Sonnett—"One Angry Juror" 3-7-69 (Judge).

Hunter, Ian (1900-9/24/75). Films: "Billy the Kid" 1941 (Eric Keating).

Hunter, Jeffrey (1926-5/27/69). Films: "Three Young Texans" 1954 (Johnny Colt); "Seven Angry Men" 1955 (Owen); "White Feather" 1955 (Little Dog); "The Great Locomotive Chase" 1956 (William A. Fuller); "The Proud Ones" 1956 (Thad); "The Searchers" 1956 (Martin Pawley); "Gun for a Coward" 1957 (Bless Keough); "The True Story of Jesse James" 1957 (Frank James); "Sergeant Rutledge" 1960 (Lt. Thomas Cantrell); "The Man from Galveston" 1964 (Timothy Higgins); "Murieta" 1965-Span./U.S. (Joaquin Murieta); "The Christmas Kid" 1966-Span./Ital. (Joe Novak); "Custer of the West" 1967-U.S./Span. (Lt. Benteen); "Find a Place to Die" 1968-Ital. (Joe Collins). ¶TV: Our American Heritage—"Destiny West" 1-24-60 (John Charles Fremont); Death Valley Days—"Suzie" 10-24-62 (Capt. Walter Reed); Temple Houston—Regular 1963-64 (Temple Houston); The Legend of Jesse James—"A Field of Wild Flowers" 4-25-66 (Jeremy Thrallkill); Daniel Boone—"Requiem for Craw Green" 12-1-66 (Roark Logan); The Monroes—"Wild Bull" 2-15-67 (Ed Stanley).

Hunter, Kim (1922-). Films:

"Money, Women and Guns" 1958 (Mary Kingman). ¶TV: *Rawhide*— "Incident of the Misplaced Indians" 5-1-59 (Amelia Spaulding); *Branded*— "Romany Roundup 12-5-65 & 12-12-65 (Lisa); *Bonanza*—"The Price of Salt" 2-4-68 (Ada Halle); *Gunsmoke*—"The Legend" 10-18-71 (Bea Colter); *Hec Ramsey*—"The Detroit Connection" 12-30-73 (Annie Kirby); *The Oregon Trail*—"The Waterhole" 9-28-77 (Liz Webster).

Hunter, Richard (1875-12/22/62). Films: "Rainbow Trail" 1932 (Horseman); "Robbers' Roost" 1933 (Horseman); "Lawless Valley" 1938 (Henchman); "The Marshal of Mesa City" 1939; "Racketeers of the Range" 1939; "Stage to Chino" 1940; "Triple Justice" 1940.

Hunter, Tab (1931-). Films: "Gun Belt" 1953 (Chip Ringo); "Track of the Cat" 1954 (Harold "Hal" Bridges); "The Burning Hills" 1956 (Trace Jordan); "Gunman's Walk" 1958 (Ed Hackett); "They Came to Cordura" 1959 (Lt. William Fowler); "Hostile Guns" 1967 (Mike Reno); "Shotgun" 1969-Ital. (Sheriff Durango); "The Life and Times of Judge Roy Bean" 1972 (Sam Dodd); "Lust in the Dust" 1985 (Abel Wood). ¶TV: *The Virginian*—"The Gift" 3-18-70 (Carl Banner); *World of Disney*—"Hacksaw" 9-26-71 & 10-3-71 (Tim Andrews).

Hunter, Virginia. Films: "The Harvey Girls" 1946 (Jane); "Last Days of Boot Hill" 1947 (Paula Thorpe); "Riders of the Lone Star" 1947; "Smoky River Serenade" 1947; "The Stranger from Ponca City" 1947; "Phantom Valley" 1948 (Janice Littlejohn).

Hunter, William. Films: "Mystery Man" 1944 (Joe); "Texas Masquerade" 1944 (Sykes); "The Moonlighter" 1953. ¶TV: *The Alaskans*—"The Devil Made Five" 6-19-60 (Sheriff).

Huntington, Joan (1938-). Films: "Young Fury" 1965 (Kathy); "The Honkers" 1972 (Rita Ferguson). ¶TV: *Bonanza*—"The Flapjack Contest" 1-3-65 (Lily); *Wild Wild West*—"The Night of the Red-Eyed Madmen" 11-26-65 (Sgt. Musk), "The Night of the Bottomless Pit" 11-4-66 (Camille Maurais), "The Night of the Circus of Death" 11-3-67 (Mary Lennox); *Laredo*—"The Last of the Caesars—Absolutely" 12-2-66 (Celeste); *Iron Horse*—"Decision at Sundown" 2-27-67 (Doris).

Huntley, Fred (1862-11/1/31). Films: "The Convert of San Clemente" 1911; "On Seperate Paths"

1911; "The Regeneration of the Apache Kid" 1911; "The Rival Stage Lines" 1911; "Told in the Sierras" 1911; "The White Medicine Man" 1911; "A Crucial Test" 1912; "The End of the Romance" 1912; "Opitsah" 1912; "The Peacemaker" 1912; "Tenderfoot Bob's Resignation" 1912; "Chip of the Flying U" 1914; "Fighting Blood" 1916 (Henry Colby); "The Only Road" 1918 (Ramon Lupo); "Rimrock Jones" 1918 (Leon Lockhart); "The Heart of Wetona" 1919 (Chief Quannah); "Johnny, Get Your Gun" 1919 (Jevne); "The Round Up" 1920 (Sagebrush Charlie); "The Crimson Challenge" 1922 (Confora); "North of the Rio Grande" 1922 (Briston); "While Satan Sleeps" 1922 (Absalom Randall); "The Call of the Canyon" 1923 (Tom Hutter); "To the Last Man" 1923 (Lee Jorth); "Thundering Hoofs" 1924 (John Marshall).

Huntley, George P. Films: "They Died with Their Boots On" 1941 (Lt. Butler); "The Great Man's Lady" 1942 (Quentin).

Huppert, Isabelle (1955-). Films: "Heaven's Gate" 1980 (Ella Watson).

Hurley, Julia (1847-6/4/27). Films: "Gold and the Woman" 1916 (Duskara's Squaw).

Hurst, Brandon (1866-7/15/47). Films: "The Enchanted Hill" 1926 (Jasper Coak); "San Antonio" 1945 (Gambler).

Hurst, James. TV: *Cheyenne*— "The Long Rope" 10-3-60 (Ed Warren); *The Rifleman*—"Woman from Hog Ridge" 10-4-60 (Sylvester); *The Virginian*—"Morgan Starr" 2-9-66 (Wilder); *Branded*—"Call to Glory" 2-27-66, 3-6-66 & 3-13-66 (Lieutenant Cable).

Hurst, Paul (1888-2/27/53). Films: "Driver of the Deadwood Coast" 1912; "Red Wing and the Paleface" 1912; "The Big Horn Massacre" 1913; "The Invaders" 1913; "The Last Blockhouse" 1913; "On the Brink of Ruin" 1913; "The Skeleton in the Closet" 1913; "The Death Sign at High Noon" 1914; "The Man in Irons" 1915; "The Pitfall" 1915; "Lass of the Lumberland" 1916-serial; "Medicine Bend" 1916 (Murray Sinclair); "Whispering Smith" 1916 (Murray Sinclair); "The Railroad Raiders" 1917; "Rimrock Jones" 1918 (Ike Bray); "Smashing Through" 1918 (Stevens); "Lightning Bryce" 1919-serial; "The High Hand" 1926 (Chris Doble); "The Outlaw Express" 1926 (Secretary); "The Devil's Saddle" 1927 (Swig Moran); "The Man from Hardpan" 1927 (Larry Lackey); "The

Overland Stage" 1927 (Hell A-Poppin' Carter); "Red Raiders" 1927 (Sergeant Murphy); "The California Mail" 1929 (Rowdy Ryand); "The Lawless Legion" 1929 (Ramirez); "The Rainbow" 1929 (Pat); "Tide of Empire" 1929 (Poppy); "Lucky Larkin" 1930 (Pete Brierson); "Mountain Justice" 1930 (Lem Harland); "The Big Stampede" 1932 (Arizona); "My Pal, the King" 1932 (Red); "Wilderness Mail" 1935 (Jules); "The Gay Desperado" 1936 (American Detective); "North of Nome" 1936 (Carlson); "Robin Hood of El Dorado" 1936 (Wilson); "Bad Lands" 1939 (Curley Tom); "The Westerner" 1940 (Chickenfoot); "The Parson of Panamint" 1941 (Jake Waldren); "Dudes Are Pretty People" 1942 (Two-Gun); "Sundown Jim" 1942 (Broderick); "Calaboose" 1943; "The Ox-Bow Incident" 1943 (Monty Smith); "Barbary Coast Gent" 1944 (Jake Compton); "Girl Rush" 1944 (Muley); "Dakota" 1945 (Capt. Spotts); "In Old Sacramento" 1946 (Stage Driver); "Plainsman and the Lady" 1946 (Al); "Angel and the Badman" 1947 (Carson); "Under Colorado Skies" 1947 (Lucky John Hawkins); "The Arizona Ranger" 1948 (Ben Riddle); "California Firebrand" 1948 (Chuck Waggoner); "Gun Smugglers" 1948 (Hasty); "Madonna of the Desert" 1948 (Pete Connors); "Son of God's Country" 1948 (Eli Walker); "Yellow Sky" 1948 (Drunk); "Law of the Golden West" 1949 (Otis Ellis); "Outcasts of the Trail" 1949 (Doc Meadowlark); "Pioneer Marshal" 1949 (Huck Homer); "Prince of the Plains" 1949 (Sheriff Hank Hartley); "Ranger of Cherokee Strip" 1949 (Jug Mason); "San Antone Ambush" 1949 (Happy Daniels); "South of Rio" 1949 (Andrew Jackson Weems); "The Missourians" 1950 (John X. Finn); "The Old Frontier" 1950 (Skipper Horton); "The Vanishing Westerner" 1950 (Waldorf Worthington); "Toughest Man in Arizona" 1952 (Dalton).

Hurt, John (1940-). Films: "Heaven's Gate" 1980 (Billy Irvine).

Hush, Lisabeth (1937-). TV: *Two Faces West*—"Double Action" 5-8-61 (Florie); *Frontier Circus*—"The Good Fight" 4-19-62 (Hannah Cabot); *Bonanza*—"The Decision" 12-16-62 (Karen Jones); *The Virginian*—"The Payment" 12-16-64 (Rita Collins), "Star Crossed" 10-4-67 (Judith Hiller); *Rawhide*—"A Time for Waiting" 1-22-65 (Eleanor Morton); *Gunsmoke*—"The Bounty Hunter" 10-30-65 (Mal Jensen); *Laredo*—"A Prince of a Ranger" 12-9-66

(Helena); *Iron Horse*—"Welcome for the General" 1-2-67 (Amelia Henderson).

Hussenot, Olivier (1913-8/25/78). Films: "Gunmen of the Rio Grande" 1964-Fr./Ital./Span. (Judge).

Hussey, Olivia (1951-). TV: *Lonesome Dove*—"The Cattle Drive" 12-4-94 (Olivia), "Law and Order" 2-19-95 (Olivia).

Hussey, Ruth (1917-). Films: "Northwest Passage" 1940 (Elizabeth Browne); "Pierre of the Plains" 1942 (Daisy Denton); "Woman of the North Country" 1952 (Christine Powell).

Hussey, Sue. Films: "The Thundering Trail" 1951 (Sue); "The Vanishing Outpost" 1951 (Sue).

Huston, Anjelica (1953-). Films: "Lonesome Dove" TVM-1989 (Clara); "Buffalo Girls" TVM-1995 (Calamity Jane).

Huston, Carol. TV: *Paradise*—"The Women" 1-25-91 (Martha); *Adventures of Brisco County, Jr.*—"Brisco for the Defense" 10-22-93 (Cassie Crowe).

Huston, John (1906-8/28/87). Films: "The Treasure of the Sierra Madre" 1948 (White Suit); "Deserter" 1970-U.S./Ital./Yugo. (Gen. Miles); "Man in the Wilderness" 1971-U.S./Span. (Capt. Filmore Henry); "The Life and Times of Judge Roy Bean" 1972 (Grizzly Adams).

Huston, Patricia (1930-9/25/95). TV: *Gunsmoke*—"Sky" 2-14-59 (Woman); *Tales of Wells Fargo*—"The Outlaw's Wife" 3-28-60 (Marge); *Cheyenne*—"Savage Breed" 12-19-60 (Nora Kenton); *Death Valley Days*—"Bloodline" 1-9-63 (Anne Knight), "Kingdom for a Horse" 12-1-63 (Fern Mitchell), "The Man Who Wouldn't Die" 4-29-67 (Belle Monteverdi), "The Saga of Sadie Orchard" 1-13-68; *The Dakotas*—"Thunder in Pleasant Valley" 2-4-63 (Kate McNeil); *Rawhide*—"Incident at Zebulon" 3-5-64 (Luanna Day); *Daniel Boone*—"The Prophet" 1-21-65 (Amanda Dobson); *Wild Wild West*—"The Night of the Ready-Made Corpse" 11-25-66 (Leda Pellargo).

Huston, Virginia (1920-83). Films: "The Doolins of Oklahoma" 1949 (Elaine Burton); "Night Stage to Galveston" 1952 (Ann Bellamy).

Huston, Walter (1884-4/7/50). Films: "The Virginian" 1929 (Trampas); "The Bad Man" 1930 (Pancho Lopez); "Law and Order" 1932 (Frame Johnson); "The Outlaw" 1943 (Doc Holliday); "Duel in the

Sun" 1946 (the Sin Killer); "The Treasure of the Sierra Madre" 1948 (Howard); "The Furies" 1950 (T.C. Jeffords).

Hutchins, Will (1932-). Films: "The Shooting" 1966 (Coley); "The Quest" TVM-1976 (Earl). ¶TV: *Sugarfoot*—Regular 1957-60 (Tom "Sugarfoot" Brewster), "The Canary Kid" 11-11-59 (the Canary Kid), "The Return of the Canary Kid" 2-3-59 (the Canary Kid), "The Trial of the Canary Kid" 9-15-59 (the Canary Kid), "The Canary Kid, Inc." 11-10-59 (the Canary Kid); *Maverick*—"Hadley's Hunters" 9-25-60 (Sugarfoot), "Bolt from the Blue" 11-27-60 (Lawyer); *Cheyenne*—"Duel at Judas Basin" 1-30-61 (Tom "Sugarfoot" Brewster); *Bronco*—"Yankee Tornado" 3-13-61 (Tom "Sugarfoot" Brewster); *Gunsmoke*—"Blind Man's Bluff" 2-23-63 (Billy Poe).

Hutchinson, Charles (1879-5/30/49). Films: "The Little Angel of Canyon Creek" 1914 (Bishop Mills); "Fangs of the Wolf" 1924; "The Lone Ranger Rides Again" 1939-serial (Topwnsman #4); "Adventures of Red Ryder" 1940-Serial (Rancher Brown).

Hutchinson, Josephine (1904-). Films: "Many Rivers to Cross" 1955 (Mrs. Cherne); "Gun for a Coward" 1957 (Mrs. Keough); "Walk Like a Dragon" 1960 (Ma Bartlett); "Nevada Smith" 1966 (Mrs. Elvira McCanles). ¶TV: *Gunsmoke*—"Johnny Red" 10-3-59 (Mrs. Crale), "Ladies from St. Louis" 3-25-67 (Sister Ruth); *Wagon Train*—"The Tom Tuckett Story" 3-2-60 (Miss Stevenson); *The Rifleman*—"The Prodigal" 4-26-60 (Christine Havicourt); *The Deputy*—"Mother and Son" 10-29-60 (Mrs. Stanhope); *Tales of Wells Fargo*—"Lady Trouble" 4-24-61 (Agatha Webster); *Rawhide*—"Grandma's Money" 2-23-62 (Abigail Briggs); *The Rounders*—12-20-66 (Martha Frobish); *Bonanza*—"The Love Child" 11-8-70 (Martha).

Hutchinson, Ken (1948-). Films: "The Wrath of God" 1972 (Emmet Keogh).

Hutchinson, William (1869-9/7/18). Films: "The Last of Her Tribe" 1912; "The Trade Gun Bullet" 1912; "The Redemption of Railroad Jack" 1913; "The Regeneration of Jim Halsey" 1916.

Hutchison, Charles. *see* Hutchinson, Charles.

Hutton, Betty (1921-). Films: "Annie Get Your Gun" 1950 (Annie Oakley). ¶TV: *Satins and Spurs* 9-12-

54 (Cindy); *Gunsmoke*—"Bad Lady from Brookline" 5-1-65 (Molly McConnell).

Hutton, Brian (1935-). Films: "Gunfight at the O.K. Corral" 1957 (Rick); "Last Train from Gun Hill" 1959 (Lee). ¶TV: *Gunsmoke*—"Custer" 9-22-56 (Joe Trimble); *Sugarfoot*—"Yampa Crossing" 12-9-58 (the Kid); *Black Saddle*—"The Saddle" 10-9-59 (David Trench McKinney); *The Rifleman*—"Obituary" 10-20-59 (Billy Benson), "Long Gun from Tucson" 12-11-61; *The Law of the Plainsman*—"Passenger to Mescalero" 10-29-59 (Johnny Q); *Have Gun Will Travel*—"The Twins" 5-21-60 (Adam/Sam Mirakian); *Rawhide*—"Incident on the Road Back" 2-24-61; *Frontier Circus*—"Karina" 11-9-61 (Greg Andrews); *Laramie*—"Beyond Justice" 11-27-62.

Hutton, Jim (1934-6/2/79). Films: "The Hallelujah Trail" 1965 (Capt. Paul Slater); "Major Dundee" 1965 (Lt. Graham).

Hutton, Lauren (1943-). Films: "Zorro, the Gay Blade" 1981 (Charlotte).

Hutton, Leona (1892-4/1/49). Films: "The Passing of Two-Gun Hicks" 1914; "The Gun Fighter" 1915.

Hutton, Lucille. Films: "The Last Outlaw" 1919; "The Buster" 1923 (Yvonne); "The Sunset Trail" 1924 (Louise Lacharme).

Hutton, Robert (1920-8/7/94). Films: "The Younger Brothers" 1949 (Johnny Younger); "New Mexico" 1951 (Lt. Vermont); "Slaughter Trail" 1951 (Lt. Morgan); "Showdown at Boot Hill" 1958 (Sloane). ¶TV: *Wild Bill Hickok*—"The Outlaw's Portrait" 11-18-52; *Death Valley Days*—"Sego Lillies" 1-14-53 (Davis); *Wyatt Earp*—"The Toughest Judge in Arizona" 5-24-60 (Charlie Parks); *The Rebel*—"The Legacy" 11-13-60 (Prosecutor Ricker).

Hyams, John (1869-12/9/40). Films: "The Plainsman" 1936 (Schuyler Colfax).

Hyams, Leila (1905-12/4/77). Films: "The Brute" 1927 (Jennifer Duan); "The Branded Sombrero" 1928 (Connie Marsh); "Land of the Silver Fox" 1928 (Marie du Fronque); "Way Out West" 1930 (Molly); "Ruggles of Red Gap" 1935 (Nell Kenner); "Yellow Dust" 1936 (Nellis Brian).

Hyatt, Robert "Bobby". Films: "Stagecoach to Denver" 1946 (Dickie Ray); "Toughest Man in Arizona" 1952 (Davey Billings); "Gypsy Colt" 1954 (Phil Gerald). ¶TV: *The Roy*

Rogers Show—"Badman's Brother" 2-10-52 (Larry Trumbull), "Phantom Rustlers" 4-25-54 (Donnie MacGuiness); *Wild Bill Hickok*—"Rustling Stallion" 3-4-52, "Prairie Flats Land Swindle" 5-6-52, "Monster in the Lake" 8-12-52, "Buckshot Comes Home" 11-25-52; *The Californians*—"The Barber's Boy" 11-19-57 (Fritz); *Wagon Train*—"The Janet Hale Story" 5-31-61 (Jeff Hale).

Hyde, Jacqueline (1930-2/23/92). Films: "The Wild Wild West Revisited" TVM-1979 (Queen Victoria). ¶TV: *Branded*—"Call to Glory" 2-27-66, 3-6-66 & 3-13-66 (Libby Custer); *Wild Wild West*—"The Night of the Gruesome Games" 10-25-68 (La Marchessa Bellini).

Hyde-White, Alex. Films: "Wyatt Earp: Return to Tombstone" TVM-1994 (John Clum). ¶TV: *Legend*—"Custer's Next to Last Stand" 5-9-95 (General Custer).

Hyde-White, Wilfrid (1903-5/6/91). *Daniel Boone*—"They Who Will They Hang from the Yardarm if Willy Gets Away?" 2-8-68 (George Perkins); *Father Murphy*—"Matthew and Elizabeth" 3-28-82 (Willoughby).

Hyer, Martha (1924-). Films: "Thunder Mountain" 1947 (Ellen Jorth); "Gun Smugglers" 1948 (Judy); "Roughshod" 1949 (Marcia); "Rustlers" 1949 (Ruth); "Frisco Tornado" 1950 (Jean); "The Kangaroo Kid" 1950 (Mary Corbett); "Outcast of Black Mesa" 1950 (Ruth Dorn); "Salt Lake Raiders" 1950 (Helen Thornton); "Wild Stallion" 1952 (Caroline); "Yukon Gold" 1952; "Battle of Rogue River" 1954 (Brett McClain); "Kiss of Fire" 1955 (Felicia); "Wyoming Renegades" 1955 (Nancy Warren); "Red Sundown" 1956 (Caroline Murphy); "Showdown at Abilene" 1956 (Peggy Bigelow); "Once Upon a Horse" 1958 (Miss Amity Babb); "Blood on the Arrow" 1964 (Nancy Mailer); "The Sons of Katie Elder" 1965 (Mary Gordon); "The Night of the Grizzly" 1966 (Angela Cole). ¶TV: *The Lone Ranger*—"The Man Who Came Back" 1-5-50; *Wild Bill Hickok*—"The Professor's Daughter" 1-29-52; *Rawhide*—"Incident West of Lano" 2-27-59 (Hannah Haley); *The Deputy*—"Hang the Law" 1-9-60 (Joy Cartwright); *Zane Grey Theater*—"Morning Incident" 12-29-60 (Laurie Pritchard); *Branded*—"$10,000 for Durango" 11-28-65 (Callie Clay); *The Men from Shiloh*—"The West vs. Colonel MacKenzie" 9-16-70 (Amalia).

Hyke, Ray. Films: "Fort Apache" 1948 (Capt. Gates); "The Man from Colorado" 1948 (Veteran); "Red River" 1948 (Walt Jergens); "She Wore a Yellow Ribbon" 1949 (McCarthy); "The Cariboo Trail" 1950 (Jones); "Silver City" 1951 (Dacy). ¶TV: *The Cisco Kid*—"Medicine Man Story" 8-25-51, "Black Lightning" 10-6-51.

Hyland, Diana (1936-3/27/77). Films: "Scalplock" TVM-1966 (Martha Grenier); "Smoky" 1966 (Julie). ¶TV: *Stoney Burke*—"To Catch the Kaiser" 3-11-63 (Eileen Fowler); *Wagon Train*—"The Kitty Pryer Story" 11-18-63 (Kitty Pryer); *A Man Called Shenandoah*—"The Unfamiliar Tune" 4-11-66 (Nancy Pruitt); *Iron Horse*—"Joy Unconfined" 9-12-66 (Marta); *Alias Smith and Jones*—"Return to Devil's Hole" 2-25-71 (Clara Phillips); *Gunsmoke*—"Shadler" 1-15-73 (Dallas Fair).

Hyland, Jim. Films: "No Name on the Bullet" 1959. ¶TV: *Gunsmoke*—"The Preacher" 6-16-56 (Stage Driver); *Sheriff of Cochise*—"Triangle" 2-22-57 (Joe Trimble); *Have Gun Will Travel*—"Gold and Brimstone" 6-20-59; *Stagecoach West*—"Dark Return" 10-18-60 (Stanley Culver).

Hyland. Patricia. TV: *Bonanza*—"Check Rein" 12-3-67 (Kathy); *The Virginian*—"No War for the Warrior" 2-18-70 (Kgoy-Ma).

Hylands, Scott (1936-). Films: "Death Hunt" 1981 (Pilot). ¶TV: *Kung Fu*—"Blood Brother" 1-18-73 (Randy), "The Spirit Helper" 11-8-73 (Saunders); *The Quest*—"Incident at Drucker's Tavern" 1976; *Centennial*—Regular 1978-79 (Laseter).

Hylton, Richard (1920-5/12/62). Films: "The Secret of Convict Lake" 1951 (Clyde Maxwell).

Hymer, Warren (1906-3/25/48). Films: "The Lone Star Ranger" 1930 (the Bowery Kid); "The Mysterious Rider" 1933 (Jitney Smith); "The Gold Ghost" 1934-short; "Desert Justice" 1936 (Hymie); "Rhythm on the Range" 1936 (Big Brain); "Destry Rides Again" 1939 (Gyp Watson).

Hytten, Olaf (1888-3/11/55). Films: "The Last of the Mohicans" 1936 (King George II); "The Last of the Mohicans" 1936; "Allegheny Uprising" 1939 (General Gage); "Gaucho Serenade" 1940; "Bells of San Angelo" 1947 (Mr. Lionel Bates); "Unconquered" 1947; "Fancy Pants" 1950 (Stage Manager).

Iglesias, Eugene. Films: "Indian Uprising" 1951 (Sgt Ramirez); "California Conquest" 1952 (Ernest Brios); "The Duel at Silver Creek" 1952 (Johnny Sombrero); "Hiawatha" 1952 (Chibiabos); "Jack McCall, Desperado" 1953 (Grey Eagle); "Tumbleweed" 1953 (Tigre); "Taza, Son of Cochise" 1954 (Chato); "They Rode West" 1954 (Red Leaf); "The Naked Dawn" 1955 (Manuel); "Walk the Proud Land" 1956 (Chato); "Domino Kid" 1957 (Juan Cortez); "Cowboy" 1958 (Manuel Arriega); "Rio Bravo" 1959 (1st Burdette Man in Shootout); "Frontier Uprising" 1961 (Lt. Ruiz). ¶TV: *Loretta Young Show*—"The Wise One" 3-26-56 (Guitar Player); *Broken Arrow*—"Justice" 11-27-56 (Cheewaukee); *Circus Boy*—"The Knife Thrower" 2-17-57 (Marino); *Jim Bowie*—"Ursula" 2-14-58 (Esteban Caledron); *Maverick*—"Plunder of Paradise" 3-9-58 (Ricardo); *Sugarfoot*—"Vinegaroom" 3-29-60 (Johnny July); *The Outlaws*—"Rape of Red Sky" 10-27-60 (Hassini); *The Rebel*—"Don Gringo" 11-20-60 (Don Rolando), "The Uncourageous" 5-7-61 (Felipe); *The Deputy*—"The Shackled Town" 2-11-61 (Pedro O'Brien); *Laramie*—"The Perfect Gift" 1-2-62 (Jacero); *Rawhide*—"The Reunion" 4-6-62 (Wild Horse); *The Dakotas*—"One Day in Vermillion" 4-8-63 (Kicking Horse); *Bonanza*—"Woman of Fire" 1-17-65; *Wild Wild West*—"The Night of the Poisonous Posey" 10-28-66 (Galleto), "The Night of the Pistoleros" 2-21-69 (Bernal); *Hondo*—"Hondo and the Rebel Hat" 12-29-67 (Neomo).

Ihnat, Steve (1935-5/12/72). Films: "Hour of the Gun" 1967 (Andy Warshaw). ¶TV: *The Virginian*—"The Fatal Journey" 12-4-63 (Stub O'Dell), "Jed" 1-10-68 (Jed Matthews), "Last Grave at Socorro Creek" 1-22-69 (Four-Eyes); *Temple Houston*—"Seventy Times Seven" 12-5-63 (Ben Wade); *Gunsmoke*—"The Pariah" 4-17-65 (Ben Hooker), "My Father's Guitar" 2-21-66 (Jack), "The Mission" 10-8-66 (Ashe), "Noose of Gold" 3-4-67 (John Farron), "Exodus 21:22" 3-24-69 (Frank Reardon), "Jenny" 12-28-70 (Lucas Pritchard); *Death Valley Days*—"The Streets of El Paso" 5-16-64 (Rick Hubbard); *Rawhide*—"The Retreat" 3-26-65 (Kaster); *Bonanza*—"Dead and Gone" 4-4-65 (Johann), "A Dream to Dream" 4-14-68 (Josh Carter), "Terror at 2:00" 3-7-71 (Gans); *Daniel Boone*—"Perilous Journey" 12-16-65 (Tyler); *The Big Valley*—"Teacher of Outlaws" 2-2-66 (Will Hanley); *Iron Horse*—"Joy Unconfined" 9-12-66 (Luke Joy), 10-14-67 (Ray McCoy);

Shane—"The Bitter, the Lonely" 10-8-66 (R.G. Posey); *Cimarron Strip*—"The Hunted" 10-5-67 (Felix Gauge); *Dundee and the Culhane*—12-13-67 (Ben Murcheson); *The Outcasts*—"The Night Riders" 11-25-68 (Jeb Collins); *Here Come the Brides*—"The Soldier" 10-10-69 (Sgt. Noah Todd), "Absalom" 3-20-70 (Tray); *Alias Smith and Jones*—"Stagecoach Seven" 3-11-71 (Harry Downs).

Imhof, Roger (1875–4/15/58). Films: "North of Nome" 1936 (Judge Bridle); "The Three Godfathers" 1936 (Sheriff); "High, Wide and Handsome" 1937 (Pop Bowers); "Drums Along the Mohawk" 1939 (General Nicholas Herkimer); "Lady from Cheyenne" 1941 (Uncle Bill).

Ince, Ada. Films: "Frontier Days" 1934 (Beth Wilson); "Rainbow's End" 1935 (Gwen Gibson).

Ince, John (1877–4/10/47). Films: "The Girl from Sunset Pass" 1913; "On the Mountain Ranch" 1913; "The Taking of Rattlesnake Bill" 1913; "The Trapper's Revenge" 1915; "The Ropin' Fool" 1921; "Oklahoma Cyclone" 1930; "Headin' for Trouble" 1931 (Andrews); "Mounted Fury" 1931 (Big McGraw); "Wild West Whoopee" 1931; "Destry Rides Again" 1932 (the Judge); "Guns for Hire" 1932; "Human Targets" 1932 (Doctor); "The Thrill Hunter" 1933 (Mayor Thomas); "The Lucky Texan" 1934; "Call of the Wild" 1935; "Circle of Death" 1935 (Bill Carr); "Rainbow's End" 1935; "Texas Terror" 1935; "Comin' Round the Mountain" 1936 (Starting Judge); "A Tenderfoot Goes West" 1937 (Hal); "Way Out West" 1937 (Man in Audience); "Stand Up and Fight" 1939 (Man at Auction); "The Return of Wild Bill" 1940 (Sam Griffin); "Billy the Kid's Range War" 1941 (Hastings); "Code of the Outlaw" 1942; "The Lost Trail" 1945 (Bailey); "Last Frontier Uprising" 1947 (Sam Chisholm).

Ince, Ralph (1887–4/10/37). Films: "Billy the Kid" 1911; "Una of the Sierras" 1912; "Yellow Bird" 1912; "Out of the Snows" 1920 (Robert Holliday); "Law and Order" 1932 (Poe Northrup); "Men of America" 1933 (Cicero).

Inclan, Miguel (1900–7/25/56). Films: "Fort Apache" 1948 (Cochise); "Indian Uprising" 1951 (Geronimo); "Bandido" 1956 (Priest).

Incontrera, Annabella (1943–). Films: "Poker with Pistols" 1967-Ital.; "Challenge of the Mackennas" 1969-Ital./Span.; "Return of Sabata" 1972-Ital./Fr./Ger. (Maggie).

Indrisano, John (1906–7/9/68). Films: "Callaway Went Thataway" 1951 (Johnny Tarranto). ¶TV: *Rawhide*—"Incident of the Thirteenth Man" 10-23-59; *Bonanza*—"A Woman Lost" 3-17-63; *Branded*—"The Richest Man in Boot Hill" 10-31-65 (Howie); *The Big Valley*—"Price of Victory" 2-13-67; *Hondo*—"Hondo and the he Rebel Hat" 12-29-67 (Bartender).

Induni, Luis (1918–). Films: "Billy the Kid" 1962-Span.; "Gunfight at High Noon" 1963-Span./Ital.; "Shoot to Kill" 1963-Span.; "Damned Pistols of Dallas" 1964-Span./Ital./Fr.; "Ride and Kill" 1964-Ital./Span.; "Two Gunmen" 1964-Span./Ital.; "Last of the Mohicans" 1965-Ital./Span./Ger. (Hawkeye); "The Last Tomahawk" 1965-Ger./Ital./Span.; "Djurado" 1966-Ital./Span. (Tucan); "Jesse James' Kid" 1966-Span./Ital.; "One Hundred Thousand Dollars for Ringo" 1966-Ital./Span.; "Relentless Four" 1966-Span./Ital.; "The Texican" 1966-U.S./Span. (U.S. Marshal); "Woman for Ringo" 1966-Ital./Span.; "Django Does Not Forgive" 1967-Ital./Span.; "Fury of Johnny Kid" 1967-Span./Ital.; "Magnificent Texan" 1967-Ital./Span.; "The Man Who Killed Billy the Kid" 1967-Span./Ital.; "Ruthless Colt of the Gringo" 1967-Ital./Span.; "Three from Colorado" 1967-Span.; "Awkward Hands" 1968-Span./Ital.; "Cowards Don't Pray" 1968-Ital./Span.; "Cry for Revenge" 1968-Ital./Span.; "Hour of Death" 1968-Span./Ital.; "I Do Not Forgive … I Kill!" 1968-Span./Ital.; "Rattler Kid" 1968-Ital./Span.; "Adios Cjamango" 1969-Ital./Span.; "Dead Are Countless" 1969-Ital./Span.; "Killer Goodbye" 1969-Ital./Span.; "Rebels of Arizona" 1969-Span.; "Dig Your Grave, Friend … Sabata's Coming" 1970-Ital./Span./Fr.; "Sabata the Killer" 1970-Ital./Span.; "Sartana Kills Them All" 1970-Ital./Span.; "Twenty Paces to Death" 1970-Ital./Span. (Senator Cedric); "Captain Apache" 1971-Brit./Span. (Ezekiel); "Dallas" 1972-Span./Ital.; "God in Heaven … Arizona on Earth" 1972-Span./Ital.; "If One Is Born a Swine" 1972-Ital./Span.; "My Horse, My Gun, Your Widow" 1972-Ital./Span.

Inescort, Frieda (1901–2/21/76). TV: *Wagon Train*—"The Charles Maury Story" 5-7-58 (Aunt 'Toinette); *The Rebel*—"Mission—Varina" 5-14-61 (Varina Davis).

Infanti, Angelo. Films: "Four Dollars for Vengeance" 1965-Span./Ital.; "Ballad of a Gunman" 1967-Ital./Ger. (Hud).

Infuhr, Teddy. Films: "Phantom Valley" 1948; "West of El Dorado" 1949 (Larry); "Gene Autry and the Mounties" 1951; "Hills of Utah" 1951; "Valley of Fire" 1951 (Virgil). ¶TV: *The Gene Autry Show*—"Warning! Danger!" 11-10-51; *The Cisco Kid*—"Robber Crow" 11-24-51, "The Kid Brother" 2-9-52.

Ingraham, Lloyd (1874–4/4/56). Films: "Last of the Duanes" 1930 (Mr. Garrett); "Montana Moon" 1930 (Mr. Prescott); "The Spoilers" 1930 (Judge Stillman); "Cornered" 1932 (Judge Webster); "Get That Girl" 1932 (John, the Gardener); "Texas Gun Fighter" 1932 (Banty); "Silent Men" 1933 (Sheriff Vic Green); "Battle of Greed" 1934 (Virginnie); "The Dude Ranger" 1934 (Beckett); "Fighting to Live" 1934; "The Gold Ghost" 1934-short; "Branded a Coward" 1935 (Mr. Carson); "Between Men" 1935 (Sir George Thorn); "Cowboy Millionaire" 1935 (Ben); "The Ghost Rider" 1935 (Rufe); "Gunsmoke on the Guadalupe" 1935; "Northern Frontier" 1935 (Brader); "Rainbow Valley" 1935 (Powell); "The Rider of the Law" 1935; "Texas Terror" 1935 (Dan Matthews); "Timber War" 1935 (Terry O'Leary); "Trail of Terror" 1935 (Warden); "Trigger Tom" 1935 (Sheriff Pop Slater); "Westward Ho" 1935; "Everyman's Law" 1936 (Jim Morgan); "Frontier Justice" 1936 (Dr. Ralph P. Crane); "Ghost Patrol" 1936 (Prof. Brent); "Gun Smoke" 1936 (Eli Parker); "Law and Lead" 1936; "The Lawless Nineties" 1936 (Palmer); "The Lonely Trail" 1936 (Tucker); "Red River Valley" 1936; "Rogue of the Range" 1936 (Doctor); "Stormy Trails" 1936 (Curley); "Too Much Beef" 1936 (Dynamite Murray); "Undercover Man" 1936 (Judge Forbes); "Vigilantes Are Coming" 1936-serial (John Colton); "Winds of the Wasteland" 1936; "Empty Saddles" 1937 (Jim Grant); "Gun Lords of Stirrup Basin" 1937; "Lightnin' Crandall" 1937 (Judge); "Park Avenue Lodger" 1937 (Mike Curran); "Rhythm Wranglers" 1937-short; "Riders of the Dawn" 1937 (Mr. Moran); "Billy the Kid Returns" 1938; "A Buckaroo Broadcast" 1938-short; "The Feud Maker" 1938 (Hank Younger); "Gun Law" 1938; "Gun Packer" 1938 (Chief Holmes); "Man from Music Mountain" 1938 (Harmon); "The Painted Desert" 1938 (Banning); "Prairie Papas" 1938-short; "Songs and Saddles" 1938 (Judge); "A Western Welcome" 1938-short; "Destry Rides Again" 1939 (Turner, the Express Agent);

"The Marshal of Mesa City" 1939 (Mayor Sam Bentley); "Oklahoma Frontier" 1939 (Judge); "Ride 'Em, Cowgirl" 1939 (Judge); "The Singing Cowgirl" 1939 (Dr. Slocum); "Water Rustlers" 1939 (Judge); "Adventures of Red Ryder" 1940-serial (Sheriff Luke Andrews); "Bad Man from Red Butte" 1940 (Turner); "Colorado" 1940 (Henry Sanford); "Legion of the Lawless" 1940; "Melody Ranch" 1940; "My Little Chickadee" 1940 (Leading Citizen); "Pony Post" 1940 (Dr. Nesbet); "Prairie Law" 1940; "Son of Roaring Dan" 1940 (Judge); "Trail of the Vigilantes" 1940 (Rancher); "Triple Justice" 1940 (Sam); "Twenty Mule Team" 1940 (Stockholder); "Wagon Train" 1940 (Mayor); "Bad Man of Deadwood" 1941; "Dude Cowboy" 1941 (Pop Stebbens); "Jesse James at Bay" 1941; "The Musical Bandit" 1941-short; "Prairie Spooners" 1941-short; "Redskins and Redheads" 1941-short; "Robbers of the Range" 1941; "Bandit Ranger" 1942; "The Phantom Plainsmen" 1942 (Doctor); "The Silver Bullet" 1942; "The Spoilers" 1942 (Kelly); "Stagecoach Buckaroo" 1942 (Simpson); "Thundering Hoofs" 1942; "Valley of the Sun" 1942 (Man on Street); "The Avenging Rider" 1943; "Blazing Guns" 1943 (Governor); "Partners of the Trail" 1944 (Applegate); "Range Law" 1944 (Judge); "West of the Rio Grande" 1944; "Frontier Feud" 1945 (Si Peters); "Frontier Gal" 1945 (Dealer); "Springtime in Texas" 1945; "The Caravan Trail" 1946; "Lawless Empire" 1946 (Mr. Murphy); "West of Sonora" 1948; "The Savage Horde" 1950.

Ingram, Jack (1903-2/20/69). Films: "The Lonely Trail" 1936 (Trooper); "The Old Corral" 1936; "Rebellion" 1936 (Hank); "Rio Grande Ranger" 1936; "Vigilantes Are Coming" 1936-serial (Rancher); "Winds of the Wasteland" 1936 (Guard); "Doomed at Sundown" 1937; "Gunsmoke Ranch" 1937 (Jed); "Public Cowboy No. 1" 1937 (Larry); "The Rangers Step In" 1937 (Fred Warren); "The Trigger Trio" 1937; "Valley of Terror" 1937 (Spud Hayes); "Whistling Bullets" 1937 (Tim Raymond); "Wild Horse Rodeo" 1937 (Jim Travis); "Wild Horse Round-Up" 1937; "Yodelin' Kid from Pine Ridge" 1937 (LLoyd); "Zorro Rides Again" 1937-serial (Carter); "Black Bandit" 1938; "Call the Mesquiteers" 1938; "Code of the Rangers" 1938 (Hank); "Desert Patrol" 1938 (Chet); "Durango Valley Raiders" 1938 (Slade); "Gunsmoke

Trail" 1938 (Ed); "In Early Arizona" 1938 (Marshal Jeff Bowers); "The Lone Ranger" 1938-serial (Trooper); "Outlaw Express" 1938; "Outlaws of Sonora" 1938 (Nick); "Phantom Gold" 1938 (Pete); "Riders of the Black Hills" 1938 (Lefty); "Stagecoach Days" 1938 (Virg); "Two-Gun Justice" 1938; "Under Western Stars" 1938; "Western Jamboree" 1938; "Western Trails" 1938; "The Arizona Kid" 1939; "The Adventures of the Masked Phantom" 1939 (Outlaw); "Blue Montana Skies" 1939 (Frazier); "Colorado Sunset" 1939 (Clanton); "Days of Jesse James" 1939; "Down the Wyoming Trail" 1939 (Monte); "Feud of the Range" 1939 (Baxton); "Frontier Scout" 1939 (Folsom); "Frontiers of '49" 1939; "Home on the Prairie" 1939 (Wilson); "The Law Comes to Texas" 1939; "Lone Star Pioneers" 1939 (John Coe); "Mexicali Rose" 1939; "Mountain Rhythm" 1939 (Carney); "New Frontier" 1939 (Harmon); "The Night Riders" 1939 (Wilkins); "The Pal from Texas" 1939; "Rovin' Tumbleweeds" 1939 (Blake); "Saga of Death Valley" 1939 (Brace); "Southward Ho!" 1939; "Straight Shooter" 1939; "Two-Gun Troubador" 1939; "Wall Street Cowboy" 1939 (McDermott); "Wyoming Outlaw" 1939 (Sheriff); "Billy the Kid Outlawed" 1940; "The Carson City Kid" 1940; "Deadwood Dick" 1940-serial (Buzz); "Ghost Valley Raiders" 1940 (Sam Kennelly); "Melody Ranch" 1940; "One Man's Law" 1940; "Rancho Grande" 1940; "Ridin' the Trail" 1940 (Tex Walters); "Under Texas Skies" 1940 (Finley); "Young Bill Hickok" 1940 (Red); "King of Dodge City" 1941; "King of the Texas Rangers" 1941-serial (Shorty); "Law of the Wolf" 1941; "The Lone Rider Ambushed" 1941 (Charlie Davis); "The Lone Rider in Ghost Town" 1941; "Lone Star Law Men" 1941; "Nevada City" 1941; "Prairie Pioneers" 1941 (Wade); "Sheriff of Tombstone" 1941 (Bill Starr); "The Son of Davy Crockett" 1941; "Texas" 1941 (Henchman); "White Eagle" 1941-serial (Cantro); "Code of the Outlaw" 1942; "Arizona Roundup" 1942; "Along the Sundown Trail" 1942; "Arizona Stagecoach" 1942; "Bad Men of the Hills" 1942; "Billy the Kid Trapped" 1942 (Harton); "The Lone Rider and the Bandit" 1942; "The Lone Rider in Cheyenne" 1942; "Man from Cheyenne" 1942 (Jack); "The Mysterious Rider" 1942; "Perils of the Royal Mounted" 1942-serial (Baptiste); "Raiders of the Range" 1942; "Rolling Down the Great Divide" 1942

(Dale); "South of Santa Fe" 1942; "The Sundown Kid" 1942; "Sunset Serenade" 1942; "Valley of Vanishing Men" 1942-serial (Butler); "Arizona Trail" 1943 (Ace Vincent); "Bad Men of Thunder Gap" 1943; "Border Buckaroos" 1943 (Cole Melford); "Frontier Law" 1943 (Hawkins); "Fugitive of the Plains" 1943; "Idaho" 1943; "The Lone Star Trail" 1943 (Dan Jason); "The Man from Thunder River" 1943; "Raiders of San Joaquin" 1943 (Lear); "Raiders of Sunset Pass" 1943 (Rustler); "Riders of the Northwest Mounted" 1943; "Riders of the Rio Grande" 1943 (Berger); "Saddles and Sagebrush" 1943; "Santa Fe Scouts" 1943 (Frank Howard); "Silver City Raiders" 1943 (Dirk); "Wagon Tracks West" 1943; "West of Texas" 1943 (Blackie); "Wolves of the Range" 1943 (Hammond); "Beneath Western Skies" 1944; "Boss of Boomtown" 1944 (Ridgeway); "Boss of Rawhide" 1944 (Sam Barrett); "Devil Riders" 1944 (Turner); "The Drifter" 1944 (Dirk Trent); "Frontier Outlaws" 1944 (Taylor); "Ghost Guns" 1944; "Guns of the Law" 1944; "Gunsmoke Mesa" 1944 (Henry Black); "Mojave Firebrand" 1944; "Oath of Vengeance" 1944; "Oklahoma Raiders" 1944 (Arnold Drew); "Outlaw Roundup" 1944 (Trigger); "Partners of the Trail" 1944 (Trigger); "The Pinto Bandit" 1944; "Raiders of Ghost City" 1944-serial; "Range Law" 1944 (Phil Randall); "Sundown Valley" 1944 (Bart Adams); "Thundering Gun Slingers" 1944 (Vic); "Trail of Terror" 1944 (Nevada Simmons); "Trigger Law" 1944; "Trigger Trail" 1944; "Valley of Vengeance" 1944 (Brett); "Bandits of the Badlands" 1945; "Beyond the Pecos" 1945; "Enemy of the Law" 1945 (Steve Martin); "Flame of the West" 1945 (Slick); "Frontier Feud" 1945 (Don Graham); "Frontier Fugitives" 1945; "Frontier Gal" 1945 (Henchman); "Marked for Murder" 1945; "Rough Ridin' Justice" 1945 (Nick Dunham); "Saddle Serenade" 1945; "Sheriff of Cimarron" 1945 (Brace McCord); "Strange from Santa Fe" 1945; "Under Western Skies" 1945 (Red Hutchins); "Canyon Passage" 1946 (Pack Train Leader); "Moon Over Montana" 1946; "The Scarlet Horseman" 1946-serial (Tragg); "West of Alamo" 1946 (Clay Bradford); "The Fabulous Texan" 1947; "Ghost Town Renegades" 1947 (Sharpe); "Pioneer Justice" 1947 (Bill Judd); "South of the Chisholm Trail" 1947; "The Vigilante" 1947-serial (Silver); "Blazing Across the Pecos" 1948; "The Gallant Legion" 1948;

"The Strawberry Roan" 1948 (Pete Lucas); "Sundown Riders" 1948 (Tug Wilson); "Tex Granger" 1948-serial (Reno); "Whirlwind Raiders" 1948 (Buff Tyson); "Calamity Jane and Sam Bass" 1949 (Mayes); "Desert Vigilante" 1949 (Sergeant); "Law of the West" 1949 (Burke); "Roaring Westward" 1949 (Marshal Braden); "Son of a Badman" 1949 (Rocky); "Bandit Queen" 1950 (Barton); "Cody of the Pony Express" 1950-serial (Pecos); "Desperadoes of the West" 1950-serial (Todd); "Gold Strike" 1950-short; "Roar of the Iron Horse" 1950-serial (Homer Lathrop); "Short Grass" 1950 (Jack); "Sierra" 1950; "Streets of Ghost Town" 1950 (Kirby); "The Texan Meets Calamity Jane" 1950 (Matt Baker); "Don Daredevil Rides Again" 1951-serial (Jack); "Fort Dodge Stampede" 1951 (Cox); "The Battle at Apache Pass" 1952 (Johnny Ward); "Fargo" 1952; "Lost in Alaska" 1952 (Henchman); "Cow Country" 1953 (Terrell); "The Great Sioux Uprising" 1953 (Sam); "Law and Order" 1953 (Man); "Son of the Renegade" 1953 (Three Fingers); "Riding with Buffalo Bill" 1954-serial (Ace); "Five Guns West" 1955 (Jethro); "Man Without a Star" 1955 (Jessup); "Utah Blaine" 1957 (Clel Miller). ¶TV: *The Gene Autry Show*— "Blackwater Valley Feud" 9-3-50, "The Raiders" 4-14-51, "Double Barrelled Vengeance" 4-21-51; *The Lone Ranger*—"Double Jeopardy" 9-7-50, "Triple Cross" 5-21-53; *The Cisco Kid*—"Big Switch" 2-10-51, "Railroad Land Rush" 3-17-51, "Renegade Son" 4-7-51, "Monkey Business" 1-26-52, "The Ventriloquist" 2-7-53, "Gold Strike" 3-14-53, "The Hospital" 5-16-53; *Annie Oakley*—"Annie and the Chinese Puzzle" 2-13-55 (Mob Leader); *Tales of Wells Fargo*—"The Break" 5-19-58 (Jake Norton).

Ingram, Jean. Films: "Tickle Me" 1965 (Evelyn). ¶TV: *Tales of Wells Fargo*—"The Canyon" 2-1-60 (Jane); *Overland Trail*—"Daughter of the Sioux" 3-20-60 (Diana); *Gunsmoke*—"Ben Toliver's Stud" 11-26-60 (Nancy Creed).

Ingram, Rex (1893-7/21/50). Films: "Escort West" 1959 (Nelson); "Journey to Shiloh" 1968 (Jacob). ¶TV: *Black Saddle*—"Client: McQueen" 1-24-59 (Alex Booth); *The Rifleman*—"Closer Than a Brother" 2-21-61 (Thaddeus); *Branded*—"This Stage of Fools" 1-16-66 (Hannibal); *Cowboy in Africa*—"The Kasubi Death" 4-1-68 (Dr. Tom Merar); *Gunsmoke*—"The Good Samaritans" 3-10-69 (Juba).

Ingrassia, Ciccio (1923-). Films: "For a Fist in the Eye" 1965-Ital./Span.; "Two Gangsters in the Wild West" 1965-Ital./Span. (Ciccio); "Two Sergeants of General Custer" 1965-Ital./Span.; "Two Sons of Ringo" 1966-Ital.; "The Handsome, the Ugly, and the Stupid" 1967-Ital.; "Two R-R-Ringos from Texas" 1967-Ital.; "Ciccio Forgives, I Don't" 1968-Ital.; "Grandsons of Zorro" 1968-Ital. (Ciccio); "Nephews of Zorro" 1969-Ital. (Ciccio); "Paths of War" 1969-Ital.; "Two Sons of Trinity" 1972-Ital.

Inkijnoff, Valery. Films: "The Legend of Frenchie King" 1971-Fr./Ital./Span./Brit. (Spitting Bull).

Inness, Jean (1902-12/27/78). Films: "Mrs. Mike" 1949 (Mrs. Mathers); "Friendly Persuasion" 1956 (Mrs. Purdy); "Gun Fever" 1958 (Martha). ¶TV: *The Lone Ranger*—"Rendezvous at Whipsaw" 11-11-54; *Gunsmoke*—"Reward for Matt" 1-28-56 (Mrs. Reeves), "The Deserter" 6-4-60 (Maddie); *Wagon Train*—"Chuck Wooster, Wagonmaster" 5-20-59 (Sarah Duncan), "The Sam Spicer Story" 10-28-63 (Ma Adams); *Rawhide*—"Incident of the Dry Drive" 5-22-59 (Carrie Hode), "Judgment at Hondo Seco" 10-20-61 (Hattie); *Wichita Town*—"Passage to the Enemy" 12-2-59 (Mrs. Warren); *Texas John Slaughter*—"The Robber Stallion" 12-4-59 (Mrs. Scanlon); *Johnny Ringo*—"The Vindicator" 3-31-60 (Melissa); *Tales of Wells Fargo*—"Pearl Hart" 5-9-60 (Martha); *The Rebel*—"The Hostage" 6-11-61 (Martha Randall); *Bonanza*—"The Miracle Worker" 5-20-62 (Aunt Celia), "The Pursued" 10-2-66 & 10-9-66 (Mrs. Lang); *Have Gun Will Travel*—"The Knight" 6-2-62 (Pegine); *Empire*—"Breakout" 4-16-63 (Rose Serrato); *The Virginian*—"The Return of Golden Tom" 3-9-66 (Widow Hazard), "Doctor Pat" 3-1-67, "The Deadly Past" 9-20-67 (Mrs. Peterson), "Fox, Hound, and the Widow McCloud" 4-2-69 (Clarissa McCloud); *Daniel Boone*—"Heroes Welcome" 2-22-68; *The Big Valley*—"Top of the Stairs" 1-6-69 (Grace Newcomb).

Innocent, Harold (1933-9/12/93). TV: *Have Gun Will Travel*—"An International Affair" 4-2-60 (Gateshead); *Gunsmoke*—"Chesterland" 11-18-61 (William), "Catawomper" 2-10-62 (George), "Reprisal" 3-10-62 (Bank Teller).

Inslee, Charles. Films: "The Call of the Wild" 1908; "The Girl and the Outlaw" 1908; "The Red Girl" 1908; "The Redman and the Child" 1908; "The Vaquero's Vow" 1908; "Davy Crockett in Hearts United" 1909; "A True Indian's Heart" 1909; "Little Dove's Romance" 1911; "The Sheriff's Brother" 1911; "Tribal Law" 1912; "A Frontier Providence" 1913; "The Desert's Sting" 1914; "Desperate Trails" 1921 (Doc Higgins); "The Man Who Woke Up" 1921; "The Valley of the Rogues" 1921.

Ipale, Aharon (1941-). Films: "Madron" 1970-U.S./Israel (Singer).

Ireland, Jill (1936-5/18/90). Films: "Robbery Under Arms" 1958-Brit. (Jean); "Villa Rides" 1968 (Girl in Restaurant); "Chino" 1973-Ital./Span./Fr. (Louise); "Breakheart Pass" 1976 (Marcia Scoville); "From Noon to Three" 1976 (Amanda Starbuck). ¶TV: *Shane*—Regular 1966 (Marian Starrett); *Daniel Boone*—"The Traitor" 10-30-69 (Angela).

Ireland, John (1915-3/21/92). Films: "My Darling Clementine" 1946 (Billy Clanton); "Red River" 1948 (Cherry Valance); "The Doolins of Oklahoma" 1949 (Bitter Creek); "I Shot Jesse James" 1949 (Bob Ford); "Roughshod" 1949 (Lednov); "The Walking Hills" 1949 (Frazee); "The Return of Jesse James" 1950 (Johnny); "Little Big Horn" 1951 (Lt. John Haywood); "Red Mountain" 1951 (Quantrell); "Vengeance Valley" 1951 (Hub Fasken); "The Bushwackers" 1952 (Jeff Waring); "Hannah Lee" 1953 (Rochelle); "Southwest Passage" 1954 (Clint McDonald); "Gunslinger" 1956 (Cane Miro); "Gunfight at the O.K. Corral" 1957 (Johnny Ringo); "Fort Utah" 1967 (Tom Horn); "Hate for Hate" 1967-Ital. (Cooper); "Run Man, Run" 1967-Ital./Fr.; "Arizona Bushwackers" 1968 (Dan Shelby); "All Out" 1968-Ital./Span.; "Cost of Dying" 1968-Ital./Fr. (Bill Ramson); "Dead for a Dollar" 1968-Ital.; "Machine Gun Killers" 1968-Ital./Span. (Tapos); "Pistol for a Hundred Coffins" 1968-Ital./Span. (Garff); "Revenge for Revenge" 1968-Ital. (Major Bower); "Villa Rides" 1968 (Dave, the Man in the Barber Shop); "Challenge of the Mackennas" 1969-Ital./Span.; "Blood River" 1974-Ital.; "Kino, the Padre on Horseback" 1977; "Bonanza: The Next Generation" TVM-1988 (Aaron Cartwright). ¶TV: *Zane Grey Theater*—"Return to Nowhere" 12-7-56 (Marshal Phillips); *Riverboat*—"The Fight Back" 10-18-59 (Chris Slade); *Rawhide*—"Incident in the Garden of Eden" 6-17-60 (Winch), "Incident of the Portrait"

10-5-62 (Frank Trask), "The Spanish Camp" 5-7-65 (Merritt), Regular 1965-66 (Jed Colby); *Branded*—"Leap Upon Mountains..." 2-28-65 (Renger), "Cowards Die Many Times" 4-17-66 (Tad Evers); *A Man Called Shenandoah*—"Marlee" 3-14-66 (Sheriff Vernon Cole); *Gunsmoke*—"Stage Stop" 11-26-66 (Jed Coombs), "Vengeance" 10-2-67 & 10-9-67 (Parker); *Iron Horse*—"Appointment with an Epitaph" 2-13-67 (Carl Mobley); *Bonanza*—"Judgment at Red Creek" 2-26-67 (Rimbau); *Daniel Boone*—"The Fallow Land" 4-13-67 (Hiram Manville); *The Men from Shiloh*—"Jenny" 9-30-70 (Kinroy); *The Quest*—"Portrait of a Gunfighter" 12-22-76 (Jack Bell).

Irish, Tom. Films: "Hondo" 1953 (Lt. McKay); "Seven Angry Men" 1955 (Watson); "Friendly Persuasion" 1956 (Young Rebel). ¶TV: *The Lone Ranger*—"Sheriff of Gunstock" 7-27-50; *The Cisco Kid*—"The Kidnapped Cameraman" 10-24-53, "The Two Wheeler" 11-21-53.

Ironside, Michael. Films: "Dead Man's Revenge" TVM-1994 (Luck Hatcher).

Irvin, Gregory. TV: *Fury*—"Packy's Dilemma" 2-13-60 (Ken); *Zane Grey Theater*—"The Ox" 11-3-60; *Wagon Train*—"The Annie Duggan Story" 3-13-63 (Johnnie Leeds); *Temple Houston*—"The Guardian" 1-2-64 (Robert Ballard).

Irving, Amy (1953-). Films: "An American Tail: Fievel Goes West" 1991 (voice of Miss Kitty).

Irving, Buster. Films: "The Desert Man" 1917 (Joey); "Breed of Men" 1919 (Bobby Fellows).

Irving, Charles (1912-2/15/81). TV: *The Dakotas*—"Sanctuary at Crystal Springs" 5-6-63 (Reverend Spencer); *Bonanza*—"A Passion for Justice" 9-29-63 (Rogers), "The Emperor Norton" 2-27-66 (Judge), "Ballad of the Ponderosa" 11-13-66 (Judge Borman); "The Bottle Fighter" 5-12-68 (Judge); *Lancer*—"Blind Man's Bluff" 9-23-69 (Doctor), "Zee" 9-30-69 (Doctor).

Irving, George (1874-9/11/61). Films: "North of '36" 1924 (Pattison); "The Wanderer of the Wasteland" 1924 (Mr. Virey); "The Golden Princess" 1925 (Bill Kent); "Wild Horse Mesa" 1925 (Lige Melberne); "Desert Gold" 1926 (Richard Stanton Gale); "Three Bad Men" 1926 (Gen. Neville); "Broncho Twister" 1927 (Ned Mason); "Drums of the desert" 1927 (Prof. Elias Manton); "The Spoilers" 1930 (William Wheaton); "Cisco Kid" 1931; "The Vanishing Frontier" 1932 (Gen Winfield); "Under the Pampas Moon" 1935 (Don Bennett); "Sutter's Gold" 1936; "Border Cafe" 1937 (Senator Henry Whitney); "The Outcasts of Poker Flat" 1937 (Doctor); "The Law West of Tombstone" 1938 (Mort Dixon); "The Great Man's Lady" 1942 (Dr. Adams); "King of the Mounties" 1942-serial (Professor Marshall Brent).

Irving, Hollis. TV: *Colt .45*—"Final Payment" 11-22-57; *Man from Blackhawk*—"Death by Northwest" 3-25-60 (Shelly); *Wanted—Dead or Alive*—"Baa-Baa" 1-4-61 (Helen Wood); *Stagecoach West*—"The Outcasts" 3-7-61 (Cora Temple); *The Tall Man*—"The Impatient Brides" 2-3-62 (Jane).

Irving, Margaret. Films: "The Outcasts of Poker Flat" 1937 (the Duchess).

Irving, Mary Jane (1913-7/17/83). Films: "The Square Deal Man" 1917 (Blossom); "Desert Gold" 1919 (the Child); "The Westerners" 1919 (Little Molly Welch); "Travelin' On" 1922 (Mary Jane Morton); "When Romance Rides" 1922 (Bostie Bostil); "The Splendid Road" 1925 (Hester Gephart); "The Flaming Forest" 1926 (Ruth McTavish); "Without Honor" 1932 (Bernie Donovan); "Gunfire" 1935 (Sally Moore).

Irving, William (1893-12/25/43). Films: "Rough Waters" 1930 (Bill); "Song of the Cabellero" 1930 (Bernardo).

Irwin, Boyd (1880-1/22/57). Films: "The Long Chance" 1922 (Boston/T. Morgan Carey); "North of the Rockies" 1942; "In Old Sacramento" 1946; "King of the Bandits" 1947 (Col. Wayne).

Irwin, Charles (1888-1/12/69). Films: "The Curse of the Great Southwest" 1913; "The Cowpuncher" 1915; "Susannah of the Mounties" 1939 (Sgt. McGregor); "Wolf Call" 1939 (Police Sergeant); "Rangers of Fortune" 1940; "Montana" 1950 (MacKenzie); "Fort Vengeance" 1953 (Saxon); "The Sheriff of Fractured Jaw" 1958-Brit. (Luke). ¶TV: *The Adventures of Rin Tin Tin*—"Wind-Wagon McClanahan" 4-4-58 (Terrance X. McClanahan); *The Restless Gun*—"The Lady and the Gun" 1-19-59.

Isabell, Henry. Films: "Wild Horse Rodeo" 1937 (Slim); "Zorro Rides Again" 1937-serial (Raider #1); "The Lone Ranger" 1938-serial (Trooper).

Ishimoto, Dale (1923-). TV: *Wanted—Dead or Alive*—"The Long Search" 3-15-61 (Taro); *Kung Fu*—"Alethea" 3-15-73 (Chinese Sergeant), "The Devil's Champion" 11-29-74 (Weapon Maker), "The Thief of Chendo" 3-29-75 (Palace Guard).

Isley, Phyllis. *see* Jones, Jennifer.

Israel, Victor (1929-). Films: "A Place Called Glory" 1966-Span./Ger. (Clerk); "Sugar Colt" 1966-Ital./Span.; "The Texican" 1966-U.S./Span. (Station Master); "Up the MacGregors!" 1967-Ital./Span. (Trevor, the Dentist); "White Comanche" 1967-Ital./Span./U.S.; "Yankee" 1967-Ital./Span.; "Pistol for a Hundred Coffins" 1968-Ital./Span.; "Killer Goodbye" 1969-Ital./Span.; "Companeros" 1970-Ital./Span./Ger.; "His Name Was Holy Ghost" 1970-Ital./Span.; "Forewarned, Half-Killed ... The Word of the Holy Ghost" 1971-Ital./Span. (the Preacher); "Return of Halleluja" 1972-Ital./Ger.; "What Am I Doing in the Middle of the Revolution?" 1973-Ital.; "Don't Turn the Other Cheek" 1974-Ital./Ger./Span.; "The White, the Yellow, and the Black" 1974-Ital./Span./Fr.

Ito, Robert (1931-). Films: "Kung Fu" TVM-1972 (Fong). ¶TV: *Kung Fu*—"The Assassin" 10-4-73 (Blacksmith), "The Raiders" 1-24-74 (Captain Lee); *How the West Was Won*—"China Girl" 4-16-79 (Chuk).

Ivar, Stan. Films: "Little House on the Prairie: Look Back to Yesterday" TVM-1983 (John Carter); "Little House: The Last Farewell" TVM-1984 (John Carter); "The Alamo: 13 Days to Glory" TVM-1987. ¶TV: *Little House: A New Beginning*—Regular 1982-83 (John Carter).

Ivers, Robert. Films: "Cattle King" 1963 (Webb Carter); "Town Tamer" 1965 (Vagrant). ¶TV: *Gunsmoke*—"Print Asper" 5-23-59 (Johnny Asper); *Tombstone Territory*—3-11-60 (Eddie Casper); *Bat Masterson*—"The Snare" 3-17-60 (the Yaqui Kid), "The Good and the Bad" 3-23-61 (Charley Boy); *The Virginian*—"The Payment" 12-16-64 (Vance Clayton).

Ives, Burl (1909-4/14/95). Films: "Smoky" 1946 (Bill); "Green Grass of Wyoming" 1948 (Gus); "Station West" 1948 (Hotel Clerk); "Sierra" 1950 (Lonesome); "The Big Country" 1958 (Rufus Hannassey); "Day of the Outlaw" 1959 (Jack Bruhn); "The McMasters" 1970 (Neal McMasters); "Baker's Hawk" 1976 (Mr. McGraw). ¶TV: *Zane Grey Theater*—"The Ox" 11-3-60 (Ox);

Daniel Boone—"A Tall Tale of Prater Beasely" 1-16-69 (Prater Beasley), "Love and Equity" 3-13-69 (Pratr Beasely); *Alias Smith and Jones*—"The McCreedy Bush" 1-21-71 (Big Mac), "The McCreedy Bust — Going, Going Gone" 1-13-72 (McCreedy), "Which Way to the O.K. Corral?" 2-10-72 (McCreedy), "The McCreedy Feud" 9-30-72 (McCreedy).

Ives, Kenneth (1934-). TV: *Masterpiece Theatre*—"The Last of the Mohicans" 1972 (Hawkeye).

Ivins, Perry (1895-8/22/63). Films: "Call of the Wild" 1935 (2nd Faro Player); "Red River Range" 1938 (Hartley); "Streets of Laredo" 1949 (Mayor Towson); "The Missourians" 1950 (Judge); "The Redhead and the Cowboy" 1951 (Mr. Barrett). ¶TV: *Wild Bill Hickok*—"Vigilante Story" 1-22-52; *Wagon Train*—"The Mark Hanford Story" 2-26-58 (Lawyer); *Black Saddle*—"The Long Rider" 10-16-59; *Have Gun Will Travel*—"The Lady on the Wall" 2-20-60 (Double G. Phillips); *Gunsmoke*—"Colleen So Green" 4-2-60 (Employee); *The Deputy*—"Last Gunfight" 4-30-60 (Haskins).

Ivo, Tommy (1936-). Films: "Song of Arizona" 1946 (Jimmy); "Smoky Mountain Melody" 1948 (Tommy Darkin); "Song of Idaho" 1948 (Junior); "Trail to Laredo" 1948; "Laramie" 1949 (Ronald Dennison, Jr.); "Outcasts of the Trail" 1949 (Chad White); "Horsemen of the Sierras" 1950 (Robin Grant); "Trail of the Rustlers" 1950; "Hills of Utah" 1951; "Snake River Desperadoes" 1951 (Billy); "Whirlwind" 1951 (Johnny Evans); "The Rough, Tough West" 1952 (Bill); "The Treasure of Lost Canyon" 1952 (David). ¶TV: *The Gene Autry Show*—"The Doodle Bug" 8-13-50; *Wild Bill Hickok*—"The Dog Collar Story" 7-17-51, "Johnny Deuce" 9-4-51, "Blake's Kid" 12-23-52; *The Adventures of Rin Tin Tin*—"The Gentle Kingdom" 6-7-57 (Josh); *26 Men*—"Bounty Hunter" 4-15-58; *The Tall Man*—"A Kind of Courage" 4-8-61 (Jody Latimer).

Izay, Victor (1923-). Films: "Billy Jack" 1971 (Doctor); "The Trial of Billy Jack" 1974 (Doc); "Little House on the Prairie: Look Back to Yesterday" TVM-1983 (Thomas Hall); "Young Guns" 1988 (Justice Wilson); "Gunsmoke: The Long Ride" TVM-1993 (Pastor Zach). ¶TV: *The Westerner*—"Brown" 10-21-60 (Bartender), "Treasure" 11-18-60; *The Rebel*—"The Promise" 1-15-61 (Abel Hawkins); *Gunsmoke*—"The

Storm" 9-25-65 (Bartender), "The Bounty Hunter" 10-30-65 (Bartender). "The Wrong Man" 10-29-66 (Dutch), "Luke" 11-2-70 (Bill), "The Scavengers" 11-16-70 (Barkeep), "The Legend" 10-18-71 (Bull), "The Boy and the Sinner" 10-1-73, "Like Old Times" 1-21-74 (Bull), "Thirty a Month a Found" 10-7-74 (Bull); *Branded*—"The Greatest Coward on Earth" 11-21-65 (Hotel Clerk), "Yellow for Courage" 2-20-66; *Cimarron Strip*—"The Deputy" 12-21-67; *Bonanza*—"The Twenty-Sixth Grave" 10-31-72 (Foreman).

Jaccard, Jacques (1886-7/24/60). Films: "Crossed Clues" 1921.

Jack, T.C. (1882-10/4/54). Films: "Daring Days" 1925 (Eli Carson); "Treason" 1933 (Buck Donohoe); "Wells Fargo" 1937; "Union Pacific" 1939 (Irish Paddy).

Jackie, William (1894-9/19/54). Films: "The Two Gun Man" 1931 (Monty).

Jackman, Jr., Fred. Films: "The Devil Horse" 1926 (Young Dave).

Jackson, Anne (1926-). Films: "Dirty Dingus Magee" 1970 (Belle). ¶TV: *Gunsmoke*—"Phoebe" 2-21-72 (Phoebe Preston).

Jackson, Barry. Films: "The Web of the Law" 1923 (Sundown Brown).

Jackson, Bradford. Films: "War Arrow" 1953 (Lieutenant). ¶TV: *Death Valley Days*—"Pay Dirt" 6-23-56 (MacGordon), "Mercer Girl" 2-10-57; *The Adventures of Rin Tin Tin*—"Forward Ho" 9-7-56 (Lt. Craig), "Sorrowful Joe Returns" 2-1-57 (Bart Grew); *Circus Boy*—"The Masked Marvel" 12-9-56 (Billy Stanton); *The Lone Ranger*—"The Angel and the Outlaw" 5-23-57.

Jackson, Ethel (1883-7/27/52). Films: "Six Gun Justice" 1935; "The Vanishing Riders" 1935 (Joan Stanley).

Jackson, Eugene. Films: "Cimarron" 1931 (Isaiah); "Tumbling Tumbleweeds" 1935 (Eightball); "Guns and Guitars" 1936 (Eightball); "The Lonely Trail" 1936 (Dancer); "Red River Valley" 1936 (Iodine).

Jackson, Jr., Eugene. Films: "Shenandoah" 1965 (Gabriel).

Jackson, Freda (1909-10/20/90). Films: "The Valley of Gwangi" 1969 (Tia Zorina).

Jackson, Jenie (1921-3/14/76). Films: "Ride the High Country" 1962 (Kate). ¶TV: *Wild Wild West*—"The Night of the Bars of Hell" 3-4-66 (Kitten), "The Night of the Murderous Spring" 4-15-66 (Kitten Twitty).

Jackson, Kate (1949-). TV: *Bonanza*—"One Ace Too Many" 4-2-72 (Ellen).

Jackson, Mary (1910-). Films: "Friendly Persuasion" 1956 (Country Woman); "Wild Rovers" 1971 (Sada's Mother); "Kid Blue" 1973 (Mrs. Evans). ¶TV: *Stoney Burke*—"Five by Eight" 12-10-62 (Matty); *Lancer*—"Child of Rock and Sunlight" 4-1-69 (Hotel Keeper), "Jelly Hoskins' American Dream" 11-11-69.

Jackson, Peaches. Films: "Lahoma" 1920 (Lahoma as a Child); "Rio Grande" 1920 (Maria at Age 6); "While Justice Waits" 1922 (Daughter).

Jackson, Sammy (1937-4/25/95). Films: "The Fabulous Texan" 1947; "The Night of the Grizzly" 1966 (Cal Curry); "The Fastest Guitar Alive" 1967 (Steve). ¶TV: *Sugarfoot*—"Short Range" 5-13-58 (Leonard Ryan); *The Adventures of Rin Tin Tin*—"Apache Stampede" 3-20-59 (Bill Masters); *Maverick*—"Trooper Maverick" 11-29-59 (Albert Heaven), "Greenbacks Unlimited" 3-13-60 (Junior Kallikak), "A Bullet for the Teacher" 10-30-60 (Walter Burch); *G.E. Theater*—"Aftermath" 4-17-60 (Galoot); *Temple Houston*—"The Guardian" 1-2-64 (Sodbuster), "Miss Katherina" 4-2-64 (Wick); *The Virginian*—"Jed" 1-10-68 (Ron Kiefer).

Jackson, Selmer (1888-3/30/71). Films: "South of the Border" 1939 (Consul); "Stand Up and Fight" 1939 (Whittingham Talbot); "Union Pacific" 1939 (Jerome); "Brigham Young—Frontiersman" 1940 (Caleb Kent); "The Man from Dakota" 1940 (Surgeon); "Santa Fe Trail" 1940 (Officer); "Wagons Westward" 1940 (Major Marlowe); "The Shepherd of the Hills" 1941 (Doctor); "They Died with Their Boots On" 1941 (Capt. McCook); "Sheriff of Las Vegas" 1944; "Dakota" 1945 (Dr. Judson); "Royal Mounted Rides Again" 1945-serial (Superintendent MacDonald); "Renegades of the Sage" 1949 (Brown); "Gunmen of Abilene" 1950 (Dr. Johnson); "Buckaroo Sheriff of Texas" 1951 (Governor); "Jack McCall, Desperado" 1953 (Col. Braud). ¶TV: *Wyatt Earp*—"Dodge City Gets a New Marshal" 9-4-56 (Town Councilman), "A Quiet Day in Dodge City" 10-9-56 (Mayor Hoover), "The Lonesomest Man in the World" 11-27-56 (Mayor Hoover), "Take Back Your Town" 12-4-56 (Mayor Hoover), "They Hired Some Guns" 2-26-57 (Mayor Hoover); *The Adventures of Rin Tin Tin*—"Return to Fort Apache" 9-20-57 (General);

The Restless Gun—"Remember the Dead" 11-17-58 (Judge Wayne); *Bonanza*—"Elizabeth, My Love" 5-27-61, "Gabrielle" 12-24-61.

Jackson, Sherry (1942-). Films: "Covered Wagon Raid" 1950 (Susie); "The Lion and the Horse" 1952 (Jenny); "Wild Women" TVM-1970 (Nancy Delacourt). ¶TV: *The Gene Autry Show*—"The Kid Comes West" 12-8-51, "Rocky River Feud" 1-18-52; *The Roy Rogers Show*—"The Unwilling Outlaw" 3-8-52 (Lucy Collins); *Maverick*—"Naked Gallows" 12-15-57 (Annie Haines), "Red Dog" 3-5-61 (Erma); *The Rifleman*—"The Sister" 11-25-58 (Rebecca Snipe); *Riverboat*—"The Water of Gorgeous Springs" 11-7-60 (Inez Cox); *The Tall Man*—"Apache Daughter" 12-30-61 (White Moon); *Gunsmoke*—"Lacey" 1-13-62 (Lacey Parcher), "Root Down" 10-6-62 (Aggie Dutton); *Wagon Train*—"The Geneva Balfour Story" 1-20-64; *Rawhide*—"Moment in the Sun" 1-29-65; *The Virginian*—"Show Me a Hero" 11-17-65 (Lois Colter); *Branded*—"Barbed Wire" 2-13-66 (Nell Beckwith); *Death Valley Days*—"Lady of the Plains" 7-23-66 (Kate Turner); *Wild Wild West*—"The Night of the Vicious Valentine" 2-10-67 (Michelle LeMaster), "The Night of the Gruesome Games" 10-25-68 (Lola Cortez); *Barbary Coast*—"Crazy Cats" 9-15-75 (Sherry).

Jackson, Thomas (1886-9/8/7). Films: "Call of the Wild" 1935 (Tex Rickard); "Blazing Across the Pecos" 1948; "The Lawless Breed" 1952 (McNelly). ¶TV: *Have Gun Will Travel*—"The Trial" 6-11-60; *The Tall Man*—"One of One Thousand" 12-31-60 (Jaeggar); *The Loner*—"Escort for a Dead Man" 12-18-65 (Old Man).

Jackson, Valerie. Films: "Law and Order" 1953 (Clarissa); "Take Me to Town" 1953 (Dancehall Girl).

Jackson, Warren (1893-5/10/50). Films: "Call the Mesquiteers" 1938 (Mac); "Hollywood Roundup" 1938 (Perry King); "Mexican Spitfire Out West" 1940 (Stranger); "The Gunman from Bodie" 1941; "Alaska" 1944; "Under Western Skies" 1945 (Young Buck); "Trail Street" 1947 (Henchman); "Coroner Creek" 1948 (Ray Flanders); "Return of the Badmen" 1948 (George Mason); "Montana" 1950 (Curley Bennett).

Jacobi, Lou (1913-). TV: *The Texan*—"The Peddler" 1-26-59 (Joseph Varga).

Jacobsson, Ulla (1929-8/20/82). TV: *The Virginian*—"The Final Hour" 5-1-63 (Polcia).

Jacques, Ted. Films: "Powder River Rustlers" 1949 (Blacksmith); "Western Pacific Agent" 1950; "Flaming Star" 1960 (Hornsby); "Black Patch" 1957 (Maxton). ¶TV: *Sergeant Preston of the Yukon*—"Phantom of Phoenixville" 1-26-56 (Big Red Brawley), "Lost Patrol" 10-18-56 (Pete Dexter), "The Williwaw" 12-20-56 (Abel Frame); *Rough Riders*—"Killers at Chocktaw Valley" 12-4-58 (Charles Darke); *Bat Masterson*—"Buffalo Kills" 7-29-59 (J.J. Carver); *Gunsmoke*—"Durham Bull" 3-31-62 (Brakeman); *The Tall Man*—"A Time to Run" 4-7-62 (Hank Boudine); *The Legend of Jesse James*—"The Hunted and the Hunters" 4-11-66 (Mitchum).

Jacquet, Frank (1885-5/11/58). Films: "Shine on Harvest Moon" 1938 (Homer Sheldon); "Stand Up and Fight" 1939 (Bartender); "Call of the Canyon" 1942; "In Old California" 1942; "Raiders of the Range" 1942 (Sam Daggett); "Beneath Western Skies" 1944 (Samuel Webster); "Call of the Rockies" 1944; "Silver City Kid" 1944; "Beyond the Pecos" 1945; "The Cherokee Flash" 1945; "Colorado Pioneers" 1945; "In Old New Mexico" 1945; "Oregon Trail" 1945 (George Layton); "Santa Fe Saddlemates" 1945; "The Topeka Terror" 1945 (Trent Parker); "Trail to Vengeance" 1945 (Foster Felton); "The Daring Caballero" 1949 (Judge Perkins); "Riders in the Sky" 1949 (Coroner); "King of the Bullwhip" 1950; "Mule Train" 1950 (Clayton Hodges); "Outlaw Gold" 1950; "Over the Border" 1950 (Doc Foster); "Six Gun Mesa" 1950; "Winning of the West" 1953 (Manager). ¶TV: *The Lone Ranger*—"Bullets for Ballots" 5-11-50; *The Roy Rogers Show*—"Haunted Mine of Paradise Valley" 5-18-52; *The Gene Autry Show*—"Outlaw Stage" 7-21-53.

Jaeckel, Richard (1926-). Films: "The Gunfighter" 1950 (Eddie); "Wyoming Mail" 1950 (Nafe); "Apache Ambush" 1955 (Lee Parker); "The Violent Men" 1955 (Wade Matlock); "3:10 to Yuma" 1957 (Charlie Prince); "Cowboy" 1958 (Paul Curtis); "Flaming Star" 1960 (Angus Pierce); "Four for Texas" 1964 (Mancini); "Town Tamer" 1965 (Honsinger); "Chisum" 1970 (Evans); "Ulzana's Raid" 1972 (Sergeant); "Pat Garrett and Billy the Kid" 1973 (Sheriff Kip McKinney); "Go West, Young Girl" TVM-1978 (Billy). ¶TV: *Stories of the Century*—"Billy the Kid" 4-1-55; *Luke and the Tenderfoot*—Pilot 8-6-55 & 8-13-55 (Hardin's Sidekick); *Cimarron City*—"The Bloodline" 12-13-58 (Webb Martin); *The*

Texan—"The Man Behind the Star" 2-9-59 (Clint Gleason); *Trackdown*—"The Protector" 4-1-59 (Frank Wilson); *Zane Grey Theater*—"Man in the Middle" 2-11-60 (Tod Mulvey); *Tales of Wells Fargo*—"The Kinfolk" 9-26-60 (Len Lassiter); *The Rebel*—"Run, Killer, Run" 10-30-60 (Traskel); *The Tall Man*—"The Grudge Fight" 1-21-61 (Denver); *Lawman*—"Blue Boss and Willie Shay" 3-12-61 (Al Janaker); *Wagon Train*—"The Chalice" 5-24-61 (Barker), "The Lily Legend Story" 2-13-63 (Piper); *Frontier Circus*—Regular 1961-62 (Tony Gentry); *Have Gun Will Travel*—"The Predators" 11-3-62; *The Dakotas*—"Fargo" 2-25-63 (Cal Storm); *Gunsmoke*—"Two of a Kind" 3-16-63 (Sean O'Ryan), "The Raid" 1-22-66 & 1-29-66 (Pence Fraley), "Larkin" 1-20-75 (Larkin); *Temple Houston*—"The Case for William Gotch" 2-6-64 (Coley); *The Virginian*—"A Matter of Destiny" 2-19-64 (Pat Wade); *Bonanza*—"Between Heaven and Earth" 11-15-64 (Mitch), "Night of Reckoning" 10-15-67 (Dibbs); *Wild Wild West*—"The Night of the Grand Emir" 1-28-66 (Christopher Cable), "The Night of the Cadre" 3-24-67 (Sgt. Stryker); *Walt Disney Presents*—"Kit Carson and the Mountain Men" 1-9-77 & 1-16-77 (Ed Kern); *Big Hawaii*—"You Can't Lose 'Em All" 11-30-77 (Cal Seward).

Jaffe, Allen (1928-3/18/89). Films: "The Firebrand" 1962 (Torres). ¶TV: *Bat Masterson*—"A Picture of Death" 1-14-60 (Colman), "Law of the Land" 10-6-60 (Wolff), "Death by Decree" 12-22-60 (Bolo), "A Lesson in Violence" 2-23-61 (Cross); *Wanted—Dead or Alive*—"The Twain Shall Meet" 10-19-60 (Sid Gonda); *Death Valley Days*—"The White Healer" 11-30-60 (Hamaz), *Wagon Train*—"The River Crossing" 12-14-60; *Rawhide*—"Incident of the Captive" 12-16-60; *Gunslinger*—"Rampage" 3-16-61 (Waldhorn)."The Red Petticoat" 3-29-61; *Tales of Wells Fargo*—"Incident at Crossbow" 2-3-62 (Case); *The Dakotas*—"Trouble at French Creek" 1-28-63 (Foster); *Gunsmoke*—"Winner Take All" 2-20-65 (Gunman), "Seven Hours to Dawn" 9-18-65 (Jack Dawn), "Clayton Thaddeus Greenwood" 10-2-65 (Webster), "The Pretender" 11-20-65 (John Neers), "The Whispering Tree" 11-12-66 (Ryan), "The Pillagers" 11-6-67 (Johns), "MacGraw" 12-8-69 (Ed Crawford), "The Cage" 3-23-70 (Gresley); *Branded*—"Coward Step Aside" 3-7-65 (Topaz); *The Big Valley*—"Forty Rifles" 9-22-65 (Cota); *The Loner*—"The Ordeal of Bud

Windom" 12-25-65 (Sid Loomis); *Wild Wild West*—"The Night of the Steel Assassin" 1-7-66 (Guthrie), "The Night of the Braine" 2-17-67 (Leeto); *Shane*—"The Wild Geese" 9-24-66 (Casey Driscoll); *Laredo*—"Road to San Remo" 11-25-66; *Iron Horse*—"Dry Run to Glory" 1-6-68 (Dink); *Here Come the Brides*—"A Hard Card to Play" 10-23-68 (Bear); *The Guns of Will Sonnett*—"Time Is the Rider" 1-10-69 (Charlie).

Jaffe, Chappelle. Films: "Silence of the North" 1981 (John's Girlfriend).

Jaffe, Robert. Films: "The Magnificent Seven Ride" 1972 (Bob Allan).

Jaffe, Sam (1897-3/24/84). Films: "Guns for San Sebastian" 1967-U.S./Fr./Mex./Ital. (Father Joseph); "The Great Bank Robbery" 1969 (Brother Lilac); "Sam Hill: Who Killed the Mysterious Mr. Foster?" TVM-1971 (Toby). ¶TV: *The Westerner*—"The Old Man" 11-25-60 (Old Man McKeen); *Daniel Boone*—"The First Beau" 12-9-65 (Jed Tolson); *Bonanza*—"The Emperor Norton" 2-27-66 (Emperor Norton); *Alias Smith and Jones*—"The Great Shell Game" 2-18-71 (Dr. Sylvester), "A Fistful of Diamonds" 3-4-71 (Soapy Saunders), "Bad Night in Big Butte" 3-2-72.

Jagger, Dean (1903-2/5/91). Films: "Home on the Range" 1935 (Boyd Thurman); "Wanderer of the Wasteland" 1935 (Adam Larey); "Brigham Young—Frontiersman" 1940 (Brigham Young); "Western Union" 1941 (Edward Creighton); "The Omaha Trail" 1942 (Pipestone Ross); "Valley of the Sun" 1942 (Jim Sawyer); "Alaska" 1944; "Pursued" 1947 (Gran Callum); "Sierra" 1950 (Jeff Hassard); "Rawhide" 1951 (Yancy); "Warpath" 1951 (Storekeeper Sam Quade); "Denver and Rio Grande" 1952 (General Palmer); "Bad Day at Black Rock" 1955 (Tim Horn); "Red Sundown" 1956 (Sheriff Jade Murphy); "Forty Guns" 1957 (Ned Logan); "The Proud Rebel" 1958 (Harry Burleigh); "Day of the Evil Gun" 1968 (Jimmy Noble); "Firecreek" 1968 (Whittier); "Smith" 1969 (Judge); "The Hanged Man" TVM-1974 (Josiah Lowe). ¶TV: *Zane Grey Theater*—"They Were Four" 3-15-57 (Bert); *Bonanza*—"Shadow of a Hero" 2-21-71 (Gen. Ira Cloninger); *Kung Fu*—"Dark Angel" 11-11-72 (Henry Caine); *Alias Smith and Jones*—"Only Three to a Bed" 1-13-73 (Mark Tisdale).

Jagger, Mick (1939-). Films: "Ned Kelly" 1970-Brit. (Ned Kelly).

Jak, Lisa. TV: *The Monroes*—"Incident at Hanging Tree" 10-12-66 (Lorna Wales), "Silent Night, Deathly Night" 11-23-66 (Lorna Wales), "Race for the Rainbow" 1-18-67 (Lorna Wales); *Lancer*—"The High Riders" 9-24-68.

Jalbert, Pierre (1925-). TV: *Custer*—"Suspicion" 10-18-67 (Auguste Grule).

James, Alf (1865-10/9/46). Films: "White Eagle" 1932; "The Thrill Hunter" 1933 (Mesbit); "Unknown Valley" 1933; "The Fighting Code" 1934 (Judge Williams); "Rocky Rhodes" 1934 (John Street); "The Singing Cowboy" 1936 (Justice of Peace).

James, Anne. Films: "Barbed Wire" 1952 (Cay Kendall).

James, Anthony (1942-). Films: "Sam Whiskey" 1969 (Cousin Leroy); "The Culpepper Cattle Company" 1972 (Nathaniel); "High Plains Drifter" 1973 (Cole Carlin); "Hearts of the West" 1975 (Lean Crook); "Ransom for Alice!" TVM-1977 (James); "Unforgiven" 1992 (Skinny Dubois). ¶TV: *The Big Valley*—"Ladykiller" 10-16-67 (Bart Bleeck), "Danger Road" 4-21-69 (Samuels); *The High Chaparral*—"The Fillibusteros" 10-22-67 (Harley Deever); *Gunsmoke*—"Hard Luck Henry" 10-23-67 (Reb Dooley), "Hill Girl" 1-29-68 (Elbert Moses), "Uncle Finney" 10-14-68 (Elbert Moses), "O'Quillian" 10-28-68 (Chickenfoot), "The Gold Mine" 1-27-69 (Elbert Moses), "The Still" 11-10-69 (Elbert Moses), "The Innocent" 11-24-69 (Loyal Yewker); *Cimarron Strip*—"The Deputy" 12-21-67 (Benji); *Bonanza*—"The Imposters" 12-13-70 (Willie); *Outlaws*—"Hymn" 1-31-87 (Joshua).

James, Brion (1945-). Films: "The Ballad of Gregorio Cortez" 1983 (Capt. Rogers); "The Gambler, Part II—The Adventure Continues" TVM-1983 (Reece); "Desperado: The Outlaw Wars" TVM-1989 (Grimes); "Rio Diablo" TVM-1993 (Jake Walker). ¶TV: *Gunsmoke*—"Manolo" 3-17-75 (Joe Barnes).

James, Claire (1920-1/18/86). Films: "Saddle Serenade" 1945.

James, Clifton (1921-). Films: "Invitation to a Gunfighter" 1964 (Tuttle); "Will Penny" 1968 (Catron); "Kid Blue" 1973 (Mr. Hendricks); "Friendly Persuasion" TVM-1975 (Sam Jordan); "Rancho Deluxe" 1975 (John Brown). ¶TV: *Gunsmoke*—"Letter of the Law" 10-11-58 (Brandon Teek), "The Lady" 3-27-65 (Sam Hare), "The Wrong Man" 10-29-66 (Tenner Jackson), "Snow Train" 10-19-70 & 10-26-70 (Sam Wickes); *The Virginian*—"Linda" 11-30-66 (Big Ben Albright); *Cimarron Strip*—"Till the End of the Night" 11-16-67 (Sheriff Hawkes); *Bonanza*—"The Real People of Muddy Creek" 10-6-68 (Lawson), "Winter Kill" 3-28-71 (Mr. Quarry); *Young Maverick*—"A Fistful of Oats" 12-5-79 (Judge Stebbins).

James, Gardner (1903-6/23/53). Films: "Silent Sanderson" 1925 (Art Parsons); "The Flaming Forest" 1926 (Roger Audemard); "The Great Meadow" 1931 (Joe Tandy); "Adventures of Red Ryder" 1940-Serial (H.S. Barnett).

James, Gladden (1892-8/28/48). Films: "The Heart of Wetona" 1919 (Tony Wells); "Channing of the Northwest" 1922 (Jim Franey); "Marry in Haste" 1924 (Monte Brett); "Tex" 1926; "Driftin Sands" 1928 (Benton); "Branded Men" 1931.

James, Harry (1916-7/5/83). Films: "Outlaw Queen" 1957.

James, J. Wharton. Films: "Wild and Woolly" 1917; "The Mysterious Witness" 1923 (Jim Garland).

James, James. Films: "Westward Ho" 1942 (Jimmy Henderson); "Hidden Valley Outlaws" 1944; "The Wild Frontier" 1947 (Jimmy Lane).

James, Jr., Jesse (1876-3/26/51). Films: "Jesse James as the Outlaw" 1921 (Jesse James, Jr./Jesse James); "Jesse James Under the Black Flag" 1921 (Jese James, Jr./Jesse James).

James, John (1914-5/20/60). Films: "King of the Texas Rangers" 1941-serial (Dave); "Outlaws of the Cherokee Trail" 1941; "West of Cimarron" 1941; "The Cyclone Kid" 1942 (Dr. Dawson); "The Sombrero Kid" 1942 (Tommy Holden); "The Man from Thunder River" 1943; "Riders of the Rio Grande" 1943; "Santa Fe Scouts" 1943 (Tim Clay); "Thundering Trails" 1943; "Beneath Western Skies" 1944; "Bordertown Trail" 1944; "The Laramie Trail" 1944; "Great Stagecoach Robbery" 1945; "Lonesome Trail" 1945; "Renegades of the Rio Grande" 1945 (Johnny Emerson); "Riders of the Dawn" 1945 (Dusty); "Saddle Serenade" 1945; "Homesteaders of Paradise Valley" 1947; "Ridin' Down the Trail" 1947; "Song of the Wasteland" 1947; "Outlaw Brand" 1948; "Range Renegades" 1948; "The Valiant Hombre" 1948 (Paul Mason); "Gun Law Justice" 1949; "Son of Billy the Kid" 1949 (Colt); "Topeka" 1953 (Marv Ronsom); "Vigilante Terror" 1953.

James, Kyle. *see* Anderson, James.

James, Lisa. TV: *Laredo*—"A Question of Guilt" 3-10-67 (Adeline Foster).

James, Ralph (1924-3/14/92). TV: *Gunsmoke*—"The Money Store" 12-30-68, "The Intruders" 3-3-69 (Hall); *Bonanza*—"The Lady and the Mark" 2-1-70 (Alderman), "A Deck of Aces" 1-31-71 (1st Poker Player), "Rock-a-Bye, Hoss" 10-10-71 (Gambler).

James, Rosemond. Films: "Along the Navajo Trail" 1945; "Bells of Rosarita" 1945; "The Man from Oklahoma" 1945.

James, Sidney (1913-4/26/76). Films: "The Sheriff of Fractured Jaw" 1958-Brit. (the Drunk).

James, Vera. Films: "McGuire of the Mounted" 1923 (Katie Peck).

James, Walter (1886-6/27/46). Films: "The Seventh Bandit" 1926 (Ben Goring); "Hell's Heroes" 1930 (Sheriff); "Arizona Bad Man" 1935 (Cowboy); "Custer's Last Stand" 1936-serial (Judge Hooker); "Oh, Susanna!" 1936; "White Fang" 1936 (Posse Member); "The Lone Ranger" 1938-serial (Joe Cannon); "Adventures of Red Ryder" 1940-serial (Judge #2).

Jameson, Adair. Films: "Cain's Way" 1969 (Cain's Girl); "Smoke in the Wind" 1975 (Hannah). ¶TV: *Laredo*—"The Golden Trail" 11-4-65 (Flame Burns); *Gunsmoke*—"Wishbone" 2-19-66 (Stage Passenger).

Jameson, Joyce (1932-1/16/87). Films: "Run, Simon, Run" TVM-1970 (Clarice); "The Outlaw Josey Wales" 1976 (Rose); "The Wild Wild West Revisited" TVM-1979 (Lola). ¶TV: *The Cisco Kid*—"Roundup" 4-17-54; *Yancy Derringer*—"Gone But Not Forgotten" 5-28-59 (Bonnie Mason); *Stagecoach West*—"Come Home Again" 1-10-61 (Angie La Jay); *The Outlaws*—"The Dark Sunrise of Griff Kincaid" 1-4-62 (Lotus); *Gunsmoke*—"The Summons" 4-21-62 (Pearl); *The Big Valley*—"The Haunted Gun" 2-6-67 (Blonde); *F Troop*—"Marriage, Fort Courage Style" 3-9-67 (Sally Tyler); *The Virginian*—"The Long Ride Home" 9-17-69 (Millie); *Alias Smith and Jones*—"The Reformation of Harry Briscoe" 11-11-71 (Madge); *Barbary Coast*—"Guns for a Queen" 10-6-75 (Mame).

Jamison, Bob. Films: "Lawless Riders" 1935; "Vigilantes Are Coming" 1936-serial (Rancher); "Zorro Rides Again" 1937-serial; "Adventures

of Red Ryder" 1940-serial (Gus); "King of the Royal Mounted" 1940-serial (Pete); "King of the Texas Rangers" 1941-serial (Dam Guard); "King of the Mounties" 1942-serial (Pete); "Canadian Mounties vs. Atomic Invaders" 1953-serial.

Jamison, Bud (1894-9/30/44). Films: "A Texas Steer" 1927 (Othello); "The Fugitive Sheriff" 1936; "Heroes of the Range" 1936; "The Unknown Ranger" 1936; "Whoops, I'm an Indian" 1936-short (Pierre); "Back to the Woods" 1937-short (Prosecutor); "Melody of the Plains" 1937 (Cook); "Pest from the West" 1939-short; "Teacher's Pest" 1939-short; "Phony Express" 1943-short (Red Morgan).

Jan and Dean (Jan Berry & Dean Torrence). TV: *Redigo*—"Papa-San" 11-12-63.

Janes, Enid. TV: *Wichita Town*—"Bought" 1-13-60 (Thursday); *Wyatt Earp*—"My Enemy—John Behan" 5-31-60; *Wanted—Dead or Alive*—"Epitaph" 2-8-61 (Martha Boyd).

Janis, Conrad (1926-). Films: "The Duchess and the Dirtwater Fox" 1976 (Gladstone). ¶TV: *Zane Grey Theater*—"The Long Road Home" 10-19-56 (Ben Gracie); *Stoney Burke*—"A Matter of Pride" 11-5-62 (Penn Hudson).

Janis, Dorothy. Films: "Kit Carson" 1928 (Sings-in-the-Clouds); "The Overland Telegraph" 1929 (Dorothy).

Janiss, Vivi (1923-9/7/88). TV: *Gunsmoke*—"The Cover-Up" 1-12-57 (Sara Baxton); *Trackdown*—"The Kid" 12-12-58 (Summer York); *Wagon Train*—"The Kitty Angel Story" 1-7-59 (Cassie Holden), "The Dick Jarvis Story" 5-18-60 (Mrs. Jarvis), "The Cathy Eckhardt Story" 11-9-60 (Sarah), "The Nancy Palmer Story" 3-8-61 (Madge), "The Saul Bevins Story" 4-12-61 (Martha), "The Terry Morrell Story" 4-25-62 (Letty Morse); *Lawman*—"The Visitor" 3-15-59 (Mrs. Welch); *Tales of Wells Fargo*—"End of a Legend" 11-23-59 (Elsie); *Laramie*—"Ride the Wild Wind" 10-11-60 (Hanna Moore); *The Outlaws*—"Shorty" 11-3-60 (Chloe Duane); *Have Gun Will Travel*—"The Exiles" 1-27-62 (Countess Casares); *The Virginian*—"The Devil's Children" 12-5-62 (Ivy Flood), "The Girl on the Pinto" 3-29-67 (Miriam Harley).

Jann, Gerald. Films: "Red Tomahawk" 1967 (Wu Sing). ¶TV: *Kung Fu*—"The Devil's Champion" 11-29-74 (Village Inn Man).

Janney, Leon (Laon Ramon) (1917-10/28/80). Films: "The Wind" 1928 (Cora's Child).

Janney, William. Films: "Cimarron" 1931 (Worker); "The King of the Wild Horses" 1933 (Red Wolf); "Hopalong Cassidy Returns" 1936 (Buddy Cassidy); "Sutter's Gold" 1936 (John Sutter, Jr.).

Jans, Harry (1900-2/4/62). Films: "The Last Outlaw" 1936 (Joe); "Two in Revolt" 1936 (Crane).

Janssen, David (1931-2/13/80). Films: "Chief Crazy Horse" 1955 (Lt. Cartwright); "Showdown at Abilene" 1956 (Verne Ward); "Macho Callahan" 1970 (Diego "Macho" Callahan); "Pioneer Woman" TVM-1973 (Robert Douglas). ¶TV: *Sheriff of Cochise*—"The Farmers" 9-21-56 (Arnie Hix); *Zane Grey Theater*—"They Were Four" 3-15-57 (Danny Ensign), "Trial by Fear" 1-20-58 (Tod Owen), "Trail to Nowhere" 10-2-58 (Seth Larker), "Hang the Heart High" 1-15-59 (Dix Porter); *You Are There*—"The End of the Dalton Gang" 5-12-57 (Grat Dalton); *Death Valley Days*—"Deadline at Austin" 2-8-61 (Bill Breckinridge); *Centennial*—Regular 1978-79 (Paul Garrett/Narrator).

Janssen, Eilene (1937-). Films: "Renegades" 1946 (Janina Jackorski); "Arizona Manhunt" 1951 (Judy); "Buckaroo Sheriff of Texas" 1951 (Judy Dawson); "The Dakota Kid" 1951 (Judy); "Wild Horse Ambush" 1952 (Judy); "Escape from Red Rock" 1958 (Janie Acker). ¶TV: *The Gene Autry Show*—"T.N.T." 12-31-50, "Ghost Mountain" 7-28-53; *Tales of Wells Fargo*—"Shotgun Messenger" 5-6-57 (Julie Taylor), "The Kid" 11-18-57 (Julie Taylor); *Sugarfoot*—"Mule Team" 6-10-58 (Nancy Boggs).

January, Bob. TV: *Tate*—"Voices of the Town" 7-6-60 (Frank Turner); *Wanted—Dead or Alive*—"The Trial" 9-21-60.

January, Lois. Films: "Arizona Bad Man" 1935 (Lucy Dunstan); "Skull and Crown" 1935 (Barbara Franklin); "Border Caballero" 1936 (Goldie Ralph); "Lightning Bill Carson" 1936 (Dolores); "Rogue of the Range" 1936 (Stella Lamb); "Bar Z Bad Men" 1937 (Beth Harvey); "Courage of the West" 1937 (Beth Andrews); "Lightnin' Crandall" 1937 (Sheila Shannon); "Moonlight on the Range" 1937 (Wanda Brooks); "The Red Rope" 1937 (Betty Duncan); "The Roaming Cowboy" 1937 (Jeanie); "The Trusted Outlaw" 1937 (Molly).

Jara, Maurice. Films: "Pals of

the Golden West" 1951 (Lopez); "The Nebraskan" 1953 (Wingfoot); "Jubilee Trail" 1954 (Vaquero); "They Rode West" 1954 (Spotted Wolf); "Giant" 1956 (Dr. Guerra); "Walk the Proud Land" 1956 (Alchise); "The Lone Ranger and the Lost City of Gold" 1958 (Redbird); "They Came to Cordura" 1959 (Mexican Federale); "Powderkeg" TVM-1971. ¶TV: *The Lone Ranger*—"The Condemned Man" 12-11-52, "Enfield Rifle" 1-13-55, "The Courage of Tonto" 1-17-57; *Death Valley Days*—"The Saint's Portrait" 10-11-54 (Felipe); *Broken Arrow*—"Apache Dowry" 1-15-57 (Oreste); *Rawhide*—"Incident of the Day of the Dead" 9-18-59; *Lawman*—"The Surface of Truth" 4-17-60 (Tonkawa); *Bonanza*—"The Savage" 12-3-60 (Tolka).

Jarman, Jr., Claude (1934-). Films: "Roughshod" 1949 (Steve); "The Outriders" 1950 (Roy Gort); "Rio Grande" 1950 (Trooper Jeff Yorke); "Inside Straight" 1951 (Rip MacCool at Age 16); "Hangman's Knot" 1952 (Jamie Groves); "The Great Locomotive Chase" 1956 (Jacob Parrott). ¶TV: *Centennial*—Regular 1978-79 (Earl Grebe).

Jarmyn, Jill. Films: "Lay That Rifle Down" 1955 (Betty); "The Twinkle in God's Eye" 1955 (Millie); "War Drums" 1957 (Nona); "Man or Gun" 1958 (Mrs. Pinch Corley). ¶TV: *Death Valley Days*—"The Diamond Babe" 10-28-53; "The Invaders" 3-17-59 (Lucia); *Cheyenne*—"Born Bad" 3-26-57 (Francy); *Broken Arrow*—"Apache Child" 10-15-57 (Sanza).

Jarrett, Art (1884-6/12/60). Films: "Trigger Pals" 1939 (Lucky Morgan).

Jarrett, Dan (1894-3/13/38). Films: "Cowboy Millionaire" 1935 (Edward Doyle).

Jarvis, Francesca. Films: "The Life and Times of Judge Roy Bean" 1972 (Mrs. Jackson); "High Noon, Part II: The Return of Will Kane" TVM-1980 (Mrs. Garver). ¶TV: *The High Chaparral*—"For What We Are About to Receive" 11-29-68 (Martha Carter); *Gunsmoke*—"Women for Sale" 9-10-73 & 9-17-73, "A Town in Chains" 9-16-74 (Martha); *Young Riders*—"Born to Hang" 9-22-90 (Helga).

Jarvis, Graham (1930-). Films: "The New Maverick" TVM-1978 (Lambert, the Undertaker); "Draw" CTVM-1984 (Willy Blodgett). ¶TV: *Gunsmoke*—"The Sharecroppers" 3-31-75 (Rupert Silverton); *Father Mur-*

phy—"State Aid" 12-15-81 (Simpson); *Paradise*—"See No Evil" 2-22-91 (Gus).

Jarvis, Jean (1903-3/16/33). Films: "Fear-Bound" 1925 (Fluffy Ralston).

Jarvis, Sam. TV: *The Big Valley*—"The River Monarch" 4-6-66 (Sam Jorter); *The High Chaparral*—"It Takes a Smart Man" 10-23-70; *Bonanza*—"The Lady and the Mark" 2-1-70 (Walt), "A Deck of Aces" 1-31-71 (Telegraph Operator), "Shanklin" 2-13-72 (McLaughlin), "The Initiation" 9-26-72 (Bailiff).

Jarvis, Sidney (1881-6/6/39). Films: "The Prairie King" 1927 (Jim Gardner); "The Upland Rider" 1928 (Ross Cheswick); "The Wagon Show" 1928 (Sayre); "The Plainsman" 1936 (Gideon Welles); "The Bad Man of Brimstone" 1937 (Jury Foreman); "Wild and Woolly" 1937 (Referee).

Jasmin, Paul. TV: *Have Gun Will Travel*—"Three Sons" 5-10-58 (Hank Bosworth); *Zane Grey Theater*—"Trail Incident" 1-29-59 (Tom Brannigan); *The Rifleman*—"The Legacy" 12-8-59 (Alison Mitchell); *Wyatt Earp*—"Roscoe Turns Detective" 5-3-60 (Louis Vanik).

Jasmine, Arthur. Films: "Broncho Billy's Parents" 1915; "Lasca" 1919 (Ricardo); "The Son of the Wolf" 1922 (the Fox); "Lure of the Yukon" 1924 (Kuyak).

Jason, Harvey (1940-). Films: "Oklahoma Crude" 1973 (Wilcox). ¶TV: *Cowboy in Africa*—"John Henry's Eden" 3-18-68 (Albert); *The Outcasts*—"And Then There Was One" 3-3-69 (Limey).

Jason, Peter (1944-). Films: "Rio Lobo" 1970 (Lt. Forsythe); "The Long Riders" 1980; "Sunset" 1988 (Frank Coe). ¶TV: *Cimarron Strip*—"The Assassin" 1-11-68, "The Greeners" 3-7-68 (David Arlyn); *Here Come the Brides*—"None to a Customer" 2-19-69 (Adam Wilson); *Daniel Boone*—"Bickford's Bridge" 2-20-69 (Clint); *Gunsmoke*—"The Judas Gun" 1-19-70 (Culy Haimes), "Gentry's Law" 10-12-70 (Colt Gentry), "Talbot" 2-26-73 (Bob Pope); *Dr. Quinn, Medicine Woman*—"Crossing the Line" 1-1-94 (Stone).

Jason, Rick (1923-). Films: "Sierra Baron" 1958 (Miguel Delmonte). ¶TV: *Stories of the Century*—"Joaquin Murieta" 6-17-55; *Rawhide*—"Incident of the Coyote Weed" 3-20-59 (Rivera), "Incident of the Valley in Shadow" 11-20-59 (Chief Manse); *Prudence and the Chief*—Pilot 8-26-70 (Chief Snow Eagle);

The Men from Shiloh—"Jump-Up" 3-24-71 (Fuller).

Jaspe, Jose Rivas (1906-). Films: "Sign of Coyote" 1964-Ital./Span.; "Two Gunmen" 1964-Span./Ital.; "Jesse James' Kid" 1966-Span./Ital.; "Relentless Four" 1966-Span./Ital.; "Rojo" 1966-Ital./Span.; "Savage Pampas" 1966-U.S./Span./Arg. (Luis); "Thompson 1880" 1966-Ital./Ger. (Blackie); "Ringo, the Lone Rider" 1967-Ital./Span.; "Cowards Don't Pray" 1968-Ital./Span.; "One After Another" 1968-Span./Ital.; "Stranger in Paso Bravo" 1968-Ital.; "Killer Goodbye" 1969-Ital./Span. (Bill Bragg); "Heads or Tails" 1969-Ital./Span.; "Django Challenges Sartana" 1970-Ital.; "More Dollars for the MacGregors" 1970-Ital./Span.; "Light the Fuse ... Sartana Is Coming" 1971-Ital./Fr.; "Durango Is Coming, Pay or Die" 1972-Ital./Span.; "Thunder Over El Paso" 1972-Ital./Span. (Corbancho); "The Man Called Noon" 1973-Brit./Span./Ital. (Henneker); "Don't Turn the Other Cheek" 1974-Ital./Ger./Span.

Jauregui, Eddie. Films: "The Old Wyoming Trail" 1937; "The Rangers Step In" 1937; "The Lone Ranger" 1938-serial (Trooper); "Adventures of Red Ryder" 1940-serial (Driver #2); "Bells of Capistrano" 1942; "Cattle Empire" 1958; "The Young Land" 1959 (Drifter). ¶TV: *Bonanza*—"Top Hand" 1-17-71 (Bones).

Jay, Helen. Films: "Frontier Gambler" 1956; "The Naked Gun" 1956; "Badlands of Montana" 1957 (2nd Girl). ¶TV: *Sergeant Preston of the Yukon*—"Littlest Rookie" 10-11-56 (Beth Lawson); *Wanted—Dead or Alive*—"Miracle at Pot Hole" 10-25-58 (Martha).

Jay, Tony. TV: *Adventures of Brisco County, Jr.*—"Brisco for the Defense" 10-22-93 (Judge Silot Gatt).

Jaynes, Enid. Films: "Geronimo" 1962 (Huera). ¶TV: *The Rifleman*—"Panic" 11-10-59 (Amy), "The Wyoming Story" 2-7-61 & 2-14-61 (Aggie), "The Quiet Fear" 1-22-62 (Abbey Striker), "Waste" 10-1-62 & 10-8-62 (Young Woman); *The Law of the Plainsman*—"The Comet" 1-21-60, "Cavern of the Wind" 4-21-60 (Lilly McGrath); *Johnny Ringo*—"The Derelict" 5-26-60 (Carrie); *Have Gun Will Travel*—"Face of a Shadow" 4-20-63 (Darkilis).

Jean, Gloria (1928-). TV: *Death Valley Days*—"Lotta Crabtree" 12-9-53 (Lotta Crabtree).

Jeanette, Gertrude (1918-). Films: "The Legend of Nigger Charley" 1972 (Theo).

Jefferson, Thomas (1859-4/2/32). Films: "Good Men and True" 1922 (Simon Hibbler); "The Son of the Wolf" 1922 (Chief Thing Tinner).

Jeffreys, Anne (1923-). Films: "Billy the Kid Trapped" 1942 (Sally); "Bordertown Gunfighters" 1943 (Anita Shelby); "Calling Wild Bill Elliott" 1943 (Edith Richards); "Death Valley Manhunt" 1943 (Nicky Nobart); "The Man from Thunder River" 1943; "Overland Mail Robbery" 1943 (Judy Goodrich); "Wagon Tracks West" 1943 (Moonbush); "Hidden Valley Outlaws" 1944; "Mojave Firebrand" 1944; "Nevada" 1944 (Julie Dexter); "Trail Street" 1947 (Ruby Stone); "Return of the Badmen" 1948 (Cheyenne). ¶TV: *Wagon Train*—"The Julia Gage Story" 12-18-57 (Julia Gage), "The Mary Beckett Story" 5-9-62 (Mary Beckett); *Bonanza*—"The Unwritten Commandment" 4-10-66 (Lily).

Jeffries, Fran. Films: "Talent for Loving" 1969-Brit./Span.

Jeffries, Herbert (1912-). Films: "Two Gun Man from Harlem" 1938 (Bob Blake/the Deacon); "The Bronze Buckaroo" 1939 (Bob Blake); "Harlem Rides the Range" 1939 (Bob Blake). ¶TV: *The Virginian*—"Stopover" 1-8-69 (Frank Hammel).

Jeffries, Lang (1931-2/12/87). Films: "Duel in the Eclipse" 1967-Span. (Gringo). ¶TV: *Overland Trail*—"The Most Dangerous Gentleman" 6-5-60 (Mike Day).

Jeffries, Will A. Films: "Faith Endurin'" 1918 (Jim Lee); "The Law of the Great Northwest" 1918 (Jamieson); "Wolves of the Border" 1918; "The Flip of a Coin" 1919; "The Fighting Shepherdess" 1920 (the Engineer); "Lahoma" 1920 (Red Feather).

Jellison, Bob. TV: *Bat Masterson*—"River Boat" 2-18-59 (Mr. Perry); *Have Gun Will Travel*—"Blind Circle" 12-16-61 (Parsons).

Jenkins, Allen (1890-7/20/74). Films: "Heart of the North" 1938 (Bill Hardsock); "Destry Rides Again" 1939 (Bugs Watson); "Go West, Young Lady" 1941 (Hank); "Singin' in the Corn" 1946 (Glen Cummings); "Oklahoma Annie" 1952 (Bartender). ¶TV: *Wagon Train*—"The Horace Best Story" 10-5-60 (Gillespie).

Jenkins, Dal. Films: "Invitation to a Gunfighter" 1964 (Dancer);

"Young Fury" 1965 (Sam); "Will Penny" 1968 (Sambo); "Lock, Stock and Barrel" TVM-1971 (Butcher). ¶TV: *The Rifleman*—"Requiem at Mission Springs" 3-4-63 (Smiley); *Temple Houston*—"The Town That Trespassed" 3-26-64 (Wade); *Destry*—"Ride to Rio Verde" 4-10-64 (Yarrow); *Bonanza*—"A Dime's Worth of Glory" 11-1-64 (Raymond); *Rawhide*—"Encounter at Boot Hill" 9-14-65 (Lodi); *The Legend of Jesse James*—"One Too Many Mornings" 11-22-65 (Amos Todd); *Wild Wild West*—"The Night of the Fatal Trap" 12-24-65 (Luke Dawson); *Iron Horse*—"High Devil" 9-26-66 (Razor Joe); *Here Come the Brides*—"The Road to the Cradle" 11-7-69 (Pinkie); *Lancer*—"Legacy" 12-9-69 (Bill Degan).

Jenkins, Jackie "Butch" (1937-). Films: "Boy's Ranch" 1946 (Butch).

Jenkins, Mark. TV: *The High Chaparral*—"Apache Trust" 11-7-69 (Mulvaney); *Death Valley Days*—"The Dragon of Gold Hill" 1-24-70.

Jenkins, Terry. Films: "Bandidos" 1967-Ital. (Ricky Shot); "Paint Your Wagon" 1969 (Joe Mooney).

Jenks, Frank (1902-5/13/62). Films: "The Last Outlaw" 1936 (Tom); "Pecos River" 1951 (Sheriff Dennig); "Silver City Bonanza" 1951 (Theatre Owner); "Utah Wagon Train" 1951 (Hap); "Outlaw Treasure" 1955; "Dig That Uranium" 1956 (Olaf); "Friendly Persuasion" 1956 (Shell Game Man). ¶TV: *The Cisco Kid*—"The Photo Studio" 7-5-52; *Wild Bill Hickok*—"The Right of Way" 8-5-52; *The Roy Rogers Show*—"The Knockout" 12-28-52 (Art Gauley); *The Gene Autry Show*—"The Million Dollar Fiddle" 10-1-55; *Circus Boy*—"Hortense the Hippo" 6-2-57 (Flash); *Wagon Train*—"Princess of a Lost Tribe" 11-2-60 (Dutch Anders); *Laramie*—"The Betrayers" 1-22-63.

Jenks, Si (1876-1/6/70). Films: "The Man from Death Valley" 1931 (Bank Teller); "Near the Trail's End" 1931; "Oklahoma Jim" 1931 (Driver); "Two-Fisted Justice" 1931; "Lawless Valley" 1932; "Galloping Thru" 1932; "Ghost City" 1932 (Henchman); "Lawless Valley" 1932 (Zeb Huff); "Crashing Broadway" 1933; "Riders of Destiny" 1933; "The Dude Ranger" 1934; "Lightning Range" 1934 (Hezekiah Simmons); "Rawhide Romance" 1934 (Ranch Cook); "Big Calibre" 1935 (Dance Caller); "Coyote Trails" 1935; "Desert Gold" 1935 (Driver); "Fighting Shadows" 1935 (Hank Bascom); "Gun Play" 1935 (Cowpoke); "Law Beyond the Range" 1935 (Zeke); "The Outlaw Deputy"

1935 (Charlie); "The Rider of the Law" 1935; "Riding Wild" 1935; "Arizona Mahoney" 1936 (Stagecoach Driver); "The Cowboy Star" 1936 (Buckshot); "Dodge City Trail" 1937 (Rawhide); "The Old Wyoming Trail" 1937 (Old Jed); "The Outcasts of Poker Flat" 1937 (Kentuck); "A Tenderfoot Goes West" 1937; "Rawhide" 1938 (Pop Mason); "Drums Along the Mohawk" 1939 (Jacobs); "Frontier Marshal" 1939 (Prospector); "Stagecoach" 1939; "Union Pacific" 1939 (Old Prospector); "My Little Chickadee" 1940 (Deputy); "The Ranger and the Lady" 1940 (Purdy); "Ride, Tenderfoot, Ride" 1940 (Sheriff); "The Trail Blazers" 1940 (Dr. T.L. Johnson); "Gauchos of El Dorado" 1941; "Cowboy Serenade" 1942; "Wild Horse Stampede" 1943 (Rawhide); "Song of Nevada" 1944; "Zorro's Black Whip" 1944-serial (Zeke Haydon); "Bandits of the Badlands" 1945; "The Man from Oklahoma" 1945 (Jeff Whittaker); "Oregon Trail" 1945 (Andy); "San Antonio" 1945 (Station Boss); "Duel in the Sun" 1946 (Dancer); "God's Country" 1946; "Singin' in the Corn" 1946 (Old Man); "Son of Zorro" 1947-serial (Fred); "Trail Street" 1947 (Charlie Thorne, Publisher); "Unconquered" 1947 (Farmer); "The Dude Goes West" 1948 (Horse Trader); "Fury at Furnace Creek" 1948 (Jury Foreman); "Rawhide" 1951 (Old Timer); "Oklahoma Annie" 1952 (Old Man). ¶TV: *The Lone Ranger*—"Stage to Tishomingo" 10-28-54.

Jennings, Al (1864-12/26/61). Films: "The Bank Robbery" 1908 (Al Jennings); "Beating Back" 1914 (Al Jennings); "The Frame-Up" 1915; "Bond of Blood" 1916; "The Captain of the Gray Horse Troop" 1917 (Cut Finger); "The Lady of the Dugout" 1918 (Al Jennings); "The Canyon Holdup" 1919; "Fighting Fury" 1924 (Splain); "The Demon" 1926 (Dan Carroll); "The Ridin' Rascal" 1926; "Loco Luck" 1927 (Jesse Turner); "The Land of Missing Men" 1930 (Ex-Sheriff John Evans); "At the Ridge" 1931 (Mike Logan); "Song of the Gringo" 1936 (Judge).

Jennings, DeWitt (1879-3/1/37). Films: "Blinky" 1923 (Col. "Raw Meat" Islip); "Out of Luck" 1923 (Captain Bristol); "The Deadwood Coach" 1924 (Jim Shields); "The Desert Outlaw" 1924 (Doc McChesney; "The Splendid Road" 1925 (Capt. Bashford); "Chip of the Flying U" 1926 (J.G. Whitmore); "The Big Trail" 1930 (Boat Captain); "The Squaw Man" 1931 (Sheriff Bud Handy); "Fighting with Kit Carson"

1933-serial; "Massacre" 1934 (Sheriff Jennings).

Jennings, Frank. Films: "Beating Back" 1914 (Morris Foster); "The Lady of the Dugout" 1918 (Frank Jennings); "The Three Outcasts" 1929 (Sheriff).

Jennings, S.E. (1880-2/3/32). Films: "Dead Shot Baker" 1917 (Cherokee Hall); "Vengeance and the Woman" 1917-serial; "The Home Trail" 1918 (Sheriff); "Lucky Dan" 1922 (Slim Connors); "The Sunset Trail" 1924 (Silent Saunders); "The Border Sheriff" 1926 (Carter Brace); "Western Pluck" 1926 (Buck Zaney).

Jennings, Waylon (1937-). Films: "Stagecoach" TVM-1986 (Hatfield); "Maverick" 1994 (Man with Concealed Gun).

Jens, Salome (1935-). TV: *Stoney Burke*—"Spin a Golden Web" 11-26-62 (Mavis); *Bonanza*—"The Wagon" 10-5-70 (Madge Tucker); *Gunsmoke*—"Captain Sligo" 1-4-71 (Josephine Burney), "Talbot" 2-26-73 (Katherine); *The New Land*—"The Word Is: Mortal" 10-5-74.

Jensen, Eulalie (1884-10/7/52). Films: "West Wind" 1915; "Britton of the Seventh" 1916 (Frances Granson); "Ranger of the Big Pines" 1925 (Lize Weatherford); "The Thundering Herd" 1925 (Mrs. Randall Jett).

Jensen, Johnny. TV: *Branded*—"The Vindicator" 1-31-65 (Johnny Pritchett); *Cimarron Strip*—"Nobody" 12-7-67; *Daniel Boone*—"A Very Small Rifle" 9-18-69 (Sandy).

Jensen, Karen (1944-). Films: "Ballad of Josie" 1968 (Deborah Wilkes). ¶TV: *The Virginian*—"A Bald-Faced Boy" 4-13-66 (Glory Claiborne); *Wild Wild West*—"The Night of the Legion of Death" 11-24-67 (Catherine Kittridge).

Jenson, Roy (1935-). Films: "Buchanan Rides Alone" 1958 (Hemp); "The Missouri Traveler" 1958 (Simpson); "Ride Lonesome" 1959 (Outlaw); "North to Alaska" 1960 (Logger); "How the West Was Won" 1962 (Henchman); "Law of the Lawless" 1964 (Johnson Brother); "Stage to Thunder Rock" 1964; "Hostile Guns" 1967; "Red Tomahawk" 1967 (Prospector); "Waterhole No. 3" 1967 (Doc Quinley); "Five Card Stud" 1968 (Mace Jones); "Will Penny" 1968 (Boetius Sullivan); "Paint Your Wagon" 1969 (Hennessey); "Powderkeg" TVM-1971; "Count Your Bullets" 1972 (Blacksmith); "Journey Through Rosebud" 1972 (Park Ranger); "The Life and Times of Judge Roy Bean" 1972

(Outlaw); "Breakheart Pass" 1976 (Banlon); "The Duchess and the Dirtwater Fox" 1976 (Bloodworth); "Tom Horn" 1980 (Mendenhour); "The Gambler, Part II—The Adventure Continues" TVM-1983 (Hatch); "Kung Fu: The Movie" TVM-1986. ¶TV: *Bonanza*—"The Prime of Life" 12-29-63, "The Brass Box" 9-26-65 (Harry), "The Wish" 3-9-69 (Craig), "Forever" 9-12-72 (Hanley); *Daniel Boone*—"The Trek" 10-21-65 (Jensen), "The High Cumberland" 4-14-66 & 4-21-66 (Cash Doyle), "Heroes Welcome" 2-22-68, "The Road to Freedom" 10-2-69 (Crane Hawkins); *Wild Wild West*—"The Night of the Eccentrics" 9-16-66 (Vance Markham); *Gunsmoke*—"The Goldtakers" 9-24-66 (Troy), "The Victim" 1-1-68 (Crow), "Railroad" 11-25-68 (Larnen), "The Badge" 2-2-70 (Keller), "The Scavengers" 11-16-70 (Rath), "The Colonel" 12-16-74 (Jeff Higgins); *The Monroes*—"The Hunter" 10-26-66 (Vorhees); *Cimarron Strip*—"The Legend of Jud Starr" 9-14-67 (Bloody Bob Agnew), "The Greeners" 3-7-68; *The Big Valley*—"Ladykiller" 10-16-67; *Hondo*—"Hondo and the Judas" 11-3-67 (Bob Ford); *The High Chaparral*—"Follow Your Heart" 10-4-68 (Frank Lynch), "The Guns of Johnny Rondo" 2-6-70 (Jed); *The Virginian*—"The Storm Gate" 11-13-68 (Lueder); *The Outcasts*—"My Name Is Jemal" 11-18-68 (Ben); *Nichols*—"The One Eyed Mule's Time Has Come" 11-23-71 (Bull); *Kung Fu*—"Superstition" 4-5-73 (Rupp); *How the West Was Won*—Episode One 2-6-77 (Sergeant Macklin), "The Slavers" 4-23-79 (Trako); *Father Murphy*—Pilot 11-3-81 (Hogan); *Bret Maverick*—"Dateline: Sweetwater" 1-12-82 (Monte).

Jergens, Adele (1922-). Films: "Black Arrow" 1944-serial (Mary); "Law of the Barbary Coast" 1949 (Lita); "Sugarfoot" 1951 (Reva Cairn); "Overland Pacific" 1954 (Jessie Lorraine); "The Lonesome Trail" 1955; "Outlaw Treasure" 1955; "Strange Lady in Town" 1955 (Bella Brown).

Jergens, Diane. Films: "Friendly Persuasion" 1956 (Elizabeth, the Young Girl). ¶TV: *Wagon Train*—"The Steele Family" 6-17-59 (Prudence), "The Prairie Story" 2-1-61 (Sally); *Walt Disney Presents*—"Daniel Boone" 1960-61 (Maybelle Yancy); *Wyatt Earp*—"The Shooting Starts" 4-18-61 (Edith Rickabaugh).

Jerome, Edwin (1884-9/10/59). TV: *Jim Bowie*—"The Bridegroom" 11-29-57 (Maurice Delacroix); *The*

Californians—"Mutineers from Hell" 9-30-58 (Poke); *Zane Grey Theater*—"Make It Look Good" 2-5-59 (Doc Kendall).

Jerome, Elmer (1872-8/10/47). Films: "False Colors" 1943 (Jed Stevers).

Jerome, Jerry. Films: "Sunset Trail" 1938; "King of the Texas Rangers" 1941-serial (Ed); "Stardust on the Sage" 1942; "Romance of the West" 1946 (Marks); "The Wistful Widow of Wagon Gap" 1947 (Cowboy); "Phantom Valley" 1948; "River Lady" 1948 (Croupier); "Silver River" 1948 (Soldier).

Jesters, The (Dwight Latham, Walter Carlson, Guy Bonham). Films: "Cowboy in the Clouds" 1943; "Both Barrels Blazing" 1945; "Return of the Durango Kid" 1945.

Jeter, James (1921-). Films: "Oklahoma Crude" 1973 (Stapp). ¶TV: *Bonanza*—"A Question of Strength" 10-27-63, "Sweet Annie Laurie" 1-5-69 (Duncan), "The Clarion" 2-9-69 (Cotton), "Caution: Easter Bunny Crossing" 3-29-70 (Blacksmith), "The Younger Brothers' Younger Brother" 3-12-72 (Stage Guard); *Wild Wild West*—"The Night of the Human Trigger" 12-3-65 (Harry); *Gunsmoke*—"Shadler" 1-15-73 (Creech), "The Town Tamers" 1-28-74 (Barker).

Jewel, Betty. Films: "Mile-A-Minute Romeo" 1924 (Molly); "Arizona Bound" 1927 (Ann Winslow); "The Last Outlaw" 1927 (Janet Lane); "The Mysterious Rider" 1927 (Dorothy King).

Jewell, Isabell (1910-4/5/72). Films: "Northwest Passage" 1940 (Jennie Coit); "Badman's Territory" 1946 (Belle Star); "Belle Starr's Daughter" 1947 (Belle Starr); "Drum Beat" 1954 (Lily White). ¶TV: *Gunsmoke*—"Circus Trick" 2-6-65 (Mme. Ahr).

Jewkes, Delos (1895-7/17/84). Films: "Rose Marie" 1936 (Butcher at Hotel).

Jillian, Ann (1951-). TV: *Wagon Train*—"The Hobie Redman Story" 1-17-62 (Sandra Carlson).

Jiminez, Soledad (1874-10/17/66). Films: "In Old Arizona" 1929 (Cook); "Romance of the Rio Grande" 1929 (Catalina); "The Arizona Kid" 1930 (Pulga); "Billy the Kid" 1930; "The Texan" 1930 (the Duenna); "The Broken Wing" 1932 (Maria); "Cyclone Ranger" 1935 (Donna Castelar); "Under the Pampas Moon" 1935 (Senora Campo); "The Bold Caballero" 1936; "Law and Lead" 1936 (Senora Gonzales); "The Phantom of the Range" 1936; "Robin Hood of El Dorado" 1936 (Madre Murrieta); "The Traitor" 1936 (Juana); "California Frontier" 1938 (Mama Cantova); "Forbidden Valley" 1938 (Meetah); "The Oklahoma Kid" 1939 (Indian Woman); "The Return of the Cisco Kid" 1939 (Mama Soledad); "Rough Riders' Round-Up" 1939 (Old Woman); "Northwest Mounted Police" 1940 (Grandmother); "Bad Men of the Border" 1945; "South of the Rio Grande" 1945 (Mama Maria); "Black Bart" 1948 (Teresa); "Dakota Lil" 1950; "Seminole" 1953 (Mattie Sue Thomas).

Jimmy Wakely Trio, The (Jimmy Wakely, Johnny Bond & Scotty Harrell). Films: "Little Joe, the Wrangler" 1942; "Cheyenne Roundup" 1943; "Cyclone Prairie Rangers" 1944.

Jobson, Edward (1864-2/7/25). Films: "The Mints of Hell" 1919 (Bill Weed).

Joby, Hans (1884-4/30/43). Films: "Border Phantom" 1937 (Dr. Von Kurtz).

Jocelyn, Sylvia. Films: "Three Gold Coins" 1920 (Peggy Benson).

Jochim, Anthony (1892-4/10/78). Films: "Fighting Man of the Plains" 1949 (Holz); "Western Pacific Agent" 1950; "Three Desperate Men" 1951 (Farmer); "City of Badmen" 1953 (Blister); "Star in the Dust" 1956 (Doc Quinn); "Drango" 1957 (Stryker); "Gunfight at the O.K. Corral" 1957 (Old Man); "Joe Dakota" 1957 (Claude Henderson); "The Legend of Tom Dooley" 1959 (Preacher). ¶TV: *The Adventures of Rin Tin Tin*— "Top Gun" 1-24-58 (Abel Caution); *Bonanza*—"Death at Dawn" 4-30-60, "A Dime's Worth of Glory" 11-1-64 (Deputy); *The High Chaparral*—"Bad Day for a Thirst" 2-18-68 (Prospector); *Wild Wild West*—"The Night of the Sedgewick Curse" 10-18-68 (Prisoner).

Jodorowsky, Alexandro. Films: "El Topo" 1971-Mex. (El Topo).

John, Errol (1924-7/10/88). Films: "Buck and the Preacher" 1972 (Joshua).

Johnny Bond and His Red River Valley Boys (Johnny Bond, Paul Sells, Wesley Tuttle & Jimmie Dean). Films: "Frontier Law" 1943.

Johns, Bertram (1874-5/9/34). Films: "Colorado Pluck" 1921 (Lord Featherstone).

Johns, Larry. Films: "Belle Starr's Daughter" 1947 (Jed Purdy);

"Dakota Lil" 1950 (Sheriff); "Rio Grande Patrol" 1950 (Doctor); "Law of the Badlands" 1951 (Simms). ¶TV: *The Lone Ranger*—"Outlaw's Revenge" 10-5-50; *The Adventures of Rin Tin Tin*—"Brave Bow" 4-18-58 (Chief Chonose); *Death Valley Days*—"The Newspaper That Went to Jail" 3-31-59 (Judge Clinton); *The Deputy*—"The Return of Simon Fry" 2-13-60 (Silas Jones).

Johnson, Arch (1923-). Films: "Gun Glory" 1957 (Gunn); "The Cheyenne Social Club" 1970 (Marshal Anderson). ¶TV: *Maverick*—"Royal Four-Flush" 9-20-59 (Placer Jack Mason), "A Bullet for the Teacher" 10-30-60 (Ephrim Burch), "The Bold Fenian Men" 12-18-60 (Col. Gaylor Summers); *The Law of the Plainsman*—"Dangerous Barriers" 3-10-60 (Cass Marby); *Bronco*—"Tangled Trail" 5-3-60 (Mark Tanner); *Bat Masterson*—"The Big Gamble" 6-16-60 (Mr. Smith); *Laramie*—Regular 1960-63 (Wellman); *Lawman*—"The Old War Horse" 10-9-60 (Jason McQuade), "The Lords of Darkness" 12-3-61 (Andrew Lord), "The Hold-Out" 2-18-62 (Logan); *Rawhide*—"Incident of the Captive" 12-16-60, "Incident on the Road Back" 2-24-61 (James Cronin), "Incident of the Reluctant Bridegroom" 11-30-62 (John Landy), "Incident at Crooked Hat" 2-1-63 (Big Sam Talbot), "Incident at Paradise" 10-24-63 (Harry Johanson), "Incident of the Pied Piper" 2-6-64 (Sheriff Andrews); *Zane Grey Theater*—"Ambush" 1-5-61 (Dutch); *Wagon Train*—"The Hobie Redman Story" 1-17-62 (Glen Andrews); *Gunsmoke*—"Wagon Girls" 4-7-62 (Karl Feester), "Hammerhead" 12-26-64 (Big Jim Ponder), "The Mission" 10-8-66 (Sergeant Macklin), "Sam McTavish, M.D." 10-5-70 (Barnaby Bascomb); *Tales of Wells Fargo*—"The Angry Sky" 4-21-62 (Swede Lowell); *Cheyenne*—"A Man Called Ragan" 4-23-62 (Ben Stark); *Bonanza*—"The Artist" 10-7-62 (Gavin), "Return to Honor" 3-22-64 (Butler), "Judgment at Olympus" 10-8-67 (Wheelock); *Empire*—"Season of Growth" 2-19-63 (Brad Hollister); *Redigo*—"Privilege of a Man" 12-17-63 (Stuart Graham); *The Virginian*—"A Killer in Town" 10-9-63 (Dr. Ashley), "Timberland" 3-10-65 (Charles Daniels); *The Travels of Jaimie McPheeters*—"The Day of the Tin Trumpet" 2-2-64 (Lize Daggett); *Daniel Boone*—"Ken-Tuck-E" 9-24-64 (Judson), "The Williamsburg Cannon" 1-12-67 & 1-19-67 (Tavern Proprietor), "For Want of a Hero" 3-6-69 (Hanks); *Laredo*—"That's Noway, Thataway" 1-20-66; *F*

Troop—"Guns, Guns, Who's Got the Guns?" 3-2-67; *The Big Valley*—"Showdown in Limbo" 3-27-67 (Frank Sawyer), "The Twenty-five Graves of Midas" 2-3-69 (Webb Dutton); *Cimarron Strip*—"Broken Wing" 9-21-67 (Parson Endicott); *Death Valley Days*—"Out of the Valley of Death" 5-25-68 (Landusky); *The Men from Shiloh*—"Nan Allen" 1-6-71 (Sheriff); *Kung Fu*—"The Passion of Chen Yi" 2-28-74 (Larkin); *Young Maverick*—"A Fistful of Oats" 12-5-79.

Johnson, Arte (1934-). TV: *Frontier Circus*—"Journey from Hannibal" 11-16-61 (Charles Gippner); *Destry*—"Deputy for a Day" 4-3-64 (Lester).

Johnson, Arthur (1876-1/17/16). Films: "The Girl and the Outlaw" 1908; "The Greaser's Gauntlet" 1908; "The Vaquero's Vow" 1908; "Comata, the Sioux" 1909; "The Indian Runner's Romance" 1909; "The Mended Lute" 1909; "The Mountaineer's Honor" 1909; "The Renunciation" 1909; "In Old California" 1910; "Over Silent Paths" 1910; "A Romance of the Western Hills" 1910; "The Tenderfoot's Triumph" 1910; "The Thread of Destiny" 1910; "The Twisted Trails" 1910; "Two Brothers" 1910; "Unexpected Help" 1910.

Johnson, Ben (1919-). Films: "The Three Godfathers" 1948 (Posse Member); "She Wore a Yellow Ribbon" 1949 (Sgt. Tyree); "Rio Grande" 1950 (Trooper Tyree); "Wagonmaster" 1950 (Travis Blue); "Fort Defiance" 1951 (Ben Shelby); "Wild Stallion" 1952 (Dan Light); "Shane" 1953 (Chris); "Oklahoma!" 1955 (Cowboy at Train Depot); "Rebel in Town" 1956 (Frank Mason); "Slim Carter" 1957 (Montana Burris); "War Drums" 1957 (Luke Fargo); "Fort Bowie" 1958 (Capt. Thompson); "Ten Who Dared" 1960 (George Bradley); "One-Eyed Jacks" 1961 (Bob Amroy); "Tomboy and the Champ" 1961 (Uncle Jim); "Cheyenne Autumn" 1964 (Trooper Plumtree); "Major Dundee" 1965 (Sgt. Chillum); "The Rare Breed" 1966 (Jeff Harter); "Hang 'Em High" 1968 (Sheriff Dave Bliss); "Will Penny" 1968 (Alex); "Ride a Northbound Horse" 1969; "The Undefeated" 1969 (Short Grub); "The Wild Bunch" 1969 (Tector Gorch); "Chisum" 1970 (James Pepper); "Something Big" 1971 (Jesse Bookbinder); "Junior Bonner" 1972 (Buck Roan); "Kid Blue" 1973 (Sheriff Mean John Simpson); "The Train Robbers" 1973 (Wil Jesse); "Bite the Bullet" 1975

(Mister); "Breakheart Pass" 1976 (Nathan Pearce); "Grayeagle" 1977 (John Colter); "The Sacketts" TVM-1979 (Cap Roundtree); "Wild Times" TVM-1980 (Doc Bogardus); "The Shadow Riders" TVM-1982 (Uncle Jack Traven); "Wild Horses" TVM-1985 (Bill Ward); "Dream West" TVM-1986 (Jim Bridger); ; "My Heroes Have Always Been Cowboys" 1991 (Jesse Dalton); "Bonanza: The Return" TVM-1993 (Bronc Evans); "Bonanza: Under Attack" TVM-1995 (Bronc Evans). ¶TV: *The Restless Gun*—"No Way to Kill" 11-24-58 (Sheriff Tim Malachy); *Laramie*—"Hour After Dawn" 3-15-60 (Billy Pardee), "A Sound of Bells" 12-27-60 (Driver), "Widow in White" 6-13-61 (Tarp); *Have Gun Will Travel*—"A Head of Hair" 9-24-60 (John Anderson), "The Race" 10-28-61 (Sam Crabbe), "The Fifth Bullet" 9-29-62 (John Bartlett); *Bonanza*—"The Gamble" 4-1-62 (Stan), "The Deserter" 3-16-69 (Sam Bellis), "Top Hand" 1-17-71 (Kelly James); *Stoney Burke*—"Point of Honor" 10-22-62 (Rex Donally); *The Virginian*—"Duel at Shiloh" 1-2-63 (Spinner), "Dangerous Road" 3-17-65 (Brandt), "Johnny Moon" 10-11-67 (Hogan), "Vision of Blindness" 10-9-68 (Jed Cooper); *Gunsmoke*—"Quint-Cident" 4-27-63 (Ben Crown), "Quaker Girl" 12-10-66 (Vern Morland), "Drago" 11-22-71 (Hannon); *Branded*—"McCord's Way" 1-30-66 (Bill Latigo); *The Monroes*—Regular 1966-67 (Sleeve).

Johnson, Brad (1925-4/4/81). Films: "Outlaw Women" 1952 (Chuck); "The Marksman" 1953. ¶TV: *The Cisco Kid*—"Water Toll" 9-22-51; *The Range Rider*—"Bullets and Badmen" 3-29-52; *Annie Oakley*—Regular 1954-57 (Deputy Sheriff Lofty Craig); *The Adventures of Rin Tin Tin*—"The Iron Horse" 10-28-55 (John Quinn), "Rin Tin Tin and the Second Chance" 6-1-56 (Tom Buckner); *Wyatt Earp*—"The Nice Ones Always Die First" 4-2-57 (Ed Masterson), "The Underdog" 4-22-58 (Hurley Abbott); *The Lone Ranger*—"The Law and Miss Aggie" 4-11-57; *Circus Boy*—"The Cub Reporter" 4-21-57 (Frank Dillard); *Tales of Wells Fargo*—"Wild Cargo" 1-19-59 (Joe Shields); *Maverick*—"The Saga of Waco Williams" 2-15-59 (Karl Bent, Jr.), "A Bullet for the Teacher" 10-30-60 (Jim Reardon); *Death Valley Days*—"Stagecoach Spy" 2-17-59 (Tom Fuller), "The Blonde King" 3-24-59 (John Trask), "A Wedding Dress" 2-9-60 (Bill Tilghman), "Dead Man's Tale" 3-8-61 (Noble);

Zane Grey Theater—"Trouble at Tres Cruces" 3-26-59; *Cheyenne*—"Home Is the Brave" 3-14-60 (Dan Blaisdell); *Gunsmoke*—"Cattle Barons" 9-18-67 (Laskin).

Johnson, Brad. TV: *Ned Blessing: The Story of My Life and Times*—Regular 1993 (Ned Blessing).

Johnson, Casey. Films: "Hurricane Smith" 1942 (Johnny Smith).

Johnson, Chubby (1903-10/31/74). Films: "Rocky Mountain" 1950 (Gil Craigie); "Fort Dodge Stampede" 1951 (Skeeter); "Fort Worth" 1951 (Sheriff); "Night Riders of Montana" 1951 (Sheriff Davis); "Wells Fargo Gunmaster" 1951 (Skeeter Davis); "Bend of the River" 1952 (Cap'n Mello); "Last of the Comanches" 1952 (Henry Ruppert); "The Treasure of Lost Canyon" 1952 (Baltimore Dan); "Back to God's Country" 1953 (Billy Shorter); "Calamity Jane" 1953 (Rattlesnake); "Gunsmoke" 1953 (Doc Farrell); "Law and Order" 1953 (Denver Dahoon); "Cattle Queen of Montana" 1954 (Nat); "Overland Pacific" 1954 (Sheriff Blaney); "The Far Country" 1955 (Dusty); "Rage at Dawn" 1955 (Hyronemus); "Tennessee's Partner" 1955 (Grubstake McNiven); "Fastest Gun Alive" 1956 (Frank Stringer); "The First Texan" 1956 (Deaf Smith); "The Rawhide Years" 1956 (Gif Lessing); "Tribute to a Badman" 1956 (Baldy); "The Young Guns" 1956 (Grandpa); "Drango" 1957 (Zeb); "Gunfire at Indian Gap" 1957 (Samuel); "The True Story of Jesse James" 1957 (Askew); "The Firebrand" 1962 (Tampico); "Sam Whiskey" 1969 (the Blacksmith). ¶TV: *The Lone Ranger*—"The Woman from Omaha" 7-2-53; *The Adventures of Rin Tin Tin*—"Rusty Meets Mr. Nobody" 5-4-56 (Jake Wallace), "The Best Policy" 12-5-58 (Jake Appleby); *Circus Boy*—"The Pawnee Strip" 4-14-57 (Harry Garth); *Sugarfoot*—"Brannigan's Boots" 9-17-57 (Wally Higgins); *Maverick*—"Stage West" 10-27-57 (Simmons), "Pappy" 9-13-59 (Miller), "The Sheriff of Duck 'n' Shoot" 9-27-59 (Billy Walker), "The Misfortune Teller" 3-6-60 (Jailer), "The Maverick Line" 10-20-60 (Dutch Wilcox), "Destination Devil's Flat" 12-25-60 (Oscar), "The Cactus Switch" 1-15-61 (Andy Gish); *Jim Bowie*—"Silk Purse" 12-27-57 (Capt. Bildag Creel); *Buckskin*—"Tell Me, Leonardo" 9-25-58 (Leonardo); *Wagon Train*—"The Millie Davis Story" 11-26-58 (Judd), "The Cathy Eckhardt Story" 11-9-60 (Lieutenant); *Tales of Wells Fargo*—"Lola Montez"

2-16-59 (Pete); *The Rifleman*—"The Horse Traders" 2-9-60, "The Spoiler" 2-16-60 (Mr. Avery), "Guilty Conscience" 4-2-62 (Old Man); *Wanted-Dead or Alive*—"Black Belt" 3-19-60 (Chalmly Cove); *Man from Blackhawk*—"The Last Days of Jessie Turnbull" 4-1-60 (Jessie Turnbull); *Lawman*—"The Break-In" 5-21-61 (Cactus Gates); *Bonanza*—"The Ride" 1-21-62 (Toby Barker), "Gallagher Sons" 12-9-62, "The Last Haircut" 2-3-63, "Hound Dog" 3-21-65 (Abner), "Ponderosa Explosion" 1-1-67 (Clyde), "The Gold Detector" 12-24-67 (Cash), "Search in Limbo" 2-20-72 (Old Man); *Rawhide*—"Incident of the Pale Rider" 3-15-63 (Sam Mayhew); *Temple Houston*—Regular 1963-64 (Concho Charlie); *Gunsmoke*—"Chicken" 12-5-64, Gunsmoke—"Hammerhead" 12-26-64 (Wohaw Simmons), "The Gold Mine" 1-27-69 (Old Timer); *The Big Valley*—"Night of the Wolf" 12-1-65 (Dr. Borland); *Wild Wild West*—"The Night of the Tartar" 2-3-67 (Old Prospector), "The Night Dr. Loveless Died" 9-29-67 (Sheriff Quayle), "The Night of the Simian Terror" 2-16-68 (Sheriff); *Pistols 'n' Petticoats*—3-11-67 (Stage Driver); *Death Valley Days*—"The Other Side of the Mountain" 4-13-68 (Davis), "The Tenderfoot" 11-15-69 (Jake; *The Guns of Will Sonnett*—"Reunion" 9-27-68.

Johnson, Claude (1938-). Films: "How the West Was Won" 1962 (Jeremiah Rawlings). ¶TV: *Bonanza*—"Springtime" 10-1-61 (Paul); *Redigo*—"Horns of Hate" 11-19-63 (Bud); *Gunsmoke*—"Jonah Hutchison" 11-21-64 (Aaron Hutchison); *Daniel Boone*—"The King's Shilling" 10-19-67 (Jack Weaver), "Big, Black and Out There" 11-14-68 (Joe), "Perilous Passage" 1-15-70.

Johnson, Dale R. TV: *The Restless Gun*—"The Englishman" 6-8-59 (Sheriff); *Colt .45*—"Queen of Dixie" 10-4-59; *Wyatt Earp*—"Wyatt's Brothers Join Up" 6-6-61; *The Virginian*—"The Mountain of the Sun" 4-17-63; *The Big Valley*—"Alias Nellie Handley" 2-24-69 (Onlooker).

Johnson, Don (1950-). Films: "Zachariah" 1971 (Matthew); "Law of the Land" TVM-1976 (Quirt). ¶TV: *Kung Fu*—"The Spirit Helper" 11-8-73 (Nashebo); *Big Hawaii*—"Gandy" 9-21-77 (Gandy).

Johnson, Doug. Films: "Buck and the Preacher" 1972 (Sam).

Johnson, Dyke. Films: "Ride Lonesome" 1959 (Charlie); "Comanche Station" 1960 (Mr. Lowe).

¶TV: *The Virginian*—"The Man from the Sea" 12-26-62.

Johnson, Edith (1894-9/6/69). Films: "The Lore O' the Windigo" 1914; "A Fight for Millions" 1918-serial; "The Fighting Grin" 1918 (Margie Meredith); "Smashing Barriers" 1919-serial; "Steelheart" 1921 (Ethel Kendall); "Where Men Are Men" 1921 (Princess/Eileen); "The Fighting Guide" 1922 (Ethel MacDonald); "When Danger Smiles" 1922 (Frania Caravalle); "Playing It Wild" 1923 (Beth Webb); "The Steel Trail" 1923-serial; "Wolves of the North" 1924-serial.

Johnson, Edward. Films: "Stepping Fast" 1923 (Commodore Simpson).

Johnson, Emory (1894-4/18/60). Films: "Broncho Billy's Bible" 1912; "The Calling of Jim Barton" 1914; "A Gambler's Way" 1914; "The Warning" 1914; "Two Men of Sandy Bar" 1916 (Sandy Morton); "The Yaqui" 1916 (Flores); "A Yoke of Gold" 1916 (Jose Garcia); "Put Up Your Hands" 1919 (Leonard Hewitt).

Johnson, Georgann (1926-). TV: *Dr. Quinn, Medicine Woman*—"Where the Heart Is" 11-20-93 (Elizabeth Quinn).

Johnson, Gray (1939-). Films: "The Hired Hand" 1971 (Will).

Johnson, Harvey. TV: *The Rifleman*—"Trail of Hate" 9-27-60 (Noley); *Maverick*—"The Bold Fenian Men" 12-18-60 (Charles Donovan), "Deadly Image" 3-12-61 (Sergeant Rafferty); *Empire*—"Between Friday and Monday" 5-7-63 (Desk Clerk).

Johnson, J. Louis (1878-4/29/54). Films: "Surrender" 1950 (Butler).

Johnson, J.S. TV: *Wild Wild West*—"The Night of the Fugitives" 11-8-68 (Plank); *Bonanza*—"Mrs. Wharton and the Lesser Breeds" 1-19-69 (Carmody).

Johnson, Jason (1907-11/24/77). Films: "The Persuader" 1957 (Morse Fowler); "The Legend of Tom Dooley" 1959 (Frank). ¶TV: *Sergeant Preston of the Yukon*—"Dog Race" 1-19-56 (Daggett); *Circus Boy*—"The Pawnee Strip" 4-14-57 (Luke Simmons); *Zane Grey Theater*—"The Freighter" 1-17-58 (Ez Williams), "Threat of Violence" 5-23-58 (Dr. Harris), "Day of the Killing" 1-8-59 (Ricker), "Man in the Middle" 2-11-60 (Mat); *Gunsmoke*—"Claustrophobia" 1-25-58 (Judge), "The Bounty Hunter" 10-30-65 (Homesteader); *Tales of Wells Fargo*—"Special Deliv-

ery" 3-31-58 (Keener), "The Easterner" 1-11-60 (Steve), "Frightened Witness" 12-26-60 (Sheriff); *Jim Bowie*—"A Night in Tennessee" 4-25-58 (Ralph Corlett); *The Rifleman*—"The Deadeye Kid" 2-10-59 (Cramer), "The Money Gun" 5-12-59; *Hotel De Paree*—"Sundance and the Hostiles" 12-11-59 (Orie); *Have Gun Will Travel*—"Never Help the Devil" 4-16-60; *The Tall Man*—"Bad Company" 9-24-60 (Paul Appel); *Bonanza*—"The Hopefuls" 10-8-60, "A Man to Admire" 12-6-64 (Doctor); *The Virginian*—"The Big Deal" 10-10-62 (Workman); *Laramie*—"Protective Custody" 1-15-63; *Empire*—"A House in Order" 3-5-63 (Ranger); *Wagon Train*—"The Sandra Cummings Story" 12-2-63; *The Big Valley*—"Ladykiller" 10-16-67, "They Called Her Delilah" 9-30-68 (Buggy Driver).

Johnson, June (1918-7/14/87). Films: "The Big Show" 1937; "Lone Star Raiders" 1940 (Linda Cameron); "Gangs of Sonora" 1941 (June Conners); "Pals of the Pecos" 1941 (June).

Johnson, Kay (1905-11/17/75). Films: "Billy the Kid" 1930 (Claire); "The Spoilers" 1930 (Helen Chester).

Johnson, Lamont (1920-). TV: *The Big Valley*—"Last Stage to Salt Flats" 12-5-66 (Anson Cross); *Gunsmoke*—"The Prodigal" 9-25-67 (Stoner).

Johnson, Laraine. see Day, Laraine.

Johnson, LeRoy (1919-10/95). Films: "Colt .45" 1950; "The Hawk of Wild River" 1952 (Smoky); "Smoky Canyon" 1952 (Ace); "Pony Express" 1953; "The Far Horizons" 1955; "Texas Lady" 1955 (Rancher); "Badman's Country" 1958; "Shenandoah" 1965 (Rider); "The Rare Breed" 1966 (Stunts); "Monte Walsh" 1970 (Marshal); "The Life and Times of Judge Roy Bean" 1972. ¶TV: *Tales of Wells Fargo*—"Home Town" 11-16-59 (Lasser); *Bonanza*—"Danger Road" 1-11-70 (Ed).

Johnson, Les. TV: *Tales of Wells Fargo*—"Tom Horn" 10-26-59 (Tom Horn); *Wanted—Dead or Alive*—"Reckless" 11-7-59 (Tony Egan).

Johnson, Linda. Films: "The Sundown Kid" 1942 (Lynn Parsons); "Wild Horse Rustlers" 1943 (Ellen); "The Haunted Mine" 1946; "Bandits of Dark Canyon" 1947 (Joan Shaw). ¶TV: *The Lone Ranger*—"Drink of Water" 10-26-50; *The Cisco Kid*—"The Kid Brother" 2-9-52, "Dutchman's Flat" 3-15-52, "Commodore Goes West" 7-12-52.

Johnson, Melodie (1943-). Films: "The Ride to Hangman's Tree" 1967 (Lillie Malone); "Powderkeg" TVM-1971 (Miss Baker). ¶TV: *Laredo*—"Any Way the Wind Blows" 10-28-66 (Eve); *The Rounders*—12-27-66 (Laura Jean Layton); *The Road West*—"Charade of Justice" 3-27-67 (Millie Peters).

Johnson, Michelle. Films: "Far and Away" 1992 (Grace).

Johnson, Noble (1897-1/9/78). Films: "A Western Governor's Humanity" 1915; "Fighting for Love" 1917 (Johnny Little Bear); "The Indian's Lament 1917; "The Red Ace" 1917-serial; "Bull's Eye" 1918-serial; "The Human Tiger" 1918; "Sunset Sprague" 1920 (the Crow); "The Wallop" 1921 (Espinol); "The Loaded Door" 1922 (Blackie Lopez); "Tracks" 1922 (Leon Serrano); "The Gold Hunters" 1925 (Wabigoon); "Flaming Frontier" 1926 (Sitting Bull); "Hands Up!" 1926 (Sitting Bull); "Red Clay" 1927 (Chief Bear Paw); "The Black Ace" 1928; "The Yellow Cameo" 1928-serial; "Redskin" 1929 (Pueblo Jim); "Mystery Ranch" 1932 (Mudo); "The Plainsman" 1936; "Frontier Pony Express" 1939 (Cantrell); "Union Pacific" 1939 (Indian Brave); "Northwest Mounted Police" 1940; "The Ranger and the Lady" 1940 (El Lobo); "Shut My Big Mouth" 1942 (Chief Standing Bull); "Plainsman and the Lady" 1946 (Wassao); "Unconquered" 1947 (Big Ottawa Indian); "The Gallant Legion" 1948; "She Wore a Yellow Ribbon" 1949 (Red Shirt); "North of the Great Divide" 1950 (Nogura).

Johnson, Rafer (1935-). Films: "The Red, White and Black" 1970 (Pvt. Armstrong). ¶TV: *Daniel Boone*—"My Name Is Rawls" 10-7-65 (Rawls).

Johnson, Rita (1913-10/31/65). Films: "My Friend Flicka" 1943 (Nell); "The Michigan Kid" 1947 (Sue).

Johnson, Russell (1924-). Films: "Column South" 1953 (Corp. Biddle); "Law and Order" 1953 (Jimmy Johnson); "Ride Clear of Diablo" 1953 (Ringer); "Seminole" 1953 (Lt. Hamilton); "The Stand at Apache River" 1953 (Greiner); "Tumbleweed" 1953 (Lam); "Many Rivers to Cross" 1955 (Banks); "Strange Lady in Town" 1955 (Shadduck); "Badman's Country" 1958 (the Sundance Kid); "The Saga of Hemp Brown" 1958 (Hook); "A Distant Trumpet" 1964 (Capt. Brinker). ¶TV: *The Adventures of Rin Tin Tin*—"The Tin Soldier" 1-27-56 (Lt.

Greene); *Circus Boy*—"Corky and the Circus Doctor" 10-21-56 (Ben Osgood); *Gunsmoke*—"Bloody Hands" 2-16-57 (Joe Stanger), "The Bear" 2-28-59 (Harry Webb), "The Long Night" 2-17-69 (Diggs), "The Fugitives" 10-23-72 (Link Parrin); *Tales of Wells Fargo*—"Rio Grande" 6-3-57 (William Dodd), "To Kill a Town" 3-21-62 (Normalie Hall); *Wagon Train*—"The Cliff Grundy Story" 12-25-57 (Clint McCullough), "The Beauty Jamison Story" 12-17-58 (Steve Marshall), "The Shiloh Degnan Story" 11-7-62 (Major Dan Marriott); *Jefferson Drum*—"A Very Deadly Game" 5-30-58 (the Sundown Kid); *The Californians*—"Overland Mail" 10-28-58; *Lawman*—"The Encounter" 1-18-59 (Ward Horgan); *Black Saddle*—Regular 1959 (Marshal Gib Scott); *Laramie*—"Killer's Odds" 4-25-61 (Stanton), "The Perfect Gift" 1-2-62 (Wayne Cady), "The Dynamiters" 3-6-62 (Bob Murkland), "Double Eagles" 11-20-62 (Al Denning), "Badge of Glory" 5-7-63; *The Deputy*—"Lawman's Conscience" 7-1-61 (Albee Beckett); *Wide Country*—"Who Killed Edde Gannon?" 10-11-62 (Arch McHugh); *The Dakotas*—"Mutiny at Fort Mercy" 1-21-63 (Lt. Clyde Mariot); *Empire*—"Arrow in the Sky" 4-9-63 (Bill Carey); *Rawhide*—"Incident at Alkali Sink" 5-24-63 (Burt Harvey); *The Big Valley*—"The Good Thieves" 1-1-68 (Davey Dunigan).

Johnson, Sander. TV: *The Quest*—"The Longest Drive" 12-1-76 & 12-8-76 (Billy Donn); *How the West Was Won*—Episode One 2-6-77 (Charlie Judson), Episode Two 2-7-77 (Charlie Judson), Episode Three 2-14-77 (Charlie Judson).

Johnson, Tefft (1887-10/56). Films: "Billy the Kid" 1911; "Una of the Sierras" 1912; "Yellow Bird" 1912.

Johnson, Tor (1903-5/12/71). Films: "The San Francisco Story" 1952 (Buck). ¶TV: *Bonanza*—"San Francisco Holiday" 4-2-60 (Busthead Brannigan).

Johnson, Van (1916-). Films: "The Siege at Red River" 1954 (Jim Farraday); "The Price of Power" 1969-Ital./Span. (President Garfield). ¶TV: *Zane Grey Theater*—"Deadfall" 2-19-59 (Frank Gilette); *The Men from Shiloh*—"The Angus Killer" 2-10-71 (Alonzo).

Johnson, Vida. Films: "The Desert Scorpion" 1920 (the Cattle King's Daughter).

Johnston, J.W. (1876-8/1/46). Films: "The Trail of the Hanging Rock" 1913; "The Caballero's Wife"

1914; "Rose of the Rancho" 1914 (Kearney); "The Stirrup Brother" 1914; "The Virginian" 1914 (Steve); "Where the Trail Divides" 1914 (Clayton Craig); "The Cost of Hatred" 1917 (Robert Amory); "Speedy Meade" 1919 (Henry Dillman); "Channing of the Northwest" 1922 (Buddy); "Partners of the Sunset" 1922 (Jim Worth); "The Valley of Silent Men" 1922 (Jacques Radison); "Desert Valley" 1926 (Timothy Dean); "Union Pacific" 1939.

Johnston, John Dennis. Films: "Pale Rider" 1985 (Deputy Tucker); "Longarm" TVM-1988; "Sunset" 1988 (Ed); "Miracle in the Wilderness" TVM-1991 (Sam Webster); "Wyatt Earp" 1994 (Frank Stillwell). ¶TV: *Best of the West*—1-21-82 (Curtis); *Bret Maverick*—"The Hidalgo Thing" 5-4-82 (Burt Full Moon); *Ned Blessing: The Story of My Life and Times*—"The Smink Brothers" 9-1-93 (Albert Smink).

Johnston, Lorimer (1858-2/20/41). Films: "Ruth of the Range" 1923-serial.

Johnstone, Lamar (1886-5/21/19). Films: "Grease Paint Indians" 1913; "Ben Blair" 1916 (Scott Winthrop); "Last of the Duanes" 1919 (Captain Neil); "The Lone Star Ranger" 1919 (Jeff Lawson); "A Man in the Open" 1919 (Bull Brookes); "The Sheriff's Son" 1919 (Brad Charlton); "Tapering Fingers" 1919.

Johnstone, William. Films: "Riding Shotgun" 1954 (Col. Flynn).

Joiner, Pat (1929-10/30/78). TV: *Death Valley Days*—"The Homeliest Man in Nevada" 11-7-55.

Jolley, Charles. Films: "Rancho Notorious" 1952 (Deputy Warren).

Jolley, I. Stanford (1900-12/7/78). Films: "The Big Show" 1937; "Ghost Town Gold" 1937; "Arizona Bound" 1941; "Rollin' Home to Texas" 1941 (Red); "Trail of the Silver Spurs" 1941 (Jingler); "Arizona Roundup" 1942; "Boot Hill Bandits" 1942 (the Mesquite Kid); "Border Roundup" 1942; "Dawn on the Great Divide" 1942; "Outlaws of Boulder Pass" 1942; "Prairie Pals" 1942 (Ace Shannon); "The Rangers Take Over" 1942 (Rance Blair); "The Sombrero Kid" 1942 (Taggart); "Valley of Vanishing Men" 1942-serial; "Bad Men of Thunder Gap" 1943; "Frontier Fury" 1943 (Nick Dawson); "Frontier Law" 1943 (Weasel); "The Kid Rides Again" 1943 (Mort); "Man from Music Mountain" 1943; "The Return of the Rangers" 1943; "Wild Horse Stampede" 1943; "Wolves of

the Range" 1943 (Dorn); "Black Arrow" 1944-serial; "Blazing Frontier" 1944 (Sharp); "Brand of the Devil" 1944; "Cyclone Prairie Rangers" 1944; "Death Rides the Plains" 1944 (Rogan); "Gangsters of the Frontier" 1944; "Oklahoma Raiders" 1944 (Colonel); "Outlaw Roundup" 1944; "Swing, Cowboy, Swing" 1944; "Trail of Terror" 1944 (Hank); "Trouble at Melody Mesa" 1944; "The Whispering Skull" 1944; "Fighting Bill Carson" 1945; "Flaming Bullets" 1945; "Frontier Fugitives" 1945; "Gangster's Den" 1945 (Horace Black); "Outlaws of the Rockies" 1945 (Ace Lanning); "Prairie Rustlers" 1945 (Matt); "Stagecoach Outlaws" 1945 (Steve); "Ambush Trail" 1946 (Hatch Bolton); "Border Bandits" 1946; "Lightning Raiders" 1946 (Kane); "'Neath Canadian Skies" 1946; "North of the Border" 1946; "Silver Range" 1946; "Six Gun Man" 1946 (Matt Haley); "Terrors on Horseback" 1946 (Grant Barlow); "Two-Fisted Ranger" 1946; "Land of the Lawless" 1947; "Prairie Express" 1947 (Sheriff); "West of Dodge City" 1947; "Wild Country" 1947 (Rif Caton); "The Adventures of Frank and Jesse James" 1948-serial (Ward); "Check Your Guns" 1948 (Brad); "Dangers of the Canadian Mounted" 1948-serial (J.P. Belanco); "The Fighting Ranger" 1948; "Gunning for Justice" 1948; "Oklahoma Blues" 1948 (Beasley); "Tex Granger" 1948-serial (Dance Carson); "Bandit King of Texas" 1949 (Willets); "Desert Vigilante" 1949; "Ghost of Zorro" 1949-serial (Paul Hobson); "Gun Law Justice" 1949; "Haunted Trails" 1949 (Joe Rankin); "Roll, Thunder, Roll" 1949 (El Conejo); "Rimfire" 1949 (Toad); "Son of Billy the Kid" 1949 (Fergus); "Stampede" 1949 (Link Spain); "Hostile Country" 1950 (Bartender); "The Baron of Arizona" 1950 (Secretary of Interior); "Colorado Ranger" 1950 (Bartender); "Curtain Call at Cactus Creek" 1950 (Pecow); "Desperadoes of the West" 1950-serial (J.B. "Dude" Dawson); "Fast on the Draw" 1950; "Sierra" 1950 (Snake Willens); "Trigger, Jr." 1950 (Doc Brown); "Canyon Raiders" 1951; "Cattle Queen" 1951 (Scarface); "Don Daredevil Rides Again" 1951-serial (Sheriff); "Lawless Cowboys" 1951 (Sheriff); "The Longhorn" 1951 (Robinson); "Nevada Badmen" 1951; "Oklahoma Justice" 1951; "Stage to Blue River" 1951 (Westbrook); "Texans Never Cry" 1951 (Red); "Texas Lawmen" 1951 (Bart Morrow); "Whistling Hills" 1951 (Chet Norman); "Dead Man's

Trail" 1952; "Fargo" 1952; "Fort Osage" 1952 (Sam Winfield); "The Gunman" 1952; "Kansas Territory" 1952 (Slater); "The Lawless Breed" 1952 (2nd Bartender); "Leadville Gunslinger" 1952 (Cliff Saunders); "The Man from Black Hills" 1952 (Pete Ingram); "Rodeo" 1952 (Pete Adkins); "Waco" 1952 (Curly Ivers); "Wagons West" 1952 (Slocum); "Wild Stallion" 1952 (Bill Cole); "Wyoming Roundup" 1952 (Earl Craven); "Yukon Gold" 1952; "The Marksman" 1953; "Rebel City" 1953 (Perry); "Son of Belle Star" 1953 (Rocky); "Topeka" 1953 (Doctor); "Tumbleweed" 1953 (Ted); "Vigilante Terror" 1953; "The Desperado" 1954 (Mr. Garner); "The Forty-Niners" 1954 (Everett); "Man with the Steel Whip" 1954-serial (Sloane); "Silver Lode" 1954 (Searcher); "Two Guns and a Badge" 1954 (Allen); "I Killed Wild Bill Hickok" 1956 (Henry Longtree); "Kentucky Rifle" 1956; "The Proud Ones" 1956 (Crooked Card Player); "The Rawhide Years" 1956 (Man); "The Wild Dakotas" 1956; "The Young Guns" 1956 (Felix Briggs); "Gun Battle at Monterey" 1957 (Idwall); "Gunsight Ridge" 1957 (Daggett); "The Halliday Brand" 1957; "The Iron Sheriff" 1957 (Walden); "The Oklahoman" 1957 (Storekeeper); "Outlaw Queen" 1957; "Lone Texan" 1959 (Trades); "The Miracle of the Hills" 1959 (Dr. Tuttle); "Thirteen Fighting Men" 1960 (Pvt. Ebb); "The Firebrand" 1962; "Terror at Black Falls" 1962; "The Bounty Killer" 1965 (Sheriff Jones). ¶TV: *The Lone Ranger*— "Rifles and Renegades" 5-4-50, "Lady Killer" 12-21-50, "Trader Boggs" 1-15-53, "Hidden Fortune" 6-18-53; *The Gene Autry Show*—"The Breakup" 11-5-50, "Twisted Trails" 11-12-50, "Talking Guns" 8-10-54, "Civil War at Deadwood" 9-14-54; *The Cisco Kid*—"Lynching Story" 4-28-51, "Confession for Money" 5-26-51, "Pancho Hostage" 6-23-51, "Hidden Valley Pirates" 10-27-51, "Quarter Horse" 12-8-51, "Freedom of the Press" 9-27-52, "The Raccoon Story" 11-15-52, "Trouble in Tonopah" 3-21-53, "Stolen River" 10-3-53, "Montezuma's Treasure" 11-7-53; *Sky King*—"The Plastic Ghost 9-30-51 (Fallon); *The Roy Rogers Show*—"The Unwilling Outlaw" 3-8-52 (Jed Collins), "Ghost Gulch" 3-30-52, "His Weight in Wildcats" 11-11-56; *Wild Bill Hickok*—"A Joke on Sir Antony" 4-1-52, "Ol' Pardner Rides Again" 9-16-52; *Tales of the Texas Rangers*—"West of Sonora" 9-17-55; *Death Valley Days*—"California's First

Ice Man" 1-14-56 (Colby), "Gold Rush in Reverse" 10-21-57, "Eruption at Volcano" 2-24-59 (Taylor); *Sergeant Preston of the Yukon*—"Fancy Dan" 4-5-56 (Sam Haley), "Gold Rush Patrol" 1-16-58 (Frisco); *Wyatt Earp*—"The Hanging Judge" 12-18-56, "Last Stand at Smoky Hill" 1-20-59 (Charlie Andrews), "The Ring of Death" 11-3-59 (Limey Parkhamp), "The Toughest Judge in Arizona" 5-24-60 (Mine Foreman), "A Papa for Butch and Ginger" 5-9-61; *Maverick*—"Diamond in the Rough" 1-26-58 (McClure), "Alias Bart Maverick" 10-5-58 (Sheriff), "Holiday at Hollow Rock" 12-28-58 (Stableman), "Trooper Maverick" 11-29-59 (Dakota Cadman), "Bundle from Britain" 9-18-60 (Kratkovitch), "Poker Face" 1-7-62 (Chauncey); *26 Men*—"Panic at Bisbee" 2-4-58, "My Brother's Keeper" 12-2-58, "Redskin" 5-5-59, "Terror in Paradise" 5-19-59; *Fury*—"The Horse Nobody Wanted" 2-15-58 (Jake); *Wagon Train*—"The Mark Hanford Story" 2-26-58 (Martin), "The Saul Bevins Story" 4-12-61 (Jed), "The John Turnbull Story" 5-30-62 (Burro Beedle), "The Clarence Mullins Story" 5-1-63 (Harvey Mullins), "The Myra Marshall Story" 10-21-63, "The Fenton Canaby Story" 12-30-63, "The Ben Engel Story" 3-16-64 (Jenks); *The Restless Gun*—"The Gold Star" 5-19-58 (Sam Baggott); *Decision*—"The Tall Man" 7-27-58 (Russ); *Wanted—Dead or Alive*—"Shawnee Bill" 10-4-58; *Lawman*—"Wanted" 11-16-58, "Firehouse Lil" 1-8-61 (Bandit); *Have Gun Will Travel*—"Death of a Gunfighter" 3-14-59; *Bonanza*—"The Paiute War" 10-3-59, "The Gamble" 4-1-62, "A Question of Strength" 10-27-63, "Return to Honor" 3-22-64 (Bixby), "Peace Officer" 2-6-66 (Jonesy), "Company of Forgotten Men" 2-2-69 (Jackson); *The Alaskans*—"Contest at Gold Bottom" 11-15-59 (Beriah Jackson); *Bronco*—"Shadow of Jesse James" 1-12-60 (Old Man Shirley); *Wichita Town*—"Paid in Full" 3-23-60 (Smokey); *Tales of Wells Fargo*— "The Hand That Shook the Hand" 2-6-61 (Perfesser); *Cheyenne*—"Winchester Quarantine" 9-25-61 (Smokey), "Cross Purpose" 10-9-61 (Corporal McCauley); *Rawhide*—"The Peddler" 1-19-62 (Caretaker), "Incident of the Four Horsemen" 10-26-62 (Justice of the Peace), "Incident of the Pale Rider" 3-15-63 (Doctor), "Incident at Alkali Sink" 5-24-63 (Preacher), "Incident at Zebulon" 3-5-64; *The Tall Man*—"Quarantine" 3-17-62 (Stranger); *Wide Country*— "The Girl in the Sunshine Smile"

11-15-62 (Woody); *The Rifleman*— "Hostages to Fortune" 2-4-63 (Joe Fogner); *The Virginian*—"Run Away Home" 4-24-63; *Gunsmoke*—"Carter Caper" 11-16-63 (Mims), "The Hostage" 12-4-65 (Sheriff Foley), "Prairie Wolfers" 11-13-67 (Grandpa), "Lyle's Kid" 9-23-68 (Attendant), "The Reprisal" 2-10-69 (Jeb), "The Devil's Outpost" 9-22-69 (Tilman), "Morgan" 3-2-70 (Zack), "The Witness" 11-23-70 (Beecher); *Daniel Boone*—"A Place of 1000 Spirits" 2-4-65 (Tavern Keeper); *Laredo*—"A Matter of Policy" 11-11-65 (Jarvis); *Branded*—"The Greatest Coward on Earth" 11-21-65 (Enos Scoggins); *The Big Valley*—"A Noose Is Waiting" 11-13-67; *The High Chaparral*—"The Widow from Red Rock" 11-26-67 (Foreman); *Cimarron Strip*—"The Judgment" 1-4-68.

Jolley, Norman. Films: "Flashing Guns" 1947 (Foley); "Pursued" 1947 (Callum); "Silver River" 1948 (Scout); "Two-Gun Lady" 1956 (Gruber).

Jones, Allan (1907-6/27/92). Films: "Rose Marie" 1936 (Romeo/ Mario Cavaradossi); "Senorita from the West" 1945; "Stage to Thunder Rock" 1964 (Mayor Ted Dollar).

Jones, Beulah Hall. Films: "Drums Along the Mohawk" 1939 (Daisy).

Jones, Bill. Films: "The Lone Ranger" 1938-serial (Trooper); "Santa Fe Marshal" 1940; "Gunsmoke" 1947; "She Wore a Yellow Ribbon" 1949 (Courier).

Jones, Billy "Red" (1889-11/23/40). Films: "The Phantom Flyer" 1928 (Nick Crandall); "Get That Girl" 1932.

Jones, Buck (1889-11/30/42). Films: "Riders of the Purple Sage" 1918; "True Blue" 1918; "Western Blood" 1918; "The Sheriff's Son" 1919; "Firebrand Trevison" 1920 (Firebrand Trevison); "Forbidden Trails" 1920 (Quinton "Squint" Taylor); "Just Pals" 1920 (Bim); "The Last Straw" 1920 (Tom Beck); "The Square Shooter" 1920 (Chick Crandall); "Sunset Sprague" 1920 (Sunset Sprague); "Two Moons" 1920 (Bill Blunt); "Bar Nothin'" 1921 (Duke Travis); "The Big Punch" 1921; "Get Your Man" 1921 (Jock MacTier); "The One-Man Trail" 1921; "Riding with Death" 1921 (Dynamite Steve Dorsey); "Straight from the Shoulder" 1921 (the Mediator); "To a Finish" 1921 (Jim Blake); "Bells of San Juan" 1922 (Roerick Norton); "The Fast Mail" 1922 (Stanley Carson); "Rough Shod" 1922 (Steel Brannon); "Trooper O'Neil" 1922 (Trooper

O'Neil); "Western Speed" 1922 (Red Kane); "The Footlight Ranger" 1923 (Bill Moreland); "Hell's Hole" 1923 (Tod Musgrave); "Snowdrift" 1923 (Carter Brent); "Against All Odds" 1924 (Chick Newton); "Circus Cowboy" 1924 (Buck Saxon); "The Desert Outlaw" 1924 (Sam Langdon); "Not a Drum Was Heard" 1924 (Jack Mills); "The Vagabond Trail" 1924 (Donnegan); "The Arizona Romeo" 1925 (Tom Long); "The Desert's Price" 1925 (Wils McCann); "Durand of the Bad Lands" 1925 (Dick Durand); "Gold and the Girl" 1925 (Dan Prentiss); "Hearts and Spurs" 1925 (Hal Emory); "The Man Who Played Square" 1925 (Matt Black); "The Timber Wolf" 1925 (Bruce Standing); "The Trail Rider" 1925 (Tex Hartwell); "The Cowboy and the Countess" 1926 (Jerry Whipple); "Desert Valley" 1926 (Fitzsmith); "The Fighting Buckaroo" 1926 (Larry Crawford); "The Flying Horseman" 1926 (Mark Winton); "The Gentle Cyclone" 1926 (Absolem Wells); "A Man Four-Square" 1926 (Craig Norton); "Black Jack" 1927 (Phil Dolan); "Chain Lightning" 1927 (Steve Lannon); "Good as Gold" 1927 (Buck Brady); "Hills of Peril" 1927 (Laramie); "The War Horse" 1927 (Buck Thomas); "Whispering Sage" 1927 (Buck Kildare); "The Big Hop" 1928 (Buck Bronson); "Blood Will Tell" 1928 (Buck Peters); "The Branded Sombrero" 1928 (Starr Hallett); "The Dawn Trail" 1930 (Larry); "The Lone Rider" 1930 (Jim Lanning); "Men Without Law" 1930 (Buck Healy); "Shadow Ranch" 1930 (Sim Baldwin); "Border Law" 1931 (Jim Houston); "Branded" 1931 (Tom Dale); "The Avenger" 1931 (Joaquin Murieta); "Desert Vengeance" 1931 (Jim Cardew); "The Fighting Sheriff" 1931 (Bob Terry); "The Range Feud" 1931 (Sheriff Buck Gordon); "The Texas Ranger" 1931 (Ranger Jim Logan); "The Deadline" 1932 (Buck Donlin); "Forbidden Trail" 1932 (Tom Devlin); "Hello Trouble" 1932 (Ranger Jeff Douglas); "McKenna of the Mounted" 1932 (Sgt. Tom McKenna); "One-Man Law" 1932 (Brand Thompson); "Ridin' for Justice" 1932 (Buck Randall); "South of the Rio Grande" 1932 (Carlos); "White Eagle" 1932 (John Harvey/White Eagle); "The California Trail" 1933 (Santa Fe Stewart); "Gordon of Ghost City" 1933-serial (Buck Gordon); "The Sundown Rider" 1933 (Camp O'Neill); "The Thrill Hunter" 1933 (Buck Crosby); "Treason" 1933 (Jeff Connors); "Unknown Valley" 1933 (Joe Gordon); "The

Fighting Code" 1934 (Ben Halliday/Grover Jones); "The Fighting Ranger" 1934 (Jim Houston); "The Man Trailer" 1934 (Dan Lee/Track Ames); "The Red Rider" 1934-serial (Red Davidson); "Rocky Rhodes" 1934 (Rocky Rhodes); "When a Man Sees Red" 1934 (Buck Benson); "Border Brigands" 1935 (Lt. Tim Barry); "The Crimson Trail" 1935 (Billy Carter); "Ivory-Handled Gun" 1935 (Buck Ward); "Outlawed Guns" 1935 (Reece Rivers); "The Roaring West" 1935-serial (Montana Larkin); "Stone of Silver Creek" 1935 (T. William Stone); "The Throwback" 1935 (Buck Saunders); "Boss Rider of Gun Creek" 1936 (Larry Day/Gary Elliott); "The Cowboy and the Kid" 1936 (Steve Davis); "For the Service" 1936 (Buck O'Bryan); "The Phantom Rider" 1936-serial (Buck Grant); "Ride 'Em Cowboy" 1936 (Jess Burns); "Silver Spurs" 1936 (Jim Fentriss); "Sunset of Power" 1936 (Cliff Lea); "Black Aces" 1937 (Ted Ames); "Boss of Lonely Valley" 1937 (Steve Hanson); "Empty Saddles" 1937 (Buck Devlin); "Headin' East" 1937 (Buck Benson); "Law for Tombstone" 1937 (Alamo Bowie); "Left-Handed Law" 1937 (Alamo Bowie); "Sandflow" 1937 (Buck Hallett); "Smoke Tree Range" 1937 (Lee Cary); "Sudden Bill Dorn" 1937 (Sudden Bil Dorn); "California Frontier" 1938 (Buck Pearson); "Hollywood Roundup" 1938 (Buck Kennedy); "Law of the Texan" 1938 (Sergeant Buck Weaver); "The Overland Express" 1938 (Buck Dawson); "The Stranger from Arizona" 1938 (Buck Weylan); "Wagons Westward" 1940 (Sheriff Jim McDaniels); "Arizona Bound" 1941; "Forbidden Trails" 1941 (Buck Roberts); "The Gunman from Bodie" 1941; "Riders of Death Valley" 1941-serial (Tombstone); "White Eagle" 1941-serial (White Eagle); "Below the Border" 1942 (Buck Roberts); "Dawn on the Great Divide" 1942 (Buck Roberts); "Down Texas Way" 1942 (Buck); "Ghost Town Law" 1942 (Buck Roberts); "Riders of the West" 1942 (Buck Roberts); "West of the Law" 1942.

Jones, Carolyn (1933-8/3/83). Films: "Three Hours to Kill" 1954 (Polly); "Last Train from Gun Hill" 1959 (Linda); "How the West Was Won" 1962 (Julie Rawlings); "Heaven with a Gun" 1969 (Madge McCloud). ¶TV: *Zane Grey Theater*—"Until the Man Dies" 1-25-57 (Ella), "Picture of Sal" 1-28-60 (Sal), "Blood Red" 1-29-61 (Julie Whiting); *Wagon Train*—"The John Cameron Story" 10-2-57 (Julie Cameron), "The Jenna Dou-

glas Story" 11-1-61 (Jenna Douglas), "The Molly Kincaid Story" 9-16-63; *Frontier Circus*—"Stopover in Paradise" 2-22-62 (Amy Tyson); *Rango*—"What's a Nice Girl Like You Doing Holding Up a Place Like This?" 2-17-67 (Belle Starker); *The Men from Shiloh*—"The Legacy of Spencer Flats" 1-27-71 (Annie).

Jones, Charles. Films: "Pardon My Nerve!" 1922 (Racey Dawson); "West of Chicago" 1922 (Conroy Daly); "Western Luck" 1924 (Larry Campbell).

Jones, Chester (1899-6/27/75). TV: *Jim Bowie*—"Thieves' Market" 3-29-57 (Scipio).

Jones, Chris (1941-). TV: *The Legend of Jesse James*—Regular 1965-66 (Jesse James).

Jones, Claude Earl. TV: *Centennial*—Regular 1978-79 (Matt).

Jones, Darby (1910-11/30/86). Films: "Wells Fargo" 1937 (Black Man).

Jones, Dean (1933-). TV: *Zane Grey Theater*—"The Sunday Man" 2-25-60 (Bill Devlin); *The Outlaws*—"Beat the Drum Slowly" 10-20-60 (Danny Cannon); *Stagecoach West*—"Red Sand" 11-22-60 (Brady); *Bonanza*—"The Friendship" 11-12-61 (Danny Kidd); *Tales of Wells Fargo*—"A Killing in Calico" 12-16-61 (Jamie Coburn); *Wagon Train*—"The Lieutenant Burton Story" 2-28-62 (Lieutenant Burton).

Jones, Dickie (1927-). Films: "Moonlight on the Prairie" 1935 (Dickie Roberts); "Trail of the Hawk" 1935 (Dickie); "Westward Ho" 1935 (Young Jim Wyatt); "Daniel Boone" 1936 (Jerry); "Renfrew of the Royal Mounted" 1937 (Tommy MacDonald); "Smoke Tree Range" 1937 (Teddy Page); "Wild Horse Round-Up" 1937 (Dickie Williams); "Border Wolves" 1938 (Jimmie Benton); "The Frontiersman" 1938 (Artie Peters); "The Great Adventures of Wild Bill Hickok" 1938 (Bud); "Hollywood Roundup" 1938 (Dickie Stevens); "Land of Fighting Men" 1938 (Jimmy Mitchell); "Destry Rides Again" 1939 (Eli Whitney Claggett); "Brigham Young—Frontiersman" 1940 (Henry Kent); "Hi-Yo Silver" 1940; "Virginia City" 1940 (Cobby); "The Vanishing Virginian" 1941 (Robert Yancey, Jr.); "The Outlaw" 1943 (Boy); "The Strawberry Roan" 1948 (Joe Bailey); "Sons of New Mexico" 1949 (Randy Pryor); "Redwood Forest Trail" 1950 (Mighty Mite); "Rocky Mountain" 1950 (Jim Wheat); "Fort Worth" 1951 (Luther

Wick); "The Old West" 1952 (Pinto); "Wagon Team" 1952 (Dave Weldon); "Last of the Pony Riders" 1953 (Johnny Blair); "The Wild Dakotas" 1956; "Requiem for a Gunfighter" 1965 (Fletcher). ¶TV: *The Lone Ranger*—"Rustler's Hideout" 10-13-49, "Man Without a Gun" 6-15-50; *The Gene Autry Show*—"Gun Powder Range" 10-29-50, "The Sheriff of Santa Rosa" 12-24-50, "Warning! Danger!" 11-10-51, "Bandits of Boulder Bluff" 11-24-51 (Tom Colby), "Horse Sense" 1-11-52, "The Western Way" 2-1-52, "The Sheriff Is a Lady" 3-23-52, "Santa Fe Raiders" 7-6-54, "Sharpshooter" 8-3-54 (Randy Barker), "Outlaw of Blue Mesa" 9-7-54; *The Range Rider*—Regular 1951-53 (Dick West); *Buffalo Bill, Jr.*—Regular 1955-56 (Buffalo Bill, Jr.).

Jones, Edgar "King Fisher". Films: "The Deputy's Peril" 1912; "The Minister and the Outlaw" 1912; "Ranch-Mates" 1912; "On the Mountain Ranch" 1913; "Men of the Mountain" 1915; "On Bitter Creek" 1915; "The Trapper's Revenge" 1915; "Wild Honey" 1918 (Dick Hadding); "The Ace of the Saddle" 1919; "By Indian Post" 1919; "The Last Outlaw" 1919; "The Boss of Copperhead" 1920; "Action" 1921 (Art Smith); "The Big Punch" 1921 (the Sheriff).

Jones, Edward. Films: "The Girl from Sunset Pass" 1913; "The Girl of Gold Gulch" 1916; "Cheyenne's Pal" 1917; "The Texas Sphinx" 1917; "Wild Women" 1918 (Pelon); "A Woman's Fool" 1918 (Honey Wiggins); "Sundown Slim" 1920 (Sheriff); "The Black Ace" 1928; "45 Calibre War" 1929 (Sheriff Henshaw).

Jones, Elizabeth "Tiny" (1875-3/22/52). Films: "Drums Along the Mohawk" 1939 (Mrs. Reall); "Melody Ranch" 1940; "Unconquered" 1947 (Bondswoman).

Jones, Fenton. Films: "Beyond the Purple Hills" 1950; "Slaughter Trail" 1951 (Caller); "One-Eyed Jacks" 1961 (Square Dance Caller). ¶TV: *Rawhide*—"Incident of His Brother's Keeper" 3-31-61 (Square Dance Caller).

Jones, Fred C. Films: "Flower of No Man's Land" 1916 (Pedro); "God's Country and the Law" 1922 (Andre); "The Man Who Paid" 1922 (Louis Duclor); "Don Quickshot of the Rio Grande" 1923 (George Vivian).

Jones, George Washington. Films: "The Struggle" 1921 (Pumpkins).

Jones, Gordon (1911-6/20/63). Films: "Beau Bandit" 1930 (Cow-

hand); "Three Rogues" 1931 (Teamster); "Forlorn River" 1937 (Lem Watkins); "Out West with the Hardys" 1938 (Ray Holt); "Henry Goes Arizona" 1939 (Tug Evans); "Texas Rangers Ride Again" 1940 (Announcer); "The Wistful Widow of Wagon Gap" 1947 (Jake Frame); "Black Eagle" 1948 (Benjy Laughton); "Sons of Adventure" 1948 (Andy); "The Untamed Breed" 1948 (Happy Keegan); "The Arizona Cowboy" 1950 (I.Q. Barton); "North of the Great Divide" 1950 (Splinters); "The Palomino" 1950 (Bill); "Sunset in the West" 1950 (Splinters); "Trail of Robin Hood" 1950 (Splinters McGonigle, the Blacksmith); "Trigger, Jr." 1950 (Splinters); "Heart of the Rockies" 1951 (Splinters); "Spoilers of the Plains" 1951 (Splinters); "Wagon Team" 1952 (U.S. Marshal Jones); "The Woman They Almost Lynched" 1953 (Sergeant); "The Outlaw Stallion" 1954 (Wagner); "Smoke Signal" 1955 (Cpl. Rogers); "Treasure of Ruby Hills" 1955 (Voyle); "Shoot-Out at Medicine Bend" 1957 (Clegg); "McClintock" 1963 (Matt Douglas). ¶TV: *Wild Bill Hickok*—"Tax Collecting Story" 8-7-51; *The Gene Autry Show*—"Warning! Danger!" 11-10-51, "Bandits of Boulder Bluff" 11-24-51; *Wyatt Earp*—"Marshal Earp Plays Cupid" 1-3-56; *Fury*—"Wonder Horse" 3-24-56 (Jeff); *Jim Bowie*—"Counterfeit Dixie" 9-27-57 (Pat Donovan); *Broken Arrow*—"Smoke Signal" 12-10-57 (Sgt. Temby); *Death Valley Days*—"The Rival Hash House" 12-30-58; *Lawman*—"The Gunmen" 2-15-59 (Chalk Hennessey); *The Rifleman*—"The Wrong Man" 3-31-59 (Carnival Barker), "Stopover" 4-25-61 (Medford); *Maverick*—"Full House" 10-25-59 (Marshal), "The Troubled Heir" 4-1-62 (Ward Quillan); *Colt .45*—"Chain of Command" 4-5-60 (Sergeant O'Hickey); *Frontier Circus*—"Lippizan" 10-19-61 (Rousty), "The Good Fight" 4-19-62 (Jase); *Have Gun Will Travel*—"Marshal of Sweetwater" 11-24-62 (Brawley).

Jones, Grace (1952-). Films: "Straight to Hell" 1987-Brit. (Sonya).

Jones, Henry (1912-). Films: "3:10 to Yuma" 1957 (Alex Potter); "Something for a Lonely Man" TVM-1968 (R.J. Hoferkamp); "Butch Cassidy and the Sundance Kid" 1969 (Bike Salesman); "Support Your Local Sheriff" 1969 (Preacher Henry Jackson); "The Cockeyed Cowboys of Calico County" 1970 (Hanson); "Dirty Dingus Magee" 1970 (Rev. Green); "Skin Game" 1971 (Sam); "Support Your Local

Gunfighter" 1971 (Ez); "The Daughters of Joshua Cabe" TVM-1972 (Codge Collier); "California Gold Rush" TVM-1981 (Joe Gillis). ¶TV: *Frontier Circus*—"The Courtship" 2-15-62 (Marshal Longstreet); *The Outlaws*—"Ride the Man Down" 3-8-62 (Henry Plummer); *Wagon Train*—"The Terry Morrell Story" 4-25-62 (Ben Morrell); *Bonanza*—"A Knight to Remember" 12-20-64 (King Arthur), "The Younger Brothers' Younger Brother" 3-12-72; *A Man Called Shenandoah*—"Town on Fire" 11-8-65 (Arnold Shaw); *Daniel Boone*—"The Spanish Horse" 11-23-67 (Landers), "Minnow for a Shark" 1-2-69 (Jonas Morgan); *The Big Valley*—"Court Martial" 3-6-67 (General Alderson); *Gunsmoke*—"Stranger in Town" 11-20-67 (Harvey Cagle), "The Badge" 2-2-70 (Papa Steiffer), "No Tomorrow" 1-3-72 (J. Luther Gross); *The Guns of Will Sonnett*—"Chapter and Verse" 10-11-68 (Preacher); *Here Come the Brides*—"Mr. and Mrs. J. Bolt" 3-12-69 (Jebediah); *The Virginian*—"No War for the Warrior" 2-18-70 (Ned Cochran); *Alias Smith and Jones*—"The Day They Hanged Kid Curry" 9-16-71; *Hec Ramsey*—"The Mystery of Chalk Hill" 2-18-73 (Doc Kirby); *Gun Shy*—Regular 1983 (Homer McCoy).

Jones, Ivy. TV: *Gunsmoke*—"Homecoming" 1-8-73 (Martha Beal).

Jones, J. Parks (1890-1/11/50). Films: "Hawk of the Hills" 1927-serial (Lieutenant MacCready).

Jones, James Earl (1931-). Films: "Grim Prairie Tales" 1990 (Morrison); "Sommersby" 1993 (Court Bailiff).

Jones, Jay. TV: *The High Chaparral*—"Alliance" 12-12-69 (Lieutenant Cooper); *Bonanza*—"Danger Road" 1-11-70 (Willard), "Kingdom of Fear" 4-4-71 (1st Gunman), "A Place to Hide" 3-19-72 (Twohy), "Forever" 9-12-72 (Carver); *Kung Fu*—"One Step to Darkness" 1-25-75 (the Demon).

Jones, Jeffrey. Films: "The Gambler, Part III—The Legend Continues" TVM-1987 (Buffalo Bill); "The Avenging Angel" TVM-1995.

Jones, Jennifer (Phyllis Isley) (1919-). Films: "New Frontier" 1939 (Celia); "Duel in the Sun" 1946 (Pearl Chavez).

Jones, John Paul. Films: "The Devil Horse" 1932-serial; "The California Trail" 1933 (Lopez); "White Eagle" 1941-serial.

Jones, Karen. Films: "The Good

Old Boys" TVM-1995 (Cora Law-dermilk).

Jones, Kevin. TV: *Death Valley Days*—"Man on the Road" 4-5-60 (Pete Rawson); *Zane Grey Theater*—"Morning Incident" 12-29-60 (Jason).

Jones, L.Q. (1936-) Films: "Love Me Tender" 1956 (Fleming); "Buchanan Rides Alone" 1958 (Pecos Bill); "Warlock" 1959 (Jiggs); "Cimarron" 1960 (Mills); "Flaming Star" 1960 (Tom Howard); "Ten Who Dared" 1960 (Billy Hawkins); "Ride the High Country" 1962 (Sylvus Hammond); "Showdown" 1963 (Foray); "Apache Rifles" 1964 (Mike Greer); "Major Dundee" 1965 (Arthur Hadley); "Hang 'Em High" 1968 (Loomis); "The Wild Bunch" 1969 (T.C.); "The Ballad of Cable Hogue" 1970 (Taggart); "The Mc-Masters" 1970 (Russell); "The Hunting Party" 1971-Brit./Ital./Span. (Hog Warren); "The Bravos" TVM-1972 (Ben Lawler); "Pat Garrett and Billy the Kid" 1973 (Black Harris); "Mrs. Sundance" TVM-1974 (Charles Siringo); "Winterhawk" 1975 (Gates); "Banjo Hackett: Roamin' Free" TVM-1976 (Sheriff Tadlock); "Standing Tall" TVM-1978 (Nate Rackley); "The Sacketts" TVM-1979 (Beldon); "Wild Times" TVM-1980 (Wild Bill Hickok); "Timerider" 1983 (Ben Potter); "Lightning Jack" 1994-Australia (Sheriff). ¶TV: *Cheyenne*—Regular 1955-56 (Smitty); *Jefferson Drum*—"The Keeney Gang" 10-3-58 (Burdette); *Tales of Wells Fargo*—"The Cleanup" 1-26-59 (Wes), "Defiant at the Gate" 11-25-61 (Striker); *Wagon Train*—"The Old Man Charvanaugh Story" 2-18-59 (Squirrell Charvanaugh), "The Christopher Hale Story" 3-15-61 (Lenny), "Charlie Wooster—Outlaw" 2-20-63 (Esdras), "The Duncan McIvor Story" 3-9-64; *Black Saddle*—"Client: Banke" 4-11-59 (Jack Shepherd); *Wichita Town*—"Drifting" 10-28-59 (Walter); *Laramie*—"Dark Verdict" 11-24-59 (John McLane), "Cactus Lady" 2-21-61 (Homer), "Siege at Jubilee" 10-10-61 (Truk), "The Replacement" 3-27-62 (Johnny Duncan), "Among the Missing" 9-25-62, "Shadow of the Past" 10-16-62 (Frank Keefer), "The Stranger" 4-23-63 (Sergeant); *Johnny Ringo*—"Four Came Quietly" 1-28-60 (Billy Boy Jethro); *The Rebel*—"The Earl of Durango" 6-12-60 (Otis), "Explosion" 11-27-60 (Roy); *Klondike*—"River of Gold" 10-24-60 (Joe Teel), "Saints and Stickups" 10-31-60 (Joe Teel), "The Unexpected Candidate" 11-7-60 (Joe Teel); *Two Faces West*—"The Last Man" 12-19-60, "The Noose" 5-15-61; *Wyatt Earp*—"Casey and the Clowns" 2-21-61 (Tex); *Have Gun Will Travel*—"Justice in Hell" 1-6-62 (Little Fontana), "The Debutante" 1-19-63 (Hector); *Lawman*—"The Bride" 4-1-62 (Ollie Earnshaw); *The Rifleman*—"Day of Reckoning" 4-9-62 (Charley Breen); *Empire*—"The Convention" 5-14-63 (L.Q.); *Rawhide*—"Incident at El Crucero" 10-10-63 (George Cornelius), "Incident at Gila Flats" 1-30-64 (Corporal Wayne), "The Race" 9-25-64 (Luke); *Gunsmoke*—"Tobe" 10-19-63 (Skinner), "Chicken" 12-5-64 (Brady), "Dry Road to Nowhere" 4-3-65 (Wally), "The Good Samaritans" 3-10-69 (Kittridge), "Albert" 2-9-70 (Nix), "The Gun" 11-19-70 (Sumner Pendleton), "Tara" 1-17-72 (Gecko Ridley); *The Virginian*—Regular 1964-67 (Andy Belden); *Branded*—"Elsie Brown" 2-14-65 (Miles); *A Man Called Shenandoah*—"Rope's End" 1-17-66 (Ben Lloyd); *The Big Valley*—"By Force and Violence" 3-30-66 (Cort), "Court Martial" 3-6-67, "Showdown in Limbo" 3-27-67 (Earl Vaughn), "Ambush" 9-18-67 (Hutch), "Fall of a Hero" 2-5-68 (Gus Vandiver); *Cimarron Strip*—"The Battleground" 9-28-67, "The Search" 11-9-67 (Lummy); *Hondo*—"Hondo and the Death Drive" 12-1-67 (Allie); *Lancer*—"Blind Man's Bluff" 9-23-69 (Slate Meek); *Alias Smith and Jones*—"Stagecoach Seven" 3-11-71 (Clint Weaver), "McGuffin" 12-9-72 (Peterson); *Kung Fu*—"An Eye for an Eye" 1-25-73 (Sgt. Straight), "The Last Raid" 4-26-75 (Major Clarke Bealson); *The Buffalo Soldiers*—Pilot 5-26-79 (Renegade).

Jones, Marcia Mae (1924-). Films: "Tucson" 1949 (Polly Johnson). ¶TV: *Wild Bill Hickok*—"Yellow Haired Kid" 8-28-51; *The Cisco Kid*—"Hypnotist Murder" 11-10-51, "Ghost Town Story" 12-22-51.

Jones, Marilyn. Films: "Support Your Local Sheriff" 1969 (Bordello Girl). ¶TV: *Paradise*—"The News from St. Louis" 10-27-88 (Gloria Benning).

Jones, Marshal (1927-). Films: "Indian Paint" 1965 (Comanche Leader).

Jones, Mickey. Films: "Lacy and the Mississippi Queen" TVM-1978; "Tom Horn" 1980 (Brown's Hole Rustler); "Gunsmoke: Return to Dodge" TVM-1987 (Oakum). ¶TV: *Father Murphy*—"The Piano" 1-19-82 (Leon).

Jones, Miranda. TV: *Lawman*—"The Outsider" 1-4-59 (Rene Lebeau), "Marked Man" 1-22-61 (Murial), "Explosion" 6-3-62 (Bobbie Desmond); *Have Gun Will Travel*—"Juliet" 1-31-59 (Juliet Harper), "Fight at Adobe Wells" 3-12-60 (Juliana Guilder); *Sugarfoot*—"The Mountain" 3-31-59 (Jean Bradley); *Bat Masterson*—"Flume to the Mother Lode" 1-28-60 (Nancy Wilkerson); *Gunsmoke*—"Abe Blocker" 11-24-62 (Mary Groves).

Jones, Morgan (1879-9/21/51). Films: "The Man from New York" 1923 (Dad Crawford).

Jones, Morgan. Films: "Apache Woman" 1955 (Macey). ¶TV: *Wild Bill Hickok*—"The Rainmaker" 4-14-53; *Death Valley Days*—"The Crystal Gazer" 4-11-55; *Judge Roy Bean*—"The Elopers" 4-11-56 (Adam Brimmer), "Spirit of the Law" 4-11-56 (Ed Hart), "Luck O' the Irish" 7-1-56 (Jim Devers); *Death Valley Days*—"Head of the House" 4-7-57; *Tombstone Territory*—"Shoot Out at Dark" 1-8-58 (Sandy); *Maverick*—"Betrayal" 3-22-59 (Buck Wilkerson); *Rawhide*—"Incident of the Sharpshooter" 2-26-60; *Bat Masterson*—"Masterson's Arcadia Club" 4-28-60 (Mace Gunnison); *Gunsmoke*—"Killer at Large" 2-5-66 (Coor); *Daniel Boone*—"Bitter Mission" 3-30-67, "The Fallow Land" 4-13-67, "The King's Shilling" 10-19-67 (Keller).

Jones, Pamela. Films: "Buck and the Preacher" 1972 (Delilah).

Jones, Podner. Films: "Without Honor" 1932 (Mac McLain); "The Arizonian" 1935; "Sunset Range" 1935; "Thunder Trail" 1937 (Cowboy).

Jones, Ray. Films: "Cornered" 1932; "Breed of the Border" 1933; "The Westerner" 1934 (Posse Member); "Gallant Defender" 1935; "Justice of the Range" 1935; "The Outlaw Deputy" 1935; "Rio Grande Ranger" 1936; "Fugitive from Sonora" 1937; "Guns of the Pecos" 1937; "The Old Wyoming Trail" 1937; "Outlaws of the Prairie" 1937; "The Rangers Step In" 1937; "Two-Fisted Sheriff" 1937; "California Frontier" 1938; "The Great Adventures of Wild Bill Hickok" 1938; "Gun Law" 1938; "Outlaw Express" 1938; "The Painted Desert" 1938 (Man in Bar); "Utah Trail" 1938; "West of Rainbow's End" 1938; "Pioneers of the West" 1940; "Gauchos of El Dorado" 1941; "Jesse James at Bay" 1941; "Sheriff of Tombstone" 1941; "The Son of Davy Crockett" 1941; "Wrangler's Roost" 1941; "Bells of Capistrano" 1942; "Dawn on the Great Divide" 1942; "Deep in the Heart of Texas" 1942;

"Prairie Gunsmoke" 1942; "Stagecoach Buckaroo" 1942; "Texas Justice" 1942; "West of Tombstone" 1942; "Westward Ho" 1942; "Arizona Trail" 1943; "Black Hills Express" 1943; "Cowboy Commandos" 1943; "Daredevils of the West" 1943-serial (Barn Heavy #1); "Overland Mail Robbery" 1943; "Robin Hood of the Range" 1943; "Saddles and Sagebrush" 1943; "Tenting Tonight on the Old Camp Ground" 1943; "Wagon Tracks West" 1943; "Boss of Boomtown" 1944; "Law Men" 1944; "The Old Texas Trail" 1944; "Riders of the Santa Fe" 1944; "Trigger Trail" 1944; "Frontier Feud" 1945; "Border Bandits" 1946; "The Haunted Mine" 1946; "Lawless Empire" 1946, "Moon Over Montana" 1946; "Six Gun Man" 1946; "Song of the Sierras" 1946; "Trigger Fingers" 1946; "Under Arizona Skies" 1946; "West of Alamo" 1946; "Code of the Saddle" 1947; "Flashing Guns" 1947 (Stirrup); "Raiders of the South" 1947; "Song of the Wasteland" 1947; "Tornado Range" 1948; "Brand of Fear" 1949; "Gun Law Justice" 1949; "Gun Runner" 1949; "Riders of the Dusk" 1949; "Cowboy and the Prizefighter" 1950; "The Fargo Phantom" 1950-short; "The Fighting Redhead" 1950; "Hostile Country" 1950; "Law of the Panhandle" 1950; "Outlaw Gold" 1950; "Over the Border" 1950; "The Texan Meets Calamity Jane" 1950; "Man from Sonora" 1951; "Wanted Dead or Alive" 1951; "Whistling Hills" 1951; "Waco" 1952.

Jones, Richard. Films: "The Good Old Boys" TVM-1995 (Alvin Lawdermilk). ¶TV: *Ned Blessing: The Story of My Life and Times*—Regular 1993 (Leopole Siddons).

Jones, Sam J. (1954-). Films: "No Man's Land" TVM-1984 (Eli Howe).

Jones, Shirley (1934-). Films: "Oklahoma!" 1955 (Laurey); "Two Rode Together" 1961 (Marty Purcell); "The Cheyenne Social Club" 1970 (Jenny).

Jones, Stanley (1914-12/13/63). Films: "Rio Grande" 1950 (Sergeant); "Whirlwind" 1951; "The Last Musketeer" 1952 (Sheriff Blake); "The Great Locomotive Chase" 1956 (Wilson Brown); "The Rainmaker" 1956 (Townsman); "The Horse Soldiers" 1959 (Gen. U.S. Grant); "Ten Who Dared" 1960 (Seneca Howland). ¶TV: *Frontier*—"The Suspects" 11-6-55; *Sheriff of Cochise*—Regular 1956-58 (Deputy Olsen).

Jones, T.C. (1920-9/25/71). TV: *Wild Wild West*—"The Night of the

Running Death" 12-15-67 (Enzo/Miss Tyler).

Jones, Tiny. *see* Jones, Elizabeth.

Jones, Tommy Lee (1946-). Films: "Lonesome Dove" TVM-1989 (Capt. Woodrow F. Call); "The Good Old Boys" TVM-1995 (Hewey Calloway).

Jones, Wallace (1883-10/7/36). Films: "Red Love" 1925 (Bill Mosher).

Jones, Wharton. Films: "When a Girl Loves" 1919 (the Minister).

Jones-Moreland, Betsy (-4/3/82). Films: "Day of the Outlaw" 1959 (Mrs. Preston). ¶TV: *Zane Grey Theater*—"To Sit in Judgment" 11-13-58 (Mrs. Parney); *Man from Blackhawk*—"Incident at Tupelo" 4-29-60 (Mrs. Thornton); *Have Gun Will Travel*—"The Poker Friend" 11-12-60 (Mrs. Neal), "My Brother's Keeper" 5-6-61 (Topaz); *Bonanza*—"Five into the Wind" 4-21-63 (Nora Whitley); *Gunsmoke*—"Kate Heller" 9-28-63 (Tess).

Jons, Beverly. Films: "Ridin' Down the Trail" 1947; "Carson City Raiders" 1948 (Mildred Drew); "The Gay Amigo" 1949 (Girl).

Jordan, Betty. Films: "Trail of the Hawk" 1935 (Betty King).

Jordan, Bobbi. Films: "The Barbara Coast" TVM-1975 (Flame). ¶TV: *The Rounders*—Regular 1966-67 (Ada); *Wild Wild West*—"The Night of the Death Masks" 1-26-68 (Fleur Fogerty).

Jordan, Bobby (1923-9/10/65). Films: "Bowery Buckaroos" 1947 (Bobby). ¶TV: *Wild Bill Hickok*—"Outlaw Flats" 10-9-51, "Marriage Feud of Ponca City" 5-13-52, "Jingles on Jail Road" 7-14-53; *Tales of Wells Fargo*—"Jesse James" 7-1-57 (Bob Ford), "Man in the Box" 11-11-57 (Sonny Stillwell), "Ride with the Killer" 12-2-57 (Ernie Handsfelt).

Jordan, Dorothy (1906-12/7/88). Films: "The Searchers" 1956 (Martha Edwards).

Jordan, Judy. Films: "The Gatling Gun" 1972 (Martha Bland).

Jordan, Nick. Films: "Sabata" 1969-Ital. (Alley Cat).

Jordan, Richard (1938-8/30/93). Films: "Lawman" 1971 (Crowe Wheelwright); "Valdez Is Coming" 1971 (R.L. Davis); "Chato's Land" 1972 (Earl Hooker); "Rooster Cogburn" 1975 (Hawk); "Posse" 1993 (Sheriff Bates). ¶TV: *Empire*—"Long Past, Long Remembered" 10-23-62 (Jay Bee Fowler), "End of an Image" 1-15-63 (Jay Bee Fower); *Wide Coun-*

try—"Our Ernie Kills People" 11-1-62 (Ernie Stannard); *Hec Ramsey*—"The Detroit Connection" 12-30-73 (Charles Clavell).

Jordan, Robert. TV: *The Adventures of Rin Tin Tin*—"Top Gun" 1-24-58 (Bart Desay); *Maverick*—"The Judas Mask" 11-2-58 (Willy); "The Many Faces of Gideon Flinch" 11-5-61.

Jordan, Sid (1889-9/30/70). Films: "A Militant School Ma'am" 1914; "The Rival Stage Lines" 1914; "An Arizona Wooing" 1915; "Athletic Ambitions" 1915; "Bad Man Bobbs" 1915; "Bill Haywood, Producer" 1915; "The Chef at Circle G" 1915; "The Child, the Dog, and the Villain" 1915; "Forked Trails" 1915; "The Conversion of Smiling Tom" 1915; "Getting a Start in Life" 1915; "The Gold Dust and the Squaw" 1915; "The Grizzly Gulch Chariot Race" 1915; "How Weary Went Wooing" 1915; "The Impersonation of Tom" 1915; "A Lucky Deal" 1915; "The Man from Texas" 1915; "Never Again" 1915; "On the Eagle Trail" 1915; "Pals in Blue" 1915; "The Race for a Gold Mine" 1915; "The Range Girl and the Cowboy" 1915; "Roping a Bride" 1915; "The Stagecoach Driver and the Girl" 1915; "The Stagecoach Guard" 1915; "The Tenderfoot's Triumph" 1915; "A Bear of a Story" 1916; "The Canby Hill Outlaws" 1916; "A Close Call" 1916; "Crooked Trails" 1916; "The Desert Calls Its Own" 1916; "The Golden Thought" 1916; "Local Color" 1916; "The Man Within" 1916; "A Mistake in Rustlers" 1916; "Mistakes Will Happen" 1916; "A Mix-Up in Movies" 1916; "The Passing of Pete" 1916; "The Pony Express Rider" 1916; "Roping a Sweetheart" 1916; "The Sheriff's Blunder" 1916; "The Sheriff's Duty" 1916; "Shooting Up the Movies" 1916; "Starring in Western Stuff" 1916; "The Taming of Groucho Bill" 1916; "Twisted Trails" 1916; "A Western Masquerade" 1916; "Hearts and Saddles" 1917; "The Heart of Texas Ryan" 1917; "The Luck That Jealousy Brought" 1917; "The Saddle Girth" 1917; "A Soft Tenderfoot" 1917; "The Coming of the Law" 1919 (Neal Norton); "The Feud" 1919 (Bill Brady); "Fighting for Gold" 1919 (Jim Bleyer); "Rough-Riding Romance" 1919 (Pat Leary); "The Wilderness Trail" 1919 (Sergius); "The Daredevil" 1920 (Black Donlin); "Prairie Trails" 1920 (Jack Purdy); "The Texan" 1920 (Jack Purdy); "Three Gold Coins" 1920 (Boots); "The Untamed" 1920 (Hal Purvis); "Hands Off" 1921 (Pete Dinsmore); "The Night Horsemen"

1921 (Buck Daniels); "A Ridin' Romeo" 1921 (Jack Walters); "The Rough Diamond" 1921 (Manuel Garcia); "Trailin'" 1921 (Steve Nash); "Bells of San Juan" 1922 (Tom Cutter); "Fighting Streak" 1922 (Bill Dozier); "For Big Stakes" 1922 (Scott Mason); "Sky High" 1922 (Bates); "Trooper O'Neil" 1922 (Rodd); "Up and Going" 1922 (Louis Patie); "Eyes of the Forest" 1923 (Horgan); "Men in the Raw" 1923 (Bill Spray); "Where Is This West?" 1923 (Buck Osborn); "The Deadwood Coach" 1924 (Need); "The Ridin 'Kid from Powder River" 1924 (Buzzard Davis); "Rustlin' for Cupid" 1926 (Jack Mason); "The Dude Ranger" 1934 (Dunk); "Thunder Mountain" 1935; "Hollywood Cowboy" 1937 (Morgan); "The Marshal of Mesa City" 1939; "Lucky Cisco Kid" 1940.

Jordan, Ted (1925-). Films: "Sierra" 1950 (Jim Coulter); "Bonanza Town" 1951 (Bob Dillon); "The Bushwackers" 1952 (Soldier); "The Marshal's Daughter" 1953 (Augie); "The Apple Dumpling Gang Rides Again" 1979. ¶TV: *Gunsmoke*— "Perce" 9-30-61 (Del), "Durham Bull" 3-31-62 (Kearny), "The Ditch" 10-27-62 (Foreman), "Old Comrade" 12-29-62 (Lounger), "Louie Pheeters" 1-5-62 (Gus Thompson), "Kate Heller" 9-28-63 (Bo), "Comanches Is Safe" 3-7-64, "Caleb" 3-28-64 (Chad), "Twenty Miles from Dodge" 4-10-65 (Bolen), "Outlaw's Woman" 12-11-65 (Hank Wheeler), "The Raid" 1-22-66 & 1-29-66 (Shiloh), "Honor Before Justice" 3-5-66 (Policeman), "Harvest" 3-26-66 (Leemer), Regular 1966-75 (Nathan Burke, the Freight Agent); *Branded*— "Now Join the Human Race" 9-19-65 (Sergeant Mayhew), "Barbed Wire" 2-13-66; *The Road West*— "Lone Woman" 11-7-66 (Trooper), "Charade of Justice" 3-27-67 (Blacksmith); *Hondo*—"Hondo and the Ghost of Ed Dow" 11-24-67 (Gruder); *The High Chaparral*—"North to Tucson" 11-8-68 (Bayliss); *Kung Fu*— "Barbary House" 2-15-75 (Head Guard), "Flight to Orion" 2-22-75 (Head Guard), "The Brothers Cain" 3-1-75 (Head Guard), "Full Circle" 3-15-75 (Head Guard); *How the West Was Won*—Episode One 2-12-78 (Charlie).

Jordan, William. Films: "A Man Called Horse" 1970 (Bent). ¶TV: *The Big Valley*—"A Stranger Everywhere" 12-9-68 (Carr); *Bonanza*—"Night of Reckoning" 10-15-67 (Rusher), "The Clarion" 2-9-69 (Leek); *The High Chaparral*—"The Buffalo Soldiers" 11-22-68 (Pearsall); *Barbary Coast*—

"Arson and Old Lace" 11-14-75 (James Carr); *Paradise*—"Vengeance" 3-16-89 (Curtis Ivey).

Jory, Victor (1902-2/12/82). Films: "Smoky" 1933 (Clint Peters); "Dodge City" 1939 (Yancy); "Man of Conquest" 1939 (William Travis); "Rangle River" 1939-Australia (Dick Drake); "Susannah of the Mounties" 1939 (Wolf Pelt); "Cherokee Strip" 1940 (Coy Barrett); "Knights of the Range" 1940 (Malcolm Lascalles); "The Light of Western Stars" 1940 (Gene Stewart); "River's End" 1940 (Norman Talbot); "Bad Men of Missouri" 1941 (William Merrick); "Border Vigilantes" 1941 (Henry Logan); "Riders of the Timberline" 1941 (Baptiste); "Wide Open Town" 1941 (Steve Fraser); "Shut My Big Mouth" 1942 (Buckskin Bill); "Tombstone, the Town Too Tough to Die" 1942 (Ike Clanton); "Bar 20" 1943 (Mark Jackson); "Buckskin Frontier" 1943 (Champ Clanton); "Colt Comrades" 1943 (Jebb Hardin); "Hoppy Serves a Writ" 1943 (Tom Jordan); "The Kansan" 1943 (Jeff Barat); "The Leather Burners" 1943 (Dan Slack); "Canadian Pacific" 1949 (Dirk Rourke); "Fighting Man of the Plains" 1949 (Dave Oldham); "South of St. Louis" 1949 (Luke Cottrell); "The Capture" 1950 (Father Gomez); "The Cariboo Trail" 1950 (Frank Walsh); "Cave of Outlaws" 1951 (Ben Cross); "Flaming Feather" 1952 (Lucky Lee); "Toughest Man in Arizona" 1952 (Frank Girard); "The Man from the Alamo" 1953 (Jess Wade); "Blackjack Ketchum, Desperado" 1956 (Jared Tetlow); "The Last Stagecoach West" 1957 (Rand McCord); "Cheyenne Autumn" 1964 (Tall Tree); "MacKenna's Gold" 1969 (Narrator); "Flap" 1970 (Wounded Bear Mr. Smith); "A Time for Dying" 1971 (Judge Roy Bean); "Kino, the Padre on Horseback" 1977; "The Mountain Men" 1980 (Iron Belly). ¶TV: *Stories of the Century*—"Last Stagecoach West" 1954 (Rand McCord); *Wanted—Dead or Alive*—"The Legend" 3-7-59 (Sam McGarrett); *Rawhide*—"Incident of the Dry Drive" 5-22-59 (Jess Hode), "Gold Fever" 5-4-62 (Hosea Brewer); *Empire*—"Ride to a Fall" 10-16-62 (Milo Dahlbeck); *Wide Country*—"Step Over the Sky" 1-10-63 (Johny Prewitt); *Temple Houston*—"The Twisted Rope" 9-19-63 (Claude Boley); *Great Adventure*—"The Testing of Sam Houston" 1-31-64 (Andrew Jackson); *The Virginian*—"The Dark Challenge" 9-23-64 (Carl Hendricks), "The Return of Golden Tom" 3-9-66 (Tom Brant), "Melanie" 2-22-67

(Jim Kohler), "A Bad Place to Die" 11-8-67 (Luke), "Fox, Hound, and the Widow McCloud" 4-2-69 (Buke); *Gunsmoke*—"Chief Joseph" 1-30-65 (Chief Joseph); *Bonanza*— "Ride the Wind" 1-16-66 & 1-23-66 (Charles Ludlow); *The Loner*—"The Burden of the Badge" 3-5-66 (Simon Ridley); *The Legend of Jesse James*— "Things Don't Just Happen" 3-14-66 (Judge Parker); *F Troop*—"Indian Fever" 4-5-66 (Chief Mean Buffalo); *Iron Horse*—"Pride at the Bottom of the Barrel" 10-10-66 (Captain Anderson); *The Road West*—"Beyond the Hill" 1-16-67 (Collier); *The High Chaparral*—"The Peacemaker" 3-3-68 (Kelly); *Nakia*—"The Non-Person" 9-21-74 (Ben Redearth), "The Fire Dancer" 12-28-74 (Ben Redearth); *Kung Fu*—"Cry of the Night Beast" 10-19-74 (Fred); *Young Maverick*—"Makin' Tracks" 1-9-80 (Pony-That Waits).

Jose, Edward (-/12/18/30). Films: "The Perils of Pauline" 1914-serial.

Joseph, Allen (1919-). TV: *Wagon Train*—"The Kitty Pryer Story" 11-18-63, "The Story of Cain" 12-16-63 (Benny); *Alias Smith and Jones*—"Everything Else You Can Steal" 12-16-71, "McGuffin" 12-9-72.

Joseph, Jackie (1936-). Films: "The Cheyenne Social Club" 1970 (Annie Jo). ¶TV: *F Troop*—"Our Hero—What's His Name" 1-4-66 (Betty Lou).

Joslin, Howard (1908-8/1/75). Films: "The Texas Rangers" 1936 (Ranger); "High Lonesome" 1950 (Jim Shell); "Silver City" 1951 (Freed); "Son of Paleface" 1952 (Sam); "Pony Express" 1953; "The Vanquished" 1953; "Run for Cover" 1955.

Joslyn, Allyn (1905-1/21/81). Films: "Fastest Gun Alive" 1956 (Harvey Maxwell); "The Brothers O'Toole" 1973. ¶TV: *The Alaskans*— "Gold Sled" 10-4-59; *Hotel De Paree*—"Sundance and the Hostiles" 12-11-59 (Josh); *Gunsmoke*—"I Thee Wed" 4-16-60 (Sam Lackett); *Have Gun Will Travel*—"The Fatal Flaw" 2-25-61 (Marshal McKendrick); *Rawhide*—"Incident of the Banker" 4-2-64 (Albert Ashton-Warner); *F Troop*—"Iron Horse Go Home" 12-28-65 (Colonel Parmenter).

Josol, Sandy (1940-1/25/80). TV: *Wild Wild West*—"The Night of the Raven" 9-30-66 (Chawtaw).

Joston, Darwin. Films: "Cain's Way" 1969. TV: *The Virginian*— "The Gentle Tamers" 1-24-68 (Dan Moss).

Jostyn, Jay (1901-7/24/76). TV: *Jim Bowie*—"Country Cousin" 5-3-57 (Capt. Slocum); *Tales of Wells Fargo*—"The Manuscript" 9-15-58 (Paul Moran); *Gunslinger*—"Golden Circle" 4-13-61 (Warden); *Branded*—"Very Few Heroes" 4-11-65 (Judge), "A Proud Town" 12-19-65 (Dr. Coats); *Wild Wild West*—"The Night of the Pistoleros" 2-21-69 (Major).

Jovovich, Milla. TV: *Paradise*—"Childhood's End" 12-29-88 (Katie).

Joy, Ernest (1880-2/12/24). Films: "Salomy Jane" 1914 (Marbury); "Chimmie Fadden Out West" 1915 (Mr. Van Cortland); "Nan of Music Mountain" 1917 (Lefever); "Rimrock Jones" 1918 (Jepson); "Johnny, Get Your Gun" 1919 (Lawyer Cotter).

Joy, Leatrice (1897-5/13/85). Films: "The Bachelor Daddy" 1922 (Sally Lockwood); "Red Stallion in the Rockies" 1949 (Martha Simpson).

Joyce, Alice (1890-10/9/55). Films: "The Blackfoot Half-Breed" 1911; "The Indian Maid's Sacrifice" 1911; "The Outlaw" 1912; "The Suffragette Sheriff" 1912; "The Brand" 1914.

Joyce, Elaine (1945-). TV: *Here Come the Brides*—"Here Come the Brides" 9-25-68, "Man of the Family" 10-16-68.

Joyce, Jean. Films: "Outlaws of Sonora" 1938 (Miss Burke); "Prairie Papas" 1938-short; "Overland Mail" 1939 (Mary); "Riders of the Frontier" 1939 (Martha); "Sagebrush Serenade" 1939-short.

Joyce, Jimmy (1923-1/5/79). TV: *Laredo*—"The Land Slickers" 10-14-66 (Bellhop).

Joyce, Marty (1915-1/2/37). Films: "Border Vengeance" 1935 (Jim Benson); "Fighting Caballero" 1935 (Agent); "Trail of the Hawk" 1935; "Custer's Last Stand" 1936-serial (Buzz).

Joyce, Natalie (1902-11/9/92). Films: "The Circus Ace" 1927 (Millie Jane Raleigh); "Whispering Sage" 1927 (Mercedes); "Daredevil's Reward" 1928 (Ena Powell); "Law of the Plains" 1929; "The Man from Nevada" 1929 (Virginia Watkins); "Pals of the Prairie" 1929 (Dolores).

Joyce, Stephen (1930-). TV: *Decision*—"The Virginian" 7-6-58 (Steve); *Rawhide*—"Incident of the Shambling Men" 10-9-59, "Incident of the Murder Steer" 5-13-60 (Hanson Buck), "Incident on the Road to Yesterday" 11-18-60 (Wilbur), "Incident of the Wager on Payday" 6-16-61 (Sidney Porter); *Bronco*—"Death

of an Outlaw" 3-8-60 (Billy the Kid); *G.E. Theater*—"Aftermath" 4-17-60 (Murray); *The Rebel*—"The Ballad of Danny Brown" 4-9-61 (Isham), "The Hostage" 6-11-61 (Frank Dagget); *Bonanza*—"The Secret" 5-6-61 (Jerome Bell); *The Outlaws*—"Walk Tall" 11-16-61 (Wace); *The Dakotas*—"Trouble at French Creek" 1-28-63 (Billy Dancer).

Joyce, William (1930-). TV: *The Restless Gun*—"Quiet City" 2-3-58 (Buzz Partridge), "The Last Grey Man" 2-23-59 (Capt. Clayton); *Tales of Wells Fargo*—"The Legacy" 3-9-59 (Tom Casement); *Rawhide*—"Incident Below the Brazos" 5-15-59; *Stripe Playhouse*—"Ballad to Die By" 7-31-59 (Johnny Guitar); *The Rifleman*—"Panic" 11-10-59 (Barker); *Have Gun Will Travel*—"The Day of the Bad Men" 1-9-60 (Laredo); *Lawman*—"Heritage of Hate" 3-18-62 (Bill Fells).

Joyner, Henry. Films: "Davy Crockett, King of the Wild Frontier" 1955 (Swaney).

Joyner, Michelle. Films: "Grim Prairie Tales" 1990 (Jenny). ¶TV: *Young Riders*—"Bad Company" 12-1-90 (Jennifer).

Joyzelle (Joyner). Films: "Song of the Cabellero" 1930 (Conchita); "The Vanishing Frontier" 1932 (Dolores); "Whistlin' Dan" 1932 (Carmelita).

Judd, John (1893-10/7/50). Films: "Headin' South" 1918; "Double Crossers" 1921; "The Movie Trail" 1921; "Who Was That Man?" 1921; "The Wild Wild West" 1921; "The Kingfisher's Roost" 1922 (Chief of the Rurales); "Blinky" 1923 (Husk Barton); "Out of Luck" 1923 (Pig Hurley); "Forty-Horse Hawkins" 1924 (Wild Bill Bailey); "Texas Trail" 1937 (Lieutenant); "Cowboy and the Lady" 1938 (Rodeo Rider); "Riders of Pasco Basin" 1940 (Trick Roper); "The Texas Kid" 1943 (Roy).

Judels, Charles (1882-2/14/69). Films: "Captain Thunder" 1931 (El Comandante Ruiz); "The Plainsman" 1936 (Tony the Barber); "The Big Show" 1937 (Swartz); "Viva Cisco Kid" 1940 (Pancho); "In Old Sacramento" 1946 (Marchetti); "Plainsman and the Lady" 1946 (Manuel Lopez); "Panhandle" 1948 (Barber).

Judge, Arline (1912-2/7/74). Films: "Song of Texas" 1943 (Hildegarde).

Judge, Neoma. Films: "The Man from Arizona" 1932 (Lupita); "Young Blood" 1932 (Lola Montaine,

the Countess); "Terror Trail" 1933 (Norma Laird).

Julia, Raul (1940-10/24/94). Films: "The Alamo: 13 Days to Glory" TVM-1987 (Santa Anna).

Julian, Rupert (1889-12/27/43). Films: "The Desperado" 1916; "The Desire of the Moth" 1917 (John Wesley Pringle); "Hands Down" 1918 (Tom Flynn); "Hungry Eyes" 1918 (John Silver).

Julien, Max (1940-). Films: "Thomasine and Bushrod" 1974 (Bushrod).

Jump, Gordon (1933-). TV: *Daniel Boone*—"The Devil's Four" 3-4-65 (Marcus Clements); *Here Come the Brides*—"Here Come the Brides" 9-25-68.

Junco, Victor (1918-). Films: "Bandido" 1956 (Lorenzo); "The Undefeated" 1969 (Maj. Tapia).

June, Mildred (1906-6/19/40). Films: "Hook and Ladder" 1924 (Sally Drennan).

Jung, Allen (1909-82). Films: "King of the Mounties" 1942-serial (Sato). ¶TV: *Man from Blackhawk*—"Logan's Policy" 10-9-59 (Ying Lee); *Have Gun Will Travel*—"The Hatchet Man" 3-5-60 (Loo Sam); *Wagon Train*—"The John Augustus Story" 10-17-62 (Din Pau Yee); *Gunsmoke*—"Hackett" 3-16-70 (Chinese Proprietor).

Junkermann, Kelly. Films: "Rio Diablo" TVM-1993 (Carson); "The Gambler V: Playing for Keeps" TVM-1994 (Caldwell).

Jurado, Katy (1927-). Films: "High Noon" 1952 (Helen Ramirez); "Arrowhead" 1953 (Nita); "San Antone" 1953 (Mistania Figueroa); "Broken Lance" 1954 (Senora Devereaux); "Man from Del Rio" 1956 (Estella); "Dragoon Wells Massacre" 1957 (Mara Fay); "The Badlanders" 1958 (Anita); "One-Eyed Jacks" 1961 (Maria); "Smoky" 1966 (Maria); "Pat Garrett and Billy the Kid" 1973 (Mrs. Baker). ¶TV: *The Rifleman*—"The Boarding House" 2-24-59 (Julia Massini); *The Westerner*—"Ghost of a Chance" 12-2-60; *Death Valley Days*—"La Tules" 6-27-62 (La Tules); *The Men from Shiloh*—"The Best Man" 9-23-70 (Mama Fe); *Alias Smith and Jones*—"The McCreedy Feud" 9-30-72 (Carlotta).

Jury, Richard "Rick". Films: "The Brothers O'Toole" 1973; "Donner Pass: The Road to Survival" TVM-1978; "Conagher" TVM-1991.

Justice, Katharine (1942-). Films: "The Way West" 1967 (Amanda Mack); "Five Card Stud"

1968 (Nora Evers). ¶TV: *The Big Valley*—"The River Monarch" 4-6-66 (Melanie); *Preview Tonight*—"Roaring Camp" 9-4-66 (Rachel); *Iron Horse*—"The Bride at Forty-Mile" 1-23-67 (Kat Preston); *Gunsmoke*—"A Matter of Honor" 11-17-69 (Lydia Fletcher), "Luke" 11-2-70 (Doris Prebble), "The Bullet" 11-29-71, 12-6-71 & 12-13-71 (Beth Tilton), "The Sodbusters" 11-20-72 (Clarabelle Callahan); *The Virginian*—"Ride the Misadventure" 11-6-68 (Ruby); *Lancer*—"Legacy" 12-9-69 (Julie); *Bearcats!*—10-7-71 (Hilda).

Justice, William. Films: "King of the Royal Mounted" 1940-serial (Hallett); "Here Comes the Cavalry" 1941-short.

Kaaren, Suzanne. Films: "Undercover Man" 1936 (Linda Forbes); "Phantom Ranger" 1938 (Joan Doyle); "Yes, We Have No Bonanza" 1939-short (Saloon Girl).

Kabott, Frankie. TV: *Bonanza*—"The Unseen Wound" 1-29-67 (Timmy); *Daniel Boone*—"The Young Ones" 2-23-67 (Little Tom); *The Big Valley*—"Guilty" 10-30-67 (Stevie Becker).

Kadler, Karen (1934-11/15/84). Films: "Kiss of Fire" 1955 (Shining Moon). ¶TV: *Cheyenne*—"Fury at Rio Hondo" 4-17-56 (Isabella Montalban); *Rough Riders*—"The Scavengers" 1-8-59 (Mary Ellen Lee).

Kahn, Madeline (1943-). Films: "Blazing Saddles" 1974 (Lili Von Shtupp).

Kalisz, Armand (1887-2/1/41). Films: "The Siren" 1917 (Armand).

Kallman, Dick (1934-2/22/80). Films: "Hell Canyon Outlaws" 1957. ¶TV: *The Californians*—"Deadly Tintype" 3-31-59 (Armand); *The Texan*—"The Gunfighter" 6-8-59 (Grady Fenton), "Dangerous Ground" 12-14-59 (Ben Howell).

Kamaryt, Joseph (1890-6/14/77). Films: "Riders of Pasco Basin" 1940 (Rancher).

Kamber, Stan (1935-). Films: "Warlock" 1959 (Hutchinson).

Kamel, Joe. Films: "Man from the Cursed Valley" 1964-Ital./Span.; "Minnesota Clay" 1964-Ital./Fr./Span. (Millicet); "Seven Guns from Texas" 1964-Span./Ital.; "Few Dollars for Django" 1966-Ital./Span.; "Jesse James' Kid" 1966-Span./Ital.

Kamm, Kris. Films: "The Gambler V: Playing for Keeps" TVM-1994 (Jeremiah Hawkes); "Wyatt Earp" 1994 (Bill Claborne).

Kanaly, Steve (1946-). Films:

"The Life and Times of Judge Roy Bean" 1972 (Whorehouse Lucky Jim); "My Name Is Nobody" 1973-Ital. (Flase Barber).

Kane, Big Daddy. Films: "Posse" 1993 (Father Time).

Kane, Carol (1952-). TV: *The Virginian*—"The Return of Golden Tom" 3-9-66 (Ellen), "Outcast" 10-26-66 (Charlotte).

Kane, Eddie (1889-4/30/69). Films: "The Thrill Hunter" 1933 (Levine); "Hollywood Roundup" 1938 (Henry Westcott); "Rovin' Tumbleweeds" 1939 (Congressman); "Dude Cowboy" 1941 (Gordon West); "Bells of Rosarita" 1945; "The Man from Oklahoma" 1945 (Club Manager). ¶TV: *Wild Bill Hickok*—"Mexican Rustlers Story" 10-23-51.

Kane, Gail (1885-2/17/66). Films: "Arizona" 1913 (Bonita Canby); "The Red Woman" 1917 (Marie Temosach).

Kane, Jackson D. Films: "Showdown" 1973 (Clem); "Thomasine and Bushrod" 1974 (Adolph).

Kane, Jimmy. Films: "Mystery Valley" 1928; "Beyond the Law" 1930 (Ted).

Kane, Marjorie. Films: "The Great Divide" 1929; "Border Romance" 1930 (Nina).

Kane, Sid. Films: "Frontier Uprising" 1961. ¶TV: *Maverick*—"The Ice Man" 1-29-61 (Carl Stone); *Nichols*—"Flight of the Century" 2-22-72.

Kapp, Joe (1938-). Films: "Nakia" TVM-1974 (Deputy Hubbel Martin).

Kaquitts, Frank. Films: "Buffalo Bill and the Indians, or Sitting Bull's History Lesson" 1976 (Sitting Bull).

Karamensinis, Wassilli. *see* Karis, Vassili.

Karath, Jimmy. Films: "Take Me to Town" 1953 (Boy). ¶TV: *Fury*—"Junior Rodeo" 12-24-55 (Tuck Wilson); *The Adventures of Rin Tin Tin*—"The Big Top" 2-3-56 (Daisy); *My Friend Flicka*—"The Foundlings" 6-1-56 (Paul).

Kardell, Lili. TV: *Annie Oakley*—"Annie and the Bicycle Riders" 7-8-56 (Helga King); *Rawhide*—"Incident of the Music Maker" 5-20-60 (Maria Zwahlen).

Karen, Anna (1921-). TV: *Jefferson Drum*—"Return" 10-30-58 (Bess); *The Rebel*—"Shriek of Silence" 3-19-61 (Mrs. Warren); *Gunsmoke*—"Quaker Girl" 12-10-66 (Woman #1); *Iron Horse*—"The Red Tornado" 2-20-67 (Amy Hobart).

Karen, James (1923-). Films: "Little House: The Last Farewell" TVM-1984 (Nathan Lassiter); "Bonanza: Under Attack" TVM-1995 (Mr. Stewart).

Karis, Vassili (Wassilli Karamensinis). Films: "Five Giants from Texas" 1966-Ital./Span.; "Wanted Sabata" 1970-Ital.; "His Name Was King" 1971-Ital.; "Death Is Sweet from the Soldier of God" 1972-Ital.; "He Was Called the Holy Ghost" 1972-Ital. (Holy Ghost); "Magnificent West" 1972-Ital.; "Animal Called Man" 1973-Ital. (Bill Masson); "Gunmen and the Holy Ghost" 1973-Ital. (Holy Ghost); "Scalps" 1986-Ital./Ger.

Kark, Raymond (1937-6/28/86). TV: *Here Come the Brides*—"Democracy in Action" 2-5-69.

Karlan, Richard (1919-). Films: "Snow Dog" 1950 (Birof); "Sierra Passage" 1951 (Bart); "Blowing Wind" 1953 (Henderson). ¶TV: *Wild Bill Hickok*—"The Music Teacher" 12-2-52, "Jingles on Jail Road" 7-14-53; *Frontier*—"Ferdinand Meyer's Army" 12-18-55 (Ferdinand Meyer); *Fury*—"Ghost Town" 12-31-55 (Rocky), "A Fish Story" 3-8-58 (Lucky); *Tales of the Texas Rangers*—"The Kid from Amarillo" 11-17-57 (Jonathan Cole); *Buckskin*—"Tree of Death" 8-21-58 (Abraham Taliaferro); *Northwest Passage*—"Trial by Fire" 3-6-59 (Capt. Bracque); *Zane Grey Theater*—"Checkmate" 4-30-59; *Pony Express*—"The Renegade" 5-3-60 (Lafe Carlin).

Karlen, John (1933-). Films: "Last Ride of the Dalton Gang" TVM-1979 (Charlie Powers). ¶TV: *Stoney Burke*—"Joby" 3-18-63 (Mickey).

Karloff, Boris (1887-2/2/69). Films: "The Last of the Mohicans" 1920 (Indian Chief); "The Prairie Wife" 1925 (Diego); "The Meddlin' Stranger" 1927 (Al Meggs); "The Phantom Buster" 1927 (Ramon); "Burning the Wind" 1928 (Pug Doran); "Phantom of the North" 1929 (Jules Gregg); "The Utah Kid" 1930 (Baxter); "Unconquered" 1947 (Guyasuta, Chief of the Senecas). ¶TV: *Wild Wild West*—"The Night of the Golden Cobra" 9-23-66 (Maharajah Singh).

Karnes, Robert (1917-12/4/79). Films: "Hills of Oklahoma" 1950 (Brock Stevens); "Utah Wagon Train" 1951 (Scully); "Rodeo" 1952 (Charles Olenick); "Seminole" 1953 (Corporal); "Stagecoach to Fury" 1956 (Talbot); "Five Guns to Tombstone" 1961 (Matt Wade); "Apache Rifles" 1964;

"Charro!" 1969 (Harvey); "The Oregon Trail" TVM-1976 (Hatcher); "Last Ride of the Dalton Gang" TVM-1979 (Poker Player). ¶TV: *Zane Grey Theater*—"The Fearful Courage" 10-12-56 (Rider); *Gunsmoke*—"What the Whiskey Drummer Heard" 4-27-57 (Roberts), "Fawn" 4-4-59 (Jep Hunter), "Moo Moo Raid" 2-13-60 (Bert), "Hard Virtue" 5-6-61 (Ed Fallon), "Colorado Sheriff" 6-17-61 (Ben Witter), "Cale" 5-5-62 (Sterret), "The Twisted Heritage" 1-6-69 (Driver #2), "The Night Riders" 2-24-69 (Ross), "Roots of Fear" 12-15-69 (Charlie), "The Iron Blood of Courage" 2-18-74 (Chandler); *Have Gun Will Travel*—"Winchester Quarantine" 10-5-57, "The Lady" 11-15-58 (Rancher), "The Taffeta Mayor" 1-10-59 (Clay Morrow), "Shadow of a Man" 1-28-61, "The Siege" 4-1-61 (Tyler), "Odds for a Big Red" 10-7-61; *The Californians*—"The Marshal" 3-11-58 (George Cook); *Broken Arrow*—"Blood Brothers" 5-13-58 (Sergeant Xavier); *Wagon Train*—"The Dan Hogan Story" 5-14-58; *The Texan*—"Outpost" 1-19-59; *Rawhide*—"Incident of the Shambling Men" 10-9-59; *Bat Masterson*—"The Disappearance of Bat Masterson" 3-10-60 (Landry), "Last Stop to Austin" 12-1-60 (Marshal); *The Deputy*—"Mother and Son" 10-29-60 (Sam Nelson); *Klondike*—"The Golden Burro" 1-16-61 (Jack Wells); *The Outlaws*—"Chalk's Lot" 10-5-61 (Betts); *Tales of Wells Fargo*—"Reward for Gaine" 1-20-62 (Corporal Lark); *Bonanza*—"The Jacknife" 2-18-62, "The First Born" 9-23-62 (Miner), "The Pressure Game" 5-10-64 (Jeff), "Check Rein" 12-3-67 (Sheriff Buhler), "A Home for Jamie" 12-19-71 (Jess McLean); *The Big Valley*—"Earthquake!" 11-10-65 (Padre), "Legend of a General" 9-19-66 & 9-26-66 (Father Estaban), "The Man from Nowhere" 11-14-66 (Priest), "Ambush" 9-18-67; *The Virginian*—"Long Ride to Wind River" 1-19-66 (Hobey Kendall), "Paid in Full" 11-22-67 (Jeffers); *Cimarron Strip*—"Nobody" 12-7-67; *The Guns of Will Sonnett*—"Find a Sonnett, Kill a Sonnett" 12-8-67 (Sheriff McCall), "Guilt" 11-29-68 (Sheriff Barlow); *The Men from Shiloh*—"Hannah" 12-30-70 (Hendricks); *Kung Fu*—"The Well" 9-27-73 (Parkes).

Karns, Roscoe (1891-2/6/70). Films: "A Western Governor's Humanity" 1915; "The Vanishing Pioneer" 1928 (Ray Hearn); "Riding High" 1943 (Shorty); "Vigilantes of Boomtown" 1947 (Delaney).

Karr, Darwin (1875-12/31/45).

Films: "The Story of the Indian Lodge" 1911; "West Wind" 1915.

Karr, H.S. Films: "Big Stakes" 1922 (Skinny Fargo).

Karras, Alex (1935-). Films: "Hardcase" TVM-1972 (Booker Llewellyn); "Blazing Saddles" 1974 (Mongo). ¶TV: *Daniel Boone*—"The Cache" 12-4-69 (Williams); *Centennial*—Regular 1978-79 (Hans Brumbaugh).

Karroll, Dot. Films: "The Adventures of the Masked Phantom" 1939 (Grandma Mary Barton).

Kartalian, Buck (1922-). TV: *Here Come the Brides*—"Here Come the Brides" 9-25-68, "A Crying Need" 10-2-68, "Letter of the Law" 10-30-68, "Stand Off" 11-27-68, "None to a Customer" 2-19-69, "A Dream That Glitters" 2-26-69; *Wild Wild West*—"The Night of the Pelican" 12-27-68 (Police Lt. Tom Bengston).

Kasday, David. Films: "The Marauders" 1955 (Albie Ferber); "Red Sundown" 1956 (Hughie Clore). ¶TV: *Fury*—"Scorched Earth" 11-12-55 (Tom).

Kashfi, Anna. Films: "Cowboy" 1958 (Maria Vidal). ¶TV: *The Deputy*—"The Border Between" 3-12-60 (Felipa); *Bronco*—"Seminole War Pipe" 12-12-60 (Princess Natula).

Kastner, Peter (1944-). TV: *Cimarron Strip*—"Whitey" 10-19-67 (Robert "Whitey" White).

Kasznar, Kurt (1913-8/6/79). Films: "Ride, Vaquero!" 1953 (Father Antonio). ¶TV: *The Men from Shiloh*—"Crooked Corner" 10-28-70 (August Hansch); *Young Dan'l Boone*—"The Game" 10-10-77 (Emil Van Diben).

Katch, Kurt (1893-8/14/58). Films: "Salome, Where She Danced" 1945 (Prince Otto von Bismarck). ¶TV: *The Adventures of Rin Tin Tin*—"The Lost Puppy" 11-9-56 (Siegfried Kurtz).

Katchenaro, Pete. Films: "King of the Mounties" 1942-serial (Falcon Pilot); "Song of Old Wyoming" 1945 (Ling).

Katcher, Aram (1921-). TV: *Daniel Boone*—"Benvenuto ... Who?" 10-9-69 (Thibaud).

Katsulas, Andreas. Films: "Sunset" 1988 (Arthur).

Katt, William (1955-). Films: "The Daughters of Joshua Cabe" TVM-1972 (Billy Jack); "Butch and Sundance: The Early Days" 1979 (the Sundance Kid). ¶TV: *Kung Fu*—"The Ancient Warrior" 5-3-73 (Andy).

Kaufman, Al. Films: "The Black Sheep" 1921 (Jim McGowan); "The Dangerous Coward" 1924 (Battling Benson); "Marry in Haste" 1924 (Jack Dugan); "Red Hot Hoofs" 1926 (Battling Jack Rice); "Walloping Kid" 1926 (Wild Cat McKee).

Kay, Beatrice (1917-11/8/86). Films: "A Time for Dying" 1971 (Mamie). ¶TV: *The Alaskans*—"The Golden Fleece" 11-29-59; *Bonanza*—"The Burma Rarity" 10-22-61 (Clementine Hawkins); *The Rifleman*—"Which Way'd They Go?" 4-1-63 (Goldie Drain).

Kay, Bernard (1928-). Films: "The Hunting Party" 1971-Brit./Ital./Span. (Buford King).

Kay, Bernice. Films: "Wide Open Town" 1941 (Joan Stuart).

Kay, Jean. Films: "The Riding Kid" 1931 (Miss Barton).

Kay, Joyce. Films: "Rio Grande Romance" 1936 (Patricia Carter).

Kay, Kathleen. Films: "Flaming Frontier" 1926 (Lucretia).

Kay, Mary Ellen. Films: "Streets of Ghost Town" 1950 (Doris Donner); "Desert of Lost Men" 1951 (Nan Webster); "Fort Dodge Stampede" 1951 (Natalie Bryan); "Rodeo King and the Senorita" 1951 (Janet Wells); "Silver City Bonanza" 1951 (Katie McIntosh); "Thunder in God's Country" 1951 (Dell Stafford); "Wells Fargo Gunmaster" 1951 (Carol Hines); "Border Saddlemates" 1952 (Jane Richards); "Colorado Sundown" 1952 (Jackie Reynolds); "The Last Musketeer" 1952 (Sue); "Vigilante Terror" 1953; "Thunder Pass" 1954; "Yukon Vengeance" 1954; "Buffalo Gun" 1961 (Clementine). ¶TV: *The Roy Rogers Show*—"Pat's Inheritance" 11-11-53 (Mary); *Annie Oakley*—Semi-Regular 1954-57 (Miss Curtis); *Circus Boy*—"The Little Gypsy" 12-2-56 (Tula); *The Lone Ranger*—"Trouble at Tylerville" 12-13-56, "Outlaws in Grease Paint" 6-6-57.

Kaye, Celia (1943-). TV: *Wagon Train*—"The Clay Shelby Story" 12-6-64 (Ann Shelby); *Iron Horse*—"Decision at Sundown" 2-27-67 (Emily).

Kaye, Clarissa (1931-). Films: "Ned Kelly" 1970-Brit. (Mrs. Kelly).

Kaye, Stubby (1928-). Films: "Cat Ballou" 1965 (Singer); "The Way West" 1967 (Sam Fairman); "The Cockeyed Cowboys of Calico County" 1970 (Bartender).

Kazan, Lanie (1940-). Films: "Lust in the Dust" 1985 (Marguerita Ventura).

Kazann, Zitto. Films: "Ghost Town" 1988 (Blacksmith). ¶TV: *Barbary Coast*—"Crazy Cats" 9-15-75 (Garvey).

Keach, James. Films: "Comes a Horseman" 1978 (Kroegh); "Lacy and the Mississippi Queen" TVM-1978 (Parker); "The Long Riders" 1980 (Jesse James); "The Legend of the Lone Ranger" 1981 (Voice of the Lone Ranger). ¶TV: *Kung Fu*—"The Assassin" 10-4-73 (Abe Jones); *The Quest*—"Day of Outrage" 10-27-76 (Blue); *Big Bend Country*—Pilot 8-27-81 (Ian McGregor).

Keach, Stacy (1941-). Films: "Doc" 1971 (Doc Holliday); "The Life and Times of Judge Roy Bean" 1972 (Bad Bob); "The Long Riders" 1980 (Frank James); "Rio Diablo" TVM-1993 (Kansas); "James A. Michener's Texas" TVM-1995 (Sam Houston). ¶TV: *The Deputy*—"The Return of Simon Fry" 2-13-60 (Vic Rufus); *Shotgun Slade*—"Lost Gold" 8-30-60.

Keach, Sr., Stacy (1914-). TV: *The Lone Ranger*—"Trigger Finger 4-7-55, "Showdown at Sand Creek" 5-26-55; *Maverick*—"Ghost Riders" 10-13-57 (Sheriff), "The Lass with the Poisonous Air" 11-1-59 (Deevers), "Family Pride" 1-8-61 (Marshal); *The Californians*—"Truce of the Tree" 12-17-57, "The Coward" 1-7-58; *Colt .45*—"Last Chance" 12-6-57 (Sheriff Ben Mason); *Cheyenne*—"Lone Patrol" 4-10-61 (Sergeant O'Bannion); *Wagon Train*—"The Traitor" 12-13-61 (Major Hansen); *Bonanza*—"The Weary Willies" 9-27-70 (Farmer), "The Twenty-Sixth Grave" 10-31-72 (Prentiss); *Young Riders*—"The Initiation" 11-25-91 (Quimby).

Kean, Richard (1881-12/29/59). Films: "Storm Over Wyoming" 1950 (Watson).

Keane, Charles. Films: "The Lone Cowboy" 1934 (2nd Station Agent); "Hannah Lee" 1953 (2nd Loafer); "Seven Guns to Mesa" 1958 (Marsh)). ¶TV: *The Restless Gun*—"The Red Blood of Courage" 2-2-59, "Dead Man's Hand" 3-16-59.

Keane, Edward (1884-10/12/59). Films: "Border Brigands" 1935 (Comm. Jim Barry); "Whispering Smith Speaks" 1935 (Edward Rebstock); "For the Service" 1936 (Capt. Murphy); "The California Mail" 1937 (Thompson); "The Californian" 1937 (Marshal Morse); "High, Wide and Handsome" 1937 (Jones); "Wells Fargo" 1937 (Secretary of Treasury); "Westbound Mail" 1937 (Gun Barlow); "Border G-Man" 1938 (Col. Christie); "Hollywood Roundup"

1938 (Lew Wallach); "Frontier Pony Express" 1939 (Senator Lassiter); "Stand Up and Fight" 1939 (Donnelly); "Union Pacific" 1939; "Virginia City" 1940 (Officer); "Winners of the West" 1940-serial (Johyn Hartford); "Riders of the Timberline" 1941 (Yatos); "They Died with Their Boots On" 1941 (Congressman); "Bordertown Gunfighters" 1943; "California Joe" 1943 (Gou Glynn); "Death Valley Manhunt" 1943; "Out California Way" 1946 (E.J. Pearson); "Roll on, Texas Moon" 1946 (Frank J. Wilson); "Saddle Pals" 1947; "Trail to San Antone" 1947 (Sheriff Jones); "Hellfire" 1949; "The Baron of Arizona" 1950 (Surveyor Miller); "Twilight in the Sierras" 1950 (Judge Wiggins). ¶TV: *The Cisco Kid*—"Postal Inspector" 8-4-51, "Kid Sister Trouble" 9-15-51.

Keane, Kerrie. Films: "Kung Fu: The Movie" TVM-1986 (Sarah Perkins).

Keane, Robert Emmett (1885-7/2/81). Films: "Captain Thunder" 1931 (Don Miguel Salazar); "Billy the Kid Returns" 1938 (Page); "Henry Goes Arizona" 1939 (Bentley); "The Border Legion" 1940 (Officer Willets); "The Cowboy and the Blonde" 1941 (Mr. Gregory); "Fool's Gold" 1946 (Professor Dixon); "Rainbow Over Texas" 1946 (Wooster Dalrymple); "The Timber Trail" 1948 (Jordan Weatherbee); "Frontier Investigator" 1949 (Erskine Doubleday); "Navajo Trail Raiders" 1949 (John Blanford); "Susanna Pass" 1949 (Martin Masters); "Hills of Oklahoma" 1950 (Charles Stevens).

Kearney, Carolyn. TV: *Zane Grey Theater*—"The Doctor Keeps a Promise" 3-21-58 (Jenny Bechdolt); *Buckskin*—"The Lady from Bismarck" 7-3-58 (Marietta Flynn), "The Monkey's Uncle" 1-12-59 (Marietta Flynn); *Wanted—Dead or Alive*—"The Voice of Silence" 2-15-61 (Carol Hagen); *Stagecoach West*—"The Bold Whip" 5-23-61 (Anne Marston); *Frontier Circus*—"The Patriarch of Purgatory" 11-30-61 (Susannah Hedges); *The Virginian*—"Big Day, Great Day" 10-24-62 (Maxine); *Empire*—"Pressure Lock" 12-4-62 (Charlotte); *Wagon Train*—"The Annie Duggan Story" 3-13-63 (Annie Duggan); *Bonanza*—"My Brother's Keeper" 4-7-63 (Sheila).

Kearns, Geraldine. Films: "The Outlaw Josey Wales" 1976 (Little Moonlight).

Kearns, Joe (1907-2/17/62). TV: *Gunsmoke*—"The Big Con" 5-3-58 (Banker Papp), "Murder Warrant" 4-

18-59 (Dobie), "The Constable" 5-30-59 (Botkin).

Keast, Paul. Films: "Hannah Lee" 1953 (1st Villager); "Snowfire" 1958. ¶TV: *The Lone Ranger*—"A Broken Match" 12-2-54, "Code of the Pioneers" 2-17-55, "Sawtelle Saga's End" 3-24-55; *The Adventures of Rin Tin Tin*—"Connecticut Yankees" 11-4-55, "Homer the Great" 4-20-56; *Circus Boy*—"The Lady and the Circus" 3-31-57 (Mike Anderson); *Tales of Wells Fargo*—"Alias Jim Hardie" 3-10-58 (Sheriff Carlson); *Sugarfoot*—"The Wizard" 10-14-58 (Judge Wilson); *The Restless Gun*—"Bonner's Squaw" 11-3-58 (Sam Tapley); *The Texan*—"The Invisible Noose" 5-16-60 (Parson); *Whispering Smith*—"Poet and Peasant Case" 8-28-61 (Summers).

Keating, Larry (1896-8/26/63). Films: "Carson City" 1952 (William Sharon); "Gypsy Colt" 1954 (Wade Y. Gerald).

Keaton, Buster (1895-2/1/66). Films: "The Paleface" 1922; "Go West" 1925 (Friendless Homer Holiday); "The Gold Ghost" 1934-short; "Pest from the West" 1939-short; "God's Country" 1946.

Keaton, Harry (1896-6/18/66). Films: "Desert Mesa" 1935 (Killer).

Keats, Steven (1945-5/8/94). Films: "The Awakening Land" TVM-1978 (Jake Tench).

Keckley, Jane (1876-8/14/63). Films: "The Chief's Daughter" 1911; "A Frontier Girl's Courage" 1911; "John Oakhurst—Gambler" 1911; "McKee Rankin's '49" 1911; "A Broken Spur" 1912; "The Massacre of Santa Fe Trail" 1912; "The Parson of Panamint" 1916 (Arabella Randall); "Aflame in the Sky" 1927 (Cordelia Murdoch); "Tonto Kid" 1935 (Mrs. Fritch); "The Plainsman" 1936; "Roarin' Lead" 1936; "Gunsmoke Ranch" 1937 (Mathilda); "Lightning Carson Rides Again" 1938 (Katherine); "The Lone Ranger" 1938-serial (Mrs. Clark); "Six Shootin' Sheriff" 1938 (Mrs. Morgan); "In Old Montana" 1939 (Pocohantas); "Union Pacific" 1939 (Official's Wife); "Melody Ranch" 1940; "Northwest Mounted Police" 1940; "The Musical Bandit" 1941-short; "Redskins and Redheads" 1941-short.

Keefe, Cornelius (Jack Hill) (1900-12/11/72). Films: "Tumbling Tumbleweeds" 1935 (Harry Brooks); "Western Courage" 1935 (Eric Simpson); "The Old Corral" 1936 (Martin Simms); "The Big Show" 1937; "The Trigger Trio" 1937 (Tom Brent);

"Way Out West" 1937 (Worker at Mickey Finn's); "Stagecoach" 1939 (Capt. Whitney); "Saddlemates" 1941 (Lt. Manning); "Gunplay" 1951 (Sheriff); "The Vanquished" 1953. ¶TV: *Sergeant Preston of the Yukon*—"Golden Gift" 6-14-56 (Stoner).

Keefe, Zena (1896-11/16/77). Films: "Out of the Snows" 1920 (Anitah).

Keefer, Don (1916-). Films: "Butch Cassidy and the Sundance Kid" 1969 (Fireman). ¶TV: *Gunsmoke*—"Wrong Man" 4-13-57 (Sam Rickers), "Bad Sheriff" 1-7-61 (Chet), "Coventry" 3-17-62 (Pete Rankin), "Quint-Cident" 4-27-63 (Nally), "The Pariah" 4-17-65 (Newspaper Editor), "Taps for Old Jeb" 10-16-65 (Milty Sims), "Champion of the World" 12-24-66 (Wally), "Gentry's Law" 10-12-70 (Floyd Babcock), "Kitty's Love Affair" 10-22-73 (Turner); *Have Gun Will Travel*—"Winchester Quarantine" 10-5-57, "The Solid Gold Patrol" 12-13-58 (Col. Barlowe), "The Tender Gun" 10-22-60 (Corcoran); *Rawhide*—"Incident of the Druid's Curse" 1-8-60; *Wagon Train*—"The Tom Tuckett Story" 3-2-60; *Hotel De Paree*—"Sundance and the Barren Soil" 5-20-60 (Red Porterfield); *Whispering Smith*—"The Deadliest Weapon" 6-19-61 (Dr. Johnson); *The Dakotas*—"Feud at Snake River" 4-29-63 (Minister); *The Loner*—"The Homecoming of Lemuel Stove" 11-20-65 (the Minister); *The Virginian*—"The Return of Golden Tom" 3-9-66 (Ross Tedler), "Last Grave at Socorro Creek" 1-22-69 (Undertaker); *Iron Horse*—"Sister Death" 4-3-67 (Blake); *Dundee and the Culhane*—"The Dead Man's Brief" 10-4-67 (Johnson); *Cimarron Strip*—"The Judgment" 1-4-68 (Bolt); *The Guns of Will Sonnett*—"End of the Rope" 1-12-68 (Prosecutor), "One Angry Juror" 3-7-69; *The Outcasts*—"The Man from Bennington" 12-16-68 (Case); *Alias Smith and Jones*—"The Man Who Murdered Himself" 3-18-71; *Bonanza*—"The Running Man" 3-30-69 (Billy Harris), "The Rattlesnake Brigade" 12-5-71 (Tobias Temple); *The High Chaparral*—"Spokes" 9-25-70 (Telegrapher); *Nichols*—"The Dirty Half Dozen Run Amuck" 10-28-71 (Burt Lincoln); *Kung Fu*—"Cry of the Night Beast" 10-19-74 (Stripper), "Barbary House" 2-15-75 (Station Keeper), "Flight to Orion" 2-22-75 (Station Keeper), "The Brothers Cain" 3-1-75 (Station Keeper), "Full Circle" 3-15-75 (Station Keeper).

Keefer, Phil. Films: "'Neath the Arizona Skies" 1934 (Jameson Hodges); "The New Frontier" 1935.

Keel, Howard (1919-). Films: "Annie Get Your Gun" 1950 (Frank Butler); "Callaway Went Thataway" 1951 (Stretch Barnes/Smoky Callaway); "Calamity Jane" 1953 (Wild Bill Hickok); "Ride, Vaquero!" 1953 (King Cameron); "Rose Marie" 1954 (Mike Malone); "The Man from Button Willow" 1965 (Voice); "Waco" 1966 (Waco); "Red Tomahawk" 1967 (Capt. Tom York); "The War Wagon" 1967 (Levi Walking Bear); "Arizona Bushwhackers" 1968 (Lee Travis). ¶TV: *Zane Grey Theater*—"Gift from a Gunman" 12-13-57 (Will Gorman); *Tales of Wells Fargo*—"Casket 7.3" 9-30-61 (Justin Brox); *Death Valley Days*—"Diamond Jim Brady" 6-2-63 (Diamond Jim Brady); *The Quest*—"Seventy-Two Hours" 11-3-76 (Shanghai Pierce).

Keeler, Wee Willie (1891-1/17/64). Films: "Cheyenne Wildcat" 1944; "Covered Wagon Raid" 1950.

Keen, Noah (1927-). Films: "A Big Hand for the Little Lady" 1966 (Sparrow). ¶TV: *Have Gun Will Travel*—"The Gospel Singer" 10-21-61 (Harry Durbin), "A Drop of Blood" 12-2-61 (Billy Buckstone); *Empire*—"Long Past, Long Remembered" 10-23-62 (Dr. Phelps), "Duet for Eight Wheels" 4-30-63 (Dr. Phelps); *The Virginian*—"The Accomplice" 12-19-62 (Samuel Cole), "Vengeance Trail" 1-4-67 (Judge Benson), "The Barren Ground" 12-6-67 (Arnold Page); *Wide Country*—"To Cindy, with Love" 2-28-63 (Mr. Hopkins); *Stoney Burke*—"Forget Me More" 3-25-63 (Ed Larkin); *A Man Called Shenandoah*—"The Onslaught" 9-23-65 (Dr. Maghee); *The Big Valley*—"The Invaders" 12-29-65 (Doc), "The Prize" 12-16-68; *Bonanza*—"The Prince" 4-2-67 (Dixon), "To Die in Darkness" 5-5-68 (Warden); *The High Chaparral*—"Tiger by the Tail" 2-25-68 (Travers).

Keenan, Frank (1858-2/24/29). Films: "The Long Chance" 1915 (Harley P. Hennage); "Jim Grimsby's Boy" 1916 (Jim Grimsby); "The Midnight Stage" 1919 (John Lynch/Bige Rivers).

Keene, Mike. TV: *The Californians*—"Act of Faith" 5-26-59 (Cal Dobbs); *Wyatt Earp*—"Wyatt Wins One" 11-10-59; *Bronco*—"The Devil's Spawn" 12-1-59 (Pete Donner), "The Mustangers" 10-17-60 (Abner Shelton); *Wagon Train*—"The Ruth Marshall Story" 12-30-59 (Amos Marshall).

Keene, Richard (1890-3/11/71).

TV: *Wichita Town*—"The Long Night" 1-20-60 (Man); *The Rifleman*—"The Hero" 2-2-60 (Jethroe); *Gunsmoke*—"Durham Bull" 3-31-62 (Dan Binny).

Keene, Tom (George Duryea, Richard Powers) (1898-8/4/63). Films: "In Old California" 1929 (Lt. Tony Hopkins); "Tide of Empire" 1929 (Dermod D'Arcy); "Beau Bandit" 1930 (Howard); "The Dude Wrangler" 1930 (Wally McCann); "Pardon My Gun" 1930 (Ted Duncan); "Sundown Trail" 1931 (Robert "Buck" Sawyer); "Beyond the Rockies" 1932 (Blackjack); "Come on, Danger!" 1932 (Larry Madden); "Freighters of Destiny" 1932 (Steve Macey); "Ghost Valley" 1932 (Jerry Long); "Partners" 1932 (Dick Barstow); "Renegades of the West" 1932 (Tom Bigby); "The Saddle Buster" 1932 (Montana); "The Cheyenne Kid" 1933 (Tom Larkin); "Crossfire" 1933 (Tom Allen); "Scarlet River" 1933 (Tom Baxter); "Son of the Border" 1933 (Tom Owens); "Sunset Pass" 1933 (Jack Rock/Jim Collins); "Battle of Greed" 1934 (John Storm); "Desert Gold" 1936 (Dick Gale); "Drift Fence" 1936 (Jim Travis); "Rebellion" 1936 (Capt. John Carroll); "Drums of Destiny" 1937 (Capt. Jerry Crawford); "The Glory Trail" 1937 (John Morgan); "God's Country and the Man" 1937 (Jim Reed); "The Law Commands" 1937 (Dr. Keith Kenton); "Old Louisiana" 1937 (John Colfax); "Raw Timber" 1937 (Tom Corbin); "Romance of the Rockies" 1937 (Tom); "Under Strange Flags" 1937 (Tom Kenyon); "Where Trails Divide" 1937 (Tom Allen); "The Painted Trail" 1938 (Tom Gray/the Pecos Kid); "The Driftin' Kid" 1941; "Dynamite Canyon" 1941 (Tom Evans); "Lone Star Law Men" 1941 (Tom); "Riding the Sunset Trail" 1941 (Tom Sterling); "Wanderers of the West" 1941 (Tom Mallory/Arizona); "Arizona Roundup" 1942; "Western Mail" 1942; "Where Trails End" 1942; "The Lights of Old Santa Fe" 1944 (Frank Madden); "Thunder Mountain" 1947 (Johnny Blue); "Under the Tonto Rim" 1947 (Dennison); "Wild Horse Mesa" 1947 (Hod Slack); "Blood on the Moon" 1948 (Ted Eiser); "Indian Agent" 1948 (Hutchins); "Return of the Badmen" 1948 (Jim Younger); "Western Heritage" 1948 (Spade); "Brothers in the Saddle" 1949 (Nash Prescott); "Desperadoes of the West" 1950-serial (Ward Gordon); "Storm Over Wyoming" 1950 (Tug Caldwell); "Trail of Robin Hood" 1950; "Texans Never Cry" 1951 (Tracy

Wyatt); "The Outlaw's Daughter" 1954 (Bank Manager); "Dig That Uranium" 1956 (Frank Loomis); "Once Upon a Horse" 1958 (Tom Keene). ¶TV: *Judge Roy Bean*—"The Runaway" 10-15-55 (Kenyon), "Slightly Prodigal" 10-15-55 (Ab Hanlon), "Vinegarone" 12-1-55 (Raymodn Murton); *Sergeant Preston of the Yukon*—"Skagway Secret" 2-16-56 (Cap Higsby), "Golden Gift" 6-14-56 (Furman); *Tales of the Texas Rangers*—"Traitor's Gold" 10-2-58 (Morgan Thorpe).

Keene, Valley. Films: "Son of the Renegade" 1953 (Dusty). ¶TV: *Judge Roy Bean*—"Four Ladies from Laredo" 7-1-56 (Melissa).

Keene, William. TV: *Wild Bill Hickok*—"Counterfeit Ghost" 8-11-53; *Gunsmoke*—"Kitty Caught" 1-18-58 (Mr. Botkin); *Wagon Train*—"Around the Horn" 10-1-58 (Alfie); *The Californians*—"Old Sea Dog" 12-16-58; *Tales of Wells Fargo*—"Return of Doc Bell" 11-30-59 (Huggins); *Wyatt Earp*—"Roscoe Turns Detective" 5-3-60; *Bonanza*—"The Burma Rarity" 10-22-61, "The Artist" 10-7-62 (Stevens), "Five Candles" 3-2-69 (Doc Hill); *The Big Valley*—"Point and Counterpoint" 5-19-69 (Judge).

Keener, Hazel (1904-8/7/79). Films: "The Mask of Lopez" 1923 (Doris Hampton); "The Dangerous Coward" 1924 (Hazel McGuinn); "The Fighting Sap" 1924 (Marjorie Stoddard); "Galloping Gallagher" 1924 (Evelyn Churchill); "Hard Hittin' Hamilton" 1924 (Mary Downing); "North of Nevada" 1924 (Marion Ridgeway); "The Silent Stranger" 1924 (Lillian Warner); "Vanishing Hoofs" 1926 (Edith Marsh); "One Hour of Love" 1927 (Vi); "The Silent Partner" 1927; "Whispering Sage" 1927 (Mercedes' Friend); "The Scarlet Arrow" 1928-serial; "Wells Fargo" 1937.¶TV: *Judge Roy Bean*—"The Wedding of Old Sam" 10-1-55 (Emma Perkins).

Keenlyside, Eric. Films: "Children of the Dust" TVM-1995 (Boss Beeson).

Keep, Michael. Films: "40 Guns to Apache Pass" 1967 (Cochise); "The Way West" 1967 (Sioux Brave); "Wild Women" TVM-1970. ¶TV: *Wrangler*—"Incident of the Wide Lop" 9-1-60 (Jensen); *Zane Grey Theater*—"The Last Bugle" 11-24-60 (Natchez); *Wagon Train*—"The River Crossing" 12-14-60 (Dark Eagle); *Bronco*—"The Buckbrier Trail" 2-20-61 (Walter Ruick); *Gunsmoke*—"Quint Asper Comes Home" 9-29-62 (Chief), "Chief Joseph" 1-30-65;

Have Gun Will Travel—"Brotherhood" 1-5-63 (Abe Redrock); *Death Valley Days*—"With Honesty and Integrity" 4-21-63 (Crow Dog), "Honor the Name Dennis Driscoll" 10-25-64, "Hero of Fort Halleck" 6-27-65 (Indian Chief), "The Journey" 6-13-65 (Wolf), "Let My People Go" 10-21-67 (Pacomio), "The Lady Doctor" 10-11-69, "The Great Pinto Bean Gold Hunt" 12-13-69; *Bonanza*—"The Toy Soldier" 10-20-63, "Erin" 1-26-69 (Bear Hunter), "The Lady and the Mountain Lion" 2-23-69 (Brett Rankin); *The Travels of Jaimie McPheeters*—"The Day of the Taboo Man" 10-27-63 (Indian Chief); *Rawhide*—"Incident at Gila Flats" 1-30-64 (Cado); *Branded*—"The Test" 2-7-65 (Bold Eagle), "Fill No Glass for Me" 11-7-65 & 11-14-65 (Chief Wateekah); *Daniel Boone*—"The Tamarack Massacre Affair" 12-30-65 (Rain Cloud), "The Kidnaping" 1-22-70; *Laredo*—"Hey Diddle Diddle" 2-24-67 (Yaqui); *The High Chaparral*—"The Stallion" 9-20-68 (Natchez), "The Last Hundred Miles" 1-24-69, "Mi Casa, Su Casa" 2-20-70 (Chiopana), "Too Many Chiefs" 3-27-70 (Chiopana), "A Man to Match the Land" 3-12-71 (Red Eagle); *The Cowboys*—4-3-74 (Chief).

Kehoe, Jack (1938-). Films: "Young Guns II" 1990 (Ashmun Upson).

Keim, Betty Lou. TV: *The Deputy*—Regular 1959-60 (Fran McCord); *Riverboat*—"The Wichita Arrows" 2-29-60 (Holly Andrews).

Keitel, Harvey (1939-). Films: "Buffalo Bill and the Indians, or Sitting Bull's History Lesson" 1976 (Ed); "Eagle's Wing" 1979-Brit./Span. (Henry).

Keith, Brian (Robert Keith, Jr.) (1921-). Films: "Arrowhead" 1953 (Capt. North); "Drum Beat" 1954 (Bill Satterwhite); "The Violent Men" 1955 (Cole Wilkison); "Hell Canyon Outlaws" 1957; "Run of the Arrow" 1957 (Capt. Clark); "Fort Dobbs" 1958 (Clett); "Sierra Baron" 1958 (Jack McCracken); "Villa!" 1958 (Bill Harmon); "Ten Who Dared" 1960 (William Dunn); "The Deadly Companions" 1961 (Yellowleg); "Savage Sam" 1963 (Uncle Beck Coates); "The Raiders" 1964 (John G. McElroy); "The Hallelujah Trail" 1965 (Frank Willingham); "Nevada Smith" 1966 (Jonas Cord); "The Rare Breed" 1966 (Alexander Bowen); "Scandalous John" 1971 (John McCanless); "Something Big" 1971 (Col. Morgan); "Joe Panther" 1976 (Capt. Harper); "The Quest" TVM-1976

(Tank Logan); "The Chisholms" TVM-1979 (Andrew Blake); "The Mountain Men" 1980 (Henry Frapp); "The Alamo: 13 Days to Glory" TVM-1987 (Davy Crockett); "Young Guns" 1988 (Buckshot Roberts); "The Gambler Returns: The Luck of the Draw" TVM-1991 (the Westerner). ¶TV: *Walt Disney Presents*—"Elfego Baca" Regular 1958-60 (Shadrock); *Zane Grey Theater*—"Trouble at Tres Cruces" 3-26-59 (Dave Blasingame); *Rawhide*—"Incident in No Man's Land" 6-12-59 (Tod Macauley); *Laramie*—"General Delivery" 11-3-59 (Capt. Whit Malone), "The General Must Die" 11-17-59 (Capt. Whit Malone); *The Westerner*—Regular 1960 (Dave Blasingame); *Frontier Circus*—"The Smallest Target" 10-12-61 (Dan); *The Outlaws*—"My Friend, the Horse Thief" 10-19-61 (Whip), "The Bitter Swede" 1-18-62 (Sven Johannsen); *The Virginian*—"Duel at Shiloh" 1-2-63 (Johnny Wade); *Wagon Train*—"The Tom Tuesday Story" 4-3-63 (Tom Tuesday), "The Robert Harrison Clarke Story" 10-14-63 (Gault); *Redigo*—"Hostage Hero Riding" 12-10-63; *Hallmark Hall of Fame*—"The Court-Martial of General George Armstrong Carter" 12-1-77 (Allan Jacobson); *How the West Was Won*—Episode One 2-12-78 (General Stoneciper), Episode Two 2-19-78 (General Stoneciper); *Centennial*—Regular 1978-79 (Sheriff Axel Dumire); *The Chisholms*—Regular 1979 (Andrew Blake); *Young Riders*—"Star Light, Star Bright" 12-15-90 (Cyrus).

Keith, Byron. Films: "Dallas" 1950 (Jason Trask); "The Black Lash" 1952 (Leonard); "The Great Bank Robbery" 1969 (Deputy). ¶TV: *The Adventures of Rin Tin Tin*—"The Iron Horse" 10-28-55 (Robert Quinn); *Bronco*—"The Prince of Darkness" 11-6-61 (Colonel Traver); *The Virginian*—"The Challenge" 10-19-66 (Dr. Manning).

Keith, David (1954-). Films: "James A. Michener's Texas" TVM-1995 (Jim Bowie).

Keith, Donald (1903-8/1/69). Films: "Baree, Son of Kazan" 1925 (Jim Carvel); "Phantom of the North" 1929 (Bob Donald); "Branded Men" 1931 (the Brother); "White Renegade" 1931; "Outlaw Justice" 1933.

Keith, Ian (1899-3/26/60). Films: "The Great Divide" 1929 (Stephen Ghent); "The Sundown Kid" 1942 (J. Richard Spencer); "Bordertown Gunfighters" 1943 (Cameo Shelby); "The Man from Thunder River" 1943; "Wild Horse

Stampede" 1943 (Carson); "Arizona Whirlwind" 1944 (Polini); "Cowboy from Lonesome River" 1944; "Northwest Trail" 1945; "Phantom of the Plains" 1945; "Song of Old Wyoming" 1945 (Landow); "Under Western Skies" 1945 (Prof. Moffett); "Singing on the Trail" 1946; "Border Feud" 1947. ¶TV: *The Adventures of Rin Tin Tin*—"Rin Tin Tin Meets Shakespeare" 9-16-55.

Keith, Isabelle (1898-7/20/79). Films: "The Desert Flower" 1925 (Inga Hulverson).

Keith, Richard (1905-9/16/76). TV: *Gunsmoke*—"Custer" 9-22-56 (Major Banker); *Zane Grey Theater*—"Ride a Lonely Trail" 11-2-57 (Mayor); *Death Valley Days*—"California's First Schoolmarm" 11-4-57.

Keith, Robert (1898-12/22/66). Films: "Branded" 1951 (Leffingwell); "Devil's Canyon" 1953 (Steve Morgan); "Cimarron" 1960 (Sam Pegler); "Posse from Hell" 1961 (Capt. Brown). ¶TV: *Fury*—"The Scientists" 2-23-57 (Freddie); *Sheriff of Cochise*—"Approach with Caution" 4-19-57 (Col. Evans).

Keith, Robert. Films: "Cowboy" TVM-1983 (Rusty). ¶TV: *Adventures of Brisco County, Jr.*—"AKA Kansas" 12-17-93 (Kansas).

Keith, Jr., Robert. *see* Keith, Brian.

Keith, Rosalind. Films: "King of the Royal Mounted" 1936 (Helen Lawton); "Westbound Mail" 1937 (Marion Saunders); "Trouble in Sundown" 1939 (Jewell Cameron).

Keith, Sherwood (1912-2/21/72). TV: *Have Gun Will Travel*—"Love and a Bad Woman" 3-26-60 (Dandy).

Keith-Johnston, Colin (1896-1/3/80). Films: "Fancy Pants" 1950 (Twombley), "The Left-Handed Gun" 1958 (Tunstall).

Kellard, Robert. *see* Stevens, Robert.

Kellaway, Cecil (1893-2/28/73). Films: "Mexican Spitfire Out West" 1940 (Chumley); "Unconquered" 1947 (Jeremy Love); "The Proud Rebel" 1958 (Dr. Enos Davis); "The Adventures of Bullwhip Griffin" 1967 (Mr. Pemberton). ¶TV: *Johnny Ringo*—"The Cat" 12-3-59 (Cyrus); *Rawhide*—"Incident in the Middle of Nowhere" 4-7-61 (MacKay).

Keller, Betty. Films: "Across the Sierras" 1912; "The Girl and the Sheriff" 1912; "The Love Trail" 1912; "The Sheriff Outwitted" 1912; "An Eventful Evening" 1916; "The Passing of Pete" 1916; "The Sheriff's

Duty" 1916; "Tom's Strategy" 1916; "Trilby's Love Disaster" 1916; "Superstition" 1920.

Keller, Sam. Films: "Jesse James' Women" 1954 (Cole Younger); "Frontier Woman" 1956.

Kellerman, Sally (1938-). Films: "September Gun" TVM-1983 (Mama Queen). ¶TV: *Cheyenne*—"The Durango Brothers" 9-24-62 (Lottie Durango); *A Man Called Shenandoah*—"Run, Killer, Run" 1-10-66 (Phil Bartlett); *The Legend of Jesse James*—"The Lonely Place" 2-21-66 (Kate Mason); *Bonanza*—"A Dollar's Worth of Trouble" 5-15-66 (Kathleen Walker), "Return Engagement" 3-1-70 (Lotta Crabtree); *Dundee and the Culhane*—"The Dead Man's Brief" 10-4-67 (Cynthia); *Centennial*—Regular 1978-79 (Lise Bockweiss).

Kellerman, Susan. Films: "The Wild Women of Chastity Gulch" TVM-1982 (Betsy).

Kellett, Pete. Films: "Blazing the Overland Trail" 1956-serial; "Reprisal!" 1956 (Foreman). ¶TV: *Wild Bill Hickok*—"The Gorilla of Owl Hoot Mesa" 9-23-52; *Branded*—"The Bounty" 2-21-65 (Gil Starrett), "The First Kill" 4-4-65 (Bartender); *Gunsmoke*—"The Well" 11-19-66 (Monk), "Champion of the World" 12-24-66 (Mac), "Mail Drop" 1-28-67 (Al), "Stranger in Town" 11-20-67, "Uncle Finney" 10-14-68 (Joe), "9:12 to Dodge" 11-11-68 (Joe), "The Gold Mine" 1-27-69 (Spectator), "Coreyville" 10-6-69 (Guard #1), "The War Priest" 1-5-70 (Shotgun), "Doctor Herman Schultz, M.D." 1-26-70 (Stoney), "McCabe" 11-30-70 (Bartender), "Lijah" 11-8-71 (Frank), "The Bullet" 11-29-71, 12-6-71 & 12-13-71 (Baker), "The River" 9-11-72 & 9-18-72 (Hodad), "Jessie" 2-19-73 (Drucker), "Kitty's Love Affair" 10-22-73 (Curt), "A Child Between" 12-24-73 (1st Hide Cutter), "The Colonel" 12-16-74 (Biggs); *The Big Valley*—"Bounty on a Barkley" 2-26-68, "The Secret" 1-27-69 (Smith), "Lightfoot" 2-17-69; *The Virginian*—"The Long Ride Home" 9-17-69 (Purty).

Kelley, Alice. Films: "Buckaroo Sheriff of Texas" 1951 (Betty Dawson); "Take Me to Town" 1953 (Heroine).

Kelley, Barry (1908-6/15/91). Films: "Fighting Man of the Plains" 1949 (Slocum); "The Capture" 1950 (Mahoney); "Singing Guns" 1950 (Mike); "The Great Missouri Raid" 1951 (Mr. Bauer); "Woman of the North Country" 1952 (O'Hara);

"Law and Order" 1953 (Fin Elder); "Gunfire at Indian Gap" 1957 (Sheriff Daniel Harris); "The Tall Stranger" 1957 (Hardy Bishop); "Buchanan Rides Alone" 1958 (Lou Agry); "Rio Conchos" 1964 (Croupier). ¶TV: *The Lone Ranger*—"Texas Draw" 11-5-54 (Brother John Thorpe); *Gunsmoke*—"Romeo" 11-9-57 (Jake Pierce); *Tales of Wells Fargo*—"The Inscrutable Man" 12-9-57 (Bill Bolliver), "Clay Allison" 6-15-59 (Pat Hendrix); *Maverick*—"Prey of the Cat" 12-7-58 (Sheriff), "One of Our Trains Is Missing" 4-22-62 (Diamond Jim Brady); *Lawman*—"The Outsider" 1-4-59 (Josh Teller), "Owny O'Reilly, Esq." 10-15-61 (Governor Johnson); *Bronco*—"Backfire" 4-7-59 (Sheriff Linc McKeever), "Game at the Beacon Club" 9-22-59 (G.J. Harkness), "Flight from an Empire" 12-15-59 (Goddard); *Bonanza*—"A Rose for Lotta" 9-12-59 (Aaron Hooper), "The War Comes to Washoe" 11-4-62 (Stewart); *Cheyenne*—"Blind Spot" 9-21-59 (Sheriff Henshaw), "Dark Decision" 11-5-62 (Nathan Alston); *Walt Disney Presents*—"Elfego Baca: Mustang Men, Mustang Maid" 11-20-59 (Sheriff Holman); *Wanted—Dead or Alive*—"Jason" 1-30-60 (Sheriff), "Payoff at Pinto" 5-21-60 (Sheriff Luke Deaver); *Johnny Ringo*—"Killer, Choose a Card" 6-9-60 (Bill Jacobs); *Have Gun Will Travel*—"The Prisoner" 12-17-60 (Sheriff), "Everyman" 3-25-61 (Danceman), "Trial at Tablerock" 12-15-62 (Judge Bryant); *Bat Masterson*—"Ledger of Guilt" 4-6-61 (Frank Williams); *Rango*—"If You Can't Take It with You, Don't Go" 4-21-67 (Mayor); *Laramie*—"A Grave for Cully Brown" 2-13-62 (Sheriff); *The Dakotas*—"Feud at Snake River" 4-29-63 (Amish); *Temple Houston*—"Fracas at Kiowa Flats" 12-12-63 (Col. Jim Shepard); *Death Valley Days*—"The Paper Dynasty" 2-29-64, "No Gun Behind His Badge" 3-28-65 (Prentiss); *The Virginian*—"The Girl from Yesterday" 11-11-64 (Commissioner Todd), "The Showdown" 4-14-65 (Sheriff Jim Brady); *F Troop*—"Scourge of the West" 9-14-65 (General); *Laredo*—"The Would-Be Gentleman of Laredo" 4-14-66 (Quinn O'Connell).

Kelley, DeForest (1920-). Films: "Tension at Table Rock" 1956 (Breck); "Gunfight at the O.K. Corral" 1957 (Morgan Earp); "The Law and Jake Wade" 1958 (Wexler); "Warlock" 1959 (Curley Burns); "Gunfight at Comanche Creek" 1964 (Troop); "Black Spurs" 1965 (First Sheriff); "Town Tamer" 1965 (Guy Tavenner);

"Apache Uprising" 1966 (Toby Jack Saunders); "Waco" 1966 (Bill Rile). ¶TV: *The Lone Ranger*—"Legion of Old Timers" 10-6-49, "Gold Train" 3-16-50, "Death in the Forest" 6-4-53; *Gunsmoke*—"Indian Scout" 3-31-56 (Will Bailey); *Zane Grey Theater*—"Stage to Tucson" 11-16-56 (Les Porter), "Village of Fear" 3-1-57 (Pickard), "Shadow of a Dead Man" 4-11-58 (Logan Wheeler), "The Accuser" 10-30-58, "Calico Bait" 3-31-60 (Swain); *Trackdown*—"End of an Outlaw" 11-29-57 (Deputy), "The Jailbreak" 5-2-58 (Childers), "Hard Lines" 3-11-59 (Ed Crow), "Blind Alley" 9-16-59 (Tom Dooley), "Quiet Night in Porter" 9-23-59 (Tom); *Boots and Saddles*—"The Marquis of Donnybrook" 12-26-57 (Merriweather); *Rough Riders*—"The Nightbinders" 11-20-58 (Lance); *26 Men*—"Trail of Revenge" 1-13-59; *Northwest Passage*—"Death Rides the Wind" 1-23-59 (David Cooper); *Wanted—Dead or Alive*—"Secret Ballot" 2-14-59 (Steve Pax), "The Hostage" 10-10-59 (Ollie Tate); *Rawhide*—"Incident at Barker Springs" 2-20-59 (Slate Prell); *Black Saddle*—"Apache Trail" 11-20-59 (Sam King); *Lawman*—"The Thimblerigger" 2-28-60 (Sam White), "The Squatters" 1-29-61 (Brent Carr); *Two Faces West*—"Fallen Gun" 11-21-60; *Tales of Wells Fargo*—"Captain Scoville" 1-9-61 (Cole Scoville); *Stagecoach West*—"Image of a Man" 1-31-61 (Clay), "The Big Gun" 4-25-61 (Lieutenant Clarke); *The Deputy*—"The Means and the End" 3-18-61 (Farley Styles); *Bat Masterson*—"No Amnesty for Death" 3-30-61 (Brock Martin); *Bonanza*—"The Honor of Cochise" 10-8-61 (Captain Johnson), "The Decision" 12-16-62 (Dr. Jones), "Ride the Wind" 1-16-66 & 1-23-66 (Tully); *Death Valley Days*—"The Breaking Point" 6-13-62 (Shad Cullen), "Coffin for a Coward" 2-6-63 (Clint Rogers), "Lady of the Plains" 7-23-66 (Elliot Webster); *Laramie*—"Gun Duel" 12-25-62 (Bart Collins), "The Unvanquished" 3-12-63; *Have Gun Will Travel*—"The Treasure" 12-29-62 (Deakin); *The Virginian*—"Duel at Shiloh" 1-2-63 (Ben Tully), "Man of Violence" 12-25-63 (Blden); *The Dakotas*—"Reformation at Big Nose Butte" 4-1-63 (Martin Volet); *A Man Called Shenandoah*—"The Riley Brand 2-21-66 (Egan); *Laredo*—"Sound of Terror" 4-7-66 (Dr. David Ingram); *The Cowboys*—"David Done It" 5-15-74 (Jack Potter).

Kelley, Walter (1922-). Films: "Pat Garrett and Billy the Kid" 1973 (Rupert).

Kellin, Mike (1922-8/26/83). Films: "The Wonderful Country" 1959 (Pancho Gil); "Invitation to a Gunfighter" 1964 (Tom); "Fools' Parade" 1971 (Steve Mystic). ¶TV: *Have Gun Will Travel*—"The Solid Gold Patrol" 12-13-58 (Sergeant Siebert), "Shadow of a Man" 1-28-61 (Logan Adcock), "The Siege" 4-1-61 (Alvah Brent), "A Drop of Blood" 12-2-61 (Raivel Melamed); *Black Saddle*—"Apache Trail" 11-20-59 (Ulzana); *The Rifleman*—"Surveyors" 12-29-59 (Len Sommers); *The Outlaws*—"No More Horses" 3-1-62 (Bates); *Rawhide*—"A Man Called Mushy" 10-23-64 (Vassily); *Gunsmoke*—"The Moonstone" 12-17-66 (Chad Timpson).

Kellogg, Bruce. Films: "Deerslayer" 1943 (Deerslayer); "Barbary Coast Gent" 1944 (Bradford Bellamy III).

Kellogg, Cecil. Films: "Gordon of Ghost City" 1933-serial; "The Roaring West" 1935-serial; "Stormy" 1935 (Lark); "Arizona Mahoney" 1936 (Player); "End of the Trail" 1936; "The Mysterious Avenger" 1936 (Posse); "The Texas Rangers" 1936 (Ranger); "Thunder Trail" 1937 (Cowboy); "Rawhide" 1938 (Gilliam); "Chip of the Flying U" 1939 (Red); "The Lone Ranger Rides Again" 1939-serial (Raider #6); "The Thundering West" 1939; "Geronimo" 1940 (Soldier Kells); "The Outlaw" 1943 (Officer).

Kellogg, Frances. Films: "Red Blood" 1926 (Carlotta); "Lawless Land" 1937.

Kellogg, Gayle. Films: "Tough Assignment" 1949 (Rancher); "Canadian Mounties vs. Atomic Invaders" 1953-serial (Corporal Guy Sanders); "Thunder Over the Plains" 1953.

Kellogg, John (1916-). Films: "King of the Wild Horses" 1947; "Robin Hood of Texas" 1947 (Nick Castillo); "Borrowed Trouble" 1948 (Lee Garvin); "Sinister Journey" 1948 (Lee Garvin); "Station West" 1948 (Ben); "Bad Men of Tombstone" 1949 (Curly); "Kansas Raiders" 1950 (Red Leg Leader); "The Raiders" 1952 (Welch); "Rancho Notorious" 1952 (Factor); "The Fighting Lawman" 1953; "The Silver Whip" 1953 (Slater); "Those Redheads from Seattle" 1953 (Mike Yurkil); "The Bravos" TVM-1972 (Sergeant Marcy); "A Knife for the Ladies" 1973 (Hollyfield). ¶TV: *Black Saddle*—"The Return" 4-8-60 (Chance Crawford); *Tate*—"The Return of Jessica Jackson" 9-14-60 (Milo Jackson); *Stagecoach West*—"Dark Return" 10-18-60 (Jed Culver), "The Bold Whip" 5-23-61

(Rupe Larned); *Maverick*—"The Ice Man" 1-29-61 (Ben Stricker); *Lawman*—"Mark of Cain" 3-26-61 (Chad), "The Appointment" 11-26-61 (Lochard); *Gunsmoke*—"Durham Bull" 3-31-62 (Silva), "Ex-Con" 11-30-63 (Leo Pitts), "The Raid" 1-22-66 & 1-29-66 (T.R. Stark), "The Victim" 1-1-68 (Sheriff Joe Wood), "The Intruders" 3-3-69 (Henry Decker); *Stoney Burke*—"The Scavenger" 11-12-62 (Voit); *The Dakotas*—"Trouble at French Creek" 1-28-63 (Kirk); *Rawhide*—"Incident of Judgment Day" 2-8-63 (Leslie Bellamy); *Bonanza*—"A Question of Strength" 10-27-63 (Stager), "No Less a Man" 3-15-64 (Wagner), "Logan's Treasure"10-18-64 (Frank Reed), "The Conquistadors" 10-1-67 (Anderson), "Salute to Yesterday" 9-29-68 (Sergeant Ordy); *The Virginian*—"All Nice and Legal" 11-25-64 (Seth Potter), "Lost Yesterday" 2-3-65 (Barton), "Stopover" 1-8-69 (Mel Dover); *Laredo*—"Above the Law" 1-13-66 (Brad Scanlon); *Daniel Boone*—"Gun-Barrel Highway" 2-24-66 (Cassady), "The Cache" 12-4-69 (Swanson); *Wild Wild West*—"The Night of the Amnesiac" 2-9-68 (Rusty); *Lancer*—"Julie" 10-29-68 (Sheriff Cutler); *Alias Smith and Jones*—"Stagecoach Seven" 3-11-71 (Joe), "What's in It for Mia?" 2-24-72 (Dealer), "The Strange Fate of Conrad Meyer Zulick" 12-2-72.

Kellogg, Lynn (1945-). Films: "Charro!" 1969 (Marcie).

Kellogg, Ray (1906-7/5/76). Films: "Apache Warrior" 1957 (Bounty Man). ¶TV: *Wyatt Earp*—"One of Jesse's Gang" 3-13-56, "Hunt the Man Down" 5-3-56, "The Almost Dead Cowhand" 10-23-56, "Command Performance" 2-19-57 (Buffalo Bill), "Wells Fargo Calling Marshal Earp" 12-29-59 (Todd), "He's My Brother" 11-29-60 (Marshal Pritchard); *The Californians*—"The Regulators" 11-5-57 (James Sloat); *Wagon Train*—"The Honorable Don Charlie Story" 1-22-58 (Big Frank); *Rough Riders*—"The Maccabites" 10-16-58 (Seth); *Bat Masterson*—"The Fighter" 11-5-58 (Brock), "The Disappearance of Bat Masterson" 3-10-60 (Deputy); *Fury*—"The Witch" 1-16-60; *The Law of the Plainsman*—"Dangerous Barriers" 3-10-60; *The Tall Man*—"Garrett and the Kid" 9-10-60 (Witness); *The Deputy*—"Enemy of the Town" 5-6-61 (Quent Hall); *The Rifleman*—"Incident at Line Shack Six" 1-7-63 (Vale Croton); *Wild Wild West*—"The Night of the Red-Eyed Madmen" 11-26-65 (Capt. Sandy O'Brien); *Laredo*—"Meanwhile, Back at the Reservation" 2-10-

66; *Lancer*—"The Prodigal" 11-12-68, "Yesterday's Vendetta" 1-28-69, "The Lion and the Lamb" 2-3-70.

Kellogg, William. Films: "King of the Royal Mounted" 1940-serial (MacCloud); "One Man's Law" 1940; "The Return of Wild Bill" 1940 (Hep); "Trailing Double Trouble" 1940 (Walt); "West of Abilene" 1940 (Deputy); "Young Buffalo Bill" 1940; "Kansas Cyclone" 1941; "King of the Texas Rangers" 1941-serial (Hank Breen); "Bells of Capistrano" 1942; "Home in Wyomin'" 1942.

Kelly, Bebe. TV: *Daniel Boone*—"The Reunion" 3-11-65 (Mary Barnes); *Death Valley Days*—"The Courtship of Carrie Huntington" 6-4-66 (Sister); *How the West Was Won*—Episode Three 2-14-77 (Alva).

Kelly, Brian (1931-). Films: "Shoot, Gringo … Shoot!" 1968-Ital./Fr. (Stark).

Kelly, Carol. Films: "The Desperados Are in Town" 1956 (Hattie); "Daniel Boone, Trail Blazer" 1957 (Jemima Boone); "Terror in a Texas Town" 1958 (Molly). ¶TV: *Sugarfoot*—"The Stallion Trail" 12-24-57 (Elaine White); *The Deputy*—"The Orphans" 12-26-59 (Mrs. Bean).

Kelly, Claire (1935-). Films: "The Badlanders" 1958 (Ada Winston); "Snowfire" 1958 (Carol Hampton). ¶TV: *The Adventures of Rin Tin Tin*—"Frontier Angel" 11-22-57; *Northwest Passage*—"The Killers" 3-13-59 (Lucy); *The Texan*—"Lady Tenderfoot" 5-9-60 (Gail Henshaw).

Kelly, Craig. Films: "The Furies" 1950 (Young Anaheim).

Kelly, Don (1924-10/2/66). Films: "Buzzy Rides the Range" 1940 (Deck); "Cyclone on Horseback" 1941; "The Big Land" 1957 (Billy). ¶TV: *Frontier*—"The Well" 4-8-56 (Jim), "A Somewhere Voice" 5-6-56 (Jim); *Death Valley Days*—"The Sinbuster" 6-2-56; *Maverick*—"Trail West to Fury" 2-16-58 (Jett), "Holiday at Hollow Rock" 12-28-58 (Ira Swain); *Broken Arrow*—"War Trail" 4-8-58 (Capt. Baker); *Lawman*—"The Oath" 10-26-58 (Lou Menke), "The Souvenir" 4-5-59 (Virgil Carey); *The Texan*—"A Quart of Law" 1-12-59; *Black Saddle*—"Client: Reynolds" 5-23-59 (Harry Briggs); *Tales of Wells Fargo*—"The Daltons" 5-25-59 (Bob Dalton); *The Restless Gun*—"A Very Special Investigation" 6-15-59 (Blair Weeks); *Bonanza*—"El Toro Grande" 1-2-60.

Kelly, Dorothy (1894-5/31/66). Films: "The Battle of Frenchman's Run" 1915; "From Out of the Big Snows" 1915 (Marie).

Kelly, Grace (1929-9/14/82). Films: "High Noon" 1952 (Amy Kane).

Kelly, Helen. Films: "M'Liss" 1918 (Clytemnestra Veronica McSnagley).

Kelly, Jack (1927-11/7/92). Films: "New Mexico" 1951 (Pvt. Clifton); "Column South" 1953 (Trooper Vaness); "Gunsmoke" 1953 (Curly Mather); "Law and Order" 1953 (Jed); "The Redhead from Wyoming" 1953 (Sandy); "The Stand at Apache River" 1953 (Hatcher); "They Rode West" 1954 (Lt. Raymond); "The Violent Men" 1955 (DeRosa); "Young Billy Young" 1969 (John Behan); "The New Maverick" TVM-1978 (Bart Maverick); "The Gambler Returns: The Luck of the Draw" TVM-1991 (Bart Maverick). ¶TV: *Stories of the Century*—"Black Bart" 7-8-55, "Clay Allison" 9-16-55; *Frontier*—"The Hunted" 5-13-56, "The Return of Jubal Dolan" 8-26-56 (Jubal Dolan), "The Hostage" 9-9-56; *Gunsmoke*—"Jealousy" 7-6-57 (Cam Durbin); *Maverick*—Regular 1957-62 (Bart Maverick), "Deadly Image" 3-12-61 (Rod Claxton); *Wagon Train*—"The Fenton Canaby Story" 12-30-63 (Fenton Canaby); *Laredo*—"The Deadliest Kid in the West" 3-31-66 (Lancy Mabray), "Enemies and Brother" 2-17-67 (Bart Cutler/Frank Parmalee); *The High Chaparral*—"The Doctor from Dodge" 10-29-67 (Doc Henry); *Iron Horse*—"T Is for Traitor" 12-2-67 (Logan); *Alias Smith and Jones*—"The Night of the Red Dog" 11-4-71 (Doc Beauregard); *Bret Maverick*—"The Hidalgo Thing" 5-4-82 (Bart Maverick).

Kelly, James (1854-11/12/33). Films: "Cyclone Bliss" 1921 (Jimmie Donahue); "Man Rustlin'" 1926 (Angus MacGregor); "Men of Daring" 1927 (Piney).

Kelly, Jeanne. *see* Brooks, Jean.

Kelly, Jim (1948-). Films: "Take a Hard Ride" 1974-Ital./Brit./Ger. (Kashtok).

Kelly, John (1901-12/9/47). Films: "Wolf Call" 1939 (Bull Nelson); "Trail to Vengeance" 1945 (Bully).

Kelly, John (-1973). Films: "The Last Rebel" 1961-Mex.; "Two Mules for Sister Sara" 1970 (2nd American); "Something Big" 1971 (Barkeeper); "Buck and the Preacher" 1972 (Sheriff); "Jory" 1972 (Thatcher); "The Revengers" 1972-U.S./Mex. (Whitcomb).

Kelly, Kitty (1902-6/29/68). Films: "Geronimo" 1940 (Daisy Devine). ¶TV: *Bonanza*—"The Quality of Mercy" 11-17-63 (Mrs. Gibbons).

Kelly, Lee. Films: "The Branded Sombrero" 1928 (Lane Hallett).

Kelly, Lew (1879-6/10/44). Films: "The Devil Horse" 1932-serial; "Man of the Forest" 1933 (Matt Hawkins); "Wanderer of the Wasteland" 1935 (Guide); "Rose of the Rancho" 1936 (Coach Driver); "Wild Brian Kent" 1936 (Bill Harris); "Winds of the Wasteland" 1936 (Rocky O'Brien); "Forlorn River" 1937 (Sheriff Jim Warner); "High, Wide and Handsome" 1937 (Carpenter); "It Happened Out West" 1937 (Gus); "Western Gold" 1937 (Ezra); "Gold Mine in the Sky" 1938; "Lawless Valley" 1938 (Fresno); "Man from Music Mountain" 1938 (Bowdie Bill); "The Overland Express" 1938 (Fred Greeley); "The Painted Desert" 1938 (Pete, the Bartender); "The Arizona Wildcat" 1939 (Miner); "Saga of Death Valley" 1939; "Three Texas Steers" 1939 (Postman); "Lucky Cisco Kid" 1940 (Stage Dispatcher); "Shooting High" 1940 (John); "Trail of the Vigilantes" 1940; "Twenty Mule Team" 1940; "The Westerner" 1940 (Ticket Man); "Cyclone on Horseback" 1941; "Last of the Duanes" 1941 (Old Timer); "Road Agent" 1941 (Luke); "Shut My Big Mouth" 1942 (Westerner).

Kelly, Nancy (1921-1/2/95). Films: "Frontier Marshal" 1939 (Sarah Allen); "Jesse James" 1939 (Zee).

Kelly, Patsy (1910-9/24/81). Films: "Cowboy and the Lady" 1938 (Katie Callahan); "In Old California" 1942 (Helga). ¶TV: *Laramie*—"The Legend of Lily" 1-26-60 (Bee); *Wild Wild West*—"The Night of the Big Blast" 10-7-66 (Prudence Fortune), "The Night of the Bogus Bandits" 4-7-67 (Mrs. Bancroft); *Bonanza*—"A Girl Named George" 1-14-68 (Mrs. Neely).

Kelly, Paul (1899-11/6/56). Films: "When a Man's a Man" 1935 (Phil Acton); "The Country Beyond" 1936 (Sgt. Cassidy); "It Happened Out West" 1937 (Dick Howe); "Wyoming" 1940 (Gen. George Armstrong Custer); "Man from Music Mountain" 1943 (Victor Marsh); "San Antonio" 1945 (Roy Stuart); "Frenchie" 1950 (Pete Lambert); "The Painted Hills" 1951 (Jonathan Harvey); "Springfield Rifle" 1952 (Lt. Col. Hudson); "Gunsmoke" 1953 (Dan Saxon).

Kelly, Sean. Films: "The Cowboys" 1972 (Stuttering Bob). ¶TV: *Lancer*—"A Scarecrow at Hacket's" 12-16-69 (Silas); *Bonanza*—"He Was Only Seven" 3-5-72 (Billy), "The Initiation" 9-26-72 (Josh Adams), "The Twenty-Sixth Grave" 10-31-72 (Petey); *The Cowboys*—Regular 1974 (Jimmy).

Kelly, Tommy (1928-). Films: "The Fabulous Texan" 1947.

Kelman, Ricky Williams. Films: "Once Upon a Horse" 1958 (Small Boy)."Last Train from Gun Hill" 1959 (Boy). ¶TV: *Buckskin*—"Tell Me, Leonardo" 9-25-58 (Homer Foley), "The Bullnappers" 11-6-58 (Homer Foley), "The Better Mouse Trap" 5-25-59 (Homer Foley); *Bonanza*—"The Many Faces of Gideon Flinch" 11-5-61; *Gunsmoke*—"Durham Bull" 3-31-62 (Little Bit).

Kelman, Terry. TV: *Sky King*—"Sleight of Hand" 5-25-53 (Davey), "Stop That Train" 6-8-52; *Wagon Train*—"The Ella Lindstrom Story" 2-4-59 (Lennard), "The Duke LeMay Story" 4-29-59 (Davey).

Kelsey, Fred (1884-9/2/61). Films: "Arms and the Gringo" 1914; "Dan Morgan's Way" 1914; "Captain Fly-By-Night" 1922 (Gomez); "Men Without Law" 1930 (Deputy Sheriff); "Horses' Collars" 1935-short (Detective Hyden Zeke); "Sagebrush Troubador" 1935 (Hank Polk); "Wild and Woolly" 1937; "Rough Riders' Round-Up" 1939 (Agitator); "Deadwood Dick" 1940-serial; "Mexican Spitfire Out West" 1940 (Cop); "They Died with Their Boots On" 1941 (Bartender); "Riding High" 1943 (Honest John Kelsey); "Silver River" 1948 (Townsman); "Dallas" 1950 (Carter). ¶TV: *Wild Bill Hickok*—"Civilian Clothes Story" 12-18-51, "Rustling Stallion" 3-4-52, "Prairie Flats Land Swindle" 5-6-52.

Kelsey, Linda (1946-). TV: *The Texas Wheelers*—7-24-75 (Mavis).

Kelso, Mayme (1867-6/5/46). Films: "The Cost of Hatred" 1917 (Elsie's Companion); "Johnny, Get Your Gun" 1919 (Mrs. Tupper).

Kelton, Pert (1907-10/30/68). Films: "Annie Oakley" 1935 (Vera Delmar); "Rhythm of the Saddle" 1938 (Aunt Hattie).

Kelton, Richard (1943-11/27/78). Films: "Wild Women" TVM-1970 (Captain Charring); "Go West, Young Girl" TVM-1978 (Griff). ¶TV: *Gunsmoke*—"Snow Train" 10-19-70 & 10-26-70 (Bud), "The Legend" 10-18-71 (Clayt Colter), "Spratt" 10-2-72 (Ab Craddock), "Homecoming" 1-8-73 (Rick Wilson); *The Cow-*

boys—"The Long Rider" 2-20-74 (Carl Rivers); *Nakia*—"The Sand Trap" 10-5-74 (Carl); *Kung Fu*—"My Brother, My Executioner" 10-12-74 (Curly Bill Graham); *Barbary Coast*—"The Ballad of Redwing Jail" 9-29-75 (Cad Shugrue); *How the West Was Won*—"Hillary" 2-26-79 (Clay Hollingsworth).

Kemmer, Edward (1921-). Films: "Sierra Stranger" 1957 (Sonny Grover). ¶TV: *Maverick*—"Naked Gallows" 12-15-57 (Clete Overton), "A Tale of Three Cities" 10-18-59 (Sherwood Hampton); *Gunsmoke*—"Innocent Broad" 4-26-58 (Lou Paxon); *Sugarfoot*—"The Wizard" 10-14-58 (Sheriff Collins), "The Ghost" 1-28-58 (Deputy Sheriff); *Tombstone Territory*—"The Gatling Gun" 8-27-58 (Lt. Crane); *Trackdown*—"Deadly Decoy" 11-14-58 (Stan Elliott); *Bronco*—"Trail to Taos" 12-2-58 (George Dowling); *Wanted—Dead or Alive*—"Reunion for Revenge" 1-24-59 (Aben Starr), "The Inheritance" 4-30-60 (Adam Smith/William Davis); *Cheyenne*—"Gold, Glory and Custer—Prelude" 1-4-60 (Capt. Fred Benteen), "Gold, Glory and Custer—Requiem" 1-11-60 (Capt. Fred Benteen); *Hotel De Paree*—"Sundance and the Boat Soldier" 2-5-60 (Lieutenant Booth); *Overland Trail*—"Westbound Stage" 3-6-60 (Jody Cabel); *Tales of Wells Fargo*—"The Great Bullion Robbery" 3-21-60 (Joe); *The Alaskans*—"A Barrel of Gold" 4-3-60 (Vess Owen); *Laramie*—"Midnight Rebellion" 4-5-60 (Vern Jamison), "The Renegade Brand" 2-26-63; *Colt .45*—"Trial by Rope" 5-3-60 (Ben Anderson); *The Rebel*—"Lady of Quality" 6-5-60 (Dr. Curtis), "The Champ" 10-2-60 (Jake Wiley), "The Hostage" 6-11-61 (Jesse Wilks); *Shotgun Slade*—"Major Trouble" 10-10-60; *Stagecoach West*—"The Renegades" 6-20-61 (Dan Pollier); *Death Valley Days*—"The Truth Teller" 1-31-62 (Stanley); *Rawhide*—"The Hostage Child" 3-9-62 (Major Harper), "Incident of the Midnight Cave" 1-16-64 (Dr. Jethro Manning); *The Virginian*—"Vengeance Is the Spur" 2-27-63.

Kemmerling, Warren (1928-). Films: "Gun Street" 1961 (Frank Bogan); "Navajo Run" 1966 (Luke Grog); "The Cheyenne Social Club" 1970 (Kohler). ¶TV: *Shotgun Slade*—"Backtrack" 7-26-60 (Trumbo); *Lawman*—"The Robbery" 1-1-61 (Tay Roach), "The Actor" 5-27-62 (Bill Carson); *Gunsmoke*—"The Love of Money" 5-27-61 (Nate Tatham), "Harper's Blood" 10-21-61 (Carr), "The Moonstone" 12-17-66 (Del

Phillips), "The Bullet" 11-29-71, 12-6-71 & 12-13-71 (Conductor), "Lynch Town" 11-19-73 (Sheriff Ridder); *Laramie*—"The High Country" 2-6-62 (Reb); *Tales of Wells Fargo*—"The Traveler" 2-24-62 (Morgan); *The Virginian*—"It Tolls for Thee" 11-21-62 (Sharkey), "Nightmare" 1-21-70 (Frank); *Bonanza*—"The Colonel" 1-6-63 (Asa Flanders), "Amigo" 2-12-67 (Hartley), "To Stop a War" 10-19-69 (Slater), "Heritage of Anger" 9-19-72 (Sheriff Garth); *Destry*—"Law and Order Day" 2-28-64 (Badger); *Laredo*—"It's the End of the Road, Stanley" 3-10-66 (Jack Hanks), "A Double Shot of Nepenthe" 9-30-66 (Jake Murdock); *The Monroes*—"Court Martial" 11-16-66 (Colonel Malcomm); *Daniel Boone*—"Thirty Pieces of Silver" 3-28-68 (Dekker); *The High Chaparral*—"A Matter of Vengeance" 11-27-70 (Reese); *How the West Was Won*—Episode Four 3-5-78 (Judge Rensen), Episode Five 3-12-78 (Judge Rensen), Episode Eight 4-16-78 (Judge Rensen), Episode Nine 4-23-78 (Judge Rensen), Episode Twelve 5-14-78 (Judge Rensen).

Kemp, Daniel. Films: "Cry Blood, Apache" 1970 (Vittorio); "Cahill, United States Marshal" 1973 (Joe Meehan). ¶TV: *Bonanza*—"Silence at Stillwater" 9-28-69 (Jim Hale), "The Reluctant American" 2-14-71 (Bolton); *The High Chaparral*—"Fiesta" 11-20-70 (Tim); *Gunsmoke*—"McCabe" 11-30-70 (McCabe); *Alias Smith and Jones*—"Escape from Wickenberg" 1-28-71 (Al Gorman).

Kemp, Matty. Films: "Rustlers' Ranch" 1926 (Clem Allen); "Law of the Texan" 1938 (Bryant); "The Adventures of the Masked Phantom" 1939 (Stanley Barton).

Kemp, Sally. TV: *Bonanza*—"The Witness" 1-2-73 (Kate); *Gunsmoke*—"Women for Sale" 9-10-73 & 9-17-73 (Rachel).

Kemper, Charles (1900-5/12/50). Films: "Belle Starr's Daughter" 1947 (Gaffer); "The Gunfighters" 1947 (Sheriff Lacaden); "King of the Wild Horses" 1947; "Fury at Furnace Creek" 1948 (Peaceful Jones); "Yellow Sky" 1948 (Walrus); "The Doolins of Oklahoma" 1949 (Arkansas); "California Passage" 1950 (Willy); "The Nevadan" 1950 (Dyke Merrick); "Stars in My Crown" 1950 (Prof. Sam Houston Jones); "Ticket to Tomahawk" 1950 (Deputy Chickity); "Wagonmaster" 1950 (Uncle Shiloh Clegg).

Kemper, Doris. Films: "The Tall Men" 1955 (Mrs. Robbins); "The Oklahoman" 1957 (Woman). ¶TV:

Wagon Train—"The John Bernard Story" 11-21-62 (Mrs. Budgen).

Kendall, Cyris W. (1898-7/22/53). Films: "King of the Pecos" 1936 (Alexander Stiles); "The Lonely Trail" 1936 (Benedict Holden); "Land Beyond the Law" 1937 (Slade Henaberry); "Gold Is Where You Find It" 1938 (Kingan); "The Girl of the Golden West" 1938 (Hank, the Gambler); "Rawhide" 1938 (Sheriff Kale); "Frontier Marshal" 1939 (Mine Owner); "Stand Up and Fight" 1939 (Foreman Ross); "Trouble in Sundown" 1939 (Ross); "The Fargo Kid" 1940 (Nick Kane); "Prairie Law" 1940 (Peter Gore); "Billy the Kid" 1941 (Sheriff Cass McAndrews); "Honky Tonk" 1941 (Man with Tar); "Robin Hood of the Pecos" 1941 (Ballard); "Silver Queen" 1942 (Sheriff); "A Lady Takes a Chance" 1943 (Gambling House Boss); "Girl Rush" 1944 (Bartlan); "Outlaw Trail" 1944 (Honest John Travers); "Tall in the Saddle" 1944 (Cap the Bartender); "The Cisco Kid Returns" 1945 (Jennings); "The Scarlet Horseman" 1946-serial (Amigo).

Kendall, Harry (1898-6/9/62). Films: "Jamestown" 1923 (Capt. George Yeardley).

Kendall, Lee. Films: "Young Jesse James" 1960 (Jennison). ¶TV: *Yancy Derringer*—"The Quiet Firecracker" 5-21-59 (Blackjack Benson), "Two Tickets to Promontory" 6-4-59 (Blackjack Benson).

Kendall, Tony (Luciano Stella). Films: "Pirates of the Mississippi" 1963-Ger./Ital./Fr.; "Black Eagle of Santa Fe" 1964-Ger./Ital./Fr. (Chief Black Eagle); "Hatred of God" 1967-Ital./Ital. (Carl); "Django Challenges Sartana" 1970-Ital. (Django); "Fighters from Ave Maria" 1970-Ital./Ger.; "Brother Outlaw" 1971-Ital. (Dakota Thompson); "Gunman of One Hundred Crosses" 1972-Ger./Ital. (Django).

Kendis, William. TV: *Gunsmoke*—"Joe Phy" 1-4-58 (Cary Post); *Man from Blackhawk*—"Gold Is Where You Find It" 6-24-60 (Frank Owen); *The Rifleman*—"Death Trap" 5-9-61.

Kendrick, Henry Max (1933-). Films: "High Noon, Part II: The Return of Will Kane" TVM-1980 (Martin Garver); "California Gold Rush" TVM-1981 (C.C. Smith); "September Gun" TVM-1983 (Lawyer); "Calamity Jane" TVM-1984 (Station Boss); "Poker Alice" TVM-1987; "Desperado: The Outlaw Wars" TVM-1989 (Bartender); "El Diablo" TVM-1990 (Town Fool). ¶TV: *The*

High Chaparral—"The Buffalo Soldiers" 11-22-68 (Wetlow); *Gunsmoke*—"Thirty a Month a Found" 10-7-74 (Sheriff); *The Life and Times of Grizzly Adams*—2-9-77 (Jed).

Kennard, Pop. Films: "Outlawed" 1921 (Howard Gordon).

Kenneally, Robert W. Films: "Two Rode Together" 1961 (Officer). ¶TV: *Wanted—Dead or Alive*—"Surprise Witness" 11-2-60, "The Long Search" 3-15-61 (Bill Timmons).

Kenneally, Philip (1923-). Films: "Little Big Man" 1971 (Mr. Kane). ¶TV: *Bonanza*—"The Clarion" 2-9-69 (Sheriff Knox), "The Twenty-Sixth Grave" 10-31-72 (McNabb).

Kennedy, Adam. Films: "The Tall Stranger" 1957 (Red). ¶TV: *Gunsmoke*—"Kite's Reward" 11-12-55 (Andy Travis), "Gentleman's Disagreement" 4-30-60 (Bert Wells); *Zane Grey Theater*—"A Man on the Run" 6-21-57 (Adam Dempster); *Frontier Circus*—"Stopover in Paradise" 2-22-62 (Sam Hagen).

Kennedy, Arthur (1914-1/5/90). Films: "They Died with Their Boots On" 1941 (Ned Sharp, Jr.); "The Walking Hills" 1949 (Chalk); "Red Mountain" 1951 (Lane Waldron); "The Lusty Men" 1952 (Wes Merritt); "Rancho Notorious" 1952 (Vern Haskell); "The Man from Laramie" 1955 (Vic Hansbro); "The Naked Dawn" 1955 (Santiago); "The Rawhide Years" 1956 (Rick Harper); "Murieta" 1965-Span./U.S. (Capt. Love); "Nevada Smith" 1966 (Bill Bowdre); "A Minute to Pray, a Second to Die" 1967-Ital. (Roy Colby). ¶TV: *Zane Grey Theater*—"Make It Look Good" 2-5-59 (Sam Carter); *Nakia*—Regular 1974 (Sheriff Sam Jericho).

Kennedy, Bill. Films: "Royal Mounted Rides Again" 1945-serial (Wayne Decker); "Overland Trails" 1948; "The Sheriff of Medicine Bow" 1948; "Triggerman" 1948; "Law of the West" 1949 (Nixon); "Shadows of the West" 1949 (Ward); "Trail of the Yukon" 1949 (Constable); "Border Outlaws" 1950 (Carson); "I Shot Billy the Kid" 1950 (Poe); "Storm Over Wyoming" 1950 (Rawlins); "Train to Tombstone" 1950; "Abilene Trail" 1951 (Colter); "Canyon Raiders" 1951; "Nevada Badmen" 1951; "Silver City Bonanza" 1951 (Monk Monroe). ¶TV: *The Lone Ranger*—"Barnaby Boggs, Esquire" 2-2-50, "White Man's Magic" 7-13-50, "Drink of Water" 10-26-50, "Code of the Pioneers" 2-17-55; *The Gene Autry Show*—"The Raiders" 4-14-51,

"Double Barrelled Vengeance" 4-21-51, "Warning! Danger!" 11-10-51, "Bandits of Boulder Bluff" 11-24-51; *The Cisco Kid*—"Haven for Heavies" 5-19-51, "Phony Sheriff" 6-16-51, "Uncle Disinherits Niece" 7-14-51, "The Fugitive" 11-1-52, "Pot of Gold" 4-25-53; *Death Valley Days*—"Eleven Thousand Miners Can't Be Wrong" 9-13-54, "Halfway Girl" 11-22-54.

Kennedy, Dennis. Films: "The Chisholms" TVM-1979 (Benjamin Lowery). ¶TV: *The Chisholms*—Regular 1979 (Benjamin Lowery).

Kennedy, Don. Films: "Hell's Outpost" 1954; "Walk Like a Dragon" 1960 (Masters). ¶TV: *Death Valley Days*—"Snowshoe Thompson" 4-7-54; *My Friend Flicka*—"Refuge for the Night" 4-20-56; *Frontier*—"Patrol" 4-29-56 (Sgt. Casey); *Zane Grey Theater*—"The Three Graves" 1-4-57 (Stony Fields); *The Californians*—Regular 1957-58 (Dion Patrick), "The Painted Lady" 1-13-59 (Big Corny); *Tales of the Texas Rangers*—"The Kid from Amarillo" 11-17-57 (Dirk); *Wyatt Earp*—"Wyatt Earp Rides Shotgun" 2-18-58, "Wells Fargo Calling Marshal Earp" 12-29-59 (Sharkey); *The Rifleman*—"Home Ranch" 10-7-58 (Clyde); *The Restless Gun*—"No Way to Kill" 11-24-58 (Wade Calley); *Tales of Wells Fargo*—"The Counterfeiters" 12-8-58 (Bill), "Portrait of Teresa" 2-10-62 (Deputy); *Bat Masterson*—"Wanted—Dead" 10-15-59 (Gunman), "Death and Taxes" 11-26-59 (Tim Lockhart); *Tombstone Territory*—10-30-59 (Ed Chandler); *Maverick*—"The White Widow" 1-24-60 (Sheriff Jim Vaughan), "Three Queens Full" 11-12-61 (Humbolt); *Wanted—Dead or Alive*—"The Inheritance" 4-30-60 (Marc); *Stagecoach West*—"The Land Beyond" 10-11-60 (Bret); *Laramie*—"Drifter's Gold" 11-29-60 (Nick), "The Betrayers" 1-22-63 (Deputy), "No Place to Run" 2-5-63; *The Tall Man*—"Bitter Ashes" 12-3-60 (Palen), "A Tombstone for Billy" 12-16-61 (Garth Cumpson); *Bonanza*—"A Woman Lost" 3-17-63; *The Dakotas*—"The Chooser of the Slain" 4-22-63 (McNally); *Temple Houston*—"Sam's Boy" 1-23-64 (Ike Hobbs); *Wild Wild West*—"The Night of the Howling Light" 12-17-65 (Junior Officer); *Here Come the Brides*—"Man of the Family" 10-16-68.

Kennedy, Douglas (1915-8/10/73). Films: "Northwest Mounted Police" 1940 (Constable Carter); "The Round Up" 1941 (Trooper); "Fighting Man of the Plains" 1949 (Ken Vedder); "Ranger of Cherokee Strip" 1949 (Joe Bearclaws); "South of Rio"

1949 (Bob Mitchell); "South of St. Louis" 1949 (Lee Price); "The Cariboo Trail" 1950 (Murphy); "Montana" 1950 (Rodney Ackroyd); "Callaway Went Thataway" 1951 (Drunk); "Indian Uprising" 1951 (Cliff Taggert); "Oh! Susanna" 1951 (Trooper Emers); "The Texas Rangers" 1951 (Dave Rudabaugh); "Fort Osage" 1952 (George Keane); "Ride the Man Down" 1952 (Harve Garrison); "Gun Belt" 1953 (Dixon); "Jack McCall, Desperado" 1953 (Wild Bill Hickok); "San Antone" 1953 (Capt. Garfield); "War Paint" 1953 (Clancy); "The Lone Gun" 1954 (Gad Moran); "Massacre Canyon" 1954 (Sgt. James Marlowe); "Rails into Laramie" 1954 (Telegraph Operator); "Sitting Bull" 1954 (Col. G.A. Custer); "Strange Lady in Town" 1955 (Slade Wickstrom); "Wyoming Renegades" 1955 (Charlie Veer); "The Last Wagon" 1956 (Col. Normand); "Hell's Crossroads" 1957 (Frank James); "Last of the Badmen" 1957 (Hawkins); "The Lone Ranger and the Lost City of Gold" 1958 (Ross Bardy); "Lone Texan" 1959 (Phillip Harvey); "The Fastest Guitar Alive" 1967 (Joe). ¶TV: The Lone Ranger—"Pardon for Curley" 6-22-50, "Desperado at Large" 10-2-52, "Ranger in Danger" 10-30-52, "Right to Vote" 2-12-53, "Trigger Finger 4-7-55; Stories of the Century—"Bill Langley" 7-22-55; Steve Donovan, Western Marshal—Regular 1955-56 (Marshal Steve Donovan); Cheyenne—"The Spanish Grant" 5-7-57 (Blake Holloway); Jim Bowie—"Gone to Texas" 5-24-57 (Col. Bradford); Tales of Wells Fargo—"The Silver Bullets" 7-8-57 (Martin Yates); Maverick—"The Burning Sky" 2-23-58 (Connors), "Easy Mark" 11-15-59 (McFearson); Wagon Train—"The Major Adams Story" 4-23-58 & 4-30-58 (Col. Hillery), "Chuck Wooster, Wagonmaster" 5-20-59 (John Loring); Tombstone Territory—"The Gatling Gun" 8-27-58 (Sam Colby); Rough Riders—"Breakout" 10-9-58 (Sergeant True); Bronco—"Four Guns and a Prayer" 11-4-58 (Paul Duquesne); Wanted—Dead or Alive—"The Favor" 11-15-58 (Sheriff Bedloe); Cimarron City—"Kid on a Calico Horse" 11-22-58 (Sam Thaw); Northwest Passage—"The Long Rifle" 11-23-58 (Eli Dillon); Jefferson Drum—"Thicker Than Water" 11-27-58 (Dallas); The Restless Gun—"Shadow of a Gunfighter" 1-12-59 (Cal Winfield), "Lady by Law" 5-11-59 (Sheriff); Bat Masterson—"License to Cheat" 2-4-59 (Jeb Crater); Zorro—"The Captain Regrets" 5-28-59, "Masquerade for Murder" 6-4-

59, "Long Live the Governor" 6-11-59; Colt .45—"Law West of the Pecos" 6-7-59 (Jay Brisco); Wyatt Earp—"The Trail to Tombstone" 9-8-59 (Dave Mather); Bonanza—"The Paiute War" 10-3-59, "A Natural Wizard" 12-12-65 (Stoney), "The Oath" 11-20-66 (Big Charlie), "Second Chance" 9-17-67, "The Bottle Fighter" 5-12-68 (Sheriff); Rawhide—"Incident at Dangerfield Dip" 10-2-59 (Ewan Dangerfield); Laramie—"Man of God" 12-1-59 (Parker); The Texan—"Border Incident" 12-7-59, "Buried Treasure" 2-15-60; Have Gun Will Travel—"The Misguided Father" 2-27-60 (Loring); The Rifleman—"Smoke Screen" 4-5-60 (Crandell); Pony Express—"Payoff" 4-13-60 (Marshal Jeb Loring); Sugarfoot—"Blue Bonnet Stray" 4-26-60 (Sheriff Williams); Gunsmoke—"Speak Me Fair" 5-7-60 (Traych), "Cherry Red" 6-11-60 (Yancey), "Prime of Life" 5-7-66 (John Stoner); The Deputy—"Ma Mack" 7-9-60 (Bates); The Big Valley—"Forty Rifles" 9-22-65 (McColl), "Day of the Comet" 12-26-66 (Alexander Morrison), Regular 1967-69 (Sheriff Fred Madden); The Legend of Jesse James—"One Too Many Mornings" 11-22-65 (Ben Todd); The Virginian—"Men with Guns" 1-12-66 (Sheriff), "Paid in Full" 11-22-67 (Oliver); Iron Horse—"The Bride at Forty-Mile" 1-23-67 (Adam Preston).

Kennedy, Duane. Films: "Girl Rush" 1944 (Troupe Member); "Royal Mounted Rides Again" 1945-serial (June Bailey); "Salome, Where She Danced" 1945 (Salome Girl).

Kennedy, Edgar (1890-11/9/48). Films: "The Blue Streak" 1917; "The Golden Princess" 1925 (Gewilliker Hay); "Crossfire" 1933 (Ed Wimpy); "Scarlet River" 1933 (Sam Gilroy); "Son of the Border" 1933 (Windy); "Cowboy Millionaire" 1935 (Persimmon Bates); "Robin Hood of El Dorado" 1936 (Sheriff Judd); "Westward Ho-Hum" 1941-short; "In Old California" 1942 (Kegs McKeever); "Heaven Only Knows" 1947 (Jud).

Kennedy, Fred (1910-12/5/58). Films: "She Wore a Yellow Ribbon" 1949 (Badger); "Rio Grande" 1950 (Heinze); "The Charge at Feather River" 1953 (Leech); "The Searchers" 1956 (Stunts); "The Horse Soldiers" 1959 (Cavalryman).

Kennedy, George (1925-). Films: "Lonely Are the Brave" 1962 (Guitierrez); "Shenandoah" 1965 (Col. Fairchild); "The Sons of Katie Elder" 1965 (Curley); "Ballad of Josie" 1968 (Arch Ogden); "Bandolero!" 1968 (Sheriff Johnson); "The

Good Guys and the Bad Guys" 1969 (McKay); "Guns of the Magnificent Seven" 1969 (Chris); "Dirty Dingus Magee" 1970 (Hoke); "Fools' Parade" 1971 (Doc Council); "Cahill, United States Marshal" 1973 (Fraser); "A Cry in the Wilderness" TVM-1974 (Sam Hadley); "The Gambler, Part III—The Legend Continues" TVM-1987. ¶TV: Colt .45—"The Rival Gun" 10-25-59 (Hank); Cheyenne—"Prisoner of Moon Mesa" 11-16-59; Laramie—"Duel at Alta Mesa" 2-23-60 (Gene); Gunsmoke—"The Blacksmith" 9-17-60 (Emil), "Kitty Shot" 2-11-61 (Jake Bayloe), "Big Man" 3-25-61 (Pat Swarner), "The Boys" 5-26-62 (Hug), "The Warden" 5-16-64 (Stark), "Crooked Mile" 10-3-64 (Cyrus Degler), "Harvest" 3-26-66 (Ben Payson); Have Gun Will Travel—"A Head of Hair" 9-24-60 (Lieutenant Bryson), "The Legacy" 12-10-60 (Sam Tarnitzer), "The Road" 5-27-61, "The Vigil" 9-16-61 (Deke), "A Proof of Love" 10-14-61 (Rud Saxon), "Don't Shoot the Piano Player" 3-10-62 (Big Jim), "The Eve of St. Elmo" 3-23-63 (Brother Grace); Maverick—"Hadley's Hunters" 9-25-60 (Deputy Jones); Riverboat—"Rive Champion" 10-10-60 (Gunner Slagle); Klondike—"Swing Your Partner" 1-9-61 (Ira Shallop); Bat Masterson—"The Fourth Man" 4-27-61 (Zeke Armitage); The Tall Man—"Trial by Hanging" 11-4-61 (Jake Newton), "Three for All" 3-10-62 (Hyram Killgore); Rawhide—"The Peddler" 1-19-62 (George Wales); Tales of Wells Fargo—"Assignment in Gloribee" 1-27-62 (Hawk); The Outlaws—"Farewell Performance" 3-15-62 (Joe Ferris); Bonanza—"The Infernal Machine" 4-11-62 (Pete Long), "The Scapegoat" 10-25-64 (Waldo Watson); Death Valley Days—"Miracle at Whiskey Gulch" 5-16-62 (Steamboat Sully); The Travels of Jaimie McPheeters—"The Day of the Long Night" 11-10-63 (Angus); The Virginian—"A Gallows for Sam Horn" 12-2-64 (Jack Marshman), "Nobility of Kings" 11-10-65 (Bear Suchette); Daniel Boone—"A Rope for Mingo" 12-2-65 (Zach Morgan); A Man Called Shenandoah—"Special Talent for Killing" 12-6-65 (Mitchell); Laredo—"Pride of the Rangers" 12-16-65 (Jess Moran); The Legend of Jesse James—"Return to Lawrence" 1-31-66 (Blodgett); The Big Valley—"Barbary Red" 2-16-66 (Thatcher); Lonesome Dove—"The Trial" 10-30-94 (Judge J.T. "Rope" Calder).

Kennedy, Harold (1914-). Films: "Hannah Lee" 1953 (Bainbridge); "Run for Cover" 1955.

Kennedy, Jack (-11/6/60). Films: "McKenna of the Mounted" 1932; "The Westerner" 1934 (Bucking Horse Rider); "Nevada" 1935 (Mac Turk); "Red River Valley" 1936 (Mike); "Born to the West" 1937 (Sheriff); "Western Trails" 1938; "Union Pacific" 1939.

Kennedy, Lindsay. Films: "Little House on the Prairie: Look Back to Yesterday" TVM-1983 (Jeb Carter); "Little House: The Last Farewell" TVM-1984 (Jeb Carter). ¶TV: *Little House: A New Beginning*—Regular 1982-83 (Jeb Carter).

Kennedy, Madge (1892-6/9/87). Films: "Leave It to Susan" 1919 (Susan Burbridge; "Plunderers of Painted Flats" 1959 (Mary). ¶TV: *Wyatt Earp*—"Don't Get Tough with a Sailor" 2-23-60 (Mrs. Rowland); *The Tall Man*—"The Hunt" 1-27-62 (Elizabeth Van Doren).

Kennedy, Mary Jo. TV: *The High Chaparral*—"Ride the Savage Land" 2-11-68 (Ann); *Here Come the Brides*—"Mr. and Mrs. J. Bolt" 3-12-69; *Lancer*—"The Gifts" 10-28-69 (Trina).

Kennedy, Merna (1908-12/20/44). Films: "The Gay Buckaroo" 1932 (Mildred Field); "Ghost Valley" 1932 (Jane Worth); "Come on Tarzan" 1933 (Patricia Riley).

Kennedy, Richard. Films: "J.W. Coop" 1971 (Sheriff); "Tom Horn" 1980 (John Cleveland).

Kennedy, Ron. Films: "The Moonlighter" 1953; "Hidden Guns" 1956 (Burt Miller). ¶TV: *Wyatt Earp*—"Wyatt and the Captain" 1-15-57 (Sgt. Craig).

Kennedy, Sarah (1948-). TV: *Dirty Sally*—2-22-74.

Kennedy, Tom (1884-10/6/65). Films: "With Naked Fists" 1923; "The Best Bad Man" 1925 (Dan Ellis); "Born to the West" 1926 (Dinkey Hooley); "Man of the Forest" 1926 (Sheriff); "The Mysterious Rider" 1927 (Lem Spooner); "Silver Valley" 1927 (Hayfever Hawkins); "Caught" 1931 (Jard Harmon); "Man of the Forest" 1933 (Kennedy); "The Yankee Senor" 1926 (Luke Martin); "Mexican Spitfire Out West" 1940 (Taxi Driver); "Riding High" 1943 (Wilson); "Moonlight and Cactus" 1944 (Lucky); "The Paleface" 1948 (Bartender); "Thunder in the Pines" 1948 (Station Master); "Square Dance Jubilee" 1949 (Bartender); "Border Rangers" 1950 (Station Agent); "Gold Fever" 1952 (Big Tom); "Road Agent" 1952; "The Bounty Killer" 1965 (Waiter).

Kenneth, Arthur. Films: "Bad Men of Missouri" 1941 (Jim Younger); "Cheyenne" 1947 (Sundance Kid); "Bend of the River" 1952 (Cole Garret); "Cheyenne Autumn" 1964 (Doc Holliday); "Day of the Evil Gun" 1968 (Forbes).

Kenneth, Harry (1854-1/18/29). Films: "The Eagle's Nest" 1915 (Geoffrey Milford).

Kenneth, Keith (Keith Hitchcock) (1887-4/11/66). Films: "Daniel Boone" 1936 (Commissioner); "Hudson Bay" 1941 (Footman).

Kenney, Jack (1888-5/26/64). Films: "Hidden Loot" 1925 (Big Bill Angus); "Beauty and Bullets" 1928 (Joe Kemp); "The Mysterious Avenger" 1936 (Cowboy); "The Old Barn Dance" 1938; "Wyoming Outlaw" 1939 (Amos); "King of the Mounties" 1942-serial (Plant Guard); "Cattle Town" 1952 (Storekeeper); "The Tin Star" 1957 (Sam Hodges); "Toughest Gun in Tombstone" 1958 (Purdy); "The Gambler Wore a Gun" 1961 (Bartender); "Gun Fight" 1961 (Jake); "The Man Who Shot Liberty Valance" 1962. ¶TV: *The Lone Ranger*—"Sheriff of Gunstock" 7-27-50.

Kenney, June. TV: *Bonanza*—"The Infernal Machine" 4-11-62 (Robin); *The Tall Man*—"G.P." 5-19-62 (Mary Curtis).

Kenney, Sean (1942-). Films: "Journey to Shiloh" 1968 (Custis Claiborne); "Machismo—40 Graves for 40 Guns" 1970 (Wichita).

Kenny, Colin (1888-12/2/68). Films: "The Last Straw" 1920 (Dick Hilton); "Silent Pal" 1925 (Randall Phillips); "The Oregon Trail" 1939-serial (Slade).

Kent, Barbara (1906-). Films: "Prowlers of the Night" 1926 (Anita Parsons); "No Man's Law" 1927 (Toby Belcher); "Freighters of Destiny" 1932 (Ruth).

Kent, Carole. TV: *Hotel De Paree*—"Sundance and the Black Widow" 4-1-60 (Flora); *Rawhide*—"Incident of the Woman Trap" 1-26-62.

Kent, Charles (1852-5/21/23). FIlms: "Britton of the Seventh" 1916 (Lt. Tony Britton at Age 70).

Kent, Crauford (1881-5/14/53). Films: "The Eagle's Feather" 1923 (Count De Longe); "Morganson's Finish" 1926 (G.T. Williams); "Daniel Boone" 1936 (Attorney General); "O'Malley of the Mounted" 1936 (McGregor); "Rovin' Tumbleweeds" 1939.

Kent, David. Films: "Two Rode Together" 1961 (Running Wolf);

"Hud" 1963 (Donald). ¶TV: *Gunsmoke*—"Love Thy Neighbor" 1-28-61 (Peter); *The Tall Man*—"A Kind of Courage" 4-8-61 (Skip); *Stoney Burke*—"Joby" 3-18-63 (Ray).

Kent, Dorothea. Films: "Horses' Collars" 1935-short (Nell); "Danger Ahead" 1940 (Genevieve); "Call of the Canyon" 1942 (Jane Oakley); "King of the Cowboys" 1943 (Ruby Smith).

Kent, Larry (1900-11/7/67). Films: "Treachery Rides the Range" 1936 (Clerk). ¶TV: *Rawhide*—"Incident on the Road Back" 2-24-61, "Incient of the Wager on Payday" 6-16-61, "The Pitchwagon" 3-2-62.

Kent, Leon D. (1880-6/12/43). Films: "By Right of Possession" 1917 (Trimble); "All for Gold" 1918; "Captured Alive" 1918; "Riddle Gawne" 1918 (Jess Cass); "The Robber" 1918; "Horse Sense" 1924 (Sheriff Crawford); "Ten Scars Make a Man" 1924-serial; "Pals" 1925 (Obediah Dillwater); "Triple Action" 1925 (Bandit); "The Lost Trail" 1926; "Sitting Bull at the Spirit Lake Massacre" 1927 (John Mulcain); "Human Targets" 1932 (Pop Snyder).

Kent, Mary. Films: "Canadian Pacific" 1949 (Mrs. Gautier); "The Cariboo Trail" 1950 (Mrs. Winters).

Kent, Robert (1908-5/4/55). Films: "The Country Beyond" 1936 (Corp. Robert King); "King of the Royal Mounted" 1936 (Sergeant King); "Sunset in Wyoming" 1941; "Twilight on the Trail" 1941 (Drake); "Range Rhythm" 1942-short; "Stagecoach Express" 1942 (Griff Williams); "The Phantom Rider" 1946-serial (Dr. Jim Sterling/the Phantom Rider); "Rebel City" 1953 (Capt. Ramsey). ¶TV: *The Lone Ranger*—"Rifles and Renegades" 5-4-50, "Lady Killer" 12-21-50.

Kenton, Erle C. (1896-1/28/80). Films: "End of the Trail" 1936 (Theodore Roosevelt).

Kenton, James "Pop" (1867-2/11/52). Films: "Wagon Wheels" 1934 (Masters); "Law Beyond the Range" 1935 (Pete); "End of the Trail" 1936 (Newman).

Kenworthy, Katherine. Films: "Wyoming Outlaw" 1939 (Mrs. Parker); "Twenty Mule Team" 1940.

Kenyon, Doris (1897-9/1/79). Films: "Wild Honey" 1918 (Wild Honey/Mrs. Holbrook); "The Love Bandit" 1924 (Amy Van Clayton); "Beau Bandit" 1930.

Kenyon, Gwen. Films: "Wells Fargo" 1937 (Girl); "Lawless Plainsmen" 1942 (Madge Mason); "Riding

High" 1943 (Ginger); "In Old New Mexico" 1945 (Ellen).

Kenyon, Robert (1889-12/19/28). Films: "The Hidden Law" 1916 (Carl Holmes).

Kenyon, Sandy (1924-). Films: "Nevada Smith" 1966 (Bank Clerk); "Something for a Lonely Man" TVM-1968 (Bleeck); "Rancho Deluxe" 1975 (Skinny Face). ¶TV: *Northwest Passage*—"Break Out" 10-19-58 (Nathan Hill); *Gunsmoke*—"Stage Holdup" 10-25-58 (Green), "Big Man" 3-25-61 (Ak), "I Call Him Wonder" 3-23-63 (Docker), "The New Society" 5-22-65 (Bennings), "Lobo" 12-16-68 (Catlin); *Rawhide*—"Incident of the Power and the Plow" 2-13-59; *Colt .45*—"The Escape" 4-5-59; *Riverboat*—"About Roger Mowbray" 9-27-59 (Jeb Grant), "No Bridge on the River" 10-24-60 (Abraham Lincoln); *The Rifleman*—"Mail Order Groom" 1-12-60 (Jim Prophet); *Have Gun Will Travel*—"Fight at Adobe Wells" 3-12-60 (Rio Jones), "Out at the Old Ball Park" 10-1-60 (Oudry), "The Mountebank" 8-3-63 (Jeb); *Gunslinger*—"The Zone" 3-2-61 (Willoughby); *The Tall Man*—"An Item for Auction" 10-14-61 (Sam Nayfack); *Wide Country*—"The Royce Bennett Story" 9-20-62 (Walt); *The Travels of Jaimie McPheeters*—Regular 1963-64 (Shep Baggott); *Bonanza*—"Square Deal Sam" 11-8-64 (Gibson), "Caution: Easter Bunny Crossing" 3-29-70 (Elijah Meek); *Wild Wild West*—"The Night of the Sudden Death" 10-8-65 (Hugo); *A Man Called Shenandoah*—"Run, Killer, Run" 1-10-66 (Matthew Crawson); *Kung Fu*—"The Gunman" 1-3-74 (Sheriff); *Barbary Coast*—"Irish Coffee" 10-13-75 (Sorensen).

Kerby, Marian (1878-12/16/75). Films: "Tumbledown Ranch in Arizona" 1941 (Mother Rogers).

Kercheval, Ken (1936-). Films: "Calamity Jane" TVM-1984 (Buffalo Bill Coy).

Kern, Cecil (1892-6/28). Films: "The Gray Towers Mystery" 1919 (Miss Sutherland).

Kern, Roger. Films: "Young Pioneers" TVM-1976 (David Beaton); "Young Pioneers' Christmas" TVM-1976 (David Beaton). ¶TV: *The Young Pioneers*—Regular 1978 (David Beaton).

Kerr, Arthur. Films: "Secret Patrol" 1936 (Jordan); "Stampede" 1936 (Bill Gans); "Death Goes North" 1939 (Bart Norton).

Kerr, Donald (1891-1/25/77). Films: "West of Carson City" 1940 (John Manners); "Rollin' Home to Texas" 1941; "Under Western Skies" 1945 (Stable Owner); "Shadows of the West" 1949 (Baker); "Flaming Feather" 1952; "Lost in Alaska" 1952 (Multolah); "Four Guns to the Border" 1954 (Town Loafer); "Friendly Persuasion" 1956 (Manager); "Yaqui Drums" 1956. ¶TV: *Wild Bill Hickok*—"Mountain Men" 2-3-53, "Halley's Comet" 2-17-53, "The Steam Wagon" 5-12-53; *Klondike*—"88 Keys to Trouble" 11-14-60 (Pianist).

Kerr, John (1931-). Films: "Yuma" TVM-1971 (Captain White). ¶TV: *Riverboat*—"The Barrier" 9-20-59 (Jefferson Carruthers); *Walt Disney Presents*—"Elfego Baca: Friendly Enemies at Law" 3-18-60 (Dibler); *Rawhide*—"Incident of the Last Chance" 6-10-60 (Bert Eaton); *Gunsmoke*—"Half Straight" 2-17-62 (Lute Willis); *The Virginian*—"The Judgment" 1-16-63 (Oliver Smith); *Wagon Train*—"The Jim Whitlow Story" 5-29-63 (Jim Whitlow); *The High Chaparral*—"Sudden Country" 11-5-67 (Creed Hallock); *Alias Smith and Jones*—"Only Three to a Bed" 1-13-73 (George Sterling).

Kerr, Lorence (-2/25/68). TV: *Wagon Train*—"The Shiloh Degnan Story" 11-7-62 (Shiloh Degnan).

Kerr, Sondra. TV: *Gunsmoke*—"Chesterland" 11-18-61 (Daisy Fair); *Rawhide*—"A Man Called Mushy" 10-23-64 (Teya); *The Legend of Jesse James*—"The Lonely Place" 2-21-66 (Linda Davis).

Kerrick, Tom (1895-4/27/27). Films: "Men in the Raw" 1923 (Les Edler).

Kerrigan, J.M. (1887-4/29/64). Films: "Rainbow Trail" 1932 (Paddy Harrington); "The Lone Cowboy" 1934 (Mr. Curran); "The Barrier" 1937 (Sgt. Thomas); "The Kid from Texas" 1939 (Farr); "Union Pacific" 1939 (Monahan); "The Vanishing Virginian" 1941 (John Phelps); "The Big Bonanza" 1944 (Jasper Kincaid); "Mrs. Mike" 1949 (Uncle John); "The Wild North" 1952 (Callahan); "The Silver Whip" 1953 (Riley); "Fastest Gun Alive" 1956 (Kevin McGovern). ¶TV: *Frontier*—"The Devil and Doctor O'Hara" 2-5-56 (Doc O'Hara); *Union Pacific*—"Iron West" 1-24-59; *Wagon Train*—"The St. Nicholas Story" 12-23-59.

Kerrigan, J. Warren (1889-6/9/47). Films: "The Actress and the Cowboys" 1911; "The Call of the Open Range" 1911; "Cattle, Gold and Oil" 1911; "The Cowboy and the Artist" 1911; "$5,000 Reward, Dead or Alive" 1911; "The Land Thieves" 1911; "A New York Cowboy" 1911; "The Poisoned Flame" 1911; "The Ranch Girl" 1911; "The Ranchman's Nerve" 1911; "The Rustler Sheriff" 1911; "The Sheriff's Sisters" 1911; "The Stranger at Coyote" 1911; "The Test" 1911; "Three Million Dollars" 1911; "A Trooper's Heart" 1911; "The Agitator" 1912; "A Bad Investment" 1912; "The Brand" 1912; "The Coward" 1912; "The Daughters of Senor Lopez" 1912; "Driftwood" 1912; "The Eastern Girl" 1912; "End of the Feud" 1912; "For the Good of Her Men" 1912; "From the Four Hundred to the Herd" 1912; "The Girl and the Gun" 1912; "The Intrusion of Compoc" 1912; "The Jack of Diamonds" 1912; "The Jealous Rage" 1912; "The Land Baron of San Tee" 1912; "The Land of Death" 1912; "The Law of God" 1912; "Maiden and Men" 1912; "A Man's Calling" 1912; "The Mormon" 1912; "Nell of the Pampas" 1912; "The New Cowpuncher" 1912; "Objections Overruled" 1912; "The Outlaw Cowboy" 1912; "The Pensioner" 1912; "The Power of Love" 1912; "The Promise" 1912; "The Real Estate Fraud" 1912; "Reformation of Sierra Smith" 1912; "The Reward of Valor" 1912; "The Thief's Wife" 1912; "The Thread of Life" 1912; "The Tramp's Gratitude" 1912; "Where Broadway Meets the Mountain" 1912; "The Angel of the Canyons" 1913; "Calamity Anne Takes a Trip" 1913; "Calamity Anne's Beauty" 1913; "Calamity Anne's Inheritance" 1913; "An Eastern Flower" 1913; "The Girl and the Greaser" 1913; "Hidden Treasure Ranch" 1913; "High and Low" 1913; "Jack Meets His Waterloo" 1913; "Mission Bells" 1913; "Quicksands" 1913; "The Reward of Courage" 1913; "The Romance" 1913; "Tom Blake's Redemption" 1913; "Truth in the Wilderness" 1913; "Woman's Honor" 1913; "Women Left Alone" 1913; "Out of the Valley" 1914; "The Sheep Herder" 1914; "A Bogus Bandit" 1915; "The Beckoning Trail" 1916; "The Code of the Mounted" 1916; "Prisoner of the Pines" 1918 (Hillaire Latour); "The End of the Game" 1919 (Burke Allister); "The White Man's Courage" 1919 (Donald Joseph Blenhorn/Don Jose Alvarez); "The Coast of Opportunity" 1920 (Dick Bristow); "The Covered Wagon" 1923 (Will Banion); "The Girl of the Golden West" 1923 (Ramarez).

Kerry, Norman (1889-1/12/56). Films: "Under Western Skies" 1926 (Robert Erskine); "Phantom of Santa Fe" 1937 (Miguel Morago/the Hawk).

Kershaw, Doug (1936-). Films: "Zachariah" 1971 (the Fiddler); "The Chisholms" TVM-1979 (Fiddler Ephraim). ¶TV: *The Chisholms*—Regular 1979 (Fiddler Ephraim).

Kerwin, Brian (1949-). Films: "The Chisholms" TVM-1979 (Gideon Chisholm). ¶TV: *The Busters*—Pilot 5-28-78 (Albie McRae); *The Chisholms*—Regular 1979 (Gideon Chisholm).

Kerwin, Lance (1960-). TV: *Gunsmoke*—"The First of Ignorance" 1-27-75 (Tommy Harker); *Sara*—2-20-76 (Derek).

Kesterson, George. *see* Mix, Art.

Ketchum, Cliff. Films: "The Young Land" 1959 (Ben Stroud) ¶TV: *Tales of Wells Fargo*—"Wild Cargo" 1-19-59 (Frank); *Gunsmoke*—"Jayhawkers" 1-31-59 (Cowboy), "Cherry Red" 6-11-60 (Nightshire).

Kevin, Sandy (1936-). Films: "The Man Who Loved Cat Dancing" 1973 (Ben). ¶TV: *Bonanza*—"The Legacy" 12-15-63 (Billy); *Iron Horse*—"Sister Death" 4-3-67 (Krause); *Gunsmoke*—"Vengeance" 10-2-67 & 10-9-67 (Floyd Binnes); *The Guns of Will Sonnett*—"A Son for a Son" 10-20-67.

Key, Kathleen (1906-12/22/54). Films: "Bells of San Juan" 1922 (Florrie Engel); "West of Chicago" 1922 (Senorita Gonzales); "Hell's Hole" 1923 (Mabel Grant); "North of Hudson Bay" 1924 (Estelle McDonald); "The Desert's Toll" 1926 (Muriel Cooper); "Hey! Hey! Cowboy" 1927 (Emily Decker); "Phantom of the North" 1929 (Colette).

Keyes, Evelyn (1919-). Films: "Union Pacific" 1939 (Mrs. Calvin); "Beyond the Sacramento" 1940 (Lynn Perry); "The Desperadoes" 1943 (Allison MacLeod); "Renegades" 1946 (Hannah Brockway); "Mrs. Mike" 1949 (Kathy O'Fallon).

Keyes, Irwin. TV: *Outlaws*—"Potboiler" 2-28-87 (Buford).

Keyes, Stephen. Films: "Land of the Outlaws" 1944; "Oklahoma Raiders" 1944; "Dead Man's Gold" 1948 (Morgan); "Deadline" 1948; "Fighting Mustang" 1948; "Sunset Carson Rides Again" 1948; "Battling Marshal" 1950; "Mustang" 1959 (Lou).

Keymas, George. Films: "Border Rangers" 1950 (Raker); "The Black Dakotas" 1954 (Spotted Deer); "They Rode West" 1954 (Torquay); "Apache Ambush" 1955 (Tweedy); "Santa Fe Passage" 1955 (Satank); "The Vanishing American" 1955 (Coshonta); "Wyoming Renegades" 1955 (George Curry); "Fury at Gunsight Pass" 1956

(Daley); "Kentucky Rifle" 1956; "The Maverick Queen" 1956 (Muncie); "Thunder Over Arizona" 1956; "The White Squaw" 1956 (Yotah); "Apache Warrior" 1957 (Chato); "Gunfire at Indian Gap" 1957 (Sculy); "The Storm Rider" 1957 (Apache Kid); "Utah Blaine" 1957 (Rink Witter); "Cole Younger, Gunfighter" 1958 (Price); "Gunsmoke in Tucson" 1958 (Hondo); "Arizona Raiders" 1965 (Montana); "Winchester '73" TVM-1967; "The Oregon Trail" TVM-1976 (Trenchard). ¶TV: *Stories of the Century*—"Chief Crazy Horse" 7-1-55; *Frontier*—"The Shame of a Nation" 10-23-55; *The Adventures of Rin Tin Tin*—"Rin Tin Tin and the Christmas Story" 12-23-55 (Soho), "The Silent Battle" 10-5-56 (Jaga), "Boone's Grandpappy" 11-2-56 (Yellow Wolf), "Star of India" 1-2-59 (Yussef Husein), "Pillajohn's Progress" 3-6-59 (Red Wolf); *Tales of Wells Fargo*—"Belle Starr" 9-9-57 (Blue Duck), "The Killer" 12-1-58 (Les Walker), "Cole Younger" 1-4-60 (Charlie Pitts), "Portrait of Teresa" 2-10-62 (Miguel); *The Restless Gun*—"Rink" 10-14-57 (Trager), "The Outlander" 4-21-58 (Clague); *Circus Boy*—"Return of Casey Perkins" 10-17-57 (Two Knives); *Zorro*—"Agent of the Eagle" 2-20-58, "Zorro Springs a Trap" 2-27-58, "The Unmasking of Zorro" 3-6-58; *Jim Bowie*—"Apache Silver" 2-21-58 (Three Hands); *Colt .45*—"The Manbuster" 4-4-58 (Pete Cerrilos); *Wagon Train*—"The Charles Maury Story" 5-7-58 (Luke Goslett), "The Dr. Denker Story" 1-31-62 (Ed Beaufort), "The Nancy Davis Story" 5-16-62 (Pitts), "The Lisa Raincloud Story" 10-31-62 (Grey Wolf), "The Robert Harrison Clarke Story" 10-14-63 (Warbow), "The Santiago Quesada Story" 3-30-64 (Stitch); *Trackdown*—"Day of Vengeance" 11-28-58 (Stratton); *Tales of the Texas Rangers*—"The Fifth Plague" 12-19-58 (Billy Joe Hammer); *26 Men*—"Profane Masquerade" 3-10-59; *Maverick*—"The Strange Journey of Jenny Hill" 3-29-59 (Sam), "Thunder from the North" 11-13-60 (War Shirt); *Black Saddle*—"Client: Vardon" 5-30-59 (Mace); *Zane Grey Theater*—"Lone Woman" 10-8-59 (Indian); *Bonanza*—"The Paiute War" 10-3-59, "The Deserter" 10-21-62 (Running Wolf), "The Last Mission" 5-8-66 (George Elkoro); *Overland Trail*—"Westbound Stage" 3-6-60 (Pace Kyber); *The Texan*—"Borrowed Time" 3-7-60 (Lud Galloway); *The Law of the Plainsman*—"Cavern of the Wind" 4-21-60; *Johnny Ringo*—"The Derelict" 5-26-60 (Chaco); *Death*

Valley Days—"Mission to the Mountains" 6-14-60, "Little Cayuse" 2-8-64; *Shotgun Slade*—"Charcoal Bullet" 8-16-60 (Hack); *Wyatt Earp*—"Miss Sadie" 12-20-60 (Jacob Birch), "Apache Gold" 3-7-61 (Chief Natchez); *Laramie*—"The Lost Dutchman" 2-14-61 (Clint Mocassin), "Widow in White" 6-13-61 (Stover), "The Runt" 2-20-62 (Cobey Catlin); *Gunsmoke*—"Old Faces" 3-18-61 (Ed Ivers), "Durham Bull" 3-31-62 (Polk), "The Quest for Asa Janin" 6-1-63 (Pardee), "Friend" 1-25-64 (Frank Gore), "Honor Before Justice" 3-5-66 (Thunder Man), "Sarah" 10-16-72 (Deering), "A Family of Killers" 1-14-74 (Tobin Pitchford); *Rawhide*—"Incident in the Middle of Nowhere" 4-7-61 (Siko); *The Tall Man*—"The Cloudbusters" 4-29-61 (Victorio); *Laredo*—"A Question of Discipline" 10-28-65 (Padilla), "Leave It to Dixie" 12-30-66 (Mace); *Shane*—"Killer in the Valley" 10-15-66 (Danko); *Wild Wild West*—"The Night of the Poisonous Posey" 10-28-66 (Sergei Kaminsk), "The Night of the Deadly Blossom" 3-17-67 (Doctor), "The Night of the Falcon" 11-10-67 (Silvio Balya); *Pistols 'n' Petticoats* 1-21-67 (Hangman); *Hondo*—"Hondo and the Gladiators" 12-15-67 (Nakka); *Daniel Boone*—"Faith's Way" 4-4-68, "Minnow for a Shark" 1-2-69 (Portugee); *The High Chaparral*—"Ride the Savage Land" 2-11-68 (Medicine Man); *The Big Valley*—"The Long Ride" 11-25-68; *Lancer*—"The Last Train for Charlie Poe" 11-26-68 (Slaughter), "Jelly Hoskins' American Dream" 11-11-69; *Alias Smith and Jones*—"The Long Chase" 9-16-72 (Hank Silvers); *Dirty Sally*—4-19-74 (Taos).

Keys, Peggy. Films: "Raw Timber" 1937 (Dale McFarland); "Riders of the Dawn" 1937 (Jean Porter).

Keys, Robert. Films: "Kansas Pacific" 1953 (Lt. Stanton); "Son of Belle Star" 1953 (Bart Wren); "The Bounty Hunter" 1954 (George Williams); "Revolt at Fort Laramie" 1957 (Sgt. Darrach). ¶TV: *The Adventures of Rin Tin Tin*—"The Third Rider" 3-16-56 (Pat McGrath); *Sheriff of Cochise*—"Helldorado" 12-7-56 (Deputy #2); *Gunsmoke*—"The Executioner" 2-2-57 (Abe Curry).

Kibbee, Guy (1886-5/24/56). Films: "The Conquerors" 1932 (Dr. Daniel Blake); "The Bad Man of Brimstone" 1938 (Eight Ball Harrison); "Henry Goes Arizona" 1939 (Judge Van Treece); "Let Freedom Ring" 1939 (Judge David Bronson); "Let Freedom Ring" 1939 (David

Bronson); "Cowboy Blues" 1946; "Lone Star Moonlight" 1946; "Singing on the Trail" 1946; "Over the Santa Fe Trail" 1947; "The Red Stallion" 1947 (Dr. Thompson); "Fort Apache" 1948 (Dr. Wilkens); "The Three Godfathers" 1948 (Judge).

Kibbee, Milton (1896-4/17/70). Films: "Moonlight on the Prairie" 1935 (Pete); "Song of the Saddle" 1936 (Chesty); "Trailin' West" 1936 (Bandit); "Treachery Rides the Range" 1936 (Eph Billings); "Blazing Sixes" 1937 (Mort); "The California Mail" 1937 (Bard Banton); "Cherokee Strip" 1937 (Blade Simpson); "The Devil's Saddle Legion" 1937 (Spane); "Empty Holsters" 1937 (Jim Hall); "Guns of the Pecos" 1937 (Carlos); "Land Beyond the Law" 1937 (Sheriff Spence); "Gold Is Where You Find It" 1938 (Guest); "Overland Stage Raiders" 1938; "Dodge City" 1939 (Printer); "Trigger Smith" 1939; "Lucky Cisco Kid" 1940 (Wells Fargo Man); "The Return of Frank James" 1940 (Reporter); "West of Abilene" 1940 (Land Agent); "Across the Sierras" 1941 (Sheriff); "Billy the Kid's Range War" 1941 (Leonard); "Kansas Cyclone" 1941 (Cal Chambers); "Two-Gun Sheriff" 1941 (Jones); "Billy the Kid Trapped" 1942 (Judge Clark); "Billy the Kid's Smoking Guns" 1942; "Heart of the Rio Grande" 1942; "In Old California" 1942 (Mr. Tompkins); "The Lone Rider and the Bandit" 1942; "The Lone Rider in Cheyenne" 1942; "Raiders of the West" 1942; "Westward Ho" 1942; "Black Hills Express" 1943; "Western Cyclone" 1943 (Senator Peabody); "Blazing Frontier" 1944 (Barslow); "Conquest of Cheyenne" 1946; "Desert Fury" 1947 (Mike, the Bartender); "Homesteaders of Paradise Valley" 1947; "River Lady" 1948 (Limpy); "Daughter of the West" 1949; "Three Desperate Men" 1951 (Cashier); "When the Redskins Rode" 1951 (Davey); "Rodeo" 1952; "Born to the Saddle" 1953.

Kibrick, Leonard (1925-1/4/93). Films: "The Lone Cowboy" 1934 (Irving); "Jesse James" 1939 (Boy).

Kidd, Jim (1846-12/9/16). Films: "Jordan Is a Hard Road" 1915.

Kidd, John. Films: "Plunderers of Painted Flats" 1959 (Glenn).

Kidd, Jonathan (1914-12/15/87). Films: "Young Pioneers" TVM-1976 (Dr. Thorne). ¶TV: *Sugarfoot*—"The Giant Killer" 3-3-59 (Clarence); *Tales of Wells Fargo*—"Remember the Yazoo" 4-14-62 (Dunbar Burnett); *Rawhide*—"A Man Called Mushy" 10-23-

64 (Seth Parker); *Gunsmoke*—"Bad Lady from Brookline" 5-1-65 (Harper); *The Loner*—"The House Rules at Mrs. Wayne's" 11-6-65 (Barber).

Kidder, Margot (1948-). Films: "Bounty Man" TVM-1972 (Mae); "Honky Tonk" TVM-1974 (Lucy Cotton). ¶TV: *Nichols*—Regular 1971-72 (Ruth).

Kidman, Nicole (1967-). Films: "Far and Away" 1992 (Shannon Christie).

Kieffer, Philip (1886-7/13/62). Films: "Wells Fargo" 1937 (Top Sergeant); "Fort Apache" 1948 (Man); "Pillars of the Sky" 1956 (Maj. Randall).

Kiel, Richard (1939-). Films: "The Barbara Coast" TVM-1975 (Moose Moran); "Pale Rider" 1985 (Club); "The Giant of Thunder Mountain" 1991 (Eli). ¶TV: *Klondike*—"Bare Knuckles" 12-12-60; *The Rifleman*—"The Decision" 11-6-61; *Wild Wild West*—"The Night the Wizard Shook the Earth" 10-1-65 (Voltaire), "The Night That Terror Stalked the Town" 11-19-65 (Voltaire), "The Night of the Whirring Death" 2-18-66 (Voltaire); *The Monroes*—"Ghosts of Paradox" 3-15-67 (Casmir); *Daniel Boone*—"Benvenuto … Who?" 10-9-69 (Lemouche); *Barbary Coast*—Regular 1975-76 (Moose Moran); *Young Dan'l Boone*—"The Game" 10-10-77.

Kieling, Wolfgang (1924-). Films: "Duel at Sundown" 1965-Fr./Ger. (Punch).

Kikume, Al (1894-3/27/72). Films: "Kit Carson" 1940 (Indian Chief).

Kilbane, Dennis. Films: "The Christmas Kid" 1966-Span./Ital. (Luke Acker); "The Valley of Gwangi" 1969 (Rowdy).

Kilbride, Percy (1888-12/11/64). Films: "The Woman of the Town" 1943 (Rev. Samuel Small); "Black Bart" 1948 (Jersey Brady).

Kilburn, Terry (1926-). Films: "Only the Valiant" 1951 (Trooper Saxton).

Kiley, Richard (1922-). Films: "Friendly Persuasion" TVM-1975 (Jess Birdwell); "The Macahans" TVM-1976 (Timothy Macahan); "Gunsmoke: The Last Apache" TVM-1990 (Chalk Brighton). ¶TV: *Gunsmoke*—"Stark" 9-28-70 (Lewis Stark), "Lynott" 11-1-71 (Tom Lynott), "Bohannan" 9-25-72 (Bohannan), "Kitty's Love Affair" 10-22-73 (Will Stambridge); *Bonanza*—"Gideon the Good" 10-18-70 (Sheriff Yates).

Kilgas, Nancy. TV: *Sergeant Preston of the Yukon*—"Lost River Roundup" 12-12-57 (Dora Lloyd); *Tales of Wells Fargo*—"Wild Cargo" 1-19-59 (Gee Gee); *26 Men*—"The Unwanted" 3-31-59.

Kilian, Victor (1898-3/11/79). Films: "Ramona" 1936 (Father Gaspare); "Fair Warning" 1937 (Sam); "Jesse James" 1939 (Preacher); "The Return of the Cisco Kid" 1939 (Bartender); "Mark of Zorro" 1940 (Boatman); "Out West with the Peppers" 1940 (Jim Anderson); "The Return of Frank James" 1940 (Preacher); "Santa Fe Trail" 1940 (Dispatch Rider); "Virginia City" 1940 (Abraham Lincoln); "Western Union" 1941 (Charlie); "The Ox-Bow Incident" 1943 (Darby); "Barbary Coast Gent" 1944 (Curry Slake); "Belle of the Yukon" 1944 (the Professor); "Duel in the Sun" 1946 (Gambler); "Smoky" 1946 (Junk Man); "Northwest Stampede" 1948 (Mel Saunders); "Yellow Sky" 1948 (Bartender); "Colorado Territory" 1949 (Sheriff); "I Shot Jesse James" 1949 (Soapy); "Rimfire" 1949 (Sheriff Jordan); "The Wyoming Bandit" 1949 (Ross Tayler); "Bandit Queen" 1950 (Jose Montalve); "The Old Frontier" 1950 (Judge Ames); "The Return of Jesse James" 1950 (Rigby); "The Showdown" 1950 (Hemp). ¶TV: *Gunsmoke*—"The Fourth Victim" 11-4-74 (Homer Jones).

Killmond, Frank. Films: "Hud" 1963 (Dumb Billy). ¶TV: *Death Valley Days*—"Old Blue" 4-7-59 (John); *Wichita Town*—"The Frontiersman" 3-2-60 (Eddie Davners); *The Tall Man*—"The Shawl" 10-1-60 (Martin Roberts).

Kilmer, Val (1959-). Films: "Tombstone" 1993 (Doc Holliday).

Kilpatrick, Lincoln (1932-). Films: "The Red, White and Black" 1970 (Sgt. Hatch); "The Master Gunfighter" 1975 (Jacques). ¶TV: *Bearcats!*—11-11-71 (Jake).

Kimball, Ann. Films: "Fort Osage" 1952; "Wagons West" 1952 (Alice Lawrence). ¶TV: *Wild Bill Hickok*—"The Outlaw's Son" 2-12-52; *The Cisco Kid*—"The Devil's Deputy" 5-10-52, "Fear" 6-28-52.

Kimbley, Bill. Films: "Raiders of Tomahawk Creek" 1950 (Billy Calhoun); "Silver City Bonanza" 1951 (Jimmy McIntosh). ¶TV: *The Gene Autry Show*—"Killer Horse" 12-10-50 (Chuck).

Kimbrough, Clint (1935-). TV: *Iron Horse*—"The Bride at Forty-Mile" 1-23-67 (Rafe Wheeler).

Kimbrough, John. Films: "Lone Star Ranger" 1942 (Buck Duane); "Sundown Jim" 1942 (Jim Majors).

Kimmell, Leslie. Films: "Coyote Canyon" 1949-short; "The Vanquished" 1953 (Col. Ellansby); "Outlaw's Son" 1957 (Kessler). ¶TV: *Jim Bowie*—"Jackson's Assassination" 3-15-57 (Andrew Jackson).

King, Andrea (1915-). Films: "Mark of the Renegade" 1951 (Anita Gonzales); "Outlaw Queen" 1957. ¶TV: *Fireside Theater*—"Man of the Comstock" 11-3-53 (Annie Foote); *Cheyenne*—"The Law Man" 11-6-56 (Julie); *Maverick*—"Two Tickets to Ten Strike" 3-15-59 (Mae Miller); *The Alaskans*—"The Blizzard" 10-18-59 (Duchess), "The Devil Made Five" 6-19-60 (Duchess).

King, Anita (1889-6/10/63). Films: "The Virginian" 1914 (Mrs. Ogden); "The Girl of the Golden West" 1915 (Wowkle); "The Girl Angle" 1917 (Maud Wainwright); "The Golden Fetter" 1917 (Faith Miller); "The Squaw Man's Song" 1917 (Wah-na-gi); "Petticoats and Politics" 1918 (Ann Murdock); "Whatever the Cost" 1918 (Jess Farley).

King, Billy. Films: "Hopalong Rides Again" 1937 (Artie Peters); "Texas Trail" 1937 (Boots); "Heart of Arizona" 1938 (Artie); "Pride of the West" 1938 (Dick Martin).

King, Brad (1918-1/1/91). Films: "Outlaws of the Desert" 1941 (Johnny Nelson); "Riders of the Timberline" 1941 (Johnny Nelson); "Secrets of the Wastelands" 1941 (Johnny Nelson); "Stick to Your Guns" 1941 (Johnny Nelson); "Twilight on the Trail" 1941 (Johnny Nelson); "Trouble at Melody Mesa" 1944; "Pistol Packin' Nitwits" 1945-short; "San Antonio" 1945 (Cowboy).

King, Brett. Films: "Jesse James Versus the Daltons" 1954 (Joe Branch). ¶TV: *The Roy Rogers Show*—"The Outlaw's Girl" 2-17-52, "Outlaws' Town" 3-1-52; *Gunsmoke*—"Cooter" 5-19-56 (Pate), "Kitty Lost" 12-21-57 (Pate), "Buffalo Hunter" 5-2-59 (Duff), "False Front" 12-22-62 (Hank); *Tombstone Territory*—"Gunslinger from Galeville" 10-16-57 (Monk); *Zane Grey Theater*—"Man of Fear" 3-14-58 (Sheriff), "Let the Man Die" 12-18-58 (Dolf Akins), "Cry Hope! Cry Hate!" 10-20-60 (Luke French); *MacKenzie's Raiders*—Regular 1958-59; *Wyatt Earp*—"Truth About Gunfighting" 11-18-58 (Conroy), "Loyalty" 2-7-61 (Marlin); *Bat Masterson*—"License to Cheat" 2-4-59 (Hub Elliott), "The Hunter" 10-

27-60 (Johnny Hillman); *Lawman*—"The Souvenir" 4-5-59; *Yancy Derringer*—"Outlaw at Liberty" 5-7-59; *Johnny Ringo*—"Die Twice" 1-21-60 (Florey Tamlin), "Judgment Day" 4-14-60 (Jessie); *Death Valley Days*—"The Devil's Due" 1-26-60 (Cassidy); *Klondike*—"Bathhouse Justice" 12-26-60 (Colly Boyd); *Wagon Train*—"The Lieutenant Burton Story" 2-28-62 (Cpl. Ben Rawlings), "The George B. Hanrahan Story" 3-28-62 (Haynes), "The Sandra Cummings Story" 12-2-63; *Laramie*—"The Last Battleground" 4-16-63 (Hall).

King, Burton (1887-5/4/44). "The Half-Breed's Treachery" 1912; "Parson James" 1912; "Ranch-Mates" 1912; "The Ranger's Reward" 1912; "The Salted Mine" 1912; "The Girl from Sunset Pass" 1913.

King, Carlton (1881-7/6/32). Films: "Loaded Dice" 1925; "The Texas Bearcat" 1925 (Sethman); "Law of the Rio Grande" 1931 (Cookie); "Partners" 1932 (Mr. Morgan).

King, Charles (1889-1/11/44). Films: "The Miracle Rider" 1935-serial; "The Singing Vagabond" 1935 (Red); "Tumbling Tumbleweeds" 1935 (Blaze); "Guns and Guitars" 1936 (Sam); "The Lawless Nineties" 1936 (Hartley); "Red River Valley" 1936 (Sam); "Santa Fe Bound" 1936 (Steve Denton); "A Lawman Is Born" 1937 (Bert Moscrip); "The Trusted Outlaw" 1937 (Bert Gilmore); "Ridin' the Lone Trail" 1937 (Dusty Williams); "Gold Mine in the Sky" 1938; "Santa Fe Stampede" 1938; Thunder in the Desert" 1938 (Curt Harris); "South of the Border" 1939; "Shadows of Death" 1945.

King, Sr., Charles L. (1899-5/7/57). Films: "Singing River" 1921 (Grimes); "Hearts of the West" 1925; "Triple Action" 1925 (Dick Clayton); "Range Courage" 1927 (Red Murphy); "Beyond the Law" 1930 (Brand); "The Dawn Trail" 1930 (Skeets); "Fighting Thru" 1930 (Fox Tyson); "Oklahoma Cyclone" 1930 (McKim); "Alias the Bad Man" 1931 (Black); "Arizona Terror" 1931 (Hite); "Branded Men" 1931 (Mace); "The Mystery Trooper" 1931-serial; "The Pocatello Kid" 1931 (Trinidad); "Range Law" 1931 (Legal); "The Two Gun Man" 1931 (Thorne); "Between Fighting Men" 1932; "Cornered" 1932; "Fighting Champ" 1932 (Jock Malone); "Fighting for Justice" 1932; "The Gay Buckaroo" 1932 (Faro Parker); "Ghost City" 1932 (Buck); "Honor of the Mounted" 1932; "The Man from Arizona" 1932 (Collins); "A Man's Land" 1932 (Joe); "Vanish-

ing Men" 1932; "Young Blood" 1932 (Sheriff Jake Sharpe); "Crashing Broadway" 1933 (Gus Jeffries); "The Dude Bandit" 1933; "The Fighting Parson" 1933 (Mike); "The Lone Avenger" 1933 (Tuck); "Outlaw Justice" 1933; "Son of the Border" 1933 (Tupper); "Strawberry Roan" 1933 (Curley); "The Fighting Trooper" 1934 (Landeau); "The Law of the Wild" 1934-serial; "Mystery Ranch" 1934 (Sam); "The Prescott Kid" 1934 (J. Bones); "Born to Battle" 1935; "Courage of the North" 1935; "His Fighting Blood" 1935; "Ivory-Handled Gun" 1935 (Tom); "Law Beyond the Range" 1935 (Townsman); "The Man from Guntown" 1935; "Northern Frontier" 1935 (Mountie); "Outlawed Guns" 1935 (Frank Davilla); "Red Blood of Courage" 1935 (Joe); "The Revenge Rider" 1935 (Sykes); "The Roaring West" 1935-serial; "Silent Valley" 1935 (Harry Kellar); "The Silver Bullet" 1935 (Luke Hargrave); "Trail of Terror" 1935 (Hashknife); "Brand of the Outlaws" 1936 (Rufe Matlock); "The Crooked Trail" 1936 (Lanning); "Fast Bullets" 1936; "The Last of the Warrens" 1936 (Kent); "The Law Rides" 1936 (Hank Davis); "The Kid Ranger" 1936 (Joe); "Lucky Terror" 1936 (Lawyer Wheeler); "Men of the Plains" 1936 (Johnson); "O'Malley of the Mounted" 1936 (Brody); "The Phantom of the Range" 1936; "The Phantom Rider" 1936-serial; "Pinto Rustlers" 1936; "Rip Roarin' Buckaroo" 1936; "Sundown Saunders" 1936; "Sunset of Power" 1936 (Coley); "Valley of the Lawless" 1936 (Regan); "Black Aces" 1937 (Less); "Danger Valley" 1937 (Dana); "Desert Phantom" 1937 (Dan); "Doomed at Sundown" 1937; "The Fighting Deputy" 1937 (Scar Adams); "The Gambling Terror" 1937 (Brett); "God's Country and the Man" 1937 (Red Gentry); "Headin' for the Rio Grande" 1937 (Tick); "Hittin' the Trail" 1937 (Slug); "The Idaho Kid" 1937 (Bib Slagel); "Lightnin' Crandall" 1937 (Carson Blaine); "The Luck of Roaring Camp" 1937 (Sandy); "The Mystery of the Hooded Horseman" 1937 (Blackie Devlin); "The Painted Stallion" 1937-serial (Bull Smith); "The Red Rope" 1937 (Red Mike); "Riders of the Rockies" 1937 (Butch Regan); "Rootin' Tootin' Rhythm" 1937 (Black Jim); "Sing, Cowboy, Sing" 1937 (Red Holman); "Smoke Tree Range" 1937; "Tex Rides with the Boy Scouts" 1937 (Stark); "Trouble in Texas" 1937 (Pinto); "Flaming Frontier" 1938-serial; "Frontier

Town" 1938 (Pete Denby); "Gun Packer" 1938 (Chance Moore); "In Early Arizona" 1938; "The Lone Ranger" 1938-serial (Morely); "Man's Country" 1938 (Guard); "Panamint's Bad Man" 1938; "Phantom Ranger" 1938 (Dan); "Renfrew the Great White Trail" 1938 (LeGrange); "Rollin' Plains" 1938 (Trigger Gargan); "Songs and Bullets" 1938 (Sheriff); "Songs and Saddles" 1938 (Falcon); ""Utah Trail" 1938 (Badger); "Wild Horse Canyon" 1938 (Red); "Cowboys from Texas" 1939 (Beau); "Down the Wyoming Trail" 1939 (Red Becker); "Feud of the Range" 1939 (Dirk); "Frontier Pony Express" 1939; "Frontiers of '49" 1939 (Howard Brunon); "The Law Comes to Texas" 1939 (Kaintucky); "Lone Star Pioneers" 1939 (Pete Pike); "The Man from Texas" 1939; "Mesquite Buckaroo" 1939 (Trigger); "Oklahoma Frontier" 1939 (Soapy); "The Oregon Trail" 1939-serial (Dirk); "Riders of the Frontier" 1939; "Rollin' Westward" 1939 (Haines); "Song of the Buckaroo" 1939 (Max Groat); "Sundown on the Prairie" 1939 (Dorgan); "The Taming of the West" 1939 (Jackson); "Zorro's Fighting Legion" 1939-serial (Valdez); "Billy the Kid in Texas" 1940 (Dave); "Billy the Kid's Gun Justice" 1940 (Ed Baker); "The Cheyenne Kid" 1940 (Carson); "Deadwood Dick" 1940-serial (Tex); "Death Rides the Range" 1940 (Joe Larkin); "Law and Order" 1940; "Lightning Strikes West" 1940 (Jed Larkin); "One Man's Law" 1940; "Pony Post" 1940 (Hamilton); "Riders from Nowhere" 1940 (Trigger); "Roll, Wagons, Roll" 1940; "West of Carson City" 1940 (Drag); "Wild Horse Range" 1940 (Stoner); "The Apache Kid" 1941; "Billy the Kid in Santa Fe" 1941 (Steve Barton); "Billy the Kid Wanted" 1941 (Saunders); "Billy the Kid's Fighting Pals" 1941 (Badger); "Billy the Kid's Range War" 1941; "Billy the Kid's Roundup" 1941 (Ed); "Bury Me Not on the Lone Prairie" 1941; "Desert Bandit" 1941; "Forbidden Trails" 1941 (Fulton); "The Gunman from Bodie" 1941; "Law of the Range" 1941; "The Lone Rider Ambushed" 1941 (Foreman); "The Lone Rider Crosses the Rio" 1941 (Jarvis); "The Lone Rider Fights Back" 1941; "The Lone Rider in Ghost Town" 1941 (Roberts); "Lone Star Law Men" 1941 (Dude); "Outlaws of the Rio Grande" 1941 (Trigger); "Roaring Frontiers" 1941; "The Texas Marshal" 1941 (Titus); "White Eagle" 1941-serial (Brace); "Along the Sundown Trail" 1942; "Arizona Stagecoach" 1942; "Below the Border"

1942 (Slade); "Boot Hill Bandits" 1942 (Outlaw); "Border Roundup" 1942; "Ghost Town Law" 1942 (Gus); "Law and Order" 1942 (Crawford); "Outlaws of Boulder Pass" 1942; "Overland Stagecoach" 1942; "Pirates of the Prairie" 1942; "Prairie Pals" 1942 (Mitchell); "Raiders of the West" 1942; "The Rangers Take Over" 1942 (Kip Lane); "Riders of the West" 1942; "Sheriff of Sage Valley" 1942 (Sloane); "Trail Riders" 1942 (Cole); "Where Trails End" 1942; "Bad Men of Thunder Gap" 1943; "Blazing Guns" 1943; "Border Buckaroos" 1943 (Rance Daggett); "Bordertown Gunfighters" 1943; "California Joe" 1943 (Ashley); "Calling Wild Bill Elliott" 1943; "Cattle Stampede" 1943 (Coulter); "Cowboy in the Clouds" 1943; "The Desperadoes" 1943 (Outlaw); "Fighting Valley" 1943 (Slim); "The Ghost Rider" 1943; "The Haunted Ranch" 1943; "The Kid Rides Again" 1943 (Vic); "King of the Cowboys" 1943 (Henchman); "Land of Hunted Men" 1943; "The Man from Thunder River" 1943; "Outlaws of Stampede Pass" 1943; "Raiders of Red Gap" 1943 (Bennett); "The Return of the Rangers" 1943; "Riders of the Rio Grande" 1943 (Thunder); "The Stranger from Pecos" 1943 (Harmond); "The Texas Kid" 1943; "Two Fisted Justice" 1943 (Trigger); "Western Cyclone" 1943 (Ace Harmon); "Arizona Whirlwind" 1944 (Duke Rollins); "The Big Bonanza" 1944; "Boss of Rawhide" 1944 (Frank Hade); "Brand of the Devil" 1944; Code of the Prairie" 1944 (Election Informer); "Dead or Alive" 1944; "Death Valley Rangers" 1944 (Blackie); "Devil Riders" 1944 (Del Stone); "Frontier Outlaws" 1944 (Barlow); "Fuzzy Settles Down" 1944; "Gangsters of the Frontier" 1944; "Guns of the Law" 1944; "Land of the Outlaws" 1944; "Law of the Valley" 1944; "Marshal of Reno" 1944; "Oath of Vengeance" 1944; "Outlaw Roundup" 1944; "Outlaw Trail" 1944 (Chuck Walters); "The Pinto Bandit" 1944; "Rustlers' Hideout" 1944 (Buck Shaw); "Sonora Stagecoach" 1944 (Blackie Reed); "Thundering Gun Slingers" 1944 (Steve Kirby); "Valley of Vengeance" 1944 (Burke); "Border Badmen" 1945 (Merritt); "Both Barrels Blazing" 1945; "Enemy of the Law" 1945 (Charlie); "Fighting Bill Carson" 1945; "Flaming Bullets" 1945; "Frontier Feud" 1945; "Frontier Fugitives" 1945; "Gangster's Den" 1945 (Butch); "His Brother's Ghost" 1945 (Thorne); "Marked for Murder" 1945; "The Navajo Trail"

1945; "Three in the Saddle" 1945; "Ambush Trail" 1946 (Al Craig); "The Caravan Trail" 1946 (Joe King); "Colorado Serenade" 1946 (Deputy); "Ghost of Hidden Valley" 1946 (Dawson); "The Lawless Breed" 1946; "Outlaw of the Plains" 1946; "Prairie Badmen" 1946 (Cal); "Thunder Town" 1946 (Bill Rankin); "Jesse James Rides Again" 1947-serial (Trent); "Law of the Lash" 1947 (Sheriff); "Ridin' Down the Trail" 1947; "Son of Zorro" 1947-serial (Dow); "White Stallion" 1947 (Jim Sorrell); "The Wistful Widow of Wagon Gap" 1947 (Gunman); "Wyoming" 1947 (Cowboy); "The Hawk of Powder River" 1948; "Oklahoma Blues" 1948 (Gabe); "Ghost of Zorro" 1949-serial (Joe).

King, Jr., Charles. Films: "Starlight Over Texas" 1938 (Hank Boston); "Where the Buffalo Roam" 1938 (Bull); "Spook Town" 1944; "The Navajo Kid" 1945 (Lee Hedges).

King, Chris. TV: *The Outlaws*—"Charge!" 3-22-62 (Ree); *The Virginian*—"Duel at Shiloh" 1-2-63 (Morgan); *Have Gun Will Travel*—"Bob Wire" 1-12-63 (Dane).

King, Claude (1879–9/18/41). Films: "McKenna of the Mounted" 1932; "The Last of the Mohicans" 1936 (Duke of Marlborough); "Three on the Trail" 1936 (J.P. Ridley).

King, Jr., Dennis (-8/24/86). Films: "The Restless Breed" 1957 (Hotel Clerk).

King, Diana (-7/21/86). Films: "Girl Rush" 1944 (Martha).

King, Emmett C. (1866-4/21/53). Films: "Fightin' Mad" 1921 (Howard Graham); "Don Quickshot of the Rio Grande" 1923 (Jim Hellier); "Arizona Sweepstakes" 1926 (Col. Tom Savery); "The Man in the Saddle" 1926 (Tom Stewart).

King, George. Films: "The Ramblin' Kid" 1923 (Sing Pete).

King, Henry (1886-1/29/82). Films: "The Mainspring" 1917 (Ned Gillett).

King, Jack (1883-10/8/43). Films: "Western Courage" 1935; "Avenging Waters" 1936; "The Cattle Thief" 1936; "Heroes of the Range" 1936; "The Traitor" 1936 (Ranger); "Code of the Cactus" 1939; "The Gunman from Bodie" 1941.

King, Joe (1883-4/11/51). Films: "The Ball Player and the Bandit" 1912; "The Charmed Arrow" 1914; "In Defiance of the Law" 1914; "The Wilderness Mail" 1914; "The Ring of Destiny" 1915; "Until They Get Me" 1917 (Selwyn); "The Valley of Silent

Men" 1922 (Buck O'Connor); "Moonlight on the Prairie" 1935 (Sheriff); "Romance of the West" 1935-short; "God's Country and the Woman" 1937 (Red Munro); "Land Beyond the Law" 1937 (Governor Lew Wallace); "Destry Rides Again" 1939; "Pony Express Days" 1940-short; "Trail of the Vigilantes" 1940 (Ellery).

King, John (1909-11/11/87). Films: "Outlaws' Highway" 1934 (Jack McKenzie); "The Gentleman from Arizona" 1939 (Pokey); "The Range Busters" 1940 (Dusty); "Trailing Double Trouble" 1940 (Dusty); "West of Pinto Basin" 1940 (Dusty); "Fugitive Valley" 1941 (Dusty); "The Kid's Last Ride" 1941 (Dusty); "Saddle Mountain Roundup" 1941 (Dusty); "Tonto Basin Outlaws" 1941 (Dusty); "Trail of the Silver Spurs" 1941 (Dusty); "Tumbledown Ranch in Arizona" 1941 (Dusty); "Underground Rustlers" 1941 (Dusty); "Wrangler's Roost" 1941 (Dusty); "Arizona Stagecoach" 1942; "Boot Hill Bandits" 1942 (Dusty); "Rock River Renegades" 1942 (Dusty); "Texas to Bataan" 1942 (Dusty); "Texas Trouble Shooters" 1942 (Dusty); "Thunder River Feud" 1942 (Dusty); "Trail Riders" 1942 (Dusty); "The Haunted Ranch" 1943; "Two Fisted Justice" 1943 (Dusty); "Renegade Girl" 1946.

King, Joseph (1883-4/11/51). Films: "They Died with Their Boots On" 1941 (Chairman).

King, Judy. Films: "The Best Bad Man" 1925 (Molly Jones); "The Bonanza Buckaroo" 1926 (Cleo Gordon).

King, Kewpie. Films: "Battling Buddy" 1924 (Ginger); "Fast and Fearless" 1924 (Fatty Doolittle); "Hurricane Horseman" 1926 (Kewpie Cook).

King, Kip (1937-). TV: *The Rifleman*—"The Deadeye Kid" 2-10-59 (Donnel O'Mahoney).

King, Louis (1898-9/7/62). Films: "The Secret of Black Mountain" 1917 (Jake Dewitt); "Singing River" 1921 (Kane); "Straight from the Shoulder" 1921 (Rogers); "Quicksands" 1923 (Barfly).

King, Mollie (1898-12/28/81). Films: "All Man" 1916 (Alice Maynard).

King, Nellie (1895-7/1/35). Films: "Wild Honey" 1918 (Minnie Lou).

King, Pee Wee (and His Gold West Cowboys). Films: "Flame of the West" 1945; "Ridin' the Outlaw Trail" 1951; "The Rough, Tough West" 1952;

King, Russell. Films: "Heart of the North" 1938 (Mac Drummond).

King, Ruth. Films: "The Land of Long Shadows" 1917 (Jeanne Verrette); "Men of the Desert" 1917 (May); "Open Places" 1917 (Mollie Andrews); "The Range Boss" 1917 (Ruth Harkness); "Dangerous Love" 1920 (the Other Woman); "Driftin' Thru" 1926 (Stella Dunn); "The Lady from Hell" 1926 (Lucy Wallace).

King, Walter Woolf (1899-10/24/84). Films: "Go West" 1940 (Mr. Beecher). ¶TV: *My Friend Flicka*—"Rough and Ready" 3-9-56; *Fury*—"Fury Runs to Win" 3-10-56 (Jack Kingsley); *Wagon Train*—"The Barbara Lindquist Story" 10-18-64 (Ed Everest); *The Virginian*—"Two Men Named Laredo" 1-6-65 (Judge), "Hideout" 1-13-65 (Judge); *Wild Wild West*—"The Night of the Inferno" 9-17-65 (Col. Kelly Shear); *The Big Valley*—"The Murdered Party" 11-17-65 (Judge), "Target" 10-31-66; *Laredo*—"The Sweet Gang" 11-4-66.

King, Wright (1927-). Films: "Stagecoach to Fury" 1956 (Ralph Slader); "The Young Guns" 1956 (Jonesy); "Cast a Long Shadow" 1959 (Noah); "The Gunfight at Dodge City" 1959 (Billy); "Journey Through Rosebud" 1972 (Indian Agent). ¶TV: *Gunsmoke*—"Home Surgery" 10-8-55 (Ben Walling), "Born to Hang" 11-2-57 (Joe Digger), "False Witnes" 12-12-59 (Rumey Crep), "Little Girl" 4-1-61 (Hi Stevens), "Colorado Sheriff" 6-17-61 (Rod Ellison), "Abe Blocker" 11-24-62 (Bud Groves), "No Hands" 2-8-64 (Lon Ginnis), "The Bounty Hunter" 10-30-65 (Lon Jensen); *Cheyenne*—"Born Bad" 3-26-57 (Blaney Wilcox), "Ghost of Cimarron" 3-25-58 (the Kiowa Kid); *Boots and Saddles*—"The Obsession" 10-3-57 (Pvt. Bennett); *Maverick*—"Hostage!" 11-10-57 (Rick); *Have Gun Will Travel*—"Helen of Abajinian" 12-28-57 (O'Reilly), "The Chase" 4-11-59 (Gyppo), "The Search" 6-18-60 (Lane Kilner), "My Brother's Keeper" 5-6-61 (Cull), "A Knight to Remember" 12-9-61 (Alessandro Caloca); *The Texan*—"Desert Passage" 12-1-58 (Mac Kernin); *Tombstone Territory*—"Warrant for Death" 5-8-59; *Sugarfoot*—"Wolf" 6-9-59 (Wolf Wilkes); *The Rebel*—"The Vagrants" 12-20-59 (Woody); *Johnny Ringo*—"Judgment Day" 4-14-60 (Junior); *Wanted—Dead or Alive*—Regular 1960-61 (Jason Nichols), "No Trail Back" 11-28-59 (Joe Hooker); *The Outlaws*—"The Bill Doolin Story" 3-2-61 (Little

Dick), "No Luck on Friday" 11-30-61 (Sondberg); *Tales of Wells Fargo*—"Man of Another Breed" 12-2-61 (Will Norris); *Bronco*—"The Harrigan" 12-25-61 (Allen Miller); *Rawhide*—"Incident of the Rawhiders" 11-14-63 (Collie Quade); *The Outcasts*—"Act of Faith" 2-10-69 (Fred Willard); *Lancer*—"The Knot" 3-18-69 (Zack Blake).

King, Zalman (1942-). Films: "The Dangerous Days of Kiowa Jones" TVM-1966 (Jesse); "Stranger on the Run" TVM-1967; "The Intruders" TVM-1970 (Bob Younger). ¶TV: *Gunsmoke*—"Ten Little Indians" 10-9-65 (Billy Coe), "My Father, My Son" 4-23-66 (Joey Jeffords), "The Jailor" 10-1-66 (Jack Stone), "Muley" 1-21-67 (Muley), "Death Train" 11-27-67 (Willie Groom); *The Legend of Jesse James*—"The Judas Boot" 11-8-65 (Cincy); *The Loner*—"To the West of Eden" 1-1-66 (Red Segus); *Bonanza*—"The Code" 2-13-66 (Pete); *Cimarron Strip*—"The Search" 11-9-67 (Strawdy Vardeman); *Daniel Boone*—"The Terrible Tarbots" 12-11-69 (Meshach).

Kingi, Henry (1943-). Films: "Smoke in the Wind" 1975 (Smoky). ¶TV: *Daniel Boone*—"Run for the Money" 2-19-70.

Kingsford, Guy. Films: "Stagecoach Express" 1942 (Sam Elkins); "Texas to Bataan" 1942 (Miller); "Fort Vengeance" 1953 (MacRea). ¶TV: *Sergeant Preston of the Yukon*—"The Rebel Yell" 10-10-57 (Jerry Carter).

Kingsford, Walter (1882-2/7/58). Films: "The Pathfinder" 1952 (Col. Duncannon).

Kingsley, Martin. Films: "Gunslinger" 1956 (Gideon Polk); "The Oklahoma Woman" 1956 (Sheriff Bill Peters). ¶TV: *Gunsmoke*—"20-20" 2-25-56 (Lee Polen).

Kingston, Harry (1914-7/4/51). Films: "Viva Zapata!" 1952 (Don Garcia).

Kingston, Lenore (1914-5/5/93). TV: *Wagon Train*—"Clyde" 12-27-61 (Mrs. Sherman).

Kingston, Natalie (1905-2/2/91). Films: "Painted Post" 1928 (Barbara Lane); "Under Texas Skies" 1930 (Joan Prescott).

Kingston, Tommy (1902-1/27/59). Films: "The Man from Sundown" 1939 (Roulette Dealer).

Kingston, Winifred (1895-2/3/67). Films: "The Call of the North" 1914 (Virginia, Factor's Daughter); "The Squaw Man" 1914 (Diana, Countess of Kerhill); "The Virginian"

1914 (Molly Wood); "Where the Trail Divides" 1914 (Bess Lander); "Captain Courtesy" 1915 (Eleanor); "The Love Route" 1915 (Allene Houston); "Ben Blair" 1916 (Florence Winthrop); "Davy Crockett" 1916 (Eleanor Vaughn); "The Parson of Panamint" 1916 (Buckskin Liz); "Durand of the Bad Lands" 1917 (Molly Gore); "North of '53" 1917 (Hazel Weir); "The Light of Western Stars" 1918 (Majesty Hammond); "The Trail of the Axe" 1922 (Betty Somer); "The Squaw Man" 1931.

Kinney, Clyde (1892-5/15/62). Films: "Flaming Guns" 1932; "Texas Trail" 1937 (Courier); "I'm from the City" 1938 (Butch).

Kinney, Jack. Films: "Vigilantes Are Coming" 1936-serial (Rancher); "Billy the Kid Trapped" 1942; "Prairie Pals" 1942; "The Desperadoes" 1943; "Gun to Gun" 1944-short; "Badman's Country" 1958.

Kino, Goro. Films: "Little Red Decides" 1918 (Duck Sing).

Kino, Lloyd (1919-). Films: "The Outlaws Is Coming!" 1965 (Japanese Moe). ¶TV: *Laredo*—"The Bitter Yen of General Ti" 2-3-67; *Kung Fu*—"One Step to Darkness" 1-25-75 (Doctor).

Kino, Robert. TV: *Wagon Train*—"The Sakae Ito Story" 12-3-58 (Matsu); *Wanted—Dead or Alive*—"Black Belt" 3-19-60 (Sammy Wong); *Laramie*—"Dragon at the Door" 9-26-61 (Tomomi).

Kinsella, Walter (1901-5/11/75). TV: *Stagecoach West*—"The Guardian Angels" 6-6-61 (Abel Morgan); *The Tall Man*—"Trial by Hanging" 11-4-61 (Sheriff Cy Clayer).

Kinskey, Leonid (1903-). Films: "Rhythm on the Range" 1936 (Mischa); "The Three Godfathers" 1936 (Poker Player). ¶TV: *The Alaskans*—"Sign of the Kodiak" 5-29-60 (Ivan); *Have Gun Will Travel*—"The Hunt" 2-3-62 (Prince Radachev).

Kinski, Klaus (1926-9/23/91). Films: "For a Few Dollars More" 1965-Ital./Ger./Span. (Hunchback); "A Bullet for the General" 1966-Ital. (Santo); "Last of the Renegades" 1966-Fr./Ital./Ger./Yugo. (Luke); "Man: His Pride and His Vengeance" 1967-Ital./Ger. (Garcia); "Great Silence" 1968-Ital./Fr. (Tigero); "The Ruthless Four" 1968-Ital./Ger. (Blond); "Sartana" 1968-Ital./Ger. (Morgan); "Twice a Judas" 1968-Span./Ital. (Victor Barrett); "And God Said to Cain" 1969-Ital.; "I Am Sartana, Your Angel of Death" 1969-Ital./Fr.; "Last Ride to Santa Cruz"

1969-Ger./Fr.; "Beast" 1970-Ital. (Machete); "Black Killer" 1971-Ital./Ger. (James Webb); "Fistful of Death" 1971-Ital. (Reverend Cotton); "His Name Was King" 1971-Ital. (Sheriff Foster); "Return of Clint the Stranger" 1971-Ital./Span.; "Shoot the Living ... Pray for the Dead" 1971-Ital. (Ken Hogan); "Vengeance Is a Dish Served Cold" 1971-Ital./Span.; "Price of Death" 1972-Ital. (Chester Conway); "Showdown for a Badman" 1972-Ital.; "Fighting Fists of Shanghai Joe" 1973-Ital. (Staurt); "Return of Shanghai Joe" 1974-Ger./Ital.; "Genius" 1975-Ital./Fr./Ger. (Doc Foster).

Kinsolving, Lee (1938-12/4/74). TV: *Black Saddle*—"Client: Banke" 4-11-59 (Dick Banks); *Have Gun Will Travel*—"The Sons of Aaron Murdock" 5-9-59 (Jamie Murdock); *The Rifleman*—"Boomerang" 6-23-59 (Tim Elder); *Zane Grey Theater*—"The Release" 4-17-61 (Dee Pritcher); *Gunsmoke*—"The Other Half" 5-30-64 (Jay Bartell/Jess Bartell).

Kipling, Richard (1880-3/11/65). Films: "Santa Fe Trail" 1940 (Army Doctor); "The Furies" 1950.

Kippen, Manart (1892-10/12/47). Films: "Flame of the Barbary Coast" 1945 (Dr. Gorman).

Kirby, Bruce (1925-). Films: "J.W. Coop" 1971 (Diesel Driver); "Bad Jim" 1990 (Customer). ¶TV: *Bonanza*—"Child" 9-22-68 (Chad), "The Big Jackpot" 1-18-70 (Simms).

Kirby, Bruno (1949-). Films: "City Slickers" 1991 (Ed Furillo).

Kirby, David (1880-4/4/54). Films: "Marked Men" 1919 (Warden "Bruiser" Kelly); "The Ranger and the Law" 1921 (Bootlegger); "The Mask of Lopez" 1923 (Angel Face Harry); "The Dangerous Coward" 1924 (Red O'Hara); "Lightning Romance" 1924 (Red Taylor); "The Dangerous Dude" 1925; "The Man Who Played Square" 1925 (Piggy); "Ridin' the Wind" 1925 (Sheriff Lacy); "Burning Brides" 1928 (Crabs); "The Upland Rider" 1928 (Red).

Kirby, Jay. Films: "Undercover Man" 1942 (Breezy Travers); "Border Patrol" 1943 (Johnny Travers); "Colt Comrades" 1943 (Johnny Nelson); "Hoppy Serves a Writ" 1943 (Johnny Travers); "The Leather Burners" 1943 (John Travers); "Lost Canyon" 1943 (Breezy Travers); "Marshal of Reno" 1944; "Sheriff of Las Vegas" 1944; "Zorro's Black Whip" 1944-serial (Randolph Meredith); "Rockin' in the Rockies" 1945 (Rusty); "Wagon Wheels Westward" 1945; "Conquest

of Cheyenne" 1946; "Days of Buffalo Bill" 1946; "King of the Forest Rangers" 1946-serial (Hale); "Oklahoma Badlands" 1948 (Ken Rawlins); "Outlaw Brand" 1948; "Partners of the Sunset" 1948; "Son of God's Country" 1948 (Frank Thornton); "Sundown Riders" 1948 (Sundown Rider).

Kirby, Newt. Films: "Roarin' Lead" 1936; "Rough Ridin' Rhythm" 1937 (Detective Thomas); "Wildcat of Tucson" 1941.

Kirk, Jack (1895-9/3/48). Films: "The Stolen Ranch" 1926 (Slim); "Fighting Thru" 1930; "Riders of the Rio" 1931 (Tim); "The Cheyenne Cyclone" 1932; "Gold" 1932; "Lawless Valley" 1932; "Tombstone Canyon" 1932; "Gun Law" 1933; "King of the Arena" 1933; "The Lone Avenger" 1933; "Outlaw Justice" 1933; "The Telegraph Trail" 1933; "The Trail Drive" 1933; "When a Man Rides Alone" 1933 (Man in Saloon); "The Dude Ranger" 1934; "Fighting Through" 1934 (Singer); "Honor of the Range" 1934; "In Old Santa Fe" 1934; "The Sundown Trail" 1934; "Terror of the Plains" 1934 (Cowboy); "Thunder Over Texas" 1934; "Between Men" 1935 (Henchman); "Circle of Death" 1935; "The Cowboy and the Bandit" 1935; "Gallant Defender" 1935; "His Fighting Blood" 1935; "Law of the 45's" 1935 (Singing Wrangler); "Lawless Range" 1935; "Lawless Riders" 1935; "Moonlight on the Prairie" 1935; "The New Frontier" 1935; "Outlaw Rule" 1935 (Tubby Jones); "The Rider of the Law" 1935; "Rough Riding Ranger" 1935; "Stormy" 1935; "Thunderbolt" 1935; "Westward Ho" 1935; "Bold Caballero" 1936; "The Cattle Thief" 1936; "The Fugitive Sheriff" 1936; "Guns and Guitars" 1936; "King of the Pecos" 1936; "The Lawless Nineties" 1936; "The Lonely Trail" 1936 (Trooper); "Oh, Susanna!" 1936; "The Singing Cowboy" 1936 (Lane); "Song of the Gringo" 1936 (Cowboy); "Sundown Saunders" 1936; "Too Much Beef" 1936 (Player); "The Traitor" 1936 (Outlaw); "Valley of the Lawless" 1936; "Vigilantes Are Coming" 1936-serial (Rancher); "Arizona Gunfighter" 1937; "The California Mail" 1937; "Cherokee Strip" 1937; "Come on Cowboys" 1937; "Courage of the West" 1937; "Doomed at Sundown" 1937; "Git Along, Little Dogies" 1937; "Gun Lords of Stirrup Basin" 1937 (Jack); "The Gun Ranger" 1937; "Guns of the Pecos" 1937; "Gunsmoke Ranch" 1937 (Sheriff); "Hit the Saddle" 1937 (Rancher); "Outlaws of the Prairie"

1937; "Range Defenders" 1937; "Riders of the Whistling Skull" 1937 (Deputy); "Ridin' the Lone Trail" 1937 (Henchman); "Round-Up Time in Texas" 1937; "Springtime in the Rockies" 1937; "Trail of Vengeance" 1937 (Rancher); "Wild Horse Rodeo" 1937; "Yodelin' Kid from Pine Ridge" 1937 (Cattleman); "Zorro Rides Again" 1937-serial; "Billy the Kid Returns" 1938; "Border Wolves" 1938; "Ghost Town Riders" 1938 (Slim); "Guilty Trails" 1938 (Stage Driver); "Heroes of the Hills" 1938; "The Last Stand" 1938 (Ed); "The Lone Ranger" 1938-serial (Gunman #1); "Outlaw Express" 1938 (Phelps); "Outlaws of Sonora" 1938; "Overland Stage Raiders" 1938; "Pals of the Saddle" 1938 (Sheriff); "Prairie Justice" 1938 (Boots); "Prairie Moon" 1938; "Rhythm of the Saddle" 1938; The Singing Outlaw" 1938; "Under Western Stars" 1938; "Colorado Sunset" 1939; "Come on, Rangers" 1939; "Cowboys from Texas" 1939; "Frontier Pony Express" 1939; "Henry Goes Arizona" 1939 (Squinty Potts); "Honor of the West" 1939 (Heck Clayborn); "The Lone Ranger Rides Again" 1939-serial (Sam Lawson); "The Night Riders" 1939; "The Phantom Stage" 1939 (Stage Driver); "Rough Riders' Round-Up" 1939 (Jim Horn); "Rovin' Tumbleweeds" 1939; "Wyoming Outlaw" 1939; "Adventures of Red Ryder" 1940-serial (Hank); "The Carson City Kid" 1940; "Covered Wagon Days" 1940; "Gaucho Serenade" 1940; "Lone Star Raiders" 1940 (Bixby); "Melody Ranch" 1940; "One Man's Law" 1940; "Pioneers of the Frontier" 1940; "Pioneers of the West" 1940; "Ride, Tenderfoot, Ride" 1940; "Rocky Mountain Rangers" 1940 (Harris); "Texas Terrors" 1940; "The Trail Blazers" 1940; "The Tulsa Kid" 1940 (Sheriff); "Under Texas Skies" 1940; "Young Bill Hickok" 1940; "Bad Man of Deadwood" 1941 (Clem); "Gangs of Sonora" 1941; "In Old Cheyenne" 1941; "Jesse James at Bay" 1941 (Rufe Balder); "Kansas Cyclone" 1941 (Jim Turner); "Nevada City" 1941; "Pals of the Pecos" 1941; "Prairie Pioneers" 1941 (Al); "Sheriff of Tombstone" 1941; "Sierra Sue" 1941 (Sheriff); "The Singing Hill" 1941; "Under Fiesta Stars" 1941; "Home in Wyomin'" 1942; "In Old California" 1942; "Jesse James, Jr." 1942 (Sheriff); "The Lone Prairie" 1942; "Man from Cheyenne" 1942; "Pardon My Gun" 1942; "The Phantom Plainsmen" 1942 (Joe); "Romance on the Range" 1942; "Sheriff of Sage Valley" 1942; "South of Santa Fe" 1942 (Benton);

"Sunset Serenade" 1942 (Sheriff Praskins); "A Tornado in the Saddle" 1942; "Valley of Hunted Men" 1942; "West of Tombstone" 1942 (Sheriff); "Westward Ho" 1942 (Deputy); "Beyond the Last Frontier" 1943; "Canyon City" 1943; "Carson City Cyclone" 1943 (Dave); "Death Valley Manhunt" 1943 (Ward); "Hail to the Rangers" 1943 (Sheriff Ward); "Hands Across the Border" 1943; "In Old Oklahoma" 1943; "King of the Cowboys" 1943 (Bartender); "The Man from the Rio Grande" 1943 (Curyl Wells); "Overland Mail Robbery" 1943; "Raiders of Sunset Pass" 1943 (George Meehan); "Santa Fe Scouts" 1943; "Silver Spurs" 1943; "Beneath Western Skies" 1944 (Wainwright); "Bordertown Trail" 1944; "Call of the Rockies" 1944; "Cheyenne Wildcat" 1944; "Code of the Prairie" 1944 (Boggs); "Cowboy and the Senorita" 1944 (Sheriff); "Death Valley Rangers" 1944 (Johnson); "Firebrands of Arizona" 1944 (Memphis); "Hidden Valley Outlaws" 1944; "The Lights of Old Santa Fe" 1944; "Marshal of Reno" 1944; "Mojave Firebrand" 1944; "Outlaws of Santa Fe" 1944; "Pride of the Plains" 1944 (Steve Craig); "The San Antonio Kid" 1944; "Sheriff of Las Vegas" 1944; "Sheriff of Sundown" 1944 (Andy Craig); "Silver City Kid" 1944; "Stagecoach to Monterey" 1944; "Tucson Raiders" 1944; "The Vigilantes Ride" 1944 (Lafe Andrews); "Zorro's Black Whip" 1944-serial (Marshal Wetherby); "Bandits of the Badlands" 1945; "Colorado Pioneers" 1945; "Corpus Christi Bandits" 1945 (Alonzo Adams); "Lone Texas Ranger" 1945; "Phantom of the Plains" 1945; "Sheriff of Cimarron" 1945 (John Burton); "Sunset in El Dorado" 1945; "Texas Panhandle" 1945; "The Topeka Terror" 1945 (Mr. Green); "Trail of Kit Carson" 1945; "Wagon Wheels Westward" 1945; "California Gold Rush" 1946; "Conquest of Cheyenne" 1946; "The Desert Horseman" 1946 (Sheriff); "Gunning for Vengeance" 1946; "Home on the Range" 1946 (Benson); "King of the Forest Rangers" 1946-serial (Holmes); "The Phantom Rider" 1946-serial (Deputy Sheriff Turner); "Sun Valley Cyclone" 1946; "Terrors on Horseback" 1946; "Homesteaders of Paradise Valley" 1947; "Law of the Canyon" 1947; "Oregon Trail Scouts" 1947 (Stage Coach Driver); "Son of Zorro" 1947-serial (Charlie Grimes/Blake); "The Adventures of Frank and Jesse James" 1948-serial (Casey, the Stage Driver); "The Bold Frontiersman" 1948

(Rancher); "Dangers of the Canadian Mounted" 1948-serial (A.L. Thomas); "The Gallant Legion" 1948; "Oklahoma Badlands" 1948 (Marsden).

Kirk, Joe (1903-4/16/75). Films: "The Big Sombrero" 1949; "Lost in Alaska" 1952 (Henchman).

Kirk, Phyllis (1926-). Films: "The Iron Mistress" 1952 (Ursula de Veramendi); "Thunder Over the Plains" 1953 (Norah); "Canyon Crossroads" 1955 (Katherine Rand); "Johnny Concho" 1956 (Mary Dark). ¶TV: *Western Theatre*—Host 1959; *Zane Grey Theater*—"Setup" 3-3-60 (Ann Bagley).

Kirk, Tommy (1941-). Films: "Old Yeller" 1957 (Travis Coates); "Savage Sam" 1963 (Travis Coates); "My Name Is Legend" 1975. ¶TV: *Frontier*—"The Devil and Doctor O'Hara" 2-5-56 (Mike Austin); *Gunsmoke*—"Cow Doctor" 9-8-56 (Jerry Pitcher); *The Californians*—"Little Lost Man" 12-3-57 (Billy Kilgore).

Kirke, Donald (1902-5/18/71). Films: "The Fourth Horseman" 1933 (Thad Hurley); "Hidden Gold" 1933 (Edward Mortimer "Doc" Griffin); "Oh, Susanna!" 1936 (Flash Baldwin); "Ride 'Em Cowboy" 1936 (Sam Parker, Jr.); "Sunset of Power" 1936 (Page Cothran); "Range Defenders" 1937; "Smoke Tree Range" 1937 (Wirt Stone/El Capitan); "The Showdown" 1940 (Harry Cole); "Outlaws of Pine Ridge" 1942 (Jeff Cardeen); "Hoppy's Holiday" 1947 (Sheriff). ¶TV: *Maverick*—"The War of the Silver Kings" 9-22-57 (Crane), "Rope of Cards" 1-19-58 (1st Juror), "The People's Friend" 2-7-60 (Clayton).

Kirkham, Kathleen (1895-11/7/61). Films: "A Modern Musketeer" 1917 (Mrs. Moran); "The Sky Pilot" 1921 (Lady Charlotte); "Back to Yellow Jacket" 1922 (Carmen Ballantyne); "One-Eighth Apache" 1922 (Norma Biddle).

Kirkland, David (1878-10/27/64). Films: "Western Hearts" 1912; "Broncho Billy Gets Square" 1913.

Kirkland, Hardee (1864-2/20/29). Films: "Without Compromise" 1922 (Judge Gordon Randolph); "Hell's Hole" 1923 (Warden); "Quicksands" 1923 (Farrell); "The Arizona Romeo" 1925 (John Wayne).

Kirkland, Muriel (1903-9/26/71). Films: "To the Last Man" 1933 (Molly Hayden).

Kirkland, Sally (1953-). Films: "Blue" 1968 (Sara Lambert); "Bite the Bullet" 1975 (Honey).

Kirkpatrick, Jess (1898-8/9/76). Films: "Star in the Dust" 1956 (Ed Pardee); "Tomboy and the Champ" 1961 (Model T. Parson). ¶TV: *Gunsmoke*—"How to Cure a Friend" 11-10-56 (Mr. Teeters), "Poor Pearl" 12-22-56 (Frank Teeters), "Crackup" 9-14-57 (Mr. Teeters), "Laughing Gass" 3-29-58 (Mr. Teeters), "The Dealer" 4-14-62 (Barney), "Carter Caper" 11-16-63 (Teeters); *Have Gun Will Travel*—"The Colonel and the Lady" 11-23-57; *Zane Grey Theater*—"A Man to Look Up To" 11-29-57 (Clem), "Threat of Violence" 5-23-58 (William Newman); *Fury*—"The Witch" 1-16-60; *The Law of the Plainsman*—"Common Ground" 2-11-60 (Timmins), "The Show-Off" 3-17-60 (Deputy Timmins); *Wagon Train*—"The Ah Chong Story" 6-14-61 (Proprietor), "The Fenton Canaby Story" 12-30-63, "The Duncan McIvor Story" 3-9-64; *The Virginian*—"Run Away Home" 4-24-63; *Branded*—"Price of a Name" 5-23-65 (Pete); *Laredo*—"The Heroes of San Gill" 12-23-65; *Iron Horse*—"Dry Run to Glory" 1-6-68 (Engineer).

Kirkwood, Jack (1895-8/2/64). Films: "Fancy Pants" 1950 (Mike Floud).

Kirkwood, James (1883-8/21/63). Films: "Comata, the Sioux" 1909; "Fools of Fate" 1909; "The Honor of the Family" 1909; "The Indian Runner's Romance" 1909; "Leather Stocking" 1909; "The Mended Lute" 1909; "The Mountaineer's Honor" 1909; "The Redman's View" 1909; "The Renunciation" 1909; "The Mountain Rat" 1914; "The Branding Iron" 1920 (Pierre Landis); "Bob Hampton of Placer" 1921 (Bob Hampton); "The Eagle's Feather" 1923 (John Trent); "The Spoilers" 1930 (Joe Dextry); "A Holy Terror" 1931 (William Drew); "My Pal, the King" 1932 (Count DeMar); "Rainbow Trail" 1932 (Venters); "Lady from Cheyenne" 1941 (Politician); "The Untamed Breed" 1948 (Sheriff); "The Doolins of Oklahoma" 1949 (Rev. Mears); "Red Stallion in the Rockies" 1949; "The Nevadan" 1950 (Tex); "Stage to Tucson" 1950 (Sheriff Pete Deuce); "Man in the Saddle" 1951 (Sheriff Medary); "Santa Fe" 1951; "The Last Posse" 1953 (Judge Parker); "Winning of the West" 1953; "The Woman They Almost Lynched" 1953 (Old Man); "Passion" 1954 (Don Rosendo). ¶TV: *The Lone Ranger*—"Double Jeopardy" 9-7-50; *The Cisco Kid*—"Vigilante Story" 10-20-51, "Quicksilver Murder" 1-12-52; *The Roy Rogers Show*—"The Hermit's Secret" 5-1-52, "Blind

Justice" 12-14-52; *Lawman*—"The Runaway" 2-1-59 (Ben); *The Rifleman*—"The Horse Traders" 2-9-60 (Colonel Bourbon).

Kirtley, Virginia (1883-8/19/56). Films: "On the Border" 1915; "A Law Unto Himself" 1916; "The Regeneration of Jim Halsey" 1916.

Kiser, Terry (1939-). Films: "Last Ride of the Dalton Gang" TVM-1979 (Nafius).

Kitchen, Dorothy. Films: "Barely Reasonable" 1926; "The Horse Trader" 1927; "Broncho Twister" 1927 (Daisy Mason); "The Pride of Peacock" 1927; "The Rest Cure" 1927; "The Bantam Cowboy" 1928 (Nan Briggs); "Breed of the Sunsets" 1928 (Marie Alvaro); "The Riding Renegade" 1928 (Janet Reynolds).

Kitosch, Cole. *see* Dell'Acqua, Alberto.

Kjellin, Alf (1920-4/5/88). Films: "The Iron Mistress" 1952 (Philippe de Cabanal); "Zandy's Bride" 1974.

Kleeb, Helen (1907-). Films: "A Day of Fury" 1956 (Mrs. McLean); "Friendly Persuasion" 1956 (Old Lady); "Curse of the Undead" 1959 (Dora); "The Hallelujah Trail" 1965 (Henrietta); "Blue" 1968 (Elizabeth Parker). ¶TV: *Frontier*—"The Texicans" 1-8-56 (Mrs. Reed); *Gunsmoke*—"Unmarked Grave" 8-18-56 (Mrs. Randolph), "Hanging Man" 4-19-58 (Mrs. Sawyer), "Doctor's Wife" 10-24-64 (Mrs. Gort), "Bohannan" 9-25-72 (Dorcas Wentzel); *Rough Riders*—"Paradise Gap" 4-16-59 (Sister Eugenia); *Wanted—Dead or Alive*—"The Healing Woman" 9-12-59 (Mag Blake); *Trackdown*—"Quiet Night in Porter" 9-23-59 (Mrs. Dooley); *The High Chaparral*—"Ebenezer" 11-1-68 (Mr. Mulroy); *Here Come the Brides*—"Marriage Chinese Style" 4-9-69; *Bonanza*—"A Lawman's Lot Is Not a Happy One" 10-5-69 (Mrs. Franklin), "Forever" 9-12-72 (Miss Grayson).

Klein, Ricky. TV: *The Restless Gun*—"Strange Family in Town" 1-20-58 (Peter Hoffman), "Multiply One Boy" 12-8-58 (Michael); *Tales of Wells Fargo*—"Scapegoat" 5-5-58 (Stan Tyles); *Wagon Train*—"The Old Man Charvanaugh Story" 2-18-59 (Duane Lerner).

Klein, Robert (1880-12/21/60). Films: "The Senor's Silver Buckle" 1915; "The Challenge of the Law" 1920 (Proprietor of General); "Do and Dare" 1922 (Yellow Crow); "The Man from Hell's River" 1922 (Lo-

pente); "The Desert Outlaw" 1924 (Mad McTavish).

Klein, Robert (1941-). TV: *Bonanza*—"The Hanging Posse" 11-28-59; *Rawhide*—"Incident at Quivira" 12-14-62 (Bugler); *Laramie*—"The Betrayers" 1-22-63.

Klemperer, Werner (1919-). TV: *Maverick*—"Comstock Conspiracy" 12-29-57 (Alex Jennings); *Gunsmoke*—"Sunday Supplement" 2-8-58 (Clifton Bunker); *Have Gun Will Travel*—"Fragile" 10-31-59 (Etienne Ledoux), "The Uneasy Grave" 6-3-61 (Leander Johnson); *The Alaskans*—"Gold Fever" 1-17-60 (Baron); *Overland Trail*—"Vigilantes of Montana" 4-3-60 (Arnold Braun); *Rawhide*—"Incident of the Music Maker" 5-20-60 (Kessle); *The Dakotas*—"Trial at Grand Forks" 3-25-63 (Colonel von Bleist).

Kleven, Max (1934-). Films: "Billy the Kid vs. Dracula" 1966.

Kline, Brady (1892-11/18/46). Films: "The Painted Desert" 1931; "Wanderer of the Wasteland" 1935 (Dealer at Dice Game).

Kline, James. Films: "Comes a Horseman" 1978 (Ralph Cole); "The Electric Horseman" 1979 (Tommy); "Tom Horn" 1980 (Arlo Chance). ¶TV: *Laramie*—"Trapped" 5-14-63 (Mills.

Kline, Kevin (1947-). Films: "Silverado" 1985 (Paden).

Klugman, Jack (1922-). TV: *Gunsmoke*—"Buffalo Man" 1-11-58 (Earl Ticks); *The Virginian*—"Roar from the Mountain" 1-8-64 (Charles Mayhew).

Knaggs, Skelton (1911-4/30/55). Films: "The Paleface" 1948 (Pete).

Knapp, Charles (1919-10/22/95). Films: "Butch and Sundance: The Early Days" 1979 (the Telegrapher); "The Gambler" TVM-1980 (Shuster).

Knapp, Evelyn (1908-6/10/81). Films: "River's End" 1930 (Miriam); "The Vanishing Frontier" 1932 (Carol Winfield); "In Old Santa Fe" 1934 (Lila Miller); "Speed Wings" 1934 (Mary Stuart); "Hawaiian Buckaroo" 1938 (Paula Harrington); "Rawhide" 1938 (Peggy Gehrig).

Knapp, Robert (1924-). Films: "Outlaw's Son" 1957 (Deputy Marshal Ralph Striker); "Tomahawk Trail" 1957 (Pvt. Barrow); "The Rawhide Trail" 1958 (Farley Durand); "Gunmen from Laredo" 1959 (Gil Reardon). ¶TV: *The Roy Rogers Show*—"Head for Cover" 10-21-56, "Paleface Justice" 11-18-56, "Fighting Sire" 12-16-56; *Broken Arrow*—"Son of Cochise" 12-17-57 (Lt. Neal); *Bonanza*—"The Newcomers" 9-26-59 (John Pennington), "Winter Kill" 3-28-71 (Denman); *Laramie*—"Night of the Quiet Man" 12-22-59 (Brodie), "The Last Battleground" 4-16-63 (Gibbs); *Death Valley Days*—"The Devil's Due" 1-26-60 (Tom Dixon); *Black Saddle*—"Means to an End" 1-29-60 (Emory Parsons); *The Rifleman*—"A Time for Singing" 3-8-60 (Dan Hewitt); *Gunsmoke*—"Cody's Code" 1-20-62 (Sam Dukes), "Old York" 5-4-63 (Clayton), "Kate Heller" 9-28-63 (Driver), "The Hanging" 12-31-66 (Warren), "Time of the Jackals" 1-13-69 (Dan Foley), "Chato" 9-14-70 (Surgeon), "Mirage" 1-11-71 (Deputy); *Cheyenne*—"Wanted for the Murder of Cheyenne Bodie" 12-10-62 (Rankin).

Knapp, Shorty Jack. Films: "Flaming Snow" 1927; "King of the Rodeo" 1929 (Shorty).

Knapp, Wilfred. Films: "Johnny Concho" 1956 (Pearson). ¶TV: *Gunsmoke*—Regular 1955-56 (Mr. Botkin).

Knell, David. Films: "Belle Starr" TVM-1980 (Ed Reed); "September Gun" TVM-1983 (Jason Farragut). ¶TV: *Best of the West*—11-5-81 (Jimmy-Jack); *Bret Maverick*—Regular 1981-82 (Rodney).

Knight, Charles (1885-1/24/79). Films: "Pals of the Saddle" 1938 (English Musician).

Knight, Charlotte (1894-5/16/77). TV: *Ford Theater*—"Sudden Silence" 10-10-56; *Maverick*—"Ghost Riders" 10-13-57 (Mrs. Clemmer), "A Rage for Vengeance" 1-12-58 (Mrs. Walker); *Zane Grey Theater*—"Blood Red" 1-29-61 (Mrs. Scully); *The Big Valley*—"Boy into Man" 1-16-67.

Knight, Don (1933-). Films: "Something Big" 1971 (Tommy MacBride); "Hitched" TVM-1973 (Reese); "The Apple Dumpling Gang" 1975 (John Wintle). ¶TV: *The Big Valley*—"In Silent Battle" 9-23-68 (Sgt. Sean McQuade), "The Other Face of Justice" 3-31-69 (Sam Jester); *The Virginian*—"The Mustangers" 12-4-68 (Cal Hobson), "A King's Ransom" 2-25-70 (Henry); *Bonanza*—"Five Candles" 3-2-69 (Bristol Toby),"Blind Hunch" 11-21-71 (Clayton), "The Bucket Dog" 12-19-72 (Tim Riley); *Lancer*—"Lifeline" 5-19-70 (McGovern); *Kung Fu*—"A Praying Mantis Kills" 3-22-73 (Hap Darrow); *The Buffalo Soldiers*—Pilot 5-26-79 (Renegade); *Father Murphy*—"The Piano" 1-19-82 (Toby).

Knight, Edward. Films: "The Night Rider" TVM-1979. ¶TV: *Cheyenne*—"The Young Fugitives" 10-23-61 (Kinsey); *Great Adventure*—"Wild Bill Hickok—the Legend and the Man" 1-3-64 (Brady); *Wild Wild West*—"The Night of the Falcon" 11-10-67 (Gen. Lassiter); *Bonanza*—"A Place to Hide" 3-19-72 (Sgt. Brown).

Knight, Fuzzy (1901-2/23/76). Films: "Sunset Pass" 1933 (Willie Willard); "To the Last Man" 1933 (Jeff Morley); "Under the Tonto Rim" 1933 (Tex); "The Last Round-Up" 1934 (Bunko McGee); "Home on the Range" 1935 (Cracker Williams); "Trails of the Wild" 1935 (Windy); "Wanderer of the Wasteland" 1935 (Deputy Scott); "Arizona Mahoney" 1936; "The Plainsman" 1936 (Dave); "Rio Grande Romance" 1936 (Elmer); "Song of the Gringo" 1936 (Tony); "Song of the Trail" 1936 (Pudge); "Wildcat Trooper" 1936 (Pat); "Courage of the West" 1937 (Hank Givens); "Border Wolves" 1938 (Clem Barrett); "Cowboy and the Lady" 1938 (Buzz); "The Last Stand" 1938 (Pepper); "The Singing Outlaw" 1938 (Longhorn); "Where the West Begins" 1938 (Buzzy); "Chip of the Flying U" 1939 (Weary); "Desperate Trails" 1939 (Cousin Willie); "Oklahoma Frontier" 1939 (Windy Day); "The Oregon Trail" 1939-serial (Deadwood Hawkins); "Union Pacific" 1939 (Cookie); "Bad Man from Red Butte" 1940 (Spud Jenkins); "Brigham Young—Frontiersman" 1940 (Pete); "Law and Order" 1940 (Deadwood); "My Little Chickadee" 1940 (Cousin Zeb); "Pony Post" 1940 (Shorty); "Ragtime Cowboy Joe" 1940 (Joe Bushberry); "Riders of Pasco Basin" 1940 (Luther); "The Singing Dude" 1940-short; "Son of Roaring Dan" 1940 (Tick Belden); "West of Carson City" 1940 (Banjo); "Arizona Cyclone" 1941 (Muleshoe); "Badlands of Dakota" 1941 (Hurricane Harry); "Boss of Bullion City" 1941 (Burt); "Bury Me Not on the Lone Prairie" 1941; "The Cowboy and the Blonde" 1941 (Skeeter); "Law of the Range" 1941 (Chaparral); "Man from Montana" 1941 (Grubby); "The Masked Rider" 1941 (Patches); "Rawhide Rangers" 1941 (Porky); "The Shepherd of the Hills" 1941 (Mr. Palestrom); "Boss of Hangtown Mesa" 1942 (Dr. J. Wellington Dingle); "Deep in the Heart of Texas" 1942 (Happy T. Snodgrass); "Fighting Bill Fargo" 1942 (Grubby); "Little Joe, the Wrangler" 1942 (Little Joe Smith); "Old Chisholm Trail" 1942 (Polario); "The Silver Bullet" 1942; "Stagecoach Buckaroo" 1942 (Clem); "Arizona

Trail" 1943 (Kansas); "Apache Trail" 1943 (Juke); "Cheyenne Roundup" 1943 (Cal Cawkins); "Frontier Law" 1943 (Ramblin' Rufe Randall); "The Lone Star Trail" 1943 (Angus MacAngus); "Raiders of San Joaquin" 1943 (Eustace Clairmont); "Tenting To-night on the Old Camp Ground" 1943 (Si Dugan); "Boss of Boomtown" 1944 (Chatter); "Cowboy and the Senorita" 1944 (Fuzzy); "Marshal of Gunsmoke" 1944 (Glow-Worm); "Oklahoma Raiders" 1944 (Banjo); "The Old Texas Trail" 1944 (Pinky); "Riders of the Santa Fe" 1944 (Bullseye); "The Singing Sheriff" 1944 (Fuzzy); "Trail to Gunsight" 1944 (Horatius); "Trigger Trail" 1944 (Echo); "Bad Men of the Border" 1945; "Beyond the Pecos" 1945; "Code of the Lawless" 1945 (Bonanza); "Frisco Sal" 1945 (Hallelujah); "Frontier Gal" 1945 (Fuzzy); "Renegades of the Rio Grande" 1945 (Trigger Bidwell); "Senorita from the West" 1945; "Trail to Vengeance" 1945 (Hungry); "Gun Town" 1946 (Ivory); "Gunman's Code" 1946; "The Lawless Breed" 1946; "Rustler's Roundup" 1946 (Pinky); "Adventures of Gallant Bess" 1948 (Woody); "Apache Chief" 1949 (Nevada Smith); "Rimfire" 1949 (Porky); "Colorado Ranger" 1950 (Tony); "Crooked River" 1950 (Deacon); "Fast on the Draw" 1950 (Deacon); "Hills of Oklahoma" 1950 (Jigg); "Hostile Country" 1950 (Deacon); "Marshal of Heldorado" 1950 (Mayor Deacon); "West of the Brazos" 1950 (Deacon); "Canyon Raiders" 1951; "Gold Raiders" 1951 (Sheriff Wade); "Lawless Cowboys" 1951 (Smithers); "Nevada Badmen" 1951; "Skipalong Rosenbloom" 1951 (Sneaky Pete); "Stage to Blue River" 1951 (Texas); "Stagecoach Driver" 1951; "Wanted Dead or Alive" 1951; "Fargo" 1952; "The Gunman" 1952; "Kansas Territory" 1952 (Fuzzy); "Night Raiders" 1952 (Texas); "Oklahoma Annie" 1952 (Larry); "Rancho Notorious" 1952 (Barber); "Rodeo" 1952 (Jazbo Davis); "Topeka" 1953 (Pop Harrison); "Vigilante Terror" 1953; "The Naked Hills" 1956 (Pitch Man); "Three Thousand Hills" 1959 (Sally the Cook); "The Bounty Killer" 1965 (Luther); "Waco" 1966 (Telegraph Operator); "Hostile Guns" 1967 (Buck). ¶TV: *The Gene Autry Show*—"The Sheriff of Santa Rosa" 12-24-50 (Sagebrush), "T.N.T." 12-24-50 (Sagebrush), "The Raiders" 4-14-51 (Sagebrush), "Double Barrelled Vengeance" 4-21-51 (Sagebrush); *Wild Bill Hickok*—"Old Cowboys Never Die" 12-16-52, "Battle Line" 1-6-53;

The Outlaws—"The Quiet Killer" 12-29-60 (Isaac Miller); *Lawman*—"The Inheritance" 3-5-61 (Morris); *The Tall Man*—"Trial by Fury" 4-14-62 (Johnny Red).

Knight, Gladys (1944-). Films: "Desperado" TVM-1987 (Mona Lisa).

Knight, Harlan. Films: "The Fighting Sheriff" 1931 (Calico); "Whistlin' Dan" 1932 (July); "To the Last Man" 1933 (Grandpa Spelvin); "The Roaring West" 1935-serial (Clem Morgan).

Knight, Lillian (1881-5/16/46). Films: "Margy of the Foothills" 1916.

Knight, Patricia. Films: "The Fabulous Texan" 1947 (Josie Allen).

Knight, Sandra. Films: "Terror at Black Falls" 1962. ¶TV: *The Restless Gun*—"Better Than a Cannon" 2-9-59 (Heide); *Tales of Wells Fargo*—"The Legacy" 3-9-59 (Sally Gannon); *Man from Blackhawk*—"The Search for Cope Borden" 4-15-60 (Jenny); *Tate*—"Home Town" 6-8-60 (Mary Eden); *Laramie*—"Drifter's Gold" 11-29-60 (Wilma), "The Last Journey" 10-31-61 (Mary Cole); *The Rebel*—"The Actress" 2-5-61 (Ruth Revere); *The Tall Man*—"A Time to Run" 4-7-62 (Lucy Potter).

Knight, Shirley (1937-). Films: "Friendly Persuasion" TVM-1975 (Eliza Birdwell); "Children of the Dust" TVM-1995 (Aunt Bertha). ¶TV: *Buckskin*—Regular 1958-59 (Mrs. Newcomb); *Bronco*—"The Baron of Broken Lance" 1-13-59 (Kathy), "The Invaders" 1-23-61 (Molly Durrock); *Rawhide*—"Incident in No Man's Land" 6-12-59; *The Texan*—"Stampede" 11-2-59, "Showdown at Abilene" 11-9-59; *Maverick*—"The Ice Man" 1-29-61 (Nancy Powers); *Lawman*—"The Trial" 5-7-61 (Tandis); *The Virginian*—"The Man from the Sea" 12-26-62 (Susan Morrow), "Lost Yesterday" 2-3-65 (Clara Malone); *Alias Smith and Jones*—"The Ten Days That Shook Kid Curry" 11-4-72 (Amy Martin); *Nakia*—"Pete" 12-21-74 (Faye Arnold).

Knight, Ted (1924-8/26/86). Films: "Thirteen Fighting Men" 1960 (Samuel); "Two Rode Together" 1961 (Lt. Upton). ¶TV: *Gunsmoke*—"Print Asper" 5-23-59 (Jay Rabb); *Lawman*—"The Ugly Man" 2-14-60 (the Ugly Man); *Bonanza*—"Elizabeth, My Love" 5-27-61, "Peace Officer" 2-6-66 (Mayor); *The Virginian*—"Throw a Long Rope" 10-3-62 (Skelly), "The Final Hour" 5-1-63; *Wild Wild West*—"The Night of the Kraken" 11-1-68 (Daniel).

Knott, Adelbert (1859-5/3/33). Films: "Danger" 1923 (Blance).

Knott, Lydia (1866-3/30/55). Films: "The Whipping Boss" 1924 (Jim's Mother); "Overland Bound" 1929 (Ma Winters); "Men Without Law" 1930 (Mrs. Healy); "Rocky Rhodes" 1934 (Mrs. Rhodes); "Fair Warning" 1937 (Miss Willoughby).

Knotts, Don (1924-). Films: "The Shakiest Gun in the West" 1968 (Jesse W. Heywood); "The Apple Dumpling Gang" 1975 (Theodore Ogilvie); "Hot Lead and Cold Feet" 1978 (Denver Kid); "The Apple Dumpling Gang Rides Again" 1979 (Theodore). ¶TV: *Bob Hope Chrysler Theatre*—"The Reason Nobody Hardly Ever Seen a Fat Outlaw in the Old West Is as Follows:" 3-8-67 (the Curley Kid).

Knowland, Alice (1879-5/27/30). Films: "Rustling a Bride" 1919 (School Mistress).

Knowles, Patrick (1911-). Films: "Heart of the North" 1938 (Jim Montgomery); "Sin Town" 1942 (Wade Crowell); "The Way West" 1967 (Col. Grant); "Chisum" 1970 (Tunstall). ¶TV: *Maverick*—"The Wrecker" 12-1-57 (Paul Carthew), "Guatemala City" 1-31-60 (Sam Bishop); *Walt Disney Presents*—"Elfego Baca: The Griswold Murder" 2-20-59 (Mr. Cunningham); *Wagon Train*—"The Vivian Carter Story" 3-11-59 (Bert Johnson); *Have Gun Will Travel*—"Chapagne Safari" 12-5-59 (Trevington), "Fogg Bound" 12-3-60 (Phileas Fogg), "The Savages" 3-16-63 (August Pireaux); *Klondike*—"Sitka Madonna" 2-6-61 (Carson); *Whispering Smith*—"Stain of Justice" 6-12-61 (Judge Wilbur Harrington).

Knox, Alexander (1907-4/25/95). Films: "Man in the Saddle" 1951 (Will Isham); "Shalako" 1968-Brit./Fr. (Henry Clarke); "Villa Rides" 1968 (President Francisco Madero).

Knox, Elyse (1917-). Films: "Sheriff of Tombstone" 1941 (Mary Carson); "Moonlight and Cactus" 1944 (Louise Ferguson).

Knox, Mona. Films: "Thundering Caravans" 1952 (Alice Scott).

Knox, Patricia. Films: "Border Roundup" 1942; "Trail of Terror" 1944 (Belle Blaine); "Flaming Bullets" 1945; "Gentlemen with Guns" 1946 (Matilda); "Prairie Badmen" 1946 (Linda Latimar); "Singing Spurs" 1948; "The James Brothers of Missouri" 1950-serial (Belle Calhoun).

Knudsen, Peggy (1923-7/11/80). Films: "Copper Canyon" 1950

(Cora). ¶TV: *Wyatt Earp*—"The Kansas Lily" 2-11-58 (Lily Reeve); *Bat Masterson*—"A Personal Matter" 1-28-59 (Louisa Carey), "The Court Martial of Major Mars" 1-12-61 (Lottie Tremaine); *Tombstone Territory*—"Payroll to Tombstone" 3-27-59 (Amy Ward).

Knudson, Barbara. Films: "The Lady from Texas" 1951 (Mabel). ¶TV: *Sky King*—"Triple Exposure" 5-11-52 (Gloria Blane); *Hopalong Cassidy*—"Frontier Law" 6-21-52; *Death Valley Days*—"Jimmy Dayton's Treasure" 3-10-54; *The Gene Autry Show*—"Stage to San Dimas" 10-8-55; *The Lone Ranger*—"The Wooden Rifle" 9-23-56, "Hot Spell in Panamint" 11-22-56; *Sergeant Preston of the Yukon*—"Out of the Night" 11-28-57 (Laura Hope); *Fury*—"The Baby Sitters" 2-8-58 (Martha Mitchell); *Daniel Boone*—"Crisis by Fire" 1-27-66 (Kate Tolliver).

Kobe, Gail. Films: "Gunsmoke in Tucson" 1958 (Katy Porter). ¶TV: *Cheyenne*—"The Bounty Killer" 10-23-56 (Della), "The Long Search" 4-22-58 (Dell Carver); *Sugarfoot*—"The Ghost" 1-28-58 (Molly); *Gunsmoke*—"Dirt" 3-1-58 (Polly Troyman), "Bank Baby" 3-20-65 (Grace Fisher), "The Moonstone" 12-17-66 (Madge), "The Intruders" 3-3-69 (Ellie Decker); *Trackdown*—"The House" 3-21-58 (Penny Adams), "The Boy" 3-28-58 (Penny Adams), "Sunday's Child" 11-21-58 (Cindy); *Tombstone Territory*—"The Assassin" 5-21-58 (Nellie Cashman); *Zane Grey Theater*—"The Accuser" 10-30-58 (Widow); *The Californians*—"Bella Union" 1-20-59 (Charlotte Tuttle); *Wagon Train*—"The Vincent Eaglewood Story" 4-15-59 (Ericka Hennepin); *The Law of the Plainsman*—"Full Circle" 10-8-59; *Tales of Wells Fargo*—"The Lat Mayor Brown" 3-7-60 (Kate Brown); *The Rebel*—"Night on a Rainbow" 5-29-60 (Carrie Evans), "The Ballad of Danny Brown" 4-9-61 (Emily); *Maverick*—"Marshal Maverick" 3-11-62 (Theodora Rush); *Rawhide*—"A Woman's Place" 3-30-62 (Dr. Louise Amadon), "Incident of Judgment Day" 2-8-63 (Agnes); *Laramie*—"Gun Duel" 12-25-62, "The Dispossessed" 2-19-63 (Madge); *Empire*—"End of an Image" 1-15-63 (Janet Rainey); *Have Gun Will Travel*—"Two Plus One" 4-6-63 (Francine); *The Virginian*—"Run Quiet" 11-13-63 (Ruth Ferris); *A Man Called Shenandoah*—"End of a Legend" 2-7-66 (Ellie); *Cimarron Strip*—"The Beast That Walks Like a Man" 11-30-67; *Daniel Boone*—"The Plague That Came to Ford's Run" 10-

31-68 (Amanda Wharton), "The Kidnaping" 1-22-70 (Letitia).

Kobi, Michi. TV: *The Californians*—"The Lost Queue" 10-29-57 (Wan), "Deaty by Proxy" 3-18-58 (Lili), "Gold-Tooth Charlie" 3-10-59 (Mai Sung).

Koch, Marianne. Films: "A Fistful of Dollars" 1964-Ital./Ger./Span. (Marisol); "A Place Called Glory" 1966-Span./Ger. (Jade Grande); "Sunscorched" 1966-Span./Ger. (Anna-Lisa); "Who Killed Johnny R.?" 1966-Ital./Span. (Jill); "Clint the Stranger" 1968-Ital./Span./Ger. (Julie); "Last Ride to Santa Cruz" 1969-Ger./Fr.

Koenig, Walter (1936-). TV: *The Men from Shiloh*—"Crooked Corner" 10-28-70 (Paul Erlich).

Kohler, Jr., Fred (-1/7/93). Films: "The Pecos Kid" 1935 (Donald Ellis/the Pecos Kid); "Toll of the Desert" 1936 (Bill Carson); "Roaring Timber" 1937 (Curley); "Billy the Kid Returns" 1938 (Matson); "Lawless Valley" 1938 (Jeff Marsh); "Texas Stampede" 1939 (Wayne Cameron); "Two-Gun Sheriff" 1941 (Keller); "Boss of Hangtown Mesa" 1942 (Clem); "Nevada City" 1941; "Lone Star Ranger" 1942 (Red); "Raiders of the Range" 1942 (Plummer); "Western Mail" 1942 (Lucky); "Calling Wild Bill Elliott" 1943 (John Culver); "The Big Bonanza" 1944 (Roberts); "Unconquered" 1947 (Sergeant); "The Gallant Legion" 1948; "Loaded Pistols" 1948 (Bill Otis); "The Gay Amigo" 1949 (Brack); "Range Justice" 1949 (Stoner); "Tough Assignment" 1949 (Grant); "The Baron of Arizona" 1950 (Demming); "Desperadoes of the West" 1950-serial (Plummer); "Gold Strike" 1950-short; "Twilight in the Sierras" 1950 (Mason); "Spoilers of the Plains" 1951 (Brooks); "Born to the Saddle" 1953; "Daniel Boone, Trail Blazer" 1957 (Kenton); "Terror in a Texas Town" 1958 (Weed); "Thirteen Fighting Men" 1960 (Corey). ¶TV: *The Lone Ranger*—"Rustler's Hideout" 10-13-49; *The Cisco Kid*—"Counterfeit Money" 1-27-51, "Big Switch" 2-10-51, "Convict Story" 2-17-51, "Oil Land" 2-24-51, "Railroad Land Rush" 3-17-51, "The Will" 3-24-51, "Cattle Quarantine" 3-31-51, "Renegade Son" 4-7-51, "False Marriage" 4-14-51, "Wedding Blackmail" 4-21-51; *Wild Bill Hickok*—"Homer Atchison" 9-11-51, "Pony Express vs. Telegraph" 9-25-51, "Medicine Show" 12-25-51, "Sheriff of Buckeye" 6-30-53; *Judge Roy Bean*—"The Defense Rests" 6-1-56 (Prosecutor), "Lone Star Killer" 8-

1-56 (Kell); *The Restless Gun*—"The Torn Flag" 5-5-58 (Sheriff Tornwell); *The Texan*—"Private Account" 4-6-59 (Fred Jackson).

Kohler, Sr., Fred (1888-10/28/38). Films: "The Great Round Up" 1920; "The Honor of the Range" 1920; "The Lone Ranger" 1920; "The Red Hot Trail" 1920; "Cyclone Bliss" 1921 (Jack Hall); "The Stampede" 1921 (Steve Morton); "His Back Against the Wall" 1922 (Arizona Pete); "The Son of the Wolf" 1922 (Malemute Kid); "Trimmed" 1922 (Young Bill Young); "Without Compromise" 1922 (Cass Blake); "Hell's Hole" 1923 (Prisoner); "The Red Warning" 1923 (Tom Jeffries); "Shadows of the North" 1923 (Ray Brent); "Three Who Paid" 1923 (Jim Quade); "Fighting Fury" 1924 (Two-Finger Larkin); "The Iron Horse" 1924 (Deroux); "North of Hudson Bay" 1924 (Armand LeMoire); "The Prairie Pirate" 1925 (Aguilar); "Riders of the Purple Sage" 1925 (Metzger); "The Thundering Herd" 1925 (Follansbee); "The Devil's Masterpiece" 1927 (Reckless Jim Regan); "The Gay Defender" 1927 (Jake Hamby); "Open Range" 1927 (Sam Hardman); "Shootin' Irons" 1927 (Dick Hardman); "The Vanishing Pioneer" 1928 (Sheriff Murdock); "Stairs of Sand" 1929 (Boss Stone); "Tide of Empire" 1929 (Cannon); "Hell's Heroes" 1930 (Wild Bill Kearney); "The Lash" 1930 (Peter Harkness); "The Light of the Western Stars" 1930 (Stack); "Under a Texas Moon" 1930 (Bad Man); "Fighting Caravans" 1931 (Lee Murdock); "99 Wounds" 1931 (Monty Vale); "Woman Hungry" 1931 (Jampen); "Rider of Death Valley" 1932 (Lew Grant); "Texas Bad Man" 1932 (Gore Hampton); "Wild Horse Mesa" 1932 (Rand, the Horse Trapper); "The Fourth Horseman" 1933 (Softy Jones); "Under the Tonto Rim" 1933 (Murther); "The Fiddlin' Buckaroo" 1934 (Wolf); "Honor of the Range" 1934 (Rawhide); "The Last Round-Up" 1934 (Sam Gulden); "West of the Pecos" 1934 (Breen Sawtelle); "The Man from Hell" 1934 (Mayor Anse McCloud/Trig Kelso); "Border Brigands" 1935 (Conyda); "Horses' Collars" 1935-short (Double Deal Decker); "Lightning Triggers" 1935 (Bull Thompson/Big Bill Russell); "Stormy" 1935 (Craig); "Trails End" 1935 (Wild Bill Holman); "Wilderness Mail" 1935 (Lobo McBain); "Arizona Mahoney" 1936 (Gil Blair); "For the Service" 1936 (Bruce Howard); "The Plainsman" 1936 (Jack); "The Texas Rangers" 1936 (Higgins);

"Vigilantes Are Coming" 1936-serial (Jason Burr); "Heart of the West" 1937 (Barton); "Forbidden Valley" 1938 (Matt Regan); "Lawless Valley" 1938 (Tom Marsh); "The Painted Desert" 1938 (Fawcett).

Kohlmar, Lee (1873-5/14/46). Films: "Ruggles of Red Gap" 1935 (Red Gap Jailer); "Ramona" 1936 (Woodcarver Lang).

Kohner, Susan (1936-). Films: "The Last Wagon" 1956 (Jolie); "Trooper Hook" 1957 (Consuela). ¶TV: *Wagon Train*—"The Charles Avery Story" 12-13-57 (the Chief's Daughter); *Temple Houston*—"Toll the Bell Slowly" 10-17-63 (Ellena Romolo); *Rawhide*—"Incident at Ten Trees" 1-2-64 (Abbie Bartlett).

Kolb, Clarence (1875-11/25/64). Films: "Wells Fargo" 1937 (John Butterfield); "Gold Is Where You Find It" 1938 (Sen. Walsh); "The Law West of Tombstone" 1938 (Sam Kent).

Kolker, Henry (1874-7/15/47). Films: "Gloria's Romance" 1916-serial; "Massacre" 1934 (Senator Woolsey); "Cowboy and the Lady" 1938 (Mr. Smith); "Union Pacific" 1939 (Asa M. Barrows); "The Parson of Panamint" 1941 (Judge Arnold Mason).

Komack, Jimmie (1930-). TV: *Zane Grey Theater*—"They Were Four" 3-15-57 (Whitey); *Wagon Train*—"The Julia Gage Story" 12-18-57 (Buck).

Komant, Carolyn. TV: *Maverick*—"The Cactus Switch" 1-15-61 (Flossie); *Lawman*—"The Promise" 6-11-61 (Nancy Fuller).

Komai, Tetsu (1894-8/10/70). Films: "Border Devils" 1932 (the General); "Texas Bad Man" 1932 (Yat Gow).

Konopka, Magda (1943-). Films: "A Sky Full of Stars for a Roof" 1968-Ital.; "Night of the Serpent" 1969-Ital.; "Blindman" 1971-Ital. (Sweet Mama).

Konrad, Dorothy (1912-). Films: "Tickle Me" 1965 (Mrs. Dabney); "Blue" 1968 (Alma Wishoff). ¶TV: *Lawman*—"The Four" 10-1-61 (Mrs. Bangle); *Gunsmoke*—"Lover Boy" 10-5-63 (Mom); *Bonanza*—"The Stalker" 11-2-69 (Mrs. Pardee); *Daniel Boone*—"Run for the Money" 2-19-70.

Koock, Guich (1944-). Films: "Mackintosh & T.J." 1975; "Substitute Wife" TVM-1994 (Mr. Van Der Meer). ¶TV: *The Chisholms*—2-9-80 (Frank O'Neal).

Kopecky, Milos. Films: "Lemonade Joe" 1966-Czech. (Horace Bad-man).

Kopins, Karen. Films: "The Tracker" TVM-1988.

Korda, Maria (1940-). Films: "The Fastest Guitar Alive" 1967 (Tanya).

Korff, Arnold (1871-6/2/44). Films: "Men of the North" 1930 (John Ruskin).

Korman, Harvey (1927-). Films: "Blazing Saddles" 1974 (Hedley Lamarr). ¶TV: *Empire*—"Pressure Lock" 12-4-62 (Bunce); *Walt Disney Presents*—"Gallegher" 1965-67 (Brownie); *F Troop*—"Bye, Bye, Balloon" 9-22-66 (Von Zeppel); *Wild Wild West*—"The Night of the Big Blackmail" 9-27-68 (Baron Hinterstoisser).

Kornman, Mary (1917-6/1/73). Films: "Desert Trail" 1935 (Anne); "Smokey Smith" 1935 (Bess).

Kortman, Robert "Bob" (1887-3/13/67). Films: "Desert Gold" 1914; "The Golden Trail" 1915; "The Narrow Trail" 1918 (Moose Halloran); "Hell's Hinges" 1919 (Henchman); "Montana Bill" 1921; "Another Man's Boots" 1922 (Sly Stevens); "Gun Shy" 1922 (Buck Brady); "The Lone Hand" 1922 (Curly); "Travelin' On" 1922 (Gila); "Wolf Pack" 1922 (the Wolf); "The Devil Horse" 1926 (Chief Prowling Wolf); "Hills of Peril" 1927 (Red); "Blood Will Tell" 1928 (Carloon); "The Lone Rider" 1929; "Perilous Paths" 1929; "A Rider of the Sierras" 1929; "The Thrill Hunter" 1929; "The Virginian" 1929 (Henchman); "The Lone Defender" 1930-serial (Jenkins); "Branded" 1931; "Cimarron" 1931 (Killer); "The Conquering Horde" 1931 (Digger Hale); "Lightning Warrior" 1931-serial (Wells); "The Vanishing Legion" 1931-serial (Larno); "Between Fighting Men" 1932; "Cornered" 1932 (Pete Fleming, the Foreman); "The Fighting Fool" 1932 (Dutch Charley); "Gold" 1932 (Outlaw); "The Last of the Mohicans" 1932-serial; "The Night Rider" 1932 (Steve); "White Eagle" 1932 (Sheriff); "Come on Tarzan" 1933 (Spike Collins); "The Fugitive" 1933 (Dutch Walton); "King of the Arena" 1933 (Bargoff); "The Phantom Thunderbolt" 1933 (One Shot Mallory); "Rainbow Ranch" 1933 (Marvin Black); "Sunset Pass" 1933 (Dick); "Terror Trail" 1933 (Tim McPherson); "The Trail Drive" 1933 (Blake); "The Fiddlin' Buckaroo" 1934; "The Fighting Code" 1934 (Carter); "Mystery Mountain" 1934-serial (Hank); "Smoking Guns" 1934 (Biff); "When a Man Sees Red" 1934

(Spook); "The Arizonian" 1935; "Branded a Coward" 1935; "The Crimson Trail" 1935 (Tom); "Ivory-Handled Gun" 1935 (Alf Steen); "Lawless Range" 1935; "The Miracle Rider" 1935-serial (Longboat); "Swifty" 1935 (Clam Givens); "Wild Mustang" 1935 (Utah Evans); "Feud of the West" 1936 (Hawk Decker); "Heroes of the Range" 1936 (Slick); "The Lonely Trail" 1936 (Hays); "Romance Rides the Range" 1936 (Clem Allen); "Rose of the Rancho" 1936 (Kincaid Henchman); "Song of the Saddle" 1936; "The Unknown Ranger" 1936; "Vigilantes Are Coming" 1936-serial (Boris Petroff); "Winds of the Wasteland" 1936 (Cherokee Joe); "Black Aces" 1937 (Wolf Whalen); "Ghost Town Gold" 1937 (Monk); "Law for Tombstone" 1937; "The Luck of Roaring Camp" 1937 (Yuba Bill); "Ranger Courage" 1937 (Toady); "The Rangers Step In" 1937; "Sandflow" 1937 (Quayle); "Smoke Tree Range" 1937 (Paso Wells); "Texas Trail" 1937 (Hawks); "Wild West Days" 1937-serial (Trigger); "Zorro Rides Again" 1937-serial (Trelliger); "Forbidden Valley" 1938 (Cowboy); "Law of the Texan" 1938 (Quinn); "The Law West of Tombstone" 1938; "The Lone Ranger" 1938-serial (Trooper); "The Mysterious Rider" 1938 (Morris); "The Painted Trail" 1938; "Panamint's Bad Man" 1938; "Renegade Ranger" 1938 (Idaho); "Stagecoach Days" 1938; "West of Rainbow's End" 1938 (Speck); "Arizona Legion" 1939; "Oklahoma Frontier" 1939 (J.W. Sanders); "The Oklahoma Kid" 1939 (Juryman); "Renegade Trail" 1939 (Haskins); "Timber Stampede" 1939 (Pete Larkin); "Adventures of Red Ryder" 1940-Serial (One-Eye Chapin); "Hidden Gold" 1940; "Law and Order" 1940 (Henchman); "Stagecoach War" 1940; "Boss of Bullion City" 1941; "Bury Me Not on the Lone Prairie" 1941; "Fugitive Valley" 1941 (Langdon); "Law of the Range" 1941; "The Lone Rider Rides On" 1941; "Rawhide Rangers" 1941 (Dirk); "The Shepherd of the Hills" 1941 (Hand); "Twilight on the Trail" 1941; "Wide Open Town" 1941; "Bandit Ranger" 1942; "Fighting Bill Fargo" 1942; "Jesse James, Jr." 1942; "The Sundown Kid" 1942 (Luke Reed); "Thundering Hoofs" 1942; "The Avenging Rider" 1943 (Harris); "Black Hills Express" 1943 (Dutch); "California Joe" 1943 (Bradshaw); "Days of Old Cheyenne" 1943 (Slim Boyd); "The Leather Burners" 1943; "Boss of Rawhide" 1944; "Call of the Rockies" 1944; "Death Valley

Rangers" 1944; "Forty Thieves" 1944 (Joe Garms); "Guns of the Law" 1944; "Outlaws of Santa Fe" 1944 (Ed); "The Pinto Bandit" 1944; "Saddle Leather Law" 1944; "The Vigilantes Ride" 1944 (Drag); "West of the Rio Grande" 1944; "The Whispering Skull" 1944; "Wyoming Hurricane" 1944; "Along Came Jones" 1945 (Posse); "Border Badmen" 1945; "Marked for Murder" 1945; "Rough Ridin' Justice" 1945 (Pete); "Stagecoach Outlaws" 1945 (Matt); "Frontier Gunlaw" 1946; "Gunning for Vengeance" 1946; "Landrush" 1946 (Sackett); "Unconquered" 1947 (Frontiersman); "The Paleface" 1948 (Onlooker); "Whispering Smith" 1948 (Gabby Barton); "Streets of Laredo" 1949 (Ranger); "Copper Canyon" 1950 (Bill Newton); "Fancy Pants" 1950 (Henchman); "Flaming Feather" 1952 (Lafe).

Korvin, Charles (1907-). TV: *Zorro*—Regular 1958 (the Eagle).

Kosleck, Martin (1907-1/16/94). TV: *The Rifleman*—"Old Tony" 4-8-63 (Joe); *Wild Wild West*—"The Night of the Diva" 3-7-69 (Igor).

Koslo, Paul (1944-). Films: "Scandalous John" 1971 (Pipes); "The Daughters of Joshua Cabe" TVM-1972 (Deke Wetherall); "Joe Kidd" 1972 (Roy); "Rooster Cogburn" 1975 (Luke); "Scott Free" TVM-1976 (Al); "The Sacketts" TVM-1979 (Kid Newton); "Heaven's Gate" 1980 (Mayor); "The Gambler, Part II— The Adventure Continues" TVM-1983 (Holt); "Conagher" TVM-1991. ¶TV: *Bearcats!*—9-16-71 (Billy Joe); *Gunsmoke*—"In Performance of Duty" 11-18-74 (Cory); *How the West Was Won*—"The Enemy" 2-5-79 (Jobe); *Bret Maverick*—"A Night at the Red Ox" 2-23-82 (Fletcher).

Kosslyn, Jack. Films: "High Plains Drifter" 1973 (Saddlemaker). ¶TV: *Rawhide*—"Incident of the Reluctant Bridegroom" 11-30-62 (Bert the Bartender).

Kotto, Yaphet (1937-). Films: "Five Card Stud" 1968 (Little George); "Man and Boy" 1971 (Nate Hodges); "Desperado" TVM-1987 (Bede). ¶TV: *The Big Valley*—"The Iron Box" 11-28-66 (Lobo Brown); "The Buffalo Man" 12-25-67 (Damien); *Death Valley Days*—"A Man Called Abraham" 3-11-67 (Abraham); *Cowboy in Africa*—"Incident at Derati Wells" 9-25-67 (Musa); *Bonanza*—"Child" 9-22-68 (Child Barnett); *Daniel Boone*—"Big, Black and Out There" 11-14-68 (Luke), "Jonah" 2-13-69 (Jonah); *The High Chaparral*—"The Buffalo Soldiers" 11-22-68

(Sergeant Major Creason); *Gunsmoke*—"The Scavengers" 11-16-70 (Piney Biggs).

Koufax, Sandy (1935-). TV: *Colt .45*—"Impasse" 1-31-60 (Johnny).

Kovack, Nancy (1935-). Films: "The Wild Westerners" 1962 (Rose Sharon); "The Great Sioux Massacre" 1965 (Libbie Custer); "The Outlaws Is Coming!" 1965 (Annie Oakley).

Kovacs, Ernie (1919-1/12/62). Films: "North to Alaska" 1960 (Frankie Canon). ¶TV: *Shotgun Slade*—"The Salted Mine" 11-24-59 (Hack).

Kove, Martin (1947-). Films: "The White Buffalo" 1977 (Jack McCall); "The Gambler V: Playing for Keeps" TVM-1994 (Black Jack Ketchum); "Wyatt Earp" 1994 (Ed Ross); "Wyatt Earp: Return to Tombstone" TVM-1994 (Bad Jack Dupree). ¶TV: *Gunsmoke*—"In Performance of Duty" 11-18-74.

Kowal, Jon. TV: *Gunsmoke*—"The Bounty Hunter" 10-30-65 (Rancher), "Stranger in Town" 11-20-67 (Shamrock Casey), "The Avenger" 11-27-72 (Barfly Joe); *Iron Horse*—"The Dynamite Driver" 9-19-66 (Trailman).

Kowal, Mitchell (1916-5/2/71). Films: "River of No Return" 1954. ¶TV: *The Lone Ranger*—"Drink of Water" 10-26-50; *The Cisco Kid*—"Extradition Papers" 9-12-53, "Son of a Gunman" 10-10-53; *Maverick*—"Point Blank" 9-29-57 (Fletcher); *The Restless Gun*—"The Outlander" 4-21-58 (Waco); *Rough Riders*—"Shadows of the Past" 11-27-58 (Buller); *Have Gun Will Travel*—"Love and a Bad Woman" 3-26-60 (Cowboy).

Kozak, Heidi. TV: *Dr. Quinn, Medicine Woman*—Pilot 1-1-93 (Emily), "Law of the Land" 1-16-93 (Emily), "Portraits" 5-22-93 (Emily).

Krah, Marc (1906-9/25/73). Films: "Call of the Klondike" 1950 (Mencheck).

Kramer, Al. Films: "The Oklahoman" 1957 (Wild Line). ¶TV: *Maverick*—"The Wrecker" 12-1-57 (Jerome Braus); *The Rebel*—"Panic" 11-1-59 (Dobbs), "The Guard" 1-8-61 (Jake).

Kramer, Bert. TV: *Sara*—Regular 1976 (Emmet Ferguson); *Paradise*—"The Holstered Gun" 11-3-88 (Marshal Walker).

Kramer, Stepfanie (1956-). TV: *Cliffhangers*—"The Secret Empire" 1979 (Tara).

Kramer, Wright (1875-10/20/59). Films: "The Showdown" 1940 (Colonel White).

Kray, Walter (-7/3/89). Films: "Apache Warrior" 1957; "Fort Massacre" 1958 (Chief). ¶TV: *Two Faces West*—"The $10,000 Reward" 4-17-61; *Daniel Boone*—"The Allegiances" 9-22-66 (Chenrogan); *Bonanza*—"The Wormwood Cup" 4-23-67 (Caleb).

Krebs, Nita (1905-1/18/91). Films: "The Terror of Tiny Town" 1938 (the Vampire).

Kreig, Frank. Films: "Dallas" 1950 (Politician). ¶TV: *Wanted—Dead or Alive*—"Jason" 1-30-60 (Bartender); *Lawman*—"Cornered" 12-11-60 (Waters); *Gunsmoke*—"Friend" 1-25-64 (Barkeep).

Kreski, Connie (1949-). Films: "The Trackers" TVM-1971 (Becky Paxton).

Kreuger, Kurt (1917-). TV: *Wild Wild West*—"The Night of the Falcon" 11-10-67 (Alex Heindorf).

Krieger, Lee (1919-12/22/67). TV: *Gunsmoke*—"Innocence" 12-12-64 (Carl Beck), "The Prodigal" 9-25-67 (Eli); *The Big Valley*—"The Great Safe Robbery" 11-21-66 (Station Agent), "The Haunted Gun" 2-6-67 (Hodges), "Price of Victory" 2-13-67 (O'Rafferty), "Night in a Small Town" 10-9-67, "Shadow of a Giant" 1-29-68; *The Virginian*—"Stacey" 2-28-68 (Janie), "Incident at Diablo Crossing" 3-12-69 (Marcy).

Krige, Alice (1955-). Films: "Dream West" TVM-1986 (Jessie Benton Fremont).

Kristen, Marta (1945-). Films: "Savage Sam" 1963 (Lisbeth Searcy). ¶TV: *Wagon Train*—"The Wanda Snow Story" 1-17-65 (Wanda Snow).

Kristofferson, Kris (1936-). Films: "Pat Garrett and Billy the Kid" 1973 (Billy the Kid); "Heaven's Gate" 1980 (Marshal James Averill); "The Last Days of Frank and Jesse James" TVM-1986 (Jesse James); "Stagecoach" TVM-1986 (Billy "Ringo" Williams); "The Tracker" TVM-1988 (Nobel Adams); "Miracle in the Wilderness" TVM-1991 (Jericho Adams).

Kriza, John (1919-8/18/75). TV: *Omnibus*—"Billy the Kid" 11-8-53 (Billy the Kid).

Kroeger, Berry (1912-1/4/91). Films: "Fighting Man of the Plains" 1949 (Cliff Bailey); "The Battles of Chief Pontiac" 1952 (Col. Von Weber); "Yellowneck" 1955 (Plunkett). ¶TV: *Bronco*—"The Burning Spring" 10-6-59 (Carl Hugo); *The Rifleman*—"Closer Than a Brother" 2-21-61 (Ansel Bain); *Bonanza*—"Elizabeth, My Love" 5-27-61 (Man-

dible); *The Tall Man*—"Legend of Billy" 12-9-61 (Dean Almond); *Daniel Boone*—"Bitter Mission" 3-30-67 (Governor of Virginia), "A Matter of Blood" 12-28-67 (William Creighton).

Kroger, John. TV: *Rawhide*—"Incident of the Haunted Hills" 11-6-59 (Phillips); *Wagon Train*—"The Albert Farnsworth Story" 10-12-60.

Krone, Fred. Films: "Apache Territory" 1958 (Styles); "Badman's Country" 1958; "The Firebrand" 1962 (Dickens); "Young Guns of Texas" 1963 (Pike); "Arizona Raiders" 1965 (Matt Edwards); "Convict Stage" 1965; "Fort Courageous" 1965; "War Party" 1965; "Young Fury" 1965; "The Great Bank Robbery" 1969; "The Life and Times of Judge Roy Bean" 1972 (Outlaw). ¶TV: *The Range Rider*—"The Border City Affair" 4-26-52; *The Texan*—"Law of the Gun" 9-29-58 (Fred Bray); *Johnny Ringo*—"The Gunslinger" 3-24-60 (Bill Broger); *Zane Grey Theater*—"Desert Flight" 10-13-60 (Clerk), "The Ox" 11-3-60; *Wyatt Earp*—"Miss Sadie" 12-20-60; *Maverick*—"Benefit of Doubt" 4-9-61 (Walt); *Laredo*—"Scourge of San Rosa" 1-20-67 (George McCord); *The High Chaparral*—"Shadow of the Wind" 1-10-69 (Ike Simes).

Kronen, Ben. TV: *Paradise*—"The Valley of Death" 2-8-91 (Minister).

Kruger, Fred (1913-12/5/61). TV: *The Restless Gun*—"Rink" 10-14-57 (Bank Clerk); *Maverick*—"The Brasada Spur" 2-22-59 (Cecil Barnes), "Cruise of the Cynthia B" 1-10-60 (Meacham); *The Deputy*—"The World Against Me" 11-26-60 (Grisby).

Kruger, Hardy (1928-). Films: "Montana Trap" 1976-Ger. (Potato Fritz).

Kruger, Harold "Stubby" (1897-10/7/65). Films: "Devil's Canyon" 1953 (Prisoner).

Kruger, Otto (1885-9/6/74). Films: "The Barrier" 1937 (Stark); "Duel in the Sun" 1946 (Mr. Langford); "High Noon" 1952 (Percy Mettrick); "The Last Command" 1955 (Stephen Austin). ¶TV: *The Rebel*—"Gun City" 12-27-59 (Ben Tully); *Frontier Circus*—"Lippizan" 10-19-61 (Gen. Fredric Jellich); *Bonanza*—"Elegy for a Hangman" 1-20-63 (Judge Harry Whitaker).

Kruger, Paul (1895-11/6/60). Films: "High, Wide and Handsome" 1937 (Man); "Wells Fargo" 1937 (Coachman); "Texas Rangers Ride

Again" 1940 (Laborer); "Viva Cisco Kid" 1940 (Jack); "They Died with Their Boots On" 1941 (Officer); "Broken Lance" 1954 (Bailiff).

Krugman, Lou (1914-8/8/92). TV: *Zane Grey Theater*—"Black Creek Encounter" 3-8-57 (Paco Morales); *Maverick*—"Relic of Fort Tejon" 11-3-57 (Ferguson), "Game of Chance" 1-4-59 (Murdock), "The Art Lovers" 10-1-61 (Larouche); *The Restless Gun*—"Imposter for a Day" 2-17-58 (Pat Kellway); *The Adventures of Rin Tin Tin*—"Border Incident" 3-28-58 (Sanchez); *Gunsmoke*—"Amy's Good Deed" 4-12-58 (Emmett Gold), "Buffalo Hunter" 5-2-59 (Tom Mercer), "Old York" 5-4-63 (Barkeep); *Zorro*—"The Fortune Teller" 6-18-59 (Defense Attorney); *Wyatt Earp*—"Lineup for Battle" 9-29-59; *Have Gun Will Travel*—"Chapagne Safari" 12-5-59; *Wanted—Dead or Alive*—"Triple Vise" 2-27-60; *Man from Blackhawk*—"The Harpoon Story" 5-6-60 (Dr. Trout); *Two Faces West*—"The Drought" 1-9-61; *The Loner*—"An Echo of Bugles" 9-18-65 (Bartender); *F Troop*—"The Day the Indians Won" 5-3-66 (Snake Eyes); *Pistols 'n' Petticoats*—1-28-67 (Smoking Horse); *Wild Wild West*—"The Night of the Deadly Bubble" 2-24-67 (Felix), "The Night of the Avaricious Actuary" 12-6-68 (Maitre'd).

Kruschen, Jack (1922-). Films: "Untamed Heiress" 1954 (Louie); "Carolina Cannonball" 1955 (Hogar); "Badlands of Montana" 1957 (Cavalry Sergeant); "Seven Ways from Sundown" 1960 (Becker); "McClintock" 1963 (Birnbaum); "Guardian of the Wilderness" 1976 (Madden, the Surveyor); "The Incredible Rocky Mountain Race" TVM-1977 (Jim Bridger). TV: *Gunsmoke*—"Spring Team" 12-15-56 (Jed); *Trackdown*—"The Kid" 12-12-58 (Milo York); *Sugarfoot*—"The Desperadoes" 1-6-59 (Sam Bolt); *The Rifleman*—"The Retired Gun" 1-20-59 (Clyde), "One Went to Denver" 3-17-59 (Sammy), "Trail of Hate" 9-27-60, "Baranca" 11-1-60; *Wanted—Dead or Alive*—"Railroaded" 3-14-59 (Fig), "The Hostage" 10-10-59 (Hunt Willis); *Rough Riders*—"Ransom of Rita Renee" 6-11-59 (Tully); *Bat Masterson*—"The Desert Ship" 7-15-59 (Ben Tarko); *The Law of the Plainsman*—"Clear Title" 12-17-59 (Doctor); *Death Valley Days*—"Eagle in the Rocks" 5-24-60 (Manuel Garcie); *The Westerner*—"Going Home" 12-16-60; *Bonanza*—"Big Shadow on the Land" 4-17-66 (Giorgio Rossi), "The Deed and the Dilemma" 3-26-67 (Giorgio Rossi), "The Sound of

Drums" 11-17-68 (Giorgio Rossi); *The Life and Times of Grizzly Adams*—5-4-77 (Metcalf), "Once Upon a Starry Night" 12-19-78 (Frostbite Foley).

Kubik, Alex. Films: "Stagecoach" TVM-1986 (Ike Plummer). TV: *Riding for the Pony Express*—Pilot 9-3-80 (Blue Hawk); *Paradise*—"A Gather of Guns" 9-10-89 (Deputy Virgil).

Kuenstle, Charles. Films: "Death of a Gunfighter" 1969 (Roy Brandt). TV: *Have Gun Will Travel*—"The Knight" 6-2-62 (Waco); *Gunsmoke*—"Pa Hack's Brood" 12-28-63 (Lonnie Hack), "My Father, My Son" 4-23-66 (Bernie Jeffords), "The Wrong Man" 10-29-66 (Wilton Kyle), "The Wreckers" 9-11-67 (Luke), "Hard Luck Henry" 10-23-67 (Homer Haggen), "Slocum" 10-21-68 (2nd Cowboy), "The Twisted Heritage" 1-6-69 (Elan Dagget), "The Devil's Outpost" 9-22-69 (Kelly), "MacGraw" 12-8-69 (Wilkes), "The Lost" 9-13-71 (Valjean Mather), "Phoebe" 2-21-72 (Hank McCall); *Shane*—"An Echo of Anger" 10-1-66 (Boon).

Kuhn, Mickey. Films: "Roaring Rangers" 1946; "Red River" 1948 (Matt as a Boy); "Broken Arrow" 1950 (Chip Slade); "The Last Frontier" 1955 (Luke).

Kulkovich, Henry. *see* Kulky, Henry.

Kulky, Henry (Henry Kulkovich) (1911-2/12/65). Films: "Northwest Outpost" 1947 (Peasant); "Jiggs and Maggie Out West" 1950 (Bomber); "Bandits of El Dorado" 1951 (Spade); "The Kid from Amarillo" 1951 (Zeno); "The Charge at Feather River" 1953 (Smiley); "Powder River" 1953 (Bartender); "Yukon Vengeance" 1954; "Sierra Stranger" 1957 (Matt); "The Gunfight at Dodge City" 1959 (Bartender); "Guns of the Timberland" 1960 (Logger). TV: *Wild Bill Hickok*—"Wrestling Story" 4-8-52, "Indians and the Delegates" 7-8-52, "Mountain Men" 2-3-53; *Sky King*—"Danger at the Saw Mill" 5-18-52 (Moose Tanner); *The Lone Ranger*—"Dan Reid's Fight for Life" 11-18-54 (Gus Gotwals); *The Texan*—"The Man Hater" 6-15-59; *Bonanza*—"Old Sheba" 11-22-64 (Bearcat).

Kulp, Nancy (1921-2/3/91). Films: "Shane" 1953 (Mrs. Howell); "Count Three and Pray" 1955 (Matty); "Shoot-Out at Medicine Bend" 1957; "The Night of the Grizzly" 1966 (Wilhelmina Peterson). TV: *Maverick*—"Full House" 10-25-59 (Waitress).

Kuluva, Will (1917-11/6/90). Films: "Viva Zapata!" 1952 (Lazaro). TV: *Bonanza*—"The Deadly Ones" 12-2-62 (General Diaz); *Wagon Train*—"The Link Cheney Story" 4-13-64 (Euchre Jones); *Death Valley Days*—"The Water Bringer" 4-23-66 (Martinez), "The Firebrand" 4-30-66 (Pio Pico); *Laredo*—"A Double Shot of Nepenthe" 9-30-66 (Doc Duvain); *Wild Wild West*—"The Night of the Infernal Machine" 12-23-66 (Zeno Barota); *Lancer*—"The Gifts" 10-28-69 (James Mumford).

Kunde, Al (1887-8/10/52). Films: "Santa Fe" 1951.

Kunde, Ann (1896-6/14/60). Films: "Hollywood Barn Dance" 1947 (Ma Tubb); "Jubal" 1956 (Girl).

Kunkel, George (1867-11/8/37). Films: "The Horse Thief" 1914; "The Navajo Ring" 1914; "Wards Claim" 1914; "The Legend of the Lone Tree" 1915; "The Man from the Desert" 1915; "The Sage Brush Girl" 1915; "The Dawn of Understanding" 1918 (Sheriff Jack Scott); "Unclaimed Goods" 1918 (Uncle Placer Jim Murphy); "Leave It to Susan" 1919 (Two-Gun Smith); "Forbidden Trails" 1920 (Sheriff Danforth); "Where Men Are Men" 1921 (Sheriff Grimes).

Kupcinet, Karyn (1941-11/30/63). TV: *Wide Country*—"A Cry from the Mountain" 1-17-63 (Barbara Rice).

Kurihara, Thomas. Films: "The Square Deal Man" 1917 (Anastacio); "Wolves of the Rail" 1918 (Pasquale Trilles).

Kusatsu, Clyde (1948-). Films: "The Frisco Kid" 1979. TV: *Kung Fu*—"Sun and Cloud Shadow" 2-22-73 (Ying's Son), "Arrogant Dragons" 3-14-74 (Lo Sing), "Blood of the Dragon" 9-14-74 (Han Su Lok), "Forbidden Kingdom" 1-18-75 (Po San); *Adventures of Brisco County, Jr.*—"The Brooklyn Dodgers" 2-11-94.

Kuter, Kay E. (1925-). Films: "A Time for Killing" 1967 (Owelson); "The Intruders" TVM-1970. TV: *Jim Bowie*—"Thieves' Market" 3-29-57 (Sykes), "The Lion's Cub" 3-14-58 (Molichucky); *Zorro*—"The Fortune Teller" 6-18-59 (Hernando); *Tales of Wells Fargo*—"The Train Robbery" 10-12-59 (Slim); *Bonanza*—"The Julia Bulette Story" 10-17-59; *The Texan*—"Trouble on the Trail" 11-23-59 (Shooter); *Riverboat*—"Landlubbers" 1-10-60 (Hoskins); *Overland Trail*—"First Stage to Denver" 5-1-60 (Saunders); *The Rifleman*—"The Lonesome Ride" 5-2-61 (Charv Banner); *Two Faces West*—"Day of Violence" 7-10-61; *The Tall Man*—"The Woman" 10-28-61 (Clarence); *Maverick*—"Marshal Maverick" 3-11-62 (1st Creditor); *Redigo*—"The Blooded Bull" 10-1-63 (Vulture); *Wild Wild West*—"The Night of the Howling Light" 12-17-65 (Caged Man); *Laredo*—"Sound of Terror" 4-7-66 (Ernie Venner); *The Virginian*—"A Bald-Faced Boy" 4-13-66 (Razz); *Cowboy in Africa*—"To Build a Beginning" 12-11-67 (B'Kuma); *Gunsmoke*—"Sarah" 10-16-72 (Warren), "The Town Tamers" 1-28-74 (McCurdy); *Kung Fu*—"Blood of the Dragon" 9-14-74 (Vinnie), "Ambush" 4-5-75 (Marshal).

Kuwa, George (1885-10/13/31). Films: "Rimrock Jones" 1918 (Woe Chong); "The Round Up" 1920 (Chinese Boy); "The Half-Breed" 1922 (Kito); "The Eternal Struggle" 1923 (Wo Long); "The Man from Wyoming" 1924 (Sing Lee Wah); "A Son of His Father" 1925 (Wing); "The Enchanted Hill" 1926 (Chan).

Kuznetzoff, Adia (1890-8/10/54). Films: "Let Freedom Ring" 1939 (Pole).

Kwan, Nancy (1938-). Films: "The McMasters" 1970 (Robin). ¶TV: *Kung Fu*—"The Centoph" 4-4-74 & 4-11-74 (Mayli Ho).

La Badie, Florence (1894-10/13/17). "Comata, the Sioux" 1909; "Fighting Blood" 1911; "The Indian Brothers" 1911.

LaBissoniere, Erin (1901-9/22/76). Films: "Gypsy of the North" 1928 (Jane); "The Storm" 1930.

Laborteaux, Matthew (1966-). Films: "Little House on the Prairie: Look Back to Yesterday" TVM-1983 (Albert Ingalls). ¶TV: *Little House on the Prairie*—Regular 1978-82 (Albert); *Paradise*—"The Coward" 4-7-90 (Sam DeWitt).

Laborteaux, Patrick (1965-). TV: *Little House on the Prairie*—Regular 1977-81 (Andy Garvey); *Paradise*—"The Gates of Paradise" 1-6-90 (Jerome), "Shadow of a Doubt" 3-3-90 (Jerome), "The Coward" 4-7-90 (Jerome).

Lacey, Adele (1914-7/3/53). Films: "Vanishing Men" 1932; "When a Man Rides Alone" 1933 (Ruth Davis).

Lacher, Taylor. Films: "Santee" 1973; "Nakia" TVM-1974 (Eddie); "Baker's Hawk" 1976 (Sweeney); "Last Ride of the Dalton Gang" TVM-1979 (Bill Dalton). ¶TV: *Nakia*—Regular 1974 (Deputy Hubbel Martin); *How the West Was Won*—

"The Rustler" 1-22-79 (Ferris); *Father Murphy*—"The Failed Priest" 1-26-82 (O'Bannion).

Lackaye, Ruth. Films: "The Girl Angle" 1917 (Mrs. Millikin); "The Yellow Bullet" 1917 (Mrs. Black); "Petticoats and Politics" 1918 (Mrs. Lou Winters).

Lackteen, Frank (1895-7/8/68). Films: "The Avenging Arrow" 1921-serial; "The Timber Queen" 1922-serial; "White Eagle" 1922-serial; "Leatherstocking" 1924-serial; "Idaho" 1925-serial; "The Pony Express" 1925 (Charlie Bent); "Desert Gold" 1926 (Yaqui); "The Last Frontier" 1926 (Pawnee Killer); "The Unknown Cavalier" 1926 (Bad Man); "Hawk of the Hills" 1927-serial (the Hawk); "Hell's Valley" 1931 (Don Francisco Fernando); Come on, Danger!" 1932 (Piute); "Heroes of the West" 1932-serial (Buckskin Joe); "Land of Wanted Men" 1932 (Lonie); "The Last Frontier" 1932-serial; "Texas Pioneers" 1932 (Scout); "Clancy of the Mounted" 1933-serial; "Rustlers' Roundup" 1933 (Bayhorse); "Treason" 1933 (Chet Dawson); "Wanderer of the Wasteland" 1935 (Half-Breed Indian); "Comin' Round the Mountain" 1936; "Rose of the Rancho" 1936 (Peon Spy); "Left-Handed Law" 1937; "The Girl and the Gambler" 1939 (Tomaso); "The Kansas Terrors" 1939 (Capt. Gonzales); "Union Pacific" 1939 (Indian); "The Gay Caballero" 1940 (Peon); "Lucky Cisco Kid" 1940 (Bandit); "Stagecoach War" 1940 (Twister Maxwell); "Frontier Badman" 1943 (Cherokee); "Moonlight and Cactus" 1944 (Ogala); "Frontier Gal" 1945 (Cherokee); "Under Western Skies" 1945 (Dan Boone); "Singin' in the Corn" 1946 (Medicine Man); "Oregon Trail Scouts" 1947 (Running Fox); "Trail of the Mounties" 1947; "The Cowboy and the Indians" 1949 (Blue Eagle); "The Mysterious Desperado" 1949 (Pedro); "Son of a Badman" 1949 (Piute); "Dakota Lil" 1950; "Indian Territory" 1950; "The Big Sky" 1952; "Desert Pursuit" 1952; "Flaming Feather" 1952; "Northern Patrol" 1953 (Dancing Horse); "Flesh and the Spur" 1957 (Indian Chief); "Requiem for a Gunfighter" 1965. ¶TV: *The Roy Rogers Show*—"The Silver Fox Hunt" 4-19-53; *Wild Bill Hickok*—"Daughter of Casey O'-Grady" 7-21-53; *The Adventures of Rin Tin Tin*—"Running Horse" 10-24-58 (Chieftain).

La Croix, Emile. Films: "A Woman's Man" 1920 (Joshua Bushby).

Lacy, Alva Marie. Films: "Fancy Pants" 1950 (Daisy); "Jack McCall, Desperado" 1953 (Hisega).

Lacy, Tom (1933-). Films: "The Mark of Zorro" TVM-1974 (Frey Felipe). ¶TV: *Gunsmoke*—"I Have Promises to Keep" 3-3-75 (Reverend Atkins).

Ladd, Alan (1913-1/29/64). Films: "Born to the West" 1937 (Inspector); "The Light of Western Stars" 1940 (Danny); "Whispering Smith" 1948 (Luke "Whispering" Smith); "Branded" 1951 (Choya); "Red Mountain" 1951 (Capt. Brett Sherwood); "The Iron Mistress" 1952 (Jim Bowie); "Shane" 1953 (Shane); "Drum Beat" 1954 (Johnny MacKay); "Saskatchewan" 1954 (Sgt. Thomas O'Rourke); "The Big Land" 1957 (Morgan); "The Badlanders" 1958 (Peter Van Hock); "The Proud Rebel" 1958 (John Chandler); "Guns of the Timberland" 1960 (Jim Hadley); "One Foot in Hell" 1960 (Mitch Barrett).

Ladd, Alana. Films: "Guns of the Timberland" 1960 (Jane Peterson); "Young Guns of Texas" 1963 (Lily Glendenning).

Ladd, David (1947-). Films: "The Big Land" 1957 (David Johnson); "The Proud Rebel" 1958 (David Chandler); "The Sad Horse" 1959 (Jackie Connors); "Catlow" 1971-Span. (Caxton). ¶TV: *Bonanza*—"Feet of Clay" 4-16-60 (Billy); *Zane Grey Theater*—"The Broken Wing" 2-9-61 (Thalian Kihlgren); *Wagon Train*—"The Terry Morrell Story" 4-25-62 (Terry Morrell); *The Quest*—"Dynasty of Evil" 1976.

Ladd, Diane (1932-). Films: "Macho Callahan" 1970 (Girl). ¶TV: *Wide Country*—"Step Over the Sky" 1-10-63 (Alma Prewitt); *Gunsmoke*—"Blue Heaven" 9-26-64 (Elena), "The Reward" 11-6-65 (Brian Forbes), "Sweet Billy, Singer of Songs" 1-15-66 (Lulu), "The Favor" 3-11-67 (Bonnie Mae Haley); *Daniel Boone*—"Seminole Territory" 1-13-66 (Ronda Cameron); *Shane*—"The Distant Bell" 9-10-66 (Amy Sloate); *The Big Valley*—"Boy into Man" 1-16-67 (Muriel Akely); *Dr. Quinn, Medicine Woman*—Pilot 1-1-93 (Charlotte Cooper), "Mike's Dream—A Christmas Tale" 12-18-93 (Charlotte Cooper).

Lafayette, Ruby (1844-4/3/35). Films: "Three Mounted Men" 1918 (Mrs. Masters); "Rustling a Bride" 1919 (Ruby); "Catch My Smoke" 1922 (Mrs. Archer); "The Phantom Horseman" 1924 (Maxwell's Mother).

Lafferty, Marcy. TV: *Barbary Coast*—"The Ballad of Redwing Jail" 9-29-75 (Tranquility Smith); *Big Hawaii*—"Graduation Eve" 10-26-77 (Susan Barlow).

La Fleur, Art. Films: "Maverick" 1994 (Poker Player). ¶TV: *Bret Maverick*—"The Not So Magnificent Six" 3-2-82 (Deacon Tippett); *Young Riders*—"Shadowmen" 5-21-92 (Pinkerton).

La Grasse, Jerome. Films: "Blue Blazes" 1926 (Matt Bunker); "The Grey Devil" 1926; "A Gentleman Preferred" 1928 (Lord Stanweight).

Lahr, Bert (1895-12/4/67). Films: "Rose Marie" 1954 (Barney McGorkle).

Laidlaw, Ethan (1899-5/25/63). Films: "No Man's Law" 1925 (Nick Alby); "The Wyoming Wildcat" 1925 (Rudy Kopp); "Born to Battle" 1926 (Trube); "The Masquerade Bandit" 1926 (Duncan); "Out of the West" 1926 (Bide Goodrich); "Wild to Go" 1926 (Jake Trumbull); "The Silent Rider" 1927 (Red Wender); "The Sonora Kid" 1927 (Tough Ryder); "Thunderbolt's Tracks" 1927 (Buck Moulton); "Danger Patrol" 1928 (Regina Jim Lawlor); "Rough Ridin' Red" 1928 (Cal Rogers); "The Big Diamond Robbery" 1929 (Chick); "Bride of the Desert" 1929 (Tom Benton); "The Little Savage" 1929 (Blake); "Outlawed" 1929 (McCasky); "The Virginian" 1929 (Posse Man); "Pardon My Gun" 1930 (Tex); "Dugan of the Badlands" 1931 (Dan Kirk); "The Fighting Marshal" 1931; "Gordon of Ghost City" 1933-serial (Pete); "Rainbow Riders" 1934; "Fighting Shadows" 1935 (Brannon); "Powdersmoke Range" 1935 (Fin Sharkey); "Ramona" 1936 (Bill); "Song of the Gringo" 1936; "Two in Revolt" 1936 (Bill Donlan); "Yellow Dust" 1936 (Bogan); "Fugitive from Sonora" 1937 (Hack Roberts); "Goofs and Saddles" 1937-short (Man); "One Man Justice" 1937; "Two-Fisted Sheriff" 1937 (Burke); "Border G-Man" 1938 (Curly); "Call the Mesquiteers" 1938; "Gun Law" 1938; "I'm from the City" 1938 (Jeff); "Law of the Plains" 1938 (J.N. Rider); "Rhythm of the Saddle" 1938 (Tex Robinson); "Allegheny Uprising" 1939 (Jim's Man); "Colorado Sunset" 1939; "Cowboys from Texas" 1939 (Duke Plummer); "Frontier Marshal" 1939 (Tough); "Home on the Prairie" 1939 (Carter); "Jesse James" 1939 (Barshee's Cohort); "The Night Riders" 1939 (Andrews); "The Return of the Cisco Kid" 1939; "Spoilers of the Range" 1939 (Bartender); "Three Texas Steers" 1939 (Morgan); "Union Pacific" 1939 (Irish Paddy); "Western Caravans" 1939 (Tip); "The Gay Caballero" 1940 (Bandit); "Law and Order" 1940 (Kurt Daggett); "Lucky Cisco Kid" 1940 (Henchman); "Northwest Mounted Police" 1940; "Son of Roaring Dan" 1940 (Matt Gregg); "Stage to Chino" 1940 (Wheeler); "The Tulsa Kid" 1940 (Nick); "Two-Fisted Rangers" 1940 (Joe); "Wagon Train" 1940 (Pat Hays); "Bury Me Not on the Lone Prairie" 1941; "Hands Across the Rockies" 1941; "Last of the Duanes" 1941 (Henchman); "Law of the Range" 1941 (Hobart); "Riders of Death Valley" 1941-serial; "Riders of the Badlands" 1941 (Bill); "Texas" 1941 (Henry's Handler); "Westward Ho-Hum" 1941-short; "Wyoming Wildcat" 1941; "Cowboy Serenade" 1942; "Keep Shooting" 1942-short; "Little Joe, the Wrangler" 1942 (Bit); "The Lone Star Vigilantes" 1942 (Benson); "Overland Mail" 1942-serial; "Riding Through Nevada" 1942; "Stagecoach Express" 1942 (Lou Hawkins); "Valley of the Sun" 1942 (Johnson); "Border Buckaroos" 1943 (Hank Dugan); "The Desperadoes" 1943 (Cass); "The Lone Star Trail" 1943 (Steve Bannister); "The Outlaw" 1943 (Deputy); "Marshal of Gunsmoke" 1944 (Larkin); "Oklahoma Raiders" 1944 (Williams); "Bad Men of the Border" 1945; "Blazing the Western Trail" 1945; "The Daltons Ride Again" 1945 (Trailer); "Renegades of the Rio Grande" 1945; "West of the Pecos" 1945 (Lookout); "Badman's Territory" 1946; "California" 1946 (Reb); "Lawless Empire" 1946 (Duke Flinders); "Rustler's Roundup" 1946 (Louie Todd); "Singin' in the Corn" 1946 (Silk Stevens); "Three Troubledoers" 1946-short (Henchman); "Cheyenne" 1947 (Barfly); "The Fabulous Texan" 1947; "The Wistful Widow of Wagon Gap" 1947 (Cowboy); "Buckaroo from Powder River" 1948 (Ben Trask); "The Paleface" 1948 (Henchman); "Relentless" 1948 (Miner); "Six-Gun Law" 1948 (Sheriff Brackett); "Station West" 1948 (Man); "Trail to Laredo" 1948; "Laramie" 1949; "South of Santa Fe" 1949-short; "Copper Canyon" 1950 (Deputy); "Winchester '73" 1950 (Station Master); "The Great Missouri Raid" 1951 (Jim Cummings); "Ridin' the Outlaw Trail" 1951; "Flaming Feather" 1952 (Ed Poke); "The Lawless Breed" 1952 (Clerk); "Montana Territory" 1952 (Frank Parrish); "Law and Order" 1953 (Man); "Powder River" 1953 (Lame Jack Banner); "The Violent Men" 1955 (Barfly); "Gunfight at the O.K. Corral" 1957 (Bartender). ¶TV: *Wyatt Earp*—"He's My Brother" 11-29-60 (Cowhand).

Laidlaw, Roy (1883-2/2/36). Films: "In the Cow Country" 1914; "The Darkening Trail" 1915; "The Roughneck" 1915; "The Gunfighter" 1916 (El Salvador); "The Patriot" 1916 (Pancho Zapilla); "With Hoops of Steel" 1919 (Albert Wellesley); "Cupid, the Cowpuncher" 1920 (Dr. Billy Trowbridge); "The Ridin' Streak" 1925 (Judge Howells); "The Splendid Road" 1925 (Capt. Sutter); "Where Romance Rides" 1925 (Andrew J. Thompson); "Beyond the Rockies" 1926 (Dave Heep); "The Devil's Gulch" 1926 (Seth Waverly); "Cactus Trails" 1927 (Jeb Poultney); "The Wild West Show" 1928 (Joe Henson).

Laine, Frankie (1913-). TV: *Rawhide*—"Incident on the Road to Yesterday" 11-18-60 (Ralph Bartlet).

Laird, Effie. Films: "Beneath Western Skies" 1944 (Carrie Stokes); "Wagons West" 1952 (Old Maid). ¶TV: *Wild Bill Hickok*—"Jingles Becomes a Baby Sitter" 4-15-52; *The Gene Autry Show*—"Rio Renegades" 9-29-53.

Laire, Judson (1902-7/5/79). TV: *Stoney Burke*—"Child of Luxury" 10-15-62 (Charley Fitch).

Lake, Alice (1895-11/15/67). Films: "The Texas Sphinx" 1917; "I Am the Law" 1922 (Joan Cameron); "The Spider and the Rose" 1923 (Paula); "Untamed Justice" 1929 (Ann).

Lake, Florence (1905-4/11/80). Films: "Stagecoach" 1939 (Mrs. Nancy Whitney); "Union Pacific" 1939; "Fargo" 1952; "The Man from Black Hills" 1952 (Martha); "The Maverick" 1952 (Grandma Watson); "Bitter Creek" 1954 (Mrs. Hammond); "The Desperado" 1954 (Mrs. Cameron). ¶TV: *Cowboy G-Men*—"Pixilated" 11-8-52; *Wild Bill Hickok*—"Spurs for Johnny" 5-26-53; *My Friend Flicka*—"Refuge for the Night" 4-20-56; *The Lone Ranger*—"The Law and Miss Aggie" 4-11-57, "Mission for Tonto" 5-2-57, "The Angel and the Outlaw" 5-23-57; *Wanted—Dead or Alive*—"The Giveaway Gun" 10-11-58; *Nichols*—Pilot 9-16-71, "Flight of the Century" 2-22-72.

Lake, Janet. TV: *Have Gun Will Travel*—"The Unforgiven" 11-7-59, "The Revenger" 9-30-61 (Mrs. Turner); *Colt .45*—"Bounty List" 5-31-60 (Harriet Potts); *Maverick*—

"Thunder from the North" 11-13-60 (Kitty O'Hearn), "Mr. Muldoon's Partner" 4-15-62 (Bonnie Shay); *Sugarfoot*—"Welcome Enemy" 12-26-60 (Jane Watson); *Wyatt Earp*—"The Convict's Revenge" 4-4-61 (Marge Davies); *Bonanza*—"The Friendship" 11-12-61 (Ann Carter).

Lake, Veronica (1919-7/7/73). Films: "Ramrod" 1947 (Connie Dickason).

LaLanne, Jack (1914-). Films: "More Wild Wild West" TVM-1980 (Physical Fitness Instructor).

Lally, Mike (1902-2/15/85). Films: "Desert Fury" 1947 (Dealer); "Streets of Laredo" 1949 (Townsman).

Lally, William. TV: *Circus Boy*—"The Good Samaritans" 12-23-56 (John McNair); *Colt .45*—"Law West of the Pecos" 6-7-59 (Sergeant Webster).

Lamar, Billy. Films: "Hi-Jacking Rustlers" 1926; "West of the Rainbow's End" 1926 (Red); "Thunderbolt's Tracks" 1927 (Red).

LaMarr, Barbara (1896-1/30/26). Films: "Desperate Trails" 1921 (Lady Lou); "The Eternal Struggle" 1923 (Camille Lenoir).

Lamarr, Hedy (1915-). Films: "Copper Canyon" 1950 (Lisa Roselle). ¶TV: *Zane Grey Theater*—"Proud Woman" 10-25-57 (Consuela Bowers).

Lamas, Fernando (1915-10/8/82). Films: "Rose Marie" 1954 (James Severn Duval); "100 Rifles" 1969 (Verdugo); "Powderkeg" TVM-1971 (Chucho Morales). ¶TV: *Zane Grey Theater*—"The Last Raid" 2-26-59 (Miguel), "Guns for Garibaldi" 2-18-60 (Guilio Mandati); *The Virginian*—"We've Lost a Train" 4-21-65 (Captain Estrada); *Laredo*—"It's the End of the Road, Stanley" 3-10-66 (Paco Romero); *Hondo*—"Hondo and the Commancheros" 11-10-67 (Rodrigo); *The High Chaparral*—"The Firing Wall" 12-31-67 (El Caudillo); *Alias Smith and Jones*—"Return to Devil's Hole" 2-25-71 (Jim Santana); *How the West Was Won*—"The Slavers" 4-23-79 (Fierro).

Lamb, Betty. Films: "The Man from Montana" 1917 (Mrs. Summers).

Lamb, Gil (1904-). Films: "Riding High" 1943 (Bob "Foggy" Day); "Terror in a Texas Town" 1958 (Barnaby); "The Adventures of Bullwhip Griffin" 1967. ¶TV: *Gunsmoke*—"The Bad One" 1-26-63 (Porter); *Pistols 'n' Petticoats*—"No Sale" 9-24-66 (Town Drunk), 10-29-66 (Alfred); *Wild*

Wild West—"The Night of the Amnesiac" 2-9-68 (Claude Cooper).

Lambert, Douglas (1936-12/17/86). TV: *Rawhide*—"Incident of the Lost Idol" 4-28-61 (Billy Manson), "Incident of Decision" 12-28-62 (Johnny Calvin); *Bonanza*—"Look to the Stars" 3-18-62 (Albert Michelson); *Have Gun Will Travel*—"Invasion" 4-28-62 (Danny Mahoney); *Wagon Train*—"The Madame Sagittarius Story" 10-3-62 (Dennis); *The Loner*—"Escort for a Dead Man" 12-18-65 (Libbett).

Lambert, Jack (1920-). Films: "Abilene Town" 1946 (Jet Younger); "The Harvey Girls" 1946 (Marty Peters); "Plainsman and the Lady" 1946 (Sival); "Belle Starr's Daughter" 1947 (Brone); "The Vigilantes Return" 1947 (Ben); "River Lady" 1948 (Swede); "Big Jack" 1949 (Bud Valentine); "Brimstone" 1949 (Luke Courteen); "Dakota Lil" 1950 (Dummy); "North of the Great Divide" 1950 (Stagg); "Stars in My Crown" 1950 (Perry Lokey); "The Secret of Convict Lake" 1951 (Matt Anderson); "Bend of the River" 1952 (Red); "Montana Belle" 1952 (Ringo); "Vera Cruz" 1954 (Charlie); "At Gunpoint" 1955 (Kirk); "Run for Cover" 1955 (Larsen); "Canyon River" 1956 (Kincaid); "Day of the Outlaw" 1959 (Tex); "How the West Was Won" 1962 (Gaunt Henchman); "Four for Texas" 1964 (Monk); "Winchester '73" TVM-1967. ¶TV: *The Adventures of Rin Tin Tin*—"Return of the Chief" 9-28-56 (Bull Brando); *Wagon Train*—"The Mary Halstead Story" 11-20-57 (Creegar), "The Sakae Ito Story" 12-3-58 (Tom Revere), "The Benjamin Burns Story" 2-17-60, "The Myra Marshall Story" 10-21-63 (Nick); *Lawman*—"Short Straw" 12-14-58 (Lon Haggert); *Tales of Wells Fargo*—"Cow Town" 12-15-58 (Luke Stevens); *Sugarfoot*— "The Extra Hand" 1-20-59 (Hank Bremer); *The Californians*—"A Turn in the Trail" 2-17-59 (Shaster Poe), "The Fur Story" 5-5-59 (Harte); *Bat Masterson*—"Incident in Leadville" 3-18-59 (King Fisher), "The Rage of Princess Ann" 10-20-60 (Ulbrecht), "Bullwhacker's Bounty" 2-16-61 (Wancho Tully); *Colt .45*—"Law West of the Pecos" 6-7-59; *Frontier Doctor*—"Bitter Creek Gang" 6-20-59; *The Deputy*—"Back to Glory" 9-26-59 (Keever); *Riverboat*—Regular 1959-61 (Joshua); *The Texan*—"The Dishonest Posse" 10-5-59 (Jack Proddy); *The Rifleman*—"The Spiked Rifle" 11-24-59; *Have Gun Will Travel*—"Never Help the Devil" 4-16-60 (Doggie Kramer); *Bonanza*—

"Showdown" 9-10-60 (Pardo), "The Unseen Wound" 1-29-67 (Landers); *Gunsmoke*—"Stolen Horses" 4-8-61 (Hank Tebow), "The Renegades" 1-12-63 (Brice), "The Quest for Asa Janin" 6-1-63 (Scotsman), "Abelia" 11-18-68 (Gar), "The Reprisal" 2-10-69 (Garth), "The Badge" 2-2-70 (Locke); *Frontier Circus*—"The Shaggy Kings" 12-7-61 (Hark Baker); *The Virginian*—"The Awakening" 10-13-65 (Pine); *Branded*—"The Richest Man in Boot Hill" 10-31-65 (Marty Slater); *Death Valley Days*—"A City Is Born" 1-29-66 (Curly Burke), "Doc Holliday's Gold Bard" 12-31-66 (Creek Johnson); *Daniel Boone*—"The Scalp Hunter" 3-17-66 (Rafe Todd), "The Williamsburg Cannon" 1-12-67 & 1-19-67 (Alexander McAfee), "The Desperate Raid" 11-16-67 (Stronk); *Bob Hope Chrysler Theatre*—"The Reason Nobody Hardly Ever Seen a Fat Outlaw in the Old West Is as Follows:" 3-8-67 (Sid Swine); *Iron Horse*—"Consignment, Betsy the Boiler" 9-23-67; *The Big Valley*—"Night in a Small Town" 10-9-67.

Lambert, Jane (-7/6/80). TV: *Kung Fu*—"The Well" 9-27-73 (Bess Hawkins).

Lambert, Lee Jay. TV: *Daniel Boone*—"The Flaming Rocks" 2-1-68, "To Slay a Giant" 1-9-69 (Hemit); *Gunsmoke*—"Slocum" 10-21-68 (Paul Riker); *Bonanza*—"Another Windmill to Go" 9-14-69 (Shack), "The Wagon" 10-5-70 (Jase); *Kung Fu*—"Alethea" 3-15-73 (Tork Wittner).

Lambert, Paul (1922-). Films: "A Gunfight" 1971 (Ed Fleury). ¶TV: *Gunsmoke*—"Brush at Elkador" 9-15-56 (Lou Shipen), "Kick Me" 1-26-57 (Harry Bent), "There Never Was a Horse" 5-16-59 (Kin Creed); *Tombstone Territory*—"The Tin Gunman" 4-16-58 (Dick); *The Californians*—"Lola Montez" 10-7-58 (Duane Parker); *Bat Masterson*—"The Tumbleweed Wagon" 3-25-59 (Luke Steiger), "Flume to the Mother Lode" 1-28-60 (Charles Hamilton); *Gunslinger*—"Road of the Dead" 3-30-61 (Pritchard); *Rawhide*—"Mrs. Harmon" 4-16-65 (Fred Harmon); *Wild Wild West*—"The Night of the Firebrand" 9-15-67 (Andre Durain); *The Big Valley*—"They Called Her Delilah" 9-30-68 (Ross Parker), "A Passage of Saints" 3-10-69 (Arthur W. Denby); *Bonanza*—"Queen High" 12-1-68 (Renfro); *Here Come the Brides*—"The Fetching of Jenny" 12-5-69.

Lamey, Tommy. TV: *Wildside*—Regular 1985 (Parks Ritche).

Lamond, Don. Films: "The

Outlaws Is Coming!" 1965 (Rance Roden).

Lamont, Dixie. Films: "The Great Round Up" 1920; "The Pony Express Rider" 1921; "The Western Musketeer" 1922; "Wolf's Trail" 1927 (Jane Drew).

Lamont, Duncan (1918-). TV: *The Texan*—"Border Incident" 12-7-59 (David MacMorris), "Dangerous Ground" 12-14-59 (David MacMorris), "End of Track" 12-21-59 (David MacMorris), "Quarantine" 2-8-60 (David MacMorris), "Buried Treasure" 2-15-60 (David MacMorris), "Captive Crew" 2-22-60 (David MacMorris), "Showdown" 2-29-60 (David MacMorris), "The Mountain Man" 5-23-60 (Mack); *Wyatt Earp*—"The Big Fight at Total Wreck" 1-12-60 (Jock Welsh); *Gunsmoke*—"The Night Riders" 2-24-69.

LaMont, Harry (1887-5/8/57). Films: "Peaceful Peters" 1922 (Jim Blalock); "Diamond Trail" 1933 (Spike); "Rose of the Rancho" 1936 (Vigilante); "Valley of the Sun" 1942 (Man on Street); "Pursued" 1947.

Lamour, Dorothy (1914-). Films: "High, Wide and Handsome" 1937 (Molly Fuller); "Riding High" 1943 (Ann Castle).

Lampert, Zohra (1936-). Films: "Posse from Hell" 1961 (Helen Caldwell).

Lamphier, James. TV: *Wyatt Earp*—"Bat Masterson for Sheriff" 3-3-57 (Jerry); *The Adventures of Rin Tin Tin*—"The Old Man of the Mountain" 6-21-57 (Pointed Thorn); *The Deputy*—"Lady with a Mission" 3-5-60 (Sloan); *Death Valley Days*—"The Paper Dynasty" 2-29-64; *Wild Wild West*—"The Night of the Grand Emir" 1-28-66 (Dr. Mohammed Bey), "The Night of the Plague" 4-4-69 (Malcolm Lansing).

Lampkin, Charles (1913-4/17/89). Films: "Rider on a Dead Horse" 1962 (Taylor); "The Rare Breed" 1966 (Porter); "Journey to Shiloh" 1968 (Edward). ¶TV: *Cowboy in Africa*—"Little Boy Lost" 11-27-67 (Dr. Mehrar); *Father Murphy*—"The Newlyweds" 9-28-82 (Jed Matthews).

Lancaster, Burt (1913-10/20/94). Films: "Desert Fury" 1947 (Tom Hanson); "Vengeance Valley" 1951 (Owen Daybright); "Apache" 1954 (Massai); "Vera Cruz" 1954 (Joe Erin); "The Kentuckian" 1955 (Big Eli); "The Rainmaker" 1956 (Starbuck); "Gunfight at the O.K. Corral" 1957 (Wyatt Earp); "The Unforgiven" 1960 (Ben Zachary); "The Hallelujah Trail" 1965 (Col. Thadeus Gearhart); "The Professionals" 1966 (Bill Dolworth); "The Scalphunters" 1968 (Joe Bass); "Lawman" 1971 (Marshal Jared Maddox); "Valdez Is Coming" 1971 (Bob Valdez); "Ulzana's Raid" 1972 (McIntosh); "Buffalo Bill and the Indians, or Sitting Bull's History Lesson" 1976 (Ned Buntline); "Cattle Annie and Little Britches" 1981 (Bill Doolin).

Lancaster, Iris. Films: "The Trail Beyond" 1934 (Marie La Fleur); "Ridin' the Trail" 1940 (Carmencita).

Lanchester, Elsa (1902-12/26/86). Films: "Northwest Outpost" 1947 (Princess Tanya Tatiana); "Frenchie" 1950 (Countess).

Land, Geoffrey. Films: "The Female Bunch" 1971 (Jim); "Against a Crooked Sky" 1975 (Temkai); "Jessi's Girls" 1976 (Sheriff Clay).

Landa, Miguel. TV: *Broken Arrow*—"Apache Girl" 5-7-57 (Togan); *Maverick*—"The Jeweled Gun" 11-24-57 (Henrique Fillipe), "Thunder from the North" 11-13-60 (Swift River); *The Adventures of Rin Tin Tin*—"The Matador" 2-6-59 (Miguel Guitierrez); *Colt .45*—"The Cause" 2-28-60 (Ramon); *Jim Bowie*—"Country Girl" 12-13-57 (Carlos); *Riverboat*—"Forbidden Island" 1-24-60 (Raoul Duprez); *Bat Masterson*—"Three Bullets for Bat" 3-24-60 (Jorge); *Wide Country*—"Yanqui, Go Home!" 4-4-63 (Carlos); *Gunsmoke*—"Extradition" 12-7-63 & 12-14-63 (Rivera); *The High Chaparral*—"A Piece of Land" 10-10-69 (Jaime), "Friends and Partners" 1-16-70.

Landau, David (1878-9/20/35). Films: "Heritage of the Desert" 1932 (Judson Holderness).

Landau, Martin (1931-). Films: "Stagecoach to Dancer's Rock" 1962 (Dade Coleman); "The Hallelujah Trail" 1965 (Chief Walks-Stooped Over); "Nevada Smith" 1966 (Jesse Coe); "A Town Called Hell" 1971-Span./Brit. (the Colonel); "Kung Fu: The Movie" TVM-1986 (John Martin Perkins III). ¶TV: *Gunsmoke*—"The Patsy" 9-20-58 (Thorp), "The Goldtakers" 9-24-66 (Britton); *Maverick*—"High Card Hangs" 10-19-58 (Mike Manning); *Lawman*—"The Outcast" 11-2-58 (Bob Ford); *Tales of Wells Fargo*—"Doc Holliday" 5-4-59 (Doc Holliday); *Rawhide*—"Incident Below the Brazos" 5-15-59 (Cort); *Wanted—Dead or Alive*—"The Monsters" 1-16-60 (Khorba); *Johnny Ringo*—"The Derelict" 5-26-60 (Wes Tymon); *Tate*—"Tigero" 8-3-60 (John Chess); *Wagon Train*—"The Cathy Eckhardt Story" 11-9-60

(Preacher); *The Tall Man*—"Dark Moment" 2-11-61 (Francisco), "The Black Robe" 5-5-62 (Father Gueselin); *Bonanza*—"The Gift" 4-1-61 (Emeliano); *The Outlaws*—"The Avenger" 4-13-61 (Rankin); *The Rifleman*—"The Vaqueros" 10-2-61 (Miguel); *The Travels of Jaimie McPheeters*—"The Day of the Killer" 11-17-63 (Cochio); *A Man Called Shenandoah*—"The Locket" 11-22-65 (Jace Miller); *The Big Valley*—"The Way to Kill a Killer" 11-24-65 (Mariano Montoya); *Wild Wild West*—"The Night of the Red-Eyed Madmen" 11-26-65 (Gen. Grimm); *Branded*—"This Stage of Fools" 1-16-66 (Edwin Booth).

Lander, Stephen. TV: *Sugarfoot*—"Stranger in Town" 3-27-61 (Ollie Bernstrom).

Landers, Audrey (1959-). TV: *Young Maverick*—"Hearts O'Gold" 12-12-79 (Sara Lou Mullins).

Landers, Harry (1921-). Films: "Jack Slade" 1953; "The Indian Fighter" 1955 (Grey Wolf); "The Black Whip" 1956 (Fiddlers); "Charro!" 1969 (Heff). ¶TV: *Cavalry Patrol*—Pilot 1956 (Pvt. Danny Quintana); *The Roy Rogers Show*—"Fighting Sire" 12-16-56; *Have Gun Will Travel*—"The Yuma Treasure" 12-14-57 (Lt. Harvey), "Love and a Bad Woman" 3-26-60 (Cowboy); *Johnny Ringo*—"East Is East" 1-7-60 (Arch Ganzer); *The Law of the Plainsman*—"The Imposter" 2-4-60 (Kid Remick); *Black Saddle*—"Burden of Guilt" 3-18-60 (Rand); *Wanted—Dead or Alive*—"Three for One" 12-21-60 (Lafe Martin); *Iron Horse*—"Hellcat" 12-26-66 (Yancey).

Landers, Muriel (1921-2/19/77). Films: "Pony Soldier" 1952 (Poks-Ki). ¶TV: *The Gene Autry Show*—"Go West, Young Lady" 11-19-55; *Rango*—"You Can't Scalp a Bald Indian" 4-28-67 (Little Sparrow).

Landesberg, Steve (1945-). TV: *Black Bart*—Pilot 4-4-75 (Reb Jordan).

Landey, Clayton. Films: "The Cisco Kid" CTVM-1994 (Van Booze).

Landgard, Janet (1945-). Films: "Land Raiders" 1969-U.S./Span. (Kate Mayfield).

Landin, Hope (1893-2/22/73). Films: "Sugarfoot" 1951 (Mary).

Landis, Carole (1919-7/5/48). Films: "Cowboys from Texas" 1939 (June Jones); "Reno" 1939.

Landis, Cullen (1898-8/26/75). Films: "The Mainspring" 1917 (Bellamy Hardor); "The Outcasts of

Poker Flat" 1919 (Billy Lanyon/ Tommy Oakhurst); "Where the West Begins" 1919 (Ned Caldwell); "Getting Some" 1920; "Crashin' Thru" 1923 (Kid Allison); "Pioneer Trails" 1923 (Jack Dale/Jack Plains); "One Law for the Woman" 1924 (Ben Martin); "Buffalo Bill on the U.P. Trail" 1926 (Gordon Kent); "Davy Crockett at the Fall of the Alamo" 1926 (Davy Crockett); "The Fighting Failure" 1926 (Denny O'Brien).

Landis, Margaret (1890-4/1/81). Films: "Code of the Yukon" 1918 (Dorothy Nolan); "The Love Brand" 1923; "The Miracle Baby" 1923 (Judy Stanton); "Fighter's Paradise" 1924; "Her Man" 1924; "Trigger Finger" 1924 (Ruth Deering); "The Western Wallop" 1924 (Anita Stillwell).

Landis, Monte (1936-). TV: *The High Chaparral*—"Too Many Chiefs" 3-27-70 (Tailor).

Landis, Winifred. Films: "Double Fisted" 1925; "The Bandit Buster" 1926 (Mrs. Morton); "The Bonanza Buckaroo" 1926 (Mrs. Gordon); "The Border Whirlwind" 1926 (Mrs. Blake); "A Gentleman Preferred" 1928 (Mrs. Clark Carter).

Lando, Brian. TV: *Paradise*—Regular 1988-91 (Benjamin Cord).

Lando, Joe. TV: *Dr. Quinn, Medicine Woman*—Regular 1993- (Byron Sully).

Landon, Hal. Films: "Rollin' Home to Texas" 1941; "Springtime in the Sierras" 1947 (Bert Baker); "Carson City Raiders" 1948 (Jimmy Davis); "The Gallant Legion" 1948 (Chuck Conway); "Navajo Trail Raiders" 1949 (Tom Stanley); "Roar of the Iron Horse" 1950-serial (Tom Lane).

Landon, Leslie. Films: "Little House on the Prairie: Look Back to Yesterday" TVM-1983 (Etta Plum); "Little House: Bless All the Dear Children" TVM-1984 (Etta Plum). ¶TV: *Little House: A New Beginning*—Regular 1982-83 (Etta Plum).

Landon, Michael (1937-7/1/91). Films: "The Legend of Tom Dooley" 1959 (Tom Dooley); "Little House on the Prairie" TVM-1974 (Charles Ingalls); "Little House on the Prairie: Look Back to Yesterday" TVM-1983 (Charles Ingalls); "Little House: The Last Farewell" TVM-1984 (Charles Ingalls). ¶TV: *Luke and the Tenderfoot*—Pilot 8-6-55 & 8-13-55 (Tough); *Jim Bowie*—"Deputy Sheriff" 9-28-56 (Jerome), "The Swordsman" 12-14-56 (Armand De Nivernais); *Schlitz Playhouse of the Stars*—"The Restless Gun" 3-29-57

(Sandy), "Way of the West" 6-6-58 (Don Burns); *Tales of Wells Fargo*—"Shotgun Messenger" 5-6-57 (Tad Cameron), "Sam Bass" 6-10-57 (Jackson), "The Kid" 11-18-57 (Tad Cameron); *Zane Grey Theater*—"Gift from a Gunman" 12-13-57 (Dan), "Living Is a Lonesome Thing" 1-1-59 (Vance Coburn); *Cheyenne*—"White Warrior" 3-11-58 (Alan Horn); *Wanted—Dead or Alive*—"The Martin Poster" 9-6-58 (Carl Martin), "The Legend" 3-7-59 (Clay McGarrett); *Tombstone Territory*—"Rose of the Rio Bravo" 9-17-58 (Barton Clark), "The Man from Brewster" 4-24-59 (Chris Anderson); *The Rifleman*—"End of a Young Gun" 10-14-58 (Will Fulton), "The Mind Reader" 6-30-59 (Bill Mathis); *The Texan*—"The Hemp Tree" 11-17-58 (Nick Ahearn); *Trackdown*—"Day of Vengeance" 11-28-58 (Jack Summers); *Frontier Doctor*—"Shadows of Belle Starr" 1-3-59; *Bonanza*—Regular 1959-73 (Little Joe Cartwright), "Alias Joe Cartwright" 1-26-64 (Borden); *Little House on the Prairie*—Regular 1974-82 (Charles Ingalls).

Landon, Jr., Michael. Films: "Bonanza: The Next Generation" TVM-1988 (Benj Cartwright); "Bonanza: The Return" TVM-1993 (Benj Cartwright); Bonanza: Under Attack" TVM-1995 (Benj Cartwright).

Landowska, Yona. Films: "The Sacrifice of Jonathan Gray" 1915; "Two Men of Sandy Bar" 1916 (Don Jovita Castro); "The Yaqui" 1916 (Ysobel).

Landry, Gerard. Films: "Seven Pistols for a Gringo" 1967-Ital./Span. (Dr. Clapper); "Trinity Is Still My Name" 1974-Ital.

Landy, Hanna. "Convict Stage" 1965 (Ma Simes); "Fort Courageous" 1965 (Woman).

Lane, Abbe (1933-). Films: "Ride Clear of Diablo" 1953 (Kate); "Wings of the Hawk" 1953 (Elena); "The Americano" 1955 (Teresa). ¶TV: *F Troop*—"Spy, Counterspy, Counter Counterspy" 2-15-66 (Lorelei).

Lane, Adele (1877-10/24/57). Films: "An Indian's Gratitude" 1912; "The Redemption of Railroad Jack" 1913; "The Trail of Cards" 1913; "The Valley of Regeneration" 1915.

Lane, Allan "Rocky" (1904-10/27/73). Films: "The Galloping Kid" 1932 (Tom Farley); "The Law West of Tombstone" 1938 (Danny Sanders); "King of the Royal Mounted" 1940-serial (Sergeant Dave King); "King of the Mounties" 1942-

serial (Sergeant Dave King); "Daredevils of the West" 1943-serial (Duke Cameron); "Sheriff of Sundown" 1944 (Tex Jordan); "Silver City Kid" 1944; "Stagecoach to Monterey" 1944; "Bells of Rosarita" 1945; "Corpus Christi Bandits" 1945 (Capt. James Christie/Corpus Christi Jim); "The Topeka Terror" 1945 (Chad Stevens); "Trail of Kit Carson" 1945; "Out California Way" 1946; "Santa Fe Uprising" 1946 (Red Ryder); "Stagecoach to Denver" 1946 (Red Ryder); "Bandits of Dark Canyon" 1947 (Rocky Lane); "Homesteaders of Paradise Valley" 1947; "The Marshal of Cripple Creek" 1947 (Red Ryder); "Oregon Trail Scouts" 1947 (Red Ryder); "Rustlers of Devil's Canyon" 1947 (Red Ryder); "Vigilantes of Boomtown" 1947 (Red Ryder); "The Wild Frontier" 1947 (Rocky Lane); "The Bold Frontiersman" 1948 (Rocky Lane); "Carson City Raiders" 1948 (Rocky Lane); "The Denver Kid" 1948; "Desperadoes of Dodge City" 1948 (Rocky Lane); "Marshal of Amarillo" 1948 (Rocky Lane); "Oklahoma Badlands" 1948 (Rocky Lane); "Renegades of Sonora" 1948; "Sundown in Santa Fe" 1948; "Bandit King of Texas" 1949 (Rocky Lane); "Death Valley Gunfighter" 1949 (Rocky Lane); "Frontier Marshal" 1949 (Rocky Lane); "Navajo Trail Raiders" 1949 (Rocky Lane); "Powder River Rustlers" 1949 (Rocky Lane); "Sheriff of Wichita" 1949 (Rocky Lane); "The Wyoming Bandit" 1949 (Rocky Lane); "Code of the Silver Sage" 1950 (Rocky Lane); "Covered Wagon Raid" 1950 (Rocky Lane); "Frisco Tornado" 1950 (Rocky Lane); "Gunmen of Abilene" 1950 (Rocky Lane); "Rustlers on Horseback" 1950 (Rocky Lane); "Salt Lake Raiders" 1950 (Rocky Lane); "Trail of Robin Hood" 1950; "Vigilante Hideout" 1950 (Rocky Lane); "Desert of Lost Men" 1951 (Rocky Lane); "Fort Dodge Stampede" 1951 (Rocky Lane); "Night Riders of Montana" 1951 (Rocky Lane); "Rough Riders of Durango" 1951 (Rocky Lane); "Wells Fargo Gunmaster" 1951 (Rocky Lane); "Black Hills Ambush" 1952 (Rocky Lane); "Captive of Billy the Kid" 1952 (Rocky Lane); "Desperadoes' Outpost" 1952 (Rocky Lane); "Leadville Gunslinger" 1952 (Rocky Lane); "Thundering Caravans" 1952 (Rocky Lane); "Bandits of the West" 1953 (Rocky Lane); "El Paso Stampede" 1953 (Rocky Lane); "Marshal of Cedar Rock" 1953 (Rocky Lane); "Savage Frontier" 1953 (Rocky Lane); "The Saga of Hemp Brown" 1958 (Sheriff); "Hell Bent for

Leather" 1960 (Kelsey); "Posse from Hell" 1961 (Burt Hogan). ¶TV: *Gunsmoke*—"Texas, Cowboys" 4-5-58 (Kin Talley), "The Badge" 11-12-60 (Mac), "Long Hours, Short Pay" 4-29-61 (Captain Graves); *Wagon Train*—"The Daniel Barrister Story" 4-16-58 (Mr. Miller); *Tales of Wells Fargo*—"The Reward" 4-21-58 (Chet); *Colt .45*—"Arizona Anderson" 2-14-60 (Gilby); *Texas John Slaughter*—"Kentucky Gunslick" 2-26-60 (John Ringo); *Bonanza*—"The Blood Line" 12-31-60 (Luke Grayson).

Lane, Brenda. Films: "Rip Roarin' Roberts" 1924 (Estelle Morgan).

Lane, Bruce. Films: "Silver Spurs" 1936 (Yuma Kid); "Two-Fisted Sheriff" 1937 (Bob Pearson).

Lane, Carol. Films: "Lightnin' Shot" 1928; "Mystery Valley" 1928; "The Arizona Kid" 1929 (Mary Grant); "Bullets and Justice" 1929.

Lane, Charles (1869-10/17/45). Films: "Ruggles of Red Gap" 1918 (Earl of Brinstead); "The Winning of Barbara Worth" 1926 (Jefferson Worth).

Lane, Charles (1905-). Films: "Buck Benny Rides Again" 1940 (Charlie Graham); "Texas Rangers Ride Again" 1940 (Train Passenger); "The Great Man's Lady" 1942 (Pierce); "Home in Wyomin'" 1942 (Editor); "Ride 'Em, Cowboy" 1942 (Martin Manning); "Hitched" TVM-1973; "Posse" 1993 (Weezie). ¶TV: *Maverick*—"Mr. Muldoon's Partner" 4-15-62 (Proprietor); *Lawman*—"The Doctor" 5-6-62 (Morris Weeks); *Temple Houston*—"Thy Name Is Woman" 1-9-64 (Amos Riggs), "Last Full Moon" 2-27-64 (Amos Riggs); *F Troop*—"Reach for the Sky, Pardner" 9-29-66 (Maguire).

Lane, Diane (1963-). Films: "Cattle Annie and Little Britches" 1981 (Jenny); "Lonesome Dove" TVM-1989 (Lorena Wood).

Lane, Jocelyn (1940-). Films: "Tickle Me" 1965 (Pam Merritt); "Incident at Phantom Hill" 1966 (Memphis); "Land Raiders" 1969-U.S./Span. (Luisa Rojas). ¶TV: *Wild Wild West*—"The Night of the Watery Death" 11-11-66 (Demonique).

Lane, Leela. Films: "The Half-Breed" 1922 (Isabelle Pardeau).

Lane, Lillian. Films: "Cimarron" 1931 (Cousin Bella).

Lane, Lola (1906-6/22/81). Films: "Buckskin Frontier" 1943 (Rita Molyneux); "Lost Canyon" 1943 (Laura).

Lane, Magda. Films: "Ace High"

1919; "The Best Bad Man" 1919; "By Indian Post" 1919; "Captive Bride" 1919; "The Counterfeit Trail" 1919; "Dynamite" 1919; "The Fighting Sheriff" 1919; "The Four Gun Bandit" 1919; Gun Magic" 1919; "The Gun Packer" 1919; "The Hidden Badge" 1919; "Neck and Noose" 1919; "To the Tune of Bullets" 1919; "The Trail of the Hold-Up Man" 1919; "A Western Wooing" 1919; "The Wild Westerner" 1919; "Bought and Fought For" 1920; "Fighting Pals" 1920; "The Red Hot Trail" 1920; "The Smoke Signal" 1920; "When the Cougar Called" 1920; "Both Barrels" 1921; "In the Nick of Time" 1921; "Range Rivals" 1921; "The Rim of the Desert" 1921.

Lane, Michael (1931-). Films: "Hell Canyon Outlaws" 1957; "The Way West" 1967 (Sioux Chief); "The Master Gunfighter" 1975 (Frewen). ¶TV: *Wild Bill Hickok*—"Daughter of Casey O'Grady" 7-21-53; *Maverick*—"Stampede" 11-17-57 (Noah Perkins), "Yellow River" 2-8-59 (Horace Cuseck); *Sugarfoot*—"The Hunted" 11-25-58 (John Allman); *Rough Riders*—"The Last Rebel" 7-16-59; *Have Gun Will Travel*—"The Black Handkerchief" 11-14-59; *Hotel De Paree*—"Sundance and the Bare-Knuckled Fighters" 1-8-60 (Jackson); *Man from Blackhawk*—"The Hundred Thousand Dollar Policy" 1-22-60 (Lembrick); *Branded*—"Mightier Than the Sword" 9-26-65 (Trask); *Hondo*—"Hondo and the Superstition Massacre" 9-29-67 (Moon Dog); *Daniel Boone*—"Jonah" 2-13-69; *Gunsmoke*—"Sarah" 10-16-72 (Digby).

Lane, Nora (1905-10/16/48). Films: "Arizona Nights" 1927 (Ruth Browning); "The Flying U Ranch" 1927 (Sally Denson); "Jesse James" 1927 (Zerelda Mimms); "Kit Carson" 1928 (Josefa); "The Pioneer Scout" 1928 (Mary Baxter); "The Texas Tornado" 1928 (Ellen Briscoe); "The Lawless Legion" 1929 (Mary Keiver); "Sunset Pass" 1929 (Leatrice Preston); "Lucky Larkin" 1930 (Emmy Lou Parkinson); "Cisco Kid" 1931 (Sally Benton); "The Western Code" 1932 (Polly Lumas); "The Outlaw Deputy" 1935 (Joyce Rutledge); "Western Frontier" 1935 (Goldie/Gail Masters); "Borderland" 1937 (Grace Rand); "Hopalong Rides Again" 1937 (Nora Blake); "Cassidy of Bar 20" 1938 (Nora Blake); "Six-Gun Trail" 1938; "The Gentleman from Arizona" 1939 (Martha); "Texas Renegades" 1940 (Ruth Rand); "Heart of the Rio Grande" 1942; "Undercover Man" 1942 (Louise Saunders).

Lane, Priscilla (1917-4/4/95). Films: "Cowboy from Brooklyn" 1938 (Jane Hardy); "Silver Queen" 1942 (Coralie Adams).

Lane, Richard (1900-9/5/82). Films: "The Outcasts of Poker Flat" 1937 (High-Grade); "I'm from the City" 1938 (Ollie); "Union Pacific" 1939 (Sam Reed); "The Cowboy and the Blonde" 1941 (Gilbert); "Riders of the Purple Sage" 1941 (Oldring); "Romance of the Rio Grande" 1941; "Ride 'Em, Cowboy" 1942 (Peter Conway); "Sioux City Sue" 1946 (Jefferson Lang); "I Shot Billy the Kid" 1950. ¶TV: *Bonanza*—"The Running Man" 3-30-69 (Tracy).

Lane, Rosemary (1914-11/25/74). Films: "The Oklahoma Kid" 1939 (Jane Hardwick); "Sing Me a Song of Texas" 1945.

Lane, Rusty (1913-10/10/86). Films: "Fury at Showdown" 1957 (Riley); "The Rawhide Trail" 1958 (Captain). ¶TV: *Zane Grey Theater*—"Stage to Tucson" 11-16-56 (Tharpe); *Tales of Wells Fargo*—"The Hasty Gun" 3-25-57 (Tom Ogburn); *Have Gun Will Travel*—"In an Evil Time" 9-13-58 (Judge); *The Restless Gun*—"The Nowhere Kid" 10-20-58 (Josiah Austin); *Wanted—Dead or Alive*—"The Fourth Headstone" 11-1-58 (Sheriff Gladstone); *Buckskin*—"Cousin Casey" 3-9-59 (Moose); *Wagon Train*—"The Clara Duncan Story" 4-22-59 (Ron Waldron), "The Emmett Lawton Story" 3-6-63 (Del Masters); *The Texan*—"The Smiling Loser" 5-25-59 (W.J. Morgan); *Bronco*—"The Masquerade" 1-26-60 (Luke Davis); *The Alaskans*—"The Long Pursuit" 1-31-60 (Doc Williams); *Tate*—"Quiet After the Storm" 9-7-60 (Jesse); *Bonanza*—"The Friendship" 11-12-61 (Warden), "The Oath" 11-20-66 (Fielding), "Judgment at Olympus" 10-8-67 (Judge); *Death Valley Days*—"Coffin for a Coward" 2-6-63 (Billy Johnson); *The Virginian*—"The Money Cage" 3-6-63 (Ezra Griswold), "Seth" 3-20-68 (Sheriff Calder); *Temple Houston*—"Toll the Bell Slowly" 10-17-63 (Poag); *Gunsmoke*—"Seven Hours to Dawn" 9-18-65 (Johnson), "The Pretender" 11-20-65 (Will Baker), "Stark" 9-28-70 (Bo), "Alias Festus Haggen" 3-6-72 (Sheriff Buckley), "The Hanging of Newly O'Brien" 11-26-73 (Grandpa); *Branded*—"Nice Day for a Hanging" 2-6-66 (Sheriff).

Lane, Sara. TV: *The Virginian*—Regular 1966-70 (Elizabeth Grainger).

Lane, Tracy. Films: "The Man from Hell" 1934 (Gillis); "Melody

Trail" 1935 (Slim); "Comin' Round the Mountain" 1936 (Butch); "The Lawless Nineties" 1936 (Belden).

Lane, Vicky. Films: "The Cisco Kid Returns" 1945 (Mrs. Page).

Lane, Yancie. Films: "Trail of the Hawk" 1935 (Jack King/Jay Price).

Laneuville, Eric (1952-). TV: *Nichols*—"Eddie Joe" 1-4-72 (Danny).

Lang, Barbara. TV: *Death Valley Days*—"The Seventh Day" 3-14-55, "Bill Bottle's Birthday" 5-19-56; *Maverick*—"Escape to Tampico" 10-26-58 (Amy Lawrence).

Lang, Christa. Films: "Charro!" 1969 (Christa).

Lang, Doreen. TV: *Rawhide*—"Incident of the Dust Flower" 3-4-60; *Gunsmoke*—"Snow Train" 10-19-70 & 10-26-70 (Mae), "Kimbro" 2-12-73 (Mary Bentley); *Kung Fu*—"Empty Pages of a Dead Book" 1-10-74 (Grandma McNelly); *Dirty Sally*—3-22-74 (Sarah Brewster).

Lang, Howard (1923-11/16/70). Films: "The Judgement Book" 1935 (Bill Williams); "Bar 20 Rides Again" 1936 (Jim Arnold); "Call of the Prairie" 1936 (Buck Peters).

Lang, Judy. TV: *Wild Wild West*—"The Night of the Deadly Bubble" 2-24-67 (Prof. Abigail J. Pringle); *The Virginian*—"Dark Corridor" 11-27-68 (Girl).

Lang, Melvin (1894-11/14/40). Films: "Boss of Bullion City" 1941 (Steve); "The Durango Kid" 1940 (Marshal Trayboe); "Queen of the Yukon" 1940 (Thorne).

Lang, Perry. Films: "Cattle Annie and Little Britches" 1981 (Elrod). ¶TV: *How the West Was Won*—"The Innocent" 2-12-79 (Willie Johnson).

Lang, Peter (1867-8/20/32). Films: "The Valley of Lost Hope" 1915 (James Ewing).

Lang, Richard. Films: "Code of the Northwest" 1926 (Sgt. Jerry Tyler).

Lang, Stephen. Films: "Tombstone" 1993 (Ike Clanton); "Tall Tales: The Unbelievable Adventures of Pecos Bill" 1995 (Jonas Hackett).

Langan, Glenn (1917-1/19/91). Films: "Riding High" 1943 (Jack Holbrook); "Fury at Furnace Creek" 1948 (Rufe); "The Iroquois Trail" 1950 (Capt. West); "Hangman's Knot" 1952 (Capt. Peterson); "Outlaw Treasure" 1955; "Chisum" 1970 (Dudley). ¶TV: *Hondo*—"Hondo and the War Hawks" 10-20-67 (Victor Tribolet), "Hondo and the Com-

mancheros" 11-10-67 (Victor Tribolet), "Hondo and the Sudden Town" 11-17-67 (Victor Tribolet), "Hondo and the Ghost of Ed Dow" 11-24-67 (Victor Tribolet), "Hondo and the Death Drive" 12-1-67 (Victor Tribolet).

Langdon, Harry (1884-12/22/44). Films: "The Fighting Parson" 1930-short; "Pistol Packin' Nitwits" 1945-short.

Langdon, Lillian (1862-2/8/43). Films: "The Lamb" 1915; "Getting Some" 1920; "Fools of Fortune" 1922 (Mrs. DePuyster); "Lights of the Desert" 1922 (Susan Gallant); "The Footlight Ranger" 1923 (Nellis Andrews).

Langdon, Roy. Films: "Riders of the Range" 1923 (Bob Randall).

Langdon, Ruth. Films: "The Firebrand" 1922 (Alice Acker).

Langdon, Sue Ane (1936-). Films: "The Rounders" 1965 (Mary); "The Cheyenne Social Club" 1970 (Opal Ann). ¶TV: *Shotgun Slade*—"Crossed Guns" 9-19-60 (Lydia); *The Outlaws*—"Culley" 2-16-61 (Miss Julie); *Tales of Wells Fargo*—"Fraud" 3-13-61 (Jessica Brown); *Bonanza*—"The Many Faces of Gideon Flinch" 11-5-61 (Jennifer), "Hound Dog" 3-21-65 (Tracey); *Gunsmoke*—"Catawomper" 2-10-62 (Kate Tassel); *Wild Wild West*—"The Night of the Steel Assassin" 1-7-66 (Nina Gilbert).

Lange, Carl. Films: "The Desperado Trail" 1965-Ger./Yugo. (Governor); "Duel at Sundown" 1965-Fr./Ger.; "The Last Tomahawk" 1965-Ger./Ital./Span.; "Machine Gun Killers" 1968-Ital./Span.

Lange, Claudie. Films: "For One Hundred Thousand Dollars Per Killing" 1967-Ital.; "To Hell and Back" 1968-Ital./Span.; "My Horse, My Gun, Your Widow" 1972-Ital./Span. (Donovan).

Lange, Hope (1931-). Films: "The True Story of Jesse James" 1957 (Zee).

Langella, Frank (1940-). Films: "The Wrath of God" 1972 (Tomas De La Plata); "The Mark of Zorro" TVM-1974 (Don Diego/Zorro).

Langford, Frances (1914-). Films: "Girl Rush" 1944 (Flo Daniels); "Deputy Marshal" 1949 (Janet Masters).

Langrishe, Caroline. Films: "Eagle's Wing" 1979-Brit./Span. (Judith).

Langton, Paul (1913-4/15/80). Films: "Gentle Annie" 1944 (Violet Goss); "Jack Slade" 1953 (Dan Tra-

vers); "Utah Blaine" 1957 (Rip Coker); "Advance to the Rear" 1964 (Maj. Forsythe); "Four for Texas" 1964 (Beauregard). ¶TV: *Broken Arrow*—"Renegades Return" 12-3-57 (Col. Horn), "Massacre" 1-28-58 (Col. Horn); *Gunsmoke*—"Gunsmuggler" 9-27-58 (Major Evans), "Tag, You're It" 12-19-59 (Karl Killion), "The Imposter" 5-13-61 (Ab Stringer); *Wagon Train*—"The Juan Ortega Story" 10-8-58 (Father Martin), "The Terry Morrell Story" 4-25-62 (Ralph Morse); *Lawman*—"Bloodline" 11-30-58 (Matt Saint); *Zane Grey Theater*—"Deadfall" 2-19-59 (Tom Lamont); *Rough Riders*—"Forty-Five Calibre Law" 5-14-59 (Rudabaugh); *Tales of Wells Fargo*—"The Trading Post" 4-11-60 (Frisbee); *The Law of the Plainsman*—"Cavern of the Wind" 4-21-60 (Sgt. Sean McGrath); *Rawhide*—"Incident of the Silent Web" 6-3-60 (Henry Porter); *Bat Masterson*—"Debt of Honor" 9-29-60 (Marshal); *Cheyenne*—"The Young Fugitives" 10-23-61 (Sheriff); *The Virginian*—"Say Goodbye to All That" 1-23-63; *The Travels of Jaimie McPheeters*—"The Day of the Lame Duck" 2-9-64 (Beaufoy); *The Outcasts*—"Three Ways to Die" 10-7-68 (Gregg Jeremy).

Langtry, Hugh. TV: *Branded*—"The Greatest Coward on Earth" 11-21-65 (Preston); *Daniel Boone*—"Beaumarchais" 10-12-67 (Bartolo).

LaNiece, Ed. Films: "The Double O" 1921 (Jim); "Two-Fisted Jefferson" 1922; "The Desert Hawk" 1924 (Sheriff Carson); "Sell 'Em Cowboy" 1924 (Sheriff Fowler); "The Range Riders" 1927 (Henry Fellows); "Riders of the West" 1927; "Western Courage" 1927; "Thundering Thompson" 1929.

Lanin, Jay. TV: *The Outlaws*—"Charge!" 3-22-62 (Burling); *Gunsmoke*—"The Ditch" 10-27-62 (Trent Hawkins), "Scot-Free" 5-9-64 (Rob Scot); *Wide Country*—"The Man Who Ran Away" 2-7-63 (Robert Lund); *Bonanza*—"Rich Man, Poor Man" 5-12-63 (Slauson). "The Pure Truth" 3-8-64.

Lanning, Frank (1872-6/17/45). Films: "Indian Pete's Gratitude" 1910; "The Legend of Scar Face" 1910; "Winona" 1910; "My Hero" 1912; "Buckshot John" 1915 (Bad Jake Kennedy); "The Three Godfathers" 1916 (Bill Kearney); "North of '53" 1917 (Nig Geroux); "Bull's Eye" 1918-serial; "The Goddess of Lost Lake" 1918 (Eagle); "The Human Tiger" 1918; "Bare-Fisted Gallagher" 1919 (Aliso Pete); "The Blue Bandanna"

1919 (Ben Cowan); "Desert Gold" 1919 (Papago Indian Son); "The Mints of Hell" 1919 (Maung); "The Prodigal Liar" 1919 (Steve Logan); "A Sage Brush Hamlet" 1919 (Two-Gun Dan); "Fighting Cressy" 1920 (Old Man Harrison); "The Third Woman" 1920 (Tonawanna); "That Girl Montana" 1921 (Jim Harris); "Another Man's Boots" 1922 (Injun Jim); "Cameron of the Royal Mounted" 1922; "Hellounds of the West" 1922 (Black Joe); "Out of the Silent North" 1922 (Jean Cour); "Step on It!" 1922 (Pidge Walters); "The Storm" 1922 (Manteeka); "Unmasked" 1922; "The Bad Man" 1923 (Indian Cook); "The Fighting Ranger" 1925-serial; "The Red Rider" 1925 (Medicine Man); "Black Jack" 1927 (Kentuck); "The Unknown Rider" 1929; "The Lone Defender" 1930-serial (Burke); "Rough Romance" 1930 (Pop Nichols); "Lightning Warrior" 1931-serial (Indian George); "The Phantom of the West" 1931-serial (Cortez); "Clancy of the Mounted" 1933-serial.

Lannom, Les. Films: "Lacy and the Mississippi Queen" TVM-1978 (Webber). ¶TV: *Kung Fu*—"The Soul Is the Warrior" 2-8-73 (Billy Thoms); *Centennial*—Regular 1978-79 (Bufe Coker); *The Chisholms*—2-9-80 (Jerry O'Neal).

Lansbury, Angela (1925-). Films: "The Harvey Girls" 1946 (Em); "A Lawless Street" 1955 (Tally Dickinson). ¶TV: *Stage 7*—"Billy and the Bride" 5-8-55 (Vanessa Peters).

Lansford, T.C. "Sonny" (Bob Wills and the Texas Playboys) (1914-7/31/89). Films: "Take Me Back to Oklahoma" 1940; "Go West, Young Lady" 1941; "Silver City Raiders" 1943; "The Last Horseman" 1944.

Lansing, Joi (1934-8/7/72). TV: *Sugarfoot*—"Bullet Proof" 1-21-58 (Peaches); *Maverick*—"Seed of Deception" 4-13-58 (Doll Hayes); *Bat Masterson*—"No Funeral for Thorn" 10-22-59 (Sapphira Gardiner); *Klondike*—Regular 1960-61 (Goldie); *Rawhide*—"Incident at El Crucero" 10-10-63 (Dance Hall Girl).

Lansing, Robert (1929-10/23/94). Films: "An Eye for an Eye" 1966 (Talion). ¶TV: *The Outlaws*—"The Daltons Must Die" 1-26-61 & 2-2-61 (Frank Dalton); *Bonanza*—"Cut-Throat Junction" 3-18-61, "Danger Road" 1-11-70 (Gunny Riley), "Heritage of Anger" 9-19-72 (Dundee); *The Tall Man*—"Rovin' Gambler" 3-18-61 (Doc Holliday); *Temple Houston*—"Gallows in Galilee" 10-31-63 (Judge Galen Stanke); *The Virgin-*

ian—"The Fatal Journey" 12-4-63 (George Calhoun), "The Brothers" 9-15-65 (Matt Denning), "Execution at Triste" 12-13-67 (Lee Knight); *Wagon Train*—"The Geneva Balfour Story" 1-20-64 (Judge Arthur Forbes); *Gunsmoke*—"The Bounty Hunter" 10-30-65 (Luke Frazer), "The Devil's Outpost" 9-22-69 (Yancy Tyce); *Daniel Boone*—"The Tamarack Massacre Affair" 12-30-65 (Captain Robert Ives); *The Loner*—"The Trial in Paradise" 1-22-66 (Hibbard); *Branded*—"Call to Glory" 2-27-66, 3-6-66 & 3-13-66 (General George Armstrong Custer); *The Monroes*—"Manhunt" 3-1-67 (Jonas Prine); *The High Chaparral*—"Mark of the Turtle" 12-10-67 (Marshal Packer); *Cimarron Strip*—"The Assassin" 1-11-68 (Darcy).

Lansing, Sherry (1944-). Films: "Rio Lobo" 1970 (Amelita).

Lanteau, William (1922-11/3/93). Films: "From Noon to Three" 1976 (Rev. Cabot).

Lantieri, Franco (Frank Liston). Films: "Johnny Colt" 1966-Ital. (Curry); "Johnny Yuma" 1966-Ital.; "A Minute to Pray, a Second to Die" 1967-Ital. (Butler); "Heads or Tails" 1969-Ital./Span. (Serpiente).

LaPlanche, Rosemary (1925-5/6/79). Films: "Prairie Chickens" 1943; "Girl Rush" 1944 (Troupe Member).

La Plante, Laura (1904-). Films: "The Alarm" 1921; "Big Town Round-Up" 1921 (Mildred Hart); "The Brand of Courage" 1921; "The Call of the Blood" 1921; "The Deputy's Double Cross" 1921; "Old Dynamite" 1921; "The Big Ranger" 1922; "The Call of Courage" 1922; "Desperation" 1922; "Fighting Back" 1922; "Matching Wits" 1922; "Perils of the Yukon" 1922-serial; "The Ranger's Reward" 1922; "The Trail of the Wolf" 1922; "Dead Game" 1923 (Alice Mason); "Out of Luck" 1923 (Mae Day); "The Ramblin' Kid" 1923 (Carolyn June); "Shootin' for Love" 1923 (Mary Randolph); "True Gold" 1923; "Ride for Your Life" 1924 (Betsy Burke).

La Plante, Violet (1908-6/1/84). Films: "Battling Buddy" 1924 (Dorothy Parker); "His Majesty the Outlaw" 1924; "Walloping Wallace" 1924 (Carol Grey); "The Hurricane Kid" 1925 (Joan's Friend); "The Ramblin' Galoot" 1926 (Pansy Price); "The Haunted Homestead" 1927.

Lapp, Richard. Films: "Duel at Diablo" 1966 (Forbes); "Barquero" 1970 (Poe); "A Time for Dying" 1971 (Cass Bunning). ¶TV: *Iron Horse*—

"The Dynamite Driver" 9-19-66 (Small Wolf); *Cimarron Strip*—"The Battle of Blood Stone" 10-12-67; *Bonanza*—"Salute to Yesterday" 9-29-68 (Trooper Kelly); *The High Chaparral*—"The Lost Ones" 11-21-69 (Nemo); *Gunsmoke*—"Kitowa!" 2-16-70 (Tomani), "Snow Train" 10-19-70 & 10-26-70 (Running Fox).

Lara, Joe. Films: "Gunsmoke: The Last Apache" TVM-1990 (Wolf).

Laramy, Grant. Films: "Adios Gringo" 1965-Ital./Fr./Span. (Stan Clevenger); "Colt Is the Law" 1965-Ital./Span.; "I'll Sell My Skin Dearly" 1968-Ital. (Father Dominique).

Larch, John (1924-). Films: "Bitter Creek" 1954 (Gunman); "Man from Del Rio" 1956 (Bill Dawson); "Seven Men from Now" 1956 (Pete Bodeen); "Gun for a Coward" 1957 (Stringer); "Man in the Shadow" 1957 (Ed Yates); "Quantez" 1957 (Heller); "From Hell to Texas" 1958 (Hal Carmody); "The Saga of Hemp Brown" 1958 (Jed Givens); "How the West Was Won" 1962 (Grimes); "The Great Bank Robbery" 1969 (Sheriff); "Cannon for Cordoba" 1970 (Harry Warner); "Santee" 1973. ¶TV: *Gunsmoke*—"Smoking Out the Nolans" 11-5-55 (Clay), "Fingered" 11-23-57 (Jim Corbett), "The Constable" 5-30-59 (Rance), "The Boots" 11-14-59 (Zeno), "Jailbait Janet" 2-27-60 (Dan Everly), "Long Hours, Short Pay" 4-29-61 (Serpa), "All That" 10-28-61 (Cliff Chanks); *You Are There*—"The Gunfight at the O.K. Corral" 11-6-55; *Zane Grey Theater*—"Death Watch" 11-9-56 (Quine), "A Time to Live" 4-5-57 (Cole Gentry), "The Broken Wing" 2-9-61 (Magnus Kihlgren); *Broken Arrow*—"Ordeal" 4-16-57; *The Restless Gun*—"The Shooting of Jett King" 10-28-57 (Wyoming Kid), "Hornitas Town" 2-10-58 (Sheriff Riker), "The Crisis at Easter Creek" 4-7-58 (Redeye Kirk), "Thunder Valley" 10-13-58 (Anse Newton); *Telephone Time*—"Trail Blazer" 4-1-58 (Oliver Loving); *Jefferson Drum*—"The Bounty Man" 5-2-58 (John Larkin); *Wagon Train*—"The Dan Hogan Story" 5-14-58 (Human Ranse), "The Ben Courtney Story" 1-28-59 (John Ramsey), "The Cathy Eckhardt Story" 11-9-60 (Ben Harness), "The Baylor Crowfoot Story" 3-21-62 (Jethro Creech); *The Texan*—"Law of the Gun" 9-29-58 (Les Torbert); *Have Gun Will Travel*—"The Hanging of Roy Carter" 10-4-58 (Chaplain April), "Out at the Old Ball Park" 10-1-60 (McNagle);

Wanted—Dead or Alive—"Die by the Gun" 12-6-58 (Kale); *Rawhide*—"Incident of the Tumbleweed Wagon" 1-9-59, "Incident at Sugar Creek" 11-23-62 (Sam Garrett); *Rough Riders*—"Death Sentence" 3-12-59 (Ed Mackin); *Black Saddle*—"Client: Northrup" 3-14-59 (Ty Northrup); *Bat Masterson*—"The Secret Is Death" 5-27-59 (Garrickson); *Yancy Derringer*—"Two Tickets to Promontory" 6-4-59 (Wayland Farr); *Riverboat*—"Payment in Full" 9-13-59 (Touhy); *Bonanza*—"The Newcomers" 9-26-59 (Blake McCall); *Wichita Town*—"Drifting" 10-28-59 (Gant); *Tales of Wells Fargo*—"End of a Legend" 11-23-59 (Johnny), "A Killing in Calico" 12-16-61 (Beaker); *The Law of the Plainsman*—"Fear" 1-7-60 (Jaster Mullen); *Johnny Ringo*—"The Liars" 2-4-60 (Mills Walter); *The Outlaws*—"Last Chance" 11-10-60 (Tillitson); *The Deputy*—"The Higher Law" 11-12-60 (Jack Rivers); *Laramie*—"Day of Vengeance" 1-19-60 (Cabe Reynolds), "The Confederate Express" 1-30-62 (Matt Grundy); *The Rifleman*—"Six Years and a Day" 1-3-61 (Jack Cooke); *The Virginian*—"The Executioners" 9-19-62 (Sheriff Neil Brandon), "The Good-Hearted Badman" 2-7-68 (Ben Hicks), "Train of Darkness" 2-4-70 (Charles Neeley); *Stoney Burke*—"Gold-Plated Maverick" 1-7-63 (Byron Latimer); *Daniel Boone*—"Chief Mingo" 12-7-67 (Sam Hawken); *The Men from Shiloh*—"The West vs. Colonel MacKenzie" 9-16-70 (Sheriff); *Alias Smith and Jones*—"The Girl in Boxcar Number Three" 2-11-71 (Griffin); *Big Hawaii*—"Sun Children" 9-28-77 (Waltah Morrison), "The Sugar War" 1977.

La Reno, Richard "Dick" (1873-7/26/45). Films: "Rose of the Rancho" 1914 (Ezra Kinkaid); "The Squaw Man" 1914 (Big Bill); "The Virginian" 1914 (Ballam); "The Buzzard's Shadow" 1915 (Colonel Sears); "The Cactus Blossom" 1915; "The Love Route" 1915 (Colonel Houston); "The Human Tiger" 1918; "Mr. Logan, U.S.A." 1918; "Naked Fists" 1918; "Quick Triggers" 1918; "The Trail of No Return" 1918; "Unclaimed Goods" 1918 (Sheriff Bill Blake); "The Blue Bandanna" 1919 (Sheriff); "Go Get 'Em Garringer" 1919 (Red McCarty); "A Man's Fight" 1919 (Logan); "The Midnight Stage" 1919 (Boggs); "Rustling a Bride" 1919 (Sheriff); "Isobel, or the Trail's End" 1920 (Jim Blake); "Kaintuck's Ward" 1920; "Two Moons" 1920 (Blacksmith); "One-Eighth Apache" 1922 (Joseph Murdock); "Out of the Silent North" 1922 (Lazy Lester); "Trimmed" 1922 (Judge William Dandridge); "Playing It Wild" 1923 (Sheriff Gideon); "Singled-Handed" 1923 (Wheriff Simpel); "Crashin' Thru" 1924 (Mr. Rankin); "Oh, You Tony!" 1924 (Mark Langdon); "Ridin' Mad" 1924 (Thornton Hawks); "Drug Store Cowboy" 1925 (Sheriff); "Flashing Steeds" 1925 (Captain Randall); "Blue Blazes" 1926 (Jess Macy); "Buffalo Bill on the U.P. Trail" 1926 (William Rose); "The High Hand" 1926 (Sheriff); "Border Cavalier" 1927 (Dave Lawton); "Gold from Weepah" 1927; "The Long Loop on the Pecos" 1927; "The Silent Rider" 1927 (Sheriff); "The Apache Raider" 1928.

Largay, Raymond (1886-9/28/74). Films: "Four Faces West" 1948 (Dr. Eldredge); "Jesse James Versus the Daltons" 1954 (Corey Bayless). ¶TV: *The Lone Ranger*—"A Matter of Courage" 4-26-50, "Through the Wall" 10-9-52.

Larkin, Dolly. Films: "Breed of the West" 1913; "The Gun Men of Plumas" 1914; "Under Arizona Skies" 1914.

Larkin, George (1888-3/27/46). Films: "The Trey O'Hearts" 1914-serial (Alan); "The Primitive Call" 1917 (Percy Malcolm); "The Border Raiders" 1918; "Hands Up" 1918-serial; "The Devil's Trail" 1919 (Sgt. MacNair); "The Terror of the Range" 1919-serial; "Beauty and the Bandit" 1921; "The Call of Duty" 1921; "Fair Fighting" 1921; "The Fight Within" 1921; "The Honor of the Mounted" 1921; "The Man Trackers" 1921 (Jimmy Hearn); "The Raiders of the North" 1921; "Roaring Waters" 1921; "Barriers of Folly" 1922 (Jim Buckely); "Bulldog Courage" 1922 (Jimmy Brent); "Cameron of the Royal Mounted" 1922.

Larkin, John (1912-1/29/65). TV: *Gunsmoke*—"Louie Pheeters" 1-5-63 (Murphy Moody); *Bonanza*—"The Colonel" 1-6-63 (Col. Frank Medford); *Wagon Train*—"The Duncan McIvor Story" 3-9-64 (Colonel Lipton).

Larkin, Mary (1948-). TV: *The Cherokee Trail*—Pilot 11-28-81 (Matty Aginnis).

Larkin, Sheila (1944-). TV: *Bonanza*—"Showdown at Tahoe" 11-19-67 (Julie); *The Virginian*—"Death Wait" 1-15-69 (Ellen Jones); *Gunsmoke*—"The Devil's Outpost" 9-22-69 (Abby Tilman), "Tatum" 11-13-72 (Marion).

LaRoche, Mary. TV: *Jefferson Drum*—"Band of Iron" 10-23-58 (Laura Comstock); *Yancy Derringer*—"Nightmare on Bourbon Street" 1-8-59 (Barbara Kent); *Black Saddle*—"Client: Frome" 4-25-59 (Lydia Frome); *Man from Blackhawk*—"Station Six" 11-13-59 (Grace Arthur); *Tales of Wells Fargo*—"Long Odds" 12-14-59 (Lorna Terret), "Long Odds" 6-27-60 (Lrona Terret); *Zane Grey Theater*—"Guns for Garibaldi" 2-18-60 (Liz Randall); *Wagon Train*—"The Jud Steele Story" 5-2-62 (Ursula); *Gunsmoke*—"Quint-Cident" 4-27-63 (Willa Devlin), "Tobe" 10-19-63 (Hannah Young); *The Virginian*—"First to Thine Own Self" 2-12-64 (Alma).

LaRoche, William. Films: "Bucking the Truth" 1926 (Eben Purkiss).

LaRocque, Rod (1898-10/15/69). Films: "Ruggles of Red Gap" 1918 (Belknap Jackson); "Braveheart" 1925 (Braveheart); "Beau Bandit" 1930 (Montero); "Hi Gaucho!" 1936 (Escurra).

LaRoux, Carmen (1909-8/24/42). Films: "Don Mike" 1927 (Carmen); "Cavalier of the West" 1931 (Dolores Fernandez); "Two Gun Caballero" 1931; "Son of Oklahoma" 1932 (Anita); "The California Trail" 1933 (Juan's Wife); "A Demon for Trouble" 1934 (Maya); "Desert Trail" 1935 (Juanita); "Ramona" 1936 (Dancer); "Cheyenne Rides Again" 1937 (Pamela); "Starlight Over Texas" 1938 (Rosita).

La Roy, Rita. Films: "A Holy Terror" 1931 (Kitty Carroll); "Border G-Man" 1938 (Rita Browning).

Larrabee, Louise. Films: "Five Bad Men" 1935 (Marie).

Larrain, Michael (1947-). Films: "Buckskin" 1968 (Jimmy Cody). ¶TV: *Gunsmoke*—"MacGraw" 12-8-69 (Dave Wilson); *The Virginian*—"Rich Man, Poor Man" 3-11-70 (Whit).

Larsen, Keith (1926-). Films: "Hiawatha" 1952 (Pau Puk Keewis); "Fort Vengeance" 1953 (Carey); "Son of Belle Star" 1953 (the Kid); "War Paint" 1953 (Taslik); "Arrow in the Dust" 1954 (Lt. King); "Chief Crazy Horse" 1955 (Flying Hawk); "Wichita" 1955 (Bat Masterson); "Apache Warrior" 1957 (Apache Kid); "Badlands of Montana" 1957 (Rick); "Last of the Badmen" 1957 (Roberts); "Trap on Cougar Mountain " 1972. ¶TV: *Brave Eagle*—Regular 1955-56 (Brave Eagle); *Northwest Passage*—Regular 1958-59 (Major Robert Rogers); *Wichita Town*—"Seed of

Hate" 1-27-60 (Blue Raven); *Tombstone Territory*—4-8-60 (John Edwards).

Larson, Bobby. Films: "Out West with the Peppers" 1940 (David Pepper); "Jackass Mail" 1942 (Boy); "Riders of the Northland" 1942 (Buddy Taylor); "The Leather Burners" 1943 (Bobby Longstreet); "Redwood Forest Trail" 1950 (Chips).

Larson, Christine. Films: "The Fighting Ranger" 1948; "Outlaw Brand" 1948; "Partners of the Sunset" 1948; "Silver Trails" 1948 (Diane); "Crashing Thru" 1949; "Hidden Danger" 1949 (Valerie); "Valley of Fire" 1951 (Bee Laverne); "Brave Warrior" 1952 (Laura Macgregor). ¶TV: *The Lone Ranger*—"Double Jeopardy" 9-7-50, "The Silent Voice" 1-11-51; *The Cisco Kid*—"Cattle Rustling" 2-3-51, "Medicine Flats" 3-10-51, "Bandaged Badman" 10-11-52, "The Black Terror" 11-29-52; *Wild Bill Hickok*—"Widow Muldane" 8-14-51.

Larson, Darrell (1950-). Films: "The Magnificent Seven Ride" 1972 (Shelly Donavan); "The Gambler V: Playing for Keeps" TVM-1994 (Kershaw). ¶TV: *Bonanza*—"Thorton's Account" 11-1-70 (Brian); *Gunsmoke*—"The Fugitives" 10-23-72 (Danny Stalcup); *Young Riders*—"A House Divided" 9-28-91 (Fitzgerald).

Larson, Jack (1933-). Films: "Redwood Forest Trail" 1950 (Dusty); "Star of Texas" 1953 (John Jenkins).

Lartigue, Gerard (1942-). Films: "Arizona Colt" 1965-Ital./Fr./Span. (John).

LaRue, Al. *see* LaRue, Lash.

LaRue, Ashley. TV: *Wild Wild West*—"The Night of the Circus of Death" 11-3-67 (Harry Holmes).

LaRue, Bart (1932-1/5/90). TV: *Wild Wild West*—"The Night of the Juggernaut" 10-11-68 (Maddox); *Bonanza*—"Another Windmill to Go" 9-14-69 (Walters); *Here Come the Brides*—"The Last Winter" 3-27-70 (Drummer).

LaRue, Fontaine. Films: "The Bearcat" 1922 (Mary Lang); "Trigger Finger" 1924 (Wetona); "Gold from Weepah" 1927; "West of the Rockies" 1929 (Celia de la Costa).

LaRue, Frank (1878-9/26/60). Films: "Human Stuff" 1920 (Boka); "Forbidden Trail" 1932 (Collins); "Fighting Texans" 1933; "The Sundown Rider" 1933 (Sheriff Rand); "The Thrill Hunter" 1933 (Hall); "The Fighting Ranger" 1934 (Pegleg Barnes); "When a Man Sees Red" 1934 (Radcliffe); "Heir to Trouble"

1935; "His Fighting Blood" 1935; "The Singing Vagabond" 1935 (Colonel Seward); "The Throwback" 1935 (Tom Fergus); "The Phantom Rider" 1936-serial (Judge Holmes); "Red River Valley" 1936 (Hartley Moore); "Bar Z Bad Men" 1937 (Hamp Harvey); "Boothill Brigade" 1937 (Jeff Reynolds); "Danger Valley" 1937 (Pappy Temple); "The Fighting Deputy" 1937 (Sheriff Bentley); "Fighting Texan" 1937 (Joe Walton); "Gun Lords of Stirrup Basin" 1937 (Boone Dawson); "It Happened Out West" 1937 (Sheriff); "A Lawman Is Born" 1937 (Graham); "Left-Handed Law" 1937; "Lightnin' Crandall" 1937 (Wes Shannon); "Moonlight on the Range" 1937; "Public Cowboy No. 1" 1937 (Justice); "Trail of Vengeance" 1937 (Tilden); "Code of the Rangers" 1938 (Dave Sage); "Colorado Kid" 1938 (Toles); "Flaming Frontier" 1938-serial; "Knight of the Plains" 1938 (J.C. Rand); "Lightning Carson Rides Again" 1938; "Mexicali Kid" 1938; "Outlaws of Sonora" 1938 (Coroner); "Overland Stage Raiders" 1938 (Milton); "Songs and Bullets" 1938 (Morgan); "West of Rainbow's End" 1938 (Ed); "Code of the Fearless" 1939 (Morrison); "Down the Wyoming Trail" 1939 (Chattan McClellan); "Feud of the Range" 1939 (Harvey Allen); "Frontier Scout" 1939; "In Old Montana" 1939 (Theodore Jason); "The Law Comes to Texas" 1939; "Lone Star Pioneers" 1939 (Joe Cribben); "Mesquite Buckaroo" 1939 (Jim Bond); "The Oregon Trail" 1939-serial; "Riders of the Sage" 1939 (Jim Martin); "Smoky Trails" 1939 (Sheriff); "Song of the Buckaroo" 1939 (Rev Bayliss); "Sundown on the Prairie" 1939; "Trigger Pals" 1939 (Gates); "Trigger Smith" 1939 (Marshal Smith); "Westbound Stage" 1939 (Colonel Hale); "Arizona Frontier" 1940 (Captain Farley); "Beyond the Sacramento" 1940 (Jeff Adams); "Billy the Kid in Texas" 1940 (Jim Morgan); "Brigham Young—Frontiersman" 1940 (Sheriff); "The Durango Kid" 1940 (Sam Lowry); "Frontier Crusader" 1940; "The Golden Trail" 1940; "Land of the Six Guns" 1940 (Howard); "The Range Busters" 1940 (Doc Stengle); "The Return of Wild Bill" 1940 (Ole Mitch); "Riders on Black Mountain" 1940 (Judge Harper); "Riders of Pasco Basin" 1940 (Joe Madison); "Roll, Wagons, Roll" 1940 (Benson); "West of Abilene" 1940 (Kendall); "The Gunman from Bodie" 1941; "Hands Across the Rockies" 1941; "A Missouri Outlaw" 1941 (Randell);

"Prairie Stranger" 1941 (Jim Dawson); "Robbers of the Range" 1941 (Higgins); "The Son of Davy Crockett" 1941; "The Cyclone Kid" 1942 (Marshall); "Lawless Plainsmen" 1942 (Bill Mason); "Stardust on the Sage" 1942; "Trail Riders" 1942 (Banker); "Frontier Fury" 1943; "Frontier Law" 1943 (Vernon); "Robin Hood of the Range" 1943 (Carter); "Saddles and Sagebrush" 1943; "Devil Riders" 1944 (Tom Farrell); "Ghost Guns" 1944; "The Last Horseman" 1944 (Rance Williams); "Saddle Leather Law" 1944; "West of the Rio Grande" 1944; "Blazing the Western Trail" 1945; "Frontier Feud" 1945 (Chalmers); "The Lost Trail" 1945 (Jones); "Song of Old Wyoming" 1945 (Cheyenne Kid); "Border Bandits" 1946 (John Halliday); "The Fighting Frontiersman" 1946; "Frontier Gunlaw" 1946; "The Gay Cavalier" 1946; "Gunning for Vengeance" 1946; "The Haunted Mine" 1946; "Silver Range" 1946; "Under Arizona Skies" 1946; "Flashing Guns" 1947 (Judge); "Gun Talk" 1947 (Simpson); "Law Comes to Gunsight" 1947; "Over the Santa Fe Trail" 1947; "Prairie Express" 1947; "Prairie Raiders" 1947; "Raiders of the South" 1947; "South of the Chisholm Trail" 1947; "Courtin' Trouble" 1948 (Judge); "Crossed Trails" 1948 (Judge); "Frontier Agent" 1948; "Oklahoma Blues" 1948 (Judge); "Range Renegades" 1948; "The Sheriff of Medicine Bow" 1948; "Song of the Drifter" 1948.

LaRue, Jack (1903-1/11/84). Films: "To the Last Man" 1933 (Jim Daggs); "Under the Pampas Moon" 1935 (Bazan); "A Tenderfoot Goes West" 1937 (Killer Madden); "In Old Caliente" 1939 (Delgado); "American Empire" 1942 (Pierre); "The Law Rides Again" 1943 (Dillon); "Dakota" 1945 (Slade); "In Old Sacramento" 1946 (Laramie); "Santa Fe Uprising" 1946; "Robin Hood of Monterey" 1947; "Ride the Man Down" 1952 (Kennedy). ¶TV: *Cheyenne*—"Devil's Canyon" 11-19-57 (Senor Beloze); *Frontier Doctor*—"Storm Over King City" 2-21-59; *Tombstone Territory*—11-13-59 (Padre Miguel).

LaRue, Lash (Al LaRue) (1921-). Films: "The Caravan Trail" 1946 (Ezra); "Wild West" 1946 (Stormy); "Border Feud" 1947 (the Cheyenne Kid); "Cheyenne Takes Over" 1947 (Cheyenne); "The Fighting Vigilantes" 1947 (Marshal Cheyenne Davis); "Ghost Town Renegades" 1947 (Cheyenne); "Law of the Lash" 1947 (Cheyenne); "Pioneer Justice" 1947 (Cheyenne); "Return of the Lash" 1947 (Cheyenne); "Stage to Mesa

City" 1947 (Marshal Cheyenne Davis); "Dead Man's Gold" 1948 (Lash LaRue); "Frontier Revenge" 1948 (Lash LaRue); "Mark of the Lash" 1948; "Prairie Outlaws" 1948; "Outlaw Country" 1949 (Lash La-Rue/the Frontier Phantom); "Son of a Badman" 1949 (Lash); "Son of Billy the Kid" 1949 (Jack Garrett); "The Daltons' Women" 1950; "King of the Bullwhip" 1950 (Lash LaRue); "The Thundering Trail" 1951 (U.S. Marshal); "The Vanishing Outpost" 1951 (U.S. Marshal); "The Black Lash" 1952 (U.S. LaRue); "The Frontier Phantom" 1952; "Hard Trail" 1969 (Slade); "Stagecoach" TVM-1986 (Lash). ¶TV: Lash of the West—Regular 1953 (Host); Judge Roy Bean— "Gunman's Bargain" 1-1-56 (John Wesley Hardin), "The Katcina Doll" 1-1-56 (Storts), "Outlaw's Son" 1-1-56 (Matt Logan), "The Reformer" 1-1-56 (Duke Castle), "Bad Medicine" 6-1-56 (Todd Malone/Will Malone), "The Defense Rests" 6-1-56 (Cashier), "Lone Star Killer" 8-1-56 (Bass); 26 Men—"Chain Gang" 5-6-58; Wyatt Earp—Regular 1959 (Sheriff John Behan).

LaRue, Walt. Films: "New Frontier" 1939 (Man at Dance); "The Phantom Rider" 1946-serial (Ambusher #2); "Cow Town" 1950; "Man with the Steel Whip" 1954-serial (Townsman #2). ¶TV: The High Chaparral—"The Terrorist" 12-17-67 (2nd Bandit).

LaRusso, Adrianna. TV: Centennial—Regular 1978-79 (Clemma Zendt).

La Savio, Jo Jo. Films: "Law of the Pampas" 1939 (Ernesto "Tito" Valdez).

Lascoe, Henry (1914-9/1/64). TV: Man from Blackhawk—"The Trouble with Tolliver" 10-16-59; Bonanza—"The Saga of Annie O'Toole" 10-24-59 (Gregory Spain); Sugarfoot—"The Gitanos" 10-27-59 (Bulu), "Outlaw Island" 11-24-59 (Montes).

Lasell, John (1928-). TV: Wagon Train—"The Jed Polke Story" 3-1-61 (Jed Polke), "The Eleanor Culhane Story" 5-17-61 (Riker Culhane); Tales of Wells Fargo—"A Show from Silver Lode" 3-6-61 (Arthur Phillips); The Tall Man—"A Scheme of Hearts" 4-22-61 (Ben Jardine); Gunsmoke—"Miss Kitty" 10-14-61 (Tucker); Rawhide—"The Retreat" 3-26-65 (Captain Wayly).

Lasses. see White, Lee.

La Starza, Roland (1927-). TV: Wild Wild West—"The Night of the Bogus Bandits" 4-7-67 (Joe Kirby),

"The Night of Montezuma's Hordes" 10-27-67 (Jake).

Lastretti, Adolfo. Films: "Find a Place to Die" 1968-Ital. (Reverend Riley); "Deaf Smith and Johnny Ears" 1972-Ital.

Latell, Lyle (1905-10/24/67). Films: "Texas" 1941 (Dutch Henry, the Boxer); "At Gunpoint" 1955 (Man in Saloon).

Latham, Louise (1922-). Films: "Firecreek" 1968 (Dulcie); "The Awakening Land" TVM-1978 (Jary Luckett). ¶TV: A Man Called Shenandoah—"The Death of Matthew Eldridge" 3-21-66 (Cora Eldridge); Bonanza—"A Real Nice, Friendly Little Town" 11-27-66 (Willie Mae Rikeman), "The Silent Killers" 2-28-71 (Harriet Clinton); Gunsmoke—"Waco" 12-9-68 (Polly Cade), "The Mark of Cain" 2-3-69 (Louise), "Hawk" 10-20-69 (Phoebe Clifford), "Roots of Fear" 12-15-69 (Emilie Sadler), "Gentry's Law" 10-12-70 (Claire Gentry), "To Ride a Yellow Horse" 3-18-74 (Joan Sheperd); Hec Ramsey—"The Mystery of Chalk Hill" 2-18-73 (Willa Hollister); Sara—Regular 1976 (Martha Higgins).

Latimer, Cherie. TV: Bonanza—"In Defense of Honor" 4-28-68 (Bright Moon); The Guns of Will Sonnett—"First Love" 11-3-67 (Diantha Banning).

Latimer, Louise. Films: "Two in Revolt" 1936 (Gloria Benton).

Latimore, Frank (1925-). Films: "Shadow of Zorro" 1963-Span./Ital. (Don Jose/El Zorro); "Shoot to Kill" 1963-Span. (Lance); "Cavalry Charge" 1964-Span.; "Fury of the Apaches" 1966-Span./Ital. (Major Loman).

LaTorre, Charles (1894-2/2/90). Films: "Panhandle" 1948 (Juan); "Sunset in the West" 1950 (Nick Corella).

Latta, Dorothy. Films: "Roll, Thunder, Roll" 1949 (Dorothy Culvert).

Lattell, Ed. Films: "West Is West" 1920 (Herman Mendenhall).

Lau, Wesley (1921-8/30/84). Films: "The Alamo" 1960 (Emil); "Journey to Shiloh" 1968 (Col. Boykin). ¶TV: Lawman—"The Badge" 11-23-58 (Rick Andrews); Gunsmoke—"Young Love" 1-3-59 (Rod Allison), "Miguel's Daughter" 11-28-59 (Ab Cole), "The Blacksmith" 9-17-60 (Willy); Black Saddle—"Client: Tagger" 2-14-59 (Jesse Britt), "Burden of Guilt" 3-18-60 (Harris); Have Gun Will Travel—"The Sons of Aaron Murdock" 5-9-59 (Lew Murdock),

"Saturday Night" 10-8-60 (Stub); Pony Express—"The Peace Offering" 11-18-59; Tales of Wells Fargo—"The English Woman" 2-15-60 (Hank), "Leading Citizen" 11-14-60 (Morgan Bates); Bonanza—"Desert Justice" 2-20-60 (Billy Walker), "Her Brother's Keeper" 3-6-66 (Carl); Johnny Ringo—"Uncertain Vengeance" 3-10-60 (Red); The Law of the Plainsman—"Stella" 3-31-60 (Staff Meeker); Wyatt Earp—"He's My Brother" 11-29-60 (Dave Dray); Wagon Train—"The Christopher Hale Story" 3-15-61 (Stevens); The Tall Man—"Ladies of the Town" 5-20-61 (Jason Cleary); The Big Valley—"Earthquake!" 11-10-65 (Ralph Snyder); The Virginian—"Nobody Said Hello" 1-5-66 (McClain), "Vengeance Trail" 1-4-67 (Sheriff Ben Morris), "The Gentle Tamers" 1-24-68 (Hoyt); Laredo—"The Callico Kid" 1-6-66 (Jacobus Carson), "The Seventh Day" 1-6-67 (Rev. Egan Thomas); Time Tunnel—Regular 1966-67 (Sgt. Jiggs).

Laughlin, Tom (1931-). Films: "Billy Jack" 1971 (Billy Jack); "The Trial of Billy Jack" 1974 (Billy Jack); "The Master Gunfighter" 1975 (Finley); "The Legend of the Lone Ranger" 1981 (Neeley). ¶TV: Wagon Train—"The Mary Halstead Story" 11-20-57 (the Laramie Kid); The Deputy—"Like Father" 10-17-59 (Jim Stanton); Tales of Wells Fargo—"The Quiet Village" 11-2-59 (Jess Wilson).

Laughton, Charles (1899-12/15/62). Films: "Ruggles of Red Gap" 1935 (Col. Marmaduke "Bill" Ruggles). ¶TV: Wagon Train—"The Albert Farnsworth Story" 10-12-60 (Colonel Albert Farnsworth).

Laughton, Eddie (1903-3/21/52). Films: "One Man Justice" 1937; "Pest from the West" 1939-short; "Blazing Six Shooters" 1940 (Bunyon); "Bullets for Rustlers" 1940 (Shorty); "The Man from Tumbleweeds" 1940 (Jackson); "Out West with the Peppers" 1940 (Lumberjack); "Texas Stagecoach" 1940 (Workman); "Thundering Frontier" 1940 (Tyler); "West of Abilene" 1940 (Poke); "Across the Sierras" 1941; "Hands Across the Rockies" 1941; "Outlaws of the Panhandle" 1941 (Chad); "Bullets for Bandits" 1942; "Lawless Plainsmen" 1942 (Slim); "Vengeance of the West" 1942; "West of Tombstone" 1942; "Hail to the Rangers" 1943; "Sundown Valley" 1944 (Tom Carleton).

Launders, Perc (1904-10/2/52). Films: "Twilight on the Prairie" 1944; "Under Western Skies" 1945 (Hank); "West of the Pecos" 1945 (Sam

Sawtelle); "River Lady" 1948 (Man); "Western Heritage" 1948 (Sheriff).

Launer, S. John (1919-). Films: "Apache Rifles" 1964; "The Girl Called Hatter Fox" TVM-1977 (Mr. Winton). ¶TV: *Gunsmoke*—"Robin Hood" 2-4-56 (Judge), "Fingered" 11-23-57 (Jim Dobie), "Tobe" 10-19-63 (Townsman); *Zane Grey Theater*—"Man Unforgiving" 1-3-58 (Wilkins); *Have Gun Will Travel*—"Three Sons" 5-10-58; *The Texan*—"The Hemp Tree" 11-17-58 (Ben Cushman); *The Restless Gun*—"Lady by Law" 5-11-59 (Judge); *Bonanza*—"The Truckee Strip" 11-21-59 (Jason Cauter), "The Artist" 10-7-62 (Buyer); *Man from Blackhawk*—"Gold Is Where You Find It" 6-24-60 (Rodney); *Stoney Burke*—"Gold-Plated Maverick" 1-7-63 (Dr. Telford); *The Big Valley*—"Danger Road" 4-21-69 (Ted).

Laurel, Stan (1890-2/23/65). Films: "Way Out West" 1937 (Stan).

Lauren, Rod (1940). Films: "The Gun Hawk" 1963 (Roan); "Law of the Lawless" 1964 (Deputy Tim Ludlow).

Laurenz, John (1909-11/7/58). Films: "Black Arrow" 1944-serial; "In Old New Mexico" 1945 (Brady); "Sunset Pass" 1946 (Chito); "Apache Rose" 1947 (Pete); "Code of the West" 1947 (Chito); "Border Outlaws" 1950 (Kevin).

Laurie, Piper (1932-). Films: "Dawn at Socorro" 1954 (Rannah Hayes); "Smoke Signal" 1955 (Laura Evans).

Lauter, Ed (1940-). Films: "The Badge of Marshal Brennan" 1957 (Dr. Steve Hale); "Bad Company" 1972 (Big Joe's Gang Member); "Dirty Little Billy" 1972 (Tyler); "The Magnificent Seven Ride" 1972 (Scott Elliott); "The Godchild" TVM-1974 (Crees); "Breakheart Pass" 1976 (Major Claremont); "The White Buffalo" 1977 (Capt. Tom Custer); "Death Hunt" 1981 (Hazel); "Timerider" 1983 (Padre); "Wagons East!" 1994 (John Slade). ¶TV: *The New Land*—"The Word Is: Growth" 9-21-74; *How the West Was Won*—Episode Eight 4-16-78 (Martin Stillman), Episode Twelve 5-14-78 (Martin Stillman), Episode Thirteen 5-21-78 (Martin Stillman).

Lauter, Harry (1920-10/30/90). Films: "Bandit King of Texas" 1949 (Tremm Turner); "Frontier Marshal" 1949 (Kenny); "Prince of the Plains" 1949 (Tom Owens); "Tucson" 1949 (George Reeves, Jr.); "Ready to Ride" 1950-short; "Hills of Utah" 1951 (Evan Fox); "The Kid from Amarillo" 1951 (Tom Mallory); "Silver City Bonanza" 1951 (Peter); "Thunder in God's Country" 1951 (Tim Gallery); "Valley of Fire" 1951 (Tod Rawlings); "Whirlwind" 1951 (Wade Trimble); "Apache Country" 1952 (Dave Kilrain); "Bugles in the Afternoon" 1952 (Cpl. Jackson); "Night Stage to Galveston" 1952 (Evans); "Yukon Gold" 1952; "Canadian Mounties vs. Atomic Invaders" 1953-serial (Mountie Clark); "The Fighting Lawman" 1953; "The Marshal's Daughter" 1953 (Russ Mason); "Pack Train" 1953 (Roy Wade); "Topeka" 1953 (Mack Wilson); "The Forty-Niners" 1954 (Gambler); "Apache Ambush" 1955 (Bailey); "At Gunpoint" 1955 (Federal Marshal); "Outlaw Treasure" 1955; "Dig That Uranium" 1956 (Haskell); "The Oklahoman" 1957 (Grant); "Raiders of Old California" 1957; "Shoot-Out at Medicine Bend" 1957; "Good Day for a Hanging" 1958 (Matt Fletcher); "Return to Warbow" 1958 (1st Deputy); "Toughest Gun in Tombstone" 1958 (Barger); "The Gunfight at Dodge City" 1959 (Ed); "Buffalo Gun" 1961 (Telegrapher); "Posse from Hell" 1961 (Russell); "The Wild Westerners" 1962 (Judas); "Convict Stage" 1965 (Ben Lattimore); "Fort Courageous" 1965 (Joe); "Fort Utah" 1967 (Britches); "Barquero" 1970 (Steele). ¶TV: *The Lone Ranger*—"Rustler's Hideout" 10-13-49, "Trouble Waters" 3-9-50, "Dead Man's Chest" 9-28-50, "Paid in Full" 12-28-50, "Diamond in the Rough" 8-27-53, "Code of the Pioneers" 2-17-55, "White Hawk's Decision" 10-18-56, "Quarter Horse War" 11-8-56, "Ghost Canyon" 12-27-56; *The Gene Autry Show*—"Blackwater Valley Feud" 9-3-50, "Doublecross Valley" 9-10-50, "Hot Lead" 11-26-50, "Warning! Danger!" 11-10-51, "Bandits of Boulder Bluff" 11-24-51, "The Western Way" 2-1-52, "Hot Lead and Old Lace" 2-15-52, "Thunder Out West" 7-14-53, "Bandidos" 9-1-53, "Johnny Jackaroo" 7-13-54, "Talking Guns" 8-10-54, "The Carnival Comes West" 8-24-54, "Civil War at Deadwood" 9-14-54, "The Million Dollar Fiddle" 10-1-55, "The Golden Chariot" 10-29-55; *The Range Rider*—"Ambush in Coyote Canyon" 3-15-52, "Convict at Large" 10-4-52, "Marked for Death" 11-8-52, "Marshal from Madero" 1-24-53; *The Roy Rogers Show*—"The Double Crosser" 6-1-52 (Ralph Colton), "Hidden Treasure" 12-19-54 (Vic), "The Big Chance" 1-23-55 (Mart Sellers); *Wild Bill Hickok*—"Treasure Trail" 12-30-52, "Jingles Wins a Friend" 4-28-53; *Annie Oak-*ley—"Annie and the Silver Ace" 2-27-54, "Annie and the First Phone" 7-22-56 (Sam Johnson), "Indian Justice" 7-29-56 (Quint Kelly); *Tales of the Texas Rangers*—Regular 1955-57 (Clay Morgan); *Wyatt Earp*—"The Assassins" 1-10-56 (Baumer); *Fury*—"Tungsten Queen" 1-14-56 (Haylor), "The Timber Walkers" 11-14-59; *Zane Grey Theater*—"A Quiet Sunda in San Ardo" 11-23-56 (Maurie), "Village of Fear" 3-1-57, "Decision at Wilson's Creek" 5-17-57 (Sgt. Stone), "Threat of Violence" 5-23-58 (Hake Morris), "The Accuser" 10-30-58; *Jim Bowie*—"The Intruder" 4-26-57; *Tombstone Territory*—"The Rebels' Last Charge" 1-15-58; *Sergeant Preston of the Yukon*—"Gold Rush Patrol" 1-16-58 (Curly); *Jefferson Drum*—"The Hanging of Joe Lavetti" 8-1-58 (Vince Meeker); *Northwest Passage*—"Fight at the River" 9-14-58 (Mason); *Wichita Town*—"Day of Battle" 1-18-59 (Jim Dudley); *Rawhide*—"Incident of the Widowed Dove" 1-30-59 (Billy Grant), "Incident of the Haunted Hills" 11-6-59 (Garrison), "Incident of the Painted Lady" 5-12-61, "The Blue Sky" 12-8-61 (Kirby), "The Devil and the Deep Blue" 5-11-62 (Reagan), "Incident of the Reluctant Bridegroom" 11-30-62 (Hank), "Incident of the Clown" 3-29-63 (Captain Ross), "Incident at Confidence Creek" 11-28-63 (Orville Tippet), "Incident at Gila Flats" 1-30-64 (Major Blaine), "The Diehard" 4-9-65 (Lenny); *Death Valley Days*—"Gold Lake" 2-3-59 (Mel Hardin), "Wheelbarrow Johnny" 2-10-59 (Mel Hardin); *Maverick*—"The Saga of Waco Williams" 2-15-59 (Bernie Adams), "Three Queens Full" 11-12-61 (Brazo); *Rough Riders*—"Gunpoint Persuasion" 4-30-59 (Jacob Nibley); *Colt .45*—"The Sanctuary" 5-10-59 (Johnny Tyler), "Impasse" 1-31-60 (Rafe Larson); *The Texan*—"The Smiling Loser" 5-25-59; *Laramie*—"The Run to Rumavaca" 11-10-59 (Roy Crystal), "The Legend of Lily" 1-26-60 (Alamo), "Run of the Hunted" 4-4-61 (Harry), "Deadly Is the Night" 11-7-61 (Rafe Andrews), "The Killer Legend" 12-12-61 (Joe Bartell), "Fall into Darkness" 4-17-62 (Ben Frances), "Edge of Evil" 4-2-63 (Bert Lewis); *Gunsmoke*—"Big Tom" 1-9-60 (Clay Cran), "The Lady Killer" 4-23-60 (Sy), "Say Uncle" 10-1-60 (Martin Nagle), "All That" 10-28-61, "Ex-Con" 11-30-63 (Kelly), "Big Man, Big Target" 11-28-64, "Honey Pot" 5-15-65 (Gregory Bellow), "Baker's Dozen" 12-25-67 (Henry Rucker), "9:12 to Dodge" 11-11-68 (Michael Drennan); *Cheyenne*—

"Riot at Arroyo Soco" 2-1-60 (Harry Tobin); *Bat Masterson*—"The Reluctant Witness" 3-31-60 (Sheriff Conners); *Riverboat*—"The Long Trail" 4-4-60 (Colonel Tryker); *Death Valley Days*—"Mission to the Mountains" 6-14-60 (Henry Schmidtlein), "By the Book" 5-4-68 (Bennett); *Klondike*—"Taste of Danger" 12-5-60 (Collins); *Stagecoach West*—"Three Wise Men" 12-20-60 (Doyle), "Songs My Mother Told Me" 2-21-61 (North), "The Dead Don't Cry" 5-2-61 (Sheriff Woods); *Have Gun Will Travel*—"The Legacy" 12-10-60 (Crawford); *The Deputy*—"The Lesson" 1-14-61 (Lex Danton); *Lawman*—"The Stalker" 10-29-61 (Compton Schaeffer); *Bonanza*—"Day of the Dragon" 12-3-61 (Barrett), "The Quest" 9-30-62; *Tales of Wells Fargo*—"To Kill a Town" 3-21-62 (Pete); *The Rifleman*—"The Bullet" 2-25-63 (Hired Gun); *Temple Houston*—"Thunder Gap" 11-21-63 (Sheriff Macon); *The Virginian*—"Six Graves at Cripple Creek" 1-27-65 (McGraw), "The Gauntlet" 2-8-67 (Lund), "The Lady from Wichita" 9-27-67 (Roy Kane), "Nora" 12-11-68 (Captain Sam Harris); *Branded*—"Fill No Glass for Me" 11-7-65 & 11-14-65 (Dart); *Wild Wild West*—"The Night of the Double-Edged Knife" 11-12-65, "The Night of the Headless Woman" 1-5-68 (Marshal); *Time Tunnel*—"Billy the Kid" 2-10-67 (Wilson); *Cimarron Strip*—"The Search" 11-9-67 (Wisler); *Daniel Boone*—"Thirty Pieces of Silver" 3-28-68; *The Guns of Will Sonnett*—"Pariah" 10-18-68 (Elihu Long), "A Town in Terror" 2-7-69 & 2-14-69 (Frank Corbett); *The Big Valley*—"Lightfoot" 2-17-69 (Ben Watson); *The High Chaparral*—"Pale Warrior" 12-11-70 (Mobley); *Alias Smith and Jones*—"Smiler with a Gun" 10-7-71.

La Varre, Bob. TV: *Sergeant Preston of the Yukon*—"The Skull in the Stone" 11-7-57 (Uluk); *The Restless Gun*—"The Peddler" 6-9-58 (Spook Sanford).

LaVerne, Lucille (1872-3/4/45). Films: "The Great Meadow" 1931 (Elvira Jarvis); "Wild Horse Mesa" 1932 (Ma Melberne); "The Last Trail" 1933 (Mrs. Wilson).

Laverre, Morton. see Merton, John.

Lavi, Daliah (1940-). Films: "Old Shatterhand" 1968-Ger./Yugo./Fr./Ital. (Paloma); "Catlow" 1971-Span. (Rosita).

Law, Burton C. (1877-11/2/63). Films: "Winners of the West" 1921-serial (Captain John C. Fremont); "In the Days of Buffalo Bill" 1922-serial

(Allan Pinkerton); "The Oregon Trail" 1923-serial.

Law, John Phillip (1937-). Films: "Death Rides a Horse" 1967-Ital. (Bill).

Law, Walter (1876-8/8/40). Films: "Between Fighting Men" 1932 (Winchester Thompson).

Lawford, Peter (1923-12/24/84). Films: "Kangaroo" 1952 (Richard Connor); "Sergents 3" 1962 (Sgt. Larry Barrett). ¶TV: *Ruggles of Red Gap* 2-3-57 (Lord George Vane-Brinstead); *Wild Wild West*—"The Night of the Flying Pie Plate" 10-21-66 (Carl Jackson); *The Men from Shiloh*—"The Town Killer" 3-10-71 (Ben Hunter).

Lawler, Anderson (-1959). Films: "The Cheyenne Kid" 1933 (Tate); "Empty Holsters" 1937 (Buck Govern); "Heart of the North" 1938 (Burgoon).

Lawless, Patrick. Films: "Drum Beat" 1954 (O'Brien); "The Firebrand" 1962. ¶TV: *The Lone Ranger*—"The Banker's Son" 5-16-57; *Sergeant Preston of the Yukon*—"Lost River Roundup" 12-12-57 (Hank Lloyd); *The Californians*—"The First Gold Brick" 1-6-59 (Daniels).

Lawliss, Joe. Films: "Flying Lariats" 1931 (Dad Starr); "Riders of the Cactus" 1931 (Bill).

Lawrence, Babe. Films: "Frontier Town" 1938 (Clem Brooks).

Lawrence, Barbara (1928-). Films: "Arena" 1953 (Sylvia Morgan); "Jesse James Versus the Daltons" 1954 (Kate Manning); "Man with the Gun" 1955 (Ann Wakefield); "Oklahoma!" 1955 (Gertie); "Joe Dakota" 1957 (Myrna Weaver); "Man in the Shadow" 1957 (Helen Sadler). ¶TV: *Cheyenne*—"The Last Train West" 5-29-56 (Lola McQuillan); *Jim Bowie*—"Up the Creek" 3-7-58 (Millie); *Cimarron City*—"Terror Town" 10-18-58 (Cora Budinger); *Trackdown*—"The Avenger" 10-31-58 (Grace Marsden); *Riverboat*—"Witness No Evil" 11-1-59 (Abby Saunders); *Man from Blackhawk*—"The Hundred Thousand Dollar Policy" 1-22-60 (Evelyn Marquis); *Bat Masterson*—"Law of the Land" 10-6-60 (Melanie Haywood); *Bonanza*—"The Abduction" 10-29-60 (Della); *The Tall Man*—"Trial by Fury" 4-14-62 (Sadie Wren); *Cimarron Strip*—"The Greeners" 3-7-68.

Lawrence, Carol (1934-). TV: *Wagon Train*—"The Widow O'Rourke Story" 10-7-63 (Princess Mei Ling); *Rawhide*—"The Vasquez Woman" 10-26-65 (Maria Vasquez); *Kung Fu*—

"My Brother, My Executioner" 10-12-74 (Ada Caine).

Lawrence, Del (1874-4/1/65). Films: "Overland with Kit Carson" 1939-serial; "The Pioneers" 1941 (Ames).

Lawrence, Delphi (1932-). Films: "The Last Challenge" 1967 (Marie Webster). ¶TV: *Wild Wild West*—"The Night of the Poisonous Posey" 10-28-66 (Lucrece Posey); *Gunsmoke*—"Old Friend" 2-4-67 (Willa).

Lawrence, Edna. Films: "The Lone Ranger" 1938-serial (Marina); "Drums of Destiny" 1937 (Rosa Maria Dominguez); "Rancho Grande" 1940 (Rita Ross).

Lawrence, Florence (1888-12/27/38). Films: "Daniel Boone" 1907; "The Call of the Wild" 1908; "The Girl and the Outlaw" 1908; "The Red Girl" 1908; "The Vaquero's Vow" 1908; "The Mended Lute" 1909; "Hard Hombre" 1931; "Secrets" 1933.

Lawrence, Hugh (-7/13/69). TV: *Empire*—"Breakout" 4-16-63 (Driver).

Lawrence, Jay (1924-6/18/87). Films: "The Man from Tumbleweeds" 1940 (Ranger); "King of Dodge City" 1941; "Riding Shotgun" 1954 (Lewellyn); "A Lawless Street" 1955; "The Halliday Brand" 1957.

Lawrence, Jody (1931-7/10/86). Films: "Captain John Smith and Pocahontas" 1953 (Pocahontas); "Stagecoach to Dancer's Rock" 1962 (Dr. Ann Thompson). ¶TV: *The Rebel*—"The Scavengers" 11-8-59 (Kate), "The Earl of Durango" 6-12-60 (Lorena).

Lawrence, John (1910-6/26/74). Films: "In Old New Mexico" 1945; "Nevada Smith" 1966 (Hogg). ¶TV: *Pony Express*—"The Killer" 3-23-60 (Wes McPhail); *Gunsmoke*—"Panacea Sykes" 4-13-63; *Laredo*—"The Would-Be Gentleman of Laredo" 4-14-66; *The Outcasts*—"Alligator King" 1-20-69 (Burns).

Lawrence, Lillian (1870-5/7/26). Films: "The Mysterious Avenger" 1936; "Texas Stagecoach" 1940.

Lawrence, Mady. Films: "Heart of the Rio Grande" 1942; "Oath of Vengeance" 1944; "The Pinto Bandit" 1944; "Spook Town" 1944; "Lightning Raiders" 1946 (Jane).

Lawrence, Marc (1910-). Films: "The Cowboy Star" 1936 (Johnny Sampson); "Robin Hood of El Dorado" 1936 (Manuel); "Brigham Young—Frontiersman" 1940 (Prosecutor); "The Shepherd of the Hills"

1941 (Pete Matthews); "Call of the Canyon" 1942 (Horace Dunston); "Calaboose" 1943; "The Ox-Bow Incident" 1943 (Farnley); "Don't Fence Me In" 1945 (Cliff Anson); "Flame of the Barbary Coast" 1945 (Disko); "The Virginian" 1946 (Pete); "Unconquered" 1947 (Sioto, Medicine Man); "Yankee Fakir" 1947 (Duke); "Calamity Jane and Sam Bass" 1949 (Dean); "Tough Assignment" 1949 (Vince); "Jubal" 1956 (Tolliver Boy); "Savage Pampas" 1966-U.S./Span./Arg. (Sgt. Barril); "Custer of the West" 1967-U.S./Span. (Goldminer); "The Five Man Army" 1969-Ital. (Carnival Barker). ¶TV: *Wagon Train*—"Around the Horn" 10-1-58 (Ferris); *The Rifleman*—"The Safe Guard" 11-18-58 (Gavin), "Trail of Hate" 9-27-60 (Cougar); *Zane Grey Theater*—"Killer Instinct" 3-17-60 (Wade Migill); *Bronco*—"Tangled Trail" 5-3-60 (Joe Russo); *The Deputy*—"The Hard Decision" 1-28-61 (Alvy Burke); *Lawman*—"Homecoming" 2-5-61 (Frank Walker); *Whispering Smith*—"Death at Even Money" 7-10-61 (Frankie Wilson); *Bonanza*—"Caution: Easter Bunny Crossing" 3-29-70 (Red Gaskell); *Nichols*—"Zachariah" 1-11-72 (Prouty).

Lawrence, Marjory. Films: "Anything Once" 1917 (Dorothy Stuart).

Lawrence, Mary (1918-9/24/91). TV: *Casey Jones*—Regular 1958-59 (Alice Jones); *Northwest Passage*—"War Sign" 11-30-58 (Ruth Martin).

Lawrence, Muriel. Films: "Belle Le Grand" 1951 (Nan Henshaw).

Lawrence, Peter Lee (1943-73). Films: "Days of Violence" 1967-Ital. (John); "Fury of Johnny Kid" 1967-Span./Ital. (Johnny Kid); "Killer Caliber .32" 1967-Ital. (Silver); "The Man Who Killed Billy the Kid" 1967-Span./Ital. (Billy Bonney); "Awkward Hands" 1968-Span./Ital. (Kitt); "One Against One … No Mercy" 1968-Span./Ital. (Chico); "Pistol for a Hundred Coffins" 1968-Ital./Span. (the Kid); "Dead Are Countless" 1969-Ital./Span. (Johnny); "Death on High Mountain" 1969-Ital./Span. (Lorring Vanderbuilt); "Killer Goodbye" 1969-Ital./Span. (Jess Frank); "More Dollars for the MacGregors" 1970-Ital./Span. (Blondie); "Sabata the Killer" 1970-Ital./Span. (Peter); "Four Gunmen of the Holy Trinity" 1971-Ital. (Lincoln); "Raise Your Hands, Dead Man … You're Under Arrest" 1971-Ital./Span. (the Sando Kid); "God in Heaven … Arizona on Earth" 1972-Span./Ital. (Arizona); "Prey of Vultures" 1973-Span./Ital. (Kit).

Lawrence, Rosina. Films: "Way Out West" 1937 (Mary Roberts).

Lawrence, Terry. Films: "Trooper Hook" 1957 (Quito).

Lawrence, William E. (1896-11/28/47). Films: "The Deputy's Chance That Won" 1915; "The Outlaw's Revenge" 1916 (Federal Officer); "Fightin' Mad" 1921 (Francisco Lazaro); "Get Your Man" 1921 (Arthur Whitman); "The Love Gambler" 1922 (Tom Gould); "Blinky" 1923 (Lt. Rawkins); "The Thrill Chaser" 1923; "Blue Wing's Revenge" 1924; "The Boss of Bar 20" 1924; "Flying Eagle" 1924; "The King's Command" 1924; "A Sagebrush Vagabond" 1924; "The Traitor" 1924; "Hard-Boiled" 1926 (Gordon Andrews); "A Man Four-Square" 1926 (Jim Clanton); "Boss Rider of Gun Creek" 1936; "Ride 'Em Cowboy" 1936 (Sandy Adams); "Silver Spurs" 1936 (Snell); "Sunset of Power" 1936 (Bud Rolfe); "Empty Saddles" 1937; "Black Aces" 1937 (Boyd Loomis); "Sudden Bill Dorn" 1937 (Hank Smith).

Lawson, Bobby. Films: "Down the Wyoming Trail" 1939 (Jerry Parker).

Lawson, Carol. TV: *Bonanza*—"It's a Small World" 1-4-70 (Alice), "The Love Child" 11-8-70 (Etta), "The Sound of Loneliness" 12-5-72 (Mrs. Holcombe).

Lawson, Eric. Films: "Last Ride of the Dalton Gang" TVM-1979 (Willie Powers); "Bonanza: Under Attack" TVM-1995 (Morgan).

Lawson, Kate Drain (1894-11/14/77). Films: "The Nevadan" 1950 (Mama Lito); "Rock Island Trail" 1950 (Mrs. McCoy); "The First Traveling Saleslady" 1956 (Annie Peachpit).

Lawson, Linda (1935-). Films: "Apache Rifles" 1964 (Dawn Gillis). ¶TV: *Tales of the Texas Rangers*—"Edge of Danger" 10-23-58 (Dolores); *Maverick*—"Duel at Sundown" 2-1-59 (Lily); *Have Gun Will Travel*—"The Unforgiven" 11-7-59 (Reva); *Colt .45*—"Impasse" 1-31-60 (Barbara); *Tombstone Territory*—2-5-60 (Jeannie); *Wagon Train*—"Princess of a Lost Tribe" 11-2-60 (Lia); *Bonanza*—"The Trail Gang" 11-26-60 (Melinda), "To Own the World" 4-18-65 (Maria Hackett); *Tales of Wells Fargo*—"Escort to Santa Fe" 12-19-60 (Kate Fallon); *Stagecoach West*—"The Root of Evil" 2-28-61 (Stella Smith); *The Rifleman*—"Assault" 3-21-61 (Vashti Croxton); *The Virginian*—"Chaff in the Wind" 1-26-66 (Becky Ellis).

Lawson, Louise. TV: *Wild Wild West*—"The Night of the Glowing Corpse" 10-29-65 (Blonde), "The Night of the Underground Terror" 1-19-68 (Slave Girl); *Laredo*—"Coup de Grace" 10-7-66 (Betsy).

Lawson, Priscilla (1915-60). Films: "The Phantom Rider" 1936-serial; "Sutter's Gold" 1936; "The Girl of the Golden West" 1938 (Nina Martinez); "Heroes of the Hills" 1938 (Madelyn Reynolds).

Lawson, Richard. TV: *The Buffalo Soldiers*—Pilot 5-26-79 (Caleb Holiday).

Lawson, Wilfred (1900-10/10/66). Films: "Allegheny Uprising" 1939 (MacDougle).

Lawton, Alma. TV: *Sergeant Preston of the Yukon*—"Blind Justice" 1-17-57 (Molly Andrews).

Lawton, Don. TV: *Sergeant Preston of the Yukon*—"Blind Justice" 1-17-57 (Jim Andrews); *Tales of the Texas Rangers*—"Edge of Danger" 10-23-58 (Escobar).

Lawton, Frank (1904-6/10/69). Films: "Bar 20 Rides Again" 1936 (Elbows).

Layman, Gene (1889-6/6/46). Films: "White Renegade" 1931.

Layne, Tracy. Films: "Arizona Bad Man" 1935 (Cowboy); "Gunsmoke on the Guadalupe" 1935; "Tumbling Tumbleweeds" 1935 (Henchman); "Gun Smoke" 1936 (Pecos); "Guns and Guitars" 1936 (Henchman); "King of the Pecos" 1936 (Trooper); "The Lonely Trail" 1936 (Kirk); "The Singing Cowboy" 1936 (Kirk); "Vigilantes Are Coming" 1936-serial (Clem Peters); "Winds of the Wasteland" 1936; "The Big Show" 1937; "Galloping Dynamite" 1937 (Mosby); "Riders of the Whistling Skull" 1937 (Henchman).

Layton, Dru. Films: "Valley of Wanted Men" 1935 (Sally Sanderson).

Lazareff, Serge (1944-). Films: "Ned Kelly" 1970-Brit. (Wild Wright).

LaZarre, Jerry. TV: *Wagon Train*—"The Don Alvarado Story" 6-21-61 (Edwardo); *The Deputy*—"Lawman's Conscience" 7-1-61 (Zack Tanby).

Lazer, Peter (1946-). Films: "Hombre" 1967 (Billy Lee). ¶TV: *Riverboat*—"Strange Request" 12-13-59 (Bobby).

Lea, Jennifer. Films: "The Oklahoman" 1957 (Girl); "The Tall Stranger" 1957 (Mary). ¶TV: *Ser-*

geant Preston of the Yukon—"Escape to the North" 1-9-58 (Rita O'Day); Wanted—Dead or Alive—"The Martin Poster" 9-6-58 (Louise Martin); Tales of Wells Fargo—"The Deserter" 11-24-58 (Ellen Rath); Wichita Town—"Man on the Hill" 11-4-59 (Marianne); Colt .45—"Tar and Feathers" 11-22-59 (Louise Porter); The Rebel—"Glory" 1-24-60 (Glory); The Rifleman—"Smoke Screen" 4-5-60 (Marge Crandell); Have Gun Will Travel—"The Twins" 5-21-60 (Beth Mirakian); Gunsmoke—"Twenty Miles from Dodge" 4-10-65 (Mrs. Rucker).

Leach, Britt. Films: "Banjo Hackett: Roamin' Free" TVM-1976 (the Carpenter); "Young Pioneers' Christmas" TVM-1976 (Loftus); "Goin' South" 1978 (Parson Weems); "High Noon, Part II: The Return of Will Kane" TVM-1980 (Virgil). ¶TV: Bonanza—"The Twenty-Sixth Grave" 10-31-72 (Postal Clerk).

Leachman, Cloris (1926-). Films: "Butch Cassidy and the Sundance Kid" 1969 (Agnes). ¶TV: Zane Grey Theater—"You Only Run Once" 10-5-56 (Martha), "The Hanging Tree" 2-22-57 (Martha); Gunsmoke—"Legal Revenge" 11-17-56 (Flory Tebbs), "The Love of Money" 5-27-61 (Boni Van Demar); Rawhide—"Incident of the Arana Sacar" 4-22-60 (Mary Ann Belden); Wanted—Dead or Alive—"The Medicine Man" 11-23-60 (Ann Barchester); The Outlaws—"Starfall" 11-24-60 & 12-1-60 (Maddy); Frontier Circus—"The Hunter and the Hunted" 11-2-61 (Anna); Laramie—"Trial by Fire" 4-10-62 (Zoie Carter); Wagon Train—"The Nancy Davis Story" 5-16-62 (Loretta); Stoney Burke—"Cousin Eunice" 12-24-62 (Eunice Stocker); A Man Called Shenandoah—"The Caller" 10-11-65; The Virginian—"Requiem for a Country Doctor" 1-25-67 (Clara), "The Land Dreamer" 2-26-69 (Ellen McKinley); The Big Valley—"Plunder at Hawk's Grove" 3-13-67 (Fay); The Road West—"The Eighty-Seven Dollar Bride" 4-3-67 (Amadee); The Guns of Will Sonnett—"And a Killing Rode into Town" 12-1-67 (Vera); Lancer—"Angel Day and Her Sunshine Girls" 2-25-69 (Angel Day), "Little Darling of the Sierras" 12-30-69 (Hester).

Lear, Evelyn. Films: "Buffalo Bill and the Indians, or Sitting Bull's History Lesson" 1976 (Nina).

Learn, Bessie (1888-2/5/87). Films: "Across the Great Divide" 1915.

Learned, Michael (1929-). Films: "Gunsmoke: The Last

Apache" TVM-1990 (Mike Yardner). ¶TV: Gunsmoke—"Matt's Love Story" 9-24-73 (Mike Yardner), "A Game of Death…An Act of Love" 11-5-73 & 11-12-73 (May Lassiter).

Leary, Mildred. Films: "Wild Honey" 1918 (Letty Noon).

Leary, Nolan (1891-12/12/87). Films: "Days of Old Cheyenne" 1943 (Higgins); "Code of the Prairie" 1944 (Rancher); "Outlaws of Santa Fe" 1944 (Mayor Ward); "Saddle Leather Law" 1944; "Saddle Leather Law" 1944; "Sheriff of Sundown" 1944 (Dineem); "Zorro's Black Whip" 1944-serial (Payne); "Blazing the Western Trail" 1945; "Lone Texas Ranger" 1945; "Santa Fe Saddlemates" 1945; "Galloping Thunder" 1946; "Heading West" 1946; "Out California Way" 1946 (George Sheridan); "That Texas Jamboree" 1946; "The Last Round-Up" 1947; "Over the Santa Fe Trail" 1947; "The Sea of Grass" 1947 (Homesteader); "West of Dodge City" 1947; "Outlaw Brand" 1948; "The Cowboy and the Indians" 1949 (Sheriff Don Payne); "Riders of the Whistling Pines" 1949; "Roaring Westward" 1949 (Mossy); "The Blazing Sun" 1950; "The Furies" 1950 (Drunk Guest); "The James Brothers of Missouri" 1950-serial (Pop Keever); "Gene Autry and the Mounties" 1951 (Dr. Sawyer); "The Big Sky" 1952; "High Noon" 1952 (Lewis); "Tall Man Riding" 1955 (Dr. William Stone); "The Persuader" 1957 (Dan); "Money, Women and Guns" 1958 (Job Kingman). ¶TV: The Roy Rogers Show—"Haunted Mine of Paradise Valley" 5-18-52, "Deadlock at Dark Canyon" 1-6-57; Fury—"Joey Sees It Through" 1-21-56 (Mr. Adams); Wanted—Dead or Alive—"The Corner" 2-21-59; Have Gun Will Travel—"The Hatchet Man" 3-5-60 (Clarence Magruder); Laramie—"Justice in a Hurry" 3-20-62, "The Violent Ones" 3-5-63; Bonanza—"Inger, My Love" 4-15-62, "Riot!" 10-3-72 (Old Charlie); The Virginian—"The Horse Fighter" 12-15-65 (Doctor).

Leary, Timothy (1921-). TV: Adventures of Brisco County, Jr.—"Stagecoach" 4-1-94 (Dr. Milo).

Lease, Maria. Films: "The Scavengers" 1969 (Faith).

Lease, Rex (1901-1/3/66). Films: "The Outlaw Dog" 1927 (Bill Brady); "The Law of the Range" 1928 (the Solitaire Kid); "Red Riders of Canada" 1928 (Pierre Duval); "Riders of the Dark" 1928 (Jim Graham); "The Utah Kid" 1930 (Cal Reynolds); "Wings of Adventure" 1930 (Dave

Kent); "In Old Cheyenne" 1931 (Jim); "The Sign of the Wolf" 1931-serial (Tom Lanning); "The Cowboy and the Bandit" 1935 (Bill); "Cyclone of the Saddle" 1935 (Andy Thomas); "Fighting Caballero" 1935; "The Ghost Rider" 1935 (Dave Danford); "The Man from Guntown" 1935 (Alan McArthur); "Pals of the Range" 1935 (Steve Barton); "Rough Riding Ranger" 1935 (Corporal Daniels/the Tombstone Kid); "Aces and Eights" 1936 (Jose Hernendez); "Cavalcade of the West" 1936 (Ace Carter/Asa Knox); "Custer's Last Stand" 1936-serial (Kit Cardigan); "Fast Bullets" 1936 (Jimmy); "Lightning Bill Carson" 1936 (the Pecos Kid); "Ridin' On" 1936 (Danny O'Neill); "Roarin' Guns" 1936 (Jerry); "The Silver Trail" 1937 (Bob Crandall); "Code of the Rangers" 1938 (Jack Strong); "Desert Patrol" 1938 (Dan Drury); "Heroes of the Alamo" 1938 (William B. Travis); "Land of Fighting Men" 1938 (Ed); "In Old Monterey" 1939; "The Lone Ranger Rides Again" 1939-serial (Evans); "South of the Border" 1939 (Flint); "Billy the Kid's Gun Justice" 1940 (Buck Mason); "Lone Star Raiders" 1940 (Fisher); "One Man's Law" 1940 (Frank Hudkins); "Rancho Grande" 1940 (Travis); "Riders on Black Mountain" 1940 (Sheriff Clay); "The Trail Blazers" 1940 (Reynolds); "Under Texas Skies" 1940 (Marsden); "Billy the Kid in Santa Fe" 1941 (Jeff); "Billy the Kid's Range War" 1941 (Buck); "Jesse James at Bay" 1941; "Nevada City" 1941; "Outlaws of the Cherokee Trail" 1941; "Outlaws of the Rio Grande" 1941 (Luke); "The Phantom Cowboy" 1941 (Jeffers); "Sierra Sue" 1941 (Rancher); "Tonto Basin Outlaws" 1941 (Editor); "Arizona Terrors" 1942 (Briggs); "Boss of Hangtown Mesa" 1942 (Bert Lawler); "The Cyclone Kid" 1942 (Rankin); "Home in Wyomin'" 1942; "In Old California" 1942; "Raiders of the West" 1942; "Shadows on the Sage" 1942; "The Silver Bullet" 1942; "Stardust on the Sage" 1942; "Sunset Serenade" 1942; "Daredevils of the West" 1943-serial (Jack/Barn Heavy #2); "Dead Man's Gulch" 1943 (Steve Barker); "The Haunted Ranch" 1943; "Idaho" 1943; "Santa Fe Scouts" 1943; "Tenting Tonight on the Old Camp Ground" 1943 (Zeke Larkin); "Bordertown Trail" 1944; "Call of the Rockies" 1944; "Cheyenne Wildcat" 1944; "Code of the Prairie" 1944 (Outlaw on Trail); "Cowboy and the Senorita" 1944; "Death Valley Rangers" 1944 (Jim Collins); "Firebrands of Arizona" 1944 (Deputy Sheriff); "Sheriff of Sundown" 1944 (Murdock); "The Yellow Rose of Tesas" 1944; "Bells of Rosarita" 1945; "Code of the Lawless" 1945 (Crenshaw); "Dakota" 1945 (Railroad Conductor); "Flame of the Barbary Coast" 1945 (Headwaiter); "Frontier Gal" 1945 (Henchman); "Lone Texas Ranger" 1945; Oregon Trail" 1945 (Cowboy); "Rough Riders of Cheyenne" 1945; "Santa Fe Saddlemates" 1945; "Springtime in Texas" 1945; "Canyon Passage" 1946 (Player); "Days of Buffalo Bill" 1946; "Heldorado" 1946 (Charlie); "King of the Forest Rangers" 1946-serial (Toler); "The Phantom Rider" 1946-serial (Randall); "Plainsman and the Lady" 1946 (Croupier); "Rustler's Roundup" 1946 (Saloon Proprietor); "Sun Valley Cyclone" 1946; "The Wistful Widow of Wagon Gap" 1947 (Hank); "Wyoming" 1947 (Clerk); "The Gallant Legion" 1948; "The Plunderers" 1948; "The Last Bandit" 1949; "Bells of Coronado" 1950 (Foreman); "Code of the Silver Sage" 1950 (Charlie Speed); "Copper Canyon" 1950 (Southerner); "Covered Wagon Raid" 1950 (Bob Davis); "Curtain Call at Cactus Creek" 1950 (Yellowstone); "Frisco Tornado" 1950 (Mac); "Hills of Oklahoma" 1950 (Joe Brant); "Singing Guns" 1950 (Stage Driver); "Lone Star" 1952 (Senator); "Lost in Alaska" 1952 (Old-Timer); "The Man Behind the Gun" 1952; "Montana Belle" 1952 (Barfly); "The Wild North" 1952 (Quarlette Member); "Ride, Vaquero!" 1953 (Deputy); "Perils of the Wilderness" 1956-serial (Sergeant Rodney); "The Rawhide Years" 1956 (Card Player). ¶TV: *The Lone Ranger*—"Backtrail" 1-25-51; *Wild Bill Hickok*—"Ex-Convict Story" 11-20-51; *The Roy Rogers Show*—"The Young Defenders" 10-3-54 (Fred Topp), "Hard Luck Story" 10-31-54 (Slip Macon); *Wyatt Earp*—"Command Performance" 2-19-57 (Cagle), "Call Me Your Honor" 9-17-57, "Woman Trouble" 12-17-57 (Brother William), "Cattle Thieves" 10-28-59 (Rance); *Jefferson Drum*—"The Cheater" 5-23-58 (Tobin); *Maverick*—"The People's Friend" 2-7-60 (Poker Player #2).

Leaud, Jean-Pierre (1944-). Films: "A Girl Is a Gun" 1970-Fr. (Billy).

Leavitt, Douglas (1883-3/3/50). Films: "Law of the Northwest" 1943 (George Bradley).

Leavitt, Norman (1903-76). Films: "The Harvey Girls" 1946 (Cowboy); "Yellow Sky" 1948 (Bank Teller); "Mule Train" 1950; "Ven-

geance Valley" 1951 (Cowhand); "The Bushwackers" 1952 (Yale); "Hannah Lee" 1953 (Miller); "The Moonlighter" 1953 (Tidy); "Ride, Vaquero!" 1953 (Dentist); "The Brass Legend" 1956 (Cooper); "Friendly Persuasion" 1956 (Clem); "Stagecoach to Fury" 1956 (Customer); "Fury at Showdown" 1957 (Swamper); "Showdown at Boot Hill" 1958 (Photographer); "Young Jesse James" 1960 (Foolsom). ¶TV: *The Roy Rogers Show*—"Bullets and a Burro" 11-15-53; *The Adventures of Rin Tin Tin*—"The Wild Stallion" 9-23-55; *Wagon Train*—"The John Darro Story" 11-6-57, "The Ella Lindstrom Story" 2-4-59 (Bartender), "The Frank Carter Story" 5-23-62 (Joe Casper), "The Myra Marshall Story" 10-21-63, "The Sandra Cummings Story" 12-2-63; *Trackdown*—Regular 1958-59 (Ralph); *The Texan*—"The Edge of the Cliff" 10-27-58, "Reunion" 5-4-59 (Man); *Rawhide*—"Incident of the Sharpshooter" 2-26-60, "Incident of His Brother's Keeper" 3-31-61 (Telegraph Operator), "Incident of the Night on the Town" 6-2-61, "Grandma's Money" 2-23-62 (Deputy), "Incident at Confidence Creek" 11-28-63 (Miner), "Incident at the Odyssey" 3-26-64; *Bonanza*—"Showdown" 9-10-60 (Telegrapher), "The Blood Line" 12-31-60 (Bert), "The Countess" 11-19-61, "The Auld Sod" 2-4-62, "The Cheating Game" 2-9-64, "Her Brother's Keeper" 3-6-66 (Clerk), "Clarissa" 4-30-67 (Telegrapher); *Stagecoach West*—"High Lonesome" 10-4-60 (Gabe), "The Raider" 5-9-61 (Adam); *Wyatt Earp*—"Horse Thief" 1-10-61, "The Good Mule and the Bad Mule" 3-14-61 (Phillips); *Laramie*—"Riders of the Night" 3-7-61 (Ben Yuma), "Ladies Day" 10-3-61, "The Killer Legend" 12-12-61 (Freddie), "The Dynamiters" 3-6-62, "Shadow of the Past" 10-16-62, "Double Eagles" 11-20-62, "Vengeance" 1-8-63, "Broken Honor" 4-9-63; *Tales of Wells Fargo*—"Prince Jim" 3-27-61 (Willy Zane); *The Rifleman*—"Short Rope for a Tall Man" 3-28-61, "The Bullet" 2-25-63 (Hotel Clerk); *Gunslinger*—"Road of the Dead" 3-30-61 (Bank Clerk); *Maverick*—"Substitute Gun" 4-2-61 (Ezra Gouch); *Frontier Circus*—"Dr. Sam" 10-26-61 (Willoughby); *Wide Country*—"The Quest for Jacob Blaufus" 3-7-63 (Ike Bieler); *The Virginian*—"Timberland" 3-10-65 (Proprietor), "Johnny Moon" 10-11-67 (Storekeeper), "The Masquerade" 10-18-67 (Charles Colton); *Daniel Boone*—"Daughter of the Devil" 4-15-65 (Clyde Devon), "Thirty Pieces of Silver" 3-28-68, "Is-

rael and Love" 5-7-70; *Laredo*—"A Question of Discipline" 10-28-65 (Farmer), "The Land Grabbers" 12-9-65; *The Guns of Will Sonnett*—"Reunion" 9-27-68, "Sunday in Paradise" 12-15-67 (Chelby Witty); *Cimarron Strip*—"The Blue Moon Train" 2-15-68; *Kung Fu*—"The Soul Is the Warrior" 2-8-73 (Burt Proctor).

LeBaron, Bert (1900-3/3/56). Films: "The Bandit Trail" 1941; "King of the Texas Rangers" 1941-serial (Dock Heavy); "Stardust on the Sage" 1942; "Girl Rush" 1944; "Jesse James Rides Again" 1947-serial (Raider #1); "The Michigan Kid" 1947 (Rifleman); "Desperadoes of the West" 1950-serial (Bart); "The James Brothers of Missouri" 1950-serial (Price); "Don Daredevil Rides Again" 1951-serial (Tex). ¶TV: *The Roy Rogers Show*—"Flying Bullets" 6-15-52, "Death Medicine" 9-7-52, "Hard Luck Story" 10-31-54 (Lee Jennings), "Violence in Paradise Valley" 11-2-55.

Lebeau, Madeleine. Films: "Gunmen of the Rio Grande" 1964-Fr./Ital./Span. (Jennie Lee).

Lebedeff, Ivan (1894-3/31/53). Films: "Sin Town" 1929 (Pete Laguerro); "Fair Warning" 1937 (Count Andre Lukacha); "California Conquest" 1952 (Alexander Fotcheff).

LeBrun, Mignon (1888-9/20/41). Films: "The Secret of Black Mountain" 1917 (Sarah Stanley).

Leckner, Brian. Films: "Bonanza: The Return" TVM-1993 (Josh Cartwright); "Bonanza: Under Attack" TVM-1995 (Josh Cartwright).

LeClair, Michael. TV: *Gunsmoke*—"Larkin" 1-20-75 (Jess Cass); *Centennial*—Regular 1978-79 (Young Jim Lloyd).

Ledebur, Friedrich (1900-86). Films: "Montana Trap" 1976-Ger.

Lederer, Francis (1906-). Films: "Surrender" 1950 (Henry Vaan).

Lederer, Gretchen (1891-12/20/55). Films: "Desert Thieves" 1914; "Two Men of Sandy Bar" 1916 (the Duchess); "The Yaqui" 1916 (Senora Estaban); "A Yoke of Gold" 1916; "The Greater Law" 1917 (Seattle Lou); "Hungry Eyes" 1918 (Bessie Dupont); "The Red, Red Heart" 1918 (Katherine Newman); "Riddle Gawne" 1918 (Blanche Dillon).

Lederer, Otto (1886-9/3/65). Films: "The Little Angel of Canyon Creek" 1914 (Doc Casey); "A Child of the North" 1915; "The Legend of the Lone Tree" 1915; "The Man from the Desert" 1915; "By Right of Possession" 1917 (Bells); "The Captain of the Gray Horse Troop" 1917; "Dead

Shot Baker" 1917 (Old Baldwin); "Cavanaugh of the Forest Rangers" 1918 (Ed Wetherford); "The Avenging Arrow" 1921-serial; "White Eagle" 1922-serial; "Behind Two Guns" 1924; "Gun Law" 1933.

Ledig, Howard. TV: *The Rifleman*—"The Blowout" 10-13-59 (Jake Porter); *Colt .45*—"Alias Mr. Howard" 12-6-59 (Woodie Keene); *Wanted—Dead or Alive*—"The Twain Shall Meet" 10-19-60 (Jack Torrance); *Bonanza*—"Crucible" 4-8-62 (Frank Preston).

Lee, Alberta. Films: "Beyond the Shadows" 1918 (Mrs. DuBois); "Closin' In" 1918 (Mrs. Carlton); "Keith of the Border" 1918 (Mrs. Murphy).

Lee, Allan (1875-2/5/51). Films: "Three Rogues" 1931 (Teamster); "Crashing Broadway" 1933; "Stagecoach" 1939; "West of the Pecos" 1945 (Four-Up Driver).

Lee, Alta. Films: "Swing, Cowboy, Swing" 1944; "Trouble at Melody Mesa" 1944.

Lee, Anna (1914-). Films: "Lariats and Sixshooters" 1933 (Tessie); "Fort Apache" 1948 (Mrs. Emily Collingwood); "The Horse Soldiers" 1959 (Mrs. Buford); "Two Rode Together" 1961 (Mrs. Malaprop); "The Man Who Shot Liberty Valance" 1962 (Passenger); "The Night Rider" TVM-1979 (Lady Earl). ¶TV: *Wagon Train*—"The Colter Craven Story" 11-23-60 (Alarice Craven); *Maverick*—"Diamond Flush" 2-5-61 (Helene Ferguson); *Daniel Boone*—"The Ben Franklin Encounter" 3-18-65 (Clara Merivale); *Gunsmoke*—"Rope Fever" 12-4-67 (Amy Bassett).

Lee, Annabelle (-9/8/89). Films: "Ridin' Mad" 1924 (Beth Carlson); "Hearts of the West" 1925.

Lee, Billy (1929-11/17/89). Films: "Wagon Wheels" 1934 (Sonny Wellington); "Arizona Mahoney" 1936 (Kid); "Thunder Trail" 1937 (Bob Ames as a Child); "In Old Monterey" 1939 (Jimmy Whittaker); "Jeepers Creepers" 1939 (Skeeter); "Nevada City" 1941.

Lee, Brandon (1965-3/31/93). Films: "Kung Fu: The Movie" TVM-1986 (Chung Wang).

Lee, Bruce (1940-7/20/73). TV: *Here Come the Brides*—"Marriage Chinese Style" 4-9-69 (Lin Sung).

Lee, Carl (1933-4/17/86). TV: *Barbary Coast*—"Jesse Who?" 9-22-75 (Currier).

Lee, Charles (1882-3/14/27). Films: "Girl of the Timber Claims" 1917 (Homesteader).

Lee, Chen. Films: "Fighting Fists of Shanghai Joe" 1973-Ital. (Shanghai Joe); "Return of Shanghai Joe" 1974-Ger./Ital. (Shanghai Joe).

Lee, Christopher (1922-). Films: "Hannie Calder" 1971-Brit./Span./Fr. (Bailey). ¶TV: *How the West Was Won*—Episode One 2-12-78 (the Grand Duke).

Lee, Doris. Films: "The Law of the North" 1918 (Therese LeNoir); "Playing the Game" 1918 (Moya Shannon).

Lee, Dorothy. Films: "The Man from the Rio Grande" 1926; "Salt Lake Trail" 1926.

Lee, Duke R. (1881-4/1/59). Films: "The Savage" 1917 (Pierre); "The Soul Herder" 1917; "Straight Shooting" 1917 (Thunder Flint); "Hell Bent" 1918 (Cimmaron Bill); "At the Point of the Gun" 1919; "The Ace of the Saddle" 1919 (Sheriff Faulkner of Pinkerton County); "By Indian Post" 1919; "Dynamite" 1919; "The Face in the Watch" 1919; "The Fighting Brothers" 1919; "The Fighting Sheriff" 1919; "A Gun Fightin' Gentleman" 1919; "The Gun Packer" 1919; "The Outcasts of Poker Flat" 1919; "The Rider of the Law" 1919 (Captain Saltire); "Just Pals" 1920 (Sheriff); "The Line Runners" 1920; "Sundown Slim" 1920 (Loring); "Vanishing Trails" 1920-serial; "The Cactus Kid" 1921; "If Only Jim" 1921 (Keno); "Trailin'" 1921 (Butch Conklin); "In the Days of Buffalo Bill" 1922-serial (Buffalo Bill Cody); "Just Tony" 1922 (Manuel Cordova); "Tracked to Earth" 1922 (Stub Lou Tate); "The Verdict" 1922; "In the Days of Daniel Boone" 1923-serial; "The Oregon Trail" 1923-serial; "Fighting Fury" 1924 (Scarface Denton); "Mile-A-Minute Romeo" 1924 (Sheriff); "The Western Wallop" 1924 (Bandit); "The Call of Courage" 1925 (Sam Caldwell); "Don Dare Devil" 1925 (Bud Latham); "Flying Hoofs" 1925 (the Raven); "The Red Rider" 1925 (Indian Chief); "The White Outlaw" 1925 (James Hill); "The Canyon of Light" 1926; "The Little Warrior" 1926; "The Man in the Saddle" 1926 (Snell); "Man of the Forest" 1926 (Martin Mulvery); "Rustlers' Ranch" 1926 (Boggs); "Sky High Coral" 1926 (Whitey Durk); "Tony Runs Wild" 1926 (Bender); "The Circus Ace" 1927 (Job Jasper); "Galloping Fury" 1927 (Henchman); "Land of the Lawless" 1927 (Bartender); "Outlaws of Red River" 1927 (Dick Williams); "The Terror of Bar X" 1927 (Jim Ashland); "The Big Hop" 1928 (Ranch Foreman); "Clear-

ing the Trail" 1928 (Cook); "Crashing Through" 1928 (Sheriff); "Son of the Golden West" 1928 (Slade); "45 Calibre War" 1929 (Nick Darnell); "The Concentratin' Kid" 1930 (Moss Blaine); "Headin' for Trouble" 1931 (Jake); "Flaming Guns" 1932 (Red McIntyre); "Scarlet Brand" 1932 (Sheriff); "Deadwood Pass" 1933 (Deputy Sheriff); "The Fourth Horseman" 1933 (Jim); "Man of the Forest" 1933 (Jake); "When a Man Rides Alone" 1933 (Hiram Jones); "Five Bad Men" 1935 (Sheriff); "Swifty" 1935 (Posse Member); "The Whirlwind Rider" 1935; "Desert Guns" 1936 (Steve Logan); "Santa Fe Stampede" 1938; "Feud of the Range" 1939 (Sheriff Cal Winters); "The Lone Ranger Rides Again" 1939-serial (Deputy); "Mountain Rhythm" 1939; "Stagecoach" 1939 (Sheriff of Lordsburg); "My Darling Clementine" 1946 (Townsman).

Lee, Eddie. Films: "Sunset Range" 1935 (Ling Fo); "The Cowboy and the Kid" 1936 (Chinese Laundryman); "The Man from Thunder River" 1943; "Frontier Gal" 1945 (Wing Lee, the Candy-Shop Proprietor); "Bells of Coronado" 1950 (Shanghai).

Lee, Florence (1888-9/1/62). Films: "Red Blood and Yellow" 1919; "Blood Test" 1923; "Between Fires" 1924; "A Sagebrush Vagabond" 1924; "Way of a Man" 1924-serial; "Across the Deadline" 1925 (Mrs. Revelle); "Luck and Sand" 1925 (Roy's Mother); "The High Hand" 1926 (Mrs. Oaks); "Man Rustlin'" 1926 (Mary Wilson); "Road Agent" 1926; "The Bronc Stomper" 1928 (Mrs. Hollister); "The Little Buckaroo" 1928 (Mrs. Durking).

Lee, Frances. Films: "Good as Gold" 1927 (Jane Laurier); "The Tabasco Kid" 1932-short; "The Phantom Thunderbolt" 1933 (Judy Lane).

Lee, Frankie. Films: "Durand of the Bad Lands" 1917 (Jimmy); "One Touch of Sin" 1917 (Little Billy); "Boss of the Lazy Y" 1918 (Bob Clayton); "The Dead Shot" 1918; "The Westerners" 1919 (Dennis); "The Killer" 1921 (Bobby Emory); "The Primal Law" 1921 (Bobbie Carson); "Flaming Hearts" 1922; "While Justice Waits" 1922 (Joe); "Code of the West" 1925 (Bud); "The Golden Strain" 1925 (Milt, as a Boy).

Lee, Frederick. Films: "Thundering Through" 1925 (Aaron Austin); "The Ramblin' Galoot" 1926 (Roger Farnley); "Twin Triggers" 1926 (Dan Wallace).

Lee, George (1929-). Films: "Fort Ti" 1953 (Capt. Delecroix).

Lee, Georgia (1925-). Films: "The Persuader" 1957 (Cora Nicklin).

Lee, Gita. Films: "Riders of Vengeance" 1919 (Virginia).

Lee, Gloria. Films: "The Pinto Kid" 1928 (Janet Bruce).

Lee, Guy (1927-11/22/93). Films: "One More Train to Rob" 1971 (Sen). TV: *Bonanza*—"The Fear Merchants" 1-30-60 (Jimmy Chong), "The Meredith Smith" 10-31-65 (Ah Chow); *Wild Wild West*—"The Night the Dragon Screamed" 1-14-66 (Coolie #1).

Lee, Gwen (1904-8/20/61). Films: "Broadway to Cheyenne" 1932 (Myrna).

Lee, Gypsy Rose (1914-4/26/70). Films: "Belle of the Yukon" 1944 (Belle Devalle); "The Over-the-Hill Gang" TVM-1969 (Cassie).

Lee, Harry (1872-12/8/32). Films: "Channing of the Northwest" 1922 (McCool's Man); "The Man She Brought Back" 1922 (Sgt. Hawkins).

Lee, Jack (1907-4/24/69). Films: "River Lady" 1948 (Man); "Broken Arrow" 1950 (Boucher); "Two Flags West" 1950 (Courier).

Lee, Jennie (1850-8/4/25). Films: "Two Men of the Desert" 1913; "Madame Bo-Peep" 1917 (Housekeeper); "The Rider of the Law" 1919 (Jim's Mother); "Riders of Vengeance" 1919; "The Big Punch" 1921 (Buck's Mother); "Under Pressure" 1922; "North of Hudson Bay" 1924 (Dane's Mother).

Lee, Jennifer (1949-). Films: "The Duchess and the Dirtwater Fox" 1976 (Trollop). ¶TV: *Kung Fu*—"The Devil's Champion" 11-29-74 (Daughter).

Lee, Johnny (1898-12/12/65). Films: "The First Traveling Saleslady" 1956 (Amos); "North to Alaska" 1960 (Coachman). ¶TV: *Jim Bowie*—"The Return of the Alciblade" 12-21-56.

Lee, Johnny. TV: *Prudence and the Chief*—Pilot 8-26-70 (Fergus MacKenzie); *Alias Smith and Jones*—"Escape from Wickenberg" 1-28-71 (Tommy Cuningham); *Bonanza*—"Fallen Woman" 9-26-71 (Petey).

Lee, Laura. Films: "Jesse James' Women" 1954 (Angel Botts).

Lee, Lila (1905-11/13/73). Films: "A Daughter of the Wolf" 1919 (Annette Ainsworth); "Rustling a Bride" 1919 (Emily); "Woman Hungry" 1931 (Judith Temple); "The Lone Cowboy" 1934 (Eleanor Jones).

Lee, Margaret (1943-). Films: "Two Sergeants of General Custer" 1965-Ital./Span.; "Djurado" 1966-Ital./Span.

Lee, Mary. Films: "South of the Border" 1939 (Patsy); "Carolina Moon" 1940 (Patsy); "Gaucho Serenade" 1940 (Patsy Halloway); "Melody Ranch" 1940 (Penny); "Rancho Grande" 1940 (Patricia Fairfield Dodge); "Ride, Tenderfoot, Ride" 1940 (Patsy Randolph); "Back in the Saddle" 1941 (Pasty); "Meet Roy Rogers" 1941-short; "Ridin' on a Rainbow" 1941 (Patsy); "The Singing Hill" 1941; "Cowboy and the Senorita" 1944 (Chip Williams); "Song of Nevada" 1944 (Kitty Hanley).

Lee, Michelle (1942-). TV: *Alias Smith and Jones*—"Which Way to the O.K. Corral?" 2-10-72 (Georgette Sinclair), "Don't Get Mad, Get Even" 2-17-72 (Georgette Sinclair), "Bad Night in Big Butte" 3-2-72 (Georgette Sinclair).

Lee, Palmer. see Palmer, Gregg.

Lee, Pinky (1916-4/3/93). Films: "In Old Amarillo" 1951 (Pinky); "Pals of the Golden West" 1951 (Pinky); "South of Caliente" 1951 (Pinky Lee).

Lee, Raymond (1910-6/26/74). Films: "Six-Shooter Andy" 1918.

Lee, Richard (1870-7/24/31). Films: "The Cyclone Cowboy" 1927 (Gerald Weith).

Lee, Rudy. Films: "Son of Paleface" 1952 (Boy); "Lay That Rifle Down" 1955 (Billy). ¶TV: *Wild Bill Hickok*—"The Sheriff's Secret" 10-21-52.

Lee, Ruta (1936-). Films: "The Twinkle in God's Eye" 1955 (3rd Girl); "Sergents 3" 1962 (Amelia Parent); "The Gun Hawk" 1963 (Marleen); "Bullet for a Badman" 1964 (Lottie). ¶TV: *Maverick*—"Comstock Conspiracy" 12-29-57 (Ellen Bordeen), "Plunder of Paradise" 3-9-58 (Sally), "Betrayal" 3-22-59 (Laura Dillon); *Sugarfoot*—"The Dead Hills" 3-4-58 (Lucy Barron); *Gunsmoke*—"Carmen" 5-24-58 (Jennie Lane), "Jenny" 10-13-62 (Jenny); *The Restless Gun*—"The Painted Beauty" 1-5-59 (Lucy); *Wagon Train*—"The Kate Parker Story" 5-6-59 (Evie Finley), "The Bleeker Story" 12-9-63 (Jenny); *Colt .45*—"The Hothead" 11-1-59 (Dottie Hampton), "Showdown at Goldtown" 6-14-60 (Molly Perkins); *The Alaskans*—"The Abominable Snowman" 12-13-59 (Alabama), "The Long Pursuit" 1-31-60 (Amy); *Man from Blackhawk*—"The Legacy" 12-25-59 (Ginnie Thompson); *The Rebel*—"Grant of Land" 5-22-60

(Ellen Barton); *Shotgun Slade*—"Killer Brand" 8-2-60 (Lilly); *Zane Grey Theater*—"Man from Everywhere" 4-13-61 (Jenny Aldrich); *Stagecoach West*—"Blind Man's Bluff" 5-16-61 (Della Bell), "The Marker" 6-27-61 (Jenny Forbes); *Laramie*—"Siege at Jubilee" 10-10-61 (Opal); *Rawhide*—"Incident of the Reluctant Bridegroom" 11-30-62 (Sheila Delancey), "Incident at Alkali Sink" 5-24-63 (Lorraine Stanton); *The Outlaws*—"Farewell Performance" 3-15-62 (Alice); *Cheyenne*—"Wanted for the Murder of Cheyenne Bodie" 12-10-62 (Lenore Hanford); *Bonanza*—"A Woman Lost" 3-17-63 (Rita Marlow); *Temple Houston*—"Enough Rope" 12-19-63 (Lucy Tolliver); *The Travels of Jaimie McPheeters*—"The Day of the Lame Duck" 2-9-64 (Zoe Pigalle); *The Virginian*—"The Long Quest" 4-8-64 (Judith Holly), "The Girl from Yesterday" 11-11-64 (Jane Carlyle); *Wild Wild West*—"The Night of the Casual Killer" 10-15-65 (Laurie Morgan), "The Night of the Gypsy Peril" 1-20-67 (Zoe); *The Guns of Will Sonnett*—"Trail's End" 1-31-69 (Fan).

Lee, Ruth (1896-8/3/75). Films: "Tucson Raiders" 1944; "Corpus Christi Bandits" 1945 (Mom Christie); "The Daltons Ride Again" 1945 (Mrs. Bohannon); "Hell's Outpost" 1954 (Mrs. Moffit). ¶TV: *The Roy Rogers Show*—"The Feud" 11-16-52, "The High-Graders of Paradise Valley" 2-28-54 (Sarah Granby); *The Californians*—"A Turn in the Trail" 2-17-59; *Bat Masterson*—"The Death of Bat Masterson" 5-20-59 (Nellie Fontana).

Lee, Scott. Films: "The Kid from Amarillo" 1951 (Snead); "Wild Horse Ambush" 1952 (Shorty); "Seminole" 1953 (Trooper); "Dawn at Socorro" 1954 (Vince McNair).

Lee, Sheryl. TV: *Dr. Quinn, Medicine Woman*—"Another Woman" 1-22-94.

Lee, Stephen. TV: *Paradise*—"A Matter of Honor" 4-8-89 & 4-15-89 (Jacob Brandt).

Lee, Tommy (1900-6/19/76). Films: "Rooster Cogburn" 1975 (Chen Lee). ¶TV: *Cimarron Strip*—"Nobody" 12-7-67; *Kung Fu*—"Arrogant Dragons" 3-14-74 (Apothecary), "Forbidden Kingdom" 1-18-75 (Bystander).

Lee, Virginia. Films: "Beyond the Law" 1918 (Ruth Lane); "Oh, Johnny!" 1918 (Adele Butler); "Sandy Burke of the U-Bar-U" 1919 (Molly Kirby); "The White Masks" 1921 (Olga Swenson); "It Happened Out West" 1923.

Lee, Virginia. TV: *Annie Oakley*—Semi-Regular 1954 (Marge Hardy); *Death Valley Days*—"Million Dollar Wedding" 1-31-55 (Aggie Filene), "Thorn of the Rose" 6-16-57 (Rose), "Empire of Youth" 1-27-58.

Lee, Wendy (1923-8/23/68). Films: "I Shot Billy the Kid" 1950 (Francesca).

Lee Chasing His Horse, Nathan. Films: "Dances with Wolves" 1990 (Smiles a Lot).

Leeds, Andrea (Antoinette Lees) (1914-5/21/84). Films: "Song of the Trail" 1936 (Betty Hobson).

Leeds, Elissa. Films: "The Legend of the Golden Gun" TVM-1979 (Sara Powell).

Leeds, Maureen. TV: *Johnny Ringo*—"The Killing Bug" 4-18-60 (Mary); *Cheyenne*—"One Way Ticket" 2-19-62 (Laura Barrington).

Leeds, Nancy. Films: "The Human Tornado" 1925 (Marion Daley).

Leeds, Peter (1918-). Films: "Saddle Tramp" 1950. ¶TV: *The Cisco Kid*—"The Devil's Deputy" 5-10-52, "The Fire Engine" 5-31-52, "Fear" 6-28-52; *Trackdown*—Regular 1958-59 (Tenner Smith); *Wichita Town*—"The Long Night" 1-20-60 (Dan Sommers); *Have Gun Will Travel*—"Jenny" 1-23-60 (Wilson); *Bonanza*—"Death at Dawn" 4-30-60 (Norton), "Blood Tie" 2-18-68; *Wagon Train*—"The Countess Baranof Story" 5-11-60 (Alex Foster); *Wide Country*—"The Girl in the Sunshine Smile" 11-15-62 (Vince Dekker); *Rawhide*—"Incident of the Swindler" 2-20-64 (Samson); *The Monroes*—"Ride with Terror" 9-21-66 (Cobb); *F Troop*—"Bring on the Dancing Girls" 12-22-66 (Dan Carson); *Rango*—"What's a Nice Girl Like You Doing Holding Up a Place Like This?" 2-17-67 (Raven); *The Virginian*—"With Help from Ulysses" 1-17-68 (Peterson); *The Guns of Will Sonnett*—"Jim Sonnett's Lady" 2-21-69 (Milhoan).

Leegant, Dan. Films: "Grim Prairie Tales" 1990 (Dr. Lenderman).

Lees, Antoinette. *see* Leeds, Andrea.

Lees, Paul. Films: "Copper Canyon" 1950 (Bat Laverne); "The Great Missouri Raid" 1951 (Bob Younger); "Warpath" 1951 (Cpl. Stockbridge). ¶TV: *Whispering Smith*—"The Deadliest Weapon" 6-19-61 (Vince Posdell).

Lee-Sung, Richard. Films: "The Apple Dumpling Gang" 1975 (Oh So). ¶TV: *Kung Fu*—"The Devil's Champion" 11-29-74 (Fourth Master); *How the West Was Won*—"China Girl" 4-16-79 (Sentinel).

LeFever, Ralph (1916-12/9/74). Films: "The Lone Star Ranger" 1930 (Stage Driver); "The Lone Ranger" 1938-serial (Trooper); "The Lone Ranger Rides Again" 1939-serial (Bill).

Leftwich, Alexander (1885-1/13/47). Films: "Union Pacific" 1939 (Official).

LeGault, Lance (1940-). Films: "Pioneer Woman" TVM-1973 (Joe Wormser); "This Was the West That Was" TVM-1974 (Hearts); "Donner Pass: The Road to Survival" TVM-1978 (Charles Stanton); "The Gambler" TVM-1980 (Doc Palmer). ¶TV: *Gunsmoke*—"A Town in Chains" 9-16-74 (Oregon); *Barbary Coast*—"Jesse Who?" 9-22-75 (Ben Sharpe); *The Busters*—Pilot 5-28-78 (Mel Drew); *How the West Was Won*—"The Scavengers" 3-12-79 (Zachary); *Paradise*—"Vengeance" 3-16-89 (Harlan Ivey).

LeGay, Sheila. Films: "Call of the Desert" 1930 (Jean Walker); "The Canyon of Missing Men" 1930 (Inez Sepulveda).

Legge-Willis, Arthur. Films: "Secret Patrol" 1936 (Old Man); "Stampede" 1936 (Doc).

LeGros, James. Films: "Bad Girls" 1994 (William Tucker).

Lehman, Trent (1961-1/18/82). TV: *Gunsmoke*—"The Still" 11-10-69 (Chester).

Lehmann, John. Films: "Fury at Gunsight Pass" 1956 (Forrest); "The Phantom Stagecoach" 1957 (Williams). ¶TV: *Sergeant Preston of the Yukon*—"Fancy Dan" 4-5-56 (Mike), "Revenge" 10-4-56 (Constable Duggan).

Lehmann, Ted (1922-). TV: *Wild Bill Hickok*—"Spurs for Johnny" 5-26-53; *The Law of the Plainsman*—"The Imposter" 2-4-60; *Black Bart*—Pilot 4-4-75 (Mrs. Swenson).

Lehne, John. TV: *Paradise*—"A Gathering of Guns" 2-17-90 (General Benson).

Lehr, Anna. Films: "Colorado" 1915 (Mary Doyle); "The Bugle Call" 1916 (Mary); "Ramona" 1916 (Ramona as a Child); "Laughing Bill Hyde" 1918 (Ponotah); "The Valley of Doubt" 1920 (Annice); "Ruggles of Red Gap" 1923 (Mrs. Belknap Jackson); "Unconquered" 1947.

Leiber, Fritz (1882-10/14/49). Films: "The Primitive Call" 1917 (Brain Elkhorn); "The Cisco Kid Returns" 1945 (Padre); "Bells of San Angelo" 1947 (the Padre); "Dangerous Venture" 1947 (Xeoli); "The Devil's Doorway" 1950 (Mr. Poole).

Leibman, Ron (1937-). Films: "Zorro, the Gay Blade" 1981 (Esteban).

Leicester, William (1915-1/9/69). Films: "Strange Gamble" 1948; "The Secret of Convict Lake" 1951 (Luke Haggerty). ¶TV: *Zane Grey Theater*—"Dangerous Orders" 2-8-57 (Maj. Carr), "Badge of Honor" 5-3-57 (Ranger); *Broken Arrow*—"Smoke Signal" 12-10-57 (Maj. Henderson); *Lawman*—"The Salvation of Owny O'Reilly" 4-24-60 (Samson); *The Alaskans*—"Calico" 5-22-60 (Red).

Leigh, Barbara (1946-). Films: "Junior Bonner" 1972 (Charmagne); "Boss Nigger" 1974 (Miss Pruitt).

Leigh, Carol. TV: *Jim Bowie*—"Bayou Tontine" 2-15-57 (Odile Broussard); *The Deputy*—"Back to Glory" 9-26-59 (Lily); *The Rifleman*—"Quiet Night, Deadly Night" 10-22-62 (Betty Lind).

Leigh, Frank (1876-5/9/48). Films: "Rose of the West" 1919 (Pierre Labelle); "The Sleeping Lion" 1919; "Bob Hampton of Placer" 1921 (Silent Murphy); "Out of the Silent North" 1922 (Ashleigh Nefferton); "North of Hudson Bay" 1924 (Jeffrey Clough); "The Flaming Forest" 1926 (Lupin); "Somewhere in Sonora" 1927 (Monte Black); "King Cowboy" 1928 (Abdul El Hassan).

Leigh, George (-12/11/88). Films: "Salome, Where She Danced" 1945 (Bayard Taylor).

Leigh, Janet (1927-). Films: "The Naked Spur" 1953 (Lina Patch); "Kid Rodelo" 1966-U.S./Span. (Nora). ¶TV: *The Men from Shiloh*—"Jenny" 9-30-70 (Jenny).

Leigh, Nelson (1914-67). Films: "Texas Masquerade" 1944 (James Corwin); "Yukon Manhunt" 1951; "Bugles in the Afternoon" 1952 (Maj. Reno); "Jack Slade" 1953 (Alf Slade); "Texas Bad Man" 1953 (Bradley); "Jesse James Versus the Daltons" 1954 (Father Kerrigan); "The Outlaw's Daughter" 1954 (Dalton); "The First Texan" 1956 (Hockley); "Friendly Persuasion" 1956 (Minister); "Gunfight at the O.K. Corral" 1957 (Mayor Kelley); "Three Thousand Hills" 1959 (Brother Van). ¶TV: *The Cisco Kid*—"Big Switch" 2-10-51, "Railroad Land Rush" 3-17-51, "Renegade Son" 4-7-51; *Wild Bill Hickok*—"Marriage Feud of Ponca City" 5-13-52; *Bonanza*—"The Pursued" 10-2-66 & 10-9-66 (Dr. Bingham), "Black Friday" 1-22-67 (Dr. Geis).

Leighton, Lillian (1874-3/19/

56). Films: "The Call of the Canyon" 1923 (Mrs. Hutter); "Ruggles of Red Gap" 1923 (Ma Pettingill); "$50,000 Reward" 1924 (Mrs. Miller); "Code of the West" 1925 (Ma Thurman); "The Thundering Herd" 1925 (Mrs. Clark Hudnall); "Tumbleweeds" 1925 (Mrs. Riley); "California" 1927 (Duenna); "The Frontiersman" 1927 (Mrs. Andrew Jackson); "The Fighting Sheriff" 1931 (Aunt Sally); "The Man from Monterey" 1933 (Juanita).

Leipnitz, Harald (1926-). Films: "Rampage at Apache Wells" 1965-Ger./Yugo. (the Oil Prince); "Thunder at the Border" 1967-Ger./Yugo.; "Prairie in the City" 1971-Ger.

Leith, Virginia (1932-). Films: "White Feather" 1955 (Ann Magruder).

Leland, David (1921-4/17/87). TV: *Have Gun Will Travel*—"Hey Boy's Revenge" 4-12-58; *Wagon Train*—"The Liam Fitzmorgan Story" 10-28-58 (Michael Dermoth), "The Kitty Angel Story" 1-7-59 (Sam Hogg), "Trial for Murder" 4-27-60 & 5-4-60; *The Restless Gun*—"Dead Man's Hand" 3-16-59; *Buckskin*—"The Venus Adjourner" 3-30-59 (Melton); *The Rifleman*—"The Woman" 5-5-59; *Laredo*—"The Other Cheek" 2-10-67; *Masterpiece Theatre*—"The Last of the Mohicans" 1972 (David).

Lemaire, Philippe (1927-). Films: "Massacre at Marble City" 1964-Ger./Ital./Fr. (Donovan).

LeMaire, William (1892-11/11/33). Films: "The Light of the Western Stars" 1930 (Grif Meeker); "The Painted Desert" 1931; "The Lone Cowboy" 1934 (Buck).

LeMat, Paul (1945-). TV: *Lonesome Dove*—Pilot 10-2-94, 10-9-94 & 10-16-94 (Josiah), 3-5-95.

Lembeck, Harvey (1923-1/5/82). Films: "The Command" 1953 (Gottschalk).

Lemmon, Jack (1925-). Films: "Cowboy" 1958 (Frank Harris). ¶TV: *Zane Grey Theater*—"The Three Graves" 1-4-57 (Cass Kendall).

Lemoine, Michel. Films: "The Road to Fort Alamo" 1966-Fr./Ital. (Slim).

LeMoyne, Charles (1880-9/13/56). Films: "The Country That God Forgot" 1916 (Sheriff Grantwell); "Mr. Logan, U.S.A." 1918; "The Coming of the Law" 1919 (Ten Spot); "Marked Men" 1919 (Sheriff Pete Cushing); "Treat 'Em Rough" 1919 (Dave Leviatt); "Blue Streak McCoy" 1920 (Mulhall); "Bullet Proof" 1920 (Bandit); "Hearts Up" 1920 (Bob

Harding); "Human Stuff" 1920 (Bull Elkins); "The Last Straw" 1920 (Hepburn); "Overland Red" 1920 (Silent Saunders); "Sundown Slim" 1920 (Fadeaway); "West Is West" 1920 (Connors); "The Fox" 1921 (Black Mike); "The Freeze-Out" 1921 (Denver Red); "The Wallop" 1921 (Matt Lisner); "Good Men and True" 1922 (Bowerman); "Headin' West" 1922 (Mark Rivers); "The Kick Back" 1922 (Chalk Eye); "Man to Man" 1922 (Joe Blenham); "Rough Shod" 1922 (Denver); "Brass Commandments" 1923 (Dave De Vake); "Canyon of the Fools" 1923 (Swasey); "Crashin' Thru" 1923 (Allison); "Desert Driven" 1923 (Leary); "The Miracle Baby" 1923 (Hopeful Mason); "Riders of the Purple Sage" 1925 (Richard Tull); "Dynamite Ranch" 1932; "Hell Fire Austin" 1932 (Henchman); "The Cowboy and the Kid" 1936 (Sheriff Stanton); "The Phantom Rider" 1936-serial (Roscoe); "Ride 'Em Cowboy" 1936 (Sheriff Stanton); "Black Aces" 1937 (Sheriff Potter); "The Devil's Saddle Legion" 1937 (Callope); "Empty Holsters" 1937 (Tom Raines); "Empty Saddles" 1937 (Mace); "Law for Tombstone" 1937; "Left-Handed Law" 1937; "Outlaws of the Prairie" 1937; "Sudden Bill Dorn" 1937 (Sheriff).

Lemp, James. Films: "Valdez Is Coming" 1971 (Bony Man).

Lenard, Grace (1921-4/7/87). Films: "The Silver Bullet" 1942; "Sundown Valley" 1944 (Sally Jenks). ¶TV: *The Rebel*—"Dark Secret" 11-22-59 (Cora Trask).

Lenard, Mark (1927-). Films: "Hang 'Em High" 1968. ¶TV: *Iron Horse*—"Sister Death" 4-3-67 (Charlie Duke); *Wild Wild West*—"The Night of the Iron Fist" 12-8-67 (Count Draja); *Gunsmoke*—"Nowhere to Run" 1-15-68 (Ira Stonecipher); *Cimarron Strip*—"The Greeners" 3-7-68 (Jared Arlyn); *Here Comes the Brides*—Regular 1968-70 (Aaron Stempel); *Alias Smith and Jones*—"Escape from Wickenberg" 1-28-71 (Jim Plummer); *Cliffhangers*—"The Secret Empire" 1979 (Thorval).

Lenhart, Billy. Films: "Melody of the Plains" 1937; "Man from Montana" 1941 (Butch).

Lenhart, Buddy "Bull Fiddle Bill". Films: "Two-Gun Troubador" 1939 (Fred, Jr.).

Lenz, Kay (1953-). Films: "The Great Scout and Cathouse Thursday" 1976 (Thursday). ¶TV: *Gunsmoke*—"The Foundling" 2-11-74 (Lettie); *Nakia*—"The Hostage" 10-12-74 (Barbara); *How the West Was Won*—

Episode Ten 4-30-78 (Doreen), Episode Eleven 5-7-78 (Doreen), Episode Thirteen 5-21-78 (Doreen).

Lenz, Rick (1939-). Films: "Scandalous John" 1971 (Jimmy Whittaker); "Hec Ramsey" TVM-1972 (Chief Oliver Stamp); "The Shootist" 1976 (Dobkins). ¶TV: *Hec Ramsey*—Regular 1972-74 (Oliver B. Stamp).

Leo, Melissa. TV: *Young Riders*—Regular 1989-90 (Emma Shannon).

Leon, Connie (1880-5/10/55). Films: "The Westerner" 1940 (Langtry's Maid).

Leon, Pedro (1876-7/14/31). Films: "Neola, the Sioux" 1915; "Love's Lariat" 1916 (Cowboy); "Vanishing Trails" 1920-serial.

Leonard, Archie (1917-2/7/59). Films: "Mrs. Mike" 1949 (Trader Henderson).

Leonard, David (1892-4/2/67). Films: "Don Ricardo Returns" 1946; "The Bells of San Fernando" 1947 (Padre); "The Daring Caballero" 1949 (Del Rio); "Border Treasure" 1950 (Padre). ¶TV: *The Gene Autry Show*—"Guns Below the Border" 11-5-55; *Sergeant Preston of the Yukon*—"Ten Little Indians" 4-18-57 (Father Michael).

Leonard, Marion (1880-1/9/56). Films: "The Greaser's Gauntlet" 1908; "The Tavern-Keeper's Daughter" 1908; "Comata, the Sioux" 1909; "Fools of Fate" 1909; "The Indian Runner's Romance" 1909; "Leather Stocking" 1909; "In Old California" 1910; "Over Silent Paths" 1910; "The Seal of Time" 1912.

Leonard, Robert (1889-8/27/68). Films: "An Arrowhead Romance" 1914; "The Mistress of Deadwood Basin" 1914.

Leonard, Sheldon (1907-). Films: "Klondike Kate" 1942 (Sometime Smith); "Pierre of the Plains" 1942 (Clerou); "Frontier Gal" 1945 (Blackie); "Rainbow Over Texas" 1946 (Kirby Haynes); "Madonna of the Desert" 1948 (Nick Julian); "The Iroquois Trail" 1950 (Ogane).

Leonard, Terry (1940-). Films: "Barquero" 1970 (Hawk); "The Mountain Men" 1980. ¶TV: *Wild Wild West*—"The Night of the Underground Terror" 1-19-68 (Corporal Quist).

Leone, Sergio (1921-4/30/89). Films: "Cemetery Without Crosses" 1968-Ital./Fr.

Leong, James (1900-10/24/63). TV: *Have Gun Will Travel*—"The Hatchet Man" 3-5-60.

Lepore, Richard. TV: *Frontier Circus*—"Mr. Grady Regrets" 1-25-62 (Jake Gard); *The Virginian*—"The Mark of a Man" 4-20-66 (Will Rountree), "Seth" 3-20-68 (Cully).

Lerner, Fred. Films: "The Legend of Nigger Charley" 1972 (Ollokot); "The Soul of Nigger Charley" 1973 (Woods); "Posse" 1993 (Stunts). ¶TV: *Rawhide*—"Incident of the Sharpshooter" 2-26-60, "The Greedy Town" 2-16-62 (Lon); *Kung Fu*—"The Spirit Helper" 11-8-73 (Comanchero), "A Dream Within a Dream" 1-17-74 (Blaney); *Gunsmoke*—"Hard Labor" 2-24-75 (Guard).

Lerner, Michael (1937-). Films: "Scott Free" TVM-1976 (Santini).

Leroy, Allan. Films: "Massacre at Fort Holman" 1972-Ital./Fr./Span./Ger. (Confederate Sergeant).

Le Roy, Gloria (1925-). TV: *Gunsmoke*—"The Guns of Cibola Blanca" 9-23-74 & 9-30-74 (Mady).

LeRoy, Mervyn (1900-9/13/87). Films: "The Call of the Canyon" 1923 (Jack Rawlins).

Leroy, Phillippe (1930-). Films: "Yankee" 1967-Ital./Span. (Yankee); "Calibre .38" 1971-Ital.; "Man Called Blade" 1977-Ital. (McGowan).

LeSaint, Edward J. (1871-9/10/40). Films: "The Dawn Trail" 1930 (Amos); "Caught" 1931 (Haverstraw); "The Fighting Marshal" 1931 (Mark Hollister); "The Range Feud" 1931 (John Walton); "Daring Danger" 1932 (Boss); "The Deadline" 1932; "Destry Rides Again" 1932 (Mr. Dangerfield); "One-Man Law" 1932; "Texas Bad Man" 1932 (Chester Bigelow); "The Last Trail" 1933 (Judge Wilson); "The Thrill Hunter" 1933 (Jackson); "Treason" 1933 (Judge); "Frontier Marshal" 1934 (Judge Walters); "The Westerner" 1934 (Zack Addison); "Fighting Shadows" 1935 (Duncan); "Gallant Defender" 1935 (Harvey Campbell); "Justice of the Range" 1935 (John McLean); "Riding Wild" 1935 (McCabe); "Ruggles of Red Gap" 1935 (Patron); "Square Shooter" 1935 (Rancher); "Thunder Mountain" 1935 (Samuel Blair); "End of the Trail" 1936 (Jim Watrous); "The Mysterious Avenger" 1936 (Lockhart); "The Oregon Trail" 1936 (Gen. Ferguson); "Code of the Range" 1937 (Adams); "The Old Wyoming Trail" 1937 (Jeff Halliday); "Outlaws of the Prairie" 1937 (Lafe Garfield); "Trapped" 1937 (Doctor); "Two Gun Law" 1937 (Ben Hammond); "Wells Fargo" 1937 (Doctor); "Westbound Mail" 1937 (Doctor); "Wild West Days" 1937-serial; "Call of the Rockies" 1938 (Judge Stockton); "Cattle Raiders" 1938 (John Reynolds); "Colorado Trail" 1938 (Jeff Randall); "Law of the Plains" 1938 (William Norton); "Rio Grande" 1938 (Sanborn); "The Texans" 1938 (Confederate Soldier); "West of Cheyenne" 1938 (J.B. Wayne); "West of Santa Fe" 1938 (Jeff Conway); "The Oregon Trail" 1939-serial (John Mason); "Arizona Legion" 1939 (Judge Clayton L. Meade); "Frontier Marshal" 1939 (Man); "Jesse James" 1939 (Judge Rankin); "The Man from Sundown" 1939 (Judge Townsend); "Overland with Kit Carson" 1939-serial; "Spoilers of the Range" 1939 (Dan Patterson); "The Stranger from Texas" 1939 (Dan Murdock); "The Thundering West" 1939 (Judge Patterson); "Union Pacific" 1939 (Father Ryan); "Bullets for Rustlers" 1940 (Judge Baxter); "The Man from Tumbleweeds" 1940 (Jeff Cameron); "Rangers of Fortune" 1940 (Minister); "The Return of Wild Bill" 1940 (Lige Saunders); "Texas Stagecoach" 1940 (Jim Kincaid).

LeSaint, Stella (Stella Razetto) (1881-9/21/48). Films: "Outwitted by Billy" 1913; "Ye Vengeful Vagabonds" 1914; "His Father's Rifle" 1915; "The Three Godfathers" 1916 (Ruby Merrill); "Law of the Plains" 1938; "The Taming of the West" 1939 (Mrs. Gardner).

Lescoulie, Jack (1912-7/9/87). Films: "Oklahoma Renegades" 1940 (Bob Wallace).

Leslie, Bethel (1929-). TV: *Maverick*—"The Thirty-Ninth Star" 11-16-58 (Janet Kilmer); *Wanted—Dead or Alive*—"Secret Ballot" 2-14-59 (Carole Easter); *Trackdown*—"False Witness" 4-8-59; *The Texan*—"Reunion" 5-4-59 (Julie Bofert); *Bat Masterson*—"Wanted—Dead" 10-15-59 (Mildred Conrad); *Riverboat*—"The Faithless" 11-22-59 (Cathy), "Trunk Full of Dreams" 10-31-60 (Juliet); *Man from Blackhawk*—"A Matter of Conscience" 12-11-59 Sheila Downey), "The Lady in Yellow" 6-17-60 (Mrs. Menzies); *Wagon Train*—"The Joshua Gilliam Story" 3-30-60 (Greta Haldstadt), "The Janet Hale Story" 5-31-61 (Helen Martin), "The Miss Mary Lee McIntosh Story" 2-28-65 (Mary Lee McIntosh); *Death Valley Days*—"A Woman's Rights" 5-10-60; *Shotgun Slade*—"Ring of Death" 7-19-60 (Kate); *Stagecoach West*—"The Unwanted" 10-25-60 (Mary Kelly); *The Rifleman*—"Stopover" 4-25-61 (Tess); *Frontier Circus*—"The Depths of Fear" 10-5-61 (Millie Carno); *Rawhide*—"The Long Count" 1-5-62 (Martha Hastings); *Bonanza*—"The Jacknife" 2-18-62 (Ann Grant); *Gunsmoke*—"The Summons" 4-21-62 (Rose-Ellen), "Innocence" 12-12-64 (Elsa Poe); *Empire*—"The Tall Shadow" 11-20-62 (Charlotte Robbins); *The Virginian*—"The Money Cage" 3-6-63 (Lydia Turner), "A Woman of Stone" 12-17-69 (Cath); *Have Gun Will Travel*—"The Lady of the Fifth Moon" 3-30-63 (Kim Sing); *Daniel Boone*—"The Family Fluellen" 10-15-64 (Zerelda Fleullen); *The Loner*—"Mantrap" 1-8-66 (Ellen Jameson); *Wild Wild West*—"The Night of the Sabatini Death" 2-2-69 (Melanie Nolan/Laura Samples); *The High Chaparral*—"No Bugles, No Women" 3-14-69 (Anne Simmons); *Kung Fu*—"The Passion of Chen Yi" 2-28-74 (Rita Coblenz).

Leslie, Edith (1905-4/9/73). TV: *The Adventures of Rin Tin Tin*—"The Blushing Brides" 3-18-55; *Maverick*—"Black Fire" 3-16-58 (Elizabeth); *Wyatt Earp*—"The Shooting Starts" 4-18-61 (Big Dora); *The Big Valley*—"Alias Nellie Handley" 2-24-69 (Big Mary); *Nichols*—"The One Eyed Mule's Time Has Come" 11-23-71.

Leslie, Gladys (1899-10/2/76). Films: "Ranson's Folly" 1915 (Miss Perry); "The Gray Towers Mystery" 1919 (June Wheeler); "God's Country and the Law" 1922 (Marie).

Leslie, Joan (1925-). Films: "Northwest Stampede" 1948 (Chris Johnson); "Man in the Saddle" 1951 (Laure Bidwell); "Hellgate" 1952 (Ellen Hanley); "Toughest Man in Arizona" 1952 (Mary Kimber); "The Woman They Almost Lynched" 1953 (Sally Maris); "Hell's Outpost" 1954 (Sarah Moffit); "Jubilee Trail" 1954 (Gernet Hale).

Leslie, Lila (1892-9/8/40). Films: "Blue Streak McCoy" 1920 (Eileen Marlowe).

Leslie, Maxine. Films: "Overland Mail" 1939 (Blondie); "Riders of the Frontier" 1939 (Goldie); "The Lone Rider Ambushed" 1941 (Linda); "Sheriff of Sage Valley" 1942 (Janet); "Fugitive of the Plains" 1943.

Leslie, Nan (1926-). Films: "Under Western Skies" 1945 (Prudence); "Sunset Pass" 1946 (Jane); "Under the Tonto Rim" 1947 (Lucy); "Wild Horse Mesa" 1947 (Sue Melbern); "The Arizona Ranger" 1948 (Laura Butler); "Guns of Hate" 1948 (Judy); "Indian Agent" 1948 (Ellen); "Western Heritage" 1948 (Beth Winston); "Pioneer Marshal" 1949 (Susan Forester); "Rim of the Canyon" 1949 (Ruth Lambert); "Train to Tombstone" 1950 (Marie); "Iron Mountain Trail" 1953 (Nancy Sawyer); "The Miracle of the Hills" 1959 (Joanne Tashman). ¶TV: *The Lone Ranger*—"Lady Killer" 12-21-50, "Special Edition" 9-25-52, "The Durango Kid" 4-16-53, "A Broken Match" 12-2-54; *The Gene Autry Show*—"The Sheriff of Santa Rosa" 12-24-50, "The Raiders" 4-14-51, "Double Barrelled Vengeance" 4-21-51, "Go West, Young Lady" 11-19-55; *The Roy Rogers Show*—"Jailbreak" 12-30-51 (Bess Walton); *The Cisco Kid*—"The Fugitive" 11-1-52, "Outlaw's Gallery" 11-22-52, "Pot of Gold" 4-25-53, "Doorway to Nowhere" 9-26-53; *Annie Oakley*—Semi-Regular 1954-57 (Alias Annie Oakley); *Fury*—Regular 1955-60 (Harriet Newton); *The Adventures of Rin Tin Tin*—"Rin Tin Tin and the Second Chance" 6-1-56 (Claire Corbin), "Wagon Train" 11-23-56 (Joan Lambert), "Fort Adventure" 11-30-56 (Joan Lambert); *Zane Grey Theater*—"The Three Graves" 1-4-57 (Nancy Barnett); *Circus Boy*—"Death Defying Donzetti" 5-12-57 (Muriel); *The Californians*—Regular 1957-59 (Martha McGiern); *Wichita Town*—"Day of Battle" 1-18-59 (Margaret Cook); *Wanted—Dead or Alive*—"The Legend" 3-7-59 (Beth McGarrett); *Riverboat*—"The Quick Noose" 4-11-60 (Amy Carson); *The Tall Man*—"The Female Artillery" 9-30-61 (Beth).

Leslie, William. Films: "Scorching Fury" 1952; "Taza, Son of Cochise" 1954 (Cavalry Sergeant); "Seventh Cavalry" 1956; "The White Squaw" 1956 (Thor Swanson); "Buchanan Rides Alone" 1958 (Roy Agry); "Cowboy" 1958 (Tucker); "Return to Warbow" 1958 (Johnny); "The Horse Soldiers" 1959 (Maj. Richard Gray). ¶TV: *The Adventures of Rin Tin Tin*—"Rusty's Romance" 1-20-56 (Dave Stanford); *Fury*—"The Pulling Contest" 1-3-59; *Wichita Town*—"The Hanging Judge" 3-9-60 (Dan Upham).

Lesser, Len (1922-). Films: "Dirty Little Billy" 1972 (Slits); "Death Hunt" 1981 (Lewis). ¶TV: *The Texan*—"The Widow of Paradise" 11-24-58 (Brad); *Hotel De Paree*—"Hard Luck for Sundance" 2-19-60; *Bat Masterson*—"Blood on the Money" 6-23-60 (Frank Holloway); *Stoney Burke*—"Bandwagon" 12-17-62 (Leo); *The Travels of Jaimie McPheeters*—"The Day of the Giants" 11-3-63 (Wes Matlock); *Temple Houston*—"Billy Hart" 11-28-63 (Orley

Baldwin); *Great Adventure*—"Wild Bill Hickok—the Legend and the Man" 1-3-64 (Varnes); *Wild Wild West*—"The Night of the Casual Killer" 10-15-65 (Mason); *Laredo*—"A Very Small Assignment" 3-17-66 (Dirk); *Bonanza*—"Caution: Easter Bunny Crossing" 3-29-70 (Fred), "Heritage of Anger" 9-19-72 (Fancher); *Barbary Coast*—"Crazy Cats" 9-15-75 (the Clerk).

Lessey, George (1880-6/3/47). Films: "Durand of the Bad Lands" 1925 (John Boyd); "Scar Hanan" 1925 (Bart Hutchins); "White Thunder" 1925 (Sheriff Richards); "Go West" 1940 (Railroad President); "Buffalo Bill" 1944 (Mr. Vandevere).

Lessing, Arnold. TV: *The Virginian*—"The Executioners" 9-19-62 (Cowboy Guitarist), "Woman from White Ting" 9-26-62 (Mickey), "Throw a Long Rope" 10-3-62 (Mickey).

Lessy, Ben (1915-). Films: "The Fastest Guitar Alive" 1967 (Indian Chief).

Lester, Bruce (1912-). Films: "The Pathfinder" 1952 (Capt. Bradford).

Lester, Buddy (1915-). Films: "Sergents 3" 1962 (Willie Sharpknife). ¶TV: *Alias Smith and Jones*—"Dreadful Sorry, Clementine" 11-18-71.

Lester, Jack (1915-). Films: "The Sheriff of Fractured Jaw" 1958-Brit. (Coach Driver); "Deadwood '76" 1965 (Tennessee Thompson). ¶TV: *Bat Masterson*—"Lottery of Death" 5-13-59 (Bartender), "Debt of Honor" 9-29-60 (Eddy); *Tales of Wells Fargo*—"The Quiet Village" 11-2-59 (Henry); *Bonanza*—"Denver McKee" 10-15-60 (Johnson); *The Rifleman*—"The Promoter" 12-6-60; *The Rebel*—"Shriek of Silence" 3-19-61 (Warren).

Lester, Kate (1857-10/12/24). Films: "The Meddler" 1925 (Mrs. Gilmore).

Lester, Ketty (1938-). TV: *Here Come the Brides*—"A Bride for Obie Brown" 1-9-70.

Lester, Louise (1867-11/18/52). Films: "Calamity Anne's Ward" 1912; "From the Four Hundred to the Herd" 1912; "Maiden and Men" 1912; "Nell of the Pampas" 1912; "Calamity Anne, Detective" 1913"; "Calamity Anne, Heroine" 1913; "Calamity Anne Parcel Post" 1913; "Calamity Anne Takes a Trip" 1913; "Calamity Anne's Beauty" 1913; "Calamity Anne's Inheritance" 1913; "Calamity Anne's Sacrifice" 1913; "Calamity

Anne's Trust" 1913; "Calamity Anne's Vanity" 1913; "Woman's Honor" 1913; "Calamity Anne in Society" 1914; "Calamity Anne's Love Affair" 1914; "Redbird Wins" 1914; "Broadcloth and Buckskin" 1915; "The Purple Hills" 1915; "The Sheriff of Willow Creek" 1915; "Two Spot Joe" 1915; "The Desert Hawk" 1924 (Bridget); "Galloping On" 1925 (Mrs. Moore).

Lester, Terry. Films: "The Barbara Coast" TVM-1975 (Bret Hollister).

Lester, William "Billy". Films: "The Double O" 1921 (Mat Haley); "Barb Wire" 1922 (Bart Moseby); "The Crow's Nest" 1922 (Pecos); "The Firebrand" 1922 (Sheriff Harding); "The Marshal of Moneymint" 1922 (Slick Boyle); "The Forbidden Trail" 1923 (Rufe Trent); "Wolf Tracks" 1923 (Laroque); "Wolves of the Border" 1923; "The Back Trail" 1924 (Jim Lawton); "The Girl from San Lorenzo" 1950 (Jerry); "Twilight in the Sierras" 1950 (Paul Clifford). ¶TV: *The Lone Ranger*—"Pete and Pedro" 10-27-49.

L'Estrange, Dick (1889-11/19/63). Films: "The Squaw Man" 1914 (Grouchy); "The Girl of the Golden West" 1915 (Senor Slim); "How Callahan Cleaned Up Little Hell" 1915; "Fighting Blood" 1916 (Deacon Flint); "Neck and Noose" 1919; "The Unbroken Promise" 1919 (Sundown Slim); "Blazing Days" 1927 (Turtle Neck Pete); "Border Cavalier" 1927 (Lazy); "Desert Dust" 1927 (Slim Donovan); "One Glorious Scrap" 1927 (Lazy); "The Silent Rider" 1927 (Blondy); "Arizona Cyclone" 1928 (Lazy Lester); "Made-to-Order Hero" 1928 (Lazy); "Quick Triggers" 1928 (Lazy); "Thunder Riders" 1928 (Rider).

Letondal, Henri (1902-2/14/55). Films: "Across the Wide Missouri" 1951 (Lucien Chennault); "The Big Sky" 1952 (Ladadie); "The Wild North" 1952 (John Mudd); "The Gambler from Natchez" 1954 (Renard).

Lettieri, Al (1928-10/18/75). Films: "A Town Called Hell" 1971-Span./Brit. (La Bomba); "Deadly Trackers" 1973 (Gutierrez).

Lettieri, Louis. Films: "Cyclone Fury" 1951 (Johnny); "The Buckskin Lady" 1957 (Ralphy). ¶TV: *Wild Bill Hickok*—"Stolen Church Funds" 9-9-52, "The Steam Wagon" 5-12-53; *The Roy Rogers Show*—"Uncle Steve's Finish" 2-3-55, "Quick Draw" 3-20-55 (Billy Hanley), "And Sudden Death" 10-9-55; *Fury*—"Joey and the Gypsies" 11-26-55 (Karol); *The Adventures of Rin Tin Tin*—"The Third Rider" 3-16-56 (Jimmy), "The Silent Battle" 10-5-56 (Chief Pokiwah), "Major Mockingbird" 1-30-59 (Otoma); *The Lone Ranger*—"White Hawk's Decision" 10-18-56; *Circus Boy*—"The Little Gypsy" 12-2-56 (Prado); *Jim Bowie*—"The Bounty Hunter" 5-17-57 (Luigi); *Broken Arrow*—"Devil's Eye" 11-12-57 (Taneya), "The Teacher" 11-19-57 (Pedro); *Tales of the Texas Rangers*—"Gypsy Boy" 11-24-57 (Julio Conzog), "Warpath" 10-9-58.

Letz, George. see Montgomery, George.

Leverington, Shelby. Films: "The Long Riders" 1980 (Annie Ralston); "The Return of Desperado" TVM-1988.

Leversee, Loretta (1928-). TV: *Here Come the Brides*—"Man of the Family" 10-16-68 (Polly Blake); *Daniel Boone*—"Bringing Up Josh" 4-16-70 (Abigail); *Bonanza*—"Blind Hunch" 11-21-71 (Laurie Hewitt).

Levy, Weaver (1925-). TV: *Sergeant Preston of the Yukon*—"Pack Ice Justice" 9-27-56 (Ooluk); *Here Come the Brides*—"Marriage Chinese Style" 4-9-69.

Lewis, Al (1910-). TV: *Best of the West*—"They're Hanging Parker Tillman" 10-15-81 & 10-22-81 (Judge).

Lewis, Artie (1917-). Films: "The Silent Gun" TVM-1969. ¶TV: *Man from Blackhawk*—"Death by Northwest" 3-25-60 (Harvey); *Wide Country*—"The Quest for Jacob Blaufus" 3-7-63 (Skelly).

Lewis, Ben. Films: "Beyond the Shadows" 1918 (Black Fagan); "The Fighting Shepherdess" 1920 (Lingle).

Lewis, Cathy (1918-11/20/68). TV: *Empire*—"A Place to Put a Life" 10-9-62 (Grace Koenig); *Death Valley Days*—"Graydon's Charge" 1-12-64 (Mamie); *Wagon Train*—"The Captain Sam Story" 3-21-65 (Captain Sam); *F Troop*—"Johnny Eagle Eye" 4-12-66 (Whispering Breeze).

Lewis, David (1916-). Films: "Standing Tall" TVM-1978 (Judge Lang). ¶TV: *Iron Horse*—"Gallows for Bill Pardew" 9-30-67 (Wilson); *The Dakotas*—"Crisis at High Banjo" 2-11-63 (Logan Ames); *Bonanza*—"Six Black Horses" 11-26-67 (Giblin).

Lewis, Edgar (1872-5/21/38). Films: "The Sage Hen" 1921; "Human Targets" 1932 (Recorder); "Texas Gun Fighter" 1932 (Frank Adams); "Law Beyond the Range" 1935 (Townsman).

Lewis, Fiona (1946-). Films: "Wanda Nevada" 1979 (Dorothy Deerfield).

Lewis, Forrest (1900-6/2/77). Films: "The Lawless Breed" 1952 (Zeke Jenkins); "Escape from Fort Bravo" 1953 (Dr. Miller); "Gun Fury" 1953; "The Stand at Apache River" 1953 (Deadhorse); "Take Me to Town" 1953 (Ed Higgins); "Apache Ambush" 1955 (Silas Parker); "The Spoilers" 1955 (Banty Jones); "Man in the Shadow" 1957 (Jake Kelley); "Posse from Hell" 1961 (Dr. Welles); "Skin Game" 1971. ¶TV: *My Friend Flicka*—"One Man's Horse" 9-30-55; *Zane Grey Theater*—"A Time to Live" 4-5-57 (Dr. Bishop); *Maverick*—"Naked Gallows" 12-15-57 (Alec Fall), "The Resurrection of Joe November" 2-28-60 (Captain Nelson), "The Town That Wasn't Thrree" 10-2-60 (Old Timer); *Jim Bowie*—"The Lion's Cub" 3-14-58 (Gunsmith), "The Brothers" 4-4-58 (Team); *Wanted—Dead or Alive*—"Die by the Gun" 12-6-58 (Prospector), "No Trail Back" 11-28-59 (Doc Blake); *Trackdown*—"Guilt" 12-19-58 (Abe Perkins); *Colt .45*—"The Devil's Godson" 10-18-59 (Mr. Van Rensselaer); *Man from Blackhawk*—"Death by Northwest" 3-25-60 (Ward); *Wyatt Earp*—"The Court vs. Doc Holliday" 4-26-60; *Wrangler*—"Incident of the Wide Lop" 9-1-60 (Calvin); *Klondike*—"River of Gold" 10-24-60 (Charlie Morrison); *F Troop*—"Corporal Agarn's Farewell to the Troops" 10-5-65 (Doc Emmett); *Wild Wild West*—"The Night of the Watery Death" 11-11-66 (Captain Pratt).

Lewis, Frederick (1874-3/19/47). Films: "The Lily of Poverty Flat" 1915 (Joe).

Lewis, Garrett. Films: "The Good Guys and the Bad Guys" 1969 (Hawkins).

Lewis, Gene (1888-3/27/79). Films: "Flaming Feather" 1952.

Lewis, Geoffrey (1935-). Films: "Bad Company" 1972 (Big Joe's Gang Member); "The Culpepper Cattle Company" 1972 (Russ); "High Plains Drifter" 1973 (Stacey Bridges); "My Name Is Nobody" 1973-Ital. (Scape); "The Gun and the Pulpit" TVM-1974 (Jason McCoy); "Honky Tonk" TVM-1974 (Roper); "The New Daughters of Joshua Cabe" TVM-1976 (Dutton); "The Return of a Man Called Horse" 1976 (Zenas Morro); "Belle Starr" TVM-1980 (Reverend Weeks); "Bronco Billy" 1980 (John Arlington); "Heaven's Gate" 1980 (Trapper); "Tom Horn" 1980 (Walter Stoll); "The Shadow Riders" TVM-1982 (Major Ashbury); "September Gun" TVM-1983 (Sheriff Bill Johnson); "Lust in the Dust" 1985 (Hard Case Williams); "Desperado: The Outlaw Wars" TVM-1989; "Gunsmoke: The Last Apache" TVM-1990 (Bodine); "The Gambler V: Playing for Keeps" TVM-1994 (Lynch); "Maverick" 1994 (Matthew Wicker); "White Fang 2: Myth of the White Wolf" 1994 (Heath). ¶TV: *Bonanza*—"A Matter of Faith" 9-20-70 (Rogers); *Alias Smith and Jones*—"Stagecoach Seven" 3-11-71, "The Bounty Hunter" 12-9-71, "What Happened at the XST?" 10-28-72 (Deputy Burk Stover); *Gunsmoke*—"The Gang" 12-11-72 (Lafitte); *Kung Fu*—"Chains" 3-8-73 (Johnson); *Centennial*—Regular 1978-79 (Sheriff Bogardus); *Bret Maverick*—"Hallie" 2-9-82 (Barney Broomick); *Gun Shy*—Regular 1983 (Amos); *Wildside*—4-25-85; *Paradise*—"The Burial Ground" 11-4-89 (Colonel Jack Russell).

Lewis, George J. (1904-). Films: "South of the Rio Grande" 1932 (Ramon); "The Pecos Dandy" 1934 (the Pecos Dandy); "Under the Pampas Moon" 1935 (Aviator); "Ride, Ranger, Ride" 1936 (Lt. Bob Cameron); "Kansas Cyclone" 1941; "Outlaws of the Desert" 1941 (Yussuf); "Riders of the Badlands" 1941; "Outlaws of Pine Ridge" 1942 (Ross); "Sin Town" 1942 (Oil Man); "Black Hills Express" 1943 (Vic Fowler); "The Blocked Trail" 1943; "Daredevils of the West" 1943-serial (Turner); "The Texas Kid" 1943; "Black Arrow" 1944-serial (Snake-That-Walks); "Death Valley Rangers" 1944; "The Laramie Trail" 1944; "Zorro's Black Whip" 1944-serial (Vic Gordon); "South of the Rio Grande" 1945 (Sanchez); "Wagon Wheels Westward" 1945; "Beauty and the Bandit" 1946; "The Phantom Rider" 1946-serial (Blue Feather); "Rainbow Over Texas" 1946 (Jim Pollard); "South of Monterey" 1946; "Under Nevada Skies" 1946 (Flying Eagle); "Pirates of Monterey" 1947 (Pirate); "Twilight on the Rio Grande" 1947 (Capt. Gonzales); "The Wistful Widow of Wagon Gap" 1947 (Cow Puncher); "The Adventures of Frank and Jesse James" 1948-serial (Rafe Helney); "Oklahoma Blues" 1948 (Slip Drago); "Renegades of Sonora" 1948; "The Sheriff of Medicine Bow" 1948; "Silver Trails" 1948 (Jose); "The Big Sombrero" 1949 (Juan Vazcaro); "Crashing Thru" 1949; "The Dalton Gang" 1949 (Chief Irahu); "Ghost of Zorro" 1949-serial (Moccasin); "Cody of the Pony Express" 1950-serial (Mort Black); "Crooked River"

1950 (Gentry); "Fast on the Draw" 1950 (Pedro); "Hostile Country" 1950 (Knowlton); "King of the Bullwhip" 1950 (Rio); "Marshal of Heldorado" 1950 (Nate); "Short Grass" 1950 (Diego); "West of the Brazos" 1950 (Manuel); "Al Jennings of Oklahoma" 1951 (Sammy Page); "Bandits of El Dorado" 1951 (Jose Vargas); "The Kid from Amarillo" 1951 (Don Jose Figaroa); "Saddle Legion" 1951 (Rurales Captain); "South of Caliente" 1951; "The Iron Mistress" 1952 (Col. Wells); "The Raiders" 1952 (Vicente); "Viva Zapata!" 1952 (Rurale); "Wagon Team" 1952 (Carlos de la Torre); "Cow Country" 1953 (Sanchez); "Devil's Canyon" 1953 (Col. Gomez); "Shane" 1953 (Ryker Man); "Border River" 1954 (Sanchez); "Drum Beat" 1954 (Capt. Alonzo Clark); "Saskatchewan" 1954 (Lawson); "Davy Crockett and the River Pirates" 1956 (Black Eagle); "The Big Land" 1957 (Dawson); "The Tall Stranger" 1957 (Chavez); "The Comancheros" 1961 (Iron Shirt); "Indian Paint" 1965 (Nopawallo). ¶TV: *The Lone Ranger*—"Enter the Lone Ranger" 9-15-49 (Collins), "The Lone Ranger Fights On" 9-22-49 (Collins), "The Lone Ranger's Triumph" 9-29-49 (Collins), "Pay Dirt" 3-23-50, "Gold Fever" 4-13-50, "Trouble at Black Rock" 2-8-51; *The Gene Autry Show*—"Head for Texas" 7-23-50, "Silver Arrow" 8-6-50, "The Star Toter" 8-20-50, "Gun Powder Range" 10-29-50, "Fight at Peaceful Mesa" 11-19-50, "Ghost Town Raiders" 10-6-51, "Silver Dollars" 10-20-51, "Galloping Hoofs" 12-22-51, "Melody Mesa" 1-4-52, "Stage to San Dimas" 10-8-55, "Guns Below the Border" 11-5-55; *Wild Bill Hickok*—"Homer Atchison" 9-11-51, "Border City" 11-13-51, "Vigilante Story" 1-22-52; *The Roy Rogers Show*—"The Unwilling Outlaw" 3-8-52, "Ghost Gulch" 3-30-52, "Go for Your Gun" 11-23-52; *The Range Rider*—"Outlaw Pistols" 4-5-52; *Annie Oakley*—"The Dude Stagecoach" 1-30-54, "Annie Rides the Navajo Trail" 11-18-56 (Chief Angry Owl); *Wyatt Earp*—"Trail's End for a Cowboy" 12-6-55, "Bat Masterson Wins His Star" 11-20-56 (Dave Pollock); *Sergeant Preston of the Yukon*—"Crime at Wounded Moose" 1-12-56 (Butte Howser); *The Adventures of Rin Tin Tin*—"Circle of Fire" 5-11-56 (Marango); *Broken Arrow*—"The Broken Wire" 5-14-57; *Zorro*—Regular 1957-59 (Don Alejandro de la Vega); *Bonanza*—"The Newcomers" 9-26-59 (Jose Moreno); *Daniel Boone*—"The Returning" 1-14-65 (Menewa); *La-*redo—"The Treasure of San Diablo" 2-17-66 (Don Julio).

Lewis, Harrison. Films: "The Proud Ones" 1956 (Editor); "Face of a Fugitive" 1959 (Bartender). ¶TV: *Sergeant Preston of the Yukon*—"Revenge" 10-4-56 (Doctor); *Lawman*—"Cornered" 12-11-60 (Blake), "Detweiler's Kid" 2-26-61 (Blake); *Have Gun Will Travel*—"Blind Circle" 12-16-61 (Simpson), "Hobson's Choice" 4-7-62 (Barber).

Lewis, Ida (1871-4/21/35). Films: "The Law of Fear" 1928.

Lewis, Jarma (1931-11/11/85). Films: "River of No Return" 1954 (Dancer); "The Marauders" 1955 (Hanna Ferber).

Lewis, Jerry (1926-). Films: "Pardners" 1956 (Wade Kingsley, Jr.).

Lewis, Jimmie (and his Texas Cowboys). Films: "Carolina Moon" 1940.

Lewis, Joshua Hill. Films: "Bad Company" 1972 (Boog Bookin).

Lewis, Judy. TV: *The Outlaws*—Regular 1961-62 (Connie).

Lewis, Mitchell (1880-8/24/56). Films: "Flower of No Man's Land" 1916 (Kahoma); "Code of the Yukon" 1918 (Jean Dubois); "The Sign Invisible" 1918 (Lone Deer); "Calibre 38" 1919 (Austin Brandt); "Jacques of the Silver North" 1919 (Jacques La Rouge); "The Last of His People" 1919 (Wolf); "The Siren Call" 1922 (Beauregard); "The Spoilers" 1923 (Marshal Voorhees); "The Mine with the Iron Door" 1924 (Sonora Jack); "Frivolous Sal" 1925 (Osner); "Tracked in the Snow Country" 1925 (Jules Renault); "The Last Frontier" 1926 (Lige); "Beau Bandit" 1930 (Coloso); "The Squaw Man" 1931 (Tabywanna); "McKenna of the Mounted" 1932 (Pierre); "Sutter's Gold" 1936 (King Kamehameha); "The Bad Man of Brimstone" 1937 (Jake Mulligan); "Henry Goes Arizona" 1939; "Let Freedom Ring" 1939 (Joe); "Stand Up and Fight" 1939 (Sport); "Go West" 1940 (Halfbreed); "Twenty Mule Team" 1940 (Barfly); "Billy the Kid" 1941 (Bart Hodges); "The Harvey Girls" 1946 (Sandy); "The Kissing Bandit" 1948 (Fernando).

Lewis, Monica (1925-). Films: "Inside Straight" 1951 (Cafe Singer). ¶TV: *Tales of Wells Fargo*—"Wild Cargo" 1-19-59 (Moll); *Riverboat*—"Race to Cincinnati" 10-4-59 (M'Liss McCabe); *The Deputy*—"Last Gunfight" 4-30-60 (Helen Ivers); *The Tall Man*—"Ladies of the Town" 5-20-61 (Sal), "The Four Queens" 3-24-62 (Babette); *Overland Trail*—"The Reckoning" 5-29-60 (Anne Michaels); *Laramie*—"The Debt" 4-18-61 (Clovis); *The Virginian*—"Lost Yesterday" 2-3-65 (Martha Winslow), "The Decision" 3-13-68 (Emily Porter); *Laredo*—"Split the Difference" 4-7-67 (Belle Bronson); *Barbary Coast*—"The Day Cable Was Hanged" 12-26-75 (Mrs. Cushman).

Lewis, Ralph (1872-12/4/37). Films: "Jordan Is a Hard Road" 1915; "Revenge" 1918 (Sudden Duncan); "The Lady from Hell" 1926 (Earl of Kennet); "McKenna of the Mounted" 1932; "Somewhere in Sonora" 1933 (Kelly Burton); "Fighting Hero" 1934 (Judge)"Terror of the Plains" 1934 (Dad Lansing); "Born to Battle" 1935; "Outlaw Rule" 1935 (John Lathrop); "Sunset Range" 1935 (Sheriff); "Swifty" 1935 (Alec McNeil); "The Singing Outlaw" 1938 (Colonel Bixer).

Lewis, Ralph. Films: "Marked Trails" 1944 (Jed); "Trigger Law" 1944; "The Utah Kid" 1944; "The Scarlet Horseman" 1946-serial (Pecos).

Lewis, Richard (1869-4/30/35). Films: "Yankee Speed" 1924 (Pedro Ramirez).

Lewis, Richard. Films: "Wagons East!" 1994 (Phil Taylor).

Lewis, Robert Q. (1924-12/11/91). Films: "Ride Beyond Vengeance" 1966 (Hotel Clerk). ¶TV: *Branded*—"The Mission" 3-14-65, 3-21-65 & 3-28-65 (Ray Hatch), "Headed for Doomsday" 4-10-66 (Satteffield).

Lewis, Ronald (1928-1/11/82). Films: "Robbery Under Arms" 1958-Brit. (Dick Marston).

Lewis, Sheldon (1869-5/7/58). Films: "Kit Carson Over the Great Divide" 1925 (Flint Bastille); "Silent Sanderson" 1925 (Single Tooth Wilson); "Beyond the Trail" 1926 (Cal, the Foreman); "Buffalo Bill on the U.P. Trail" 1926 (Maj. Mike Connel); "Moran of the Mounted" 1926 (Lamont); "Senor Daredevil" 1926 (Ratburn); "The Two-Gun Man" 1926 (Ivor Johnson); "Born to Battle" 1927 (Hank Tollivar); "The Overland Stage" 1927 (Jules); "Code of the Scarlet" 1928 (Bartender); "Untamed Justice" 1929 (Sheriff); "Firebrand Jordan" 1930 (David Hampton); "Riders of the Rio" 1931 (Tony); "Tex Takes a Holiday" 1932; "Tombstone Canyon" 1932 (the Phantom); "Gun Justice" 1934; "The Cattle Thief" 1936 (Dolson).

Lewis, Texas Jim (and His Lone Star Cowboys). Films: "Bad Man from Red Butte" 1940; "Swingin' in the Barn" 1940-short; "Pardon My Gun" 1942 (Tex); "Law of the Canyon" 1947; "My Pal Ringeye" 1947-short; "The Stranger from Ponca City" 1947.

Lewis, Vera (1873-2/8/56). Films: "As the Sun Went Down" 1919 (Ike's Wife); "Ramona" 1928 (Senora Moreno); "Dodge City" 1939 (Woman); "They Died with Their Boots On" 1941 (Head Nurse).

Lewis, Walter P. (1871-1/30/32). Films: "The Gambler of the West" 1914; "The Arizona Kid" 1930 (Sheriff Andrews).

Leyva, Frank (1897-2/25/81). Films: "Ramona" 1936 (Servant); "The Painted Stallion" 1937-serial (Captain of the Guard); "Zorro Rides Again" 1937-serial (Gonzalez); "The Lone Ranger" 1938-serial (Pedro); "The Tall Men" 1955 (Waiter); "El Dorado" 1967.

Lezana, Sara. Films: "Last of the Mohicans" 1965-Ital./Span./Ger.; "Murieta" 1965-Span./U.S. (Rosita Murieta).

Li, Alicia. Films: "Stagecoach to Dancer's Rock" 1962 (Mai Lei).

Libby, Freddy. Films: "My Darling Clementine" 1946 (Phin Clanton); "Belle Starr's Daughter" 1947 (Slim); "The Three Godfathers" 1948 (Deputy Sheriff Curly); "She Wore a Yellow Ribbon" 1949 (Col. Krumrein); "The Cariboo Trail" 1950 (Chief White Buffalo); "Wagonmaster" 1950 (Reese Clegg); "Sergeant Rutledge" 1960 (Chandler Hubble). ¶TV: *The Lone Ranger*—"Crime in Time" 10-19-50, "Lady Killer" 12-21-50, "The Outcast" 1-18-51, "The Durango Kid" 4-16-53, "Homer with a High Hat" 12-16-54, "Gold Freight" 4-28-55; *Wild Bill Hickok*—"The Lady Mayor" 7-10-51, "Prairie Flats Land Swindle" 5-6-52.

Libertini, Richard (1933-). TV: *Bret Maverick*—"Faith, Hope and Clarity" 4-13-82 & 4-20-82 (Fingers Wachefsky).

Liddell, Jane. Films: "Rogue River" 1950 (Eileen Reid); "Westward Ho the Wagons" 1956 (Ruth Benjamin).

Lieb, Robert P. (1914-). Films: "The Intruders" TVM-1970. ¶TV: *Jefferson Drum*—"Law and Order" 5-9-58 (Stoker); *The Californians*—"The Inner Circle" 5-13-58 (Albert Bender); *Bonanza*—"The Outcast" 1-9-60, "Enter Thomas Bowers" 4-26-64, "The Trackers" 1-7-68; *The Deputy*—"The Deadly Breed" 9-24-60 (Baker); *Tales of Wells Fargo*—"All That Glitters" 10-24-60 (Sam); *Death*

Valley Days—"Measure of a Man" 11-17-63 (Judge Barnes); *The Virginian*—"Nobility of Kings" 11-10-65 (Howell), "Harvest of Strangers" 2-16-66 (Stacey); *F Troop*—"Spy, Counterspy, Counter Counterspy" 2-15-66 (Assistant); *The Road West*—"The Lean Years" 10-3-66 (Nat); *Alias Smith and Jones*—"The McCreedy Bust—Going, Going Gone" 1-13-72.

Lightfoot, Gordon (1938-). Films: "Harry Tracy—Desperado" 1982 (Morrie Nathan).

Lightner, Richard. Films: "Springfield Rifle" 1952 (Lt. Johnson).

Ligon, Tom (1945-). Films: "Paint Your Wagon" 1969 (Horton Fenty).

Lilburn, James. Films: "San Antone" 1953 (Jim); "Hell's Outpost" 1954; "Jubilee Trail" 1954 (Sgt. Aherne); "At Gunpoint" 1955 (Wally); "Fort Yuma" 1955 (Cpl. Taylor); "Mohawk" 1956 (Sergeant). ¶TV: *Death Valley Days*—"Lola Montez" 12-20-54.

Lilley, Jack. Films: "Little House on the Prairie: Look Back to Yesterday" TVM-1983 (Townsman); "Little House: The Last Farewell" TVM-1984 (Stagecoach Driver); "Little House: Bless All the Dear Children" TVM-1984 (Stagecoach Driver); "Bonanza: The Next Generation" TVM-1988; "The Gambler V: Playing for Keeps" TVM-1994 (Frisco).

Lime, Yvonne (1938-). Films: "The Rainmaker" 1956 (Snookie). ¶TV: *Wichita Town*—"Biggest Man in Town" 12-30-59 (Fran).

Linaker, Kay. Films: "Black Aces" 1937 (Sandy McKenzie); "Drums Along the Mohawk" 1939 (Mrs. Demooth); "Buck Benny Rides Again" 1940 (Brenda Tracy); "Men of Texas" 1942 (Mrs. Olsen).

Lince, John. Films: "The Bond of Fear" 1917; "The Devil Dodger" 1917 (Ricketts); "Beyond the Shadows" 1918 (Du Longpre); "By Proxy" 1918 (Shorty Stokes); "Untamed" 1918 (Mike); "Tempest Cody Backs the Trust" 1919; "All Around the Frying Pan" 1925 (Jim Dawson).

Lincoln, Caryl (1908-2/20/83). Films: "Hello Cheyenne" 1928 (Diana Cody); "Tracked" 1928 (Molly Butterfield); "Wild West Romance" 1928; "The Land of Missing Men" 1930 (Nita Madero); "At the Ridge" 1931 (Pola Valdez); "Cyclone Kid" 1931 (Rose Comstock); "Quick Trigger Lee" 1931 (Rose Campbell); "The Man from New Mexico" 1932 (Sally Langton); "Man of Action" 1933

(Irene Summers); "War on the Range" 1933 (the Rancher's Daughter).

Lincoln, E.K. (1884-1/9/58). Films: "Una of the Sierras" 1912; "Desert Gold" 1919 (Dick Gale); "Fighting Through" 1919 (Robert Carr); "The Inner Voice" 1920; "Man of Courage" 1922 (William Gregory).

Lincoln, Elmo (1889-6/27/52). Films: "Jordan Is a Hard Road" 1915; "The Big Ranger" 1922; "Desperation" 1922; "Fighting Back" 1922; "All Around the Frying Pan" 1925 (Foreman Slade); "Blue Montana Skies" 1939; "Colorado Sunset" 1939 (Burns); "Timber Stampede" 1939 (Townsman); "Union Pacific" 1939 (Card Player); "Wyoming Outlaw" 1939 (U.S. Marshal); "Stage to Chino" 1940; "Return of the Durango Kid" 1945; "Rough Ridin' Justice" 1945 (Guard).

Lincoln, Lar Park. TV: *Outlaws*—"Pursued" 3-7-87 (Grady).

Lincoln, Pamela. TV: *Bronco*—"Four Guns and a Prayer" 11-4-58 (Marcy Lake); *Have Gun Will Travel*—"First, Catch a Tiger" 9-12-59; *Man from Blackhawk*—"Execution Day" 3-4-60 (Kathy).

Lind, Myrtle. Films: "Winners of the West" 1921-serial (Elizabeth Edwards).

Lind, Rex. Films: "Wyatt Earp" 1994 (Frank McLaury).

Lindan, Tove. Films: "Circle of Death" 1935 (Mary Carr); "Senor Jim" 1936 (Adele Thorne).

Linden, Eric (1909-7/14/94). Films: "Robin Hood of El Dorado" 1936 (Johnnie Warren).

Linden, Hal (1931-). TV: *Ruggles of Red Gap* 2-3-57 (Man).

Linden, Judith. Films: "King of Dodge City" 1941 (Janice Blair).

Linder, Alfred (1902-7/4/57). Films: "Trooper Hook" 1957 ¶TV: *Gunsmoke*—"Brush at Elkador" 9-15-56 (Clerk).

Linder, Cecil (1921-). Films: "Flaming Frontier" 1958-Can. (Capt. Dan Carver).

Linder, Christa. Films: "Day of Anger" 1967-Ital./Ger. (Judge's Daughter); "Trinity Plus the Clown and a Guitar" 1975-Ital./Austria/Fr.

Lindfors, Viveca (1920-10/25/95). Films: "The Raiders" 1952 (Elena Ortega); "Run for Cover" 1955 (Helga Swenson); "The Halliday Brand" 1957 (Aleta). ¶TV: *Rawhide*—"Incident of the Day of the Dead" 9-18-59 (Luisa Hadley); *Bonanza*—"The Spotlight" 5-16-65 (Angela Drake).

Lindgren, Orley. Films: "Saddle

Tramp" 1950; "The Savage" 1952 (Whopper Aherne); "Wild Stallion" 1952 (Young Dan Light). ¶TV: *Wild Bill Hickok*—"The Silver Mine Protection Story" 7-24-51.

Lindley, Bert (1873-9/12/53). Films: "The Hidden Badge" 1919; "Fightin' Mad" 1921 (Micah Higgins); "The Crow's Nest" 1922 (John Benton); "Bringin' Home the Bacon" 1924; "$50,000 Reward" 1924 (Anthony Jordan); "Rip Roarin' Roberts" 1924 (Poker Dick); "Men of Daring" 1927 (Colonel Murphy); "Pals in Peril" 1927 (Luther Fox); "The Pocatello Kid" 1931; "Law Beyond the Range" 1935 (Townsman); "The Revenge Rider" 1935 (Townsman); "Tonto Kid" 1935 (Ranch Foreman); "Rose Marie" 1936 (Pop); "Wells Fargo" 1937 (Townsman).

Lindsay, Les. Films: "The Man from Arizona" 1932 (Jerry Sutton).

Lindsay, Margaret (1910-5/9/81). Films: "The Fourth Horseman" 1933 (Molly O'Rourke); "Gold Is Where You Find It" 1938 (Rosanne Ferris); "The Spoilers" 1942 (Helen Chester); "Alaska" 1944; "The Vigilantes Return" 1947 (Kitty). ¶TV: *Buckskin*—"The Ballad of Gabe Pruitt" 7-24-58 (Leora); *Pistols 'n' Petticoats*—2-25-67 (Maggie Lawson).

Lindsey, George (1933-). TV: *The Rifleman*—"Requiem at Mission Springs" 3-4-63 (Dove); *Gunsmoke*—"Pa Hack's Brood" 12-28-63 (Orville Hack), "Hung High" 11-14-64 (Bud Evans), "Two Tall Men" 5-8-65 (Bill Yaeger), "Which Doctor" 3-19-66 (Skeeter), "Mad Dog" 1-14-67 (Pinto Watson), "Phoebe" 2-21-72 (Charlie Clavin); *Daniel Boone*—"Ken-Tuck-E" 9-24-64 (Wigeon).

Line, Helga. Films: "Seven Hours of Gunfire" 1964-Span./Ital.; "Sign of Zorro" 1964-Ital./Span.; "In a Colt's Shadow" 1965-Ital./Span.; "Have a Good Funeral, My Friend… Sartana Will Pay" 1971-Ital.; "Raise Your Hands, Dead Man… You're Under Arrest" 1971-Ital./Span.; "Those Dirty Dogs!" 1973-U.S./Ital./Span.; "China 9, Liberty 37" 1978-Ital./Span./U.S.

Lineback, Richard. Films: "Sommersby" 1993 (Timothy Fry). ¶TV: *Riding for the Pony Express*—Pilot 9-3-80 (Willy Gomes); *Paradise*—"Home Again" 9-16-89 (Drummer).

Lingham, Thomas G. (1870-2/19/50). Films: "The Man in Irons" 1915; "The Pitfall" 1915 (Deering); "Lass of the Lumberland" 1916-serial; "Medicine Bend" 1916 (Ed Banks); "Whispering Smith" 1916 (Sheriff Ed Banks); "The Lost Express" 1917-serial; "The Railroad Raiders" 1917; "Ruth of the Rockies" 1920-serial; "The Fire Eater" 1921 (Jacob Lemar); "The Crow's Nest" 1922 (Beaugard); "Desert Driven" 1923 (Sheriff); "The Desert Rider" 1923 (Dan Baird); "Eyes of the Forest" 1923 (Dr. Jerry MacGinnity); "The Forbidden Trail" 1923 (John Anthony Todd); "The Lone Star Ranger" 1923 (Chaptain McNally); "Wolf Tracks" 1923 (Lemuel Blatherwick); "Huntin' Trouble" 1924; "The Lightning Rider" 1924 (Sheriff Alvarez); "Western Luck" 1924 (Lem Pearson); "Across the Deadline" 1925 (Martin Revelle); "Don Dare Devil" 1925 (Felipe Berengo); "Riders of Mystery" 1925 (John Arliss); "The Border Sheriff" 1926 (Henry Belden); "Davy Crockett at the Fall of the Alamo" 1926 (Dandy Dick Heston); "The Set-Up" 1926 (Seth Tolliver); "Sky High Coral" 1926 (Bill Hayden); "The Bandit's Son" 1927 (Dan McCall); "The Desert Pirate" 1927 (Shorty Gibbs); "Sitting Bull at the Spirit Lake Massacre" 1927 (Parson Rogers); "Splitting the Breeze" 1927 (Tom Rand); "Tom's Gang" 1927 (George Daggett); "The Bantam Cowboy" 1928 (John Briggs); "Man in the Rough" 1928 (Cale Winters); "Orphan of the Sage" 1928 (Jeff Perkins); "The Rawhide Kid" 1928 (Deputy); "Son of the Golden West" 1928 (Jim Calhoun); "The Trail of Courage" 1928 (Jack Tobin); "Young Whirlwind" 1928 (Sheriff); "The Amazing Vagabond" 1929 (George Hobbs); "The Cowboy and the Outlaw" 1929 (Tom Bullhead); "The Freckled Rascal" 1929 (Follansbee); "The Invaders" 1929; "Pals of the Prairie" 1929 (Don Jose Valencia); "The Oklahoma Sheriff" 1930; "The Star Packer" 1934 (Sheriff Davis).

Linkletter, Art (1912-). TV: *Zane Grey Theater*—"The Bible Man" 2-23-61 (Albert Pierce); *Wagon Train*—"The Sam Darland Story" 12-26-62 (Sam Darland).

Linkletter, Jack. TV: *Zane Grey Theater*—"The Bible Man" 2-23-61 (Jimmy Pierce).

Linn, Bambi (1926-). Films: "Oklahoma!" 1955 (Dream Laurey).

Linn, James. Films: "Alias Billy the Kid" 1946 (Jack); "The Phantom Rider" 1946-serial (Thompson); "Calamity Jane and Sam Bass" 1949; "Gold Strike" 1950-short; "Don Daredevil Rides Again" 1951-serial (Thompson).

Linn, Rex. Films: "Desperado: The Outlaw Wars" TVM-1989 (Logan); "The Gambler Returns: The Luck of the Draw" TVM-1991 (Henry); "Iron Will" 1994 (Joe McPherson). ¶TV: *Adventures of Brisco County, Jr.*—"Bounty Hunter's Convention" 1-7-94 (Mountain McClain).

Linow, Ivan. Films: "In Old Arizona" 1929 (Russian Immigrant); "The Silver Horde" 1930 (Svenson).

Linville, Albert (1918-3/1/85). TV: *Gunsmoke*—"The Gypsum Hills Feud" 12-27-58 (Jack Cade).

Linville, Joanne (1928-). TV: *Hotel De Paree*—"Sundance and the Barren Soil" 5-20-60 (Jennifer Wheatley); *Have Gun Will Travel*—"Saturday Night" 10-8-60 (Maggie); *Gunsmoke*—"Old Yellow Boots" 10-7-61 (Beulah Parker), "The Ditch" 10-27-62 (Susan Bart), "9:12 to Dodge" 11-11-68 (Elizabeth Devon); *Laramie*—"The Accusers" 11-14-61 (Carla Morton); *Empire*—"Walk Like a King" 10-30-62 (Leona Spence); *Bonanza*—"The Bridegroom" 12-4-66 (Maggie Dowling), "The Fence" 4-27-69 (Will Tyler); *Shane*—"The Big Fifty" 12-10-66 (Lydia Montgomery); *Lancer*—"Welcome to Genesis" 11-18-69 (Sarah); *Nakia*—"A Beginning in the Wilderness" 10-26-74 (Helen).

Linville, Larry (1939-). TV: *Here Come the Brides*—"Break the Bank of Tacoma" 1-16-70 (Harry Miles).

Lippe, Jonathan (1938-). Films: "Hang 'Em High" 1968. ¶TV: *Gunsmoke*—"Killer at Large" 2-5-66 (Ira), "Prime of Life" 5-7-66 (Kyle Stoner), "The Returning" 2-18-67 (Billy Judd), "Zavala" 10-7-68 (Alex Rawlins), "Time of the Jackals" 1-13-69 (Lucas Brant), "The Devil's Outpost" 9-22-69 (Cody Tyce), "Morgan" 3-2-70 (Carter), "Lynott" 11-1-71 (Wallace), "The Bullet" 11-29-71, 12-6-71 & 12-13-71 (Roper), "Sarah" 10-16-72 (Sonny), "Matt's Love Story" 9-24-73 (Monte Rupert), "Cowtown Hustler" 3-11-74 (Dave Rope); *The Road West*—"The Gunfighter" 9-26-66 (Billy Joe); *Wild Wild West*—"The Night of the Wolf" 3-31-67 (Capt. Adam Douchen); *Cimarron Strip*—"The Search" 11-9-67 (Kerwin Vardeman); *The High Chaparral*—"Auld Lang Syne" 4-10-70 (Lark), "The Badge" 12-18-70 (Mobley); *Bonanza*—"The Wagon" 10-5-70 (Kyte); *Nichols*—"Sleight of Hand" 2-1-72 (Ralph).

Lipson, Jack "Tiny" (1901-11/28/47). Films: "One Man Justice" 1937 (Slim); "Brothers of the West" 1938.

Lipton, Michael (1925-). TV: *Buckskin*—Regular 1958-59 (Ben Newcomb); *The Restless Gun*—"The Dead Ringer" 2-16-59 (Arch Tatum); *Wanted—Dead or Alive*—"The Twain Shall Meet" 10-19-60 (Arthur Pierce Madison).

Lipton, Peggy (1948-). TV: *The Virginian*—"The Wolves Up Front, the Jackals Behind" 3-23-66 (Ducie Colby); *The Road West*—"Elizabeth's Odyssey" 5-1-67 (Jenny Grimmer).

Lipton, Robert (1944-). Films: "Blue" 1968 (Antonio); "Tell Them Willie Boy Is Here" 1969 (Newcombe); "God's Gun" 1976-Ital./Israel. ¶TV: *The Virginian*—"The Sins of the Father" 3-4-70 (Adam Randall).

Liss, Stephen. TV: *Gunsmoke*—"Cattle Barons" 9-18-67 (Boy); *The Big Valley*—"Guilty" 10-30-67 (Ollie).

Lister, Jr., Tiny. Films: "Posse" 1993 (Obobo).

Liston, Frank. *see* Lantieri, Franco.

Liszt, Margie. Films: "Callaway Went Thataway" 1951 (Phone Girl); "Valley of Fire" 1951 (Widow Blanche). ¶TV: *Rawhide*—"Incident of the Roman Candles" 7-10-59, "Incident of His Brother's Keeper" 3-31-61.

Litel, John (1894-2/3/72). Films: "Gold Is Where You Find It" 1938 (Ralph Ferris); "Dodge City" 1939 (Matt Cole); "Santa Fe Trail" 1940 (Harlan); "Virginia City" 1940 (Marshal); "They Died with Their Boots On" 1941 (Gen. Phil Sheridan); "Men of Texas" 1942 (Col. Scott); "The Daltons Ride Again" 1945 (Bohannon); "Northwest Trail" 1945; "Salome, Where She Danced" 1945 (Gen. Robert E. Lee); "San Antonio" 1945 (Charlie Bell); "Heaven Only Knows" 1947 (Reverend); "The Valiant Hombre" 1948 (Lon Lansdell); "The Sundowners" 1950 (John Gaul); "The Texas Rangers" 1951 (Maj. John D. Jones); "Montana Belle" 1952 (Matt Towner); "Jack Slade" 1953 (Judge); "Sitting Bull" 1954 (Gen. Howell); "The Kentuckian" 1955 (Babson); "Texas Lady" 1955 (Mead Moore); "Comanche" 1956 (Gen. Miles); "The Wild Dakotas" 1956; "Decision at Sundown" 1957 (Charles Summerton); "The Hired Gun" 1957 (Mace Beldon); "The Gun Hawk" 1963 (Drunk); "The Sons of Katie Elder" 1965 (Minister); "Nevada Smith" 1966 (Doctor). ¶TV: *Maverick*—"The War of the Silver Kings" 9-22-57 (Joshua Thayer), "The Thirty-Ninth Star" 11-

16-58 (Judge Somervell), "The People's Friend" 2-7-60 (Ellsworth Greeley); *Sugarfoot*—"Quicksilver" 11-26-57 (Hank Tatum), "The Giant Killer" 3-3-59 (Mr. Crenshaw); *Colt .45* - "Ghost Town" 2-21-58 (Hosea Tillery); *Trackdown*—"The Judge" 3-14-58 (Judge Henry); *The Restless Gun*—"Gratitude" 6-16-58, "A Bell for Santo Domingo" 12-22-58 (Father Luke), "Incident at Bluefield" 3-30-59 (Tom Cauter); *Zorro*—"An Eye for an Eye" 11-20-58 (Governor), "Zorro and the Flag of Truce" 11-27-58 (Governor), "Ambush" 12-4-58 (Governor), "Amnesty for Zorro" 1-1-59 (Governor), "Invitation to Death" 5-21-59 (Governor), "The Captain Regrets" 5-28-59 (Governor), "Masquerade for Murder" 6-4-59 (Governor), "Long Live the Governor" 6-11-59 (Governor); *Cimarron City*—"Kid on a Calico Horse" 11-22-58 (Judge Platt); *Wanted—Dead or Alive*—"Sheriff of Red Rock" 11-29-58 (Jude Healy), "The Corner" 2-21-59, "The Inheritance" 4-30-60 (Clint Davis); *Zane Grey Theater*—"Day of the Killing" 1-8-59 (Sheriff Martin Calder); *Cheyenne*—"Blind Spot" 9-21-59 (Vincent Claiborne); *Bonanza*—"Enter Mark Twain" 10-10-59 (Judge Yerrington), "The Tin Badge" 12-17-61 (Mayor Goshen); *Bronco*—"Winter Kill" 5-31-60 (Marshal Matt Sample); *Rawhide*—"Incident of the Running Iron" 3-10-61 (Jim Rye), "Incident at Sugar Creek" 11-23-62 (James Whitcomb); *Stagecoach West*—"The Land Beyond" 10-11-60 (Dan Murchison), "The Unwanted" 10-25-60 (Dan Murchison), "The Saga of Jeremy Boone" 11-29-60 (Dan Murchison), "Come Home Again" 1-10-61 (Dan Murchison), "The Brass Lily" 1-17-61 (Dan Murchison), "The Swindler" 6-13-61 (Don Murchison); *Have Gun Will Travel*—"Ben Jalisco" 11-18-61 (Sheriff Armstedder); *Wide Country*—"Our Ernie Kills People" 11-1-62 (Fred Winkler); *Wagon Train*—"The Whipping" 3-23-64 (Dr. Burke); *Branded*—"The Vindicator" 1-31-65 (Gen. James Reed); *The Virginian*—"Legend for a Lawman" 3-3-65 (Wade Hammill); *The Road West*—"No Sanctuary" 2-6-67 (Judge).

Little, Anna (1891-5/21/84). Films: "Cowgirls' Pranks" 1911; "The Crisis" 1912; "Custer's Last Fight" 1912; "For the Honor of the 7th" 1912; "His Better Self" 1912; "His Punishment" 1912; "The Indian Massacre" 1912; "The Invaders" 1912; "Mary of the Mines" 1912; "The Post Telegrapher" 1912; "The Prospector's Daughter" 1912; "The Reckoning"

1912; "Past Redemption" 1913; "The Sergeant's Secret" 1913; "On the Rio Grande" 1914; "Broadcloth and Buckskin" 1915; "The Cactus Blossom" 1915; "Man-Afraid-of-His-Wardrobe" 1915; "The Sheriff of Willow Creek" 1915; "There's Good in the Worst of Us" 1915; "Two Spot Joe" 1915; "The Valley Feud" 1915; "According to St. John" 1916 (Bessie); "Immediate Lee" 1916 (Beulah); "The Land O' Lizards" 1916 (Bobbie Moore); "Nan of Music Mountain" 1917 (Nan Morgan); "Under Handicap" 1917 (Agryl Crawford); "The Man from Funeral Range" 1918 (Janice Williams); "Rimrock Jones" 1918 (Mary Fortune); "The Squaw Man" 1918 (Naturich); "Lightning Bryce" 1919-serial; "Prowlers of the Wild" 1919; "Square Deal Sanderson" 1919 (Mary Bransford); "Told in the Hills" 1919 (Rachel Hardy); "The Blue Fox" 1921; "Nan of the North" 1922-serial.

Little, Cleavon (1939-10/22/92). Films: "Blazing Saddles" 1974 (Bart).

Little, Eddie. *see* Little Sky, Eddie.

Little, Mickey. Films: "Pursued" 1947; "The Daring Caballero" 1949 (Bobby Del Rio); "Callaway Went Thataway" 1951 (Kid); "Take Me to Town" 1953 (Boy). ¶TV: *Annie Oakley*—"The Tomboy" 7-17-54 (Andy Evans); *The Gene Autry Show*—"Outlaw Warning" 10-2-54.

Little, Rich (1938-). Films: "Lucky Luke" 1971-Fr./Belg. (Voice of Lucky Luke).

Little Billy (Billy Rhodes) (1894-7/24/67). Films: "The Terror of Tiny Town" 1938 (Pat Haines, the Villain).

Little Sky, Dawn. Films: "Cimarron" 1960 (Arita Red Feather); "Ten Who Dared" 1960 (Indian Woman); "Duel at Diablo" 1966 (Chata's Wife); "Billy Two Hats" 1973-Brit. (Squaw); "The Apple Dumpling Gang" 1975 (Big Foot). ¶TV: *Gunsmoke*—"Long Hours, Short Pay" 4-29-61 (the Squaw), "Indian Ford" 12-2-61 (Indian Woman); *Have Gun Will Travel*—"Brotherhood" 1-5-63 (Mrs. Jim Redrock).

Little Sky, Eddie. Films: "Apache Warrior" 1957 (Apache); "Revolt at Fort Laramie" 1957 (Red Cloud); "Tomahawk Trail" 1957 (Johnny Dogwood); "Gun Fever" 1958 (2nd Indian Chief); "The Missouri Traveler" 1958 (Red Poole); "Ride a Crooked Trail" 1958 (Jimmy); "Cimarron" 1960 (Ben Red

Feather); "Hell Bent for Leather" 1960 (William); "Heller in Pink Tights" 1960 (Indian); "Buffalo Gun" 1961; "Sergents 3" 1962 (Ghost Dancer); "Duel at Diablo" 1966 (Alchise); "The Professionals" 1966 (the Prisoner); "The Last Challenge" 1967; "The Way West" 1967 (Sioux Brave); "Paint Your Wagon" 1969 (Indian); "A Man Called Horse" 1970 (Black Eagle); "Run, Simon, Run" TVM-1970 (Santana); "Journey Through Rosebud" 1972 (Stanley Pike); "Breakheart Pass" 1976 (White Hand); "The Oregon Trail" TVM-1976 (Sioux Brave); "The Villain" 1979. ¶TV: *Gunsmoke*—"Sunday Supplement" 2-8-58 (Chief Little Hawk), "Cheyennes" 6-13-59 (Warrior), "Stolen Horses" 4-8-61 (Brave), "Chester's Indian" 5-12-62 (Indian), "I Call Him Wonder" 3-23-63 (Charlie), "Deadman's Law" 1-8-68 (Indian), "The First People" 2-19-61 (Policeman), "The Innocent" 11-24-69 (Indian Chief), "The Scavengers" 11-16-70 (Scarface), "A Child Between" 12-24-73 (Goriko); *Have Gun Will Travel*—"The Solid Gold Patrol" 12-13-58, "The Prophet" 1-2-60 (Indian Scout), "Crowbait" 11-19-60 (Indian Chief); *The Rifleman*—"The Indian" 2-17-59 (Apache); *Rawhide*—"Incident of the Blue Fire" 12-11-59 (Comanche Brave); *The Rebel*—"Gold Seeker" 1-17-60 (Touch the Clouds); *Zane Grey Theater*—"Blood Red" 1-29-61 (Cherokee); *Gunslinger*—"The Death of Yellow Singer" 5-11-61 (Navajo Policeman); *Great Adventure*—"The Death of Sitting Bull"/ "Massacre at Wounded Knee" 10-4-63 & 10-11-63 (Left Hand); *Wagon Train*—"The Miss Mary Lee McIntosh Story" 2-28-65 (Man Who Steals Ponies); *Branded*—"One Way Out" 4-18-65 (Blue Hawk); *Daniel Boone*—"Doll of Sorrow" 4-22-65 (Grey Eagle), "A Very Small Rifle" 9-18-69 (Eagle); *Laredo*—"A Question of Discipline" 10-28-65, "Miracle at Massacre Mission" 3-3-66 (Red Cloud); *The Road West*—"Lone Woman" 11-7-66 (Jaro); *The High Chaparral*—"Gold Is Where You Leave It" 1-21-68 (Alacran); *Death Valley Days*—"The Visitor" 12-27-69 (White Wolf); *The Men from Shiloh*— "The Regimental Line" 3-3-71 (Grey Bull); *Bonanza*—"Shanklin" 3-13-72 (Gaviotta); *Royce*—Pilot 5-21-76 (White Bull); *How the West Was Won*—Episode One 2-12-78 (Drives-His-Horses).

Littlefeather, Sacheen (1946-). Films: "The Trial of Billy Jack" 1974 (Patsy Littlejohn); "Winterhawk" 1975 (Paleflower).

Littlefield, Jack. Films: "Black-jack Ketchum, Desperado" 1956 (Burl Tetlow). ¶TV: *Wild Bill Hickok*—"Town Without Law" 6-23-53; *The Cisco Kid*—"The Epidemic" 4-3-54; *Tales of the Texas Rangers*— "Ransom Flight" 8-27-55 (Al Barrows); *My Friend Flicka*—"The Little Secret" 12-2-55 (Watanah); *Sergeant Preston of the Yukon*—"Old Ben's Gold" 10-3-57 (Bart); *Tales of Wells Fargo*—"The Break" 5-19-58 (Cal Turner); *The Adventures of Rin Tin Tin*—"Running Horse" 10-24-58 (Second Chieftain), "The Cloudbusters" 10-31-58 (Walking Wolf), "Grandpappy's Love Affair" 11-14-58 (Karl), "The Luck of O'Hara" 4-3-59 (Leaning Rock).

Littlefield, Lucien (1895-6/4/60). Films: "The Cost of Hatred" 1917; "The Golden Fetter" 1917 (Pete); "The Jaguar's Claws" 1917; "The Squaw Man's Song" 1917 (Lord Yester); "The Round Up" 1920 (Parenthesis); "The Siren Call" 1922 (Irishman); "The Deadwood Coach" 1924 (Charlie Winter); "Teeth" 1924 (Under Sheriff); "Gold and the Girl" 1925 (Weasel); "The Rainbow Trail" 1925 (Joe Lake); "Tumbleweeds" 1925 (Kentucky Rose); "Tony Runs Wild" 1926 (Red); "A Texas Steer" 1927 (Yell); "The Great Divide" 1929 (Texas Tommy); "Ruggles of Red Gap" 1935 (Charles Balknap-Jackson); "Rose Marie" 1936 (Storekeeper); "Born to the West" 1937 (John, the Cattle Buyer); "High, Wide and Handsome" 1937 (Mr. Lippincott); "Wells Fargo" 1937 (San Francisco Postmaster); "Jeepers Creepers" 1939 (Grandpa); "The Westerner" 1940 (Stranger); "Bells of Capistrano" 1942 (Pa McCracken); "The Great Man's Lady" 1942 (City Editor); "Cowboy and the Senorita" 1944 (Judge Loomis); "The Lights of Old Santa Fe" 1944 (the Judge); "Zorro's Black Whip" 1944-serial (Tenpoint Jackson); "In Old Sacramento" 1946; "Bad Men of Tombstone" 1949; "Susanna Pass" 1949 (Russell Masters). ¶TV: *The Lone Ranger*—"Death Trap" 4-20-50, "Million Dollar Wallpaper" 9-14-50; *Wild Bill Hickok*—"Golden Rainbow" 12-9-52, "The Steam Wagon" 5-12-53; *The Roy Rogers Show*—"Money Is Dangerous" 1-29-56 (Eli Carson); *Circus Boy*—"Uncle Cyrus" 11-28-57 (Uncle Cyrus); *The Texan*—"No Way Out" 9-14-59 (John Partland).

Littlefield, Ralph. Films: "Along Came Jones" 1945 (Townsman); "The Sea of Grass" 1947 (Homesteader); "Swing the Western Way" 1947; "Smoky Mountain Melody"

1948. ¶TV: *The Lone Ranger*—"Enter the Lone Ranger" 9-15-49 (Jim Blane), "The Lone Ranger Fights On" 9-22-49 (Jim Blane), "The Lone Ranger's Triumph" 9-29-49 (Jim Blane).

Littler, Craig. Films: "Buckskin" 1968; "More Dead Than Alive" 1968 (Rafe Karma); "Barquero" 1970 (Pitney).

Liu, Kalen. Films: "Welcome to Hard Times" 1967 (China).

Lively, Jason. Films: "Gunsmoke: To the Last Man" TVM-1991 (Rusty Dover).

Lively, Robin. Films: "Buckeye and Blue" 1988 (Baby Lou).

Livermore, Paul. Films: "The Woman They Almost Lynched" 1953 (Bill Anderson). ¶TV: *The Cisco Kid*—"Talking Dog" 2-23-52, "Big Steal" 4-12-52.

Livesy, Jack (1901-10/12/61). TV: *Maverick*—"Cruise of the Cynthia B" 1-10-60 (Gillespie MacKenzie), "The Bold Fenian Men" 12-18-60 (Patrick Hunter).

Livingston, Jack. Films: "Ashes of Hope" 1917 (Jim Gordon); "The Desert Man" 1917 (Dr. Howard); "His Enemy, the Law" 1918 (Arthur Mason); "The Golden Trail" 1920 (Dave Langdon); "Judge Her Not" 1921 (Ned Hayes); "Wolves of the Range" 1921; "The Range Patrol" 1923; "Scars of Hate" 1923; "The Vow of Vengeance" 1923; "Beaten" 1924.

Livingston, Margaret (1895-12/13/84). Films: "Colorado Pluck" 1921 (Angela Featherstone); "The Yankee Senor" 1926 (Flora), "Lightning" 1927 (Dot Dean/Little Eva).

Livingston, Patricia. Films: "The Guns of Fort Petticoat" 1957 (Stella Leatham).

Livingston, Robert "Bob" (1908-3/7/88). Films: "Bold Caballero" 1936 (Don Diego Vega/Zorro); "Roarin' Lead" 1936 (Stoney Brooke); "The Three Godfathers" 1936 (Frank Benson); "The Three Mesquiteers" 1936 (Stoney Brooke); "Vigilantes Are Coming" 1936-serial (Don Loring/the Eagle); "Come on Cowboys" 1937 (Stoney Brooke); "Ghost Town Gold" 1937 (Stoney Brooke); "Gunsmoke Ranch" 1937 (Stoney Brooke); "Heart of the Rockies" 1937 (Stoney Brooke); "Hit the Saddle" 1937 (Stoney Brooke); "Range Defenders" 1937 (Stoney Brooke); "Riders of the Whistling Skull" 1937 (Stoney Brooke); "Wild Horse Rodeo" 1937 (Stony Brooke); "Call the Mesquiteers" 1938 (Stony

Brooke); "Heroes of the Hills" 1938 (Stoney Brooke); "Outlaws of Sonora" 1938 (Stoney Brooke); "The Purple Vigilantes" 1938 (Stoney Brooke); "Riders of the Black Hills" 1938 (Stoney Brooke); "Cowboys from Texas" 1939 (Stoney Brooke); "The Kansas Terrors" 1939 (Stoney Brooke); "The Lone Ranger Rides Again" 1939-serial (Bill Andrews/the Lone Ranger); "Covered Wagon Days" 1940 (Stoney Brooke); "Heroes of the Saddle" 1940 (Stoney Brooke); "Lone Star Raiders" 1940 (Stony Brooke); "Oklahoma Renegades" 1940 (Stoney Brooke); "Pioneers of the West" 1940 (Stoney Brooke); "Rocky Mountain Rangers" 1940 (Stoney Brooke/the Laredo Kid); "The Trail Blazers" 1940 (Stoney Brooke); "Under Texas Skies" 1940 (Stony Brooke); "Gangs of Sonora" 1941 (Stoney Brooke); "Pals of the Pecos" 1941 (Stoney Brooke); "Prairie Pioneers" 1941 (Stoney Brooke); "Saddlemates" 1941 (Stony Brooke); "Overland Stagecoach" 1942; "Law of the Saddle" 1943 (Rocky Cameron); "Raiders of Red Gap" 1943 (Rocky Cameron); "Wild Horse Rustlers" 1943 (Lone Rider Tom Cameron); "Wolves of the Range" 1943 (Rocky Cameron); "Beneath Western Skies" 1944; "The Big Bonanza" 1944 (Sam Ballou); "Death Rides the Plains" 1944 (Rocky Cameron); "The Laramie Trail" 1944; "Pride of the Plains" 1944 (Johnny Revere); "Bells of Rosarita" 1945; "Dakota" 1945 (Lieutenant); "Don't Fence Me In" 1945 (Jack Chandler); "Grand Canyon Trail" 1948 (Bill Regan); "The Mysterious Desperado" 1949 (Jordan); "Riders in the Sky" 1949 (Rock Mc-Cleary); "Mule Train" 1950 (Sam Brady); "Law of the Badlands" 1951 (Dirkin); "Night Stage to Galveston" 1952 (Adj. Gen. Slaydon); "Once Upon a Horse" 1958 (Bob Livingston); "Saddle Legion" 1951 (Regan); "Winning of the West" 1953 (Art Selby). ¶TV: *The Gene Autry Show*— "Silver Arrow" 8-6-50, "The Star Toter" 8-20-50; *The Cisco Kid*— "Counterfeit Money" 1-27-51, "Convict Story" 2-17-51, "Oil Land" 2-24-51, "The Will" 3-24-51, "False Marriage" 4-14-51; "Wedding Blackmail" 4-21-51, "Pancho and the Wolf Dog" 9-13-52, "Faded General" 10-25-52; *Wild Bill Hickok*—"Mexican Rustlers Story" 10-23-51, "Blacksmith Story" 1-1-52; *The Lone Ranger*— "Frame for Two" 10-23-52, "Message to Fort Apache" 9-23-54; *Stories of the Century*—"Little Britches" 8-19-55.

Lloyd, Albert S. (1886-6/16/41).

Films: "The Half-Breed" 1922 (Hops).

Lloyd, Betty. Films: "Wild Horse Round-Up" 1937 (Ruth Williams).

Lloyd, Christopher (1938-). Films: "Goin' South" 1978 (Towfield); "Lacy and the Mississippi Queen" TVM-1978 (Jennings); "Butch and Sundance: The Early Days" 1979 (Bill Carver); "The Legend of the Lone Ranger" 1981 (Cavendish); "September Gun" TVM-1983 (Jack Brian); "Back to the Future, Part III" 1990 (Dr. Emmet Brown). ¶TV: *Best of the West*—9-10-81 (Calico Kid), 10-1-81 (Calico Kid), "The Calico Kid Goes to School" 1-14-82 (Calico Kid).

Lloyd, Doris (1900-5/21/68). Films: "The Man from Red Gulch" 1925 (Madame LeBlanc); "Broncho Twister" 1927 (Teresa Brady); "The Trail of '98" 1929; "Robbers' Roost" 1933 (Prossie); "Secrets" 1933 (Susan Channing). ¶TV: *Maverick*—"Poker Face" 1-7-62 (Lady Florentine Bleakly); *Wide Country*—"The Girl from Nob Hill" 3-8-63 (Aunt Cora).

Lloyd, Frank (1886-8/10/60). Films: "On the Rio Grande" 1914; "Prowlers of the Wild" 1919.

Lloyd, George H. Films: "The Oklahoma Kid" 1939 (Bartender); "Gaucho Serenade" 1940; "The Return of Wild Bill" 1940 (Matt Kilgore); "Bad Man of Deadwood" 1941; "In Old Cheyenne" 1941 (Smitty); "Wildcat of Tucson" 1941 (Marshall); "In Old California" 1942; "Valley of the Sun" 1942 (Sergeant); "The Ox-Bow Incident" 1943 (Moore); "Frisco Sal" 1945 (Judge); "Royal Mounted Rides Again" 1945-serial (Kent); "Under Western Skies" 1945 (Proprietor); "Home in Oklahoma" 1946 (Sheriff Barclay); "Swing the Western Way" 1947; "Vigilantes of Boomtown" 1947 (Thug); "The Denver Kid" 1948; "Red River" 1948 (Gambler); "Under California Stars" 1948 (Jonas "Pop" Jordan); "Bandit King of Texas" 1949 (Dobson); "Death Valley Gunfighter" 1949 (George); "Frontier Marshal" 1949 (Milton Leffingwell); "Laramie" 1949 (Sgt. Duff); "Outcasts of the Trail" 1949 (Horace Rysen); "The Pecos Pistol" 1949-short; "The Arizona Cowboy" 1950 (Fogarty); "Don Daredevil Rides Again" 1951-serial (Martin); "Man in the Saddle" 1951 (Tom Croker); "Iron Mountain Trail" 1953 (Brockway). ¶TV: *The Gene Autry Show*—"The Devil's Brand" 9-24-50; *The Lone Ranger*—"Dead Man's Chest" 9-28-50.

Lloyd, Jimmy (1919-8/25/88). Films: "Riders of the Whistling Pines" 1949 (Joe Lucas); "Battle of Rogue River" 1954 (Hamley). ¶TV: *The Lone Ranger*—"Devil's Pass" 5-25-50.

Lloyd, Kathleen. Films: "The Missouri Breaks" 1976 (Jane Braxton); "Lacy and the Mississippi Queen" TVM-1978 (Kate Lacy). ¶TV: *Bearcats!*—9-16-71 (Sister Catalina).

Lloyd, Suzanne (1939-). Films: "Seven Ways from Sundown" 1960 (Lucinda). ¶TV: *Zorro*—"The New Commandante" 3-20-58 (Raquel Toledano), "The Fox and the Coyote" 3-26-58 (Raquel Toledano), "Adios, Senor Magistrado" 4-3-58 (Raquel Toledano), "The Eagle's Brood" 4-10-58 (Raquel Toledano), "Zorro by Proxy" 4-17-58 (Raquel Toledano), "Quintana Makes a Choice" 4-24-58 (Raquel Toledano), "Zorro Lights a Fuse" 5-1-58 (Raquel Toledano); *The Texan*—"A Time of the Year" 12-22-58 (Maria Sammett); *Rawhide*—"Incident at Alabaster Plain" 1-16-59 (Verbena Cardin); *Buckskin*—"Fry's Wife" 2-9-59 (Nora Fry); *Gunsmoke*—"Target" 9-5-59 (Nayomi), "Harriet" 3-4-61 (Harriet Horne); *Bronco*—"The Burning Spring" 10-6-59 (Marcia Colby); *The Law of the Plainsman*—"The Hostiles" 10-22-59, "Jeb's Daughter" 4-14-60 (Bertha Wickens); *Sugarfoot*—"The Gitanos" 10-27-59 (Gaya), "Welcome Enemy" 12-26-60 (White Fawn); *Maverick*—"Trooper Maverick" 11-29-59 (Catherine), "Last Stop: Olivion" 2-12-61 (Laura Nelson); *Colt .45*—"Under False Pretenses" 1-10-60 (Julie Gannon); *Wichita Town*—"Afternoon in Town" 2-17-60 (Laura), "Sidekicks" 4-6-60 (Laura Canfield); *Overland Trail*—"Westbound Stage" 3-6-60 (Anne Camber); *Bat Masterson*—"Three Bullets for Bat" 3-24-60 (Linda); *Lawman*—"Girl from Grantsville" 4-10-60 (Jenny Miles); *Have Gun Will Travel*—"Black Sheep" 4-30-60 (Chita); *Wrangler*—"Affair at the Trading Post" 8-18-60 (Monacita); *Wyatt Earp*—"Johnny Ringo's Girl" 12-13-60 (Mary Turner); *Walt Disney Presents: Zorro*—"Auld Acquaintance" 4-2-61 (Isabella); *Tales of Wells Fargo*—"Casket 7.3" 9-30-61 (Christine); *Bonanza*—"The Bride" 1-21-61 (Jennifer); *Laramie*—"Edge of Evil" 4-2-63 (Ann Rhodes).

Lloyd, William. Films: "Bloodhounds of the North" 1913; "The Unlawful Trade" 1914; "West Is Best" 1920.

Loback, Marvin (1898-8/18/38). Films: "Hands Off" 1921 (Jumbo).

Locher, Charles. *see* Hall, Jon.

Locher, Felix (1882-3/13/69). Films: "Thunder in the Sun" 1959 (Danielle); "Walk Tall" 1960 (Chief Black Feather); "The Firebrand" 1962 (Ramirez); "California" 1963 (Don Pablo Hernandez). ¶TV: *Jim Bowie*—"Apache Silver" 2-21-58 (Don Ramon Gonzalez); *Have Gun Will Travel*—"The Ballad of Oscar Wilde" 12-6-58; *Wagon Train*—"The Vincent Eaglewood Story" 4-15-59 (Zonn); *Wyatt Earp*—"The Fugitive" 11-17-59 (Ricardo); *Gunsmoke*—"The First People" 2-19-61 (Grey Feather); *Branded*—"Call to Glory" 2-27-66, 3-6-66 & 3-13-66 (Sitting Bull).

Locke, Jon. Films: "Westward Ho the Wagons" 1956 (Ed Benjamin); "Five Guns to Tombstone" 1961 (Kolloway); "Gun Fight" 1961 (Saunders). ¶TV: *The Texan*—"Desert Passage" 12-1-58 (Pete Masters); *26 Men*—"Live and Let Die" 4-7-59; *Tales of Wells Fargo*—"The Last Stand" 4-13-59 (Reese); *Bonanza*—"House Divided" 1-16-60 (Southern Miner); *Wagon Train*—"Trial for Murder" 4-27-60 & 5-4-60, "The Amos Billings Story" 3-14-62 (Gabe Billings), "The Sam Spicer Story" 10-28-63 (Cam), "The Fenton Canaby Story" 12-30-63 (Gabe), "The Andrew Elliott Story" 2-10-64; *Frontier Circus*—"Dr. Sam" 10-26-61 (Jerry Jones); *The Virginian*—"Day of the Scorpion" 9-22-65 (Abel Tercell); *Laredo*—"A Matter of Policy" 11-11-65 (Giles), "The Legend of Midas Mantee" 9-16-66 (Deputy); *Daniel Boone*—"The Symbol" 12-29-66 (Tate), "Then Who Will They Hang from the Yardarm if Willy Gets Away?" 2-8-68 (Corporal Harrison); *Gunsmoke*—"Spratt" 10-2-72 (Orval); *Dirty Sally*—"Right of Way" 1-11-74 (Sykes).

Locke, Sondra (1946-). Films: "The Outlaw Josey Wales" 1976 (Laura Lee); "Shadow of Chikara" 1978 (Drusilla Wilcox); "Bronco Billy" 1980 (Antoinette). ¶TV: *Kung Fu*—"This Valley of Terror" 9-28-74 (Gwyneth).

Locke, Tammy. TV: *The Monroes*—Regular 1966-67 (Amy Monroe).

Lockhart, Anne (1953-). Films: "Jory" 1972 (Dora). ¶TV: *Dr. Quinn, Medicine Woman*—"Where the Heart Is" 11-20-93 (Maureen).

Lockhart, Gene (1891-4/1/57). Films: "Geronimo" 1940 (Gillespie); "Billy the Kid" 1941 (Dan Hickey); "They Died with Their Boots On" 1941 (Samuel Bacon); "The Lady from Texas" 1951 (Judge George Jeffers); "Apache War Smoke" 1952 (Cyril R. Snowden); "The Vanishing American" 1955 (Blucher).

Lockhart, June (1925-). Films: "The Capture of Grizzly Adams" TVM-1982 (Liz Hawkins). ¶TV: *Have Gun Will Travel*—"No Visitors" 11-30-57 (Dr. Phyllis Thackery), "Twenty-Four Hours to North Fork" 5-17-58 (Dr. Phyllis Thackeray); *Gunsmoke*—"Dirt" 3-1-58 (Crazy Beula); *Wagon Train*—"The Sarah Drummond Story" 4-2-58 (Sarah Drummond), "The Ricky and Laura Bell Story" 2-24-60 (Laurie Bell); *Zane Grey Theater*—"A Handful of Ashes" 5-2-58; *Cimarron City*—"Medicine Man" 11-8-58 (Emily Newton); *Rawhide*—"Incident at Barker Springs" 2-20-59 (Rainy Dawson); *Branded*—"The Vindicator" 1-31-65 (Sue Pritchett); *Death Valley Days*—"Magic Locket" 5-16-65 (Ina Coolbrith), "A City Is Born" 1-29-66.

Lockhart, Kathleen (1894-2/18/78). Films: "Man of Conquest" 1939 (Mrs. Allen).

Lockhart, Laura. Films: "Twin Triggers" 1926 (Muriel Trigger).

Lockney, John P. Films: "The Gunfighter" 1916 (Colonel Ellis Lawton); "Jim Grimsby's Boy" 1916 (Doctor); "The Return of Draw Egan" 1916 (Mat Buckton); "Golden Rule Kate" 1917; "The Silent Man" 1917 (Grubstake Higgins); "The Son of His Father" 1917 (Peter McSwain); "A Desert Wooing" 1918 (Keno Clark); "Flare-Up Sal" 1918 (Tin Cup Casey); "The Tiger Man" 1918 (Dick Hawkins); "Partners Three" 1919 (Hassayampa Hardy); "The Sheriff's Son" 1919 (Dave Dingwell); "A Broadway Cowboy" 1920 (Cal Jordan); "Just Tony" 1922 (Oliver Jordan); "Western Speed" 1922 (Ben Lorimer); "While Satan Sleeps" 1922 (Chuckawalla Bill); "Eyes of the Forest" 1923 (Jaol Fierro); "McGuire of the Mounted" 1923 (Andre Montreau); "Cyclone Buddy" 1924 (Luke Noels); "Thundering Romance" 1924 (Mark Jennings); "Double Action Daniels" 1925 (Old Bill Daniels); "Where the Worst Begins" 1925; "The Desperate Game" 1926 (Adam Grayson); "Deuce High" 1926 (Mandell Armstrong); "Double Daring" 1926 (Banker Wells); "Twisted Triggers" 1926 (Hiram Weston); "Galloping Thunder" 1927 (Oliver Lamb); "The Ore Raiders" 1927; "Soda Water Cowboy" 1927 (Prof. Beerbum); "The Flying Buckaroo" 1928 (Mr. Matthews); "Smoke Bellew" 1929; "Law Beyond the Range" 1935 (Townsman).

Lockwood, Alexander (1901-1/25/90). Films: "Hell Canyon Outlaws" 1957. ¶TV: *Gunsmoke*—"Indian White" 10-27-56 (Colonel Honeyman), "The Widow" 3-24-62 (Colonel); *Sheriff of Cochise*—"Wyatt Earp" 6-7-57 (Insp. Boland); *The Legend of Jesse James*—"Reunion" 1-10-66 (Clint Bethard); *The Big Valley*—"The Fallen Hawk" 3-2-66 (Dr. Merar), "Hazard" 3-9-66 (Doc), "Rimfire" 2-19-68 (Judge Power).

Lockwood, Alyn. Films: "Badman's Gold" 1951 (Bess Benson); "Cattle Queen" 1951 (Rosa).

Lockwood, Gary (1937-). Films: "Firecreek" 1968 (Earl). ¶TV: *Gunsmoke*—"The Raid" 1-22-66 & 1-29-66 (Jim Stark); *The Quest*—"The Longest Drive" 12-1-76 & 12-8-76 (Lucas); *Walt Disney Presents*—"Kit Carson and the Mountain Men" 1-9-77 & 1-16-77 (Bret Haskell).

Lockwood, Harold (1887-10/19/18). Films: "The Law of the Range" 1911; "A True Westerner" 1911; "The White Medicine Man" 1911; "The White Red Man" 1911; "The Ball Player and the Bandit" 1912; "The Deserter" 1912; "For the Honor of the 7th" 1912; "His Better Self" 1912; "The Reckoning" 1912; "The Sergeant's Boy" 1912; "When Thieves Fall Out" 1914; "The Buzzard's Shadow" 1915 (Sgt. Barnes); "The Love Route" 1915 (John Ashby); "The Hidden Children" 1917 (Evan Loskiel); "The Hidden Spring" 1917 (Donald Keeth); "The Promise" 1917 (Bill Carmody); "Under Handicap" 1917 (Greek Conniston).

Lockwood, Margaret (1916-7/15/90). Films: "Susannah of the Mounties" 1939 (Vicky Standing).

Loder, John (1898-1/2/89). Films: "Sunset Pass" 1929 (Ashleigh Preston).

Lodge, David (1921-). Films: "Charley One-Eye" 1973-Brit. (Colonel).

Lodge, John (1903-10/29/85). Films: "Under the Tonto Rim" 1933 (Joe Gilbert). ¶TV: *Laramie*—"No Place to Run" 2-5-63; *The Virginian*—"Farewell to Honesty" 3-24-65 (Doctor); *The Road West*—"Reap the Whirlwind" 1-9-66 (Daniel Bethel); *Daniel Boone*—"The Fallow Land" 4-13-67 (Harris); *Bonanza*—"The Thirteenth Man" 1-21-68 (Terry), "The Crime of Johnny Mule" 2-25-68 (Deputy), "In

Defense of Honor" 4-28-68 (Deputy).

Loff, Jeanette (1906-8/4/42). Films: "The Black Ace" 1928; "45 Calibre War" 1929 (Ruth Walling); "Fighting Thru" 1930 (Alice Madden).

Loft, Arthur (1897-1/1/47). Films: "Kid Courageous" 1935; "Western Justice" 1935 (Clem Slade); "King of the Royal Mounted" 1936 (Sneed); "Public Cowboy No. 1" 1937 (Jack Shannon); "Rawhide" 1938 (Ed Saunders); "Rhythm of the Saddle" 1938 (Clyde Chase); "The Arizona Wildcat" 1939 (Bailiff); "Days of Jesse James" 1939 (Sam Wyatt); "Southward Ho!" 1939 (Captain Jeffries); "The Carson City Kid" 1940 (Kirke); "Colorado" 1940 (Jim Macklin); "Riders of Pasco Basin" 1940 (Matt Kirby); "Texas Terrors" 1940 (Blake); "Back in the Saddle" 1941 (E.G. Blaine); "Down Mexico Way" 1941 (Gerard); "North from the Lone Star" 1941 (Flash Kirby); "They Died with Their Boots On" 1941 (Tillaman); "South of Santa Fe" 1942 (Moreland); "Frontier Badman" 1943 (Lindsay); "In Old Oklahoma" 1943 (Man on Train); "My Friend Flicka" 1943 (Charley Sargent); "The Outlaw" 1943 (Salesman); "Silver Spurs" 1943; "Buffalo Bill" 1944 (Barker); "The Lights of Old Santa Fe" 1944 (Bill Wetherbee); "Along Came Jones" 1945 (Sheriff); "The Man from Oklahoma" 1945 (J.J. Cardigan); "Rhythm Round-Up" 1945; "Lone Star Moonlight" 1946; "Sheriff of Redwood Valley" 1946; "Whirlwind Raiders" 1948.

Loftin, Carey (1914-). Films: "Zorro's Black Whip" 1944-serial (Dirk); "Trail to Vengeance" 1945; "King of the Forest Rangers" 1946-serial (Forbes); "Jesse James Rides Again" 1947-serial (Harlan); "The Adventures of Frank and Jesse James" 1948-serial (Carlson/Pete); "Dangers of the Canadian Mounted" 1948-serial (Clerk/Porter); "Don Daredevil Rides Again" 1951-serial (Owens); "Canadian Mounties vs. Atomic Invaders" 1953-serial (Launch Heavy #2). ¶TV: *Laredo*—"That's Noway, Thataway" 1-20-66.

Logan, Frank (1925-3/28/92). TV: *The Tall Man*—"The Girl from Paradise" 1-13-62 (Deputy).

Logan, Jacqueline (1903-4/4/83). Films: "Salome Jane" 1923 (Salomy Jane); "Tony Runs Wild" 1926 (Grace Percival); "One Hour of Love" 1927 (Jerry McKay).

Logan, James E. Films: "Flashing Guns" 1947 (Ainsworth); "Rose Marie" 1954 (Clerk).

Logan, John (1924-12/7/72). Films: "The Man Behind the Gun" 1952; "Tall Man Riding" 1955.

Logan, Phoebe. Films: "The Fighting Deputy" 1937 (Alice Denton).

Logan, Robert (1940-). Films: "Across the Great Divide" 1976 (Zachariah). ¶TV: *Maverick*—"The Cactus Switch" 1-15-61 (Ben Daniels); *Daniel Boone*—"The Courtship of Jericho Jones" 4-19-65 (Jericho Jones).

Logan, Stanley (1885-1/30/53). Films: "Young Daniel Boone" 1950 (Col. Benson).

Logan, Sydney. Films: "Gangster's Den" 1945 (Ruth Lane).

Loggia, Robert (1930-). Films: "Cattle King" 1963 (Johnny Quatro); "Scott Free" TVM-1976 (James Donaldson); "Bad Girls" 1994 (Frank Jarrett). ¶TV: *Walt Disney Presents*—"Elfego Baca" Regular 1958-60 (Elfego Baca); *Wagon Train*—"The Jose Maria Moran Story" 5-27-59 (Jose Maria Moran); *Overland Trail*—"Mission to Mexico" 4-24-60 (Porfirio Diaz); *Rawhide*—"Incident of the Comanchero" 3-22-63 (Maria Jose Chappala); *Gunsmoke*—"Chief Joseph" 1-30-65 (Lieutenant Cal Tripp); *Wild Wild West*—"The Night of the Sudden Death" 10-8-65 (Warren Trevor), "The Night of the Assassin" 9-22-67 (Col. Barbossa); *A Man Called Shenandoah*—"The Lost Diablo" 1-24-66 (Manuel Rojas); *Custer*—"Suspicion" 10-18-67 (Lt. Carlos Moreno); *The High Chaparral*—"The Deceivers" 11-15-68 (Chio), "The Forge of Hate" 11-13-70 (Grey Wolf); *The Big Valley*—"The Profit and the Lost" 12-2-68 (Vern Hickson); *Big Hawaii*—"The Sugar War" 1977.

Lollobrigida, Gina (1927-). Films: "Bad Man's River" 1971-Span./Ital./Fr. (Alicia).

Lollobrigida, Guido. *see* Burton, Lee.

Lom, Herbert (1917-). Films: "Treasure of Silver Lake" 1963-Fr./Ger./Yugo. (Brinkley); "Villa Rides" 1968 (Gen. Huerta).

Lomas, Jack M. (1911-5/13/59). Films: "Seven Angry Men" 1955 (Doyle); "Reprisal!" 1956 (Bartender); "Copper Sky" 1957 (Lawson); "Cattle Empire" 1958 (Sheriff Brewster); "Last Train from Gun Hill" 1959 (Charlie). ¶TV: *Sky King*—"Fight for Oil" 2-3-52; *Tales of the Texas Rangers*—"Home in San Antone" 10-22-55 (Mac), "Jail Bird" 10-29-55 (Jeeter), "Bandits of El Dorado" 2-18-56 (Morgan), "Quarter

Horse" 10-6-57 (Jay Breen); *The Adventures of Rin Tin Tin*—"Mother O'Hara's Marriage" 10-25-57, "The Ming Vase" 3-13-59 (Gibby); *The Restless Gun*—"Thicker Than Water" 12-9-57; *Broken Arrow*—"Water Witch" 1-7-58 (Lt. Foley); *Wagon Train*—"The Honorable Don Charlie Story" 1-22-58 (Bartender), "The Dick Richardson Story" 12-31-58 (Sheriff); *Tales of Wells Fargo*—"The Pickpocket" 4-28-58 (Duckbill); *Maverick*—"Alias Bart Maverick" 10-5-58 (Mayor), "The Jail at Junction Flats" 11-9-58 (Bartender); *Death Valley Days*—"Gold Lake" 2-3-59 (Tom Stoddard); *Lawman*—"Riding Shotgun" 4-19-59 (Jesse Brubaker).

Lombard, Carol (1909-1/16/42). Films: "Durand of the Bad Lands" 1925 (Ellen Boyd); "Hearts and Spurs" 1925 (Sybil Estabrook); "The Arizona Kid" 1930 (Virginia Hoyt).

Lomond, Britt. Films: "Tonka" 1958 (Gen. George Armstrong Custer). ¶TV: *Death Valley Days*—"Faro Bill's Layout" 10-7-56 (Faro Bill), "A Piano Goes West" 1-6-59; *Cheyenne*—"Test of Courage" 1-29-57 (Lieutenant Poole); *Zorro*—Regular 1957-59 (Captain Monastario); *Colt .45*—"A Legend of Buffalo Bill" 11-8-59 (Buffalo Bill Cody); *Tombstone Territory*—11-20-59 (Jay Pell); *Tales of Wells Fargo*—"The Journey" 1-25-60 (Haggerty); *Wyatt Earp*—Regular 1960-61 (Johnny Ringo); *Klondike*—"Bathhouse Justice" 12-26-60 (Clete Slade); *Zane Grey Theater*—"The Atoner" 4-6-61 (Logan Drew); *Rawhide*—"The Prairie Elephant" 11-17-61 (Dario); *The Virginian*—"If You Have Tears" 2-13-63 (Kyle Lawson).

Loncar, Beba (1943-). Films: "Sheriff Was a Lady" 1965-Ger.; "Days of Violence" 1967-Ital.

London, Babe (1901-11/29/80). Films: "When Romance Rides" 1922 (Sally Brackton); "Jackass Mail" 1942 (Dance Hall Girl); "The Paleface" 1948 (Woman on Wagon Train). ¶TV: *Sergeant Preston of the Yukon*—"Trouble at Hogback" 7-19-56 (Mrs. Martin).

London, Dirk. Films: "The Lonely Man" 1957; "Ambush at Cimarron Pass" 1958 (Johnny Willows). ¶TV: *Sergeant Preston of the Yukon*—"Totem Treasure" 3-1-56 (Ted Sheridan), "Girl from Vancouver" 6-28-56 (Larry Cushing), "Eye of Evil" 11-8-56 (Jerry Traynor); *The Adventures of Rin Tin Tin*—"Return of the Chief" 9-28-56 (Crane); *Tales of the Texas Rangers*—"Streamlined Rustlers" 12-8-57; *Wyatt Earp*—Regular 1958-61 (Morgan Earp).

London, Julie (1926-). Films: "Return of the Frontiersman" 1950 (Janie Martin); "Drango" 1957 (Shelby); "Man of the West" 1958 (Billie Ellis); "Saddle the Wind" 1958 (Joan Blake); "The Wonderful Country" 1959 (Ellen Colton). ¶TV: *Zane Grey Theater*—"A Time to Live" 4-5-57 (Julie); *Laramie*—"Queen of Diamonds" 9-20-60 (June Brown); *Rawhide*—"Incident at Rojo Canyon" 9-30-60 (Anne Danders); *The Big Valley*—"They Called Her Delilah" 9-30-68 (Julia Saxon).

London, Steve. TV: *Sky King*—"Dead Man's Will" 4-6-52 (Dr. Dan Vickers); *Sugarfoot*— "The Avengers" 5-12-59 (Pike); *Branded*—"A Destiny Which Made Us Brothers" 1-23-66.

London, Tom (1893-12/5/63). Films: "The Great Train Robbery" 1903; "Dropped from the Clouds" 1917; "Lone Larry" 1917; "Cyclone Smith Plays Trumps" 1919; "Big Stakes" 1920; "The Forest Runners" 1920; "The Girl and the Law" 1920; "Her Five-Foot Higness" 1920 (Slim Higgins); "'In Wrong' Wright" 1920; "Masked" 1920; "Ransom" 1920; "A Son of the North" 1920; "The Timber Wolf" 1920; "Under Northern Lights" 1920 (Jacques Foucharde); "When the Devil Laughed" 1920; "Wolf Tracks" 1920; "Ghost City" 1921; "The Pony Express Rider" 1921; "The Cowboy and the Lady" 1922 (Joe); "The Long Chance" 1922 (John Corbaly); "Nan of the North" 1922-serial; "The Call of the Canyon" 1923 (Lee Stanton); "God's Law" 1923; "The Guilty Hand" 1923; "To the Last Man" 1923 (Guy); "With Naked Fists" 1923; "The Loser's End" 1924 (Barney Morris); "Headin' Through" 1924 (Roy Harlan); "Heritage of the Desert" 1924; "Not Guilty for Runnin'" 1924 (Lem Dodge); "The Perfect Alibi" 1924 (Ollie Summers); "Riding Double" 1924; "The Demon Rider" 1925 (Black Hawk); "Ranchers and Rascals" 1925 (Simons); "Border Vengeance" 1925 (Sanger); "Luck and Sand" 1925 (Sanger); "The Shield of Silence" 1925 (Harry Ramsey); "Silent Sheldon" 1925 (Bill Fadden); "Three in Exile" 1925 (Jed Hawkins); "The Trouble Buster" 1925 (Larry Simons); "Win, Lose or Draw" 1925 (Fred Holt); "Chasing Trouble" 1926 (Jerome Garrett); "Code of the Northwest" 1926 (Pvt. Frank Stafford); "The Grey Devil" 1926; "West of the Rainbow's End" 1926 (Harry Palmer); "Border Blackbirds" 1927; "The Devil's Twin" 1927 (Otis Dilbre); "The Long Loop on the Pecos" 1927 (Laird); "The Return of the Riddle Rider" 1927-serial; "The Apache Raider" 1928 (Griffin Dawson); "The Border Wildcat" 1928 (Joe Kern); "The Boss of Rustler's Roost" 1928 (Pronto Giles, the Foreman); "The Bronc Stomper" 1928 (Alan Riggs); "The Mystery Rider" 1928-serial (the Claw); "Put 'Em Up" 1928 (Jake Lannister); "The Yellow Cameo" 1928-serial; "Harvest of Hate" 1929 (Martin Trask); "Untamed Justice" 1929; "Firebrand Jordan" 1930 (Ed Burns); "Romance of the West" 1930 (K.O. Mooney); "The Storm" 1930; "Under Texas Skies" 1930 (Hartford); "Westward Bound" 1930 (Dick); "Arizona Terror" 1931 (Chuck Wallace); "Lightnin' Smith Returns" 1931 (Lightnin' Smith); "Lightnin' Smith Returns" 1931; "Range Law" 1931; "Trails of the Golden West" 1931; "The Two Gun Man" 1931 (Tulliver); "Beyond the Rockies" 1932 (Kirk Tracy); "The Boiling Point" 1932 (Pete Maltus); "Cornered" 1932 (Ranch Hand); "Gold" 1932 (Sheriff); "Hidden Valley" 1932; "Honor of the Mounted" 1932; "Human Targets" 1932; "The Night Rider" 1932 (Jeff Barton); "Trailing the Killer" 1932 (Sheriff); "Without Honor" 1932 (Sholt Fletcher); "Clancy of the Mounted" 1933-serial (Constable MacGregor); "The Fugitive" 1933 (Foreman); "Outlaw Justice" 1933; "Sunset Pass" 1933 (Ben); "The Cactus Kid" 1934 (Sheriff); "The Ferocious Pal" 1934 (Dave Brownell); "Fighting Hero" 1934 (Sheriff); "Mystery Mountain" 1934-serial; "Mystery Ranch" 1934 (Blake); "Outlaws' Highway" 1934 (Chet); "The Prescott Kid" 1934 (Slim); "Rawhide Mail" 1934; "The Thundering Herd" 1934; "Courage of the North" 1935 (Morden); "Five Bad Men" 1935 (Gangster); "Gallant Defender" 1935; "Gun Play" 1935 (Meeker); "Justice of the Range" 1935; "The Last of the Clintons" 1935 (Jim Elkins); "Law Beyond the Range" 1935 (Grant); "The Miracle Rider" 1935-serial; "The Revenge Rider" 1935 (Peters); "Rio Rattler" 1935 (Bob Adams); "The Roaring West" 1935-serial; "Sagebrush Troubador" 1935; "Skull and Crown" 1935 (Jennings); "Timber Terrors" 1935 (Burke); "Trails End" 1935 (Ranch Hands); "Tumbling Tumbleweeds" 1935 (Sykes); "Avenging Waters" 1936 (Hoppy); "The Border Patrolman" 1936 (Johnson); "Guns and Guitars" 1936 (Conner); "Heroes of the Range" 1936 (Bud); "The Lawless Nineties" 1936 (Ward); "The Mysterious Avenger" 1936; "O'Malley of the Mounted" 1936 (Lefty); "The Phantom Rider" 1936-serial; "Ramona" 1936 (American Settler); "The Riding Avenger" 1936; "Rio Grande Ranger" 1936 (Sneed); "Toll of the Desert" 1936 (Sheriff Jackson); "Wildcat Saunders" 1936 (Hawkins); "Bar Z Bad Men" 1937 (Sig Bostell); "Courage of the West" 1937; "Law of the Ranger" 1937 (Pete); "The Old Wyoming Trail" 1937; "Reckless Ranger" 1937; "Roaring Timber" 1937 (Duke); "Secret Valley" 1937; "The Silver Trail" 1937 (Looney); "Springtime in the Rockies" 1937 (Tracy); "Western Gold" 1937 (Clem); "Zorro Rides Again" 1937-serial (O'Shea); "Black Bandit" 1938; "California Frontier" 1938; "The Colorado Trail" 1938 (Townsman); "In Early Arizona" 1938; "The Lone Ranger" 1938-serial (Felton); "Outlaws of Sonora" 1938 (Sheriff Trask); "The Painted Trail" 1938 (Mr. Towers); "Phantom Ranger" 1938 (Reynolds); "Pioneer Trail" 1938 (Sam Harden); "Prairie Moon" 1938 (Steve); "Renegade Ranger" 1938 (Red); "Rhythm of the Saddle" 1938; "Riders of the Black Hills" 1938 (Rod); "Santa Fe Stampede" 1938 (Marshal Wood); "Six Shootin' Sheriff" 1938 (Furman); "Sunset Trail" 1938 (Patrol Captain); "Allegheny Uprising" 1939 (Frontiersman); "Flaming Lead" 1939 (Daggett); "Frontier Marshal" 1939; "Jesse James" 1939 (Soldier); "Lure of the Wasteland" 1939 (Ranch Foreman); "The Man from Texas" 1939 (Slim); "Mexicali Rose" 1939; "Mountain Rhythm" 1939 (Deputy); "The Night Riders" 1939 (Wilson); "North of the Yukon" 1939 (Carter); "The Oregon Trail" 1939-serial; "Rollin' Westward" 1939 (Sheriff); "Song of the Buckaroo" 1939 (Sheriff Wade); "Southward Ho!" 1939 (Hadley); "Timber Stampede" 1939 (Hunter); "Westbound Stage" 1939 (Parker); "Covered Wagon Days" 1940 (Martin); "The Dark Command" 1940 (Messenger); "Deadwood Dick" 1940-serial; "Gaucho Serenade" 1940; "The Gay Caballero" 1940 (Rancher); "Ghost Valley Raiders" 1940 (Sheriff); "The Kid from Santa Fe" 1940 (Bill Stewart); "Lone Star Raiders" 1940 (Jones); "Melody Ranch" 1940 (Joe); "Northwest Passage" 1940 (Ranger); "Phantom Rancher" 1940 (Parker); "Riders from Nowhere" 1940 (Mason); "Roll, Wagons, Roll" 1940 (Grimes); "Shooting High" 1940 (Eph Carson); "Stage to Chino" 1940 (Dolan); "Trailing Double Trouble" 1940 (Kirk); "Viva Cisco Kid" 1940 (Town Marshal); "Wagon Train" 1940; "When the Dalton's

Rode" 1940 (Lyncher); "Wild Horse Range" 1940 (Arnold); "Across the Sierras" 1941; "Bad Man of Deadwood" 1941; "Dude Cowboy" 1941 (Sheriff); "Dynamite Canyon" 1941 (John Reed); "Fugitive Valley" 1941 (Warren); "Last of the Duanes" 1941 (Deputy); "The Lone Rider in Frontier Fury" 1941; "The Lone Rider Rides On" 1941; "Pals of the Pecos" 1941 (Sheriff); "Ridin' on a Rainbow" 1941; "Riding the Sunset Trail" 1941 (Sheriff Hays); "Robbers of the Range" 1941 (Monk); "Romance of the Rio Grande" 1941 (Marshal); "The Son of Davy Crockett" 1941; "Stick to Your Guns" 1941 (Waffles); "Twilight on the Trail" 1941 (Gregg); "Underground Rustlers" 1941 (Tom); "Wanderers of the West" 1941 (Sheriff); "American Empire" 1942; "Arizona Terrors" 1942 (Wade); "Bandit Ranger" 1942; "Cowboy Serenade" 1942; "Down Texas Way" 1942 (Pete); "Ghost Town Law" 1942; "Land of the Open Range" 1942 (Tonton); "Lone Star Ranger" 1942; "Riders of the West" 1942; "Shadows on the Sage" 1942 (Franklin); "Sons of the Pioneers" 1942; "Stardust on the Sage" 1942 (MacGowan); "Valley of the Sun" 1942 (Trooper Parker); "Valley of Vanishing Men" 1942-serial (Slater); "West of Tombstone" 1942 (Morris); "Bad Men of Thunder Gap" 1943; "California Joe" 1943; "Canyon City" 1943; "Carson City Cyclone" 1943; "Daredevils of the West" 1943-serial (Miller); "False Colors" 1943 (Townsman); "Fighting Frontier" 1943 (Snap); "Hail to the Rangers" 1943 (Jessup); "Idaho" 1943; "In Old Oklahoma" 1943 (Tom); "The Man from the Rio Grande" 1943; "Overland Mail Robbery" 1943 (Sheriff); "The Ox-Bow Incident" 1943 (Deputy); "Red River Robin Hood" 1943; "The Renegade" 1943; "Santa Fe Scouts" 1943 (Billy Dawson); "Silver Spurs" 1943; "Song of Texas" 1943; "The Stranger from Pecos" 1943; "Wagon Tracks West" 1943 (Lem Martin); "West of Texas" 1943 (Steve London); "Wild Horse Stampede" 1943 (Outlaw); "The Woman of the Town" 1943 (Cowboy); "Beneath Western Skies" 1944 (Earl Phillips); "Call of the Rockies" 1944; "Cheyenne Wildcat" 1944; "Code of the Prairie" 1944 (Loomis); "Firebrands of Arizona" 1944 (Wagon Driver); "Hidden Valley Outlaws" 1944; "Marshal of Reno" 1944; "Mojave Firebrand" 1944; "The San Antonio Kid" 1944; "Sheriff of Sundown" 1944 (Tom Carpenter); "Silver City Kid" 1944; "Stagecoach to Monterey" 1944; "Tucson Raiders" 1944;

"Vigilantes of Dodge City" 1944; "The Yellow Rose of Texas" 1944 (Sheriff Allen); "Zorro's Black Whip" 1944-serial (Commissioner Jams Bradley); "Bells of Rosarita" 1945; "The Cherokee Flash" 1945; "Colorado Pioneers" 1945; "Corpus Christi Bandits" 1945 (Rocky); "Don't Fence Me In" 1945 (the Sheriff); "Great Stagecoach Robbery" 1945; "Marshal of Laredo" 1945; "Oregon Trail" 1945 (Marshal); "Phantom of the Plains" 1945; "Rough Riders of Cheyenne" 1945; "Sheriff of Cimarron" 1945 (Frank Holden); "Sunset in El Dorado" 1945 (Sheriff Gridley); "The Topeka Terror" 1945 (William Hardy); "Trail of Kit Carson" 1945; "Wagon Wheels Westward" 1945; "Alias Billy the Kid" 1946 (Dakota); "California Gold Rush" 1946; "Conquest of Cheyenne" 1946; "Days of Buffalo Bill" 1946; "King of the Forest Rangers" 1946-serial (Tom Judson); "The Man from Rainbow Valley" 1946 (Healey); "Out California Way" 1946 (Johnny Archer); "The Phantom Rider" 1946-serial (Ceta); "Red River Renegades" 1946; "Rio Grande Raiders" 1946; "Roll on, Texas Moon" 1946 (Bert Morris); "Santa Fe Uprising" 1946; "Sheriff of Redwood Valley" 1946; "Stagecoach to Denver" 1946; "Sun Valley Cyclone" 1946; "Along the Oregon Trail" 1947; "Homesteaders of Paradise Valley" 1947; "Jesse James Rides Again" 1947-serial (Sam Bolton); "Last Frontier Uprising" 1947 (Skillet); "The Marshal of Cripple Creek" 1947 (Baker); "Rustlers of Devil's Canyon" 1947 (Sheriff); "Saddle Pals" 1947 (Dad Gardner); "Son of Zorro" 1947-serial (Mark Daniels); "Under Colorado Skies" 1947 (Sheriff Blanchard); "The Wild Frontier" 1947 (Patrick MacSween); "Wyoming" 1947 (Jennings); "Mark of the Lash" 1948; "Marshal of Amarillo" 1948 (Snodgrass); "Overland Trails" 1948; "Brand of Fear" 1949; "The Far Frontier" 1949; "Frontier Marshal" 1949 (Jed); "Red Desert" 1949 (Col. McMasters); "Riders in the Sky" 1949 (Old Man Roberts); "San Antone Ambush" 1949 (Bartender); "South of Rio" 1949 (Weston); "The Blazing Sun" 1950 (Tom Ellis); "Cody of the Pony Express" 1950-serial (Doc Laramie); "The Old Frontier" 1950 (Banker); "Hills of Utah" 1951 (Mayor Donovan); "Rough Riders of Durango" 1951 (Evans); "The Secret of Convict Lake" 1951 (Jerry); "Apache Country" 1952 (Patches); "Blue Canadian Rockies" 1952 (Pop Phillips); "High Noon" 1952 (Sam); "The Old West"

1952 (Chadwick); "Trail Guide" 1952 (Old Timer); "The Marshal's Daughter" 1953 (Sheriff Flynn); "Pack Train" 1953 (Dan Coleman); "Tribute to a Badman" 1956 (Cowboy); "The Storm Rider" 1957 (Todd); "The Tall Stranger" 1957 (Worker); "Good Day for a Hanging" 1958 (Farmer); "Lone Texan" 1959 (Old Dan). ¶TV: *The Gene Autry Show*—"Gold Dust Charlie" 7-30-50, "The Doodle Bug" 8-13-50, "Double Switch" 8-27-50, "The Black Rider" 10-1-50, "The Poisoned Waterhole" 10-8-50, "The Black Rider" 10-22-50, "Steel Ribbon" 9-22-53, "Ransom Cross" 10-6-53, "Santa Fe Raiders" 7-6-54; *The Cisco Kid*—"Pancho and the Pachyderm" 2-2-52, "Laughing Badman" 3-8-52; *The Roy Rogers Show*—"Ghost Town Gold" 5-25-52 (Webb Jenkins), "Carnival Killer" 6-8-52, "Outlaw's Return" 9-28-52, "Huntin' for Trouble" 10-5-52 (Sheriff Ira Gilmore), "Pat's Inheritance" 11-11-53 (Jim), "The Deputy Sheriff" 2-7-54, "Treasure of Paradise Valley" 12-11-55; *The Lone Ranger*—"Tumblerock Law" 2-26-53, "The Red Mark" 9-3-53; *Annie Oakley*—"The Dude Stagecoach" 1-30-54; *Schlitz Playhouse of the Stars*—"Flowers for Jenny" 8-3-56 (Curt Sawyer); *Sergeant Preston of the Yukon*—"The Stolen Malamute" 4-4-57 (Sam Barker); *Broken Arrow*—"Smoke Signal" 12-10-57 (Scout); *Fury*—"The Baby Sitters" 2-8-58 (Matthews); *Have Gun Will Travel*—"The Silver Queen" 5-3-58; *Wyatt Earp*—"The Mysterious Cowhand" 10-14-58 (Nate Strathearn), "Love and Shotgun Gibbs" 4-21-59; *Bat Masterson*—"A Personal Matter" 1-28-59 (Sheriff), "The Lady Plays Her Hand" 12-29-60 (Pop); *The Texan*—"The Marshal of Yellow Jacket" 3-2-59 (Grandpa Avery), "No Love Wasted" 3-9-59, "The Man Hater" 6-15-59 (Jess), 9-12-60; *Tombstone Territory*—"The Man from Brewster" 4-24-59 (Jeriah Hoskins); *The Tall Man*—"Forty-Dollar Boots" 9-17-60 (Saddle Bum), "Rovin' Gambler" 3-18-61 (Stage Driver); *Laramie*—"Three Roads West" 10-4-60 (Old Man), "Cactus Lady" 2-21-61 (Charlie), "Rimrock" 3-21-61 (Tim); *Maverick*—"A Bullet for the Teacher" 10-30-60 (Farmer).

Lonergan, Lenore. Films: "Westward the Women" 1951 (Margaret O'Malley).

Long, Audrey (1924–). Films: "Tall in the Saddle" 1944 (Clara Cardell); "Wanderer of the Wasteland" 1945 (Jean Collinshaw); "Adventures of Gallant Bess" 1948 (Penny Gray); "Cavalry Scout" 1951

(Claire); "Indian Uprising" 1951 (Norma Clemson).

Long, Ed. Films: "Wild Rovers" 1971 (Cassidy). ¶TV: *Bonanza*—"The Real People of Muddy Creek" 10-6-68 (Deputy), "The Running Man" 3-30-69 (Sheriff Daniels), "Heritage of Anger" 9-19-72 (Anders); *Gunsmoke*—"9:12 to Dodge" 11-11-68 (Karns), "The Devil's Outpost" 9-22-69 (Farley), "Morgan" 3-2-70 (Trent), "Kitty's Love Affair" 10-22-73 (Morg).

Long, Jack (-8/7/38). Films: "The Man from New Mexico" 1932 (Hank); "Mark of the Spur" 1932 (Slim); "Mason of the Mounted" 1932; "Scarlet Brand" 1932 (Pete); "Speed Wings" 1934 (Nick Haley); "The Whirlwind Rider" 1935; "End of the Trail" 1936; "Cattle Raiders" 1938 (Posse Man); "Law of the Plains" 1938.

Long, Richard (1927-12/22/74). Films: "Kansas Raiders" 1950 (Frank James); "Saskatchewan" 1954 (Scanlon); "Fury at Gunsight Pass" 1956 (Roy Hanford). ¶TV: *Wagon Train*—"The Annie MacGregor Story" 2-5-58 (Jason); *Have Gun Will Travel*—"The Singer" 2-8-58 (Rod Blakely); *Maverick*—"Alias Bart Maverick" 10-5-58 (Gnetleman Jack Darby), "Shady Deal at Sunny Acres" 11-23-58 (Gentleman Jack Darby), "The Spanish Dancer" 12-14-58 (Gentleman Jack Darby), "The Goose-Drownder" 12-13-59 (Gentleman Jack Darby); *Sugarfoot*—"The Vultures" 4-28-59 (Capt. Clayton Raymond); *Lawman*—"The Ring" 5-24-59 (Zachary Adams); *Tales of Wells Fargo*—"Hometown Doctor" 2-17-62 (Dr. Jeremy Wilson); *The Outlaws*—"No More Horses" 3-1-62 (Morgan Mayberry); *The Big Valley*—Regular 1965-69 (Jarrod Barkley).

Long, Ronald (1911-10/23/86). TV: *Wild Wild West*—"The Night of the Gypsy Peril" 1-20-67 (Sultan of Ramapur); *Bonanza*—"The Reluctant American" 2-14-71 (Gore Stanhope).

Long, Sally (1901-8/12/87). Films: "The Border Whirlwind" 1926 (Isabella Cordova); "The Fighting Buckaroo" 1926 (Betty Gregory); "The Man in the Saddle" 1926 (Laura Mayhew).

Long, Walter (1879-7/4/52). Films: "The Deerslayer" 1913; "Jordan Is a Hard Road" 1915; "A Man and His Mate" 1915; "The Martyrs of the Alamo" 1915 (Santa Anna); "The Outlaw's Revenge" 1916 (Federal Officer); "The Cost of Hatred" 1917 (Jefe Politico); "The Golden Fetter" 1917 (McGill); "A Romance of the Redwoods" 1917 (the Sheriff); "Chas-

ing Rainbows" 1919 (Lacy); "Desert Gold" 1919 (Rojas); "Scarlet Days" 1919 (King Bagley, the Dancehall Proprietor); "The Fighting Shepherdess" 1920 (Pete Mullendore); "The Third Woman" 1920 (Scar Norton); "Call of the Wild" 1923 (Hagin); "The Huntress" 1923; "Quicksands" 1923 (Ring Member); "The Ridin 'Kid from Powder River" 1924 (Steve Lanning); "The Reckless Sex" 1925; "West of Broadway" 1926 (Bad Willie); "Jim the Conqueror" 1927 (Hank Milford); "Forbidden Grass" 1928; "Beau Bandit" 1930 (Bobcat); "Cornered" 1932 (Slade); "Bold Caballero" 1936 (Chat); "Drift Fence" 1936 (Bev Wilson); "The Glory Trail" 1937 (Riley); "North of the Rio Grande" 1937 (Bull); "Bar 20 Justice" 1938 (Pierce); "Man's Country" 1938 (Lex Crane/Buck Crane); "The Painted Trail" 1938 (Driscoll); "Six Shootin' Sheriff" 1938 (Chuck); "Wild Horse Canyon" 1938 (Rosco); "Fighting Mad" 1939 (Frenchy); "Flaming Lead" 1939 (Jim Greeley); "Union Pacific" 1939 (Irishman); "Hidden Gold" 1940; "When the Dalton's Rode" 1940 (Deputy on Train); "Silver Stallion" 1941 (Benson).

Longet, Claudine (1941-). TV: *Alias Smith and Jones*—"Journey from San Juan" 4-8-71 (Michelle Monet).

Longo, Malisa Luisa (1950-). Films: "Once Upon a Time in the Wild, Wild West" 1969-Ital.; "Zorro, the Navarra Marquis" 1969-Ital./Span. (Carmen); "Django Challenges Sartana" 1970-Ital.; "More Dollars for the MacGregors" 1970-Ital./Span.; "Zorro, Rider of Vengeance" 1971-Span./Ital.; "Desperado" 1972-Span./Ital. (Barbara); "California" 1976-Ital./Span. (Helen); "Macho Killers" 1977-Ital.

Lono, James (1890-8/18/54). Films: "Call of the Yukon" 1938 (Topek).

Lonsdale, Harry (-7/12/23). Films: "Battle-Ground" 1912; "The Fall of Black Hawk" 1912; "Fighting for Gold" 1919 (Babyan Verender); "The Last of His People" 1919 (Anthony Briggs); "Vanishing Trails" 1920-serial; "The Night Horsemen" 1921 (Old Joe Cumberland); "Where Men Are Men" 1921 (R.C. Cavendish); "The Fighting Guide" 1922 (Lord Chumleigh Winston); "The Last of the Duanes" 1924 (Jenny's Father); "The Vagabond Trail" 1924 (Colonel Macon); "Brand of Cowardice" 1925.

Lontoc, Leon (1909-1/22/74). TV: *Bonanza*—"The Big Jackpot" 1-

18-70 (Ah Yee); *Here Come the Brides*—"Debt of Honor" 1-23-70.

Loo, Richard (1903-11/20/83). Films: "Secrets of the Wastelands" 1941 (Quan); "One More Train to Rob" 1971 (Mr. Chang); "Kung Fu" TVM-1972 (Master Sun). ¶TV: *Maverick*—"The Golden Fleecing" 10-8-61 (Lee Hong Chang); *Bonanza*—"Day of the Dragon" 12-3-61 (General Tsung); *The Dakotas*—"The Chooser of the Slain" 4-22-63 (George Yang); *Wagon Train*—"The Widow O'Rourke Story" 10-7-63 (Lin Yang); *Wild Wild West*—"The Night the Dragon Screamed" 1-14-66 (Wang Chung); *Here Come the Brides*—"Marriage Chinese Style" 4-9-69 (Chi Pei); *Kung Fu*—"Dark Angel" 11-11-72 (Master Sun), "Blood Brother" 1-18-73 (Master Sun), "The Tong" 11-15-73 (Chen), "Arrogant Dragons" 3-14-74 (Wu Chang), "Besieged: Death on Cold Mountain" 11-15-74 (Weapons Master), "Besieged: Cannon at the Gate" 11-22-74 (Weapons Master), "The Devil's Champion" 11-29-74 (Weapons Master); *The Quest*—"Welcome to America, Jade Snow" 11-24-76.

Lookinland, Todd. TV: *Gunsmoke*—"P.S. Murry Christmas" 12-27-71 (Jake), "The Schoolmarm" 2-25-74 (Lester Pruitt), "The Colonel" 12-16-74 (Corporal); *The New Land*—Regular 1974 (Tuliff Larsen); *How the West Was Won*—Episode One 2-6-77 (Joshua Hanks), Episode Two 2-7-77 (Joshua Hanks), Episode Three 2-14-77 (Joshua Hanks); *Father Murphy*—"Buttons and Beaux" 11-30-82 (T.J.).

Loomis, Margaret. Films: "Told in the Hills" 1919 (Talapa); "Three Gold Coins" 1920 (Betty Reed).

Loos, Ann (1916-5/3/86). Films: "Hannah Lee" 1953 (Sheriff's Wife). ¶TV: *Laramie*—"Dragon at the Door" 9-26-61; *The Virginian*—"The Man Who Couldn't Die" 1-30-63; *Gunsmoke*—"Caleb" 3-28-64 (Dorcas Marr); *A Man Called Shenandoah*—"Care of General Delivery" 5-9-66 (Sarah).

Lopert, Tanya (1943-). Films: "Navajo Joe" 1966-Ital./Span. (Maria).

Lopez, Augustina. Films: "The Crow's Nest" 1922 (the Squaw); "Redskin" 1929 (Yina); "Wolf Song" 1929 (Louisa).

Lopez, Danny. TV: *Zorro*—"The New Order" 11-13-58 (Joaquin Castenada), "An Eye for an Eye" 11-20-58 (Joaquin Castenada), "Zorro and the Flag of Truce" 11-27-58 (Joaquin Castenada), "Ambush" 12-4-58 (Joaquin Castenada).

Lopez, Manuel (-1/31/76). Films: "Jubilee Trail" 1954 (Senor Silva). ¶TV: *Sheriff of Cochise*—"Bandit Chief" 2-15-57 (Capt. Perado); *Maverick*—"Plunder of Paradise" 3-9-58 (Diego); *Tales of the Texas Rangers*—"The Fifth Plague" 12-19-58 (Ruiz); *The Law of the Plainsman*—"Desperate Decision" 11-12-59 (Bandit); *Wyatt Earp*—"Requiem for Old Man Clanton" 5-30-61 (Vaquero); *The Tall Man*—"Sidekick" 12-23-61 (Fosforito).

Lopez, Paul. Films: "The Painted Stallion" 1937-serial (Secretary); "Riders of the Rockies" 1937 (Pete); "Zorro Rides Again" 1937-serial (Captain of Rurales).

Lopez, Perry (1931-). Films: "Drum Beat" 1954 (Bogus Charlie); "Jubilee Trail" 1954 (Silva's Son); "The Lone Ranger" 1956 (Ramirez); "The Young Guns" 1956 (San Antone); "Flaming Star" 1960 (Two Moons); "McClintock" 1963 (Davey Elk); "The Rare Breed" 1966 (Juan); "Bandolero!" 1968 (Frisco); "Hec Ramsey" TVM-1972 (Sgt. Juan Mendoza). ¶TV: *Jim Bowie*—"Jackson's Assassination" 3-15-57 (Jethro Humphrey); *Tombstone Territory*—"Legacy of Death" 6-11-58 (Juan); *The Rifleman*—"The Gaucho" 12-30-58 (Manolo); *The Rebel*—"Yellow Hair" 10-18-59 (Iron Hand); *Riverboat*—"The Long Trail" 4-4-60 (James Evans); *Wagon Train*—"The Jed Polke Story" 3-1-61 (Jeff), "The Madame Sagittarius Story" 10-3-62, "The John Bernard Story" 11-21-62 (Mitsina), "The Santiago Quesada Story" 3-30-64 (Lance Starbuck); *Have Gun Will Travel*—"The Siege" 4-1-61 (Theo Brent); *Bonanza*—"The Last Haircut" 2-3-63 (Duke Miller); *Redigo*—"The Hunters" 12-31-63 (Afraid of His Own Horses); *The Virginian*—"Ring of Silence" 10-27-65 (Shotgun); *Time Tunnel*—"Massacre" 10-28-66 (Dr. Whitebird); *Wild Wild West*—"The Night of the Feathered Fury" 1-13-67 (Dodo le Blanc), "The Night of the Pistoleros" 2-21-69 (Sanchez); *Hondo*—"Hondo and the Singing Wire" 9-22-67 (Delgado); *Hec Ramsey*—"Hangman's Wages" 10-29-72 (Juan Mendoza).

Lopez, Rafael (1946-). TV: *Death Valley Days*—"Death Ride" 3-15-61 (Miguelito); *Rawhide*—"Twenty-Five Santa Clauses" 12-22-61 (Danny); *Bonanza*—"The Last Haircut" 2-3-63; *The Loner*—"Widow on the Evening Stage" 10-30-65 (Indian Captive).

Lora, Joan. TV: *Sugarfoot*—"Small Hostage" 5-26-59 (Estrella);

Man from Blackhawk—"Vendetta for the Lovelorn" 11-20-59; *Colt .45*—"The Gandy Dancers" 5-10-60 (Anna Ziegler).

Lorch, Theodore (1880-11/11/47). Films: "The Last of the Mohicans" 1920 (Chingachgook); "Westbound" 1924; "Where the Worst Begins" 1925; "Black Jack" 1927 (Sam Vonner); "Tracked by the Police" 1927 (Bull Storm); "The Canyon of Adventure" 1928 (Don Alfredo Villegas); "The Royal Rider" 1929 (Prime Minister); "Wild Blood" 1929 (Luke Conner); "Lightning Warrior" 1931-serial (La Farge); "Honor of the Mounted" 1932; "The Man from Arizona" 1932 (Bartender); "Texas Bad Man" 1932 (Art); "The Fugitive" 1933 (Parker); "The Gallant Fool" 1933 (Ramey); "The Whirlwind" 1933 (Jude); "Annie Oakley" 1935 (Announcer); "Gunfire" 1935; "His Fighting Blood" 1935; "The New Frontier" 1935; "Rustlers' Paradise" 1935; "Tonto Kid" 1935 (Samuel Creech); "Rebellion" 1936 (Gen. Vallejo); "Rip Roarin' Buckaroo" 1936; "Romance Rides the Range" 1936 (Jonas Allen); "Wildcat Trooper" 1936 (Rogers); "Aces Wild" 1937 (Kelton); "Back to the Woods" 1937-short (Chief Rain in the Puss); "Cheyenne Rides Again" 1937 (Rollin); "Goofs and Saddles" 1937-short (Gen. Muster); "Lost Ranch" 1937 (Merkle); "Orphan of the Pecos" 1937 (Jeremiah Mathews); "Red River Range" 1938; "Stagecoach" 1939; "Stand Up and Fight" 1939; "Zorro's Fighting Legion" 1939-serial (Carlos).

Lord, Dorothea. TV: *Buckskin*—"The Gold Watch" 8-28-58 (Mrs. Clausen); *The Restless Gun*—"The Hill of Death" 6-22-59 (Ruth); *Maverick*—"The People's Friend" 2-7-60 (Mrs. McCoy), "The Witch of Hound Dog" 11-6-60 (Miz Turner), "Family Pride" 1-8-61 (Mrs. Hale); *Sugarfoot*—"Man from Medora" 11-21-60 (Ella Larson).

Lord, Harry. Films: "Deuce High" 1926 (Jim Blake).

Lord, Jack (1928-). Films: "Man of the West" 1958 (Coaley); "The Hangman" 1959 (Johnny Bishop); "Walk Like a Dragon" 1960 (Line Bartlett); "The Ride to Hangman's Tree" 1967 (Guy Russell). ¶TV: *Have Gun Will Travel*—"Three Bells to Perdido" 9-14-57 (Dave Enderby); *Gunsmoke*—"Doc's Reward" 12-14-57 (Nate Brandell/Myles Brandell); *Rawhide*—"Incident of the Calico Gun" 4-24-59 (Blake), "Incident of His Brother's Keeper" 3-31-61 (Paul

Evans); *Bonanza*—"The Outcast" 1-9-60 (Clay Renton); *The Outlaws*—"The Bell" 3-9-61 (Jim Houston); *Stagecoach West*—"House of Violence" 3-21-61 (Russ Doty), "The Butcher" 3-28-61 (Johnny Kane); *Stoney Burke*—Regular 1962-63 (Stoney Burke); *Wagon Train*—"The Echo Pass Story" 1-3-65 (Lee Barton); *The Loner*—"The Vespers" 9-25-65 (the Rev. Mr. Booker); *Laredo*—"Above the Law" 1-13-66 (Jab Heller); *The Virginian*—"High Stakes" 11-16-66 (Roy Dallman); *The High Chaparral*—"The Kinsman" 1-28-68 (Dan Brookes).

Lord, Marjorie (1918-). Films: "Border Cafe" 1937 (Janet); "Masked Raiders" 1949 (Gale); "Down Laredo Way" 1953 (Valerie); "Rebel City" 1953 (Jane Dudley). ¶TV: *The Lone Ranger*—"Bullets for Ballots" 5-11-50, "The Law Lady" 2-24-55; *Zane Grey Theater*—"Decision at Wilson's Creek" 5-17-57 (Amy Marr); *Wagon Train*—"The Willy Moran Story" 9-18-57 (Mary Palmer).

Lorde, Athena (1915-5/23/73). Films: "Firecreek" 1968 (Mrs. Littlejohn); "Skin Game" 1971 (Margaret). ¶TV: *Gunsmoke*—"The Pretender" 11-20-65 (Mrs. Dano); *Cimarron Strip*—"The Beast That Walks Like a Man" 11-30-67; *Bonanza*—"The Trouble with Trouble" 10-25-70 (2nd Lady), "Face of Fear" 11-14-71 (Miss Griggs).

Loren, Sophia (1934-). Films: "Heller in Pink Tights" 1960 (Angela Rossini).

Lorenzon, Livio (1926-12/23/71). Films: "Terror of Oklahoma" 1961-Ital.; "Last Gun" 1964-Ital.; "The Avengers" 1966-Ital.; "The Good, the Bad, and the Ugly" 1966-Ital.; "Savage Gringo" 1966-Ital.; "Texas, Adios" 1966-Ital./Span.; "Ace High" 1967-Ital./Span. (Paco Rosa); "Cjamango" 1967-Ital. (El Tigre); "Two R-R-Ringos from Texas" 1967-Ital.; "Piluk, the Timid One" 1968-Ital.; "Chrysanthemums for a Bunch of Swine" 1968-Ital.; "Winchester Does Not Forgive" 1968-Ital. (Lasch); "God Will Forgive My Pistol" 1969-Ital.

Lorimer, Elsa. Films: "The Good for Nothing" 1914 (Gertrude Chapin).

Lorimer, Louise (1898-8/12/95). Films: "Pack Train" 1953; "Strange Lady in Town" 1955 (Mrs. Wallace); "Five Card Stud" 1968 (Mrs. Wells). ¶TV: *The Gene Autry Show*—"Silver Dollars" 10-20-51, "Prize Winner" 7-27-54; *Wild Bill Hickok*—"Marriage Feud of Ponca City" 5-13-52;

Wanted—Dead or Alive—"Call Your Shot" 2-7-59; *Wyatt Earp*—"The Actress" 4-14-59 (Mrs. Calloway); *Bonanza*—"Clarissa" 4-30-67 (Mrs. Peterson).

Loring, Ann. Films: "Robin Hood of El Dorado" 1936 (Juanita de la Cuesta).

Loring, Lynn (1944–). Films: "Black Noon" TVM-1971 (Lorna Keyes). ¶TV: *Wagon Train*—"The Lonnie Fallon Story" 2-7-62 (Kathy Jennings); *Gunsmoke*—"Pa Hack's Brood" 12-28-63 (Maybelle Hack); *Daniel Boone*—"Tekawitha McLeod" 10-1-64 (Tekawitha); *Wild Wild West*—"The Night of the Flaming Ghost" 2-4-66 (Carma Vasquez); *A Man Called Shenandoah*—"Run and Hide" 2-14-66 (Jocelyn); *Bonanza*—"Something Hurt, Something Wild" 9-11-66 (Laurie Ferguson); *The Big Valley*—"Judgement in Heaven" 12-22-65 (Maybelle); *Lancer*—"Foley" 10-15-68 (Polly), "Shadow of a Dead Man" 1-6-70 (Jessamie).

Lormer, Jon (1905-3/19/86). Films: "The Comancheros" 1961; "The Gun and the Pulpit" TVM-1974 (Luther); "Rooster Cogburn" 1975 (Rev. Godnight). ¶TV: *Maverick*—"Day of Reckoning" 2-2-58 (Summers), "Lonesome Reunion" 9-28-58 (Newspaperman), "The Town That Wasn't There" 10-2-60 (Sam Bradford); *Have Gun Will Travel*—"Three Sons" 5-10-58; *Wanted—Dead or Alive*—"The Giveaway Gun" 10-11-58, "Railroaded" 3-14-59; *Sugarfoot*—"The Wizard" 10-14-58, "Outlaw Island" 11-24-59 (Doc); *Gunsmoke*—"Young Love" 1-3-59 (Jesse Wheat), "Jailbait Janet" 2-27-60 (Clerk), "McCabe" 11-30-70 (Judge Clairborne), "New Doctor in Town" 10-11-71 (Cody Sims), "Trafton" 10-25-71 (Storekeeper), "Alias Festus Haggen" 3-6-72 (Judge Clayborne); *Lawman*—"The Big Hat" 2-22-59 (Harry Tate); *Bonanza*—"The Newcomers" 9-26-59 (Dr. Riley), "The Scapegoat" 10-25-64 (Collins), "The Thirteenth Man" 1-21-68 (Lamar), "The Bottle Fighter" 5-12-68 (Winter), "The Real People of Muddy Creek" 10-6-68 (Jody), "Is There Any Man Here?" 2-8-70 (Preacher); *Riverboat*—"About Roger Mowbray" 9-27-59 (Dr. Landers); *The Rebel*—"Night on a Rainbow" 5-29-60 (Doctor), "The Legacy" 11-13-60 (Judge Ricker); *Rawhide*—"Incident of the Last Chance" 6-10-60 (Harry Gillespie); *Tate*—"The Return of Jessica Jackson" 9-14-60 (Indian Chief); *Two Faces West*—"The Accused" 2-27-61; *Tales of Wells Fargo*—"The Dodger"

10-7-61 (Clerk); *The Tall Man*—5-26-62 (Medford); *The Virginian*—"Vengeance Is the Spur" 2-27-63; *Empire*—"Breakout" 4-16-63 (Sam Richmond); *Temple Houston*—"Billy Hart" 11-28-63 (Matt Turner); *Branded*—"The Mission" 3-14-65, 3-21-65 & 3-28-65 (Colonel Snow), "Now Join the Human Race" 9-19-65 (Jud Markham); *Walt Disney Presents*—"Gallegher" 1965-67 (Pete); *Laredo*—"Meanwhile, Back at the Reservation" 2-10-66; *Wild Wild West*—"The Night of the Infernal Machine" 12-23-66 (Judge Vickerman), "The Night of the Spanish Curse" 1-3-69 (Elder), "The Night of Bleak Island" 3-14-69 (Boatman); *The Big Valley*—"The Stallion" 1-30-67, "Days of Wrath" 1-8-68 (Doc Saxton), "They Called Her Delilah" 9-30-68 (Dr. Thomas J. Merar), "Run of the Cat" 10-21-68, "A Stranger Everywhere" 12-9-68 (Senator Roberts); *Daniel Boone*—"The Flaming Rocks" 2-1-68; *Lancer*—"Blood Rock" 10-1-68; *The Men from Shiloh*—"Nan Allen" 1-6-71 (Dr. Walker); *Alias Smith and Jones*—"Return to Devil's Hole" 2-25-71, "Jailbreak at Junction City" 9-30-71, "The Biggest Game in the West" 2-3-72; *Dirty Sally*—2-8-75 (Miller).

Loros, George (1944–). Films: "The New Maverick" TVM-1978 (Vinnie).

Lorraine, Harry (1886-8/21/34). Films: "The Last of the Mohicans" 1920 (Hawkeye); "Man of the Forest" 1921 (Al Auchincloss).

Lorraine, Jean (1907-1/24/58). Films: "The Great Divide" 1929 (Polly).

Lorraine, Leota (1893-7/9/75). Films: "The Promise" 1917 (Miss Baker); "A Daughter of the West" 1918 (Sarah Malcomb); "Desert Law" 1918 (Julia Wharton); "Playing the Game" 1918 (Babe Bleur de Lis); "Her Five-Foot Higness" 1920 (Chorus Girl); "Ruggles of Red Gap" 1935 (Mrs. Belknap-Jackson); "The Sea of Grass" 1947 (Bit).

Lorraine, Louise (1901-2/2/81). Films: "Bib Bob" 1921; "The Danger Man" 1921; "Fighting Blood" 1921; "The Fire Eater" 1921 (Martha McCarthy); "The Knockout Man" 1921; "The Midnight Raiders" 1921; "The Outlaw" 1921; "Stand Up and Fight" 1921; "The Valley of the Rogues" 1921; "Headin' West" 1922 (Ann Forest); "McGuire of the Mounted" 1923 (Julie Montreau); "The Oregon Trail" 1923-serial; "Pals" 1925 (Molly Markham); "Three in Exile" 1925 (Lorraine Estes); "The Wild Girl" 1925

(Pattie); "The Silent Guardian" 1926 (Jessie Stevens); "The Stolen Ranch" 1926 (Mary Jane); "The Frontiersman" 1927 (Athalie Burgoyne); "Hard Fists" 1927 (Betty Barnes); "Winners of the Wilderness" 1927 (Mimi); "Beyond the Law" 1930 (Barbara Reingold); "The Mounted Stranger" 1930 (Bonita Coy); "Near the Rainbow's End" 1930 (Ruth Wilson).

Lorre, Peter (1904-3/23/64). TV: *Wagon Train*—"The Christine Elliot Story" 3-23-60 (Mr. Snipple); *Rawhide*—"Incident of the Slavemaster" 11-11-60 (Victor Laurier).

Lorys, Diana (1940–). Films: "Cavalry Charge" 1964-Span.; "Twins from Texas" 1964-Ital./Span.; "Gunfighters of Casa Grande" 1965-U.S./Span. (Gitana); "Murieta" 1965-Span./U.S. (Kate); "He Who Shoots First" 1966-Ital.; "The Texican" 1966-U.S./Span. (Kit O'Neal); "Three from Colorado" 1967-Span.; "Sartana Does Not Forgive" 1968-Span./Ital.; "Villa Rides" 1968 (Emilita); "Canadian Wilderness" 1969-Span./Ital.; "Bad Man's River" 1971-Span./Ital./Fr. (Dolores); "Kill Django... Kill First" 1971-Ital.; "Chino" 1973-Ital./Span./Fr. (Indian); "Get Mean" 1975-Ital. (Princess Elizabeth Maria); "California" 1976-Ital./Span.

Losby, Donald (1951–). TV: *Tate*—"The Return of Jessica Jackson" 9-14-60 (Wovoka); *The Deputy*—"Tension Point" 4-8-61 (Mark Baker); *The Rebel*—"Decision at Sweetwater" 4-23-61 (Rodney); *Bonanza*—"The Jacknife" 2-18-62 (Jody Grant); *Wide Country*—"A Devil in the Chute" 11-8-62 (Tommy); *Rawhide*—"Incident at Quivira" 12-14-62 (Boy); *Wagon Train*—"The Michael McGoo Story" 3-20-63 (Homer); *Great Adventure*—"Teeth of the Lion" 1-17-64 (Billy); *Temple Houston*—"Miss Katherina" 4-2-64 (Tommy Rivers); *Daniel Boone*—"The Family Fluellen" 10-15-64 (Rhys Fluellen); *Gunsmoke*—"The Pariah" 4-17-65 (Thomas Scanzano), "The Whispering Tree" 11-12-66 (Bryant).

Losch, Tilly (1902-12/24/75). Films: "Duel in the Sun" 1946 (Mrs. Chavez).

Losee, Frank (1856-11/14/37). Films: "The Man She Brought Back" 1922 (Fenton).

Loti, Elisa (1936–). Films: "Villa!" 1958 (Manuela).

Loughery, Jacqueline "Jackie" (1930–). Films: "Take Me to Town" 1953 (Dancehall Girl); "Pardners" 1956 (Dolly Riley). ¶TV: *Judge Roy*

Bean—Regular 1955-56 (Letty Bean); *26 Men*—"Runaway Stage" 6-17-58; *Wanted—Dead or Alive*—"The Showdown" 10-26-60 (Kitty Conners); *Bat Masterson*—"Farmer with a Badge" 5-18-61 (Martha Phelps); *Wagon Train*—"The Jeff Hartfield Story" 2-14-62 (Jenny Hartfield); *Bonanza*—"The Waiting Game" 12-8-63 (Rita); *F Troop*—"Play, Gypsy, Play" 3-1-66 (Tanya).

Louie, Bebe. TV: *Wild Wild West*—"The Night of the Inferno" 9-17-65 (Mei Mei), "The Night of the Turncoat" 12-1-67 (Song).

Louis, Jean. Films: "Ramon the Mexican" 1966-Ital./Span. (Ramon the Mexican); "May God Forgive You ... But I Won't" 1968-Ital.; "No Graves on Boot Hill" 1968-Ital. (Paco); "Winchester Does Not Forgive" 1968-Ital.; "Django the Bastard" 1969-Ital./Span.; "Ringo, It's Massacre Time" 1970-Ital.; "Halleluja to Vera Cruz" 1973-Ital.

Louis, Willard (1886-7/22/26). Films: "The End of the Trail" 1916 (Devil Cabot); "Fighting Blood" 1916 (Big Bill); "The Man from Bitter Roots" 1916 (J. Winfield Harrah); "One Touch of Sin" 1917 (Watt Tabor); "Jubilo" 1919 (Punt); "What Am I Bid?" 1919 (Abner Grimp); "McGuire of the Mounted" 1923 (Bill Lusk).

Louise, Anita (1915-4/25/70). Films: "The Great Meadow" 1931 (Betty Hall); "Reno" 1939 (Mrs. Ryder); "Wagons Westward" 1940 (Phyllis O'Conover). ¶TV: *My Friend Flicka*—Regular 1955-56 (Nell McLaughlin).

Louise, Tina (1934-). Films: "Day of the Outlaw" 1959 (Helen Crane); "The Hangman" 1959 (Selah Jennison); "The Good Guys and the Bad Guys" 1969 (Carmel). ¶TV: *Tales of Wells Fargo*—"New Orleans Trackdown" 12-23-61 (Helene Montclair); *Bonanza*—"Desperate Passage" 11-5-67 (Mary Burns); *Kung Fu*—"A Dream Within a Dream" 1-17-74 (Carol Mercer).

Louisiana Lou. Films: "Wall Street Cowboy" 1939 (Louisiana Lou).

Love, Bessie (1898-4/26/86). Films: "The Aryan" 1916 (Mary Jane); "The Good Bad Man" 1916 (Amy); "The Dawn of Understanding" 1918 (Sue Prescott); "Penny of Top Hill Trail" 1921 (Penny); "Bulldog Courage" 1922 (Gloria Phillips); "Three Who Paid" 1923 (Virginia Cartwright/John Caspar); "Sundown" 1924 (Ellen Crawley); "Tongues of Flame" 1924 (Lahleet); "A Son of His Father" 1925 (Nora); "Catlow" 1971-Span. (Mrs. Frost).

Love, Courtney. Films: "Straight to Hell" 1987-Brit. (Velma).

Love, June. Films: "Courage of the North" 1935 (Yvonne Travis).

Love, Lucretia. Films: "Go with God, Gringo" 1966-Ital./Span.; "Colt in the Hand of the Devil" 1967-Ital.; "Blindman" 1971-Ital.; "Two Sons of Trinity" 1972-Ital.

Love, Montague (1877-5/17/43). Films: "The Challenge" 1916 (Quarrier); "The Desert's Price" 1925 (Jim Martin); "Hands Up!" 1926 (Union General); "Jesse James" 1927 (Frederick Mimms); "One Hour of Love" 1927 (J.W. McKay); "Rose of the Golden West" 1927 (Gen. Vallero); "The Wind" 1928 (Roddy); "The Riding Tornado" 1932 (Walt Carson); "Hi Gaucho!" 1936 (Hilario); "Sutter's Gold" 1936 (Capt. Kettleson); "Mark of Zorro" 1940 (Don Alejandro Vega); "Northwest Mounted Police" 1940 (Inspector Cabot); "Northwest Passage" 1940 (Wiseman Clagett); "Hudson Bay" 1941 (Governor d'Argenson).

Love, Phyllis. Films: "Friendly Persuasion" 1956 (Mattie Birdwell). ¶TV: *Laramie*—"Three Roads West" 10-4-60 (Mrs. Adams); *Have Gun Will Travel*—"A Quiet Night in Town" 1-7-61 & 1-14-61 (Dot); *The Deputy*—"The Means and the End" 3-18-61 (Josie Styles); *Gunsmoke*—"Bless Me Till I Die" 4-22-61 (Beth Treadwell), "Doctor's Wife" 10-24-64 (Jennifer May); *The Tall Man*—"Fool's Play" 12-2-61 (Sarah Wilson); *Shane*—"Poor Tom's A-Cold" 11-5-66 (Ada Gary); *Bonanza*—"A Home for Jamie" 12-19-71 (Miss Griggs), "The Initiation" 9-26-72 (Miss Griggs).

Lovejoy, Frank (1914-10/2/62). Films: "Black Bart" 1948 (Lorimer); "The Charge at Feather River" 1953 (Sgt. Baker); "The Americano" 1955 (Bento Hermanny); "Cole Younger, Gunfighter" 1958 (Cole Younger). ¶TV: *Zane Grey Theater*—"No Man Living" 1-11-57 (Jim Todd), "Hanging Fever" 3-12-59 (Sam Walton), "Shadows" 11-5-59 (Loy Bannister); *Wichita Town*—"The Hanging Judge" 3-9-60 (Judge Parker).

Lovelock, Raymond. Films: "Django Kill" 1967-Ital./Span.

Lovely, Louise (1896-3/18/80). Films: "The Outlaw and the Lady" 1917; "The Wolf and His Mate" 1917 (Bess Nolan); "The Girl Who Wouldn't Quit" 1918 (Joan Tracy); "Nobody's Wife" 1918 (Hope Ross); "Last of the Duanes" 1919 (Jenny Lee); "The Lone Star Ranger" 1919 (Ray Longstreth); "The Joyous Troublemaker" 1920 (Beatrice Corlin); "The Orphan" 1920 (Helen Shields); "The Third Woman" 1920 (Eleanor Steele); "Twins of Suffering Creek" 1920; "Heart of the North" 1921 (Patricia Graham).

Loveridge, Margarita. *see* Marsh, Marguerite.

Lovitz, Jon (1957-). Films: "Three Amigos" 1986 (Morty); "An American Tail: Fievel Goes West" 1991 (voice of T.R. Chula); "City Slickers II: The Legend of Curly's Gold" 1994 (Glen Robbins).

Lovsky, Celia (1897-10/12/79). Films: "Texas Lady" 1955 (Mrs. Gantz); "Trooper Hook" 1957 (Senora). ¶TV: *Wagon Train*—"A Man Called Horse" 3-26-58; *Bonanza*—"The Spanish Grant" 2-6-60; *The Texan*—"Badman" 6-20-60 (Grandma Branden); *Riverboat*—"The Two Faces of Grey Holden" 10-3-60 (Grandma Joe); *Gunslinger*—"The Death of Yellow Singer" 5-11-61 (Aunt Kayenta); *The Big Valley*—"Hide the Children" 12-19-66 (Salishka).

Low, Carl (1917-10/19/88). TV: *Dupont Show of the Week*—"The Silver Burro" 11-3-63 (Jim Wardner).

Low, Jack (1898-2/21/58). Films: "The Westerner" 1934 (Hotel Clerk); "Beyond the Sacramento" 1940 (Prison Guard); "The Dark Command" 1940; "Outlaws of the Panhandle" 1941 (Dogger); "The Proud Ones" 1956 (Guard).

Lowe, Edmund (1892-4/21/71). Films: "In Old Arizona" 1929 (Sgt. Mickey Dunne); "Cisco Kid" 1931 (Sgt. Mickey Dunn); "Plunderers of Painted Flats" 1959 (Ned East); "Heller in Pink Tights" 1960 (Manfred "Doc" Montague). ¶TV: *Maverick*—"The War of the Silver Kings" 9-22-57 (Phineas King).

Lowe, Ellen. Films: "Rancho Grande" 1940 (Effie Tinker); "Wagon Train" 1940 (Amanthy); "Saddlemates" 1941 (Aunt Amanda); "Bordertown Trail" 1944.

Lowe, James (1880-5/18/63). Films: "The Demon Rider" 1925 (Cook); "Blue Blazes" 1926 (Rastus).

Lowe, Rob (1964-). Films: "Frank and Jesse" TVM-1995 (Jesse James).

Lowell, Helen (1866-6/28/37). Films: "Wild Brian Kent" 1936 (Sue Prentice); "High, Wide and Handsome" 1937 (Mrs. Lippincott).

Lowell, Joan (1900-11/7/67). Films: "Cold Nerve" 1925.

Lowell, John (1875-9/19/37). Films: "Red Love" 1925 (Thunder Cloud); "Headin' Westward" 1928 (Ed Benson); "The Silent Trail" 1928; "Bad Man's Money" 1929; "Captain Cowboy" 1929; "Fighters of the Saddle" 1929 (Henry "Bulldog" Weatherby).

Lowell, Tom (1941-). TV: *Gunsmoke*—"Kate Heller" 9-28-63 (Andy Heller), "Homecoming" 5-23-64 (Ethan Lowell); *The Loner*—"The Kingdom of McComb" 10-9-65 (Young Townsend); *Bonanza*—"Ride the Wind" 1-16-66 & 1-23-66 (Jabez Ludlow); *The Big Valley*—"Showdown in Limbo" 3-27-67 (Chad Sawyer); *Daniel Boone*—"The Patriot" 12-5-68 (Davy Gist).

Lowens, Curt (1925-). Films: "The Night Rider" TVM-1979 (Hans Klaus).

Lowery, Robert (1914-12/26/71). Films: "Drums Along the Mohawk" 1939 (John Weaver); "Mark of Zorro" 1940 (Rodrigo); "Shooting High" 1940 (Bob Merritt); "Ride on, Vaquero" 1941 (Carlos); "Dawn on the Great Divide" 1942 (Terry); "Death Valley" 1946; "God's Country" 1946; "Call of the Forest" 1949; "The Dalton Gang" 1949 (Blackie Mullet); "Border Rangers" 1950 (Mugo); "Gunfire" 1950 (Kelly); "I Shot Billy the Kid" 1950 (Garrett); "Train to Tombstone" 1950 (Staley); "Western Pacific Agent" 1950; "Cow Country" 1953 (Harry Odell); "The Homesteaders" 1953 (Clyde Moss); "Lay That Rifle Down" 1955 (Nick Stokes); "Two-Gun Lady" 1956 (Big Mike Dougherty); "The Parson and the Outlaw" 1957 (Col. Morgan); "McClintock" 1963 (Gov. Cuthbert H. Humphrey); "Young Guns of Texas" 1963 (Jesse Glendenning); "Stage to Thunder Rock" 1964 (Seth Harrington); "Johnny Reno" 1966 (Jake Reed); "Waco" 1966 (Mayor Ned West); "Ballad of Josie" 1968 (Whit Minick). ¶TV: *The Gene Autry Show*—"Steel Ribbon" 9-22-53, "Ransom Cross" 10-6-53; *Death Valley Days*—"Whirlwind Courtship" 1-13-54; *Judge Roy Bean*—"Family Ties" 10-1-55 (Bartlett), "The Horse Thief" 10-1-55 (Devlin), "The Wedding of Old Sam" 10-1-55 (Waco); *Wyatt Earp*—"The Bank Robbers" 11-8-55 (Clem Parker), "Mr. Buntline's Vacation" 11-19-57 (Slade); *Circus Boy*—Regular 1956-58 (Big Tim Champion); *The Adventures of Rin Tin Tin*—"Fort Adventure" 11-30-56 (Maj. Arden), "The Last Navajo" 10-18-57 (Col. Stone), "The Best Policy" 12-5-58 (Jim Carstairs); *Wagon Train*—"The Marie Dupree Story" 3-19-58 (Bill Howard), "The Candy O'Hara Story" 12-7-60; *Tales of Wells Fargo*—"Special Delivery" 3-31-58 (Maj. Keel), "Dealer's Choice" 5-2-60 (Galena); *26 Men*—"Parrish Gang" 4-1-58, "Bounty Hunter" 4-15-58, "Killer's Trail" 7-15-58; *The Texan*—"A Quart of Law" 1-12-59 (Coy Benner); *Bronco*—"Riding Solo" 2-10-59 (Mike Kirk); *Cimarron City*—"Chinese Invasion" 3-21-59 (Harris); *Maverick*—"Burial Ground of the Gods" 3-30-59 (Paul Asher), "Full House" 10-25-59 (Foxy Smith); *Colt .45*—"Return to El Paso" 6-21-59 (Richard Delgado); *Riverboat*—"Race to Cincinnati" 10-4-59 (Carstairs); *Rawhide*—"Incident of the Shambling Men" 10-9-59 (Lou Thompson), "Incident of the Wanted Painter" 1-29-60 (Major Sinclair), "The Captain's Wife" 1-12-62 (Captain Holloway); *Man from Blackhawk*—"Portrait of Cynthia" 1-29-60 (Gordon Hull); *Walt Disney Presents*—"Elfego Baca: Friendly Enemies at Law" 3-18-60 (Cather); *The Alaskans*—"Kangaroo Court" 5-8-60 (John Ryan); *Hotel De Paree*—"Sundance and the Cattlemen" 5-13-60 (Trent); *Cheyenne*—"Counterfeit Gun" 10-10-60 (Giff Murdock/Richard Scott); *Whispering Smith*—"Death at Even Money" 7-10-61 (Dave Markson); *Frontier Circus*—"Incident at Pawnee Gun" 9-6-62 (Tigard); *Gunsmoke*—"The Trappers" 11-3-62 (Idaho Smith); *Pistols 'n' Petticoats*—Regular 1966-67 (Buss Courtney).

Lowery, William A. (1885-11/15/41). Films: "A Ticket to Red Horse Gulch" 1914; "Big Jim's Heart" 1915; "The Lamb" 1915; "The Man from Painted Post" 1917 (Charles Ross); "The Primal Law" 1921 (Meacham); "Her Half Brother" 1922; "Pals of the West" 1922; "Dangerous Trails" 1923 (Jean Le Fere); "McGuire of the Mounted" 1923 (Major Cordwell); "Men in the Raw" 1923 (Marshal Flynn); "Battling Buddy" 1924 (Pete Hall); "Thundering Hoofs" 1924 (Luke Sever); "A Daughter of the Sioux" 1925 (Big Bill Hay); "Tricks" 1925 (Buck Barlow); "Call of the Klondike" 1926 (Harkness).

Lowry, Morton (1908-). Films: "Hudson Bay" 1941 (Gerald Hall).

Loy, Barbara. Films: "Last of the Mohicans" 1965-Ital./Span./Ger.; "Magnificent Texan" 1967-Ital./Span.

Loy, Myrna (1905-12/14/93). Films: "The Great Divide" 1929 (Manuella); "The Bad Man" 1930; "Last of the Duanes" 1930 (Lola); "Rogue of the Rio Grande" 1930 (Carmita); "Under a Texas Moon" 1930 (Lolita Romero); "Scarlet River" 1933 (Herself). ¶TV: *The Virginian*—"Lady of the House" 4-5-67 (Mrs. Miles).

Lozano, Margarita (1931-). Films: "A Fistful of Dollars" 1964-Ital./Ger./Span. (Consuela Baxter).

Lozano, Mario. Films: "Savage Pampas" 1966-U.S./Span./Arg. (Santiago).

Lu, Lisa (1931-). Films: "Rider on a Dead Horse" 1962 (Ming). ¶TV: *Yancy Derringer*—"An Ace Called Spade" 10-30-58 (Miss Mandarin), "The Quiet Firecracker" 5-21-59 (Miss Mandarin); *Tales of the Texas Rangers*—"The Fifth Plague" 12-19-58 (Betty Lee); *Cimarron City*—"Chinese Invasion" 3-21-59 (Mei Ling); *The Rebel*—"Blind Marriage" 4-17-60 (Quong Lia); *Have Gun Will Travel*—Regular 1960-61 (Hey Girl); *Bat Masterson*—"Terror on the Trinity" 3-9-61 (Hsieh-Lin); *Bonanza*—"Day of the Dragon" 12-3-61 (Su Ling); *Cheyenne*—"Pocketful of Stars" 11-12-62 (Mai Ling); *The Big Valley*—"Rimfire" 2-19-68 (Ling), "Run of the Cat" 10-21-68 (Chinese Girl).

Lucas, Jimmy (1888-2/21/49). Films: "Riders of Death Valley" 1941-serial (Bartender); "Call of the Canyon" 1942.

Lucas, Loyal "Doc". TV: *The Tall Man*—"One of One Thousand" 12-31-60 (Old Bill); *Have Gun Will Travel*—"Everyman" 3-25-61 (Miner); *Tales of Wells Fargo*—"Reward for Gaine" 1-20-62 (Boulanger); *Branded*—"Coward Step Aside" 3-7-65 (Stoner); *The Virginian*—"The Brothers" 9-15-65 (Gunny).

Lucas, Wilfred (1871-12/13/40). Films: "The Greaser's Gauntlet" 1908; "The Vaquero's Vow" 1908; "The Man" 1910; "Billy's Stratagem" 1911; "The Heart of a Savage" 1911; "The Indian Brothers" 1911; "The Squaw's Love" 1911; "Was He a Coward?" 1911; "The Chief's Blanket" 1912; "Fate's Interception" 1912; "Goddess of Sagebrush Gulch" 1912; "The Massacre" 1912; "A Pueblo Legend" 1912; "Under Burning Skies" 1912; "A Chance Deception" 1913; "The Desert's Sting" 1914; "Hands Up!" 1917 (John Houston); "The Westerners" 1919 (Jim Buckley); "The Fighting Breed" 1921 (John MacDonald); "Barriers of Folly" 1922 (Wallace Clifton); "The Girl of the Golden West" 1923 (Ashby); "The Mask of Lopez" 1923 (Richard O'Neil); "The Fighting Sap" 1924 (Charles Richmond); "Lightning

Romance" 1924 (Richard Wade); "North of Nevada" 1924 (C. Hanaford); "The Bad Lands" 1925 (Col. Owen); "Cyclone Cavalier" 1925 (Hugh Clayton); "Riders of the Purple Sage" 1925 (Oldring); "The Arizona Kid" 1930 (Hoboken Hooker's Manager); "The Tabasco Kid" 1932-short; "Breed of the Border" 1933; "Lucky Larrigan" 1933; "The Phantom Thunderbolt" 1933 (Mr. Eaton); "Stormy" 1935 (Horse Trainer); "Blazing Sixes" 1937 (Oneye); "The California Mail" 1937 (Sheriff); "Empty Holsters" 1937 (John Ware); "Land Beyond the Law" 1937; "Prairie Thunder" 1937 (Nate Temple); "Gold Is Where You Find It" 1938 (Man at Stock Exchange); "Arizona Legion" 1939; "Dodge City" 1939 (Bartender); "The Marshal of Mesa City" 1939 (Marshal Thompson); "Racketeers of the Range" 1939; "Legion of the Lawless" 1940; "Ragtime Cowboy Joe" 1940 (Sam Osborne); "Santa Fe Trail" 1940 (Weiner); "Triple Justice" 1940 (Constable); "Virginia City" 1940 (Southerner).

Lucero, Enrique (1920-5/9/89). Films: "Sierra Baron" 1958 (Anselmo); "Villa!" 1958 (Tenorio); "Major Dundee" 1965 (Dr. Aguilar); "Guns for San Sebastian" 1967-U.S./ Fr./Mex./Ital. (Renaldo); "Two Mules for Sister Sara" 1970 (3rd American); "Something Big" 1971 (Indian Spy); "Buck and the Preacher" 1972 (Indian Chief); "The Wrath of God" 1972 (Nacho, Chela's Father); "The Return of a Man Called Horse" 1976 (Raven); "Eagle's Wing" 1979-Brit./Span. (Shaman); "Mr. Horn" TVM-1979 (Geronimo).

Luckinbill, Laurence (1934-). TV: *Bonanza*—"Shadow of a Hero" 2-21-71 (Freed).

Lucking, William. Films: "Wild Rovers" 1971 (Ruff); "The Magnificent Seven Ride" 1972 (Walt Drummond); "Oklahoma Crude" 1973 (Marion); "The Return of a Man Called Horse" 1976 (Tom Gryce); "The Mountain Men" 1980 (Jim Walker); "Kung Fu: The Movie" TVM-1986 (Deputy Wyatt); "Outlaws" TVM-1986 (Harland Pike). ¶TV: *Lancer*—"Juniper's Camp" 3-11-69 (Crocker Cooper); *Here Come the Brides*—"His Sister's Keeper" 12-12-69 (Stacy); *The Virginian*—"The Sins of the Father" 3-4-70 (Sam); *The High Chaparral*—"A Matter of Vengeance" 11-27-70 (Galt); *Bonanza*—"The Imposters" 12-13-70 (Gabe); *Kung Fu*—"The Stone" 4-12-73 (Quade); *Gunsmoke*—"Matt Dillon

Must Die!" 9-9-74 (Esau); *Big Hawaii*—Regular 1977 (Oscar); *How the West Was Won*—"L'Affaire Riel" 3-5-79 (Kenyou); *Outlaws*—Regular 1986-87 (Harland Pike); *Young Riders*—"The Blood of Others" 10-12-91 (John Gilmore).

Luddy, Barbara (1908-4/1/79). Films: "Born to Battle" 1927 (Barbara Barstow); "Headin' North" 1930 (Mary Jackson).

Luden, Jack (1902-2/15/51). Films: "Aflame in the Sky" 1927 (Terry Owen); "The Last Outlaw" 1927 (Ward Lane); "Shootin' Irons" 1927 (Pan Smith); "Under the Tonto Rim" 1928 (Bud Watson); "King of the Royal Mounted" 1936 (Smith); "Phantom Gold" 1938 (Breezy Larkin); "Pioneer Trail" 1938 (Breezy Larkin); "Rolling Caravans" 1938 (Breezy Larkin); "Stagecoach Days" 1938 (Breezy Larkin); "Susannah of the Mounties" 1939 (Williams); "Northwest Mounted Police" 1940 (Constable Douglas); "Bordertown Trail" 1944; "Rough Riders of Cheyenne" 1945.

Luez, Laurette. Films: "Ballad of a Gunfighter" 1964 (Felina).

Lufkin, Sam (1892-2/19/52). Films: "The Fighting Boob" 1926 (Jeff Randall); "Rose of the Rancho" 1936 (Bystander); "Goofs and Saddles" 1937-short (Colonel); "Way Out West" 1937 (Stagecoach Baggage Man); "Trail Street" 1947 (Farmer); "Law of the Badlands" 1951.

Luisi, James (1928-). Films: "Honky Tonk" TVM-1974. ¶TV: *The Rifleman*—"Sporting Chance" 1-29-62 (Chuley Carr); *Bonanza*—"Any Friend of Walter's" 3-24-63 (Willard), "Walter and the Outlaws" 5-24-64 (Willard); *Gunsmoke*—"The Guns of Cibola Blanca" 9-23-74 & 9-30-74 (Ivers).

Lukas, Karl (1919-1/16/95). Films: "There Was a Crooked Man" 1970; "Oklahoma Crude" 1973 (Hobo); "Blazing Saddles" 1974 (Tough). ¶TV: *Tombstone Territory*—"Skeleton Canyon Massacre" 4-2-58 (Bandit); *The Rifleman*—"The Brother-in-Law" 10-28-58; *Lawman*—"The Runaway" 2-1-59; *Yancy Derringer*—"The Wayward Warrior" 4-16-59 (Warrior); *The Deputy*—"The Orphans" 12-26-59; *Man from Blackhawk*—"Execution Day" 3-4-60 (Boyd); *Wagon Train*—"The Kurt Davos Story" 11-28-62 (Dr. Parnell); *Gunsmoke*—"Hung High" 11-14-64 (Hardy), "Death Watch" 1-8-66 (Williams), "The Well" 11-19-66 (Lake); *Rawhide*—"The Calf Women" 4-30-65 (Cole Wallace); *Shane*—"The

Distant Bell" 9-10-66 (Howell); *Bonanza*—"Devil on Her Shoulder" 10-17-65 (Brother), "Shanklin" 2-13-72 (Irons); *Here Come the Brides*—"Man of the Family" 10-16-68; *Nichols*—1-25-72 (Harry Carmichael); *Barbary Coast*—"Sharks Eat Sharks" 11-21-75 (Hobie).

Lukas, Paul (1894-8/15/71). TV: *The Slowest Gun in the West* 7-29-63 (Jack Dalton).

Lukather, Paul (1936-). Films: "Alvarez Kelly" 1966 (Capt. Webster); "The Way West" 1967 (Turley); "Hot Lead and Cold Feet" 1978. ¶TV: *Have Gun Will Travel*—"The Five Books of Owen Deaver" 4-26-58; *Buckskin*—"Lament for Durango" 8-14-58 (Job); *The Restless Gun*—"A Trial for Jenny May" 5-25-59 (Randolph Clayton); *Rawhide*—"Incident of the Murder Steer" 5-13-60 (Gus Price); *Bonanza*—"Breed of Violence" 11-5-60, "The Trap" 3-28-65 (Cletus); *Bat Masterson*—"End of the Line" 1-26-61 (Lieutenant); *Laramie*—"Trapped" 5-14-63 (Park).

Luke, Jorge. Films: "Eye for an Eye" 1972-Ital./Span./Ital. (Judd); "The Revengers" 1972-U.S./Mex. (Chamaco); "Ulzana's Raid" 1972 (Ke-Ni-Tay); "Nevada Smith" TVM-1975 (Two Moon); "The Return of a Man Called Horse" 1976 (Running Bull); "Eagle's Wing" 1979-Brit./Span. (Red Sky).

Luke, Keye (1904-1/12/91). Films: "North to the Klondike" 1942 (Wellington Wong); "Kung Fu" TVM-1972 (Master Po); "Kung Fu: The Movie" TVM-1986 (Master Po). ¶TV: *Annie Oakley*—"Annie and the Chinese Puzzle" 2-13-55 (Li Wong); *Gunsmoke*—"The Queue" 12-3-55 (Chen); *Trackdown*—"Chinese Cowboy" 9-19-58 (Wong); *The Big Valley*—"The Emperor of Rice" 2-12-68; *Kung Fu*—Regular 1972-75 (Master Po); *How the West Was Won*—"China Girl" 4-16-79 (Leong Chung Hua); *Bret Maverick*—"The Yellow Rose" 12-22-81 (Lu Sung).

Luke, Norman W. Films: "Boots and Saddles" 1916 (William Briscoe).

Lukes, Oldrich. Films: "Lemonade Joe" 1966-Czech. (Sheriff).

Lukschy, Wolfgang (1905-). Films: "A Fistful of Dollars" 1964-Ital./Ger./Span. (John Baxter); "Flaming Frontier" 1965-Ger./Yugo. (Judge Edwards); "Lost Treasure of the Incas" 1965-Ger./Ital./Fr./Span.; "A Place Called Glory" 1966-Span./Ger. (Barman).

Lulli, Folco (1912-5/24/70). Films: "Sign of Zorro" 1964-Ital./

Span.; "Between God, the Devil and a Winchester" 1968-Ital./Span. (Bob Ford); "Shoot, Gringo... Shoot!" 1968-Ital./Fr. (Don Francisco).

Lulli, Piero (1923-). Films: "Shadow of Zorro" 1963-Span./Ital.; "Sign of Coyote" 1964-Ital./Span.; "Hands of a Gunman" 1965-Ital./Span.; "Adios Hombre" 1966-Ital./Span.; "Savage Gringo" 1966-Ital.; "Big Ripoff" 1967-Span./Ital.; "Cjamango" 1967-Ital.; "Django Kill" 1967-Ital./Span.; "For One Hundred Thousand Dollars Per Killing" 1967-Ital.; "Fury of Johnny Kid" 1967-Span./Ital.; "Kitosch, the Man who Came from the North" 1967-Ital./Span.; "Ringo, the Lone Rider" 1967-Ital./Span. (Bill Anderson); "Cry for Revenge" 1968-Ital./Span.; "Find a Place to Die" 1968-Ital.; "God Made Them ... I Kill Them" 1968-Ital.; "Pistol for a Hundred Coffins" 1968-Ital./Span.; "The Boldest Job in the West" 1969-Ital.; "Shotgun" 1969-Ital.; "Forgotten Pistolero" 1970-Ital./Span.; "The Dirty Outlaws" 1971-Ital. (Sam); "Forewarned, Half-Killed ... The Word of the Holy Ghost" 1971-Ital./Span.; "Light the Fuse ... Sartana Is Coming" 1971-Ital./Fr. (Grand Full); "Fighting Fists of Shanghai Joe" 1973-Ital.; "My Name Is Nobody" 1973-Ital. (Sheriff); "Carambola's Philosophy: In the Right Pocket" 1975-Ital.; "Trinity Plus the Clown and a Guitar" 1975-Ital./Austria/Fr.

Lum, Benjamin. TV: *Paradise*—Regular 1988-91 (Mr. Lee).

Lummis, Dayton (1903-6/23/88). Films: "The Yellow Mountain" 1954 (Geraghty); "The Spoilers" 1955 (Wheaton); "A Day of Fury" 1956; "The First Texan" 1956 (Austin); "Showdown at Abilene" 1956 (Jack Bedford). ¶TV: *The Lone Ranger*—"Mrs. Banker" 3-26-53; *Jim Bowie*—"The General's Disgrace" 4-12-57 (Gen. Rogers); *Buckskin*—"Hunter's Moon" 9-11-58 (Jabez Lord); *Yancy Derringer*—"Gone But Not Forgotten" 5-28-59; *The Law of the Plainsman*—Regular 1959-60 (Marshal Morrison); *Wagon Train*—"The Martha Barham Story" 11-4-59 (Major Barham), "The John Turnbull Story" 5-30-62 (T.J. Gingle), "The Myra Marshall Story" 10-21-63; *Riverboat*—"Path of an Eagle" 2-1-60 (Gideon Templeton); *Death Valley Days*—"Shadow on the Window" 2-23-60 (Lew Wallace), "City of Widows" 12-21-60 (John De La Mar); *Bonanza*—"Escape to the Ponderosa" 3-5-60 (Colonel Metcalfe), "The Secret" 5-6-61 (Hiram), "The Legacy" 12-15-

63, "The Dilemma" 9-19-65 (Judge O'Hara); *The Rifleman*—"The Lariat" 3-29-60 (Colonel Craig), "The Illustrator" 12-13-60 (Jake Shaw); *Laramie*—"Killer Without Cause" 1-24-61 (the Judge); *Sugarfoot*—"Trouble at Sand Springs" 4-17-61 (Silas Rigsby); *Cheyenne*—"The Young Fugitives" 10-23-61 (Frank Collins); *Empire*—"Green, Green, Hills" 12-25-62 (Jason Simms), "Down There, the World" 3-12-63 (Thomas Fenton Giler); *The Virginian*—"The Money Cage" 3-6-63 (Horatio Turner); *The Dakotas*—"The Chooser of the Slain" 4-22-63 (Clayton Emory); *Temple Houston*—"Fracas at Kiowa Flats" 12-12-63 (Col. Bob Grainger); *Gunsmoke*—"The Angry Land" 2-3-75 (Mr. Holmby).

Luna, Barbara (1939-). Films: "Mail Order Bride" 1964 (Marietta); "Winchester '73" TVM-1967 (Meriden); "Firecreek" 1968 (Meli); "The Gatling Gun" 1972 (Leona); "The Hanged Man" TVM-1974 (Soledad Villeas). ¶TV: *Zorro*—"The New Order" 11-13-58 (Theresa Modesto), "An Eye for an Eye" 11-20-58 (Theresa Modesto), "Zorro and the Flag of Truce" 11-27-58 (Theresa Modesto), "Ambush" 12-4-58 (Theresa Modesto); *The Texan*—"Showdown at Abilene" 11-9-59, "The Reluctant Bridegroom" 11-16-59; *Bonanza*—"El Toro Grande" 1-2-60 (Cayetena); *Overland Trail*—"Mission to Mexico" 4-24-60 (Estrellita); *Tales of Wells Fargo*—"Vasquez" 5-16-60 (Rosita); *Death Valley Days*—"Pete Kitchen's Wedding Night" 6-21-60 (Dona Rosa); *Stagecoach West*—"The Big Gun" 4-25-61 (Chiquita); *Gunslinger*—"The Death of Yellow Singer" 5-11-61 (Elise); *Gunsmoke*—"He Learned About Women" 2-24-62 (Chavela); *Wide Country*—"Farewell to Margarita" 3-21-63 (Margarita Diaz); *Wild Wild West*—"Night of the Deadly Bed" 9-24-65 (Gatilla); *Laredo*—"Coup de Grace" 10-7-66 (Carmella Alveraz); *Cimarron Strip*—"The Legend of Jud Starr" 9-14-67 (Roseanne Todd); *The High Chaparral*—"The Firing Wall" 12-31-67 (Conchita); *Lancer*—"Lifeline" 5-19-70 (Anna); *Kung Fu*—"A Lamb to the Slaughter" 1-11-75 (Isela).

Luna, Margarito. Films: "The Treasure of the Sierra Madre" 1948 (Pancho); "Bandido" 1956 (Santos); "The Beast of Hollow Mountain" 1956 (Jose).

Lund, Art (1920-). Films: "The Quest" TVM-1976 (Blanchard). ¶TV: *Wagon Train*—"The Hiram Winthrop Story" 6-6-62 (Laif Riatt);

Gunsmoke—"False Front" 12-22-62 (Nick Heber), "Susan Was Evil" 12-3-73 (Norman Boswell); *Calamity Jane* 11-12-63 (Wild Bill Hickock); *Custer*—"To the Death" 9-27-67 (Sgt. John Tuvey); *Here Come the Brides*—"A Wild Colonial Boy" 10-24-69 (Flynn); *Hec Ramsey*—"Dead Heat" 2-3-74 (Major Holliday).

Lund, Deanna (1937-). TV: *The Loner*—"The Trial in Paradise" 1-22-66 (Susan); *The Road West*—"Ashes and Tallow and One True Love" 10-24-66; *Laredo*—"The Sweet Gang" 11-4-66.

Lund, John (1913-5/10/92). Films: "The Battle at Apache Pass" 1952 (Maj. Jim Colton); "Bronco Buster" 1952 (Tom Moody); "The Woman They Almost Lynched" 1953 (Lance Horton); "Chief Crazy Horse" 1955 (Major Twist); "Five Guns West" 1955 (Govern Sturges); "White Feather" 1955 (Col. Lindsay); "Dakota Incident" 1956 (Carter Hamilton).

Lund, Lucille (1912-). Films: "Fighting Through" 1934 (Lucille); "Range Warfare" 1935 (Little Feather); "Timber War" 1935 (Sally Martin); "The Cowboy Star" 1936 (Mother); "Rio Grande Romance" 1936 (Rose Carter).

Lund, O.A.C. (1890-1963) Films: "The Devil Fox of the North" 1914; "The First Nugget" 1914; "M'Liss" 1915 (Don Jose).

Lundigan, William (1914-12/20/75). Films: "Dodge City" 1939 (Lee Irving); "Santa Fe Trail" 1940 (Bob Halliday); "Northwest Rangers" 1942 (James Kevin Gardiner); "Apache Trail" 1943 (Tom Folliard); "The Way West" 1967 (Michael Moynihan). ¶TV: *Death Valley Days*—"Dangerous Crossing" 3-22-61 (Nathaniel Norgate).

Lundin, Richard. TV: *Gunsmoke*—"Patricia" 1-22-73 (Driver), "Matt's Love Story" 9-24-73 (Canoot), "The Widow and the Rogue" 10-29-73 (Stage Driver), "Like Old Times" 1-21-74 (Stage Driver), "The Schoolmarm" 2-25-74.

Lundin, Vic. TV: *Gunsmoke*—"The Constable" 5-30-59 (Hank); *Hondo*—"Hondo and the War Cry" 9-15-67 (Silva).

Lundmark, William. TV: *Buckskin*—"Lament for Durango" 8-14-58 (Durango); *Wagon Train*—"The Conchita Vasquez Story" 3-18-59 (Dan Jaeger); *The Restless Gun*—"Incident at Bluefield" 3-30-59 (Junior Cauter).

Lundy, Ken. Films: "Sioux City Sue" 1946 (Jody).

Lung, Clarence. Films: "The Rawhide Years" 1956 (Chinese Steward). ¶TV: *Tales of Wells Fargo*—"The Golden Owl" 9-29-58 (Mr. Soo).

Lupi, Rolando (1909-8/13/89). Films: "Buffalo Bill, Hero of the Far West" 1964-Ital./Ger./Fr. (Colonel Peterson).

Lupino, Ida (1914-8/3/95). Films: "The Gay Desperado" 1936 (Jane); "Lust for Gold" 1949 (Julia Thomas); "Junior Bonner" 1972 (Elvira Bonner); "Female Artillery" TVM-1973 (Martha Lindstrom). ¶TV: *Zane Grey Theater*—"The Fearful Courage" 10-12-56 (Louise Brandon); *Bonanza*—"The Saga of Annie O'Toole" 10-24-59 (Annie O'Toole); *Death Valley Days*—"Pamela's Oxen" 9-28-60 (Pamela Mann); *The Virginian*—"A Distant Fury" 3-20-63 (Helen Blaine), "We've Lost a Train" 4-21-65 (Mama Dolores); *Wild Wild West*—"The Night of the Big Blast" 10-7-66 (Dr. Faustina); *The Outcasts*—"The Thin Edge" 2-17-69 (Mrs. Blake); *Alias Smith and Jones*—"What's in It for Mia?" 2-24-72 (Mia Bronson).

Lupino, Richard. Films: "The Marauders" 1955 (Perc Kettering). ¶TV: *Great Adventure*—"Kentucky's Bloody Ground"/"The Siege of Boonesborough" 4-3-64 & 4-10-64 (Lieutenant Brown).

Lupo, Alberto. Films: "He Who Shoots First" 1966-Ital.

Lupton, John (1928-11/3/93). Films: "Escape from Fort Bravo" 1953 (Bailey); "Man with the Gun" 1955 (Jeff Castle); "The Great Locomotive Chase" 1956 (William Pittenger); "Drango" 1957 (Marc); "Gun Fever" 1958 (Simon); "Jesse James Meets Frankenstein's Daughter" 1966 (Jesse James). ¶TV: *20th Century Fox Hour*—"Broken Arrow" 5-2-56 (Tom Jeffords); *Broken Arrow*—Regular 1956-58 (Tom Jeffords); *Wanted—Dead or Alive*—"Secret Ballot" 2-14-59 (Ned Easter); *The Restless Gun*—"Ricochet" 3-9-59 (Peter Garrick); *Yancy Derringer*—"A State of Crisis" 4-30-59 (Maj. Alvin); *U.S. Marshal*—"Anything for a Friend" 10-17-59 (Jack Barker); *Black Saddle*—"Client: Peter Warren" 10-30-59 (Peter Warren); *Tales of Wells Fargo*—"Day of Judgment" 9-5-60 (Eli Fisher); *Death Valley Days*—"The Grand Duke" 11-10-59 (Bill Cody), "South of Horror Flats" 2-1-61 (Hodges), "The Private Mint of Clark, Gruber and Company" 2-13-63 (Milton Clark); *Gunsmoke*—"Ben Toliver's Stud" 11-26-60 (Ben Toliver), "Chicken" 12-5-64 (Carl); *Laramie*—"Killer's Odds" 4-

25-61 (Fred Powers), "The Day of the Savage" 3-13-62 (Glen Colton); *Wagon Train*—"The Jenna Douglas Story" 11-1-61 (Dr. David Mille), "The Trace McCloud Story" 3-2-64 (Ernie Weaver); *Rawhide*—"Incident at Zebulon" 3-5-64 (Roy Cutter); *Temple Houston*—"Miss Katherina" 4-2-64 (Sinclair); *The Virginian*—"A Gallows for Sam Horn" 12-2-64 (Sam Horn), "Bitter Harvest" 3-15-67 (Frank Adams), "A Small Taste of Justice" 12-20-67 (John Cooper); *Daniel Boone*—"The Trek" 10-21-65 (Chadwick); *Time Tunnel*—"The Alamo" 12-9-66 (Capt. Reynerson); *The Men from Shiloh*—"Tate, Ramrod" 2-24-71 (Floyd Ramon); *Kung Fu*—"Barbary House" 2-15-75 (McCord), "Flight to Orion" 2-22-75 (McCord), "The Brothers Cain" 3-1-75 (McCord), "Full Circle" 3-15-75 (McCord).

Lurie, Allen. Films: "Plunderers of Painted Flats" 1959 (Cass). ¶TV: *The Texan*—"The Hemp Tree" 11-17-58 (Gus Phelan); *Gunsmoke*—"Wind" 3-21-59 (Singer).

Lusk, Freeman (1906-8/25/70). TV: *Sergeant Preston of the Yukon*—"Storm the Pass" 10-24-57 (Insp. Ward); *Buckskin*—"Fry's Wife" 2-9-59 (Dr. Samuel Woodson), "Act of Faith" 3-23-59 (Dr. Samuel Woodson), "Charlie, My Boy" 4-6-59 (Dr. Samuel Woodson); *The Restless Gun*—"The Hill of Death" 6-22-59 (Mayor Baxter); *Wyatt Earp*—"The Outlaws Cry Murder" 6-27-61 (Colonel Herring).

Lussier, Robert. Films: "The Gambler" TVM-1980 (Businessman); "Dream West" TVM-1986 (Dr. Harris).

Luster, Robert. Films: "Will Penny" 1968 (Shem Bodine); "Charro!" 1969 (Will Joslyn). ¶TV: *The High Chaparral*—"Ebenezer" 11-1-68 (Camel); *Gunsmoke*—"The Twisted Heritage" 1-6-69 (Cookie); *Bonanza*—"Easy Come, Easy Go" 12-12-71 (Garvey).

Luther, Johnny (1909-7/31/60). Films: "The Phantom Thunderbolt" 1933; "Rough Riding Ranger" 1935; "Stormy" 1935 (Wrangler).

Luxford, Nola (1897-10/10/94). Films: "Border Justice" 1925 (Mary Maitland); "That Devil Quemado" 1925 (Conchita Rameriz); "Forlorn River" 1926 (Magda Lee); "King of the Herd" 1927 (Nancy Dorrance); "The Meddlin' Stranger" 1927 (Mildred Crawford).

Lycan, George. Films: "Dynamite Jack" 1963-Fr.; "The Tramplers" 1965-Ital. (Longfellow Wiley).

Lyden, Pierce. Films: "Fugitive from Sonora" 1937 (Slade); "King of Dodge City" 1941 (Reynolds); "Undercover Man" 1942 (Bert); "Black Hills Express" 1943 (Carl); "The Blocked Trail" 1943; "Border Patrol" 1943; "California Joe" 1943 (Harper); "Canyon City" 1943; "Daredevils of the West" 1943-serial (Citizen #4); "Dead Man's Gulch" 1943 (Curley Welch); "Death Valley Manhunt" 1943 (Clayton); "False Colors" 1943 (Lefty); "Riders of the Deadline" 1943 (Sanders); "Firebrands of Arizona" 1944 (Gopher); "Lumberjack" 1944; "Mystery Man" 1944 (Red); "Outlaws of Santa Fe" 1944; "San Fernando Valley" 1944; "Texas Masquerade" 1944 (Al); "Trigger Law" 1944; "West of the Rio Grande" 1944; "Bad Men of the Border" 1945; "The Cherokee Flash" 1945; "Code of the Lawless" 1945 (Pete); "Flame of the West" 1945; "Trail to Vengeance" 1945 (Sam); "Alias Billy the Kid" 1946 (Sam); "Gentleman from Texas" 1946; "Rainbow Over Texas" 1946 (Iverson); "Roll on, Texas Moon" 1946 (Stuhler); "Shadows on the Range" 1946; "Trigger Fingers" 1946; "Wild Beauty" 1946 (Roy); "Adventures of Don Coyote" 1947 (Jeff); "The Fabulous Texan" 1947; "Raiders of the South" 1947; "Rustlers of Devil's Canyon" 1947 (Matt); "Six Gun Serenade" 1947; "Son of Zorro" 1947-serial (Lem Carter); "Song of the Wasteland" 1947; "Valley of Fear" 1947; "Back Trail" 1948 (Gilmore); "Blazing Across the Pecos" 1948; "Crossed Trails" 1948 (Whitfield); "Dead Man's Gold" 1948 (Silver); "Overland Trails" 1948; "The Rangers Ride" 1948; "Silver Trails" 1948 (Ramsay); "Six-Gun Law" 1948 (Jack Reed); "The Big Sombrero" 1949 (Farmer); "Calamity Jane and Sam Bass" 1949 (Deputy); "Shadows of the West" 1949 (Jordon); "Sons of New Mexico" 1949 (Watson); "Cody of the Pony Express" 1950-serial (Slim); "Covered Wagon Raid" 1950 (Brag); "Roar of the Iron Horse" 1950-serial (Erv); "Twilight in the Sierras" 1950 (Blake); "Man from Sonora" 1951; "Nevada Badmen" 1951; "Stage to Blue River" 1951 (Preston); "Texas Lawmen" 1951; "Whistling Hills" 1951; "Canyon Ambush" 1952; "Carson City" 1952; "Kansas Territory" 1952 (Johnson); "Montana Belle" 1952 (Deputy); "Texas City" 1952 (Markham); "Waco" 1952 (Farley); "Wagon Team" 1952 (Mangrum); "Gunfighters of the Northwest" 1954-serial (Dakota); "Riding with Buffalo Bill" 1954-serial (Darr); "Blazing the Overland Trail" 1956-

serial (Bragg); "The First Traveling Saleslady" 1956 (Official); "Frontier Gambler" 1956; "Perils of the Wilderness" 1956-serial (Amby); "The Wild Westerners" 1962 (Jake). ¶TV: *The Cisco Kid*—"Stolen Bonds" 7-28-51, "Protective Association" 9-8-51, "Mr. X" 4-10-54; *Wild Bill Hickok*—"Rustling Stallion" 3-4-52, "Blind Alley" 2-24-53; *The Roy Rogers Show*—"The Feud" 11-16-52, "The Run-A-Round" 2-22-53 (Carl Saunders), "His Weight in Wildcats" 11-11-56; *The Gene Autry Show*—"Outlaw Stage" 7-21-53, "Border Justice" 8-18-53, "Talking Guns" 8-10-54, "Civil War at Deadwood" 9-14-54; *Judge Roy Bean*—"Family Ties" 10-1-55 (Stevens), "The Horse Thief" 10-1-55 (Morango), "The Wedding of Old Sam" 10-1-55 (Slim); *Sergeant Preston of the Yukon*—"Limping King" 9-13-56 (Larry Bates), "Fantastic Creatures" 11-1-56 (Prospector); *26 Men*—"The Bells of St. Thomas" 5-13-58; *Bat Masterson*—"A Personal Matter" 1-28-59 (Blacksmith); *Wyatt Earp*—"Study of a Crooked Sheriff" 10-25-60 (Saloon Owner).

Lydon, James (1923-). Films: "Tucson" 1949 (Andy Bryant); "Oh! Susanna" 1951 (Trumpeter Benton); "The Desperado" 1954 (Tall Cameron); "Death of a Gunfighter" 1969 (Luke Mills); "Scandalous John" 1971 (Grotch); "The New Daughters of Joshua Cabe" TVM-1976 (Jim Pickett); "Peter Lundy and the Medicine Hat Stallion" TVM-1977 (Muggeridge). ¶TV: *Sergeant Preston of the Yukon*—"The Williwaw" 12-20-56 (Johnny Lane); *Trackdown*—"Law in Lampasas" 10-11-57 (Sam Devlin), "The Feud" 2-11-59 (Mark Turley), "False Witness" 4-8-59; *Colt .45*—"Sign in the Sand" 1-3-58 (Frank Harper), "Return to El Paso" 6-21-59 (Willy); *Tales of the Texas Rangers*—"Warpath" 10-9-58 (Lt. Jared Evans); *Maverick*—"The Brasada Spur" 2-22-59 (Terry McKenna); *Wanted—Dead or Alive*—"Twelve Hours to Crazy Horse" 11-21-59 (Dan Murdock), "Dead Reckoning" 3-22-61 (Paul Decker); *Wagon Train*—"The Vittorio Bottecelli Story" 12-16-59 (Tod), "The Sam Livingston Story" 6-15-60 (Hotel Clerk), "The Jeremy Dow Story" 12-28-60 (Clete Millikan), "The Dr. Denker Story" 1-31-62 (George Blair); *Hotel De Paree*—"Sundance and the Barren Soil" 5-20-60 (Lowell Wheatley); *The Texan*—"The Accuser" 6-6-60 (Smitty); *Bronco*—"End of a Rope" 6-14-60 (Allen Brierly); *Gunsmoke*—"The First People" 2-19-61 (Baines), "Tarnished Badge" 11-11-74 (Charlie Boggs);

Wyatt Earp—"Until Proven Guilty" 4-11-61; *Stagecoach West*—"The Raider" 5-9-61 (Gil Soames); *Whispering Smith*—"The Devil's Share" 5-22-61 (Frank Whalen).

Lyman, Abe (1897-10/23/57). Films: "Pardon My Gun" 1930.

Lyman, Jr., Frank. Films: "Trail of Terror" 1935 (Kent Baxter).

Lyn, Dawn (1963-). TV: *Gunsmoke*—"The Sodbusters" 11-20-72 (Maria Callahan), "Women for Sale" 9-10-73 & 9-17-73 (March).

Lynch, Hal. Films: "Stagecoach" 1966 (Bartender); "The Way West" 1967 (Big Henry); "Wild Rovers" 1971 (Mack). ¶TV: *Gunsmoke*—"The Bounty Hunter" 10-30-65 (Cowboy), "Mistaken Identity" 3-18-67 (Mel Gates); *The Loner*—"Escort for a Dead Man" 12-18-65 (Copley); *The Big Valley*—"The Midas Man" 4-13-66, "Last Train to the Fair" 4-27-66 (Ab Stullman); *Wild Wild West*—"The Night of the Poisonous Posey" 10-28-66 (Sam Colbern); *Shane*—"The Great Invasion" 12-17-66 & 12-24-66 (Gunderson); *Custer*—"Blazing Arrows" 11-29-67 (Cpl. Thomas Hagen); *Bonanza*—"Commitment at Angelus" 4-7-68 (Steve), "The Real People of Muddy Creek" 10-6-68 (Haines).

Lynch, Helen (1900-3/2/65). Films: "A Tough Tenderfoot" 1920; "Bustin' Thru" 1925 (Helen Merritt); "Arizona Sweepstakes" 1926 (Nell Savery); "My Own Pal" 1926 (Trixie Tremaine); "Tom and His Pals" 1926 (Pandora Golden); "Avenging Fangs" 1927 (Mary Kirkham); "General Custer at the Little Big Horn" 1927 (Betty Rossman); "Little Big Horn" 1927 (Betty Rossman); "In Old Arizona" 1929 (Woman).

Lynch, Ken (1911-2/13/90). Films: "Man or Gun" 1958 (Buckstorm); "The Legend of Tom Dooley" 1959 (Father); "Seven Ways from Sundown" 1960 (Graves); "Apache Rifles" 1964 (Hodges); "Run, Simon, Run" TVM-1970. ¶TV: *Gunsmoke*—"The Bureaucrat" 3-16-57 (Will Stroud), "Born to Hang" 11-2-57 (Ed Glick), "Dooley Surrenders" 3-8-58 (Colpitt), "The Patsy" 9-20-58, "Bad Sheriff" 1-7-61 (Gance), "Love Thy Neighbor" 1-28-61 (Leroy Galloway), "Perce" 9-30-61 (Seeber), "Snow Train" 10-19-70 & 10-26-70 (Lucas), "Shadler" 1-15-73 (McKee), "The Boy and the Sinner" 10-1-73 (Jess Bradman); *Zane Grey Theater*—"A Time to Live" 4-5-57 (Collins), "The Doctor Keeps a Promise" 3-21-58 (Hod Strosnidor); *Wagon Train*—"The Riley Gratton Story" 12-4-57,

"The Alice Whitetree Story" 11-1-64 (Morton); *The Californians*—"Gentleman from Philadelphia" 3-4-58 (Benedict), "Hangtown" 11-18-58 (Wes Neeley); *Zorro*—"Zorro Rides Alone" 10-16-58, "Horse of Another Color" 10-23-58, "The Senorita Makes a Choice" 10-30-58, "Rendezvous at Sundown" 11-6-58; *Have Gun Will Travel*—"The Wager" 1-3-59 (Shawcross), "Fight at Adobe Wells" 3-12-60 (Commodore Guilder), "The Marshal's Boy" 11-26-60 (Marshal); *Maverick*—"The Brasada Spur" 2-22-59 (Rufus Elgree), "Dade City Dodge" 9-18-61 (Sheriff Clark); *Bat Masterson*—"Deadline" 4-8-59 (Tim Minto); *Bronco*—"The Last Resort" 11-17-59 (Marshal Gaffney), "The Harrigan" 12-25-61 (Wallace), "The Last Letter" 3-5-62; *The Rifleman*—"Letter of the Law" 12-1-59; *Hotel De Paree*—"Sundance and the Bare-Knuckled Fighters" 1-8-60 (Matlock); *Bonanza*—"Blood on the Land" 2-13-60, "The Beginning" 11-25-62 (Milton Tanner), "My Brother's Keeper" 4-7-63 (Doud), "Journey Remembered" 11-11-63 (Welks), "The Lonely Runner" 10-10-65 (Sam Whipple), "Joe Cartwright, Detective" 3-5-67 (Simms), "Commitment at Angelus" 4-7-68 (Garrett), "The Company of Forgotten Men" 2-2-69 (Gibson), "The Younger Brothers' Younger Brother" 3-12-72 (Warden); *Overland Trail*—"The Baron Comes Back" 5-15-60 (Quint); *Tales of Wells Fargo*—"Man for the Job" 5-30-60 (Parker), "All That Glitters" 10-24-60 (Joe Brass); *The Tall Man*—"Forty-Dollar Boots" 9-17-60 (Andy Gorman), "The Lonely Star" 10-8-60 (Andy Gorman), "First Blood" 1-7-61 (Andy Gorman); *The Outlaws*—"Starfall" 11-24-60 & 12-1-60 (Aberforth), "The Outlaw Marshals" 12-14-61 (Slater); *Lawman*—"The Escape of Joe Kilmer" 12-18-60, "The Promise" 6-11-61 (Jed Barrister); *Rawhide*—"Abilene" 5-18-62 (Grenfell), "Incident of the Wild Deuces" 12-12-63 (Walt Fuller); *Stoney Burke*—"Spin a Golden Web" 11-26-62 (Lyle Sweet); *The Virginian*—"The Exiles" 1-9-63 (Sheriff Morino), "A Portrait of Marie Valonne" 11-6-63 (Big Jay), "Ride a Cock-Horse to Laramie Cross" 2-23-66 (Johnson), "The Substitute" 12-5-69 (Sheriff Stoddard); *Laramie*—"The Renegade Brand" 2-26-63 (Tindall); *Destry*—"Deputy for a Day" 4-3-64 (Barnes); *The Big Valley*—"Young Marauders" 10-6-65 (Jacobsen), "The Brawlers" 12-15-65 (Storekeeper), "Teacher of Outlaws" 2-2-66 (Sheriff), "Into the Widow's

Web" 3-23-66 (Sheriff); *A Man Called Shenandoah*—"Obion—1866" 10-25-65 (Nester); *Laredo*—"A Very Small Assignment" 3-17-66 (Anson Jones), "Finnegan" 10-21-66 (John Clayton); *Wild Wild West*—"The Night of the Flying Pie Plate" 10-21-66 (Tom Kellogg); *Iron Horse*—10-14-67 (Klate); *The Outcasts*—"A Ride to Vengeance" 9-30-68 (Sheriff Lansford); *Lancer*—"Jelly" 11-19-68 (Charlker); *Alias Smith and Jones*—"Something to Get Hung About" 10-21-71; *Kung Fu*—"King of the Mountain" 10-14-72 (McCoy); *The Life and Times of Grizzly Adams*—1-4-78 (Harry).

Lynd, Helen (1900-3/2/65). Films: "The Kid from Texas" 1939 (Mabel); "The Great Man's Lady" 1942 (Bettina).

Lynde, Paul (1926-1/9/82). Films: "The Villain" 1979 (Nervous Elk). ¶TV: *Ruggles of Red Gap* 2-3-57 (Charles Belknap-Jackson); *F Troop*—"The Singing Mountie" 9-8-66 (Sergeant Ramsden).

Lynley, Carol (1942-). Films: "The Light in the Forest" 1958 (Shenandoe Hastings); "The Last Sunset" 1961 (Missy Breckenridge). ¶TV: *The Virginian*—"The Man from the Sea" 12-26-62 (Judith Morrow); *The Big Valley*—"Hell Hath No Fury" 11-18-68 (Dilly Shanks).

Lynn, Betty. Films: "Gun for a Coward" 1957 (Claire). ¶TV: *Texas John Slaughter*—Regular 1958-61 (Viola Slaughter); *Lawman*—"The Oath" 10-26-58 (Edna Phillips); *Wagon Train*—"The Dick Richardson Story" 12-31-58 (Molly Richardson); *Bronco*—"The Baron of Broken Lance" 1-13-59; *Sugarfoot*—"The Royal Raiders" 3-17-59 (Sarah Sears), "The Twister" 4-14-59 (Miss Fenton); *Tales of Wells Fargo*—"The Bounty Hunter" 6-1-59 (Mary Francis).

Lynn, Diana (1926-12/18/71). Films: "Track of the Cat" 1954 (Gwen Williams); "The Kentuckian" 1955 (Susie). ¶TV: *The Virginian*—"You Take the High Road" 2-17-65 (Peggy Shannon).

Lynn, Emmett "Pappy" (1897-10/20/58). Films: "The Fargo Kid" 1940 (Whopper); "Wagon Train" 1940 (Whopper); "Along the Rio Grande" 1941 (Whopper); "California or Bust" 1941-short; "Road Agent" 1941; "Robbers of the Range" 1941 (Whopper); "Cactus Capers" 1942-short; "In Old California" 1942 (Whitey); "Outlaws of Pine Ridge" 1942 (Jackpot McGraw); "Sons of the Pioneers" 1942; "Stagecoach Express" 1942 (Charles Haney); "The Sundown Kid" 1942 (Pop Tanner); "Westward Ho" 1942 (Sheriff); "Carson City Cyclone" 1943 (Tombstone); "Days of Old Cheyenne" 1943 (Tombstone Boggs); "Dead Man's Gulch" 1943 (Fiddlefoot); "The Law Rides Again" 1943 (Eagle Eye); "The Return of the Rangers" 1943; "Cowboy Canteen" 1944 (Hank); "Frontier Outlaws" 1944 (Judge); "The Laramie Trail" 1944; "Nevada" 1944 (Comstock); "Outlaws of Santa Fe" 1944 (Saloon Drunk); "Both Barrels Blazing" 1945; "The Cisco Kid Returns" 1945 (Sheriff); "Gangster's Den" 1945 (Webb); "Shadows of Death" 1945; "Song of Old Wyoming" 1945 (Uncle Ezra); "Wagon Wheels Westward" 1945; "The Caravan Trail" 1946 (Cherokee); "Conquest of Cheyenne" 1946; "The Fighting Frontiersman" 1946; "Landrush" 1946 (Jake Parker); "The Man from Rainbow Valley" 1946 (Locoweed); "Romance of the West" 1946 (Ezra); "Santa Fe Uprising" 1946; "Stagecoach to Denver" 1946 (Coon-Skin); "Throw a Saddle on a Star" 1946; "Code of the West" 1947 (Doc Quinn); "Jesse James Rides Again" 1947-serial (Drunk); "Oregon Trail Scouts" 1947 (Bear Trap); "Rustlers of Devil's Canyon" 1947 (Blizzard); "Trail of the Mounties" 1947; "The Wistful Widow of Wagon Gap" 1947 (Old Codger); "Grand Canyon Trail" 1948 (Ed Carruthers); "Relentless" 1948 (Nester); "West of Sonora" 1948 (Jack Bascom); "Western Heritage" 1948; "The Last Bandit" 1949; "Ride, Ryder, Ride" 1949 (Buckskin); "Roll, Thunder, Roll" 1949 (Buckskin); "Cowboy and the Prizefighter" 1950 (Buckskin); "The Fighting Redhead" 1950 (Buckskin); "Badman's Gold" 1951 (Miner); "Best of the Badmen" 1951 (Oscar); "Callaway Went Thataway" 1951 (Desert Rat); "Apache War Smoke" 1952 (Les); "Desert Pursuit" 1952 (Leatherface); "Lone Star" 1952 (Josh); "The Lusty Men" 1952 (Travis White); "Oklahoma Annie" 1952 (Paydirt); "Sky Full of Moon" 1952 (Otis); "The Homesteaders" 1953 (Grimer); "Northern Patrol" 1953 (Old Timer); "Jubilee Trail" 1954 (Drunk Man with Little Hat); "Shot in the Frontier" 1954-short (Lem). ¶TV: *The Lone Ranger*—"Legion of Old Timers" 10-6-49, "The Man Who Came Back" 1-5-50, "Pay Dirt" 3-23-50, "Million Dollar Wallpaper" 9-14-50, "Paid in Full" 12-28-50, "Trouble at Black Rock" 2-8-51, "Stage for Mademoiselle" 3-12-53, "The Frightened Woman" 9-30-54; *Wild Bill Hickok*—"Town Without Law" 6-23-53; *The Gene Autry Show*—"Talking Guns" 8-10-54, "Civil War at Deadwood" 9-14-54; *The Californians*—"J. Jimmerson Jones, Inc" 4-1-58; *The Restless Gun*—"More Than Kin" 5-26-58 (Town Drunk); *The Adventures of Rin Tin Tin*—"The Luck of O'Hara" 4-3-59 (Borrowin' Sam).

Lynn, George (-1967). Films: "Under Nevada Skies" 1946 (LeBlane); "The Bushwackers" 1952 (Guthrie); "The Halliday Brand" 1957. ¶TV: *The Lone Ranger*—"Pay Dirt" 3-23-50, "Through the Wall" 10-9-52; *Tales of the Texas Rangers*—"Horseman on the Sierras" 1-14-56 (Cy McCord); *The Adventures of Rin Tin Tin*—"The Big Top" 2-3-56 (Red); *Sergeant Preston of the Yukon*—"The Devil's Roost" 4-11-57 (Bascom); *The Deputy*—"The Hard Decision" 1-28-61 (Hangman).

Lynn, Jeffrey (1909-). Films: "Cowboy from Brooklyn" 1938 (Chronicle Reporter); "Black Bart" 1948 (Lance Hardeen).

Lynn, Jenny. TV: *Tales of Wells Fargo*—"Gunman's Revenge" 5-22-61 (Neil); *Rawhide*—"Incident of the Pied Piper" 2-6-64; *The Virginian*—"Felicity's Springs" 10-14-64 (Tessie).

Lynn, Peter. Films: "Wolf Call" 1939 (Father Devlin); "Kit Carson" 1940 (James King); "Northwest Passage" 1940 (Turner); "Saddlemates" 1941 (LeRoque/Wanechee).

Lynn, Rita (1921-). Films: "Code of the West" 1947 (Pepita); "Joe Dakota" 1957 (Rosa Vizzini); "Cast a Long Shadow" 1959 (Hortensia). ¶TV: *Wyatt Earp*—"The Bank Robbers" 11-8-55 (Bonnie Dawson), "Woman of Tucson" 11-15-60 (Amy Jones); *Jim Bowie*—"Jim Bowie and His Slave" 11-30-56 (Madeline Duprez), "Outlaw Kingdom" 12-7-56 (Madeline Duprez); *Have Gun Will Travel*—"Bitter Wine" 2-15-58 (Teresa), "The Campaign of Billy Banjo" 5-28-60 (Elsie Banjo); *Jefferson Drum*—"Bad Day for a Tinhorn" 5-16-58 (Birdy Thornton); *Zane Grey Theater*—"Trouble at Tres Cruces" 3-26-59, "Lonesome Road" 11-19-59 (Peggy); *The Californians*—"The Bell Tolls" 5-19-59 (Bella Ryan); *Yancy Derringer*—"Two Tickets to Promontory" 6-4-59 (Vinnie Farr); *Wanted—Dead or Alive*—"Estrelita" 10-3-59 (Estrelita); *Desilu Playhouse*—"Border Justice" 11-13-59 (Elena); *Maverick*—"The Devil's Necklace" 4-16-61 & 4-23-61 (Edith Reidinger); *The Big Valley*—"Hide the Children" 12-19-66 (Angelina); *The Virginian*—"Sue Ann" 1-11-67 (Mrs. Crandall); *Bo-*

nanza—"Dark Enough to See the Stars" 3-12-67 (Angel).

Lynn, Robert (1897-12/18/69). Films: "Texas Lady" 1955 (Rev. Callander); "Shoot-Out at Medicine Bend" 1957. ¶TV: *Fury*—"The Choice" 2-4-56 (Doc Bennett); *Sergeant Preston of the Yukon*—"Incident at Gordon Landing" 7-26-56 (Jim Carver); *Jim Bowie*—"The Secessionist" 11-9-56 (Maj. Jordan); *Maverick*—"Rope of Cards" 1-19-58 (Doctor); *Bat Masterson*—"Double Trouble in Trinidad" 1-7-59 (Transfer Clerk), "A Personal Matter" 1-28-59 (Inn Clerk), "The Lady Plays Her Hand" 12-29-60 (Zach); *Rough Riders*—"Death Sentence" 3-12-59 (Judge Burns); *Wanted—Dead or Alive*—"Double Fee" 3-21-59.

Lynn, Sharon (1904-5/26/63). Films: "Aflame in the Sky" 1927 (Inez Carillo); "The Cherokee Kid" 1927 (Helen Flynne); "Tom's Gang" 1927 (Lucille Rogers); "Son of the Golden West" 1928 (Alice Calhoun).

Lynne, Sharon (1910-5/26/63). Films: "Way Out West" 1937 (Lola Marcel).

Lyon, Ben (1901-3/22/79). Films: "Call of the Rockies" 1931 (Matthew).

Lyon, Earle. Films: "The Lonesome Trail" 1955; "The Silver Star" 1955 (Gregg); "Two-Gun Lady" 1956 (Ben Ivers).

Lyon, Sue (1946-). Films: "Four Rode Out" 1969-Ital./Span./U.S. ¶TV: *The Men from Shiloh*—"Experiment at New Life" 11-18-70 (Belinda).

Lyons, Cliff "Tex" (1902-1/6/74). Films: "Road Agent" 1926; "West of the Law" 1926 (Sheriff); "Across the Plains" 1928 (Chuck Lang); "Flashing Hoofs" 1928; "Headin' Westward" 1928 (Pat Carle); "Law of the Mounted" 1928; "Manhattan Cowboy" 1928; "Master of the Range" 1928; "The Old Code" 1928 (Jacques de Long); "The Riddle Trail" 1928; "The Arizona Kid" 1929 (Ned Hank); "Captain Cowboy" 1929; "Code of the West" 1929; "The Cowboy and the Outlaw" 1929 (Slim Saxon); "Fighters of the Saddle" 1929 (Weatherby Henchman); "The Fighting Terror" 1929; "The Galloping Lover" 1929; "The Last Roundup" 1929; "The Saddle King" 1929 (Rance Baine); "The Sheriff's Lash" 1929; "West of the Rockies" 1929 (Snakey Rogers); "Breezy Bill" 1930 (Bandit); "Call of the Desert" 1930 (Nate Thomas); "Canyon Hawks" 1930 (Tom Hardy); "The Canyon of

Missing Men" 1930 (Brill Lonergan); "Crusaders of the West" 1930; "Firebrand Jordan" 1930 (Pete); "Oklahoma Cyclone" 1930; "The Oklahoma Sheriff" 1930; "O'Malley Rides Alone" 1930; "Red Gold" 1930; "Red Fork Range" 1931 (Skeet Beldon); "Three Rogues" 1931 (Deputy); "Dynamite Ranch" 1932; "The Night Rider" 1932 (Burt Logan); "Rainbow Trail" 1932; "Gun Justice" 1934; "In Old Santa Fe" 1934; "Outlawed Guns" 1935; "The Roaring West" 1935-serial; "Rustlers of Red Dog" 1935-serial; "Tumbling Tumbleweeds" 1935 (Henchman); "The Lawless Nineties" 1936 (Davis); "The Phantom Rider" 1936-serial; "The Big Show" 1937; "North of the Rio Grande" 1937; "Desperate Trails" 1939; "The Dark Command" 1940; "Wagon Tracks West" 1943 (Matt); "Zorro's Black Whip" 1944-serial (Ambusher #1/Rock Heavy #1); "Dakota" 1945 (Bouncers); "Frontier Gal" 1945 (Brawler in Candy Shop); "San Antonio" 1945 (Flynn's Double); "The Phantom Rider" 1946-serial (Dick); "The Three Godfathers" 1948 (Guard at Mojave Tanks); "She Wore a Yellow Ribbon" 1949 (Trooper Cliff); "Rio Grande" 1950 (Soldier); "Wagonmaster" 1950 (Sheriff of Crystal City); "Bend of the River" 1952 (Willie); The Searchers" 1956 (Col. Greenhill); "The Horse Soldiers" 1959 (Sergeant); "The Young Land" 1959 (Jury Foreman); "Sergeant Rutledge" 1960 (Sam Beecher); "Two Rode Together" 1961 (William McCandless). ¶TV: *Wagon Train*—"The Colter Craven Story" 11-23-60.

Lyons, Collette (1908-10/5/86). Films: "Three Texas Steers" 1939 (Lillian); "Frisco Sal" 1945 (Mickey). ¶TV: *Wyatt Earp*—"Wyatt Earp Comes to Wichita" 10-4-55, "The Bribe" 1-31-56 (Rowdy Kate), "Little Brother" 12-23-58 (Kate Holliday), "The Reformation of Doc Holliday" 12-30-58 (Kate Holliday).

Lyons, Gene (1921-7/8/74). TV: *Have Gun Will Travel*—"Episode in Laredo" 9-19-59 (Sam Tuttle), "The Road" 5-27-61 (Merton); *Gunsmoke*—"Brother Love" 12-31-60 (Frank Cumbers), "Bently" 4-11-64; *The Outlaws*—"All in a Day's Work" 5-10-62 (Wim Squires); *Stoney Burke*—"The Mob Riders" 10-29-62 (Clyde Lampert); *The Virginian*—"If You Have Tears" 2-13-63 (Sheriff Ballard); *The Dakotas*—"Terror at Heart River" 4-15-63 (John Volk); *Wide Country*—"The Lucky Punch" 4-18-63 (Jack Higby); *Death Valley Days*—"The Captain Dick Mine" 11-27-65;

Bonanza—"Shining in Spain" 3-27-66 (Taylor Dant).

Lyons, Lurline. Films: "Ramona" 1916 (Senora Moreno); "The Gray Wolf's Ghost" 1919 (Dona Maria Saltonstall); "Lahoma" 1920 (Mrs. Gledware).

Lyons, Robert F. (1940-). Films: "Shoot Out" 1971 (Bobby Jay). ¶TV: *Iron Horse*—"Broken Gun" 10-17-66 (Sam Ringer); *Pistols 'n' Petticoats*—1-7-67 (Virgil Hoeffer); *Bonanza*—"The Deed and the Dilemma" 3-26-67 (Sandy); *Gunsmoke*—"Major Glory" 10-30-67 (Maxwell); *The Outcasts*—"The Town That Wouldn't" 3-31-69 (Pollard).

Lys, Agatha. Films: "In the Name of the Father, the Son and the Colt" 1972-Fr./Ital.; "Tequila" 1974-Ital./Span.; "Three Supermen of the West" 1974-Ital./Span.

Lytell, Bert (1885-9/28/54). Films: "The Trail to Yesterday" 1918 (Ned "Dakota" Keegles); "Steele of the Royal Mounted" 1925 (Philip Steele).

Lytell, Ed. Films: "Sell 'Em Cowboy" 1924 (Frank Mathewson, Sr.).

Lytell, Wilfred (1892-9/10/54). Films: "The Man Who Paid" 1922 (Oliver Thornton).

Lytton, Debbie. Films: "Hot Lead and Cold Feet" 1978 (Roxanne). ¶TV: *The New Land*—Regular 1974 (Annaliese Larsen); *Sara*—Regular 1976 (Debbie Higgins).

Lytton, Herbert C. (1897-6/26/81). Films: "Marshal of Cedar Rock" 1953 (John Harper). ¶TV: *The Lone Ranger*—"Backtrail" 1-25-51, "The Woman from Omaha" 7-2-53; *Gunsmoke*—"No Handcuffs" 1-21-56 (Hunter), "How to Die for Nothing" 6-23-56 (Stranger), "Custer" 9-22-56 (Judge), "Joke's on Us" 3-15-58 (Tom Benson), "Blind Man's Bluff" 2-23-63 (Bud Hays); *Sheriff of Cochise*—"Closed for Repairs" 11-30-56 (Fred Baxter); *Maverick*—"The Quick and the Dead" 12-8-57 (Gus), "Seed of Deception" 4-13-58 (Dr. Teller); *Sergeant Preston of the Yukon*—"Battle at Bradley's" 12-26-57 (Doc Miller); *The Restless Gun*—"Better Than a Cannon" 2-9-59 (Marshal Gavin Brandon); *Wagon Train*—"The Danny Benedict Story" 12-2-59 (Doctor), "The John Bernard Story" 11-21-62 (Dr. Porter); *The Deputy*—"Silent Gun" 1-23-60 (Parnell Locke); *Bonanza*—"The Last Viking" 11-12-60, "Rain from Heaven" 10-6-63; *Whispering Smith*—"Death at Even Money" 7-10-61 (Dr. Henderson);

The Tall Man—"Petticoat Crusade" 11-18-61 (Judge), "A Tombstone for Billy" 12-16-61 (Judge).

Lytton, J. Courtland. Films: "Last Days of Boot Hill" 1947 (Dan McCoy); "Oklahoma Blues" 1948 (State Commissioner Walton); "Partners of the Sunset" 1948.

Mabe, Byron. Films: "Mrs. Sundance" TVM-1974 (Merkle). ¶TV: *The Virginian*—"The Barren Ground" 12-6-67 (Dobie Keogh); *Bonanza*—"Terror at 2:00" 3-7-71 (Hunter), "The Witness" 1-2-73 (Louis Gardner); *Gunsmoke*—"The Wedding" 3-13-72 (Sandy Carr); *Kung Fu*—"Alethea" 3-15-73 (Cranch), "One Step to Darkness" 1-25-75 (Sergeant Craig).

McAdams, Heather. TV: *Father Murphy*—"The Reluctant Runaway" 11-16-82 & 11-23-82 (Polly).

McAllister, Mary (1909-5/1/91). Films: "The Kill-Joy" 1917 (Billie); "The Measure of a Man" 1924 (Pattie Batch); "Ace of Spades" 1925-serial; "The Red Rider" 1925 (Lucille Cavanaugh); "A Roaring Adventure" 1925 (Gloria Carpenter).

McAllister, Paul (1875-7/8/55). Films: "Jamestown" 1923 (Don Diego de Molina); "The Winning of Barbara Worth" 1926 (the Seer).

McArthur, Alex. Films: "Desperado" TVM-1987 (Duell McCall); "Desperado: Avalanche at Devil's Rider" TVM-1988 (Duell McCall); "The Return of Desperado" TVM-1988 (Duell McCall); "Desperado: Badlands Justice" TVM-1989 (Duell McCall); "Desperado: The Outlaw War" TVM-1989 (Duell McCall).

MacArthur, Charles. TV: *Jim Bowie*—"The Brothers" 4-4-58 (Jefferson Davis); *Gunsmoke*—"The Bobsy Twins" 5-21-60 (Taylor).

MacArthur, James (1937-). Films: "The Light in the Forest" 1958 (Johnny Butler/True Son); "Ride Beyond Vengeance" 1966 (Delahay, the Census Taker); "Hang 'Em High" 1968 (Preacher). ¶TV: *Wagon Train*—"The Dick Pederson Story" 1-10-62 (Dick Pederson); *The Virginian*—"Jennifer" 11-3-65 (Johnny); *Branded*—"A Destiny Which Made Us Brothers" 1-23-66 (Lt. Jed Laurance); *Gunsmoke*—"Harvest" 3-26-66 (David McGovern); *Hondo*—"Hondo and the Mad Dog" 10-27-67 (Judd Barton); *Bonanza*—"Check Rein" 12-3-67 (Jace Fredericks); *Death Valley Days*—"The Indian Girl" 1-20-68 (Kit Carson).

Macaulay, Charles (1927-). TV: *The Rifleman*—"Sheer Terror" 10-16-

61 (Sloan); *Destry*—"Stormy Is a Lady" 3-6-64 (Travers); *Daniel Boone*—"The Desperate Raid" 11-16-67; *Wild Wild West*—"The Night of Fire and Brimstone" 11-22-68 (Zack Morton); *Gunsmoke*—"Milligan" 11-6-72 (Doleny), "Talbot" 2-26-73 (Dofeny); *Barbary Coast*—"Funny Money" 9-8-75.

McAuliffe, Leon (1917-8/22/88). Films: "Take Me Back to Oklahoma" 1940; "A Tornado in the Saddle" 1942; "Riders of the Northwest Mounted" 1943.

McAvoy, Charles (1885-4/20/53). Films: "The Singing Cowboy" 1936 (Johnson); "Wells Fargo" 1937 (Miner); "Union Pacific" 1939 (Engineer); "Salome, Where She Danced" 1945 (Policeman); "The Sea of Grass" 1947 (Homesteader); "Return of the Badmen" 1948 (Elmer).

McAvoy, May (1901-4/26/84). Films: "Gun Glory" 1957 (Woman).

McBain, Diane (1941-). Films: "A Distant Trumpet" 1964 (Laura); "Donner Pass: The Road to Survival" TVM-1978 (Margaret Reed). ¶TV: *Maverick*—"Passage to Fort Doom" 3-8-59 (Charlotte), "A Fellow's Brother" 11-22-59 (Holly); *The Alaskans*—"Behind the Moon" 3-6-60 (Harriet Pemberton); *Sugarfoot*—"Return to Boot Hill" 3-15-60 (Joan); *Lawman*—"The Judge" 5-15-60 (Lilac Allen); *Wild Wild West*—"The Night of a Thousand Eyes" 10-22-65 (Jennifer Wingate), "The Night of the Vicious Valentine" 2-10-67 (Elaine Dodd); *Barbary Coast*—"Sauce for the Goose" 10-20-75 (Myra).

McBan, Mickey. Films: "Not a Drum Was Heard" 1924 (Jack Loupel, Jr.); "The Splendid Road" 1925 (Billy Gephart).

MacBride, Donald (1889-6/21/57). Films: "The Girl and the Gambler" 1939 (Mike Bascom); "Northwest Passage" 1940 (Sgt. McNott); "Wyoming" 1940 (Bart).

McBride, Thomas (-7/29/74). TV: *Have Gun Will Travel*—"One Came Back" 12-26-59; *Stagecoach West*—"Object: Patrimony" 1-3-61 (Steve McLord).

McBroom, Amanda. TV: *Gunsmoke*—"Brides and Grooms" 2-10-75 (Fran).

McBroom, Marcia (1947-). Films: "The Legend of Nigger Charley" 1972 (Julia).

McCabe, Harry (1881-2/11/25). Films: "Immediate Lee" 1916; "A Western Thoroughbred" 1922; "The No-Gun Man" 1925 (Snooper).

McCaffrie, Pat. TV: *Wanted—*

Dead or Alive—"The Looters" 10-12-60; *The Deputy*—"Duty Bound" 1-7-61 (Trooper); *The Outlaws*—"The Outlaw Marshals" 12-14-61 (Doctor); *The Virginian*—"The Man Who Couldn't Die" 1-30-63 (Tom Rodell).

McCall, William (1879-1/10/38). Films: "Smashing Barriers" 1919-serial; "Where Men Are Men" 1921 (Mike Regan); "Across the Border" 1922 (Phillip Landers); "The Fighting Guide" 1922 (Tubbs); "Rounding Up the Law' 1922 (Judge Hyland); "When Danger Smiles" 1922 (Marshal); "The Back Trail" 1924 (Judge Talent); "Daring Chances" 1924 (Sheriff); "The Phantom Horseman" 1924 (Deputy Sheriff); "Sell 'Em Cowboy" 1924 (John Atwood); "The Red Rider" 1925 (John Cavanaugh); "Ridin' Thunder" 1925 (Sheriff); "A Clean Sweep" 1928; "A Close Call" 1929; "The Range of Fear" 1929; "Ridin' Leather" 1929; "Two-Gun Morgan" 1929; "The Lonesome Tail" 1930 (Rankin); "Trailin' Trouble" 1930 (Father); "Under Texas Skies" 1930 (Marshal Walsh); "The Whirlwind" 1933 (Pa Curtis); "Lightning Bill" 1934 (Ross); "Lightning Bill" 1934; "Desert Mesa" 1935 (Sam Kent); "The Last of the Clintons" 1935; "Law of the 45's" 1935 (Doctor); "Lawless Borders" 1935; "Lightning Triggers" 1935 (Sheriff Stewart); "Cavalcade of the West" 1936; "The Mysterious Avenger" 1936 (Rancher); "Oh, Susannah!" 1936; "Outlaws of the Range" 1936 (Mr. Wilson); "Aces Wild" 1937 (Sheriff); "The Idaho Kid" 1937; "Moonlight on the Range" 1937; "Whistling Bullets" 1937; "Heroes of the Alamo" 1938.

McCalla, Irish (1929-). Films: "Five Bold Women" 1960 (Big Pearl). ¶TV: *Have Gun Will Travel*—"Bob Wire" 1-12-63 (Anna).

McCallion, James (1918-7/11/91). Films: "Vera Cruz" 1954 (Little Bit); "Tribute to a Badman" 1956 (Shorty); "Gunfight in Abilene" 1967 (Smoke Staub); "The Cockeyed Cowboys of Calico County" 1970 (Dr. Henry); "Skin Game" 1971 (Stanfil). ¶TV: *Gunsmoke*—"Robin Hood" 2-4-56 (Vince Butler), "Railroad" 11-25-68 (Amos Billings), "Tara" 1-17-72 (Fletcher); *Maverick*—"Day of Reckoning" 2-2-58 (Charlie); *Wagon Train*—"The Martin Gatsby Story" 10-10-62 (Caleb Lefton), "The Trace McCloud Story" 3-2-64, "The John Gillman Story" 10-4-64 (Gorman); *Stoney Burke*—"The Weapons Man" 4-8-63 (Lieutenant Bolan); *The Big Valley*—"Last Train to the Fair" 4-27-66 (Charlie Wellman),

"The Royal Road" 3-3-69 (Eli Owens); *Pistols 'n' Petticoats*—12-31-66 (Big Shorty); *Custer*—"Under Fire" 11-15-67 (Jason Talbert); *The Guns of Will Sonnett*—"Find a Sonnett, Kill a Sonnett" 12-8-67 (Bartender), "A Difference of Opinion" 11-15-68, "Jim Sonnett's Lady" 2-21-69 (Peter); *Here Come the Brides*—"The Firemaker" 1-15-69 (Omar Freeman); *Bonanza*—"Long Way to Ogden" 2-22-70 (Luther); *Alias Smith and Jones*—"The Bounty Hunter" 12-9-71.

McCallister, Lon (1923-). Films: "Montana Territory" 1952 (John Malvin). ¶TV: *The Rebel*— "The Hostage" 6-11-61 (Coley Wilks).

McCallum, David (1933-). Films: "Robbery Under Arms" 1958-Brit. (Jim Marston). ¶TV: *The Travels of Jaimie McPheeters*—"The Day of the Search" 1-19-64 (Prophet); *Great Adventure*—"Kentucky's Bloody Ground"/"The Siege of Boonesborough" 4-3-64 & 4-10-64 (Captain Hanning).

McCalman, Macon. Films: "Comes a Horseman" 1978 (Hoverton); "The New Maverick" TVM-1978; "The Gambler, Part II—The Adventure Continues" TVM-1983 (Rawlins Sheriff); "Timerider" 1983 (Dr. Sam); "Independence" TVM-1987 (Angus Thurston). ¶TV: *Best of the West*—Regular 1981-82 (Mayor); *Paradise*—"A Proper Stranger" 11-11-89 (Warren Turtle); *Adventures of Brisco County, Jr.*—"High Treason" 5-13-94 & 5-20-94.

McCambridge, Mercedes (1918-). Films: "Inside Straight" 1951 (Ada Stritch); "Johnny Guitar" 1954 (Emma Small); "Giant" 1956 (Luz Benedict); "Cimarron" 1960 (Sarah Wyatt); "Run Home Slow" 1965; "The Sacketts" TVM-1979 (Ma Sackett). ¶TV: *Wagon Train*—"The Emily Rossiter Story" 10-30-57 (Emily Rossiter); *Rawhide*—"Incident at the Curious Street" 4-10-59 (Mrs. Miller), "Incident of the Captive" 12-16-60 (Martha Mushgrove), "The Greedy Town" 2-16-62 (Ada Randolph), "Hostage for Hanging" 10-19-65 (Ma Gufler); *Riverboat*—"Jessie Quinn" 12-6-59 (Jessie Quinn); *Overland Trail*—"Sour Annie" 5-8-60 (Sour Annie); *Bonanza*—"The Lady from Baltimore" 1-14-62 (Deborrah Banning), "The Law and Billy Burgess" 2-15-70 (Matilda Curtis); *The Dakotas*—"Trouble at French Creek" 1-28-63 (Jay French); *Gunsmoke*—"The Lost" 9-13-71 (Mrs. Mather).

McCann, Chuck (1936-). TV: *Bonanza*—"The Younger Brothers' Younger Brother" 3-12-72 (Lonnie Younger).

McCann, John. TV: *Colt .45*— "The Hothead" 11-1-59 (Outlaw), "Phantom Trail" 3-13-60 (Dan Thorne); *Sugarfoot*—"The Long Dry" 4-10-60 (Mark Baylor); *Lawman*— "Dilemma" 10-30-60 (Fen Carmody); *Laredo*—"Anybody Here Seen Billy?" 10-21-65 (Billy Harker); *Daniel Boone*—"Three Score and Ten" 2-6-69 (Jesse); *Bonanza*—"The Iron Butterfly" 11-28-71 (Bennett).

McCargo, Marian. *see* Moses, Marian.

McCarroll, Frank (1892-3/8/54). Films: "Fighting Through" 1934 (Frank); "Big Calibre" 1935; "Blazing Guns" 1935 (Duke Craven/Slugs Raton); "Branded a Coward" 1935; "Tombstone Terror" 1935 (Swede); "Border Caballero" 1936; "Song of the Trail" 1936; "The Traitor" 1936 (Lyncher at Fence); "Treachery Rides the Range" 1936; "West of Nevada" 1936 (Slade Sangree); "Fugitive from Sonora" 1937 (Harris); "Guns of the Pecos" 1937; "Land Beyond the Law" 1937; "Law for Tombstone" 1937; "Outlaws of the Prairie" 1937 (Outlaw); "Prairie Thunder" 1937; "Valley of Terror" 1937 (Hank Taylor); "Wild Horse Round-Up" 1937; "Zorro Rides Again" 1937-serial; "Code of the Rangers" 1938 (Al); "The Arizona Kid" 1939; "Come on, Rangers" 1939; "Desperate Trails" 1939; "Rough Riders' Round-Up" 1939 (Rough Rider); "Southward Ho!" 1939; "Covered Wagon Days" 1940; "Covered Wagon Trails" 1940; "Law and Order" 1940 (Townsman); "Pony Post" 1940; "Ragtime Cowboy Joe" 1940; "Son of Roaring Dan" 1940; "Three Men from Texas" 1940; "The Driftin' Kid" 1941; "Fugitive Valley" 1941; "A Missouri Outlaw" 1941; "Prairie Pioneers" 1941; "Tumbledown Ranch in Arizona" 1941; "Underground Rustlers" 1941; "Wrangler's Roost" 1941; "Down Rio Grande Way" 1942; "Heart of the Golden West" 1942; "Pirates of the Prairie" 1942; "Prairie Pals" 1942 (Henchman); "Riding the Wind" 1942; "Bordertown Gunfighters" 1943; "Calling Wild Bill Elliott" 1943; "Carson City Cyclone" 1943; "Daredevils of the West" 1943-serial (Gulch Heavy #1); "Land of Hunted Men" 1943; "The Man from Thunder River" 1943; "Overland Mail Robbery" 1943; "Raiders of Sunset Pass" 1943 (Rustler); "Robin Hood of the Range" 1943; "Sagebrush Law" 1943; "Wagon Tracks West" 1943; "Western Cyclone" 1943; "Call of the Rock-

ies" 1944; "Firebrands of Arizona" 1944 (Outlaw); "Fuzzy Settles Down" 1944; "Guns of the Law" 1944; "Hidden Valley Outlaws" 1944; "Outlaw Roundup" 1944; "Outlaws of Santa Fe" 1944 (Bill); "Rustlers' Hideout" 1944 (Squint); "Sheriff of Las Vegas" 1944; "Silver City Kid" 1944; "Song of Nevada" 1944; "Tucson Raiders" 1944; "Wild Horse Phantom" 1944; "Along Came Jones" 1945 (Posse); "Corpus Christi Bandits" 1945; "Flame of the West" 1945; "Gangster's Den" 1945 (Gambler); "His Brother's Ghost" 1945 (Madison); "Lonesome Trail" 1945; "The Lost Trail" 1945 (Joe); "Rustlers of the Badlands" 1945; "Saddle Serenade" 1945; "Shadows of Death" 1945; "Conquest of Cheyenne" 1946; "Gunman's Code" 1946; "Heading West" 1946; "Sheriff of Redwood Valley" 1946; "Trigger Fingers" 1946; "Adventures of Don Coyote" 1947 (Steve); "Buffalo Bill Rides Again" 1947 (Hank); "Twilight on the Rio Grande" 1947; "Blazing Across the Pecos" 1948; "Buckaroo from Powder River" 1948 (McCall); "Outlaw Brand" 1948; "Silver River" 1948 (Soldier); "The Blazing Trail" 1949; "Brand of Fear" 1949; "Calamity Jane and Sam Bass" 1949; "Challenge of the Range" 1949 (Dugan); "Lawless Code" 1949; "Renegades of the Sage" 1949 (Drew); "Cow Town" 1950; "Dallas" 1950 (Citizen); "Fence Riders" 1950; "Gunslingers" 1950 (Parsons); "Over the Border" 1950 (Carl); "West of Wyoming" 1950; "Don Daredevil Rides Again" 1951-serial (Deputy #2); "Captive of Billy the Kid" 1952 (1st Deputy Marshall). ¶TV: *The Cisco Kid*—"Dog Story" 5-12-51, "The Old Bum" 6-9-51, "Water Rights" 7-7-51.

McCarthy, Dennis. TV: *Wagon Train*—"The Tent City Story" 12-10-58 (Clyde Parker), "The River Crossing" 12-14-60, "The George B. Hanrahan Story" 3-28-62 (Burton), "Alias Bill Hawks" 5-15-63 (Harvey York), "The Barnaby West Story" 6-5-63 (Palmer), "The Sam Spicer Story" 10-28-63, "The Duncan McIvor Story" 3-9-64, "The Miss Mary Lee McIntosh Story" 2-28-65 (Curt); *Cimarron City*—Regular 1959 (Doc Hodges); *Black Saddle*—"Means to an End" 1-29-60 (Mike Whitney); *Laredo*— "The Land Grabbers" 12-9-65; *The Virginian*—"The Return of Golden Tom" 3-9-66 (Frank Shaw), "Legacy of Hate" 9-14-66 (Cooper), "Image of an Outlaw" 10-23-68 (Editor), "Fox, Hound, and the Widow McCloud" 4-2-69 (Editor).

McCarthy, Earl (1906-5/28/33).

Films: "Clancy of the Mounted" 1933-serial (Steve Clancy).

McCarthy, Julianna. TV: *Paradise*—"Founder's Day" 11-10-88 (Bank Teller), "Hard Choices" 1-12-89 (Margaret), "Crossroads" 1-26-89 (Margaret), "The Traveler" 2-2-89 (Margaret), "The Secret" 2-8-89 (Margaret).

McCarthy, Kevin (1914-). Films: "The Gambler from Natchez" 1954 (Andre Rivage); "Stranger on Horseback" 1955 (Tom Bannerman); "The Misfits" 1961 (Raymond Taber); "A Big Hand for the Little Lady" 1966 (Otto Habershaw); "Ace High" 1967-Ital./Span. (Drake); "Dan Candy's Law" 1975-U.S./Can.; "Buffalo Bill and the Indians, or Sitting Bull's History Lesson" 1976 (Maj. Burke); "Once Upon a Texas Train" TVM-1988 (Governor). ¶TV: *Satins and Spurs* 9-12-54 (Tony); *The Rifleman*—"The Shattered Idol" 12-4-61 (Mark Twain), "Suspicion" 1-14-63 (Winslow Quince); *The Legend of Jesse James*—"A Burying for Rosey" 5-9-66 (Sheriff Dockery); *The Road West*—"Never Chase a Rainbow" 3-6-67 (Rando); *The Guns of Will Sonnett*—"Ride the Man Down" 11-17-67 (Sheriff); *Wild Wild West*—"The Night of the Doomsday Formula" 10-4-68 (Maj. Gen. Walter Kroll); *The High Chaparral*—"North to Tucson" 11-8-68 (James Forrest); *Bearcats!*—"Conqueror's Gold" 10-28-71 (Carter Gladstone); *The Oregon Trail*—"The Army Deserter" 10-19-77 (Levering).

McCarthy, Lin. Films: "Yellowneck" 1955 (the Sergeant); "Face of a Fugitive" 1959 (Mark Riley). ¶TV: *Death Valley Days*—"The Scalpel and the Gun" 11-17-59 (Dr. Tom Bell); *The Rifleman*—"Surveyors" 12-29-59 (Charley Burn); *Laramie*—"Siege at Jubilee" 10-10-61 (Hobey Devon), "Badge of Glory" 5-7-63 (John Holby); *Wagon Train*—"The Hobie Redman Story" 1-17-62 (Hobie Redman); *Tales of Wells Fargo*—"End of a Minor God" 4-7-62 (Billy Trent); *The Virginian*—"The Accomplice" 12-19-62 (Malcolm Brent); *Stoney Burke*—"Color Him Lucky" 4-1-63 (Brad Cullman); *Rawhide*—"A Time for Waiting" 1-22-65 (Lt. Scot MacIntosh); *Lancer*—"Yesterday's Vendetta" 1-28-69 (Judd Haney); *Gunsmoke*—"The Schoolmarm" 2-25-74 (Carl Pruitt); *The New Land*—"The Word Is: Mortal" 10-5-74.

McCarthy, Miles (1874-9/27/28). Films: "A Man's Fight" 1919 (Oliver Dale); "Oh, You Tony!" 1924 (Senator from Arizona); "Tricks" 1925 (William Varden).

McCarthy, Nobu (1932-). Films: "Walk Like a Dragon" 1960 (Kim Sung). ¶TV: *Laramie*—"Dragon at the Door" 9-26-61 (Haru); *Wagon Train*—"The John Augustus Story" 10-17-62 (Mayleen); *Wild Wild West*—"The Night of the Sudden Plague" 4-22-66 (Anna Kirby); *Kung Fu*—"The Assassin" 10-4-73 (Mrs. Swan).

McCarty, Mary (1923-4/3/80). Films: "Bells of Rosarita" 1945.

McCarty, Patti (1921-7/7/85). Films: "Prairie Stranger" 1941 (Sue Evans); "Fighting Valley" 1943 (Joan Manning); "Devil Riders" 1944 (Sally Farrell); "Fuzzy Settles Down" 1944; "Gangsters of the Frontier" 1944; "Gunsmoke Mesa" 1944 (Joan Royal); "Rustlers' Hideout" 1944 (Barbara); "Outlaw of the Plains" 1946; "Overland Riders" 1946; "Terrors on Horseback" 1946 (Roxie).

McCauley, Wilbur. Films: "Cheyenne Rides Again" 1937; "Outlaw Express" 1938; "Desperate Trails" 1939 (Joe).

McCay, Peggy. TV: *Jim Bowie*—"Epitaph for an Indian" 9-6-57 (Nekeeta), "Silk Purse" 12-27-57 (Malvina Creel); *Maverick*—"The Sheriff of Duck 'n' Shoot" 9-27-59 (Melissa Maybrook), "The Maverick Line" 10-20-60 (Polly Goodin), "Kiz" 12-4-60 (Melissa Bouchet); *Lawman*—"Whiphand" 4-23-61 (Cassie Nickerson); *Wide Country*—"The Bravest Man in the World" 12-6-62 (Mildred Price); *Laramie*—"Broken Honor" 4-9-63 (Martha Halloran); *Redigo*—"Privilege of a Man" 12-17-63 (Jessie Graham); *The Virginian*—"Man of Violence" 12-25-63; *Great Adventure*—"Kentucky's Bloody Ground"/"The Siege of Boonesborough" 4-3-64 & 4-10-64 (Mrs. Callaway); *Profiles in Courage*—"Sam Houston" 12-13-64 (Margaret Houston); *Bonanza*—"Bushwacked" 10-3-71 (Mrs. Griswold); *Gunsmoke*—"Lynott" 11-1-71 (Rene Lynott).

Macchi, Valentino. Films: "Arizona Colt" 1965-Ital./Fr./Span.; "A Bullet for the General" 1966-Ital. (Pedrito); "The Tall Women" 1966-Austria/Ital./Span.

McClary, Clyde (1895-6/30/39). Films: "The Lone Rider" 1922 (Bull Davidson); "Double Action Daniels" 1925 (the Sheriff); "Galloping Jinx" 1925; "Speedy Spurs" 1926 (City Father); "Twin Triggers" 1926 (Bugs); "Fighting Cowboy" 1933 (Irishman); "Circle Canyon" 1934 (Jim Black); "Boss Cowboy" 1934 (Ranch Hand); "Lightning Range" 1934 (Miner); "The Pecos Dandy" 1934; "Range Riders" 1934; "Rawhide Romance" 1934 (Rancher); "Riding Speed" 1934 (Joe); "Between Men" 1935 (Bralwer); "Cheyenne Tornado" 1935; "No Man's Range" 1935; "The Pecos Kid" 1935 (Townsman); "Rough Riding Ranger" 1935; "Timber Terrors" 1935; "The Whirlwind Rider" 1935; "Brand of the Outlaws" 1936; "Valley of the Lawless" 1936; "Border Phantom" 1937; "The Gambling Terror" 1937; "Range Defenders" 1937; "Riders of the Rockies" 1937; "Sing, Cowboy, Sing" 1937; "Trail of Vengeance" 1937 (Rancher); "The Trusted Outlaw" 1937; "Rollin' Plains" 1938; "Whirlwind Horseman" 1938; "Code of the Cactus" 1939.

McCleod, Catherine. TV: *Maverick*—"A Rage for Vengeance" 1-12-58 (Margaret Ross); *Colt .45*—"Arizona Anderson" 2-14-60 (Mrs. Anderson).

McClory, Sean (1924-). Films: "The Guns of Fort Petticoat" 1957 (Kettle); "Cheyenne Autumn" 1964 (Dr. O'Carberry); "Bandolero!" 1968 (Bobbie); "The New Daughters of Joshua Cabe" TVM-1976 (Codge Collier). ¶TV: *Frontier*—"Tomas and the Widow" 10-2-55; *Broken Arrow*—"Passage Deferred" 10-30-56 (Shawn); *Jim Bowie*—"Convoy Gold" 2-1-57 (Pat Donovan), "The Irishman" 9-20-57; *The Californians*—Regular 1957-59 (Jack McGivern); *The Restless Gun*—"Silver Threads" 12-16-57 (Mike O'Hara); *Zane Grey Theater*—"The Tall Shadow" 11-20-58 (Graham Pogue); *Have Gun Will Travel*—"The Solid Gold Patrol" 12-13-58 (Corporal Callahan); *Man from Blackhawk*—"The Savage" 1-15-60 (Matt Clovis); *Wanted—Dead or Alive*—"Jason" 1-30-60 (Doc Phillips); *Overland Trail*—"The O'Mara's Ladies" 2-14-60 (the O'Mara), "All the O'Mara's Horses" 3-13-60 (the O'Mara); *Wagon Train*—"The Charlene Brenton Story" 6-8-60 (Casey); *Stagecoach West*—"Finn McColl" 1-24-61 (Finn McCool); *Wyatt Earp*—"Wyatt Earp's Baby" 4-25-61 (Muley Boles); *The Rifleman*—"Knight Errant" 11-13-61 (Colonel Black), "I Take This Woman" 11-5-62 (Dennis O'Flarrety); *Bronco*—"The Harrigan" 12-25-61 (Terrence Harrigan); *Bonanza*—"The Tall Stranger" 1-7-62 (Mark Connors), "Hoss and the Leprechauns" 12-22-63 (Prof. McCarthy); *Tales of Wells Fargo*—"Incident at Crossbow" 2-3-62 (Con Toole); *Laramie*—"The Turn of the Wheel" 4-3-62 (Gordon); *The Dakotas*—"Terror at Heart River" 4-15-63 (Fallain); *Rawhide*—"Damon's Road"

11-13-64 & 11-20-64 (Finn); *Daniel Boone*—"The Devil's Four" 3-4-65 (Liam O'Hara), "Be Thankful for the Fickleness of Women" 9-19-68 (Ephron Marsh); *Death Valley Days*—"Magic Locket" 5-16-65 (Joaquin Miller), "Talk to Me, Charley" 12-20-69; *The Virginian*—"Day of the Scorpion" 9-22-65 (Cobb); *Iron Horse*—"Right of Way Through Paradise" 10-3-66 (Beau Slidell); *The Monroes*—"The Hunter" 10-26-66 (Miner); *Lancer*—"The High Riders" 9-24-68; *The Outcasts*—"They Shall Rise Up" 1-6-69 (Welch); *The High Chaparral*—"The Glory Soldiers" 1-31-69 (Sandy McIntire); *The Guns of Will Sonnett*—"A Town in Terror" 2-7-69 & 2-14-69 (Pat Murphy); *Gunsmoke*—"The Judas Gun" 1-19-70 (Clete Bolden), "The Town Tamers" 1-28-74 (Sham).

McClung, Bob (1921-1/27/45). TV: "Wild West Days" 1937-serial; "The Lone Ranger Rides Again" 1939-serial (Danny Daniels).

McClure, Bud "Tarzan" (1886-11/2/42). Films: "The Flying Buckaroo" 1928 (Sheriff); "Fighting Thru" 1930; "Branded Men" 1931; "Hell Fire Austin" 1932; "The Sunset Trail" 1932; "Texas Gun Fighter" 1932; "Tombstone Canyon" 1932; "Whistlin' Dan" 1932; "Come on Tarzan" 1933; "Fargo Express" 1933; "King of the Arena" 1933; "The Lone Avenger" 1933; "The Phantom Thunderbolt" 1933; "Strawberry Roan" 1933 (Cowboy); "The Trail Drive" 1933; "The Fiddlin' Buckaroo" 1934; "Gun Justice" 1934; "Gun Justice" 1934; "Honor of the Range" 1934; "The Law of the Wild" 1934-serial; "Smoking Guns" 1934; "Wheels of Destiny" 1934; "Coyote Trails" 1935; "Gallant Defender" 1935; "Heir to Trouble" 1935; "Lawless Riders" 1935; "Tumbling Tumbleweeds" 1935; "Western Courage" 1935; "Avenging Waters" 1936; "The Cattle Thief" 1936; "The Fugitive Sheriff" 1936; "Gun Smoke" 1936; "Heroes of the Range" 1936 (Lem); "The Lione's Den" 1936 (Henchman); "The Unknown Ranger" 1936; "Winds of the Wasteland" 1936 (Guard); "Overland Stage Raiders" 1938; "Panamint's Bad Man" 1938; "Santa Fe Stampede" 1938; "Destry Rides Again" 1939 (Stage Driver); "Texas Renegades" 1940 (Tom); "Two-Gun Sheriff" 1941; "The Wild Frontier" 1947.

McClure, Doug (1935-2/5/95). Films: "The Unforgiven" 1960 (Andy Zachary); "Shenandoah" 1965 (Sam); "Wild and Wooly" TVM-1978 (Delaney Burke); "The Gambler Returns:

The Luck of the Draw" TVM-1991 (Doug); "Maverick" 1994 (Riverboat Poker Player); "Riders of the Storm" 1995 (Hamilton Monroe). ¶TV: *Death Valley Days*—"Gold Rush in Reverse" 10-21-57, "Fifteen Paces to Fame" 11-25-57; *Jim Bowie*—"Bad Medicine" 4-18-58 (Luke); *26 Men*—"The Hellion" 1-20-59; *Riverboat*—"Face of Courage" 12-27-59 (Corporal Jenkins); *Overland Trail*—Regular 1960 (Flip Flippen); *The Virginian*—Regular 1962-70 (Trampas); *The Men from Shiloh*—Regular 1970-71 (Trampas); *Barbary Coast*—Regular 1975-76 (Cash Conover).

McClure, Greg. Films: "Thunder in the Pines" 1948 (Hammerhead Hogan); "The Dalton Gang" 1949 (Missouri Ganz); "The Golden Stallion" 1949 (Ben).

McClure, Mark (1957-). Films: "Back to the Future, Part III" 1990 (Dave McFly); "Grim Prairie Tales" 1990 (Tom).

McClure, Tipp. TV: *Bat Masterson*—"Murder Can Be Dangerous" 11-3-60 (Shad); *Maverick*—"Destination Devil's Flat" 12-25-60 (Guard).

McConnell, Gladys (1907-3/4/79). Films: "The Devil Horse" 1926 (Marion Morrow); "The Flying Horseman" 1926 (June Savary); "The Bullet Mark" 1928; "Code of Scarlet" 1928 (Helen Morgan); "The Glorious Trail" 1928 (Alice Harper); "Cheyenne" 1929 (Violet Wentworth); "Parade of the West" 1930 (Mary Owens).

McConnell, Judy (1945-). TV: *Wild Wild West*—"The Night of the Death Masks" 1-26-68 (Amanda Vale/Morrison).

McConnell, Keith (1923-). Films: "Border Saddlemates" 1952 (Gene Dalton); "Breakheart Pass" 1976 (Gabriel). ¶TV: *Rawhide*—"The Retreat" 3-26-65 (Sergeant).

McConnell, Molly (1865-12/9/20). Films: "A Ticket to Red Horse Gulch" 1914; "The Girl Angle" 1917 (Maud's Aunt); "Go West, Young Man" 1918 (Amos Latham); "Bare Fists" 1919 (Conchita's Mother); "The Feud" 1919 (Mrs. Summers); "Roped" 1919 (Mrs. Judson-Brown).

McCord, Evan. TV: *Maverick*—"Red Dog" 3-5-61 (Kid Curran), "Three Queens Full" 11-12-61 (Small Paul); *Lawman*—"The Persecuted" 4-9-61 (Roy), "The Four" 10-1-61 (Lee Darragh), "The Youngest" 4-22-62 (Jim Martin, Jr.); *Cheyenne*—"Lone Patrol" 4-10-61 (Trooper Dailey), "Day's Pay" 10-30-61 (Billy Fipps); *Bronco*—"Cousin from Atlanta" 10-

16-61 (Tommy Dancer), "Trail of Hatred" 2-5-62 (Private Foster), "The Last Letter" 3-5-62 (Rob).

McCord, Mrs. Lewis (-/12/24/17). Films: "The Virginian" 1914 (Mrs. Ballam); "Chimmie Fadden Out West" 1915 (Mother Fadden); "The Golden Fetter" 1917 (Big Annie).

McCord, III, Robert. TV: *Yancy Derringer*—"The Gun That Murdered Lincoln" 3-19-59 (Senator Yardley), "Duel at the Oaks" 4-9-59 (Captain Fry), "The Wayward Warrior" 4-16-59 (Captain Fry), "V As in Voodoo" 5-14-59 (Captain Fry); *Wild Wild West*—"The Night of the Human Trigger" 12-3-65 (Sidney), "The Night of the Sedgewick Curse" 10-18-68 (Prisoner).

McCormack, Frank (1876-5/22/41). Films: "Fighting Texan" 1937 (Bart Green).

McCormack, Patty (1945-). TV: *Wagon Train*—"The Mary Ellen Thomas Story" 12-24-58 (Mary Ellen Thomas); *Death Valley Days*—"A Girl Named Virginia" 12-28-60 (Virginia Reed); *Rawhide*—"Incident of the Wolvers" 11-16-62 (Julie Cannon), "Incident at Paradise" 10-24-63 (Sarah Higgins); *Wild Wild West*—"The Night of the Death Masks" 1-26-68 (Beltsy Cole/Stark); *Lancer*—"Child of Rock and Sunlight" 4-1-69 (Pearl Sickles).

McCormick, Gilmer. Films: "Squares" 1972 (Chase Lawrence).

McCormick, Maureen (1956-). Films: "Pony Express Rider" 1976 (Rose).

McCormick, Myron (1908-7/30/62). TV: *The Outlaws*—"The Outlaw Marshals" 12-14-61 (Logan Henry), "Farewell Performance" 3-15-62 (Thomas Hardy).

McCormick, Pat (1934-). Films: "Buffalo Bill and the Indians, or Sitting Bull's History Lesson" 1976 (Grover Cleveland); "Mr. Horn" TVM-1979 (John Noble). ¶TV: *Gun Shy*—Regular 1983 (Colonel Mound).

McCormick, William Merrill (1892-8/19/53). Films: "Hands Off" 1921 (Tony Alviro); "Red Courage" 1921 (Percy Gibbons); "Danger" 1923 (Jose); "Good Men and Bad" 1923 (Don Pedro Martinez); "Fangs of Fate" 1925 (Red Mack); "Flashing Steeds" 1925 (Lord Rathburne); "Reckless Courage" 1925 (Chuck Carson); "Vic Dyson Pays" 1925 (Albert Stacey); "The Desperate Game" 1926 (Luke Grayson); "Arizona Nights" 1927 (Speed Lester); "The Long Loop on the Pecos" 1927;

"Whispering Smith Rides" 1927-serial; "The Apache Raider" 1928 (Ray Wharton); "The Fighting Forester" 1928; "A Son of the Desert" 1928 (Sheik Hammid Zayad); "Born to the Saddle" 1929 (Amos Judd); "Romance of the Rio Grande" 1929 (Luca); "Riders of the Rio Grande" 1929 (Tough Hawkins); "Near the Rainbow's End" 1930; "The Spoilers" 1930 (Miner); "Fighting Caravans" 1931 (Townsman); "The Nevada Buckaroo" 1931; "Trails of the Golden West" 1931; "The Boiling Point" 1932; "Border Devils" 1932 (Jose Lopez); "Cornered" 1932; "A Man's Land" 1932; "Tombstone Canyon" 1932; "Whistlin' Dan" 1932; "Cowboy Counsellor" 1933 (Prisoner); "Deadwood Pass" 1933 (Felipe); "The Dude Bandit" 1933; "The Fighting Parson" 1933; "King of the Arena" 1933; "The Lone Avenger" 1933; "Man of the Forest" 1933; "Boss Cowboy" 1934 (Slim); "The Fighting Trooper" 1934; "Lightning Range" 1934; "Range Riders" 1934; "West on Parade" 1934; "The Westerner" 1934; "Wheels of Destiny" 1934; "Gallant Defender" 1935; "Law of the 45's" 1935 (Gunman); "Lawless Borders" 1935; "The Old Corral" 1936 (Joe); "Rebellion" 1936 (Dr. Semple); "Rose of the Rancho" 1936 (Kincaid Henchman); "The Unknown Ranger" 1936; "Winds of the Wasteland" 1936 (Pete); "Boots and Saddles" 1937 (Neale's Henchman); "Cheyenne Rides Again" 1937 (Gang Member); "Come on Cowboys" 1937; "Danger Valley" 1937; "Empty Holsters" 1937; "Fighting Texan" 1937 (Bart); "Forlorn River" 1937 (Chet Parker); "God's Country and the Man" 1937 (Henchman); "Guns in the Dark" 1937; "One Man Justice" 1937; "Phantom of Santa Fe" 1937; "Range Defenders" 1937; "Trail of Vengeance" 1937 (Deputy); "Two-Fisted Sheriff" 1937 (Hank); "Wells Fargo" 1937 (Dealer); "Zorro Rides Again" 1937-serial (Raider #3); "Cattle Raiders" 1938; "Ghost Town Riders" 1938; "Heroes of the Alamo" 1938; "Outlaws of Sonora" 1938 (Pete); "Prairie Moon" 1938; "The Adventures of the Masked Phantom" 1939 (Outlaw); "Dodge City" 1939 (Man); "In Old Caliente" 1939 (Pedro); "The Kansas Terrors" 1939; "Lone Star Pioneers" 1939; "Mexicali Rose" 1939; "Overland Mail" 1939 (Squint); "Ride 'Em, Cowgirl" 1939 (Deputy Sheriff); "Riders of the Frontier" 1939 (Boney); "The Singing Cowgirl" 1939 (Deputy Sheriff); "Stagecoach" 1939 (Ogler); "Water Rustlers" 1939 (Sheriff); "Adventures

of Red Ryder" 1940-serial; "Hidden Gold" 1940; "Melody Ranch" 1940; "Prairie Schooners" 1940; "Desert Bandit" 1941; "In Old Cheyenne" 1941 (Townsman); "The Lone Rider Fights Back" 1941; "The Son of Davy Crockett" 1941; "White Eagle" 1941-serial; "Below the Border" 1942; "Boot Hill Bandits" 1942; "Fighting Bill Fargo" 1942; "In Old California" 1942; "Pirates of the Prairie" 1942; "The Silver Bullet" 1942; "The Sombrero Kid" 1942; "South of Santa Fe" 1942; "Stardust on the Sage" 1942; "Texas Justice" 1942; "Border Patrol" 1943; "The Kansan" 1943; "Lost Canyon" 1943; "Raiders of Red Gap" 1943; "Robin Hood of the Range" 1943; "Silver City Raiders" 1943; "Gun Town" 1946; "The Gallant Legion" 1948; "The Blazing Trail" 1949; "Gun Law Justice" 1949; "Beyond the Purple Hills" 1950; "Desperadoes of the West" 1950-serial; "The Fighting Stallion" 1950 (Yancy); "Lightning Guns" 1950; "Outlaw Gold" 1950; "Six Gun Mesa" 1950; "Santa Fe" 1951; "Whistling Hills" 1951; "The Man from Black Hills" 1952. ¶TV: *The Cisco Kid*—"Foreign Agent" 8-18-51, "Bates Story" 9-29-51; *Wild Bill Hickok*—"Blacksmith Story" 1-1-52; *The Roy Rogers Show*—"Flying Bullets" 6-15-52, "Death Medicine" 9-7-52, "Violence in Paradise Valley" 11-2-55.

McCoy, Gertrude (1890-7/17/67). Films: "When the Cartridges Failed" 1914.

McCoy, Kay. Films: "Tombstone Terror" 1935 (Jean Adams).

McCoy, Matt. Films: "Dream West" TVM-1986 (Louis Freniere); "Samurai Cowboy" 1993 (Colt Wingate).

McCoy, Tim (1891-1/29/78). Films: "The Covered Wagon" 1923 (Rider); "The Thundering Herd" 1925 (Burn Hudnall); "War Paint" 1926 (Lt. Tim Marshall); "California" 1927 (Capt. Archibald Gillespie); "The Frontiersman" 1927 (John Dale); "Winners of the Wilderness" 1927 (Colonel Sir Dennis O'Hara); "The Adventurer" 1928 (Jim McClellan); "Beyond the Sierras" 1928 (the Masked Stranger); "The Law of the Range" 1928 (Jim Lockheart); "Riders of the Dark" 1928 (Lt. Carne); "Spoilers of the West" 1928 (Lt. Lang); "Wyoming" 1928 (Lt. Jack Colton); "The Desert Rider" 1929 (Jed Tyler); "Morgan's Last Raid" 1929 (Capt. Daniel Clairbourne); "The Overland Telegraph" 1929 (Capt. Allen); "Sioux Blood" 1929 (Flood); "The Indians Are

Coming" 1930-serial (Jack Manning); "The Fighting Marshal" 1931 (Tim Benton); "The One Way Trail" 1931 (Tim Allen); "Shotgun Pass" 1931 (Tim Walker); "Cornered" 1932 (Tim Laramie); "Daring Danger" 1932 (Tim Madigan); "End of the Trail" 1932 (Captain Tim Travers); "The Fighting Fool" 1932 (Tim Collins); "Fighting for Justice" 1932 (Tim Keane); "The Riding Tornado" 1932 (Tim Torrant); "Texas Cyclone" 1932 (Texas Grant/Jim Rawlins); "Two-Fisted Law" 1932 (Tim Clark); "The Western Code" 1932 (Tim Barrett); "Man of Action" 1933 (Tim Barlowe); "Rusty Rides Alone" 1933 (Tim "Rusty" Burke); "Silent Men" 1933 (Tim Richards); "The Whirlwind" 1933 (Tim Reynolds); "The Prescott Kid" 1934 (Tim Hamlin); "Speed Wings" 1934 (Tim Robertson); "The Westerner" 1934 (Tim Addison); "Bulldog Courage" 1935 (Slim Braddock/Tim Braddock); "Fighting Shadows" 1935 (Tim O'Hara); "Justice of the Range" 1935 (Tim Condon); "Law Beyond the Range" 1935 (Tim McDonald); "The Man from Guntown" 1935 (Tim Hanlon); "The Outlaw Deputy" 1935 (Tim Mallory); "The Revenge Rider" 1935 (Tim O'Neil); "Riding Wild" 1935 (Tim Malloy/Tex Ravelle); "Square Shooter" 1935 (Tim Baxter); "Aces and Eights" 1936 (Wild Bill Hickok); "Border Caballero" 1936 (Tim Ross); "Ghost Patrol" 1936 (Tim Caverly); "Lightning Bill Carson" 1936 (Lightning Bill Carson); "The Lion's Den" 1936 (Tim Barton); "Roarin' Guns" 1936 (Tim Corwin); "The Traitor" 1936 (Tim Vallance); "Code of the Rangers" 1938 (Tim Strong); "Lightning Carson Rides Again" 1938 (Capt. William "Lighting Bill" Carson/Jose Hernandez); "Phantom Ranger" 1938 (Tim Hayes); "Six-Gun Trail" 1938 (Captain William "Lightning Bill" Carson); "Two-Gun Justice" 1938 (Tim Carson); "West of Rainbow's End" 1938 (Tim); "Code of the Cactus" 1939 (Lightning Bill Carson/Miguel); "Fighting Renegade" 1939 (Lightning Bill Carson/El Puma); "Outlaw's Paradise" 1939 (Trigger Mallory/Capt. William Carson); "Straight Shooter" 1939 (Lightning Bill Carson); "Texas Wildcats" 1939 (Lightning Bill Carson); "Trigger Fingers" 1939 (Lightning Bill Carson); "Arizona Gangbusters" 1940 (Trigger Tim); "Frontier Crusader" 1940 (Trigger Tim Rand); "Gun Code" 1940 (Tim Hammond); "Riders on Black Mountain" 1940 (Tim Donovan); "Texas Renegades" 1940 (Silent Tim Smith);

"Arizona Bound" 1941; "Forbidden Trails" 1941 (Colonel); "The Gunman from Bodie" 1941; "Outlaws of the Rio Grande" 1941 (Tim); "The Texas Marshal" 1941 (Tim Rand); "Below the Border" 1942 (Tim McCall); "Down Texas Way" 1942 (Tim); "Ghost Town Law" 1942 (Tim); "Riders of the West" 1942 (Tim); "West of the Law" 1942; "Run of the Arrow" 1957 (Gen. Allan); "Requiem for a Gunfighter" 1965 (Judge Irving Short).

McCoy, Tony. Films: "The Naked Gun" 1956. ¶TV: *The Adventures of Rin Tin Tin*—"Wagon Train" 11-23-56 (Grey Cloud).

McCrea, Ann (1931-). Films: "River of No Return" 1954; "Pardners" 1956 (Dance Hall Girl); "The War Wagon" 1967 (Felicia); "Welcome to Hard Times" 1967 (Flo). ¶TV: *Death Valley Days*—"Mr. Bigfoot" 3-24-56, "Pirates of San Francisco" 4-26-60; *Cheyenne*—"Wagon Tongue North" 4-8-58 (Faith Swain); *Rawhide*—"Incident of the Shambling Men" 10-9-59; *Black Saddle*—"Burden of Guilt" 3-18-60 (Liz); *The Deputy*—"The Standoff" 6-11-60 (Helen Swayde).

McCrea, Jody (1934-). Films: "The First Texan" 1956 (Baker); "The Naked Gun" 1956; "Gunsight Ridge" 1957 (Groom); "Trooper Hook" 1957; "The Broken Land" 1962 (Deputy); "Young Guns of Texas" 1963 (Jeff Shelby); "Law of the Lawless" 1964 (George Stapleton); "Young Fury" 1965 (Stone); "Cry Blood, Apache" 1970 (Pitcalin). ¶TV: *Sergeant Preston of the Yukon*—"The Criminal Collie" 2-27-58 (Jerry Turner); *Wichita Town*—Regular 1959-60 (Ben Matheson); *Death Valley Days*—"To Walk with Greatness" 11-14-62 (John F. Pershing).

McCrea, Joel (1905-10/20/90). Films: "The Silver Horde" 1930 (Boyd Emerson); "Scarlet River" 1933 (Himself); "Wells Fargo" 1937 (Ramsay MacKay); "Union Pacific" 1939 (Jeff Butler); "The Great Man's Lady" 1942 (Ethan Hoyt); "Buffalo Bill" 1944 (Buffalo Bill); "The Virginian" 1946 (the Virginian); "Ramrod" 1947 (Dave Nash); "Four Faces West" 1948 (Ross McEwen); "Colorado Territory" 1949 (Wes McQueen); "South of St. Louis" 1949 (Kip Davis); "Frenchie" 1950 (Tom Banning); "The Outriders" 1950 (Will Owen); "Saddle Tramp" 1950 (Chuck Conner); "Stars in My Crown" 1950 (Josiah Doziah Gray); "Cattle Drive" 1951 (Dan Mathews); "The San Francisco Story" 1952 (Rick

Nelson); "The Lone Hand" 1953 (Zachary Hallock); "Black Horse Canyon" 1954 (Del Rockwell); "Border River" 1954 (Clete Mattson); "Stranger on Horseback" 1955 (Rick Thorne); "Wichita" 1955 (Wyatt Earp); "The First Texan" 1956 (Sam Houston); "Gunsight Ridge" 1957 (Mike); "The Oklahoman" 1957 (Dr. John Brighton); "The Tall Stranger" 1957 (Ned Bannon); "Trooper Hook" 1957 (Sgt. Hook); "Cattle Empire" 1958 (John Cord); "Fort Massacre" 1958 (Vinson); "The Gunfight at Dodge City" 1959 (Bat Masterson); "Ride the High Country" 1962 (Steve Judd); "Cry Blood, Apache" 1970 (Older Pitcalin); "The Great American Cowboy" 1974; "Mustang Country" 1976 (Dan). ¶TV: *Wichita Town*—Regular 1959-60 (Marshal Mike Dunbar); *Wagon Train*—"The Betsy Blee Smith Story" 3-28-65 (Calvin).

McCready, Ed. Films: "Heaven with a Gun" 1969 (Charlie). ¶TV: *Branded*—"Mightier Than the Sword" 9-26-65 (Anders); *Gunsmoke*—"The Pretender" 11-20-65 (Waiter), "Judge Calvin Strom" 12-18-65 (Freight Agent), "Quaker Girl" 12-10-66 (Henry), "A Hat" 10-16-67 (Villager), "Baker's Dozen" 12-25-67 (Fred Remick), "Alias Festus Haggen" 3-6-72 (Scotty), "I Have Promises to Keep" 3-3-75 (Freight Agent); *Cimarron Strip*—"The Roarer" 11-2-67; *Hondo*—"Hondo and the Superstition Massacre" 9-29-67 (Sergeant), "Hondo and the War Hawks" 10-20-67 (Sergeant), "Hondo and the Apache Trail" 12-22-67 (Sergeant Hurst); *Bonanza*—"The Clarion" 2-9-69 (Purdy); *Here Come the Brides*—"A Dream That Glitters" 2-26-69; *Kung Fu*—"The Hoots" 12-13-73 (Schroeder).

McCubbin, Russ (1935-). Films: "Waco" 1966; "Cain's Way" 1969; "High Plains Drifter" 1973 (Fred Short); "Santee" 1973; "James A. Michener's Texas" TVM-1995 (Panther Komax). ¶TV: *Wide Country*—"The Girl in the Sunshine Smile" 11-15-62 (Mort Lamson); *Daniel Boone*—"The Courtship of Jericho Jones" 4-19-65 (Jubal Markham), "The Tamarack Massacre Affair" 12-30-65 (Sergeant), "The Search" 3-3-66 (Armand), "The Spanish Horse" 11-23-67; *Laredo*—"No Bugles, One Drum" 2-24-66, "The Other Cheek" 2-10-67, "Like One of the Family" 3-24-67; *Branded*—"Headed for Doomsday" 4-10-66 (Fred Turner); *Iron Horse*—"The Dynamite Driver" 9-19-66 (Pettyman); *Wild Wild West*—"The

Night of the Firebrand" 9-15-67 (Briscoe); *World of Disney*—"Hacksaw" 9-26-71 & 10-3-71 (Dusty Trent); *Nichols*—3-14-72 (Donnie); *Paradise*—"Shield of Gold" 4-12-91 (Brody).

McCue, Mathew (1895-4/10/66). TV: *Gunsmoke*—"Big Man" 3-25-61 (Joe), "Minnie" 4-15-61 (Joe).

McCulley, W.T. Films: "Blinky" 1923 (the Adjutant); "The Ramblin' Kid" 1923 (Sheriff Tom Poole); "Shootin' for Love" 1923 (Sandy); "Singled-Handed" 1923 (Ringmaster); "The Sawdust Trail" 1924 (Red McLaren).

McCullough, Philo (1890-6/5/81). Films: "The Secret of Black Mountain" 1917 (Blake Stanley); "The Girl Who Wouldn't Quit" 1918 (Jim Younger); "The Untamed" 1920 (Lee Haines); "The Primal Law" 1921 (Travers); "West of Chicago" 1922 (John Hampton); "Hook and Ladder" 1924 (Gus Henshaw); "The Calgary Stampede" 1925 (Callahan); "Arizona Sweepstakes" 1926 (Jonathan Carey); "The Bar C Mystery" 1926-serial (Robbins); "Chip of the Flying U" 1926 (Duncan Whittaker); "Silver Valley" 1927 (Black Jack Lundy); "Clearing the Trail" 1928 (Silk Cardross); "Painted Post" 1928 (Ben Tuttle); "Untamed Justice" 1929 (Herbert Winslow); "Spurs" 1930 (Tom Marsden); "Branded" 1931 (Sheriff Mac); "The Phantom of the West" 1931-serial (Royce Macklin); "The Vanishing Legion" 1931-serial (Stevens); "White Renegade" 1931; "Heroes of the West" 1932-serial (Rance Judd); "South of the Rio Grande" 1932 (Clark); "The Sunset Trail" 1932 (Weller); "The Cactus Kid" 1934 (Duncan); "The Lone Bandit" 1934; "Mystery Mountain" 1934-serial; "Outlaws' Highway" 1934 (Frank Carter); "Thunder Over Texas" 1934 (Tom Collier); "West on Parade" 1934; "Wheels of Destiny" 1934 (Rocky); "Annie Oakley" 1935 (Officer); "Gunfire" 1935 (Dan McGregor); "Gunsmoke on the Guadalupe" 1935; "Ridin' Thru" 1935 (Winthrop); "Wanderer of the Wasteland" 1935 (Squid); "Gun Smoke" 1936 (Abner Sneed); "The Lawless Nineties" 1936 (Outlaw Leader); "Texas Trail" 1937 (Jordan); "Renfrew on the Great White Trail" 1938 (Williams); "Frontier Marshal" 1939 (Tough); "Let Freedom Ring" 1939 (Gagan's Henchman); "Stampede" 1949 (Charlie); "Montana" 1950 (Bystander); "Sugarfoot" 1951; "Horizons West" 1952 (Rancher); "The Treasure of Lost Canyon" 1952 (Miner); "The

Redhead from Wyoming" 1953 (Aldrich); "Dawn at Socorro" 1954 (Rancher); "Cheyenne Autumn" 1964 (Man); "The Great Bank Robbery" 1969.

McCullough, Ralph Fee (1895-12/25/43). Films: "Fighting Pals" 1920; "Across the Divide" 1921 (Wallace Layson); "The Man Trackers" 1921 (Morgan); "The Red Warning" 1923 (Harry Williams); "The Bloodhound" 1925 (Constable Ray Fitzgerald); "Galloping Vengeance" 1925 (Jack Reeves); "A Man of Nerve" 1925 (Art Gatlin); "No Man's Law" 1925 (Donald Moore); "Davy Crockett at the Fall of the Alamo" 1926 (Colonel Bonham); "The Stolen Ranch" 1926 (Frank Wilcox); "The Cowboy Star" 1936 (Pretty Boy Hogan); "Code of the Range" 1937 (Quigley); "Wells Fargo" 1937 (Clerk); "The Thundering West" 1939 (Clerk); "Pioneers of the Frontier" 1940 (Lem Watkins).

McCutcheon, Wallace (1894-1/27/28). Films: "The Phantom Foe" 1920-serial.

McDaniel, Etta (1890-1/13/46). Films: "Smoking Guns" 1934 (Clementine); "The Arizonian" 1935; "Cavalry" 1936 (Mammy); "The Lawless Nineties" 1936 (Mandy Lou); "The Lonely Trail" 1936 (Mammy); "The Glory Trail" 1937 (Mandy); "Carolina Moon" 1940 (Mammny); "American Empire" 1942 (Wida May); "The Great Man's Lady" 1942 (Delilah).

McDaniel, George (1886-8/20/44). Films: "The Hidden Children" 1917 (Amochol); "Hell's Crater" 1918 (Jim Shamrick); "Hungry Eyes" 1918 (Pinto Dupont); "The Man from Funeral Range" 1918 (Mark Brenton); "Unclaimed Goods" 1918 (Gentleman Joe Slade).

McDaniel, Hattie (1895-10/26/52). Films: "The Boiling Point" 1932; "The Golden West" 1932 (Mammy Lou); "They Died with Their Boots On" 1941 (Callie).

McDaniel, Sam "Deacon" (1886-9/24/62). Films: "The Vanishing Frontier" 1932 (Whistlin' Six); "Wagon Wheels" 1934 (Black Coachman); "Stormy" 1935 (Hostler); "Cavalry" 1936 (Mose); "Rhythm on the Range" 1936 (Porter); "The Three Godfathers" 1936 (Cook); "Git Along, Little Dogies" 1937 (Sam Brown); "Bad Men of Missouri" 1941 (Wash); "They Died with Their Boots On" 1941 (Waiter); "Silver Queen" 1942 (Toby).

McDermott, Dylan. Films:

"Into the Badlands" TVM-1991 (John McComas).

McDermott, Hugh (1908-1/30/72). Films: "Captain Apache" 1971-Brit./Span. (Gen. Ryland); "Lawman" 1971 (Moss); "Chato's Land" 1972 (Bartender).

McDermott, Joe (1890-3/6/23). Films: "Three Friends" 1912; "Just Gold" 1913; "A Misunderstood Boy" 1913; "The Sheriff's Story" 1915; "Barb Wire" 1922 (Nick Lazarre); "Perils of the Yukon" 1922-serial; "The Forbidden Trail" 1923 (Red "Hawk" Dugan).

MacDermott, Marc (1881-1/5/29). Films: "The House of Cards" 1909; "The Story of the Indian Lodge" 1911; "A Cowboy's Stratagem" 1912; "When East Met West in Boston" 1914; "Ranson's Folly" 1915 (Patrick Cahill); "California" 1927 (Drachano).

McDevitt, Ruth (1895-5/27/76). Films: "The Shakiest Gun in the West" 1968 (Olive). ¶TV: *Pistols 'n' Petticoats*—Regular 1966-67 (Grandma Hanks); *Gunsmoke*—"Tarnished Badge" 11-11-74 (Gramma Boggs).

Macdonald, Donald. Films: "The Indian Vestal" 1911; "A Tale of the West" 1913; "A Desert Wooing" 1918 (Dr. Fortescue Van Fleet); "The Sky Pilot" 1921 (the Duke); "Stepping Fast" 1923 (Fabian).

McDonald, Donald (1898-12/9/59). Films: "The Kentuckian" 1955 (Little Eli); "Lay That Rifle Down" 1955 (Johnny); "The Brass Legend" 1956 (Clay); "Great Day in the Morning" 1956 (Gary Lawford). ¶TV: *Fury*—"The Horse Coper" 10-29-55 (Ted); *My Friend Flicka*—"Wind from Heaven" 2-3-56; *Frontier*—"The Hanging at Thunder Butte Creek" 3-11-56.

MacDonald, Edmund (1908-9/2/51). Films: "Destry Rides Again" 1939 (Rockwell); "Brigham Young—Frontiersman" 1940 (Elger); "The Gay Caballero" 1940 (Joe Turner); "Trail of the Vigilantes" 1940 (Ed Wheeler); "Texas" 1941 (Comstock); "Call of the Canyon" 1942 (Thomas McCoy); "Heart of the Golden West" 1942 (Ross Lambert); "Black Eagle" 1948 (Si); "Red Canyon" 1949 (Farlane).

McDonald, Francis J. (1891-9/18/68). Films: "As in the Days of Old" 1915; "The Gun Woman" 1918 (the Gent); "Nomads of the North" 1920 (Buck McDougall); "The Call of the North" 1921 (Achille Picard); "Captain Fly-By-Night" 1922 (Second Stranger); "Trooper O'Neil" 1922 (Pierre); "The Buster" 1923

(Swing); "The Desert's Toll" 1926 (Frank Darwin); "The Yankee Senor" 1926 (Juan Gutierrez); "Outlaws of Red River" 1927 (Ben Tanner); The Valley of Hell" 1927 (Creighton Steele); "Hidden Valley" 1932 (Frank Gavin); "Honor of the Mounted" 1932; "Texas Buddies" 1932 (Blake); "Trailing the Killer" 1932 (Pierre La-Plant); "Terror Trail" 1933 (Tad McPherson); "Cheyenne Tornado" 1935; "The Plainsman" 1936 (Boat Gambler); "Robin Hood of El Dorado" 1936 (Pedro, the Spy); "White Fang" 1936 (Suds); "Wild West Days" 1937-serial (Purvis); "Gun Law" 1938 (Nevada); "The Texans" 1938; "Bad Lands" 1939 (Manuel Lopez); "Range War" 1939 (Dave Morgan); "Union Pacific" 1939 (Gen. Grenville M. Dodge); "The Carson City Kid" 1940 (Laramie); "Northwest Mounted Police" 1940 (Louis Riel); "Wyoming" 1940 (Dawson); "The Kid from Kansas" 1941 (Cesar); "Men of the Timberland" 1941; "Girl from Alaska" 1942 (Pelly); "Valley of the Sun" 1942 (Interpreter); "Wild Bill Hickok Rides" 1942; "Bar 20" 1943 (One Eye Quirt); "Buckskin Frontier" 1943 (Duvall); "The Kansan" 1943 (Gil Hatton); "Bordertown Trail" 1944; "Cheyenne Wildcat" 1944; "Lumberjack" 1944 (Fenwick); "Mystery Man" 1944 (Bert Rogan); "Texas Masquerade" 1944 (Sam Nolan); "Zorro's Black Whip" 1944-serial (Dan Hammond); "Bad Men of the Border" 1945; "Corpus Christi Bandits" 1945 (Dad Christie); "Great Stagecoach Robbery" 1945; "South of the Rio Grande" 1945 (Torres); "Canyon Passage" 1946 (Cobb); "The Devil's Playground" 1946 (Roberts); "Duel in the Sun" 1946 (Gambler); "My Pal Trigger" 1946 (Storekeeper); "Roll on, Texas Moon" 1946 (Steve Anders); "Dangerous Venture" 1947 (Kane); "Saddle Pals" 1947 (Sheriff); "Unconquered" 1947; "The Bold Frontiersman" 1948 (Adam Post); "The Dead Don't Dream" 1948 (Bert Lansing); "The Paleface" 1948 (Lance); "Panhandle" 1948 (Crump); "Son of God's Country" 1948 (Tom Ford); "Apache Chief" 1949 (Mohaska); "Brothers in the Saddle" 1949; "Calamity Jane and Sam Bass" 1949 (Starter); "Powder River Rustlers" 1949 (Shears Williams); "Rim of the Canyon" 1949 (Charlie Lewis); "Rustlers" 1949; "Son of a Badman" 1949 (Joe Christ); "California Passage" 1950 (Kane/Recorder); "Gene Autry and the Mounties" 1951 (Batiste); "Red Mountain" 1951 (Marshal Roberts); "Santa Fe" 1951; "Desert Passage" 1952; "Fort

Osage" 1952 (Indian Chief); "The Raiders" 1952 (John Cummings); "Rancho Notorious" 1952 (Harbin); "The Stranger Wore a Gun" 1953; "Three Hours to Kill" 1954 (Vince); "Shotgun" 1955 (Dishwasher); "Ten Wanted Men" 1955 (Warner); "Dig That Uranium" 1956 (Chief); "Raw Edge" 1956 (Chief Kiyuva); "Thunder Over Arizona" 1956; "Duel at Apache Wells" 1957 (Hank); "The Last Stagecoach West" 1957; "Pawnee" 1957 (Tip); "Fort Massacre" 1958 (Piute Man); "The Saga of Hemp Brown" 1958 (Prosecutor). ¶TV: *The Lone Ranger*—"Finders Keepers" 12-8-49, "The Quiet Highwayman" 1-27-55, "Trouble at Tylerville" 12-13-56, "The Avenger" 1-10-57, "The Courage of Tonto" 1-17-57; *The Gene Autry Show*—"Blackwater Valley Feud" 9-3-50, "Doublecross Valley" 9-10-50, "Frontier Guard" 10-13-51, "Killer's Trail" 10-27-51, "Trouble at Silver Creek" 3-9-52, "Trail of the Witch" 3-30-52, "Battle Axe" 8-31-54, "Outlaw Warning" 10-2-54, "Dynamite" 12-24-55; *Wild Bill Hickok*—"Papa Antinelli" 11-27-51; *The Roy Rogers Show*—"Badman's Brother" 2-10-52 (Mr. Trumbull), "The Kid from Silver City" 1-17-54 (Peter Miner), "Phantom Rustlers" 4-25-54 (Sam MacGuiness), "The Lady Killer" 9-12-54, "Strangers" 12-5-54, "Fishing for Fingerprints" 10-28-56; *The Cisco Kid*—"Pancho and the Wolf Dog" 9-13-52, "Faded General" 10-25-52; *The Adventures of Champion*—Regular 1955-56 (Will Calhoun); *My Friend Flicka*—"Rebels in Hiding" 3-30-56 (Thundercloud); *Fury*—"The Feud" 1-5-57 (Adam Hayes), "The Claim Jumpers" 4-5-58 (Carty); *Broken Arrow*—"The Desperado" 3-26-57 (Nochay), "Black Moment" 10-29-57 (Hobe), "Massacre" 1-28-58 (Nana); *Wyatt Earp*—"Old Jake" 4-9-57 (Jake Caster), "The Muleskinner" 1-27-59 (Sam McGuffin), "Terror in the Desert" 1-24-61 (Pat Few); *Tales of Wells Fargo*—"Renegade Raiders" 5-20-57 (Aaron Ross); *Have Gun Will Travel*—"Three Bells to Perdido" 9-14-57; *Wagon Train*—"The John Cameron Story" 10-2-57 (Squawman), "The Amos Gibbon Story" 4-20-60 (Tom Duncan), "The Dr. Swift Cloud Story" 5-25-60; *Tombstone Territory*—"Strange Vengeance" 4-9-58 (Winnie Joe Westerby); *Wanted—Dead or Alive*—"The Bounty" 9-20-58 (Juan Hernandez), "Reckless" 11-7-59; *Man Without a Gun*—"The Last Hunt" 11-8-58 (Clam Tabor); *Trackdown*—"Day of Vengeance" 11-28-58 (Milo); *The Texan*—"The Lord Will Provide" 12-29-58 (Sheriff), "Ruthless Woman" 4-11-60 (Colton); *Lawman*—"Red Ransom" 6-21-59 (Chief Red Horse); *Maverick*—"The Lass with the Poisonous Air" 11-1-59 (Pop Talmadge); *Wichita Town*—"Seed of Hate" 1-27-60 (Medicine Chief); *The Law of the Plainsman*—"The Imposter" 2-4-60 (Cavour Watkins); *Sugarfoot*—"The Long Dry" 4-10-60 (Jerich Dooley); *Bat Masterson*—"High Card Loses" 11-10-60 (Winkler); *The Deputy*—"The Dream" 2-4-61 (Roy Wilkins); *Laramie*—"Shadows in the Dust" 1-16-62 (Gimp); *The Virginian*—"Echo from Another Day" 3-27-63 (Saul Weintraub).

MacDonald, Ian. Films: "Secrets of the Wastelands" 1941 (Hollister); "They Died with Their Boots On" 1941 (Soldier); "North of the Rockies" 1942; "Ramrod" 1947 (Walt Shipley); "The Man from Colorado" 1948 (Jack Rawson); "Colt .45" 1950 (Miller); "Comanche Territory" 1950 (Walsh); "Montana" 1950 (Slim Reeves); "New Mexico" 1951 (Pvt. Daniels); "The Texas Rangers" 1951 (the Sundance Kid); "Thunder in God's Country" 1951 (Smitty); "Flaming Feather" 1952 (Tombstone Jack); "Hiawatha" 1952 (Megissogwon); "High Noon" 1952 (Frank Miller); "The Savage" 1952 (Yellow Eagle); "Toughest Man in Arizona" 1952 (Steve Girard); "Blowing Wind" 1953 (Jackson); "A Perilous Journey" 1953 (Sprague); "The Silver Whip" 1953 (Hank); "Apache" 1954 (Glagg); "Johnny Guitar" 1954 (Pete); "Taza, Son of Cochise" 1954 (Geronimo); "The Lonesome Trail" 1955; "Timberjack" 1955 (Pauguette); "Stagecoach to Fury" 1956 (Sheriff Ross); "Two-Gun Lady" 1956 (Jud Ivers); "Duel at Apache Wells" 1957 (Marcus Wolf); "Money, Women and Guns" 1958 (Nibbs); "Warlock" 1959 (MacDonald). ¶TV: *The Lone Ranger*—"Stage to Estacado" 7-23-53; *The Adventures of Rin Tin Tin*—"Higgins Rides Again" 11-11-55; *Zane Grey Theater*—"Stage to Tucson" 11-16-56 (Ed Loomis); *Wyatt Earp*—"Dull Knife Strikes for Freedom" 5-7-57 (Dull Knife); *Trackdown*—"Alpine, Texas" 11-15-57 (Jed Burroughs), "The Brothers" 5-16-58 (Sheriff); *Gunsmoke*—"Dirt" 3-1-58 (Mr. Troyman); *The Rebel*—"Angry Town" 1-10-60 (Storekeeper); *Man from Blackhawk*—"The Savage" 1-15-60 (Guard).

MacDonald, Inez. Films: "The Man Who Waited" 1922 (June Rance).

MacDonald, J. Farrell (1875-8/2/52). Films: "On Burning Sands" 1913; "A Fight for Love" 1919 (the Priest); "Marked Men" 1919 (Tom "Placer" McGraw); "The Outcasts of Poker Flat" 1919; "Riders of Vengeance" 1919 (Buell); "Roped" 1919 (Butler); "This Hero Stuff" 1919 (Softnose Smith); "The Boss of Copperhead" 1920; "Bullet Proof" 1920 (Jim Boone); "Hitchin's Posts" 1920; "Action" 1921 (Mormon Peters); "The Freeze-Out" 1921 (Bobtail McGuire); "Riding with Death" 1921 (Sheriff Pat Garrity); "The Wallop" 1921 (Neuces River); "The Bachelor Daddy" 1922 (Joe Pelton); "Over the Border" 1922 (Peter Galbraith); "Sky High" 1922 (Jim Halloway); "Tracks" 1922 (Jack Bess); "Under Pressure" 1922; "Quicksands" 1923 (Col. Patterson); "The Iron Horse" 1924 (Corporal Casey); "Western Luck" 1924 (Chuck Campbell); "The Lucky Horseshoe" 1925 (Mack); "Three Bad Men" 1926 (Mike Costigan); "In Old Arizona" 1929 (Ted); "Girl of the Golden West" 1930 (Sonora Slim); "River's End" 1930 (O'Toole); "The Painted Desert" 1931 (Jeff Cameron); "The Squaw Man" 1931 (Big Bill); "Woman Hungry" 1931 (Buzzard); "Heritage of the Desert" 1932 (Adam Nash); "The Vanishing Frontier" 1932 (Hornet); "The Fighting Parson" 1933; "The Arizonian" 1935; "Northern Frontier" 1935 (Insp. Stevens); "Square Shooter" 1935 (Sheriff); "Stormy" 1935 (Trinidad Dorn); "Courage of the West" 1937 (Buck Saunders); "Roaring Timber" 1937 (Andrew MacKinley); "Come on, Rangers" 1939 (Col. Forbes); "The Gentleman from Arizona" 1939 (Coburn); "The Lone Ranger Rides Again" 1939-serial (Craig Dolan); "Susannah of the Mounties" 1939 (Pat O'Hannegan); "The Dark Command" 1940 (Dave); "Knights of the Range" 1940 (Cappy); "The Light of Western Stars" 1940 (Bill Stillwell); "Pony Express Days" 1940-short; "Prairie Law" 1940 (Sheriff Austin); "Stagecoach War" 1940 (Jeff Chapman); "In Old Cheyenne" 1941 (Tim Casey); "Riders of the Timberline" 1941 (Kerrigan); "Wild Bill Hickok Rides" 1942 (Judge Hathaway); "Texas Masquerade" 1944 (John Martindale); "My Darling Clementine" 1946 (Mac the Bartender); "Smoky" 1946 (Jim, the Cook); "Belle Starr's Daughter" 1947; "Fury at Furnace Creek" 1948 (Pops); "Panhandle" 1948 (Doc Cooper); "Whispering Smith" 1948 (Bill Baggs); "The Dalton Gang" 1949 (Judge Price); "Fighting Man of the Plains" 1949 (Partridge); "Law of the Barbary

Coast" 1949 (Sgt. O'Leary); "Tough Assignment" 1949; "Dakota Lil" 1950 (Expert); "The Daltons' Women" 1950; "Hostile Country" 1950 (Mr. Lane).

McDonald, Jack (1886-12/26/52). Films: "The Spoilers" 1914 (Slap-Jack); "When the West Was Young" 1914; "One Touch of Sin" 1917 (Hard-luck Danvers); "Code of the Yukon" 1918 (Justice Breen); "The Great Redeemer" 1920 (the Sheriff); "The Last of the Mohicans" 1920 (Tamenund); "The Big Punch" 1921 (Jed's Friend); "Singing River" 1921 (Bert Condon); "Western Speed" 1922 (Brad Usher); "The Interferin' Gent" 1927 (Joe Luke); "A California Romance" 1923 (Don Manuel Casca); "Against All Odds" 1924 (Warner's Uncle); "Circus Cowboy" 1924 (Ezra Bagley); "The Trail Rider" 1925 (Dee Winch); "The Flame of the Yukon" 1926 (Sour Dough Joe); "Phantom City" 1928 (Simon); "Pursued" 1947 (Callum).

MacDonald, Jeanette (1906-1/14/65). Films: "Rose Marie" 1936 (Marie de Flor); "The Girl of the Golden West" 1938 (Mary Robbins).

MacDonald, Katherine (1894-6/4/56). Films: "Headin' South" 1918 (the Girl); "Riddle Gawne" 1918 (Kathleen Harkless); "The Squaw Man" 1918 (Diana, Henry's Wife); "High Pockets" 1919 (Joy Blyth); "Speedy Meade" 1919 (Mary Dillman).

MacDonald, Kenneth (1901-5/5/72). Films: "Yankee Speed" 1924 (Dick Vegas); "Avenging Fangs" 1927 (Dick Mansfield); "The Little Buckaroo" 1928 (Jack Pemberton); "Border Vengeance" 1935 (Flash Burdue); "Outpost of the Mounties" 1939 (R.A. Kirby); "Overland with Kit Carson" 1939-serial (Winchester); "Spoilers of the Range" 1939 (Cash Fenton); "The Taming of the West" 1939 (Carp Blaisdale); "Bullets for Rustlers" 1940 (Ed Brock); "The Durango Kid" 1940 (Mace Ballard); "Texas Stagecoach" 1940 (John Appleby); "Hands Across the Rockies" 1941; "Prairie Pioneers" 1941 (Fields); "The Son of Davy Crockett" 1941 (King Canfield); "Wildcat of Tucson" 1941 (McNee); "Perils of the Royal Mounted" 1942-serial (Ransome); "Riders of the Northland" 1942 (Matt Taylor); "Valley of Vanishing Men" 1942-serial (Kincaid); "Robin Hood of the Range" 1943 (Henry Marlowe); "Six Gun Gospel" 1943; "Black Arrow" 1944-serial (Jake Jackson); "Cowboy from Lonesome River" 1944; "Pride of the Plains"

1944 (Hurley); "West of the Rio Grande" 1944; "The Lost Trail" 1945 (John Corbett); "That Texas Jamboree" 1946; "Cheyenne" 1947 (Gambler); "The Fabulous Texan" 1947; "False Paradise" 1948; "Frontier Agent" 1948; "Return of the Badmen" 1948 (Col. Markham); "The Gay Amigo" 1949 (Capt. Lewis); "Hellfire" 1949; "The Mysterious Desperado" 1949 (Sheriff); "South of Santa Fe" 1949-short; "Stagecoach Kid" 1949 (Sheriff); "Border Treasure" 1950 (Sheriff); "Dakota Lil" 1950 (Sentry); "Punchy Cowpunchers" 1950-short (Dillon); "Salt Lake Raiders" 1950 (Deputy Marshal); "Storm Over Wyoming" 1950 (Dawson); "Along the Great Divide" 1951 (Crowley, the Rancher); "Desert of Lost Men" 1951 (Bill Hackett); "Hot Lead" 1951 (Sheriff); "Law of the Badlands" 1951 (Capt. McVey); "Sugarfoot" 1951; "Carson City" 1952; "Leadville Gunslinger" 1952 (Sheriff Nichols); "Montana Belle" 1952 (Sheriff Irving); "Trail Guide" 1952 (Wheeler); "Marshal of Cedar Rock" 1953 (Sheriff); "Savage Frontier" 1953 (Bradley); "Shot in the Frontier" 1954-short (Noonan); "Southwest Passage" 1954 (Sheriff Morgan); "The Gun That Won the West" 1955 (Col. E.M. Still); "Seminole Uprising" 1955 (Dinker); "Perils of the Wilderness" 1956-serial (Bart Randall); "Three Violent People" 1956 (Croupier); "Gunfighters of Abilene" 1960 (Harker); "40 Guns to Apache Pass" 1967 (Harry Malone). ¶TV: *The Lone Ranger*—"The Renegades" 11-3-49, "Outlaw's Revenge" 10-5-50, "Gold Freight" 4-28-55; *The Gene Autry Show*—"Gun Powder Range" 10-29-50, "Fight at Peaceful Mesa" 11-19-50; *The Cisco Kid*—"The Caution of Curley Thompson" 5-2-53, "Doorway to Nowhere" 9-26-53, "Juggler's Silver" 10-17-53, "Vendetta" 11-14-53, "Gold, Death and Dynamite" 2-13-54; *My Friend Flicka*—"The Foundlings" 6-1-56 (Brady); *Cheyenne*—"The Trap" 12-18-56 (Sheriff Gaffey); *Zane Grey Theater*—"They Were Four" 3-15-57 (Jury Foreman); *Colt .45*—"A Time to Die" 10-25-57 (Col. Parker), "Sign in the Sand" 1-3-58 (Col. Parker), "Dead Reckoning" 1-24-58 (Col. Parker); *Trackdown*—"The Bounty Hunter" 3-7-58 (Sheriff); *Wanted—Dead or Alive*—"Drop to Drink" 12-27-58 (Sheriff); *Rough Riders*—"Wilderness Trace" 1-29-59 (Oliver Wentworth); *The Texan*—"The Marshal of Yellow Jacket" 3-2-59 (Ed Grover); *Frontier Doctor*—"Danger Valley" 4-11-59; *The Restless Gun*—"One on the House" 4-20-59;

Bat Masterson—"A Matter of Honor" 4-29-59 (Tack Colby); *Rawhide*—"Incident of a Burst of Evil" 6-26-59, "Incident of the Running Iron" 3-10-61 (Morgan Shaw); *Laramie*—"The General Must Die" 11-17-59 (Mose), "Wolf Cub" 11-21-61 (Captain Reeces); *Maverick*—"A Cure for Johnny Rain" 12-20-59 (Sheriff); *Bonanza*—"House Divided" 1-16-60; *Man from Blackhawk*—"The Search for Cope Borden" 4-15-60 (Jess); *Wyatt Earp*—"Casey and the Clowns" 2-21-61; *The Deputy*—"Two-way Deal" 3-11-61 (the Sheriff); *Wide Country*—"Speckle Bird" 1-31-63 (Doctor); *Temple Houston*—"Enough Rope" 12-19-63 (Official), "Sam's Boy" 1-23-64 (Jury Foreman); *Daniel Boone*—"Cry of Gold" 11-4-65.

McDonald, Marie (1923-10/21/65). Films: "Riding High" 1943.

MacDonald, Sam (1887-9/25/70). Films: "Branded" 1931.

MacDonald, Wallace (1891-10/30/78). Films: "Nanette of the Wilds" 1916 (Harry Jennings); "Leave It to Susan" 1919 (Jimmy Dawson); "The Fighting Shepherdess" 1920 (Hughie); "Two from Texas" 1920; "The Sage Hen" 1921 (John Croft); "Youth Must Have Love" 1922 (Earl Stanndard); "The Spoilers" 1923 (Broncho Kid); "The Bar C Mystery" 1926-serial (Nevada); "Fighting with Buffalo Bill" 1926-serial; "Drums of the Desert" 1927 (Will Newton); "Tumbling River" 1927 (Keechie); "Whispering Smith Rides" 1927-serial; "Fighting Thru" 1930 (Tennessee Malden); "Branded" 1931 (Starett); "The Range Feud" 1931 (Hank); "Between Fighting Men" 1932 (Wally Thompson); "Daring Danger" 1932 (Jughandle); "Hello Trouble" 1932 (Le Tange); "The Riding Tornado" 1932 (Dick Stark); "Tex Takes a Holiday" 1932 (Tex); "Texas Cyclone" 1932 (Nick Lawlor); "Two-Fisted Law" 1932 (Artie); "The Vanishing Frontier" 1932 (Capt. Rogers Kearney); "The King of the Wild Horses" 1933 (Clint Bolling); "Frontier Vengeance" 1940 (Slash); "Two-Fisted Rangers" 1940 (Jack Rand); "Belle Starr's Daughter" 1947 (Jim Davis).

McDonell, Arch. TV: *Hawkeye and the Last of the Mohicans*—"The Witch" 5-22-57.

McDonnell, Ed T. Films: "The Outlaws Is Coming!" 1965 (Bat Masterson).

McDonnell, Mary. Films: "Dances with Wolves" 1990 (Stands With a Fist).

McDonough, Tom. Films: "The Stranger from Ponca City" 1947; "Dangers of the Canadian Mounted" 1948-serial (Frank); "Desperadoes of the West" 1950-serial (Larkin); "City of Badmen" 1953 (Deputy Tex); "The Woman They Almost Lynched" 1953 (Quantrill's Henchman). ¶TV: *Tales of Wells Fargo*—"Sam Bass" 6-10-57 (Ranger Clark), "Two Cartridges" 9-16-57 (Buck); *Schlitz Playhouse of the Stars*—"A Tale of Wells Fargo" 12-14-58 (Rosser); *The Law of the Plainsman*—"Desperate Decision" 11-12-59 (Neeley); *Cimarron Strip*—"The Legend of Jud Starr" 9-14-67.

McDormand, Frances (1957-). Films: "The Good Old Boys" TVM-1995 (Eve Calloway).

McDougall, Alistair. Films: "Bonanza: The Return" TVM-1993 (Adam "A.C." Cartwright, Jr.).

MacDouglas, John (Giuseppe Addobatti) (1909-). Films: "Ride and Kill" 1964-Ital./Span.; "Joe Dexter" 1965-Span./Ital. (Burton); "Man from Oklahoma" 1965-Ital./Span./Ger.; "Deguello" 1966-Ital. (Colonel Crook); "Massacre Time" 1966-Ital./Span./Ger. (Scott); "Django, Last Killer" 1967-Ital. (Barrett); "Hole in the Forehead" 1968-Ital./Span.; "God Will Forgive My Pistol" 1969-Ital.

McDowall, Roddy (1928-). Films: "My Friend Flicka" 1943 (Ken McLaughlin); "The Adventures of Bullwhip Griffin" 1967 (Bullwhip Griffin); "Five Card Stud" 1968 (Nick Evers); "The Life and Times of Judge Roy Bean" 1972 (Frank Gass).

MacDowell, Andie (1958-). Films: "Bad Girls" 1994 (Eileen Spenser).

McDowell, Claire (1877-10/23/66). Films: "A Mohawk's Way" 1910; "Billy's Stratagem" 1911; "In the Days of '49" 1911; "The Female of the Species" 1912; "In the Aisles of the Wild" 1912; "The Massacre" 1912; "A Temporary Truce" 1912; "The Ranchero's Revenge" 1913; "The Stolen Treaty" 1913; "The Tenderfoot's Money" 1913; "The Indian" 1914; "The Gambler's I.O.U." 1915; "The Sheriff's Dilemma" 1915; "Mixed Blood" 1916 (Nita Valyez); "The Empty Gun" 1917; "Fighting Back" 1917 (the Fury); "Closin' In" 1918; "Man Above the Law" 1918 (Natchah); "Chasing Rainbows" 1919 (Mrs. Walters); "The Feud" 1919 (Mary Lynch); "Rosalind at Red Gate" 1919; "Mark of Zorro" 1920 (Donna Catalina); "In the North Woods" 1921; "The Reckless Sex" 1925 (Concha); "The Flaming Forest" 1926 (Mrs. McTavish); "Cor-

nered" 1932 (Aunt Caroline); "High, Wide and Handsome" 1937 (Seamstress); "Two-Fisted Sheriff" 1937 (Miss Herrick); "Stand Up and Fight" 1939 (Woman); "Black Market Rustlers" 1943.

McDowell, James. Films: "Jacques of the Silver North" 1919 (Tennessee Jake).

McDowell, Malcolm (1943-). Films: "Sunset" 1988 (Alfie Alperin).

MacDowell, Melbourne (1857-2/18/41). Films: "The Bond of Fear" 1917; "The Flame of the Yukon" 1917 (Black Jack Hovey); "Go West, Young Man" 1918 (Amos Latham); "Playing the Game" 1918; "Wolves of the Rail" 1918 (Murray Lemantier); "Nomads of the North" 1920 (Duncan McDougall); "Fighting Courage" 1925 (Kinglsey, Sr.); "The Outlaw Express" 1926 (Sheriff); "Code of the Cow Country" 1927 (John Calhoun); "The Old Code" 1928 (Steve MacGregor).

McDowell, Nelson (1875-11/3/47). Films: "The Feud" 1919 (McFadden); "Cupid, the Cowpuncher" 1920 (Sheriff Bergin); "The Last of the Mohicans" 1920 (David Gamut); "Masked" 1920; "Ransom" 1920; "Riders of the Dawn" 1920; "Shod with Fire" 1920 (Parson); "Shadows of Conscience" 1921 (Wesley Coburn); "The Silent Call" 1921 (Dad Kinney); "The Girl Who Ran Wild" 1922 (Deacon McSnagley); "Blood Test" 1923; "The Girl of the Golden West" 1923 (Sonora Slim); "Pioneer Trails" 1923 (Parson); "Galloping Gallagher" 1924 (Leon I. Berry); "Rainbow Rangers" 1924 (Deacon Slim); "The Ridin' Kid from Powder River" 1924 (Luke Meggary); "Gold and Grit" 1925 (Horation Jeferson Blaabs); "Idaho" 1925-serial; "Kit Carson Over the Great Divide" 1925 (Windy Bill Sharp); "On the Go" 1925 (Philip Graves); "A Streak of Luck" 1925 (Big Ben Tuttle); "The Frontier Trail" 1926 (Pawnee Jack); "Blind Trail" 1926 (Hank O'Hara); "The Iron Rider" 1926 (Dunk); "The Outlaw Express" 1926 (Chaw Egan); "The Phantom Bullet" 1926 (Zack Peters); "The Valley of Bravery" 1926 (Missouri); "Whispering Smith" 1926 (Seagrue); "The Bugle Call" 1927 (Luke); "Code of the Range" 1927; "Danger Ahead" 1927; "Blind Man's Bluff" 1927; "Border Blackbirds" 1927 (Mournful Luke); "Hands Off" 1927 (Prof. Hawley); "The Outlaw Breaker" 1927; "A Clean Sweep" 1928; "Kit Carson" 1928 (Jim Bridger); "The Vanishing Rider" 1928-serial; "Born to the Saddle"

1929 (Pop Healy); "Grit Wins" 1929 (John Deering); "Wild Blood" 1929 (John Ellis); "Billy the Kid" 1930 (Hatfield); "Law of the Rio Grande" 1931 (Wolf Hardy); "The Texas Ranger" 1931 (High Pocketts); "Guns for Hire" 1932; "The Last of the Mohicans" 1932-serial; "Law and Order" 1932 (Parker Brother); "Mason of the Mounted" 1932; "Scarlet Brand" 1932 (Slim Grand); "Come on Tarzan" 1933 (Slim); "The Phantom Thunderbolt" 1933; "Rustlers' Roundup" 1933 (Sheriff Brass); "Sunset Pass" 1933; "The Ferocious Pal" 1934 (Charlie); "Fighting Hero" 1934 (Bailiff); "Fighting Through" 1934 (Parson); "The Fighting Trooper" 1934 (Woodsman); "Honor of the Range" 1934; "Lightning Bill" 1934 (Barney); "Lightning Bill" 1934; "Rawhide Mail" 1934 (Judge); "Terror of the Plains" 1934 (Parson Jones); "Wheels of Destiny" 1934 (Trapper); "Border Guns" 1935 (Diganburywell); "Born to Battle" 1935; "The Dawn Rider" 1935 (Undertaker); "Gunsmoke on the Guadalupe" 1935; "Horses' Collars" 1935-short (Bartender); "The Laramie Kid" 1935 (Convict); "Northern Frontier" 1935; "Powdersmoke Range" 1935; "Rio Rattler" 1935; "The Silver Bullet" 1935; "Texas Jack" 1935 (Barney); "Western Frontier" 1935; "Wilderness Mail" 1935 (Mailman); "Fast Bullets" 1936; "Feud of the West" 1936 (Wild Horse Henderson); "Gun Smoke" 1936 (Long Distance Jones); "Lucky Terror" 1936; "Ride, Ranger, Ride" 1936; "Ridin' On" 1936 (Pete); "Rose of the Rancho" 1936 (Decrepit Old Man); "Boots and Saddles" 1937; "Desert Phantom" 1937 (Doc Simpson); "Heart of the Rockies" 1937; "Santa Fe Rides" 1937; "Wild Horse Round-Up" 1937; "Santa Fe Stampede" 1938; "The Lone Ranger Rides Again" 1939-serial (Johnny); "The Man from Texas" 1939; "Riders of the Frontier" 1939; "Westbound Stage" 1939 (Rawhide); "Pioneer Days" 1940 (Judge); "The Return of Frank James" 1940 (Confederate Veteran/Juror); "Riders from Nowhere" 1940 (Undertaker); "Roll, Wagons, Roll" 1940 (Lucky); "Lone Texas Ranger" 1945.

MacDuff, Tyler. Films: "The Bounty Hunter" 1954 (Vance); "The Boy from Oklahoma" 1954 (Billy the Kid); "The Burning Hills" 1956 (Wes Parker); "Fury at Showdown" 1957 (Tom Williams). ¶TV: *Death Valley Days*—"The Hoodoo Mine" 4-7-56 (Norman Berry); *Annie Oakley*—"The Saga of Clement O'Toole" 11-4-56 (Clement O'Toole); *The Lone*

Ranger—"The Twisted Track" 11-29-56, "Mission for Tonto" 5-2-57; *Maverick*—"Relic of Fort Tejon" 11-3-57 (Drake); *Sergeant Preston of the Yukon*—"Lost River Roundup" 12-12-57 (Bill Corey); *Tales of Wells Fargo*—"The Witness" 12-30-57 (Jed Copeland), "The Newspaper" 3-24-58 (Cleve Hepburn); *Lawman*—"Conditional Surrender" 5-28-61 (Ernie Beason); *Gunsmoke*—"Baker's Dozen" 12-25-67 (Bailiff).

Mace, Fred (1879-2/21/17). Films: "A Knot in the Plot" 1910; "Some Bull's Daughter" 1914.

Mace, Patricia. Films: "Riding High" 1943 (Jean Holbrook).

Mace, Wynn (1890-1/15/55). Films: "Sky High" 1922 (Patterson); "Romance Land" 1923 (Sheriff); "King Cowboy" 1928 (Ben Suliman Ali); "Son of the Golden West" 1928 (Slade's Henchman); "The Drifter" 1929 (Henchman).

McEachin, James (1930-). Films: "The Undefeated" 1969 (Jimmy Collins); "Buck and the Preacher" 1972 (Kingston). ¶TV: *Cowboy in Africa*—"Stone Age Safari" 10-16-67 (Dr. Lee Matsis).

McElhern, James. Films: "Captain Fly-By-Night" 1922 (Padre Michael); "The Freshie" 1922 (Prof. Noyes).

McElroy, Bob (1890-1/29/76). Films: "Code of the Saddle" 1947; "Gun Talk" 1947 (Pete); "Prairie Express" 1947 (Joe).

McEntire, Reba (1955-). Films: "The Gambler Returns: The Luck of the Draw" TVM-1991 (Burgundy Jones); "Buffalo Girls" TVM-1995 (Annie Oakley).

McEvoy, Renny. Films: "Senorita from the West" 1945; "Star in the Dust" 1956 (Timothy Brown); "Gun Street" 1961 (Operator). ¶TV: *Broken Arrow*—"Hired Killer" 3-4-58 (Dexter); *Wagon Train*—"The Major Adams Story" 4-23-58 & 4-30-58 (Clerk); *Tales of Wells Fargo*—"The Pickpocket" 4-28-58 (Lute); *Wanted—Dead or Alive*—"Double Fee" 3-21-59; *The Rifleman*—"The Grasshopper" 3-1-60; *Bonanza*—"A Time to Step Down" 9-25-66 (Flint); *The Big Valley*—"Boy into Man" 1-16-67 (Railroad Clerk), "Guilty" 10-30-67 (Townsman); *Iron Horse*—"Shadow Run" 1-30-67 (Julius); *Cimarron Strip*—"The Judgment" 1-4-68.

McFadden, Barney. Films: "The Awakening Land" TVM-1978 (Louie Scurrah). ¶TV: *Centennial*—Regular 1978-79 (Abel Tanner); *How the West Was Won*—"The Innocent" 2-12-79

(Esau Kelsay); *Young Riders*—"Mask of Fear" 5-28-92 (Elroy).

MacFadden, Hamilton (1901-). Films: "Shooting High" 1940 (J. Wallace Rutledge).

McFadden, Ivor (1887-8/14/42). Films: "The Testing Block" 1920 (Slim); "Three Word Brand" 1921 (Solly); "The Wolverine" 1921 (Buck Olney); "Fangs of Fate" 1925 (Sheriff Dan Dodo Briggs); "The Two-Gun Man" 1926 (Texas Pete); "Treason" 1933 (O'Leary); "Riders of Death Valley" 1941-serial.

McFadden, Tom. Films: "Hot Spur" 1968. ¶TV: *Gunsmoke*—"Alias Festus Haggen" 3-6-72 (Luke); *Young Maverick*—"A Fistful of Oats" 12-5-79 (Jubal Moffit).

McFarland, Robert. Films: "Silent Sheldon" 1925 (Sheriff).

MacFarlane, Bruce (1910-11/25/67). Films: "Come on, Rangers" 1939 (Lt. Nelson). ¶TV: *Lawman*—"Mark of Cain" 3-26-61 (Cooper); *Bonanza*—"King of the Mountain" 2-23-64, "Something Hurt, Something Wild" 9-11-66 (Clerk).

McGarity, Blanche. Films: "Rangeland" 1922 (Betty Howard).

McGaugh, Wilbur (1895-1/31/65). Films: "The Broken Spur" 1921 (Pierre LeBac); "Cupid's Brand" 1921 (Spike Crowder); "Dead or Alive" 1921 (Tom Stone); "The Sheriff of Hope Eternal" 1921 (Marybelle's Brother); "One-Eighth Apache" 1922 (Charlie Longdeer); "Peaceful Peters" 1922 (Sad Simpson); "At Devil's Gorge" 1923 (Clayton's Partner Dav); "The Devil's Dooryard" 1923 (Bill Bowers); "The Law Rustlers" 1923 (John Cale); "The Santa Fe Trail" 1923-serial; "Branded a Bandit" 1924 (Horse Williamson); "Bringin' Home the Bacon" 1924; "Cupid's Rustler" 1924 (Ranch Foreman); "Days of '49" 1924-serial; "Ridin' Mad" 1924 (Allen Walker); "Branded a Thief" 1925; "The Cactus Cure" 1925 (Buck Lowry); "The Fugitive" 1925 (Yaqui Kid); "Bad Man's Bluff" 1926 (Joe Slade); "The Indians Are Coming" 1930-serial (Rance Carter).

McGavin, Darren (1922-). Films: "Bullet for a Badman" 1964 (Sam Ward); "The Great Sioux Massacre" 1965 (Capt. Benton); "Hot Lead and Cold Feet" 1978 (Mayor Ragsdale). ¶TV: *Riverboat*—Regular 1959-61 (Grey Holden); *Death Valley Days*—"The Stolen City" 4-19-61 (Zacharias Gurney); *Rawhide*—"The Sendoff" 10-6-61 (Jed Hadley); *The Virginian*—"The Intruders" 3-4-64 (Mark Troxel), "The Deadly Past" 9-

20-67 (Sam Evans); *Gunsmoke*—"Twenty Miles from Dodge" 4-10-65 (Will Helmick), "The Hostage" 12-4-65 (Lon Gorman), "Gunfighter, R.I.P." 10-22-66 (Joe Bascome); *Cimarron Strip*—"The Legend of Jud Starr" 9-14-67 (Jud Starr); *Custer*—"Desperate Mission" 11-8-67 (Jeb Powell).

McGee, Vonetta (1948-). Films: "Great Silence" 1968-Ital./Fr.; "Thomasine and Bushrod" 1974 (Thomasine).

McGhee, Gloria (1922-5/4/64). Films: "Sierra Stranger" 1957 (Meg Anderson). ¶TV: *Judge Roy Bean*—"Four Ladies from Laredo" 7-1-56 (Hannah); *Gunsmoke*—"Mr. and Mrs. Amber" 8-4-56 (Sarah Amber), "Big Girl Lost" 4-20-57 (Laura Simmons), "Louie Pheeters" 1-5-62 (Clara Felder).

McGeehan, Pat (1907-1/3/88). Films: "Son of the Renegade" 1953 (Narrator).

McGill, Bruce. Films: "The Ballad of Gregorio Cortez" 1983 (Bill Blakely); "The Good Old Boys" TVM-1995 (City Marshal).

McGill, Lawrence. Films: "Pierre of the Plains" 1914 (Father Coraine).

McGiver, John (1913-9/9/75). Films: "Once Upon a Horse" 1958 (Mr. Tharp); "Lawman" 1971 (Mayor Sam Bolden); "Sam Hill: Who Killed the Mysterious Mr. Foster?" TVM-1971 (Judge Hathaway); "The Apple Dumpling Gang" 1975 (Leonard Sharpe). ¶TV: *Bonanza*—"Land Grab" 12-31-61 (Colonel Bragg); *DuPont Show of the Week*—"Big Deal in Laredo" 10-7-62 (C.P. Ballinger); *Destry*—"The Nicest Girl in Gomorrah" 3-13-64 (Spink); *Wild Wild West*—"The Night of the Turncoat" 12-1-67 (Elisha Calamander); *The High Chaparral*—"Ebenezer" 11-1-68 (Ebenezer Binns); *Alias Smith and Jones*—"A Fistful of Diamonds" 3-4-71 (August Binford), "Witness to a Lynching" 12-16-72 (Doc Snively); *The Men from Shiloh*—"Jump-Up" 3-24-71 (John Timothy Driscoll).

McGivney, Maura (1935-). TV: *The Virginian*—"Day of the Scorpion" 9-22-65 (Reagan Tercell); *Laredo*—"The Legend of Midas Mantee" 9-16-66 (Rita Silver); *Death Valley Days*—"The Lady Doctor" 10-11-69.

McGlynn, Sr., Frank (1867-5/17/51). Films: "Across the Great Divide" 1915; "Gloria's Romance" 1916-serial; "Rough and Ready" 1918 (the Siwash); "The Golden Strain" 1925

(Zeb); "Rustlin' for Cupid" 1926 (Dave Martin); "Riders of the Purple Sage" 1931 (Jeff Tull); "Unknown Valley" 1933 (Debbs); "Massacre" 1934 (Missionary); "Lawless Range" 1935 (Frank Carter/Butch Martin); "Outlawed Guns" 1935 (Slim Gordon); "The Roaring West" 1935-serial (Jinglebob Morgan); "Arizona Mahoney" 1936 (Sleepy); "The Eagle's Brood" 1936; "For the Service" 1936 (Jim); "King of the Royal Mounted" 1936 (Dundas); "The Last of the Mohicans" 1936 (David Gamut); "North of Nome" 1936 (Marshall); "The Plainsman" 1936 (Abraham Lincoln); "Sudden Bill Dorn" 1937 (Cap Jinks); "Wells Fargo" 1937 (Lincoln); "Western Gold" 1937 (President Abraham Lincoln); "Wild West Days" 1937-serial (Larry); "The Girl of the Golden West" 1938 (Pete, the Gambler); "The Lone Ranger" 1938-serial (Lincoln); "In Old California" 1942; "Hollywood Barn Dance" 1947 (Pa Tubb); "Trail Street" 1947 (Tim McKeon).

McGlynn, Jr., Frank (1904-3/29/39). Films: "Man of the Forest" 1933 (Pegg); "Hopalong Cassidy" 1935 (Red Conners); "Lawless Range" 1935 (Carter); "Westward Ho" 1935 (Jim Wyatt); "Bar 20 Rides Again" 1936 (Red Conners); "Custer's Last Stand" 1936-serial (General Custer).

McGoohan, Patrick (1928-). Films: "Genius" 1975-Ital./Fr./Ger. (Maj. Cabot).

McGovern, Johnny. Films: "Tumbleweed Trail" 1946 (Freckles Ryan).

McGovern, Terrence. Films: "No Man's Land" TVM-1984 (Everett Vanders).

McGowan, J.P. (1880-3/26/52) Films: "The Identification" 1914; "The Oil Well Conspiracy" 1914; "The Girl and the Game" 1915-serial; "The Mettle of Jerry McGuire" 1915; "Medicine Bend" 1916 (Whispering Smith); "Whispering Smith" 1916 (Whispering Smith); "A Crook's Romance" 1921; "The Ruse of the Rattlesnake" 1921 (the Rattler); "Hills of Missing Men" 1922 (Captain Brandt/the Dragon); "Crossed Trail" 1924 (Pepper Baldwin/Bandy Dawson); "The Whipping Boss" 1924 (Livingston); "Border Intrigue" 1925 (Tough Tidings); "Moran of the Mounted" 1926 (Sgt. Churchill); "Red Blood" 1926 (Eagle Custer); "Senor Daredevil" 1926 (Jesse Wilks); "The Texas Terror" 1926; "Arizona Nights" 1927 (Jeff Decker); "Gun Gospel" 1927 (Bill Brogan); "Red

Raiders" 1927 (Captain Ortwell); "Whispering Smith Rides" 1927-serial; "Arizona Days" 1928 (Villain); "The Black Ace" 1928; "Code of the Scarlet" 1928 (Blake); "The Devil's Tower" 1928 (George Stillwell); "Headin' Westward" 1928 (Sneezer Clark); "Law of the Mounted" 1928; "Lightnin' Shot" 1928; "The Old Code" 1928 (Raoul de Valle); "On the Divide" 1928; "Plunging Hoofs" 1928 (Jim Wales); "The Silent Trail" 1928; "West of Santa Fe" 1928; "Bad Man's Money" 1929; "The Two Outlaws" 1928 (Abner Whitcomb); "The Cowboy and the Outlaw" 1929 (Pepper Hardcastle); "The Fighting Terror" 1929; "The Invaders" 1929; "The Last Roundup" 1929; "Law of the Plains" 1929; "The Lawless Legion" 1929 (Matson); "The Lone Horseman" 1929; "'Neath Western Skies" 1929 (Dugan); "The Oklahoma Kid" 1929; "The Phantom Rider" 1929; "Pioneers of the West" 1929 (Tom Dorgan); "Senor Americano" 1929 (Maddux); "A Texas Cowboy" 1929; "Breezy Bill" 1930 (Sheriff); "The Canyon of Missing Men" 1930; "Covered Wagon Trails" 1930 (King Kincaid); "O'Malley Rides Alone" 1930 (McGregor); "Son of the Plains" 1931 (Buck Brokoff); "Lawless Valley" 1932 (Big Mike Carter/El Lobo); "Somewhere in Sonora" 1933 (Monte Black); "Fighting Hero" 1934 (Morales); "The Outlaw Tamer" 1934 (Sheriff Jim Porter); "The Red Rider" 1934-serial (Scott McKee); "Wagon Wheels" 1934 (Couch); "Border Brigands" 1935 (Comm. Winston); "Rustlers of Red Dog" 1935-serial (Captain Trent); "The Silent Code" 1935 (Commissioner); "Bar 20 Rides Again" 1936 (Buck Peters); "Guns and Guitars" 1936 (Dave Morgan); "Ride 'Em Cowboy" 1936 (Jim Howard); "Robin Hood of El Dorado" 1936 (Danglong); "Secret Patrol" 1936 (Blacksmith Barstow); "Silver Spurs" 1936 (Webb Allison); "Stampede" 1936 (Matt Stevens); "The Three Mesquiteers" 1936 (Brack Canfield); "Empty Holsters" 1937 (Billy O'Neill); "Heart of the Rockies" 1937 (Dawson); "Hit the Saddle" 1937 (Rance McGowan); "Prairie Thunder" 1937 (Col. Stanton); "Rough Ridin' Rhythm" 1937 (Hobart); "Flaming Frontier" 1938-serial; "The Great Adventures of Wild Bill Hickok" 1938 (Scudder).

McGowan, Molly. Films: "Snowfire" 1958 (Molly McGowan). ¶TV: *Death Valley Days*—"The Capture" 4-14-57, "The Talking Wire" 4-21-59 (Susie).

McGowan, Oliver (1907-8/23/

71). Films: "Stagecoach" 1966 (Mr. Haines). ¶TV: *Maverick*—"Comstock Conspiracy" 12-29-57 (Jerome Horne); *Sugarfoot*—"Deadlock" 2-4-58 (Laurin), "The Wizard" 10-14-58; *Rough Riders*—"Witness Against the Judge" 2-26-59 (Governor); *Yancy Derringer*—"Thunder on the River" 3-12-59; *Hotel De Paree*—"Sundance and the Marshal of Water's End" 3-18-60 (Doc), "Sundance and the Man in the Shadows" 4-15-60 (Doc); *Man from Blackhawk*—"The Money Machine" 6-10-60 (Taylor); *Laramie*—"The Barefoot Kid" 1-9-62 (Judge Craik); *Gunsmoke*—"Lacey" 1-13-62 (Cyrus Parcher); *Empire*—"The Day the Empire Stood Still" 9-25-62 (Harvey Welk), "End of an Image" 1-15-63 (Harvey Welk), "A House in Order" 3-5-63 (Harvey Welk), "Down There, the World" 3-12-63 (Harvey Welk); *Wild Wild West*—"The Night of the Feathered Fury" 1-13-67 (Armstrong).

McGowan, Robert (1882-1/27/55). Films: "The Rip Snorter" 1925 (Cole Slaw Randall).

McGrail, Walter (1899-3/19/70). Films: "Suzanna" 1922 (Ramon); "The Yosemite Trail" 1922 (Ned Henderson); "The Bad Man" 1923 (Morgan Pel); "The Scarlet West" 1925 (Lt. Harper); "A Son of His Father" 1925 (Holdbrook); "The Old Code" 1928 (Pierre Belleu); "Last of the Duanes" 1930 (Bland); "The Lone Star Ranger" 1930 (Phil Lawson); "River's End" 1930 (Martin); "The Last of the Mohicans" 1932-serial; "McKenna of the Mounted" 1932 (Inspector Oliver P. Logan); "Robbers' Roost" 1933 (Brad); "A Demon for Trouble" 1934 (Dyer); "Sunset Range" 1935 (Grant); "Renfrew on the Great White Trail" 1938 (Garou); "West of Rainbow's End" 1938 (Johnson); "Code of the Fearless" 1939 (Captain Rowlins); "In Old Montana" 1939 (Joe Allison); "Stagecoach" 1939 (Capt. Sickels); "Billy the Kid Outlawed" 1940 (John Fitzgerald); "My Little Chickadee" 1940; "Last of the Duanes" 1941 (Ranger Guard); "Billy the Kid Trapped" 1942 (Judge McConnell); "Riders of the West" 1942 (Miller).

McGrath, Douglas. Films: "Bronco Billy" 1980 (Lt. Wiecker); "Pale Rider" 1985 (Spider Conway).

McGrath, Frank (1903-5/13/67). Films: "Rainbow Trail" 1932; "Robbers' Roost" 1933 (Mexican); "Riders of the Purple Sage" 1941 (Pete); "Sundown Jim" 1942 (Outlaw); "The Ox-Bow Incident" 1943; "She Wore a Yellow Ribbon" 1949 (Trumpeter/Indian); "Ride, Vaquero!" 1953 (Pete); "The Searchers" 1956 (Stunts); "The Tin Star" 1957 (Jim Clark); "Gunfight in Abilene" 1967 (Ned Martin); "The Last Challenge" 1967 (Ballard Weeks); "The War Wagon" 1967 (Bartender); "The Shakiest Gun in the West" 1968 (Mr. Remington). ¶TV: *Wagon Train*— Regular 1957-63 (Charlie Wooster); *Tales of Wells Fargo*—"The Most Dangerous Man Alive" 11-10-58 (Jake Rivers); *The Virginian*—"Linda" 11-30-66 (Neddie Henshaw); *The Big Valley*—"Plunder at Hawk's Grove" 3-13-67 (Buster).

McGrath, James. Films: "Secret Patrol" 1936 (Tim Arnold); "Stampede" 1936 (Henry Brooks); "Death Goes North" 1939 (Puffet).

McGrath, Larry (1888-7/6/60). Films: "The Arizona Kid" 1930 (Homer Sook); "Under the Pampas Moon" 1935; "The Bad Man of Brimstone" 1937 (Gang Member); "Twenty Mule Team" 1940; "Sin Town" 1942 (Stick Man); "Renegades of the Rio Grande" 1945 (Villager); "Trail Street" 1947 (Henchman); "Return of the Badmen" 1948 (Scout); "Dallas" 1950 (Citizen); "Kansas Raiders" 1950 (Man in Crowd); "Flaming Feather" 1952.

MacGraw, Ali (1938-). Films: "Gunsmoke: The Long Ride" TVM-1993 (Uncle Jane Merckel).

McGraw, Charles (1914-7/29/80). Films: "On the Old Spanish Trail" 1947 (Harry Blaisdell); "Blood on the Moon" 1948 (Milo Sweet); "Thunder Over the Plains" 1953 (Ben Westman); "War Paint" 1953 (Sgt. Clarke); "Joe Dakota" 1957 (Cal Moore); "Saddle the Wind" 1958 (Larry Venables); "The Wonderful Country" 1959 (Doc Stovall); "Cimarron" 1960 (Bob Younts); "Tell Them Willie Boy Is Here" 1969 (Frank Wilson); "The Devil and Miss Sarah" TVM-1971 (Marshal Duncan). ¶TV: *Hotel De Paree*—"The Man Who Believed in Law" 11-27-59 (Martin Wood); *Man from Blackhawk*—"Death at Noon" 1-8-60 (Matt Clovis); *Wyatt Earp*—"The Scout" 3-1-60 (Tom Barrows); *The Deputy*—"Last Gunfight" 4-30-60 (Johnny Dean); *Laramie*—"The Mark of the Maneaters" 3-14-61 (Marshal Craig); *Wagon Train*—"The Lieutenant Burton Story" 2-28-62 (Sergeant Kile); *Bonanza*—"The Gamble" 4-1-62 (Sheriff Gains), "The Unwanted" 4-6-69 (Luke Mansfield); *The Virginian*—"Say Goodbye to All That" 1-23-63 (Big John Belden); *The Travels of Jaimie McPheeters*—"The Day of the Search" 1-19-64 (Dan Carver);

Destry—"Ride to Rio Verde" 4-10-64 (Hatch); *Gunsmoke*—"Bently" 4-11-64 (Albert Calvin), "Prairie Wolfers" 11-13-67 (Dolen), "My Brother's Keeper" 11-15-71 (Squaw Man); *A Man Called Shenandoah*—"The Debt" 10-18-65 (Sheriff Hobbs); *Hondo*—"The Savage" 10-6-67 (General Rutledge); *The Outcasts*—"A Ride to Vengeance" 9-30-68 (Mose Skinner); *Wild Wild West*—"The Night of the Fugitives" 11-8-68 (Sheriff Baggs); *Nichols*—"Gulley vs. Hansen" 10-7-71 (Hansen), "About Jesse James" 2-15-72 (Luke).

McGraw, William "Bill". Films: "Copper Sky" 1957 (Man #1); "Blood Arrow" 1958 (Norm); "Cattle Empire" 1958 (Jim Whittaker). ¶TV: *Gunsmoke*—"Romeo" 11-9-57 (Ab Drain).

McGreevey, Michael (1948-). Films: "Day of the Outlaw" 1959 (Bobby); "The Way West" 1967 (Brownie Evans); "Death of a Gunfighter" 1969 (Dan Joslin). ¶TV: *Riverboat*—Regular 1959-61 (Chip); *Black Saddle*—"Murdock" 11-13-59 (Tad Murdock); *Bonanza*—"Gabrielle" 12-24-61; *Wagon Train*— "Clyde" 12-27-61 (Sonny Sherman); *The Men from Shiloh*—"Experiment at New Life" 11-18-70 (Toby).

MacGregor, Casey. Films: "Canyon Passage" 1946 (Poker Player); "Border Feud" 1947 (Jed Young); "Jesse James Rides Again" 1947-serial (Jim Doyle); "West to Glory" 1947; "Buckaroo from Powder River" 1948 (Dave Ryland); "Man Without a Star" 1955 (Hammer); "The First Traveling Saleslady" 1956 (Oldtimer). ¶TV: *Wild Bill Hickok*—"Kangaroo Kapers" 3-10-53; *Sergeant Preston of the Yukon*—"One Good Turn" 3-8-56 (Mike Ferguson); *Rawhide*—"Incident of the Sharpshooter" 2-26-60.

McGregor, Charles. Films: "Blazing Saddles" 1974; "Take a Hard Ride" 1974-Ital./Brit./Ger. (Cloyd).

McGregor, Gordon. Films: "A Deal in Indians" 1915; "The Ruse of the Rattlesnake" 1921 (Henry Morgan); "Singled-Handed" 1923 (the Boss).

MacGregor, Katherine. TV: *Little House on the Prairie*—Regular 1974-82 (Harriet Oleson).

MacGregor, Lee (1927-6/61). Films: "Ticket to Tomahawk" 1950 (Gilo); "Two Flags West" 1950 (Cal); "Best of the Badmen" 1951 (Lieutenant); "Hot Lead" 1951 (Bob); "The Half-Breed" 1952 (Lt. Mon-

roe); "Toughest Man in Arizona" 1952 (Jerry Girard).

McGregor, Malcolm (1892-4/29/45). Films: "Broken Chains" 1922 (Peter Wyndham); "The Vanishing American" 1925 (Earl Ramsdale).

MacGregor, Park (1907-12/5/62). Films: "Yukon Vengeance" 1954. ¶TV: *Wild Bill Hickok*—"Behind Southern Lines" 6-26-51, "Pony Express vs. Telegraph" 9-25-51, "A Joke on Sir Antony" 4-1-52, "Golden Rainbow" 12-9-52.

MacGregor, Warren. Films: "Distant Drums" 1951 (Pvt. Sullivan); "Lone Star" 1952 (Rancher).

McGuinn, Joe (1904-9/22/71). Films: "The Marshal of Mesa City" 1939 (Pete); "Zorro's Fighting Legion" 1939-serial (Soldier #4); "Billy the Kid Outlawed" 1940 (Pete Morgan); "The Dark Command" 1940; "Pals of the Silver Sage" 1940 (Cowhide); "Pioneers of the West" 1940 (Sheriff Gorham); "Ride, Tenderfoot, Ride" 1940 (Martin); "Texas Renegades" 1940 (Jeff); "Wagons Westward" 1940; "Back in the Saddle" 1941 (Sheriff Simpson); "Roaring Frontiers" 1941; "Thunder Over the Prairie" 1941 (Hartley); "Bells of Capistrano" 1942; "Bullets for Bandits" 1942; "The Cyclone Kid" 1942 (Ames); "The Devil's Trail" 1942; "Prairie Gunsmoke" 1942; "Riders of the Northland" 1942 (Stacy); "Shut My Big Mouth" 1942 (Hank); "The Sundown Kid" 1942; "Saddles and Sagebrush" 1943; "The Cherokee Flash" 1945; "Sunset in El Dorado" 1945; "Colorado Ambush" 1951; "South Pacific Trail" 1952 (Ace); "Hannah Lee" 1953 (3rd Villager); "Jack McCall, Desperado" 1953 (U.S. Marshal); "Showdown at Boot Hill" 1958 (Mr. Creavy); "The Gambler Wore a Gun" 1961 (Hastings); "The Wild Westerners" 1962 (Sam Clay). ¶TV: *The Gene Autry Show*—"Dry Gulch at Devil's Elbow" 9-8-53; *The Texan*—"The Hemp Tree" 11-17-58 (Sam Chase); *Wichita Town*—"The Long Night" 1-20-60 (Sheriff); *Wyatt Earp*—"The Doctor" 10-4-60 (Harms); *The Legend of Jesse James*—"The Pursuers" 10-11-65 (Storekeeper).

McGuire, Barry (1937-). TV: *Gunsmoke*—"Dirt" 3-1-58 (Henry Troyman), "Kitty's Rebellion" 2-7-59 (Billy Chris); *Hotel De Paree*—"Sundance and the Delayed Gun" 6-3-60 (Ferguson); *The Virginian*—"Big Day, Great Day" 10-24-62.

McGuire, Biff (1926-). TV: *Gunsmoke*—"The Fourth Victim" 11-

4-74 (Potter); *Hallmark Hall of Fame*—"The Court-Martial of General George Armstrong Carter" 12-1-77 (General Terry).

McGuire, Dorothy (1918-). Films: "Callaway Went Thataway" 1951 (Deborah Patterson); "Friendly Persuasion" 1956 (Eliza Birdwell); "Old Yeller" 1957 (Katie Coates).

McGuire, Harp (1921-10/21/66). TV: *Colt .45*—"Bounty List" 5-31-60; *Tales of Wells Fargo*—"Rifles for Red Hand" 5-15-61 (Matt Taylor), "Don't Wake a Tiger" 5-12-62 (Deputy); *The Tall Man*—"The Long Way Home" 3-31-62 (Joe Touhy).

McGuire, J.A. Films: "The Angel of the Desert" 1913; "The Sage Brush Girl" 1915; "The Untamed" 1920 (Morgan).

McGuire, John (-10/2/80). Films: "Guns for Hire" 1932; "Outlaw Rule" 1935 (Danny Taylor); "End of the Trail" 1936 (Larry Pearson); "Bells of San Angelo" 1947 (Rex Gridley); "River Lady" 1948 (Collins); "The Strawberry Roan" 1948 (Bud Williams). ¶TV: *The Lone Ranger*—"Man of the House" 1-26-50.

McGuire, Kathryn (1904-10/10/78). Films: "The Silent Call" 1921 (Betty Houston); "The Gold Hunters" 1925 (Miss Drew); "Two-Fisted Jones" 1925 (Mary Mortimer); "Buffalo Bill on the U.P. Trail" 1926 (Millie); "Davy Crockett at the Fall of the Alamo" 1926 (Alice Blake); "The Border Wildcat" 1928 (Mary Bell); "The Big Diamond Robbery" 1929 (Ellen Brooks); "The Long, Long Trail" 1929 (Ophelia).

McGuire, Paul. Films: "Raiders of Tomahawk Creek" 1950 (Sheriff); "Bonanza Town" 1951 (Marshall Reed); "Sierra Passage" 1951 (Andy); "Yukon Manhunt" 1951; "Son of Belle Star" 1953 (Pinkly); "Thunder Pass" 1954; "Seminole Uprising" 1955 (Spence); "The Spoilers" 1955 (Thompson); "Reprisal!" 1956 (Whitey); "Secret of Treasure Mountain" 1956 (Sheriff). ¶TV: *Wild Bill Hickok*—"Marriage Feud of Ponca City" 5-13-52, "The Gorilla of Owl Hoot Mesa" 9-23-52, "Great Obstacle Race" 3-3-53; *The Range Rider*—"Buckskin" 9-27-52; *Sergeant Preston of the Yukon*—"Luck of the Trail" 1-5-56, "The Assassins" 6-7-56 (Gordon), "Vindication of Yukon" 7-5-56 (Bascom), "Turnabout" 8-22-56 (Jack Garfield), "Boy Alone" 2-20-58 (Inspector); *Death Valley Days*—"Pay Dirt" 6-23-56 (Don Daley); *Tales of the Texas Rangers*—"Kickback" 12-12-58 (J.F.); *Rawhide*—"Incident of the Judas Trap" 6-5-59; *Wyatt Earp*—"China Mary" 3-15-60 (Ferguson).

McGuire, Tom (1874-5/6/54). Films: "Singled-Handed" 1923 (Macklin); "The Spoilers" 1923 (Captain Stevens); "Her Man" 1924; "My Own Pal" 1926 (Pat McGuire).

McGuire, Tucker (1913-8/88). Films: "The Sheriff of Fractured Jaw" 1958-Brit. (Luke's Wife).

McHattie, Stephen (1947-). Films: "Geronimo: An American Legend" 1993 (Schoonover). ¶TV: *Centennial*—Regular 1978-79 (Jacques Pasquinel).

Machiavelli, Nicoletta (1945-). Films: "The Hills Run Red" 1966-Ital. (Mary Ann); "Navajo Joe" 1966-Ital./Span. (Estella); "Face to Face" 1967-Ital.; "Garter Colt" 1967-Ital./Span./Ger. (Lulu); "A Minute to Pray, a Second to Die" 1967-Ital. (Laurinda); "Hate Thy Neighbor" 1969-Ital.; "No Room to Die" 1969-Ital.

Macht, Stephen (1942-). Films: "The Mountain Men" 1980 (Heavy Eagle). ¶TV: *Big Hawaii*—"Pipeline" 10-12-77 (Max Gentry).

McHugh, Charles (1870-10/21/31). Films: "Nan of Music Mountain" 1917; "Fame and Fortune" 1918 (Judge Quinn); "The Eagle's Feather" 1923 (the Irishman); "The Girl of the Golden West" 1923 (Trinidad Joe); "Brand of Cowardice" 1925; "Phantom of the Range" 1928 (Tim O'Brien).

McHugh, Frank (1899-9/11/81). Films: "Wide Open Spaces" 1932-short; "The Telegraph Trail" 1933 (Sgt. Tippy); "Dodge City" 1939 (Joe Clemens); "Virginia City" 1940 (Mr. Upjohn). ¶TV: *Studio One*—"The Silent Gun" 2-6-56; *The Outlaws*—"Outrage at Pawnee Bend" 4-6-61 (John Buttery); *Wagon Train*—"The Duke Shannon Story" 4-26-61 (Henry Shannon); *F Troop*—"Will the Real Captain Try to Stand Up" 5-10-66 (Charlie Charles); *Lancer*—"The Fix-It Man" 2-11-69 (Charlie Wingate).

McHugh, Grace (1898-7/1/14). Films: "Across the Border" 1914.

McHugh, Matt (1894-2/22/71). Films: "The Last Trail" 1933 (Looney McCann); "The Country Beyond" 1936 (Constable Weller); "The Phantom Rider" 1936-serial; "Heroes of the Saddle" 1940; "Rangers of Fortune" 1940 (Horatio Wells); "Riding High" 1943 (Murphy); "Salome, Where She Danced" 1945 (Lafe); "Return of the Frontiersman" 1950 (Harvey). ¶TV: *The Lone Ranger*—"Billie the Great" 3-30-50.

McIllwain, William (1863-5/27/33). Films: "Reckless Courage" 1925 (Butler).

McIntire, Holly. TV: *Wagon Train*—"The Sara Proctor Story" 2-27-63 (Jenny Graham), "The Bleeker Story" 12-9-63 (Holly Bleeker); *Gunsmoke*—"Prairie Wolfer" 1-18-64 (Sarah Guthrie); *Rawhide*—"The Backshooter" 11-27-64 (Miss Tasker).

McIntire, John (1907-1/30/91). Films: "Black Bart" 1948 (Clark); "River Lady" 1948 (Mr. Morrison); "Red Canyon" 1949 (Floyd Cordt); "Ambush" 1950 (Frank Holly); "Saddle Tramp" 1950 (Hess Higgins); "Winchester '73" 1950 (Joe Lamont); "Westward the Women" 1951 (Roy Whitman); "Horizons West" 1952 (Ira Hammond); "The Lawless Breed" 1952 (J.C. Hardin/John Clements); "War Arrow" 1953 (Col. Jackson Meade); "Apache" 1954 (Al Sieber); "Four Guns to the Border" 1954 (Dutch); "The Yellow Mountain" 1954 (Bannon); "The Far Country" 1955 (Mr. Gannon); "The Kentuckian" 1955 (Zack); "The Spoilers" 1955 (Dextry); "Stranger on Horseback" 1955 (Josiah Bannerman); "Backlash" 1956 (Jim Bonniwell); "The Tin Star" 1957 (Dr. McCord); "The Light in the Forest" 1958 (John Elder); "The Gunfight at Dodge City" 1959 (Doc); "Flaming Star" 1960 (Pa Burton); "Seven Ways from Sundown" 1960 (Sgt. Hennessey); "Two Rode Together" 1961 (Maj. Frazer); "Rough Night in Jericho" 1967 (Ben Hicman); "Powderkeg" TVM-1971 (Cyrus Davenport); "Rooster Cogburn" 1975 (Judge Parker); "The New Daughters of Joshua Cabe" TVM-1976 (Sheriff Joshua Cabe). ¶TV: *Cimarron City*—"Chinese Invasion" 3-21-59 (Judson); *Wanted—Dead or Alive*—"Crossroad" 4-11-59 (Bannister); *Zane Grey Theater*—"Mission to Marathon" 5-14-59 (Major Samuels); *Wagon Train*—"The Andrew Hale Story" 6-3-59 (Andrew Hale), Regular 1961-65 (Chris Hale), "The Levi Hale Story" 4-18-62 (Levi Hale); *Laramie*—"The Lawbreakers" 10-20-59 (Judge Cade), "The Passing of Kuba Smith" 1-3-61 (Kuba Smith); *Wichita Town*—"Drifting" 10-28-59 (Frank Matheson), "Paid in Full" 3-23-60 (Frank); *Overland Trail*—"The Most Dangerous Gentleman" 6-5-60 (William Palmer); *Bonanza*—"The Bride" 1-21-61 (Sheriff Mike Latimer), "Old Charlie" 11-6-66 (Charlie); *Daniel Boone*—"The Reunion" 3-11-65 (Timothy Patrick Bryan), "The Thanksgiving Story" 11-25-65 (Timothy Patrick Bryan); *A Man Called Shenandoah*—"Care of General

Delivery" 5-9-66 (Simon); *Dundee and the Culhane*—"The Dead Man's Brief" 10-4-67 (Sheriff Moss); *The Virginian*—Regular 1967-70 (Clay Grainger); *Dirty Sally*—"Right of Way" 1-11-74; *Young Maverick*—"Dead Man's Hand" 12-26-79 & 1-2-80 (Vernon Maywood).

McIntire, Tim (1944-4/15/86). Films: "Shenandoah" 1965 (Henry Anderson). ¶TV: *Wagon Train*—"The Bleeker Story" 12-9-63 (Dave Bleeker), "The Last Circle Up" 4-27-64 (Dewey Jameson), "Herman" 2-14-65 (William Temple); *Bonanza*—"Logan's Treasure" 10-18-64 (Mike), "A Dublin Lad" 1-2-66 (Jeb), "Old Charlie" 11-6-66 (Billy Barker/George Barker); *Gunsmoke*—"The Storm" 9-25-65 (Claude Benteen); *Death Valley Days*—"The Lawless Have Laws" 11-6-65 (Lorenzo Oatman), "Traveling Trees" 11-13-65; *Rawhide*—"Brush War at Buford" 11-23-65 (Court Buford); *The Big Valley*—"Last Train to the Fair" 4-27-66 (Andy Moyers); *Iron Horse*—"The Pembrooke Blood" 1-9-67 (Harlan Pembrooke); *The Virginian*—"Sue Ann" 1-11-67 (Milt), "The Death Wagon" 1-3-68 (Marcus Veda), "Nora" 12-11-68 (Lt. Tim O'Hara), "The Sins of the Father" 3-4-70 (John Wesley Hardin); *Kung Fu*—"An Eye for an Eye" 1-25-73 (Samuel Buchanan), "The Well" 9-27-73 (Deputy Mitchell), "Barbary House" 2-15-75 (Danny Caine), "Flight to Orion" 2-22-75 (Danny Caine), "The Brothers Cain" 3-1-75 (Danny Caine), "Full Circle" 3-15-75 (Danny Caine).

McIntosh, Burr (1862-4/28/42). Films: "The Buckaroo Kid" 1926 (Henry Radigan); "The Golden Stallion" 1927-serial.

MacIntosh, Jay W. TV: *Bonanza*—"Saddle Stiff" 1-16-72 (Sally); *Gunsmoke*—"Tatum" 11-13-72 (Gwen); *Centennial*—Regular 1978-79 (Emma Lloyd).

MacIntyre, Christine (1916-7/8/84). Films: "The Rangers' Roundup" 1938 (Mary); "Forbidden Trails" 1941 (Mary); "The Gunman from Bodie" 1941; "Dawn on the Great Divide" 1942 (Mary); "Riders of the West" 1942 (Hope); "Rock River Renegades" 1942; "Border Buckaroos" 1943 (Betty Clark); "The Stranger from Pecos" 1943 (Ruth); "Partners of the Trail" 1944 (Kate); "West of the Rio Grande" 1944; "Frontier Feud" 1945 (Blanche); "Pistol Packin' Nitwits" 1945-short; "Gentleman from Texas" 1946; "Three Trouble-doers" 1946-short (Nell); "Gun Talk"

1947 (Daisy); "Land of the Lawless" 1947; "Out West" 1947-short (Nell); "Valley of Fear" 1947; "Punchy Cow-punchers" 1950-short (Nell); "Colorado Ambush" 1951 (Mae Star); "Wanted Dead or Alive" 1951; "Pals and Gals" 1954-short (Nell).

McIntyre, Leila (1892-1/9/53). Films: "The Plainsman" 1936 (Mary Todd Lincoln).

McIntyre, Marvin J. Films: "Pale Rider" 1985 (Jagou); "Silverado" 1985 (Clerk); "Back to the Future, Part III" 1990 (Mortician).

McIntyre, Peggy. Films: "El Paso" 1949 (Mary "Lizbeth" Fletcher).

McIvor, Mary (1901-2/28/41). Films: "The Square Deal Man" 1917 (Virginia Ransome); "The Mints of Hell" 1919 (Kit Hibbing); "The Burning Trail" 1925 (Nell Loring).

Mack, Betty (1901-11/5/80). Films: "God's Country and the Man" 1931 (Rose); "Headin' for Trouble" 1931 (Mary Courtney); "Law of the Rio Grande" 1931 (Judy Lanning); "The Man from Death Valley" 1931 (Ann); "Partners of the Trail" 1931 (Ruby Gerard); "The Forty-Niners" 1932 (Virginia Hawkins); "Galloping Thru" 1932; "Scarlet Brand" 1932 (Ellen Walker); "The Fighting Texans" 1933 (Rita Walsh); "The Last of the Clintons" 1935 (Edith Elkins); "Outlaw Rule" 1935 (Kay Lathrop); "The Reckless Buckaroo" 1935; "Hair-Trigger Casey" 1936 (Jane Elkins); "Senor Jim" 1936 (Bunny Stafford); "Toll of the Desert" 1936 (Jean Streeter); "Rough Ridin' Rhythm" 1937 (Ethyle Horne); "The Pal from Texas" 1939 (Queenie).

Mack, Bobby. Films: "The Red Ace" 1917-serial; "Human Stuff" 1920 (Butler); "While Satan Sleeps" 1922 (Bones); "The Range Terror" 1925 (Sims); "The Bandit's Son" 1927 (Jake Kirby).

Mack, Cactus (Curtis McPeters, Taylor MacPeters) (1899-4/17/62). Films: "The Western Code" 1932; "Moonlight on the Prairie" 1935; "Rough Riding Ranger" 1935; "Stormy" 1935 (Wrangler); "Avenging Waters" 1936; "Custer's Last Stand" 1936-serial (Lieutenant Weir); "The Phantom Rider" 1936-serial; "The Unknown Ranger" 1936; "Blazing Sixes" 1937; "Knight of the Plains" 1938; "Man from Music Mountain" 1938; "The Rangers' Roundup" 1938 (Art); "Rolling Caravans" 1938 (Happy); "The Fighting Gringo" 1939 (Utah Jones); "In Old Montana" 1939; "The Lone Ranger

Rides Again" 1939-serial (Townsman #2); "The Marshal of Mesa City" 1939 (Deputy); "New Frontier" 1939; "The Night Riders" 1939; "The Oregon Trail" 1939-serial; "Racketeers of the Range" 1939 (Flash); "Saga of Death Valley" 1939; "Timber Stampede" 1939 (Frank); "Two-Gun Troubador" 1939; "Zorro's Fighting Legion" 1939-serial (Cisco); "Bullet Code" 1940 (Cowhand); "Corralling a School Marm" 1940-short; "Molly Cures a Cowboy" 1940-short; "One Man's Law" 1940; "Prairie Law" 1940; "The Trail Blazers" 1940; "The Tulsa Kid" 1940; "The Apache Kid" 1941; "In Old Cheyenne" 1941; "Kansas Cyclone" 1941; "Outlaws of the Cherokee Trail" 1941; "Prairie Pioneers" 1941; "Prairie Spooners" 1941-short; "The Singing Hill" 1941; "West of Cimarron" 1941; "Wyoming Wildcat" 1941; "Code of the Outlaw" 1942; "Heart of the Golden West" 1942; "Outlaws of Pine Ridge" 1942; "Raiders of the Range" 1942; "The Sundown Kid" 1942; "Sunset on the Desert" 1942; "Beyond the Last Frontier" 1943; "Outlaws of Stampede Pass" 1943; "Overland Mail Robbery" 1943; "Sagebrush Law" 1943; "Thundering Trails" 1943; "Hidden Valley Outlaws" 1944; "Sheriff of Sundown" 1944; "Stagecoach to Monterey" 1944; "Oregon Trail" 1945; "Rough Riders of Cheyenne" 1945; "The Phantom Rider" 1946-serial (Joe); "Shadows on the Range" 1946; "Silver Range" 1946; "Trigger Fingers" 1946; "Trail to Mexico" 1946; "Gun Talk" 1947 (Marshal Wetherby); "Land of the Lawless" 1947; "Raiders of the South" 1947; "Six Gun Serenade" 1947; "Son of Zorro" 1947-serial (Green/Raider #2); "Trailing Danger" 1947; "Valley of Fear" 1947; "The Gallant Legion" 1948; "Range Renegades" 1948; "The Rangers Ride" 1948; "Sundown Riders" 1948 (Walker); "The Dalton Gang" 1949 (Stage Driver); "Desperadoes of the West" 1950-serial (Drake); "The James Brothers of Missouri" 1950-serial (Heavy #2); "Don Daredevil Rides Again" 1951-serial (Turner); "The Big Sky" 1952; "The First Traveling Saleslady" 1956 (Rancher); "Heller in Pink Tights" 1960. ¶TV: *The Cisco Kid*—"Medicine Man Story" 8-25-51, "Black Lightning" 10-6-51, "Talking Dog" 2-23-52; *Gunsmoke*—"Marry Me" 12-23-61 (Pa Cathcart).

Mack, Charles W. (1878-11/29/56). Films: "The Bandit's Baby" 1925 (Doctor); "Silent Pal" 1925 (Lazarus).

Mack, Fred. Films: "Jacques of the Silver North" 1919 (Malamute Mike).

Mack, Hayward (1879-12/24/21). Films: "The Goddess of Lost Lake" 1918 (Chester Martin); "The Winding Trail" 1918 (Alvin Steele); "Fighting Through" 1919 (Raymond Haynes); "Put Up Your Hands" 1919 (Alvin Thorne); "Some Liar" 1919 (Sheldon Lewis Kellard); "The Gamesters" 1920 (Jim Welch).

Mack, Helen (1913-8/13/86). Films: "The California Trail" 1933 (Dolores Ramirez); "Fargo Express" 1933 (Helen Clark).

Mack, Hughie (1884-10/13/27). Films: "Some Duel" 1915; "The Riddle Rider" 1924-serial; "The Arizona Whirlwind" 1927 (Gonzales).

Mack, James T. (1871-8/12/48). Films: "The Texans" 1938 (Moody Citizen).

Mack, Joseph P. (1878-4/8/46). Films: "Wild Honey" 1918 (Jim Belcher); "Canyon Passage" 1946 (Miner).

Mack, Robert (1877-5/2/49). Films: "The Cowboy and the Lady" 1922 (Justice of the Peace); "The Timber Wolf" 1925 (Billy Winch).

Mack, Stanley. Films: "Gun Smoke" 1931 (Jassy Quinn).

Mack, Tommy. Films: "Law of the Texan" 1938 (Juan); "The Kid from Texas" 1939 (Indian).

Mack, Wayne. Films: "The Outlaws Is Coming!" 1965 (Jesse James).

Mack, Wilbur (1873-5/13/64). Films: "Gold and Grit" 1925 (Jack Crawford); "The Love of Paquita" 1927; "Shooting Straight" 1927 (Black Brody); "Straight Shootin'" 1927 (Black Brody); "Beauty and Bullets" 1928 (Frank Crawford); "The Crimson Canyon" 1928 (Sam Slade); "The Death's Head" 1928; "Quick Triggers" 1928 (Jeff Thorne); "A Tenderfoot Hero" 1928; "Just in Time" 1929; "Red Romance" 1929; "The Thrill Hunter" 1929; "The Plainsman" 1936; "New Frontier" 1939 (Dodge); "Union Pacific" 1939 (Bartender); "Trail of the Yukon" 1949. ¶TV: *Trackdown*—"The Governor" 5-23-58 (Ben Morgan).

Mack, Willard (1879-11/18/34). Films: "Nanette of the Wilds" 1916 (Constable Thomas O'Brien).

Mackaill, Dorothy (1904-8/12/90). Films: "The Mine with the Iron Door" 1924 (Marta); "Ranson's Folly" 1926 (Mary Cahill); "The Great Divide" 1929 (Ruth Jordan).

McKay, Allison (1938-). TV: *Here Come the Brides*—"The Fetching of Jenny" 12-5-69.

McKay, Ann. Films: "Gold and Grit" 1925 (Helen Mason); "Roarin' Broncs" 1927 (Rose Tracy).

McKay, Belva. Films: "Comin an' Going" 1926 (Rose Brown).

Mackay, Charles (1867-11/19/35). Films: "The Man She Brought Back" 1922 (Major Shanley).

McKay, Doreen. Films: "Pals of the Saddle" 1938 (Ann); "The Night Riders" 1939 (Soledad).

McKay, Gardner (1932-). TV: *Boots and Saddles*—Regular 1957-59 (Lieutenant Kelly); *Death Valley Days*—"The Big Rendezvous" 4-15-58; *Jefferson Drum*—"Showdown" 9-26-58 (Simon Easton).

McKay, George (1880-12/3/45). Films: "End of the Trail" 1936 (Ben Parker); "Beyond the Sacramento" 1940 (Bartender); "Klondike Kate" 1942 (Bartender).

MacKay, Jeff. Films: "The Wild Wild West Revisited" TVM-1979 (Hugo Kaufman). ¶TV: *Outlaws*—"Madrid" 2-7-87 (Redman).

McKay, Peggy. TV: *Gunsmoke*—"Bottleman" 3-22-58 (Flora Clell), "Chato" 9-14-70 (Mrs. Cooper); *How the West Was Won*—Episode One 2-12-78 (Maggie Taylor).

McKay, Scotty (1915-3/16/87). Films: "Duel in the Sun" 1946 (Sid).

McKay, Wanda. Films: "The Pioneers" 1941 (Suzanna); "The Royal Mounted Patrol" 1941 (Betty Duvalle); "Twilight on the Trail" 1941 (Lucy); "Law and Order" 1942 (Linda); "Rolling Down the Great Divide" 1942 (Rita); "Texas Justice" 1942 (Kate Stewart); "Deerslayer" 1943 (Hetty); "Belle of the Yukon" 1944 (Cherie Atterbury); "Raiders of Ghost City" 1944-serial (Cathy Haines). ¶TV: *The Lone Ranger*—"Paid in Full" 12-28-50, "Trouble at Black Rock" 2-8-51; *The Cisco Kid*—"Medicine Man Story" 8-25-51, "Black Lightning" 10-6-51.

MacKaye, Fred. Films: "King of the Arena" 1933; "Gun Justice" 1934 (Imposter); "Honor of the Range" 1934; "Smoking Guns" 1934; "Wheels of Destiny" 1934 (Red); "Rustlers of Red Dog" 1935-serial (Snakey); "Black Aces" 1937 (Len Stoddard).

McKee, Blaisdell. TV: *The Big Valley*—"Pursuit" 10-10-66 (Nameh), "Flight from San Miguel" 4-28-69 (Francisco); *Iron Horse*—"The Red Tornado" 2-20-67 (Gato); *Daniel Boone*—"The Flaming Rocks" 2-1-68; *Hondo*—"Hondo and the Commancheros" 11-10-67 (Paco).

McKee, John. Films: "Loaded Pistols" 1948; "Challenge of the Range" 1949 (Cowpuncher); "Rim of the Canyon" 1949 (Tex Rawlins); "Indian Territory" 1950; "Mule Train" 1950; "Gene Autry and the Mounties" 1951; "Silver Canyon" 1951; "Texans Never Cry" 1951 (Ed Durham); "Vengeance Valley" 1951 (Player); "Thunder Over the Plains" 1953; "The Big Country" 1958 (Terrill Cowboy); "Showdown" 1963 (Marshal Beaudine); "Cheyenne Autumn" 1964 (Trooper); "The Hallelujah Trail" 1965 (Rafe Pike); "The Professionals" 1966 (Sheriff); "Monte Walsh" 1970 (Petey Williams); "Rio Lobo" 1970 (Official); "Ulzana's Raid" 1972; "Nevada Smith" TVM-1975 (McLane); "Banjo Hackett: Roamin' Free" TVM-1976 (Official). ¶TV: *The Roy Rogers Show*—"Fishing for Fingerprints" 10-28-56, "Mountain Pirates" 11-4-56; *Maverick*—"The Spanish Dancer" 12-14-58 (3rd Miner); *The Texan*—"The Marshal of Yellow Jacket" 3-2-59 (Ranch Hand), "The Smiling Loser" 5-25-59 (Ranch Hand); *The Deputy*—"Shadow of the Noose" 10-3-59 (Hollister); *Riverboat*—"Three Graves" 3-14-60 (Stoneman); *Laramie*—"Ladies Day" 10-3-61; *The Tall Man*—"The Long Way Home" 3-31-62 (Marshal Thomas); *The Virginian*—"The Man from the Sea" 12-26-62; *Wagon Train*—"The Bleeker Story" 12-9-63 (Quincy); *Rawhide*—"Incident of the Gilded Goddess" 4-30-64 (Posse Leader); *Cimarron Strip*—"The Roarer" 11-2-67, "Without Honor" 2-29-68; *Iron Horse*—"Dry Run to Glory" 1-6-68 (Pops); *Lancer*—"Foley" 10-15-68; *The High Chaparral*—"The Little Thieves" 12-26-69; *The Cowboys*—"The Accused" 3-13-74 (Foley).

McKee, Lafe (1872-8/10/59). Films: "The Fifty Man" 1914; "How Callahan Cleaned Up Little Hell" 1915; "The Silent Rider" 1918 (Jim Carson); "The Daredevil" 1920 (Sheriff of Coyote Flats); "Blazing Arrows" 1922 (Elias Thornby); "Blood Test" 1923; "The Lone Wagon" 1923; "Bringin' Home the Bacon" 1924; "Hard Hittin' Hamilton" 1924 (Jim Downing); "Rainbow Rangers" 1924 (Luke Warner); "Thundering Romance" 1924 (Sheriff); "Western Grit" 1924 (Jed Black); "Double Action Daniels" 1925 (the Banker); "Fort Frayne" 1925 (Col. John Farrar); "The Human Tornado" 1925 (Peter Daley); "The Mystery Box" 1925-serial; "On the Go" 1925 (Mr. Hall); "Saddle Cyclone" 1925 (Burns); "Triple Action" 1925 (Don

Pio Mendez); "Warrior Gap" 1925 (John Folsom); "Baited Trap" 1926 (Bobbie's Father); "The Bandit Buster" 1926 (Henry Morton); "The Bonanza Buckaroo" 1926 (Andrew Gordon); "Rawhide" 1926 (the Law); "Twin Triggers" 1926 (Silas Trigger); "West of the Law" 1926 (Jim Armstrong); "The Ridin' Rowdy" 1927 (Doc); "Roarin' Broncs" 1927; "The Ballyhoo Buster" 1928; "Desperate Courage" 1928 (Brannon Brother); "Manhattan Cowboy" 1928; "On the Divide" 1928; "The Painted Trail" 1928 (Dan Winters); "The Riding Renegade" 1928 (Sheriff Jim Taylor); "Saddle Mates" 1928 (Grouchy Ferris); "The Trail Riders" 1928; "Trailin' Back" 1928; "The Upland Rider" 1928 (John Graham); "The Amazing Vagabond" 1929 (Phil Dunning); "The California Mail" 1929 (William Butler); "Breed of the West" 1930 (Mr. Sterner); "Code of Honor" 1930 (Dad Bradfield); "The Lone Defender" 1930-serial (Sheriff Billings); "The Lonesome Trail" 1930 (Sheriff); "Men Without Law" 1930; "Near the Rainbow's End" 1930 (Tom Bledsoe); "Shadow Ranch" 1930; "Under Montana Skies" 1930 (Pinky); "The Utah Kid" 1930 (Parson Joe); "Alias the Bad Man" 1931 (Clem Neville); "Branded" 1931; "Cyclone Kid" 1931 (Harvey Comstock); "The Fighting Marshal" 1931 (Clint Wheeler); "Hell's Valley" 1931; "Hurricane Horseman" 1931 (Senor Roberto); "Lightning Warrior" 1931-serial (Hayden); "Partners of the Trail" 1931 (Sheriff McWade); "The Pocatello Kid" 1931; "Range Law" 1931 (Frisco); "Red Fork Range" 1931 (Charles Farrell); "The Two Gun Man" 1931 (Joe Kearney); "The Vanishing Legion" 1931-serial (Hornback); "West of Cheyenne" 1931 (Lafe Langdon); "Battling Buckaroo" 1932 (Don Felipe Mendoza); "The Big Stampede" 1932 (Cal Brett); "The Boiling Point" 1932 (Tom Kirk); "Dynamite Ranch" 1932; "End of the Trail" 1932 (Colonel Burke); "Fighting Champ" 1932 (Sheriff Jim Cosgrove); "Fighting for Justice" 1932 (Sam Tracey); "The Gay Buckaroo" 1932 (Sporty Bill Field); "Gold" 1932 (Jeff Sellers); "Hell Fire Austin" 1932 (Uncle Joe); "Hello Trouble" 1932 (Sheriff Edwards); "Klondike" 1932 (Seth); "The Man from New Mexico" 1932 (Sheriff); "Mark of the Spur" 1932 (Hardshell Beckett); "Ride Him, Cowboy" 1932; "Ridin' for Justice" 1932; "The Riding Tornado" 1932 (Hiram Olcott); "Spirit of the West" 1932 (Bowie Moore); "The Texan" 1932; "Tombstone Canyon"

1932 (Colonel Lee); "Without Honor" 1932 (Frank Henderson); "Young Blood" 1932 (Colonel Bondage); "Crossfire" 1933 (Daniel Plummer); "Deadwood Pass" 1933 (Sheriff Rawlins); "The Dude Bandit" 1933 (Brown); "The Fighting Texans" 1933 (Sheriff Carver); "Fighting with Kit Carson" 1933-serial; "Galloping Romeo" 1933 (Marshal); "Jaws of Justice" 1933 (Seeker Dean); "King of the Arena" 1933; "Lariats and Sixshooters" 1933; "The Man from Monterey" 1933 (Don Jose Castanares); "Man of Action" 1933 (Matt Sherman); "Riders of Destiny" 1933 (Sheriff Bill Baxter); "The Telegraph Trail" 1933 (Lafe, the Old-timer); "Terror Trail" 1933 (Shay); "The Trail Drive" 1933 (Jameson); "War on the Range" 1933; "Blue Steel" 1934 (Dad Mason); "The Border Menace" 1934; "Boss Cowboy" 1934 (Nolan); "A Demon for Trouble" 1934 (Sheriff); "The Dude Ranger" 1934; "The Fighting Trooper" 1934 (Trapper); "Frontier Days" 1934 (Grandpa Wilson); "Gun Justice" 1934; "Honor of the Range" 1934; "The Law of the Wild" 1934-serial; "Lightning Bill" 1934 (Tom Ross); "Lightning Bill" 1934; "Lightning Range" 1934 (Judge Williams); "The Man from Utah" 1934 (Judge Carter); "Mystery Mountain" 1934-serial (Mr. Corwin); "Mystery Ranch" 1934; "Nevada Cyclone" 1934; "Outlaws' Highway" 1934 (Sheriff Hibbs); "Rawhide Mail" 1934 (Sheriff); "Rawhide Romance" 1934 (Roger Whitney); "Ridin' Gent" 1934-short; "Riding Speed" 1934 (John Vale); "West of the Divide" 1934 (Winters); "The Westerner" 1934; "Big Boy Rides Again" 1935 (Tap Smiley); "Blazing Guns" 1935 (John Rickard); "Cheyenne Tornado" 1935; "The Cowboy and the Bandit" 1935; "Coyote Trails" 1935 (John Baker); "Desert Trail" 1935 (Sheriff Barker); "The Ghost Rider" 1935 (Jake); "Gunsmoke on the Guadalupe" 1935; "Heir to Trouble" 1935; "Ivory-Handled Gun" 1935 (Sheriff Crane); "Kid Courageous" 1935; "The Last of the Clintons" 1935; "Law of the 45's" 1935 (Hayden); "The Miracle Rider" 1935-serial; "Northern Frontier" 1935; "Rainbow Valley" 1935 (Storekeeper); "Range Warfare" 1935; "The Revenge Rider" 1935 (Minister); "Ridin' Thru" 1935 (Dan Brooks); "Riding Wild" 1935; "Rio Rattler" 1935 (Pop); "The Roaring West" 1935-serial; "Rustlers of Red Dog" 1935-serial (Bob Lee); "The Silver Bullet" 1935 (Dad Kane); "Swifty" 1935 (Sandy McGregor);

"Thunderbolt" 1935; "Tracy Rides" 1935 (Jim Green); "Trail of the Hawk" 1935 (Jim King); "Western Justice" 1935 (Sheriff); "Wolf Riders" 1935 (Clark); "The Cowboy and the Kid" 1936 (Sheriff Bailey); "Custer's Last Stand" 1936-serial (Captain Benteen); "Frontier Justice" 1936 (Gordon); "The Fugitive Sheriff" 1936; "Gun Smoke" 1936 (Sheriff); "Heroes of the Range" 1936; "The Kid Ranger" 1936 (Jim Burton); "The Last of the Warrens" 1936 (Sheriff); "Lightning Bill Carson" 1936 (Costillo); "Men of the Plains" 1936 (Ed Green); "The Mysterious Avenger" 1936 (Maitland); "The Phantom Rider" 1936-serial; "Roamin' Wild" 1936 (Dad Parker); "Santa Fe Bound" 1936 (Sheriff); "The Fighting Deputy" 1937 (Frank Denton); "The Idaho Kid" 1937 (John Endicott); "Law of the Ranger" 1937 (Polk); "Lost Ranch" 1937 (Carroll); "Melody of the Plains" 1937 (Langley); "The Mystery of the Hooded Horseman" 1937 (Tom Wilson); "Mystery Range" 1937 (Jed Travis); "North of the Rio Grande" 1937 (Joe); "Orphan of the Pecos" 1937 (Hank Gelbert); "The Painted Stallion" 1937-serial (Boat Officer); "Ranger Courage" 1937; "The Rangers Step In" 1937 (Jed Warren); "Reckless Ranger" 1937; "Santa Fe Rides" 1937; "Wild West Days" 1937-serial; "Brothers of the West" 1938 (Sheriff Bob Bain); "Feud of the Trail" 1938 (John Granger); "Heroes of the Alamo" 1938 (Storekeeper); "I'm from the City" 1938 (Bixby); "Knight of the Plains" 1938 (John Lane); "The Lone Ranger" 1938-serial (Rancher); "Rawhide" 1938 (McDonnell); "Rolling Caravans" 1938 (Henry Rankin); "The Singing Outlaw" 1938; "Six Shootin' Sheriff" 1938 (Zeke); "South of Arizona" 1938 (Lafe Brown); "Stagecoach Days" 1938 (Tom Larkin); "Arizona Legion" 1939; "The Lone Ranger Rides Again" 1939-serial (Townsman #3); "The Man from Sundown" 1939 (Doc Sprague); "The Oregon Trail" 1939-serial; "Trouble in Sundown" 1939; "Bad Man from Red Butte" 1940 (Dan Todhunter); "The Cheyenne Kid" 1940 (Roberts); "Covered Wagon Trails" 1940 (John Bradford); "Pioneer Days" 1940 (Agent); "Pioneers of the Frontier" 1940 (Mort Saunders); "Riders of Pasco Basin" 1940 (Uncle Dan); "Santa Fe Trail" 1940 (Minister); "Son of Roaring Dan" 1940 (Frank Brooks); "When the Dalton's Rode" 1940 (Doctor); "Wild Horse Valley" 1940 (Mr. Kimball); "Wells Fargo Days" 1944-short.

McKee, Raymond (1892-10/3/84). Films: "Capturing Bad Bill" 1915; "Blind Hearts" 1921 (Paul Thomas); "King of the Herd" 1927 (Paul Garrison).

McKee, Scott (1881-4/17/45). Films: "West Is West" 1920 (Nagle).

McKee, Tom (1917-6/20/60). Films: "Fury at Showdown" 1957 (Sheriff of Buckhorn); "Valerie" 1957 (Dave Carlin). ¶TV: *Wild Bill Hickok*—"Wild Bill's Odyssey" 3-31-53; *Tales of the Texas Rangers*—"Return of the Rough Riders" 11-26-55 (Ben Fowler); *The Adventures of Rin Tin Tin*—"Attack on Fort Apache" 4-13-56 (Capt. Davis), "The Silent Battle" 10-5-56 (Davis), "Mother O'Hara's Marriage" 10-25-57, "The Epidemic" 11-21-58 (Captain Davis), "Stagecoach to Phoenix" 1-23-59 (Capt. Davis); *Circus Boy*—"The Knife Thrower" 2-17-57 (Dr. Adams); *Tales of Wells Fargo*—"Alder Gulch" 4-8-57 (Sheriff), "The Governor's Visit" 1-18-60 (Sheriff); *Cheyenne*—"Devil's Canyon" 11-19-57 (Sheriff Pickering); *Maverick*—"The Jeweled Gun" 11-24-57 (La Mesa Sheriff); *Bat Masterson*—"Dynamite Blows Two Ways" 10-22-58 (Swede), "Marked Deck" 3-11-59 (Derelict); *Wagon Train*—"The Ben Courtney Story" 1-28-59 (Vinson); *Yancy Derringer*—"The Gun That Murdered Lincoln" 3-19-59 (General Cochran); *The Deputy*—"The X Game" 5-28-60 (Coyle).

MacKellar, Helen. Films: "The Dark Command" 1940 (Mrs. Hale); "Northwest Passage" 1940 (Sarah Hadden); "Three Faces West" 1940 (Mrs. Welles); "Down Mexico Way" 1941; "Gangs of Sonora" 1941 (Kansas Kate Conners); "The Sundown Kid" 1942 (Lucy Randall).

McKellen, Ian (1935-). Films: "The Ballad of Little Jo" 1993 (Percy Corcoran).

MacKenna, Kenneth (1899-1/15/62). TV: *Bonanza*—"Silent Thunder" 12-10-60 (Sam Croft).

McKennon, Dallas (1919-). Films: "The Glory Guys" 1965 (Gunsmith); "Hot Lead and Cold Feet" 1978. ¶TV: *Wagon Train*—"The Jeremy Dow Story" 12-28-60, "The Will Santee Story" 5-3-61 (Lee), "The Lisa Raincloud Story" 10-31-62 (Jethro), "The Eli Bancroft Story" 11-11-63, "The Kitty Pryer Story" 11-18-63, "The Zebedee Titus Story" 4-20-64; *The Tall Man*—"The Judas Palm" 10-21-61 (Bartender); *Gunsmoke*—"Chesterland" 11-18-61 (Neighbor), "Call Me Dodie" 9-22-62 (Jake); *Laramie*—"Justice in a Hurry" 3-20-62, "Gun Duel" 12-25-62; *The Virginian*—"The Big Deal" 10-10-62 (Lumberyard Owner), "The Small Parade" 2-20-63; *The Rifleman*—"The Bullet" 2-25-63 (Judge Hopkins), "Which Way'd They Go?" 4-1-63 (Judge Moze); *The Big Valley*—"Palms of Glory" 9-15-65 (Abner Wirth); *Bonanza*—"The Oath" 11-20-66 (Jenkins); *Dundee and the Culhane*—11-22-67 (Al); *Daniel Boone*—Regular 1968-70 (Cincinnatus).

MacKenzie, Donald (1879-7/21/72). Films: "The Perils of Pauline" 1914-serial; "Fighting Caravans" 1931 (Gus).

McKenzie, Ella (-4/23/87). Films: "Broncho Billy Begins Life Anew" 1915; "Fade Away Foster" 1926; "The Rest Cure" 1927; "The Man from Guntown" 1935 (Aunt Sarah); "The Mysterious Avenger" 1936 (Miss Gates); "Riders of the Dawn" 1937.

McKenzie, Eva (Eva Heazlit) (1889-9/15/67). Films: "The Book Agent's Romance" 1916; "Boss Cowboy" 1934 (Ranch Woman); "Lightning Bill" 1934 (Mathilda); "Lightning Bill" 1934; "The Mysterious Avenger" 1936 (Mrs. Gates); "The Phantom Rider" 1936-serial; "The Unknown Ranger" 1936; "Pioneer Trail" 1938 (Ma Allen); "Death Rides the Range" 1940 (Letty Morgan); "Triple Justice" 1940; "Down Mexico Way" 1941 (Maria Elena); "Wells Fargo Days" 1944-short.

McKenzie, Fay (1917-). Films: "A Knight of the West" 1921 (Fay Murten); "Boss Cowboy" 1934 (Sally Nolan); "The Sundown Trail" 1934; "When the Dalton's Rode" 1940 (Hannah); "Sierra Sue" 1941 (Sue Larrabee); "Cowboy Serenade" 1942; "Heart of the Rio Grande" 1942 (Alice Bennett); "Home in Wyomin'" 1942 (Clem Benson); "The Singing Sheriff" 1944 (Caroline).

McKenzie, Ida (1912-6/29/86). Films: "Shadows of Conscience" 1921 (Winnie Coburn).

MacKenzie, Joyce. Films: "Broken Arrow" 1950 (Terry); "Ticket to Tomahawk" 1950 (Ruby); "Rails into Laramie" 1954 (Helen Shanessy).

MacKenzie, Patch. TV: *Young Maverick*—"Have I Got a Girl for You" 1-16-80 (Alice).

McKenzie, Richard (1930-). Films: "Doc" 1971 (Sheriff Beham).

McKenzie, Robert "Bob" (1883-7/8/49). Films: "Bullet Proof" 1920 (Dick Wilbur); "The Sheriff of Sun-Dog" 1922 (Harp Harris); "The Devil's Dooryard" 1923 (Windy Woods); "Don Quickshot of the Rio Grande" 1923 (Sheriff Littlejohn); "Singled-Handed" 1923 (Manager); "Where Is This West?" 1923 (Bimbo McGuire); "The Covered Trail" 1924 (Sheriff); "In the West" 1924; "Bad Man's Bluff" 1926 (Hank Dooley); "Fade Away Foster" 1926; "The Fighting Peacemaker" 1926 (Hanna); "One Wild Time" 1926; "A Six Shootin' Romance" 1926 (Ricketts); "One Glorious Scrap" 1927 (Prof. Parkinson); "The Rest Cure" 1927; "Set Free" 1927 (Sam Cole); "Shadow Ranch" 1930 (Fatty); "Cimarron" 1931 (Pat Leary); "The Man from Arizona" 1932; "Rider of Death Valley" 1932; "Ridin' for Justice" 1932 (Spears); "The Fiddlin' Buckaroo" 1934 (Jailer); "Frontier Days" 1934 (Casey); "Gun Justice" 1934; "Thunder Over Texas" 1934 (Judge Blake); "Alias John Law" 1935 (Judge); "Defying the Law" 1935; "Desert Gold" 1935; "Lawless Riders" 1935; "The Man from Guntown" 1935 (Eric McGillis); "Powdersmoke Range" 1935; "Stone of Silver Creek" 1935 (Hotel Proprietor); "Thunderbolt" 1935; "Border Caballero" 1936; "Cavalcade of the West" 1936 (Judge Beasley); "Comin' Round the Mountain" 1936 (Marshal John Hawkins); "The Cowboy and the Kid" 1936 (Hank Simmons); "End of the Trail" 1936 (Town Official); "Feud of the West" 1936; "Lucky Terror" 1936 (Sheriff); "The Mysterious Avenger" 1936 (Horner); "Rebellion" 1936 (Judge Moore); "Rhythm on the Range" 1936 (Farmer); "Ridin' On" 1936 (Doc Onderdonk); "Senor Jim" 1936 (Sheriff Bob Arnett); "Silver Spurs" 1936; "Song of the Trail" 1936 (Bartender); "Sundown Saunders" 1936; "The Unknown Ranger" 1936; "Valley of the Lawless" 1936 (Coupier); "Black Aces" 1937 (Hank Farnum); "God's Country and the Man" 1937 (Storekeeper); "Gunsmoke Ranch" 1937; "Heart of the West" 1937 (Tim Grady); "The Luck of Roaring Camp" 1937 (Tuttle); "Reckless Ranger" 1937; "Smoke Tree Range" 1937; "Sing, Cowboy, Sing" 1937 (Judge Roy Dean); "Stars Over Arizona" 1937; "Wells Fargo" 1937 (U.S. Postmaster Batabia); "Billy the Kid Returns" 1938; "Heart of Arizona" 1938; "Lawless Valley" 1938; "Phantom Ranger" 1938 (Charles); "Pioneer Trail" 1938; "Red River Range" 1938; "The Singing Outlaw" 1938; "A Western Welcome" 1938-short; "The Arizona Wildcat" 1939 (Miner); "Cupid Rides the Range" 1939-short; "Destry Rides Again" 1939 (Doctor); "Frontier Pony Express" 1939; "Ranch House Romeo"

1939-short; "Bullet Code" 1940 (Doctor); "My Little Chickadee" 1940; "The Return of Frank James" 1940 (Old Man on Rocker); "Take Me Back to Oklahoma" 1940 (Ames); "Trail of the Vigilantes" 1940 (Proprietor); "Triple Justice" 1940 (Agent); "Wagon Train" 1940 (Ed); "When the Dalton's Rode" 1940 (Photographer); "A Missouri Outlaw" 1941; "Prairie Spooners" 1941-short; "Sierra Sue" 1941; "In Old California" 1942 (Mr. Bates); "The Sombrero Kid" 1942 (Judge Tater); "The Spoilers" 1942 (Restaurateur); "Red River Robin Hood" 1943; "Sagebrush Law" 1943; "Wild Horse Stampede" 1943; "Death Valley Rangers" 1944 (Doc Blake); "Tall in the Saddle" 1944 (Doc Riding); "Texas Masquerade" 1944 (Rowbottom); "Code of the Lawless" 1945 (Amos Judd); "Wagon Wheels Westward" 1945; "Colorado Serenade" 1946 (Col. Blake); "Duel in the Sun" 1946 (Bartender); "Romance of the West" 1946 (Matthews); "White Stallion" 1947 (Pop Martin).

McKeon, Doug (1966-). TV: *Centennial*—Regular 1978-79 (Philip Wendell).

McKim, Harry. Films: "Days of Old Cheyenne" 1943 (Bobby); "Mojave Firebrand" 1944; "Nevada" 1944 (Marvie Ide); "Wanderer of the Wasteland" 1945 (Adam as a Boy).

McKim, Robert (1887-6/2/27). Films: "The Disciple" 1915 (Doc Hardy); "The Devil's Double" 1916 (Van Dyke Tarleton); "Jim Grimsby's Boy" 1916 (Waldo Whittier); "The Primal Lure" 1916 (Richard Sylvester); "The Return of Draw Egan" 1916 (Arizona Joe); "The Silent Man" 1917 (Handsome Jack Presley); "The Son of His Father" 1917 (David Slosson); "Blue Blazes Rawden" 1918 (Ladyfingers Hilgard); "The Law of the North" 1918 (Caesar LeNoir); "Playing the Game" 1918 (Flash Purdy); "Hell's Hinges" 1919 (Clergyman); "Partners Three" 1919 (Grant Haywood); "Wagon Tracks" 1919 (Donald Washburn); "The Westerners" 1919 (Black Mike Lafond); "Bullet Proof" 1920 (McGuirk); "Mark of Zorro" 1920 (Captain Juan Ramon); "Out of the Dust" 1920 (Brett Arnold); "Riders of the Dawn" 1920 (Henry Neuman); "The U.P. Trail" 1920 (Jose Durade); "Man of the Forest" 1921 (Harvey Riggs); "The Mysterious Rider" 1921 (Hell Bent Wade); "Without Compromise" 1922 (David Ainsworth); "Dead Game" 1923 (Prince Tetlow); "The Spider and the Rose" 1923 (Men-

doza); "The Spoilers" 1923 (Struve); "The Galloping Ace" 1924 (David Kincaid); "Ride for Your Life" 1924 (Gentleman Jim Slade); "Spook Ranch" 1925 (Don Ramies); "The Dead Line" 1926 (Silver Sam McGee); "A Regular Scout" 1926 (Ed Powell); "Tex" 1926; "The Tough Guy" 1926 (Con Carney); "The Wolf Hunters" 1926; "Aflame in the Sky" 1927 (Joseph Murdoch); "The Denver Dude" 1927 (Bob Flint).

McKim, Sammy. Films: "Annie Oakley" 1935 (Boy at Shooting Gallery); "Gunsmoke Ranch" 1937 (Jimmy); "Heart of the Rockies" 1937 (Davey); "Hit the Saddle" 1937 (Tim Miller); "The Old Wyoming Trail" 1937 (Boy); "The Painted Stallion" 1937-serial (Kit Carson); "The Trigger Trio" 1937 (Mickey Evans); "Call the Mesquiteers" 1938 (Tim Irving); "The Great Adventures of Wild Bill Hickok" 1938 (Boots); "The Lone Ranger" 1938-serial (Sammy); "The Old Barn Dancer" 1938 (Johnny Dawson); "Red River Range" 1938 (Tommy Jones); "New Frontier" 1939 (Stevie); "The Night Riders" 1939 (Tim); "Rovin' Tumbleweeds" 1939 (Eddie); "Western Caravans" 1939 (Matt Winters); "Rocky Mountain Rangers" 1940 (Daniel Burke); "Texas Terrors" 1940 (Bob as a Boy).

Mackin, Harry. Films: "Sons of New Mexico" 1949; "Texans Never Cry" 1951 (Bill Ross); "Last of the Pony Riders" 1953 (Cliff Patrick). ¶TV: *The Roy Rogers Show*—"Badman's Brother" 2-10-52 (Stu Trumbull); "Phantom Rustlers" 4-25-54; *The Gene Autry Show*—"Outlaw Stage" 7-21-53 (Johnny Peters); *The Adventures of Rin Tin Tin*—"Rin Tin Tin Meet's O'Hara's Mother" 2-17-56 (Pvt. Carson); *Death Valley Days*—"Two Bits" 5-5-56 (Pvt. Sam Loomis); *Annie Oakley*—"Annie and the Bicycle Riders" 7-8-56 (Bicycle Rider).

McKinley, J. Edward (1917-). Films: "A Thunder of Drums" 1961 (Capt. Alan Scarborough); "How the West Was Won" 1962 (Auctioneer); "Charro!" 1969 (Henry Carter); "Flap" 1970 (Harris); "There Was a Crooked Man" 1970 (Governor). ¶TV: *Tales of Wells Fargo*—"The Branding Iron" 2-23-59 (Sheriff Welk); *Buckskin*—"The Knight Who Owned Buckskin" 3-2-59 (Thomas); *Sugarfoot*—"Welcome Enemy" 12-26-60 (President Grant); *Lawman*—"The Promoter" 2-19-61 (Clifford North); *Bonanza*—"Cut-Throat Junction" 3-18-61; *Maverick*—"Triple Indemnity" 3-19-61 (Sam Landry), "The Golden

Fleecing" 10-8-61 (Loftus Jaeggers); *The Deputy*—"Brand of Honesty" 6-10-61 (John Gardner); *Gunsmoke*—"Half Straight" 2-17-62 (Grant Hatcher), "The Widow" 3-24-62 (Emil Peck), "The Still" 11-10-69 (Rancher Bishop); *Bronco*—"The Immovable Object" 4-16-62 (Governor); *Colt .45*—"Bounty List" 5-31-60; *Bonanza*—"Enter Thomas Bowers" 4-26-64, "To Own the World" 4-18-65 (Mayor); *The Legend of Jesse James*—"1863" 3-28-66 (Jason Smith); *Wild Wild West*—"The Night of the Vicious Valentine" 2-10-67 (Curtis Langley Dodd); *Bret Maverick*—"The Rattlesnake Brigade" 4-27-82 (Snow).

McKinney, Florine (1912-7/28/75). Films: "Oklahoma Renegades" 1940 (Marian Carter); "Little Joe, the Wrangler" 1942 (Mary Brewster).

McKinney, Myra (-5/2/78). Films: "Blazing Sixes" 1937 (Aunt Sarah); "Prairie Moon" 1938; "Bad Man from Red Butte" 1940 (Miss Woods); "Santa Fe Trail" 1940 (Woman); "Rough Riders of Cheyenne" 1945; "Trail to Laredo" 1948; "Kansas Raiders" 1950 (Woman); "Trail of the Rustlers" 1950; "Heart of the Rockies" 1951 (Mrs. Edsel); "The Last Posse" 1953 (Mrs. Mitchell). ¶TV: *The Lone Ranger*—"The Man with Two Faces" 2-23-50, "Sheriff of Gunstock" 7-27-50, "The Silent Voice" 1-11-51, "The Hooded Men" 2-22-51, "Stage to Tishomingo" 10-28-54; *The Gene Autry Show*—"The Sheriff of Santa Rosa" 12-24-50, "The Western Way" 2-1-52, "Hot Lead and Old Lace" 2-15-52 (Maude), "Battle Axe" 8-31-54, "Boots and Ballots" 9-25-54.

McKinney, Nina Mae (1913-5/3/67). Films: "Copper Canyon" 1950 (Theresa).

McKinney, William "Bill" (1931-). Films: "Alias Smith and Jones" TVM-1971 (Lobo); "Junior Bonner" 1972 (Red Terwillger); "The Life and Times of Judge Roy Bean" 1972 (Fermel Parlee); "The Godchild" TVM-1974 (Crawley); "This Was the West That Was" TVM-1974 (Osvar Wellman); "Breakheart Pass" 1976 (Rev. Peabody); "The Outlaw Josey Wales" 1976 (Terrill); "The Shootist" 1976 (Cobb); "Bronco Billy" 1980 (Lefty LeBow); "Back to the Future, Part III" 1990 (Engineer); "City Slickers II: The Legend of Curly's Gold" 1994 (Matt). ¶TV: *Alias Smith and Jones*—"Return to Devil's Hole" 2-25-71 (Lobo), "The Man Who Murdered Himself" 3-18-71, "The Biggest Game in the West"

2-3-72; *Sara*—2-13-76 (Tom Sellers); *Young Maverick*—"Hearts O'Gold" 12-12-79 (Smoky Trumbull); *Ned Blessing: The Story of My Life and Times*—Regular 1993 (Verlon Borgers).

McKinnon, Neil. Films: "The Phantom Horseman" 1924 (Fred Mason).

McKinsey, Beverlee. Films: "Bronco Billy" 1980 (Irene). ¶TV: *The Virginian*—"The Substitute" 12-5-69 (Abby Clayton); *Death Valley Days*—"The Wizard of Aberdeen" 1-17-70.

Mackley, Arthur (1865-12/21/26). Films: "The Ranchmen's Feud" 1910; "The Sheriff's Brother" 1911; "The Sheriff's Decision" 1911; "Broncho Billy and the Indian Maid" 1912; "Broncho Billy for Sheriff" 1912; "Broncho Billy's Heart" 1912; "Broncho Billy's Pal" 1912; "The Dead Man's Claim" 1912; "The Loafer's Mother" 1912; "Love on Tough Luck Ranch" 1912; "A Moonshiner's Heart" 1912; "An Outlaw's Sacrifice" 1912; "The Ranch Girl's Mistake" 1912; "A Road Agent's Love" 1912; "The Sheepman's Escape" 1912; "The Sheriff's Luck" 1912; "The Shotgun Ranchman" 1912; "The Smuggler's Daughter" 1912; "A Wife of the Hills" 1912; "A Woman of Arizona" 1912; "Broncho Billy and the Sheriff's Kid" 1913; "The Call of the Plains" 1913; "The Housekeeper of Circle C" 1913; "A Montana Mix-Up" 1913; "The Ranch Feud" 1913; "The Ranchman's Blunder" 1913; "The Sheriff and the Rustler" 1913; "The Sheriff's Story" 1913; "The Sheriff's Wife" 1913; "The Story the Desert Told" 1913; "This Life We Live" 1913; "Deputy Sheriff's Star" 1914; "Out of the Deputy's Hands" 1914; "The Sheriff's Choice" 1914; "The Deputy's Chance That Won" 1915; "The Crow" 1919; "The Feud" 1919 (William Lynch); "The Sheriff's Oath" 1920; "Shootin' for Love" 1923 (Sheriff Bludsoe); "The Hurricane Kid" 1925 (Col. Langdon).

Mackley, Julia. Films: "The Mother of the Ranch" 1912; "An Outlaw's Sacrifice" 1912; "A Road Agent's Love" 1912; "The Sheriff's Luck" 1912; "The Sheriff's Wife" 1913.

Macklin, David. Films: "Gunpoint" 1966 (Mark Emerson). ¶TV: *Bonanza*—"The Blood Line" 12-31-60 (Todd Grayson); *Wide Country*—"The Quest for Jacob Blaufus" 3-7-63 (Jacob Blaufus); *Stoney Burke*—"Kincaid" 4-22-63 (Frank Sommers); *The Virginian*—"The Fortunes of J. Jimerson Jones" 1-15-64 (Eddie Tighe), "Dead Eye Dick" 11-9-66 (Bob Foley); *Gunsmoke*—"Jonah Hutchison" 11-21-64 (Steven Hutchison); *Iron Horse*—"Welcome for the General" 1-2-67 (Wade Henderson); *The Guns of Will Sonnett*—"The Turkey Shoot" 11-24-67 (Cleve Atwood); *Lancer*—"Welcome to Genesis" 11-18-69; *Barbary Coast*—"Funny Money" 9-8-75 (Phillip Van Cleve).

Macklin, Harry. Films: "The Cowboy and the Indians" 1949 (Bob Collins).

McKuen, Rod (1933-). Films: "Wild Heritage" 1958 (Dirk Breslin).

McLaglen, Victor (1886-11/7/59). Films: "Three Rogues" 1931 (Bull Stanley); "The Gay Caballero" 1932 (Don Bob Harkness); "Let Freedom Ring" 1939 (Chris Mulligan); "The Michigan Kid" 1947 (Curley); "Fort Apache" 1948 (Sgt. Festus Mulcahy); "She Wore a Yellow Ribbon" 1949 (Sgt. Quincannon); "Rio Grande" 1950 (Sgt. Maj. Quincannon); "Many Rivers to Cross" 1955 (Cadmus Cherne). ¶TV: *Have Gun Will Travel*—"The O'Hare Story" 3-1-58 (Mike O'Hare); *Rawhide*—"Incident of the Shambling Men" 10-9-59 (Harry Wittman).

MacLaine, Shirley (1934-). Films: "The Sheepman" 1958 (Dell Payton); "Two Mules for Sister Sara" 1970 (Sister Sara).

MacLane, Barton (1900-1/1/69). Films: "Man of the Forest" 1933 (Mulvey); "To the Last Man" 1933 (Neil Standing); "The Last Round-Up" 1934 (Charley Benson); "The Lone Cowboy" 1934 (J.J. Baxter); "The Thundering Herd" 1934 (Pruitt); "God's Country and the Woman" 1937 (Bullhead); "Gold Is Where You Find It" 1938 (Slag Minton); "Stand Up and Fight" 1939 (Crowder); "Melody Ranch" 1940 (Mark Wildhack); "Western Union" 1941 (Jack Slade); "Song of Texas" 1943 (Jim Calvert); "Gentle Annie" 1944 (Sheriff Tatum); "Santa Fe Uprising" 1946 (Yancey); "Cheyenne" 1947 (Yancey); "The Dude Goes West" 1948 (Texas Jack); "Relentless" 1948 (Tex Brandow); "Silver River" 1948 (Banjo Sweeney); "The Treasure of the Sierra Madre" 1948 (McCormick); "Bandit Queen" 1950 (Jim Harden); "Best of the Badmen" 1951 (Joad); "Drums in the Deep South" 1951 (McCardle); "Bugles in the Afternoon" 1952 (Capt. Myles Moylan); "The Half-Breed" 1952 (Marshal); "Jack Slade" 1953 (Jules Reni); "Kansas Pacific" 1953 (Calvin Bruce); "Cow Country" 1953 (Parker); "Hell's Outpost" 1954 (Sheriff Olson); "Jubilee Trail" 1954 (Deacon Bartlett); "Rails into Laramie" 1954 (Lee Graham); "Last of the Desperadoes" 1955 (Mosby); "The Silver Star" 1955 (Tiny); "Treasure of Ruby Hills" 1955 (Reynolds); "Backlash" 1956 (George Lake); "The Naked Gun" 1956; "Three Violent People" 1956 (Yates); "Hell's Crossroads" 1957 (Clyde O'Connell); "Naked in the Sun" 1957; "Sierra Stranger" 1957 (Lem Gotch); "Frontier Gun" 1958 (Simon Crayle); "Gunfighters of Abilene" 1960 (Seth); "Noose for a Gunman" 1960 (Carl Avery); "Law of the Lawless" 1964 (Big Tom Stone); "The Rounders" 1965 (Tanner); "Town Tamer" 1965 (James Fenimore Fell); "Arizona Bushwhackers" 1968 (Sheriff Grover); "Buckskin" 1968 (Do Raymond). ¶TV: *Cheyenne*—"The Storm Riders" 2-7-56 (Storm); *Circus Boy*—"The Tumbling Clown" 5-5-57 (Nolan); *Black Saddle*—"Client: Braun" 4-4-59 (Gen. Fowler); *Desilu Playhouse*—"Border Justice" 11-13-59 (Wentworth); *Texas John Slaughter*—"The Robber Stallion" 12-4-59 (Scanlon); *Laramie*—"Street of Hate" 3-1-60 (Cameron Gault), "The High Country" 2-6-62 (Mel Bishop), "The Wedding Party" 1-29-63 (Ed Bishop), "Trapped" 5-14-63 (Owen Richards); *Walt Disney Presents*—"Elfego Baca: Friendly Enemies at Law" 3-18-60 (Rauls Kettrick); *Overland Trail*—"Lawyer in Petticoats" 3-27-60 (Jed Braddock); *The Outlaws*—Regular 1960-62 (Marshal Frank Caine); *Gunsmoke*—"Honor Before Justice" 3-5-66 (Herkimer Crawford), "Noose of Gold" 3-4-67 (Willard F. Kerner); *Hondo*—"Hondo and the Gladiators" 12-15-67 (Markham).

MacLane, Kerry (1958-). TV: *The Virginian*—"Sue Ann" 1-11-67 (Jim); *Bonanza*—"Journey to Terror" 2-5-67 (Benjie); *Cimarron Strip*—"The Beast That Walks Like a Man" 11-30-67; *The Cowboys*—Regular 1974 (Homer); *Kung Fu*—"Blood of the Dragon" 9-14-74 (Richie).

MacLaren, Ian (1875-4/10/52). Films: "The Conquering Horde" 1931 (Marvin Fletcher); "The Last of the Mohicans" 1936 (William Pitt).

MacLaren, Mary (1900-11/9/85). Films: "The Plow Woman" 1917 (Mary MacTavish); "The New Frontier" 1935 (Minister's Wife); "Saddle Aces" 1935; "King of the Pecos" 1936 (Mrs. Clayborn); "A Lawman Is Born" 1937 (Martha Lance); "Reckless Ranger" 1937 (Mary Allen); "Union Pacific" 1939 (Official's Wife); "The Fargo Kid" 1940 (Sarah Winters); "Prairie Pioneers" 1941

(Martha Nelson); "Fighting Valley" 1943 (Ma Donovan); "Six Gun Gospel" 1943; "Frontier Feud" 1945 (Sarah Moran); "The Navajo Trail" 1945; "Crossed Trails" 1948 (Mrs. Laswell).

McLaren, Mary. Films: "Westward Ho" 1935 (Hannah Wyatt).

McLaren, Wayne (1941-7/22/92). Films: "The Honkers" 1972 (Everett). ¶TV: *Gunsmoke*—"The Golden Land" 3-5-73 (Homer).

McLarty, Gary (1941-). Films: "The Way West" 1967 (Cattleman); "Rooster Cogburn" 1975 (Gang Member); "The Apple Dumpling Gang Rides Again" 1979. ¶TV: *Bearcats!*—"Hostages" 10-14-71 (Herrera); *Kung Fu*—"King of the Mountain" 10-14-72 (Frank McCoy).

McLaughlin, Harry (-9/21/20). Films: "Honeymoon Ranch" 1920 (Tom Van Hess Creighton); "West of the Rio Grande" 1921 (Tom Norton).

McLaughlin, James. Films: "The Secret of Black Mountain" 1917 (Jim Vale); "The Black Sheep" 1921 (Jose); "South of the Northern Lights" 1922 (Cpl. McAllister).

McLaughlin, William. Films: "The Devil's Bowl" 1923 (Sgt. Jerry O'Neill).

McLean, Billy. TV: *Bonanza*—"The Gunmen" 1-23-60; *Gunsmoke*—"Little Girl" 4-1-61 (Rafe); *The Virginian*—"If You Have Tears" 2-13-63, "Legend for a Lawman" 3-3-65 (Telegrapher); *Wild Wild West*—"The Night of the Murderous Spring" 4-15-66 (Hotel Clerk); *Kung Fu*—"Dark Angel" 11-11-72 (Poker Player), "The Salamander" 12-6-73 (Brew).

McLean, David (1922-10/12/95). Films: "Nevada Smith" 1966 (Romero). ¶TV: *Tate*—Regular 1960 (Tate); *Laramie*—"A Grave for Cully Brown" 2-13-62 (Cully Brown), "Beyond Justice" 11-27-62 (Steven Collier), "The Marshals" 4-30-63 (Branch McGary); *The Virginian*—"The Judgment" 1-16-63 (Burt Adams), "The Fatal Journey" 12-4-63 (Fred Troy), "Letter of the Law" 12-22-65 (Governor); *Death Valley Days*—"Stubborn Mule Hill" 3-31-63 (Kit Carson), "A Book of Spanish Grammar" 4-18-64 (Stephen Austin), "Death in the Desert" 5-9-65 (Luke Lundy), "A Saint of Travellers" 2-14-70 (Jean Baptiste Lamy), "A Gift from Father Tapis" 5-9-70 (McGrath); *Gunsmoke*—"The Twisted Heritage" 1-6-69 (Webb); *Lancer*—"Angel Day and Her Sunshine Girls" 2-25-69 (Sheriff), "Jelly Hoskins' American Dream" 11-11-69, "The Buscaderos"

3-17-70; *Bonanza*—"Emily" 3-23-69 (Marhsal Calhoun), "Return Engagement" 3-1-70 (Fallon); *Daniel Boone*—"A Matter of Vengeance" 2-26-70 (Smith).

MacLean, Douglas (1890-7/9/67). Films: "The Sunshine Trail" 1923 (James Henry MacTavish).

McLeod, Catherine (1924-). Films: "The Harvey Girls" 1946 (Louise); "The Fabulous Texan" 1947 (Alice Sharp); "Old Los Angeles" 1948 (Marie Marlowe); "The Outcast" 1954 (Alice Austin); "Return to Warbow" 1958 (Kathleen Fallam). ¶TV: *Frontier*—"Georgia Gold" 6-10-56 (Elizabeth Masters); *Zane Grey Theater*—"Back Trail" 2-1-57 (Effie Fallon); *Gunsmoke*—"Wrong Man" 4-13-57 (Letty), "Quint-Cident" 4-27-63 (Lizzie); *Lawman*—"Battle Scar" 3-22-59 (Cynthia Rogers), "The Payment" 5-8-60 (Judith Manning), "Fugitive" 4-2-61 (Meg Cormack), "The Prodigal Mother" 12-17-61 (Margaret Coleson); *Hotel De Paree*—"Bounty for Sundance" 4-29-60 (Hannah); *Stagecoach West*—"By the Deep Six" 12-27-60 (Mrs. Walker); *Bonanza*—"The Smiler" 9-24-61 (Mrs. McClure); *Have Gun Will Travel*—"Cream of the Jest" 5-5-62 (Nora); *The Virginian*—"To Make This Place Remember" 9-25-63 (Amy Sturgis), "Six Graves at Cripple Creek" 1-27-65 (Mrs. Mallory).

McLeod, Duncan (1918-). TV: *Black Saddle*—"Four from Stillwater" 11-27-59 (Ben Thompson); *Branded*—"Fill No Glass for Me" 11-7-65 & 11-14-65 (Major Brackham); *The Legend of Jesse James*—"Benjamin Bates" 2-28-66 (Darby Craile).

MacLeod, Gavin (1931-). Films: "A Man Called Gannon" 1969 (Lou); "The Intruders" TVM-1970; "Ransom for Alice!" TVM-1977 (Yankee Sullivan). ¶TV: *The Big Valley*—"Brother Love" 2-20-67 (Mace), "Presumed Dead" 10-7-68 (O'Leary), "Alias Nellie Handley" 2-24-69 (Clute); *The Road West*—"The Eighty-Seven Dollar Bride" 4-3-67 (Nick Marteen); *Iron Horse*—"Six Hours to Sky High" 11-25-67 (Merv); *Death Valley Days*—"The Great Diamond Mines" 3-9-68 (Arnold); *Lancer*—"The Black Angel" 10-21-69 (Bateman).

MacLeod, Murray. Films: "Cahill, United States Marshal" 1973 (Deputy Gordine). ¶TV: *Pistols 'n' Petticoats*—"A Crooked Line" 9-17-66 (Kenny Turner); *The High Chaparral*—"Ride the Savage Land" 2-11-68 (Lieutenant Tobar); *The Virginian*—"Death Wait" 1-15-69 (Lorne

Buchanan); *Here Come the Brides*—"The Deadly Trade" 4-16-69 (Dorne); *Death Valley Days*—"A Simple Question of Justice" 11-22-69; *Daniel Boone*—"Noblesse Oblige" 3-26-70 (Edgar); *Bonanza*—"Ambush at Rio Lobo" 10-24-72 (Zachariah); *Kung Fu*—"A Praying Mantis Kills" 3-22-73 (Arnold).

McLerie, Allyn Ann (1926-). Films: "Calamity Jane" 1953 (Katie Brown); "Monte Walsh" 1970 (Mary Eagle); "The Cowboys" 1972 (Ellen Price); "Jeremiah Johnson" 1972 (Crazy Woman); "The Magnificent Seven Ride" 1972 (Mrs. Donavan). ¶TV: *Bonanza*—"Caution: Easter Bunny Crossing" 3-29-70 (Charity); *Nichols*—3-7-72.

McLiam, John (1918-4/16/94). Films: "Monte Walsh" 1970 (Fightin' Joe Hooker); "The Culpepper Cattle Company" 1972 (Pierce); "Hitched" TVM-1973 (Pete Hutter); "Showdown" 1973 (P.J. Wilson); "The Call of the Wild" TVM-1976 (Prospector); "The Missouri Breaks" 1976 (David Braxton); "The Legend of the Golden Gun" TVM-1979 (Jake Powell); "Bret Maverick" TVM-1981 (Doc Holliday). ¶TV: *Wagon Train*—"The Bleymier Story" 11-16-60 (Larch); *Riverboat*—"Chicota Landing" 12-5-60 (Sheriff Matson); *Tales of Wells Fargo*—"Jeff Davis' Treasure" 12-5-60 (Henry Moore); *Gunsmoke*—"Big Man" 3-25-61 (Jud Sloan), "Big Man, Big Target" 11-28-64, "My Father, My Son" 4-23-66 (Doherty), "Parson Comes to Town" 4-30-66 (Dougherty), "Champion of the World" 12-24-66 (Dougherty), "The Gunrunners" 2-5-68 (Bender), "O'Quillian" 10-28-68 (Leary O'Quillian); *Two Faces West*—"Trail to Indian Wells" 4-24-61; *Have Gun Will Travel*—"The Gospel Singer" 10-21-61 (Mayor Harper); *Stoney Burke*—"Five by Eight" 12-10-62 (Fred); *Empire*—"No Small Wars" 2-5-63 (Pat Sullivan); *Rawhide*—"A Man Called Mushy" 10-23-64 (Bartender); *Daniel Boone*—"Mountain of the Dead" 12-17-64 (Charles Bane), "The Fifth Man" 2-17-66 (Mathew Elbridge), "The Lost Colony" 12-8-66 (Jedediah Corbett); *The Virginian*—"Day of the Scorpion" 9-22-65 (John Pierce), "The Mark of a Man" 4-20-66 (Eben McDevitt), "Stopover" 1-8-69 (O'Neill); *The Big Valley*—"Heritage" 10-20-65 (Paddy the Ghoul); *The Legend of Jesse James*—"Wanted: Dead and Only" 5-2-66 (Perkins); *Death Valley Days*—"The Fight San Francisco Never Forgot" 5-14-66 (Walter Watson), "Early Candle Lighten" 11-8-69, "The Solid Gold

Pie" 11-29-69; *The Road West*—"Piece of Tin" 10-31-66; *The Monroes*—"Court Martial" 11-16-66 (Sgt. Duncan McMurdoch); *Wild Wild West*—"The Night of the Headless Woman" 1-5-68 (Tucker); *Bonanza*—"Is There Any Man Here?" 2-8-70 (Harry Carlis); *Lancer*—"The Experiment" 2-17-70; *The Men from Shiloh*—"The West vs. Colonel MacKenzie" 9-16-70 (Parker), "The Mysterious Mr. Tate" 10-14-70 (Parker).

McLuke, Luke. Films: "Trail of the Hawk" 1935.

MacMahon, Aline (1899-10/12/91). Films: "The Man from Laramie" 1955 (Kate Canaday); "Cimarron" 1960 (Mrs. Pegler).

McMahon, David (1909-1/27/72). Films: "The Peacemaker" 1956 (Sam Davis). ¶TV: *The Lone Ranger*—"Thieves' Money" 11-2-50, "Mr. Trouble" 3-8-51; *Maverick*—"Black Fire" 3-16-58 (Sheriff); *Rawhide*—"Incident of the Roman Candles" 7-10-59 (Larch), "Incident of the Lost Idol" 4-28-61 (Doc Crowder), "Incident of the Wager on Payday" 6-16-61; *Wagon Train*—"The Estaban Zamora Story" 10-21-59, "The Bleymier Story" 11-16-60 (Ed Cowan), "The Pearlie Garnet Story" 2-24-64 (Stimson), "The Miss Mary Lee McIntosh Story" 2-28-65 (Sergeant O'Rourke); *Lawman*—"Yawkey" 10-23-60 (Man); *Laramie*—"The Fatal Step" 10-24-61; *Wide Country*—"My Candle Burns at Both Ends" 12-20-62 (Jimmy); *Temple Houston*—"Miss Katherina" 4-2-64 (Doc Burgess); *The Virginian*—"Portrait of a Widow" 12-9-64 (Conductor).

McMahon, Horace (1907-8/17/71). Films: "Melody Ranch" 1940 (Bud Wildhack); "Texas Lady" 1955 (Stringy Winfield). ¶TV: *The Alaskans*—"Counterblow" 4-24-60 (Tim Carstairs); *Sugarfoot*—"The Captive Locomotive" 6-7-60 (Cameron); *Bronco*—"End of a Rope" 6-14-60 (Tom Merrick).

McMahon, Leo. Films: "Hills of Old Wyoming" 1937 (Steve); "North of the Rio Grande" 1937; "Texas Trail" 1937 (Corporal); "Heart of Arizona" 1938 (Twister); "The Mysterious Rider" 1938 (Montana); "Pride of the West" 1938 (Johnson); "Station West" 1948 (Rider); "Dakota Lil" 1950; "Colt .45" 1950; "Storm Over Wyoming" 1950 (Zeke); "Gunplay" 1951 (Zeke); "Silver City" 1951 (Townsman); "Son of Paleface" 1952 (Crag).

McManus, Don. Films: "Gunsmoke: The Long Ride" TVM-1993 (Jules Braxton, Jr.).

McManus, George (1884-10/22/54). Films: "Jiggs and Maggie Out West" 1950 (George McManus).

McManus, Mark (1935-6/6/94). Films: "Ned Kelly" 1970-Brit. (Joe Byrne).

MacMichael, Florence (1921-). TV: *Gunsmoke*—"Annie Oakley" 10-24-59 (Kate Kinsman); *Bonanza*—"Tax Collector" 2-18-61.

McMillan, Roddy (1923-7/9/79). Films: "Chato's Land" 1972 (Gavin Malechie).

McMullan, Jim (1936-). Films: "The Raiders" 1964 (William F. "Buffalo Bill" Cody); "Shenandoah" 1965 (John Anderson); "Desperate Mission" TVM-1971 (Arkansaw). ¶TV: *Frontier Circus*—"The Race" 5-3-62 (Charlie); *Wide Country*—"A Guy for Clementine" 9-27-62 (Spence Roebuck), "Don't Cry for Johnny Devlin" 1-24-63 (Johnny Devlin); *Laramie*—"The Long Road Back" 10-23-62 (Virgil Walker), "Beyond Justice" 11-27-62; *The Virginian*—"Impasse" 11-14-62 (Jes Kroeger), "The Invaders" 1-1-64 (Tom Tyrone); *Wagon Train*—"The Clarence Mullins Story" 5-1-63 (Barker); *Destry*—"Blood Brother-in-Law" 4-17-64 (Morgan Motley); *The Big Valley*—"The Death Merchant" 2-23-66 (Frank Craddock); *Preview Tonight*—"Roaring Camp" 9-4-66 (Cain); *Iron Horse*—"The Prisoners" 12-30-67 (Frank Gurney); *Daniel Boone*—"The Blackbirder" 10-3-68 (Mason Pruitt), "The Fleeing Nuns" 10-24-68 (Mason Pruitt), "A Matter of Vengeance" 2-26-70 (Mason Pruitt); *Centennial*—Regular 1978-79 (Prosecutor).

McMullen, Denis. TV: *Gunsmoke*—"Johnny Red" 10-3-59 (Ponca City Kid); *Johnny Ringo*—"The Assassins" 2-18-60 (Josh).

McMurphy, Charles (1894-10/24/69). Films: "The Thundering Herd" 1934 (Andrews); "Song of the Trail" 1936 (Curtis); "My Little Chickadee" 1940; "Man from Montana" 1941 (Dugan); "The Spoilers" 1942 (Deputy); "Law of the Valley" 1944.

MacMurray, Fred (1907-11/5/91). Films: "The Texas Rangers" 1936 (Jim Hawkins); "Rangers of Fortune" 1940 (Gil Farra); "Smoky" 1946 (Clint Barkley); "Callaway Went Thataway" 1951 (Mike Frye); "The Moonlighter" 1953 (Wes Anderson); "At Gunpoint" 1955 (Jack Wright); "The Far Horizons" 1955 (Meriwether Lewis); "Gun for a Coward" 1957 (Will Keough); "Quantez" 1957 (Gentry/John Coventry); "Day of the

Bad Man" 1958 (Judge Jim Scott); "Good Day for a Hanging" 1958 (Ben Cutler); "Face of a Fugitive" 1959 (Jim Larson/Roy Kincaid); "The Oregon Trail" 1959 (Neal Harris). ¶TV: *Cimarron City*—"I, the People" 10-11-58 (Laird Garner).

McMurray, Lucky. Films: "Once Upon a Time in the Wild, Wild West" 1969-Ital. (Enzo); "Hero Called Allegria" 1971-Ital.; "One Damned Day at Dawn … Django Meets Sartana" 1971-Ital. (Joe "the Worm" Smith); "Reach You Bastard!" 1971-Ital.; "Go Away! Trinity Has Arrived in Eldorado" 1972-Ital.; "They Called Him Trinity" 1972-Ital./Span. (Sheriff Ryan).

McMyler, Pamela (1946-). Films: "Chisum" 1970 (Sally Chisum); "One More Train to Rob" 1971 (Cora May Jones). ¶TV: *The Virginian*—"A Flash of Darkness" 9-24-69; *The Men from Shiloh*—"Lady at the Bar" 11-4-70 (Ellie); *Gunsmoke*—"No Tomorrow" 1-3-72 (Elizabeth Justin), "Tarnished Badge" 11-11-74 (Jenny Blair).

McNair, Heather. TV: *Young Riders*—"Lessons Learned" 7-9-92 (Mrs. Hutchins).

McNally, Edward (1923-). TV: *Jefferson Drum*—"Bad Day for a Tinhorn" 5-16-58 (Rogers).

McNally, Stephen (Horace McNally) (1913-6/4/94). Films: "The Harvey Girls" 1946 (Goldust McClean); "Winchester '73" 1950 (Dutch Henry Brown); "Wyoming Mail" 1950 (Steve Davis); "Apache Drums" 1951 (Sam Leeds); "The Duel at Silver Creek" 1952 (Lightning); "Devil's Canyon" 1953 (Jesse Gorman); "The Stand at Apache River" 1953 (Sheriff Lane Dakota); "A Bullet Is Waiting" 1954 (Sheriff Munson); "The Man from Bitter Ridge" 1955 (Alec Black); "Tribute to a Badman" 1956 (McNulty); "Hell's Crossroads" 1957 (Vic Rodell); "The Fiend Who Walked the West" 1958 (Emmett); "Hell Bent for Leather" 1960 (Deckett); "Requiem for a Gunfighter" 1965 (Red Zimmer); "Nakia" TVM-1974 (Alva Chambers); "Kino, the Padre on Horseback" 1977. ¶TV: *Loretta Young Show*—"The Wise One" 3-26-56 (Garson); *Zane Grey Theater*—"Return to Nowhere" 12-7-56 (Steve), "Mission to Marathon" 5-14-59 (Big Luke Meredith), "The Reckoning" 1-14-60 (Mace), "The Mormons" 12-15-60 (Matt Rowland); *Wagon Train*—"The Ben Courtney Story" 1-28-59 (Ben Courtney); *Texas John Slaughter*—"The Man from Bitter

Creek" 3-6-59 (Bill Gallagher); *The Texan*—"Badlands" 5-11-59 (Clay Thompson); *Riverboat*—"Hang the Men High" 3-21-60 (Jeb Randell); *Laramie*—"The Track of the Jackal" 9-27-60 (Luke Wiley); *Rawhide*—"Incident of the Blackstorms" 5-26-61 (Sky Blackstorm); *The Virginian*—"No Tears for Savannah" 10-2-63 (Sheriff Avedon); *Branded*—"The Bar Sinister" 10-10-65 (Caleb Reymer); *Iron Horse*—"War Cloud" 10-31-66 (Wilkens); *The Big Valley*—"Hide the Children" 12-19-66 (Corso); *Gunsmoke*—"The Lure" 2-25-67 (Dal Neely); *The Guns of Will Sonnett*—"The Favor" 11-10-67 (Ben Colter); *The Men from Shiloh*—"The Angus Killer" 2-10-71 (Muller).

McNally, Terrence (1939-). TV: *Dr. Quinn, Medicine Woman*—"Father's Day" 1-30-93 (Harriet's Husband).

McNamara, James (1913-5/18/80). Films: "Union Pacific" 1939 (Mr. Mills); "One Man's Law" 1940 (Martin); "Home in Wyomin'" 1942.

McNamara, John (-10/27/68). TV: *The Californians*—"J. Jimmerson Jones, Inc" 4-1-58 (Paul Saunders), "One Ton of Peppercorns" 5-12-59 (Capt. Whitehead).

McNamara, Ted (1892-2/3/28). Films: "Chain Lightning" 1927 (Shorty).

McNear, Howard (1905-1/3/69). Films: "Escape from Fort Bravo" 1953 (Watson); "Drums Across the River" 1954 (Stilwell); "Good Day for a Hanging" 1958 (Olson); "Heller in Pink Tights" 1960 (Photographer). TV: *Gunsmoke*—"The Pest Hold" 4-14-56 (Bradley), "Box O'Rocks" 12-5-59 (Pete), "The Tragedian" 1-23-60 (Joe), "Root Down" 10-6-62 (Howard), "Aunt Thede" 12-19-64 (Howard); *Jim Bowie*—"Country Cousin" 5-3-57 (Colonel); *Maverick*—"Hadley's Hunters" 9-25-60 (Copes), "Dodge City or Bust" 12-11-60 (Sheriff of Dangerfield); *Have Gun Will Travel*—"The Prisoner" 12-17-60 (Samuels); *Klondike*—"The Golden Burro" 1-16-61 (Augustus Brown); *The Tall Man*—"A Tombstone for Billy" 12-16-61 (Cyrus Skinner); *Frontier Circus*—"Calamity Circus" 3-8-62 (Judge); *Wide Country*—"Straightjacket for an Indian" 10-25-62 (Agent Carmody).

Macnee, Patrick (1922-). Films: "The Gambler Returns: The Luck of the Draw" TVM-1991 (Sir Colin Douglas). TV: *Northwest Passage*—"The Red Coat" 9-21-58 (Col. Trent); *Black Saddle*—"Client: McQueen" 1-24-59 (Michael Kent);

Rawhide—"Incident of the Thirteenth Man" 10-23-59; *The Virginian*—"A King's Ransom" 2-25-70 (Connor); *Alias Smith and Jones*—"The Man Who Murdered Himself" 3-18-71 (Norman Alexander).

McNeil, Claudia (1917-11/25/93). Films: "There Was a Crooked Man" 1970 (Madam).

McNeil, Norman (1891-12/17/38). Films: "Girl of the Golden West" 1930 (Happy Holiday).

McNichol, Kristie (1963-). TV: *Sara*—5-7-76.

McNulty, Kevin. Films: "Blood River" TVM-1994; "Children of the Dust" TVM-1995 (Sheriff Harriman).

Macollum, Barry (1889-2/22/71). Films: "Arkansas Judge" 1941 (Mr. Melvany).

McPeak, Sandy. Films: "Belle Starr" TVM-1980 (Pratt); "Independence" TVM-1987 (Sterling Mott). TV: *Big Hawaii*—"Graduation Eve" 10-26-77 (Charley Woodman); *Centennial*—Regular 1978-79 (Soren Sorenson); *Bret Maverick*—"The Ballad of Bret Maverick" 2-16-82 (Voorsanger); *Wildside*—Regular 1985 (Governor J.W. Summerhayes); *Outlaws*—"Orleans" 1-17-87 (Malet).

McPeters, Curtis. see Mack, Cactus.

MacPeters, Taylor. see Mack, Cactus.

McPhail, Addie. Films: "Northwest Passage" 1940 (Jane Browne).

Macpherson, Jeanie (1887-8/26/46). Films: "The Last Drop of Water" 1911; "On Burning Sands" 1913; "The Desert's Sting" 1914; "The Outlaw Reforms" 1914 (Mary); "Rose of the Rancho" 1914 (Isabelita); "The Girl of the Golden West" 1915 (Nina).

MacQuarrie, Albert (1882-2/17/50). Films: "Colorado" 1915 (Mr. Staples); "Prayer of a Horse" 1915; "The Almost Good Man" 1917; "Arizona" 1918 (Lt. Hatton); "Under False Pretenses" 1918; "The Knickerbocker Buckaroo" 1919 (Manuel Lopez, the Bandit); "Rosalind at Red Gate" 1919; "Mark of Zorro" 1920; "The Mollycoddle" 1920 (Desert Yacht Driver); "Bulldog Courage" 1922 (John Morton); "Crimson Gold" 1923 (David Ellis); "Don Q, Son of Zorro" 1925 (Col. Matsado).

MacQuarrie, Frank (1875-12/25/50). Films: "Two Men of Sandy Bar" 1916 (Old Morton); "The Almost Good Man" 1917; "A 45 Calibre Mystery" 1917; "Boss of the Lazy

Y" 1918 (Tom Taggart); "Little Red Decides" 1918 (Parson Jones); "Wolves of the Border" 1918; "The Lone Hand" 1919.

McQuarrie, George. Films: "All Man" 1916 (Gillette Barker); "The Price of Pride" 1917 (Ben Richardson); "Call of the Wild" 1935 (Mounted Policeman); "The Border Patrolman" 1936 (Riker); "The Plainsman" 1936 (Gen. Merritt); "Robin Hood of El Dorado" 1936 (Smithers); "Lawless Valley" 1938 (Tim Wade); "Trail of the Vigilantes" 1940 (Rancher).

MacQuarrie, Murdock (1878-8/22/42). Films: "Bloodhounds of the North" 1913; "The Honor of the Mounted" 1914; "A Ranch Romance" 1914; "The Tragedy of Whispering Creek" 1914; "The Unlawful Trade" 1914; "Babbling Tongues" 1915; "The Flag of Fortune" 1915; "Prayer of a Horse" 1915; "The Sacrifice of Jonathan Gray" 1915; "The Sheriff of Red Rock Gulch" 1915; "The Trap That Failed" 1915; "The Accusing Evidence" 1916; "The Stain in the Blood" 1916 (Bill Jenkins); "Riders of the Purple Sage" 1918 (Tull); "Jacques of the Silver North" 1919 (Jim Blake); "Sure Fire" 1921 (Major Parker); "Canyon of Fools" 1923 (Sproul); "Hair Trigger Baxter" 1926 (Joe Craddock); "The High Hand" 1926 (Martin Shaler); "Black Jack" 1927 (Holbrook); "The Long Loop on the Pecos" 1927; "The Man from Hardpan" 1927 (Henry Hardy); "The Apache Raider" 1928 (Don Felix Beinal); "45 Calibre War" 1929 (Mark Blodgett); "Arizona Terror" 1931 (Joe Moore); "Near the Trail's End" 1931; "Sundown Trail" 1931 (Judge Lawlor); "The Two Gun Man" 1931 (Rancher Markham); "Border Devils" 1932; "Daring Danger" 1932 (Norris); "Fighting for Justice" 1932 (Sheriff); "One-Man Law" 1932 (Grimm); "Crossfire" 1933 (Sheriff Jim Wells); "Fighting Hero" 1934 (Prosecutor); "The Man from Hell" 1934 (Sheriff Jake); "Potluck Pards" 1934; "Terror of the Plains" 1934 (Foreman); "The Laramie Kid" 1935 (Dad Bland); "Nevada" 1935 (Watson); "The New Frontier" 1935 (Tom Lewis); "North of Arizona" 1935 (Marshal Elmer Harron); "Silent Valley" 1935 (Elmer Barnes); "Stone of Silver Creek" 1935 (George J Mason); "Tonto Kid" 1935 (Pop Slawson); "Pinto Rustlers" 1936 (Dad); "Song of the Gringo" 1936; "Stormy Trails" 1936 (Sheriff); "Sunset of Power" 1936; "Fighting Texan" 1937 (Slim Perkins); "Git Along, Little Dogies" 1937; "Zorro Rides Again" 1937-serial (Jones); "Ghost Town Riders" 1938 (Tax Collector); "Guilty Trails" 1938 (Judge); "The Lone Ranger" 1938-serial (Matt Clark); "Man from Music Mountain" 1938; "Prairie Justice" 1938; "Western Trails" 1938; "Colorado Sunset" 1939; "Honor of the West" 1939 (Rancher); "The Phantom Stage" 1939 (Scott); "Smoky Trails" 1939 (Will Archer); "Stand Up and Fight" 1939 (Engineer); "Death Rides the Range" 1940; "Konga, the Wild Stallion" 1940 (Clerk); "Pinto Canyon" 1940 (Elmer Barnes); "Man from Montana" 1941 (Preston); "The Return of Daniel Boone" 1941; "Wildcat of Tucson" 1941; "Ghost Town Law" 1942 (Judge Crail); "Jackass Mail" 1942 (Hickory Jake).

McQueen, Butterfly (1911-). Films: "Flame of the Barbary Coast" 1945 (Beulah); "Duel in the Sun" 1946 (Vashti).

McQueen, Steve (1930-11/7/ 80). Films: "The Magnificent Seven" 1960 (Vin); "Nevada Smith" 1966 (Nevada Smith/Max Sand); "Junior Bonner" 1972 (Junior Bonner); "Tom Horn" 1980 (Tom Horn). ¶TV: *Tales of Wells Fargo*—"Bill Longley" 2-10-58 (Bill Longley); *Trackdown*—"The Bounty Hunter" 3-7-58 (Josh Randall), "The Brothers" 5-16-58 (Mal Cody/Wes Cody); *Wanted—Dead or Alive*—Regular 1958-61 (Josh Randall).

McQueeney, Robert. Films: "The Glory Guys" 1965 (Marcus). ¶TV: *Wagon Train*—"The Emily Rossiter Story" 10-30-57 (Si); *Gunsmoke*—"Romeo" 11-9-57 (Pete Knight); *Colt .45*—"The Man Who Loved Lincoln" 5-3-59 (Edwin Booth), "The Rival Gun" 10-25-59 (Duke); *Lawman*—"Shackled" 10-18-59 (Bench Ryan), "The Truce" 3-6-60 (O.C. Coulsen), "The Payment" 5-8-60 (Ron Fallon), "Tarot" 12-10-61 (Joe Wyatt); *Cheyenne*—"The Imposter" 11-2-59 (Derwent), "Lone Patrol" 4-10-61 (Captain Duquesne), "Sweet Sam" 10-8-62 (Sam Pridemore); *Overland Trail*—"High Bridge" 2-28-60 (Jim); *The Alaskans*—"Counterblow" 4-24-60 (Van Peyton); *The Tall Man*—"Night Train to Tularosa" 11-5-60 (Bragg); *Bonanza*—"The Rival" 4-15-61 (Gideon), "The Strange One" 11-14-65 (Jeremy), "Black Friday" 1-22-67 (Enos Low), "False Witness" 10-22-67 (Sheriff Dunkel); *Bronco*—"One Came Back" 11-27-61 (Jeremy), "Destinies West" 2-26-62 (Major Creighton); *Temple Houston*—"Do Unto Others, Then Gallop" 3-19-64

(Robert Sangster); *The Legend of Jesse James*—"Three Men from Now" 9-13-65 (Haynes).

McRae, Duncan (1881-2/4/31). Films: "Flower of No Man's Land" 1916 (Roy Talbot).

McRae, Ellen. *see* Burstyn, Ellen.

MacRae, Elizabeth (1936-). Films: "The Wild Westerners" 1962 (Crystal Plummer). ¶TV: *Maverick*—"Benefit of Doubt" 4-9-61 (Emily Todd); *Gunsmoke*—"Half Straight" 2-17-62 (Fanny Fields), "Us Haggens" 12-8-62 (April), "Once a Haggen" 2-1-64 (April), "Now That April's There" 3-21-64 (April), "Circus Trick" 2-6-65 (April); *Stoney Burke*—"A Matter of Percentage" 1-28-63 (Paula); *Rawhide*—"Incident at Hourglass" 3-12-64 (Sally Ann Rankin); *The Virginian*—"Two Men Named Laredo" 1-6-65 (Molly Weems), "Last Grave at Socorro Creek" 1-22-69 (Kate Burden); *Bonanza*—"Star Crossed" 3-10-68 (Lila Holden).

McRae, Frank (1942-). Films: "Lightning Jack" 1994-Australia (Mr. Doyle). ¶TV: *The Quest*—"The Freight Train Rescue" 12-29-76.

MacRae, Gordon (1921-1/24/ 86). Films: "Return of the Frontiersman" 1950 (Logan Barrett); "Oklahoma!" 1955 (Curly).

MacRae, Meredith (1945-). TV: *Alias Smith and Jones*—"Something to Get Hung About" 10-21-71 (Sarah Henderson).

McRaney, Gerald (1947-). Films: "Where the Hell's That Gold?!!!" TVM-1988 (Jones). ¶TV: *Alias Smith and Jones*—"The Day the Amnesty Came Through" 11-25-72; *Gunsmoke*—"Whelan's Men" 2-5-73 (Gentry), "Kitty's Love Affair" 10-22-73 (Lonnie Colby), "Hard Labor" 2-24-75 (Pete Murphy); *How the West Was Won*—"Luke" 4-2-79 (Thorne).

Macready, George (1909-7/2/ 73). Films: "Coroner Creek" 1948 (Younger Miles); "The Doolins of Oklahoma" 1949 (Sam Hughes); "The Nevadan" 1950 (Edward Galt); "The Stranger Wore a Gun" 1953 (Jules Mourret); "Vera Cruz" 1954 (Emperor Maximilian); "Thunder Over Arizona" 1956; "Gunfire at Indian Gap" 1957 (Pike/Mr. Jefferson); "Plunderers of Painted Flats" 1959 (Ed Sampson). ¶TV: *The Rifleman*—"Eight Hours to Die" 11-4-58 (Judge Zephaniah Burgess), "The Lariat" 3-29-60; *Gunsmoke*—"Lynching Man" 11-15-58 (Charlie Drain); *Wanted—Dead or Alive*—"Rawhide Breed" 12-13-58 (Jefferson Klingsmith); *The*

Texan—"A Time of the Year" 12-22-58 (Big Jim Sammett); *Rough Riders*—"The Last Rebel" 7-16-59; *Bonanza*—"A Rose for Lotta" 9-12-59 (Alpheus Troy); *The Rebel*— "Vicious Circle" 10-25-59 (General Pollack), "Johnny Yuma at Appomattox" 9-18-60 (Gen. Robert E. Lee); *Riverboat*—"Guns for Empire" 12-20-59 (Anthony Lorrimer); *Have Gun Will Travel*—"Ambush" 4-23-60 (Gundar); *The Tall Man*—"Counterfeit Law" 11-19-60 (Roy A. Barlow), 5-26-62 (Cyrus Canfield); *Bat Masterson*—"Tempest at Tioga Pass" 1-5-61 (Clyde Richards); *Laramie*—"Handful of Fire" 12-5-61 (Colonel John Barrington); *Frontier Circus*—"The Good Fight" 4-19-62 (John Duncan); *The Dakotas*—"Mutiny at Fort Mercy" 1-21-63 (Captain Ridgeway); *Lancer*—"Legacy" 12-9-69 (Harlan Garrett).

Macready, Michael (1932-). TV: *The Texan*—"A Time of the Year" 12-22-58 (Jody Sammett); *Lawman*—"The Posse" 3-8-59 (Tracy Hunter); *The Virginian*—"Legend for a Lawman" 3-3-65 (Coby).

McReynolds, Dexter. Films: "Fear-Bound" 1925 (Alkali Red); "Red Love" 1925 (Scar-Face).

McTaggart, Malcolm "Bud" (1910-5/29/49). Films: "Six-Gun Rhythm" 1939 (Don Harper); "Trigger Fingers" 1939 (Jerry); "Wyoming Outlaw" 1939; "Triple Justice" 1940 (Tom Payson); "Wagon Train" 1940 (Coe Gardner); "Gangs of Sonora" 1941 (David Conners); "Robbers of the Range" 1941 (Curly); "Billy the Kid Trapped" 1942 (Jeff); "Come on, Danger!" 1942 (Russ); "West of the Law" 1942; "The Avenging Rider" 1943 (Baxter); "Dead Man's Gulch" 1943 (Tommy Logan); "Red River Robin Hood" 1943; "Sagebrush Law" 1943.

McVeagh, Eve (1923-). Films: "High Noon" 1952 (Mildred Fuller); "Reprisal!" 1956 (Nora Shipley); "Sierra Stranger" 1957 (Ruth Gaines); "The Way West" 1967 (Mrs. Masters). ¶TV: *Rawhide*—"Incidcnt of a Burst of Evil" 6-26-59; *Lawman*—"The Ugly Man" 2-14-60 (Josie); *Have Gun Will Travel*—"One, Two, Three" 2-17-62 (Katherine); *Wagon Train*—"The Terry Morrell Story" 4-25-62 (Yolanda), "The Cassie Vance Story" 12-23-63 (Mrs. Sharp); *The Tall Man*—5-26-62 (Lily Varnell); *Daniel Boone*—"The Quietists" 2-25-65 (Kate Bothwell), "The Christmas Story" 12-23-65 (Eleanor Tully); *F Troop*—"Reunion for O'Rourke" 3-8-66 (Wilma McGee); *The Virginian*—"The Deadly Past" 9-20-67 (Maude);

Bonanza—"Night of Reckoning" 10-15-67 (Harriet); *Alias Smith and Jones*—"What Happened at the XST?" 10-28-72; *The Texas Wheelers*—7-17-75 (Mrs. Klate).

McVey, Patrick (1910-7/6/73). Films: "They Died with Their Boots On" 1941 (Jones); "Pierre of the Plains" 1942 (Sgt. Dugan). ¶TV: *Cheyenne*—"Decision at Gunsight" 4-23-57 (Dave Beaton), "Ghost of Cimarron" 3-25-58 (Sheriff Kim Younger), "Trouble Street" 10-2-61 (Marshal Bailey); *Boots and Saddles*—Regular 1957-59 (Lieutenant Colonel Hays); *The Restless Gun*—"Strange Family in Town" 1-20-58 (John Durant); *Sugarfoot*—"Price on His Head" 4-29-58 (Sheriff Dunbar); *Tombstone Territory*—"Pick Up the Gun" 5-14-58 (Lisa's Father), "Day of the Amnesty" 4-3-59 (Fred Tanner); *Bat Masterson*—"Two Graves for Swan Valley" 10-15-58 (Angus McLarnin), "Dynamite Blows Two Ways" 10-22-58 (Thompson); *Maverick*—"The Jail at Junction Flats" 11-9-58 (Sheriff Morrison Pyne), "The Brasada Spur" 2-22-59 (Roy Stafford); *Lawman*—"Wanted" 11-16-58 (Red Barrington); *Rough Riders*—"Shadows of the Past" 11-27-58 (Andy); *The Texan*—"Outpost" 1-19-59 (Marshal Dodson); *Zane Grey Theater*—"Hanging Fever" 3-12-59 (Jack Lathrop); *Wanted—Dead or Alive*—"Bounty for a Bride" 4-4-59 (Damon Albright); *The Rifleman*—"The Hawk" 4-14-59 (Walt Hake), "The Quiet Fear" 1-22-62 (Jake Striker); *Black Saddle*—"Client: Nelson" 5-2-59 (Tom Nelson); *Bonanza*—"Enter Mark Twain" 10-10-59 (Bill Raleigh); *Have Gun Will Travel*—"Shootout at Hogtooth" 11-10-62 (Clanahan); *Gunsmoke*—"Quint's Indian" 3-2-63 (Houser).

McVey, Paul. Films: "The Country Beyond" 1936 (Fred Donaldson); "Fair Warning" 1937 (Mr. Berkhardt); "Drums Along the Mohawk" 1939 (Captain Mark Demooth); "Stagecoach" 1939 (Express Agent); "King of the Royal Mounted" 1940-serial (Excellency Zernoff); "Shane" 1953 (Grafton).

McVey, Tyler (1912-). Films: "Horizons West" 1952 (Player); "Terror in a Texas Town" 1958 (Sheriff Stoner); "Lone Texan" 1959 (Henry Biggs); "Sidekicks" TVM-1974. ¶TV: *The Lone Ranger*—"Ex-Marshal" 9-16-54; *My Friend Flicka*—"The Wild Horse" 11-18-55; *Gunsmoke*—"Hack Prine" 5-12-56, "Prairie Happy" 7-7-56 (Father), "The Cover-Up" 1-12-57 (Sam Baxton), "Romeo" 11-9-57 (Emmett Bowers), "Dirt" 3-1-58,

"The Choice" 5-9-59, "Moo Moo Raid" 2-13-60 (Gib); *Broken Arrow*—"The Assassin" 4-23-57 (Simmons); *Maverick*—"The War of the Silver Kings" 9-22-57 (Kriedler), "According to Hoyle" 10-6-57 (Hayes); *Wyatt Earp*—"Ballad and Truth" 3-4-58 (Mrs. Bates), "When Sherman Marched Through Kansas" 3-18-58 (Bates), "Santa Fe War" 12-2-58 (Dan Christy), "Shoot to Kill" 10-18-60; *The Restless Gun*—"The Hand Is Quicker" 3-17-58 (Foreman), "The Nowhere Kid" 10-20-58 (Sheriff Jackson), "The Pawn" 4-6-59; *Have Gun Will Travel*—"The Five Books of Owen Deaver" 4-26-58 (Jim Morris); *Wagon Train*—"The John Wilbot Story" 6-11-58 (Thaddeus Field), "The Cappy Darrin Story" 11-11-59, "Trial for Murder" 4-27-60 & 5-4-60, "The Bleeker Story" 12-9-63; *Rough Riders*—"The Double Dealers" 3-19-59 (Col. Thompson); *Zane Grey Theater*—"Legacy of a Legend" 11-6-58 (Bartender); *Buckskin*—"Act of Faith" 3-23-59 (Ben Gordon); *Wanted—Dead or Alive*—"The Empty Cell" 10-17-59; *The Rebel*—"Dark Secret" 11-22-59 (Sheriff); *The Law of the Plainsman*—"The Imposter" 2-4-60; *Colt .45*—"Absent Without Leave" 4-19-60 (Col. Ben Williams); *Riverboat*—"No Bridge on the River" 10-24-60 (Judge); *Klondike*—"Sure Thing, Men" 11-28-60 (Emil Watkins); *The Deputy*—"Day of Fear" 12-17-60 (Stu Collins); *Gunslinger*—"Golden Circle" 4-13-61 (Harris); *Bat Masterson*—"Dead Man's Claim" 5-4-61 (Vernon Ellwood); *Rawhide*—"Incident at Rio Salado" 9-29-61; *Death Valley Days*—"The Third Passenger" 12-6-61 (Lew Sayres), "Abel Duncan's Dying Wish" 2-21-62 (Priest); *Tales of Wells Fargo*—"The Traveler" 2-24-62 (Max Andrews); *Bonanza*—"Knight Errant" 11-18-62 (Townsman), "The Late Ben Cartwright" 3-3-68, "Anatomy of a Lynching" 10-12-69 (Al Crane); *Redigo*—"Hostage Hero Riding" 12-10-63; *Wild Wild West*—"The Night of the Double-Edged Knife" 11-12-65 (Parnell), "The Night of the Plague" 4-4-69; *The Road West*—"The Insider" 2-13-67; *Daniel Boone*—"Mamma Cooper" 2-5-70; *The High Chaparral*—"Wind" 10-9-70.

McWade, Edward (1865-5/17/43). Films: "Her Half Brother" 1922; "The Return of Frank James" 1940 (Col. Fentridge Jackson).

McWade, Margaret (1872-4/1/56). Films: "Sundown" 1924 (Mrs. Brent); "Partners of the Trail" 1931 (Mary Lopez); "Forbidden Valley" 1938 (Mrs. Scudd); "The Texans" 1938 (Middle-Aged Lady).

McWade, Robert (1882-1/20/38). Films: "Cimarron" 1931 (Louie Heffner); "Gold Is Where You Find It" 1938 (Crouch).

Macy, Carleton (1861-10/18/46). Films: "Gold and the Woman" 1916 (Dugald Chandor).

Madden, Dave (1933-). Films: "More Wild Wild West" TVM-1980 (German Ambassador).

Madden, Goldie (1886-10/26/60). Films: "The Marshal of Moneymint" 1922 (Mandie St. Claire).

Maddern, Victor (1926-6/22/93). TV: *Bonanza*—"A Passion for Justice" 9-29-63 (Dan).

Maddock, Burt. Films: "The Masked Avenger" 1922 (Lariat Bill Williams); "A Rodeo Mixup" 1924 (Arizona Dick).

Maddock, Jeanne. Films: "The Light of Western Stars" 1918 (Florence Kingsley).

Madison, Cleo (1883-3/11/64). Films: "Under the Black Flag" 1913; "The Trey O'Hearts" 1914-serial (Rose); "The Ring of Destiny" 1915; "The Flame of the West" 1918.

Madison, Guy (1922-). Films: "Massacre River" 1949 (Larry Knight); "Drums in the Deep South" 1951 (Will Denning); "The Charge at Feather River" 1953 (Miles Archer); "The Command" 1953 (Capt. Mac-Claw); "The Last Frontier" 1955 (Capt. Riordan); "The Beast of Hollow Mountain" 1956 (Jimmy Ryan); "Reprisal!" 1956 (Frank Madden); "The Hard Man" 1957 (Steve Burden); "Bullwhip" 1958 (Steve); "Gunmen of the Rio Grande" 1964-Fr./Ital./Span. (Wyatt Earp/Laramie); "Legacy of the Incas" 1965-Ger./Ital. (Wutuma); "Five Giants from Texas" 1966-Ital./Span.; "Son of Django" 1967-Ital. (Reverend Fleming); "The Bang Bang Kid" 1968-U.S./Span./Ital. (Bear Bullock); "Old Shatterhand" 1968-Ger./Yugo./Fr./Ital. (Bradley); "Payment in Blood" 1968-Ital. (Col. Blake); "This Man Can't Die" 1968-Ital. (Martin Benson); "Reverend Colt" 1970-Ital./Span. (Reverend Miller). ¶TV: *Wild Bill Hickok*—Regular 1951-53 (U.S. Marshal James Butler "Wild Bill" Hickok); *Wagon Train*—"The Riley Gratton Story" 12-4-57 (Riley Gratton); *Death Valley Days*—"Extra Guns" 11-23-60 (Luke Short); *Zane Grey Theater*—"Jericho" 5-18-61 (Jericho).

Madison, Julian. Films: "Wagon Wheels" 1934 (Lester); "The Last of the Warrens" 1936; "Guns in the Dark" 1937 (Dick Martin); "Desert

Patrol" 1938 (Carson); "Durango Valley Raiders" 1938; "Death Rides the Range" 1940 (Jim Morgan).

Madison, Mae. Films: "The Big Stampede" 1932 (Ginger Malloy).

Madison, Virginia. Films: "His Back Against the Wall" 1922 (Mrs. Welling).

Madoc, Philip (1934-). TV: *Masterpiece Theatre*—"The Last of the Mohicans" 1972 (Magua).

Madsen, Michael. Films: "Montana" TVM-1990 (Pierce).

Magalo, Paolo. *see* Carter, Peter.

Magalotti, Paolo. *see* Carter, Peter.

Magee, Gordon. Films: "Tiger Rose" 1929 (Hainey).

Maggart, Brandon (1933-). TV: *Adventures of Brisco County, Jr.*—"The Orb Scholar" 9-3-93 (Prof. Ogden Coles), "Fountain of Youth" 1-14-94 (Prof. Ogden Coles).

Magill, James. Films: "Trail of Robin Hood" 1950 (Murtagh); "Don Daredevil Rides Again" 1951-serial (Carson); "Silver Canyon" 1951.

Magnus, Annabelle. Films: "Orphan of the Sage" 1928 (Mary Jane Perkins).

Magrill, George (1900-5/31/52). Films: "The Mask of Lopez" 1923 (Pancho); "Fast and Fearless" 1924 (Pedro Gomez); "North of Nevada" 1924 (Joe Deerfoot); "The Fighting Smile" 1925; "Wild Horse Mesa" 1925 (Bert Manerube); "The Enchanted Hill" 1926 (1st Killer); "The Lone Prairie" 1926; "The Cyclone Cowboy" 1927; "The Desert of the Lost" 1927; "Hawk of the Hills" 1927-serial; "Ride 'Em High" 1927 (Paul Demming); "Roarin' Broncs" 1927 (Henry Ball); "The Ballyhoo Buster" 1928 (Brooks Mitchell); "Texas Bad Man" 1932 (Harry); "The Gay Desperado" 1936; "Wells Fargo" 1937 (Northerner); "The Lone Ranger" 1938-serial (Sentry #2); "Oklahoma Frontier" 1939 (Trooper); "The Gay Caballero" 1940 (Deputy Sheriff); "The Man from Dakota" 1940 (Confederate Sergeant); "Daredevils of the West" 1943-serial (Citizen #2); "Santa Fe Saddlemates" 1945; "Pirates of Monterey" 1947 (Pirate); "The Sea of Grass" 1947 (Homesteader); "River Lady" 1948 (Logger); "Twilight on the Rio Grande" 1947; "Valley of Fire" 1951 (Bartender).

Mahan, Larry. Films: "J.W. Coop" 1971 (Himself); "The Honkers" 1972 (Larry Mahan); "The Great American Cowboy" 1974; "Mackin-tosh & T.J." 1975; "The Good Old Boys" TVM-1995 (Hannigan).

Maharis, George (1928-). Films: "The Desperados" 1969 (Jacob Galt); "Land Raiders" 1969-U.S./Span. (Paul Cardenas). ¶TV: *Nakia*—"Pete" 12-21-74 (Joe Arnold).

Mahoney, Jock (Jock O'Mahoney) (1919-12/14/89). Films: "The Fighting Frontiersman" 1946; "Out West" 1947-short (Johnny, the Arizona Kid); "South of the Chisholm Trail" 1947; "The Stranger from Ponca City" 1947; "Blazing Across the Pecos" 1948; "Smoky Mountain Melody" 1948; "The Blazing Trail" 1949 (Full House Patterson); "The Doolins of Oklahoma" 1949 (Tulsa Jack); "Renegades of the Sage" 1949 (Lt. Hunter); "Rim of the Canyon" 1949 (Pete Reagan); "Cody of the Pony Express" 1950-serial (Lt. Jim Archer); "Cow Town" 1950 (Tod Jeffreys); "Frontier Outpost" 1950 (Lt. Peck); "Hoedown" 1950 (Stoney Rhodes); "Horsemen of the Sierras" 1950 (Bill Grant); "The Kangaroo Kid" 1950 (Tex Kinnane); "Lightning Guns" 1950 (Rob Saunders); "The Nevadan" 1950 (Sandy); "Punchy Cowpunchers" 1950-short (Elmer, the Arizona Kid); "Roar of the Iron Horse" 1950-serial (Jim Grant); "Texas Dynamo" 1950 (Bill Beck); "Bandits of El Dorado" 1951 (Starling); "Pecos River" 1951 (Jock Mahoney); "Santa Fe" 1951 (Crake); "The Texas Rangers" 1951 (Duke Fisher); "The Hawk of Wild River" 1952 (Jock Mahoney); "Junction City" 1952 (Jock Mahoney); "The Kid from Broken Gun" 1952 (Jock Mahoney); "Laramie Mountains" 1952 (Swift Eagle); "The Rough, Tough West" 1952 (Big Jack Mahoney); "Smoky Canyon" 1952 (Jock Mahoney); "Gunfighters of the Northwest" 1954-serial (Joe Ward); "Overland Pacific" 1954 (Rose Granger); "Pals and Gals" 1954-short (Johnny, the Arizona Kid); "A Day of Fury" 1956 (Marshal Allan Burnett); "Showdown at Abilene" 1956 (Jim Trask); "Joe Dakota" 1957 (the Stranger); "Slim Carter" 1957 (Slim Carter/Hughie Mack); "The Last of the Fast Guns" 1958 (Brad Ellison); "Money, Women and Guns" 1958 (Hogan); "California" 1963 (Don Michael O'Casey); "Bandolero!" 1968 (Stoner). ¶TV: *The Range Rider*—Regular 1951-53 (the Range Rider); *Death Valley Days*—"Husband Pro Tem" 4-21-54; *Wagon Train*—"The Dan Hogan Story" 5-14-58 (Dan Hogan); *Yancy Derringer*—Regular 1958-59 (Yancy Derringer); *Rawhide*—"Incident of the Sharpshooter" 2-26-60 (Vance/Jonathan Williams), "Incident of the Phantom Burglar" 4-14-61 (Captain Donahoe); *Laramie*—"Man from Kansas" 1-10-61 (Clay Jackson), "Ladies Day" 10-3-61, "The Unvanquished" 3-12-63; *Gunslinger*—"Rampage" 3-16-61 (Halsey Roland); *Daniel Boone*—"The Secret Code" 12-14-67; *Kung Fu*—"The Hoots" 12-13-73 (Kyle Davidson).

Mahoney, Maggie. Films: "Blackjack Ketchum, Desperado" 1956 (Nita Riordan); "Slim Carter" 1957 (Hat Check Girl). ¶TV: *Wagon Train*—"The Rex Montana Story" 5-28-58 (Loaitha); *Tombstone Territory*—"The Gatling Gun" 8-27-58 (Sarah Medford); *Yancy Derringer*—"A Bullet for Bridget" 11-6-58 (Bridget Malone), "Three Knaves from New Haven" 12-11-58 (Bridget Malone); *Wild Wild West*—"The Night of the Tycoons" 3-28-69; *U.S. Marshal*—"Honeymoon" 12-26-59 (Gloria); *The Rebel*—"Paint a House with Scarlet" 5-15-60 (Sara Bodine); *The Westerner*—"School Days" 10-7-60 (Eleanor); *Lawman*—"Cold Fear" 6-4-61 (Ann Turner); *Bonanza*—"A Dublin Lad" 1-2-66 (Molly).

Mahoney, Tom (1890-11/5/58). Films: "The Girl of the Golden West" 1938 (Handsome Charlie).

Mailes, Charles Hill (1870-2/17/37). Films: "Fate's Interception" 1912; "Goddess of Sagebrush Gulch" 1912; "A Lodging for the Night" 1912; "Man's Lust for Gold" 1912; "A Tale of the Wilderness" 1912; "A Temporary Truce" 1912; "The Battle at Elderbrush Gulch" 1913; "The Sheriff's Baby" 1913; "The Fighting Grin" 1918 (Otis Kennedy); "The Girl Who Wouldn't Quit" 1918 (Robert Carter); "Three Mounted Men" 1918 (Warden); "The Outcasts of Poker Flat" 1919; "The Wild Rider" 1919; "Mark of Zorro" 1920 (Don Carlos Pulido); "Crashin' Thru" 1923 (Uncle Benedict); "Soft Boiled" 1923 (Lawyer); "Thundering Hoofs" 1924 (Don Juan Estrada); "When a Man's a Man" 1924 (Jim Reid); "The Frontier Trail" 1926 (Major Mainard); "The Man in the Saddle" 1926 (Jeff Morgan, Sr.); "Somewhere in Sonora" 1927 (Mexicali Burton); "Phantom City" 1928 (Benedict); "Treason" 1933 (General Frank Hawthorne).

Main, Laurie (1922-). TV: *Maverick*—"Bundle from Britain" 9-18-60 (Marquis of Bognor), "The Art Lovers" 10-1-61 (Crimmins); *Wagon Train*—"The Odyssey of Flint McCullough" 2-15-61; *Daniel Boone*—"The Ben Franklin Encounter" 3-18-65 (Benjamin Franklin), 9-23-65

(Stinch), "The Matchmaker" 10-27-66 (Stinch), "The Necklace" 3-9-67 (Stinch), "The Kidnaping" 1-22-70 (Sir George Peacham); *Iron Horse*—"Grapes of Grass Valley" 10-21-67 (Jean Louis); *The Guns of Will Sonnett*—"Look for the Hound Dog" 1-26-68.

Main, Marjorie (1890-4/10/75). Films: "The Dark Command" 1940 (Mrs. Cantrell); "Wyoming" 1940 (Mehitabel); "Honky Tonk" 1941 (Reverend Mrs. Varner); "The Shepherd of the Hills" 1941 (Granny Becky); "Jackass Mail" 1942 (Clemtine "Tiny" Tucker); "Gentle Annie" 1944 (Annie Goss); "Bad Bascomb" 1946 (Abbey Hanks); "The Harvey Girls" 1946 (Sonora Cassidy); "The Wistful Widow of Wagon Gap" 1947 (Widow Hawkins); "Big Jack" 1949 (Flapjack Kate); "Ricochet Romance" 1954 (Pansy Jones); "Rose Marie" 1954 (Lady Jane Dunstock); "Friendly Persuasion" 1956 (Widow Hudspeth). ¶TV: *Wagon Train*—"The Cassie Tanner Story" 6-4-58 (Cassie Tanner), "The Sacramento Story" 6-25-58 (Cassie Tanner).

Maines, Dan (1869-1/2/34). Films: "The Man Who Waited" 1922 (Sandy).

Majalca, Ana Maria. Films: "Giant" 1956 (Petra). ¶TV: *The Roy Rogers Show*—"Paleface Justice" 11-18-56; *Colt .45*—"The Mirage" 1-10-58 (Maurita); *Tales of Wells Fargo*—"The Most Dangerous Man Alive" 11-10-58 (Jeanie Two Eagles); *Cheyenne*—"The Wedding Rings" 1-8-62 (Mariquita).

Majeroni, Mario (1870-11/18/31). Films: "The Valley of Silent Men" 1922 (Pierre Radison).

Majors, Eddie. Films: "Lonesome Trail" 1945; "Moon Over Montana" 1946; "West of Alamo" 1946 (Dean); "Outlaw Brand" 1948; "Gun Law Justice" 1949; "Gun Runner" 1949 (Joe); "Haunted Trails" 1949 (Deputy Jed); "Trail's End" 1949 (Luke).

Majors, Lee (1942-). Films: "Will Penny" 1968 (Blue); "High Noon, Part II: The Return of Will Kane" TVM-1980 (Will Kane). ¶TV: *Gunsmoke*—"Song for Dying" 2-13-65 (Dave Lukens); *The Big Valley*—Regular 1965-69 (Heath); *The Men from Shiloh*—Regular 1970-71 (Roy Tate); *Alias Smith and Jones*—"The McCreedy Bust—Going, Going Gone" 1-13-72 (Joe Briggs).

Mako (Iwamatsu) (1933-). Films: "The Great Bank Robbery" 1969 (Secret Service Agent Elliot Fong). ¶TV:

F Troop—"From Karate with Love" 1-5-67 (Samurai Warrior); *The Big Valley*—"Rimfire" 2-19-68 (Wong Lo); *Kung Fu*—"The Tide" 2-1-73 (Wong Ti Liu); *Paradise*—"Dangerous Cargo" 1-20-90 (Kao).

Mala, Ray (1906-9/23/52). Films: "Call of the Yukon" 1938 (Olee John); "The Great Adventures of Wild Bill Hickok" 1938 (Little Elk); "Union Pacific" 1939 (Indian Brave); "Northwest Mounted Police" 1940 (Indian); "Girl from Alaska" 1942 (Charley).

Malan, William (1868-2/13/41). Films: "Flashing Spurs" 1924 (John Holden); "Red Hot Leather" 1926 (Daniel Lane); "The Broncho Buster" 1927 (Maj. John Furth); "The Fighting Three" 1927 (John D'Arcy); "Men of Daring" 1927 (Jasper Morton); "A One Man Game" 1927 (John Starke); "The Overland Stage" 1927 (John Marshall); "The Border Wildcat" 1928 (John Bell).

Malatesta, Fred (1889-4/8/52). Films: "The Claim" 1918 (Ted "Blackie" Jerome); "The Devil's Trail" 1919 (Dubec); "The Terror of the Range" 1919-serial; "The Challenge of the Law" 1920 (Jules Lafitte); "Broadway or Bust" 1924 (Count Dardanelle); "The Night Hawk" 1924 (Jose Valdez); "The Wagon Show" 1928 (Vicarino); "Wings of Adventure" 1930 (La Panthera); "Get That Girl" 1932 (Dr. Sandro Tito); "Fighting Shadows" 1935 (Dusquesne); "Under the Pampas Moon" 1935 (Doorman); "Senor Jim" 1936 (Nick Zellini); "The Arizona Wildcat" 1939 (Battista); "Mark of Zorro" 1940 (Sentry); "Rangers of Fortune" 1940 (Genoa).

Malcolm, Christopher (1946-). Films: "The Desperados" 1969 (Greg); "Rustler's Rhapsody" 1985 (Jud).

Malcolm, Robert. Films: "The Caravan Trail" 1946 (Jim Bristol); "The Sea of Grass" 1947 (Man); "Blood on the Moon" 1948; "The Blazing Trail" 1949 (Old Williams); "Annie Get Your Gun" 1950. ¶TV: *Sergeant Preston of the Yukon*—"Cinderella of the Yukon" 3-22-56 (Grandpa Atwater).

Malden, Karl (1914-). Films: "The Gunfighter" 1950 (Mac); "The Hanging Tree" 1959 (Frenchy Plante); "One-Eyed Jacks" 1961 (Dad Longworth); "How the West Was Won" 1962 (Zebulon Prescott); "Cheyenne Autumn" 1964 (Capt. Oscar Wessels); "Nevada Smith" 1966 (Tom Fitch); "The Adventures of Bullwhip Griffin" 1967 (Judge Hig-

gins); "Blue" 1968 (Doc Morton); "Wild Rovers" 1971 (Walter Buckman).

Malet, Arthur (1927-). Films: "The Man from Galveston" 1964 (Barney); "The Culpepper Cattle Company" 1972 (Doctor). ¶TV: *The Rifleman*—"Sporting Chance" 1-29-62 (Jeremy Pennebroke); *Gunsmoke*—"The Boys" 5-26-62 (Farnum), "Run, Sheep, Run" 1-9-65 (Cox), "The Hanging of Newly O'Brien" 11-26-73 (Old Timer); *Temple Houston*—"The Man from Galveston" 1963 (Barney); *Destry*—"The Infernal Triangle" 5-1-64 (Hanock); *Wild Wild West*—"The Night of the Steel Assassin" 1-7-66 (Dr. Meyer), "The Night of the Janus" 2-15-69 (Prof. Montague); *The Guns of Will Sonnett*—"The Trap" 10-4-68 (Pickett); *Bonanza*—"Catch as Catch Can" 10-27-68 (Tingle); *Lancer*—"The Lorelei" 1-27-70 (Footman).

Maley, Dutch. Films: "Beyond All Odds" 1926 (Hard Rock Jordan); "The Bonanza Buckaroo" 1926 (Spike); "Cyclone Bob" 1926 (Skeeter Thompson); "Lure of the West" 1928.

Maley, Peggy. Films: "The Harvey Girls" 1946 (Dance Hall Girl); "Gypsy Colt" 1954 (Pat); "The Guns of Fort Petticoat" 1957 (Lucy Conover). ¶TV: *Tombstone Territory*—"The Lady Gambler" 5-28-58 (Belle Winters); *The Texan*—"A Time of the Year" 12-22-58 (Dolly Mathews); *The Rifleman*—"The Boarding House" 2-24-59; *Wanted—Dead or Alive*—"Double Fee" 3-21-59; "Littlest Giant" 4-25-59 (Dolly Cleary).

Malfatti, Marina. Films: "Return of Clint the Stranger" 1971-Ital./Span.

Mallette, Arthur. Films: "Bare-Fisted Gallagher" 1919 (Selby Mason).

Mallinson, Rory (1913-3/26/76). Films: "Frontier Days" 1945-short; "King of the Bandits" 1947 (Burl); "The Denver Kid" 1948; "Last of the Wild Horses" 1948 (Hank); "Panhandle" 1948 (Sheriff); "Bad Men of Tombstone" 1949; "El Dorado Pass" 1949 (Sheriff Tom Wright); "Prince of the Plains" 1949 (James Taylor); "Rim of the Canyon" 1949; "South of Rio" 1949 (Bob Mitchell); "Salt Lake Raiders" 1950 (Sheriff); "Short Grass" 1950 (Jim Westafall); "Cavalry Scout" 1951 (Corporal); "Fort Dodge Stampede" 1951 (Sheriff); "Rodeo King and the Senorita" 1951 (Sheriff); "Three Desperate Men" 1951 (Ed Larkin); "Brave Warrior" 1952 (Barker); "Hellgate"

1952 (Banta); "Laramie Mountains" 1952 (Paul Drake); "The Man Behind the Gun" 1952; "Montana Belle" 1952 (Grat Dalton); "Scorching Fury" 1952; "Springfield Rifle" 1952 (Barfly); "Waco" 1952 (Crawford); "Cow Country" 1953 (Tim Sykes); "The Great Jesse James Raid" 1953 (Cavalry Officer); "Jesse James Versus the Daltons" 1954 (Bob Ford); "Seminole Uprising" 1955 (Toby Wilson); "Shotgun" 1955 (Frank); "Kentucky Rifle" 1956; "Shoot-Out at Medicine Bend" 1957; "King of the Wild Stallions" 1959 (Sheriff); "Westbound" 1959. ¶TV: *The Cisco Kid*—"Postal Inspector" 8-4-51, "Kid Sister Trouble" 9-15-51, "Battle of Bad Rock" 10-4-52, "Outlaw's Gallery" 11-22-52, "The Haunted Stage Stop" 3-7-53, "Stolen River" 10-3-53; *Wild Bill Hickok*—"The Lady School Teacher" 10-2-51, "School Teacher Story" 1-15-52, "Hands Across the Border" 7-22-52, "Stolen Church Funds" 9-9-52, "Jingles Gets the Bird" 3-24-53; *The Roy Rogers Show*—"Flying Bullets" 6-15-52, "Death Medicine" 9-7-52, "Violence in Paradise Valley" 11-2-55; *The Lone Ranger*—"Jeb's Gold Mine" 10-16-52, "Outlaw's Trail" 10-21-54; *The Gene Autry Show*—"The Hold-Up" 12-14-52, "The Hoodoo Canyon" 8-17-54; *Maverick*—"The Long Hunt" 10-20-57 (Local Sheriff); *The Tall Man*—"Full Payment" 9-9-61 (Jack Barron); *Cheyenne*—"Winchester Quarantine" 9-25-61 (Burt).

Mallory, Ed. TV: *Wagon Train*—"Princess of a Lost Tribe" 11-2-60 (Mike Kelly); *Death Valley Days*—"Lieutenant Bungle" 10-25-61 (Ross); *Laramie*—"Wolf Cub" 11-21-61; *Tales of Wells Fargo*—"Trackback" 12-30-61 (Ron); *The Tall Man*—"An Hour to Die" 2-17-62 (Johnny Pride).

Mallory, Patricia "Boots" (1913-12/1/58). Films: "Powdersmoke Range" 1935 (Carolyn Sibley).

Mallory, Wayne. Films: "Reprisal!" 1956 (Tom Shipley); "The Storm Rider" 1957 (Hanks); "Bullwhip" 1958 (Larry). ¶TV: *Wild Bill Hickok*—"Treasure Trail" 12-30-52, "Halley's Comet" 2-17-53, "Wild Bill's Odyssey" 3-31-53; *The Cisco Kid*—"Arroyo Millionaire's Castle" 12-12-53, "Stevens Gang and Telegraph" 1-2-54; *Death Valley Days*—"Death and Taxes" 1-17-55; *The Roy Rogers Show*—"The Scavenger" 11-27-55 (Mack), "Treasure of Paradise Valley" 12-11-55; *Sergeant Preston of the Yukon*—"Dog Race" 1-19-56 (Dave Daggett), "The Coward" 4-12-56 (Andy Hewitt).

Malone, Dorothy (1925-). Films: "Frontier Days" 1945-short; "Two Guys from Texas" 1948 (Joan Winston); "Colorado Territory" 1949 (Julie Ann); "South of St. Louis" 1949 (Deborah Miller); "The Nevadan" 1950 (Karen Galt); "Saddle Legion" 1951 (Dr. Ann Rollins); "The Bushwackers" 1952 (Cathy Sharpe); "Jack Slade" 1953 (Virginia Dale); "Law and Order" 1953 (Jeannie Bristow); "The Lone Gun" 1954 (Charlotte Downing); "At Gunpoint" 1955 (Martha Wright); "Five Guns West" 1955 (Shalee); "Tall Man Riding" 1955 (Corinna Ordway Willard); "Pillars of the Sky" 1956 (Calla Gaxton); "Tension at Table Rock" 1956 (Lorna Miller); "Quantez" 1957 (Chaney); "Warlock" 1959 (Lilly Dollar); "The Last Sunset" 1961 (Belle Breckenridge). ¶TV: *Cimarron City*—"A Respectable Girl" 12-6-58 (Nora Atkins); *Death Valley Days*—"The Watch" 1-16-63 (Mary Parker).

Malone, Molly (1888-2/15/52). Films: "Birds of a Feather" 1916; "Mountain Blood" 1916; "The Red Stain" 1916; "The Timber Wolf" 1916; "Bucking Broadway" 1917 (Molly); "A Marked Man" 1917 (Molly Young); "The Soul Herder" 1917; "Straight Shooting" 1917 (Joan Sims); "The Phantom Riders" 1918 (Molly); "The Scarlet Drop" 1918 (Molly Calvert); "Thieves' Gold" 1918 (Alice Norris); "Wild Women" 1918 (the Princess); "A Woman's Fool" 1918 (Jessamine Buckner); "Red Courage" 1921 (Jane Reedly); "Sure Fire" 1921 (Marian Hoffman); "Blaze Away" 1922 (Molly Melody); "The Freshie" 1922 (Violet Blakely); "Jaws of Steel" 1922; "Never Let Go" 1922; "Trail of Hate" 1922 (Mary Stockdale); "Westbound" 1924 (Evelyn Vaughn); "Double Fisted" 1925; "The Knockout Kid" 1925 (Jenny Jenkins); "Bad Man's Bluff" 1926 (Alice Hardy); "The Bandit Buster" 1926 (Sylvia Morton); "Rawhide" 1926 (Nan); "The Girl in the Garrett" 1927; "The Golden Stallion" 1927-serial.

Malone, Nancy (1935-). Films: "The Man Who Loved Cat Dancing" 1973 (Sudie). ¶TV: *Bonanza*—"The Unseen Wound" 1-29-67 (Catherine Rowen); *Hondo*—"Hondo and the Superstition Massacre" 9-29-67 (Mary Davis); *The Big Valley*—"The Secret" 1-27-69 (Marcy Howard); *The Outcasts*—"Give Me Tomorrow" 4-21-69 (Mavis).

Malone, Violet. Films: "The Little Angel of Canyon Creek" 1914 (Mary Morrison).

Maloney, James (1915-8/19/78). Films: "Hell Canyon Outlaws" 1957. ¶TV: *Zane Grey Theater*—"A Gun Is for Killing" 10-18-57 (Will Parr); *Gunsmoke*—"Jesse" 10-19-57 (Karl), "Dooley Surrenders" 3-8-58 (Faber), "Hard Virtue" 5-6-61 (Jenkins); *Colt .45*—"Dead Aim" 4-12-59 (Clark Lingle); *Have Gun Will Travel*—"Bear Bait" 5-13-61 (Jimmy).

Maloney, Leo (1888-11/2/29). Films: "The Reckoning" 1912; "Santa Fe Max" 1912; "The Battle at Fort Laramie" 1913; "Cactus Jake, Heart-Breaker" 1914; "Jimmy Hayes and Muriel" 1914; "The Man from the East" 1914; "The Mexican" 1914; "A Militant School Ma'am" 1914; "The Rival Stage Lines" 1914; "Saved by a Watch" 1914; "The Scapegoat" 1914; "The Sheriff's Reward" 1914; "The Telltale Knife" 1914; "The Way of the Redman" 1914; "Why the Sheriff Is a Bachelor" 1914; "The Brave Deserve the Fair" 1915; "A Desperate Leap" 1915; "The Girl and the Game" 1915-serial; "Harold's Bad Man" 1915; "Her Slight Mistake" 1915; "How Weary Went Wooing" 1915; "The Man from Texas" 1915; "The Mettle of Jerry McGuire" 1915; "Never Again" 1915; "The Range Girl and the Cowboy" 1915; "Lass of the Lumberland" 1916-serial; "The Manager of the B & A" 1916; "Medicine Bend" 1916 (Du Sang); "A Mistake in Rustlers" 1916; "Whispering Smith" 1916 (Du Sang); "The Heart of Texas Ryan" 1917; "The Lost Express" 1917-serial; "The Railroad Raiders" 1917; "Wolves of the Range" 1918; "The Arizona Catclaw" 1919 (Asa Harris); "Captive Bride" 1919; "A Pistol Point Proposal" 1919; "Riding Wild" 1919; "The Secret Peril" 1919; "The Great Round Up" 1920; "The Honor of the Range" 1920; "The Lone Ranger" 1920; "One Law for All" 1920; "The Red Hot Trail" 1920; "Ghost City" 1921; "No Man's Woman" 1921 (Cullen); "The Wolverine" 1921 (Charlie Fox); "The Bar Cross War" 1922; "Come and Get Me" 1922; "Deputized" 1922; "The Drifter" 1922; "Here's Your Man" 1922; "His Enemy's Friend" 1922; "His Own Law" 1922; "Nine Points of the Law" 1922 (Fred Cullum); "One Jump Ahead" 1922; "Rough Going" 1922; "Under Suspicion" 1922; "The Western Musketeer" 1922 (Ranger); "The Extra Seven" 1923; "Hyde and Zeke" 1923; "In Wrong Right" 1923; "King's Creek Law" 1923 (Tom Hardy); "Lost, Strayed or Stolen" 1923; "100% Nerve" 1923; "Partners Three" 1923; "The Rum Runners" 1923; "Smoked Out" 1923; "Steel Shod

Evidence" 1923; "Tom, Dick and Harry" 1923; "The Unsuspecting Stranger" 1923; "Warned in Advance" 1923; "When Fighting's Necessary" 1923; "Wings of the Storm" 1923; "Yellow Gold and Men" 1923; "Built for Running" 1924; "Headin' Through" 1924 (Bob Baxter); "The Loser's End" 1924 (Bruce Mason); "Not Guilty for Runnin'" 1924 (Sonny-Jack Parr); "Payable on Demand" 1924 (Buck McDavid); "The Perfect Alibi" 1924 (Mack MacGregor); "Riding Double" 1924 (Hoss Martin); "Across the Deadline" 1925 (Clem Wainwright); "The Blood Bond" 1925 (Burr Evans); "Flash O'-Lightning" 1925 (Flash Lightnin'/Richard Coakley); "Luck and Sand" 1925 (Jim Blake); "Ranchers and Rascals" 1925 (Harvey Martin); "The Shield of Silence" 1925 (Nathan Holden); "The Trouble Buster" 1925 (Harvey Martin); "Win, Lose or Draw" 1925 (Ward Austin/Ben Austin); "Blind Trail" 1926 (Bob Carson); "The High Hand" 1926 (Sandy Sands); "The Outlaw Express" 1926 (Miles Wayburn); "Without Orders" 1926 (Dale Monroe); "Border Blackbirds" 1927 (Bart Evans); "The Devil's Twin" 1927 (Honest John Andrews/George Andrews); "Don Desperado" 1927 (Leo McHale); "The Long Loop on the Pecos" 1927 (Jim Rutledge); "The Man from Hardpan" 1927 (Robert Alan); "Two-Gun of the Tumbleweed" 1927 (Two-Gun Calder); "The Apache Raider" 1928 (Apache Bob); "The Vanishing West" 1928-serial; "Overland Bound" 1929 (Lucky Lorimer).

Malooly, Maggie. TV: *Cimarron Strip*—"The Last Wolf" 12-14-67; *Gunsmoke*—"Larkin" 1-20-75 (Woman); *Bret Maverick*—"The Vulture Also Rises" 3-16-82 (Irish Annie).

Malvern, Paul (1902-5/29/93). Films: "Gun-Hand Garrison" 1927; "The Trail Riders" 1928.

Maly, Walter. Films: "Ridin' Wild" 1925 (Fred Blake); "Prowlers of the Night" 1926 (Bell); "Bulldog Pluck" 1927 (Gillen); "Code of the Cow Country" 1927 (Dutch Moore); "The Fighting Hombre" 1927 (Lone Badger); "The Galloping Gobs" 1927 (Outlaw Leader); "The Phantom Buster" 1927 (Jack); "The Terror of Bar X" 1927 (Hoke Channing); "White Pebbles" 1927 (Sam Harvey); "The Little Buckaroo" 1928 (Sam Baxter); "The White Outlaw" 1929 (Deputy Bud Mason).

Malyon, Eily (1879-9/26/61). Films: "God's Country and the

Woman" 1937 (Mrs. Higginbottom); "Arkansas Judge" 1941 (Widow Smithers).

Mamakos, Peter (1918-). Films: "Trail of the Yukon" 1949 (Rand); "Silver Canyon" 1951 (Laughing Jack); "Horizons West" 1952 (Lt. Salazar); "Viva Zapata!" 1952 (Soldier); "The Gambler from Natchez" 1954 (Etienne); "The Marauders" 1955 (Ramos); "Quincannon, Frontier Scout" 1956 (Blackfoot Sara); "The Searchers" 1956 (Futterman); "Fort Bowie" 1958 (Sgt. Kukus); "Terror at Black Falls" 1962 (Father). ¶TV: *The Lone Ranger*—"Jim Tyler's Luck" 2-16-50, "The Black Widow" 8-24-50, "The Squire" 11-9-50, "Son of Adoption" 3-19-53, "The Gentleman from Julesburg" 6-11-53, "Enfield Rifle" 1-13-55, "Uncle Ed" 3-3-55; *The Cisco Kid*—"Quick on the Trigger" 2-6-54; *Broken Arrow*—"Apache Massacre" 1-1-57 (Tigre), "Conquistador" 10-8-57; *Jim Bowie*—"A Horse for Old Hickory" 1-4-57 (Jean Lafitte), "Master at Arms" 1-25-57 (Jean Lafitte), "The Captain's Chimp" 3-8-57 (Jean Lafitte), "Mexican Adventure" 12-20-57 (Jean Lafitte); *Zorro*—"Zorro by Proxy" 4-17-58; *Gunsmoke*—"Overland Express" 5-31-58 (Al Carp); *Wyatt Earp*—"The Frame-Up" 6-3-58 (Cy Johnson), "The Actress" 4-14-59 (Clay Bronson), "The Posse" 5-10-60 (Hoodlum), "Terror in the Desert" 1-24-61 (Baxter); *The Adventures of Rin Tin Tin*—"The Cloudbusters" 10-31-58 (Geronimo); *Maverick*—"The Thirty-Ninth Star" 11-16-58 (Watchman); *Rawhide*—"Incident at Alabaster Plain" 1-16-59 (Kellum), "Incident of the Devil and His Due" 1-22-60 (Eddie), "Incident of the Running Man" 5-5-61 (Slade); *The Texan*—"South of the Border" 5-18-59; *The Deputy*—"The Return of Simon Fry" 2-13-60 (Jubba); *The Virginian*—"The Final Hour" 5-1-63, "Walk in Another's Footsteps" 3-11-64 (Smudge); *Wagon Train*—"The Widow O'Rourke Story" 10-7-63 (Auctioneer); *Daniel Boone*—9-23-65 (Indian Chief), "The Matchmaaker" 10-27-66 (Chief Two Shots), "Run for the Money" 2-19-70 (Indian Chief).

Mamo, John. TV: *The Rifleman*—"The Sixteenth Cousin" 1-28-63 (Hikaru Yamanaka); *Kung Fu*—"Sun and Cloud Shadow" 2-22-73 (Ying), "The Hoots" 12-13-73 (Old Hunter).

Manard, Biff. Films: "Machismo—40 Graves for 40 Guns" 1970 (Harris Gang Member); "Bo-

nanza: Under Attack" TVM-1995 (Luke). ¶TV: *Bonanza*—"The Rattlesnake Brigade" 12-5-71 (Suggins), "A Place to Hide" 3-19-72 (Hartsfield), "Riot!" 10-3-72 (Scoggins).

Mancini, Carla. Films: "Calibre .38" 1971-Ital.; "Bounty Hunter In Trinity" 1972-Ital.; "Go Away! Trinity Has Arrived in Eldorado" 1972-Ital.; "Pistol Packin' Preacher" 1972-Ital./Fr.; "Sometimes Life Is Hard, Right Providence?" 1972-Ital./Fr./Ger.; "Sting of the West" 1972-Ital.; "Trinity and Sartana Are Coming" 1972-Ital.; "Animal Called Man" 1973-Ital.; "Anything for a Friend" 1973-Ital.; "Fighting Fists of Shanghai Joe" 1973-Ital.; "Man Called Invincible" 1973-Ital.; "Don't Turn the Other Cheek" 1974-Ital./Ger./Span.; "Patience Has a Limit, We Don't" 1974-Span./Ital.

Mancuso, Nick (1956-). Films: "The Legend of Walks Far Woman" TVM-1982 (Horses Ghost).

Mandan, Robert (1932-). TV: *Sara*—2-20-76.

Mander, Miles (1888-2/8/46). Films: "Apache Trail" 1943 (James V. Thorne).

Mando, Peggy. TV: *Laredo*—"Oh Careless Love" 12-23-66 (Lost Bird).

Mandy, Jerry (1892-5/1/45). Films: "The Gay Defender" 1927 (Chombo); "Rainbow's End" 1935.

Mankuma, Blu. Films: "Davy Crockett: Rainbow in the Thunder" TVM-1988.

Manley, David. TV: *Two Faces West*—"The Prisoner" 2-6-61; *Wanted—Dead or Alive*—"Monday Morning" 3-8-61 (Joseph Richards); *Bonanza*—"The Tin Badge" 12-17-61 (Virgil).

Manley, Stephen (1965-). TV: *Kung Fu*—"A Lamb to the Slaughter" 1-11-75 (Boy Caine), "One Step to Darkness" 1-25-75 (Boy Caine).

Mann, Delbert. Films: "The Iron Horse" 1924 (Charles Crocker).

Mann, Hank (1887-11/25/71). Films: "The Arizona Romeo" 1925 (Deputy); "The Man Who Played Square" 1925 (the Cook); "The Flying Horseman" 1926 (Newton Carey); "Wings of the Storm" 1926 (Red Jones); "Morgan's Last Raid" 1929 (Tex); "The Arizona Kid" 1930 (Bartender Bill); "The Dawn Trail" 1930 (Cock Eye); "Ridin' for Justice" 1932 (Pete); "The Fourth Horseman" 1933; "Smoky" 1933 (Buck); "Fair Warning" 1937; "Call of the Prairie" 1936 (Tom); "Goofs and Saddles" 1937-short (Lem); "The Stranger from Arizona" 1938 (Garrison); "Frontier Marshal" 1939 (Man); "Son of Paleface" 1952 (Bartender); "Three Hours to Kill" 1954 (Man); "Pardners" 1956 (Townsman); "Last Train from Gun Hill" 1959 (Storekeeper).

Mann, Jack. TV: *Gunsmoke—*"Jealousy" 7-6-57 (Jack Davis), "Kitty's Outlaw" 10-5-57 (1st Man); *Tombstone Territory—*"Johnny Ringo's Last Ride" 2-19-58 (Sidney Farrell).

Mann, Larry D. (1922-). Films: "Flaming Frontier" 1958-Can. (Bradford); "The Appaloosa" 1966 (Priest); "There Was a Crooked Man" 1970; "Scandalous John" 1971 (Bartender); "The Wild Country" 1971 (Marshal); "Oklahoma Crude" 1973 (Deke Watson); "Pony Express Rider" 1976 (Blackmore). ¶TV: *The Dakotas—*"Justice at Eagle's Nest" 3-11-63 (Ed Jarvis); *The Big Valley—*"The Murdered Party" 11-17-65 (Jake Kyles); *The Legend of Jesse James—*"One Too Many Mornings" 11-22-65 (Union Sergeant); *Shane—*Regular 1966 (Harve); *Iron Horse—*"A Dozen Ways to Kill a Man" 12-19-66 (Kellam); *Gunsmoke—*"Saturday Night" 1-7-67 (Chick), "Major Glory" 10-30-67 (Lanny), "Zavala" 10-7-68 (Bakman), "Waco" 12-9-68 (Gamble), "A Matter of Honor" 11-17-69 (Prosecutor), "Women for Sale" 9-10-73 & 9-17-73; *Rango—*"Requiem for a Ranger" 2-24-67 (Purcell); *Here Come the Brides—*"Letter of the Law" 10-30-68 (Judge Cody), "A Man's Errand" 3-19-69 (Kimberly); *The Guns of Will Sonnett—*"Guilt" 11-29-68 (Mort Lucas); *The High Chaparral—*"Spokes" 9-25-70 (Boggs); *Bonanza—*"An Earthquake Called Callahan" 4-11-71 (Alex Steiner)

Mann, Leonard. Films: "Chuck Moll" 1970-Ital. (Chuck Moll); "Forgotten Pistolero" 1970-Ital./Span.; "Vengeance Is a Dish Served Cold" 1971-Ital./Span. (Jeremiah Bridger)

Mann, Margaret (1868-2/4/41). Films: "Secret Menace" 1931; "The Law Rides" 1936 (Mrs. Lewis).

Manners, Dorothy (-7/5/49). Films: "Across the Divide" 1921 (Helen); "Snowdrift" 1923 (Snowdrift).

Manners, Marjorie. Films: "Outlaws of Boulder Pass" 1942; "Texas to Bataan" 1942 (Dallas); "Western Cyclone" 1943 (Mary Arnold); "Blazing Frontier" 1944 (Helen).

Manners, Mickey. TV: *The Rifleman—*"Which Way'd They Go?" 4-1-63 (Moss Jackman).

Manners, Sheila (1911-). Films:

"Land of Wanted Men" 1932 (Cynthia); "Texas Gun Fighter" 1932 (Jane Adams); "Texas Pioneers" 1932 (Nancy Thomas); "Cowboy Counsellor" 1933 (Ruther Avery); "The Prescott Kid" 1934 (Dolores Ortega); "Lawless Range" 1935 (Anne Mason); "Moonlight on the Prairie" 1935 (Barbara Roberts); "Westward Ho" 1935 (Mary Gordon); "Desert Phantom" 1937 (Jean Haloran).

Manni, Ettore (1927-7/27/79). Films: "Ringo and His Golden Pistol" 1966-Ital.; "Born to Kill" 1967-Ital.; "The Stranger Returns" 1967-U.S./Ital./Ger./Span. (Stafford); "Bury Them Deep" 1968-Ital. (Chaleco Hunter); "I Am Sartana, Your Angel of Death" 1969-Ital./Fr.; "Django and Sartana Are Coming ... It's the End" 1970-Ital.; "Stranger That Kneels Beside the Shadow of a Corpse" 1971-Ital. (Solinas); "Chino" 1973-Ital./Span./Fr. (Sheriff); "Silver Saddle" 1978-Ital.

Manning, Aileen (1886-3/25/46). Films: "Range Law" 1931.

Manning, Buck. Films: "The Winding Trail" 1921 (Laughing Larry).

Manning, Hope. Films: "The Old Corral" 1936 (Eleanor Spenser).

Manning, Jack (1916-). Films: "The Great Northfield, Minnesota Raid" 1972 (Heywood). ¶TV: *Bonanza—*"Rock-a-Bye, Hoss" 10-10-71 (Henry Clagger); *Alias Smith and Jones—*"McGuffin" 12-9-72 (Dr. O'Connell).

Manning, Mildred. Films: "A Chance Deception" 1913; "The Westerners" 1919 (Prue Welch/Molly Lafond).

Manning, Robert. Films: "Single-Handed Sanders" 1932; "Vanishing Men" 1932; "The Ferocious Pal" 1934 (Dr. Elliott).

Manon, Gloria. Films: "Poker Alice" TVM-1987. ¶TV: *Daniel Boone—*"A Rope for Mingo" 12-2-65 (Kutawarl).

Manon, Marcia (-4/12/73). Films: "The Border Wireless" 1918 (Esther Meier); "A Daughter of the Wolf" 1919 (Jean Burroughs); "The Vanishing Pioneer" 1928 (the Apron Woman).

Mansell, Barbara. Films: "Frontier Uprising" 1961; "The Firebrand" 1962 (Cassie); "Young Guns of Texas" 1963 (Martha Jane Canary). ¶TV: *Wide Country—*"The Care and Handling of Tigers" 4-25-63 (Winifred Garner).

Mansfield, David. Films: "The Last Chance" 1921 (Dynamite Dan).

Mansfield, Jayne (1933-6/29/67). Films: "The Sheriff of Fractured Jaw" 1958-Brit. (Kate).

Mansfield, John (1919-9/18/56). Films: "Silver City" 1951 (Townsman); "Warpath" 1951 (Sub-Chief); "Pony Express" 1953; "Tennessee's Partner" 1955 (Clifford). ¶TV: *The Lone Ranger—*"Sunstroke Mesa" 3-17-55.

Mansfield, Marian (1905-11/16/88). Films: "Wanderer of the Wasteland" 1935 (Lady at Card Game).

Mansfield, Rankin (-1/22/69). Films: "Badlands of Montana" 1957 (Travis); "The Oklahoman" 1957 (Doctor); "Face of a Fugitive" 1959 (Minister). ¶TV: *The Cisco Kid—*"The Powder Trail" 2-14-53; *The Restless Gun—*"The Gold Star" 5-19-58 (Fred); *Tales of Wells Fargo—*"Portrait of Teresa" 2-10-62 (Storekeeper).

Mansfield, Sally. TV: *Wild Bill Hickok—*"The Maverick" 8-19-52; *Death Valley Days—*"Sego Lillies" 1-14-53 (Wilhelmina); *The Gene Autry Show—*"Saddle Up" 12-3-55, "Ride, Rancheros" 12-10-55, "The Rangerette" 12-17-55.

Manson, Maurice (1913-). TV: *Gunsmoke—*"Reunion '78" 3-3-56 (Andy Culley), "How to Die for Nothing" 6-23-56 (Reisling); *Zane Grey Theater—*"The Open Cell" 11-22-57 (Ben McCready); *Maverick—*"The Wrecker" 12-1-57 (Bellairs), "Cruise of the Cynthia B" 1-10-60 (Rutherford Carr), "Last Stop: Oblivion" 2-12-61 (Bascombe Sunday); *Rawhide—*"Incident of the Tumbleweed Wagon" 1-9-59; *Colt .45—*"The Magic Box" 4-19-59 (Brady); *Sugarfoot—*"Journey to Provision" 1-5-60 (Mayor); *Cheyenne—*"The Return of Mr. Grimm" 2-13-61 (Mayor Stanley); *Lawman—*"The Break-In" 5-21-61 (Harold G. Berliner); *Laramie—*"Handful of Fire" 12-5-61, "War Hero" 10-2-62; *The Virginian—*"The Devil's Children" 12-5-62.

Mantee, Paul (1936-). Films: "Blood on the Arrow" 1964 (Segura). ¶TV: *The Rifleman—*"Assault" 3-21-61, "Incident at Line Shack Six" 1-7-63 (Johnny Wing); *Laredo—*"A Very Small Assignment" 3-17-66 (Ed); *Rango—*"The Spy Who Was Out Cold" 2-10-67 (Carter); *Bonanza—*"The Stronghold" 5-26-68 (Mike Farrell); *Cimarron Strip—*"Without Honor" 2-29-68 (Lane Bardeen); *The Virginian—*"The Handy Man" 3-6-68 (Roy Havens); *The Outcasts—*"Alligator King" 1-20-69 (Julbuta Mekko); *Daniel Boone—*"How to Become a Goddess" 4-30-70 (Atawa).

Mantegna, Joe (1947-). Films: "Three Amigos" 1986 (Harry Flugleman).

Mantell, Joe (1920-). TV: *Wanted—Dead or Alive*—"Sheriff of Red Rock" 11-29-58 (Orv Daniels); *Man from Blackhawk*—"The Biggest Legend" 1-1-60 (Wayne Weedy); *The Travels of Jaimie McPheeters*—"The Day of the Lame Duck" 2-9-64 (Piggy Trewblood); *The Virginian*—"Beyond the Border" 11-24-65 (Aaron); *The Loner*—"The Trial in Paradise" 1-22-66 (Allerdyce).

Mantley, Jon Jason. TV: *Gunsmoke*—"The Gun" 11-19-70 (Tom), "Pike" 3-1-71 & 3-8-71 (Billy), "The Lost" 9-13-71 (Boy Jon).

Mantley, Maria. TV: *Gunsmoke*—"The Gun" 11-19-70 (Anne), "Pike" 3-1-71 & 3-8-71 (Girl #1), "The Lost" 9-13-71 (Girl).

Mantooth, Randolph (1945-). Films: "The Bravos" TVM-1972 (Lieutenant Lewis); "Testimony of Two Men" TVM-1977 (Father Frank McNulty). ¶TV: *The Men from Shiloh*—"The Regimental Line" 3-3-71 (Lieutenant Dorn); *Alias Smith and Jones*—"Stagecoach Seven" 3-11-71 (Dan Loomis).

Manx, Kate (1930-11/15/64). TV: *Tales of Wells Fargo*—"The Little Man" 5-18-59 (Julie); *Stoney Burke*—"The Contender" 10-1-62 (Erlie Bristol).

Many Treaties, Chief (William Hazlett) (1875-2/29/48). Films: "Rustlers of Red Dog" 1935-serial (Chief); "Drums of Destiny" 1937; "Flaming Frontier" 1938-serial; "Outlaw Express" 1938; "Go West, Young Lady" 1941 (Chief Big Thunder); "The Pioneers" 1941 (Warcloud); "Saddlemates" 1941; "King of the Stallions" 1942; "Overland Mail" 1942-serial; "Daredevils of the West" 1943-serial (Blue Eagle); "Deerslayer" 1943 (Chief Brave Eagle); "The Law Rides Again" 1943 (Barking Fox); "Buffalo Bill" 1944 (Tall Bull); "Buffalo Bill Rides Again" 1947 (Chief Brave Eagle); "Last of the Redmen" 1947; "The Sea of Grass" 1947 (Indian); "Black Bart" 1948 (Indian); "Sundown Riders" 1948 (Indian Charlie).

Manz, Linda (1961-). Films: "Orphan Train" TVM-1979 (Sarah).

Manza, Ralph (1921-). Films: "The Apple Dumpling Gang Rides Again" 1979. ¶TV: *Judge Roy Bean*—"Citizen Romeo" 12-1-55 (Gasparo); *The Outlaws*—"The Little Colonel" 5-18-61 (Colonel); *The Virginian*—"If You Have Tears" 2-13-63; *Wide Country*—"Yanqui, Go Home!" 4-4-63 (Lupo); *Laredo*—"Jinx" 12-2-65 (Blue Dog), "No Bugles, One Drum" 2-24-66 (Blue Dog), "Split the Difference" 4-7-67 (Blue Dog); *The High Chaparral*—"Only the Bad Come to Sonora" 10-2-70.

Mapes, Ted (1902-9/9/84). Films: "The Silent Code" 1935 (Constable); "End of the Trail" 1936; "The Law Rides" 1936; "Secret Patrol" 1936 (Man); "Stampede" 1936 (Whitey); "One Man Justice" 1937; "Rio Grande" 1938; "The Arizona Kid" 1939; "The Lone Ranger Rides Again" 1939-serial (Merritt); "Three Texas Steers" 1939 (Willie); "Wall Street Cowboy" 1939; "Zorro's Fighting Legion" 1939-serial; "The Border Legion" 1940; "The Carson City Kid" 1940; "King of the Royal Mounted" 1940-serial (Blake); "The Ranger and the Lady" 1940 (Kramer); "Under Texas Skies" 1940; "Gauchos of El Dorado" 1941; "In Old Cheyenne" 1941; "Red River Valley" 1941; "Riders of the Badlands" 1941; "The Royal Mounted Patrol" 1941; "Tonto Basin Outlaws" 1941 (Ricks); "Below the Border" 1942 (Max); "Home in Wyomin'" 1942; "Pardon My Gun" 1942 (Ace); "Prairie Gunsmoke" 1942; "Texas Trouble Shooters" 1942 (Slim); "Thunder River Feud" 1942 (Buck); "A Tornado in the Saddle" 1942; "Valley of Vanishing Men" 1942-serial; "Vengeance of the West" 1942; "Calling Wild Bill Elliott" 1943; "Cowboy in the Clouds" 1943; "Frontier Fury" 1943 (Jim Wallace); "Land of Hunted Men" 1943; "The Outlaw" 1943 (Guard); "Black Arrow" 1944-serial; "Cyclone Prairie Rangers" 1944; "Dead or Alive" 1944; "Death Rides the Plains" 1944; "Fuzzy Settles Down" 1944; "The Last Horseman" 1944 (Cudlow); "Law Men" 1944 (Curley); "Partners of the Trail" 1944; "Flame of the West" 1945; "Frontier Feud" 1945; "Return of the Durango Kid" 1945; "Rustlers of the Badlands" 1945; "Texas Panhandle" 1945; "Conquest of Cheyenne" 1946; "Drifting Along" 1946 (Ed); "My Pal Trigger" 1946; "The Phantom Rider" 1946-serial (Riot Leader); "Roaring Rangers" 1946; "Terror Trail" 1946; "Two-Fisted Ranger" 1946; "Under Arizona Skies" 1946; "The Fabulous Texan" 1947; "Jesse James Rides Again" 1947-serial (Bass/Dale); "Riders of the Lone Star" 1947; "Son of Zorro" 1947-serial (Larkin); "The Stranger from Ponca City" 1947; "The Wild Frontier" 1947 (Gunman); "Black Eagle" 1948 (Sam); "Dangers of the Canadian Mounted" 1948-serial (Mac); "Desperadoes of Dodge City" 1948 (Jake); "Fury at Furnace Creek" 1948 (Man); "The Paleface" 1948 (Horseman); "The Strawberry Roan" 1948 (Smitty); "Sundown Riders" 1948 (Gilson); "Bad Men of Tombstone" 1949; "Desert Vigilante" 1949; "El Dorado Pass" 1949 (Dodd); "Outcasts of the Trail" 1949 (Fred Smith); "Cow Town" 1950 (Ed Loomis); "Punchy Cowpunchers" 1950-short (Red); "Raiders of Tomahawk Creek" 1950; "Winchester '73" 1950 (Bartender); "Topeka" 1953 (Cully); "The Far Country" 1955 (Deputy); "Night Passage" 1957 (Leary); "The Man Who Shot Liberty Valance" 1962 (Highpockets); "Cheyenne Autumn" 1964 (Trooper); "The Rare Breed" 1966 (Liveryman). ¶TV: *The Cisco Kid*—"Carrier Pigeon" 11-3-51, "Jewelry Hold-Up" 12-15-51, "The Puppeteer" 1-19-52, "Canyon City Kit" 3-1-52, "Mining Madness" 4-11-53, "Three Suspects" 5-23-53; *The Gene Autry Show*—"Cold Decked" 9-15-53; *Wagon Train*—"The John Cameron Story" 10-2-57, "The Les Rand Story" 10-16-57, "The Tracy Sadler Story" 3-9-60; *Rough Riders*—"The Holdout" 6-25-59.

Maple, Christine. Films: "Roarin' Lead" 1936 (Doris Moore); "The Big Show" 1937 (Elizabeth).

Mara, Adele (1923-). Films: "Shut My Big Mouth" 1942 (Conchita Montoya); "Vengeance of the West" 1942; "Riders of the Northwest Mounted" 1943; "Bells of Rosarita" 1945 (Patty Phillips); "Flame of the Barbary Coast" 1945 (Marie); "Robin Hood of Texas" 1947 (Julie Reeves); "Twilight on the Rio Grande" 1947 (Elena Del Rio); "The Gallant Legion" 1948 (Catalina); "Night Time in Nevada" 1948 (Joan Andrews); "California Passage" 1950 (Beth Martin); "Rock Island Trail" 1950 (Constance Strong); "The Black Whip" 1956 (Ruthie). ¶TV: *Cheyenne*—"Border Showdown" 11-22-55, "Star in the Dust" 5-1-56 (Claire), "The Angry Sky" 6-17-58 (Rose); *The Adventures of Rin Tin Tin*—"Rusty's Romance" 1-20-56 (Rose Marlowe), "Circle of Fire" 5-11-56 (Crystal Ramsey); *Maverick*—"Seed of Deception" 4-13-58 (June Mundy), "The Spanish Dancer" 12-14-58 (Elena Grande), "The Marquesa" 1-3-60 (Marquesa Luisa de Ruisenor); *Wyatt Earp*—"Dig a Grave for Ben Thompson" 5-20-58 (Girl), "Wyatt's Brothers Join Up" 6-6-61 (Thelma Callum); *Bat Masterson*—"Double Showdown" 10-8-58 (Maria); *Tales of Wells Fargo*—"Wild Cargo" 1-19-59 (Theo); *Laramie*—"Day of Vengeance" 1-19-60 (Alice Goren); *Stagecoach West*—"The Arsonist" 2-14-61 (Sally Burke); *The Tall Man*—"The Woman in Black" 5-12-62 (Rosa).

Maranda, Evi. Films: "Damned Pistols of Dallas" 1964-Span./Ital./Fr. ¶TV: *Dundee and the Culhane*—10-18-67 (Antonia).

Marano, Ezio. Films: "They Call Me Trinity" 1970-Ital. (Weasel).

Maranzana, Mario. Films: "Dollar of Fire" 1967-Ital./Span.; "Two Sides of the Dollar" 1967-Fr./Ital.; "Ciccio Forgives, I Don't" 1968-Ital.; "A Long Ride from Hell" 1968-Ital. (Bobcat).

Marba, Joe (1879-9/7/38). Films: "Under Texas Skies" 1930 (Sheriff); "The Sheriff's Secret" 1931; "Shotgun Pass" 1931 (Spider Mitchell).

Marburgh, Bertran (1875-8/22/56). Films: "A Streak of Luck" 1925 (Mr. Burton).

Marc, Alice. Films: "Nan of Music Mountain" 1917 (Nita).

March, Eve (1910-9/18/74). Films: "Calling Wild Bill Elliott" 1943; "Song of Texas" 1943 (Miss Murray).

March, Fredric (1897-4/14/75). Films: "Hombre" 1967 (Favor).

March, Linda. TV: *Bonanza*—"A World Full of Cannibals" 12-22-68 (Harriet Ball).

March, Lori. TV: *Rough Riders*—"The Last Rebel" 7-16-59; *The Tall Man*—"The Frame" 4-21-62 (Isobel Stewart).

Marchal, Arlette (1902-2/9/84). Films: "Born to the West" 1926 (Belle of Paradise Bar); "Forlorn River" 1926 (Ina Blaine).

Marchand, Corinne (1937-). Films: "Arizona Colt" 1965-Ital./Fr./Span. (Jane).

Marchent, Carlos Romero. *see* Romero Marchent, Carlos.

Marco, Jose. Films: "Man from the Cursed Valley" 1964-Ital./Span.; "Last of the Mohicans" 1965-Ital./Span./Ger.; "Django, A Bullet for You" 1966-Span./Ital.; "Taste for Killing" 1966-Ital./Span.; "Quinta: Fighting Proud" 1969-Ital./Span.; "Cry for Revenge" 1968-Ital./Span.

Marcus, James (1868-10/15/37). Films: "Blue Blood and Red" 1916; "The Mediator" 1916 (Big Bill); "Evangeline" 1919 (Basil); "Broken Chains" 1922 (Pat Mulcahy); "Quicksands" 1923 (Ring Member); "The Iron Horse" 1924 (Judge Haller); "All Around the Frying Pan" 1925 (Sheriff); "The Texas Streak" 1926 (Col.

Hollis); "The Meddlin' Stranger" 1927 (Big Bill Dawson); "Border Patrol" 1928 (Captain Bonham); "In Old Arizona" 1929 (Blacksmith); "Billy the Kid" 1930 (Donovan); "The Texan" 1930 (John Brown); "Fighting Caravans" 1931 (the Blacksmith); "The Great Meadow" 1931 (James Harrod); "Land of Wanted Men" 1932 (Judge); "The Man from Arizona" 1932 (Judge McSweeny); "Mason of the Mounted" 1932 (Sheriff); "Vanishing Men" 1932; "King of the Arena" 1933 (Colonel Hiller); "The Lone Avenger" 1933 (Joel Winters); "Strawberry Roan" 1933 (Big Jim Edwards); "Honor of the Range" 1934 (Turner); "The Trail Beyond" 1934 (Henchman); "Wagon Wheels" 1934 (Jed); "Western Frontier" 1935 (Marshal Bat Manning); "The Cattle Thief" 1936 (Cal); "The Lonely Trail" 1936 (Mayor); "Rose of the Rancho" 1936 (Old Spaniard).

Marcus, Vitina. TV: *Gunslinger*—"The Death of Yellow Singer" 5-11-61 (Clea); *Gunsmoke*—"The Squaw" 11-11-61 (Natacea), "Old Comrade" 12-29-62 (Missy); *Rawhide*—"The Peddler" 1-19-62 (Wahkshum); *The Travels of Jaimie McPheeters*—"The Day of the Wizard" 1-12-64 (Irina).

Marcuse, Theodore (1920-11/29/67). TV: *Gunsmoke*—"The Cover-Up" 1-12-57 (Zack Ritter); *Have Gun Will Travel*—"Three Bells to Perdido" 9-14-57, "High Wire" 11-2-57, "The Return of the Lady" 2-21-59 (B.G.); *The Alaskans*—"The Golden Fleece" 11-29-59; *U.S. Marshal*—"The Assassins" 4-9-60 (Bo Collins); *Bonanza*—"The Abduction" 10-29-60; *Laredo*—"The Heroes of San Gill" 12-23-65 (Waldo); *Wild Wild West*—"The Night of the Sudden Plague" 4-22-66 (Dr. Kirby), "The Night of the Bottomless Pit" 11-4-66 (Gustave Maurais/Hubert Crandell), "The Night of the Headless Woman" 1-5-68 (Abdul Hassan); *Daniel Boone*—"Fort New Madrid" 2-15-68 (Hugo Dopfer).

Marden, Adrienne (1909-11/9/78). Films: "Count Three and Pray" 1955 (Mrs. Swallow); "Man from Del Rio" 1956 (Mrs. Tilman). ¶TV: *Trackdown*—"Terror" 2-4-59 (Annabelle); *Rawhide*—"Incident in the Garden of Eden" 6-17-60 (Oneewa); *Wagon Train*—"The Sam Elder Story" 1-18-61 (Lila Allen), "The Cassie Vance Story" 12-23-63 (Mrs. Jenkins); *Lawman*—"Homecoming" 2-5-61 (Mary Walker); *Bonanza*—"No Less a Man" 3-15-64, "Devil on Her Shoulder" 10-17-65 (Emma Morgan);

Kung Fu—"Dark Angel" 11-11-72 (Coralee), "My Brother, My Executioner" 10-12-74 (Coralee).

Marfield, Dwight (1908-8/15/78). TV: *Wagon Train*—"The Clayton Tucker Story" 2-10-60.

Margetts, Monty (1912-). TV: *The Alaskans*—"Contest at Gold Bottom" 11-15-59 (Sara McTavish); *The Texas Wheelers*—7-3-75 (Mrs. Swope).

Margo (1918-7/17/85). Films: "Robin Hood of El Dorado" 1936 (Rosita Murrieta); "Viva Zapata!" 1952 (La Soldadera); "From Hell to Texas" 1958 (Mrs. Bradley). ¶TV: *Wagon Train*—"The John Darro Story" 11-6-57 (Aline Darro); *Rawhide*—"A Man Called Mushy" 10-23-64 (Selena).

Margolin, Janet (1943-12/17/93). Films: "Nevada Smith" 1966 (Neesa).

Margolin, Stuart (1939-). Films: "The Intruders" TVM-1970 (Jesse James); "This Was the West That Was" TVM-1974 (Blind Pete); "Bret Maverick" TVM-1981 (Philo Sandine). ¶TV: *Branded*—"A Taste of Poison" 5-2-65 (Officer); *Gunsmoke*—"The Storm" 9-25-65 (Sheriff), "Homecoming" 1-8-73 (John Mophet), "A Family of Killers" 1-14-74 (Brownie); *Pistols 'n' Petticoats*—12-3-66 (Rafe Blanton); *The Virginian*—"Jed" 1-10-68 (Abe Yeager); *Nichols*—Regular 1971-72 (Mitchell); *Bret Maverick*—Regular 1981-82 (Philo Sandine).

Margotta, Michael (1946-). TV: *The Outcasts*—"The Heroes" 11-11-68 (Matt); *Death Valley Days*—"A Simple Question of Justice" 11-22-69.

Mari, George. Films: "The Eagle's Brood" 1936 (Pablo); "Zorro Rides Again" 1937-serial (Jose); "The Lone Ranger" 1938-serial (Pepito).

Marie, Rose. *see* Rose Marie.

Marievsky, Joseph (1888-4/27/71). Films: "The Three Godfathers" 1936 (Pedero).

Marihugh, Tammy. Films: "A Thunder of Drums" 1961 (Laurie). ¶TV: *Wagon Train*—"The Jess MacAbbee Story" 11-25-59 (Cora Belle); *Stagecoach West*—"The Unwanted" 10-25-60 (Sara Kelly).

Marin, Luis. Films: "Great Treasure Hunt" 1967-Ital./Span. (Felipe); "Canadian Wilderness" 1969-Span./Ital.; "More Dollars for the MacGregors" 1970-Ital./Span.

Marin, Richard "Cheech" (1946-). Films: "The Cisco Kid" CTVM-1994 (Pancho).

Marin, Russ (1934-). TV: *Bonanza*—"Warbonnet" 12-26-71 (Sheriff); *Bret Maverick*—"Welcome to Sweetwater" 12-8-81 (Garrick).

Marion, Beth (1913-). Films: "Between Men" 1935 (Gale Winters); "Trail of Terror" 1935 (Judy Baxter); "Avenging Waters" 1936 (Mary Mortimer); "Everyman's Law" 1936 (Marian Henley); "For the Service" 1936 (Penny Carson); "The Fugitive Sheriff" 1936 (Jane Roberts); "The Phantom of the Range" 1936 (Jeanne Moore); "Rip Roarin' Buckaroo" 1936 (Betty Rose Hayden); "Silver Spurs" 1936 (Peggy Wyman); "Phantom Gold" 1938 (Mary Davis); "Frontier Scout" 1939 (Mary).

Marion, Edna (1908-12/2/57). Films: "The Desert's Price" 1925 (Nora); "Romance of the West" 1930 (Mary Winter).

Marion, George F. (1860-11/30/45). Films: "Gun Shy" 1922 (Undertaker); "Bringin' Home the Bacon" 1924; "On the Go" 1925 (Eb Moots); "Tumbleweeds" 1925 (Old Man); "Loco Luck" 1927 (Dad Perkins, the Postmaster); "Skedaddle Gold" 1927 (George F.); "A Texas Steer" 1927 (Fishback); "Rocky Mountain Mystery" 1935 (Jim Ballard/Adolph Borg).

Marion, Paul. Films: "In Old Caliente" 1939 (Carlos); "Zorro's Fighting Legion" 1939-serial (Kala); "Covered Wagon Days" 1940 (Carlos); "Bandit Queen" 1950 (Manuel); "Raiders of Tomahawk Creek" 1950 (Chief Flying Arrow); "Hot Lead" 1951 (Dakota); "The Fighter" 1952 (Rivas); "Fort Vengeance" 1953 (Eagle Heart); "Shotgun" 1955 (Delgadito). ¶TV: *The Cisco Kid*—"Face of Death" 2-16-52, "Freedom of the Press" 9-27-52, "The Racoon Story" 11-15-52.

Marion, Sidney (1900-6/29/65). Films: "The Outlaws Is Coming!" 1965 (Hammond).

Maris, Mona (1903-3/23/91). Films: "Romance of the Rio Grande" 1929 (Manuelita); "The Arizona Kid" 1930 (Lorita); "Under a Texas Moon" 1930 (Lolita Roberto); "South of the Rio Grande" 1932 (Consuella); "Secrets" 1933 (Senora Martinez); "When Love Laughs" 1933-Mex.

Mark, Flip. TV: *Have Gun Will Travel*—"Squatter's Rights" 12-23-61 (Silver Strike); *The Big Valley*—"The Good Thieves" 1-1-68 (Jerry Frye).

Mark, Michael (1886-2/3/75). Films: "Northwest Outpost" 1947 (Small Convict); "Desert Passage" 1952 (Burley). ¶TV: *The Cisco Kid*—

"Jewelry Store Fence" 8-11-51, "Water Toll" 9-22-51; *Sergeant Preston of the Yukon*—"Old Ben's Gold" 10-3-57 (Hans Weber); *Rawhide*—"Incident of the Dancing Death" 4-8-60 (Gypsy).

Mark, Robert. Films: "Kill or Be Killed" 1966-Ital. (Johnny Ringo/Gerry); "God Does Not Pay on Saturday" 1968-Ital. (Wyatt).

Markey, Enid (1896-11/16/81). Films: "The Colonel's Ward" 1912; "The Days of '49" 1913; "In the Cow Country" 1914; "Shorty's Sacrifice" 1914; "The Darkening Trail" 1915 (Ruby McGraw); "The Roughneck" 1915; "The Taking of Luke McVane" 1915; "The Devil's Double" 1916 (Naomi Tarleton); "Jim Grimsby's Boy" 1916 (Bill Grimsby); "Lieutenant Danny, U.S.A." 1916 (Senorita Ysobel); "Six-Shooter Andy" 1918 (Susan Allenby).

Markham, Monte (1935-). Films: "Hour of the Gun" 1967 (Sherman McMasters); "Guns of the Magnificent Seven" 1969 (Keno). ¶TV: *Iron Horse*—"Death by Triangulation" 3-20-67 (Dan Patrick); *Here Come the Brides*—"The Firemaker" 1-15-69 (Redmond Bass); *The Men from Shiloh*—"Gun Quest" 10-21-70 (Boss Cooper); *The High Chaparral*—"Too Late the Epitaph" 11-6-70 (Dave Redman); *Alias Smith and Jones*—"Something to Get Hung About" 10-21-71 (Jim Stokely); *The Quest*—"The Freight Train Rescue" 12-29-76 (Nelson Story); *Bret Maverick*—"The Vulture Also Rises" 3-16-82 (Captain Dawkins).

Markland, Ted. Films: "The Hallelujah Trail" 1965 (Bandmaster); "Waterhole No. 3" 1967 (Soldier); "The Hired Hand" 1971 (Luke); "Jory" 1972 (Evans); "Ulzana's Raid" 1972; "Wanda Nevada" 1979 (Strap Pangburn); "Bonanza: Under Attack" TVM-1995 (Cole). ¶TV: *The Restless Gun*—"Peligroso" 12-15-58 (Collie Smith); *Buckskin*—"Coup Stick" 2-2-59 (Nestor); *Have Gun Will Travel*—"Incident at Borasca Bend" 3-21-59 (Patterson); *Man from Blackhawk*—"Death Is the Best Policy" 12-18-59 (Early Schuler); *Tate*—"Tigero" 8-3-60 (Bill Towey); *The Outlaws*—"The Little Colonel" 5-18-61 (Cass); *Wild Wild West*—"The Night of the Red-Eyed Madmen" 11-26-65 (Jack Talbot); *Bonanza*—"Credit for a Kill" 10-23-66 (Boone); *The High Chaparral*—Regular 1967-71 (Reno); *How the West Was Won*—Episode One 2-12-78 (Nugget); *Father Murphy*—Regular 1981-82 (Frank); *Adventures of Brisco County, Jr.*—"Wild Card" 4-8-94 (Duster #1).

Markoff, Diane. TV: *Cliffhangers*—"The Secret Empire" 1979 (Tara).

Marks, Guy. TV: *Rango*—Regular 1967 (Pink Cloud).

Marks, Willis (1865-12/6/52). Films: "The Man from Funeral Range" 1918 (Joe Budlong); "When a Girl Loves" 1919 (William Wiatt); "The Beautiful Gambler" 1921 (Mark Hanlon); "Travelin' On" 1922 (Know-It-All Haskins); "Silent Pal" 1925 (Daniel Winters); "Desert Gold" 1935 (J.T. Winters).

Marlen, Gloria. Films: "Border Feud" 1947 (Carol Condon).

Marletta, Franco. Films: "Sabata" 1969-Ital. (Captain).

Marley, Florence (1919-11/9/78). TV: *Have Gun Will Travel*—"The Prophet" 1-2-60.

Marley, John (1916-5/22/84). Films: "Cat Ballou" 1965 (Frankie Ballou); "Man Called Sledge" 1971-Ital./U.S. (the Old Man); "Jory" 1972 (Roy); "Kid Vengeance" 1976-Ital./U.S./Israel. ¶TV: *Cheyenne*—"The Rebellion" 10-12-59 (Sgt. Pedro Castillo); *The Law of the Plainsman*—"Desperate Decision" 11-12-59 (Walt); *Black Saddle*—"Burden of Guilt" 3-18-60 (Morgan Ames); *Rawhide*—"Incident of the Last Chance" 6-10-60 (Little Cloud); *Wrangler*—"A Time for Hanging" 8-11-60 (Towne); *Sugarfoot*—"Toothy Thompson" 1-16-61 (Jon Brice); *The Rebel*—"Jerkwater" 1-22-61 (George Campbell); *Two Faces West*—"Hand of Vengeance" 4-3-61 (Josiah Brady); *The Deputy*—"Tension Point" 4-8-61 (Zeb Baker); *Great Adventure*—"The Special Courage of Captain Pratt" 2-14-64 (Grey Beard); *Branded*—"The Vindicator" 1-31-65 (Ritter), "The Greatest Coward on Earth" 11-21-65 (Coutts); *Laredo*—"I See By Your Outfit" 9-23-65 (Alvar de Avelas); *Gunsmoke*—"Ten Little Indians" 10-9-65 (Ben Pringle); *The Legend of Jesse James*—"Manhunt" 11-29-65 (John Wills); *Wild Wild West*—"The Night of the Wolf" 3-31-67 (King Stefan IX); *Iron Horse*—"Gallows for Bill Pardew" 9-30-67 (Albert); *The Virginian*—"The Crooked Pat" 2-21-68 (Rondell); *Bonanza*—"Child" 9-22-68 (Sheriff Millet); *Here Come the Brides*—"Letter of the Law" 10-30-68 (Sheriff Emmett Wade); *The Outcasts*—"My Name Is Jemal" 11-18-68 (Bricker).

Marlo, Frank. see Marlowe, Frank.

Marlo, Steven. Films: "The Hanged Man" TVM-1974 (Joe Janney). ¶TV: *The Rifleman*—"The

Patsy" 9-29-59 (Doke Marvin), "The Assailants" 11-12-62 (Sergeant Will), "The Anvil Chorus" 12-17-62 (Stagg); *The Rebel*—"The Death of Gray" 1-3-60 (Cass); *The Law of the Plainsman*—"Dangerous Barriers" 3-10-60 (Manuel); *Johnny Ringo*—"Soft Cargo" 5-5-60 (Dolan); *Wanted—Dead or Alive*—"El Gato" 2-22-61 (Coyote); *Great Adventure*—"Teeth of the Lion" 1-17-64 (Red Deer); *Gunsmoke*—"Hung High" 11-14-64 (Corporal Miller); *Branded*—"The Mission" 3-14-65, 3-21-65 & 3-28-65 (Private Tyler); *Death Valley Days*—"The Journey" 6-13-65 (Swift Knife); *Bonanza*—"Horse of a Different Hue" 9-18-66 (MacKaye), "Dark Enough to See the Stars" 3-12-67 (Barclay).

Marlow, Rex. Films: "Deadwood '76" 1965 (Sam Bass).

Marlow, Ric. TV: *Bonanza*—"Death at Dawn" 4-30-60, "The Last Viking" 11-12-60 (Morgan); *Two Faces West*—"The Crisis" 3-6-61; *Lawman*—"The Cold One" 11-12-61 (Willis).

Marlowe, Frank (Frank Marlo) (1904-3/30/64). Films: "Buzzy Rides the Range" 1940 (Mesa); "Buzzy and the Phantom Pinto" 1941; "Rustler's Roundup" 1946 (Jules Todd); "Sioux City Sue" 1946; "Jesse James Rides Again" 1947-serial (Joe #1); "Riding the California Trail" 1947; "The Vigilante" 1947-serial; "The Wistful Widow of Wagon Gap" 1947 (Cowboy); "Barricade" 1950 (Brandy); "Cattle Queen" 1951 (Driver); "The Bushwackers" 1952 (Peter Sharpe); "Johnny Guitar" 1954 (Frank); "The Americano" 1955 (Captain of Ship); "Escape from Red Rock" 1958 (Manager); "Lone Texan" 1959 (Charlie). ¶TV: *The Lone Ranger*—"Rifles and Renegades" 5-4-50; *The Restless Gun*—"The New Sheriff" 11-18-57; *Wanted—Dead or Alive*—"Miracle at Pot Hole" 10-25-58 (Land Agent); *The Texan*—"Jail for the Innocents" 11-3-58 (Bartender).

Marlowe, Gene. Films: "Apache Woman" 1955 (White Star).

Marlowe, Hugh (1914-5/2/82). Films: "Rawhide" 1951 (Zimmerman); "Bugles in the Afternoon" 1952 (Garnett); "Way of a Gaucho" 1952 (Miguel); "The Stand at Apache River" 1953 (Col. Morsby); "Garden of Evil" 1954 (John Fuller); "The Black Whip" 1956 (Lorn); "The Long Rope" 1961 (Jonas Stone). ¶TV: *Rawhide*—"Incident of the Champagne Bottles" 3-18-60 (James Parker), "The Pitchwagon" 3-2-62 (Sam Garner); *Tales of Wells Fargo*—"The Wayfarers" 5-19-62 (George Adams);

The Virginian—"The Intruders" 3-4-64 (Billings), "Trail to Ashley Mountain" 11-2-66 (Ed Wells).

Marlowe, Jerry. Films: "Man from Montreal" 1940 (Jim Morris).

Marlowe, Jo Ann. Films: "The Man from Rainbow Valley" 1946 (Ginny Hale).

Marlowe, June (1903-3/10/84). Films: "When a Man's a Man" 1924 (Kitty Reid); "Clash of the Wolves" 1925 (May Barstowe); "Tracked in the Snow Country" 1925 (Joan Hardy); "Night Cry" 1926 (Mrs. John Martin); "The Lone Defender" 1930-serial (Dolores Valdez); "Riddle Ranch" 1936 (Helene).

Marlowe, Lucy. TV: *Gunsmoke*—"Change of Heart" 4-25-59 (Bella Grant); *Overland Trail*—"The Baron Comes Back" 5-15-60 (Sandra Kale); *Tales of Wells Fargo*—"Kid Brother" 5-23-60 (Laurie).

Marlowe, Nora (1915-12/7/77). Films: "Texas Across the River" 1966 (Emma); "Westworld" 1973 (Hostess). ¶TV: *Gunsmoke*—"Robin Hood" 2-4-56 (Mrs. Bowen), "Love Thy Neighbor" 1-28-61 (Jennie), "Double Entry" 1-2-65 (Woman Passenger), "The Twisted Heritage" 1-6-69 (Ma Dagget), "The Tycoon" 1-25-71 (Ma Fowler); *The Law of the Plainsman*—Regular 1959-60 (Martha); *Hotel De Paree*—"A Rope Is for Hanging" 11-6-59 (Mrs. Fleethill); *Texas John Slaughter*—"Range War at Tombstone" 12-18-59 (Ma Howell), "Apache Friendship" 2-19-60 (Ma Howell); *Klondike*—"Bathhouse Justice" 12-26-60 (Marnie Bronson); *Wagon Train*—"The Maud Frazer Story" 10-11-61 (Bessie), "Clyde" 12-27-61 (Mrs. Sherman), "The Levy-McGowan Story" 11-14-62 (Nancy McGowan), "The Trace McCloud Story" 3-2-64; *The Big Valley*—"Last Train to the Fair" 4-27-66 (Cora Wellman), "The Lady from Mesa" 4-3-67; *The Guns of Will Sonnett*—"Meeting in a Small Town" 12-6-68; *Here Come the Brides*—"Marriage Chinese Style" 4-9-69.

Marlowe, Scott (1931-). Films: "The Young Guns" 1956 (Knox Cutler); "The Restless Breed" 1957 (Allan). ¶TV: *Wagon Train*—"The Gabe Carswell Story" 1-15-58 (Jess Carswell); *Have Gun Will Travel*—"The Hanging of Roy Carter" 10-4-58 (Roy Carter), "Charley Red Dog" 12-12-59 (Charley Red Dog), "Duke of Texas" 4-22-61 (Prince Franz); *Bronco*—"The Turning Point" 10-21-58 (John Wesley Hardin); *Hotel De Paree*—"Sundance and the Kid from Nowhere" 1-15-60 (Kid); *Cheyenne*—

"Apache Blood" 2-8-60 (Mickey Free); *The Law of the Plainsman*—"The Show-Off" 3-17-60 (Clancy Jones); *Zane Grey Theater*—"The Long Shadow" 1-19-61 (Jimmy Budd); *Stoney Burke*—"Point of Honor" 10-22-62 (Soames Hewitt); *Gunsmoke*—"Legends Don't Sleep" 10-12-63 (Britt), "Hung High" 11-14-64 (Tony Serpa), "Thursday's Child" 3-6-65 (Lon Blane), "The Brothers" 3-12-66 (Ed); *Bonanza*—"The Roper" 4-5-64 (Lee Hewitt); *Rawhide*—"Canliss" 10-30-64; *Wild Wild West*—"The Night of the Howling Light" 12-17-65 (Ahkeema); *Lancer*—"The Experiment" 2-17-70 (Billy Kells).

Maross, Joe (1923-). TV: *Gunsmoke*—"Claustrophobia" 1-25-58 (Jim Branch), "Coventry" 3-17-62 (Dean Beard), "Chief Joseph" 1-30-65 (Charlie Britton); *The Restless Gun*—"Hang and Be Damned" 1-27-58 (Kalell); *Jefferson Drum*—"A Matter of Murder" 7-11-58 (Peter Norse); *Walt Disney Presents*—"Elfego Baca: Elfego—Lawman or Gunman" 11-28-58 (Horace Towne); *Northwest Passage*—"War Sign" 11-30-58 (Will Martin); *Wanted—Dead or Alive*—"Drop to Drink" 12-27-58 (Frank Parish); *Rough Riders*—"Reluctant Hostage" 6-18-59 (Johnny Dime); *Bonanza*—"Escape to the Ponderosa" 3-5-60 (Sutton); *The Outlaws*—"The Bill Doolin Story" 3-2-61 (Bill Doolin); *Texas John Slaughter*—"A Trip to Tucson" 4-16-61 (Jimmy Deuce); *Wagon Train*—"The Mary Beckett Story" 5-9-62 (Robert Waring); *Frontier Circus*—"Incident at Pawnee Gun" 9-6-62 (Al Buchanan); *Stoney Burke*—"Gold-Plated Maverick" 1-7-63 (Whitey Kilgore), "Kelly's Place" 4-15-63 (Vince Patterson); *The Virginian*—"Echo from Another Day" 3-27-63 (Landegger), "Brother Thaddeus" 10-30-63 (Homer Slattery), "Ride the Misadventure" 11-6-68 (Buck Stargil); *Time Tunnel*—"Massacre" 10-28-66 (Gen. Custer); *Iron Horse*—"Six Hours to Sky High" 11-25-67 (Jess); *The High Chaparral*—"The Promised Land" 10-25-68; *Kung Fu*—"Battle Hymn" 2-8-75 (Sheriff Mike Barrow).

Marquand, Serge (1930-). Films: "Black Eagle of Santa Fe" 1964-Ger./Ital./Fr.; "Massacre at Marble City" 1964-Ger./Ital./Fr. (Burning Arrow); "Cemetery Without Crosses" 1968-Ital./Fr.; "Wanted" 1968-Ital./Fr. (Lloyd); "Drop Them or I'll Shoot" 1969-Fr./Ger./Span.

Marquand, Tina. *see* Aumont, Tina.

Marques, Maria Elena. Films: "Across the Wide Missouri" 1951 (Kamiah); "Ambush at Tomahawk Gap" 1953 (Indian Girl).

Marquis, Margaret. Films: "Brand of the Outlaws" 1936 (Verna Matlock); "The Last of the Warrens" 1936 (Mary Burns); "Cassidy of Bar 20" 1938 (Mary Dillon).

Marr, Eddie (-8/25/87). TV: *Circus Boy*—"Meet Circus Boy" 9-23-56 (Barker); *Maverick*—"Betrayal" 3-22-59 (Drummer).

Marr, Sally (1906-). TV: *The Men from Shiloh*—"Hannah" 12-30-70 (Martha).

Marriott, Ronald. Films: "The Texan Meets Calamity Jane" 1950 (Nick).

Marriott, Sylvia (1917-). TV: *Wagon Train*—"The Sister Rita Story" 3-25-59 (Sister Monica), "The Maggie Hamilton Story" 4-6-60 (Marie Louise Hamilton).

Mars, Bruce. Films: "Stagecoach" 1966 (Trooper). ¶TV: *Bonanza*—"Five Sundowns to Sunup" 12-5-65 (Johnny), "The Fighters" 4-24-66 (Bert).

Mars, Kenneth (1936-). Films: "The Apple Dumpling Gang Rides Again" 1979 (Marshall); "Butch Cassidy and the Sundance Kid" 1969 (Marshal). ¶TV: *Gunsmoke*—"The Returning" 2-18-67 (Clyde Hayes).

Marsac, Maurice (1920-). TV: *Jim Bowie*—"Deputy Sheriff" 9-28-56 (Jacques Juventin), "Jim Bowie and His Slave" 11-30-56 (Pierre Jouvin), "Outlaw Kingdom" 12-7-56 (Pierre Jouvin), "Curfew Cannon" 1-24-58 (Maxim); *Northwest Passage*—"The Secret of the Cliff" 1-9-59 (Colonel Giroux); *Daniel Boone*—"Cain's Birthday" 4-1-65 & 4-8-65 (Telesphore Gagne), "The Fleeing Nuns" 10-24-68.

Marsh, Anthony. Films: "Overland Stage Raiders" 1938 (Ned Hoyt); "Call of the Canyon" 1942.

Marsh, Caren. Films: "The Navajo Kid" 1945 (Winifred McMasters).

Marsh, Linda (1939-). TV: *Wild Wild West*—"The Night of the Howling Light" 12-17-65 (Indra); *Death Valley Days*—"No Place for a Lady" 1-8-66 (Susan Magoffin); *Iron Horse*—"Consignment, Betsy the Boiler" 9-23-67 (Constance); *Here Come the Brides*—"A Jew Named Sullivan" 11-20-68 (Rachel); *The Big Valley*—"The Twenty-five Graves of Midas" 2-3-69 (Nora); *Daniel Boone*—"A Matter of Vengeance" 2-26-70 (Amy); *Alias Smith and Jones*—

"Twenty-One Days to Tenstrike" 1-6-72 (Elizabeth Tynan); *Gunsmoke*—"Survival" 1-10-72 (Lucero), "Bohannan" 9-25-72 (Lydia Walden).

Marsh, Mae (1895-2/13/68). Films: "The Indian Uprising at Santa Fe" 1912; "Three Friends" 1912; "The Battle at Elderbrush Gulch" 1913; "The Broken Ways" 1913; "Two Men of the Desert" 1913; "Meg of the Mines" 1914; "Big Jim's Heart" 1915; "The Outlaw's Revenge" 1916 (the Lover); "Drums Along the Mohawk" 1939; "Belle Starr" 1941 (Preacher's Wife); "My Darling Clementine" 1946 (Woman); "Fort Apache" 1948 (Mrs. Martha Gates); "The Three Godfathers" 1948 (Mrs. Perley Sweet); "The Fighting Kentuckian" 1949 (Sister Hattie); "The Gunfighter" 1950 (Mrs. O'Brien); "The Searchers" 1956 (Woman at Fort); "Sergeant Rutledge" 1960 (Nellie); "Two Rode Together" 1961 (Hanna Clay). ¶TV: *Bonanza*—"The Diedeshiemer Story" 10-31-59.

Marsh, Marguerite (Margarita Loveridge) (1892-12/8/25). FIlms: "Buck Richard's Bride" 1913; "Some Bull's Daughter" 1914; "Iron to Gold" 1922 (Anne Kirby).

Marsh, Michele (1949-). Films: "Last of the Mohicans" TVM-1977 (Cora Morgan). ¶TV: *Gunsmoke*—"The Wiving" 10-14-74 (Sarah Lynn), "Brides and Grooms" 2-10-75 (Sarah).

Marsh, Myra (1894-1964). Films: "The Kansas Terrors" 1939 (Duenna); "The Man from the Alamo" 1953 (Ma Anders); "The Moonlighter" 1953 (Mrs. Anderson). ¶TV: *Hopalong Cassidy*—"Guns Across the Border" 3-1-52.

Marsh, Tiger Joe (1911-5/9/89). Films: "Vengeance" 1964 (Bully). ¶TV: *Laredo*—"Sound of Terror" 4-7-66, "Any Way the Wind Blows" 10-28-66 (Hercules); *Barbary Coast*—"Sharks Eat Sharks" 11-21-75 (Bear).

Marshal, Alan (1909-7/9/61). Films: "Day of the Outlaw" 1959 (Hal Crane). ¶TV: *Buckskin*—"The Ghost of Balaclava" 9-4-58 (Richard Norton-Basett); *Wagon Train*—"The Doctor Willoughby Story" 11-5-58 (Bart Grover); *Rawhide*—"Incident at the Edge of Madness" 2-6-59 (Warren Millett); *Sugarfoot*—"The Vultures" 4-28-59 (Col. Lucius Starkey).

Marshall, Adam. Films: "The True Story of Jesse James" 1957 (Dick Liddell).

Marshall, Brenda (1915-7/30/92). Films: "Whispering Smith" 1948 (Marian Sinclaire); "The Iroquois Trail" 1950 (Marion Thorne).

Marshall, Bryan (1938-). Films: "Man in the Wilderness" 1971-U.S./Span. (Smith).

Marshall, Connie. Films: "Saginaw Trail" 1953 (Flora Tourney).

Marshall, Don (1934-). TV: *Rawhide*—"Incident at Seven Fingers" 5-7-64 (Private Goodlove).

Marshall, E.G. (1910-). Films: "Broken Lance" 1954 (the Governor). ¶TV: *20th Century Fox Hour*—"The Ox-Bow Incident" 11-2-55 (Davies); *Rawhide*—"Incident of the Broken Word" 1-20-61 (Ben Foley); *The Men from Shiloh*—"Lady at the Bar" 11-4-70 (Judge Carver), "Nan Allen" 1-6-71 (Judge Carver).

Marshall, Ellye. Films: "Rogue River" 1950 (Judy Haven).

Marshall, George (1891-2/17/75). Films: "The Code of the Mounted" 1916; "Timberjack" 1955 (Fireman).

Marshall, Gloria (-12/18/94). TV: *Death Valley Days*—"Husband Pro Tem" 4-21-54; *Gunsmoke*—"Bloody Hands" 2-16-57 (Linda Hawkins).

Marshall, Herbert (1890-1/22/66). Films: "Duel in the Sun" 1946 (Scott Chavez). ¶TV: *Zane Grey Theater*—"The Atoner" 4-6-61 (Simon Baker).

Marshall, Joan. TV: *Maverick*—"Rope of Cards" 1-19-58 (Lucy Sutter), "Substitute Gun" 4-2-61 (Connie Malone); *Tombstone Territory*—"Fight for a Fugitive" 6-4-58 (Laura Coleman); *Bat Masterson*—"Stampede at Tent City" 10-29-58 (Laura Hopkins); *Rough Riders*—"The Governor" 11-6-58 (Lydia Kimbrough); *Lawman*—"The Lady Belle" 5-1-60 (Lady Belle Smith); *Bronco*—"End of a Rope" 6-14-60 (Rouge Carter), "The Invaders" 1-23-61, "Stage to the Sky" 4-24-61 (Molly Rawlins); *Tales of Wells Fargo*—"The Barefoot Banit" 1-30-61 (Lisa Lindsey); *Gunsmoke*—"Wagon Girls" 4-7-62 (Emma); *Laredo*—"Limit of the Law Larkin" 1-27-66 (Ivy Vine); *The Road West*—"The Predators" 1-23-67 (Judith Devery); *Bonanza*—"A Man Without Land" 4-9-67 (Millie Perkins).

Marshall, Marion (1926-). Films: "Ticket to Tomahawk" 1950 (Annie). ¶TV: *Have Gun Will Travel*—"Maggie O'Bannion" 4-4-59 (Maggie O'Bannion).

Marshall, Mike (1944-). Films: "Death Rides Alone" 1968-Ital./Span. (Bobby); "I'll Sell My Skin Dearly" 1968-Ital. (Shane).

Marshall, Penny (1942-). Films:

"Evil Roy Slade" TVM-1972 (Bank Teller).

Marshall, Peter (1930-). TV: *Big Hawaii*—"Gandy" 9-21-77 (Fred Whipple).

Marshall, Sarah. TV: *Stoney Burke*—"Kincaid" 4-22-63 (Diane Banner); *Daniel Boone*—"Cry of Gold" 11-4-65 (Anne Denning), "Take the Southbound Stage" 4-6-67 (Nancy Bedloe), "Heroes Welcome" 2-22-68 (Elizabeth); *F Troop*—"Wrongo Starr and the Lady in Black" 1-11-66 (Hermione Gooderly); *Wild Wild West*—"The Night of the Hangman" 10-20-67 (Eugenia Rawlins).

Marshall, Sean. Films: "Deadly Trackers" 1973. ¶TV: *Kung Fu*—"The Stone" 4-12-73 (Abel Lovitt).

Marshall, Shary. TV: *Gunsmoke*—"False Front" 12-22-62 (Rita), "Father Love" 3-14-64 (Cora Prell); *Destry*—"Blood Brother-in-Law" 4-17-64 (Jenny Jellico); *Death Valley Days*—"No Gun Behind His Badge" 3-28-65 (Millie), "The Lawless Have Laws" 11-6-65 (Olive); *Wild Wild West*—"The Night of the Red-Eyed Madmen" 11-26-65 (Jenny).

Marshall, Tully (1864-3/10/43). Films: "The Golden Fetter" 1917 (Henry Slade); "A Modern Musketeer" 1917 (Phillip Marden); "A Romance of the Redwoods" 1917 (Sam Sparks); "Arizona" 1918; "The Man from Funeral Range" 1918 (Frank Beekman); "M'Liss" 1918 (Judge McSnagley); "The Squaw Man" 1918 (Sir John Applegate); "The Lady of Red Butte" 1919 (Spanish Ed); "Honest Hutch" 1920 (Thomas Gunnison); "Fools of Fortune" 1922 (Scenery Simms); "Good Men and True" 1922 (Fite); "Without Compromise" 1922 (Samuel McAllister); "The Covered Wagon" 1923 (Bridger); "Dangerous Trails" 1923 (Steve Bradley); "The Ridin' Kid from Powder River" 1924 (the Spider); "Jim the Conqueror" 1927 (Dave Mahler); "Redskin" 1929 (Navajo Jim); "Tiger Rose" 1929 (Hector McCollins); "The Trail of '98" 1929 (Salvation Jim); "The Big Trail" 1930 (Zeke); "Under a Texas Moon" 1930 (Gus Aldrich); "Fighting Caravans" 1931 (Jim Bridger); "Klondike" 1932 (Editor Hinman); "The Last of the Mohicans" 1932-serial; "Two-Fisted Law" 1932 (Sheriff Malcolm); "Fighting with Kit Carson" 1933-serial; "Massacre" 1934; "Blue Montana Skies" 1939 (Steve); "The Kid from Texas" 1939 (Adam Labert); "Brigham Young—Frontiersman" 1940 (Judge); "Go West" 1940 (Dan Wilson).

Marshall, William (1918-6/8/94). Films: "Santa Fe Trail" 1940 (George Pickett); "Belle of the Yukon" 1944 (Steve).

Marshall, William (1924-). Films: "Maverick" 1994 (Riverboat Poker Player). ¶TV: *Bonanza*—"Enter Thomas Bowers" 4-26-64 (Thomas Bowers); *Rawhide*—"Incident at Seven Fingers" 5-7-64 (Sergeant Sam Turner); *Daniel Boone*—"The Long Way Home" 2-16-67 (Birch Kendall); *Wild Wild West*—"The Night of the Egyptian Queen" 11-15-68 (Amalek).

Marshe, Vera (1905-3/25/84). Films: "Way Out West" 1930 (La Belle Rosa); "The Big Sombrero" 1949 (Angie Burke); "Davy Crockett, Indian Scout" 1950 (Mrs. Simms); "Western Pacific Agent" 1950.

Marstini, Rosita (1894-4/24/48). Films: "The Primal Law" 1921 (LaBelle).

Marston, Joel (1922-). Films: "Old Oklahoma Plains" 1952 (Lt. Spike Connors). ¶TV: *The Cisco Kid*—"The Puppeteer" 1-19-52, "Canyon City Kit" 3-1-52; *Branded*—"Seward's Folly" 10-17-65.

Marston, John (1890-9/2/62). Films: "Wagon Wheels" 1934 (Orator); "Union Pacific" 1939 (Dr. Durant); "Broken Arrow" 1950 (Maury).

Marta, Lynne (1946-). Films: "Joe Kidd" 1972 (Elma). ¶TV: *Gunsmoke*—"Homecoming" 1-8-73 (Prudence).

Martan, Nita. Films: "Border Romance" 1930 (Gloria); "Under Montana Skies" 1930 (Blondie); "The Two Gun Man" 1931 (Kitty).

Martel, Alphonse (1890-3/18/76). Films: "Strings of Steel" 1926-serial; "Grinning Guns" 1927 (Tony, the Dude); "The Cowboy and the Bandit" 1935; "Wells Fargo" 1937 (Headwaiter).

Martel, Arlene. TV: *Iron Horse*—"Hellcat" 12-26-66 (Noshima); *Wild Wild West*—"The Night of the Circus of Death" 11-3-67 (Erika); *Here Come the Brides*—"To the Victor" 2-27-70 (Astasia); *Gunsmoke*—"The Squaw" 1-6-75 (Quanah).

Martel, Jeanne. Films: "Santa Fe Bound" 1936 (Molly Bates); "Lost Ranch" 1937 (Rita Carroll); "Orphan of the Pecos" 1937 (Ann Gelbert).

Martel, June (1909-11/23/78). Films: "Arizona Mahoney" 1936 (Sue Beatrice Bixby); "Forlorn River" 1937 (Ina Blaine); "Wild Horse Rodeo" 1937 (Alice Harkley); "Santa Fe Stampede" 1938 (Nancy Carson).

Martell, Donna (1923-86). Films: "Twilight on the Rio Grande" 1947; "Coyote Canyon" 1949-short; "The Girl from Gunsight" 1949-short; "South of Santa Fe" 1949-short; "Ready to Ride" 1950-short; "Hills of Utah" 1951 (Nola); "Last of the Desperadoes" 1955 (Paulita); "Ten Wanted Men" 1955 (Maria Segura). ¶TV: *The Gene Autry Show*—"Frontier Guard" 10-13-51, "Killer's Trail" 10-27-51; *Frontier*—"Ferdinand Meyer's Army" 12-18-55 (Elena Meyer); *Broken Arrow*—"Apache Girl" 5-7-57 (Marsheela); *Bat Masterson*—"One Bullet from Broken Bow" 1-21-59 (Barbara Rafferty); *Cheyenne*—"Home Is the Brave" 3-14-60 (Maria); *Tales of Wells Fargo*—"John Jones" 6-26-61 (Zita Lopez); *Bonanza*—"The Toy Soldier" 10-20-63 (Esther).

Martell, Gregg (1914-). Films: "Sierra" 1950 (Hogan); "Winchester '73" 1950 (Mossman); "Devil's Canyon" 1953 (Tower Guard); "Masterson of Kansas" 1954 (Mitch); "Gunfight at the O.K. Corral" 1957 (Cowboy); "Tonka" 1958 (Cpl. Korn). ¶TV: *The Restless Gun*—"The New Sheriff" 11-18-57 (Gus Cotten); *Bonanza*—"The Paiute War" 10-3-59; *Rawhide*—"Incident of the Running Man" 5-5-61; *Wild Wild West*—"The Night of the Red-Eyed Madmen" 11-26-65 (Otto), "The Night of the Bottomless Pit" 11-4-66 (Guard), "The Night of the Underground Terror" 1-19-68 (Cajun); *The Virginian*—"The Deadly Past" 9-20-67 (Blacksmith).

Martell, Peter. Films: "Black Tigress" 1967-Ital.; "Fury of Johnny Kid" 1967-Span./Ital.; "Ringo, the Lone Rider" 1967-Ital./Span. (Ringo); "Death Rides Alone" 1968-Ital./Span.; "Dollars for a Fast Gun" 1968-Ital./Span.; "God Made Them ... I Kill Them" 1968-Ital.; "Long Day of the Massacre" 1968-Ital.; "May God Forgive You ... But I Won't" 1968-Ital.; "This Man Can't Die" 1968-Ital. (Tony Guy); "Two Crosses at Danger Pass" 1968-Ital./Span. (the Kid); "Chuck Moll" 1970-Ital.; "Forgotten Pistolero" 1970-Ital./Span.; "Ringo, It's Massacre Time" 1970-Ital.; "Hero Called Allegria" 1971-Ital. (Pot); "Patience Has a Limit, We Don't" 1974-Span./Ital. (Bill).

Marth, Frank (1930-). Films: "Young Pioneers" TVM-1976 (Mr. Swenson) ¶TV: *Philco Television Playhouse*—"The Death of Billy the Kid" 7-24-55 (2nd Guard); *The Big Valley*—"A Time to Kill" 1-19-66 (Monroe), "Hazard" 3-9-66 (Marshal Lanson), "The Iron Box" 11-28-66

(Sheriff Barnes), "The Lady from Mesa" 4-3-67 (Walter Meeder), "Deathtown" 10-28-68 (Sheriff Tom Hayes); *A Man Called Shenandoah*— "Run and Hide" 2-14-66 (Doctor); *Shane*—"The Great Invasion" 12-17-66 & 12-24-66 (Ball); *Iron Horse*— "Shadow Run" 1-30-67 (Wiley); *Cowboy in Africa*—"The New World" 9-11-67 (Kurt Neumann); *The Outcasts*—"A Ride to Vengeance" 9-30-68 (Roy Tanner); *Gunsmoke*—"9:12 to Dodge" 11-11-68 (Leitner), "Danny" 10-13-69 (Ed Wickes), "Celia" 2-23-70 (Martin Blake), "Disciple" 4-1-74 (Loveday); *Lancer*—"The Last Train for Charlie Poe" 11-26-68 (Marks), "Jelly Hoskins' American Dream" 11-11-69; *The Virginian*—"The Gift" 3-18-70 (Rawlings); *The Quest*—"Portrait of a Gunfighter" 12-22-76 (Sheriff Coe); *Best of the West*— "They're Hanging Parker Tillman" 10-15-81 & 10-22-81 (Kinkaid).

Martin, Andrea (1947-). Films: "Yellowstone Kelly" 1959 (Wahleeah). ¶TV: *Maverick*—"Gun-Shy" 1-11-59 (Virginia Adams), "Hadley's Hunters" 9-25-60 (Molly Brewster), "Thunder from the North" 11-13-60 (Pale Moon); *Bronco*—"Borrowed Glory" 2-24-59 (Nancy Currier); *Lawman*—"The Huntress" 5-3-59; *Colt .45*—"The Sanctuary" 5-10-59 (Lorelei Chadwick), "Absent Without Leave" 4-19-60 (Mary Steele); *Cheyenne*—"Gold, Glory and Custer—Prelude" 1-4-60 (Singing Waters), "Gold, Glory and Custer—Requiem" 1-11-60 (Singing Waters); *The Alaskans*—"Behind the Moon" 3-6-60 (Kerano), "The Last Bullet" 3-27-60, "White Vengeance" 6-5-60 (Lily); *Wagon Train*—"The Don Alvarado Story" 6-21-61 (Teresa Gervado).

Martin, Barney (1927-). TV: *Zorro and Son*—Regular 1983 (Brother Napa/Borther Sonoma).

Martin, Buzz. Films: "Cimarron" 1960 (Cim Cravet). ¶TV: *Wagon Train*—"The Flint McCullough Story" 1-14-59 (Hibbs); *Wanted—Dead or Alive*—"Railroaded" 3-14-59 (Sam Cole); *Rawhide*—"Incident of the Coyote Weed" 3-20-59 (Roy Evans); *Colt .45*—"The Reckoning" 10-11-59 (Billy Gibson); *The Deputy*— "Three Brothers" 12-10-60 (Gary Bennett); *Have Gun Will Travel*— "The Prisoner" 12-17-60 (Justin Groton), "Darwin's Man" 4-21-62 (Tully Coombs); *The Tall Man*—"The Legend and the Gun" 4-1-61 (Bedloe); *Bronco*—"Beginner's Luck" 1-1-62 (Lew Gant).

Martin, Chris-Pin (King Martin) (1894-6/27/53). Films: "Cisco Kid" 1931 (Gordito); "The Squaw Man" 1931 (Zeke); "The Broken Wing" 1932 (Mexican Husband); "South of Sante Fe" 1932 (Pedro); "The California Trail" 1933 (Pancho); "The Man from Monterey" 1933; "Outlaw Justice" 1933; "Rawhide Mail" 1934 (Esteban); "Under the Pampas Moon" 1935 (Pietro); "The Gay Desperado" 1936 (Pancho); "Boots and Saddles" 1937 (Juan); "A Tenderfoot Goes West" 1937 (Stubby); "Under Strange Flags" 1937 (Lopez); "Zorro Rides Again" 1937-serial (Pedro); "Billy the Kid Returns" 1938; "Renegade Ranger" 1938 (Felipe); "The Texans" 1938 (Juan Rodriguez); "The Arizona Wildcat" 1939 (Pedro); "The Cisco Kid and the Lady" 1939 (Gordito); "The Fighting Gringo" 1939 (Felipe); "Frontier Marshal" 1939 (Pete); "The Girl and the Gambler" 1939 (Pasqual); "The Llano Kid" 1939 (Sixton); "The Return of the Cisco Kid" 1939 (Gordito); "Rough Riders' Round-Up" 1939 (Hotel Keeper); "Stagecoach" 1939 (Chris); "The Gay Caballero" 1940 (Gordito); "Lucky Cisco Kid" 1940 (Gordito); "Mark of Zorro" 1940 (Turnkey); "Viva Cisco Kid" 1940 (Gordito); "The Bad Man" 1941 (Pedro); "Ride on, Vaquero" 1941 (Gordito); "Romance of the Rio Grande" 1941 (Gordito); "American Empire" 1942 (Augustin); "Tombstone, the Town Too Tough to Die" 1942 (Chris); "Undercover Man" 1942 (Miguel); "The Ox-Bow Incident" 1943 (Poncho); "Along Came Jones" 1945 (Store Proprietor); "San Antonio" 1945 (Hymie Rosas); "Belle Starr's Daughter" 1947; "King of the Bandits" 1947 (Pancho); "Pirates of Monterey" 1947 (Caretta Man); "Robin Hood of Monterey" 1947 (Pancho); "Blood on the Moon" 1948; "The Return of Wildfire" 1948 (Pancho); "Rimfire" 1949 (Chico); "The Arizona Cowboy" 1950 (Pedro Morales); "The Lady from Texas" 1951 (Jose); "Ride the Man Down" 1952 (Chris). ¶TV: *The Lone Ranger*—"Eye for an Eye" 6-29-50.

Martin, Daniel. Films: "Gringo" 1963-Span./Ital.; "A Fistful of Dollars" 1964-Ital./Ger./Span. (Julian); "Man Called Gringo" 1964-Ger./Span. (Gringo) "Last of the Mohicans" 1965-Ital./Span./Ger. (Luncan); "The Last Tomahawk" 1965-Ger./Ital./Span. (Chinga); "Seven Guns for Timothy" 1966-Span./Ital.; "A Minute to Pray, a Second to Die" 1967-Ital. (Father Santana); "Dead Men Ride" 1970-Ital./Span.; "Bad Man's River" 1971-Span./Ital./Fr. (False Montero); "Return of Clint the Stranger" 1971-Ital./Span.; "Watch Out Gringo! Sabata Will Return" 1972-Ital./Span.; "Blood River" 1974-Ital.; "None of the Three Were Called Trinity" 1974-Span. (Jim); "Too Much Gold for One Gringo" 1974-Ital./Span.

Martin, Dean (1917-). Films: "Pardners" 1956 (Slim Mosely, Jr.); "Rio Bravo" 1959 (Dude); "Sergents 3" 1962 (Sgt. Chip); "Four for Texas" 1964 (Joe Jarrett); "The Sons of Katie Elder" 1965 (Tom Elder); "Texas Across the River" 1966 (Sam Hollis); "Rough Night in Jericho" 1967 (Alex Flood); "Five Card Stud" 1968 (Van Morgan); "Bandolero!" 1968 (Dee Bishop); "Something Big" 1971 (Joe Baker); "Showdown" 1973 (Billy Massey). ¶TV: *Rawhide*—"Canliss" 10-30-64 (Gurd Canliss).

Martin, Dean Paul (1951-3/25/ 87). Films: "Rough Night in Jericho" 1967 (Cowboy).

Martin, Deana (1942-). Films: "Young Billy Young" 1969 (Evvie Cushman).

Martin, Dewey (1923-). Films: "Kansas Raiders" 1950 (James Younger); "The Big Sky" 1952 (Boone); "Savage Sam" 1963 (Lester White); "Seven Alone" 1974 (Henry). ¶TV: *Cavalry Patrol*—Pilot 1956 (Lt. Johnny Reardon); *Zane Grey Theater*—"Episode in Darkness" 11-15-57 (Ethan Boyan), "Man of Fear" 3-14-58 (Doc Holliday), "Stagecoach to Yuma" 5-5-60 (Jack Harmon); *Walt Disney Presents*—"Daniel Boone" 1960-61 (Daniel Boone); *Laramie*— "The Stranger" 4-23-63 (Vanton Madox); *Death Valley Days*—"The Bigger They Are" 4-4-64 (John Wheeler).

Martin, Diana. Films: "Minnesota Clay" 1964-Ital./Fr./Span. (Nancy); "Taste for Killing" 1966-Ital./Span.

Martin, Dick (1923-). Films: "Once Upon a Horse" 1958 (Doc Logan).

Martin, D'Urville (1939-5/28/ 84). Films: "The Legend of Nigger Charley" 1972 (Toby); "The Soul of Nigger Charley" 1973 (Toby); "Boss Nigger" 1974 (Amos).

Martin, Eugene. Films: "Terror in a Texas Town" 1958 (Pepe Mirada). ¶TV: *Broken Arrow*—"Quarantine" 4-9-57 (Teeahbay); *Wagon Train*— "The Les Rand Story" 10-16-57, "The Tracy Sadler Story" 3-9-60 (Arthur); *Jefferson Drum*—Regular 1958-59 (Joey); *Sugarfoot*—"The Desperadoes" 1-6-59 (Pedro); *The Texan*— "No Love Wasted" 3-9-59 (Jody);

Wanted—Dead or Alive—"The Monsters" 1-16-60 (Indian Boy); *Bonanza*—"The Avenger" 3-19-60, "Mirror of a Man" 3-31-63 (Tobey), "Napoleon's Children" 4-16-67 (J.W.); *The Rifleman*—"Sins of the Father" 4-19-60 (Bobby); *Bat Masterson*—"The Last of the Night Raiders" 11-24-60 (Jimmy); *The Rebel*—"The Burying of Sammy Hart" 3-5-61 (Billy Wallace); *Rawhide*—"The Captain's Wife" 1-12-62 (Tonio), "Deserter's Patrol" 2-9-62 (Acoma); *Custer*—"Spirit Woman" 12-13-67.

Martin, Frank. Films: "The Lone Star Vigilantes" 1942 (Cannonball). ¶TV: *Wild Wild West*—"The Night of the Arrow" 12-29-67 (Col. Theodore Rath); *Bonanza*—"Silence at Stillwater" 9-28-69 (Barnum).

Martin, Fred S. Films: "Riders of the Whistling Pines" 1949 (Freddie); "Wagon Team" 1952 (Fred Cass); "On Top of Old Smoky" 1953 (Freddie Cass).

Martin, George (Jorge Martin). Films: "Billy the Kid" 1962-Span.; "Two Gunmen" 1964-Span./Ital. (Cassidy); "A Pistol for Ringo" 1965-Ital./Span. (Sheriff); "Fury of the Apaches" 1966-Span./Ital.; "The Return of Ringo" 1966-Ital./Span.; "Taste for Killing" 1966-Ital./Span.; "Thompson 1880" 1966-Ital./Ger. (Raymond Thompson); "Three from Colorado" 1967-Span.; "Clint the Stranger" 1968-Ital./Span./Ger. (Clint Harrison); "Fifteen Scaffolds for the Killer" 1968-Ital./Span.; "Red Blood, Yellow Gold" 1968-Ital./Span. (Fidel Ramirez); "Sartana Does Not Forgive" 1968-Span./Ital. (Sartana); "Canadian Wilderness" 1969-Span./Ital.; "Return of Clint the Stranger" 1971-Ital./Span.; "Let's Go and Kill Sartana" 1972-Ital./Span. (Clay); "Watch Out Gringo! Sabata Will Return" 1972-Ital./Span.; "Three Supermen of the West" 1974-Ital./Span.

Martin, James. Films: "The Pinto Bandit" 1944; "King of the Forest Rangers" 1946-serial (Todd); "Renegade Girl" 1946; "The Thundering Trail" 1951 (Clinton); "Garter Colt" 1967-Ital./Span./Ger.

Martin, Janet. Films: "Hands Across the Border" 1943 (Rosita Morales); "The Yellow Rose of Texas" 1944 (Speciality Singer); "Bells of Rosarita" 1945 (Rosarita).

Martin, Jared (1943-). Films: "Westworld" 1973 (Technician). ¶TV: *Nakia*—"A Matter of Choice" 12-7-74 (Atterbury); *How the West Was Won*—Episode Eleven 5-7-78 (Frank Grayson), Episode Thirteen 5-21-78 (Frank Grayson), "The Gunfighter" 1-15-79 (Frank Grayson).

Martin, Jean. Films: "Adios Gringo" 1965-Ital./Fr./Span. (Murphy); "My Name Is Nobody" 1973-Ital. (Sullivan); "Genius" 1975-Ital./Fr./Ger.

Martin, Jill. Films: "Trigger Fingers" 1939 (Jessie Bolton).

Martin, Jimmy. Films: "Strange from Santa Fe" 1945; "'Neath Canadian Skies" 1946; "Six Gun Man" 1946 (Tim Hager); "Six Gun Serenade" 1947; "West to Glory" 1947 (Cory); "Frontier Revenge" 1948 (Pete); "Mark of the Lash" 1948; "Colorado Ranger" 1950 (Sandy); "Crooked River" 1950 (Dick); "The Daltons' Women" 1950; "Hostile Country" 1950 (Fred); "King of the Bullwhip" 1950; "Marshal of Heldorado" 1950 (Ben); "West of the Brazos" 1950 (Joe); "The Black Lash" 1952 (Pete).

Martin, Jorge. see Martin, George.

Martin, Jose Manuel. Films: "The Savage Guns" 1961-U.S./Span.; "Bullets Don't Argue" 1964-Ital./Ger./Span.; "Minnesota Clay" 1964-Ital./Fr./Span.; "Four Dollars for Vengeance" 1965-Span./Ital.; "Gunfighters of Casa Grande" 1965-U.S./Span. (Don Luis); "Last of the Mohicans" 1965-Ital./Span./Ger.; "Man from Canyon City" 1965-Span./Ital.; "A Pistol for Ringo" 1965-Ital./Span.; "A Bullet for the General" 1966-Ital. (Raimundo); "God Forgives—I Don't" 1966-Ital./Span. (Bud); "He Who Shoots First" 1966-Ital.; "A Minute to Pray, a Second to Die" 1967-Ital. (El Bailarin); "Fifteen Scaffolds for the Killer" 1968-Ital./Span.; "I Want Him Dead" 1968-Ital./Span. (Jackson Blood); "One After Another" 1968-Span./Ital.; "Seven Dollars on the Red" 1968-Ital./Span.; "100 Rifles" 1969 (Sarita's Father); "Arizona" 1970-Ital./Span.; "A Bullet for Sandoval" 1970-Ital./Span. (Guerico); "Bastard, Go and Kill" 1971-Ital.

Martin, Kiel (1944-12/28/90). Films: "The Undefeated" 1969 (Union Runner). ¶TV: *The Virginian*—"Star Crossed" 10-4-67 (Tony Barnes), "The Hell Wind" 2-14-68 (Cal Dorsey), "Incident at Diablo Crossing" 3-12-69 (Pat Rankin); *Gunsmoke*—"The Drummer" 10-9-72 (Ike Daggett); *Kung Fu*—"The Stone" 4-12-73 (Marshal).

Martin, King. see Martin, Chris-Pin.

Martin, Lewis (1894-2/21/69). Films: "Star in the Dust" 1956 (Pastor Harris); "The Blazing Sun" 1950; "Drums in the Deep South" 1951 (Gen. Johnston); "The Wild North" 1952 (Sergeant); "Pony Express" 1953 (Sgt. Russell); "Arrowhead" 1953 (Col. Weybright); "The Last Stagecoach West" 1957; "The Quiet Gun" 1957 (Hardy); "Badman's Country" 1958. ¶TV: *Wild Bill Hickok*—"Sagebrush Manhunt" 11-11-52; *Maverick*—"A Rage for Vengeance" 1-12-58 (Andrew Wiggins); *Jim Bowie*—"Deaf Smith" 2-7-58 (Scholar); *Northwest Passage*—"The Traitor" 12-7-58 (Capt. Morgan); *Have Gun Will Travel*—"Homecoming" 5-23-59 (Will Stanhope), "Never Help the Devil" 4-16-60 (Doctor), "Pandora's Box" 5-19-62 (Official); *Fury*—"The Vanishing Blacksmith" 12-19-59 (Dr. Ellis); *The Deputy*—"The Higher Law" 11-12-60 (Judge Wilkins).

Martin, Marcella. Films: "West of Tombstone" 1942 (Carol Barnet).

Martin, Margaret. Films: "The Desert Demon" 1925 (Squaw); "Viva Cisco Kid" 1940 (Helena's Mother); "Buffalo Bill" 1944 (Indian Servant); "My Darling Clementine" 1946 (Woman); "The Eagle and the Hawk" 1950.

Martin, Maria. Films: "The Hellbenders" 1966-U.S./Ital./Span. (Kitty); "Bandidos" 1967-Ital.; "Cry for Revenge" 1968-Ital./Span. (Mrs. Reed); "Four Rode Out" 1969-Ital./Span./U.S.; "Reverend Colt" 1970-Ital./Span.; "My Colt, Not Yours" 1972-Span./Fr./Ital.

Martin, Marion (1916-8/13/85). Films: "Lady from Cheyenne" 1941 (Gertie); "The Woman of the Town" 1943 (Daisy Davenport); "Thunder in the Pines" 1948 (Pearl); "Dakota Lil" 1950 (Blonde); "Merry Mavericks" 1951-short (Gladys); "Oklahoma Annie" 1952 (Le Belle La Tour). ¶TV: *The Lone Ranger*—"Pardon for Curley" 6-22-50.

Martin, Mary (1913-11/4/90). TV: *Annie Get Your Gun* 11-25-57 (Annie Oakley).

Martin, Mickey (1921-7/25/73). Films: "The Throwback" 1935 (Spike as a Boy); "The Sea of Grass" 1947 (Newsboy).

Martin, Nan (1927-). Films: "Proud Men" TVM-1987 (Laura). ¶TV: *Lancer*—"Goodbye, Lizzie" 4-28-70 (Lizzie Cramer); *Adventures of Brisco County, Jr.*—"Mail Order Brides" 12-10-93 (Lil Swill).

Martin, Nora Lou. Films: "Rovin' Tumbleweeds" 1939; "Boss of

Hangtown Mesa" 1942; "The Silver Bullet" 1942.

Martin, Pamela Sue (1954-). Films: "The Gun and the Pulpit" TVM-1974 (Sally Underwood). ¶TV: *The Quest*—"Day of Outrage" 10-27-76 (Ginger).

Martin, Pepper (1936-). Films: "The Over-the-Hill Gang Rides Again" TVM-1970 (Drifter); "The Animals" 1971 (Jamie); "Cahill, United States Marshal" 1973 (Hard Case). ¶TV: *The Guns of Will Sonnett*—"Alone" 2-9-68 (Ed Collins); *Bonanza*—"Yonder Man" 12-8-68 (Hawkface); *Bearcats!*—"Conqueror's Gold" 10-28-71 (Gus Bailey); *Alias Smith and Jones*—"Only Three to a Bed" 1-13-73 (Head Gunman).

Martin, Richard (1919-9/4/94). Films: "Nevada" 1944 (Chito Rafferty); "Wanderer of the Wasteland" 1945 (Chito Rafferty); "West of the Pecos" 1945 (Chito Rafferty); "Adventures of Don Coyote" 1947 (Don Coyote); "Thunder Mountain" 1947 (Chito Rafferty); "Under the Tonto Rim" 1947 (Chito Rafferty); "Wild Horse Mesa" 1947 (Chito Rafferty); "The Arizona Ranger" 1948 (Chito Rafferty); "Gun Smugglers" 1948 (Chito Rafferty); "Guns of Hate" 1948 (Chito Rafferty); "Indian Agent" 1948 (Chito Rafferty); "Western Heritage" 1948 (Chito Rafferty); "Brothers in the Saddle" 1949 (Chito Rafferty); "Masked Raiders" 1949 (Chito Rafferty); "The Mysterious Desperado" 1949 (Chito Rafferty); "Rustlers" 1949 (Chito Rafferty); "Stagecoach Kid" 1949 (Chito Rafferty); "Border Treasure" 1950 (Chito Rafferty); "Dynamite Pass" 1950 (Chito Rafferty); "Rider from Tucson" 1950 (Chito Rafferty); "Riders of the Range" 1950 (Chito Rafferty); "Rio Grande Patrol" 1950 (Chito Rafferty); "Storm Over Wyoming" 1950 (Chito Rafferty); "Gunplay" 1951 (Chito Rafferty); "Hot Lead" 1951 (Chito Rafferty); "Law of the Badlands" 1951 (Chito Rafferty); "Overland Telegraph" 1951 (Chito Rafferty); "Pistol Harvest" 1951 (Chito Rafferty); "Saddle Legion" 1951 (Chito Rafferty); "Desert Passage" 1952 (Chito Rafferty); "The Raiders" 1952 (Felipe Ortega); "Road Agent" 1952 (Chito Rafferty); "Target" 1952 (Chito Rafferty); "Trail Guide" 1952 (Chito Rafferty); "Four Fast Guns" 1959 (Quijano).

Martin, Ross (1920-7/3/81). Films: "Geronimo" 1962 (Mangus); "The Man from Button Willow" 1965 (Voice); "Wild and Wooly" TVM-1978 (Otis Bergen); "The Wild Wild West Revisited" TVM-1979 (Artemus Gordon); "More Wild Wild West" TVM-1980 (Artemus Gordon); "I Married Wyatt Earp" TVM-1983 (Jacob Spiegler). ¶TV: *Sheriff of Cochise*—"The Check Artist" 9-14-56; *Gunsmoke*—"Bottleman" 3-22-58 (Dan Clell), "Land Deal" 11-8-58 (Keppert); *Texas John Slaughter*—Regular 1958-61 (Cesario Lucero); *Bat Masterson*—"The Treasure of Worry Hill" 12-3-58 (Caulder Larson); *Laramie*—"A Sound of Bells" 12-27-60 (Angel); *Walt Disney Presents: Zorro*—"Auld Acquaintance" 4-2-61 (Marcos); *Bonanza*—"Little Man—Ten Feet Tall" 5-26-63 (Nick Biancci); *Wagon Train*—"The Sam Pulaski Story" 11-4-63 (Sam Pulaski); *Wild Wild West*—Regular 1965-69 (Artemus Gordon).

Martin, Scoop. Films: "The Phantom Rider" 1936-serial; "The Texans" 1938 (Cowboy); "Law and Order" 1940 (Henchman); "Son of Roaring Dan" 1940 (Stage Driver); "Raiders of San Joaquin" 1943 (Tripp); "Crooked River" 1950.

Martin, Steve (1945-). Films: "Three Amigos" 1986 (Lucky Day).

Martin, Strother (1919-8/1/80). Films: "Drum Beat" 1954 (Scotty); "The Black Whip" 1956 (Thorny); "Black Patch" 1957 (Petey); "Copper Sky" 1957 (Pokey); "The Horse Soldiers" 1959 (Virgil); "The Wild and the Innocent" 1959 (Ben Stocker); "The Deadly Companions" 1961 (Parson); "The Man Who Shot Liberty Valance" 1962 (Floyd); "McClintock" 1963 (Agard); "Showdown" 1963 (Charlie Reeder); "Invitation to a Gunfighter" 1964 (Fiddler); "Shenandoah" 1965 (Engineer); "The Sons of Katie Elder" 1965 (Jeb Ross); "An Eye for an Eye" 1966 (Trumbull); "Butch Cassidy and the Sundance Kid" 1969 (Percy Garris); "True Grit" 1969 (Col. G. Stonehill); "The Wild Bunch" 1969 (Coffer); "The Ballad of Cable Hogue" 1970 (Bowen); "Fools' Parade" 1971 (Lee Cottrill); "Hannie Calder" 1971-Brit./Span./Fr. (Rufus Clemens); "Pocket Money" 1972 (Garrett); "Rooster Cogburn" 1975 (McCoy); "The Great Scout and Cathouse Thursday" 1976 (Billy); "The Villain" 1979 (Parody Jones). ¶TV: *Gunsmoke*—"Professor Lute Bone" 1-7-56 (Mr. Stooler), "Cooter" 5-19-56 (Cooter), "Liar from Blackhawk" 6-22-57, "Dooley Surrenders" 3-8-58 (Emmett Dooley), "The Constable" 5-30-59 (Dillard Band), "Tall Trapper" 1-21-61 (Rowley), "The Do-Badder" 1-6-62 (Gene Bunch), "The Trappers" 11-3-62 (Billy Logan), "No Hands" 2-8-64 (Will Timble), "Island in the Desert" 12-2-74 & 12-9-74 (Ben Snow); *Frontier*—"The Well" 4-8-56 (Mayes), "Patrol" 4-29-56; *Broken Arrow*—"Apache Dowry" 1-15-57 (Renton), "Shadow of Cochise" 2-4-58 (Joe Roman); *Zane Grey Theater*—"The Necessary Breed" 2-15-57 (Joby); *Have Gun Will Travel*—"A Matter of Ethics" 10-12-57, "High Wire" 11-2-57 (Dooley Delaware), "One Came Back" 12-26-59 (Carew), "Justice in Hell" 1-6-62 (Boise Peabody); *Jim Bowie*—"The Close Shave" 1-10-58 (Leopold Vaupel); *Trackdown*—"A Stone for Benny French" 10-3-58 (Benny French); *Jefferson Drum*—"Pete Henke" 11-20-58 (Pete Henke); *Black Saddle*—"Client: Mowery" 3-28-59 (Pit Thatcher); *The Texan*—"No Place to Stop" 4-27-59 (Polk); *Hotel De Paree*—Regular 1959-60 (Aaron); *The Rebel*—"Johnny Yuma" 10-4-59 (Jess); *Lawman*—"The Hunch" 10-11-59 (Jack Roley); *Rawhide*—"Incident of the Haunted Hills" 11-6-59 (Meeker), "The Gray Rock Hotel" 5-21-65 (Bates); *Stoney Burke*—"Sidewinder" 11-12-62 (Buckley); *The Dakotas*—"Walk Through the Badlands" 3-18-63 (Pvt. Anton Copang); *Bonanza*—"The Saga of Muley Jones" 3-29-64 (Urey), "The Meredith Smith" 10-31-65 (Little Meredith), "Silence at Stillwater" 9-28-69 (Lonnie), "The Imposters" 12-13-70 (Joad Bruder), "The Younger Brothers' Younger Brother" 3-12-72 (Cole Younger); *Death Valley Days*—"The Bigger They Are" 4-4-64 (Arkie Monson), "There Was Another Dalton Brother" 6-6-65 (Barfly), "The Four Dollar Law Suit" 4-16-66, "Silver Tombstone" 2-25-67 (Ed Schiefelin); *The Virginian*—"The Claim" 10-6-65 (Finley), "You Can Lead a Horse to Water" 1-7-70 (Luther); *The Legend of Jesse James*—"Return to Lawrence" 1-31-66 (Meeker); *A Man Called Shenandoah*—"Aces and Kings" 3-28-66; *Iron Horse*—"Broken Gun" 10-17-66 (Johnny Burke), "Diablo" 9-16-67 (Applegate); *The Big Valley*—"Target" 10-31-66 (Daniel Hawks), "Brother Love" 2-20-67 (Fludd); *The Rounders*—11-29-66 (Cousin Fletch), 12-13-66 (Cousin Fletch); *The Road West*—"A Mighty Hunter Before the Lord" 1-30-67 (Grady Couts); *The Guns of Will Sonnett*—"Message at Noon" 10-13-67 (Harvey Bains), "Joby" 11-1-68 (Joby); *Daniel Boone*—"The Terrible Tarbots" 12-11-69 (Tarbot); *Nichols*—"Zachariah" 1-11-72 (Zachariah).

Martin, Todd (1927-). Films: "Finger on the Trigger" 1965-Span./

Ital./U.S. (Hillstrom); "Powderkeg" TVM-1971; "Bad Company" 1972 (Sergeant); "Jory" 1972 (Barron); "The Barbara Coast" TVM-1975 (Gibbon). ¶TV: *The Legend of Jesse James*—"As Far as the Sea" 3-21-66 (Stagecoach Guard); *Cowboy in Africa*—"Little Boy Lost" 11-27-67 (Staub); *Bonanza*—"The Deserter" 3-16-69 (Denton); *The High Chaparral*—"New Hostess in Town" 3-20-70 (Gideon); *Alias Smith and Jones*—"Bushwack!" 10-21-72.

Martin, Tony (1914-). Films: "Quincannon, Frontier Scout" 1956 (Linus Quincannon). ¶TV: *Death Valley Days*—"The Unshakable Man" 5-9-62 (Amadeo Giannini).

Martin, Vivian (1891-3/16/87). Films: "The Sunset Trail" 1917 (Bess Aiken); "Unclaimed Goods" 1918 (Betsey Burke).

Martindel, Edward (1876-5/4/55). Films: "The Call of the North" 1921 (Graham Stewart); "Tony Runs Wild" 1926 (Mr. Johnson); "Song of the West" 1930 (Colonel).

Martinelli, Elsa (1932-). Films: "The Indian Fighter" 1955 (Onahti); "Belle Starr Story" 1968-Ital. (Belle Starr).

Martinez, A. (1948-). Films: "The Cowboys" 1972 (Cimarron); "Starbird and Sweet William" 1975; "Joe Panther" 1976 (Billy Tiger). ¶TV: *The Outcasts*—"A Time of Darkness" 3-24-69 (Indian); *Bonanza*—"Gideon the Good" 10-18-70 (Luis); *The Cowboys*—Regular 1974 (Cimarron); *Nakia*—"The Non-Person" 9-21-74 (George); *Kung Fu*—"My Brother, My Executioner" 10-12-74 (Slade), "Barbary House" 2-15-75 (Tigre), "Flight to Orion" 2-22-75 (Tigre), "The Brothers Cain" 3-1-75 (Tigre), "Full Circle" 3-15-75 (Tigre); *Centennial*—Regular 1978-79 (Tranquilino Marquez); *Born to the Wind* 1982 (Low Wolf).

Martinez, Claudio. Films: "Bridger" TVM-1976 (David Bridger). ¶TV: *Nichols*—"Deer Crossing" 10-21-71; *Gunsmoke*—"Manolo" 3-17-75 (Vitorio); *Born to the Wind* 1982 (Night Eyes).

Martinez, Gisela. Films: "Villa!" 1958 (Bailarina Flamenca).

Martinez, Joaquin (1930-). Films: "The Stalking Moon" 1969 (Julio); "The Bravos" TVM-1972 (Santana); "Jeremiah Johnson" 1972 (Paints His Shirt Red); "Joe Kidd" 1972 (Manolo); "Ulzana's Raid" 1972 (Ulzana); "Dream West" TVM-1986 (Sagundai); "Gunsmoke: The Last Apache" TVM-1990 (Geronimo).

¶TV: *The High Chaparral*—"The Ghost of Chaparral" 9-17-67 (Little Cloud), "The Promised Land" 10-25-68 (Innocente), "A Way of Justice" 12-13-68 (Luis), "Only the Bad Come to Sonora" 10-2-70; *Dundee and the Culhane*—"The 3:10 to a Lynching Brief" 11-8-67 (Jesus Padilla); *Bonanza*—"The Sound of Drums" 11-17-68 (Red Sky), "Decision at Los Robles" 3-22-70 (Sanchez), "The Rattlesnake Brigade" 12-5-71 (Chavez); *Gunsmoke*—"The Cage" 3-23-70 (Pepe); *Death Valley Days*—"A Gift from Father Tapis" 5-9-70 (Joaquin); *Alias Smith and Jones*—"Journey from San Juan" 4-8-71; *Centennial*—Regular 1978-79 (Colonel Salcedo); *How the West Was Won*—"The Slavers" 4-23-79 (Perez); *Young Riders*—"Pride and Prejudice" 10-27-90 (Running Bear).

Martinez De Hoyos, Jorge (1920-). Films: "The Magnificent Seven" 1960 (Hilario); "The Professionals" 1966 (Padilla); "Smoky" 1966 (Pepe); "Guns for San Sebastian" 1967-U.S./Fr./Mex./Ital. (Cayetano); "The Revengers" 1972-U.S./Mex. (Cholo).

Martinez, Mina. Films: "One-Eyed Jacks" 1961 (Margarita, the Castilian Girl); "Dirty Dingus Magee" 1970 (Belle's Girl). ¶TV: *Redigo*—Regular 1963 (Lenda); *The Virginian*—"The Mustangers" 12-4-68 (Querida).

Martinez, Nana. *see* Woodbury, Joan.

Martinez, Patrice. Films: "Three Amigos" 1986 (Carmen); "Gunsmoke: Return to Dodge" TVM-1987 (Bright Water).

Martini, Nino (1904-12/9/76). Films: "The Gay Desperado" 1936 (Chivo).

Marturano, Gino (1931-). Films: "Sabata" 1969-Ital. (McCallum); "Jesse and Lester, Two Brothers in a Place Called Trinity" 1972-Ital.

Marvin, Frankie. Films: "In Old Santa Fe" 1934; "Sagebrush Troubador" 1935; "Tumbling Tumbleweeds" 1935 (Shorty); "Comin' Round the Mountain" 1936; "Guns and Guitars" 1936 (Shorty); "Oh, Susanna!" 1936 (Hank); "The Old Corral" 1936 (1st Prisoner); "Red River Valley" 1936 (Becker); "Ride, Ranger, Ride" 1936; "The Singing Cowboy" 1936 (Shorty); "Vigilantes Are Coming" 1936-serial (Rancher); "The Big Show" 1937 (Shorty); "Boots and Saddles" 1937 (Shorty); "Git Along, Little Dogies" 1937; "The Painted Stallion"

1937-serial (Clerk); "Public Cowboy No. 1" 1937 (Stubby); "Rootin' Tootin' Rhythm" 1937 (Hank); "Round-Up Time in Texas" 1937 (Second Cape Cop); "Springtime in the Rockies" 1937 (Frankie); "Yodelin' Kid from Pine Ridge" 1937 (Luke); "Zorro Rides Again" 1937-serial; "Gold Mine in the Sky" 1938 (Joe); "The Lone Ranger" 1938-serial (Rancher); "Man from Music Mountain" 1938 (Larry); "The Old Barn Dancer" 1938 (Cowboy); "Prairie Moon" 1938; "Under Western Stars" 1938 (Deputy Pete); "Colorado Sunset" 1939 (Frankie); "Heritage of the Desert" 1939; "Mountain Rhythm" 1939 (Burt); "Racketeers of the Range" 1939 (Skeeter); "Saga of Death Valley" 1939; "Adventures of Red Ryder" 1940-serial (Water Heavy #4); "Corralling a School Marm" 1940-short; "Gaucho Serenade" 1940; "Melody Ranch" 1940; "Down Mexico Way" 1941; "The Musical Bandit" 1941-short; "Sierra Sue" 1941; "Under Fiesta Stars" 1941; "Bells of Capistrano" 1942; "Call of the Canyon" 1942; "Cowboy Serenade" 1942; "Heart of the Rio Grande" 1942; "Range Rhythm" 1942-short; "Stardust on the Sage" 1942; "Sioux City Sue" 1946; "The Last Round-Up" 1947; "Robin Hood of Texas" 1947; "Twilight on the Rio Grande" 1947; "Rim of the Canyon" 1949; "Sons of New Mexico" 1949 (Joe); "Beyond the Purple Hills" 1950; "The Blazing Sun" 1950 (Deputy Sheriff); "Cow Town" 1950; "Indian Territory" 1950; "Silver Canyon" 1951; "Valley of Fire" 1951; "Whirlwind" 1951; "Barbed Wire" 1952; "The Old West" 1952 (Watkins); "Pack Train" 1953. ¶TV: *The Gene Autry Show*—"Gold Dust Charlie" 7-30-50, "The Star Toter" 8-20-50, "Double Switch" 8-27-50, "Doublecross Valley" 9-10-50, "The Posse" 9-17-50, "Six Shooter Sweepstakes" 10-1-50, "The Poisoned Waterhole" 10-8-50, "Lost Chance" 10-15-55, "Gun Powder Range" 10-29-50, "Hot Lead" 11-26-50, "Killer Horse" 12-10-50, "The Lawless Press" 1-25-52, "Ruthless Renegade" 2-8-52, "Six Gun Romeo" 3-16-52, "Narrow Escape" 8-11-53, "Steel Ribbon" 9-22-53, "Ransom Cross" 10-6-53, "Santa Fe Raiders" 7-6-54, "The Hold-Up" 12-14-52, "Prize Winner" 7-27-54, "Sharpshooter" 8-3-54, "Battle Axe" 8-31-54, "Civil War at Deadwood" 9-14-54, "Boots and Ballots" 9-25-54, "Stage to San Dimas" 10-8-55, "The Golden Chariot" 10-29-55.

Marvin, Grace. Films: "The Long Chance" 1922 (Soft Wind); "A

Horseman of the Plains" 1928 (Esmerelda).

Marvin, Lee (1925-8/29/87). Films: "The Duel at Silver Creek" 1952 (Tinhorn Burgess); "Hangman's Knot" 1952 (Rolph Bainter); "Gun Fury" 1953 (Blinky); "Seminole" 1953 (Sgt. Magruder); "The Stranger Wore a Gun" 1953 (Dan Kurth); "Bad Day at Black Rock" 1955 (Hector David); "Pillars of the Sky" 1956 (Sgt. Lloyd Carracart); "Seven Men from Now" 1956 (Big Masters); "The Missouri Traveler" 1958 (Tobias Brown); "Ride Lonesome" 1959; "The Man Who Shot Liberty Valance" 1962 (Liberty Valance); "Cat Ballou" 1965 (Kid Shelleen/Tim Strawn); "The Professionals" 1966 (Henry Rico Farden); "Paint Your Wagon" 1969 (Ben Rumson); "Monte Walsh" 1970 (Monte Walsh); "Pocket Money" 1972 (Leonard); "The Spikes Gang" 1974 (Harry Spikes); "The Great Scout and Cathouse Thursday" 1976 (Sam Longwood); "Death Hunt" 1981 (Sergeant Edgar Millen). ¶TV: *Wagon Train*—"The Jose Morales Story" 10-19-60 (Jose Morales), "The Christopher Hale Story" 3-15-61 (Jud Benedict); *Bonanza*—"Crucible" 4-8-62 (Peter Kane); *The Virginian*—"It Tolls for Thee" 11-21-62 (Martin Kalig).

Marvin, Marion. Films: "Cactus Crandall" 1918 (Helen Ware).

Marx, Chico (Leonard Marx) (1891-10/11/61). Films: "Go West" 1940 (Joseph Panello).

Marx, Groucho (Julius Marx) (1890-8/19/77). Films: "Go West" 1940 (S. Quentin Quale).

Marx, Harpo (Arthur Marx) (1893-9/28/64). Films: "Go West" 1940 (Rusty Panello).

Marx, Max (-1925). Films: "Zorro's Fighting Legion" 1939-serial (Presidio Guard); "Man from Montreal" 1940 (Simmons).

Marx, Neyle. Films: "Three Men from Texas" 1940; "The Phantom Cowboy" 1941 (Lobo); "The Cisco Kid Returns" 1945.

Mascolo, Joseph (1935-). Films: "Hot Spur" 1968 (Carlo).

Mase, Marino (1939-). Films: "The Five Man Army" 1969-Ital. (Train Engineer).

Maslow, Walter. TV: *Wyatt Earp*—"One" 4-15-58 (Dick Averill), "Two" 4-29-58 (Dick Averill), "Three" 5-13-58 (Dick Averill), "The Hole Up" 9-16-58 (Blackie Sanders), "The Peacemaker" 9-23-58 (Blackie Saunders); *Tales of Wells Fargo*—"The Renegade" 5-12-58 (Judd); *26 Men*—

"Long Trail Home" 2-10-59; *Fury*—"The Relay Station" 2-21-59 (Slit); *Colt .45*—"Phantom Trail" 3-13-60 (Burke); *Daniel Boone*—"Perilous Passage" 1-15-70, "Readin', Ritin', and Revolt" 3-12-70.

Mason, Buddy (1903-4/15/75). Films: "The Lone Ranger Rides Again" 1939-serial (Luke).

Mason, Dan (1853-7/6/29). Films: "Laughing Bill Hyde" 1918 (Danny Dorgan); "Iron to Gold" 1922 (Lem Baldwin, the Hotel Keeper); "The Plunderer" 1924 (Bells Parks); "Hard-Boiled" 1926 (Abrue Boyden).

Mason, James (1890-11/7/59). Films: "Nan of Music Mountain" 1917 (Scott); "On the Level" 1917 (Pike); "The Border Wireless" 1918 (Carl Miller); "Headin' South" 1918 (Aide); "The Squaw Man" 1918 (Grouchy); "A Daughter of the Wolf" 1919 (Roe); "The Hidden Badge" 1919; "Jubilo" 1919 (Bert Rooker); "The Knickerbocker Buckaroo" 1919; "The Mysterious Rider" 1921 (Jack Bellounds); "The Sage Hen" 1921 (Craney); "The Silent Call" 1921 (Luther Nash); "The Fast Mail" 1922 (Lee Martin); "Lights of the Desert" 1922 (Slim Saunders); "The Footlight Ranger" 1923 (Al Brownley); "The Old Fool" 1923 (Henry Steele); "Heritage of the Desert" 1924; "Mile-A-Minute Romeo" 1924 (Morgan); "The Plunderer" 1924 (the Wolf); "The Wanderer of the Wasteland" 1924 (Guerd Larey); "The Flaming Forties" 1925 (Jay Bird Charley); "The Unknown Cavalier" 1926 (Henry Suggs); "Whispering Canyon" 1926 (Medbrook); "Whispering Smith" 1926 (Du Sang); "Phantom City" 1928 (Joe Bridges); "The Long, Long Trail" 1929 (Mike Wilson); "Sunset Pass" 1929; "The Virginian" 1929 (Jim); "The Concentratin' Kid" 1930 (Campbell); "Last of the Duanes" 1930 (Morgan); "Border Law" 1931 (Shag Smith); "Call of the Rockies" 1931 (Tony); "Caught" 1931 (Scully); "The Painted Desert" 1931; "Renegades of the West" 1932 (Blackie); "Texas Gun Fighter" 1932 (Drag Kells); "Drum Taps" 1933 (Sheriff); "Scarlet River" 1933 (Dummy); "Sunset Pass" 1933 (Harry); "The Dude Ranger" 1934 (Hawk Selbert); "The Last Round-Up" 1934 (2nd Outlaw); "Mystery Mountain" 1934-serial; "The Westerner" 1934 (Henchman); "Fighting Shadows" 1935 (Horn); "Hopalong Cassidy" 1935 (Tom Shaw); "Powdersmoke Range" 1935 (Jordan); "Arizona Mahoney" 1936 (Ramsey);

"Call of the Prairie" 1936 (Hoskins); "The Phantom Rider" 1936-serial (Dirk); "The Plainsman" 1936; "Rose Marie" 1936 (Trapper); "Headin' for the Rio Grande" 1937; "Hills of Old Wyoming" 1937 (Deputy); "Public Cowboy No. 1" 1937; "Way Out West" 1937 (Anxious Patron); "Where Trails Divide" 1937; "Cattle Raiders" 1938; "Gun Law" 1938; "The Painted Desert" 1938 (Hank); "Renegade Ranger" 1938 (Hank); "Rhythm of the Saddle" 1938; "Utah Trail" 1938; "Arizona Legion" 1939; "In Old Monterey" 1939; "Stagecoach" 1939 (Jim, the Expressman); "Twenty Mule Team" 1940; "Viva Cisco Kid" 1940 (Lem); "Billy the Kid's Roundup" 1941; "Billy the Kid Trapped" 1942; "Santa Fe" 1951.

Mason, James (1909-7/27/84). Films: "Bad Man's River" 1971-Span./Ital./Fr. (Montero).

Mason, Larry. see Davis, Art.

Mason, LeRoy (1903-10/13/47). Films: "The Arizona Streak" 1926 (Velvet Hamilton); "Born to Battle" 1926 (Daley); "Tom and His Pals" 1926 (Courtney); "Bride of the Desert" 1929 (Fugitive); "The Last Frontier" 1932-serial (Buch); "Mason of the Mounted" 1932 (Calhoun); "Texas Pioneers" 1932 (Mark Collins); "Smoky" 1933 (Lefty); "The Dude Ranger" 1934 (Dale Hyslip); "The Fighting Trooper" 1934 (La Farge); "When a Man Sees Red" 1934 (Dick Brady); "Call of the Wild" 1935 (Pimp in Marie's Room); "Northern Frontier" 1935 (Bull Stone); "Rainbow Valley" 1935 (Rogers); "Texas Terror" 1935 (Joe Dickson); "Valley of Wanted Men" 1935 (Larry Doyle); "The Border Patrolman" 1936 (Courtney Maybrook); "Comin' Round the Mountain" 1936 (Matt Ford); "Ghost Town Gold" 1937 (Barrington); "It Happened Out West" 1937 (Burt Travis); "The Painted Stallion" 1937-serial (Alfredo Dupreay); "Round-Up Time in Texas" 1937 (John Cardigan); "Western Gold" 1937 (Fred Foster); "Yodelin' Kid from Pine Ridge" 1937 (Len Parker); "Gold Mine in the Sky" 1938 (Sykes); "Heroes of the Hills" 1938 (Red); "Outlaw Express" 1938 (Summers); "The Painted Trail" 1938 (Duke Prescott); "Rhythm of the Saddle" 1938 (Jack Pomeroy); "Santa Fe Stampede" 1938 (Mayor Gil Byron); "The Singing Outlaw" 1938 (Teton Joe); "West of Santa Fe" 1938 (U.S. Marshal McLain); "The Fighting Gringo" 1939 (John Courtney); "Lure of the Wasteland" 1939 (Butch); "Mexicali Rose" 1939

(Blythe); "New Frontier" 1939 (M.C. Gilbert); "Overland with Kit Carson" 1939-serial (John Baxter); "Wyoming Outlaw" 1939 (Balsinger); "The Gay Caballero" 1940 (Deputy); "Ghost Valley Raiders" 1940 (Frank Ewing); "The Range Busters" 1940 (Torrence); "Rocky Mountain Rangers" 1940 (King Barton); "Shooting High" 1940 (2nd Crook); "Triple Justice" 1940 (Sheriff Bill Gregory); "Viva Cisco Kid" 1940 (Outlaw Leader); "The Apache Kid" 1941 (Nick Barter); "Across the Sierras" 1941 (Stanley); "Last of the Duanes" 1941 (Henchman); "Riders of the Purple Sage" 1941 (Jerry Card); "Robbers of the Range" 1941 (Rankin); "Silver Stallion" 1941 (Pascal); "Six Gun Gold" 1941 (Marshal); "Bandit Ranger" 1942; "Jackass Mail" 1942 (Vigilante); "The Silver Bullet" 1942; "Sundown Jim" 1942 (Brick Brand); "Western Mail" 1942 (Gordon); "Black Hills Express" 1943; "Blazing Guns" 1943; "California Joe" 1943 (Breck Colton); "Canyon City" 1943 (Webb Hepburn); "Hands Across the Border" 1943 (Mac Marclay); "In Old Oklahoma" 1943 (Man on Train); "The Man from the Rio Grande" 1943; "Overland Mail Robbery" 1943; "Raiders of Sunset Pass" 1943 (Henry Judson); "Beneath Western Skies" 1944 (Bull Bricker); "Firebrands of Arizona" 1944 (Bailey); "Hidden Valley Outlaws" 1944; "Lucky Cowboy" 1944-short; "Marshal of Reno" 1944; "Mojave Firebrand" 1944; "Outlaws of Santa Fe" 1944 (Trigger McGurn); "The San Antonio Kid" 1944; "San Fernando Valley" 1944 (Matt); "Song of Nevada" 1944 (Ferguson); "Stagecoach to Monterey" 1944; "Tucson Raiders" 1944 (Banker); "Vigilantes of Dodge City" 1944; "Lone Texas Ranger" 1945; "Heldorado" 1946 (Ranger); "Home on the Range" 1946 (Dan Long); "King of the Forest Rangers" 1946-serial (Flush Haliday); "My Pal Trigger" 1946 (Carson); "The Phantom Rider" 1946-serial (Fred Carson); "Red River Renegades" 1946; "Sioux City Sue" 1946; "Under Nevada Skies" 1946 (Marty Fields); "Along the Oregon Trail" 1947 (John Fremont); "Apache Rose" 1947 (Hilliard); "Bandits of Dark Canyon" 1947 (Guard); "Jesse James Rides Again" 1947-serial (Finlay); "Saddle Pals" 1947; "Under Colorado Skies" 1947 (Faro); "California Firebrand" 1948 (Luke Hartell); "The Gay Ranchero" 1948 (Mike Ritter).

Mason, Louis (1888-11/12/59). Films: "Stagecoach" 1939 (Sheriff); "The Return of Frank James" 1940

(Wilson, the Watchman); "Jackass Mail" 1942 (Slim); "The Nevadan" 1950 (Duke); "Santa Fe" 1951.

Mason, Marilyn (1940-). TV: *Bonanza*—"Bullet for a Bride" 2-16-64 (Tessa Caldwell), "Ponderosa Birdman" 2-7-65 (Amanda); *Destry*—"The Infernal Triangle" 5-1-64 (J.P. Crane); *Laredo*—"A Question of Discipline" 10-28-65 (Marianne Montaigne), "That's Noway, Thataway" 1-20-66 (Belleflower); *The Big Valley*—"The Fallen Hawk" 3-2-66 (Nora), "Ladykiller" 10-16-67 (Belle Bleeck).

Mason, Martin. Films: "Shane" 1953 (Howell). TV: *Bonanza*—"The Newcomers" 9-26-59 (1st Miner).

Mason, Mary (1911-10/13/80). Films: "The Cheyenne Kid" 1933 (Hope Winters).

Mason, Michael. Films: "Showdown at Boot Hill" 1958 (Patton).

Mason, Shirley (1901-7/27/79). Films: "Lights of the Desert" 1922 (Yvonne Laraby); "Youth Must Have Love" 1922 (Della Marvin); "Desert Gold" 1926 (Mercedes Castanada).

Mason, Sidney (1886-3/1/23). Films: "The Unbroken Promise" 1919 (John Corliss).

Mason, Sydney (1905-4/11/76). Films: "Apache Country" 1952 (Walter Rayburn); "Blackjack Ketchum, Desperado" 1956 (Matt Riordan); "A Day of Fury" 1956 (Beemans); "Frontier Gun" 1958 (Doc Studdeford). TV: *The Roy Rogers Show*—"The Feud" 11-16-52 (Les Harris), "The Run-A-Round" 2-22-53 (Lewis Colby), "M Stands for Murder" 12-6-53, "Backfire" 10-10-54 (Rev. Ezra Loomis); *The Cisco Kid*—"Schoolmarm" 1-23-54, "Kilts and Sombreros" 5-1-54; *My Friend Flicka*—Regular 1955-56 (Sheriff Downey); *The Gene Autry Show*—"Law Comes to Scorpion" 10-22-55, "Feuding Friends" 11-26-55; *The Lone Ranger*—"The Wooden Rifle" 9-23-56, "Hot Spell in Panamint" 11-22-56, "Clover in the Dust" 3-7-57; *Sergeant Preston of the Yukon*—"Eye of Evil" 11-8-56 (Martin); *Maverick*—"The Seventh Hand" 3-2-58 (Mr. Lockridge); *Jefferson Drum*—"The Captive" 11-6-58 (Marshal Regan); *Tales of Wells Fargo*—"The Town That Wouldn't Talk" 2-9-59 (Phin Teller).

Mason, Vivian. Films: "The Charge at Feather River" 1953; "Shot in the Frontier" 1954-short (Ella). TV: *The Cisco Kid*—"Phony Heiress" 7-21-51.

Massari, Lea (1933-). Films: "I Want Him Dead" 1968-Ital./Span.

Massen, Osa (1915-). TV: *Wagon Train*—"Around the Horn" 10-1-58 (Osa Massen).

Massey, Daniel (1933-). TV: *Bonanza*—"The Reluctant American" 2-14-71 (Leslie Harwood).

Massey, Daria. Films: "The Iron Mistress" 1952 (Teresa de Veramendi). TV: *Death Valley Days*—"The Rosebush of Tombstone" 3-3-57, "The Man Who Was Never Licked" 6-2-57; *The Restless Gun*—"Bonner's Squaw" 11-3-58 (Running Fawn); *Cimarron City*—"The Evil One" 4-4-59 (Nooma); *Wagon Train*—"The Greenhorn Story" 10-7-59 (Melanie Pumphret); *The Tall Man*—"The Shawl" 10-1-60 (Maria).

Massey, Ilona (1910-8/20/74). Films: "The Plunderers" 1948 (Lin Conner); "Northwest Outpost" 1947 (Natalia Alanova).

Massey, Raymond (1896-7/29/83). Films: "Santa Fe Trail" 1940 (John Brown); "Barricade" 1950 (Boss Kruger); "Dallas" 1950 (Will Marlow); "Sugarfoot" 1951 (Jacob Stint); "Carson City" 1952 (Big Jack Davis); "Seven Angry Men" 1955 (John Brown); "How the West Was Won" 1962 (Abraham Lincoln). TV: *Zane Grey Theater*—"Seed of Evil" 4-7-60 (Malachi West); *Riverboat*—"Trunk Full of Dreams" 10-31-60 (Sir Oliver Garrett); *Wagon Train*—"Princess of a Lost Tribe" 11-2-60 (Montezuma).

Masters, Howard. Films: "Billy the Kid Wanted" 1941 (Stan); "Billy the Kid's Range War" 1941 (Jenkins); "The Lone Rider Crosses the Rio" 1941 (Francisco); "Along the Sundown Trail" 1942; "Ghost Town Law" 1942 (Tom Cook).

Masters, Michael. Films: "Macho Callahan" 1970; "The Hanged Man" TVM-1974; "The Apple Dumpling Gang Rides Again" 1979. TV: *Tales of Wells Fargo*—"The Break" 5-19-58 (Cass); *Man from Blackhawk*—"Portrait of Cynthia" 1-29-60 (Willie Fry); *The Tall Man*—"Hard Justice" 3-25-61 (Kramer); *Branded*—"Leap Upon Mountains…" 2-28-65 (Sheriff), "Headed for Doomsday" 4-10-66; *Wild Wild West*—"The Night the Wizard Shook the Earth" 10-1-65 (Wrestler), "The Night of the Human Trigger" 12-3-65 (Hercules Cadwallader), "The Night of the Eccentrics" 9-16-66 (Titan), "The Night of the Poisonous Posey" 10-28-66 (Cyril the Firebug), "The Night of the Skulls" 12-16-66 (Shanto the Beard); *Laredo*—"The Sweet Gang" 11-4-66 (West Sweet); *Hondo*—"Hondo and the Gladiators"

12-15-67 (Bully); *The Virginian*—"The Ordeal" 2-19-69 (Morgan); *The Men from Shiloh*—"Last of the Comancheros" 12-9-70 (Owens); *Bearcats!*—9-16-71 (Coley Wyatt).

Masters, Natalie. TV: *Buckskin*—"A Picture of Pa" 10-2-58 (Ella Meadows); *Johnny Ringo*—"The Gunslinger" 3-24-60 (Martha); *The Rebel*—"Absolution" 4-24-60 (Nurse), "The Bequest" 9-25-60 (Ma Silvers); *Gunsmoke*—"Wishbone" 2-19-66 (Stage Passenger), "Albert" 2-9-70 (Mrs. Bodkin); *The Legend of Jesse James*—"Benjamin Bates" 2-28-66.

Masterson, Mary Stuart (1967-). Films: "Mad at the Moon" 1992 (Jenny Hill); "Bad Girls" 1994 (Anita Crown).

Mastroianni, Marcello (1923-). Films: "Don't Touch White Women!" 1974-Ital. (George Armstrong Custer).

Masur, Richard (1948-). Films: "Mr. Horn" TVM-1979 (Sheriff Ed Smalley); "Heaven's Gate" 1980 (Cully); "Timerider" 1983 (Claude Dorsett); "Wild Horses" TVM-1985 (Bob Browne).

Matchinga, Toian. TV: *Wild Wild West*—"The Night of the Red-Eyed Madmen" 11-26-65 (Lola Bracer), "The Night of the Legion of Death" 11-24-67 (Henriette Faure), "The Night of the Spanish Curse" 1-3-69 (Cosina); *Iron Horse*—"Explosion at Waycrossing" 11-21-66 (Serafina); *Rango*—"Viva Rango" 3-24-67 (Carmelita); *The Big Valley*—"Ambush" 9-18-67 (Seataki).

Mateos, Julian (1943-). Films: "The Hellbenders" 1966-U.S./Ital./Span. (Ben); "Return of the Seven" 1966-Span. (Chico); "Shalako" 1968-Brit./Fr. (Rojas); "Three Silver Dollars" 1968-Ital. (Hondo); "Four Rode Out" 1969-Ital./Span./U.S.; "Catlow" 1971-Span. (Recalde).

Mather, George Edward. Films: "Blackjack Ketchum, Desperado" 1956 (Andy Tetlow). ¶TV: *Judge Roy Bean*—"Citizen Romeo" 12-1-55 (Pick), "Murder in Langtry" 12-1-55 (Drake); *Sergeant Preston of the Yukon*—"Treasure of Fifteen Mile Creek" 8-2-56 (Jim Dallas); *The Lone Ranger*—"Quarter Horse War" 11-8-56; *The Roy Rogers Show*—"Tossup" 12-2-56.

Mather, Jack (1908-8/15/66). Films: "Broken Lance" 1954 (Gateman); "River of No Return" 1954 (Croupier); "The Tall Men" 1955 (Cavalry Lieutenant); "The Bravados" 1958 (Quinn); "Squares" 1972 (Roth's Father). ¶TV: *The Adventures of Rin Tin Tin*—"Brave Bow" 4-18-58 (Chief Tucuman); *Maverick*—"The Sheriff of Duck 'n' Shoot" 9-27-59 (Judge Hardy), "Maverick and Juliet" 1-17-60 (Mr. Carteret), "Thunder from the North" 11-13-60 (Colonel O'Hearn), "The Forbidden City" 3-26-61 (Mayor Moss); *Colt .45*—"The Reckoning" 10-11-59 (Father Knox); *Bonanza*—"Mr. Henry Comstock" 11-7-59 (Heck Turner); *Death Valley Days*—"His Brother's Keeper" 1-19-60 (Hite Rogan); *Lawman*—"The Wolfer" 1-24-60 (Carl Haydn); *The Alaskans*—"A Barrel of Gold" 4-3-60 (Ed Stevenson); *Riverboat*—"The Quick Noose" 4-11-60 (Sheriff); *Bronco*—"La Rubia" 5-17-60 (Brother Paul); *The Tall Man*—"One of One Thousand" 12-31-60 (Sheriff); *Wagon Train*—"The Daniel Clay Story" 2-21-62 (Frank Lathrop).

Mathes, Marissa. Films: "Ride Beyond Vengeance" 1966 (Maria).

Matheson, Don. TV: *Death Valley Days*—"The Girl Who Walked the West" 11-4-67 (Clark); *The Quest*—"Day of Outrage" 10-27-76 (Sam Grant).

Matheson, Murray (1912-4/25/85). TV: *Laramie*—"Duel at Parkison Town" 12-13-60 (Alexander); *The Tall Man*—"The Reversed Blade" 2-4-61 (John Tundall); *Hec Ramsey*—"Hangman's Wages" 10-29-72 (Lionel Harlock).

Matheson, Tim (1948-). Films: "Lock, Stock and Barrel" TVM-1971 (Clarence Bridgeman); "Hitched" TVM-1973 (Clare Bridgeman); "The Quest" TVM-1976 (Quentin Baudine); "The Apple Dumpling Gang Rides Again" 1979 (Private Jeff Reid). ¶TV: *The Virginian*—Regular 1969-70 (Jim Horn); *Bonanza*—Regular 1972-73 (Griff King); *Kung Fu*—"The Soldier" 11-29-73 (Lt. Bill Wyland); *The Quest*—Regular 1976 (Quentin); *How the West Was Won*—Episode Two 2-19-78 (Curt), Episode Three 2-26-78 (Curt), Episode Four 3-5-78 (Curt).

Mathews, Carl (1899-5/3/59). Films: "Fighting Caballero" 1935; "Red Blood of Courage" 1935 (Indian in Store/Mountie); "Rough Riding Ranger" 1935 (Cinch Clemons); "The Silent Code" 1935 (Lobo); "Custer's Last Stand" 1936-serial (Curley/True Eagle); "Boots of Destiny" 1937; "Melody of the Plains" 1937; "Moonlight on the Range" 1937; "North of the Rio Grande" 1937; "The Roaming Cowboy" 1937; "The Singing Buckaroo" 1937; "California Frontier" 1938; "Gunsmoke Trail" 1938; "Heroes of the Alamo" 1938; "Knight of the Plains" 1938; "The Rangers' Roundup" 1938 (Durk); "Renfrew on the Great White Trail" 1938; "Rollin' Plains" 1938; "Six Shootin' Sheriff" 1938 (Henchman); "Songs and Bullets" 1938; "Whirlwind Horseman" 1938; "Code of the Cactus" 1939; "Code of the Fearless" 1939 (Henchman); "Feud of the Range" 1939; "Fighting Renegade" 1939; "Flaming Lead" 1939; "Frontier Scout" 1939 (Crandall); "In Old Montana" 1939; "Outlaw's Paradise" 1939; "Six-Gun Rhythm" 1939 (Jake); "Straight Shooter" 1939 (Lane); "Texas Wildcats" 1939; "Trigger Fingers" 1939; "Trigger Pals" 1939 (Hank); "Two-Gun Troubador" 1939 (Kirk Dean); "Arizona Gangbusters" 1940; "Covered Wagon Trails" 1940 (Nixon); "Frontier Crusader" 1940; "Gun Code" 1940; "The Kid from Santa Fe" 1940 (George); "Land of the Six Guns" 1940 (Drake); "Lightning Strikes West" 1940; "Phantom Rancher" 1940 (Hank); "Pinto Canyon" 1940 (Clem); "The Range Busters" 1940 (Rocky); "Riders from Nowhere" 1940; "Riders on Black Mountain" 1940; "Ridin' the Trail" 1940; "The Sagebrush Family Trails West" 1940 (Zeke); "Trailing Double Trouble" 1940 (Drag); "West of Pinto Basin" 1940 (Joe); "Wild Horse Range" 1940 (Frank); "Fugitive Valley" 1941 (Slick); "The Kid's Last Ride" 1941; "The Lone Rider Ambushed" 1941; "Saddle Mountain Roundup" 1941 (Bill); "Tonto Basin Outlaws" 1941 (Ed); "Trail of the Silver Spurs" 1941; "Tumbledown Ranch in Arizona" 1941; "Underground Rustlers" 1941; "Wrangler's Roost" 1941; "Arizona Stagecoach" 1942; "Billy the Kid Trapped" 1942; "Boot Hill Bandits" 1942; "Heart of the Golden West" 1942; "Lawless Plainsmen" 1942 (Outlaw); "Prairie Pals" 1942; "The Rangers Take Over" 1942 (Weir Slocum); "Rock River Renegades" 1942; "Texas to Bataan" 1942 (Engel); "Texas Trouble Shooters" 1942; "Thunder River Feud" 1942 (Tex); "Black Market Rustlers" 1943; "The Blocked Trail" 1943; "Bullets and Saddles" 1943; "Cheyenne Roundup" 1943; "Fighting Valley" 1943; "The Haunted Ranch" 1943; "The Lone Star Trail" 1943 (Townsman); "Two Fisted Justice" 1943; "Song of the Range" 1944; "The Cisco Kid Returns" 1945; "The Lost Trail" 1945; "Stars Over Texas" 1946 (Two Horn); "Tumbleweed Trail" 1946; "Buffalo Bill Rides Again" 1947 (Pete); "Cheyenne Takes Over" 1947 (Messenger); "The Fighting Vigilantes" 1947 (Shanks); "Gun

Talk" 1947 (Pepper); "Law of the Lash" 1947 (Blackie); "Prairie Express" 1947 (Collins); "Return of the Lash" 1947; "Shadow Valley" 1947 (Tucker); "Stage to Mesa City" 1947 (Jim); "West to Glory" 1947 (Vincente); "Black Hills" 1948; "The Hawk of Powder River" 1948 (Heavy); "Overland Trails" 1948; "Partners of the Sunset" 1948; "Range Renegades" 1948; "Song of the Drifter" 1948; "The Westward Trail" 1948 (Bart); "Haunted Trails" 1949 (Red); "Range Land" 1949 (Spike); "Arizona Territory" 1950 (Steve); "Crooked River" 1950 (Cherokee); "Gunslingers" 1950 (Kerner); "Marshal of Heldorado" 1950; "Outlaw Gold" 1950; "Six Gun Mesa" 1950; "West of Wyoming" 1950 (Ray); "Blazing Bullets" 1951; "The Longhorn" 1951; "Montana Desperado" 1951; "Nevada Badmen" 1951; "Oklahoma Justice" 1951; "Skipalong Rosenbloom" 1951; "Treasure of Ruby Hills" 1955 (Sherry).

Mathews, Carmen (1918-8/31/95). Films: "Sam Hill: Who Killed the Mysterious Mr. Foster?" TVM-1971 (Abigail Booth); "Charlie Cobb: Nice Night for a Hanging" TVM-1977 (Miss Cumberland). ¶TV: *Alias Smith and Jones*—"Six Strangers at Apache Springs" 10-28-71 (Caroline Rangely).

Mathews, Carole (1920-). Films: "Swing in the Saddle" 1944; "Blazing the Western Trail" 1945; "Outlaws of the Rockies" 1945 (Jane Stuart); "Sing Me a Song of Texas" 1945; "Massacre River" 1949 (Laura Jordan); "City of Badmen" 1953 (Cynthia London); "Shark River" 1953 (Jane Daugherty); "Showdown at Boot Hill" 1958 (Jill); "Thirteen Fighting Men" 1960 (Carole). ¶TV: *Wild Bill Hickok*—"The Slocum Family" 12-4-51, "Blacksmith Story" 1-1-52; *The Cisco Kid*—"Pancho and the Pachyderm" 2-2-52, "Laughing Badman" 3-8-52; *Jim Bowie*—"The General's Disgrace" 4-12-57 (Dellie Hartford); *Trackdown*—"The Farrand Story" 1-10-58 (Millie Gwynn); *Zane Grey Theater*—"This Man Must Die" 1-24-58 (Libby); *Tales of Wells Fargo*—"The Pickpocket" 4-28-58 (Lola); *The Californians*—Regular 1958-59 (Wilma Fansler); *The Texan*—"No Tears for the Dead" 12-8-58 (Bess Corbin); *Northwest Passage*—"The Deserter" 2-27-59 (Lila Jason); *Rough Riders*—"Lesson in Violence" 3-26-59 (Dora Thackeray); *Death Valley Days*—"A Bullet for the D.A." 11-22-61 (Belle Starr); *Rawhide*—"Incident at the Odyssey" 3-26-64 (Lucey).

Mathews, George (1911-11/7/84). Films: "Last of the Comanches" 1952 (Romany O'Rattigan); "The Last Wagon" 1956 (Bull Harper); "The Proud Ones" 1956 (Dillon, the Saloon Manager); "Gunfight at the O.K. Corral" 1957 (John Shanssey); "Heller in Pink Tights" 1960 (Sam Pierce). ¶TV: *Death Valley Days*—"Gold Is Where You Find It" 1-28-56; *The Rifleman*—"The Angry Man" 4-28-59 (Abel MacDonald); *Have Gun Will Travel*—"One Came Back" 12-26-59 (Ben Harvey), "The Bird of Time" 10-20-62 (Ahab Tyson); *Gunsmoke*—"The Dealer" 4-14-62 (Champ); *Empire*—"Ballard Number One" 10-2-62 (Kelly Biggs).

Mathews, June. Films: "Circle Canyon" 1934 (Clara Moore).

Mathews, Kerwin (1926-). Films: "Barquero" 1970 (Marquette).

Mathews, Walter (1926-). TV: *The Virginian*—"The Brazen Bell" 10-17-62; *Temple Houston*—"Seventy Times Seven" 12-5-63 (Prosecutor).

Matieson, Otto (1873-2/20/32). Films: "The Golden Trail" 1920 (Dick Sunderlin); "Bells of San Juan" 1922 (Antone).

Matranga, Leo V. Films: "Heller in Pink Tights" 1960 (2nd Gunslinger). ¶TV: *Branded*—"Headed for Doomsday" 4-10-66 (Menafee); *Daniel Boone*—"The Williamsburg Cannon" 1-12-67 & 1-19-67 (Tavern Landlord).

Mattea, Kathy. Films: "Maverick" 1994 (Woman with Concealed Gun).

Matthau, Walter (1920-). Films: "The Indian Fighter" 1955 (Wes Todd); "The Kentuckian" 1955 (Bodine); "Ride a Crooked Trail" 1958 (Judge Kyle); "Lonely Are the Brave" 1962 (Sheriff Johnson). ¶TV: *DuPont Show of the Week*—"Big Deal in Laredo" 10-7-62 (Meredith).

Matthews, Dorcas (1890-1/24/69). Films: "The Silent Man" 1917 (Topaz); "Out of the Dust" 1920 (Martha Evans).

Matthews, Forrest (1908-11/22/51). Films: "Trail to Mexico" 1946; "Wild Country" 1947 (Sam); "Deadline" 1948; "Fighting Mustang" 1948; "Frontier Revenge" 1948; "Sunset Carson Rides Again" 1948; "Triggerman" 1948; "Battling Marshal" 1950; "Red Rock Outlaw" 1950.

Matthews, John. Films: "Blood on the Arrow" 1964 (Mike); "The Great Sioux Massacre" 1965 (Dakota). ¶TV: *Have Gun Will Travel*—"Marshal of Sweetwater" 11-24-62 (Farmer); *Empire*—"Hidden Asset" 3-26-63 (Matt Christopher); *Bo-*

nanza—"Bullet for a Bride" 2-16-64 (Clergyman), "Sense of Duty" 9-24-67 (Col. Brill); *Wild Wild West*—"Night of the Bubbling Death" 9-8-67 (Driver).

Matthews, Junius (1892-1/18/78). TV: *The Gene Autry Show*—"The Golden Chariot" 10-29-55; *Have Gun Will Travel*—"The Gentleman" 9-27-58 (Clem).

Matthews, Lester (1900-6/6/75). Films: "Susannah of the Mounties" 1939 (Harlan Chambers); "Gaucho Serenade" 1940 (Alfred Willoughby); "Northwest Passage" 1940 (Sam Livermore); "Montana" 1950 (George Forsythe); "Fort Ti" 1953 (Lord Jeffrey Amherst); "The Far Horizons" 1955 (Mr. Hancock); "Ten Wanted Men" 1955 (Adam Stewart). ¶TV: *Yancy Derringer*—"Old Dixie" 12-25-58 (Jerrison Ames); *Rawhide*—"The House of the Hunter" 4-20-62 (Larkins); *Bonanza*—"The Actress" 2-24-63 (Forrester); *Daniel Boone*—"The Desperate Raid" 11-16-67.

Mattingly, Hedley (1915-). TV: *Hudson's Bay*—"Montgomery Velvet" 3-15-58 (Factor Balfour), "The Drummer Boy" 3-22-58 (Captain); *The Travels of Jaimie McPheeters*—Regular 1963-64 (Coe); *Death Valley Days*—"The $25,000 Wager" 2-7-65 (Muybridge), "An Organ for Brother Brigham" 7-16-66 (Joseph Ridges).

Mattox, Martha (1879-5/2/33). Films: "The Scarlet Drop" 1918 (Mammy); "Thieves' Gold" 1918 (Mrs. Larkin); "Wild Women" 1918 (the Queen); "Ace High" 1919; "Firebrand Trevison" 1920 (Aunt Agatha); "The Sheriff's Oath" 1920; "The Conflict" 1921 (Miss Labo); "The Yankee Senor" 1926 (Aunt Abagail); "The Big Diamond Robbery" 1929 (Aunt Effie); "Dynamite Ranch" 1932 (Aunt Sarah); "Haunted Gold" 1932 (Mrs. Herman); "Heroes of the West" 1932-serial (Martha Blaine); "The Fourth Horseman" 1933.

Mattraw, Scotty (1885-11/9/46). Films: "One Glorious Scrap" 1927 (Scotty); "The Return of the Riddle Rider" 1927-serial; "Arizona Cyclone" 1928 (Scotty); "Made-to-Order Hero" 1928 (Scotty); "Quick Triggers" 1928 (Scotty); "Captain Cowboy" 1929.

Matts, Frank. Films: "The Capture" 1950 (Juan); "Silver Canyon" 1951; "Apache Country" 1952 (Steve); "Montana Territory" 1952 (Jack Gallagher); "Son of Geronimo" 1952-serial; "Escape from Fort Bravo" 1953 (Kiowa Indian); "Thunder Over the Plains" 1953 (Jurgens). ¶TV: *The Gene Autry Show*—"Gun Powder

Range" 10-29-50; *The Cisco Kid*—"Cattle Rustling" 2-3-51, "Medicine Flats" 3-10-51, "Lynching Story" 4-28-51, "Confession for Money" 5-26-51, "Pancho Hostage" 6-23-51.

Mattson, Robin (1956-). TV: *Daniel Boone*—"Israel and Love" 5-7-70 (Brae Secord); *Nakia*—"The Moving Target" 11-9-74 (Donna).

Mature, Victor (1916-). Films: "My Darling Clementine" 1946 (Doc Holliday); "Fury at Furnace Creek" 1948 (Cash); "Chief Crazy Horse" 1955 (Crazy Horse); "The Last Frontier" 1955 (Jed); "Escort West" 1959 (Ben Lassiter).

Maude, Beatrice. Films: "Arkansas Judge" 1941 (Mrs. Neill); "Lawless Code" 1949.

Mauldin, John. TV: *Have Gun Will Travel*—"Vernon Good" 12-31-60 (Vernon Good); *Rawhide*—"The Immigrants" 3-16-62 (Karl).

Maunder, Wayne (1942-). Films: "Kung Fu" TVM-1972 (McKay). ¶TV: *Custer*—Regular 1967 (Lieutenant Colonel George A. Custer); *Lancer*—Regular 1968-70 (Scott Lancer).

Maupain, Ernest (1881-1/10/49). Films: "The Trail to Yesterday" 1918 (David Langford).

Maurey, Nicole (1925-). Films: "The Jayhawkers" 1959 (Jeanne Dubois).

Max, Edwin (1909-10/17/80). Films: "Law of the Barbary Coast" 1949 (Arnold); "Ride, Ryder, Ride" 1949 (Frenchy). ¶TV: *The Big Valley*—"Price of Victory" 2-13-67.

Maxam, Louella (1896-9/4/70). Films: "A Child of the Prairie" 1915; "The Child, the Dog, and the Villain" 1915; "The Conversion of Smiling Tom" 1915; "The Foreman of the Bar-Z Ranch" 1915; "Getting a Start in Life" 1915; "In the Sunset Country" 1915; "The Man from Texas" 1915; "Ma's Girls" 1915; "A Matrimonial Boomerang" 1915; "Mrs. Murphy's Cooks" 1915; "Saved by Her Horse" 1915; "The Stagecoach Driver and the Girl" 1915; "The Taking of Mustang Pete" 1915; "The Luck That Jealousy Brought" 1917; "The Saddle Girth" 1917; "Deuce Duncan" 1918 (Ann Tyson); "The Uphill Climb" 1920; "Vengeance and the Girl" 1920 (Henrietta Mitchell).

Maxey, Paul (1908-6/3/63). Films: "River Lady" 1948 (Mr. Miller); "Calamity Jane and Sam Bass" 1949 (Underwood); "The Return of Jesse James" 1950; "The Stranger Wore a Gun" 1953 (Poley); "Ten Wanted Men" 1955; "Show-down at Boot Hill" 1958 (Judge); "North to Alaska" 1960. ¶TV: *Tales of the Texas Rangers*—"Ransom Flight" 8-27-55 (Constable Dawes); *Wagon Train*—"The Jennifer Churchill Story" 10-15-58 (Mr. Churchill).

Maxwell, Charles (-8/7/93). TV: *The Cisco Kid*—"New York's Priest 1-9-54, "He Couldn't Quit" 4-24-54, "Magician of Jamesville" 5-22-54; *Bat Masterson*—"Double Showdown" 10-8-58 (Ed Caulder), "One Bullet from Broken Bow" 1-21-59 (Gen. Phil Sheridan), "Dead Man's Claim" 5-4-61 (Harvey Mason); *Gunsmoke*—"Snakebite" 12-20-58 (Walt Moorman), "The Choice" 5-9-59 (Kerrick), "Honey Pot" 5-15-65 (Hy Evers), "Time of the Jackals" 1-13-69 (Del Rainey); *Rough Riders*—"The Double Dealers" 3-19-59 (Duprez); *The Texan*—"Blood Money" 4-20-59 (Lew Cade), "The Sheriff of Boot Hill" 6-1-59 (Luke Stricker), "The Invisible Noose" 5-16-60 (Jeff); *The Restless Gun*—"The Cavis Boy" 6-1-59 (Pike Duncan); *Bonanza*—"The Newcomers" 9-26-59 (Krug), "The Hopefuls" 10-8-60 (Shenandoah), "The Guilty" 2-25-62 (Jack Groat), "A Dime's Worth of Glory" 11-1-64 (Pickard), "Credit for a Kill" 10-23-66 (Virgil), "Check Rein" 12-3-67 (Rio), "Child" 9-22-68 (Buck), "Company of Forgotten Men" 2-2-69 (Jeb), "The Law and Billy Burgess" 2-15-70 (Billings), "Blind Hunch" 11-21-71 (Keeley); *Maverick*—"A Fellow's Brother" 11-22-59 (Russ Ankerman), "The Resurrection of Joe November" 2-28-60 (Baron Thor Von Und Zu Himmelstern); *Rawhide*—"Incident of the Wanted Painter" 1-29-60 (Chaffee), "Incident of the Silent Web" 6-3-60 (John Taggart), "The Long Count" 1-5-62 (Staley), "A Woman's Place" 3-30-62 (Sheriff Barker); *Overland Trail*—"Vigilantes of Montana" 4-3-60 (Tex Tobey); *Zane Grey Theater*—"Seed of Evil" 4-7-60 (Lance); *Two Faces West*—"The Challenge" 10-7-60 (Frank Turner); *Lawman*—"The Unmasked" 6-17-62 (Sam Davidson); *Laramie*—"Naked Steel" 1-1-63 (McKeever); *The Rifleman*—"The Sixteenth Cousin" 1-28-63 (Gus Torpin); *Branded*—"The Bounty" 2-21-65 (Andy Starrett), "Seward's Folly" 10-17-65 (Sobel); *Pistols 'n' Petticoats*—12-3-66 (Ike Blanton); *Hondo*—"Hondo and the Judas" 11-3-67 (Look Harker); *The High Chaparral*—"Threshold of Courage" 3-31-68 (Hank), "The Buffalo Soldiers" 11-22-68 (MacAteer), "Sangre" 2-26-71 (Sergeant Smith); *The Outcasts*—"Gideon" 2-24-69 (Obie).

Maxwell, Edwin (1886-8/12/48). Films: "The Plainsman" 1936 (Stanton); "Drums Along the Mohawk" 1939 (Pastor); "Kit Carson" 1940 (John Sutter); "Ride On, Vaquero" 1941 (Clark).

Maxwell, Frank (1916-). TV: *Gunsmoke*—"Robber and Bridegroom" 12-13-58 (Stage Driver); *Black Saddle*—"The Freight Line" 11-6-59; *Rawhide*—"Incident at Rojo Canyon" 9-30-60 (Anderson), "Grandma's Money" 2-23-62 (Sheriff), "Texas Fever" 2-5-65; *The Virginian*—"First to Thine Own Self" 2-12-64 (Silas Burkett); *The Deputy*—"Duty Bound" 1-7-61 (Mel Ricker); *Alias Smith and Jones*—"The Day They Hanged Kid Curry" 9-16-71.

Maxwell, Jenny (1942-6/10/81). TV: *Bonanza*—"The Gunmen" 1-23-60; *Wagon Train*—"The Lieutenant Burton Story" 2-28-62 (Susan Lane); *Empire*—"When the Gods Laugh" 12-18-62 (Collin Haskel); *Death Valley Days*—"Peter the Hunter" 2-14-65; *Wild Wild West*—"The Night of the Avaricious Actuary" 12-6-68 (Billie).

Maxwell, John. Films: "Honky Tonk" 1941 (Kendall); "Arizona Terrors" 1942 (Larry Madden); "The Lone Prairie" 1942; "Alaska" 1944; "The Last Horseman" 1944 (Cash Watson); "The Paleface" 1948 (Village Gossip); "Johnny Guitar" 1954 (Jake); "Masterson of Kansas" 1954 (Merrick); "Showdown at Abilene" 1956 (Frank Scovie); "Gunfight at the O.K. Corral" 1957 (Merchant). ¶TV: *The Texan*—"The Hemp Tree" 11-17-58 (Dr. Graybill); *The Rifleman*—"The Challenge" 4-7-59; *Wyatt Earp*—"Get Shotgun Gibbs" 12-22-59, "The Arizona Lottery" 2-16-60 (Shiloh Smith); *Riverboat*—"Fight at New Canal" 2-22-60 (Sam Harper); *The Rebel*—"Absolution" 4-24-60 (Doctor); *Johnny Ringo*—"The Derelict" 5-26-60 (Doc Bardell); *Bonanza*—"Showdown" 9-10-60 (Tom Clure).

Maxwell, Lucien (1898-9/17/72). Films: "Prairie Schooners" 1940 (Indian Boy).

Maxwell, Marilyn (1922-3/20/72). Films: "New Mexico" 1951 (Cherry); "Stage to Thunder Rock" 1964 (Leah Parker); "Arizona Bushwhackers" 1968 (Molly); "Wild Women" TVM-1970 (Maude Webber). ¶TV: *Gunsmoke*—"Old Flame" 5-28-60 (Dolly Winters); *Wagon Train*—"The Pearlie Garnet Story" 2-24-64 (the Duchess); *Bob Hope Chrysler Theatre*—"Have Girls—Will Travel" 10-16-64 (Charity); *Branded*—"Price of a Name" 5-23-65 (Lucy Benson).

Maxwell, Paul (1920-1/92). TV: *Bronco*—"The Masquerade" 1-26-60 (Lou Drum).

May, Ann (1899-7/26/85). Films: "The Half-Breed" 1922 (Doll Pardeau); "Thundering Hoofs" 1924 (Carmelita); "O.U. West" 1925 (Tina Jones).

May, Donald (1947-). TV: *Colt .45*—Regular 1959-60 (Sam Colt, Jr.); *Sugarfoot*—"Funeral at Forty Mile" 5-24-60 (Luke Condon); *Cheyenne*—"The Long Rope" 10-3-60 (Fred Baker).

May, Doris (1902-5/12/84). Films: "The Gunfighter" 1923 (Nellie Camp); "The Deadwood Coach" 1924 (Helen Shields).

May, Ida. Films: "Union Pacific" 1939 (Goldie).

May, Marta. Films: "Massacre at Fort Grant" 1963-Span. (Jane); "The Texican" 1966-U.S./Span. (Elena); "Seven Pistols for a Gringo" 1967-Ital./Span.

May, Princess Neola. Films: "Neola, the Sioux" 1915; "The Captain of the Gray Horse Troop" 1917 (Cut Finger's Wife); "A Fight for Love" 1919 (Indian Girl).

May, Vivian. Films: "The White Outlaw" 1929 (Janice Holbrook).

Mayall, Herschel (1863-6/10/41). Films: "Days of '49" 1913; "Shorty's Sacrifice" 1914; "Keno Bates—Liar" 1915; "The Man from Oregon" 1915 (William Landers); "On the Night Stage" 1915 (Handsome Jack Malone); "The Renegade" 1915; "The Aryan" 1916 (Trixie's Lover); "Carmen of the Klondike" 1918 (Silk McDonald); "A Man in the Open" 1919 (Trevor); "The Money Corral" 1919 (Carl Bruler); "The Sleeping Lion" 1919 (Durant); "The Coast of Opportunity" 1920 (Julien Marr); "Drag Harlan" 1920 (Lane Morgan); "The Beautiful Gambler" 1921 (Judge Rand); "Straight from the Shoulder" 1921 (Joseph Martin); "Three Word Brand" 1921 (Carrol); "To a Finish" 1921 (Joe Blake); "Wild Bill Hickok" 1923 (Gambler).

Mayama, Miko (1939-). TV: *F Troop*—"From Karate with Love" 1-5-67 (Kimo Mayama).

Mayberry, Mary. Films: "The Texas Terror" 1926; "Headin' Westward" 1928 (Mary Benson); "Manhattan Cowboy" 1928.

Maye, Hazel. Films: "The Heart of a Texan" 1922 (June Jackson); "Table Top Ranch" 1922 (Kate Bowers); "West of the Pecos" 1922 (Irene Osborne).

Mayer, Charles (1904-). Films: "Rootin' Tootin' Rhythm" 1937.

Mayer, Ken (1919-1/30/85). Films: "Ambush at Cimarron Pass" 1958 (Corporal Schwitzer); "The Miracle of the Hills" 1959 (Milo Estes); "Frontier Uprising" 1961 (Beaver); "Gun Fight" 1961 (Joe Emery). ¶TV: *Wild Bill Hickok*—"Money Shines" 6-2-53; *Gunsmoke*—"Sweet and Sour" 3-2-57 (Hank), "Widow's Mite" 5-10-58 (Zack Morton), "The Cook" 12-17-60 (Ed Fisher), "Deputy Festus" 1-16-65 (Tiplett), "Mistaken Identity" 3-18-67 (Timmons), "Rope Fever" 12-4-67 (Shad), "Lyle's Kid" 9-23-68 (Tuttle), "The Cage" 3-23-70 (Blake), "The Gun" 11-19-70 (Greenwood), "The Legend" 10-18-71 (Farmer), "Tara" 1-17-72 (Pudge), "Arizona Midnight" 1-1-73 (Ed); *Tales of the Texas Rangers*—"Key Witness" 9-29-57 (Frankie); *The Adventures of Rin Tin Tin*—"Hostage of War Bonnet" 11-1-57 (Jeb Hogarth), "The Misfit Marshal" 1-9-59 (Ken Sterling); *Tombstone Territory*—"Postmarked for Death" 2-12-58 (Rigg Quade), "Death Is to Write About" 5-29-59 (Deke Reardon); *Tales of Wells Fargo*—"Special Delivery" 3-31-58 (Stelman), "The Traveler" 2-24-62 (Sunderman); *Have Gun Will Travel*—"The Protege" 10-18-58 (Man); *Jefferson Drum*—"Simon Pitt" 12-11-58 (Jingo); *Wagon Train*—"The Beauty Jamison Story" 12-17-58 (Judge Bascombe), "The Colonel Harris Story" 1-13-60 (Shegan), "The Lisa Raincloud Story" 10-31-62 (Pearson), "The Gus Morgan Story" 9-30-63 (Jesse), "The Pearlie Garnet Story" 2-24-64 (Norton), "The Wanda Snow Story" 1-17-65 (Junius Hotstatter); *Maverick*—"The Saga of Waco Williams" 2-15-59 (Sheriff Boyd Tait), "Maverick at Law" 2-26-61 (Sheriff Starrett); *The Texan*—"No Love Wasted" 3-9-59, "Ruthless Woman" 4-11-60 (Tom Bolt), "The Mountain Man" 5-23-60 (Ace Morgan); *Rough Riders*—"The Injured" 4-9-59 (Jake); *Bronco*—"Hero of the Town" 6-2-59 (Sheriff Turner), "Then the Mountains" 4-30-62 (Horse Trader); *Frontier Doctor*—"The Counterfeiters" 6-13-59; *Wanted—Dead or Alive*—"Vanishing Act" 12-26-59 (Charlie Trace); *Rawhide*—"Incident of the Devil and His Due" 1-22-60 (Sam Burton), "Incident at Poco Tiempo" 12-9-60, "Incident of the Phantom Burglar" 4-14-61 (Thompson), "Incident of the Wager on Payday" 6-16-61 (Joe Stapp); *Johnny Ringo*—"The Liars" 2-4-60 (Wally Borman); *Overland Trail*—"West of Boston" 2-21-60

(Sheriff); *The Law of the Plainsman*—"The Question of Courage" 2-25-60 (Burt Kolb); *Bonanza*—"The Last Trophy" 3-26-60 (Whitey), "Denver McKee" 10-15-60 (Miles), "The Dowry" 4-29-62 (Crusty), "Gallagher Sons" 12-9-62, "Rich Man, Poor Man" 5-12-63, "The Jonah" 5-9-65 (Kern), "The Last Mission" 5-8-66 (Poker), "Clarissa" 4-30-67 (Baker), "The Clarion" 2-9-69 (North), "Thorton's Account" 11-1-70 (Sheriff); *Bat Masterson*—"Come Out Fighting" 4-7-60 (Largo Morgan), "Dagger Dance" 4-20-61 (Major Whitsett); *Death Valley Days*—"The Man Everyone Hated" 4-12-60 (Blanchard), "Girl with a Gun" 6-6-62 (Martin); *Tate*—"The Gunfighters" 8-31-60 (Lathrop); *The Rebel*—"To See the Elephant" 10-16-60 (Bull Hollingsworth), "Miz Purdy" 4-2-61 (Preacher), "The Executioner" 6-18-61 (Andrews); *Two Faces West*—"The Hanging" 12-12-60; *Cheyenne*—"Duel at Judas Basin" 1-30-61 (Hank Lutz); *Wyatt Earp*—"The Convict's Revenge" 4-4-61 (Dapper Courtney); *Whispering Smith*—"Three for One" 7-3-61 (Carter); *The Virginian*—"The Accomplice" 12-19-62 (Clay Friendly), "Legend for a Lawman" 3-3-65 (Gaynor), "Morgan Starr" 2-9-66 (McDuff); *The Dakotas*—"Justice at Eagle's Nest" 3-11-63 (Crawford); *Laramie*—"The Unvanquished" 3-12-63; *Destry*—"The Solid Gold Girl" 2-14-64 (Sheriff Blane), "Law and Order Day" 2-28-64 (Conductor); *Temple Houston*—"Do Unto Others, Then Gallop" 3-19-64 (Sam); *The Big Valley*—"The Odyssey of Jubal Tanner" 10-13-65 (Crowell), "Last Train to the Fair" 4-27-66 (Deakes); *The Legend of Jesse James*—"The Celebrity" 12-6-65 (Sheriff); *Branded*—"A Proud Town" 12-19-65 (Martin Stoddard); *Laredo*—"Miracle at Massacre Mission" 3-3-66 (Dan Rodden); *Death Valley Days*—"Lady of the Plains" 7-23-66 (Seth Bremen), "A Man Called Abraham" 3-11-67 (Marshal), "Biscuits and Billy the Kid" 11-1-69, "The Tenderfoot" 11-15-69; *Daniel Boone*—"The Enchanted Gun" 11-17-66 (Flint); *Pistols 'n' Petticoats*—1-28-67 (Dirty Dan); *Hondo*—"Hondo and the Judas" 11-3-67 (Sam Bragg); *Iron Horse*—"Steel Chain to a Music Box" 11-18-67; *Wild Wild West*—"The Night of Fire and Brimstone" 11-22-68 (Hannon); *The High Chaparral*—"Stinky Flanagan" 2-21-69 (Sergeant Cochrane), "Fiesta" 11-20-70; *Alias Smith and Jones*—"The Great Shell Game" 2-18-71.

Mayer, Ray (1901-11/22/48). Films: "The Arizonian" 1935 (Mc-

Closky); "Powdersmoke Range" 1935 (Chap Bell); "The Last Outlaw" 1936 (Jess); "The Oklahoma Kid" 1939 (Professor).

Mayhew, Kate (1853-6/16/44). Films: "Tongues of Flame" 1924 (Mrs. Vickers).

Maynard, Ken (1895-3/23/73). Films: "The Man Who Won" 1923 (Cowboy); "$50,000 Reward" 1924 (Tex Sherwood); "The Demon Rider" 1925 (Billy Dennis); "Fighting Courage" 1925 (Richard Kingsley); "The Haunted Range" 1926 (Terry Baldwin); "Senor Daredevil" 1926 (Don Luis O'Flagherty); "The Unknown Cavalier" 1926 (Tom Drury); "The Devil's Saddle" 1927 (Harry Morrell); "Gun Gospel" 1927 (Granger Hume); "The Land Beyond the Law" 1927 (Jerry Steele); "The Overland Stage" 1927 (Jack Jessup); "Red Raiders" 1927 (Lieutenant John Scott); "Somewhere in Sonora" 1927 (Bob Bishop); "The Canyon of Adventure" 1928 (Steve Bancroft); "The Glorious Trail" 1928 (Pat O'Leary); "Phantom City" 1928 (Tim Kelly); "The Upland Rider" 1928 (Dan Dailey); "The Wagon Show" 1928 (Bob Mason); "The California Mail" 1929 (Bob Scott); "Cheyenne" 1929 (Cal Roberts); "The Lawless Legion" 1929 (Cal Stanley); "The Royal Rider" 1929 (Dick Scott); "Senor Americano" 1929 (Michael Banning); "The Wagon Master" 1929 (the Rambler); "The Fighting Legion" 1930 (Dave Hayes); "Fighting Thru" 1930 (Dan Barton); "Lucky Larkin" 1930 (Lucky Larkin); "Mountain Justice" 1930 (Ken McTavish); "Parade of the West" 1930 (Bud Rand); "Song of the Caballero" 1930 (Juan); "Sons of the Saddle" 1930 (Jim Brandon); "Alias the Bad Man" 1931 (Ken Neville); "Branded Men" 1931 (Rod Whitaker); "Arizona Terror" 1931 (the Arizonan); "The Pocatello Kid" 1931 (Jim Bledsoe/the Pocatello Kid); "Range Law" 1931 (Hap Connors); "The Two Gun Man" 1931 (Blackie Weed); "Between Fighting Men" 1932 (Ken Lanning); "Dynamite Ranch" 1932 (Blaze Howell); "Hell Fire Austin" 1932 (Ken Austin); "The Sunset Trail" 1932 (Jim Brandon)"Texas Gun Fighter" 1932 (Bill Dane); "Tombstone Canyon" 1932 (Ken Mason); "Whistlin' Dan" 1932 (Dan Savage); "Come on Tarzan" 1933 (Ken Benson); "Drum Taps" 1933 (Ken Cartwright); "Fargo Express" 1933 (Ken); "King of the Arena" 1933 (Firebrand Kenton); "The Lone Avenger" 1933 (Cal Weston); "The Phantom Thunderbolt" 1933 (Ken Petes/the Thunderbolt

Kid); "Strawberry Roan" 1933 (Ken Masters); "The Trail Drive" 1933 (Ken); "The Fiddlin' Buckaroo" 1934 (Fiddlin'); "Gun Justice" 1934 (Ken Lance); "Honor of the Range" 1934 (Ken/Clem); "In Old Santa Fe" 1934 (Ken Maynard); "Mystery Mountain" 1934-serial (Ken Williams); "Smoking Guns" 1934 (Ken Masters); "Wheels of Destiny" 1934 (Ken Manning); "Heir to Trouble" 1935 (Ken Armstrong); "Lawless Riders" 1935 (Ken Manley); "Western Courage" 1935 (Ken Baxter); "Western Frontier" 1935 (Ken Masters); "Avenging Waters" 1936 (Ken Morley); "The Cattle Thief" 1936 (Ken Martin); "The Fugitive Sheriff" 1936 (Ken Marshall); "Heroes of the Range" 1936 (Ken Smith); "Boots of Destiny" 1937 (Ken Crawford); "Galloping Dynamite" 1937 (Jim Dillon); "Trailing Trouble" 1937 (Friendly Fielding/Blackie Burke); "Six Shootin' Sheriff" 1938 (Trigger); "Whirlwind Horseman" 1938 (Ken Morton); "Flaming Lead" 1939 (Ken Clark); "Death Rides the Range" 1940 (Ken Baxter); "Lightning Strikes West" 1940 (Lightning Ken Morgan); "Phantom Rancher" 1940 (Ken Mitchell); "Perils of the Royal Mounted" 1942-serial (Collins); "Blazing Guns" 1943 (Ken); "Border Buckaroos" 1943; "The Law Rides Again" 1943 (Ken); "Wild Horse Stampede" 1943 (Ken); "Arizona Whirlwind" 1944 (Ken Maynard); "Brand of the Devil" 1944; "Death Valley Rangers" 1944 (Ken); "Westward Bound" 1944 (Ken); "White Stallion" 1947 (Ken Maynard); "Buck and the Preacher" 1972 (Little Henry).

Maynard, Kermit "Tex" (1902-1/16/71). Films: "Gun-Hand Garrison" 1927 (Garrison); "Prince of the Plains" 1927; "Ridin' Luck" 1927; "Wanderer of the West" 1927; "Wild Born" 1927; "Code of the Scarlet" 1928 (Bruce Kenton); "The Drifting Kid" 1928; "Lightning Warrior" 1931-serial; "The Phantom of the West" 1931-serial (Peter Drake); "Dynamite Ranch" 1932; "Drum Taps" 1933 (Earl Cartwright); "Outlaw Justice" 1933; "The Fighting Trooper" 1934 (Burke); "Code of the Mounted" 1935 (Jim Wilson); "His Fighting Blood" 1935 (Tom Elliott); "Northern Frontier" 1935 (Trooper MacKenzie); "Red Blood of Courage" 1935 (Jim Sullivan/James Anderson); "Timber War" 1935 (Jim Dolan); "Trails of the Wild" 1935 (McKenna); "Wilderness Mail" 1935 (Rance Raine/Keith Raine); "Phantom Patrol" 1936 (Sergeant Jim Mc-

Gregor); "Song of the Trail" 1936 (Jim Carter); "Wildcat Trooper" 1936 (Gale Farrell); "Fighting Texan" 1937 (Glenn Oliver); "Roaring Six Guns" 1937 (Buck Sinclair); "Rough Ridin' Rhythm" 1937 (Jim Langley); "Valley of Terror" 1937 (Bob Wilson); "Whistling Bullets" 1937 (Larry Graham); "Wild Horse Rodeo" 1937; "Wild Horse Round-Up" 1937 (Jack Benson); "The Great Adventures of Wild Bill Hickok" 1938 (Kit Lawson); "The Law West of Tombstone" 1938; "Western Jamboree" 1938 (Slim); "Chip of the Flying U" 1939; "Code of the Cactus" 1939; "Colorado Sunset" 1939 (Drake); "The Night Riders" 1939 (Sheriff Pratt); "Heroes of the Saddle" 1940; "Law and Order" 1940 (Henchman); "Northwest Mounted Police" 1940 (Constable Porter); "Pony Post" 1940 (Whitmore); "Ragtime Cowboy Joe" 1940; "The Range Busters" 1940 (Wyoming); "The Return of Frank James" 1940 (Man in Courtroom); "Riders of Pasco Basin" 1940; "The Showdown" 1940 (Johnson); "West of Carson City" 1940 (2nd Bandit); "Arizona Cyclone" 1941; "Billy the Kid" 1941 (Thad Decker); "Boss of Bullion City" 1941 (Cowboy); "Bury Me Not on the Lone Prairie" 1941; "King of the Texas Rangers" 1941-serial (Wichita Bates); "Man from Montana" 1941 (Chris); "A Missouri Outlaw" 1941; "The Royal Mounted Patrol" 1941 (Sgt. Coburn); "Sierra Sue" 1941 (Jarvis); "Stick to Your Guns" 1941; "Trail of the Silver Spurs" 1941; "Wyoming Wildcat" 1941; "Along the Sundown Trail" 1942; "Arizona Stagecoach" 1942; "Down Rio Grande Way" 1942; "Fighting Bill Fargo" 1942; "Home in Wyomin'" 1942; "Jesse James, Jr." 1942; "Law and Order" 1942; "The Lone Prairie" 1942; "The Mysterious Rider" 1942; "The Omaha Trail" 1942; "Prairie Pals" 1942 (Crandall); "Riders of the West" 1942; "Riding Through Nevada" 1942; "Rock River Renegades" 1942; "Sheriff of Sage Valley" 1942 (Slim); "Stagecoach Buckaroo" 1942; "Texas Trouble Shooters" 1942 (Pete); "Trail Riders" 1942 (Ace); "Beyond the Last Frontier" 1943 (Clyde Barton); "The Blocked Trail" 1943; "Cheyenne Roundup" 1943; "Frontier Badman" 1943 (Townsman); "Fugitive of the Plains" 1943; "Raiders of Red Gap" 1943 (Bradley); "Santa Fe Scouts" 1943 (Ben Henderson); "Silver Spurs" 1943; "The Stranger from Pecos" 1943; "The Texas Kid" 1943 (Alex); "Two Fisted Justice" 1943; "Western Cyclone" 1943 (Hank); "Blazing

Frontier" 1944 (Pete); "Death Rides the Plains" 1944 (Jed); "Devil Riders" 1944 (Red); "The Drifter" 1944 (Jack); "Frontier Outlaws" 1944 (Wallace); "Gunsmoke Mesa" 1944 (Sam Sneed); "Oath of Vengeance" 1944; "Raiders of the Border" 1944; "Thundering Gun Slingers" 1944 (Ed); "Wild Horse Phantom" 1944; "Enemy of the Law" 1945 (Mike); "Fighting Bill Carson" 1945; "Flaming Bullets" 1945; "Gangster's Den" 1945 (Curt); "Marked for Murder" 1945; "Prairie Rustlers" 1945 (Vic); "Rough Ridin' Justice" 1945 (Guard); "Stagecoach Outlaws" 1945 (Vic); "Ambush Trail" 1946 (Walter Gordon); "Badman's Territory" 1946; "Galloping Thunder" 1946; "'Neath Canadian Skies" 1946; "Prairie Badmen" 1946 (Lon); "Rustler's Roundup" 1946; "Stars Over Texas" 1946 (Knuckles); "Terrors on Horseback" 1946 (Wagner); "Tumbleweed Trail" 1946 (Bill Ryan); "Under Arizona Skies" 1946; "Along the Oregon Trail" 1947; "Law Comes to Gunsight" 1947; "Return of the Lash" 1947; "Ridin' Down the Trail" 1947; "Buckaroo from Powder River" 1948; "Frontier Revenge" 1948 (Outlaw); "Fury at Furnace Creek" 1948 (Scout); "The Gallant Legion" 1948; "Northwest Stampede" 1948; "The Paleface" 1948 (Horseman); "Lust for Gold" 1949 (Man in lobby); "Massacre River" 1949 (Scout); "Range Land" 1949 (Shad); "Riders in the Sky" 1949; "Law of the Panhandle" 1950 (Luke Winslow); "The Savage Horde" 1950; "Short Grass" 1950; "Silver Raiders" 1950 (Larkin); "Trail of Robin Hood" 1950; "Fort Dodge Stampede" 1951 (Settler); "In Old Amarillo" 1951; "Three Desperate Men" 1951 (Guard); "The Black Lash" 1952 (Woodruff); "Law and Order" 1953 (Onlooker); "Pack Train" 1953; "Blazing the Overland Trail" 1956-serial; "Perils of the Wilderness" 1956-serial; "Flesh and the Spur" 1957 (Outlaw); "The Oklahoman" 1957 (Townsman); "Once Upon a Horse" 1958 (Kermit Maynard); "Westbound" 1959; "Noose for a Gunman" 1960 (Carter); "North to Alaska" 1960 (Townsman). ¶TV: *The Lone Ranger*—"Greed for Gold" 1-19-50, "Desert Adventure" 11-30-50; *The Gene Autry Show*—"Gray Dude" 12-3-50, "The Peace Maker" 12-17-50, "Ghost Town Raiders" 10-6-51, "Silver Dollars" 10-20-51, "Blazeaway" 2-22-52, "Six Gun Romeo" 3-16-52, "Outlaw Stage" 7-21-53; *The Cisco Kid*—"Robber Crow" 11-24-51, "Spanish Dagger" 1-5-52, "The Kid Brother" 2-9-52, "Dutch-

man's Flat" 3-15-52, "Commodore Goes West" 7-12-52, "Steel Plow" 1-31-53, "The Caution of Curley Thompson" 5-2-53, "The Kidnapped Cameraman" 10-24-53, "Gold, Death and Dynamite" 2-13-54.

Maynard, Mary. Films: "Return of the Lash" 1947 (Kay).

Maynard, Tex. *see* Maynard, Kermit.

Mayne, Eric (1866-2/10/47). Films: "Suzanna" 1922 (Don Diego); "Cyclone Cavalier" 1925 (President Gonzales); "Beyond the Trail" 1926 (Ranch Owner); "The Canyon of Adventure" 1928 (Don Miguel); "Wells Fargo" 1937.

Maynor, Asa (1937-). TV: *Lawman*—"The Mad Bunch" 10-2-60 (Dory); *Wagon Train*—"The Bettina May Story" 12-20-61 (Rose); *The Rifleman*—"The Bullet" 2-25-63 (Molly).

Mayo, Alfredo (1911-5/19/85). Films: "Bullets and the Flesh" 1965-Ital./Fr./Span.; "Magnificent Brutes of the West" 1965-Ital./Span./Fr.; "Great Treasure Hunt" 1967-Ital./Span. (Sam); "Sabata the Killer" 1970-Ital./Span. (Mangusta).

Mayo, Frank (1886-7/9/63). Films: "Lasca" 1919 (Anthony Moreland); "Hitchin's Posts" 1920 (Jefferson Todd); "Out of the Silent North" 1922 (Pierre Baptiste); "Tracked to Earth" 1922 (Charles Cranner); "Wolf Law" 1922; "The Plunderer" 1924 (Bill Matthews); "Alias the Bad Man" 1931 (Rance Collins); "Range Law" 1931 (Jim Blont); "Arizona Mahoney" 1936 (Lefty); "Desert Gold" 1936 (Bert Lash); "Fair Warning" 1937 (Headwaiter); "Phantom of Santa Fe" 1937 (Steve Gant); "Dodge City" 1939; "Oklahoma Frontier" 1939 (Marshal); "The Oklahoma Kid" 1939 (Land Agent); "River's End" 1940 (Bartender); "Santa Fe Trail" 1940 (Engineer); "They Died with Their Boots On" 1941 (Orderly).

Mayo, Harry (18989-1/6/64). TV: *Hotel De Paree*—"Sundance and the Fallen Sparrow" 5-27-60 (Bartender).

Mayo, Jacqueline. TV: *Wagon Train*—"A Man Called Horse" 3-26-58 (Lucinda); *Have Gun Will Travel*—"Three Sons" 5-10-58 (Janie Bosworth); *Rawhide*—"Incident West of Lano" 2-27-59 (Margaret Haley).

Mayo, Raymond. TV: *Lawman*—"The Actor" 5-27-62 (George Carson); *Gunsmoke*—"A Noose for Dobie Price" 3-4-68 (Harry Walden); *The High Chaparral*—"The Forge of Hate" 11-13-70 (Longly).

Mayo, Virginia (1920-). Films: "Colorado Territory" 1949 (Colorado Carson); "Along the Great Divide" 1951 (Ann Keith); "The Iron Mistress" 1952 (Judalon de Bornay); "Devil's Canyon" 1953 (Abby Nixon); "Great Day in the Morning" 1956 (Ann Merry Alaine); "The Proud Ones" 1956 (Sally); "The Big Land" 1957 (Helen); "The Tall Stranger" 1957 (Ellen); "Fort Dobbs" 1958 (Celia Gray); "Westbound" 1959 (Norma Putnam); "Young Fury" 1965 (Sara McCoy); "Fort Utah" 1967 (Linda Lee). ¶TV: *Wagon Train*—"The Beauty Jamison Story" 12-17-58 (Beauty Jamison).

Mazurki, Mike (1909-10/9/90). Films: "Dakota" 1945 (Bigtree Collins); "Unconquered" 1947 (Dave Bone); "Relentless" 1948 (Jake); "Davy Crockett, King of the Wild Frontier" 1955 (Bigfoot Mason); "Comanche" 1956 (Flat Mouth); "Cheyenne Autumn" 1964 (1st Sgt. Stanislaus Wichowsky); "Four for Texas" 1964 (Chad); "Requiem for a Gunfighter" 1965 (Ivy Bliss); "The Adventures of Bullwhip Griffin" 1967 (Mountain Ox); "The Incredible Rocky Mountain Race" TVM-1977 (Crazy Horse). ¶TV: *Walt Disney Presents*—"Davy Crockett"—Regular 1954-55 (Big Foot Mason); *My Friend Flicka*—"The Old Champ" 5-4-56 (Hercules); *Jim Bowie*—"Outlaw Kingdom" 12-7-56 (Butcher of Barbados); *Have Gun Will Travel*—"Ella West" 1-4-58 (Half Breed), "Love's Young Dream" 9-17-60 (Power), "Don't Shoot the Piano Player" 3-10-62 (Jo Jo); *The Texan*—"The Accuser" 6-6-60; *Laredo*—"Pride of the Rangers" 12-16-65; *F Troop*—"Our Hero—What's His Name" 1-4-66 (Geronimo); *Wagon Train*—"The Duncan McIvor Story" 3-9-64; *Daniel Boone*—"Gabriel" 1-6-66 (El Toro); *The Loner*—"Pick Me Another Time to Die" 2-26-66 (Rufe Vernon); *Rango*—"Diamonds Look Better Around Your Neck Than a Rope" 3-3-67 (Jake Downey); *Bonanza*—"Stage Door Johnnies" 7-28-68 (Big Man), "Dead Wrong" 12-7-69 (Bic Jack); *Gunsmoke*—"Trafton" 10-25-71 (Whale); *Kung Fu*—"Superstition" 4-5-73 (Hannibal).

Mazursky, Paul (1930-). TV: *The Rifleman*—"Shotgun Man" 4-12-60 (Shorty), "Hostages to Fortune" 2-4-63 (Sylvester).

Mazza, Marc. Films: "Big Showdown" 1972-Ital./Fr.

Meacham, Anne (1925-). TV: *The Virginian*—"The Brazen Bell" 10-17-62 (Sarah Lilley); *The Road West*—"Shaman" 11-14-66 (Miss Welch).

Mead, Phillip L. Films: "The Cheyenne Social Club" 1970 (Cook); "A Gunfight" 1971 (Kyle); "Showdown" 1973 (Jack Bonney); "The Tracker" TVM-1988. ¶TV: *Nakia*—"The Moving Target" 11-9-74 (Lieutenant Grimes).

Meade, Claire (1883-1/14/68). TV: *Whispering Smith*—"Three for One" 7-3-61 (Mrs. Hopper).

Meader, George (1888-12/17/63). Films: "Shoot-Out at Medicine Bend" 1957. ¶TV: *The Lone Ranger*—"Billie the Great" 3-30-50; *The Cisco Kid*—"The Epidemic" 4-3-54; *The Adventures of Rin Tin Tin*—"Rin Tin Tin and the Rainmaker" 3-30-56 (Prof. Pluvius).

Meader, William (-4/15/79). Films: "The Lonely Man" 1957. ¶TV: *Gunsmoke*—"Wishbone" 2-19-66 (Stage Passenger).

Meadows, Audrey (1922-). TV: *Wagon Train*—"The Nancy Palmer Story" 3-8-61 (Nancy Palmer).

Meadows, Dennis. see Moore, Dennis.

Meadows, Jayne (1923-). Films: "City Slickers" 1991. ¶TV: *Here Come the Brides*—"Next Week, East Lynne" 10-17-69 (Eleanor Tangiers).

Meadows, Joyce. Films: "Flesh and the Spur" 1957 (Rena); "Frontier Gun" 1958 (Peg Barton); "Walk Tall" 1960 (Sally Medford). ¶TV: *The Restless Gun*—"Sheriff Billy" 3-10-58 (Annie White); *Wagon Train*—"The Conchita Vasquez Story" 3-18-59 (Martha Williams), "The Jed Polke Story" 3-1-61 (Rheba Polke), "The Artie Matthewson Story" 11-8-61 (Melanie Sanders); *Tombstone Territory*—"Day of the Amnesty" 4-3-59 (Ellen); *Rough Riders*—"Hired Gun" 4-23-59 (Rosemarie), "The Last Rebel" 7-16-59; *The Texan*—"South of the Border" 5-18-59, "Ruthless Woman" 4-11-60 (Helen Castle); *Johnny Ringo*—"Border Town" 3-17-60 (Julie); *Wanted—Dead or Alive*—"One Mother Too Many" 12-7-60 (Beth Morrison); *Lawman*—"Detweiler's Kid" 2-26-61 (Elfrieda Detweiler), "The Cold One" 11-12-61 (Barbara Harris); *Two Faces West*—"The Stilled Gun" 3-20-61, "The Noose" 5-15-61, "The Lesson" 5-22-61, "Doctor's Orders" 6-5-61; *Cheyenne*—"Cross Purpose" 10-9-61 (Madaline De Vier); *Maverick*—"Epitaph of a Gambler" 2-11-62 (Linda Storey).

Meakin, Charles (1879-1/17/61). Films: "Lightning Bill" 1926 (Daniel Carson).

Meaney, Colm. Films: "The Gambler, Part III—The Legend Continues" TVM-1987; ."Far and Away" 1992 (Kelly). ¶TV: *Dr. Quinn, Medicine Woman*—Pilot 1-1-93 (Jake Slicker).

Means, Russell (1939-). Films: "The Last of the Mohicans" 1992 (Chingachgook); "Wagons East!" 1994 (the Chief); "Buffalo Girls" TVM-1995 (Sitting Bull).

Mears, Charles. Films: "Ace of Cactus Range" 1924 (Quosmo).

Medeiros, Michael. Films: "Son of the Morning Star" TVM-1991 (Reno).

Medin, Harriet (1914-). Films: "Squares" 1972 (Roth's Mother). ¶TV: *Bonanza*—"The Survivors" 11-10-68 (Elizabeth Bauer), "The Trouble with Amy" 1-25-70 (Mrs. Ocher).

Medina, Hazel. TV: *Gunsmoke*—"The Good Samaritans" 3-10-69 (Erlene).

Medina, Julio. TV: *Gunsmoke*—"The Reward" 11-6-65 (Pedro), "The Noonday Devil" 12-7-70 (Rodriguez), "Survival" 1-10-72 (Fermin); *Wild Wild West*—"The Night of the Camera" 11-29-68 (Don Carlos); *The High Chaparral*—"A Time to Laugh, a Time to Cry" 9-26-69 (Sanchez), "Fiesta" 11-20-70; *Bearcats!*—9-16-71 (Ramirez); *Kung Fu*—"The Brujo" 10-25-73 (Father Salazar), "A Lamb to the Slaughter" 1-11-75 (Padre).

Medina, Patricia (1920-). Films: "The Beast of Hollow Mountain" 1956 (Sarita); "Stranger at My Door" 1956 (Peg Jarret); "The Buckskin Lady" 1957 (Angela Medley). ¶TV: *The Californians*—"Lola Montez" 10-7-58 (Lola Montez); *Have Gun Will Travel*—"The Lady" 11-15-58 (Diana Coulter), "The Return of the Lady" 2-21-59 (Diana Coulter), "Unforgiving Minute" 1-26-63 (Sabina); *Zorro*—"The Gay Caballero" 1-22-59 (Margarita Cortazar), "Tornado Is Missing" 1-29-59 (Margarita Cortazar), "Zorro Versus Cupid" 2-5-59 (Margarita Cortazar), "The Legend of Zorro" 2-12-59 (Margarita Cortazar); *Rawhide*—"Incident at Jacob's Well" 10-16-59 (Illona Calvin), "Incident of the Boomerang" 3-24-61 (Ruthanne Harper); *Black Saddle*—"Change of Venue" 12-11-59 (Carla); *Bonanza*—"The Spanish Grant" 2-6-60 (Rosita Morales); *The Rebel*—"Fair Game" 3-27-60 (Belle Kenyon), "The Earl of Durango" 6-12-60 (Lupe); *Riverboat*—"The Night of the Faceless Men" 3-28-60 (Eileen Mason); *Hotel De Paree*—"Sundance and the Black Widow" 4-1-60 (Sabrina); *Whispering Smith*—"The Hemp Reeger Case" 7-17-61 (Flo); *Branded*—"Yellow for Courage" 2-20-66 (Dr. Karen Miller).

Meehan, Jack. Films: "The Broken Law" 1924; "The Passing of Wolf MacLean" 1924; "Hurricane Hal" 1925; "The Son of Sontag" 1925.

Meehan, Lew (1890-8/10/51). Films: "Crossing Trails" 1921 (Red Murphy); "Daring Danger" 1922 (Steve Harris); "Blazing Arrows" 1922 (Bart McDermott); "Ace of the Law" 1924 (Black Muller); "Battlin' Buckaroo" 1924 (Buck Wheeler); "Huntin' Trouble" 1924; "Lightnin' Jack" 1924 (Spike Jordan); "The Man from God's Country" 1924 (Pete Hurley); "Rainbow Rangers" 1924 (Manual Lopez); "Ridgeway of Montana" 1924 (Steve Pelton); "Thundering Romance" 1924 (Hank Callahan); "Travelin' Fast" 1924 (Red Sampson); "Walloping Wallace" 1924 (Squinty Burnt); "Double Fisted" 1925; "Kit Carson Over the Great Divide" 1925 (Josef La Rocque); "Silent Sheldon" 1925 (Joe Phillips); "Thundering Through" 1925 (Rufe Gorman); "White Thunder" 1925 (Black Morgan); "Beyond All Odds" 1926 (Corey Forbes); "The Desert's Toll" 1926; "The Desperate Game" 1926 (Bat Grayson); "Fighting Luck" 1926; "Hair Trigger Baxter" 1926 (Mont Blake); "Red Blood" 1926 (Dick Willis); "Road Agent" 1926; "Cactus Trails" 1927 (Angel); "Code of the Range" 1927; "King Cowboy" 1928 (Ralph Bennett); "Gun Law" 1929 (Big Bill Driscoll); "Idaho Red" 1929 (Sheriff George Wilkins); "The Pride of Pawnee" 1929 (Andrew Jeel); "The White Outlaw" 1929 (Jed Izbell); "Firebrand Jordan" 1930 (Spike); "Pardon My Gun" 1930 (Denver); "South of Sonora" 1930; "Trails of Danger" 1930 (Joe Fenton); "Cavalier of the West" 1931 (Tim Slade); "The Pocatello Kid" 1931; "The Range Feud" 1931; "The Texas Ranger" 1931; "The Boiling Point" 1932; "Hell Fire Austin" 1932; "The Sunset Trail" 1932; "Whistlin' Dan" 1932; "The Lone Avenger" 1933 (Burl Adams' Henchman); "The Lone Avenger" 1933; "The Phantom Thunderbolt" 1933; "Treason" 1933 (Cowboy in Bar); "The Cactus Kid" 1934; "Fighting Hero" 1934 (Henchman); "The Fighting Ranger" 1934; "Fighting Through" 1934; "The Man Trailer" 1934; "Mystery Mountain" 1934-serial; "Nevada Cyclone" 1934; "The Prescott Kid" 1934; "Range Riders" 1934; "Rawhide Mail" 1934 (Tim, the Bartender); "Wagon Wheels" 1934 (Listener); "Border

Brigands" 1935; "Desert Mesa" 1935 (El Garto/Lynx Merson); "Desert Trail" 1935; "Five Bad Men" 1935 (Gangster); "Gallant Defender" 1935; "Gunfire" 1935 (Les Daggett); "Gunsmoke on the Guadalupe" 1935; "The Last of the Clintons" 1935; "Law Beyond the Range" 1935 (Cowboy); "Lightning Triggers" 1935; "The Phantom Cowboy" 1935 (Rancher Mason); "The Reckless Buckaroo" 1935; "Ridin' Thru" 1935 (Joe); "The Silver Bullet" 1935 (Pete); "Stone of Silver Creek" 1935; "Texas Jack" 1935 (Biff); "The Unconquered Bandit" 1935; "Wagon Trail" 1935; "The Cowboy Star" 1936; "Fast Bullets" 1936; "Feud of the West" 1936 (Lew); "The Fugitive Sheriff" 1936; "Gun Smoke" 1936; "Law and Lead" 1936; "The Lawless Nineties" 1936; "Roarin' Guns" 1936 (Sanderson); "Three on the Trail" 1936; "The Unknown Ranger" 1936; "Arizona Gunfighter" 1937 (Snake Bralt); "Boothill Brigade" 1937 (Sheriff); "The California Mail" 1937; "Dodge City Trail" 1937 (Joe); "Doomed at Sundown" 1937; "Gun Lords of Stirrup Basin" 1937 (Blackie Fallon); "The Gun Ranger" 1937; "Guns in the Dark" 1937; "A Lawman Is Born" 1937 (General Store Customer); "Lightnin' Crandall" 1937 (Bull Prescott); "Melody of the Plains" 1937 (Starr); "Moonlight on the Range" 1937; "One Man Justice" 1937; "The Rangers Step In" 1937; "The Red Rope" 1937 (Rattler Hayne); "Ridin' the Lone Trail" 1937 (Sparks); "The Roaming Cowboy" 1937 (Ranch Hand); "Springtime in the Rockies" 1937; "Trail of Vengeance" 1937 (Bill O'Donnell); "Trapped" 1937 (Moose Nelson); "Yodelin' Kid from Pine Ridge" 1937 (Parker's Henchman); "The Feud Maker" 1938 (Jake Slaben); "Panamint's Bad Man" 1938; "Prairie Moon" 1938; "Thunder in the Desert" 1938 (Mike); "Whirlwind Horseman" 1938 (Hank); "Cowboys from Texas" 1939; "The Lone Ranger Rides Again" 1939-serial (Lynch); "Riders of the Black River" 1939 (Rustler); "Law and Order" 1940 (Vote Counter); "Bullet Code" 1940 (Seeley Johnson); "The Return of Frank James" 1940 (Bailiff); "Triple Justice" 1940; "The Bandit Trail" 1941; "Roaring Frontiers" 1941; "The Son of Davy Crockett" 1941; "Frontier Fury" 1943.

Meek, Donald (1878-11/18/46). Films: "Jesse James" 1939 (McCoy); "Stagecoach" 1939 (Mr. Samuel Peacock); "The Man from Dakota" 1940 (Mr. Vestry); "My Little Chickadee"

1940 (Amos Budget, Cardsharp); "The Return of Frank James" 1940 (McCoy); "The Omaha Trail" 1942 (Jonah McCleod); "Barbary Coast Gent" 1944 (Bradford Bellamy).

Meeker, George (1903-8/19/84). Films: "The Girl-Shy Cowboy" 1928 (Harry Lasser); "The Kid from Texas" 1939 (Henry Smith Harrington); "Rough Riders' Round-Up" 1939 (Lanning); "The Singing Hill" 1941; "The Ox-Bow Incident" 1943 (Mr. Swanson); "Song of Nevada" 1944 (Calahan); "Northwest Trail" 1945; "Home in Oklahoma" 1946 (Steve McClory); "Apache Rose" 1947 (Reed Calhoun); "The Denver Kid" 1948; "The Dude Goes West" 1948 (Gambler); "The Gay Ranchero" 1948 (Vance Brados); "Silver Trails" 1948 (Jackson); "Ranger of Cherokee Strip" 1949 (Eric Parsons); "Twilight in the Sierras" 1950 (Matt Brunner); "Spoilers of the Plains" 1951 (Scientist); "Wells Fargo Gunmaster" 1951 (Croupier).

Meeker, Ralph (1920-8/5/88). Films: "The Naked Spur" 1953 (Roy Anderson); "Run of the Arrow" 1957 (Lt. Driscoll). ¶TV: *Zane Grey Theater*—"A Time to Live" 4-5-57 (Steve Elkins); *Wagon Train*—"A Man Called Horse" 3-26-58 (Horse); *Wanted—Dead or Alive*—"Reunion for Revenge" 1-24-59 (Ash); *The Texan*—"Blood Money" 4-20-59 (Sam Kerrigan); *Texas John Slaughter*—"Frank Clell Is in Town" 4-23-61 (Frank Clell); *Empire*—"Walk Like a King" 10-30-62 (Barney Swanton); *Custer*—"Glory Rider" 9-20-67 (Kermit Teller); *Dundee and the Culhane*—10-25-67 (Maximus Tobin); *The High Chaparral*—"The Pride of Revenge" 11-19-67 (Tracy Conlin); *The Men from Shiloh*—"Experiment at New Life" 11-18-70 (August Cruber); *Barbary Coast*—"The Ballad of Redwing Jail" 9-29-75 (Big Lou Hobart).

Megehee, Patrick. Films: "Rangeland" 1922 (Sheriff John Hampton).

Megowan, Don (1922-6/26/81). Films: "The Kid from Amarillo" 1951 (Rakim); "Davy Crockett, King of the Wild Frontier" 1955 (Col. Billy Travis); "A Lawless Street" 1955 (Dooley Brion); "The Great Locomotive Chase" 1956 (Marion A. Ross); "Gun the Man Down" 1957 (Ralph Farley); "Hell Canyon Outlaws" 1957; "Money, Women and Guns" 1958 (John Briggs); "Snowfire" 1958 (Mike McGowan); "The Jayhawkers" 1959 (China); "Blazing Saddles" 1974. ¶TV: *Walt Disney Presents*—"Davy Crockett"—Regular

1954-55 (William Travis); *The Lone Ranger*—"Stage to Tishomingo" 10-28-54; *Death Valley Days*—"To Big Charlie from Little Charlie" 1-3-55, "Forty Steps to Glory" 5-19-59 (Buff McCloud); *Cheyenne*—"Star in the Dust" 5-1-56 (Sheriff Wes Garth), "Hired Gun" 12-17-57 (Kiley Rand), "Dead to Rights" 5-20-58 (Gregg Dewey), "Reprieve" 10-5-59 (Wed McQueen), "The Beholden" 2-27-61 (Tom Grant), "Storm Center" 11-20-61 (Matt Nelson); *Wagon Train*—"The Julia Gage Story" 12-18-57 (Jess), "The Nellie Jefferson Story" 4-5-61 (Sean Hennessey); *Colt .45*—"The Gypsies" 12-27-57 (Deputy Pete Dawson); *Tales of Wells Fargo*—"Hide Jumpers" 1-27-58 (Ben Thompson), "The Warrior's Return" 9-21-59 (Soldier O'Malley); *Have Gun Will Travel*—"The Prize Fight Story" 4-5-58 (Oren Gilliam), "Something to Live For" 12-20-58 (Wichita Walker), "Homecoming" 5-23-59 (Ben Stacy), "First, Catch a Tiger" 9-12-59 (Huston); *Trackdown*—"Chinese Cowboy" 9-19-58 (Les Morgan); *Cimarron City*—"Terror Town" 10-18-58 (Grant Budinger), "The Beast of Cimarron" 11-29-58 (the Beast); *The Californians*—"The First Gold Brick" 1-6-59 (Clay Kendall); *Wyatt Earp*—"The Actress" 4-14-59 (Tom Tanner), "A Papa for Butch and Ginger" 5-9-61 (Ginger); *Rawhide*—"Incident in No Man's Land" 6-12-59, "Deserter's Patrol" 2-9-62 (Corporal Cochran), "Incident of the Rusty Shotgun" 1-9-64 (Abraham Claybank); *Bonanza*—"The Magnificent Adah" 11-14-59 (John C. Regan), "A Woman Lost" 3-17-63 (Mase Sindell); *Laramie*—"Bare Knuckles" 12-8-59 (Terrible Terry Mulligan), "Men of Defiance" 4-19-60 (Clint Gentry); *Gunsmoke*—"Big Tom" 1-9-60 (Hob Creel), "Phoebe Strunk" 11-10-62 (Oliver Strunk), "Comanches Is Safe" 3-7-64 (Big Hardy), "The Town Tamers" 1-28-74 (Michael), "Hard Labor" 2-24-75 (Mike); *The Rifleman*—"Seven" 10-11-60 (Dorf); *The Deputy*—"Bitter Foot" 11-5-60 (Tim Brandon); *Lawman*—"Chantay" 11-13-60 (Rafe Curry); *Two Faces West*—"Trail to Indian Wells" 4-24-61; *The Tall Man*—"The Leopard's Spots" 11-11-61 (Galt); *The Travels of Jaimie McPheeters*—"The Day of the Giants" 11-3-63 (Ed Matlock); *Daniel Boone*—"The Sisters O'Hannrahan" 12-3-64 (Hermann Boehm); *Death Valley Days*—"Death in the Desert" 5-9-65 (Dan Burgess), "A Wrangler's Last Ride" 4-8-67 (Drifter), "Halo for a Badman" 4-15-67 (Clay), "The Contract" 3-14-70;

Branded—"Price of a Name" 5-23-65 (Carruthers); *A Man Called Shenandoah*—"Town on Fire" 11-8-65 (Johnny Kyle); *Cowboy in Africa*—"To Build a Beginning" 12-11-67 (Sims); *Kung Fu*—"The Elixir" 12-20-73 (Quinn).

Mehaffey, Blanche (Janet Morgan) (1908-3/31/68). Films: "The Texas Streak" 1926 (Amy Hollis); "The Denver Dude" 1927 (Patricia La Mar); "The Silent Rider" 1927 (Marian Faer); "Smilin' Guns" 1929 (Helen Van Smythe); "Dugan of the Badlands" 1931 (June Manning); "Mounted Fury" 1931 (Enid Marsh); "The Mystery Trooper" 1931-serial; "Riders of the North" 1931 (Ann); "Sunrise Trail" 1931 (Goldie); "White Renegade" 1931; "Border Guns" 1934 (Jane Wilson); "The Outlaw Tamer" 1934 (Jean Bennett); "The Cowboy and the Bandit" 1935 (Alice); "North of Arizona" 1935 (Madge Harron); "The Silent Code" 1935 (Helen Brent); "Wildcat Saunders" 1936 (June Lawson).

Meighan, Thomas (1879-7/8/36). Films: "Heart of the Wilds" 1918 (Sgt. Tom Gellatly); "M'Liss" 1918 (Charles Gray); "The Heart of Wetona" 1919 (John Hardin); "The Bachelor Daddy" 1922 (Richard Chester); "Tongues of Flame" 1924 (Harry Harrington).

Meigs, William. Films: "The Glory Guys" 1965 (Treadway). ¶TV: *Have Gun Will Travel*—"The Protege" 10-18-58 (Sheriff); *The Rifleman*—"The Sheridan Story" 1-13-59 (Col. Cushman), "The Second Witness" 3-3-59, "The Anvil Chorus" 12-17-62; *Gunsmoke*—"Buffalo Hunter" 5-2-59 (Agent).

Meiklejohn, Linda. Films: "Ballad of Josie" 1968 (Jenny).

Meillon, John (1933-8/11/89). Films: "Bullseye!" 1986-Australia (Merritt).

Melesh, Alex (1890-3/4/49). Films: "The Adventurer" 1928 (John Milton Gibbs); "A Lady Takes a Chance" 1943 (Bartender).

Melford, George (1877-4/25/61). Films: "The Blackfoot Half-Breed" 1911; "The Bugler of Battery B" 1912; "Frontier Marshal" 1939 (Man); "Brigham Young—Frontiersman" 1940 (John Taylor); "Buck Benny Rides Again" 1940 (Bartender); "My Little Chickadee" 1940 (Sheriff); "Belle Starr" 1941; "Robbers of the Range" 1941 (Col. Lodge); "Lone Star Ranger" 1942 (Hardin); "Valley of the Sun" 1942 (Dr. Thomas); "California" 1946 (Delegate); "City of Badmen" 1953 (Old Timer).

Mell, Joseph (1915-8/31/77). TV: *Gunsmoke*—"The Guitar" 7-21-56 (Pence), "How to Cure a Friend" 11-10-56 (Bill Pence), "Kitty Shot" 2-11-61 (Bill Pence), "Potshot" 3-11-61 (Bill Pence), "Minnie" 4-15-61 (Bill Pence); *Trackdown*—"The Mistake" 4-18-58 (Farrow); *Wanted—Dead or Alive*—"The Giveaway Gun" 10-11-58; *The Rifleman*—"The Retired Gun" 1-20-59 (Mr. Moody); *Wagon Train*—"The Elizabeth McQueeney Story" 10-28-59, "The Larry Hanify Story" 1-27-60; *Klondike*—"Halliday's Club" 12-19-60 (Ed); *Death Valley Days*—"Out of the Valley of Death" 5-25-68 (Ashby).

Mell, Marisa (1939-5/16/92). Films: "Last Ride to Santa Cruz" 1969-Ger./Fr.; "Ben and Charlie" 1970-Ital.; "Miss Dynamite" 1972-Ital./Fr.

Mellinger, Max (1906-2/25/68). TV: *Zorro*—"The Fortune Teller" 6-18-59 (Judge); *Rawhide*—"Incident of the Fish Out of the Water" 2-17-61; *Have Gun Will Travel*—"Brotherhood" 1-5-63 (Mossman).

Mellish, Fuller (1865-12/7/36). Films: "The Trail of the Shadow" 1917 (Padre Constantine); "The Inner Voice" 1920.

Melton, Frank (1907-3/19/51). Films: "The Cowboy Star" 1936 (Denny); "The Traitor" 1936 (Jimmy); "The Glory Trail" 1937 (Gilchrist); "Wild and Woolly" 1937 (Barton Henshaw); "Riders of the Black Hills" 1938 (Don Weston); "The Return of Frank James" 1940 (Reporter).

Melton, Sid (1920-). Films: "Tough Assignment" 1949 (Herman); "The Return of Jesse James" 1950; "Western Pacific Agent" 1950; "Three Desperate Men" 1951 (Connors); "Alias Jesse James" 1959 (Fight Fan); "Lone Texan" 1959 (Gus Pringle).

Melton, Troy (1921-11/15/95). Films: "Davy Crockett and the River Pirates" 1956; "The Firebrand" 1962 (Walker); "Young Guns of Texas" 1963 (Luke); "Wild Women" TVM-1970; "A Cry in the Wilderness" TVM-1974. ¶TV: *The Cisco Kid*—"Battle of Bad Rock" 10-4-52, "Cisco Meets the Gorilla" 12-13-52, "Not Guilty" 12-20-52, "The Haunted Stage Stop" 3-7-53; *The Roy Rogers Show*—"Empty Saddles" 3-10-56 (Hal Parker), "Sheriff Missing" 3-17-56, "The Morse Mixup" 3-24-56 (Wade), "Head for Cover" 10-21-56, "Paleface Justice" 11-18-56, "Fighting Sire" 12-16-56, "Deadlock at Dark Canyon" 1-6-57, "End of the Trail" 1-27-57 (Bill Scranton), "Brady's Bonanza" 3-31-57; *Zane Grey Theater*—"Village of Fear" 3-1-57, "The Accuser" 10-30-58; *Maverick*—"The Long Hunt" 10-20-57 (1st Pursuer), "Day of Reckoning" 2-2-58 (Harry); *Bat Masterson*—"Stampede at Tent City" 10-29-58 (the Wrangler); *Rough Riders*—"Blood Feud" 11-13-58 (Ed Maddox); *Wanted—Dead or Alive*—"Secret Ballot" 2-14-59; *Bonanza*—"The Newcomers" 9-26-59 (Merrill), "The Scapegoat" 10-25-64 (Reese), "The Jonah" 5-9-65 (Charlie), "The Genius" 4-3-66 (Draves), "Credit for a Kill" 10-23-66 (Walt), "Amigo" 2-12-67 (Carson), "Showdown at Tahoe" 11-19-67 (Houston), "In Defense of Honor" 4-28-68 (Skinner), "Salute to Yesterday" 9-29-68 (Cpl. Jensen), "El Jefe" 11-15-70 (Graves), "Winter Kill" 3-28-71 (Gorley), "Frenzy" 1-30-72 (Slim); *Klondike*—"Swing Your Partner" 1-9-61 (Ferris); *Wyatt Earp*—"The Shooting Starts" 4-18-61 (Barkeep), "Wyatt's Brothers Join Up" 6-6-61 (Hoodlum); *Whispering Smith*—"Stakeout" 5-29-61 (Dugan); *The Rifleman*—"First Wages" 10-9-61 (Wally Pierson); *Laredo*—"The Golden Trail" 11-4-65 (Andy), "Enemies and Brother" 2-17-67; *The Virginian*—"Legacy of Hate" 9-14-66 (Ed); *Gunsmoke*—"Champion of the World" 12-24-66 (Zac), "The Lure" 2-25-67 (Hemmington), "The Favor" 3-11-67 (Stage Driver), "Blood Money" 1-22-68 (Jake Walker), "9:12 to Dodge" 11-11-68 (Miles), "The Devil's Outpost" 9-22-69 (Mike Lennox), "Captain Sligo" 1-4-71 (Rackley), "The Wedding" 3-13-72 (Pete Calder), "The Fugitives" 10-23-72 (Curley Danzig); *The Big Valley*—"Legend of a General" 9-19-66 & 9-26-66 (Morgan), "Image of Yesterday" 1-9-67, "A Flock of Trouble" 9-25-67 (Macklin), "Shadow of a Giant" 1-29-68; *Rango*—"The Daring Holdup of the Deadwood Stage" 1-20-67 (Stage Driver); *Wild Wild West*—"The Night of the Iron Fist" 12-8-67 (Harry); *The Guns of Will Sonnett*—"The Straw Man" 11-8-68; *Prudence and the Chief*—Pilot 8-26-70 (Sergeant).

Melville, Sam (1936-3/9/89). Films: "Hour of the Gun" 1967 (Morgan Earp). ¶TV: *Shane*—"The Hant" 9-17-66 (Shane's Companion), "The Day the Wolf Laughed" 11-19-66 (Len); *The Big Valley*—"Image of Yesterday" 1-9-67 (Jack); *Gunsmoke*—"Mistaken Identity" 3-18-67 (Dunster), "Death Train" 11-27-67 (Zack Hodges), "Lyle's Kid" 9-23-68 (Jack

Garvin), "The Good Samaritans" 3-10-69 (Croyden), "MacGraw" 12-8-69 (Garvey), "The War Priest" 1-5-70 (Lt. Snell), "The Gun" 11-19-70 (Wade Pasco), "The Bullet" 11-29-71, 12-6-71 & 12-13-71 (Nebo); *The Guns of Will Sonnett*—"Message at Noon" 10-13-67 (Kirk); *Iron Horse*—"Leopards Try, But Leopard's Can't" 10-28-67 (Lloyd Barrington); *Dundee and the Culhane*—12-13-67; *Here Come the Brides*—"The Log Jam" 1-8-69 (Lew); *Bonanza*—"The Law and Billy Burgess" 2-15-70 (Coulter); *Death Valley Days*—"Clum's Constabulary" 4-11-70 (Clum).

Melvin, Allan. TV: *Empire*—"The Loner" 1-22-63 (Dr. Benjamin Walls); *Kung Fu*—"One Step to Darkness" 1-25-75 (Voice of the Demon).

Melvoin, Don. TV: *Bonanza*—"A Darker Shadow" 11-23-69 (Sweeney), "Is There Any Man Here?" 2-8-70 (Morris); *The High Chaparral*—"The Little Thieves" 12-26-69, "Jelks" 1-23-70 (Hendricks).

Menard, Tina. Films: "The Cactus Kid" 1934 (Rosie); "Loser's End" 1934 (Lolita Carlos); "Cheyenne Tornado" 1935 (Rita Farley); "The Traitor" 1936 (Maria); "Surrender" 1950 (Flower Vendor); "Jubilee Trail" 1954 (Isabel); "Giant" 1956 (Lupe); "Escape from Red Rock" 1958 (Maria Chavez); "Man of the West" 1958 (Mexican Woman). TV: *The Roy Rogers Show*—"The Ride of the Ranchers" 4-20-52 (Maria); *Gunsmoke*—"Thick 'n' Thin" 12-26-59 (Summer Dove); *Bonanza*—"El Toro Grande" 1-2-60, "Knight Errant" 11-18-62 (Francesca), "The Power of Life and Death" 10-11-70 (Mexican Woman); *The Rebel*—"The Hunted" 11-6-60 (Elena); *The Big Valley*—"Legend of a General" 9-19-66 & 9-26-66 (Mexican Woman); *The Virginian*—"The Captive" 9-28-66 (Elk Woman); *Pistols 'n' Petticoats*—10-1-66 (Whispering Water).

Mendez, Guillermo. Films: "Two Thousand Dollars for Coyote" 1965-Span.; "The Christmas Kid" 1966-Span./Ital. (Karl Humber); "The Mercenary" 1968-Ital./Span. (Captain).

Mendoza, George. Films: "Clearing the Range" 1931 (Juan Conares); "The Conquering Horde" 1931 (Cinco Centavos); "Spirit of the West" 1932 (Ricardo); "Ramona" 1936 (Dancer); "Triple Justice" 1940 (Manuelo).

Mendoza, Harry (1900-2/15/70). Films: "The Stranger Wore a Gun" 1953.

Mendoza, Henry B. Films: "Gunfight at the O.K. Corral" 1957 (Cockeyed Frank Loving).

Mendoza, Victor Manuel. Films: "Garden of Evil" 1954 (Vicente Madariaga); "Cowboy" 1958 (Mendoza); "The Wonderful Country" 1959 (Gen. Castro).

Meniconi, Furio (Men Fury). Films: "Kill or Be Killed" 1966-Ital.; "John the Bastard" 1967-Ital.; "Kill Them All and Come Back Alone" 1967-Ital./Span.; "Two Pistols and a Coward" 1967-Ital.; "God Does Not Pay on Saturday" 1968-Ital.; "Machine Gun Killers" 1968-Ital./Span.; "Shoot, Gringo … Shoot!" 1968-Ital./Fr.; "Time and Place for Killing" 1968-Ital.; "Django the Bastard" 1969-Ital./Span.; "Bastard, Go and Kill" 1971-Ital.; "Kill Django … Kill First" 1971-Ital.; "Deadly Trackers" 1972-Ital.; "Don't Turn the Other Cheek" 1974-Ital./Ger./Span.

Menjou, Adolphe (1890-10/29/63). Films: "The Fast Mail" 1922 (Cal Baldwin); "Across the Wide Missouri" 1951 (Pierra); "Timberjack" 1955 (Swiftwater Tilton).

Menken, Shepard. Films: "Captain John Smith and Pocahontas" 1953 (Nantaquas). TV: *The Big Valley*—"The Time After Midnight" 10-2-67 (Sanders).

Menzies, Heather (1949-). TV: *The High Chaparral*—"The Little Thieves" 12-26-69 (Bet); *Bonanza*—"Thorton's Account" 11-1-70 (Martha); *Alias Smith and Jones*—"The Girl in Boxcar Number Three" 2-11-71 (Annabelle).

Mercer, Beryl (1882-7/28/39). Films: "Broken Chains" 1922 (Mrs. Mulcahy).

Mercer, Mae (1932-). TV: *Kung Fu*—"The Well" 9-27-73 (Elizabeth Brown), "The Last Raid" 4-26-75 (Elizabeth).

Mercer, Marilyn. Films: "Guns of Hate" 1948 (Mabel).

Mercier, Louis (1901-). Films: "Tiger Rose" 1929 (Frenchie); "Rose Marie" 1936 (Admirer in Hall); "My Darling Clementine" 1946 (Francois). TV: *Maverick*—"Diamond in the Rough" 1-26-58 (Beaujean), "Escape to Tampico" 10-26-58 (Raoul Girreaux); *Zane Grey Theater*—"Picture of Sal" 1-28-60 (Raoul Libiche); *Bonanza*—"The Last Viking" 11-12-60 (Duzzaq).

Mercier, Michele (1939-). Films: "Cemetery Without Crosses" 1968-Ital./Fr.

Meredith, Burgess (1908-). Films: "A Big Hand for the Little

Lady" 1966 (Doc Scully); "There Was a Crooked Man" 1970 (the Missouri Kid); "Lock, Stock and Barrel" TVM-1971 (Reverend Willie Pursle); "Kate Bliss and the Ticker Tape Kid" TVM-1978 (William Blackstone). TV: *Rawhide*—"The Little Fishes" 11-24-61 (Tom Gwynn), "Incident at Paradise" 10-24-63 (Matthew Higgins), "Incident at Dead Horse" 4-16-64 & 4-23-64 (Hannible Plew); *The Travels of Jaimie McPheeters*—"The Day of the Wizard" 1-12-64 (Saracen); *Wagon Train*—"The Grover Allen Story" 2-3-64 (Grover Allen); *Laredo*—"Lazyfoot, Where Are You?" 9-16-65 (Grubby Sully); *Wild Wild West*—"The Night of the Human Trigger" 12-3-65 (Prof. Orkney Cadwallader); *The Loner*—"Hunt the Man Down" 12-11-65 (Siedry); *Branded*—"Headed for Doomsday" 4-10-66 (Horace Greeley); *Bonanza*—"Six Black Horses" 11-26-67 (Ownie Dugan); *The Virginian*—"The Orchard" 10-2-68 (Tim Bradbury); *Daniel Boone*—"Three Score and Ten" 2-6-69 (Alex Hemmings); *The Men from Shiloh*—"Flight from Memory" 2-17-71 (Muley).

Meredith, Charles (1894-11/28/64). Films: "Al Jennings of Oklahoma" 1951 (Judge Evans); "Along the Great Divide" 1951 (the Judge); "Santa Fe" 1951; "The Big Trees" 1952 (Elder Bixby); "Cattle Town" 1952 (Governor); "Giant" 1956 (Minister); "The Lone Ranger" 1956 (the Governor); "The Quick Gun" 1964 (Rev. Staley). TV: *The Lone Ranger*—"Message to Fort Apache" 9-23-54; *20th Century Fox Hour*—"Gun in His Hand" 4-4-56 (Judge Blanton); *Jim Bowie*—"The Bridegroom" 11-29-57 (Father Manet), "The Close Shave" 1-10-58 (Father Manet); *The Texan*—"The Hemp Tree" 11-17-58 (Eli Townsend); *Bonanza*—"The Sisters" 12-12-59; *Maverick*—"The Golden Fleecing" 10-8-61 (Seth Carter).

Meredith, Cheerio (1890-12/25/64). TV: *The Adventures of Rin Tin Tin*—"The Courtship of Marshal Higgins" 9-27-57 (Effie Trindle); *Bronco*—"Brand of Courage" 12-16-58 (Sister Anna); *Rawhide*—"The Long Count" 1-5-62 (Old Woman); *Bonanza*—"The Auld Sod" 2-4-62 (Nellie Lynch).

Meredith, Don (1938-). Films: "Banjo Hackett: Roamin' Free" TVM-1976 (Banjo Hackett); "Kate Bliss and the Ticker Tape Kid" TVM-1978 (Clint Allison); "Wyatt Earp: Return to Tombstone" TVM-1994 (Reily, the Bartender). TV: *The Quest*—"Shanklin" 10-13-76 (Shanklin).

Meredith, Iris (1915-1/22/80). Films: "The Cowboy Star" 1936 (May Baker); "Rio Grande Ranger" 1936 (Sandra Cullen); "The Gambling Terror" 1937 (Betty Garrett); "A Lawman Is Born" 1937 (Beth Graham); "The Mystery of the Hooded Horseman" 1937 (Nancy); "Outlaws of the Prairie" 1937 (Judy Garfield); "Trail of Vengeance" 1937 (Jean Warner); "Call of the Rockies" 1938 (Ann Bradford); "Cattle Raiders" 1938 (Nancy Grayson); "Colorado Trail" 1938 (Joan Randall); "Law of the Plains" 1938 (Marion); "South of Arizona" 1938 (Ann Madison); "West of Cheyenne" 1938 (Jean Wayne); "West of Santa Fe" 1938 (Madge Conway); "The Man from Sundown" 1939 (Barbara Kellogg); "Outpost of the Mounties" 1939 (Norma Daniels); "Overland with Kit Carson" 1939-serial (Carmelita); "Riders of the Black River" 1939 (Linda Holden); "Spoilers of the Range" 1939 (Madge Patterson); "The Taming of the West" 1939 (Pepper); "Texas Stampede" 1939 (Joan Cameron); "The Thundering West" 1939 (Helen Patterson); "Western Caravans" 1939 (Joyce Thompson); "Blazing Six Shooters" 1940 (Janet Kenyon); "The Man from Tumbleweeds" 1940 (Spunky Cameron); "The Return of Wild Bill" 1940 (Sammy Lou Griffin); "Texas Stagecoach" 1940 (Jean Harper); "Thundering Frontier" 1940 (Norma Belknap); "Two-Fisted Rangers" 1940 (Betty Webster); "The Son of Davy Crockett" 1941 (Doris Mathews); "The Rangers Take Over" 1942 (Jean Lorin); "The Kid Rides Again" 1943 (Joan).

Meredith, Joan (1905-10/13/80). Films: "The Fighting Boob" 1926 (Dolores); "King of the Saddle" 1926 (Mary).

Meredith, JoAnne (1932-). Films: "Peace for a Gunfighter" 1967 (Melody).

Meredith, Judi (1937-). Films: "Money, Women and Guns" 1958 (Sally Gunston); "Wild Heritage" 1958 (Callis Bascomb); "The Raiders" 1964 (Martha "Calamity Jane" Canary); "Something Big" 1971 (Carrie Standall). ¶TV: *The Restless Gun*—"Tomboy" 11-10-58 (Lettie Belknap); *Cimarron City*—"A Legacy for Ossie Harper" 1-10-59 (Martha Fenton); *Wagon Train*—"The Last Man" 2-11-59 (Ellen Emerson), "The Antone Rose Story" 5-22-63 (Judy Ludlow), "The Michael Malone Story" 1-6-64 (Beth); *Tales of Wells Fargo*—"Terry" 4-6-59 (Terry); *Yancy Derringer*—"V As in Voodoo" 5-14-59 (Charlotte Dubois); *Hotel De Paree*—Regular 1959-60 (Monique Devereaux); *Riverboat*—"Salvage Pirates" 1-31-60 (Louise Harrison); *Laramie*—"Drifter's Gold" 11-29-60 (Marcie Benson); *Have Gun Will Travel*—"Bear Bait" 5-13-61 (Sally), "Memories of Monica" 10-27-62 (Monica), "The Savages" 3-16-63 (Gina); *The Tall Man*—"Time of Foreshadowing" 11-25-61 (Mattie Arnold); *Gunsmoke*—"The Dealer" 4-14-62 (Lily Baskin); *The Virginian*—"Trail to Ashley Mountain" 11-2-66 (Ruth); *Bonanza*—"Knight Errant" 11-18-62 (Lotty), "The Wormwood Cup" 4-23-67 (Linda Roberts); *Rawhide*—"Texas Fever" 2-5-65 (Kate Wentworth); *Death Valley Days*—"The Saga of Dr. Davis" 3-18-67 (Jenny).

Meredith, Lucille (1916-). TV: *The Oregon Trail*—"Hannah's Girls" 10-26-77 (Mrs. Thatcher).

Meredith, Madge. Films: "Trail Street" 1947 (Susan Pritchett); "Tumbleweed" 1953 (Sarah); "The Guns of Fort Petticoat" 1957 (Hazel McCasslin). ¶TV: *Cowboy G-Men*—"Center Fire" 10-18-52; *The Lone Ranger*—"The School Story" 1-20-55; *Judge Roy Bean*—"Lock O' the Irish" 7-1-56 (Kate O'Hara); *Northwest Passage*—"Surprise Attack" 10-5-58 (Mary Broom).

Meredyth, Bess (1890-7/13/69). Films: "Bred in the Bone" 1913; "The Desert's Sting" 1914.

Merenda, Luc (1943-). Films: "Red Sun" 1971-Fr./Ital./Span.; "Man Called Amen" 1972-Ital. (Horacio); "They Still Call Me Amen" 1972-Ital. (Horacio).

Meril, Macha (1940-). Films: "Rampage at Apache Wells" 1965-Ger./Yugo. (Lizzy).

Meriwether, Lee (1935-). Films: "The Undefeated" 1969 (Margaret Langdon); "The Brothers O'Toole" 1973; "True Grit" TVM-1978 (Annie). ¶TV: *F Troop*—"O'Rourke vs. O'Reilly" 12-7-65 (Lilly O'Reilly); *Time Tunnel*—Regular 1966-67 (Dr. Ann MacGregor); *Iron Horse*—"T Is for Traitor" 12-2-67 (Anne).

Merkel, Una (1903-1/2/86). Films: "Destry Rides Again" 1939 (Lily Belle Callahan); "The Man from Texas" 1947 (Widow Weeks); "The Kentuckian" 1955 (Sophie). ¶TV: *Destry*—"Law and Order Day" 2-28-64 (Granny Farrell).

Merli, Maurizio (1939-3/10/89). Films: "Man Called Blade" 1977-Ital. (Blade).

Merlin, Jan (1924-). Films: "A Day of Fury" 1956 (Billy Brand); "The Peacemaker" 1956 (Viggo Tomlin); "Cole Younger, Gunfighter" 1958 (Frank); "Hell Bent for Leather" 1960 (Travers); "Gunfight at Comanche Creek" 1964 (Nielson); "Guns of Diablo" 1964 (Rance Macklin). ¶TV: *Frontier*—"The Captivity of Joe Long" 2-12-56 (Joe Long), "The Hunted" 5-13-56; *Wyatt Earp*—"Vengeance Trail" 2-12-57 (Fred Colby); *Zane Grey Theater*—"Black Creek Encounter" 3-8-57 (Davey Harper); *Broken Arrow*—"Apache Girl" 5-7-57 (Pete); *Trackdown*—"Marple Brothers" 10-4-57; *Tombstone Territory*—"Guilt of a Town" 3-19-58 (Billy Clyde); *Rough Riders*—Regular 1958-59 (Lieutenant Kirby); *Tales of Wells Fargo*—"The Great Bullion Robbery" 3-21-60 (Johnny), "End of a Minor God" 4-7-62 (Johnny Fullen); *Laramie*—"Three Roads West" 10-4-60 (Chris), "Stolen Tribute" 1-31-61 (Clint Wade), "Trial by Fire" 4-10-62 (Garth), "Among the Missing" 9-25-62 (Milo Gordon), "The Fugitives" 2-12-63 (Joel Greevy); *Bat Masterson*—"Last Stop to Austin" 12-1-60 (Kid Jimmy Fresh); *The Tall Man*—"First Blood" 1-7-61 (Hendry Grant); *Whispering Smith*—"The Blind Gun" 5-8-61 (Thad Janeck); *The Outlaws*—"The Verdict" 12-28-61 (Jed Evans); *Bonanza*—"The Ride" 1-21-62 (Bill Enders); *Rawhide*—"Incident at Crooked Hat" 2-1-63 (Little Sam Talbot); *The Virginian*—"First to Thine Own Self" 2-12-64 (Reese), "Ryker" 9-16-64 (Lake); *The Travels of Jaimie McPheeters*—"The Day of the Reckoning" 3-15-64 (Rance Macklin); *Gunsmoke*—"Blue Heaven" 9-26-64 (Sykes); *The Legend of Jesse James*—"The Celebrity" 12-6-65 (Jesse's Imposter); *Branded*—"A Destiny Which Made Us Brothers" 1-23-66 (Jim Darcy); *Paradise*—"The Bounty" 1-11-91 (Joe Miller).

Merman, Ethel (1909-12/15/84). TV: *Annie Get Your Gun* 3-19-67 (Annie Oakley).

Merriam, Charlotte (1906-7/10/72). Films: "The Flip of a Coin" 1919; "A Sagebrush Gentleman" 1920; "Code of the Wilderness" 1924 (Hagar); "Steele of the Royal Mounted" 1925 (Isobel Becker).

Merrick, Doris. Films: "The Fighting Stallion" 1950 (Jeanne Barton). ¶TV: *The Cisco Kid*—"Hypnotist Murder" 11-10-51, "Ghost Town Story" 12-22-51.

Merrick, John. Films: "Yaqui Drums" 1956; "Ride Out for Revenge" 1957 (Lieutenant); "Ambush at Cimarron Pass" 1958 (Private

Nathan); "Seven Guns to Mesa" 1958 (Brown); "Toughest Gun in Tombstone" 1958 (Ranger Burgess); "Thirteen Fighting Men" 1960 (Lee). ¶TV: *Wild Bill Hickok*—"Missing Diamonds" 3-17-53; *Frontier*—"The Voyage of Captain Castle" 2-19-56 (Crane); *Tales of Wells Fargo*—"The Hasty Gun" 3-25-57 (Webb McCloy), "The Happy Tree" 12-22-58 (Tenny Jackson); *Tales of the Texas Rangers*—"Both Barrels Blazing" 10-20-57 (Red Adams); *The Restless Gun*—"The New Sheriff" 11-18-57; *Wagon Train*—"The Clara Beauchamp Story" 12-11-57 (Sergeant), "The Dan Hogan Story" 5-14-58; *Schlitz Playhouse of the Stars*—"A Tale of Wells Fargo" 12-14-58 (Beal); *Death Valley Days*—"Vlley of Danger" 5-12-59 (John Warner); *Bonanza*—"The Truckee Strip" 11-21-59, "The Spanish Grant" 2-6-60.

Merrick, Lynn (Marilyn Merrick). Films: "Fugitive from Sonora" 1937 (Dixie Martin); "Ragtime Cowboy Joe" 1940 (Mary Curtis); "The Apache Kid" 1941 (Barbara Taylor); "Desert Bandit" 1941 (Sue Martin); "Kansas Cyclone" 1941 (Martha); "A Missouri Outlaw" 1941 (Virginia Randall); "Two-Gun Sheriff" 1941 (Ruth); "Arizona Terrors" 1942 (Lila Adams); "The Cyclone Kid" 1942 (Mary Phillips); "Jesse James, Jr." 1942 (Joan Perry); "Outlaws of Pine Ridge" 1942 (Ann Hollister); "The Sombrero Kid" 1942 (Dorothy Russell); "Stagecoach Express" 1942 (Ellen Bristol); "Carson City Cyclone" 1943 (Linda Wade); "Days of Old Cheyenne" 1943 (Nancy Carlyle); "Dead Man's Gulch" 1943 (Mary Logan); "Death Valley Rangers" 1944 (Carolyn).

Merrick, Marilyn. *see* Merrick, Lynn.

Merrill, Dina (1925-). Films: "Running Wild" 1973. ¶TV: *Rawhide*—"Incident of the Gilded Goddess" 4-30-64 (Lisa Temple); *Daniel Boone*—"The Tamarack Massacre Affair" 12-30-65 (Madeline Lorne); *Bonanza*—"The Pursued" 10-2-66 & 10-9-66 (Susannah); *The Men from Shiloh*—"The Angus Killer" 2-10-71 (Laura Duff).

Merrill, Gary (1914-3/5/90). Films: "The Black Dakotas" 1954 (Brock Marsh); "The Missouri Traveler" 1958 (Doyle Magee); "The Wonderful Country" 1959 (Maj. Stark Colton); "The Dangerous Days of Kiowa Jones" TVM-1966 (Marshal Duncan); "Ride Beyond Vengeance" 1966 (Dub Stokes); "The Last Challenge" 1967 (Squint Calloway). ¶TV:

Zane Grey Theater—"Badge of Honor" 5-3-57 (Col. Boyd Nelson), "The Promise" 11-8-57 (Noah), "Utopia, Wyoming" 6-6-58 (Luke Cannon), "The Release" 4-17-61 (Ken Kenyon); *Wagon Train*—"The Zeke Thomas Story" 11-27-57 (Zeke Thomas); *Cimarron City*—"Medicine Man" 11-8-58 (Joshua Newton); *Rawhide*—"Incident of Fear in the Streets" 5-8-59 (Jed Mason); *Laramie*—"The Lonesome Gun" 12-15-59 (Ed Farrell); *The Outlaws*—"Blind Spot" 3-30-61 (Frank Denton); *Branded*—"Romany Roundup 12-5-65 & 12-12-65 (Aaron Shields); *A Man Called Shenandoah*—"Macauley's Cure" 5-16-66 (Sheriff Ben Sumner); *Hondo*—"Hondo and the Eagle Claw" 9-8-67 (General Sheridan); *Kung Fu*—"The Raiders" 1-24-74 (Dan Hoyle).

Merrill, Louis "Lew". (1912-4/7/63). Films: "Kit Carson" 1940 (Gen. Vallejo); "Northwest Mounted Police" 1940 (Leisure); "Fort Ti" 1953 (Raoul de Moreau).

Merrill, Walter "Tony" (1906-1/10/85. Films: "Sagebrush Politics" 1930; "End of the Trail" 1936; "The Rainmaker" 1956 (Townsman); "Gunfight at the O.K. Corral" 1957 (Barber); "Last Train from Gun Hill" 1959 (Conductor); "Sergents 3" 1962 (Telegrapher).

Merritt, Arnold. Films: "The Unforgiven" 1960 (Jude Rawlins). ¶TV: *Maverick*—"Bolt from the Blue" 11-27-60 (Junior); *Bonanza*—"Bank Run" 1-28-61.

Merrow, Jane (1941-). TV: *Bearcats!*—"Conqueror's Gold" 10-28-71 (Samantha Burke); *Alias Smith and Jones*—"The Reformation of Harry Briscoe" 11-11-71 (Molly/Sister Isabel).

Mersch, Mary. Films: "The Rainbow Trail" 1918 (Jane Withersteen); "Riders of the Purple Sage" 1918 (Jane); "Rimrock Jones" 1918 (Mrs. Hardesty); "Song of the Saddle" 1936 (Frontiersman's Wife); "Empty Saddles" 1937 (Mrs. Mills); "Wells Fargo" 1937 (Pioneer Woman).

Mersereau, Violet. Films: "At Sunset Ranch" 1911; "Alias Yellowstone Joe" 1911; "The Cowpuncher" 1911; "The Sheriff's Mistake" 1911; "The Shot That Failed" 1912; "A Western Girl's Dream" 1912; "Cupid's Round Up" 1918 (Peggy Blair); "The Midnight Flyer" 1918; "A Proxy Husband" 1919; "Out of the Depths" 1921 (Chuckie Knowles).

Merton, Ivy. Films: "Hell Fire Austin" 1932 (Judy Brooks).

Merton, John (Morton Laverre) (1901-9/18/59). Films: "The Red Rider" 1934-serial (Banty); "Hopalong Cassidy" 1935 (Party Guest); "Aces and Eights" 1936 (Gambler); "Bar 20 Rides Again" 1936 (Carp); "Bold Caballero" 1936 (Sergeant); "Border Caballero" 1936 (Runnyian); "Call of the Prairie" 1936 (Arizona); "The Crooked Trail" 1936 (Harve Tarlton); "The Eagle's Brood" 1936 (Ed); "Lightning Bill Carson" 1936 (Breed Hawkins); "The Lion's Den" 1936 (Single-Shot Smith); "The Three Mesquiteers" 1936 (Bull); "Vigilantes Are Coming" 1936-serial (Rance Talbot); "Wildcat Trooper" 1936 (Henry McClain); "Arizona Gunfighter" 1937 (Farley); "Blazing Sixes" 1937 (Jim Hess); "Drums of Destiny" 1937 (Fiske's Henchman); "Fighting Texan" 1937; "Galloping Dynamite" 1937 (Reed); "The Gun Ranger" 1937 (Kemper Mills); "Gunsmoke Ranch" 1937; "The Law Commands" 1937 (Clark); "Law of the Ranger" 1937 (Nash); "Range Defenders" 1937 (Crag); "The Rangers Step In" 1937 (Martin); "Roaring Six Guns" 1937 (Mileaway); "A Tenderfoot Goes West" 1937 (Butch); "Valley of Terror" 1937 (Mark Flemming); "Wild Horse Round-Up" 1937 (Charlie Doan); "Colorado Kid" 1938 (Court Clerk); "Gunsmoke Trail" 1938 (Bill Larsen); "Knight of the Plains" 1938 (Dan Carson/Pedro de Cordova); "Land of Fighting Men" 1938 (Flint); "The Lone Ranger" 1938-serial (Kester); "Phantom Ranger" 1938 (Bud); "Riders of the Black Hills" 1938 (Man in Theater); "Songs and Saddles" 1938 (Rocky); "Where the Buffalo Roam" 1938; "Code of the Fearless" 1939 (Red Kane); "In Old Montana" 1939 (Ed Brandt); "Flaming Lead" 1939; "Renegade Trail" 1939 (Traynor); "Rough Riders' Round-Up" 1939 (Patrolman); "Three Texas Steers" 1939 (Mike Abbott); "Two-Gun Troubador" 1939 (Bill Barton); "Union Pacific" 1939 (Laborer); "Union Pacific" 1939 (Laborer); "Zorro's Fighting Legion" 1939-serial (Manuel); "Billy the Kid in Texas" 1940 (Flash); "Billy the Kid Outlawed" 1940 (Lije Ellis); "Covered Wagon Days" 1940 (Gregg); "The Dark Command" 1940 (Cantrell Man); "Frontier Crusader" 1940 (Hippo Potts); "Lone Star Raiders" 1940 (Dixon); "Melody Ranch" 1940 (Wildhack's Cohort); "Northwest Passage" 1940 (Lt. Dunbar); "Pals of the Silver Sage" 1940; "Queen of the Yukon" 1940 (Charlie); "Rainbow Over the Range" 1940; "The Return of Wild Bill" 1940 (Dusty Donahue); "The Trail Blazers" 1940 (Mason); "The Bandit Trail" 1941; "Gauchos of El Dorado" 1941; "The Gunman from Bodie" 1941; "A Missouri Outlaw" 1941 (Bancroft); "Two-Gun Sheriff" 1941; "Under Fiesta Stars" 1941; "White Eagle" 1941-serial (Ronimo); "Along the Sundown Trail" 1942; "Arizona Terrors" 1942; "Billy the Kid's Smoking Guns" 1942; "Boot Hill Bandits" 1942 (Brand Bolton); "Law and Order" 1942 (Turtle); "The Lone Prairie" 1942; "The Mysterious Rider" 1942; "Prairie Pals" 1942 (Ed Blair); "Sheriff of Sage Valley" 1942 (Nick); "A Tornado in the Saddle" 1942; "Black Market Rustlers" 1943 (Parry); "Bullets and Saddles" 1943; "Cowboy Commandos" 1943 (Fraser); "Fighting Valley" 1943 (Dan Wakely); "The Kid Rides Again" 1943; "Land of Hunted Men" 1943; "The Law Rides Again" 1943; "Phony Express" 1943-short (Joe); "Sagebrush Law" 1943; "Devil Riders" 1944 (Jim Higgins); "Fuzzy Settles Down" 1944; "Gentle Annie" 1944 (Engineer); "Ghost Guns" 1944; "Girl Rush" 1944 (Scully); "Land of the Outlaws" 1944; "Mystery Man" 1944 (Bill); "Rustlers' Hideout" 1944 (Harry Stanton); Texas Masquerade" 1944 (Jeff); "Valley of Vengeance" 1944 (Kurt); "West of the Rio Grande" 1944; "Zorro's Black Whip" 1944-serial (Ed Harris); "Bandits of the Badlands" 1945; "Along Came Jones" 1945 (Card Player); "The Cherokee Flash" 1945; "Oregon Trail" 1945; "Stranger from Santa Fe" 1945; "Border Bandits" 1946 (Spike); "The Desert Horseman" 1946 (Rex Young); "Ghost of Hidden Valley" 1946 (Henry); "Galloping Thunder" 1946; "The Gay Cavalier" 1946; "The Haunted Mine" 1946; "Heading West" 1946; "Shadows on the Range" 1946; "Cheyenne Takes Over" 1947 (McCord); "Raiders of the South" 1947; "Unconquered" 1947 (Corporal); "Trail to Laredo" 1948; "The Blazing Trail" 1949; "Haunted Trails" 1949 (Sheriff Charley Coons); "Outlaw Country" 1949 (Marshal Clark); "Riders of the Dusk" 1949 (Art); "Western Renegades" 1949 (Blacksmith); "Bandit Queen" 1950 (Hank); "Arizona Territory" 1950 (Kilborn); "Border Rangers" 1950 (Gans); "Fence Riders" 1950; "I Shot Billy the Kid" 1950 (Ollinger); "West of Wyoming" 1950 (Sheriff); "Gold Raiders" 1951 (Clete); "Man from Sonora" 1951; "Silver Canyon" 1951; "Blue Canadian Rockies" 1952 (Frenchie); "The Old West" 1952; "Trail Guide" 1952 (Dale); "Frontier

Gambler" 1956. ¶TV: *The Lone Ranger*—"War Horse" 10-20-49, "Banker's Choice" 11-23-50; *The Cisco Kid*—"Foreign Agent" 8-18-51, "Bates Story" 9-29-51, "Chinese Gold" 10-18-52; *Wild Bill Hickok*—"Civilian Clothes Story" 12-18-51, "The Boy and the Bandit" 3-25-52, "Heading for Trouble" 6-10-52, "Blake's Kid" 12-23-52; *The Roy Rogers Show*—"The Last of the Larrabee Kid" 10-17-54 (Hank Rogers), "Boys' Day in Paradise Valley" 11-7-54.

Mervyn, William (1912-8/6/76). Films: "Charley One-Eye" 1973-Brit. (Honeydew).

Messenger, Buddy (1907-10/25/65). Films: "Six-Shooter Andy" 1918; "The Lone Ranger Rides Again" 1939-serial (Rance).

Messinger, Gertrude. Films: "Hidden Valley" 1932 (Joyce Lanners); "Lawless Valley" 1932 (Rosita); "Riders of the Desert" 1932 (Barbara Reynolds); "Melody Trail" 1935 (Cuddles); "The Rider of the Law" 1935; "Rustlers' Paradise" 1935 (Connie Kincaid); "Wagon Trail" 1935 (Joan Collins); "Blazing Justice" 1936 (Virginia Peterson); "Aces Wild" 1937 (Martha Woods); "Feud of the Range" 1939 (Madge Allen).

Metcalfe, Jr., Bradley. Films: "Westward Ho" 1935 (Young John Wyatt); "King of the Pecos" 1936 (Little John).

Metcalfe, Burt. Films: "The Canadians" 1961-Brit. (Constable Springer). ¶TV: *Death Valley Days*—"Indian Emily" 12-8-59 (Tom); *Fury*—"The Skin Divers" 2-27-60 (Dick Thompson).

Metcalfe, Earl (1889-1/26/28). Films: "The Mexican Spy" 1913; "Back to Yellow Jacket" 1922 (Flush Kirby, the Gambler); "While Justice Waits" 1922 (George Carter); "White Eagle" 1922-serial; "The Lone Wagon" 1923; "Kit Carson Over the Great Divide" 1925 (Basil Morgan); "Buffalo Bill on the U.P. Trail" 1926 (Sheriff); "Call of the Klondike" 1926 (Petrov); "Outlaw Love" 1926; "The Devil's Saddle" 1927 (Gentle Ladley).

Metrano, Art (1935-). TV: *The Outcasts*—"The Candidates" 1-27-69 (Sheriff Calloway); *Bonanza*—"Caution: Easter Bunny Crossing" 3-29-70 (LeRoy); *Centennial*—Regular 1978-79 (Muerice).

Metzetti, Otto (1891-1/31/49). Films: "The Lone Defender" 1930-serial (Butch).

Metzetti, Victor (1895-8/21/49). Films: "Bulldog Pluck" 1927 (Curley

Le Baste); "The Lone Defender" 1930-serial (Red).

Metzler, Jim. Films: "The Alamo: 13 Days to Glory" TVM-1987 (Major Bonham); "Old Gringo" 1989 (Ron).

Meyer, Emile (1910-3/19/87). Films: "Cattle Queen" 1951 (Shotgun Thompson); "The Wild North" 1952 (Jake); "Shane" 1953 (Ryker); "Drums Across the River" 1954 (Marlowe); "Silver Lode" 1954 (Sheriff Wooley); "Man with the Gun" 1955 (Saul Atkins); "Stranger on Horseback" 1955 (Sheriff Nat Bell); "The Tall Men" 1955 (Chickasaw); "White Feather" 1955 (Magruder); "The Maverick Queen" 1956 (Malone); "Raw Edge" 1956 (Pop Penny); "Badlands of Montana" 1957 (Hammer); "Gun the Man Down" 1957 (Sheriff Morton); "The Fiend Who Walked the West" 1958 (Ames); "Good Day for a Hanging" 1958 (Marshal Hiram Cain); "King of the Wild Stallions" 1959 (Matt); "Young Jesse James" 1960 (William Quantrill); "Taggart" 1964 (Ben Blazer); "Hostile Guns" 1967 (Uncle Joe); "A Time for Killing" 1967 (Col. Harries); "Buckskin" 1968. ¶TV: *Death Valley Days*—"Death Valley Scott" 5-9-55 (Marcus Delafield); *The Gene Autry Show*—"Ride, Rancheros" 12-10-55 (Big Jim Weston), "The Rangerette" 12-17-55 (Big Jim Weston); *Zane Grey Theater*—"Back Trail" 2-1-57 (Eldredge); *The Restless Gun*—"Man and Boy" 11-25-57 (Sheriff Lawson), "Friend in Need" 1-13-58 (Sheriff Vail); *Broken Arrow*—"Water Witch" 1-7-58 (Bert Kellems); *Maverick*—"Rope of Cards" 1-19-58 (Pike), "Holiday at Hollow Rock" 12-28-58 (Colonel Arnold Taylor); *Colt .45*—"Point of Honor" 3-21-58 (Tom Shannon); *Northwest Passage*—"The Bound Women" 10-12-58 (Ben Klagg); *Bat Masterson*—"Battle of the Pass" 2-25-59 (General Moran), "Garrison Finish" 12-10-59 (General Moran); *Tales of Wells Fargo*—"The Legacy" 3-9-59 (Bob Gannon); *Wichita Town*—"The Avengers" 2-3-60 (Pa); *Lawman*—"Belding's Girl" 4-3-60 (Ben Belding); *Laramie*—"The Debt" 4-18-61 (Pierson); *The Tall Man*—"Legend of Billy" 12-9-61 (Jared Cobb); *The Outlaws*—"The Outlaw Marshals" 12-14-61 (Root); *Rawhide*—"Incident of the Portrait" 10-5-62 (Raymond Curtis); *The Legend of Jesse James*—"A Real Tough Town" 1-24-66 (Cap Walters); *Bonanza*—"Decision at Los Robles" 3-22-70 (John Walker), "Frenzy" 1-30-72 (Cherokee).

Meyerink, Victoria Paige (1960-). Films: "The Night of the Grizzly" 1966 (Gypsy Cole).

Meyler, Fintan. Films: "Showdown at Boot Hill" 1958 (Sally). ¶TV: *Gunsmoke*—"No Indians" 12-8-56 (Arie O'Dell), "Miguel's Daughter" 11-28-59 (Chavela Ramirez), "Gentleman's Disagreement" 4-30-60 (Jeanne Wells); *Have Gun Will Travel*—"The Girl from Piccadilly" 2-22-58 (the Girl), "An International Affair" 4-2-60 (Pegeen), "Don't Shoot the Piano Player" 3-10-62 (Emily Eubanks); *Zorro*—"Finders Keepers" 7-2-59 (Senorita Celesta Villagrana); *The Texan*—"Badlands" 5-11-59; *Wagon Train*—"The Andrew Hale Story" 6-3-59 (Marilee Hamplar), "The St. Nicholas Story" 12-23-59; *The Rebel*—"School Days" 11-15-59 (Peggy O'Shea); *Hotel De Paree*—"Sundance and the Man in Room Seven" 2-12-60 (Julia); *Bonanza*—"Desert Justice" 2-20-60 (Andrea).

Micale, Paul. TV: *Bonanza*—"To Bloom for Thee" 10-16-66 (Barber); *Laredo*—"A Prince of a Ranger" 12-9-66; *Gunsmoke*—"Roots of Fear" 12-15-69 (Assistant Teller); *Alias Smith and Jones*—"The Great Shell Game" 2-18-71, "The McCreedy Bust — Going, Going Gone" 1-13-72 (Little Man).

Michael, Gertrude (1911-12/31/64). Films: "Bugles in the Afternoon" 1952 (May).

Michael, Peter. Films: "Overland Mail Robbery" 1943 (Jimmy Hartley); "Yankee Fakir" 1947 (Walker).

Michael, Ralph (1907-11/9/94). Films: "No Man's Land" TVM-1984 (Doc Haviland).

Michaels, Dolores. Films: "The Fiend Who Walked the West" 1958; "Warlock" 1959 (Jessie Marlow); "One Foot in Hell" 1960 (Julie Reynolds). ¶TV: *Laramie*—"Among the Missing" 9-25-62 (Nona).

Michaels, Shawn. TV: *Have Gun Will Travel*—"Hobson's Choice" 4-7-62 (Husband); *Wild Wild West*—"The Night of the Bars of Hell" 3-4-66 (Convict Painter).

Michaelsen, Melissa. Films: "Orphan Train" TVM-1979 (J.P.); "No Man's Land" TVM-1984 (Missy Wilder).

Michelena, Beatriz (1890-10/10/42). Films: "Salomy Jane" 1914 (Salomy Jane); "The Lily of Poverty Flat" 1915 (Lily Folinsbee); "The Heart of Juanita" 1919 (Juanita); "Just Squaw" 1919 (Fawn); "The Flame of Hellgate" 1920 (Star Dowell).

Michelle, Donna (1943-). TV: *The Big Valley*—"Barbary Red" 2-16-66 (Dolly).

Michenaud, Gerald (1956-). Films: "A Big Hand for the Little Lady" 1966 (Jackie); "Buckskin" 1968 (Akii). ¶TV: *The Outcasts*—"The Man from Bennington" 12-16-68 (Benjuie).

Michon, Pat. TV: *The Range Rider*—"Baron of Broken Bow" 2-21-53; *The Californians*—"The Long Night" 12-23-58 (Gertrude); *26 Men*—"Profane Masquerade" 3-10-59; *Riverboat*—"Forbidden Island" 1-24-60 (Caroline Duprez), "No Bridge on the River" 10-24-60 (Marie Maret); *Bonanza*—"The Fear Merchants" 1-30-60 (Sally Ridley), "The Secret" 5-6-61 (Betty May); *Rawhide*—"Incident of the One Hundred Amulets" 5-6-60 (Polly); *Wrangler*—"Incident of the Wide Lop" 9-1-60 (Florrie Barton); *Tales of Wells Fargo*—"Captain Scoville" 1-9-61 (Susan Kellogg), "Tanoa" 10-28-61 (Tanoa); *The Tall Man*—"Maria's Little Lamb" 2-25-61 (Maria); *Laramie*—"Killer's Odds" 4-25-61 (Sue Fenton).

Middlemass, Robert (1885-9/10/49). Films: "The Bad Man of Brimstone" 1937 (Schurz); "Guns of the Pecos" 1937 (Judge Blake); "Trapped" 1937 (Sol Rothert); "The Arizona Kid" 1939 (General Stark); "Stand Up and Fight" 1939 (Harkrider).

Middleton, Charles B. (1879-4/22/49). Films: "Beau Bandit" 1930 (Perkins); "Way Out West" 1930 (Buck); "Mystery Ranch" 1932 (Henry Steele); "Sunset Pass" 1933 (Williams); "The Last Round-Up" 1934 (Sheriff); "The Lone Cowboy" 1934 (Marshal); "Massacre" 1934; "Hopalong Cassidy" 1935 (Buck Peters); "The Miracle Rider" 1935-serial (Zaroff); "Square Shooter" 1935 (Jed Miller); "Ramona" 1936 (American Settler); "Rose of the Rancho" 1936 (Horse Doctor); "Song of the Saddle" 1936 (Phineas P. Hook); "Sunset of Power" 1936 (Neil Brannum); "Empty Saddles" 1937 (Cim White); "Hollywood Cowboy" 1937 (Doc Kramer); "Two Gun Law" 1937 (Wolf Larson); "Yodelin' Kid from Pine Ridge" 1937 (Arthur Autry); "Flaming Frontier" 1938-serial (Ace Dagett); "Allegheny Uprising" 1939 (Doctor); "Cowboys from Texas" 1939 (Kansas Jones); "Jesse James" 1939 (Doctor); "The Oklahoma Kid" 1939 (Alec Martin); "Wyoming Outlaw" 1939 (Luke Parker); "Brigham Young—Frontiersman" 1940 (Henchman); "Rangers of Fortune" 1940;

"Santa Fe Trail" 1940 (Gentry); "Shooting High" 1940 (Hod Carson); "Virginia City" 1940 (Jefferson Davis); "Belle Starr" 1941 (Carpetbagger); "The Shepherd of the Hills" 1941 (Blacksmith); "Western Union" 1941 (Stagecoach Rider); "Wild Bill Hickok Rides" 1942; "Oklahoma Outlaws" 1943-short; "Wagon Wheels West" 1943-short; "Black Arrow" 1944-serial (Tom Whitney); "Northwest Trail" 1945; "The Sea of Grass" 1947 (Charley); "Unconquered" 1947 (Mulligan); "Wyoming" 1947 (Doctor); "Station West" 1948 (Sheriff); "The Last Bandit" 1949 (Circuit Rider).

Middleton, Ray (1907-4/10/84). Films: "Girl from Alaska" 1942 (Steve Bentley); "Hurricane Smith" 1942 (Hurricane Smith); "Jubilee Trail" 1954 (Charles Hale); "The Road to Denver" 1955 (John Sutton); "Hec Ramsey" TVM-1972 (Judge Leroy Tate).

Middleton, Robert (1911-6/14/77). Films: "Friendly Persuasion" 1956 (Sam Jordan); "Love Me Tender" 1956 (Siringo); "The Proud Ones" 1956 (Honest John Barrett); "Red Sundown" 1956 (Rufus Henshaw); "The Lonely Man" 1957 (Ben Ryerson); "Day of the Bad Man" 1958 (Charlie Hayes); "The Law and Jake Wade" 1958 (Ortero); "Hell Bent for Leather" 1960 (Ambrose); "Gold of the Seven Saints" 1961 (Gondora); "Cattle King" 1963 (Clay Mathews); "A Big Hand for the Little Lady" 1966 (Dennis Wilcox); "The Cheyenne Social Club" 1970 (Great Plains Saloon Barkeep); "The Mark of Zorro" TVM-1974 (Don Luis Quintero). ¶TV: *Gunsmoke*—"Word of Honor" 10-1-55 (Jake Worth), "Dutch George" 6-30-56 (Dutch George), "The Hunger" 11-17-62 (Claude Dorf); *Bat Masterson*—"Double Showdown" 10-8-58 (Big Keel Roberts); *Texas John Slaughter*—"Texas John Slaughter" 10-31-58 (Frank Davis), "Ambush in Laredo" 11-14-58 (Frank Davis); *Wichita Town*—"Bought" 1-13-60 (Sam Buhl); *Wagon Train*—"The Tom Tuckett Story" 3-2-60 (Nat Burkett); *Tales of Wells Fargo*—"Threat of Death" 4-25-60 (Kreegar), "Leading Citizen" 11-14-60 (Bodie Seaton), "The Diamond Dude" 2-27-61 (Bodie Seaton), "Man of Another Breed" 12-2-61 (Caleb Timmons); *Bonanza*—"Death at Dawn" 4-30-60 (Sam Bryant), "King of the Mountain" 2-23-64 (Grizzly), "The Greedy Ones" 5-14-67 (Shasta); *Wrangler*—"A Time for Hanging" 8-11-60 (Josiah Cunningham); *The Tall Man*—"Garrett and the Kid" 9-10-60 (Paul Masson); *The Rebel*—"The Road to Jericho" 2-19-61 (Sutro); *Zane Grey Theater*—"Storm Over Eden" 5-4-61 (Whitney Gaynor); *Rawhide*—"Incident of the Mountain Man" 1-25-63 (Josh Green), "Incident of the Travellin' Man" 10-17-63 (Matt Harger), "Incident at Dead Horse" 4-16-64 & 4-23-64 (Judge Hogan), "Brush War at Buford" 11-23-65 (Duke Aberdeen); *Wild Wild West*—"The Night of the Grand Emir" 1-28-66 (Emir El Emid); *Daniel Boone*—"The Gun" 2-3-66 (Simon Brasher); *The Monroes*—"Incident at Hanging Tree" 10-12-66 (Barney Wales), "Silent Night, Deathly Night" 11-23-66 (Barney Wales), "Range War" 12-21-66 (Barney Wales), "Mark of Death" 1-4-67 (Barney Wales); *The Big Valley*—"Down Shadow Street" 1-23-67 (Judge Tyrone), "Rimfire" 2-19-68 (Sidney Glover); *Alias Smith and Jones*—"The Bounty Hunter" 12-9-71, "Don't Get Mad, Get Even" 2-17-72 (Wheelwright); *Kung Fu*—"The Passion of Chen Yi" 2-28-74 (Marshal Ford).

Middleton, Tom. Films: "Bridger" TVM-1976 (Doctor). ¶TV: *Maverick*—"Trooper Maverick" 11-29-59 (O'Dell); *Young Maverick*—"Clancy" 11-28-79.

Midgley, Fanny (1877-1/4/32). Films: "Shorty Escapes Marriage" 1914 (Mrs. Simms); "The Bad Buck of Santa Ynez" 1915; "The Man from Oregon" 1915 (Mother Martin); "Jim Grimsby's Boy" 1916 (Mrs. Grimsby); "The Apostle of Vengeance" 1916 (Marm Hudson); "The Vigilantes" 1918; "Blue Blazes" 1922 (Mrs. Lee); "Ace of Action" 1926; "The Dangerous Dub" 1926 (Mrs. Cooper); "Hair Trigger Baxter" 1926 (Mrs. Craddock); "The Cowboy Cavalier" 1928.

Midgley, Florence (1890-11/16/49). Films: "The Fighting Cheat" 1926 (Mrs. Wells); "Burning Brides" 1928 (Widow Wilkins); "The Flying Buckaroo" 1928 (Mrs. Matthews); "The Three Outcasts" 1929 (Mrs. Slavin).

Mifune, Toshiro (1920-). Films: "Red Sun" 1971-Fr./Ital./Span. (Kuroda, Samurai Bodyguard); "Shadow of the Wolf" 1993-Can./Fr. (Kroomak).

Mikler, Michael T. Films: "Gunfight at Comanche Creek" 1964; "War Party" 1965 (Johnny Hawk); "Pat Garrett and Billy the Kid" 1973 (Denver); "Westworld" 1973 (Black Knight). ¶TV: *Zane Grey Theater*—"Man in the Middle" 2-11-60 (Luke), "Knife of Hate" 12-8-60

(Lacey); *The Rebel*—"A Grave for Johnny Yuma" 5-1-60 (Zack); *The Westerner*—"Brown" 10-21-60, "Dos Pinos" 11-4-60, "The Old Man" 11-25-60, "Going Home" 12-16-60; *The Virginian*—"It Tolls for Thee" 11-21-62; *Gunsmoke*—"The Badge" 11-12-60, "False Front" 12-22-62 (Bill), "The Bad One" 1-26-63 (Cowpoke), "Ash" 2-16-63 (Frank); *Empire*—"Where the Hawk Is Wheeling" 1-29-63 (Ben); *Laramie*—"The Marshals" 4-30-63; *Stoney Burke*—"Tigress by the Tail" 5-6-63 (Cy Lewton); *Bonanza*—"Twilight Town" 10-13-63 (Mathews), "The Desperado" 2-7-71 (Thad); *Death Valley Days*—"Hero of Fort Halleck" 6-27-65 (Hank Keith); *Iron Horse*—"Explosion at Waycrossing" 11-21-66 (the Stranger); *Cimarron Strip*—"Whitey" 10-19-67 (Beau Tinker); *Alias Smith and Jones*—"The Strange Fate of Conrad Meyer Zulick" 12-2-72.

Milan, Frank (1906-4/8/77). Films: "Hollywood Cowboy" 1937 (Westbrook Courtney); "Roll Along, Cowboy" 1937 (Arthur J. Hathaway); "Pals of the Saddle" 1938 (Frank Paige); "Rangers of Fortune" 1940 (Sam Todd).

Milan, Lita. Films: "The Violent Men" 1955 (Elena); "Gun Brothers" 1956 (Meeteetse); "Naked in the Sun" 1957; "The Ride Back" 1957 (Elena); "The Left-Handed Gun" 1958 (Celsa). ¶TV: *Jim Bowie*—"The Captain's Chimp" 3-8-57 (Paola); *Have Gun Will Travel*—"The Silver Queen" 5-3-58 (Annette); *Jefferson Drum*—"Bandidos" 6-13-58 (Chuli Ornitiz).

Milar, Adolph (1886-5/25/50). Films: "The Girl from Porcupine" 1922 (Red McTavish); "Sudden Bill Dorn" 1937 (Tony).

Milasch, Robert (1885-11/14/54). Films: "Grinning Guns" 1927 (Buckaroo Bob); "Men of Daring" 1927 (King); "The Upland Rider" 1928 (Slim); "Texas Bad Man" 1932 (Cheerful Charlie); "Santa Fe Stampede" 1938.

Miles, Art (1901-11/6/55). Films: "Silent Valley" 1935 (George Hull); "Fighting Texan" 1937 (Carter); "The Roaming Cowboy" 1937 (Red); "Honky Tonk" 1941 (Dealer); "Riders of Death Valley" 1941-serial (Evergreen); "The Return of Daniel Boone" 1941; "Perils of the Royal Mounted" 1942-serial (Flying Cloud); "Sin Town" 1942 (Man); "The Spoilers" 1942 (Deputy); "Gentle Annie" 1944 (Conductor); "Dakota" 1945 (Ciano); "Colt .45" 1950.

Miles, Betty. Films: "The

Driftin' Kid" 1941; "Lone Star Law Men" 1941 (Betty); "The Return of Daniel Boone" 1941 (Ellen Brandon); "Ridin' the Cherokee Trail" 1941 (Ruth); "Riding the Sunset Trail" 1941 (Betty Dawson); "Wanderers of the West" 1941 (Laura Lee); "Law of the Saddle" 1943 (Gayle); "The Law Rides Again" 1943 (Betty); "Wild Horse Stampede" 1943 (Betty Wallace); "Gangsters of the Frontier" 1944; "Sonora Stagecoach" 1944 (Betty); "Westward Bound" 1944 (Enid Barrett).

Miles, Joanna (1940-). TV: *Barbary Coast*—"Crazy Cats" 9-15-75 (Renata).

Miles, John. Films: "San Antonio" 1945 (Cowboy); "The Fabulous Texan" 1947 (Sim Clayton); "The Gunfighters" 1947 (Johnny O'Neil).

Miles, General Nelson (1839-5/15/25). Films: "The Adventures of Buffalo Bill" 1914.

Miles, Peter. Films: "Heaven Only Knows" 1947 (Speck O'Donnell); "California Passage" 1950 (Tommy Martin); "Trigger, Jr." 1950 (Larry). ¶TV: *Maverick*—"Yellow River" 2-8-59 (Jean Baxter); *Colt .45*—"The Escape" 4-5-59.

Miles, Robert J. Films: "Riders of the Plains" 1924-serial; "The Water Hole" 1928 (Joe); "The Last Round-Up" 1934 (Scarface); "Pony Express" 1953.

Miles, Jr., Robert. Films: "Young Fury" 1965. ¶TV: *Bonanza*—"Badge Without Honor" 9-24-60 (Bill Clevenger), "Cut-Throat Junction" 3-18-61, "The Gift" 4-1-61, "The Law Maker" 3-11-62, "The Quality of Mercy" 11-17-63 (Card Player), "No Less a Man" 3-15-64; *Gunsmoke*—"Mail Drop" 1-28-67 (Chuck).

Miles, Sherry (1951-). TV: *The High Chaparral*—"Too Many Chiefs" 3-27-70 (Margaret Louise).

Miles, Sylvia (1932-). Films: "The Man Who Loved Cat Dancing" 1973 (Catherine Crocker); "The Great Scout and Cathouse Thursday" 1976 (Mike).

Miles, Vera (1929-). Films: "The Charge at Feather River" 1953 (Jennie McKeever); "Wichita" 1955 (Laurie); "The Searchers" 1956 (Laurie Jorgensen); "The Man Who Shot Liberty Valance" 1962 (Hallie Stoddard); "The Wild Country" 1971 (Kate Tanner); "Molly and Lawless John" 1972 (Molly Parker); "One Little Indian" 1973 (Doris); "The Castaway Cowboy" 1974 (Henrietta MacAvoy). ¶TV: *Wagon Train*—"The

Sister Rita Story" 3-25-59 (Sister Rita), "The Bob Stuart Story" 9-30-64 (Janice Stuart), "The Silver Lady" 4-25-65 (Anne Read); *Riverboat*—"About Roger Mowbray" 9-27-59 (Jeanette Mowbray); *Rawhide*—"Incident at the Buffalo Smokehouse" 10-30-59 (Helen Walsh); *Zane Grey Theater*—"Miss Jenny" 1-7-60 (Jenny Breckenridge); *Laramie*—"Three Roads West" 10-4-60 (Anne Andrews); *Frontier Circus*—"Lippizan" 10-19-61 (Maureen McBride); *The Virginian*—"The Man Who Couldn't Die" 1-30-63 (Mrs. Wallace), "Portrait of a Widow" 12-9-64 (Maggie Benken); *Bonanza*—"Four Sisters from Boston" 10-30-66 (Ara Lowell), "A Time to Die" 3-21-71 (April Christopher); *Gunsmoke*—"Sam Mc-Tavish, M.D." 10-5-70 (Dr. Sam Mc-Tavish); *The Men from Shiloh*—"Experiment at New Life" 11-18-70 (Amelia); *Alias Smith and Jones*—"The Posse That Wouldn't Quit" 10-14-71 (Belle Jordon); *How the West Was Won*—Episode Three 2-26-78 (Beth), Episode Four 3-5-78 (Beth), Episode Five 3-12-78 (Beth).

Milford, John (1929-). Films: "The Persuader" 1957 (Clint); "Face of a Fugitive" 1959 (Haley); "Gunfight at Comanche Creek" 1964; "The Last Challenge" 1967 (Turpin). ¶TV: *The Texan*—"Jail for the Innocents" 11-3-58 (Max), "Traildust" 10-19-59; *The Restless Gun*—"Shadow of a Gunfighter" 1-12-59 (Pete Lawson), "The Englishman" 6-8-59 (Shotgun); *Wyatt Earp*—"Death for a Stolen Horse" 1-13-59 (Pete Hendell), Regular 1959-61 (Ike Clanton); *Wanted—Dead or Alive*—"Call Your Shot" 2-7-59; *Buckskin*—"Charlie, My Boy" 4-6-59 (Tink Fallon); *Tales of Wells Fargo*—"The Daltons" 5-25-59 (Cowley), "Frightened Witness" 12-26-60 (Walt Corbin); *The Rifleman*—"The Blowout" 10-13-59, "The Coward" 12-22-59, "The Horse Traders" 2-9-60 (Jonah Winters), "A Time for Singing" 3-8-60 (Bro Hadley), "Meeting at Midnight" 5-17-60 (Morgan), "The Pitchman" 10-18-60, "Baranca" 11-1-60 (Hadley), "Dark Day at North Fork" 3-7-61 (Jack Solby), "The Clarence Bibbs Story" 4-4-61 (Reade), "The Journey Back" 10-30-61 (Jess), "The Assailants" 11-12-62 (Lieutenant Price); *Fury*—"Trail Drive" 10-24-59; *Zane Grey Theater*—"The Grubstake" 12-24-59 (Bart Nelin); *The Law of the Plainsman*—"The Rawhiders" 1-28-60 (Lije Wesley); *Wichita Town*—"The Avengers" 2-3-60 (Hazen); *Have Gun Will Travel*—"The Shooting of Jesse May" 10-20-60 (Abe Sinclair), "Long Way

Home" 2-4-61 (Hutton); *Two Faces West*—"The Operation" 11-14-60 (Will); *Sugarfoot*—"Man from Medora" 11-21-60 (Jed Carter); *Gunsmoke*—"The Cook" 12-17-60 (Joe Grisim), "Winner Take All" 2-20-65 (Pinto Renner), "Cattle Barons" 9-18-67 (Blair Smith), "The Badge" 2-2-70 (John Dawson), "Snow Train" 10-19-70 & 10-26-70 (Clay Foreman), "The Iron Blood of Courage" 2-18-74 (Hutchinson); *Riverboat*—"Zigzag" 12-26-60 (Egan); *The Outlaws*—"Culley" 2-16-61 (Leo Kirk); *Stagecoach West*—"The Orphans" 5-30-61 (Hogan); *Cheyenne*—"Man Alone" 10-15-62 (Johnny Dugan); *Laramie*—"Vengeance" 1-8-63 (Joe Morgan); *Bonanza*—"Half a Rogue" 1-27-63 (Jelke), "A World Full of Cannibals" 12-22-68 (Rodgers); *The Virginian*—"If You Have Tears" 2-13-63 (Perry Allen), "Shadows of the Past" 2-24-65 (Will Gar), "A Bad Place to Die" 11-8-67 (Kiley); *Stoney Burke*—"Webb of Fear" 2-18-63 (Pete Simmons); *Empire*—"Burnout" 3-19-63 (Tom Barton); *Destry*—"Red Brady's Kid" 4-24-64 (Butch Jenkins); *The Big Valley*—"Forty Rifles" 9-22-65 (Barrett), "Lost Treasure" 9-12-66 (Atteridge), "The Disappearance" 11-6-67 (Hearn), "Run of the Cat" 10-21-68 (Giles); *A Man Called Shenandoah*—"The Young Outlaw" 12-27-65 (Pendleton); *Iron Horse*—"The Man from New Chicago" 11-14-66 (Johnny Spanish); *Cimarron Strip*—"The Battleground" 9-28-67, "Sound of a Drum" 2-1-68; *The High Chaparral*—"A Quiet Day in Tucson" 10-1-67 (Hardicker); *Lancer*—"The Lawman" 10-22-68 (Thompkins); *The Guns of Will Sonnett*—"One Angry Juror" 3-7-69 (Ben Stoll); *Daniel Boone*—"The Road to Freedom" 10-2-69 (Jud Baker).

Milford, Mary Beth. Films: "The Bashful Whirlwind" 1925; "The Bloodhound" 1925 (Marie Rambo); "Galloping Vengeance" 1925 (Marion Reeves); "That Man Jack!" 1925 (Anita Leland).

Milian, Tomas (1936-). Films: "The Big Gundown" 1966-Ital. (Cuchilo); "The Ugly Ones" 1966-Ital./Span. (Jose Gomez); "Death Sentence" 1967-Ital.; "Django Kill" 1967-Ital./Span. (Django); "Face to Face" 1967-Ital. (Beauregard Bennet; "Run Man, Run" 1967-Ital./Fr. (Cuchillo); "Blood and Guns" 1968-Ital./Span; "The Magnificent Bandits" 1969-Ital./Span. (Miguein); "Companeros" 1970-Ital./Span./Ger. (Vasco); "Sometimes Life Is Hard, Right Providence?" 1972-Ital./Fr./Ger. (Providence); "Bandera Bandits"

1973-Ital./Span./Ger. (Jed); "Here We Go Again, Eh Providence?" 1973-Ital./Fr./Span. (Providence); "The White, the Yellow, and the Black" 1974-Ital./Span./Fr. (Yellow); "Four Horsemen of the Apocalpyse" 1975-Ital. (Chaco).

Miljan, John (1893-1/24/60). Films: "Romance Ranch" 1924 (Clifton Venable); "Silent Sanderson" 1925 (Jim Downing); "Land of the Silver Fox" 1928 (James Crawford); "Under the Pampas Moon" 1935 (Graham Scott); "Arizona Mahoney" 1936 (Cameron Lloyd); "North of Nome" 1936 (Ralph Dawson); "The Plainsman" 1936 (Gen. George Armstrong Custer); "Sutter's Gold" 1936 (Gen. Juan Batista Alvarado); "Border G-Man" 1938 (Louis Rankin); "The Oklahoma Kid" 1939 (Ringo); "Texas Rangers Ride Again" 1940 (Carter Dangerfield); "Young Bill Hickok" 1940 (Nicholas Tower); "The Cowboy and the Blonde" 1941 (Bob Roycroft); "North of the Rockies" 1942; "Wildfire" 1945 (Pete Fanning); "Unconquered" 1947 (Prosecutor); "Mrs. Mike" 1949 (Mr. Howard); "Stampede" 1949 (Furman); "Mule Train" 1950 (Judd Holbrook); "The Savage" 1952 (White Thunder); "Run for Cover" 1955 (Mayor Walsh); "The Wild Dakotas" 1956; "Apache Warrior" 1957 (Nantan); "The Lone Ranger and the Lost City of Gold" 1958 (Tomache). ¶TV: *Frontier*—"The Captivity of Joe Long" 2-12-56 (Chief); *Jim Bowie*—"Master at Arms" 1-25-57 (Jean Dubois).

Millais, Hugh (1929-). Films: "McCabe and Mrs. Miller" 1971 (Dog Butler).

Millan, Lynne. TV: *Wyatt Earp*—"The Equalizer" 4-16-57 (Martha McCallum); *The Californians*—"Little Lost Man" 12-3-57 (Mrs. Kilgore).

Millan, Victor (1920-). Films: "Apache Ambush" 1955 (Manoel); "Giant" 1956 (Angel Obregon I); "Walk the Proud Land" 1956 (Santos); "The Ride Back" 1957 (Padre); "Terror in a Texas Town" 1958 (Jose Mirada). ¶TV: *Wild Bill Hickok*—"The Gatling Gun" 5-5-53; *Annie Oakley*—"Annie Rides the Navajo Trail" 11-18-56 (Brave Rider); *Tales of Wells Fargo*—"The Lynching" 5-13-57; *Sheriff of Cochise*—"Good Indian" 12-6-57; *Trackdown*—"Man and Money" 12-27-57 (Rodolfo); *Broken Arrow*—"Doctor" 2-12-57 (Dr. Luke), "Escape" 2-18-58 (Tahzay); *Wichita Town*—"Compadre" 11-25-59 (Rafael); *Bonanza*—"The Savage" 12-

3-60 (Dako); *Wanted—Dead or Alive*—"Witch Woman" 12-28-60 (Rafael Guerra); *Iron Horse*—"Grapes of Grass Valley" 10-21-67 (Manuel); *The Big Valley*—"Flight from San Miguel" 4-28-69 (Juan); *Kung Fu*—"The Chalice" 10-11-73 (Padre Benito).

Milland, Gloria. Films: "Gunfight at High Noon" 1963-Span./Ital.; "Three Swords of Zorro" 1963-Ital./Span.; "Seven Guns from Texas" 1964-Span./Ital. (Mary); "Seven Hours of Gunfire" 1964-Span./Ital. (Calamity Jane); "Hands of a Gunman" 1965-Ital./Span. (Laura); "Man with the Golden Pistol" 1966-Span./Ital. (Lily); "Hate for Hate" 1967-Ital.; "Man and a Colt" 1967-Span./Ital.; "The Man Who Killed Billy the Kid" 1967-Span./Ital. (Billy's Mother); "Hour of Death" 1968-Span./Ital.

Milland, Ray (1908-3/10/86). Films: "California" 1946 (Jonathan Trumbo); "Copper Canyon" 1950 (Johnny Carter); "Bugles in the Afternoon" 1952 (Kern Shafter); "A Man Alone" 1955 (Wes Steele); "Black Noon" TVM-1971 (Caleb Hobbs); "Testimony of Two Men" TVM-1977 (Jonas Witherby). ¶TV: *Trails West*—Host 1958-61; *Dupont Show of the Week*—"The Silver Burro" 11-3-63 (Investigator).

Millar, Lee (1888-12/24/41). Films: "Konga, the Wild Stallion" 1940 (Randall).

Millard, Harry (1928-9/2/69). TV: *Lawman*—"The Journey" 4-26-59 (Phillip).

Millay, Diana (1938-). TV: *The Westerner*— "Jeff" 9-30-60 (Jeff); *Wyatt Earp*—"Shoot to Kill" 10-18-60; *Stagecoach West*—"Red Sand" 11-22-60 (Martha); *Maverick*—"Dodge City or Bust" 12-11-60 (Diana Dangerfield); *The Rifleman*—"The Actress" 1-24-61 (Beth Black); *Bonanza*—"The Dream Riders" 5-20-61 (Diana Cayley); *Gunsmoke*—"Melinda Miles" 6-3-61 (Melinda Miles); *Whispering Smith*—"Dark Circle" 9-4-61 (Ellen Philo); *Rawhide*—"The Greedy Town" 2-16-62 (Honey Lassiter), "Incident of the White Eyes" 5-3-63 (Rachel Shay); *Laramie*—"Justice in a Hurry" 3-20-62 (Julie Keleher); *Wagon Train*—"The Cole Crawford Story" 4-11-62 (Helen Crawford); *Tales of Wells Fargo*—"The Gold Witch" 5-5-62 (Ruth Reardon); *The Travels of Jaimie McPheeters*— "The Day of the Skinners" 10-20-63 (Tassie); *Redigo*—"Horns of Hate" 11-19-63 (Val Cresco); *Temple Houston*— "Thunder Gap" 11-21-63 (Marcey

Bannister); *The Virginian*—"Rope of Lies" 3-25-64 (Alva Lowell).

Miller, Ann (1919-). Films: "Melody Ranch" 1940 (Julie Shelton); "Go West, Young Lady" 1941 (Lola); "The Kissing Bandit" 1948 (Dancer).

Miller, Bill (1887-11/12/39). Films: "The Fighting Ranger" 1922 (Ranger Bill); "The Web of the Law" 1923 (Bill Barton); "A Pair of Hellions" 1924; "Heartbound" 1925 (Ranger Bill).

Miller, Billy. Films: "The Restless Breed" 1957; "Run of the Arrow" 1957 (Silent Tongue). ¶TV: *Sergeant Preston of the Yukon*—"Ten Little Indians" 4-18-57 (Napoleon); *The Adventures of Rin Tin Tin*—"Bitter Medicine" 4-26-57.

Miller, Carl (1893-2/79). Films: "Tempest Cody Plays Detective" 1919; "Tempest Cody Turns the Table" 1919; "The Canyon of Light" 1926; "The Great K & A Train Robbery" 1926 (Burton); "The Power of the Weak" 1926 (Raymond); "Good as Gold" 1927 (Thomas Tilford); "Whispering Sage" 1927 (Esteban Bengoa); "Renegades of the West" 1932 (Rankin).

Miller, Charles (1891-6/5/55). Films: "The Phantom Plainsmen" 1942 (Capt. Marvin); "Raiders of the Range" 1942 (Pop Travers); "South of Santa Fe" 1942 (McMahon); "Beyond the Last Frontier" 1943 (Raymond Harper); "Black Hills Express" 1943 (Raymond Harper); "The Blocked Trail" 1943; "Daredevils of the West" 1943-serial (Foster); "Days of Old Cheyenne" 1943 (John Carlyle); "Raiders of Sunset Pass" 1943 (Dad Mathews); "Thundering Trails" 1943; "Wagon Tracks West" 1943 (Brown Baer); "Beneath Western Skies" 1944 (Lem Toller); "Hidden Valley Outlaws" 1944; "Pride of the Plains" 1944 (Grant Bradford); "The Daltons Ride Again" 1945 (Haines); "Gunman's Code" 1946; "Rustler's Roundup" 1946 (Judge Wayne); "The Lawless Breed" 1952.

Miller, Cheryl (1943-). Films: "Guardian of the Wilderness" 1976 (Kathleen Clark).

Miller, Colleen. Films: "Four Guns to the Border" 1954 (Lolly Bhumer); "The Rawhide Years" 1956 (Zoe); "Man in the Shadow" 1957 (Skippy Renchler); "Gunfight at Comanche Creek" 1964 (Abbie).

Miller, David. Films: "Tomahawk" 1951 (Capt. Ten Eyck); "Chief Crazy Horse" 1955 (Lieutenant); "Cheyenne Autumn" 1964 (Trooper).

Miller, Denny (1935-). Films:

"Buck and the Preacher" 1972 (Floyd). ¶TV: *Northwest Passage*— "Fight at the River" 9-14-58 (Cooper); *Laramie*—"Men of Defiance" 4-19-60 (Toby), "License to Kill" 11-22-60 (Wilkie); *Overland Trail*—"The Reckoning" 5-29-60 (Nicky); *Have Gun Will Travel*—"Saturday Night" 10-8-60 (Svenska); *The Rifleman*—"The Promoter" 12-6-60 (Reuben Miles); *The Deputy*— "Brother in Arms" 4-15-61 (Bill Jason); *Stagecoach West*—"Finn McColl" 1-24-61 (Dunn); *Wagon Train*—Regular 1961-63 (Duke Shannon); *Death Valley Days*—"The Leprechaun of Last Chance" 10-26-68 (Tomy); *The High Chaparral*—"A Way of Justice" 12-13-68 (Kolos); *The Men from Shiloh*—"The Politician" 1-13-71 (Joe Terry); *Gunsmoke*—"Lijah" 11-8-71 (Lijah); *Young Maverick*—"Clancy" 11-28-79 (Clancy Flannery); *Outlaws*—"Orleans" 1-17-87; *Lonesome Dove*—"Law and Order" 2-19-95 (Sheriff Owen Kearny), 3-5-95 (Sheriff Owen Kearny).

Miller, Diana (1902-12/18/27). Films: "The Rainbow Trail" 1925 (Anne); "The Cowboy and the Countess" 1926 (Nanette).

Miller, Dick (1928-). Films: "Apache Woman" 1955 (Tall Tree); "Gunslinger" 1956 (Jimmy Tonto)."The Oklahoma Woman" 1956; "A Time for Killing" 1967 (Zollicoffer). ¶TV: *Bonanza*—"A Woman Lost" 3-17-63 (Sam); *Wagon Train*— "The Brian Conlin Story" 10-25-64 (Michael); *Branded*—"Nice Day for a Hanging" 2-6-66 (Wrangler).

Miller, Eve (1933-3/27/77). Films: "Buckaroo from Powder River" 1948 (Molly Parnell); "The Big Trees" 1952 (Alicia Chadwick); "Kansas Pacific" 1953 (Barbara Bruce). ¶TV: *The Range Rider*— "Stage to Rainbow's End" 9-2-51; *Zane Grey Theater*—"A Man on the Run" 6-21-57 (Kate Longstreth); *Trackdown*—"Self-Defense" 11-22-57 (Sally McDermit).

Miller, Flournoy E. (1887-6/6/71). Films: "The Bronze Buckaroo" 1939 (Jim Pecklat); "Harlem Rides the Range" 1939 (Slim Perkins).

Miller, Harold (1894-7/18/72). Films: "Her Five-Foot Higness" 1920 (Sir Gerald Knowlton); "Leatherstocking" 1924-serial; "Way of a Man" 1924-serial.

Miller, Hope (1929-7/25/92). Films: "The Bounty Hunter" 1954.

Miller, Ivan (1888-9/27/67). Films: "Robin Hood of El Dorado" 1936 (Marshal); "High, Wide and

Handsome" 1937 (Marble); "Call of the Yukon" 1938 (O'Malley); "Man from Music Mountain" 1938 (John Scanlon); "The Old Barn Dancer" 1938 (Tornton); "The Cisco Kid and the Lady" 1939 (Post Commander); "Cowboys from Texas" 1939 (Clay Allison); "Wall Street Cowboy" 1939 (Niles); "Frontier Vengeance" 1940 (Frank Blackburn); "Geronimo" 1940 (Hamilton Fish); "Shooting High" 1940 (Sanders); "Twenty Mule Team" 1940 (Alden); "Jesse James at Bay" 1941 (Judge Rutherford); "Under Fiesta Stars" 1941.

Miller, Jack "Shorty" (1895-2/28/41). Films: "Moonlight on the Range" 1937; "The Singing Buckaroo" 1937; "Trouble in Texas" 1937 (Henchman).

Miller, Jane (-9/20/36). Films: "Heart of the Sunset" 1918 (Rosa); "The Forfeit" 1919 (Elvine Van Blooren); "The Unbroken Promise" 1919 (Nell Loring).

Miller, John "Skins". Films: "The Devil's Saddle Legion" 1937 (Spooks); "Heritage of the Desert" 1939 (John Twerk); "Texas Rangers Ride Again" 1940 (Station Attendant); "The Paleface" 1948 (Bellhop); "Valley of Fire" 1951; "Shane" 1953 (Atkey).

Miller, Kristine. Films: "Desert Fury" 1947 (Claire Lindquist); "High Lonesome" 1950 (Abbey Davis); "Young Daniel Boone" 1950 (Rebecca Bryan); "Hell's Outpost" 1954 (Beth Hodes); "Thunder Over Arizona" 1956; "Domino Kid" 1957 (Barbara Ellison); "The Persuader" 1957 (Kathryn Bonham). ¶TV: *Wild Bill Hickok*—"Outlaw Flats" 10-9-51; *Stories of the Century*—Regular 1955 (Jonsey Jones); *The Restless Gun*—"The Torn Flag" 5-5-58 (Mrs. Wheeler); *Wagon Train*—"The Rex Montana Story" 5-28-58 (Milly); *The Texan*—"The Gunfighter" 6-8-59 (Ruth Fenton), "The Accuser" 6-6-60 (Mattie); *Tales of Wells Fargo*—"Prince Jim" 3-27-61 (Ruth Hudson).

Miller, Lorraine (1929-2/6/78). Films: "Beyond the Last Frontier" 1943 (Susan Cook); "Riders of the Rio Grande" 1943 (Janet Owens); "Riding High" 1943 (Blanche); "Border Badmen" 1945 (Helen); "Fighting Bill Carson" 1945; "Frontier Fugitives" 1945; "Lonesome Trail" 1945; "Three in the Saddle" 1945; "Ambush Trail" 1946 (Alice Rhodes).

Miller, Mark (1925-). TV: *Gunsmoke*—"Wind" 3-21-59 (Frank Paris); *Zane Grey Theater*—"Checkmate" 4-30-59 (Ward Pendleton); *The Tall Man*—"Property of the

Crown" 2-24-62 (Sam Kirby); *Stoney Burke*—"Sidewinder" 11-12-62 (Morgan Julian); *Kung Fu*—"A Dream Within a Dream" 1-17-74 (Horace Mercer).

Miller, Marvin (1913-2/8/85). TV: *Bat Masterson*—"The Marble Slab" 5-11-61 (John Kelso).

Miller, Michael (1931-5/4/83). TV: *Gunsmoke*—"Carter Caper" 11-16-63 (Harry).

Miller, Mirta. Films: "The White, the Yellow, and the Black" 1974-Ital./Span./Fr.; "Get Mean" 1975-Ital.

Miller, Patsy Ruth (1904-7/16/95). Films: "Fighting Streak" 1922 (Ann Withero); "For Big Stakes" 1922 (Dorothy Clark); "Trimmed" 1922 (Alice Millard); "Singer Jim McKee" 1924 (Betty Gleason); "Red Riders of Canada" 1928 (Joan Duval).

Miller, Peter (1933-). Films: "The Iron Sheriff" 1957 (Jackson). ¶TV: *Wyatt Earp*—"The Clantons' Family Row" 12-8-59; *The Tall Man*—"The Runaway Groom" 4-28-62 (Luke Tugwell).

Miller, Richard. *see* Miller, Dick.

Miller, Roger (1936-10/25/92). TV: *Daniel Boone*—"A Very Small Rifle" 9-18-69 (Jonny Appleseed).

Miller, Shorty. *see* Miller, Jack "Shorty".

Miller, Ty. TV: *Young Riders*—Regular 1990-92 (the Kid).

Miller, W. Christie (1843-9/23/22). Films: "The Dancing Girl of Butte" 1909; "The Redman's View" 1909; "Over Silent Paths" 1910; "The Tenderfoot's Triumph" 1910; "That Chink at Golden Gulch" 1910; "The Thread of Destiny" 1910; "The Twisted Trails" 1910; "Two Brothers" 1910; "The Last Drop of Water" 1911; "A Temporary Truce" 1912; "The Battle at Elderbrush Gulch" 1913.

Miller, Walter (1892-3/30/40). Films: "In the Days of '49" 1911; "Two Men of the Desert" 1913; "The Yaqui Cur" 1913; "Hawk of the Hills" 1927-serial (Laramie); "Queen of the Northwoods" 1929-serial; "The Lone Defender" 1930-serial (Ramon); "Rogue of the Rio Grande" 1930 (Sheriff Rankin); "Rough Waters" 1930 (Morris); "The Utah Kid" 1930 (Sheriff Bentley); "Hell's Valley" 1931; "Hurricane Horseman" 1931 (Pancho Gomez); "Ghost City" 1932 (Jim Blane); "The Last of the Mohicans" 1932-serial; "Ridin' for Justice" 1932 (Deputy Marshal Alec Frame); "Gordon of Ghost City" 1933-serial (Rance Radigan); "The Fighting

Trooper" 1934 (Sgt. Leyton); "Gun Justice" 1934 (Chris Hogan); "The Red Rider" 1934-serial (Jim Breen); "Rocky Rhodes" 1934 (Dan Murtch); "Smoking Guns" 1934 (Dick Adams); "Ivory-Handled Gun" 1935 (Wolverine Kid); "The Roaring West" 1935-serial (Gil Gillespie); "Rustlers of Red Dog" 1935-serial (Deacon); "Valley of Wanted Men" 1935 (Ralph Dexter); "Desert Gold" 1936 (Hank Lade); "The Fugitive Sheriff" 1936 (Flamer); "Ghost Patrol" 1936 (Ted Dawson); "Border Cafe" 1937 (Evans); "Boss of Lonely Valley" 1937 (Jake Wagner); "Heart of the West" 1937 (Whitey); "Ranger Courage" 1937 (Bull); "Wild Horse Rodeo" 1937 (Colonel Nye); "Wild West Days" 1937-serial (Doc Hardy); "The Great Adventures of Wild Bill Hickok" 1938; "Lawless Valley" 1938 (Bob North); "Home on the Prairie" 1939 (Belknap); "Bullet Code" 1940 (Samuel Gorman); "Gaucho Serenade" 1940; "Virginia City" 1940 (Sergeant).

Milletaire, Carl (1924-5/4/94). TV: *The Cisco Kid*—"Foreign Agent" 8-18-51, "Bates Story" 9-29-51; *Broken Arrow*—"Devil's Eye" 11-12-57 (Hoteko); *Lawman*—"Conclave" 6-14-59 (Ramirez); *Maverick*—"Easy Mark" 11-15-59 (Hakime); *Bonanza*—"Bank Run" 1-28-61.

Millett, Arthur (1874-2/24/52). Films: "Humanizing Mr. Winsby" 1916; "The Land Just Over Yonder" 1916 (Sheriff Toilable Tom Jennings); "The Hidden Spring" 1917 (Olaf Erickson); "The Good Loser" 1918 (Doctor Jim); "Paying His Debt" 1918 (Sheriff of Rubio); "Drag Harlan" 1920 (John Haydon); "Hearts Up" 1920 (Jim Drew); "West Is West" 1920 (J.C. Armstrong); "Tracked to Earth" 1922 (Big Bill Angus); "The Two-Gun Man" 1926 (Sheriff Dalton); "Range Courage" 1927 (John Martin); "Shootin' Irons" 1927 (Sheriff); "Hidden Valley" 1932 (Sheriff Dave Bristow); "Honor of the Mounted" 1932; "The Fugitive Sheriff" 1936 (John); "The Lion's Den" 1936 (Merwin); "Winds of the Wasteland" 1936.

Millhollin, James (1920-5/23/93). TV: *Tales of Wells Fargo*—"The Diamond Dude" 2-27-61 (Leroy Finch).

Millican, James (1910-11/24/55). Films: "North of the Yukon" 1939 (Orderly); "Adventures of Gallant Bess" 1948 (Bud Mellerick); "Last of the Wild Horses" 1948 (Sheriff Harrison); "The Man from Colorado" 1948 (Sgt. Jericho Howard);

"The Return of Wildfire" 1948 (Frank Keller); "The Dalton Gang" 1949 (Sheriff Jeb Marvin); "Fighting Man of the Plains" 1949 (Cummings); "Grand Canyon" 1949 (Tex Hartford); "Rimfire" 1949 (Capt. Tom Harvey); "Beyond the Purple Hills" 1950 (Rocky Morgan); "The Devil's Doorway" 1950 (Ike Stapleton); "The Gunfighter" 1950 (Pete); "Winchester '73" 1950 (Wheeler); "Al Jennings of Oklahoma" 1951 (Ed Jennins); "Cavalry Scout" 1951 (Martin Gavin); "The Great Missouri Raid" 1951 (Sgt. Trowbridge); "Rawhide" 1951 (Tex Squires); "Warpath" 1951 (Gen. George Armstrong); "Bugles in the Afternoon" 1952 (Sgt. Hines); "Carson City" 1952 (Jim Squires); "Springfield Rifle" 1952 (Matthew Quint); "Cow Country" 1953 (Fritz Warner); "Gun Belt" 1953 (Wyatt Earp); "The Silver Whip" 1953 (Bowen); "The Stranger Wore a Gun" 1953; "Dawn at Socorro" 1954 (Harry McNair); "Jubilee Trail" 1954 (Rinardi); "The Outcast" 1954 (Cal Prince); "Riding Shotgun" 1954 (Dan Marady); "Chief Crazy Horse" 1955 (Gen. Crook); "The Man from Laramie" 1955 (Tom Quigby); "Top Gun" 1955 (Bat Davis); "The Vanishing American" 1955 (Walker); "Red Sundown" 1956 (Purvis). ¶TV: *Wild Bill Hickok*—"Heading for Trouble" 6-10-52, "The Avenging Gunman" 7-29-52; *The Westerner*—Pilot 11-53.

Milligan, Spencer. TV: *Gunsmoke*—"Brides and Grooms" 2-10-75 (Jinx Tobin); *Barbary Coast*—"The Dawson Marker" 1-9-76 (Williams); *Father Murphy*—Pilot 11-3-81 (Arnie Winkler).

Millman, William LeStrange (1883-7/19/37). Films: "Secret Patrol" 1936 (C.J. McCord); "Stampede" 1936 (John Milford).

Millner, Marietta (1906-6/26/27). Films: "Drums of the Desert" 1927 (Mary Manton).

Mills, Donna (1943-). TV: *Lancer*—"The Lion and the Lamb" 2-3-70 (Lucy); *Gunsmoke*—"A Game of Death ... An Act of Love" 11-5-73 & 11-12-73 (Cora Sanderson); *The Oregon Trail*—"The Scarlet Ribbon" 1977; *Young Maverick*—"Dead Man's Hand" 12-26-79 & 1-2-80 (Lila).

Mills, Edith (1894-5/16/62). Films: "Cherokee Uprising" 1950 (Mrs. Strongbow).

Mills, Edwin (-5/23/81). Films: "Stagecoach" 1966 (Sergeant Major). ¶TV: *Have Gun Will Travel*—"Love and a Bad Woman" 3-26-60 (Dandy); *Wanted—Dead or Alive*—"The Trial" 9-21-60 (Atkins); *Great*

Adventure—"The Testing of Sam Houston" 1-31-64 (Secretary); *Daniel Boone*—"The Inheritance" 10-26-67 (Ostler).

Mills, Frank (1870-6/11/21). Films: "The Price of Pride" 1917 (Jeffrey Arnold Black); "Wild Honey" 1918 (Rev. Jim Brown/Pastor Holbrook).

Mills, Frank (1891-8/18/73). Films: "Hi Gaucho!" 1936; "Way Out West" 1937 (Bartender); "Wells Fargo" 1937; "Union Pacific" 1939 (Irish Paddy); "Stage to Chino" 1940; "Honky Tonk" 1941 (Pallbearer); "Western Union" 1941 (Man); "Heart of the Rio Grande" 1942.

Mills, Gordon. Films: "Daniel Boone, Trail Blazer" 1957 (John Holder). ¶TV: *Tales of the Texas Rangers*—"Carnival Criss-Cross" 9-3-55 (Duke Bishop); *Sheriff of Cochise*—"Closed for Repairs" 11-30-56 (Chase); *Gunsmoke*—"The Big Con" 5-3-58 (Varden).

Mills, Grace (1883-1/7/72). Films: "Vengeance Valley" 1951 (Mrs. Burke).

Mills, Hayley (1946-). Films: "Africa—Texas Style!" 1967-U.S./Brit. (Girl).

Mills, Hazel. Films: "The Fighting Terror" 1929; "The Last Roundup" 1929 (Lucy Graves).

Mills, Joe (1875-10/19/35). Films: "Two-Fisted Justice" 1931 (Abraham Lincoln).

Mills, John (1908-). Films: "The Singer Not the Song" 1961-Brit. (Father Keogh); "Africa—Texas Style!" 1967-U.S./Brit. (Wing Commander Howard Hayes); "Chuka" 1967 (Col. Stuart Valois); "Oklahoma Crude" 1973 (Cleon Doyle). ¶TV: *Dundee and the Culhane*—Regular 1967 (Dundee).

Mills, Juliet (1941-). Films: "The Rare Breed" 1966 (Hilary Price). ¶TV: *A Man Called Shenandoah*—"The Imposter" 4-4-66 (Paula); *Alias Smith and Jones*—"The Man Who Murdered Himself" 3-18-71 (Julia Finney).

Mills, Marilyn. Films: "A Western Demon" 1922 (Rose Dale); "Come on Cowboys!" 1924 (Priscilla); "Horse Sense" 1924 (Molly McLane); "Riders of the Plains" 1924-serial; "Sell 'Em Cowboy" 1924 (Milly Atwood); "Two Fisted Justice" 1924 (Mort Landeau's Wife); "The Cactus Cure" 1925 (Poppy Saunders); "My Pal" 1925; "The Rip Snorter" 1925 (Betty Saunders); "Tricks" 1925 (Angelica "Trix" Varden); "Where Romance Rides" 1925 (Muriel Thompson); "The Love of Paquita" 1927.

Mills, Mort (1919-6/6/93). Films: "Hannah Lee" 1953 (Deputy); "Texas Bad Man" 1953 (Bartender); "The Marauders" 1955 (Cormack); "Davy Crockett and the River Pirates" 1956 (Sam Mason); "The Iron Sheriff" 1957 (Sutherland); "Man in the Shadow" 1957 (Gateman); "Ride a Crooked Trail" 1958 (Pecos); "Bullet for a Badman" 1964; "Gunfight at Comanche Creek" 1964; "The Quick Gun" 1964 (Cagle); "The Outlaws Is Coming!" 1965 (Trigger Mortis); "Return of the Gunfighter" TVM-1967 (Will Parker); "Soldier Blue" 1970 (Sgt. O'Hearn). ¶TV: *The Cisco Kid*—"Sky Sign" 12-6-52, "Marriage by Mail" 1-3-53, "Arroyo Millionaire's Castle" 12-12-53, "Stevens Gang and Telegraph" 1-2-54; *Walt Disney Presents*—"Davy Crockett"—Regular 1954-55 (Sam Mason); *Gunsmoke*—"No Handcuffs" 1-21-56 (Brake), "How to Die for Nothing" 6-23-56 (Howard Bulow), "Born to Hang" 11-2-57 (Robie), "Murder Warrant" 4-18-59 (Jake Harbin), "Take Her, She's Cheap" 10-31-64 (Loren Billings), "Honey Pot" 5-15-65, "Death Train" 11-27-67 (Jack Marple); *20th Century Fox Hour*—"Gun in His Hand" 4-4-56 (Kirby); *Cheyenne*—"Johnny Bravo" 5-15-56 (Ben Taggart); *Sheriff of Cochise*—"Fire on Chiricahua Mountains" 11-2-56 (Barlett); *Zane Grey Theater*—"Time of Decision" 1-18-57 (Bart Miller), "The Scar" 3-2-61 (Foreman); *Broken Arrow*—"Legacy of a Hero" 2-26-57 (Connell), "Black Moment" 10-29-57 (Halley); *Wyatt Earp*—"The Vultures" 3-19-57 (Sam Watts), "The Fanatic" 11-22-60 (Odie Cairns); *Maverick*—"The Quick and the Dead" 12-8-57 (Parker), "Day of Reckoning" 2-2-58 (Red Scanlon); *Sugarfoot*—"Man Wanted" 2-18-58 (Smiley), "Journey to Provision" 1-5-60 (Sheriff Len Gogarty); *Wanted—Dead or Alive*—"The Bounty" 9-20-58 (Clark Daimier), "Eight Cent Record" 12-20-58 (Harmon Stone), "Railroaded" 3-14-59 (Ed Bruner), "The Healing Woman" 9-12-59 (Tom Summers), "The Most Beautiful Woman" 1-23-60 (Frank); *Man Without a Gun*—Regular 1958-59 (Marshal Frank Tallman); *Bronco*—"The Long Ride Back" 11-18-58 (Jacob Stint), "Apache Treasure" 11-7-60 (Hickins); *The Rifleman*—"The Sister" 11-25-58 (Josh), "Jealous Man" 3-26-62 (Jake Owens); *Trackdown*—"Bad Judgment" 1-28-59 (Rafe Borden); *Have Gun Will Travel*—"Hunt the Man Down" 4-25-59 (Ben Coey); *Tales of Wells Fargo*—"The Bounty Hunter" 6-1-59 (Jeff Briscoe), "The Trading

Post" 4-11-60 (Robson); *Wichita Town*—"Man on the Hill" 11-4-59 (Pete Bennett); *Bat Masterson*—"Who'll Bury My Violence?" 11-12-59 (Barney Kaster); *Man from Blackhawk*—"Station Six" 11-13-59; *The Law of the Plainsman*—"The Gibbet" 11-26-59; *Bonanza*—"Vendetta" 12-5-59 (Carl Morgan), "Day of the Dragon" 12-3-61 (Gordon), "The Miracle Worker" 5-20-62 (Thorne), "Song in the Dark" 1-13-63 (Deputy), "Joe Cartwright, Detective" 3-5-67 (Perkins); *The Alaskans*—"Million Dollar Kid" 1-3-60 (Wilkes); *The Texan*—"Thirty Hours to Kill" 2-1-60 (Ben Dawson/Blackie Dawson); *Johnny Ringo*—"Killer, Choose a Card" 6-9-60 (Jed); *Stagecoach West*—"By the Deep Six" 12-27-60, "The Remounts" 3-14-61 (Griz), "The Marker" 6-27-61 (Mingo); *Laramie*—"Rimrock" 3-21-61 (Rink Banners), "The Last Journey" 10-31-61 (Damon Johntry), "The Last Journey" 10-31-61, "War Hero" 10-2-62 (Obie Loomis); *Lawman*—"Owny O'Reilly, Esq." 10-15-61 (Jack Saunders); *The Virginian*—"Duel at Shiloh" 1-2-63 (Deputy Bender); *Wagon Train*—"The Clay Shelby Story" 12-6-64 (Sergeant Bragan), "The Jarbo Pierce Story" 5-2-65 (Grant); *The Big Valley*—"Young Marauders" 10-6-65 (Sheriff), "The Odyssey of Jubal Tanner" 10-13-65 (Sheriff), "My Son, My Son" 11-3-65 (Sheriff), "Earthquake!" 11-10-65 (Sheriff), "Hazard" 3-9-66 (Sheriff); *Wild Wild West*—"The Night of the Casual Killer" 10-15-65 (Harper); *A Man Called Shenandoah*—"The Locket" 11-22-65 (Sheriff); *Laredo*—"Finnegan" 10-21-66 (Muldoon); *Iron Horse*—"Explosion at Waycrossing" 11-21-66 (Sheriff Harkness); *Daniel Boone*—"The King's Shilling" 10-19-67 (Andrew Hubbard), "Flag of Truce" 11-21-68 (General Grosscup); *The Outcasts*—"They Shall Rise Up" 1-6-69 (Tauber); *The Guns of Will Sonnett*—"A Town in Terror" 2-7-69 & 2-14-69 (Ben Adams); *Alias Smith and Jones*—"McGuffin" 12-9-72.

Mills, Thomas R. (1878-11/29/53). Films: "The Arizona Romeo" 1925 (Sam Barr); "Gold Is Where You Find It" 1938 (Man at Stock Exchange).

Milner, Martin (1927-). Films: "Last of the Comanches" 1952 (Billy Creel); "Springfield Rifle" 1952 (Olie Larsen); "Pillars of the Sky" 1956 (Waco); "Gunfight at the O.K. Corral" 1957 (James Earp). ¶TV: *The Lone Ranger*—"Pay Dirt" 3-23-50; *Wagon Train*—"The Sally Potter Story" 4-9-58 (Matt Trumbull);

Rawhide—"Incident with an Executioner" 1-23-59 (Johnny Doan); *Hotel De Paree*—"Vein of Ore" 10-16-59 (Pat Williams); *U.S. Marshal*—"Trigger Happy" 10-31-59 (Bob Baxter); *The Virginian*—"Timberland" 3-10-65 (Dave Ferguson), "Trail to Ashley Mountain" 11-2-66 (Case); *Laredo*—"Yahoo" 9-30-65 (Clendon MacMillan); *A Man Called Shenandoah*—"Requiem for the Second" 5-2-66 (Neal Henderson).

Milo, Sandra. Films: "The Bang Bang Kid" 1968-U.S./Span./Ital. (Gwenda Skaggel).

Miltern, John (1870-1/15/37). Films: "Tongues of Flame" 1924 (Scanlon).

Milton, Gerald. Films: "Forty Guns" 1957 (Shotgun Spangler); "The Quiet Gun" 1957 (Lesser); "The Restless Breed" 1957 (Bartender); "Toughest Gun in Tombstone" 1958 (Ike Clanton). ¶TV: *Tales of Wells Fargo*—"The Bounty" 4-15-57 (Lon Ellwood); *Gunsmoke*—"Big Girl Lost" 4-20-57 (Ed Doolin); *Have Gun Will Travel*—"Strange Vendetta" 10-26-57, "Coming of the Tiger" 4-14-62 (Sam); *Jefferson Drum*—"A Very Deadly Game" 5-30-58 (Moose Miklos); *Bat Masterson*—"The Black Pearls" 7-1-59 (Sheriff Gowdy), "Welcome to Paradise" 5-5-60 (John Whelan); "The Hunter" 10-27-60 (Middleswirth); *Rawhide*—"Incident of the Roman Candles" 7-10-59 (Mooney); *The Texan*—"No Way Out" 9-14-59 (Tod Cannon); *The Deputy*—"The Big Four" 11-14-59 (Curly Bill Brocius); *Wanted—Dead or Alive*—"Baa-Baa" 1-4-61 (Moose).

Mimieux, Yvette (1939-). Films: "The Reward" 1965 (Sylvia); "Black Noon" TVM-1971 (Deliverance); "Ransom for Alice!" TVM-1977 (Jenny Cullen).

Mims, William (1927-4/9/91). Films: "I Killed Wild Bill Hickok" 1956 (Dan); "Walk Tall" 1960 (Jake); "Lonely Are the Brave" 1962 (1st Deputy in Bar); "Gunfight in Abilene" 1967 (Ed Scovie); "Paint Your Wagon" 1969 (Frock-Coated Man); "The Ballad of Cable Hogue" 1970 (Jensen); "Flap" 1970 (Steve Gray). ¶TV: *Have Gun Will Travel*—"The Sons of Aaron Murdock" 5-9-59, "Chapagne Safari" 12-5-59 (Gravely), "Trial at Tablerock" 12-15-62 (Adams); *Rough Riders*—"The Wagon Raiders" 6-4-59; *Wyatt Earp*—"The Nugget and the Epitaph" 10-6-59, "Woman of Tucson" 11-15-60 (Dameron), "The Good Mule and the Bad Mule" 3-14-61 (Editor Dameron);

Bronco—"The Magnificent Adah" 11-14-59, "Legacy of Twisted Creed" 4-19-60 (Sheriff); *Tate*—"Voices of the Town" 7-6-60 (Hotel Clerk); *Death Valley Days*—"Devil's Bar" 10-5-60 (Jake Higgins); *The Westerner*—"School Days" 10-7-60; *Cheyenne*—"Counterfeit Gun" 10-10-60 (Tully); *Lawman*—"The Frame-Up" 1-15-61 (Rich Matthews), "The Bride" 4-1-62 (Frank Farnum); *Bonanza*—"The Bride" 1-21-61 (Eb Bailey), "A Man to Admire" 12-6-64 (Evans), "One Ace Too Many" 4-2-72 (Williams); *Tales of Wells Fargo*—"The Remittance Man" 4-3-61 (Dan Gillette), "Vignette of a Sinner" 6-2-62 (Lucius Kramm); *Wagon Train*—"The Johnny Masters Story" 1-16-63 (Waters), "The Adam MacKenzie Story" 3-27-63 (Esteban Perez), "The Jed Whitmore Story" 1-13-64 (Jennings); *Empire*—"Between Friday and Monday" 5-7-63 (Perry Wilmot); *The Virginian*—"Legend for a Lawman" 3-3-65 (Cole); *Wild Wild West*—"The Night the Wizard Shook the Earth" 10-1-65 (Governor of California); *Daniel Boone*—"Forty Rifles" 3-10-66 (Scraps), "The Desperate Raid" 11-16-67 (Malloy); *The Big Valley*—"The Martyr" 10-17-66, "Wagonload of Dreams" 1-2-67 (Senator Bridger); *Rango*—"The Not So Great Train Robbery" 3-17-67; *Cowboy in Africa*—"The Adopted One" 10-23-67 (Arne Petesen); *The Guns of Will Sonnett*—"The Turkey Shoot" 11-24-67; *The Outcasts*—"The Understanding" 10-14-68 (Murphy); *Lancer*—"Splinter Group" 3-3-70 (Sheriff Jayson); *Alias Smith and Jones*—"The Wrong Train to Brimstone" 2-4-71 (Grady), "Which Way to the O.K. Corral?" 2-10-72; *Gunsmoke*—"Pike" 3-1-71 & 3-8-71 (Hawkins); *Kung Fu*—"Alethea" 3-15-73 (Luke Jezdale), "Ambush" 4-5-75 (Sheriff).

Minardos, Nico (1930-). Films: "Day of the Evil Gun" 1968 (DeLeon); "Cannon for Cordoba" 1970 (Peter Andros). ¶TV: *Broken Arrow*—"Fathers and Sons" 4-2-57 (Nachise); *Wagon Train*—"The Charles Avery Story" 12-13-57 (Big Bear); *Maverick*—"The Judas Mask" 11-2-58 (Enrico); *Sugarfoot*—"Fernando" 2-16-60 (Fernando); *Riverboat*—"The Two Faces of Grey Holden" 10-3-60 (Sebastian); *The Rebel*—"The Liberators" 1-1-61 (Comandante); *Frontier Circus*—"Calamity Circus" 3-8-62 (the Great Roberto); *Redigo*—"Prince Among Men" 10-15-63 (Luis Guardino); *Branded*—"Romany Roundup" 12-5-65 & 12-12-65 (Kolyan); *The Big Valley*—"The Martyr" 10-17-66 (Paulino); *Hondo*—"The Savage" 10-

6-67 (Ponce Coloradas); *The Outcasts*—"The Understanding" 10-14-68 (Lieutenant); *Alias Smith and Jones*— "Journey from San Juan" 4-8-71 (El Clavo), "Miracle at Santa Marta" 12-30-71 (Alcaide).

Mineo, Sal (1939-2/12/76). Films: "Giant" 1956 (Angel Obregon III); "Tonka" 1958 (White Bull); "Cheyenne Autumn" 1964 (Red Shirt); "The Dangerous Days of Kiowa Jones" TVM-1966 (Bobby Jack Wilkes); "Stranger on the Run" TVM-1967 (George Blaylock).

Ministeri, George (1913-1/29/ 86). Films: "The Terror of Tiny Town" 1938 (B. Armstrong, the Blacksmith).

Minner, Kathryn (1892-5/26/ 69). TV: *Gunsmoke*—"The Gold Mine" 1-27-69 (Grandma).

Minor, Bob (1942-). Films: "The Soul of Nigger Charley" 1973 (Fred); "Friendly Persuasion" TVM-1975 (Burk); "Posse" 1993 (Alex). ¶TV: *Paradise*—"Ghost Dance" 11-24-88 (Walbash).

Minter, Mary Miles (1902-8/4/ 84). Films: "The Cowboy and the Lady" 1922 (Jessica Weston).

Mintz, Eli (1905-6/8/88). Films: "The Proud Rebel" 1958 (Gorman).

Mioni, Fabrizio (1930-). TV: *Bronco*—"La Rubia" 5-17-60 (Salazar); *Death Valley Days*—"Hangtown Fry" 10-3-62 (Paul Duval); *Bonanza*—"The Deadliest Game" 2-21-65 (Carlo Alfieri); *The Virginian*— "Harvest of Strangers" 2-16-66 (Jean); *The Big Valley*—"Joaquin" 9-11-67 (Juan Molina); *The High Chaparral*—"Shadow of the Wind" 1-10-69 (Nickanora).

Miou-Miou (1950-). Films: "Genius" 1975-Ital./Fr./Ger. (Lucy).

Miracle, Irene. TV: *Paradise*— "Childhood's End" 12-29-88 (Sarah Hamilton).

Miranda, John. TV: *Paradise*— Regular 1988-91 (Baxter).

Miranda, Soledad (1943-). Films: "Sugar Colt" 1966-Ital./Span.; "100 Rifles" 1969 (Girl in Hotel).

Miranda, Susana (1947-). Films: "Flap" 1970 (Ann Looking Deer). ¶TV: *The Men from Shiloh*— "The Best Man" 9-23-70 (Teresa Zaragosa).

Miroslava (1926-3/10/55). Films: "Stranger on Horseback" 1955 (Amy Lee Bannerman).

Mistral, Jorge (1923-4/20/72). Films: "Gunfighters of Casa Grande" 1965-U.S./Span. (the Traveler).

Mitchell, Barry. Films: "Heldorado" 1946 (Alex Baxter).

Mitchell, Belle (1888-2/12/79). Films: "Mark of Zorro" 1940 (Maria); "Unconquered" 1947; "Viva Zapata!" 1952 (Nacio's Wife); "Passion" 1954 (Senora Carrisa); "The First Traveling Saleslady" 1956 (Emily); "The Lone Ranger and the Lost City of Gold" 1958 (Caulama); "High Plains Drifter" 1973 (Mrs. Lake). ¶TV: *The Gene Autry Show*—"Galloping Hoofs" 12-22-51, "Melody Mesa" 1-4-52; *Sergeant Preston of the Yukon*—"The Devil's Roost" 4-11-57 (Nirana); *Maverick*—"The Marquesa" 1-3-60 (Bufemia).

Mitchell, Beth. Films: "The Fighting Strain" 1923 (Bess Barlow).

Mitchell, Bruce (1880-9/26/52). Films: "Fighting to Live" 1934; "The Phantom Empire" 1935-serial; "Wanderer of the Wasteland" 1935 (Dealer in Big Jo's Place); "Oh, Susanna!" 1936; "White Fang" 1936; "Fighting Texan" 1937 (Sheriff Bart Widner); "Galloping Dynamite" 1937; "Wells Fargo" 1937 (Miner); "Whistling Bullets" 1937 (Capt. John Saunders); "Wild West Days" 1937-serial; "The Mysterious Rider" 1938 (Baker); "Pride of the West" 1938 (Detective); "The Arizona Wildcat" 1939 (Bartender); "Dodge City" 1939; "Riders of the Frontier" 1939 (Marshal); "Silver on the Sage" 1939 (Bartender); "Stage to Chino" 1940; "Triple Justice" 1940.

Mitchell, Cameron (1918-7/6/ 94). Films: "Adventures of Gallant Bess" 1948 (Ted Daniels); "Man in the Saddle" 1951 (George Virk); "The Outcasts of Poker Flat" 1952 (Ryker); "Pony Soldier" 1952 (Konah); "Powder River" 1953 (Mitch Hardin); "Garden of Evil" 1954 (Luke Daly); "Strange Lady in Town" 1955 (David Garth); "The Tall Men" 1955 (Clint Allison); "Tension at Table Rock" 1956 (Sheriff Miller); "Last Gun" 1964-Ital.; "Minnesota Clay" 1964-Ital./Fr./Span. (Minnesota); "Ride in the Whirlwind" 1966 (Vern); "Hombre" 1967 (Braden); "Buck and the Preacher" 1972 (Deshay); "Eye for an Eye" 1972-Ital./Span./Ital. (Huck); "The Hanged Man" TVM-1974 (Lew Halleck); "The Quest" TVM-1976 (Shadrack Peltzer); "Testimony of Two Men" TVM-1977 (Jeremiah Hadley); "Wild Times" TVM-1980 (Harry Dreier); "The Gambler, Part II—The Adventure Continues" TVM-1983 (Colonel Greeley); "Dream West" TVM-1986 (Commodore Robert Stockton). ¶TV: *20th Century Fox Hour*—"The Ox-Bow Incident" 11-2-55 (Donald Martin); *Colt .45*—"Point of Honor" 3-21-58

(Dr. Alan McMurdo); *Zane Grey Theater*—"The Doctor Keeps a Promise" 3-21-58 (Dr. Allan McMurdo), "Trail Incident" 1-29-59 (Charlie Patch), "The Grubstake" 12-24-59 (Jim Goad); *Wagon Train*—"The Duke LeMay Story" 4-29-59 (Duke LeMay); *Bonanza*—"House Divided" 1-16-60 (Fred Kyle); *Death Valley Days*—"Pete Kitchen's Wedding Night" 6-21-60 (Pete Kitchen); *Daniel Boone*—"The Fifth Man" 2-17-66 (Major George R. Clark/Catahecassa), "The Loser's Race" 11-10-66 (James Dorsey); *The High Chaparral*—Regular 1967-71 (Buck Cannon); *Alias Smith and Jones*—"Which Way to the O.K. Corral?" 2-10-72 (Wyatt Earp); *Gunsmoke*—"The Iron Man" 10-21-74 (Chauncey Demon); *Nakia*—"A Beginning in the Wilderness" 10-26-74 (Bob Polk); *The Quest*—"Seventy-Two Hours" 11-3-76 (Marshal Horne); *How the West Was Won*—Episode One 2-12-78 (Coulee John Brinkerhoff), Episode Two 2-19-78 (Coulee John Brinkerhoff).

Mitchell, Carlyle. TV: *Zane Grey Theater*—"The Necessary Breed" 2-15-57 (Dr. Asher); *Cheyenne*—"Incident at Indian Springs" 9-24-57 (Hug Powell), "Savage Breed" 12-19-60 (Sen. Leland Carr); *Maverick*— "Diamond in the Rough" 1-26-58 (General Marvin); *Tales of Wells Fargo*—"The Newspaper" 3-24-58 (John Sayers); *Tombstone Territory*— "The Lady Gambler" 5-28-58 (Val Slater); *The Restless Gun*—"The Manhunters" 6-2-58 (Newt Bascomb), "Jebediah Bonner" 9-22-58 (Dr. Ken Ludlow); *Rough Riders*—"The Governor" 11-6-58 (Gov. Martin Kimbrough), "The Electioners" 1-1-59 (Carlson); *Bonanza*—"The Last Hunt" 12-19-59 (Doctor); *Bat Masterson*—"Run for Your Money" 3-2-61 (Theo Stebbins).

Mitchell, Chuck (1928-6/22/ 92). Films: "Bret Maverick" TVM-1981 (Joe Dakota).

Mitchell, Dallas. TV: *Colt .45*— "The Confession" 4-26-59 (Joe Donnelly), "Night of Decision" 6-28-59 (Ben); *Gunsmoke*—"Odd Man Out" 11-21-59 (Cowboy), "Potshot" 3-11-61 (Bert); *Have Gun Will Travel*— "The Naked Gun" 12-19-59 (Kew); *Riverboat*—"Hang the Men High" 3-21-60 (Jerry Madden); *Cimarron Strip*—"Without Honor" 2-29-68.

Mitchell, Ewing (1910-9/2/88). Films: "The Last Outpost" 1951 (Major Riordan); "Springfield Rifle" 1952 (Spencer); "Winning of the West" 1953 (Ranger Capt. Hickson); "Black Horse Canyon" 1954 (Sheriff); "Man Without a Star" 1955 (Johnson). ¶TV: *Sky King*—Regular 1951-53 (Mitch); *The Gene Autry Show*—"Frontier Guard" 10-13-51, "Killer's Trail" 10-27-51, "Outlaw Escape" 12-1-51, "The Return of Maverick Dan" 12-15-51, "Melody Mesa" 1-4-52, "The Old Prospector" 8-4-53, "Gypsy Woman" 8-25-53; *Wild Bill Hickok*—"Chain of Events" 6-24-52; *The Roy Rogers Show*—"The Showdown" 5-22-55 (Wayne Corbin), "Ranch War" 10-23-55, "Accessory to Crime" 3-3-57, "Portrait of Murder" 3-17-57; *The Adventures of Champion*—Regular 1955-56 (Sheriff Powers); *The Lone Ranger*—"The Courage of Tonto" 1-17-57, "The Banker's Son" 5-16-57; *Annie Oakley*—"Dude's Decision" 2-10-57 (Col. Granger); *Wyatt Earp*—"Old Jake" 4-9-57 (Colonel); *Death Valley Days*—"The Red Flannel Shirt" 6-9-57 (Fred Gerlock); *Tales of the Texas Rangers*—"Whirlwind Raiders" 10-13-57 (Tom Weldon); *Sergeant Preston of the Yukon*—"Out of the Night" 11-28-57 (Inspector Graham); *The Restless Gun*—"Bonner's Squaw" 11-3-58 (Sheriff Frank Kemper).

Mitchell, Frank. Films: "Rhythm of the Rio Grande" 1940 (Shorty); "West of Carson City" 1940 (Breed); "Roaring Frontiers" 1941; "Bullets for Bandits" 1942; "The Devil's Trail" 1942; "North of the Rockies" 1942; "Prairie Gunsmoke" 1942; "Vengeance of the West" 1942; "Advance to the Rear" 1964 (Belmont). ¶TV: *Lawman*—"Old Stefano" 12-25-60 (Hank Buel); *Wagon Train*—"The Sam Spicer Story" 10-28-63 (Stoney).

Mitchell, Geneva (1907-3/10/49). Films: "Get That Girl" 1932 (Nedra Tito); "Fighting Shadows" 1935 (Martha Harrison); "Lawless Riders" 1935 (Edith Adams); "Western Courage" 1935 (Gloria Hanley); "The Cattle Thief" 1936 (Alice).

Mitchell, George (1905-1/18/72). Films: "3:10 to Yuma" 1957 (Bartender); "The Wild and the Innocent" 1959 (Uncle Hawkes); "Nevada Smith" 1966 (Paymaster); "Ride in the Whirlwind" 1966 (Evan). ¶TV: *Death Valley Days*—"One in a Hundred" 12-23-53 (Sam Dorrance), "Fair Exchange" 11-24-59 (Charlie Stoner); "Davy's Friend" 11-28-62 (Mr. McAllister), "Little Cayuse" 2-8-64; *Philco Television Playhouse*—"The Death of Billy the Kid" 7-24-55 (Pete Maxwell); *Have Gun Will Travel*—"The Protege" 10-18-58 (Joe Sprague), "The Prisoner" 12-17-60 (Keel); *The Californians*—"A Turn in

the Trail" 2-17-59 (Asa Deane); *Gunsmoke*—"Annie Oakley" 10-24-59 (Jeff Kinsman), "Distant Drummer" 11-19-60 (Grade); *The Law of the Plainsman*—"The Gibbet" 11-26-59; *Bonanza*—"The Gunmen" 1-23-60 (Jubal), "Land Grab" 12-31-61 (Mike Sullivan); *Laramie*—"Rope of Steel" 2-16-60 (Bowden), "Man from Kansas" 1-10-61 (August Willoughby), "Justice in a Hurry" 3-20-62; *Tales of Wells Fargo*—"The Lat Mayor Brown" 3-7-60 (Fogarty); *Tate*—"Voices of the Town" 7-6-60 (Grizzled Man); *The Tall Man*—"Counterfeit Law" 11-19-60 (Moffitt); *Frontier Circus*—"Quick Shuffle" 2-1-62 (Sheriff); *Stoney Burke*—"Fight Night" 10-8-62 (Clay Bristol), "A Matter of Pride" 11-5-62 (Cal Bristol), "Cousin Eunice" 12-24-62 (Cal Bristol); *A Man Called Shenandoah*—"The Siege" 12-13-65 (Billings); *The Virginian*—"Morgan Starr" 2-9-66 (Noah MacMillian); *Time Tunnel*—"Massacre" 10-28-66 (Sitting Bull); *Lancer*—"The Black McGloins" 1-21-69 (Talbot); *The Men from Shiloh*—"Jump-Up" 3-24-71 (Stanton).

Mitchell, Gordon (Charles Pendleton). Films: "Kill or Be Killed" 1966-Ital. (Hired Gunman); "Thompson 1880" 1966-Ital./Ger.; "Three Graves for a Winchester" 1966-Ital.; "Born to Kill" 1967-Ital. (Gordon); "John the Bastard" 1967-Ital.; "Rita of the West" 1967-Ital.; "Beyond the Law" 1968-Ital.; "Dead for a Dollar" 1968-Ital.; "If One Is Born a Swine ... Kill Him" 1968-Ital.; "Saguaro" 1968-Ital.; "Finders Killers" 1969-Ital.; "I Am Sartana, Your Angel of Death" 1969-Ital./Fr.; "Once Upon a Time in the Wild, Wild West" 1969-Ital. (Bill); "Django and Sartana Are Coming ... It's the End" 1970-Ital. (Black Burt); "Fistful of Death" 1971-Ital.; "Hero Called Allegria" 1971-Ital. (Ray); "Reach You Bastard!" 1971-Ital.; "Stranger That Kneels Beside the Shadow of a Corpse" 1971-Ital.; "Go Away! Trinity Has Arrived in Eldorado" 1972-Ital.; "Let's Go and Kill Sartana" 1972-Ital./Span. (Greg); "Magnificent West" 1972-Ital.; "Showdown for a Badman" 1972-Ital. (Hagen); "They Called Him Trinity" 1972-Ital./Span.; "Anything for a Friend" 1973-Ital. (Muller); "Fighting Fists of Shanghai Joe" 1973-Ital.; "Arizona Kid" 1974-Ital./Phil. (Coyote); "Drummer of Vengeance" 1974-Brit./Ital.

Mitchell, Guy (1925-). Films: "Those Redheads from Seattle" 1953 (Joe Keenan); "Red Garters" 1954 (Reb Randall); "The Wild Western-

ers" 1962 (Deputy Johnny Silver). ¶TV: *Overland Trail*—"West of Boston" 2-21-60 (Murdock); *Whispering Smith*—Regular 1961 (Detective George Romack).

Mitchell, Howard (1888-10/9/58). Films: "Wells Fargo" 1937; "Dodge City" 1939; "Wyoming" 1940 (Conductor); "Heart of the Rio Grande" 1942; "Colorado Pioneers" 1945; "Jesse James Rides Again" 1947-serial (Ward); "Son of Zorro" 1947-serial (Louie Wells).

Mitchell, Irving (1891-8/3/69). TV: *Maverick*—"Relic of Fort Tejon" 11-3-57 (Doe Nelson); *The Rifleman*—"Eight Hours to Die" 11-4-58 (Judge Harlow); *Hotel De Paree*—"Hard Luck for Sundance" 2-19-60.

Mitchell, James. Films: "Colorado Territory" 1949 (Duke Harris); "The Devil's Doorway" 1950 (Red Rock); "Stars in My Crown" 1950 (Dr. D.K. Harris, Jr.); "Oklahoma!" 1955 (Dream Curly); "The Peacemaker" 1956 (Terrall Butler).

Mitchell, Johnny. see Newland, Douglass.

Mitchell, Keith (1970-). TV: *Gun Shy*—Regular 1983 (Clovis).

Mitchell, Laurie (1922-). Films: "The Oklahoman" 1957 (Girls). ¶TV: *Wanted—Dead or Alive*—"Chain Gang" 12-12-59 (Belle Colter); *Man from Blackhawk*—"El Patron" 2-5-60 (Carol); *The Deputy*—"The Border Between" 3-12-60 (Lorrie); *Wagon Train*—"The Shad Bennington Story" 6-22-60 (Princess Fatima), "The Pearlie Garnet Story" 2-24-64 (June); *Bonanza*—"The Abduction" 10-29-60, "King of the Mountain" 2-23-64 (Julie); *Maverick*—"Triple Indemnity" 3-19-61 (Ellen); *Two Faces West*—"The Coward" 6-26-61; *Rawhide*—"The Prairie Elephant" 11-17-61 (Rosette); *Bronco*—"Moment of Doubt" 4-2-62 (Bess); *Laredo*—"Above the Law" 1-13-66; *The Virginian*—"Girl on the Glass Mountain" 12-28-66.

Mitchell, Les (1885-10/25/65). TV: *The Roy Rogers Show*—"Head for Cover" 10-21-56, "Paleface Justice" 11-18-56, "Fighting Sire" 12-16-56; *Sergeant Preston of the Yukon*—"Emergency on Scarface Flat" 12-13-56 (Basil Ogden).

Mitchell, Millard (1903-10/13/53). "The Gunfighter" 1950 (Sheriff Mark Street); "Winchester '73" 1950 (Johnny "High Spade" Williams); "The Naked Spur" 1953 (Jesse Tate).

Mitchell, Pat. Films: "Northwest Territory" 1951 (Billy Kellogg). ¶TV: *Wild Bill Hickok*—"The Lady

School Teacher" 10-2-51, "Civilian Clothes Story" 12-18-51; *The Range Rider*—"Outlaw Masquerade" 12-27-52; *The Gene Autry Show*—"The Carnival Comes West" 8-24-54.

Mitchell, Rhea (1893-9/16/57). Films: "The Colonel's Ward" 1912; "The Hidden Trail" 1912; "His Squaw" 1912; "A Frontier Wife" 1913; "An Indian's Gratitude" 1913; "An Indian's Honor" 1913; "Shorty Escapes Marriage" 1914 (Nell Holden); "In the Sage Brush Country" 1915; "Molly of the Mountains" 1915; "Mr. Silent Haskins" 1915; "On the Night Stage" 1915 (Belle Shields); "The Operator at Big Sandy" 1915; "The Scourge of the Desert" 1915; "Tools of Providence" 1915; "Overalls" 1916 (Bettina Warren); "The Ghost of the Rancho" 1918 (Mary Drew); "The Money Corral" 1919 (Janet Collins); "The Sleeping Lion" 1919 (Kate Billings); "A Ridin' Romeo" 1921 (Mabel Brentwood); "Danger Patrol" 1928 (Gladys Lawlor); "The Texas Rangers" 1936 (Passenger).

Mitchell, Steve (1926-). Films: "Seven Men from Now" 1956 (Fowler); "Terror in a Texas Town" 1958 (Keeno); "Nevada Smith" 1966 (Buckshot). ¶TV: *Sergeant Preston of the Yukon*—"Love and Honor" 5-3-56 (Barney); *Have Gun Will Travel*—"The Outlaw" 9-21-57; *Rawhide*—"Incident of the Calico Gun" 4-24-59 (Dave); *Tales of Wells Fargo*—"The Little Man" 5-18-59 (Frank Lucas); *The Deputy*—"The Border Between" 3-12-60 (Zimmer); *Bat Masterson*—"The Last of the Night Raiders" 11-24-60 (Tulsa Jack); *Gunslinger*—"Rampage" 3-16-61 (Corporal Blaney); *Hondo*—"Hondo and the Hanging Town" 12-8-67 (Morrison); *Wild Wild West*—"The Night of the Headless Woman" 1-5-68 (Ringo).

Mitchell, Thomas (1892-12/17/62). Films: "Stagecoach" 1939 (Dr. Josiah Boone); "The Outlaw" 1943 (Pat Garrett); "Buffalo Bill" 1944 (Ned Buntline); "Silver River" 1948 (John Plato Beck); "High Noon" 1952 (Jonas Henderson); "Destry" 1954 (Rags Barnaby). ¶TV: *Zane Grey Theater*—"A Handful of Ashes" 5-2-58, "Man Alone" 3-5-59 (Cason Thomas), "A Warm Day in Heaven" 3-23-61 (Nick Finn); *Laramie*—"Dark Verdict" 11-24-59 (Judge Hedrick); *Stagecoach West*—"Image of a Man" 1-31-61 (Ethan Blount).

Mitchell, Yvette. Films: "The Red Ace" 1917-serial; "The Robber" 1918; "The Border Terror" 1919; "The Fighting Brothers" 1919; "His Buddy" 1919; "The Last of His People" 1919

(Na-Ta-Le); "The Broncho Kid" 1920; "The Fightin' Terror" 1920; "Lahoma" 1920 (Red Fawn); "Straight from the Shoulder" 1921 (Gladys Martin); "The Kingfisher's Roost" 1922 (Betty Brownlee).

Mitchlll, Scoey (1930-). TV: *Here Come the Brides*—"A Far Cry from Yesterday" 9-26-69 (Sheriff Bond).

Mitchum, Christopher (1943-). Films: "Young Billy Young" 1969 (Kane's Son); "Chisum" 1970 (O'-Folliard); "Rio Lobo" 1970 (Tuscarora); "Big Jake" 1971 (Michael McCandles); "The Last Hard Men" 1976 (Hal Brickman); "Tombstone" 1993 (Ranch Hand).

Mitchum, James (1940-). Films: "Massacre at Grand Canyon" 1963-Ital. (Wes Evans); "Young Guns of Texas" 1963 (Morgan Coe); "The Tramplers" 1965-Ital. (Hoby Cordeen). ¶TV: *The High Chaparral*—"Time of Your Life" 9-19-69 (Johnny Keogh).

Mitchum, John (1919-). Films: "Perils of the Wilderness" 1956-serial (Brent); "Cole Younger, Gunfighter" 1958 (Bartender); "Cattle King" 1963 (Tex); "El Dorado" 1967 (Jason's Saloon Bartender); "The Way West" 1967 (Little Henry); "Bandolero!" 1968 (Bath House Customer); "Paint Your Wagon" 1969 (Jacob Woodling); "Chisum" 1970 (Baker); "One More Train to Rob" 1971 (Guard); "High Plains Drifter" 1973 (Warden); "The Hanged Man" TVM-1974 (Eubie Turpin); "Breakheart Pass" 1976 (Red Beard). ¶TV: *Sergeant Preston of the Yukon*—"Go Fever" 3-29-56 (Lefty Lamong); *Judge Roy Bean*—"Spirit of the Law" 4-11-56 (Clint Hammer); "Luck O' the Irish" 7-1-56 (Mac Larsen); *Gunsmoke*—"Sweet and Sour" 3-2-57 (Joe), "Texas Cowboys" 4-5-58 (Bob), "The Constable" 5-30-59 (Joe), "Perce" 9-30-61 (Norm), "Two of a Kind" 3-16-63 (Wills); *The Adventures of Rin Tin Tin*—"Boone's Commission" 3-22-57 (Sergeant); *Wyatt Earp*—"The Nice Ones Always Die First" 4-2-57 (Jake Stevens); *The Restless Gun*—"The Coward" 1-6-58 (Red), "Hiram Grover's Strike" 5-12-58 (Len); *Wagon Train*—"The Bill Tawnee Story" 2-12-58 (Norden); *Maverick*—"The Spanish Dancer" 12-14-58 (2nd Miner); *Riverboat*—Regular 1959-61 (Pickalong); *Bonanza*—"The Dark Gate" 3-11-62 (Lou Palmer), "A Hot Day for a Hanging" 10-14-62, "The Legacy" 12-15-63, "Thanks for Everything, Friend" 10-11-64 (Grimes), "An Earthquake Called Callahan" 4-

11-71 (Myers); *Tales of Wells Fargo*—"Who Lives by the Gun" 3-24-62 (Bartender); *Have Gun Will Travel*—"The Hunt" 2-3-62, "Genesis" 9-15-62 (Roderick Jefferson); *The Virginian*—"Echo from Another Day" 3-27-63 (Madison), "Walk in Another's Footsteps" 3-11-64 (Pooch), "Nobility of Kings" 11-10-65 (Bartender), "Blaze of Glory" 12-29-65 (Bartender); *Rawhide*—"Incident of the Rawhiders" 11-14-63 (Luke Rose); *Destry*—"Big Deal at Little River" 3-20-64 (Swanee); *F Troop*—Regular 1965-67 (Hoffenmueller); *The Legend of Jesse James*—"The Dead Man's Hand" 9-20-65 (Bartender); *Laredo*—"Yahoo" 9-30-65 (George); *Branded*—"Salute the Soldier Briefly" 10-24-65 (Slate); *The Road West*—"Pariah" 12-5-66 (Prisoner); *Pistols 'n' Petticoats*—12-17-66 (Claw); *Iron Horse*—"Grapes of Grass Valley" 10-21-67 (Zekel).

Mitchum, Robert (1917-). Films: "Bar 20" 1943 (Richard Adams); "Beyond the Last Frontier" 1943 (Trigger Dolan); "Border Patrol" 1943; "Colt Comrades" 1943; "False Colors" 1943 (Rip Austin); "Hoppy Serves a Writ" 1943 (Rigney); "The Leather Burners" 1943 (Randall); "The Lone Star Trail" 1943 (Ben Slocum); "Riders of the Deadline" 1943 (Drago); "Girl Rush" 1944 (Jimmy Smith); "Nevada" 1944 (Jim "Nevada" Lacy); "West of the Pecos" 1945 (Pecos Smith); "Pursued" 1947 (Jeb Rand); "Blood on the Moon" 1948 (Jim Garry); "Rachel and the Stranger" 1948 (Jim Fairways); "The Lusty Men" 1952 (Jeff McCloud); "River of No Return" 1954 (Matt Calder); "Track of the Cat" 1954 (Curt Bridges); "Man with the Gun" 1955 (Clint Tollinger); "Bandido" 1956 (Wilson); "The Wonderful Country" 1959 (Martin Brady); "El Dorado" 1967 (J.P. Harrah); "The Way West" 1967 (Dick Summers); "Five Card Stud" 1968 (Rev. Rudd); "Villa Rides" 1968 (Lee Arnold); "The Good Guys and the Bad Guys" 1969 (Flagg); "Young Billy Young" 1969 (Ben Kane); "The Wrath of God" 1972 (Van Horne); "Tombstone" 1993 (Narrator); "Dead Man" 1995 (John Dickinson).

Mitsoras, Demetrius J. Films: "Salomy Jane" 1914 (Gallaher); "The Lily of Poverty Flat" 1915 (Sanchez); "Just Squaw" 1919 (Romney); "When a Man Rides Alone" 1919 (Fernando); "The Challenge of the Law" 1920 (Fourchette); "The Flame of Hellgate" 1920 (Blunt's Gunman).

Mix, Art (Art Smith; George

Kesterson) (1896-12/7/72). Films: "Ace of Cactus Range" 1924 (U.S. Marshal Bob Cullen); "Rider of Mystery Ranch" 1924; "Romance of the Wasteland" 1924; "The Terror of Pueblo" 1924; "Riders of Border Bay" 1925; "Roped by Radio" 1925; "The Man from the Rio Grande" 1926; "Salt Lake Trail" 1926; "Shadow Ranger" 1926; "Wild Horse Stampede" 1926 (Henchman); "Loco Luck" 1927; "West of the Rockies" 1929 (Bob Strong); "Breed of the West" 1930; "Desert Vultures" 1930; "Fighting Thru" 1930; "The Lonesome Tail" 1930 (Slim); "Men Without Law" 1930; "Sagebrush Politics" 1930; "Battling with Buffalo Bill" 1931-serial; "Border Law" 1931; "Pueblo Terror" 1931 (Buck Peters); "The Boiling Point" 1932; "Border Devils" 1932 (Bud Brandon); "Cornered" 1932; "Daring Danger" 1932 (Gang Member); "Destry Rides Again" 1932 (Thomas J. Destry, Jr.); "Law and Order" 1932; "Lawless Valley" 1932; "Mason of the Mounted" 1932; "The Riding Tornado" 1932; "The Texan" 1932; "Young Blood" 1932 (Ed); "The Dude Bandit" 1933 (Art); "The King of the Wild Horses" 1933 (Cowboy); "Lariats and Six-shooters" 1933; "Sagebrush Trail" 1933 (Henchman); "Strawberry Roan" 1933 (Cowboy); "The Trail Drive" 1933; "Treason" 1933 (1st Lieutenant); "The Fighting Ranger" 1934 (Kelso); "Honor of the Range" 1934; "The Law of the Wild" 1934-serial; "Mystery Mountain" 1934-serial; "The Prescott Kid" 1934; "Rawhide Terror" 1934 (Al Blake); "The Red Rider" 1934-serial; "The Way of the West" 1934 (Tim); "The Westerner" 1934 (Deputy); "The Cowboy and the Bandit" 1935 (Luke Short); "Cyclone of the Saddle" 1935 (Pioneer); "Five Bad Men" 1935 (Bad Man); "The Ghost Rider" 1935 (Guard); "Heir to Trouble" 1935; "Pals of the Range" 1935 (Dick); "Powdersmoke Range" 1935 (Rube); "Rustlers of Red Dog" 1935-serial (Waiter/Henchman); "Square Shooter" 1935; "Swifty" 1935 (Squid); "Western Frontier" 1935; "Code of the Range" 1936 (Gunman); "End of the Trail" 1936 (Red Allen); "The Fugitive Sheriff" 1936; "Lucky Terror" 1936 (Scooter); "The Phantom Rider" 1936-serial; "Rio Grande Ranger" 1936; "The Unknown Ranger" 1936; "Winds of the Wasteland" 1936; "Yellow Dust" 1936; "The Big Show" 1937; "Code of the Range" 1937; "The Devil's Saddle Legion" 1937; "Dodge City Trail" 1937 (Blackie); "Empty Hol-

sters" 1937; "The Old Wyoming Trail" 1937 (Carson); "One Man Justice" 1937 (Bull); "Outlaws of the Prairie" 1937 (Lawton); "Prairie Thunder" 1937; "Trapped" 1937; "Two-Fisted Sheriff" 1937 (Bud); "Two Gun Law" 1937 (Cullen); "Way Out West" 1937 (Man in Audience); "Westbound Mail" 1937 (Shorty); "Yodelin' Kid from Pine Ridge" 1937; "The Bad Man of Brimstone" 1938; "Call of the Rockies" 1938 (Trigger); "Cattle Raiders" 1938 (Keno); "The Great Adventures of Wild Bill Hickok" 1938; "Law of the Plains" 1938 (Grant); "Rio Grande" 1938 (Durkin); "The Singing Outlaw" 1938; "South of Arizona" 1938 (Santos); "West of Cheyenne" 1938 (Cinch); "Arizona Legion" 1939; "Overland with Kit Carson" 1939-serial; "Rovin' Tumbleweeds" 1939; "Spoilers of the Range" 1939 (Santos); "The Stranger from Texas" 1939; "The Taming of the West" 1939 (Blackie); "The Thundering West" 1939 (Kirk); "Adventures of Red Ryder" 1940-serial; "Bad Man from Red Butte" 1940 (Townsman); "Beyond the Sacramento" 1940 (1st Henchman); "Covered Wagon Days" 1940; "Covered Wagon Trails" 1940; "The Golden Trail" 1940; "Melody Ranch" 1940; "The Westerner" 1940 (Seth Tucker); "Across the Sierras" 1941; "Hands Across the Rockies" 1941; "Nevada City" 1941; "North from the Lone Star" 1941; "Bad Men of the Hills" 1942; "Bullets for Bandits" 1942; "Down Rio Grande Way" 1942; "In Old California" 1942; "Overland Stagecoach" 1942; "Overland to Deadwood" 1942; "Pardon My Gun" 1942; "Prairie Gunsmoke" 1942; "Ridin' Down the Canyon" 1942; "Riding Through Nevada" 1942; "Shut My Big Mouth" 1942 (Bandit); "A Tornado in the Saddle" 1942; "Hail to the Rangers" 1943; "Hoppy Serves a Writ" 1943; "Outlaws of Stampede Pass" 1943; "Saddles and Sagebrush" 1943; "Silver City Raiders" 1943 (Slim); "Thundering Trails" 1943; "Mystery Man" 1944 (Bank Robber); "Gangster's Den" 1945 (Customer); "Roaring Westward" 1949; "The Painted Hills" 1951 (Pilot Pete).

Mix, Olive. Films: "The Cowboy's Best Girl" 1912; "The Scapegoat" 1912; "Saved from a Vigilantes" 1913.

Mix, Ruth (1912-9/21/77). Films: "Tex" 1926; "That Girl Oklahoma" 1926; "The Little Boss" 1927; "Red Fork Range" 1931 (Ruth Farrel); "Fighting Pioneers" 1935 (Wa-No-Na); "Gunfire" 1935 (Mary Vance);

"Saddle Aces" 1935 (Jane Langdon); "Tonto Kid" 1935 (Nancy Cahill); "Custer's Last Stand" 1936-serial (Mrs. Elizabeth Custer); "The Riding Avenger" 1936 (Chita).

Mix, Tom (1880-10/12/40). Films: "On the Little Big Horn or Cuser's Last Stand" 1909; "Ranch Life in the Great Southwest" 1909; "An Indian Wife's Devotion" 1910; "The Long Trail" 1910; "Pride of the Range" 1910; "The Range Rider" 1910; "The Trimming of Parradise Gulch" 1910; "The Bully of Bingo Gulch" 1911 (Pop Lynd); "The Cowboy and the Shrew" 1911 (Hank Wilson); "Dad's Girls" 1911; "In Old California When the Gringos Came" 1911; "In the Days of Gold" 1911; "Kit Carson's Wooing" 1911; "The Man from the East" 1911; "Romance of the Rio Grande" 1911; "The Rose of Old St. Augustine" 1911 (Black Hawk); "Saved by the Pony Express" 1911; "The Schoolmaster of Mariposa" 1911; "The Telltale Knife" 1911; "Told in Colorado" 1911; "The Totem Mark" 1911; "Western Hearts" 1911; "Wheels of Justice" 1911; "Why the Sheriff Is a Bachelor" 1911 (Sheriff Joe Davis); "The Cowboy's Best Girl" 1912; "A Reconstructed Rebel" 1912; "The Scapegoat" 1912; "An Apache Gratitude" 1913; "Buster's Little Game" 1913; "A Child of the Prairies" 1913 (Fred Watson); "Cupid in the Cow Camp" 1913; "Dishwash Dick's Counterfeit" 1913; "The Escape of Jim Dolan" 1913; "The Good Indian" 1913; "His Father's Deputy" 1913; "How Betty Made Good" 1913; "How It Happened" 1913; "Howlin' Jones" 1913; "Juggling with Fate" 1913; "The Law and the Outlaw" 1913; "The Life Timer" 1913; "Local Color" 1913; "Made a Coward" 1913; "The Marshal's Capture" 1913; "Mother Love vs. Gold" 1913; "A Muddle in Horse Thieves" 1913; "The Noisy Six" 1913; "Physical Culture on the Quarter Circle V Bar" 1913; "The Range Law" 1913; "The Rejected Lover's Luck" 1913 (the Indian); "Religion and Gun Practice" 1913 (Kill Kullen); "Sallie's Sure Shot" 1913; "Saved from a Vigilantes" 1913 (Squire Beasley); "The Schoolmarm's Shooting Match" 1913; "The Sheriff and the Rustler" 1913; "The Sheriff of Yawapai County" 1913; "The Shotgun Man and the Stage Driver" 1913; "The Silver Grindstone" 1913; "The Stolen Moccasins" 1913; "Taming a Tenderfoot" 1913; "The Taming of Texas Pete" 1913; "That Mail Order Suit" 1913; "Buffalo Hunting" 1914; "Cactus Jake, Heart-Breaker" 1914; "Chip of the Flying U" 1914 (Chip);

"The Fifty Man" 1914; "The Flower of Faith" 1914; "A Friend in Need" 1914; "The Going of the White Swan" 1914; "His Fight" 1914; "In Defiance of the Law" 1914; "In the Days of the Thundering Herd" 1914 (Tom Mingle); "Jimmy Hayes and Muriel" 1914 (Jimmy Hayes); "The Lonesome Trail" 1914; "The Man from the East" 1914; "The Mexican" 1914; "A Militant School Ma'am" 1914; "The Moving Picture Cowboy" 1914; "The Ranger's Romance" 1914; "The Real Thin in Cowboys" 1914 (Wallace Carey); "The Rival Stage Lines" 1914; "Saved by a Watch" 1914; "The Scapegoat" 1914; "The Sheriff's Reward" 1914; "The Telltale Knife" 1914; "Wade Brent Pays" 1914; "The Way of the Redman" 1914; "When the Cook Fell Ill" 1914; "When the West Was Young" 1914; "Why the Sheriff Is a Bachelor" 1914; "The Wilderness Mail" 1914; "An Arizona Wooing" 1915; "Athletic Ambitions" 1915; "The Auction Sale of Run-Down Ranch" 1915; "Bad Man Bobbs" 1915; "Bill Haywood, Producer" 1915 (Bill Haywood); "The Brave Deserve the Fair" 1915; "Cactus Jim's Shopgirl" 1915; "The Chef at Circle G" 1915; "A Child of the Prairie" 1915; "The Child, the Dog, and the Villain" 1915; "The Conversion of Smiling Tom" 1915; "The Face at the Window" 1915; "The Foreman of the Bar-Z Ranch" 1915; "Forked Trails" 1915; "Getting a Start in Life" 1915; "The Girl and the Mail Bag" 1915; "The Gold Dust and the Squaw" 1915; "The Grizzly Gulch Chariot Race" 1915; "Harold's Bad Man" 1915; "The Heart of the Sheriff" 1915; "Heart's Desire" 1915; "Her Slight Mistake" 1915; "How Weary Went Wooing" 1915; "The Impersonation of Tom" 1915; "Jack's Pals" 1915; "A Lucky Deal" 1915; "The Man from Texas" 1915; "Ma's Girls" 1915; "A Matrimonial Boomerang" 1915; "Mrs. Murphy's Cooks" 1915; "Never Again" 1915; "On the Eagle Trail" 1915; "The Outlaw's Bride" 1915; "Pals in Blue" 1915; "The Parson Who Fled West" 1915; "The Puny Soul of Peter Rand" 1915; "The Race for a Gold Mine" 1915; "The Range Girl and the Cowboy" 1915; "Roping a Bride" 1915; "Sagebrush Tom" 1915; "Saved by Her Horse" 1915; "The Stagecoach Driver and the Girl" 1915; "The Stagecoach Guard" 1915; "The Taking of Mustang Pete" 1915; "The Tenderfoot's Triumph" 1915; "With the Aid of the Law" 1915; "An Angelic Attitude" 1916; "Along the Border" 1916; "A Bear of a Story" 1916; "The Canby Hill Outlaws" 1916; "A Close Call" 1916; "A Corner in Water" 1916; "The Cowpuncher's Peril" 1916; "Crooked Trails" 1916; "The Desert Calls Its Own" 1916; "An Eventful Evening" 1916; "The Girl of Gold Gulch" 1916; "Going West to Make Good" 1916; "The Golden Thought" 1916; "In the Days of Daring" 1916; "Legal Advice" 1916; "Local Color" 1916; "Making Good" 1916; "The Man Within" 1916; "A Mistake in Rustlers" 1916; "Mistakes Will Happen" 1916; "A Mix-Up in Movies" 1916; "The Passing of Pete" 1916; "The Pony Express Rider" 1916; "The Raiders" 1916; "Roping a Sweetheart" 1916; "The Sheriff's Blunder" 1916; "The Sheriff's Duty" 1916; "Shooting Up the Movies" 1916; "Starring in Western Stuff" 1916; "Taking a Chance" 1916; "The Taming of Groucho Bill" 1916; "Tom's Sacrifice" 1916; "Tom's Strategy" 1916; "Too Many Chefs" 1916; "Trilby's Love Disaster" 1916; "Twisted Trails" 1916; "A Western Masquerade" 1916; "When Cupid Slipped" 1916; "Durand of the Bad Lands" 1917 (Clem Allison); "The Heart of Texas Ryan" 1917 (Jack Parker); "Hearts and Saddles" 1917; "The Luck That Jealousy Brought" 1917; "The Saddle Girth" 1917; "A Soft Tenderfoot" 1917; "Tom and Jerry Mix" 1917; "Ace High" 1918 (Jean Rivard); "Cupid's Round Up" 1918 (Larry Kelly); "Fame and Fortune" 1918 (Clay Burgess); "Mr. Logan, U.S.A." 1918 (Mr. Logan); "Six-Shooter Andy" 1918 (Andy Crawford); "Western Blood" 1918 (Tex Wilson); "The Coming of the Law" 1919 (Kent Hollis); "The Feud" 1919 (Jere Lynch/Jere Smith); "Fighting for Gold" 1919 (Jack Kilmeny); "Hell Roarin' Reform" 1919 (Tim); "Rough-Riding Romance" 1919 (Phineas Dobbs); "Slim Higgins" 1919; "Treat 'Em Rough" 1919 (Ned Ferguson); "The Wilderness Trail" 1919 (Donald MacTavish); "The Cyclones" 1920 (Sgt. Tim Ryerson); "The Daredevil" 1920 (Timothy Atkinson); "Days of Daring" 1920; "Desert Love" 1920 (Buck Marston, Jr.); "Prairie Trails" 1920 (Tex Benton); "The Terror" 1920 (Bat Carson); "The Texan" 1920 (Tex Benton); "Three Gold Coins" 1920 (Bob Fleming/Bad Pat Dugan); "The Untamed" 1920 (Whistling Dan); "Big Town Round-Up" 1921 (Larry McBride); "Hands Off" 1921 (Tex Roberts); "The Night Horsemen" 1921 (Whistling Dan); "A Ridin' Romeo" 1921 (Jim Rose); "The Rough Diamond" 1921 (Hank Sherman); "Trailin'" 1921 (Anthony Woodbury); "Arabia" 1922 (Billy Evans); "Catch My Smoke" 1922 (Bob Stratton); "Do and Dare" 1922 (Kit Carson Boone/Henry Boone); "Fighting Streak" 1922 (Andrew Lanning); "For Big Stakes" 1922 (Clean-Up Sudden); "Just Tony" 1922 (Red Ferris); "Sky High" 1922 (Grant Newburg); "Up and Going" 1922 (David Brandon); "Eyes of the Forest" 1923 (Bruce Thornton); "The Lone Star Ranger" 1923 (Duane); "Romance Land" 1923 (Pep Hawkins); "Soft Boiled" 1923 (Tom Steele); "Stepping Fast" 1923 (Grant Malvern); "Three Jumps Ahead" 1923 (Steve Clancy); "The Deadwood Coach" 1924 (Orphan); "The Heart Buster" 1924 (Tod Walton); "The Last of the Duanes" 1924 (Buck Duane); "Mile-A-Minute Romeo" 1924 (Lucky Bill); "North of Hudson Bay" 1924 (Michael Dane); "Oh, You Tony!" 1924 (Tom Masters); "Teeth" 1924 (Dave Deering); "The Best Bad Man" 1925 (Hugh Nichols); "A Child of the Prairie" 1925 (Square Deal Tom); "The Everlasting Whisper" 1925; "The Lucky Horseshoe" 1925 (Tom Foster); "The Rainbow Trail" 1925 (John Shefford/Lassiter); "Riders of the Purple Sage" 1925 (Jim Lassiter); "The Canyon of Light" 1926; "The Great K & A Train Robbery" 1926 (Tom Gordon); "Hard-Boiled" 1926 (Tom Bouden); "My Own Pal" 1926 (Tom O'Hara); "No Man's Gold" 1926 (Tom Stone); "Tony Runs Wild" 1926 (Tom Trent); "The Yankee Senor" 1926 (Paul Wharton); "Arizona Wildcat" 1927 (Tom Phelan); "Broncho Twister" 1927 (Tom Mason); "The Circus Ace" 1927 (Tom Terry); "The Last Trail" 1927 (Tom Dane); "Outlaws of Red River" 1927 (Tom Morley); "Silver Valley" 1927 (Tom Tracey); "Tumbling River" 1927 (Tom Gier); "Daredevil's Reward" 1928 (Tom Hardy); "Hello Cheyenne" 1928 (Tom Remington); "A Horseman of the Plains" 1928 (Tom Swift); "King Cowboy" 1928 (Tex Rogers); "Painted Post" 1928 (Tom Blake); "Son of the Golden West" 1928 (Tom Handy); "The Big Diamond Robbery" 1929 (Tom Markham); "The Drifter" 1929 (Tom McCall); "Outlawed" 1929 (Tom Manning); "Flaming Guns" 1932 (Tom Malone); "My Pal, the King" 1932 (Tom Reed); "Rider of Death Valley" 1932 (Tom Rigby); "Texas Bad Man" 1932 (Tom Logan); "The Fourth Horseman" 1933 (Tom Martin); "Hidden Gold" 1933 (Tom); "Rustlers' Roundup" 1933 (Tom Lawson); "Terror Trail" 1933 (Tom Munroe); "The

Miracle Rider" 1935-serial (Tom Mogan).

Mobley, Mary Ann (1938-). TV: *The Virginian*—"Vengeance Trail" 1-4-67 (Ellie Willard); *Iron Horse*—"Shadow Run" 1-30-67 (Susan); *Custer*—"Sabres in the Sun" 9-6-67 (Ann L'Andry).

Mobley, Roger. Films: "The Comancheros" 1961 (Bub Schofield); "The Apple Dumpling Gang Rides Again" 1979. ¶TV: *Fury*—Regular 1955-60 (Packy Lambert); *Buckskin*—"Mr. Rush's Secretary" 1-19-59 (Noah Wesley); *Wagon Train*—"The Ben Courtney Story" 1-28-59 (Michael), "The Sam Elder Story" 1-18-61 (Tod), "The Nancy Palmer Story" 3-8-61, "The Clementine Jones Story" 10-25-61 (Homer), "The Jeff Hartfield Story" 2-14-62 (Stevey Brewster), "The Caroline Casteel Story" 9-26-62 (Jamie Casteel), "The Michael McGoo Story" 3-20-63 (Humphrey); *The Outlaws*—"Blind Spot" 3-30-61 (Davey Morgan); *Gunsmoke*—"Miss Kitty" 10-14-61 (Thad); *The Tall Man*—"St. Louis Woman" 1-20-62 (David Harper); *Cheyenne*—"The Idol" 1-29-62 (Gabe Morse), "Sweet Sam" 10-8-62 (Billy); *Alcoa Premiere*—"Second Chance" 3-13-62 (Lonnie Dunlap); *Frontier Circus*—"Mighty Like Rogues" 4-5-62 (Andrew Jackson Jukes); *The Virginian*—"Throw a Long Rope" 10-3-62 (Homer Tatum); *Wide Country*—"Journey Down a Dusty Road" 10-4-62 (Billy Joe Perry); *Empire*—"When the Gods Laugh" 12-18-62 (Kieran Haskell); *Death Valley Days*—"Deadly Decision" 10-13-63 (Steve McKinney); *The Dakotas*—"Feud at Snake River" 4-29-63 (Christopher); *Destry*—"Red Brady's Kid" 4-24-64 (Toby Brady); *Walt Disney Presents*—"Gallegher" 1965-67 (Gallegher).

Mock, Laurie (1946-). Films: "War Party" 1965 (Nicoma). ¶TV: *Great Adventure*—"Kentucky's Bloody Ground"/"The Siege of Boonesborough" 4-3-64 & 4-10-64 (Frances Callaway); *Cimarron Strip*—"The Last Wolf" 12-14-67 (Mary Varner); *The High Chaparral*—"A Joyful Noise" 3-24-68 (Maria); *Gunsmoke*—"The Judas Gun" 1-19-70 (Janie Bolden).

Modio, Jolando. Films: "A Stranger in Town" 1966-U.S./Ital. (Cica); "Face to Face" 1967-Ital.; "One After Another" 1968-Span./Ital.; "Sartana in the Valley of Death" 1970-Ital. (Esther); "He Was Called the Holy Ghost" 1972-Ital.

Moede, Titus. TV: *Have Gun Will Travel*—"Hobson's Choice" 4-7-62 (Thurber's Helper).

Moehring, Kansas (1897-10/3/68). Films: "Out of Luck" 1923 (Kid Hogan); "Shootin' for Love" 1923 (Tex Carson); "Heart of the North" 1938 (Trapper); "Down Texas Way" 1942 (Luke); "The Man from the Rio Grande" 1943 (Art Homas); "Outlaws of Stampede Pass" 1943; "Wild Horse Rustlers" 1943; "Land of the Outlaws" 1944; "Gun Smoke" 1945; "Trailing Danger" 1947; "Frontier Agent" 1948; "The Cariboo Trail" 1950 (Stage Driver); "Colt .45" 1950.

Moffatt, Donald (1930-). Films: "The Devil and Miss Sarah" TVM-1971 (Appleton); "The Great Northfield, Minnesota Raid" 1972 (Manning); "Showdown" 1973 (Art Williams); "The Call of the Wild" TVM-1976 (Simpson); "Houston: The Legend of Texas" TVM-1986 (Colonel John Allen); "Desperado" TVM-1987 (Malloy). ¶TV: *Here Come the Brides*—"Next Week, East Lynne" 10-17-69 (Marlowe); *Bonanza*—"The Trouble with Amy" 1-25-70 (Judge), "Face of Fear" 11-14-71 (Thatcher); *Lancer*—"The Lion and the Lamb" 2-3-70 (Porter); *The High Chaparral*—"The Lieutenant" 2-27-70 (Simmonds); *Gunsmoke*—"The Foundling" 2-11-74 (Joseph Graham); *The New Land*—Regular 1974 (Lundstrom); *The Chisholms*—2-2-80 (Enos), "Death in the Sierras" 2-16-80 (Enos).

Mohica, Victor (1933-). Films: "Showdown" 1973 (Big Eye); "Little House on the Prairie" TVM-1974 (Sodat Du Chene); "The Macahans" TVM-1976 (Vic); "The Deerslayer" TVM-1978 (Rivenoak); "California Gold Rush" TVM-1981 (Joaquin Murieta).

Mohner, Carl (1921-). Films: "Last Gun" 1964-Ital.; "Man with the Golden Pistol" 1966-Span./Ital. (Larry Kling); "Thirty Winchesters for El Diablo" 1967-Ital. (Jeff Benson).

Mohr, Gerald (1914-11/10/68). Films: "King of the Cowboys" 1943 (Maurice); "Heaven Only Knows" 1947 (Treason); "Two Guys from Texas" 1948 (Link Jessup); "The Duel at Silver Creek" 1952 (Rod Lacey); "The Buckskin Lady" 1957 (Slinger). ¶TV: *Cheyenne*—"Rendezvous at Red Rock" 2-21-56 (Pat Keogh), "Incident at Dawson Flats" 1-9-61 (Elmer Bostrum); *Zane Grey Theater*—"A Quiet Sunda in San Ardo" 11-23-56 (Veringo); *Maverick*—"The Quick and the Dead" 12-8-57 (Doc Holliday), "The Burning Sky" 2-23-58 (Johnny Bolero), "Seed of Deception" 4-13-58 (Doc Holliday), "Es-

cape to Tampico" 10-26-58 (Steve Corbett), "You Can't Beat the Percentage" 10-4-59 (Dave Lindell), "Mano Nera" 10-23-60 (Giacomo Beretti), "Deadly Image" 3-12-61 (Gus Tellson); *The Californians*—"The Coward" 1-7-58; *Sugarfoot*—"Hideout" 4-1-58 (Jasper Monday), "Outlaw Island" 11-24-59 (Baron); *Tombstone Territory*—"The Outcast" 4-23-58 (Doc Holliday); *Wanted—Dead or Alive*—"Till Death Do Us Part" 11-8-58 (Leo); *Bronco*—"The Long Ride Back" 11-18-58 (Ricky Cortez), "The Invaders" 1-23-61 (Mace Tilsey), "Then the Mountains" 4-30-62 (Bohannon); *The Texan*—"The Duchess of Denver" 1-5-59 (Col. Garson); *Rough Riders*—"The Injured" 4-9-59 (Ben Sabier); *Rawhide*—"Incident of the Judas Trap" 6-5-59 (Brad Morgan); *Bat Masterson*—"Promised Land" 6-10-59 (Courtney Shepherd), "Run for Your Money" 3-2-61 (Crimp Ward); *Johnny Ringo*—"Love Affair" 12-17-59 (Barney Guisom); *Tales of Wells Fargo*—"The Easterner" 1-11-60 (Dan Mulvaney); *The Alaskans*—"Gold Fever" 1-17-60 (Swiftwater Charlie); *The Deputy*—"Final Payment" 3-19-60 (Dustin Groat); *Overland Trail*—"The Baron Comes Back" 5-15-60 (James Addison Reavis); *Stagecoach West*—"The Unwanted" 10-25-60 (Ben Marble); *The Outlaws*—"Rape of Red Sky" 10-27-60 (Beau Latimer), "The Fortune Stone" 12-15-60 (Beau Latimer), "No Luck on Friday" 11-30-61 (Lopez); *Bonanza*—"The Abduction" 10-29-60 (Phil Reed), "Found Child" 10-24-65 (Collins), "A Girl Named George" 1-14-68 (Cato Troxell); *The Rifleman*—"Squeeze Play" 12-3-62 (Willard Prescott); *Laredo*—"Split the Difference" 4-7-67 (Gypsy John Guente); *Death Valley Days*—"The Firebrand" 4-30-66 (Andres Pico); *Pistols 'n' Petticoats*—11-12-66 (1st Card Player); *Iron Horse*—"The Golden Web" 3-27-67 (Prescott Webb); *The Big Valley*—"Flight from San Miguel" 4-28-69 (Raoul Mendez).

Mojave, King (-/3/23/73). Films: "Public Cowboy No. 1" 1937 (Steve).

Mojica, Jose (1896-9/20/74). Films: "When Love Laughs" 1933-Mex.

Molieri, Lillian. Films: "South of the Rio Grande" 1945 (Dolores); "South of Caliente" 1951 (Gypsy Dancer); "Horizons West" 1952 (Teresa); "The Three Outlaws" 1956. ¶TV: *The Cisco Kid*—"He Couldn't Quit" 4-24-54.

Molina, Alfred. Films: "Maverick" 1994 (Angel); "White Fang 2:

Myth of the White Wolf" 1994 (Rev. Leland Drury); "Dead Man" 1995 (Trading Post Missionary).

Molina, Joe (1899-12/16/77). Films: "Zorro's Fighting Legion" 1939-serial (Tarmac); "Comanche Station" 1960 (Comanche Chief).

Molina, Mariano Vidal. Films: "Secret of Captain O'Hara" 1965-Span. (Major Brooks); "Two Thousand Dollars for Coyote" 1965-Span.; "Five Giants from Texas" 1966-Ital./ Span.; "White Comanche" 1967-Ital./Span./U.S.; "Awkward Hands" 1968-Span./Ital.; "Challenge of the Mackennas" 1969-Ital./Span.; "Gentleman Killer" 1969-Span./Ital.; "More Dollars for the MacGregors" 1970-Ital./Span.; "Reverend Colt" 1970-Ital./Span.; "My Colt, Not Yours" 1972-Span./Fr./Ital.

Moll, Richard (1943-). Films: "Bret Maverick" TVM-1981 (Sloate). ¶TV: *How the West Was Won*—"The Enemy" 2-5-79 (Mose); *Best of the West*—"The Prisoner" 9-17-81 (Prisoner).

Moncries, Edward (1859-3/22/ 38). Films: "Western Hearts" 1921 (George Adams).

Mondo, Peggy. TV: *Lawman*—"The Man Behind the News" 5-13-62 (Flora).

Mong, William V. (1875-12/10/ 40). Films: "Told in the Rockies" 1915; "Two Men of Sandy Bar" 1916 (Don Jose de Castro); "The Flame of the West" 1918; "The Law of the Great Northwest" 1918 (Petain Monest); "Put Up Your Hands" 1919 (Highball Hazelitt); "The Coast of Opportunity" 1920 (Old Miner); "The Winding Trail" 1921; "The Big Trail" 1930 (Wellmore); "Gun Smoke" 1931 (Strike Jackson); "The Fighting Fool" 1932 (Uncle John Lyman); "Fighting for Justice" 1932 (Gafford); "Silent Men" 1933 (Oscar Sikes); "Massacre" 1934 (Grandy); "Square Shooter" 1935 (Root); "Whispering Smith Speaks" 1935 (Blake); "The Last of the Mohicans" 1936 (Sacham); "The Painted Desert" 1938 (Heist); "Ridin' on a Rainbow" 1941.

Monk, Thomas (1877-10/28/ 56). Films: "Courage of the West" 1937 (Secretary Seward).

Monroe, Del. TV: *Wyatt Earp*—"John Clum, Fighting Editor" 4-12-60 (Pete Spence); *The Dakotas*—"Justice at Eagle's Nest" 3-11-63 (Bailiff); *The Legend of Jesse James*—"The Man Who Killed Jesse" 12-27-65 (Tron); *Gunsmoke*—"My Father, My Son" 4-23-66 (Will Jeffords), "Drago" 11-22-

71 (Flagg), "Kitty's Love Affair" 10-22-73 (Coots); *Lancer*—"The Prodigal" 11-12-68, "Warburton's Edge" 2-4-69 (Driscoll), "Dream of Falcons" 4-7-70 (2nd Cowboy).

Monroe, Marilyn (1926-8/5/ 62). Films: "Ticket to Tomahawk" 1950 (Clara); "River of No Return" 1954 (Kay Weston); "The Misfits" 1961 (Roslyn Taber).

Monroe, Tom. Films: "Powder River Rustlers" 1949 (Guard); "Border Rangers" 1950 (Hackett); "Border Treasure" 1950 (Dimmick); "The Cariboo Trail" 1950 (Bartender); "I Shot Billy the Kid" 1950 (Maxwell); "Rustlers on Horseback" 1950 (Guard); "The Half-Breed" 1952 (Russell); "Horizons West" 1952 (Jim Clawson); "Rose of Cimarron" 1952 (Mike Finch); "The Command" 1953 (Nikirk); "El Paso Stampede" 1953 (Marty); "The Homesteaders" 1953 (Jake); "Man with the Steel Whip" 1954-serial (Road Worker); "The Far Horizons" 1955; "Giant" 1956 (Guard); "Shoot-Out at Medicine Bend" 1957; "War Drums" 1957 (Dutch Herman); "Rio Bravo" 1959 (Henchman); "Westbound" 1959. ¶TV: *The Gene Autry Show*—"Gray Dude" 12-3-50, "The Peace Maker" 12-17-50, "Frontier Guard" 10-13-51, "Killer's Trail" 10-27-51; *Wild Bill Hickok*—"Medicine Show" 12-25-51, "Golden Rainbow" 12-9-52; *The Cisco Kid*—"Face of Death" 2-16-52, "Lost City of the Incas" 3-29-52; *The Range Rider*—"The Holy Terror" 3-22-52; *Wyatt Earp*—"The Pinkertons" 3-20-56, "Siege at Little Alamo" 2-5-57 (Henchman), "Wyatt Earp Rides Shotgun" 2-18-58 (Dan Purvis), "Frontier Woman" 11-25-58 (Jed Carney), "The Arizona Lottery" 2-16-60 (Dade); *Judge Roy Bean*—"Bad Medicine" 6-1-56 (Stage Driver), "The Defense Rests" 6-1-56 (Marshal), "Lone Star Killer" 8-1-56 (Curley); *Maverick*—"Rope of Cards" 1-19-58 (Slim); *Tales of Wells Fargo*—"The Break" 5-19-58 (Gill); *Wagon Train*—"The Ruttledge Munroe Story" 5-21-58 (Henshaw); *The Tall Man*—"Where Is Sylvia?" 9-23-61 (Jake); *The Big Valley*—"A Day of Terror" 12-12-66, "Presumed Dead" 10-7-68 (Guard #2).

Monroe, Vaughn (1911-5/21/ 73). Films: "Singing Guns" 1950 (Rhiannon/John Gwenn); "Toughest Man in Arizona" 1952 (Matt Landry). ¶TV: *Bonanza*—"The Wooing of Abigail Jones" 3-4-62 (Hank Meyers).

Monson, Bee. Films: "The Sheriff of Hope Eternal" 1921 (Marybelle Sawyer).

Montague, Fred (1864-7/3/19). Films: "The Call of the North" 1914 (Jock Wilson); "The Squaw Man" 1914 (Mr. Petrie); "Where the Trail Divides" 1914 (Rev. John Eaton); "The Hidden Law" 1916 (Henry Richter); "The Red Stain" 1916; "The Fighting Grin" 1918 (Amos Meredith); "A Western Wooing" 1919.

Montague, Lee (1927-). Films: "The Singer Not the Song" 1961-Brit. (Pepe).

Montague, Monte (1891-4/6/ 59). Films: "Peaceful Peters" 1922 (Cactus Collins); "The Three Buckaroos" 1922 (Athor); "A Western Demon" 1922 (Joe Dalton); "The Secret of the Pueblo" 1923; "Wild Horse Stampede" 1926 (Henchman); "Hey! Hey! Cowboy" 1927 (Hank Mander, Decker's Foreman); "The One-Man Trail" 1927; "The Rambling Ranger" 1927 (Sheriff Boy); "Range Courage" 1927 (Bart Allan); "Rough and Ready" 1927 (Rawhide Barton); "Somewhere in Sonora" 1927 (Kettle Belly Simpson); "Spurs and Saddles" 1927 (Stage Driver); "Clearing the Trail" 1928 (Tramp); "The Danger Rider" 1928 (Scar Bailey); "The Wild West Show" 1928 (the Goof); "Courtin' Wildcats" 1929 (McLaren); "King of the Rodeo" 1929 (Weasel); "The Lonesome Tail" 1930 (Gila Red); "Trigger Tricks" 1930 (Nick Dalgus); "Quick Trigger Lee" 1931 (Sammy Wales); "Come on, Danger!" 1932; "Clancy of the Mounted" 1933-serial; "The Red Rider" 1934-serial (Al Abel); "Rocky Rhodes" 1934 (Jack); "Outlawed Guns" 1935; "Rustlers of Red Dog" 1935-serial (Kruger); "Stormy" 1935 (Cowboy); "Song of the Saddle" 1936 (Simon Bannion); "Treachery Rides the Range" 1936 (Nebraska Bill); "The Californian" 1937 (Bradford); "Git Along, Little Dogies" 1937; "Guns of the Pecos" 1937 (Luke); "The Painted Stallion" 1937-serial (Tanner); "Phantom of Santa Fe" 1937; "Roll Along, Cowboy" 1937 (Bixby); "Wells Fargo" 1937 (Prospector); "The Law West of Tombstone" 1938 (Clayt McQuinn); "Pals of the Saddle" 1938; "Renegade Ranger" 1938 (Monte); "Riders of the Black Hills" 1938 (Sam); "Arizona Legion" 1939 (Dawson); "Allegheny Uprising" 1939 (Morris); "The Lone Ranger Rides Again" 1939-serial (Tucker); "Racketeers of the Range" 1939 (Larkin); "Timber Stampede" 1939 (Jake); "Trouble in Sundown" 1939 (Hartman); "Legion of the Lawless" 1940 (Borden); "Prairie Law" 1940 (Abe Sully); "Virginia City" 1940 (Stage Driver); "Wagon Train" 1940

(Kurt); "Young Bill Hickok" 1940 (Majors); "Along the Rio Grande" 1941 (Kirby); "The Apache Kid" 1941 (Sheriff); "Cyclone on Horseback" 1941; "King of the Texas Rangers" 1941-serial (Dade); "The Singing Hill" 1941; "The Cyclone Kid" 1942 (Sheriff); "The Phantom Plainsmen" 1942 (Muller); "Raiders of the Range" 1942; "Stardust on the Sage" 1942; "Thundering Hoofs" 1942 (Slick); "Westward Ho" 1942; "Fighting Frontier" 1943 (Pete); "Jesse James Rides Again" 1947-serial (Green); "The Vigilantes Return" 1947 (Henchman); "Station West" 1948 (Man); "Brothers in the Saddle" 1949; "The Pecos Pistol" 1949-short; "Rustlers" 1949 (Hawkins); "The Fargo Phantom" 1950-short; "The Savage Horde" 1950; "Vengeance Valley" 1951 (Man); "Horizons West" 1952 (Doctor); "The Last Musketeer" 1952 (Matt Becker); "Thunder Over the Plains" 1953

Montague, Jr., Monte. Films: "The Rambling Ranger" 1927 (Royal Highness).

Montaigne, Lawrence (1931-). TV: *Daniel Boone*—"My Name Is Rawls" 10-7-65 (Mawson), "The Long Way Home" 2-26-67 (Hayes Fuller); *Time Tunnel*—"Massacre" 10-28-66 (Yellow Elk); *Laredo*—"The Bitter Yen of General Ti" 2-3-67 (Rocco Calvelli); *Hondo*—"Hondo and the War Hawks" 10-20-67 (Soldado); *Bearcats!*—11-25-71 (Koster); *Bonanza*—"Search in Limbo" 2-20-72 (Sid Langley).

Montalbano, Renato. Films: "Zorro, the Navarra Marquis" 1969-Ital./Span. (King Ferdinand VII).

Montalban, Ricardo (1920-). Films: "The Kissing Bandit" 1948 (Dancer); "Across the Wide Missouri" 1951 (Ironshirt); "Mark of the Renegade" 1951 (Marcos); "Cheyenne Autumn" 1964 (Little Wolf); "Blue" 1968 (Ortega); "Deserter" 1970-U.S./Ital./Yugo. (Natchai); "Desperate Mission" TVM-1971 (Joaquin Murieta); "The Train Robbers" 1973 (Pinkerton Man); "The Mark of Zorro" TVM-1974 (Captain Esteban); "Joe Panther" 1976 (Turtle George); "Kino, the Padre on Horseback" 1977. ¶TV: *20th Century Fox Hour*—"Broken Arrow" 5-2-56 (Cochise); *Wagon Train*—"The Jean LeBec Story" 9-25-57 (Jean LeBec); *Riverboat*—"A Night at Trapper's Landing" 11-8-59 (Lt. Andre Baptiste Devereaux); *Death Valley Days*—"Eagle in the Rocks" 5-24-60 (Joaquin Murietta); *Bonanza*—"Day of Reckoning" 10-22-60 (Indian Mat-

sou); *Walt Disney Presents: Zorro*—"Auld Acquaintance" 4-2-61 (Ramon Castillo); *The Virginian*—"The Big Deal" 10-10-62 (Enrique Cuellar), "The Wind of Outrage" 10-16-68 (Louis Boissevain); *Great Adventure*—"The Death of Sitting Bull"/"Massacre at Wounded Knee" 10-4-63 & 10-11-63 (Philip Crow); *Daniel Boone*—"The Symbol" 12-29-66 (Count Alfonso De Borba); *Wild Wild West*—"The Night of the Lord of Limbo" 12-30-66 (Vautrain); *The High Chaparral*—"Tiger by the Tail" 2-25-68 (El Tigre), "Our Lady of Guadalupe" 12-20-68 (Father Sanchez); *Gunsmoke*—"Chato" 9-14-70 (Chato); *The Men from Shiloh*—"Last of the Comancheros" 12-9-70 (Sosentes); *Nichols*—"The Siege" 9-23-71 (Alcazar); *How the West Was Won*—Episode One 2-12-78 (Satangkai), Episode Two 2-19-78 (Satangkai).

Montana, Bull (1887-1/24/50). Films: "Snap Judgment" 1917 (Bull); "Wild and Woolly" 1917; "The Border Legion" 1918 (Red Pierce); "The Timber Queen" 1922-serial; "The Gold Hunters" 1925 (Hairy Grimes); "Tiger Rose" 1929 (Joe).

Montana, Monte (1910-). Films: "Circle of Death" 1935 (Little Buffalo); "Riders of the Deadline" 1943 (Calhoun); "Down Dakota Way" 1949 (Sheriff Holbrook); "The Man Who Shot Liberty Valance" 1962 (Politician on Horseback); "Arizona Bushwhackers" 1968 (Stage Driver). ¶TV: *26 Men*—"Trail of Revenge" 1-13-59; *Frontier Doctor*—"The Big Gamblers" 3-7-59; *The Rifleman*—"Mail Order Groom" 1-12-60; *Gunsmoke*—"Jenny" 10-13-62 (Joe).

Montana, Patsy. Films: "Colorado Sunset" 1939 (Patsy Montana).

Monte, Alberto. Films: "Walk Tall" 1960 (Carlos). ¶TV: *Branded*—"The Test" 2-7-65; *The High Chaparral*—"The Lion Sleeps" 3-28-69 (Bandito).

Montefiori, Luigi. *see* Eastman, George.

Monteil, Beatriz. TV: *The High Chaparral*—"The Glory Soldiers" 1-31-69 (Carla); *The Big Valley*—"Flight from San Miguel" 4-28-69 (Rose Valdez).

Montell, Lisa. Films: "The Wild Dakotas" 1956; "Tomahawk Trail" 1957 (Tula); "The Lone Ranger and the Lost City of Gold" 1958 (Paviva); "The Long Rope" 1961 (Alicia Alarez); "The Firebrand" 1962 (Clarita Vasconcelos). ¶TV: *The Gene Autry Show*—"Law Comes to Scorpion" 10-

22-55; *Cheyenne*—"Border Showdown" 11-22-55, "Apache Blood" 2-8-60 (Rheba Garcia); *Broken Arrow*—"Apache Dowry" 1-15-57 (Tesalbe); *Tales of Wells Fargo*—"Rio Grande" 6-3-57 (Juanita); *Colt .45*—"One Good Turn" 11-29-57 (Teresa Valdez); *Jim Bowie*—"Curfew Cannon" 1-24-58 (Lisette Rochambeau); *Sugarfoot*—"Hideout" 4-1-58 (Konoee), "Outlaw Island" 11-24-59 (Carmencita); *Walt Disney Presents*—"Elfego Baca: The Nine Lives of Elfego Baca" 10-3-58 (Anita), "Elfego Baca: Four Down and Five Lives to Go" 10-17-58 (Anita); *Northwest Passage*—"Stab in the Back" 2-20-59 (Emily Duren); *Bat Masterson*—"Pigeon and Hawk" 1-21-60 (Selena Thorn); *Maverick*—"The Forbidden City" 3-26-61 (Andalucia Rubio); *The Deputy*—"Chechez la Femme" 4-1-61 (Rosaria Martinez).

Montenegro, Conchita. Films: "Cisco Kid" 1931 (Carmencita); "The Gay Caballero" 1932 (Adela Morales).

Monteros, Rosenda. Films: "Villa!" 1958 (Mariana); "The Magnificent Seven" 1960 (Petra); "Savage Pampas" 1966-U.S./Span./Arg. (Rucu).

Montes, Elisa. Films: "The Avengers" 1966-Ital.; "Mutiny at Fort Sharp" 1966-Ital.; "Outlaw of Red River" 1966-Ital. (Francisca); "Return of the Seven" 1966-Span. (Petra); "Texas, Adios" 1966-Ital./Span.; "Cowards Don't Pray" 1968-Ital./Span. (Julie); "Seven Dollars on the Red" 1968-Ital./Span.; "Captain Apache" 1971-Brit./Span. (Rosita).

Montez, Maria (1920-9/7/51). Films: "Boss of Bullion City" 1941 (Linda Calhoun); "Pirates of Monterey" 1947 (Marguerita).

Montgomery, Belinda (1950-). Films: "Lock, Stock and Barrel" TVM-1971 (Roselle Bridgeman); "The Bravos" TVM-1972 (Heller Chase). ¶TV: *The Virginian*—"A Touch of Hands" 12-3-69 (Peg Halstead); *Alias Smith and Jones*—"The Day They Hanged Kid Curry" 9-16-71 (Penny Roach); *The New Land*—"The Word Is: Alternative" 10-12-74; *How the West Was Won*—"Luke" 4-2-79 (Florrie Thompson).

Montgomery, Elizabeth (1933-5/18/95). Films: "Mrs. Sundance" TVM-1974 (Etta Place); "The Awakening Land" TVM-1978 (Sayward Luckett Wheeler); "Belle Starr" TVM-1980 (Belle Starr). ¶TV: *Cimarron City*—"Hired Hand" 11-15-58 (Ellen Wilson); *Riverboat*—"The Barrier" 9-20-59 (Abigail Carruthers); *Wagon Train*—"The Vittorio Bottecelli Story" 12-16-59 (Julie Carson); *Frontier Circus*—"Karina" 11-9-61; *Rawhide*—"Incident at El Crucero" 10-10-63 (Rose Cornelius).

Montgomery, Frank (1870-7/19/44). Films: "The Man Who Paid" 1922 (Songo, the Indian Guide); "Red Love" 1925 (Two Crows); "Way Out West" 1937 (Man in Audience).

Montgomery, George (George Letz) (1916-). Films: "The Singing Vagabond" 1935; "Springtime in the Rockies" 1937; "Billy the Kid Returns" 1938; "Come on, Ranger" 1938 (Ranger); "Gold Mine in the Sky" 1938; "The Lone Ranger" 1938-serial (Jim Clark); "Shine on Harvest Moon" 1938 (Cowboy); "The Cisco Kid and the Lady" 1939 (Tommy Bates); "Frontier Pony Express" 1939; "Rough Riders' Round-Up" 1939 (Telegrapher); "The Cowboy and the Blonde" 1941 (Lank Garrett); "Last of the Duanes" 1941 (Buck Duane); "Riders of the Purple Sage" 1941 (Jim Lassiter); "Belle Starr's Daughter" 1947 (Tom Jackson); "Dakota Lil" 1950 (Tom Horn); "Davy Crockett, Indian Scout" 1950 (Davy Crockett); "The Iroquois Trail" 1950 (Hawkeye); "Indian Uprising" 1951 (Capt. McCloud); "The Texas Rangers" 1951 (Johnny Carver); "Cripple Creek" 1952 (Bret Ivers); "The Pathfinder" 1952 (Pathfinder); "Fort Ti" 1953 (Capt. Pedediah Horn); "Gun Belt" 1953 (Billy Ringo); "Jack McCall, Desperado" 1953 (Jack McCall); "Battle of Rogue River" 1954 (Maj. Frank Archer); "The Lone Gun" 1954 (Cruz); "Masterson of Kansas" 1954 (Bat Masterson); "Robbers' Roost" 1955 (Tex); "Seminole Uprising" 1955 (Lt. Cam Elliott); "Canyon River" 1956 (Steve Patrick); "Black Patch" 1957 (Clay Morgan); "Gun Duel in Durango" 1957 (Dan); "Last of the Badmen" 1957 (Dan Barton); "Pawnee" 1957 (Paul); "Badman's Country" 1958 (Pat Garrett); "Man from God's Country" 1958 (Dan Beattie); "Toughest Gun in Tombstone" 1958 (Matt Sloane); "King of the Wild Stallions" 1959 (Randy); "Outlaw of Red River" 1966-Ital. (Reese O'Brien); "Hostile Guns" 1967 (Gid McCool). ¶TV: *Wagon Train*—"The Jessie Cowan Story" 1-8-58 (Jessie Cowan); *Cimarron City*—Regular 1958-59 (Matt Rockford); *Bonanza*—"The Code" 2-13-66 (Dan Taggert); *Alias Smith and Jones*—"Jailbreak at Junction City" 9-30-71 (Clitterhouse).

Montgomery, Jack (1891-1/21/62). Films: "The New Frontier" 1935; "The Outlaw Deputy" 1935 (Stibes); "Outlawed Guns" 1935; "The Texas Rangers" 1936 (Ranger); "Courage of the West" 1937 (U.S. Marshall); "The Gambling Terror" 1937; "Yodelin' Kid from Pine Ridge" 1937; "Black Bandit" 1938; "Border Wolves" 1938 (MacKay); "The Last Stand" 1938; "Red River Range" 1938; "The Singing Outlaw" 1938 (Marshal Sam Fairfax); "Western Trails" 1938; "The Lone Ranger Rides Again" 1939-serial (Smith); "Western Caravans" 1939 (Joe); "Covered Wagon Days" 1940; "Covered Wagon Trails" 1940; "The Dark Command" 1940; "Ghost Valley Raiders" 1940; "Melody Ranch" 1940; "Son of Roaring Dan" 1940; "Desert Bandit" 1941; "Westward Ho" 1942; "Red River Robin Hood" 1943; "Wagon Tracks West" 1943; "Gunman's Code" 1946; "Pursued" 1947; "Run for Cover" 1955; "Gun Glory" 1957 (Farmer).

Montgomery, Lee Harcourt (1961-). Films: "Female Artillery" TVM-1973 (Brian Townsend); "A Cry in the Wilderness" TVM-1974 (Gus Hadley); "Baker's Hawk" 1976 (Billy Baker); "True Grit" TVM-1978 (Daniel). ¶TV: *Hec Ramsey*—"Hangman's Wages" 10-29-72 (Billy McCarty).

Montgomery, Peggy. Films: "Rainbow Rangers" 1924 (Rose Warner); "Fighting Courage" 1925 (Marjorie Crenshaw); "Tricked" 1925; "The Ace of Clubs" 1926 (June); "The Dangerous Dub" 1926 (Rose Cooper); "The Fighting Failure" 1926; "Looking for Trouble" 1926 (Laura Buckhold); "The Desert of the Lost" 1927 (Dolores Wolfe); "Hoof Marks" 1927 (Alice Dixon); "The Sonora Kid" 1927 (Phyllis Butterworth); "Splitting the Breeze" 1927 (Janet Rand); "Two-Gun of the Tumbleweed" 1927 (Doris Gibson); "Arizona Days" 1928 (Dolly Martin); "The Brand of Courage" 1928; "On the Divide" 1928 (Sally Martin); "Saddle Mates" 1928 (Betty Shelby); "The Silent Trail" 1928; "West of Santa Fe" 1928 (Helen); "Wolves of the Range" 1928; "Bad Man's Money" 1929; "Fighters of the Saddle" 1929 (Nesta).

Montgomery, Ralph (1912-5/10/80). TV: *Bonanza*—"The Artist" 10-7-62, "Return to Honor" 3-22-64 (Bartender), "Her Brother's Keeper" 3-6-66 (Charlie); *Daniel Boone*—"Perilous Passage" 1-15-70.

Montgomery, Ray (1919-). Films: "Tomahawk" 1951 (Balir Streeter); "Bugles in the Afternoon" 1952 (Osborne); "Bandits of the West" 1953 (Steve Edrington); "Column South" 1953 (Keit). ¶TV: *The Lone Ranger*—"Dead Man's Chest" 9-28-50, "Lady Killer" 12-21-50; *Wyatt Earp*—"The Assassins" 1-10-56 (Virgil Earp); *Fury*—"Trial by Jury" 10-27-56; *Rawhide*—"Incident at Tinker's Dam" 2-5-60, "Incident of the Buffalo Soldier" 1-1-61 (Lieutenant Howard), "Incident of the Woman Trap" 1-26-62 (Lieutenant Keown); *Wide Country*—"Speckle Bird" 1-31-63 (Deputy); *The Virginian*—"The Money Cage" 3-6-63 (John Dales); *Daniel Boone*—"A Rope for Mingo" 12-2-65 (Hank).

Montgomery, Jr., Robert. TV: *Gunsmoke*—"Lynching Man" 11-15-58 (Billy Drico); *The Deputy*—"The Two Faces of Bob Claxton" 2-27-60 (Bob Claxton); *Death Valley Days*—"The Gentle Sword" 11-9-60; *The Tall Man*—"First Blood" 1-7-61 (Jimmy Carter).

Monti, Carlotta (1907-12/8/93). Films: "In Old California" 1929 (Juanita); "Cavalier of the West" 1931 (Chiquita); "Deadwood Pass" 1933 (Lolita); "Robin Hood of El Dorado" 1936 (Dancer).

Monti, Maria. Films: "Duck, You Sucker!" 1971-Ital. (Adolita).

Monti, Silva (1946-). Films: "Judge Roy Bean" 1970-Fr.

Montiel, Sarita (1927-). Films: "Vera Cruz" 1954 (Nina); "Run of the Arrow" 1957 (Yellow Moccasin).

Montoya, Alex (1907-9/25/70). Films: "Beauty and the Bandit" 1946; "Trail to Mexico" 1946; "The Last Round-Up" 1947; "Riding the California Trail" 1947; "Robin Hood of Monterey" 1947; "Twilight on the Rio Grande" 1947; "West to Glory" 1947 (Juan); "The Big Sombrero" 1949; "Ghost of Zorro" 1949-serial (Yellow Hawk); "Square Dance Jubilee" 1949 (2nd Indian); "Dallas" 1950 (Vaquero); "California Conquest" 1952 (Juan); "Wild Horse Ambush" 1952 (Pedro); "Conquest of Cochise" 1953 (Garcia); "Escape from Fort Bravo" 1953 (Chavez); "Son of Belle Star" 1953 (Mexican); "Passion" 1954 (Manuel Felipe); "Three Young Texans" 1954 (Tomas); "Apache Ambush" 1955 (Joaquin Jironza); "Stagecoach to Fury" 1956 (Oro); "War Drums" 1957 (Manuel); "Toughest Gun in Tombstone" 1958 (Sergeant); "The Appaloosa" 1966 (Squint Eye). ¶TV: *Broken Arrow*—"The Archaeologist" 4-30-57 (Nogalo); *The Californians*—"Skeleton in the Closet" 4-8-58 (Dom); *Rawhide*—"Incident of the Day of the

Dead" 9-18-59, "Incident of the One Hundred Amulets" 5-6-60, "Incident at Rio Salado" 9-29-61 (Segundo); *Wagon Train*—"The Jose Morales Story" 10-19-60 (Paco), "The Traitor" 12-13-61 (Bandit); *Tales of Wells Fargo*—"Escort to Santa Fe" 12-19-60 (Ortega); *The Tall Man*—"Rio Doloroso" 2-10-62 (Comingo); *The Rifleman*—"Waste" 10-1-62 & 10-8-62 (Ear Digger); *Bonanza*—"The Fugitive" 2-4-61, "The Last Haircut" 2-3-63 (Carlos); *Gunsmoke*—"Extradition" 12-7-63 & 12-14-63 (Captain Diaz), "The Jackals" 2-12-68 (Bandito); *The Virginian*—"Ride a Cock-Horse to Laramie Cross" 2-23-66 (Dom); *The High Chaparral*—"Young Blood" 10-8-67 (Miguel), "The Promised Land" 10-25-68 (Miguel), "Ebenezer" 11-1-68 (Miguel).

Montoya, Julia. Films: "Lost in Alaska" 1952 (Eskimo Woman); "Viva Zapata!" 1952 (Wife); "The Great Sioux Uprising" 1953 (Heyoka); "They Rode West" 1954 (Maria); "The Far Horizons" 1955 (Crow Woman); "Raw Edge" 1956 (Indian Squaw). ¶TV: *Wild Bill Hickok*—"Bold Raven Rodeo" 4-7-53; *Colt .45*—"The Cause" 2-28-60 (Senora Martinez); *Wanted—Dead or Alive*—"Witch Woman" 12-28-60 (Esperanza); *The Tall Man*—"Rio Doloroso" 2-10-62 (Maria); *The High Chaparral*—"Shadow of the Wind" 1-10-69.

Montt, Christina (1897-4/22/69). Films: "Rose of the Golden West" 1927 (Senorita Gonzalez).

Monty, Harry. Films: "Ride 'Em, Cowboy" 1942 (Midget). ¶TV: *Bonanza*—"Hoss and the Leprechauns" 12-22-63.

Moody, Harry. Films: "The Arrow Maiden" 1915; "The Huron Converts" 1915; "The Haunted Range" 1926 (Alex Forester); "Under Fire" 1926.

Moody, Jeanne. TV: *Frontier*—"A Somewhere Voice" 5-6-56 (Susan); *Jim Bowie*—"The Squatter" 9-14-56 (Regina), "The Swordsman" 12-14-56, "The Bound Girl" 5-10-57.

Moody, King (1929-). TV: *Bonanza*—"El Toro Grande" 1-2-60, "The Conquistadors" 10-1-67 (Charlie), "The Sure Thing" 11-12-67 (Carter), "Stage Door Johnnies" 7-28-68 (Man); *The High Chaparral*—"Sudden Country" 11-5-67.

Moody, Lynne (1948-). TV: *Outlaws*—"Orleans" 1-17-87 (Nicole).

Moody, Ralph (1886-9/16/71). Films: "Square Dance Jubilee" 1949 (Indian Chief); "Red Mountain" 1951 (Meredyth); "Column South"

1953 (Joe Copper Face); "Seminole" 1953 (Kulak); "Tumbleweed" 1953 (Aguila); "The Far Horizons" 1955 (Le Borgne); "Many Rivers to Cross" 1955 (Sandak); "Rage at Dawn" 1955; "Strange Lady in Town" 1955 (Gen. Lew Wallace); "The Last Hunt" 1956 (Indian Agent); "Reprisal!" 1956 (Matara); "Pawnee" 1957 (Wise Eagle); "The Lone Ranger and the Lost City of Gold" 1958 (Padre Vincente Esteban); "The Legend of Tom Dooley" 1959 (Doc Henry). ¶TV: *The Lone Ranger*—"The Renegades" 11-3-49, "Man Without a Gun" 6-15-50, "White Man's Magic" 7-13-50; *The Marshal of Gunsight Pass*—Regular 1950; *The Adventures of Rin Tin Tin*—"The Bugle Call" 9-9-55 (Sgt. Ed Fallon), "Attack on Fort Apache" 4-13-56 (Wynoki), "Return of Rin Tin Tin" 10-26-56 (Walking Bear), "Racing Rails" 12-28-56 (Tom Dunnegan), "The Old Soldier" 4-12-57 (Silas Gunn), "Ol' Betsy" 1-16-59 (Chief White Water); *The Roy Rogers Show*—"False Faces" 2-5-56, "Smoking Guns" 3-3-56 (Kumaska); *Cheyenne*—"Fury at Rio Hondo" 4-17-56 (Pete); *Circus Boy*—"Casey Rides Again" 11-4-56 (Casey Perkins), "White Eagle" 11-25-56 (Chief Spotted Horse), "Corky's Big Parade" 3-24-57 (Ezra Hillman), "Return of Casey Perkins" 10-17-57 (Casey Perkins); *Zane Grey Theater*—"Return to Nowhere" 12-7-56 (Cluny), "A Gun for Willie" 10-6-60 (George); *Telephone Time*—"Sam Houston's Decision" 12-10-57 (Deaf Smith); *Broken Arrow*—"White Savage" 12-24-57 (Nachato), "Bear Trap" 4-29-58 (Nochalo); *Jim Bowie*—"A Grave for Jim Bowie" 2-28-58 (Rev. Rudsill); *Have Gun Will Travel*—"The Silver Queen" 5-3-58, "The Monster of Moon Ridge" 2-28-59 (Jake), "The Lady on the Wall" 2-20-60, "The Long Weekend" 4-8-61 (Valentine Collins); *Wanted—Dead or Alive*—"Fatal Memory" 9-13-58 (Victor Flamm); *The Texan*—"Law of the Gun" 9-29-58, "A Race for Life" 3-16-59, "The Reluctant Bridegroom" 11-16-59; *Bat Masterson*—"Deadline" 4-8-59 (Garth); *Rawhide*—"Incident at the Curious Street" 4-10-59 (Ed Corey), "Incident of Iron Bull" 10-3-63 (Yellow Elk); *Gunsmoke*—"Cheyennes" 6-13-59 (Long Robe), "The Bobsy Twins" 5-21-60 (Harvey Finney), "Old Comrade" 12-29-62 (Gen. Kip Marston), "Friend" 1-25-64 (Finley), "Honor Before Justice" 3-5-66 (Joseph); *Black Saddle*—"The Saddle" 10-9-59 (Judge Tenifree), "Murdock" 11-13-59 (Judge Tennifree); *The Law of the Plainsman*—"The Dude" 12-3-

59; *The Rifleman*—"The Visitors" 1-26-60, "The Spoiler" 2-16-60 (Roy Merrick), "The Hangman" 5-31-60, Regular 61-63 (Doc Burrage); *The Rebel*—"Land" 2-21-60 (Judge Parks); *Wagon Train*—"The Tom Tuckett Story" 3-2-60; *The Deputy*—"Lucifer Urge" 5-14-60 (Conroy); *Johnny Ringo*—"Cave-In" 6-30-60 (Cobb); *Klondike*—"The Man Who Owned Skagway" 1-30-61 (Indian Chief); *The Tall Man*—"Apache Daughter" 12-30-61 (Chief Nanay); *Lawman*—"The Wanted Man" 4-8-62 (Doc Greer), "Cort" 4-29-62 (Doc Jessup); *Bonanza*—"The Prime of Life" 12-29-63, "The Saga of Muley Jones" 3-29-64, "To Kill a Buffalo" 1-9-66 (Old Indian), "It's a Small World" 1-4-70 (Clarke), "The Grand Swing" 9-19-71 (Tall Pony); *Great Adventure*—"The Testing of Sam Houston" 1-31-64 (Do-Loo-Techka); *Daniel Boone*—"The Sound of Wings" 11-12-64 (Charlie Crow); *Death Valley Days*—"Tribute to the Dog" 12-27-64 (Andrew Cody); *Wild Wild West*—"The Night of the Howling Light" 12-17-65 (Ho-Tami); *The Monroes*—"The Forest Devil" 9-28-66 (the Shaman).

Moody, Ron (1924-). TV: *Gunsmoke*—"The Boy and the Sinner" 10-1-73 (Noah Beal).

Mooers, De Sacia (1888-1/11/60). Films: "The Arizona Kid" 1930 (Molly).

Moon, Arthur. Films: "Babbling Tongues" 1915; "The Flag of Fortune" 1915; "The Sacrifice of Jonathan Gray" 1915; "The Sheriff of Red Rock Gulch" 1915; "The Trap That Failed" 1915.

Moore, Alvy (1925-). Films: "The Persuader" 1957 (Willy Williams); "Lacy and the Mississippi Queen" TVM-1978 (Reverend); "Little House: The Last Farewell" TVM-1984 (First Mayor). ¶TV: *Johnny Ringo*—"The Liars" 2-4-60 (Gordie Fields), "Single Debt" 5-12-60 (Billy Joe Scanlon); *Zane Grey Theater*—"The Bible Man" 2-23-61 (Cox); *Stagecoach West*—"A Place of Still Waters" 4-11-61 (J.J. Brewster); *Wide Country*—"Straightjacket for an Indian" 10-25-62 (Rex); *Death Valley Days*—"The Grass Man" 11-21-62; "The Race at Cherry Creek" 3-7-65; *The Virginian*—"Run Away Home" 4-24-63, "The Brazos Kid" 10-21-64, "Man of the People" 12-23-64 (Ray Harris); *Daniel Boone*—"Four-Leaf Clover" 3-25-65 (Amos Truro); *The Legend of Jesse James*—"The Man Who Killed Jesse" 12-27-65 (Joe T. Alcorn).

Moore, Archie (1916-). Films: "Breakheart Pass" 1976 (Carlos). ¶TV: *Wagon Train*—"The Geneva Balfour Story" 1-20-64 (Ishmael); *Shane*—"The Great Invasion" 12-17-66 & 12-24-66 (Dan).

Moore, Candy. Films: "Tomboy and the Champ" 1961 (Tommy Jo); "The Night of the Grizzly" 1966 (Meg). ¶TV: *Rawhide*—"Incident of the Fish Out of the Water" 2-17-61 (Gillian Favor), "The Bosses' Daughter" 2-2-62 (Gillian Favor); *Wagon Train*—"Wagon to Fort Anderson" 6-7-61 (Sue).

Moore, Jr., Carlyle (1909-3/3/77). Films: "Trailin' West" 1936 (Hotel Clerk); "Treachery Rides the Range" 1936 (Little Big Wolf); "The Devil's Saddle Legion" 1937 (Chip Carter); "Outlaw Express" 1938 (Bill Cody); "The Overland Express" 1938 (Tom Furness); "Western Trails" 1938 (Rudd).

Moore, Charles R. (1893-7/20/47). Films: "Southward Ho!" 1939 (Skeeter); "Desert Bandit" 1941 (T-Bone); "Kansas Cyclone" 1941 (T-Bone); "Riding High" 1943.

Moore, Clayton (1908-). Films: "Arizona Legion" 1939 (Lt. Ives); "Kit Carson" 1940 (Paul Terry); "Outlaws of Pine Ridge" 1942 (Lane Hollister); "Heldorado" 1946; "Along the Oregon Trail" 1947 (Gregg Thurston); "Jesse James Rides Again" 1947-serial (Jesse James/John C. Howard); "The Adventures of Frank and Jesse James" 1948-serial (Jesse James/John Howard); "Marshal of Amarillo" 1948 (Art Crandall); "The Cowboy and the Indians" 1949 (Luke); "The Far Frontier" 1949 (Tom Sharper); "Frontier Marshal" 1949 (Scott Garnett); "The Gay Amigo" 1949 (Lieutenant); "Ghost of Zorro" 1949-serial (Ken Mason/Zorro); "Masked Raiders" 1949 (Matt); "Riders of the Whistling Pines" 1949 (Pete); "Sheriff of Wichita" 1949 (Raymond D'Arcy); "Sons of New Mexico" 1949 (Rufe Burns); "South of Death Valley" 1949 (Bead); "Bandits of El Dorado" 1951 (Morgan); "Cyclone Fury" 1951 (Grat Hanlon); "Barbed Wire" 1952 (Bailey); "Buffalo Bill in Tomahawk Territory" 1952 (Buffalo Bill); "Captive of Billy the Kid" 1952 (Paul Howarth); "Desert Passage" 1952 (Warwick); "The Hawk of Wild River" 1952 (the Hawk); "Montana Territory" 1952 (George Ives); "Night Stage to Galveston" 1952 (Clyde Chambers); "Son of Geronimo" 1952-serial (Jim Scott); "Down Laredo Way" 1953 (Chip Wells); "Kansas Pacific" 1953 (Stone); "The Black

Dakotas" 1954 (Stone); "Gunfighters of the Northwest" 1954-serial (Bram Nevin); "The Lone Ranger" 1956 (the Lone Ranger); "The Lone Ranger and the Lost City of Gold" 1958 (the Lone Ranger). ¶TV: *The Lone Ranger*—Regular 1949-57 (The Lone Ranger); *The Range Rider*—"Ambush in Coyote Canyon" 3-15-52; *Wild Bill Hickok*—"Trapper's Story" 3-18-52; *The Gene Autry Show*—"Ghost Mountain" 7-28-53, "Dry Gulch at Devil's Elbow" 9-8-53, "The Carnival Comes West" 8-24-54.

Moore, Cleo (1924-10/25/73). Films: "Dynamite Pass" 1950 (Lulu); "Rio Grande Patrol" 1950 (Peppie).

Moore, Colleen (1902-11/25/88). Films: "Hands Up!" 1917 (Marjorie Houston); "The Savage" 1917 (Lizette); "The Wilderness Trail" 1919 (Jeanne Fitzpatrick); "The Cyclones" 1920 (Sylvia Sturgis); "The Sky Pilot" 1921 (Gwen); "Broken Chains" 1922 (Mercy Boone); "The Huntress" 1923 (Bela); "The Desert Flower" 1925 (Maggie Fortune).

Moore, Constance (1922-). Films: "Border Wolves" 1938 (Mary Jo Benton); "The Last Stand" 1938 (Nancy Drake); "In Old Sacramento" 1946 (Belle Malone). ¶TV: *Laramie*—"The Legend of Lily" 1-26-60 (Lily Langford).

Moore, Del (1917-8/30/70). Films: "Stagecoach to Dancer's Rock" 1962 (Hiram Best). ¶TV: *Wagon Train*—"Trial for Murder" 4-27-60 & 5-4-60, "The Beth Pearson Story" 2-22-61 (Johnson); *F Troop*—"Go for Broke" 1-25-66 (Dapper Dan Fulbright); *Bonanza*—"Maestro Hoss" 5-7-67 (Hank); *The Men from Shiloh*—"Last of the Comancheros" 12-9-70 (Deputy).

Moore, Dennis (Dennis Meadows) (1908-3/1/64). Films: "The Red Rider" 1934-serial (Cowboy); "West on Parade" 1934; "Dawn Rider" 1935 (Rudd); "Sagebrush Troubador" 1935 (Lon Dillon); "Desert Justice" 1936; "Hair-Trigger Casey" 1936 (Brooks); "The Lonely Trail" 1936 (Dick Terry); "Silver Spurs" 1936 (Dude); "Too Much Beef" 1936 (Cowhand); "Valley of the Lawless" 1936 (Cliff Graves); "Wildcat Saunders" 1936; "Cowboy from Brooklyn" 1938 (Abby Pitts); "Wild Horse Canyon" 1938 (Pete Hall); "Across the Plains" 1939 (Kansas Kid); "Overland Mail" 1939 (Duke); "Trigger Smith" 1939 (Bud); "Rainbow Over the Range" 1940 (Manners); "Rocky Mountain Rangers" 1940 (Jim Barton); "Arizona Bound" 1941 (Silent Don Vincent); "Billy

the Kid's Roundup" 1941; "Cyclone on Horseback" 1941; "Law of the Wolf" 1941; "The Lone Rider Fights Back" 1941; "Pals of the Pecos" 1941 (Larry Burke); "Pirates on Horseback" 1941 (Jud Carter); "Bandit Ranger" 1942; "Below the Border" 1942 (Joe); "Border Roundup" 1942; "Dawn on the Great Divide" 1942 (Tony Corkle); "The Lone Rider and the Bandit" 1942; "The Lone Rider in Cheyenne" 1942; "Outlaws of Boulder Pass" 1942; "Overland Stagecoach" 1942; "Raiders of the Range" 1942 (Ned Foster); "Riders of the West" 1942 (Steve); "Rolling Down the Great Divide" 1942; "Texas Justice" 1942 (Smokey); "Texas Man Hunt" 1942 (Jim Rogers); "Arizona Trail" 1943 (Wayne Trent); "Black Market Rustlers" 1943 (Dennis); "Bullets and Saddles" 1943; "Cowboy Commandos" 1943 (Denny); "Frontier Law" 1943 (Dusty); "Land of Hunted Men" 1943; "Oklahoma Raiders" 1944 (Todd); "Raiders of Ghost City" 1944-serial (Captain Steve Clark); "Song of the Range" 1944 (Denny); "Twilight on the Prairie" 1944; "Wells Fargo Days" 1944-short; "West of the Rio Grande" 1944; "Frontier Feud" 1945 (Joe); "Springtime in Texas" 1945; "Colorado Serenade" 1946 (Duke Dillon); "Driftin' River" 1946 (Marino); "Rainbow Over the Rockies" 1947; "Frontier Agent" 1948; "The Gay Ranchero" 1948 (Tex); "Range Renegades" 1948; "The Tioga Kid" 1948 (Morino); "Across the Rio Grande" 1949 (Carson); "Haunted Trails" 1949 (Phil Rankin); "Navajo Trail Raiders" 1949 (Frank Stanley); "Riders in the Sky" 1949 (Bud Dwyer); "Roaring Westward" 1949 (Sanders); "Arizona Territory" 1950 (Lance); "Crooked River" 1950 (Bob); "Desperadoes of the West" 1950-serial (Ned Foster); "Fast on the Draw" 1950; "Gunslingers" 1950 (Brad Brasser); "Hostile Country" 1950 (Pete); "I Killed Geronimo" 1950 (Luke); "King of the Bullwhip" 1950 (Joe Chester); "Marshal of Heldorado" 1950 (Doc); "Silver Raiders" 1950 (Boland); "West of the Brazos" 1950 (Ricco); "West of Wyoming" 1950 (Dorsey); "Abilene Trail" 1951 (Brandon); "Blazing Bullets" 1951; "Fort Defiance" 1951 (Lt. Lucas); "Man from Sonora" 1951; "Canyon Ambush" 1952; "The Lusty Men" 1952 (Cashier); "Montana Belle" 1952 (Messenger); "Blazing the Overland Trail" 1956-serial (Ed Marr); "Perils of the Wilderness" 1956-serial (Laramie); "Tribute to a Badman" 1956 (Cowboy); "Gunfight at the

O.K. Corral" 1957 (Cowboy); "Utah Blaine" 1957 (Ferguson). ¶TV: *The Cisco Kid*—"Newspaper Crusade" 5-5-51, "Freight Line Feud" 6-2-51, "Performance Bond" 6-30-51, "Medicine Man Story" 8-25-51, "Black Lightning" 10-6-51, "A Six-Gun for No Pain" 2-28-53 (No Pain Norton), "Harry the Heir" 3-28-53, "Cisco and the Giant" 10-31-53; *Sky King*—"The Crystal Trap" 10-7-51, "Showdown" 1-27-52 (Rick Varney); *The Gene Autry Show*—"Frame for Trouble" 11-3-51, "Revenge Trail" 11-17-51, "The Lawless Press" 1-25-52, "Ruthless Renegade" 2-8-52, "Feuding Friends" 11-26-55; *Wild Bill Hickok*—"Halley's Comet" 2-17-53; *The Lone Ranger*—"Two from Juan Ringo" 12-23-54, "The Letter Bride" 11-15-56, "The Avenger" 1-10-57, "The Law and Miss Aggie" 4-11-57, "The Angel and the Outlaw" 5-23-57; *The Roy Rogers Show*—"The Brothers O'Dell" 11-20-55, "Three Masked Men" 12-18-55 (Phil Kent), "Ambush" 1-15-56, "Johnny Rover" 6-9-57 (Dan Cass); *Judge Roy Bean*—"Gunman's Bargain" 1-1-56 (Starkey), "Outlaw's Son" 1-1-56 (Frank Donovan), "The Feformer" 1-1-56 (Memphis); *Sergeant Preston of the Yukon*—"All Is Not Gold" 5-10-56 (Paddy Lambert), "Ten Little Indians" 4-18-57 (Mike Donovan); *The Adventures of Rin Tin Tin*—"Stagecoach Sally" 4-19-57 (Marty); *Wyatt Earp*—"Beautiful Friendship" 4-30-57 (Frank Loving), "The Underdog" 4-22-58 (Hugh Jackson); *Tales of the Texas Rangers*—"Panhandle" 9-22-57 (Jim Webb); *Tombstone Territory*—"Reward for a Gunslinger" 10-23-57, "Skeleton Canyon Massacre" 4-2-58 (Deputy), "The Tin Gunman" 4-16-58 (Deputy), "Fight for a Fugitive" 6-4-58 (Deputy Lee); *The Restless Gun*—"The Manhunters" 6-2-58 (Adam Paxton); *Buckskin*—"The Gold Watch" 8-28-58 (Mr. Finley), "A Permanent Juliet" 10-23-58 (Jeb); *Trackdown*—"The Avenger" 10-31-58 (Lance Garth); *Wagon Train*—"The Sakae Ito Story" 12-3-58 (Burt Rake); *Bat Masterson*—"A Personal Matter" 1-28-59 (Tim Clovis), "Wanted—Dead" 10-15-59 (Tom), "A Picture of Death" 1-14-60 (Sheriff), "Run for Your Money" 3-2-61 (Hacker); *Fury*—"Joey's Jalopy 4-4-59; *Rough Riders*—"The Holdout" 6-25-59 (Jeff); *Have Gun Will Travel*—"Tiger" 11-28-59; *Tales of Wells Fargo*—"Something Pretty" 4-17-61 (Marshal Buxton).

Moore, Dickie (1925-). Films: "The Squaw Man" 1931 (Little Hal); "Cody of the Pony Express" 1950-serial (Bill Cody).

Moore, Eunice Murdock. Films: "Fighting Cressy" 1920 (Ma McKinstry); "Just Pals" 1920 (Mrs. Stone); "Two Moons" 1920 (Wooly Ann).

Moore, Frederick. Films: "The Man from Nowhere" 1920 (Duke Fuller); "Cyclone Bliss" 1921 (Bill Turner); "The Stampede" 1921 (Jim Henderson).

Moore, Gladys (1864-9/5/37). Films: "His Greatest Battle" 1925; "Tricks" 1925 (Aunt Angelica).

Moore, Hilda (1886-5/18/29). Films: "Law and Lawless" 1932 (Rosita Lopez).

Moore, Ida (1882-9/26/64). Films: "Riders of the Santa Fe" 1944 (Luella Tucker); "Return of the Badmen" 1948 (Mrs. Moore); "Fancy Pants" 1950 (Betsy).

Moore, Jack. Films: "Forlorn River" 1926 (Deputy); "Thunder Trail" 1937 (Cowboy); "The Texans" 1938 (Slim); "Zorro's Fighting Legion" 1939-serial (Fernando).

Moore, Joanna (1933-). Films: "Slim Carter" 1957 (Charlene Carroll); "Ride a Crooked Trail" 1958 (Little Brandy); "The Man from Galveston" 1964 (Rita Dillard). ¶TV: *Wagon Train*—"The Jean LeBec Story" 9-25-57 (Mary Clairborne), "The Duncan McIvor Story" 3-9-64 (Lucinda Carter); *Rough Riders*—"Reluctant Hostage" 6-18-59 (Faye Scarlet); *The Rifleman*—"Obituary" 10-20-59 (Elinor Claremont); *Maverick*—"The Lass with the Poisonous Air" 11-1-59 (Linda Burke); *Bat Masterson*—"Who'll Bury My Violence?" 11-12-59 (Sharon Stabler), "The Canvas and the Cane" 12-17-59 (Teresa Renaut); *Riverboat*—"Face of Courage" 12-27-59 (Kitty McGuire); *Tales of Wells Fargo*—"The Easterner" 1-11-60 (Arlene Howell); *Gunsmoke*—"Colleen So Green" 4-2-60 (Colleen Tawney), "Cherry Red" 6-11-60 (Cherry O'Dell), "Honey Pot" 5-15-65 (Honey Dare); *The Rebel*—"Lady of Quality" 6-5-60 (Barbara Dyer); *Empire*—"Green, Green, Hills" 12-25-62 (Althea Dodd); *The Virginian*—"The Money Cage" 3-6-63 (Jenny), "No Tears for Savannah" 10-2-63 (Jane Dent), "A Father for Toby" 11-4-64 (Ellen), "To Bear Witness" 11-29-67 (Carol Fisk); *The Dakotas*—"Justice at Eagle's Nest" 3-11-63 (Doll Harvey); *Temple Houston*—"The Man from Galveston" 1963 (Rita Dillard); *Wild Wild West*—"The Night of the Fatal Trap" 12-24-65 (Linda Medford); *Daniel Boone*—"The Accused" 3-24-66 (Lacey Lowe); *Cowboy in Africa*—"Kifaru! Kifaru!" 9-18-67 (Peggy Fisher); *Iron

Horse*—"Wild Track" 12-16-67 (Maggie Briggs); *The High Chaparral*—"Lady Fair" 11-14-69 (Charly Converse).

Moore, Joe (1896-8/22/26). Films: "The White Rider" 1920 (Chauncey Day); "False Brands" 1922 (Joe Sullivan); "Wolf Pack" 1922 (Joe Hammond).

Moore, Juanita (1922-). Films: "Skin Game" 1971 (Viney); "Thomasine and Bushrod" 1974 (Pecolia). ¶TV: *Wagon Train*—"The Blane Wessels Story" 4-17-63 (Essie); *Kung Fu*—"Barbary House" 2-15-75 (Lula), "Flight to Orion" 2-22-75 (Lula), "The Brothers Cain" 3-1-75 (Lula), "Full Circle" 3-15-75 (Lula).

Moore, Kieron (1925-). Films: "Son of a Gunfighter" 1966-U.S./Span. (Deputy Fenton); "Custer of the West" 1967-U.S./Span. (Cheyenne Chief Dull Knife).

Moore, Mary (1861-4/6/31). Films: "The Great Divide" 1915 (Phil's Wife).

Moore, Mary Tyler (1937-). TV: *Bronco*—"Flight from an Empire" 12-15-59 (Marilee); *Riverboat*—"Trunk Full of Dreams" 10-31-60 (Lily Belle); *Wanted—Dead or Alive*—"The Twain Shall Meet" 10-19-60 (Sophie Anderson); *The Deputy*—"Day of Fear" 12-17-60 (Amy Collins).

Moore, Matt (1888-1/20/60). Films: "Heart of the Wilds" 1918 (Val Galbraith); "The Storm" 1922 (Dave Stewart); "Where the Worst Begins" 1925 (Donald Van Dorn); "Call of the West" 1930 (Lon Dixon); "Range War" 1939 (Jim Marlow); "Santa Fe Marshal" 1940.

Moore, Michael. Films: "Silver City" 1951 (Taff); "Pony Express" 1953 (Rance Hastings). ¶TV: *Death Valley Days*—"Dear Teacher" 10-14-53, "The Seventh Day" 3-14-55.

Moore, Mickey. Films: "Out of the Dust" 1920 (Evan's Grandchild); "The Man from Red Gulch" 1925 (Jimmy); "The Lady from Hell" 1926 (Billy Boy); "No Man's Gold" 1926 (Jimmy); "Good as Gold" 1927 (Buck as a Boy).

Moore, Mildred. Films: "The Crow" 1919; "The Fighting Line" 1919; "The Kid and the Cowboy" 1919; "Hair-Trigger Stuff" 1920; "Held Up for the Makin's" 1920; "The Moon Riders" 1920-serial; "The Prospector's Vengeance" 1920; "The Rattler's Hiss" 1920; "The Texas Kid" 1920.

Moore, Norma. TV: *Tombstone Territory*—"The Return of the Outlaw" 3-12-58 (Kay Danbury); *Sugar-foot*—"The Wizard" 10-14-58 (Olivia); *Texas John Slaughter*—Regular 1958-61 (Adeline Harris).

Moore, Owen (1886-6/9/39). Films: "The Dancing Girl of Butte" 1909; "The Indian Runner's Romance" 1909; "Leather Stocking" 1909; "The Mended Lute" 1909; "The Mountaineer's Honor" 1909; "The Redman's View" 1909; "The Broken Doll" 1910; "The Fugitive" 1910; "Behind the Stockade" 1911; "Jordan Is a Hard Road" 1915 (Mark Sheldon); "Code of the West" 1925 (Cal Thurman).

Moore, Pat. Films: "The Squaw Man" 1918 (Little Hal); "A Prisoner for Life" 1919; "The Sleeping Lion" 1919 (Little Tony); "Out of the Dust" 1920 (Jimmie Evans).

Moore, Pauline. Films: "Wagon Wheels" 1934; "Wild and Woolly" 1937 (Ruth Morris); "Arizona Wildcat" 1938 (Caroline Reed); "Days of Jesse James" 1939 (Mary Whittaker); "The Carson City Kid" 1940 (Joby Gilby); "Colorado" 1940 (Lylah Sanford); "The Trail Blazers" 1940 (Marcia Kelton); "Young Buffalo Bill" 1940 (Tonia Regas); "Arkansas Judge" 1941 (Margaret); "King of the Texas Rangers" 1941-serial (Sally Crane).

Moore, Rex (1900-4/21/75). Films: "Shane" 1953 (Ryker Man).

Moore, Roger (1928-). Films: "Gold of the Seven Saints" 1961 (Shaun Garrett). ¶TV: *Maverick*—"The Rivals" 1-25-59 (Jack Vandergelt III), Regular 1960-62 (Beau Maverick); *The Alaskans*—Regular 1959-60 (Silky Harris).

Moore, Sue (1904-4/10/66). Films: "Gold Is Where You Find It" 1938 (Guest).

Moore, Terry (1929-). Films: "Cast a Long Shadow" 1959 (Janet Calvert); "Black Spurs" 1965 (Anna); "Town Tamer" 1965 (Susan Tavenner); "Waco" 1966 (Dolly). ¶TV: *Rawhide*—"Incident of the Tumbleweed Wagon" 1-9-59 (Mrs. Storm); *The Rebel*—"The Executioner" 6-18-61 (Janice); *Empire*—Regular 1962-63 (Connie); *The Virginian*—"High Stakes" 11-16-66 (Alma Wilson); *Bonanza*—"Gideon the Good" 10-18-70 (Lydia Yates).

Moore, Thomas. Films: "Black Eagle of Santa Fe" 1964-Ger./Ital./Fr.; "Bullets and the Flesh" 1965-Ital./Fr./Span.; "Few Dollars for Django" 1966-Ital./Span. (Logan); "Reverend Colt" 1970-Ital./Span.

Moore, Tom (1883-2/12/55). Films: "The Brand" 1914; "The Ja-

guar's Claws" 1917 (Phil Jordan); "Go West, Young Man" 1918 (Dick Latham); "The Cowboy and the Lady" 1922 (Teddy North); "Over the Border" 1922 (Sgt. Flaherty); "The Yellowback" 1929 (O'Mara); "Robin Hood of El Dorado" 1936 (Sheriff Hannan); "The Redhead and the Cowboy" 1951 (Gus); ¶TV: *Wild Bill Hickok*—"The Avenging Gunman" 7-29-52.

Moore, Victor (1876-7/23/62). Films: "Chimmie Fadden Out West" 1915 (Chimmie Fadden); "Riding High" 1943 (Mortimer J. Slocum).

Moore, Vin (1878-12/5/49). Films: "Lazy Lightning" 1926 (Sheriff Dan Boyd); "The Man from the West" 1926 (Lloyd Millard).

Moorehead, Agnes (1906-4/30/74). Films: "Station West" 1948 (Mrs. Caslon); "Those Redheads from Seattle" 1953 (Mrs. Edmonds); "Pardners" 1956 (Mrs. Matilda Kingsley); "The True Story of Jesse James" 1957 (Mrs. Samuel); "How the West Was Won" 1962 (Rebecca Prescott). ¶TV: *Wagon Train*—"The Mary Halstead Story" 11-20-57 (Mary Halstead); *The Rebel*—"In Memorian" 12-6-59 (Martha Lassiter); *Rawhide*—"Incident at Poco Tiempo" 12-9-60 (Sister Frances); *The Rifleman*—"Miss Bertie" 12-27-60 (Miss Bertie); *Wild Wild West*—"The Night of the Vicious Valentine" 2-10-67 (Emma Valentine); *Custer*—"Spirit Woman" 12-13-67 (Watoma); *Lancer*—"A Person Unknown" 11-25-69 (Mrs. Normile); *The Men from Shiloh*—"Gun Quest" 10-21-70 (Ma Garvey).

Moorehead, Jean. Films: "Gunmen from Laredo" 1959 (Katy Reardon). ¶TV: *Death Valley Days*—"The Last Bad Man" 12-16-57; *Northwest Passage*—"The Ambush" 2-6-59 (Eliabeth Browne).

Moorhead, Natalie (1901-10/6/92). Films: "Captain Thunder" 1931 (Bonita Salazar); "Heart of Arizona" 1938 (Belle Starr).

Moorhouse, Bert (1894-1/26/54). Films: "Rough Ridin' Red" 1928 (Sheriff Jerry Martin); "Wells Fargo" 1937 (Clerk); "Nevada" 1944.

Mora, Bradley. Films: "Annie Get Your Gun" 1950 (Little Jake); "Return of the Texan" 1952 (Spiller Boy); "The Vanquished" 1953.

Moran, Betty. Films: "Range War" 1939 (Ellen Marlow); "Frontier Vengeance" 1940 (Ruth Hunter).

Moran, Erin (1960-). TV: *Death Valley Days*—"Biscuits and Billy the Kid" 11-1-69, "The Tender-

foot" 11-15-69 (Mary); *Bearcats!*—"Hostages" 10-14-71 (Elisa Tillman); *Gunsmoke*—"Lijah" 11-8-71 (Rachel), "P.S. Murry Christmas" 12-27-71 (Jenny).

Moran, Francisco. Films: Overland with Kit Carson" 1939-serial; "For a Fist in the Eye" 1965-Ital./Span.; "Shots Ring Out!" 1965-Ital./Span.; "Ringo's Big Night" 1966-Ital./Span.

Moran, Frank (1887-12/14/67). Films: "Call of the Wild" 1935 (Dawson Bartender); "Six Gun Justice" 1935; "End of the Trail" 1936 (Drunk); "Dudes Are Pretty People" 1942.

Moran, George (1881-8/1/49). Films: "My Little Chickadee" 1940 (Clarence).

Moran, Lee (1888-4/24/61). Films: "The Sheriff Outwitted" 1912; "Pardon My Gun" 1930 (Jeff).

Moran, Neil. Films: "High Pockets" 1919 (Henry Allison); "Speedy Meade" 1919 (Robert Bridges).

Moran, Patsy (1903-12/10/68). Films: "The Golden Trail" 1940 (Patsy); "Song of the Drifter" 1948. ¶TV: *The Cisco Kid*—"Fool's Gold" 5-9-53.

Moran, Peggy (1918-). Films: "Rhythm of the Saddle" 1938 (Maureen McClune); "Trail of the Vigilantes" 1940 (Barbara Thornton); "West of Carson City" 1940 (Millie Harkins); "King of the Cowboys" 1943 (Judy Mason).

Moran, Polly (1883-1/25/52). Films: "Hogan Out West" 1915; "Beyond the Sierras" 1928 (Inez); "Way Out West" 1930 (Pansy); "Red River Range" 1938 (Mrs. Maxwell).

Morante, Milburn (1887-1/28/64). Films: "Hearts O' the Range" 1921 (Beldon); "Rainbow Rangers" 1924 (English Charlie); "Don X" 1925 (Frank Paget); "The Range Terror" 1925 (Sam Lee); "The Rip Snorter" 1925 (Tom Moffitt); "Triple Action" 1925 (Scaby MacGonigal); "Buffalo Bill on the U.P. Trail" 1926 (Hearts Farrel); "The Desperate Game" 1926 (Shinney); "The Grey Devil" 1926; "Lawless Trails" 1926 (Lafe Sturgess); "West of the Rainbow's End" 1926 (Tim); "Cactus Trails" 1927 (Jack Mason); "The Fightin' Redhead" 1928 (Sidewinder Steve); "The Little Buckaroo" 1928 (Toby Jones); "The Pinto Kid" 1928 (Pat Logan); "Wizard of the Saddle" 1928 (Hank Robbins); "The Freckled Rascal" 1929 (Hank Robbins); "The Little Savage" 1929 (Hank

Robbins); "Pals of the Prairie" 1929 (Pedro Terrazzes); "The Vagabond Cub" 1929 (Dan Morgan); "The Fighting Trooper" 1934; "Between Men" 1935 (Doctor); "Cyclone of the Saddle" 1935 (Pa); "Defying the Law" 1935 (Tex Parker); "Fighting Caballero" 1935 (Alkali); "Gunfire" 1935 (Bud McGuire); "The Irish Gringo" 1935 (Gold Dust); "The Pecos Kid" 1935; "The Phantom Cowboy" 1935; "The Reckless Buckaroo" 1935; "Red Blood of Courage" 1935 (Gunman); "Rough Riding Ranger" 1935 (Drunk); "Skull and Crown" 1935 (Dad Miller); "The Vanishing Riders" 1935 (Hank); "Wild Mustang" 1935; "Blazing Justice" 1936 (Bob); "Cavalcade of the West" 1936; "Custer's Last Stand" 1936-serial (Buckskin); "Lucky Terror" 1936; "The Old Corral" 1936 (Snodgrass); "Pinto Rustlers" 1936; "Ridin' On" 1936; "Roarin' Guns" 1936; "Sundown Saunders" 1936 (Smokey); "Valley of the Lawless" 1936 (Ed Reynolds); "Bar Z Bad Men" 1937 (Deputy); "Come on Cowboys" 1937; "Ghost Town Gold" 1937 (Jake); "Gun Lords of Stirrup Basin" 1937; "Mystery Range" 1937 (Jim); "Public Cowboy No. 1" 1937 (Ezra); "Range Defenders" 1937 (Citizen); "Sing, Cowboy, Sing" 1937; "Trouble in Texas" 1937 (1st Townsman); "Feud of the Trail" 1938 (Jerry MacLaine); "Gold Mine in the Sky" 1938 (Mugsy Malone); "Heroes of the Alamo" 1938; "Riders of the Black Hills" 1938; "Six Shootin' Sheriff" 1938 (Shorty); "Buzzy and the Phantom Pinto" 1941; "Trail of the Silver Spurs" 1941 (Nordick); "Boot Hill Bandits" 1942 (Cameron); "Dawn on the Great Divide" 1942; "Riders of the West" 1942; "West of the Law" 1942; "The Ghost Rider" 1943; "Outlaws of Stampede Pass" 1943; "Six Gun Gospel" 1943; "The Stranger from Pecos" 1943; "The Lost Trail" 1945 (Zeke); "Drifting Along" 1946 (Zeke); "Ridin' Down the Trail" 1947; "Song of the Wasteland" 1947; "Cowboy Cavalier" 1948; "Crossed Trails" 1948 (Anderson); "The Fighting Ranger" 1948; "Oklahoma Blues" 1948 (Amos); "Overland Trails" 1948; "Range Renegades" 1948; "The Rangers Ride" 1948; "Haunted Trails" 1949 (Cookie); "Hidden Danger" 1949 (Clerk); "West of El Dorado" 1949 (Brimstone); "Western Renegades" 1949 (Jenkins); "Law of the Panhandle" 1950 (Ezra Miller); "Outlaw Gold" 1950 (Sandy Barker); "Over the Border" 1950 (Mason); "Six Gun Mesa" 1950; "West of

Wyoming" 1950 (Panhandle); "Abilene Trail" 1951 (Chuck); "Blazing Bullets" 1951. ¶TV: *The Cisco Kid*—"Carrier Pigeon" 11-3-51, "Romany Caravan" 11-17-51.

Moray, Yvonne. Films: "The Terror of Tiny Town" 1938 (Nancy, the Girl).

Mordant, Edwin (1868-2/16/42). Films: "Outlaws of Sonora" 1938 (Pierce).

More, Kenneth (1914-7/12/82). Films: "The Sheriff of Fractured Jaw" 1958-Brit. (Jonathan Tibbs).

Moreau, Jeanne (1928-). Films: "Viva Maria" 1965-Fr./Ital. (Maria); "Monte Walsh" 1970 (Martine Bernard).

Morehead, Dick. Films: "Cavalcade of the West" 1936; "Undercover Man" 1936 (Rusty Wilson); "Roaring Six Guns" 1937 (Bill); "The Adventures of the Masked Phantom" 1939 (Outlaw).

Moreland, Mantan (1902-9/28/73). Films: "Two Gun Man from Harlem" 1938 (Bill); "Frontier Scout" 1939; "Riders of the Frontier" 1939 (Cookie); "Viva Cisco Kid" 1940 (Memphis).

Moreland, Sherry. Films: "When the Redskins Rode" 1951 (Morna). ¶TV: *The Cisco Kid*—"Carrier Pigeon" 11-3-51, "Jewelry Hold-Up" 12-15-51.

Morell, Ann (1941-). Films: "Tickle Me" 1965 (Sibyl). ¶TV: *Gunsmoke*—"A Man a Day" 12-30-61 (Ana); *Branded*—"Now Join the Human Race" 9-19-65 (Snow Child).

Moreno, Antonio (1887-2/15/67). Films: "A Misunderstood Boy" 1913; "Strongheart" 1914; "By Right of Possession" 1917 (Tom Baxter); "The Captain of the Gray Horse Troop" 1917 (Capt. George Curtis); "The Perils of Thunder Mountain" 1919-serial; "The Border Legion" 1924 (Jim Cleve); "The Flaming Forest" 1926 (Sgt. David Carrigan); "Romance of the Rio Grande" 1929 (Juan); "Rough Romance" 1930 (Loup LaTour); "Wide Open Spaces" 1932-short; "Rose of the Rio Grande" 1938 (Lugo); "The Kid from Kansas" 1941 (Chief of Police); "Undercover Man" 1942 (Tomas Gonzales); "Valley of the Sun" 1942 (Chief Cochise); "Lust for Gold" 1949 (Ramon Peralta); "Dallas" 1950 (Felipe); "Saddle Tramp" 1950; "Mark of the Renegade" 1951 (Jose De Vasquez); "Untamed Frontier" 1952 (Bandera); "Wings of the Hawk" 1953 (Father Perez); "Saskatchewan" 1954 (Chief Dark

Cloud); "The Searchers" 1956 (Emilio Figueroa).

Moreno, Jorge (-4/10/92). Films: "One-Eyed Jacks" 1961 (Bouncer in Shack); "Young Fury" 1965; "Donner Pass: The Road to Survival" TVM-1978; "Last Ride of the Dalton Gang" TVM-1979 (Archulleta). ¶TV: *Maverick*—"Plunder of Paradise" 3-9-58 (Ubaldo), "Poker Face" 1-7-62 (Captain Renaldo); *El Coyote Rides*—Pilot 1958 (Lopez); *Rawhide*—"Incident of the Coyote Weed" 3-20-59 (Sanchez), "Incident at Spanish Rock" 12-18-59; *Bonanza*—"Tommy" 12-18-66 (Waiter); *Wild Wild West*—"The Night of the Surreal McCoy" 3-3-67 (Bartender); *The High Chaparral*—"The High Chaparral" 9-10-67 (Chico), "The Promised Land" 10-25-68 (Bartender), "The Glory Soldiers" 1-31-69 (Ramon); *Gunsmoke*—"The Jackals" 2-12-68 (Perino), "The Cage" 3-23-70 (Alfonso); *The Outcasts*—"The Understanding" 10-14-68 (Captain).

Moreno, Paco (1885-10/15/41). Films: "Mark of Zorro" 1940 (Peon).

Moreno, Rita (1931-). Films: "Cattle Town" 1952 (Queli); "Fort Vengeance" 1953 (Bridget); "Garden of Evil" 1954 (Singer); "The Yellow Tomahawk" 1954 (Honey Bear); "The Deerslayer" 1957 (Hetty). ¶TV: *20th Century Fox Hour*—"Broken Arrow" 5-2-56 (Sonseeahray); *Cimarron City*—"The Town Is a Prisoner" 3-28-59 (Gutterez's Fiancee); *Tales of Wells Fargo*—"Lola Montez" 2-16-59 (Lola Montez); *Trackdown*—"The Samaritan" 2-18-59 (Tina); *Zane Grey Theater*—"The Last Raid" 2-26-59 (Linda); *Walt Disney Presents: Zorro*—"El Bandito" 10-30-60 (Chulita), "Adios El Cuchillo" 11-6-60 (Chulita); *Hec Ramsey*—"A Hard Road to Vengeance" 11-25-73 (Lina).

Moreno, Rosita. Films: "The Santa Fe Trail" 1930 (Maria Castinado).

Moreno, Ruben. Films: "El Dorado" 1967; "Little Big Man" 1971 (Shadow That Comes at Night); "The Deerslayer" TVM-1978 (Tamenund); "Outlaws" TVM-1986 (Deputy Graza). ¶TV: *Wanted—Dead or Alive*—"Witch Woman" 12-28-60; *Wyatt Earp*—"Requiem for Old Man Clanton" 5-30-61 (Marcia); *The Virginian*—"We've Lost a Train" 4-21-65; *Gunsmoke*—"The Mission" 10-8-66 (Captain), "The Jackals" 2-12-68 (2nd Bandito); *Rango*—"What's a Nice Girl Like You Doing Holding Up a Place Like This?" 2-17-67 (Cisco); *The Big Valley*—"Ambush" 9-

18-67; *Death Valley Days*—"Let My People Go" 10-21-67 (Captain), "A Gift from Father Tapis" 5-9-70 (Soldier); *The Guns of Will Sonnett*—"The Secret of Hangtown Mine" 12-22-67 (Vasquez); *Lancer*—"The High Riders" 9-24-68; *Bonanza*—"Shadow of a Hero" 2-21-71 (Sam Greybuck); *Black Bart*—Pilot 4-4-75 (Moonwolf); *The Chisholms*—3-1-80 (Andres).

Morey, Harry T. (1873-1/24/36). Films: "Indian Romeo and Juliet" 1912; "The Deerslayer" 1913; "Under the Tonto Rim" 1928 (Sam Spralls).

Morgan, Boyd "Red" (1915-1/8/88). Films: "Lucky Cisco Kid" 1940 (Soldier); "Desert of Lost Men" 1951 (Frank); "Silver City" 1951 (Townsman); "Snake River Desperadoes" 1951 (Brandt); "Cattle Town" 1952 (Bayo); "The Last Musketeer" 1952 (Barney); "Smoky Canyon" 1952 (Joe); "Thundering Caravans" 1952 (Joe); "The Command" 1953 (Cpl. Fleming); "The Great Sioux Uprising" 1953 (Ray); "Gun Belt" 1953 (Texas Jack); "The Nebraskan" 1953 (Sgt. Phillips); "Thunder Over the Plains" 1953; "Winning of the West" 1953; "Riding Shotgun" 1954 (Red); "Robbers' Roost" 1955 (Brad); "Ten Wanted Men" 1955 (Red Dawes); "The Dalton Girls" 1957 (Stage Driver); "Gun Duel in Durango" 1957 (Burt); "War Drums" 1957 (Trooper Teal); "Ride Lonesome" 1959 (Outlaw); "The Alamo" 1960; "Gunfighters of Abilene" 1960 (Gene); "Five Guns to Tombstone" 1961 (Hoagie); "The Gambler Wore a Gun" 1961 (Luke); "How the West Was Won" 1962; "Arizona Raiders" 1965 (Tex); "The Bounty Killer" 1965 (Seddon); "Requiem for a Gunfighter" 1965; "The Sons of Katie Elder" 1965 (Burr Sandeman); "Waco" 1966; "The War Wagon" 1967 (Early); "Five Card Stud" 1968 (Fred Carson); "The Stalking Moon" 1969 (Shelby, the Stage Driver); "True Grit" 1969 (Red, the Ferryman); "The Cheyenne Social Club" 1970 (Hansen); "Rio Lobo" 1970 (Train Engineer); "Wild Rovers" 1971 (Sheepman); "Deadly Trackers" 1973; "One Little Indian" 1973; "Santee" 1973; "The Soul of Nigger Charley" 1973 (Donovan). ¶TV: *The Roy Rogers Show*—"The Set-Up" 1-20-52, "The Treasure of Howling Dog Canyon" 1-27-52, "The Double Crosser" 6-1-52, "The Mayor of Ghost Town" 11-30-52, "Money to Burn" 6-28-53, "The Milliner from Medicine Hat" 10-11-53, "Gun Trouble" 11-22-53, "Doc Stevens' Traveling Store" 7-25-

54; *The Gene Autry Show*—"The Hold-Up" 12-14-52; *Maverick*—"Comstock Conspiracy" 12-29-57 (Stagecoach Driver); *The Texan*—"The Marshal of Yellow Jacket" 3-2-59 (Pete Nolan), "The Smiling Loser" 5-25-59, "Stampede" 11-2-59; *Bonanza*—"Showdown" 9-10-60, "The Reluctant American" 2-14-71 (Stokely), "Riot!" 10-3-72 (Kelly); *The Westerner*—"Dos Pinos" 11-4-60 (Red Coons); *The Tall Man*—"First Blood" 1-7-61 (Toby); *The Rebel*—"The Threat" 2-12-61 (Garth), "Miz Purdy" 4-2-61 (Jack Tarr); *Wagon Train*—"The Christopher Hale Story" 3-15-61 (Wash); *Wyatt Earp*—"Wyatt Takes the Primrose Path" 3-28-61; *Whispering Smith*—"Double Edge" 8-7-61 (Molloy); *Lawman*—"The Locket" 1-7-62 (Scar); *Rawhide*—"The Bosses' Daughter" 2-2-62 (Cowhand); *Tales of Wells Fargo*—"Portrait of Teresa" 2-10-62 (Cowboy); *Destry*—"Destry Had a Little Lamb" 2-21-64 (Stan), "Go Away, Little Sheba" 3-27-64 (Rider); *Branded*—"Yellow for Courage" 2-20-66; *Daniel Boone*—"The Search" 3-3-66 (Kidder); *Laredo*—"The Would-Be Gentleman of Laredo" 4-14-66; *Hondo*—"Hondo and the Singing Wire" 9-22-67 (Morgan); *Cimarron Strip*—"The Assassin" 1-11-68; *The Virginian*—"Silver Image" 9-25-68; *The High Chaparral*—"Shadow of the Wind" 1-10-69 (Buckskin Frank); *Gunsmoke*—"Captain Sligo" 1-4-71 (Tanner); "The River" 9-11-72 & 9-18-72 (Suggs); *Alias Smith and Jones*—"The Fifth Victim" 3-25-71 (Augie Helms); *Kung Fu*—"Forbidden Kingdom" 1-18-75 (1st Guard).

Morgan, Buck (-8/81). Films: "The Lone Avenger" 1933; "A Demon for Trouble" 1934 (Killer); "Border Guns" 1935; "The Cyclone Ranger" 1935 (Outlaw); "Danger Trails" 1935; "Law of the 45's" 1935; "The Outlaw Deputy" 1935; "Ridin' Thru" 1935 (Cowboy); "Six Gun Justice" 1935; "The Texas Rambler" 1935; "The Vanishing Riders" 1935 (Red Kelley); "Blazing Justice" 1936; "Ridin' On" 1936; "Roamin' Wild" 1936; "The Traitor" 1936 (Lyncher); "Valley of the Lawless" 1936; "The Gambling Terror" 1937; "The Idaho Kid" 1937; "Law of the Ranger" 1937; "North of the Rio Grande" 1937; "Sing, Cowboy, Sing" 1937; "Six Shootin' Sheriff" 1938.

Morgan, Clarence. Films: "The Joyous Troublemaker" 1920 (Turk Smith).

Morgan, Claudia (1911-9/17/

74). Films: "Stand Up and Fight" 1939 (Carolyn Talbot).

Morgan, Del. Films: "Outlaws' Highway" 1934 (Sally Carter).

Morgan, Dennis (1910-9/7/94). Films: "Ride, Cowboy, Ride" 1939-short; "River's End" 1940 (John Keith/Sgt. Derry Conniston); "The Singing Dude" 1940-short; "Bad Men of Missouri" 1941 (Cole Younger); "Cheyenne" 1947 (James Wylie); "Two Guys from Texas" 1948 (Steve Carroll); "Raton Pass" 1951 (Marc Challon); "Cattle Town" 1952 (Mike McGann); "The Gun That Won the West" 1955 (Jim Bridger).

Morgan, Frank (1890-9/18/49). Films: "The Gray Towers Mystery" 1919 (Billy Durland); "Henry Goes Arizona" 1939 (Henry Conway); "Honky Tonk" 1941 (Judge Cotton); "The Vanishing Virginian" 1941 (Robert Yancey).

Morgan, Gary (1950-). TV: *Bonanza*—"The Law and Billy Burgess" 2-15-70 (Chip).

Morgan, Gene (1893-8/15/40). Films: "Rogue of the Rio Grande" 1930 (Seth Landport); "End of the Trail" 1936 (Cheyenne); "Gaucho Serenade" 1940.

Morgan, Harry (Henry Morgan) (1915-). Films: "The Omaha Trail" 1942 (Nat); "The Ox-Bow Incident" 1943 (Art Croft); "Gentle Annie" 1944 (Cottonwood Goss); "Silver River" 1948 (Tailor); "Yellow Sky" 1948 (Half Pint); "The Showdown" 1950 (Rod Main); "Belle Le Grand" 1951 (Abel Stone); "Apache War Smoke" 1952 (Ed Cotten); "Bend of the River" 1952 (Shorty); "High Noon" 1952 (William Fuller); "Toughest Man in Arizona" 1952 (Verne Kimber); "Arena" 1953 (Lew Hutchins); "The Forty-Niners" 1954 (Alf Billings); "The Far Country" 1955 (Ketchum); "Backlash" 1956 (Tony Welker); "Star in the Dust" 1956 (Lew Hogan); "Cimarron" 1960 (Jesse Rickey); "How the West Was Won" 1962 (Gen. Ulysses S. Grant); "Support Your Local Sheriff" 1969 (Mayor Olly Perkins); "Scandalous John" 1971 (Sheriff Pippin); "Support Your Local Gunfighter" 1971 (Taylor Barton); "Hec Ramsey" TVM-1972 (Doc Amos C. Coogan); "Sidekicks" TVM-1974 (Sheriff Jenkins); "The Apple Dumpling Gang" 1975 (Homer McCoy); "The Shootist" 1976 (Marshall Thibido); "Kate Bliss and the Ticker Tape Kid" TVM-1978 (Hugo Peavey); "The Apple Dumpling Gang Rides Again" 1979 (Major Gaskill); "The Wild Wild West Revisited" TVM-1979 (Robert T. Malone); "More Wild Wild West" TVM-1980 (Robert T. Malone). ¶TV: *Have Gun Will Travel*—"A Score for Murder" 11-22-58 (Fred Braus), "American Primitive" 2-2-63 (Sheriff Ernie Backwater); *The Virginian*—"Strangers at Sundown" 4-3-63 (Kendall Jones); *Gunsmoke*—"The Witness" 11-23-70 (Osgood Pickett), "Milligan" 11-6-72 (John Milligan), "The Wiving" 10-14-74 (Jed Hockett), "Brides and Grooms" 2-10-75 (Jed Hockett); *Hec Ramsey*—Regular 1972-74 (Doc Coogan).

Morgan, Horace. Films: "The Border Legion" 1918 (Sam Gulden).

Morgan, Janet. *see* Mehaffey, Blanche.

Morgan, Kewpie. Films: "Dropped from the Clouds" 1917; "Drag Harlan" 1920 (Red Linton).

Morgan, Lee (1902-1/30/67). Films: "Cheyenne Takes Over" 1947 (Delhaven); "The Fighting Vigilantes" 1947 (Sheriff); "Return of the Lash" 1947 (Clark); "Shadow Valley" 1947 (Sheriff); "Stage to Mesa City" 1947 (Sheriff); "Black Hills" 1948 (Sheriff); "Dangers of the Canadian Mounted" 1948-serial (Dale); "Frontier Revenge" 1948 (Jake); "The Westward Trail" 1948 (Sheriff); "Roll, Thunder, Roll" 1949 (Happy Loomis); "Raiders of Tomahawk Creek" 1950 (Saunders); "Border Fence" 1951; "Hills of Utah" 1951; "Ridin' the Outlaw Trail" 1951 (Sam Barton); "The Vanishing Outpost" 1951 (Outlaw Guard); "The Man Behind the Gun" 1952; "Blazing the Overland Trail" 1956-serial (Alby); "Daniel Boone, Trail Blazer" 1957 (Smitty); "The Last of the Fast Guns" 1958 (Johnny Ringo); "Sierra Baron" 1958 (Frank Goheen); "Villa!" 1958 (Rancher); "The Last Rebel" 1961-Mex. (Lang). ¶TV: *The Gene Autry Show*—"Outlaw Escape" 12-1-51, "The Return of Maverick Dan" 12-15-51; *The Cisco Kid*—"Roundup" 4-17-54, "Tangled Trails" 5-29-54.

Morgan, Maxwell. Films: "The Ranger and the Law" 1921 (Daniel Ferguson).

Morgan, Melissa. Films: "Deadwood '76" 1965 (Poker Kate).

Morgan, Michael. Films: "The Gun That Won the West" 1955 (Afraid of Horses). ¶TV: *Tombstone Territory*—"Mexican Bandito" 1-29-58 (Bandit), 11-20-59 (Sam Crane); *The Rifleman*—"The Sister" 11-25-58; *Stripe Playhouse*—"Ballad to Die By" 7-31-59 (Gyte); *The Westerner*—"Treasure" 11-18-60; *Gunslinger*—"The Death of Yellow Singer" 5-11-61 (Wounded Face).

Morgan, Patsy. Films: "Cowboy from Sundown" 1940 (Prunella Wallaby).

Morgan, Ralph (1883-6/11/56). Films: "Wells Fargo" 1937 (Mr. Pryor); "Out West with the Hardys" 1938 (Bill Northcote); "Man of Conquest" 1939 (Stephen Austin); "Geronimo" 1940 (Gen. Steele); "The Last Round-Up" 1947 (Mason); "Heart of the Rockies" 1951 (Andrew Willard); "Gold Fever" 1952 (Nugget Jack).

Morgan, Ray (-1/5/75). Films: "Desperadoes of the West" 1950-serial (Townsman #3); "The James Brothers of Missouri" 1950-serial (Driver/Townsman #4); "The Old West" 1952 (Duffield); "Hidden Guns" 1956 (Emmett).

Morgan, Read (1931-). Films: "Black Spurs" 1965; "Deadwood '76" 1965; "Fort Utah" 1967 (Cavalry Lieutenant); "Hostile Guns" 1967 (Tubby); "Return of the Gunfighter" TVM-1967 (Wid Boone); "Breakheart Pass" 1976 (Capt. Oakland); "Maverick" 1994 (Dealer). ¶TV: *Wild Bill Hickok*—"Monster in the Lake" 8-12-52; *Have Gun Will Travel*—"The Prize Fight Story" 4-5-58, "A Drop of Blood" 12-2-61 (Frank); *The Restless Gun*—"Jebediah Bonner" 9-22-58; *Gunsmoke*—"Passive Resistance" 1-17-59 (Joe Kell), "Dry Road to Nowhere" 4-3-65 (Pete Moreland), "Morgan" 3-2-70 (Lieutenant), "Sam McTavish, M.D." 10-5-70 (Dan Slade), "Sergeant Holly" 12-14-70 (Roy Gast), "The Legend" 10-18-71 (Eddie), "The Predators" 1-31-72 (Brown), "Milligan" 11-6-72 (Potter), "The Boy and the Sinner" 10-1-73 (Jack Beaver), "Trail of Bloodshed" 3-4-74 (Bartender); *Wagon Train*—"The Vincent Eaglewood Story" 4-15-59 (Ben Denike), "The Martha Barham Story" 11-4-59 (Curly Horse), "The Myra Marshall Story" 10-21-63; *Tales of Wells Fargo*—"The Little Man" 5-18-59 (Jeff); *Riverboat*—"The Barrier" 9-20-59 (Clint Casey); *The Deputy*—"Powder Keg" 10-10-59 (Vince), Regular 1960-61 (Sergeant Tasker); *Laramie*—"The General Must Die" 11-17-59, "Night of the Quiet Man" 12-22-59 (Ames), "Cemetery Road" 4-12-60 (Glen Bentley); *Hotel De Paree*—"Sundance and Useless" 3-4-60 (Jesse Hobbs); *Zane Grey Theater*—"A Gun for Willie" 10-6-60 (Clayton); *Whispering Smith*—"The Jodie Tyler Story" 8-21-61 (Hob Tyler); *Wide Country*—"Good Old Uncle Walt" 12-13-62 (Ed Squires); *Bonanza*—"The Ballerina" 1-24-65; *The Big Valley*—"The Way to Kill a Killer" 11-24-65;

Custer—"Spirit Woman" 12-13-67; *Pistols 'n' Petticoats*—"The Triangle" 10-22-66 (Moose Dreyfus); *Cimarron Strip*—"The Last Wolf" 12-14-67 (Jess Daley); *The Men from Shiloh*—"Nan Allen" 1-6-71 (Luke); *Alias Smith and Jones*—"The Day They Hanged Kid Curry" 9-16-71, "The Reformation of Harry Briscoe" 11-11-71 (Charley); *Paradise*—"The Coward" 4-7-90 (Harrington).

Morgan, Robert "Bob" (1915-). Films: "Dakota Lil" 1950; "Shotgun" 1955 (Sam); "The Big Country" 1958 (Terrill Cowboy); "The Man Who Shot Liberty Valance" 1962 (Roughrider); "Alvarez Kelly" 1966 (Capt. Williams); "Macho Callahan" 1970 (McIntyre); "The Culpepper Cattle Company" 1972 (Old John). ¶TV: *The Restless Gun*—"The Peddler" 6-9-58 (Duke Ballinger); *Gunsmoke*—"Stage Holdup" 10-25-58 (Charley), "Sergeant Holly" 12-14-70 (Lomax).

Morgan, Stafford. Films: "Mr. Horn" TVM-1979 (Gen. Nelson Miles). ¶TV: *Daniel Boone*—"Readin', Ritin', and Revolt" 3-12-70, "Bringing Up Josh" 4-16-70.

Morgan, Tracy (1939-). TV: *The Loner*—"The Lonely Calico Queen" 10-2-65 (Francine); *Lancer*—"Blood Rock" 10-1-68.

Morgan, Wesley. Films: "The Lone Hand" 1953 (Daniel Skaggs).

Moriarity, Marcus (-6/21/16). Films: "Flower of No Man's Land" 1916 (Potter, the Butler).

Moriarity, Pat (1896-10/21/62). Films: "The Plainsman" 1936 (Sgt. McGinnis); "God's Country and the Woman" 1937 (Tim O'Toole); "Union Pacific" 1939 (Mike); "Arizona" 1940 (Terry); "Texas" 1941 (Matthews); "Valley of the Sun" 1942 (Mickey Maguire); "Ambush" 1950 (Sgt. Mack).

Moriarty, Michael (1941-). Films: "Pale Rider" 1985 (Hull Barret); "Children of the Dust" TVM-1995 (Maxwell).

Morick, Dave (1934-). TV: *Daniel Boone*—"The Williamsburg Cannon" 1-12-67 & 1-19-67 (Coach Driver); *Alias Smith and Jones*—"Don't Get Mad, Get Even" 2-17-72, "What Happened at the XST?" 10-28-72.

Morin, Alberto (1902-4/7/89). Films: "The Girl of the Golden West" 1938 (Juan); "Outpost of the Mounties" 1939 (Jacques Larue); "Outlaws of the Desert" 1941 (Nickie Karitza); "The Kissing Bandit" 1948 (Lotso); "Strange Gamble" 1948; "Dakota Lil" 1950 (Rurales); "The Gunfighter"

1950 (Pablo); "Rio Grande" 1950 (Lieutenant); "Under Mexicali Stars" 1950 (Capt. Gomez); "Mark of the Renegade" 1951 (Cervera); "Horizons West" 1952 (M. Auriel); "The Man Behind the Gun" 1952; "Pillars of the Sky" 1956 (Sgt. Major Desmonde); "The Cheyenne Social Club" 1970 (Ranch Foreman); "Chisum" 1970 (Delgado); "Two Mules for Sister Sara" 1970 (Gen. LeClaire); "The Wild Wild West Revisited" TVM-1979 (Spanish King). ¶TV: *Maverick*—"Bundle from Britain" 9-18-60 (Hotel Clerk), "Triple Indemnity" 3-19-61 (Chef); *Tales of Wells Fargo*—"The Border Renegade" 1-2-61 (Manuel); *The Virginian*—"We've Lost a Train" 4-21-65; *Wild Wild West*—"The Night of the Inferno" 9-17-65 (Major Domo); *Lancer*—"The High Riders" 9-24-68.

Morison, Patricia (1915-). Films: "Rangers of Fortune" 1940 (Sharon McCloud); "Romance of the Rio Grande" 1941 (Rosita); "The Round Up" 1941 (Janet); "The Return of Wildfire" 1948 (Pat Marlowe). ¶TV: *Have Gun Will Travel*—"The Moor's Revenge" 12-27-58 (Victoria Vestris).

Morita, Miki. Films: "North of Nome" 1936 (Sato); "Border Phantom" 1937 (Chang Lu); "Wild West Days" 1937-serial.

Morita, Pat (1928-). Films: "The Shakiest Gun in the West" 1968 (Wong); "Evil Roy Slade" TVM-1972 (Turhan). ¶TV: *Kung Fu*—"Ambush" 4-5-75 (Arthur Chan).

Morley, Jay (1890-11/9/76). Films: "The Legend of the Poisoned Pool" 1915; "Ace High" 1918 (Harvey Wright); "Who Knows?" 1918 (Surgeon Thomas Rawn); "In the Days of Buffalo Bill" 1922-serial (Lambert Ashley); "The Man Who Waited" 1922 (Joe Rance); "The Verdict" 1922; "Crimson Gold" 1923 (Clem Bisbee); "Face to Face" 1923; "No Tenderfoot" 1923; "Out of Luck" 1923 (Boggs); "Rustlin'" 1923; "The Twilight Trail" 1923; "The Wolf Trapper" 1923; "Behind Two Guns" 1924; "Reckless Courage" 1925 (Jim Allen); "Buffalo Bill on the U.P. Trail" 1926 (Jim); "Davy Crockett at the Fall of the Alamo" 1926 (Zachary Kennedy); "The Mojave Kid" 1927 (Bull Dugan); "Sitting Bull at the Spirit Lake Massacre" 1927 (Pat Mulcain); "The Slingshot Kid" 1927 (Santa Fe Sullivan); "Driftin Sands" 1928; "Man in the Rough" 1928 (Buck Helm); "The Trail of Courage" 1928 (Chili Burns); "The Amazing Vagabond" 1929 (Bill Wharton); "Near the Trail's End" 1931.

Morley, Karen (1910-). Films: "Born to the Saddle" 1953. ¶TV: *Kung Fu*—"A Praying Mantis Kills" 3-22-73 (Mrs. Roper).

Morley, Kay. Films: "Code of the Saddle" 1947; "Six Gun Serenade" 1947; "Outlaw Brand" 1948; "Trail's End" 1949 (Laurie). ¶TV: *The Lone Ranger*—"Rustler's Hideout" 10-13-49; *The Cisco Kid*—"Jewelry Store Fence" 8-11-51, "Water Toll" 9-22-51, "Trouble in Tonopah" 3-21-53, "Pancho's Niece" 9-5-53, "West of the Law" 5-8-54.

Morley, Robert (1908-6/3/92). Films: "The Sheriff of Fractured Jaw" 1958-Brit. (Uncle Lucius).

Moroni, Fabrizio. Films: "Kill or Be Killed" 1966-Ital.; "Shoot, Gringo … Shoot!" 1968-Ital./Fr.

Morphy, Louis (1904-11/7/58). Films: "Son of Paleface" 1952 (Posse). ¶TV: *The Gene Autry Show*—"Six Shooter Sweepstakes" 10-1-50, "Lost Chance" 10-15-55.

Morrell, George (1872-4/28/55). Films: "Heart of the North" 1921 (Father Ormounde); "The Virginian" 1929 (Rev. Dr. McBride); "Crashing Broadway" 1933 (Ernie Tupper); "The Dude Bandit" 1933; "The Cactus Kid" 1934; "The Fighting Trooper" 1934; "The Lucky Texan" 1934; "Between Men" 1935 (Townsman); "Bulldog Courage" 1935; "Circle of Death" 1935 (Drunk); "Courageous Avenger" 1935; "Cyclone of the Saddle" 1935; "Danger Trails" 1935; "Fighting Caballero" 1935 (Beetle); "Law of the 45's" 1935 (Wounded Townsman); "North of Arizona" 1935 (Dancer in Bar); "Pals of the Range" 1935; "Paradise Canyon" 1935; "Rough Riding Ranger" 1935; "Thunderbolt" 1935; "Timber War" 1935; "Tombstone Terror" 1935; "Trail of the Hawk" 1935; "Tumbling Tumbleweeds" 1935; "Wild Mustang" 1935; "Wolf Riders" 1935; "Border Caballero" 1936; "Custer's Last Stand" 1936-serial (Sergeant Flannigan); "Everyman's Law" 1936 (Bartender); "Guns and Guitars" 1936; "Lucky Terror" 1936; "The Law Rides" 1936; "Lightning Bill Carson" 1936 (Gambler); "Oh, Susanna!" 1936; "Red River Valley" 1936; "Rogue of the Range" 1936 (Stage Driver); "Stormy Trails" 1936; "Undercover Man" 1936; "Valley of the Lawless" 1936 (Gambler); "Bar Z Bad Men" 1937; "Boots of Destiny" 1937 (Pedro); "Come on Cowboys" 1937; "The Gambling Terror" 1937; "Git Along, Little Dogies" 1937; "The Gun Ranger" 1937; "Hit the Saddle" 1937 (Patron); "The Idaho Kid" 1937

(Storekeeper); "Melody of the Plains" 1937; "Moonlight on the Range" 1937; "North of the Rio Grande" 1937; "Outlaws of the Prairie" 1937; "Range Defenders" 1937; "Riders of the Rockies" 1937 (Man in Cantina); "The Roaming Cowboy" 1937; "Round-Up Time in Texas" 1937; "Two-Fisted Sheriff" 1937; "Trouble in Texas" 1937 (2nd Townsman); "The Trusted Outlaw" 1937; "Two Gun Law" 1937; "Valley of Terror" 1937 (Man in Saloon); "Yodelin' Kid from Pine Ridge" 1937; "Brothers of the West" 1938; "California Frontier" 1938; "Cattle Raiders" 1938; "The Frontiersman" 1938 (Townsman); "Ghost Town Riders" 1938; "Gunsmoke Trail" 1938; "Heroes of the Alamo" 1938; "Knight of the Plains" 1938; "Overland Stage Raiders" 1938; "Phantom Ranger" 1938; "Pride of the West" 1938 (Townsman); "Rio Grande" 1938; "Santa Fe Stampede" 1938; "Six-Gun Trail" 1938; "Six Shootin' Sheriff" 1938; "South of Arizona" 1938; "Utah Trail" 1938; "Whirlwind Horseman" 1938; "Outlaw's Paradise" 1939; "Silver on the Sage" 1939; "The Taming of the West" 1939; "Texas Wildcats" 1939; "Buzzy Rides the Range" 1940 (Dude Bates); "Phantom Rancher" 1940; "Prairie Schooners" 1940; "Texas Stagecoach" 1940; "Three Men from Texas" 1940; "Bad Man of Deadwood" 1941; "Buzzy and the Phantom Pinto" 1941; "Hands Across the Rockies" 1941; "The Kid's Last Ride" 1941; "Prairie Stranger" 1941; "The Royal Mounted Patrol" 1941; "Dawn on the Great Divide" 1942; "Pardon My Gun" 1942; "Pirates of the Prairie" 1942; "Riders of the West" 1942; "A Tornado in the Saddle" 1942; "West of Tombstone" 1942; "Cattle Stampede" 1943; "False Colors" 1943 (Denton Townsman); "The Ghost Rider" 1943; "Lost Canyon" 1943; "Raiders of Red Gap" 1943; "Silver City Raiders" 1943; he Stranger from Pecos 1943; "Ghost Guns" 1944; "Land of the Outlaws" 1944; "Law Men" 1944; "Law of the Valley" 1944; "Marked Trails" 1944 (Liveryman); "Mystery Man" 1944 (Townsman); "Range Law" 1944; "Texas Masquerade" 1944 (Oldtimer); "Trigger Law" 1944; "The Utah Kid" 1944; "The Whispering Skull" 1944; "Colorado Pioneers" 1945; "His Brother's Ghost" 1945 (Foster); "The Lost Trail" 1945; "Prairie Rustlers" 1945; "Salome, Where She Danced" 1945 (Miner); "Gentlemen with Guns" 1946; "Ghost of Hidden Valley" 1946; "Gun Town" 1946 (Townsman);

"Rustler's Roundup" 1946 (Doc Davitt); "Silver Range" 1946; "Trigger Fingers" 1946; "The Prairie" 1947 (Luke); "Raiders of the South" 1947; "Back Trail" 1948; "Gun Law Justice" 1949; "Mule Train" 1950.

Morrill, Priscilla (1927-11/9/94). TV: *Wild Wild West*—"The Night of the Undead" 2-2-68 (Pahlah); *Bret Maverick*—Regular 1981-82 (Mrs. Springer).

Morris, Adrian (1907-11/30/41). Films: "Powdersmoke Range" 1935 (Brose Glascow); "The Cisco Kid and the Lady" 1939 (Drunk); "The Return of the Cisco Kid" 1939 (Deputy Johnson); "Union Pacific" 1939 (Brakeman); "Wall Street Cowboy" 1939 (Gillespie); "Lucky Cisco Kid" 1940 (Stagecoach Passenger); "The Return of Frank James" 1940 (Detective).

Morris, Aubrey (1930-). TV: *Outlaws*—"Potboiler" 2-28-87 (Whitlow Basset).

Morris, Ben. TV: *Have Gun Will Travel*—"Killer's Widow" 3-22-58; *Wagon Train*—"The Major Adams Story" 4-23-58 & 4-30-58 (Walt Bradley), "The Kitty Angel Story" 1-7-59 (Ben Holden); *Buckskin*—"A Picture of Pa" 10-2-58 (Pike Meadows); *Maverick*—"The Spanish Dancer" 12-14-58 (Harry); *The Rifleman*—"One Went to Denver" 3-17-59; *Wanted—Dead or Alive*—"The Medicine Man" 11-23-60.

Morris, Chester (1901-9/11/70). Films: "The Three Godfathers" 1936 (Bob Sangster); "Wagons Westward" 1940 (David Cook/Tom Cook). ¶TV: *Zane Grey Theater*—"Black Is for Grief" 4-12-57 (Frank Simmons); *Rawhide*—"Incident on the Road to Yesterday" 11-18-60 (Hugh Clements); *Cimarron Strip*—"Without Honor" 2-29-68 (George Deeker).

Morris, Clara. Films: "Where Romance Rides" 1925 (Imogene Harris).

Morris, Corbet (1881-3/10/51). Films: "The Westerner" 1940 (Orchestra Leader).

Morris, Dave (1897-6/8/60). Films: "Tracked by the Police" 1927 (Wyoming Willie).

Morris, Dorothy. TV: *Rawhide*—"Incident at Dangerfield Dip" 10-2-59 (Mrs. Kincaid), "The Child Woman" 3-23-62 (LaVerne Mushgrove); *Wagon Train*—"The Kate Crawley Story" 1-27-64.

Morris, Frances (Francis Wright). Films: "The Ridin' Fool" 1931 (Sally Warren); "Guns for Hire" 1932; "Trailing North" 1933; "Boss Cowboy" 1934 (Mary Ross); "Nevada Cyclone" 1934; "Rawhide Terror" 1934 (Betty Blake); "Pals of the Range" 1935 (Peggy); "The Big Show" 1937; "The Woman of the Town" 1943 (Mrs. Logan); "Lumberjack" 1944 (Mrs. Williams); "Mrs. Mike" 1949 (Mrs. Howard); "Fury at Showdown" 1957 (Mrs. Williams); "Gun for a Coward" 1957 (Mrs. Anderson); "Shoot-Out at Medicine Bend" 1957. ¶TV: *Wild Bill Hickok*—"The Lady Mayor" 7-10-51 (David Sharpe; *Wagon Train*—"The Mark Hanford Story" 2-26-58 (Mother); *Maverick*—"Seed of Deception" 4-13-58 (Mrs. Pearce); *The Restless Gun*—"Bonner's Squaw" 11-3-58 (Mrs. Tapley); *Rawhide*—"Incident at Red River Station" 1-15-60 (Hannah Junkin); *The Deputy*—"Dark Reward" 3-26-60 (Mrs. Carter); *The Virginian*—"If You Have Tears" 2-13-63.

Morris, Greg (1934-). TV: *Branded*—"Fill No Glass for Me" 11-7-65 & 11-14-65 (Cpl. Johnny Macon).

Morris, Happy. Films: "Yodelin' Kid from Pine Ridge" 1937 (Tennessee Rambler).

Morris, Jeffrey (1937-). Films: "The Legend of Tom Dooley" 1959 (Confederate Soldier); "The Long Rope" 1961 (Will Matthews); "Banjo Hackett: Roamin' Free" TVM-1976 (Jack O'Spades); "Goin' South" 1978 (Big Abe). ¶TV: *Death Valley Days*—"After the O.K. Corral" 5-2-64 (Morgan Earp); *Hondo*—"Hondo and the Death Drive" 12-1-67 (Galin); *Bonanza*—"Mrs. Wharton and the Lesser Breeds" 1-19-69 (Dunne), "The Trouble with Trouble" 10-25-70 (Matthew Brody), "A Deck of Aces" 1-31-71 (Turk), "He Was Only Seven" 3-5-72 (Hal), "New Man" 10-10-72 (Tulsa); *Barbary Coast*—"Funny Money" 9-8-75 (Tully).

Morris, John (1886-10/7/69). Films: "The Gentleman from Arizona" 1939 (Peewee); "Queen of the Yukon" 1940 (Runt).

Morris, Kirk. Films: "Rita of the West" 1967-Ital.; "Saguaro" 1968-Ital. (Jeff).

Morris, Lee (1863-2/6/33). Films: "Durand of the Bad Lands" 1917 (Kingdom Come Knapp).

Morris, Margaret (1898-6/7/68). Films: "Face to Face" 1923; "Ghost City" 1923-serial; "Rustlin'" 1923; "The Twilight Trail" 1923; "The Galloping Ace" 1924 (Anne Morse); "Horseshoe Luck" 1924; "Wild Horse Mesa" 1925 (Sosie); "Born to the West" 1926 (Nell Worstall); "Single-Handed Sanders" 1932; "Desert Guns" 1936 (Roberta Enright).

Morris, Philip (1893-12/18/49). Films: "Home on the Range" 1935 (Benson); "Desert Gold" 1936 (Sentry); "High, Wide and Handsome" 1937 (Teamster); "Wells Fargo" 1937 (Express Driver); "The Texans" 1938 (Fen); "Brigham Young—Frontiersman" 1940 (Henchman); "Nevada" 1944 (Ed Nolan); "West of the Pecos" 1945 (Marshal); "Buckaroo from Powder River" 1948 (Sheriff Barnell); "Whirlwind Raiders" 1948 (Homer Ross).

Morris, Phyllis (1894-2/9/82). TV: *The Lone Ranger*—"Banker's Choice" 11-23-50.

Morris, Robert. Films: "In Mizzoura" 1919 (Colonel Bollinger).

Morris, Robert. TV: *The Law of the Plainsman*—"Toll Road" 12-24-59 (Davey); *Wanted—Dead or Alive*—"The Partners" 2-6-60 (Billy Joe Henry); *The Texan*—9-12-60 (Chuck Cameron).

Morris, Roland (1922-5/14/86). Films: "Cactus Cut-Up" 1949-short.

Morris, Rusty (1923-). TV: *Death Valley Days*—"Mr. Godiva" 9-26-54, "Death Valley Scotty" 5-9-55 (Sam Swift).

Morris, Stephen. *see* Ankrum, Morris.

Morris, Wayne (1914-9/14/59). Films: "Land Beyond the Law" 1937 (Dave Massey); "Bad Men of Missouri" 1941 (Bob Younger); "The Younger Brothers" 1949 (Cole Younger); "Stage to Tucson" 1950 (Barney Broderick); "Sierra Passage" 1951 (Johnny Yorke); "The Bushwackers" 1952 (John Harding); "Desert Pursuit" 1952 (Ford Smith); "The Fighting Lawman" 1953; "The Marksman" 1953; "Star of Texas" 1953 (Ed Ryan); "Texas Bad Man" 1953 (Walt); "The Desperado" 1954 (Sam Garrett); "Riding Shotgun" 1954 (Tub Murphy); "Two Guns and a Badge" 1954 (Jim Blake); "The Lonesome Trail" 1955; "Buffalo Gun" 1961 (Rocca). ¶TV: *Colt .45*—"A Time to Die" 10-25-57 (Jim Girad); *Gunsmoke*—"Dirt" 3-1-58 (Nat Siberts); *Maverick*—"Prey of the Cat" 12-7-58 (Pete Stillman); *Wagon Train*—"The Tent City Story" 12-10-58 (Will Hardisty); *Lawman*—"The Master" 12-28-58 (Tod Horgan); *Wanted—Dead or Alive*—"Secret Ballot" 2-14-59 (Barney Pax); *Bat Masterson*—"Battle of the Pass" 2-25-59 (Mace Pomeroy); *Bronco*—"Shadow of a Man" 5-19-59 (Clete Rayner); *They*

Went Thataway—Pilot 8-15-60 (Sheriff Sam Claggert).

Morrison, Albert. Films: "Just Squaw" 1919 (the Half-Breed); "The Flame of Hellgate" 1920 (Blunt).

Morrison, Ann (1916-4/18/78). Films: "The Tall Stranger" 1957 (Mrs. Judson). ¶TV: *Tales of Wells Fargo*—"Run for the River" 11-7-60 (Nora Benson); *Gunsmoke*—"Little Girl" 4-1-61 (Mrs. Henry); *Have Gun Will Travel*—"Genesis" 9-15-62.

Morrison, Arthur (1877-2/20/50). Films: "The Border Legion" 1918 (Sheriff Roberts); "Code of the Yukon" 1918 (Faro Telford); "Desert Gold" 1919 (Lash); "The Heart of Juanita" 1919 (Jim Brandt); "The Challenge of the Law" 1920 (Trooper Tom Wallace); "The Iron Rider" 1920 (Jim Mason); "Riders of the Dawn" 1920; "The Sagebrusher" 1920 (Wid Gardner); "The Sage Hen" 1921 (Grote); "Singing River" 1921 (Sam Hemp); "The Gunfighter" 1923 (Jacob Benchley); "In the West" 1924; "Cold Nerve" 1925; "Riders of the Purple Sage" 1925 (Frank Erne); "Lazy Lightning" 1926 (Henry S. Rogers); "Riding Romance" 1926; "Tony Runs Wild" 1926 (Auto Stage Driver); "Grinning Guns" 1927 (Harvey Purcell); "The Silent Rider" 1927 (Green); "The Lone Defender" 1930-serial (Limpy); "The Sting of the Scorpion" 1923.

Morrison, Barbara (1907-3/12/92). Films: "Three Thousand Hills" 1959 (Miss Fran). ¶TV: *Rawhide*—"Incident of the Devil and His Due" 1-22-60 (Mrs. Gary); *Bonanza*—"The Roper" 4-5-64; *The Outcasts*—"The Long Ride" 4-28-69 (Mrs. Baylis).

Morrison, Chick (1878-6/20/24). Films: "Immediate Lee" 1916 (John Masters); "The Wild Rider" 1919; "The Big Catch" 1920; "Finger Prints" 1920; "A Gamblin' Fool" 1920; "When the Cougar Called" 1920; "Duke of Chimney Butte" 1921 (Kerr).

Morrison, Chuck. Films: "Fighting Pioneers" 1935 (Sgt. O'Shaughnessy); "Gunfire" 1935 (Chuck); "Rustlers' Paradise" 1935; "Saddle Aces" 1935; "Wagon Trail" 1935 (Collins' Henchman); "Wild Mustang" 1935; "Ghost Town" 1936 (Blackie Hawks); "Ridin' On" 1936; "Stormy Trails" 1936; "Aces Wild" 1937 (Heck); "Law for Tombstone" 1937; "Chip of the Flying U" 1939; "Rovin' Tumbleweeds" 1939; "The Golden Trail" 1940; "Rainbow Over the Range" 1940 (Buck); "The Return of Wild Bill" 1940 (Bart); "Ride, Tenderfoot, Ride" 1940; "Riders of

Pasco Basin" 1940 (Johnson); "Son of Roaring Dan" 1940; "Winners of the West" 1940-serial; "Arizona Cyclone" 1941; "Border Vigilantes" 1941; "Jesse James at Bay" 1941; "North from the Lone Star" 1941 (Spike); "Outlaws of the Cherokee Trail" 1941; "Pals of the Pecos" 1941; "The Singing Hill" 1941; "Code of the Outlaw" 1942; "Raiders of the Range" 1942.

Morrison, James (1888-11/15/74). Films: "The Sheriff's Sisters" 1911; "From Out of the Big Snows" 1915 (Edwin Harris); "Sacred Silence" 1919; "The Seventh Bandit" 1926 (Paul Scanlon).

Morrison, Kenny. Films: "The Quick and the Dead" CTVM-1987 (Tom McKaskel).

Morrison, Louis (1866-4/22/46). Films: "The Prodigal Liar" 1919 (Jim Rainey); "His Back Against the Wall" 1922 (Foutch).

Morrison, Palmer. Films: "Scar Hanan" 1925 (Dr. Craig Fleming).

Morrison, Pete (1890-2/5/73). Films: "The Little Doctor of the Foothills" 1910; "Truth or Fiction" 1915; "Fighting Back" 1917 (Mournful Pete); "Cactus Crandall" 1918 (Carter); "The Good Loser" 1918 (Long William); "Keith of the Border" 1918 (Bill Scott); "The Law's Outlaw" 1918 (Carey Tait); "Ace High" 1919; "At the Point of the Gun" 1919; "The Best Bad Man" 1919; "The Black Horse Bandit" 1919; "By Indian Post" 1919; "The Canyon Mystery" 1919; "Captive Bride" 1919; "Dynamite" 1919; "Even Money" 1919; "The Fighting Brothers" 1919; "The Fighting Sheriff" 1919; "The Flip of a Coin" 1919; "The Four Gun Bandit" 1919; "Gun Law" 1919; "Gun Magic" 1919; "The Gun Packer" 1919 (Pearl Handle Wiley); "The Hidden Badge" 1919; "His Buddy" 1919; "The Jaws of Justice" 1919; "Kingdom Come" 1919; "Neck and Noose" 1919; "Riding Wild" 1919; "The Rustlers" 1919; "To the Tune of Bullets" 1919; "A Western Wooing" 1919; "Call of the West" 1920; "The Cowboy's Sweetheart" 1920; "Dangerous Love" 1920 (Ben Warman); "The Fiddler of the Little Big Horn" 1920; "Ranch and Range" 1920; "Vulture of the West" 1920; "Crossing Trails" 1921 (Jim Warren); "The Long Trail" 1921; "The Better Man Wins" 1922 (Bill Harrison); "Daring Danger" 1922 (Cal Horton); "Duty First" 1922; "Headin' North" 1922 (Bob Ryan); "West vs. East" 1922 (Harry Atterridge); "False Play" 1923; "Gentlemen of the West" 1923; "Ghost City" 1923-serial; "Hard Luck Jack" 1923;

"The Homeward Trail" 1923; "Making Good" 1923; "Shootin' em Up" 1923; "Smilin' On" 1923; "The Strike of the Rattler" 1923; "Western Blood" 1923; "Black Gold" 1924 (Don Endicott); "Buckin' the West" 1924; "The Bull Tosser" 1924; "False Trails" 1924 (Stewart "Wolf" Larsen); "Hats Off" 1924; "The Little Savage" 1924; "Pioneer's Gold" 1924; "Pot Luck Pards" 1924; "The Powerful Eye" 1924; "Rainbow Rangers" 1924 (Buck Adams); "Red Raymond's Girl" 1924; "Always Ridin' to Win" 1925 (Hackamore); "Cowboy Grit" 1925; "The Empty Sadle" 1925 (Bob Kingston); "The Ghost Rider" 1925 (Jim Powers); "The Mystery of Lost Ranch" 1925; "One Shot Ranger" 1925; "Range Buzzards" 1925 (Dave Weston); "A Ropin' Ridin' Fool" 1925 (Jim Warren); "Santa Fe Pete" 1925; "Stampede Thunder" 1925; "Triple Action" 1925 (Dave Mannion); "West of Arizona" 1925; "Blue Blazes" 1926 (Dee Halloran); "Bucking the Truth" 1926 (Slim Duane); "Chasing Trouble" 1926 (Blizz Ballard); "The Desperate Game" 1926 (Jim Wesley); "The Escape" 1926 (Johnny Bowers); "Courtin' Wildcats" 1929 (Huxley); "The Three Outcasts" 1929 (Bruce Slavin); "Beyond the Rio Grande" 1930 (Al Mooney); "Phantom of the Desert" 1930 (Jim); "Ridin' Law" 1930; "Spurs" 1930 (Blackie); "Trailin' Trouble" 1930 (Buck Saunders); "Trails of Danger" 1930 (Tom Weld); "Trigger Tricks" 1930; "Westward Bound" 1930; "Three Rogues" 1931 (Teamster); "The Vanishing Legion" 1931-serial (Dopey); "The Last Frontier" 1932-serial (Hank); "Rider of Death Valley" 1932 (Citizen); "Riders of the Golden Gulch" 1932 (Pete); "The Dude Bandit" 1933; "Outlaw Justice" 1933; "Five Bad Men" 1935 (Bad Man).

Morrison, Shelley (1936-). Films: "MacKenna's Gold" 1969 (the Pima Squaw); "Man and Boy" 1971 (Rosita). ¶TV: *Laredo*—"Yahoo" 9-30-65 (Linda Little Trees), "Jinx" 12-2-65 (Linda Little Trees), "No Bugles, One Drum" 2-24-66 (Linda Little Trees), "Split the Difference" 4-7-67 (Linda Little Trees); *Gunsmoke*—"Which Doctor" 3-19-66 (Addie).

Morrissey, Betty (1908-4/20/44). Films: "The Desert Demon" 1925 (Nita Randall).

Morrow, Brad. Films: "The Wild North" 1952 (Boy). ¶TV: *Wild Bill Hickok*—"Cry Wolf" 10-7-52, "The Steam Wagon" 5-12-53; *The Roy Rogers Show*—"Backfire" 10-10-54 (Johnny Loomis); *The Gene Autry*

Show—"Feuding Friends" 11-26-55; Wyatt Earp—"A Quiet Day in Dodge City" 10-9-56 (Toby), "When Sherman Marched Through Kansas" 3-18-58 (Link Hanson); Jim Bowie—"Natchez Trace" 10-19-56 (Peter Jelkins); The Lone Ranger—"The Breaking Point" 1-24-57; Tales of Wells Fargo—"A Time to Kill" 4-22-57 (Finley), "The Happy Tree" 12-22-58 (Jimmy Kramer); Wagon Train—"The Dr. Swift Cloud Story" 5-25-60 (Dabbs Hargrove), "The Barnaby West Story" 6-5-63 (Karl Roberts); Rawhide—"Incident at El Toro" 4-9-64 (Jones).

Morrow, Byron. Films: "40 Guns to Apache Pass" 1967 (Col. Reed). ¶TV: Tombstone Territory—2-5-60 (Bert Magraw); Gunslinger—"Golden Circle" 4-13-61 (Sheriff); Bat Masterson—"Dagger Dance" 4-20-61 (Amos Judd); Rawhide—"Incident of the Painted Lady" 5-12-61, "The Bosses' Daughter" 2-2-62 (Sheriff Crowell); The Virginian—"The Accomplice" 12-19-62 (Bertram Cornwall); Empire—"Burnout" 3-19-63 (Lloyd Halstead); Redigo—"Lady War-Bonnet" 9-24-63; Wagon Train—"The Jed Whitmore Story" 1-13-64; Wild Wild West—"The Night of the Dancing Death" 11-5-65 (Major Domo), "The Night of Miguelito's Revenge" 12-13-68 (Judge Alonzo Farley); A Man Called Shenandoah—"The Death of Matthew Eldridge" 3-21-66 (Matthew Eldridge); Death Valley Days—"An Organ for Brother Brigham" 7-16-66 (Brigham Young); Bonanza—"The Pursued" 10-2-66 & 10-9-66 (Rev. Mr. Blaisdale), "Justice Deferred" 12-17-67 (Belden), "The Sound of Drums" 11-17-68 (Sam Kettle), "A Lawman's Lot Is Not a Happy One" 10-5-69 (Mr. Franklin), "Shanklin" 2-13-72 (Whitlock); The Big Valley—"A Stranger Everywhere" 12-9-68 (Patton), "Top of the Stairs" 1-6-69; Lancer—"The Black McGloins" 1-21-69; Here Come the Brides—"The Fetching of Jenny" 12-5-69; Riding for the Pony Express—Pilot 9-3-80 (Rev. Slaughter); Bret Maverick—"Dateline: Sweetwater" 1-12-82 (Shaw).

Morrow, Doug (1913-9/9/94). Films: "Along Came Jones" 1945 (Rifleman).

Morrow, Jeff (1913-12/26/93). Films: "The Siege at Red River" 1954 (Frank Kelso); "The First Texan" 1956 (Bowie); "Pardners" 1956 (Pete Rio); "Copper Sky" 1957 (Hack Williams); "Five Bold Women" 1960 (Kirk Reed). ¶TV: Frontier—"The

Founding of Omaha, Nebraska" 10-30-55; My Friend Flicka—"The Stranger" 11-11-55 (Mason); Ford Theater—"Sudden Silence" 10-10-56 (Sheriff Tom Frazier); Zane Grey Theater—"Blood in the Dust" 10-11-57 (Jim Horncuff), "The Reckoning" 1-14-60 (Luke); Union Pacific—Regular 1958-59 (Bart McClelland); Wagon Train—"The Clayton Tucker Story" 2-10-60 (Clayton Tucker); The Deputy—"The Jason Harris Story" 10-8-60 (Marshal Jason Harris); Bonanza—"The Honor of Cochise" 10-8-61 (Cochise); Cheyenne—"The Idol" 1-29-62 (Ben Shelby); Tales of Wells Fargo—"Vignette of a Sinner" 6-2-62 (Les Caldwell); The Virginian—"The Man Who Couldn't Die" 1-30-63 (William Bradford); The Rifleman—"End of the Hunt" 2-18-63 (Reef Jackson); Iron Horse—"No Wedding Bells for Tony" 11-7-66 (Sheriff Tom Judson); Daniel Boone—"The Symbol" 12-29-66 (Major Neville Hughes), "Faith's Way" 4-4-68 (Jody Brown).

Morrow, Jo (1939-). Films: "The Legend of Tom Dooley" 1959 (Laura); "He Rides Tall" 1964 (Kate McCloud). ¶TV: Maverick—"The Maverick Report" 3-4-62 (Jeanie Porter); Lawman—"The Bride" 4-1-62 (Melanie Wells); Laramie—"Badge of Glory" 5-7-63 (Helen).

Morrow, Neyle. Films: "Dangerous Venture" 1947 (Jose); "Pirates of Monterey" 1947 (Manuel); "The Big Sombrero" 1949 (Tico); "Ranger of Cherokee Strip" 1949 (Tokata); "The Raiders" 1952 (Juan Castillo); "Goldtown Ghost Raiders" 1953 (Teeno); "The White Squaw" 1956 (Swift Arrow); "Forty Guns" 1957 (Wiley); "Run of the Arrow" 1957 (Lt. Stockwell). ¶TV: Wild Bill Hickok—"Indian Bureau Story" 7-31-51, "Mexican Gun Running Story" 1-8-52; Sugarfoot—"The Desperadoes" 1-6-59 (Pedro's Father).

Morrow, Patricia. TV: Annie Get Your Gun 11-27-57 (Jessie Oakley); The Virginian—"Rich Man, Poor Man" 3-11-70 (Ellen); Gunsmoke—"The Gun" 11-19-70 (Stella Felton).

Morrow, Scott. Films: "Toughest Gun in Tombstone" 1958 (Terry Sloane). ¶TV: Wild Bill Hickok—"Wild Bill's Odyssey" 3-31-53; The Roy Rogers Show—"Junior Outlaw" 2-10-57 (Specs); Circus Boy—"The Pawnee Strip" 4-14-57 (Matt); Buckskin—"The Gold Watch" 8-28-58 (Floyd Worthington), "The Monkey's Uncle" 1-12-59 (Floyd Worthington), "Annie's Old Beau" 4-13-59 (Floyd Worthington); The Restless Gun—"A

Trial for Jenny May" 5-25-59 (Gordon); Wagon Train—"The Christine Elliot Story" 3-23-60, "The Barnaby West Story" 6-5-63 (Kenny Roberts).

Morrow, Susan (1932-). Films: "The Savage" 1952 (Tally Hathersall); "Canadian Mounties vs. Atomic Invaders" 1953-serial (Kay Conway). ¶TV: Sheriff of Cochise—"Helldorado" 12-7-56 (Darlene); Gunsmoke—"Skid Row" 2-23-57 (Ann Cabot), "The Last Fling" 3-23-57 (Melanie), "Cheap Labor" 5-4-57 (Melanie); The Alaskans—"Gold Fever" 1-17-60 (Sarah); Bronco—"Volunteers from Aberdeen" 2-9-60 (Molly Corley); Maverick—"The Iron Hand" 2-21-60 (Connie Coleman); Lawman—"Belding's Girl" 4-3-60 (Meg Belding).

Morrow, Vic (1932-7/23/82). Films: "Tribute to a Badman" 1956 (Lars Peterson); "Cimarron" 1960 (Keith); "Posse from Hell" 1961 (Crip); "Wild and Wooly" TVM-1978 (Warden Willis). ¶TV: The Restless Gun—"Duel at Lockwood" 9-23-57 (Wes Singer); Trackdown—"Man and Money" 12-27-57 (Stoney Buckram); The Rifleman—"The Angry Gun" 12-23-58 (Johnny Cotton), "Letter of the Law" 12-1-59; Wichita Town—"They Won't Hang Jimmy Relson" 10-21-59 (Jimmy Relson); Johnny Ringo—"Kid with a Gun" 12-24-59 (Bill); Bonanza—"The Avenger" 3-19-60 (Lassiter), "The Tin Badge" 12-17-61 (Ab Brock); The Outlaws—"Beat the Drum Slowly" 10-20-60 (Joe Cannon), "The Avenger" 4-13-61 (Tommy Dodge), "No Luck on Friday" 11-30-61 (Sawyer); The Tall Man—"Time of Foreshadowing" 11-25-61 (Skip Farrell); Death Valley Days—"A Matter of Duty" 4-4-62 (Lt. Robert Benson), "Matter of Honor" 4-28-63 (Lt. Robert Benson).

Morse, Barry (1919-). Films: "Welcome to Blood City" 1977-Brit./Can. (Supervisor). ¶TV: Hudson's Bay—"Montgomery Velvet" 3-15-58 (Montgomery Velvet); Wagon Train—"The Shiloh Degnan Story" 11-7-62 (Fogarty).

Morse, David (1953-). Films: "Tecumseh: The Last Warrior" TVM-1995 (Galloway).

Morse, Freeman. Films: "The Vanquished" 1953 (Randy Williams); "Battle of Rogue River" 1954 (Pvt. Reed). ¶TV: Wyatt Earp—"Doc Fabrique's Greatest Case" 4-7-59.

Morse, Robert (1931-). TV: Alias Smith and Jones—"The Day They Hanged Kid Curry" 9-16-71 (Fred Philpotts).

Morse, Robin (1915-12/11/58). Films: "The Great Jesse James Raid" 1953 (Anderson); "Hannah Lee" 1953 (2nd Villager); "True Grit" 1969.

Mortimer, Henry (1875-8/20/52). Films: "Their Compact" 1917 (Robert Forrest).

Morton, Charles (1908-10/26/66). Films: "The Dawn Trail" 1930 (Mart); "Man from Music Mountain" 1943; "Cheyenne Wildcat" 1944; "Firebrands of Arizona" 1944 (Stunts); "Hidden Valley Outlaws" 1944; "Lumberjack" 1944 (Big Joe); "Outlaws of Santa Fe" 1944 (Jim Hackett); "Trail to Gunsight" 1944 (Reb Tanner); "Along Came Jones" 1945 (Fat Card Player); "Plainsman and the Lady" 1946 (Doctor); "Jesse James Rides Again" 1947-serial (Farmer #1); "Wyoming" 1947 (Settler); "River Lady" 1948 (Logger); "Scorching Fury" 1952; "Son of Paleface" 1952 (Ned); "At Gunpoint" 1955 (Bartender); "Shotgun" 1955 (Cavalryman); "Westbound" 1959 (Stock Tender); "The Man Who Shot Liberty Valance" 1962 (Drummer). ¶TV: *Wagon Train*—"The Grover Allen Story" 2-3-64 (Watchman).

Morton, Danny. Films: "Royal Mounted Rides Again" 1945-serial (Danner); "Gunman's Code" 1946; "The Scarlet Horseman" 1946-serial (Ballou); "Eyes of Texas" 1948 (Frank Dennis).

Morton, Gregory (1911-1/28/86). Films: "The Fiend Who Walked the West" 1958 (Gage). ¶TV: *Tate*—"A Lethal Pride" 7-20-60 (Manuel Arriega); *Sugarfoot*—"Toothy Thompson" 1-16-61 (Governor Lee Dandridge); *Death Valley Days*—"The Stolen City" 4-19-61 (Jose Limantour); *The Tall Man*—"The Cloudbusters" 4-29-61 (John Forrest), "The Woman in Black" 5-12-62 (Don Diego); *Daniel Boone*—"Ken-Tuck-E" 9-24-64 (Brayton), "The Prisoners" 2-10-66 (Col. Richard Callaway); *A Man Called Shenandoah*—"Muted Fifes, Muffled Drums" 2-28-66 (Colonel); *Wild Wild West*—"The Night of the Lord of Limbo" 12-30-66 (Levering).

Morton, Howard. Films: "Scalplock" TVM-1966; "The Life and Times of Judge Roy Bean" 1972 (Photographer). ¶TV: *The High Chaparral*—"Too Many Chiefs" 3-27-70 (Proprietor).

Morton, James C. (1884-10/24/42). Films: "Arizona Mahoney" 1936 (Bald-Headed Man); "Song of the Saddle" 1936; "Public Cowboy No. 1" 1937 (Eustace P. Quackenbush); "Way Out West" 1937 (Bartender);

"Brothers of the West" 1938; "California Frontier" 1938; "Bad Man from Red Butte" 1940 (Baldy); "My Little Chickadee" 1940; "The Return of Frank James" 1940 (Bartender); "When the Daltons Rode" 1940 (Juror Ed Pickett); "In Old California" 1942.

Morton, Judee. TV: *Bonanza*—"The Boss" 5-19-63 (Karen Slayden); *Great Adventure*—"Kentucky's Bloody Ground"/"The Siege of Boonesborough" 4-3-64 & 4-10-64 (Jemima Brown).

Morton, Mickey (1935-8/8/93). TV: *Yancy Derringer*—"The Quiet Firecracker" 5-21-59 (Wee Willie Benson); *Maverick*—"Dodge City or Bust" 12-11-60 (Sheriff of Rockford), "Dade City Dodge" 9-18-61 (Sheriff Hiram Tiray); *Bat Masterson*—"Terror on the Trinity" 3-9-61 (Bearded Man); *Rawhide*—"The Prairie Elephant" 11-17-61 (Orlando); *Gunsmoke*—"The Search" 9-15-62 (Coot); *Here Come the Brides*—"The Legend of Big Foot" 11-14-69.

Moschin, Gaston (1929-). Films: "Drop Them Or I'll Shoot" 1969-Fr./Ger./Span.

Moscovich, Maurice (1871-6/18/40). Films: "Susannah of the Mounties" 1939 (Chief Big Eagle).

Moses, Marian (Marian McCargo) (1935-). Films: "The Undefeated" 1969 (Ann Langdon). ¶TV: *Laredo*—"It's the End of the Road, Stanley" 3-10-66 (Letty Willburn); *The Virginian*—"The Gauntlet" 2-8-67 (May Keets).

Moses, Rick. TV: *Young Dan'l Boone*—Regular 1977 (Dan'l Boone).

Mosley, Roger (1943-). TV: *Kung Fu*—"In Uncertain Bondage" 2-7-74 (Seth Packard); *The Life and Times of Grizzly Adams*—2-22-78 (Isaac).

Moss, Arnold (1910-12/15/89). Films: "Viva Zapata!" 1952 (Don Nacio). ¶TV: *The Rifleman*—"The Schoolmaster" 11-29-60 (Stevan Griswald); *Laredo*—"Coup de Grace" 10-7-66 (Captain Henri Declair); *Daniel Boone*—"Take the Southbound Stage" 4-6-67 (Anthony Bedloe); *Bonanza*—"In Defense of Honor" 4-28-68 (Chief Lone Spear).

Moss, Ellen. TV: *The Virginian*—"The Crooked Pat" 2-21-68 (Melissa); *Bonanza*—"Rock-a-Bye, Hoss" 10-10-71 (Elaine Summers).

Moss, Jimmy. Films: "Davy Crockett, Indian Scout" 1950 (Jimmy Simms); "Border Saddlemates" 1952 (Danny Richards).

Moss, Stewart (1937-). Films:

"Bonanza: The Return" TVM-1993; "Gunsmoke: The Long Ride" TVM-1993 (Dr. Stader). ¶TV: *The Loner*—"To the West of Eden" 1-1-66 (Hank Prescott); *Bonanza*—"Ride the Wind" 1-16-66 & 1-23-66 (Aaron).

Mostel, Josh (1946-). Films: "City Slickers" 1991 (Barry Sahlowitz); "City Slickers II: The Legend of Curly's Gold" 1994 (Barry Shalowitz).

Mostel, Zero (1915-9/8/77). Films: "The Great Bank Robbery" 1969 (Reverend Pious Blue).

Moulton, Buck (1891-5/7/59). Films: "A Man of Nerve" 1925 (Bandit); "That Man Jack!" 1925 (Bill Stearns); "The Border Sheriff" 1926 (Limpy Peel); "The Devil's Gulch" 1926 (Heavy); "Black Jack" 1927 (2nd Deputy); "Grit Wins" 1929 (Jake); "Ghost Valley" 1932 (Henchman); "Texas Bad Man" 1932 (Messenger); "The Fighting Code" 1934 (Bond); "Avenging Waters" 1936; "Code of the Range" 1936 (Harrigan); "The Kid Ranger" 1936; "The Unknown Ranger" 1936; "Dodge City Trail" 1937 (Rider); "Empty Saddles" 1937 (Sam); "Outlaws of the Prairie" 1937 (Calvin); "Whistling Bullets" 1937; "Cattle Raiders" 1938 (Jury Foreman); "The Arizona Wildcat" 1939 (Deputy); "Bad Man from Red Butte" 1940 (Jitters); "Ragtime Cowboy Joe" 1940 (Buck Edwards); "The Westerner" 1940 (Charles Evans); "Arizona Cyclone" 1941; "The Apache Kid" 1941; "Hands Across the Rockies" 1941; "Two-Gun Sheriff" 1941; "The Devil's Trail" 1942.

Mountford, Diane. TV: *Fury*—"The Will" 12-27-58 (Penny Blaine); *Bonanza*—"Gabrielle" 12-24-61 (Gabrielle Wickham); *Gunsmoke*—"Call Me Dodie" 9-22-62 (Lady); *Wide Country*—"The Quest for Jacob Blaufus" 3-7-63 (Hildy Blaufus); *Wagon Train*—"The Eli Bancroft Story" 11-11-63 (Milly).

Moustache (1928-3/25/87). Films: "Zorro" 1974-Ital./Fr.

Movita (Castenada) (1915-). Films: "Rose of the Rio Grande" 1938 (Rosita de la Torre); "Wolf Call" 1939 (Towanah); "Fort Apache" 1948 (Guadalupe); "The Mysterious Desperado" 1949 (Luisa); "The Furies" 1950 (Chiquita); "Wagonmaster" 1950 (Navajo Woman); "Saddle Legion" 1951 (Mercedes); "Wild Horse Ambush" 1952 (Lita Espinosa); "Ride, Vaquero!" 1953 (Hussy); "Apache Ambush" 1955 (Rosita).

Mowbray, Alan (1896-3/25/69). Films: "Rose Marie" 1936 (Premier);

"The Llano Kid" 1939 (John Travers); "The Cowboy and the Blonde" 1941 (Phineas Johnson); "My Darling Clementine" 1946 (Granville Thorndyke); "Wagonmaster" 1950 (Dr. A. Locksley Hall). ¶TV: *Maverick*—"The Misfortune Teller" 3-6-60 (Luke Abigor); *Whispering Smith*—"Poet and Peasant Case" 8-28-61 (Lord Hillary).

Mower, Jack (1890-1/6/65). Films: "The Navajo Ring" 1914; "The Worthier Man" 1915; "The Beautiful Gambler" 1921 (Miles Rand); "Cotton and Cattle" 1921 (Jack Hardin); "A Cowboy Ace" 1921 (Bill Gaston); "Flowing Gold" 1921; "Out of the Clouds" 1921; "The Range Pirate" 1921; "Riding with Death" 1921 (Val Nelson); "Rustlers of the Night" 1921; "The Trail to Red Dog" 1921; "The Crimson Challenge" 1922 (Billy); "In the Days of Daniel Boone" 1923-serial; "The Payroll Thief" 1923; "Pure Grit" 1923 (Frank Bolling); "The Rustlin' Buster" 1923; "Stolen Gold" 1923; "Western Skies" 1923; "Ten Scars Make a Man" 1924-serial; "The Crook Buster" 1925; "Cyclone Cavalier" 1925 (El Diablo); "Kit Carson Over the Great Divide" 1925 (Kit Carson); "The Rattler" 1925 (Chick McGuire); "Don't Shoot" 1926; "The Fire Barrier" 1926; "The Gunless Bad Man" 1926; "The Pinnacle Rider" 1926; "Ridin' for Love" 1926; "Sky High Coral" 1926 (Burns); "The Water Hole" 1928 (Mojave); "The Cheyenne Kid" 1930; "Ridin' Law" 1930 (Ricardo); "The Sign of the Wolf" 1931-serial (Butch Kohler); "The Devil Horse" 1932-serial; "The Texan" 1932; "Come on Tarzan" 1933 (Skeeter Holmes); "Fighting with Kit Carson" 1933-serial; "King of the Arena" 1933; "The Fiddlin' Buckaroo" 1934 (Buck); "Bulldog Courage" 1935; "Fighting Shadows" 1935 (Orderly); "Law Beyond the Range" 1935 (Cal); "The Revenge Rider" 1935 (Vance); "Skull and Crown" 1935 (King/Zorro); "Blazing Sixes" 1937 (Wells Fargo Agent); "The Devil's Saddle Legion" 1937 (Dawson); "Cherokee Strip" 1937 (Bill Tidewell); "Empty Holsters" 1937 (Hampton); "Phantom of Santa Fe" 1937 (Captain Rubio); "Prairie Thunder" 1937 (Foreman); "Cowboy from Brooklyn" 1938 (Station Manager); "Dodge City" 1939; "The Oklahoma Kid" 1939 (Mail Clerk); "River's End" 1940; "Santa Fe Trail" 1940 (Surveyor); "They Died with Their Boots On" 1941 (Telegrapher); "San Antonio" 1945 (Wild Cowman); "Cheyenne" 1947 (Deputy); "Montana" 1950 (Rancher); "Spring-field Rifle" 1952 (Guard). ¶TV: *The Lone Ranger*—"Banker's Choice" 11-23-50.

Mower, Patrick (1940-). Films: "Charley One-Eye" 1973-Brit. (Richard).

Mowery, Helen. Films: "The Fighting Frontiersman" 1946; "Range Beyond the Blue" 1947 (Margie Rodgers); "Across the Badlands" 1950 (Eileen Carson). ¶TV: *The Californians*—"The Golden Bride" 5-20-58 (Melissa).

Muellerleile, Marianne. TV: *Ned Blessing: The Story of My Life and Times*—"The Smink Brothers" 9-1-93 (Etta).

Muir, Esther (1903-8/1/95). Films: "The Law West of Tombstone" 1938 (Mme. Mustache); "Western Jamboree" 1938 (Duchess); "The Girl and the Gambler" 1939 (Madge); "Honky Tonk" 1941 (Blonde on Train).

Muir, Gavin (1909-5/24/72). Films: "Fair Warning" 1937 (Herbert Willett); "Salome, Where She Danced" 1945 (Henderson); "California" 1946 (Booth Pennock); "Unconquered" 1947 (Lt. Fergus McKenzie). ¶TV: *Northwest Passage*—"The Long Rifle" 11-23-58 (Col. Benson); *Bat Masterson*—"Man of Action" 4-22-59 (Oliver Jenkins).

Muir, Jean (1911-). Films: "White Fang" 1936 (Syulvia Burgess); "The Outcasts of Poker Flat" 1937 (Helen Colby).

Muldaur, Diana (1938-). Films: "One More Train to Rob" 1971 (Katy). ¶TV: *Gunsmoke*—"Fandango" 2-11-67 (Laurel Tyson); *The Virginian*—"The Masquerade" 10-18-67 (Laura Messinger); *The Outcasts*—"A Ride to Vengeance" 9-30-68 (Peg Skinner); *Bonanza*—"The Passing of a King" 10-13-68 (Mary); *The Men from Shiloh*—"The Politician" 1-13-71 (Rachel Bonham); *Alias Smith and Jones*—"The Great Shell Game" 2-18-71 (Grace Turner); *Hec Ramsey*—"The Mystery of the Yellow Rose" 1-28-73 (Savannah); *Kung Fu*—"The Elixir" 12-20-73 (Theodora).

Mule, Francesco. Films: "Rick and John, Conquerors of the West" 1967-Ital.

Mulhall, Jack (1887-6/1/79). Films: "The Sheriff's Trap" 1915; "Fighting for Love" 1917 (Jim); "The Grand Passion" 1918 (Jack Ripley); "The Bad Man" 1923 (Gilbert Jones); "Call of the Wild" 1923 (John Thornton); "Wild West" 1925-serial; "Skull and Crown" 1935 (Ed); "The Country Beyond" 1936 (Mountie);

"Custer's Last Stand" 1936-serial (Lieutenant Cook); "Secret Valley" 1937 (Russell Parker); "Outlaws of Sonora" 1938 (Dr. Martin); "Home on the Prairie" 1939 (Dr. Sommers); "Outlaw's Paradise" 1939 (Warden); "Saddle Mountain Roundup" 1941 (Freeman); "Sin Town" 1942 (Hanson); "'Neath Canadian Skies" 1946; "North of the Border" 1946.

Mulhare, Edward (1923-). TV: *Daniel Boone*—"The Ben Franklin Encounter" 3-18-65 (Admiral Lord Clydesdale), "Empire of the Lost" 9-16-65 (Col. Marcus Worthing), "The Secret Code" 12-14-67 (Colonel Burton); *Cowboy in Africa*—"The Man Who Has Everything" 12-4-67; *Custer*—"The Gauntlet" 12-20-67 (Col. Sean Redmond).

Mulkey, Chris. Films: "The Long Riders" 1980; "Timerider" 1983 (Daniels).

Mullaney, Jack (1932-6/27/82). Films: "Tickle Me" 1965 (Stanley Potter); "Little Big Man" 1971 (Card Player); "When the Legends Die" 1972 (Gas Station Attendant). ¶TV: *The Outlaws*—"Last Chance" 11-10-60 (Harry Gannon).

Mullavey, Greg (1939-). Films: "The Shakiest Gun in the West" 1968 (Phelps). ¶TV: *Bonanza*—"Commitment at Angelus" 4-7-68 (Kabe), "One Ace Too Many" 4-2-72 (Jordan); *The Big Valley*—"Joshua Watson" 1-20-69 (J.P. Morton); *The Virginian*—"The Girl in the Shadows" 3-26-69 (William McGraw); *Alias Smith and Jones*—"How to Rob a Bank in One Hard Lesson" 9-23-71 (Deputy Lee Harper); *Gunsmoke*—"The Legend" 10-18-71 (Virgil Colter); *Centennial*—Regular 1978-79 (Mule Canby).

Mullen, Virginia. Films: "Lust for Gold" 1949 (Matron); "Winchester '73" 1950 (Mrs. Jameson); "The Treasure of Lost Canyon" 1952 (Mrs. Crabtree).

Muller, Paul (1923-). Films: "Last of the Mohicans" 1965-Ital./Span./Ger. (Colonel Munro); "Thompson 1880" 1966-Ital./Ger.; "To Hell and Back" 1968-Ital./Span.; "Sometimes Life Is Hard, Right Providence?" 1972-Ital./Fr./Ger.

Mulligan, Marina. Films: "Black Killer" 1971-Ital./Ger. (Consuela); "Gunman of One Hundred Crosses" 1972-Ger./Ital. (Marianne).

Mulligan, Richard (1932-). Films: "The Undefeated" 1969 (Dan Morse); "Little Big Man" 1971 (Gen. George A. Custer); "Poker Alice" TVM-1987 (Jake Sears). ¶TV: *Gun-*

smoke—"Wonder" 12-18-67 (Jud Pryor); *Bonanza*—"Kingdom of Fear" 4-4-71 (Farley), "Don't Cry, My Son" 10-31-71 (Dr. Mark Sloan).

Mulock, Al (-1970). Films: "The Hellbenders" 1966-U.S./Ital./Span. (the Beggar).

Mulqueen, Kathleen. Films: "Texas Lady" 1955 (Nanny Winfield); "Toughest Gun in Tombstone" 1958 (Mrs. Oliver). ¶TV: *Sky King*—"Man Hunt" 9-23-51 (Judith Beldon); *Sheriff of Cochise*—"Stepfather" 11-15-57; *Tales of Wells Fargo*—"The Inscrutable Man" 12-9-57 (Mrs. Harper); *The Rifleman*—"The Sharpshooter" 9-30-58 (Nancy Havanan), "The Angry Gun" 12-23-58 (Mrs. Peterson), "Eddie's Daughter" 11-3-59, "The Actress" 1-24-61.

Mulroney, Dermot (1963-). Films: "Sunset" 1988 (Michael Alperin); "Young Guns" 1988 (Dirty Steve Stephens); "Silent Tongue" 1993 (Reeves McCree); "Bad Girls" 1994 (Josh McCoy).

Mummert, Dan. Films: "Thunder Over the Prairie" 1941 (Timmy); "Senorita from the West" 1945; "Bitter Creek" 1954 (Jerry Bonner).

Mumy, Billy (1954-). TV: *Wide Country*—"The Royce Bennett Story" 9-20-62 (David Bennett); *Wagon Train*—"The Sam Darland Story" 12-26-62 (Toddy); *Empire*—"End of an Image" 1-15-63 (Freddy); *The Virginian*—"The Old Cowboy" 3-31-65 (Willy); *Lancer*—"The Kid" 10-7-69 (Andy); *Here Come the Brides*—"Break the Bank of Tacoma" 1-16-70 (Simon).

Munday, Mary (1930-). TV: *Bonanza*—"The Julia Bulette Story" 10-17-59; *Black Saddle*—"Blood Money" 12-18-59 (Grace Baker); *The Deputy*—"The Dream" 2-4-61 (Mildred Lawson); *Gunsmoke*—"About Chester" 2-25-61 (Lilymae), "May Blossoms" 2-15-64 (Nellie); *Have Gun Will Travel*—"El Paso Stage" 4-15-61 (Lena), "Pandora's Box" 5-19-62 (Decora); *Stoney Burke*—"Spin a Golden Web" 11-26-62 (Betty Austin).

Mundy, Ed (1888-2/25/62). Films: "The Gunfighter" 1950 (Street Loafer); "The Proud Ones" 1956 (Saloon Barker); "Gun Glory" 1957 (Ancient).

Muni, Paul (1895-8/25/67). Films: "Hudson Bay" 1941 (Pierre Radisson).

Munier, Ferdinand (1889-5/27/45). Films: "Ruggles of Red Gap" 1918 (Sen. Floud); "Bold Caballero" 1936 (Landlord); "Wells Fargo" 1937

(Mr. Langley); "Northwest Passage" 1940 (Stoodley).

Munro, Caroline (1950-). Films: "Talent for Loving" 1969-Brit./Span.

Munsel, Patrice (1925-). TV: *Wild Wild West*—"The Night of the Diva" 3-7-69 (Rosa Montebello).

Munson, Byron (1900-7/28/89). Films: "Honest Hutch" 1920 (Thomas Gunni-son, Jr.); "Action" 1921 (Henry Meekin).

Munson, Ona (1906-2/11/55). Films: "Wagons Westward" 1940 (Julie O'Conover); "Idaho" 1943 (Belle Bonner); "Dakota" 1945 (Jersey Thomas).

Munson, Warren. TV: *The Big Valley*—"Hide the Children" 12-19-66 (Man); *Daniel Boone*—"The Traitor" 11-2-67; *Here Come the Brides*—"The Crimpers" 3-5-69; *Father Murphy*—"Will's Surprise" 1-12-82 (Doc Thompson), "The Reluctant Runaway" 11-16-82 & 11-23-82 (Doc Thompson); *Paradise*—"Long Lost Lawson" 5-20-89 (Henderson), "Home Again" 9-16-89 (Henderson), "Common Good" 9-23-89 (Henderson), "All the Pretty Little Horses" 10-14-89 (Henderson), "Orphan Train" 10-28-89 (Henderson), "The Burial Ground" 11-4-89 (Henderson), "Boomtown" 11-18-89 (Henderson), "The Return of Johnny Ryan" 12-2-89 (Henderson).

Murdock, George. Films: "The Forfeit" 1919 (Dug McFarlane).

Murdock, George (1930-). Films: "He Rides Tall" 1964 (Burt); "Taggart" 1964 (Army Scout); "The Bravos" TVM-1972 (Captain Macdowall); "Thomasine and Bushrod" 1974 (Bogardie). ¶TV: *Destry*—"Go Away, Little Sheba" 3-27-64 (George Washington Bedloe); *Wild Wild West*—"The Night of the Feathered Fury" 1-13-67 (Luther Coyle); *Gunsmoke*—"Mad Dog" 1-14-67 (Jim Travers), "Rope Fever" 12-4-67 (Bret Gruber), "The Predators" 1-31-72 (Cole Matson), "The Iron Man" 10-21-74 (Luke); *Iron Horse*—"Death by Triangulation" 3-20-67 (Walcott); *Cimarron Strip*—"Knife in the Darkness" 1-25-68 (Bladgey); *Bonanza*—"Different Pines, Same Wind" 9-15-68 (Marks), "The Wagon" 10-5-70 (Luis Getty); *The Virginian*—"A Love to Remember" 10-29-69 (Barton).

Murdock, Jack (1933-). Films: "Calamity Jane" TVM-1984 (Rev. Warren).

Murdock, James. TV: *Rawhide*—Regular 1959-65 (Mushy); *The Monroes*—"The Intruders" 9-7-66;

Gunsmoke—"The Newcomers" 12-3-66 (Pony).

Murdock, Kermit (1909-2/11/81). Films: "Belle Starr" 1941 (Union Officer); "The Godchild" TVM-1974 (Mony). ¶TV: *The High Chaparral*—"The Hostage" 3-5-71 (Seechrist); *Alias Smith and Jones*—"Everything Else You Can Steal" 12-16-71 (Henry Blodgett); *Kung Fu*—"Blood Brother" 1-18-73 (Coroner).

Murdock, Perry. Films: "The Amazing Vagabond" 1929 (Haywire); "A Texas Cowboy" 1929; "Breezy Bill" 1930 (Gabe's Son); "Covered Wagon Trails" 1930 (Chet Clayton); "Headin' North" 1930 (Snicker); "The Man from Nowhere" 1930 (Smiley McCloud); "The Oklahoma Sheriff" 1930; "O'Malley Rides Alone" 1930; "Man from Hell's Edges" 1932 (Drake Brother); "Young Blood" 1932 (Hank); "Breed of the Border" 1933 (Red); "Crashing Broadway" 1933 (Eddie Tupper); "The Gallant Fool" 1933 (Bart Connors); "Trailing North" 1933; "A Demon for Trouble" 1934; "Big Calibre" 1935 (Otto Zenz/Gadski); "Kid Courageous" 1935; "Paradise Canyon" 1935 (Ike); "Western Justice" 1935 (Rufe); "Cavalry" 1936 (Gang Member); "Border Phantom" 1937 (Slim Barton).

Murphy, Al. Films: "Dakota" 1945 (Trainman); "Flame of the Barbary Coast" 1945 (Horseshoe Brown); "Trail Street" 1947 (Dealer); "Blood on the Moon" 1948; "The Bold Frontiersman" 1948; "Surrender" 1950 (Cashier).

Murphy, Audie (1924-5/28/71). Films: "Kansas Raiders" 1950 (Jesse James); "The Kid from Texas" 1950 (Billy the Kid); "Sierra" 1950 (Ring Hassard); "The Cimarron Kid" 1951 (the Cimarron Kid); "The Duel at Silver Creek" 1952 (the Silver Kid); "Column South" 1953 (Lt. Jed Sayre); "Gunsmoke" 1953 (Reb Kittredge); "Ride Clear of Diablo" 1953 (Clay O'Mara); "Tumbleweed" 1953 (Jim Harvey); "Destry" 1954 (Tom Destry); "Drums Across the River" 1954 (Gary Brannon); "Walk the Proud Land" 1956 (John P. Clum); "The Guns of Fort Petticoat" 1957 (Lt. Frank Hewitt); "Night Passage" 1957 (the Utica Kid); "Ride a Crooked Trail" 1958 (Joe Maybe); "Cast a Long Shadow" 1959 (Matt Brown); "No Name on the Bullet" 1959 (John Gant); "The Wild and the Innocent" 1959 (Yancey); "Hell Bent for Leather" 1960 (Clay); "Seven Ways from Sundown" 1960 (Seven Jones); "The Unforgiven" 1960 (Cash

Zachary); "Posse from Hell" 1961 (Banner Cole); "Six Black Horses" 1962 (Ben Lane); "Showdown" 1963 (Chris Foster); "Apache Rifles" 1964 (Jef Stanton); "Bullet for a Badman" 1964 (Logan Kelliher); "Gunfight at Comanche Creek" 1964 (Bob Gifford); "The Quick Gun" 1964 (Clint Cooper); "Arizona Raiders" 1965 (Clint); "Gunpoint" 1966 (Chad Lucas); "The Texican" 1966-U.S./Span. (Jess Carlin); "40 Guns to Apache Pass" 1967 (Capt. Coburn); "A Time for Dying" 1971 (Jesse James). ¶TV: *Whispering Smith*—Regular 1961 (Tom "Whispering" Smith).

Murphy, Ben (1941-). Films: "Alias Smith and Jones" TVM-1971 (Jed "Kid" Curry/Thaddeus Jones); "This Was the West That Was" TVM-1974 (Wild Bill Mickok); "Bridger" TVM-1976 (Kit Carson); "The Chisholms" TVM-1979 (Will Chisholm). ¶TV: *The Virginian*—"The Decision" 3-13-68 (Wes Manning), "The Orchard" 10-2-68 (Mike Bradbury); *Alias Smith and Jones*—Regular 1971-73 (Kid Curry/Thaddeus Jones); *The Chisholms*—Regular 1979-80 (Will Chisholm); *Dr. Quinn, Medicine Woman*—"Father's Day" 1-30-93 (Ethan Cooper).

Murphy, Bill. Films: "The Prairie" 1947 (Jess Bush); "Unconquered" 1947. ¶TV: *Judge Roy Bean*—"The Judge of Pecos Valley" 9-10-55 (Johnny Dillon); *Gunsmoke*—"Blue Horse" 6-6-59 (Lieutenant Eldridge), "Baker's Dozen" 12-25-67 (Monk), "9:12 to Dodge" 11-11-68 (Hugh), "Lobo" 12-16-68 (Ethen), "Pike" 3-1-71 & 3-8-71 (Loomis).

Murphy, Bob (1889-8/5/48). Films: "The Girl of the Golden West" 1938 (Sonora Slim).

Murphy, Charles B. (1881-6/11/42). Films: "When California Was Wild" 1915; "Riders of the Dawn" 1920; "The U.P. Trail" 1920 (Larry "Red" King); "Man of the Forest" 1921 (Snake Anson); "Singled-Handed" 1923 (Foreman); "Rustlers of Red Dog" 1935-serial (Kruger); "Stormy" 1935 (Bartender); "North of the Rio Grande" 1937; "Romance of the Rockies" 1937 (Sheriff); "Panamint's Bad Man" 1938; "Santa Fe Stampede" 1938; "New Frontier" 1939 (Zeke, the Mailman); "Zorro's Fighting Legion" 1939-serial (Pepito); "Adventures of Red Ryder" 1940-serial (Driver #1); "The Tulsa Kid" 1940.

Murphy, Donald. Films: "Masterson of Kansas" 1954 (Virgil Earp). ¶TV: *Frontier*—"The Voyage of Captain Castle" 2-19-56 (Tom); *Wyatt Earp*—"Warpath" 10-22-57 (Lt.

Clark), "The Peacemaker" 9-23-58 (John Ringgold), "Little Gray Home in the West" 5-5-59; *Tombstone Territory*—1-1-60 (Anson Gurney); *Pony Express*—"The Station Keeper's Bride" 3-2-60; *Bat Masterson*—"The Reluctant Witness" 3-31-60 (Charlie Ryan); *Lawman*—"The Salvation of Owny O'Reilly" 4-24-60 (Jack O'Reilly).

Murphy, Edna (1899-8/3/74). Films: "The Galloping Kid" 1922 (Helen Arnett); "Ridin' Wild" 1922 (Grace Nolan); "The King of the Wild Horses" 1924 (Mary Fielding); "Leatherstocking" 1924-serial; "The Silent Hero" 1927 (Mary Stoddard); "Silver Comes Through" 1927 (Lucindy); "The Valley of Hell" 1927 (Mary Calvert); "The Sunset Legion" 1928 (Susan).

Murphy, Horace (1880-1/20/75). Films: "Alias John Law" 1935; "Between Men" 1935 (Burton); "Timber War" 1935 (Charlie); "Brand of the Outlaws" 1936; "The Crooked Trail" 1936 (Carter); "Everyman's Law" 1936 (Sheriff Chris Bradley); "The Fugitive Sheriff" 1936; "Gun Grit" 1936 (Sully); "The Law Rides" 1936; "Lucky Terror" 1936 (Townsman); "The Mine with the Iron Door" 1936 (Garage Man); "Rogue of the Range" 1936 (Sheriff Tom); "Song of the Trail" 1936 (Sheriff); "Sundown Saunders" 1936; "Too Much Beef" 1936 (Sheriff); "Undercover Man" 1936 (Sheriff Pegg); "Valley of the Lawless" 1936; "Arizona Days" 1937 (Sheriff Brown); "Bar Z Bad Men" 1937 (Jake, the Bartender); "Boothill Brigade" 1937 (Calico Haynes); "Border Phantom" 1937 (Sheriff); "Come On, Cowboys" 1937 (Jeff Harris); "Doomed at Sundown" 1937; "The Gambling Terror" 1937 (Missouri Bill); "Ghost Town Gold" 1937; "Gun Lords of Stirrup Basin" 1937; "The Gun Ranger" 1937 (Cook); "Lawless Land" 1937 (Lafe); "Lightnin' Crandall" 1937 (Travis); "The Mystery of the Hooded Horseman" 1937 (Stubby); "Ranger Courage" 1937 (Doc); "The Red Rope" 1937 (Eddy Horner); "Riders of the Rockies" 1937 (Doc Thornton); "Sing, Cowboy, Sing" 1937 (Henchman); "Stars Over Arizona" 1937 (Grizzly); "Tex Rides with the Boy Scouts" 1937 (Stubby); "Trail of Vengeance" 1937 (Rancher); "Trouble in Texas" 1937 (Lucky); "Western Gold" 1937 (Squatter); "Billy the Kid Returns" 1938 (Moore); "Colorado Kid" 1938 (Col. Gifford); "Durango Valley Raiders" 1938 (Matt Tanner); "Flaming Frontier" 1938-serial (Sheriff); "Frontier Town" 1938 (Stubby);

"Paroled to Die" 1938 (Lucky Gosden); "Rollin' Plains" 1938 (Ananias); "Rolling Caravans" 1938; "Starlight Over Texas" 1938 (Ananias); "The Stranger from Arizona" 1938 (Sheriff); "Thunder in the Desert" 1938 (Sheriff); "Utah Trail" 1938 (Ananias); "Where the Buffalo Roam" 1938 (Ananias); "Cowboys from Texas" 1939; "Desperate Trails" 1939 (Nebraska); "Down the Wyoming Trail" 1939 (Missouri); "Fighting Mad" 1939 (Smith); "Oklahoma Frontier" 1939 (Mushy); "The Oklahoma Kid" 1939 (Bartender); "The Oregon Trail" 1939-serial; "Rollin' Westward" 1939 (Missouri); "Rovin' Tumbleweeds" 1939 (Sheriff); "Saga of Death Valley" 1939; "Song of the Buckaroo" 1939 (Cashaway); "Sundown on the Prairie" 1939 (Ananias); "Union Pacific" 1939 (Irishman); "Ghost Valley Raiders" 1940 (Ringleader); "Melody Ranch" 1940 (Loco); "The Range Busters" 1940 (Homer); "Arizona Bound" 1941; "Bad Man of Deadwood" 1941 (Seth Belden); "Honky Tonk" 1941 (Butler); "Lonesome Trail" 1945; "Riders of the Dawn" 1945 (Sheriff); "Song of Old Wyoming" 1945 (Meeks).

Murphy, Jack. Films: "Tumbleweeds" 1925 (Bart Lassiter); "The Texas Streak" 1926 (Jimmy Hollis); "Union Pacific" 1939 (Terry/Fireman).

Murphy, Jimmy (1931-). Films: "Curse of the Undead" 1959 (Tim Carter); "Lone Texan" 1959 (Ric); "California" 1963 (Jacinto); "The Good Guys and the Bad Guys" 1969 (Buckshot). ¶TV: *Buckskin*—"Cousin Casey" 3-9-59 (Casey); *Wyatt Earp*—"Miss Sadie" 12-20-60 (Joe); *Daniel Boone*—"The Spanish Horse" 11-23-67.

Murphy, John Daly (1873-11/20/34). Films: "Oh, Johnny!" 1918 (Van Pelt Butler).

Murphy, Mary (1931-). Films: "Sitting Bull" 1954 (Kathy); "A Man Alone" 1955 (Nadine Corrigan); "The Maverick Queen" 1956 (Lucy Lee); "Junior Bonner" 1972 (Ruth Bonner). ¶TV: *Wagon Train*—"The Luke O'Malley Story" 1-1-58 (Martha); *The Restless Gun*—"Four Lives" 4-13-59 (Mary Clayton); *Black Saddle*—"The Cabin" 4-1-60 (Laurie); *The Westerner*—"Going Home" 12-16-60; *Laramie*—"Riders of the Night" 3-7-61 (Sandy), "Trigger Point" 5-16-61 (Lottie); *The Rebel*—"Ben White" 5-28-61 (T); *Redigo*—"Lady War-Bonnet" 9-24-63 (Laura McAdams); *Laredo*—"Enemies and Brother" 2-17-67 (Jessica Boyd); *Death Valley*

Days—"Shanghai Kelly's Birthday Party" 10-7-67 (Marianne).

Murphy, Maura. Films: "Drango" 1957 (Young Woman). ¶TV: *Annie Oakley*—"The Dude Stagecoach" 1-30-54 (Patricia Dennis); *Frontier*—"The Big Dry" 3-18-56 (Louise Hart), "Salt War" 4-22-56 (Mrs. Shaw); *Death Valley Days*—"The Jackass Mail" 6-30-57.

Murphy, Maurice (1913-11/23/78). Films: "Call of the Heart" 1928 (Josh O'Day); "The Shepherd of the Hills" 1928 (Little Pete); "The Three Outcasts" 1929 (Dick as a Boy).

Murphy, Melissa. Films: "The Magnificent Seven Ride" 1972 (Madge Buchanan). ¶TV: *Bonanza*—"Yonder Man" 12-8-68 (Noreen), "The Witness" 9-21-69 (Jenny Winters), "The Hidden Enemy" 11-28-72 (Nancy Agar); *Lancer*—"Blind Man's Bluff" 9-23-69 (Mattie Cable); *Gunsmoke*—"Celia" 2-23-70 (Celia Madden), "One for the Road" 1-24-72 (Elsie), "The Wedding" 3-13-72 (Donna Clayton).

Murphy, Michael (1949-). Films: "McCabe and Mrs. Miller" 1971 (Sears). ¶TV: *Bonanza*—"The Burning Sky" 1-28-68 (Web Holt); *Here Come the Brides*—"Letter of the Law" 10-30-68 (Ethan); *Alias Smith and Jones*—"The McCreedy Bush" 1-21-71 (Delgado).

Murphy, Pamela (1945-). TV: *The Guns of Will Sonnett*—"Stopover in a Troubled Town" 2-2-68; *The Virginian*—"A Time of Terror" 2-11-70 (Emily).

Murphy, William. Films: "Outlaw Queen" 1957; "The Rawhide Trail" 1958 (Elbe Rotter). ¶TV: *Laramie*—"Deadly Is the Night" 11-7-61 (Dave).

Murray, Charles (1872-7/29/41). Films: "Hogan Out West" 1915; "The Mine with the Iron Door" 1924 (Thad Groves); "Sundown" 1924 (Pat Meech).

Murray, Jr., Charles. Films: "Death Valley Manhunt" 1943 (Danny); "The Law Rides Again" 1943 (Marshal); "Arizona Whirlwind" 1944 (Ted Hodges); "Sonora Stagecoach" 1944 (Weasel); "Two-Fisted Ranger" 1946.

Murray, Don (1929-). Films: "From Hell to Texas" 1958 (Tod Lohman); "Three Thousand Hills" 1959 (Lat Evans); "One Foot in Hell" 1960 (Dan Keats); "Kid Rodelo" 1966-U.S./Span. (Kid Rodelo); "The Plainsman" 1966 (Wild Bill Hickok); "The Intruders" TVM-1970 (Sam Garrison). ¶TV: *The Outcasts*—Reg-

ular 1968-69 (Earl Corey); *How the West Was Won*—Episode One 2-6-77 (Anderson), Episode Two 2-7-77 (Anderson), Episode Three 2-14-77 (Anderson).

Murray, Forbes. Films: "Wells Fargo" 1937; "The Lone Ranger" 1938-serial (Marcus Jeffries); "Cowboys from Texas" 1939; "Pest from the West" 1939-short; "Spoilers of the Range" 1939 (David Rowland); "Ride, Tenderfoot, Ride" 1940 (Henry Walker); "The Apache Kid" 1941 (Commissioner); "Prairie Stranger" 1941 (Jud Evans); "Saddlemates" 1941 (Col. Langley); "Cowboy Serenade" 1942; "Jesse James, Jr." 1942; "Calling Wild Bill Elliott" 1943; "Canyon City" 1943; "Hoppy Serves a Writ" 1943 (Ben Hollister); "The Leather Burners" 1943 (Bart); "Thundering Trails" 1943; "Hidden Valley Outlaws" 1944; "Bells of Rosarita" 1945; "Santa Fe Saddlemates" 1945; "Cowboy Blues" 1946; "Fool's Gold" 1946 (Col. Jed Landy); "Romance of the West" 1946 (Commissioner Wright); "The Wistful Widow of Wagon Gap" 1947; "The Dead Don't Dream" 1948 (Sheriff Thompson); "Silent Conflict" 1948 (Randall); "Horizons West" 1952 (Player); "Road Agent" 1952 (Adams).

Murray, Gary. Films: "Ghost Town" 1956 (Alex); "Escape from Red Rock" 1958 (Cal Bowman). ¶TV: *Maverick*—"Arizona Black Maria" 10-9-60 (Red Feather).

Murray, Ian. TV: *The Cisco Kid*—"Kilts and Sombreros" 5-1-54; *The Rifleman*—"The Challenge" 4-7-59, "Brood Brothers" 5-26-59 (Harley), "Obituary" 10-20-59, "Meeting at Midnight" 5-17-60, "The Hangman" 5-31-60, "The Illustrator" 12-13-60.

Murray, James (1901-7/11/36). Films: "Skull and Crown" 1935 (Brent).

Murray, Jan (1917-). Films: "Banjo Hackett: Roamin' Free" TVM-1976 (Jethro Swain). ¶TV: *Zane Grey Theater*—"The Empty Shell" 3-30-61 (Cletis Madden); *Cowboy in Africa*—"African Rodeo" 1-15-68 & 1-22-68 (Trevor Wellington).

Murray, John T. (1886-2/12/57). Films: "Call of the Wild" 1935 (Heavy on Stage); "The Bad Man of Brimstone" 1937 (Preacher); "High, Wide and Handsome" 1937 (Mr. Green); "Cowboy from Brooklyn" 1938 (Col. Rose).

Murray, Ken (1903-10/12/88).

Films: "The Marshal's Daughter" 1953 (Sliding Bill Murray); "The Man Who Shot Liberty Valance" 1962 (Doc Willoughby); "The Way West" 1967 (Hank). ¶TV: *Death Valley Days*—"Gamble with Death" 2-22-61 (Dave Eldridge), "Little Cayuse" 2-8-64 (Whipsaw McGee).

Murray, Mae (1889-3/23/65). Films: "What Am I Bid?" 1919 (Betty Yarnell).

Murray, Rick. TV: *The Lone Ranger*—"The Frightened Woman" 9-30-54; *Sergeant Preston of the Yukon*—"The Stolen Malamute" 4-4-57 (Jimmy Gibbs); *Zane Grey Theater*—"Day of the Killing" 1-8-59 (Kim Sutton); *The Virginian*—"The Brazen Bell" 10-17-62; *Gunsmoke*—"The Glory and the Mud" 1-4-64 (Young Buck).

Murray, Tom (1874-8/27/35). Films: "White Renegade" 1931.

Murray, Zon (-3/2/79). Films: "Lonesome Trail" 1945; "The El Paso Kid" 1946 (Moyer); "The Fighting Frontiersman" 1946; "Ghost of Hidden Valley" 1946 (Arnold); "Song of the Sierras" 1946; "Terror Trail" 1946; "Code of the Saddle" 1947; "Gun Talk" 1947 (Nolan); "Law Comes to Gunsight" 1947; "Law of the Canyon" 1947; "Rainbow Over the Rockies" 1947; "Trail of the Mounties" 1947; "West of Dodge City" 1947; "West to Glory" 1947 (Avery); "The Wistful Widow of Wagon Gap" 1947 (Cowboy); "Blood on the Moon" 1948 (Nels Titterton); "Crossed Trails" 1948 (Curtin); "False Paradise" 1948; "Grand Canyon Trail" 1948; "Oklahoma Blues" 1948 (Matt Drago); "Phantom Valley" 1948 (Frazer); "Grand Canyon" 1949 (Morgan); "Gun Law Justice" 1949; "Son of a Badman" 1949 (Horn); "Trail's End" 1949 (Kettering); "Dallas" 1950 (Cullen Marlow); "The Kid from Texas" 1950 (Lucas); "Outlaws of Texas" 1950 (Wilkins); "Along the Great Divide" 1951 (Wilson, the Witness); "The Longhorn" 1951 (Tyler); "Night Riders of Montana" 1951 (Joe); "Oklahoma Justice" 1951; "Pecos River" 1951 (Mose); "Wanted Dead or Alive" 1951; "Barbed Wire" 1952; "Border Saddlemates" 1952 (Matt Lacey); "Carson City" 1952; "Cripple Creek" 1952 (Lefty); "Desperadoes' Outpost" 1952 (Tony); "Laramie Mountains" 1952 (Carson); "Son of Geronimo" 1952-serial (Bat); "Down Laredo Way" 1953 (Joe); "Old Overland Trail" 1953 (Mack); "On Top of Old Smoky" 1953 (Bud); "Powder River" 1953 (Henchman); "Vigilante Terror" 1953; "Bitter

Creek" 1954 (2nd Rider); "The Outlaw's Daughter" 1954 (Duke, the Bartender); "Passion" 1954 (Barca); "The Phantom Stallion" 1954; "Riding with Buffalo Bill" 1954-serial; "The Lone Ranger" 1956 (Goss); "The Lonely Man" 1957; "Escape from Red Rock" 1958 (Krug); "Gunsmoke in Tucson" 1958 (Bragg); "Requiem for a Gunfighter" 1965. ¶TV: *The Lone Ranger*—"Pay Dirt" 3-23-50, "Trader Boggs" 1-15-53, "The Frightened Woman" 9-30-54; *The Gene Autry Show*—"Six Shooter Sweepstakes" 10-1-50, "Lost Chance" 10-15-55; *The Cisco Kid*—"Dog Story" 5-12-51, "The Old Bum" 6-9-51, "Water Rights" 7-7-51, "Hypnotist Murder" 11-10-51, "Ghost Town Story" 12-22-51, "Monkey Business" 1-26-52, "The Ventriloquist" 2-7-53, "Cisco Plays the Ghost" 2-21-53, "A Six-Gun for No Pain" 2-28-53, "Stolen River" 10-3-53, "Montezuma's Treasure" 11-7-53, "Bounty Men" 1-30-54; *Wild Bill Hickok*—"The Border City Election" 9-18-51; *The Roy Rogers Show*—"The Set-Up" 1-20-52, "The Mayor of Ghost Town" 11-30-52, "The Milliner from Medicine Hat" 10-11-53, "Doc Stevens' Traveling Store" 7-25-54; *The Adventures of Rin Tin Tin*—"Rusty Meets Mr. Nobody" 5-4-56 (Art Dawson); *Wyatt Earp*—"The Nice Ones Always Die First" 4-2-57 (Alf Walker), "The Kansas Lily" 2-11-58 (Gus), "Casey and the Clowns" 2-21-61 (Sam Newton); *Tales of the Texas Rangers*—"Panhandle" 9-22-57 (Ross Pardee); *Maverick*—"Point Blank" 9-29-57 (Callahan); *Sergeant Preston of the Yukon*—"Boy Alone" 2-20-58, "The Stolen Malamute" 4-4-57 (John Gibbs); *Have Gun Will Travel*—"Gun Shy" 3-29-58; *Rawhide*—"Incident of the Roman Candles" 7-10-59 (Harv), "Grandma's Money" 2-23-62; *Bonanza*—"The Sun Mountain Herd" 9-19-59 (Miner), "My Son, My Son" 1-19-64; *The Deputy*—"Bitter Foot" 11-5-60 (Joe Foss); *Gunslinger*—"Rampage" 3-16-61 (Hix).

Murrell, Alys. Films: "Branded a Bandit" 1924 (Jeanne); "Branded a Thief" 1925; "Flying Hoofs" 1925 (Mary Conner); "Rough Going" 1925 (La Rosita).

Murtagh, Kate (1920-). Films: "Gun Fight" 1961 (Molly). ¶TV: *Wagon Train*—"The Geneva Balfour Story" 1-20-64; *Laredo*—"I See By Your Outfit" 9-23-65; *A Man Called Shenandoah*—"The Reward" 11-29-65 (Maude); *Daniel Boone*—"The Jasser Ledbedder Story" 2-2-67 (Lucy Ledbedder).

Murton, Lionel (1915-). Films: "Cannon for Cordoba" 1970.

Musante, Tony (1936-). Films: "The Mercenary" 1968-Ital./Span. (Eufemio).

Muse, Clarence (1889-10/13/79). Films: "The Fighting Sheriff" 1931 (Curfew); "Massacre" 1934 (Sam); "Daniel Boone" 1936 (Pompey); "Belle Starr" 1941; "Sin Town" 1942 (Porter); "Unconquered" 1947 (Jason); "Apache Drums" 1951 (Jehu); "The First Traveling Saleslady" 1956 (Amos); "Buck and the Preacher" 1972 (Cudjo).

Mustin, Burt (1882-1/28/77). Films: "The Lusty Men" 1952 (Jeremiah); "The Moonlighter" 1953; "The Silver Whip" 1953 (Uncle Ben); "Cattle Queen of Montana" 1954 (Dan); "Silver Lode" 1954 (Spectator); "Cat Ballou" 1965 (Accuser); "The Adventures of Bullwhip Griffin" 1967; "The Great Bank Robbery" 1969 (Glazier); "The Over-the-Hill Gang Rides Again" TVM-1970 (Best Man); "A Time for Dying" 1971 (Seth); "Baker's Hawk" 1976 (General). ¶TV: *The Adventures of Kit Carson*—"Fury at Red Gulch" 10-27-51 (Bill Lowery); *The Lone Ranger*—"Heritage of Treason" 2-3-55; *The Adventures of Rin Tin Tin*—"The Legacy of Sean O'Hara" 3-4-55 (Jameson Penrose); *Tales of the Texas Rangers*—"Home in San Antone" 10-22-55 (Ned Watkins); *Maverick*—"The Day They Hanged Bret Maverick" 9-21-58 (Henry); *Tombstone Territory*—"The Black Diamond" 4-17-59 (Lucky Oliver); *G.E. Theater*—"Aftermath" 4-17-60; *The Texan*—"Twenty-Four Hours to Live" 9-5-60; *Bonanza*—"The Many Faces of Gideon Flinch" 11-5-61, "The Saga of Whizzer McGee" 4-28-63 (Mashburn), "The Meredith Smith" 10-31-65 (Jake Smith), "A Real Nice, Friendly Little Town" 11-27-66 (Old Man); *Wagon Train*—"The Jed Whitmore Story" 1-13-64; *Destry*—"Blood Brother-in-Law" 4-17-64 (the Rev. Mr. Simpson); *Pistols 'n' Petticoats*—11-12-66 (Old Man); *Cimarron Strip*—"The Deputy" 12-21-67 (Ruckles),"Big Jessie" 2-8-68; *Gunsmoke*—"Hill Girl" 1-29-68, "Uncle Finney" 10-14-68 (Uncle Finney); *Alias Smith and Jones*—"Never Trust an Honest Man" 4-15-71 (Jeweler).

Musy, Gianni (1931-). Films: "Grandsons of Zorro" 1968-Ital. (Ramirez).

Muzquiz, Carlos (1906-2/60). Films: "Sierra Baron" 1958 (Andrews); "Ten Days to Tulara" 1958 (Dario); "Villa!" 1958 (Cobb).

Myers, Carmel (1901-11/9/80). Films: "Breaking Through" 1921-serial; "The Love Gambler" 1922 (Jean McClelland).

Myers, Cynthia. Films: "Molly and Lawless John" 1972 (Dolly).

Myers, Harry (1882-12/25/38). Films: "The Masked Rider" 1919-serial; "On the High Card" 1921 (Harry Holt); "The Bad Man" 1923 (Red Gittings); "Zander the Great" 1925 (Texas); "Potluck Pards" 1934; "Ridin' Gent" 1934-short.

Myers, Kathleen. Films: "Cyclone Smith's Vow" 1921; "Flaming Hearts" 1922; "Go West" 1925 (Gloria Thompson); "The Gentle Cyclone" 1926 (Mary Wilkes); "A Gentleman Preferred" 1928 (Maryann Carter).

Myers, Otto. Films: "Gun Law" 1919; "Sundown Slim" 1920 (Bud Shoop); "The Gambling Fool" 1925 (Stringy Hawkins).

Myers, Pauline (1913-). TV: *Jim Bowie*—"The General's Disgrace" 4-12-57 (Lulu); *Gunsmoke*—"The Good Samaritans" 3-10-69 (Mama Olabelle).

Myers, Ray. Films: "The Invaders" 1912; "The Law of the West" 1912; "The Prospector's Daughter" 1912; "The Sergeant's Boy" 1912; "War on the Plains" 1912; "The Battle of Bull Run" 1913; "Wynona's Vengeance" 1913; "The Boundary Line" 1915; "The Race War" 1915.

Myhers, John (1924-5/27/92). TV: *The High Chaparral*—"Too Late the Epitaph" 11-6-70 (Stoker).

Myles, Norbert A. (1887-3/15/66). Films: "The Girl Stage Driver" 1914; "The Squatter" 1914; "Avarice" 1915; "The Dawn Road" 1915; "The Oath of Smoky Joe" 1915; "The Code of the Mounted" 1916; "The Stain in the Blood" 1916 (Joe Thompson); "Truthful Tulliver" 1917 (York Cantrell); "Saddle Cyclone" 1925 (Frank Lowery); "A Streak of Luck" 1925 (Sam Kellman); "Under Fire" 1926; "A One Man Game" 1927 (Stephen Laban); "The Return of the Riddle Rider" 1927-serial; "The Two Fister" 1927; "The Ambuscade" 1928.

Mylong, John (1892-9/7/75). Films: "Unconquered" 1947 (Col. Henry Bouquet); "Annie Get Your Gun" 1950 (Kaiser Wilhelm II); "Young Daniel Boone" 1950 (Col. von Arnheim). ¶TV: *Black Saddle*—"Client: Starkey" 2-7-59 (Karl Borgen).

Myrtil, Odette (1898-11/18/78). Films: "The Fighting Kentuckian" 1949 (Madame DeMarchand).

Nace, Anthony. Films: "Sunset Trail" 1938 (Steve Dorman).

Nader, George (1921-). Films: "Rustlers on Horseback" 1950 (Jack Reynolds); "Overland Telegraph" 1951 (Paul Manning); "Four Guns to the Border" 1954 (Bronco); "Nakia" TVM-1974 (McMasters). ¶TV: *Sergeant Preston of the Yukon*—"Golden Gift" 6-14-56 (Bob); *Laramie*—".45 Calibre" 11-15-60 (Wells Clark).

Nader, Michael (1945-). Films: "Blue" 1968 (Mexican Assassin).

Nadja. Films: "The Night Rider" 1932 (Tula Fernandez).

Nagel, Anne (1915-7/6/66). Films: "The Devil's Saddle Legion" 1937 (Karen Ordley); "Guns of the Pecos" 1937 (Alice Burton); "My Little Chickadee" 1940 (Miss Ermingarde Foster); "Winners of the West" 1940-serial (Claire Hartford); "Road Agent" 1941 (Lola); "Stagecoach Buckaroo" 1942 (Nina). ¶TV: *Circus Boy*—"The Return of Buffalo Bill" 12-12-57 (Louisa Cody).

Nagel, Conrad (1897-2/24/70). TV: *Bat Masterson*—"Sharpshooter" 2-11-59 (Harry Varden); *Gunsmoke*—"The Prisoner" 5-19-62 (Major Emerson Owen).

Nail, Joanne. TV: *Young Maverick*—"Clancy" 11-28-79 (Rose).

Nails, Shirley. Films: "Riders of the Purple Sage" 1931 (Fay Larkin).

Naish, Herbert. Films: "Young Daniel Boone" 1950 (Pvt. Haslet).

Naish, J. Carroll (1897-1/24/73). Films: "Gun Smoke" 1931 (Mink Gordon); "The Conquerors" 1932; "The Last Trail" 1933 (John Ross); "Silent Men" 1933 (Jack Wilder); "The Whirlwind" 1933 (Injun); "Under the Pampas Moon" 1935 (Tito); "Ramona" 1936 (Juan Can); "Robin Hood of El Dorado" 1936 (Three-Fingered Jack); "Border Cafe" 1937 (Rocky Alton); "Thunder Trail" 1937 (Rafael Lopez); "Jackass Mail" 1942 (Signor O'Sullivan); "Bad Bascomb" 1946 (Bart Yancy); "The Kissing Bandit" 1948 (Chico); "Canadian Pacific" 1949 (Dynamite Dawson); "Annie Get Your Gun" 1950 (Chief Sitting Bull); "Rio Grande" 1950 (Gen. Philip Sheridan); "Across the Wide Missouri" 1951 (Looking Glass); "Mark of the Renegade" 1951 (Luis); "Denver and Rio Grande" 1952 (Harkness); "Ride the Man Down" 1952 (Joe Kneen); "Woman of the North Country" 1952 (Mulholland); "Saskatchewan" 1954 (Batoche); "Sitting Bull" 1954 (Chief Sitting Bull); "The Last Command" 1955 (Santa Anna); "Rage at Dawn" 1955 (Sim

Reno); "Rebel in Town" 1956 (Bedloe Mason); "Yaqui Drums" 1956; "Cutter's Trail" TVM-1970 (Froteras). ¶TV: *The Texan*—"The First Notch" 10-20-58 (Walt Pearce); *Wanted—Dead or Alive*—"Ricochet" 11-22-58 (Miguel Ramirez); *Cimarron City*—"The Bloodline" 12-13-58 (Rafe Crowder); *The Restless Gun*—"The Red Blood of Courage" 2-2-59 (Maj. Quint Langley); *Wagon Train*—"The Old Man Charvanaugh Story" 2-18-59 (Charvanaugh), "The Benjamin Burns Story" 2-17-60 (Benjamin Burns); *Bonanza*—"A Severe Case of Matrimony" 7-7-68 (Anselmo).

Naismith, Laurence (1908-6/5/92). Films: "The Singer Not the Song" 1961-Brit. (Old Uncle); "Robbery Under Arms" 1958-Brit. (Ben Marston); "The Valley of Gwangi" 1969 (Prof. Horace Bromley). ¶TV: *Lancer*—"Glory" 12-10-68 (Collier); *Bonanza*—"Another Windmill to Go" 9-14-69 (Don Q. Hought).

Nakadai, Tatsuya (1930-). Films: "Today It's Me … Tomorrow You!" 1968-Ital.

Naldi, Nita (1897-2/17/61). Films: "Channing of the Northwest" 1922 (Cicily Varden).

Namath, Joe (1943-). Films: "The Last Rebel" 1971-Ital./U.S./Span. (Burnside Hollis).

Nanasi, Anna Marie. TV: *The Adventures of Rin Tin Tin*—"Hubert's Niece" 5-10-57; *Circus Boy*—"The Return of Buffalo Bill" 12-12-57 (Irma Cody); *Sugarfoot*—"Short Range" 5-13-58 (Willie Ann Miles); *Buckskin*—"The Gold Watch" 8-28-58 (Sara); *Trackdown*—"McCallin's Daughter" 1-2-59 (Debby McCallin).

Napier, Alan (1903-8/8/88). Films: "Unconquered" 1947 (Sir William Johnson); "Across the Wide Missouri" 1951 (Capt. Humberstone Lyon). ¶TV: *Tales of Wells Fargo*—"The Dowry" 7-10-61 (Bertram La Tour), "Remember the Yazoo" 4-14-62 (Colonel Decatur); *Daniel Boone*—"Cain's Birthday" 4-1-65 & 4-8-65 (Sir Hubert Crater), "Perilous Journey" 12-16-65 (Lord Brisbane); *Laredo*—"The Land Grabbers" 12-9-65 (Major Donaldson).

Napier, Charles (1935-). Films: "Ransom for Alice!" TVM-1977 (Pete Phelan); "Outlaws" TVM-1986 (Wolf Lucas). ¶TV: *The Oregon Trail*—Regular 1977 (Luther Sprague); *Outlaws*—Regular 1986-87 (Wolf Lucas); *Paradise*—"A Gather of Guns" 9-10-89 (Sheriff Cochran).

Napier, Elmer. Films: "The Lone Ranger" 1938-serial (Trooper);

"The Cisco Kid Returns" 1945; "Gun Smoke" 1945; "Saddle Serenade" 1945; "Sundown Riders" 1948 (Pioneer).

Napier, John (1916-). Films: "The Great Sioux Massacre" 1965 (Tom Custer); "Rough Night in Jericho" 1967 (McGivern). ¶TV: *Bonanza*—"The Emperor Norton" 2-27-66 (Chris Milner).

Napier, Russell (1910-75). Films: "Robbery Under Arms" 1958-Brit. (Mr. Green).

Naranjo, Ivan. Films: "Windwalker" 1980 (Crooked Leg); "The Mystic Warrior" TVM-1984 (Ogle). ¶TV: *Gunsmoke*—"A Game of Death … An Act of Love" 11-5-73 & 11-12-73 (2nd Renegade); *Kung Fu*—"The Centoph" 4-4-74 & 4-11-74 (Tall Pot).

Narciso, Grazia (-12/10/67). Films: "Madonna of the Desert" 1948 (Mama Baravellia). ¶TV: *Wagon Train*—"The Marie Dupree Story" 3-19-58 (Mrs. Caserti).

Nardini, Tom (1945-). Films: "Cat Ballou" 1965 (Jackson Two-Bears); "Africa—Texas Style!" 1967-U.S./Brit. (John Henry). ¶TV: *Death Valley Days*—"Death in the Desert" 5-9-65 (Steve Avote); *Gunsmoke*—"Gold Mine" 12-25-65 (Richard Danby); *Cowboy in Africa*—Regular 1967-68 (John Henry); *Cimarron Strip*—"The Battle of Blood Stone" 10-12-67 (John Wolf); *Bearcats!*—"Conqueror's Gold" 10-28-71 (Father Librerto); *Kung Fu*—"The Vanishing Image" 12-20-74 (Matoska).

Narita, Richard. TV: *Kung Fu*—"The Predators" 10-5-74 (Disciple), "Besieged: Death on Cold Mountain" 11-15-74 (Kang Li), "Besieged: Cannon at the Gate" 11-22-74 (Kang Li).

Naschy, Paul (Jacinto Molina) (1936-). Films: "Fury of Johnny Kid" 1967-Span./Ital. (Blackie).

Nash, Clarence (1904-2/20/85). Films: "The Man from Button Willow" 1965 (Voice).

Nash, George (1873-12/31/44). Films: "The Valley of Silent Men" 1922 (Inspector Kedsty); "The Man from Arizona" 1932; "The Fighting Texans" 1933 (Albert); "The Fugitive" 1933 (Smith); "The Gallant Fool" 1933 (Rube); "Galloping Romeo" 1933 (Henchman); "Rainbow Ranch" 1933 (Pete); "The Ranger's Code" 1933 (Danny Clayton); "Blue Steel" 1934 (Bridegroom).

Nash, Mary (1885-12/3/76). Films: "Wells Fargo" 1937 (Mrs. Pryor).

Nash, Noreen. Films: "The Red

Stallion" 1947 (Ellen Reynolds); "Storm Over Wyoming" 1950 (Chris); "Road Agent" 1952 (Cora Drew); "Giant" 1956 (Lorna Lane); "The Lone Ranger and the Lost City of Gold" 1958 (Frances Henderson). ¶TV: *Yancy Derringer*—"The Belle from Boston" 11-13-58 (Agatha Colton), "Fire on the Frontier" 4-2-59 (Agatha Colton).

Nash, Robert. Films: "Pawnee" 1957 (Carter); "Gun Fight" 1961 (Vance); "How the West Was Won" 1962 (Lawyer). ¶TV: *Wild Bill Hickok*—"Counterfeit Ghost" 8-11-53; *Annie Get Your Gun* 11-27-57 (Pawnee Bill); *Maverick*—"The Belcastle Brand" 10-12-58 (Foreman); *Laramie*—"The General Must Die" 11-17-59 (Sheriff McCord); *Hotel De Paree*—"Sundance Goes to Kill" 1-22-60 (Lawman); *Wanted—Dead or Alive*—"Criss Cross" 11-16-60 (Sheriff); *Gunsmoke*—"Panacea Sykes" 4-13-63; *Branded*—"Coward Step Aside" 3-7-65 (Jenkins).

Nathan, Stephen. Films: "Scott Free" TVM-1976 (Kevin Southerland). ¶TV: *Bonanza*—"The Witness" 1-2-73 (Oscar Hamner).

Natheaux, Louis (1894-8/23/42). Films: "The Fighting Code" 1934 (Barry); "Wells Fargo" 1937 (Jonathan, the Proprietor); "Union Pacific" 1939 (Card Player).

Natoli, Ric. TV: *Laredo*—"The Short, Happy Fatherhood of Reese Bennett" 1-27-67 (Black Wing); *Daniel Boone*—"The Renegade" 9-28-67; *Here Come the Brides*—"Hosanna's Way" 10-31-69 (Hosanna).

Natwick, Mildred (1908-10/25/94). Films: "The Kissing Bandit" 1948 (Isabella); "The Three Godfathers" 1948 (the Mother); "She Wore a Yellow Ribbon" 1949 (Mrs. Abby Allshard). ¶TV: *Bonanza*—"Mrs. Wharton and the Lesser Breeds" 1-19-69 (Mrs. Wharton).

Navarro, Anna. Films: "Jack Slade" 1953; "Jubilee Trail" 1954 (Conchita); "Female Artillery" TVM-1973 (Sarah Gallado). ¶TV: *The Cisco Kid*—"New York's Priest 1-9-54; *Death Valley Days*—"The Hidden Treasure of Cucamonga" 12-2-56; *Trackdown*—"Man and Money" 12-27-57 (Juanita); *The Californians*—"Murietta" 5-27-58 (Maria), "Hangtown" 11-18-58 (Florita Bowan), "Guns for King Joseph" 3-24-59 (Little Cloud); *Wanted—Dead or Alive*—"Dead End" 9-27-58 (Conchita); *U.S. Marshal*—"The Reservation" 10-18-58; *Wyatt Earp*—"The Fugitive" 11-17-59 (Felicia); *Bat Masterson*—"The Good and the Bad" 3-23-61

(Teresa Martinez); *The Outlaws*—"The Little Colonel" 5-18-61 (Monique); *Tales of Wells Fargo*—"Moneyrun" 1-6-62 (Carl); *Temple Houston*—"Find Angel Chavez" 9-26-63 (Donna Lennox); *Gunsmoke*—"Extradition" 12-7-63 & 12-14-63 (Marguerita), "The Hanging" 12-31-66 (Maria Oro); *The Monroes*—"War Arrow" 11-2-66 (Wahkonda); *Bonanza*—"Amigo" 2-12-67 (Consuela), "The Thirteenth Man" 1-21-68 (Prudence), "Danger Road" 1-11-70 (Serafina), "El Jefe" 11-15-70 (Sara); *The High Chaparral*—"A Hanging Offense" 11-12-67 (Indian Girl).

Navarro, George. Films: "Black Arrow" 1944-serial; "Pirates of Monterey" 1947 (Lieutenant); "Jubilee Trail" 1954 (Orosco Guest); "The Americano" 1955 (Tuba).

Navarro, Mario. Films: "The Beast of Hollow Mountain" 1956 (Panchito); "Villa!" 1958 (Pajarito); "Geronimo" 1962 (Giantah).

Navarro, Nieves. Films: "A Pistol for Ringo" 1965-Ital./Span. (Dolores); "The Big Gundown" 1966-Ital. (Widow); "The Return of Ringo" 1966-Ital./Span.; "Rojo" 1966-Ital./Span.; "Long Days of Vengeance" 1967-Ital./Span.

Nazarro, Cliff (1904-2/18/61). Films: "Romance Rides the Range" 1936 (Shorty); "The Singing Buckaroo" 1937; "In Old Colorado" 1941 (Nosey Haskins); "Call of the Canyon" 1942 (Pete Murphy); "'Neath Canadian Skies" 1946.

Neal, Patricia (1926-). Films: "Raton Pass" 1951 (Ann); "Hud" 1963 (Alma). ¶TV: *Kung Fu*—"Blood of the Dragon" 9-14-74 (Sara Kingsley).

Neal, Tom (1914-8/7/72). Films: "Rodeo Dough" 1940-short; "Klondike Kate" 1942 (Jefferson Braddock); "Apache Chief" 1949 (Lt. Brown); "Red Desert" 1949 (John Williams); "Call of the Klondike" 1950 (Mallory); "The Daltons' Women" 1950; "I Shot Billy the Kid" 1950 (Bowdre); "King of the Bullwhip" 1950 (Benson); "Train to Tombstone" 1950 (Dr. Willoughby); "The Great Jesse James Raid" 1953 (Arch Clements). ¶TV: *The Gene Autry Show*—"Six Shooter Sweepstakes" 10-1-50, "Lost Chance" 10-15-55; *Wild Bill Hickok*—"Vigilante Story" 1-22-52; *Tales of Wells Fargo*—"Faster Gun" 10-6-58 (Johnny Reno).

Nedell, Bernard J. (1893-11/23/72). Films: "Rangers of Fortune" 1940 (Tod Shelby); "The Desperadoes" 1943 (Jack Lester); "Lucky Cowboy" 1944-short; "Albuquerque"

1948 (Sheriff Linton); "Heller in Pink Tights" 1960 (Stunt Double).

Needham, Hal (1931-). Films: "McClintock" 1963 (Carter); "The War Wagon" 1967 (Hite); "One More Train to Rob" 1971 (Bert Gant); "The Culpepper Cattle Company" 1972 (Burgess). ¶TV: *Have Gun Will Travel*—"Episode in Laredo" 9-19-59, "The Naked Gun" 12-19-59 (Mabry), "The Day of the Bad Men" 1-9-60 (Gandy Dancer), "Jenny" 1-23-60 (Gunman), "Ambush" 4-23-60 (Morgan), "Full Circle" 5-14-60, "The Campaign of Billy Banjo" 5-28-60, "The Calf" 10-15-60 (Cowhand), "The Marshal's Boy" 11-26-60 (Cal), "The Princess and the Gunfighter" 1-21-61 (Guide), "The Tax Gatherer" 2-11-61, "Broken Image" 4-29-61 (Lookout), "The Hanging of Aaron Gibbs" 11-4-61 (Turner), "The Brothers" 11-25-61, "Dream Girl" 2-10-62 (Buddy), "Bandit" 5-12-62, "Memories of Monica" 10-27-62 (Dick), "Be Not Forgetful to Strangers" 12-22-62 (Harry), "Caravan" 2-23-63 (Indian), "The Walking Years" 3-2-63 (Wigen), "The Mountebank" 8-3-63 (Simms); *The Rebel*—"The Scalp Hunter" 12-11-60 (Apache); *Wagon Train*—"Wagon to Fort Anderson" 6-7-61 (Warrior), "The Race Town Story" 10-11-64 (Digger); *Rawhide*—"Deserter's Patrol" 2-9-62 (Corporal Williams), "The Race" 9-25-64 (Tom); *Tales of Wells Fargo*—"Portrait of Teresa" 2-10-62 (Cowboy); *The Virginian*—"Riff-Raff" 11-7-62; *Stoney Burke*—"Webb of Fear" 2-18-63 (Stan Fremont); *Laramie*—"The Renegade Brand" 2-26-63; *Laredo*—"A Matter of Policy" 11-11-65 (Cole); *Cimarron Strip*—"The Battleground" 9-28-67; *Gunsmoke*—"Hawk" 10-20-69 (Renegade #3).

Needham, J. Conrad. Films: "Western Firebrands" 1921 (Tom Fargo).

Needham, James. Films: "Ramona" 1916 (Jim Farrar).

Needham, Leo. TV: *The Cisco Kid*—"The Epidemic" 4-3-54, "West of the Law" 5-8-54; *Bat Masterson*—"Battle of the Pass" 2-25-59 (Bartender); *Rawhide*—"Incident of the Thirteenth Man" 10-23-59 (Nate Harmon); *Bonanza*—"The Mission" 9-17-60 (Bank Clerk).

Neeley, Ted (1943-). Films: "Shadow of Chikara" 1978 (Amos "Teach" Richmond).

Neff, Pauline. Films: "Ranson's Folly" 1926 (Mrs. Bolland).

Neff, Ralph (1907-1/28/73). Films: "The Last of the Fast Guns"

1958 (Bartender); "Something for a Lonely Man" TVM-1968. ¶TV: *Wild Bill Hickok*—"Wild Bill's Odyssey" 3-31-53; *Sergeant Preston of the Yukon*—"Follow the Leader" 3-15-56 (Hod), "Pack Ice Justice" 9-27-56 (Vic Sealy); *Maverick*—"The Brasada Spur" 2-22-59 (Horace Hogan); *Have Gun Will Travel*—"Tiger" 11-28-59; *The Tall Man*—"Counterfeit Law" 11-19-60 (Nathan Talby); *Death Valley Days*—"3-7-77" 12-14-60 (Ben); *Temple Houston*—"Fracas at Kiowa Flats" 12-12-63 (Two Finger Bill); *Gunsmoke*—"The Judas Gun" 1-19-70 (Town Bum).

Negley, Howard. Films: "Smoky" 1946 (Nelson); "Twilight on the Rio Grande" 1947 (Jake Short); "Fury at Furnace Creek" 1948 (Defense Counsel); "River Lady" 1948 (McKenzie); "Canadian Pacific" 1949 (Mallis); "Colt .45" 1950; "The Missourians" 1950 (Lucius Valentine); "Rawhide" 1951 (Chickenring); "Silver City" 1951 (Spence Fuller); "Lost in Alaska" 1952 (Higgins); "The Savage" 1952 (Col. Ellis); "Shane" 1953 (Pete); "The Gun That Won the West" 1955 (General Carveth); "A Man Alone" 1955 (Wilson); "Shoot-Out at Medicine Bend" 1957. ¶TV: *Wyatt Earp*—"Marshal Earp Plays Cupid" 1-3-56 (Fog MacMurray), "Lineup for Battle" 9-29-59; *The Roy Rogers Show*—"Sheriff Missing" 3-17-56, "The Morse Mixup" 3-24-56 (Henry Hawkins); *Zane Grey Theater*—"Black Creek Encounter" 3-8-57 (Sheriff Sloane); *Tales of Wells Fargo*—"Sam Bass" 6-10-57 (Merchant), "White Indian" 9-22-58 (Sheriff), "The Killing of Johnny Lash" 11-21-60 (Marshal); *Maverick*—"Stage West" 10-27-57 (Sheriff Tibbs); *Broken Arrow*—"The Arsenal" 11-5-57 (Cal); *The Restless Gun*—"General Gilford's Widow" 11-11-57 (Sheriff Jessup); *The Texan*—"Desert Passage" 12-1-58; *Wichita Town*—"Death Watch" 12-16-59 (Luke Connors); *Wanted—Dead or Alive*—"Man on Horseback" 12-5-59, "Tolliver Bender" 2-13-60; *Walt Disney Presents*—"Elfego Baca: Gus Tomlin Is Dead" 3-25-60 (Sheriff Matt Arnold); *The Deputy*—"A Time to Sow" 4-23-60 (Hank Bridges); *The Tall Man*—"The Great Western" 6-3-61 (Mayor Blount).

Negrete, Jorge (1911-12/5/53). Films: "The Devil's Godmother" 1938-Mex.

Neilan, Marshall (1891-10/26/58). Films: "The Stranger at Coyote" 1911; "The Bugler of Battery B" 1912; "The Reward of Valor" 1912; "The Weaker Brother" 1912; "The Tenderfoot's Luck" 1913; "Two Men of the Desert" 1913; "The Love Route" 1915.

Neill, James (1860-3/15/31). Films: "Bloodhounds of the North" 1913; "The Honor of the Mounted" 1914; "Rose of the Rancho" 1914 (Padre Antonio); "Where the Trail Divides" 1914 (Sam Rowland); "Tennessee's Pardner" 1916 (the Padre); "On the Level" 1917 (Mr. Warner); "A Daughter of the Wolf" 1919 (Judge Burroughs); "Salome Jane" 1923 (Larabee); "The Thrill Chaser" 1923; "Born to the West" 1926 (Sheriff Haverill); "Border Patrol" 1928 (Lefty Waterman).

Neill, Noel. Films: "Over the Santa Fe Trail" 1947; "The Adventures of Frank and Jesse James" 1948-Serial (Judy Powell); "Cactus Cut-Up" 1949-short; "Gun Runner" 1949 (Jessica); "Son of a Badman" 1949 (Vicki); "The James Brothers of Missouri" 1950-serial (Peggy Howard); "Abilene Trail" 1951 (Mary Dawson); "Whistling Hills" 1951 (Beth Fairchild); "Montana Incident" 1952; "The Lawless Rider" 1954 (Nancy Jones). ¶TV: *The Lone Ranger*—"Letter of the Law" 1-4-51; *The Cisco Kid*—"Chain Lightning" 3-3-51.

Neill, Richard R. (1875-4/8/70). Films: "A Perilous Ride" 1911; "The El Dorado Lode" 1913; "Heritage of the Desert" 1924; "The Wanderer of the Wasteland" 1924 (Collishaw); "Tumbleweeds" 1925 (Bill Freel); "Satan Town" 1926 (Cherokee Charlie); "Whispering Smith" 1926 (Lance Dunning); "Bulldog Pluck" 1927 (Destin); "Code of the Cow Country" 1927 (Bill Jackson); "The Desert of the Lost" 1927; "The Fightin' Comeback" 1927 (Three-Card Spencer); "Galloping Thunder" 1927 (Dallas); "Somewhere in Sonora" 1927 (Ramon Bistula); "Beyond the Sierras" 1928 (Carlos); "The Last Frontier" 1932-serial (Tiger Morris).

Neise, George (1917-). Films: "Valley of Hunted Men" 1942 (Schiller); "The Tall Stranger" 1957 (Harper); "Tomahawk Trail" 1957 (Lt. Jonathan Davenport); "Fort Massacre" 1958 (Pendleton). ¶TV: *Cheyenne*—"Test of Courage" 1-29-57 (McCool); *Trackdown*—"The Bounty Hunter" 3-7-58, "The Avenger" 10-31-58 (Kels Gregory); *Northwest Passage*—"The Ambush" 2-6-59 (Vance Stark); *Death Valley Days*—"Stagecoach Spy" 2-17-59 (Ed Chase); *Zorro*—"Invitation to Death" 5-21-59 (Captain Felipe Arrellano), "The Captain Regrets" 5-28-59 (Captain Felipe Arrellano), "Masquerade for Murder" 6-4-59 (Captain Felipe Arrellano), "Long Live the Governor" 6-11-59 (Captain Felipe Arrellano); *Bat Masterson*—"The Secret Is Death" 5-27-59 (Calhoun); *Wichita Town*—Regular 1959-60 (Doc Nate Wyndham); *Have Gun Will Travel*—"The Gladiators" 3-19-60 (Graham Beckley); *Laramie*—"Saddle and Spur" 3-29-60 (Earl Durbin); *The Rifleman*—"Smoke Screen" 4-5-60 (Roger Quenton); *Man from Blackhawk*—"The Search for Cope Borden" 4-15-60 (John Fuller); *Stagecoach West*—"Object: Patrimony" 1-3-61 (Lionel Chambers); *Maverick*—"The Maverick Report" 3-4-62 (Jonesy); *Bronco*—"The Immovable Object" 4-16-62 (Major Moore); *Death Valley Days*—"The Solid Gold Pie" 11-29-69.

Nelkin, Stacey. Films: "The Chisholms" TVM-1979 (Bonnie Sue Chisholm). ¶TV: *The Chisholm*—Regular 1979 (Bonnie Sue Chisholm).

Nell, Krista. Films: "Kitosch, the Man who Came from the North" 1967-Ital./Span.; "To Hell and Back" 1968-Ital./Span.; "Django and Sartana Are Coming ... It's the End" 1970-Ital.; "You're Jinxed, Friend, You Just Met Sacramento" 1970-Ital./Span.; "Kill Django ... Kill First" 1971-Ital.; "God Is My Colt .45" 1972-Ital. (Mary); "Paid in Blood" 1972-Ital. (Cora).

Nelson, Arvid. TV: *Black Saddle*—"Client: Meade" 1-17-59 (Ed Tibbett); *Have Gun Will Travel*—"Gold and Brimstone" 6-20-59; *Two Faces West*—"Portrait of Bravery" 3-13-61.

Nelson, Barry (1920-). Films: "The First Traveling Saleslady" 1956 (Charles Masters). ¶TV: *Hudson's Bay*—Regular 1958 (Jonathan Banner); *Zane Grey Theater*—"Deception" 4-14-60 (Mark Bigelow).

Nelson, Bek. Films: "Cowboy" 1958 (Charlie's Girl). ¶TV: *Tales of the Texas Rangers*—"Panhandle" 9-22-57 (Claire Tatum); *Lawman*—Regular 1958-59 (Dru Lemp); *The Restless Gun*—"Take Me Home" 12-29-58 (Dixie Starr), "The Way Back" 7-13-59; *Buckskin*—"I'll Sing at Your Wedding" 5-4-59 (Melissa Jenkins); *Bonanza*—"The Sun Mountain Herd" 9-19-59 (Glory); *Wanted—Dead or Alive*—"The Monsters" 1-16-60 (Hannah); *The Deputy*—"The Chain of Action" 5-7-60 (Claudia); *Bat Masterson*—"Episode in Eden" 3-16-61 (Martha Yale).

Nelson, Billy (1904-6/12/79). Films: "Senorita from the West"

1945. ¶TV: *Wild Bill Hickok*—"Great Obstacle Race" 3-3-53; *Death Valley Days*—"Man on the Run" 2-10-58; *Tombstone Territory*—"Fight for a Fugitive" 6-4-58 (Man), "Surrender at Sunglow" 5-15-59 (Murphy); *Bat Masterson*—"A Noose Fits Anybody" 11-19-58 (Ringmaster).

Nelson, Bobby. Films: "Dangerous Days" 1919 (the Pioneer Kid); "The Border Whirlwind" 1926 (Petie); "The Fighting Boob" 1926 (Bobby); "Bulldog Pluck" 1927 (Danny Haviland); "The Boy and the Bad Man" 1929 (the Pioneer Kid); "The Kid Comes Through" 1929; "Orphan of the Wagaon Trails" 1929; "Waif of the Wilderness" 1929; "Alias the Bandit" 1930 (the Pioneer Kid); "The Battling Kid" 1930 (the Pioneer Kid); "The Danger Claim" 1930; "The Last Stand" 1930; "The Pony Express Kid" 1930; "The Post of Honor" 1930; "Roaring Ranch" 1930 (Teddie); "Six-Gun Justice" 1930; "Son of Courage" 1930; "Battling with Buffalo Bill" 1931-serial; "Two-Fisted Justice" 1931 (Danny); "Two Gun Caballero" 1931; "Daring Danger" 1932; "Partners" 1932 (Bud Roach); "The Texan" 1932 (Bobby); "Cowboy Counsellor" 1933 (Bobby Avery); "King of the Arena" 1933; "The Way of the West" 1934 (Bobbie Parker); "The Cowboy and the Bandit" 1935 (Bobbie Barton); "Cyclone of the Saddle" 1935 (Dick); "The Ghost Rider" 1935 (Bobby Bullard); "Rough Riding Ranger" 1935 (Bobby Francis); "Texas Terror" 1935; "The Throwback" 1935 (Milt as a Boy); "Thunderbolt" 1935 (the Boy); "Custer's Last Stand" 1936-serial (Bobby); "Valley of the Lawless" 1936 (Billy Jenkins); "Boothill Brigade" 1937 (Tug Murdock); "The Gambling Terror" 1937 (Jerry Garrett); "Gun Lords of Stirrup Basin" 1937; "The Red Rope" 1937 (Jimmy Duncan).

Nelson, Burt. Films: "Bullwhip" 1958 (Pine Hawk); "Seven Guns to Mesa" 1958 (Bear); "Massacre at Grand Canyon" 1963-Ital. ¶TV: *The Restless Gun*—"The Peddler" 6-9-58 (Jeff Jackson); *Wyatt Earp*—"The Mysterious Cowhand" 10-14-58 (Red).

Nelson, David (1936-). Films: "Day of the Outlaw" 1959 (Gene). ¶TV: *Hondo*—"Hondo and the Apache Trail" 12-22-67 (Jeff).

Nelson, Ed (1926-). Films: "The Man from Galveston" 1964 (Cole Marteen). ¶Television: *Maverick*—"The Rivals" 1-25-59 (Classmate), "Triple Indemnity" 3-19-61 (Bill Parker), "The Maverick Report"

3-4-62 (Gary Harrison); *Zane Grey Theater*—"Make It Look Good" 2-5-59 (Jack Bowen), "The Reckoning" 1-14-60 (Albie), "Ransom" 11-17-60 (Tantasi), "Honor Bright" 2-2-61 (Vince Harwell); *Bat Masterson*—"Marked Deck" 3-11-59 (Jedrow), "The Fatal Garment" 5-25-61 (Browder); *Gunsmoke*—"Murder Warrant" 4-18-59 (Lee Prentice), "Miguel's Daughter" 11-28-59 (Rusk Davis), "Perce" 9-30-61 (Perce McCally), "The Prisoner" 5-19-62 (Seth), "Uncle Sunday" 12-15-62 (Burt Cury), "Father Love" 3-14-64 (Tom King); *Have Gun Will Travel*—"Hunt the Man Down" 4-25-59 (Will Gage), "Homecoming" 5-23-59 (Ed Stacy), "The Black Handkerchief" 11-14-59 (Pierre Deverall), "Ambush" 4-23-60 (Carl), "My Brother's Keeper" 5-6-61 (Rack); *Rawhide*—"Incident of Fear in the Streets" 5-8-59 (Kels Morgan), "Incident of the One Hundred Amulets" 5-6-60, "Incident of the Painted Lady" 5-12-61 (Lt. Corey Clemens), "Incident of the Reluctant Bridegroom" 11-30-62 (Sam Weber); *Black Saddle*—"Client: Vardon" 5-30-59 (Roy Corey), "Client: Peter Warren" 10-30-59 (Lee Coogan); *The Rebel*—"Vicious Circle" 10-25-59 (Matt), "Grant of Land" 5-22-60 (Chad), "Johnny Yuma at Appomattox" 9-18-60 (Doug), "Run, Killer, Run" 10-30-60 (Stalker), "The Guard" 1-8-61 (Clint Maowbree); *Johnny Ringo*—"Border Town" 3-17-60 (Kirk); *Riverboat*—"The Quick Noose" 4-11-60 (Jim Tyler); *The Rifleman*—"Dead Cold Cash" 11-22-60 (Stacy Baldin), "The Illustrator" 12-13-60 (Ben Travis), "First Wages" 10-9-61 (Ben Vargas); *Wyatt Earp*—"The Too Perfect Crime" 12-6-60 (Hal Babcock); *The Deputy*—"Judas Town" 12-31-60 (Pete McCurdy); *Tales of Wells Fargo*—"The Jealous Man" 4-10-61 (Andy Thorpe), "A Fistful of Pride" 11-18-61 (Frisco Kid); *Laramie*—"Bitter Glory" 5-2-61 (Cal Mason), "Dragon at the Door" 9-26-61, "The Wedding Party" 1-29-63 (Gil Harrison); *Wagon Train*—"The Don Alvarado Story" 6-21-61 (Donovan), "Alias Bill Hawks" 5-15-63 (Burke Clayton), "The Bleeker Story" 12-9-63 (Al Bleeker); *The Tall Man*—"G.P." 5-19-62 (Dr. Wade Parsons); *Bonanza*—"The Miracle Worker" 5-20-62 (Garth); *Death Valley Days*—"Fort Bowie: Urgent" 10-10-62 (Frank Girard); *Wide Country*—"Who Killed Edde Gannon?" 10-11-62 (Paul Corbello); *Stoney Burke*—"Five by Eight" 12-10-62 (Nick Martin); *The Virginian*—"The Exiles" 1-9-63; *The Dakotas*—"Walk Through the Badlands"

3-18-63 (Lt. John Schwimmer); *Temple Houston*—"The Man from Galveston" 1963 (Cole Marteen); *Redigo*—"Hostage Hero Riding" 12-10-63 (Danny Kilpatrack); *Alias Smith and Jones*—"What Happened at the XST?" 10-28-72 (Sheriff Frank Canton); *Kung Fu*—"The Third Man" 4-26-73 (Sheriff Raha); *Bret Maverick*—"Dateline: Sweetwater" 1-12-82 (Andrew Tyndall).

Nelson, Evelyn (1900-6/16/23). Films: "The Broken Spur" 1921 (Angel Lambert); "Cyclone Bliss" 1921 (Helen Turner); "Dead or Alive" 1921 (Beulah); "The Double O" 1921 (Frances Powell); "The Crow's Nest" 1922 (Patricia Benton); "A Desert Bridegroom" 1922 (Matilda Ann Carter); "Peaceful Peters" 1922 (Mary Langdon); "Two-Fisted Jefferson" 1922; "The Forbidden Trail" 1923 (Isobel Lorraine).

Nelson, Felix. Films: "The Ballad of Cable Hogue" 1970 (William). ¶TV: *Death Valley Days*—"Land of the Free" 2-11-53.

Nelson, Frank (1872-11/27/32). Films: "The Last of the Duanes" 1924 (Euchre); "The Vagabond Trail" 1924 (Slippy); "In Old Arizona" 1929 (Cowboy); "The Fighting Parson" 1933.

Nelson, Gene (1920-). Films: "Oklahoma!" 1955 (Will Parker); "The Purple Hills" 1961 (Gil Shepard). ¶TV: *Maverick*—"Trail West to Fury" 2-16-58 (Jim Hazlit); *Northwest Passage*—"The Fourth Brother" 1-30-59 (Dane Wade); *Have Gun Will Travel*—"The Return of the Lady" 2-21-59 (Vance); *Bat Masterson*—"Brunette Bombshell" 4-1-59 (Whit Morrison); *Gunsmoke*—"Blue Horse" 6-6-59 (Hob Cannon), "Saludos" 10-31-59 (Joe Foss), "Say Uncle" 10-1-60 (Hutch); *Rawhide*—"Incident of the Shambling Men" 10-9-59 (Dave Thompson); *Black Saddle*—"The Cabin" 4-1-60 (Wicks); *The Law of the Plainsman*—"Trojan Horse" 5-5-60 (Hardy Mullins).

Nelson, Gordon (1898-2/19/56). Films: "The Iron Mistress" 1952 (Dr. Maddox); "City of Badmen" 1953 (Doctor).

Nelson, Herbert (1913-). Films: "The Great Northfield, Minnesota Raid" 1972 (Chief Detective); "When the Legends Die" 1972 (Dr. Wilson). ¶TV: *Kung Fu*—"The Gunman" 1-3-74 (Sam Cogan).

Nelson, Jack. Films: "The Long Chance" 1915 (Bob McGraw); "The Sheriff's Streak of Yellow" 1915; "Mountain Blood" 1916; "The Red

Stain" 1916; "The Timber Wolf" 1916; "Winner Takes All" 1918 (Banjo Gibson); "Fighting for Gold" 1919 (Curley Brandon); "Rose of the West" 1919 (Jules); "Rough-Riding Romance" 1919 (Pietro, the Spy); "The Wilderness Trail" 1919 (Halfbreed); "The Reckless Buckaroo" 1935.

Nelson, Jessica. Films: "Plainsong" 1982 (Mary Jessop); "Calamity Jane" TVM-1984 (Patty).

Nelson, Kristin (1945-). Films: "The Over-the-Hill Gang" TVM-1969 (Hannah Rose).

Nelson, Lloyd. Films: "Bullet for Billy the Kid" 1963; "Bronco Billy" 1980 (Sanatorium Policeman); "Pale Rider" 1985 (Bank Teller). ¶TV: Gunsmoke—"The Legend" 10-18-71 (Slater), "Alias Festus Haggen" 3-6-72 (Shorty), "Tatum" 11-13-72 (Clergyman), "Jessie" 2-19-73 (Dr. Miller), "The Iron Blood of Courage" 2-18-74 (Norris), "A Town in Chains" 9-16-74 (Welch), "Hard Labor" 2-24-75 (Jury Foreman).

Nelson, Lori (1933-). Films: "Bend of the River" 1952 (Marjie); "Tumbleweed" 1953 (Laura); "Destry" 1954 (Martha Phillips); "Mohawk" 1956 (Cynthia Stanhope); "Pardners" 1956 (Carol Kingsley); "Outlaw's Son" 1957 (Lila Costain). ¶TV: Wanted—Dead or Alive—"Bounty for a Bride" 4-4-59 (White Antelope); The Texan—"The Man Hater" 6-15-59 (Elizabeth); Wagon Train—"The Steele Family" 6-17-59 (Charity); Sugarfoot—"The Gaucho" 12-22-59 (Ellen Conway); Tales of Wells Fargo—"Relay Station" 12-28-59 (Susan); Laramie—"Trigger Point" 5-16-61 (Grace); Whispering Smith—"Double Edge" 8-7-61 (Venetia Molloy).

Nelson, Otto. Films: "The Gun Game" 1920; "West Is West" 1920 (Sim Wigfall); "The Black Sheep" 1921 (Capt. Morran); "Kickaroo" 1921; "A Knight of the West" 1921 (Daniel McKitrick); "The Midnight Raiders" 1921; "The Outlaw" 1921; "Sweet Revenge" 1921; "In the Days of Buffalo Bill" 1922-serial (Alden Carter); "Thorobred" 1922 (Pop Martin).

Nelson, Ralph (1916-). Films: "Soldier Blue" 1970 (Indian Agent); "The Wrath of God" 1972 (Executed Prisoner).

Nelson, Ricky (1940-12/31/85). Films: "Rio Bravo" 1959 (Colorado Ryan); "The Over-the-Hill Gang" TVM-1969 (Jeff Rose). ¶TV: Hondo—"Hondo and the Judas" 11-3-67 (Jesse James).

Nelson, Ruth (1905-9/12/92). Films: "The Sea of Grass" 1947 (Selina Hall).

Nelson, Sam (1896-5/1/63). Films: "The Bantam Cowboy" 1928 (Jim Thornton); "The Law of Fear" 1928 (Bud Hardy); "Tracked" 1928 (Jed Springer); "The Little Savage" 1929 (Norton); "The One Man Dog" 1929 (Larry); "The Vagabond Cub" 1929 (Bob McDonald).

Nelson, Willie (1933-). Films: "The Electric Horseman" 1979 (Wendell); "Barbarosa" 1982 (Barbarosa); "The Last Days of Frank and Jesse James" TVM-1986 (General Jo Shelby); "Stagecoach" TVM-1986 (Doc Holliday); "Red Headed Stranger" 1987 (Rev. Julian Shay); "Once Upon a Texas Train" TVM-1988 (John Henry Lee); "Where the Hell's That Gold?!!!" TVM-1988 (Cross).

Neola, Princess. Films: "The Red, Red Heart" 1918 (Molly); "Perils of the Yukon" 1922-serial; "Reckless Courage" 1925 (Winona); "Land of the Silver Fox" 1928 (the Squaw); "Girl of the Golden West" 1930 (Wowkle).

Neri, Rosalba (Sarah Bay) (1946-). Films: "Arizona Colt" 1965-Ital./Fr./Span. (Dolores); "Dynamite Jim" 1966-Span./Ital.; "Johnny Yuma" 1966-Ital. (Samantha Felton); "Days of Violence" 1967-Ital.; "Great Treasure Hunt" 1967-Ital./Span.; "A Long Ride from Hell" 1968-Ital. (Prostitute); "Sartana Does Not Forgive" 1968-Span./Ital.; "This Man Can't Die" 1968-Ital. (Jenny Benson); "Killer Goodbye" 1969-Ital./Span. (Fannie); "Arizona" 1970-Ital./Span. (Sheena); "The Reward's Yours, the Man's Mine" 1970-Ital.; "Wanted Johnny Texas" 1971-Ital.; "Watch Out Gringo! Sabata Will Return" 1972-Ital./Span.; "And They Smelled the Strange, Exciting, Dangerous Scent of Dollars" 1973-Ital.; "Man Called Invincible" 1973-Ital.; "Blood River" 1974-Ital.; "Drummer of Vengeance" 1974-Brit./Ital.;

Nero, Franco (1941-). Films: "The Tramplers" 1965-Ital. (Charley Garvey); "The Avengers" 1966-Ital.; "Django" 1966-Ital./Span. (Django); "Massacre Time" 1966-Ital./Span./Ger. (Tom); "Texas, Adios" 1966-Ital./Span. (Burt); "Man: His Pride and His Vengeance" 1967-Ital./Ger. (Jose); "The Mercenary" 1968-Ital./Span. (Bill Douglas); "Companeros" 1970-Ital./Span./Ger. (Yod the Swede); "Deaf Smith and Johnny Ears" 1972-Ital. (Johnny Ears); "Don't Turn the Other Cheek" 1974-Ital./Ger./Span.; "Cipolla Colt"

1975-Ital./Ger. (Stark); "Keoma" 1975-Ital./Span. (Keoma); "Mexico in Flames" 1982-Rus./Mex./Ital. (John Reed)."Django Strikes Again" 1987-Ital./Span./Ger. (Django); "Jonathan of the Bears" 1994-Ital./Rus. (Jonathan).

Nesbitt, Cathleen (1889-8/2/82). TV: Wagon Train—"The Matthew Lowry Story" 4-1-59 (Rebecca); Empire—"Pressure Lock" 12-4-62 (Hettie Burton).

Nesbitt, Miriam (1873-8/11/54). Films: "The Story of the Indian Lodge" 1911.

Nesmith, Ottola (1889-2/7/72). Films: "The Girl-Shy Cowboy" 1928 (College Teacher); "The Great Man's Lady" 1942 (Mrs. Frisbee); "Unconquered" 1947. ¶TV: Cheyenne—"Alibi for a Scalped Man" 3-7-60 (Liza Marley); Rawhide—"Josh" 1-15-65 (Mrs. Beech); Wild Wild West—"The Night of the Howling Light" 12-17-65 (Madame Lafarge).

Nestell, William "Bill" (1893-10/18/66). Films: "Cheyenne Trails" 1928; "Texas Flash" 1928; "The Thrill Chaser" 1928; "When the Law Rides" 1928 (Snake Arnold); "The Trail of the Horse Thieves" 1929 (Babcock); "The Fighting Legion" 1930 (Ed Hook); "Fighting Thru" 1930; "The Man from Nowhere" 1930 (Dan McCloud); "The Last Frontier" 1932-serial; "Deadwood Pass" 1933 (Forty-Four); "Robbers' Roost" 1933 (Mac)."North of the Rio Grande" 1937; "Yodelin' Kid from Pine Ridge" 1937; "The Old Barn Dance" 1938; "The Night Riders" 1939 (Allen); "Adventures of Red Ryder" 1940-serial (Bartender #2); "The Trail Blazers" 1940; "Boss of Bullion City" 1941 (Cowboy); "The Sombrero Kid" 1942; "Stagecoach Buckaroo" 1942; "Stardust on the Sage" 1942; "Buckskin Frontier" 1943 (Whiskers); "Wagon Tracks West" 1943; "Call of the Rockies" 1944.

Nettleton, Lois (1927-). Films: "Mail Order Bride" 1964 (Annie Boley); "The Good Guys and the Bad Guys" 1969 (Mary)."Dirty Dingus Magee" 1970 (Prudence); "The Honkers" 1972 (Linda Lathrop). ¶TV: Gunsmoke—"Nina's Revenge" 12-16-61 (Nina Sharky), "The Returning" 2-18-67 (Amy Todd); The Virginian—"Nobility of Kings" 11-10-65 (Mary), "The Wind of Outrage" 10-16-68 (Suzanne); Bonanza—"The Pursued" 10-2-66 & 10-9-66 (Elizabeth Anne); Daniel Boone—"The Bait" 11-7-68 (Sulie); Kung Fu—"Barbary House" 2-15-75 (Delonia Cartell), "Flight to Orion" 2-22-75

(Delonia Cartell), "The Brothers Cain" 3-1-75 (Delonia Cartell), "Full Circle" 3-15-75 (Delonia Cartell); *Centennial*—Regular 1978-79 (Maude Wendell).

Neumann, Dorothy (1914-5/20/94). Films: "Take Me to Town" 1953 (Felice Pickett); "The Oklahoman" 1957 (Woman); "The Shakiest Gun in the West" 1968; "The Missouri Breaks" 1976 (Madame). ¶TV: *Wild Bill Hickok*—"Sheriff of Buckeye" 6-30-53; *Bonanza*—"The Gunmen" 1-23-60, "The Tall Stranger" 1-7-62, "Enter Thomas Bowers" 4-26-64, "A Man Without Land" 4-9-67; *Bronco*—"Ordeal at Dead Tree" 1-2-61 (Prudence Harrod); *Gunsmoke*—"Old Dan" 1-27-62 (Mrs. Bales), "Old York" 5-4-63 (Mrs. Finney), "Doctor's Wife" 10-24-64 (Old Woman), "Albert" 2-9-70 (Emily Cushing), "One for the Road" 1-24-72 (Old Woman); *The Virginian*—"Big Day, Great Day" 10-24-62.

Nevins, Claudette. Films: "Mrs. Sundance" TVM-1974 (Mary Lant). ¶TV: *Young Riders*—"A Tiger's Tale" 12-28-91 (Sister Katherine).

Newberg, Frank (1886-11/4/69). Films: "The Sign of the Cactus" 1925 (Earl of Chico).

Newell, David (1905-1/25/80). Films: "Woman Hungry" 1931 (Dr. Neil Cranford); "Wells Fargo" 1937; "Heart of the North" 1938 (Pilot); "Union Pacific" 1939 (Reporter).

Newell, Marie. Films: "Dangerous Trails" 1920; "The Unknown Ranger" 1920 (Jo).

Newell, William (1894-2/21/67). Films: "The Big Show" 1937 (Wilson); "The Outlaw" 1943 (Drunk Cowboy); "High Noon" 1952 (Drunk); "Escape from Fort Bravo" 1953 (Symore); "The Missouri Traveler" 1958 (Pos Neely); "Last Train from Gun Hill" 1959 (Hotel Clerk). ¶TV: *Wild Bill Hickok*—"Runaway Wizard" 6-9-53; *The Texan*—"The Lord Will Provide" 12-29-58; *Hotel De Paree*—"Sundance and the Hero of Bloody Blue Creek" 3-11-60 (Carl); *Gunsmoke*—"Distant Drummer" 11-19-60 (Green).

Newill, Jim (1911-7/31/75). Films: "Renfrew of the Royal Mounted" 1937 (Sergeant Renfrew); "Renfrew on the Great White Trail" 1938 (Renfrew); "Crashing Thru" 1939 (Sgt. Renfrew); "Fighting Mad" 1939 (Renfrew); "Danger Ahead" 1940 (Renfrew); "Murder on the Yukon" 1940 (Renfrew); "Sky Bandits" 1940 (Sgt. Renfrew); "Yukon Flight" 1940 (Renfrew); "The Rangers Take

Over" 1942 (Jim Steele); "Bad Men of Thunder Gap" 1943; "Border Buckaroos" 1943 (Jim Steele); "Fighting Valley" 1943 (Jim Steele); "The Return of the Rangers" 1943; "West of Texas" 1943 (Jim Steele); "Boss of Rawhide" 1944 (Jim Steele); "Brand of the Devil" 1944 (Jim Steele); "Guns of the Law" 1944; "Gunsmoke Mesa" 1944 (Jim Steele); "Outlaw Roundup" 1944; "The Pinto Bandit" 1944; "Spook Town" 1944; "Trail of Terror" 1944 (Jim Steele).

Newlan, Paul "Tiny" (1903-11/23/73). Films: "Arizona Mahoney" 1936 (Boots); "Wells Fargo" 1937 (Zeke Martin); "Rangers of Fortune" 1940; "The Devil's Trail" 1942; "Down Rio Grande Way" 1942 (Sam Houston); "Jackass Mail" 1942 (Rancher)."Girl Rush" 1944 (Miner); "The Bells of San Fernando" 1947 (Gueyon); "Fury at Furnace Creek" 1948 (Bartender); "Colt .45" 1950; "Sugarfoot" 1951; "The Lawless Breed" 1952 (Race Track Judge); "Lost in Alaska" 1952 (Captain Chisholm); "The Treasure of Lost Canyon" 1952 (Coach Driver); "River of No Return" 1954 (Prospector); "Davy Crockett and the River Pirates" 1956 (Big Harpe); "Badlands of Montana" 1957 (Marshal); "The Lonely Man" 1957 (Fence Green); "Trooper Hook" 1957; "The Outrage" 1964 (Juan Carrasco); "There Was a Crooked Man" 1970. ¶TV: *Walt Disney Presents*—"Davy Crockett"—Regular 1954-55 (Big Harp); *Gunsmoke*—"Reward for Matt" 1-28-56 (Jeremy Stoner), "Spring Team" 12-15-56 (Danch); *Tales of Wells Fargo*—"Barbara Coast" 11-25-57; *Buckskin*—"The Manager" 4-27-59 (Dan Stevens); *Frontier Circus*—"Never Won Fair Lady" 4-12-62 (General Youngblood); *Wide Country*—"Whose Hand at My Throat?" 2-14-63 (Eugene Walston); *Wagon Train*—"The Trace McCloud Story" 3-2-64; *Destry*—"Blood Brother-in-Law" 4-17-64 (Anse Motley).

Newland, Douglass (Johnny Mitchell) (1919-1/19/51). Films: "The Vanishing Virginian" 1941 (Jim Shirley).

Newland, John (1916-). Films: "Sons of Adventure" 1948 (Peter Winslow). ¶TV: *Schlitz Playhouse of the Stars*—"The Bitter Land" 4-13-56 (Wesley Hammond).

Newley, Anthony (1931-). Films: "Stagecoach" TVM-1986 (Trevor Peacock).

Newman, Hank (and the Georgia Crackers) (1905-7/25/78). Films: "The Fighting Frontiersman"

1946; "South of the Chisholm Trail" 1947.

Newman, James. Films: "Wanted Johnny Texas" 1971-Ital. (Johnny Texas).

Newman, Melissa (1951-). Films: "The Undefeated" 1969 (Charlotte Langdon). ¶TV: *Bonanza*—"A Time to Die" 3-21-71 (Lori).

Newman, Paul (1925-). Films: "The Left-Handed Gun" 1958 (Billy Bonney); "Hud" 1963 (Hud Bannon); "Hombre" 1967 (John Russell); "Butch Cassidy and the Sundance Kid" 1969 (Butch Cassidy); "The Life and Times of Judge Roy Bean" 1972 (Judge Roy Bean); "Pocket Money" 1972 (Jim Kane); "Buffalo Bill and the Indians, or Sitting Bull's History Lesson" 1976 (Buffalo Bill). ¶TV: *Philco Television Playhouse*—"The Death of Billy the Kid" 7-24-55 (Billy the Kid).

Newman, Phyllis (1935-). TV: *Wild Wild West*—"The Night of the Raven" 9-30-66 (Princess Wanakee).

Newman, Scott (1951-11/20/79). Films: "Breakheart Pass" 1976 (Rafferty).

Newman, Walter. Films: "The Long Chance" 1915 (Borax O'Rourke).

Newmar, Julie (1930-). Films: "MacKenna's Gold" 1969 (Heshke); "Blood River" 1974-Ital.; "Oblivion" 1994 (Miss Kitty). ¶TV: *F Troop*—"Yellow Bird" 10-20-66 (Yellow Bird).

Newmark, Matthew. TV: *Paradise*—Regular 1988-91 (Joseph Cord).

Newton, Charles (1874-1926). Films: "The Senor's Silver Buckle" 1915; "This Is the Life" 1915; "The Warning" 1915; "Immediate Lee" 1916; "Snap Judgment" 1917 (Henry Page); "The Crow" 1919; "The Fighting Line" 1919; "The Kid and the Cowboy" 1919; "Double Danger" 1920; "Fight It Out" 1920; "Hair-Trigger Stuff" 1920; "The Man with the Punch" 1920; "Marryin' Marion" 1920; "The Moon Riders" 1920-serial; "A Pair of Twins" 1920; "The Prospector's Vengeance" 1920; "Superstition" 1920; "Tipped Off" 1920; "The Trail of the Hound" 1920; "The Two-Fisted Lover" 1920; "Wolf Tracks" 1920; "Action" 1921 (Sheriff Dupple); "Bandits Beware" 1921; "The Cactus Kid" 1921; "The Movie Trail" 1921; "Red Courage" 1921 (Tom Caldwell); "The Saddle King" 1921; "Sure Fire" 1921 (Leo Ballinger); "Who Was That Man?" 1921; "The Loaded Door" 1922 (Dad Stewart); "Western Speed" 1922 (Express Agent); "Danger" 1923 (Dry Walsh Jake); "$50,000 Reward" 1924 (Pa Miller); "The Iron Horse" 1924 (Collins P. Hutgton); "Riders of the Purple Sage" 1925 (Herd); "Western Pluck" 1926 (Sheriff Dan Wayne).

Newton, Dodo. Films: "The Big Trail" 1930 (Abigail).

Newton, Frank. Films: "The Wanderer's Pledge" 1915; "Rough and Ready" 1918 (Ed Brown).

Newton, John. TV: *The Law of the Plainsman*—"The Innocents" 12-10-59; *Black Saddle*—"Mr. Simpson" 1-22-60 (Secret Service Agent), "The Penalty" 4-22-60 (Stamp); *Zane Grey Theater*—"The Sunday Man" 2-25-60; *Johnny Ringo*—"The Derelict" 5-26-60 (Riker); *Gunsmoke*—"Indian Ford" 12-2-61 (Sergeant Cromwell), "Tobe" 10-19-63 (Cowman); *Stoney Burke*—"Cousin Eunice" 12-24-62 (Desk Clerk).

Newton, Mary. Films: "Last Days of Boot Hill" 1947 (Mrs. Forrest Brent); "The Lone Hand Texan" 1947 (Mrs. Adams); "The Marauders" 1947 (Mrs. Crowell); "Bad Men of Tombstone" 1949 (Ma Brown); "Desert Vigilante" 1949 (Angel); "Junction City" 1952 (Ella Sanderson); "The Stranger Wore a Gun" 1953; "Pardners" 1956 (Laura); "Toughest Gun in Tombstone" 1958 (Mrs. Beasley). ¶TV: *Sky King*—"Triple Exposure" 5-11-52 (Mrs. Van Kamp); *The Lone Ranger*—"Christmas Story" 12-20-56; *Bronco*—"Ordeal at Dead Tree" 1-2-61 (Mrs. Lloyd); *Bonanza*—"Rain from Heaven" 10-6-63.

Newton, Richard. TV: *Zane Grey Theater*—"Until the Man Dies" 1-25-57 (Ranch Hand); *Tales of the Texas Rangers*—"Deadfall" 11-6-58 (Joe Taylor); *Johnny Ringo*—"The Liars" 2-4-60 (Lon McClinton).

Newton, Theodore. Films: "Friendly Persuasion" 1956 (Army Major); "The Saga of Hemp Brown" 1958 (Murphy). ¶TV: *The Californians*—"The Alice Pritchard Case" 2-4-58 (John Selwyn); *Gunsmoke*—"Sunday Supplement" 2-8-58 (Major); *Wagon Train*—"The Flint McCullough Story" 1-14-59 (Jim Bridger), "The Hunter Malloy Story" 1-21-59 (Daryl Grant), "The C.L. Harding Story" 10-14-59 (Buzz), "The Ricky and Laura Bell Story" 2-24-60 (Jacob); *Rawhide*—"Incident of the Slavemaster" 11-11-60 (Somers), "Twenty-Five Santa Clauses" 12-22-61 (Doctor); *Gunslinger*—"Rampage" 3-16-61 (Dave Cameron); *Lawman*—"Mark of Cain" 3-26-61 (Aaron Kennedy).

Newton, Wayne (1942-). TV: *Bonanza*—"The Unwritten Commandment" 4-10-66 (Andy Walker), "A Christmas Story" 12-25-66 (Andy Walker).

Ney, Richard (1917-). TV: *Northwest Passage*—"Court Martial" 10-26-58 (Lt. Chambers); *Hotel De Paree*—"Sundance and the Greenhorn Trader" 2-26-60 (Oliver Weatherford); *Have Gun Will Travel*—"Odds for a Big Red" 10-7-61 (Guy Fremont); *The Tall Man*—"The Hunt" 1-27-62 (Edward Van Doren).

Nicholas, Denise (1944-). Films: "The Soul of Nigger Charley" 1973 (Elena).

Nicholas, George. Films: "Fame and Fortune" 1918 (Big Dave Dawley).

Nicholas, Robert. Television: *Tales of Wells Fargo*—"Young Jim Hardie" 9-7-59 (Butler); *The Big Valley*—"Guilty" 10-30-67 (Sam Becker); *Alias Smith and Jones*—"Bad Night in Big Butte" 3-2-72.

Nichols, Barbara (1932-10/5/76). Films: "River of No Return" 1954 (Blonde Dancer); "King and Four Queens" 1956 (Birdie). ¶TV: *Maverick*—"The Third Rider" 1-5-58 (Blanche); *Stagecoach West*—"A Time to Run" 11-15-60 (Sadie Wren); *The Travels of Jaimie McPheeters*—"The Day of the Dark Deeds" 3-8-64 (Mamie); *Laredo*—"A Question of Discipline" 10-28-65 (Princess); *Wild Wild West*—"The Night of the Whirring Death" 2-18-66 (Bessie Bowen).

Nichols, George (1865-9/20/27). Films: "Leather Stocking" 1909; "The Mountaineer's Honor" 1909; "A Mohawk's Way" 1910; "The Twisted Trails" 1910; "Two Brothers" 1910; "Unexpected Help" 1910; "Fighting Blood" 1911; "Heredity" 1912; "Iola's Promise" 1912; "The Silent Man" 1917 (Preaching Bill Hardy); "The Son of His Father" 1917 (Silas Mallinsbee); "The Coming of the Law" 1919 (Big Bill Dunlavey); "The Iron Rider" 1920 (John Lannigan); "The Joyous Troublemaker" 1920 (Cash Truit); "The Orphan" 1920 (Sheriff Jim Shields); "The Fox" 1921 (Sheriff Mart Fraser); "Suzanna" 1922 (Don Fernando); "The Silent Stranger" 1924 (Silas Horton); "The Light of Western Stars" 1925 (Billy Stillwell); "Senor Daredevil" 1926 (Tiger O'Flagherty); "White Gold" 1927 (Carson).

Nichols, Robert (1928-). Films: "The Command" 1953 (O'Hirons); "Giant" 1956 (Pinky Snyuthe). ¶TV:

Wyatt Earp—"Killing at Cowskin Creek" 2-14-56 (Simp Sheldon), "Doc Holliday Rewrites History" 5-6-58 (Prof. Jordan), "The Noble Outlaws" 11-24-59 (Spencer); *Trackdown*—"Matter of Justice" 10-17-58 (Cotti); *Wanted—Dead or Alive*—"The Spur" 1-17-59 (Deputy Sheriff), "Angels of Vengeance" 4-18-59 (John Evans); *Maverick*—"The Goose-Drownder" 12-13-59 (Red Herring), "Greenbacks Unlimited" 3-13-60 (Driscoll); *Bonanza*—"San Francisco Holiday" 4-2-60 (Johnny); *The Big Valley*—"They Called Her Delilah" 9-30-68 (Chet Staley); *Gunsmoke*—"No Tomorrow" 1-3-72 (Warden), "The Golden Land" 3-5-73 (Barkeep).

Nicholson, Carol. TV: *Maverick*—"A Bullet for the Teacher" 10-30-60 (Elvira); *Cheyenne*—"The Bad Penny" 3-12-62 (Nancy McConnell).

Nicholson, Jack (1937-). Films: "The Broken Land" 1962; "Ride in the Whirlwind" 1966 (Wes); "The Shooting" 1966 (Billy Spear); "The Missouri Breaks" 1976 (Tom Logan); "Goin' South" 1978 (Henry Moon). ¶TV: *Tales of Wells Fargo*—"That Washburn Girl" 2-13-61 (Tom Washburn); *Bronco*—"The Equalizer" 12-18-61 (Bob Doolin); *The Guns of Will Sonnett*—"A Son for a Son" 10-20-67.

Nicholson, Nick. TV: *Bat Masterson*—"Flume to the Mother Lode" 1-28-60 (Stock Exchange Agent); *Laramie*—"The Day of the Savage" 3-13-62, "Gun Duel" 12-25-62 (Ray Vincent); *Empire*—"Season of Growth" 2-19-63 (Sig Torvald).

Nicholson, Paul (1877-2/2/35). Films: "Broncho Twister" 1927 (Black Jack Brady); "The Brute" 1927 (Square Deal Felton).

Nicol, Alex (1929-). Films: "Tomahawk" 1951 (Lt. Rob Dancy); "Law and Order" 1953 (Lute Johnson); "The Lone Hand" 1953 (Jonah Varden); "The Redhead from Wyoming" 1953 (Stan Blaine); "Dawn at Socorro" 1954 (Jimmy Rapp); "The Man from Laramie" 1955 (Dave Waggoman); "Great Day in the Morning" 1956 (Stephen Kirby); "The Savage Guns" 1961-U.S./Span. (Danny Post); "Ride and Kill" 1964-Ital./Span. (Brandy); "Gunfighters of Casa Grande" 1965-U.S./Span. (Joe Daylight). ¶TV: *U.S. Marshal*—"Cop Hater" 11-8-58.

Nielsen, Hans. Films: "Bullets Don't Argue" 1964-Ital./Ger./Span.; "Five Thousand Dollars on One Ace" 1965-Span./Ital.; "Pyramid of the Sun God" 1965-Ger./Ital./Fr.; "A Place Called Glory" 1966-Span./Ger.

(Judge of Glory); "Prairie in the City" 1971-Ger.

Nielsen, Leslie (1926-). Films: "The Sheepman" 1958 (Johnny Bledsoe/Col. Stephen Bedford); "The Plainsman" 1966 (Col. George A. Custer); "Gunfight in Abilene" 1967 (Grant Evers); "Four Rode Out" 1969-Ital./Span./U.S. ¶TV: *Rawhide*—"Incident Below the Brazos" 5-15-59 (Eli Becker); *Wagon Train*—"The Jeremy Dow Story" 12-28-60 (Jeff Durant), "The Brian Conlin Story" 10-25-64 (Brian Conlin); *The Virginian*—"Ryker" 9-16-64 (Hagen), "The Laramie Road" 12-8-65 (Lightfoot), "No Drums, No Trumpets" 4-6-66 (Cleve Mason), "The Fortress" 12-27-67 (Winthrop), "The Long Ride Home" 9-17-69 (Ben Stratton); *Daniel Boone*—"Mountain of the Dead" 12-17-64 (William Russell); *The Loner*—"The Kingdom of McComb" 10-9-65 (McComb); *Wild Wild West*—"The Night of the Double-Edged Knife" 11-12-65 (Maj. Gen. Ball); *Bonanza*—"The Unseen Wound" 1-29-67 (Sheriff Rowen); *Cimarron Strip*—"The Beast That Walks Like a Man" 11-30-67 (Rowan Houston); *Gunsmoke*—"Time of the Jackals" 1-13-69 (Jess Trevor); *The Big Valley*—"Town of No Exit" 4-7-69 (Conway); *Bearcats!*—12-2-71; *Kung Fu*—"Barbary House" 2-15-75 (Vincent Corbino), "Flight to Orion" 2-22-75 (Vincent Corbino), "The Brothers Cain" 3-1-75 (Vincent Corbino), "Full Circle" 3-15-75 (Vincent Corbino); *The Chisholms*—3-1-80 (Sinclair).

Nieto, Jose (1902-8/9/82). Films: "The Savage Guns" 1961-U.S./Span. (Ortega); "Man from the Cursed Valley" 1964-Ital./Span. (Sam Burnett); "The Hellbenders" 1966-U.S./Ital./Span. (Sheriff); "Kid Rodelo" 1966-U.S./Span. (Thomas Reese); "Outlaw of Red River" 1966-Ital. (Gen. Miguel Camargo); "Savage Pampas" 1966-U.S./Span./Arg. (Gen. Chavez); "Red Sun" 1971-Fr./Ital./Span.; "Scandalous John" 1971 (Mariachi Band Member).

Nigh, Jane (1925-10/5/93). Films: "Unconquered" 1947 (Evelyn); "Fighting Man of the Plains" 1949 (Florence Peel); "Border Treasure" 1950 (Stella); "Rio Grande Patrol" 1950 (Sherry); "Fort Osage" 1952 (Ann Pickett); "Rodeo" 1952 (Nancy Cartwright). ¶TV: *Tales of Wells Fargo*—"The General" 12-16-57; *Rawhide*—"Incident of the Judas Trap" 6-5-59 (Paula Wilcox); *Shotgun Slade*—"Freight Line" 11-17-59; *Colt .45*—"Alias Mr. Howard" 12-6-59

(Zee); *Wichita Town*—"Second Chance" 3-16-60 (Myra Henderson).

Nigh, William (1881-11/27/55). Films: "Salomy Jane" 1914 (Rufe Warren); "The Blue Streak" 1917 (Blue Streak); "Fear-Bound" 1925 (Jim Tumble).

Niles, Wendell (1904-3/28/94). Films: "Cowboy from Brooklyn" 1938 (Announcer); "Gaucho Serenade" 1940; "Three Faces West" 1940 (Radio Announcer). ¶TV: *Circus Boy*—"Daring Young Man" 12-30-56 (Chester Blake).

Nilsson, Anna Q. (1888-2/11/74). Films: "The Toll Gate' 1920 (Mary Brown); "The Fraud at the Hope Mine" 1912; "Heart of the Sunset" 1918 (Alaire Austin); "The Trail to Yesterday" 1918 (Sheila Langford); "The Spoilers" 1923 (Cherry Malotte); "The Splendid Road" 1925 (Sandra De Hault); "Wanderer of the Wasteland" 1935 (Mrs. Virey); "Riders of the Timberline" 1941 (Donna); "They Died with Their Boots On" 1941 (Mrs. Taipe); "The Great Man's Lady" 1942 (Paula Wales).

Nimoy, Leonard (1931-). Films: "Old Overland Trail" 1953 (Black Hawk); "Catlow" 1971-Span. (Miller); "Bonanza: Under Attack" TVM-1995 (Frank James). ¶TV: *26 Men*—"Trail of Revenge" 1-13-59, "Long Trail Home" 2-10-59, "Ricochet" 2-24-59; *Rough Riders*—"Gunpoint Persuasion" 4-30-59 (Jeff Baker); *Colt .45*—"Night of Decision" 6-28-59 (Luke Reid); *Wagon Train*—"The Esteban Zamora Story" 10-21-59 (Bernabe), "The Maggie Hamilton Story" 4-6-60, "The Tiburcio Mendez Story" 3-22-61 (Judge Alfred Black); *Tombstone Territory*—11-13-59 (Little Hawk); *Tate*—"Comanche Scalps" 8-10-60 (Comanche); *The Tall Man*—"A Bounty for Billy" 10-15-60 (Deputy Johnny Swift), "A Gun Is for Killling" 1-14-61 (Johnny Swift); *The Rebel*—"The Hunted" 11-6-60 (Jim Colburn); *Bonanza*—"The Ape" 12-17-60 (Freddie); *Tales of Wells Fargo*—"Something Pretty" 4-17-61 (Coleman); *Rawhide*—"Incident Before Black Pass" 5-19-61 (Anko); *Two Faces West*—"Doctor's Orders" 6-5-61; *Gunsmoke*—"A Man a Day" 12-30-61 (Grice), "The Search" 9-15-62 (Arnie), "I Call Him Wonder" 3-23-63 (Holt), "Treasure of John Walking Fox" 4-16-66 (John Walking Fox); *Laramie*—"The Runt" 2-20-62 (Rix Catlin); *The Virginian*—"Man of Violence" 12-25-63 (Wismer), "The Showdown" 4-14-65 (Benjamin Frome), "Show Me a Hero" 11-17-65 (Keith Bentley); *Death Valley Days*—

"The Journey" 6-13-65 (Yellow Bear); *A Man Called Shenandoah*—"Run, Killer, Run" 1-10-66 (Del Hillman); *Daniel Boone*—"Seminole Territory" 1-13-66 (Oontah).

Nipar, Yvette. Television: *Adventures of Brisco County, Jr.*—"Socrates' Sister" 9-24-93 (Ellie), "Pirates" 10-8-93 (Ellie), "Senior Spirit" 10-15-93 (Ellie).

Nisbet, Stuart (1934-). Films: "The Night Rider" TVM-1979 (Doc Ellis). ¶TV: *Bonanza*—"The Dream Riders" 5-20-61 (Sergeant Hines), "The Survivors" 11-10-68 (Paul Fletcher), "Meena" 11-16-69 (Charlie), "It's a Small World" 1-4-70 (Wiley), "Danger Road" 1-11-70 (Storekeeper), "The Night Virginia City Died" 9-13-70 (Evans), "Winter Kill" 3-28-71 (Fred Tyson), "Fallen Woman" 9-26-71 (Colter); *The Virginian*—"It Tolls for Thee" 11-21-62, "Harvest of Strangers" 2-16-66 (Bartender), "The Mark of a Man" 4-20-66 (Tolliver), "A Small Taste of Justice" 12-20-67, "The Good-Hearted Badman" 2-7-68 (Bartender), "Stopover" 1-8-69 (Bartender), "The Girl in the Shadows" 3-26-69 (Bart), "The Sins of the Father" 3-4-70 (Bartender); *Empire*—"The Four Thumbs Story" 1-8-63 (Fred); *Laredo*—"That's Noway, Thataway" 1-20-66, "A Very Small Assignment" 3-17-66 (Doc Stevernson); *The Road West*—"Pariah" 12-5-66 (Deputy Gibson).

Nissen, Greta (1906-5/15/88). Films: "Life in the Raw" 1922 (Belle).

Niven, David (1910-7/29/83). Films: "Rose Marie" 1936 (Teddy). ¶TV: *Zane Grey Theater*—"Village of Fear" 3-1-57 (Allan Raikes), "The Accuser" 10-30-58 (Milo Brant).

Niven, Kip (1945-). Films: "Dream West" TVM-1986 (Senator John Crittenden). ¶TV: *How the West Was Won*—"The Enemy" 2-5-79 (Lieutenant Ayeless).

Nixon, Allan (1915-4/13/95). Films: "Outlaw Women" 1952 (Dr. Bob Ridgeway); "Apache Warrior" 1957 (Bounty Man). ¶TV: *Wild Bill Hickok*—"The Right of Way" 8-5-52; *Judge Roy Bean*—"Black Jack" 1-1-55 (Will Brock/Black Jack Ketchum), "Judge Declares a Holiday" 1-1-55 (Karl Grafton), "Connie Comes to Town" 12-1-55 (Miller); *Tales of the Texas Rangers*—"The Devil's Deputy" 1-7-56 (Zeke), "The Man from Sundown" 1-21-56 (Lobo Mackinson); *Sergeant Preston of the Yukon*—"Escape to the North" 1-9-58 (Vance Tatum); *Maverick*—"The People's Friend" 2-7-60 (Cosgrove Crony #1); *Rawhide*—"Incident at Poco Tiempo"

12-9-60, "Incident of the Night on the Town" 6-2-61.

Nixon, Marian (1904-2/13/83). Films: "Circus Cowboy" 1924 (Bird Taylor); "The Last of the Duanes" 1924 (Jenny); "The Vagabond Trail" 1924 (Lou Macon); "Durand of the Bad Lands" 1925 (Molly Gore); "The Hurricane Kid" 1925 (Joan Langdon); "Let 'Er Buck" 1925 (Jacqueline McCall); "Riders of the Purple Sage" 1925 (Bess Erne); "The Saddle Hawk" 1925 (Rena Newhall); "Hands Up!" 1926 (the Girl); "The Lash" 1930 (Dolores Delfino).

Noble, Leighton (1911-3/6/94). Films: "At Gunpoint" 1955 (Bob, the New Teller).

Noble, Trish (1946-). Films: "Testimony of Two Men" TVM-1977 (Edna Beamish); "The Wild Wild West Revisited" TVM-1979 (Penelope). ¶TV: *How the West Was Won*—Episode One 2-12-78 (Valerie).

Noe, Annamaria. Films: "Seven Guns for the MacGregors" 1965-Ital./Span. (Mamie MacGregor); "Up the MacGregors!" 1967-Ital./Span. (Mamie); "Matalo!" 1971-Ital./Span.

Noel, Chris (1941-). Films: "Wild Times" TVM-1980 (Dolly).

Noiret, Philippe (1931-). Films: "Don't Touch White Women!" 1974-Ital. (Terry).

Nokes, George. Films: "Buffalo Bill" 1944 (Boy); "Return of the Badmen" 1948 (Donald Webster); "The Cowboy and the Indians" 1949 (Rona).

Nolan, Bob (1908-6/16/80). Films: "Gallant Defender" 1935; "The Mysterious Avenger" 1936; "Rhythm on the Range" 1936; "Song of the Saddle" 1936; "The California Mail" 1937; "The Old Wyoming Trail" 1937; "Outlaws of the Prairie" 1937 (Bob Nolan); "Cattle Raiders" 1938 (Bob); "Colorado Trail" 1938 (Bob); "Law of the Plains" 1938 (Bob); "Rio Grande" 1938 (Bob Stevens); "South of Arizona" 1938 (Bob); "West of Cheyenne" 1938 (Bob Nolan); "West of Santa Fe" 1938 (Bob); "The Man from Sundown" 1939 (Bob); "North of the Yukon" 1939 (Bob Cameron); "Outpost of the Mounties" 1939 (Bob); "Riders of the Black River" 1939 (Bob); "Spoilers of the Range" 1939 (Bob); "The Stranger from Texas" 1939 (Bob); "Texas Stampede" 1939 (Bob); "The Thundering West" 1939 (Bob); "Western Caravans" 1939 (Bob); "Blazing Six Shooters" 1940 (Bob); "Bullets for Rustlers" 1940 (Bob); "The Durango Kid" 1940

(Bob); "Texas Stagecoach" 1940 (Bob Harper); "Thundering Frontier" 1940 (Bob); "Two-Fisted Rangers" 1940 (Bob); "West of Abilene" 1940 (Bob); "Outlaws of the Panhandle" 1941 (Bob); "The Pinto Kid" 1941 (Bob); "Red River Valley" 1941; "Call of the Canyon" 1942; "Heart of the Golden West" 1942; "Man from Cheyenne" 1942; "Ridin' Down the Canyon" 1942; "Romance on the Range" 1942; "Sunset on the Desert" 1942; "Sunset Serenade" 1942; "Hands Across the Border" 1943; "Idaho" 1943; "King of the Cowboys" 1943; "Man from Music Mountain" 1943; "Silver Spurs" 1943; "Song of Texas" 1943; "Cowboy and the Senorita" 1944; "San Fernando Valley" 1944; "Song of Nevada" 1944; "The Yellow Rose of Tesas" 1944; "Along the Navajo Trail" 1945; "Bells of Rosarita" 1945; "Don't Fence Me In" 1945; "The Man from Oklahoma" 1945; "Sunset in El Dorado" 1945; "Utah" 1945; "Heldorado" 1946; "Home in Oklahoma" 1946; "Home on the Range" 1946; "My Pal Trigger" 1946; "Rainbow Over Texas" 1946; "Roll on, Texas Moon" 1946; "Song of Arizona" 1946; "Under Nevada Skies" 1946; "Apache Rose" 1947; "Bells of San Angelo" 1947; "On the Old Spanish Trail" 1947; "Springtime in the Sierras" 1947; "Eyes of Texas" 1948; "The Gay Ranchero" 1948; "Melody Time" 1948; "Night Time in Nevada" 1948; "Under California Stars" 1948.

Nolan, Dani Sue. Films: "Bandit King of Texas" 1949 (Emily Baldwin); "Smoky Canyon" 1952 (Roberta Woodstock).

Nolan, Herman. Films: "The Fourth Horseman" 1933 (Bill Thrasher); "Triple Justice" 1940 (Driver); "Two-Gun Sheriff" 1941.

Nolan, James (1916-7/9/85). Films: "The Arizona Ranger" 1948 (Nimino); "Guns of Hate" 1948 (Sheriff); "Night Time in Nevada" 1948 (Jim Andrews); "Son of God's Country" 1948 (Bill Sanger); "Bandit King of Texas" 1949 (Dan McCabe); "Death Valley Gunfighter" 1949 (Shad Booth). ¶TV: *Gunsmoke*—"How to Die for Nothing" 6-23-56 (Zack); *Schlitz Playhouse of the Stars*—"The Restless Gun" 3-29-57 (Gib); *Colt .45*—"Final Payment" 11-22-57 (Ben Bluestone); *Wanted—Dead or Alive*—"Railroaded" 3-14-59; *Wyatt Earp*—"Woman of Tucson" 11-15-60; *The Virginian*—"The Mountain of the Sun" 4-17-63 (Helen Dryer), Regular 1968-70 (Holly Grainger); *Wild Wild West*—"The Night of the Amnesiac" 2-9-68 (War-

den); *The High Chaparral*—"The Guns of Johnny Rondo" 2-6-70.

Nolan, Jeanette (1911-). Films: "Saddle Tramp" 1950 (Ma Higgins); "The Secret of Convict Lake" 1951 (Harriet); "Hangman's Knot" 1952 (Mrs. Harris); "A Lawless Street" 1955 (Mrs. Dingo Brion); "Seventh Cavalry" 1956 (Mrs. Reynolds); "Tribute to a Badman" 1956 (Mrs. L.A. Peterson); "The Guns of Fort Petticoat" 1957 (Cora Melavan); "The Halliday Brand" 1957 (Nante); "Wild Heritage" 1958 (Ma Bascomb); "Two Rode Together" 1961 (Mrs. McCandless); "The Man Who Shot Liberty Valance" 1962 (Nora Ericson); "Alias Smith and Jones" TVM-1971 (Miss Birdie); "The New Daughters of Joshua Cabe" TVM-1976 (Essie Cargo); "The Winds of Autumn" 1976; "The Awakening Land" TVM-1978 (Granny McWhirter); "The Wild Women of Chastity Gulch" TVM-1982 (Gertrude). ¶TV: *Gunsmoke*—"Potato Road" 10-12-57 (Ma Grilk), "Amy's Good Deed" 4-12-58 (Amy Slater), "Love Thy Neighbor" 1-28-61 (Rose Galloway), "Aunt Thede" 12-19-64 (Aunt Thede), "Pike" 3-1-71 & 3-8-71 (Sally Fergus), "P.S. Murry Christmas" 12-27-71 (Emma Grundy), "One for the Road" 1-24-72 (Sally Fergus); *Have Gun Will Travel*—"Gun Shy" 3-29-58 (Mrs. Warren), "The Tender Gun" 10-22-60 (Maude Smuggley), "The Trap" 3-3-62 (Jeri Marcus), "Alive" 3-17-62 (Alice); *Tales of Wells Fargo*—"The Gun" 4-14-58 (Mrs. Borkman); *Decision*—"The Virginian" 7-6-58 (Dora); *The Restless Gun*—"The Sweet Sisters" 3-23-59 (Abigail Sweet); *Lawman*—"The Souvenir" 4-5-59 (Ma Carey); *Rough Riders*—"Paradise Gap" 4-16-59 (Sister Celestine); *Black Saddle*—"Client: Jessup" 4-18-59 (Alice Jessup); *Hotel De Paree*—Regular 1959-60 (Annette); *The Rebel*—"Johnny Yuma" 10-4-59 (Emmy); *Klondike*—"Swoger's Mules" 11-21-60 (Hattie Swoger); *Wanted—Dead or Alive*—"Witch Woman" 12-28-60 (La Curandera); *Bat Masterson*—"The Good and the Bad" 3-23-61 (Sister Mary Paul); *The Outlaws*—"The Avenger" 4-13-61; *Wagon Train*—"The Janet Hale Story" 5-31-61 (Janet Hale), "Charlie Wooster—Outlaw" 2-20-63 (Bella McKavitch), "The Chottsie Gubenheimer Story" 1-10-65 (Chottsie Gubbenheimer); *Frontier Circus*—"The Courtship" 2-15-62 (Amanda Curtis); *Laramie*—"The Renegade Brand" 2-26-63 (Ellen McGovern); *Laredo*—"The Golden Trail" 11-4-65 (Ma Burns), "It's the End of the Road, Stanley" 3-10-66 (Martha

Tuforth), "Like One of the Family" 3-24-67 (Vita Rose); *F Troop*—"A Fort's Best Friend Is Not a Mother" 4-19-66 (Mrs. Parmenter); *A Man Called Shenandoah*—"Care of General Delivery" 5-9-66 (Matilda Coleman); *Bonanza*—"Old Charlie" 11-6-66 (Annie); *Here Come the Brides*—"The Last Winter" 3-27-70 (Ma Oates); *Hec Ramsey*—"The Mystery of Chalk Hill" 2-18-73 (Rody Claiborne); *Dirty Sally*—Regular 1974 (Sally Fergus).

Nolan, Kathleen (1933-). Films: "The Desperados Are in Town" 1956 (Alice Rutherford); "The Iron Sheriff" 1957 (Kathi); "Testimony of Two Men" TVM-1977 (Myrtle Heger). ¶TV: *Broken Arrow*—"The Rescue" 1-8-57 (Cathy Mason); *Tombstone Territory*—"Rose of the Rio Bravo" 9-17-58 (Rose); *Gunsmoke*—"Call Me Dodie" 9-22-62 (Dodie), "Comanches Is Safe" 3-7-64 (Liz), "Susan Was Evil" 12-3-73 (Nellie); *The Big Valley*—"Into the Widow's Web" 3-23-66 (Liberty Keane); *Custer*—"Breakout" 11-1-67 (Nora Moffett).

Nolan, Lloyd (1902-9/27/85). Films: "The Texas Rangers" 1936 (Sam McGee); "Wells Fargo" 1937 (Del Slade); "Apache Trail" 1943 (Trigger Bill); "Green Grass of Wyoming" 1948 (Rob McLaughlin); "The Last Hunt" 1956 (Woodfoot). ¶TV: *Zane Grey Theater*—"The Homecoming" 10-23-58 (Adam Larkin), "Knife of Hate" 12-8-60 (Dr. Elisha Pittman); *Wagon Train*—"The Hunter Malloy Story" 1-21-59 (Hunter Malloy); *Laramie*—"The Star Trail" 10-13-59 (Tully Hatch), "Deadly Is the Night" 11-7-61 (Matt Dyer), "War Hero" 10-2-62 (Gen. George Barton); *Desilu Playhouse*—"Six Guns for Donegan" 10-16-59 (Sheriff Orville Darrow); *Bonanza*—"The Stranger" 2-27-60 (Charles Leduque); *The Outlaws*—"Buck Breeson Rides Again" 1-25-62 (Buck Breeson); *Great Adventure*—"The Death of Sitting Bull"/"Massacre at Wounded Knee" 10-4-63 & 10-11-63 (Colonel Fraser); *The Virginian*—"It Takes a Big Man" 10-23-63 (Wade Anders), "The Payment" 12-16-64 (Abe Clayton), "The Masquerade" 10-18-67 (Tom Foster); *Daniel Boone*—"The Price of Friendship" 2-18-65 (Ben Hanks); *The Road West*—"A Mighty Hunter Before the Lord" 1-30-67 (Jed Daniell).

Nolan, Tommy (1947-). Films: "Something for a Lonely Man" TVM-1968 (Rafe Runkel). ¶TV: *Buckskin*—Regular 1958-59 (Jody

O'Connell); *Wagon Train*—"The Cappy Darrin Story" 11-11-59 (Tuck Hardy), "The Dick Jarvis Story" 5-18-60 (Dick Jarvis), "The Sam Darland Story" 12-26-62 (Billy); *Riverboat*—"The Boy from Pittsburgh" 11-29-59 (Tommy Jones); *Rawhide*—"Incident of the Night Visitor" 11-4-60 (Joey Gardner); *The Rifleman*—"Guilty Conscience" 4-2-62 (Hab Carraway); *The High Chaparral*—"Tornado Frances" 10-11-68 (Wilbur); *Gunsmoke*—"The Innocent" 11-24-69 (Sonny).

Nolan, Valera (1942-). Films: "The War Wagon" 1967 (Kate Catlin). ¶TV: *The Rifleman*—"The High Country" 12-18-61; *Laramie*—"Double Eagles" 11-20-62; *Wagon Train*—"The Last Circle Up" 4-27-64; *The Virginian*—"The Girl on the Pinto" 3-29-67 (Amanda Harley).

Nolte, Bill. Films: "The Man from Nevada" 1929 (Bowery Walker); "The Man from New Mexico" 1932 (Slink); "Scarlet Brand" 1932 (Lefty).

Nolte, Nick (1941-). TV: *Gunsmoke*—"Tarnished Badge" 11-11-74 (Barney Austin).

Nomkeena, Keena (1942-). TV: *Brave Eagle*—Regular 1955-56 (Keena).

Noonan, Tom (1922-4/24/68). Films: "I Shot Jesse James" 1949 (Charles Ford); "The Return of Jesse James" 1950 (Charlie Ford). ¶TV: *The Rebel*—"Shriek of Silence" 3-19-61 (Paul).

Noonan, Tom. Films: "Heaven's Gate" 1980 (Jake).

Norcross, Frank (1857-9/12/26). Films: "The Flaming Forties" 1925 (Col. Starbottle); "The Man from Red Gulch" 1925 (Col. Starbuttle); "The Escape" 1926 (Jeremiah Grant).

Norden, Eric. Films: "Border Rangers" 1950 (George Standish).

Norell, Henry. Films: "One Foot in Hell" 1960 (George Caldwell). ¶TV: *The Tall Man*—"The Lonely Star" 10-8-60 (Mayor Baldwin).

Noriega, Eduardo (1918-). Films: "El Paso" 1949 (Nacho Vasquez); "The Eagle and the Hawk" 1950 (Roberto); "The Far Horizons" 1955 (Cameahwait); "Fury in Paradise" 1955-U.S./Mex.; "The Beast of Hollow Mountain" 1956 (Enrique Rios); "Daniel Boone, Trail Blazer" 1957 (Squire Boone); "The Last of the Fast Guns" 1958 (Cordoba); "The Last Rebel" 1961-Mex.; "Geronimo" 1962 (Col. Morales); "Zorro, the Gay Blade" 1981 (Don Francisco). ¶TV: *Man from Blackhawk*—"El Patron" 2-

5-60 (El Patron); *The Texan*—"Mission to Monteray" 6-13-60 (Captain Ortega).

Norman, Amber (1901-10/21/72). Films: "The Dude Cowboy" 1926 (Mabel La Rue).

Norman, Bruce G. Films: "The Gunfighter" 1950 (Jimmie); "Callaway Went Thataway" 1951 (Kid); "The Marshal's Daughter" 1953 (Little Boy); "Pack Train" 1953 (Ted). ¶TV: *The Lone Ranger*—"The Beeler Gang" 8-10-50, "Jeb's Gold Mine" 10-16-52, "The New Neighbor" 12-18-52; *The Gene Autry Show*—"The Lawless Press" 1-25-52, "Ruthless Renegade" 2-8-52, "Johnny Jackaroo" 7-13-54 (Johnny); *The Cisco Kid*—"The Runaway Kid" 6-21-52, "Harry the Heir" 3-28-53; *The Roy Rogers Show*—"The Secret of Indian Gap" 1-24-54 (Jiggers Riley), "The Young Defenders" 10-3-54 (Mike Tobin); *Trackdown*—"The Governor" 5-23-58 (Ronnie).

Norman, Hal Jon. TV: *Wagon Train*—"Around the Horn" 10-1-58 (Indian Chief); *The Restless Gun*—"A Bell for Santo Domingo" 12-22-58 (Indian Chief); *Tales of Wells Fargo*—"Vasquez" 5-16-60 (Indian George); *The Rifleman*—"The Pet" 1-6-59 (Father), "Seven" 10-11-60 (Frost); *The Tall Man*—"Night of the Hawk" 3-3-62 (Chatto); *Bonanza*—"The Savage" 12-3-60 (Chato), "The Deserter" 10-21-62; *Rawhide*—"The Peddler" 1-19-62 (Mumush), "The House of the Hunter" 4-20-62 (Walker), "Incident of the Peyote Cup" 5-14-64 (Yulca); *Daniel Boone*—10-14-65 (Gray Elk), "Crisis by Fire" 1-27-66 (Quonah); *Wild Wild West*—"The Night of Montezuma's Hordes" 10-27-67 (Juan); *The High Chaparral*—"For What We Are About to Receive" 11-29-68 (Chief Koso).

Norman, Jack. *see* Willis, Norman.

Norman, Lucille (1926-). Films: "Carson City" 1952 (Susan Mitchell).

Norman, Maidie (1912-). TV: *Wide Country*—"Speckle Bird" 1-31-63 (Pecos Smith); *Death Valley Days*—"No Place for a Lady" 1-8-66 (Martha); *Kung Fu*—"Barbary House" 2-15-75 (Omar's Mother), "Flight to Orion" 2-22-75 (Omar's Mother), "The Brothers Cain" 3-1-75 (Omar's Mother), "Full Circle" 3-15-77 (Omar's Mother).

Norman, Olah. Films: "The Conflict" 1921 (Letty Piggott); "Barb Wire" 1922 (Martha Harding).

Normand, Mabel (1894-2/23/

30). Films: "The Squaw's Love" 1911; "The Tourists" 1912; "Suzanna" 1922 (Suzanna).

Norris, Edward (1910-). Films: "Wagon Trail" 1935 (Clay Hartley); "Frontier Marshal" 1939 (Dan Blackmore); "Back in the Saddle" 1941 (Tom Bennett); "The Singing Sheriff" 1944 (Vance); "The Mysterious Desperado" 1949 (Ramon); "The Wolf Hunters" 1949 (Henri); "The Blazing Sun" 1950 (Doc Taylor); "Surrender" 1950 (Wilbur); "The Man from the Alamo" 1953 (Mapes); "The Kentuckian" 1955 (Gambler). ¶TV: *Wild Bill Hickok*—"Cry Wolf" 10-7-52.

North, Jay (1952-). Films: "The Miracle of the Hills" 1959 (Davey Leonard). ¶TV: *Wanted—Dead or Alive*—"Eight Cent Record" 12-20-58 (Laddie Stone); *Sugarfoot*—"The Giant Killer" 3-3-59 (Bobby); *Wagon Train*—"Those Who Stay Behind" 11-8-64 (Tom Blake).

North, Michael. see Ted North.

North, Sheree (1930-). Films: "Lawman" 1971 (Laura Shelby); "The Shootist" 1976 (Serepta). ¶Television: *Gunsmoke*—"Lover Boy" 10-5-63 (Avis Fisher); *Great Adventure*—"Wild Bill Hickok—the Legend and the Man" 1-3-64 (Agnes Lake); *The Virginian*—"Walk in Another's Footsteps" 3-11-64 (Karen), "That Saunders Woman" 3-30-66 (Della Saunders); *The Loner*—"Escort for a Dead Man" 12-18-65 (Cora); *The Big Valley*—"The Man from Nowhere" 11-14-66 (Libby Mathews); *Iron Horse*—"A Dozen Ways to Kill a Man" 12-19-66 (Alix); *Here Come the Brides*—"A Hard Card to Play" 10-23-68 (Felicia); *Alias Smith and Jones*—"The Man Who Corrupted Hadleyburg" 1-27-72 (Bess Tapscott); *Kung Fu*—"The Third Man" 4-26-73 (Noreen Gallagher); *Hec Ramsey*—"Dead Heat" 2-3-74 (Widow Helpinstall).

North, Ted (Michael North). Films: "Mark of Zorro" 1940 (Michael); "The Ox-Bow Incident" 1943 (Joyce).

North, Wilfred (1863-6/3/35). Films: "The Love Brand" 1923; "Tracked by the Police" 1927 (Tom Bradley); "The Dude Wrangler" 1930 (the Snorer).

North, Zeme. TV: *Wagon Train*—"The Madame Sagittarius Story" 10-3-62 (Fessie); *Temple Houston*—"Ten Rounds for Baby" 1-30-64 (Babe Dale); *Rawhide*—"No Dogs or Drovers" 12-18-64 (Claire Dennis); *Bonanza*—"A Knight to Remember" 12-20-64 (Phoebe); *The Legend of*

Jesse James—"Manhunt" 11-29-65 (Zee Wills); *Branded*—"The Wolfers" 1-9-66 (White Fawn).

Northon, Al. see Caltabiano, Alfio.

Northrup, Harry E. (1940-). Films: "Tom Horn" 1980 (Burke). ¶Television: *Alias Smith and Jones*—"The Man Who Murdered Himself" 3-18-71.

Northrup, Harry S. (1875-7/2/36). Films: "West Wind" 1915; "Britton of the Seventh" 1916 (Capt. Gransom); "Their Compact" 1917 (Ace High Horton); "The Trail of the Shadow" 1917 (Jack Leslie/the Shadow); "Arizona" 1918 (Estrella); "The Trail to Yesterday" 1918 (Jack Duncan); "As the Sun Went Down" 1919 (Arbuthnot); "The Gambling Fool" 1925 (Lightning Cass); "The Squaw Man" 1931 (Butler).

Northwesterners, The (Merle Scobee, A.J. Brier, Wilson D. Rasch, Ray Scobee & Charles Davis). Films: "Starlight Over Texas" 1938; "Down the Wyoming Trail" 1939.

Norton, Barry (1905-8/24/56). Films: "Twilight on the Rio Grande" 1947.

Norton, Cliff (1919-). TV: *Death Valley Days*—"Out of the Valley of Death" 5-25-68 (Wirt); *Wild Wild West*—"The Night of the Plague" 4-4-69 (Drummer); *Young Maverick*—"Half-Past Noon" 1-30-80 (Ambrose).

Norton, Edgar (1868-2/6/53). Films: "The Lady from Hell" 1926 (Honorable Charles Darnely); "When a Man's a Man" 1935 (Gibbs).

Norton, Fletcher (1877-10/3/41). Films: "The Cowboy and the Countess" 1926 (Duke de Milos); "Davy Crockett at the Fall of the Alamo" 1926 (General Santa Anna).

Norton, Jack (1889-10/15/58). Films: "Ruggles of Red Gap" 1935 (Barfly); "Rose of the Rancho" 1936 (Croupier); "The Spoilers" 1942 (Mr. Skinner); "The Kansan" 1943; "Prairie Chickens" 1943; "Alaska" 1944; "Flame of the Barbary Coast" 1945 (Blyline Conners).

Norton, Jr., Ken. Television: *Adventures of Brisco County, Jr.*—"High Treason" 5-13-94 & 5-20-94 (Aldo Buttuchi).

Norton, Tony. Films: "Sartana Does Not Forgive" 1968-Span./Ital. (Jose); "Dick Luft in Sacramento" 1974-Ital. (Valeno); "Trinity Is Still My Name" 1974-Ital.

Norwick, Natalie. TV: *Death Valley Days*—"The Crystal Gazer" 4-

11-55; *Boots and Saddles*—"The Obsession" 10-3-57 (Lucy); *Have Gun Will Travel*—"The Monster of Moon Ridge" 2-28-59 (Emily Bella), "Ambush" 4-23-60 (Sarah), "The Puppeteer" 12-24-60 (Maryanne Croft), "Soledad Crossing" 6-10-61 (Jody Strickland), "Bandit" 5-12-62 (Sandy), "The Mountebank" 8-3-63 (Mrs. Clemenceau); *The Law of the Plainsman*—"Amnesty" 4-7-60 (Clara).

Nova, Hedda. Films: "The Sign Invisible" 1918 (Winona); "Calibre 38" 1919 (Joan); "Shadows of the West" 1921 (Mary); "Golden Silence" 1923; "The Miracle Baby" 1923 (Violet); "The Gold Hunters" 1925 (Minnetake); "My Own Pal" 1926 (Mrs. Jud McIntire).

Nova, Lou (1915-). Films: "Cowboy and the Prizefighter" 1950 (Bull); "Inside Straight" 1951 (Connegan).

Novack, Shelly (1945-5/27/78). Films: "Tell Them Willie Boy Is Here" 1969 (Finney); "The Intruders" TVM-1970 (Theron Pardo). ¶TV: *The Virginian*—"Bitter Autumn" 11-1-67 (Stone), "The Stranger" 4-9-69 (Garrison), "A Time of Terror" 2-11-70 (Frank); *Gunsmoke*—"Stark" 9-28-70 (Adam Bramley); *Kung Fu*—"The Soul Is the Warrior" 2-8-73 (Breck Rankin), "The Nature of Evil" 3-21-74 (Bounty Hunter).

Novak, Eva (1898-4/17/88). Films: "The Feud" 1919 (Betty Summers/Betty Brown); "The Daredevil" 1920 (Alice Spencer); "Desert Love" 1920 (Dolly Remington); "The Testing Block" 1920 (Nellie Gray); "The Last Trail" 1921 (Winifred Samson); "O'Malley of the Mounted" 1921 (Rose Lanier); "The Rough Diamond" 1921 (Gloria Gomez); "Trailin'" 1921 (Sally Fortune); "Barriers of Folly" 1922 (May Gordon); "The Man from Hell's River" 1922 (Marballa); "Sky High" 1922 (Estelle Halloway); "Up and Going" 1922 (Jackie McNab); "Lure of the Yukon" 1924 (Sue McGraig); "No Man's Gold" 1926 (Jane Rogers); "Phantom of the Desert" 1930 (Mary Van Horn); "The Topeka Terror" 1945 (Mrs. Green); "Robin Hood of Texas" 1947; "Four Faces West" 1948 (Mrs. Winston); "Tall Man Riding" 1955; "Ride a Violent Mile" 1957 (Townswoman); "Sergeant Rutledge" 1960 (Spectator); "The Man Who Shot Liberty Valance" 1962. ¶TV: *Laredo*—"That's Noway, Thataway" 1-20-66.

Novak, Jane (1896-2/6/90). Films: "The Greater Courage" 1915; "The Worthier Man" 1915; "Selfish

Yates" 1918 (Mary Adams); "The Tiger Man" 1918 (Ruth Ingram); "The Money Corral" 1919 (Rose); "Treat 'Em Rough" 1919 (Mary Radford); "Wagon Tracks" 1919 (Jane Washburn); "The Golden Trail" 1920 (Faro Kate/Jane Sunderlin); "Isobel, or the Trail's End" 1920 (Isobel Dean); "Kazan" 1921 (Joan Radisson); "Three Word Brand" 1921 (Ethel Barton); "Belle of Alaska" 1922 (Ruth Harkin); "The Snowshoe Trail" 1922 (Virginia Tremont); "The Lure of the Wild" 1925 (Agnes Belmont); "Whispering Canyon" 1926 (Antonia Lee); "Redskin" 1929 (Judy); "Ghost Town" 1936 (Rose); "Desert Fury" 1947 (Mrs. Lindquist); "The Furies" 1950 (Woman).

Novak, Kim (1933-). Films: "The Great Bank Robbery" 1969 (Lyda Kabanov); "The White Buffalo" 1977 (Poker Jenny Schermerhorn).

Novarro, Ramon (1899-10/31/68). Films: "The Outriders" 1950 (Don Antonio Chaves); "Heller in Pink Tights" 1960 (De Leon). ¶TV: *Walt Disney Presents*—"Elfego Baca" Regular 1958-60 (Don Estevan Miranda); *Rawhide*—"Canliss" 10-30-64; *Bonanza*—"The Brass Box" 9-26-65 (Jose Ortega); *Wild Wild West*—"The Night of the Assassin" 9-22-67 (Don Tomas); *The High Chaparral*—"A Joyful Noise" 3-24-68 (Padre Guillermo).

Novello, Jay (1905-9/2/82). Films: "Bandits and Ballads" 1939-short; "The Border Legion" 1940 (Santos); "Colorado" 1940; "Bad Man of Deadwood" 1941 (Monte); "Robin Hood of the Pecos" 1941 (Stacy); "Sheriff of Tombstone" 1941 (Joe Martinez/John Anderson); "Two-Gun Sheriff" 1941 (Albo); "Bells of Capistrano" 1942 (Jed Johnson); "King of the Mounties" 1942-serial (Lewis); "Man from Music Mountain" 1943 (Barker); "The Big Sky" 1952; "Cattle Town" 1952 (Felipe Rojas); "The Iron Mistress" 1952 (Judge Crain); "The Gambler from Natchez" 1954 (Garonne); "The Wonderful Country" 1959 (Diego Casas); "Powderkeg" TVM-1971. ¶TV: *Frontier*—"The Texicans" 1-8-56 (Dalgo); *The Adventures of Rin Tin Tin*—"The Gentle Kingdom" 6-7-57 (Carlos De La Marca), "Spanish Gold" 3-7-58 (Enrique Contreres); *Maverick*—"According to Hoyle" 10-6-57 (Henry Tree), "Plunder of Paradise" 3-9-58 (Paco Torres), "The Day They Hanged Bret Maverick" 9-21-58 (Coroner Oliver Poole), "The Marquesa" 1-3-60 (Pepe); *Colt .45*—

"Small Man" 11-15-57 (John Barnett), "The Cause" 2-28-60; *Trackdown*—"The Reward" 1-3-58 (Robert Murchison); *Zorro*—"The Tightening Noose" 6-5-58 (Senor Greco), "The Sergeant Regrets" 6-12-58 (Senor Greco), "The Eagle Leaves the Nest" 6-19-58 (Senor Greco), "Day of Decision" 7-3-58 (Senor Greco); *Bronco*—"Quest of the Thirty Dead" 10-7-58 (Paco); *Northwest Passage*—"The Vulture" 12-28-58 (Link); *Sugarfoot*—"Small Hostage" 5-26-59 (Pepe Valdez); *Wagon Train*—"The Lita Foladaire Story" 1-6-60; *Wichita Town*—"Brothers of the Knife" 2-10-60 (Ruzzo); *The Rebel*—"Unsurrendered Sword" 4-3-60 (Morales); *Lawman*—"The Witness" 6-24-62 (Beetee); *F Troop*—"La Dolce Courage" 11-24-66 (Emilio Barberini); *Bonanza*—"A Lawman's Lot Is Not a Happy One" 10-5-69 (Fairfax); "Woman of Fire" 1-17-65 (Don Miguel); *Bat Masterson*—"Barbary Castle" 6-30-60 (Captain MacLeod); *Have Gun Will Travel*—"The Exiles" 1-27-62 (Count Casares), "The Knight" 6-2-62 (Otto von Albrecht); *Wide Country*—"What Are Friends For?" 10-18-62 (Julio Perez); *Death Valley Days*—"A Bell for Volcano" 1-24-65 (Jack Harris), "Let My People Go" 10-21-67 (Padre Rodriguez); *The Guns of Will Sonnett*—"A Grave for James Sonnett" 9-22-67 (Father Felipe), "The Man Who Killed James Sonnett" 3-21-69 (Morris).

Nowell, Wedgwood (1878-6/17/57). Films: "The Deserter" 1916 (Captain Turner); "A Man's Fight" 1919 (Norman Evans); "Virginia City" 1940 (Prosecuting Officer).

Nowlin, Herman (1892-9/2/51). Films: "Rainbow Trail" 1932 (Horseman); "The Fargo Kid" 1940 (Hank); "Stage to Chino" 1940; "Flaming Feather" 1952.

Noyes, Skeets (1868-4/18/36). Films: "Rough Waters" 1930 (Davis).

Nugent, Carol. Films: "The Sea of Grass" 1947 (Sarah Beth at Age 7); "Trail of Robin Hood" 1950 (Sis McGonigle); "The Lusty Men" 1952 (Rusty Davis). ¶TV: *The Gene Autry Show*—"The Return of Maverick Dan" 12-15-51; *Wild Bill Hickok*—"Town Without Law" 6-23-53; *Death Valley Days*—"The Calico Dog" 12-2-57 (Nancy Drake); *The Rebel*—"Yellow Hair" 10-18-59 (Indian Girl).

Nugent, Judy (1947-). Films: "Night Stage to Galveston" 1952 (Cathy Evans); "Down Laredo Way" 1953 (Taffy). ¶TV: *The Lone Ranger*—"Triple Cross" 5-21-53; *Annie Oakley*—Semi-Regular 1954-57

(Penny); *Sugarfoot*—"Wolf" 6-9-59 (Charonne); *Rawhide*—"Incident of the Night Horse" 2-19-60 (Willie); *The Tall Man*—"Larceny and Young Ladies" 11-12-60 (June McBean), "McBean Rides Again" 12-10-60 (June McBean), "The Reluctant Bridegroom" 2-18-61 (June McBean), "Millionaire McBean" 4-15-61 (June McBean), "Substitute Sheriff" 1-6-62 (June McBean).

Numkena, Anthony Earl. *see* Holliman, Earl.

Nunn, Alice (1927-). Films: "Evil Roy Slade" TVM-1972 (Claire Beckendorf). ¶TV: *Alias Smith and Jones*—"McGuffin" 12-9-72 (Hotel Clerk).

Nusciak, Lorendana. Films: "Man from Canyon City" 1965-Span./Ital.; "Django" 1966-Ital./Span.; "10,000 Dollars Blood Money" 1966-Ital.; "Revenge for Revenge" 1968-Ital.; "Seven Dollars on the Red" 1968-Ital./Span.; "God Will Forgive My Pistol" 1969-Ital.

Nusser, Jim (1905-6/9/79). Films: "Hell Canyon Outlaws" 1957; "Cahill, United States Marshal" 1973 (Doctor). ¶TV: *Gunsmoke*—"Helping Hand" 3-17-56 (Wilkins), "Dooley Surrenders" 3-8-58 (Nelson), "The Peace Officer" 10-15-60 (Crowe), "Big Man" 3-25-61 (Dick), Regular 1963-75 (Louie Pheeters); *Broken Arrow*—"The Missionaries" 1-29-57 (Perkins); *Temple Houston*—"Billy Hart" 11-28-63 (Flytrap); *The Road West*—"The Gunfighter" 9-26-66 (Amos); *Cimarron Strip*—"Till the End of the Night" 11-16-67; *Wild Wild West*—"The Night of the Legion of Death" 11-24-67 (Reeves).

Nutter, Mayf. TV: *Gunsmoke*—"Hard Luck Henry" 10-23-67 (Heathcliffe Haggen); *Bonanza*—"The Weary Willies" 9-27-70 (Pelletin); *The High Chaparral*—"Too Late the Epitaph" 11-6-70 (Roy).

Nuyen, France (1939-). Films: "One More Train to Rob" 1971 (Ah Toy). ¶TV: *Gunsmoke*—"Honor Before Justice" 3-5-66 (Sarah), "Gunfighter, R.I.P." 10-22-66 (Ching Lee); *Kung Fu*—"A Small Beheading" 9-21-74 (Lady Ching).

Nye, Carroll (1901-3/17/74). Films: "The Brute" 1927 (the Eel); "Death Valley" 1927 (the Boy); "Land of the Silver Fox" 1928 (Carroll); "Sons of the Saddle" 1930 (Harvey, the Cowhand); "The One Way Trail" 1931 (Terry Allen); "The Trail Blazers" 1940 (Jim Chapman).

Nye, G. Raymond. Films: "A Bogus Bandit" 1915; "Liberty" 1916-

serial; "The Branded Man" 1918; "The Fast Mail" 1918; "The Midnight Flyer" 1918; "Play Straight or Fight" 1918; "True Blue" 1918 (Hank Higgins); "Last of the Duanes" 1919 (Poggin); "The Lone Star Ranger" 1919 (Bully Brome); "Drag Harlan" 1920 (Luke Deveny); "The Joyous Troublemaker" 1920 (Bill Rice); "The Orphan" 1920 (Bill Howland); "Sand!" 1920 (Joseph Garber); "Straight from the Shoulder" 1921 (Big Ben Williams); "To a Finish" 1921 (Bill Terry); "Pardon My Nerve!" 1922 (Bill McFluke); "The Ramblin' Kid" 1923 (Mike Sabota); "Salome Jane" 1923 (Ned Pete); "Snowdrift" 1923 (Johnnie Claw); "Do It Now" 1924; "The Sawdust Trail" 1924 (Gorilla Lawson); "Let 'Er Buck" 1925 (James Ralston); "Nine and Three-Fifths Seconds" 1925 (Link Edwards); "The Saddle Hawk" 1925 (Zach Marlin); "Driftin' Thru" 1926 (Joe Walters); "Hard Hombre" 1931 (Joe Barlow); "The Deadline" 1932 (Sheriff Grady); "The Reckless Rider" 1932.

Nye, G. William. Films: "The Rainbow Trail" 1918 (Shad); "A Man's Land" 1932 (Pudge); "Git Along, Little Dogies" 1937.

Oakie, Jack (1903-1/23/78). Films: "Sin Town" 1929 (Chicken O'Toole); "Dude Ranch" 1931 (Jennifer); "Call of the Wild" 1935 (Shorty Hoolihan); "The Texas Rangers" 1936 (Wahoo Jones); "Northwest Stampede" 1948 (Mike Kirby); "Tomahawk" 1951 (Col. Beckworth); "Once Upon a Horse" 1958 (Fireman); "The Wonderful Country" 1959 (Travis Hight). ¶TV: *Daniel Boone*—"Goliath" 9-29-66 (Otis Cobb); *Bonanza*—"A Christmas Story" 12-25-66 (Thadeus Cade).

Oakland, Simon (1922-8/29/83). Films: "The Raiders" 1964 (Sgt. Austin Tremaine); "The Plainsman" 1966 (Chief Black Kettle); "The Hunting Party" 1971-Brit./Ital./Span. (Matthew Gun); "Scandalous John" 1971 (Barton Whittaker); "Chato's Land" 1972 (Jubal Hooker). ¶TV: *Sheriff of Cochise*—"Question of Honor" 10-26-56; *Gunsmoke*—"How to Cure a Friend" 11-10-56 (Enoch Mills), "Overland Express" 5-31-58 (Jim Nation), "Miguel's Daughter" 11-28-59 (Miguel Ramirez), "The Hostage" 12-4-65 (Carl Mandee); *Have Gun Will Travel*—"The Statue of San Sebastian" 6-14-58 (Sancho Fernandez); *Black Saddle*—"Client: Mowery" 3-28-59 (Grat Mowery); *The Alaskans*—"Doc Booker" 12-6-59 (Doc Booker); *Zane Grey Theater*—"Death in a Wood" 12-17-59

(Townsend), "Sundown Smith" 3-24-60 (Jesse Harp); *Bronco*—"Every Man a Hero" 2-23-60 (Sergeant Ross); *Laramie*—"Ride or Die" 3-8-60 (Vernon Kane); *Wagon Train*—"The Countess Baranof Story" 5-11-60 (Colonel Vasily), "The Donna Fuller Story" 12-19-62 (Alonzo Galezio); *The Outlaws*—"The Bell" 3-9-61 (Neil Gwinner); *Tales of Wells Fargo*—"Portrait of Teresa" 2-10-62 (Poderio); *Wild Wild West*—"The Night of the Fugitives" 11-8-68 (Diamond Dave Desmond); *Stoney Burke*—"Image of Glory" 2-4-63 (Sam Hagen); *Bonanza*—"The Thunder Man" 5-5-63 (William Poole), "Justice Deferred" 12-17-67 (Mel Barnes/Frank Scott), "The Clarion" 2-9-69 (Seth Tabor); *Rawhide*—"Incident of the Travellin' Man" 10-17-63 (Bolivar Jagger), "Encounter at Boot Hill" 9-14-65 (Sheriff Blaine); *The Virginian*—"Dangerous Road" 3-17-65 (Coulter), "Letter of the Law" 12-22-65 (Sanders); *Daniel Boone*—9-30-65 (Dull Knife), "Bitter Mission" 3-30-67 (General James Wilkerson), "Bickford's Bridge" 2-20-69 (Bickford); *Cimarron Strip*—"The Beast That Walks Like a Man" 11-30-67 (Joshua Broom); *The Big Valley*—"The Secret" 1-27-69 (Adam Howard); *Bret Maverick*—"Horse of Yet Another Color" 1-5-82 (Delwood Crestmore).

Oakland, Vivien (1895-8/1/58). Films: "The Rainbow Trail" 1925 (Bessie Erne); "Tony Runs Wild" 1926 (Mrs. Johnson); "Way Out West" 1937 (Stagecoach Passenger/Molly, the Sheriff's Wife); "Utah" 1945 (Stella Mason).

Oakley, Annie (1860-11/3/26). Films: "Buffalo Bill" 1893.

Oakley, Laura (1879-1/30/57). Films: "A Cowgirl Cinderella" 1912; "Two-Gun Betty" 1919 (Miss Ambrose).

Oakman, Wheeler (1890-3/19/49). Films: "The God of Gold" 1912; "The Last of Her Tribe" 1912; "The Little Indian Martyr" 1912; "Opitsah" 1912; "Sergeant Byrne of the N.W.M.P." 1912; "In the Long Ago" 1913; "Vengeance Is Mine" 1913; "A Wild Ride" 1913; "Chip of the Flying U" 1914; "In Defiance of the Law" 1914; "In the Days of the Thundering Herd" 1914 (Chief Swift Wing); "The Lonesome Trail" 1914; "Shotgun Jones" 1914; "The Spoilers" 1914 (Broncho Kid); "When the Cook Fell Ill" 1914; "When the West Was Young" 1914; "The Wilderness Mail" 1914; "The Golden Spurs" 1915; "The Claim" 1918 (John MacDonald); "Revenge" 1918 (Dick Randall);

"Penny of Top Hill Trail" 1921 (Kurt Walters); "The Half-Breed" 1922 (Delmar Spavinaw); "The Son of the Wolf" 1922 (Scruff Mackenzie); "Hey! Hey! Cowboy" 1927 (John Evans); "Danger Patrol" 1928 (George Gambier); "Morgan's Last Raid" 1929 (John Bland); "Roaring Ranch" 1930 (Ramsey Kane); "The Boiling Point" 1932 (Nobro); "Cornered" 1932 (Deputy Red); "End of the Trail" 1932 (Major Jenkins); "The Riding Tornado" 1932 (Hetch Engall); "Texas Cyclone" 1932 (Utah Becker); "Two-Fisted Law" 1932 (Bob Russell); "The Western Code" 1932 (Nick Grindell); "Man of Action" 1933 (Sheriff Norton); "Rusty Rides Alone" 1933 (Poe Powers); "Silent Men" 1933 (Ed Wilder); "The Sundown Rider" 1933 (Laughing Maxey); "Frontier Days" 1934 (Sheriff Barnes); "In Old Santa Fe" 1934 (Tracy); "Code of the Mounted" 1935 (Duval); "The Man from Guntown" 1935 (De Long); "The Phantom Empire" 1935-serial (Argo); "Square Shooter" 1935 (Jim Thorne); "Timber War" 1935 (Murdock); "Trails of the Wild" 1935 (Hardy); "Undercover Men" 1935; "Aces and Eights" 1936 (Ace Morgan); "Ghost Patrol" 1936 (Kincaid); "Roarin' Guns" 1936 (Walton); "Song of the Trail" 1936 (Bob Arnold); "Code of the Rangers" 1938 (Blackie Miller); "The Mysterious Avenger" 1936 (Brophy); "Land of Fighting Men" 1938 (Wallace); "The Texans" 1938 (U.S. Captain); "In Old Montana" 1939 (Jim Dawson); "The Lone Ranger Rides Again" 1939-serial (Manny); "Wolf Call" 1939 (Carson); "The Medico of Painted Springs" 1941 (Fred Burns); "The Fighting Buckaroo" 1943 (Sam Thacher); "Saddles and Sagebrush" 1943; "Riding West" 1944 (Capt. Amos Karnes); "Sundown Valley" 1944 (Cab Baxter); "Rough Ridin' Justice" 1945 (Virgil Trent).

Oates, Warren (1932-4/3/82). Films: "Yellowstone Kelly" 1959 (Corporal); "Ride the High Country" 1962 (Henry Hammond); "Mail Order Bride" 1964 (Jace); "Major Dundee" 1965 (O.W. Hadley); "Shenandoah" 1965 (Billy Packer); "Return of the Seven" 1966-Span. (Colbee); "The Shooting" 1966 (Willet Gashade); "Welcome to Hard Times" 1967 (Jenks); "Something for a Lonely Man" TVM-1968 (Angus Duren); "Smith" 1969 (Walter Charles); "The Wild Bunch" 1969 (Lyle Gorch); "Barquero" 1970 (Jake Remy); "There Was a Crooked Man" 1970 (Floyd Moon); "The Hired Hand" 1971 (Arch Harris); "Kid

Blue" 1973 (Reese Ford); "China 9, Liberty 37" 1978-Ital./Span./U.S. (Sebanek); "True Grit" TVM-1978 (Rooster Cogburn). ¶TV: *Have Gun Will Travel*—"Three Sons" 5-10-58 (Half-Brother), "The Poker Friend" 11-12-60 (Harrison); *The Rifleman*—"The Marshal" 10-21-58 (Andrew Sheltin), "Bloodlines" 10-6-59, "The Prodigal" 4-26-60 (Santos), "Miss Milly" 11-15-60 (Marty Ryan), "Day of Reckoning" 4-9-62 (Willie Breen); *The Adventures of Rin Tin Tin*—"The Epidemic" 11-21-58 (Deke); *Wanted—Dead or Alive*—"Die by the Gun" 12-6-58 (Cox), "The Legend" 3-7-59 (Billy Clegg), "Amos Carter" 5-9-59 (Seth Blake), "Angela" 1-9-60 (George Aswell), "The Last Retreat" 1-11-61 (Clem Robinson); *Gunsmoke*—"Snakebite" 12-20-58 (Jed Hakes), "Small Water" 9-24-60 (Leroy Pickett), "Love Thy Neighbor" 1-28-61 (Peter Scooper), "Marry Me" 12-23-61 (Sweet Billy Cathcart), "The Do-Badder" 1-6-62 (Chris Kelly), "The Bassops" 2-22-64 (Deke Bassop), "Circus Trick" 2-6-65 (Speeler), "Ten Little Indians" 10-9-65 (Al Tresh), "The Mission" 10-8-66 (Lafe), "The Wreckers" 9-11-67 (Tate Crocker); *Trackdown*—"Bad Judgment" 1-28-59 (Lute Borden), "Fear" 3-18-59 (Kelly), "Back to Crawford" 9-9-59 (Norvil); *Tombstone Territory*—"Whipsaw" 3-13-59 (Bob Pickett), 1-29-61 (Vic Reel); *Black Saddle*—"Client: Steele" 3-21-59 (Simms); *Buckskin*—"Charlie, My Boy" 4-6-59 (Charlie); *Rough Riders*—"The Rifle" 5-7-59 (Frank Day); *Bat Masterson*—"Lottery of Death" 5-13-59 (Sonny Parsons), "Meeting at Mimbers" 4-13-61 (Cat Crail); *Wagon Train*—"The Martha Barham Story" 11-4-59 (Silas Carpenter); *The Rebel*—"School Days" 11-15-59 (Troy Armbruster); *Rawhide*—"Incident of the Dancing Death" 4-8-60 (Marco), "Incident of the Prophecy" 11-21-63 (Rabbit Waters), "The Race" 9-25-64 (Weed), "Hostage for Hanging" 10-19-65 (Jesse Gufler); *Johnny Ringo*—"Single Debt" 5-12-60 (Burt Scanlon); *Tate*—"Before Sunup" 8-17-60 (Cowpoke); *Wrangler*—"Affair at the Trading Post" 8-18-60 (Shep Martin); *The Outlaws*—"Thirty a Month" 9-29-60 (Billy Hooton); *The Westerner*—"Jeff" 9-30-60; *Lawman*—"The Second Son" 11-27-60 (Al May); *Laramie*—"Two for the Gallows" 4-11-61 (Pete); *Stagecoach West*—"The Renegades" 6-20-61 (Tom Lochlin); *Bonanza*—"The Mountain Girl" 5-13-62 (Paul); *Stoney Burke*—Regular 1962-63 (Ves Painter); *The Travels of Jaimie*

McPheeters—"The Day of the First Suitor" 9-29-63 (Eldon Bishop); *The Virginian*—"Stopover in a Western Town" 11-27-63 (Corbie), "One Spring Like Long Ago" 3-2-66 (Bowers), "Ride to Delphi" 9-21-66 (Buxton); *Branded*—"Judge Not" 9-12-65 (Perce Clampett/Frank Clampett); *A Man Called Shenandoah*—"The Fort" 9-27-65 (Sergeant Ryder); *Shane*—"An Echo of Anger" 10-1-66 (Kemp Spicer); *Dundee and the Culhane*—"The Turn the Other Cheek Brief" 9-6-67 (Lafe Doolin); *Cimarron Strip*—"The Battleground" 9-28-67 (Mobeetie), "Nobody" 12-7-67 (Mobeetie); *The Big Valley*—"The Murdered Party" 11-17-65 (Korby Kyles), "The Great Safe Robbery" 11-21-66 (Duke); *The Monroes*—"The Forest Devil" 9-28-66 (Nick Beresford); *Iron Horse*—"The Return of Hode Avery" 11-4-67 (Hode Avery); *Lancer*—"The Man Without a Gun" 3-25-69 (Sheriff Val Crawford), "The Buscaderos" 3-17-70 (Drago).

Obeck, Ferdinand (1881-1/31/29). Films: "The Great Divide" 1915 (Dutch).

Ober, Philip (1902-9/13/82). Films: "Broken Lance" 1954 (Van Cleve). ¶TV: *Sugarfoot*—"The Vultures" 4-28-59 (Gen. Humphrey); *Bat Masterson*—"The Prescott Campaign" 2-2-61 (Silas Guild); *Death Valley Days*—"Lieutenant Bungle" 10-25-61 (Major Galloway); *Empire*—"Down There, the World" 3-12-63 (Walter Kenner); *Bonanza*—"The Boss" 5-19-63 (Oliver); *Temple Houston*—"Billy Hart" 11-28-63 (Bert Clarke); *Walt Disney Presents*—"Gallegher" 1965-67 (Hade); *Iron Horse*—"Broken Gun" 10-17-66 (Cal Diver).

Oberdiear, Karen. TV: *The Texas Wheelers*—Regular 1974-75 (Boo Wheeler); *Gunsmoke*—"The First of Ignorance" 1-27-75 (Sallie Harker).

Oberon, Merle (1911-11/23/79). Films: "Cowboy and the Lady" 1938 (Mary Smith).

O'Brian, Hugh (1925-). Films: "The Return of Jesse James" 1950 (Lem); "Buckaroo Sheriff of Texas" 1951 (Ted Gately); "Cave of Outlaws" 1951 (Garth); "The Cimarron Kid" 1951 (Red Buck); "Little Big Horn" 1951 (Pvt. Al DeWalt); "Vengeance Valley" 1951 (Dick Fasken); "The Lawless Breed" 1952 (Ike Hanley); "The Raiders" 1952 (Hank Purvis); "Back to God's Country" 1953 (Frank Hudson); "The Man from the Alamo" 1953 (Lt. Lamar); "Seminole" 1953 (Kajeck); "The Stand at Apache River" 1953 (Tom Kenyon);

"Broken Lance" 1954 (Mike Devereaux); "Drums Across the River" 1954 (Morgan); "Saskatchewan" 1954 (Marshal Smith); "The Twinkle in God's Eye" 1955 (Marty); "White Feather" 1955 (American Horse); "The Brass Legend" 1956 (Sheriff Wade Adams); "The Fiend Who Walked the West" 1958 (Dan Hardy); "Alias Jesse James" 1959 (Wyatt Earp); "Africa—Texas Style!" 1967-U.S./Brit. (Jim Sinclair); "Wild Women" TVM-1970 (Killian); "The Shootist" 1976 (Pulford); "Gunsmoke: The Last Apache" TVM-1990 (Gen. Nelson Miles); "The Gambler Returns: The Luck of the Draw" TVM-1991 (Wyatt Earp); "Wyatt Earp: Return to Tombstone" TVM-1994 (Wyatt Earp). ¶TV: *Stage 7*—"Billy and the Bride" 5-8-55 (Billy the Kid); *Wyatt Earp*—Regular 1955-61 (Wyatt Earp); *The Virginian*—"The Executioners" 9-19-62 (Paul Taylor); *Paradise*—"A Gather of Guns" 9-10-89 (Wyatt Earp), "Home Again" 9-16-89 (Wyatt Earp).

O'Brien, Billy. Films: "The Sign of the Wolf" 1931-serial (Bud); "West of the Divide" 1934 (Spuds).

O'Brien, Clay (1961-). Films: "The Cowboys" 1972 (Hardy Fimps); "Cahill, United States Marshal" 1973 (Billy Joe Cahill); "One Little Indian" 1973 (Mark); "The Apple Dumpling Gang" 1975 (Bobby Bradley); "Mackintosh & T.J." 1975 (T.J.). ¶TV: *Gunsmoke*—"The River" 9-11-72 & 9-18-72 (Tuttle Kinkaid), "The Widow and the Rogue" 10-29-73 (Caleb Cunningham); *The Cowboys*—Regular 1974 (Weedy).

O'Brien, Cubby. Films: "Westward Ho the Wagons" 1956 (Jerry Stephen). ¶TV: *Zane Grey Theater*—"The Man from Yesterday" 12-22-60 (Ted Duncan).

O'Brien, Dave "Tex" (David Barclay) (1912-11/8/69). Films: "Lightnin' Crandall" 1937 (Tommy Shannon); "Renfrew of the Royal Mounted" 1937 (Dreamy Charles Nolan); "Rough Ridin' Rhythm" 1937 (Detective Waters); "Brothers of the West" 1938 (Davy); "Law of the Texan" 1938; "Man's Country" 1938 (Bert); "Starlight Over Texas" 1938; "Utah Trail" 1938 (Mason); "Where the Buffalo Roam" 1938 (Jeff Grey); "Whirlwind Horseman" 1938 (Slade); "Code of the Cactus" 1939 (Bob Swane); "Crashing Thru" 1939 (Fred Chambers); "Drifting Westward" 1939 (Trigger); "Fighting Mad" 1939 (Constable Kelly); "Fighting Renegade" 1939 (Jerry Leonard); "Flaming Lead" 1939 (Frank Gordon); "Frontier Scout" 1939 (Steve Hickok); "New Frontier" 1939 (Jason); "Outlaw's Paradise" 1939 (Meggs); "Riders of the Sage" 1939 (Tom Martin); "Rollin' Westward" 1939 (Red); "The Singing Cowgirl" 1939 (Dick Williams); "Song of the Buckaroo" 1939 (Alden); "Sundown on the Prairie" 1939 (Denny); "Texas Wildcats" 1939 (Ed Arden); "Trigger Smith" 1939 (Duke); "Water Rustlers" 1939 (Bob Lawson); "Wyoming Outlaw" 1939; "Buzzy Rides the Range" 1940 (Ken Blair); "Cowboy from Sundown" 1940 (Steve Davis); "Danger Ahead" 1940 (Kelly); "Gun Code" 1940 (Gale); "The Kid from Santa Fe" 1940 (Chester); "Murder on the Yukon" 1940 (Constable Kelly); "Phantom Rancher" 1940 (Luke); "Queen of the Yukon" 1940 (Bob Adams); "Sky Bandits" 1940 (Kelly); "Yukon Flight" 1940 (Constable Kelly); "Billy the Kid in Santa Fe" 1941 (Texas Joe Vincent); "Billy the Kid Wanted" 1941 (Jeff); "Buzzy and the Phantom Pinto" 1941; "Forbidden Trails" 1941 (Jim Cramer); "The Gunman from Bodie" 1941; "The Texas Marshal" 1941 (Buzz); "Billy the Kid's Smoking Guns" 1942; "Down Texas Way" 1942 (Dave); "King of the Stallions" 1942; "Law and Order" 1942 (Jeff); "The Rangers Take Over" 1942 (Tex Wyatt); "Sheriff of Sage Valley" 1942 (Jeff); "Bad Men of Thunder Gap" 1943; "Border Buckaroos" 1943 (Tex Wyatt); "Fighting Valley" 1943 (Tex Wyatt); "The Return of the Rangers" 1943; "West of Texas" 1943 (Tex Wyatt); "Boss of Rawhide" 1944 (Tex Wyatt); "Brand of the Devil" 1944 (Tex Wyatt); "Dead or Alive" 1944; "Gangsters of the Frontier" 1944; "Guns of the Law" 1944; "Gunsmoke Mesa" 1944 (Tex Wyatt); "Outlaw Roundup" 1944; "The Pinto Bandit" 1944; "Spook Town" 1944; "Trail of Terror" 1944 (Tex Wyatt/Curly Wyatt); "The Whispering Skull" 1944; "Enemy of the Law" 1945 (Dave Wyatt); "Flaming Bullets" 1945; "Frontier Fugitives" 1945; "Marked for Murder" 1945; "Three in the Saddle" 1945; "The Desperados Are in Town" 1956 (Doc Lapman).

O'Brien, Donald. Films: "Run Man, Run" 1967-Ital./Fr. (Cassidy); "Finders Killers" 1969-Ital. (Jack); "Sheriff of Rock Spring" 1971-Ital.; "Thirteenth Is a Judas" 1971-Ital.; "God Is My Colt .45" 1972-Ital. (Collins); "Jesse and Lester, Two Brothers in a Place Called Trinity" 1972-Ital. (Lester); "Paid in Blood" 1972-Ital. (Lee Rastus); "Kung Fu

Brothers in the Wild West" 1973-Ital./Hong Kong; "Four Horsemen of the Apocalypse" 1975-Ital.; "Keoma" 1975-Ital./Span.; "Man Called Blade" 1977-Ital. (Burt Craven); "Silver Saddle" 1978-Ital. (Luke).

O'Brien, Edmond (1915-5/9/85). Films: "The Redhead and the Cowboy" 1951 (Dunn Jeffers); "Silver City" 1951 (Larkin Moffatt); "Warpath" 1951 (John Vickers); "Denver and Rio Grande" 1952 (Jim Vesser); "Cow Country" 1953 (Ben Anthony); "The Big Land" 1957 (Jagger); "The Man Who Shot Liberty Valance" 1962 (Dutton Peabody); "Rio Conchos" 1964 (Col. Theron Pardee); "The Wild Bunch" 1969 (Sykes); "The Intruders" TVM-1970 (Col. William Bodeen). ¶TV: *Zane Grey Theater*—"A Gun Is for Killing" 10-18-57 (Russell Andrews), "Lonesome Road" 11-19-59 (Marshal Ben Clark); *Laramie*—"The Iron Captain" 10-26-59 (Capt. Sam Prado); *Walt Disney Presents*—"Gallegher" 1965-67 (Editor Crowley); *The Virginian*—"Ah Sing vs. Wyoming" 10-25-67 (Thomas Manstead); *The High Chaparral*—"The Hostage" 3-5-71 (MacQuarie).

O'Brien Moore, Erin (1902-5/3/79). TV: *My Friend Flicka*—"The Recluse" 5-25-56; *Colt .45*—"The Peacemaker" 10-18-57 (Sister Helen MacGregor); *Maverick*—"Stage West" 10-27-57 (Linda Harris), "Island in the Swamp" 11-30-58 (Victoria Forge); *Cheyenne*—"Border Affair" 11-5-57 (Maria Felitzia); *Sugarfoot*—"A Wreath for Charity Lloyd" 3-18-58 (Charity), "Short Range" 5-13-58 (Princess Tania); *Bat Masterson*—"The Disappearance of Bat Masterson" 3-10-60 (Jenie Landry), "The Marble Slab" 5-11-61 (Marie); *Tombstone Territory*—4-29-60 (Isabelle/Gwen Rand); *Death Valley Days*—"Emma Is Coming" 6-7-60 (Emma Nevada); *Laramie*—"The Jailbreakers" 12-19-61 (Gina Ross), "The Turn of the Wheel" 4-3-62 (Abbey O'Neill).

O'Brien, Eugene (1880-4/29/66). Films: "Channing of the Northwest" 1922 (Channing); "Frivolous Sal" 1925 (Roland Keene).

O'Brien, George (1900-9/4/85). Films: "Life in the Raw" 1922 (Jim Barry); "The Iron Horse" 1924 (Davy Brandon); "Rustlin' for Cupid" 1926 (Bradley Blatchford); "Three Bad Men" 1926 (Dan O'Malley); "Last of the Duanes" 1930 (Buck Duane); "The Lone Star Ranger" 1930 (Buck Duane); "Rough Romance" 1930 (Billy West); "Fair Warning" 1931

(Whistlin' Dan Barry); "A Holy Terror" 1931 (Tony Bard/Tony Woodbury); "Riders of the Purple Sage" 1931 (Jim Lassiter); "The Gay Caballero" 1932 (Ted Radcliffe); "The Golden West" 1932 (David Lynch/Motano); "Mystery Ranch" 1932 (Bob Sanborn); "Rainbow Trail" 1932 (Shefford); "The Last Trail" 1933 (Tom Daley); "Robbers' Roost" 1933 (Jim Wall); "Smoke Lightning" 1933 (Smoke Mason); "The Dude Ranger" 1934 (Ernest Selby); "Frontier Marshal" 1934 (Michael Wyatt); "Cowboy Millionaire" 1935 (Bob Walker); "Thunder Mountain" 1935 (Cal Emerson); "When a Man's a Man" 1935 (Larry Knight); "Whispering Smith Speaks" 1935 (Gordon D. Harrington, Jr./Whispering Smith); "The Border Patrolman" 1936 (Bob Wallace); "Daniel Boone" 1936 (Daniel Boone); "O'Malley of the Mounted" 1936 (O'Malley); "Hollywood Cowboy" 1937 (Jeffery Carson); "Park Avenue Lodger" 1937 (Grant Curran); "Border G-Man" 1938 (Jim Galloway); "Gun Law" 1938 (Tom O'Malley); "Lawless Valley" 1938 (Larry Rhodes); "The Painted Desert" 1938 (Bob McVey); "Renegade Ranger" 1938 (Capt. Jack Steele); "Arizona Legion" 1939 (Boone Yeager); "The Fighting Gringo" 1939 (Wade Barton); "The Marshal of Mesa City" 1939 (Cliff Mason); "Racketeers of the Range" 1939 (Barney O'Dell); "Timber Stampede" 1939 (Scott Baylor); "Trouble in Sundown" 1939 (Clint Bradford); "Bullet Code" 1940 (Steve Holden); "Legion of the Lawless" 1940 (Jeff Toland); "Prairie Law" 1940 (Brill); "Stage to Chino" 1940 (Dan Clark); "Triple Justice" 1940 (Brad Henderson); "Fort Apache" 1948 (Capt. Sam Collingwood); "She Wore a Yellow Ribbon" 1949 (Maj. Mack Allshard); "Gold Raiders" 1951 (George); "Cheyenne Autumn" 1964 (Maj. Braden).

O'Brien, Jack. Films: "Action Galore" 1925 (Strike Carney); "The Desert Demon" 1925 (Bugs); "Galloping Jinx" 1925; "Reckless Courage" 1925 (Scar Degan); "A Streak of Luck" 1925 (Jack Hurst).

O'Brien, Joan. Films: "The Alamo" 1960 (Mrs. Dickinson); "The Comancheros" 1961 (Melinda); "Six Black Horses" 1962 (Kelly). ¶TV: *Bat Masterson*—"One Bullet from Broken Bow" 1-21-59 (Dolores Clark), "Shakedown at St. Joe" 10-29-59 (Dora Miller), "High Card Loses" 11-10-60 (Eileen); *Riverboat*—"The Fight Back" 10-18-59 (Sonja Torgin); *The Alaskans*—"Kangaroo Court" 5-

8-60 (Fay Campbell); *Bronco*—"La Rubia" 5-17-60 (Judith Castle); *Wagon Train*—"The Luke Grant Story" 6-1-60 (Victoria Fleming), "The Candy O'Hara Story" 12-7-60 (Candy O'Hara); *The Deputy*—"Meet Sergeant Tasker" 10-1-60 (Emily Price); *The Westerner*—"The Courting of Libby" 11-11-60 (Libby); *Cheyenne*—"Incident at Dawson Flats" 1-9-61 (Selma Dawson); *Whispering Smith*—"The Idol" 9-18-61 (Marilyn); *The Outlaws*—"A Bit of Glory" 2-1-62 (Laurie); *The Tall Man*—"The Impatient Brides" 2-3-62 (Marilee); *Rawhide*—"The Pitchwagon" 3-2-62 (Melinda); *The Virginian*—"The Dark Challenge" 9-23-64 (Joan).

O'Brien, John. Films: "Vigilantes Are Coming" 1936-serial (Robert Loring).

O'Brien, Kenneth (1935-1/19/85). TV: *Kung Fu*—"The Tide" 2-1-73 (Jenkins), "The Ancient Warrior" 5-3-73 (Arlo), "Cry of the Night Beast" 10-19-74 (Landry).

O'Brien, Margaret (1937-). Films: "Bad Bascomb" 1946 (Emmy); "Heller in Pink Tights" 1960 (Della Southby); "Testimony of Two Men" TVM-1977 (Flora Bumpstead Eaton). ¶TV: *Wagon Train*—"The Sacramento Story" 6-25-58 (Julie); *Rawhide*—"Incident of the Town in Terror" 3-6-59 (Betsy Stauffer).

O'Brien, Pat (1899-10/15/83). Films: "Shadows of the West" 1921 (Jim Kern); "The Freckled Rascal" 1929 (Jim Kane); "Outlawed Guns" 1935 (Babe Rivers); "The Roaring West" 1935-serial (Steve); "Bar 20 Justice" 1938 (Frazier); "Cowboy from Brooklyn" 1938 (Roy Chadwick); "Flaming Frontier" 1938-serial; "Hawaiian Buckaroo" 1938 (Stephen Wainwright); "Panamint's Bad Man" 1938 (Carl Adams); "Bury Me Not on the Lone Prairie" 1941; "Doomed Caravan" 1941 (Jim Ferber); "Jubilee Trail" 1954 (Ernest "Texas" Conway); "Town Tamer" 1965 (Judge Murcott); "The Over-the-Hill Gang" TVM-1969 (Capt. Oren Hayes). ¶TV: *The Virginian*—"The Fortunes of J. Jimerson Jones" 1-15-64 (J. Jimerson Jones), "Yesterday's Timepiece" 1-18-67 (Doc Bigelow); *Branded*—"The Greatest Coward on Earth" 11-21-65 (P.T. Barnum); *Alias Smith and Jones*—"Shootout at Diablo Station" 12-2-71 (Hayfoot).

O'Brien, Richard (1918-3/29/83). Films: "Rough Night in Jericho" 1967 (Ryan); "The Honkers" 1972 (Matt Weber). ¶TV: *The Big Valley*—"Under a Dark Sea" 2-9-66, "The Midas Man" 4-13-66 (Jace), "The

Man from Nowhere" 11-14-66 (Jed Cameron), "Presumed Dead" 10-7-68 (Mosley), "Alias Nellie Handley" 2-24-69 (Sheriff Bannock); *Cimarron Strip*—"The Search" 11-9-67 (Ben Lorton), "Big Jessie" 2-8-68 (Chandler); *Wild Wild West*—"The Night of the Vipers" 1-12-68 (Sheriff Tenney), "The Night of the Pistoleros" 2-21-69 (Sgt. Charlie Tobin), "The Night of the Tycoons" 3-28-69 (Mr. Van Cleeve); *Gunsmoke*—"The Twisted Heritage" 1-6-69 (Simpson), "The Avenger" 11-27-72 (Deputy Carter), "Cowtown Hustler" 3-11-74 (Adam Keraney); *Lancer*—"The Measure of a Man" 4-8-69 (Owen Wilson); *Bonanza*—"Bushwacked" 10-3-71 (Griswold); *Centennial*—Regular 1978-79 (Judge); *Bret Maverick*—"Dateline: Sweetwater" 1-12-82 (Stephen A. Hennessey).

O'Brien, Rory (1955-). Films: "Little Big Man" 1971 (Assassin). ¶TV: *Bonanza*—"Blessed Are They" 4-22-62 (Kenny); *The Virginian*—"The Small Parade" 2-20-63; *Daniel Boone*—"The Ordeal of Israel Boone" 9-21-67 (3rd Boy), "Readin', Ritin', and Revolt" 3-12-70 (Jonathan).

O'Brien, Tom (1890-6/8/47). Films: "The Mints of Hell" 1919; "The Sagebrusher" 1920 (Charlie Dornewald); "Up and Going" 1922 (Sgt. Langley); "The Flaming Forest" 1926 (Mike); "The Bugle Call" 1927 (Sgt. Doolan); "The Frontiersman" 1927 (Abner Hawkins); "Winners of the Wilderness" 1927 (Timothy); "Call of the West" 1930 (Bull Clarkson); "Phantom of Santa Fe" 1937 (Kilbaine).

O'Brien, Virginia (1922-). Films: "The Harvey Girls" 1946 (Alma).

O'Byrne, Bryan (1931-). Films: "Gunfight in Abilene" 1967 (Frobisher); "The Apple Dumpling Gang Rides Again" 1979. ¶TV: *The Virginian*—"The Accomplice" 12-19-62 (Ned Carlin), "Letter of the Law" 12-22-65 (Caldwell); *Rawhide*—"No Dogs or Drovers" 12-18-64 (Hotel Manager); *The Loner*—"The Ordeal of Bud Windom" 12-25-65 (Editor); *Daniel Boone*—"First in War, First in Peace" 10-13-66 (Portman); *The Big Valley*—"Boy into Man" 1-16-67; *Iron Horse*—"Six Hours to Sky High" 11-25-67; *Gunsmoke*—"The Legend" 10-18-71 (Mr. Palmer).

O'Byrne, Patsy (1886-4/18/68). Films: "Under Western Skies" 1945 (Mrs. Bassett).

O'Callahan, Fox (1900-4/14/76). Films: "Three Rogues" 1931 (Teamster); "Trouble in Texas" 1937.

O'Connell, Arthur (1908-5/18/81). Films: "The Proud Ones" 1956 (Deputy Jim Dexter); "Man of the West" 1958 (Sam Beasley); "Cimarron" 1960 (Tom Wyatt); "A Thunder of Drums" 1961 (Sgt. Rodermill); "Ride Beyond Vengeance" 1966 (Narrator); "There Was a Crooked Man" 1970 (Mr. Lomax); "Shootout in a One-Dog Town" TVM-1974 (Henry Gillis). ¶TV: *Zane Grey Theater*—"The Broken Wing" 2-9-61 (Lyman); *Stagecoach West*—"Songs My Mother Told Me" 2-21-61 (Matt Dexter); *Empire*—"Green, Green, Hills" 12-25-62 (Clayton Dodd); *Wagon Train*—"The Wanda Snow Story" 1-17-65 (Dabney Pitts), "The Silver Lady" 4-25-65 (Charlie Loughlin); *The Big Valley*—"The Odyssey of Jubal Tanner" 10-13-65 (Jubal Tanner); *Wild Wild West*—"The Night of the Bars of Hell" 3-4-66 (Warden Ragan); *A Man Called Shenandoah*—"The Clown" 4-18-66 (Professor); *The Men from Shiloh*—"Wolf Track" 3-17-71 (Emmitt); *Bonanza*—"Fallen Woman" 9-26-71 (Dr. Hubert); *Alias Smith and Jones*—"Bad Night in Big Butte" 3-2-72 (Sheriff).

O'Connell, Peggy. Films: "Too Much Beef" 1936 (Sheila Murray).

O'Connell, Susan. Films: "The Ballad of Cable Hogue" 1970 (Claudia). ¶TV: *The Big Valley*—"Hunter's Moon" 12-30-68 (Juliet); *Lancer*—"Warburton's Edge" 2-4-69 (Tallie Warburton).

O'Connell, William (1929-). Films: "Paint Your Wagon" 1969 (Horace Tabor); "Scandalous John" 1971 (Men's Store Clerk); "The Culpepper Cattle Company" 1972 (Piercetown Bartender); "High Plains Drifter" 1973 (Barber); "The Outlaw Josey Wales" 1976 (Carstairs). ¶TV: *Daniel Boone*—"Hannah Comes Home" 12-25-69 (Pickering), "Readin', Ritin', and Revolt" 3-12-70 (Pickering); *Rawhide*—"The Photographer" 12-11-64 (Poet); *Wild Wild West*—"The Night of the Pistoleros" 2-21-69 (Dr. Winterich); *Gunsmoke*—"The Badge" 2-2-70 (Jackson).

O'Connor, Carroll (1925-). Films: "Lonely Are the Brave" 1962 (Hinton); "Waterhole No. 3" 1967 (Sheriff John Copperud); "Death of a Gunfighter" 1969 (Lester Locke); "Ride a Northbound Horse" 1969. ¶TV: *Stoney Burke*—"Webb of Fear" 2-18-63 (Harry Clark); *Death Valley Days*—"A Gun Is Not a Gentleman" 4-14-63 (Broderick); *Bonanza*—"The Boss" 5-19-63 (Tom Slayden); *Dupont Show of the Week*—"The Silver Burro" 11-3-63 (Noah Kellogg); *Great*

Adventure—"The Pathfinder" 3-6-64 (Johann Sutter); *Bob Hope Chrysler Theatre*—"Massacre at Fort Phil Kearny" 10-26-66 (Capt. Ted Eyck); *Gunsmoke*—"The Wrong Man" 10-29-66 (Hootie Kyle), "Major Glory" 10-30-67 (Major Vanscoy); *Wild Wild West*—"The Night of the Ready-Made Corpse" 11-25-66 (Fabian Lavendor); *Dundee and the Culhane*—11-1-67 (McJames).

O'Connor, Donald (1925-). Films: "Curtain Call at Cactus Creek" 1950 (Edward Timmons).

O'Connor, Edward (1862-5/14/32). Films: "The Daisy Cowboy" 1911.

O'Connor, Frank (1882-11/22/59). Films: "His Fighting Blood" 1935; "Ruggles of Red Gap" 1935 (Station Agent); "Drift Fence" 1936 (Bartender); "King of the Royal Mounted" 1936; "Gun Law" 1938 (Parson Ross); "The Purple Vigilantes" 1938 (Deputy Tracy); "Riders of the Black Hills" 1938 (Doctor); "Santa Fe Stampede" 1938; "Honor of the West" 1939 (Butch); "Racketeers of the Range" 1939; "Silver on the Sage" 1939; "Prairie Law" 1940; "Ride, Tenderfoot, Ride" 1940; "Triple Justice" 1940 (Doctor); "Bury Me Not on the Lone Prairie" 1941; "Wyoming Wildcat" 1941; "Stardust on the Sage" 1942; "Beyond the Last Frontier" 1943; "Hidden Valley Outlaws" 1944; "Saddle Leather Law" 1944; "Silver City Kid" 1944; "Lone Texas Ranger" 1945; "Days of Buffalo Bill" 1946; "Sun Valley Cyclone" 1946; "Sunset Pass" 1946 (Station Agent); "Buffalo Bill Rides Again" 1947 (Mr. Jordan); "Last Frontier Uprising" 1947 (Rancher); "Saddle Pals" 1947; "Son of Zorro" 1947-serial (Jailer); "The Adventures of Frank and Jesse James" 1948-Serial (Doctor); "Dangers of the Canadian Mounted" 1948-serial (U.S. Commissioner Barton); "Loaded Pistols" 1948; "Ghost of Zorro" 1949-serial (Doctor); "Beyond the Purple Hills" 1950; "Desperadoes of the West" 1950-serial (Bartender); "The James Brothers of Missouri" 1950-serial (Citizen); "Mule Train" 1950; "Cyclone Fury" 1951 (Doc); "Fort Dodge Stampede" 1951; "Santa Fe" 1951; "Pack Train" 1953.

O'Connor, Glynnis (1956-). Films: "Kid Vengeance" 1976-Ital./U.S./Israel; "The Chisholms" TVM-1979 (Elizabeth Chisholm). ¶TV: *The Chisholms*—Regular 1979 (Elizabeth Chisholm).

O'Connor, Harry (1873-7/10/71). Films: "Flashing Steeds" 1925

(Joe Stern); "Red Hot Hoofs" 1926 (Jim Morris); "Cyclone of the Range" 1927 (Seth Butler); "When the Law Rides" 1928 (Henry Blaine); "The Trail of the Horse Thieves" 1929 (Clint Taggart).

O'Connor, Kathleen (1894-6/24/57). Films: "Fame and Fortune" 1918 (Della Bowen); "A Gun Fightin' Gentleman" 1919 (Helen Merritt); "Hell Roarin' Reform" 1919 (Doris Jenkins); "Bullet Proof" 1920 (Mary Brown); "Prairie Trails" 1920 (Janet McWhorter); "Sunset Jones" 1921 (Molly Forbes); "Wild Bill Hickok" 1923 (Elaine Hamilton).

O'Connor, Louis J. (1879-8/7/59). Films: "Rarin' to Go" 1924 (John Taylor); "Thundering Through" 1925 (Ezra Hendrix); "Out of the West" 1926 (Jim Rollins); "The Silent Guardian" 1926 (Red Collins).

O'Connor, Ray. Films: "Bad Kids of the West" 1967-Ital.; "Requiem for a Bounty Hunter" 1970-Ital. (Tony); "Calibre .38" 1971-Ital.; "Gunmen and the Holy Ghost" 1973-Ital.

O'Connor, Robert Emmett (1885-9/4/62). Films: "Park Avenue Lodger" 1937 (Police Sergeant); "Wells Fargo" 1937 (Sea Captain); "Jackass Mail" 1942 (Peter Lawson); "Boy's Ranch" 1946 (Druggist); "The Harvey Girls" 1946 (Conductor).

O'Connor, Tim (1924-). TV: *Gunsmoke*—"Blue Heaven" 9-26-64 (Kip Gilman), "The Witness" 11-23-70 (Arnie Sprague), "Spratt" 10-2-72 (Gideon); *Lancer*—"Splinter Group" 3-3-70 (Samuel); *Daniel Boone*—"Israel and Love" 5-7-70 (James Secord); *Nakia*—"The Driver" 11-2-74 (Carlyle).

O'Connor, Una (1880-2/4/59). Films: "Rose Marie" 1936 (Anna); "Unexpected Guest" 1947 (Miss Hackett, the Housekeeper).

O'Crotty, Peter. Films: "The Deadly Companions" 1961 (Mayor). ¶TV: *Bonanza*—"The Hunter" 1-16-73 (Old Man).

O'Dare, Peggy. *see* O'Day, Peggy.

O'Day, Dawn (Anne Shirley) (1918-7/4/93). Films: "Moonshine Valley" 1922 (Nancy); "Riders of the Purple Sage" 1925 (Fay Larkin); "Gun Smoke" 1931 (Isabelle, Horton's Daughter).

O'Day, Mary. Films: "The Fighting Hombre" 1927 (Rose Martin).

O'Day, Molly (1911-12/5/87). Films: "The Shepherd of the Hills" 1928 (Sammy Lane); "Law of the

45's" 1935 (Jean Hayden); "Lawless Borders" 1935; "Skull and Crown" 1935 (Ann Morton).

O'Day, Nell (1909-1/3/89). Films: "Smoke Lightning" 1933 (Dorothy Bailey); "Law and Order" 1940 (Sally Dixon); "Pony Post" 1940 (Norma Reeves); "Ragtime Cowboy Joe" 1940 (Helen Osborne); "Son of Roaring Dan" 1940 (Jane Belden); "Arizona Cyclone" 1941 (Claire); "Boss of Bullion City" 1941 (Martha); "Bury Me Not on the Lone Prairie" 1941; "Law of the Range" 1941 (Mary); "Man from Montana" 1941 (Sally); "The Masked Rider" 1941 (Jean); "Rawhide Rangers" 1941 (Patti); "Arizona Stagecoach" 1942; "Fighting Bill Fargo" 1942 (Julie); "Perils of the Royal Mounted" 1942-serial (Diana); "Pirates of the Prairie" 1942; "Stagecoach Buckaroo" 1942 (Molly); "The Return of the Rangers" 1943; "Thundering Trails" 1943; "Boss of Rawhide" 1944 (Mary Colby).

O'Day, Peggy (1900-11/25/64). Films: "Blind Chance" 1920; "Kaintuck's Ward" 1920; "Angel Citizens" 1922 (Isabelle Bruner); "The Three Buckaroos" 1922 (Constance Kingsley); "Trail's End" 1922 (Edith Kilgallen); "Ace of the Law" 1924 (Mildred Mitchell); "Battlin' Buckaroo" 1924 (Mary Stevens); "Shootin' Square" 1924; "Moccasins" 1925 (Wright Avery); "Travelin' Fast" 1924 (Ora Perdue); "Red Blood and Blue" 1925 (Leona Lane); "Riders of Mystery" 1925 (Helen Arliss); "Riders of the Sand Storm" 1925; "Sporting West" 1925; "Whistling Jim" 1925; "Hoof Marks" 1927 (Henrietta Bowers); "The Lone Ranger" 1927; "South of the Northern Lights" 1927; "The Clean-Up Man" 1928 (Jane Brooks).

Oddie, Gov. Tasker L. (1870-1950). Films: "The Tonopah Stampede for Gold" 1913 (Himself).

Oddo, Jerry. Films: "Copper Sky" 1957 (Juror); "From Hell to Texas" 1958 (Morgan). ¶TV: *The Californians*—"Murietta" 5-27-58, "Guns for King Joseph" 3-24-59 (Jose Rey); *The Rifleman*—"New Orleans Menace" 12-2-58 (Sam Schuette); *Bonanza*—"Blood on the Land" 2-13-60, "The Abduction" 10-29-60 (Gerner); *Zane Grey Theater*—"The Last Bugle" 11-24-60 (Martine).

O'Dell, Doye. Films: "Fugitive Valley" 1941 (Jim); "The Pioneers" 1941 (Doye); "Heldorado" 1946 (Tickettaker); "The Man from Rainbow Valley" 1946 (Jim); "Last Frontier Uprising" 1947 (Rancher);

"Whirlwind Raiders" 1948; "Home in San Antone" 1949; "Son of a Bad-man" 1949 (Tex James). ¶TV: *Maverick*—"Island in the Swamp" 11-30-58 (Herbert Forge); *Sugarfoot*—"The Return of the Canary Kid" 2-3-59 (Clanker); *The Tall Man*—"Night Train to Tularosa" 11-5-60 (Conductor); *Bronco*—"The Last Letter" 3-5-62 (Marsten); *Empire*—"The Convention" 5-14-63 (Announcer).

O'Dell, Garry. Films: "Where Romance Rides" 1925 (Thomas Lapsley); "Shooting Straight" 1927 (Malpai Joe); "Straight Shootin'" 1927 (Malpai Joe).

Odell, George R. Films: "The Wolf and His Mate" 1917 (Steve Nolan).

O'Dell, Georgia (1893-9/6/50). Films: "Big Calibre" 1935 (Arabella); "West of Nevada" 1936 (Rose Gilhuly); "Guilty Trails" 1938 (Aunt Martha); "The Singing Outlaw" 1938 (Lucy Harris).

Odell, Kent. Films: "Stagecoach" 1939 (Billy Pickett, Jr.).

Odetta (1930-). TV: *Have Gun Will Travel*—"The Hanging of Aaron Gibbs" 11-4-61 (Sarah Gibbs).

Odin, Susan (-10/17/75). Films: "Annie Get Your Gun" 1950 (Jessie); "Wild Stallion" 1952 (Caroline as a Child). ¶TV: *Wild Wild West*—"The Night of the Tartar" 2-3-67 (Anastasia Rimsky).

Odney, Douglas. TV: *Gunsmoke*—"Unmarked Grave" 8-18-56 (Tolliver); *Sheriff of Cochise*—"Border Sanctuary" 12-27-57; *Death Valley Days*—"Pioneer Circus" 3-10-59 (Dan Rowland); *Lawman*—"Marked Man" 1-22-61 (Arnie Steele).

O'Donnell, Cathy (1923-4/11/70). Films: "The Man from Laramie" 1955 (Barbara Waggoman); "The Deerslayer" 1957 (Judith). ¶TV: *Zane Grey Theater*—"Sundown at Bitter Creek" 2-14-58 (Jennie Parsons); *The Californians*—"Skeleton in the Closet" 4-8-58 (Grace Adams); *The Rebel*—"You Steal My Eyes" 3-20-60 (Blind Girl), "The Hope Chest" 12-25-60 (Felicity Bowman); *Tate*—"Quiet After the Storm" 9-7-60 (Amy); *Sugarfoot*—"Angel" 3-6-61 (Angel); *Bonanza*—"The Lila Conrad Story" 1-5-64.

O'Donnell, Erin. TV: *Temple Houston*—"The Case for William Gotch" 2-6-64 (Laura Jean); *Bonanza*—"The Jonah" 5-9-65 (Susan); *The High Chaparral*—"The High Chaparral" 9-10-67.

O'Donnell, Gene (1911-11/22/92). Films: "Queen of the Yukon" 1940 (Young Man). ¶TV: *Gunsmoke*—"The Mistake" 11-24-56 (Haney), "A Hat" 10-16-67 (Waiter); *Death Valley Days*—"Fifteen Paces to Fame" 11-25-57; *The Big Valley*—"A Day of Terror" 12-12-66.

O'Donnell, Walter "Spec" (1911-10/14/86). Films: "Hard-Boiled" 1926 (Eddie Blix); "Hello Trouble" 1932.

O'Driscoll, Martha (1922-). Films: "Wagon Train" 1940 (Helen Lee); "The Daltons Ride Again" 1945 (Mary); "Under Western Skies" 1945 (Katie).

O'Farrell, Broderick. Films: "The Golden Trail" 1920 (Bill Lee); "Ridin' Thunder" 1925 (Governor); "Law of the 45's" 1935 (Sir Henry Sheffield); "Call of the Canyon" 1942.

Offerman, Jr., George (1917-1/14/63). "The Outlaw Deputy" 1935 (Chuck Adams); "Frontier Vengeance" 1940 (Clay Blackburn); "The Vigilante" 1947-serial (Stuff). ¶TV: *The Cisco Kid*—"Jewelry Store Fence" 8-11-51, "Water Toll" 9-22-51; *Bat Masterson*—"A Noose Fits Anybody" 11-19-58 (Dealer), "Marked Deck" 3-11-59 (Dealer).

O'Flynn, Damian. Films: "The Great Man's Lady" 1942 (Burns); "Saddle Pals" 1947 (Brad Collins); "Pioneer Marshal" 1949 (Bruce Burnett); "Riders of the Whistling Pines" 1949 (Bill Wright); "Young Daniel Boone" 1950 (Capt. Fraser); "The Half-Breed" 1952 (Capt. Jackson); "Two Guns and a Badge" 1954 (Wilson); "The Far Country" 1955 (Second Mate); "Hidden Guns" 1956 (Kingsley); "Apache Warrior" 1957 (Major); "Daniel Boone, Trail Blazer" 1957 (Andy Callaway); "Drango" 1957 (Blackford); "Gunfight at Comanche Creek" 1964 (Winton). ¶TV: *Wild Bill Hickok*—"Great Obstacle Race" 3-3-53; *Death Valley Days*—"The Big Team Rolls" 5-23-55; *Wyatt Earp*—Regular 1956-59 (Judge Tobin), Regular 1959-61 (Dr. Goodfellow); *Broken Arrow*—"The Trial" 1-22-57 (Hawkins); *Maverick*—"The Seventh Hand" 3-2-58 (Mr. Taber); *Wagon Train*—"The Last Man" 2-11-59 (Mr. Emerson); *Rawhide*—"Incident of the Calico Gun" 4-24-59.

O'Flynn, Paddy (1896-12/11/61). Films: "The Fighting Ranger" 1934 (Bob Houston).

Ogg, Jimmy. Films: "Redwood Forest Trail" 1950 (Two Bits); "The Treasure of Lost Canyon" 1952 (Guard). ¶TV: *The Lone Ranger*—"Sheep Thieves" 2-9-50; *Broken Arrow*—"Son of Cochise" 12-17-57 (Corporal).

Ogg, Sammy. Films: "Navajo" 1952 (Narrator); "Jack Slade" 1953 (Joey Slade); "Frontier Gun" 1958 (Virgil Barton). ¶TV: *The Gene Autry Show*—"Saddle Up" 12-3-55, "Ride, Rancheros" 12-10-55, "The Rangerette" 12-17-55; *Fury*—"Junior Rodeo" 12-24-55 (Ty Jones); *Wagon Train*—"The Riley Gratton Story" 12-4-57; *Maverick*—"Day of Reckoning" 2-2-58 (Boy).

Ogilvy, Ian (1943-). TV: *Adventures of Brisco County, Jr.*—"Bounty Hunter's Convention" 1-7-94 (Trevor Furlong).

Ogle, Charles (1865-10/11/40). Films: "The Ranch Owner's Love-Making" 1913; "The Cost of Hatred" 1917 (McCabe); "Nan of Music Mountain" 1917 (Sassoon); "A Romance of the Redwoods" 1917 (Jim Lyn); "The Sunset Trail" 1917 (Judd Aiken); "M'Liss" 1918 (Yuba Bill); "Rimrock Jones" 1918 (Hassayamp Hicks); "The Squaw Man" 1918 (Bull Cowan); "Told in the Hills" 1919 (Davy MacDougall); "North of the Rio Grande" 1922 (Col. Haddington); "The Covered Wagon" 1923 (Mr. Wingate); "Ruggles of Red Gap" 1923 (Jeff Tuttle); "Salome Jane" 1923 (Madison Clay); "The Border Legion" 1924 (Harvey Roberts); "Code of the West" 1925 (Henry Thurman); "The Thundering Herd" 1925 (Clark Hudnall); "The Flaming Forest" 1926 (Donald McTavish).

O'Grady, Lani (Tammy August). TV: *The High Chaparral*—"Time of Your Life" 9-19-69 (Penny).

Oh, Soon-Taik (1943-). Films: "One More Train to Rob" 1971 (Yung). ¶TV: *Death Valley Days*—"The Dragon of Gold Hill" 1-24-70 (Masu); *Kung Fu*—"Sun and Cloud Shadow" 2-22-73 (Kwan Chen), "The Passion of Chen Yi" 2-28-74 (Chen Yi), "The Devil's Champion" 11-29-74 (Yi Lien); *How the West Was Won*—"China Girl" 4-16-79 (Kee).

O'Hanlon, George (1917-2/11/89). Films: "Cattle Town" 1952 (Shiloh); "The Lion and the Horse" 1952 (Shorty Cameron); "So You Want to Be a Cowboy" 1951-short. ¶TV: *Maverick*—"Rope of Cards" 1-19-58 (Caldwell), "Black Fire" 3-16-58 (Cousin Elmo), "Holiday at Hollow Rock" 12-28-58 (Morton Connors); *Sugarfoot*—"Short Range" 5-13-58 (Dick).

O'Hara, Barry (1926-9/5/79). Films: "Chuka" 1967 (Slim). ¶TV: *The Virginian*—"A Bald-Faced Boy" 4-13-66 (Bartender).

O'Hara, Brian. Films: "California Joe" 1943 (Delancey Cartaret); "The Last Round-Up" 1947; "Valerie" 1957.

O'Hara, Catherine. Films: "Wyatt Earp" 1994 (Allie Earp); "Tall Tales: The Unbelievable Adventures of Pecos Bill" 1995 (Calamity Jane).

O'Hara, George (1899-10/16/66). Films: "Jesse James" 1939 (Tiller); "The Cowboy and the Blonde" 1941 (Melvyn).

O'Hara, James (1927-). Films: "The Deadly Companions" 1961 (Cal); "Cheyenne Autumn" 1964 (Trooper); "The Rare Breed" 1966 (Sagamon); "Death of a Gunfighter" 1969 (Father Sweeney). ¶TV: *Maverick*—"The Bold Fenian Men" 12-18-60 (Sean Flaherty); *Daniel Boone*—"The Tamarack Massacre Affair" 12-30-65 (British Officer); *Gunsmoke*—"The Good People" 10-15-66 (Sutton).

O'Hara, Jenny. TV: *Bret Maverick*—"The Mayflower Women's Historical Society" 2-2-82 (Samantha Dunne); *Young Riders*—"Pride and Prejudice" 10-27-90 (Sally Tompkins).

O'Hara, Maureen (1920-). Films: "Buffalo Bill" 1944 (Louisa Cody); "Comanche Territory" 1950 (Katie); "Rio Grande" 1950 (Mrs. Kathleen Yorke); "Kangaroo" 1952 (Dell McGuire); "The Redhead from Wyoming" 1953 (Kate Maxwell); "War Arrow" 1953 (Elaine Corwin); "The Deadly Companions" 1961 (Kit); "McClintock" 1963 (Katherine McLintock); "The Rare Breed" 1966 (Martha Price); "Big Jake" 1971 (Martha McCandles).

O'Hara, Pat. Films: "Outpost of the Mounties" 1939 (Inspector Wainwright); "The Miracle of the Hills" 1959 (Lucky). ¶TV: *Death Valley Days*—"Emperor Norton, 1st" 11-4-56 (Franklyn Duffy).

O'Hara, Shirley (1911-5/5/79). Films: "Blind Man's Bluff" 1927; "Dangerous Double" 1927; "The Bells of San Fernando" 1947 (Nita); "Ballad of Josie" 1968 (Elizabeth); "Banjo Hackett: Roamin' Free" TVM-1976 (the Postmistress). ¶TV: *Have Gun Will Travel*—"The Monster of Moon Ridge" 2-28-59, "Comanche" 5-16-59 (Geraldine Carver), "The Princess and the Gunfighter" 1-21-61 (Duchess), "A Proof of Love" 10-14-61 (Mrs. Grey); *Gunsmoke*—"Crowbait Bob" 3-26-60 (Martha), "Stolen Horses" 4-8-61 (Mrs. Kurtch), "Quint's Trail" 11-9-63 (Florie Neff); *Rawhide*—"Incident on the Road to Yesterday" 11-18-60 (Mrs. Slocum); *Bonanza*—"The Witness" 1-2-73 (Ella Peterson).

O'Herlihy, Dan (1919-). Films: "The Iroquois Trail" 1950 (Lt. Blakely); "The Young Land" 1959 (Judge Isham); "One Foot in Hell" 1960 (Harry Ivers); "100 Rifles" 1969 (Grimes); "Banjo Hackett: Roamin' Free" TVM-1976 (Tip Conaker). ¶TV: *Zane Grey Theater*—"The Bitter Land" 12-6-57; *Rawhide*—"Incident at Dragoon Crossing" 10-21-60 (John Cord); *Bonanza*—"The Artist" 10-7-62 (Mathew Raine); *Empire*—"The Earth Mover" 11-27-62 (Glenn Kassin); *The Travels of Jaimie McPheeters*—Regular 1963-64 (Doc Sardius McPheeters); *The Road West*—"Have You Seen the Aurora Borealis?" 12-12-66 (Seamas O'Flaherty); *The Big Valley*—"Image of Yesterday" 1-9-67 (David Wyncop); *The High Chaparral*—"The Fillibusteros" 10-22-67 (Lanier); *Hondo*—"Hondo and the Hanging Town" 12-8-67 (Prof. Phineas Blackstone); *The Quest*—"The Longest Drive" 12-1-76 & 12-8-76 (Hatcher); *Hunter's Moon*—Pilot 12-1-79 (Hobble).

O'Herlihy, Gavin. Films: "Lonesome Dove" TVM-1989; "Conagher" TVM-1991.

Ohmart, Carol (1928-). Films: "Born Reckless" 1959 (Liz). ¶TV: *Northwest Passage*—"The Assassin" 11-16-58 (Nora Clayton); *Bronco*—"Backfire" 4-7-59 (Laurie Callen); *Wyatt Earp*—"The Actress" 4-14-59 (Cora Campbell); *Bat Masterson*—"Promised Land" 6-10-59 (Linda Beaudine), "Six Feet of Gold" 2-25-60 (Lisa Truex); *Branded*—"Headed for Doomsday" 4-10-66 (Laureen Macklin).

O'Keefe, Dennis (Bud Flanagan) (1908-8/31/68). Films: "Cimarron" 1931; "The Red Rider" 1934-serial (Wedding Guest); "The Plainsman" 1936; "Rhythm on the Range" 1936 (Heckler); "The Bad Man of Brimstone" 1938 (Jeffrey Burton); "The Kid from Texas" 1939 (William Quincy Malone); "The Eagle and the Hawk" 1950 (Whitney Randolph); "Passage West" 1951 (Jacob Karns); "Dragoon Wells Massacre" 1957 (Capt. Matt Riordan). ¶TV: *Riverboat*—"Rive Champion" 10-10-60 (Dan Muldoon).

O'Keefe, Michael. Films: "Friendly Persuasion" TVM-1975 (Josh).

O'Kelly, Don. Films: "Frontier Uprising" 1961 (Kilpatrick); "Shoot Out at Big Sag" 1962 (Fargo). ¶TV: *Have Gun Will Travel*—"The Day of the Bad Men" 1-9-60 (Amos Saint); *The Alaskans*—"The Trial of Reno McKee" 1-10-60 (Carl), "Black Sand" 2-14-60; *Laramie*—"Duel at Alta Mesa" 2-23-60 (Rick); *Lawman*—"The Truce" 3-6-60 (Jess Hahn); *Overland Trail*—"Fire in the Hole" 4-17-60 (Red); *Bat Masterson*—"The Elusive Baguette" 6-2-60 (Reed Morgan), "The Last of the Night Raiders" 11-24-60 (Jack Doolin), "Meeting at Mimbers" 4-13-61 (Tom Smith); *The Deputy*—"Lady for a Hanging" 12-3-60 (Hunter); *Riverboat*—"Zigzag" 12-26-60 (Clyde); *The Dakotas*—"Fargo" 2-25-63 (Paul Young); *The Virginian*—"The Evil That Men Do" 10-16-63 (Deke); *Bonanza*—"The Lila Conrad Story" 1-5-64; *Gunsmoke*—"Eliab's Aim" 2-27-65 (Dealer); *Wild Wild West*—"The Night of a Thousand Eyes" 10-22-65 (Poavey).

O'Kelly, Tim (1942-). TV: *Gunsmoke*—"Killer at Large" 2-5-66 (Sandy), "The Victim" 1-1-68 (Billy Martin); *The Big Valley*—"Caesar's Wife" 10-3-66 (Will Marvin); *The Monroes*—"Incident at Hanging Tree" 10-12-66 (Billy Dan Wales), "Silent Night, Deathly Night" 11-23-66 (Billy Dan Wales), "Range War" 12-21-66 (Billy Dan Wales), "Mark of Death" 1-4-67 (Billy Dan Wales); *Shane*—"The Great Invasion" 12-17-66 & 12-24-66 (Eddy); *Cimarron Strip*—"Broken Wing" 9-21-67 (Jing McQueen); *The Guns of Will Sonnett*—"Reunion" 9-27-68 (Billy Delver).

Oland, Warner (1880-8/6/38). Films: "The Phantom Foe" 1920-serial; "Don Q, Son of Zorro" 1925 (Archduke Paul of Austria); "Riders of the Purple Sage" 1925 (Lew Walters/Judge Dyer); "Man of the Forest" 1926 (Clint Beasley).

Olandt, Ken. Films: "Gunsmoke: Return to Dodge" TVM-1987 (Lieutenant Dexter).

O'Leary, John E. (1926-). Films: "Banjo Hackett: Roamin' Free" TVM-1976 (Mr. Cred); "Bonanza: The Next Generation" TVM-1988. ¶TV: *The Quest*—"The Freight Train Rescue" 12-29-76 (Struthers).

Oliver, Clarence. Films: "Laughing Bill Hyde" 1918 (Dr. Evan Thomas).

Oliver, Edna May (1883-11/9/42). Films: "Cimarron" 1931 (Mrs. Tracy Wyatt); "The Conquerors" 1932 (Matilda Blake); "Drums Along the Mohawk" 1939 (Mrs. McKlennan).

Oliver, Gordon (1910-12/26/94). Films: "Sunset Pass" 1929

(Clark); "Station West" 1948 (Prince).

Oliver, Guy (1878–9/1/32). Films: "Outwitted by Billy" 1913; "Ye Vengeful Vagabonds" 1914; "His Father's Rifle" 1915; "The Regeneration of Jim Halsey" 1916; "The Golden Fetter" 1917 (Edson); "Nan of Music Mountain" 1917 (Bull Page); "M'Liss" 1918 (Snakebite Saunders); "Rimrock Jones" 1918 (Andrew McBain); "The Squaw Man" 1918 (Kid Clarke); "In Mizzoura" 1919 (Esrom); "Rustling a Bride" 1919 (Ezry); "Told in the Hills" 1919 (Captain Holt); "The Round Up" 1920 (Uncle Jim); "The Cowboy and the Lady" 1922 (Ross); "The Covered Wagon" 1923 (Kit Carson); "Ruggles of Red Gap" 1923 (Judge Ballard); "To the Last Man" 1923 (Bill); "North of '36" 1924 (Maj. McCoyne); "The Vanishing American" 1925 (Kit Carson); "Man of the Forest" 1926 (Deputy); "Arizona Bound" 1927 (Sheriff); "Drums of the Desert" 1927 (Indian Agent); "The Mysterious Rider" 1927 (Jack Wilson); "Nevada" 1927 (Sheriff of Lineville); "Open Range" 1927 (Jim Blake); "Shootin' Irons" 1927 (Judge Mathews); "Avalanche" 1928 (Mr. Mains); "The Vanishing Pioneer" 1928 (Mr. Shelby); "Stairs of Sand" 1929 (Sheriff Collishaw); "The Light of the Western Stars" 1930 (Sheriff Jarvis); "Caught" 1931 (McNeill); "Dude Ranch" 1931 (Simonson); "Gun Smoke" 1931 (Posey Meed).

Oliver, Henry. TV: *Zane Grey Theater*—"Utopia, Wyoming" 6-6-58 (Joe Esmond); *Bonanza*—"Meena" 11-16-69 (Firman), "The Horse Traders" 4-5-70 (Firman), "Heritage of Anger" 9-19-72 (Telegrapher); *Daniel Boone*—"Perilous Passage" 1-15-70.

Oliver, Steven (1942–). Films: "Savage Red—Outlaw White" 1974; "The Great Gundown" 1977 (Arden); "Tom Horn" 1980 (Gentleman Jim Corbett).

Oliver, Susan (1937–5/20/90). Films: "Guns of Diablo" 1964 (Maria); "A Man Called Gannon" 1969 (Matty). ¶TV: *Wagon Train*—"The Emily Rossiter Story" 10-30-57 (Judy), "The Maggie Hamilton Story" 4-6-60 (Maggie Hamilton), "The Cathy Eckhardt Story" 11-9-60 (Cathy Eckhardt), "The Lily Legend Story" 2-13-63 (Lily Legend); *Trackdown*—"Blind Alley" 9-16-59 (Rebecca Ford); *Bonanza*—"The Outcast" 1-9-60 (Leta Malvet); *Wanted—Dead or Alive*—"The Parish" 3-26-60 (Bess Wilson); *Wrangler*—"Incident at the Bar M" 8-4-60 (Helen McQueen); *The Deputy*—

"The Deadly Breed" 9-24-60 (Julie); *Zane Grey Theater*—"Knife of Hate" 12-8-60 (Susan Pittman), "Image of a Drawn Sword" 5-11-61 (Hannah); *Rawhide*—"Incident of His Brother's Keeper" 3-31-61 (Laurie Evans), "Incident at Spider Rock" 1-18-63 (Judy Hall); *Laramie*—"Shadows in the Dust" 1-16-62 (Jean Lavelle); *The Travels of Jaimie McPheeters*—"The Day of the Reckoning" 3-15-64 (Maria); *Destry*—"One Hundred Bibles" 5-8-64 (Rebecca Fairhaven); *The Virginian*—"A Little Learning…" 9-29-65 (Martha Perry), "A Small Taste of Justice" 12-20-67 (Ellen Cooper), "The Storm Gate" 11-13-68 (Anne Crowder); *A Man Called Shenandoah*—"Rope's End" 1-17-66 (Virginia Harvey); *Wild Wild West*—"The Night Dr. Loveless Died" 9-29-67 (Triste); *The Big Valley*—"Alias Nellie Handley" 2-24-69 (Kate Wilson); *The Men from Shiloh*—"Hannah" 12-30-70 (Carole Carson); *Alias Smith and Jones*—"Journey from San Juan" 4-8-71 (Blanche Graham); *Gunsmoke*—"Eleven Dollars" 10-30-72 (Sarah Elkins).

Oliver, Ted (1892–6/30/57). Films: "Daring Days" 1925 (Boggs); "Triple Action" 1925 (Assistant Chief); "The Fighting Peacemaker" 1926 (Jefferson Carne); "The Lone Ranger" 1927; "Robbers' Roost" 1933 (Latimer); "The Arizonian" 1935; "The Plainsman" 1936; "Rose of the Rancho" 1936 (Kincaid Henchman); "Yellow Dust" 1936 (McLearney); "Trapped" 1937 (Ike Brett); "Stand Up and Fight" 1939 (Deputy Cochran); "Geronimo" 1940 (Officer); "The Man from Dakota" 1940 (Officer); "Northwest Passage" 1940 (Farrington).

Oliveras, Frank. *see* Pesce, Franco.

Olkewicz, Walter. Films: "Calamity Jane" TVM-1984 (Will Lull); "The Good Old Boys" TVM-1995 (Fat Gerwin).

Olmi, Corrado. Films: "Apache Woman" 1975-Ital. (Honesty Jeremy).

Olmos, Edward James (1947–). Films: "The Ballad of Gregorio Cortez" 1983 (Gregorio Cortez).

Olmstead, Gertrude (1904–1/18/75). Films: "Marryin' Marion" 1920; "Tipped Off" 1920; "The Driftin' Kid" 1921; "The Fox" 1921 (Stella Fraser); "Kickaroo" 1921; "Out O' Luck" 1921; "Shadows of Conscience" 1921 (Winifred Coburn); "Sweet Revenge" 1921; "The Loaded Door" 1922 (Molly Grainger); "Better Than Gold" 1923; "God's Law" 1923; "The Guilty Hand" 1923.

Olmsted, Nelson (1914–4/8/92). Films: "Butch Cassidy and the Sundance Kid" 1969 (Photographer). ¶TV: *Sky King*—Regular 1951-53 (Bob Carey); *Maverick*—"The Ice Man" 1-29-61 (Eli Sayles); *Wild Wild West*—"The Night of the Red-Eyed Madmen" 11-26-65 (Senator Rawls), "The Night of the Puppeteer" 2-25-66 (Dr. Lake); *Bonanza*—"The Big Jackpot" 1-18-70 (Appleton).

O'Loughlin, Gerald S. (1921–). TV: *Gunsmoke*—"Twenty Miles from Dodge" 4-10-65 (Grant Shay); *Cimarron Strip*—"Sound of a Drum" 2-1-68 (Sgt. Maj. Boyd Chambers); *The Virginian*—"Train of Darkness" 2-4-70 (Dormer); *Nichols*—"The Marrying Fool" 12-28-71 (Roarke).

Olsen, Chris. Films: "The Naked Hills" 1956 (Billy as a Boy); "The Tall T" 1957 (Jeff); "Return to Warbow" 1958 (David Fallam). ¶TV: *Cheyenne*—"Incident at Indian Springs" 9-24-57 (Kenny Powell).

Olsen, Merlin (1940–). Films: "The Undefeated" 1969 (Big George); "One More Train to Rob" 1971 (Eli Jones); "Something Big" 1971 (Sgt. Fitzsimmons). ¶TV: *Kung Fu*—"Nine Lives" 2-15-73 (Perlee Skowrin); *Little House on the Prairie*—Regular 1977-81 (Jonathan Garvey); *Father Murphy*—Regular 1981-82 (Father John Michael Murphy).

Olsen, Moroni (1889–11/22/54). Films: "Annie Oakley" 1935 (Buffalo Bill); "Two in Revolt" 1936 (Cyrus Benton); "Yellow Dust" 1936 (Missouri); "Gold Is Where You Find It" 1938 (Sen. Hearst); "Allegheny Uprising" 1939 (Calhoon); "Susannah of the Mounties" 1939 (Superintendent Andrew Standing); "Brigham Young—Frontiersman" 1940 (Doc Richards); "Santa Fe Trail" 1940 (Robert E. Lee); "Virginia City" 1940 (Dr. Cameron); "Sundown Jim" 1942 (Andrew Barr); "Buffalo Bill" 1944 (Sen. Frederici); "Don't Fence Me In" 1945 (Henry Bennett); "Boy's Ranch" 1946 (Judge Henderson); "Lone Star" 1952 (Sam Houston).

Olsen, Ole (1892–1/26/63). Films: "Fighting Mad" 1939 (Joe).

Olsen, Tracy (1940–). Films: "Johnny Reno" 1966 (Maria Yates); "Waco" 1966 (Patricia West); "Red Tomahawk" 1967 (Sal). ¶TV: *Bonanza*—"The Trouble with Jamie" 3-20-66 (Elizabeth).

Olson, Eric (1962–). TV: *Gunsmoke*—"The Iron Man" 10-21-74 (Johnny Carter).

Olson, James (1930–). Films: "Wild Rovers" 1971 (Joe Billings).

¶TV: *Have Gun Will Travel*—"The Five Books of Owen Deaver" 4-26-58 (Sheriff Owen Deaver); *Bonanza*—"Sweet Annie Laurie" 1-5-69 (Kelly Adams); "Ambush at Rio Lobo" 10-24-72 (Vance); *Lancer*—"Death Bait" 1-14-69 (Alton Gannett); *The Virginian*—"The Land Dreamer" 2-26-69 (Hosea McKinley); *Gunsmoke*—"The Fugitives" 10-23-72 (Bede Stalcup); *The New Land*—"The Word Is: Persistence" 9-14-74; *Kung Fu*—"The Garments of Rage" 11-8-74 (Damion); *Big Hawaii*—"Blind Rage" 1977; *Hallmark Hall of Fame*—"The Court-Martial of General George Armstrong Carter" 12-1-77 (General Custer).

Olson, Nancy (1928-). Films: "Canadian Pacific" 1949 (Cecile Gautier); "The Boy from Oklahoma" 1954 (Katie Brannigan); "Smith" 1969 (Norah Smith). ¶TV: *The Big Valley*—"Night of the Wolf" 12-1-65 (Julia); *Gunsmoke*—"Yankton" 2-7-72 (Henrietta Donavan).

O'Mahoney, Jock. *see* Mahoney, Jock.

O'Malley, Charles (1897-7/29/58). Films: "The Iron Horse" 1924 (Major North); "Gun-Hand Garrison" 1927; "Ridin' Luck" 1927.

O'Malley, J. Pat (1901-2/27/85). Films: "Frontier Marshal" 1939 (Customer); "The Kid from Broken Gun" 1952 (Doc Handy); "The Cheyenne Social Club" 1970 (Dr. Foy); "Skin Game" 1971 (William). ¶TV: *Gunsmoke*—"Monopoly" 10-4-58 (Joe Trimble), "Print Asper" 5-23-59 (Print Asper), "The Dreamers" 4-28-62 (Jake Fogle), "Old Comrade" 12-29-62 (Col. Gabe Wilson), "A Quiet Day in Dodge" 1-29-73 (Drummer); *Zane Grey Theater*—"Legacy of a Legend" 11-6-58 (Pete), "Picture of Sal" 1-28-60 (Inspector MacNeil), "Stagecoach to Yuma" 5-5-60 (Will MacNeil); *Maverick*—"Shady Deal at Sunny Acres" 11-23-58 (Ambrose Callahan), "Betrayal" 3-22-59 (Mr. Dillon); *The Californians*—"The First Gold Brick" 1-6-59 (Walter Morgan); *Black Saddle*—"Client: Tagger" 2-14-59 (Judge Caleb Marsh), "Client: Martinez" 3-7-59 (Judge Caleb Marsh), "Client: Jessup" 4-18-59 (Judge Caleb Marsh), "Client: Reynolds" 5-23-59 (Judge Caleb Marsh), "Client: Vardon" 5-30-59 (Judge Caleb Marsh), "The Freebooters" 10-2-59 (Judge Caleb Marsh), "Client: Peter Warren" 10-30-59 (Judge Caleb Marsh); *Lawman*—"The Journey" 4-26-59 (Owen Muldoon), "The Swamper" 6-5-60 (Jim Phelan); *Have Gun Will Travel*—"Episode in Laredo" 9-19-59 (Kovac), "Out at the Old Ball Park" 10-1-60 (Marcus Goodbaby); *The Law of the Plainsman*—"Prairie Incident" 10-1-59, "Endurance" 1-14-60, "Cavern of the Wind" 4-21-60; *The Rebel*—"Judgment" 10-11-59 (Judge Russell), "Panic" 11-1-59 (Sam), "Johnny Yuma at Appomattox" 9-18-60 (McCune); *Rawhide*—"Incident at the Buffalo Smokehouse" 10-30-59 (Mart Peeler), "Incident in the Garden of Eden" 6-17-60 (Oliver), "The Greedy Town" 2-16-62 (George Emory), "Incident at Confidence Creek" 11-28-63 (Judge Fillmore); *Hotel De Paree*—"Vengeance for Sundance" 4-8-60 (Matt Hollis); *Wanted—Dead or Alive*—"The Medicine Man" 11-23-60 (Doc); *Klondike*—"Bare Knuckles" 12-12-60 (Uncle Johan); *Stagecoach West*—"The Storm" 12-13-60 (Doc Apperson); *The Outlaws*—"The Quiet Killer" 12-29-60 (Kels Nickels); *Tales of Wells Fargo*—"The Has-Been" 1-16-61 (Cedric Manning), "Prince Jim" 3-27-61 (Dan Mallory), "Treasure Coach" 10-14-61 (Dr. Cobb); *Bonanza*—"The Duke" 3-11-61 (Limey), "Rich Man, Poor Man" 5-12-63 (Clancy); *Laramie*—"The Fatal Step" 10-24-61; *Frontier Circus*—"Dr. Sam" 10-26-61 (Duffy), "Karina" 11-9-61 (Duffy), "Quick Shuffle" 2-1-62 (Townsman), "The Inheritance" 3-15-62, "Mighty Like Rogues" 4-5-62 (Duffy); *The Tall Man*—"Apache Daughter" 12-30-61 (Sam Bartlett); *The Virginian*—"The Small Parade" 2-20-63 (Charlie Dell), "The Long Quest" 4-8-64 (Samuel Bowman), "With Help from Ulysses" 1-17-68 (Joe Keller); *Stoney Burke*—"The Test" 5-13-63 (Sam Blake); *Temple Houston*—"Fracas at Kiowa Flats" 12-12-63 (Joshua C. Merry); *Wagon Train*—"The Ben Engel Story" 3-16-64 (Colin Dunn), "The Last Circle Up" 4-27-64; *Destry*—"Deputy for a Day" 4-3-64 (Whit Hansen); *Branded*—"Seward's Folly" 10-17-65 (Rufus I. Pitkin), "The Richest Man in Boot Hill" 10-31-65 (Rufus I. Pitkin); *The Big Valley*—"The Brawlers" 12-15-65 (Grandpa), "Boy into Man" 1-16-67 (Wiley); *Laredo*—"Meanwhile, Back at the Reservation" 2-10-66 (Stan Greevy); *The Legend of Jesse James*—"South Wind" 2-14-66 (Dooley); *Death Valley Days*—"The Four Dollar Law Suit" 4-16-66, "The World's Greatest Swimming Horse" 2-8-69 (Pete); *Shane*—"The Silent Gift" 11-26-66 (Jingles); *The Guns of Will Sonnett*—"The Guns of Will Sonnett" 9-8-67 (Drummer); *Hondo*—"Hondo and the Death Drive" 12-1-67 (Rufus); *Wild Wild West*—"The Night of the Death-Maker" 2-23-68 (Brother Angelo); *Daniel Boone*—"Copperhead Izzy" 1-30-69 (Uncle Brian); *The Outcasts*—"The Long Ride" 4-28-69 (Northingest Jim); *Alias Smith and Jones*—"The Wrong Train to Brimstone" 2-4-71 (H.T. McDuff); *Bonanza*—"The Reluctant American" 2-14-71 (Big Mac); *Young Maverick*—"A Fistful of Oats" 12-5-79 (Uncle Malachy).

O'Malley, John. Films: "Black Patch" 1957 (Colonel). ¶TV: *Have Gun Will Travel*—"The Ballad of Oscar Wilde" 12-6-58 (Oscar Wilde), "The Unforgiven" 11-7-59; *Gunsmoke*—"The Bobsy Twins" 5-21-60 (Man).

O'Malley, Kathleen (1924-). Films: "Salome, Where She Danced" 1945 (Salome Girl); "Wagonmaster" 1950 (Prudence Perkins); "Night Stage to Galveston" 1952; "The Shootist" 1976 (School Teacher). ¶TV: *Maverick*—"Gun-Shy" 1-11-59 (Amy Ward); *Bronco*—"Backfire" 4-7-59 (Mrs. Graham); *Rawhide*—"Incident at Jacob's Well" 10-16-59 (Mrs. Henry), "Incident of the Dogfaces" 11-9-62 (Beard's Wife); *Laramie*—"Man of God" 12-1-59 (Wife); *Wagon Train*—"The Albert Farnsworth Story" 10-12-60 (Sharry O'Toole), "The Dr. Denker Story" 1-31-62 (Emma Beaufort); *Stoney Burke*—"Cat's Eyes" 2-11-63 (Nurse); *Bonanza*—"Mirror of a Man" 3-31-63 (Janey), "Journey Remembered" 11-11-63 (Mrs. Payne); *The Legend of Jesse James*—"The Pursuers" 10-11-65 (Mrs. Bentley); *Gunsmoke*—"The Whispering Tree" 11-12-66 (Mother), "Sam McTavish, M.D." 10-5-70 (Bridget O'Reilly).

O'Malley, Pat (1890-5/21/66). Films: "The Prospector's Vengeance" 1920; "Bob Hampton of Placer" 1921 (Lt. Brant); "The Eternal Struggle" 1923 (Bucky O'Hara); "The Virginian" 1923 (Steve); "The Mine with the Iron Door" 1924 (Hugh Edwards); "The Fighting Marshal" 1931 (Ed Myers); "Lightning Warrior" 1931-serial (Sheriff); "Klondike" 1932 (Burke); "The Sundown Rider" 1933 (Lafe Armstrong); "The Whirlwind" 1933 (Pat); "Heir to Trouble" 1935 (Dwyer); "The Miracle Rider" 1935-serial (Sam Morgan); "Wanderer of the Wasteland" 1935 (Jed); "The Country Beyond" 1936 (Mountie); "Dodge City" 1939 (Conductor); "Wolf Call" 1939 (Sergeant); "Lucky Cisco Kid" 1940; "River's End" 1940 (Turnkey); "Rocky Mountain Rangers" 1940 (Capt. Taylor);

"Shooting High" 1940 (Sam Pritchard); "Law of the Range" 1941 (Steve's Father); "Pals of the Pecos" 1941 (Jim Burke); "Deep in the Heart of Texas" 1942 (Jonathan Taylor); "The Great Man's Lady" 1942 (Murphy the Policeman); "Singin' in the Corn" 1946 (O'Rourke); "Blazing Across the Pecos" 1948; "The Man from Colorado" 1948 (Citizen); "Riders in the Sky" 1949; "Beyond the Purple Hills" 1950; "The Blazing Sun" 1950; "Cow Town" 1950; "Mule Train" 1950 (Charley Stewart); "Silver Canyon" 1951; "Valley of Fire" 1951; "Whirlwind" 1951; "Barbed Wire" 1952; "The Old West" 1952; "Blackjack Ketchum, Desperado" 1956 (Doc Blaine).

O'Mara, Kate (1939-). Films: "The Desperados" 1969 (Adah). ¶TV: *Gunsmoke*—"The Night Riders" 2-24-69.

Omen, Judd. Films: "Outlaws" TVM-1986 (Carlos Diaz).

O'Moore, Patrick (1909-12/10/83). Films: "The Black Whip" 1956 (Governor); "Copper Sky" 1957 (Col. Thurston); "Ride a Violent Mile" 1957 (Bartender); "Trooper Hook" 1957 (Col. Weaver); "Blood Arrow" 1958 (McKenzie); "Cattle Empire" 1958 (Cogswell). ¶TV: *Gunsmoke*—"The Pest Hold" 4-14-56 (Pelzer); *Rawhide*—"Incident of the Town in Terror" 3-6-59 (Matt Novak), "Incident of the Silent Web" 6-3-60, "Incident in the Garden of Eden" 6-17-60 (Tompkins); *Daniel Boone*—"The Traitor" 11-2-67; *Death Valley Days*—"The Biggest Little Post Office in the World" 2-7-70.

O'Neal, Anne (1893-11/24/71). Films: "In Old California" 1942 (Mrs. Tompkins); "The Sombrero Kid" 1942 (Mrs. Barnett); "In Old Oklahoma" 1943 (Mrs. Peabody); "Cheyenne" 1947 (Miss Kittredge); "Black Bart" 1948 (Mrs. Harmon); "Annie Get Your Gun" 1950 (Miss Willoughby); "Wells Fargo Gunmaster" 1951 (Mrs. Feathergill). ¶TV: *The Gene Autry Show*—"Bandits of Boulder Bluff" 11-24-51; *Gunsmoke*—"The Last Fling" 3-23-57 (Sabina Peavy).

O'Neal, Kevin (1945-). Films: "Young Fury" 1965 (Curly). ¶TV: *The Deputy*—"The Lesson" 1-14-61 (Johnny); *Wagon Train*—"The Miss Mary Lee McIntosh Story" 2-28-65 (Efram); *Gunsmoke*—"The Wrong Man" 10-29-66 (James Kyle); *Bonanza*—"Napoleon's Children" 4-16-67 (Reb); *Daniel Boone*—"The Man" 10-16-69 (Webster); *Lancer*—"Cut the Wolf Loose" 11-4-69.

O'Neal, Patrick (1927-9/19/94). Films: "Alvarez Kelly" 1966 (Maj. Albert Stedman); "El Condor" 1970 (Chavez). ¶TV: *Alias Smith and Jones*—"Everything Else You Can Steal" 12-16-71 (Kenneth Blake).

O'Neal, Ron (1937-). Films: "The Master Gunfighter" 1975 (Paulo).

O'Neal, Ryan (1941-). Films: "Wild Rovers" 1971 (Frank Post). ¶TV: *Two Faces West*—"Doctor's Orders" 6-5-61; *Empire*—Regular 1962-63 (Tal); *The Virginian*—"It Takes a Big Man" 10-23-63 (Ben Anders); *Wagon Train*—"The Nancy Styles Story" 11-22-64 (Paul Phillips).

O'Neal, William (1898-5/12/61). Films: "Law and Order" 1953 (Ben Wiley). ¶TV: *Death Valley Days*—"To Big Charlie from Little Charlie" 1-3-55, "Two-Gun Nan" 3-10-58 (Buffalo Bill); *Annie Get Your Gun* 11-27-57 (Buffalo Bill Cody).

O'Neil, Nance (1875-2/7/65). Films: "Cimarron" 1931 (Felice Venable).

O'Neil, Robert (1911-10/8/51). Films: "The Baron of Arizona" 1950 (Brother Paul).

O'Neil, Tricia (1945-). Films: "The Legend of Nigger Charley" 1972 (Sarah Lyons); "Charlie Cobb: Nice Night for a Hanging" TVM-1977 (Angelica). ¶TV: *Big Hawaii*—"Sun Children" 9-28-77 (Dr. Ericka Bergen).

O'Neill, Dick (1928-). Films: "Posse" 1975 (Wiley). ¶TV: *Young Maverick*—"Clancy" 11-28-79 (Hobbs).

O'Neill, Henry (1891-5/18/61). Films: "Massacre" 1934 (Mr. Dickinson); "Wells Fargo" 1937 (Henry Wells); "Gold Is Where You Find It" 1938 (Judge); "Dodge City" 1939 (Col. Dodge); "Santa Fe Trail" 1940 (Cyrus Halliday); "Billy the Kid" 1941 (Tim Ward); "Honky Tonk" 1941 (Daniel Wells); "Barbary Coast Gent" 1944 (Colonel Watrous); "Bad Bascomb" 1946 (Governor Winter); "The Virginian" 1946 (Mr. Taylor).

O'Neill, James (1863-10/8/38). Films: "Miss Arizona" 1919 (Will Norman); "The Sheriff's Oath" 1920; "Two Moons" 1920 (the Killer); "West Is West" 1920 (Black Beard); "Blazing Arrows" 1922 (Scarface); "Sitting Bull at the Spirit Lake Massacre" 1927 (Little Bear).

O'Neill, Jennifer (1948-). Films: "Rio Lobo" 1970 (Shasta Delaney).

O'Neill, Johnny. Films: "Young Jesse James" 1960 (Jim Younger).

O'Neill, Robert (1911-10/8/51). Films: "The Fargo Phantom" 1950-short.

Ong, Dana (1874-12/31/48). Films: "Broadway, Arizona" 1917 (Press Agent).

Ontiveros, Lupe. Films: "Rio Diablo" TVM-1993 (Duena).

Ontkean, Michael (1946-). TV: *Hudson's Bay*—"Warrant's Depot" 3-29-58 (Jeremy).

Onyx, Narda. Films: "Jesse James Meets Frankenstein's Daughter" 1966 (Maria Frankenstein). ¶TV: *Jim Bowie*—"Land Jumpers" 11-16-56 (Marcella); *The Tall Man*—"Bitter Ashes" 12-3-60 (Teresa Oberon); *Have Gun Will Travel*—"The Prisoner" 12-17-60 (the Marquesa).

Opatoshu, David (1918-). Films: "Cimarron" 1960 (Sol Levy); "Death of a Gunfighter" 1969 (Edward Rosenbloom). ¶TV: *Zane Grey Theater*—"Wire" 1-31-58 (Dave Purcell); *The Loner*—"Westward the Shoemaker" 11-27-65 (Hyman Rabinovitch); *Daniel Boone*—"The Secret Code" 12-14-67 (Philip Cobb), "The Homecoming" 4-9-70 (Tamenund).

Oppenheimer, Alan (1930-). Films: "Little Big Man" 1971 (Major). ¶TV: *Lancer*—"The Great Humbug" 3-4-69 (Dan'l Drew); *Here Come the Brides*—"Loggerheads" 3-26-69 (Victor), "How Dry We Are" 3-6-70 (Benet); *The High Chaparral*—"The Badge" 12-18-70 (Sweets); *Bonanza*—"A Deck of Aces" 1-31-71 (Wentworth), "Customs of the Country" 2-6-72 (Ernesto), "A Visit to Upright" 3-26-72 (Dalrymple); *Nichols*—"Ketcham Power" 11-11-71 (Avarill).

Opper, Don Keith. TV: *Adventures of Brisco County, Jr.*—"Bad Luck Betty" 4-29-94 (Riley).

Opperman, Frank. Films: "The Indian Brothers" 1911; "Fate's Interception" 1912; "A Lodging for the Night" 1912; "Man's Lust for Gold" 1912.

O'Quinn, Terry. Films: "Heaven's Gate" 1980 (Capt. Minardi); "Young Guns" 1988 (Alex McSween); "Son of the Morning Star" TVM-1991 (Gen. Terry); "Tombstone" 1993 (Mayor Clum).

Orbach, Jerry (1935-). Films: "Dream West" TVM-1986 (John Sutter). ¶TV: *Annie Get Your Gun* 3-19-67 (Charles Davenport).

Orbison, Roy (1936-12/6/88). Films: "The Fastest Guitar Alive" 1967 (Johnny).

Orchard, John (1930-). Films: "Rustler's Rhapsody" 1985 (Town

Sheriff). ¶TV: *Walt Disney Presents*—"Gallegher" 1965-67 (Butler); *Daniel Boone*—"Perilous Journey" 12-16-65 (Stone), "Delo Jones" 3-2-67 (British Sergeant), "The King's Shilling" 10-19-67 (Sergeant Braddock), "The Traitor" 10-30-69 (Perkins); "Perilous Passage" 1-15-70; *The Big Valley*—"Barbary Red" 2-16-66 (Banks); *Cimarron Strip*—"The Judgment" 1-4-68; *Gunsmoke*—"Sarah" 10-16-72 (Taylor).

O'Rear, James (1914-). Films: "The Sea of Grass" 1947 (Piano Tuner). ¶TV: *Gunsmoke*—"General Parsley Smith" 12-10-55 (Drew Holt).

O'Reilly, James D. Films: "The Awakening Land" TVM-1978 (Angus Witherspoon); "The Chisholms" TVM-1979 (Luke Cassidy). ¶TV: *The Chisholms*—3-29-79 (Luke Cassidy).

O'Reilly, Robert. Films: "Desperado: Badlands Justice" TVM-1989 (Pike). ¶TV: *Father Murphy*—"The Robber" 12-14-82 (Clete); *Paradise*—"Stray Bullet" 12-8-88 (Hugh); *Adventures of Brisco County, Jr.*—"Pirates" 10-8-93 (Sketch).

O'Reilly, Tex (1880-12/8/46). Films: "Honeymoon Ranch" 1920 (Wild Bill Devlin); "On the High Card" 1921 (Hank Saunders); "West of the Rio Grande" 1921 (Pecos Bill Sinto).

Orfei, Liana. Films: "Django Kills Softly" 1968-Ital. (Linda).

Orfei, Moira. Films: "Two Sergeants of General Custer" 1965-Ital./Span.

Orlamond, William (1867-4/23/57). Films: "Vanishing Trails" 1920-serial; "Broken Chains" 1922 (Slog Sallee); "Doubling for Romeo" 1922 (Movie Director); "The Eagle's Feather" 1923 (the Swede); "The Great Divide" 1925 (Lon); "A Texas Steer" 1927 (Blow); "The Wind" 1928 (Sourdough); "Cimarron" 1931 (Grat Gotch).

Orlandi, Felice (1925-). Films: "The Long Riders" 1980 (Mr. Reddick). ¶TV: *Wild Wild West*—"The Night of the Lord of Limbo" 12-30-66 (Capt. Vincent Schofield), "The Night of the Simian Terror" 2-16-68 (Benjamin Buckley); *Gunsmoke*—"The Jackals" 2-12-68 (Emilio); *The High Chaparral*—"No Trouble at All" 5-5-70 (Felipe).

Orlando, Don (1912-12/10/87). Films: "The Irish Gringo" 1935; "Trail of the Hawk" 1935; "The Painted Stallion" 1937-serial (Jose); "Romance of the Rockies" 1937 (Mike); "Pals of the Saddle" 1938 (Italian Musician); "Domino Kid"

1957 (Ramon); "Run of the Arrow" 1957 (Vinci); "The Broken Land" 1962.

Ormond, Ron (1911-5/11/81). Films: "Sunset Carson Rides Again" 1948.

Orr, Owen (1934-). Films: "The Hired Hand" 1971 (Mace); "Kid Blue" 1973 (Train Robber); "The Great Gundown" 1977 (Happy Hogan); "The Shadow Riders" TVM-1982 (Frank King). ¶TV: *Cheyenne*—"The Brahma Bull" 12-11-61 (Harrison Hawker).

Orrick, David (1914-8/18/79). Films: "Blackjack Ketchum, Desperado" 1956 (Bob Early).

Orrison, Bob. Films: "The Culpepper Cattle Company" 1972 (Rutter).

Orrison, George. Films: "Bronco Billy" 1980 (Cowboy at Bar). ¶TV: *Tate*—"A Lethal Pride" 7-20-60 (Sheriff); *The Tall Man*—"A Gun Is for Killing" 1-14-61 (Chullo); *Laramie*—"The Last Journey" 10-31-61 (Brad Hartley), "Handful of Fire" 12-5-61, "The Dynamiters" 3-6-62, "The Betrayers" 1-22-63; *Laredo*—"Which Way Did They Go?" 11-18-65.

Orsatti, Frank (1941-). Films: "Maverick" 1994 (Unshaven Man). ¶TV: *Kung Fu*—"Blood Brother" 1-18-73 (Cole).

Ortego, Artie (Art Ardigan) (1890-7/24/60). Films: "Big Rock's Last Stand" 1912; "A Red Man's Love" 1912; "An Indian Maid's Strategy" 1913; "The Spring in the Desert" 1913; "The Call of the Tribe" 1914; "The Navajo Blanket" 1914; "The Girl of the Golden West" 1915; "The Indian Trapper's Vindication" 1915; "Skyfire" 1920 (Little Wolf); "The Driftin' Kid" 1921; "The Man Who Woke Up" 1921; "Riding with Death" 1921 (Tony Carilla); "Two-Fisted Jones" 1925 (Buck Oxford); "The Fighting Boob" 1926 (Ortega); "The Valley of Bravery" 1926 (Joe); "Spurs" 1930 (Eagle-Claw); "God's Country and the Man" 1931; "Near the Trail's End" 1931; "The Nevada Buckaroo" 1931 (Alex); "Oklahoma Jim" 1931; "Partners of the Trail" 1931; "The Ridin' Fool" 1931; "The Squaw Man" 1931 (Naturich's Brother); "The Boiling Point" 1932; "Cornered" 1932; "Galloping Thru" 1932; "The Riding Tornado" 1932; "Gordon of Ghost City" 1933-serial; "King of the Arena" 1933; "The Fighting Trooper" 1934 (Little Moose); "The Lawless Frontier" 1934; "The Lucky Texan" 1934; "The Man from Utah" 1934 (Hench-

man); "The Man Trailer" 1934; "'Neath the Arizona Skies" 1934 (Shorty); "The Prescott Kid" 1934 (Cowboy); "Randy Rides Alone" 1934 (Henchman); "The Red Rider" 1934-serial (Player); "The Star Packer" 1934 (Henchman); "The Trail Beyond" 1934; "West of the Divide" 1934; "Wheels of Destiny" 1934; "Between Men" 1935 (Henchman); "Circle of Death" 1935; "The Code of the Mounted" 1935 (Trapper); "Desert Trail" 1935; "Heir to Trouble" 1935; "The Laramie Kid" 1935 (Henchman); "Lightning Triggers" 1935; "North of Arizona" 1935 (Red Cloud); "Northern Frontier" 1935 (Slink Garu); "Pals of the Range" 1935 (Rod); "Rough Riding Ranger" 1935 (Duce); "Rustlers of Red Dog" 1935-serial (Chief/Scout/Henchman); "Tombstone Terror" 1935; "Code of the Range" 1936 (Posse); "The Crooked Trail" 1936; "Custer's Last Stand" 1936-serial (Quirk); "Ghost Patrol" 1936 (Ramon); "King of the Royal Mounted" 1936 (Indian Joe); "Lightning Bill Carson" 1936 (Henchman); "Roarin' Guns" 1936; "Song of the Trail" 1936; "Three on the Trail" 1936; "Treachery Rides the Range" 1936; "Blazing Sixes" 1937; "Cherokee Strip" 1937; "The Devil's Saddle Legion" 1937; "Empty Holsters" 1937; "Hopalong Rides Again" 1937; "Land Beyond the Law" 1937; "Heart of the North" 1938 (Chink Wooley); "The Kansas Terrors" 1939; "The Kid from Texas" 1939; "Stagecoach" 1939 (Barfly in Lordsburg); "Pioneers of the West" 1940; "Arizona Bound" 1941; "Dawn on the Great Divide" 1942; "Pirates of the Prairie" 1942; "Bad Men of Thunder Gap" 1943; "Cowboy Commandos" 1943; "Fugitive of the Plains" 1943; "The Ghost Rider" 1943; "Outlaws of Stampede Pass" 1943; "Six Gun Gospel" 1943; "The Stranger from Pecos" 1943 (Ed); "Western Cyclone" 1943; "Devil Riders" 1944; "Trail of Terror" 1944; "Trigger Trail" 1944; "Beyond the Pecos" 1945; "In Old New Mexico" 1945; "Rough Riders of Cheyenne" 1945; "Beauty and the Bandit" 1946; "The Gay Cavalier" 1946; "Gentleman from Texas" 1946; "Gunman's Code" 1946; "The Lawless Breed" 1946; "North of the Border" 1946; "Rustler's Roundup" 1946; "Song of the Sierras" 1946; "Sunset Pass" 1946 (Posse Man); "Law Comes to Gunsight" 1947; "Prairie Express" 1947 (Torgo); "Raiders of the South" 1947; "Six Gun Serenade" 1947; "Trailing Danger" 1947; "Where the North Begins" 1947; "Crossed Trails" 1948;

"Gunning for Justice" 1948; "Overland Trails" 1948; "The Big Sombrero" 1949; "Stampede" 1949; "West of El Dorado" 1949 (Indian); "Colt .45" 1950; "Over the Border" 1950; "Six Gun Mesa" 1950; "Nevada Badmen" 1951; "Skipalong Rosenbloom" 1951.

Orth, Frank (1880-3/17/62). Films: "The Devil's Saddle Legion" 1937 (Judge); "Land Beyond the Law" 1937 (Shorty); "Prairie Thunder" 1937 (Wichita); "Mexican Spitfire Out West" 1940 (Window Cleaner); "They Died with Their Boots On" 1941 (Barfly); "Buffalo Bill" 1944 (Sherman); "Tall in the Saddle" 1944 (Ferdy Davis); "Fury at Furnace Creek" 1948 (Evans).

Ortiz, Angel. Films: "Fury of the Apaches" 1966-Span./Ital.; "Navajo Joe" 1966-Ital./Span. (El Cojo); "Savage Gringo" 1966-Ital.; "Blood and Guns" 1968-Ital./Span.; "I Do Not Forgive ... I Kill!" 1968-Span./Ital.; "Here We Go Again, Eh Providence?" 1973-Ital./Fr./Span.

Ortiz, Peter. Films: "Rio Grande" 1950 (Capt. St. Jacques); "Jubilee Trail" 1954 (Horseman); "A Lawless Street" 1955 (Hiram Hayes); "Seventh Cavalry" 1956 (Pollock).

Osborn, Lyn (1926-8/30/58). TV: *Jim Bowie*—"Epitaph for an Indian" 9-6-57 (2nd Gunman), "A Grave for Jim Bowie" 2-28-58 (Criminal).

Osborne, Bud (1884-2/2/64). Films: "A Knight of the Range" 1916 (Sheriff); "Love's Lariat" 1916 (Cowboy); "Bill Brennan's Claim" 1917; "The Getaway" 1917; "Squaring It" 1917; "The Galloping Devil" 1920 (Chip); "Vengeance and the Girl" 1920 (Sheriff); "The Struggle" 1921 (Sheriff); "Barriers of Folly" 1922 (Perry Wilson); "The Prairie Mystery" 1922; "Rough Going" 1922; "White Eagle" 1922-serial; "Cyclone Buddy" 1924 (Steve Noels); "The Loser's End" 1924 (Lucky Hamish); "Not Guilty for Runnin'" 1924 (Jess Raglan); "The Silent Stranger" 1924 (Law Sleeman); "Way of a Man" 1924-serial; "Across the Deadline" 1925 (Ben Larrago); "The Fighting Ranger" 1925-serial; "Flash O'Lightning" 1925 (Ed Wiley); "The Knockout Kid" 1925 (Piut Sam); "Ranchers and Rascals" 1925 (Yates); "The Trouble Buster" 1925 (Slim Yates); "Win, Lose or Draw" 1925 (Barney Sims); "Blind Trail" 1926 (Mort Van Vleck); "Hi-Jacking Rustlers" 1926; "Lawless Trails" 1926 (Slim Lamont); "Looking for Trouble" 1926 (Lou Burkhold); "The Outlaw Express" 1926

(Blackie Lewis); "The Texas Terror" 1926; "Three Bad Men" 1926; "Without Orders" 1926 (Ranger); "Border Blackbirds" 1927 (McWraight); "Cactus Trails" 1927 (Draw Egan); "The Devil's Twin" 1927 (Tom Todd); "Don Desperado" 1927 (Frenchy); "King of the Herd" 1927 (Barry Kahn); "The Long Loop on the Pecos" 1927; "A One Man Game" 1927; "The Ore Raiders" 1927; "Pioneers of the West" 1927; "Riders of the West" 1927; "Sky-High Saunders" 1927 (George Delatour); "Two-Gun of the Tumbleweed" 1927; "The Bronc Stomper" 1928 (Slim Garvey); "Cheyenne Trails" 1928; "The Danger Rider" 1928 (Sheriff); "The Fighting Forester" 1928; "A Fighting Tenderfoot" 1928; "Forbidden Trails" 1928; "Law of the Mounted" 1928; "The Mystery Rider" 1928-serial; "On the Divide" 1928; "Secrets of the Range" 1928; "Texas Flash" 1928; "The Thrill Chaser" 1928; "The Vanishing Rider" 1928-serial; "West of Santa Fe" 1928; "Where the West Begins" 1928; "Bad Man's Money" 1929; "Code of the West" 1929; "The Cowboy and the Outlaw" 1929 (Lefty Lawson); "Days of Daring" 1929; "Far Western Trails" 1929; "The Fighting Terror" 1929; "The Go Get 'Em Kid" 1929; "The Invaders" 1929; "The Lariat Kid" 1929 (Trigger Finger); "The Last Roundup" 1929 (Villain); "Ridin' Leather" 1929; "The Smiling Terror" 1929 (Ned); "A Texas Cowboy" 1929; "West of the Rockies" 1929 (Juan Escobar); "The Apache Kid's Escape" 1930; "Breezy Bill" 1930 (Bandit); "Call of the Desert" 1930 (Todd Walker); "Call of the West" 1930; "The Canyon of Missing Men" 1930 (Slug Slagel); "The Indians Are Coming" 1930-serial (Bull McGee); "O'Malley Rides Alone" 1930; "The Utah Kid" 1930 (Deputy); "Battling with Buffalo Bill" 1931-serial (Joe Tempas); "The One Way Trail" 1931; "The Pocatello Kid" 1931; "Red Fork Range" 1931 (Whip Reden); "Come on, Danger!" 1932; "Flaming Guns" 1932 (Rustler); "Mark of the Spur" 1932 (Buzzard); "McKenna of the Mounted" 1932; "The Riding Tornado" 1932; "The Sunset Trail" 1932; "Texas Bad Man" 1932; "The Western Code" 1932; "Deadwood Pass" 1933 (the Hawk); "Diamond Trail" 1933 (Bill Miller); "The Fourth Horseman" 1933; "Gordon of Ghost City" 1933-serial (Hank); "Rustlers' Roundup" 1933 (Sodden); "When a Man Rides Alone" 1933; "Boss Cowboy" 1934 (Sheriff); "Circle Canyon" 1934 (Sheriff); "The Fighting Ranger"

1934; "The Last Round-Up" 1934; "The Law of the Wild" 1934-serial; "Lightning Bill" 1934 (Landis); "The Prescott Kid" 1934 (Ames); "The Red Rider" 1934-serial (Kelsey); "Riding Speed" 1934 (Bill Dirky); "Rocky Rhodes" 1934 (Red); "Between Men" 1935 (Ranch Hand); "Big Boy Rides Again" 1935 (Windy); "Bulldog Courage" 1935; "The Crimson Trail" 1935 (Jack); "Fighting Shadows" 1935 (Randall); "Gallant Defender" 1935; "Gunsmoke on the Guadalupe" 1935; "Justice of the Range" 1935 (Sykes); "Moonlight on the Prairie" 1935; "The Outlaw Deputy" 1935 (Cash); "Pals of the Range" 1935; "Ridin' Thru" 1935 (Sheriff); "Riding Wild" 1935 (Billings); "Rustlers of Red Dog" 1935-serial (Jake); "Saddle Aces" 1935; "The Silent Code" 1935 (Sergeant of Police); "Square Shooter" 1935 (Guard); "Stormy" 1935 (Cowboy); "Trigger Tom" 1935 (Scarface Taylor); "The Vanishing Riders" 1935; "Western Racketeers" 1935 (Blackie Morgan); "Brand of the Outlaws" 1936; "End of the Trail" 1936 (Mason's Man); "The Fugitive Sheriff" 1936; "Gun Smoke" 1936 (Haws McGee); "Heroes of the Range" 1936 (Jame); "Pinto Rustlers" 1936 (Buck); "The Plainsman" 1936; "Roamin' Wild" 1936 (Rand); "Song of the Saddle" 1936 (Porter); "Trailin' West" 1936 (Stagecoach Driver); "Treachery Rides the Range" 1936; "Vigilantes Are Coming" 1936-serial (Harris); "Wildcat Saunders" 1936; "Blazing Sixes" 1937 (Dave); "Boots and Saddles" 1937 (Joe Larkins); "The Californian" 1937 (Murphy); "Cherokee Strip" 1937; "Danger Valley" 1937; "The Devil's Saddle Legion" 1937 (Boreland); "Ghost Town Gold" 1937; "Guns of the Pecos" 1937 (Jake); "Headin' for the Rio Grande" 1937 (Cactus); "Land Beyond the Law" 1937; "Law of the Ranger" 1937; "Ranger Courage" 1937 (Steve); "Reckless Ranger" 1937; "Roll Along, Cowboy" 1937 (Burgen); "Western Gold" 1937 (Steve); "Where Trails Divide" 1937; "Wild West Days" 1937-serial; "Yodelin' Kid from Pine Ridge" 1937 (Carter); "In Early Arizona" 1938; "The Lone Ranger" 1938-serial (Hobart); "Man's Country" 1938 (Jed); "Mexicali Kid" 1938 (Chris); "The Overland Express" 1938 (Overland Wilson); "Overland Stage Raiders" 1938; "The Painted Trail" 1938 (Spud); "Pioneer Trail" 1938; "Prairie Moon" 1938 (Pete); "Riders of the Black Hills" 1938; "Rolling Caravans" 1938 (Groucher); "Santa Fe Stampede" 1938; "Six Shootin' Sheriff" 1938

(Ted); "Utah Trail" 1938 (Hank); "West of Santa Fe" 1938; "Whirlwind Horseman" 1938; "Across the Plains" 1939 (Lex); "Allegheny Uprising" 1939 (Jim's Man); "Cowboys from Texas" 1939 (Plummer's Henchman); "Days of Jesse James" 1939; "Dodge City" 1939 (Stagecoach Driver/Waiter); "Frontier Pony Express" 1939; "Frontiers of '49" 1939; "The Law Comes to Texas" 1939 (Judge Dean); "The Man from Sundown" 1939 (Ranger); "New Frontier" 1939 (Dickson); "The Night Riders" 1939; "Racketeers of the Range" 1939 (Hank); "Riders of the Sage" 1939 (Sheriff); "Rovin' Tumbleweeds" 1939; "Sundown on the Prairie" 1939; "Timber Stampede" 1939 (Brady); "Trigger Smith" 1939; "Two-Gun Troubador" 1939; "Cowboy from Sundown" 1940 (Pronto); "Deadwood Dick" 1940-serial; "Death Rides the Range" 1940; "Ghost Valley Raiders" 1940 (Gang Member); "Land of the Six Guns" 1940 (Sheriff); "Legion of the Lawless" 1940 (Jim Holmes); "Lone Star Raiders" 1940 (Blake); "One Man's Law" 1940; "Pioneer Days" 1940 (Saunders); "Prairie Law" 1940; "Ragtime Cowboy Joe" 1940 (Clements); "Rancho Grande" 1940; "Ridin' the Trail" 1940; "The Trail Blazers" 1940; "Virginia City" 1940 (Stage Driver); "Viva Cisco Kid" 1940 (Kennedy); "Wagon Train" 1940; "West of Abilene" 1940 (Wilson); "West of Pinto Basin" 1940 (Sheriff); "Wild Horse Valley" 1940 (Winton); "The Bandit Trail" 1941 (Tint); "Beyond the Sacramento" 1941 (2nd Henchman); "Bury Me Not on the Lone Prairie" 1941; "Gangs of Sonora" 1941; "Law of the Range" 1941; "The Medico of Painted Springs" 1941 (Karns); "Outlaws of the Cherokee Trail" 1941; "Outlaws of the Panhandle" 1941 (Mart Monahan); "Pals of the Pecos" 1941; "The Phantom Cowboy" 1941 (Dreer); "Riders of Death Valley" 1941-serial (Stage Driver); "The Return of Daniel Boone" 1941 (Red); "Robbers of the Range" 1941 (Blackie); "Underground Rustlers" 1941 (Sheriff): "White Eagle" 1941-serial; "Below the Border" 1942 (Scully); "Bullets for Bandits" 1942; "Code of the Outlaw" 1942; "Dawn on the Great Divide" 1942; "The Devil's Trail" 1942; "Fighting Bill Fargo" 1942; "In Old California" 1942; "Overland to Deadwood" 1942; "The Rangers Take Over" 1942 (Pete Dawson); "Riders of the West" 1942 (Red); "Riding the Wind" 1942 (Chuck Brown); "The Spoilers" 1942 (Marshal); "Trail Riders" 1942; "Valley of the Sun" 1942

(Rose); "West of the Law" 1942; "Westward Ho" 1942; "The Avenging Rider" 1943 (Wade); "Bad Men of Thunder Gap" 1943; "The Blocked Trail" 1943; "Border Buckaroos" 1943; "Canyon City" 1943; "Carson City Cyclone" 1943 (Sheriff Wells); "Cowboy Commandos" 1943 (Hans); "Fighting Frontier" 1943; "The Ghost Rider" 1943; "The Haunted Ranch" 1943; "Raiders of Red Gap" 1943; "Riders of the Rio Grande" 1943; "Robin Hood of the Range" 1943 (Thompson); "Silver Spurs" 1943; "Six Gun Gospel" 1943; "The Stranger from Pecos" 1943 (Gus); "Tenting Tonight on the Old Camp Ground" 1943 (Deputy Snell); "The Texas Kid" 1943 (Streve); "Cheyenne Wildcat" 1944; "Dead or Alive" 1944; "Devil Riders" 1944; "Girl Rush" 1944; "Guns of the Law" 1944; "The Laramie Trail" 1944; "Law Men" 1944 (Handy); "Marshal of Gunsmoke" 1944; "Marked Trails" 1944 (Sheriff); "Mojave Firebrand" 1944; "Outlaw Roundup" 1944; "Outlaw Trail" 1944 (Blackie); "Pride of the Plains" 1944; "Range Law" 1944 (Davis); "Rustlers' Hideout" 1944; "Song of the Range" 1944; "Sonora Stagecoach" 1944 (Steve Martin); "Trigger Law" 1944; "Trigger Trail" 1944; "The Utah Kid" 1944; "Valley of Vengeance" 1944 (Dad Carson); "West of the Rio Grande" 1944; "Border Badmen" 1945; "The Cherokee Flash" 1945; "The Cisco Kid Returns" 1945; "Fighting Bill Carson" 1945; "Flame of the West" 1945 (Pircell); "Flaming Bullets" 1945; "His Brother's Ghost" 1945 (Magill); "In Old New Mexico" 1945; "The Navajo Kid" 1945 (Abe Murdock); "The Navajo Trail" 1945; "Northwest Trail" 1945; "Oregon Trail" 1945; "Prairie Rustlers" 1945 (Bart); "Rough Ridin' Justice" 1945 (Driver); "Salome, Where She Danced" 1945 (Gambler); "Stranger from Santa Fe" 1945; "Sunset in El Dorado" 1945; "Three in the Saddle" 1945; "Badman's Territory" 1946; "Border Bandits" 1946 (Dutch); "California Gold Rush" 1946; "The Caravan Trail" 1946; "Colorado Serenade" 1946; "The Desert Horseman" 1946 (Walt Jarvis); "Landrush" 1946 (Sheriff Collins); "Outlaw of the Plains" 1946; "Overland Riders" 1946; "Rainbow Over Texas" 1946; "Rustler's Roundup" 1946 (Jury Foreman); "Six Gun Man" 1946 (Sam Elkins); "Thunder Town" 1946 (Henry Carson); "Wild West" 1946 (Cactus); "Border Feud" 1947; "Bowery Buckaroos" 1947 (Spike); "Code of the Saddle" 1947; "The Last Round-Up" 1947; "Over the Santa Fe

Trail" 1947; "Return of the Lash" 1947; "Six Gun Serenade" 1947; "Trailing Danger" 1947; "Twilight on the Rio Grande" 1947; "White Stallion" 1947 (Tip); "The Adventures of Frank and Jesse James" 1948-serial (Bat Kelsey); "Black Hills" 1948; "Blood on the Moon" 1948 (Cap Willis); "Courtin' Trouble" 1948 (Sheriff); "Cowboy Cavalier" 1948; "Crossed Trails" 1948 (Sheriff Cook); "Frontier Revenge" 1948 (Dawson Brother); "The Gallant Legion" 1948; "Gunning for Justice" 1948; "Indian Agent" 1948 (Sheriff); "Outlaw Brand" 1948; "Panhandle" 1948; "Prairie Outlaws" 1948; "The Rangers Ride" 1948; "Return of the Badmen" 1948 (Steve, the Stagecoach Driver); "Silver River" 1948 (Posse Man); "Silver Trails" 1948; "Six-Gun Law" 1948 (Barton); "Song of the Drifter" 1948; "Station West" 1948 (Man); "Sundown Riders" 1948 (Loco); "Across the Rio Grande" 1949 (Stage Driver); "The Gay Amigo" 1949 (Driver); "Gun Law Justice" 1949; "Gun Runner" 1949 (Burt); "Haunted Trails" 1949 (Tom Craig); "Law of the West" 1949 (Brook); "Lawless Code" 1949; "Riders in the Sky" 1949; "Roaring Westward" 1949 (Deputy Blake); "Shadows of the West" 1949 (Jones); "Son of Billy the Kid" 1949 (Guard); "West of El Dorado" 1949 (Jerry); "Arizona Territory" 1950 (Stableman); "Border Outlaws" 1950 (Sheriff); "Border Rangers" 1950 (Driver); "Cow Town" 1950 (George Copeland); "Cowboy and the Prizefighter" 1950; "Crooked River" 1950 (Stage Driver); "The Daltons' Women" 1950; "Desperadoes of the West" 1950-serial (Joe); "Fast on the Draw" 1950; "Frontier Outpost" 1950 (Stage Driver); "Hostile Country" 1950 (Agate); "Marshal of Heldorado" 1950 (Brad); "Outlaw Gold" 1950 (Sheriff); "Over the Border" 1950 (Stableman); "Roar of the Iron Horse" 1950-serial; "The Savage Horde" 1950; "Six Gun Mesa" 1950; "West of the Brazos" 1950 (Stage Driver); "West of Wyoming" 1950; "Winchester '73" 1950 (Man); "Don Daredevil Rides Again" 1951-serial (Bartender); "Nevada Badmen" 1951; "Stage to Blue River" 1951; "The Thundering Trail" 1951 (Stage Driver); "Valley of Fire" 1951 (Beardsley); "The Vanishing Outpost" 1951 (Outlaw Chief); "Whirlwind" 1951; "Whistling Hills" 1951 (Pete); "Barbed Wire" 1952; "The Black Lash" 1952 (Operator); "Bugles in the Afternoon" 1952 (Teamster); "The Frontier Phantom" 1952; "Last of the Comanches" 1952 (Wagon Driver);

"The Man from Black Hills" 1952; "Son of Geronimo" 1952-serial (Tulsa); "Texas City" 1952 (Birk); "The Lawless Rider" 1954 (Tulso); "Fastest Gun Alive" 1956 (Rancher); "Perils of the Wilderness" 1956-serial (Jake); "Tribute to a Badman" 1956 (Cowboy); "Flesh and the Spur" 1957 (Outlaw); "Gun Glory" 1957 (Clem); "The Storm Rider" 1957 (Toby); "Escape from Red Rock" 1958; "The Hanging Tree" 1959 (Horseman). ¶TV: *The Lone Ranger*—"The Whimsical Bandit" 8-31-50, "Banker's Choice" 11-23-50, "Backtrail" 1-25-51, "The Empty Strongbox" 1-8-53; *The Gene Autry Show*—"The Posse" 9-17-50, "The Devil's Brand" 9-24-50; *The Cisco Kid*—"Dog Story" 5-12-51, "The Old Bum" 6-9-51. "Uncle Disinherits Niece" 7-14-51, "Stolen Bonds" 7-28-51, "Protective Association" 9-8-51, "Lodestone" 4-26-52, "Gun Totin' Papa" 5-24-52; *Wild Bill Hickok*—"Marvins' Mix-Up" 5-19-53; *Annie Oakley*—"Annie and the Silver Ace" 2-27-54; *The Roy Rogers Show*—"Treasure of Paradise Valley" 12-11-55; *The Adventures of Rin Tin Tin*—"The Southern Colonel" 10-18-57 (Driver), "Bitter Bounty" 3-14-58 (Casey); *Wyatt Earp*—"The Imitation Jesse James" 2-4-58 (Sam Landale); *Maverick*—"The Judas Mask" 11-2-58 (Stagecoach Driver), "A Cure for Johnny Rain" 12-20-59 (Stagecoach Driver), "Last Stop: Olivion" 2-12-61 (Sam Overman); *The Rifleman*—"Eight Hours to Die" 11-4-58 (Hangman), "The Shattered Idol" 12-4-61 (Driver); *The Law of the Plainsman*—"Passenger to Mescalero" 10-29-59; *Have Gun Will Travel*—"Jenny" 1-23-60 (Driver), "The Revenger" 9-30-61, "Darwin's Man" 4-21-62; *Bonanza*—"Desert Justice" 2-20-60 (Charlie); *The Texan*—"The Mountain Man" 5-23-60; *Rawhide*—"Incident of the Captive" 12-16-60, "The Pitchwagon" 3-2-62.

Osborne, Jefferson (1871-6/11/32). Films: "A Deal in Indians" 1915.

Osborne, Vivienne (1896-6/10/61). Films: "Cameron of the Royal Mounted" 1922.

Oscar, John. Films: "Courtin' Wildcats" 1929 (Quid Johnson); "Branded" 1931 (Olaf "Swede" Hanson); "The Man from Death Valley" 1931 (Hank).

Oscarsson, Per (1927-). Films: "The New Land" 1973-Swed. (Pastor Torner).

O'Shea, Jack (1906-10/1/67). Films: "Guns for Hire" 1932; "The Red Rider" 1934-serial; "The Big Show" 1937; "Range Defenders" 1937; "In Early Arizona" 1938; "Outlaws of Sonora" 1938; "The Painted Desert" 1938 (Miner); "Renegade Ranger" 1938 (Henchman); "Riders of the Black Hills" 1938; "Cowboys from Texas" 1939; "Frontier Pony Express" 1939; "In Old Monterey" 1939; "Six-Gun Rhythm" 1939; "South of the Border" 1939; "Zorro's Fighting Legion" 1939-serial (Cave Heavy #1); "Adventures of Red Ryder" 1940-serial (Lem); "Prairie Law" 1940; "Stage to Chino" 1940; "Young Buffalo Bill" 1940; "Bad Man of Deadwood" 1941; "Back in the Saddle" 1941; "Desert Bandit" 1941; "Down Mexico Way" 1941; "In Old Cheyenne" 1941 (Barfly); "Jesse James at Bay" 1941; "The Lone Rider Fights Back" 1941; "The Phantom Cowboy" 1941; "The Singing Hill" 1941; "White Eagle" 1941-serial; "Bells of Capistrano" 1942; "The Cyclone Kid" 1942; "In Old California" 1942; "Outlaws of Pine Ridge" 1942; "Romance on the Range" 1942; "The Sombrero Kid" 1942; "Sons of the Pioneers" 1942; "South of Santa Fe" 1942; "Westward Ho" 1942; "California Joe" 1943; "Carson City Cyclone" 1943; "Daredevils of the West" 1943-serial (Citizen #1); "Hands Across the Border" 1943; "King of the Cowboys" 1943 (Henchman); "Man from Music Mountain" 1943; "The Man from the Rio Grande" 1943; "The Man from Thunder River" 1943; "Overland Mail Robbery" 1943; "Raiders of San Joaquin" 1943 (Detective); "Riders of the Rio Grande" 1943; "Silver Spurs" 1943; "Thundering Trails" 1943; "Wagon Tracks West" 1943; "Bordertown Trail" 1944; "Call of the Rockies" 1944; "Cheyenne Wildcat" 1944; "Code of the Prairie" 1944 (Townsman); "Cowboy and the Senorita" 1944; "Firebrands of Arizona" 1944 (Ranch Hand); "Marshal of Reno" 1944; "Outlaws of Santa Fe" 1944; "The San Antonio Kid" 1944; "Sheriff of Sundown" 1944; "Song of Nevada" 1944; "Stagecoach to Monterey" 1944; "The Yellow Rose of Tesas" 1944; "Bandits of the Badlands" 1945; "Frontier Gal" 1945 (Barfly); "Marshal of Laredo" 1945; "Rough Riders of Cheyenne" 1945; "Santa Fe Saddlemates" 1945; "Sheriff of Cimarron" 1945 (Brody); "The Caravan Trail" 1946 (Poker Face); "In Old Sacramento" 1946; "Outlaw of the Plains" 1946; "Overland Riders" 1946; "The Phantom Rider" 1946-serial (Ace); "Plainsman and the Lady" 1946 (Bartender); "Rio Grande Raiders" 1946; "Romance of the West" 1946 (Marshal); "Stars Over Texas" 1946 (Ringo Evans); "Tumbleweed Trail" 1946 (Gringo); "Bowery Buckaroos" 1947 (Jose); "Flashing Guns" 1947 (Sagebrush); "King of the Bandits" 1947; "Law of the Lash" 1947 (Decker); "Oregon Trail Scouts" 1947; "Son of Zorro" 1947-serial (Hood); "Twilight on the Rio Grande" 1947; "Vigilantes of Boomtown" 1947 (Referee); "Wyoming" 1947 (Bartender); "Ghost of Zorro" 1949-serial (Freight Agent); "The Last Bandit" 1949; "Outlaw Country" 1949 (Senor Cordova); "Ride, Ryder, Ride" 1949 (Keno); "Roll, Thunder, Roll" 1949 (Bartender); "Sheriff of Wichita" 1949 (Joe); "The Savage Horde" 1950; "Twenty Mule Team" 1940 (Conductor); "Silver Canyon" 1951; "Wanted Dead or Alive" 1951; "The Frontier Phantom" 1952; "A Perilous Journey" 1953 (Cook); "Jubilee Trail" 1954 (Corporal); "The Maverick Queen" 1956 (Waiter). ¶TV: *The Roy Rogers Show*—"Money to Burn" 6-28-53, "The Outlaws of Paradise Valley" 11-8-53, "The Peddler from the Pecos" 12-13-53 (Bonimo), "Bad Company" 12-27-53, "The High-Graders of Paradise Valley" 2-28-54, "The Last of the Larrabee Kid" 10-17-54, "Outcasts of Paradise Valley" 1-9-55, "Treasure of Paradise Valley" 12-11-55, "Smoking Guns" 3-3-56, "Paleface Justice" 11-18-56, "Junior Outlaw" 2-10-57; *Maverick*—"Shady Deal at Sunny Acres" 11-23-58 (1st Rube).

O'Shea, Michael (1906-12/4/73). Films: "Last of the Redmen" 1947 (Hawk-Eye).

O'Shea, Milo (1925-). Films: "Peter Lundy and the Medicine Hat Stallion" TVM-1977 (Brisly).

O'Shea, Oscar (1881-4/5/60). Films: "Border Wolves" 1938 (Judge Coleman); "Riders of the Purple Sage" 1941 (Judkins); "Sin Town" 1942 (Conductor); "Senorita from the West" 1945; "Fury at Furnace Creek" 1948 (Jailer).

Osmond, Cliff (1937-). Films: "The Raiders" 1964 (Duchamps); "Oklahoma Crude" 1973 (Massive Man); "Guardian of the Wilderness" 1976 (McCollough, the Lumber Foreman); "Joe Panther" 1976 (Rance); "The Apple Dumpling Gang Rides Again" 1979 (Wes Hardin); "California Gold Rush" TVM-1981 (Harry Love). ¶TV: *The Rifleman*—"None So Blind" 3-19-62 (Lafayette Bly); *Wagon Train*—"The Jud Steele Story" 5-2-62 (Simmons), "The John Bernard Story" 11-21-62 (Ben Gill), "Alias Bill Hawks" 5-15-63 (Chester Cole); *The Dakotas*—"Thunder in Pleasant Valley" 2-4-63

(Telford); *Have Gun Will Travel*—"Caravan" 2-23-63 (Koro); *Laredo*—"Yahoo" 9-30-65 (Running Antelope), "The Legend of Midas Mantee" 9-16-66 (Midas Mantee); *Shane*—"An Echo of Anger" 10-1-66 (Joshua); *Gunsmoke*—"The Victim" 1-1-68 (Bo Remick), "The Hide Cutters" 9-30-68 (Chunk), "Roots of Fear" 12-15-69 (Daniel Sadler), "Celia" 2-23-70 (Ben Sommars), "Pike" 3-1-71 & 3-8-71 (Tom Malcomb); *Cowboy in Africa*—"Search and Destroy" 3-4-68 (Frank Bentley); *Paradise*—"Orphan Train" 10-28-89 (Travis).

Osmond, Donny (1957-). Films: "The Wild Women of Chastity Gulch" TVM-1982 (Frank Isaacs).

Osmond, Ken (1943-). TV: *Circus Boy*—"Corky's Big Parade" 3-24-57 (Skinny).

Osmond, Marie (1959-). Films: "I Married Wyatt Earp" TVM-1983 (Josephine Marcus).

Osterhage, Jeffrey. Films: "True Grit" TVM-1978 (Christopher); "The Legend of the Golden Gun" TVM-1979 (John Colton); "The Sacketts" TVM-1979 (Tye Sackett); "The Shadow Riders" TVM-1982 (Jesse Traven); "Buckeye and Blue" 1988 (Blue Duck).

Osterloh, Robert (1918-). Films: "The Doolins of Oklahoma" 1949 (Wichita); "The Palomino" 1950 (Sam); "Drums in the Deep South" 1951 (Harper); "The Great Missouri Raid" 1951 (August); "New Mexico" 1951 (Pvt. Parsons); "Johnny Guitar" 1954 (Sam); "Man with the Gun" 1955 (Virg Trotter); "Seven Angry Men" 1955 (Col. Robert E. Lee); "The Desperados Are in Town" 1956 (Deputy Sheriff Groome); "Johnny Concho" 1956 (Duke Lang); "Star in the Dust" 1956 (Rigdon); "Fort Massacre" 1958 (Schwabacker); "Warlock" 1959 (Professor). ¶TV: *Tales of Wells Fargo*—"The Newspaper" 3-24-58 (Tom Sutton), "Reward for Gaine" 1-20-62 (Corporal Simon); *Gunsmoke*—"Hanging Man" 4-19-58 (Dan Dresslar); *Wagon Train*—"The Juan Ortega Story" 10-8-58 (Ransome Jarvis), "The Andrew Elliott Story" 2-10-64; *The Deputy*—"The Deal" 12-5-59 (Quincannon), "Day of Fear" 12-17-60 (Sam Nathan), "Brand of Honesty" 6-10-61 (Nathans); *The Law of the Plainsman*—"Endurance" 1-14-60; *The Rifleman*—"A Time for Singing" 3-8-60 (Walt Durkins); *Laramie*—"Hour After Dawn" 3-15-60 (Sheriff); *Wanted—Dead or Alive*—"Payoff at Pinto" 5-21-60; *Whispering Smith*—

"The Blind Gun" 5-8-61 (Ben Avery); *The Legend of Jesse James*—"The Widow Fay" 12-20-65 (Sheriff).

Osterwald, Bibi (1920-). TV: *Preview Tonight*—"Roaring Camp" 9-4-66 (Mary).

O'Sullivan, Anthony (-7/5/20). Films: "The Renunciation" 1909; "The Tourists" 1912.

O'Sullivan, Jerry. Films: "Springfield Rifle" 1952 (Lt. Evans); "North to Alaska" 1960 (Sergeant). ¶TV: *Riverboat*—"Landlubbers" 1-10-60 (Captain Clegg); *Tales of Wells Fargo*—"A Show from Silver Lode" 3-6-61 (Lou Kendall); *Maverick*—"The Devil's Necklace" 4-16-61 & 4-23-61 (Lieutenant Torrance).

O'Sullivan, Maureen (1911-). Films: "Robbers' Roost" 1933 (Helen Herrick); "The Tall T" 1957 (Doretta Mims); "Wild Heritage" 1958 (Emma Breslin).

O'Sullivan, Michael (1934-7/24/71). Films: "Hang 'Em High" 1968 (Francis Duffy).

Otho, Henry (1888-6/6/40). Films: "The Beaded Buckskin Bag" 1913; "The Trail of Cards" 1913; "The Outlaw Express" 1926 (John Mills); "Trailin' West" 1936 (Hawk); "Treachery Rides the Range" 1936 (Burley Barton); "Blazing Sixes" 1937 (Hank); "The Devil's Saddle Legion" 1937; "Empty Holsters" 1937 (Jerry); "God's Country and the Woman" 1937 (Logger); "Guns of the Pecos" 1937 (Hank); "It Happened Out West" 1937; "Land Beyond the Law" 1937 (Kirby); "Prairie Thunder" 1937 (Chris); "Overland Stage Raiders" 1938 (Sheriff Mason); "Pride of the West" 1938 (Slim); "Dodge City" 1939 (Conductor); "The Lone Ranger Rides Again" 1939-serial (Pa Daniels); "Mexicali Rose" 1939 (Alcalde).

Otis, Oleta (1851-8/10/27). Films: "Under Northern Lights" 1920 (Madge Carson).

Otis, Ted. TV: *Maverick*—The Ghost Soldiers" 11-8-59 (Corporal Daggott); *The Rifleman*—"Surveyors" 12-29-59 (Elliot Hodgins); *Death Valley Days*—"Forbidden Wedding" 3-22-60 (Henry).

O'Toole, Annette (1953-). TV: *The Men from Shiloh*—"The Mysterious Mr. Tate" 10-14-70 (Lark Walters); *Gunsmoke*—"The Witness" 11-23-70 (Edda Sprague); *Dirty Sally*—"My Fair Laddie" 3-29-74 (George).

O'Toole, Ollie (1912-2/25/92). Films: "The Oregon Trail" 1959 (James G. Bennett); "North to

Alaska" 1960 (Mack). ¶TV: *Circus Boy*—"The Return of Colonel Jack" 2-10-57 (Mr. Meeker); *Maverick*—"Stage West" 10-27-57 (McLean); *Tombstone Territory*—"Mexican Bandito" 1-29-58 (Jonas), "The Lady Gambler" 5-28-58 (Clerk); *Bat Masterson*—"Marked Deck" 3-11-59 (Rinehart); *Bonanza*—"The Saga of Annie O'Toole" 10-24-59 (Simpson), "Mrs. Wharton and the Lesser Breeds" 1-19-69 (Bartender), "To Stop a War" 10-19-69 (Bartender), "Danger Road" 1-11-70 (Bartender); *The Rifleman*—"The Promoter" 12-6-60 (John Crabtree); *Wyatt Earp*—"Wyatt Earp's Baby" 4-25-61 (Hotel Clerk); *Have Gun Will Travel*—"Bear Bait" 5-13-61 (Telegraph Operator), "Odds for a Big Red" 10-7-61, "Squatter's Rights" 12-23-61 (Barber), "Hobson's Choice" 4-7-62 (Drunk); *Tales of Wells Fargo*—"Gunman's Revenge" 5-22-61 (Al Willey); *Gunsmoke*—"The Gallows" 3-3-62 (Milt), "Root Down" 10-6-62 (Clerk), "Panacea Sykes" 4-13-63 (Telegrapher), "The Bassops" 2-22-64 (Telegrapher), "Journey for Three" 6-6-64 (Telegrapher), "Bad Lady from Brookline" 5-1-65 (Herb); *The Virginian*—"The Man Who Couldn't Die" 1-30-63; *Laredo*—"Which Way Did They Go?" 11-18-65; *Daniel Boone*—"Be Thankful for the Fickleness of Women" 9-19-68 (Auctioneer), "The Fleeing Nuns" 10-24-68 (Toy Merchant); *The High Chaparral*—"Spokes" 9-25-70 (Store Keeper).

Otto, Henry (1877-8/3/52). Films: "When Thieves Fall Out" 1914.

Ouspenskaya, Maria (1876-12/3/49). Films: "Wyoming" 1947 (Maria).

Overall, Park. Films: "The Gambler Returns: The Luck of the Draw" TVM-1991 (Melody O'Rourke); "The Good Old Boys" TVM-1995 (Florence). ¶TV: *Young Riders*—"Judgment Day" 1-5-91 (Millie Owens).

Overholts, Jay. TV: *Gunsmoke*—"Catawomper" 2-10-62 (Sergeant).

Overman, Jack (1916-1/4/50). Films: "Nevada" 1944 (Red Barry); "Frontier Gal" 1945 (Buffalo).

Overman, Lynn (1887-2/19/43). Films: "Union Pacific" 1939 (Leach Overmile); "Northwest Mounted Police" 1940 (Tod McDuff); "Silver Queen" 1942 (Hector Bailey).

Overton, Frank (1918-4/23/67). Films: "The True Story of Jesse James" 1957 (Maj. Cobb); "Posse from Hell" 1961 (Burt Hogan). ¶TV:

Philco Television Playhouse—"The Death of Billy the Kid" 7-24-55 (Pat Garrett); *Black Saddle*—"The Deal" 12-4-59 (Pete Hooker); *Riverboat*—"The Sellout" 4-18-60 (Nick Logan); *Tate*—"Comanche Scalps" 8-10-60 (Amos Dundee); *The Rebel*—"Two Weeks" 3-26-61 (John Galt); *Lawman*—"Cold Fear" 6-4-61 (Brad Turner); *The Deputy*—"Lorinda Belle" 6-24-61 (Bill Corman); *Bonanza*—"The Storm" 1-28-62 (Captain White), "The Wormwood Cup" 4-23-67 (Amos Crenshaw); *Laramie*—"The High Country" 2-6-62 (Jason Duncan), "The Last Battleground" 4-16-63 (James Courtland); *Wagon Train*—"The Lonnie Fallon Story" 2-7-62 (Martin Jennings), "The Story of Cain" 12-16-63; *Empire*—"The Tall Shadow" 11-20-62 (Charles Pierce); *The Virginian*—"Fifty Days to Moose Jaw" 12-12-62 (Sam Cafferty), "Smile of a Dragon" 2-26-64 (Umber), "The Welcoming Town" 3-22-67 (Sam Atkins); *The Dick Powell Show*—"Colossus" 3-12-63 (Dan Corbett); *Stoney Burke*—"Joby" 3-18-63 (Chief Ramsey).

Ovey, George (1870-9/23/51). Films: "A Deal in Indians" 1915; "Arizona Sweepstakes" 1926 (Stuffy McGee); "Strings of Steel" 1926-serial; "Desert Dust" 1927 (Shorty Benson); "Pals in Peril" 1927 (Shorty Gilmore); "Moonlight on the Prairie" 1935 (Short Cowboy); "The Roaring West" 1935-serial; "The Phantom Rider" 1936-serial; "Wells Fargo" 1937 (Townsman); "The Arizona Wildcat" 1939; "Stand Up and Fight" 1939 (Conductor); "West of Abilene" 1940 (Varner).

Owen, Beverley. Films: "Bullet for a Badman" 1964 (Susan). ¶TV: *Wagon Train*—"The Myra Marshall Story" 10-21-63 (Grace Marshall); *The Virginian*—"The Invaders" 1-1-64 (Margaret Tyrone).

Owen, Garry (1897-6/1/51). Films: "Call of the Yukon" 1938 (Conner); "Heart of the North" 1938 (Tom Ryan); "The Woman of the Town" 1943 (Dealer).

Owen, Michael. Films: "King of the Texas Rangers" 1941-serial (Ronnie Nelson); "Death Valley Rangers" 1944 (Bill Weston); "Gangster's Den" 1945 (Jimmy Lane).

Owen, Milton (1891-10/1/69). Films: "Rose Marie" 1936 (Stage Manager).

Owen, Reginald (1887-11/5/72). Films: "Robbers' Roost" 1933 (Cecil Herrick).; "Call of the Wild" 1935 (Smith); "Rose Marie" 1936 (Myerson); "Pierre of the Plains" 1942

(Noah Glenkins); "Red Garters" 1954 (Judge Winthrop). ¶TV: *Maverick*—"The Belcastle Brand" 10-12-58 (Norbert), "Gun-Shy" 1-11-59 (Freddie Hawkins), "A Technical Error" 11-26-61 (Major Holbrook Sims).

Owen, Seena (1894-8/15/66). Films: "The Lamb" 1915 (Mary); "Madame Bo-Peep" 1917 (Octavia); "Branding Broadway" 1918 (Mary Lee); "Breed of Men" 1919 (Ruth Fellows); "Riders of Vengeance" 1919 (Lola Madison); "The Sheriff's Son" 1919 (Beulah Rutherford); "The Flame of the Yukon" 1926 (the Flame).

Owen, Tudor (1898-3/13/79). Films: "Montana" 1950 (Jock); "Back to God's Country" 1953 (Fitzsimmons); "Arrow in the Dust" 1954 (Tillotson); "The Oklahoma Woman" 1956 (Ed Grant); "The Lonely Man" 1957; "North to Alaska" 1960 (Purser); "Frontier Uprising" 1961; "How the West Was Won" 1962 (Scotsman). ¶TV: *The Lone Ranger*—"Greed for Gold" 1-19-50, "The Sheriff of Smoke Tree" 9-20-56, "The Letter Bride" 11-15-56; *My Friend Flicka*—"Cavalry Horse" 10-28-55 (Sergeant Tim O'Gara), "Lock, Stock and Barrel" 4-6-56 (Sergeant Tim O'Gara), "When Bugles Blow" 5-18-56 (Sergeant Tim O'Gara); *The Adventures of Rin Tin Tin*—"The Lost Puppy" 11-9-56 (Sandy MacDonald); *Wagon Train*—"The Annie MacGregor Story" 2-5-58 (Angus MacGregor), "The Jose Maria Moran Story" 5-27-59 (Tim Naughton), "The Eve Newhope Story" 12-5-62 (Patrick O'Shaughnessy), "The Bleeker Story" 12-9-63 (McFerren); *Black Saddle*—"Client: Starkey" 2-7-59 (Dr. MacAdam); *The Texan*—"The Eyes of Captain Wylie" 2-23-59 (Judge Moffett); *Sugarfoot*—"MacBrewster the Bold" 10-13-59 (Angus MacBrewster); *Rawhide*—"Incident of the Devil and His Due" 1-22-60 (Riley); *Maverick*—"Guatemala City" 1-31-60 (Sim Carter); *Klondike*—"Queen of the Klondike" 1-23-61 (Brock).

Owen, Virginia. Films: "Thunder Mountain" 1947 (Ginger Kelly).

Owens, Buck (1929-). Films: "Pals of the Prairie" 1934-short.

Owens, Marjorie. TV: *Gunsmoke*—"No Handcuffs" 1-21-56 (Woman); *Frontier*—"Patrol" 4-29-56; *Sheriff of Cochise*—"Fire on Chiricahua Mountains" 11-2-56 (Mrs. Simpson); *Broken Arrow*—"Return from the Shadows" 12-4-56 (Mrs. Pilgrim); *Wyatt Earp*—"Sweet Revenge" 1-28-58 (Barbara); *Zane Grey Theater*—"Man of Fear" 3-14-58; *Track-*

down—"The Avenger" 10-31-58 (Bess Garth).

Owens, Patricia (1925-). Films: "The Law and Jake Wade" 1958 (Peggy Carter); "Three Thousand Hills" 1959 (Joyce); "Black Spurs" 1965 (Clare Grubbs). ¶TV: *Tales of Wells Fargo*—"Assignment in Gloribee" 1-27-62 (Katherine Anne Murdock); *Gunsmoke*—"Scot-Free" 5-9-64 (Nora Brand).

Pace, Judy (1946-). TV: *Kung Fu*—"In Uncertain Bondage" 2-7-74 (Jenny Mabry).

Packer, Doris (1904-79). TV: *Maverick*—"Maverick Springs" 12-6-59 (Kate Dawson).

Packer, Netta (1897-11/7/62). Films: "Prairie Schooners" 1940 (Cora Gibbs); "Adventures in Silverado" 1948. ¶TV: *Gunsmoke*—"Doc's Reward" 12-14-57 (1st Lady).

Padden, Sarah (1881-12/4/67). Films: "The Bugle Call" 1927 (Luke's Wife); "The Great Meadow" 1931 (Mistress Hall); "Forbidden Valley" 1938 (Mrs. Ragona); "Let Freedom Ring" 1939 (Ma Logan); "Man of Conquest" 1939 (Mrs. Houston); "Lone Star Raiders" 1940 (Lydia "Granny" Phelps); "In Old Colorado" 1941 (Ma Woods); "Outlaws of the Cherokee Trail" 1941; "The Devil's Trail" 1942; "Heart of the Rio Grande" 1942 (Mrs. Forbes); "Law and Order" 1942 (Aunt Mary); "Riders of the West" 1942 (Ma Turner); "Wild Bill Hickok Rides" 1942; "Ghost Guns" 1944; "Girl Rush" 1944 (Emma); "Range Law" 1944 (Boots Annie); "Trail to Gunsight" 1944 (Ma Wagner); "Dakota" 1945 (Mrs. Plummer); "Marshal of Laredo" 1945; "Riders of the Dawn" 1945 (Melinda); "Song of Old Wyoming" 1945 (Ma Conway); "Wildfire" 1945 (Aunt Agatha); "Wild West" 1946 (Carrio); "Ramrod" 1947 (Mrs. Parks); "Trail Street" 1947 (Mrs. Ferguson); "The Dude Goes West" 1948 (Mrs. Hallahan); "Frontier Revenge" 1948 (Widow Owens); "Prairie Outlaws" 1948; "Range Justice" 1949 (Ma Curtis); "Gunslingers" 1950 (Rawhide Rose); "The Missourians" 1950 (Mother); "Utah Wagon Train" 1951 (Sarah Wenover). ¶TV: *The Lone Ranger*—"The Star Witness" 8-17-50; *The Cisco Kid*—"Big Switch" 2-10-51, "False Marriage" 4-14-51, "Wedding Blackmail" 4-21-51; *The Roy Rogers Show*—"The Knockout" 12-28-52 (Gradma Conley), "The Last of the Larrabee Kid" 10-17-54 (Martha Crosswick), "Boys' Day in Paradise Valley" 11-7-54.

Paddock, Charles (1900-7/21/43). Films: "Nine and Three-Fifths Seconds" 1925 (Charles Raymond).

Padgett, Slim. Films: "Just Pals" 1920 (Outlaw); "Two Moons" 1920 (Rogers); "Western Grit" 1924 (Black's Stage Driver).

Padgett, H.W. Films: "The Last Straw" 1920 (Sam McKee).

Padilla, Jr., Manuel (1956-). Films: "Black Spurs" 1965 (Manuel); "Cutter's Trail" TVM-1970 (Paco Avila); "A Man Called Horse" 1970 (Leaping Buck). ¶TV: *Rawhide*—"El Hombre Bravo" 5-14-65 (Pepe); *Gunsmoke*—"Zavala" 10-7-68 (Paco Avila), "The Innocent" 11-24-69 (Indian Boy), "The Pack Rat" 1-12-70 (Sancho), "Trafton" 10-25-71 (Manuel); *Lancer*—"The Man Without a Gun" 3-25-69, "Lamp in the Wilderness" 3-10-70 (Running Fox); *Bonanza*—"The Prisoners" 10-17-71 (Pedro).

Padilla, Robert. Films: "Machismo—40 Graves for 40 Guns" 1970 (Hidalgo); "Scandalous John" 1971 (Paco's Cousin); "Savage Red—Outlaw White" 1974; "The Great Gundown" 1977 (Mario Ochoa, the Savage). ¶TV: *Bonanza*—"Little Girl Lost" 11-3-68 (Charley), "What Are Pardners For?" 4-12-70 (Running Cloud); *How the West Was Won*—Episode One 2-6-77 (Mountain-Is-Long), Episode Two 2-7-77 (Mountain-Is-Long), Episode Three 2-14-77 (Mountain-Is-Long).

Padilla, Ruben (1910-6/16/91). Films: "The Alamo" 1960 (Gen. Santa Anna).

Padjan, Jack (Jack Duane) (1887-2/1/60). Films: "The Iron Horse" 1924 (Wild Bill Hickok); "The Little Warrior" 1926; "Tony Runs Wild" 1926 (Deputy Sheriff); "Land of the Lawless" 1927 (Jim Catlin); "Crashing Through" 1928 (Tex); "Forbidden Grass" 1928; "Redskin" 1929 (Barrett); "Three Rogues" 1931 (Deputy); "The Gay Desperado" 1936; "Gunsmoke Ranch" 1937 (Duke); "One Man Justice" 1937 (Whitey); "The Painted Stallion" 1937-serial.

Padula, Marguerita (1891-2/22/57). Films: "Billy the Kid" 1930 (Nicky Whoosiz).

Padula, Vincent (1900-1/16/67). Films: "The Three Outlaws" 1956; "Hell Canyon Outlaws" 1957; "Escape from Red Rock" 1958. ¶TV: *Jim Bowie*—"Gone to Texas" 5-24-57 (Don Ignacio); *The Adventures of Rin Tin Tin*—"The Matador" 2-6-59 (Pedro); *Rawhide*—"Incident at Span-

ish Rock" 12-18-59; *The Tall Man*—"The Judas Palm" 10-21-61 (Rompero); *The Outlaws*—"A Day to Kill" 2-22-62 (Ambassador).

Pagan, William. Films: "Lucky Cisco Kid" 1940 (Stagecoach Passenger); "Santa Fe Marshal" 1940 (Gardner); "Riders of Death Valley" 1941-serial (Marshall).

Page, Bradley (1904-86). Films: "The Sundown Rider" 1933 (Jim Hunter); "The Fighting Ranger" 1934 (Cougar); "The Outcasts of Poker Flat" 1937 (Sonoma); "The Law West of Tombstone" 1938 (Doc Howard); "Beyond the Sacramento" 1940 (Cord Crowley); "Badlands of Dakota" 1941 (Chapman); "Roaring Frontiers" 1941; "King of the Mounties" 1942-serial (Charles Blake); "Sons of the Pioneers" 1942 (Frank Bennett).

Page, Dorothy. Films: "Ride 'Em, Cowgirl" 1939 (Helen Rickson); "The Singing Cowgirl" 1939 (Dorothy Hendrick); "Water Rustlers" 1939 (Shirley Martin).

Page, Gale (1918-1/8/83). Films: "Heart of the North" 1938 (Elizabeth Spaulding).

Page, Genevieve (1930-). Films: "Talent for Loving" 1969-Brit./Span.

Page, Geraldine (1924-6/13/87). Films: "Hondo" 1953 (Angie); "J.W. Coop" 1971 (Mama).

Page, Harrison (1941-). TV: *Kung Fu*—"The Garments of Rage" 11-8-74 (Pete).

Page, Joy. Films: "Conquest of Cochise" 1953 (Consuelo de Cordova); "Tonka" 1958 (Prairie Flower). ¶TV: *Loretta Young Show*—"The Wise One" 3-26-56 (Ellen); *Cheyenne*—"Border Affair" 11-5-57 (Empress Carlotta), "Standoff" 5-6-58 (Maria Vargas); *Wagon Train*—"The Bill Tawnee Story" 2-12-58 (Leeana).

Paget, Alfred (-1925). Films: "The Redman's View" 1909; "The Broken Doll" 1910; "A Mohawk's Way" 1910; "A Romance of the Western Hills" 1910; "Fighting Blood" 1911; "The Indian Brothers" 1911; "The Last Drop of Water" 1911; "Black Sheep" 1912; "The Chief's Blanket" 1912; "Goddess of Sagebrush Gulch" 1912; "Heredity" 1912; "In the Aisles of the Wild" 1912; "Iola's Promise" 1912; "A Temporary Truce" 1912; "The Battle at Elderbrush Gulch" 1913; "The Broken Ways" 1913; "Just Gold" 1913; "A Misunderstood Boy" 1913; "The Sheriff's Baby" 1913; "The Tenderfoot's Money" 1913; "Two Men of the Desert" 1913; "The Yaqui Cur" 1913;

"The Gambler of the West" 1914; "The Lamb" 1915; "The Martyrs of the Alamo" 1915 (James Bowie); "Cupid's Round Up" 1918 (Jim Cocksey); "When a Girl Loves" 1919 (Ben Grant).

Paget, Debra (1933-). Films: "Broken Arrow" 1950 (Sonseeahray); "The Gambler from Natchez" 1954 (Melanie Barbee); "Seven Angry Men" 1955 (Elizabeth); "White Feather" 1955 (Appearing Day); "The Last Hunt" 1956 (Indian Girl); "Love Me Tender" 1956 (Cathy). ¶TV: *20th Century Fox Hour*—"Gun in His Hand" 4-4-56 (Mary); *Wagon Train*—"The Marie Dupree Story" 3-19-58 (Marie Dupree), "The Stagecoach Story" 9-30-59 (Angela deVarga); *Cimarron City*—"The Beauty and the Sorrow" 2-7-59 (Margaret); *Riverboat*—"The Unwilling" 10-11-59 (Lela Candida); *Johnny Ringo*—"East Is East" 1-7-60 (Agnes St. John); *Rawhide*—"Incident in the Garden of Eden" 6-17-60 (Laura Ashley), "The Hostage Child" 3-9-62 (Azuela); *Tales of Wells Fargo*—"Man of Another Breed" 12-2-61 (Kate Timmons).

Paggett, Gary (1941-). Films: "Little House: The Last Farewell" TVM-1984 (Turner). ¶TV: *Gunsmoke*—"Seven Hours to Dawn" 9-18-65 (Simpson).

Pagliani, Ugo (Ugo Paplisi). Films: "The Magnificent Bandits" 1969-Ital./Span. (Heffen).

Paige, Janis (1922-). Films: "Cheyenne" 1947 (Emily Carson); "The Younger Brothers" 1949 (Kate); "Welcome to Hard Times" 1967 (Adah); "Bret Maverick" TVM-1981 (Mandy Packer); "No Man's Land" TVM-1984 (Maggie Hodiak). ¶TV: *Wagon Train*—"The Nellie Jefferson Story" 4-5-61 (Nellie Jefferson); *Gun Shy*—Regular 1983 (Nettie McCoy).

Paige, LeRoy "Satchel" (1906-6/8/82). Films: "The Wonderful Country" 1959 (Sgt. Tobe Sutton).

Paige, Robert (1910-12/21/87). Films: "Frontier Badman" 1943 (Steve); "The Red Stallion" 1947 (Andy McBride).

Paiva, Nestor (1905-9/9/66). Films: "Union Pacific" 1939 (C.P. Conductor); "Northwest Mounted Police" 1940 (Half Breed); "Santa Fe Trail" 1940 (Agitator); "The Kid from Kansas" 1941 (Jamaica); "Girl from Alaska" 1942 (Geroux); "King of the Mounties" 1942-serial (Count Baroni); "Along the Navajo Trail" 1945 (Janza); "Salome, Where She Danced" 1945 (Panatella); "Badman's Territory" 1946 (Sam Bass); "Ramrod" 1947 (Curley); "Robin Hood of Monterey" 1947; "The Paleface" 1948 (Patient); "South Pacific Trail" 1952 (Carlos Alvarez); "Viva Zapata!" 1952 (New General); "The Desperado" 1954 (Capt. Thornton); "Four Guns to the Border" 1954 (Greasy); "Thunder Pass" 1954; "Comanche" 1956 (Puffer); "The Guns of Fort Petticoat" 1957 (Tortilla); "The Left-Handed Gun" 1958 (Maxwell); "Frontier Uprising" 1961 (Montalvo); "The Wild Westerners" 1962 (Gov. John Bullard); "California" 1963 (Gen. Micheltorena); "Ballad of a Gunfighter" 1964 (Padre); "Jesse James Meets Frankenstein's Daughter" 1966. ¶TV: *The Lone Ranger*—"The Whimsical Bandit" 8-31-50, "Dan Reid's Fight for Life" 11-18-54 (Juan Pedro Cardoza); *The Adventures of Rin Tin Tin*—"The Barber of Seville" 3-11-55, "O'Hara Gets Culture" 3-8-57; *The Gene Autry Show*—"The Million Dollar Fiddle" 10-1-55; *Jim Bowie*—"The Secessionist" 11-9-56 (Bouchar); *Cheyenne*—"The Mustang Trail" 11-20-56 (Esteban), "Born Bad" 3-26-57 (Black Frank), "The Wedding Rings" 1-8-62 (the Padre); *Tombstone Territory*—"Revenge Town" 11-6-57; *Sugarfoot*—"Quicksilver" 11-26-57 (Senor Contreras); *Wagon Train*—"The Dan Hogan Story" 5-14-58, "The Colonel Harris Story" 1-13-60 (Sergeant Boehmer), "The Jane Hawkins Story" 11-30-60, "The Jim Bridger Story" 5-10-61 (Sergeant Hoag), "The Clementine Jones Story" 10-25-61 (Gip), "The Eli Bancroft Story" 11-11-63 (Money Joe); *Walt Disney Presents*—"Elfego Baca" Regular 1958-60 (Justice of the Peace); *Maverick*—"The Thirty-Ninth Star" 11-16-58 (Louie); *Death Valley Days*—"The Invaders" 3-17-59 (Rosselli); *Lawman*—"The Friend" 6-28-59 (Jack Gorman); *The Texan*—"The Dishonest Posse" 10-5-59 (Jose Taffola); *Wanted—Dead or Alive*—"Triple Vise" 2-27-60 (Pedro); *Bonanza*—"The Avenger" 3-19-60 (Thornton), "The Burma Rarity" 10-22-61, "Ponderosa Matador" 1-12-64 (Senor Tenino); *Rawhide*—"The Captain's Wife" 1-12-62 (Hagerty); *Have Gun Will Travel*—"Face of a Shadow" 4-20-63 (Dan Tibner); *The Virginian*—"Siege" 12-18-63 (Charley Sanchez); *Gunsmoke*—"Winner Take All" 2-20-65 (Barman); *Daniel Boone*—"The Peace Tree" 11-11-65 (Menewa).

Pak, Jacquelyn. Television: *Annie Oakley*—Semi-Regular 1954-57 (Helen Lacey).

Pakula, Joanna. Films: "Tombstone" 1993 (Kate).

Palacios, Begonia. Films: "Major Dundee" 1965 (Linda).

Palacios, Ricardo. Films: "Return of the Seven" 1966-Span.; "Seven for Pancho Villa" 1966-Span. (General Pancho Villa); "The Ugly Ones" 1966-Ital./Span.; "Kitosch, the Man Who Came from the North" 1967-Ital./Span.; "El Condor" 1970 (Chief Mexican Bandit); "With Friends, Nothing Is Easy" 1971-Span./Ital.; "The Man Called Noon" 1973-Brit./Span./Ital. (Brakeman); "None of the Three Were Called Trinity" 1974-Span.; "The Spikes Gang" 1974 (Doctor); "Take a Hard Ride" 1974-Ital./Brit./Ger. (Calvera); "Comin' at Ya" 1981-Ital. (Polk).

Palance, Cody. Films: "God's Gun" 1976-Ital./Israel; "Young Guns" 1988 (Baker).

Palance, Holly (1950-). TV: *Bret Maverick*—"Horse of Yet Another Color" 1-5-82 (Dolly O'Hare).

Palance, Jack (1920-). Films: "Arrowhead" 1953 (Toriano); "Shane" 1953 (Wilson); "Kiss of Fire" 1955 (El Tigre); "The Lonely Man" 1957 (Jacob Wade); "The Professionals" 1966 (Capt. Jesus Raza); "The Mercenary" 1968-Ital./Span. (Ricciolo); "The Desperados" 1969 (Parson Josiah Galt); "Companeros" 1970-Ital./Span./Ger. (Jack); "The McMasters" 1970 (Kolby); "Monte Walsh" 1970 (Chet Rollins); "The Big and the Bad" 1971-Ital./Fr./Span.; "It Can be Done ... Amigo" 1971-Ital./Fr./Span. (Sonny Bronston); "Chato's Land" 1972 (Quincey Whitmore); "Sting of the West" 1972-Ital. (Father Jackleg); "Brothers Blue" 1973-Ital./Fr. (Helliman); "Oklahoma Crude" 1973 (Hellman); "The Godchild" TVM-1974 (Rourke); "God's Gun" 1976-Ital./Israel (Sam Clayton); "Welcome to Blood City" 1977-Brit./Can. (Sheriff Frendlander); "Last Ride of the Dalton Gang" TVM-1979 (Will Smith); "Young Guns" 1988 (Lawrence G. Murphy); "City Slickers" 1991 (Curly); "City Slickers II: The Legend of Curly's Gold" 1994 (Duke Washburn); "Buffalo Girls" TVM-1995 (Bartle Boone). ¶TV: *Zane Grey Theater*—"The Lariat" 11-2-56 (Dan Morgan).

Palange, Inez (1889-10/16/62). Films: "Men of America" 1933 (Mrs. Garboni); "Robin Hood of El Dorado" 1936 (Nurse); "Viva Cisco Kid" 1940 (Mexican Mother); "Romance of the Rio Grande" 1941 (Mama Lopez); "Under Fiesta Stars" 1941; "Unconquered" 1947.

Palasthy, Alex (1877-3/16/48). Films: "Wild and Woolly" 1937 (Orchestra Leader).

Pallante, Aladdin (1913-6/9/70). TV: *The Rebel*—"The Threat" 2-12-61 (Ambrose Pack), "The Hostage" 6-11-61 (Judge Baylon).

Pallavicino, Gianni. Films: "Find a Place to Die" 1968-Ital.; "Shoot, Gringo ... Shoot!" 1968-Ital./Fr.; "Beast" 1970-Ital.

Pallette, Eugene (1889-9/3/54). Films: "The Gunman" 1914; "The Horse Wrangler" 1914; "On the Border" 1914; "The Sheriff's Prisoner" 1914; "The World Apart" 1917 (Clyde Holt); "Two Kinds of Women" 1922 (Old Carson); "Without Compromise" 1922 (Tommy Ainsworth); "Hell's Hole" 1923 (Pablo); "To the Last Man" 1923 (Slim Bruce); "North of Hudson Bay" 1924 (Peter Dane); "The Light of Western Stars" 1925 (Stub); "Desert Valley" 1926 (Deputy); "Whispering Canyon" 1926 (Harvey Hawes); "Whispering Smith" 1926 (Bill Dancing); "The Virginian" 1929 (Honey Wiggin); "The Border Legion" 1930 (Bunco Davis); "The Santa Fe Trail" 1930 (Doc Brady); "Dude Ranch" 1931 (Judd); "Fighting Caravans" 1931 (Seth Higgins); "Gun Smoke" 1931 (Stub Wallack); "Mark of Zorro" 1940 (Fra Felipe); "Silver Queen" 1942 (Steve Adams); "The Kansan" 1943 (Tom Waggoner); "In Old Sacramento" 1946 (Jim Wales).

Palmer, Anthony (1934-). Films: "Rancho Deluxe" 1975 (Karl); "Lacy and the Mississippi Queen" TVM-1978 (Sam Lacy). ¶TV: *How the West Was Won*—Episode Two 2-7-77 (Russell), Episode Three 2-14-77 (Russell).

Palmer, Betsy (1929-). Films: "The Tin Star" 1957 (Nona Mayfield).

Palmer, Dick. see Palmera, Mimmo.

Palmer, Gregg (Palmer Lee) (1927-). Films: "The Cimarron Kid" 1951 (Grat Dalton); "The Battle at Apache Pass" 1952 (Joe Bent); "The Raiders" 1952 (Marty Smith); "Column South" 1953 (Charlmers); "The Redhead from Wyoming" 1953 (Hal Jessup); "Taza, Son of Cochise" 1954 (Capt. Burnett); "Revolt at Fort Laramie" 1957 (Capt. James Tenslip); "The Sad Horse" 1959 (Bart Connors); "The Comancheros" 1961; "Five Guns to Tombstone" 1961; "Gun Fight" 1961 (Brad Santley); "Advance to the Rear" 1964 (Gambler); "The Quick Gun" 1964 (Donovan); "Shenandoah" 1965 (Union Guard); "The Rare Breed" 1966 (Rodenbush); "The Undefeated" 1969 (Parker); "Chisum" 1970 (Riker);

"Big Jake" 1971 (John Goodfellow); "Sometimes Life Is Hard, Right Providence?" 1972-Ital./Fr./Ger. (Hurricane Kid); "The Shootist" 1976 (Burly Man); "Go West, Young Girl" TVM-1978 (Payne); "Hot Lead and Cold Feet" 1978 (Jeff). ¶TV: *Sergeant Preston of the Yukon*—"Littlest Rookie" 10-11-56 (Ed McQuade); *Death Valley Days*—"The Loggerheads" 12-16-56, "The Trial of Red Haskell" 2-24-57, "Lady Engineer" 5-5-57, "Perilous Cargo" 6-23-57, "Empire of Youth" 1-27-58 (William T. Coleman), "Perilous Refuge" 4-14-59 (John Brewster), "Forty Steps to Glory" 5-19-59 (Randall), "Paid in Full" 1-3-65, "Kate Melville and the Law" 6-20-65 (Gabe), "The Indian Girl" 1-20-68 (Shunar), "Son of Thunder" 10-25-69; *Tales of the Texas Rangers*—"Panhandle" 9-22-57 (Pete Hackett); *Tales of Wells Fargo*—"Chips" 11-4-57, "The Warrior's Return" 9-21-59 (Deputy), "Death Raffle" 10-21-61 (Steger); *Wagon Train*—"The Mary Halstead Story" 11-20-57 (Groton), "The Riley Gratton Story" 12-4-57 (Paul Dawson), "The Jose Morales Story" 10-19-60 (Raleigh); *Broken Arrow*—"White Savage" 12-24-57 (Lieutenant Fielding); *The Restless Gun*—"The Hand Is Quicker" 3-17-58 (Joe Kruger), "Four Lives" 4-13-59 (Bill Clayton); *26 Men*—"Runaway Stage" 6-17-58; *The Texan*—"The Troubled Town" 10-13-58 (Player); *Frontier Doctor*—"The Crooked Circle" 10-18-58; *Jefferson Drum*—"Band of Iron" 10-23-58 (Grant); *Buckskin*—"A Man from the Mountains" 10-30-58 (Jackel); *Cimarron City*—"The Bitter Lesson" 1-3-59 (Tom Hiller); *Have Gun Will Travel*—"Fragile" 10-31-59 (Drunk), "The Misguided Father" 2-27-60 (Brogan), "Fight at Adobe Wells" 3-12-60, "Trial at Tablerock" 12-15-62 (Sheriff); *Shotgun Slade*—"Freight Line" 11-17-59; *Hotel De Paree*—"Sundance and the Bare-Knuckled Fighters" 1-8-60 (Cooper); *Gunsmoke*—"Big Tom" 1-9-60 (Harry), "Phoebe Strunk" 11-10-62 (Hulett Strunk), "Blind Man's Bluff" 2-23-63 (Wells), "The Odyssey of Jubal Tanner" 5-18-63 (Collie Fletcher), "Eliab's Aim" 2-27-65 (Jake), "The Bounty Hunter" 10-30-65 (Doak), "The Pretender" 11-20-65 (Sheriff Jackson), "South Wind" 11-27-65 (Blacksmith), "Which Doctor" 3-19-66 (Herk), "The Victim" 1-1-68 (Deputy Reed), "Deadman's Law" 1-8-68 (Fry), "The Hide Cutters" 9-30-68 (Clete Davis), "Abelia" 11-18-68 (Wales), "The Cage" 3-23-70 (Benson), "Sergeant Holly" 12-14-70 (Bo-

dine), "Lynott" 11-1-71 (Nicols), "Alias Festus Haggen" 3-6-72 (Guthrie), "The Busters" 3-10-75 (Simeon Reed); *Overland Trail*—"Vigilantes of Montana" 4-3-60 (Will Purdue); *Man from Blackhawk*—"The Harpoon Story" 5-6-60 (Gil Harrison); *The Deputy*—"Trail of Darkness" 6-18-60 (Tully); *Lawman*—"Old Stefano" 12-25-60 (Tracy McNeil); *Sugarfoot*—"Welcome Enemy" 12-26-60 (Captain McKinley); *The Tall Man*—"A Gun Is for Killing" 1-14-61 (Blanchard); *Wyatt Earp*—"Doc Holliday Faces Death" 2-28-61 (Tom McLowery), "The Law Must Be Fair" 5-2-61 (Tom McLowery), "Just Before the Battle" 6-13-61 (Tom McLowery), "Gunfight at the O.K. Corral" 6-21-61 (Tom McLowery); *Cheyenne*—"The Frightened Town" 3-20-61 (Dillard); *The Outlaws*—"Sam Bass" 5-4-61 (Heff); *Two Faces West*—"The Dead Ringer" 7-24-61; *Laramie*—"The Long Road Back" 10-23-62 (Duke Walker), "Badge of Glory" 5-7-63 (Chuck Logan); *The Virginian*—"The Drifter" 1-29-64 (Sunday), "Beyond the Border" 11-24-65 (Cal), "The Inchoworm's Got No Wings at All" 2-2-66 (Peters); *Bonanza*—"Return to Honor" 3-22-64 (Gannett), "Speak No Evil" 4-20-69 (Terrell), "Another Windmill to Go" 9-14-69 (Benson); *Rawhide*—"The Violent Land" 3-5-65 (Mace); *The Loner*—"An Echo of Bugles" 9-18-65 (Adjutant); *The Big Valley*—"Winner Lose All" 10-27-65 (Coombs); *Laredo*—"The Golden Trail" 11-4-65 (Curly), "The Dance of the Laughing Death" 9-23-66; *Branded*—"$10,000 for Durango" 11-28-65 (Doc); *Wild Wild West*—"The Night of the Human Trigger" 12-3-65 (Thaddeus Cadwallader), "The Night of the Gruesome Games" 10-25-68 (Dr. Walter DeForrest); *The Legend of Jesse James*—"A Real Tough Town" 1-24-66 (Moose Walters); *Cimarron Strip*—"Journey to a Hanging" 9-7-67, "The Deputy" 12-21-67 (Buford), "The Greeners" 3-7-68; *The High Chaparral*—"Ride the Savage Land" 2-11-68 (Colonel); *The Men from Shiloh*—"Hannah" 12-30-70 (O'Shea); *Alias Smith and Jones*—"Don't Get Mad, Get Even" 2-17-72.

Palmer, Jasper. Films: "Lonesome Trail" 1945; "The Navajo Trail" 1945; "Salome, Where She Danced" 1945 (Cowhand); "King of the Bandits" 1947 (U.S. Marshal); "Rainbow Over the Rockies" 1947; "Song of the Sierras" 1946; "The Big Sombrero" 1949.

Palmer, Lorna (1907-6/14/28). Films: "Double Action Daniels" 1925 (Ruth Fuller).

Palmer, Maria (1924-9/6/81). Films: "Surrender" 1950 (Janet Barton). ¶TV: *The Californians*—"Act of Faith" 5-26-59 (Mme. Jouvais); *Rawhide*—"Incident of the Woman Trap" 1-26-62 (Emilie), "The Immigrants" 3-16-62 (Elsa).

Palmer, Max (1928-5/7/84). TV: *Bat Masterson*—"A Noose Fits Anybody" 11-19-58 (1st Bartender).

Palmer, Patricia (Margaret Gibson) (1895-10/21/64). Films: "The Outlaw" 1913; "Sunny or the Cattle Thief" 1913; "Anne of the Mines" 1914; "The Horse Thief" 1914; "The Navajo Ring" 1914; "A Child of the North" 1915; "The Golden Trail" 1915; "The Hidden Law" 1916 (Wanda Holmes); "The Home Trail" 1918 (Elsie); "The Money Corral" 1919 (Chicago Kate); "Sand!" 1920 (Josie Kirkwood); "Across the Border" 1922 (Margie Landers); "The Cowboy and the Lady" 1922 (Midge); "The Cowboy King" 1922; "Rounding Up the Law" 1922 (Doris Hyland); "The Web of the Law" 1923 (Mollie Barbee); "A Pair of Hellions" 1924; "The Little Savage" 1929 (Kitty).

Palmer, Paul. Films: "The Roaring West" 1935-serial; "Canadian Mounties vs. Atomic Invaders" 1953-serial (Turner).

Palmer, Peter (1931-). TV: *Custer*—Regular 1967 (Sergeant James Bustard); *Lancer*—"The Black McGloins" 1-21-69 (Sorley Boy McGloin), "Lifeline" 5-19-70 (Charlie).

Palmer, Renzo (1930-). Films: "Sting of the West" 1972-Ital.

Palmer, Robert. Films: "Heller in Pink Tights" 1960 (McAllister); "Thirteen Fighting Men" 1960 (Pvt. Jensen); "Young Jesse James" 1960 (Bob Younger). ¶TV: *Bronco*—"Seminole War Pipe" 12-12-60 (John Jumper); *The Rebel*—"Paperback Hero" 1-29-61 (Jack Slater); *Lawman*—"The Promise" 6-11-61 (Geoff Washburn); *Death Valley Days*—"The Third Passenger" 12-6-61 (Bill Gentry); *Gunsmoke*—"Shona" 2-9-63; *The Big Valley*—"A Flock of Trouble" 9-25-67 (Chambers).

Palmer, Shirley. Films: "Code of the Northwest" 1926 (Lorna McKenna); "Sitting Bull at the Spirit Lake Massacre" 1927 (Ceila Moore); "Somewhere in Sonora" 1933 (Mary Burton).

Palmer, Tex. Films: "Three Rogues" 1931 (Teamster); "The Riding Tornado" 1932; "Crashing Broadway" 1933; "Outlaw Justice" 1933; "Rainbow Ranch" 1933; "Riders of

Destiny" 1933; "The Lucky Texan" 1934; "The Outlaw Tamer" 1934; "Randy Rides Alone" 1934 (Henchman); "The Star Packer" 1934 (Stagecoach Driver); "West of the Divide" 1934; "The Fighting Parson" 1935; "Coyote Trails 1935; "The Dawn Rider" 1935 (Henchman); "The Last of the Clintons" 1935; "Law of the 45's" 1935 (Henchman); "Lawless Range" 1935; "Paradise Canyon" 1935; "The Pecos Kid" 1935; "The Rider of the Law" 1935; "Smokey Smith" 1935; "Westward Ho" 1935; "The Whirlwind Rider" 1935; "The Crooked Trail" 1936; "Everyman's Law" 1936 (Saloon Man); "The Fugitive Sheriff" 1936; "King of the Pecos" 1936; "The Last of the Warrens" 1936; "The Law Rides" 1936; "The Lawless Nineties" 1936; "Rogue of the Range" 1936 (Stage Bandit); "The Unknown Ranger" 1936; "Arizona Gunfighter" 1937 (Monty); "Arizona Days" 1937; "Bar Z Bad Men" 1937; "Boothill Brigade" 1937 (McGee); "The California Mail" 1937; "Danger Valley" 1937; "The Gambling Terror" 1937; "Gun Lords of Stirrup Basin" 1937 (Hammond's Man); "The Gun Ranger" 1937; "Guns in the Dark" 1937; "Headin' for the Rio Grande" 1937; "Law of the Ranger" 1937; "A Lawman Is Born" 1937; "Lightnin' Crandall" 1937; "Moonlight on the Range" 1937; "The Mystery of the Hooded Horseman" 1937; "Ranger Courage" 1937; "The Rangers Step In" 1937; "Reckless Ranger" 1937; "The Red Rope" 1937; "Riders of the Rockies" 1937 (Jeffries' Lookout Man); "Romance of the Rockies" 1937; "Sing, Cowboy, Sing" 1937; "Stars Over Arizona" 1937; "Trail of Vengeance" 1937 (Henchman); "Trailing Trouble" 1937; "Black Bandit" 1938; "Desert Patrol" 1938; "The Feud Maker" 1938; "In Early Arizona" 1938; "Man's Country" 1938; "Outlaw Express" 1938; "Pals of the Saddle" 1938; "Pioneer Trail" 1938; "Prairie Justice" 1938; "Rolling Caravans" 1938; "Starlight Over Texas" 1938; "Western Trails" 1938; "Lone Star Pioneers" 1939; "The Phantom Stage" 1939 (Runt); "The Cheyenne Kid" 1940; "Colorado" 1940; "Covered Wagon Days" 1940; "The Golden Trail" 1940; "The Kid from Santa Fe" 1940; "Lightning Strikes West" 1940; "Wild Horse Range" 1940; "Billy the Kid in Santa Fe" 1941 (Outlaw); "Billy the Kid's Range War" 1941; "Billy the Kid's Roundup" 1941; "The Kid's Last Ride" 1941; "The Lone Rider in Frontier Fury" 1941; "Rawhide Rangers" 1941; "Sad-

dle Mountain Roundup" 1941; "Tonto Basin Outlaws" 1941; "Tumbledown Ranch in Arizona" 1941; "Underground Rustlers" 1941; "Wrangler's Roost" 1941; "Arizona Roundup" 1942; "Along the Sundown Trail" 1942; "Boot Hill Bandits" 1942; "Fighting Bill Fargo" 1942; "Rock River Renegades" 1942; "Rolling Down the Great Divide" 1942; "Texas to Bataan" 1942 (Grob); "Thunder River Feud" 1942; "Trail Riders" 1942; "Western Mail" 1942; "Where Trails End" 1942; "The Haunted Ranch" 1943; "Silver City Raiders" 1943; "Two Fisted Justice" 1943; "Wild Horse Stampede" 1943 (Outlaw); "Fuzzy Settles Down" 1944; "Outlaw Trail" 1944; "Range Law" 1944; "Texas Panhandle" 1945; "Jesse James Rides Again" 1947-serial (Doty); "The Hawk of Powder River" 1948 (Stage Driver); "The Tioga Kid" 1948; "Law of the Panhandle" 1950.

Palmer, Tom. TV: *Gunsmoke*— "Moon" 5-11-57 (Jack Salter); *Wyatt Earp*—"The Wicked Widow" 5-21-57 (Ted Styles), "Cattle Thieves" 10-28-59 (Rep Cantwell), "Silver Dollar" 2-2-60; *Death Valley Days*—"The Little Trooper" 12-15-59; *Have Gun Will Travel*—"Ransom" 6-4-60 (Sutton); *Stoney Burke*—"Color Him Lucky" 4-1-63 (Kitner); *Great Adventure*—"The Testing of Sam Houston" 1-31-64 (Tom Allen); *Wild Wild West*—"The Night of the Grand Emir" 1-28-66 (Willard Drapeau); *Bonanza*—"The Emperor Norton" 2-27-66 (Harris); *Cimarron Strip*—"The Hunted" 10-5-67 (Booth); *The Outcasts*—"The Town That Wouldn't" 3-31-69 (Jessup).

Palmer, Violet. Films: "The Blue Streak" 1917 (the Flegling); "Rough and Ready" 1918 (Evelyn Durant); "Tangled Trails" 1921 (Milly); "The Fighting Boob" 1926 (Helen Hawksby).

Palmera, Mimmo (Dick Palmer) (1928-). Films: "Bullets Don't Argue" 1964-Ital./Ger./Span. (Billy Clanton); "Left Handed Johnny West" 1965-Span./Ital. (Johnny West); "For One Thousand Dollars Per Day" 1966-Ital./Span. (Steve); "Two Sons of Ringo" 1966-Ital.; "The Handsome, the Ugly, and the Stupid" 1967-Ital.; "Poker with Pistols" 1967-Ital. (Masters); "Black Jack" 1968-Ital.; "Dead for a Dollar" 1968-Ital.; "Execution" 1968-Ital./Fr. (Chips); "A Long Ride from Hell" 1968-Ital. (Freeman); "Time and Place for Killing" 1968-Ital.; "Paths of War" 1969-Ital.; "Shotgun" 1969-Ital.; "Deserter" 1970-U.S./Ital./Yugo.

(Chief Durango); "Calibre .38" 1971-Ital.; "Gunman of One Hundred Crosses" 1972-Ger./Ital. (Frank Dawson); "He Was Called the Holy Ghost" 1972-Ital.; "Gunmen and the Holy Ghost" 1973-Ital. (Weston).

Palomino, Carlos. Films: "Geronimo: An American Legend" 1993 (Sgt. Turkey).

Palter, Lew. TV: *Gunsmoke*— "Lyle's Kid" 9-23-68 (Hillman); *The High Chaparral*—"Mi Casa, Su Casa" 2-20-70 (Jorge).

Paluzzi, Luciana (1937-). Films: "Chuka" 1967 (Veronica Kleitz); "Forgotten Pistolero" 1970-Ital./ Span. (Anna); "Powderkeg" TVM-1971 (Juanita Sierra-Perez). ¶TV: *Bonanza*—"The Dowry" 4-29-62 (Michele Dubois).

Pani, Corrado (1936-). Films: "Matalo!" 1971-Ital./Span. (Bart).

Pantoliano, Joe. Films: "El Diablo" CTVM-1990 (Kid Durango).

Panzer, Paul (1872-8/16/58). Films: "The Maid of Niagara" 1910; "The Arrowmaker's Daughter" 1912; "The Cowboy and the Baby" 1912; "On the Brink of the Chasm" 1912; "The Sheriff's Brother" 1912; "The Perils of Pauline" 1914-serial; "The Masked Rider" 1919-serial; "The Mohican's Daughter" 1922 (Father LaClaire); "The Best Bad Man" 1925 (Sheriff); "Hawk of the Hills" 1927-serial (Manson); "Redskin" 1929; "Cavalier of the West" 1931 (Don Fernandez); "The Montana Kid" 1931 (Gabby Gable); "Secrets" 1933; "Moonlight on the Prairie" 1935 (Townsman); "Cherokee Strip" 1937 (Henry Coleman); "Guns of the Pecos" 1937 (Stranger); "Land Beyond the Law" 1937 (Blake); "Prairie Thunder" 1937 (Jed); "Heart of the North" 1938 (Trapper).

Papas, Irene (1926-). Films: "Tribute to a Badman" 1956 (Jocasta Constantine).

Pape, Lionel (1877-10/21/44). Films: "Drums Along the Mohawk" 1939 (General).

Paplisi, Ugo. *see* Pagliani, Ugo.

Pardee, C.W. "Doc" (1885-7/17/75). Films: "The Gentleman from Arizona" 1939 (Doc).

Pardee, Ida. Films: "Beyond the Law" 1918 (Mother Dalton).

Parfrey, Woodrow (1923-7/29/84). Films: "Cattle King" 1963 (Stafford); "Scalplock" TVM-1966; "Sam Whiskey" 1969 (Mint Inspector Thornton Bromley); "Sam Hill: Who Killed the Mysterious Mr. Foster?" TVM-1971; "Oklahoma Crude" 1973

(Lawyer); "This Was the West That Was" TVM-1974; "The Outlaw Josey Wales" 1976 (Carpetbagger); "The New Maverick" TVM-1978 (Leveque); "Bronco Billy" 1980 (Dr. Canterbury). ¶TV: *The Virginian*—"The Accomplice" 12-19-62 (Joe Darby), "The Hell Wind" 2-14-68 (Hobie Simpson); *Gunsmoke*—"Louie Pheeters" 1-5-63 (Tom Wiggins); *Have Gun Will Travel*—"Bob Wire" 1-12-63 (Bob Fire); *Empire*—"65 Miles Is a Long, Long Way" 4-23-63 (Gates); *Temple Houston*—"Find Angel Chavez" 9-26-63 (Fred Bell); *Bonanza*— "Shining in Spain" 3-27-66 (Huber), "Napoleon's Children" 4-16-67 (Professor), "My Friend, My Enemy" 1-12-68 (Theodore Scott), "Shanklin" 2-13-72 (Dr. Ingram); *The Dakotas*— "Sanctuary at Crystal Springs" 5-6-63; *Laredo*—"Rendezvous at Arillo" 10-7-65 (Sam Burns); *The Legend of Jesse James*—"Manhunt" 11-29-65 (Clagett); *A Man Called Shenandoah*—"The Death of Matthew Eldridge" 3-21-66 (Cliff Eldridge); *Death Valley Days*—"The Four Dollar Law Suit" 4-16-66; *Iron Horse*—"Joy Unconfined" 9-12-66 (Holmes), "Big Deal" 12-12-66, "The Golden Web" 3-27-67 (Holmes), "T Is for Traitor" 12-2-67 (Holmes); *Lancer*—"The Man Without a Gun" 3-25-69 (Zeek); *Daniel Boone*—"The Printing Press" 10-23-69 (Quartermaster); *The High Chaparral*—"The Hostage" 3-5-71 (Pruitt); *Alias Smith and Jones*— "The Fifth Victim" 3-25-71 (Sam Winters); *Kung Fu*—"Superstition" 4-5-73 (Denver Peck).

Paris, Jerry (1925-3/31/86). Films: "No Name on the Bullet" 1959 (Miller); "Evil Roy Slade" TVM-1972 (Souvenir Salesman). ¶TV: *Colt .45*— "Blood Money" 1-17-58 (Joe Bullock); *Sugarfoot*—"Brink of Fear" 6-30-58 (Cully Abbot); *The Alaskans*—"Peril at Caribou Crossing" 2-28-60 (Walter Collier); *Death Valley Days*—"The Private Mint of Clark, Gruber and Company" 2-13-63 (Emmanuel Gruber).

Paris, Manuel (1894-11/19/59). Films: "Jubilee Trail" 1954 (Mexican).

Park, Jacquelyn. TV: *The Cisco Kid*—"The Lowest Bidder" 4-4-53, "Sundown's Gun" 4-18-53; *Wild Bill Hickok*—"Daughter of Casey O'-Grady" 7-21-53; *The Gene Autry Show*—"Stage to San Dimas" 10-8-55; *Tales of the Texas Rangers*—"Streamlined Rustlers" 12-8-57.

Park, Post (1899-9/18/55). Films: "Moonlight on the Prairie" 1935 (Driver); "The Lone Ranger" 1938-serial (Trooper); "Frontier Mar-shal" 1939 (Driver); "The Lone Ranger Rides Again" 1939-serial (Stage Driver); "Adventures of Red Ryder" 1940-Serial (Seldeen); "The Border Legion" 1940; "The Pioneers" 1941 (Benton); "Zorro's Black Whip" 1944-serial (Rock Heavy #2); "The El Paso Kid" 1946; "The Phantom Rider" 1946-serial (Driver #1/Tom); "Ridin' Down the Trail" 1947; "Son of Zorro" 1947-serial (Driver); "Overland Trails" 1948; "Ghost of Zorro" 1949-serial (Driver #1/Zeke); "She Wore a Yellow Ribbon" 1949 (Noncommissioned Officer); "The James Brothers of Missouri" 1950-serial (Farrow/Wagoner); "Hangman's Knot" 1952; "Gun Fury" 1953; "Powder River" 1953 (Stage Coach Driver); "The Woman They Almost Lynched" 1953 (Driver); "The Tall Men" 1955 (Stagecoach Driver).

Parker, Andy (and the Plainsmen). Films: "Shadow Valley" 1947; "Black Hills" 1948; "Check Your Guns" 1948; "The Hawk of Powder River" 1948; "The Tioga Kid" 1948; "Tornado Range" 1948; "The Westward Trail" 1948.

Parker, Carol. Films: "Wells Fargo" 1937 (Girl); "The Drifter" 1944 (Sally Dawson).

Parker, Cecilia (1905-7/25/93). Films: "Mystery Ranch" 1932 (Jane Emory); "Rainbow Trail" 1932 (Fay Larkin); "Tombstone Canyon" 1932 (Jenny Lee); "The Fugitive" 1933 (Georgia Stevens); "Rainbow Ranch" 1933 (Molly Burke); "Riders of Destiny" 1933 (Fay Denton); "The Trail Drive" 1933 (Virginia); "Unknown Valley" 1933 (Sheila O'Neill); "Gun Justice" 1934 (Ray Harsh); "Honor of the Range" 1934 (Mary); "The Man Trailer" 1934 (Sally Ryan); "The Mine with the Iron Door" 1936 (Marta Hill); "Hollywood Cowboy" 1937 (Joyce Butler); "Roll Along, Cowboy" 1937 (Janet Blake); "Out West with the Hardys" 1938 (Marian Hardy).

Parker, Dorothea. Films: "Pirates of the Mississippi" 1963-Ger./Ital./Fr.; "Massacre at Marble City" 1964-Ger./Ital./Fr.

Parker, Earl. TV: *Hudson's Bay*— "Warrant's Depot" 3-29-58 (Thorne); *Have Gun Will Travel*—"The Lady" 11-15-58 (Chief's Son), "The Princess and the Gunfighter" 1-21-61 (Morton); *Gunsmoke*—"Marshal Proudfoot" 1-10-59 (Ben), "Jayhawkers" 1-31-59 (Snyder); *Wyatt Earp*—"Bat Jumps the Reservation" 2-10-59 (Officer); *The Rebel*—"The Scalp Hunter" 12-11-60 (Masi).

Parker, Edwin "Eddie" (1900-1/20/60). Films: "The Lawless Frontier" 1934; "The Lucky Texan" 1934 (Al Miller); "'Neath the Arizona Skies" 1934 (Henchman); "The Star Packer" 1934 (Parker); "The Trail Beyond" 1934 (Ryan, the Mountie); "The Ghost Rider" 1935 (Wirt); "Border Vengeance" 1935; "The Courageous Avenger" 1935 (Welford); "Rainbow Valley" 1935; "Westward Ho" 1935; "Git Along, Little Dogies" 1937; "God's Country and the Man" 1937 (Bill Briggs); "Heart of the North" 1938 (Gonzales); "Desperate Trails" 1939; "The Lone Ranger Rides Again" 1939-serial (Hank); "Mexicali Rose" 1939; "Northwest Passage" 1940 (Ranger); "Ragtime Cowboy Joe" 1940; "Virginia City" 1940 (Lieutenant); "They Died with Their Boots On" 1941 (Sentry); "Daredevils of the West" 1943-serial (Monk Mason/Attacker #2/Indian Rustler #1/Rock Heavy/Jim); "Days of Old Cheyenne" 1943; "The Lone Star Trail" 1943 (Lynch); "Thundering Trails" 1943; "Black Arrow" 1944-serial; "Flame of the West" 1945 (Murphy); "Frontier Feud" 1945 (Murphy); "The Lost Trail" 1945 (Bill); "Stranger from Santa Fe" 1945; "Days of Buffalo Bill" 1946; "King of the Forest Rangers" 1946-serial (Stover); "The Phantom Rider" 1946-serial (Martin); "Silver Range" 1946; "Trigger Fingers" 1946; "Adventures of Don Coyote" 1947 (Joe); "Jesse James Rides Again" 1947-serial (Captain Flint); "Raiders of the South" 1947; "Riders of the Lone Star" 1947; "Shadow Valley" 1947 (Foster); "Son of Zorro" 1947-serial (Melton); "South of the Chisholm Trail" 1947; "Trailing Danger" 1947; "Valley of Fear" 1947; "The Vigilante" 1947-serial (Doc); "The Adventures of Frank and Jesse James" 1948-serial (Jergens/Joe); "Black Hills" 1948; "Dangers of the Canadian Mounted" 1948-serial (Lowry); "The Fighting Ranger" 1948; "The Hawk of Powder River" 1948 (Cochrane); "Silver River" 1948 (Bugler); "The Strawberry Roan" 1948 (Jake); "The Tioga Kid" 1948 (Clem); "Whirlwind Raiders" 1948 (Red Jordan); "Ghost of Zorro" 1949-serial (Jim Cleaver); "Law of the West" 1949 (Mike); "Powder River Rustlers" 1949; "Range Justice" 1949 (Lacey); "Desperadoes of the West" 1950-serial (Martin); "Mule Train" 1950; "Al Jennings of Oklahoma" 1951 (Doc Wrightmire); "Barbed Wire" 1952 (Ed Parker); "The Hawk of Wild River" 1952 (Skeeter); "Horizons West" 1952 (Northerner); "The Kid from Broken Gun" 1952; "Law and

Order" 1953 (Man); "Winning of the West" 1953; "The Far Country" 1955 (Carson); "Curse of the Undead" 1959 (Henchman). ¶TV: *The Cisco Kid*—"The Will" 3-24-51, "Mad About Money" 3-22-52, "The Caution of Curley Thompson" 5-2-53, "Pancho's Niece" 9-5-53, "Gold, Death and Dynamite" 2-13-54; Colt .45—"A Time to Die" 10-25-57 (Clete); *Tales of the Texas Rangers*—"The Man from Sundown" 1-21-56, "Jace and Clay" 12-5-58 (Tucker).

Parker, Eleanor (1922-). Films: "Escape from Fort Bravo" 1953 (Carla Forester); "Many Rivers to Cross" 1955 (Mary Stuart Cherne); "King and Four Queens" 1956 (Sabina).

Parker, Fess (1927-). Films: "Springfield Rifle" 1952 (Jim Randolph); "Untamed Frontier" 1952 (Clem McCloud); "Take Me to Town" 1953 (Long John); "Thunder Over the Plains" 1953 (Kirby); "The Bounty Hunter" 1954; "Davy Crockett, King of the Wild Frontier" 1955 (Davy Crockett); "Davy Crockett and the River Pirates" 1956 (Davy Crockett); "The Great Locomotive Chase" 1956 (James J. Andrews); "Westward Ho the Wagons" 1956 (John "Doc" Grayson); "Old Yeller" 1957 (Jim Coates); "The Light in the Forest" 1958 (Del Hardy); "Alias Jesse James" 1959 (Davey Crockett); "The Hangman" 1959 (Sheriff Buck Weston); "The Jayhawkers" 1959 (Cam Bleeker); "Smoky" 1966 (Clint). ¶TV: *Annie Oakley*—Semi-Regular 1954 (Tom Conrad); *Death Valley Days*—"The Kickapoo Run" 5-12-54, "Miracle at Whiskey Gulch" 5-16-62 (Rev. Joel Todd); *Walt Disney Presents*—"Davy Crockett"—Regular 1954-55 (Davy Crockett); *Stories of the Century*—"The Dalton Gang" 5-20-55; *G.E. Theater*—"Aftermath" 4-17-60 (Jonathan West); *Destry*—"Destry Had a Little Lamb" 2-21-64 (Clarence Jones); *Daniel Boone*—Regular 1964-70 (Daniel Boone).

Parker, Franklin (1900-6/12/62). Films: "Wells Fargo" 1937 (Reporter); "Texas Rangers Ride Again" 1940 (Gas Station Attendant); "Cactus Caravan" 1950-short.

Parker, Fred. Films: "The Dude Wrangler" 1930 (Dude Guest); "Six Shootin' Sheriff" 1938; "Lightnin' Smith Returns" 1931 (Storekeeper); "Riders of the Rio" 1931 (Dad Lane); "The Galloping Kid" 1932; "Arizona Cyclone" 1934; "The Lone Rider" 1934; "Pals of the West" 1934-short; "Range Riders" 1934; "Rawhide Terror" 1934; "The Way of the West" 1934 (Dad Parker); "West of the

Law" 1934-short; "Arizona Trails" 1935; "Border Guns" 1935 (Bartender); "The Dawn Rider" 1935 (Doctor); "Courageous Avenger" 1935; "The Cowboy and the Bandit" 1935; "Lawless Range" 1935; "Paradise Canyon" 1935; "Timber Terrors" 1935 (Trapper Parker); "The Crooked Trail" 1936; "End of Trail" 1936; "Roamin' Wild" 1936 (Dad Sommers); "Valley of the Lawless" 1936; "Range Defenders" 1937; "The Red Rope" 1937; "Trouble in Texas" 1937 (Sheriff); "The Trusted Outlaw" 1937; "Two-Fisted Sheriff" 1937; "Mexicali Kid" 1938; "Pals of the Silver Sage" 1940.

Parker, Jack. Films: "Throw a Saddle on a Star" 1946; "Stampede" 1949 (Jake); "The Man Behind the Gun" 1952; "Seventh Cavalry" 1956.

Parker, Jameson (1950-). TV: *Bret Maverick*—"Faith, Hope and Clairty" 4-12-82 & 4-20-82 (Whitney Delaworth III).

Parker, Jean (1916-). Films: "The Texas Rangers" 1936 (Amanda Bailey); "The Barrier" 1937 (Necia); "Knights of the Range" 1940 (Holly Ripple); "Girl from Alaska" 1942 (Mary "Pete" McCoy); "Deerslayer" 1943 (Judith); "The Gunfighter" 1950 (Molly); "Toughest Man in Arizona" 1952 (Della); "Those Redheads from Seattle" 1953 (Liz); "A Lawless Street" 1955 (Cora Dean); "The Parson and the Outlaw" 1957 (Mrs. Jones); "Apache Uprising" 1966 (Mrs. Hawkes). ¶TV: *Stories of the Century*—"Cattle Kate" 4-29-55.

Parker, Kathleen. Films: "Sheriff with the Gold" 1966-Ital./Span.; "Up the MacGregors!" 1967-Ital./Span. (Belfast).

Parker, Lara (1942-). TV: *Kung Fu*—"King of the Mountain" 10-14-72 (Amy Allender).

Parker, Lew (1907-10/27/72). TV: *F Troop*—"The Ballot of Corporal Agarn" 10-27-66 (George Bagan).

Parker, Lloyd "Sunshine". Films: "Mr. Horn" TVM-1979. ¶TV: *Bonanza*—"My Friend, My Enemy" 1-12-69, "Dead Wrong" 12-7-69 (Bum #1), "The Trouble with Trouble" 10-25-70 (Wally); *Adventures of Brisco County, Jr.*—Pilot 8-27-93 (Stagecoach Driver #2).

Parker, Mary (1915-6/1/66). Films: "Ranch House Romeo" 1939-short.

Parker, Murray (1896-10/18/65). Films: "Sin Town" 1942 (Juggler). ¶TV: *Wanted—Dead or Alive*—"A House Divided" 2-20-60.

Parker, Warren (-7/31/76). TV:

Have Gun Will Travel—"The Outlaw" 9-21-57, "Lady on the Stagecoach" 1-17-59 (Clerk); *Wild Wild West*—"The Night of the Inferno" 9-17-65 (Train Engineer).

Parker, Willard (1912-). Films: "The Devil's Saddle Legion" 1937 (Hub Ordley); "Renegades" 1946 (Dr. Sam Martin); "Relentless" 1948 (Jeff Moyer); "Calamity Jane and Sam Bass" 1949 (Sheriff Will Egan); "Bandit Queen" 1950 (Dan Hinsdale); "Apache Drums" 1951 (Joe Madden); "The Great Jesse James Raid" 1953 (Jesse James); "The Vanquished" 1953 (Capt. Kirby); "The Naked Gun" 1956; "Lone Texan" 1959 (Clint Banister); "Walk Tall" 1960 (Capt. Ed Trask); "Young Jesse James" 1960 (Cole Younger); "Waco" 1966 (Pete Jenner). ¶TV: *Tales of the Texas Rangers*—Regular 1955-57 (Jace Pearson).

Parkes, Eddie (1893-7/24/85). Films: "The Gunfighter" 1950 (Barber).

Parkes, Gerard (1924-). Films: "Draw" CTVM-1984 (Judge Nat Fawcett).

Parkins, Barbara (1942-). Films: "Law of the Land" TVM-1976 (Jane Adams); "Testimony of Two Men" TVM-1977 (Marjorie Ferrier/Hilda Eaton). ¶TV: *Wagon Train*—"The Mark Miner Story" 11-15-61; *Wide Country*—"Our Ernie Kills People" 11-1-62 (Sharon Crosley); *Laramie*—"The Wedding Party" 1-29-63 (Marilee Bishop).

Parkinson, Cliff (1898-10/1/50). Films: "Borderland" 1937; "North of the Rio Grande" 1937; "Rough Ridin' Rhythm" 1937 (Hank); "Whistling Bullets" 1937 (Bart); "In Old Mexico" 1938; "Rawhide" 1938 (Pete); "Santa Fe Stampede" 1938; "Six-Gun Rhythm" 1939; "Law and Order" 1940 (Henchman); "Santa Fe Marshal" 1940; "Border Patrol" 1943 (Don Enrique); "Calling Wild Bill Elliott" 1943; "Riders of the Deadline" 1943; "Bordertown Trail" 1944; "The San Antonio Kid" 1944; "Zorro's Black Whip" 1944-serial (Ed/Trail Heavy #2); "Colorado Pioneers" 1945; "The Phantom Rider" 1946-serial (Ambusher #3/Road Heavy); "Ramrod" 1947 (Tom Peebles); "Sundown Riders" 1948 (Evans).

Parkison, Chuck (1945-11/23/76). Films: "The Honkers" 1972 (Announcer).

Parks, Andrew (1951-). TV: *The Men from Shiloh*—"The Angus Killer" 2-10-71 (Jimmy).

Parks, Eddie. Films: "Plainsman and the Lady" 1946 (Drunk); "Slaughter Trail" 1951 (Rufus Black); "The Bushwackers" 1952 (Funeral Franklin); "Forty Guns" 1957 (Sexton).

Parks, Larry (1914-4/13/75). Films: "North of the Rockies" 1942; "Deerslayer" 1943 (Jing-Good); "Renegades" 1946 (Ben "Taylor" Dembrow).

Parks, Michael (1938-). Films: "Stranger on the Run" TVM-1967 (Vincent McKay); "The Last Hard Men" 1976 (Sheriff Noel Nye); "The Return of Josey Wales" 1987 (Josey Wales). ¶TV: *Zane Grey Theater*— "Ransom" 11-17-60 (Juanito); *Gunsmoke*—"The Boys" 5-26-62 (Park); *Stoney Burke*—"The Mob Riders" 10-29-62 (Tack Reynolds); *Wagon Train*—"Heather and Hamish" 4-10-63 (Hamish), "The Michael Malone Story" 1-6-64 (Michael Malone); *Royce*—Pilot 5-21-76 (Blair Mabry); *Big Hawaii*—"Yesterdays" 1977.

Parnell, Emory (1892-6/22/79). Films: "Call of the Yukon" 1938 (Swede Trapper); "Let Freedom Ring" 1939 (Swede); "Union Pacific" 1939 (Foreman); "Northwest Mounted Police" 1940 (Constable Higgins); "Out West with the Peppers" 1940 (Ole); "Lady from Cheyenne" 1941 (Crowley); "The Outlaw" 1943 (Dolan); "Tall in the Saddle" 1944 (Sheriff Jackson); "Badman's Territory" 1946 (Bitter Creek); "Gas House Kids Go West" 1947 (Sgt. Casey); "Song of Idaho" 1948 (J. Chester Nottingham); "Hellfire" 1949 (Sheriff Duffy); "Massacre River" 1949 (Sgt. Johanssen); "Rock Island Trail" 1950 (Sen. Wells); "Trail of Robin Hood" 1950 (J. Corwin Aldridge); "The Lawless Breed" 1952 (Bartender); "Lost in Alaska" 1952 (Sherman); "Oklahoma Annie" 1952 (Judge Byrnes); "Fort Vengeance" 1953 (Fitzgibbon); "Shadows of Tombstone" 1953 (Sheriff Webb); "Battle of Rogue River" 1954 (Sgt. McClain); "Pardners" 1956 (Col. Hart); "Man of the West" 1958 (Gribble); "The Bounty Killer" 1965 (Sam). ¶TV: *Wild Bill Hickok*—"Johnny Deuce" 9-4-51, "School Teacher Story" 1-15-52, "The Rainmaker" 4-14-53; *The Lone Ranger*—"Diamond in the Rough" 8-27-53; *Maverick*—"The Jeweled Gun" 11-24-57 (Sheriff), "Black Fire" 3-16-58 (Cousin Lonnie), "A Fellow's Brother" 11-22-59 (Bill Anders), "The Misfortune Teller" 3-6-60 (Fred Grady), "Kiz" 12-4-60 (Hank), "One of Our Trains Is Missing" 4-22-62 (Clarence); *The Texan*—"The

Duchess of Denver" 1-5-59 (Samuel Dickens), "Lady Tenderfoot" 5-9-60 (Hugh Henshaw); *Lawman*—"The Gang" 3-29-59 (Hank), "The Wayfarer" 6-7-59 (Hank), "The Friend" 6-28-59 (Hank), "The Swamper" 6-5-60 (Hank); *Cheyenne*—"Outcast of Cripple Creek" 2-29-60 (Luther Cannon); *The Alaskans*—"Heart of Gold" 5-1-60 (Swede), "The Devil Made Five" 6-19-60 (Manager); *Klondike*—"The Man Who Owned Skagway" 1-30-61 (Mr. Sykes); *Bat Masterson*—"The Prescott Campaign" 2-2-61 (Ira Ponder).

Parnell, James (1923-12/27/61). Films: "War Paint" 1953 (Martin); "The Yellow Mountain" 1954 (Joe); "Shotgun" 1955 (Cavalryman); "Pardners" 1956 (Bank Teller); "Running Target" 1956 (Pryor); "Star in the Dust" 1956 (Marv Tremain); "Outlaw's Son" 1957 (Jorgenson); "War Drums" 1957 (Arizona); "Gun Fight" 1961 (Moose). ¶TV: *Wild Bill Hickok*—"Vigilante Story" 1-22-52; *The Lone Ranger*—"Frame for Two" 10-23-52; *Sheriff of Cochise*—"Helldorado" 12-7-56 (Tex); *Have Gun Will Travel*—"Winchester Quarantine" 10-5-57, "A Sense of Justice" 11-1-58; *The Texan*—"A Tree for Planting" 11-10-58 (Jake); *The Rifleman*— "The Blowout" 10-13-59; *The Deputy*—"Silent Gun" 1-23-60; *Wanted— Dead or Alive*—"The Most Beautiful Woman" 1-23-60 (Fat Man); *Bonanza*—"Escape to the Ponderosa" 3-5-60 (Mertz); *Bat Masterson*—"Welcome to Paradise" 5-5-60 (Sheriff); *The Alaskans*—"The Ballad of Whitehorse" 6-12-60 (Robert Howard).

Parr, Thelma. Films: "The Devil's Tower" 1928 (Doris Stilwell).

Parrish, Helen (1924-2/22/59). Films: "The Big Trail" 1930 (Honey Girl); "Cimarron" 1931 (Young Donna Cravat); "In Old California" 1942 (Ellen Sanford); "Overland Mail" 1942-serial (Barbara Gilbert); "Sunset Serenade" 1942 (Sylvia Clark); "Quick on the Trigger" 1948 (Nora Reed); "The Wolf Hunters" 1949 (Marcia).

Parrish, John. Films: "Unexpected Guest" 1947 (David Potter, the Attorney); "The Dead Don't Dream" 1948 (Jeff Potter); "Four Faces West" 1948 (Frenger); "Canadian Pacific" 1949 (Mr. Gautier); "Riders in the Sky" 1949; "Wagons West" 1952 (Chief Black Kettle); "Saginaw Trail" 1953 (Walt Curry). ¶TV: *The Lone Ranger*—"Pete and Pedro" 10-27-49; *My Friend Flicka*— "Lost River" 6-15-56; *Annie Oakley*— "Annie and the Bicycle Riders" 7-8-

56 (Hank); *Rough Riders*—"The Imposters" 10-30-58 (Col. Anson); *Death Valley Days*—"A Bullet for the Captain" 1-13-59; *Wanted—Dead or Alive*—"Mental Lapse" 1-2-60 (Sheriff Persall), "The Medicine Man" 11-23-60.

Parrish, Julie (1940-). TV: *Temple Houston*—"The Guardian" 1-2-64 (Maggie Ballard); *Gunsmoke*—"The Warden" 5-16-64 (Cool Dawn); *Bonanza*—"Horse of a Different Hue" 9-18-66 (Patty Lou Fairchild); *Pistols 'n' Petticoats*—10-1-66 (Bitter Blossom); *Death Valley Days*—"Along Came Mariana" 5-27-67 (Mariana Jaramilio).

Parrish, Leslie (1935-). TV: *Bat Masterson*—"The Elusive Baguette" 6-2-60 (Lucy Carter), "A Time to Die" 12-15-60 (Lisa Anders); *Wild Wild West*—"The Night the Wizard Shook the Earth" 10-1-65 (Greta Lundquist); *Iron Horse*—"Dry Run to Glory" 1-6-68 (Eve Lewis); *The Big Valley*— "Bounty on a Barkley" 2-26-68 (Layle Johnson).

Parrott, Charles. *see* Chase, Charley.

Parry, Harvey (1900-9/18/85). Films: "Silver City" 1951 (Townsman); "How the West Was Won" 1962 (Henchman); "Paint Your Wagon" 1969 (Higgins); "Oklahoma Crude" 1973 (Bliss); "Blazing Saddles" 1974. ¶TV: *Laredo*—"The Land Grabbers" 12-9-65.

Parry, Ivan. Films: "Red River" 1948 (Bunk Kenneally).

Parsons, Estelle (1927-). Films: "The Gun and the Pulpit" TVM-1974 (Sadie Underwood).

Parsons, Milton (1904-5/15/80). Films: "Girl from Alaska" 1942 (Sanderson); "The Great Man's Lady" 1942 (Froman); "Outcasts of the Trail" 1949 (Elias Dunkenscold); "The Capture" 1950 (Thin Man); "Last of the Comanches" 1952 (Prophet Satterlee). ¶TV: *The Rifleman*—"Letter of the Law" 12-1-59, "The Vision" 3-22-60 (Perkins), "Strange Town" 10-25-60; *Lawman*— "Chantay" 11-13-60 (Grimshaw), "Explosion" 6-3-62 (Murdoch); *Rawhide*—"Incident of the Blackstorms" 5-26-61 (Williams); *The Dakotas*— "Requiem at Dancer's Hill" 2-18-63 (Cal Jackson); *Wild Wild West*—"The Night of the Bars of Hell" 3-4-66 (Executioner), "The Night of the Tycoons" 3-28-69 (Kessel); *Bonanza*— "Dead Wrong" 12-7-69 (Undertaker); *Kung Fu*—"The Centoph" 4-4-74 & 4-11-74 (Rev. Mr. Stekel).

Parsons, William "Smiling

Billy" (1878-9/29/19). Films: "His Partner's Sacrifice" 1915; "The Vigilantes" 1918 (Don Enrico Felipe).

Parton, Reg. Films: "Four Guns to the Border" 1954 (Cashier); "Backlash" 1956 (Tom Welker); "The Hired Gun" 1957 (Clint); "Apache Territory" 1958 (Conley); "Law of the Lawless" 1964 (Johnson Brother); "Young Fury" 1965 (Jeb); "Johnny Reno" 1966 (Bartender); "Waco" 1966 (Ike Jenner); "Fort Utah" 1967 (Rafe); "Hostile Guns" 1967 (Chig); "Red Tomahawk" 1967 (Prospector); "Arizona Bushwhackers" 1968 (Curly). ¶TV: *The Texan*—"Law of the Gun" 9-29-58 (Pete Bray), "The Ringer" 2-16-59 (Warren Mastes), "Dangerous Ground" 12-14-59, "End of Track" 12-21-59, "Rough Track to Payday" 12-28-59, "Friend of the Family" 1-4-60, "The Invisible Noose" 5-16-60 (Pete), "The Mountain Man" 5-23-60, "The Accuser" 6-6-60; *Stripe Playhouse*—"Ballad to Die By" 7-31-59 (Harry Shay); *Rawhide*—"Incident of the Running Man" 5-5-61, "Incident Before Black Pass" 5-19-61, "The Blue Sky" 12-8-61 (Callaway), "A Woman's Place" 3-30-62; *The Rifleman*—"The Bullet" 2-25-63 (Victim); *Branded*—"The Bounty" 2-21-65 (Vince Starrett); *Cimarron Strip*—"The Legend of Jud Starr" 9-14-67; *Barbary Coast*—"Guns for a Queen" 10-6-75 (Dundee).

Partridge, Joseph. Films: "Convict Stage" 1965; "Fort Courageous" 1965. ¶TV: *Sky King*—"Dead Man's Will" 4-6-52 (Sam Driver); *Jim Bowie*—"The Puma" 5-23-58 (Jess Miller); *Maverick*—"You Can't Beat the Percentage" 10-4-59 (Dealer); *Wanted—Dead or Alive*—"Angela" 1-9-60 (Sheriff Wilson); *Colt .45*—"Under False Pretenses" 1-10-60 (Dade Wagner); *Wichita Town*—"The Legend of Tom Horn" 3-30-60 (Joe Moss); *Rawhide*—"Incident of the Silent Web" 6-3-60; *Bonanza*—"The Rescue" 2-25-61 (Gus Tatum).

Pasco, Richard (1926-). Films: "Six Black Horses" 1962 (Charlie).

Pasha, Kalla (1879-6/10/33). Films: "Ruggles of Red Gap" 1923 (Herr Schwitz).

Pasolini, Pier Paolo (1922-11/1/75). Films: "Let Them Rest" 1967-Ital./Ger.

Pastorelli, Robert. Films: "Dances with Wolves" 1990 (Timmons).

Pataki, Michael (1938-). Films: "The Call of the Wild" TVM-1976 (Stranger); "High Noon, Part II: The Return of Will Kane" TVM-1980

(Darold); "Cowboy" TVM-1983 (Sheriff Grover). ¶TV: *Rawhide*—"A Man Called Mushy" 10-23-64 (Anselmo); *Dundee and the Culhane*—10-25-67 (Charlie Hughes); *Bonanza*—"Frenzy" 1-30-72 (Nick); *Kung Fu*—"The Centoph" 4-4-74 & 4-11-74 (Buskirk); *Father Murphy*—Pilot 11-3-81 (Mr. Adams), "Will's Surprise" 1-12-82 (Mr. Adams).

Pate, Michael (1920-). Films: "Hondo" 1953 (Vittoro); "A Lawless Street" 1955 (Harley Baskam); "Reprisal!" 1956 (Bert Shipley); "Seventh Cavalry" 1956 (Capt. Benteen); "The Oklahoman" 1957 (Charlie Smith); "The Tall Stranger" 1957 (Charley); "Curse of the Undead" 1959 (Drake Robey); "Westbound" 1959 (Mace); "Walk Like a Dragon" 1960 (Will Allen); "The Canadians" 1961-Brit. (Chief Four Horns); "Sergents 3" 1962 (Watanka); "California" 1963 (Don Francisco Hernandez); "McClintock" 1963 (Puma); "Advance to the Rear" 1964 (Thin Elk); "The Great Sioux Massacre" 1965 (Sitting Bull); "Major Dundee" 1965 (Sierra Charriba); "Return of the Gunfighter" TVM-1967 (Frank Boone); "Mad Dog Morgan" 1975-Australia (Superintement Winch). ¶TV: *Broken Arrow*—"The Mail Riders" 9-25-56 (Gokliya), "Battle at Apache Pass" 10-2-56 (Gokliya), "Indian Agent" 10-9-56 (Geronimo); *Zane Grey Theater*—"The Fearful Courage" 10-12-56 (Gunman), "To Sit in Judgment" 11-13-58 (Charlie Spawn), "Trouble at Tres Cruces" 3-26-59 (Miguel), "The Last Bugle" 11-24-60 (Geronimo); *Gunsmoke*—"Big Girl Lost" 4-20-57 (Philip Locke), "Renegade White" 4-11-59 (Wild Hog), "Blue Horse" 6-6-69 (Blue Horse), "The Violators" 10-17-64 (Buffalo Calf); *Have Gun Will Travel*—"Strange Vendetta" 10-26-57 (Don Miguel Rojas), "The Race" 10-28-61 (Tamasun), "Silent Death" 3-31-62 (Indian Chief); *Cheyenne*—"Border Affair" 11-5-57 (Colonel Rissot), "Johnny Brassbuttons" 12-3-62 (Chief Chato); *Sugarfoot*—"The Ghost" 1-28-58 (Ross Garrett); *Wagon Train*—"A Man Called Horse" 3-26-58 (Yellow Robe), "The Indian Girl Story" 4-18-65; *Zorro*—"The Eagle's Brood" 4-10-58 (Salvadore Quintana), "Zorro by Proxy" 4-17-58 (Salvadore Quintana), "Quintana Makes a Choice" 4-24-58 (Salvadore Quintana), "Zorro Lights a Fuse" 5-1-58 (Salvadore Quintana); *The Rifleman*—"New Orleans Menace" 12-2-58 (Xavier), "The Second Witness" 3-3-59 (Brad Davis), "The Visitors" 1-26-60 (Pete), "The Mescalero

Curse" 4-18-61 (Mogollan), "The Executioner" 5-7-62 (Sanchez); *The Texan*—"No Tears for the Dead" 12-8-58 (George Brandon), "End of Track" 12-21-59 (Emory), "Captive Crew" 2-22-60; *Rawhide*—"Incident of the Power and the Plow" 2-13-59 (Taslatch), "Incident of the Challenge" 10-14-60 (Mitla), "Incident at Superstition Prairie" 12-2-60 (Sankeno), "Incident of the Boomerang" 3-24-61 (Richard Goffage), "Incident at Ten Trees" 1-2-64 (Cheyenne Chief Running Horse); *The Adventures of Rin Tin Tin*—"The Devil Rides Point" 2-27-59 (Sleeping Dog); *Wanted—Dead or Alive*—"Bounty for a Bride" 4-4-59 (Victorio), "The Conquerers" 5-2-59 (Capt. Manuel Herrara); *Black Saddle*—"Client: Frome" 4-25-59 (Garnie Starrit); *The Law of the Plainsman*—"Common Ground" 2-11-60 (Frank Deegan); *Wichita Town*—"The Legend of Tom Horn" 3-30-60 (Kotana); *Laramie*—"Midnight Rebellion" 4-5-60 (Loren Corteen), "The Perfect Gift" 1-2-62, "The Day of the Savage" 3-13-62 (Toriano); *Tales of Wells Fargo*—"Pearl Hart" 5-9-60 (Hogan), "Kelly's Clover Girls" 12-9-61 (Kalo); *Maverick*—"Flood's Folly" 2-19-61 (Chet Whitehead); *The Tall Man*—"The Legend and the Gun" 4-1-61 (Harry Young); *Lawman*—"The Cold One" 11-12-61 (King Harris); *Frontier Circus*—"The Shaggy Kings" 12-7-61 (Quanah Parker); *Death Valley Days*—"Feud at Dome Rock" 3-21-62 (Harry), "Measure of a Man" 11-17-63 (Chacun), "Samaritans, Mountain Style" 11-19-66 (Frenchy Godey); *The Dakotas*—"Crisis at High Banjo" 2-11-63 (Hal Regis); *The Virginian*—"Man of Violence" 12-25-63 (Mike McGoff), "A King's Ransom" 2-25-70 (Alf); *Temple Houston*—"The Gun That Swept the West" 3-5-64 (Nat Cramer); *Daniel Boone*—"The Sound of Wings" 11-12-64 (Pushta), "The Allegiances" 9-22-66 (Raccuwan); *Branded*—"Call to Glory" 2-27-66, 3-6-66 & 3-13-66 (Crazy Horse); *Wild Wild West*—"The Night of the Infernal Machine" 12-23-66 (Bledsoe); *Rango*—"My Teepee Runneth Over" 3-10-67 (Burning Arrow); *Hondo*—Regular 1967 (Vittoro).

Patric, Jason (1966-). Films: "Geronimo: An American Legend" 1993 (Lt. Charles Gatewood).

Patrick, Butch (1953-). TV: *Death Valley Days*—"Kingdom for a Horse" 12-1-63 (Tommy); *Bonanza*—"The Prime of Life" 12-29-63; *Pistols 'n' Petticoats*—"A Crooked Line" 9-17-66 (Chad Turner); *Gunsmoke*—"Friend" 1-25-64 (Runt), "Mad Dog"

1-14-67 (Tom John); *Rawhide*—"Incident of the Pied Piper" 2-6-64; *Daniel Boone*—"Copperhead Izzy" 1-30-69 (Black Cat Jack).

Patrick, Cynthia. TV: *Death Valley Days*—"Loophole" 4-5-61 (Lisbeth).

Patrick, Dennis (1918-). TV: *The Lone Ranger*—"Prisoner in Jeopardy" 8-20-53; *Gunsmoke*—"Land Deal" 11-8-58 (Trumbill); *Sugarfoot*—"The Royal Raiders" 3-17-59 (Cal Sears); *Buckskin*—"Mail-Order Groom" 4-20-59 (Dennis Wainwright); *The Deputy*—"Focus of Doom" 11-7-59 (Regan); *Riverboat*—"Guns for Empire" 12-20-59 (Lancing); *Laramie*—"Cemetery Road" 4-12-60 (Ross), "Stolen Tribute" 1-31-61 (Deke Belden), "Men in Shadows" 5-30-61 (Kramer), "The Fatal Step" 10-24-61 (Wes Darrin), "Shadows in the Dust" 1-16-62 (Rolph), "The Betrayers" 1-22-63 (Ray Thatcher), "The Marshals" 4-30-63 (Vern Buckner); *Bonanza*—"The Hopefuls" 10-8-60 (Sam Bord); *Wanted—Dead or Alive*—"The Looters" 10-12-60 (Eli); *Tales of Wells Fargo*—"The Killing of Johnny Lash" 11-21-60 (Nevada); *Stagecoach West*: *Object: Patrimony*" 1-3-61 (Pasquindice), "The Swindler" 6-13-61 (Hollis Collier); *The Outlaws*—"Sam Bass" 5-4-61 (Joel Collins); *The Tall Man*—"Rio Doloroso" 2-10-62 (Curtis); *Wagon Train*—"The Amos Billings Story" 3-14-62 (Josh Anders); *The Virginian*—"Big Day, Great Day" 10-24-62; *Empire*—"The Tiger Inside" 2-12-63 (Hoot Hinkley); *The Dakotas*—"Incident at Rapid City" 3-4-63 (Sergeant Bonner); *A Man Called Shenandoah*—"Survival" 9-20-65 (Red); *Custer*—"The Gauntlet" 12-20-67 (Finn MacDiarmuid); *The Big Valley*—"Fall of a Hero" 2-5-68 (Daniel Mannis), "A Stranger Everywhere" 12-9-68 (Ted Halyard), "The Battle of Mineral Springs" 3-24-69 (Crawford); *Barbary Coast*—"Arson and Old Lace" 11-14-75 (Peter Dunn); *Paradise*—"A Matter of Honor" 4-8-89 & 4-15-89 (Clay Jennings).

Patrick, Dorothy (1922-5/31/87). Films: "Boy's Ranch" 1946 (Susan Walker); "Under Mexicali Stars" 1950 (Madeline Wellington); "Desert Passage" 1952 (Rosa); "Road Agent" 1952 (Sally Clayton); "Savage Frontier" 1953 (Elizabeth Webb); "The Outlaw Stallion" 1954 (Mary Saunders); "Thunder Pass" 1954; "The Peacemaker" 1956 (Ben Seale). ¶TV: *Wild Bill Hickok*—"Photographer Story" 2-5-52, "Sundown Valley" 11-4-52; *Cowboy G-Men*—"Sidewinder" 5-2-53.

Patrick, Gail (1911-7/6/80). Films: "The Mysterious Rider" 1933 (Mary Foster); "To the Last Man" 1933 (Ann Hayden Standing); "Wagon Wheels" 1934 (Nancy Wellington); "Wanderer of the Wasteland" 1935 (Ruth Virey); "Man of Conquest" 1939 (Margaret Lea); "Reno" 1939 (Jessie Gibbs); "Plainsman and the Lady" 1946 (Cathy Arnesen); "King of the Wild Horses" 1947.

Patrick, Gil (1896-2/21/71). Films: "Cheyenne Roundup" 1943 (Perkins); "'Neath Canadian Skies" 1946; "Buffalo Bill Rides Again" 1947 (Simpson); "Hoppy's Holiday" 1947 (Jay).

Patrick, John. TV: *Gunsmoke*—"Tape Day for Kitty" 3-24-56 (Jonas), "The Roundup" 9-29-56 (Dad); *The Restless Gun*—"Silver Threads" 12-16-57 (Sean O'Hara); *Bonanza*—"The Saga of Annie O'-Toole" 10-24-59 (Kevin O'Toole).

Patrick, Lee (1906-11/21/82). Films: "Border Cafe" 1937 (Ellie); "Singing Spurs" 1948; "The Doolins of Oklahoma" 1949 (Melissa Price); "Take Me to Town" 1953 (Rose). ¶TV: *Circus Boy*—"Counterfeit Clown" 4-7-57 (Mrs. Minerva Murdock); *Lawman*—"The Chef" 3-1-59 (Mrs. Young), "The Old War Horse" 10-9-60 (Bess Harper); *Wagon Train*—"The Steele Family" 6-17-59 (Mrs. Steele); *The Rifleman*—"Guilty Conscience" 4-2-62 (Leota Carraway).

Patrick, Lory. TV: *Tales of Wells Fargo*—Regular 1961-62 (Tina); *Wagon Train*—"The Nancy Davis Story" 5-16-62 (Nancy Davis), "The Levy-McGowan Story" 11-14-62 (Rachel Levy), "The Blane Wessels Story" 4-17-63 (Laura); *Wide Country*—"Straightjacket for an Indian" 10-25-62 (Georgina); *Laramie*—"The Renegade Brand" 2-26-63 (Laurie); *Death Valley Days*—"The Paper Dynasty" 2-29-64; *Bonanza*—"Journey to Terror" 2-5-67 (Rita).

Patrick, Millicent. Films: "Man Without a Star" 1955 (Box Car Alice). ¶TV: *The Roy Rogers Show*—"The Ride of the Ranchers" 4-20-52 (Elena); *The Restless Gun*—"Hornitas Town" 2-10-58 (Rosita); *Laramie*—"The Jailbreakers" 12-19-61.

Patten, Luana (1938-). Films: "Melody Time" 1948; "Joe Dakota" 1957 (Jody Weaver); "A Thunder of Drums" 1961 (Tracey Hamilton); "Shoot Out at Big Sag" 1962 (Hannah Hawker). ¶TV: *The Restless Gun*—"The Nowhere Kid" 10-20-58 (Celia Austin); *Cimarron City*—"Twelve Guns" 11-1-58 (Elizabeth Buckley); *Wagon Train*—"The Hunter

Malloy Story" 1-21-59 (Natalie Garner), "The Ruth Marshall Story" 12-30-59 (Ruth Marshall); *Wanted—Dead or Alive*—"Call Your Shot" 2-7-59 (Abbie Fenton); *Rawhide*—"Incident of the Druid's Curse" 1-8-60 (Naeve); *Bonanza*—"Credit for a Kill" 10-23-66 (Lorna); *F Troop*—"The Ballot of Corporal Agarn" 10-27-66 (Mindy).

Patten, Robert (1924-). Films: "Westworld" 1973 (Technician). ¶TV: *Wagon Train*—"The Mary Halstead Story" 11-20-57 (Kermit); *Wyatt Earp*—"Sweet Revenge" 1-28-58, "Kill the Editor" 12-16-58 (Jim Murdock); *Gunsmoke*—"Carmen" 5-24-58 (Nate Brand); *The Tall Man*—"A Bounty for Billy" 10-15-60 (Burt Summers); *The Virginian*—"Big Day, Great Day" 10-24-62; *Bonanza*—"The Price of Salt" 2-4-68 (Pardee).

Patterson, Elizabeth (1874-1/31/66). Films: "The Lone Star Ranger" 1930 (Sarah Martin); "High, Wide and Handsome" 1937 (Grandma Cortlandt); "Belle Starr" 1941 (Sarah); "The Vanishing Virginian" 1941 (Grandma); "The Oregon Trail" 1959 (Maria Cooper). ¶TV: *Jim Bowie*—"A Fortune for Madame" 10-18-57 (Mme. De Vaux).

Patterson, Floyd (1935-). TV: *Wild Wild West*—"The Night of the Juggernaut" 10-11-68 (Lyle Dixon); *Daniel Boone*—"The Road to Freedom" 10-2-69 (George Hill).

Patterson, Hank (1888-8/23/75). Films: "Abilene Town" 1946 (Doug Neil); "The El Paso Kid" 1946 (Jeff Winters); "Santa Fe Uprising" 1946; "Wild Beauty" 1946 (Ed); "Bells of San Angelo" 1947 (the Old Timer); "Robin Hood of Texas" 1947; "Springtime in the Sierras" 1947 (Old Timer); "Under Colorado Skies" 1947 (Slim); "The Denver Kid" 1948; "Night Time in Nevada" 1948 (2nd Tramp); "Oklahoma Badlands" 1948 (Fred); "Relentless" 1948 (Bob Pliny); "The Cowboy and the Indians" 1949 (Tom Garber); "Red Canyon" 1949 (Osborne); "Riders in the Sky" 1949 (Luke); "Desperadoes of the West" 1950-serial (Hardrock Haggerty); "The Gunfighter" 1950 (Jake); "The James Brothers of Missouri" 1950-serial (Duffy/Waller); "Don Daredevil Rides Again" 1951-serial (Buck Bender); "Indian Uprising" 1951 (Jake Wilson); "Silver City Bonanza" 1951 (Postman); "California Conquest" 1952 (Sam Lawrence); "Canadian Mounties vs. Atomic Invaders" 1953-serial (Jed Larson, the Trapper); "The First Traveling Saleslady" 1956 (1st Cowhand); "The Storm Rider" 1957

(Milstead); "Escape from Red Rock" 1958 (Grover); "Terror in a Texas Town" 1958 (Brady); "Lone Texan" 1959 (Jack Stone); "Gunfighters of Abilene" 1960 (Andy Ferris). ¶TV: *The Lone Ranger*—"Legion of Old Timers" 10-6-49, "Gold Train" 3-16-50; *The Cisco Kid*—"Dog Story" 5-12-51, "The Old Bum" 6-9-51, "Water Rights" 7-7-51, "The Devil's Deputy" 5-10-52, "The Fire Engine" 5-31-52, "Pot of Gold" 4-25-53; *The Adventures of Kit Carson*—Regular 1951-55; *The Roy Rogers Show*—"Outlaws' Town" 3-1-52, "The Hermit's Secret" 5-1-52, "Haunted Mine of Paradise Valley" 5-18-52, "The Young Defenders" 10-3-54 (Hermit); *Death Valley Days*—"Sego Lillies" 1-14-53 (Nephi), "Ten Feet of Nothing" 1-5-60 (Abe); *Wild Bill Hickok*—"Wild Bill's Odyssey" 3-31-53; *The Gene Autry Show*—"Outlaw of Blue Mesa" 9-7-54; *Wyatt Earp*—"Siege at Little Alamo" 2-5-57 (Dunbar), "One" 4-15-58; *Annie Oakley*—"Desperate Men" 2-24-57 (Jake Wilkin); *Broken Arrow*—"The Teacher" 11-19-57 (Stagecoach Driver); *Have Gun Will Travel*—"The Hanging Cross" 12-21-57, "Gun Shy" 3-29-58, "The Man Who Wouldn't Talk" 9-20-58 (Pappy French), "Duel at Florence" 10-11-58, "The Unforgiven" 11-7-59 (Ronson), "The Lady on the Wall" 2-20-60 (Rafe Adams), "El Paso Stage" 4-15-61 (the Judge), "Blind Circle" 12-16-61 (Jess Larker), "The Hunt" 2-3-62 (Jesse), "The Sanctuary" 6-22-63 (William Barton); *The Restless Gun*—"Sheriff Billy" 3-10-58 (Milt Hatten); *Trackdown*—"Three Legged Fox" 12-5-58 (Taverner); *Bat Masterson*—"Trail Pirate" 12-31-58 (Prospector), "Tempest at Tioga Pass" 1-5-61 (Soda Smith); *Maverick*—"The Saga of Waco Williams" 2-15-59 (Perkins); *Tales of Wells Fargo*—"Lola Montez" 2-16-59 (Larson), "Kelly's Clover Girls" 12-9-61 (Coleman Flagg), "End of a Minor God" 4-7-62 (Benson), "Don't Wake a Tiger" 5-12-62 (Stage Driver); *Bronco*—"Prairie Skipper" 5-5-59 (Chips); *Riverboat*—"About Roger Mowbray" 9-27-59 (Rafe); *The Alaskans*—"Gold Sled" 10-4-59; *Zane Grey Theater*—"The Sunday Man" 2-25-60, "A Warm Day in Heaven" 3-23-61 (Jonas Mulvey); *Gunsmoke*—"Crowbait Bob" 3-26-60 (Crowbait Bob), "I Thee Wed" 4-16-60 (Judge), "The Bobsy Twins" 5-21-60 (Carl), "The Blacksmith" 9-17-60 (Spooner), "Ben Toliver's Stud" 11-26-60 (Carl), "Durham Bull" 3-31-62 (Cowboy), Regular 1960-75 (Hank Miller, the Stableman); *Rawhide*—"Incident of the Last Chance"

6-10-60 (Dan Simmons), "Incident of the Wager on Payday" 6-16-61; *Johnny Ringo*—"Coffin Sam" 6-16-60 (Old Man); *The Tall Man*—"Garrett and the Kid" 9-10-60 (Jake), "The Hunt" 1-27-62 (Amos); *Lawman*—"The Town Boys" 9-18-60 (Harrison Lester); *Bonanza*—"The Hopefuls" 10-8-60; *The Westerner*—"Line Camp" 12-9-60; *Klondike*—"Queen of the Klondike" 1-23-61 (Spunky); *Wagon Train*—"The Eleanor Culhane Story" 5-17-61 (Old Man); *The Rifleman*—"The Debit" 3-5-62 (Abe Mercer); *Laramie*—"The Replacement" 3-27-62; *Empire*—"65 Miles Is a Long, Long Way" 4-23-63 (Hughes); *Daniel Boone*—"The Reunion" 3-11-65 (Jed Harper), "The Inheritance" 10-26-67 (Gray), "The Bait" 11-7-68 (Fiddler); *A Man Called Shenandoah*—"The Reward" 11-29-65 (Godey); *Wild Wild West*—"The Night of the Human Trigger" 12-3-65 (Mr. Porter); *The Legend of Jesse James*—"Benjamin Bates" 2-28-66 (Porter); *Laredo*—"A Very Small Assignment" 3-17-66 (Stationmaster); *Cimarron Strip*—"The Battle of Blood Stone" 10-12-67; *The Guns of Will Sonnett*—"First Love" 11-3-67 (Stableman).

Patterson, Herbert. Films: "The Peacemaker" 1956 (Gray Arnett). ¶TV: *Have Gun Will Travel*—"Return to Fort Benjamin" 1-30-60 (Sergeant Kern), "The Tender Gun" 10-22-60 (Heck); *Rawhide*—"Incident at Tinker's Dam" 2-5-60, "Incident of the Painted Lady" 5-12-61 (Clint Coffee), "A Woman's Place" 3-30-62 (Harv Carter), "Incident of the Querencias" 12-7-62 (Lieutenant), "Incident at Zebulon" 3-5-64.

Patterson, James (1932-8/19/72). TV: *Stoney Burke*—"Joby" 3-18-63 (Mark); *The Big Valley*—"Young Marauders" 10-6-65 (Jamie Drumm); *Bonanza*—"A World Full of Cannibals" 12-22-68 (Charles Ball).

Patterson, John. Films: "Born to the West" 1937 (Hardy); "Forlorn River" 1937 (Ben Ide).

Patterson, Kenneth. Films: "The Lady from Texas" 1951; "The Violent Men" 1955 (1st Farmer); "The Plunderers" 1960 (2nd Citizen). ¶TV: *The Lone Ranger*—"Stage to Tishomingo" 10-28-54; *Telephone Time*—"Sam Houston's Decision" 12-10-57 (George Hockley); *Black Saddle*—"Client: Neal Adams" 5-9-59; *Johnny Ringo*—"The Derelict" 5-26-60 (Theodore Polk); *Zane Grey Theater*—"A Gun for Willie" 10-6-60 (Tim), "The Black Wagon" 12-1-60 (Quint); *Stoney Burke*—"Death Rides a Pale Horse" 1-14-63 (Doc Sterling);

The Virginian—"A Distant Fury" 3-20-63 (Mr. Colby).

Patterson, Lee (1929-). Films: "Chato's Land" 1972 (George Dunn). ¶TV: *The Alaskans*—"Behind the Moon" 3-6-60 (Tom Kirk), "Sign of the Kodiak" 5-29-60 (Jeff Warren); *The Deputy*—"The Chain of Action" 5-7-60 (Lige Schofield); *The Virginian*—"Show Me a Hero" 11-17-65 (Midge Conway); *Bonanza*—"The Crime of Johnny Mule" 2-25-68 (Virgil Lowden).

Patterson, Melody (1947-). TV: *F Troop*—Regular 1965-67 (Wrangler Jane).

Patterson, Neva (1922-). Films: "Skin Game" 1971 (Mrs. Claggart). ¶TV: *Satins and Spurs* 9-12-54 (Ursula); *Nichols*—Regular 1971-72 (Ma Ketcham); *Bret Maverick*—"The Mayflower Women's Historical Society" 2-2-82 (Mrs. Emma Crittenson).

Patterson, Pat (1920-). Films: "Rustlers" 1949. ¶TV: *The Guns of Will Sonnett*—"Sunday in Paradise" 12-15-67 (Matthew).

Patterson, Shirley (Shawn Smith) (1921-4/11/95). Films: "North of the Rockies" 1942; "Riders of the Northland" 1942 (Sheila Taylor); "Riding Through Nevada" 1942; "Law of the Northwest" 1943 (Michel Darcy); "Phony Express" 1943-short (Lola); "The Texas Kid" 1943 (Nancy); "Riding West" 1944 (Alice Morton); "The Vigilantes Ride" 1944 (Jane Andrews); "Driftin' River" 1946 (J.C. Morgan); "Stars Over Texas" 1946 (Terry Lawrence); "Tumbleweed Trail" 1946 (Robin Ryan); "Black Hills" 1948 (Janet). ¶TV: *Wyatt Earp*—"Four" 5-27-58 (Blanche).

Patterson, Walter. Films: "Lightning Bryce" 1919-serial; "Triple Action" 1925 (Bandit); "Red Blood" 1926 (Sodapop); "The Oklahoma Kid" 1929; "The Mounted Stranger" 1930 (Lookout); "Wild West Whoopee" 1931; "Flaming Guns" 1932 (Rustler); "Boots of Destiny" 1937 (Pasquale); "Ride 'Em, Cowgirl" 1939.

Pattison, Gerry. Films: "Law of the West" 1949 (Tennessee).

Patton, Bill (1894-12/12/51). Films: "Boss of the Lazy Y" 1918 (Dade); "Wild Life" 1918 (Bill); "Bare-Fisted Gallagher" 1919 (Driver #1); "Leave It to Susan" 1919; "A Sage Brush Hamlet" 1919 (Larry's Pal); "Blazing the Way" 1920; "Sand!" 1920 (Pete Beckett); "Outlawed" 1921 (Bob Fleming); "Bulldog Courage" 1922 (Sheriff Weber); "Tracks" 1922

(Norman Draper); "Cyclone Jones" 1923 (Kirk Davis); "Ace of the Law" 1924 (Bill Kennedy); "Battlin' Buckaroo" 1924; "The Desert Secret" 1924; "Fightin' Thru" 1924; "A Game Fighter" 1924; "The Last Man" 1924; "The Smoking Trail" 1924; "Fangs of Fate" 1925 (Bob Haynes); "Fightin' Odds" 1925 (Bruce Martin); "Flashing Steeds" 1925 (Bill Swift); "Fort Frayne" 1925 (Royle Farrar/Graice); "Warrior Gap" 1925 (Courier); "Beyond the Trail" 1926 (Bill); "The Last Chance" 1926; "Temporary Sheriff" 1926; "Under Fire" 1926 (Lt. Tom Brennan); "Western Trails" 1926; "The Flying U Ranch" 1927 (Happy Jack); "Lucky Spurs" 1927; "The Bantam Cowboy" 1928 (Chuck Rogers); "Orphan of the Sage" 1928 (Nevada Naldene); "The Pinto Kid" 1928 (Rufe Sykes); "Young Whirlwind" 1928 (Bart); "A Close Call" 1929; "The Freckled Rascal" 1929 (Bill Latham); "In Line of Duty" 1929; "The One Man Dog" 1929 (Gadsky); "Pals of the Prairie" 1929 (Pete Sanger); "Two-Gun Morgan" 1929; "The Vagabond Cub" 1929 (Pete Hogan); "The White Outlaw" 1929 (Ted Williams); "Beau Bandit" 1930 (Texas); "Three Rogues" 1931 (Henchman); "Battling Buckaroo" 1932 (Duke Lawson); "Guns for Hire" 1932; "Strawberry Roan" 1933 (Cowboy); "Brand of Hate" 1934; "Fighting Through" 1934 (Bill); "Honor of the Range" 1934; "Rawhide Terror" 1934 (Blake Cowboy); "The Way of the West" 1934; "The Westerner" 1934 (Cowboy); "Arizona Trails" 1935; "The Ghost Rider" 1935 (Max); "The Cowboy and the Bandit" 1935 (Whitey); "Desert Mesa" 1935 (Pete); "Five Bad Men" 1935 (Bad Man); "Justice of the Range" 1935; "Law of the 45's" 1935 (Barfly); "Pals of the Range" 1935 (Stranger); "Rustlers of Red Dog" 1935-serial; "Border Caballero" 1936; "Gun Smoke" 1936; "Dodge City Trail" 1937 (Dawson's Gang Member); "Law for Tombstone" 1937; "Little Joe, the Wrangler" 1942 (Miner); "Prairie Pals" 1942.

Patton, Mary. Films: "A Distant Trumpet" 1964 (Jessica Prescott). ¶TV: *Zane Grey Theater*—"Blood Red" 1-29-61 (Woman); *Gunsmoke*—"Call Me Dodie" 9-22-62 (Addie Bagge).

Patton, Virginia. Films: "Roaring Guns" 1944-short; "Canyon Passage" 1946 (Liza Stone); "Black Eagle" 1948 (Ginny Long).

Paul, Eugenia. Films: "Apache Warrior" 1957 (Liwana); "Gun-

fighters of Abilene" 1960 (Raquel). ¶TV: *Cavalcade of America*—"Mountain Man" 9-28-54; *Death Valley Days*—"The Saint's Portrait" 10-11-54 (Sabita); *Sky King*—"The Geiger Detective" 11-4-51; *The Gene Autry Show*—"Guns Below the Border" 11-5-55; *Circus Boy*—"White Eagle" 11-25-56 (Nitika); *The Lone Ranger*—"Two Against Two" 3-21-57; *Zorro*—"Zorro's Romance" 11-7-57 (Elena Torres), "The Unmasking of Zorro" 3-6-58 (Elena Torres); *Broken Arrow*—"Kingdom of Terror" 1-14-58 (Serafina); *Jim Bowie*—"Ursula" 2-14-58 (Ursula de Veramendi), "Horse Thief" 3-21-58 (Ursula de Veramendi); *Rough Riders*—"The End of Nowhere" 2-12-59 (Donna Marriot).

Paul, Gloria (1941-). Films: "For a Few Dollars Less" 1966-Ital.; "Two Sons of Ringo" 1966-Ital.; "Two R-R-Ringos from Texas" 1967-Ital.

Paul, Graham. Films: "Pale Rider" 1985 (Ev Gossage).

Paul, John (1921-2/95). Films: "The Desperados" 1969 (Lacey).

Paul, Lee (1939-). Films: "The Gambler" TVM-1980 (George); "The Gambler, Part II—The Adventure Continues" TVM-1983 (Pettibone); "Desperado: Avalanche at Devil's Rider" TVM-1988 (Joshua Barrens). ¶TV: *Hec Ramsey*—"The Mystery of Chalk Hill" 2-18-73 (Rance Claiborne); *Kung Fu*—"The Chalice" 10-11-73 (Gilchrist).

Paul, Logan (1849-1//15/32). Films: "Britton of the Seventh" 1916 (Rain-in-the-Face).

Paul, Nick. TV: *The Texan*—"The Peddler" 1-26-59; *Colt .45*—"The Devil's Godson" 10-18-59; *Rawhide*—"The Pitchwagon" 3-2-62 (Nonie Matthews).

Paul, Rene (-10/21/68). TV: *Our American Heritage*—"Destiny West" 1-24-60 (Nicollet).

Paul, Val (1886-3/23/62). Films: "The Law of the Range" 1914; "The Trail Breakers" 1914; "The End of the Rainbow" 1916 (Jerry Smpson); "The Perilous Leap" 1917; "Fame and Fortune" 1918 (Flash Denby); "The Fast Mail" 1918; "M'Liss" 1918 (Jim Peterson); "Mr. Logan, U.S.A." 1918; "The Red, Red Heart" 1918 (Jack Newman); "Treat 'Em Rough" 1919 (Ben Radford); "The Timber Queen" 1922-serial.

Paulette, Ezra. Films: "Boss of Lonely Valley" 1937; "Law for Tombstone" 1937; "Sudden Bill Dorn" 1937 (Curly O'Connor); "Trail to

Gunsight" 1944 (Bar-6 Cowboy); "Trigger Trail" 1944.

Paulin, Scott. Films: "Grim Prairie Tales" 1990 (Martin); "The Gambler V: Playing for Keeps" TVM-1994 (Butch Cassidy).

Paull, Morgan (1944-). Films: "Fools' Parade" 1971 (Junior Kilfong); "Cahill, United States Marshal" 1973 (Struther); "The Last Hard Men" 1976 (Portugee Shiraz); "The Apple Dumpling Gang Rides Again" 1979 (Corporal #1); "Belle Starr" TVM-1980 (Latham). ¶TV: *Bearcats!*—12-2-71; *Gunsmoke*—"A Family of Killers" 1-14-74 (Hamilton Pitchford), "The Squaw" 1-6-75 (Brinker); *Centennial*—Regular 1978-79 (Philip Wendell as an Adult).

Paulsen, Albert (1927-). TV: *Frontier Circus*—"Karina" 11-9-61 (Rodales); *The High Chaparral*—"The New Lion of Sonora" 2-19-71 (Nervo).

Paulson, George. TV: *Death Valley Days*—"Early Candle Lighten" 11-8-69; *Bonanza*—"The Gold-Plated Rifle" 1-10-71 (Frank); *The Men from Shiloh*—"Tate, Ramrod" 2-24-71 (Mal Donner).

Pavan, Marisa (1932-). Films: "Drum Beat" 1954 (Toby); "Cutter's Trail" TVM-1970 (Amelita Avila).

Pawl, Nick. TV: *Maverick*—"Triple Indemnity" 3-19-61 (Slim), "A Technical Error" 11-26-61 (the Durango Kid); *Bat Masterson*—"Jeopardy at Jackson Hole" 6-1-61 (Al Stowe); *Destry*—"Go Away, Little Sheba" 3-27-64 (Abraham Lincoln Bedloe).

Pawley, Edward (1903-1/27/88). Films: "Gun Law" 1938 (the Raven); "The Oklahoma Kid" 1939 (Doolin); "River's End" 1940 (Frank Crandall); "Texas Rangers Ride Again" 1940 (Palo Pete); "Romance on the Range" 1942 (Banning); "The Desperadoes" 1943 (Blackie).

Pawley, William (1905-6/15/52). Films: "Robbers' Roost" 1933 (Hank Hays); "Prairie Moon" 1938 (Jim "Legs" Barton); "Frontier Marshal" 1939 (Cowardly Man); "Rough Riders' Round-Up" 1939 (Arizona Jack); "Union Pacific" 1939; "The Return of Frank James" 1940 (Jesse James Actor); "Sky Bandits" 1940 (Morgan); "West of Abilene" 1940 (Chris Matson); "Yukon Flight" 1940 (Yuke).

Pawn, Doris. Films: "On Desert Sands" 1915; "Blue Blood and Red" 1916; "Fightin' Mad" 1921 (Eileen Graham); "The Buster" 1923 (Charlotte Rowland).

Paxton, Bill. Films: "Tombstone" 1993 (Morgan Earp); "Frank and Jesse" TVM-1995 (Frank James).

Paxton, Richard. Films: "Little Big Horn" 1951 (Pvt. Ralph Hall); "Hellgate" 1952 (George Nye); "The Iron Mistress" 1952 (John Bowie); "Waco" 1952 (Ace Logan); "Arrowhead" 1953. ¶TV: *Gunsmoke*—"Word of Honor" 10-1-55 (Rudy).

Paymer, David. Films: "City Slickers" 1991 (Ira Shalowitz); "City Slickers II: The Legend of Curly's Gold" 1994 (Ira Shalowitz).

Payne, Bruce. Films: "Texas Lady" 1955; "The Cisco Kid" CTVM-1994 (St. Martin Dupre). ¶TV: *The Cisco Kid*—"Talking Dog" 2-23-52, "Big Steal" 4-12-52, "Dangerous Shoemaker" 5-15-54; *The Lone Ranger*—"Hidden Fortune" 6-18-53.

Payne, Edna (1891-1/31/53). Films: "The Half-Breed's Treachery" 1912; "The Silent Signal" 1912; "The Uprising" 1912; "Down the Rio Grande" 1913; "The Mexican Spy" 1913; "The Caballero's Wife" 1914; "The Girl Stage Driver" 1914; "The Squatter" 1914; "A Tale of the Desert" 1914; "Avarice" 1915; "Babbling Tongues" 1915; "The Dawn Road" 1915; "The Flag of Fortune" 1915; "Lure of the West" 1915; "The Oath of Smoky Joe" 1915; "The Sacrifice of Jonathan Gray" 1915; "The Sheriff of Red Rock Gulch" 1915; "The Trap That Failed" 1915.

Payne, John (1912-12/6/89). Films: "Fair Warning" 1937 (Jim Preston); "Bad Lands" 1939; "The Royal Rodeo" 1939-short; "El Paso" 1949 (Clayton Fletcher); "The Eagle and the Hawk" 1950 (Todd Croyden); "Passage West" 1951 (Pete Black); "The Vanquished" 1953 (Rock Grayson); "Rails into Laramie" 1954 (Jefferson Harder); "Silver Lode" 1954 (Don Ballard); "The Road to Denver" 1955 (Bill Mayhew); "Santa Fe Passage" 1955 (Kirby Randolph); "Tennessee's Partner" 1955 (Tennessee); "Rebel in Town" 1956 (John Willoughby). ¶TV: *Zane Grey Theater*—"Until the Man Dies" 1-25-57 (Clint Belmet); *Schlitz Playhouse of the Stars*—"The Restless Gun" 3-29-57 (Britt Ponset); *The Restless Gun*—Regular 1957-59 (Vint Bonner), "Jebediah Bonner" 9-22-58 (Jeb Bonner), "The Dead Ringer" 2-16-59 (Gene Baroda); *Call of the West*—Host 1969-70; *Gunsmoke*—"Gentry's Law" 10-12-70 (Amos Gentry).

Payne, Julie (1940-). TV: *The Restless Gun*—"The Pawn" 4-6-59 (Peggy McGiven); *The Big Valley*—"Young Marauders" 10-6-65 (Fran-

cie); *Wild Wild West*—"The Night of the Sudden Death" 10-8-65 (Corinne Foxx).

Payne, Laurence (1919-). Films: "The Singer Not the Song" 1961-Brit. (Pablo).

Payne, Louis (1876-8/14/53). Films: "The Dude Wrangler" 1930 (Dude Guest).

Payne, Sally. Films: "The Big Show" 1937 (Toodles); "Man from Music Mountain" 1938 (Patsy); "Rodeo Dough" 1940-short; "When the Daltons Rode" 1940 (Annabella); "Young Bill Hickok" 1940 (Calamity Jane); "Bad Man of Deadwood" 1941 (Sally Blackstone); "In Old Cheyenne" 1941 (Squeak); "Jesse James at Bay" 1941 (Polly Morgan); "Lady from Cheyenne" 1941 (Chorus Girl); "Nevada City" 1941; "Red River Valley" 1941; "Robin Hood of the Pecos" 1941 (Belle Starr); "Sheriff of Tombstone" 1941 (Queenie); "Westward Ho-Hum" 1941-short; "Man from Cheyenne" 1942 (Sally); "Romance on the Range" 1942 (Sally).

Payson, Ed. Films: "Wyoming Outlaw" 1939; "Riders of Death Valley" 1941-serial (Buck Hansen).

Payton, Barbara (1927-5/8/67). Films: "The Pecos Pistol" 1949-short; "Silver Butte" 1949-short; "Dallas" 1950 (Flo); "Drums in the Deep South" 1951 (Kathy); "Only the Valiant" 1951 (Cathy Eversham); "The Great Jesse James Raid" 1953 (Kate).

Payton, Claude (Claude Peyton) (1882-3/1/55). Films: "A Knight of the West" 1921 (Ralph Barton); "Bells of San Juan" 1922 (Jim Garson); "Catch My Smoke" 1922 (Tex Lynch); "The Desert's Crucible" 1922 (Tex Fuller); "Do and Dare" 1922 (Cordoba); "The Marshal of Moneymint" 1922 (Velvet Joe Sellers); "The Masked Avenger" 1922 (Bruno Douglas); "Trooper O'Neil" 1922 (Black Flood); "Two-Fisted Jefferson" 1922; "The Desert Rider" 1923 (Rufe Kinkaid); "The Devil's Dooryard" 1923 (Fred Bradley); "The Law Rustlers" 1923 (Doc Jordan); "The Back Trail" 1924 (Harry King); "Daring Chances" 1924 (Sampson Burke); "The Desert Outlaw" 1924 (Black Loomis); "The Man from Wyoming" 1924 (Jack Halloway); "The Riddle Rider" 1924-serial; "The Ridin' Streak" 1925 (Sheriff); "Gold and the Girl" 1925 (Rankin); "The Texas Trail" 1925 (Dan Merrill); "The Yellow Back" 1926 (Bruce Condon); "Set Free" 1927 (Burke Tanner); "The Western Whirlwind" 1927 (Jeff Taylor); "Dodging Danger" 1929; "The Last Frontier" 1932-serial; "Tex Takes

a Holiday" 1932 (Saunders); "Fargo Express" 1933 (Tom); "Thunder Over Texas" 1934 (Bruce Laird).

Payton, Ethel. Films: "The Fighting Breed" 1921 (Enid MacDonald).

Payton, Gloria (1897-8/1/89). Films: "The Yellow Bullet" 1917 (Spanish Nell); "Sunset Sprague" 1920 (Lolita).

Payton, Lucy (1877-1/15/69). Films: "The Yellow Bullet" 1917 (Theresa Fowler).

Payton-Wright, Pamela (1941-). TV: *Gunsmoke*—"Yankton" 2-7-72 (Emma Donavan); *Bonanza*—"Search in Limbo" 2-20-72 (Zeena).

Pazzafini, Giovanni. Films: "Arizona Colt" 1965-Ital./Fr./Span. (Kay); "Killer Caliber .32" 1967-Ital.; "If One Is Born a Swine ... Kill Him" 1968-Ital.; "It Can Be Done ... Amigo" 1971-Ital./Fr./Span.; "Carambola's Philosophy: In the Right Pocket" 1975-Ital.

Pazzafini, Nello (Ted Carter). Films: "Blood for a Silver Dollar" 1965-Ital./Fr.; "Adios Hombre" 1966-Ital./Span.; "Fort Yuma Gold" 1966-Ital./Fr./Span.; "Days of Violence" 1967-Ital.; "Face to Face" 1967-Ital.; "Run Man, Run" 1967-Ital./Fr.; "Two Pistols and a Coward" 1967-Ital. (Coleman); "Find a Place to Die" 1968-Ital.; "A Long Ride from Hell" 1968-Ital. (Shorty); "Wanted" 1968-Ital./Fr.; "Death on High Mountain" 1969-Ital./Span.; "Killer Goodbye" 1969-Ital./Span. (Sheriff); "His Name Was Holy Ghost" 1970-Ital./Span.; "Calibre .38" 1971-Ital.; "They Call Him Cemetery" 1971-Ital./Span.; "Vendetta at Dawn" 1971-Ital.; "I Am Sartana, Trade Your Guns for a Coffin" 1972-Ital.; "Return of Halleluja" 1972-Ital./Ger.; "Man Called Invincible" 1973-Ital.; "Dick Luft in Sacramento" 1974-Ital.; "Man Called Blade" 1977-Ital.

Peabody, Jack. Films: "The Big Trail" 1930 (Bill Gillis).

Peabody, Richard (1925-). Films: "The Good Guys and the Bad Guys" 1969 (Boyle); "MacKenna's Gold" 1969 (Avila); "Support Your Local Sheriff" 1969 (Luke Danby); "Sidekicks" TVM-1974 (Ed). ¶TV: *Gunsmoke*—"Phoebe Strunk" 11-10-62 (Simsie Strunk), "The Gunrunners" 2-5-68 (Patch); *Bonanza*—"Destiny's Child" 1-30-66 (Sonny); *The Big Valley*—"Journey into Violence" 12-18-67 (Cyrus); *Daniel Boone*—"A Touch of Charity" 2-27-69 (Samuel Stone), "The Cache" 12-4-69 (Dawson); *Here Come the Brides*—"The Eyes of London Bob" 11-28-69 (Zach); *Lancer*—"The Experiment" 2-17-70 (Ox).

Pearce, Adele. *see* Blake, Pamela.

Pearce, George (1865-8/12/40). Films: "The Gambler of the West" 1914; "'49-'17" 1917 (Pa Bobbett); "Closin' In" 1918 (Mr. Carlton); "Desert Law" 1918 (the Stranger); "Little Red Decides" 1918 (Dr. Kirk); "Three Word Brand" 1921 (John Murray); "The Twilight Trail" 1923; "The Lone Rider" 1930 (Judge); "Dynamite Ranch" 1932 (Andrew Collins); "The Lone Cowboy" 1934 (Doctor); "Fighting Shadows" 1935 (Father O'Donovan); "Law Beyond the Range" 1935 (Doc Pearce); "The Man from Guntown" 1935 (Wells); "The Revenge Rider" 1935 (Dr. Lindsay); "The Singing Cowboy" 1936 (Dr. Hill); "Heart of the Rockies" 1937; "The Thundering West" 1939 (Doctor).

Pearce, John (1931-). Films: "The Culpepper Cattle Company" 1972 (Spectator); "Ulzana's Raid" 1972 (Corporal); "The Great Northfield, Minnesota Raid" 1972 (Frank James); "Billy Two Hats" 1973-Brit. (Spencer).

Pearce, Peggy. Films: "The Good Loser" 1918 (Evelyn Haselton); "The Red Haired Cupid" 1918; "The Ace of the Saddle" 1919 (Madeline Faulkner).

Pearce, Wynn. Films: "Pocket Money" 1972 (Border Patrolman). ¶TV: *Gunsmoke*—"The Boots" 11-14-59 (Hank Fergus); *Maverick*—"Easy Mark" 11-15-59 (Cornelius Van Rensselaer, Jr.); *Tales of Wells Fargo*—"Relay Station" 12-28-59 (Logan), "The Dowry" 7-10-61 (Roel La Tour); *The Alaskans*—"Gold Fever" 1-17-60 (Danny); *Cheyenne*—"Riot at Arroyo Soco" 2-1-60 (Jess Tobin); *Sugarfoot*—"Blue Bonnet Stray" 4-26-60 (Utah Kid); *Lawman*—"The Escape of Joe Kilmer" 12-18-60 (Joe Killmer); *Bonanza*—"Bank Run" 1-28-61 (Teller), "Love Me Not" 3-1-64, "The Meredith Smith" 10-31-65 (Ozzie), "Three Brides for Hoss" 2-20-66 (Jed); *The Road West*—"No Sanctuary" 2-6-67 (Charlie).

Pearson, Brett. Films: "Stagecoach" 1966 (Sergeant). ¶TV: *The Road West*—"The Gunfighter" 9-26-66 (Deputy); *Daniel Boone*—"The Long Way Home" 2-16-67 (Seymour Coot); *Custer*—"The Gauntlet" 12-20-67 (Deasy).

Pearson, Jesse (1930-12/5/79). Films: "Advance to the Rear" 1964 (Cpl. Silas Geary). ¶TV: *Great Adventure*—"Teeth of the Lion" 1-17-64 (Tom Jethro); *Death Valley Days*—"The Last Stagecoach Robbery" 3-21-64 (Joe), "The Rider" 12-4-65 (Jim

Barnes), "The Courtship of Carrie Huntington" 6-4-66 (Henry), "The World's Greatest Swimming Horse" 2-8-69 (Frank), "The Mezcla Man" 1-3-70"The Visitor" 12-27-69 (Jess Ivy); *The Road West* and Thirsty Land" 10-10-66 (Neil Brubaker); *The Guns of Will Sonnett*—"Join the Army" 1-3-69 (Lieutenant Elder); *Bonanza*—"Mrs. Wharton and the Lesser Breeds" 1-19-69 (Ed).

Pearson, Virginia (1888-6/6/58). Films: "Smilin' Guns" 1929 (Mrs. Van Smythe).

Peary, Harold (1908-3/30/85). Films: "Outlaw Queen" 1957. ¶TV: *Circus Boy*—"Hortense the Hippo" 6-2-57 (Al Garson); *Tombstone Territory*—5-20-60 (Metcalf); *The Loner*—"The Sheriff of Fetterman's Crossing" 11-13-65 (Peabody).

Peck, Ed (1917-9/12/92). Films: "The Ride to Hangman's Tree" 1967 (Sheriff Stewart); "The Shakiest Gun in the West" 1968 (Sheriff); "A Man Called Gannon" 1969 (Delivery Rider). ¶TV: *Have Gun Will Travel*—"The Gospel Singer" 10-21-61 (Sims), "The Trap" 3-3-62 (Roy Bissell); *Death Valley Days*—"Trial by Fear" 1-10-62 (Chris), "A Calamity Called Jane" 2-11-67 (Charlie Utter); *Gunsmoke*—"Quint Asper Comes Home" 9-29-62 (Semple), "Old Man" 10-10-64 (Joe Silva); *The Dakotas*—"Crisis at High Banjo" 2-11-63 (Johnny Fox); *Redigo*—"Papa-San" 11-12-63 (Bryce); *The Virginian*—"The Payment" 12-16-64 (Ben Clayton), "The Challenge" 10-19-66 (Sheriff Milt Hayle); *Daniel Boone*—"Mountain of the Dead" 12-17-64 (John Hawkins), "Goliath" 9-29-66 (Smedley); *The Loner*—"The Kingdom of McComb" 10-9-65 (Lowden), "Pick Me Another Time to Die" 2-26-66 (Charlie); *Wild Wild West*—"The Night of the Double-Edged Knife" 11-12-65 (Merritt); *Laredo*—"A Question of Guilt" 3-10-67 (Frank Foster); *The High Chaparral*—"No Irish Need Apply" 1-17-69 (Captain Slater); *The Outcasts*—"Hung for a Lamb" 3-10-69 (Jenner); *Bonanza*—"Speak No Evil" 4-20-69 (Pollard).

Peck, Gregory (1916-). Films: "Duel in the Sun" 1946 (Lewt McCanles); "Yellow Sky" 1948 (Stretch); "The Gunfighter" 1950 (Jimmy Ringo); "Only the Valiant" 1951 (Capt. Richard Lance); "The Big Country" 1958 (James McKay); "The Bravados" 1958 (Jim Douglas); "How the West Was Won" 1962 (Cleve Van Valen); "MacKenna's Gold" 1969 (Mackenna); "The Stalking Moon" 1969 (Sam Varner); "Shoot Out" 1971

(Clay Lomax); "Billy Two Hats" 1973-Brit. (Deans); "Old Gringo" 1989 (Ambrose Bierce).

Peck, J. Eddie. TV: *Wildside*—Regular 1985 (Sutton Hollister).

Peck, Steve (1928-). Films: "The Lion and the Horse" 1952 (Jiggs Dalton).

Peckinpah, Matthew. Films: "Junior Bonner" 1972 (Tim Bonner).

Peckinpah, Sam (1925-12/28/84). Films: "Pat Garrett and Billy the Kid" 1973 (Will); "China 9, Liberty 37" 1978-Ital./Span./U.S. (Wilber Olsen).

Pedersoli, Carlo. *see* Spencer, Bud.

Peebles, Nia (1961-). Films: "Return to Lonesome Dove" TVM-1993 (Agostina Vega).

Peel, David (1920-82). TV: *Daniel Boone*—"The Symbol" 12-29-66 (Dick), "Then Who Will They Hang from the Yardarm If Willy Gets Away?" 2-8-68 (Corporal Barton).

Peel, Richard (-10/11/88). TV: *The High Chaparral*—"Too Many Chiefs" 3-27-70.

Pegg, Vester (1889-2/19/51). Films: "The Caballero's Wife" 1914; "Mountain Blood" 1916; "The Timber Wolf" 1916; "The Almost Good Man" 1917; "Bucking Broadway" 1917 (Thornton); "Cheyenne's Pal" 1917; "The Fighting Gringo" 1917 (Pedro); "A 45 Calibre Mystery" 1917; "The Golden Bullet" 1917; "Hair-Trigger Burk" 1917; "A Marked Man" 1917 (Kent); "The Secret Man" 1917 (Bill); "Straight Shooting" 1917 (Placer Fremont); "Sure Shot Morgan" 1917; "The Texas Sphinx" 1917; "The Wrong Man" 1917; "Hell Bent" 1918 (Jack Thurston); "The Phantom Riders" 1918 (the Unknown); "The Scarlet Drop" 1918 (Marley Calvert); "Thieves' Gold" 1918 (Curt Simmons); "Wild Women" 1918 (Pegg); "A Woman's Fool" 1918 (Tommy Lusk); "The Ace of the Saddle" 1919 (Gambler); "Bare Fists" 1919 (Lopez); "The Black Horse Bandit" 1919; "The Border Terror" 1919 (the Cisco Kid); "The Canyon Mystery" 1919; "The Outcasts of Poker Flat" 1919; "The Rider of the Law" 1919 (Nick Kyneton); "Riders of Vengeance" 1919; "The Galloping Devil" 1920 (Pink); "Vanishing Trails" 1920-serial; "Vengeance and the Girl" 1920 (Black Arno); "The Fighting Stranger" 1921 (Joe Kilburn); "The Last Chance" 1921 (Black Sparr); "The Struggle" 1921 (Diamond Joe); "The Kick Back" 1922 (Ramon Pinellos); "Canyon of the Fools" 1923 (Knute);

"Crashin' Thru" 1923 (Saunders); "The Lone Fighter" 1923 (Harvey Bates); "The Rattler" 1925 (Blin Dudley); "Rough Going" 1925 (Jim Benton); "The Shield of Silence" 1925; "Tearin' Loose" 1925 (Jim, the Tramp); "Bucking the Truth" 1926 (Sheriff Findlay); "The Flying Horseman" 1926; "Hurricane Horseman" 1926 (Jim Marden); "Man of the Forest" 1926 (Moses); "Three Bad Men" 1926; "The Dawn Trail" 1930 (Mac); "Three Rogues" 1931 (Henchman); "The Revenge Rider" 1935 (Connors); "Born to the West" 1937 (Bartender); "Forlorn River" 1937 (Hank Gordon); "Thunder Trail" 1937 (Lee); "Wells Fargo" 1937 (Fargo Rider); "Wild and Woolly" 1937 (Man on Street); "Stagecoach" 1939 (Hank Plummer); "Colorado" 1940 (Sam Smith); "My Little Chickadee" 1940 (Gambler); "Under Texas Skies" 1940; "West of Abilene" 1940 (Kennedy); "Sheriff of Tombstone" 1941.

Peil, Sr., Edward (1888-12/29/58). Films: "The Golden Spurs" 1915; "The Man from Montana" 1917 (Warren Summers); "Captured Alive" 1918; "The Fly God" 1918 (Bob Aliers); "The Robber" 1918; "A Sage Brush Hamlet" 1919 (Claude Dutton); "Fighting Cressy" 1920 (John Ford); "Isobel, or the Trail's End" 1920 (Scottie Dean); "The Rose of Nome" 1920 (Tim Donnay); "Two Moons" 1920 (Lang Whistler); "The Killer" 1921 (Ramon); "That Girl Montana" 1921 (Lee Holly); "Arabia" 1922 (Ibrahim Bulamar); "Broken Chains" 1922 (Burglar); "The Lone Star Ranger" 1923 (Kane); "Stepping Fast" 1923 (Sun Yat); "Three Jumps Ahead" 1923 (Taggit); "$50,000 Reward" 1924 (Buck Schofield); "The Iron Horse" 1924 (Old Chinaman); "Teeth" 1924 (Sheriff); "Double Action Daniels" 1925 (Jack Monroe); "The Great K & A Train Robbery" 1926 (Bandit Leader); "Tumbling River" 1927 (Roan Tibbets); "In Old Arizona" 1929 (Man); "The Avenger" 1931 (Ike Mason); "Clearing the Range" 1931 (Sheriff Jim Burke); "The Texas Ranger" 1931 (Lanning); "Wild Horse" 1931 (Sheriff); "Cornered" 1932; "Destry Rides Again" 1932 (Frank Warren); "The Devil Horse" 1932-serial; "The Gay Buckaroo" 1932 (Hi Low Jack); "Local Bad Man" 1932 (Sheriff Hickory Dale); "Tombstone Canyon" 1932 (Henchman); "Blue Steel" 1934 (Melgrove); "The Man from Utah" 1934 (Barton); "Branded a Coward" 1935; "The Phantom Empire" 1935-serial; "The Revenge Rider" 1935; "The Cowboy Star" 1936 (Clem Baker); "Oh, Su-

sanna!" 1936 (Sheriff Briggs); "White Fang" 1936; "Code of the Range" 1937 (Sheriff); "Come On Cowboys" 1937; "Ghost Town Gold" 1937; "Gunsmoke Ranch" 1937; "The Old Wyoming Trail" 1937 (Sheriff); "The Painted Stallion" 1937-serial (Marshal); "Riders of the Whistling Skull" 1937 (Sheriff); "Trapped" 1937 (Bill Ashley); "Two-Fisted Sheriff" 1937 (Judge Webster); "Westbound Mail" 1937 (Judge); "Cattle Raiders" 1938 (Sheriff); "Code of the Rangers" 1938 (Ranger Captain); "Colorado Trail" 1938 (Hobbs); "Heroes of the Alamo" 1938 (Sam Houston); "Law of the Plains" 1938 (Bernard); "Rio Grande" 1938; "The Singing Outlaw" 1938; "Six Shootin' Sheriff" 1938 (Andy); "West of Cheyenne" 1938 (Jed); "Dodge City" 1939; "The Man from Sundown" 1939 (Sheriff Wiley); "The Night Riders" 1939 (Harper); "Racketeers of the Range" 1939; "The Singing Cowgirl" 1939 (Tom Harkins); "Spoilers of the Range" 1939 (Harper); "Sundown on the Prairie" 1939 (John); "The Thundering West" 1939 (Hayes); "Union Pacific" 1939 (Laborer); "Water Rustlers" 1939 (Lawyer); "Billy the Kid's Gun Justice" 1940 (Barlow); "Deadwood Dick" 1940-serial; "Geronimo" 1940 (John Cresswell); "Legion of the Lawless" 1940; "One Man's Law" 1940 (Joe Winters); "Riders on Black Mountain" 1940 (Harris); "Riders of Pasco Basin" 1940 (Rancher); "Santa Fe Trail" 1940 (Guard); "Billy the Kid's Fighting Pals" 1941 (Hardy); "Fugitive Valley" 1941 (Jailer); "In Old Cheyenne" 1941 (Conductor); "Jesse James at Bay" 1941; "Kansas Cyclone" 1941; "The Lone Rider in Frontier Fury" 1941; "The Lone Rider in Ghost Town" 1941 (Clark); "Red River Valley" 1941; "The Texas Marshal" 1941 (Adams); "Tonto Basin Outlaws" 1941 (Photographer); "Underground Rustlers" 1941; "White Eagle" 1941-serial; "Border Roundup" 1942; "Code of the Outlaw" 1942; "Down Rio Grande Way" 1942; "Riders of the West" 1942; "Shut My Big Mouth" 1942 (Hotel Proprietor); "Sin Town" 1942 (Hedges); "Texas Justice" 1942; "Canyon City" 1943; "The Kid Rides Again" 1943 (Ainsley); "The Outlaw" 1943 (Swanson); "Robin Hood of the Range" 1943 (Grady); "Silver City Kid" 1944; "Shadows of Death" 1945; "The Last Round-Up" 1947; "Saddle Pals" 1947; "Valley of Fear" 1947; "The Wistful Widow of Wagon Gap" 1947 (Townsman); "Wyoming" 1947 (Nester); "Colt .45" 1950; "Kansas Raiders" 1950 (Bank Teller).

Peil, Jr., Ed (1908-1/7/62). Films: "The Pony Express" 1925 (Billy Cody).

Pelikan, Lisa. Films: "True Grit" TVM-1978 (Mattie); "Into the Badlands" TVM-1991 (Sarah Carstairs).

Pelish, Thelma (1928-3/6/83). TV: *Dirty Sally*—"The Hanging of Cyrus Pike" 4-5-74 (Mabel).

Pelletier, Andrea. Films: "Marie-Ann" 1978-Can. (Marie-Ann).

Pelletier, Yvonne. Films: "Riders of the Purple Sage" 1931 (Bess); "Lightning Triggers" 1935 (Marion).

Pellicer, Pilar. Films: "Day of the Evil Gun" 1968 (Lydia); "Zorro, the Gay Blade" 1981 (Francisco's Wife).

Pellicer, Pina (1935-12/10/64). Films: "One-Eyed Jacks" 1961.

Peloquin, Jean. TV: *The Virginian*—"The Gentle Tamers" 1-24-68 (Gene), "Stacey" 2-28-68 (Gene), "The Saddle Warmer" 9-18-68 (Gene), "The Orchard" 10-2-68 (Gene).

Peluce, Meeno (1970-). TV: *Best of the West*—Regular 1981-82 (Daniel West).

Pembroke, George (1900-6/11/72). Films: "Cowboy from Sundown" 1940 (Cylus Cuttler); "Daredevils of the West" 1943-serial (Powers); "Hell Canyon Outlaws" 1957; "Outlaw's Son" 1957 (Paul Wentworth); "Shoot-Out at Medicine Bend" 1957; "Showdown at Boot Hill" 1958 (Sheriff). ¶TV: *The Lone Ranger*—"The Black Hat" 5-18-50, "The Black Widow" 8-24-50; *The Gene Autry Show*—"The Lawless Press" 1-25-52, "Trouble at Silver Creek" 3-9-52, "Trail of the Witch" 3-30-52, "Narrow Escape" 8-11-53, "Prize Winner" 7-27-54; *Annie Oakley*—"Sharpshooting Annie" 6-12-54; *The Roy Rogers Show*—"Boys' Day in Paradise Valley" 11-7-54.

Pembroke, Jerry. Films: "The Cherokee Kid" 1927 (Ralphe McPherson).

Pembroke, Percy. Films: "Lone Larry" 1917; "The Girl in the Saddle" 1921; "The Heart of Arizona" 1921; "The Shadow of Suspicion" 1921; "Winners of the West" 1921-serial (Louis Blair); "The Call of Courage" 1922; "The Night Attack" 1922; "The Trail of the Wolf" 1922; "Two Men" 1922.

Pembroke, Stanley. Films: "Whatever the Cost" 1918 (Steve Douglas).

Pena, Julio (1912-7/22/72). Films: "Minnesota Clay" 1964-Ital./

Fr./Span. (Lt. Evans); "Bullets and the Flesh" 1965-Ital./Fr./Span.; "Magnificent Brutes of the West" 1965-Ital./Span./Fr.; "The Hellbenders" 1966-U.S./Ital./Span. (Sgt. Tolt); "Kid Rodelo" 1966-U.S./Span. (Balsas); "Mutiny at Fort Sharp" 1966-Ital.; "Savage Pampas" 1966-U.S./Span./Arg. (Chicha); "Sunscorched" 1966-Span./Ger.; "Cowards Don't Pray" 1968-Ital./Span.; "Pistol for a Hundred Coffins" 1968-Ital./Span.; "Alive or Preferably Dead" 1969-Span./Ital.; "Red Sun" 1971-Fr./Ital./Span.

Pena, Pascual Garcia. Films: "City of Badmen" 1953 (Pig); "The Treasure of Pancho Villa" 1955 (Ricardo); "The Beast of Hollow Mountain" 1956 (Pancho).

Pendleton, Austin (1940-). Films: "Four Eyes and Six-Guns" TVM-1992 (Moustached Passenger).

Pendleton, Charles. see Mitchell, Gordon.

Pendleton, Jack. Films: "The Judgement Book" 1935 (Tim Osborne).

Pendleton, Nat (1899-10/11/67). Films: "Last of the Duanes" 1930 (Bossamer); "Fair Warning" 1931 (Purvis); "Hell Fire Austin" 1932 (Bouncer); "Northwest Passage" 1940 (Capt. Huff); "Death Valley" 1946.

Pendleton, Steve Gaylord (1908-10/3/84). Films: "Life in the Raw" 1933 (Tom Halloway); "Unknown Valley" 1933 (Bennson); "Fighting to Live" 1934; "Trails End" 1935 (Ed "Kid" Malloy); "Geronimo" 1940 (Pvt. Young); "Triple Justice" 1940 (Tommy); "Young Buffalo Bill" 1940 (Jerry); "Men of the Timberland" 1941; "The Blazing Trail" 1949 (Kirk Brady); "Ride, Ryder, Ride" 1949 (Gerry); "Roll, Thunder, Roll" 1949 (Marshal Bill Faugh); "Sons of New Mexico" 1949; "Gunfire" 1950 (Charlie Ford); "Rio Grande" 1950 (Capt. Prescott); "Sunset in the West" 1950 (Walter Kimball); "Buckaroo Sheriff of Texas" 1951 (Sam White); "Desert of Lost Men" 1951 (Evans); "The Great Missouri Raid" 1951 (Arch Clements); "The Great Jesse James Raid" 1953 (Todd); "Once Upon a Horse" 1958 (Milligan). ¶TV: *Wild Bill Hickok*—"Indian Bureau Story" 7-31-51, "Border City" 11-13-51, "School Teacher Story" 1-15-52, "Hands Across the Border" 7-22-52; *The Cisco Kid*—"Postal Inspector" 8-4-51, "Kid Sister Trouble" 9-15-51; *The Gene Autry Show*—"The Kid Comes West" 12-8-51, "Rocky River Feud" 1-18-52; *The Roy Rogers Show*—"Flying Bullets" 6-15-52 (Joe Slade),

"Outlaw's Return" 9-28-52 (Spade Oakley), "Huntin' for Trouble" 10-5-52 (Bart Hollister), "Loaded Guns" 4-15-53 (Bill Eaton), "Empty Saddles" 3-10-56 (Sid Morgan), "Fishing for Fingerprints" 10-28-56, "Mountain Pirates" 11-4-56, "Deadlock at Dark Canyon" 1-6-57; *Wyatt Earp*—"The Man Who Rode with Custer" 1-8-57, "Dull Knife Strikes for Freedom" 5-7-57 (Major Benteen), "The Bounty Killer" 9-30-58 (Col. Benteen), "His Life in His Hands" 3-22-60 (Thacker), "Behan's Double Game" 3-29-60 (Thacker), "The Court vs. Doc Holliday" 4-26-60, "My Enemy—John Behan" 5-31-60 (Thacker), "Wyatt's Bitterest Enemy" 6-7-60 (Thacker), "Until Proven Guilty" 4-11-61; *Tales of the Texas Rangers*—"Traitor's Gold" 10-2-58 (Ed Handson); *U.S. Marshal*—"The Fugitives" 10-11-58; *26 Men*—"Dog Eat Dog" 11-18-58; *Lawman*—"Man on a Mountain" 6-12-60 (Kelsey); *Maverick*—"The Town That Wasn't There" 10-2-60 (Marshal McCoy); *The Rifleman*—"Death Trap" 5-9-61.

Penman, Lea (1895-10/12/62). Films: "Fancy Pants" 1950 (Effie Floud).

Penn, Christopher. Films: "Pale Rider" 1985 (Josh LaHood).

Penn, Leonard (1907-5/20/75). Films: "The Girl of the Golden West" 1938 (Pedro); "Hoppy's Holiday" 1947 (Danning); "Courtin' Trouble" 1948 (Dawson); "The Dead Don't Dream" 1948 (Earl Wesson); "Outlaw Brand" 1948; "Partners of the Sunset" 1948; "Range Land" 1949 (Bart); "The Girl from San Lorenzo" 1950 (McCarger); "Gunfire" 1950 (Simons); "Silver Raiders" 1950 (Cobry); "Six Gun Mesa" 1950; "Law of the Badlands" 1951 (Cash); "South of Caliente" 1951 (Commandante); "Stagecoach Driver" 1951; "Wanted Dead or Alive" 1951; "Barbed Wire" 1952 (Steve Ruttledge); "Outlaw Women" 1952 (Samn Bass); "Fangs of the Arctic" 1953. ¶TV: *The Lone Ranger*—"War Horse" 10-20-49; *The Gene Autry Show*—"The Poisoned Waterhole" 10-8-50, "The Black Rider" 10-22-50, "Warning! Danger!" 11-10-51, "Bandits of Boulder Bluff" 11-24-51, "Trouble at Silver Creek" 3-9-52, "Trail of the Witch" 3-30-52, "Saddle Up" 12-3-55 (Martin Pickett), "Ride, Rancheros" 12-10-55 (Martin Pickett), "The Rangerette" 12-17-55 (Martin Pickett); *Wild Bill Hickok*—"Mexican Rustlers Story" 10-23-51, "Civilian Clothes Story" 12-18-51, "The Iron Major" 4-21-53, "Jingles on Jail Road" 7-14-53; *The*

Cisco Kid—"Carrier Pigeon" 11-3-51, "Jewelry Hold-Up" 12-15-51, "The Puppeteer" 1-19-52, "Canyon City Kit" 3-1-52, "Trouble in Tonopah" 3-21-53, "Juggler's Silver" 10-17-53, "Vendetta" 11-14-53; *The Roy Rogers Show*—"The Knockout" 12-28-52 (Gil Tolland), "The Silver Fox Hunt" 4-19-53; *The Range Rider*—"Baron of Broken Bow" 2-21-53; *Wyatt Earp*—"The Bank Robbers" 11-8-55 (Tarp Anders), "Vengeance Trail" 2-12-57 (Burleigh), "Wyatt Fights" 2-25-68 (Jim Cockrell); *Judge Roy Bean*—"Citizen Romeo 12-1-55 (Martin), "Murder in Langtry" 12-1-55 (Burt); *Sergeant Preston of the Yukon*—"Trouble at Hogback" 7-19-56 (Greig); *Death Valley Days*—"Emperor Norton, 1st" 11-4-56 (Thomas King); *Zane Grey Theater*—"Courage Is a Gun" 12-14-56 (Walter Blake); *Have Gun Will Travel*—"The Poker Friend" 11-12-60 (Cavage).

Pennell, Larry (1928-). Films: "The Far Horizons" 1955 (Wild Eagle); "Seven Angry Men" 1955 (Oliver); "Flaming Frontier" 1965-Ger./Yugo. (the General); "Journey Through Rosebud" 1972 (Sheriff); "The Revengers" 1972-U.S./Mex. (Arny). ¶TV: *Tombstone Territory*—"The Assassin" 5-21-58 (Bill Doolin); *Rough Riders*—"Blood Feud" 11-13-58 (Creed Pearce); *Cimarron City*—"McGowan's Debt" 12-27-58 (Drew McGowan); *Have Gun Will Travel*—"Commanche" 5-16-59 (Henry Carver); *The Alaskans*—"Kangaroo Court" 5-8-60 (Harry Seattle); *Tales of Wells Fargo*—"Kid Brother" 5-23-60 (Ben Hardie); *Death Valley Days*—"Queen of the High-Graders" 10-12-60 (Romer Maxwell); *Klondike*—"Sure Thing, Men" 11-28-60 (Rufe Lukas); *Zane Grey Theater*—"The Black Wagon" 12-1-60 (Tully); *The Outlaws*—"The Daltons Must Die" 1-26-61 & 2-2-61 (Bob Dalton); *Bat Masterson*—"Jeopardy at Jackson Hole" 6-1-61 (Cal Beamus); *Wagon Train*—"The Trace McCloud Story" 3-2-64 (Trace McCloud); *The Virginian*—"The Dark Challenge" 9-23-64 (Wally), "Bitter Harvest" 3-15-67 (Carl Rand); *Branded*—"I Killed Jason McCord" 10-3-65 (Tuck Fraser); *The Big Valley*—"Price of Victory" 2-13-67 (Jack Kilbain); *Rango*—"Requiem for a Ranger" 2-24-67 (Larkin); *Custer*—"To the Death" 9-27-67 (Chief Yellow Hawk); *Cimarron Strip*—"The Deputy" 12-21-67 (Rapp); *Gunsmoke*—"Mr. Sam'l" 2-26-68 (Ben Akins), "Trail of Bloodshed" 3-4-74 (John Woolfe).

Penner, Joe (1905-1/10/41). Films: "I'm from the City" 1938 (Pete).

Pennick, Jack (1895-8/16/64). Films: "Broncho Twister" 1927 (Jinx Johnson); "The Virginian" 1929 (Slim); "Way Out West" 1930 (Pete); "Hell Fire Austin" 1932; "Renegades of the West" 1932 (Dave); "Drift Fence" 1936 (Weary); "Rose Marie" 1936 (Brawler); "Drums Along the Mohawk" 1939 (Amos); "Mountain Rhythm" 1939 (Rocky); "Stagecoach" 1939 (Jerry the Bartender); "Union Pacific" 1939 (Harmonica Player); "Northwest Mounted Police" 1940 (Sgt. Field); "The Westerner" 1940 (Bantry); "My Darling Clementine" 1946 (Stagecoach Driver); "Unconquered" 1947 (Joe Lovat); "Fort Apache" 1948 (Sgt. Shattuck); "The Three Godfathers" 1948 (Luke, the Train Conductor); "The Fighting Kentuckian" 1949 (Captain Dan Carroll); "She Wore a Yellow Ribbon" 1949 (Sergeant Major); "Rio Grande" 1950 (Sergeant); "The Last Frontier" 1955 (Corporal); "The Searchers" 1956 (Private); "The Horse Soldiers" 1959 (Sgt. Maj. Mitchell); "Two Rode Together" 1961 (Sergeant); "How the West Was Won" 1962 (Cpl. Murphy); "The Man Who Shot Liberty Valance" 1962 (Jack the Bartender). ¶TV: *Wagon Train*—"The Colter Craven Story" 11-23-60.

Pennington, Ann (1892-11/4/71). Films: "The Golden Strain" 1925 (Lucy Sulter); "The Lucky Horseshoe" 1925 (Dancer); "Texas Terrors" 1940 (Dancer).

Penny, Hank (and his Plantation Boys) (1919-4/17/92). Films: "Heading West" 1946; "The Blazing Trail" 1949; "Frontier Outpost" 1950 (Musician); "Webb Pierce and His Wanderin' Boys" 1955-short.

Penny, Sydney. Films: "The Night Rider" TVM-1979; "The Capture of Grizzly Adams" TVM-1982 (Peg Adams); "Pale Rider" 1985 (Megan Wheeler).

Penrose, Allen. Films: "Dangerous Trails" 1923 (Roland St. Clair).

Peppard, George (1929-5/8/94). Films: "How the West Was Won" 1962 (Zeb Rawlings); "Rough Night in Jericho" 1967 (Dolan); "Cannon for Cordoba" 1970 (Capt. Rod Douglas); "One More Train to Rob" 1971 (Harker Fleet); "The Bravos" TVM-1972 (Maj. John Harkness).

Pepper, Barbara (1916-7/18/69). Films: "Sagebrush Troubador" 1935 (Joan Martin); "The Singing Vagabond" 1935 (Honey); "The Outcasts of Poker Flat" 1937 (Tavern Lady); "Colorado Sunset" 1939 (Ginger); "The Return of Frank James" 1940 (Nellie Blane); "Terror Trail" 1946.

¶TV: *Tales of Wells Fargo*—"Butch Cassidy" 10-13-58 (Boxcar Annie); *Wagon Train*—"The Mary Ellen Thomas Story" 12-24-58 (Mrs. Gifford); *The Texan*—"The Telegraph Story" 10-26-59 (Mary Devlin); *Bonanza*—"The Hanging Posse" 11-28-59; *The Tall Man*—"Shadow of the Past" 10-7-61 (Sue Wiley); *Have Gun Will Travel*—"One, Two, Three" 2-17-62; *Wide Country*—"To Cindy, with Love" 2-28-63 (Waitress).

Pepper, Jack (1903-3/31/79). Films: "Silver Canyon" 1951; "Son of Paleface" 1952 (Customer in Restaurant).

Pepperell, Ethel. Films: "The Mainspring" 1917 (Frances Hardor).

Pera, Lisa. TV: *Wild Wild West*—"The Night of the Tottering Tontine" 1-6-67 (Amelia), "The Night of the Iron Fist" 12-8-67 (Countess Zorana); *Cowboy in Africa*—"The Adopted One" 10-23-67 (Signe Petersen).

Pera, Radames. Films: "Kung Fu" TVM-1972 (Boy Caine). ¶TV: *Kung Fu*—Regular 1972-75 (Young Caine).

Percival, Walter (1887-1/28/34). Films: "The Flying Horseman" 1926 (Bert Ridley); "The Avenger" 1931 (Al Goss).

Percy, Eileen (1901-7/29/73). Films: "The Man from Painted Post" 1917 (Jane Forbes); "Wild and Woolly" 1917 (Nell); "Desert Gold" 1919 (Nell); "In Mizzoura" 1919 (Kate Vernon); "Some Liar" 1919 (Celie Sterling); "Told in the Hills" 1919 (Tillie Hardy); "Where the West Begins" 1919 (Prudence Caldwell); "The Fast Mail" 1922 (Virginia Martin); "Pardon My Nerve!" 1922 (Molly Dale); "Western Speed" 1922 (Dot Lorimer); "Tongues of Flame" 1924 (Billie Boland); "The Phantom Bullet" 1926 (Jane Terrill).

Perdue, Derelyn (1902-9/30/89). Films: "Where the Worst Begins" 1925 (Annice's Friend); "The Mystery Rider" 1928-serial (Grace Wentworth); "Quick Triggers" 1928 (Jeanne Landis); "The Range of Fear" 1929; "The Smiling Terror" 1929 (Mabel).

Perez, Jose (1940-). Films: "The Godchild" TVM-1974 (Sanchez).

Periolat, George (1876-2/20/40). Films: "From the Four Hundred to the Herd" 1912; "Nell of the Pampas" 1912; "The Thread of Life" 1912; "Calamity Anne's Beauty" 1913; "Quicksands" 1913; "The Sheep Herder" 1914; "A Bogus Bandit" 1915; "Put Up Your Hands" 1919 (Peter Barton); "Mark of Zorro" 1920 (Gov-

ernor Alvarado); "Fangs of Destiny" 1927 (Col. Shelby); "The Prairie King" 1927 (Don Fernandez).

Perkins, Anthony (1932-9/12/92). Films: "Friendly Persuasion" 1956 (Josh Birdwell); "The Lonely Man" 1957 (Riley Wade); "The Tin Star" 1957 (Sheriff Ben Owens); "The Life and Times of Judge Roy Bean" 1972 (Rev. LaSalle); "Lovin' Molly" 1974 (Gid). ¶TV: *Studio One*—"The Silent Gun" 2-6-56.

Perkins, Gilbert V. (1907-). Films: "God's Country and the Woman" 1937 (1st Man at Boundary); "Riders of Death Valley" 1941-serial; "Jesse James Rides Again" 1947-serial (Cody); "Son of Zorro" 1947-serial (Cole); "Twilight on the Rio Grande" 1947; "Brave Warrior" 1952 (English Lieutenant); "City of Badmen" 1953 (Bob Fitzsimmons); "Shoot-Out at Medicine Bend" 1957. ¶TV: *Wild Bill Hickok*—"Spurs for Johnny" 5-26-53; *The Californians*—"The Marshal" 3-11-58 (Hogan); *Colt .45*—"The Manbuster" 4-4-58 (Hank Lawler); *Wagon Train*—"Around the Horn" 10-1-58 (Freddy), "The Orly French Story" 12-12-62 (Bates); *Bonanza*—"Knight Errant" 11-18-62 (Whitey), "The Prince" 4-2-67 (Porter); *The Virginian*—"Vengeance Is the Spur" 2-27-63; *Laredo*—"A Matter of Policy" 11-11-65 (Will Brannigan); *Cimarron Strip*—"The Last Wolf" 12-14-67 (Swede).

Perkins, Jack. Films: "A Man Called Gannon" 1969 (Railroad Lineman); "The Apple Dumpling Gang Rides Again" 1979. ¶TV: *Rawhide*—"Incident of the New Start" 3-3-61, "The Child Woman" 3-23-62; *Laredo*—"That's Noway, Thataway" 1-20-66; *Wild Wild West*—"The Night of the Ready-Made Corpse" 11-25-66 (Golo); *Cimarron Strip*—"Nobody" 12-7-67; *Lancer*—"The Heart of Pony Alice" 12-17-68; *Here Come the Brides*—"The Crimpers" 3-5-69, "Marriage Chinese Style" 4-9-69; *Gunsmoke*—"Lavery" 2-22-71 (Trapper), "One for the Road" 1-24-72 (Bouncer), "Kitty's Love Affair" 10-22-73 (Drummer).

Perkins, Leslie. TV: *Wagon Train*—"The Captain Sam Story" 3-21-65 (Mary Anne); *The Virginian*—"The Showdown" 4-14-65 (Junie).

Perkins, Millie (1938-). Films: "Ride in the Whirlwind" 1966 (Abby); "The Shooting" 1966 (Woman). ¶TV: *Wagon Train*—"The Will Santee Story" 5-3-61 (Jessie McDermott); *Dirty Sally*—2-1-74 (Martha).

Perkins, Peter. Films: "Riders of

the Lone Star" 1947; "The Fighting Ranger" 1948; "The Gallant Legion" 1948; "Marshal of Amarillo" 1948 (Sam); "The Sheriff of Medicine Bow" 1948.

Perkins, Voltaire (1897-10/10/77). Films: "The Vanquished" 1953 (Harvey Giddens); "The Far Horizons" 1955.

Perkins, Walter (1870-6/3/25). Films: "Faith Endurin'" 1918 (Sol Durkee); "The Gun Woman" 1918 (Sheriff Joe Harper); "Paying His Debt" 1918 (Father Kelly); "The Pretender" 1918 (Ezra Hoskish); "When Romance Rides" 1922 (Thomas Brackton).

Perley, Charles (1886-2/10/33). Films: "The Gambler of the West" 1914 (Lucky Jack Gordon); "The Bandit and the Baby" 1915; "The Man Who Took a Chance" 1917 (Duke of Cannister); "Playing the Game" 1918 (Hickey Trent).

Perlman, Ron (1950-). Films: "The Cisco Kid" CTVM-1994 (Delacroix).

Perna, David. Films: "Hour of the Gun" 1967 (Frank McLowery). ¶TV: *Bat Masterson*—"The Reluctant Witness" 3-31-60 (Hub Mason); *Laramie*—"The Renegade Brand" 2-26-63; *Wagon Train*—"The Barbara Lindquist Story" 10-18-64 (Johnny); *Laredo*—"Lazyfoot, Where Are You?" 9-16-65, "Which Way Did They Go?" 11-18-65, "The Deadliest Kid in the West" 3-31-66 (Espada), "A Double Shot of Nepenthe" 9-30-66; *The Legend of Jesse James*—"Dark Side of the Moon" 4-18-66 (Rafe Butler).

Perreau, Gigi (1941-). Films: "Wild Heritage" 1958 (Missouri Breslin). ¶TV: *The Rifleman*—"Heller" 2-23-60 (Heller Chase), "Death Trap" 5-9-61 (Carrie Battle); *Stagecoach West*—"The Land Beyond" 10-11-60 (Sarah Lou Proctor); *Laramie*—"The Dark Trail" 11-1-60 (Celie Bronson); *The Rebel*—"Don Gringo" 11-20-60 (Senorita Demetria), "The Promise" 1-15-61 (Laurie); *Rawhide*—"Incident at Poco Tiempo" 12-9-60 (Sister Joan); *Gunsmoke*—"Chicken" 12-5-64 (Lucy Benton); *Iron Horse*—"Death by Triangulation" 3-20-67 (Teresa).

Perreau, Janine (1942-). Films: "The Redhead and the Cowboy" 1951 (Mary Brrett).

Perrin, Jack (Richard Terry, Jack Gable) (1896-12/17/67). Films: "Toton, the Apache" 1917; "The Fighting Heart" 1919; "The Four-Bit Man" 1919; "The Jack of Hearts" 1919; "Two Men of Tainted Butte" 1919;

"The Wild Rider" 1919; "Lahoma" 1920 (Will Compton); "One He Man" 1920; "Bib Bob" 1921; "Both Barrels" 1921; "The Danger Man" 1921; "Fighting Blood" 1921; "The Grip of the Law" 1921; "In the Nick of Time" 1921; "The Knockout Man" 1921; "The Midnight Raiders" 1921; "The Outlaw" 1921; "The Pony Express Rider" 1921; "The Rim of the Desert" 1921; "Stand Up and Fight" 1921; "The Valley of the Rogues" 1921; "Golden Silence" 1923; "The Lone Horseman" 1923; "The Santa Fe Trail" 1923-serial; "Coyote Fangs" 1924 (Jack Burroughs); "Crashin' Thru" 1924 (Jack Lawton); "Lightnin' Jack" 1924 (Lightnin' Jack Hardy); "Riders of the Plains" 1924-serial; "Ridin' West" 1924; "Shootin' Square" 1924; "Travelin' Fast" 1924 (Jack Foster); "Border Vengeance" 1925 (Wes Channing); "Cactus Trails" 1925; "Canyon Rustlers" 1925; "Desert Madness" 1925; "Double Fisted" 1925; "The Knockout Kid" 1925 (Jack Lanning); "Silent Sheldon" 1925 (Jack Sheldon); "Starlight, the Untamed" 1925; "Winning a Woman" 1925; "The Grey Devil" 1926; "Hi-Jacking Rustlers" 1926; "The Man from Oklahoma" 1926; "A Ridin' Gent" 1926; "Starlight's Revenge" 1926; "The Thunderbolt Strikes" 1926; "West of the Rainbow's End" 1926 (Don Brandon); "Blind Man's Bluff" 1927; "Code of the Range" 1927; "Danger Ahead" 1927; "King of Hearts" 1927; "The Laffin' Fool" 1927; "South of the Northern Lights" 1927; "Thunderbolt's Tracks" 1927 (Sgt. Larry Donovan); "Where the North Holds Sway" 1927; "Bare Fists" 1928; "Code of the Mounted" 1928; "A Dangerous Trail" 1928; "Guardians of the Wild" 1928 (Jerry Lane); "The Iron Code" 1928; "Madden of the Mounted" 1928; "Plunging Hoofs" 1928 (Parson Jed Campbell); "The Ring Leader" 1928; "The Ruse" 1928; "Sealed Orders" 1928; "The Two Outlaws" 1928 (Phil Manners/the Lone Rider); "The Vanishing West" 1928-serial; "The Water Hole" 1928 (Ray); "Yukon Gold" 1928; "Harvest of Hate" 1929 (Jack Merritt); "Hoofbeats of Vengeance" 1929 (Sgt. Jack Gordon); "Overland Bound" 1929 (Larry Withers/Jimmy Withers); "Wild Blood" 1929 (Jack Crosby); "The Apache Kid's Escape" 1930; "Beyond the Rio Grande" 1930 (Bert Allen); "Phantom of the Desert" 1930 (Jack Saunders); "Ridin' Law" 1930 (Jack Rowland); "Romance of the West" 1930 (Jack Walsh); "Trails of Danger" 1930 (Sheriff Johnson); "The Kid from

Arizona" 1931; "Rider of the Plains" 1931; "The Sheriff's Secret" 1931; "The Sign of the Wolf" 1931-serial (Jack); "Wild West Whoopee" 1931; "Between Fighting Men" 1932; "Dynamite Ranch" 1932 (Henchman Blackie); "Forty-Five Calibre Echo" 1932; "Hell Fire Austin" 1932 (Curly); "Tex Takes a Holiday" 1932; "Girl Trouble" 1933; "Jaws of Justice" 1933 (Sgt. Kinkaid); "Lariats and Sixshooters" 1933 (Jack Saunders); "Arizona Nights" 1934; "The Cactus Kid" 1934 (Cactus Kid Jack); "Loser's End" 1934 (Jack Fenrod); "Mystery Ranch" 1934 (George Andrews); "Rainbow Riders" 1934; "Rawhide Mail" 1934 (Jack Reed); "Ridin' Gent" 1934-short; "North of Arizona" 1935 (Jack Loomis); "Texas Jack" 1935 (Texas Jack Carrol); "Wolf Riders" 1935 (Jack Jennings); "Arizona Mahoney" 1936 (Stevens); "Desert Justice" 1936 (Jack Franklin); "Gun Grit" 1936 (Bob Blake); "Hair-Trigger Casey" 1936 (Captain Jim Casey); "Wildcat Saunders" 1936 (Wildcat Saunders); "The Painted Stallion" 1937-serial (Davy Crockett); "Reckless Ranger" 1937 (Chet Newton); "Wells Fargo" 1937 (Scout); "The Lone Ranger" 1938-serial (Morgan); "The Purple Vigilantes" 1938 (Duncan); "The Texans" 1938 (Private Soldier); "Western Jamboree" 1938; "The Pal from Texas" 1939 (Sheriff); "Land of the Six Guns" 1940 (Davis); "Texas Rangers Ride Again" 1940 (Radio Technician); "West of Pinto Basin" 1940 (Ware); "Riders of Death Valley" 1941-serial; "Shadows on the Range" 1946; "Bandit Queen" 1950 (Mr. Grayson); "I Shot Billy the Kid" 1950 (Man); "The Treasure of Lost Canyon" 1952 (Sheriff); "Ten Wanted Men" 1955; "Westbound" 1959 (Man).

Perrin, Vic (1916-7/4/89). Films: "Riding Shotgun" 1954 (Bar-M Rider). ¶TV: *Gunsmoke*—"No Handcuffs" 1-21-56 (Hank Springer), "What the Whiskey Drummer Heard" 4-27-57 (Wilbur Hawkins), "Bless Me Till I Die" 4-22-61 (Nate Bush), "Not That April's There" 3-21-64 (Argus), "The Promoter" 4-25-64 (Henry Huckaby); *Frontier*—"The Hanging at Thunder Butte Creek" 3-11-56; *Have Gun Will Travel*—"Winchester Quarantine" 10-5-57, "Show of Force" 11-9-57 (Bernard), "The Night the Town Died" 2-6-60, "The Campaign of Billy Banjo" 5-28-60 (Cooley), "Everyman" 3-25-61 (Drunk); *Jim Bowie*—"Deaf Smith" 2-7-58 (Deaf Smith); *Wanted—Dead or Alive*—"Fatal Memory" 9-13-58 (Willie Joe Weems); *Wagon Train*—

"The Juan Ortega Story" 10-8-58 (Tuck Edwards); *Tales of Wells Fargo*—"The Dealer" 12-29-58 (Langford Peel), "The Lat Mayor Brown" 3-7-60 (Ben Locust); *Rawhide*—"Incident of the Widowed Dove" 1-30-59, "Incident of the Captive" 12-16-60, "Prairie Fire" 3-19-65 (Vinnie Pitts); *Black Saddle*—"Client: Braun" 4-4-59 (Ernie Weems); *Lancer*—"Glory" 12-10-68 (Pete), "The Kid" 10-7-69 (Whitley Scroggs); *The Deputy*—"Focus of Doom" 11-7-59 (Madden); *The Rebel*—"The Actress" 2-5-61 (Will Arvid); *Empire*—"The Day the Empire Stood Still" 9-25-62 (Matt Webster); *A Man Called Shenandoah*—"Rope's End" 1-17-66 (Station Master); *The Big Valley*—"Down Shadow Street" 1-23-67 (Albert Pruitt); *Wild Wild West*—"The Night of the Winged Terror" 1-17-68 & 1-24-68 (Professor); *Kung Fu*—"The Third Man" 4-26-73 (Eldon Riddle).

Perrine, Valerie (1944-). Films: "The Electric Horseman" 1979 (Charlotta).

Perron, Larry. TV: *Broken Arrow*—"Power" 4-22-58; *Tales of the Texas Rangers*—"Edge of Danger" 10-23-58 (Johnny Ryan); *Wagon Train*—"The Felezia Kingdom Story" 11-18-59 (Snare); *The Rifleman*—"Baranca" 11-1-60 (Eddie), "Death Trap" 5-9-61 (Sag); *Whispering Smith*—"The Idol" 9-18-61 (Tom Jerson); *The Tall Man*—"Time of Foreshadowing" 11-25-61 (Posseman); *Laramie*—"The High Country" 2-6-62 (Clay); *The Virginian*—"The Intruders" 3-4-64 (Indio).

Perrott, William. Films: "Son of Billy the Kid" 1949 (Billy the Kid); "Dakota Lil" 1950 (Cashier).

Perry, Barbara. Films: "Fort Bowie" 1958 (Mrs. Maywood). ¶TV: *Wyatt Earp*—"Love and Shotgun Gibbs" 4-21-59 (Phronsie LaTour); *Daniel Boone*—"The Loser's Race" 11-10-66 (Lydia Dorsey).

Perry, Elizabeth. Films: "The Silent Gun" TVM-1969; "Banjo Hackett: Roamin' Free" TVM-1976 (Grace Nye). ¶TV: *Tate*—"The Gunfighters" 8-31-60 (Maggie); *Great Adventure*—"The Pathfinder" 3-6-64 (Mrs. Chiles); *Gunsmoke*—"The New Society" 5-22-65 (Vera Scanlon); *Bonanza*—"The Dilemma" 9-19-65 (Ruth).

Perry, Felton (1942-). TV: *Here Come the Brides*—"The Wealthiest Man in Seattle" 10-3-69 (Mark), "Break the Bank of Tacoma" 1-16-70; *Adventures of Brisco County, Jr.*—"Brisco for the Defense" 10-22-93 (Sheriff Bumper W. Crosswaite).

Perry, Jack (-10/7/71). Films: "Rose of the Rancho" 1936 (Vigilante).

Perry, Jean. Films: "The Ruse of the Rattlesnake" 1921 (Bud Sanderson); "Hills of Missing Men" 1922 (Crando).

Perry, Jessie (1876-7/6/44). Films: "Law of the Plains" 1938 (Mrs. Bowen).

Perry, Joan. Films: "Gallant Defender" 1935 (Barbara McGrall); "Heir to Trouble" 1935 (Jane Parker); "The Mysterious Avenger" 1936 (Alice Lockhart).

Perry, John Bennett. Films: "The Legend of the Lone Ranger" 1981 (Dan Reid); "I Married Wyatt Earp" TVM-1983 (John Behan); "Independence" TVM-1987 (Sheriff); "Poker Alice" TVM-1987. ¶TV: *Nakia*—"The Moving Target" 11-9-74 (Cal Terman); *Kung Fu*—"Battle Hymn" 2-8-75 (Deputy Hank Archer); *Barbary Coast*—"An Iron-Clad Plan" 10-31-75.

Perry, Joseph (1931-). TV: *Gunsmoke*—"Reunion '78" 3-3-56 (Witness), "Bloody Hands" 2-16-57 (Clay), "The Deserter" 6-4-60 (Radin), "The Cousin" 2-2-63 (Moran), "Seven Hours to Dawn" 9-18-65 (Buck); *Broken Arrow*—"Shadow of Cochise" 2-4-58 (Coffee); *Maverick*—"The Seventh Hand" 3-2-58 (Pritchard); *Have Gun Will Travel*—"The Prize Fight Story" 4-5-58, "In an Evil Time" 9-13-58 (Brother), "The Moor's Revenge" 12-27-58 (Drunk), "The Black Handkerchief" 11-14-59 (Sheriff); *Wanted—Dead or Alive*—"The Favor" 11-15-58 (Gabe Justin), "Bounty for a Bride" 4-4-59 (Black Horse), "The Conquerers" 5-2-59 (Juan), "Tolliver Bender" 2-13-60; *Black Saddle*—"Client: Meade" 1-17-59 (Cass Tibbett); *Death Valley Days*—"Tribal Justice" 12-22-59 (Yellow Bear), "The Hero of Apache Pass" 1-14-67 (Cherokee Bob), "Major Horace Bell" 5-20-67 (King), "The Contract" 3-14-70; *Johnny Ringo*—"The Killing Bug" 4-18-60 (Deke Lewis), "Lobo Lawman" 6-23-60 (Joe); *The Law of the Plainsman*—"Trojan Horse" 5-5-60 (Ben); *Stagecoach West*—"A Fork in the Road" 11-1-60 (Somerset); *The Rifleman*—"The Illustrator" 12-13-60; *Zane Grey Theater*—"The Mormons" 12-15-60 (Frank); *Stoney Burke*—"Five by Eight" 12-10-62 (Captain Bender); *Rawhide*—"Incident of the Comanchero" 3-22-63 (Carlos), "Incident of the Hostages" 4-19-63 (Ulzana), "Incident of the Geisha" 12-19-63 (Santana); *Daniel Boone*—

"Pompey" 12-10-64 (Tabuka), "The Return of Sidewinder" 12-12-68 (Kinch); *Branded*—"A Taste of Poison" 5-2-65 (Jimmie Boy); *Iron Horse*—"The Execution" 3-13-67 (Bart Hobson); *The Guns of Will Sonnett*—"The Turkey Shoot" 11-24-67; *Wild Wild West*—"The Night of the Undead" 2-2-68 (Bartender); *Lancer*—"Foley" 10-15-68, "The Great Humbug" 3-4-69 (Bartender), "The Buscaderos" 3-17-70; *Here Come the Brides*—"Hosanna's Way" 10-31-69 (Billy Gumm); *Bonanza*—"He Was Only Seven" 3-5-72 (Sheriff Tyson).

Perry, Linda. Films: "The California Mail" 1937 (Mary Tolliver); "Land Beyond the Law" 1937 (Louise).

Perry, Luke (1967-). Films: "8 Seconds" 1994.

Perry, Pascale (1889-7/11/53). Films: "The Gallant Fool" 1933 (Layton); "King of the Arena" 1933; "The Fiddlin' Buckaroo" 1934; "Gun Justice" 1934; "Honor of the Range" 1934; "Gallant Defender" 1935; "Lawless Range" 1935; "Lawless Riders" 1935; "Bold Caballero" 1936; "Guns and Guitars" 1936 (Frank Hall); "Oh, Susannah!" 1936; "Roarin' Lead" 1936; "Vigilantes Are Coming" 1936-serial (Rancher); "The Painted Stallion" 1937-serial (Joe); "Days of Jesse James" 1939; "Saga of Death Valley" 1939; "Billy the Kid in Texas" 1940; "Oklahoma Renegades" 1940; "The Trail Blazers" 1940; "Bad Man of Deadwood" 1941; "Desert Bandit" 1941; "Under Fiesta Stars" 1941; "Shadows on the Sage" 1942; "The Sombrero Kid" 1942; "Carson City Cyclone" 1943; "California Gold Rush" 1946; "Thunder Town" 1946; "Jesse James Rides Again" 1947-serial (Raider #3); "Son of Zorro" 1947-serial; "Springtime in the Sierras" 1947 (Henchman); "Eyes of Texas" 1948 (Pete); "Gun Runner" 1949 (Allen).

Perry, Robert "Bob" (1879-1/8/62). Films: "Iron to Gold" 1922 (Creel); "The Light of Western Stars" 1925 (Nelse); "The Thundering Herd" 1925 (Joe Dunn); "Jaws of Steel" 1927 (the Sheriff); "White Gold" 1927 (Bucky O'Neill); "Sin Town" 1929 (Slippery Simpson); "Trailin' Trouble" 1930; "The Fighting Marshal" 1931 (Joe Stevens); "Call of the Wild" 1935 (Stage Manager); "Robin Hood of El Dorado" 1936 (Miner at Grave); "The Bad Man of Brimstone" 1937 (Gang Member); "Twenty Mule Team" 1940; "They Died with Their Boots On" 1941 (Officer); "The Great Man's

Lady" 1942 (Miner); "Jackass Mail" 1942 (Miner); "Calamity Jane and Sam Bass" 1949.

Perry, Roger (1933-). Films: "Heaven with a Gun" 1969 (Ned Hunter). ¶TV: *Desilu Playhouse*—"Ballad for a Badman" 1-26-59 (Danny Cash); *U.S. Marshal*—"Paper Bullets" 12-5-59 (Ted Jarvis); *The Texan*—"Friend of the Family" 1-4-60 (Robin Randolph); *Hondo*—"Hondo and the Judas" 11-3-67 (Johnny Ringo); *Lancer*—"The Measure of a Man" 4-8-69 (Ben Cameron); *Alias Smith and Jones*—"Something to Get Hung About" 10-21-71.

Perry, Walter (1868-1/22/54). Films: "The Learnin' of Jim Benton" 1917 (Joe); "Truthful Tulliver" 1917 (Silver Lode Thompson); "Until They Get Me" 1917 (Sergeant Blaney); "By Proxy" 1918 (Aleck); "Faith Endurin'" 1918 (King); "The Fly God" 1918 (Wind River); "Little Red Decides" 1918 (Two Pair Smith); "Prisoner of the Pines" 1918 (Spud Lafferty); "The Red Haired Cupid" 1918; "The End of the Game" 1919 (Wild Bill); "The Mints of Hell" 1919 (Reirdon); "The Prodigal Liar" 1919 (Paddy Donohue); "A Sage Brush Hamlet" 1919 (Sheriff John Doe); "Fighting Cressy" 1920 (Uncle Ben Dabney); "The U.P. Trail" 1920 (Casey); "The Fire Eater" 1921 (Jim O'Neil); "Three Bad Men" 1926 (Pat Monahan); "Trigger Tricks" 1930 (Ike); "The Two Gun Man" 1931 (Riggs); "Spirit of the West" 1932 (Toby).

Perryman, Lloyd (1917-3/31/77). Films: "Santa Fe Rides" 1937; "Law of the Plains" 1938 (Lloyd); "South of Arizona" 1938; "Rio Grande" 1950 (Regimental Singer). ¶TV: *Gunsmoke*—"The Fourth Victim" 11-4-74 (Henry Meeker).

Perschy, Maria (1938-). Films: "The Tall Women" 1966-Austria/Ital./Span.

Pershing, Marcella. Films: "Bandits Beware" 1921; "Beating the Game" 1921; "Crossed Clues" 1921; "Double Crossers" 1921; "The Man Who Woke Up" 1921; "The Movie Trail" 1921; "The Showdown" 1921; "Who Was That Man?" 1921; "The Wild Wild West" 1921; "Looped for Life" 1924 (Mary Baker).

Persoff, Nehemiah (1920-). Films: "The Badlanders" 1958 (Vincente); "Day of the Outlaw" 1959 (Dan); "The Comancheros" 1961 (Amflung); "The Dangerous Days of Kiowa Jones" TVM-1966 (Skoda); "Cutter's Trail" TVM-1970 (Santillo); "An American Tail: Fievel Goes West" 1991 (voice of Papa Mousekewitz).

¶TV: *Wagon Train*—"The Tiburcio Mendez Story" 3-22-61 (Tiburcio Mendez); *Frontier Circus*—"The Daring Durandos" 5-17-62; *Rawhide*—"Incident of the White Eyes" 5-3-63 (Domingo), "Incident of the Wanderer" 2-27-64 (Michob); *Wild Wild West*—"The Night of the Inferno" 9-17-65 (Juan Manola/Gen. Andreas Cassinello), "The Night of the Deadly Blossom" 3-17-67 (Adam Barclay), "The Night of the Underground Terror" 1-19-68 (Major Hazzard); *Gunsmoke*—"Ten Little Indians" 10-9-65 (Jack Pinto), "The Pretender" 11-20-65 (Dano), "Blood Money" 1-22-68 (Alex Skouras), "The Mark of Cain" 2-3-69 (Timothy Driscoll), "Like Old Times" 1-21-74 (Ben Rando), "Manolo" 3-17-75 (Alejo Etchahoun); *A Man Called Shenandoah*—"The Bell" 12-20-65 (Father Rodriguez); *The Legend of Jesse James*—"The Empty Town" 1-3-66 (El Carnicero); *The Big Valley*—"Legend of a General" 9-19-66 & 9-26-66 (General Vicente Ruiz); *The High Chaparral*—"Fiesta" 11-20-70 (Jose).

Pesce, Franco (Frank Oliveras). Films: "A Pistol for Ringo" 1965-Ital./Span.; "Seven Guns for Timothy" 1966-Span./Ital.; "Sunscorched" 1966-Span./Ger. (Luke); "Blood at Sundown" 1967-Span./Ital.; "Shango" 1969-Ital.; "Roy Colt and Winchester Jack" 1970-Ital.; "Gold of the Heroes" 1971-Ital./Fr.; "Have a Good Funeral, My Friend ... Sartana Will Pay" 1971-Ital.; "Miss Dynamite" 1972-Ital./Fr.

Peters, Brock (1927-). Films: "Major Dundee" 1965 (Aesop); "Ace High" 1967-Ital./Span. (Thomas); "The McMasters" 1970 (Benjie). ¶TV: *Daniel Boone*—"Pompey" 12-10-64 (Pompey); *Rawhide*—"The Spanish Camp" 5-7-65 (Phinn); *The Loner*—"The Homecoming of Lemuel Stove" 11-20-65 (Lemuel Stove); *The Outcasts*—"Act of Faith" 2-10-69 (Ben Pritchard); *Gunsmoke*—"The Good Samaritans" 3-10-69 (Cato), "Jessie" 2-19-73 (Jesse Dillard); *The Men from Shiloh*—"Crooked Corner" 10-28-70 (Ivers).

Peters, Erika. TV: *Sugarfoot*—"Stranger in Town" 3-27-61 (Inga Bernstrom); *Bonanza*—"The Frenchman" 12-10-61 (Eloise); *The Outlaws*—"The Bitter Swede" 1-18-62 (Hulda Christianson); *Wide Country*—"Whose Hand at My Throat?" 2-14-63 (Ilona Lukins).

Peters, Frederic (1884-4/23/63). Films: "The Millionaire Cowboy" 1924 (Grafter Torso).

Peters, House (1880-12/7/67). Films: "Salomy Jane" 1914 (Jack Dart); "The Girl of the Golden West" 1915 (Ramerez); "The Great Divide" 1915 (Stephen Ghent); "The Highway of Hope" 1917 (Steve King); "The Forfeit" 1919 (Jeffrey Masters); "The Great Redeemer" 1920 (Dan Malloy); "Isobel, or the Trail's End" 1920 (Sergeant William McVeigh); "The Storm" 1922 (Burr Winton); "The Old West" 1952 (Prson Brooks).

Peters, Jr., House. Films: "Public Cowboy No. 1" 1937 (Jim Shannon); "The Adventures of Frank and Jesse James" 1948-Serial (Sheriff Towey); "Courtin' Trouble" 1948 (Larsen); "Dangers of the Canadian Mounted" 1948-serial (Ford); "Desperadoes of Dodge City" 1948 (Henry); "Gunning for Justice" 1948; "Oklahoma Badlands" 1948 (Wilkins); "Renegades of Sonora" 1948; "Under California Stars" 1948 (Ed); "Outlaw Country" 1949 (Col. Saunders); "Sheriff of Wichita" 1949 (Jack Thorne); "Son of Billy the Kid" 1949 (1st Outlaw); "Border Treasure" 1950 (Rod); "Cow Town" 1950 (Gil Saunders); "Over the Border" 1950 (Wade Shelton); "Twilight in the Sierras" 1950 (Williams); "Blazing Bullets" 1951; "The Dakota Kid" 1951 (Sam Dawson); "Gene Autry and the Mounties" 1951 (Hogan); "Man from Sonora" 1951; "Spoilers of the Plains" 1951 (Scheller); "Three Desperate Men" 1951 (Dick Cable); "Carson City" 1952; "Fargo" 1952; "Kansas Territory" 1952 (Carruthers); "The Lion and the Horse" 1952 (Rocky Steuber); "Oklahoma Annie" 1952 (Tullett); "The Old West" 1952 (Saunders); "Waco" 1952 (Doctor); "Wyoming Roundup" 1952 (Randolph); "Winning of the West" 1953 (Marshal Hackett); "Overland Pacific" 1954 (Perkins); "Black Patch" 1957 (Holman); "Man from God's Country" 1958 (Curt Warren); "Terror at Black Falls" 1962 (Sheriff); "Rio Conchos" 1964 (Pardee Officer); "The Great Sioux Massacre" 1965 (Reporter). ¶TV: *The Lone Ranger*—"Jim Tyler's Luck" 2-16-50, "Man Without a Gun" 6-15-50, "Desert Adventure" 11-30-50, "Mr. Trouble" 3-8-51, "Best Laid Plans" 12-25-52, "Prisoner in Jeopardy" 8-20-53, "Ex-Marshal" 9-16-54, "Gold Freight" 4-28-55, "The Breaking Point" 1-24-57, "Ghost Town Fury" 3-28-57; *The Gene Autry Show*—"Head for Texas" 7-23-50, "The Star Toter" 8-20-50; *Annie Oakley*—"The Dude Stagecoach" 1-30-54; *The Cisco Kid*—"Pancho and the Pachyderm" 2-2-52,

"Laughing Badman" 3-8-52; *Colt .45*—"The Saga of Sam Bass" 5-17-59 (Sheriff); *Wild Bill Hickok*—"Wrestling Story" 4-8-52; *Wyatt Earp*—"The Man Who Lied" 10-11-55 (Dave Bennett), "The Gambler" 10-18-55, "The Killer" 10-25-55; *Fury*—"Joey Sees It Through" 1-21-56 (Bill Adams); *The Roy Rogers Show*—"His Weight in Wildcats" 11-11-56 (Lou Driggs), "Tossup" 12-2-56 (Bill Wheeling), "Portrait of Murder" 3-17-57; *Sergeant Preston of the Yukon*—"Scourge of the Wilderness" 1-11-57 (Monk Larson); *Telephone Time*—"Elfego Baca" 4-18-57 (McCarthy); *Tales of Wells Fargo*—"The Feud" 10-14-57; *Broken Arrow*—"Bear Trap" 4-29-58 (Capt. Rowan); *Wagon Train*—"The Charles Maury Story" 5-7-58 (Matt Goslett), "The Artie Matthewson Story" 11-8-61 (Ick Fears), "The Jeff Hartfield Story" 2-14-62 (Link Hartfield); *Northwest Passage*—"Break Out" 10-19-58 (Zach Miller); *Rough Riders*—"The Counterfeiters" 12-11-58 (Pete Terrell); *Buckskin*—"Who Killed Pat Devlin?" 2-16-59 (Pat Devlin); *Gunsmoke*—"The Coward" 3-7-59 (Nat Swan), "About Chester" 2-25-61 (Jake Wirth); *Bat Masterson*—"Shakedown at St. Joe" 10-29-59 (Marshal); *Lawman*—"Trapped" 9-17-61 (Joe Poole); *Laramie*—"The Marshals" 4-30-63.

Peters, Jan. TV: *Have Gun Will Travel*—"Hobson's Choice" 4-7-62 (Carriage Maker); *Gunsmoke*—"Bad Lady from Brookline" 5-1-65 (Curley), "The Prisoner" 3-17-69 (Cardplayer); *The Legend of Jesse James*—"Things Don't Just Happen" 3-14-66 (Sherif).

Peters, Jean (1927-). Films: "Viva Zapata!" 1952 (Josefa Espejo); "Apache" 1954 (Nalinle); "Broken Lance" 1954 (Barbara).

Peters, John (1894-11/7/63). Films: "Ranson's Folly" 1926 (Judge Advocate); "The Frontiersman" 1927 (Col. Coffee); "Northwest Outpost" 1947 (Officer); "Tomahawk" 1951 (Pvt. Osborne); "Chief Crazy Horse" 1955 (Sgt. Guthrie).

Peters, Kelly Jean (1940-). Films: "Little Big Man" 1971 (Olga); "Pocket Money" 1972 (Wife); "Deadly Trackers" 1973 (Katharine). ¶TV: *Iron Horse*—"Broken Gun" 10-17-66 (Lee Diver); *The Virginian*—"Yesterday's Timepiece" 1-18-67 (Elaine); *Gunsmoke*—"Ladies from St. Louis" 3-25-67 (Sister John), "Prairie Wolfers" 11-13-67 (Adele), "Johnny Cross" 12-23-68 (Vera Cross); *Bonanza*—"A Lonely Man" 1-2-72

(Missy); *Kung Fu*—"The Stone" 4-12-73 (Martha Lovitt).

Peters, Laurie (1943-). TV: *Gunsmoke*—"May Blossoms" 2-15-64 (May Blossom), "Take Her, She's Cheap" 10-31-64 (Allie Carp); *The Road West*—"Reap the Whirlwind" 1-9-66 (Sarah).

Peters, Lyn (1943-). TV: *Laredo*—"The Short, Happy Fatherhood of Reese Bennett" 1-27-67; *Daniel Boone*—"The Traitor" 11-2-67 (Julia Cartwright).

Peters, Page (1890-6/22/16). Films: "Davy Crockett" 1916 (Neil Crampton).

Peters, Ralph (1903-6/5/59). Films: "Gun Grit" 1936 (Dopey); "Rough Ridin' Rhythm" 1937 (Scrubby); "Call the Mesquiteers" 1938; "Man's Country" 1938 (Snappy); "Outlaws of Sonora" 1938 (Gabby); "Santa Fe Stampede" 1938; "The Stranger from Arizona" 1938; "Where the West Begins" 1938 (Hawkins); "Colorado Sunset" 1939; "The Man from Sundown" 1939 (Bradley); "Oklahoma Terror" 1939 (Reb); "Rovin' Tumbleweeds" 1939 (Satchel); "Six-Gun Rhythm" 1939 (Spud Donovan); "Trigger Fingers" 1939 (Mort); "Wyoming Outlaw" 1939; "Death Rides the Range" 1940 (Panhandle); "The Durango Kid" 1940 (Taylor); "Ghost Valley Raiders" 1940 (Deputy Sheriff); "Pioneers of the Frontier" 1940; "Riders on Black Mountain" 1940 (Tombstone); "Son of Roaring Dan" 1940 (Casey Waters); "Across the Sierras" 1941; "Billy the Kid's Range War" 1941 (Jailer); "Honky Tonk" 1941 (Pallbearer); "The Lone Rider Ambushed" 1941 (Bartender); "Outlaws of the Rio Grande" 1941 (Monty); "Sunset in Wyoming" 1941; "Texas" 1941 (Deputy); "Bells of Capistrano" 1942; "In Old California" 1942; "Ride 'Em, Cowboy" 1942 (1st Henchman); "Shut My Big Mouth" 1942 (Butch); "Twilight on the Prairie" 1944; "Canyon Passage" 1946 (Stutchell); "Desert Fury" 1947 (Pete, the Cafe Owner); "Trail to San Antone" 1947 (Sam); "The Valiant Hombre" 1948; "Cactus Cut-Up" 1949-short; "Beyond the Purple Hills" 1950 (Tim); "Slaughter Trail" 1951 (Stage Driver); "Destry" 1954 (Bartender); "Badlands of Montana" 1957 (Sammy). ¶TV: *The Lone Ranger*—"The Beeler Gang" 8-10-50; *Wyatt Earp*—"County Seat War" 4-8-58 (Honky).

Peters, Scott (-1/23/94). Films: "Outlaw's Son" 1957 (Randall); "The Canadians" 1961-Brit. ¶TV: *The Texan*—"Outpost" 1-19-59 (Charley

Arno); *Gunsmoke*—"The Constable" 5-30-59 (Pete); *Wyatt Earp*—"The Trail to Tombstone" 9-8-59 (Lucas); *Bonanza*—"The Lila Conrad Story" 1-5-64; *The Big Valley*—"Tunnel of Gold" 4-20-66 (Lou Stone).

Peters, Susan (Suzanne Carnahan) (1921-10/23/52). Films: "Santa Fe Trail" 1940 (Charlotte Davis).

Peters, Tom. TV: *Zane Grey Theater*—"The Freighter" 1-17-58 (Gil Murdock); *Rawhide*—"Incident of the Night on the Town" 6-2-61; *Death Valley Days*—"The Solid Gold Cavity" 10-1-66, "The Duke of Tombstone" 1-10-70; *Bonanza*—"What Are Pardners For?" 4-12-70 (Ray Stahl).

Peters, Wayne. Films: "Stage to Thunder Rock" 1964 (Toby Sawyer).

Peters, Werner (1919-3/31/71). Films: "Black Eagle of Santa Fe" 1964-Ger./Ital./Fr. (Morton).

Petersen, Paul (1944-). Films: "A Time for Killing" 1967 (Blue Lake); "Journey to Shiloh" 1968 (J.C. Sutton); "Something for a Lonely Man" TVM-1968 (Pete Duren). ¶TV: *F Troop*—"Johnny Eagle Eye" 4-12-66 (Johnny Eagle Eye); *Custer*—"Suspicion" 10-18-67 (Lieutenant Cox); *Iron Horse*—"Steel Chain to a Music Box" 11-18-67 (Frank); *The Big Valley*—"The Long Ride" 11-25-68 (Roy Sanders).

Petersen, Robert. TV: *Wanted—Dead or Alive*—"Call Your Shot" 2-7-59; *The Virginian*—"The Inchoworm's Got No Wings at All" 2-2-66 (Gully).

Petersen, Stewart. Films: "Seven Alone" 1974 (John); "Against a Crooked Sky" 1975 (Sam Sutter); "Pony Express Rider" 1976 (Jimmy).

Petersen, William. Films: "Young Guns II" 1990 (Pat Garrett); "Return to Lonesome Dove" TVM-1993.

Peterson, Arthur (1912-). Films: "Invitation to a Gunfighter" 1964 (Schoop); "The Great Northfield, Minnesota Raid" 1972 (Jefferson Jones). ¶TV: *Gunsmoke*—"The Peace Officer" 10-15-60 (Parks), "Chesterland" 11-18-61 (Arny), "A Man a Day" 12-30-61 (Frazer), "Champion of the World" 12-24-66 (Drunk), "Roots of Fear" 12-15-69 (Judge Brooker); *The Rebel*—"Berserk" 12-18-60 (Doc Jones), "The Executioner" 6-18-61 (Sheriff); *Bonanza*—"Blessed Are They" 4-22-62, "The Trackers" 1-7-68, "In Defense of Honor" 4-28-68 (Judge), "The Clarion" 2-9-69 (Dr. Adams), "Long Way to Ogden" 2-22-70 (Lloyd Walsh), "The Luck of

Pepper Shannon" 11-22-70 (Donavan), "The Twenty-Sixth Grave" 10-31-72 (Martin); *The Big Valley*—"Palms of Glory" 9-15-65 (Swenson); *Iron Horse*—"Volcano Wagon" 1-16-67 (the Rev. Mr. Sparrow); *Death Valley Days*—"Along Came Mariana" 5-27-67 (Judge); *The Guns of Will Sonnett*—"Meeting at Devil's Fork" 10-27-67 (Stevens).

Peterson, Dorothy (-1979). Films: "Out West with the Peppers" 1940 (Mrs. Pepper); "Canyon Passage" 1946 (Mrs. Dance).

Peterson, Nan. TV: *Zane Grey Theater*—"Checkmate" 4-30-59; *Lawman*—"The Return" 5-10-59, "Lily" 10-4-59 (Annette); *The Texan*—"Traildust" 10-19-59; *Rawhide*—"Incident of the Thirteenth Man" 10-23-59 (Janet Hennig); *Black Saddle*—"The Indian Tree" 2-19-60 (Dallas Carver); *Gunsmoke*—"Unwanted Deputy" 3-5-60 (Janet).

Petit, Michael. TV: *The Rifleman*—"The Princess" 1-8-62 (Charles); *The Travels of Jaimie McPheeters*—"The Day of the Toll Takers" 1-5-64 (Tubal), "The Day of the Pretenders" 3-1-64 (Paul); *Bonanza*—"A Man to Admire" 12-6-64 (Benjie); *Gunsmoke*—"Deputy Festus" 1-16-65 (Glen); *Rawhide*—"Blood Harvest" 2-12-65 (Boy); *Branded*—"The Bar Sinister" 10-10-65 (Jimmy Whitlaw).

Petit, Pascale (1938-). Films: "Find a Place to Die" 1968-Ital. (Lisa).

Petit, Wanda. *see* Hawley, Wanda.

Petri, Mario (1921-1/26/85). Films: "Lost Treasure of the Incas" 1965-Ger./Ital./Fr./Span.

Petrie, George. Films: "Hud" 1963 (Joe Scanlon); "He Rides Tall" 1964 (Crowley). ¶TV: *Rawhide*—"Judgment at Hondo Seco" 10-20-61; *Bronco*—"Ride the Whirlwind" 1-15-62 (Tom Egan); *Temple Houston*—"The Third Bullet" 10-24-63 (Newton Fountain); *Destry*—"Big Deal at Little River" 3-20-64 (Gambler); *Bonanza*—"Enter Thomas Bowers" 4-26-64; *The Virginian*—"The Brazos Kid" 10-21-64 (Delaney); *Branded*—"The Ghost of Murrieta" 3-20-66; *Wild Wild West*—"The Night of the Amnesiac" 2-9-68 (Col. Petrie); *Barbary Coast*—"The Dawson Marker" 1-9-76 (Samuels); *Gunsmoke*—"Celia" 2-23-70 (Cashier); *How the West Was Won*—"The Innocent" 2-12-79 (Dr. Baker); *Young Riders*—"The Littlest Cowboy" 11-23-90 (Sims).

Petrie, Howard (1907-3/26/68). Films: "Fancy Pants" 1950 (Secret

Service Man); "Rocky Mountain" 1950 (Cole Smith); "Cattle Drive" 1951 (Cap); "Bend of the River" 1952 (Tom Hendricks); "Pony Soldier" 1952 (Inspector Frazer); "The Wild North" 1952 (Brody); "Woman of the North Country" 1952 (Rick Barton); "Fort Ti" 1953 (Maj. Rogers); "Border River" 1954 (Newlund); "The Bounty Hunter" 1954 (Sheriff Brand); "Rage at Dawn" 1955 (Lattimore); "The Return of Jack Slade" 1955 (Ryan); "Timberjack" 1955 (Axe-Handle Ole); "Johnny Concho" 1956 (Helgeson); "The Maverick Queen" 1956 (Butch Cassidy); "The Tin Star" 1957 (Harvey King). ¶TV: *Gunsmoke*—"Yorky" 2-18-56 (Brant); *Zane Grey Theater*—"You Only Run Once" 10-5-56 (Kroll), "The Hanging Tree" 2-22-57 (Kroll), "Killer Instinct" 3-17-60 (Killegrew); *Cheyenne*—"The Bounty Killer" 10-23-56 (Sheriff Barnes), "Wagon Tongue North" 4-8-58; *Broken Arrow*—"Apache Dowry" 1-15-57 (Sam Carson); *The Californians*—"Pipeline" 4-22-58 (Stryker); *Bonanza*—"The Paiute War" 10-3-59; *Lawman*—"The Hunch" 10-11-59 (Hal Mead); *Maverick*—"The Lass with the Poisonous Air" 11-1-59 (Mike Burke); *Colt .45*—"Tar and Feathers" 11-22-59 (John Porter); *Wanted—Dead or Alive*—"No Trail Back" 11-28-59 (Sheriff Akers), "Angela" 1-9-60 (Sam Prior); *Bat Masterson*—"A Picture of Death" 1-14-60 (Hugh Blain), "Pigeon and Hawk" 1-21-60 (Hugh Blaine), "A Grave Situation" 5-12-60 (Hugh Blaine), "Law of the Land" 10-6-60 (Hugh Blaine); *Have Gun Will Travel*—"The Lady on the Wall" 2-20-60 (Jack Foster); *Johnny Ringo*—"The Gunslinger" 3-24-60 (Blanchard); *Death Valley Days*—"The General Who Disappeared" 5-3-60; *Rawhide*—"Incident of the Murder Steer" 5-13-60 (Abner Carter), "Incident of the Broken Word" 1-20-61; *Wyatt Earp*—"The Truth About Old Man Clanton" 9-27-60, "Shoot to Kill" 10-18-60 (Governor Gibbs).

Petrucci, Giovanni. Films: "Big Ripoff" 1967-Span./Ital.; "Death Rides a Horse" 1967-Ital.; "Cost of Dying" 1968-Ital./Fr. (Tony); "The Dirty Outlaws" 1971-Ital.

Pette, Graham. Films: "Up or Down? 1917 (Sheriff); "Beyond the Shadows" 1918 (Leon DuBois); "Boss of the Lazy Y" 1918 (Jim Marston); "Closin' In" 1918 (Sour Dough Green); "Faith Endurin'" 1918 (Old Jerry); "The Good Loser" 1918 (McCoy); "His Enemy, the Law" 1918 (Jim Dawson); "The Pretender" 1918 (Seth Higgins); "Untamed" 1918

(Pancho); "Wild Life" 1918 (Al); "The Westerners" 1919 (Prof. Welch).

Pettet, Joanna (1944-). Films: "Blue" 1968 (Joanne Morton); "Pioneer Woman" TVM-1973 (Maggie Sergeant); "A Cry in the Wilderness" TVM-1974 (Delda Hadley). ¶TV: *A Man Called Shenandoah*—"The Riley Brand 2-21-66 (Rulia Riley).

Petti, Giovanni. Films: "Canadian Wilderness" 1969-Span./Ital.; "Requiem for a Bounty Hunter" 1970-Ital. (Lassiter); "The White, the Yellow, and the Black" 1974-Ital./Span./Fr.

Pettyjohn, Angelique (1944-2/14/92). Films: "Heaven with a Gun" 1969 (Emily).

Peyser, Penny (1951-). Films: "The Frisco Kid" 1979 (Rosalie); "Wild Times" TVM-1980 (Libby Tyree).

Peyton, Claude. *see* Payton, Claude

Peyton, Lawrence (-10/18). Films: "Buck Parvin and the Movies" 1915; "Buck's Lady Friend" 1915; "Film Tempo" 1915; "A Life at Stake" 1915; "Man-Afraid-of-His-Wardrobe" 1915; "This Is the Life" 1915; "Margy of the Foothills" 1916; "The Golden Fetter" 1917 (Buck Hanson); "The Greater Law" 1917 (Cort Dorian); "The Red Ace" 1917-serial; "Ace High" 1918 (Jack Keefe).

Peyton, Robert. Films: "Night Stage to Galveston" 1952 (T.J. Wilson). ¶TV: *The Adventures of Kit Carson*—"Fury at Red Gulch" 10-27-51 (Red Barrows); *The Gene Autry Show*—"Outlaw Escape" 12-1-51, "The Return of Maverick Dan" 12-15-51.

Pflug, Jo Ann (1940-). Films: "Catlow" 1971-Span. (Christina). ¶TV: *The Big Valley*—"Down Shadow Street" 1-23-67 (Rothie Murphy); *Alias Smith and Jones*—"Only Three to a Bed" 1-13-73 (Beegee).

Pharr, Frank (1890-3/10/69). Films: "The Cherokee Strip" 1937; "Gold Is Where You Find It" 1938 (Rancher); "Dodge City" 1939; "Wild West" 1946 (Doctor); "The Sea of Grass" 1947 (Station Loafer); "The Texan Meets Calamity Jane" 1950 (Sheriff Atwood).

Phelps, Lee (1894-3/19/53). Films: "The Freshie" 1922 (Tom); "Boss Rider of Gun Creek" 1936 (Sheriff Marsden); "Robin Hood of El Dorado" 1936 (Hank); "Rose Marie" 1936 (Barfly); "Boss of Lonely Valley" 1937 (Peter Starr); "God's Country and the Woman" 1937 (Brakeman); "Left-Handed Law"

1937 (Sheriff Grant); "Raw Timber" 1937 (Bull); "Sandflow" 1937 (the Kid); "Smoke Tree Range" 1937; "Sudden Bill Dorn" 1937 (Ben Fairchild); "Wells Fargo" 1937 (Printer); "Gun Law" 1938; "The Great Adventures of Wild Bill Hickok" 1938; "Heart of Arizona" 1938; "The Fargo Kid" 1940 (Bartender); "Hidden Gold" 1940 (Sheriff Cameron); "The Return of Frank James" 1940 (Bartender); "Wyoming" 1940 (Man); "Honky Tonk" 1941 (Man in Meeting House); "The Great Man's Lady" 1942; "Riders of the West" 1942; "Gentle Annie" 1944 (Expressman); "Girl Rush" 1944 (Mac); "Along Came Jones" 1945 (Deputy); "Duel in the Sun" 1946 (Engineer); "Red River" 1948; "Gun Law Justice" 1949; "Shadows of the West" 1949 (Hart); "Desperadoes of the West" 1950-serial (Rusty Steele); "The Girl from San Lorenzo" 1950 (Sheriff); "Hills of Oklahoma" 1950 (Scotty Davis); "Western Pacific Agent" 1950; "Don Daredevil Rides Again" 1951-serial (Uncle Michael Doyle); "Pistol Harvest" 1951; "Oklahoma Annie" 1952 (Taylor); "The Outcasts of Poker Flat" 1952 (Man); "The Marshal's Daughter" 1953 (Sheriff Barnes). ¶TV: *The Lone Ranger*—"Never Say Die" 4-6-50; *The Gene Autry Show*—"Gun Powder Range" 10-29-50, "Fight at Peaceful Mesa" 11-19-50; *The Cisco Kid*—"Boomerang" 1-20-51; *Wild Bill Hickok*—"The Silver Mine Protection Story" 7-24-51.

Phelps Guthrie, Tani. TV: *Gunsmoke*—"McCabe" 11-30-70 (Amy), "Drago" 11-22-71 (Clara); *Bonanza*—"The Law and Billy Burgess" 2-15-70 (Nora Burgess); *The High Chaparral*—"The Hostage" 3-5-71 (Meelie); *Hec Ramsey*—"Dead Heat" 2-3-74 (Anna Carmody).

Phelps, Tex. Films: "Young Whirlwind" 1928 (Bandit); "One-Man Law" 1932; "Sagebrush Trail" 1933; "The Lucky Texan" 1934; "'Neath the Arizona Skies" 1934 (Henchman); "Randy Rides Alone" 1934 (Deputy); "Between Men" 1935 (Henchman); "The Dawn Rider" 1935 (Henchman); "Smokey Smith" 1935; "Border Caballero" 1936; "The Lonely Trail" 1936 (Trooper); "Roarin' Guns" 1936; "Valley of the Lawless" 1936 (Henchman); "California Frontier" 1938; "Ghost Town Riders" 1938; "Heroes of the Alamo" 1938; "Man from Music Mountain" 1938; "Santa Fe Marshal" 1940.

Phelps Brothers, The (Willie Phelps, Norman Phelps & Earl Phelps). Films: "The Mystery of the Hooded Horseman" 1937; "Rhythm Wranglers" 1937-short; "A Buckaroo Broadcast" 1938-short; "The Painted Desert" 1938; "Prairie Papas" 1938-short; "Renegade Ranger" 1938; "A Western Welcome" 1938-short; "Where the West Begins" 1938; "Bandits and Ballads" 1939-short; "Cupid Rides the Range" 1939-short; "Ranch House Romeo" 1939-short; "Sagebrush Serenade" 1939-short; "Trouble in Sundown" 1939.

Philbin, John. Films: "Tombstone" 1993 (Tom McLaury).

Philbin, Mary (1903-5/7/93). Films: "Red Courage" 1921 (Eliza Fay); "Where Is This West?" 1923 (Sallie Summers).

Philbin, Regis. TV: *The Big Valley*—"The Challenge" 3-18-68 (Reporter).

Philbrook, James (1924-10/24/82). Films: "Warlock" 1959 (Cade); "The Wild Westerners" 1962 (U.S. Marshal Jim McDowell); "Finger on the Trigger" 1965-Span./Ital./U.S. (Adam Hyde); "Two Thousand Dollars for Coyote" 1965-Span. (Coyote); "Django, A Bullet for You" 1966-Span./Ital. (Django); "Seven for Pancho Villa" 1966-Span.; "Son of a Gunfighter" 1966-U.S./Span. (Ketchum); "I Do Not Forgive ... I Kill!" 1968-Span./Ital.; "If You Shoot ... You Live!" 1974-Span. ¶TV: *Wagon Train*—"The Les Rand Story" 10-16-57; *Maverick*—"The Seventh Hand" 3-2-58 (Simon Sloan); *Sugarfoot*—"A Wreath for Charity Lloyd" 3-18-58 (Smokey); *Broken Arrow*—"Manhunt" 6-3-58 (Clem Harrison); *The Texan*—"Return to Friendly" 2-2-59 (Yancey Lewis); *Bonanza*—"Inger, My Love" 4-15-62 (McWhorter).

Philippe, Andre (1927-). TV: *Bonanza*—"The Frenchman" 12-10-61 (Francois Villon), "A Severe Case of Matrimony" 7-7-68 (Poco); *Wild Wild West*—"The Night of the Freebooters" 4-1-66 (Enrique Leon), "The Night of the Poisonous Posey" 10-28-66 (Ascot Sam), "The Night of the Tartar" 2-3-67 (Feodor Rimsky), "The Night of the Pelican" 12-27-68 (Jean Paul).

Philliber, John (1872-11/6/44). Films: "A Lady Takes a Chance" 1943 (Storekeeper); "Gentle Annie" 1944 (Barrow).

Phillips, Art. Films: "So This Is Arizona" 1922 (Bob Thompson); "Galloping On" 1925 (Storekeeper).

Phillips, Augustus. Films: "Joyce of the North Woods" 1913; "The Man from the West" 1913.

Phillips, Barney (1914-8/17/82). Films: "The True Story of Jesse James" 1957 (Dr. Samuel); "Drango" 1957 (Cameron); "Run, Simon, Run" TVM-1970 (Detective); "Law of the Land" TVM-1976. ¶TV: *Gunsmoke*—"The Roundup" 9-29-56 (Ed Summers), "The Coward" 3-7-59 (Pence), "Renegade White" 4-11-59 (Ord Spicer), "Don Mateo" 10-22-60 (Bill Pence), "Big Man" 3-25-61 (Pence); *Have Gun Will Travel*—"The Monster of Moon Ridge" 2-28-59 (Dan Bella), "The Prophet" 1-2-60 (Major Ferber), "The Night the Town Died" 2-6-60, "The Shooting of Jesse May" 10-20-60 (Ergo); *Black Saddle*—"Client: Jessup" 4-18-59 (Thompson), "Four from Stillwater" 11-27-59 (Charlie Johnson); *Wyatt Earp*—"Shoot to Kill" 10-18-60, "Billy Buckett, Incorporated" 1-3-61, "The Shooting Starts" 4-18-61 (Lou Rickabaugh); *Death Valley Days*—"The Truth Teller" 1-31-62 (Hancock); *Wild Wild West*—"The Night of a Thousand Eyes" 10-22-65 (Captain Tenney); *Bonanza*—"Riot!" 10-3-72 (Asa Calhoun); *Young Maverick*—"Hearts O'Gold" 12-12-79.

Phillips, Carmen (1897-1973). Films: "The Sunset Trail" 1917 (Camilla Aiken); "Unclaimed Goods" 1918 (Idaho Ina); "The Fire Eater" 1921 (Marie Roselli); "A Six Shootin' Romance" 1926 (Mrs. King).

Phillips, Carmen (1937-). Films: "Ride the High Country" 1962 (Saloon Girl). ¶TV: *The Deputy*—"Three Brothers" 12-10-60 (Suzy); *Laramie*—"The Accusers" 11-14-61 (Sally); *Destry* "The Infernal Triangle" 5-1-64 (Marie); *Laredo*—"The Treasure of San Diablo" 2-17-66 (Lupita).

Phillips, Charles (1904-5/25/58). Films: "Rollin' Home to Texas" 1941; "Raiders of the Range" 1942.

Phillips, Doris. Films: "Son of the Plains" 1931 (Anne Farrell).

Phillips, Dorothy (1889-5/1/80). Films: "The Trail of the Upper Yukon" 1915; "The Valley of Silent Men" 1915; "Pay Me!" 1917 (Marta); "The Grand Passion" 1918 (Viola Argus); "The Bar C Mystery" 1926-serial (Jane Cortelyou); "The Man Who Shot Liberty Valance" 1962.

Phillips, Edward "Eddie" (1868-10/7/44). Films: "The Plunderer" 1924 (Richard Townsend); "The Whipping Boss" 1924 (Jim); "Silent Pal" 1925 (David Kingston); "Wild West" 1925-serial; "Burning Brides" 1928 (Tommy Wilkins); "Crossfire" 1933 (Bert King); "Fighting to Live" 1934; "Border Vengeance" 1935 (John Preston); "The Code of the Mounted" 1935 (Louis); "Ivory-Handled Gun" 1935 (Young Bill Ward); "The Throwback" 1935 (Milt Fergus); "Ambush Valley" 1936 (Clay Morgan); "Phantom Patrol" 1936 (Emile); "Vengeance of Rannah" 1936 (Macklin); "Wildcat Trooper" 1936 (Bob Reynolds); "Smoke Tree Range" 1937; "Billy the Kid Trapped" 1942 (Dave); "Texas Man Hunt" 1942 (Nate Winters); "Texas Trouble Shooters" 1942 (Wade); "Death Valley Manhunt" 1943 (Blaine); "Cyclone Prairie Rangers" 1944; "Dangers of the Canadian Mounted" 1948-serial (Barker); "Buffalo Bill in Tomahawk Territory" 1952 (Lt. Bryan).

Phillips, Edna (1878-2/26/52). Films: "Ruggles of Red Gap" 1918 (Klondike Kate Kenner).

Phillips, Jean (1914-12/15/70). Films: "Outlaws of the Desert" 1941 (Susan Grant).

Phillips, Jeff. Films: "Bonanza: Under Attack" TVM-1995 (Adam "A.C." Cartwright, Jr.). ¶TV: *Adventures of Brisco County, Jr.*—"Hard Rock" 2-4-94 (Whip), "Wild Card" 4-8-94 (Whip), "And Baby Makes Three" 4-22-94 (Whip), "Bad Luck Betty" 4-29-94 (Whip), "High Treason" 5-13-94 & 5-20-94 (Whip).

Phillips, Joe (1913-10/19/72). Films: "Son of Zorro" 1947-serial (Deputy #2/Sniper); "The Adventures of Frank and Jesse James" 1948-serial; "Crooked River" 1950 (Rancher); "Desperadoes of the West" 1950-serial; "The James Brothers of Missouri" 1950-serial (Jackson); "Don Daredevil Rides Again" 1951-serial (Attacker #2).

Phillips, John. Films: "Heldorado" 1946 (Sheriff); "The Kid from Texas" 1950 (Sid Curtis); "Seminole" 1953 (Maj. Lawrence); "Seven Men from Now" 1956 (Jed). ¶TV: *The Lone Ranger*—"The New Neighbor" 12-18-52; *Tales of the Texas Rangers*—"Double Edge" 10-8-55 (Tom Dawson), "The Shooting of Sam Bass" 10-15-55 (Tom Nixon); *Fury*—"Joey's Father" 12-3-55.

Phillips, Lee. TV: *Death Valley Days*—"The White Healer" 11-30-60 (Lt. Wood); *Wagon Train*—"The Bonnie Brooke Story" 2-21-65 (Jack Evans), "The Jarbo Pierce Story" 5-2-65 (Fortune); *The Loner*—"The House Rules at Mrs. Wayne's" 11-6-65 (Gibson).

Phillips, Lou Diamond (1962-). Films: "Young Guns" 1988 (Chavez Y. Chavez), "Young Guns II" 1990

(Chavez Y. Chavez); "Shadow of the Wolf" 1993-Can./Fr. (Agaguk).

Phillips, Minna (1885-1/17/63). Films: "Bandit Queen" 1950 (Mrs. Grayson); "Train to Tombstone" 1950 (Abbie).

Phillips, Robert (1930-). Films: "Cat Ballou" 1965 (Klem); "Hour of the Gun" 1967 (Frank Stilwell); "MacKenna's Gold" 1969 (Monkey); "Yuma" TVM-1971 (Sanders); "The Gun and the Pulpit" TVM-1974 (Tom Underwood); "Adios Amigo" 1975. ¶TV: *Temple Houston*—"Fracas at Kiowa Flats" 12-12-63 (Shotgun Guard), "Miss Katherina" 4-2-64 (Private Keller); *The Loner*—"The Kingdom of McComb" 10-9-65 (Sloan); *Wild Wild West*—"The Night of the Human Trigger" 12-3-65 (Sam), "The Night of the Sudden Plague" 4-22-66 (Lafe), "The Night of the Arrow" 12-29-67 (Oconee), "The Night of Fire and Brimstone" 11-22-68 (Frank Roach); *Laredo*—"A Medal for Reese" 12-30-65 (Sergeant); *Bonanza*—"Black Friday" 1-22-67 (Jakes); *The High Chaparral*—"Survival" 1-14-68 (Klosen); *Cimarron Strip*—"Heller" 1-18-68 (Matt Sherman); *The Outcasts*—"The Stalking Devil" 4-7-69; *Gunsmoke*—"The Gun" 11-19-70 (Vance Jessop), "Disciple" 4-1-74 (Bill Jim); *Kung Fu*—"The Predators" 10-5-74 (Mutala the Navajo); *The Quest*—"Portrait of a Gunfighter" 12-22-76 (Slavens).

Phillips, William "Bill" (1908-6/27/57). Films: "The Harvey Girls" 1946 (Cowboy); "The Sea of Grass" 1947 (Santy); "The Man from Colorado" 1948 (York); "Big Jack" 1949 (Teddy); "Al Jennings of Oklahoma" 1951 (Bill Mertz); "Cavalry Scout" 1951 (Sgt. Wilkins); "Bugles in the Afternoon" 1952 (Tinney); "High Noon" 1952 (Barber); "Devil's Canyon" 1953 (Red); "Gun Belt" 1953 (Curly); "Jesse James Versus the Daltons" 1954 (Bill Dalton); "The Law vs. Billy the Kid" 1954 (Charlie Bowdre); "Fort Yuma" 1955 (Sgt. Halleck); "Man Without a Star" 1955; "Top Gun" 1955 (Hank); "The Broken Star" 1956 (Doc Mott); "Fastest Gun Alive" 1956 (Lars Toomey); "Ghost Town" 1956 (Kerry McCabe); "The Last Hunt" 1956 (Man); "The Naked Gun" 1956; "Stagecoach to Fury" 1956 (Bartender); "Revolt at Fort Laramie" 1957 (Lt. Waller). ¶TV: *Sergeant Preston of the Yukon*—"Justice at Goneaway Creek" 2-9-56 (Flint); *Dundee and the Culhane*—10-25-67 (Turpin); *Here Come the Brides*—"Next Week, East Lynne" 10-17-69.

Phipps, Charles (1877-2/12/50). Films: "Riding the Wind" 1942 (Ezra Westfall); "Thundering Hoofs" 1942 (Kellogg).

Phipps, Jack. Films: "Lightnin' Jack" 1924 (Knowles Brother); "Hell's Valley" 1931 (Jose Valdez).

Phipps, Sally (1909-3/17/78). Films: "Broncho Billy and the Baby" 1915.

Phipps, William (1923-). Films: "Belle Starr's Daughter" 1947 (Yuma); "The Arizona Ranger" 1948 (Mae); "Desperadoes of Dodge City" 1948 (Ted Loring); "Station West" 1948 (Sergeant); "Rider from Tucson" 1950 (Tug/Caldwell); "The Vanishing Westerner" 1950 (Bud); "Fort Osage" 1952 (Nathan Goodspeed); "Rose of Cimarron" 1952 (Jeb Dawley); "Northern Patrol" 1953 (Frank Stevens); "Red River Shore" 1953 (Ned Barlow); "Savage Frontier" 1953 (Johnny Webb); "Two Guns and a Badge" 1954 (Allen); "The Far Horizons" 1955; "Fort Yuma" 1955; "The Indian Fighter" 1955 (Lt. Blake); "Man Without a Star" 1955 (Cookie); "Smoke Signal" 1955 (Pvt. Porter); "The Violent Men" 1955 (Bud Hinkleman); "The First Texan" 1956; "Badlands of Montana" 1957 (Walt); "Escape from Red Rock" 1958 (Arky Shanks); "Cavalry Command" 1963-U.S./Phil. (Pvt. Haines); "Incident at Phantom Hill" 1966 (Trader); "Gunfight in Abilene" 1967 (Frank Norton); "The Intruders" TVM-1970. ¶TV: *Wild Bill Hickok*—"Yellow Haired Kid" 8-28-51; *The Cisco Kid*—"Double Deal" 1-17-53, "Fool's Gold" 5-9-53; *The Westerner*—Pilot 11-53; *The Adventures of Rin Tin Tin*—"The Poor Little Rich Boy" 10-7-55 (Wesley Parish); *Broken Arrow*—"The Raiders" 12-25-56 (Frank Krohl), "Black Moment" 10-29-57 (Summerfield); *Annie Oakley*—"Dude's Decision" 2-10-57 (Earl Wallace); *Wagon Train*—"The Jean LeBec Story" 9-25-57 (Bill Hammond), "The Emily Rossiter Story" 10-30-57 (Hank), "The Santiago Quesada Story" 3-30-64; *Colt .45*—"One Good Turn" 11-29-57 (Trumbull); *Circus Boy*—"The Judge's Boy" 12-5-57 (Dirk Keyes); *Trackdown*—"Look for the Woman" 12-6-57 (Bud Crome); *Wyatt Earp*—"One-Man Army" 1-7-58, Regular 1959-61 (Curly Bill Brocius); *Tombstone Territory*—"Gun Fever" 1-22-58 (Neal Weaton), 1-15-60 (Kyle Dodge); *Decision*—"The Tall Man" 7-27-58 (Leslie Henderson); *Maverick*—"The Thirty-Ninth Star" 11-16-58 (Hazelton); *Cimarron City*—"McGowan's

Debt" 12-27-58 (Rand Scoville); *Bat Masterson*—"License to Cheat" 2-4-59 (Ken Wills); *Wanted—Dead or Alive*—"The Corner" 2-21-59 (Fred Teton), "Breakout" 9-26-59, "Triple Vise" 2-27-60; *Gunsmoke*—"The Coward" 3-7-59 (Lou), "Odd Man Out" 11-21-59 (Hody Peel), "The Prisoner" 5-19-62 (Ham Owen), "Carter Caper" 11-16-63 (Joe Stark), "Gilt Guilt" 4-24-65 (Drifter); *The Rifleman*—"The Money Gun" 5-12-59 (Asa Manning); *Riverboat*—"The Faithless" 11-22-59 (Abner Crane); *Texas John Slaughter*—"Wild Horse Revenge" 12-11-59 (Gabe); *Laramie*—"The Protectors" 3-22-60 (Allen); *Johnny Ringo*—"Black Harvest" 4-7-60 (Paul Connell); *G.E. Theater*—"Aftermath" 4-17-60 (Hicks); *The Rebel*—"The Guard" 1-8-61 (Ben Mowbree), "Decision at Sweetwater" 4-23-61 (Mr. Bishop); *Cheyenne*—"The Greater Glory" 5-15-61 (Smiler Jones); *The Tall Man*—"Full Payment" 9-9-61 (Bert); *Rawhide*—"The Greedy Town" 2-16-62 (Floyd Peters); *The Virginian*—"Impasse" 11-14-62 (Jock Wheeler), "The Orchard" 10-2-68 (Ritt); *Stoney Burke*—"Cat's Eyes" 2-11-63 (Gene Yates); *Temple Houston*—"Ten Rounds for Baby" 1-30-64 (Sandy Dale); *Daniel Boone*—"The Price of Friendship" 2-18-65 (Dink), "The Fleeing Nuns" 10-24-68 (Horn); *The Legend of Jesse James*—"The Dead Man's Hand" 9-20-65 (Buck); *Laredo*—"The Heroes of San Gill" 12-23-65 (Hollen), "A Prince of a Ranger" 12-9-66; *Branded*—"The Golden Fleece" 1-2-66 (Captain Brooks); *The Road West*—"Power of Fear" 12-26-66 (Cleary), "Reap the Whirlwind" 1-9-66 (Charlie); *Wild Wild West*—"The Night of the Falcon" 11-10-67 (Marshal); *Cimarron Strip*—"Knife in the Darkness" 1-25-68; *The Guns of Will Sonnett*—"Look for the Hound Dog" 1-26-68, "Chapter and Verse" 10-11-68, "One Angry Juror" 3-7-69; *Bonanza*—"The Law and Billy Burgess" 2-15-70 (Tom Burgess); *Sara*—Regular 1976 (Claude Barstow); *The Oregon Trail*—"The Waterhole" 9-28-77.

Phoenix, River (1970-10/31/93). Films: "Silent Tongue" 1993 (Talbot Roe).

Piaget, Paul. Films: "Magnificent Three" 1963-Span./Ital.; "Charge of the Seventh Cavalry" 1964-Ital./Span./Fr.; "Seven Guns from Texas" 1964-Span./Ital. (Clifford); "Shots Ring Out!" 1965-Ital./Span. (Frank Dalton); "Hour of Death" 1968-Span./Ital.

Piazza, Ben (1934-9/7/91).

Films: "The Hanging Tree" 1959 (Rune). ¶TV: *Zane Grey Theater*—"The Grubstake" 12-24-59 (Coley); *Stoney Burke*—"A Matter of Pride" 11-5-62 (Dayton Hill); *Gunsmoke*—"Hard Labor" 2-24-75 (Fifer); *The Chisholms*—"Death in the Sierras" 2-16-80 (Sutter), "Chains" 3-8-80 (Sutter); *Outlaws*—"Madrid" 2-7-87 (Joseph Conlon).

Pica, Antonio. Films: "The Man Who Killed Billy the Kid" 1967-Span./Ital.; "Bandidos" 1967-Ital.; "Ringo, the Lone Rider" 1967-Ital./Span.; "Two Crosses at Danger Pass" 1968-Ital./Span.; "A Bullet for Sandoval" 1970-Ital./Span. (Sam); "Who's Afraid of Zorro?" 1975-Ital./Span. (the Governor).

Picardo, Robert. Films: "Wagons East!" 1994 (Ben Wheeler). ¶TV: *Adventures of Brisco County, Jr.*—"The Orb Scholar" 9-3-93 (Puel).

Piccoli, Michel (1925-). Films: "Don't Touch White Women!" 1974-Ital. (Buffalo Bill).

Picerni, Charles. Films: "The Barbary Coast" TVM-1975. ¶TV: *Daniel Boone*—"A Pinch of Salt" 5-1-69.

Picerni, Paul (1922-). Films: "Saddle Tramp" 1950; "Fort Worth" 1951 (Castro); "Cattle Town" 1952 (Pepe); "The Bounty Hunter" 1954 (Jud); "Riding Shotgun" 1954 (Bob Purdee); "Return to Warbow" 1958 (2nd Deputy); "The Scalphunters" 1968 (Frank); "Land Raiders" 1969-U.S./Span. (Carney). ¶TV: *Cavalcade of America*—"Mountain Man" 9-28-54; *Circus Boy*—"Little Vagabond" 6-23-57 (Julio Gaetano); *Broken Arrow*—"Apache Child" 10-15-57 (Zele), "White Savage" 12-24-57 (Major Markson); *Boots and Saddles*—"The Deserter" 11-14-57 (Trooper Grimes); *Tales of the Texas Rangers*—"Gypsy Boy" 11-24-57 (Philip Conzog); *Colt .45*—"The Gypsies" 12-27-57 (Quito), "Return to El Paso" 6-21-59 (Jose), "Martial Law" 5-17-60 (Duke Blaine); *26 Men*—"Gun Hand" 2-25-58; *Zorro*—"The Deadly Bolas" 5-22-58 (Pietro Murietta), "The Well of Death" 5-29-58 (Pietro Murietta); *Maverick*—"Escape to Tampico" 10-26-58 (Rene); *The Adventures of Rin Tin Tin*—"Star of India" 1-2-59 (Jaffar Husein); *Fury*—"An Old Indian Trick" 2-14-59 (Shunatona), "Packy, the Lion Tamer" 1-2-60 (Tupelo); *Northwest Passage*—"Stab in the Back" 2-20-59 (Guy Perro); *Wyatt Earp*—"Horse Race" 3-3-59 (Chief Bullhead); *Bonanza*—"The Spanish Grant" 2-6-60 (Sanchez); *The Rebel*—"Unsurrendered" (chez); "Two Crosses at Danger Pass"

Sword" 4-3-60 (Manuel), "The Legacy" 11-13-60 (Lee Ricker); *Rawhide*—"Incident of the Dancing Death" 4-8-60 (Bahari); *Sugarfoot*—"The Corsican" 4-12-60 (Gian-Paola); *The Big Valley*—"The Iron Box" 11-28-66 (Peterson); *Gunsmoke*—"The Lure" 2-25-67 (William McGee), "The Pillagers" 11-6-67 (Ganns), "Kitty's Love Affair" 10-22-73 (Grimes), "Disciple" 4-1-74 (Virgil Orcutt); *The Virginian*—"The Fortress" 12-27-67 (Parks); *Lancer*—"The Prodigal" 11-12-68.

Pichel, Irving (1891-7/13/54). Films: "The Mysterious Rider" 1933 (Cliff Harkness); "High, Wide and Handsome" 1937 (Mr. Stark); "She Wore a Yellow Ribbon" 1949 (Narrator); "Santa Fe" 1951 (Harned).

Pickard, John (1913-8/4/93). Films: "The Gunfighter" 1950 (3rd Brother); "Stage to Tucson" 1950 (Sam Granger); "Little Big Horn" 1951 (Sgt. Vet McCloud); "Oh! Susanna" 1951 (Rennie); "Snake River Desperadoes" 1951 (Dodds); "Bugles in the Afternoon" 1952 (McDermott); "Hellgate" 1952 (Gundy Boyd); "Trail Guide" 1952 (Dawson); "Arrowhead" 1953 (John Gunther); "The Fighting Lawman" 1953; "Arrow in the Dust" 1954 (Lybarger); "Bitter Creek" 1954 (Oak Mason); "Black Horse Canyon" 1954 (Duke); "Massacre Canyon" 1954 (Lt. Ridgeford); "Rose Marie" 1954 (Orderly); "Two Guns and a Badge" 1954 (Sharkey); "At Gunpoint" 1955 (Alvin); "Fort Yuma" 1955; "Seminole Uprising" 1955 (Sgt. Chris Zanoba); "Seven Angry Men" 1955 (Wilson); "Shotgun" 1955 (Perez); "The Black Whip" 1956 (Sheriff Persons); "The Broken Star" 1956 (Van Horn); "Friendly Persuasion" 1956 (Ex-Sergeant); "Kentucky Rifle" 1956; "The Lone Ranger" 1956 (Sheriff Kimberley); "Badlands of Montana" 1957 (Vince); "Copper Sky" 1957 (Trooper Hadley); "The Oklahoman" 1957 (Marshal Bill); "Outlaw's Son" 1957 (Ed Wyatt); "Ride a Violent Mile" 1957 (Marshal Thorne); "War Drums" 1957 (Sheriff Bullard); "Gun Street" 1961 (Dr. Knudson); "Charro!" 1969 (Jerome Selby); "True Grit" 1969 (Frank Ross); "Chisum" 1970 (Aggressive Sergeant); "The Hanged Man" TVM-1974; "Shootout in a One-Dog Town" TVM-1974 (Preston). ¶TV: *The Cisco Kid*—"The Runaway Kid" 6-21-52, "New Evidence" 9-19-53; *The Lone Ranger*—"Best Laid Plans" 12-25-52, "Sunstroke Mesa" 3-17-55, "Trouble at Tylerville" 12-13-56, "Outlaws in Grease Paint" 6-6-57; *Tales of the Texas Rangers*—"Ransom Flight" 8-

27-55 (Frank Warren); *The Adventures of Rin Tin Tin*—"Wolf Cry" 10-22-55 (Sam), "Rinty Finds a Bone" 4-27-56 (Morrison), "The Frame-Up" 3-15-57; *Cavalry Patrol*—Pilot 1956 (Sgt. Gilchrist); *My Friend Flicka*—"Wind from Heaven" 2-3-56; *Fury*—"Timber" 3-17-56 (Rusty), "Trail Drive" 10-24-59; *Sergeant Preston of the Yukon*—"Remember the Maine" 4-26-56 (Sid Helm), "Rebellion in the North" 7-12-56 (Jim Dark), "King of Herschel Island" 10-25-56 (Jim Dark), "Old Ben's Gold" 10-3-57 (Red Brody); *Zane Grey Theater*—"Back Trail" 2-1-57 (Tom Clauson), "Legacy of a Legend" 11-6-58 (Deputy), "Desert Flight" 10-13-60 (Sheriff), "The Long Shadow" 1-19-61; *Wyatt Earp*—"The Equalizer" 4-16-57 (Johnny Ringgold), "They Think They're Immortal" 5-28-57 (John Ringgold), "The Trail to Tombstone" 9-8-59 (Whitey); *Tales of Wells Fargo*—"Shotgun Messenger" 5-6-57 (Sheriff Lyons), "The Kid" 11-18-57 (Sheriff Lyons), "The Stage Line" 10-5-59 (Langer); *Boots and Saddles*—Regular 1957-59 (Captain Shank Adams); *Death Valley Days*—"The Jackass Mail" 6-30-57, "Honor the Name Dennis Driscoll" 10-25-64, "Hero of Fort Halleck" 6-27-65 (Major Breen), "The Red Shawl" 2-5-66 (Will Dundy), "The Resurrection of Deadwood Dick" 10-22-66 (Sheriff McKittrick), "The Saga of Sadie Orchard" 1-13-68, "The Other Cheek" 11-16-68 (Lafe Ellsworth), "Old Stape" 10-18-69; *Rawhide*—"Incident of the Golden Calf" 3-13-59 (Clint Crowley), "Incident of the Devil and His Due" 1-22-60 (Owens), "Incident at Rojo Canyon" 9-30-60 (Mattson), "Incident at Rio Salado" 9-29-61 (Sheriff), "The Devil and the Deep Blue" 5-11-62 (Sheriff), "Abilene" 5-18-62 (Sheriff), "Incident at Farragut Pass" 10-31-63 (Sheriff), "Incident at the Odyssey" 3-26-64, "The Race" 9-25-64 (Morgan), "Josh" 1-15-65 (Sam Parks); *Wagon Train*—"The Matthew Lowry Story" 4-1-59 (Jed Otis); *Lawman*—"The Huntress" 5-3-59; *The Texan*—"The Gunfighter" 6-8-59 (Ben Kirby), "Borrowed Time" 3-7-60 (Jess Walton); *Laramie*—"Circle of Fire" 9-22-59 (Calvin Dalyrumple), "The Pass" 12-29-59 (Will Cooper), "Men of Defiance" 4-19-60 (Gabe Kett), ".45 Calibre" 11-15-60 (Sloane), "Handful of Fire" 12-5-61, "The Marshals" 4-30-63, "The Road to Helena" 5-21-63 (Bradford); *The Law of the Plainsman*—"Passenger to Mescalero" 10-29-59; *Hotel De Paree*—"Sundance and the Hostiles" 12-11-59 (Matt);

Johnny Ringo—"East Is East" 1-7-60 (Riley Criswell); *Gunsmoke*—"Kitty's Killing" 2-20-60 (Ollie Radford), "The Cook" 12-17-60 (Jack Purdy), "The Renegades" 1-12-63 (Poole), "Killer at Large" 2-5-66 (Gabin), "The Newcomers" 12-3-66 (Head Vigilante), "The Lure" 2-25-67 (John Vanner), "The Reprisal" 2-10-69 (Forbes), "Milligan" 11-6-72 (Bob Power), "A Game of Death … An Act of Love" 11-5-73 & 11-12-73 (Captain Sykes), "The First of Ignorance" 1-27-75 (Bud); *Wichita Town*—"Second Chance" 3-16-60 (Bain); *The Rebel*—"The Captive of Tremblor" 4-10-60 (Marshal Drown), "The Bequest" 9-25-60 (Sheriff Cahill), "Run, Killer, Run" 10-30-60 (Sheriff Pruett); *Overland Trail*—"Fire in the Hole" 4-17-60 (Cavanaugh); *Wanted—Dead or Alive*—"The Trial" 9-21-60 (Langley); *Two Faces West*—"The Last Man" 12-19-60 (Laird Willoughby); *The Westerner*—"Hand on the Gun" 12-23-60; *The Rifleman*—"Death Trap" 5-9-61 (Stacey); *Gunslinger*—Regular 1961 (Sergeant Major Murdock); *Frontier Circus*—"Incident at Pawnee Gun" 9-6-62 (Murdoch); *Branded*—"The Vindicator" 1-31-65 (Sergeant), "The First Kill" 4-4-65 (Rand), "Salute the Soldier Briefly" 10-24-65 (Lieutenant Stanley), "Call to Glory" 2-27-66, 3-6-66 & 3-13-66 (General Phil Sheridan); *Daniel Boone*—"The Price of Friendship" 2-18-65 (Telly), "Tanner" 10-5-67 (Beckitt); *The Loner*—"The Homecoming of Lemuel Stove" 11-20-65; *Wild Wild West*—"The Night of the Steel Assassin" 1-7-66 (R.L. Gilbert), "The Night of the Hangman" 10-20-67 (Amos Rawlins), "The Night of the Running Death" 12-15-67 (Governor Ireland), "The Night of the Pistoleros" 2-21-69 (Duty Sergeant); *The Virginian*—"Chaff in the Wind" 1-26-66 (Sheriff), "Family Man" 10•15-69 (Nathan Rigby); *The Road West*—"Long Journey to Leavenworth" 10-17-66 (Earl Collins); *Iron Horse*—"War Cloud" 10-31-66 (Sergeant Terry), "Through Ticket to Gunsight" 11-28-66 (Bulwer); *The Big Valley*—"Cage of Eagles" 4-24-67 (Sheriff); *The High Chaparral*—"Shadows on the Land" 10-15-67 (Jack Coffin), "Sea of Enemies" 1-3-69 (Sergeant Williams); *Dundee and the Culhane*—10-25-67 (Watchman); *Cimarron Strip*—"The Last Wolf" 12-14-67 (Carl Kersey); *Bonanza*—"Company of Forgotten Men" 2-2-69 (Perkins), "Winter Kill" 3-28-71 (Griggs); *Kung Fu*—"The Soul Is the Warrior" 2-8-73 (Benson); *How the West Was Won*—Episode One 2-6-77 (Colonel Caine), Episode Two 2-6-77 (Colonel Caine), Episode

2-7-77 (Colonel Caine), Episode Three 2-14-77 (Colonel Caine).

Pickard, Obed "Dad" (1874-9/24/54). Films: "Frontier Vengeance" 1940 (Rocky); "Riders of the Dawn" 1945 (Dad Pickard); "The Sea of Grass" 1947 (Man).

Pickens, Slim (1919-12/8/83). Films: "Rocky Mountain" 1950 (Plank); "Border Saddlemates" 1952 (Slim Pickens); "Colorado Sundown" 1952 (Slim); "The Last Musketeer" 1952 (Slim); "Old Oklahoma Plains" 1952 (Slim); "South Pacific Trail" 1952 (Slim Pickens); "Down Laredo Way" 1953 (Slim Pickens); "Iron Mountain Trail" 1953 (Slim); "Old Overland Trail" 1953 (Slim); "Red River Shore" 1953 (Slim); "Shadows of Tombstone" 1953 (Slim); "The Boy from Oklahoma" 1954 (Shorty); "The Outcast" 1954 (Boone Polsen); "The Phantom Stallion" 1954; "The Last Command" 1955 (Abe); "Santa Fe Passage" 1955 (Sam Beekman); "The Great Locomotive Chase" 1956 (Pete Bracken); "Gun Brothers" 1956 (Moose MacLain); "Stranger at My Door" 1956 (Ben Silas, Horse Trader); "Gunsight Ridge" 1957 (Hank Moss); "The Sheepman" 1958 (Marshall); "Tonka" 1958 (Ace); "Escort West" 1959 (Wheeler); "One-Eyed Jacks" 1961 (Lon); "A Thunder of Drums" 1961 (Trooper Erschick); "Savage Sam" 1963 (Wily Crup); "The Glory Guys" 1965 (Gregory); "Major Dundee" 1965 (Wiley); "An Eye for an Eye" 1966 (Ike Slant); "Stagecoach" 1966 (Buck); "Rough Night in Jericho" 1967 (Yarbrough); "Will Penny" 1968 (Ike Wallerstein, the Trail Cook); "The Ballad of Cable Hogue" 1970 (Ben); "Deserter" 1970-U.S./Ital./Yugo. (Tattinger); "Desperate Mission" TVM-1971 (Three-Finger Jack); "The Devil and Miss Sarah" TVM-1971 (Stoney); "Sam Hill: Who Killed the Mysterious Mr. Foster?" TVM-1971 (Kilpatrick); "The Cowboys" 1972 (Anse); "The Honkers" 1972 (Clete); "Hitched" TVM-1973 (Sam/Bart Dawson); "Pat Garrett and Billy the Kid" 1973 (Sheriff Baker); "Blazing Saddles" 1974 (Taggard); "The Gun and the Pulpit" TVM-1974 (Billy One-Eye); "The Legend of Earl Durand" 1974; "The Apple Dumpling Gang" 1975 (Frank Stillwell); "Rancho Deluxe" 1975 (Henry Beige); "Banjo Hackett: Roamin' Free" TVM-1976 (Lijah Tuttle); "Hawmps!" 1976 (Naman Tucker); "Pony Express Rider" 1976 (Bob); "The White Buffalo" 1977 (Abel Pinkney); "Shadow of Chikara" 1978 (Virgil Cane); "The Sacketts" TVM-1979 (Jack Bigelow); "The

Sweet Creek County War" 1979 (Jitters Pippin); "Tom Horn" 1980 (Sam Creedmore). ¶TV: *Annie Oakley*— "Annie and the Leprechauns" 9-2-56 (Sundown), "The Waco Kid" 10-28-56 (Slim); *The Lone Ranger*—"The Sheriff of Smoke Tree" 9-20-56, "The Letter Bride" 11-15-56; *Circus Boy*— "The Proud Pagliacci" 11-18-56 (Curly); *Disneyland*—"The Saga of Andy Burnett"—Regular 1957-58 (Old Bill Williams); *Sugarfoot*— "Short Range" 5-13-58 (Harry); *Wagon Train*—"The Tent City Story" 12-10-58 (Rafe Jeffers), "The Eve Newhope Story" 12-5-62; *Maverick*— "The Spanish Dancer" 12-14-58 (Jed), "A State of Siege" 1-1-61 (Stagecoach Driver), "Benefit of Doubt" 4-9-61 (Roscoe); *Frontier Doctor*—"Bitter Creek Gang" 6-20-59; *Overland Trail*—"Sour Annie" 5-8-60 (Allard); *Riverboat*—"Rive Champion" 10-10-60 (Porter Slagle); *The Westerner*— "Line Camp" 12-9-60; *The Outlaws*— Regular 1961-62 (Slim); *The Tall Man*—"The Black Robe" 5-5-62 (Starr); *Wide Country*—Regular 1962-63 (Slim Walker); *Bonanza*—"Half a Rogue" 1-27-63 (Jim Leyton), "King of the Mountain" 2-23-64 (Jim Leyton), "Catch as Catch Can" 10-27-68 (Sheriff Gant), "What Are Pardners For?" 4-12-70 (Sheriff); *The Virginian*—"Run Quiet" 11-13-63 (Slim), "Big Image ... Little Man" 10-28-64 (Hogy); *The Travels of Jaimie McPheeters*—"The Day of the Homeless" 12-8-63 (Bly); *Gunsmoke*— "Once a Haggen" 2-1-64 (Bucko Taos), "Sweet Billy, Singer of Songs" 1-15-66 (Pony Beal), "The Scavengers" 11-16-70 (Colley), "The River" 9-11-72 & 9-18-72 (Charlie Utter); *Rawhide*—"The Backshooter" 11-27-64 (Sheriff); *Profiles in Courage*—"Sam Houston" 12-13-64 (William Rogers); *Daniel Boone*—"The Deserter" 1-20-66 (Simon Harman), "Dan'l Boone Shot a B'ar" 9-15-66 (Cletus Mott); *Custer*—Regular 1967 (California Joe Milner); *The Legend of Jesse James*—"Wanted: Dead and Only" 5-2-66 (Sheriff Homer Brinks); *Cimarron Strip*—"The Assassin" 1-11-68 (Grimes); *The Outcasts*— "The Outcasts" 9-23-68 (Sergeant); *Alias Smith and Jones*—"Escape from Wickenberg" 1-28-71 (Mike), "The Man Who Murdered Himself" 3-18-71 (Sheriff Benton), "The Day They Hanged Kid Curry" 9-16-71 (Sheriff Whittaker), "The Strange Fate of Conrad Meyer Zulick" 12-2-72 (Sheriff); *The Men from Shiloh*—"The Angus Killer" 2-10-71 (Sheriff); *Kung Fu*—"Empty Pages of a Dead Book" 1-10-74 (Bart Fisher); *The Life and*

Times of Grizzly Adams—"The Unholy Beast" 4-20-77 (Findhope); *The Busters*—Pilot 5-28-78 (Wister Kane); *How the West Was Won*—Regular 1978 (Tap Henry); *Best of the West*—"The Prisoner" 9-17-81 (Sheriff).

Pickering, Rita. Films: "Hands Down" 1918 (Marina); "Hungry Eyes" 1918 (Nellis); "Skyfire" 1920 (Marette); "The Man from New York" 1923 (Trini).

Pickett, Bobby (1940-). TV: *Bonanza*—"Five Candles" 3-2-69 (Gibson).

Pickett, Cindy (1947-). TV: *The Cherokee Trail*—Pilot 11-28-81 (Mary Breydon).

Pickford, Jack (1896-1/3/33). Films: "Black Sheep" 1912; "Heredity" 1912; "The Massacre" 1912; "The Love Route" 1915 (Billy Ball); "Jack and Jill" 1917 (Jack Ranney).

Pickford, Lottie (1895-12/9/36). Films: "The Redman's View" 1909; "The Tenderfoot's Triumph" 1910; "Unexpected Help" 1910; "On the Level" 1917 (Eleanore Duke); "The Man from Funeral Range" 1918 (Dixie); "Don Q, Son of Zorro" 1925 (Lola).

Pickford, Mary (1893-5/29/79). Films: "The Indian Runner's Romance" 1909; "Mexican Sweethearts" 1909; "The Mountaineer's Honor" 1909; "The Renunciation" 1909; "Ramona" 1910 (Ramona); "A Romance of the Western Hills" 1910; "The Song of the Wildwood Flute" 1910; "That Chink at Golden Gulch" 1910; "The Thread of Destiny" 1910; "The Twisted Trails" 1910; "Two Brothers" 1910; "Behind the Stockade" 1911; "The Stampede" 1911; "Fate's Interception" 1912; "The Female of the Species" 1912; "Iola's Promise" 1912; "A Lodging for the Night" 1912; "A Pueblo Legend" 1912; "A Romance of the Redwoods" 1917 (Jenny Lawrence); "M'Liss" 1918 (M'Liss Smith); "Secrets" 1933 (Mary Marlowe/Mary Carlton).

Pidgeon, Walter (1898-9/25/84). Films: "The Girl of the Golden West" 1938 (Sheriff Jack Rance); "The Dark Command" 1940 (William Cantrell). ¶TV: *Zane Grey Theater*—"Pressure Point" 12-4-58 (Jess Clark), "King of the Valley" 11-26-59 (Dave King); *Rawhide*—"The Reunion" 4-6-62 (Gen. Augustus Perry); *Daniel Boone*—"Not in Our Stars" 12-31-64 (Lord Dunsmore).

Piel, Sr., Edward. see Peil, Sr., Edward.

Pierce, Charles B. (1938-). Films: "Winterhawk" 1975 (Cotton);

"The Winds of Autumn" 1976; "Grayeagle" 1977 (Bugler).

Pierce, Charlotte. Films: "Man of the Forest" 1921 (Bo Raynor); "Queen of Spades" 1925; "Sheep Trail" 1926.

Pierce, Evelyn (1908-8/9/60). Films: "Border Cavalier" 1927 (Anne Martin).

Pierce, George. see Pearce, George.

Pierce, Jack (1889-7/19/68). Films: "The Man Who Waited" 1922 (Black Pete); "The Golden Trail" 1940.

Pierce, Jim (1900-11/12/83). Films: "Her Man" 1924; "Jesse James" 1927 (Frank James); "Phantom of the Range" 1928 (Flash Corbin); "Border Guns" 1934; "Timber War" 1935 (Braden); "Union Pacific" 1939 (Card Player); "Zorro's Fighting Legion" 1939-serial (Moreno); "Arizona Frontier" 1940 (Kansas); "The Gay Caballero" 1940 (Bandit); "Northwest Mounted Police" 1940 (Corporal); "Rainbow Over the Range" 1940 (Jim Rader); "Texas Rangers Ride Again" 1940 (Higboots); "Across the Sierras" 1941; "Cattle Queen" 1951 (Bad Bill Smith).

Pierce, Maggie (1937-). Films: "Cattle King" 1963 (June Carter); "The Fastest Guitar Alive" 1967 (Flo). ¶TV: *Wagon Train*—"The Elizabeth McQueeney Story" 10-28-59 (Roxanne), "The Shad Bennington Story" 6-22-60 (Jenny), "The Daniel Clay Story" 2-21-62 (Frances Cole), "The Indian Girl Story" 4-18-65; *The Law of the Plainsman*—"Toll Road" 12-24-59 (Ellen Dawson); *Overland Trail*—"The O'Mara's Ladies" 2-14-60 (Kathy); *Bat Masterson*—"Bat Trap" 10-13-60 (Amber Mason); *Bronco*—"The Immovable Object" 4-16-62 (Melvina Streeter); *The Dakotas*—"Incident at Rapid City" 3-4-63 (Catherine Mitchell); *Laramie*—"The Road to Helena" 5-21-63 (Ruth Franklin).

Pierce, Preston. Films: "Young Fury" 1965 (Tiger McCoy). ¶TV: *Bonanza*—"A Dime's Worth of Glory" 11-1-64 (Mike); *Gunsmoke*—"The Raid" 1-22-66 & 1-29-66 (Jeff Fraley).

Pierce, Webb (1926-2/24/91). Films: "Webb Pierce and His Wanderin' Boys" 1955-short; "Buffalo Gun" 1961 (Webb Pierce).

Pierlot, Francis (1876-5/11/55). Films: "The Dude Goes West" 1948 (Mr. Brittle); "Copper Canyon" 1950 (Moss Balfour).

Pierson, Arthur (1891-1/1/75).

Films: "The Golden West" 1932 (Robert Summers).

Pierson, Leo (1888-10/2/43). Films: "McKee Rankin's '49" 1911; "Across the Desert" 1915; "'49-'17" 1917 (Tom Robbins); "Desert Law" 1918 (Dick); "Wagon Tracks" 1919 (Billy Hamilton).

Pignozzi, Luciano. *see* Collins, Alan.

Pigott, Tempe (1884-10/13/62). Films: "The Masked Avenger" 1922 (Aunt Phoebe Dyer); "Man of the Forest" 1933 (Madame).

Pike, William. Films: "Salomy Jane" 1914 (Red Pete); "The Heart of Juanita" 1919 (Calvert); "Just Squaw" 1919 (Hollister); "The Flame of Hellgate" 1920 (Page).

Pileggi, Mitch. TV: *Paradise*—"The Valley of Death" 2-8-91 (Rafe).

Piltz, George (1908-4/18/68). Films: "Riders of the Northland" 1942 (Luke).

Pinal, Silvia. Films: "Guns for San Sebastian" 1967-U.S./Fr./Mex./Ital. (Felcia).

Pine, Philip (1925-). Films: "I Shot Jesse James" 1949 (Man in Saloon). ¶TV: *Wyatt Earp*—"John Wesley Hardin" 11-1-55 (John Wesley Hardin), "Plague Carrier" 12-9-58 (Dr. Carl McDowell); *Gunsmoke*—"Moon" 5-11-57 (Vint); *Zane Grey Theater*—"Episode in Darkness" 11-15-57 (Joe Fletcher); *U.S. Marshal*—"The Arraignment" 11-15-58; *Wagon Train*—"The Ben Courtney Story" 1-28-59 (Marty Craig), "The Estaban Zamora Story" 10-21-59 (Manuel), "The Dr. Swift Cloud Story" 5-25-60 (Straight Arrow); *Tales of Wells Fargo*—"Kid Curry" 5-11-59; *Have Gun Will Travel*—"Gold and Brimstone" 6-20-59 (Mason Baird); *Wanted—Dead or Alive*—"Breakout" 9-26-59 (Tom Dunn); *Rawhide*—"Incident at Dangerfield Dip" 10-2-59 (Reese Dangerfield); *Wichita Town*—"Death Watch" 12-16-59 (Charlie Wilkes); *Laramie*—"Day of Vengeance" 1-19-60 (Juan Mendoza); *The Deputy*—"Lawman's Blood" 2-6-60 (Jack Burch); *The Outlaws*—"Last Chance" 11-10-60 (Quinsey); *Klondike*—"Taste of Danger" 12-5-60 (Dr. Jarver); *Bonanza*—"The Legacy" 12-15-63 (Gannon), "The Fighters" 4-24-66 (Ross Dugan), "The Running Man" 3-30-69 (Stead Butler); *Wild Wild West*—"The Night of the Glowing Corpse" 10-29-65 (Lt. Armand Renard), "The Night of the Pistoleros" 2-21-69 (Lt. Murray); *Death Valley Days*—"Samaritans, Mountain Style" 11-19-66 (Kit Carson); *The*

Guns of Will Sonnett—"The Trial" 2-28-69 (Granger); *Barbary Coast*—"Mary Had More Than a Little" 1-2-76 (Hungerford); *The Quest*—"Shanklin" 10-13-76.

Pine, Robert (1941-). Films: "Gunpoint" 1966 (Mitch); "Journey to Shiloh" 1968 (Collins); "One Little Indian" 1973 (Lt. Cummins); "The Apple Dumpling Gang Rides Again" 1979 (Lt. Ravencroft). ¶TV: *The Virginian*—"Six Graves at Cripple Creek" 1-27-65 (Orderly), "Dangerous Road" 3-17-65 (Bob Coulter, Jr.), "Jacob Was a Plain Man" 10-12-66 (Curley), "The Ordeal" 2-19-69 (Scott Austin); *Pistols 'n' Petticoats*—10-8-66 (Boy Bunnoy); *Bob Hope Chrysler Theatre*—"Massacre at Fort Phil Kearny" 10-26-66 (Lieutenant Brown); *Gunsmoke*—"Lyle's Kid" 9-23-68 (Jeffery Lyle), "The Night Riders" 2-24-69 (Eliot Proctor), "Gentry's Law" 10-12-70 (Ben Gentry), "Jessie" 2-19-73 (Link); *The Guns of Will Sonnett*—"Join the Army" 1-3-69 (Kit Torrey); *The High Chaparral*—"The Lieutenant" 2-27-70 (Lt. Jason Adams); *The Oregon Trail*—"The Race" 1977.

Pingree, Earl (1887-7/12/58). Films: "A Holy Terror" 1931 (Jim Lawler); "The Throwback" 1935 (Jim Saunders).

Pinsent, Gordon (1933-). Films: "Silence of the North" 1981 (John Fredrickson). ¶TV: *Lonesome Dove*—"The Road Home" 2-26-95 (Shaw).

Pinson, Allen. Films: "Advance to the Rear" 1964 (Pvt. Long); "Desperate Mission" TVM-1971 (Croncracker). ¶TV: *The Cisco Kid*—"Talking Dog" 2-23-52; *Zane Grey Theater*—"Man of Fear" 3-14-58; *Man from Blackhawk*—"Logan's Policy" 10-9-59 (Drunk); *Tales of Wells Fargo*—"Reward for Gaine" 1-20-62 (Moore); *Alias Smith and Jones*—"What's in It for Mia?" 2-24-72 (Karl).

Pisani, Remo. TV: *Bonanza*—"Another Windmill to Go" 9-14-69 (Bartender), "A Lawman's Lot Is Not a Happy One" 10-5-69 (Bartender), "The Medal" 10-26-69 (Bartender), "The Big Jackpot" 1-18-70 (Bartender), "Long Way to Ogden" 2-22-70 (Bartender), "The Weary Willies" 9-27-70 (Bartender), "The Law and Billy Burgess" 2-15-70 (Bartender), "Winter Kill" 3-28-71 (Bartender), "Rock-a-Bye, Hoss" 10-10-71 (Joel Sawyer).

Pistilli, Luigi (1929-). Films: "For a Few Dollars More" 1965-Ital./Ger./Span. (Indio's Gang Member);

"The Good, the Bad, and the Ugly" 1966-Ital.; "Texas, Adios" 1966-Ital./Span.; "Bandidos" 1967-Ital.; "Death Rides a Horse" 1967-Ital. (Wolcott); "Dollars for a Fast Gun" 1968-Ital./Span.; "Great Silence" 1968-Ital./Fr.; "Night of the Serpent" 1969-Ital. (the Serpent).

Pitcairn, Jack. Films: "Western Firebrands" 1921 (Victor Lanning).

Pitlik, Noam (1932-). Films: "The Hallelujah Trail" 1965 (Interpreter). ¶TV: *The Rifleman*—"The Assailants" 11-12-62 (Trooper Dalt); *Gunsmoke*—"Twenty Miles from Dodge" 4-10-65 (Dobbs); *The Virginian*—"Blaze of Glory" 12-29-65 (March), "The Handy Man" 3-6-68 (Walt Hardesty); *Iron Horse*—"The Execution" 3-13-67 (Gabe Randall); *The Guns of Will Sonnett*—"Alone" 2-9-68 (John Darby); *Here Come the Brides*—"The Legend of Big Foot" 11-14-69 (Frobes); *Nichols*—"The Unholy Alliance" 1-18-72 (Jack Stone).

Pitt, Ingrid (1944-). TV: *Dundee and the Culhane*—10-25-67 (Tallie Montreaux).

Pitti, Carl (1916-). Films: "Billy the Kid" 1941 (Bat Smithers); "Bandit Queen" 1950 (McWilliams); "The Lawless Breed" 1952 (Sheriff Conlon); "The Woman They Almost Lynched" 1953 (Hangman); "Tribute to a Badman" 1956 (Tom); "Gun Glory" 1957 (Joel); "The Hallelujah Trail" 1965 (Phillips); "High Plains Drifter" 1973 (Teamster). ¶TV: *Bonanza*—"The Trouble with Amy" 1-25-70 (David).

Pittman, Thomas "Tom" (1933-10/31/58). Films: "Black Patch" 1957 (Flytrap); "The True Story of Jesse James" 1957 (Hughie); "Apache Territory" 1958 (Lonnie Foreman); "The Proud Rebel" 1958 (Tom Burleigh). ¶TV: *Gunsmoke*—"Dutch George" 6-30-56 (Jimmy McQueen), "Potato Road" 10-12-57 (Budge Grilk); *Cheyenne*—"The Long Winter" 9-25-56 (Bushrod); *Zane Grey Theater*—"The Deserters" 10-4-57 (John Harris); *Wagon Train*—"The Mary Halstead Story" 11-20-57 (Tom); *Telephone Time*—"Trail Blazer" 4-1-58 (Wes Sheek); *Trackdown*—"The Winter Boys" 4-11-58 (Red Bolton); *Tombstone Territory*—"Pick Up the Gun" 5-14-58 (Billy Clanton); *The Restless Gun*—"The Manhunters" 6-2-58 (Jason Teal); *Buckskin*—"The Ballad of Gabe Pruitt" 7-24-58 (Dan Pruitt); *Tales of Wells Fargo*—"The Gambler" 9-8-58 (Bill Dowd); *Zorro*—"The Runaways" 1-8-59 (Romaldo); *Cimarron City*—"Child of Fear" 1-17-59 (Jesse Stainback).

Pitts, ZaSu (1898-6/7/63). Films: "A Modern Musketeer" 1917; "As the Sun Went Down" 1919 (Sal Sue); "The Great Divide" 1925 (Polly Jordan); "River's End" 1930 (Louise); "Destry Rides Again" 1932 (Temperance Worker); "The Vanishing Frontier" 1932 (Aunt Sylvia); "Ruggles of Red Gap" 1935 (Mrs. Judson); "Denver and Rio Grande" 1952 (Jane).

Pizzuti, Riccardo. Films: "A Man from the East" 1974-Ital./Fr. (Morton Clayton).

Planchard, Phyllis. Films: "The Westward Trail" 1948 (Ann).

Platt, Alma (1892-1980). TV: *Maverick*—"A Technical Error" 11-26-61 (Mrs. Hennessey); *Gunsmoke*—"Harvest" 3-26-66 (Gran McGovern).

Platt, Billy. Films: "The Terror of Tiny Town" 1938 (Jim "Tex" Preston, the Rich Uncle).

Platt, Edward C. (1916-3/20/74). Films: "The Old Corral" 1936 (Oscar); "Gunsmoke Ranch" 1937 (Elmer); "The Painted Stallion" 1937-serial (Oscar); "Backlash" 1956 (Sheriff Marson); "The Proud Ones" 1956 (Dr. Barlow); "Reprisal!" 1956 (Neil Shipley); "Gunman's Walk" 1958 (Purcell Avery); "The Last of the Fast Guns" 1958 (Samuel Grypton); "Oregon Passage" 1958 (Roland Dane); "They Came to Cordura" 1959 (Col. DeRose); "Bullet for a Badman" 1964 (Tucker); "The Man from Button Willow" 1965 (Voice). ¶TV: *Gunsmoke*—"Smoking Out the Nolans" 11-5-55 (Mr. Burgess), "Bloody Hands" 2-16-57; *Tales of Wells Fargo*—"Doc Bell" 1-6-58 (Doc Ballon), "Return of Doc Bell" 11-30-59 (Doc Bell), "Vignette of a Sinner" 6-2-62 (Doc Bell); *Trackdown*—"Right of Way" 1-17-58 (Sheriff Harper), "Every Man a Witness" 12-26-58 (George Mason), "The Eyes of Jerry Kelson" 4-22-59; *Zane Grey Theater*—"Trial by Fear" 1-20-58 (Sheriff Galt), "The Ox" 11-3-60 (Marshal Mays); *Have Gun Will Travel*—"The Taffeta Mayor" 1-10-59 (Arnold Oaklin); *Bat Masterson*—"Incident in Leadville" 3-18-59 (Roy Evans); *Wagon Train*—"The Duke LeMay Story" 4-29-59 (Matthew Sinclair), "The Marine Brant Story" 1-20-60 (Orobio Da Costa), "The Frank Carter Story" 5-23-62 (Cyrus Bolton); *Rawhide*—"Incident of the Thirteenth Man" 10-23-59 (Jason Clark); *Bonanza*—"The Outcast" 1-9-60 (Harvey Bufford), "The Guilty" 2-25-62 (Wade), "The Colonel" 1-6-63 (Will Flanders); *Overland Trail*—"Westbound Stage" 3-6-60 (Dr. Jacob Bronson); *Death*

Valley Days—"A Girl Named Virginia" 12-28-60 (Frank Graves); *The Deputy*—"Chechez la Femme" 4-1-61 (Noah Harper); *Whispering Smith*—"The Hemp Reeger Case" 7-17-61 (Sheriff Aiken); *Bronco*—"Ride the Whirlwind" 1-15-62 (Sheriff Lockwood); *The Rifleman*—"The Assailants" 11-12-62 (Senator Jim Borden).

Platt, Howard (1938-). Films: "Westworld" 1973 (Supervisor); "The Great Scout and Cathouse Thursday" 1976 (Vishniac). ¶TV: *Young Maverick*—"Half-Past Noon" 1-30-80 (Mayor Waldo Leggett).

Platt, Louise. Films: "Stagecoach" 1939 (Lucy Mallory).

Platt, Marc. Films: "Oklahoma!" 1955 (Dancer). ¶TV: *Sky King*—"Sleight of Hand" 5-25-53 (Bob); *Wyatt Earp*—"Big Brother Virgil" 3-25-58 (Mel Herrick); *Hotel De Paree*—"Sundance and the Barren Soil" 5-20-60 (Gaskins).

Platt, Oliver. Films: "Tall Tales: The Unbelievable Adventures of Pecos Bill" 1995 (Paul Bunyon).

Playdon, Paul. TV: *Jim Bowie*—"Monsieur Francois" 12-28-56 (Francois de Gravien), "The Beggar of New Orleans" 1-11-57 (Francois de Gravien), "Master at Arms" 1-25-57 (Francois de Gravien), "Thieves' Market" 3-29-57 (Francois de Gravien), "The Intruder" 4-26-57 (Francois de Gravien), "The Quarantine" 10-11-57 (Francois de Gravien); *Sergeant Preston of the Yukon*—"Boy Alone" 2-20-58 (Tommy Smith).

Playter, Wellington (1879-7/15/37). Films: "The War of the Wild" 1915.

Pleasence, Donald (1919-2/2/95). Films: "The Hallelujah Trail" 1965 (Oracle Jones); "Will Penny" 1968 (Preacher Quint); "Soldier Blue" 1970 (Isaac Q. Cumber); "Hearts of the West" 1975 (A.J. Nietz); "Django Strikes Again" 1987-Ital./Span./Ger. ¶TV: *Centennial*—Regular 1978-79 (Samuel Purchase).

Pleshette, Suzanne (1937-). Films: "A Distant Trumpet" 1964 (Kitty); "Nevada Smith" 1966 (Pilar); "The Adventures of Bullwhip Griffin" 1967 (Arabella Flagg); "Support Your Local Gunfighter" 1971 (Patience Barton); "Kate Bliss and the Ticker Tape Kid" TVM-1978 (Kate Bliss). ¶TV: *Have Gun Will Travel*—"Death of a Gunfighter" 3-14-59 (Maria); *Black Saddle*—"The Long Rider" 10-16-59 (Nedda Logan); *Riverboat*—"The Two Faces of Grey Holden" 10-3-60 (Marie Tourette);

Wagon Train—"The Myra Marshall Story" 10-21-63 (Myra Marshall); *Wild Wild West*—"The Night of the Inferno" 9-17-65 (Lydia Monteran); *Cimarron Strip*—"Till the End of the Night" 11-16-67 (Sarah Lou Burke); *Gunsmoke*—"Stark" 9-28-70 (Glory Bramley); *Bonanza*—"A Place to Hide" 3-19-72 (Rose).

Plimpton, George (1927-). Films: "Rio Lobo" 1970 (Whitey's Henchman).

Plowman, Melinda. Films: "Pack Train" 1953 (Judy); "Billy the Kid vs. Dracula" 1966. ¶TV: *The Cisco Kid*—"Witness" 12-19-53; *Annie Oakley*—"The Tomboy" 7-17-54 (Penny); *The Gene Autry Show*—"Outlaw Warning" 10-2-54; *Wagon Train*—"The Danny Benedict Story" 12-2-59 (Prissy), "Trial for Murder" 4-27-60 & 5-4-60 (Eileen), "Path of the Serpent" 2-8-61 (Penelope); *Wanted—Dead or Alive*—"Detour" 3-1-61 (Patience Fairweather); *The Virginian*—"A Time Remembered" 12-11-63 (Karen); *Bonanza*—"Four Sisters from Boston" 10-30-66 (Heather); *Wild Wild West*—"The Night of the Doomsday Formula" 10-4-68 (Wilma Crane).

Plowright, Hilda (1890-10/9/73). Films: "Partners of the Plains" 1938 (Aunt Martha).

Plues, George (1895-8/16/53). Films: "Call of the Heart" 1928; "Bold Caballero" 1936; "Guns and Guitars" 1936; "The Mysterious Avenger" 1936 (Mailman); "The Phantom Rider" 1936-serial; "Roarin' Lead" 1936; "Come on Cowboys" 1937; "Hit the Saddle" 1937 (Henchman); "Public Cowboy No. 1" 1937; "The Rangers Step In" 1937; "Reckless Ranger" 1937; "Flaming Frontier" 1938-serial; "The Lone Ranger" 1938-serial (Trooper); "Overland Stage Raiders" 1938; "New Frontier" 1939 (Henchman); "The Oregon Trail" 1939-serial; "Zorro's Fighting Legion" 1939-serial (Garcia); "King of the Royal Mounted" 1940-serial (Brakeman); "Law and Order" 1940 (Stage Driver); "Ragtime Cowboy Joe" 1940 (Roy Gordon); "Two-Gun Sheriff" 1941; "Daredevils of the West" 1943-serial (Citizen #5); "The Ox-Bow Incident" 1943 (Alec Small); "Tenting Tonight on the Old Camp Ground" 1943 (Stage Driver); "Sunset Pass" 1946 (Posse Man).

Plumb, Eve (1957-). TV: *The Big Valley*—"Hide the Children" 12-19-66 (Sara Jane), "Brother Love" 2-20-67; *Lancer*—"The Heart of Pony Alice" 12-17-68 (Pony Alice); *Gunsmoke*—"The Gold Mine" 1-27-69 (Sue).

Plumer, Lincoln (1876-2/14/28). Films: "The Bullet Mark" 1928.

Plumer, Rose (1876-3/3/55). Films: "Law of the West" 1932 (Mrs. Carruthers); "Brand of Hate" 1934 (Mrs. Kent); "The Pecos Kid" 1935 (Townswoman); "Git Along, Little Dogies" 1937; "Rovin' Tumbleweeds" 1939; "Adventures of Red Ryder" 1940-serial; "Take Me Back to Oklahoma" 1940; "The Cyclone Kid" 1942; "Bordertown Gunfighters" 1943; "Bullets and Saddles" 1943; "Trail of Terror" 1944; "Phantom of the Plains" 1945; "Duel in the Sun" 1946 (Dancer); "Son of Paleface" 1952 (Townswoman).

Plummer, Amanda (1957-). Films: "Cattle Annie and Little Britches" 1981 (Annie).

Plyler, Montie. TV: *Branded*—"The Mission" 3-14-65, 3-21-65 & 3-28-65 (Angulia), "$10,000 for Durango" 11-28-65 (Morgan); *Hondo*—"Hondo and the Gladiators" 12-15-67 (Jake).

Pocath, Werner. Films: "Vengeance" 1968-Ital./Ger.; "Bandera Bandits" 1973-Ital./Span./Ger.

Poff, Lon (1870-8/8/52). Films: "The Light of Western Stars" 1918 (Monty Price); "The Last Straw" 1920 (Rev. Beal); "Sand!" 1920 (Jim Kirkwood); "The Square Shooter" 1920 (Sandy); "The Night Horsemen" 1921 (Haw Haw); "Suzanna" 1922 (Alvarez); "Tracked to Earth" 1922 (Meenie Wade); "Brass Commandments" 1923 (Slim Lally); "The Man Who Won" 1923 (Sandy Joyce); "The Man from Wyoming" 1924 (Jim McWilliams); "The Fighting Texan" 1927; "The Silent Rider" 1927 (Baldy); "Silver Valley" 1927 (Slim Snitzer); "Greased Lightning" 1928 (Beauty Jones); "Caught" 1931 (Clem); "The Texans" 1938 (Moody Citizen).

Poggi, Nando. Films: "Massacre at Grand Canyon" 1963-Ital.; "Minnesota Clay" 1964-Ital./Fr./Span. (Tubbs); "Johnny Yuma" 1966-Ital.

Pohlmann, Eric (1913-79). Films: "The Singer Not the Song" 1961-Brit. (Presidente).

Pointer, Priscilla. TV: *The High Chaparral*—"A Matter of Vengeance" 11-27-70 (Mrs. Colton).

Poitier, Sidney (1924-). Films: "Duel at Diablo" 1966 (Toller); "Buck and the Preacher" 1972 (Buck); "Children of the Dust" TVM-1995 (Gypsy Smith).

Polesello, Franca. Films: "Navajo Joe" 1966-Ital./Span. (Barbara); "Shoot Joe, and Shoot Again" 1972-Ital.

Poli, Maurice (Monty Greenwood). Films: "Two Sides of the Dollar" 1967-Fr./Ital. (Matematica); "Shango" 1969-Ital. (Martinez); "Thirteenth Is a Judas" 1971-Ital.; "Sometimes Life Is Hard, Right Providence?" 1972-Ital./Fr./Ger. (Colonel Albert James).

Poli, Mimmo. Films: "Sabata" 1969-Ital. (Hotel Workman).

Polk, Gordon (1924-6/9/60). TV: *Trackdown*—"A Stone for Benny French" 10-3-58 (Adrian Zach), "The Gang" 2-25-59 (Lafe), "Fear" 3-18-59 (Garth); *Wanted—Dead or Alive*—"Sheriff of Red Rock" 11-29-58 (Evans), "The Most Beautiful Woman" 1-23-60 (Skeek); *Black Saddle*—"Client: Brand" 5-16-59 (Eddie Dime); *Have Gun Will Travel*—"The Unforgiven" 11-7-59, "The Black Handkerchief" 11-14-59 (Luss), "Crowbait" 11-19-60 (Jubal); *Johnny Ringo*—"Four Came Quietly" 1-28-60 (Frank Jethro); *Hotel De Paree*—"Sundance and the Barren Soil" 5-20-60 (Turkey Crowder).

Pollack, Sydney (1930-). TV: *Have Gun Will Travel*—"A Quiet Night in Town" 1-7-61 & 1-14-61 (Joe Culp); *The Deputy*—"Spoken in Silence" 4-29-61 (Chuck Johnson).

Pollard, Bud (1887-12/16/52). Films: "The Broken Land" 1962.

Pollard, Michael J. (1939-). Films: "The Legend of Frenchie King" 1971-Fr./Ital./Span./Brit. (Marshal); "Dirty Little Billy" 1972 (Billy Bonney); "Four Horsemen of the Apocalypse" 1975-Ital. (Josh). ¶TV: *Gunsmoke*—"Journey for Three" 6-6-64 (Cyrus Gifford); *Branded*—"Romany Roundup 12-5-65 & 12-12-65 (Digby Popham); *The Virginian*—"The Wolves Up Front, the Jackals Behind" 3-23-66 (Georgie Sam); *Cimarron Strip*—"The Battle of Blood Stone" 10-12-67 (Bert); *Paradise*—"A Study in Fear" 3-29-91 (Lester Barr).

Pollard, Snub (1886-1/19/62). Films: "The Laramie Kid" 1935 (Shorty); "Arizona Days" 1937 (Cook); "Headin' for the Rio Grande" 1937 (Cookie); "Hittin' the Trail" 1937 (Bartender); "Riders of the Rockies" 1937 (Pee Wee McDougall); "Santa Fe Rides" 1937; "Sing, Cowboy, Sing" 1937 (Henchman); "Tex Rides with the Boy Scouts" 1937 (Pee Wee); "Frontier Town" 1938 (Peewee); "Rollin' Plains" 1938 (Pee Wee); "Starlight Over Texas" 1938 (Pee Wee); "Utah Trail" 1938 (Pee Wee); "Where the Buffalo Roam" 1938 (Pee Wee); "Lure of the Wasteland" 1939 (Cookie);

"Mesquite Buckaroo" 1939 (Suds); "Song of the Buckaroo" 1939 (Perky); "Murder on the Yukon" 1940 (Archie); "The Kid Rides Again" 1943; "Phony Express" 1943-short (Sheriff); "San Antonio" 1945 (Dancer); "Cheyenne" 1947 (Barfly); "Back Trail" 1948 (Goofy); "Loaded Pistols" 1948; "One-Eyed Jacks" 1961 (Townsman).

Pollick, Teno. TV: *Gunsmoke*—"Kioga" 10-23-65 (Kioga), "My Father, My Son" 4-23-66 (David Barrett); *Bonanza*—"Night of Reckoning" 10-15-67 (Carew); *Lancer*—"Legacy" 12-9-69 (Carl Degan).

Pollock, Channing. TV: *Great Adventure*—"The Pathfinder" 3-6-64 (Kit Carson); *Daniel Boone*—"Seminole Territory" 1-13-66 (Fletcher Cameron); *Bonanza*—"Easy Come, Easy Go" 12-12-71 (Carter).

Pollock, Dee (1937-). Films: "The Old West" 1952 (Eddie Jamison); "The Legend of Tom Dooley" 1959 (Abel); "The Plunderers" 1960 (Davy); "Captain Apache" 1971-Brit./Span. (Ben). ¶TV: *The Lone Ranger*—"Sinner by Proxy" 3-5-53; *The Gene Autry Show*—"Talking Guns" 8-10-54; *Wagon Train*—"The Bill Tawnee Story" 2-12-58 (Steve Barry); *The Law of the Plainsman*—"The Gibbet" 11-26-59; *Johnny Ringo*—"The Vindicator" 3-31-60 (Tommy); *The Westerner*—"The Old Man" 11-25-60; *The Rebel*—"The Guard" 1-8-61 (Charles Mowbree); *Rawhide*—"Incident of the Blackstorms" 5-26-61 (Inger Jeffries), "Incident at Farragut Pass" 10-31-63 (Cass); *Gunslinger*—Regular 1961 (Billy); *Tales of Wells Fargo*—"Man of Another Breed" 12-2-61 (Arly Timmons); *The Outlaws*—"A Bit of Glory" 2-1-62 (Billy); *Laramie*—"The Last Battleground" 4-16-63 (Will Courtland); *Bonanza*—"My Son, My Son" 1-19-64 (Eden), "Peace Officer" 2-6-66 (Chuck); *The Virginian*—"The Return of Golden Tom" 3-9-66 (Willie Cade); *Shane*—"Day of the Hawk" 10-22-66 (Hoke).

Polo, Eddie (1875-6/14/61). Films: "Liberty" 1916-serial; "The Plow Woman" 1917 (Bill Mathews); "Bull's Eye" 1918-serial; "Cyclone Smith Plays Trumps" 1919 (Cyclone Smith); "Cyclone Smith's Comeback" 1919 (Cyclone Smith); "Cyclone Smith's Partner" 1919 (Cyclone Smith); "Down But Not Out" 1919; "The Missing Bullet" 1919; "The Phantom Fugitive" 1919; "A Pistol Point Proposal" 1919 (Cyclone Smith); "A Prisoner for Life" 1919 (Cyclone Smith); "The Wild Rider" 1919; "A Battle Against Odds" 1921

(Cyclone Smith); "Cyclone Smith's Vow" 1921 (Cyclone Smith); "Heritage of Hate" 1921; "A Race for a Rancho" 1921 (Cyclone Smith); "Square Deal" 1921; "The Yellow Streak" 1921; "The Verdict" 1922; "The White Messenger" 1922; "Son of Roaring Dan" 1940 (Charlie Gregg); "Deep in the Heart of Texas" 1942.

Polo, Sam (1873-100/3/66). Films: "The Man from Nowhere" 1920 (Miner).

Pomerantz, Jeffrey (1945-). TV: *Daniel Boone*—"The King's Shilling" 10-19-67 (Davey Hubbard); *The High Chaparral*—"Follow Your Heart" 10-4-68 (Tom Lynch); *The Outcasts*—"The Night Riders" 11-25-68 (Clay); *Here Come the Brides*—"A Man's Errand" 3-19-69 (Ward); *Gunsmoke*—"Johnny Cross" 12-23-68 (Johnny Cross), "Tatum" 11-13-72 (Dirk Mitchell).

Ponder, Jack (1903-8/5/70). Films: "Arizona Days" 1928 (Detective); "The Silent Trail" 1928; "Fighters of the Saddle" 1929 (Tom Wayne).

Ponedel, Dorothy. Films: "Border Justice" 1925 (Annona Wetona); "Galloping Vengeance" 1925 (Little Wolf).

Ponti, Sal (1934-1/28/88). TV: *Colt .45*—"Tar and Feathers" 11-22-59 (Andrew Bourdette).

Poole, Roy (1924-7/1/86). Films: "A Cry in the Wilderness" TVM-1974 (Rex Millard). ¶TV: *Dundee and the Culhane*—9-27-67 (Zack Carson).

Poore, Dan. Films: "Bronco Buster" 1952 (Elliott); "Horizons West" 1952 (Henchman); "The Man from the Alamo" 1953.

Pop, Iggy (1947-). Films: "Dead Man" 1995 (Salvatore "Sally" Jenko).

Pope, Bud. Films: "Ranson's Folly" 1926 (Abe Fisher); "Guns for Hire" 1932; "The Cyclone Ranger" 1935 (Outlaw); "The Man from Guntown" 1935; "The Outlaw Deputy" 1935; "Sagebrush Troubador" 1935; "Six Gun Justice" 1935; "The Texas Rambler" 1935; "Tonto Kid" 1935 (Cowboy); "Tumbling Tumbleweeds" 1935 (Henchman); "The Vanishing Riders" 1935; "King of the Pecos" 1936; "The Lonely Trail" 1936 (Trooper); "Ride, Ranger, Ride" 1936; "Rip Roarin' Buckaroo" 1936; "Valley of the Lawless" 1936; "Vigilantes Are Coming" 1936-serial (Ivan); "Cheyenne Rides Again" 1937 (Shayne); "Wild Horse Round-Up" 1937; "Rollin' Plains" 1938; "Six Shootin' Sheriff" 1938; "The Man from Texas" 1939.

Poppe, Herman. Films: "Pale Rider" 1985 (Ulrik Lindquist); "Gunsmoke: To the Last Man" TVM-1991 (John Tewksbury). ¶TV: *Gunsmoke*—"The Tycoon" 1-25-71 (Clarence Carver), "The Wiving" 10-14-74 (Luke); *How the West Was Won*—Episode One 2-6-77 (Jake Judson), Episode Two 2-7-77 (Jake Judson), Episode Three 2-14-77 (Jake Judson); *Adventures of Brisco County, Jr.*—"The Orb Scholar" 9-3-93 (Sheriff Worth).

Popwell, Albert (1926-). Films: "Journey to Shiloh" 1968 (Samuel). ¶TV: *Cowboy in Africa*—"Lake Sinclair" 11-13-67 (Lukora), "African Rodeo" 1-15-68 & 1-22-68.

Porcasi, Paul (1880-8/8/46). Films: "Under the Pampas Moon" 1935 (Headwaiter); "Hi Gaucho!" 1936 (General Ortegas); "Rose Marie" 1936 (Emil, the Chef); "The Border Legion" 1940 (Tony).

Porter, Don (1912-). Films: "Wild Beauty" 1946 (Dave Morrow); "Cripple Creek" 1952 (Denver Jones); "The Savage" 1952 (Running Dog).

Porter, Ed (1884-7/29/39). Films: "Guns for Hire" 1932; "Cheyenne Tornado" 1935 (Farley); "Lightning Triggers" 1935 (Bartender); "Range Warfare" 1935.

Porter, J. Robert (1939-). Films: "Firecreek" 1968 (Arthur); "MacKenna's Gold" 1969 (the Young Englishman). ¶TV: *Gunsmoke*—"Nowhere to Run" 1-15-68 (Mark Stonecipher).

Porter, Jean. Films: "Barb Wire" 1922 (Joan Lorne); "Heart of the Rio Grande" 1942 (Pudge); "Home in Wyomin'" 1942; "Calaboose" 1943; "San Fernando Valley" 1944 (Betty Lou).

Portugal, Jose (1908-12/28/76). Films: "The Big Sombrero" 1949.

Post, Buddy (1897-12/20/52). Films: "M'Liss" 1918 (Butch Saunders); "Bob Hampton of Placer" 1921 (Jack Moffet).

Poston, Tom (1921-). TV: *Dr. Quinn, Medicine Woman*—"Halloween" 10-30-93 (Man).

Potel, Victor (1889-3/8/47). Films: "Broncho Billy—Guardian" 1914; "Broncho Billy's Wild Ride" 1914; "The Good for Nothing" 1914 (Old Clerk); "Broncho Billy and the Vigilante" 1915; "Hearts and Saddles" 1917; "In Mizzoura" 1919 (Dave); "The Outcasts of Poker Flat" 1919; "Bob Hampton of Placer" 1921 (Willie McNeil); "The Loaded Door" 1922 (Slim); "Step on It!" 1922 (Noisy Johnson); "The Bar C Mys-

tery" 1926-serial; "Morganson's Finish" 1926 (Ole Jensen); "The Virginian" 1929 (Nebraskey); "Border Romance" 1930 (Slim); "Call of the West" 1930 (Trig Peters); "The Squaw Man" 1931 (Andy); "Partners" 1932 (Deputy Lem); "Frontier Days" 1934 (Deputy Fox); "Thunder Over Texas" 1934; "Big Boy Rides Again" 1935 (Scarface); "The Cowboy and the Bandit" 1935; "The Last of the Clintons" 1935 (Jed Clinton); "Moonlight on the Prairie" 1935 (Tall Cowboy); "Ruggles of Red Gap" 1935 (Curly); "Trails End" 1935 (Red); "Whispering Smith Speaks" 1935 (Bill Prouty); "Arizona Mahoney" 1936 (Stagecoach Helper); "O'Malley of the Mounted" 1936 (Gabby); "Song of the Saddle" 1936 (Little Casino); "The Three Godfathers" 1936 (Buck Tooth); "Yellow Dust" 1936 (Jugger); "God's Country and the Woman" 1937 (Turpentine); "Two Gun Law" 1937 (Cassius); "Western Gold" 1937 (Jasper); "The Girl of the Golden West" 1938 (Stage Driver); "Renfrew on the Great White Trail" 1938 (Parker); "Chip of the Flying U" 1939; "Let Freedom Ring" 1939 (2nd Swede); "Rovin' Tumbleweeds" 1939 (Zeke); "Stand Up and Fight" 1939 (Coach Driver); "Trail of the Vigilantes" 1940 (Conductor); "West of Carson City" 1940 (Heavy); "Rhythm Round-Up" 1945.

Potter, Bill. Films: "Courtin' Trouble" 1948 (Graves); "Gunning for Justice" 1948; "Across the Rio Grande" 1949; "Brand of Fear" 1949; "Haunted Trails" 1949 (Deputy); "Hidden Danger" 1949 (Perry); "Range Justice" 1949 (Bill); "West of El Dorado" 1949 (Phil); "Western Renegades" 1949 (Bob).

Potter, Cliff. Films: "A Man Called Gannon" 1969 (Ike). ¶TV: *The Virginian*—"Johnny Moon" 10-11-67 (Wes).

Potts, Annie. Films: "Cowboy" TVM-1983 (D.G.).

Potts, Cliff (1942-). Films: "Count Your Bullets" 1972 (Billy); "Nevada Smith" TVM-1975 (Nevada Smith); "Last Ride of the Dalton Gang" TVM-1979 (Bob Dalton); "Belle Starr" TVM-1980 (Cole Younger). ¶TV: *Hec Ramsey*—"Only Birds and Fools" 4-7-74 (Ton Bailey); *Big Hawaii*—Regular 1977 (Mitch Fears); *Bret Maverick*—"The Eight Swords of Cyrus and Other Illusions of Grandeur" 3-23-83 (the Great Malooley).

Potts, Hank (1896-4/1/80). Films: "Beau Bandit" 1930 (Cowhand); "The Crimson Trail" 1935 (Shorty);

Pouget, Ely. TV: *Adventures of Brisco County, Jr.*—"High Treason" 5-13-94 & 5-20-94 (Jennifer Hart).

Poule, Ezelle. Films: "Calamity Jane and Sam Bass" 1949 (Woman Customer); "Border Rangers" 1950 (Aunt Priscilla). ¶TV: *The Cisco Kid*—"The Fire Engine" 5-31-52, "Fear" 6-28-52; *Maverick*—"The Jeweled Gun" 11-24-57 (Mrs. Adams).

Pounder, CCH. Films: "Return to Lonesome Dove" TVM-1993.

Powell, Addison (1921-). TV: *Gunsmoke*—"Kitty's Rebellion" 2-7-59 (Tal).

Powell, David (1885-4/16/25). Films: "Gloria's Romance" 1916-serial; "The Siren Call" 1922 (Ralph Stevens).

Powell, Dick (1904-1/2/63). Films: "Cowboy from Brooklyn" 1938 (Elly Jordan); "Riding High" 1943 (Steve Baird); "Station West" 1948 (Haven); "Mrs. Mike" 1949 (Sgt. Mike Flannigan). ¶TV: *Four Star Playhouse*—"Trail's End" 1-29-53; *Zane Grey Theater*—Regular 1956-62 (Host), "The Long Road Home" 10-19-56 (Sam Gracie), "Courage Is a Gun" 12-14-56 (Marshal Jess Brackett), "Back Trail" 2-1-57 (John Fallon), "The Deserters" 10-4-57 (Sgt. Maj. Dravo), "The Open Cell" 11-22-57 (Sheriff Morgan Winter), "Sundown at Bitter Creek" 2-14-58 (Dan Case), "The Scaffold" 10-9-58 (Sheriff Ross Conners), "Let the Man Die" 12-18-58 (Dr. Mike Reynolds), "Welcome Home a Stranger" 1-15-59 (Ben Sanderson), "Confession" 10-15-59 (Sheriff Agate Slade), "Death in a Wood" 12-17-59 (Lawrence), "A Small Town That Died" 3-10-60 (Dave Cameron), "Desert Flight" 10-13-60 (Brenner), "Ambush" 1-5-61 (Colonel Blackburn), "The Silent Sentry" 2-16-61 (Rebel).

Powell, Frank. Films: "Fools of Fate" 1909; "Leather Stocking" 1909; "A Knot in the Plot" 1910; "The Man" 1910; "Over Silent Paths" 1910.

Powell, Jack (1901-4/6/76). Films: "Kid Courageous" 1935.

Powell, Jane (1929-). TV: *Ruggles of Red Gap* 2-3-57 (Clementine).

Powell, Lee (1908-7/8/44). Films: "Forlorn River" 1937 (Duke); "The Lone Ranger" 1938-serial (Allen King/the Lone Ranger); "Come on, Rangers" 1939 (Earp); "Trigger Pals" 1939 (Stormy); "The Lone Rider Rides On" 1941; "The Return of Daniel Boone" 1941 (Tax Collector Fuller); "Along the Sundown Trail" 1942; "Prairie Pals" 1942 (Lee);

"Raiders of the West" 1942; "Texas Man Hunt" 1942 (Lee Clark).

Powell, Patricia. TV: *Tales of Wells Fargo*—"The Most Dangerous Man Alive" 11-10-58 (Ellen Nagel); *Bat Masterson*—"River Boat" 2-18-59 (Nora).

Powell, Randolph (1950-). TV: *Father Murphy*—"False Blesing" 2-9-82 (Warren Collier).

Powell, Russ (1875-11/28/50). Films: "The Big Trail" 1930 (Windy Bill); "Mystery Ranch" 1932 (Sheriff Bill Burnap); "To the Last Man" 1933 (Greaves); "Call of the Wild" 1935 (Bartender); "Rose of the Rancho" 1936 (Bartender); "Sutter's Gold" 1936; "Hit the Saddle" 1937 (Rancher); "Cowboy and the Lady" 1938 (Rodeo Rider); "Santa Fe Stampede" 1938; "The Arizona Wildcat" 1939; "Union Pacific" 1939 (Vendor); "The Return of Frank James" 1940 (Juror); "When the Daltons Rode" 1940 (Engineer); "Prairie Stranger" 1941 (Whittling Jones).

Powell, William (1892-3/5/84). Films: "Desert Gold" 1926 (Landree); "Nevada" 1927 (Clan Dillon); "The Vanishing Pioneer" 1928 (John Murdock); "The Treasure of Lost Canyon" 1952 (Doc Homer Brown).

Power, Paul (1902-4/5/68). Films: "Under California Stars" 1948 (Director). ¶TV: *Maverick*—"Diamond in the Rough" 1-26-58 (Pyne).

Power, Jr., Tyrone (1914-11/15/58). Films: "Northern Frontier" 1935 (Mountie); "Jesse James" 1939 (Jesse James); "Brigham Young—Frontiersman" 1940 (Jonathan Kent); "Mark of Zorro" 1940 (Diego Vega); "Rawhide" 1951 (Tom Owens); "Pony Soldier" 1952 (Duncan MacDonald).

Power, Sr., Tyrone (1869-12/30/31). Films: "A Texas Steer" 1915 (Maverick Brander); "Braveheart" 1925 (Standing Rock); "Hands Across the Border" 1926 (John Drake); "The Big Trail" 1930 (Red Flack).

Powers, Francis (1865-5/10/40). Films: "Out of the Dust" 1920 (Sgt. Burns); "The White Rider" 1920 (Major Drake); "Playing It Wild" 1923 (Old Man Web).

Powers, Hunt. Films: "Sugar Colt" 1966-Ital./Span. (Tom Cooper); "The Greatest Robbery in the West" 1968-Ital. (Billy Rum); "Django and Sartana Are Coming ... It's the End" 1970-Ital. (Sartana); "Fistful of Death" 1971-Ital. (Macho Callaghan); "One Damned Day at Dawn ... Django Meets Sartana" 1971-Ital. (Django); "Reach You Bastard!" 1971-Ital. (Django); "Stranger

That Kneels Beside the Shadow of a Corpse" 1971-Ital. (Lazar); "He Was Called the Holy Ghost" 1972-Ital.; "Showdown for a Badman" 1972-Ital. (Nevada Kid).

Powers, John (1885-1/17/41). Films: "Hills of Old Wyoming" 1937 (Smiley, the Cook); "Rustler's Valley" 1937 (Stuttering Man); "Union Pacific" 1939 (Irishman); "Twilight on the Trail" 1941 (Drummer); "Ramrod" 1947 (Pokey).

Powers, Lucille. Films: "Billy the Kid" 1930; "The Two Gun Man" 1931 (Joan Markham); "Texas Bad Man" 1932 (Nancy Keefe).

Powers, Mala (1931-). Films: "Rose of Cimarron" 1952 (Rose of Cimarron); "The Yellow Mountain" 1954 (Nevada Wray); "Rage at Dawn" 1955 (Laura Reno); "The Storm Rider" 1957 (Tay Rorick); "Sierra Baron" 1958 (Sue Russell). ¶TV: *Zane Grey Theater*—"Black Is for Grief" 4-12-57 (Barbara Anderson); *Wagon Train*—"The Ruttledge Munroe Story" 5-21-58 (Ruth Hadley); *Wanted—Dead or Alive*—"Till Death Do Us Part" 11-8-58 (Stacy Torrance); *The Restless Gun*—"Take Me Home" 12-1-58 (Lee Laney), "The Lady and the Gun" 1-19-59 (Myra Baker), "The Way Back" 7-13-59; *Bonanza*—"The Diedeshiemer Story" 10-31-59 (Helene); *Tombstone Territory*—2-12-60 (Renee Carter); *The Rebel*—"Take Dead Aim" 3-6-60 (Cassie); *Cheyenne*—"Alibi for a Scalped Man" 3-7-60 (Celia Marley), "Trouble Street" 10-2-61 (Sharon Colton); *Bronco*—"Montana Passage" 4-5-60 (Ruth Miller); *Sugarfoot*—"The Corsican" 4-12-60 (Roberta Shipman); *Walt Disney Presents*—"Daniel Boone" 1960-61 (Rebecca Boone); *Maverick*—"Dutchman's Gold" 1-22-61 (Charlotte Simmons); *Lawman*—"Blind Hate" 5-14-61 (Lucy Pastor); *Rawhide*—"A Woman's Place" 3-30-62 (Loretta Opel); *Wide Country*—"The Man Who Ran Away" 2-7-63 (Georgia Lund); *Daniel Boone*—"When I Became a Man, I Put Away Childish Things" 2-9-67 (Polly Cooper); *Wild Wild West*—"The Night of the Big Blast" 10-7-66 (Lily Fortune); *Here Come the Brides*—"The Fetching of Jenny" 12-5-69 (Jenny Lind).

Powers, Richard. *see* Keene, Tom.

Powers, Stefanie (1942-). Films: "McClintock" 1963 (Becky McLintock); "Stagecoach" 1966 (Mrs. Lucy Mallory); "Hardcase" TVM-1972 (Rozaline); "The Magnificent Seven Ride" 1972 (Laurie Gunn); "Shootout in a One-Dog Town" TVM-1974

(Letty Crandell). ¶TV: *Bonanza*— "Calamity Over the Comstock" 11-3-63 (Calamity Jane); *Lancer*—"The Black McGloins" 1-21-69 (Moira Mc-Gloin), "Zee" 9-30-69 (Zee); *Kung Fu*—"Cry of the Night Beast" 10-19-74 (Edna).

Powers, Tom (1890-11/9/55). Films: "Angel and the Badman" 1947 (Dr. Mangrum); "Station West" 1948 (Capt. Iles); "The Nevadan" 1950 (Bill Martin); "Denver and Rio Grande" 1952 (Sloan); "Horizons West" 1952 (Frank Tarleton); "Hannah Lee" 1953 (Sheriff); "The Last Posse" 1953 (Frank White); "The Marksman" 1953; "The Americano" 1955 (Jim Rogers); "Ten Wanted Men" 1955 (Green). ¶TV: *The Lone Ranger*—"Two Gold Lockets" 2-15-51.

Prada, Jose Maria (1943-8/13/78). Films: "Villa Rides" 1968; "Pancho Villa" 1975-Span.

Prange, Laurie. Films: "Ransom for Alice!" TVM-1977 (Alice Halliday); "Testimony of Two Men" TVM-1977 (Jenny Heger). ¶TV: *Gunsmoke*—"The Lost" 9-13-71 (Girl); *Kung Fu*—"The Hoots" 12-13-73 (Gretchen Klempt); *How the West Was Won*—"The Forgotten" 3-19-79 (Prudence Willow).

Prather, Joan (1951-). Films: "The Deerslayer" TVM-1978 (Judith Hutter).

Prather, Lee (1890-1/3/58). Films: "End of the Trail" 1936; "Born to the West" 1937 (Stranger); "Two-Fisted Sheriff" 1937 (Herrick); "Two Gun Law" 1937 (Sheriff Bill Collier); "Rio Grande" 1938 (Goulding); "West of Santa Fe" 1938 (Jackson); "Overland with Kit Carson" 1939-serial; "Texas Stampede" 1939 (Jeff Cameron); "Bullets for Rustlers" 1940 (Tom Andrews); "Konga, the Wild Stallion" 1940 (Allen); "Texas Renegades" 1940 (Jim Bates); "King of Dodge City" 1941; "Outlaws of the Panhandle" 1941 (Elihu Potter); "Rolling Down the Great Divide" 1942 (Lee Powell).

Pratt, Gil (1891-12/10/54). Films: "Law of the North" 1932.

Pratt, Jack (1878-12/24/38). Films: "Back to Yellow Jacket" 1922 (William Carson); "The Lone Hand" 1922 (Jack Maltrain); "Daring Chances" 1924 (Joe Slavin); "The Western Wallop" 1924 (Convict Leader); "Ace of Spades" 1925-serial; "The Red Rider" 1925 (Black Panther); "Ridin' Thunder" 1925 (Cal Watson); "A Roaring Adventure" 1925 (Brute Kilroy); "The Sign of the

Cactus" 1925 (Sheriff); "Wild Horse Stampede" 1926 (Henchman); "Hawk of the Hills" 1927-serial (Colonel Jennings); "Rough and Ready" 1927 (Parson Smith); "The Western Whirlwind" 1927 (Jim Blake); "Made-to-Order Hero" 1928 (Fred Van Ratt).

Pratt, Judson (1916-). Films: "The Horse Soldiers" 1959 (Sgt. Maj. Kirby); "Sergeant Rutledge" 1960 (Lt. Mulqueen); "Cheyenne Autumn" 1964 (Mayor Dog Kelly); "A Distant Trumpet" 1964 (Capt. Cedric Gray). ¶TV: *Zane Grey Theater*—"No Man Living" 1-11-57 (Ramsey); *Gunsmoke*—"Big Girl Lost" 4-20-57 (Bill Pence), "Daddy-O" 6-1-57, "Blind Man's Bluff" 2-23-63; *Have Gun Will Travel*—"Three Bells to Perdido" 9-14-57, "The Statue of San Sebastian" 6-14-58; *Union Pacific*—Regular 1958-59 (Bill Kincaid); *Jefferson Drum*—"Prison Hill" 12-4-58 (Father Andrew Damon); *Texas John Slaughter*—"Killers from Kansas" 1-9-59 (Capt. Cooper); *Rough Riders*—"The Rifle" 5-7-59 (Jack McCoy); *Riverboat*—"A Night at Trapper's Landing" 11-8-59 (Sgt. Ned Bolger); *Hotel De Paree*—"Sundance and the Boat Soldier" 2-5-60 (Cappy); *Man from Blackhawk*—"Drawing Acount" 2-12-60 (Thomas Cash); *Overland Trail*—"First Stage to Denver" 5-1-60 (Abner Dutton); *Klondike*—"The Unexpected Candidate" 11-7-60 (Dan Sheean); *The Outlaws*—"Culley" 2-16-61 (Dagget); *Bonanza*—"Thunderhead Swindle" 4-29-61 (Jim Bronson), "Half a Rogue" 1-27-63 (Nelson); *Rawhide*—"The Reunion" 4-6-62 (Sergeant Morgan), "Incident of the Gallows Tree" 2-22-63 (Sheriff Ben Devlin), "Incident at Alkali Sink" 5-24-63 (Reb), "Incident of Iron Bull" 10-3-63 (Sergeant Grogan); *The Virginian*—"Riff-Raff" 11-7-62, "All Nice and Legal" 11-25-64 (Jerd), "A Small Taste of Justice" 12-20-67; *Stoney Burke*—"Color Him Lucky" 4-1-63 (Ed Mitchner); *Daniel Boone*—"The Family Fluellen" 10-15-64 (Amos Whythe), "Seminole Territory" 1-13-66 (John Bridger); *Death Valley Days*—"The Left Hand Is Damned" 11-1-64, "Raid on the San Francisco Mint" 5-23-65 (General); *Walt Disney Presents*—"Gallegher" 1965-67 (Police Chief O'Malley); *Iron Horse*—"Wild Track" 12-16-67 (Brady); *The Guns of Will Sonnett*—"One Angry Juror" 3-7-69 (Hardwick); *Nichols*—"The Indian Giver" 9-30-71; *Kung Fu*—"An Eye for an Eye" 1-25-73 (Cotton).

Pratt, Purnell (1886-7/25/41). Films: "The Silver Horde" 1930

(Wayne Wayland); "The Plainsman" 1936 (Capt. Wood); "Forlorn River" 1937 (David Ward); "High, Wide and Handsome" 1937 (Colonel Blake); "Colorado Sunset" 1939 (Mr. Hall); "Come on, Rangers" 1939 (Sen. Harvey).

Pratt, Robert. Films: "The Hired Hand" 1971 (Dan Griffin); "Hec Ramsey" TVM-1972 (Steve Ritt). ¶TV: *Alias Smith and Jones*— "The Night of the Red Dog" 11-4-71 (Billy Boggs); *Gunsmoke*—"Homecoming" 1-8-73 (Raymond Wilson).

Pravda, George (1919-4/30/85). TV: *Masterpiece Theatre*—"The Last of the Mohicans" 1972 (General Montcalm).

Prendes, Luis (1913-). Films: "The Christmas Kid" 1966-Span./ Ital. (George Perkins); "The Tall Women" 1966-Austria/Ital./Span. (Pope); "Django Does Not Forgive" 1967-Ital./Span.; "The Man Who Killed Billy the Kid" 1967-Span./Ital. (Mark Liston); "White Comanche" 1967-Ital./Span./U.S.; "China 9, Liberty 37" 1978-Ital./Span./U.S.

Prentice, Keith (1940-). Films: "The Legend of Nigger Charley" 1972 (Nils Fowler).

Prentiss, Ann (1941-). TV: *The Virginian*—"Crime Wave at Buffalo Spring" 1-29-69 (Geraldine); *Bonanza*—"Meena" 11-16-69 (Meena), "The Horse Traders" 4-5-70 (Meena), "Easy Come, Easy Go" 12-12-71 (Meena).

Prentiss, Ed (1908-). Films: "Westbound" 1959 (James Fuller). ¶TV: *Maverick*—"Comstock Conspiracy" 12-29-57 (John Bordeen); *Cheyenne*—"Top Hand" 12-31-57 (Ben Gentry), "Duel at Judas Basin" 1-30-61 (Mayor Grant); *Broken Arrow*—"Power" 4-22-58 (Captain Farrell); *Jim Bowie*—"The Cave" 5-9-58 (Dr. Rufus Wiley); *Wanted—Dead or Alive*—"Mental Lapse" 1-2-60 (Sheriff Truxton); *Laramie*—"Ride the Wild Wind" 10-11-60 (Sheriff Simms), "Widow in White" 6-13-61 (Bailey), "Siege at Jubilee" 10-10-61, "Shadows in the Dust" 1-16-62, "Gun Duel" 12-25-62, "The Unvanquished" 3-12-63, "The Stranger" 4-23-63 (Doc), "The Marshals" 4-30-63; *The Tall Man*—"The Parson" 10-29-60 (Mr. Colby), "Enough Rope" 12-19-63 (Burton); *Bronco*—"Apache Treasure" 11-7-60 (Major Keever); *The Deputy*—"Judas Town" 12-31-60 (the Mayor); *Bonanza*—"The Blood Line" 12-31-60, "The Tall Stranger" 1-7-62, "The Quality of Mercy" 11-17-63 (Minister), "No Less a Man" 3-15-64, "Joe Cartwright, Detective" 3-5-67 (Barnes); *The Virginian*—"The Devil's Children" 12-5-62 (Simon Pingree), "Legacy of Hate" 9-14-66 (Parker), "Girl on the Glass Mountain" 12-28-66 (Winner), "The Masquerade" 10-18-67 (Carl Jensen), "Paid in Full" 11-22-67 (Jensen), "Last Grave at Socorro Creek" 1-22-69 (Dave Owens); *The Dakotas*—"Crisis at High Banjo" 2-11-63 (the Governor); *F Troop*—"The New I.G." 2-8-66 (General Morgan); *Wild Wild West*—"The Night of the Lord of Limbo" 12-30-66 (Col. Fairchild).

Prescott, Guy (1884-1968). Films: "Rage at Dawn" 1955; "Shotgun" 1955 (Thompson); "Outlaw's Son" 1957 (Phil Costain); "The Tall Stranger" 1957 (Barrett); "Fort Massacre" 1958 (Tucker); "Quantrill's Raiders" 1958 (Maj. Mathews). ¶TV: *Death Valley Days*—"The Longest Beard in the World" 7-7-56, "Gold Rush in Reverse" 10-21-57; *Bat Masterson*—"Bat Plays a Dead Man's Hand" 12-3-59 (Phil Hood); *Bonanza*—"Feet of Clay" (4-16-60); *Gunsmoke*—"Cody's Code" 1-20-62 (Frank).

Presle, Micheline (1922-). Films: "The Legend of Frenchie King" 1971-Fr./Ital./Span./Brit.

Presley, Elvis (1935-8/16/77). Films: "Love Me Tender" 1956 (Clint); "Flaming Star" 1960 (Pacer Burton); "Tickle Me" 1965 (Lonnie Beale); "Charro!" 1969 (Jess Wade).

Presnell, Harve (1933-). Films: "The Glory Guys" 1965 (Sol Rogers); "Paint Your Wagon" 1969 (Rotten Luck Willie).

Press, Marvin (1915-3/17/68). Films: "The Treasure of Lost Canyon" 1952 (Paddy). ¶TV: *Wild Bill Hickok*—"The Fortune Telling Story" 4-22-52; *Wyatt Earp*—"It's a Wise Calf" 1-17-56.

Preston, J.A. Films: "High Noon, Part II: The Return of Will Kane" TVM-1980 (Alonzo). ¶TV: *The Chisholms*—"Chains" 3-8-80 (Morgan).

Preston, John. Films: "Courage of the North" 1935 (Sergeant Bruce Morton); "Timber Terrors" 1935 (Sgt. Bruce Morton).

Preston, Kelly (1962-). Films: "Cheyenne Warrior" 1994 (Rebecca Carver).

Preston, Lew (and His Ranch Hands). Films: "Prairie Stranger" 1941.

Preston, Robert (1918-3/21/87). Films: "Union Pacific" 1939 (Dick Allen); "Northwest Mounted Police"

1940 (Constable Ronnie Logan); "Lady from Cheyenne" 1941 (Steve); "Blood on the Moon" 1948 (Tate Biling); "Whispering Smith" 1948 (Murray Sinclaire); "The Sundowners" 1950 (Kid Wichita); "Best of the Badmen" 1951 (Matthew Fowler); "My Brother, the Outlaw" 1951 (Joe Warnder); "Face to Face" 1952 ("The Bride Comes to Yellow Sky" segment—the Sheriff); "The Last Frontier" 1955 (Col. Frank Marston); "How the West Was Won" 1962 (Roger Morgan); "Junior Bonner" 1972 (Ace Bonner); "The Chisholms" TVM-1979 (Hadley Chisholm); "September Gun" TVM-1983 (Ben Sunday). ¶TV: *The Chisholms*—Regular 1979-80 (Hadley Chisholm).

Preston, Wayde (1930-2/6/92). Films: "Death Knows No Time" 1968-Span./Ital.; "A Long Ride from Hell" 1968-Ital. (Mayner); "Today It's Me ... Tomorrow You!" 1968-Ital.; "Wrath of God" 1968-Ital./Span.; "God Will Forgive My Pistol" 1969-Ital. (Johnny Brennan); "Sartana in the Valley of Death" 1970-Ital.; "Hey Amigo! A Toast to Your Death!" 1971-Ital.; "Man Called Sledge" 1971-Ital./U.S. (Ripley). ¶TV: *Colt .45*—Regular 1957-60 (Christopher Colt); *Sugarfoot*—"The Return of the Canary Kid" 2-3-59 (Christopher Colt), "The Trial of the Canary Kid" 9-15-59 (Christopher Colt), "The Canary Kid, Inc." 11-10-59 (Christopher Colt); *Maverick*—"The Saga of Waco Williams" 2-15-59 (Waco Williams), "The Witch of Hound Dog" 11-6-60 (Luke Baxter); *Bonanza*—"The Waiting Game" 12-8-63 (Frank Dayton).

Prete, Giancarlo. see Brent, Timothy.

Pretty, Arline (1893-4/14/78). Films: "The Challenge of Chance" 1919 (Fay Calvert); "The Valley of Doubt" 1920 (Marion); "Bucking the Barrier" 1923 (Blanche Cavendish).

Prevost, Francoise (1930-). Films: "Johnny Hamlet" 1966-Ital. (Gertrude).

Prevost, Marie (1898-1/21/37). Films: "If Only Jim" 1921 (Squaw); "The Girl of the Golden West" 1923 (the Squaw); "Call of the Rockies" 1931 (Arleta).

Price, Alonzo (1888-6/5/62). Films: "Forbidden Valley" 1938 (Indian Joe); "Riders of Death Valley" 1941-serial (Wilson).

Price, Hal (Harry F. Price) (1886-4/15/64). Films: "Breed of the Border" 1933; "The Ranger's Code" 1933 (Sheriff); "Riders of Destiny" 1933; "Sagebrush Trail" 1933; "West

of the Divide" 1934; "Heir to Trouble" 1935; "Wanderer of the Wasteland" 1935 (Bartender); "Cavalry" 1936 (Horace Leeds); "The Crooked Trail" 1936; "End of the Trail" 1936 (Deputy); "The Fugitive Sheriff" 1936 (Louder Lucas); "The Mysterious Avenger" 1936 (Sheriff); "Sundown Saunders" 1936 (Lewis); "Wildcat Trooper" 1936 (Buyer); "Arizona Gunfighter" 1937; "Danger Valley" 1937 (Lucky); "Desert Phantom" 1937 (Jim Day); "Melody of the Plains" 1937 (Gorman); "Public Cowboy No. 1" 1937 (Bidwell); "Reckless Ranger" 1937; "Ridin' the Lone Trail" 1937 (Furman); "Stars Over Arizona" 1937 (Hashknife); "Trouble in Texas" 1937 (G-Man); "The Trusted Outlaw" 1937 (Pember); "Valley of Terror" 1937; "Wells Fargo" 1937 (Townsman); "Where Trails Divide" 1937 (Happy); "Call the Mesquiteers" 1938 (Sheriff); "Code of the Rangers" 1938 (Stevens); "Gunsmoke Trail" 1938 (Scroggins); "Heroes of the Alamo" 1938; "Man from Music Mountain" 1938; "Mexicali Kid" 1938; "Pioneer Trail" 1938 (Baron Waite); "Prairie Moon" 1938; "Wild Horse Canyon" 1938; "Across the Plains" 1939 (Buckskin); "Home on the Prairie" 1939 (Sheriff); "In Old Monterey" 1939; "The Man from Texas" 1939 (Sheriff Missouri); "New Frontier" 1939 (Sheriff); "The Night Riders" 1939; "Overland Mail" 1939 (Lugo); "South of the Border" 1939; "Stand Up and Fight" 1939; "Arizona Frontier" 1940 (Joe Lane); "The Carson City Kid" 1940; "Frontier Crusader" 1940 (Sheriff Sam Dolan); "Lone Star Raiders" 1940 (Sheriff); "Out West with the Peppers" 1940 (Bill); "Texas Renegades" 1940 (Mr. Lee); "Arizona Bound" 1941; "Billy the Kid in Santa Fe" 1941 (Sheriff); "Billy the Kid's Fighting Pals" 1941 (Burroughs); "Forbidden Trails" 1941 (Bunion); "Gangs of Sonora" 1941 (Sheriff); "The Lone Rider Ambushed" 1941 (Sheriff); "The Lone Rider Fights Back" 1941; "The Parson of Panamint" 1941; "Riders of the Badlands" 1941 (Warden James); "Ridin' the Cherokee Trail" 1941; "Secrets of the Wastelands" 1941 (Prof. Stubbs); "Sierra Sue" 1941; "The Singing Hill" 1941; "Arizona Roundup" 1942; "Along the Sundown Trail" 1942; "Cowboy Serenade" 1942; "The Cyclone Kid" 1942; "Home in Wyomin'" 1942 (Sheriff); "Law and Order" 1942 (Simms); "The Lone Rider and the Bandit" 1942; "Prairie Gunsmoke" 1942; "Raiders of the Range" 1942 (Sheriff); "Raiders of the West" 1942; "Sheriff of Sage Valley" 1942 (Harrison); "Thunder River Feud" 1942; "Valley of Hunted Men" 1942; "Black Market Rustlers" 1943 (Bartender); "The Blocked Trail" 1943; "Fugitive of the Plains" 1943; "Outlaws of Stampede Pass" 1943; "Robin Hood of the Range" 1943 (Sheriff); "Two Fisted Justice" 1943 (Sam); "Wagon Tracks West" 1943; "Western Cyclone" 1943 (Sheriff); "Fuzzy Settles Down" 1944; "Law Men" 1944 (Haynes); "Law of the Valley" 1944; "Marshal of Reno" 1944; "Mojave Firebrand" 1944; "Oath of Vengeance" 1944; "Outlaw Trail" 1944 (H.A. Fraser); "Partners of the Trail" 1944 (Dobbey); "Range Law" 1944 (Zeke); "Rustlers' Hideout" 1944 (Dave Crockett); "Silver City Kid" 1944; "Sonora Stagecoach" 1944; "West of the Rio Grande" 1944; "Westward Bound" 1944 (Jasper Tuttle); "Wild Horse Phantom" 1944; "Wyoming Hurricane" 1944; "Corpus Christi Bandits" 1945; "Return of the Durango Kid" 1945; "Sheriff of Cimarron" 1945 (Stage Passenger); "Stranger from Santa Fe" 1945; "Wildfire" 1945; "The Phantom Rider" 1946-serial (Simpson); "Sun Valley Cyclone" 1946; "White Stallion" 1947 (Mr. Hodges); "Sundown Riders" 1948 (Yeager); "Frisco Tornado" 1950 (Thompson); "Rough Riders of Durango" 1951 (Johnson); "Junction City" 1952 (Sheriff); "Oklahoma Annie" 1952 (Sheriff). ¶TV: *The Lone Ranger*—"Six Gun Legacy" 11-24-49, "Barnaby Boggs, Esquire" 2-2-50, "Trader Boggs" 1-15-53; *The Roy Rogers Show*—"The Mayor of Ghost Town" 11-30-52, "The Milliner from Medicine Hat" 10-11-53.

Price, Harry F. *see* Price, Hal.

Price, Kate (1872-1/4/43). Films: "Some Duel" 1915; "Arizona" 1918 (Mrs. Canby); "The Perils of Thunder Mountain" 1919-serial; "Put Up Your Hands" 1919 (Bridget); "That Girl Montana" 1921 (Mrs. Huzzard); "The Spoilers" 1923 (Landlady); "Wolf Tracks" 1923 (Kitty Blatherwick); "The Desert Flower" 1925 (Mrs. McQuade); "Arizona Sweepstakes" 1926 (Mrs. McGuire); "Shadow Ranch" 1930 (Maggie Murphy).

Price, Nanci (1880-3/31/70). Films: "Human Targets" 1932 (Marjorie Stockton).

Price, Sherwood (1928-). Films: "Nevada Badmen" 1951; "Night Raiders" 1952 (Telegraph Man); "Scorching Fury" 1952; "The Man from Galveston" 1964 (George Taggart). ¶TV: *Desilu Playhouse*—"Six

Guns for Donegan" 10-16-59; *Wichita Town*—"The Long Night" 1-20-60 (Chet); *Bonanza*—"Escape to the Ponderosa" 3-5-60 (Corporal), "Silent Thunder" 12-10-60 (Eb), "The Secret" 5-6-61 (Pete Parson), "My Son, My Son" 1-19-64 (Miller), "A Time to Step Down" 9-25-66 (Sand); *Overland Trail*—"Vigilantes of Montana" 4-3-60 (Sam Kemp); *Wyatt Earp*—"Big Brother" 11-1-60 (McLowery); *Wagon Train*—"The Jane Hawkins Story" 11-30-60, "The Martin Onyx Story" 1-3-62 (1st Killer); *Cheyenne*—"The Return of Mr. Grimm" 2-13-61 (Hardy Russell), "Massacre at Gunsight Pass" 5-1-61 (Johnny Eldorado), "Man Alone" 10-15-62 (Jimmy Dugan); *Whispering Smith*—"Death at Even Money" 7-10-61 (Rios); *Lawman*—"The Doctor" 5-6-62 (Will Evans); *Have Gun Will Travel*—"Trial at Tablerock" 12-15-62 (Virge Beech); *Temple Houston*—"The Man from Galveston" 1963 (George Taggart), "The Gun That Swept the West" 3-5-64 (Dan Sheldon); *Rawhide*—"Corporal Dasovik" 12-4-64 (Willoughby); *Gunsmoke*—"Clayton Thaddeus Greenwood" 10-2-65 (Frank Band); *The Big Valley*—"Heritage" 10-20-65 (Dion O'Doul), "Target" 10-31-66 (Frank Wesley); *Death Valley Days*—"Brute Angel" 10-15-66 (Sam Bolt); *Iron Horse*—"Six Hours to Sky High" 11-25-67 (Gore).

Price, Stanley (1900-7/13/55). Films: "The Miracle Rider" 1935-serial; "Range War" 1939 (Agitator); "Ride 'Em, Cowgirl" 1939 (Robert Weylan); "The Singing Cowgirl" 1939 (John Tolen); "Water Rustlers" 1939 (Robert Weylan); "The Golden Trail" 1940 (Prader); "One Man's Law" 1940; "Texas Rangers Ride Again" 1940 (Nevers); "The Driftin' Kid" 1941; "Dynamite Canyon" 1941 (Duke Rand); "Lone Star Law Men" 1941 (Mason); "Outlaws of the Desert" 1941 (Charles Grant); "Wanderers of the West" 1941 (Jack Benson); "Arizona Stagecoach" 1942; "King of the Mounties" 1942-serial (McGee); "Outlaws of Pine Ridge" 1942 (Steve Mannion); "Black Market Rustlers" 1943; "Fighting Valley" 1943 (Tucson Jones); "Frontier Badman" 1943 (Blackie); "Riding High" 1943 (Train Conductor); "The Texas Kid" 1943 (Ed); "Wild Horse Rustlers" 1943 (Collins); "Black Arrow" 1944-serial; "Raiders of the Border" 1944 (Blackie); "Range Law" 1944 (Dawson); "Zorro's Black Whip" 1944-serial (Hedges); "Flame of the West" 1945; "Frontier Feud" 1945; "Sunset in El Dorado" 1945 (Lyle Fish); "Alias Billy the Kid" 1946

(Frank Pearson); "Frontier Gunlaw" 1946; "Heading West" 1946; "Romance of the West" 1946 (Rockwood); "Stagecoach to Denver" 1946; "Son of Zorro" 1947-serial (Pancho); "The Dalton Gang" 1949; "Grand Canyon" 1949 (Makeup Man); "Rimfire" 1949 (Lamson); "Tough Assignment" 1949 (Foster); "Cherokee Uprising" 1950 (Smokey); "Colorado Ranger" 1950 (Sheriff); "Crooked River" 1950 (Sheriff); "The Daltons' Women" 1950; "Fast on the Draw" 1950 (Carter); "Hostile Country" 1950 (Sheriff); "Marshal of Heldorado" 1950 (Marshal); "Outlaws of Texas" 1950 (Moore); "Punchy Cowpunchers" 1950-short (Lefty); "The Sundowners" 1950 (Fletcher); "West of the Brazos" 1950 (Marshal); "Abilene Trail" 1951 (Sheriff Warner); "Blazing Bullets" 1951; "Hills of Utah" 1951; "Lawless Cowboys" 1951; "Man from Sonora" 1951; "Oklahoma Justice" 1951; "Stage to Blue River" 1951 (Martin); "Stagecoach Driver" 1951; "Texas Lawmen" 1951; "Wanted Dead or Alive" 1951; "Dead Man's Trail" 1952; "Fargo" 1952; "Hellgate" 1952 (Col. Telsen); "The Man from Black Hills" 1952 (Shealey); "Montana Incident" 1952; "Texas City" 1952 (2nd Sergeant); "Waco" 1952 (Sheriff of Waco); "Wyoming Roundup" 1952 (Clark); "The Homesteaders" 1953 (Van); "The Marksman" 1953; "Rebel City" 1953 (Herb); "Star of Texas" 1953 (Hank Caldwell); "Perils of the Wilderness" 1956-serial.

Price, Vincent (1911-10/25/93). Films: "Brigham Young—Frontiersman" 1940 (Joseph Smith); "Hudson Bay" 1941 (King Charles); "The Baron of Arizona" 1950 (James Addison Reaves); "Curtain Call at Cactus Creek" 1950 (Tracy Holland); "More Dead Than Alive" 1968 (Dan Ruffalo). ¶TV: *Have Gun Will Travel*—"The Moor's Revenge" 12-27-58 (Charles Matthews); *Riverboat*—"Witness No Evil" 11-1-59 (Otto Justin); *F Troop*—"V Is for Vampire" 2-2-67 (Count Sforza); *Daniel Boone*—"Copperhead Izzy" 1-30-69 (Dr. Thaddeus Morton).

Prickett, Maudie (1915-4/14/76). Films: "Gold Mine in the Sky" 1938; "The Fighting Frontiersman" 1946; "Two-Fisted Ranger" 1946; "The Lone Hand Texan" 1947 (Hattie Hatfield); "Song of Idaho" 1948 (Millie); "The Cowboy and the Indians" 1949 (Miss Summers); "Beyond the Purple Hills" 1950 (Montana" 1950 (Rancher's Wife); "Pecos River" 1951 (Mrs. Peck); "Lost in Alaska" 1952 (Woman in Window); "Man with the Gun" 1955 (Mrs. Elderhorn); "The Phantom Stagecoach" 1957 (Mrs. Wiggins); "The Legend of Tom Dooley" 1959 (2nd Old Maid). ¶TV: *Schlitz Playhouse of the Stars*—"Way of the West" 6-6-58 (Miss Piper); *Fury*—"Aunt Harriet" 10-8-58 (Aunt Harriet), "Trottin' Horse" 2-6-60 (Aunt Harriet); *Zane Grey Theater*—"Legacy of a Legend" 11-6-58 (Mils Howland); *The Texan*—"Private Account" 4-6-59; *Bonanza*—"Tax Collector" 2-18-61, "The Pure Truth" 3-8-64; *Wagon Train*—"The Duke Shannon Story" 4-26-61 (Ethel); *Daniel Boone*—"The Sisters O'Hannrahan" 12-3-64 (Flavia Tillridge); *Walt Disney Presents*—"Gallegher" 1965-67 (Maid); *Gunsmoke*—"By Line" 4-9-66 (Mrs. Preeker), "P.S. Murry Christmas" 12-27-71 (Mrs. Pretch), "The River" 9-11-72 & 9-18-72 (Aunt Ida); *Dirty Sally*—"Wimmen's Rights" 3-15-74 (Mabel).

Priest, Pat (1936-). TV: *Death Valley Days*—"The Wild West's Biggest Train Holdup" 5-2-65 (Nora).

Priestley, Jason. Films: "Tombstone" 1993 (Billy Breckenridge).

Prieto, Antonio (1915-4/14/76). Films: "Three Swords of Zorro" 1963-Ital./Span.; "A Fistful of Dollars" 1964-Ital./Ger./Span. (Benito Rojo).

Prima, Louis (1911-8/24/78). Films: "Rhythm on the Range" 1936.

Primus, Barry (1938-). Films: "Heartland" 1980 (Jack). ¶TV: *The Virginian*—"The Mark of a Man" 4-20-66 (Johnny Younce).

Prince, John T. (1871-12/24/37). Films: "The Call of Courage" 1925 (Jeff Hazleton); "The Gold Hunters" 1925 (John Ball); "The Phantom Bullet" 1926 (Tom Farlane, Sr.); "Prowlers of the Night" 1926 (George Moulton); "Hawk of the Hills" 1927-serial (the Hermit); "Ramona" 1928 (Father Salvierderra).

Prince, William (1913-). Films: "Lust for Gold" 1949 (Barry Storm); "Secret of Treasure Mountain" 1956 (Robert Kendall); "Bronco Billy" 1980 (Edgar).

Principal, Victoria (1945-). Films: "The Life and Times of Judge Roy Bean" 1972 (Marie Elena).

Prine, Andrew (1935-). Films: "Advance to the Rear" 1964 (Pvt. Owen Selous); "Texas Across the River" 1966 (Lt. Sibley); "Bandolero!" 1968 (Roscoe Bookbinder); "Chisum" 1970 (Alex McSween); "Squares" 1972 (Austin Roth); "One Little Indian" 1973 (Chaplain); "Law

of the Land" TVM-1976 (Travis Carrington); "The Winds of Autumn" 1976; "Last of the Mohicans" TVM-1977 (Major Heyward); "Donner Pass: The Road to Survival" TVM-1978 (Keyser); "The Avenging Angel" TVM-1995. ¶TV: *Overland Trail*—"Sour Annie" 5-8-60 (Paulson); *Have Gun Will Travel*—"The Marshal's Boy" 11-26-60 (Billy), "Fandango" 3-4-61 (Bobby Olson); *Alcoa Premiere*—"Second Chance" 3-13-62 (Andy Guthrie); *Gunsmoke*—"The Prisoner" 5-19-62 (Billy Joe Arlen), "Flase Front" 12-22-62 (Clay Tatum), "Easy Come" 10-26-63 (Elmo Sippy); *Wide Country*—Regular 1962-63 (Andy Guthrie); *Great Adventure*—"The Outlaw and the Nun" 12-6-63 (Billy the Kid); *Wagon Train*—"The Bob Stuart Story" 9-30-64 (Felix Colton), "Thye Isaiah Quickfox Story" 1-31-65 (Eric Camden); *Bonanza*—"The Jonah" 5-9-65 (George Whitman); *The Virginian*—"Hideout" 1-13-65 (Clint Evers), "The Brothers" 9-15-65 (Will Denning), "A Bald-Faced Boy" 4-13-66 (Brett Benton), "The Strange Quest of Claire Bingham" 4-12-67 (Chuck Larson), "The Power Seekers" 10-8-69 (Tobe Larkin); *The Road West*—Regular 1966-67 (Tim Pride); *Daniel Boone*—"Thirty Pieces of Silver" 3-28-68 (Amos Fargo); *Lancer*—"The Heart of Pony Alice" 12-17-68 (Wilf Guthrie), "The Lion and the Lamb" 2-3-70 (Gabe Lincoln); *Kung Fu*—"The Gunman" 1-3-74 (White); *Barbary Coast*—"Crazy Cats" 9-15-75 (Fitzgerald); *Dr. Quinn, Medicine Woman*—"Progress" 2-27-93 (Thaddeus Birch), "The Prisoner" 3-13-93 (Thaddeus Birch).

Pring, Gerald. Films: "Broken Chains" 1922 (Butler); "Fighting Streak" 1922 (Charles Merchant).

Pringle, Aileen (1895-12/16/89). Films: "They Died with Their Boots On" 1941 (Mrs. Sharp).

Pringle, John (1862-8/12/29). Films: "Travelin' Fast" 1924 (William Conway); "His Greatest Battle" 1925.

Prior, Herbert (1867-10/3/54). Films: "Ranson's Folly" 1910; "A Perilous Ride" 1911; "The Disputed Claim" 1912; "At Bear Track Gulch" 1913; "The Ranch Owner's Love-Making" 1913; "A Tale of Old Tucson" 1914; "When East Met West in Boston" 1914; "The Rose of Nome" 1920 (Jack Hilton); "The Snowshoe Trail" 1922 (Kenly Lounsbury); "The Taming of the West" 1925 (Old Manking); "The Wild Bull's Lair" 1925 (James Harbison); "Rustlin' for Cupid" 1926 (Tom Martin); "The Last Outlaw" 1927 (Bert Wagner);

"The Winged Horseman" 1929 (Eben Matthews).

Prisco, Albert. Films: "That Devil Quemado" 1925 (Jose Rameriz); "Lone Hand Saunders" 1926 (Charlie); "Don Mike" 1927 (Don Louis Ybara); "The Prairie King" 1927 (Dan Murdock).

Pritchard, David. Films: "Winchester '73" TVM-1967 (Dan McAdam) ¶TV: *Bonanza*—"Ride the Wind" 1-16-66 & 1-23-66 (Pat), "Something Hurt, Something Wild" 9-11-66 (Bret), "The Price of Salt" 2-4-68 (Ned).

Prival, Lucien (1900-). Films: "King of the Royal Mounted" 1940-serial (Admiral Johnson); "King of the Texas Rangers" 1941-serial (Captain); "High Noon" 1952 (Bartender).

Proach, Henry (1920-6/22/86). Films: "Dirty Little Billy" 1972 (Lloyd).

Proctor, Marland (1941-10/8/88). Films: "Fandango" 1970 (Sissy Sam).

Proctor, Philip (1940-). TV: *Daniel Boone*—"Noblesse Oblige" 3-26-70 (Bernard).

Prohoska, Janos (1921-3/13/74). Films: "Advance to the Rear" 1964 (Flag Pole Sitter).

Prokop, Paul. Films: "There Was a Crooked Man" 1970. ¶TV: *Wild Wild West*—"The Night of the Firebrand" 9-15-67 (Clint Goxi); *Gunsmoke*—"The Sodbusters" 11-20-72 (Dan Underwood).

Prosky, Robert (1930-). Films: "Far and Away" 1992 (Daniel Christie).

Prosser, Hugh (1906-11/8/52). Films: "The Night Riders" 1939; "Hands Across the Rockies" 1941; "Sierra Sue" 1941; "West of Cimarron" 1941; "Boss of Hangtown Mesa" 1942 (the Utah Kid); "Lost Canyon" 1943; "Riders of the Deadline" 1943 (Martin); "Land of the Outlaws" 1944; "Range Law" 1944 (Sheriff); "Song of the Range" 1944; "West of the Rio Grande" 1944; "Code of the Lawless" 1945 (Lester Ward); "The Phantom Rider" 1946-serial (Keeler); "Prairie Raiders" 1947; "Unconquered" 1947 (Soldier at Gilded Beaver); "The Vigilante" 1947-serial (Captain Reilly); "Six-Gun Law" 1948 (Boss Decker); "Trail to Laredo" 1948; "Western Renegades" 1949 (Laren); "Across the Badlands" 1950 (Jeff Carson); "Outlaw Gold" 1950 (Bigsby); "Roar of the Iron Horse" 1950-serial (Lefty); "Canyon Ambush" 1952; "Montana Incident" 1952; "The Treasure of Lost Canyon"

1952 (Fire Captain). ¶TV: *The Lone Ranger*—"The Beeler Gang" 8-10-50, "The Devil's Bog" 2-5-53, "Hidden Fortune" 6-18-53; *The Gene Autry Show*—"Heir to the Lazy L" 12-29-51, "Horse Sense" 1-11-52; *The Cisco Kid*—"Quicksilver Murder" 1-12-52.

Prouty, Jed (1879-5/10/56). Films: "The Girl of the Golden West" 1923 (Nick); "The Conquerors" 1932 (Auctioneer); "The Texas Rangers" 1936 (Prosecuting Attorney); "Go West, Young Lady" 1941 (Judge Harmon).

Provine, Dorothy (1937-). TV: *Man Without a Gun*—"Man Missing" 12-6-58; *Lawman*—"Lady in Question" 12-21-58 (Julie); *Sugarfoot*—"The Giant Killer" 3-3-59, "The Avengers" 5-12-59; *Rough Riders*—"Lesson in Violence" 3-26-59 (Holly Morrow); *Wagon Train*—"The Matthew Lowry Story" 4-1-59; *The Texan*—"Blood Money" 4-20-59 (Chalmers); *Colt .45*—"The Confession" 4-26-59 (Ann Donnelly); *Bronco*—"Red Water North" 6-16-59 (Gilda Harper); *Cimarron City*—"The Bitter Lesson" 1-3-59 (Laura Winfield); *The Alaskans*—Regular 1959-60 (Rocky Shaw).

Prowse, Juliet (1937-). Films: "The Second Time Around" 1961 (Rena, the Dancehall Girl).

Prud'Homme, Cameron (1892-11/27/67). Films: "The Rainmaker" 1956 (H.C. Curry). ¶TV: *Riverboat*—"About Roger Mowbray" 9-27-59 (Jonathan Reed).

Prud'homme, George. *see* Pembroke, George.

Pryor, Ainslie (1921-5/27/58). Films: "The Last Hunt" 1956 (1st Buffalo Hunter); "Walk the Proud Land" 1956 (Capt. Larsen); "The Guns of Fort Petticoat" 1957 (Col. Chilvington); "Cole Younger, Gunfighter" 1958 (Follyward); "The Left-Handed Gun" 1958 (Joe Grant). ¶TV: *Gunsmoke*—"Smoking Out the Nolans" 11-5-55 (Josh Nolan), "Doc's Revenge" 6-9-56 (George Maddow), "Mr. and Mrs. Amber" 8-4-56 (Peak Fletcher), "Kitty's Outlaw" 10-5-57 (Cole Yankton); *Zane Grey Theater*—"The Long Road Home" 10-19-56 (Kimbal Hatton); *Sheriff of Cochise*—"Wyatt Earp" 6-7-57 (Matt Davis); *Cheyenne*—"Devil's Canyon" 11-19-57 (King Forest).

Pryor, Herbert. Films: "The Half-Breed" 1922 (Ned Greenwood).

Pryor, Richard (1940-). Films: "Adios Amigo" 1975 (Sam). ¶TV: *Wild Wild West*—"The Night of the Eccentrics" 9-16-66 (Villar, the Ventriloquist).

Pryor, Roger (1901-1/31/74). Films: "The Cisco Kid Returns" 1945 (Harris); "The Man from Oklahoma" 1945 (Jim Gardner).

Puente, Jesus. Films: "Seven Guns from Texas" 1964-Span./Ital. (Ringo); "Adios Gringo" 1965-Ital./Fr./Span. (Tex Slaughter); "Behind the Mask of Zorro" 1965-Ital./Span.; "For a Fist in the Eye" 1965-Ital./Span.; "Hands of a Gunman" 1965-Ital./Span.; "Seven Guns for the MacGregors" 1965-Ital./Span.; "Fury of the Apaches" 1966-Span./Ital.; "Ringo, the Lone Rider" 1967-Ital./Span.; "Dollars for a Fast Gun" 1968-Ital./Span.; "Hour of Death" 1968-Span./Ital.; "Rattler Kid" 1968-Ital./Span.; "Two Crosses at Danger Pass" 1968-Ital./Span.

Puglia, Frank (1892-10/25/75). Films: "The Gay Desperado" 1936 (Lopez); "The Girl and the Gambler" 1939 (Gomez); "In Old Caliente" 1939 (Don Miguel); "Mark of Zorro" 1940 (Proprietor); "Rangers of Fortune" 1940 (Stefan); "Billy the Kid" 1941 (Pedro Gonzales); "The Parson of Panamint" 1941 (Joaquin); "Tall in the Saddle" 1944 (Juan Tala); "Colorado Territory" 1949 (Brother Thomas); "Son of Belle Star" 1953 (Manuel); "Jubilee Trail" 1954 (Don Orosco); "The Burning Hills" 1956 (Tio Perico); "The First Texan" 1956 (Pepe); "Duel at Apache Wells" 1957 (Senor Valdez). ¶TV: *Colt .45*—"The Mirage" 1-10-58 (Ramon Esperanza); *The Law of the Plainsman*—"Dangerous Barriers" 3-10-60 (Don Esteban); *The Texan*—"The Governor's Lady" 3-14-60 (Carlos Moreno); *Rawhide*—"Incident at Poco Tiempo" 12-9-60 (Father Sebastian); *Wide Country*—"Farewell to Margarita" 3-21-63 (Papa Viejo); *Bonanza*—"Tommy" 12-18-66 (Padre); *The High Chaparral*—"Threshold of Courage" 3-31-68 (Miguel).

Puig, Eva (1894-10/6/68). Films: "Northwest Mounted Police" 1940 (Ekawo); "Texas Rangers Ride Again" 1940 (Maria); "Romance of the Rio Grande" 1941 (Marta); "Below the Border" 1942 (Aunt Maria); "Undercover Man" 1942 (Rosita Lopez); "Vengeance of the West" 1942; "The Cisco Kid Returns" 1945 (Tia); "Plainsman and the Lady" 1946 (Anita Lopez); "Wild Beauty" 1946 (Winnie).

Pullen, William. Films: "The Lawless Breed" 1952 (Joe Hardin); "Ride Clear of Diablo" 1953 (Meredith); "Those Redheads from Seattle" 1953 (Rev. Petrie); "War Paint" 1953 (Jeb); "Canyon Crossroads" 1955

(A.E.C. Clerk); "Hell Canyon Outlaws" 1957. ¶TV: *Wild Bill Hickok*—"Blake's Kid" 12-23-52; *The Cisco Kid*—"Choctaw Justice" 12-26-53; *Wyatt Earp*—"The Man Who Rode with Custer" 1-8-57, "The Gatling Gun" 10-21-58 (Capt. Stewart), "The Toughest Judge in Arizona" 5-24-60; *Death Valley Days*—"The Last Letter" 1-13-57 (Alex Todd); *Yancy Derringer*—"The Wayward Warrior" 4-16-59 (Major Henri); *Bonanza*—"Vendetta" 12-5-59 (Sheriff Toller).

Pullman, Bill. Films: "Sommersby" 1993 (Orin); "Wyatt Earp" 1994 (Ed Masterson).

Puppo, Romano. Films: "The Tramplers" 1965-Ital. (Paine Cordeen); "The Big Gundown" 1966-Ital. (Rocky); "Death Rides a Horse" 1967-Ital.; "Sabata" 1969-Ital. (Rocky Bendato); "Dead Men Ride" 1970-Ital./Span.; "Deaf Smith and Johnny Ears" 1972-Ital.; "Cipolla Colt" 1975-Ital./Ger.

Purcell, Dick (1908-4/10/44). Films: "In Old California" 1942 (Joe Dawson); "Idaho" 1943 (Duke Springer); "The Old Texas Trail" 1944.

Purcell, Lee (1947-). Films: "Dirty Little Billy" 1972 (Berle); "Kid Blue" 1973 (Molly Ford); "The Gambler" TVM-1980 (Jennie Reed). ¶TV: *Bonanza*—"The Weary Willies" 9-27-70 (Angie).

Purdom, Edmund (1924-). Films: "Shoot to Kill" 1963-Span. (Tom Jameson); "Charge of the Seventh Cavalry" 1964-Ital./Span./Fr. (Sugar); "Chrysanthemums for a Bunch of Swine" 1968-Ital. (the Monk); "Piluk, the Timid One" 1968-Ital. (Piluk); "Last Ride to Santa Cruz" 1969-Ger./Fr.

Purdy, Constance (1885-4/1/60). Films: "Unconquered" 1947. ¶TV: *The Lone Ranger*—"Trouble at Black Rock" 2-8-51.

Purl, Linda (1955-). Films: "Jory" 1972 (Amy); "The Oregon Trail" TVM-1976 (Deborah Randal); "Young Pioneers" TVM-1976 (Molly Beaton); "Young Pioneers' Christmas" TVM-1976 (Molly Beaton); "Testimony of Two Men" TVM-1977 (Mavis Eaton). ¶TV: *The Young Pioneers*—Regular 1978 (Molly Beaton).

Putch, John. Films: "The Gambler, Part II—The Adventure Continues" TVM-1983 (Hanging Deputy).

Pyle, Denver (1920-). Films: "Where the North Begins" 1947; "The Man from Colorado" 1948 (Easy Jarrett); "Marshal of Amarillo"

1948 (Night Clerk); "Hellfire" 1949 (Rex); "Red Canyon" 1949 (Hutch); "Rim of the Canyon" 1949; "Dynamite Pass" 1950 (Whip); "The Old Frontier" 1950 (George); "Hills of Utah" 1951 (Bowie French); "Rough Riders of Durango" 1951 (Lacey); "Canyon Ambush" 1952; "Desert Passage" 1952 (Allen); "Fargo" 1952; "The Lusty Men" 1952 (Niko); "The Man from Black Hills" 1952 (Hartley); "The Maverick" 1952 (Bud Karnes); "Oklahoma Annie" 1952 (Skip); "Goldtown Ghost Raiders" 1953 (Bernie Malloy); "A Perilous Journey" 1953 (Bartender); "Texas Bad Man" 1953 (Tench); "Topeka" 1953 (Jonas Bailey); "Red Canyon" 1949 (Hutch); "Rebel City" 1953 (Greeley); "Ride Clear of Diablo" 1953 (Rev. Moorehead); "Texas Bad Man" 1953 (Tench); "Vigilante Terror" 1953; "Johnny Guitar" 1954 (Posse); "Rage at Dawn" 1955 (Clint Reno); "Run for Cover" 1955 (Harvey); "Ten Wanted Men" 1955 (Dave Weed); "Top Gun" 1955; "I Killed Wild Bill Hickok" 1956 (Jim Bailey); "The Naked Hills" 1956 (Bert Killian); "Seventh Cavalry" 1956 (Dixon); "Yaqui Drums" 1956; "Domino Kid" 1957 (Bill Dragger); "Gun Duel in Durango" 1957 (Ranger Captain); "The Lonely Man" 1957 (Sheriff); "Fort Massacre" 1958 (Collins); "Good Day for a Hanging" 1958 (Moore); "The Left-Handed Gun" 1958 (Ollinger); "Cast a Long Shadow" 1959 (Harrison); "The Horse Soldiers" 1959 (Jagger Joe); "King of the Wild Stallions" 1959 (Doc); "The Alamo" 1960 (Gambler); "Geronimo" 1962 (Sen. Conrad); "The Man Who Shot Liberty Valance" 1962 (Amos Carruthers); "Cheyenne Autumn" 1964 (Sen. Henry); "Mail Order Bride" 1964 (Preacher Pope); "The Rounders" 1965 (Bull); "Shenandoah" 1965 (Pastor Bjoeriling); "Gunpoint" 1966 (Cap Hold); "Incident at Phantom Hill" 1966 (1st Hunter); "Welcome to Hard Times" 1967 (Alfie); "Bandolero!" 1968 (Muncie Carter); "Five Card Stud" 1968 (Sig Evers); "Something Big" 1971 (Junior Frisbee); "Cahill, United States Marshal" 1973 (Denver); "Hitched" TVM-1973 (Ben Barnstable); "Sidekicks" TVM-1974 (Drunk); "Winterhawk" 1975 (Arkansas); "The Adventures of Frontier Fremont" 1976 (Old Mountainman); "Buffalo Bill and the Indians, or Sitting Bull's History Lesson" 1976 (McLaughlin); "Guardian of the Wilderness" 1976 (Galen Clark); "Hawmps!" 1976 (Col. Seymour Hawkins); "Maverick" 1994 (Old Gambler). ¶TV: *The Lone Ranger*—"The Outcast" 1-18-51, "The Hooded Men" 2-22-51, "The Fugitive" 9-9-54, "The Woman in the White Mask" 5-12-55, "The Cross of Santo Domingo" 10-11-56; *The Gene Autry Show*—"Frontier Guard" 10-13-51, "Killer's Trail" 10-27-51, "Galloping Hoofs" 12-22-51, "Melody Mesa" 1-4-52, "Bullets and Bows" 3-2-52, "The Sheriff Is a Lady" 3-23-52, "Johnny Jackaroo" 7-13-54, "Sharpshooter" 8-3-54, "The Carnival Comes West" 8-24-54, "Outlaw of Blue Mesa" 9-7-54; *The Cisco Kid*—"Hypnotist Murder" 11-10-51, "Ghost Town Story" 12-22-51; *The Roy Rogers Show*—"The Treasure of Howling Dog Canyon" 1-27-52, "The Double Crosser" 6-1-52, "Flying Bullets" 6-15-52 (Zeke Miller), "Loaded Guns" 4-15-53 (Tom Larrabee); *Wild Bill Hickok*—"Hands Across the Border" 7-22-52; *Wyatt Earp*—Regular 1955-56 (Ben Thompson), "A Good Man" 1-6-59 (Oliver Tittle), "A Murderer's Return" 1-5-60 (Dobie Jenner), "The Too Perfect Crime" 12-6-60 (Hoss Mackey); *My Friend Flicka*—"The Wild Horse" 11-18-55, "Big Red" 6-22-56 (Clint Taylor); *Fury*—"Joey's Father" 12-3-55 (Carter); *Frontier*—"Mother of the Brave" 1-15-56; *Gunsmoke*—"Poor Pearl" 12-22-56 (Willie Calhoun), "Liar from Blackhawk" 6-22-57 (Hank Shinn), "The Bear" 2-28-59 (Mike Blocker), "The Wake" 12-10-60 (Gus Mather), "Us Haggens" 12-8-62 (Black Jack Haggen), "The Odyssey of Jubal Tanner" 5-18-63 (Aaron Larker), "No Hands" 2-8-64 (Pa Ginnis), "The Violators" 10-17-64 (Caleb Nash), "Deputy Festus" 1-16-65 (Claudius), "By Line" 4-9-66 (Clab Chummer), "The Goldtakers" 9-24-66 (Caleb Nash), "Mad Dog" 1-14-67 (Dr. Henry Rand), "Baker's Dozen" 12-25-67 (Judge Blent), "Shadler" 1-15-73 (Cyrus Himes); *Jim Bowie*—"A Horse for Old Hickory" 1-4-57 (Sam Houston), "Master at Arms" 1-25-57 (Sam Houston); *Tales of Wells Fargo*—"Renegade Raiders" 5-20-57 (Jack Powers), "Double Reverse" 10-19-59; *Zane Grey Theater*—"Blood in the Dust" 10-11-57 (Sheriff), "The Stranger" 2-28-58 (Sheriff), "A Thread of Respect" 2-12-59 (Seth Robson), "A Small Town That Died" 3-10-60 (Marshal Joe Sully), "The Empty Shell" 3-30-61 (Nat Sledge); *The Restless Gun*—"Rink" 10-14-57 (Sheriff Jay), "The Pawn" 4-6-59 (Jeb); *Have Gun Will Travel*—"The Colonel and the Lady" 11-23-57 (Clay Sommers), "The Singer" 2-8-58 (Pete Hollister), "The Wager" 1-3-59 (Sid Morgan), "The Posse" 10-3-59 (McKay), "Ransom" 6-4-60 (The Calf" 10-15-60 (George Advent), "The Puppeteer" 12-24-60 (Gen. George Croft); *Broken Arrow*—"Bad Boy" 1-21-58 (Fred); *Tales of the Texas Rangers*—"Texas Flyer" 11-28-58 (Noah Reed); *Jefferson Drum*—"Prison Hill" 12-4-58 (Bart Resdake); *Man Without a Gun*—"Shadow of a Gun" 1-31-59; *Bat Masterson*—"Marked Deck" 3-11-59 (Dan Morgan), "End of the Line" 1-26-61 (Walsh); *The Texan*—"No Place to Stop" 4-27-59 (Houston), "The Sheriff of Boot Hill" 6-1-59 (Joe Lufton), "The Telegraph Story" 10-26-59 (Chip Andrews), "The Guilty and the Innocent" 3-28-60 (Sheriff); *26 Men*—"Fighting Man" 5-26-59; *Lawman*—"Conclave" 6-14-59 (Glen Folsom), "Explosion" 6-3-62 (Sam Brackett); *The Deputy*—"Shadow of the Noose" 10-3-59 (Akins), "The Example" 3-25-61 (Frank Barton); *The Rifleman*—"Bloodlines" 10-6-59, "The Legacy" 12-8-59, "The Hangman" 5-31-60 (Harold Tenner), "The Clarence Bibbs Story" 4-4-61 (George Tanner), "The Decision" 11-6-61 (Frank Hazlett); *The Law of the Plainsman*—"The Matriarch" 2-18-60 (Burke); *Overland Trail*—"Lawyer in Petticoats" 3-27-60 (Sheriff), "The Baron Comes Back" 5-15-60 (Jonathan Kale); *Wichita Town*—"The Legend of Tom Horn" 3-30-60 (Aaron Faber); *Pony Express*—"Special Delivery" 4-20-60 (Hank Watson); *Hotel De Paree*—"Sundance and the Long Trek" 4-22-60 (Taylor); *Man from Blackhawk*—"The Man Who Wanted Everything" 6-3-60 (Arthur White); *The Tall Man*—"Garrett and the Kid" 9-10-60 (Dave Leggett); *Laramie*—"Three Roads West" 10-4-60 (Sheriff), "Strange Company" 6-6-61 (Bailey), "Siege at Jubilee" 10-10-61, "Vengeance" 1-8-63 (Al Morgan); *Riverboat*—"No Bridge on the River" 10-24-60 (Jim Bledsoe); *Stagecoach West*—"Three Wise Men" 12-20-60 (Hewitt); *Maverick*—"Family Pride" 1-8-61 (Jerry O'Brien); *Bronco*—"The Buckbrier Trail" 2-20-61 (Norton Gillespie), "Guns of the Lawless" 5-8-61 (Petrie Munger), "The Prince of Darkness" 11-6-61 (Mason); *Two Faces West*—"Hand of Vengeance" 4-3-61; *Cheyenne*—"Winchester Quarantine" 9-25-61, "Sweet Sam" 10-8-62; *Bonanza*—"Springtime" 10-1-61 (Theodore), "A Hot Day for a Hanging" 10-14-62 (Sheriff Stedman), "The Boss" 5-19-63 (Sheriff), "Little Man—Ten Feet Tall" 5-26-63 (Sheriff), "Bullet for a Bride" 2-16-64 (Mr. Caldwell), "The Passing of a King" 10-13-68 (Claude), "The Wagon" 10-5-70

(Price Buchanan), "Riot!" 10-3-72 (Warden); *Empire*—"The Day the Empire Stood Still" 9-25-62 (Tom Rawlings); *The Virginian*—"Vengeance Is the Spur" 2-27-63 (Pico Brown); *Death Valley Days*—"With Honesty and Integrity" 4-21-63 (Lucius Barkey), "Grandon's Charge" 1-12-64 (Ortho Williams), "Big John and the Rainmaker" 12-6-64 (Fenimore Bleek), "The Resurrection of Deadwood Dick" 10-22-66 (Deadwood Dick); *Rawhide*—"Incident of the Rawhiders" 11-14-63 (Daddy Quade); *Temple Houston*—"The Case for William Gotch" 2-6-64 (Phineas Fallon); *Great Adventure*—"The Special Courage of Captain Pratt" 2-14-64 (General Miles); *The High Chaparral*—"A Hanging Offense" 11-12-67 (General Warren); *Hondo*—"Hondo and the Hanging Town" 12-8-67 (Judge Blunt); *Cimarron Strip*—"The Last Wolf" 12-14-67 (Charley Austin); *The Guns of Will Sonnett*—"The Warriors" 3-1-68 (Sam Cochran); *Here Come the Brides*—"Bolt of Kilmaren" 3-13-70 (Uncle Duncan); *Kung Fu*—"The Ancient Warrior" 5-3-73 (Mayor Simms), "Cross-ties" 2-21-74 (Dr. Colton); *Dirty Sally*—2-8-75 (Parker); *The Life and Times of Grizzly Adams*—Regular 1977-78 (Mad Jack); *How the West Was Won*—"The Enemy" 2-5-79 (Sergeant Tripp).

Pyne, Francine. TV: *Laredo*—"The Heroes of San Gill" 12-23-65 (Dora); *Pistols 'n' Petticoats*—"No Sale" 9-24-66 (Flossie).

Pyper-Ferguson, John. Films: "Children of the Dust" TVM-1995 (Sonny Boy); "Frank and Jesse" TVM-1995 (Clell Miller). ¶TV: *Adventures of Brisco County, Jr.*—Pilot 8-27-93 (Pete Hutter), "Brisco in Jalisco" 9-17-93 (Pete Hutter), "Socrates' Sister" 9-24-93 (Pete Hutter), "Riverboat" 10-1-93 (Pete Hutter), "Stagecoach" 4-1-94 (Pete Hutter), "And Baby Makes Three" 4-22-94 (Pete Hutter), "High Treason" 5-13-94 & 5-20-94 (Pete Hutter); *Legend*—"The Life, Death, and Life of Wild Bill Hickok" 5-16-95.

Quabius, Faith. Films: "Banjo Hackett: Roamin' Free" TVM-1976 (Ruttles); "Standing Tall" TVM-1978 (Anne Klinger).

Quade, John (1938-). Films: "Bad Company" 1972 (Big Joe's Gang Member); "High Plains Drifter" 1973 (Jake Ross); "The Godchild" TVM-1974 (Denton); "Honky Tonk" TVM-1974; "Rancho Deluxe" 1975 (Circular Face); "The Last Hard Men" 1976 (Will Gant); "The Out-

law Josey Wales" 1976 (Comanchero Leader); "Peter Lundy and the Medicine Hat Stallion" TVM-1977 (Adam); "Go West, Young Girl" TVM-1978 (Ingalls); "Cattle Annie and Little Britches" 1981 (Morgan); "No Man's Land" TVM-1984 (Henry Lambert); "Dream West" TVM-1986 (Big Fallon); "Houston: The Legend of Texas" TVM-1986 (Senator Stanbury); "Longarm" TVM-1988; "The Tracker" TVM-1988 (Lomax). ¶TV: *Bonanza*—"Catch as Catch Can" 10-27-68 (Telegrapher), "The Rattlesnake Brigade" 12-5-71 (Tallman); *The High Chaparral*—"The Glory Soldiers" 1-31-69; *Nichols*—Pilot 9-16-71 (Scully One), 3-14-72 (Zeb); *Kung Fu*—"This Valley of Terror" 9-28-74 (Johnson); *The Quest*—"The Buffalo Hunters" 9-29-76 (Neeley); *Hunter's Moon*—Pilot 12-1-79 (Ora Bowen); *Big Bend Country*—Pilot 8-27-81 (Hart).

Quaid, Dennis (1953-). Films: "The Long Riders" 1980 (Ed Miller); "Wyatt Earp" 1994 (Doc Holliday).

Quaid, Randy (1950-). Films: "The Missouri Breaks" 1976 (Little Tod); "Last Ride of the Dalton Gang" TVM-1979 (Grat Dalton); "The Long Riders" 1980 (Clell Miller); "Cowboy" TVM-1983 (Evan Coleman).

Qualen, John (1899-9/12/87). Films: "The Bad Man of Brimstone" 1938 (Loco); "The Texans" 1938 (Swede); "Stand Up and Fight" 1939 (Davey); "The Shepherd of the Hills" 1941 (Coot Royal); "Belle Le Grand" 1951 (Corky McGee); "Ambush at Tomahawk Gap" 1953 (Jonas P. Travis); "Passion" 1954 (Gaspar Melo); "At Gunpoint" 1955 (Livingstone); "Johnny Concho" 1956 (Jake); "The Searchers" 1956 (Lars Jorgensen); "The Big Land" 1957 (Sven Johnson); "Hell Bent for Leather" 1960 (Old Ben); "North to Alaska" 1960 (Logger); "Two Rode Together" 1961 (Ole Knudsen); "The Man Who Shot Liberty Valance" 1962 (Peter Ericson); "Cheyenne Autumn" 1964 (Svenson); "The Sons of Katie Elder" 1965 (Charlie Biller); "A Big Hand for the Little Lady" 1966 (Jesse Buford); "The Adventures of Bullwhip Griffin" 1967; "Firecreek" 1968 (Hall). ¶TV: *Cheyenne*—"Deadline" 2-26-57 (Charley Dolan); *The Californians*—"J. Jimmerson Jones, Inc" 4-1-58 (J. Jimmerson Jones), "Stampede at Misery Flats" 3-17-59 (Vinegar Pete Jones); *Maverick*—"Lonesome Reunion" 9-28-58 (Leland Mills), "The Golden Fleecing" 10-8-61 (Henry Albright); *Yancy Der-*

ringer—"Gallatin Street" 10-9-58 (Larsen); *Bronco*—"The Burning Spring" 10-6-59 (Mr. Colby); *The Alaskans*—"Starvation Stampede" 11-1-59 (Jack Despain); *Overland Trail*—"Lawyer in Petticoats" 3-27-60 (Circuit Judge); *Sugarfoot*—"Funeral at Forty Mile" 5-24-60 (Jens Jensen); *Lawman*—"Old Stefano" 12-25-60 (Doc Shannon), "Blind Hate" 5-14-61 (Doc Marston), "Explosion" 6-3-62 (Doc Shay); *Klondike*—"Queen of the Klondike" 1-23-61 (Larsen); *Bonanza*—"Springtime" 10-1-61 (Parley); *Laramie*—"Shadow of the Past" 10-16-62; *Wide Country*—"Whose Hand at My Throat?" 2-14-63 (Henry Demeter); *Shane*—"The Hant" 9-17-66 (the Old Man).

Quarry, Robert (1928-). TV: *The Lone Ranger*—"A Broken Match" 12-2-54; *Frontier Doctor*—"Fury in the Big Top" 11-22-58.

Quartaro, Nena (1908-11/23/85). Films: "The Virginian" 1929 (Girl in Bar); "Men of the North" 1930 (Woolie-Woolie); "Arizona Terror" 1931 (Lola); "The Fighting Sheriff" 1931 (Tiana); "The Man from Monterey" 1933 (Anita Garcia); "Cyclone Ranger" 1935 (Nita Garcia); "The Three Mesquiteers" 1936 (Rosita); "Left-Handed Law" 1937; "Phantom of Santa Fe" 1937 (Teresa Valarde); "A Lady Takes a Chance" 1943 (Carmencita); "The Outlaw" 1943 (Chita).

Quayle, Anthony (1913-10/20/89). Films: "MacKenna's Gold" 1969 (the Older Englishman).

Quesada, Milo (1930-). Films: "Savage Pampas" 1966-U.S./Span./Arg. (Alfonso); "Django Kill" 1967-Ital./Span.; "The Mercenary" 1968-Ital./Span. (Marco); "Red Blood, Yellow Gold" 1968-Ital./Span.; "Twice a Judas" 1968-Span./Ital.

Quick, Eldon (1937-). TV: *The Big Valley*—"The Twenty-five Graves of Midas" 2-3-69; *Bret Maverick*—"Hallie" 2-9-82 (Clerk).

Quigley, Charles (1906-8/5/64). Films: "The Saddle Buster" 1932 (Cladgett); "Mexican Spitfire Out West" 1940 (Roberts); "The Cowboy and the Indians" 1949 (Henderson).

Quigley, Juanita (1930-). Films: "The Vanishing Virginian" 1941 (Caroline Yancey).

Quillan, Marie. Films: "Hurricane Horseman" 1931 (Tonita); "The Cheyenne Cyclone" 1932; "The Saddle Buster" 1932 (Rita); "Melody Trail" 1935 (Perdita); "The Singing Vagabond" 1935 (Show Girl).

Quillen, Eddie (1907-7/19/90).

Films: "Allegheny Uprising" 1939 (Anderson); "Moonlight and Cactus" 1944 (Stubby); "Twilight on the Prairie" 1944; "Advance to the Rear" 1964 (Smitty); "Gunfight at Comanche Creek" 1964; "The Bounty Killer" 1965 (Pianist). ¶TV: *The Texan*—"The Smiling Loser" 5-25-59 (Slick Parker); *The Law of the Plainsman*—"Passenger to Mescalero" 10-29-59 (Horace Arnold); *The Alaskans*—"Contest at Gold Bottom" 11-15-59 (Kid Johns); *Death Valley Days*—"Gamble with Death" 2-22-61 (Job Darius), "Trial by Fear" 1-10-62 (Hill Beachy); *The Rifleman*—"Mark's Rifle" 11-19-62 (Angus Evans), "Conflict" 12-24-62 (Harvey Evans); *Bonanza*—"The Decision" 12-16-62 (Culp); *Daniel Boone*—"The Accused" 3-24-66 (Ephriam Smith), "First in War, First in Peace" 10-13-66 (Inn Landlord), "Then Who Will They Hang from the Yardarm If Willy Gets Away?" 2-8-68 (Stokey), "Noblesse Oblige" 3-26-70; *Cimarron Strip*—"Till the End of the Night" 11-16-67; *Wild Wild West*—"The Night of the Cut Throats" 11-17-67 (Hogan), "The Night of the Sabatini Death" 2-2-69 (Snidley); *The Guns of Will Sonnett*—"And a Killing Rode into Town" 12-1-67 (Clerk), "A Difference of Opinion" 11-15-68; *The Virginian*—"The Girl in the Shadows" 3-26-69 (Edmunds); *Father Murphy*—"John Michael Murphy, R.I.P." 12-7-82 (Grizzly Bates).

Quimby, Margaret (1905-8/26/65). Films: "The Western Whirlwind" 1927 (Molly Turner); "Trailin' Trouble" 1930 (Molly).

Quine, Don. TV: *The Virginian*—Regular 1966-68 (Stacy Grainer); *Lancer*—"Foley" 10-15-68 (Corey).

Quiney, Charles. Films: "Rebels of Arizona" 1969-Span.; "More Dollars for the MacGregors" 1970-Ital./Span.; "Zorro, Rider of Vengeance" 1971-Span./Ital. (Zorro)

Quinlan, Kathleen (1954-). Films: "Sunset" 1988 (Nancy Shoemaker).

Quinlivan, Charles (1923-11/12/74). Films: "Seven Guns to Mesa" 1958 (John Trey). ¶TV: *Maverick*—"The Seventh Hand" 3-2-58 (Mr. Beaker); *Cheyenne*—"Noose at Noon" 6-3-58 (Jim O'Neill).

Quinn, Anthony (1915-). Films: "The Plainsman" 1936 (Cheyenne Warrior); "Union Pacific" 1939 (Jack Cordray); "Texas Rangers Ride Again" 1940 (Joe Yuma); "They Died with Their Boots On" 1941 (Crazy Horse); "The Ox-Bow Incident" 1943 (Juan Martinez); "Buffalo Bill"

1944 (Yellow Hand); "California" 1946 (Don Luis); "Viva Zapata!" 1952 (Eufemio Zapata); "Blowing Wind" 1953 (Paco); "Ride, Vaquero!" 1953 (Jose Esqueda); "Seminole" 1953 (Osceola/John Powell); "Man from Del Rio" 1956 (Dave Robles); "The Ride Back" 1957 (Kallen); "Last Train from Gun Hill" 1959 (Craig Belden); "Warlock" 1959 (Tom Morgan); "Heller in Pink Tights" 1960 (Tom Healy); "Guns for San Sebastian" 1967-U.S./Fr./Mex./Ital. (Leon Alastray); "Flap" 1970 (Flapping Eagle); "Deaf Smith and Johnny Ears" 1972-Ital. (Erastus "Deaf" Smith).

Quinn, Bill (1912-4/29/94). TV: *The Californians*—"Murietta" 5-27-58 (Carter); *The Rifleman*—Regular 1958-63 (Sweeney, the Bartender); *Bonanza*—"The Marshal" 10-21-58, "Vendetta" 12-5-59 (Doc Travis), "Elizabeth, My Love" 5-27-61, "The Miracle Worker" 5-20-62, "The Thunder Man" 5-5-63 (Doctor), "The Waiting Game" 12-8-63 (Clinton), "The Thirteenth Man" 1-21-68 (Allison); *The Westerner*—"School Days" 10-7-60; *Wanted—Dead or Alive*—"Surprise Witness" 11-2-60 (Sheriff), "Monday Morning" 3-8-61 (Porter Fairchild), "Barney's Bounty" 3-29-61 (Bartender); *Zane Grey Theater*—"The Release" 4-17-61 (Hibbens); *Empire*—"Down There, the World" 3-12-63 (Lupak); *The Virginian*—"The Brothers" 9-15-65 (Prosecutor), "The Mark of a Man" 4-20-66 (Doctor Stanton); *The Loner*—"The Vespers" 9-25-65 (Doctor); *The Big Valley*—"The Murdered Party" 11-17-65, "A Time to Kill" 1-19-66 (Hyatt), "Target" 10-31-66, "The Great Safe Robbery" 11-21-66 (Lou Johnson), "A Stranger Everywhere" 12-9-68 (Mr. Simmons), "Lightfoot" 2-17-69; *A Man Called Shenandoah*—"A Long Way Home" 1-31-66 (Doctor); *Pistols 'n' Petticoats*—"A Crooked Line" 9-17-66 (Mr. Stebbins); *Laredo*—"Any Way the Wind Blows" 10-28-66 (Warburton); *The Rounders*—11-1-66 (Paul Canfield); *Shane*—"The Great Invasion" 12-17-66 & 12-24-66 (Shaw); *Iron Horse*—"T Is for Traitor" 12-2-67 (the Preacher); *Wild Wild West*—"The Night of the Death Masks" 1-26-68 (Dr. Pryor), "The Night of Fire and Brimstone" 11-22-68 (Dr. Emmett Sloan); *The Guns of Will Sonnett*—"Stopover in a Troubled Town" 2-2-68; *Alias Smith and Jones*—"The Fifth Victim" 3-25-71 (Doctor), "Which Way to the O.K. Corral?" 2-10-72, "The Ten Days That Shook Kid Curry" 11-4-72.

Quinn, Jack (-12/10/29). Films: "The Set-Up" 1926 (Bert Tolliver).

Quinn, James (1885-8/22/40). Films: "Mile-A-Minute Romeo" 1924 (Coroner); "Wells Fargo" 1937 (Miner); "The Texans" 1938 (Confederate Soldier).

Quinn, Jimmie (1885-8/22/40). Films: "Soft Shoes" 1925 (Majel).

Quinn, Joe (1917-2/2/71). TV: *The Rifleman*—"The Angry Gun" 12-23-58 (Marshal); *Pistols 'n' Petticoats*—"The Triangle" 10-22-66 (Townsman).

Quinn, Louis (1915-9/14/88). TV: *The Virginian*—"The Dark Challenge" 9-23-64 (Perkins); *Wild Wild West*—"The Night of the Death Masks" 1-26-68 (Mr. Goff).

Quinn, Pat (1937-). Films: "Shoot Out" 1971 (Juliana Farrell); "Zachariah" 1971 (Belle Starr).

Quinn, Teddy (1959-). Films: "Ballad of Josie" 1968 (Luther Minick). ¶TV: *Bonanza*—"Tommy" 12-18-66 (Tommy), "Silence at Stillwater" 9-28-69 (Peter); *Lancer*—"Jelly" 11-19-68 (Sawdust); *Prudence and the Chief*—Pilot 8-26-70 (Gavin MacKenzie).

Quinn, Tom. Films: "Ghost Guns" 1944; "Land of the Outlaws" 1944; "Law of the Valley" 1944; "Flame of the West" 1945 (Ed); "The Navajo Trail" 1945; "Stranger from Santa Fe" 1945; "Border Bandits" 1946 (Pepper); "Song of Arizona" 1946 (Tom); "Under Nevada Skies" 1946 (Hoffman); "The Michigan Kid" 1947 (Hank); "Crashing Thru" 1949.

Quinn, William. Films: "Love's Lariat" 1916 (Allan Landers); "A Daughter of the West" 1918 (Rawhide Pete); "The Arizona Catclaw" 1919 (Frank Stimpson); "The Devil's Trail" 1919 (Dutch Vogel); "Hell's Oasis" 1920 (Wolf Sims); "Skyfire" 1920 (Jean Beaupre); "The Heart of a Texan" 1922 (Pete Miller); "The Kingfisher's Roost" 1922 (Bull Keeler); "Lure of Gold" 1922 (Chuck Wallace); "Rangeland" 1922 (Buck Kelley); "Table Top Ranch" 1922 (Palque Powell); "West of the Pecos" 1922 (Chuck Wallace); "Wolf Law" 1922; "The Fighting Strain" 1923 (Jim Black); "The No-Gun Man" 1925 (Bill Kilgore); "Gypsy of the North" 1928 (Baptiste); "Law and Lawless" 1932; "Big Calibre" 1935 (Rusty Hicks).

Quirk, Billy (1881-4/20/26). Films: "The Dancing Girl of Butte" 1909; "Leather Stocking" 1909; "Mexican Sweethearts" 1909; "The

Renunciation" 1909; "A Knot in the Plot" 1910; "Salome Jane" 1923 (Col. Starbottle).

Quirk, Charles. Films: "Gunsmoke" 1947; "Son of Paleface" 1952 (Zeke); "Shane" 1953 (Clerk).

Quo, Beulah (1923-). TV: *Have Gun Will Travel*—"Coming of the Tiger" 4-14-62 (Mrs. Osata); *Wild Wild West*—"The Night the Dragon Screamed" 1-14-66 (May Li); *Kung Fu*—"Blood Brother" 1-18-73 (Soong's Wife), "My Brother, My Executioner" 10-12-74 (Mai Chi, the Seeress), "The Thief of Chendo" 3-29-75 (Mme. Chun).

Raaf, Vici. Films: "The Man Behind the Gun" 1952. ¶TV: *Wyatt Earp*—"Witness for the Defense" 1-22-57 (Marcia); *Colt .45*—"Small Man" 11-15-57 (Madge); *The Californians*—"Second Trial" 5-6-58 (Ivy); *Rawhide*—"Incident of the Challenge" 10-14-60, "The Bosses' Daughter" 2-2-62 (Hostess), "Incident of the Swindler" 2-20-64; *Gunsmoke*—"Kitty Cornered" 4-18-64 (Fay).

Rabal, Francisco (1925-). Films: "Legacy of the Incas" 1965-Ger./Ital.; "Long Days of Vengeance" 1967-Ital./Span.; "The Big and the Bad" 1971-Ital./Fr./Span.; "It Can be Done ... Amigo" 1971-Ital./Fr./Span.

Racette, Francine (1947-). Films: "Dan Candy's Law" 1975-U.S./Can.

Racimo, Victoria (1945-). Films: "Journey Through Rosebud" 1972 (Shirley); "The Mountain Men" 1980 (Running Moon); "The Mystic Warrior" TVM-1984 (Napewaste); "White Fang 2: Myth of the White Wolf" 1994 (Katrin). ¶TV: *Nakia*—"The Driver" 11-2-74 (Jean); *Kung Fu*—"The Devil's Champion" 11-29-74 (Lady Mei); *The Chisholms*—Regular 1980 (Kewedinok Chisholm).

Radcliff, Violet (1908-26). Films: "Six-Shooter Andy" 1918.

Radcliffe, E.J. *see* Ratcliffe, E.J.

Rader, Jack (1937-). Films: "Wild Horses" TVM-1985 (Dick Post). ¶TV: *Gunsmoke*—"Larkin" 1-20-75 (Angus).

Radilac, Charles (1907-7/19/72). TV: *Temple Houston*—"Seventy Times Seven" 12-5-63 (Gustav Bergen); *Wild Wild West*—"The Night of the Wolf" 3-31-67 (Priest); *The Virginian*—"The Storm Gate" 11-13-68 (Doctor).

Rado, Ivan J. Films: "Bret Maverick" TVM-1981 (Wolfgang Miter).

Rafferty, Chips (1909-5/27/71). Films: "Kangaroo" 1952 (Trooper Leonard). ¶TV: *Whiplash*—"Day of the Hunter" 6-5-61, "The Adelaide Arabs" 10-14-61; *The Big Valley*—"The River Monarch" 4-6-66 (Jock); *Gunsmoke*—"By Line" 4-9-66 (Angus McTabbott).

Rafferty, Frances (1922-). Films: "Adventures of Don Coyote" 1947 (Maggie); "Rodeo" 1952 (Dixie Benson).

Raffetto, Michael (1899-5/31/90). Films: "Pirates of Monterey" 1947 (Sgt. Gomara). ¶TV: *The Law of the Plainsman*—"Appointment in Sante Fe" 11-19-59; *Klondike*—"The Hostages" 2-13-61 (Arnold Jackson).

Ragan, Michael. *see* Bane, Holly.

Ragin, John S. (1929-). TV: *Laredo*—"A Prince of a Ranger" 12-9-66 (Karl); *Alias Smith and Jones*—"Six Strangers at Apache Springs" 10-28-71 (Edward Fielding).

Rahmn, Knute (1876-7/23/57). Films: "The Apache Renegade" 1912; "The Indian Uprising at Santa Fe" 1912; "Red Wing and the Paleface" 1912; "The Tragedy of Big Eagle Mine" 1912; "The Last Blockhouse" 1913.

Raho, Umberto. Films: "Man with the Golden Pistol" 1966-Span./Ital.; "Pecos Cleans Up" 1967-Ital.

Railsback, Steve (1947-). TV: *Young Riders*—"The Peacemakers" 1-19-91 (Tyler).

Raimbourg, Lucien (1903-73). Films: "Dynamite Jack" 1963-Fr.

Rain, Douglas (1928-). TV: *Hudson's Bay*—"The Accounting" 3-1-58 (Martin Cobb).

Rainboth, Frank (1874-2/17/51). Films: "The Big Trail" 1930 (Ohio Man).

Raine, Jack (1897-5/30/79). Films: "Scandalous John" 1971 (Switchman).

Raines, Cristina (1952-). TV: *Centennial*—Regular 1978-79 (Lucinda McKeag Zendt).

Raines, Ella (1921-5/30/88). Films: "Tall in the Saddle" 1944 (Arly Harolday); "The Walking Hills" 1949 (Chris Jackson); "Singing Guns" 1950 (Nan Morgan); "Ride the Man Down" 1952 (Celia Evarts).

Raines, Steve. Films: "Under Colorado Skies" 1947 (Pony); "Frontier Revenge" 1948 (Dawson Brother); "Sheriff of Wichita" 1949 (Will); "Son of a Badman" 1949 (Larson); "Border Fence" 1951; "Shane" 1953 (Ryker Man); "Count Three and Pray" 1955 (Jake); "The Naked Gun" 1956; "Cattle Empire" 1958 (Corbo). ¶TV: *The Roy Rogers Show*—"Dead Men's Hills" 3-15-52, "The Ride of the Ranchers" 4-20-52, "The Hijackers" 10-24-54, "The Morse Mixup" 3-24-56, "Tossup" 12-2-56; *The Gene Autry Show*—"The Portrait of White Cloud" 10-15-55; *Gunsmoke*—"The F.U." 3-14-59 (1st Cowboy), "Stage Stop" 11-26-66 (Trivers), "Mail Drop" 1-28-67 (Steve), "Deadman's Law" 1-8-68 (Trail Boss), "The Hide Cutters" 9-30-68 (Lawson), "Uncle Finney" 10-14-68 (Wagon Driver), "O'Quillian" 10-28-68 (Brigs), "The Twisted Heritage" 1-6-69 (Driver #1), "Danny" 10-13-69 (Stage Driver), "The Scavengers" 11-16-70 (Driver), "Jenny" 12-28-70 (Ed Reilly); *Rawhide*—Regular 1959-66 (Quince); *The Tall Man*—"Hard Justice" 3-25-61 (Carl); *Maverick*—"Benefit of Doubt" 4-9-61 (Sims); *Wyatt Earp*—"The Shooting Starts" 4-18-61 (Hoodlum); *Bonanza*—"Destiny's Child" 1-30-66 (Darrel), "A Girl Named George" 1-14-68 (Deputy); *Iron Horse*—"Broken Gun" 10-17-66 (Sheriff O'Moore); *Laredo*—"One Too Many Voices" 11-18-66, "Road to San Remo" 11-25-66; *The Virginian*—"Girl on the Glass Mountain" 12-28-66 (Winky), "Execution at Triste" 12-13-67 (Morgan Oliver), "Nora" 12-11-68 (Charley Kroeger); *The High Chaparral*—"Best Man for the Job" 9-24-67 (1st Cowboy), "The Long Shadow" 1-2-70, "Wind" 10-9-70; *The Guns of Will Sonnett*—"Reunion" 9-27-68; *Wild Wild West*—"The Night of the Plague" 4-4-69.

Rainey, Ford (1906-). Films: "3:10 to Yuma" 1957 (Marshal); "The Badlanders" 1958 (Warden); "Flaming Star" 1960 (Doc Phillips); "Two Rode Together" 1961 (Henry Clay); "Gunpoint" 1966 (Emerson); "Guardian of the Wilderness" 1976 (Abraham Lincoln); "The New Daughters of Joshua Cabe" TVM-1976 (the Judge). ¶TV: *The Tall Man*—"Forty-Dollar Boots" 9-17-60 (Sheriff Brady), "The Lonely Star" 10-8-60 (Sheriff Brady); *Bonanza*—"Sam Hill" 6-3-61 (Colonel Tyson), "Blessed Are They" 4-22-62 (Clarke), "Mirror of a Man" 3-31-63 (Luke), "The Debt" 9-12-65 (Sam Kane), "Black Friday" 1-22-67 (Judge Wyllit), "Check Rein" 12-3-67 (Bingham), "The Deserter" 3-16-69 (Arnholt), "Fallen Woman" 9-26-71 (Judge Simms), "A Home for Jamie" 12-19-71 (Judge Taylor); *Rawhide*—"Incident of the Wager on Payday" 6-16-61 (Sheriff), "Incident of the Dogfaces" 11-9-62 (Broken Bow), "The Retreat" 3-26-65 (Colonel Hart); *Gunsmoke*—"Cale" 5-5-62 (Tate

Gifford), "The Search" 9-15-62 (Tate Gifford), "Song for Dying" 2-13-65 (Hode Embry), "Thirty a Month a Found" 10-7-74 (George Newton); *Stoney Burke*—"The Mob Riders" 10-29-62 (Frank Hughes); *Empire*—"Pressure Lock" 12-4-62 (Josh); *Wide Country*—"The Bravest Man in the World" 12-6-62 (Mike Callahan); *Laramie*—"The Fugitives" 2-12-63; *The Virginian*—"The Small Parade" 2-20-63, "Two Men Named Laredo" 1-6-65 (the Prosecutor), "Legend for a Lawman" 3-3-65 (Marshal Floyd Buckman), "The Awakening" 10-13-65 (Claypool), "Requiem for a Country Doctor" 1-25-67 (Sheriff), "The Hell Wind" 2-14-68 (Marcus Van Owen), "The Land Dreamer" 2-26-69 (Amos Wardlow); *Daniel Boone*—"My Brother's Keeper" 10-8-64 (Matawa), "The Patriot" 12-5-68 (John Gist), "Hannah Comes Home" 12-25-69 (Jonas); *The Big Valley*—"Heritage" 10-20-65 (Murdoch); *Iron Horse*—"A Dozen Ways to Kill a Man" 12-19-66 (Ross); *Cimarron Strip*—"The Legend of Jud Starr" 9-14-67; *The Guns of Will Sonnett*—"A Bell for Jeff Sonnett" 9-15-67 (Doc Sales), "Meeting in a Small Town" 12-6-68; *Wild Wild West*—"The Night of the Iron Fist" 12-8-67 (Pa Garrison), "The Night of the Kraken" 11-1-68 (Admiral Charles Hammond); *Alias Smith and Jones*—"Escape from Wickenberg" 1-28-71 (Warren Epps), "Never Trust an Honest Man" 4-15-71 (Father), "The Man Who Broke the Bank at Red Gap" 1-20-72 (Collins), "The Biggest Game in the West" 2-3-72, "Bushwack!" 10-21-72 (Teshmacher); *Kung Fu*—"Superstition" 4-5-73 (Jacob Sterne); *Sara*—4-9-76 (Jake Willis).

Rains, Claude (1889-5/30/67). Films: "Gold Is Where You Find It" 1938 (Col. Ferris). ¶TV: *Wagon Train*—"The Daniel Clay Story" 2-21-62 (Judge Daniel Clay); *Rawhide*—"Incident of Judgment Day" 2-8-63 (Alexander Langford).

Rainwater, Gregg. TV: *Young Riders*—Regular 1990-92 (Buck Cross).

Raisch, Bill (1905-7/31/84). Films: "Lonely Are the Brave" 1962 (One Arm).

Raiter, Frank (1932-). Films: "The McMasters" 1970 (Grant).

Raitt, John (1917-). TV: *Annie Get Your Gun* 11-25-57 (Frank Butler); *Death Valley Days*—"Man on the Road" 4-5-60 (Jim Dandy).

Raker, Lorin (1891-12/25/59). Films: "Call of the Canyon" 1942; "Cowboy Serenade" 1942.

Ralli, Giovanna (1935-). Films: "Taste of Violence" 1961-Fr.; "The Mercenary" 1968-Ital./Span. (Columba); "Cannon for Cordoba" 1970 (Leonora).

Ralli, Paul (1903-9/4/53). Films: "The Water Hole" 1928 (Diego).

Ralph, Jessie (1865-5/30/44). Films: "Yellow Dust" 1936 (Mrs. Brian); "Drums Along the Mohawk" 1939 (Mrs. Weaver); "The Kid from Texas" 1939 (Aunt Minetta); "Lady from Cheyenne" 1941 (Mrs. McGuinness).

Ralph, Sheryl Lee. Films: "The Gambler Returns: The Luck of the Draw" TVM-1991 (Miss Rosalee).

Ralston, Esther (1902-1/14/94). Films: "Crossing Trails" 1921 (Helen Stratton); "Daring Danger" 1922 (Ethel Stanton); "The Gypsy Trail" 1922; "Her Half Brother" 1922; "Pals of the West" 1922; "Timberland Treachery" 1922; "Unmasked" 1922; "Blinky" 1923 (Mary Lou Kileen); "Pure Grit" 1923 (Stella Bolling); "$50,000 Reward" 1924 (Carolyn Jordan); "The Heart Buster" 1924 (Rose Hillyer); "Wolves of the North" 1924-serial; "To the Last Man" 1933 (Ellen Colby).

Ralston, Jobyna (1900-1/22/67). Films: "Lightning" 1927 (Mary Warren/Topsy); "The Big Hop" 1928 (June Halloway); "Rough Waters" 1930 (Mary).

Ralston, Marcia. Films: "Gold Is Where You Find It" 1938 (Molly Featherstone); "The Kid from Kansas" 1941 (Linda).

Ralston, Vera Hruba (1921-). Films: "Dakota" 1945 (Sandy); "Plainsman and the Lady" 1946 (Ann Arnesen); "Wyoming" 1947 (Karen Alderson); "The Fighting Kentuckian" 1949 (Fleurette De Marchand); "Surrender" 1950 (Violet Barton); "Belle Le Grand" 1951 (Belle Le Grand); "A Perilous Journey" 1953 (Francie Landreaux); "Jubilee Trail" 1954 (Florinda Grove/Julie Latour); "Timberjack" 1955 (Lynne Tilton); "Gunfire at Indian Gap" 1957 (Cheel).

Rambeau, Marjorie (1889-7/7/70). Films: "Santa Fe Marshal" 1940 (Ma Burton); "Twenty Mule Team" 1940 (Josie Johnson); "In Old Oklahoma" 1943 (Bessie Baxter); "Salome, Where She Danced" 1945 (Madam).

Rambo, Dack (1941-3/21/94). Films: "No Man's Land" TVM-1984 (Connell). ¶TV: *The Guns of Will Sonnett*—Regular 1967-69 (Jeff Sonnett); *Gunsmoke*—"The Witness" 11-

23-70 (Ira Pickett), "Pike" 3-1-71 & 3-8-71 (Cyrus Pike); *Dirty Sally*—Regular 1974 (Cyrus Pike).

Rambo, Dirk (1941-2/5/67). TV: *The Virginian*—"High Stakes" 11-16-66 (Wesley Hedges).

Ramirez, Frank. Films: "Smith" 1969 (Gabriel Jimmyboy); "The Wrath of God" 1972 (Moreno, the Cantina Operator); "The Sacketts" TVM-1979. ¶TV: *The Outcasts*—"They Shall Rise Up" 1-6-69 (Martinez); *The High Chaparral*—"The Glory Soldiers" 1-31-69, "Feather of an Eagle" 2-7-69 (Santos); *Gunsmoke*—"Whelan's Men" 2-5-73 (Breed).

Ramon, Laon. *see* Janney, Leon.

Ramondetta, John. TV: *Cheyenne*—"The Frightened Town" 3-20-61 (Matt Cooper), "Day's Pay" 10-30-61 (Augie McCracken); *Bronco*—"One Came Back" 11-27-61.

Ramos, Fernando (1913-11/21/69). Films: "Bells of Capistrano" 1942.

Ramos, Rudy. TV: *The High Chaparral*—Regular 1967-71 (Wind); *The Men from Shiloh*—"The Animal" 1-20-71 (Indian).

Ramsay, Anne (1929-8/11/88). Films: "Goin' South" 1978.

Ramsay, Logan (1921-). Films: "The Devil and Miss Sarah" TVM-1971 (Holmes); "Testimony of Two Men" TVM-1977. ¶TV: *The Outcasts*—"The Heady Wine" 12-2-68 (Ab); *Here Come the Brides*—"Democracy in Action" 2-5-69 (Leonard Spence), "The She-Bear" 3-10-70 (Evans); *The Big Valley*—"Danger Road" 4-21-69 (Lawyer); *Alias Smith and Jones*—"The Root of It All" 4-1-71 (Oscar Rosewood), "Six Strangers at Apache Springs" 10-28-71; *Kung Fu*—"The Squaw Man" 11-1-73 (Abel).

Ramsey, George. TV: *Rawhide*—"Incident at Spanish Rock" 12-18-59; *Tales of Wells Fargo*—"The Great Bullion Robbery" 3-21-60 (Trager); *Wanted—Dead or Alive*—"To the Victor" 11-9-60; *The Loner*—"Incident in the Middle of Nowhere" 2-19-66 (Cook).

Ramsey, Quen. Films: "Prairie Law" 1940 (Murphy); "When the Daltons Rode" 1940 (Wilson); "Tumbledown Ranch in Arizona" 1941 (Gallop).

Ramsey, Ward (1925-). Films: "Seven Ways from Sundown" 1960 (Fogarty); "Posse from Hell" 1961 (Marshal Webb).

Ramus, Nick. Films: "I Will

Fight No More Forever" TVM-1975 (Rainbow); "The Apple Dumpling Gang Rides Again" 1979; "Wind-walker" 1980 (Smiling Wolf/Twin Brother/Narrator); "The Legend of Walks Far Woman" TVM-1982 (Left Hand Bull); "The Mystic Warrior" TVM-1984 (Olepi); "Son of the Morning Star" TVM-1991 (Red Cloud); "Geronimo" TVM-1993. ¶TV: *Gunsmoke*—"The Iron Blood of Courage" 2-18-74 (Lynit); *Centennial*—Regular 1978-79 (Lost Eagle); *The Chisholms*—1-26-80; *Born to the Wind* 1982 (Grey Cloud); *Paradise*—"The Burial Ground" 11-4-89 (Black Cloud); *Dr. Quinn, Medicine Woman*—Regular 1993- (Chief Black Kettle).

Rand, Edwin. Films: "Broken Arrow" 1950 (Sergeant); "The Capture" 1950 (Tevlin); "Return of the Frontiersman" 1950 (Kearney); "Column South" 1953 (Sabbath); "Those Redheads from Seattle" 1953 (Jacobs). ¶TV: *The Lone Ranger*—"Death in the Forest" 6-4-53.

Rand, John (1872-1/25/40). Films: "Western Caravans" 1939 (Jennings).

Rand, Sally (1904-8/31/79). Films: "Braveheart" 1925 (Sally Vernon); "The Texas Bearcat" 1925 (Jean Crawford); "Galloping Fury" 1927 (Dorothy Shelton); "Crashing Through" 1928 (Rita Bayne); "The Big Show" 1937.

Randall, Anne (1944-). Films: "A Time for Dying" 1971 (Nellie Winters); "Westworld" 1973 (Servant Girl).

Randall, Bernard (1884-12/17/54). Films: "Sundown" 1924 (William Dickson).

Randall, Jack (1906-7/16/45). Films: "His Greatest Battle" 1925; "Danger Valley" 1937 (Jack); "Riders of the Dawn" 1937 (Marshal Jack Preston); "Stars Over Arizona" 1937 (Jack Dawson); "Gun Packer" 1938 (Jack Dinton); "Gunsmoke Trail" 1938 (Jack Lane); "Land of Fighting Men" 1938 (Jack Lambert); "Man's Country" 1938 (Jack Hale); "Mexicali Kid" 1938 (Jack Wood); "Where the West Begins" 1938 (Jack Manning); "Wild Horse Canyon" 1938 (Jack); "Across the Plains" 1939 (Cherokee); "Drifting Westward" 1939 (Jack Clark); "Oklahoma Terror" 1939 (Jack); "Overland Mail" 1939 (Jack); "Trigger Smith" 1939 (Trigger Smith); "The Cheyenne Kid" 1940 (the Cheyenne Kid); "Covered Wagon Trails" 1940 (Jack Cameron); "The Kid from Santa Fe" 1940 (Santa Fe); "Land of the Six

Guns" 1940 (Jack Rowan); "Pioneer Days" 1940 (Jack Dunham); "Riders from Nowhere" 1940 (Jack Rankin); "Wild Horse Range" 1940 (Jack Wallace).

Randall, Lorraine. Films: "North of the Rio Grande" 1937 (Mary Cassidy); "Where Trails Divide" 1937 (Bess Lane).

Randall, Monica (1944-). Films: "For a Fist in the Eye" 1965-Ital./Span.; "Five Giants from Texas" 1966-Ital./Span. (Rosaria); "One Hundred Thousand Dollars for Ringo" 1966-Ital./Span.; "Ringo and Gringo Against All" 1966-Ital./Span.; "All Out" 1968-Ital./Span.; "Red Blood, Yellow Gold" 1968-Ital./Span.; "Red Sun" 1971-Fr./Ital./Span.

Randall, Stuart. Films: "Bells of Coronado" 1950 (Sheriff); "Rider from Tucson" 1950 (Slim); "Rustlers on Horseback" 1950 (Clune); "Arizona Manhunt" 1951 (Scar); "Rough Riders of Durango" 1951 (Jed); "Tomahawk" 1951 (Sgt. Newell); "Wells Fargo Gunmaster" 1951 (John Thorton); "Bugles in the Afternoon" 1952 (Bannack Bill); "The Bushwackers" 1952 (Slocum); "Hiawatha" 1952 (Mudjekeewis); "Pony Soldier" 1952 (Standing Bear); "Rancho Notorious" 1952 (Starr); "Arena" 1953 (Eddie Elstead); "Captain John Smith and Pocahontas" 1953 (Opechanco); "Hannah Lee" 1953 (Montgomery); "Pony Express" 1953 (Pemberton); "Man with the Steel Whip" 1954-serial (Harris); "Southwest Passage" 1954 (Lt. Owens); "They Rode West" 1954 (Satanta); "Chief Crazy Horse" 1955 (Old Man Afraid); "The Far Country" 1955 (Capt. Benson); "Pardners" 1956 (Carol's Cowhand); "Star in the Dust" 1956 (Jess Ryman); "Run of the Arrow" 1957 (Col. Taylor); "Frontier Uprising" 1961 (Ben Wright); "The Long Rope" 1961 (Henchman); "Posse from Hell" 1961 (Luke Gorman); "Taggart" 1964 (Sheriff). ¶TV: *The Lone Ranger*—"The Squire" 11-9-50, "Heritage of Treason" 2-3-55; *Frontier*—"Cattle Drive to Casper" 11-27-55; *Zane Grey Theater*—"You Only Run Once" 10-5-56 (Sayers), "Until the Man Dies" 1-25-57 (Ed Bentley), "The Hanging Tree" 2-22-57 (Sayers); *The Restless Gun*—"Jenny" 10-21-57 (Sheriff York), "Aunt Emma" 4-14-58 (Sheriff Tinsley), "Take Me Home" 12-29-58 (Marshal Powers), "The Way Back" 7-13-59 (Marshal Powers); *Colt .45*—"Gallows at Granite Gap" 11-8-57 (Sheriff Monohan); *Wyatt Earp*—"Two" 4-29-58 (Rufe Prentice), "Four" 5-27-58 (Rufe Prentice),

"Horse Race" 3-3-59 (Milt Canyon), "The Ring of Death" 11-3-59 (Stake Brown); *Sugarfoot*—"The Bullet and the Cross" 5-27-58 (Sheriff Olson), "The Canary Kid" 11-11-59 (Sheriff); *The Texan*—"The Hemp Tree" 11-17-58 (Marshal Ike Masters), "Letter of the Law" 3-23-59 (Sheriff Rangel), "No Way Out" 9-14-59 (Lee Tatlock); *Schlitz Playhouse of the Stars*—"A Tale of Wells Fargo" 12-14-58 (Marshal); *The Rifleman*—"The Gaucho" 12-30-58 (Palmer), "The Grasshopper" 3-1-60 (Marshal Dixon); *Northwest Passage*—"The Deserter" 2-27-59 (Bailiff Rankin); *Rough Riders*—"The Promise" 4-2-59 (James Kirby); *Wagon Train*—"The Estaban Zamora Story" 10-21-59 (Sheriff Hixon), "The Lita Foladaire Story" 1-6-60; *Maverick*—The Ghost Soldiers" 11-8-59 (Red Wing); *Bonanza*—"The Spanish Grant" 2-6-60, "Breed of Violence" 11-5-60, "The Lila Conrad Story" 1-5-64, "The Real People of Muddy Creek" 10-6-68 (Sheriff Walker), "The Wagon" 10-5-70 (Sheriff Brody), "Shadow of a Hero" 2-21-71 (Sheriff Baker); *Riverboat*—"Fort Epitaph" 3-7-60 (Chief Running Bear), "The Quota" 11-28-60 (Gen. Winfield Scott); *Wanted—Dead or Alive*—"Black Belt" 3-19-60 (Mr. Cummings), "Baa-Baa" 1-4-61 (Watkins); *Laramie*—"The Violent Ones" 3-5-63, "The Unvanquished" 3-12-63, "Broken Honor" 4-9-63, "The Last Battleground" 4-16-63, "The Stranger" 4-23-63, "Badge of Glory" 5-7-63; *The Virginian*—"Ride a Dark Trail" 9-18-63 (Dailey), "Lost Yesterday" 2-3-65 (Sheriff), "The Brothers" 9-15-65 (Judge), "That Saunders Woman" 3-30-66 (Judge Franklin), "Fox, Hound, and the Widow McCloud" 4-2-69 (Rancher); *Destry*—"Big Deal at Little River" 3-20-64 (Sheriff Denton); *The Big Valley*—"Shadow of a Giant" 1-29-68; *The High Chaparral*—"The Lieutenant" 2-27-70; *Alias Smith and Jones*—"Dreadful Sorry, Clementine" 11-18-71.

Randall, Sue (1935-10/26/84). TV: *Bronco*—"The Besieged" 9-23-58 (Hope Cabot); *The Rifleman*—"The Mind Reader" 6-30-59 (Lucy Hallager); *Have Gun Will Travel*—"Shot by Request" 10-10-59 (Anna), "The Day of the Bad Men" 1-9-60 (Ruth); *The Rebel*—"Judgment" 10-11-59 (Elaine); *Wagon Train*—"The St. Nicholas Story" 12-23-59; *Bat Masterson*—"The Hunter" 10-27-60 (Elizabeth); *Wyatt Earp*—"Big Brother" 11-1-60 (Lucy Tedder); *Gunsmoke*—"The Cook" 12-17-60 (Effie), "Milly" 11-25-61 (Laura); *Bonanza*—"The Horse

Breaker" 11-26-61 (Ann Davis), "Patchwork Man" 5-23-65 (Ann), "Mighty Is the Word" 11-7-65 (Sue Watson); *Death Valley Days*—"The Man Who Died Twice" 12-22-63 (Virginia Slade), "See the Elephant and Hear the Owl" 5-9-64, "A Bargain Is for Keeping" 2-28-65, "The Courtship of Carrie Huntington" 6-4-66 (Carrie Huntington); *The Dakotas*—"Reformation at Big Nose Butte" 4-1-63 (Hardi Masters); *Daniel Boone*—"The Courtship of Jericho Jones" 4-19-65 (Chief Kawita).

Randall, Tony (1920-). Films: "Kate Bliss and the Ticker Tape Kid" TVM-1978 (Lord Seymour Devery).

Randell, Ron (1918-). Films: "Quincannon, Frontier Scout" 1956 (Capt. Bell); "Savage Pampas" 1966-U.S./Span./Arg. (Padron). ¶TV: *Gunsmoke*—"Thoroughbreds" 10-18-58 (Jack Portis); *Overland Trail*—"The Most Dangerous Gentleman" 6-5-60 (Bill Jordan); *Tales of Wells Fargo*—"The Gold Witch" 5-5-62 (Arthur Reardon); *Bonanza*—"The Spotlight" 5-16-65 (Carleton); *Rawhide*—"Clash at Broken Bluff" 11-2-65 (Mal Thorner); *Wild Wild West*—"The Night of the Fatal Trap" 12-24-65 (Col. Vasquez).

Randle, Karen. Films: "Frontier Gal" 1945 (Hostess); "Salome, Where She Danced" 1945 (Salome Girl); "Cowboy and the Prizefighter" 1950 (Sue).

Randles, Larry. Films: "The Cowboys" 1972 (Ben); "Ulzana's Raid" 1972 (Mulkearn); "The Legend of the Lone Ranger" 1981 (Stacy). ¶TV: *Gunsmoke*—"Drago" 11-22-71 (Larry), "The Town Tamers" 1-28-74 (Texan Rider); *Kung Fu*—"The Raiders" 1-24-74 (Deputy).

Randolf, Anders (1870-7/2/30). Films: "The Eternal Struggle" 1923 (Capt. Jack Scott); "Ranson's Folly" 1926 (the Post Trader); "Call of the Rockies" 1931 (Jim Vance).

Randolph, Amanda (1896-8/24/67). Films: "The Iron Mistress" 1952 (Maria); "Heller in Pink Tights" 1960 (Maid); "The Last Challenge" 1967 (Lisa's Maid). ¶TV: *Man from Blackhawk*—"The Ghost of Lafitte" 2-26-60 (Auntie Cotton).

Randolph, Clay. Films: "Revolt at Fort Laramie" 1957 (Caswell). ¶TV: *Death Valley Days*—"Jerkline Jitters" 1-6-58 (Brad Tyson); *Tales of Wells Fargo*—"The Gun" 4-14-58 (Matt Borkman), "The Tall Texan" 4-27-59 (Will Carver); *Bronco*—"The Masquerade" 1-26-60 (Joe Bush);

Wagon Train—"The Odyssey of Flint McCullough" 2-15-61.

Randolph, Donald (1905-3/16/93). Films: "Gunsmoke" 1953 (Matt Telford); "The Gambler from Natchez" 1954 (Pierre Bonet); "Chief Crazy Horse" 1955 (Aaron Cartwright); "The Rawhide Years" 1956 (Carrico); "Cowboy" 1958 (Senor Vidal). ¶TV: *Broken Arrow*—"The Mail Riders" 9-25-56 (Col. Bernall); *Wagon Train*—"The Willy Moran Story" 9-18-57 (Robinson); *Jim Bowie*—"Pirate on Horseback" 1-17-58 (John Murrel), "The Puma" 5-23-58 (Col. Mendoza); *Have Gun Will Travel*—"Silver Convoy" 5-31-58, "The Last Judgment" 3-11-61 (Dr. Simeon Loving); *Gunsmoke*—"Robber and Bridegroom" 12-13-58 (Reeves); *Yancy Derringer*—"Panic in Town" 2-12-59 (Bert Ogilvie); *The Californians*—"The Fur Story" 5-5-59.

Randolph, Isabel (1889-1/11/73). Films: "Ride, Tenderfoot, Ride" 1940 (Miss Spencer); "Ride 'Em, Cowboy" 1942 (Lady); "Thundering Caravans" 1952 (Deborah Cranston). ¶TV: *Wild Bill Hickok*—"Border City" 11-13-51; *Wyatt Earp*—"Wyatt Earp Rides Shotgun" 2-18-58 (Grandma Wilkins); *Cimarron City*—"Runaway Train" 1-31-59 (Amy Howard).

Randolph, Jane (1919-). Films: "Fool's Gold" 1946 (Jessie Dixon).

Randolph, John (1915-). Films: "Smith" 1969 (Mr. Edwards); "There Was a Crooked Man" 1970 (Cyrus McNutt). ¶TV: *Bonanza*—"Different Pines, Same Wind" 9-15-68 (Doc), "Shadow of a Hero" 2-21-71 (Donavan), "The Sound of Loneliness" 12-5-72 (Dawson); *Best of the West*—"The Railroad" 11-19-81 (Chairman); *Bret Maverick*—"Welcome to Sweetwater" 12-8-81 (Austin).

Random, Bob (1944-). Films: "Scalplock" TVM-1966 (Barnabus Rogers); "Cutter's Trail" TVM-1970 (Kyle Bowen); "A Time for Dying" 1971 (Billy Pimple). ¶TV: *Daniel Boone*—"The Quietists" 2-25-65 (Stephen Bothwell), "A Rope for Mingo" 12-2-65 (Johnny Morgan); *The Legend of Jesse James*—"Three Men from Now" 9-13-65 (Jeremy); *The Virginian*—"Nobility of Kings" 11-10-65 (Will Justin), "Silver Image" 9-25-68 (Jeremy Sheppard); *Gunsmoke*—"South Wind" 11-27-65 (Verlyn Print), "Sweet Billy, Singer of Songs" 1-15-66 (Sweet Billy Haggen), "The Mission" 10-8-66 (Reb Jessup), "Nowhere to Run" 1-15-68 (Bishop), "The Night Riders" 2-24-69 (Jay

Proctor), "Albert" 2-9-70 (Tom Clark), "Murdoch" 2-8-71 (Scott Murdoch); *A Man Called Shenandoah*—"The Young Outlaw" 12-27-65 (Tommy); *Iron Horse*—Regular 1966-68 (Barnabas Rogers), "Banner with a Strange Device" 2-6-67 (Jeff Clayborne); *Cimarron Strip*—"The Assassin" 1-11-68 (the Kid).

Rangel, Arturo Soto (1882-5/25/65). Films: "The Treasure of the Sierra Madre" 1948 (Presidente).

Rangno, Terry. TV: *Frontier*—"Mother of the Brave" 1-15-56 (Joseph Horn); *Bronco*—"The Besieged" 9-23-58 (David Platt); *Bat Masterson*—"Death by the Half Dozen" 2-4-60 (Johnny).

Rankin, Arthur (1896-3/23/47). Films: "The Call of the Canyon" 1923 (Virgil Rust); "The Fighting Fool" 1932 (Bud Collins); "Terror Trail" 1933 (Bernie "Little Casino" Laird); "The Thrill Hunter" 1933 (Roy Lang); "Trailing North" 1933 (Lucky); "The Westerner" 1934 (Bank Clerk); "The Cisco Kid and the Lady" 1939 (Telegraph Operator).

Rankin, Caroline (1889-2/2/53). Films: "Bare-Fisted Gallagher" 1919 (Old Maid); "The Lone Star Ranger" 1930 (Mrs. Parker).

Rankin, Gil (1911-10/31/93). Films: "Ghost Town" 1956 (Simon Peter Wheedle); "Black Patch" 1957 (Judge Parnell). ¶TV: *Frontier*—"Patrol" 4-29-56; *Broken Arrow*—"Doctor" 2-12-57 (Tawanga); *Cheyenne*—"The Mutton Puncher" 10-22-57 (Ringo), "Trouble Street" 10-2-61; *Tales of Wells Fargo*—"Tom Horn" 10-26-59 (Foreman); *Laramie*—"The General Must Die" 11-17-59 (General Sherman); *Have Gun Will Travel*—"Chapagne Safari" 12-5-59; *The Alaskans*—"Disaster at Gold Hill" 3-20-60 (Tully); *Overland Trail*—"Daughter of the Sioux" 3-20-60 (Sioux Chieftain); *Man from Blackhawk*—"The Harpoon Story" 5-6-60 (Thornlee); *The Texan*—"Badman" 6-20-60; *Riverboat*—"That Taylor Affair" 9-26-60 (Pierce); *Gunsmoke*—"The Peace Officer" 10-15-60 (Shay), "I Call Him Wonder" 3-23-63 (Waiter), "The Reward" 11-6-65 (Hank Purvis), "Killer at Large" 2-5-66 (Horse Trader), "The Wrong Man" 10-29-66 (Purvis), "Larkin" 1-20-75 (Waiter); *Two Faces West*—"The Decision" 4-10-61; *Empire*—"Duet for Eight Wheels" 4-30-63 (Ben).

Ranous, William V. (1857-4/1/15). Films: "The Easterner" 1907; "Hiawatha" 1909 (Hiawatha); "Yellow Bird" 1912; "The Little Angel of

Canyon Creek" 1914 (Sheriff Four Eyes).

Ransom, Lois. Films: "Under Texas Skies" 1940 (Helen); "Pierre of the Plains" 1942 (Clara).

Ransome, Prunella (1943-). Films: "Man in the Wilderness" 1971-U.S./Span. (Grace).

Rapp, Carl. Films: "The Christmas Kid" 1966-Span./Ital. (Sheriff Anderson).

Raquello, Edward (1900-8/24/76). Films: "Western Jamboree" 1938 (Don Carlos); "The Girl and the Gambler" 1939 (Rodolfo).

Rasputin, Ivan (-9/25/76). Films: "Friendly Persuasion" 1956 (Billy Goat).

Rassimov, Ivan (Sean Todd). Films: "Cjamango" 1967-Ital. (Cjamango); "If You Want to Live ... Shoot!" 1967-Ital./Span. (Marlow); "Cowards Don't Pray" 1968-Ital./Span. (Daniel); "Don't Wait, Django ... Shoot!" 1969-Ital. (Django); "Vengeance Is a Dish Served Cold" 1971-Ital./Span. (Perkins).

Rassimov, Rada. Films: "The Good, the Bad, and the Ugly" 1966-Ital.; "Taste for Killing" 1966-Ital./Span.; "Machine Gun Killers" 1968-Ital./Span.; "Django the Bastard" 1969-Ital./Span.; "Don't Wait, Django ... Shoot!" 1969-Ital. (Mary).

Rasulala, Thalmus (1939-10/9/91). Films: "Adios Amigo" 1975 (Noah); "The Last Hard Men" 1976 (George Weed).

Rasumny, Mikhail (1890-2/17/56). Films: "Pirates of Monterey" 1947 (Pio); "The Kissing Bandit" 1948 (Don Jose).

Ratcliffe, E.J. (1863-9/28/48). Films: "Sundown" 1924 (Pres. Theodore Roosevelt); "The Fighting Buckaroo" 1926 (Judge Richard Gregory); "The Winning of Barbara Worth" 1926 (James Greenfield).

Rathbone, Basil (1892-7/21/67). Films: "Mark of Zorro" 1940 (Esteban Pasquale).

Rattenberry, Harry (1857-12/9/25). Films: "'49-'17" 1917 (Col. Hungerford); "The Learnin' of Jim Benton" 1917; "A Marked Man" 1917 (Mr. Young); "The Law's Outlaw" 1918 (Oscar Davison); "Playing the Game" 1918 (Matt Shannon); "The Best Bad Man" 1919; "The Broken Spur" 1921 (Andy MacGregor); "Daring Days" 1925 (Uncle Johnny Catter).

Rattray, Heather. Films: "Across the Great Divide" 1976 (Holly).

Ravaioli, Isarco. Films: "Charge

of the Seventh Cavalry" 1964-Ital./Span./Fr.; "Djurado" 1966-Ital./Span.; "Let's Go and Kill Sartana" 1972-Ital./Span.

Ravenscroft, Thurl. "Rose Marie" 1954 (Indian Medicine Man). ¶TV: *Wagon Train*—"The Annie MacGregor Story" 2-5-58 (Singer).

Rawlings, Judith. TV: *The Rebel*—"To See the Elephant" 10-16-60 (Mavis); *Bat Masterson*—"The Lady Plays Her Hand" 12-29-60 (Elsie); *Wanted—Dead or Alive*—"Baa-Baa" 1-4-61 (Hazel).

Rawlins, Monte (1907-7/13/88). Films: "The Adventures of the Masked Phantom" 1939 (Alamo).

Rawlins, Phil. Films: "Fort Defiance" 1951 (Jake); "Gun Fury" 1953 (Jim Morse).

Rawlinson, Herbert (1885-7/12/53). Films: "The Cowboy and the Shrew" 1911; "Heart of John Barlow" 1911; "How Algy Captured a Wild Man" 1911; "In the Shadow of the Pines" 1911; "It Happened in the West" 1911; "Little Injin" 1911; "A New York Cowboy" 1911; "On Seperate Paths" 1911; "Range Pals" 1911; "The Regeneration of the Apache Kid" 1911; "The Rival Stage Lines" 1911; "Told in the Sierras" 1911; "The Ace of Spades" 1912; "The Bandit's Mask" 1912; "A Crucial Test" 1912; "Darkfeather's Strategy" 1912; "The End of the Romance" 1912; "The Girl and the Cowboy" 1912; "The God of Gold" 1912; "John Colter's Escape" 1912; "The Legend of the Lost Arrow" 1912; "The Old Stage Coach" 1912; "The Peacemaker" 1912; "Sergeant Byrne of the N.W.M.P." 1912; "The Shrinking Rawhide" 1912; "The Trade Gun Bullet" 1912; "The Vow of Ysobel" 1912; "The Beaded Buckskin Bag" 1913; "Buck Richard's Bride" 1913; "The Rancher's Failing" 1913; "The Trail of Cards" 1913; "Me an' Bill" 1914; "On the Rio Grande" 1914; "Smashing Through" 1918 (Jack "Hod" Mason); "Prowlers of the Wild" 1919; "The Conflict" 1921 (Jevons); "The Prairie Wife" 1925 (Duncan MacKail); "The Bugle Call" 1927 (Capt. Randolph); "God's Country and the Woman" 1937 (Doyle); "King of the Royal Mounted" 1940-serial (Inspector Ross King); "Arizona Cyclone" 1941 (Randolph); "Bad Man of Deadwood" 1941 (Judge Gary); "King of the Texas Rangers" 1941-serial (Colonel Lee Avery); "Perils of the Royal Mounted" 1942-serial (Winton); "Silver Queen" 1942 (Judge); "Stagecoach Buckaroo" 1942 (Kincaid); "Colt Comrades" 1943 (Var-

ney); "Daredevils of the West" 1943-serial (T.M. Sawyer); "Days of Old Cheyenne" 1943 (Gov. Shelby); "Lost Canyon" 1943 (Clark); "Riders of the Deadline" 1943 (Capt. Jennings); "The Woman of the Town" 1943 (Doc Sears); "Forty Thieves" 1944 (Buck Peters); "Lumberjack" 1944 (Buck); "Marshal of Gunsmoke" 1944 (Garrett); "Marshal of Reno" 1944; "Oklahoma Raiders" 1944 (Colonel); "Sheriff of Sundown" 1944 (Governor Brainerd); "The Gallant Legion" 1948 (Maj. Grant); "Silent Conflict" 1948 (Yardman); "Sinister Journey" 1948; "Strange Gamble" 1948; "Brimstone" 1949 (Storekeeper); "Fighting Man of the Plains" 1949 (Lawyer); "Gene Autry and the Mounties" 1951 (Inspector Wingate); "The Stranger Wore a Gun" 1953.

Rawls, Lou (1935-). TV: *The Big Valley*—"Joshua Watson" 1-20-69 (Joshua Watson).

Ray, Albert (1884-2/5/44). Films: "The Night Rider" 1920 (John Tresler).

Ray, Aldo (1926-3/27/91). Films: "Welcome to Hard Times" 1967 (Man from Bodie); "Seven Alone" 1974 (Dr. Dutch); "Kino, the Padre on Horseback" 1977. ¶TV: *Riverboat*—"Payment in Full" 9-13-59 (Hunk Farber); *Frontier Circus*—"The Depths of Fear" 10-5-61 (Toby Mills); *Bonanza*—"The Wild One" 10-4-64 (Lafe Jessup), "Riot!" 10-3-72 (Heiser); *The Virginian*—"Big Day, Great Day" 10-24-62 (Frank Krause), "Jacob Was a Plain Man" 10-12-66 (Jake); *Bob Hope Chrysler Theatre*—"Have Girls—Will Travel" 10-16-64 (Moose); *Daniel Boone*—"The Trek" 10-21-65 (John Benton); *The Quest*—"Seventy-Two Hours" 11-3-76 (Chippy).

Ray, Allan. Films: "The Far Country" 1955 (Bosun); "Frontier Uprising" 1961. ¶TV: *Sky King*—"Double Trouble" 2-24-52 (Mason); *The Tall Man*—"Three for All" 3-10-62 (Bartender).

Ray, Allene (1901-5/5/79). Films: "Honeymoon Ranch" 1920 (Blue Bonnet); "West of the Rio Grande" 1921 (Eileen Nawn); "Partners of the Sunset" 1922 (Patricia Moreland); "Galloping Hoofs" 1924-serial; "Ten Scars Make a Man" 1924-serial; "Way of a Man" 1924-serial; "Hawk of the Hills" 1927-serial (Mary Selby); "The Yellow Cameo" 1928-serial; "Overland Bound" 1929 (Mary Winters); "The Indians Are Coming" 1930-serial (Mary Woods); "Westward Bound" 1930 (Marge Holt).

Ray, Andrew (Andrea Aureli).

Films: "Colorado Charlie" 1965-Ital./Span.; "Ringo and His Golden Pistol" 1966-Ital.; "Rojo" 1966-Ital./Span.; "Dollars for a Fast Gun" 1968-Ital./Span.; "Sabata" 1969-Ital. (Daniel); "Chuck Moll" 1970-Ital.

Ray, Anthony. Films: "The True Story of Jesse James" 1957 (Bob Younger). ¶TV: *The Restless Gun*—"Cheyenne Express" 12-2-57 (Tough); *Tombstone Territory*—4-8-60 (Sam Edwards).

Ray, Charles (1891-11/23/43). Films: "The Quakeress" 1913; "The Sergeant's Secret" 1913; "A Slave's Devotion" 1913; "Desert Gold" 1914 (Jim Hardy); "Desert Thieves" 1914; "In the Cow Country" 1914; "Shorty's Sacrifice" 1914; "Shorty's Strategy" 1914; "The Words of His People" 1914; "The Conversion of Frosty Blake" 1915; "The Grudge" 1915; "The Renegade" 1915; "The Deserter" 1916 (Lieutenant Parker); "The Son of His Father" 1917 (Gordon Carbhoy); "The Law of the North" 1918 (Alain de Montcalm); "Playing the Game" 1918 (Larry Prentiss); "Staking His Life" 1918 (Frank Hamilton).

Ray, Joe. Films: "The Vigilantes" 1918 (Rip Speckman); "The White Man's Courage" 1919 (Augustin Gonzalez); "Firebrand Trevison" 1920 (Mullarkey); "Twins of Suffering Creek" 1920; "Over the Border" 1922 (Borden).

Ray, Joey. Films: "Son of the Golden West" 1928 (Keller); "Three Rogues" 1931 (Deputy); "Pals of the Range" 1935 (Tom); "The Phantom Rider" 1936-serial (Steve); "Station West" 1948 (Stickman); "Ride, Vaquero!" 1953 (Croupier); "Toughest Gun in Tombstone" 1958 (Hellman). ¶TV: *The Cisco Kid*—"Cisco Plays the Ghost" 2-21-53, "A Six-Gun for No Pain" 2-28-53.

Ray, Michael. Films: "The Tin Star" 1957 (Kip Mayfield).

Ray, Nita. Films: "Oklahoma Cyclone" 1930 (Carmelita).

Ray, Rex. Films: "Dangerous Trails" 1920 (the Cactus Kid); "The Unknown Ranger" 1920 (Manning).

Ray, Vivian. Films: "The Oklahoma Kid" 1929; "Parting of the Trails" 1930 (Corliss Fiske).

Raybould, Harry. TV: *The Outlaws*—"The Brathwaite Brothers" 11-9-61 (Levi Brathwaite); *Gunsmoke*—"Phoebe Strunk" 11-10-62 (Casper Strunk), "Mirage" 1-11-71 (Maddox); *Wide Country*—"Memory of a Filly" 1-3-63 (Orval Caruthers); *Daniel Boone*—"Run a Crooked Mile" 10-20-

66 (Hoad); *Pistols 'n' Petticoats*—1-7-67 (Cowhand); *Iron Horse*—"Diablo" 9-16-67 (Luft).

Raye, Martha (1916-10/19/94). Films: "Rhythm on the Range" 1936 (Emma).

Rayford, Alma (1903-2/14/87). Films: "The Lone Rider" 1922 (Ruth Harrison); "The Passing of Wolf MacLean" 1924; "The Smoking Trail" 1924; "The Demon Rider" 1925 (Mary Bushman); "The Rattler" 1925 (Arline Warner); "Ace of Action" 1926 (June Darcy); "Cyclone Bob" 1926 (Molly Mallory); "Deuce High" 1926 (Nell Clifton); "The Fighting Strain" 1926; "The Haunted Range" 1926 (Judith Kellerd); "The Lone Prairie" 1926; "The Lost Trail" 1926; "Speedy Spurs" 1926 (Marie Tuttle); "Trumpin' Trouble" 1926 (Molly Rankin); "Vanishing Hoofs" 1926 (Lucy Bowers); "When Bonita Rides" 1926; "Between Dangers" 1927 (Sue Conway); "Galloping Justice" 1927; "The Phantom Buster" 1927 (Babs); "Tenderfoot Courage" 1927; "Speed and Spurs" 1928; "The Valley of Hunted Men" 1928 (Valita); "Young Whirlwind" 1928 (Molly); "Law and Lawless" 1932; "Lightning Bill" 1934 (Sally Ross).

Raymond, Felice. Films: "Trail of the Mounties" 1947; "Fighting Mustang" 1948; "Loaded Pistols" 1948; "Cow Town" 1950.

Raymond, Frances "Frankie" (1869-6/18/61). Films: "Last of the Duanes" 1919 (Buck Duane's Mother); "The Grail" 1923 (Mrs. Bledsoe); "The Gay Defender" 1927 (Aunt Emily).

Raymond, Francis. Films: "A Law Unto Himself" 1916 (Paul Belleau).

Raymond, Gene (1908-). Films: "The Way of the West" 1934; "Five Blood Graves" 1969 (Voice of Death). ¶TV: *Johnny Ringo*—"Poster Incident" 1-14-60 (Arthur Tobias); *Laredo*—"The Land Slickers" 10-14-66 (Conrad Fletcher); *Hondo*—"Hondo and the Sudden Town" 11-17-67 (Senator Knight).

Raymond, Guy (1911-). Films: "Ballad of Josie" 1968 (Doc); "Bandolero!" 1968 (Ossie Grimes); "The Undefeated" 1969 (Giles). ¶TV: *Satins and Spurs* 9-12-54 (Tex); *Gunsmoke*—"Stolen Horses" 4-8-61 (Abe Kurtch), "All That" 10-28-61 (Jim Redfield), "The Well" 11-19-66 (Dr. Tobias); *Here Come the Brides*—"Debt of Honor" 1-23-70 (Amos); *The Men from Shiloh*—"Jump-Up" 3-24-71 (Mapes); *Alias Smith and Jones*—"The

Legacy of Charlie O'Rourke" 4-22-71 (Sheriff Carver); *Young Maverick*—"Half-Past Noon" 1-30-80 (Leander Berry).

Raymond, Helen (1885-11/26/65). Films: "The Able-Minded Lady" 1922 (Widow McGee).

Raymond, Jack (1892-3/20/53). Films: "Points West" 1929 (His Nibs); "Scarlet River" 1933 (Benny). ¶TV: *The Cisco Kid*—"Ghost Story" 9-1-51.

Raymond, Paula (1923-). Films: "Powder River Gunfire" 1948-short; "Challenge of the Range" 1949 (Judy Barton); "The Devil's Doorway" 1950 (Orrie Masters); "Inside Straight" 1951 (Zoe Carnot); "The Gun That Won the West" 1955 (Maxine Gaines); "Five Blood Graves" 1969 (Kansas Kelly). ¶TV: *The Californians*—"Shanghai Queen" 6-3-58 (Lottie Goth); *Yancy Derringer*—"Gallatin Street" 10-9-58 (Lucy Maridale); *Rough Riders*—"The Double Dealers" 3-19-59 (Charlotta Drake); *Bat Masterson*—"A Matter of Honor" 4-29-59 (Millie Wilkins), "Mr. Fourpaws" 2-18-60 (Linda Wills), "The Last of the Night Raiders" 11-24-60 (Angie Pierce); *Wyatt Earp*—"The Paymaster" 12-1-59 (Miss Crystal); *The Deputy*—"Backfire" 1-2-60 (Peg Marlowe); *Cheyenne*—"Home Is the Brave" 3-14-60 (Ruth Thompson); *Have Gun Will Travel*—"Lady with a Gun" 4-9-60 (Miss MacIntosh); *The Texan*—9-12-60 (Gloria Cameron); *Maverick*—"The Golden Fleecing" 10-8-61 (Adele Jaeggers); *Rawhide*—"The House of the Hunter" 4-20-62 (Franny Wells); *Death Valley Days*—"The Wooing of Perilous Pauline" 2-22-64 (Pauline); *Temple Houston*—"Miss Katherina" 4-2-64 (Miss Katherina).

Raymond, Robin (1921-). TV: *Trackdown*—"Alpine, Texas" 11-15-57 (Sal Hendricks), "The Reward" 1-3-58 (Sal Hendricks); *The Guns of Will Sonnett*—"Joby" 11-1-68; *Kung Fu*—"The Soul Is the Warrior" 2-8-73 (Molly).

Rayner, John (1934-). TV: *The Big Valley*—"The River Monarch" 4-6-66 (Peter Doolin); *Bonanza*—"Judgment at Red Creek" 2-26-67 (Morgan); *The Men from Shiloh*—"The Mysterious Mr. Tate" 10-14-70 (Rex Phillips); *Kung Fu*—"Barbary House" 2-15-75 (2nd Gunfighter), "Flight to Orion" 2-22-75 (2nd Gunfighter), "The Brothers Cain" 3-1-75 (2nd Gunfighter), "Full Circle" 3-15-75 (2nd Gunfighter).

Raynor, Grace. Films: "Ten Days to Tulara" 1958 (Teresa). ¶TV:

Have Gun Will Travel—"The Gentleman" 9-27-58 (Maria DeCastro); *The Californians*—"Overland Mail" 10-28-58 (Millie); *Sugarfoot*—"Devil to Pay" 12-23-58 (Monah); *Bronco*—"Freeze-Out" 12-30-58 (Mary Brown); *Trackdown*—"The Protector" 4-1-59 (Ann Jackson); *Two Faces West*—"Portrait of Bravery" 3-13-61.

Razeto, Stella. *see* LeSaint, Stella.

Re, Gustavo (1908-7/79). Films: "None of the Three Were Called Trinity" 1974-Span.

Rea, Isabel. Films: "The Sheriff's Trap" 1915; "The Wanderer's Pledge" 1915; "The Siren" 1917 (Rose Langdon).

Rea, Mabel (1932-12/24/68). TV: *Death Valley Days*—"Gold Rush in Reverse" 10-21-57; *Man from Blackhawk*—"The Savage" 1-15-60 (Barmaid).

Rea, Peggy (1921-). TV: *Have Gun Will Travel*—"The Colonel and the Lady" 11-23-57, "Maggie O'Bannion" 4-4-59 (Cookie), "The Search" 6-18-60, "The Hanging of Aaron Gibbs" 11-4-61 (Widow), "American Primitive" 2-2-63 (Maggie); *Gunsmoke*—"Chester's Indian" 5-12-62 (Miss Peggity), "Outlaw's Woman" 12-11-65 (Dress Shop Owner), "Baker's Dozen" 12-25-67 (Mrs. Roniger), "O'Quillian" 10-28-68 (Rosey), "The Lost" 9-13-71 (Mrs. Roniger); *Wild Wild West*—"The Night of the Green Terror" 11-18-66 (Bright Star's Wife); *Bonanza*—"For a Young Lady" 12-27-70 (Clara); *Death Valley Days*—"Old Stape" 10-18-69; *How the West Was Won*—Episode One 2-6-77 (Mother Tice), Episode Two 2-7-77 (Mother Tice), Episode Three 2-14-77 (Mother Tice).

Reach, John. Films: "The Bounty Killer" 1965 (Jeb). ¶TV: *Wild Bill Hickok*—"Good Indian" 8-4-53; *The Adventures of Rin Tin Tin*—"Rin Tin Tin and the Second Chance" 6-1-56 (Mike Buckner), "Spanish Gold" 3-7-58 (Rex Gregor); *Circus Boy*—"The Masked Marvel" 12-9-56 (Earl Stanton); *Tales of the Texas Rangers*—"Quarter Horse" 10-6-57 (Hogan); *Jefferson Drum*—"The Captive" 11-6-58 (Grosset); *The Texan*—"Desert Passage" 12-1-58; *Rough Riders*—"Double Cross" 1-22-59 (Dan); *Tombstone Territory*—"Payroll to Tombstone" 3-27-59 (King Cahoon); *Tales of Wells Fargo*—"The Tall Texan" 4-27-59 (Kilpatrick); *Maverick*—"The Lass with the Poisonous Air" 11-1-59 (Phil Dana); *The Alaskans*—"Black Sand" 2-14-60 (Pete Yeager).

Reade, Charles. TV: *Bat Masterson*—"The Reluctant Witness" 3-31-60 (Clerk), "Welcome to Paradise" 5-5-60 (Jeriah Smith), "Last Stop to Austin" 12-1-60 (Teller); *Klondike*—"River of Gold" 10-24-60 (Little Man); *The Rifleman*—"Knight Errant" 11-13-61.

Ready, Mike (1858-3/26/36). Films: "Rough Ridin'" 1924 (Nolan).

Reagan, Ronald (1911-). Films: "Cowboy from Brooklyn" 1938 (Pat Dunn); "Santa Fe Trail" 1940 (George Halliday); "The Bad Man" 1941 (Gil Jones); "The Last Outpost" 1951 (Vance Britten); "Law and Order" 1953 (Frame Johnson); "Cattle Queen of Montana" 1954 (Farrell); "Tennessee's Partner" 1955 (Cowpoke). ¶TV: *Zane Grey Theater*—"The Long Shadow" 1-19-61 (Maj. Will Sinclair); *Wagon Train*—"The Fort Pierce Story" 9-23-63 (Capt. Paul Winters); *Death Valley Days*—"Tribute to the Dog" 12-27-64 (George Vest), "No Gun Behind His Badge" 3-28-65 (Bear River Smith), "The Battle of San Francisco Bay" 4-11-65 (David Farragut), "Raid on the San Francisco Mint" 5-23-65 (Ralston), Host 1965-66, "The Lawless Have Laws" 11-6-65 (Lt. Col. Martin Burke), "No Place for a Lady" 1-8-66 (William Bent), "A City Is Born" 1-29-66 (Charles Poston).

Reason, Rex (1928-). Films: "Kiss of Fire" 1955 (Duke of Montera); "Smoke Signal" 1955 (Lt. Wayne Ford); "Raw Edge" 1956 (John Randolph); "Badlands of Montana" 1957 (Steve); "The Rawhide Trail" 1958 (Jess Brady); "The Miracle of the Hills" 1959 (Scott Macauley); "The Sad Horse" 1959 (Bill MacDonald). ¶TV: *Cheyenne*—"The Trap" 12-18-56 (Les Shore), "Outcast of Cripple Creek" 2-29-60 (Bill Lockhart); *Trackdown*—"The San Saba Incident" 10-18-57 (Stranger); *Man Without a Gun*—Regular 1958-59 (Adam MacLean); *The Alaskans*—"Spring Fever" 2-7-60 (Gordon Talbot), "Disaster at Gold Hill" 3-20-60 (Paul Loomis), "Calico" 5-22-60 (Stony McBride), "The Ballad of Whitehorse" 6-12-60 (Joe Holland); *Bronco*—"Montana Passage" 4-5-60 (Amory Tate); *Sugarfoot*—"The Captive Locomotive" 6-7-60 (Simon March); *Wagon Train*—"The Myra Marshall Story" 10-21-63 (Colin); *The Big Valley*—"Plunder at Hawk's Grove" 3-13-67 (Dave Cannon).

Reason, Rhodes (1928-). Films: "The Desperados Are in Town" 1956 (Frank Bonner); "Yellowstone Kelly" 1959 (Maj. Towns). ¶TV: *Tales of the*

Texas Rangers—"Uranium Pete" 10-1-55, "Hail to the Rangers" 12-17-55 (Dave); *Death Valley Days*—"California's First Ice Man" 1-14-56 (Peter Jeffries), "A Calamity Called Jane" 2-11-67 (Wild Bill Hickok); *TV Reader's Digest*—"Cochise–Greatest of All the Apaches" 1-30-56; *Frontier*—"The Ballad of Pretty Polly" 4-1-56 (Will); *Maverick*—"Ghost Riders" 10-13-57 (Hank Foster); *Sugarfoot*—"The Strange Land" 10-15-57 (Burr Fulton); *Tombstone Territory*—"Ambush at Gila Gulch" 12-18-57 (Nate Crandall); *Frontier Doctor*—"The Homesteaders" 4-4-59; *Bronco*—"The Burning Spring" 10-6-59 (Lt. John Stoddard), "Death of an Outlaw" 3-8-60 (Pat Garrett); *Colt .45*—"Appointment in Agoura" 6-7-60 (Ben Thompson); *Laramie*—"Riders of the Night" 3-7-61 (Phil Yuma); *The Rifleman*—"Conflict" 12-24-62 (Ben Kendrick); *Daniel Boone*—"The Hostages" 1-7-65 (Captain William Butler), "Crisis by Fire" 1-27-66 (Dr. Jedrick); *Time Tunnel*—"The Alamo" 12-9-66 (Col. William Travis); *Prudence and the Chief*—Pilot 8-26-70 (Major O'Toole).

Rector, Josephine. Films: "The Dance at Silver Gulch" 1912; "Broncho Billy's Reason" 1913; "The Cast of the Die" 1914.

Red River Dave. Films: "Swing in the Saddle" 1944; "Echo Ranch" 1948-short; "Hidden Valley Days" 1948-short.

Red Wing (Lillian St. Cyr) (1873-3/12/74). Films: "The White Squaw" 1908; "The Mended Lute" 1909; "The Flight of Red Wing" 1910; "Ramona" 1910; "Red Wing's Loyalty" 1910; "Back to the Prairie" 1911; "Little Dove's Romance" 1911; "The Frame-Up" 1912; "The Penalty Paid" 1912; "A Redskin's Appeal" 1912; "The Unwilling Bride" 1912; "An Indian's Honor" 1913; "The Pioneer's Recompense" 1913; "The Squaw Man" 1914 (Nat-U-Rich); "The Cowpuncher" 1915; "Ramona" 1916 (Phail's Wife).

Redd, Ivalou (-4/13/75). Films: "Blue" 1968 (Helen Buchanan). ¶TV: *Death Valley Days*—"Son of Thunder" 10-25-69, "The Visitor" 12-27-69.

Redd, Mary-Robin (1940-). Films: "J.W. Coop" 1971 (Bonnie May); "The Great Northfield, Minnesota Raid" 1972 (Kate). ¶TV: *Rough Riders*—"Shadows of the Past" 11-27-58 (Molly); *Bob Hope Chrysler Theatre*—"The Reason Nobody Hardly Ever Seen a Fat Outlaw in the Old West Is as Follows:" 3-8-67 (Pauline); *The Virginian*—"The

Deadly Past" 9-20-67 (Emily Williams); *Father Murphy*—"Buttons and Beaux" 11-30-82 (Miss Emma).

Redeker, Quinn (1936-). Films: "The Electric Horseman" 1979 (Bud Broderick). ¶TV: *The Virginian*—"Impasse" 11-14-62 (Daniel Kroeger), "Long Ride to Wind River" 1-19-66 (Benjy Davis), "Family Man" 10-15-69 (C.J.); *Wide Country*—"The Man Who Ran Away" 2-7-63 (Detective Kelson); *Laramie*—"Edge of Evil" 4-2-63 (Jack Lewis); *Bonanza*—"The Toy Soldier" 10-20-63; *Here Come the Brides*—"How Dry We Are" 3-6-70 (Tom).

Redfearn, Linda Moon. Films: "I Will Fight No More Forever" TVM-1975 (Toma); "The White Buffalo" 1977 (Black Shawl). ¶TV: *The Quest*—"The Buffalo Hunters" 9-29-76 (Motaheva'e); *How the West Was One*—Episode Two 2-7-77 (Little Tree), Episode Three 2-14-77 (Little Tree); *Born to the Wind* 1982 (Prairie Woman).

Redfield, Dennis (1943-). Films: "The Gambler V: Playing for Keeps" TVM-1994 (Abernathy). ¶TV: *Kung Fu*—"A Praying Mantis Kills" 3-22-73 (Victor); *Gunsmoke*—"Disciple" 4-1-74 (Lem Rawlins), "The Wiving" 10-14-74 (Shep), "Brides and Grooms" 2-10-75 (Luke Hockett).

Redfield, William (1927-8/17/76). Films: "Duel at Diablo" 1966 (Sgt. Ferguson). ¶TV: *Wrangler*—"The Affair with Browning's Woman" 8-25-60 (Clint Browning); *Gunsmoke*—"Unloaded Gun" 1-14-61 (Joe Lime).

Redford, Robert (1936-). Films: "Butch Cassidy and the Sundance Kid" 1969 (the Sundance Kid); "Tell Them Willie Boy Is Here" 1969 (Christopher Cooper); "Jeremiah Johnson" 1972 (Jeremiah Johnson); "The Electric Horseman" 1979 (Sonny Steele). ¶TV: *Maverick*—"The Iron Hand" 2-21-60 (Jimmy Coleman); *The Deputy*—"Last Gunfight" 4-30-60 (Bill Johnson); *Tate*—"The Bounty Hunter" 6-22-60 (John Torsett), "Comanche Scalps" 8-10-60 (Tad Dundee); *Whispering Smith*—"The Grudge" 5-15-61 (Johnny Gates); *The Virginian*—"The Evil That Men Do" 10-16-63 (Matthew Cordell).

Redgrave, Lynn (1943-). Films: "Don't Turn the Other Cheek" 1974-Ital./Ger./Span. ¶TV: *Centennial*—Regular 1978-79 (Charlotte Buckland).

Redgrave, Michael (1908-3/21/85). TV: *Ruggles of Red Gap* 2-3-57 (Alfred Ruggles).

Reding, Judi. TV: *Branded*—"The Bounty" 2-21-65 (Liz); *The Big Valley*—"Four Days to Furnace Hill" 12-4-67.

Redman, Minna. Films: "The Lone Star Ranger" 1923 (Mrs. Laramie); "Stepping Fast" 1923 (Mrs. Malvern); "Border Vengeance" 1925 (Mrs. Jackson); "The Ace of Clubs" 1926 (Widow Horton).

Redmond, Liam (1913-11/89). Films: "The Adventures of Bullwhip Griffin" 1967 (Capt. Swain). ¶TV: *Gunsmoke*—"The Dreamers" 4-28-62 (Henry Cairn); *Wagon Train*—"The Levy-McGowan Story" 11-14-62 (Patrick McGowan), "Heather and Hamish" 4-10-63 (MacIntosh); *Daniel Boone*—"The Peace Tree" 11-11-65 (Roderick MacIntosh).

Redmond, Marge (1926-). TV: *The Virginian*—"A Portrait of Marie Valonne" 11-6-63 (Hazel), "The Laramie Road" 12-8-65; *Nichols*—3-14-72 (Bertha).

Redwing, Roderick "Rod" (1904-5/30/71). Films: "Daredevils of the West" 1943-serial (Indian #3); "Sonora Stagecoach" 1944; "Singin' in the Corn" 1946 (Brave); "The Last Round-Up" 1947; "Apache Chief" 1949 (Tewa); "Riders of the Pony Express" 1949; "Little Big Horn" 1951 (Cpl. Arika); "Buffalo Bill in Tomahawk Territory" 1952 (Chief White Cloud); "Hellgate" 1952 (Pima); "Last of the Comanches" 1952 (Indian); "The Pathfinder" 1952 (Chief Arrowhead); "Rancho Notorious" 1952 (Rio); "Son of Geronimo" 1952-serial (Porico); "Conquest of Cochise" 1953 (Red Knife); "Saginaw Trail" 1953 (the Huron); "Winning of the West" 1953 (Pete Littlewolf); "Cattle Queen of Montana" 1954 (Powhani); "Gunfighters of the Northwest" 1954-serial (Bear Tooth); "Copper Sky" 1957 (Indian); "Flaming Star" 1960 (Indian Brave); "Heller in Pink Tights" 1960 (Indian); "Sergents 3" 1962 (Irregular); "Johnny Reno" 1966 (Indian); "Shalako" 1968-Brit./Fr. (Chato's Father); "Charro!" 1969 (Lige). ¶TV: *The Cisco Kid*—"Medicine Man Story" 8-25-51, "Juggler's Silver" 10-17-53; *Frontier*—"Mother of the Brave" 1-15-56; *Wyatt Earp*—Regular 1956-57 (Mr. Brother); *Wagon Train*—"The Rex Montana Story" 5-28-58 (Tahzan), "The Cappy Darrin Story" 11-11-59, "The Luke Grant Story" 6-1-60 (the Mojave Chief); *Rawhide*—"Incident of the Misplaced Indians" 5-1-59 (Indian); *Bonanza*—"El Toro

Grande" 1-2-60; *Zane Grey Theater*—"The Last Bugle" 11-24-60 (Kaeta); *The Road West*—"Shaman" 11-14-66 (Chief); *Custer*—"Blazing Arrows" 11-29-67 (Brave Dog).

Reed, Alan (1907-6/14/77). Films: "The Redhead and the Cowboy" 1951 (Lamartine); "Viva Zapata!" 1952 (Pancho Villa); "The Far Horizons" 1955 (Charboneau); "Kiss of Fire" 1955 (Diego). ¶TV: *Jim Bowie*—"The Bridegroom" 11-29-57 (Bill Sedley); *Man from Blackhawk*—"Vendetta for the Lovelorn" 11-20-59 (Drago); *The Law of the Plainsman*—"The Matriarch" 2-18-60 (Dev Valeri).

Reed, Jr., Alan (1938-). TV: *Gunsmoke*—"Tail to the Wind" 10-17-59 (Harlow Reese), "The Widow" 3-24-62 (Corporal Jennings); *Have Gun Will Travel*—"Gold and Brimstone" 6-20-59 (Dirks); *Death Valley Days*—"The Reluctant Gun" 10-27-59 (Bill), "The Trouble with Taxes" 4-18-65 (Billy Slade); *Bonanza*—"The Hanging Posse" 11-28-59; *Zane Grey Theater*—"Never Too Late" 2-4-60 (Kirk Smith), "The Atoner" 4-6-61 (Matt Tompkins); *The Dakotas*—"Requiem at Dancer's Hill" 2-18-63 (Morgan Jackson).

Reed, Barbara. Films: "Death Valley" 1946; "Coroner Creek" 1948 (Abbie Miles).

Reed, David. Films: "Deadwood '76" 1965 (Fancy Poggin).

Reed, Dean (1939-6/17/86). Films: "God Made Them ... I Kill Them" 1968-Ital. (Compton); "Winchester Does Not Forgive" 1968-Ital. (Buckaroo); "Nephews of Zorro" 1969-Ital. (Raphael); "Adios, Sabata" 1970-Ital./Span. (Ballantine); "The Bounty Hunters" 1970-Ital.; "Twenty Paces to Death" 1970-Ital./Span. (Saranda).

Reed, Donald (1901-2/28/73). Films: "The Texan" 1930 (Nick Ibarra); "The Man from Monterey" 1933 (Don Luis Gonzales); "Cyclone Ranger" 1935 (Juan Castelar); "Six Gun Justice" 1935; "The Vanishing Riders" 1935 (Frank Stanley); "Law and Lead" 1936 (Pancho Gonzales); "Ramona" 1936 (Vaquero); "Renfrew of the Royal Mounted" 1937 (Sergeant McDonald); "Under Strange Flags" 1937 (Garcia).

Reed, Donna (1921-1/14/86). Films: "Apache Trail" 1943 (Rosalia Martinez); "Gentle Annie" 1944 (Mary Lingen); "Hangman's Knot" 1952 (Molly Hull); "Gun Fury" 1953 (Jennifer Ballard); "They Rode West" 1954 (Laurie MacKaye); "Three

Hours to Kill" 1954 (Laurie Mastin); "The Far Horizons" 1955 (Sacajawea); "Backlash" 1956 (Karyl Orton); "Ride Lonesome" 1959.

Reed, George (1866-11/6/52). Films: "The Vagabond Trail" 1924 (George Romain); "The Golden Strain" 1925 (Butler); "The Clean-Up Man" 1928 (Sambo); "Trails of the Golden West" 1931; "The Last Trail" 1933 (Japonica Jones); "The Country Beyond" 1936 (Porter); "Belle Starr" 1941; "The Sea of Grass" 1947 (Uncle Nat); "They Died with Their Boots On" 1941 (Charles).

Reed, Ione. Films: "Bucking the Truth" 1926 (Anne); "Chasing Trouble" 1926 (Emily Gregg); "Desperate Chance" 1926; "Fighting Luck" 1926; "Road Agent" 1926; "Across the Plains" 1928 (Helene Williams); "Texas Flash" 1928; "Captain Cowboy" 1929; "An Oklahoma Cowboy" 1929; "Riders of the Storm" 1929; "West of the Rockies" 1929 (Beth Lee); "The Man from Nowhere" 1930 (Grace McCloud); "Melody Trail" 1935 (Mamie).

Reed, Jim. *see* Giuliano, Luigi.

Reed, Marshall (1918-4/15/80). Films: "Black Hills Express" 1943; "Bordertown Gunfighters" 1943; "Death Valley Manhunt" 1943; "The Texas Kid" 1943 (the Texas Kid); "Wagon Tracks West" 1943; "Gangsters of the Frontier" 1944; "Ghost Guns" 1944; "The Laramie Trail" 1944; "Law Men" 1944 (Killifer); "Law of the Valley" 1944; "Marshal of Reno" 1944; "Mojave Firebrand" 1944; "Partners of the Trail" 1944 (Baker); "Range Law" 1944 (Jim Bowen); "Tucson Raiders" 1944; "Zorro's Black Whip" 1944-serial (Citizens #1); "Bandits of the Badlands" 1945; "Gun Smoke" 1945; "Drifting Along" 1946 (Slade); "Gentleman from Texas" 1946; "The Haunted Mine" 1946; "In Old Sacramento" 1946; "Shadows on the Range" 1946; "Angel and the Badman" 1947 (Nelson); "Cheyenne Takes Over" 1947 (Companion); "The Fighting Vigilantes" 1947 (Check); "Land of the Lawless" 1947; "On the Old Spanish Trail" 1947 (Gus); "Song of the Wasteland" 1947; "Stage to Mesa City" 1947 (Baxter); "Trailing Danger" 1947; "West of Dodge City" 1947; "Wyoming" 1947 (Man); "Back Trail" 1948 (Lacey); "The Bold Frontiersman" 1948 (Sam); "Courtin' Trouble" 1948 (Cody); "Dead Man's Gold" 1948; "Dangers of the Canadian Mounted" 1948-serial (Dave/Douglas/Jim/Williams); "The Fighting Ranger" 1948;

"The Gallant Legion" 1948 (Bowling); "The Hawk of Powder River" 1948; "Mark of the Lash" 1948; "Overland Trails" 1948; "Partners of the Sunset" 1948; "The Rangers Ride" 1948; "Renegades of Sonora" 1948; "Song of the Drifter" 1948; "Sundown Riders" 1948 (Bob Casey); "Tornado Range" 1948 (Wilson); "Triggerman" 1948; "Brand of Fear" 1949; "The Dalton Gang" 1949 (Joe); "Frontier Marshal" 1949 (Outlaw); "Ghost of Zorro" 1949-serial (Fowler); "Gun Runner" 1949 (Riley); "Hidden Danger" 1949 (Mason); "Law of the West" 1949 (Drago); "Navajo Trail Raiders" 1949 (Jed); "Riders of the Dusk" 1949 (Bradshaw); "Roaring Westward" 1949 (Jorgen); "Square Dance Jubilee" 1949 (Charlie); "Stampede" 1949 (Shires); "West of El Dorado" 1949 (Barstow); "Western Renegades" 1949 (Frank); "Cactus Caravan" 1950-short; "Cherokee Uprising" 1950 (Sheriff); "Covered Wagon Raid" 1950; "Cowboy and the Prizefighter" 1950 (Osborne); "The James Brothers of Missouri" 1950-serial (Dutch); "Law of the Panhandle" 1950 (Rance); "Outlaw Gold" 1950 (Jackson); "Over the Border" 1950 (Bart Calhoun); "Rider from Tucson" 1950 (Jackson); "The Savage Horde" 1950; "Silver Raiders" 1950 (Horn); "Six Gun Mesa" 1950; "Texas Dynamo" 1950; "Abilene Trail" 1951 (Slavens); "Canyon Raiders" 1951; "Gunplay" 1951 (Dobbs); "Lawless Cowboys" 1951 (Paul Maxwell); "The Longhorn" 1951 (Latimer); "Montana Desperado" 1951 (Hal Jackson); "Nevada Badmen" 1951; "Oh! Susanna" 1951 (Trooper Murray); "Oklahoma Justice" 1951; "Stagecoach Driver" 1951; "Texas Lawmen" 1951 (Potter); "Wanted Dead or Alive" 1951; "Whistling Hills" 1951 (Claine); "Canyon Ambush" 1952; "Kansas Territory" 1952 (Bob Jethro); "Laramie Mountains" 1952 (Lt. Pierce); "The Lusty Men" 1952 (Jim-Bob); "Montana Incident" 1952; "Night Raiders" 1952 (Sheriff Hodkins); "The Rough, Tough West" 1952 (Fulton); "Son of Geronimo" 1952-serial (Rance Rankin); "Texas City" 1952 (Varnell); "Cow Country" 1953 (Riley); "Gunfighters of the Northwest" 1954-serial (Lynch); "Prairie Express" 1947 (Burke); "Raiders of the South" 1947; "Riding with Buffalo Bill" 1954-serial (Bill Cody); "Rose Marie" 1954 (Mountie); "The Wild Westerners" 1962 (Sheriff Henry Plummer); "The Hallelujah Trail" 1965 (Carter); "A Time for Killing" 1967 (Stedner). ¶TV: The

Gene Autry Show—"Hot Lead" 11-26-50, "Killer Horse" 12-10-50, "Frame for Trouble" 11-3-51, "Revenge Trail" 11-17-51, "Narrow Escape" 8-11-53, "Prize Winner" 7-27-54; *The Cisco Kid*—"Lynching Story" 4-28-51, "Confession for Money" 5-26-51, "Pancho Hostage" 2-23-51, "Monkey Business" 1-26-52, "Church in Town" 5-17-52, "Rodeo" 12-27-52, "Steel Plow" 1-31-53, "The Ventriloquist" 2-7-53, "The Lowest Bidder" 4-4-53, "Mining Madness" 4-11-53, "Sundown's Gun" 4-18-53, "Three Suspects" 5-23-53, "Schoolmarm" 1-23-54; *Wild Bill Hickok*—"The Dog Collar Story" 7-17-51, "Trapper's Story" 3-18-52, "A Joke on Sir Antony" 4-1-52, "The Maverick" 8-19-52; *The Roy Rogers Show*—"Carnival Killer" 6-8-52; *The Range Rider*—"Sealed Justice" 12-6-52; *The Lone Ranger*—"False Accusations" 4-21-55; *Bat Masterson*—"The Snare" 3-17-60 (Alf Hayman), "High Card Loses" 11-10-60 (Romer); *Wagon Train*—"The River Crossing" 12-14-60; *Bonanza*—"The Courtship" 1-7-61 (Hammond), "The War Comes to Washoe" 11-4-62; *Lawman*—"The Tarnished Badge" 1-28-62 (Jake); *Gunsmoke*—"Abe Blocker" 11-24-62 (Sam Vestal); *Laramie*—"The Last Battleground" 4-16-63; *Death Valley Days*—"Tracy's Triumph" 10-4-69, "The Mezcla Man" 1-3-70"The Visitor" 12-27-69.

Reed, Maxwell (1919-10/31/74). TV: *Bonanza*—"The Duke" 3-11-61 (Duke); *Daniel Boone*—"Cry of Gold" 11-4-65 (Thomas Cromwell).

Reed, Oliver (1938-). Films: "The Hunting Party" 1971-Brit./Ital./Span. (Frank Calder); "The Great Scout and Cathouse Thursday" 1976 (Joe Knox); "Return to Lonesome Dove" TVM-1993 (Gregor Dunnegan).

Reed, Pamela. Films: "The Long Riders" 1980 (Belle Starr).

Reed, Paul (1909-). Films: "The Ride to Hangman's Tree" 1967 (Corbett).

Reed, Phillip (1900-). Films: "The Last of the Mohicans" 1936 (Uncas); "Pirates of Monterey" 1947 (Lt. Carlos Ortega); "Daughter of the West" 1949 (Navo); "Bandit Queen" 1950 (Joaquin Murietta); "Davy Crockett, Indian Scout" 1950 (Red Hawk); "Take Me to Town" 1953 (Newton Cole). ¶TV: *Riverboat*—"Escape to Memphis" 10-25-59 (Raleigh).

Reed, Ralph. Films: "High Noon" 1952 (Johnny); "Lone Star" 1952 (Bud Yoakum); "Saginaw Trail" 1953 (Randy Lane); "The Tall

Stranger" 1957 (Murray). ¶TV: *20th Century Fox Hour*—"Broken Arrow" 5-2-56 (Chip Slade); *Wyatt Earp*—"Young Guns" 3-26-57 (Jimmy Craig), "Truth About Gunfighting" 11-18-58 (Mitch Hallam), "The Truth About Old Man Clanton" 9-27-60, "Horse Thief" 1-10-61 (Billy Clanton), "Just Before the Battle" 6-13-61 (Billy Clanton), "Gunfight at the O.K. Corral" 6-21-61 (Billy Clanton); *Tombstone Territory*—"The Youngest Gun" 1-1-58 (Jett Sergeant); *Wagon Train*—"The Annie MacGregor Story" 2-5-58, "The Rex Montana Story" 5-28-58 (Young Man); *Lawman*—"Wanted" 11-16-58 (Roy Barrington); *Zane Grey Theater*—"Let the Man Die" 12-18-58 (Nick Reynolds); *Rawhide*—"Incident at the Edge of Madness" 2-6-59 (Boston), "Incident of the Devil and His Due" 1-22-60 (Hal Burton), "The Pitchwagon" 3-2-62, "Incident at Farragut Pass" 10-31-63 (Jared); *Have Gun Will Travel*—"The Man Who Lost" 2-7-59, "Bear Bait" 5-13-61 (Burt); *Tales of Wells Fargo*—"Lola Montez" 2-16-59 (Milt); *The Rebel*—"The Pit" 3-12-61 (Slip); *Riverboat*—"Rive Champion" 10-10-60 (Bates); *Temple Houston*—"Gallows in Galilee" 10-31-63 (Roy Julian).

Reed, Robert (1932-5/12/92). TV: *Bronco*—"Volunteers from Aberdeen" 2-9-60 (Tom Fuller); *Lawman*—"Left Hand of the Law" 3-27-60 (Jim Malone); *Hondo*—"Hondo and the Superstition Massacre" 9-29-67 (Frank Davis); *Walt Disney Presents*—"Kit Carson and the Mountain Men" 1-9-77 & 1-16-77 (Capt. John C. Fremont).

Reed, Walter. Films: "Return of the Badmen" 1948 (Bob Dalton), "Western Heritage" 1948 (Joe Powell); "The Eagle and the Hawk" 1950 (Jones); "Wells Fargo Gunmaster" 1951 (Ed Hines); "Desert Passage" 1952 (Carver); "Horizons West" 1952 (Layton); "Target" 1952 (Conroy); "Seminole" 1953 (Farmer); "Those Redheads from Seattle" 1953 (Whitey Marks); "War Paint" 1953 (Allison); "The Yellow Tomahawk" 1954 (Keats); "The Far Horizons" 1955 (Cruzatte); "Seven Men from Now" 1956 (John Greer); "Slim Carter" 1957 (Richard L. Howard); "The Lawless Eighties" 1958; "The Horse Soldiers" 1959 (Union Officer); "Westbound" 1959 (Doctor); "Sergeant Rutledge" 1960 (Capt. MacAfee); "Thirteen Fighting Men" 1960 (Col. Jeffers); "How the West Was Won" 1962 (Union Soldier); "Cheyenne Autumn" 1964 (Lt. Peterson); "Convict Stage" 1965; "Fort Coura-

geous" 1965. ¶TV: *Hopalong Cassidy*—"Death by Proxy" 6-14-52; *The Lone Ranger*—"The Gentleman from Julesburg" 6-11-53, "Code of the Pioneers" 2-17-55; *Fury*—"Killer Stallion" 10-22-55 (Stevens), "Sonic Boom" 2-7-59 (Miles Jackson); *Wyatt Earp*—"Hunt the Man Down" 5-3-56 (Turner Ashby), "Winning Streak" 12-27-60 (Ace Hudson); *Annie Oakley*—"Annie and the Leprechauns" 9-2-56 (Ben Cobey), "Annie Rides the Navajo Trail" 11-18-56 (Henry Hayden),"The Dutch Gunmaker" 2-17-57 (Steve Scribner); *Sergeant Preston of the Yukon*—"Return Visit" 11-22-56 (Walt Daniels), "Emergency on Scarface Flat" 12-13-56 (Dr. Godfrey); *Gunsmoke*—"Sweet and Sour" 3-2-57 (Joe Garrett); *The Adventures of Rin Tin Tin*—"The Frame-Up" 3-15-57 (Capt. James); *Have Gun Will Travel*—"The Great Mojave Chase" 9-28-57; *Maverick*—"According to Hoyle" 10-6-57 (Bledsoe), "The Cactus Switch" 1-15-61 (Ed Spencer); *Zane Grey Theater*—"A Gun Is for Killing" 10-18-57 (Sam Cluny); *The Restless Gun*—"Jenny" 10-21-57 (Ned Landy); *Buckskin*—"Hunter's Moon" 9-11-58 (Sam Kirby); *Wagon Train*—"The Danny Benedict Story" 12-2-59 (Harrison), "The Fenton Canaby Story" 12-30-63; *Colt .45*—"Breakthrough" 3-27-60 (Harry Dodson); *Hotel De Paree*—"Sundance and the Man in Room Seven" 2-12-60 (Shelby Adams); *Cheyenne*—"Two Trails to Santa Fe" 10-28-60 (Jack Riggs); *Lawman*—"The Threat" 4-30-61 (James Chase); *Bonanza*—"The Way Station" 10-29-62; *The Virginian*—"Six Graves at Cripple Creek" 1-27-65 (Major Mallory), "High Stakes" 11-16-66 (Caleb), "Image of an Outlaw" 10-23-68 (Stephens).

Reese, Della (1932-). TV: *Young Riders*—"Born to Hang" 9-22-90 (Stagecoach Sally).

Reese, Samuel (1930-). TV: *The Law of the Plainsman*—"The Dude" 12-3-59; *Gunsmoke*—"Mad Dog" 1-14-67 (Buff Watson); *The Big Valley*—"Down Shadow Street" 1-23-67 (Ollie Patten); *Iron Horse*—"Decision at Sundown" 2-27-67 (Ferris).

Reese, Tom (1930-). Films: "Flaming Star" 1960 (Jute); "Blood on the Arrow" 1964 (Charlie); "Taggart" 1964 (Vince August); "Stranger on the Run" TVM-1967 (Leo Weed). ¶TV: *Bonanza*—"Blood on the Land" 2-13-60 (Burton), "The Underdog" 12-13-64 (Lee Burton), "The Last Mission" 5-8-66 (Sergeant Devlin); *Man from Blackhawk*—"The Last Days of Jessie Turnbull" 4-1-60 (Carl

Mayhew); *The Law of the Plainsman*—"Jeb's Daughter" 4-14-60 (Cal Cyder); *Gunsmoke*—"Gentleman's Disagreement" 4-30-60 (Tulsa), "Friend's Pay-Off" 9-3-60 (Joe Leeds), "Tall Trapper" 1-21-61 (Ben), "Harriet" 3-4-61 (Dan Scorp), "Reprisal" 3-10-62 (Wellman), "Friend" 1-25-64 (Judd Nellis), "The Pariah" 4-17-65 (Wayne Hooker), "The Hostage" 12-4-65 (Wade Keys), "Judge Calvin Strom" 12-18-65, "The Brothers" 3-12-66 (Oakie), "Quaker Girl" 12-10-66 (Dave Westerfield), "Nitro!" 4-8-67 & 4-15-67 (Ben Stearman), "Waco" 12-9-68 (Slick Regan), "The Squaw" 1-6-75 (Charlie Dent); *The Virginian*—"Woman from White Ting" 9-26-62 (Wid), "Dangerous Road" 3-17-65 (Woolsack); *Great Adventure*—"Wild Bill Hickok—the Legend and the Man" 1-3-64 (Mike Williams); *Destry*—"The Infernal Triangle" 5-1-64 (Joe); *Rawhide*—"Piney" 10-9-64 (Bert); *Wild Wild West*—"The Night of the Inferno" 9-17-65 (Wagon Driver); *Laredo*—"The Golden Trail" 11-4-65 (Tom Baker), "That's Noway, Thataway" 1-20-66 (Tom Baker); *Branded*—"McCord's Way" 1-30-66 (Jess Muhler); *Iron Horse*—"The Dynamite Driver" 9-19-66 (Gage); *The Guns of Will Sonnett*—"Meeting at Devil's Fork" 10-27-67 (Lando); *Hondo*—"Hondo and the Sudden Town" 11-17-67 (Wilson); *Cimarron Strip*—"The Last Wolf" 12-14-67 (Pete Spurber); *The High Chaparral*—"Ebenezer" 11-1-68 (Judson); *Kung Fu*—"Blood of the Dragon" 9-14-74 (Sheriff); *The Quest*—"Prairie Woman" 11-10-76 (Sheriff); *Father Murphy*—"Stopover in a One-Way Horse Town" 10-26-82 (Packard).

Reeve, Christopher (1952-) Films: "Black Fox" TVM 1995 (Alan Johnson).

Reeves, Charles E. Films: "Jim's Vindication" 1912; "A Rough Ride with Nitroglycerine" 1912; "So-Jun-Wah and the Tribal Law" 1912; "The Whiskey Runners" 1912; "Why Jim Reformed" 1912.

Reeves, Del (1933-). Films: "Sam Whiskey" 1969 (Fisherman).

Reeves, George (1914-6/16/59). Films: "Ride, Cowboy, Ride" 1939-short; "Pony Express Days" 1940-short; "Virginia City" 1940 (Telegrapher); "Bar 20" 1943 (Lin Bradley); "Border Patrol" 1943 (Mexican Officer); "Buckskin Frontier" 1943 (Jeff Collins); "Colt Comrades" 1943 (Lin Whitlock); "Hoppy Serves a Writ" 1943 (Steve Jordan); "The Leather Burners" 1943 (Harrison Brooke); "Thunder in the Pines"

1948 (Jeff Collins); "Bugles in the Afternoon" 1952 (Lt. Smith); "Rancho Notorious" 1952 (Wilson); "Westward Ho the Wagons" 1956 (James Stephen).

Reeves, Richard (1912-3/17/67). Films: "Fargo" 1952; "The Maverick" 1952 (Frank Bullitt); "Jack Slade" 1953; "A Perilous Journey" 1953 (Stewart, the Sailor); "Destry" 1954 (Mac); "Top Gun" 1955 (Willetts); "Running Target" 1956 (Jaynes); "The Buckskin Lady" 1957 (Porter); "Gunsmoke in Tucson" 1958 (Notches); "Billy the Kid vs. Dracula" 1966. ¶TV: *The Roy Rogers Show*—"Shoot to Kill" 4-27-52, "The Peddler from the Pecos" 12-13-53 (Hal Burnside), "Bad Company" 12-27-53 (Ham Murray), "Little Dynamite" 1-3-54 (Piney Yokum), "The Land Swindle" 3-14-54 (Mike Pool); "The Young Defenders" 10-3-54 (Joel Tobin), "Hard Luck Story" 10-31-54 (Ralph Graham); *The Lone Ranger*—"The Woman in the White Mask" 5-12-55, "The Bounty Hunter" 5-19-55; *Fury*—"Ghost Town" 12-31-55 (Ox); *Schlitz Playhouse of the Stars*—"Flowers for Jenny" 8-3-56 (Red Heron); *Annie Oakley*—"The Waco Kid" 10-28-56 (Dixie); *Maverick*—"The Long Hunt" 10-20-57, "Lonesome Reunion" 9-28-58 (Monty), "Alias Bart Maverick" 10-5-58 (Rafe Plummer), "Island in the Swamp" 11-30-58 (Anthony Offord), "Last Wire from Stop Gap" 10-16-60 (Prospector), "Destination Devil's Flat" 12-25-60 (Bull Crumpett); *Trackdown*—"The Town" 12-13-57 (Saul McCready); *Tales of Wells Fargo*—"Doc Bell" 1-6-58 (Tibbs); *Tombstone Territory*—"The Rebels' Last Charge" 1-15-58, "The Man from Brewster" 4-24-59 (Deputy Tom Hatch); *Sugarfoot*—"Bullet Proof" 1-21-58 (Pete), "The Return of the Canary Kid" 2-3-59 (Blackie); *Jim Bowie*—"Patron of the Arts" 4-11-58 (Stokes); *Jefferson Drum*—"The Hanging of Joe Lavetti" 8-1-58 (Paul Meeker); *Wanted—Dead or Alive*—"Eight Cent Record" 12-20-58; *Bat Masterson*—"Double Trouble in Trinidad" 1-7-59 (George Swift); *The Texan*—"Letter of the Law" 3-23-59; *Zorro*—"The Sergeant Sees Red" 5-14-59; *Rough Riders*—"The Highgraders" 5-28-59 (Bart Michaels); *26 Men*—"Abandoned" 6-16-59; *Bonanza*—"The Saga of Annie O'Toole" 10-24-59 (Clayton), "The Hopefuls" 10-8-60; *Wyatt Earp*—"Get Shotgun Gibbs" 12-22-59, "Terror in the Desert" 1-24-61 (Bucko); *Gunsmoke*—"Hinka Do" 1-30-60 (Drunk); *The Alaskans*—"Black Sand" 2-14-60;

Lawman—"The Thimblerigger" 2-28-60 (Ed Shafter); *Rawhide*—"Incident of the One Hundred Amulets" 5-6-60 (Sheriff), "Incident of the Blackstorms" 5-26-61 (Long), "The Little Fishes" 11-24-61 (Higgins), "Incident of the Swindler" 2-20-64 (Jess Carmody); *Wagon Train*—"The Dick Jarvis Story" 5-18-60 (Sam Hulsey), "The Eve Newhope Story" 12-5-62 (Orv Bassett), "The Barnaby West Story" 6-5-63 (Roberts), "The Molly Kincaid Story" 9-16-63 (Wells), "The Kate Crawley Story" 1-27-64 (Pop Harmon); *Two Faces West*—"Hot Water" 10-17-60, "The Coward" 6-26-61 (Klien); *Have Gun Will Travel*—"The Piano" 11-11-61 (Jerris); *Frontier Circus*—"Quick Shuffle" 2-1-62 (Gruber), "Never Won Fair Lady" 4-12-62 (Customer); *The Tall Man*—"G.P." 5-19-62 (Santee); *The Virginian*—"West" 11-20-62 (Munsy); *The Travels of Jaimie McPheeters*—"The Day of the Flying Dutchman" 12-1-63 (Bullie); *Laredo*—"Three's Company" 10-14-65 (Coke), "A Taste of Money" 4-28-66, "A Double Shot of Nepenthe" 9-30-66; *The Legend of Jesse James*—"The Judas Boot" 11-8-65 (Dan Mitchell); *Wild Wild West*—"The Night of the Whirring Death" 2-18-66; *F Troop*—"Reunion for O'Rourke" 3-8-66 (Jim Sweeney); *Pistols 'n' Petticoats*—11-5-66 (Cowhand).

Reeves, Robert "Bob" (1892-4/13/60). Films: "To the Tune of Bullets" 1919; "Finger Prints" 1920; "The Gun Game" 1920; "The Mask of Lopez" 1923 (Dick); "The Thrill Chaser" 1923; "The Twilight Trail" 1923; "Under the Border" 1923; "Gold Digger Jones" 1924; "Miscarried Plans" 1924; "The Silent Stranger" 1924 (Deputy Shorty Turner); "The No-Gun Man" 1925 (Oklahoma George); "Ambushed" 1926; "Cyclone Bob" 1926 (Cyclone Bob Flemming); "Desperate Chance" 1926; "Fighting Luck" 1926; "Iron Fist" 1926; "Ridin' Straight" 1926; "Riding for Life" 1926; "The Cherokee Kid" 1927 (Seth Daggard); "Canyon Hawks" 1930 (Sheriff Jackson); "The Lonesome Tail" 1930 (Alkali); "The Pocatello Kid" 1931; "The Range Feud" 1931; "The Trail Drive" 1933; "Smoking Guns" 1934; "Western Courage" 1935; "Heroes of the Range" 1936; "Brand of the Outlaws" 1936; "Lucky Terror" 1936; "Boots and Saddles" 1937; "Range Defenders" 1937; "Ranger Courage" 1937; "New Frontier" 1939 (Man at Dance); "My Little Chickadee" 1940 (Barfly Dandy); "Son of Roaring Dan" 1940; "When the Daltons

Rode" 1940 (Henchman); "Days of Old Cheyenne" 1943; "The Lone Star Trail" 1943 (Barfly); "The Adventures of Frank and Jesse James" 1948-serial (Tim); "Ghost of Zorro" 1949-serial (Andy); "Desperadoes of the West" 1950-serial (Jerry); "Don Daredevil Rides Again" 1951-serial (Townsman #6); "Canadian Mounties vs. Atomic Invaders" 1953-serial (Bartender).

Reeves, Steve (1926-). Films: "A Long Ride from Hell" 1968-Ital. (Mike Sturges).

Regan, Charles. Films: "The Lone Ranger Rides Again" 1939-serial (Cave Heavy #1); "Dangers of the Canadian Mounted" 1948-serial (Ralph).

Regan, Jayne. Films: "The Cactus Kid" 1934 (Beth); "West on Parade" 1934; "Ridin' Thru" 1935 (Ranch Guest); "The Silver Bullet" 1935 (Nora Kane); "Texas Jack" 1935 (Ann Hall).

Regan, Patty (1930-). TV: *F Troop*—"Miss Parmenter" 11-17-66 (Daphne Parmenter).

Regas, George (1890-12/13/40). Films: "Desert Gold" 1926 (Verd); "Redskin" 1929 (Chief Notani); "Wolf Song" 1929 (Black Wolf); "The Lonesome Tail" 1930 (Ring-Tailored Roarer); "Battling with Buffalo Bill" 1931-serial; "Mounted Fury" 1931 (Pierre LeStrange); "Riders of the North" 1931 (Leclerc); "The Golden West" 1932 (Black Wolf); "The Fighting Trooper" 1934 (Henri); "Red Blood of Courage" 1935 (Frenchy); "Daniel Boone" 1936 (Black Eagle); "Robin Hood of El Dorado" 1936 (Tomas); "Rose Marie" 1936 (Boniface); "The Bad Man of Brimstone" 1937 (Indian Chief); "The Californian" 1937 (Ruiz); "Left-Handed Law" 1937 (Sam Logan); "Hawaiian Buckaroo" 1938 (Regas); "The Oklahoma Kid" 1939 (Pedro); "Union Pacific" 1939 (Indian); "Mark of Zorro" 1940 (Sergeant Gonzales); "Northwest Mounted Police" 1940 (Freddie); "Virginia City" 1940 (Half-Breed).

Regas, Pedro (1897-8/10/74). Films: "Two-Fisted Justice" 1931 (Cheyenne Charley); "West of the Pecos" 1934 (Manuel Gomez); "Under the Pampas Moon" 1935 (Jockey); "The Phantom Rider" 1936-serial; "Sutter's Gold" 1936; "The Traitor" 1936 (Moreno); "The Girl of the Golden West" 1938 (Renegade); "South of the Rio Grande" 1945 (Luis); "Trail of the Mounties" 1947; "The Kissing Bandit" 1948 (Esteban); "Viva Zapata!" 1952 (Innocente); "Flap" 1970

(She'll-Be-Back-Pretty-Soon); "Wild Women" TVM-1970. ¶TV: *The Roy Rogers Show*—"The Ride of the Ranchers" 4-20-52 (Don Jose); *The Tall Man*—"Billy's Baby" 12-24-60 (Bartender); *Gunsmoke*—"Chato" 9-14-70 (Old Man).

Regehr, Duncan. TV: *Zorro*—Regular 1990-91 (Don Diego de la Vega/Zorro).

Reggiani, Serge (1922-). Films: "Don't Touch White Women!" 1974-Ital. (Mad One).

Regina, Paul. TV: *Zorro and Son*—Regular 1983 (Don Carlos).

Reicher, Frank (1875-1/19/65). Films: "Sutter's Gold" 1936; "South of the Border" 1939 (Don Diego Mendoza); "The Big Bonanza" 1944 (Dr. Ballou); "Home in Oklahoma" 1946 (Lawyer Cragmyle); "My Pal Trigger" 1946 (Magistrate); "Yankee Fakir" 1947 (Randall); "Carson City Raiders" 1948 (Razor Pool); "The Arizona Cowboy" 1950 (Major Sheridan).

Reichow, Otto (1904-). Films: "Arizona Gangbusters" 1940 (Haas); "King of the Texas Rangers" 1941-serial (Porter); "Silver River" 1948 (Miner); "Ulzana's Raid" 1972 (Steegmeyer). ¶TV: *Wagon Train*—"The Zebedee Titus Story" 4-20-64.

Reid, Carl Benton (1893-3/15/73). Films: "Stage to Tucson" 1950 (Doc Benteen); "Indian Uprising" 1951 (John Clemson); "The Command" 1953 (Col. Janeway); "Escape from Fort Bravo" 1953 (Col. Owens); "Broken Lance" 1954 (Clem Lawton); "The Spoilers" 1955 (Judge Stillman); "Wichita" 1955 (Mayor); "A Day of Fury" 1956 (Judge John J. Mclean); "The First Texan" 1956 (Andrew Jackson); "The Last Wagon" 1956 (Gen. Howard); "The Last of the Fast Guns" 1958 (John Forbes). ¶TV: *Zane Grey Theater*—"The Promise" 11-8-57 (Pa Rawlings), "Shadow of a Dead Man" 4-11-58 (Zachary Wheeler), "One Must Die" 1-12-61 (Thad Hobbes); *Gunsmoke*—"Passive Resistance" 1-17-59 (Gideon Seek); *Bonanza*—"The Truckee Strip" 11-21-59 (Luther Bishop), "The Mountain Girl" 5-13-62 (Josiah Harker); *Laramie*—"Night of the Quiet Man" 12-22-59 (Rogers), "Ladies Day" 10-3-61; *Wagon Train*—"The Tracy Sadler Story" 3-9-60 (Fletcher Forest); *Wichita Town*—"The Hanging Judge" 3-9-60 (Senator Gray); *The Deputy*—"Passage to New Orleans" 11-19-60 (Sameul Foreman); *Frontier Circus*—"Quick Shuffle" 2-1-62 (Judge); *The Virginian*—"Felicity's Springs" 10-14-64 (Jonah).

Reid, Elliott (1920-). "Sierra" 1950 (Duke Lafferty). ¶TV: *Wild Wild West*—"The Night of the Sudden Plague" 4-22-66 (Governor Hawthorne).

Reid, Frances. TV: *Wagon Train*—"The Daniel Clay Story" 2-21-62 (Margaret Clay), "The Frank Carter Story" 5-23-62 (Mary Carter), "The Kurt Davos Story" 11-28-62 (Florence Hastings), "The Emmett Lawton Story" 3-6-63 (Mrs. Lawton), "The Katy Piper Story" 4-11-65 (Dr. Katy Piper).

Reid, Hal (1860-5/22/20). Films: "The Deerslayer" 1913.

Reid, Jane. Films: "The Law of Fear" 1928 (Marion); "Terror Mountain" 1928 (Lucille Roberts); "When the Law Rides" 1928 (Becky Ross).

Reid, Violet. Films: "The Gambler of the West" 1914 (Mabel Grey); "The Heart of a Bandit" 1915.

Reid, Wallace (1891-1/18/23). Films: "At Cripple Creek" 1912; "The Indian Raiders" 1912; "Indian Romeo and Juliet" 1912; "Tribal Law" 1912; "The Deerslayer" 1913; "Hearts and Horses" 1913; "A Hopi Legend" 1913; "The Mystery of Yellow Aster Mine" 1913; "A Rose of Old Mexico" 1913; "Arms and the Gringo" 1914; "Sierra Jim's Reformation" 1914; "A Yankee from the West" 1915 (Billy Milford); "The Love Mask" 1916 (Dan Deering); "The Golden Fetter" 1917 (James Roger Ralston); "Nan of Music Mountain" 1917 (Henry de-Spain); "The Squaw Man's Song" 1917 (Lord Effington); "The World Apart" 1917 (Bob Fulton); "The Man from Funeral Range" 1918 (Harry Webb); "Rimrock Jones" 1918 (Rimrock Jones).

Reid, Jr., Wallace (1917-2/26/90). Films: "King of the Royal Mounted" 1940-serial (Doyle); "Northwest Mounted Police" 1940 (Constable Rankin); "The Outlaw" 1943 (Bystander).

Reid, Mrs. Wallace. see Davenport, Dorothy.

Reilly, Hugh (1921-). Films: "Chuka" 1967 (Capt. Carrol).

Reilly, John. TV: *Death Valley Days*—"The Rider" 12-4-65; *A Man Called Shenandoah*—"A Long Way Home" 1-31-66 (Jamie Brewster, Jr.); *Gunsmoke*—"To Ride a Yellow Horse" 3-18-74 (Orlo), "The Wiving" 10-14-74 (Ike); *How the West Was Won*—Episode One 2-12-78 (Jeremiah Taylor).

Reindel, Carl (1931-). Films: "He Rides Tall" 1964 (Gil); "The Cheyenne Social Club" 1970 (Pete Dodge). ¶TV: *Gunsmoke*—"Cale" 5-

5-62 (Cale), "The Search" 9-15-62 (Cale), "Easy Come" 10-26-63 (Emmett Calhoun), "Deputy Festus" 1-16-65 (Dave Carson); *Cheyenne*—"Man Alone" 10-15-62 (Terry/Billy); *Rawhide*—"Incident of the Prodigal Son" 10-19-62 (Ben Whitney); *Bonanza*—"The Beginning" 11-25-62 (Billy Horn), "Justice Deferred" 12-17-67 (Andy), "Thorton's Account" 11-1-70 (Frank Wells); *The Virginian*—"The Devil's Children" 12-5-62 (Bruce McCallum); *Laramie*—"The Dispossessed" 2-19-63 (Cass); *Wagon Train*—"The Eli Bancroft Story" 11-11-63 (Adam Bancroft); *Death Valley Days*—"Hugh Glass Meets the Bear" 6-11-66 (Jim Bridger), "The Hat That Huldah Wore" 6-25-66 (Jack Desmond); *Shane*—"The Hant" 9-17-66 (Jed).

Reineke, Gary. Films: "The Grey Fox" 1983-Can. (Detective Seavey).

Reiner, Robert (1946-). TV: *Wagon Train*—"The Lieutenant Burton Story" 2-28-62 (Thomas).

Reinhardt, Dick. Films: "Ridin' Down the Trail" 1947; "Oklahoma Blues" 1948 (Joe); "Outlaw Brand" 1948; "Song of the Drifter" 1948.

Reinhold, Judge (1958-). Films: "Four Eyes and Six-Guns" TVM-1992 (Ernest Albright). ¶TV: *Lonesome Dove*—"Wild Horses" 10-23-94.

Reischi, Geri (1960-). TV: *Gunsmoke*—"Captain Sligo" 1-4-71 (Anne Burney).

Reisner, Dean (1942-). Films: "Gunfire" 1950 (Cashier).

Reitzen, Jack. TV: *Tombstone Territory*—"Desert Survival" 12-4-57 (Slater); *Gunsmoke*—"Joe Phy" 1-4-58 (Bartender); *Bat Masterson*—"Dude's Folly" 11-26-58 (Packy), "The Canvas and the Cane" 12-17-59, "Tempest at Tioga Pass" 1-5-61 (Motto); *Tales of Wells Fargo*—"Vasquez" 5-16-60 (Moreno); *Cheyenne*—"Counterfeit Gun" 10-10-60 (Jipson).

Remar, James. Films: "The Long Riders" 1980 (Sam Starr); "Windwalker" 1980 (Windwalker as a Young Man); "The Mystic Warrior" TVM-1984 (Pesla); "Desperado: The Outlaw Wars" TVM-1989 (John Sikes); "White Fang" 1991 (Beauty Smith).

Remick, Lee (1935-7/2/91). Films: "Three Thousand Hills" 1959 (Callie); "The Hallelujah Trail" 1965 (Cora Templeton Massingale).

Remley, Ralph (1885-5/26/39). Films: "Home on the Range" 1935 (Brown); "Robin Hood of El Dorado" 1936 (Judge Perkins); "The Texans" 1938 (Town Lawyer).

Remsen, Bert (1925-). Films: "McCabe and Mrs. Miller" 1971 (Bart Coyle); "Buffalo Bill and the Indians, or Sitting Bull's History Lesson" 1976 (Crutch); "The Awakening Land" TVM-1978 (Isaac Barker); "Maverick" 1994 (Riverboat Poker Player). ¶TV: *Maverick*—"The Jail at Junction Flats" 11-9-58 (Deputy George); *Jefferson Drum*—"Pete Henke" 11-20-58 (Jim Ford); *Yancy Derringer*—"The Gun That Murdered Lincoln" 3-19-59 (Maj. Sampson); *Rawhide*—"Incident at Dangerfield Dip" 10-2-59 (Ash), "Incident Near the Promised Land" 2-3-61, "Incident of the Big Blowout" 2-10-61, "Incident at Rio Salado" 9-29-61; *Tales of Wells Fargo*—"The Town" 4-4-60 (Burkett); *Wanted—Dead or Alive*—"Vendetta" 4-9-60 (Lieutenant Pierce); *Adventures of Brisco County, Jr.*—Pilot 8-27-93 (Judge).

Renaldo, Duncan (1904-9/3/80). Films: "Pals of the Prairie" 1929 (Francisco); "Rebellion" 1936 (Ricardo Castillo); "The Painted Stallion" 1937-serial (Zamorro); "Zorro Rides Again" 1937-serial (Renaldo); "Rose of the Rio Grande" 1938 (Sebastian); "Cowboys from Texas" 1939 (Renaldo); "The Kansas Terrors" 1939 (Renaldo); "The Lone Ranger Rides Again" 1939-serial (Juan Vasquiez); "Rough Riders' Round-Up" 1939 (Alcalde); "South of the Border" 1939 (Andreo Mendoza); "Covered Wagon Days" 1940 (Rico); "Gaucho Serenade" 1940 (Gaucho); "Heroes of the Saddle" 1940 (Rico); "Oklahoma Renegades" 1940 (Rico); "Pioneers of the West" 1940 (Rico); "Rocky Mountain Rangers" 1940 (Rico); "Down Mexico Way" 1941 (Juan); "Gauchos of El Dorado" 1941 (Gaucho); "King of the Texas Rangers" 1941-serial (Pedro Garcia); "Outlaws of the Desert" 1941 (Sheik Suleiman); "King of the Mounties" 1942-serial (Pierre); "Border Patrol" 1943 (Mexican Officer); "Hands Across the Border" 1943 (Juan Morales); "The San Antonio Kid" 1944; "Sheriff of Sundown" 1944 (Chihuahua Ramirez); "The Cisco Kid Returns" 1945 (the Cisco Kid); "In Old New Mexico" 1945 (the Cisco Kid); "South of the Rio Grande" 1945 (the Cisco Kid); "The Valiant Hombre" 1948 (the Cisco Kid); "The Daring Caballero" 1949 (the Cisco Kid); "The Gay Amigo" 1949 (the Cisco Kid); "Satan's Cradle" 1949 (the Cisco Kid); "The Capture" 1950 (Carlos); "The Girl from San Lorenzo" 1950 (the Cisco Kid). ¶TV: *The Cisco Kid*—Regular 1951-55 (the Cisco Kid).

Renaldo, Tito. Films: "Ramona" 1936 (Dancer); "Apache Trail" 1943 (Cochee); "South of the Rio Grande" 1945 (Manuel); "Old Los Angeles" 1948 (Tonio Del Rey); "California Conquest" 1952 (Don Bernardo Mirana). ¶TV: *The Adventures of Rin Tin Tin*—"The New C.O." 2-14-58 (Jacillo).

Renard, David (1921-8/19/73). Films: "Frontier Uprising" 1961 (Lopez); "The Long Rope" 1961 (Louis Ortega). ¶TV: *Broken Arrow*—"Turncoat" 4-15-58; *Maverick*—"The Judas Mask" 11-2-58 (Telegrapher); *Wide Country*—"Yanqui, Go Home!" 4-4-63 (Eusebio); *Bonanza*—"Enter Thomas Bowers" 4-26-64 (Jed), "Customs of the Country" 2-6-72 (Padre); *The Big Valley*—"Legend of a General" 9-19-66 & 9-26-66 (Miguel), "Court Martial" 3-6-67 (Boreau); *Gunsmoke*—"Old Friend" 2-4-67 (Boley), "The Jackals" 2-12-68 (Policeman), "Sergeant Holly" 12-14-70 (Chico Fuentes), "Survival" 1-10-72 (Gorio), "I Have Promises to Keep" 3-3-75 (Tonkawa); *Wild Wild West*—"The Night of the Jack O'Diamonds" 10-6-67 (Enrique); *Cimarron Strip*—"Sound of a Drum" 2-1-68; *The High Chaparral*—"The Peacemaker" 3-3-68 (Prowling Dog), "North to Tucson" 11-8-68 (Pablo); *Death Valley Days*—"The Gold Mine on Main Street" 5-11-68.

Renard, Irvin. Films: "Cyclone Cavalier" 1925 (Van Blatten); "The Cowboy Cop" 1926 (Count Mirski); "The Man from the West" 1926 (Carter Blake); "Lightning Lariats" 1927 (1st Officer); "The Old Code" 1928 (Henri Langlois).

Renard, Ken (1905-11/16/93). Films: "Three Thousand Hills" 1959 (Happy); "True Grit" 1969 (Yarnell). ¶TV: *Gunsmoke*—"Kioga" 10-23-65 (Father Kioga), "Honor Before Justice" 3-5-66 (Blacksmith); *Daniel Boone*—"The Gun" 2-3-66 (Chief Red Eagle), "Run a Crooked Mile" 10-20-66 (Jason); *Cimarron Strip*—"The Legend of Jud Starr" 9-14-67 (Chief Henry Youngblood), "Heller" 1-18-68; *Cowboy in Africa*—"Lake Sinclair" 11-13-67 (Jomo); *The Virginian*—"Nora" 12-11-68 (Grey Feather); *The Men from Shiloh*—"The Mysterious Mr. Tate" 10-14-70 (Endicott); *Hec Ramsey*—"The Mystery of the Yellow Rose" 1-28-73 (Charles).

Renavent, George (1894-1/2/69). Films: "Whistlin' Dan" 1932 (Serge Karloff); "Silver Queen" 1942 (Andres, the Maitre'd).

Renella, Pat (1933-). TV: *The*

Alaskans—"White Vengeance" 6-5-60 (Evans); *The High Chaparral*—"Sangre" 2-26-71 (Sangre).

Renick, Ruth (1893-5/7/84). Films: "The Mollycoddle" 1920 (Virginia Hale); "Bar Nothin'" 1921 (Bess Lynne); "Rough Shod" 1922 (Josephine Hamilton); "Forty-Five Calibre Echo" 1932.

Rennick, Nancy. TV: *Death Valley Days*—"The Girl Who Walked with a Giran" 4-22-58 (Margaret Lea), "Hangtown Fry" 10-3-62 (Ann Alton), "The Race at Cherry Creek" 3-7-65; *Gunsmoke*—"Belle's Back" 5-14-60 (Phyllis); *Wagon Train*—"Weight of Command" 1-25-61, "The Christopher Hale Story" 3-15-61 (Mrs. Stevens), "Thye Isaiah Quickfox Story" 1-31-65 (Kate); *Bonanza*—"Mirror of a Man" 3-31-63 (Amelia), "The Quality of Mercy" 11-17-63 (Sara); *Rawhide*—"The Empty Sleeve" 4-2-65 (Jenny).

Rennie, James (1890-7/31/65). Films: "The Bad Man" 1930 (Gilbert Jones); "Girl of the Golden West" 1930 (Dick Johnson); "The Lash" 1930 (David Howard).

Rennie, Michael (1909-6/10/71). Films: "Ride Beyond Vengeance" 1966 (Brooks Durham). ¶TV: *Wagon Train*—"The John Cameron Story" 10-2-57 (John Cameron), "The Robert Harrison Clarke Story" 10-14-63 (Robert Harrison Clarke); *Zane Grey Theater*—"Three Days to Death" 4-4-58, "Living Is a Lonesome Thing" 1-1-59 (Grant Coburn), "Man in the Middle" 2-11-60 (Marshal Locke Gardner); *Decision*—"The Tall Man" 7-27-58 (Col. T.J. Allan); *The Virginian*—"Vengeance Is the Spur" 2-27-63 (Michael O'Rourke); *Daniel Boone*—"The Sound of Wings" 11-12-64 (Major Peter Wellington), "First in War, First in Peace" 10-13-66 (Edgar Newton); *Bonanza*—"Once a Doctor" 2-28-65 (Prof. Poppy); *Branded*—"Salute the Soldier Briefly" 10-24-65 (Charle Briswell); *Iron Horse*—"The Red Tornado" 2-20-67 (Johnny Hobart); *Hondo*—"Hondo and the War Cry" 9-15-67 (Tribolet).

Renno, Vincent (1914-11/5/55). Films: "Frenchie" 1950 (Tony).

Renteria, Joe. Films: "Nakia" TVM-1974 (Peter). ¶TV: *Kung Fu*—"This Valley of Terror" 9-28-74 (Tall Fire).

Rentschler, Mickey. Films: "Brand of Hate" 1934 (Buddy Orkin); "Branded a Coward" 1935; "West of Cimarron" 1941.

Repp, Stafford (1918-11/6/74). Films: "Man with the Gun" 1955

(Arthur Jackson); "Star in the Dust" 1956 (Leo Roos). ¶TV: *Cheyenne*—"The Law Man" 11-6-56 (Hammer); *Gunsmoke*—"Moon" 5-11-57 (Charlie Brewer), "Texas Cowboys" 4-5-58 (Mr. Hightower), "The Peace Officer" 10-15-60 (Styles), "Twenty Miles from Dodge" 4-10-65 (Otie), "The Gang" 12-11-72 (Sheriff Tanner); *Tales of Wells Fargo*—"Stage West" 1-13-58 (Gerson), "Pearl Hart" 5-9-60 (Henry), "Assignment in Gloribee" 1-27-62 (Major Shankford); *Texas John Slaughter*—Regular 1958-61 (Sheriff Hatch); *Rawhide*—"Incident with an Executioner" 1-23-59 (Vanryzin), "Incident of the Sharpshooter" 2-26-60, "Incident Near the Promised Land" 2-3-61 (Matt Walters); *The Californians*—"Stampede at Misery Flats" 3-17-59 (Amos Dayton); *Bonanza*—"House Divided" 1-16-60, "The Abduction" 10-29-60, "The Friendship" 11-12-61 (Carter); *Wanted—Dead or Alive*—"A House Divided" 2-20-60; *The Texan*—"Presentation Gun" 4-4-60; *Stagecoach West*—"High Lonesome" 10-4-60 (Callahan); *Gunslinger*—"The Hostage Fort" 2-16-61 (Simon Hess); *The Deputy*—"The Challenger" 2-25-61 (Collins); *The Tall Man*—"Sidekick" 12-23-61 (Barker); *The Virginian*—"The Exiles" 1-9-63; *Kung Fu*—"The Chalice" 10-11-73 (Father Clancy); *The Cowboys*—"A Matter of Honor" 3-20-74 (Zeb Warschalk).

Republic Rhythm Riders, The (Michael Barton, Darol Rice, George Bamby & Slim Duncan). Films: "Border Saddlemates" 1952; "Colorado Sundown" 1952; "The Last Musketeer" 1952; "Old Oklahoma Plains" 1952; "South Pacific Trail" 1952; "Old Overland Trail" 1953.

Requa, Charles (1892-12/11/67). Films: "South of the Rio Grande" 1932 (Andres).

Resley, Arthur. Films: "The Devil's Mistress" 1968 (Jeroboam).

Ressel, Franco (1925-). Films: "In a Colt's Shadow" 1965-Ital./Span.; "Taste for Killing" 1966-Ital./Span. (Aarons); "Bad Kids of the West" 1967-Ital.; "Man: His Pride and His Vengeance" 1967-Ital./Ger.; "The Mercenary" 1968-Ital./Span.; "Sabata" 1969-Ital. (Stengel); "Have a Good Funeral, My Friend … Sartana Will Pay" 1971-Ital.; "They Call Him Cemetery" 1971-Ital./Span.; "Two Sons of Trinity" 1972-Ital.; "Trinity Is Still My Name" 1974-Ital.; "California" 1976-Ital./Span.

Rettig, Tommy (1941-). Films: "River of No Return" 1954 (Mark Calder); "At Gunpoint" 1955 (Billy);

"The Last Wagon" 1956 (Billy). ¶TV: *Sugarfoot*—"The Ghost" 1-28-58 (Steve Carter), "Trouble at Sand Springs" 4-17-61 (Jimmy Benbow); *Wagon Train*—"Weight of Command" 1-25-61 (Billy Gentry); *Man from Blackhawk*—"The Ghost of Lafitte" 2-26-60 (Pierre); *Lawman*—"The Town Boys" 9-18-60 (Dean Bailey); *Death Valley Days*—"Davy's Friend" 11-28-62 (Joel Robinson).

Revere, Anne (1903-12/18/90). Films: "The Great Missouri Raid" 1951 (Mrs. Samuels); "Macho Callahan" 1970 (Chrystal).

Revier, Dorothy (1904-11/19/93). Films: "Border Women" 1924 (May Prentiss); "Call of the Mate" 1924; "The Cowboy and the Flapper" 1924 (Alice Allison); "Do It Now" 1924; "Down by the Rio Grande" 1924; "The Man from God's Country" 1924 (Carmencita); "Marry in Haste" 1924 (Joan Prescott); "That Wild West" 1924; "The Bad Man" 1930 (Ruth Pell); "Call of the West" 1930 (Violet LaTour); "The Avenger" 1931 (Helen Lake); "The Thrill Hunter" 1933 (Margaret Lane); "The Fighting Ranger" 1934 (Tonita); "When a Man Sees Red" 1934 (Barbara); "The Cowboy and the Kid" 1936 (June Caldwell); "The Eagle's Brood" 1936 (Dolly).

Revill, Clive (1930-). Films: "Zorro, the Gay Blade" 1981 (Garcia). ¶TV: *Young Dan'l Boone*—"The Pirate" 9-19-77 (Teague); *Centennial*—Regular 1978-79 (Finlay Perkin).

Rey, Alejandro (1930-5/21/87). TV: *The Outlaws*—"A Day to Kill" 2-22-62 (Frank Vincente); *Wide Country*—"Who Killed Edde Gannon?" 10-11-62 (Manny); *Death Valley Days*—"The Debt" 2-20-63 (Tiburcio Vasquez); *Daniel Boone*—"Cibola" 3-31-66 (Sergeant Goya); *The Monroes*—"Pawnee Warrior" 12-28-66 (Komatah); *Iron Horse*—"The Passenger" 3-6-67 (Francisco Gomez); *Cowboy in Africa*—"African Rodeo" 1-15-68 & 1-22-68 (Ruy); *The Outcasts*—"And Then There Was One" 3-3-69 (Miguel Otero); *The High Chaparral*—"An Anger Greather Than Mine" 9-18-70 (Diego De la Paula); *Gunsmoke*—"The Bullet" 11-29-71, 12-6-71 & 12-13-71 (Father Sanchez); *Alias Smith and Jones*—"The Clementine Incident" 10-7-72 (Ramon Cordoba); *Kung Fu*—"A Lamb to the Slaughter" 1-11-75 (Matteo); *Wildside*—4-18-85 (Spanish Ambassador).

Rey, Antonia (1927-). Films: "Doc" 1971 (Concha).

Rey, Araceli. TV: *The Californians*—"The Long Night" 12-23-58

(Juanita); *Gunsmoke*—"The Cage" 3-23-70 (Elderly Mexican Woman); *Kung Fu*—"The Brujo" 10-25-73 (Old Woman).

Rey, Fernando (1915-3/10/94). Films: "The Savage Guns" 1961-U.S./Span. (Don Hernan); "Legacy of the Incas" 1965-Ger./Ital.; "Navajo Joe" 1966-Ital./Span. (Parson Rattigan); "Return of the Seven" 1966-Span. (Priest); "Son of a Gunfighter" 1966-U.S./Span. (Don Furtuna); "Villa Rides" 1968 (Col. Fuentes); "Guns of the Magnificent Seven" 1969 (Quintero); "Land Raiders" 1969-U.S./Span. (Priest); "The Price of Power" 1969-Ital./Span.; "Companeros" 1970-Ital./Span./Ger. (Prof. Xantos); "A Town Called Hell" 1971-Span./Brit. (Old Blind Farmer); "Trinity Sees Red" 1971-Ital./Span.; "Rustler's Rhapsody" 1985 (Railroad Colonel).

Rey, Rosa (1892-4/7/69). Films: "Song of the Gringo" 1936; "The Great Sioux Uprising" 1953. ¶TV: *Lawman*—"The Outsider" 1-4-59 (Mrs. Lebeau); *Sugarfoot*—"The Mountain" 3-31-59 (Indian Woman).

Reyes, Patricia. Films: "The Return of a Man Called Horse" 1976 (Grey Thorn).

Reyguera, Francisco. Films: "The Last of the Fast Guns" 1958 (Pablo); "Major Dundee" 1965 (Old Apache).

Reynard, David. Films: "The Trackers" TVM-1971 (Father Gomez).

Reynolds, Adeline DeWalt (1862-6/13/61). Films: "Pony Soldier" 1952 (White Moon). ¶TV: *Have Gun Will Travel*—"The Hanging Cross" 12-21-57, "Deliver the Body" 5-24-58 (Baba Bruckner).

Reynolds, Alan (1908-6/22/76). TV: *Tales of Wells Fargo*—"The Hijackers" 6-17-57 (Agent), "The Happy Tree" 12-22-58 (John Wynfield); *The Restless Gun*—"Dragon for a Day" 9-29-58 (Dr. Kincade), "Melany" 3-2-59; *Maverick*—"The Thirty-Ninth Star" 11-16-58 (Bartender), "The Maverick Line" 10-20-60 (Phineas Cox); *Wanted—Dead or Alive*—"Reunion for Revenge" 1-24-59, "The Corner" 2-21-59; *Wagon Train*—"The Conchita Vasquez Story" 3-18-59 (Simon Williams); *Yancy Derringer*—"Duel at the Oaks" 4-9-59; *Rawhide*—"Incident Below the Brazos" 5-15-59, "Incident of His Brother's Keeper" 3-31-61 (Stableman), "The Hostage Child" 3-9-62; *Colt .45*—"Appointment in Agoura" 6-7-60; *Tate*—"The Gunfighters" 8-31-60 (Given); *Bronco*—"The Prince of Darkness" 11-6-61 (Hughes); *Bonanza*—"Commitment at Angelus" 4-7-68 (Polk).

Reynolds, Burt (1936-). Films: "Navajo Joe" 1966-Ital./Span. (Navajo Joe); "100 Rifles" 1969 (Yaqui Joe); "Sam Whiskey" 1969 (Sam Whiskey); "Run, Simon, Run" TVM-1970 (Simon Zuniga); "The Man Who Loved Cat Dancing" 1973 (Jay Grobart). ¶TV: *Riverboat*—Regular 1959-60 (Ben Frazer); *Johnny Ringo*—"The Stranger" 5-19-60 (Tad Stuart); *Zane Grey Theater*—"Man from Everywhere" 4-13-61 (Branch Taylor); *Gunsmoke*—Regular 1962-65 (Quint Asper); *Branded*—"Now Join the Human Race" 9-19-65 (Red Hand).

Reynolds, Craig (Hugh Enfield) (1907-10/22/49). Films: "Gordon of Ghost City" 1933-serial (Ed); "Treachery Rides the Range" 1936 (Wade Carter); "Gold Mine in the Sky" 1938 (Larry Cummings); "The Gentleman from Arizona" 1939 (Van Wyck); "Wall Street Cowboy" 1939 (Tony McGrath); "Nevada" 1944 (Cash Burridge); "The Man from Colorado" 1948 (Parry).

Reynolds, Debbie (1932-). Films: "The Second Time Around" 1961 (Lucretia Rogers); "How the West Was Won" 1962 (Lilith Prescott).

Reynolds, Don Kay "Little Brown Jug". Films: "The Yellow Rose of Texas" 1944 (Pinto); "Romance of the West" 1946 (Little Brown Jug); "The Last Round-Up" 1947; "Whirlwind Raiders" 1948 (Tommy Ross); "Ride, Ryder, Ride" 1949 (Little Beaver); "Roll, Thunder, Roll" 1949 (Little Beaver); "Beyond the Purple Hills" 1950 (Chip Beaumont); "Cowboy and the Prizefighter" 1950 (Little Beaver); "The Fighting Redhead" 1950 (Little Beaver); "Streets of Ghost Town" 1950 (Tommy Donner); "The Painted Hills" 1951 (Red Wing); "Snake River Desperadoes" 1951 (Little Hawk).

Reynolds, Gene (1925-). Films: "The Californian" 1937 (Ramon as a Child); "Thunder Trail" 1937 (Richard Ames at Age 14); "Santa Fe Trail" 1940 (Jason Brown). ¶TV: *The Lone Ranger*—"Outlaw Town" 1-12-50.

Reynolds, Harrington (1901-12/22/71). Films: "Ride 'Em, Cowgirl" 1939 (Boyle).

Reynolds, Jack (1900-8/7/77). Films: "Bullwhip" 1958 (Sheriff). ¶TV: *The Cisco Kid*—"Phony Heiress" 7-21-51, "Water Well Oil" 10-13-51; *Wild Bill Hickok*—"Indian Bureau

Story" 7-31-51, "Trapper's Story" 3-18-52; *Sergeant Preston of the Yukon*—"Justice at Goneaway Creek" 2-9-56 (Garrett), "Limping King" 9-13-56 (Red Roberts).

Reynolds, Kay (1940-). TV: *The Outcasts*—"The Heady Wine" 12-2-68 (Maggie).

Reynolds, Lake (1889-2/9/52). Films: "The Whirlwind Rider" 1935.

Reynolds, Lynn (1891-2/25/27). Films: "Cactus Jim's Shopgirl" 1915.

Reynolds, Marjorie (Peg Riley) (1921-). Films: "Tex Rides with the Boy Scouts" 1937 (Norma Willis); "Black Bandit" 1938 (Jane Allen); "Guilty Trails" 1938 (Jackie); "The Last Stand" 1938 (Nancy); "Man's Country" 1938 (Madge Crane); "The Overland Express" 1938 (Jean Greeley); "Six Shootin' Sheriff" 1938 (Molly Morgan); "Western Trails" 1938 (Alice); "The Phantom Stage" 1939 (Mary); "Racketeers of the Range" 1939 (Helen); "Timber Stampede" 1939 (Anne Carr, the Reporter); "Cyclone on Horseback" 1941; "Dude Cowboy" 1941 (Barbara); "Robin Hood of the Pecos 1941 (Jeanie Grayson); "Heaven Only Knows" 1947 (Ginger); "Bad Men of Tombstone" 1949 (Julie). ¶TV: *Whispering Smith*—"The Idol" 9-18-61 (Baby Doll Harris); *Tales of Wells Fargo*—"Don't Wake a Tiger" 5-12-62 (Helen Mapes); *Wide Country*—"The Quest for Jacob Blaufus" 3-7-63 (Katy Blaufus); *Laramie*—"The Last Battleground" 4-16-63.

Reynolds, Vera (1899-4/22/62). Films: "Hearts of Oak" 1923; "The Lone Rider" 1930 (Mary).

Reynolds, William (1931-). Films: "The Cimarron Kid" 1951 (Will Dalton); "The Battle at Apache Pass" 1952 (Lem Bent); "The Raiders" 1952 (Frank Morrell); "Gunsmoke" 1953 (Brazos); "A Distant Trumpet" 1964 (Lt. Theo Mainwaring). ¶TV: *Death Valley Days*—"Camel Train" 10-7-57; *Maverick*—"Rope of Cards" 1-19-58 (Bill Gregg), "Diamond in the Rough" 1-26-58 (Reynolds), "Holiday at Hollow Rock" 12-28-58 (Ted Blake), "A Cure for Johnny Rain" 12-20-59 (Johnny Rain); *Bronco*—"The Baron of Broken Lance" 1-13-59 (Pete Loomis), "Borrowed Glory" 2-24-59 (Dick Nelson); *Zane Grey Theater*—"The Last Raid" 2-26-59 (Bruce McVeigh); *Wagon Train*—"The Clara Duncan Story" 4-22-59 (Roger Garrett); *Temple Houston*—"The Siege at Thayer's Bluff" 11-7-63 (Paul Bannerman).

Rhine, William. Films: "The Devil's Twin" 1927 (Hotel Clerk); "The Terror of Bar X" 1927 (Ross Hunter).

Rhoades, Barbara (1947-). Films: "The Shakiest Gun in the West" 1968 (Penelope Cushings); "The Silent Gun" TVM-1969; "There Was a Crooked Man" 1970 (Miss Jessie Brundidge). ¶TV: *The Virginian*—"With Help from Ulysses" 1-17-68 (Josie); *Alias Smith and Jones*—"The Fifth Victim" 3-25-71; *Nakia*—"Roots of Anger" 11-30-74 (Jackie Thayer).

Rhodes, Betty Jane. Films: "The Arizona Raiders" 1936 (Lenta Lindsay); "Along the Rio Grande" 1941 (Mary).

Rhodes, Billie (1894-3/12/88). Films: "The Big Horn Massacre" 1913; "The Love Call" 1919 (Kid Allen).

Rhodes, Donnelly (1938-). Films: "Gunfight in Abilene" 1967 (Joe Slade); "Butch Cassidy and the Sundance Kid" 1969 (Macon). ¶TV: *Maverick*—"A Flock of Trouble" 2-14-60 (Cain); *Bonanza*—"San Francisco Holiday" 4-2-60, "The Mission" 9-17-60 (Latigo); *Wagon Train*—"The Wanda Snow Story" 1-17-65 (Jeremiah Stevens); *Laredo*—"Rendezvous at Arillo" 10-7-65 (Bob Jamison), "The Would-Be Gentleman of Laredo" 4-14-66 (Don Carlos); *The Virginian*—"The Wolves Up Front, the Jackals Behind" 3-23-66 (Ben Colby); *The Road West*—"Pariah" 12-5-66 (Red Eagle); *Dundee and the Culhane*—9-13-67 (Luis Montoya); *Wild Wild West*—"The Night of the Legion of Death" 11-24-67 (Capt. Dansby), "The Night of the Cossacks" 3-21-69 (Count Balkovitch); *Custer*—"Dangerous Prey" 12-6-67 (War Cloud); *Cimarron Strip*—"Big Jessie" 2-8-68 (Bill Baylor); *Here Come the Brides*—"A Wild Colonial Boy" 10-24-69 (Pat); *The Chisholms*—"The Siren Song" 3-15-80 (Padre).

Rhodes, Grandon (1905-6/9/87). Films: "Canadian Pacific" 1949 (Dr. Mason); "Streets of Laredo" 1949 (Phil Jessup); "Tucson" 1949 (Dean Sherman); "The Eagle and the Hawk" 1950 (Governor Lubbock); "Cripple Creek" 1952 (Drummond); "On Top of Old Smoky" 1953 (Doc Judson); "A Man Alone" 1955 (Luke Joiner); "Texas Lady" 1955; "Oklahoma Territory" 1960 (Blackwell). ¶TV: *U.S. Marshal*—"Inside Job" 1-3-59; *Lawman*—"The Senator" 5-17-59 (Fergus); *The Deputy*—"Silent Gun" 1-23-60 (the Mayor); *Bonanza*—"Dark Star" 4-23-60, "The Quest" 9-

30-62, "Bullet for a Bride" 2-16-64 (Doctor), "Triangle" 5-17-64, "Once a Doctor" 2-28-65, "Patchwork Man" 5-23-65 (Doctor), "The Brass Box" 9-26-65 (Doctor), "To Kill a Buffalo" 1-9-66 (Doctor), "Destiny's Child" 1-30-66 (Doctor), "Peace Officer" 2-6-66 (Doc Brown), "Three Brides for Hoss" 2-20-66 (Doctor), "Her Brother's Keeper" 3-6-66 (Doctor), "Shining in Spain" 3-27-66 (Doctor), "The Genius" 4-3-66 (Doctor), "The Fighters" 4-24-66 (Doctor), "Tommy" 12-18-66 (Doctor), "Amigo" 2-12-67 (Dr. Martin), "Dark Enough to See the Stars" 3-12-67 (Dr. Martin), "The Greedy Ones" 5-14-67, "Night of Reckoning" 10-15-67 (Dr. Martin), "Six Black Horses" 11-26-67 (Dr. Martin); *The Outlaws*—"Ballad for a Badman" 10-6-60 (Thorne); *Laramie*—"Cactus Lady" 2-21-61 (Mr. Thomson); *Laredo*—"Which Way Did They Go?" 11-18-65.

Rhodes, Hari (1932-1/14/92). TV: *Have Gun Will Travel*—"The Shooting of Jesse May" 10-20-60 (Ansel James); *The Westerner*—"Line Camp" 12-9-60; *Wagon Train*—"The Stark Bluff Story" 4-6-64 (Jefferson Washington); *Rawhide*—"Incident at Seven Fingers" 5-7-64 (Corporal Dunbar).

Rhodes, Jordan (1939-). TV: *Bonanza*—"First Love" 12-26-72 (Dan Edwards); *Father Murphy*—"State Aid" 12-15-81 (Asa Taylor).

Rhue, Madlyn (1937-). Films: "He Rides Tall" 1964 (Ellie Daniels); "Stranger on the Run" TVM-1967 (Alma Britten). ¶TV: *Have Gun Will Travel*—"The Manhunter" 6-7-58 (Mrs. Nelson), "The Man Who Lost" 2-7-59 (Elizabeth); *Black Saddle*—"Client: Reynolds" 5-23-59 (Julie Reynolds); *Riverboat*—"About Roger Mowbray" 9-27-59 (Cassie Baird); *Cheyenne*—"Prisoner of Moon Mesa" 11-16-59 (Ellen); *The Rebel*—"In Memorian" 12-6-59 (Beth); *Tales of Wells Fargo*—"Woman with a Gun" 12-7-59 (Linda); *Gunsmoke*—"Tag, You're It" 12-19-59 (Rusty); *Laramie*—"The Pass" 12-29-59 (Eve); *Hotel De Paree*—"Sundance Goes to Kill" 1-22-60 (Sarah); *The Alaskans*—"Disaster at Gold Hill" 3-20-60 (Fay Loomis); *Pony Express*—"The Last Mile" 4-6-60 (Ellen Fairchild); *The Outlaws*—"Ballad for a Badman" 10-6-60 (Rose Dabney); *Bonanza*—"Day of Reckoning" 10-22-60 (Mrs. Matsou); *Sugarfoot*—"A Noose for Nora" 10-24-60 (Nora Sutton); *Stagecoach West*—"A Place of Still Waters" 4-11-61 (Maria Larenz); *Rawhide*—"Inci-

dent at Rio Doloroso" 5-10-63 (Inez Maldenado); *The Virginian*—"A Portrait of Marie Valonne" 11-6-63 (Marie Valonne); *Daniel Boone*—"The Hostages" 1-7-65 (Ester Mancour); *A Man Called Shenandoah*—"Special Talent for Killing" 12-6-65 (Ann Clayton); *Laredo*—"The Would-Be Gentleman of Laredo" 4-14-66 (Dona Dolores); *Iron Horse*—"The Man from New Chicago" 11-14-66 (Angela); *Wild Wild West*—"Night of the Bubbling Death" 9-8-67 (Carlotta Waters); *Cowboy in Africa*—"Work of Art" 3-11-68 (Christie Blaine); *The Guns of Will Sonnett*—"The Straw Man" 11-8-68 (Marion Hagger); *The Men from Shiloh*—"Jump-Up" 3-24-71 (Frankie).

Rhys-Davies, John (1944-). Films: "No Man's Land" TVM-1984 (John Grimshaw); "Desperado: Badlands Justice" TVM-1989 (Richard Marriott).

Riano, Rennie (1899-7/3/71). Films: "Kit Carson" 1940 (Miss Genevieve Pilchard); "They Died with Their Boots On" 1941 (Nurse); "Man from Music Mountain" 1943 (Christina Kellog); "Bad Bascomb" 1946 (Lucy Lovejoy); "Jiggs and Maggie Out West" 1950 (Maggie). ¶TV: *Wild Bill Hickok*—"Hepsibah" 11-6-51.

Rice, Florence (1911-2/22/74). Films: "Cherokee Strip" 1940 (Kate Cross); "The Kid from Texas" 1939 (Margo Thomas); "Stand Up and Fight" 1939 (Susan Griffith).

Rice, Frank (1892-1/9/36). Films: "The Sagebrush Musketeers" 1921; "The Secret of Butte Ridge" 1921; "Blood Test" 1923; "The Desert Rider" 1923 (Toby Jones); "The Forbidden Trail" 1923 (Toby Jones); "The Red Warning" 1923 (Toby Jones); "The Galloping Ace" 1924 (Knack Williams); "The Ridin' Kid from Powder River" 1924 (Cal Huxley); "Wolves of the North" 1924-serial; "The Call of Courage" 1925 (Slim); "Moccasins" 1925 (Sheriff Hard Tack Avery); "Riders of Mystery" 1925 (Jerry Jones); "Ridin' Pretty" 1925 (Barbwire); "Spook Ranch" 1925 (Sheriff); "Two-Fisted Jones" 1925 (Old Bill); "The Border Sheriff" 1926 (Hewitt); "Davy Crockett at the Fall of the Alamo" 1926 (Lige Beardsley); "The Fighting Buckaroo" 1926 (Andy Parker); "The Fighting Peacemaker" 1926 (Sheriff); "The Boy Rider" 1927 (Hank Robbins); "Sky-High Saunders" 1927 (Whispering Hicks); "The Slingshot Kid" 1927 (Toby); "Tom's Gang" 1927 (Andy Barker); "The Bantam

Cowboy" 1928 (Sidewinder Steve); "Orphan of the Sage" 1928 (Hank Robbins); "The Pinto Kid" 1928 (Hank Robbins); "Rough Ridin' Red" 1928 (Hank Robbins); "The Lawless Legion" 1929 (Flapjack); "The Overland Telegraph" 1929 (Easy); "Pals of the Prairie" 1929 (Hank Robbins); "The Royal Rider" 1929 (Wild West Show Member); "Stairs of Sand" 1929 (Stage Driver); "The Vagabond Cub" 1929 (Hank Robbins); "The Wagon Master" 1929 (Grasshopper); "Parade of the West" 1930 (Swift); "Shadow Ranch" 1930 (Williams); "Song of the Cabellero" 1930 (Andrea); "Sons of the Saddle" 1930; "Border Law" 1931 (Thunder Rogers); "The Conquering Horde" 1931 (Spud Grogan); "Mounted Fury" 1931 (Sandy McNab); "Riders of the North" 1931 (Parson); "Shotgun Pass" 1931 (Sagebrush); "The Squaw Man" 1931 (Grouchy); "Forbidden Trail" 1932 (Sheriff); "Freighters of Destiny" 1932 (Rough); "Hello Trouble" 1932 (Hardpan); "The Sunset Trail" 1932 (Taterbug); "King of the Arena" 1933; "The Phantom Thunderbolt" 1933 (Nevady); "Robbers' Roost" 1933 (Daniels); "Somewhere in Sonora" 1933 (Riley); "The Trail Drive" 1933 (Thirsty); "The Fiddlin' Buckaroo" 1934 (Banty); "The Fighting Ranger" 1934 (Thunder); "The Last Round-Up" 1934 (Shrimp); "Loser's End" 1934 (Amos Butts); "The Red Rider" 1934-serial (Harp); "Terror of the Plains" 1934 (Banty); "The Thundering Herd" 1934 (Blacksmith); "Wheels of Destiny" 1934 (Pinwheel); "Border Brigands" 1935 (Roxy O'Leary); "Ivory-Handled Gun" 1935 (Pike); "Nevada" 1935 (Shorty); "Powdersmoke Range" 1935 (Sourdough Jenkins); "Ruggles of Red Gap" 1935 (Hank); "Stone of Silver Creek" 1935 (Tom Lucas); "Trails of the Wild" 1935 (Missouri); "Valley of Wanted Men" 1935 (Ned); "The Oregon Trail" 1936 (Red).

Rice, Jack (1893-12/14/68). Films: "Rhythm Wranglers" 1937-short; "A Western Welcome" 1938-short; "Men of the Timberland" 1941; "The Musical Bandit" 1941-short; "Westward Ho-Hum" 1941-short; "Under Western Skies" 1945 (Neil Matthews); "The Marksman" 1953; "The Silver Whip" 1953 (Morrison); "The First Traveling Saleslady" 1956 (Dowling). ¶TV: *Bonanza*—"Elizabeth, My Love" 5-27-61 (Van Meer).

Rice, Miriam. Films: "The Border Menace" 1934 (Helen Milette).

Rice, Roy (1887-12/29/66).

Films: "The Judgement Book" 1935 (James Burke); "Desert Guns" 1936 (Teeter).

Rice, Sam (1874-3/12/46). Films: "Moonlight on the Prairie" 1935 (Bartender); "Song of the Saddle" 1936 (Immigrant); "Trailin' West" 1936 (Bartender).

Rich, Adam (1968-). TV: *Gun Shy*—Regular 1983 (Clovis).

Rich, Allan (1927-). Films: "Scott Free" TVM-1976 (Max); "The Frisco Kid" 1979.

Rich, Christopher. Films: "The Gambler Returns: The Luck of the Draw" TVM-1991. ¶TV: *Adventures of Brisco County, Jr.*—"AKA Kansas" 12-17-93 (Doc McCoy).

Rich, Dick (1909-3/29/67). Films: "Headin' East" 1937 (Clipper); "Let Freedom Ring" 1939 (Bumper Jackson); "Brigham Young—Frontiersman" 1940 (Mob Leader); "Buck Benny Rides Again" 1940 (2nd Cowhand); "Danger Ahead" 1940 (Maxwell); "The Dark Command" 1940 (Cantrell Man); "Lucky Cisco Kid" 1940 (Stage Driver Tex); "Ride on, Vaquero" 1941 (Curly); "Western Union" 1941 (Porky); "In Old Oklahoma" 1943 (Man on Train); "The Ox-Bow Incident" 1943 (Deputy Butch Mapes); "Bugles in the Afternoon" 1952 (Biers); "The Outcasts of Poker Flat" 1952 (Drunk); "The Fighting Lawman" 1953; "Overland Pacific" 1954 (Saber); "A Man Alone" 1955 (Kincaid). ¶TV: *The Cisco Kid*—"Postal Inspector" 8-4-51, "Kid Sister Trouble" 9-15-51; Colt .45—"The Rival Gun" 10-25-59 (Butch); *The Lone Ranger*—"Prisoner in Jeopardy" 8-20-53; *The Gene Autry Show*—"The Portrait of White Cloud" 10-15-55, "Go West, Young Lady" 11-19-55; *Gunsmoke*—"No Indians" 12-8-56 (Sam Butler), "Twelfth Night" 12-28-57 (Farmer), "Hanging Man" 4-19-58 (Hank), "The Choice" 5-9-59 (Tough), "Unwanted Deputy" 3-5-60 (Rudd); *Zane Grey Theater*—"Until the Man Dies" 1-25-57 (Wade Powers), "They Were Four" 3-15-57 (Champion); *The Roy Rogers Show*—"Brady's Bonanza" 3-31-57 (Jim Morn); *Sugarfoot*—"Bullet Proof" 1-21-58 (Seven Blankets); *The Texan*—"The First Notch" 10-20-58 (Whitey Rupp); *The Rifleman*—"Young Englishman" 12-16-58 (Line Boss); *Have Gun Will Travel*—"Homecoming" 5-23-59, "Never Help the Devil" 4-16-60 (Sheriff Tobey); *Tales of Wells Fargo*—"Desert Showdown" 9-14-59 (South), "The Easterner" 1-11-60 (Scar Wilson); *The Rebel*—"School Days" 11-

15-59 (Carl Armbruster), "Land" 2-21-60 (Dan Hauser); *Bonanza*—"The Hanging Posse" 11-28-59; *Hotel De Paree*—"Sundance and the Kid from Nowhere" 1-15-60 (Pete); *The Alaskans*—"The Long Pursuit" 1-31-60 (Jeb Leary); *Bronco*—"Legacy of Twisted Creed" 4-19-60 (Sergeant Chase); *The Deputy*—"A Time to Sow" 4-23-60 (Harris); *Lawman*—"Man on a Mountain" 6-12-60 (Joe Perell); *Laramie*—"Three Roads West" 10-4-60 (Bartender); *Wanted—Dead or Alive*—"The Voice of Silence" 2-15-61 (Harry Brice); *Cheyenne*—"Cross Purpose" 10-9-61 (Starbuck).

Rich, Frances. Films: "Diamond Trail" 1933 (Lois Miller).

Rich, Gloria. Films: "Outlaws of Sonora" 1938 (Jane).

Rich, Irene (1891-4/22/88). Films: "The Lone Star Ranger" 1919 (Mrs. Laramie); "A Man in the Open" 1919 (Kate); "Desperate Trails" 1921 (Mrs. Walker); "The Ropin' Fool" 1921; "Sunset Jones" 1921 (Marion Rand); "While Justice Waits" 1922 (Nell Hunt); "The Yosemite Trail" 1922 (Eve Marsham); "Dangerous Trails" 1923 (Grace Alderson); "Snowdrift" 1923 (Kitty); "Queen of the Yukon" 1940 (Sadie Martin); "Angel and the Badman" 1947 (Mrs. Worth); "Fort Apache" 1948 (Mrs. Mary O'Rourke).

Rich, Lillian (1900-1/5/54). Films: "The Ruse of the Rattlesnake" 1921 (Helen Sanderson); "The Sage Hen" 1921 (Stella Sanson); "The Bearcat" 1922 (Alys May); "Catch My Smoke" 1922 (Mary Thorne); "Man to Man" 1922 (Terry Temple); "The Man from Wyoming" 1924 (Helen Messiter); "The Phantom Horseman" 1924 (Dorothy Mason); "Braveheart" 1925 (Dorothy Nelson); "Soft Shoes" 1925 (Faith O'Day); "Whispering Smith" 1926 (Dicksie Dunning); "The Old Code" 1928 (Marie d'Arcy); "Mark of the Spur" 1932 (Alice Beckett).

Rich, Phil (1896-2/22/56). Films: "Escape from Fort Bravo" 1953 (Barman); "Tall Man Riding" 1955.

Rich, Vernon (1906-2/7/78). Films: "The Far Horizons" 1955; "Tall Man Riding" 1955. ¶TV: *Sergeant Preston of the Yukon*—"Hidden Gold" 5-24-56 (Ezra Barton); *Wagon Train*—"The Mary Ellen Thomas Story" 12-24-58 (Jenkins); *Buckskin*—"The Monkey's Uncle" 1-12-59 (Garland); *Gunsmoke*—"Owney Tupper Had a Daughter" 4-4-64 (Art); *Lancer*—"The High Riders" 9-24-68.

Rich, Vivian (1893-11/17/57).

Films: "The Belle of the Bar Z Ranch" 1912; "The Half-Breed's Way" 1912; "The Girl and the Greaser" 1913; "Hearts and Horses" 1913; "Quicksands" 1913; "Cameo of Yellowstone" 1914; "A Child of the Desert" 1914; "The Pote Lariat of the Flying A" 1914; "Redbird Wins" 1914; "Sir Galahad of Twilight" 1914; "The Assayer of Lone Gap" 1915; "The Exile of Bar-K Ranch" 1915; "The Poet of the Peaks" 1915; "The Purple Hills" 1915; "A Question of Honor" 1915; "The Getaway" 1917; "The Man from Montana" 1917 (Meta Cooper); "Code of the Yukon" 1918 (Lola Crawford); "The Mints of Hell" 1919 (Aline Chaudiare); "The Last Straw" 1920 (Jane Hunter); "The Lone Wagon" 1923; "Idaho" 1925-serial; "Hell's Valley" 1931 (Duenna).

Richards, Addison (1902-3/22/64). Films: "The Lone Cowboy" 1934 (Dobe Jones); "Home on the Range" 1935 (Beady Pierce); "The Eagle's Brood" 1936 (Big Henry); "Song of the Saddle" 1936 (Frank Wilson, Sr.); "Sutter's Gold" 1936 (James Marshall); "Trailin' West" 1936 (Curley Thorne); "The Barrier" 1937 (Runnion); "Empty Holsters" 1937; "God's Country and the Woman" 1937 (Gaskett); "Bad Lands" 1939 (Rayburn); "Arizona" 1940 (Captain Hunter); "Cherokee Strip" 1940 (New Strawn); "Geronimo" 1940 (Frederick Allison); "The Man from Dakota" 1940 (Provost Marshal); "Man from Montreal" 1940 (Capt. Owens); "My Little Chickadee" 1940 (Judge); "Northwest Passage" 1940 (Lt. Crofton); "Pony Express Days" 1940-short; "Santa Fe Trail" 1940 (Sheriff); "Wyoming" 1940 (Kincaid); "Back in the Saddle" 1941 (Duke Winston); "Badlands of Dakota" 1941 (General Custer); "Sheriff of Tombstone" 1941 (Mayor Keeler); "Texas" 1941 (Matt Laskan); "They Died with Their Boots On" 1941 (Adjutant); "Western Union" 1941 (Capt. Harlow); "Cowboy Serenade" 1942; "Men of Texas" 1942 (Silas Hurlbert); "Ridin' Down the Canyon" 1942 (Jordan); "Deerslayer" 1943 (Mr. Hutter); "Oklahoma Outlaws" 1943-short; "Wagon Wheels West" 1943-short; "Barbary Coast Gent" 1944 (Wade Gamelin); "Bordertown Trail" 1944; "Raiders of Ghost City" 1944-serial (Colonel Sewell); "Bells of Rosarita" 1945 (Slim Phillips); "Royal Mounted Rides Again" 1945-serial (Jackson Decker); "Renegades" 1946 (Sheriff); "Rustlers" 1949 (Abbott); "Davy Crockett, Indian Scout" 1950 (Capt. Weightman); "Fort Yuma"

1955 (Gen. Crook); "The Broken Star" 1956 (Wayne Forrester); "Fastest Gun Alive" 1956 (Doc Jennings); "Fury at Gunsight Pass" 1956 (Charles Hanford); "Reprisal!" 1956 (Judge); "Walk the Proud Land" 1956 (Gov. Safford); "Gunsight Ridge" 1957 (Sheriff Jones); "Last of the Badmen" 1957 (Dillon); "The Saga of Hemp Brown" 1958 (Colonel); "The Oregon Trail" 1959 (President James K. Polk); "Frontier Uprising" 1961 (Cmdr. Kimball); "The Gambler Wore a Gun" 1961 (Doc Devlin); "The Raiders" 1964 (Huntington Lawford). ¶TV: *Sheriff of Cochise*—"The Check Artist" 9-14-56; *Zane Grey Theater*—"The Lariat" 11-2-56 (Judge Lovett); *Broken Arrow*—"Justice" 11-27-56 (Dougherty); *Jim Bowie*—"A Horse for Old Hickory" 1-4-57 (Senator Holcomb), "Hare and Tortoise" 11-22-57 (Frasier London); *Tales of Wells Fargo*—"Billy the Kid" 10-21-57, "The Killer" 12-1-58 (Keely Crawford), "Return to Yesterday" 1-13-62 (Simon Congreve); *Wanted—Dead or Alive*—"The Giveaway Gun" 10-11-58, "Payoff at Pinto" 5-21-60 (Dr. John Allen); *The Californians*—"Dangerous Journey" 11-25-58 (Durkin); *Trackdown*—"Terror" 2-4-59 (Doc Calhoun), "The Gang" 2-25-59 (Doc Jay Calhoun), "The Eyes of Jerry Kelson" 4-22-59 (Doc Jay Calhoun), "Blind Alley" 9-16-59 (Doc Jay Calhoun); *Buckskin*—"Fry's Wife" 2-9-59 (Sheriff Devlin); *The Adventures of Rin Tin Tin*—"The Accusation" 2-13-59 (Gen. Sherman); *Yancy Derringer*—"The Louisiana Dude" 2-26-59 (Judge Harper); *Rawhide*—"Incident of the Dog Days" 4-17-59 (Jed Blaine), "Incident of the Running Iron" 3-10-61 (Frank Miller), "The Greedy Town" 2-16-62 (Judge Wainright); *The Texan*—"Traildust" 10-19-59; *The Deputy*—Regular 1959-61 (Doc Landy); *Gunslinger*—"The Zone" 3-2-61 (John Pearson); *Laramie*—"Wolf Cub" 11-21-61, "The Replacement" 3-27-62; *Bonanza*—"The Horse Breaker" 11-26-61 (Dr. Kay), "A Stranger Passed This Way" 3-3-63 (Dr. Hickman); *Lawman*—"The Hold-Out" 2-18-62 (Ben Thurston); *The Virginian*—"The Exiles" 1-9-63.

Richards, Ann. Films: "Badman's Territory" 1946 (Henryette Alcott).

Richards, Charles (1899-7/29/48). Films: "The Call of the Canyon" 1923 (Roger Newton).

Richards, Cully (1910-6/17/78). Films: "Robin Hood of El Dorado" 1936 (Juan).

Richards, David. TV: *The Leg-*

end of Jesse James*—"South Wind" 2-14-66 (Jim Younger), "As Far as the Sea" 3-21-66 (Jim Younger), "Dark Side of the Moon" 4-18-66 (Jim Younger); *The Big Valley*—"The Velvet Trap" 11-7-66; *Young Riders*—"Dead Ringer" 10-6-90 (Bank Manager), "Judgment Day" 1-5-91 (Horace Pullman), "The Exchange" 5-4-91 (Mayor of Benton).

Richards, Frank (1909-4/15/92). Films: "The Cowboy and the Indians" 1949 (Smiley Martin); "Tough Assignment" 1949 (Steve); "Western Pacific Agent" 1950; "South of Caliente" 1951 (Studsy); "The Savage" 1952 (Sgt. Norris); "Destry" 1954 (Dummy); "Davy Crockett and the River Pirates" 1956 (Little Harpe); "Man from Del Rio" 1956 (Stableman); "Running Target" 1956 (Castagna); "The Hard Man" 1957 (Vince Kane); "The Persuader" 1957 (Steve); "The Storm Rider" 1957 (Will Feylan); "Escape from Red Rock" 1958 (Price). ¶TV: *The Lone Ranger*—"The Devil's Bog" 2-5-53, "Son of Adoption" 3-19-53, "The Woman from Omaha" 7-2-53, "Texas Draw" 11-5-54 (Matt); *The Cisco Kid*—"Quiet Sunday Morning" 12-5-53; *Walt Disney Presents*—"Davy Crockett"—Regular 1954-55 (Little Harp); *Fury*—"Stolen Fury" 1-28-56 (Jackson); *Annie Oakley*—"Flint and Steel" 10-14-56 (Creede); *Sergeant Preston of the Yukon*—"The Stolen Malamute" 4-4-57 (Judge Jackson); *The Restless Gun*—"Thicker Than Water" 12-9-57 (Sam Goss); *Death Valley Days*—"The Greatest Scout of All" 1-13-58; *Maverick*—"A Tale of Three Cities" 10-18-59 (Sam); *The Deputy*—"The Return of Simon Fry" 2-13-60 (Kipp); *Rawhide*—"The Photographer" 12-11-64 (Emmett).

Richards, Gordon (1893-1/13/64). Films: "Rose Marie" 1954 (Attorney). ¶TV: *The Adventures of Rin Tin Tin*—"Hubert Goes West" 5-18-56 (Hubert Twombly), "Hubert's Niece" 5-10-57; *Wyatt Earp*—"Wyatt's Love Affair" 10-2-56 (Judge Fabian); *Maverick*—"The Belcastle Brand" 10-12-58 (Butler); *Wanted—Dead or Alive*—"The Matchmaker" 9-19-59.

Richards, Grant (1911-7/4/63). Films: "Hopalong Cassidy Returns" 1936 (Bob Claiborne); "Oklahoma Territory" 1960 (Bigelow). ¶TV: *Jim Bowie*—"Rezin Bowie, Gambler" 3-22-57 (Slim Spaulding), "Home Sweet Home" 1-31-58 (Grady Sturdevant); *Sergeant Preston of the Yukon*—"The Stolen Malamute" 4-4-57 (Pete Loomis); *Tales of the Texas*

Rangers- "Both Barrels Blazing" 10-20-57 (Joe Barker); *Trackdown*—"The Farrand Story" 1-10-58 (Norval Franklin); *Wyatt Earp*—"Wyatt Fights" 2-25-58 (Luke Short); *Tombstone Territory*—"Strange Vengeance" 4-9-58 (Ben Beaumont); *Buckskin*—"Tell Me, Leonardo" 9-25-58 (Charlie Hampton); *The Texan*—"Jail for the Innocents" 11-3-58 (Dan Keyes); *The Rifleman*—"The Apprentice Sheriff" 12-9-58, "Gunfire" 1-15-62 (Dave Chester), "The Tinhorn" 3-12-62 (Keeler); *Cimarron City*—"The Beauty and the Sorrow" 2-7-59 (Jason); *Rawhide*—"Incident of the Thirteenth Man" 10-23-59 (Sheriff); *Laramie*—"Dark Verdict" 11-24-59 (Carter); *Riverboat*—"Path of an Eagle" 2-1-60 (Capt. James O'Bannion); *Johnny Ringo*—"Mrs. Ringo" 2-11-60 (King); *Death Valley Days*—"Learnin' at Dirty Devil" 11-2-60 (Hank Lanier); *Bonanza*—"The Quest" 9-30-62 (Will Poavey).

Richards, Jeff (1922-89). Films: "Many Rivers to Cross" 1955 (Fremont); "The Marauders" 1955 (Corey Everett); "Waco" 1966 (Kallen). ¶TV: *Jefferson Drum*—Regular 1958-59 (Jefferson Drum); *Laramie*—"No Second Chance" 12-6-60 (Kem Backer); *Rawhide*—"Incident of His Brother's Keeper" 3-31-61 (Jubal Evans).

Richards, Keith (1914-3/23/87). Films: "Secrets of the Wastelands" 1941 (Clay Elliott); "Lost Canyon" 1943; "Jesse James Rides Again" 1947-serial (Wynn); "Where the North Begins" 1947; "The Gay Ranchero" 1948 (Slim); "Sons of Adventure" 1948 (Harry); "Shadows of the West" 1949 (Steve); "Trail's End" 1949 (Bill); "The James Brothers of Missouri" 1950-serial (Jesse James/John Howard); "North of the Great Divide" 1950 (Dacona); "Spoilers of the Plains" 1951 (Guard); "Rebel City" 1953 (Temple); "At Gunpoint" 1955 (Man in Saloon); "Yaqui Drums" 1956; "Ambush at Cimarron Pass" 1958 (Private Lasky); "The Gambler Wore a Gun" 1961 (Het Larkin). ¶TV: *The Range Rider*—"Outlaw's Double" 9-23-51; *The Cisco Kid*—"Hidden Valley Pirates" 10-27-51, "Quarter Horse" 12-8-51, "The Kid Brother" 2-9-52, "Dutchman's Flat" 3-15-52, "Commodore Goes West" 7-12-52, "Bandaged Badman" 10-11-52, "Chinese Gold" 10-18-52, "Rodeo" 12-27-52, "Steel Plow" 1-31-53, "Trouble in Tonopah" 3-21-53, "The Kidnapped Cameraman" 10-24-53, "The Two Wheeler" 11-21-53, "Dangerous Shoemaker" 5-15-54; *The Gene Autry Show*—"The Kid Comes

West" 12-8-51, "Rocky River Feud" 1-18-52, "Stage to San Dimas" 10-8-55, "Guns Below the Border" 11-5-55; *Wild Bill Hickok*—"The Sheriff Was a Redhead" 7-15-52, "The Music Teacher" 12-2-52, "Treasure Trail" 12-30-52; *Fury*—"Joey Saves the Day" 12-10-55 (Hank); *The Roy Rogers Show*—"The Minister's Son" 3-23-52, "False Faces" 2-5-56, "Smoking Guns" 3-3-56, "Sheriff Missing" 3-17-56, "The Morse Mixup" 3-24-56 (Ed Morse); *The Lone Ranger*—"The Deserter" 4-23-53, "Trigger Finger 4-7-55, "The Breaking Point" 1-24-57; *Judge Roy Bean*—"Ah Sid, Cowboy" 1-1-56 (Keats), "The Hidden Truth" 1-1-56 (Johnnie Dexter), "The Judge's Dilemma" 1-1-56 (Connors); *Annie Oakley*—"Annie and the Bicycle Riders" 7-8-56 (Mandel); *Wyatt Earp*—"Justice" 12-25-56 (Dort), "The Imitation Jesse James" 2-4-58 (Henry Harrison Hammer), "Bat Jumps the Reservation" 2-10-59 (Al Watrous); *The Adventures of Rin Tin Tin*—"Higgins' Last Stand" 1-4-57 (Abe Tyson), "Stagecoach to Phoenix" 3-22-59 (Dan Morris); *Tales of Wells Fargo*—"The Prisoner" 2-17-58 (Curly), "Frightened Witness" 12-26-60 (Lee); *Tales of the Texas Rangers*—"Traitor's Gold" 10-2-58 (Sam Devers); *Rough Riders*—"Strand of Wire" 12-18-58 (Connolly), "The Plot to Assassinate President Johnson" 2-5-59 (Steves); *The Rebel*—"The Rattler" 3-13-60 (Tom Weed); *The Alaskans*—"The Bride Wore Black" 4-10-60 (Arlington); *Bonanza*—"The Fugitive" 2-11-61 (Willie Twilight), "The Auld Sod" 2-4-62, "The Way Station" 10-29-62; *Lawman*—"Fugitive" 4-2-61 (Casey Cormack); *Bronco*—"The Prince of Darkness" 11-6-61 (Felton), "Beginner's Luck" 1-1-62 (Jim Gant); *Wagon Train*—"The Nancy Davis Story" 5-16-62 (Lace Andrews); *Laramie*—"War Hero" 10-2-62 (Captain Winters).

Richards, Paul (1924-12/10/74). Films: "War Paint" 1953 (Perkins); "Tall Man Riding" 1955 (the Peso Kid); "The Black Whip" 1956 (Murdock); "Tension at Table Rock" 1956 (Sam Murdock); "Blood Arrow" 1958 (Brill); "Four Fast Guns" 1959 (Hoag); "The Over-the-Hill Gang Rides Again" TVM-1970 (Sam Braham). ¶TV: *Hopalong Cassidy*—"Death by Proxy" 6-14-52; *Gunsmoke*—"Matt Gets It" 9-10-55 (Don Grat), "Mr. and Mrs. Amber" 8-4-56 (Neil Amber), "Joe Phy" 1-4-58 (Joe Phy), "The Jackals" 2-12-68 (Mel Deevers); *The Adventures of Rin Tin Tin*—"Boone's Wedding Day" 11-18-55, "The Last Chance" 12-16-55;

Frontier—"The Texicans" 1-8-56 (Louis Rose), "The Big Dry" 3-18-56 (John Webb), "Salt War" 4-22-56 (Will Shaw); *Cavalry Patrol*—Pilot 1956 (Mango); *Sheriff of Cochise*—"Grandfather Grandson" 2-11-57 (Larry); *Broken Arrow*—"The Desperado" 3-26-57 (Bret Younger); *Zane Grey Theater*—"Proud Woman" 10-25-57 (Frank Frayne), "The Scaffold" 10-9-58 (John Hart), "Hang the Heart High" 1-15-59 (Jud Moore), "Hand on the Latch" 10-29-59 (Prisoner), "Blood Red" 1-29-61 (Jess Whiting); *Trackdown*—"Like Father" 11-1-57; *El Coyote Rides*—Pilot 1958 (Harvey Logan); *Tombstone Territory*—"Thicker Than Water" 9-10-58 (Milo Wade), 12-25-59 (Reed Barker); *Jefferson Drum*—"Showdown" 9-26-58 (Les Groves); *Rawhide*—"Incident at Barker Springs" 2-20-59 (Brozo), "The Bosses' Daughter" 2-2-62 (Vance Caldwell); *Black Saddle*—"Client: Martinez" 3-7-59 (Juan Martinez); *The Rifleman*—"The Trade" 3-10-59 (Sam Morley), "A Young Man's Fancy" 2-5-62; *Zorro*—"The Mountain Man" 3-19-59 (Hernando), "The Hound of the Sierras" 3-26-59 (Hernando), "Manhunt" 4-2-59 (Hernando); *Have Gun Will Travel*—"The Chase" 4-11-59 (Brazo), "Beau Beste" 10-13-62 (Sheriff John Dobbs); *Bat Masterson*—"The Conspiracy" 6-17-59 & 6-24-59 (Ned Ruggles), "Death by Decree" 12-22-60 (Marshal Corbett); *U.S. Marshal* -"One of the Ten Most Wanted Men" 11-28-59, "Kill or Be Killed" 3-12-60 (Harry Wilton); *Johnny Ringo*—"The Vindicator" 3-31-60 (Garrett); *The Rebel*—"Grant of Land" 5-22-60 (Travis); *Tate*—"Voices of the Town" 7-6-60 (Ragan); *The Westerner*—"Mrs. Kennedy" 10-28-60 (Marsh Kennedy); *The Outlaws*—"Starfall" 11-24-60 & 12-1-60 (Pepe); *Bonanza*—"The Lonely House" 10-15-61 (Trock), "A Woman in the House" 2-19-67 (Russ Wharton), "Catch as Catch Can" 10-27-68 (Parker); *Death Valley Days*—"Bloodline" 1-9-63 (Dr. Max Richter); *The Virginian*—"Strangers at Sundown" 4-3-63 (Pauk); *The Loner*—"One of the Wounded" 10-16-65 (Colonel Phelps); *Rango*—"The Town Tamer" 1-27-67 (Duke); *The Guns of Will Sonnett*—"Of Lasting Summers and Jim Sonnett" 10-6-67 (Prisoner), "The Fearless Man" 12-13-68 (Dave Henry).

Richards, Robert. TV: *Maverick*—"Yellow River" 2-8-59 (Fred Grimes); *Tales of Wells Fargo*—"Lady Trouble" 4-24-61 (Britt Kobler).

Richards, Toby. Films: "Sergeant Rutledge" 1960 (Lucy Dabney).

Richardson, Frank (1898-1/30/62). Films: "The Cowboy's Adopted Child" 1911; "Evangeline" 1911; "A Frontier Girl's Courage" 1911; "In the Days of Gold" 1911; "It Happened in the West" 1911; "The Night Herder" 1911; "On Seperate Paths" 1911; "One of Nature's Noblemen" 1911; "Range Pals" 1911; "The Regeneration of the Apache Kid" 1911; "Told in the Sierras" 1911; "The Bandit's Mask" 1912; "A Broken Spur" 1912; "Darkfeather's Strategy" 1912; "The Legend of the Lost Arrow" 1912; "A Message to Kearney" 1912; "The Old Stage Coach" 1912; "The Shrinking Rawhide" 1912; "Tenderfoot Bob's Resignation" 1912.

Richardson, Jack (1884-11/17/57). Films: "The Poisoned Flame" 1911; "The Ranchman's Nerve" 1911; "The Sheriff's Sisters" 1911; "The Brand" 1912; "The Coward" 1912; "Driftwood" 1912; "The Eastern Girl" 1912; "The Intrusion of Compoc" 1912; "The Jealous Rage" 1912; "The Land of Death" 1912; "Maiden and Men" 1912; "Nell of the Pampas" 1912; "The New Cowpuncher" 1912; "The Outlaw Cowboy" 1912; "The Pensioner" 1912; "The Power of Love" 1912; "The Promise" 1912; "Reformation of Sierra Smith" 1912; "The Reward of Valor" 1912; "The Thief's Wife" 1912; "The Thread of Life" 1912; "Under False Pretenses" 1912; "The Angel of the Canyons" 1913; "Calamity Anne Takes a Trip" 1913; "Calamity Anne's Beauty" 1913; "Calamity Anne's Inheritance" 1913; "An Eastern Flower" 1913; "The Girl and the Greaser" 1913; "Mission Bells" 1913; "Quicksands" 1913; "The Romance" 1913; "Rose of San Juan" 1913; "Woman's Honor" 1913; "Women Left Alone" 1913; "A Child of the Desert" 1914; "Redbird Wins" 1914; "Sir Galahad of Twilight" 1914; "The Assayer of Lone Gap" 1915; "Broadcloth and Buckskin" 1915; "The Purple Hills" 1915; "A Question of Honor" 1915; "The Sheriff of Willow Creek" 1915; "Two Spot Joe" 1915; "The Valley Feud" 1915; "According to St. John" 1916 (Ben Wolf); "Immediate Lee" 1916 (Kentuck Hurley); "The Land O' Lizards" 1916 (Buck Moran); "Ashes of Hope" 1917 (Ace High Lawton); "Fighting Back" 1917 (China-Mex); "Golden Rule Kate" 1917; "One Shot Ross" 1917 (Jim Butler); "The Outlaw and the Lady" 1917; "Desert Law" 1918 (Rufe Dorsey); "The Girl of Hell's Agony" 1918; "Go West, Young Man" 1918 (Hugh Godson); "His Enemy, the Law" 1918 (Capt. Jack Rogers/John Rogers); "Man Above the Law" 1918

(Duce Chalmers); "The End of the Game" 1919 (Dan Middleton); "The Mints of Hell" 1919 (Clay Hibbing); "The She Wolf" 1919 (Sheriff of Mad Dog); "Dangerous Love" 1920 (Half-Breed); "The Toll Gate" 1920 (the Sheriff); "Fightin' Mad" 1921 (Amos Rawson); "The Showdown" 1921; "Sting of the Lash" 1921 (Seeley); "Crimson Clue" 1922 (Dixon); "Girl from the West" 1923; "Border Women" 1924 (Gentleman Jack); "The Cowboy and the Flapper" 1924 (Red Carson); "Crashin' Thru" 1924 (Scarface Jordan); "Down by the Rio Grande" 1924; "Lightnin' Jack" 1924 (Knowles Brother); "Looped for Life" 1924 (Jack Hawkesby); "That Wild West" 1924; "Tiger Thompson" 1924 (Bull Dorgan); "Beyond the Border" 1925 (Brick Dawson); "Border Vengeance" 1925; "Cold Fury" 1925; "His Greatest Battle" 1925; "The Knockout Kid" 1925 (Assistant Foreman); "Ridin' Wild" 1925 (Scarface Jordan); "The Sagebrush Lady" 1925 (Tom Doyle); "The Texas Bearcat" 1925 (Watson); "Where Romance Rides" 1925 (Dave Colton); "Code of the Northwest" 1926 (Donald Stafford); "Walloping Kid" 1926 (Don Dawson); "Avenging Fangs" 1927 (Trigger Kincaid); "The Sonora Kid" 1927 (Arthur Butterworth); "Across the Plains" 1928 (Joe Steward); "The Ballyhoo Buster" 1928 (Jim Burnett); "The Dude Wrangler" 1930 (Dude Guest); "Trigger Tricks" 1930 (Joe Dixon); "Gun Smoke" 1931 (Tacy Keeler); "Lightnin' Smith Returns" 1931 (Chancey Ruggles); "Land of Wanted Men" 1932 (Thorpe); "The Man from New Mexico" 1932 (Jim Fletcher); "Without Honor" 1932 (Steve Henderson); "Gun Justice" 1934 (Sheriff); "Heart of the North" 1938 (Trapper); "Union Pacific" 1939; "Gun Code" 1940 (McClure); "Rangers of Fortune" 1940; "Romance of the West" 1946 (Smithers); "Crashing Thru" 1949.

Richardson, James G. (1945-2/20/83). TV: *Hec Ramsey*—"A Hard Road to Vengeance" 11-25-73 (Billy Jim).

Richardson, John (1934-). Films: "John the Bastard" 1967-Ital. (John Tenerico); "Execution" 1968-Ital./Fr. (John).

Richardson, Susan (1952-). TV: *Nakia*—"A Matter of Choice" 12-7-74 (Nancy).

Richardson, Sy. Films: "Straight to Hell" 1987-Brit. (Norwood); "Posse" 1993 (Shepherd).

Richman, Charles (1870-12/1/40). Films: "Cowboy and the Lady" 1938 (Dillon).

Richman, Peter Mark (1927-). Films: "Friendly Persuasion" 1956 (Gard Jordan); "Yuma" TVM-1971 (Major Lucas); "Bonanza: The Next Generation" TVM-1988 (Clel Dunston). ¶TV: *Rawhide*—"Incident at Alabaster Plain" 1-16-59 (Mastic Cardin); *Zane Grey Theater*—"Mission to Marathon" 5-14-59 (Gil Durand); *Hotel De Paree*—"Return of Monique" 10-30-59; *The Virginian*—"A Portrait of Marie Valonne" 11-6-63 (Johnny Madrid), "The Girl from Yesterday" 11-11-64 (Jack Wade), "The Gauntlet" 2-8-67 (Al Keets); *Stoney Burke*—"The Journey" 5-20-63 (Redmond); *Wild Wild West*—"The Night of the Dancing Death" 11-5-65 (Prince Gio); *The Loner*—"Incident in the Middle of Nowhere" 2-19-66 (Conway); *Iron Horse*—"The Passenger" 3-6-67 (Pierre Le Druc); *Daniel Boone*—"The Renegade" 9-28-67 (Hawk); *Gunsmoke*—"Mr. Sam'l" 2-26-68 (Norman Trainor); *Bonanza*—"A World Full of Cannibals" 12-22-68 (Vardeman); *Lancer*—"Angel Day and Her Sunshine Girls" 2-25-69 (Carl Bolton); *The Men from Shiloh*—"Tate, Ramrod" 2-24-71 (Wade).

Richmond, Al (1885-4/20/36). Films: "Biff Bang Buddy" 1924 (Nachez); "The Border Rider" 1924; "Rip Roarin' Roberts" 1924 (Red Turner); "Chasing Trouble" 1926 (Jim O'Reilly); "The Desperate Game" 1926 (Montana McGraw); "Eyes of the Desert" 1926; "Gasoline Cowboy" 1926; "Twisted Triggers" 1926 (Norris); "Deadshot Casey" 1928.

Richmond, Branscombe. Films: "The Mystic Warrior" TVM-1984 (Miyaca); "El Diablo" CTVM-1990 (Dancing Bear). ¶TV: *Paradise*—"The News from St. Louis" 10-27-88 (Howard).

Richmond, Felice. Films: "The Fighting Vigilantes" 1947 (Old Woman); "I Shot Billy the Kid" 1950 (Mrs. McSween); "Son of Paleface" 1952 (Genevieve); "Westbound" 1959. ¶TV: *Maverick*—"The Third Rider" 1-5-58 (Woman Passenger).

Richmond, John Peter. see Carradine, John.

Richmond, Kane (1906-3/22/73). Films: "Cavalier of the West" 1931 (Lieutenant Wilbur Allister); "The Silent Code" 1935 (Jerry Hale); "Thunderbolt" 1935 (the Prospector); "The Return of the Cisco Kid" 1939 (Alan Davis); "Riders of the Purple Sage" 1941 (Adam Dyer).

Richmond, Warner P. (1886-6/19/48). Films: "The Great Divide" 1915 (Dr. Newberry); "The Gray Towers Mystery" 1919 (Jean Bautiste); "Life in the Raw" 1922; "Fear-Bound" 1925 (Ed Tumble); "Billy the Kid" 1930 (Ballinger); "Life in the Raw" 1933 (H.B. Lamson); "The Courageous Avenger" 1935 (Gorman); "The New Frontier" 1935 (Ace Holmes); "The Phantom Empire" 1935-serial (Rab); "Rainbow's End" 1935 (Thomas Stark); "The Singing Vagabond" 1935 (Buck LaCrosse); "Smokey Smith" 1935 (Kent); "Song of the Gringo" 1936 (Cherokee); "Doomed at Sundown" 1937 (Jim Hatfield); "Headin' for the Rio Grande" 1937 (Ike Travis); "Heart of the West" 1937 (Johnson); "A Lawman Is Born" 1937 (Kane Briscoe); "Riders of the Dawn" 1937 (Danti); "Stars Over Arizona" 1937 (Ace Carter); "Trail of Vengeance" 1937 (Link Carson); "Where Trails Divide" 1937 (Mississippi Blackie Wilson); "Prairie Moon" 1938 (Mullens); "Six Shootin' Sheriff" 1938 (Ace Kendall); "Wild Horse Canyon" 1938 (Travers); "Fighting Mad" 1939 (Trigger); "The Oregon Trail" 1939-serial; "Ride 'Em, Cowgirl" 1939 (Wiley); "The Singing Cowgirl" 1939 (Gunhand Garrick); "Trigger Smith" 1939 (Gallop); "Water Rustlers" 1939 (Wiley); "The Golden Trail" 1940 (Chris); "Pals of the Silver Sage" 1940 (Sheriff); "Rainbow Over the Range" 1940 (Gene); "Rhythm of the Rio Grande" 1940 (Buck); "Outlaw Trail" 1944; "Colorado Serenade" 1946 (Dad Dillon); "Wild West" 1946 (Judge Templeton); "Prairie Outlaws" 1948.

Rick, Frank. Films: "Young Whirlwind" 1928 (Hank); "The Fighting Legion" 1930 (Cloudy Jones).

Ricketts, Shirley. see Rickey, Shirley Jane.

Ricketts, Thomas (1853-1/19/39). Films: "The Killer" 1921 (Tim Westmore); "Fools of Fortune" 1922 (Milton DePuyster); "Gordon of Ghost City" 1933-serial (Amos Gray); "The Red Rider" 1934-serial; "Hi Gaucho!" 1936 (Don Salvador de Aragon).

Rickey, Shirley Jane (Shirley Ricketts). Films: "'Neath the Arizona Skies" 1934 (Nina Morrell).

Rickles, Don (1926-). TV: *Wagon Train*—"Wagon to Fort Anderson" 6-7-61 (Joe Carder); *F Troop*—"The Return of Bald Eagle" 10-12-65 (Bald Eagle); *Wild Wild West*—"The Night of the Druid's Blood" 3-25-66 (Asmodeus).

Rickman, Alan. Films: "Quigley

Down Under" 1990 (Elliott Marston).

Ricks, Archie (1896-1/10/62). Films: "Ridin' Comet" 1925 (Sheriff); "The Rip Snorter" 1925 (Harry Vogelsang); "Vic Dyson Pays" 1925 (Skip); "Where Romance Rides" 1925 (Dunk Gresham); "The Long, Long Trail" 1929 (Jyp); "Branded" 1931; "Shotgun Pass" 1931; "Three Rogues" 1931 (Teamster); "Gold" 1932; "Crashing Broadway" 1933; "Gun Law" 1933; "The Phantom Thunderbolt" 1933; "Rainbow Ranch" 1933; "Sagebrush Trail" 1933; "Brand of Hate" 1934; "West of the Divide" 1934; "Between Men" 1935 (Henchman); "Dawn Rider" 1935; "Smokey Smith" 1935; "Arizona Gunfighter" 1937; "Hittin' the Trail" 1937 (Tombstone Kid); "It Happened Out West" 1937 (Red); "Mexicali Kid" 1938; "Trigger Smith" 1939; "Riders from Nowhere" 1940.

Rickson, Joseph (1880-1/8/58). Films: "The Committee on Credentials" 1916; "Love's Lariat" 1916 (Cowboy); "The Night Riders" 1916; "The Three Godfathers" 1916 (Pete Cushing); "Bill Brennan's Claim" 1917; "Double Suspicion" 1917; "The Getaway" 1917; "The Honor of Men" 1917; "The Raid" 1917; "Right-of-Way Casey" 1917; "Squaring It" 1917; "Baree, Son of Kazan" 1918 (Perriot); "Beating the Limited" 1918; "Cactus Crandall" 1918 (Mendoza); "Cavanaugh of the Forest Rangers" 1918 (Neil Ballard); "The Home Trail" 1918 (Blackie); "The Husband Hunter" 1918; "Naked Fists" 1918; "Quick Triggers" 1918; "Roped and Tied" 1918; "The Trail of No Return" 1918; "Go Get 'Em Garringer" 1919 (Bull Ross); "Outlawed" 1921 (Tom Benton); "The Purple Riders" 1921-serial; "Brass Commandments" 1923 (Tularosa); "Pioneer Trails" 1923 (Sheriff); "Code of the Wilderness" 1924 (Tom Chavis); "Rip Roarin' Roberts" 1924 (Hawk Andrews); "Rough Ridin'" 1924 (Jack Wells); "Action Galore" 1925 (Gil Kruger); "The Bad Lands" 1925 (Charlie Squirrel); "Baree, Son of Kazan" 1925 (Pierre Eustach); "The Human Tornado" 1925 (Tom Crowley); "Riders of the Purple Sage" 1925 (Slack); "A Two-Fisted Sheriff" 1925 (George Rivers); "The Buckaroo Kid" 1926; "Davy Crockett at the Fall of the Alamo" 1926 (Colonel Travis); "The Flying Horseman" 1926; "Outlaw Love" 1926; "Rawhide" 1926 (Strobel); "Border Blackbirds" 1927 (Suderman); "The Devil's Twin" 1927 (Carl Blackburn); "Land of the Lawless" 1927 (Brush Gallagher); "Two-Gun of the Tumbleweed" 1927 (Darrell); "Whispering Sage" 1927; "Code of the Scarlet" 1928 (Pete); "A Trick of Hearts" 1928; "The Drifter" 1929 (Hank); "The Lariat Kid" 1929 (Tony); "The Lone Star Ranger" 1930 (Spike); "Trails of Danger" 1930 (U.S. Marshal Bartlett); "Three Rogues" 1931 (Henchman); "Wild Horse" 1931 (Deputy); "Fargo Express" 1933 (Linn); "The Prescott Kid" 1934 (Bystander); "Under the Pampas Moon" 1935 (Bazan's Gaucho); "Bar 20 Rides Again" 1936 (Herb Layton); "Hopalong Cassidy Returns" 1936 (Buck); "Song of the Saddle" 1936; "Arizona Legion" 1939 (Dakota); "The Oklahoma Kid" 1939 (Homesteader); "Stagecoach" 1939 (Ike Plummer); "Triple Justice" 1940 (Luke).

Rickson, Lucille (1907-3/13/25). Films: "The Girl Who Ran Wild" 1922 (Clytie).

Riders of the Purple Sage, The. Films: "Twilight on the Prairie" 1944; "Sing Me a Song of Texas" 1945; "Out California Way" 1946; "Throw a Saddle on a Star" 1946; "Along the Oregon Trail" 1947; "Last Frontier Uprising" 1947; "Under Colorado Skies" 1947; "California Firebrand" 1948; "The Timber Trail" 1948; "Down Dakota Way" 1949; "The Far Frontier" 1949; "Susanna Pass" 1949; "North of the Great Divide" 1950; "Sunset in the West" 1950; "Trail of Robin Hood" 1950; "Trigger, Jr." 1950; "Twilight in the Sierras" 1950; "Heart of the Rockies" 1951; "Spoilers of the Plains" 1951.

Ridgely, Cleo (1894-8/18/62). Films: "The Love Mask" 1916 (Kate Kenner).

Ridgely, John (1909-1/17/68). Films: "Cowboy from Brooklyn" 1938 (Beacon Reporter); "Forbidden Valley" 1938 (Sheriff Lafferty); "Western Trails" 1938 (Ben); "River's End" 1940 (Constable Jeffers); "They Died with Their Boots On" 1941 (2nd Lt. Davis); "Cheyenne" 1947 (Chalkeye); "Tucson" 1949 (Ben); "Saddle Tramp" 1950; "Al Jennings of Oklahoma" 1951 (Dan Hanes); "The Last Outpost" 1951 (Sam McCloud); "Thunder in God's Country" 1951 (Bill Stafford); "When the Redskins Rode" 1951 (Christopher Gist); "Fort Osage" 1952 (Henry Travers); "The Outcasts of Poker Flat" 1952 (Bill Akeley). ¶TV: *Bonanza*—"Sam Hill" 6-3-61 (Billy Joe), "A Good Night's Rest" 4-11-65 (Wilfred), "The Imposters" 12-13-70 (Marley), "Blind Hunch" 11-21-71 (Bartender), "A Place to Hide" 3-19-72 (Liscomb).

Ridgely, Robert (1933-). TV: *Bronco*—"The Mustangers" 10-17-60 (Jimmy Smith); *Lawman*—"The Robbery" 1-1-61 (Lieutenant Davidson); *Maverick*—"Deadly Image" 3-12-61 (Lieutenant Reed); *Bonanza*—"The Countess" 11-19-61, "The Tall Stranger" 1-7-62; *Kung Fu*—"The Centoph" 4-4-74 & 4-11-74 (Whipple).

Ridges, Stanley (1892-4/22/51). Films: "Silver on the Sage" 1939 (Earl Brennan/Dave Talbot); "Union Pacific" 1939 (Gen. Casement); "They Died with Their Boots On" 1941 (Maj. Romolus Taipe); "Canyon Passage" 1946 (Jonas Overmire); "Streets of Laredo" 1949 (Maj. Bailey).

Ridgeway, Fritzi (1899-3/29/61). Films: "The Golden Bullet" 1917; "The Learnin' of Jim Benton" 1917 (Evelyn Hastings); "The Soul Herder" 1917; "Up or Down? 1917 (Esther Hollister); "The Wrong Man" 1917; "Faith Endurin'" 1918 (Helen Dryer); "The Law's Outlaw" 1918 (Rose Davison); "The Ranger of Pike's Peak" 1919; "Tapering Fingers" 1919; "Winning a Bride" 1919; "Bring Him In" 1921 (Mary Mackay); "Ruggles of Red Gap" 1923 (Emily Judson); "Son of the Golden West" 1928 (Rita); "Hell's Heroes" 1930 (Mother).

Riebe, Loren. Films: "Come on Cowboys" 1937; "Gunsmoke Ranch" 1937 (Hank); "The Painted Stallion" 1937-serial (Pedro); "Zorro Rides Again" 1937-serial (Raider #5); "Code of the Rangers" 1938 (George); "The Lone Ranger" 1938-serial (Trooper); "The Stranger from Arizona" 1938; "King of the Royal Mounted" 1940-serial (Dinwoodie); "King of the Texas Rangers" 1941-serial; "Jesse James Rides Again" 1947-serial (Haynes).

Riehl, Kay (1898-1/8/88). Films: "Hannah Lee" 1953 (Mrs. Bainbridge). ¶TV: *The Lone Ranger*—"Blind Witness" 5-30-57.

Riehle, Richard. Films: "The Gambler V: Playing for Keeps" TVM-1994 (Dimaio); "Lightning Jack" 1994-Australia (Marcus). ¶TV: *Ned Blessing: The Story of My Life and Times*—Regular 1993 (Judge Longley).

Rigaud, George "Jorge" (1906-1/17/84). Films: "Ride and Kill" 1964-Ital./Span.; "Coffin for the Sheriff" 1965-Ital./Span.; "Finger on the Trigger" 1965-Span./Ital./U.S. (Benton); "Seven Guns for the MacGregors" 1965-Ital./Span. (Alastair MacGregor); "A Place Called Glory" 1966-Span./Ger. (Seth Grand);

"Ringo's Big Night" 1966-Ital./Span.; "Savage Pampas" 1966-U.S./Span./Arg. (Old Man); "Sugar Colt" 1966-Ital./Span.; "The Tall Women" 1966-Austria/Ital./Span.; "The Texican" 1966-U.S./Span. (Mitch); "Woman for Ringo" 1966-Ital./Span. (Carl); "Up the MacGregors!" 1967-Ital./Span. (Alastair MacGregor); "Machine Gun Killers" 1968-Ital./Span.; "Alive or Preferably Dead" 1969-Span./Ital.; "Guns of the Magnificent Seven" 1969 (Gabriel); "Forewarned, Half-Killed … The Word of the Holy Ghost" 1971-Ital./Span.; "A Town Called Hell" 1971-Span./Brit. (Gato); "Valley of the Dancing Widows" 1974-Span./Ger.

Riggio, Jerry (-9/12/71). Films: "Romance of the West" 1946; "Son of Billy the Kid" 1949 (Sanchos).

Riggs, Betty. *see* Brent, Evelyn.

Riggs, Jack (-6/8/78). Films: "The Purple Hills" 1961.

Riggs, William. TV: *Wagon Train -*"A Man Called Horse" 3-26-58, "The Vincent Eaglewood Story" 4-15-59 (Ket Tam); *Rawhide*—"The Peddler" 1-19-62.

Righi, Massimo. *see* Dean, Max.

Riha, Bobby (1958-). TV: *Gunsmoke*—"Hard Luck Henry" 10-23-67 (Charlie Walsh); *Bonanza*—"The Burning Sky" 1-28-68 (Bridger), "The Trouble with Trouble" 10-25-70 (Eben); *The High Chaparral*—"The Hostage" 3-5-71 (Benjie).

Riley, Elaine. Films: "Girl Rush" 1944 (Troupe Member); "Strange Gamble" 1948 (Nora); "The Devil's Playground" 1946 (Mrs. Evans); "Dangerous Venture" 1947; "Borrowed Trouble" 1948 (Mrs. Garvin); "False Paradise" 1948; "Sinister Journey" 1948 (Mrs. Garvin); "Trailin' West" 1949; "Rider from Tucson" 1950 (Jane); "Hills of Utah" 1951 (Karen McQueen); "Leadville Gunslinger" 1952 (Carol Davis); "Texas Bad Man" 1953 (Lois); "Pardners" 1956 (Dance Hall Girl). TV: *The Gene Autry Show*—"Bullets and Bows" 3-2-52, "Six Gun Romeo" 3-16-52, "The Sheriff Is a Lady" 3-23-52; *The Range Rider*—"False Trail" 6-7-52; *Hopalong Cassidy*—"Outlaw's Reward" 7-12-52; *The Cisco Kid*—"Schoolmarm" 1-23-54; *Stories of the Century*—"Jack Slade" 12-2-55; *Fury*—"Joey Sees It Through" 1-21-56; *26 Men*—"Man in Hiding" 10-21-58; *The Texan*—"Jail for the Innocents" 11-3-58 (Dolly); *Wanted—Dead or Alive*—"The Partners" 2-6-60 (Panama).

Riley, Jack (1935-). TV: *Kung Fu*—"The Gunman" 1-3-74 (Jed Royal).

Riley, Jean. Films: "Crashin' Thru" 1924 (Eloise Hackle Penny).

Riley, Jeannine (1939-). Films: "The Wackiest Wagon Train in the West" 1976 (Lulu). TV: *Wagon Train*—"The Davey Baxter Story" 1-9-63 (Susan); *The Virginian*—"Run Away Home" 4-24-63 (Amelia Pryor); *Sheriff Who?*—Pilot 9-5-67 (Betsy); *Wild Wild West*—"The Night of the Arrow" 12-29-67 (Aimee Baldwin); *Dusty's Trail*—Regular 1973 (Lulu).

Riley, Peg. *see* Reynolds, Marjorie.

Riley, Robin. TV: *Tombstone Territory*—"Shoot Out at Dark" 1-8-58 (Slip); *Cimarron City*—"To Become a Man" 10-25-58 (Joey Conway); *Hotel De Paree*—"Sundance and the Hostiles" 12-11-59 (June); *Bat Masterson*—"Bat Trap" 10-13-60 (Eddie).

Rilla, Walter (1895-11/21/80). Films: "Day of Anger" 1967-Ital./Ger. (Murphallan).

Rimmer, Shane (1932-). Films: "Flaming Frontier" 1958-Can. (Running Bear).

Rinehart, Dick. Films: "Saga of Death Valley" 1939; "Stick to Your Guns" 1941 (Bow Wow); "Twilight on the Trail" 1941; "Heart of the Rio Grande" 1942 (Jimmy Wakely Trio); "Song of the Wasteland" 1947.

Ring, Cyril (1892-7/17/67). Films: "Tongues of Flame" 1924 (Clayton); "The Border Patrolman" 1936 (Ed Hendricks); "Wells Fargo" 1937; "Union Pacific" 1939 (Surveyor); "Home in Wyomin'" 1942; "The Texas Kid" 1943 (Atwood); "Hollywood Barn Dance" 1947 (Theater Manager); "Return of the Badmen" 1948 (Bank Clerk).

Rio, Joanne. Films: "Riding with Buffalo Bill" 1954-serial (Maria Perez); "Seminole Uprising" 1955 (Tasson Li).

Riordan, Joel. TV: *The Californians*—"Death by Proxy" 3-18-58 (Dan White); *Bat Masterson*—"License to Cheat" 2-4-59 Chuck); *Rough Riders*—"Witness Against the Judge" 2-26-59 (Albert Westcott).

Riordan, Robert (1911-1/1/68). Films: "Jesse James Rides Again" 1947-serial (Waldon). TV: *Tales of the Texas Rangers*—"The Fifth Plague" 12-19-58 (Dr. Keller); *Lawman*—"The Press" 11-29-59 (Arthur Grey); *Wyatt Earp*—"Silver Dollar" 2-2-60; *Great Adventure*—"The Testing of Sam Houston" 1-31-64 (Breckenridge).

Rios, Edward C. *see* Rios, Lalo.

Rios, Elvira (1914-11/13/87). Films: "Cupid Rides the Range" 1939-short; "Stagecoach" 1939 (Yakima, Chris' Wife).

Rios, Lalo (Edward C. Rios) (1927-3/7/73). Films: "Bandit Queen" 1950 (Juan); "Mark of the Renegade" 1951 (Paco); "Lonely Are the Brave" 1962 (Prisoner). TV: *Wagon Train*—"The Sister Rita Story" 3-25-59 (Juan), "The Stagecoach Story" 9-30-59 (Juan); *Gunsmoke*—"Long Hours, Short Pay" 4-29-61 (Little Fox); *Laredo*—"The Callico Kid" 1-6-66 (Pete); *The High Chaparral*—"The Terrorist" 12-17-67 (1st Bandit).

Ripley, Jay (1945-). Films: "Young Fury" 1965 (Slim); "Duel at Diablo" 1966 (Tech); "A Time for Killing" 1967 (Lovingwood); "True Grit" 1969 (Harold Parmalee); "Shootout in a One-Dog Town" TVM-1974 (Little Edgar); "The Apple Dumpling Gang Rides Again" 1979. TV: *Bonanza*—"A Good Night's Rest" 4-11-65 (Larry); *Gunsmoke*—"Two Tall Men" 5-8-65 (Ned Moore); *Pistols 'n' Petticoats*—"A Crooked Line" 9-17-66 (Buster Turner); *The Virginian*—"Long Journey Home" 12-14-66 (Dawkins); *How the West Was Won*—Episode One 2-12-78 (Jess Mudd).

Ripley, Ray (1891-10/7/38). Films: "Blue Streak McCoy" 1920 (Frank Otis); "Western Pluck" 1926 (Gale Collins).

Risdon, Elizabeth (1888-12/20/58). Films: "Cowboy from Brooklyn" 1938 (Mrs. Jordan); "Mexican Spitfire Out West" 1940 (Aunt Della Lindsay); "Tall in the Saddle" 1944 (Miss Martin); "Roll on, Texas Moon" 1946 (Cactus Kate Taylor); "Down Dakota Way" 1949 (Dolly Paxton); "Hills of Oklahoma" 1950 (Kate Carney); "Sierra" 1950 (Aunt Susan); "In Old Amarillo" 1951 (Granny Adams).

Risk, Linda Sue. TV: *Here Come the Brides*—"And Jason Makes Five" 10-9-68 (Melody); *Bonanza*—"Little Girl Lost" 11-3-68 (Samantha); *The Outcasts*—"The Bounty Children" 12-23-68 (Ellen).

Riss, Dan (1910-8/28/70). Films: "Wyoming Mail" 1950 (George Armstrong); "Only the Valiant" 1951 (Lt. Jerry Winters); "Three Young Texans" 1954 (Sheriff Carter); "The Yellow Tomahawk" 1954 (Sgt. Bandini); "Badman's Country" 1958 (Marshall McAfee). TV: *The Lone Ranger*—"Tenderfoot" 11-25-54; *My*

Friend Flicka—"A Good Deed" 10-21-55; *Fury*—"The Hobo" 1-7-56 (Dr. Ed Taylor), "Tungsten Queen" 1-14-56 (Doc); *Zane Grey Theater*—"Return to Nowhere" 12-7-56 (Hodges); *Sheriff of Cochise*—"Triangle" 2-22-57 (Harris); *Gunsmoke*—"Cain" 3-9-57 (Mike); *The Restless Gun*—"Cheyenne Express" 12-2-57 (Phil Waterman), "The Battle of Tower Rock" 4-28-58 (Otis Spers); *Colt .45*—"Split Second" 3-14-58 (Sheriff Milo); *The Californians*—"Mutineers from Hell" 9-30-58 (Farragut), "Deadly Tintype" 3-31-59; *Tales of Wells Fargo*—"Cow Town" 12-15-58 (Charlie), "The Kinfolk" 9-26-60 (Brian Lassiter); *Maverick*—"You Can't Beat the Percentage" 10-4-59 (Sheriff Bill Satchel); *Wagon Train*—"The Larry Hanify Story" 1-27-60, "Weight of Command" 1-25-61; *Wyatt Earp*—"Roscoe Turns Detective" 5-3-60; *Bonanza*—"The Blood Line" 12-31-60, "The Quest" 9-30-62 (Crawford), "The Prime of Life" 12-29-63, "The Return" 5-2-65 (Latham); *Wild Wild West*—"The Night of the Howling Light" 12-17-65 (Coast Guard Officer).

Ritch, Steve. Films: "Conquest of Cochise" 1953 (Tukiwah); "Battle of Rogue River" 1954 (1st Brave); "Massacre Canyon" 1954 (Black Eagle); "Riding with Buffalo Bill" 1954-serial (Elko); "Seminole Uprising" 1955 (Black Cat, Seminole Chief). ¶TV: *The Adventures of Rin Tin Tin*—"Rin Tin Tin and the Christmas Story" 12-23-55 (Tahn-Te), "The Silent Battle" 10-5-56 (Tokimaw), "Rusty's Remedy" 2-28-58 (Long Buffalo), "The Accusation" 2-13-59 (Lone Hawk); *Sergeant Preston of the Yukon*—"Trouble at Hogback" 7-19-56 (Swamp Fox); *Broken Arrow*—"Ghost Face" 3-12-57 (Nakaya), "Black Moment" 10-29-57 (Moreno), "The Bounty Hunters" 11-26-57 (Nakaya), "White Savage" 12-24-57 (Nakaya), "Water Witch" 1-7-58 (Nakaya), "Aztec Treasure" 2-25-58 (Nakaya), "Bear Trap" 4-29-58 (Nakaya), "Transfer" 6-24-58 (Bravo); *The Lone Ranger*—"Ghost Town Fury" 3-28-57; *Wagon Train*—"The Mark Hanford Story" 2-26-58 (Running Bear), "The Sakae Ito Story" 12-3-58 (Sharp Knife), "The Sam Darland Story" 12-26-62 (Red Cloud); *Tales of Wells Fargo*—"Special Delivery" 3-31-58 (Long Knife), "Terry" 4-6-59 (Homer); *The Deputy*—"The Deputy" 9-12-59 (Cowboy).

Ritchie, Clint (1939-). Films: "Alvarez Kelly" 1966 (Union Lieutenant); "Bandolero!" 1968 (Babe); "The Bravos" TVM-1972 (Corporal Love); "Joe Kidd" 1972 (Calvin); "Against a Crooked Sky" 1975. ¶TV: *Wild Wild West*—"The Night of the Inferno" 9-17-65 (Lieutenant), "The Night of the Two-Legged Buffalo" 3-11-66 (Bandit); *Daniel Boone*—"Three Score and Ten" 2-6-69 (Two Feathers); *Centennial*—Regular 1978-79 (Messmore Garrett).

Ritchie, Ethel. Films: "The Boss of Copperhead" 1920; "Two from Texas" 1920; "Hunger of the Blood" 1921 (Margaret Kenyon); "The Stranger of the Hills" 1922; "Under Pressure" 1922.

Ritter, Fred. Films: "The Forty-Niners" 1932 (Tanner); "Carolina Moon" 1940 (Thompson).

Ritter, John (1949-). Films: "Scandalous John" 1971 (Wendell); "Evil Roy Slade" TVM-1972 (Minister).

Ritter, Tex (1906-1/2/74). Films: "Song of the Gringo" 1936 (Tex); "Arizona Days" 1937 (Tex Malinson); "Headin' for the Rio Grande" 1937 (Tex); "Hittin' the Trail" 1937 (Tex Randall); "The Mystery of the Hooded Horseman" 1937 (Tex Martin); "Riders of the Rockies" 1937 (Tex Rand); "Sing, Cowboy, Sing" 1937 (Tex Archer); "Tex Rides with the Boy Scouts" 1937 (Tex Lansing); "Trouble in Texas" 1937 (Tex Masters); "Frontier Town" 1938 (Tex Lansing); "Rollin' Plains" 1938 (Tex Lawrence); "Starlight Over Texas" 1938 (Tex Newman); "Utah Trail" 1938 (Tex Stewart/the Pecos Kid); "Where the Buffalo Roam" 1938 (Tex Houston); "Down the Wyoming Trail" 1939 (Tex Yancey); "The Man from Texas" 1939 (Tex Allen); "Riders of the Frontier" 1939 (Tex Lowry); "Rollin' Westward" 1939 (Tex); "Song of the Buckaroo" 1939 (Texas Dan); "Sundown on the Prairie" 1939 (Tex); "Westbound Stage" 1939 (Tex Wallace); "Arizona Frontier" 1940 (Tex Whitedeer); "Cowboy from Sundown" 1940 (Tex Rokett); "Pals of the Silver Sage" 1940 (Tex Wright); "The Golden Trail" 1940 (Tex Roberts); "Rainbow Over the Range" 1940 (Tex Reed); "Rhythm of the Rio Grande" 1940 (Tex); "Roll, Wagons, Roll" 1940 (Tex Masters); "Take Me Back to Oklahoma" 1940 (Tex Lawton); "King of Dodge City" 1941 (Tex Rawlings); "The Pioneers" 1941 (Tex); "Ridin' the Cherokee Trail" 1941 (Tex); "Roaring Frontiers" 1941; "Rollin' Home to Texas" 1941 (Tex); "Bullets for Bandits" 1942; "Deep in the Heart of Texas" 1942 (Brent Gordon); "The Devil's Trail" 1942; "Little Joe, the Wrangler" 1942 (Bob Brewster); "The Lone Star Vigilantes" 1942 (Tex Martin); "North of the Rockies" 1942; "Old Chisholm Trail" 1942 (Montana Smith); "Prairie Gunsmoke" 1942; "Vengeance of the West" 1942; "Arizona Trail" 1943 (Johnnie); "Cheyenne Roundup" 1943 (Steve Rawlins); "Frontier Badman" 1943 (Kimball); "The Lone Star Trail" 1943 (Fargo Steele); "Raiders of San Joaquin" 1943 (Gil Blake); "Tenting Tonight on the Old Camp Ground" 1943 (Bob Courtney); "Cowboy Canteen" 1944 (Tex Coulter); "Dead or Alive" 1944; "Gangsters of the Frontier" 1944; "Marshal of Gunsmoke" 1944 (Ward); "Oklahoma Raiders" 1944 (Steve); "The Whispering Skull" 1944; "Enemy of the Law" 1945 (Tex Haines); "Flaming Bullets" 1945; "Frontier Fugitives" 1945; "Marked for Murder" 1945; "Three in the Saddle" 1945; "The Cowboy" 1954 (Narrator); "Apache Ambush" 1955 (Trager). ¶TV: *Zane Grey Theater*—"Sundown at Bitter Creek" 2-14-58 (Reydo); *Shotgun Slade*—"Gold" 10-3-60; *The Rebel*—"The Ballad of Danny Brown" 4-9-61 (Marshal).

Ritter, Thelma (1905-2/5/69). Films: "The Misfits" 1961 (Isabelle Steers); "The Second Time Around" 1961 (Aggie); "How the West Was Won" 1962 (Agatha Clegg). ¶TV: *Frontier Circus*—"Journey from Hannibal" 11-16-61 (Bertha Beecher); *Wagon Train*—"The Madame Sagittarius Story" 10-3-62 (Mme. Sagittarius).

Rivas, Carlos (1927-). Films: "Fury in Paradise" 1955-U.S./Mex.; "The Beast of Hollow Mountain" 1956 (Felipe Sanchez); "The Deerslayer" 1957 (Chingachgook); "Dalton That Got Away" 1960; "The Unforgiven" 1960 (Lost Bird); "True Grit" 1969 (Dirty Bob); "The Undefeated" 1969 (Diaz); "The Gatling Gun" 1972 (Two-Knife). ¶TV: *Cheyenne*—"Johnny Bravo" 5-15-56 (Johnny Bravo); *Zorro*—"The Missing Father" 2-26-59 (Don Miguel Cabrillo), "Please Believe Me" 3-5-59 (Don Miguel Cabrillo), "The Brooch" 3-12-59 (Don Miguel Cabrillo); *Sugarfoot*—"The Gaucho" 12-22-59 (Curro Santiago); *Maverick*—"Poker Face" 1-7-62 (Luis); *The Dakotas*—"One Day in Vermillion" 4-8-63 (Takanta); *Branded*—"The Assassins" 3-27-66 & 4-3-66 (Dr. Cuevarra), "The Conquistadors" 10-1-67 (Miguel); *Gunsmoke*—"Old Friend" 2-4-67 (Trail); *The High Chaparral*—"The Ghost of Chaparral" 9-17-67 (Jorge); *Bonanza*—"Salute to Yesterday" 9-29-68 (Angel Montana); *Daniel Boone*—"The Grand Alliance" 11-13-69 (Sergeant Ortega), "An Angel Cried" 1-8-70 (Chief Tall Fire).

Rivera, Luis (1903-). Films: "Sunscorched" 1966-Span./Ger.; "The Man Who Killed Billy the Kid" 1967-Span./Ital.; "Guns of the Magnificent Seven" 1969 (Lt. Presna); "Bad Man's River" 1971-Span./Ital./Fr. (Orozco).

Rivero, Carlos. Films: "The Raiders" 1952 (Ramon Castillo). ¶TV: *Maverick*—"The Judas Mask" 11-2-58 (Spanish Man); *Wanted—Dead or Alive*—"Triple Vise" 2-27-60 (Shepherd); *The Deputy*—"The X Game" 5-28-60 (Huerta); *Wyatt Earp*—"Requiem for Old Man Clanton" 5-30-61 (Vaquero); *The Big Valley*—"The Way to Kill a Killer" 11-24-65 (Chanter).

Rivero, Jorge (1942-). Films: "Rio Lobo" 1970 (Capt. Pierre Cordona); "Soldier Blue" 1970 (Spotted Wolf); "The Last Hard Men" 1976 (Cesar Menendez). ¶TV: *Centennial*—Regular 1978-79 (Broken Thumb).

Rivero, Julian (1890-2/24/76). Films: "Fast and Fearless" 1924 (Captain Duerta); "The Border Whirlwind" 1926 (Capt. Gonzalez); "Dugan of the Badlands" 1931 (Piedro); "God's Country and the Man" 1931 (General Pedro Gomez); "Yankee Don" 1931; "Beyond the Rockies" 1932 (Lavender Joe); "The Broken Wing" 1932 (Bassilio); "Law and Lawless" 1932 (Pancho Gonzales); "Man from Hell's Edges" 1932 (Lobo); "The Night Rider" 1932 (Manuel Alonzo Valdez); "Son of Oklahoma" 1932 (Manuel Verdugo); "The Tabasco Kid" 1932-short; "Lucky Larrigan" 1933; "Man of Action" 1933 (Don Miguel); "Via Pony Express" 1933; "Cowboy Holiday" 1934 (Pablo Escobar, the Juarez Kid); "The Westerner" 1934 (Antoine); "Born to Battle" 1935; "Gun Play" 1935 (Pedro); "Sagebrush Troubador" 1935 (Pablo); "Western Justice" 1935 (Pancho Lopez/Jack); "Hi Gaucho!" 1936; "Phantom Patrol" 1936 (French LaFarge); "Riddle Ranch" 1936 (Don Carlos); "Song of the Saddle" 1936 (Jose); "The Traitor" 1936 (Jose Ramos); "Land Beyond the Law" 1937; "Lawless Land" 1937 (Ortego); "Ridin' the Lone Trail" 1937 (Pedro); "Wells Fargo" 1937 (Candy Vendor); "Heroes of the Alamo" 1938 (Gen. Santa Ana); "Outlaw Express" 1938 (Don Diego); "The Arizona Wildcat" 1939 (Rodrigo); "Drifting Westward" 1939 (Don Careta); "The Girl and the Gambler" 1939 (Pedro); "South of the Border" 1939; "Arizona Gangbusters" 1940 (Gringo); "Billy the Kid's Gun Justice" 1940 (Carlos); "Death Rides the Range" 1940 (Pancho); "Gaucho Serenade" 1940; "Riders on Black Mountain" 1940 (Jose); "The Westerner" 1940 (Juan Gomez); "Young Buffalo Bill" 1940 (Panelio); "Billy the Kid's Fighting Pals" 1941 (Lopez); "Billy the Kid's Range War" 1941 (Romero); "Down Mexico Way" 1941 (Don Alvarado); "The Lone Rider Crosses the Rio" 1941 (Pedro); "Bells of Capistrano" 1942; "Overland Stagecoach" 1942; "Texas Justice" 1942; "Valley of Vanishing Men" 1942-serial (Jose); "Hands Across the Border" 1943 (Senor Morales); "The Outlaw" 1943 (Pablo); "Cowboy and the Senorita" 1944; "Gun to Gun" 1944-short; "Trail to Mexico" 1946; "Over the Santa Fe Trail" 1947; "Robin Hood of Monterey" 1947; "The Kissing Bandit" 1948 (Postman); "Old Los Angeles" 1948 (Diego); "The Treasure of the Sierra Madre" 1948 (Barber); "Border Treasure" 1950 (Felipe); "The Texas Rangers" 1951 (Pecos Palmer); "Wild Horse Ambush" 1952 (Enrico Espinosa); "Shadows of Tombstone" 1953 (Peon); "Broken Lance" 1954 (Manuel); "Three Hours to Kill" 1954 (Dominguez); "A Man Alone" 1955 (Tio Rubio); "Ten Wanted Men" 1955; "The Vanishing American" 1955 (Etenia); "Giant" 1956 (Old Man); "Thunder Over Arizona" 1956; "The Reward" 1965 (El Viejo). ¶TV: *The Cisco Kid*—"New Evidence" 9-19-53; *Cheyenne*—"Border Showdown" 11-22-55; *Broken Arrow*—"The Missionaries" 1-29-57 (Papago Joe); *Sheriff of Cochise*—"Taxi" 9-20-57; *The Californians*—"The Man Who Owned San Francisco" 12-30-58 (Pio Valdez); *Rawhide*—"Incident of the Day of the Dead" 9-18-59; *Lancer*—"The High Riders" 9-24-68.

Rivero, Santiago. Films: "Shoot to Kill" 1963-Span.; "Dynamite Joe" 1966-Ital./Span. (Senator Senneth); "Canadian Wilderness" 1969-Span./Ital.

Rivers, Jack. Films: "Song of the Sierras" 1946; "West of Alamo" 1946; "Song of the Wasteland" 1947; "Outlaw Brand" 1948; "Partners of the Sunset" 1948.

Riviere, Curley (1875-11/6/35). Films: "The Dangerous Dub" 1926 (the Law).

Riviere, Georges. Films: "Minnesota Clay" 1964-Ital./Fr./Span. (Fox).

Rizzo, Alfredo. Films: "Don't Wait, Django ... Shoot!" 1969-Ital. (Nico); "Paid in Blood" 1972-Ital.

Rizzo, Gianni (1920-). Films: "Face to Face" 1967-Ital.; "Sartana" 1968-Ital./Ger.; "Sabata" 1969-Ital. (Judge O'Hara); "Adios, Sabata" 1970-Ital./Span. (Folgen); "Return of Sabata" 1972-Ital./Fr./Ger. (Jeremy Sweeney).

Roach, Bert (1891-2/16/71). Films: "The Flaming Forest" 1926 (Sloppy); "Riders of the Dark" 1928 (Sheriff Snodgrass); "The Desert Rider" 1929 (Friar Bernardo); "Captain Thunder" 1931 (Pablo); "Hello Trouble" 1932; "God's Country and the Woman" 1937 (Kewpie); "Duel in the Sun" 1946 (Eater); "The Man from Rainbow Valley" 1946 (Mayor).

Roach, Margaret (1921-11/22/64). Films: "Union Pacific" 1939 (Violet); "Riders from Nowhere" 1940 (Marian Adams).

Road, Mike (1915-). TV: *Buckskin*—Regular 1958-59 (Sheriff Tom Sellers); *Lawman*—"The Exchange" 10-25-59 (Frank Quinlivan), "The Parting" 5-29-60 (Bluel), "The Man from New York" 3-19-61 (Foster); *Wagon Train*—"The Martha Barham Story" 11-4-59 (Capt. Wade Forrest); *Colt .45*—"Alias Mr. Howard" 12-6-59 (Mr. Howard), "Arizona Anderson" 2-14-60 (Anderson); *The Alaskans*—"The Long Pursuit" 1-31-60 (Marshal Wallace), "Disaster at Gold Hill" 3-20-60 (Arthur Bryant); *Gunsmoke*—"Friend's Pay-Off" 9-3-60 (Ab Butler), "Big Man, Big Target" 11-28-64 (Joe Merchant); *Bronco*—"The Buckbrier Trail" 2-20-61 (Lieutenant Blyden), "The Immovable Object" 4-16-62 (Emmet Dawson); *Maverick*—"Red Dog" 3-5-61 (Buckskin Charlie), "Dade City Dodge" 9-18-61 (Pearly Gates), "The Troubled Heir" 4-1-62 (Pearly Gates); *Cheyenne*—"The Quick and the Deadly" 10-22-62 (Jud Ainley); *Wild Wild West*—"The Night of the Tottering Tontine" 1-6-67 (Dexter); *The Outcasts*—"Hung for a Lamb" 3-10-69 (Stan Sutton); *Alias Smith and Jones*—"A Fistful of Diamonds" 3-4-71, "Shootout at Diablo Station" 12-2-71 (Sheriff Trevors).

Roadman, Betty (1889-3/24/75). Films: "Billy the Kid Returns" 1938; "The Lone Ranger Rides Again" 1939-serial (Ma Daniels); "Down Rio Grande Way" 1942 (Ma Haines); "Return of the Durango Kid" 1945.

Roan, Vinegar. Films: "Rainbow Trail" 1932 (Horseman); "Robbers' Roost" 1933 (Smoky Slocum);

"Under the Pampas Moon" 1935 (Cesar's Gaucho); "Bold Caballero" 1936; "Vigilantes Are Coming" 1936-serial (Rancher); "Gunsmoke Ranch" 1937 (Zeke); "The Painted Stallion" 1937-serial (Pete); "Zorro Rides Again" 1937-serial (Raider #6); "The Lone Ranger" 1938-serial (Trooper); "Zorro's Black Whip" 1944-serial (Trail Heavy #3).

Roark, Robert. Films: "Blackjack Ketchum, Desperado" 1956 (Ben Tetlow). ¶TV: *Sky King*—"The Haunted Castle" 4-13-52 (Clayton Jones); *Tales of the Texas Rangers*—"Carnival Criss-Cross" 9-3-55 (Anderson); *Sergeant Preston of the Yukon*—"Father of the Crime" 4-19-56 (Jeff Carson); *Tales of Wells Fargo*—"The Inscrutable Man" 12-9-57 (Hale Cameron); *Wagon Train*—"The Clara Beauchamp Story" 12-11-57 (Orderly).

Roarke, Adam (1941-). Films: "El Dorado" 1967 (Matt MacDonald). ¶TV: *The Virginian*—"A Portrait of Marie Valonne" 11-6-63 (Jimmy Raker); *The Road West*—"Ashes and Tallow and One True Love" 10-24-66 (Hanson).

Robards, Jr., Jason (1922-). Films: "A Big Hand for the Little Lady" 1966 (Henry Drummond); "Hour of the Gun" 1967 (Doc Holliday); "Once Upon a Time in the West" 1968-Ital. (Cheyenne); "The Ballad of Cable Hogue" 1970 (Cable Hogue); "Pat Garrett and Billy the Kid" 1973 (Gov. Lew Wallace); "Comes a Horseman" 1978 (Ewing); "The Legend of the Lone Ranger" 1981 (President Grant).

Robards, Sr., Jason (1892-4/4/63). Films: "Jaws of Steel" 1927 (John Warren); "Tracked by the Police" 1927 (Bob Owen); "The Conquerors" 1932 (Lane); "Klondike" 1932 (Jim Armstrong); "White Eagle" 1932 (Dave Rand); "The Miracle Rider" 1935-serial (Carlton); "Robin Hood of El Dorado" 1936 (Pancho); "Range War" 1939 (Rancher); "Zorro's Fighting Legion" 1939-serial (Cantina Owner); "Silver Queen" 1942 (Bank Teller); "Wanderer of the Wasteland" 1945 (Dealer); "Thunder Mountain" 1947 (James Gardner); "Trail Street" 1947 (Jason); "Under the Tonto Rim" 1947 (Capt. McLean); "Wild Horse Mesa" 1947 (Pop Melbern); "Guns of Hate" 1948 (Ben Jason); "Return of the Badmen" 1948 (Judge Harper); "Smoky Mountain Melody" 1948 (Josh Corby); "Son of God's Country" 1948 (John Thornton); "Western Heritage" 1948 (Judge Winston); "Haunted Trails" 1949; "Riders of the

Whistling Pines" 1949 (Charlie Carter); "Rimfire" 1949 (Banker Elkins); "South of Death Valley" 1949 (Mulen); "Horsemen of the Sierras" 1950 (Phineas Grant). ¶TV: *Philco Television Playhouse*—"The Death of Billy the Kid" 7-24-55 (Joe Grant); *Broken Arrow*—"Bad Boy" 1-21-58 (Ryder); *Colt .45*—"Dead Reckoning" 1-24-58 (Judge Hesby); *Cimarron City*—"I, the People" 10-11-58 (Cal Demming), "To Become a Man" 10-25-58 (Cal Demming), "Kid on a Calico Horse" 11-22-58 (Cal Deming); *Laramie*—"Ride into Darkness" 10-18-60 (Dan Preston); *Wagon Train*—"The Patience Miller Story" 1-11-61; *The Deputy*—"Lawman's Conscience" 7-1-61 (Rufus Hayden).

Robards, Willis (1873-11/3/21). Films: "Man to Man" 1922 (Bill Royce).

Robbins, Cindy. Films: "Gunsight Ridge" 1957 (Bride). ¶TV: *Wagon Train*—"The Ella Lindstrom Story" 2-4-59 (Inga), "The Rodney Lawrence Story" 6-10-59 (Mandy McCrea), "The Larry Hanify Story" 1-27-60 (Aggie Donovan); *The Tall Man*—"Larceny and Young Ladies" 11-12-60 (May McBean), "Substitute Sheriff" 1-6-62 (May McBean); *The Outlaws*—"Chalk's Lot" 10-5-61 (Sue Riley).

Robbins, Gale (1921-2/18/80). Films: "Calamity Jane" 1953 (Adelaide Adams); "Gunsmoke in Tucson" 1958 (Lou Crenshaw); "Quantrill's Raiders" 1958 (Kate). ¶TV: *Trackdown*—"Easton, Texas" 10-25-57 (Sherry Lamar); *Gunsmoke*—"Champion of the World" 12-24-66 (Maude).

Robbins, Marc (1868-4/5/31). Films: "Judge Not, or the Woman of Mona Diggings" 1915 (Judge Rand); "The Blue Streak" 1917; "Riders of the Purple Sage" 1918 (Dyer); "True Blue" 1918 (Henry Cottenham); "Riders of the Dawn" 1920 (Chris Dorn); "The Girl Who Ran Wild" 1922 (Bummer Smith).

Robbins, Marty (1925-12/8/82). Films: "The Badge of Marshal Brennan" 1957 (Felipe); "Raiders of Old California" 1957; "Buffalo Gun" 1961 (Marty Robbins); "Ballad of a Gunfighter" 1964 (Marty Robbins); "Guns of a Stranger" 1973.

Robbins, Peter (1956-). Films: "...And Now Miguel" 1966 (Pedro). ¶TV: *Rawhide*—"Incident of the Pied Piper" 2-6-64; *F Troop*—"The Sergeant and the Kid" 1-12-67 (Joey Walker).

Robbins, Skeeter Bill (1887-

11/28/33). Films: "Don Quickshot of the Rio Grande" 1923 (Barfly); "Chasing Trouble" 1926 (Munn); "Man Rustlin'" 1926 (Slim); "Hard Hombre" 1931 (Slim); "Wild Horse" 1931 (Skeeter Burke); "The Boiling Point" 1932 (Hi Bailey); "Local Bad Man" 1932 (Skeet); "A Man's Land" 1932 (Skeeter); "Cowboy Counsellor" 1933 (Deputy Lafe Walters); "The Dude Bandit" 1933 (Skeeter Bill); "The Fighting Parson" 1933 (Arizona Joe).

Robbins, Walt (1888-7/13/65). Films: "Three Gold Coins" 1920 (Frank); "Just Tony" 1922 (Shorty); "Western Speed" 1922 (Shorty); "Hearts and Spurs" 1925 (Jerry Clark); "Beau Bandit" 1930 (Cowhand); "The Last Frontier" 1932-serial; "The Ox-Bow Incident" 1943 (Posse).

Rober, Richard (1906-5/26/52). Films: "Sierra" 1950 (Big Matt); "Man in the Saddle" 1951 (Fay Dutcher); "Passage West" 1951 (Mike); "Outlaw Women" 1952 (Woody Callaway); "The Savage" 1952 (Capt. Arnold Vaugant).

Roberson, Charles "Chuck" (1919-6/8/88). Films: "Plainsman and the Lady" 1946 (Deputy); "Jesse James Rides Again" 1947-serial (Lafe); "Haunted Trails" 1949 (Ed); "I Shot Jesse James" 1949 (Stunt Double); "Stampede" 1949 (Sandy); "Western Renegades" 1949 (Jones); "Bandit Queen" 1950 (Deputy); "Cow Town" 1950 (Mike Grady); "Frontier Outpost" 1950 (Gopher); "The James Brothers of Missouri" 1950-serial; "Lightning Guns" 1950 (Hank Burch); "Outcast of Black Mesa" 1950 (Kramer); "Rio Grande" 1950 (Officer); "Winchester '73" 1950 (Long Tom); "Trail of the Rustlers" 1950; "Fort Dodge Stampede" 1951 (Ragan); "Ridin' the Outlaw Trail" 1951 (Reno); "The Lusty Men" 1952 (Tall Cowboy); "Gun Belt" 1953 (Oliver); "The Far Country" 1955 (Latigo); "The Rawhide Years" 1956 (Johnny); "The Searchers" 1956 (Man at Wedding); "Seven Men from Now" 1956 (Mason); "Forty Guns" 1957 (Howard Swain); "Night Passage" 1957 (Roan); "Run of the Arrow" 1957 (Sergeant); "The Big Country" 1958 (Terrill Cowboy); "Man of the West" 1958 (Rifleman); "The Wonderful Country" 1959 (Gallup); "The Alamo" 1960 (Tennessean); "Sergeant Rutledge" 1960 (Juror); "Two Rode Together" 1961 (Comanche); "How the West Was Won" 1962; "The Man Who Shot Liberty Valance" 1962 (Henchman); "McClintock" 1963 (Sheriff Lord);

"Advance to the Rear" 1964 (Monk); "Cheyenne Autumn" 1964 (Trail Hand); "Black Spurs" 1965 (Norton); "Cat Ballou" 1965 (Armed Guard); "The Sons of Katie Elder" 1965 (Townsman); "Smoky" 1966 (Cowboy); "El Dorado" 1967; "The War Wagon" 1967 (Brown); "The Scalphunters" 1968 (Scalphunter); "The Undefeated" 1969 (Yankee Officer); "Chisum" 1970 (Trail Herder); "Rio Lobo" 1970 (Corporal). ¶TV: *The Lone Ranger*—"Six Gun Legacy" 11-24-49; *The Gene Autry Show*—"Gun Powder Range" 10-29-50, "Fight at Peaceful Mesa" 11-19-50, "The Sheriff of Santa Rosa" 12-24-50, "T.N.T." 12-31-50; *The Roy Rogers Show*—"The Desert Fugitive" 2-24-52, "The Minister's Son" 3-23-52, "Bullets and a Burro" 11-15-53; *Death Valley Days*—"The Trial of Red Haskell" 2-24-57, "Splinter Station" 10-19-60 (Sgt. Jim Laughlin); *Wagon Train*—"The Bije Wilcox Story" 11-19-58 (Capt. Thorp); *Rawhide*—"Incident of the Golden Calf" 3-13-59; *Gunsmoke*—"Cheyennes" 6-13-59 (Sergeant Keller), "Speak Me Fair" 5-7-60 (Driver), "Abe Blocker" 11-24-62 (Joe); *Have Gun Will Travel*—"The Campaign of Billy Banjo" 5-28-60, "The Legacy" 12-10-60 (Pike), "Soledad Crossing" 6-10-61, "Ben Jalisco" 11-18-61 (Carly); *Laramie*—"Riders of the Night" 3-7-61 (Chet), "The Killer Legend" 12-12-61, "Among the Missing" 9-25-62; *Tales of Wells Fargo*—"The Traveler" 2-24-62 (Lee); *Wide Country*—"Straightjacket for an Indian" 10-25-62 (Stunt Rider); *Daniel Boone*—"The High Cumberland" 4-14-66 & 4-21-66 (Dutch), "The Matchmaker" 10-27-66 (Shawnee Leader); *Laredo*—"The Legend of Midas Mantee" 9-16-66 (Rafer); *Lancer*—"The High Riders" 9-24-68.

Roberson, Lou (1921-11/21/66). Films: "The Lawless Rider" 1954 (Black Jack). ¶TV: *Branded*—"Judge Not" 9-12-65 (Shotgun).

Roberts, Adelle. Films: "The Desert Horseman" 1946 (Mary Ann Jarvis); "Galloping Thunder" 1946; "Roaring Rangers" 1946; "Throw a Saddle on a Star" 1946.

Roberts, Alan. TV: *Broken Arrow*—"The Teacher" 11-19-57 (Ysidro); *The Restless Gun*—"Mme. Brimstone" 5-4-59; *The Texan*—"Border Incident" 12-7-59; *Bonanza*—"El Toro Grande" 1-2-60.

Roberts, Allene. Films: "Santa Fe" 1951 (Ella Sue).

Roberts, Barbara. Films: "Tonto Kid" 1935 (Edna Mae Cartwright).

Roberts, Beatrice. Films: "Park Avenue Lodger" 1937 (Peggy O'Shea); "Pioneers of the West" 1940 (Anna).

Roberts, Beryl. Films: "Soda Water Cowboy" 1927 (Mademoiselle Zalla); "The Valley of Hunted Men" 1928.

Roberts, Beverly (1914-). Films: "God's Country and the Woman" 1937 (Jo Barton); "Call of the Yukon" 1938 (Jean Williams).

Roberts, Charles (-9/14/27). Films: "Quicker'n Lightnin'" 1925 (Truxillo).

Roberts, Christian (1944-). Films: "The Desperados" 1969 (Adam Galt).

Roberts, Davis (1917-7/18/93). Films: "Westworld" 1973 (Supervisor); "From Noon to Three" 1976 (Amanda's Servant). ¶TV: *Branded*—"Fill No Glass for Me" 11-7-65 & 11-14-65 (Hawkins); *The Virginian*—"Nobility of Kings" 11-10-65 (Stationmaster); *Cowboy in Africa*—"The Quiet Death" 2-19-68 (Herd Owner); *Gunsmoke*—"The Good Samaritans" 3-10-69 (Ike); *How the West Was Won*—"The Scavengers" 3-12-79 (Douglas).

Roberts, Desmond (1894-1/11/68). Films: "The Squaw Man" 1931 (Hardwick).

Roberts, Edith (1899-8/20/35). Films: "Lasca" 1919 (Lasca); "Her Five-Foot Higness" 1920 (Ellen); "The Son of the Wolf" 1922 (Chook-Ra); "The Sunshine Trail" 1923 (June Carpenter); "Phantom of the North" 1929 (Doris Rayburn); "The Wagon Master" 1929 (Sue Smith).

Roberts, Florence (1861-6/6/40). Films: "Rocky Mountain Mystery" 1935 (Mrs. Ballard).

Roberts, Gordon. *see* Young, Carleton.

Roberts, Hi (1912-). Films: "The Cheyenne Social Club" 1970 (Scared Man).

Roberts, Jeremy. TV: *Ned Blessing: The Story of My Life and Times*—Regular 1993 (Hugh Bell Borgers); *Adventures of Brisco County, Jr.*—"No Man's Land" 9-10-93 (Bill Swill), "Mail Order Brides" 12-10-93 (Bill Swill).

Roberts, John Todd (1954-12/14/79). TV: *Daniel Boone*—"The Plague That Came to Ford's Run" 10-31-68 (Tim).

Roberts, Lee. Films: "Death Valley Rangers" 1944; "The Caravan Trail" 1946; "Romance of the West" 1946 (Hadley); "Stars Over Texas" 1946 (Hank Lawrence); "Tumble-weed Trail" 1946; "Wild West" 1946 (Capt. Rogers); ; "Ghost Town Renegades" 1947 (Johnson); "Wild Country" 1947 (Josh Huckings); "Law Comes to Gunsight" 1947; "Law of the Lash" 1947 (Lefty); "Deadline" 1948; "Fighting Mustang" 1948; "Mark of the Lash" 1948; "Prairie Outlaws" 1948; "The Cowboy and the Indians" 1949 (Joe); "The Dalton Gang" 1949 (Mac); "Outlaw Country" 1949 (Buck); "Riders of the Dusk" 1949 (Barney); "Rimfire" 1949 (Norton); "South of Death Valley" 1949 (Scotty Tavish); "Square Dance Jubilee" 1949 (Smokey); "Battling Marshal" 1950; "Cherokee Uprising" 1950 (Kansas); "Covered Wagon Raid" 1950 (Steve); "Desperadoes of the West" 1950-serial (Larson); "The Fighting Redhead" 1950 (Goldie); "The James Brothers of Missouri" 1950-serial (Brandy Jones); "Law of the Panhandle" 1950 (Judd); "Abilene Trail" 1951 (Red); "Colorado Ambush" 1951 (Gus); "Distant Drums" 1951 (Pvt. Tibbett); "Lawless Cowboys" 1951 (Hanson); "The Longhorn" 1951 (Clark); "Man from Sonora" 1951; "Montana Desperado" 1951 (Jackson); "Nevada Badmen" 1951; "Stage to Blue River" 1951 (Ted); "Texas Lawmen" 1951 (Steve Morrow); "Wells Fargo Gunmaster" 1951 (Townsman); "Whistling Hills" 1951 (Slade); "Canyon Ambush" 1952; "Desperadoes' Outpost" 1952 (Spec Matson); "Kansas Territory" 1952 (Larkin); "The Lion and the Horse" 1952 (Riggs); "Battle of Rogue River" 1954 (Lt. Keith Ryan); "Gunfighters of the Northwest" 1954-serial (Arnold Reed); "Riding with Buffalo Bill" 1954-serial (Zeke); "Fort Yuma" 1955; "A Man Alone" 1955 (Higgs); "Man Without a Star" 1955; "Blazing the Overland Trail" 1956-serial (Tom Bridger); "Perils of the Wilderness" 1956-serial; "Gunfight at the O.K. Corral" 1957 (Finn Clanton). ¶TV: *The Lone Ranger*—"Mission Bells" 9-21-50, "Death in the Forest" 6-4-53; *The Roy Rogers Show*—"Peril from the Past" 4-13-52, "Shoot to Kill" 4-27-52; *The Cisco Kid*—"The Devil's Deputy" 5-10-52, "The Fire Engine" 5-31-52, "Fear" 6-28-52, "Bandaged Badman" 10-11-52, "The Black Terror" 11-29-52, "Mining Madness" 4-11-53, "Three Suspects" 5-23-53; *The Adventures of Rin Tin Tin*—"The Lost Scotchman" 5-27-55 (Travis), "Hubert Goes West" 5-18-56 (Al Cross), "The Old Soldier" 4-12-57 (Aaron Depew), "The Foot Soldier" 10-10-58 (Sgt. Spike Duffy); *Broken Arrow*—"Blood Brothers" 5-13-58 (Major Spillman).

Roberts, Lenore (1931-8/14/78). TV: *Lawman*—"The Escape of Joe Kilmer" 12-18-60 (Donna Killmer); *Death Valley Days*—"The Salt War" 1-25-61 (Rachel Emory).

Roberts, Leona (1880-1/29/54). Films: "Border Cafe" 1937 (Mrs. Whitney).

Roberts, Lois. TV: *Wagon Train*—"The Jed Whitmore Story" 1-13-64 (Patsy Lewis); *Gunsmoke*—"Ladies from St. Louis" 3-25-67 (Sister Louise).

Roberts, Luanne (1942-). TV: *Daniel Boone*—"Three Score and Ten" 2-6-69 (Beulah).

Roberts, Lynne (Mary Hart) (1922-). Films: "Heart of the Rockies" 1937 (Lorna); "Billy the Kid Returns" 1938 (Ellen); "Call the Mesquiteers" 1938 (Madge Irving); "The Lone Ranger" 1938-serial (Joan Blanchard); "Shine on Harvest Moon" 1938 (Claire Brower); "Come on, Rangers" 1939 (Janice Forbes); "Frontier Pony Express" 1939 (Ann Langhorne); "In Old Caliente" 1939 (Jean); "Rough Riders' Round-Up" 1939 (Dorothy Blair); "Southward Ho!" 1939 (Ellen Denbigh); "Last of the Duanes" 1941 (Nancy Bowdrey); "Ride on, Vaquero" 1941 (Marguerita); "Riders of the Purple Sage" 1941 (Bess); "Romance of the Rio Grande" 1941 (Maria); "The Big Bonanza" 1944 (Judy Parker); "Sioux City Sue" 1946 (Sue Warner); "Robin Hood of Texas" 1947 (Virginia); "Saddle Pals" 1947 (Shelly Brooks); "Eyes of Texas" 1948 (Fanny Thatcher); "Madonna of the Desert" 1948 (Monica Dale); "Sons of Adventure" 1948 (Jean); "The Timber Trail" 1948 (Alice Baker); "The Blazing Sun" 1950 (Helen Ellis); "Call of the Klondike" 1950 (Emily); "Dynamite Pass" 1950 (Mary). ¶TV: *The Gene Autry Show*—"The Breakup" 11-5-50, "Twisted Trails" 11-12-50; *Wyatt Earp*—"King of the Cattle Trails" 11-15-55 (Alice Kennedy).

Roberts, Mark (1921-). Films: "Posse" 1975 (Mr. Cooper). ¶TV: *Cheyenne*—"Deadline" 2-26-57 (Boyd Copeland); *Gunsmoke*—"Cain" 3-9-57 (Joel Adams); *Boots and Saddles*—"The Obsession" 10-3-57 (Lt. Hagan).

Roberts, Ned (1904-3/29/73). Films: "Marshal of Heldorado" 1950 (Bartender).

Roberts, Pernell (1930-). Films: "The Sheepman" 1958 (Choctaw); "Ride Lonesome" 1959 (Sam Boone); "Four Rode Out" 1969-Ital./Span./U.S.; "The Silent Gun" TVM-1969

(Sam Benner); "The Bravos" TVM-1972 (Jackson Buckley); "Charlie Cobb: Nice Night for a Hanging" TVM-1977 (Sheriff Yates); "The Night Rider" TVM-1979 (Alex Sheridan); "High Noon, Part II: The Return of Will Kane" TVM-1980 (Marshal J.D. Ward); "Desperado" TVM-1987 (Marshal Dancey). ¶TV: *Gunsmoke*—"How to Kill a Woman" 11-30-57 (Nat Pilcher), "Stranger in Town" 11-20-67 (Dave Reeves); *Sugarfoot*—"Misfire" 12-10-57, "Man Wanted" 2-18-58 (Deuce Brade); *Trackdown*—"The Reward" 1-3-58 (Bannion); *Have Gun Will Travel*—"Hey Boy's Revenge" 4-12-58; *Tombstone Territory*—"Pick Up the Gun" 5-14-58 (Johnny Coster); *Zane Grey Theater*—"Utopia, Wyoming" 6-6-58 (Jet Mason), "Pressure Point" 12-4-58; *Northwest Passage*—"The Assassin" 11-16-58 (Capt. Jacques Chavez); *Lawman*—"The Posse" 3-8-59 (Fent Hartley); *Cimarron City*—"Have Sword, Will Duel" 3-14-59 (O'Hara); *Bronco*—"The Belles of Silver Flat" 3-24-59 (Rev. David Clayton); *Buckskin*—"Mary MacNamara" 5-18-59 (Oscar); *Bonanza*—Regular 1959-65 (Adam Cartwright); *The Virginian*—"Long Journey Home" 12-14-66 (Jim Boyer, Sr.); *The Big Valley*—"Cage of Eagles" 4-24-67 (Padraid Madigan), "Run of the Cat" 10-21-68 (Ed Tanner); *Wild Wild West*—"The Night of the Firebrand" 9-15-67 (Sean O'Reilly); *Lancer*—"Welcome to Genesis" 11-18-69 (Banning); *Alias Smith and Jones*—"Escape from Wickenberg" 1-28-71 (Sam Finrock), "Twenty-One Days to Tenstrike" 1-6-72 (Terence Tynan); *The Men from Shiloh*—"Wolf Track" 3-17-71 (the Stranger); *Nakia*—"Roots of Anger" 11-30-74 (Matt Haywood); *The Quest*—"The Last of the Mountain Men" 1976; *Centennial*—Regular 1978-79 (General Asher); *Young Riders*—"Requiem for a Hero" 11-17-90 (Hezekiah Horn).

Roberts, Rachel (1927-11/26/80). Films: "Wild Rovers" 1971 (Maybell).

Roberts, Ralph (1922-). Films: "The Misfits" 1961 (Ambulance Driver). ¶TV: *Wild Wild West*—"The Night of the Glowing Corpse" 10-29-65 (Sen. Hastings); *Gunsmoke*—"Ladies from St. Louis" 3-25-67 (Williams).

Roberts, Roy (1906-5/28/75). Films: "My Darling Clementine" 1946 (Mayor); "Smoky" 1946 (Jeff); "Fury at Furnace Creek" 1948 (Al Shanks); "Calamity Jane and Sam Bass" 1949 (Marshal Peak); "The

Palomino" 1950 (Ben Lane); "Sierra" 1950 (Sheriff Knudson); "Stage to Tucson" 1950 (Jim Maroon); "Wyoming Mail" 1950 (Charles De-Haven); "The Cimarron Kid" 1951 (Pat Roberts); "Santa Fe" 1951 (Cole Sanders); "Cripple Creek" 1952 (Marshall Thetheroe); "The Man Behind the Gun" 1952 (Mark Sheldon); "The Lone Hand" 1953 (Mr. Skaggs); "San Antone" 1953 (John Chisum); "Tumbleweed" 1953 (Nick Buckley); "Dawn at Socorro" 1954 (Doc Jameson); "The Outlaw Stallion" 1954 (Hagen); "They Rode West" 1954 (Sgt. Creever); "The Last Command" 1955 (Dr. Sutherland); "Wyoming Renegades" 1955 (Sheriff McVey); "The First Texan" 1956 (Sherman); "King and Four Queens" 1956 (Sheriff Larrabee); "The White Squaw" 1956 (Purvis); "Yaqui Drums" 1956. ¶TV: *The Adventures of Rin Tin Tin*—"Rin Tin Tin and the Flaming Forest" 10-29-54 (Tom Rogers), "The Flaming Forest" 12-7-56 (Tom Rogers); *The Lone Ranger*—"The Tell-Tale Bullet" 4-14-55; *Wyatt Earp*—"King of the Cattle Trails" 11-15-55 (Shanghai Pierce); *My Friend Flicka*—"The Phantom Herd" 12-23-55; *Schlitz Playhouse of the Stars*—"The Bitter Land" 4-13-56 (Sheriff Tom Hudson); *Zane Grey Theater*—"Proud Woman" 10-25-57 (Michael Bowers); *The Restless Gun*—"The Gold Buckle" 12-30-57 (Kit Springer); *The Deputy*—"Judas Town" 12-31-60 (Linc McCurdy); *Gunsmoke*—"Indian Ford" 12-2-61 (Tabor), "The Dealer" 4-14-62 (Billy Baskin), Regular 1963-75 (Mr. Bodkin); *Lawman*—"Heritage of Hate" 3-18-62 (John Kemper); *Have Gun Will Travel*—"Invasion" 4-28-62 (Sheriff); *Bonanza*—"A Hot Day for a Hanging" 10-14-62 (Fillmore), "Justice" 1-8-67 (Bristol); *Cheyenne*—"The Vanishing Breed" 11-19-62 (Senator Matson); *Wide Country*—"My Candle Burns at Both Ends" 12-20-62 (George Frazier); *Rawhide*—"Incident at Confidence Creek" 11-28-63 (Mayor), "Six Weeks to Bent Fork" 9-28-65 (Fletcher); *Death Valley Days*—"See the Elephant and Hear the Owl" 5-9-64; *Laredo*—"Quarter Past Eleven" 3-24-66 (Press), "Finnegan" 10-21-66 (Kelly); *The Road West*—"This Savage Land" 9-12-66 & 9-19-66 (Dr. Reynolds).

Roberts, Steve (1917-82). Films: "Rogue River" 1950 (Mayor Arthur Judson); "The Wild and the Innocent" 1959 (Bouncer); "The Quick Gun" 1964 (Dr. Stevens). ¶TV: *The Lone Ranger*—"The Red Mark" 9-3-53; *The Californians*—"Cat's Paw" 3-

3-59 (Steve Montgomery); *Have Gun Will Travel*—"The Long Hunt" 3-7-59 (John Dundee), "The Long Weekend" 4-8-61, "Bear Bait" 5-13-61 (Sheriff); *Gunsmoke*—"Wind" 3-21-59 (Hank); *Black Saddle*—"Client: Reynolds" 5-23-59 (Whit Graham); *Bonanza*—"San Francisco Holiday" 4-2-60; *Hotel De Paree*—"Sundance and the Barren Soil" 5-20-60 (Pace); *Cheyenne*—"The Return of Mr. Grimm" 2-13-61 (Judge Miller); *The Deputy*—"Enemy of the Town" 5-6-61 (Adam Crockett); *Death Valley Days*—"The Left Hand Is Damned" 11-1-64; *The Loner*—"An Echo of Bugles" 9-18-65 (Doctor); *The Virginian*—"That Saunders Woman" 3-30-66 (Alfred Krebs); *Lancer*—"The High Riders" 9-24-68.

Roberts, Thayer (1902-2/28/68). TV: *The Cisco Kid*—"Stolen River" 10-3-53, "Montezuma's Treasure" 11-7-53; *Sergeant Preston of the Yukon*—"Crime at Wounded Moose" 1-12-56 (Luke Reading), "The Coward" 4-12-56 (Caleb Jenks), "Eye of Evil" 11-8-56 (Tallin); *Wyatt Earp*—"When Sherman Marched Through Kansas" 3-18-58 (Gen. Sherman); *Death Valley Days*—"Death Ride" 3-15-61 (Doctor).

Roberts, Theodore (1861-12/14/28). Films: "The Call of the North" 1914 (Galen Albert, the Factor); "Where the Trail Divides" 1914 (Colonel Lander); "The Girl of the Golden West" 1915 (Rance); "The Cost of Hatred" 1917 (Justus Graves); "Nan of Music Mountain" 1917 (Duke Morgan); "Arizona" 1918 (Canby); "M'Liss" 1918 (Bummer Smith); "The Squaw Man" 1918 (Bib Bill).

Roberts, Tracey. Films: "Fort Defiance" 1951 (Julie); "Frontier Gambler" 1956; "Sam Whiskey" 1969. TV: *The Adventures of Rin Tin Tin*—"Boundary Busters" 12-20-57 (Ginny Anderson); *Riverboat*—"Face of Courage" 12-27-59 (Lola Duhaime); *The Deputy*—"Lawman's Conscience" 7-1-61 (Mary Hayden).

Robertson, Cliff (1925-). Films: "J.W. Coop" 1971 (J.W. Coop); "The Great Northfield, Minnesota Raid" 1972 (Cole Younger). TV: *Wagon Train*—"The Liam Fitzmorgan Story" 10-28-58 (Liam Fitzmorgan); *Riverboat*—"End of a Dream" 9-19-60 (Martinus Van Der Brigg); *The Outlaws*—"Ballad for a Badman" 10-6-60 (Chad Burns), "The Connie Masters Story" 10-12-61 (Jack Masters), "The Dark Sunrise of Griff Kincaid" 1-4-62 (Griff Kincaid); *Alcoa Premiere*—"Second Chance" 3-13-62 (Hoby Dunlap).

Robertson, Dale (1923-). Films: "Fighting Man of the Plains" 1949 (Jesse James); "The Cariboo Trail" 1950 (Will Gray); "Two Flags West" 1950 (Lem); "The Outcasts of Poker Flat" 1952 (John Oakhurst); "Return of the Texan" 1952 (Sam Crockett); "City of Badmen" 1953 (Brett Stanton); "Devil's Canyon" 1953 (Billy Reynolds); "The Silver Whip" 1953 (Race Crime); "The Gambler from Natchez" 1954 (Vance Colby); "Sitting Bull" 1954 (Parris); "Dakota Incident" 1956 (John Banner); "A Day of Fury" 1956 (Jagade); "Hell Canyon Outlaws" 1957; "Blood on the Arrow" 1964 (Wade Cooper); "Law of the Lawless" 1964 (Judge Clem Rogers); "The Man from Button Willow" 1965 (Voice of Justin Eagle); "Scalplock" TVM-1966 (Ben Calhoun); "Last Ride of the Dalton Gang" TVM-1979 (Judge Isaac Parker). TV: *Schlitz Playhouse of the Stars*—"Flowers for Jenny" 8-3-56 (Cactus Kid), "A Tale of Wells Fargo" 12-14-58 (Jim Hardie); *Tales of Wells Fargo*—Regular 1957-62 (Jim Hardie); *Iron Horse*—Regular 1966-68 (Ben Calhoun); *Death Valley Days*—Host 1968-70, "Tracy's Triumph" 10-4-69, "The Biggest Little Post Office in the World" 2-7-70, "The King of Uvalde Road" 4-25-70 (Harry).

Robertson, Dennis (1939-). Films: "War Party" 1965; "Little House: The Last Farewell" TVM-1984 (Drew Coleson). TV: *Gunsmoke*—"Caleb" 3-28-64 (Stable Boy); *Death Valley Days*—"Magic Locket" 5-16-65 (Sam Dickson); *Alias Smith and Jones*—"The Fifth Victim" 3-25-71 (Deputy); *Bonanza*—"First Love" 12-26-72 (Ranch Hand).

Robertson, Orie O. (1881-4/14/64). Films: "Bucking the Truth" 1926 (Tom Bailey).

Robertson, Willard (1886-4/5/48). Films: "Last of the Duanes" 1930 (Captain of the Rangers); "The Cisco Kid" 1931 (Enos Hankins); "Fair Warning" 1931 (Tex Calder); "The Broken Wing" 1932 (Sylvester Cross); "The Gay Caballero" 1932 (Maj. Lawrence Blount); "Rider of Death Valley" 1932 (Bill Joyce); "Texas Bad Man" 1932 (Milton Keefe); "The Last of the Mohicans" 1936 (Capt. Winthrop); "The Three Godfathers" 1936 (Reverend McLane); "Park Avenue Lodger" 1937 (Ben Morton); "Roaring Timber" 1937 (Harrigan); "Heritage of the Desert" 1939 (Nebraska); "Jesse James" 1939 (Clark); "Range War" 1939 (Buck Collins); "Union Pacific" 1939 (Oakes Ames); "Brigham Young—Frontiersman" 1940 (Heber Kimball); "Lucky Cisco Kid" 1940 (Judge McQuade); "My Little Chickadee" 1940 (Uncle John); "Northwest Mounted Police" 1940 (Supt. Harrington); "Men of the Timberland" 1941; "Texas" 1941 (Wilson); "The Ox-Bow Incident" 1943 (Sheriff); "Along Came Jones" 1945 (Luke Packard); "Renegades" 1946 (Nathan Brockway); "Fury at Furnace Creek" 1948 (Gen. Leads).

Robins, Herb. Films: "Thomasine and Bushrod" 1974 (Dodson).

Robinson, Andy (1942-). Films: "Mackintosh & T.J." 1975 (Coley Phipps); "Into the Badlands" TVM-1991 (Sheriff Anson Starrett). TV: *Bonanza*—"Forever" 9-12-72 (John Harper); *Kung Fu*—"Cross-ties" 2-21-74 (Johnny); *Young Maverick*—"Makin' Tracks" 1-9-80 (Sangree); *Big Bend Country*—Pilot 8-27-81 (Beau).

Robinson, Ann. Films: "Gun Brothers" 1956 (Rose Fargo); "Gun Duel in Durango" 1957 (Judy). TV: *Cheyenne*—"Mountain Fortress" 9-20-55, "Deadline" 2-26-57 (Paula Copeland); *Fury*—Regular 1955-60 (Helen Watkins); *The Texan*—"Borrowed Time" 3-7-60 (Anne Carter); *Rawhide*—"Incident of the Challenge" 10-14-60 (Julia Garcia); *Wyatt Earp*—"Billy Buckett, Incorporated" 1-3-61 (Hetty Doane); *Sugarfoot*—"Angel" 3-6-61 (Marie McTavish).

Robinson, Bartlett (1912-3/26/86). Films: "Warlock" 1959 (Slavin); "A Distant Trumpet" 1964 (Maj. Hiram Prescott). TV: *Gunsmoke*—"Cholera" 12-29-56 (Gabriel), "Joke's on Us" 3-15-58 (Jake Kaiser), "Doc Quits" 2-21-59 (Jake Wirth), "Kangaroo" 9-26-59 (Bowers), "Jailbait Janet" 2-27-60 (Krocker); *Maverick*—"The Wrecker" 12-1-57 (Longhurst), "Deadly Image" 3-12-61 (Captain Ranson); *Cheyenne*—"Renegades" 2-11-58 (Col. Ralph Donovan); *Tombstone Territory*—"Triangle of Death" 5-7-58 (Aaron McCalin); *The Restless Gun*—"Remember the Dead" 11-17-58 (George Mason); *The Rifleman*—"Outlaw's Inheritance" 6-16-59 (Samuel Britton); *Fury*—"Gymkhana" 1-23-60 (Fred Hughes); *Laramie*—"Rope of Steel" 2-16-60 (Sheriff), "Duel at Parkison Town" 12-13-60 (Sheriff), "The Passing of Kuba Smith" 1-3-61 (Davis), "The Fugitives" 2-12-63; *Riverboat*—"The Sellout" 4-18-60 (George Channing), "No Bridge on the River" 10-24-60 (Grimes); *Wyatt Earp*—"Billy Buckett, Incorporated" 1-3-61 (Paul Scott); *Whispering Smith*—"The

Deadliest Weapon" 6-19-61 (Ralph Miller); *The Dakotas*—"Trial at Grand Forks" 3-25-63 (Judge Elias Stone); *Wild Wild West*—"The Night of the Druid's Blood" 3-25-66 (Senator Clay Waterford); *The Virginian*—"Ah Sing vs. Wyoming" 10-25-67; *Bonanza*—"Judgment at Red Creek" 2-26-67 (Willow), "Return Engagement" 3-1-70 (Howell); *The Guns of Will Sonnett*—"The Natural Way" 9-29-67, "The Marriage" 3-14-69 (Banker); *The Men from Shiloh*—"Hannah" 12-30-70 (Doctor); *Kung Fu*—"The Nature of Evil" 3-21-74 (Bartender).

Robinson, Charles (1944-). Films: "Shenandoah" 1965 (Nathan Anderson). ¶TV: *Laramie*—"Deadly Is the Night" 11-7-61 (Bud Williams), "Double Eagles" 11-20-62 (Sam Moore); *Wide Country*—"Tears on a Painted Face" 11-29-62 (Chris Xeno); *Stoney Burke*—"Color Him Lucky" 4-1-63 (Dennis); *Wagon Train*—"The Antone Rose Story" 5-22-63 (Antone Rose); *The Travels of Jaimie McPheeters*—"The Day of the Last Bugle" 10-13-63 (Lt. Reid Beecher); *Gunsmoke*—"The Prodigal" 9-25-67 (Amos Cole); *The High Chaparral*—"Tornado Frances" 10-11-68 (Warren); *The Virginian*—"No War for the Warrior" 2-18-70 (John); *The Buffalo Soldiers*—Pilot 5-26-79 (Private Wright).

Robinson, Chris (1938-). Films: "The Long Rope" 1961 (Reb Gilroy); "Shoot Out at Big Sag" 1962 (Lee Barbee). ¶TV: *Colt .45*—"Appointment in Agoura" 6-7-60 (Cal Sanger); *Zane Grey Theater*—"So Young the Savage Land" 11-20-60 (Paul Martin); *The Outlaws*—"The Daltons Must Die" 1-26-61 & 2-2-61 (Red Buck); *Two Faces West*—"The Wayward" 3-27-61; *Empire*—"A Place to Put a Life" 10-9-62 (Arnold Koenig); *The Dakotas*—"Red Sky Over Bismarck" 1-14-63 (Chino); *Gunsmoke*—"The Bad One" 1-26-63 (Willie Jett); *Wide Country*—"Speckle Bird" 1-31-63 (Gabriel Horn); *Wagon Train*—"The Sara Proctor Story" 2-27-63 (Brad Proctor), "The Duncan McIvor Story" 3-9-64 (Lieutenant Carter), "The Hide Hunters" 9-27-64 (Gib Ryker); *Stoney Burke*—"A Girl Named Amy" 4-29-63 (Ross); *The Virginian*—"It Takes a Big Man" 10-23-63 (Hank Anders), "The Dark Challenge" 9-23-64 (Arnie Hendricks), "The Saddle Warmer" 9-18-68 (Coley); *Custer*—"Accused" 9-13-67 (Lt. Tim Rudford); *The Men from Shiloh*—"Experiment at New Life" 11-18-70 (Sandy); *The Busters*—Pilot 5-28-78 (Nick Carroll).

Robinson, Dewey (1899-12/11/50). Films: "Law and Order" 1932 (Ed Deal); "The Three Godfathers" 1936 (Horse Thief); "Rangers of Fortune" 1940; "Sky Bandits" 1940 (Swiddie); "Three Faces West" 1940 (Bartender); "Alaska" 1944; "The Wistful Widow of Wagon Gap" 1947 (Miner); "River Lady" 1948 (Bouncer); "Hellfire" 1949 (Bartender); "Tough Assignment" 1949 (Customer); "Dallas" 1950 (Prisoner); "Skipalong Rosenbloom" 1951.

Robinson, Edward G. (1893-1/26/73). Films: "The Violent Men" 1955 (Lew Wilkison); "Cheyenne Autumn" 1964 (Carl Schurz); "The Outrage" 1964 (Con Man); "MacKenna's Gold" 1969 (Old Adams). ¶TV: *Zane Grey Theater*—"Heritage" 4-2-59 (Victor Bers).

Robinson, Jr., Edward G. (1934-2/26/74). TV: *Zane Grey Theater*—"Heritage" 4-2-59 (Hunt Bers); *Gunsmoke*—"Cheyennes" 6-13-59 (Brown); *Wagon Train*—"The Allison Justis Story" 10-19-60 (Deputy); *Laramie*—"Duel at Parkison Town" 12-13-60 (Citizen).

Robinson, Fay. Films: "A Child of the Prairie" 1915; "A Child of the Prairie" 1925 (Loretta).

Robinson, Forrest (1858-1/6/24). Films: "When a Man's a Man" 1924 (the Dean).

Robinson, Frances (1916-8/16/71). Films: "Forbidden Valley" 1938 (Wilda Lanning); "Desperate Trails" 1939 (Judith Longton); "Riders of Pasco Basin" 1940 (Jean Madison); "Outlaws of the Panhandle" 1941 (Doris Burnett). ¶TV: *Circus Boy*—"The Lady and the Circus" 3-31-57 (Rosemary Anderson); *Zane Grey Theater*—"The Open Cell" 11-22-57 (Eleanor Winter).

Robinson, Gertrude (1891-3/19/62). Films: "That Chink at Golden Gulch" 1910; "At Cripple Creek" 1912; "The Gambler of the West" 1914 (Cactus Kate); "Strongheart" 1914.

Robinson, Jay (1930-). TV: *Wild Wild West*—"The Night of the Sedgewick Curse" 10-18-68 (Dr. Maitland); *The Men from Shiloh*—"Lady at the Bar" 11-4-70 (Hewitt); *Cliffhangers*—"The Secret Empire" 1979 (Demeter).

Robinson, Phillip. Films: "The Last Trail" 1933 (Frank Briggs).

Robinson, Rad (1910-9/20/88). Films: "Renegade Trail" 1939 (Rider); "Knights of the Range" 1940 (Brazos); "The Light of Western Stars" 1940 (Monty); "Stagecoach War" 1940 (Smiley).

Robinson, Robert H. Films: "Cattle Queen" 1951 (Armstrong).

Robinson, Roger (1941-). Films: "This Was the West That Was" TVM-1974.

Robinson, Ruth (1887-3/17/66). Films: "Ramona" 1936 (Patient in Doctor's Office); "Roll Along, Cowboy" 1937 (Mrs. Edwina Blake); "The Kansas Terrors" 1939 (Juanita); "Covered Wagon Days" 1940 (Mama Rinaldo); "Texas Terrors" 1940; "Across the Sierras" 1941; "Down Mexico Way" 1941 (Mercedes); "In Old California" 1942. ¶TV: *Tombstone Territory*—"Cave-In" 3-26-58 (Emily).

Robles, Richard (1902-4/21/40). Films: "Union Pacific" 1939 (Indian Brave).

Roboson, Andrew. see Robson, Andres.

Robotham, George. Films: "The Great Locomotive Chase" 1956 (William Knight); "The Deerslayer" 1957 (Stunts); "Five Card Stud" 1968 (Stoney). ¶TV: *Zane Grey Theater*—"A Gun for Willie" 10-6-60 (Navajo Jack); *Bonanza*—"Knight Errant" 11-18-62 (Frank); *Laredo*—"A Double Shot of Nepenthe" 9-30-66, "Like One of the Family" 3-24-67; *Daniel Boone*—"The Renegade" 9-28-67; *Alias Smith and Jones*—"What's in It for Mia?" 2-24-72 (Max).

Robson, Andrew (1869-4/26/61). Films: "Salomy Jane" 1914 (Yuba Bill); "The Lily of Poverty Flat" 1915 (Jack Hamlin); "Branding Broadway" 1918 (Harrington, Sr.); "Square Deal Sanderson" 1919 (Judge Graney); "The Heart of Juanita" 1919 (Sheriff Tanner); "Just Squaw" 1919 (Snake Le Gal); "Cupid, the Cowpuncher" 1920 (Zack Sewell).

Robson, May (1858-10/20/42). Films: "The Texans" 1938 (Granna); "Texas Rangers Ride Again" 1940 (Cecilia Dangerfield).

Robson, Wayne. Films: "McCabe and Mrs. Miller" 1971 (Bartender); "The Grey Fox" 1983-Can. (Shorty).

Robyns, William (1855-1/22/36). Films: "Hell Fire Austin" 1932 (Hicks); "The Phantom Thunderbolt" 1933 (Mr. Norton); "The Lone Cowboy" 1934 (Postman).

Roc, Patricia (1918-). Films: "Canyon Passage" 1946 (Caroline Marsh).

Roccardi, Albert (1864-5/14/34). Films: "Romance of the Rio Grande" 1929 (Padre Miguel)

Rocco, Alex (1936-). Films:

"Hearts of the West" 1975 (Earl, the Assistant Director).

Roccuzzo, Mario (1942-). TV: *Stoney Burke*—"Kincaid" 4-22-63 (Leader).

Roche, Eugene (1928-). Films: "The New Maverick" TVM-1978 (Judge Crupper).

Rochelle, Claire (1910-5/23/81). Films: "Boothill Brigade" 1937 (Bobbie Reynolds); "Empty Saddles" 1937 (Madge Grant); "Guns in the Dark" 1937 (Joan Williams); "Ridin' the Lone Trail" 1937 (Joan Randall); "Code of the Fearless" 1939 (Jean Morrison); "El Diablo Rides" 1939; "The Pal from Texas" 1939 (Alice Malden); "Riders of the Sage" 1939 (Mona Halsey); "Two-Gun Troubador" 1939 (Helen Bradfield); "Buzzy Rides the Range" 1940 (Myra Harding); "The Kid from Santa Fe" 1940 (Millie Logan); "Lightning Strikes West" 1940 (Mae Grant); "North from the Lone Star" 1941 (Lucy Belle); "Texas Justice" 1942 (Nora).

Rochelle, Edwin (-2/16/77). TV: *Laredo*—"A Very Small Assignment" 3-17-66.

Rock, Blossom (Marie Blake) (1899-1/14/78). Films: "Sons of New Mexico" 1949 (Hannah Dobbs); "The Second Time Around" 1961 (Mrs. Collins). ¶TV: *My Friend Flicka*—"The Medicine Man" 5-11-56.

Rocket, Charles. Films: "Dances with Wolves" 1990 (Lt. Elgin); "Wagons East!" 1994.

Rockwell, Jack (-11/10/47). Films: "Lucky Larkin" 1930; "Alias the Bad Man" 1931; "Arizona Terror" 1931; "Branded Men" 1931; "Range Law" 1931 (Sheriff); "Guns for Hire" 1932; "Hell Fire Austin" 1932; "The Sunset Trail" 1932; "Texas Gun Fighter" 1932; "Whistlin' Dan" 1932 (Cal Webster); "Come on Tarzan" 1933 (Sheriff); "Fargo Express" 1933 (Deputy); "King of the Arena" 1933 (Saunders); "The Lone Avenger" 1933 (Sheriff); "Outlaw Justice" 1933; "The Phantom Thunderbolt" 1933; "Strawberry Roan" 1933 (Beef); "The Trail Drive" 1933 (Marshal); "When a Man Rides Alone" 1933 (Red); "Brand of Hate" 1934; "The Fiddlin' Buckaroo" 1934 (Sheriff); "Gun Justice" 1934 (Hank Rivers); "Honor of the Range" 1934 (Rocky); "In Old Santa Fe" 1934 (Sheriff); "The Law of the Wild" 1934-serial (Sheriff); "The Lawless Frontier" 1934 (Sheriff); "The Lucky Texan" 1934; "The Man from Hell" 1934 (Marshal Lon Kelly); "Mystery Mountain" 1934-serial; "'Neath the Arizona Skies" 1934 (Vic Byrd); "The Prescott Kid" 1934 (Cowboy); "The Red Rider" 1934-serial; "Rocky Rhodes" 1934 (Reed); "Smoking Guns" 1934 (Captain Adams); "Wheels of Destiny" 1934 (Ed); "When a Man Sees Red" 1934 (Sheriff); "Alias John Law" 1935 (Lamar Blyth); "Bulldog Courage" 1935; "Five Bad Men" 1935 (Gunfighter); "Heir to Trouble" 1935; "Justice of the Range" 1935 (Rawhide); "Law Beyond the Range" 1935 (Garvey); "Lawless Riders" 1935 (Sheriff); "Lightning Triggers" 1935 (Butch Greer); "The Man from Guntown" 1935 (Bill Slater); "The Miracle Rider" 1935-serial; "No Man's Range" 1935 (Sheriff); "Outlaw Rule" 1935 (Whistler); "Outlawed Guns" 1935 (Harvey Daniels); "Riding Wild" 1935 (Rusty); "Tonto Kid" 1935 (Sheriff Hack Baker); "Tumbling Tumbleweeds" 1935 (McWade); "Valley of Wanted Men" 1935; "Brand of the Outlaws" 1936 (Ben Holt); "Guns and Guitars" 1936 (Sheriff Ed Miller); "Heroes of the Range" 1936 (Sheriff); "The Law Rides" 1936 (Sheriff Anderson); "The Lawless Nineties" 1936 (Smith); "Lightning Bill Carson" 1936 (Sheriff); "The Lion's Den" 1936 (Sheriff); "The Lone Den" 1936; "Lucky Terror" 1936 (Batt); "The Mysterious Avenger" 1936; "Red River Valley" 1936; "Rio Grande Ranger" 1936 (Capt. Winkler); "Roarin' Guns" 1936 (Barry); "Rogue of the Range" 1936 (Stone); "The Singing Cowboy" 1936 (Sheriff); "Sundown Saunders" 1936 (Preston); "The Traitor" 1936 (Smoky); "Valley of the Lawless" 1936 (Sheriff Graves); "Winds of the Wasteland" 1936; "Dodge City Trail" 1937 (Steve's Gang Member); "The Old Wyoming Trail" 1937 (Outlaw); "One Man Justice" 1937 (Bob); "Outlaws of the Prairie" 1937 (Sheriff); "Range Defenders" 1937; "The Rangers Step In" 1937 (Marshal J.T. Rockwell); "Reckless Ranger" 1937 (Mort); "The Red Rope" 1937 (Dotkins); "Riders of the Rockies" 1937 (Captain Hayes); "Springtime in the Rockies" 1937; "Stars Over Arizona" 1937; "Texas Trail" 1937 (Shorty); "Trapped" 1937 (Tom Haggard; "The Trusted Outlaw" 1937; "Two Gun Law" 1937 (Bledsoe); "Westbound Mail" 1937 (Sheriff); "Guilty Trails" 1938 (Brad Eason); "The Black Bandit" 1938 (Boyd Allen); "Law of the Plains" 1938 (Marshal); "The Mysterious Rider" 1938 (Lem); "The Lone Ranger" 1938-serial (Regan); "Prairie Justice" 1938 (John Benson); "Prairie Moon" 1938 (Sheriff); "Rolling Caravans" 1938; "Shine on Harvest Moon" 1938 (Jim); "The Singing Outlaw" 1938; "Sunset Trail" 1938 (Stage Driver); "Under Western Stars" 1938 (Sheriff); "West of Cheyenne" 1938 (Sheriff); "Western Trails" 1938 (Bartender); "Days of Jesse James" 1939 (McDaniels); "Lone Star Pioneers" 1939; "The Man from Sundown" 1939 (Hank Austin); "Overland with Kit Carson" 1939-serial; "Renegade Trail" 1939 (Slim); "Rough Riders' Round-Up" 1939 (Harrison); "Silver on the Sage" 1939 (City Marshal); "The Stranger from Texas" 1939 (Sheriff Fletcher); "Western Caravans" 1939 (Cole); "Bullets for Rustlers" 1940 (Sheriff Webb); "Adventures of Red Ryder" 1940-serial (Wilson); "Cherokee Strip" 1940 (Ace Eastman); "The Carson City Kid" 1940; "The Dark Command" 1940 (Assassin); "The Durango Kid" 1940 (Evans); "Hidden Gold" 1940 (Stage Driver); "Pony Post" 1940 (Mack Richards); "The Return of Wild Bill" 1940 (Sheriff); "Stagecoach War" 1940 (Mart Gunther); "Young Bill Hickok" 1940; "Border Vigilantes" 1941 (Henry Weaver); "Jesse James at Bay" 1941; "King of Dodge City" 1941 (Martin); "Law of the Range" 1941; "The Pinto Kid" 1941 (Marshal); "Rawhide Rangers" 1941; "Red River Valley" 1941; "Riders of Death Valley" 1941-serial; "Secrets of the Wastelands" 1941 (Sheriff); "Sheriff of Tombstone" 1941; "Stick to Your Guns" 1941; "Thunder Over the Prairie" 1941 (Clayton); "Twilight on the Trail" 1941 (Brent); "Wide Open Town" 1941 (Rancher); "The Cyclone Kid" 1942; "Man from Cheyenne" 1942; "Overland Mail" 1942-serial; "The Sundown Kid" 1942; "Sunset Serenade" 1942; "Undercover Man" 1942 (Capt. John Hawkins); "Daredevils of the West" 1943-serial (Sheriff Watson); "Dead Man's Gulch" 1943 (Bat Matson); "Fighting Frontier" 1943 (Ira); "Frontier Badman" 1943 (Mack); "The Man from Thunder River" 1943; "Overland Mail Robbery" 1943; "Raiders of Sunset Pass" 1943 (Sheriff Dale); "Red River Robin Hood" 1943; "The Renegade" 1943; "Silver City Raiders" 1943; "Wagon Tracks West" 1943 (Sheriff Summers); "West of Texas" 1943 (Gabe Jones); "Cowboy from Lonesome River" 1944; "Forty Thieves" 1944 (Sam Garms); "Gunsmoke Mesa" 1944 (Sheriff Horner); "Law Men" 1944; "Lumberjack" 1944 (Sheriff); "Mystery Man" 1944 (Marshal Ted Blaine); "Raiders of Ghost City" 1944-serial;

"Trigger Trail" 1944 (Joe Kincaid); "The Vigilantes Ride" 1944 (Capt. Randall); "West of the Rio Grande" 1944; "Both Barrels Blazing" 1945; "Colorado Pioneers" 1945; "Flame of the West" 1945 (Knott); "Frontier Feud" 1945 (Sheriff Clancy); "Outlaws of the Rockies" 1945 (Sheriff Hall); "Phantom of the Plains" 1945; "Rough Riders of Cheyenne" 1945; "Rough Ridin' Justice" 1945 (Sheriff Kramer); "Stranger from Santa Fe" 1945; "Canyon Passage" 1946 (Teamster); "Conquest of Cheyenne" 1946; "Cowboy Blues" 1946; "Drifting Along" 1946 (Sheriff Devers); "Frontier Gunlaw" 1946; "Gentleman from Texas" 1946; "Lawless Empire" 1946 (Jed Stevens); "Red River Renegades" 1946; "Roaring Rangers" 1946; "Two-Fisted Ranger" 1946; "Under Arizona Skies" 1946; "Flashing Guns" 1947 (Cassidy).

Rockwell, Norman (1894-11/8/78). Films: "Stagecoach" 1966 (Townsman).

Rockwell, Robert (1921-). TV: *The Lone Ranger*—"The Beeler Gang" 8-10-50, "One Jump Ahead" 12-14-50, "The Outcast" 1-18-51, "Mr. Trouble" 3-8-51; *Tales of Wells Fargo*—"A Time to Kill" 4-22-57 (Jason); *Gunsmoke*—"Fawn" 4-4-59 (Roger Phillips); *Man from Blackhawk*—Regular 1959-60 (Sam Logan); *Death Valley Days*—"Death Ride" 3-15-61 (William Thorne); *Maverick*—"Substitute Gun" 4-2-61 (Tom Blauvelt); *Bronco*—"A Town That Lived and Died" 4-9-62 (Van Dix).

Rodann, Ziva. Films: "Forty Guns" 1957 (Rio); "Last Train from Gun Hill" 1959 (Catherine Morgan). ¶TV: *Death Valley Days*—"Forbidden Wedding" 3-22-60 (Josefa); *Have Gun Will Travel*—"An International Affair" 4-2-60 (Princess Molokai); *Bonanza*—"The Fugitive" 2-4-61 (Maria); *Tales of Wells Fargo*—"Rifles for Red Hand" 5-15-61 (Leah Harper); *The Rifleman*—"The Vaqueros" 10-2-61 (Maria); *Rawhide*—"The Book" 1-8-65 (Pony).

Rodd, Marcia (1940-). TV: *Bret Maverick*—"The Yellow Rose" 12-22-81 (Captain Salter).

Rodgers, Walter (1886-4/24/51). Films: "The Law at Silver Camp" 1915; "The Fighting Trail" 1917-serial; "The Tenderfoot" 1917 (Mr. Rogers); "Vengeance and the Woman" 1917-serial; "A Fight for Millions" 1918-serial; "Smashing Barriers" 1919-serial; "Steelheart" 1921 (Steve); "Flaming Frontier" 1926 (President Ulysses S. Grant).

Rodin, Merrill Guy. Films:

"American Empire" 1942 (Paxton Bryce, Jr.); "Sagebrush Law" 1943; "Buffalo Bill" 1944 (Bellboy).

Rodman, Nancy (1931-). Films: "Daniel Boone, Trail Blazer" 1957 (Susannah Boone); "Geronimo" 1962 (Mrs. Marsh).

Rodman, Victor (1892-6/29/65). TV: *Wanted—Dead or Alive*—"Drop to Drink" 12-27-58 (Rufe Teller).

Rodney, John (1916-2/20/67). Films: "Pursued" 1947 (Adam Callum); "Calamity Jane and Sam Bass" 1949 (Morgan). ¶TV: *Cheyenne*—"Retaliation" 11-13-61 (Maxon); *Bonanza*—"The Actress" 2-24-63 (Edwin Booth).

Rodrigues, Percy (1924-). Films: "The Plainsman" 1966 (Brother John); "The Night Rider" TVM-1979 (Robert). ¶TV: *Wild Wild West*—"The Night of the Poisonous Posey" 10-28-66 (Brutus the Bonebreaker).

Rodriguez, Emilio. Films: "Terrible Sheriff" 1963-Span./Ital.; "Kid Rodelo" 1966-U.S./Span. (Warden).

Rodriguez, Estelita (1928-3/12/66). Films: "On the Old Spanish Trail" 1947 (Lola); "The Gay Ranchero" 1948 (Consuelo Belmonte); "Old Los Angeles" 1948 (Estelita Del Rey); "The Golden Stallion" 1949 (Pepita Valdez); "Susanna Pass" 1949 (Rita); "California Passage" 1950 (Maria Sanchez); "Sunset in the West" 1950 (Carmelita); "Twilight in the Sierras" 1950 (Lola Chavez); "In Old Amarillo" 1951 (Pepita); "Pals of the Golden West" 1951 (Elena Madera); "South Pacific Trail" 1952 (Lita Alvarez); "Rio Bravo" 1959 (Consuela).

Rodriguez, Orlando. Films: "Pillars of the Sky" 1956 (Malachi); "Born Reckless" 1959 (Manuel). ¶TV: *Wild Bill Hickok*—"Bold Raven Rodeo" 4-7-53; *Judge Roy Bean*—"The Eyes of Texas" 1-1-56 (Mole Eyes).

Roehn, Franz. TV: *The Adventures of Rin Tin Tin*—"Rinty Finds a Bone" 4-27-56 (Prof. Hugo Schimmel); *Jim Bowie*—"Monsieur Francois" 12-28-56 (Paul Tournay); *Have Gun Will Travel*—"Love and a Bad Woman" 3-26-60.

Roerick, William (1912-). TV: *Man from Blackhawk*—"The Gypsy Story" 11-6-59 (Jason).

Rogers, Cecile. Films: "Outlaw's Son" 1957 (Amy Wentworth).

Rogers, Charles (1887-12/20/56). Films: "A Ticket to Red Horse Gulch" 1914; "The Light of Western Stars" 1918 (Danny Marns).

Rogers, Charles "Buddy" (1904-). Films: "The Parson and the Outlaw" 1957 (Rev. Jericho Jones).

Rogers, Clyde. *see* Van Nutter, Rik.

Rogers, Elizabeth. Films: "Lacy and the Mississippi Queen" TVM-1978 (Madam Josephine). ¶TV: *Bonanza*—"Once a Doctor" 2-28-65 (Allie Lou), "Journey to Terror" 2-5-67 (Ellie Sue); *Gunsmoke*—"The Well" 11-19-66 (Mrs. Davis); *Time Tunnel*—"The Alamo" 12-9-66 (Mrs. Reynerson).

Rogers, Ginger (1911-4/25/95). Films: "The First Traveling Saleslady" 1956 (Rose Gillray). ¶TV: *Zane Grey Theater*—"Never Too Late" 2-4-60 (Angie Cartwright).

Rogers, Jean (1916-2/24/91). Films: "Stormy" 1935 (Kerry Dorn); "Brigham Young—Frontiersman" 1940 (Clara Young); "Viva Cisco Kid" 1940 (Joan Allen).

Rogers, Jimmy. Films: "Doubling for Romeo" 1922 (Jimmy Jones); "Dudes Are Pretty People" 1942 (Jimmy); "False Colors" 1943 (Jimmy Rogers); "Calaboose" 1943; "Prairie Chickens" 1943; "Riders of the Deadline" 1943 (Jimmy); "Forty Thieves" 1944 (Jimmy Rogers); "Lumberjack" 1944 (Jimmy Rogers); "Mystery Man" 1944 (Jimmy Rogers); "Texas Masquerade" 1944 (Jimmy Rogers).

Rogers, John (1888-7/31/63). Films: "Out West with the Peppers" 1940 (Ship Steward); "Hudson Bay" 1941 (Sailor); "Alaska" 1944. ¶TV: *Jim Bowie*—"The Captain's Chimp" 3-8-57 (Timmons).

Rogers, Kasey. TV: *Wyatt Earp*—"Bat Masterson Wins His Star" 11-20-56 (Nellie Wright), "Until Proven Guilty" 4-11-61; *Sergeant Preston of the Yukon*—"Underground Ambush" 4-25-57 (Sherry); *Maverick*—"The Third Rider" 1-5-58 (Dolly), "The Devil's Necklace" 4-16-61 & 4-23-61 (Angel Score), "Three Queens Full" 11-12-61 (Emma); *Colt .45*—"Rare Specimen" 2-7-58 (Molly Field), "Return to El Paso" 6-21-59 (Jessica Delgado), "Strange Encounter" 4-26-60 (Jeannie O'Mara); *Trackdown*—"Matter of Justice" 10-17-58 (Mavis), "Every Man a Witness" 12-26-58 (Stella); *Yancy Derringer*—"Marble Fingers" 12-18-58 (Blackeyed Sue); *Bat Masterson*—"Election Day" 1-14-59 (Kitty Meadows), "Masterson's Arcadia Club" 4-28-60 (Dixie Mayhew), "Dakota Showdown" 11-17-60 (Francie Wallace); *Rough Riders*—"Death Sentence" 3-12-59 (Lenore); *Wanted—Dead or Alive*—"Railroaded" 3-14-59, "The Matchmaker" 9-19-59 (Ruby Todd), "Three for One" 12-21-60; *The Restless Gun*—"A Trial for Jenny May" 5-25-59 (Jenny May); *Lawman*—"Shackled" 10-18-59 (Maggie); *Sugarfoot*—"Blackwater Swamp" 3-1-60 (Myra Crain).

Rogers, Kenny (1937-). Films: "The Gambler" TVM-1980 (Brady Hawkes); "The Gambler, Part II—The Adventure Continues" TVM-1983 (Brady Hawkes); "Wild Horses" TVM-1985 (Matt Cooper); "The Gambler, Part III—The Legend Continues" TVM-1987 (Brady Hawkes); "The Gambler Returns: The Luck of the Draw" TVM-1991 (Brady Hawkes); "Rio Diablo" TVM-1993 (Quinton Leech); "The Gambler V: Playing for Keeps" TVM-1994 (Brady Hawkes). ¶TV: *Dr. Quinn, Medicine Woman*—"Portraits" 5-22-93 (Daniel Watkins).

Rogers, Kent (-7/9/44). Films: "Northwest Passage" 1940 (Odiorne Towne).

Rogers, Lambert. Films: "Outlaws of the Prairie" 1937 (Bill Lupton).

Rogers, Linda. Films: "Tickle Me" 1965 (Clair Kinnamon).

Rogers, Mildred (1899-4/14/73). Films: "The Forty-Niners" 1932 (Lola); "The Texas Rambler" 1935 (Rosa).

Rogers, Rita. Films: "Machismo—40 Graves for 40 Guns" 1970 (Lil); "The Hired Hand" 1971 (Mexican Woman); "The Magnificent Seven Ride" 1972 (De Toro's Woman); "Showdown" 1973 (Girl). ¶TV: *Kung Fu*—"The Spirit Helper" 11-8-73 (Crucita).

Rogers, Roy (Dick Weston) (1912-). Films: "Gallant Defender" 1935; "The Mysterious Avenger" 1936; "The Old Corral" 1936; "Rhythm on the Range" 1936; "Song of the Saddle" 1936; "The Big Show" 1937; "The California Mail" 1937; "The Old Wyoming Trail" 1937; "Wild Horse Rodeo" 1937 (Singer); "Billy the Kid Returns" 1938 (Billy the Kid); "The Old Barn Dancer" 1938 (Singer); "Shine on Harvest Moon" 1938 (Roy Rogers); "Under Western Stars" 1938 (Roy Rogers); "The Arizona Kid" 1939 (Roy); "Come on, Rangers" 1939 (Roy); "Days of Jesse James" 1939 (Roy); "Frontier Pony Express" 1939 (Roy Rogers); "In Old Caliente" 1939 (Roy Rogers); "Jeepers Creepers" 1939 (Roy); "Rough Riders' Round-Up"

1939 (Roy); "Saga of Death Valley" 1939 (Roy Rogers); "Southward Ho!" 1939 (Roy Rogers); "Wall Street Cowboy" 1939 (Roy Rogers); "The Border Legion" 1940 (Steve Kells); "The Carson City Kid" 1940 (the Carson City Kid); "Colorado" 1940 (Jerry Burke); "The Dark Command" 1940 (Fletch McCloud); "The Ranger and the Lady" 1940 (Capt. Colt); "Rodeo Dough" 1940-short; "Young Bill Hickok" 1940 (Bill Hickok); "Young Buffalo Bill" 1940 (Buffalo Bill Cody); "Arkansas Judge" 1941 (Tom Martel); "Bad Man of Deadwood" 1941 (Bill Brady); "In Old Cheyenne" 1941 (Steve Blane); "Jesse James at Bay" 1941 (Jesse James/Clint Burns); "Meet Roy Rogers" 1941-short; "Nevada City" 1941; "Red River Valley" 1941; "Robin Hood of the Pecos" 1941 (Vance Corgin); "Sheriff of Tombstone" 1941 (Bret Starr); "Heart of the Golden West" 1942 (Roy); "Man from Cheyenne" 1942 (Roy); "Ridin' Down the Canyon" 1942 (Roy); "Romance on the Range" 1942 (Roy); "Sons of the Pioneers" 1942 (Roy Rogers); "South of Santa Fe" 1942 (Roy Rogers); "Sunset on the Desert" 1942 (Roy Rogers/Sloane); "Sunset Serenade" 1942 (Roy Rogers); "Hands Across the Border" 1943 (Roy); "Idaho" 1943 (Roy Rogers); "King of the Cowboys" 1943 (Roy); "Man from Music Mountain" 1943 (Roy); "Silver Spurs" 1943 (Roy Rogers); "Song of Texas" 1943 (Roy Rogers); "Cowboy and the Senorita" 1944 (Roy); "The Lights of Old Santa Fe" 1944 (Roy); "San Fernando Valley" 1944 (Roy); "Song of Nevada" 1944 (Roy Rogers); "The Yellow Rose of Tesas" 1944 (Roy); "Along the Navajo Trail" 1945 (Roy Rogers); "Bells of Rosarita" 1945 (Roy Rogers); "Don't Fence Me In" 1945 (Roy Rogers); "The Man from Oklahoma" 1945 (Roy Rogers); "Sunset in El Dorado" 1945 (Roy Rogers); "Utah" 1945 (Roy Rogers); "Heldorado" 1946 (Roy Rogers); "Home in Oklahoma" 1946 (Roy Rogers); "My Pal Trigger" 1946 (Roy Rogers); "Out California Way" 1946; "Rainbow Over Texas" 1946 (Roy Rogers); "Roll on, Texas Moon" 1946 (Roy Rogers); "Song of Arizona" 1946 (Roy Rogers); "Under Nevada Skies" 1946 (Roy Rogers); "Apache Rose" 1947 (Roy Rogers); "Bells of San Angelo" 1947 (Roy Rogers); "On the Old Spanish Trail" 1947 (Roy); "Springtime in the Sierras" 1947 (Roy Rogers); "Eyes of Texas" 1948 (Roy Rogers); "The Gay Ranchero" 1948 (Roy Rogers); "Grand Canyon Trail" 1948 (Roy

Rogers); "Melody Time" 1948; "Night Time in Nevada" 1948; "Under California Stars" 1948 (Roy Rogers); "Down Dakota Way" 1949 (Roy Rogers); "The Far Frontier" 1949 (Roy Rogers); "The Golden Stallion" 1949 (Roy Rogers); "Susanna Pass" 1949 (Roy Rogers); "Bells of Coronado" 1950 (Roy Rogers); "North of the Great Divide" 1950 (Roy Rogers); "Sunset in the West" 1950 (Roy Rogers); "Trail of Robin Hood" 1950 (Roy Rogers); "Trigger, Jr." 1950 (Roy Rogers); "Twilight in the Sierras" 1950 (Roy Rogers); "Heart of the Rockies" 1951 (Roy); "In Old Amarillo" 1951 (Roy Rogers); "Pals of the Golden West" 1951 (Roy Rogers); "South of Caliente" 1951 (Roy Rogers); "Spoilers of the Plains" 1951 (Roy Rogers); "Son of Paleface" 1952 (Roy Rogers); "Alias Jesse James" 1959 (Roy Rogers); "Mackintosh & T.J." 1975 (Mackintosh); "The Gambler, Part II—The Adventure Continues" TVM-1983 (Drunk). ¶TV: *The Roy Rogers Show*—Regular 1951-57 (Roy Rogers).

Rogers, Jr., Roy "Dusty" (1940-). Films: "Arizona Bushwhackers" 1968 (Roy). ¶TV: *The Roy Rogers Show*—"Three Masked Men" 12-18-55, "Junior Outlaw" 2-10-57 (Red).

Rogers, Ruth (1918-10/9/53). Films: "The Man from Texas" 1939 (Laddie Dennison); "The Night Riders" 1939 (Susan Randall); "Silver on the Sage" 1939 (Barbara Hamilton); "Hidden Gold" 1940 (Jane Colby); "The Light of Western Stars" 1940 (Flo Kingsley); "Take Me Back to Oklahoma" 1940; "Texas Rangers Ride Again" 1940 (Girl).

Rogers, Sandra. TV: *The Cisco Kid*—"Romany Caravan" 11-17-51, "Buried Treasure" 12-29-51; *Wagon Train*—"The Gabe Carswell Story" 1-15-58 (Mrs. Wilkes).

Rogers, Smokey. Films: "Western Whoopee" 1948-short; "Cheyenne Cowboy" 1949-short; "Coyote Canyon" 1949-short; "The Girl from Gunsight" 1949-short; "The Pecos Pistol" 1949-short; "Silver Butte" 1949-short; "Six Gun Music" 1949-short; "South of Santa Fe" 1949-short; "West of Laramie" 1949-short; "Cactus Caravan" 1950-short; "The Fargo Phantom" 1950-short; "Gold Strike" 1950-short; "Priairie Pirates" 1950-short; "Ready to Ride" 1950-short.

Rogers, Walter. Films: "Whispering Smith" 1916 (Williams); "The Iron Horse" 1924 (General Dodge); "Gold Is Where You Find It" 1938 (Gen. Grant).

Rogers, Wayne (1933-). Films: "The Glory Guys" 1965 (Moyan); "Pocket Money" 1972 (Stretch Russell). ¶TV: *The Law of the Plainsman*—"Full Circle" 10-8-59, "Calculated Risk" 12-31-59, "Dangerous Barriers" 3-10-60; *Zane Grey Theater*—"The Lonely Gun" 10-22-59 (Frank); *Gunsmoke*—"False Witness" 12-12-59 (Tom Morey), "Cody's Code" 1-20-62 (Brack Tracy), "Taps for Old Jeb" 10-16-65 (Stretch Morgan); *Wanted—Dead or Alive*—"Angela" 1-9-60 (Ash Langford); *Johnny Ringo*—"The Killing Bug" 4-18-60 (Charlie); *Stagecoach West*—Regular 1960-61 (Luke Perry); *Have Gun Will Travel*—"The Debutante" 1-19-63 (Daniel); *Death Valley Days*—"The Journey" 6-13-65 (Lt. Richard H. Pratt); *Shane*—"The Big Fifty" 12-10-66; *The Big Valley*—"The Jonah" 11-11-68 (Don Jarvis); *Lancer*—"The Escape" 12-31-68 (Lewis).

Rogers, Will (1879-8/15/35). Films: "Laughing Bill Hyde" 1918 (Laughing Bill Hyde); "Jubilo" 1919 (Jubilo); "Cupid, the Cowpuncher" 1920 (Alec Lloyd); "Honest Hutch" 1920 (Honest Hutch); "The Ropin' Fool" 1921; "Doubling for Romeo" 1922 (Sam); "A Texas Steer" 1927 (Maverick Brander).

Rogers, Jr., Will (1911-7/9/93). Films: "The Jack Rider" 1921 (Little Buster); "The Vengeance Trail" 1921 (Buddy Hicks); "The Boy from Oklahoma" 1954 (Tom Brewster); "Wild Heritage" 1958 (Judge Copeland). ¶TV: *The Pioneers*—Host 1963.

Rojas, Alfonso. Films: "Cavalry Charge" 1964-Span.; "Seven Hours of Gunfire" 1964-Span./Ital.; "Twins from Texas" 1964-Ital./Span.; "Two Thousand Dollars for Coyote" 1965-Span.; "Few Dollars for Django" 1966-Ital./Span.; "Fort Yuma Gold" 1966-Ital./Fr./Span.; "Ringo and Gringo Against All" 1966-Ital./Span.; "Savage Gringo" 1966-Ital.; "Kill Them All and Come Back Alone" 1967-Ital./Span.; "The Man Who Killed Billy the Kid" 1967-Span./Ital.; "Ringo, the Lone Rider" 1967-Ital./Span.; "I Do Not Forgive ... I Kill!" 1968-Span./Ital.; "One Against One ... No Mercy" 1968-Span./Ital.; "Dead Are Countless" 1969-Ital./Span.; "Quinta: Fighting Proud" 1969-Ital./Span.; "Reverend Colt" 1970-Ital./Span.; "Sabata the Killer" 1970-Ital./Span.

Rojas, Manuel. Films: "Buchanan Rides Alone" 1958 (Juan). ¶TV: *Broken Arrow*—"The Missionaries" 1-29-57 (Tomah), "Renegades Return" 12-3-57 (Tupai); *Telephone Time*—"Elfego Baca" 4-18-57 (Elfego Baca).

Rojo, Antonio Molino. Films: "Terrible Sheriff" 1963-Span./Ital. (the Mayor); "Seven Hours of Gunfire" 1964-Span./Ital.; "Five Thousand Dollars on One Ace" 1965-Span./Ital. (David); "Four Dollars for Vengeance" 1965-Span./Ital.; "Seven Guns for the MacGregors" 1965-Ital./Span. (Sheriff); "Five Giants from Texas" 1966-Ital./Span.; "Fort Yuma Gold" 1966-Ital./Fr./Span.; "A Place Called Glory" 1966-Span./Ger.; "Kill Them All and Come Back Alone" 1967-Ital./Span.; "A Minute to Pray, a Second to Die" 1967-Ital. (Sein); "My Colt, Not Yours" 1972-Span./Fr./Ital.

Rojo, Gustavo (1923-). Films: "Pyramid of the Sun God" 1965-Ger./Ital./Fr.; "The Christmas Kid" 1966-Span./Ital. (Mayor Louis Carrillo); "Seven for Pancho Villa" 1966-Span.; "The Tall Women" 1966-Austria/Ital./Span. (Gus McIntosh); "Django Does Not Forgive" 1967-Ital./Span.; "Kitosch, the Man Who Came from the North" 1967-Ital./Span.; "Old Shatterhand" 1968-Ger./Yugo./Fr./Ital. (Bush); "Land Raiders" 1969-U.S./Span. (Juantez); "The Valley of Gwangi" 1969 (Carlos dos Orsos); "A Bullet for Sandoval" 1970-Ital./Span. (Guadalupano); "El Condor" 1970 (Col. Aguinaldo). ¶TV: *The Law of the Plainsman*—"A Matter of Life and Death" 10-15-59; *Wagon Train*—"The Vittorio Bottecelli Story" 12-16-59 (Duke Vittorio Bottecelli); *Bronco*—"Legacy of Twisted Creed" 4-19-60; *Man from Blackhawk*—"The Sons of Don Antonio" 4-22-60 (Juan); *Lawman*—"Man on a Wire" 5-22-60 (Giuseppe Soldano).

Rojo, Ruben (1922-). Films: "For One Thousand Dollars Per Day" 1966-Ital./Span. (Jason Clark); "Duel in the Eclipse" 1967-Span.

Roland, Gilbert (1905-5/15/94). Films: "Rose of the Golden West" 1927 (Juan); "Men of the North" 1930 (Louis LeBey); "Thunder Trail" 1937 (Arizona Dick Ames); "Rangers of Fortune" 1940 (Sierra); "Beauty and the Bandit" 1946; "The Gay Cavalier" 1946; "South of Monterey" 1946; "King of the Bandits" 1947 (Cisco Kid); "Pirates of Monterey" 1947 (Maj. De Roja); "Riding the California Trail" 1947 (the Cisco Kid); "Robin Hood of Monterey" 1947 (the Cisco Kid); "The Dude Goes West" 1948 (the Pecos Kid); "The Furies" 1950 (Juan Herrera); "Mark of the Renegade" 1951 (Don Pedro Garcia); "Apache War Smoke" 1952 (Peso); "The Treasure of Pancho Villa" 1955 (Juan Castro); "Bandido" 1956 (Escobar); "Three Violent People" 1956 (Innocencio, the Foreman); "The Last of the Fast Guns" 1958 (Miles Lang); "The Wild and the Innocent" 1959 (Sheriff Paul Bartell); "Guns of the Timberland" 1960 (Monty Walker); "Cheyenne Autumn" 1964 (Dull Knife); "The Reward" 1965 (Capt. Carbajal); "Johnny Hamlet" 1966-Ital. (Horace); "Any Gun Can Play" 1968-Ital./Span. (Monetero); "Between God, the Devil and a Winchester" 1968-Ital./Span.; "The Ruthless Four" 1968-Ital./Ger. (Mason); "Sartana Does Not Forgive" 1968-Span./Ital. (Kirchner); "Running Wild" 1973; "The Mark of Zorro" TVM-1974 (Don Alejandro Vega); "The Sacketts" TVM-1979 (Don Luis Alvarado); "Barbarosa" 1982 (Don Braulio). ¶TV: *Wagon Train*—"The Bernal Sierra Story" 3-12-58 (Bernal Sierra); *Desilu Playhouse*—"Border Justice" 11-13-59 (El Patron); *Walt Disney Presents: Zorro*—"El Bandito" 10-30-60 (El Cuchillo), "Adios El Cuchillo" 11-6-60 (El Cuchillo); *Frontier Circus*—"Quick Shuffle" 2-1-62 (Luke Santos); *Death Valley Days*—"Kingdom for a Horse" 12-1-63 (Don Pedro); *Gunsmoke*—"Extradition" 12-7-63 & 12-14-63 (Julio Chavez); *Bonanza*—"The Lonely Runner" 10-10-65 (Jim Acton); *The High Chaparral*—Regular 1970-71 (Don Domingo de Montoya); *Kung Fu*—"The Chalice" 10-11-73 (Padre Braganza).

Roland, Gill (1942-). Films: "Fasthand" 1972-Ital./Span.; "For a Book of Dollars" 1973-Ital./Span.

Roland, Ruth (1894-9/22/37). Films: "Her Indian Mother" 1910; "The Indian Scout's Revenge" 1910; "Arizona Bill" 1911; "A Chance Shot" 1911; "The Bugler of Battery B" 1912; "Death Valley Scotty's Mine" 1912; "The Desert Trail" 1912; "The Mummy and the Cowpunchers" 1912; "The School Ma'am of Stone Gulch" 1912; "The Indian Maid's Warning" 1913; "The Tenderfoot's Luck" 1913; "The Medicine Show at Stone Gulch" 1914; "The Trail of Hate" 1917; "Hands Up" 1918-serial (Echo Delane); "Ruth of the Rockies" 1920-serial (Ruth); "The Avenging Arrow" 1921-serial; "The Timber Queen" 1922-serial; "White Eagle" 1922-serial; "Ruth of the Range" 1923-serial (Ruth); "Where the Worst Begins" 1925 (Jane Brower).

Rolf, Erik (1911-5/28/57).

Films: "Davy Crockett, Indian Scout" 1950 (Mr. Simms).

Rolfe, Guy (1915-). Films: "Land Raiders" 1969-U.S./Span. (Maj. Tanner).

Rollins, David. Films: "The Big Trail" 1930 (Dave Cameron).

Rollins, Jr., Howard E. (1952-). TV: *Wildside*—Regular 1985 (Bannister Sparks).

Rollins, Jack. Films: "Ruth of the Rockies" 1920-serial; "Sunset Sprague" 1920 (Red Simpson); "Do and Dare" 1922 (Jose Sanchez); "Rough Shod" 1922 (Les Artwell); "Trooper O'Neil" 1922 (Paul); "The Grail" 1923 (John Trammel).

Romaine, George (1878-5/7/29). Films: "Circus Cowboy" 1924 (Slovini).

Roman, Leticia (1939-). Films: "Gold of the Seven Saints" 1961 (Tita); "Flaming Frontier" 1965-Ger./Yugo. (Judith). ¶TV: *F Troop*—"La Dolce Courage" 11-24-66 (Gina Barberini); *The Big Valley*—"Explosion!" 11-20-67 & 11-27-67 (Michelle).

Roman, Nina. TV: *Wagon Train*—"The Santiago Quesada Story" 3-30-64 (Anitra); *Gunsmoke*—"Ten Little Indians" 10-9-65 (Nancy), "Kioga" 10-23-65 (Nancy), "The Gang" 12-11-72 (Amy Lee), "Trail of Bloodshed" 3-4-74 (Rita); *Wild Wild West*—"The Night of the Assassin" 9-22-67 (Col. Lupito Gonzalez).

Roman, Ric. Films: "Slaughter Trail" 1951 (Chief Paako); "South of Caliente" 1951 (Josef); "Last of the Comanches" 1952 (Martinez); "Lone Star" 1952 (Curau); "Springfield Rifle" 1952 (Guard); "Viva Zapata!" 1952 (Overseer); "Shadows of Tombstone" 1953 (Delgado); "Nevada Smith" 1966 (Cipriano); "Duel at Apache Wells" 1957 (Frank). ¶TV: *The Lone Ranger*—"Double Jeopardy" 9-7-50, "The Cross of Santo Domingo" 10-11-56; *Tales of Wells Fargo*—"Sam Bass" 6-10-57 (Barnes); *Trackdown*—"The Town" 12-13-57 (Deputy John Minor); *Broken Arrow*—"Backlash" 5-27-58 (Delgado); *Zorro*—"An Eye for an Eye" 11-20-58 (Briones), "Zorro and the Flag of Truce" 11-27-58 (Briones), "Ambush" 12-4-58 (Briones); *The Texan*—"The Lord Will Provide" 12-29-58 (Curley Head); *Gunsmoke*—"Hinka Do" 1-30-60 (Manuel), "Innocence" 12-12-64 (Sims); *Lawman*—"The Kids" 2-21-60, "The Frame-Up" 1-15-61 (Charlie Belmont); *Sugarfoot*—"Vinegaroom" 3-29-60 (Rufus Buck);

Maverick—"Flood's Folly" 2-19-61 (Emery); *Wagon Train*—"The Emmett Lawton Story" 3-6-63 (Jed Swairt); *Daniel Boone*—"The Prophet" 1-21-65 (Theyandaga); *Laredo*—"I See By Your Outfit" 9-23-65 (Tomas), "The Land Grabbers" 12-9-65, "The Other Cheek" 2-10-67 (Aces Brady); *The Big Valley*—"Barbary Red" 2-16-66 (Thug).

Roman, Ruth (1924-). Films: "Belle Starr's Daughter" 1947 (Rose of Cimarron); "White Stallion" 1947 (Ann Martin); "Barricade" 1950 (Judith Burns); "Colt .45" 1950 (Beth Donovan); "Dallas" 1950 (Tonia Robles); "Blowing Wind" 1953 (Sal); "The Far Country" 1955 (Ronda); "Great Day in the Morning" 1956 (Boston Grant); "Rebel in Town" 1956 (Nora Willoughby); "A Knife for the Ladies" 1973 (Elizabeth); "The Sacketts" TVM-1979 (Rosie). ¶TV: *Bonanza*—"The Magnificent Adah" 11-14-59 (Adah Menken); *The Outcasts*—"The Town That Wouldn't" 3-31-69 (Jade); *Gunsmoke*—"Coreyville" 10-6-69 (Flo Watson), "Waste" 9-27-71 & 10-4-71 (Maggie Blaisedell); *The Men from Shiloh*—"The Angus Killer" 2-10-71 (Margie); *Hec Ramsey*—"A Hard Road to Vengeance" 11-25-73 (Della); *Kung Fu*—"A Dream Within a Dream" 1-17-74 (Rhoda Norman).

Romano, Andy (1936-). TV: *Gunsmoke*—"He Learned About Women" 2-24-62 (Jose); *Laramie*—"Shadow of the Past" 10-16-62 (Will Keefer); *Here Come the Brides*—"Here Come the Brides" 9-25-68, "Lovers and Wanderers" 11-6-68.

Romano, Renato. Films: "A Minute to Pray, a Second to Die" 1967-Ital. (Cheap Charley); "The Moment to Kill" 1968-Ital./Ger.; "Shotgun" 1969-Ital.; "Deaf Smith and Johnny Ears" 1972-Ital. (Hoffman).

Romano, Tony. Films: "Robbers' Roost" 1955 (Happy Jack). ¶TV: *Maverick*—"Escape to Tampico" 10-26-58 (Chicualo), "The Spanish Dancer" 12-14-58 (Raul Onate).

Romanoff, Constantine. Films: "Wolf Song" 1929 (Rube Thatcher); "Let Freedom Ring" 1939 (Russian); "Deadwood Dick" 1940-serial; "White Eagle" 1941-serial; "Northwest Outpost" 1947 (Convict).

Romay, Lina. Films: "Cheyenne Cowboy" 1949-short; "Six Gun Music" 1949-short; "The Man Behind the Gun" 1952 (Chona Degnon).

Rome, Sydne (1947-). Films: "Alive or Preferably Dead" 1969-Span./Ital.; "Man Called Amen" 1972-Ital.; "They Still Call Me Amen" 1972-Ital.

Romero, Carlos (1927-). Films: "They Came to Cordura" 1959 (Arreaga); "The Young Land" 1959 (Quiroga); "The Professionals" 1966 (Revolutionary). ¶TV: *Broken Arrow*—"Power" 4-22-58 (Natan); *Zorro*—"Welcome to Monterey" 10-9-58 (Lieutenant Rafael), "Zorro Rides Alone" 10-16-58 (Lieutenant Rafael), "Horse of Another Color" 10-23-58 (Lieutenant Rafael), "The Senorita Makes a Choice" 10-30-58 (Lieutenant Rafael), "Rendezvous at Sundown" 11-6-58 (Lieutenant Rafael); *The Adventures of Rin Tin Tin*—"Miracle of the Mission" 12-12-58 (Strong Branch); *Wagon Train*—"The Conchita Vasquez Story" 3-18-59 (Carlos Soldareo); *Bronco*—"Prairie Skipper" 5-5-59 (Angelo), "La Rubia" 5-17-60 (Urbino); *Wichita Town*—Regular 1959-60 (Rico Rodriguez); *Rawhide*—"Incident of the Day of the Dead" 9-18-59 (Goyo), "Incident of the Silent Web" 6-3-60, "Incident at Superstition Prairie" 12-2-60 (Asunta), "Incident at Rio Salado" 9-29-61 (Antonio Marcos), "Incident of Decision" 12-28-62 (Antonio Chavez), "Incident at Rio Doloroso" 5-10-63 (Hernan Maldenado); *Cheyenne*—"The Rebellion" 10-12-59 (Lt. Jose Montez); *Wanted—Dead or Alive*—"Desert Seed" 11-14-59 (Juan Gomez); *Maverick*—"The Marquesa" 1-3-60 (Manuel Ortiz), "Dutchman's Gold" 1-22-61 (Padilla), "Substitute Gun" 4-2-61 (Clete Spain); *Riverboat*—"The Blowup" 1-17-60 (Juan Miguel); *Gunslinger*—"Road of the Dead" 3-30-61 (Colonel Delgado); *Empire*—"Where the Hawk Is Wheeling" 1-29-63 (Max); *Have Gun Will Travel*—"The Black Bull" 4-13-63 (Nino Ybarra), "The Mountebank" 8-3-63 (Quintos); *The Virginian*—"The Mountain of the Sun" 4-17-63; *Laredo*—"I See By Your Outfit" 9-23-65 (Miguel); *Daniel Boone*—"Gabriel" 1-6-66 (Captain Francisco); *The Big Valley*—"Legend of a General" 9-19-66 & 9-26-66 (Leon); *Death Valley Days*—"Along Came Mariana" 5-27-67 (Don Jose); *The High Chaparral*—"The Widow from Red Rock" 11-26-67 (Romero), "Fiesta" 11-20-70; *The Guns of Will Sonnett*—"A Town in Terror" 2-7-69 & 2-14-69 (Carlos); *The Men from Shiloh*—"Last of the Comancheros" 12-9-70 (Armendez); *Kung Fu*—"Empty Pages of a Dead Book" 1-10-74 (Doctor).

Romero, Cesar (1907-1/1/94). Films: "The Cisco Kid and the Lady" 1939 (the Cisco Kid); "Frontier Marshal" 1939 (Doc Halliday); "The Return of the Cisco Kid" 1939 (Lopez); "The Gay Caballero" 1940 (the Cisco Kid); "Lucky Cisco Kid" 1940 (the Cisco Kid); "Viva Cisco Kid" 1940 (the Cisco Kid); ; "Ride on, Vaquero" 1941 (the Cisco Kid); "Romance of the Rio Grande" 1941 (the Cisco Kid); "Vera Cruz" 1954 (Marquis de Labordere); "The Americano" 1955 (Manoel); "Villa!" 1958 (Fierro Lopez); "Talent for Loving" 1969-Brit./Span. (Alonso); "The Red, White and Black" 1970 (Col. Grierson); "Kino, the Padre on Horseback" 1977; "Lust in the Dust" 1985 (Father Garcia). ¶TV: *Wagon Train*—"The Luke O'Malley Story" 1-1-58 (Dan), "The Honorable Don Charlie Story" 1-22-58 (Don Charlie); *Zane Grey Theater*—"Threat of Violence" 5-23-58 (Carlos Gandara), "The Reckoning" 1-14-60 (Francisco), "Man from Everywhere" 4-13-61 (Tom Bowdry); *The Californians*—"The Man Who Owned San Francisco" 12-30-58 (Jose Limantour); *Zorro*—"The Gay Caballero" 1-22-59 (Senor Estevan de la Cruz), "Tornado Is Missing" 1-29-59 (Senor Estevan de la Cruz), "Zorro Versus Cupid" 2-5-59 (Senor Estevan de la Cruz), "The Legend of Zorro" 2-12-59 (Senor Estevan de la Cruz); *The Texan*—"Caballero" 4-13-59 (Joaquin); *Death Valley Days*—"Olvera" 10-13-59; *Rawhide*—"Incident of the Stalking Death" 11-13-59 (Ben Teagle), "The Child Woman" 3-23-62 (Big Tim Sloan), "Incident at Rio Doloroso" 5-10-63 (Maldenado), "The Vasquez Woman" 10-26-65 (Colonel Vasquez); *Stagecoach West*—"A Time to Run" 11-15-60 (Manola Marcial Lalanda), "The Big Gun" 4-25-61 (Francisco Martinez); *Bonanza*—"The Deadliest Game" 2-21-65 (Borelli); *Branded*—"The Mission" 3-14-65, 3-21-65 & 3-28-65 (General Arriola); *Daniel Boone*—"Gabriel" 1-6-66 (Esteban de Vaca), "Bitter Mission" 3-30-67 (Colonel Carlos Navarro), "The Grand Alliance" 11-13-69 (Buenaventura); *Alias Smith and Jones*—"The McCreedy Bush" 1-21-71 (Armendariz), "The McCreedy Bust — Going, Going Gone" 1-13-72 (Armendariz), "The McCreedy Feud" 9-30-72 (Armendariz).

Romero, Joanelle. Films: "The Girl Called Hatter Fox" TVM-1977 (Hatter Fox); "Barbarosa" 1982 (Young Whore).

Romero, Ned (1926-). Films: "The Talisman" 1966 (the Indian); "Winchester '73" TVM-1967; "Hang 'Em High" 1968; "Tell Them Willie Boy Is Here" 1969 (Tom); "I Will Fight No More Forever" TVM-1975 (Chief Joseph); "Last of the Mohicans" TVM-1977 (Chingachgook); "Peter Lundy and the Medicine Hat Stallion" TVM-1977 (Red Cloud); "The Deerslayer" TVM-1978 (Chingachgook); "The Mystic Warrior" TVM-1984 (Wisa); "Houston: The Legend of Texas" TVM-1986 (Chief John Jolly). ¶TV: *Shane*—"The Hant" 9-17-66 (1st Drover), "The Bitter, the Lonely" 10-8-66 (Chips), "Day of the Hawk" 10-22-66 (Chips); *Rango*—"Rango the Outlaw" 1-13-67 (Hocker); *Laredo*—"Enemies and Brother" 2-17-67; *The High Chaparral*—"A Quiet Day in Tucson" 10-1-67 (Carlos), "The Terrorist" 12-17-67 (Rinaldo), "For What We Are About to Receive" 11-29-68 (Carlos); *Bonanza*—"In Defense of Honor" 4-28-68 (White Wolf); *The Virginian*—"The Heritage" 10-30-68 (Tza-'Wuda); *Lancer*—"Cut the Wolf Loose" 11-4-69 (Wichita Jim); *Death Valley Days*—"A Saint of Travellers" 2-14-70, "A Gift from Father Tapis" 5-9-70 (Father De La Cuesta); *Kung Fu*—"The Centoph" 4-4-74 & 4-11-74 (Lame Dog), "Barbary House" 2-15-75 (Indian Leader), "Flight to Orion" 2-22-75 (Indian Leader), "The Brothers Cain" 3-1-75 (Indian Leader), "Full Circle" 3-15-75 (Indian Leader); *The Quest*—"Shanklin" 10-13-76 (Salcedo); *The Life and Times of Grizzly Adams*—3-22-78 (Silver Fox); *Born to the Wind* 1982 (Broken Foot).

Romero Marchent, Carlos. Films: "Seven Hours of Gunfire" 1964-Span./Ital.; "Hands of a Gunman" 1965-Ital./Span.; "Sartana Kills Them All" 1970-Ital./Span.; "Cut-Throats Nine" 1973-Span./Ital.; "Prey of Vultures" 1973-Span./Ital.

Rondell, Ronnie R. TV: *Riverboat*—"Fort Epitaph" 3-7-60 (Kicking Bear); *Wagon Train*—"The Roger Bigelow Story" 12-21-60 (Henry Tate); *Laredo*—"Rendezvous at Arillo" 10-7-65.

Rooker, Michael. Films: "Tombstone" 1993 (Sherman McMasters).

Rooney, Mickey (1920-). Films: "My Pal, the King" 1932 (King Charles V); "Out West with the Hardys" 1938 (Andy Hardy); "Rodeo Dough" 1940-short; "My Brother, the Outlaw" 1951 (Denny O'More); "The Twinkle in God's Eye" 1955 (Rev. Macklin); "The Cockeyed Cowboys of Calico County" 1970 (Indian Tom); "Evil Roy Slade" TVM-1972 (Nelson Stool); "The Gambler Returns: The Luck of the Draw" TVM-1991 (D.W.); "My Heroes Have Always Been Cowboys" 1991. ¶TV: *Wagon Train*—"The Greenhorn Story" 10-7-59 (Samuel T. Evans), "Wagons Ho!" 9-28-60 (Sam Evans); *Frontier Circus*—"Calamity Circus" 3-8-62 (Arnold); *Rawhide*—"Incident at the Odyssey" 3-26-64 (Pan Macropolous).

Rooney, Pat (1891-1/15/33). Films: "Across the Deadline" 1925 (Shifty Sands); "The Four-Footed Ranger" 1928 (Bull Becker); "Partners of the Trail" 1931 (Burke); "The Reckless Rider" 1932.

Rooney, Teddy. Films: "Seven Ways from Sundown" 1960 (Jody). ¶TV: *The Rebel*—"Johnny Yuma at Appomattox" 9-18-60 (Jimmy); *Wagon Train*—"The Candy O'Hara Story" 12-7-60 (Luther Henry); *The Rifleman*—"The Long Goodbye" 11-27-61 (Woody Fogarty).

Rooney, Timothy. (1946-). TV: *Maverick*—"Mr. Muldoon's Partner" 4-15-62 (Hatfield).

Rooney, Wallace (1910-). TV: *Maverick*—"Family Pride" 1-8-61 (Mr. Wallace); *Gunsmoke*—"Potshot" 3-11-61, "Call Me Dodie" 9-22-62 (Dan Binney), "Abe Blocker" 11-24-62 (Dan Binney), "Uncle Sunday" 12-15-62 (Dan Binney), "False Front" 12-22-62 (Dan Binney); *The Tall Man*—"Where Is Sylvia?" 9-23-61 (Peterson); *Bonanza*—"Look to the Stars" 3-18-62, "The War Comes to Washoe" 11-4-62; *The Dakotas*—"Reformation at Big Nose Butte" 4-1-63 (Guard).

Roope, Fay (1894-9/13/61). Films: "Callaway Went Thataway" 1951 (Tom Lorrison); "Indian Uprising" 1951 (Maj. Gen. Crook); "Viva Zapata!" 1952 (Diaz); "The Charge at Feather River" 1953 (Lt. Col. Kilrain); "Seminole" 1953 (Zachary Taylor); "The Black Dakotas" 1954 (John Lawrence); "The Lone Gun" 1954 (Mayor Booth); "The Proud Ones" 1956 (Markham). ¶TV: *The Lone Ranger*—"Message to Fort Apache" 9-23-54; *Jim Bowie*—"Bayou Tontine" 2-15-57 (Etienne Broussard); *The Californians*—"The Search for Lucy Manning" 10-22-57; *Tales of Wells Fargo*—"The Inscrutable Man" 12-9-57 (Mr. Harper); *Have Gun Will Travel*—"Killer's Widow" 3-22-58 (E.J. Randolf), "Alaska" 4-18-59 (Wade); *Wyatt Earp*—"The Underdog" 4-22-58 (Uncle George Jackson); *The Rifleman*—"The Brother-in-Law" 10-28-58, "Panic" 11-10-59

(Doc), "The Spiked Rifle" 11-24-59; *The Texan*—"Desert Passage" 12-1-58 (Ben Atkins), "The Accuser" 6-6-60 (Mr. Benton); *Rawhide*—"Incident at the Edge of Madness" 2-6-59; *Gunsmoke*—"The F.U." 3-14-59 (Mr. Botkin), "Murder Warrant" 4-18-59 (Mr. Botkin), "Change of Heart" 4-25-59 (Mr. Botkin); *Bonanza*—"The Magnificent Adah" 11-14-59; *Tate*—"The Gunfighters" 8-31-60 (Keefer).

Roosevelt, Buddy (Kent Sanderson) (1898-10/6/73). Films: "Battling Buddy" 1924 (Buddy West); "Biff Bang Buddy" 1924 (Buddy Walters); "Cyclone Buddy" 1924 (Buddy Blake); "Down in Texas" 1924; "Lure of the Yukon" 1924 (Bob Force); "Rip Roarin' Roberts" 1924 (Buddy Roberts); "Rough Ridin'" 1924 (Buddy Benson); "Walloping Wallace" 1924 (Buddy Wallace); "Action Galore" 1925 (Bud Lavrie); "Galloping Jinx" 1925 (Rankin); "Gold and Grit" 1925 (Buddy); "Reckless Courage" 1925 (Bud Keenan); "Thundering Through" 1925 (Bud Lawson); "The Bandit Buster" 1926 (Buddy Miller); "The Dangerous Dub" 1926 (Buddy Martin); "Easy Going" 1926; "Hoodoo Ranch" 1926; "The Ramblin' Galoot" 1926 (Buddy Royle); "Tangled Herds" 1926; "Twin Triggers" 1926 (Bud Trigger/Kenneth Trigger); "Between Dangers" 1927 (Tom Rawlins); "Code of the Cow Country" 1927 (Jim West); "The Fightin' Comeback" 1927 (Jim Jones); "The Phantom Buster" 1927 (Jeff McCloud/Bill Turner); "Ride 'Em High" 1927 (Jim Demming); "Smoking Guns" 1927; "The Cowboy Cavalier" 1928; "The Devil's Tower" 1928 (James Murdock); "Lightnin' Shot" 1928; "Mystery Valley" 1928; "The Painted Trail" 1928 (Blaze Marshall); "The Trail Riders" 1928; "Trailin' Back" 1928; "Way Out West" 1930 (Tex); "Westward Bound" 1930 (Frank); "Lightnin' Smith Returns" 1931 (John Smith); "The Riding Kid" 1931 (John Denton/the Ridin' Kid); "Valley of bad Men" 1931 (Jim Simpson); "Texas Tornado" 1932; "Wild Horse Mesa" 1932 (Horn); "The Fourth Horseman" 1933 (Fancy); "Boss Cowboy" 1934 (Dick Taylor); "Circle Canyon" 1934 (Chris Morell); "Lightning Range" 1934 (Deputy Marshal); "Range Riders" 1934 (Dick Crawford); "Powdersmoke Range" 1935 (Burnett); "The Old Corral" 1936 (Tony Pearl); "Wells Fargo" 1937 (First Lieutenant); "The Lone Ranger Rides Again" 1939-serial (Slade); "Stagecoach" 1939 (Cowboy); "Union Pacific" 1939 (Fireman);

"Buck Benny Rides Again" 1940 (Engineer); "The Man from Dakota" 1940 (Officer); "Billy the Kid's Range War" 1941 (Spike); "Kansas Cyclone" 1941; "King of the Texas Rangers" 1941-serial (Sherwood); "The Lone Rider Rides On" 1941; "King of the Forest Rangers" 1946-serial (Brooks); "The Sea of Grass" 1947 (Cowboy); "Unconquered" 1947 (Guard); "Colt .45" 1950; "Copper Canyon" 1950; "Dallas" 1950 (Northerner); "Kansas Raiders" 1950 (Another Red Leg); "Horizons West" 1952 (Bit); "The Lawless Breed" 1952 (Deputy Sheriff); "The Old West" 1952; "Law and Order" 1953; "The Redhead from Wyoming" 1953 (Man); "Riding Shotgun" 1954; "Three Hours to Kill" 1954 (Drunk); "Tall Man Riding" 1955; "Tribute to a Badman" 1956 (Cowboy); "Flesh and the Spur" 1957 (Outlaw); "Shoot-Out at Medicine Bend" 1957; "Westbound" 1959 (Stock Tender); "The Man Who Shot Liberty Valance" 1962. ¶TV: *Wild Bill Hickok*—"The Boy and the Bandit" 3-25-52.

Roper, Jack (1904-11/28/66). Films: "Flaming Frontier" 1938-serial; "Wall Street Cowboy" 1939 (Ducky); "Heroes of the Saddle" 1940 (Killer McCully); "West of Carson City" 1940 (Larkin); "North from the Lone Star" 1941 (Rawhide Fenton); "Ridin' the Cherokee Trail" 1941 (Squint); "Rolling Down the Great Divide" 1942 (Henchman); "Dakota" 1945 (Bouncer).

Roquemore, Henry (1886-6/30/43). Films: "The Fighting Three" 1927 (Revere); "Gypsy of the North" 1928 (Theater Manager); "The Wagon Show" 1928 (the Barker); "The Oklahoma Kid" 1929; "West of the Rockies" 1929; "The Apache Kid's Escape" 1930; "Parting of the Trails" 1930 (J. Addington Fiske); "Romance of the West" 1930 (Slick Graham); "Cimarron" 1931 (Jonett Goforth); "The Kid from Arizona" 1931; "Near the Trail's End" 1931; "Wild West Whoopee" 1931; "The Cheyenne Cyclone" 1932; "Fighting Champ" 1932 (Bartender); "Son of Oklahoma" 1932 (the Traveller); "Young Blood" 1932 (Beckworth); "Breed of the Border" 1933 (Dutch Krause); "Crashing Broadway" 1933 (Levi); "Trouble Busters" 1933 (Doctor); "The Ferocious Pal" 1934 (Ed Bolivar); "Nevada" 1935 (Bartender); "Powdersmoke Range" 1935 (Doctor); "Rainbow Valley" 1935; "Rainbow's End" 1935 (George Williams); "Ruggles of Red Gap" 1935 (Frank); "The Singing Vagabond" 1935 (Otto); "Texas Terror" 1935; "Drift

Fence" 1936 (Judge); "The Lion's Den" 1936 (Walker); "Battle of Greed" 1937 (Judge Albion); "Gunsmoke Trail" 1938 (Moose Walters); "Songs and Saddles" 1938 (Jed Hill); "The Girl and the Gambler" 1939; "Lure of the Wasteland" 1939 (Judge Carleton); "Lucky Cisco Kid" 1940 (Proprietor); "Texas Rangers Ride Again" 1940 (Conductor); "Triple Justice" 1940; "The Westerner" 1940 (Stage Manager); "Come on, Danger!" 1942 (Jed); "The Lone Star Trail" 1943 (Bank Teller); "Raiders of San Joaquin" 1943 (Rogers).

Rork, Ann (1908-1/24/88). Films: "A Texas Steer" 1927 (Boss Brander).

Rorke, Hayden (1910-8/19/87). Films: "Lust for Gold" 1949 (Floyd Buckley); "Inside Straight" 1951 (Carlson); "Wild Stallion" 1952 (Maj. Callen); "Drum Beat" 1954 (Gen. Grant). ¶TV: *The Lone Ranger*—"Word of Honor" 11-27-52, "The Perfect Crime" 7-30-53; *Frontier*—"The Shame of a Nation" 10-23-55; *Cheyenne*—"The Long Winter" 9-25-56 (Major Early); *Broken Arrow*—"Attack on Fort Grant" 5-21-57 (Col. Lanson); *Riverboat*—"No Bridge on the River" 10-24-60 (Ferdinand Maret); *Bronco*—"Beginner's Luck" 1-1-62 (Wigram); *Bonanza* "The Lady from Baltimore" 1-14-62; *The Dakotas*—"Reformation at Big Nose Butte" 4-1-63 (Glen Masters); *Temple Houston*—"Letter of the Law" 10-3-63 (Pinkley); *The Outcasts*—"The Man from Bennington" 12-16-68 (Doctor Ellis).

Rosanova, Rosa (1869-5/29/44). Films: "Fighting Hero" 1934 (Aunt).

Rosario, Bert. TV: *Paradise*—Regular 1988-91 (Mendez); *Hot Prospects*—Pilot 7-31-89 (Colonel Julia).

Rosato, Lucio. Films: "Navajo Joe" 1966-Ital./Span. (Jeffrey Duncan); "Days of Violence" 1967-Ital. (Clem); "Deserter" 1970-U.S./Ital./Yugo. (Jed).

Roscoe, Al (1888-3/8/33). Films: "Evangeline" 1919 (Gabriel); "A Man's Country" 1919 (Minister Ralph Bowen); "The Branding Iron" 1920 (Rev. Frank Holliwell); "The Last of the Mohicans" 1920 (Uncas); "The Spoilers" 1923 (Mexico Mullins); "The Lure of the Wild" 1925 (James Belmont); "That Devil Quemado" 1925 (Gretorix); "The Texas Streak" 1926 (Jefferson Powell); "The Wolf Hunters" 1926; "Call of the West" 1930 (Maurice Kane); "Dynamite Ranch" 1932 (Park Owens);

"Hell Fire Austin" 1932 (Mark Edmunds); "Hello Trouble" 1932 (Gregg); "The Cheyenne Kid" 1933 (Mark Hollister).

Rose, Blanche (1878-1/5/53). Films: "Call of the West" 1930 (Mrs. Burns).

Rose, Robert (1868-7/1/36). Films: "Western Pluck" 1926 (Rowdy Johnny Dyer).

Rose, Robert Films: "The Gay Ranchero" 1948 (Breezy); "Rogue River" 1950 (Carter Laney).

Rose Marie (1923-). TV: *Gunsmoke*—"Twelfth Night" 12-28-57 (Mrs. Monger); *Jim Bowie*—"Choctaw Honor" 1-3-58 (Honey Chile); *The Virginian*—"The Lady from Wichita" 9-27-67 (Belle Stephens).

Roseleigh, Jack (1887-1/5/40). Films: "Singing River" 1921 (Lew Bransom); "That Girl Montana" 1921 (Max Lyster).

Roseman, Edward F. Films: "The Blue Streak" 1917 (Butch); "The Red Woman" 1917 (Sancho); "Oh, Johnny!" 1918 (Charlie Romero); "The Sign Invisible" 1918 (Lou Baribeau); "Calibre 38" 1919 (Royce Greer); "High Pockets" 1919 (Max Manon); "Speedy Meade" 1919 (Buck Lennon); "Tangled Trails" 1921 (Phil Lawson); "Fear-Bound" 1925 (Pa Tumble).

Rosemond, Clinton (1882-3/10/66). Films: "Stand Up and Fight" 1939 (Enoch); "The Dark Command" 1940; "Santa Fe Trail" 1940 (Black); "Belle Starr" 1941.

Rosenbloom, Maxie (1904-3/6/76). Films: "Skipalong Rosenbloom" 1951 (Skipalong Rosenbloom).

Rosener, George (1879-3/29/45). Films: "Park Avenue Lodger" 1937 (Matt O'Shea); "The Carson City Kid" 1940 (Tucker); "Colorado" 1940; "Arkansas Judge" 1941 (Mr. Beaudry); "In Old Cheyenne" 1941 (Sam Drummond); "Sheriff of Tombstone" 1941.

Rosenthal, Sandy (1924-12/27/87). TV: *The High Chaparral*—"A Fella Named Kilroy" 3-7-69 (Higgins), "The Lieutenant" 2-27-70, "Too Many Chiefs" 3-27-70 (Doc); *Bonanza*—"The Desperado" 2-7-71 (Davy), "Bushwacked" 10-3-71 (Steen).

Rosing, Bodil (1877-12/31/41). Films: "The Law of the Range" 1928 (Mother Lockheart); "King of the Rodeo" 1929 (Mother).

Rosley, Adrian (1888-3/5/37). Films: "The Gay Desperado" 1936 (Radio Station Manager); "Rose Marie" 1936 (Opera Fan).

Ross, Anthony (1909-10/26/55). Films: "The Gunfighter" 1950 (Charlie); "Minnesota Clay" 1964-Ital./Fr./Span. (Scratchy).

Ross, Betsy King (1923-). Films: "Fighting with Kit Carson" 1933-serial (Joan Fargo); "Smoke Lightning" 1933 (Betsy Blake); "The Phantom Empire" 1935-serial (Betsy).

Ross, Churchill (1901-5/23/62). Films: "Blazing Days" 1927 (Jim Morgan).

Ross, Don. TV: *The Tall Man*—"Big Sam's Boy" 3-4-61 (Deputy); *Gunsmoke*—"Ten Little Indians" 10-9-65 (Lafe Cannon), "Major Glory" 10-30-67 (Cobb); *Wild Wild West*—"The Night of the Winged Terror" 1-17-68 & 1-24-68.

Ross, Earl (1888-5/21/61). Films: "Cavalry" 1936 (Colonel Lafe Harvey); "Stormy Trails" 1936 (Thurman); "Riders of the Whistling Skull" 1937 (Prof. Cleary). ¶TV: *Wild Bill Hickok*—"Ghost Town Lady" 1-27-53.

Ross, George. Films: "Rustlers" 1949; "Springfield Rifle" 1952 (Riley); "The Last Wagon" 1956 (Sarge); "Hell Canyon Outlaws" 1957; "Day of the Outlaw" 1959 (Clagett); "The Glory Guys" 1965 (Hanavan); "El Condor" 1970 (Guard for Convicts). ¶TV: *Wild Bill Hickok*—"Runaway Wizard" 6-9-53; *26 Men*—"Man on the Run" 12-10-57; *Broken Arrow*—"Backlash" 5-27-58 (Ivey); *Bat Masterson*—"The Reluctant Witness" 3-31-60 (Stage Driver).

Ross, Howard. *see* Rossini, Renato.

Ross, Katharine (1942-). Films: "Shenandoah" 1965 (Ann Anderson); "Butch Cassidy and the Sundance Kid" 1969 (Etta Place); "Tell Them Willie Boy Is Here" 1969 (Lola); "Wanted: The Sundance Woman" TVM-1976 (Etta Place); "Rodeo Girl" TVM-1980 (Sammy Garrett); "The Shadow Riders" TVM-1982 (Kate Connery); "Houston: The Legend of Texas" TVM-1986 (Woman at Alamo); "Red Headed Stranger" 1987 (Laurie); "Conagher" TVM-1991 (Evie Teale). ¶TV: *The Virginian*—"The Dark Challenge" 9-23-64 (Jenny Hendricks); *Gunsmoke*—"Crooked Mile" 10-3-64 (Susan Degler), "The Lady" 3-27-65 (Liz Beaumont); *Wagon Train*—"The Bonnie Brooke Story" 2-21-65 (Bonnie Brooke); *The Big Valley*—"Winner Lose All" 10-27-65 (Maria); *The Loner*—"Widow on the Evening Stage" 10-30-65 (Sue Sullivan); *Wild*

West—"The Night of the Double-Edged Knife" 11-12-65 (Sheila Parnell); *The Road West*—"To Light a Candle" 11-28-66 (Rachel Adams).

Ross, Lanny (1906-4/25/88). Films: "Home in Oklahoma" 1946 (Luke Lowry).

Ross, Manning. TV: *Circus Boy*—"Big Top Angel" 1-27-57 (Ken), "The Marvelous Manellis" 11-21-57 (Jean Manelli); *Jim Bowie*—"Country Cousin" 5-3-57 (Abner Bowie), "Up the Creek" 3-7-58 (Abner Bowie); *Telephone Time*—"Sam Houston's Decision" 12-10-57 (Sidney Sherman); *The Adventures of Rin Tin Tin*—"Bitter Bounty" 3-14-58 (Tampo), "The Matador" 2-6-59 (Luis Pedrosa).

Ross, Marion (1928-). TV: *The Lone Ranger*—"Texas Draw" 11-5-54 (Virginia Thorpe); *Buckskin*—"Hunter's Moon" 9-11-58 (Rose); *Zane Grey Theater*—"Seed of Evil" 4-7-60 (Mollie); *Death Valley Days*—"Death Ride" 3-15-61 (Martha Sayles), "Halo for a Badman" 4-15-67 (Emma); *Rawhide*—"Incident of the Woman Trap" 1-26-62 (Flora), "Gold Fever" 5-4-62 (Priscilla Brewer); *The Slowest Gun in the West* 7-29-63 (Elsie May); *Great Adventure*—"The Outlaw and the Nun" 12-6-63 (Sister Marcella).

Ross, Michael (-9/10/93). Films: "Lost in Alaska" 1952 (Willie); "Those Redheads from Seattle" 1953 (Mack Donahue); "The Return of Jack Slade" 1955 (Little Blue). ¶TV: *The Lone Ranger*—"The Renegades" 11-3-49; *Circus Boy*—"The Great Gambino" 10-7-56 (Ringmaster); *Bonanza*—"San Francisco Holiday" 4-2-60, "The Countess" 11-19-61; *The Virginian*—"The Accomplice" 12-19-62; *Wagon Train*—"The Jed Whitmore Story" 1-13-64.

Ross, Milton. Films: "The Darkening Trail" 1915; "The Gunfighter" 1916 (Cactus Fuller); "The Patriot" 1916 (Denman Hammond); "The Desert Man" 1917 (Tacoma Jake); "The Silent Man" 1917 (Ames Mitchell); "The Square Deal Man" 1917 (Preaching Dan); "Truthful Tulliver" 1917 (Deacon Doyle); "Flare-Up Sal" 1918 (Lige Higbee); "The Narrow Trail" 1918 (Admiral Bates); "Riddle Gawne" 1918 (Reb Butler); "The Tiger Man" 1918 (Connor Moore); "The Killer" 1921 (Buck Johnson); "Western Speed" 1922 (Kansas Casey); "Salome Jane" 1923 (Steve Lowe); "The Virginian" 1923 (Judge Henry); "The Breed of the Border" 1924 (Dad Slocum); "Call of the Mate" 1924; "The Cowboy and the Flapper" 1924 (Col. Allison);

"Down by the Rio Grande" 1924; "The Man from God's Country" 1924 (Don Manuel); "That Wild West" 1924; "O.U. West" 1925 (Cass Jones); "Beyond the Rockies" 1926 (Tex Marcy).

Ross, Robert C. Films: "Rough Ridin' Justice" 1945 (Bob); "The White Squaw" 1956 (Knute Swanson). ¶TV: *Gunsmoke*—"Who Lives by the Sword" 5-18-57 (Lew Baxter); *The Deputy*—"The Example" 3-25-61 (Gabe).

Rossellini, Isabella (1952-). Films: "Wyatt Earp" 1994 (Big Nose Kate).

Rossen, Carol (1937-). TV: *Wagon Train*—"Wagon to Fort Anderson" 6-7-61 (Fay Ellison); *Stoney Burke*—"Image of Glory" 2-4-63 (Connie); *Branded*—"A Taste of Poison" 5-2-65 (Dr. Evelyn Cole).

Rossi, Luciano. Films: "They Call Me Trinity" 1970-Ital. (Timid); "Deaf Smith and Johnny Ears" 1972-Ital.; "Watch Out Gringo! Sabata Will Return" 1972-Ital./Span.

Rossi Stuart, Giacomo (Jack Stuart) (1931-). Films: "Gringo" 1963-Span./Ital.; "Massacre at Grand Canyon" 1963-Ital.; "Five Thousand Dollars on One Ace" 1965-Span./Ital.; "Magnificent Brutes of the West" 1965-Ital./Span./Fr. (Marshal Gary Smith); "Deguello" 1966-Ital. (Norman Isaac); "The Five Man Army" 1969-Ital. (Mexican Officer); "Ben and Charlie" 1970-Ital.; "You're Jinxed, Friend, You Just Met Sacramento" 1970-Ital./Span. (Murdock); "Kill Django … Kill First" 1971-Ital. (Django); "Fighting Fists of Shanghai Joe" 1973-Ital.; "Zorro" 1974-Ital./Fr.

Rossini, Renato (Howard Ross). Films: "Johnny Colt" 1966-Ital.; "Savage Gringo" 1966-Ital.; "Wrath of God" 1968-Ital./Span. (David); "The Magnificent Bandits" 1969-Ital./Span.; "Wanted Johnny Texas" 1971-Ital. (O'Connor); "The Man Called Noon" 1973-Brit./Span./Ital. (Bayles); "Those Dirty Dogs!" 1973-U.S./Ital./Span. (Younger).

Rossington, Norman (1928-). Films: "Man in the Wilderness" 1971-U.S./Span. (Ferris).

Rossito, Angelo (1901-9/21/91). Films: "The Baron of Arizona" 1950 (Angie).

Rosson, Helene (1897-5/5/85). Films: "The Terror of Twin Mountains" 1915; "The Trail of the Serpent" 1915; "The Warning" 1915; "Get Your Man" 1921 (Margaret MacPherson); "The One-Man Trail" 1921; "At Devil's Gorge" 1923 (Mildred Morgan); "The Sting of the Scorpion" 1923; "Ridin' Mad" 1924 (Ruth Carlson); "The Fugitive" 1925 (the Sister).

Rosson, Richard (1908-2/18/66). Films: "A Case of Law" 1917; "The Good Loser" 1918 (Jack Monroe); "Chasing Rainbows" 1919 (Skinny).

Rossovich, Rick. Films: "The Gambler Returns: The Luck of the Draw" TVM-1991 (Ethan Cassidy).

Roter, Diane. TV: *The Virginian*—Regular 1965-66 (Jennifer); *Laredo*—"The Dance of the Laughing Death" 9-23-66 (Lohray).

Roth, Gene (Gene Stutenroth) (1903-7/19/76). Films: "Bad Men of the Border" 1945; "Beyond the Pecos" 1945; "Canyon Passage" 1946 (Miner); "Homesteaders of Paradise Valley" 1947; "Jesse James Rides Again" 1947-serial (Sheriff Duffie); "The Marshal of Cripple Creek" 1947 (Long John Case); "The Sea of Grass" 1947 (Homesteader); "The Adventures of Frank and Jesse James" 1948-serial (Marshal); "The Gallant Legion" 1948; "Oklahoma Badlands" 1948 (Oliver Budge); "The Big Sombrero" 1949 (Ben McBride); "Ghost of Zorro" 1949-serial (George Crane); "The Last Bandit" 1949; "Sheriff of Wichita" 1949 (Howard Thornton); "The Baron of Arizona" 1950 (Father Guardian); "Colorado Ranger" 1950 (Barber); "The James Brothers of Missouri" 1950-serial (Marshal Rand); "Trail of the Rustlers" 1950; "West of the Brazos" 1950 (Attorney); "Don Daredevil Rides Again" 1951-serial (Caleb Brown); "Blue Canadian Rockies" 1952 (Swede); "Fargo" 1952; "Gold Fever" 1952 (Bill Johnson); "The Maverick" 1952 (Fred Nixon); "Montana Belle" 1952 (Marshal Ripple); "Jack McCall, Desperado" 1953 (Attorney); "Silver Lode" 1954 (Townsman); "Running Target" 1956 (Holesworth); "Utah Blaine" 1957 (Tom Corey); "The Miracle of the Hills" 1959 (Sheriff Crane); "How the West Was Won" 1962 (Riverboat Poker Player); "Stagecoach to Dancer's Rock" 1962 (Jude). ¶TV: *The Lone Ranger*—"The Renegades" 11-3-49, "Barnaby Boggs, Esquire" 2-2-50, "Rifles and Renegades" 5-4-50, "Trouble for Tonto" 7-20-50, "Behind the Law" 2-1-51, "The Deserter" 4-23-53, "Colorado Gold" 12-9-54; *The Cisco Kid*—"Mr. X" 4-10-54; *The Roy Rogers Show*—"And Sudden Death" 10-9-55; *Sergeant Preston of the Yukon*—"Follow the Leader" 3-15-56 (Slocum), "The Skull in the Stone" 11-7-57 (Capt. Gunnar Hysted); *Have Gun Will Travel*—"Three Bells to Perdido" 9-14-57, "Young Gun" 11-8-58 (Bartender), "Ransom" 6-4-60 (Carter); *Cheyenne*—"Devil's Canyon" 11-19-57 (Karp); *The Restless Gun*—"Imposter for a Day" 2-17-58 (Olaf Ledbetter), "Tomboy" 11-10-58 (Sheriff); *Tales of Wells Fargo*—"The Break" 5-19-58 (Sheriff Lund), "The English Woman" 2-15-60 (Hodson), "That Washburn Girl" 2-13-61 (Sam Hargrove); *Bat Masterson*—"Election Day" 1-14-59 (Oliver Hinton), "The Big Gamble" 6-16-60 (Barkeep); *Tombstone Territory*—12-18-59 (Asa Sibley); *Wagon Train*—"The Larry Hanify Story" 1-27-60 (Callahan); *Wyatt Earp*—"Wyatt Takes the Primrose Path" 3-28-61 (J.B. Ayers); *The Tall Man*—"The Legend and the Gun" 4-1-61 (Blacksmith); *Laramie*—"The Last Journey" 10-31-61, "Naked Steel" 1-1-63, "The Marshals" 4-30-63; *Bonanza*—"A Hot Day for a Hanging" 10-14-62; *The Dakotas*—"Justice at Eagle's Nest" 3-11-63 (Peterson); *Death Valley Days*—"The Race at Cherry Creek" 3-7-65.

Rothwell, Robert (1930-). Films: "El Dorado" 1967 (Saul Macdonald); "Rio Lobo" 1970 (Whitey's Henchman); "Breakheart Pass" 1976 (Lt. Newell); "Hot Lead and Cold Feet" 1978. ¶TV: *Temple Houston*—"Seventy Times Seven" 12-5-63 (Joe Shivers); *Bonanza*—"A Natural Wizard" 12-12-65 (Ranch Hand); *Gunsmoke*—"Nitro!" 4-8-67 & 4-15-67 (Ben Stearman), "The Pack Rat" 1-12-70 (Shotgun), "Sam McTavish, M.D." 10-5-70 (Joe Slade); *The Virginian*—"The Good-Hearted Badman" 2-7-68 (Kelliher).

Roubert, Matty (1907-5/17/73). Films: "Rose Marie" 1936 (Newsboy); "Gold Mine in the Sky" 1938; "Shine on Harvest Moon" 1938 (Ben); "Saga of Death Valley" 1939; "Adventures of Red Ryder" 1940-serial (Pete); "Frontier Vengeance" 1940 (Pinto); "One Man's Law" 1940; "The Trail Blazers" 1940; "Romance of the West" 1946 (Wildhorse); "Stars Over Texas" 1946 (Buggsy); "Tumbleweed Trail" 1946; "Wild West" 1946 (Halfbreed Charlie); "Law of the Lash" 1947 (Pee Wee); "Valley of Fear" 1947.

Rougeul, Jean (-1978). Films: "Duck, You Sucker!" 1971-Ital. (Priest).

Roundtree, Richard (1942-). Films: "Charley One-Eye" 1973-Brit. (Black Man); "Outlaws" TVM-1986 (Isaiah "Ice" McAdams); "Bad Jim" 1990 (July); "Bonanza: Under Attack" TVM-1995 (Jacob). ¶TV: *Out-*

laws—Regular 1986-87 (Isaiah McAdams); *Young Riders*—"Kansas" 1-12-91 (Calvin).

Rourke, Mickey (1956-). Films: "Heaven's Gate" 1980.

Rousse, Dolores. Films: "Against All Odds" 1924 (Judy Malone); "Oh, You Tony!" 1924 (the Countess); "The Burning Trail" 1925 (Esther Ramsey); "The Meddler" 1925 (Gloria Canfield).

Routh, George. Films: "Two-Gun Betty" 1919 (Miguel Carballo); "The Fighting Romeo" 1925 (Henry Warner).

Rouverol, Jean. Films: "Bar 20 Rides Again" 1936 (Margaret Arnold); "The Law West of Tombstone" 1938 (Nitta Moseby); "Western Jamboree" 1938 (Betty Haskell).

Roux, Tony (1901-11/9/76). Films: "In Old Mexico" 1938 (Pancho); "Law of the Pampas" 1939 (Gaucho); "The Llano Kid" 1939 (Jose); "Gauchos of El Dorado" 1941 (Miguel); "Undercover Man" 1942 (Chavez); "Along Came Jones" 1945 (Old Mexican); "Surrender" 1950 (Chocolate Vendor); "Lone Star" 1952 (Chico). ¶TV: *Tales of the Texas Rangers*—"Blood Trail" 9-24-55 (Pedro).

Rovere, Gina (1936-). Films: "God Forgives—I Don't" 1966-Ital./Span. (Rose).

Rowan, Dan (1922-9/22/87). Films: "Once Upon a Horse" 1958 (Dan Casey).

Rowan, Don (1906-2/17/66). Films: "The Arizona Raiders" 1936 (Luke Arledge); "Oklahoma Terror" 1939 (Slade); "Riders of Death Valley" 1941-serial.

Rowe, Doug. Films: "The Legend of Nigger Charley" 1972 (Dewey Lyons). ¶TV: *Wild Wild West*—"The Night of the Legion of Death" 11-24-67 (Attendant); *Legend*—Pilot 4-18-95, "Bone of Contention" 6-20-95.

Rowe, Misty (1953-). TV: *Young Maverick*—"Have I Got a Girl for You" 1-16-80 (Betty).

Rowland, Henry (1914-4/26/84). Films: "The Phantom Plainsmen" 1942 (Lindrick); "The Showdown" 1950 (Dutch); "Wagon Team" 1952 (Mike McClure); "Wyoming Roundup" 1952 (Howard); "Captain John Smith and Pocahontas" 1953 (Turnbull); "Rebel City" 1953 (Hardy); "Topeka" 1953; "Vigilante Terror" 1953; "Two Guns and a Badge" 1954 (Jim Larkin); "Kiss of Fire" 1955 (Acosta); "Wyoming Renegades" 1955 (Elza Lay); "Friendly Persuasion" 1956 (O'Hara);

"Gun Duel in Durango" 1957 (Roy); "Shoot-Out at Medicine Bend" 1957; "Gunfighters of Casa Grande" 1965-U.S./Span. (the Kid). ¶TV: *The Lone Ranger*—"The Star Witness" 8-17-50; *The Cisco Kid*—"The Puppeteer" 1-19-52, "Lodestone" 4-26-52, "Gun Totin' Papa" 5-24-52, "Cisco Plays the Ghost" 2-21-53, "A Six-Gun for No Pain" 2-28-53, "Harry the Heir" 3-28-53, "Extradition Papers" 9-12-53, "Son of a Gunman" 10-10-53; *Wild Bill Hickok*—"The Sheriff Was a Redhead" 7-15-52, "The Kid from Red Butte" 8-26-52, "The Hideout" 1-20-53; *The Roy Rogers Show*—"The Long Chance" 5-24-53 (Pete Grundy), "M Stands for Murder" 12-6-53, "Backfire" 10-10-54 (Mel Gwyn), "Strangers" 12-5-54 (Corey), "The Brothers O'Dell" 11-20-55, "Three Masked Men" 12-18-55 (Carrie Young), "Ambush" 1-15-56, "Johnny Rover" 6-9-57 (Mack); *The Gene Autry Show*—"Cold Decked" 9-15-53, "Santa Fe Raiders" 7-6-54, "Johnny Jackaroo" 7-13-54, "Sharpshooter" 8-3-54, "The Carnival Comes West" 8-24-54, "Outlaw of Blue Mesa" 9-7-54; *Tales of the Texas Rangers*—"Buckaroo from Powder River" 2-4-56 (Pop); *Wyatt Earp*—"Killing at Cowskin Creek" 2-14-56 (Shorty Dawson), "Take Back Your Town" 12-4-56 (George Morris), "The Sharpshooter" 1-29-57 (George Morris), "Ballad and Truth" 3-4-58 (Tex McKay), "The Truth About Old Man Clanton" 9-27-60, "Study of a Crooked Sheriff" 10-25-60 (Pete Spence); *The Adventures of Rin Tin Tin*—"Lost Treasure" 5-25-56 (Crow); *Fury*—"Nature's Engineers" 2-2-57 (Steve Williams); *Tales of Wells Fargo*—"Stage to Nowhere" 6-24-57; *Broken Arrow*—"The Bounty Hunters" 11-26-57 (Lamont); *Zorro*—"Bernardo Faces Death" 6-26-58, "Day of Decision" 7-3-58; *Jefferson Drum*—"Stagecoach Episode" 10-10-58 (Bandit); *Wagon Train*—"The Sakae Ito Story" 12-3-58 (Burl Miching); *The Texan*—"The Marshal of Yellow Jacket" 3-2-59 (Deebold), "The Dishonest Posse" 10-5-59 (Dutch Slegler); *Stripe Playhouse*—"Ballad to Die By" 7-31-59; *Rawhide*—"Incident at Jacob's Well" 10-16-59 (Ludwig); *The Rifleman*—"The Baby Sitter" 12-15-59; *The Rebel*—"The Unwanted" 1-31-60 (Rollins); *The Deputy*—"The World Against Me" 11-26-60 (Brewer); *The Outlaws*—"The Sooner" 4-27-61 (Schmidt); *Laramie*—"The Barefoot Kid" 1-9-62; *Gunsmoke*—"Trip West" 5-2-64 (Frank).

Rowland, Steve (1938-). Films:

"The Moonlighter" 1953; "The Silver Star" 1955 (Shakespeare); "Gun Glory" 1957 (Young Tom Early). ¶TV: *Wyatt Earp*—"Command Performance" 2-19-57 (Prince Karl), Regular 1959-61 (Phin Clanton); *Tales of Wells Fargo*—"Bill Longley" 2-10-58 (Jeff Evans); *Wagon Train*—"The Charles Maury Story" 5-7-58 (Tom Rainey); *The Rifleman*—"Home Ranch" 10-7-58 (Billy Lehi), "The Coward" 12-22-59; *Bonanza*—"Vendetta" 12-5-59 (Billy Morgan).

Rowlands, Art (1897-5/25/44). Films: "The Devil's Tower" 1928 (Phillip Wayne); "Lightnin' Shot" 1928; "Mystery Valley" 1928; "Wells Fargo" 1937 (Townsman).

Rowlands, Gena (1934-). Films: "Lonely Are the Brave" 1962 (Jerri Bondi); "Montana" TVM-1990 (Bess Guthrie). ¶TV: *Laramie*—"The Run to Rumavaca" 11-10-59 (Laurel Demeistre); *Riverboat*—"Guns for Empire" 12-20-59 (Rose Traynor); *Bonanza*—"She Walks in Beauty" 9-22-63 (Ragan Miller); *The Virginian*—"No Tears for Savannah" 10-2-63 (Savannah); *The Road West*—"Beyond the Hill" 1-16-67 (Karen Collier).

Roy, Charles. Films: "The Sheriff's Son" 1919 (Royal Beaudry).

Roy, Gloria. Films: "Fair Warning" 1937 (Grace Hamilton); "Frontier Marshal" 1939 (Dance Hall Girl); "Lucky Cisco Kid" 1940 (Dance Hall Girl).

Roy, John (1898-5/31/75). Films: "King of the Mounties" 1942-serial (Barn Heavy #1); "The Phantom Rider" 1946-serial (Indian Rebel #2); "Shoot-Out at Medicine Bend" 1957.

Roy, Rosalie. Films: "Clancy of the Mounted" 1933-serial (Maureen Clanch).

Royal, Charles (1880-7/26/55). Films: "The Indians Are Coming" 1930-serial (Uncle Amos).

Royce, Frosty (1910-5/15/65). Films: "Bar 20 Justice" 1938; "Oklahoma Renegades" 1940 (Mort Johnson); "King of Dodge City" 1941; "Prairie Gunsmoke" 1942; "Black Market Rustlers" 1943 (Ed); "Bordertown Gunfighters" 1943; "The James Brothers of Missouri" 1950-serial; "The Outcasts of Poker Flat" 1952 (Posseman); "The Man from Laramie" 1955 (Mule Driver); "Escape from Red Rock" 1958 (Coach Driver). ¶TV: *The Cisco Kid*—"Bounty Men" 1-30-54.

Royce, Lionel (1887-4/1/46). Films: "Let Freedom Ring" 1939 (German).

Royce, Reza (1908-10/20/80). Films: "Cattle Queen of Montana" 1954. ¶TV: *Maverick*—"The Cats of Paradise" 10-11-59 (Woman); *Bonanza*—"Feet of Clay" 4-16-60.

Royce, Ruth (1893-5/7/71). Films: "Blue Streak McCoy" 1920 (Conchita); "If Only Jim" 1921 (Miss Richards); "The Man Trackers" 1921 (Lizette); "Perils of the Yukon" 1922-serial; "In the Days of Daniel Boone" 1923-serial; "Days of '49" 1924-serial; "Riders of the Plains" 1924-serial; "Action Galore" 1925 (Kate Kruger); "Fort Frayne" 1925 (Mrs. Daunton); "Tonio, Son of the Sierras" 1925 (Mrs. Bennett); "Warrior Gap" 1925 (Mrs. Fletcher); "Rawhide" 1926 (Queenie); "Code of the Cow Country" 1927 (Dolores); "Thunderbolt's Tracks" 1927 (Speedy).

Royer, Harry "Missouri" (1890-8/1/51). Films: "Sky High Coral" 1926 (Slim); "The Old Wyoming Trail" 1937 (Regan).

Roylance, Pamela. Films: "Little House on the Prairie: Look Back to Yesterday" TVM-1983 (Sarah Carter); "Little House: The Last Farewell" TVM-1984 (Sarah Carter); "Little House: Bless All the Dear Children" TVM-1984 (Sarah Carter). ¶TV: *Little House: A New Beginning*—Regular 1982-83 (Sarah Carter).

Royle, Selena (1904-4/23/83). Films: "The Harvey Girls" 1946 (Miss Bliss); "Branded" 1951 (Mrs. Lavery).

Royle, William (1887-8/9/40). Films: "Rebellion" 1936 (Harris); "The Glory Trail" 1937 (Capt. Fetterman); "Hollywood Cowboy" 1937 (Klinker); "Renfrew of the Royal Mounted" 1937 (George Hollis); "Wild West Days" 1937-serial; "Flaming Frontier" 1938-serial (Tom Crosby); "Red River Range" 1938 (Payne); "Renegade Ranger" 1938 (Ben Sanderson); "Arizona Legion" 1939 (Dutton); "The Cisco Kid and the Lady" 1939; "The Fighting Gringo" 1939 (Ben Wallace); "Frontier Pony Express" 1939 (Garrett); "Mexicali Rose" 1939 (Carruthers); "Lucky Cisco Kid" 1940 (Sheriff); "The Man from Dakota" 1940 (Supervisor); "Man from Montreal" 1940 (Luther St. Paul); "Murder on the Yukon" 1940 (George Weathers).

Rubens, Alma (1897-1/21/31). Films: "The Half Breed" 1916 (Teresa); "The Cold Deck" 1917 (Coralie); "The Firefly of Tough Luck" 1917 (Firefly); "Truthful Tulliver" 1917 (Grace Burton); "A Man's Country" 1919 (Kate Carewe); "The Valley of Silent Men" 1922 (Marette Radison).

Rubin, Benny (1899-7/15/86). Films: "Montana Moon" 1930 (the Doctor); "Fighting Mad" 1939 (Benny); "The Law vs. Billy the Kid" 1954 (Arnold Dodge); "Masterson of Kansas" 1954 (Coroner); "The Shakiest Gun in the West" 1968. ¶TV: *Brave Eagle*—"The Storm Fool" 1-18-56; *The Adventures of Rin Tin Tin*—"Lost Treasure" 5-25-56 (Cocopah Charlie); *The Rounders*—1-3-67 (Cyrus Morgan); *Wild Wild West*—"The Night of the Janus" 2-15-69 (Janus); *Gunsmoke*—"Doctor Herman Schultz, M.D." 1-26-70 (Dr. Herman Schultz).

Rubinek, Saul. Films: "Unforgiven" 1992 (W.W. Beauchamp).

Rubini, Giulia. Films: "Sign of Coyote" 1964-Ital./Span.; "Adios Hombre" 1966-Ital./Span.; "Ringo and His Golden Pistol" 1966-Ital.; "Stranger in Paso Bravo" 1968-Ital.

Rubinstein, John (1946-). Films: "Zachariah" 1971 (Zachariah). ¶TV: *The Virginian*—"The Deadly Past" 9-20-67 (Boy); *Nichols*—"The Paper Badge" 10-14-71 (Fred Buckerman); *Barbary Coast*—"The Dawson Marker" 1-9-76 (Garrison); *The Quest*—"The Longest Drive" 12-1-76 & 12-8-76 (Wakely).

Rubinstein, Zelda. Films: "The Gambler Returns: The Luck of the Draw" TVM-1991 (Butterfingers O'Malley).

Rucker, Dennis. "Hec Ramsey" TVM-1972 (Andy Muldoon); "Sunset" 1988 (Paul). ¶TV: *Alias Smith and Jones*—"The Day They Hanged Kid Curry" 9-16-71, "Everything Else You Can Steal" 12-16-71 (Billy Jack), "The Strange Fate of Conrad Meyer Zulick" 12-2-72; *Hec Ramsey*—"Dead Heat" 2-3-74 (Arne).

Rudie, Evelyn (1947-). Films: "The Restless Breed" 1957. ¶TV: *Wagon Train*—"The Millie Davis Story" 11-26-58 (Penny); *Lawman*—"The Kids" 2-21-60 (Dodie Weaver).

Rudin, Herman (1912-). Films: "Frontier Uprising" 1961 (Chief Taztay); "Run, Simon, Run" TVM-1970 (Asa). ¶TV: *The Rifleman*—"The Retired Gun" 1-20-59 (Morgan Bailey); *Death Valley Days*—"Human Sacrifice" 5-31-60 (Chief Shokab), "The Courtship of Carrie Huntington" 6-4-66 (Chief), "The Hat That Huldah Wore" 6-25-66 (Wally Denton); *Wanted—Dead or Alive*—"The Voice of Silence" 2-15-61 (Drifter); *The Rebel*—"Decision at Sweetwater" 4-23-61 (Bull).

Rudley, Herbert (1911-). Films: "Raw Edge" 1956 (Gerald Montgomery); "The Bravados" 1958 (Sheriff Elroy Sanchez); "Tonka" 1958 (Capt. Benteen); "The Jayhawkers" 1959 (Gov. William Clayton); "Hell Bent for Leather" 1960 (Perrick). ¶TV: *My Friend Flicka*—"The Silver Saddle" 12-16-55, "The Whip" 2-10-56; *Gunsmoke*—"No Indians" 12-8-56 (Captain Starr), "The Man Who Would be Marshal" 6-15-57 (Emmett Egan); *The Californians*—"The Noose" 10-8-57, "The Avenger" 10-15-57; *Boots and Saddles*—"Prussian Farmer" 10-17-57 (Franz Mueller); *Have Gun Will Travel*—"The O'Hare Story" 3-1-58 (Henry Ritchie); *The Texan*—"Jail for the Innocents" 11-3-58 (Nick Yarboro); *The Rifleman*—"The Indian" 2-17-59 (Gorman), "A Case of Identity" 1-19-60 (Capt. James Gordon); *Lawman*—"Shadow Witness" 11-15-59 (Clint Baker); *Maverick*—"Trooper Maverick" 11-29-59 (Colonel Percy); *Laramie*—"The Protectors" 3-22-60 (Luke Rawlins), "War Hero" 10-2-62 (Jeremy Thorne); *Bronco*—"The Human Equation" 3-22-60 (Major Trask); *The Virginian*—"The Exiles" 1-9-63; *Temple Houston*—"Find Angel Chavez" 9-26-63 (Paul Lennox); *Rawhide*—"Incident of the Gilded Goddess" 4-30-64 (Jeremiah Breen).

Ruggieri, Francoise. TV: *Wild Wild West*—"The Night of the Dancing Death" 11-5-65 (Baroness Nola Kolinski).

Ruggles, Charles (1886-12/23/70). Films: "Ruggles of Red Gap" 1935 (Egbert "Sourdough" Floud); "Go West, Young Lady" 1941 (Jim Pendergast); "The Parson of Panamint" 1941 (Chuckawalla Bill Redfield); n"Ramrod" 1947 (Ben Dickason). ¶TV: *Frontier Circus*—"Mr. Grady Regrets" 1-25-62 (Will Grady); *Destry*—"Deputy for a Day" 4-3-64 (Joe Finster); *Wagon Train*—"Herman" 2-14-65 (Jamison Hershey); *Laredo*—"A Taste of Money" 4-28-66 (Major John Cane); *Bonanza*—"Horse of a Different Hue" 9-18-66 (Colonel Fairchild); *Pistols 'n' Petticoats*—"The Triangle" 10-22-66 (Orville Snipe).

Ruhl, William H. (1901-3/12/56). Films: "Sutter's Gold" 1936; "Gaucho Serenade" 1940 (Cartrer); "Oklahoma Renegades" 1940 (Mace Liscomb); "Texas Terrors" 1940 (Ashley); "Gauchos of El Dorado" 1941 (Tyndal); "Days of Old Cheyenne" 1943 (Steve Brackett); "Prairie Express" 1947 (Gordon Gregg); "Cowboy Cavalier" 1948; "Frontier Agent" 1948; "Song of the Drifter" 1948; "Brand of Fear" 1949; "Haunted

Trails" 1949 (Gorman); "Shadows of the West" 1949 (Sheriff); "Western Renegades" 1949 (Curly); "Code of the Silver Sage" 1950 (Major Duncan). ¶TV: *The Lone Ranger*—"The Black Hat" 5-18-50, "The Whimsical Bandit" 8-31-50; *Wild Bill Hickok*—"Behind Southern Lines" 6-26-51, "Vigilante Story" 1-22-52.

Ruick, Barbara (1930-3/2/74). Films: "Apache War Smoke" 1952 (Nancy Dekker).

Ruick, Melville (1898-12/24/72). TV: *Branded*—"Coward Step Aside" 3-7-65 (Bates); *The Loner*—"Mantrap" 1-8-66 (Jess); *Wild Wild West*—"The Night of the Big Blast" 10-7-66 (Attorney General); *Laredo*—"Any Way the Wind Blows" 10-28-66 (Prentiss).

Ruiz, Antonio (1954-). Films: "Dollars for a Fast Gun" 1968-Ital./Span. (Frank Nolan); "Villa Rides" 1968 (Juan Gonzalez).

Ruiz, Jose Carlo. Films: "Major Dundee" 1965 (Riago); "Buck and the Preacher" 1972 (Brave); "Eagle's Wing" 1979-Brit./Span. (Lame Wolf).

Rule, Janice (1931-). Films: "Gun for a Coward" 1957 (Aud Niven); "Invitation to a Gunfighter" 1964 (Ruth Adams); "Alvarez Kelly" 1966 (Liz Pickering); "Welcome to Hard Times" 1967 (Molly Riordan); "The Devil and Miss Sarah" TVM-1971 (Sarah Turner); "Kid Blue" 1973 (Janet Conforto). ¶TV: *Have Gun Will Travel*—"Three Bells to Perdido" 9-14-57 (Nancy Reader); *Wagon Train*—"The Zeke Thomas Story" 11-27-57 (Maggie Thomas).

Ruman, Sig (1884-2/14/67). Films: "Bold Caballero" 1936 (Commandante); "Carolina Cannonball" 1955 (Stefan); "Many Rivers to Cross" 1955 (Spectacle Man). ¶TV: *Maverick*—"Diamond in the Rough" 1-26-58 (Captain Steeger), "The Strange Journey of Jenny Hill" 3-29-59 (Prof. Vegelius), "Maverick Springs" 12-6-59 (Prof. Kronkhite), "Diamond Flush" 2-5-61 (Bockenheimer), "The Money Machine" 4-8-62 (Jonckbloet); *Lawman*—"The Chef" 3-1-59 (Hans Steinmayer); *Daniel Boone*—"The Sisters O'Hannrahan" 12-3-64 (Van Coot).

Rumsey, Bert (1892-7/6/68). TV: *Gunsmoke*—"Young Man with a Gun" 10-20-56 (Bartender), "The Mistake" 11-24-56 (Bartender), "Poor Pearl" 12-22-56 (Bartender), "Pucket's New Year" 1-5-57 (Bartender), "What the Whiskey Drummer Heard" 4-27-57 (Bartender), "Doc Quits" 2-21-59 (Sam Pence).

Runningfox, Joseph. Films: "Geronimo" TVM-1993 (Geronimo). ¶TV: *Young Riders*—"Pride and Prejudice" 10-27-90 (Black Wolf).

Rupp, Sieghardt. Films: "Among Vultures" 1964-Ger./Ital./Fr./Yugo. (Preston); "A Fistful of Dollars" 1964-Ital./Ger./Span. (Esteban Rojo); "Man Called Gringo" 1964-Ger./Span.; "Who Killed Johnny R.?" 1966-Ital./Span.; "Blood at Sundown" 1969-Ital./Span.

Ruscio, Al (1924-). TV: *Zorro*—"The New Order" 11-13-58 (Luis Rico), "Zorro and the Flag of Truce" 11-27-58 (Luis Rico); *U.S. Marshal*—"The High Fence" 1-30-60; *Wrangler*—"Affair at the Trading Post" 8-18-60 (Wes Martin); *Bonanza*—"The Last Viking" 11-12-60 (Vaca), "The Honor of Cochise" 10-8-61 (Delgado); *Have Gun Will Travel*—"Unforgiving Minute" 1-26-63 (Machado); *Outlaws*—"Tintype" 1-3-87 (Martin).

Rush, Barbara (1927-). Films: "Flaming Feather" 1952 (Nora Logan); "Taza, Son of Cochise" 1954 (Oona); "Kiss of Fire" 1955 (Princess Lucia); "Hombre" 1967 (Audra Favor). ¶TV: *Frontier Circus*—"The Smallest Target" 10-12-61 (Bonnie); *Laredo*—"Miracle at Massacre Mission" 3-3-66 (Sister William); *Custer*—"The Gauntlet" 12-20-67 (Brigid O'Rourke); *Paradise*—"Bad Blood" 2-1-91 (Patricia Forrester).

Rush, Charles O. Films: "The Cold Deck" 1917 (Ace Hutton); "The Square Deal Man" 1917 (Broadway Hammersley).

Rush, Dennis. TV: *The Deputy*—"The Orphans" 12-26-59 (Timmy); *Wagon Train*—"The Christine Elliot Story" 3-23-60, "Trial for Murder" 4-27-60 & 5-4-60 (David Ivers), "The Nellie Jefferson Story" 4-5-61 (Homer), "The Jeff Hartfield Story" 2-14-62 (Davey Adams), "The Caroline Casteel Story" 9-26-62 (Ham Stryker); *Laramie*—"The Runt" 2-20-62, "The Replacement" 3-27-62.

Rush, Dick. Films: "Three Gold Coins" 1920 (Rufus Berry); "Forbidden Trail" 1932 (Wright); "Gordon of Ghost City" 1933-serial (Sheriff); "The Last Round-Up" 1934 (Rush); "The Thundering Herd" 1934 (Middlewest); "The Judgement Book" 1935 (Lee); "Justice of the Range" 1935 (Gulch Sheriff); "Law Beyond the Range" 1935 (Texas Ranger); "The Roaring West" 1935-serial; "The Cattle Thief" 1936; "Code of the Range" 1936 (Grange); "The Cowboy and the Kid" 1936 (Sheriff Morton); "The Mysterious Avenger" 1936 (Posse); "Song of the Saddle" 1936; "Two-Fisted Sheriff" 1937 (Carter); "Wells Fargo" 1937 (Conductor); "Santa Fe Stampede" 1938 (Sheriff); "Oklahoma Frontier" 1939 (Settler); "The Phantom Stage" 1939 (Blacksmith); "Union Pacific" 1939 (Irish Paddy); "My Little Chickadee" 1940; "Riders of Pasco Basin" 1940 (Rancher); "Riders of Death Valley" 1941-serial (Bartender); "Sagebrush Law" 1943; "The Sea of Grass" 1947 (Cattleman).

Ruskin, Joseph. Films: "Hell Bent for Leather" 1960 (Shad). ¶TV: *Wanted—Dead or Alive*—"Reckless" 11-7-59; *The Law of the Plainsman*—"Appointment in Sante Fe" 11-19-59; *Colt .45*—"Martial Law" 5-17-60 (Jace Kirby); *Lawman*—"The Escape of Joe Kilmer" 12-18-60, "The Hold-Out" 2-18-62 (Ed James); *Stagecoach West*—"By the Deep Six" 12-27-60 (Clye Hardisty); *Two Faces West*—"The Crisis" 3-6-61; *The Outlaws*—"The Sooner" 4-27-61 (Kopek); *Tales of Wells Fargo*—"Jeremiah" 11-11-61 (Shelby); *Gunsmoke*—"The Gallows" 3-3-62 (Judge), "Stage Stop" 11-26-66 (Curt Hansen); *Death Valley Days*—"Coffin for a Coward" 2-6-63 (Jeb Daley); *The Dakotas*—"Feud at Snake River" 4-29-63 (the Rider); *Wild Wild West*—"The Night of the Fatal Trap" 12-24-65 (Viper), "The Night of the Falcon" 11-10-67 (Fediz Munez); *The High Chaparral*—"Lady Fair" 11-14-69 (Pardee).

Russ, William. Films: "Cattle Annie and Little Britches" 1981 (Little Dick Raidler); "Houston: The Legend of Texas" TVM-1986 (Will Travis). ¶TV: *Young Riders*—"Daisy" 2-2-91 (Roger); *Adventures of Brisco County, Jr.*—"Socrates' Sister" 9-24-93 (Jack Randolph); *Legend*—"The Life, Death, and Life of Wild Bill Hickok" 5-16-95 (Wild Bill Hickok).

Russek, Jorge (1932-). Films: "Villa!" 1958 (Tniente Rurale); "Guns for San Sebastian" 1967-U.S./Fr./Mex./Ital. (Pedro); "The Wild Bunch" 1969 (Lt. Zamorra); "Soldier Blue" 1970 (Running Fox); "The Wrath of God" 1972 (Cordona); "Pat Garrett and Billy the Kid" 1973 (Silva); "The Return of a Man Called Horse" 1976 (Blacksmith); "Eagle's Wing" 1979-Brit./Span. (Gonzalo); "Zorro, the Gay Blade" 1981 (Don Fernando). ¶TV: *The High Chaparral*—"North to Tucson" 11-8-68 (Molinero), "The Lion Sleeps" 3-28-69 (El Coyote).

Russel, Tony (1925-). TV: *The*

High Chaparral—"No Trouble at All" 5-5-70 (Ricardo).

Russell, Albert (1876-4/3/46). Films: "Courage of the West" 1937 (Abraham Lincoln); "Virginia City" 1940 (Southerner).

Russell, Bing (1928-). Films: "Gunfight at the O.K. Corral" 1957 (Bartender); "Ride a Violent Mile" 1957 (Norman); "Cattle Empire" 1958 (Douglas Hamilton); "Good Day for a Hanging" 1958 (George Fletcher); "The Horse Soldiers" 1959 (Dunker); "Last Train from Gun Hill" 1959 (Skag); "Rio Bravo" 1959 (Cowboy Murdered in Saloon); "The Magnificent Seven" 1960 (Robert); "Cheyenne Autumn" 1964 (Telegrapher); "The Hallelujah Trail" 1965 (Horner); "The Ride to Hangman's Tree" 1967 (Keller); "Journey to Shiloh" 1968 (Greybeard); "A Cry in the Wilderness" TVM-1974 (Griffey); "The Apple Dumpling Gang" 1975 (Herm Dally); "Sunset" 1988 (Studio Guard). ¶TV: *Gunsmoke*— "Mr. and Mrs. Amber" 8-4-56 (Simon), "Lynching Man" 11-15-58 (Ed Shelby), "Don Mateo" 10-22-60 (Grave Tabor), "Old Yellow Boots" 10-7-61 (Head), "Mail Drop" 1-28-67 (Walsh), "The Iron Blood of Courage" 2-18-74 (Rolfing); *Cavalry Patrol*—Pilot 1956 (Jenner); *Tombstone Territory*—"Guns of Silver" 11-27-57 (Ollie Williams); *Wagon Train*—"The Charles Avery Story" 12-13-57 (Cullen); *Maverick*—"Naked Gallows" 12-15-57 (Tyler Brink), "A Fellow's Brother" 11-22-59 (Jed Hanes), "A Bullet for the Teacher" 10-30-60 (Luke Storm), "The Bold Fenian Men" 12-18-60 (Orson Holt); *Wyatt Earp*—"The General's Lady" 1-14-58 (Sgt. Turner); *Colt .45* -"Ghost Town" 2-21-58 (Jack Lowden), "Dead Aim" 4-12-59 (Jed Coy); *Tales of Wells Fargo*—"Special Delivery" 3-31-58 (Capt. Maynard), "The Train Robbery" 10-12-59 (Gig), "Wanted: Jim Hardie" 12-21-59 (Tom); *Sugarfoot*—"Hideout" 4-1-58 (Sgt. McKinnock); *Northwest Passage*—"Break Out" 10-19-58 (Ben Smith); *Have Gun Will Travel*—"A Sense of Justice" 11-1-58, "Memories of Monica" 10-27-62 (Sheriff Reagan); *Zane Grey Theater*—"Deadfall" 2-19-59 (Deputy Stover), "The Mormons" 12-15-60 (Cole); *Black Saddle*—"Client: Robinson" 2-21-59 (Ken Wilson), "The Long Rider" 10-16-59; *Bronco*—"Prairie Skipper" 5-5-59 (Jeb), "Stage to the Sky" 4-24-61 (Johnny Rawlins); *The Rifleman*—"A Matter of Faith" 5-19-59 (Hode Evans), "Seven" 10-11-60 (Sanchez); *The Texan*—"The Dishonest Posse" 10-5-

59 (Larry Boland); *Wanted—Dead or Alive*—"Desert Seed" 11-14-59, "Triple Vise" 2-27-60 (Billy Hemp); *The Alaskans*—"The Trial of Reno McKee" 1-10-60 (Edward Carse); *Laramie*—"Company Man" 2-9-60 (Tex), "Men of Defiance" 4-19-60 (Reb O'Neil), "The Sometime Gambler" 3-19-63 (Reeves); *Wrangler*—"Incident at the Bar M" 8-4-60 (Ritter); *Bonanza*—"The Long Night" 5-6-62 (Poindexter), Regular 1963-72 (Deputy Clem Poster); *Tate*—"The Reckoning" 8-24-60 (Corey); *Rawhide*—"Abilene" 5-18-62 (Jack Harris); *The Virginian*—"Riff-Raff" 11-7-62, "The Invaders" 1-1-64, "The Wolves Up Front, the Jackals Behind" 3-23-66 (Donovan), "The Challenge" 10-19-66 (Sam Fuller), "The Deadly Past" 9-20-67 (Ned Smith); *Death Valley Days*—"The Watch" 1-16-63 (Jack Short), "Measure of a Man" 11-17-63 (Jack Alvord), "By the Book" 5-4-68 (Rogers), "Son of Thunder" 10-25-69; *Stoney Burke*—"To Catch the Kaiser" 3-11-63 (Neeley); *Branded*—"Very Few Heroes" 4-11-65 (Thomas Teal), "The Golden Fleece" 1-2-66 (Sheriff Gorman); *A Man Called Shenandoah*—"The Verdict" 11-1-65 (Clem); *The Big Valley*—"Barbary Red" 2-16-66 (Clint), "The Man from Nowhere" 11-14-66 (Rancher), "Cage of Eagles" 4-24-67 (Mac), "A Flock of Trouble" 9-25-67 (Kelsey), "The Profit and the Lost" 12-2-68 (Sheriff), "The Secret" 1-27-69 (Slade), "Point and Counterpoint" 5-19-69 (Sheriff Jim Dolan); *The Monroes*—"The Hunter" 10-26-66 (Aaron); *The Guns of Will Sonnett*—"A Son for a Son" 10-20-67, "The Fearless Man" 12-13-68, "Robber's Roost" 1-17-69, "And He Shall Lead the Children" 1-19-68 (Charlie); *Dundee and the Culhane*—10-25-67 (H.P. Graham); *Hondo*—"Hondo and the Hanging Town" 12-8-67 (Thompson); *The Outcasts*—"The Glory Wagon" 2-3-69 (Grainer).

Russell, Bryan (1953-). Films: "How the West Was Won" 1962 (Zeke Prescott); "The Adventures of Bullwhip Griffin" 1967 (Jack Flagg). ¶TV: *Death Valley Days*—"The Little Trooper" 12-15-59; *The Law of the Plainsman*—"Clear Title" 12-17-59; *Wanted—Dead or Alive*—"One Mother Too Many" 12-7-60 (Davey); *Wagon Train*—"The Odyssey of Flint McCullough" 2-15-61; *Tales of Wells Fargo*—"Moment of Glory" 5-1-61 (Pete Harris), "Jeremiah" 11-11-61 (Jody).

Russell, Don (1927-5/27/81). TV: *Gunsmoke*—"Cody's Code" 1-20-62 (Harry).

Russell, Evangeline (1902-2/22/66). Films: "Red Love" 1925 (Little Antelope); "Hawk of the Hills" 1927-serial.

Russell, Gail (1924-8/26/61). Films: "Angel and the Badman" 1947 (Prudence Worth); "El Paso" 1949 (Susan Jeffers); "Seven Men from Now" 1956 (Annie Greer). ¶TV: *The Rebel*—"Noblesse Oblige" 2-14-60 (Cassandra).

Russell, George (1904-2/22/75). Films: "Spoilers of the Range" 1939 (Slim); "The Lone Hand Texan" 1947 (Second Outlaw); "Montana Territory" 1952 (Boone Helm); "Son of Paleface" 1952 (Posse); "Dalton That Got Away" 1960.

Russell, J. Buckley. Films: "The Jack Rider" 1921 (Howard Gribbon); "The Freshie" 1922 (Society Sam).

Russell, J. Gordon (1883-4/21/35). Films: "The Mediator" 1916; "Put Up Your Hands" 1919 (Three Gun Smith); "Some Liar" 1919 (High Spade McQueen); "When a Man Rides Alone" 1919 (Rodolpho); "The Sagebrusher" 1920 (Big Aleck); "The Testing Block" 1920; "Three Word Brand" 1921 (Bull Yeates); "His Back Against the Wall" 1922 (Bronc Lewis); "Trail of Hate" 1922 (Jack Beecker); "Kindled Courage" 1923 (Sheriff); "The Spoilers" 1923 (Burke); "Hard Hittin' Hamilton" 1924 (Buck Wilson); "Mile-A-Minute Romeo" 1924 (Landry); "Singer Jim McKee" 1924 (Buck Holden); "The Western Wallop" 1924 (Jefferson Bradshaw); "Flying Hoofs" 1925 (James Perdee); "Galloping Jinx" 1925 (Pete Black); "Hearts and Spurs" 1925 (Sid Thomas); "The No-Gun Man" 1925 (Tom West); "Quicker'n Lightnin'" 1925 (Mowii); "A Roaring Adventure" 1925 (Robert Carpenter); "The Sign of the Cactus" 1925 (John Henderton); "Tumbleweeds" 1925 (Noll Lassiter); "Looking for Trouble" 1926 (Jasper Murchison); "Spurs and Saddles" 1927 (Blaze Holton); "Beyond the Sierras" 1928 (Wells); "Saddle Mates" 1928 (Morgan Shelby).

Russell, Jackie (1936-). Films: "Tickle Me" 1965 (Gloria); "The Cheyenne Social Club" 1970 (Carrie Virginia). ¶TV: *Tales of Wells Fargo*—"The Rawhide Kid" 3-16-59 (Norah); *Wanted—Dead or Alive*—"Bad Gun" 10-24-59 (Cynthia Cyborn); *Bonanza*—"The Abduction" 10-29-60 (Jennifer Beale); *Wagon Train*—"The Jim Bridger Story" 5-10-61 (Mavis Beddoe); *Two Faces West*—"The Coward" 6-26-61 (Karen); *The Virginian*—"Shadows of the Past" 2-24-

65 (Bar Girl), "The Claim" 10-6-65 (Irmetta); *The Road West*—"Have You Seen the Aurora Borealis?" 12-12-66; *Gunsmoke*—"Wonder" 12-18-67 (Annie Franklin), "Hard Labor" 2-24-75 (Bar Girl); *Alias Smith and Jones*—"The Biggest Game in the West" 2-3-72.

Russell, Jane (1921-). Films: "The Outlaw" 1943 (Rio); "The Paleface" 1948 (Calamity Jane); "Montana Belle" 1952 (Belle Starr); "Son of Paleface" 1952 (Mike); "The Tall Men" 1955 (Nella Turner); "Johnny Reno" 1966 (Nona Williams); "Waco" 1966 (Jill Stone). ¶TV: *Desilu Playhouse*—"Ballad for a Badman" 1-26-59; *Death Valley Days*—"Splinter Station" 10-19-60 (Mary Taylor).

Russell, John (1920-1/19/92). Films: "Jesse James" 1939 (Jesse James, Jr.); "Yellow Sky" 1948 (Lengthy); "Frenchie" 1950 (Lance Cole); "Saddle Tramp" 1950 (Rocky); "Man in the Saddle" 1951 (Hugh Clagg); "Oklahoma Annie" 1952 (Dan Fraser); "Hell's Outpost" 1954 (Ben Hodes); "Jubilee Trail" 1954 (Oliver Hale); "The Last Command" 1955 (Lt. Dickinson); "The Dalton Girls" 1957 (W.T. "Illinois" Grey); "Fort Massacre" 1958 (Travis); "Rio Bravo" 1959 (Nathan Burdette); "Yellowstone Kelly" 1959 (Gall); "Apache Uprising" 1966 (Vance Buckner); "Fort Utah" 1967 (Eli Jonas); "Hostile Guns" 1967 (Aaron); "Buckskin" 1968 (Patch); "Cannon for Cordoba" 1970 (Brig. Gen. John J. Pershing); "Alias Smith and Jones" TVM-1971 (Marshal); "Smoke in the Wind" 1975 (Cagle); "Kino, the Padre on Horseback" 1977; "Pale Rider" 1985 (Stockburn). ¶TV: *Maverick*—"A Rage for Vengeance" 1-12-58 (John Grimes), "Lonesome Reunion" 9-28-58 (Edgar Maxwell); *Hadley's Hunters* 9-25-60 (Marshal Dan Troup); *Cheyenne*—"The Empty Gun" 2-25-58 (Matt Reardon), "Dead to Rights" 5-20-58 (Saylor Hornbrook); *Lawman*—Regular 1958-62 (Marshal Dan Troup); *Sugarfoot*—"Ring of Sand" 9-16-58 (Jeff Seward); *Northwest Passage*—"The Killers" 3-13-59; *Daniel Boone*—"The Prophet" 1-21-65 (Amos McAleer); *Alias Smith and Jones*—"Which Way to the O.K. Corral?" 2-10-72 (Bart), "The Day the Amnesty Came Through" 11-25-72 (Sheriff Lom Trevors), "Witness to a Lynching" 12-16-72 (Sheriff Lom Trevors); *Gunsmoke*—"The Iron Man" 10-21-74 (Carl Ryker).

Russell, John Lowell (1875-9/19/37). Films: "Arizona Days" 1928

(Dolly's Father); "Manhattan Cowboy" 1928.

Russell, Kurt (1951-). Films: "Guns of Diablo" 1964 (Jaimie McPheeters); "Fools' Parade" 1971 (Johnny Jesus); "The Quest" TVM-1976 (Morgan Baudine/Two Persons); "Tombstone" 1993 (Wyatt Earp). ¶TV: *The Travels of Jaimie McPheeters*—Regular 1963-64 (Jaimie McPheeters); *Gunsmoke*—"Blue Heaven" 9-26-64 (Packy Kerlin), "Trail of Bloodshed" 3-4-74 (Buck Henry); *The Virginian*—"A Father for Toby" 11-4-64 (Toby Shea), "The Brothers" 9-15-65 (Andy Denning); *Daniel Boone*—"The First Stone" 1-28-65 (William Craig), "The Price of Friendship" 2-18-65 (Matthew), "The Young Ones" 2-23-67 (Jed), "Bickford's Bridge" 2-20-69 (Paul), "Target Boone" 11-20-69 (Nathan Jarrett); *The Legend of Jesse James*—"The Colt" 1-17-66 (Elick Harte); *Laredo*—"Meanwhile, Back at the Reservation" 2-10-66 (Grey Smoke); *The Road West*—"Charade of Justice" 3-27-67 (Jay Baker); *The High Chaparral*—"The Guns of Johnny Rondo" 2-6-70 (Dan); *Hec Ramsey*—"Scar Tissue" 3-10-74 (Matthias Kane); *The New Land*—Regular 1974 (Bo Larsen); *The Quest*—Regular 1976 (Morgan Beaudine).

Russell, Lewis (1889-11/12/61). Films: "When the Redskins Rode" 1951 (Gov. Dinwiddle); "The Naked Hills" 1956 (Baxter).

Russell, Mary. Films: "Roarin' Lead" 1936 (Blondie); "The Big Show" 1937 (Mary); "Riders of Whistling Skull" 1937 (Betty Marsh); "The Silver Trail" 1937 (Molly Wellburn).

Russell, Nipsey (1924-). Films: "Posse" 1993 (Snopes).

Russell, Reb (1905-3/16/78). Films: "Fighting Through" 1934 (Reb); "Fighting to Live" 1934; "The Man from Hell" 1934 (Clint Mason); "Arizona Bad Man" 1935 (Steve Donovan); "Blazing Guns" 1935 (Bob Grady); "Border Vengeance" 1935 (Muley Kid Benson); "Cheyenne Tornado" 1935 (Cheyenne Kid); "Lightning Triggers" 1935 (Reb Russell); "Outlaw Rule" 1935 (Reb Russell); "Range Warfare" 1935 (Reb).

Russell, Ron. TV: *The Virginian*—"Ride to Delphi" 9-21-66 (Lemoine Carlson), "Vengeance Trail" 1-4-67 (Toby Willard); *Laredo*—"The Land Slickers" 10-14-66 (Ed Emerson); *The Road West*—"Long Journey to Leavenworth" 10-17-66 (Si Collins); *Pistols 'n' Petticoats*—12-24-66 (Curly Bigelow).

Russell, Tony. Films: "Behind the Mask of Zorro" 1965-Ital./Span. (Patricio/Zorro).

Russell, William (1886-2/18/29). Films: "The Last of the Mohicans" 1911; "The Forest Rose" 1912; "Lone Star" 1916 (Lone Star); "Snap Judgment" 1917 (James Page/Arizona Pete Rawley); "Eastward Ho!" 1919; "Sacred Silence" 1919; "Six Feet Four" 1919 (Buck Thornton); "Some Liar" 1919 (Robert Winchester McTabb); "This Hero Stuff" 1919 (Captain November Jones); "When a Man Rides Alone" 1919 (William Sykes); "Where the West Begins" 1919 (Cliff Redfern); "The Challenge of the Law" 1920 (Captain Bruce Cavanaugh); "The Iron Rider" 1920 (Larry Lannigan); "Shod with Fire" 1920 (Bruce Bayard); "Twins of Suffering Creek" 1920 (Lark); "Colorado Pluck" 1921 (Colorado Jim); "Singing River" 1921 (Lang Rush); "The Crusader" 1922 (Peter Brent); "Man's Size" 1923 (Tom Morse); "Wings of the Storm" 1926 (Bill Martin); "Danger Patrol" 1928 (Sgt. John Daley); "A Rough Shod Fighter" 1928.

Russo, James. Films: "Bad Girls" 1994 (Kid Jarrett).

Russo, Joey. TV: *The Virginian*—"The Small Parade" 2-20-63, "The Dream of Stavros Karas" 12-1-65 (Yanko); *Rawhide*—"Incident of the Clown" 3-29-63 (Gray Pony).

Russo, Tony. Films: "Last Train from Gun Hill" 1959 (Pinto). ¶TV: *Zorro*—"Double Trouble for Zorro" 12-19-57 (Martinez), "The Luckiest Swordsman Alive" 12-26-57 (Martinez), "An Affair of Honor" 5-7-59 (Senor Pedro Avila); *26 Men*—"Indian Gunslinger" 12-31-57; *Broken Arrow*—"Escape" 2-18-58 (Anaka).

Rust, Richard (1936-). Films: "The Legend of Tom Dooley" 1959 (Country Boy); "Comanche Station" 1960 (Dobie); "Alvarez Kelly" 1966 (Sergeant Hatcher); "Kid Blue" 1973 (Train Robbery); "Savage Red—Outlaw White" 1974; "The Great Gundown" 1977 (Joe Riles). ¶TV: *Zane Grey Theater*—"Make It Look Good" 2-5-59 (Russ Bowen); *Gunsmoke*—"Kitty's Rebellion" 2-7-59, "Kangaroo" 10-10-59 (Dal), "Say Uncle" 10-1-60 (Lee Nagle); *Buckskin*—"A Well of Gold" 3-16-59 (Mathew Gower); *Black Saddle*—"Client: Vardon" 5-30-59 (Frank Vardon), "The Apprentice" 3-11-60 (Peck); *Man from Blackhawk*—"Logan's Policy" 10-9-59 (George Blackburn); *Lawman*—"9:05 to North Platte" 12-6-59 (Rood Jute); *Sugarfoot*—"The Gaucho" 12-22-59 (Kirby Conway); *The Law of the*

Plainsman—"Toll Road" 12-24-59 (Healy); *Have Gun Will Travel*—"The Ledge" 2-13-60, "Bear Bait" 5-13-61 (Sim), "Darwin's Man" 4-21-62 (Jayce Coombs); *Johnny Ringo*—"The Vindicator" 3-31-60 (Brad); *Bronco*—"Winter Kill" 5-31-60 (Jack Crowley); *The Westerner*—"School Days" 10-7-60 (Deputy); *The Outlaws*—"The Brothers" 5-11-61 (Jimmy Kelly); *Tales of Wells Fargo*—"Trackback" 12-30-61 (Wally Lambert); *The Rifleman*—"The Quiet Fear" 1-22-62 (Brice); *Bonanza*—"The Quality of Mercy" 11-17-63 (Seth Pruitt).

Ruth, Jean (1898-12/19/55). Films: "Fancy Pants" 1950 (Miss Wilkins).

Ruth, Marshall (1898-1/17/53). Films: "Ridin' Luck" 1927; "Wild Born" 1927; "Moonlight on the Prairie" 1935 (Fat Cowboy). ¶TV: *The Lone Ranger*—"Special Edition" 9-25-52.

Ruth, Phyllis. Films: "Wild Horse Range" 1940 (Ann Morgan).

Rutherford, Ann (1924-). Films: "Melody Trail" 1935 (Millicent Thomas); "The Singing Vagabond" 1935 (Lettie Morgan/Mary Varden); "Comin' Round the Mountain" 1936 (Dolores Moreno); "The Lawless Nineties" 1936 (Janet Carter); "The Lonely Trail" 1936 (Virginia); "The Oregon Trail" 1936 (Anne Ridgley); "Public Cowboy No. 1" 1937 (Helen Morgan); "Out West with the Hardys" 1938 (Polly Benedict); "Wyoming" 1940 (Lucy Kincaid); "Badlands of Dakota" 1941 (Anne Grayson). ¶TV: *Tales of Wells Fargo*—"The Branding Iron" 2-23-59 (Etta); *U.S. Marshal*—"A Matter of Friendship" 3-14-59 (Mildred Whitley).

Rutherford, Gene. Films: "Will Penny" 1968 (Rufus Quint). ¶TV: *Gunsmoke*—"The Wreckers" 9-11-67 (Jud); *Bonanza*—"Sense of Duty" 9-24-67 (Sergeant Ankers); *The High Chaparral*—"A Quiet Day in Tucson" 10-1-67 (Bart Kellog), "The Champion of the Western World" 2-4-68 (Bart Kellog), "For What We Are About to Receive" 11-29-68 (Bart Kellog); *The Big Valley*—"A Stranger Everywhere" 12-9-68 (Lafe); *Here Come the Brides*—"The She-Bear" 1-30-70.

Rutherford, Jack (1893-8/21/82). Films: "Cowboy Counsellor" 1933 (Bill Clary); "Justice of the Range" 1935 (Lafe Brennan); "The Oregon Trail" 1936 (Benton); "Three on the Trail" 1936 (Lewis); "Hopalong Rides Again" 1937 (Blackie); "Heart of the West" 1937 (Tom Pa-

terson); "North of the Rio Grande" 1937 (Crowder); "Raw Timber" 1937 (Lane); "Rootin' Tootin' Rhythm" 1937; "Flaming Frontier" 1938-serial (Buffalo Bill); "Gold Is Where You Find It" 1938; "Riders of the Frontier" 1939 (Bart Lane); "Arizona Gangbusters" 1940 (Thorpe); "Riders on Black Mountain" 1940 (Biff); "Trailing Double Trouble" 1940 (Amos Hardy); "Rollin' Home to Texas" 1941; "Frontier Gal" 1945 (Man at Table); "Utah" 1945 (Sheriff MacBride). ¶TV: *Sergeant Preston of the Yukon*—"Last Mail from Last Chance" 5-31-56 (Meacham), "Treasure of Fifteen Mile Creek" 8-2-56 (John Dallas).

Rutherford, Kelly. TV: *Adventures of Brisco County, Jr.*—Pilot 8-27-93 (Dixie Cousins), "The Orb Scholar" 9-3-93 (Dixie Cousins), "Brisco in Jalisco" 9-17-93 (Dixie Cousins), "Riverboat" 10-1-93 (Dixie Cousins), "Deep in the Heart of Dixie" 11-5-93 (Dixie Cousins), "AKA Kansas" 12-17-93 (Dixie Cousins), "Wild Card" 4-8-94 (Dixie Cousins), "And Baby Makes Three" 4-22-94 (Dixie Cousins).

Ruud, Michael. Films: "Guardian of the Wilderness" 1976; "Donner Pass: The Road to Survival" TVM-1978; "Down the Long Hill" TVM-1987; "Geronimo: An American Legend" 1993 (Chaplain).

Ruysdael, Basil (1888-10/10/60). Films: "Colorado Territory" 1949 (Dave Rickard); "Broken Arrow" 1950 (Gen. Howard); "High Lonesome" 1950 (Horse Davis); "Raton Pass" 1951 (Pierre); "Davy Crockett, King of the Wild Frontier" 1955 (Andrew Jackson); "The Violent Men" 1955 (Tex Hinkleman); "Jubal" 1956 (Shem Hoktor); "The Horse Soldiers" 1959 (Boys School Commandant). ¶TV: *Walt Disney Presents*—"Davy Crockett"—Regular 1954-55 (General Andrew Jackson); *Black Saddle*—"Client: McQueen" 1-24-59 (Sen. McQueen).

Ryal, Richard (1935-). TV: *Nichols*—"The Paper Badge" 10-14-71; *Bonanza*—"A Place to Hide" 3-19-72 (Boardman).

Ryan, Chester "Chet" (1889-1/20/43). Films: "A Corner in Water" 1916; "The Raiders" 1916; "Across the Border" 1922 (Jim); "The Cowboy King" 1922 (Lije Butters); "The Kingfisher's Roost" 1922 (Sheriff Breen); "Rounding Up the Law' 1922 (Bull Weyman); "King's Creek Law" 1923 (Kirk Jameson); "Border Women" 1924 (the Cocas Kid); "Cyclone Buddy" 1924 (Sheriff Brady);

"Headin' Through" 1924 (Yuma Kid); "Payable on Demand" 1924 (Alf); "Way of a Man" 1924-serial; "The Long Loop on the Pecos" 1927; "The Boss of Rustler's Roost" 1928 (Ranger); "Riding for Fame" 1928.

Ryan, Dick (1896-8/12/69). Films: "Once Upon a Horse" 1958 (Henry Dick Coryell); "Law of the Lawless" 1964. ¶TV: *Rawhide*—"Incident of the Widowed Dove" 1-30-59, "Incident of the Wager on Payday" 6-16-61; *Bat Masterson*—"Bat Trap" 10-13-60 (Burt Mason).

Ryan, Edmon (1905-8/4/84). Films: "Good Day for a Hanging" 1958 (William Selby). ¶TV: *The Outlaws*—"Assassin" 2-9-61 (Tate); *Cheyenne*—"Cross Purpose" 10-9-61 (Colonel Bedlow).

Ryan, Eileen. TV: *Bonanza*—"The Wooing of Abigail Jones" 3-4-62 (Abigail Jones), "First Love" 12-26-72 (Emily); *Tales of Wells Fargo*—"End of a Minor God" 4-7-62 (Lorry).

Ryan, Fran (1926-). Films: "Scandalous John" 1971 (Farm Woman); "The Apple Dumpling Gang" 1975 (Mrs. Stockley); "The Long Riders" 1980 (Mrs. Samuel); "Pale Rider" 1985 (Ma Blankenship); "Gunsmoke: Return to Dodge" TVM-1987 (Miss Hannah). ¶TV: *Daniel Boone*—"Love and Equity" 3-13-69 (Mrs. Jones); *Nichols*—"About Jesse James" 2-15-72 (Minnie); *Gunsmoke*—"The Wedding" 3-13-72 (Mrs. Keller), "The Wiving" 10-14-74 (Hannah), "Brides and Grooms" 2-10-75 (Hannah), "I Have Promises to Keep" 3-3-75 (Hannah), "The Busters" 3-10-75 (Hannah), "Manolo" 3-17-75 (Hannah); *The Quest*—"Seventy-Two Hours" 11-3-76 (Mag Wood); *Father Murphy*—"The Piano" 1-19-82 (Toby's Mother).

Ryan, Gertrude. Films: "The Rose of Nome" 1920 (Naomi Coles); "The Devil's Bowl" 1923 (Mary Walker); "Snowdrift" 1923 (Margot McFarlane).

Ryan, Irene (1902-4/26/73). Films: "Ricochet Romance" 1954 (Miss Clay). ¶TV: *The Restless Gun*—"The Battle of Tower Rock" 4-28-58 (Thelma Taylor); *Wagon Train*—"The Malachi Hobart Story" 1-24-62 (Martha Gresham).

Ryan, Joe (1887-12/23/44). Films: "The Pirates of the Plains" 1914; "An Angelic Attitude" 1916; "Along the Border" 1916; "A Close Call" 1916; "A Corner in Water" 1916; "The Cowpuncher's Peril" 1916; "Crooked Trails" 1916; "The End of the Rainbow" 1916 (Bill Hardy); "The Girl of Gold Gulch" 1916; "Going West to Make Good" 1916; "Legal Advice" 1916; "Making Good" 1916; "The Sheriff's Duty" 1916; "Shooting Up the Movies" 1916; "Taking a Chance" 1916; "Tom's Sacrifice" 1916; "Too Many Chefs" 1916; "Trilby's Love Disaster" 1916; "The Fighting Trail" 1917-serial; "The Girl Angle" 1917 (Three-Gun Smith); "The Tenderfoot" 1917 (Smiling Jack Douglas); "A Fight for Millions" 1918-serial; "Smashing Barriers" 1919-serial; "The Purple Riders" 1921-serial; "The Lone Fighter" 1923 (Macklyn Vance); "The Vanishing American" 1925 (Jay Lord).

Ryan, John P. (1938-). Films: "The Legend of Nigger Charley" 1972 (Houston); "The Missouri Breaks" 1976 (Si); "Houston: The Legend of Texas" TVM-1986 (David Burnett); "Blood River" TVM-1994 (Logan); "Tall Tales: The Unbelievable Adventures of Pecos Bill" 1995 (Grub). ¶TV: *Adventures of Brisco County, Jr.*—"Showdown" 10-29-93 (Sheriff Bob Cavendish).

Ryan, Kelly. *see* Connelly, Sheila.

Ryan, Mary E. (1880-10/2/48). Films: "Chief White Eagle" 1912; "His Western Way" 1912; "The Uprising" 1912; "An Adventure on the Mexican Border" 1913; "Hiawanda's Cross" 1913; "The Reformed Outlaw" 1913; "The Man from the West" 1914.

Ryan, Meg (1962-). TV: *Wildside*—Regular 1985 (Cally Oaks).

Ryan, Mitchell (1928-). Films: "Monte Walsh" 1970 (Shorty Austin); "The Hunting Party" 1971-Brit./Ital./Span. (Doc Harrison); "The Honkers" 1972 (Lowell); "High Plains Drifter" 1973 (Dave Drake); "Peter Lundy and the Medicine Hat Stallion" TVM-1977 (Jethro Lundy); "The Gambler, Part II—The Adventure Continues" TVM-1983 (Charlie McCourt). ¶TV: *The High Chaparral*—"Jelks" 1-23-70 (Jelks); *The Chisholms*—Regular 1980 (Cooper Hawkins); *Young Riders*—"Lessons Learned" 7-9-92 (Territorial Marshal Murphy).

Ryan, Robert (1909-7/11/73). Films: "Northwest Mounted Police" 1940 (Constable Dumont); "Texas Rangers Ride Again" 1940 (Eddie); "Trail Street" 1947 (Allen Harper); "Return of the Badmen" 1948 (Sundance Kid); "Best of the Badmen" 1951 (Jeff Clanton); "Horizons West" 1952 (Dan Hammond); "The Naked

Spur" 1953 (Ben Vandergroat); "Bad Day at Black Rock" 1955 (Reno Smith); "The Tall Men" 1955 (Nathan Stark); "The Proud Ones" 1956 (Marshal Cass Silver); "Day of the Outlaw" 1959 (Blaise Starrett); "The Canadians" 1961-Brit. (Inspector Gannon); "The Professionals" 1966 (Hans Ehrengard); "Custer of the West" 1967-U.S./Span. (Sergeant Mulligan); "Hour of the Gun" 1967 (Ike Clanton); "A Minute to Pray, a Second to Die" 1967-Ital. (Gov. Lem Carter); "The Wild Bunch" 1969 (Deke Thornton); "Lawman" 1971 (Marshal Cotton Ryan). ¶TV: *Zane Grey Theater*—"You Only Run Once" 10-5-56 (Matt), "The Hanging Tree" 2-22-57 (Matt), "Trial by Fear" 1-20-58 (Cob Oakley), "To Sit in Judgment" 11-13-58 (Sheriff Parney), "Interrogation" 10-1-59 (Captain Kraig); *Wagon Train*—"The Madame Sagittarius Story" 10-3-62, "The John Bernard Story" 11-2162 (John Bernard), "The Bob Stuart Story" 9-30-64 (Bob Stuart).

Ryan, Sheila (1921-11/4/75). Films: "The Gay Caballero" 1940 (Susan Wetherby); "Lone Star Ranger" 1942 (Barbara Longstreth); "Song of Texas" 1943 (Sue Bennett); "The Cowboy and the Indians" 1949 (Nan Palmer); "Mule Train" 1950 (Carol Bannister); "Western Pacific Agent" 1950; "Gold Raiders" 1951 (Laura Mason); "On Top of Old Smoky" 1953 (Lila Maryland); "Pack Train" 1953 (Lola Riker). ¶TV: *The Lone Ranger*—"Pete and Pedro" 10-27-49, "The Whimsical Bandit" 8-31-50; *The Gene Autry Show*—"Gold Dust Charlie" 7-30-50, "The Doodle Bug" 8-13-50, "The Poisoned Waterhole" 10-8-50, "The Black Rider" 10-22-50, "Narrow Escape" 8-11-53, "Border Justice" 8-18-53, "Rio Renegades" 9-29-53 (Corinne Sheldon), "Prize Winner" 7-27-54, "Outlaw Warning" 10-2-54.

Ryan, Tim (1899-10/22/56). Films: "Last of the Duanes" 1941 (Bartender); "Riding High" 1943 (Jones); "Rockin' in the Rockies" 1945 (Tom Trove); "Stampede" 1949 (Drunk); "Jiggs and Maggie Out West" 1950 (Dinty Moore); "Fargo" 1952; "The Marksman" 1953.

Ryan, Tommy. Films: "Prairie Moon" 1938 (William "Brains" Barton); "Son of Zorro" 1947-serial (Messenger).

Rydbeck, Whitney. Films: "The Gambler, Part II—The Adventure Continues" TVM-1983 (Teller).

¶TV: *The Cherokee Trail*—Pilot 11-28-81 (Bob).

Rydell, Mark (1934-). TV: *Wanted—Dead or Alive*—"Criss Cross" 11-16-60 (Tom Adams).

Ryder, Alfred (1919-). Films: "Invitation to a Gunfighter" 1964 (Doc Barker); "The Raiders" 1964 (Captain Benton); "True Grit" 1969 (Goudy). ¶TV: *Gunsmoke*—"Passive Resistance" 1-17-59 (Hank Boyles), "Death Watch" 1-8-66 (Flint); *The Outlaws*—"Shorty" 11-3-60 (Jack Duane); *Wagon Train*—"The Andrew Elliott Story" 2-10-64 (Major Ogden); *Wild Wild West*—"The Night of the Torture Chamber" 12-10-65 (Horatio Bolt), "The Night of the Deadly Bubble" 2-24-67 (Captain Horatio Philo); *The Virginian*—"Jacob Was a Plain Man" 10-12-66 (Ketch); *Laredo*—"The Seventh Day" 1-6-67 (Clay Morgan); *Lancer*—"Blue Skies for Willie Sharpe" 1-13-70 (Colonel Andrews); *Bonanza*—"Kingdom of Fear" 4-4-71 (Judge); *Hec Ramsey*—"Dead Heat" 2-3-74 (Frank Carmody).

Ryder, Eddie. TV: *The Rebel*—"Vicious Circle" 10-25-59 (Sergeant), "Helping Hand" 4-30-61; *Bonanza*—"The Infernal Machine" 4-11-62 (Daniel Pettibone), "The Conquistadors" 10-1-67 (Perkins), "Silence at Stillwater" 9-28-69 (Vern), "One Ace Too Many" 4-2-72 (Clerk); *Wide Country*—"Who Killed Edde Gannon?" 10-11-62 (Ted Weiss); *Death Valley Days*—"The Wooing of Perilous Pauline" 2-22-64; *Here Come the Brides*—"To the Victor" 2-27-70; *Gunsmoke*—"The Avenger" 11-27-72 (Undertaker).

Ryder, Louis "Buck" (1912-5/2/94). Films: "Winchester '73" 1950 (Stunts); "Gunfight at the O.K. Corral" 1957 (Stunts).

Ryno, William (1864-12/3/39). Films: "The Spoilers" 1914 (Struve); "The Cowboy and the Lady" 1915; "The Heart of Texas Ryan" 1917 (Antonio Moreno); "Bullet Proof" 1920 (Father Victor); "Twins of Suffering Creek" 1920; "Kazan" 1921 (Pierre Radisson); "Daring Danger" 1922 (Bill Stanton); "The Loaded Door" 1922 (Bud Grainger); "Hard Hittin' Hamilton" 1924 (Skinflint Bressler); "Double Action Daniels" 1925 (the Wop); "Tearin' Loose" 1925 (the Philosopher); "The Bonanza Buckaroo" 1926 (the Sheriff); "Fighting Luck" 1926; "Speedy Spurs" 1926 (City Father); "Vanishing Hoofs" 1926 (Col. Bowers); "The Boy Rider" 1927 (Jim Parker); "The Cowboy Cavalier" 1928; "A Horseman of the

Plains" 1928 (Michael O'Day); "Sagebrush Politics" 1930; "Fighting Cowboy" 1933 (Cash Norton, the Miner).

Ryter, Frederick. Films: "The Man from New Mexico" 1932 (Pancho); "Scarlet Brand" 1932 (Squint).

Sabato, Antonio (1943-). Films: "Hate for Hate" 1967-Ital. (Michael); "Beyond the Law" 1968-Ital.; "I Came, I Saw, I Shot" 1968-Ital./Span. (Moses); "Twice a Judas" 1968-Span./Ital.; "Miss Dynamite" 1972-Ital./Fr.; "Thunder Over El Paso" 1972-Ital./Span. (Minnesota).

Saber, David. Films: "Drango" 1957 (Tom Randolph). ¶TV: *The Gene Autry Show*—"Guns Below the Border" 11-5-55; *Broken Arrow*—"Doctor" 2-12-57 (Jed); *Gunsmoke*—"Bloody Hands" 2-16-57 (Tom); *Fury*—"My Horse Ajax" 3-9-57 (Rocky Gray).

Sackett, Janet. Films: "Mrs. Mike" 1949 (Madeleine Beauclaire).

Sackett, Judith. Films: "Mrs. Mike" 1949 (Barbette Beauclaire).

Sackville, Gordon (1880-8/2/26). Films: "Boots and Saddles" 1916; "The Girl Angle" 1917 (Dance Hall Proprietor); "Petticoats and Politics" 1918 (Keno Bill Maguire); "Whatever the Cost" 1918 (Black Jack Fanning); "The Arizona Catclaw" 1919 (Hank Ruggles); "The Girl Who Dared" 1920 (Judd Hampton); "The One Way Trail" 1920 (William Walker); "Cowboy Courage" 1925 (Tex Miller).

Sadler, Barry (1940-11/5/89). TV: *The High Chaparral*—"For What We Are About to Receive" 11-29-68 (Robbie McLeish).

Sadler, Dudley (1918-9/25/51). Films: "Lone Star" 1952 (Ashbel Smith).

Sadoff, Fred (1926-5/6/94). TV: *Kung Fu*—"Superstition" 4-5-73 (Ward Bannack).

Safren, Dennis. TV: *The Big Valley*—"Wagonload of Dreams" 1-2-67 (Alexandros); *The High Chaparral*—"Bad Day for a Thirst" 2-18-68 (Saddleblanket).

Sage, Willard (1922-3/17/74). Films: "The Brass Legend" 1956 (Tatum); "Dirty Little Billy" 1972 (Henry McCarty). ¶TV: *Maverick*—"Ghost Riders" 10-13-57 (Bert Nicholson), "Day of Reckoning" 2-2-58 (George Buckner); *Tales of the Texas Rangers*—"A Texas Million" 10-27-57; *Trackdown*—"End of an Outlaw" 11-29-57 (Dick Wade); *Colt .45*—"Last Chance" 12-6-57 (Morgan Brent); *Gunsmoke*—"Claustrophobia" 1-25-

58 (Dever), "Take Her, She's Cheap" 10-31-64 (Mel Billings), "The Storm" 9-25-65 (Cantwell), "Death Watch" 1-8-66 (Walker); *Have Gun Will Travel*—"Treasure Trail" 1-24-59 (Gale); *Tales of Wells Fargo*—"The Branding Iron" 2-23-59 (Bravender); *Yancy Derringer*—"The Gun That Murdered Lincoln" 3-19-59 (Senator Yardley); *Black Saddle*—"Change of Venue" 12-11-59; *Two Faces West*—"The Operation" 11-14-60 (Matt), "Day of Violence" 7-10-61; *Wyatt Earp*—"Casey and the Clowns" 2-21-61 (Bill Casey); *Empire*—"Hidden Asset" 3-26-63 (Sheriff Joe Clay), "Breakout" 4-16-63 (Sheriff Joe Clay); *Branded*—"That the Brave Endure" 4-25-65, "Judge Not" 9-12-65 (Texas Ranger), "A Destiny Which Made Us Brothers" 1-23-66 (Joe Darcy), "McCord's Way" 1-30-66 (Wes Trent); *The Legend of Jesse James*—"The Pursuers" 10-11-65 (Vince); *Bonanza*—"The Strange One" 11-14-65 (Wyn), "Black Friday" 1-22-67 (Sheriff), "Dark Enough to See the Stars" 3-12-67 (Denton), "The Marriage of Theodora Duffy" 1-9-73 (Marshal Taylor); *A Man Called Shenandoah*—"Special Talent for Killing" 12-6-65 (Eldon Bennett); *The Virginian*—"Harvest of Strangers" 2-16-66 (Charlie Davis), "The Fortress" 12-27-67 (Clete); *Daniel Boone*—"The Search" 3-3-66 (Marcel Proust); *Death Valley Days*—"Mrs. Romney and the Outlaws" 4-2-66, "The Fastest Nun in the West" 4-9-66 (Tom Shelby), "The Day All Marriages Were Cancelled" 12-3-66 (Father McCabe); *The Road West*—"The Lean Years" 10-3-66 (Sykes), "The Predators" 1-23-67 (John Devery); *Hondo*—"Hondo and the Superstition Massacre" 9-29-67 (Sgt. Able); *Iron Horse*—"The Prisoners" 12-30-67 (Colonel); *The Big Valley*—"Run of the Savage" 3-11-68 (Dr. Wiggins); *The High Chaparral*—"Ebenezer" 11-1-68 (Pogue), "Too Late the Epitaph" 11-6-70 (Marshal).

Sagebrush Serenaders, The (Enright Busse, John Scott, Frank Wilder). Films: "The Man from Rainbow Valley" 1946.

Sainpolis, John. *see* St. Polis, John.

Saint, Eva Marie (1924-). Films: "The Stalking Moon" 1969 (Sarah Carver); "The Macahans" TVM-1976 (Kate Macahan).

St. Angelo, Robert. Films: "White Fang" 1936 (Posse Member); "Northwest Passage" 1940 (Solomon); "Son of Paleface" 1952 (Lem);

"Chief Crazy Horse" 1955 (Sergeant); "The Last Frontier" 1955 (Sentry).

St. Clair, Michael (1928-). TV: *Daniel Boone*—"The Aaron Burr Story" 10-28-65 (Leams O'Leary); *Cowboy in Africa*—"A Man of Value" 2-26-68 (Harry Hackett).

St. Cyr, Lillian. *see* Red Wing.

St. Cyr, Vincent. Films: "Comanche Station" 1960 (Warrior); "Bounty Man" TVM-1972 (Santana); "Billy Two Hats" 1973-Brit. (Indian); "Against a Crooked Sky" 1975; "I Will Fight No More Forever" TVM-1975 (Looking Glass). ¶TV: *The Tall Man*—"The Black Robe" 5-5-62; *Empire*—"Long Past, Long Remembered" 10-23-62 (Estoban); *Laredo*—"The Dance of the Laughing Death" 9-23-66, "Oh Careless Love" 12-23-66; *The High Chaparral*—"Bad Day for a Thirst" 2-18-68 (Apache Leader).

Saint Duval, Malila. Films: "Savage Red—Outlaw White" 1974; "The Great Gundown" 1977 (Teresa). ¶TV: *Bonanza*—"Customs of the Country" 2-6-72 (Raquel).

St. Jacques, Raymond (1930-8/27/90). TV: *Rawhide*—Regular 1965-66 (Simon Blake); *The Virginian*—"Trail to Ashley Mountain" 11-2-66 (Allerton); *Daniel Boone*—"Onatha" 11-3-66 (Nimrod).

Saint James, Susan (1946-). Films: "Alias Smith and Jones" TVM-1971 (Miss Porter); "Scott Free" TVM-1976 (Holly).

St. John, Al "Fuzzy" (1892-1/21/63). Films: "Wild West Love" 1914; "Fatty and Minnie He-Haw" 1915; "Hello Cheyenne" 1928 (Zip Coon); "Painted Post" 1928 (Joe Nimble); "The Land of Missing Men" 1930 (Buckshot); "Oklahoma Cyclone" 1930 (Slim); "At the Ridge" 1931 (Timbers); "The Painted Desert" 1931 (Buck); "Son of the Plains" 1931 (Drunk); "Law of the North" 1932; "Riders of the Desert" 1932 (Slim); "Riders of Destiny" 1933 (Bert); "Law of the 45's" 1935 (Stony Martin); "Trigger Tom" 1935 (Stub Macey); "Wanderer of the Wasteland" 1935 (Tattooer); "Bar 20 Rides Again" 1936 (Cinco); "Hopalong Cassidy Returns" 1936 (Luke); "Pinto Rustlers" 1936 (Mack); "Trail Dust" 1936 (Al); "West of Nevada" 1936 (Walla Walla Wiggins); "The Fighting Deputy" 1937 (Fuzzy); "A Lawman Is Born" 1937 (Root); "Melody of the Plains" 1937 (Fuzzy); "Moonlight on the Range" 1937 (Fuzzy Q. Jones); "The Outcasts of Poker Flat" 1937 (Uncle Billy); "The Roaming

Cowboy" 1937 (Fuzzy); "Sing, Cowboy, Sing" 1937 (Biff); "Call of the Yukon" 1938 (Joe); "Gunsmoke Trail" 1938 (Tip); "Knight of the Plains" 1938 (Fuzzy); "Prairie Papas" 1938-short; "The Rangers' Roundup" 1938 (Fuzzy); "Songs and Bullets" 1938 (Fuzzy); "Frontier Scout" 1939 (Whiney); "Oklahoma Terror" 1939 (Fuzzy); "Trigger Pals" 1939 (Fuzzy); "Billy the Kid in Texas" 1940 (Fuzzy Q. Jones); "Billy the Kid Outlawed" 1940 (Fuzzy Q. Jones); "Billy the Kid's Gun Justice" 1940 (Fuzzy Q. Jones); "Murder on the Yukon" 1940 (Bill); "Texas Terrors" 1940 (Frosty); "The Apache Kid" 1941 (Dangle); "Billy the Kid in Santa Fe" 1941 (Fuzzy Q. Jones); "Billy the Kid Wanted" 1941 (Fuzzy Q. Jones); "Billy the Kid's Fighting Pals" 1941 (Fuzzy Q. Jones); "Billy the Kid's Range War" 1941; "Billy the Kid's Roundup" 1941 (Fuzzy Q. Jones); "The Lone Rider Ambushed" 1941 (Fuzzy); "The Lone Rider Crosses the Rio" 1941 (Fuzzy); "The Lone Rider Fights Back" 1941 (Fuzzy); "The Lone Rider in Frontier Fury" 1941 (Fuzzy); "The Lone Rider in Ghost Town" 1941 (Fuzzy); "The Lone Rider Rides On" 1941 (Fuzzy); "A Missouri Outlaw" 1941 (Willoughby); "Along the Sundown Trail" 1942; "Arizona Terrors" 1942 (Hardtack); "Billy the Kid Trapped" 1942 (Fuzzy Q. Jones); "Billy the Kid's Smoking Guns" 1942 (Fuzzy Q. Jones); "Border Roundup" 1942; "Jesse James, Jr." 1942 (Pop Sawyer); "Law and Order" 1942 (Fuzzy Q. Jones); "The Lone Rider and the Bandit" 1942 (Fuzzy); "The Lone Rider in Cheyenne" 1942 (Fuzzy); "The Mysterious Rider" 1942 (Fuzzy Q. Jones); "Outlaws of Boulder Pass" 1942; "Overland Stagecoach" 1942; "Prairie Pals" 1942 (Hank Stoner); "Sheriff of Sage Valley" 1942 (Fuzzy Q. Jones); "Stagecoach Express" 1942 (Dusty Jenkins); "Texas Justice" 1942 (Fuzzy Q. Jones); "Valley of the Sun" 1942 (Man on Street); "Cattle Stampede" 1943 (Fuzzy Q. Jones); "Fugitive of the Plains" 1943 (Fuzzy Q. Jones); "The Kid Rides Again" 1943 (Fuzzy Q. Jones); "Law of the Saddle" 1943 (Fuzzy Q. Jones); "Raiders of Red Gap" 1943 (Fuzzy Q. Jones); "The Renegade" 1943; "Western Cyclone" 1943 (Fuzzy Q. Jones); "Wild Horse Rustlers" 1943 (Fuzzy); "Wolves of the Range" 1943 (Fuzzy Q. Jones); "Blazing Frontier" 1944 (Fuzzy Q. Jones); "Death Rides the Plains" 1944 (Fuzzy Q. Jones); "Devil Riders" 1944 (Fuzzy Q. Jones); "The Drifter" 1944 (Fuzzy Q. Jones); "Frontier Outlaws"

1944 (Fuzzy Q. Jones); "Fuzzy Settles Down" 1944 (Fuzzy Q. Jones); "Oath of Vengeance" 1944 (Fuzzy Q. Jones); "Rustlers' Hideout" 1944 (Fuzzy James); "Thundering Gun Slingers" 1944 (Fuzzy Q. Jones); "Valley of Vengeance" 1944 (Fuzzy Q. Jones); "Wild Horse Phantom" 1944; "Border Badmen" 1945 (Fuzzy Q. Jones); "Fighting Bill Carson" 1945 (Fuzzy Q. Jones); "Gangster's Den" 1945 (Fuzzy Q. Jones); "His Brother's Ghost" 1945 (Fuzzy Q. Jones/Andy Jones); "Prairie Rustlers" 1945 (Fuzzy Q. Jones); "Shadows of Death" 1945; "Stagecoach Outlaws" 1945 (Fuzzy Q. Jones); "Gentlemen with Guns" 1946 (Fuzzy Q. Jones); "Ghost of Hidden Valley" 1946 (Fuzzy Q. Jones); "Lightning Raiders" 1946 (Fuzzy Q. Jones); "Outlaw of the Plains" 1946; "Overland Riders" 1946 (Fuzzy Q. Jones); "Prairie Badmen" 1946 (Fuzzy Q. Jones); "Terrors on Horseback" 1946 (Fuzzy); "Border Feud" 1947 (Fuzzy Q. Jones); "Cheyenne Takes Over" 1947 (Fuzzy Q. Jones); "The Fighting Vigilantes" 1947 (Fuzzy Q. Jones); "Ghost Town Renegades" 1947 (Fuzzy Q. Jones); "Law of the Lash" 1947 (Fuzzy Q. Jones); "Pioneer Justice" 1947 (Fuzzy); "Return of the Lash" 1947 (Fuzzy); "Stage to Mesa City" 1947 (Fuzzy Q. Jones); "Dead Man's Gold" 1948 (Fuzzy Q. Jones); "Frontier Revenge" 1948 (Fuzzy Q. Jones); "Mark of the Lash" 1948; "Outlaw Country" 1949 (Fuzzy Q. Jones); "Son of a Badman" 1949 (Fuzzy Q. Jones); "Son of Billy the Kid" 1949 (Fuzzy Q. Jones); "The Daltons' Women" 1950; "King of the Bullwhip" 1950 (Fuzzy Q. Jones); "The Thundering Trail" 1951 (Fuzzy Q. Jones); "The Vanishing Outpost" 1951 (Fuzzy Q. Jones); "The Black Lash" 1952 (Fuzzy Q. Jones); "The Frontier Phantom" 1952.

St. John, Betta (1930-). Films: "The Law vs. Billy the Kid" 1954 (Nita Maxwell);"The Naked Dawn" 1955 (Maria).

St. John, Howard (1905-3/13/74). TV: *Our American Heritage*—"Destiny West" 1-24-60 (Sen. Thomas Hart Benton); *Zane Grey Theater*—"The Release" 4-17-61 (Governor).

St. John, Jill (1940-). TV: *Bob Hope Chrysler Theatre*—"Have Girls—Will Travel" 10-16-64 (Faith); *The Big Valley*—"Barbary Red" 2-16-66 (Barbara Red).

St. John, Marco (1939-). TV: *Bonanza*—"Riot!" 10-3-72 (Plank); *Gunsmoke*—"The Gang" 12-11-72

(Virgil Bonner), "Disciple" 4-1-74 (Darcy).

St. Leo, Leonard (1894-2/9/77). Films: "Riding High" 1943 (Cameron Troupe Member); "Drifting Along" 1946 (Red); "The Haunted Mine" 1946.

Sainte-Marie, Buffy (1941-). Films: "Son of the Morning Star" TVM-1991 (Voice of Kate Bighead). ¶TV: *The Virginian*—"The Heritage" 10-30-68 (Nai'Be).

St. Maur, Adele (1888-4/20/59). Films: "The Pathfinder" 1952 (Matron).

St. Pierre, Monique. Films: "The Sacketts" TVM-1979.

St. Polis, John (John Sainpolis) (1873-10/8/46). Films: "Laughing Bill Hyde" 1918 (Black Jack Burg); "Captain Thunder" 1931 (Pedro Dominguez); "King of the Arena" 1933 (Governor); "Terror Trail" 1933 (Col. Charles Ormsby); "The Border Patrolman" 1936 (Manning); "Three on the Trail" 1936 (Sheriff Sam Corwin); "Borderland" 1937 (Doctor); "Rustler's Valley" 1937; "Phantom Ranger" 1938 (Pat Doyle); "Rocky Mountain Rangers" 1940 (Manners).

Sais, Marin (1890-12/31/71). Films: "How Texas Got Left" 1911; "Days of '49" 1912; "Death Valley Scotty's Mine" 1912; "The Tenderfoot's Troubles" 1912; "The Attack at Rocky Pass" 1913; "The Big Horn Massacre" 1913; "The California Oil Crooks" 1913; "The Invaders" 1913; "The Last Blockhouse" 1913; "On the Brink of Ruin" 1913; "The Skeleton in the Closet" 1913; "The Death Sign at High Noon" 1914; "Ham Among the Redskins" 1915; "The Man in Irons" 1915; "The Pitfall" 1915 (Margaret Laird); "Man from Tiajuana" 1917; "The Secret of Lost Valley" 1917; "The Broken Spur" 1921 (Ida Hunt); "Dead or Alive" 1921 (Mrs. Lamar); "The Sheriff of Hope Eternal" 1921 (Hela Merclae); "Riders of the Law" 1922; "Good Men and Bad" 1923 (Felicia); "Wolf Tracks" 1923 (Rose Blatherwick); "Behind Two Guns" 1924; "The Measure of a Man" 1924 (Clare); "The Red Rider" 1925 (Silver Waters); "A Roaring Adventure" 1925 (Katherine Dodd); "Wild Horse Stampede" 1926 (Grace Connor); "The Fighting Three" 1927 (Clara Jones); "Men of Daring" 1927 (Mother Owen); "Rough and Ready" 1927 (Martha Bowman); "A Son of the Desert" 1928 (Helen Dobson); "Fighting Cowboy" 1933 (Mary); "Rawhide Romance" 1934 (Mrs. Whitney); "Wheels of Destiny" 1934; "Circle of Death" 1935 (Mary Gordon); "Trailing Trouble" 1937 (Mrs. Burns); "Phantom Gold" 1938 (Mag); "Pioneer Trail" 1938 (Belle); "Santa Fe Stampede" 1938; "Riders of the Frontier" 1939 (Sarah); "Deadwood Dick" 1940-serial (Calamity Jane); "The Durango Kid" 1940 (Mrs. Evans); "Wild Horse Range" 1940 (Harriet Morgan); "Billy the Kid in Santa Fe" 1941 (Pat Walker); "Saddlemates" 1941 (Mrs. Langley); "Sierra Sue" 1941; "Two-Gun Sheriff" 1941 (Mrs. McKinnon); "Frontier Outlaws" 1944 (Ma Clark); "Oath of Vengeance" 1944; "Bells of Rosarita" 1945; "Border Badmen" 1945 (Mrs. Bentley); "King of the Forest Rangers" 1946-serial (Mrs. Barton); "Lightning Raiders" 1946 (Mrs. Murray); "Terrors on Horseback" 1946 (Mrs. Bartlett); "Ride, Ryder, Ride" 1949 (Duchess); "Roll, Thunder, Roll" 1949 (Duchess); "Cowboy and the Prizefighter" 1950; "The Fighting Redhead" 1950 (Duchess); "The Great Jesse James Raid" 1953. ¶TV: *The Lone Ranger*— "Double Jeopardy" 9-7-50.

Saito, William. TV: *Iron Horse*— "The Dynamite Driver" 9-19-66 (Burati); *Kung Fu*—"The Vanishing Image" 12-20-74 (Sai Si), "The Thief of Chendo" 3-29-75 (Murderer); *Paradise*—"Dangerous Cargo" 1-20-90 (Wei).

Sakall, S.Z. (1883-2/12/55). Films: "San Antonio" 1945 (Sacha Bazic); "Montana" 1950 (Poppa Schultz); "Sugarfoot" 1951 (Don Miguel).

Salazar, Abel (1917-10/21/95). Films: "Coyote" 1964-Span./Ital. (Coyote).

Sale, Charles "Chic" (1885-11/7/36). Films: "Men of America" 1933 (Smokey Joe Miller); "Rocky Mountain Mystery" 1935 (Tex Murdock).

Sale, Virginia (1899-8/23/92). Films: "The Dude Wrangler" 1930 (Dude Guest); "Smoke Lightning" 1933 (Minnie); "They Died with Their Boots On" 1941 (Nurse); "Blazing the Western Trail" 1945; "Badman's Territory" 1946 (Meg); "Trail Street" 1947 (Hannah). ¶TV: *Wild Wild West*—"The Night of the Human Trigger" 12-3-65 (Aunt Martha).

Salem, Kario. Films: "Testimony of Two Men" TVM-1977 (Francis Campion). ¶TV: *Centennial*—Regular 1978-79 (Marcel Pasquinel); *Bret Maverick*—"The Not So Magnificent Six" 3-2-82 (Virgil La Fleur).

Salerno, Enrico Maria (1926-). Films: "Death Walks in Laredo"

1966-Ital./Span. (Giulio Cesare Fuller); "Bandidos" 1967-Ital. (Richard Martin); "Death Sentence" 1967-Ital.; "Train for Durango" 1967-Ital./Span. (Brown).

Sales, Soupy (1926-). TV: *The Rebel*—"The Hope Chest" 12-25-60 (Myers).

Salinger, Matt. Films: "Davy Crockett: Rainbow in the Thunder" TVM-1988 (Andrew Jackson).

Salisbury, Monroe (1876-8/6/35). Films: "Rose of the Rancho" 1914 (Don Luis); "The Squaw Man" 1914 (Henry, Earl of Kerhill); "The Virginian" 1914 (Mr. Ogden); "The Lamb" 1915; "Ramona" 1916 (Alessandro Assis); "The Desire of the Moth" 1917 (Christopher Roy); "The Savage" 1917 (Julio Sandoval); "The Eagle" 1918 (John Gregory); "Hands Down" 1918 (Dago Sam); "Hungry Eyes" 1918 (Dale Revenal); "The Red, Red Heart" 1918 (Kut-Lee); "Winner Takes All" 1918 (Alan MacDonald); "The Sleeping Lion" 1919 (Tony); "The Sundown Trail" 1919 (Quiet Carter).

Salmi, Albert (1928-4/23/90). Films: "The Bravados" 1958 (Ed Taylor); "The Unforgiven" 1960 (Charlie Rawlins); "The Outrage" 1964 (Sheriff); "Hour of the Gun" 1967 (Octavius Roy); "Four Rode Out" 1969-Ital./Span./U.S.; "Deserter" 1970-U.S./Ital./Yugo. (Schmidt); "Lawman" 1971 (Harvey Stenbaugh); "Something Big" 1971 (Johnny Cobb); "Kung Fu" TVM-1972 (Raif); "Female Artillery" TVM-1973 (Frank Taggert); "The Legend of Earl Durand" 1974; "The Sweet Creek County War" 1979 (George W. Breakworth). ¶TV: *Hotel De Paree*—"Sundance and the Delayed Gun" 6-3-60 (Joe Noonan); *Bonanza*—"Silent Thunder" 12-10-60 (Albie), "The Thirteenth Man" 1-21-68 (Marcus Alley), "Search in Limbo" 2-20-72 (Sheriff), "Ambush at Rio Lobo" 10-24-72 (Stretch); *Rawhide*—"Incident of the Captive" 12-16-60 (Vince Lohman), "Incident of the Pale Rider" 3-15-63 (Drover); *Have Gun Will Travel*—"Vernon Good" 12-31-60 (Father Montalvo); *Wagon Train*— "Wagon to Fort Anderson" 6-7-61 (George Carder), "The Frank Carter Story" 5-23-62 (Frank Carter); *Tales of Wells Fargo*—"Jeremiah" 11-11-61 (Jeremiah Logart); *The Virginian*—"It Tolls for Thee" 11-21-62 (Quinn), "Brother Thaddeus" 10-30-63 (Brother Thaddeus), "A Little Learning..." 9-29-65 (Rafe Simmons), "The Death Wagon" 1-3-68 (Corporal C.T. Smoot); *Stoney Burke*—"The

Wanderer" 12-3-62 (Larry Dawson); *The Travels of Jaimie McPheeters*— "The Day of the First Suitor" 9-29-63 (Frank Turner); *Redigo*—"Man in a Blackout" 11-5-63 (Ward Bennet); *Destry*—"The Nicest Girl in Gomorrah" 3-13-64 (Ed Bender); *Daniel Boone*—Regular 1964-65 (Yadkin); *Laredo*—"Jinx" 12-2-65 (Cletus Grogan); *A Man Called Shenandoah*— "The Accused" 1-3-66 (Will Turner); *Gunsmoke*—"Death Watch" 1-8-66 (Holly), "Mistaken Identity" 3-18-67 (Ed Carstairs), "Sergeant Holly" 12-14-70 (Willis Jeeter); *The Big Valley*— "Under a Dark Sea" 2-9-66 (Keno Nash), "The Buffalo Man" 12-25-67 (Birch); *The Legend of Jesse James*— "The Lonely Place" 2-21-66 (Paul Mason); *The Monroes*—"Wild Dog of the Tetons" 10-5-66 (Hasner); *The Road West*—"Elizabeth's Odyssey" 5-1-67 (Hawes Leggett); *Custer*—"Dangerous Prey" 12-6-67 (Colonel Charrington); *Cimarron Strip*—"The Last Wolf" 12-14-67 (Sam Gallatin); *The High Chaparral*—"A Man to Match the Land" 3-12-71 (White Horse); *Kung Fu*—"Nine Lives" 2-15-73 (Shawn Mulhare), "Cry of the Night Beast" 10-19-74 (Reuben Branch); *Hec Ramsey*—"Scar Tissue" 3-10-74 (John Rhodes).

Salter, Hal (1886-5/9/28). Films: "Red Raiders" 1927 (Spike Dargan); "The Canyon of Adventure" 1928 (Jake Leach); "Code of the Scarlet" 1928 (Comic).

Salter, Thelma (1909-11/17/53). Films: "The Bad Buck of Santa Ynez" 1915; "The Disciple" 1915 (Alice Houston); "Satan McAllister's Heir" 1915; "Selfish Yates" 1918 (Betty Adams).

Sam the Sham (Domingo Samudo). Films: "The Fastest Guitar Alive" 1967 (1st Expressman).

Sambrell, Aldo (Sam Brell) (1937-). Films: "Gringo" 1963-Span./Ital.; "Magnificent Three" 1963-Span./Ital.; "Massacre at Fort Grant" 1963-Span.; "Two Gunmen" 1964-Span./Ital.; "For a Few Dollars More" 1965-Ital./Ger./Span. (Indio's Gang Member); "Gunfighters of Casa Grande" 1965-U.S./Span. (Rojo); "In a Colt's Shadow" 1965-Ital./Span.; "Dynamite Jim" 1966-Span./Ital.; "The Good, the Bad, and the Ugly" 1966-Ital.; "The Hellbenders" 1966-U.S./Ital./Span. (Pedro); "Navajo Joe" 1966-Ital./Span. (Marvin "Vee" Duncan); "A Place Called Glory" 1966-Span./Ger.; "Savage Gringo" 1966-Ital.; "Son of a Gunfighter" 1966-U.S./Span. (Morales); "The Texican" 1966-U.S./Span. (Gil);

"Duel in the Eclipse" 1967-Span.; "Face to Face" 1967-Ital.; "A Minute to Pray, a Second to Die" 1967-Ital. (Jesus Maria); "Train for Durango" 1967-Ital./Span.; "Awkward Hands" 1968-Span./Ital. (El Pantera); "Dollars for a Fast Gun" 1968-Ital./Span.; "Fifteen Scaffolds for the Killer" 1968-Ital./Span.; "100 Rifles" 1969 (Sgt. Paletes); "Arizona" 1970-Ital./Span. (Keene); "Bad Man's River" 1971-Span./Ital./Fr. (Canales); "Kill Django ... Kill First" 1971-Ital.; "A Town Called Hell" 1971-Span./Brit. (Colebra); "Charley One-Eye" 1973-Brit. (Mexican Driver); "The Man Called Noon" 1973-Brit./Span./Ital. (Kissling); "Silver Saddle" 1978-Ital. (Garincha); "Tex and the Lord of the Deep" 1985-Ital.

Samms, Emma (1961-). Films: "More Wild Wild West" TVM-1980 (Merriwell Meriweather).

Sampson, Robert (1932-). Films: "The Broken Land" 1962. ¶TV: *Wyatt Earp*—"He's My Brother" 11-29-60 (Cully Dray); *Rawhide*—"Incident Before Black Pass" 5-19-61; *Frontier Circus*—"The Patriarch of Purgatory" 11-30-61 (Mark Hedges); *Tales of Wells Fargo*—"Incident at Crossbow" 2-3-62 (Arthur King); *Bonanza*—"The Gamble" 4-1-62 (Artie), "The Deserter" 10-21-62 (Bill Winters); *The Virginian*—"Woman from White Ting" 9-26-62 (Jesse); *Gunsmoke*—"Cattle Barons" 9-18-67 (McKenny); *The Big Valley*—"Joshua Watson" 1-20-69 (Zack Morton).

Sampson, Teddy (1898-11/24/70). Films: "The Boundary Line" 1915; "The Outlaw's Revenge" 1916 (the Outlaw's Younger Sister); "Fighting for Gold" 1919 (Moya); "The Bad Man" 1923 (Angela Hardy).

Sampson, Will 1935-6/3/87). Films: "Buffalo Bill and the Indians, or Sitting Bull's History Lesson" 1976 (William Halsey); "The Outlaw Josey Wales" 1976 (Ten Bears); "The White Buffalo" 1977 (Crazy Horse/Worm); "Standing Tall" TVM-1978 (Lonny Moon); "The Mystic Warrior" TVM-1984 (Wambli). ¶TV: *Born to the Wind* 1982 (Painter Bear).

Sanchez, Jaime (1938-). Films: "The Wild Bunch" 1969 (Angel). ¶TV: *Bonanza*—"El Jefe" 11-15-70 (Cardenas).

Sanchez, Pedro (Ignazio Spalla) (1924-). Films: "Blood for a Silver Dollar" 1965-Ital./Fr.; "Go with God, Gringo" 1966-Ital./Span.; "Johnny Hamlet" 1966-Ital. (Gil); "Thompson 1880" 1966-Ital./Ger.; "Two Sons of Ringo" 1966-Ital.; "Cjamango" 1967-Ital.; "Death at

Owell Rock" 1967-Ital.; "Pecos Cleans Up" 1967-Ital.; "Son of Django" 1967-Ital.; "Any Gun Can Play" 1968-Ital./Span. (Paiondo); "Death Knows No Time" 1968-Span./Ital.; "May God Forgive You ... But I Won't" 1968-Ital.; "Vengeance" 1968-Ital./Ger.; "Don't Wait, Django ... Shoot!" 1969-Ital.; "Nephews of Zorro" 1969-Ital. (Martinez); "Quintana: Dead or Alive" 1969-Ital./Span.; "Sabata" 1969-Ital. (Carrincha); "Adios, Sabata" 1970-Ital./Span. (Escudo); "The Bounty Hunters" 1970-Ital.; "Reverend Colt" 1970-Ital./Span. (Meticcio); "My Horse, My Gun, Your Widow" 1972-Ital./Span.; "Return of Sabata" 1972-Ital./Fr./Ger. (Bronco); "Seven Nuns in Kansas City" 1973-Ital. (Fatty); "Carambola" 1974-Ital.; "Three Supermen of the West" 1974-Ital./Span.; "Trinity Plus the Clown and a Guitar" 1975-Ital./Austria/Fr.

Sanchez, Ref. TV: *Maverick*—"A State of Siege" 1-1-61 (Yaquito); *Wild Wild West*—"The Night of the Jack O'Diamonds" 10-6-67 (Antonio); *Bonanza*—"The Stronghold" 5-26-68 (Pedro); *Lancer*—"The High Riders" 9-24-68; *The High Chaparral*—"The Promised Land" 10-25-68 (Emilio).

Sancho, Fernando (1916-7/31/90). Films: "Gunfight at High Noon" 1963-Span./Ital.; "Magnificent Three" 1963-Span./Ital.; "Shoot to Kill" 1963-Span.; "Gunmen of the Rio Grande" 1964-Fr./Ital./Span. (Pancho Bogan); "Minnesota Clay" 1964-Ital./Fr./Span. (Ortiz); "Seven Guns from Texas" 1964-Span./Ital.; "Sign of Coyote" 1964-Ital./Span.; "Arizona Colt" 1965-Ital./Fr./Span. (Gordon Watch); "Five Thousand Dollars on One Ace" 1965-Span./Ital. (Carrancio); "Man from Canyon City" 1965-Span./Ital. (Carrancio); "Seven Guns for the MacGregors" 1965-Ital./Span. (Miguel); "Two Gangsters in the Wild West" 1965-Ital./Span. (Rio); "Two Sergeants of General Custer" 1965-Ital./Span.; "The Big Gundown" 1966-Ital. (Capt. Segura); "Dynamite Jim" 1966-Span./Ital.; "He Who Shoots First" 1966-Ital. (Doc Gordon); "Man with the Golden Pistol" 1966-Span./Ital.; "One Hundred Thousand Dollars for Ringo" 1966-Ital./Span.; "The Return of Ringo" 1966-Ital./Span. (Esteban); "Seven Guns for Timothy" 1966-Span./Ital.; "Taste for Killing" 1966-Ital./Span.; "10,000 Dollars Blood Money" 1966-Ital.; "Duel in the Eclipse" 1967-Span.; "For One Hundred Thousand Dollars Per Killing" 1967-Ital.; "Hate for Hate" 1967-Ital.; "Killer Kid" 1967-

Ital.; "Man and a Colt" 1967-Span./Ital. (Ramon); "Rita of the West" 1967-Ital.; "All Out" 1968-Ital./Span.; "Blood Calls to Blood" 1968-Ital. (Rodriguez); "Ciccio Forgives, I Don't" 1968-Ital.; "Clint the Stranger" 1968-Ital./Span./Ger.; "Hour of Death" 1968-Span./Ital.; "If One Is Born a Swine ... Kill Him" 1968-Ital.; "Sartana" 1968-Ital./Ger.; "Seven Dollars on the Red" 1968-Ital./Span. (El Chacal); "Twenty Thousand Dollars for Seven" 1968-Ital.; "Wrath of God" 1968-Ital./Span.; "The Boldest Job in the West" 1969-Ital. (El Reyes); "A Pistol for Ringo" 1965-Ital./Span. (Sancho); "Dig Your Grave, Friend ... Sabata's Coming" 1970-Ital./Span./Fr. (Pompero); "And the Crows Will Dig Your Grave" 1971-Ital./Span.; "Return of Clint the Stranger" 1971-Ital./Span.; "Wanted Johnny Texas" 1971-Ital. (Colonel Stewart); "If One Is Born a Swine" 1972-Ital./Span. (Pepito); "Miss Dynamite" 1972-Ital./Fr.; "With Friends, Nothing Is Easy" 1971-Span./Ital. (Col. Jimenez); "Watch Out Gringo! Sabata Will Return" 1972-Ital./Span.; "Son of Zorro" 1973-Ital./Span.; "Three Supermen of the West" 1974-Ital./Span. (Cucho); "Too Much Gold for One Gringo" 1974-Ital./Span. (Rojas).

Sand, Paul (1935-). TV: *Dr. Quinn, Medicine Woman*—"Mike's Dream—A Christmas Tale" 12-18-93 (Harp).

Sande, Walter (1906-2/22/72). Films: "The Singing Sheriff" 1944 (Butch); "Along Came Jones" 1945 (Ira Waggoner); "The Daltons Ride Again" 1945 (Wilkins); "Canadian Pacific" 1949 (Mike Brannigan); "Rim of the Canyon" 1949 (Jake Fargo); "Tucson" 1949 (George Reeves); "Dakota Lil" 1950 (Butch); "The Kid from Texas" 1950 (Crowe); "Fort Worth" 1951 (Waller); "Rawhide" 1951 (Flowers); "Red Mountain" 1951 (Benjie); "Warpath" 1951 (Sgt. Parker); "The Duel at Silver Creek" 1952 (Pete Fargo); "The Great Sioux Uprising" 1953 (Joe Baird); "Powder River" 1953 (Harris); "Apache" 1954 (Lt. Col. Beck); "Overland Pacific" 1954 (Mr. Dennison); "Bad Day at Black Rock" 1955 (Sam); "Texas Lady" 1955 (Sturdy); "Wichita" 1955 (Wallace); "Canyon River" 1956 (Maddox); "Gun Brothers" 1956 (Yellowstone); "The Maverick Queen" 1956 (Sheriff Wilson); "Drango" 1957 (Dr. Blair); "The Iron Sheriff" 1957 (Ellison); "Last Train from Gun Hill" 1959 (Sheriff Bartlett); "Noose for a Gunman" 1960 (Tom Evans); "Oklahoma

Territory" 1960 (Rosslyn); "The Quick Gun" 1964 (Tom Morrison); "Death of a Gunfighter" 1969 (Paul Hammond). ¶TV: *The Lone Ranger*—"Enter the Lone Ranger" 9-15-49 (Sheriff Taylor), "The Lone Ranger Fights On" 9-22-49 (Sheriff Taylor), "The Lone Ranger's Triumph" 9-29-49 (Sheriff Taylor), "Pay Dirt" 3-23-50, "Sheriff of Gunstock" 7-27-50, "Mission Bells" 9-21-50, "The Hooded Men" 2-22-51, "The New Neighbor" 12-18-52; *My Friend Flicka*—"The Night Rider" 1-20-56; *Jim Bowie*—"The Birth of the Blade" 9-7-56 (Samuel Black); *Zane Grey Theater*—"The Unrelenting Sky" 10-26-56 (Beecher), "Time of Decision" 1-18-57 (Dan Slater), "Pressure Point" 12-4-58 (Ben Crowley), "Living Is a Lonesome Thing" 1-1-59 (Jeb Stone), "The Long Shadow" 1-19-61; *The Texan*—"The Troubled Town" 10-13-58 (Jake Talby); *Trackdown*—"Tenner Smith" 10-24-58 (Fred Creight); *Cimarron City*—"A Respectable Girl" 12-6-58 (Frank Shanley); *Black Saddle*—"Client: Tagger" 2-14-59 (Virgil Britt); *Wanted—Dead or Alive*—"Eager Man" 2-28-59, "Death, Divided by Three" 4-23-60 (Sheriff), "The Showdown" 10-26-60; *Tales of Wells Fargo*—"Young Jim Hardie" 9-7-59 (Tom Clark); *Laramie*—"The Pass" 12-29-59 (Sergeant Coffey), "The Passing of Kuba Smith" 1-3-61 (Weardon), "Shadows in the Dust" 1-16-62 (Sheriff), "Lost Allegiance" 10-30-62 (Walt Helford); *Maverick*—"The People's Friend" 2-7-60 (Sheriff Burke), "Substitute Gun" 4-2-61 (Sheriff Coleman); *The Rebel*—"The Crime" 2-7-60 (Cannon); *Riverboat*—"Hang the Men High" 3-21-60 (Tom Feller); *Overland Trail*—"Lawyer in Petticoats" 3-27-60 (Sam Morton); *The Alaskans*—"Odd Man Hangs" 4-17-60 (Tom Carter); *Johnny Ringo*—"The Derelict" 5-26-60 (Sy Bonnell); *Stagecoach West*—"By the Deep Six" 12-27-60 (Torrey); *Bronco*—"The Invaders" 1-23-61 (Marshal Steve Durrock); *Gunsmoke*—"Melinda Miles" 6-3-61 (Harry Miles), "The Lady" 3-27-65 (Charlie), "Stryker" 9-29-69 (Cal Hoskins), "A Matter of Honor" 11-17-69 (Cal Haines), "The Bullet" 11-29-71, 12-6-71 & 12-13-71 (Caldwell); *Frontier Circus*—"Winter Quarters" 11-23-61 (Jake); *Bonanza*—"Blessed Are They" 4-22-62, "The Decision" 12-16-62 (Sheriff), "The Dilemma" 9-19-65 (Hamilton), "Abner Willoughby's Return" 12-21-69 (Sheriff Brian); *Rawhide*—"Incident at Crooked Hat" 2-1-63 (Dos Crowley); *The Rifleman*—"The Guest" 3-11-63

(Ralph); *Temple Houston*—"Enough Rope" 12-19-63 (McGee), "The Town That Trespassed" 3-26-64 (Mayor); *Redigo*—"The Hunters" 12-31-63 (Curry); *Death Valley Days*—"The Race at Cherry Creek" 3-7-65; *A Man Called Shenandoah*—"The Reward" 11-29-65 (Sheriff Jack Beal); *The Rounders*—10-25-66 (Bert Larson); *Wild Wild West*—"The Night of the Tartar" 2-3-67 (Col. Crockett), "The Night of the Vicious Valentine" 2-10-67 (Col. Crockett), "The Night of the Bogus Bandits" 4-7-67 (Col. Crockett), "The Night of the Firebrand" 9-15-67 (Col. Crockett); *Rango*—"My Teepee Runneth Over" 3-10-67 (Sheriff); *The Big Valley*—"Top of the Stairs" 1-6-69 (Mike Newcomb).

Sanders, George (1906-4/25/72). Films: "Allegheny Uprising" 1939 (Captain Swanson). ¶TV: *Wild Bill Hickok*—"Behind Southern Lines" 6-26-51; *Daniel Boone*—"Crisis by Fire" 1-27-66 (Col. Roger Barr).

Sanders, Hugh (1911-1/9/66). Films: "Along the Great Divide" 1951 (Frank Newcombe); "Indian Uprising" 1951 (Ben Alsop); "Only the Valiant" 1951 (Capt. Eversham); "Sugarfoot" 1951 (Asa Goodhue); "The Fighter" 1952 (Roberts); "Last of the Comanches" 1952 (Denver Kinnaird); "Montana Territory" 1952 (Jason Waterman); "City of Badmen" 1953 (Sheriff Gifford); "Gun Belt" 1953 (Frazer); "Thunder Over the Plains" 1953 (Balfour); "Untamed Heiress" 1954 (Williams); "The Last Command" 1955 (Sam Houston); "Top Gun" 1955 (Marsh); "The Peacemaker" 1956 (Lathe Sawyer); "The Phantom Stagecoach" 1957 (Martin Maroon); "Warlock" 1959 (Sheriff Keller); "The Wild Westerners" 1962 (Chief Marshal Reuben Bernard); "Apache Rifles" 1964. ¶TV: *The Lone Ranger*—"The Godless Men" 1-29-53, "Sinner by Proxy" 3-5-53, "Outlaw's Trail" 10-21-54, "Rendezvous at Whipsaw" 11-11-54, "The Quiet Highwayman" 1-27-55, "The Sheriff's Wife" 8-18-55; *My Friend Flicka*—"One Man's Horse" 9-30-55; *Tales of Wells Fargo*—"Alder Gulch" 4-8-57 (Biedler); *Zane Grey Theater*—"A Man on the Run" 6-21-57 (Lee Bland); *Colt .45*—"Young Gun" 12-13-57 (Sheriff Powers), "The Man Who Loved Lincoln" 5-3-59 (Jameson); *Maverick*—"Rope of Cards" 1-19-58 (Blaine), "Holiday at Hollow Rock" 12-28-58 (Jed Snyder); *Broken Arrow*—"Blood Brothers" 5-13-58 (Gen. Edwards); *Wanted—Dead or Alive*— "Ransom

for a Nun" 10-18-58 (Sheriff), "Crossroad" 4-11-59 (Frank); *Northwest Passage*—"The Long Rifle" 11-23-58 (Albert Sharp); *Lawman*—"The Runaway" 2-1-59 (Army Commander); *Tombstone Territory*—"Payroll to Tombstone" 3-27-59 (Enoch Ward); *Yancy Derringer*—"Duel at the Oaks" 4-9-59 (Phillip Lorme); *Rawhide*—"Incident of the Judas Trap" 6-5-59 (Marshal McVie), "Incident of the Sharpshooter" 2-26-60, "Incident Near the Promised Land" 2-3-61 (Marshal Thorpe), "Incident of the Big Blowout" 2-10-61, "Incident of Decision" 12-28-62 (Mr. Calvin); *Bronco*—"Red Water North" 6-16-59 (Caleb White), "Montana Passage" 4-5-60 (Stratton); *The Rifleman*—"The Blowout" 10-13-59 (Ben Waller); *Hotel De Paree*—"The Man Who Believed in Law" 11-27-59 (Jenkins); *Bat Masterson*—"Pigeon and Hawk" 1-21-60 (Lee Baxter); *The Deputy*—"The Return of Simon Fry" 2-13-60 (Jake Carter); *The Texan*—"Showdown" 2-29-60; *The Alaskans*—"Behind the Moon" 3-6-60 (Douglas Pemberton); *Pony Express*—"The Last Mile" 4-6-60 (Tanner); *Bonanza*—"Death at Dawn" 4-30-60 (Dr. Brah), "Alias Joe Cartwright" 1-26-64 (Billings), "Return to Honor" 3-22-64 (Doctor), "The Ballerina" 1-24-65; *Riverboat*—"Trunk Full of Dreams" 10-31-60 (Beauregard); *Stagecoach West*—"The Saga of Jeremy Boone" 11-29-60 (Nathan Bright); *Klondike*—"Halliday's Club" 12-19-60 (Murdock); *Gunslinger*—"Road of the Dead" 3-30-61 (Marshal); *Whispering Smith*—"The Mortal Coil" 7-24-61 (Mayor Adams); *Gunsmoke*—"Old Dan" 1-27-62 (Thede); *Laramie*—"Justice in a Hurry" 3-20-62 (Ev Keleher), "Shadow of the Past" 10-16-62 (Carewe), "The Marshals" 4-30-63; *Wagon Train*—"The Levi Hale Story" 4-18-62 (Warden); *Stoney Burke*—"King of the Hill" 1-21-63 (Sager).

Sanders, Sandy. Films: "The Last Round-Up" 1947 (Jim); "Frontier Revenge" 1948 (Bart); "Loaded Pistols" 1948 (Rancher); "Outlaw Country" 1949 (Fighting Deputy); "Riders in the Sky" 1949; "Rim of the Canyon" 1949; "Son of a Badman" 1949 (Pete); "Sons of New Mexico" 1949 (Walt); "Beyond the Purple Hills" 1950 (Doghouse); "The Blazing Sun" 1950 (Carl Luber); "Cow Town" 1950 (Stormy Jones); "Desperadoes of the West" 1950-serial (Kern); "The Fighting Redhead" 1950 (Joe); "Indian Territory" 1950; "Mule Train" 1950 (Bud); "Don Daredevil Rides Again" 1951-serial

(Dirk); "Hills of Utah" 1951 (Rio); "Silver Canyon" 1951; "Texans Never Cry" 1951 (Bart Thomas); "Valley of Fire" 1951 (Banjo); "Barbed Wire" 1952 (Hendley); "The Frontier Phantom" 1952; "Night Stage to Galveston" 1952; "Smoky Canyon" 1952 (Spade); "Son of Geronimo" 1952-serial; "Wagon Team" 1952; "Masterson of Kansas" 1954 (Tyler); "The Legend of Tom Dooley" 1959 (Rand). ¶TV: *The Lone Ranger*—"Legion of Old Timers" 10-6-49, "Bad Medicine" 12-7-50; *The Gene Autry Show*—"Silver Arrow" 8-6-50, "The Kid Comes West" 12-8-51, "Heir to the Lazy L" 12-29-51, "Horse Sense" 1-11-52, "Rocky River Feud" 1-18-52, "Blazeaway" 2-22-52, "Ghost Mountain" 7-28-53, "The Old Prospector" 8-4-53, "Gypsy Woman" 8-25-53, "Dry Gulch at Devil's Elbow" 9-8-53; *The Roy Rogers Show*—"Badman's Brother" 2-10-52 (Knox), "Dead Men's Hills" 3-15-52, "Shoot to Kill" 4-27-52, "Haunted Mine of Paradise Valley" 5-18-52, "The Long Chance" 5-24-53, "The Outlaws of Paradise Valley" 11-8-53, "Phantom Rustlers" 4-25-54; *Wild Bill Hickok*—"The Avenging Gunman" 7-29-52, "The Outlaw's Portrait" 11-18-52; *The Cisco Kid*—"The Lowest Bidder" 4-4-53, "Sundown's Gun" 4-18-53, "Pancho's Niece" 9-5-53, "Dangerous Shoemaker" 5-15-54; *The Westerner*—Pilot 11-53; *The Restless Gun*—"The Gold Star" 5-19-58 (Charlie Craig); *Whispering Smith*—"Death at Even Money" 7-10-61 (Driver).

Sanders, Shepherd (1930-). Films: "The Capture of Grizzly Adams" TVM-1982 (Ranch Foreman). ¶TV: *Here Come the Brides*—"To the Victor" 2-27-70.

Sanders, Sherman. Films: "Ride 'Em, Cowboy" 1942 (Square Dance Caller); "Bowery Buckaroos" 1947 (Rufe). ¶TV: *Wyatt Earp*—"Wyatt Earp's Baby" 4-25-61 (Minister); *Sergeant Preston of the Yukon*—"All Is Not Gold" 5-10-56 (Windy Brown).

Sanderson, Kent. see Roosevelt, Buddy.

Sanderson, Lynn. Films: "Manhattan Cowboy" 1928; "The Arizona Kid" 1929 (Bud Jenkins); "Captain Cowboy" 1929; "Fighters of the Saddle" 1929 (Art Wayne).

Sanderson, William (1948-). Films: "Death Hunt" 1981 (Ned Warren); "Lonesome Dove" TVM-1989 (Lippy); "The Giant of Thunder Mountain" 1991; "Return to Lonesome Dove" TVM-1993 (Lippy); "Wagons East!" 1994 (Zeke). ¶TV: *Bret Maverick*—"Hallie" 2-9-82 (Ken-

neth Broomick); *Young Riders*—"The Debt" 7-16-92 (Emmet); *Ned Blessing: The Story of My Life and Times*—"The Smink Brothers" 9-1-93 (Alfred Smink).

Sandford, Tiny (1894-10/29/61). Films: "Fighting Caravans" 1931 (Man at Wagon Train); "Hard Hombre" 1931; "Spirit of the West" 1932 (Cook); "Rainbow Ranch" 1933 (Joe).

Sandor, Steve (1937-). Films: "Rough Night in Jericho" 1967 (Simms); "The Young Country" TVM-1970 (Parker); "One More Train to Rob" 1971 (Jim Gant). ¶TV: *Gunsmoke*—"Slocum" 10-21-68 (John Riker); *The Virginian*—"Nightmare" 1-21-70 (Billy); *The Men from Shiloh*—"Follow the Leader" 12-2-70 (Van); *Alias Smith and Jones*—"Shootout at Diablo Station" 12-2-71 (Bud); *Nakia*—"Roots of Anger" 11-30-74 (Chet Haywood).

Sandoval, Miguel. Films: "Timerider" 1983 (Emil); "Straight to Hell" 1987-Brit. (George); "El Diablo" CTVM-1990 (Zamudio); "The Cisco Kid" CTVM-1990 (Hidalgo).

Sandri, Gia. Films: "A Stranger in Town" 1966-U.S./Ital. (Maruka); "Thompson 1880" 1966-Ital./Ger.; "John the Bastard" 1967-Ital.; "Two Pistols and a Coward" 1967-Ital.; "Ciccio Forgives, I Don't" 1968-Ital.; "Wanted" 1968-Ital./Fr.

Sands, Anita. TV: *Maverick*—"The Witch of Hound Dog" 11-6-60 (Nancy Sutliff), "Family Pride" 1-8-61 (Rosanne Warren); *Bonanza*—"The Spitfire" 1-14-61 (Willow); *Cheyenne*—"The Return of Mr. Grimm" 2-13-61 (Grace Evans); *Laramie*—"Cactus Lady" 2-21-61 (Troy McCanles), "The High Country" 2-6-62 (Willow Duncan); *Wagon Train*—"The Charley Shutup Story" 3-7-62 (Marie Muskie).

Sands, Billy (1911-8/27/84). Films: "Evil Roy Slade" TVM-1972 (Billy).

Sands, Johnny. Films: "The Fabulous Texan" 1947 (Bud Clayton); "Massacre River" 1949 (Randy Reid); "Two Flags West" 1950 (Lt. Adams).

Sands, Tommy (1937-). TV: *Zane Grey Theater*—"The Promise" 11-8-57 (Jace); *Wagon Train*—"The Larry Hanify Story" 1-27-60 (Larry Hanify), "The Davey Baxter Story" 1-9-63 (Davey Baxter), "The Gus Morgan Story" 9-30-63 (Ethan Morgan), "The Bob Stuart Story" 9-30-64 (Keith Lance); *Laramie*—"Trapped" 5-14-63 (Tad Henderson); *Branded*—"That the Brave Endure"

4-25-65 (Richard Bain); *Bonanza*—"The Debt" 9-12-65 (Wiley Kane).

Sanford, Erskine (1885-7/7/69). Films: "Sierra" 1950 (Judge Prentiss).

Sanford, Garwin. TV: *Hawkeye*—Regular 1994- (Capt. Taylor Shields).

Sanford, Isabel (1917-). Films: "The Red, White and Black" 1970 (Isabel). ¶TV: *Daniel Boone*—"The Kidnaping" 1-22-70.

Sanford, Philip. Films: "The Sign Invisible" 1918 (Monihan); "Sandy Burke of the U-Bar-U" 1919 (Lafe Hinton).

Sanford, Ralph (1899-6/20/63). Films: "Dodge City" 1939 (Brawler); "Carolina Moon" 1940 (Foreman); "My Pal Trigger" 1946 (Auctioneer); "Sioux City Sue" 1946 (Big Gulliver); "Cow Town" 1950 (Martin Dalrymple); "Rogue River" 1950 (Max Bonner); "Fort Defiance" 1951 (Stage Coach Driver); "Santa Fe" 1951; "Rancho Notorious" 1952 (Politician); "Springfield Rifle" 1952 (Barfly); "Cattle Queen of Montana" 1954; "The Forty-Niners" 1954 (Bartender); "River of No Return" 1954 (Bartender); "Silver Lode" 1954 (Joe, the Bartender); "Shotgun" 1955 (Chris); "Blackjack Ketchum, Desperado" 1956 (Happy Harrow); "Friendly Persuasion" 1956 (Business Man); "Badlands of Montana" 1957 (Marshal Sloan); "The Oregon Trail" 1959 (Mr. Decker). ¶TV: *The Gene Autry Show*—"Gold Dust Charlie" 7-30-50, "The Golden Chariot" 10-29-55; *Wild Bill Hickok*—"Medicine Show" 12-25-51, "The Sheriff's Secret" 10-21-52; *The Lone Ranger*—"Best Laid Plans" 12-25-52; *The Roy Rogers Show*—"The Showdown" 5-22-55 (Bart Benton), "Ranch War" 10-23-55 (Harry Kent); *Wyatt Earp*—"Call Me Your Honor" 9-17-57, Regular 1958-59 (Mayor Jim "Dog" Kelley), "Ballad and Truth" 3-4-58 (Widdicomb); *Sergeant Preston of the Yukon*—"Ghost Mine" 11-14-57 (Lem Carslake); *The Californians*—"The Duel" 2-18-58 (Gehman); *The Restless Gun*—"The Nowhere Kid" 10-20-58 (Gallagher).

San Giacomo, Laura. Films: "Quigley Down Under" 1990 (Crazy Cora).

Sangiovanni, Vincente. Films: "Guns of the Magnificent Seven" 1969 (Manuel).

Sankey, Bessie. Films: "Broncho Billy's Promise" 1912; "At the Lariat's End" 1913; "Broncho Billy's Brother" 1913; "The Ranchman's Blunder" 1913.

Sanmartin, Conrado. Films: "In a Colt's Shadow" 1965-Ital./Span. (Jackson); "Long Days of Vengeance" 1967-Ital./Span. (Cobb); "If One Is Born a Swine" 1972-Ital./Span. (Ted Shore).

Sansberry, Hope (1896-12/14/90). Films: "Fancy Pants" 1950 (Millie).

Sanson, Yvonne (1926-). Films: "Day of Anger" 1967-Ital./Ger. (Vivien Skill).

Santley, Frederic (1888-5/14/53). Films: "Call of the Canyon" 1942; "California" 1946 (Delegate).

Santon, Penny (1916-). Films: "California" 1963 (Dona Ana Sofia Hicenta). ¶TV: *Jim Bowie*—"Counterfeit Dixie" 9-27-57 (Mlle. Benoit); *Zorro*—"The Missing Father" 2-26-59 (Chrysanthe), "Please Believe Me" 3-5-59 (Chrysanthe), "The Brooch" 3-12-59 (Chrysanthe); *Bonanza*—"El Toro Grande" 1-2-60, "Look to the Stars" 3-18-62 (Rosalie Michelson), "Big Shadow on the Land" 4-17-66 (Maria Rossi), "The Deed and the Dilemma" 3-26-67 (Maria Rossi), "The Sound of Drums" 11-17-68 (Maria); *Wyatt Earp*—"The Case of Senor Huerto" 2-9-60 (Senora Huerta); *Rawhide*—"Incident at Rio Salado" 9-29-61; *Temple Houston*—"The Dark Madonna" 12-26-63 (Senora Ortega); *The High Chaparral*—"A Joyful Noise" 3-24-68 (Sister Angelica).

Santoni, Espartaco. Films: "Raise Your Hands, Dead Man ... You're Under Arrest" 1971-Ital./Span.

Santoni, Reni (1939-). Films: "Guns of the Magnificent Seven" 1969 (Max); "Powderkeg" TVM-1971 (Ricardo Sandoval).

Santos, Bert (1937-). Films: "California Gold Rush" TVM-1981. ¶TV: *Lancer*—"Foley" 10-15-68; *Here Come the Brides*—"Wives for Wakando" 1-22-69 (Indian Sentry); *Alias Smith and Jones*—"The Strange Fate of Conrad Meyer Zulick" 12-2-72.

Santos, Joe (1931-). Films: "The Legend of Nigger Charley" 1972 (Reverend); "Zandy's Bride" 1974 (Frank Gallo). ¶TV: *Kung Fu*—"A Lamb to the Slaughter" 1-11-75 (Sanjero).

Santschi, Tom (1880-4/9/31). Films: "In the Bad Lands" 1909; "On the Border" 1909; "The Pine Ridge Feud" 1909; "The Stampede" 1909; "The Tenderfoot" 1909; "Across the Plains" 1910; "Davy Crockett" 1910; "Pride of the Range" 1910; "The Cowboy's Adopted Child" 1911; "The Curse of the Red Man" 1911; "Evangeline" 1911; "George Warrington's Escape" 1911; "How Algy Captured a Wild Man" 1911; "In Old California When the Gringos Came" 1911; "In the Days of Gold" 1911; "Kit Carson's Wooing" 1911; "Range Pals" 1911; "The Regeneration of the Apache Kid" 1911; "The Rival Stage Lines" 1911; "The Totem Mark" 1911; "Wheels of Justice" 1911; "The Bandit's Mask" 1912; "A Broken Spur" 1912; "A Crucial Test" 1912; "Darkfeather's Strategy" 1912; "The God of Gold" 1912; "The Last of Her Tribe" 1912; "Opitsah" 1912; "The Pity of It" 1912; "A Reconstructed Rebel" 1912; "Sergeant Byrne of the N.W.M.P." 1912; "The Shrinking Rawhide" 1912; "The Escape of Jim Dolan" 1913; "The Redemption of Railroad Jack" 1913; "Vengeance Is Mine" 1913; "A Wild Ride" 1913; "Etienne of the Glad Heart" 1914; "His Fight" 1914; "Me an' Bill" 1914; "The Spoilers" 1914 (Alex McNamara); "The Test" 1914; "How Callahan Cleaned Up Little Hell" 1915; "The Puny Soul of Peter Rand" 1915; "The Country That God Forgot" 1916 (Steve Brant); "The Regeneration of Jim Halsey" 1916; "Her Perilous Ride" 1917; "Code of the Yukon" 1918 (Dan Cregar); "The Hell Cat" 1918 (Jim Dyke); "Rose of the West" 1919 (Lt. Col. Bruce Knight); "Beyond the Trail" 1921; "The Death Trap" 1921; "The Desert Wolf" 1921; "The Impostor" 1921; "Larue of Phantom Valley" 1921; "Lorraine of the Timberlands" 1921; "The Sagebrush Musketeers" 1921; "The Secret of Butte Ridge" 1921; "The Sheriff of Mojave" 1921; "The Tempest" 1921; "At Large" 1922; "Come Clean" 1922; "Daring Dangers" 1922; "A Guilty Cause" 1922; "The Hour of Doom" 1922; "It Is the Law" 1922; "Seeing Red" 1922; "Two Kinds of Women" 1922 (Bud Lee); "Two Men" 1922; "Brass Commandments" 1923 (Campan); "The Plunderer" 1924 (Bill Presbey); "Beyond the Border" 1925 (Nick Perdue); "Frivolous Sal" 1925 (Steve McGregor); "The Desert's Toll" 1926 (Jasper); "Forlorn River" 1926 (Bill Hall); "Hands Across the Border" 1926 (Breen); "My Own Pal" 1926 (August Deering); "No Man's Gold" 1926 (Outlaw); "Three Bad Men" 1926 (Bill Stanley); "Jim the Conqueror" 1927 (Sam Black); "The Land Beyond the Law" 1927 (Bob Crew); "Land of the Lawless" 1927 (Kelter); "The Overland Stage" 1927 (Hank Lespard); "Tracked by the Police" 1927 (Sandy Sturgeon); "Crashing Through" 1928 (Bart Ramy); "Land of the Silver Fox" 1928 (Butch Nelson); "In Old Arizona" 1929 (Cowpuncher); "The Wagon Master" 1929 (Jake Lynch); "The Yellowback" 1929 (Jules Breton); "River's End" 1930; "The Utah Kid" 1930 (Butch); "The Phantom of the West" 1931-serial (Bud Landers); "White Renegade" 1931.

Sanz, Paco. Films: "Seven Guns from Texas" 1964-Span./Ital.; "Five Thousand Dollars on One Ace" 1965-Span./Ital.; "Hands of a Gunman" 1965-Ital./Span.; "Man from Canyon City" 1965-Span./Ital.; "A Pistol for Ringo" 1965-Ital./Span.; "God Forgives—I Don't" 1966-Ital./Span.; "Savage Gringo" 1966-Ital.; "Django Kill" 1967-Ital./Span.; "The Man Who Killed Billy the Kid" 1967-Span./Ital.; "A Minute to Pray, a Second to Die" 1967-Ital. (Barber); "Yankee" 1967-Ital./Span.; "Blood and Guns" 1968-Ital./Span.; "One Against One ... No Mercy" 1968-Span./Ital.; "Twenty Thousand Dollars for Seven" 1968-Ital.; "Sartana Kills Them All" 1970-Ital./Span.; "Fasthand" 1972-Ital./Span.; "In the Name of the Father, the Son and the Colt" 1972-Fr./Ital.; "Massacre at Fort Holman" 1972-Ital./Fr./Span./Ger.; "Fighting Fists of Shanghai Joe" 1973-Ital.

Sarandon, Susan (1946-). Films: "Lovin' Molly" 1974 (Sarah).

Sargent, Joe (1925-). TV: *Gunsmoke*—"Skid Row" 2-23-57 (Jack Stoner), "There Never Was a Horse" 5-16-59 (Drunk); *The Lone Ranger*—"Journey to San Carlos" 5-9-57; *Zane Grey Theater*—"This Man Must Die" 1-24-58 (Pete Hansen), "The Black Wagon" 12-1-60 (Sergeant).

Sargent, Lewis (1903-11/19/70). Films: "Ace High" 1918 (Jean Rivard, Age 15); "Six-Shooter Andy" 1918; "The Coming of the Law" 1919 (Jiggs); "Ridin' the Wind" 1925 (Dick Harkness); "The Man from New Mexico" 1932 (Bob Langton); "Crashing Broadway" 1933 (John Griswold).

Sargent, Richard (1933-7/8/94). TV: *Wichita Town*—"Afternoon in Town" 2-17-60 (Scott); *The Alaskans*—"The Seal Skin-Game" 2-21-60 (Joey); *Death Valley Days*—"Gamble with Death" 2-22-61 (Cliff Streeter); *Gunsmoke*—"Catawomper" 2-10-62 (Bud Bones); *Wagon Train*—"The Naomi Kaylor Story" 1-30-63 (Tom), "The Andrew Elliott Story" 2-10-64 (Andrew Elliott); *Daniel Boone*—"The Deserter" 1-20-66 (Reuben Stone), "When I Became a Man, I Put Away Childish Things" 2-9-67 (Andrew Cooper); *The Outcasts*—"Give Me Tomorrow" 4-21-69 (Reece).

Sargent, William. TV: *Cheyenne*—"The Greater Glory" 5-15-61 (Roy Wiley); *Stoney Burke*—"Forget Me More" 3-25-63 (Tom Lambert).

Saris, Marilyn. Films: "The Lawless Eighties" 1958. ¶TV: *The Cisco Kid*—"Man with the Reputation" 3-27-54; *Death Valley Days*—"Wildcat's First Piano" 12-5-55 (Deborah Lee); *Jim Bowie*—"The Secessionist" 11-9-56 (Madeline); *The Restless Gun*—"The Coward" 1-6-58 (Sarah Fetter).

Sarno, Hector V. (1880-12/16/53). Films: "The Chief's Blanket" 1912; "The Sheriff's Trap" 1915; "The Wanderer's Pledge" 1915; "The Plow Woman" 1917 (Buck Mathews); "Go West, Young Man" 1918 (Joe); "The Forfeit" 1919 (Sikem Bruce); "The Gray Wolf's Ghost" 1919 (Pereo); "Rio Grande" 1920 (Felipe Lopez); "The Conflict" 1921 (Buck Fallon); "The Rough Diamond" 1921 (Emeliano Gomez); "Arabia" (Ali Hasson) 1922; "Do and Dare" 1922 (Gen. Sanchez); "While Justice Waits" 1922 (Man); "The Girl of the Golden West" 1923 (Castro); "Stepping Fast" 1923 (Martinez); "Oklahoma Cyclone" 1930 (the Don); "Zorro Rides Again" 1937-serial (Lerda); "Mark of Zorro" 1940 (Peon at Inn); "Dakota" 1945 (Italian).

Sarracino, Ernest. Films: "Zorro's Fighting Legion" 1939-serial (Sebastian); "Adventures of Red Ryder" 1940-serial (Matt Grimes); "King of the Texas Rangers" 1941-serial (Cowan). ¶TV: *The Adventures of Rin Tin Tin*—"Rusty's Mystery" 3-9-56 (Captain Creed), "The White Wolf" 10-19-56 (Pierre), "Return of Rin Tin Tin" 10-26-56 (Pierre), "The Secret Weapon" 4-11-58 (Hamid Bey), "Running Horse" 10-24-58 (Chief Aguila); *Jim Bowie*—"A Horse for Old Hickory" 1-4-57 (Chighizola); *Rawhide*—"Incident of the Slavemaster" 11-11-60 (Francois), "Incident at Rio Doloroso" 5-10-63 (Vasquez); *Tales of Wells Fargo*—"The Border Renegade" 1-2-61 (Felipe Borras); *Gunslinger*—"The Zone" 3-2-61 (Armando Rojas); *Lawman*—"The Vintage" 1-21-62 (Lazaro Lazarino); *Bronco*—"The Last Letter" 3-5-62 (Solado); *A Man Called Shenandoah*—"The Imposter" 4-4-66 (Dr. Mendoza); *Gunsmoke*—"The Noonday Devil" 12-7-70 (Quito Vega).

Sarrazin, Michael (1940-). Films: "Gunfight in Abilene" 1967 (Cord Decker); "Journey to Shiloh" 1968 (Miller Nalls); "A Man Called Gannon" 1969 (Jess Washburn).

¶TV: *The Virginian*—"Blaze of Glory" 12-29-65 (Coates).

Satra, Sonja. Films: "Bonanza: Under Attack" TVM-1995 (Annie Stewart).

Sauers, Joseph. *see* Sawyer, Joseph.

Saum, Cliff (1882-3/5/43). Films: "Moonlight on the Prairie" 1935 (2nd Cowboy); "Trailin' West" 1936 (Jim); "Treachery Rides the Range" 1936; "The California Mail" 1937 (Jim); "The Cherokee Strip" 1937; "Guns of the Pecos" 1937 (Bartender); "Cowboy from Brooklyn" 1938 (Conductor); "Gold Is Where You Find It" 1938 (Medicine Man); "River's End" 1940 (Miner).

Saunders, Gloria (-6/4/80). Films: "Northwest Territory" 1951 (Ann DuMere). ¶TV: *Wild Bill Hickok*—"The Border City Election" 9-18-51; *The Cisco Kid*—"Face of Death" 2-16-52, "Lost City of the Incas" 3-29-52; *The Gene Autry Show*—"Santa Fe Raiders" 7-6-54; *Frontier*—"The Voyage of Captain Castle" 2-19-56 (Cristina); *Wyatt Earp*—"The Wicked Widow" 5-21-57 (Myra Malone); *Trackdown*—"The Town" 12-13-57 (Rose); *Frontier Doctor*—"Iron Trail Ambush" 12-13-58.

Saunders, J. Jay. Films: "The Return of Desperado" TVM-1988 (Ben).

Saunders, Jackie (1897-7/14/54). Films: "A Child of the West" 1916; "Drag Harlan" 1920 (Barbara Morgan).

Saunders, Lori (1941-). Films: "The Wackiest Wagon Train in the West" 1976 (Betsy). ¶TV: *Daniel Boone*—"Bringing Up Josh" 4-16-70; *Dusty's Trail*—Regular 1973 (Betsy).

Saunders, Mary Jayne. TV: *Wild Bill Hickok*—"Bold Raven Rodeo" 4-7-53; *Tales of Wells Fargo*—Regular 1961-62 (Mary Gee); *Wagon Train*—"The Mavis Grant Story" 10-24-62 (Sally Maitland); *Daniel Boone*—"The Quietists" 2-25-65 (Amantha Bothwell).

Saunders, Nancy. Films: "Law of the Canyon" 1947; "Prairie Raiders" 1947; "South of the Chisholm Trail" 1947; "West of Dodge City" 1947; "Six-Gun Law" 1948 (June Wallace); "Whirlwind Raiders" 1948 (Claire Ross); "Outlaw Country" 1949 (Jane Evans); "Arizona Territory" 1950 (Doris). ¶TV: *Jim Bowie*—"Rezin Bowie, Gambler" 3-22-57 (Rachel McCullers).

Savage, Ann (1921-). Films: "Klondike Kate" 1942 (Kathleen O'Day); "Saddles and Sagebrush"

1943; "The Last Horseman" 1944 (Judge Ware); "Renegade Girl" 1946; "Satan's Cradle" 1949 (Lil); "The Woman They Almost Lynched" 1953 (Glenda). ¶TV: *Death Valley Days*—"The Diamond Babe" 10-28-53.

Savage, Brad (1965-). Films: "The Apple Dumpling Gang" 1975 (Clovis Bradley).

Savage, John (1949-). Films: "Bad Company" 1972 (Loney); "Cattle Annie and Little Britches" 1981 (Bittercreek Newcomb).

Savage, Steve. Films: "Under the Tonto Rim" 1947 (Curly); "Gun Smugglers" 1948; "Roughshod" 1949 (Peters).

Saval, Dany (1940-). Films: "The Big and the Bad" 1971-Ital./Fr./Span.; "It Can be Done ... Amigo" 1971-Ital./Fr./Span. (Mary).

Savalas, Telly (1924-1/22/94). Films: "The Scalphunters" 1968 (Jim Howes); "Land Raiders" 1969-U.S./Span. (Vince Carden); "MacKenna's Gold" 1969 (Sgt. Tibbs); "A Town Called Hell" 1971-Span./Brit. (Don Carlos); "Massacre at Fort Holman" 1972-Ital./Fr./Span./Ger. (Major Ward); "Bandera Bandits" 1973-Ital./Span./Ger. (Franciscus); "Pancho Villa" 1975-Span. (Pancho Villa). ¶TV: *The Dakotas*—"Reformation at Big Nose Butte" 4-1-63 (Jake Volet); *Empire*—"Arrow in the Sky" 4-9-63 (Tibor); *Bonanza*—"To Own the World" 4-18-65 (Charles Hackett); *The Virginian*—"Men with Guns" 1-12-66 (Colonel Bliss); *Cimarron Strip*—"The Battleground" 9-28-67 (Beau).

Saville, Gus (1857-3/25/34). Films: "Sunset Sprague" 1920; "Two Moons" 1920 (Old Man Ring); "The Wolverine" 1921 (Jase Meilke); "Fighting Courage" 1925 (Luke Collins); "Idaho" 1925-serial; "Wild West" 1925-serial; "The High Hand" 1926 (Swamper); "The Light of the Western Stars" 1930 (Pop Skelly).

Saville, Ruth (1892-3/31/85). Films: "The Escape of Broncho Billy" 1915; "Too Much Turkey" 1915; "The Book Agent's Romance" 1916.

Sawaya, George. Films: "Convict Stage" 1965; "Fort Courageous" 1965. ¶TV: *Broken Arrow*—"Iron Maiden" 3-25-58 (Shacknasty), "Old Enemy" 5-6-58 (Shacknasty); *The Restless Gun*—"A Trial for Jenny May" 5-25-59 (Adam Gray); *Bonanza*—"The Hanging Posse" 11-28-59; *Bat Masterson*—"The Prescott Campaign" 2-2-61 (Harry Sutton); *The Rebel*—"The Found" 6-4-61 (Grooder); *The Virginian*—"We've Lost a Train" 4-21-

65; *Branded*—"A Destiny Which Made Us Brothers" 1-23-66.

Sawyer, Connie (1918-). Films: "The Way West" 1967 (Mrs. McBee); "Evil Roy Slade" TVM-1972 (Aggie Potter). ¶TV: *Bonanza*—"The Clarion" 2-9-69 (Mrs. Lewis); *Big Hawaii*—"Graduation Eve" 10-26-77.

Sawyer, Joseph (Joseph Sauers) (1901-4/21/82). Films: "The Prescott Kid" 1934 (Captain Willoughby); "The Westerner" 1934 (Bob Lockhart); "The Arizonian" 1935 (Pompey); "Moonlight on the Prairie" 1935 (Luke Thomas); The Revenge Rider" 1935; "The Last Outlaw" 1936; "Heart of the North" 1938 (Red Crocker); "Frontier Marshal" 1939 (Curly Bill); "Union Pacific" 1939 (Shamus); "The Border Legion" 1940 (Jim Gulden); "The Dark Command" 1940 (Bushropp); "Lucky Cisco Kid" 1940 (Bill Stevens); "Man from Montreal" 1940 (Biff Anders); "Melody Ranch" 1940 (Jasper Wildhack); "Santa Fe Trail" 1940 (Kitzmiller); "Belle Starr" 1941 (John Cole); "Down Mexico Way" 1941 (Allen); "Lady from Cheyenne" 1941 (Noisy); "Last of the Duanes" 1941 (Bull Lossomer); "They Died with Their Boots On" 1941 (Sgt. Doolittle); "Sundown Jim" 1942 (Moffitt); "Buckskin Frontier" 1943 (Brannigan); "The Outlaw" 1943 (Charley); "Prairie Chickens" 1943; "Raiders of Ghost City" 1944-serial (Idaho Jones); "The Singing Sheriff" 1944 (Squint); "Coroner Creek" 1948 (Frank Yord); "The Untamed Breed" 1948 (Hoy Keegan); "Deputy Marshal" 1949 (Eli Cressett); "The Gay Amigo" 1949 (Sgt. McNulty); "Stagecoach Kid" 1949 (Thatcher); "Tucson" 1949 (Tod Bryant); "Curtain Call at Cactus Creek" 1950 (Jake); "Indian Uprising" 1951 (Sgt. Keough); "Riding Shotgun" 1954 (Tom Biggert); "Taza, Son of Cochise" 1954 (Sgt. Hamma); "North to Alaska" 1960 (Land Commissioner); "How the West Was Won" 1962 (Ship's Officer). ¶TV: *The Adventures of Rin Tin Tin*—Regular 1954-59 (Sergeant Biff O'Hara); *Stories of the Century*—"Wild Bunch of Wyoming" 8-5-55; *Frontier Doctor*—"The Outlaw Legion" 11-15-58; *Maverick*—"Trooper Maverick" 11-29-59 (Sergeant Schumacher); *Sugarfoot*—"Apollo with a Gun" 12-8-59 (Sam Brown).

Sawyer, Laura (1885-9/7/70). Films: "A Perilous Ride" 1911; "The Red Man's Burden" 1912; "The El Dorado Lode" 1913.

Sax, Arline. TV: *The Restless*

Gun—"A Bell for Santo Domingo" 12-22-58 (Sister Theresa); *Death Valley Days*—"Human Sacrifice" 5-31-60 (Julia); *The Rebel*—"The Hunted" 11-6-60 (Mrs. Keller); *Have Gun Will Travel*—"The Princess and the Gunfighter" 1-21-61 (Princess Serafina); *Gunslinger*—"The Diehards" 4-20-61 (Laurie).

Saxon, Aaron. Films: "Gunslinger" 1956 (Nate Signo); "The Oklahoma Woman" 1956; "The True Story of Jesse James" 1957 (Wiley); "Gun Fever" 1958 (Trench).

Saxon, Glenn. Films: "Go with God, Gringo" 1966-Ital./Span. (Gringo); "He Who Shoots First" 1966-Ital. (Django); "Magnificent Texan" 1967-Ital./Span. (Manny); "If One Is Born a Swine ... Kill Him" 1968-Ital. (Il Mulo); "Long Day of the Massacre" 1968-Ital.

Saxon, Hugh (1869-5/14/45). Films: "Sand!" 1920 (Pop Young); "Skyfire" 1920 (Father Malloy); "Fightin' Odds" 1925 (Judge Mayhew); "The Fighting Boob" 1926 (Jasper Steele); "Hair Trigger Baxter" 1926 (Silas Brant); "Bulldog Pluck" 1927 (Pa Haviland); "King of the Herd" 1927; "Gypsy of the North" 1928 (Davey).

Saxon, John (1935-). Films: "The Plunderers" 1960 (Rondo); "The Unforgiven" 1960 (Johnny Portugal); "Posse from Hell" 1961 (Seymour Kern); "The Appaloosa" 1966 (Chuy Medina); "Winchester '73" TVM-1967 (Dakin McAdam); "I Came, I Saw, I Shot" 1968-Ital./Span. (Clay); "Death of a Gunfighter" 1969 (Lou Trinidad); "The Intruders" TVM-1970 (Billy Pye); "Joe Kidd" 1972 (Luis Chama); "The Electric Horseman" 1979 (Hunt Sears); "Jonathan of the Bears" 1994-Ital./Rus. (Fred Goodwin). ¶TV: *Gunsmoke*—"Dry Road to Nowhere" 4-3-65 (Dingo Tebbetts), "Judge Calvin Strom" 12-18-65 (Cal Strom, Jr.), "The Whispering Tree" 11-12-66 (Virgil Stanley), "The Pillagers" 11-6-67 (Manez), "The Squaw" 1-6-75 (Gristy Calhoun); *Bonanza*—"Black Friday" 1-22-67 (Friday), "The Conquistadors" 10-1-67 (Blas), "My Friend, My Enemy" 1-12-69 (Jacova); *The Virginian*—"The Modoc Kid" 2-1-67 (Dell Stetler), "Vision of Blindness" 10-9-68 (Ben Oakes); *Cimarron Strip*—"Journey to a Hanging" 9-7-67 (the Screamer); *The Men from Shiloh*—"The Regimental Line" 3-3-71 (Sergeant Mulcahy); *Kung Fu*—"King of the Mountain" 10-14-72 (Raven, the Bounty Hunter).

Sayer, Diane. Films: "Mail

Order Bride" 1964 (Lily). ¶TV: *Wide Country*—"A Cry from the Mountain" 1-17-63 (June Gladen); *The Dakotas*—"A Nice Girl from Goliah" 5-13-63 (Esther); *Here Come the Brides*—"Here Come the Brides" 9-25-68, "And Jason Makes Five" 10-9-68 (Sally), "Wives for Wakando" 1-22-69 (Sally).

Sayers, Jo Ann (1918-). Films: "The Light of Western Stars" 1940 (Madeline "Majesty" Hammond).

Sayers, Loretta. Films: "The Fighting Sheriff" 1931 (Mary Cameron); "The Deadline" 1932 (Helen Evans).

Sayles, Frances (1891-3/19/44). Films: "Texas Bad Man" 1932 (Andrews); "Home on the Range" 1935 (Hotel Clerk); "The Plainsman" 1936; "Trapped" 1937 (John); "Wells Fargo" 1937 (Townsman); "The Lone Ranger" 1938-serial (Carpetbagger); "The Purple Vigilantes" 1938 (Detective William Jones); "Dodge City" 1939; "Man of Conquest" 1939 (President James Van Buren); "Overland with Kit Carson" 1939-serial (Dr. Parker); "Riders of the Black River" 1939 (Doc Greene); "Union Pacific" 1939 (Conductor); "Riders of Pasco Basin" 1940 (Rancher); "The Son of Davy Crockett" 1941; "North of the Rockies" 1942.

Saylor, Syd (1895-12/21/62). Films: "The Mystery Rider" 1928-serial; "Red Romance" 1929; "Two-Gun Morgan" 1929; "The Border Legion" 1930 (Shrimp); "The Light of the Western Stars" 1930 (Square-Toe Boots); "Men Without Law" 1930 (Hank); "Caught" 1931 (Sergeant Weems); "Fighting Caravans" 1931 (Charlie); "Silent Men" 1933; "The Dude Ranger" 1934 (Nebraska Kemp); "Mystery Mountain" 1934-serial (Breezy); "When a Man Sees Red" 1934 (Ben); "Branded a Coward" 1935 (Oscar); "Call of the Wild" 1935; "Code of the Mounted" 1935 (Rogers); "Nevada" 1935 (Cash Burridge); "Wilderness Mail" 1935 (Mora); "Rhythm on the Range" 1936 (Gus); "The Three Mesquiteers" 1936 (Lullaby Joslin); "Arizona Days" 1937 (Grass Hopper); "Born to the West" 1937 (Dinkey Hooley); "Forlorn River" 1937 (Weary Pierce); "Guns in the Dark" 1937 (Oscar Roscoe); "Headin' for the Rio Grande" 1937 (Chile); "Roll Along, Cowboy" 1937; "Secret Valley" 1937 (Paddy); "Wild and Woolly" 1937 (Lutz); "The Kid from Texas" 1939 (Bud); "Let Freedom Ring" 1939 (1st Surveyor); "Stand Up and Fight" 1939 (Stooge); "Union Pacific" 1939 (Barker); "Arizona" 1940 (Timmins); "Geronimo" 1940 (Sergeant); "Lucky Cisco Kid" 1940 (Hotel Clerk); "Honky Tonk" 1941 (Pallbearer); "Last of the Duanes" 1941 (Man); "Nevada City" 1941; "Sierra Sue" 1941; "Sunset in Wyoming" 1941; "Wyoming Wildcat" 1941; "Buffalo Bill" 1944 (Barker); "Lucky Cowboy" 1944-short; "Bells of Rosarita" 1945; "The Navajo Kid" 1945 (Happy); "Ambush Trail" 1946 (Sam Hawkins); "Six Gun Man" 1946 (Syd McTavish); "Thunder Town" 1946 (Utah McGirk); "Unconquered" 1947 (Spieler for Dr. Diablo); "The Paleface" 1948 (Cowboy); "Big Jack" 1949 (Pokey); "Mule Train" 1950 (Skeeter); "Valley of Fire" 1951; "The Hawk of Wild River" 1952 (Yankem-out Kennedy); "The Old West" 1952; "Wagon Team" 1952; "The Redhead from Wyoming" 1953 (Drunken Settler); "The Tall Texan" 1953 (Carney); "Three Hours to Kill" 1954 (Townsman); "Shoot-Out at Medicine Bend" 1957; "Escort West" 1959 (Elwood). ¶TV: *The Lone Ranger*—"Jeb's Gold Mine" 10-16-52; *Wild Bill Hickok*—"Jingles on Jail Road" 7-14-53; *Buffalo Bill, Jr.*—"Trouble Thompson" 10-15-55; *The Adventures of Rin Tin Tin*—Regular 1956-58 (Clem Pritikin); *Wyatt Earp*—"Bat Masterson for Sheriff" 3-3-57 (Frog Face); *Sergeant Preston of the Yukon*—"Out of the Night" 11-28-57 (Zeke Gower); *Maverick*—"The Burning Sky" 2-23-58 (Depot Master), "Shady Deal at Sunny Acres" 11-23-58 (1st Townsman), "Prey of the Cat" 12-7-58 (James), "The Saga of Waco Williams" 2-15-59 (Menzies); *Fury*—"The Big Brothers" 12-26-59.

Sayre, C. Bigelow (1908-9/14/75). TV: *The Deputy*—"The Edge of Doubt" 3-4-61 (Will Jenner).

Sayre, Jeffrey (1901-9/25/74). Films: "The Oklahoma Kid" 1939 (Times Reporter).

Scala, Gia (1935-4/30/72). Films: "Ride a Crooked Trail" 1958 (Tessa Milotte).

Scannell, Frank. Films: "The Stranger Wore a Gun" 1953 (Red Glick); "A Lawless Street" 1955; "The First Traveling Saleslady" 1956 (Salesman); "Buchanan Rides Alone" 1958. ¶TV: *Wild Bill Hickok*—"Return of Chief Red Hawk" 2-10-53, "Kangaroo Kapers" 3-10-53, "Clem's Reformation" 7-7-53; *The Lone Ranger*—"The Wooden Rifle" 9-23-56; *Zane Grey Theater*—"The Necessary Breed" 2-15-57 (Stranger); *Wyatt Earp*—"Wyatt Meets Doc Holliday" 4-23-57 (Tim Riley), "County Seat War"

4-8-58 (Judge Franklin), "The Mysterious Cowhand" 10-14-58 (Cookie); *Sergeant Preston of the Yukon*—"Underground Ambush" 4-25-57 (Peters); *Wagon Train*—"The Rex Montana Story" 5-28-58 (Griff); *The Restless Gun*—"Bonner's Squaw" 11-3-58 (Shorty); *Bat Masterson*—"License to Cheat" 2-4-59 (Sandy), "Mr. Fourpaws" 2-18-60; *The Alaskans*—"The Ballad of Whitehorse" 6-12-60 (Auctioneer); *The Big Valley*—"Judgement in Heaven" 12-22-65 (Dr. Merar), "By Fires Unseen" 1-5-66 (Doctor).

Scardon, Paul (1874-1/17/54). Films: "The Fargo Kid" 1940 (Caleb Winters); "Man from Montreal" 1940; "The Son of Davy Crockett" 1941 (Zeke); "The Man from the Rio Grande" 1943 (Two-Way Hanlon).

Schaal, Richard (1928-). Films: "A Knife for the Ladies" 1973 (Ainelle).

Schable, Robert (1873-7/3/47). Films: "The Cowboy and the Lady" 1922 (Weston).

Schade, Betty. Films: "The Man from Bitter Roots" 1916; "Fighting Mad" 1917 (Faro Fanny); "The Wolf and His Mate" 1917 (Vida Burns); "All for Gold" 1918; "Nobody's Wife" 1918 (Dancing Pete); "The Scarlet Drop" 1918 (Betty Calvert); "Winner Takes All" 1918 (Nola Chadron); "A Woman's Fool" 1918 (Katie Lusk); "Bare Fists" 1919 (Conchita); "Riders of Vengeance" 1919; "Shod with Fire" 1920 (Nora Brewster).

Schaefer, Albert (1916-10/26/42). Films: "The Set-Up" 1926 (Tub Jones).

Schaefer, Anne (1870-5/3/57). Films: "Omens of the Desert" 1912; "The Angel of the Desert" 1913; "Mareea, the Half-Breed" 1914; "The Navajo Ring" 1914; "Unclaimed Goods" 1918 (Mrs. Ryal); "Six Feet Four" 1919 (Mrs. Riddell); "Ghost City" 1921; "The Wolverine" 1921 (Martha Meilke); "Heritage of the Desert" 1924; "Sitting Bull at the Spirit Lake Massacre" 1927 (Mame Mulcain); "The Arizona Wildcat" 1939.

Schaefer, Rube. Films: "Hurricane Horseman" 1931 (Cinco); "The Devil Horse" 1932-serial; "Swing the Western Way" 1947; "Seminole Uprising" 1955 (Wood). ¶TV: *Wild Bill Hickok*—"Money Shines" 6-2-53.

Schaeffer, Charles (1864-2/5/39). Films: "Gun-Hand Garrison" 1927; "Ridin' Luck" 1927; "Wild Born" 1927; "The Winged Horseman" 1929 (Col. Hobson).

Schafer, Natalie (1912-4/10/91). Films: "Callaway Went Thataway" 1951 (Martha Lorrison).

Schallert, William (1922-). Films: "Smoke Signal" 1955 (Pvt. Livingston); "Friendly Persuasion" 1956 (Young Husband); "Gunslinger" 1956 (Scott Hood); "Raw Edge" 1956 (Missionary); "Man in the Shadow" 1957 (Jim Shaney); "Day of the Outlaw" 1959 (Preston); "Lonely Are the Brave" 1962 (Harry); "Hour of the Gun" 1967 (Herman Spicer); "Will Penny" 1968 (Dr. Fraker); "Sam Whiskey" 1969 (Mint Superintendent Perkins); "Houston: The Legend of Texas" TVM-1986 (Narrator). ¶TV: *Death Valley Days*—"Reno" 10-10-55, "Hang 'Em High" 2-14-60 (Ellis Higby), "Cap'n Pegleg" 5-17-60, "The Breaking Point" 6-13-62 (Dave Meiser); *Screen Director's Playhouse*—"Arroyo" 10-26-55 (Lawyer); *Jim Bowie*—"The Captain's Chimp" 3-8-57 (Justinian Tebbs), "The Pearl and the Crown" 4-5-57 (Justinian Tebbs), "The Bounty Hunter" 5-17-57 (Justinian Tebbs), "The Close Shave" 1-10-58 (Justinian Tebbs), "Home Sweet Home" 1-31-58 (Justinian Tebbs); *Have Gun Will Travel*—"The Long Night" 11-16-57 (Firearms Salesman), "The Mark of Cain" 1-13-62 (Burchfield), "The Lady of the Fifth Moon" 3-30-63 (Chee Yan); *Gunsmoke*—"Twelfth Night" 12-28-57 (Eben Hakes), "The Gypsum Hills Feud" 12-27-58 (Alben Peavy), "Daddy Went Away" 5-11-63 (Jess Damon), "The Money Store" 12-30-68 (Ezra Thorpe), "Albert" 2-9-70 (Jake Spence), "Matt's Love Story" 9-24-73 (Cordelius); *Sugarfoot*—"Deadlock" 2-4-58 (Cole); *Zane Grey Theater*—"The Stranger" 2-28-58 (Yarbrough), "Checkmate" 4-30-59; *Jefferson Drum*—"A Matter of Murder" 7-11-58 (Polk Beauregard); *The Texan*—"The Troubled Town" 10-13-58 (Arnold Leno); *Rawhide*—"Incident with an Executioner" 1-23-59 (Salesman), "Incident of the Running Iron" 3-10-61 (Lieutenant Hill), "Incident of the White Eyes" 5-3-63 (Lieutenant Carter); *Wanted—Dead or Alive*—"Call Your Shot" 2-7-59, "Littlest Giant" 4-25-59 (Craig); *Maverick*—"The Strange Journey of Jenny Hill" 3-29-59 (Carl); *The Rifleman*—"The Mind Reader" 6-30-59, "Strange Town" 10-25-60 (Marshal Truce), "Short Rope for a Tall Man" 3-28-61 (Joe Lovering); *Johnny Ringo*—"The Accused" 10-15-59, "Killer, Choose a Card" 6-9-60 (Mr. Ferris); *Wichita Town*—"Man on the Hill" 11-4-59 (Al Watson); *Black Saddle*—"Blood Money" 12-18-59 (Mallet); *Bat Masterson*—"Deadly Diamonds" 2-11-60, "The Lady Plays Her Hand" 12-29-60 (George Winston); *Lawman*—"Reunion in Laramie" 3-13-60 (Reed Smith); *Wagon Train*—"The Amos Gibbon Story" 4-20-60, "Trial for Murder" 4-27-60 & 5-4-60; *Stagecoach West*—"A Time to Run" 11-15-60 (Aeneas Longbridge); *Gunslinger*—"Johnny Sergeant" 5-4-61 (Lieutenant Gilmore); *The Rebel*—"Mission—Varina" 5-14-61 (Ashbaugh); *Bonanza*—"Look to the Stars" 3-18-62 (Mr. Norton); *Tales of Wells Fargo*—"End of a Minor God" 4-7-62 (Paul Grieg); *Stoney Burke*—"Five by Eight" 12-10-62 (Warden Harper); *Empire*—"Breakout" 4-16-63 (Sully Mason); *The Virginian*—"Dead Eye Dick" 11-9-66 (Harry Roley); *Pistols 'n' Petticoats*—1-28-67 (Stanley Chowder); *Wild Wild West*—"Night of the Bubbling Death" 9-8-67 (Silas Grigsby), "The Night of the Gruesome Games" 10-25-68 (Rufus Draus), "The Night of the Winged Terror" 1-17-68 & 1-24-68 (Frank Harper); *The Guns of Will Sonnett*—"Look for the Hound Dog" 1-26-68 (Lawyer); *Here Come the Brides*—"Man of the Family" 10-16-68 (Rev. Mr. Gaddings), "A Far Cry from Yesterday" 9-26-69 (Sharue); *Kung Fu*—"A Praying Mantis Kills" 3-22-73 (Willis Roper).

Schanley, Tom. Films: "The Alamo: 13 Days to Glory" TVM-1987 (Danny); "Children of the Dust" TVM-1995 (Cavalary Officer).

Scharf, Sabrina. TV: *Daniel Boone*—"Requiem for Craw Green" 12-1-66 (Alkini); *Wild Wild West*—"The Night of the Underground Terror" 1-19-68 (China Hazzard); *Gunsmoke*—"The Devil's Outpost" 9-22-69 (Lora).

Schell, Maria (1926-). Films: "The Hanging Tree" 1959 (Elizabeth Mahler); "Cimarron" 1960 (Sabra Cravet); "Dust in the Sun" 1971-Fr.

Schellenberg, August. Films: "Death Hunt" 1981 (Deak); "Black Robe" 1991-Can./Australia (Chomina); "Geronimo" TVM-1993 (Cochise); "Iron Will" 1994 (Ned Dodd); "Tecumseh: The Last Warrior" TVM-1995. ¶TV: *Lonesome Dove*—"Last Stand" 11-20-94 (Chief).

Schiaffino, Rosanna (1939-). Films: "The Man Called Noon" 1973-Brit./Span./Ital. (Fan).

Schiavelli, Vincent (1947-). Films: "Butch and Sundance: The Early Days" 1979 (Guard). ¶TV: *Young Maverick*—"Half-Past Noon" 1-30-80 (Snake Speevey).

Schildkraut, Joseph (1895-1/21/64). Films: "Rangers of Fortune" 1940 (Lewis Rebstock); "The Parson of Panamint" 1941 (Bob Deming); "Flame of the Barbary Coast" 1945 (Tito Morell); "Plainsman and the Lady" 1946 (Peter Marquette); "Northwest Outpost" 1947 (Count Igor Savin); "The Gallant Legion" 1948 (Clarke Faulkner); "Old Los Angeles" 1948 (Luis Savarin).

Schiller, Norbert (1899-1/8/88). TV: *Gunsmoke*—"The Pest Hold" 4-14-56 (Berkleman); *The High Chaparral*—"Our Lady of Guadalupe" 12-20-68.

Schilling, Gus (1907-6/16/57). Films: "Mexican Spitfire Out West" 1940 (Desk Clerk); "Run for Cover" 1955 (Doc Ridgeway).

Schipa, Carlo (1900-8/26/88). Films: "The Fighting Hombre" 1927 (Tony Mendoza).

Schnabel, Stefan (1912-). Films: "Law of the Barbary Coast" 1949 (Alexis Boralof). ¶TV: *The Rifleman*—"Old Tony" 4-8-63 (Old Tony).

Schneider, Helmut (1920-). Films: "Chuck Moll" 1970-Ital.

Schneider, John (1954-). Films: "Stagecoach" TVM-1986 (Buck); "James A. Michener's Texas" TVM-1995 (Davy Crockett). ¶TV: *Paradise*—"A Gather of Guns" 9-10-89 (Pat Garrett); *Dr. Quinn, Medicine Woman*—"A Cowboy's Lullaby" 2-20-93 (Red McCall).

Schneider, Joseph. Films: "Man in the Shadow" 1957 (Juan Martin). ¶TV: *Gunsmoke*—"The Pillagers" 11-6-67 (Juan); *Alias Smith and Jones*—"The Man Who Broke the Bank at Red Gap" 1-20-72.

Schone, Reiner. Films: "Return of Sabata" 1972-Ital./Fr./Ger. (Clyde).

Schram, Violet. Films: "The Gray Wolf's Ghost" 1919 (Pequita); "Riders of the Dawn" 1920 (Olga); "Wolves of the Border" 1923; "The Bar C Mystery" 1926-serial (Wanda).

Schreck, Vicki. Films: "The Macahans" TVM-1976 (Jessie Macahan). ¶TV: *How the West Was Won*—Regular 1977-79 (Jessie Macahan).

Schreiber, Avery (1935-). Films: "More Wild Wild West" TVM-1980 (Alexyi, the Russian Ambassador); "Outlaws" TVM-1986.

Schroder, Rick (1970-). Films: "Lonesome Dove" TVM-1989 (Newt); "Call of the Wild" TVM-1993 (John Thornton); "Return to Lonesome Dove" TVM-1993 (Newt Dobbs); "Blood River" TVM-1994

(Perls); "James A. Michener's Texas" TVM-1995 (Otto MacNab).

Schrum, Walt (and the Colorado Hillbillies). Films: "The Old Barn Dancer" 1938; "Blue Montana Skies" 1939; "Rollin' Home to Texas" 1941; "Swing, Cowboy, Swing" 1944; "Trouble at Melody Mesa" 1944; "The Desert Horseman" 1946.

Schubert, Karin (1944-). Films: "Companeros" 1970-Ital./Span./Ger. (Zaira); "Three Musketeers of the West" 1972-Ital. (Dr. Alice).

Schuck, John (1941-). Films: "McCabe and Mrs. Miller" 1971 (Smalley); "Butch and Sundance: The Early Days" 1979 (Harvey Logan); "Four Eyes and Six-Guns" TVM-1992 (Charlie Winniger). ¶TV: *Gunsmoke*—"Coreyville" 10-6-69 (Amos Blake), "The Thieves" 3-9-70 (Burt Tilden); *Bonanza*—"A Single Pilgrim" 1-3-71 (Tom Brennan); *Young Riders*—"Jesse" 10-5-91 (Jarvis).

Schultz, Keith. TV: *The Monroes*—Regular 1966-67 (Jefferson "Big Twin" Monroe); *Gunsmoke*—"Baker's Dozen" 12-25-67 (Timothy).

Schultz, Kevin. TV: *The Monroes*—Regular 1966-67 (Fenimore "Little Twin" Monroe).

Schumacher, Phil (1911-1/19/75). Films: "Coroner Creek" 1948 (Bill Arnold); "The Deerslayer" 1957 (Stunts); "Duel at Diablo" 1966 (Burly Soldier). ¶TV: *Wyatt Earp*—"The Equalizer" 4-16-57 (Man).

Schumann-Heink, Ferdinand (1893-9/15/58). Films: "The Fighting Romeo" 1925 (James Warner); "My Pal, the King" 1932 (Gen. Wiedeman); "Treachery Rides the Range" 1936 (Cliff); "Guns of the Pecos" 1937 (Governor's Secretary).

Schunzel, Reinhold (1886-9/11/54). Films: "Plainsman and the Lady" 1946 (Michael Arnesen).

Schurer, Erna. Films: "Black Tigress" 1967-Ital.

Schuyler, Dorothy. Films: "The Black Whip" 1956 (Delilah); "Ride a Violent Mile" 1957 (Dance Hall Girl). ¶TV: *Gunsmoke*—"Magnus" 12-24-55 (Olive), "Tap Day for Kitty" 3-24-56 (Kate), "Alarm at Pleasant Valley" 8-25-56 (Alice Fraser), "The Photographer" 4-6-57 (Kate).

Schwarzenegger, Arnold (1947-). Films: "The Villain" 1979 (Handsome Stranger).

Schweig, Eric. Films: "The Last of the Mohicans" 1992 (Uncas).

Scipioni, Bruno. Films: "Heroes of the West" 1964-Span./Ital.; "Twins from Texas" 1964-Ital./Span.; "For One Thousand Dollars Per Day" 1966-Ital./Span.; "The Handsome, the Ugly, and the Stupid" 1967-Ital.; "Paths of War" 1969-Ital.

Scobee, Merle "Mark". Films: "Starlight Over Texas" 1938; "Down the Wyoming Trail" 1939.

Scobee, Ray. Films: "Starlight Over Texas" 1938; "Down the Wyoming Trail".

Scoggins, Jerry. Films: "Riders of the Whistling Pines" 1949 (Jerry); "Wagon Team" 1952 (Jerry Cass); "On Top of Old Smoky" 1953 (Jerry Cass).

Scollay, Fred J. (1923-). TV: *Our American Heritage*—"Destiny West" 1-24-60 (Linn); *Gunsmoke*—"The Reward" 11-6-65 (Clint Fisher), "The Favor" 3-11-67 (Morgan Haley); *Dundee and the Culhane*—"The Widow's Weeds Brief" 11-29-67 (Sheriff Bean).

Scott, Alan. Films: "Natchez Trace" 1960 (Sheriff Beesom); "Cavalry Charge" 1964-Span.; "Two Gunmen" 1964-Span./Ital. (Ranger Robert Logan).

Scott, Andrew. Films: "Two Gunmen" 1964-Span./Ital.; "In a Colt's Shadow" 1965-Ital./Span.; "Son of Django" 1967-Ital. (Clay); "Two Sides of the Dollar" 1967-Fr./Ital.

Scott, Brenda (1943-). Films: "Journey to Shiloh" 1968 (Gabrielle DuPrey). ¶TV: *Gunsmoke*—"Anybody Can Kill a Marshal" 3-9-63 (Betsy); *Wagon Train*—"The Tom O'Neal Story" 4-24-63 (Ellen Howard), "The Molly Kincaid Story" 9-16-63 (Martha Kincaid); *Temple Houston*—"Letter of the Law" 10-3-63 (Ruth); *The Virginian*—"Dark Destiny" 4-29-64 (Billie), "Men with Guns" 1-12-66 (Gina Larsen), "Jed" 1-10-68 (Abby Kiefer), "The Girl in the Shadows" 3-26-69 (Miss Claire); *Rawhide*—"The Enormous Fist" 10-2-64 (Dolly Grant); *Bonanza*—"The Far, Far Better Thing" 1-10-65 (Lucinda Melviney); *The Road West*—Regular 1966-67 (Midge Pride); *Lancer*—"Glory" 12-10-68 (Glory), "The Buscaderos" 3-17-70 (Violet); *Here Come the Brides*—"A Wild Colonial Boy" 10-24-69 (Bridget); *Alias Smith and Jones*—"Witness to a Lynching" 12-16-72 (Cybele Snively).

Scott, Bruce (1947-). Films: "Hang 'Em High" 1968 (Billy Joe).

Scott, Churchill. Films: "The Fighting Stranger" 1921 (Bob Scarritt); "The Last Chance" 1921 (Braden).

Scott, Cyril (1866-8/16/45). Films: "Arizona" 1913 (Lieutenant Denton).

Scott, Dick (1903-9/2/61). Films: "King of the Texas Rangers" 1941-serial (Derrick Heavy #1); "Alaska" 1944; "Marshal of Laredo" 1945.

Scott, Donovan. Films: "Zorro, the Gay Blade" 1981 (Paco); "Back to the Future, Part III" 1990 (Deputy).

Scott, Douglas. Films: "Cimarron" 1931 (Youngest Cim); "Wild and Woolly" 1937 (Leon Wakefield).

Scott, Ernest. Films: "Fighting Cowboy" 1933 (Desert Rat); "Circle Canyon" 1934; "Rawhide Terror" 1934; "Riding Speed" 1934.

Scott, Evelyn. TV: *Gunsmoke*—"Tape Day for Kitty" 3-24-56 (Olive), "The Pest Hold" 4-14-56 (Olive); *The Restless Gun*—"The Lady and the Gun" 1-19-59 (Zoe Alden); *Bonanza*—"The Hanging Posse" 11-28-59, "Gabrielle" 12-24-61, "The Thunder Man" 5-5-63 (Mrs. Gibson).

Scott, Fred (1902-12/16/91). Films: "The Last Outlaw" 1936 (Larry Dixon); "Romance Rides the Range" 1936 (Barry Glendon); "The Fighting Deputy" 1937 (Tom Bentley); "Melody of the Plains" 1937 (Steve Connor); "Moonlight on the Range" 1937 (Jeff Peters); "The Roaming Cowboy" 1937 (Cal Brent); "The Singing Buckaroo" 1937 (Gordon); "Knight of the Plains" 1938 (Fred "Melody" Brent); "The Rangers' Roundup" 1938 (Tex Duncan); "Songs and Bullets" 1938 (Melody Smith); "Code of the Fearless" 1939 (Fred Jamison); "In Old Montana" 1939 (Lt. Fred Dawson); "Two-Gun Troubador" 1939 (Fred Dean); "Ridin' the Trail" 1940 (Fred Martin); "Rodeo Rhythm" 1942 (Buck Knapp); "Thundering Hoofs" 1942 (Dode).

Scott, Geoffrey. TV: *Cliffhangers*—"The Secret Empire" 1979 (Marshal Jim Donner).

Scott, George C. (1926-). Films: "The Hanging Tree" 1959 (Dr. George Grubb); "Oklahoma Crude" 1973 (Noble "Mase" Mason). ¶TV: *The Virginian*—"The Brazen Bell" 10-17-62 (Arthur Lilley); *The Road West*—"This Savage Land" 9-12-66 & 9-19-66 (Jud Barker).

Scott, Gordon (1927-). Films: "Buffalo Bill, Hero of the Far West" 1964-Ital./Ger./Fr. (Buffalo Bill); "The Tramplers" 1965-Ital. (Lon Cordeen).

Scott, Jacqueline (1935-).

Films: "Firecreek" 1968 (Henrietta Cobb); "Death of a Gunfighter" 1969 (Laurie Mills). ¶TV: *Have Gun Will Travel*—"The Hanging Cross" 12-21-57, "Deliver the Body" 5-24-58 (Tildy Buckahan), "The Wager" 1-3-59 (Stacy Neal), "Fragile" 10-31-59 (Claire Ledoux), "Crowbait" 11-19-60 (Amanda), "Cage at McNaab" 2-16-63 (Nora Larson); *Gunsmoke*—"Love of a Good Woman" 1-24-59 (Abby), "Collie's Free" 10-20-62 (Francie Patten), "Kitty Cornered" 4-18-64 (Stella Damon), "The Whispering Tree" 11-12-66 (Ada Stanley), "Stranger in Town" 11-20-67 (Anne Madison), "Abelia" 11-18-68 (Abelia), "A Man Called Smith" 10-27-69 (Abelia), "The Predators" 1-31-72 (Abella); *Zane Grey Theater*—"Make It Look Good" 2-5-59 (Jenny Carter); *Bat Masterson*—"The Black Pearls" 7-1-59 (Carol Otis); *Wyatt Earp*—"Terror in the Desert" 1-24-61 (Beth Grover); *Bonanza*—"The Tall Stranger" 1-7-62 (Kathy), "The Hostage" 9-27-64 (Willa), "A Natural Wizard" 12-12-65 (Joy Dexter); *Alcoa Premiere*—"Second Chance" 3-13-62 (Oralee Dunlap); *Wide Country*—"The Royce Bennett Story" 9-20-62 (Ella Bennett); *The Virginian*—"Throw a Long Rope" 10-3-62 (Melissa Tatum); *Laramie*—"Shadow of the Past" 10-16-62 (Francie), "The Wedding Party" 1-29-63 (Stacey), "The Sometime Gambler" 3-19-63 (Ellen); *Stoney Burke*—"The Wanderer" 12-3-62 (Leora Dawson); *Temple Houston*—"Gallows in Galilee" 10-31-63 (Kate Hagadorn); *The Guns of Will Sonnett*—"The Marriage" 3-14-69 (Emily Damon); *Here Come the Brides*—"The Deadly Trade" 4-16-69 (Linda); *How the West Was Won*—"The Gunfighter" 1-15-79 (Mrs. Ferguson).

Scott, Jay (1931-). Films: "Fandango" 1970 (Billy Busby).

Scott, Jeff. TV: *The Virginian*—"A Bald-Faced Boy" 4-13-66 (Man), "Vengeance Trail" 1-4-67 (Deputy Cal Brown); *Bob Hope Chrysler Theatre*—"Massacre at Fort Phil Kearny" 10-26-66 (Lieutenant Grummond); *Custer*—"The Raiders" 12-27-67 (Blue Antelope).

Scott, Judson. TV: *Adventures of Brisco County, Jr.*—"No Man's Land" 9-10-93 (Gill Swill).

Scott, Kathryn Leigh (1943-). TV: *Paradise*—"The News from St. Louis" 10-27-88 (Lucy Cord Carroll).

Scott, Kay (1927-1/1/71). Films: "Callaway Went Thataway" 1951 (Phone Girl).

Scott, Ken (1928-12/2/86). Films: "The Bravados" 1958 (Primo);

"The Fiend Who Walked the West" 1958 (Finney); "From Hell to Texas" 1958 (Otis Boyd); "The Second Time Around" 1961 (Sheriff John Yoss). ¶TV: *Tales of Wells Fargo*—"Hometown Doctor" 2-17-62 (Stringer); *Death Valley Days*—"The Melancholy Gun" 5-12-63 (Johnny Ringo), "Trial at Belle's Springs" 5-23-64 (Virgil Earp), "The Red Shawl" 2-5-66 (Hugh Scott); *Gunsmoke*—"Circus Trick" 2-6-65 (Big Eddie); *Daniel Boone*—"The Accused" 3-24-66 (Deputy Crawford); *Laredo*—"Oh Careless Love" 12-23-66 (Jim Barnett); *Alias Smith and Jones*—"A Fistful of Diamonds" 3-4-71 (Ben Morgan), "Dreadful Sorry, Clementine" 11-18-71.

Scott, Linda Gaye (1945-). Films: "Run Home Slow" 1965. ¶TV: *Bonanza*—"A Deck of Aces" 1-31-71 (Dixie).

Scott, Lizabeth (1922-). Films: "Desert Fury" 1947 (Paula Haller); "Red Mountain" 1951 (Chris); "Silver Lode" 1954 (Rose Evans).

Scott, Mabel Julienne (1892-10/1/76). Films: "The Sign Invisible" 1918 (Jeanette Mercier); "The Round Up" 1920 (Echo Allen); "Steele of the Royal Mounted" 1925; "The Frontier Trail" 1926 (Dolly Mainard).

Scott, Mark (1915-7/13/60). TV: *Fury*—"The Baby" 4-7-56 (David Stanhope).

Scott, Martha (1914-). Films: "In Old Oklahoma" 1943 (Catherine Allen). ¶TV: *Cimarron Strip*—"The Search" 11-9-67 (Mrs. Kihlgren).

Scott, Paul (1894-11/24/44). Films: "A Lady Takes a Chance" 1943 (2nd Bartender).

Scott, Pippa (1935-). Films: "The Searchers" 1956 (Lucy Edwards). ¶TV: *Maverick*—"Easy Mark" 11-15-59 (Abigail); *The Alaskans*—"Sign of the Kodiak" 5-29-60 (Ruth Coleman); *The Outlaws*—"Starfall" 11-24-60 & 12-1-60 (Donna Pringle), "The Verdict" 12-28-61; *Stagecoach West*—"Object: Patrimony" 1-3-61 (Susan McLord); *Have Gun Will Travel*—"The Uneasy Grave" 6-3-61 (Kathy Rousseau); *Gunsmoke*—"Indian Ford" 12-2-61 (Mary Tabor), "My Brother's Keeper" 11-15-71 (Sarah Mather); *The Tall Man*—"The Girl from Paradise" 1-13-62 (Anne Drake); *The Virginian*—Regular 1962-64 (Molly Wood); *Redigo*—"The Crooked Circle" 10-22-63 (Patricia Royal); *Wagon Train*—"The Link Cheney Story" 4-13-64 (Dorothea Guilford); *F Troop*—"The Sergeant and the Kid" 1-12-67 (Molly

Walker); *The Outcasts*—"The Town That Wouldn't" 3-31-69 (Augusta Barnes); *Lancer*—"Lamp in the Wilderness" 3-10-70 (Rebecca Brown); *The Cowboys*—"A Matter of Honor" 3-20-74 (Kate Tatum).

Scott, Randolph (1903-3/2/87). Films: "The Virginian" 1929 (Rider); "Heritage of the Desert" 1932 (Jack Hare); "Wild Horse Mesa" 1932 (Chane Weymer); "Man of the Forest" 1933 (Brett Dale); "Sunset Pass" 1933 (Ash Preston); "To the Last Man" 1933 (Lynn Hayden); "The Last Round-Up" 1934 (Jim Cleve); "The Thundering Herd" 1934 (Tom Doan); "Wagon Wheels" 1934 (Clint Belmet); "Home on the Range" 1935 (Tom Hatfield); "Rocky Mountain Mystery" 1935 (Larry Sutton); "The Last of the Mohicans" 1936 (Hawkeye); "High, Wide and Handsome" 1937 (Peter Cortlandt); "The Texans" 1938 (Kirk Jordan); "Frontier Marshal" 1939 (Wyatt Earp); "Jesse James" 1939 (Will Wright); "Susannah of the Mounties" 1939 (Inspector Angus "Monty" Montague); "Virginia City" 1940 (Vance Irby); "When the Daltons Rode" 1940 (Todd Jackson); "Belle Starr" 1941 (Sam Starr); "Western Union" 1941 (Vance Shaw); "The Spoilers" 1942 (Alexander McNamara); "The Desperadoes" 1943 (Steve Upton); "Belle of the Yukon" 1944 (Honest John Calhoun); "Abilene Town" 1946 (Dan Mitchell); "Badman's Territory" 1946 (Mark Rowley); "The Gunfighters" 1947 (Brazos Kane); "Trail Street" 1947 (Bat Masterson); "Albuquerque" 1948 (Cole Armin); "Coroner Creek" 1948 (Chris Danning); "Return of the Badmen" 1948 (Vance); "Canadian Pacific" 1949 (Tom Andrews); "The Doolins of Oklahoma" 1949 (Bill Doolin); "Fighting Man of the Plains" 1949 (Jim Dancer); "The Walking Hills" 1949 (Jim Carey); "The Cariboo Trail" 1950 (Jim Refern); "Colt .45" 1950 (Steve Farrell); "The Nevadan" 1950 (Andrew Barkley); "Fort Worth" 1951 (Ned Britt); "Man in the Saddle" 1951 (Owen Merritt); "Santa Fe" 1951 (Britt Canfield); "Sugarfoot" 1951 (Sugarfoot); "Carson City" 1952 (Silent Jeff); "Hangman's Knot" 1952 (Matt Stewart); "The Man Behind the Gun" 1952 (Maj. Callicut); "The Stranger Wore a Gun" 1953 (Jeff Travis); "Thunder Over the Plains" 1953 (Capt. David Porter); "The Bounty Hunter" 1954 (Jim Kipp); "Riding Shotgun" 1954 (Larry Delong); "A Lawless Street" 1955 (Calem Ware); "Rage at Dawn" 1955 (James Barlow); "Tall Man Riding" 1955

(Larry Madden); "Ten Wanted Men" 1955 (John Stewart); "Seven Men from Now" 1956 (Ben Stride); "Seventh Cavalry" 1956 (Capt. Tom Benson); "Decision at Sundown" 1957 (Bart Allison); "Shoot-Out at Medicine Bend" 1957 (Cap Devlin); "The Tall T" 1957 (Pat Brennan); "Buchanan Rides Alone" 1958 (Buchanan); "Ride Lonesome" 1959 (Ben Brigade); "Westbound" 1959 (John Hayes); "Comanche Station" 1960 (Jefferson Cody); "Ride the High Country" 1962 (Gil Westrum).

Scott, Robert. Films: "Black Arrow" 1944-serial (Black Arrow); "Cowboy Blues" 1946; "Prairie Raiders" 1947; "Pony Express" 1953; "Last Train from Gun Hill" 1959 (Conductor).

Scott, Russ. TV: *The Roy Rogers Show*—"Peril from the Past" 4-13-52, "The Ride of the Ranchers" 4-20-52, "Carnival Killer" 6-8-52, "Flying Bullets" 6-15-52, "Outlaw's Return" 9-28-52, "Huntin' for Trouble" 10-5-52 (Deputy), "The Feud" 11-16-52, "The Mayor of Ghost Town" 11-30-52, "Blind Justice" 12-14-52, "Loaded Guns" 4-15-53, "The Silver Fox Hunt" 4-19-53, "The Mingo Kid" 4-26-53, "Money to Burn" 6-28-53, "The Milliner from Medicine Hat" 10-11-53, "The Outlaws of Paradise Valley" 11-8-53, "Gun Trouble" 11-22-53, "The Peddler from the Pecos" 12-13-53 (Deputy), "Little Dynamite" 1-3-54 (Cal Verdon), "The Kid from Silver City" 1-17-54, "The Secret of Indian Gap" 1-24-54, "The High-Graders of Paradise Valley" 2-28-54 (Jake Douglas), "The Lady Killer" 9-12-54, "The Young Defenders" 10-3-54 (Mack), "The Hijackers" 10-24-54, "Strangers" 12-5-54 (Nick), "Dead End Trail" 2-20-55 (Bat Manning), "Quick Draw" 3-20-55 (Anderson), "And Sudden Death" 10-9-55, "Ranch War" 10-23-55, "Smoking Guns" 3-3-56, "Sheriff Missing" 3-17-56, "The Morse Mixup" 3-24-56, "Fishing for Fingerprints" 10-28-56, "Mountain Pirates" 11-4-56, "His Weight in Wildcats" 11-11-56, "Paleface Justice" 11-18-56, "Tossup" 12-2-56, "End of the Trail" 1-27-57, "Junior Outlaw" 2-10-57.

Scott, Simon (1920-12/11/91). Films: "No Name on the Bullet" 1959 (Henry Reeger); "The Barbary Coast" TVM-1975 (Brant Hollister). ¶TV: *Zane Grey Theater*—"Dangerous Orders" 2-8-57 (Capt. Prentiss); *Wagon Train*—"The Dan Hogan Story" 5-14-58; *Black Saddle*—"The Freebooters" 10-2-59 (Major Pryor);

Bonanza—"Vendetta" 12-5-59 (Tom Pryor), "All Ye His Saints" 12-19-65 (Evan Thorpe), "The Late Ben Cartwright" 3-3-68 (Farraday); *The Virginian*—"The Evil That Men Do" 10-16-63 (Fred Harris), "Lost Yesterday" 2-3-65 (Holcomb); *Temple Houston*—"Seventy Times Seven" 12-5-63 (Sheriff Hab Martin), "Miss Katherina" 4-2-64 (Henry Rivers); *A Man Called Shenandoah*—"Town on Fire" 11-8-65; *Death Valley Days*—"No Place for a Lady" 1-8-66 (Samuel Magoffin); *Wild Wild West*—"The Night of the Druid's Blood" 3-25-66 (Col. Fairchild), "The Night of the Golden Cobra" 9-23-66 (Col. Stanton Mayo), "The Night of the Juggernaut" 10-11-68 (Theodore Block); *Pistols 'n' Petticoats*—11-12-66 (Sloan); *Iron Horse*—"Four Guns to Scalplock" 11-11-67 (Falconer); *Gunsmoke*—"To Ride a Yellow Horse" 3-18-74 (Mr. Rogers); *Barbary Coast*—"Sauce for the Goose" 10-20-75 (Senator).

Scott, Timothy (1937-6/14/95). Films: "The Way West" 1967 (Middle Henry); "Ballad of Josie" 1968 (Klugg); "Butch Cassidy and the Sundance Kid" 1969 (News Carver); "Lock, Stock and Barrel" TVM-1971 (Deville); "One More Train to Rob" 1971 (Slim); "Kid Vengeance" 1976-Ital./U.S./Israel.; "The Electric Horseman" 1979 (Leroy); "Wild Times" TVM-1980 (Caleb Rice); "The Ballad of Gregorio Cortez" 1983 (Sheriff Morris); "Dream West" TVM-1986 (Ezekiel Merritt); "Lonesome Dove" TVM-1989 (Pea-Eye Parker); "Return to Lonesome Dove" TVM-1993 (Pea-Eye Parker). ¶TV: *Daniel Boone*—"Gun-Barrel Highway" 2-24-66 (Phelps); *Pistols 'n' Petticoats*—2-4-67 (Cat); *The Big Valley*—"Journey into Violence" 12-18-67 (Benjamin), "A Stranger Everywhere" 12-9-68 (Jody); *Here Come the Brides*—"How Dry We Are" 3-6-70 (Turner); *The Cherokee Trail*—Pilot 11-28-81 (Wilbur Pattishal); *Ned Blessing: The Story of My Life and Times*—Regular 1993 (Sticks Packwood).

Scott, Tommy. Films: "Trail of the Hawk" 1935.

Scott, Wallace (1905-5/8/70). Films: "Canyon Passage" 1946 (MacIvar); "The Vigilantes Return" 1947 (Bartender).

Scott, Walter (1879-3/5/40). Films: "Death Valley Scotty's Mine" 1912.

Scott, Walter (1940-). Films: "The Glory Guys" 1965 (Lt. Cook); "Buck and the Preacher" 1972 (Earl); "The Cowboys" 1972; "The Culpep-

per Cattle Company" 1972 (Print); "Ulzana's Raid" 1972; "Bite the Bullet" 1975 (Steve); "The Duchess and the Dirtwater Fox" 1976 (Bloodworth Gang Member); "Another Man, Another Chance" 1977-Fr. (Bill); "Calamity Jane" TVM-1984 (Charlie Burke); "Silverado" 1985 (Swann). ¶TV: *Hondo*—"Hondo and the Hanging Town" 12-8-67 (Hoti); *Cimarron Strip*—"The Judgment" 1-4-68; *Gunsmoke*—"The Hanging of Newly O'Brien" 11-26-73 (John).

Scott, William. Films: "Riders of the Purple Sage" 1918 (Venters); "True Blue" 1918 (Stanley Brockhurst); "Chasing Rainbows" 1919 (Billy); "The Rose of Nome" 1920 (Anatole Norss); "Against All Odds" 1924 (Bill Warner); "Not a Drum Was Heard" 1924 (Bud Loupel); "Beyond the Border" 1925 (Moore); "The Light of Western Stars" 1925 (Al Hammond); "The Man Who Played Square" 1925 (Steve); "Aflame in the Sky" 1927 Saunders); "Smoke Bellew" 1929 (Stine); "Come on, Danger!" 1932 (Jim); "The Phantom Rider" 1936-serial.

Scott, Zachary (1914-10/3/65). Films: "South of St. Louis" 1949 (Charlie Burns); "Colt .45" 1950 (Jason Brett); "The Secret of Convict Lake" 1951 (Greer); "Shotgun" 1955 (Reb); "Treasure of Ruby Hills" 1955 (Haney); "Bandido" 1956 (Kennedy); "Natchez Trace" 1960 (John A. Morrow). ¶TV: *Pulitzer Prize Playhouse*—"The Raven" 11-10-50 (Sam Houston); *Rawhide*—"Incident Before Black Pass" 5-19-61 (Grey Eyes); *DuPont Show of the Week*—"Big Deal in Laredo" 10-7-62 (Habershaw).

Scotti, Andrea. Films: "Johnny Colt" 1966-Ital.; "Black Tigress" 1967-Ital.; "Get the Coffin Ready" 1968-Ital.; "I Want Him Dead" 1968-Ital./Span.; "Pistol for a Hundred Coffins" 1968-Ital./Span.; "Shango" 1969-Ital.; "The Dirty Outlaws" 1971-Ital.

Scotti, Vito (1918-). Films: "Rio Conchos" 1964 (Mexican Bandit); "When the Legends Die" 1972 (Meo). ¶TV: *The Texan*—"The Ringer" 2-16-59; *The Californians*—"Deadly Tintype" 3-31-59 (French Duclos); *Sugarfoot*—"The Avengers" 5-12-59; *Tales of Wells Fargo*—"Young Jim Hardie" 9-7-59, "The Hand That Shook the Hand" 2-6-61 (Abber Dabber), "Mr. Mute" 11-4-61 (Mr. Mute); *Bronco*—"The Last Resort" 11-17-59 (Pio Quinta), "The Last Letter" 3-5-62; *Wagon Train*—"The St. Nicholas Story" 12-23-59; *The Deputy*—"Lucifer Urge" 5-14-60 (Jose),

"The Standoff" 6-11-60 (Jose), "Trail of Darkness" 6-18-60 (Jose); *Shotgun Slade*—"The Deadly Key" 5-17-60 (Rejon); *Cheyenne*—"Counterfeit Gun" 10-10-60 (Julio); *The Outlaws*—"Culley" 2-16-61 (Paco); *Bonanza*—"Thunderhead Swindle" 4-29-61, "The Lonely House" 10-15-61 (Pooch); *Frontier Circus*—"The Depths of Fear" 10-5-61 (Jaybo); *Rawhide*—"The Long Count" 1-5-62; *The Rifleman*—"Waste" 10-1-62 & 10-8-62 (Alphonso), "The Sixteenth Cousin" 1-28-63 (Soto), "Which Way'd They Go?" 4-1-63 (Marcello Ciabini); *Stoney Burke*—"A Matter of Percentage" 1-28-63 (Polo); *Wide Country*—"Farewell to Margarita" 3-21-63 (Carlos); *Temple Houston*—"A Slight Case of Larceny" 2-13-64 (Pancho Blanca); *Laredo*—"I See By Your Outfit" 9-23-65 (Chico); *The Virginian*—"Nobility of Kings" 11-10-65 (Gilly); *Gunsmoke*—"The Hostage" 12-4-65 (Torreon), "The Pillagers" 11-6-67 (Savrin), "Danny" 10-13-69 (Indiana), "Sergeant Holly" 12-14-70 (Indian); *Wild Wild West*—"The Night of the Infernal Machine" 12-23-66 (Chef Oefali); *Rango*—"Viva Rango" 3-24-67 (El Carnicero); *Daniel Boone*—"The Ballad of Sidewinder and Cherokee" 9-14-67 (Priest); *Young Maverick*—"A Fistful of Oats" 12-5-79 (Cardenas).

Scourby, Alexander (1908-2/22/85). Films: "The Redhead from Wyoming" 1953 (Reece Duncan); "Giant" 1956 (Old Polo). ¶TV: *Rawhide*—"Incident of the Day of the Dead" 9-18-59 (Albert Hadley); *Zane Grey Theater*—"Interrogation" 10-1-59 (Interrogator); *Bonanza*—"The Julia Bulette Story" 10-17-59 (John Millain); *Wanted—Dead or Alive*—"The Empty Cell" 10-17-59; *The Rifleman*—"Obituary" 10-20-59 (Byron Claremont); *Daniel Boone*—"The Quietists" 2-25-65 (Eli Bothwell).

Scratuglia, Ivan. Films: "The Tramplers" 1965-Ital. (Adian Cordeen); "The Hellbenders" 1966-U.S./Ital./Span.; "Sheriff with the Gold" 1966-Ital./Span.; "A Stranger in Town" 1966-U.S./Ital.; "The Handsome, the Ugly, and the Stupid" 1967-Ital.; "A Minute to Pray, a Second to Die" 1967-Ital.; "Son of Django" 1967-Ital.; "A Long Ride from Hell" 1968-Ital.; "The Ruthless Four" 1968-Ital./Ger.

Seabury, Forrest (1876-2/15/44). Films: "Wild and Woolly" 1917 (Banker); "Ranson's Folly" 1926 (Drummer).

Seabury, Ynez (1907-4/11/73). Films: "Billy's Stratagem" 1911; "The

Calgary Stampede" 1925 (Neenah); "Red Clay" 1927 (Minnie Bear Paw); "The Girl of the Golden West" 1938 (Wowkle); "Union Pacific" 1939 (Shrimp); "Northwest Mounted Police" 1940 (Mrs. Shorty).

Seaforth, Susan (1943-). Films: "California" 1963 (Marianna De La Rose); "Gunfight at Comanche Creek" 1964 (Janie). ¶TV: *Wyatt Earp*—"The Sharpshooter" 1-29-57 (Annie May Hamble); *Cheyenne*—"The Bad Penny" 3-12-62 (Penelope Piper), "Satonka" 10-1-62 (Carol Dana); *Bronco*—"Then the Mountains" 4-30-62 (Julie Mae); *Redigo*—"The Black Rainbow" 12-24-63 (Gussie Leonard); *The Travels of Jaimie McPheeters*—"The Day of the Search" 1-19-64 (Louisa); *Death Valley Days*—"After the O.K. Corral" 5-2-64 (Alice); *Bonanza*—"The Dark Past" 5-3-64 (Holly Burnside); *Wagon Train*—"The Echo Pass Story" 1-3-65 (Vera); *Wild Wild West*—"The Night of Miguelito's Revenge" 12-13-68 (Delilah).

Seagram, Lisa (1936-). TV: *Wagon Train*—"The Clarence Mullins Story" 5-1-63 (Esther); *Gunsmoke*—"Extradition" 12-7-63 & 12-14-63 (Girl).

Sealy, Lewis A. (1851-3/19/31). Films: "The Primitive Call" 1917 (John Malcolm).

Seaman, Earl (1897-3/6/61). Films: "The Lawless Nineties" 1936 (T. Roosevelt); "Rangers of Fortune" 1940.

Searl, Jackie (1920-). Films: "Wild and Woolly" 1937 (Chaunce Ralston); "My Little Chickadee" 1940 (Schoolboy); "The Paleface" 1948 (Jasper Martin). ¶TV: *Bat Masterson*—"A Time to Die" 12-15-60 (Desk Clerk); *Gunslinger*—"Road of the Dead" 3-30-61 (Dorcas); *Maverick*—"Substitute Gun" 4-2-61 (Smiley); *The Rifleman*—"The Mescalero Curse" 4-18-61; *Rawhide*—"Incident of the Running Man" 5-5-61, "Incident of the Pale Rider" 3-15-63 (Hotel Clerk), "Incident at Zebulon" 3-5-64; *Lawman*—"The Tarnished Badge" 1-28-62 (Slick); *Gunsmoke*—"Call Me Dodie" 9-22-62 (Floyd Bagge), "The Gold Mine" 1-27-69 (Hale); *Empire*—"Seven Days on Rough Street" 2-26-63 (Phipps); *Wagon Train*—"The Myra Marshall Story" 10-21-63; *Destry*—"Blood Brother-in-Law" 4-17-64 (Jed Motley); *Wild Wild West*—"The Night of a Thousand Eyes" 10-22-65 (Pilot); *Laredo*—"The Golden Trail" 11-4-65; *Cimarron Strip*—"The Deputy" 12-21-67; *The High Chaparral*—"The

Kinsman" 1-28-68 (Storekeeper), "The Last Hundred Miles" 1-24-69 (Carter); *Bonanza*—"The Passing of a King" 10-13-68 (Harrison), "The Lady and the Mountain Lion" 2-23-69 (Lanky Man); *The Guns of Will Sonnett*—"Trail's End" 1-31-69 (Monk).

Sears, Alan D. (1887-8/18/42). Films: "The Martyrs of the Alamo" 1915 (David Crockett); "The Desire of the Moth" 1917 (Dick Marr); "Girl of the Timber Claims" 1917 (Francis Ames); "Madame Bo-Peep" 1917 (Teddy Westlake); "The Savage" 1917 (Captain McKeever); "The Red, Red Heart" 1918 (John Dewitt); "Two-Fisted Sheriff" 1937 (Bill Slagg); "Secrets" 1933 (Jake Houser); "Fighting Shadows" 1935 (Gavin); "Justice of the Range" 1935 (Pinto Carew); "Law Beyond the Range" 1935 (Cassidy); "The Revenge Rider" 1935 (Lynch); "The Singing Vagabond" 1935 (Utah Joe); "Boss Rider of Gun Creek" 1936; "Sunset of Power" 1936; "Trapped" 1937 (Cal); "Cattle Raiders" 1938 (Hayes); "Prairie Roundup" 1951; "Laramie Mountains" 1952 (Maj. Markham).

Sears, Fred F. (1912-11/30/57). Films: "Law of the Canyon" 1947; "The Lone Hand Texan" 1947 (Sam Jason); "West of Dodge City" 1947; "Adventures in Silverado" 1948; "Phantom Valley" 1948 (Ben Theibold); "Singing Spurs" 1948; "Smoky Mountain Melody" 1948 (Mr. Crump); "Whirlwind Raiders" 1948 (Tracy Beaumont); "The Blazing Trail" 1949 (Luke Masters); "Home in San Antone" 1949; "Laramie" 1949 (Col. Dennison); "Lust for Gold" 1949 (Hotel Clerk); "Renegades of the Sage" 1949 (Lt. Jones); "South of Death Valley" 1949 (Ashton); "Frontier Outpost" 1950 (Copeland); "Hoedown" 1950 (Sam); "Texas Dynamo" 1950 (Hawkins); "Bandits of El Dorado" 1951 (Capt. Henley); "Bonanza Town" 1951 (Henry Hardison); "Cyclone Fury" 1951 (Capt. Barham); "Fort Savage Raiders" 1951 (Col. Sutter); "The Kid from Amarillo" 1951 (Jonathan Cole); "The Rough, Tough West" 1952 (Peter Walker).

Seastrom, Dorothy (-2/30). Films: "The Call of the Canyon" 1923 (Eleanor Harmon).

Seay, James (1914-10/10/92). Films: "Northwest Mounted Police" 1940 (Constable Fenton); "Oklahoma Renegades" 1940 (Carl); "In Old Colorado" 1941 (Hank Merritt); "The Kid from Kansas" 1941 (Walker); "They Died with Their

Boots On" 1941 (Lt. Walsh); "Home in Wyomin'" 1942 (Tex Harrison); "Man from Cheyenne" 1942 (Jim); "Ride 'Em, Cowboy" 1942 (Ranger Captain); "Ridin' Down the Canyon" 1942 (Burt Wooster); "Red Canyon" 1949 (Joel Creech); "When the Redskins Rode" 1951 (George Washington); "Brave Warrior" 1952 (Gov. Harrison); "Captain John Smith and Pocahontas" 1953 (Wingfield); "Fort Ti" 1953 (Mark Chensey); "The Homesteaders" 1953 (Kroger); "Jack McCall, Desperado" 1953 (Bat McCall); "Son of Belle Star" 1953 (Clark); "Vera Cruz" 1954 (Abilene); "Friendly Persuasion" 1956 (Rebel Captain); "Gun Brothers" 1956 (Blackjack Silk). ¶TV: *The Cisco Kid*—"The Photo Studio" 7-5-52, "He Couldn't Quit" 4-24-54, "Magician of Jamesville" 5-22-54; *Fury*—Regular 1955-60 (Sheriff Davis); *Zane Grey Theater*—"Until the Man Dies" 1-25-57 (Mark Clanton); *Circus Boy*—"The Cub Reporter" 4-21-57 (Bill Logan); *Tales of Wells Fargo*—"The Silver Bullets" 7-8-57 (Gurney Cassell), "Something Pretty" 4-17-61 (Banning); *Tombstone Territory*—"Revenge Town" 11-6-57 (Hody Taylor); *Cheyenne*—"The Gamble" 1-28-58 (Duke Tavener), "Road to Three Graves" 10-31-60 (Parks); *Cimarron City*—"A Legacy for Ossie Harper" 1-10-59 (Addison); *Rough Riders*—"Lesson in Violence" 3-26-59 (Mayor Thackeray); *26 Men*—"The Unwanted" 3-31-59 (Vote); *Trackdown*—"The Vote" 5-6-59; *Wyatt Earp*—Regular 1959-61 (Judge Spicer); *The Rebel*—"The Captive of Tremblor" 4-10-60 (Jethro Gain); *Bat Masterson*—"Stage to Nowhere" 4-14-60 (Parker James), "Dakota Showdown" 11-17-60; *Maverick*—"The Ice Man" 1-29-61 (Sheriff Gil McCrary); *The Tall Man*—"Death or Taxes" 5-27-61 (Holman); *Gunsmoke*—"Owney Tupper Had a Daughter" 4-4-64 (Jay); *Death Valley Days*—"Big John and the Rainmaker" 12-6-64 (Bert Fletcher), "A City Is Born" 1-29-66 (Hermann Ehrenberg), "Clum's Constabulary" 4-11-70; *Laredo*—"Three's Company" 10-14-65; *A Man Called Shenandoah*—"Run, Killer, Run" 1-10-66 (Doctor).

Sebastian, Dorothy (1905-4/8/57). Films: "Arizona Wildcat" 1927 (Regina Schyler); "California" 1927 (Carlotta del Rey); "The Adventurer" 1928 (Dolores de Silva); "Wyoming" 1928 (Samantha Jerusha Farrell); "Morgan's Last Raid" 1929 (Judith Rogers); "The Rainbow" 1929 (Lola); "Montana Moon" 1930 (Elizabeth); "The Utah Kid" 1930 (Jenny Lee);

"Wide Open Spaces" 1932-short; "The Arizona Kid" 1939 (Bess Warren); "Rough Riders' Round-Up" 1939 (Rose); "Kansas Cyclone" 1941 (Helen King).

Seberg, Jean (1938-8/30/79). Films: "Paint Your Wagon" 1969 (Elizabeth); "Macho Callahan" 1970 (Alexandra Mountford).

Sedan, Rolfe (1896-9/16/82). Films: "The Denver Dude" 1927 (Henry Bird); "Ruggles of Red Gap" 1935 (Barber); "Rose Marie" 1936 (Admirer in Hall); "High, Wide and Handsome" 1937 (Photographer); "The Frisco Kid" 1979. ¶TV: *Wild Bill Hickok*—"Halley's Comet" 2-17-53; *Kung Fu*—"Cross-ties" 2-21-74 (Stationmaster).

Seddon, Margaret (1872-4/17/68). Films: "A Regular Scout" 1926 (Mrs. Monroe); "The Dude Wrangler" 1930 (Aunt Mary); "Three Desperate Men" 1951 (Mrs. Denton).

Sedgwick, Edward (1892-5/7/53). Films: "Forty-Horse Hawkins" 1924 (Stage Manager).

Sedgwick, Eileen (1898-3/15/91). Films: "The Eagle's Nest" 1915 (Rose Milford); "Giant Powder" 1916; "Dropped from the Clouds" 1917; "Lone Larry" 1917; "Number 10, Westbound" 1917; "All for Gold" 1918; "Hell's Crater" 1918; "The Human Tiger" 1918; "Naked Fists" 1918; "Quick Triggers" 1918; "Roped and Tied" 1918; "The Trail of No Return" 1918; "Cyclone Smith Plays Trumps" 1919; "Cyclone Smith's Comeback" 1919; "Kingdom Come" 1919; "The Phantom Fugitive" 1919; "A Pistol Point Proposal" 1919; "A Prisoner for Life" 1919; "The Wild Rider" 1919; "The White Rider" 1920 (Jewel Brand); "A Battle of Wits" 1921; "The Dream Girl" 1921; "The Girl in the Saddle" 1921; "The Heart of Arizona" 1921; "The Shadow of Suspicion" 1921; "A Woman's Wits" 1921; "False Brands" 1922 (Eileen Morgan); "The Night Attack" 1922; "The Open Wire" 1922; "Wolf Pack" 1922 (Jeanne Lamont); "In the Days of Daniel Boone" 1923-serial; "Making Good" 1923; "When Law Comes to Hades" 1923; "The Riddle Rider" 1924-serial; "The Fighting Ranger" 1925-serial; "Girl of the West" 1925; "The Sagebrush Lady" 1925 (Paula Loring); "Beyond All Odds" 1926 (Betty Mason); "Strings of Steel" 1926-serial; "Thundering Speed" 1926; "Lure of the West" 1928; "The Vanishing West" 1928-serial.

Sedgwick, Josie (1898-3/30/73). Films: "Ashes of Hope" 1917 (Belle); "Fighting Back" 1917 (Dance Hall Girl); "One Shot Ross" 1917 (Nan Sheridan); "Beyond the Shadows" 1918 (Eleanor Wyatt); "Boss of the Lazy Y" 1918 (Betty Clayton); "Keith of the Border" 1918 (Hope Waite/ Christie McClaire); "Man Above the Law" 1918 (Esther Brown); "Paying His Debt" 1918 (Nan Christy); "Wild Life" 1918 (Helen Martin); "Wolves of the Border" 1918; "Jubilo" 1919 (Rose Hardy); "The She Wolf" 1919 (Belle of the Dance Hall); "The Lone Hand" 1920 (Betty Hampton); "Duke of Chimney Butte" 1921 (Grace Kerr); "Western Hearts" 1921 (Edith Caldwell); "Crimson Clue" 1922 (Marion Gray); "The Sunshine Trail" 1923 (Woman Crook); "The Sawdust Trail" 1924 (Calamity Jane Webster); "A Battle of Wits" 1925; "The Best Man" 1925; "Daring Days" 1925 (Eve Underhill); "Dynamite's Daughter" 1925; "The Fighting Schoolmarm" 1925; "Let 'Er Buck" 1925 (Miss Mabel Thompson); "The Outlaw's Daughter" 1925 (Flora Dale); "Queen of the Roundup" 1925; "The Ropin' Venus" 1925; "The Saddle Hawk" 1925 (Mercedes); "Jim Hood's Ghost" 1926; "The Little Warrior" 1926; "Montana of the Ranges" 1926; "Mountain Molly" 1926; "Outlaw Love" 1926; "Queen of the Hills" 1926; "Son of Oklahoma" 1932 (Mary Clayton).

Sedley, Bruce. Films: "The Outlaws Is Coming!" 1965 (Cole Younger).

Sedley, Henry. Films: "One Hour of Love" 1927 (Tom Webb); "The Man from Arizona" 1932 (Buck Gallagher); "One-Man Law" 1932 (Dye).

Seel, Charles (1900-4/19/80). Films: "The Horse Soldiers" 1959 (Newton Station Bartender); "North to Alaska" 1960 (Gold Buyer); "Sergeant Rutledge" 1960 (Dr. C.J. Eckner); "The Man Who Shot Liberty Valance" 1962 (Election Council President); "Cheyenne Autumn" 1964 (Newspaper Publisher); "Westworld" 1973 (Bellhop). ¶TV: *Gunsmoke*—Regular 1955-75 (Barney Danches, the Telegraph Agent), "Stolen Horses" 4-8-61 (Jed Cuff), "Quint's Trail" 11-9-63 (Finch), "The Wreckers" 9-11-67 (Eli), "Women for Sale" 9-10-73 & 9-17-73 (Josiah); *Tombstone Territory*—"The Tin Gunman" 4-16-58 (Bartender); *Bat Masterson*—"Double Trouble in Trinidad" 1-7-59 (Barkeep); *Wanted—Dead or Alive*—"Competition" 1-31-59; *The Rifleman*—"The Boarding House" 2-24-59, "The Mind Reader" 6-30-59; *Trackdown*—"Back to Crawford" 9-9-

59 (Fred Sales); *Wichita Town*—"The Long Night" 1-20-60 (Charlie Cruter); *The Deputy*—"Final Payment" 3-19-60 (Doc Miller), "Marked for Bounty" 4-2-60 (Doc Miller); *The Tall Man*—"A Bounty for Billy" 10-15-60 (Dan); *Wagon Train*—"The Colter Craven Story" 11-23-60; *Tales of Wells Fargo*—"Royal Maroon" 4-28-62 (Dr. Fergus); *Bonanza*—"The Quest" 9-30-62 (Hawkins), "The Cheating Game" 2-9-64, "The Wish" 3-9-69 (Titus); *Laramie*—"The Sunday Shoot" 11-13-62; *The Travels of Jaimie McPheeters*—"The Day of the First Suitor" 9-29-63 (Henry Rutledge); *Temple Houston*—"Sam's Boy" 1-23-64 (Henry Hicks); *The Legend of Jesse James*—"The Man Who Killed Jesse" 12-27-65 (Old Timer); *A Man Called Shenandoah*—"Care of General Delivery" 5-9-66 (Enoch); *The Road West*—Regular 1966-67 (Tom "Grandpa" Pride); *The Guns of Will Sonnett*—"A Bell for Jeff Sonnett" 9-15-67 (Merchant), "A Town in Terror" 2-7-69 & 2-14-69; *Cimarron Strip*—"The Search" 11-9-67 (Ruckles); *The Virginian*—"The Barren Ground" 12-6-67 (Doctor); *Here Come the Brides*—"The Road to the Cradle" 11-7-69.

Seeley, James (1867-2/15/43). Films: "Channing of the Northwest" 1922 (Tom Driscol).

Seffinger, Carol. TV: *Rawhide*—"Incident of the One Hundred Amulets" 5-6-60; *The Alaskans*—"White Vengeance" 6-5-60 (Katja); *Gunsmoke*—"Call Me Dodie" 9-22-62 (Martha).

Segal, George (1934-). Films: "Invitation to a Gunfighter" 1964 (Matt Weaver); "The Duchess and the Dirtwater Fox" 1976 (Charlie Malloy).

Segal, Vivienne (1897-12/29/92). Films: "Song of the West" 1930 (Virginia).

Seidel, Tom. Films: "Riding the Sunset Trail" 1941 (Bronco West); "Wanderers of the West" 1941 (West Mack/Waco Dean); "Arizona Roundup" 1942; "Westward Ho" 1942 (Wayne Henderson); "Where Trails End" 1942; "False Colors" 1943 (Bud Lawton/Kit Mayer); "The Ghost Rider" 1943; "Moonlight and Cactus" 1944 (Tom Garrison).

Seiter, William (1892-7/26/64). Films: "Pierre of the North" 1913.

Sekka, Johnny (1939-). Films: "Charley One-Eye" 1973-Brit. (Bob).

Selbie, Evelyn (1871-12/6/50). Films: "Western Hearts" 1912; "Across the Rio Grande" 1913; "Broncho Billy and the Western Girls" 1913; "Broncho Billy Gets Square" 1913; "Broncho Billy's Capture" 1913; "The Edge of Things" 1913; "The End of the Circle" 1913; "The Man in the Cabin" 1913; "The Naming of the Rawhide Queen" 1913; "The Rustler's Step-Daughter" 1913; "A Western Sister's Devotion" 1913; "Broncho Billy—Outlaw" 1914; "The Calling of Jim Barton" 1914; "The Good for Nothing" 1914 (Mrs. Sterling); "Broncho Billy and the Baby" 1915; "Broncho Billy's Brother" 1915; "Broncho Billy's Love Affair" 1915; "Broncho Billy's Sentence" 1915; "Broncho Billy's Teachings" 1915; "Pay Me!" 1917 (Hilda Hendricks); "The Grand Passion" 1918 (Boston Kate); "A Broadway Cowboy" 1920 (Miss Howell); "The Half-Breed" 1922 (Mary); "Snowdrift" 1923 (Wananebish); "Romance Ranch" 1924 (Tessa); "The Prairie Pirate" 1925 (Madre); "Ramona" 1936 (Indian Woman); "Rose of the Rancho" 1936 (Old Woman).

Selby, David (1941-). Films: "The Night Rider" TVM-1979 (Lord Thomas Earl).

Selby, Norman (1873-4/18/40). Films: "Straight from the Shoulder" 1921 (Bill Higgins); "To a Finish" 1921 (Wolf Gary); "Arabia" 1922 (Pussy Foot Bogs).

Selby, Sarah (1906-1/7/80). Films: "The Iron Mistress" 1952 (Mrs. Bowie); "Gunfire at Indian Gap" 1957 (Mrs. Moran); "Taggart" 1964 (Maude Taggart). ¶TV: *Wagon Train*—"The Daniel Barrister Story" 4-16-58 (Mrs. Snyder); *The Restless Gun*—"A Bell for Santo Domingo" 12-22-58 (Sister Marguette); *The Rifleman*—"The Boarding House" 2-24-59 (Agnes); *Wanted—Dead or Alive*—"Littlest Giant" 4-25-59 (Sister Flavina); *Bronco*—"Red Water North" 6-16-59 (Martha Chandler); *Maverick*—"Maverick and Juliet" 1-17-60 (Mrs. Carteret); *Johnny Ringo*—"Uncertain Vengeance" 3-10-60 (Emelia Krale); *Wyatt Earp*—"The Doctor" 10-4-60 (Mrs. Mason); *Gunsmoke*—Regular 1962-75 (Ma Smalley); *Lawman*—"The Witness" 6-24-62 (Anna Prentiss); *Bonanza*—The Way of Aaron" 3-10-63, "To Kill a Buffalo" 1-9-66 (Mrs. Flanner); *Death Valley Days*—"The Red Ghost of Eagle Creek" 5-30-64 (Mrs. Davidson).

Seldes, Marian (1928-). Films: "The True Story of Jesse James" 1957 (Rowina Cobb); "The Light in the Forest" 1958 (Kate Owens). ¶TV: *Gunsmoke*—"Indian White" 10-27-56

(Mrs. Mary Cullen); *Have Gun Will Travel*—"The Bride" 10-19-57 (Christie Smith), "The Teacher" 3-15-58 (Teacher); *The Texan*—"No Love Wasted" 3-9-59 (Cora); *The Rifleman*—"The Vision" 3-22-60 (Hazel); *Branded*—"The Bar Sinister" 10-10-65 (Neela).

Self, William. Films: "The Marshal of Cripple Creek" 1947 (Dick Lambert); "Red River" 1948 (Wounded Wrangler); "Ticket to Tomahawk" 1950 (Telegrapher); "The Big Sky" 1952.

Selk, George. see Buster, Budd.

Selleck, Tom (1945-). Films: "The Sacketts" TVM-1979 (Orrin Sackett); "The Shadow Riders" TVM-1982 (Mac Traven); "Quigley Down Under" 1990 (Matthew Quigley). ¶TV: *Lancer*—"Death Bait" 1-14-69 (Cowboy in Bar).

Sellon, Charles A. (1870-6/26/37). Films: "The Bad Man" 1923 (Uncle Henry); "Sundown" 1924 (Ranchman); "The Calgary Stampede" 1925 (Regan); "Tracked in the Snow Country" 1925 (Silent Hardy); "The Mysterious Rider" 1927 (Cliff Harkness); "Painted Ponies" 1927 (Mr. Blenning); "The Prairie King" 1927 (Pop Wygant); "Under a Texas Moon" 1930 (Jose Romero); "Dude Ranch" 1931 (Spruce Meadows); "The Painted Desert" 1931 (Tonopah); "Ride Him, Cowboy" 1932 (Judge Bartlett).

Selmier, Dean. Films: "The Hunting Party" 1971-Brit./Ital./Span. (Collins); "Man in the Wilderness" 1971-U.S./Span. (Russell).

Selwyn, Edgar (1875-2/13/44). Films: "Pierre of the Plains" 1914 (Pierre).

Selwynne, Clarissa (1886-6/13/48). Films: "Smashing Through" 1918 (Mrs. Brandon); "Two Kinds of Women" 1922 (Mrs. Grimley); "The Lucky Horseshoe" 1925 (Aunt Ruth); "My Pal, the King" 1932 (Dowager Queen).

Selzer, Milton (1918-). Films: "A Big Hand for the Little Lady" 1966 (Fleeson); "Sam Hill: Who Killed the Mysterious Mr. Foster?" TVM-1971; "This Was the West That Was" TVM-1974. ¶TV: *Gunsmoke*—"Til Death Do Us" 1-16-60 (Jezra Cobb), "Anybody Can Kill a Marshal" 3-9-63 (Painter), "Pa Hack's Brood" 12-28-63 (Pa Hack), "Albert" 2-9-70 (Albert Schiller); *Have Gun Will Travel*—"A Drop of Blood" 12-2-61 (Rabbi Reb Elya), "Hobson's Choice" 4-7-62 (Alfred Nobel); *Stoney Burke*—"The Wanderer" 12-3-

62 (Dr. Laird); *A Man Called Shenandoah*—"The Fort" 9-27-65 (Captain Crowell); *Daniel Boone*—"The Gun" 2-3-66 (Isaac Delf); *The Virginian*—"Outcast" 10-26-66 (Harold Bitz); *Iron Horse*—"War Cloud" 10-31-66 (Thaddeus Bancroft); *Wild Wild West*—"The Night of the Death Masks" 1-26-68 (Emmett Star); *The High Chaparral*—"Trail to Nevermore" 10-31-69 (Sody Marcum).

Semels, Harry (1887-3/2/46). Films: "The Phantom Foe" 1920-serial; "The Demon" 1926 (Joseph Lomax); "Moran of the Mounted" 1926 (Dubuc); "Hawk of the Hills" 1927-serial (Sheckard); "Put 'Em Up" 1928 (Lloyd Turner); "The Royal Rider" 1929 (Parvene); "The Bad Man" 1930 (Jose); "Fighting Caravans" 1931 (Brawler); "Broadway to Cheyenne" 1932 (Louis); "Ghost Valley" 1932 (Henchman); "South of the Rio Grande" 1932 (Pancho); "Texas Buddies" 1932 (Kincaid); "Wyoming Whirlwind" 1932; "Young Blood" 1932 (Tony Murullu); "Drum Taps" 1933 (Pete); "The King of the Wild Horses" 1933 (Big Man); "The Thrill Hunter" 1933 (Norton); "Rocky Rhodes" 1934 (Boggs); "The Revenge Rider" 1935 (Rankin); "Stone of Silver Creek" 1935 (Simmons); "The Gay Desperado" 1936 (Manuel); "Rose of the Rancho" 1936 (Blacksmith); "High, Wide and Handsome" 1937 (Bartender); "The Trigger Trio" 1937; "Wells Fargo" 1937; "Overland Mail" 1939 (Pancho); "Rovin' Tumbleweeds" 1939; "Kit Carson" 1940 (Pioneer); "Honky Tonk" 1941 (Pallbearer); "San Antonio" 1945 (Mexican).

Semon, Larry (1889-10/8/28). Films: "Guns and Greasers" 1918.

Seneca, Joe. Films: "Silverado" 1985 (Ezra).

Sennett, Mack (1880-11/5/60). Films: "The Call of the Wild" 1908; "The Red Girl" 1908; "The Vaquero's Vow" 1908; "The Dancing Girl of Butte" 1909; "Leather Stocking" 1909; "The Mended Lute" 1909; "The Mountaineer's Honor" 1909; "The Broken Doll" 1910; "The Gold Seekers" 1910; "In Old California" 1910; "A Knot in the Plot" 1910; "A Mohawk's Way" 1910; "Over Silent Paths" 1910; "The Song of the Wildwood Flute" 1910; "The Twisted Trails" 1910; "Two Brothers" 1910; "The Last Drop of Water" 1911; "The Tourists" 1912.

Sentry, Frank. TV: *Have Gun Will Travel*—"Return to Fort Benjamin" 1-30-60; *Bonanza*—"The Savage" 12-3-60 (Iowa); *Gunsmoke*—

"Long Hours, Short Pay" 4-29-61 (Crooked Knife).

Sepulveda, Carl. Films: "Fangs of Destiny" 1927 (Hank Mitchell); "The Four-Footed Ranger" 1928 (Jake); "Code of the Cactus" 1939; "Days of Jesse James" 1939; "The Lone Ranger Rides Again" 1939-serial (Raider #7); "Riders of the Black River" 1939; "Spoilers of the Range" 1939 (Hager); "Zorro's Fighting Legion" 1939-serial (Orlando); "Billy the Kid Outlawed" 1940; "Geronimo" 1940 (Soldier Jones); "West of Abilene" 1940 (Cavalry Captain); "West of Carson City" 1940 (1st Bandit); "Arizona Cyclone" 1941; "Bad Men of the Hills" 1942; "Little Joe, the Wrangler" 1942 (Norton); "The Lone Rider and the Bandit" 1942; "Raiders of the West" 1942; "Stagecoach Buckaroo" 1942; "A Tornado in the Saddle" 1942; "Valley of the Sun" 1942 (Pickett); "Black Hills Express" 1943; "Black Market Rustlers" 1943 (Sheriff); "Bordertown Gunfighters" 1943 (Red Dailey); "Cowboy Commandos" 1943; "Fugitive of the Plains" 1943; "Land of Hunted Men" 1943; "Raiders of San Joaquin" 1943 (Tanner); "The Renegade" 1943; "Santa Fe Scouts" 1943; "Beneath Western Skies" 1944; "Marshal of Reno" 1944; "Sheriff of Sundown" 1944; "Song of the Range" 1944; "Stagecoach to Monterey" 1944; "Trouble at Melody Mesa" 1944; "Zorro's Black Whip" 1944-serial (Citizen #4); "Return of the Durango Kid" 1945; "Rough Ridin' Justice" 1945 (Guard); "Rustlers of the Badlands" 1945; "The Phantom Rider" 1946-serial (Ambusher #4); "Plainsman and the Lady" 1946 (Big Mex); "Song of the Sierras" 1946; "Jesse James Rides Again" 1947-serial (Mort); "Land of the Lawless" 1947; "Rainbow Over the Rockies" 1947; "Saddle Pals" 1947; "Son of Zorro" 1947-serial (Milt); "Partners of the Sunset" 1948; "River Lady" 1948 (Logger); "San Antone Ambush" 1949; "Annie Get Your Gun" 1950 (Rider); "Callaway Went Thataway" 1951 (Heavy). ¶TV: *The Gene Autry Show*—"The Breakup" 11-5-50, "Twisted Trails" 11-12-50.

Serato, Massimo (1916-12/22/89). Films: "Gunmen of the Rio Grande" 1964-Fr./Ital./Span. (Leo); "Dead Men Ride" 1970-Ital./Span.; "Forewarned, Half-Killed … The Word of the Holy Ghost" 1971-Ital./Span.; "Light the Fuse … Sartana Is Coming" 1971-Ital./Fr.

Serna, Pepe (1944-). Films: "Shoot Out" 1971 (Pepe); "The Bal-

lad of Gregorio Cortez" 1983 (Romaldo Cortez); "Silverado" 1985 (Scruffy); "Bad Jim" 1990 (Virgilio Seguar); "Conagher" TVM-1991. ¶TV: *Kung Fu*—"The Chalice" 10-11-73 (Los Vidrios).

Sernas, Jacques (1925-). Films: "Fort Yuma Gold" 1966-Ital./Fr./Span. (Major Sanders).

Serrano, Ramon. Films: "Guns of the Magnificent Seven" 1969 (Cesar).

Server, Eric. Films: "Hot Lead and Cold Feet" 1978. ¶TV: *Kung Fu*—"Cross-ties" 2-21-74 (Miller); *The Quest*—"Shanklin" 10-13-76 (Sgt. Rock).

Servis, Helen. Films: "The Big Show" 1937; "Daughter of the West" 1949; "The Gay Amigo" 1949 (Old Maid); "Hannah Lee" 1953 (2nd Woman). ¶TV: *The Gene Autry Show*—"Heir to the Lazy L" 12-29-51.

Sessions, Almira (1888-8/3/74). Films: "The Ox-Bow Incident" 1943 (Mrs. Sanson); "The Blazing Sun" 1950; "Fancy Pants" 1950 (Belle); "Montana" 1950 (Gaunt Woman); "The Old Frontier" 1950 (Mrs. Smedley); "Oklahoma Annie" 1952 (Mrs. Fudge); "Wagons West" 1952 (Old Maid); "Ride, Vaquero!" 1953 (Woman); "Hell's Outpost" 1954. ¶TV: *The Lone Ranger*—"Sheep Thieves" 2-9-50; *Wild Bill Hickok*—"The Lady School Teacher" 10-2-51, "Grandpa and Genie" 5-20-52; *The Gene Autry Show*—"Trail of the Witch" 3-30-52; *The Cisco Kid*—"Thunderhead" 4-5-52, "Bell of Santa Margarite" 4-19-52, "The Racoon Story" 11-15-52; *Tales of the Texas Rangers*—"Uranium Pete" 10-1-55 (Sara Norris); *Sergeant Preston of the Yukon*—"Crime at Wounded Moose" 1-12-56 (Mrs. Guffy); *Cheyenne*—"The Iron Trail" 1-1-57 (Mrs. Thatcher); *Laredo*—"The Bitter Yen of General Ti" 2-3-67.

Seurat, Pilar. TV: *Maverick*—"The White Widow" 1-24-60 (Pilar); *Stoney Burke*—"The Weapons Man" 4-8-63 (Margo Tecas); *Temple Houston*—"Last Full Moon" 2-27-64 (Bluebird); *Rawhide*—"Incident of the Peyote Cup" 5-14-64 (Maga); *Daniel Boone*—"Daughter of the Devil" 4-15-65 (Marie Bouvier); *Wild Wild West*—"The Night the Dragon Screamed" 1-14-66 (Princess Ching Ling); *The Virginian*—"Long Ride to Wind River" 1-19-66 (Hapamawa), "Nora" 12-11-68 (Tela); *The High Chaparral*—"The Terrorist" 12-17-67 (Pilar); *Bonanza*—"Customs of the Country" 2-6-72 (Ines).

Seven, Johnny (1926-). Films: "Guns of the Timberland" 1960 (Vince); "Navajo Run" 1966 (Matthew Whitehawk); "Gunfight in Abilene" 1967 (Loop). ¶TV: *The Deputy*—"The Two Faces of Bob Claxton" 2-27-60 (Pete Claxton); *Man from Blackhawk*—"The Sons of Don Antonio" 4-22-60 (Pio); *Bat Masterson*—"The Lady Plays Her Hand" 12-29-60 (Burt Comers); *Two Faces West*—"Day of Violence" 7-10-61; *Gunsmoke*—"Nina's Revenge" 12-16-61 (Harry Blucher), "Seven Hours to Dawn" 9-18-65 (Barens); *Death Valley Days*—"The Last Shot" 12-12-62 (Carlo Farelli); *Temple Houston*—"The Dark Madonna" 12-26-63 (Rio); *Bonanza*—"The Flapjack Contest" 1-3-65 (Trager); *Wild Wild West*—"The Night of the Gypsy Peril" 1-20-67 (Mikolik); *The Virginian*—"Nightmare at Fort Killman" 3-8-67 (Beale); *Lancer*—"Glory" 12-10-68 (Wade Hatcher); *Here Come the Brides*—"How Dry We Are" 3-6-70 (McKay); *Barbary Coast*—"Arson and Old Lace" 11-14-75 (Carlo).

Severinsen, Doc (1927-). TV: *Bonanza*—"The Younger Brothers' Younger Brother" 3-12-72 (Hotel Manager).

Sevilla, Carmen (1930-). Films: "The Boldest Job in the West" 1969-Ital.

Sewall, Allen (1882-1/20/54). Films: "Between Dangers" 1927; "Wells Fargo" 1937 (Northerner); "Marked Trails" 1944 (Mr. Bradley).

Seward, Billie. Films: "Branded a Coward" 1935 (Ethel Carson); "Justice of the Range" 1935 (Janet McLean); "Law Beyond the Range" 1935 (Gloria Alexander); "The Man from Guntown" 1935 (Ruth McArthur); "The Revenge Rider" 1935 (Myra Harmon); "Riding Wild" 1935 (June McCabe); "Trails of the Wild" 1935 (Jane).

Seymour, Anne (1909-12/8/88). Films: "Stage to Thunder Rock" 1964 (Myra Parker); "Waco" 1966 (Ma Jenner); "A Cry in the Wilderness" TVM-1974; "Seven Alone" 1974 (Narrator); "Triumphs of a Man Called Horse" 1984 (Elk Woman). ¶TV: *Gunsmoke*—"Kitty's Injury" 9-19-59 (Cora Judson), "The Wake" 12-10-60 (Mrs. Boggs), "Snow Train" 10-19-70 & 10-26-70 (Sarah); *Rawhide*—"Twenty-Five Santa Clauses" 12-22-61 (Mag Bateman); *Empire*—Regular 1962-63 (Lucia Garrett); *The Big Valley*—"The Man from Nowhere" 11-14-66 (Hannah Mathews); *Bonanza*—"A Visit to Upright" 3-26-

72; *Kung Fu*—"The Last Raid" 4-26-75 (Mrs. Wright).

Seymour, Carolyn. Films: "Zorro, the Gay Blade" 1981 (Dolores).

Seymour, Claire (1901-4/25/20). Films: "Scarlet Days" 1919 (Chiquita).

Seymour, Dan (1915-5/25/93). Films: "Klondike Kate" 1942 (Piano Player); "San Antonio" 1945 (Laredo Border Guard); "Trail of the Yukon" 1949 (Duval); "Face to Face" 1952 ("The Bride Comes to Yellow Sky" segment—the Drummer); "Rancho Notorious" 1952 (Comanche Paul). ¶TV: *Jim Bowie*—"Patron of the Arts" 4-11-58 (Julio); *The Restless Gun*—"Incident at Bluefield" 3-30-59.

Seymour, Harry (1891-11/11/67). Films: "San Antonio" 1945 (Bartender); "Ticket to Tomahawk" 1950 (Velvet Fingers); "The Stranger Wore a Gun" 1953; "River of No Return" 1954. ¶TV: *Maverick*—"Alias Bart Maverick" 10-5-58 (Piano Player), "Substitute Gun" 4-2-61 (Piano Player); *Bonanza*—"The Julia Bulette Story" 10-17-59 (Piano Player).

Seymour, Jane (1951-). Films: "The Awakening Land" TVM-1978 (Genny Luckett). ¶TV: *Dr. Quinn, Medicine Woman*—Regular 1993- (Dr. Michaela "Mike" Quinn).

Sha'an, Morgan. Films: "The Gambler Wore a Gun" 1961 (Thompson); "Gun Fight" 1961 (Cory). ¶TV: *Tales of Wells Fargo*—"The Inscrutable Man" 12-9-57 (Dan Cameron), "The Gun" 4-14-58 (Colby); *Death Valley Days*—"The Last Bad Man" 12-16-57; *Maverick*—"Day of Reckoning" 2-2-58 (Slim), "Prey of the Cat" 12-7-58 (2nd Deputy); *Tate*—"Before Sunup" 8-17-60 (Hobey); *The Rebel*—"The Hunted" 11-6-60 (Deputy).

Shackleford, Floyd (1905-12/17/72). Films: "The Call of Courage" 1925 (Cook); "Where the Worst Begins" 1925; "The White Outlaw" 1925 (Cook); "Sky High Coral" 1926 (Sam); "The Ballyhoo Buster" 1928; "The Lonely Trail" 1936 (Armstrong).

Shackleford, Ted (1946-). TV: *Big Hawaii*—"Sun Children" 9-28-77 (Moonstar); *Paradise*—"Long Lost Lawson" 5-20-89 (Preston McMillan).

Shackleton, Richard. Films: "Pony Soldier" 1952 (Bryan Neeley); "The Desperado" 1954 (Pat Garner). ¶TV: *The Roy Rogers Show*—"Boys' Day in Paradise Valley" 11-7-54 (Bob Miner).

Shade, Jamesson (1895-4/17/

56). Films: "The Utah Kid" 1944; "Dakota Lil" 1950.

Shadix, Glenn. Films: "Sunset" 1988 (Roscoe Arbuckle).

Shahan, Rocky. Films: "Son of Zorro" 1947-serial (Clark); "Roll, Thunder, Roll" 1949 (Red's Double); "The James Brothers of Missouri" 1950-serial (Mexican Rider); "Run for Cover" 1955; "Copper Sky" 1957; "The Deerslayer" 1957 (Stunts); "Ride a Violent Mile" 1957; "The Storm Rider" 1957 (Fred Feylan); "Blood Arrow" 1958 (Taslatch); "Cattle Empire" 1958 (Quince). ¶TV: *Gunsmoke*—"Pucket's New Year" 1-5-57 (Jim); *Have Gun Will Travel*—"Winchester Quarantine" 10-5-57; *Rawhide*—Regular 1959-65 (Joe Scarlett).

Shalet, Diane (1939-). TV: *Bonanza*—"The Imposters" 12-13-70 (Mrs. York), "Don't Cry, My Son" 10-31-71 (Ruth Sloan); *Gunsmoke*—"Eleven Dollars" 10-30-72 (Charity Spender), "The First of Ignorance" 1-27-75 (Ami Harker).

Shane, Gene. TV: *The Outcasts*—"A Ride to Vengeance" 9-30-68 (Lew); *The High Chaparral*—"Time of Your Life" 9-19-69 (Fletch); *Bonanza*—"Silence at Stillwater" 9-28-69 (John Ferson).

Shane, Sara. Films: "King and Four Queens" 1956 (Oralie).

Shank, John. Films: "Alias Smith and Jones" TVM-1971 (Outlaw); "Jessi's Girls" 1976 (Slime). ¶TV: *Gunsmoke*—"Hard Luck Henry" 10-23-67 (Truly Dooley); *Here Come the Brides*—"Hosanna's Way" 10-31-69; *Bonanza*—"The Night Virginia City Died" 9-13-70 (Tim Moss).

Shanks, Don. Films: "The Life and Times of Grizzly Adams" 1975 (Indian Brave); "Guardian of the Wilderness" 1976 (Teneiya, the Indian Friend); "Last of the Mohicans" TVM-1977 (Uncas); "The Chisholms" TVM-1979; "Down the Long Hill" TVM-1987 (Ashawakie). ¶TV: *The Life and Times of Grizzly Adams*—Regular 1977-78 (Nakuma); *The Chisholms*—Regular 1979 (Enapay).

Shannon, Cora (1869-8/27/57). Films: "Trumpin' Trouble" 1926 (Mrs. Perkins).

Shannon, Ethel (1898-7/10/51). Films: "Roarin' Dan" 1920; "Playing Dobule" 1923; "Lightning Romance" 1924 (Lila Grandon); "The Texas Trail" 1925 (Betty Foster); "The Buckaroo Kid" 1926 (Lyra Radigan).

Shannon, Frank (1874-2/1/59). Films: "The Eagle's Brood" 1936

(Mike); "End of the Trail" 1936 (Sheriff Anderson); "The Texas Rangers" 1936 (Capt. Stafford); "Outlaws of the Prairie" 1937 (Dart Collins, Sr.); "Union Pacific" 1939; "The Return of Frank James" 1940 (Sheriff Daniels); "Rawhide Rangers" 1941 (Captain).

Shannon, Harry (1890-7/27/64). Films: "In Old California" 1942 (Mr. Carlin); "Idaho" 1943 (Judge Grey); "In Old Oklahoma" 1943 (Charlie Witherspoon); "Song of Texas" 1943 (Sam Bennett); "The Yellow Rose of Tesas" 1944 (Sam Weston); "Canyon Passage" 1946 (McLane); "Northwest Stampede" 1948; "Return of the Badmen" 1948 (Wade Templeton); "Rustlers" 1949 (Sheriff); "Cow Town" 1950 (Sandy Reeves); "Curtain Call at Cactus Creek" 1950 (Clay); "The Gunfighter" 1950 (Bartender); "Singing Guns" 1950 (Judge Waller); "Al Jennings of Oklahoma" 1951 (Fred Salter); "High Noon" 1952 (Cooper); "The Outcasts of Poker Flat" 1952 (Bearded Miner); "Jack Slade" 1953 (Tom Carter); "Kansas Pacific" 1953 (Smokestack); "The Phantom Stallion" 1954; "Rails into Laramie" 1954 (Jude Pierce); "At Gunpoint" 1955 (Marshal MacKay); "The Marauders" 1955 (John Rutherford); "The Tall Men" 1955 (Sam); "The Violent Men" 1955 (Purdue); "The Peacemaker" 1956 (Cowpuncher); "Duel at Apache Wells" 1957 (Wayne Shattuck); "Hell's Crossroads" 1957 (Clay Ford); "The Lonely Man" 1957 (Dr. Fisher); "Man or Gun" 1958 (Justine Corley); "Yellowstone Kelly" 1959 (Riverboat Captain). ¶TV: *The Roy Rogers Show*—"False Faces" 2-5-56, "Smoking Guns" 3-3-56 (Greg Payne); *Cheyenne*—"Johnny Bravo" 5-15-56 (Crowley), "Storm Center" 11-20-61 (Father Paul); *Sheriff of Cochise*—"The Relatives" 3-8-57 (Caleb); *Have Gun Will Travel*—"Three Bells to Perdido" 9-14-57, "The Hanging Cross" 12-21-57, "Deliver the Body" 5-24-58 (Marty Buchanan); *The Adventures of Rin Tin Tin*—"Mother O'Hara's Marriage" 10-25-57; *The Restless Gun*—"General Gilford's Widow" 11-11-57 (Joe Kennedy); *Death Valley Days*—"Old Gabe" 12-16-58 (Jim Bridger), "Deadline at Austin" 2-8-61; *Rawhide*—"Incident of the Widowed Dove" 1-30-59, "Incident of the Blackstorms" 5-26-61 (Jeffries), "The Long Count" 1-5-62 (Sheriff Blanton), "The House of the Hunter" 4-20-62 (Kilo); *Tales of Wells Fargo*—"The Tired Gun" 3-30-59 (Tobey); *Man Without a Gun*—"Reward" 4-11-

59 (Judge); *Lawman*—"9:05 to North Platte" 12-6-59 (Pa Jute), "The Second Son" 11-27-60 (Carl May); *The Texan*—"Dangerous Ground" 12-14-59 (Jay Howell); *Sugarfoot*—"The Corsican" 4-12-60 (Henry Shipman); *Colt .45*—"Showdown at Goldtown" 6-14-60 (Clay Cooper); *Gunsmoke*—"About Chester" 2-25-61 (Emmett Bowers); *Bat Masterson*—"Meeting at Mimbers" 4-13-61 (Jobe Crail); *The Dakotas*—"Justice at Eagle's Nest" 3-11-63 (Jim Painter).

Shannon, Jack (1892-12/27/68). Films: "Square Shooter" 1935; "Stormy" 1935 (Cowboy); "Empty Holsters" 1937 (Deputy); "It Happened Out West" 1937 (Pete); "Outlaws of the Prairie" 1937 (Outlaw); "Chip of the Flying U" 1939; "Desperate Trails" 1939 (Ab); "Law and Order" 1940 (Henchman); "Son of Roaring Dan" 1940 (Tom); "West of Carson City" 1940 (Pete); "Man from Montana" 1941 (Tex); "Sundown Riders" 1948 (Jed).

Shannon, Paul. Films: "The Outlaws Is Coming!" 1965 (Wild Bill Hickok).

Shannon, Peggy (1907-5/11/41). Films: "Triple Justice" 1940 (Susan).

Shannon, Richard. Films: "Arrowhead" 1953 (Lt. Kirk); "Pony Express" 1953 (Barrett); "The Vanquished" 1953 (Lt. Adams); "Ride a Violent Mile" 1957 (Sam); "Ride Out for Revenge" 1957 (Garvin); "The Tin Star" 1957 (Buck Henderson); "Trooper Hook" 1957 (Ryan); "Cattle Empire" 1958 (Garth). ¶TV: *Zane Grey Theater*—"A Fugitive" 3-22-57 (Clay Rickert), "Shadow of a Dead Man" 4-11-58 (Mark Wilkins), "Picture of Sal" 1-28-60 (Malcolm Conway); *Tales of Wells Fargo*—"The Bounty" 4-15-57 (Sgt. Alcorn), "The Train Robbery" 10-12-59 (Dick), "Wanted: Jim Hardie" 12-21-59 (Wade); *Have Gun Will Travel*—"Bitter Wine" 2-15-58 (Tim Gorman), "The Ballad of Oscar Wilde" 12-6-58 (Jim Rook), "The Moor's Revenge" 12-27-58 (Ben Jackson), "Alaska" 4-18-59 (Carl Grimes), "The Ledge" 2-13-60 (Cass), "Alive" 3-17-62 (Morgan), "The Jonah" 5-26-62 (Dr. Weiser), "Sweet Lady of the Moon" 3-9-63 (Dr. Weiser); *Rawhide*—"Incident of the Golden Calf" 3-13-59, "Incident of the Thirteenth Man" 10-23-59 (Ed Shore), "The Gentleman's Gentleman" 12-15-61 (Bison Bob Driscoll); *Black Saddle*—"Client: Vardon" 5-30-59 (Boone); *The Deputy*—"The Wild Wind" 9-19-59 (Bull Ward), "The Return of Widow Brown" 4-22-61 (Chuck Beloyne);

Death Valley Days—"The Scalpel and the Gun" 11-17-59 (Dave Madden), "The Last Shot" 12-12-62 (Barney Sullivan); *Laramie*—"The Pass" 12-29-59 (Ben Sears), "The Dispossessed" 2-19-63 (Prentice); *Hotel De Paree*—"Bounty for Sundance" 4-29-60 (Owen); *Man from Blackhawk*—"In His Steps" 5-20-60 (Speed); *Two Faces West*—"The Stilled Gun" 3-20-61 (Buchanan); *Gunsmoke*—"The Gallows" 3-3-62 (Gamer), "The Trappers" 11-3-62 (Tug Marsh); *The Virginian*—"Big Day, Great Day" 10-24-62.

Shannon, William (1935-7/3/81). Films: "Blue" 1968 (Police Chief); "Buck and the Preacher" 1972 (Tom). ¶TV: *The High Chaparral*—"Mark of the Turtle" 12-10-67 (Sully), "A Fella Named Kilroy" 3-7-69 (Dan); *Bonanza*—"El Jefe" 11-15-70 (Brady), "The Grand Swing" 9-19-71 (Charlie Trapp); *The Cowboys*—2-13-74 (Dan Sanders).

Sharif, Omar (1932-). Films: "MacKenna's Gold" 1969 (Colorado).

Sharkey, Billy Ray. Films: "Proud Men" TVM-1987. ¶TV: *Paradise*—"The Women" 1-25-91 (Miller).

Sharkey, Tom "Sailor" (1873-4/17/53). Films: "The Range Terror" 1925 (Burke); "Fighting Jack" 1926 (Pedro Sanchez).

Sharman, Della. Films: "Five Guns to Tombstone" 1961 (Arlene). ¶TV: *Overland Trail*—"The O'Mara's Ladies" 2-14-60 (Belle); *Whispering Smith*—"Safety Value" 6-5-61 (Carrie Middleton).

Sharp, Clint. Films: "Three Rogues" 1931 (Teamster); "Rainbow Trail" 1932 (Horseman); "Robbers' Roost" 1933 (Horseman); "Racketeers of the Range" 1939; "The Ox-Bow Incident" 1943 (Posse); "Tribute to a Badman" 1956 (Red). ¶TV: *Branded*—"Judge Not" 9-12-65 (Stage Driver); *Bonanza*—"Shining in Spain" 3-27-66 (Stage Driver), "To Bloom for Thee" 10-16-66 (Stage Driver); *Lancer*—"Julie" 10-29-68 (Driver).

Sharp, Henry (1887-1/10/64). Films: "Trial by Trigger" 1944-short.

Sharpe, Alex. Films: "Rocky Mountain" 1950 (Barnes); "Seminole" 1953 (Officer); "Red Sundown" 1956; "Young Guns of Texas" 1963 (Red); "Law of the Lawless" 1964 (Drifter); "Little House: The Last Farewell" TVM-1984 (Henchman). ¶TV: *The Cisco Kid*—"The Census Taker" 6-7-52; *Gunsmoke*—"The Man Who Would Be Marshal" 6-15-

57 (Jeff Willoughby), "Stolen Horses" 4-8-61 (Acker), "Perce" 9-30-61 (Nickels), "The Ditch" 10-27-62 (Farmer), "I Call Him Wonder" 3-23-63 (Cook), "Old York" 5-4-63 (Jack), "Deadman's Law" 1-8-68 (Rustler), "Shadler" 1-15-73 (Reno), "A Child Between" 12-24-73 (3rd Hide Cutter), "The Fourth Victim" 11-4-74 (3rd Matt); *Bat Masterson*—"Come Out Fighting" 4-7-60 (Moose Morgan); *Bonanza*—"Elizabeth, My Love" 5-27-61 (Blackner), "El Jefe" 11-15-70 (Truitt); *Cheyenne*—"The Durango Brothers" 9-24-62 (Calvin); *Branded*—"I Killed Jason McCord" 10-3-65, "Cowards Die Many Times" 4-17-66.

Sharpe, David (1911-3/30/80). Films: "Desert Justice" 1936; "Ghost Town" 1936 (Bud Ellis); "Gun Grit" 1936 (Dave); "Drums of Destiny" 1937 (Crawford's Brother); "Doomed at Sundown" 1937 (Don Williams); "Galloping Dynamite" 1937 (Wilkes); "The Idaho Kid" 1937 (Kid); "The Law Commands" 1937 (Danny); "Melody of the Plains" 1937 (Bud Langley); "Santa Fe Rides" 1937; "Where Trails Divide" 1937 (Billy Allen); "Man's Country" 1938 (Ted Crane); "Shine on Harvest Moon" 1938; "Cowboys from Texas" 1939 (Courier); "The Law Comes to Texas" 1939; "The Lone Ranger Rides Again" 1939-serial (Cave Heavy #3); "Lone Star Pioneers" 1939; "The Night Riders" 1939; "Rovin' Tumbleweeds" 1939; "Three Texas Steers" 1939 (Tony); "Wyoming Outlaw" 1939 (Newt); "Adventures of Red Ryder" 1940-serial; "Covered Wagon Trails" 1940 (Ed Cameron); "King of the Royal Mounted" 1940-serial; "Riders of Pasco Basin" 1940; "King of the Texas Rangers" 1941-serial; "Silver Stallion" 1941 (Davey); "Thunder Over the Prairie" 1941 (Clay Mandan); "King of the Mounties" 1942-serial; "Texas to Bataan" 1942 (Davey); "Trail Riders" 1942 (Davy); "The Avenging Rider" 1943; "The Haunted Ranch" 1943; "Red River Robin Hood" 1943; "Two Fisted Justice" 1943 (David); "Colorado Serenade" 1946 (Nevada); "King of the Forest Rangers" 1946-serial; "Bells of San Angelo" 1947 (Gus Ulrich); "The Wistful Widow of Wagon Gap" 1947 (Man Thrown by Widow); "The Adventures of Frank and Jesse James" 1948-serial (Seth); "Dangers of the Canadian Mounted" 1948-serial; "Susanna Pass" 1949 (Vince); "The Girl from San Lorenzo" 1950 (Blackie); "The James Brothers of Missouri" 1950-serial (Bailey); "Don Daredevil Rides

Again" 1951-serial (Clark); "Tomahawk" 1951 (Pvt. Parr); "Montana Belle" 1952 (Stunts); "Canadian Mounties vs. Atomic Invaders" 1953-serial; "The Life and Times of Judge Roy Bean" 1972 (Doctor). ¶TV: *The Cisco Kid*—"Boomerang" 1-20-51, "Chain Lightning" 3-3-51; *Wild Bill Hickok*—"Lost Indian Mine" 12-11-51; *The High Chaparral*—"The Last Hundred Miles" 1-24-69.

Sharpe, Karen (1933-). Films: "The Vanquished" 1953 (Lucy Colfax); "Man with the Gun" 1955 (Stella Atkins). ¶TV: *Death Valley Days*—"Claim-Jumpin' Jennie" 7-21-56; *Gunsmoke*—"Sweet and Sour" 3-2-57 (Rena Decker), "Dry Well" 1-11-64 (Yuma Linz); *Trackdown*—"The Young Gun" 2-7-58 (Edith Collins); *Desilu Playhouse*—"Ballad for a Badman" 1-26-59 (Amy); *Rough Riders*—"Wilderness Trace" 1-29-59 (Olivia); *Yancy Derringer*—"A Game of Chance" 2-5-59 (Patricia Lee); *The Texan*—"Private Account" 4-6-59 (Jessie Martin); *Johnny Ringo*—Regular 1959-60 (Laura Thomas); *Overland Trail*—"All the O'Mara's Horses" 3-13-60 (Kathy); *Bonanza*—"The Ape" 12-17-60 (Shari); *Stagecoach West*—"Never Walk Alone" 4-18-61 (Ruby Walker); *Laramie*—"Handful of Fire" 12-5-61 (Madge); *Rawhide*—"Gold Fever" 5-4-62 (Jessica Brewer), "Incident of the Black Ace" 4-12-63 (Zia Tzgorni); *The Dakotas*—"Crisis at High Banjo" 2-11-63 (Angela Manning); *Wild Wild West*—"The Night of the Flaming Ghost" 2-4-66 (Barbara Bosley), "The Night of the Ready-Made Corpse" 11-25-66 (Rose Murphy).

Sharpe, Lester (1895-11/30/62). Films: "Rose of the Rancho" 1936 (Bystander in Saloon); "The Gallant Legion" 1948 (Matt Kirby).

Shatner, William (1931-). Films: "The Outrage" 1964 (Preacher); "White Comanche" 1967-Ital./Span./U.S. (Johnny Moon/Garvin); "Pioneer Woman" TVM-1973 (John Sergeant); "The Barbary Coast" TVM-1975 (Jeff Cable); "Testimony of Two Men" TVM-1977 (Adrian Ferrier). ¶TV: *The Outlaws*—"Starfall" 11-24-60 & 12-1-60 (Wayne Gorham); *The Dick Powell Show*—"Colossus" 3-12-63 (Eric Tegman); *The Virginian*—"The Claim" 10-6-65 (Luke Milford), "Black Jade" 12-31-69 (Henry Swann); *The Big Valley*—"A Time to Kill" 1-19-66 (Brett Schuyler); *Gunsmoke*—"Quaker Girl" 12-10-66 (Fred Batman); *Kung Fu*—"A Small Beheading" 9-21-74 (Captain Brandywine Gage); *Barbary*

Coast—Regular 1975-76 (Jeff Cable); *The Oregon Trail*—"The Scarlet Ribbon" 1977; *How the West Was Won*—Episode Four 3-5-78 (Captain Harrison), Episode Five 3-12-78 (Captain Harrison).

Shaughnessy, Mickey (1920-7/23/85). Films: "Last of the Comanches" 1952 (Rusty Potter); "Gunman's Walk" 1958 (Will Motely); "The Sheepman" 1958 (Jumbo McCall); "The Hangman" 1959 (Al Cruse); "North to Alaska" 1960 (Peter Boggs); "How the West Was Won" 1962 (Deputy Marshal). ¶TV: *Maverick*—"Mr. Muldoon's Partner" 4-15-62 (Mr. Muldoon); *The Virginian*—"Big Day, Great Day" 10-24-62 (Peter Muldoon); *Laredo*—"Pride of the Rangers" 12-16-65 (Monahan); *The Legend of Jesse James*—"South Wind" 2-14-66 (Ab Truxton); *Alias Smith and Jones*—"The Day They Hanged Kid Curry" 9-16-71 (Deputy Hollis).

Shaver, Helen (1951-). Films: "Harry Tracy—Desperado" 1982 (Catherine Tuttle).

Shaw, Al (1891-7/7/57). Films: "Danger Ahead" 1940 (Yergerson); "Skipalong Rosenbloom" 1951.

Shaw, Brinsley. Films: "The Boss of the Katy Mine" 1912; "Broncho Billy and the Indian Maid" 1912; "Broncho Billy and the Schoolmarm's Kid" 1912; "Broncho Billy's Gratitude" 1912; "Broncho Billy's Pal" 1912; "Broncho Billy's Promise" 1912; "The Dead Man's Claim" 1912; "An Indian's Friendship" 1912; "Broncho Billy's Last Deed" 1913; "Across the Rio Grande" 1913; "Broncho Billy's Love Affair" 1915; "Travelin' On" 1922 (Hi Morton); "The Last of the Duanes" 1924 (Cal Bain); "Bucking the Truth" 1926 (Coarse Gold Charlie).

Shaw, Buddy (1906-8/29/76). Films: "Riders of the North" 1931 (Tom); "Dallas" 1950 (Prisoner). ¶TV: *Maverick*—"Stage West" 10-27-57 (Dave Taylor).

Shaw, C. Montague (1882-2/6/68). Films: "The Set-Up" 1926 (Cliff Barton); "The Water Hole" 1928 (Mr. Endicott); "Morgan's Last Raid" 1929 (Gen. Rogers); "Riders of the Whistling Skull" 1937 (Faxon); "Zorro's Fighting Legion" 1939-serial (Pablo/Don del Oro); "The Gay Caballero" 1940 (George Wetherby).

Shaw, Janet. Films: "Arizona Trail" 1943 (Martha Brooks); "Bad Men of Thunder Gap" 1943; "The Scarlet Horseman" 1946-serial (Elise Halliday).

Shaw, Peggy. Films: "The Grail"

1923 (Dora Bledsoe); "The Plunderer" 1924 (Joan Presbey); "Hoof Marks" 1927 (Marie Hudson); "The Ballyhoo Buster" 1928 (Molly Burnett); "The Little Buckaroo" 1928 (Ann Crawford).

Shaw, Reta (1913-1/8/82). TV: *Annie Get Your Gun* 11-27-57 (Dolly Tate); *Wagon Train*—"The Richard Bloodgood Story" 11-29-64 (Tenney).

Shaw, Robert (1927-8/28/78). Films: "Custer of the West" 1967-U.S./Span. (Gen. George Custer); "A Town Called Hell" 1971-Span./Brit. (Town Priest).

Shaw, Stan (1952-). TV: *The Buffalo Soldiers*—Pilot 5-26-79 (Sgt. Joshua Haywood).

Shaw, Victoria (1935-8/17/88). Films: "Alvarez Kelly" 1966 (Charity Warwick); "Westworld" 1973 (Medieval Queen). ¶TV: *Walt Disney Presents*—"Gallegher" 1965-67 (Katherine Van Raalte); *Cimarron Strip*—"Knife in the Darkness" 1-25-68; *Death Valley Days*—"The Duke of Tombstone" 1-10-70.

Shaw, William. TV: *Have Gun Will Travel*—"The Taffeta Mayor" 1-10-59, "The Sons of Aaron Murdock" 5-9-59; *Maverick*—"Full House" 10-25-59 (Jesse James).

Shawhan, Paul. Films: "The Fourth Horseman" 1933 (Billy the Kid).

Shawlee, Joan (Joan Fulton) (1929-3/22/87). Films: "Frontier Gal" 1945 (Hostess); "The Michigan Kid" 1947 (Soubrette); "The Vigilantes Return" 1947 (Ben's Girl); "Something for a Lonely Man" TVM-1968; "One More Train to Rob" 1971 (Big Nellie). ¶TV: *Maverick*—"Stampede" 11-17-57 (Madame Pompoy); *Zorro*—"Death Stacks the Deck" 2-13-58 (Barmaid); *The Rifleman*—"The Lonesome Ride" 5-2-61 (Marry Woodson).

Shawn, Dick (1929-4/17/87). Films: "Evil Roy Slade" TVM-1972 (Marshal Bing Bell). ¶TV: *Sheriff Who?*—Pilot 9-5-67 (Crawford Ofwhite).

Shay, John. Films: "Bad Men of the Hills" 1942 (Marshal Upjohn); "Valley of Vanishing Men" 1942-serial (Mullins); "The Last Sunset" 1961 (Bowman). ¶TV: *Jefferson Drum*—"The Bounty Man" 5-2-58 (Will Shenandoah).

Shayne, Konstantine (1888-11/15/74). TV: *The Texan*—"Private Account" 4-6-59 (Otto Hoffner).

Shayne, Robert (1910-11/29/92). Films: "Oklahoma Outlaws" 1943-short; "Wagon Wheels West" 1943-

short; "Gun to Gun" 1944-short; "Roaring Guns" 1944-short; "Trial by Trigger" 1944-short; "Frontier Days" 1945-short; "Law of the Badlands" 1945-short; "San Antonio" 1945 (Capt. Morgan); "Loaded Pistols" 1948 (Don Mason); "Law of the Barbary Coast" 1949 (Michael Lodge); "Dynamite Pass" 1950 (Wingate); "Rider from Tucson" 1950 (Avery); "The Dakota Kid" 1951 (Ace·Crandall); "Indian Uprising" 1951 (Maj. Nathan Stark); "Marshal of Cedar Rock" 1953 (Paul Jackson). ¶TV: *Wild Bill Hickok*—"The Silver Mine Protection Story" 7-24-51; *The Lone Ranger*—"Black Gold" 4-9-53, "Colorado Gold" 12-9-54; *26 Men*—"The Hellion" 1-20-59, "Death in the Dragoons" 2-17-59; *Tombstone Territory*—"Payroll to Tombstone" 3-27-59 (Capt. Cass Emerson); *Frontier Doctor*—"Gringo Pete" 5-2-59.

Shayne, Tamara (1903-10/23/83). Films: "Northwest Outpost" 1947 (Olga, Natalia's Maid); "Pirates of Monterey" 1947 (Filomena).

Shea, Christopher. Films: "Firecreek" 1968 (Franklin); "Smith" 1969 (Albie Smith). ¶TV: *Shane*—Regular 1966 (Joey Starrett); *Bonanza*—"The Trackers" 1-7-68; *Here Come the Brides*—"The Deadly Trade" 4-16-69.

Shea, Eric (1960-). Films: "The Castaway Cowboy" 1974 (Booton MacAvoy). ¶TV: *Gunsmoke*—"Stranger in Town" 11-20-67 (Billy Madison), "The Money Store" 12-30-68 (Mike Jarvis), "The Intruders" 3-3-69 (Timmy); *Here Come the Brides*—"And Jason Makes Five" 10-9-68 (Thorn).

Shea, Gloria. Films: "The Dude Bandit" 1933 (Betty Mason); "A Demon for Trouble" 1934 (Lita Morton); "The Fiddlin' Buckaroo" 1934 (Ann Harriman); "Smoking Guns" 1934 (Alice Adams).

Shea, Michael (1952-). Films: "Welcome to Hard Times" 1967 (Jimmy Fee); "Ride a Northbound Horse" 1969. ¶TV: *The Virginian*—"Bitter Harvest" 3-15-67 (Jamie Adams); *Wild Wild West*—"The Night of the Falcon" 11-10-67 (Boy).

Shea, William (1862-11/5/18). Films: "Some Duel" 1915.

Shear, Pearl (1918-). TV: *Daniel Boone*—"Daughter of the Devil" 4-15-65 (Mrs. Bertrand).

Shearer, Norma (1900-6/12/83). Films: "Channing of the Northwest" 1922 (Jes Driscoll); "The Man Who Paid" 1922 (Jeanne Thornton).

Shearin, John. Films: "Bret Maverick" TVM-1981 (Sheriff Mitch-ell Dows). ¶TV: *Bret Maverick*—Regular 1981-82 (Sheriff Michael Dowd).

Sheehan, John (1885-2/15/52). Films: "Fair Warning" 1931 (Kelduff); "The Three Godfathers" 1936 (Ed Barrow); "Wolf Call" 1939 (Grogan); "The Outlaw" 1943 (Salesman); "The Doolins of Oklahoma" 1949 (Dunn); "Stage to Tucson" 1950 (Bartender).

Sheen, Charlie (1965-). Films: "Young Guns" 1988 (Dick Brewer).

Sheen, Martin (1940-). Films: "The Legend of Earl Durand" 1974; "Eagle's Wing" 1979-Brit./Span. (Pike). ¶TV: *Lancer*—"The Knot" 3-18-69 (Andy Blake).

Sheffield, Reginald (1901-12/8/57). Films: "Partners of the Trail" 1931 (John Durant); "Hudson Bay" 1941 (Clerk); "Secret of Treasure Mountain" 1956 (Edward Lancaster). ¶TV: *Jim Bowie*—"The Bounty Hunter" 5-17-57 (Patty McGurk).

Sheiner, David (1928-). Films: "Scalplock" TVM-1966 (Frontiersman); "A Man Called Gannon" 1969 (Sheriff Polaski); "The Alamo: 13 Days to Glory" TVM-1987 (Luis). ¶TV: *A Man Called Shenandoah*—"The Caller" 10-11-65; *The Big Valley*—"Into the Widow's Web" 3-23-66 (Phil Archer), "The Iron Box" 11-28-66 (Captain Jonathon Rizely), "Night of the Executioners" 12-11-67 (Gabe Simmons); *Iron Horse*—"Joy Unconfined" 9-12-66 (the Frontiersman), "The Golden Web" 3-27-67 (Brady); *The Virginian*—"No War for the Warrior" 2-18-70 (Cully); *Gunsmoke*—"Waste" 9-27-71 & 10-4-71 (Preacher); *Bonanza*—"The Rattlesnake Brigade" 12-5-71 (Fancher).

Sheldon, Barbara. Films: "The Lucky Texan" 1934 (Betty Benson).

Sheldon, Gene (1909-5/1/82). TV: *Zorro*—Regular 1957-59 (Bernardo).

Sheldon, Jerry (1901-4/11/62). Films: "Riders of the Sage" 1939 (Herb); "Forbidden Trails" 1941 (Sam); "The Gunman from Bodie" 1941; "Love Me Tender" 1956 (Conductor).

Sheldon, Julie. Films: "Straight Shooter" 1939 (Margaret Martin).

Sheldon, Kathryn (1879-12/25/75). Films: "Ramona" 1936 (Mrs. Scroggs); "Wells Fargo" 1937 (Wife of Captain); "I'm from the City" 1938 (Grandma); "Sunset Trail" 1938 (Abigail Snodgrass); "Frontier Marshal" 1939 (Mrs. Garvey); "Out West with the Peppers" 1940 (Abbie); "Rockin' Through the Rockies" 1940-short (Nell); "Shooting High" 1940

(Woman in Hotel); "Arizona Bound" 1941; "Return of the Texan" 1952 (Housekeeper).

Shelly, Norman (1903-8/22/80). TV: *Have Gun Will Travel*—"The Day of the Bad Men" 1-9-60 (Heath).

Shelton, · Abbagail (1936-). Films: "Mail Order Bride" 1964 (Young Old Maid). ¶TV: *Johnny Ringo*—"Coffin Sam" 6-16-60 (Ivadeen); *Bonanza*—"Broken Ballad" 10-29-61 (Sally), "A Good Night's Rest" 4-11-65 (Lucy).

Shelton, Don (1912-6/19/76). Films: "The Command" 1953 (Maj. Gibbs); "Bullwhip" 1958 (Hotel Keeper).

Shelton, Laura. TV: *Wagon Train*—"The Luke Grant Story" 6-1-60 (Chris); *Death Valley Days*—"The Red Petticoat" 3-29-61, "There Was Another Dalton Brother" 6-6-65 (Emmy Johnson).

Shelton, Maria. Films: "The Phantom Rider" 1936-serial (Mary Grayson); "Bells of Capistrano" 1942 (Jackie Laval).

Shemayme, Steve. Films: "Tell Them Willie Boy Is Here" 1969 (Johnny Hyde). ¶TV: *Bonanza*—"Shadow of a Hero" 2-21-71 (Thomas Greybuck).

Shenar, Paul (1936-10/11/89). TV: *Young Dan'l Boone*—"The Pirate" 9-19-77 (Hammond).

Shepard, Elaine. Films: "Fighting Texan" 1937 (Judy Walton); "Law of the Ranger" 1937 (Evelyn Polk).

Shepard, Iva (1886-1/26/73). Films: "The Convert of San Clemente" 1911; "Little Injin" 1911; "The Rival Stage Lines" 1911.

Shepard, Jan. TV: *Death Vally Days*—"Yaller" 1-27-54; *Tales of the Texas Rangers*—"Ransom Flight" 8-27-55 (Jeanie Warren); *Wyatt Earp*—"Marshal Earp Plays Cupid" 1-3-56 (Mamie); *Sergeant Preston of the Yukon*—"Eye of Evil" 11-8-56 (LouAnne); *Circus Boy*—"Big Top Angel" 1-27-57 (Estelle); *Rawhide*—"Incident with an Executioner" 1-23-59 (Mary Doan), "Incident at Sulphur Creek" 3-11-60 (Clara Lacey), "Incident at the Top of the World" 1-27-61 (Ann Powell); *Trackdown*—"Terror" 2-4-59 (Emily); *The Adventures of Rin Tin Tin*—"Apache Stampede" 3-20-59 (Ella Clarkson); *Wichita Town*—"Man on the Hill" 11-4-59 (Clara Bennett); *Wanted—Dead or Alive*—"Mental Lapse" 1-2-60 (Lilith Preston); *Gunsmoke*—"Tall Trapper" 1-21-61 (Tassie), "Old Faces" 3-18-61 (Tilda Cook), "Friend" 1-25-64 (Marge), "Noose of Gold" 3-4-67

(Edna Farron); *Bat Masterson*—"Bull-whacker's Bounty" 2-16-61 (Jody Reese); *Gunslinger*—"Rampage" 3-16-61 (Constance Cameron Jenks); *Stagecoach West*—"The Raider" 5-9-61 (Emily Prince); *Laramie*—"Badge of the Outsider" 5-23-61 (Cindy), "The Jailbreakers" 12-19-61 (Gina), "Bad Blood" 12-4-62; *Lawman*—"Change of Venue" 2-11-62 (Madelyn Chae); *The Virginian*—"The Brothers" 9-15-65 (Sergeant Cohane), "Harvest of Strangers" 2-16-66 (Connie Burns), "Long Journey Home" 12-14-66 (Jessica Boyer), "Stopover" 1-8-69 (Laura Cooper), "The Runaway Boy" 10-22-69 (Claire); *Bonanza*—"The Code" 2-13-66 (Sally); *A Man Called Shenandoah*—"Plunder" 3-7-66 (Ann Winters); *The Road West*—"No Sanctuary" 2-6-67 (Ellen Brewster); *The High Chaparral*—"Sudden Country" 11-5-67 (Meg Hallock), "Our Lady of Guadalupe" 12-20-68 (Mavis).

Shepard, Patty. Films: "Twenty Paces to Death" 1970-Ital./Span. (Deborah); "The Legend of Frenchie King" 1971-Fr./Ital./Span./Brit. (Petite Pluie); "The Man Called Noon" 1973-Brit./Span./Ital. (Peg).

Shepard, Sam (1943-). Films: "The Good Old Boys" TVM-1995 (Snort Yarnell).

Shepodd, Jon. Films: "The Return of Jack Slade" 1955 (Johnny Turner); "Dragoon Wells Massacre" 1957 (Tom); "Oregon Passage" 1958 (Lt. Baird Dobson). ¶TV: *Gunsmoke*—"Obie Tater" 10-15-55 (Mitch).

Sheppard, Jim (1937-8/18/77). Films: "The Wild and the Innocent" 1959 (Henchman); "Hour of the Gun" 1967 (Tom McLowery). ¶TV: *The Big Valley*—"Hide the Children" 12-19-66 (2nd Horse Thief); *Hondo*—"Hondo and the Apache Trail" 12-22-67 (Indian); *Gunsmoke*—"Chato" 9-14-70 (Case).

Sheppard, John. see Strudwick, Sheppard

Sheppard, W. Morgan. Films: "Gunsmoke: Return to Dodge" TVM-1987 (Digger).

Sherayko, Peter. Films: "Tombstone" 1993 (Texas Jack Vermillion).

Sheridan, Ann (Clara Lou Sheridan) (1915-1/21/67). Films: "The Bandit's Son" 1927 (Helen Todd); "Galloping Thunder" 1927 (Judith Lamb); "Wagon Wheels" 1934; "Home on the Range" 1935 (Elsie Brownly); "Red Blood of Courage" 1935 (Beth Henry); "Rocky Mountain Mystery" 1935 (Rita Ballard); "Cowboy from Brooklyn" 1938

(Maxine Chadwick); "Dodge City" 1939 (Ruby Gilman); "Silver River" 1948 (Georgia Moore); "Take Me to Town" 1953 (Vermilion O'Toole). ¶TV: *Wagon Train*—"The Mavis Grant Story" 10-24-62 (Mavis Grant); *Pistols 'n' Petticoats*—Regular 1966-67 (Henrietta Hanks).

Sheridan, Daniel M. (1916-6/29/63). Films: "California Firebrand" 1948 (Gunsmoke Lowry); "Horsemen of the Sierras" 1950 (Morgan Webster); "Bullwhip" 1958 (Podo); "Cole Younger, Gunfighter" 1958 (Phelps); "Seven Guns to Mesa" 1958 (Simmons); "Day of the Outlaw" 1959 (Lewis); "King of the Wild Stallions" 1959 (Woody); "Ten Who Dared" 1960 (Jack Sumner); "Lonely Are the Brave" 1962 (Deputy Glynn). ¶TV: *Maverick*—"Ghost Riders" 10-13-57 (Sideburns), "Black Fire" 3-16-58 (Luther), "High Card Hangs" 10-19-58 (Bald Bill King), "Duel at Sundown" 2-1-59 (Doc Baxter); *Gunsmoke*—"Mavis McCloud" 10-26-57 (Stage Driver), "Robber and Bridegroom" 12-13-58 (Hank), "The Constable" 5-30-59 (Dobie); *Tombstone Territory*—"Ride Out at Noon" 10-30-57; *Rough Riders*—"The Murderous Sutton Gang" 10-2-58 (Mr. Buckley); *Jefferson Drum*—"Stagecoach Episode" 10-10-58 (Leo); *The Texan*—"The First Notch" 10-20-58 (McBurney); *Tales of Wells Fargo*—"The Deserter" 11-24-58 (Sgt. Bergman), "The Train Robbery" 10-12-59 (Cy), "Incident at Crossbow" 2-3-62 (Sam Storey); *Bat Masterson*—"Election Day" 1-14-59 (Joe Rankin); *The Rifleman*—"The Trade" 3-10-59; *Colt .45*—"The Magic Box" 4-19-59 (Babcock); *Cheyenne*—"Blind Spot" 9-21-59 (Martin); *Lawman*—"Lily" 10-4-59 (Barney Tate); "Yawkey" 10-23-60 (Jake); *The Rebel*—"Gun City" 12-27-59 (Ashby), "Vindication" 12-4-60 (Jess Hosmer); *The Law of the Plainsman*—"The Comet" 1-21-60; *Overland Trail*—"All the O'Mara's Horses" 3-13-60 (Long Tom); *Sugarfoot*—"The Captive Locomotive" 6-7-60 (Marshal Garrison); *Rawhide*—"Incident of the Captive" 12-16-60 (Gottfried); *Wyatt Earp*—"Billy Buckett, Incorporated" 1-3-61 (Jack Morrow); *Bonanza*—"The Countess" 11-19-61 (Kelly); *The Virginian*—"Big Day, Great Day" 10-24-62, "Run Away Home" 4-24-63, "The Final Hour" 5-1-63.

Sheridan, Frank (1869-11/24/43). Films: "Nevada" 1935 (Tom Blaine); "The Revenge Rider" 1935 (Jed Harmon); "Whispering Smith Speaks" 1935 (Gordon Harrington, Sr.).

Sheridan, Gail. Films: "Hopalong Cassidy Returns" 1936 (Mary Saunders); "The Plainsman" 1936; "Hills of Old Wyoming" 1937 (Alice Hutchins).

Sheridan, James. see Tansey, Sherry.

Sheridan, Margaret (1926-82). TV: *Wagon Train*—"The Kate Crawley Story" 1-27-64.

Sheridan, Nicollette (1963-). TV: *Paradise*—"Twenty-Four Hours" 5-3-91 (Lilly).

Sherman, Allan (1924-11/20/73). TV: *The Loner*—"The Sheriff of Fetterman's Crossing" 11-13-65 (Walter Peterson Tetley).

Sherman, Bobby (1945-). TV: *Here Comes the Brides*—Regular 1968-70 (Jeremy Bolt).

Sherman, Evelyn (1882-4/19/74). Films: "Suzanna" 1922 (Dona Isabella); "Don Dare Devil" 1925 (Senora Berengo); "The Border Whirlwind" 1926 (Duenna); "Song of the Cabellero" 1930 (Dona Louisa); "The California Trail" 1933 (Dona Marco).

Sherman, Fred (1905-5/20/69). Films: "Valley of Fire" 1951 (Panhandle Jones); "Stranger at My Door" 1956; "Gun Battle at Monterey" 1957; "The Tall T" 1957 (Hank Parker); "War Drums" 1957 (Dr. Gordon); "Westbound" 1959 (Christy). ¶TV: *Wild Bill Hickok*—"Wrestling Story" 4-8-52, "Marvins' Mix-Up" 5-19-53; *Hopalong Cassidy*—"Death by Proxy" 6-14-52; *The Roy Rogers Show*—"Bad Company" 12-27-53 (Daniel Waller), "The Land Swindle" 3-14-54 (Jim Wilson), "The Last of the Larrabee Kid" 10-17-54, "Fishing for Fingerprints" 10-28-56, "Mountain Pirates" 11-4-56; *Sergeant Preston of the Yukon*—"Last Mail from Last Chance" 5-31-56 (Doc Merriam); *Zane Grey Theater*—"The Necessary Breed" 2-15-57 (Bartender); *Jim Bowie*—"German George" 2-22-57 (George Freiwald); *Maverick*—"The War of the Silver Kings" 9-22-57 (John Stoller), "A Bullet for the Teacher" 10-30-60 (Clerk); *Wyatt Earp*—"One-Man Army" 1-7-58 (Callum), "The Imitation Jesse James" 2-4-58 (Sloan); *Tales of Wells Fargo*—"Special Delivery" 3-31-58 (Cummings); *Wichita Town*—"The Devil's Choice" 12-23-59 (Conductor); *Man from Blackhawk*—"The Legacy" 12-25-59 (Josh Temple); *The Deputy*—"The Orphans" 12-26-59; *Wagon Train*—"The Ruth Marshall Story" 12-30-59, "The Candy O'Hara Story" 12-7-60, "The Jud

Steele Story" 5-2-62 (Attendant); *Rawhide*—"Incident of the Devil and His Due" 1-22-60 (Dooley); *Wanted—Dead or Alive*—"A House Divided" 2-20-60; *Lawman*—"Mark of Cain" 3-26-61 (Streeter); *The Tall Man*—"Ladies of the Town" 5-20-61 (Mr. Tatum); *The Rifleman*—"The Man from Salinas" 2-12-62.

Sherman, Orville (-1984). Films: "Westworld" 1973 (Supervisor). ¶TV: *Buckskin*—"Lament for Durango" 8-14-58 (Mr. Feeney), "The Ghost of Balaclava" 9-4-58 (Mr. Feeney), "Miss Pringle" 10-16-58 (Mr. Feeney), "The Bullnappers" 11-6-58 (Mr. Feeney), "The Better Mousetrap" 5-25-59 (Mr. Feeney); *Trackdown*—"The Avenger" 10-31-58 (Jed Garth); *Wagon Train*—"The Doctor Willoughby Story" 11-5-58 (Hank Simmons), "The Larry Hanify Story" 1-27-60 (Joe Hanify), "The Maggie Hamilton Story" 4-6-60 (Slim), "The Albert Farnsworth Story" 10-12-60, "The Eleanor Culhane Story" 5-17-61 (Bartender), "The Daniel Clay Story" 2-21-62 (Joe Martin); *26 Men*—"Ranger Without a Badge" 1-27-59; *Wyatt Earp*—"The Fugitive" 11-17-59, "Behan's Double Game" 3-29-60 (Cavanaugh); *Wanted—Dead or Alive*—"Jason" 1-30-60, "Journey for Josh" 10-5-60; *Rawhide*—"Incident of the Challenge" 10-14-60 (Charlie Casey); *Cheyenne*—"The Return of Mr. Grimm" 2-13-61 (Robert Garrison); *Bonanza*—"The Rival" 4-15-61, "The Countess" 11-19-61, "Three Brides for Hoss" 2-20-66 (Matt); *Gunsmoke*—"The Gallows" 3-3-62 (Sheriff), "The Far Places" 4-6-63 (Wib), "Easy Come" 10-26-63 (Wib Smith), "No Hands" 2-8-64 (Wib Smith), "Owney Tupper Had a Daughter" 4-4-64 (Wib Smith), "Snap Decision" 9-17-66 (Preacher); *The Virginian*—"The Big Deal" 10-10-62 (Doctor); *Daniel Boone*—"Daughter of the Devil" 4-15-65 (Will Camfield), "Empire of the Lost" 9-16-65 (Tupper), 9-23-65 (Tupper), "My Name Is Rawls" 10-7-65 (Tupper), "The Fifth Man" 2-17-66 (Tupper), "The Scalp Hunter" 3-17-66 (Tupper), "Grizzly" 10-6-66 (Tupper); *Alias Smith and Jones*—"The McCreedy Bush" 1-21-71 (Hank).

Sherman, Vincent. Films: "Speed Wings" 1934 (Mickey Coin).

Sherry, J. Barney (1872-2/23/44). Films: "The Great Train Robbery" 1903; "The Luck of Roaring Camp" 1910; "A Western Romance" 1910; "The Chief's Daughter" 1911; "Evangeline" 1911; "The Indian Vestal" 1911; "John Oakhurst—Gambler" 1911; "Little Dove's Romance" 1911; "The Crisis" 1912; "Custer's Last Fight" 1912; "For the Honor of the 7th" 1912; "His Punishment" 1912; "The Indian Massacre" 1912; "The Sheriff of Stony Butte" 1912; "The Sheriff's Adopted Child" 1912; "A Shadow of the Past" 1913; "The Bargain" 1914 (Phil Brent); "The Passing of Two-Gun Hicks" 1914; "The Words of His People" 1914; "The Operator at Big Sandy" 1915; "A Gun Fightin' Gentleman" 1919 (John Merritt); "A Man's Fight" 1919 (David Carr); "This Hero Stuff" 1919 (Jackson J. Joseph); "Galloping Hoofs" 1924-serial.

Sherwood, Clarence L. (1884-1/15/41). Films: "The Loaded Door" 1922 (Fatty); "Blood and Steel" 1925 (the Cook); "The Meddler" 1925 (Sheriff); "Stairs of Sand" 1929 (Waiter); "Home on the Range" 1935 (Shorty); "Wanderer of the Wasteland" 1935 (2nd Bartender); "Range Defenders" 1937; "Wells Fargo" 1937 (Miner); "Twenty Mule Team" 1940 (Barfly).

Sherwood, George. Films: "The Web of the Law" 1923 (Wolf Blake); "Overland Stage Raiders" 1938 (Clanton); "Code of the Fearless" 1939 (Jim Davis); "Wyoming Wildcat" 1941; "Stardust on the Sage" 1942; "The Man from Oklahoma" 1945 (Slade); "Salome, Where She Danced" 1945 (Bartender); "Conquest of Cheyenne" 1946; "Buffalo Bill Rides Again" 1947 (Mr. Smith); "Santa Fe" 1951; "The Lusty Men" 1952 (Vet). ¶TV: *Wild Bill Hickok*—"Medicine Show" 12-25-51.

Sherwood, Madeleine (1922-). TV: *The Outcasts*—"The Candidates" 1-27-69 (Suellen); *Bonanza*—"For a Young Lady" 12-27-70 (Vella Owens).

Sherwood, Robert. Films: "Little Big Horn" 1951 (Pvt. David Mason); "Trail Guide" 1952 (Kenny).

Sherwood, Yorke (1873-9/27/58). Films: "The Man in the Saddle" 1926 (Banker).

Shield, Bob. TV: *Tombstone Territory*—"Mexican Bandito" 1-29-58 (Deputy), "Postmarked for Death" 2-12-58 (Jim); *Bat Masterson*—"One Bullet from Broken Bow" 1-21-59 (Capt. Dayton).

Shields, Arthur (1896-4/27/70). Films: "Drums Along the Mohawk" 1939 (Father Rosenkranz); "She Wore a Yellow Ribbon" 1949 (Dr. O'Laughlin); "Apache Drums" 1951 (Rev. Griffin); "River of No Return" 1954 (the Minister); "King and Four Queens" 1956 (Padre); "For the Love of Mike" 1960 (Father Walsh). ¶TV: *Bat Masterson*—"The Conspiracy" 6-17-59 & 6-24-59 (John Surratt); *Bonanza*—"The Stranger" 2-27-60; *Rawhide*—"Incident of the Dust Flower" 3-4-60 (Sam Cartwright); *Wagon Train*—"The Amos Gibbon Story" 4-20-60 (Judge Tremayne); *Maverick*—"The Bold Fenian Men" 12-18-60 (Terence Fogarty); *Death Valley Days*—"Loophole" 4-5-61 (Jebal McSween).

Shields, Brooke (1965-). Films: "Wanda Nevada" 1979 (Wanda Nevada).

Shields, Robert. Films: "The Wild Wild West Revisited" TVM-1979 (Alan).

Shigeta, James (1933-). Films: "Walk Like a Dragon" 1960 (Cheng Lu); "Death Walks in Laredo" 1966-Ital./Span. (Lester). ¶TV: *Kung Fu*—"The Garments of Rage" 11-8-74 (Master Kwan Li), "Forbidden Kingdom" 1-18-75 (Lin Pei).

Shilling, Marion. Films: "Sundown Trail" 1931 (Dottie Beals); "A Man's Land" 1932 (Peggy Turner); "Fighting to Live" 1934 (Mary Carson); "The Red Rider" 1934-serial (Marie Maxwell); "Thunder Over Texas" 1934 (Helen Mason); "The Westerner" 1934 (Juanita Barnes); "Blazing Guns" 1935 (Betty Lou Rickard); "Gun Play" 1935 (Meg Holt); "Gunsmoke on the Guadalupe" 1935; "Rio Rattler" 1935 (Mary Adams); "Stone of Silver Creek" 1935 (Martha Mason); "Cavalcade of the West" 1936 (Mary Chrisman); "Gun Smoke" 1936 (Jean Culverson); "Romance Rides the Range" 1936 (Carol Morland); "The Idaho Kid" 1937 (Ruth Endicott).

Shimada, Teru (1905-). TV: *Laramie*—"Dragon at the Door" 9-26-61 (Kami); *Have Gun Will Travel*—"Coming of the Tiger" 4-14-62 (Takura).

Shimoda, Yuki (1922-5/21/81). TV: *The Big Valley*—"Night of the Wolf" 12-1-65 (Po); *Kung Fu*—"Sun and Cloud Shadow" 2-22-73 (Ben Tai), "The Chalice" 10-11-73 (1st Guard), "Arrogant Dragons" 3-14-74 (Bandit), "A Small Beheading" 9-21-74 (Injured Man), "Besieged: Death on Cold Mountain" 11-15-74 (Shun Low), "Besieged: Cannon at the Gate" 11-22-74 (Shun Low).

Shipman, Gwynne. Films: "Battle of Greed" 1934 (Linda Avery); "Trail Dust" 1936 (Beth Clark).

Shipman, Helen. Films: "The Phantom Rider" 1936-serial (Lizzie).

Shipman, Nell (1892-1/23/70). Films: "Baree, Son of Kazan" 1918 (Nepeese); "Cavanaugh of the Forest Rangers" 1918 (Virginia Wetherford); "The Home Trail" 1918 (Clara); "The Trials of Texas Thompson" 1919.

Shipman, Nina. Films: "The Oregon Trail" 1959 (Prudence Cooper). ¶TV: *Wyatt Earp*—"The Too Perfect Crime" 12-6-60 (Leone Simpson); *Lawman*—"The Squatters" 1-29-61 (Molly Prentice); *Maverick*—"The Forbidden City" 3-26-61 (Joanne Moss); *Tales of Wells Fargo*—"Bitter Vengeance" 6-12-61 (Jean Martin), "Hometown Doctor" 2-17-62 (Gloria Wilson); *Temple Houston*—"The Siege at Thayer's Bluff" 11-7-63 (Mary Bannerman); *The Outlaws*—"Walk Tall" 11-16-61 (Theo McClure); *Bronco*—"Trail of Hatred" 2-5-62 (Cathy Foreman); *Bonanza*—"The Mountain Girl" 5-13-62 (Trudy Harker); *Rawhide*—"Incident of the Portrait" 10-5-62 (Marion Curtis), "Incident of the Comanchero" 3-22-63 (Sister Teresa), "Incident of the Rawhiders" 11-14-63 (Valley Rose); *Daniel Boone*—"The Sisters O'Hannrahan" 12-3-64 (Molly O'Hannrahan); *A Man Called Shenandoah*—"Incident at Dry Creek" 11-15-65; *Iron Horse*—"Pride at the Bottom of the Barrel" 10-10-66 (Phyllis Anderson); *The Guns of Will Sonnett*—"A Fool and His Money" 3-8-68 (Peg); *Lancer*—"The Lorelei" 1-27-70 (Millie Barton).

Shirley, Anne. see O'Day, Dawn.

Shirley, Arthur (1853-8/22/25). Films: "Branding Broadway" 1918 (Larry Harrington); "Roped" 1919 (Ferdie Van Duzen).

Shirley, Tom (1900-1/24/62). Films: "Lightning Bill" 1926 (Lionel Jay Murphy); "Red Hot Leather" 1926 (Ross Kane).

Shockley, Marion (-12/14/81). Films: "Near the Trail's End" 1931 (Jane Rankin).

Shockley, Sallie. TV: *The Men from Shiloh*—"Gun Quest" 10-21-70 (Nellie Cooper); *Alias Smith and Jones*—"Stagecoach Seven" 3-11-71, "What's in It for Mia?" 2-24-72 (Charlotte Austin).

Shockley, William. TV: *Paradise*—"Dangerous Cargo" 1-20-90 (Gus); *Young Riders*—"Dead Ringer" 10-6-90 (Jake Colter), "The Noble Chase" 3-9-91 (Jake Colter); *Dr. Quinn, Medicine Woman*—Regular 1993- (Hank).

Shoemaker, Ann (1891-9/18/

78). TV: *Rawhide* -"Josh" 1-15-65 (Mrs. Moyer).

Sholdar, Mickey. Films: "The Intruders" TVM-1970. ¶TV: *Wagon Train*—"The Prairie Story" 2-1-61 (Garth), "Charlie Wooster—Outlaw" 2-20-63 (Scotty); *Empire*—"The Tall Shadow" 11-20-62 (Jimmy Robbins); *Bonanza*—"Rain from Heaven" 10-6-63 (Jube Weems); *Gunsmoke*—"The Bassops" 2-22-64 (Tommy Bassop); *The Road West*—"Lone Woman" 11-7-66 (Wesley Turner).

Shooting Star (1890-6/4/66). Films: "Ride, Ranger, Ride" 1936; "Buffalo Bill Rides Again" 1947 (Young Bird); "The Cowboy and the Indians" 1949; "Laramie" 1949 (Chief Eagle); "Ticket to Tomahawk" 1950 (Crazy Dog). ¶TV: *Loretta Young Show*—"The Wise One" 3-26-56 (Chief); *Wagon Train*—"The Les Rand Story" 10-16-57.

Shore, Dinah (1917-2/24/94). Films: "Belle of the Yukon" 1944 (Lettie Candless). ¶TV: *Cimarron City*—"Cimarron Holiday" 12-20-58.

Shore, Roberta (1943-). TV: *Maverick*—"Royal Four-Flush" 9-20-59 (Judy Mason); *Wagon Train*—"The Sam Elder Story" 1-18-61 (Millie Allen); *Zane Grey Theater*—"The Long Shadow" 1-19-61 (Laurie Lawson); *Lawman*—"Owny O'Reilly, Esq." 10-15-61 (Milly Cotton); *The Virginian*—Regular 1961-65 (Betsy Garth); *Laramie*—"The Replacement" 3-27-62 (Sharon Halleck); *The Tall Man*—"The Runaway Groom" 4-28-62 (Sally).

Short, Antrim (1900-11/24/72). Films: "Where the Trail Divides" 1914 (Little How); "Fighting Cressy" 1920 (Seth Davis); "O'Malley of the Mounted" 1921 (Bud Lanier); "The Big Show" 1937.

Short, Dorothy. Films: "Brothers of the West" 1938 (Annie Wade); "Heart of Arizona" 1938 (Jacqueline Starr); "Where the Buffalo Roam" 1938 (Laddie Gray); "Wild Horse Canyon" 1938 (Jean Hall); "Code of the Cactus" 1939 (Joan); "The Singing Cowgirl" 1939 (Nora Pryde); "Frontier Crusader" 1940 (Jenny Mason); "Phantom Rancher" 1940 (Ann Markham); "Pony Post" 1940 (Alice Goodwin); "Buzzy and the Phantom Pinto" 1941; "The Lone Rider Fights Back" 1941; "Trail of the Silver Spurs" 1941 (Nancy); "Bullets for Bandits" 1942.

Short, Gertrude (1902-7/31/68). Films: "Driver of the Deadwood Coast" 1912; "The Honor of the Mounted" 1914; "The Little Angel of

Canyon Creek" 1914 (Olaf Tryggvesson); "The Cowboy and the Lady" 1915; "The Only Road" 1918 (Bianca); "Riddle Gawne" 1918 (Jane Gawne); "In Mizzoura" 1919 (Lisbeth Vernon); "Headin' West" 1922 (Potato Polly); "Code of the West" 1925 (Mollie Thurman); "In Old California" 1929; "The Three Outcasts" 1929 (June); "Park Avenue Lodger" 1937 (Margy MacLean); "Sheriff of Cimarron" 1945 (Portly Woman).

Short, Lewis W. (1875-4/26/58). Films: "Three Bad Men and a Girl" 1915; "Branding Broadway" 1918 (Dick Horn); "The Three Outcasts" 1929 (Rance Slavin); "Law of the North" 1932; "Union Pacific" 1939 (Laborer).

Short, Martin (1951-). Films: "Three Amigos" 1986 (Ned Nederlander).

Short, Robin. Films: "I Shot Jesse James" 1949 (Troubadour); "Ambush" 1950 (Lt. Storrow); "The Baron of Arizona" 1950 (Lansing); "The Return of Jesse James" 1950; "The Buckskin Lady" 1957 (Nevada); "The Halliday Brand" 1957. ¶TV: *The Lone Ranger*—"Letter of the Law" 1-4-51; *The Cisco Kid*—"Quick on the Trigger" 2-6-54; *Death Valley Days*—"A Killing in Diamonds" 11-21-55.

Show, Grant. Films: "James A. Michener's Texas" TVM-1995 (William B. Travis).

Showalter, Max. see Adams, Casey.

Shrum, Cal (and His Rhythm Rangers) (Robert Hoag, Don Weston, Rusty Cline & Art Wenzel). Films: "Rollin' Home to Texas" 1941 (Cal); "Thunder Over the Prairie" 1941; "The Rangers Take Over" 1942; "Bad Men of Thunder Gap" 1943; "Swing, Cowboy, Swing" 1944; "Trouble at Melody Mesa" 1944; "The Lost Trail" 1945.

Shubert, Eddie (1898-1/23/37). Films: "Song of the Saddle" 1936 (Jake Bannion); "Trailin' West" 1936 (Happy).

Shubert, Lynn. TV: *Gunsmoke*—"Claustrophobia" 1-25-58 (Hank); *The Adventures of Rin Tin Tin*—"Bitter Bounty" 3-14-58 (Jake Carney); *The Rebel*—"Johnny Yuma at Appomattox" 9-18-60 (Penny).

Shufford, Andy. Films: "The Big Trail" 1930 (Ohio Man's Son); "Dugan of the Badlands" 1931 (Andy); "The Great Meadow" 1931; "Headin' for Trouble" 1931 (Bobbie Courtney); "The Montana Kid" 1931 (Andy Burke); "Oklahoma Jim" 1931

(Jerry); "Rider of the Plains" 1931 (Sandy); "Ghost City" 1932 (Andy Blane); "Land of Wanted Men" 1932 (Mickey); "Law of the North" 1932 (Andy); "Mason of the Mounted" 1932 (Andy Kirby); "Texas Pioneers" 1932 (Andy Thomas).

Shull, Richard B. (1929-). Films: "Hearts of the West" 1975 (Stout Crook). ¶TV: *Young Maverick*—"Have I Got a Girl for You" 1-16-80 (Montague).

Shumway, Lee C. (1884-1/4/59). Films: "When the Range Called" 1915; "The Plow Woman" 1917 (Lt. Jack Fraser); "The Silent Sentinel" 1918; "Rustling a Bride" 1919 (Pen Walton); "Two-Gun Betty" 1919 (Jack Kennedy); "The Daredevil" 1920 (Gilroy Blake); "The Gamesters" 1920 (Marshal Andrews); "The Alarm" 1921; "The Conflict" 1921 (Mark Sloane); "The Deputy's Double Cross" 1921; "Over the Border" 1922 (Cpl. Bying); "Step on It!" 1922 (Bowman); "The Gunfighter" 1923 (Joe Benchley); "The Lone Star Ranger" 1923 (Lawson); "Snowdrift" 1923 (John Reeves); "Soft Boiled" 1923 (Road House Manager); "The Vagabond Trail" 1924 (Lord Nick); "The Bad Lands" 1925 (Capt. Blake); "The Man from Red Gulch" 1925 (Lasham); "The Texas Bearcat" 1925 (Murdock); "Whispering Canyon" 1926 (Lew Selby); "The Last Trail" 1927 (Joe Pascal); "Outlaws of Red River" 1927 (Mr. Torrence); "Son of the Golden West" 1928 (Tennessee); "The Lone Defender" 1930-serial (Amos Halkey); "The Lone Star Ranger" 1930 (Red Kane); "The Santa Fe Trail" 1930 (Slaven); "The Fighting Marshal" 1931; "Partners" 1932 (Chet Jarvis); "Rocky Rhodes" 1934 (Stark); "Branded a Coward" 1935; "Ivory-Handled Gun" 1935 (Pete); "Ghost Town" 1936 (Ed Morrell); "The Phantom Rider" 1936-serial; "Robin Hood of El Dorado" 1936 (Deputy); "Song of the Trail" 1936 (Stone); "Black Aces" 1937; "Hollywood Cowboy" 1937 (Benson); "Law of the Ranger" 1937; "Left-Handed Law" 1937; "Outlaws of the Prairie" 1937 (Capt. MacMillan); "Thunder Trail" 1937 (Miner); "Two Gun Law" 1937 (Bartender); "Wells Fargo" 1937 (Townsman); "Hollywood Roundup" 1938 (Carl Dunning); "Man from Music Mountain" 1938; "The Painted Desert" 1938 (Bart Currie); "Rawhide" 1938 (Johnson); "Frontiers of '49" 1939; "The Law Comes to Texas" 1939; "Lone Star Pioneers" 1939 (Bill Ruphy); "The Night Riders" 1939; "The Return of the Cisco Kid" 1939;

"Rovin' Tumbleweeds" 1939; "Brigham Young—Frontiersman" 1940 (Henchman); "Covered Wagon Days" 1940; "Deadwood Dick" 1940-serial (Bentley); "The Gay Caballero" 1940 (Stage Driver); "Geronimo" 1940 (Captain Williams); "Bury Me Not on the Lone Prairie" 1941; "King of the Texas Rangers" 1941-serial (Coach); "A Missouri Outlaw" 1941; "Outlaws of the Cherokee Trail" 1941; "Prairie Pioneers" 1941 (Nelson); "Two-Gun Sheriff" 1941 (Sheriff Blake); "Home in Wyomin'" 1942; "Pirates of the Prairie" 1942; "Stardust on the Sage" 1942; "Dead Man's Gulch" 1943 (Fred Beecher); "The Outlaw" 1943 (Dealer); "Death Valley Rangers" 1944; "Gentle Annie" 1944 (Fireman); "Oregon Trail" 1945 (Capt. Street); "Roll on, Texas Moon" 1946 (Ned Barnes); "Buffalo Bill Rides Again" 1947 (Steve); "Jesse James Rides Again" 1947-serial (Hammond); "Wyoming" 1947 (Rancher); "Savage Frontier" 1953. ¶TV: *The Lone Ranger*—"Death Trap" 4-20-50, "Desert Adventure" 11-30-50, "The Durango Kid" 4-16-53.

Shumway, Walter (1884-1/13/65). Films: "The Fighting Sheriff" 1925 (G. Smiley); "Hi-Jacking Rustlers" 1926; "The Fighting Texan" 1927; "Prince of the Plains" 1927; "Wanderer of the West" 1927; "The Apache Raider" 1928 (Fang Jaccard); "Greased Lightning" 1928 (Dick Merrihew); "The Mystery Rider" 1928-serial; "The Pinto Kid" 1928 (Bert Lowery); "Beyond the Smoke" 1929; "Dangerous Days" 1929; "Riding for Life" 1929; "Headin' North" 1930 (Arnold); "Ghost City" 1932 (Henchman); "The Night Rider" 1932 (Sheriff Lem); "Outlaw Justice" 1933; "Fighting Shadows" 1935 (Jones); "Law Beyond the Range" 1935 (Texas Ranger); "Whirlwind Horseman" 1938 (Sheriff Blake); "Six-Gun Rhythm" 1939 (Bart); "The Showdown" 1940 (Snell); "Wrangler's Roost" 1941 (Grover).

Shutta, Ethel (1897-2/5/76). TV: *Wagon Train*—"Around the Horn" 10-1-58 (Woman), "The Doctor Willoughby Story" 11-5-58 (Mrs. Parker), "The Dick Richardson Story" 12-31-58 (Mrs. Parker), "The Kitty Angel Story" 1-7-59 (Lije's Ma), "Trial for Murder" 4-27-60 & 5-4-60, "The Countess Baranof Story" 5-11-60.

Shutta, Jack (1899-6/28/57). Films: "The Wistful Widow of Wagon Gap" 1947 (Tough Miner); "River Lady" 1948 (McGee).

Sickner, Roy. TV: *The Legend of*

Jesse James—"Put Me in Touch with Jesse" 9-27-65 (Clell); *Wild Wild West*—"The Night of the Bars of Hell" 3-4-66 (Driscoll); *Hondo*—"Hondo and the Death Drive" 12-1-67 (Cox), "Hondo and the Apache Trail" 12-22-67 (Joe).

Sidney, Scott (1872-7/20/28). Films: "Shorty's Sacrifice" 1914.

Siebert, Charles (1938-). Films: "Wild and Wooly" TVM-1978 (Sean).

Siegel, Bernard (1868-7/9/40). Films: "The Man Who Paid" 1922 (Anton Barbier); "Where Is This West?" 1923 (Indian Servant); "Against All Odds" 1924 (Lewis); "Romance Ranch" 1924 (Felipe Varillo); "The Vanishing American" 1925 (Do Etin); "Wild Horse Mesa" 1925 (Toddy Nokin); "Desert Gold" 1926 (Goat Herder); "Blazing Days" 1927 (Ezra Skinner); "Drums of the Desert" 1927 (Chief Brave Bear); "Open Range" 1927 (Brave Bear); "Guardians of the Wild" 1928 (Sing Lo); "Redskin" 1929 (Chahi); "Wells Fargo" 1937 (Pawnee).

Siegmann, George (1882-6/22/28). Films: "The Angel of Contention" 1914; "A Yankee from the West" 1915 (Sheriff Dick); "The Untamed" 1920 (Jim Silent); "The Big Punch" 1921 (Flash McGraw); "Desperate Trails" 1921 (Sheriff Price); "A California Romance" 1923 (Don Juan Diego); "The Eagle's Feather" 1923 (Van Brewen); "Hell's Hole" 1923 (Conductor); "Stepping Fast" 1923 (Red Pollock); "Singer Jim McKee" 1924 (Brute Bernstein); "Zander the Great" 1925 (Black Bart); "Born to the West" 1926 (Jesse Fillmore).

Siemaszko, Casey (1961-). Films: "Young Guns" 1988 (Charley Bowdre). ¶TV: *Adventures of Brisco County, Jr.*—"Ned Zed" 3-13-94 (Ned Zed).

Siemaszko, Nina. Films: "Lonesome Dove" TVM-1989 (Janey).

Sierra, Gregory (1937-). Films: "The Culpepper Cattle Company" 1972 (One-Eyed Thief); "Pocket Money" 1972 (Chavarin); "The Wrath of God" 1972 (Jurado, the One-Eyed Rebel); "The Castaway Cowboy" 1974 (Marrujo); "Honky Tonk" TVM-1974 (Slade); "The Gambler, Part II—The Adventure Continues" TVM-1983 (Silvera); "Where the Hell's That Gold?!!!" TVM-1988 (General); "Desperado: Badlands Justice" TVM-1989 (Jesus Gutierrez). ¶TV: *The High Chaparral*—"The Long Shadow" 1-2-70 (Arrigo); *Alias Smith and Jones*—"Journey from San Juan" 4-8-71; *Kung Fu*—"The Stone" 4-12-73 (Zolly); *Gunsmoke*—"Women for Sale" 9-10-73 & 9-17-73 (Blue Jacket), "Hard Labor" 2-24-75 (Osuna); *Zorro and Son*—Regular 1983 (Captain Paco Pico).

Sigaloff, Eugene (1887-1/13/60). Films: "Northwest Outpost" 1947 (Priest).

Sigel, Barbara (1950-). Films: "Nakia" TVM-1974 (Sally).

Sikking, James (1934-). Films: "Charro!" 1969 (Gunner); "The Magnificent Seven Ride" 1972 (Hayes); "The Electric Horseman" 1979 (Dietrich); "Desperado: Badlands Justice" TVM-1989 (Kirby Clarke). ¶TV: *Rawhide*—"Incident of the Travellin' Man" 10-17-63 (Luke Harger); *The Virginian*—"Nobility of Kings" 11-10-65 (Sanders); *Bonanza*—"The Trackers" 1-7-68 (Rimbau); *Here Come the Brides*—"The Soldier" 10-10-69 (Captain Hale), "To the Victor" 2-27-70.

Siletti, Mario (1903-4/19/64). Films: "Wings of the Hawk" 1953 (Marco); "Man in the Shadow" 1957 (Tony Santoro). ¶TV: *Cheyenne*—"Storm Center" 11-20-61 (Pepe).

Silla, Felix (1937-). TV: *Bonanza*—"Hoss and the Leprechauns" 12-22-63.

Sills, Milton (1882-9/15/30). Films: "The Hell Cat" 1918 (Sheriff Jack Webb); "The Spoilers" 1923 (Roy Glennister).

Silo, Jon. TV: *Have Gun Will Travel*—"Fogg Bound" 12-3-60 (Jean Passepartout); *The Tall Man*—"Quarantine" 3-17-62 (Amy); *Cimarron Strip*—"The Judgment" 1-4-68.

Silo, Susan. TV: *Wagon Train*—"The Joe Muharich Story" 4-19-61 (Betty Whittaker), "The David Garner Story" 5-8-63 (Susan); *Empire*—"The Fire Dancer" 11-13-62 (MacCormack); *Have Gun Will Travel*—"Two Plus One" 4-6-63 (Taymanee); *Bonanza*—"Woman of Fire" 1-17-65 (Elena); *Gunsmoke*—"The Long Night" 2-17-69 (Rita Lane); *Here Come the Brides*—"Next Week, East Lynne" 10-17-69 (Ada Moon).

Silva, David (1916-9/21/76). Films: "The First Texan" 1956 (Santa Ana).

Silva, Geno. Films: "The Chisholms" TVM-1979; "Wanda Nevada" 1979; "Belle Starr" TVM-1980 (Blue Duck); "Wild Times" TVM-1980 (Ibran); "El Diablo" TVM-1990 (Chak-Mool). ¶TV: *How the West Was One*—Episode Two 2-7-77 (Red Hawk), Episode Three 2-14-77 (Red Hawk); *The Chisholms*—Regular 1979 (Ferocious Storm).

Silva, Henry (1928-). Films: "Viva Zapata!" 1952 (Hernandez); "The Tall T" 1957 (Chink); "The Bravados" 1958 (Lujan); "The Law and Jake Wade" 1958 (Rennie); "Ride a Crooked Trail" 1958 (Sam Teeler); "The Jayhawkers" 1959 (London); "Sergents 3" 1962 (Mountain Hawk); "The Reward" 1965 (Joaquin); "The Hills Run Red" 1966-Ital. (Mendez); "The Plainsman" 1966 (Crazy Knife); "The Animals" 1971 (Chatto); "Black Noon" TVM-1971 (Moon); "Man and Boy" 1971 (Caine); "Manhunt" 1984-Ital.; "Lust in the Dust" 1985 (Bernardo). ¶TV: *Hotel De Paree*—"Sundance and the Delayed Gun" 6-3-60 (Stan Thorne); *Stagecoach West*—"The Raider" 5-9-61 (Mel Harney); *Wagon Train*—"The John Turnbull Story" 5-30-62 (John Turnbull), "The Robert Harrison Clarke Story" 10-14-63 (Ram Singh), "The Silver Lady" 4-25-65 (Doc Holliday); *Stoney Burke*—"The Weapons Man" 4-8-63 (Matt Elder); *Daniel Boone*—9-30-65 (Zapotec); *Laredo*—"The Bitter Yen of General Ti" 2-3-67 (General Shen Ti); *Cimarron Strip*—"Journey to a Hanging" 9-7-67 (Ace Coffin); *The High Chaparral*—"The Terrorist" 12-17-67 (Santos); *Bearcats!*—10-7-71 (Zavala).

Silva, Maria. Films: "Terrible Sheriff" 1963-Span./Ital.; "Cavalry Charge" 1964-Span.; "God Does Not Pay on Saturday" 1968-Ital.; "Sartana Kills Them All" 1970-Ital./Span.

Silver, Borah (1927-). Films: "The Gambler" TVM-1980 (Botkin).

Silver, Joe (1922-2/27/89). TV: *Gunsmoke*—"The Avenger" 11-27-72 (Beal Brown).

Silver, Johnny (1918-). TV: *Bat Masterson*—"Double Trouble in Trinidad" 1-7-59 (Drummer); *Bonanza*—"Horse of a Different Hue" 9-18-66 (Snowden); *Wild Wild West*—"The Night of Miguelito's Revenge" 12-13-68 (Biff Trout).

Silvera, Carl. Films: "Cyclone Smith's Partner" 1919; "The Man from God's Country" 1924 (Romero); "Way of a Man" 1924-serial; "Fangs of Fate" 1925 (Lew Sontag); "Lightning Lariats" 1927 (2nd Officer); "Lure of the West" 1928.

Silvera, Frank (1914-6/11/70). Films: "The Cimarron Kid" 1951 (Stacey Marshall); "The Fighter" 1952 (Paulino); "Viva Zapata!" 1952 (Huerta); "Heller in Pink Tights" 1960 (Santis); "The Appaloosa" 1966 (Ramos); "Hombre" 1967 (Mexican Bandit); "Guns of the Magnificent Seven" 1969 (Lobero); "The Stalking Moon" 1969 (Major); "Valdez Is Coming" 1971 (Diego). ¶TV: *Wanted—Dead or Alive*—"Sheriff of Red Rock" 11-29-58 (Sheriff Will Eckert); *Zane Grey Theater*—"Trouble at Tres Cruces" 3-26-59; *Bat Masterson*—"The Romany Knives" 7-22-59 (Grasia); *Man from Blackhawk*—"The Gypsy Story" 11-6-59 (Kiczek); *Johnny Ringo*—"The Derelict" 5-26-60 (Bevinetto); *The Rebel*—"Deathwatch" 10-23-60 (Cota); *Riverboat*—"Devil in Skirts" 11-21-60 (Colonel Ashley); *Bonanza*—"The Fugitive" 2-4-61 (El Jefe), "The Campaneros" 4-19-64 (Mateo); *The Travels of Jaimie McPheeters*—"The Day of the Taboo Man" 10-27-63 (Speaks to the Wind); *Daniel Boone*—"Daughter of the Devil" 4-15-65 (Marcel Bouvier); *Rawhide*—"El Hombre Bravo" 5-14-65 (Pajarito); *Gunsmoke*—"Death Watch" 1-8-66 (John Drago); *The High Chaparral*—Regular 1967-70 (Don Sebastian Montoya); *Wild Wild West*—"The Night of the Jack O'Diamonds" 10-6-67 (El Sordo).

Silvera, Karl. Films: "Barriers of Folly" 1922 (Wong Foo); "Bulldog Courage" 1922 (Snakey Evans).

Silverheels, Jay (Silverheels Smith) (1918-3/5/80). Films: "Valley of the Sun" 1942 (Indian); "Singin' in the Corn" 1946 (Brave); "The Last Round-Up" 1947 (Sam Luther); "Northwest Outpost" 1947 (Indian Scout); "The Prairie" 1947 (Running Deer); "Unconquered" 1947 (Indian); "Fury at Furnace Creek" 1948 (Little Dog); "Singing Spurs" 1948; "Yellow Sky" 1948 (Indian); "The Cowboy and the Indians" 1949 (Lakohna); "Laramie" 1949 (Running Wolf); "Lust for Gold" 1949 (Walter); "Trail of the Yukon" 1949 (Poleon); "Broken Arrow" 1950 (Goklia); "Red Mountain" 1951 (Little Crow); "The Battle at Apache Pass" 1952 (Geronimo); "Brave Warrior" 1952 (Chief Tecumseh); "Last of the Comanches" 1952 (Indian); "The Pathfinder" 1952 (Chingachgook); "Jack McCall, Desperado" 1953 (Red Cloud); "The Nebraskan" 1953 (Spotted Bear); "War Arrow" 1953 (Satanta); "The Black Dakotas" 1954 (Black Buffalo); "Drums Across the River" 1954 (Taos); "Four Guns to the Border" 1954 (Yaqui); "Masterson of Kansas" 1954 (Yellow Hawks); "Saskatchewan" 1954 (Cajou); "The Vanishing American" 1955 (Beeteia); "The Lone Ranger" 1956 (Tonto); "Walk the Proud Land" 1956 (Geronimo); "The Lone Ranger and the Lost City of Gold" 1958 (Tonto); "Return to Warbow" 1958 (Indian Joe); "Alias Jesse James" 1959 (Tonto); "Indian Paint" 1965 (Chief Hevatanu); "Smith" 1969 (McDonald Lasheway); "The Man Who Loved Cat Dancing" 1973 (the Chief); "One Little Indian" 1973 (Jimmy Wolfe); "Santee" 1973 (John Crow). ¶TV: *The Lone Ranger*—Regular 1949-57 (Tonto); *Wanted—Dead or Alive*—"Man on Horseback" 12-5-59 (Charley Red Cloud); *Texas John Slaughter*— "Apache Friendship" 2-19-60 (Natchez), "Geronimo's Revenge" 3-4-60 (Chief Natchez); *Wagon Train*— "Path of the Serpent" 2-8-61 (Serpent); *Gunslinger*—"The Recruit" 3-23-61 (Hopi Indian); *Rawhide*— "The Gentleman's Gentleman" 12-15-61; *Laramie*—"The Day of the Savage" 3-13-62; *Branded*—"The Test" 2-7-65; *Daniel Boone*—"The Quietists" 2-25-65 (Latawa), "The Christmas Story" 12-23-65 (Sashona); *Pistols 'n' Petticoats*—10-15-66 (Great Bear), 1-21-67 (Great Bear); *The Virginian*—"The Heritage" 10-30-68 (Den'Gwatzi).

Silvers, Phil (1912-11/1/85). Films: "A Lady Takes a Chance" 1943 (Smiley Lambert). ¶TV: *The Slowest Gun in the West* 7-29-63 (Fletcher Bissell III).

Silvestre, Armando (1926-). Films: "Wyoming Mail" 1950 (Indian Joe); "Apache Drums" 1951 (Pedro-Peter); "Mark of the Renegade" 1951 (Miguel De Gandara); "Hiawatha" 1952 (Kwasind); "For the Love of Mike" 1960 (Tony Eagle); "Geronimo" 1962 (Natchez); "Smoky" 1966 (Gordon); "The Scalphunters" 1968 (Two Crows); "Barquero" 1970 (Sawyer); "Two Mules for Sister Sara" 1970 (1st American); "Desperate Mission" TVM-1971 (Diego Campos). ¶TV: *Daniel Boone*—"The High Cumberland" 4-14-66 & 4-21-66 (Jim Santee), "A Very Small Rifle" 9-18-69 (Gabriel), "The Grand Alliance" 11-13-69 (Torres); *The Quest*— "Shanklin" 10-13-76 (Medina).

Simcox, Tom. Films: "Shenandoah" 1965 (Lt. Johnson); "Incident at Phantom Hill" 1966 (Adam Long); "One Little Indian" 1973; "Grim Prairie Tales" 1990 (Horn). ¶TV: *Gunsmoke*—"The Magician" 12-21-63 (Tom Wells), "Dry Well" 1-11-64 (Web Vickers), "Winner Take All" 2-20-65 (Curly Renner), "The Pretender" 11-20-65 (Frank Dano), "The Good People" 10-15-66 (Seth Rucker), "A Hat" 10-16-67 (Jed Conniston/Ben Conniston), "A Matter of Honor" 11-17-69 (C.V. Fletcher), "Trail of Bloodshed" 3-4-74 (Rance

Woolfe); *Wagon Train*—"The Link Cheney Story" 4-13-64 (Tom Riggs), "The Jarbo Pierce Story" 5-2-65 (Adam Pierce); *The Virginian*—"Dangerous Road" 3-17-65 (Fenton), "The Handy Man" 3-6-68 (Ward Bowden); *Bonanza*—"The Other Son" 10-3-65 (Andy Watson); *Laredo*— "Sound of Terror" 4-7-66 (Shamus McCloud); *How the West Was Won*— Episode Five 3-12-78 (Marshal Logan).

Simmons, Georgia. Films: "Heart of the Rockies" 1937 (Ma Dawson); "Rhythm Wranglers" 1937-short; "The Colorado Trail" 1938 (Mrs. Forbes); "Prairie Papas" 1938-short; "Shooting High" 1940 (Aggie); "Triple Justice" 1940; "The Fiend Who Walked the West" 1958. ¶TV: *F Troop*—"Corporal Agarn's Farewell to the Troops" 10-5-65 (Granny).

Simmons, Jean (1929-). Films: "A Bullet Is Waiting" 1954 (Cally Canham); "The Big Country" 1958 (Julie Maragon); "Rough Night in Jericho" 1967 (Molly Lang).

Simmons, Richard "Dick" (1911-). Films: "King of the Royal Mounted" 1940-serial (Carter); "King of the Texas Rangers" 1941-serial (Red Cameron); "The Woman They Almost Lynched" 1953 (Captain); "Man with the Steel Whip" 1954-serial (Jerry Randall/El Latigo); "Sergents 3" 1962 (Col. William Collingood). ¶TV: *Sergeant Preston of the Yukon*—Regular 1955-58 (Sergeant Preston); *Stories of the Century*—"Ben Thompson" 9-9-55; *Rawhide*—"Incident at El Crucero" 10-10-63 (Stranger); *Death Valley Days*—"A Bell for Volcano" 1-24-65 (Floyd Webster), "Samaritans, Mountain Style" 11-19-66 (Fremont), "Chicken Bill" 10-14-67 (George Hook), "Tracy's Triumph" 10-4-69 (Ben).

Simon, Michael (1895-5/30/75). Films: "The Girl of the Golden West" 1942-Ital.

Simon, Robert F. (1912-11/29/92). Films: "The Black Dakotas" 1954 (Marshal Collins); "Chief Crazy Horse" 1955 (Jeff Mantz); "Seven Angry Men" 1955 (Col. Washington); "The First Traveling Saleslady" 1956 (Cal); "Gunman's Walk" 1958 (Harry Brill); "The Man Who Shot Liberty Valance" 1962 (Handy Strong); "Wild Women" TVM-1970 (Colonel Donahue). ¶TV: *20th Century Fox Hour*—"Broken Arrow" 5-2-56 (Ben Slade); *Broken Arrow*— "Ghost Face" 3-12-57 (Gen. Everitt); *Cheyenne*—"Born Bad" 3-26-57 (Chad), "Prisoner of Moon Mesa" 11-

16-59 (Hub Lassiter); *Gunsmoke*— "Cheap Labor" 5-4-57 (Ben Stancil), "Potato Road" 10-12-57 (Pa Grilk), "The Cast" 12-6-58 (Shell Tucker), "Father Love" 3-14-64 (Jesse Price), "Jonah Hutchison" 11-21-64 (Jonah Hutchison), "Song for Dying" 2-13-65 (Will Lukens), "The Mission" 10-8-66 (Colonel Amos Jessup); *Have Gun Will Travel*—"The Colonel and the Lady" 11-23-57 (Col. Lathrop), "Young Gun" 11-8-58 (Frank Wellman), "The Trial" 6-11-60 (Morgan Gibbs), "One, Two, Three" 2-17-62 (Samuel H. Keel); *Walt Disney Presents*—"Elfego Baca" Regular 1958-60 (Sheriff Ed Morgan); *Wagon Train*— "The Juan Ortega Story" 10-8-58 (Jay Thornton), "The Caroline Casteel Story" 9-26-62 (Schofield); *Zane Grey Theater*—"Make It Look Good" 2-5-59 (John Hanley); *The Texan*— "Reunion" 5-4-59 (Will Crandall), "The Guilty and the Innocent" 3-28-60 (Vance); *Lawman*—"The Friend" 6-28-59 (Mr. Harmon), "Conditional Surrender" 5-28-61 (Pa Beason); *Laramie*—"Circle of Fire" 9-22-59 (Bert Bigelow); *Black Saddle*— "The Saddle" 10-9-59 (Judge Mercer McKinney); *The Law of the Plainsman*—"The Gibbet" 11-26-59; *Johnny Ringo*—"Kid with a Gun" 12-24-59 (Cason); *Rawhide*—"Incident at Red River Station" 1-15-60 (Junkin), "The House of the Hunter" 4-20-62 (Mackie); *Wichita Town*—"Second Chance" 3-16-60 (Walt McCloud); *Stagecoach West*—"High Lonesome" 10-4-60 (Tom Osgood, Sr.); *Man from Blackhawk*—"Diamond Cut Diamond" 3-18-60 (Sheriff Jim Claudious); *Bonanza*—"Bitter Water" 4-9-60 (Len Keith), "The Big Jackpot" 1-18-70 (Thurston); *Bat Masterson*— "Death by Decree" 12-22-60 (Harrison Whitney); *Klondike*—"The Golden Burro" 1-16-61 (Ed Nash); *Frontier Circus*—"Stopover in Paradise" 2-22-62 (Jess Bailey); *The Dakotas*—"Trial at Grand Forks" 3-25-63 (Charles Kimberly); *The Virginian*—"Stopover in a Western Town" 11-27-63 (Ben Wainwright), "Men with Guns" 1-12-66 (Eric Larsen), "Yesterday's Timepiece" 1-18-67 (Rafe Potter), "The Storm Gate" 11-13-68 (Sam Burmeister); *Great Adventure*—"The Pathfinder" 3-6-64 (Grief); *Daniel Boone*—"Ken-Tuck-E" 9-24-64 (Chief Blackfish); *Laredo*—"A Matter of Policy" 11-11-65 (Sen. John Sparks), "The Other Cheek" 2-10-67 (Tinker); *The Legend of Jesse James*—"The Man Who Was" 12-13-65 (Billy Clarke); *The Road West*—"Long Journey to Leavenworth" 10-17-66 (Pratt); *Custer*—Regular 1967 (General A.H. Terry); *The Outcasts*—"Act of Faith" 2-10-69 (Sheriff Lockhart); *The Guns of Will Sonnett*—"The Man Who Killed James Sonnett" 3-21-69 (Sheriff Devon); *Nichols*—"The Dirty Half Dozen Run Amuck" 10-28-71 (Slade).

Simon, Sol S. (1864-4/24/40). Films: "Desperate Courage" 1928; "Headin' North" 1930 (Palace Owner); "The Land of Missing Men" 1930 (Express Agent).

Simpson, Mickey (1913-9/23/85). Films: "Boss of Hangtown Mesa" 1942; "My Darling Clementine" 1946 (Sam Clanton); "The Wistful Widow of Wagon Gap" 1947 (Big Miner); "Fort Apache" 1948 (Non-Commissioned Officer); "River Lady" 1948 (Logger); "The Fighting Kentuckian" 1949 (Jacques); "She Wore a Yellow Ribbon" 1949 (Wagner); "Roar of the Iron Horse" 1950-serial (Cal); "Surrender" 1950 (Pete); "Wagonmaster" 1950 (Jesse Clegg); "Apache Country" 1952 (Tom Ringo); "Leadville Gunslinger" 1952 (Monk); "Lone Star" 1952 (Sen. Maynard Cole); "Saginaw Trail" 1953 (Jean Leblanc); "Star of Texas" 1953 (Tom Traynor); "Tall Man Riding" 1955 (Deputy Jeff Barkley); "Giant" 1956 (Sarge); "The Lone Ranger" 1956 (Powder); "Gunfight at the O.K. Corral" 1957 (Frank McLowery); "Warlock" 1959 (Fitzsimmons); "He Rides Tall" 1964 (Onie); "The Great Bank Robbery" 1969 (Guard). ¶TV: *The Lone Ranger*—"Drink of Water" 10-26-50, "Banker's Choice" 11-23-50, "The Outcast" 1-18-51, "Sinner by Proxy" 3-5-53, "Death in the Forest" 6-4-53, "Dan Reid's Fight for Life" 11-18-54, "Trigger Finger 4-7-55, "The Sheriff of Smoke Tree" 9-20-56; *The Cisco Kid*—"Robber Crow" 11-24-51, "Spanish Dagger" 1-5-52, "Cisco Plays the Ghost" 2-21-53, "A Six-Gun for No Pain" 2-28-53, "Bounty Men" 1-30-54; *Annie Oakley*—"Sharpshooting Annie" 6-12-54; *Gunsmoke*—"No Indians" 12-8-56 (Stapp); *Cheyenne*—"Test of Courage" 1-29-57 (Grannick), "Cross Purpose" 10-9-61 (Renant), "The Durango Brothers" 9-24-62 (Homer Durango); *Fury*—"The Strong Man" 2-16-57 (Fergus); *Maverick*—"Hostage!" 11-10-57 (Jubal), "The Thirty-Ninth Star" 11-16-58 (Tiny), "The Misfortune Teller" 3-6-60 (Charley Turple), "Bundle from Britain" 9-18-60 (Pecos), "Triple Indemnity" 3-19-61 (Cabella), "One of Our Trains Is Missing" 4-22-62 (Leroy Haod); *The Rifleman*—"The Sharpshooter" 9-30-58 (Carl Lamprey), "The Indian" 2-17-59 (Tub); *Have Gun Will Travel*—"Maggie O'Bannion" 4-4-59; *Yancy Derringer*—"The Wayward Warrior" 4-16-59 (Tennessee Slasher); *Bronco*—"Prairie Skipper" 5-5-59 (Bosum), "A Sure Thing" 1-22-62 (Jonah); *Colt .45*—"The Saga of Sam Bass" 5-17-59 (Bass's Cohort); *Rough Riders*—"The Rifle" 5-7-59 (Moose Johnson); *Desilu Playhouse*—"Six Guns for Donegan" 10-16-59; *The Deputy*—"Like Father" 10-17-59 (Gabe Willow); *The Alaskans*—"Winter Song" 11-22-59 (Steve Bonnett); *Bonanza*—"House Divided" 1-16-60 (Northern Miner), "Sam Hill" 6-3-61 (Bartender); *Lawman*—"To Capture the West" 2-7-60 (Connors), "Samson the Great" 11-20-60 (Samson); *Bat Masterson*—"The Hunter" 10-27-60 (Donovan); *Sugarfoot*—"Man from Medora" 11-21-60 (Jake Sloane); *The Dakotas*—"Reformation at Big Nose Butte" 4-1-63 (Lester Banks); *The Virginian*—"The Intruders" 3-4-64 (Bear Bristow); *Pistols 'n' Petticoats*—12-17-66 (Luke).

Simpson, Napoleon. Films: "Santa Fe Trail" 1940 (Samson).

Simpson, Russell (1880-12/12/59). Films: "Salt of the Earth" 1917 (Sinful John); "The Border Legion" 1918 (Overland Hoadley); "Oh, Johnny!" 1918 (Adele's Father); "The Blue Bandanna" 1919 (Jim Yancy); "Desert Gold" 1919 (Lad/James Warren); "The Branding Iron" 1920 (John Carver); "Fighting Cressy" 1920 (Hiram McKinstry); "Lahoma" 1920 (Brick Willock); "Out of the Dust" 1920 (Capt. John Evans); "Shadows of Conscience" 1921 (Jim Logan); "Fools of Fortune" 1922 (Magpie Simpkins); "The Girl of the Golden West" 1923 (Jack Rance); "The Huntress" 1923; "The Virginian" 1923 (Trampas); "Beauty and the Bad Man" 1925 (Chuckwalla Bill); "The Splendid Road" 1925 (Capt. Lightfoot); "Rustlin' for Cupid" 1926 (Hank Blatchford); "The Frontiersman" 1927 (Andrew Jackson); "The Trail of '98" 1929 (Old Swede); "Billy the Kid" 1930 (McSween); "The Lone Star Ranger" 1930 (Col. Aldridge); "Call of the Rockies" 1931 (Gunner Bill); "The Great Meadow" 1931 (Thomas Hall); "Hello Trouble" 1932 (Jonathan Kenyon); "Law and Order" 1932 (Judge Williams); "Ridin' for Justice" 1932 (Marshal Joseph Slyde); "The Riding Tornado" 1932 (Sheriff); "White Eagle" 1932; "Frontier Marshal" 1934 (Editor Pickett); "West of the Pecos" 1934 (Roy Neal); "Ramona" 1936 (Scroggs); "Wild West Days" 1937-serial (Keeler); "Yodelin' Kid from Pine Ridge" 1937 (Bayliss Baynum); "The Girl of the Golden West" 1938 (Pioneer); "Gold Is Where You Find It" 1938 (McKenzie); "Heart of the North" 1938 (Dave MacMillan); "The Arizona Wildcat" 1939 (Rancher); "Desperate Trails" 1939 (Big Bill Tanner); "Dodge City" 1939 (Orth); "Drums Along the Mohawk" 1939 (Dr. Petry); "Texas Stampede" 1939 (Cameron); "Western Caravans" 1939 (Winchester Thompson); "Brigham Young—Frontiersman" 1940 (Major); "Geronimo" 1940 (Scout); "Santa Fe Trail" 1940 (Shoubel Morgan); "Three Faces West" 1940 (Minister); "Virginia City" 1940 (Gaylor); "Wyoming" 1940 (Bronson); "Bad Men of Missouri" 1941 (Hank Younger); "Last of the Duanes" 1941 (Tom Duane); "Lone Star Ranger" 1942 (Tom Duane); "Shut My Big Mouth" 1942 (Mayor Potter); "The Spoilers" 1942 (Flapjack Simms); "Wild Bill Hickok Rides" 1942 (Ned Nolan); "Border Patrol" 1943 (Orestes Krebs); "Riding High" 1943 (French McQuire); "The Woman of the Town" 1943 (Sime); "The Big Bonanza" 1944 (Adam Parker); "Roaring Guns" 1944-short; "Tall in the Saddle" 1944 (Pat); "Texas Masquerade" 1944 (J.K. Trimble); "Along Came Jones" 1945 (Pop de Longpre); "Bad Bascomb" 1946 (Elijah Walker); "California Gold Rush" 1946; "Death Valley" 1946; "My Darling Clementine" 1946 (John Simpson); "Bowery Buckaroos" 1947 (Luke Barlow); "The Fabulous Texan" 1947 (Wade Clayton); "Albuquerque" 1948 (Huggins); "Coroner Creek" 1948 (Walt Hardison); "Sundown in Santa Fe" 1948; "Call of the Klondike" 1950 (McKay); "Saddle Tramp" 1950 (Pop); "Wagonmaster" 1950 (Adam Perkins); "Across the Wide Missouri" 1951 (Hoback); "Broken Lance" 1954 (Judge); "Rose Marie" 1954 (Trapper); "The Last Command" 1955 (the Parson); "The Tall Men" 1955 (Emigrant Man); "The Brass Legend" 1956 (Jackson); "Friendly Persuasion" 1956 (Elder); "The Lonely Man" 1957; "The Tin Star" 1957 (Clem Hall); "The Horse Soldiers" 1959 (Sheriff). ¶TV: *Wild Bill Hickok*—"Ghost Town Story" 8-21-51; *The Lone Ranger*—"The Old Cowboy" 6-25-53; *The Texan*—"The Man Behind the Star" 2-9-59 (Zeb Waters).

Sinatra, Frank (1915-). Films: "The Kissing Bandit" 1948 (Ricardo); "Johnny Concho" 1956 (Johnny Concho); "Sergents 3" 1962 (1st Sgt. Mike Merry); "Four for Texas" 1964

(Zack Thomas); "Dirty Dingus Magee" 1970 (Dingus Magee).

Sinatra, Jr., Frank (1944-). TV: *Alias Smith and Jones*—"The Long Chase" 9-16-72 (Deputy Wermser).

Sinatra, Nancy (1940-). TV: *The Virginian*—"If You Have Tears" 2-13-63 (Cary).

Sinclair, Diane. Films: "Rustlers' Roundup" 1933 (Mary Brand); "The Fighting Code" 1934 (Helen Jones).

Sinclair, Eric (1922-). Films: "Butch Cassidy and the Sundance Kid" 1969 (Tiffany's Salesman). ¶TV: *Sugarfoot*—"Apollo with a Gun" 12-8-59 (Roger Gillis).

Sinclair, Johnny (1900-2/13/45). Films: "Cyclone Cavalier" 1925 (Mickey); "The Royal Rider" 1929 (Wild West Show Member).

Sinclair, Ronald. Films: "Out West with the Peppers" 1940 (Jasper King).

Sindelar, Pearl. Films: "The Four-Footed Ranger" 1928 (Mary Doolittle); "Made-to-Order Hero" 1928 (Aunt Saphrona).

Singer, Marc (1948-). TV: *Nakia*—"No Place to Hide" 10-19-74.

Singer, Stuffy. TV: *Fury*—"The Boy Scout Story" 2-11-56 (Buzz); *Zane Grey Theater*—"The Ox" 11-3-60.

Singleton, Joseph. Films: "The Squaw Man" 1914 (Tabywana); "Jordan Is a Hard Road" 1915; "Judge Not, or the Woman of Mona Diggings" 1915 (Minister); "The Good Bad Man" 1916 (the Weazel); "Girl of the Timber Claims" 1917 (Leather Hermit); "Wild and Woolly" 1917 (Steve's Butler); "Desert Law" 1918 (Jim); "Deuce Duncan" 1918 (Sheriff); "The Lady of the Dugout" 1918 (the Husband); "The Pretender" 1918 (Hi Newsome); "The Great Redeemer" 1920 (the Murderer); "The Last of the Mohicans" 1920; "The Toll Gate" 1920 (Jordan); "Two Kinds of Women" 1922 (Charles Miller).

Singleton, Penny (1912-). Films: "Go West, Young Lady" 1941 (Belinda Pendergast). ¶TV: *Death Valley Days*—"The Holy Terror" 12-8-63 (Maggie Franklin).

Sinise, Gary. Films: "The Quick and the Dead" 1995 (Marshal).

Sirianni, E.A. TV: *Wild Wild West*—"The Night of the Tycoons" 3-28-69 (O'Brien); *Bonanza*—"Abner Willoughby's Return" 12-21-69 (Clerk), "The Trouble with Trouble" 10-25-70 (Jethro), "Rock-a-Bye, Hoss" 10-10-71 (Lon Meecham);

Kung Fu—"The Soul Is the Warrior" 2-8-73 (Wide Ed).

Sirola, Joseph (1929-). Films: "Chuka" 1967 (Baldwin); "Hang 'Em High" 1968. ¶TV: *Gunsmoke*—"The Quest for Asa Janin" 6-1-63 (Leroy), "Kitty Cornered" 4-18-64 (Eddie Fitch); *Death Valley Days*—"The Trouble with Taxes" 4-18-65 (Stoney); *Bret Maverick*—"The Not So Magnificent Six" 3-2-82 (Nimrod Bligh).

Sisson, Vera (1891-8/6/54). Films: "A Bogus Bandit" 1915; "The Hidden Spring" 1917 (Thora Erickson); "The Avenging Arrow" 1921-serial; "The Sagebrush Musketeers" 1921; "The Secret of Butte Ridge" 1921.

Sitka, Emil (1914-). Films: "Texas Dynamo" 1950 (Turkey); "Merry Mavericks" 1951-short (Mort, the Jailer); "A Perilous Journey" 1953 (Drunk); "Jubilee Trail" 1954 (Chair Bit); "Shot in the Frontier" 1954-short (Justice of the Peace); "The Outlaws Is Coming!" 1965 (Mr. Abernathy/Witch Doctor/Cavalry Colonel). ¶TV: *Circus Boy*—"The Tumbling Clown" 5-5-57.

Sizemore, Tom. Films: "Wyatt Earp" 1994 (Bat Masterson).

Skaggs, Jimmy F. Films: "The Gambler, Part III—The Legend Continues" TVM-1987; "Ghost Town" 1988 (Devilin); "Oblivion" 1994 (Buteo); "Tecumseh: The Last Warrior" TVM-1995 (Hardstriker).

Skala, Lilia (1907-12/18/94). Films: "Heartland" 1980 (Grandma).

Skelton, Tiny. Films: "Thunder Over Texas" 1934 (Tiny); "The Way of the West" 1934 (Tiny); "The Roaring West" 1935-serial; "Timber Terrors" 1935 (Corporal Tiny Anderson).

Skerritt, Tom (1933-). Films: "Wild Rovers" 1971 (John Buckman); "Silence of the North" 1981 (Walter Reamer); "Poker Alice" TVM-1987 (Collins). ¶TV: *The Virginian*—"Impasse" 11-14-62 (Eric Kroeger), "The Secret of Brynmar Hall" 4-1-64 (Paul), "The Showdown" 4-14-65 (Eddy Landers), "The Crooked Pat" 2-21-68 (Moran), "The Saddle Warmer" 9-18-68 (Rafe); *Laramie*—"No Place to Run" 2-5-63; *Death Valley Days*—"Three Minutes to Eternity" 1-26-64 (Emmett Dalton), "Honor the Name Dennis Driscoll" 10-25-64, "The Book" 1-15-66 (Patrick Rogan), "Sense of Justice" 12-10-66; *Wagon Train*—"The Last Circle Up" 4-27-64 (Hamish Browne); *Bonanza*—"Thanks for Everything, Friend" 10-11-64 (Jerry),

"The Hunter" 1-16-73 (Tanner); *Walt Disney Presents*—"Gallegher" 1965-67 (Corky Mardis); *Gunsmoke*—"The Pretender" 11-20-65 (Edmund Dano), "The Jailor" 10-1-66 (Ben Stone), "The Moonstone" 12-17-66 (Orv Timpson), "The Noose" 9-21-70 (Fred Garth), "Horse Fever" 12-18-72 (Tuck Frye); *Cimarron Strip*—"Knife in the Darkness" 1-25-68 (Enoch Shelton); *Lancer*—"The Knot" 3-18-69 (Bill Blake); *The Men from Shiloh*—"Nan Allen" 1-6-71 (Bobby Allen); *Nichols*—"The Marrying Fool" 12-28-71 (Charley Doyle); *Sara*—4-9-76 (Newt Johnson).

Sketchley, Leslie (1902-10/14/72). Films: "Tiger Rose" 1929 (Mounted Police Officer).

Skinner, Edna. Films: "The Kissing Bandit" 1948 (Juanita); "Friendly Persuasion" 1956 (Widow Hudspeth's Daughter). ¶TV: *Daniel Boone*—"Tekawitha McLeod" 10-1-64 (Sadie Clayburn).

Skinner, Marianne. Films: "The Cave on Thunder Cloud" 1915; "The Claim" 1918 (Pansy Bryan); "The Sleeping Lion" 1919 (Carlotta's Mother); "Billy Jim" 1922 (Mrs. Dunforth).

Slade, Mark (1939-). TV: *Rawhide*—"The Enormous Fist" 10-2-64 (Adam Grant); *Bonanza*—"A Real Nice, Friendly Little Town" 11-27-66 (Judd Rikeman); *Wild Wild West*—"The Night of the Gypsy Peril" 1-20-67 (Hilliard); *The High Chaparral*—Regular 1967-71 (Blue Cannon); *Gunsmoke*—"The Prisoner" 3-17-69; *The Life and Times of Grizzly Adams*—4-5-78 (Ulysses S. Grant).

Slate, Jeremy (1935-). Films: "The Sons of Katie Elder" 1965 (Deputy Sheriff Ben Latta); "True Grit" 1969 (Emmett Quincy); "Mr. Horn" TVM-1979 (Capt. Emmet Crawford). ¶TV: *Bat Masterson*—"Dead Men Don't Pay Debts" 11-19-59 (Bob Clements); *The Deputy*—"The Hidden Motive" 1-30-60 (Red Dawson); *Have Gun Will Travel*—"El Paso Stage" 4-15-61 (Frank DeWitt); *Gunsmoke*—"Lacey" 1-13-62 (Jess Ayley), "The Gallows" 3-3-62 (Pruit Dover), "Carter Caper" 11-16-63 (Billy Hargis), "The New Society" 5-22-65 (Sheriff Tom Scanlon), "The Raid" 1-22-66 & 1-29-66 (Web Fraley), "Abelia" 11-18-68 (Judd Ward), "Waste" 9-27-71 & 10-4-71 (Ben Rodman); *Bonanza*—"Inger, My Love" 4-15-62 (Gunnar), "A Man Without Land" 4-9-67 (Ed Phillips), "The Passing of a King" 10-13-68 (Jeremy Roman); *Empire*—"The Loner"

1-22-63 (Mike Novak); *The Virginian*—"A Man Called Kane" 5-6-64 (Johnny Kane), "Legacy of Hate" 9-14-66 (Dawson); *Bearcats!*—12-30-71 (Lassiter).

Slater, Christian (1969-). Films: "Young Guns II" 1990 (Arkansas Dave Rudabaugh).

Slater, Helen (1963-). Films: "City Slickers" 1991 (Bonnie Rayburn).

Slater, John (1916-1/9/75). Films: "Vigilantes Are Coming" 1936-serial (Rancher); "The Lone Ranger" 1938-serial (Trooper).

Slattery, Desmond. Films: "Ambush at Cimarron Pass" 1958 (Cobb); "Blood Arrow" 1958 (Ceppi).

Slattery, Page. Films: "Jesse James Meets Frankenstein's Daughter" 1966. ¶TV: *Tombstone Territory*—12-4-59 (Paul Hayden); *Bat Masterson*—"Blood on the Money" 6-23-60 (Dane Holloway), "Debt of Honor" 9-29-60 (Marc Branden).

Slattery, Richard X. (1925-) Films: "A Distant Trumpet" 1964 (Slattery); "A Time for Killing" 1967 (Cpl. Paddy Darling); "The Apple Dumpling Gang Rides Again" 1979 (Sgt. Slaughter). ¶TV: *Rawhide*—"Incident of Iron Bull" 10-3-63 (Clanton), "The Photographer" 12-11-64 (Daws), "Blood Harvest" 2-12-65; *Gunsmoke*—"May Blossoms" 2-15-64 (Greer), "The New Society" 5-22-65 (Coor), "The Judas Gun" 1-19-70 (Noah Haimes); *Temple Houston*—"Miss Katherina" 4-2-64 (Sergeant Smathers); *The Road West*—"Reap the Whirlwind" 1-9-66 (Micah Pratt); *F Troop*—"For Whom the Bugle Tolls" 11-10-66 (Colonel Bartlett); *Daniel Boone*—"The Williamsburg Cannon" 1-12-67 & 1-19-67 (Simon Foss); *Cimarron Strip*—"The Battle of Blood Stone" 10-12-67 (Max); *Iron Horse*—"The Bride at Forty-Mile" 1-23-67 (Amos Morgan); *The Virginian*—"Bitter Autumn" 11-1-67 (Kyle Jackson); *Bonanza*—"Six Black Horses" 11-26-67 (McCoy), One Ace Too Many" 4-2-72 (Henderson); *The High Chaparral*—"Stinky Flanagan" 2-21-69 (Captain Phinster); *Lancer*—"The Knot" 3-18-69 (Seth Blake), "The Kid" 10-7-69 (Dan Marvin), "Dream of Falcons" 4-7-70 (Buck Fanning); *Alias Smith and Jones*—"The Posse That Wouldn't Quit" 10-14-71 (Sheriff).

Slaven, Matthew B. see Slavin, Brad.

Slavin, Brad (Matthew B. Slaven). Films: "Moon Over Montana" 1946; "Song of the Sierras" 1946; "Trail to Mexico" 1946; "Border Feud" 1947 (Jim Condon); "Cheyenne Takes Over" 1947 (Bailey); "Law of the Lash" 1947 (Sam); "Range Beyond the Blue" 1947 (Kirk); "Ridin' Down the Trail" 1947; "Return of the Lash" 1947 (Grant); "Stage to Mesa City" 1947 (Bob Watson); "Tornado Range" 1948 (Jebby). ¶TV: *The Lone Ranger*—"Double Jeopardy" 9-7-50.

Sleeman, Philip (1891-9/19/53). Films: "Singled-Handed" 1923 (Gypsy Joe); "Come on Cowboys!" 1924 (F. Richard Worthington); "The Border Whirlwind" 1926 (Palo, the Scorpion); "Call of the Wild" 1935 (3rd Poker Player).

Sleeper, Martha (1910-3/25/83). Films: "West of the Pecos" 1934 (Terrell Lambeth); "Sunset Range" 1935; "Rhythm on the Range" 1936 (Constance).

Slezak, Walter (1902-4/21/83). Films: "Salome, Where She Danced" 1945 (Dimitroff). ¶TV: *The Outlaws*—"Masterpiece" 12-21-61 (Martin Hall); *Rawhide*—"Incident of the Black Ace" 4-12-63 (Lazio Tzgorni).

Slifer, Lizz. Films: "Hell's Outpost" 1954. ¶TV: *Wild Bill Hickok*—"Golden Rainbow" 12-9-52; *Annie Oakley*—"The Waco Kid" 10-28-56 (Junk Wagon Jenny Hutchins); *Death Valley Days*—"Auto Intoxication" 3-3-58.

Sloan, Tod (1874-12/21/33). Films: "The Killer" 1921 (Artie Brower); "When Romance Rides" 1922 (Holley).

Sloane, Everett (1909-8/6/65). Films: "Way of a Gaucho" 1952 (Falcon). ¶TV: *Wanted—Dead or Alive*—"The Giveaway Gun" 10-11-58 (Mr. Walker), "Reckless" 11-7-59 (Tate Bradley); *Wagon Train*—"The Flint McCullough Story" 1-14-59 (Col. Jase Taylor), "The Sam Elder Story" 1-18-61 (Sam Elder), "The Andrew Elliott Story" 2-10-64 (Senator Elliott); *Cimarron City*—"The Ratman" 3-7-59 (Dr. Eckhardt); *Zorro*—"The Man from Spain" 4-9-59 (Andres Felipe Basileo), "Treasure for the King" 4-16-59 (Andres Felipe Basileo), "Exposing the Tyrant" 4-23-59 (Andres Felipe Basileo), "Zorro Takes a Dare" 4-30-59 (Andres Felpe Basileo); *Laramie*—"Stage Stop" 9-15-59; *Bonanza*—"Blood on the Land" 2-13-60 (Jeb Drummond), "Right Is the Fourth R" 3-7-65 (Colonel Scott); *Zane Grey Theater*—"The Sunrise Gun" 5-19-60 (Johnny Sunrise); *Best of the Post*—"Command" 10-6-60 (Captain Brittles); *Rawhide*—"Incident at Sugar Creek" 11-23-62 (Dr.

Walter Harper), "Incident of the Pied Piper" 2-6-64 (Calvin Randolph), "The Empty Sleeve" 4-2-65 (Sam Butler); *The Virginian*—"No Tears for Savannah" 10-2-63 (Henry T. Madden); *Temple Houston*—"Toll the Bell Slowly" 10-17-63 (Daniel Forbes); *Gunsmoke*—"Quint's Trail" 11-9-63 (Cyrus Neff), "Twenty Miles from Dodge" 4-10-65 (Follansbee); *The Dakotas*—"Justice at Eagle's Nest" 3-11-63 (Judge Daniel Harvey).

Slocum, George. Films: "Red Desert" 1949 (Bartender); "Border Outlaws" 1950 (Turner); "Mule Train" 1950. ¶TV: *The Lone Ranger*—"The Beeler Gang" 8-10-50, "Through the Wall" 10-9-52; *The Roy Rogers Show*—"Dead Men's Hills" 3-15-52, "Ride in Death Wagon" 4-6-52; *Wild Bill Hickok*—"The Sheriff Was a Redhead" 7-15-52; *The Gene Autry Show*—"Thunder Out West" 7-14-53.

Sloman, Edward (1885-9/29/72). Films: "The Trey O'Hearts" 1914-serial; "The Valley of Regeneration" 1915.

Sloyan, James (1941-). TV: *Centennial*—Regular 1978-79 (Spade Larkin); *Paradise*—"Till Death Do Us Part" 2-3-90 (Joe Pratt).

Small, Louise. Films: "Melody of the Plains" 1937 (Molly Langley); "Reckless Ranger" 1937 (Mildred Newton).

Smalley, Phillips (1875-5/2/39). Films: "Border Patrol" 1928 (Conway Dix).

Smika, Gina Maria. Films: "The Oregon Trail" TVM-1976 (Rachel Thorpe). ¶TV: *The Oregon Trail*—Regular 1977 (Rachel Thorpe).

Smiley, John. Films: "Their Compact" 1917 (Peters); "The Trail to Yesterday" 1918 (Ben Doubler); "The Unbroken Promise" 1919 (Old Man Loring).

Smiley, Joseph W. (1881-12/2/45). Films: "Heart of the Wilds" 1918 (Peter Galbraith); "The Law of the Yukon" 1920 (Tim Meadows).

Smiley, Ralph (1915-9/14/77). TV: *Jim Bowie*—"A Horse for Old Hickory" 1-4-57 (Pierre); *Rawhide*—"Incident in the Middle of Nowhere" 4-7-61, "Incident of the Night on the Town" 6-2-61.

Smith, Albert J. (1894-4/12/39). Films: "A Western Romance" 1913; "The Heart of Arizona" 1921; "The Man Trackers" 1921 (Hanley); "Roaring Waters" 1921; "The Shadow of Suspicion" 1921; "Giants of the Open" 1922; "Timberland Treachery" 1922; "Hearts of Oak" 1923; "In the

Days of Daniel Boone" 1923-serial; "Wolf Tracks" 1923 (Steve "Wolf" Santell); "The Measure of a Man" 1924 (Jack Flack); "The Sunset Trail" 1924 (Dick Fenlow); "Ace of Spades" 1925-serial; "Blood and Steel" 1925 (Jurgen); "The Burning Trail" 1925 (Texas); "The Circus Cyclone" 1925 (Steve Brant); "The Meddler" 1925 (Bud Meyers); "Ridin' Through" 1925; "The Taming of the West" 1925 (Lafe Conners); "The Saddle Tramp" 1926; "Strings of Steel" 1926-serial; "Hard Fists" 1927 (Charles Crane); "Hills of Peril" 1927 (Rand); "Red Clay" 1927 (Jack Burr); "Whispering Sage" 1927 (Ed Fallows); "The Bullet Mark" 1928; "The Law of Fear" 1928 (Steve Benton); "Tracked" 1928 (Lem Hardy); "The Drifter" 1929 (Pete Lawson); "Outlawed" 1929 (Dervish); "Shadow Ranch" 1930 (Dan Blake); "Branded" 1931 (Joe Moore); "Desert Vengeance" 1931 (McBride); "Shotgun Pass" 1931; "Between Fighting Men" 1932 (Butch Martin); "Border Devils" 1932 (Inspector Bell); "Dynamite Ranch" 1932 (Red); "Forbidden Trail" 1932 (Burke); "Hello Trouble" 1932 (Vaughn); "The Telegraph Trail" 1933 (Gus Lynch); "The Thrill Hunter" 1933 (Sheriff); "Honor of the Range" 1934 (Smoiky); "The Prescott Kid" 1934 (Frazier); "The Westerner" 1934 (Sheriff); "End of the Trail" 1936 (Chief Deputy); "Sutter's Gold" 1936; "Code of the Range" 1937 (Barney Ross); "Prairie Thunder" 1937 (Lynch).

Smith, Alexis (1921-6/9/93). Films: "San Antonio" 1945 (Jeanne Starr); "South of St. Louis" 1949 (Rouge de Lisle); "Montana" 1950 (Maria Singleton); "Wyoming Mail" 1950 (Mary Williams); "Cave of Outlaws" 1951 (Liz Trent).

Smith, Arthur "Fiddlin'" (1900-2/24/73). Films: "Lonesome Trail" 1945; "Riders of the Dawn" 1945 (Arthur); "Moon Over Montana" 1946; "Trail to Mexico" 1946; "West of Alamo" 1946; "Six Gun Serenade" 1947; "Courtin' Trouble" 1948; "Oklahoma Blues" 1948 (Pete); "Partners of the Sunset" 1948; "Range Renegades" 1948; "The Rangers Ride" 1948; "Song of the Drifter" 1948; "South of St. Louis" 1949 (Bronco); "Rose of Cimarron" 1952 (Deacon).

Smith, C. Aubrey (1863-12/20/48). Films: "The Squaw Man" 1931; "Secrets" 1933 (Mr. Marlowe); "Unconquered" 1947 (Lord Chief Justice).

Smith, Charles B. (1920-12/26/88). Films: "San Fernando Valley" 1944 (Oliver Griffith); "City of Badmen" 1953 (Henry).

Smith, Charles Martin (1954-). Films: "The Culpepper Cattle Company" 1972 (Tim Slater); "Pat Garrett and Billy the Kid" 1973 (Bowdre); "The Spikes Gang" 1974 (Tod Hayhew); "Law of the Land" TVM-1976 (Dudley). ¶TV: *The Life and Times of Grizzly Adams*—3-30-77.

Smith, Cliff (1886-9/17/37). Films: "The Deserter" 1912.

Smith, Dean (1932-). Films: "El Dorado" 1967 (Charlie Hagan); "The Cheyenne Social Club" 1970 (Bannister Gang Member); "Rio Lobo" 1970 (Bitey); "Big Jake" 1971 (Kid Duffy); "The Life and Times of Judge Roy Bean" 1972 (Outlaw); "Squares" 1972; "Ulzana's Raid" 1972 (Horowitz); "Mrs. Sundance" TVM-1974 (Avery); "Seven Alone" 1974 (Kit); "Mackintosh & T.J." 1975; "Last Ride of the Dalton Gang" TVM-1979 (Deputy). ¶TV: *Tales of Wells Fargo*—"Reward for Gaine" 1-20-62 (Guard); *Have Gun Will Travel*—"One, Two, Three" 2-17-62; *The Legend of Jesse James*—"South Wind" 2-14-66 (Deke).

Smith, Earl T. Films: "The Winds of Autumn" 1976; "The Incredible Rocky Mountain Race" TVM-1977; "The Sacketts" TVM-1979; "September Gun" TVM-1983 (1st Bartender); "Desperado: The Outlaw Wars" TVM-1989 (Wilkes). ¶TV: *Cowboy in Africa*—"Lake Sinclair" 11-13-67 (Jacob's Father); *The Life and Times of Grizzly Adams*—"The Redemption of Ben" 3-23-77 (Frank).

Smith, Elizabeth. Films: "The Castaway Cowboy" 1974 (Liliha). ¶TV: *Big Hawaii*—Regular 1977 (Auntie Lu).

Smith, Gerald Oliver (1892-5/28/74). Films: "The Singing Hill" 1941; "Rainbow Over Texas" 1946 (Larkin). ¶TV: *Wild Bill Hickok*—"A Joke on Sir Antony" 4-1-52.

Smith, Hal K. (1917-1/28/94). Films: "Stars Over Texas" 1946 (Tucker); "Oklahoma Crude" 1973 (C.R. Miller). ¶TV: *Broken Arrow*—"Apache Massacre" 1-1-57 (Griffin), "The Outlaw" 6-10-58 (Dekker); *Have Gun Will Travel*—"The Great Mojave Chase" 9-28-57, "The Trial" 6-11-60; *Tombstone Territory*—"The Tin Gunman" 4-16-58 (Whitey Beck); *Jefferson Drum*—"Arrival" 4-25-58 (Hickey), "Law and Order" 5-9-58 (Hickey), "Madame Faro" 6-6-58 (Hickey), "The Post" 7-4-58 (Hickey), "The Hanging of Joe Lavetti" 8-1-58 (Hickey); *Bonanza*—"The Magnificent Adah" 11-14-59 (Watkyns); *The Texan*—"The Mountain Man" 5-23-60; *Gunsmoke*—"Old Flame" 5-28-60 (Dobie); *Laramie*—"The Killer Legend" 12-12-61 (George); *Wagon Train*—"The Daniel Clay Story" 2-21-62 (Carl Grant); *The Rounders*—10-18-66 (Orville), 11-1-66 (Orville); *Death Valley Days*—"The Man Who Didn't Want Gold" 3-25-67 (Wilson); *Sheriff Who?*—Pilot 9-5-67; *Cimarron Strip*—"Nobody" 12-7-67 (Harvey).

Smith, Harry (1911-10/25/67). Films: "Another Man's Boots" 1922 (Ned Hadley); "Daredevils of the West" 1943-serial (Kaiga).

Smith, Howard (1894-1/10/68). TV: *Wanted—Dead or Alive*—"Detour" 3-1-61 (Martin Fairweather); *The Outlaws*—"Masterpiece" 12-21-61 (Sam Porter); *The Dakotas*—"Return to Drydock" 1-7-63 (Ed Turner).

Smith, J. Lewis (1906-9/11/64). Films: "The Misfits" 1961 (Fresh Cowboy in Bar); "Advance to the Rear" 1964 (Slasher O'Toole). ¶TV: *Bat Masterson*—"Bullwhacker's Bounty" 2-16-61.

Smith, Jack C. (1896-1/14/44). Films: "Rio Grande Ranger" 1936; "Cheyenne Rides Again" 1937 (Man in Saloon); "The Fighting Deputy" 1937 (Jed); "Doomed at Sundown" 1937; "Git Along, Little Dogies" 1937; "Guns in the Dark" 1937; "Headin' for the Rio Grande" 1937; "Hittin' the Trail" 1937 (Dad Reed); "A Lawman Is Born" 1937 (Ike Manton); "Lightnin' Crandall" 1937; "The Mystery of the Hooded Horseman" 1937 (Brown); "Romance of the Rockies" 1937; "Round-Up Time in Texas" 1937; "Sing, Cowboy, Sing" 1937; "Trail of Vengeance" 1937 (Rancher); "Trouble in Texas" 1937 (Bix); "The Trusted Outlaw" 1937; "The Feud Maker" 1938 (Nelson); "Frontier Town" 1938 (Pop Pearson); "Heroes of the Alamo" 1938 (William H. Wharton); "Paroled to Die" 1938 (Prosecuting Attorney); "Where the Buffalo Roam" 1938 (Announcer); "Frontier Marshal" 1939; "Frontier Scout" 1939 (Grant); "The Oregon Trail" 1939-serial (Bull Bragg); "Outlaw's Paradise" 1939; "Bullet Code" 1940 (David Henley); "The Pioneers" 1941 (Judge); "Stick to Your Guns" 1941 (Tex); "Boss of Hangtown Mesa" 1942; "Sin Town" 1942 (Gambler); "Stagecoach Buckaroo" 1942.

Smith, Joel. TV: *Wild Bill Hickok*—"The Hideout" 1-20-53; *The Cisco Kid*—"Man with the Reputation" 3-27-54, "Kilts and Sombreros"

5-1-54; *Broken Arrow*—"Transfer" 6-24-58 (Lt. Meeker); *Laramie*—"Street of Hate" 3-1-60.

Smith, John (1931-1/25/95). Films: "Seven Angry Men" 1955 (Frederick); "Wichita" 1955 (Jim Earp); "Friendly Persuasion" 1956 (Caleb); "Ghost Town" 1956 (Duff Dailey); "Quincannon, Frontier Scout" 1956 (Lt. Hostedder); "Rebel in Town" 1956 (Wesley Mason); "Fury at Showdown" 1957 (Miles Sutton); "Tomahawk Trail" 1957 (Pvt. Reynolds); "The Lawless Eighties" 1958; "Waco" 1966 (Joe Gore). ¶TV: *Frontier*—"Paper Gunman" 9-25-55 (Willie McGill); *Stories of the Century*—"Sontage and Evans" 11-11-55; *Gunsmoke*—"Cholera" 12-29-56 (David); *Colt .45*—"Gallows at Granite Gap" 11-8-57 (the Comanche Kid), "Point of Honor" 3-21-58 (Shelby); *Cimarron City*—Regular 1958-59 (Deputy Sheriff Lane Temple); *Laramie*—Regular 1959-63 (Slim Sherman); *The Rounders*—9-20-66 (Noble Vestry); *Hondo*—"Hondo and the Eagle Claw" 9-8-67 (Ed Dow); *The Men from Shiloh*—"Gun Quest" 10-21-70 (Dee Garvey).

Smith, Justin (1919-2/27/86). TV: *Lawman*—"Clootey Hutter" 3-11-62 (Ed Cramer); *The Virginian*—"The Brazen Bell" 10-17-62; *The Dakotas*—"The Chooser of the Slain" 4-22-63 (Joe Moran); *Bonanza*—"No Less a Man" 3-15-64 (Carter); *The Guns of Will Sonnett*—"Message at Noon" 10-13-67.

Smith, Ken L. TV: *Tales of the Texas Rangers*—"Uranium Pete" 10-1-55 (Les James); *Gunsmoke*—"Helping Hand" 3-17-56 (Pence), "No Indians" 12-8-56 (Cran), "Sunday Supplement" 2-8-58 (Karl), "Hanging Man" 4-19-58 (Mrs. Sawyer); *Frontier*—"The Big Dry" 3-18-56 (Lindsay); *Zane Grey Theater*—"A Man to Look Up To" 11-29-57 (Ray Mansen); *Broken Arrow*—"Indian Medicine" 12-31-57; *Schlitz Playhouse of the Stars*—"Way of the West" 6-6-58 (Slim Enfield); *Bat Masterson*—"Double Showdown" 10-8-58 (Chuck); *Black Saddle*—"Client: Travers" 1-10-59 (Moss); *Bronco*—"The Baron of Broken Lance" 1-13-59; *Rawhide*—"Incident West of Lano" 2-27-59, "Incident at Sulphur Creek" 3-11-60, "Incident of the Lost Idol" 4-28-61 (Doug Redfern), "The Testing Post" 11-30-65 (Jackson); *Maverick*—"The Strange Journey of Jenny Hill" 3-29-59 (Starke), "Diamond Flush" 2-5-61 (Dave Dawson); *Rough Riders*—"The Highgraders" 5-28-59; *Have Gun Will Travel*—"Gold and Brimstone"

6-20-59, "The Eve of St. Elmo" 3-23-63 (Sven); *Colt .45*—"The Hothead" 11-1-59 (Outlaw); *Hotel De Paree*—"A Rope Is for Hanging" 11-6-59 (Len); *The Rebel*—"The Vagrants" 12-20-59 (Farrell); *Fury*—"Private Eyes" 1-9-60 (Cap); *Cheyenne*—"Counterfeit Gun" 10-10-60 (Morgan); *The Tall Man*—"Billy's Baby" 12-24-60 (Hartman); *Whispering Smith*—"Three for One" 7-3-61 (Ralph Malone); *Lawman*—"Tarot" 12-10-61 (Jess); *Laramie*—"Dragon at the Door" 9-26-61, "War Hero" 10-2-62; *The Virginian*—"The Mountain of the Sun" 4-17-63, "The Good-Hearted Badman" 2-7-68 (Bogen); *Wagon Train*—"The Sandra Cummings Story" 12-2-63; *The Big Valley*—"The Odyssey of Jubal Tanner" 10-13-65 (Dutton); *Laredo*—"Which Way Did They Go?" 11-18-65, "Prie of the Ranger" 12-16-65, "Meanwhile, Back at the Reservation" 2-10-66 (Charlie Stamp), "The Legend of Midas Mantee" 9-16-66 (Portrero Sheriff), "Finnegan" 10-21-66 (Tom Fox); *Bonanza*—"Five Sundowns to Sunup" 12-5-65 (Deets), "The Passing of a King" 10-13-68 (Sheriff); *Cimarron Strip*—"Big Jessie" 2-8-68.

Smith, Kent (1908-4/23/85). Films: "Comanche" 1956 (Quanah Parker); "The Badlanders" 1958 (Cyril Lounsberry); "A Distant Trumpet" 1964 (Secretary of War); "Death of a Gunfighter" 1969 (Andrew Oxley). ¶TV: *Wagon Train*—"The Ruth Owens Story" 10-9-57, "The Lita Foladaire Story" 1-6-60 (Jess Foladaire); *Have Gun Will Travel*—"The Long Night" 11-16-57 (Louis Strome), "Shadow of a Man" 1-28-61 (John Sutter), "Darwin's Man" 4-21-62 (Avery Coombs); *Rawhide*—"Incident of the Haunted Hills" 11-6-59 (Captain Loomis), "Incident at Hourglass" 3-12-64; *Lawman*—"The Appointment" 11-26-61 (Major Jason Leeds); *Bronco*—"Trail of Hatred" 2-5-62 (Dana Powell); *Wide Country*—"The Judas Goat" 2-21-63 (John Edgecomb); *Gunsmoke*—"Two of a Kind" 3-16-63 (Clay Bealton), "The Glory and the Mud" 1-4-64 (Jack Dakota); *Great Adventure*—"The Death of Sitting Bull"/"Massacre at Wounded Knee" 10-4-63 & 10-11-63 (Gen. Nelson Miles), "The Testing of Sam Houston" 1-31-64 (William Carroll); *A Man Called Shenandoah*—"The Caller" 10-11-65; *Daniel Boone*—"Fort West Point" 3-23-67 (General Hugh Scott); *Wild Wild West*—"The Night of the Legion of Death" 11-24-67 (Governor Winston E. Brubaker).

Smith, Lane (1935-). Films: "Rooster Cogburn" 1975 (Leroy).

Smith, Leonard (1933-). Films: "Take a Hard Ride" 1974-Ital./Brit./Ger. (Cangey).

Smith, Lewis. Films: "Wyatt Earp" 1994 (Curly Bill Brocius).

Smith, Lois (1930-). Films: "Strange Lady in Town" 1955 (Spurs O'Brien).

Smith, Melanie. TV: *Adventures of Brisco County, Jr.*—"Bye Bly" 2-18-94 (Carina).

Smith, Oscar (1885-3/18/56). Films: "The Golden Strain" 1925 (Snowball); "Rhythm on the Range" 1936 (Waiter); "The Texans" 1938 (Black Soldier).

Smith, Patricia. TV: *Gunsmoke*—"Buffalo Man" 1-11-58 (Abby), "Chester's Dilemma" 5-20-61 (Edna Walstrom); *Bonanza*—"Speak No Evil" 4-20-69 (Margaret Claybourne).

Smith, Paul (1929-). Films: "Shadow Valley" 1947; "Tornado Range" 1948; "The Battle at Apache Pass" 1952 (Ross); "Pillars of the Sky" 1956 (Morgan); "The Left-Handed Gun" 1958 (Bell); "Advance to the Rear" 1964 (Lieutenant). ¶TV: *Temple Houston*—"Do Unto Others, Then Gallop" 3-19-64 (Grover Clippett); *The Virginian*—"Dark Corridor" 11-27-68 (Cain Ellis).

Smith, Paul (1939-). Films: "Madron" 1970-U.S./Israel (Gabe Prince); "Carambola" 1974-Ital. (Lynn Butch); "Carambola's Philosophy: In the Right Pocket" 1975-Ital. (Lynn Butch); "Maverick" 1994 (the Archduke).

Smith, Queenie (1902-8/15/78). Films: "Massacre River" 1949 (Mrs. Johanssen).

Smith, Robert C. Films: "The Apache Raider" 1928 (Beaze La Mare); "Hurricane Horseman" 1931 (Rand); "Hit the Saddle" 1937 (Hank).

Smith, Roger (1932-). TV: *Sheriff of Cochise*—"The Kidnaper" 1-18-57 (Jim); *Wagon Train*—"The Daniel Barrister Story" 4-16-58 (Dr. Peter Culver); *Sugarfoot*—"Yampa Crossing" 12-9-58 (Gene Blair).

Smith, Sandra. Films: "Scalplock" TVM-1966 (Joanna Royce). ¶TV: *Iron Horse*—"Through Ticket to Gunsight" 11-28-66 (Nora Murphy); *The Big Valley*—"Price of Victory" 2-13-67 (Mark Kilbain), "Day of Wrath" 1-8-68 (Beth); *The Virginian*—"The Strange Quest of Claire Bingham" 4-12-67 (Claire Bingham);

Wild Wild West—"The Night of the Vipers" 1-12-68 (Nadine Conover); *Gunsmoke*—"Mr. Sam'l" 2-26-68 (Marcie), "The Miracle Man" 12-2-68 (Lorna Wright), "Tatum" 11-13-72 (Maddy); *Bonanza*—"Salute to Yesterday" 9-29-68 (Ann Harris), "A Darker Shadow" 11-23-69 (Sarah); *Nakia*—"The Non-Person" 9-21-74.

Smith, Savannah. Films: "The Long Riders" 1980 (Zee). ¶TV: *Bret Maverick*—"A Night at the Red Ox" 2-23-82 (Addie).

Smith, Shawn. *see* Patterson, Shirley.

Smith, Silverheels. *see* Silverheels, Jay.

Smith, Sydney (1910-3/4/78). Films: "Fury at Showdown" 1957 (Van Steeden); "Valerie" 1957 (Judge Frisbee); "Tonka" 1958 (Gen. Alfred Howe Terry); "Apache Rifles" 1964. ¶TV: *Cheyenne*—"The Iron Trail" 1-1-57 (Major Jonathan; *Wanted—Dead or Alive*—"Three for One" 12-21-60; *The Virginian*—"It Tolls for Thee" 11-21-62; *Bonanza*—"A Passion for Justice" 9-29-63, "The Brass Box" 9-26-65 (Ira Minton), "The Survivors" 11-10-68 (Peter Green); *Branded*—"The Golden Fleece" 1-2-66; *The Legend of Jesse James*—"Things Don't Just Happen" 3-14-66 (Paymaster).

Smith, Thomas (1892-12/3/50). Films: "If Only Jim" 1921 (Kid); "The Invaders" 1929; "The Silver Bullet" 1935.

Smith, Tom (1892-2/23/76). Films: "Gallant Defender" 1935; "The Outlaw Deputy" 1935; "Tumbling Tumbleweeds" 1935; "Aces and Eights" 1936; "Lightning Bill Carson" 1936 (Townsman); "Yodelin' Kid from Pine Ridge" 1937; "California Frontier" 1938; "Heroes of the Alamo" 1938; "Oklahoma Frontier" 1939; "The Oregon Trail" 1939-serial; "The Carson City Kid" 1940; "Melody Ranch" 1940; "Oklahoma Renegades" 1940; "The Trail Blazers" 1940; "Young Bill Hickok" 1940; "Deep in the Heart of Texas" 1942; "Down Rio Grande Way" 1942; "The Desperadoes" 1943; "False Colors" 1943; "Man from Music Mountain" 1943; "Cheyenne Wildcat" 1944; "Trail of Terror" 1944; "Roaring Westward" 1949.

Smith, Chief Tug. Films: "Shalako" 1968-Brit./Fr. (Loco); "The White Buffalo" 1977 (Old Worm); "Windwalker" 1980 (Tashina's Father).

Smith, William (1931-). Films: "Mail Order Bride" 1964 (Lank); "The Over-the-Hill Gang" TVM-

1969 (Amos); "Deadly Trackers" 1973 (Schoolboy); "Boss Nigger" 1974 (Jed); "The Frisco Kid" 1979 (Matt Diggs); "Maverick" 1994 (Riverboat Poker Player). ¶TV: *Stoney Burke*—"Point of Entry" 3-4-63 (Lieutenant Cardiff); *The Virginian*—"A Killer in Town" 10-9-63 (Andy Adams), "Dark Destiny" 4-29-64 (Bill), "Timberland" 3-10-65 (Paul), "We've Lost a Train" 4-21-65 (Riley), "Silver Image" 9-25-68 (Spector); *Wagon Train*—"The Bob Stuart Story" 9-30-64 (Thomas Lance), "The Richard Bloodgood Story" 11-29-64 (Espada); *Laredo*—Regular 1965-67 (Joe Riley); *The Guns of Will Sonnett*—"The Favor" 11-10-67, "End of the Rope" 1-12-68 (Deputy), "The Fearless Man" 12-13-68 (Luther); *Custer*—"Death Hunt" 11-22-67 (Chief Tall Knife); *Daniel Boone*—"A Matter of Blood" 12-28-67 (Catoga), "Flag of Truce" 11-21-68 (Chief Campuits); *Here Come the Brides*—"Wives for Wakando" 1-22-69 (Kitana); *Death Valley Days*—"The Dragon of Gold Hill" 1-24-70, "The Contract" 3-14-70 (Hendry Brown); *Bearcats!*—12-23-71 (Russell); *Alias Smith and Jones*—"What Happened at the XST?" 10-28-72 (Deputy Orville Larkin); *Gunsmoke*—"The Gang" 12-11-72 (Jude Bonner), "Hard Labor" 2-24-75 (Latch); *Kung Fu*—"The Chalice" 10-11-73 (Luther Staggers); *Wildside*—Regular 1985 (Brodie Hollister); *Paradise*—"Founder's Day" 11-10-88 (Quincy Bradley); *Young Riders*—"A House Divided" 9-28-91 (Marshal Ben Turner).

Smithers, William (1927-). TV: *Shane*—"The Wild Geese" 9-24-66 (Del Packard); *The Road West*—"Piece of Tin" 10-31-66 (Sam Gaskins).

Smits, Jimmy (1958-). Films: "Old Gringo" 1989 (Arroyo); "The Cisco Kid" CTVM-1994 (the Cisco Kid).

Smyrner, Ann (1934-). Films: "Beyond the Law" 1968-Ital.

Snegoff, Leonid (1883-2/22/74). Films: "Smoky" 1933 (Junkman).

Snodgrass, Carrie (1946-). Films: "Pale Rider" 1985 (Sarah Wheeler); "The Ballad of Little Jo" 1993 (Ruth Badger); "8 Seconds" 1994 (Elsie Frost). ¶TV: *The Virginian*—"Crime Wave at Buffalo Spring" 1-29-69 (Josephine).

Snow, Heber. *see* Worden, Hank.

Snow, Marguerite (1889-2/17/58). Films: "The Forest Rose" 1912; "Kit Carson Over the Great Divide" 1925 (Norma Webb).

Snow, Mortimer (1869-6/20/35). Films: "The Mohican's Daughter" 1922 (Nashinta).

Snowden, Leigh (1930-5/11/82). Films: "The Rawhide Years" 1956 (Miss Vanilla Bissell); "The Comancheros" 1961 (Hotel Girl).

Snowflake. *see* Toones, Fred.

Snyder, Arlen Dean. TV: *Bret Maverick*—"The Rattlesnake Brigae" 4-27-82 (Colonel Bang).

Snyder, Drew. Films: "The Avenging Angel" TVM-1995.

Snyder, Matt (1836-1/17/17). Films: "Salomy Jane" 1914 (Madison Clay).

Soble, Ron (1932-). Films: "Walk Tall" 1960 (Leach); "Gun Fight" 1961 (Pawnee); "Navajo Run" 1966 (Jesse Grog); "True Grit" 1969 (Capt. Boots Finch); "Chisum" 1970 (Bowdre); "Macho Callahan" 1970 (2nd Cowboy); "The Daughters of Joshua Cabe" TVM-1972 (Arnie); "Joe Kidd" 1972 (Ramon); "The Mystic Warrior" TVM-1984 (Wanagi). ¶TV: *Rawhide*—"Incident West of Lano" 2-27-59, "Incident of the Day of the Dead" 9-18-59 (Tovar), "Incident at Tinker's Dam" 2-5-60, "Corporal Dasovik" 12-4-64 (Paul Everts); *The Texan*—"Letter of the Law" 3-23-59 (Cagle), "Thirty Hours to Kill" 2-1-60 (Amos Dawson); *Lawman*—"Riding Shotgun" 4-19-59 (Jake); *Bonanza*—"The Sun Mountain Herd" 9-19-59 (Tokwa), "Elegy for a Hangman" 1-20-63; *The Deputy*—"The Two Faces of Bob Claxton" 2-27-60 (Solomon Claxton); *Have Gun Will Travel*—"Lady with a Gun" 4-9-60 (Gunslinger); *The Tall Man*—"Forty-Dollar Boots" 9-17-60 (Jerry Evers); *The Rebel*—"To See the Elephant" 10-16-60 (Josiah Boyd); *Two Faces West*—"Performance Under Fire" 1-30-61; *Gunslinger*—"The Hostage Fort" 2-16-61 (Steve Summers); *Tales of Wells Fargo*—"The Remittance Man" 4-3-61 (Gabe Adams), "Mr. Mute" 11-4-61 (Dorcus); *Wagon Train*—"The Hiram Winthrop Story" 6-6-62 (Chief Two Arrow); *The Virginian*—"It Tolls for Thee" 11-21-62 (Mungo), "Letter of the Law" 12-22-65 (Hoby Porter); *Laramie*—"Broken Honor" 4-9-63; *Temple Houston*—"Enough Rope" 12-19-63 (Fowler); *Death Valley Days*—"The Bigger They Are" 4-4-64 (Martin Beckett); *The Loner*—"The Vespers" 9-25-65 (Deneen); *The Monroes*—Regular 1966-67 (Jim); *Cimarron Strip*—"Knife in the Darkness" 1-25-68; *The Outcasts*—"Act of Faith" 2-10-69 (Joe Lennox); *Daniel Boone*—"Target Boone" 11-20-69

(Robert Jarrett); *The Men from Shiloh*—"Lady at the Bar" 11-4-70 (Deputy Wainwright); *Kung Fu*—"The Raiders" 1-24-74 (Sheriff); *Gunsmoke*—"A Town in Chains" 9-16-74 (Clatch); *Sara*—3-12-76 (Bell); *Paradise*—"Squaring Off" 5-13-89 (Wright).

Soderling, Walter (1872-4/10/48). Films: "Cherokee Strip" 1937 (Mink Abbott); "Stand Up and Fight" 1939 (Passenger); "Out West with the Peppers" 1940 (Caleb); "Ragtime Cowboy Joe" 1940 (Virgil Parker); "Santa Fe Trail" 1940 (Abolitionist); "When the Daltons Rode" 1940 (Judge Swain); "The Return of Daniel Boone" 1941 (Mayor Elwell); "The Blocked Trail" 1943; "King of the Forest Rangers" 1946-serial (Miner); "Yankee Fakir" 1947 (Sheriff).

Sofaer, Abraham (1896-1/21/88). Films: "The First Texan" 1956 (Don Carlos); "Chisum" 1970 (White Buffalo). ¶TV: *Jim Bowie*—"The Alligator" 12-6-57 (Paul); *Wagon Train*—"The Bije Wilcox Story" 11-19-58 (Bull Man), "The Stagecoach Story" 9-30-59 (Antonio); *Zane Grey Theater*—"Mission" 11-12-59 (Alou); *Wichita Town*—"Brothers of the Knife" 2-10-60 (Tomasino); *Gunsmoke*—"Kitty's Killing" 2-20-60 (Jacob Leech), "The Do-Badder" 1-6-62 (Harvey Easter); *Riverboat*—"The Long Trail" 4-4-60 (Mark Evans); *Maverick*—"Deadly Image" 3-12-61 (Papa Rambeau); *Rawhide*—"The Lost Tribe" 10-27-61 (Little Hawk); *Death Valley Days*—"Bloodline" 1-9-63 (King); *Temple Houston*—"Last Full Moon" 2-27-64 (Chief Last Full Moon); *Daniel Boone*—"Not in Our Stars" 12-31-64 (Tamend), "The Thanksgiving Story" 11-25-65 (Grey Cloud); *Laredo*—"The Dance of the Laughing Death" 9-23-66 (Tohpay); *The High Chaparral*—"Follow Your Heart" 10-4-68 (Comancho).

Sojin, K. (1891-7/28/54). Films: "Soft Shoes" 1925 (Yet Tzu); "The Dude Wrangler" 1930 (Wong).

Sokoloff, Vladimir (1889-2/15/62). Films: "The Baron of Arizona" 1950 (Pepito); "Cimarron" 1960 (Jacob Krubeckoff); "The Magnificent Seven" 1960 (Old Man). ¶TV: *Have Gun Will Travel*—"Helen of Abajinian" 12-28-57 (Gourken); *The Alaskans*—"Peril at Caribou Crossing" 2-28-60 (Chanook); *Zane Grey Theater*—"Knife of Hate" 12-8-60 (Alf); *Lawman*—"Old Stefano" 12-25-60 (Stefano); *Maverick*—"The Forbidden City" 3-26-61 (Rubio); *Wagon Train*—"The Don Alvarado Story" 6-21-61

(Felipe); *The Rifleman*—"The Vaqueros" 10-2-61 (Abuelito).

Solar, Silvia. Films: "Shoot to Kill" 1963-Span. (Mary); "Heroes of the West" 1964-Span./Ital.; "Man Called Gringo" 1964-Ger./Span. (Kate); "Two Gunmen" 1964-Span./Ital. (Mora Sheridan); "Finger on the Trigger" 1965-Span./Ital./U.S. (Violet); "Three from Colorado" 1967-Span.; "Gentleman Killer" 1969-Span./Ital. (Jill).

Solari, Rudy (1934-4/23/91). TV: *Gunsmoke*—"The Deserter" 6-4-60 (Cpl. Lurie Janus); *Have Gun Will Travel*—"Saturday Night" 10-8-60 (Ramon); *Empire*—"The Four Thumbs Story" 1-8-63 (Rabbit Stockins); *Redigo*—Regular 1963 (Frank); *The Big Valley*—"Legend of a General" 9-19-66 & 9-26-66 (Chavez).

Soldani, Charles (1893-9/10/68). Films: "The Pioneers" 1941 (Lonedeer); "Daredevils of the West" 1943-serial (Indian); "Riding High" 1943 (Indian Chief); "Arizona Whirlwind" 1944; "Belle of the Yukon" 1944 (Fire Chief); "The Man from Oklahoma" 1945 (Chief Red Feather); "Apache Chief" 1949 (Councillor); "Broken Arrow" 1950 (Skinyea); "Montana Belle" 1952 (Indian); "Winning of the West" 1953; "Escort West" 1959 (Indian); "Buffalo Gun" 1961. ¶TV: *The Cisco Kid*—"Medicine Man Story" 8-25-51.

Soldi, Steve (1899-11/14/74). Films: "Twilight on the Rio Grande" 1947.

Solinas, Marisa. Films: "Colt in the Hand of the Devil" 1967-Ital.; "Garter Colt" 1967-Ital./Span./Ger.; "Killer Goodbye" 1969-Ital./Span.

Solvay, Paul. Films: "Pirates of the Mississippi" 1963-Ger./Ital./Fr.; "Colorado Charlie" 1965-Ital./Span. (Colorado Charlie).

Somack, Jack (1919-8/24/83). Films: "The Frisco Kid" 1979 (Samuel Bender).

Somer, Yanti. Films: "A Man from the East" 1974-Ital./Fr. (Candida); "Trinity Is Still My Name" 1974-Ital. (Pioneer).

Somers, Brett (1927-). TV: *Have Gun Will Travel*—"The Poker Friend" 11-12-60 (Sarah), "The Eve of St. Elmo" 3-23-63 (Myra).

Somers, Esther. Films: "River Lady" 1948 (Mrs. Morrison); "The Iroquois Trail" 1950 (Ma Cutler). ¶TV: *The Lone Ranger*—"Man of the House" 1-26-50.

Somerset, Pat (1897-4/20/74). Films: "The Squaw Man" 1931 (Officer).

Sommars, Julie (1941-). Films: "The Great Sioux Massacre" 1965 (Carline Reno). ¶TV: *The Tall Man*—"The Woman" 10-28-61; *Great Adventure*—"Teeth of the Lion" 1-17-64 (Meg Jethro); *Bonanza*—"The Roper" 4-5-64 (Emma); *Gunsmoke*—"Scot-Free" 5-9-64 (Gert), "Dry Road to Nowhere" 4-3-65 (Bess Campbell), "The Pretender" 11-20-65 (Elsie Howell), "The Jailor" 10-1-66 (Sara Stone); *Death Valley Days*—"Peter the Hunter" 2-14-65, "The Fastest Nun in the West" 4-9-66 (Sister Blandina); *Dundee and the Culhane*—10-18-67 (Lela); *Lancer*—"The Measure of a Man" 4-8-69 (Catha Cameron); *Centennial*—Regular 1978-79 (Alice Grebe).

Sommer, Elke (1940-). Films: "Among Vultures" 1964-Ger./Ital./Fr./Yugo. (Lisa).

Sondergaard, Gale (1899-8/14/85). Films: "The Llano Kid" 1939 (Lora Travers); "Mark of Zorro" 1940 (Inez Quintero); "Pirates of Monterey" 1947 (Senorita de Sola); "The Return of a Man Called Horse" 1976 (Elk Woman). ¶TV: *Nakia*—"The Quarry" 9-28-74 (Bert); *Centennial*—Regular 1978-79 (Aunt Agusta).

Sondergaard, Quentin. Films: "Five Guns to Tombstone" 1961 (Hank). ¶TV: *Zane Grey Theater*—"Trail Incident" 1-29-59 (Barney Hollis); *Wagon Train*—"The Old Man Charvanaugh Story" 2-18-59 (Josh Charvanaugh), "The Albert Farnsworth Story" 10-12-60; *Tales of Wells Fargo*—"The Little Man" 5-18-59 (Sam); *The Deputy*—"The Deputy" 9-12-59 (Tomick); *Have Gun Will Travel*—"Jenny" 1-23-60 (Billy); *Bat Masterson*—"Dakota Showdown" 11-17-60 (Jeb Dakota); *Gunsmoke*—"Nina's Revenge" 12-16-61 (Friend), "Catawomper" 2-10-62 (Hank); *Rawhide*—"Gold Fever" 5-4-62 (Morse); *Bonanza*—"Found Child" 10-24-65 (Hank), "Four Sisters from Boston" 10-30-66 (Crocker), "The Wormwood Cup" 4-23-67 (Luke), "Emily" 3-23-69 (Hendrix); *A Man Called Shenandoah*—"A Long Way Home" 1-31-66 (Deputy); *The Virginian*—"Outcast" 10-26-66 (Zach), "A Small Taste of Justice" 12-20-67; *Wild Wild West*—"The Night of the Surreal McCoy" 3-3-67 (Gunman), "The Night of the Cut Throats" 11-17-67, "The Night of the Headless Woman" 1-5-68 (Driver); *Hondo*—"Hondo and the Hanging Town" 12-8-67 (Stoner).

Sons of the Pioneers, The (Roy Rogers, Bob Nolan, Tim Spencer, Hugh Farr and Karl Farr). Films:

"Gallant Defender" 1935; "The Old Corral" 1936; "Rhythm on the Range" 1936; "Song of the Saddle" 1936; "Outlaws of the Prairie" 1937; "Call of the Rockies" 1938; "Cattle Raiders" 1938; "Colorado Trail" 1938; "Law of the Plains" 1938; "Rio Grande" 1938; "West of Cheyenne" 1938; "West of Santa Fe" 1938; "The Man from Sundown" 1939; "North of the Yukon" 1939; "Outpost of the Mounties" 1939; "Riders of the Black River" 1939; "Spoilers of the Range" 1939; "The Stranger from Texas" 1939; "Texas Stampede" 1939; "The Thundering West" 1939; "Western Caravans" 1939; "Blazing Six Shooters" 1940; "Bullets for Rustlers" 1940; "The Durango Kid" 1940; "Texas Stagecoach" 1940; "Thundering Frontier" 1940; "Two-Fisted Rangers" 1940; "West of Abilene" 1940; "Outlaws of the Panhandle" 1941; "The Pinto Kid" 1941; "Red River Valley" 1941; "Call of the Canyon" 1942; "Heart of the Golden West" 1942; "Man from Cheyenne" 1942; "Ridin' Down the Canyon" 1942; "Romance on the Range" 1942; "Sons of the Pioneers" 1942; "South of Santa Fe" 1942; "Sunset on the Desert" 1942; "Sunset Serenade" 1942; "Hands Across the Border" 1943; "Idaho" 1943; "King of the Cowboys" 1943; "Man from Music Mountain" 1943; "Silver Spurs" 1943; "Song of Texas" 1943; "Cowboy and the Senorita" 1944; "The Lights of Old Santa Fe" 1944; "San Fernando Valley" 1944; "Song of Nevada" 1944; "The Yellow Rose of Texas" 1944; "Along the Navajo Trail" 1945; "Bells of Rosarita" 1945; "Don't Fence Me In" 1945; "The Man from Oklahoma" 1945; "Sunset in El Dorado" 1945; "Utah" 1945; "Heldorado" 1946; "Home in Oklahoma" 1946; "Home on the Range" 1946; "Roll on, Texas Moon" 1946; "Song of Arizona" 1946; "Under Nevada Skies" 1946; "Apache Rose" 1947; "Bells of San Angelo" 1947; "On the Old Spanish Trail" 1947; "Springtime in the Sierras" 1947; "Eyes of Texas" 1948; "The Gay Ranchero" 1948; "Melody Time" 1948; "Night Time in Nevada" 1948; "Under California Stars" 1948; "Legend of Lobo" 1962. ¶TV: *The Roy Rogers Show*—Regular 1951-57.

Sontag, George. Films: "The Folly of a Life of Crime" 1915 (George Sontag).

Sooter, Rudy. Films: "The Unknown Ranger" 1936; "Moonlight on the Range" 1937; "The Roaming Cowboy" 1937; "Santa Fe Rides" 1937; "Sing, Cowboy, Sing" 1937; "Trouble in Texas" 1937; "Billy the Kid Returns" 1938; "Rollin' Plains" 1938; "Rollin' Westward" 1939; "Man from Music Mountain" 1938; "Rhythm of the Saddle" 1938; "Utah Trail" 1938 (Orchestra Leader); "Riders of Pasco Basin" 1940. ¶TV: *Gunsmoke*—"The Storm" 9-25-65 (Rudy), "Taps for Old Jeb" 10-16-65 (Rudy), "The Pretender" 11-20-65 (Rudy), "Saturday Night" 1-7-67 (Rudy), "Nitro!" 4-8-67 & 4-15-67 (Rudy), "Vengeance" 10-2-67 & 10-9-67 (Rudy).

Sorel, George (1901-1/19/48). Films: "Northwest Outpost" 1947 (Baron Kruposny).

Sorel, Louise (1940-). Films: "The Mark of Zorro" TVM-1974 (Inez Quintero). ¶TV: *Bonanza*—"The Strange One" 11-14-65 (Marie); *The Virginian*—"The Dream of Stavros Karas" 12-1-65 (Eleni); *Iron Horse*—"High Devil" 9-26-66 (Jez Santeen); *The Big Valley*—"Hide the Children" 12-19-66 (Pilon); *Daniel Boone*—"Beaumarchais" 10-12-67 (Susanna); *Barbary Coast*—"An Iron-Clad Plan" 10-31-75 (Abigail McKay).

Sorenson, Linda (1942-). Films: "Draw" CTVM-1984 (Teresa).

Sorenson, Paul (1926-). Films: "Scalplock" TVM-1966; "Hang 'Em High" 1968 (Reno); "One Little Indian" 1973; "A Cry in the Wilderness" TVM-1974. ¶TV: *Wild Bill Hickok*—"Mountain Men" 2-3-53; *The Adventures of Rin Tin Tin*—"Farewell to Fort Apache" 5-20-55; *Fury*—"Timber" 3-17-56 (Matt Dixon); *Tales of the Texas Rangers*—"Whirlwind Raiders" 10-13-57 (Si Brewer); *26 Men*—"Trail of Darkness" 1-7-58; *The Restless Gun*—"The Outlander" 4-21-58 (Zack Driscoll); *Jefferson Drum*—"The Cheater" 5-23-58 (Benson); *Have Gun Will Travel*—"Maggie O'Bannion" 4-4-59, "Episode in Laredo" 9-19-59, "The Posse" 10-3-59 (Man), "The Gold Toad" 11-21-59 (Paul); *Johnny Ringo*—"Die Twice" 1-21-60 (Roy Kretcher); *Zane Grey Theater*—"Calico Bait" 3-31-60 (Gus), "A Gun for Willie" 10-6-60 (Mike); *The Law of the Plainsman*—"Amnesty" 4-7-60 (Ludwig); *Black Saddle*—"End of the Line" 5-6-60 (Luke Castleberry); *The Rifleman*—"Seven" 10-11-60, "The Sixteenth Cousin" 1-28-63; *The Deputy*—"Bitter Foot" 11-5-60 (Will Terry); *The Westerner*—"The Painting" 12-30-60; *The Virginian*—"Vengeance Is the Spur" 2-27-63; *Rawhide*—"The Violent Land" 3-5-65 (Kiley); *The Big Valley*—"The Guilt of Matt Bentell" 12-8-65 (Straw Boss), "Barbary Red" 2-16-66 (Hap),

"Target" 10-31-66, "Wagonload of Dreams" 1-2-67, "Cage of Eagles" 4-24-67 (Hammerman), "Explosion!" 11-20-67 & 11-27-67, "The Secret" 1-27-69 (Olson); *Iron Horse*—"The Dynamite Driver" 9-19-66 (Connolly), "A Dozen Ways to Kill a Man" 12-19-66 (Connolly); *F Troop*—"Reach for the Sky, Pardner" 9-29-66 (Tombstone); *Cimarron Strip*—"Whitey" 10-19-67 (Freight Agent); *The Guns of Will Sonnett*—"The Turkey Shoot" 11-24-67, "Joby" 11-1-68, "One Angry Juror" 3-7-69; *Wild Wild West*—"The Night of the Arrow" 12-29-67 (Major); *Death Valley Days*—"Son of Thunder" 10-25-69, "The Great Pinto Bean Gold Hunt" 12-13-69; *Here Come the Brides*—"Hosanna's Way" 10-31-69; *The High Chaparral*—"The Long Shadow" 1-2-70 (Beckert); *Lancer*—"The Experiment" 2-17-70; *Alias Smith and Jones*—"A Fistful of Diamonds" 3-4-71; *Gunsmoke*—"The Drummer" 10-9-72 (Trent), "The Widow and the Rogue" 10-29-73 (Farmer), "The Fourth Victim" 11-4-74 (Bill Saxbe); *The New Land*—"The Word Is: Alternative" 10-12-74.

Sorenson, Rickie (-8/25/94) Films: "The Hard Man" 1957 (Larry Thompson). ¶TV: *My Friend Flicka*—"Rough and Ready" 3-9-56; *The Restless Gun*—"Remember the Dead" 11-17-58 (Jackie Delaney), "No Way to Kill" 11-24-58 (Kyle Jepson); *The Deputy*—"The Example" 3-25-61 (Kitt).

Sorrello, Frank. TV: *Wild Wild West*—"The Night of the Eccentrics" 9-16-66 (Benito Juarez), "The Night of the Assassin" 9-22-67 (President Benito Juarez), "The Night of the Winged Terror" 1-17-68 & 1-24-68 (Ambassador Ramirez).

Sorrells, Robert (1930-). Films: "Gunfight in Abilene" 1967 (Nelson); "The Last Challenge" 1967 (Harry Bell); "The Ride to Hangman's Tree" 1967 (Blake); "Death of a Gunfighter" 1969 (Chris Hogg); "A Man Called Gannon" 1969 (Goff); "Female Artillery" TVM-1973 (Scotto). ¶TV: *Gunsmoke*—"Apprentice Doc" 12-9-61 (Augie), "The Glory and the Mud" 1-4-64 (Cloudy), "Breckinridge" 3-13-65 (Sled Grady), "Clayton Thaddeus Greenwood" 10-2-65 (Zachary), "Malachi" 11-13-65 (Cowboy), "The Jailor" 10-1-66 (Mike Stone), "The Newcomers" 12-3-66 (Handley), "A Hat" 10-16-67 (Louieville), "Zavala" 10-7-68 (Oakes), "McCabe" 11-30-70 (J.W. Hicks), "The Bullet" 11-29-71, 12-6-71 & 12-13-71 (Concho), "Larkin" 1-20-75 (Hickory); *Bonanza*—"Hoss and the

Leprechauns" 12-22-63 (Charles), "A Knight to Remember" 12-20-64 (Cyril), "The Meredith Smith" 10-31-65 (Swanson), "The Bottle Fighter" 5-12-68 (Furguson); "Dead Wrong" 12-7-69 (Sid); *Rawhide*—"Damon's Road" 11-13-64 & 11-20-64 (Barker); *Daniel Boone*—"A Short Walk to Salem" 11-19-64 (Luke Girty), "The Cache" 12-4-69 (Hogan); *A Man Called Shenandoah*—"The Bell" 12-20-65 (Rafferty); *Pistols 'n' Petticoats*—2-4-67 (Leroy); *Cimarron Strip*—"Journey to a Hanging" 9-7-67, "The Greeners" 3-7-68; *Lancer*—"Yesterday's Vendetta" 1-28-69 (Billy Joe); *Death Valley Days*—"The Wizard of Aberdeen" 1-17-70; *Kung Fu*—"The Predators" 10-5-74 (Scalp-Hunter).

Sosa, Susan (1956-). Films: "Billy Jack" 1971 (Sunshine); "The Trial of Billy Jack" 1974 (Sunshine).

Sosso, Pietro (1869-4/25/61). Films: "Western Grit" 1924 (Government Officer); "On the Go" 1925 (City Specialist); "The Broken Wing" 1932 (Pancho); "Wells Fargo" 1937; "Code of the Lawless" 1945 (Perkins).

Sothern, Ann (1909-). TV: *The Legend of Jesse James*—"The Widow Fay" 12-20-65 (Widow Fay); *The Men from Shiloh*—"The Legacy of Spencer Flats" 1-27-71 (Della); *Alias Smith and Jones*—"Everything Else You Can Steal" 12-16-71 (Blackjack Jenny).

Sothern, Hugh (1881-4/13/47). Films: "Border G-Man" 1938 (Matt Rathburn); "The Oklahoma Kid" 1939 (John Kincaid); "Legion of the Lawless" 1940 (Henry Ives); "The Man from Dakota" 1940 (General); "Northwest Passage" 1940 (Jesse Beacham); "Young Buffalo Bill" 1940 (Don Regas); "Bad Men of Missouri" 1941 (Fred Robinson); "They Died with Their Boots On" 1941 (Maj. Smith).

Soul, David (1943-). TV: *Here Comes the Brides*—Regular 1968-70 (Joshua Bolt); *Gunsmoke*—"Brides and Grooms" 2-10-75 (Ike Hockett).

Soule, Olan (1909-2/1/94). Films: "The Apple Dumpling Gang" 1975 (Rube Cluck). ¶TV: *Have Gun Will Travel*—"Hey Boy's Revenge" 4-12-58, "Three Sons" 5-10-58, "The Black Handkerchief" 11-14-59, "Jenny" 1-23-60 (Cashier), "An International Affair" 4-2-60 (Hotel Manager), "The Cure" 5-20-61 (McGinnis), "Hobson's Choice" 4-7-62 (Mr. Cartwright), "Taylor's Woman" 9-22-62; *Tales of Wells Fargo*—"The Sniper" 5-26-58 (Withers); *Tales of the Texas Rangers*—"The Steel Trap" 11-13-58 (Bill Peters); *Bat Masterson*—

"Cheyenne Club" 12-17-58 (Bartender); *Wanted—Dead or Alive*—"Eager Man" 2-28-59, "The Kovack Affair" 3-28-59 (Bartender), "Amos Carter" 5-9-59, "The Hostage" 10-10-59, "To the Victor" 11-9-60, "El Gato" 2-22-61 (Archie Warner); *Rawhide*—"Incident of Fear in the Streets" 5-8-59, "Incident of the Sharpshooter" 2-26-60, "Incident in the Middle of Nowhere" 4-7-61 (Bartender), "Grandma's Money" 2-23-62 (Hotel Clerk), "No Dogs or Drovers" 12-18-64 (Barber); *Stripe Playhouse*—"Ballad to Die By" 7-31-59; *The Rebel*—"School Days" 11-15-59 (Liam O'Shea), "A Grave for Johnny Yuma" 5-1-60 (Mr. Dover); *Wagon Train*—"The Larry Hanify Story" 1-27-60, "The Nancy Styles Story" 11-22-64 (Telegraph Operator); *Maverick*—"Family Pride" 1-8-61 (Hotel Clerk); *The Deputy*—"The Hard Decision" 1-28-61 (Dr. Stoner); *Bonanza*—"The Fugitive" 2-11-61 (Hotel Clerk), "The Pure Truth" 3-8-64, "The Flapjack Contest" 1-3-65 (Ira), "Second Chance" 9-17-67, "Judgment at Olympus" 10-8-67 (Telegrapher); *Stagecoach West*—"The Arsonist" 2-14-61 (Cal), "The Outcasts" 3-7-61 (Cal), "House of Violence" 3-21-61 (Cal), "The Bold Whip" 5-23-61 (Cal), "The Marker" 6-27-61 (Cal); *Laramie*—"The Fatal Step" 10-24-61, "Shadow of the Past" 10-16-62, "Gun Duel" 12-25-62; *The Rifleman*—"The Anvil Chorus" 12-17-62; *Wide Country*—"Memory of a Filly" 1-3-63 (Hotel Clerk), "The Man Who Ran Away" 2-7-63 (Tim); *Destry*—"Destry Had a Little Lamb" 2-21-64 (County Clerk); *The Big Valley*—"The Brawlers" 12-15-65 (Telegraph Clerk), "Danger Road" 4-21-69; *Gunsmoke*—"Judge Calvin Strom" 12-18-65 (Barber), "The Mark of Cain" 2-3-69 (Waiter); *Cimarron Strip*—"The Greeners" 3-7-68; *Daniel Boone*—"The Dandy" 10-10-68, "Copperhead Izzy" 1-30-69 (Silversmith).

Southern, Tom. Films: "Two Gun Man from Harlem" 1938; "Harlem Rides the Range" 1939 (Jim Connors).

Southwood, Charles. Films: "Three Silver Dollars" 1968-Ital. (Alan Burton); "Roy Colt and Winchester Jack" 1970-Ital. (Winchester Jack); "Heads You Die ... Tails I Kill You" 1971-Ital. (Alexi); "I Am Sartana, Trade Your Guns for a Coffin" 1972-Ital. (Sabata).

Sovine, Red (1918-4/4/80). Films: "Webb Pierce and His Wanderin' Boys" 1955-short.

Sowards, George (1888-12/20/75). Films: "The Crimson Trail" 1935 (Pete); "Sunset Range" 1935; "Daredevils of the West" 1943-serial (Indian); "Sheriff of Cimarron" 1945 (Caller); "Crooked River" 1950 (Rancher); "Hostile Country" 1950 (Rancher).

Sowards, Lem (1893-8/20/62). Films: "Sunset Range" 1935.

Spaak, Agnes (1944-). Films: "Killer Caliber .32" 1967-Ital.; "Death Knows No Time" 1968-Span./Ital.; "God Made Them ... I Kill Them" 1968-Ital.; "Death on High Mountain" 1969-Ital./Span.; "Hey Amigo! A Toast to Your Death!" 1971-Ital.

Spaak, Catherine (1945-). Films: "Take a Hard Ride" 1974-Ital./Brit./Ger. (Catherine).

Space, Arthur (1908-1/13/83). Films: "Gentle Annie" 1944 (Barker); "Bad Bascomb" 1946 (Sheriff); "Boy's Ranch" 1946 (Mr. O'Neil); "Home in Oklahoma" 1946 (Judnick); "Rustlers of Devil's Canyon" 1947 (Doctor); "The Paleface" 1948 (Zach); "Silver River" 1948 (Maj. Ross); "El Paso" 1949 (John Elkins); "Lust for Gold" 1949 (Old Man); "The Vanishing Westerner" 1950 (John Fast); "Night Riders of Montana" 1951 (Roger Brandon); "Tomahawk" 1951 (Capt. Fetterman); "Utah Wagon Train" 1951 (Hatfield); "Fargo" 1952; "Back to God's Country" 1953 (Carstairs); "Canadian Mounties vs. Atomic Invaders" 1953-serial (Marlof/Smokey Joe); "Last of the Pony Riders" 1953 (Jess Hogan); "A Man Alone" 1955 (Dr. Mason); "The Spoilers" 1955 (Bank Manager); "Day of the Outlaw" 1959 (Clay); "Gunfighters of Abilene" 1960 (Rigley); "Taggart" 1964 (Colonel); "The Shakiest Gun in the West" 1968 (Sheriff Toliver). ¶TV: *The Gene Autry Show*—"The Hold-Up" 12-14-52, "The Hoodoo Canyon" 8-17-54, "Law Comes to Scorpion" 10-22-55, "Feuding Friends" 11-26-55; *Death Valley Days*—"The Rainbow Chaser" 5-26-54, "The Talking Wire" 4-21-59 (Ben Cannon), "Hang 'Em High" 2-14-60 (Ben Hudson); *Wyatt Earp*—"Mr. Earp Becomes a Marshal" 9-6-55, "Wyatt's Decision" 9-22-59; *Broken Arrow*—"The Trial" 1-22-57 (Marshal Neilson), "Warrant for Arrest" 2-11-58 (Marshal Gary); *Trackdown*—"Like Father" 11-1-57; *The Restless Gun*—"Friend in Need" 1-13-58 (Sam Ditley); *Colt .45* -"Ghost Town" 2-21-58 (Jud), "Arizona Anderson" 2-14-60 (Marshal Len Jennings), "The Trespasser" 6-21-60

(Colonel Tomkin); *Wagon Train*—"The Daniel Barrister Story" 4-16-58 (Guard), "The Ben Courtney Story" 1-28-59 (Mayor Storey), "The Kurt Davos Story" 11-28-62 (Will Hershey), "Alias Bill Hawks" 5-15-63 (Martin Wells), "The Last Circle Up" 4-27-64 (Dewhirst Jameson); *Tales of Wells Fargo*—"Scapegoat" 5-5-58 (Hank Tyles), "Dealer's Choice" 5-2-60 (Arnold); *Wanted—Dead or Alive*—"The Corner" 2-21-59; *Zorro*—"The Missing Father" 2-26-59, "Please Believe Me" 3-5-59, "The Brooch" 3-12-59; *Bat Masterson*—"Promised Land" 6-10-59 (Doc Ferguson); *Wichita Town*—"The Devil's Choice" 12-23-59 (Sid Durant); *Bonanza*—"The Fear Merchants" 1-30-60, "The Jury" 12-30-62 (Judge Crane); *Have Gun Will Travel*—"The Night the Town Died" 2-6-60 (Sayer); *The Rifleman*—"The Grasshopper" 3-1-60; *Bronco*—"The Last Letter" 3-5-62; *The Virginian*—"Man of the People" 12-23-64 (Ownie Francis); *The Big Valley*—"The Way to Kill a Killer" 11-24-65 (Prof. Hawthorne), "The Man from Nowhere" 11-14-66; *Daniel Boone*—"Gun-Barrel Highway" 2-24-66 (Sawyer); *Wild Wild West*—"The Night of the Tottering Tontine" 1-6-67 (Applegate), "The Night of the Sedgewick Curse" 10-18-68 (A.T. Redmond); *Here Comes the Brides*—"A Crying Need" 10-2-68.

Spacek, Sissy (1949-). Films: "The Good Old Boys" TVM-1995 (Spring Renfro).

Spain, Fay (1933-5/83). Films: "Welcome to Hard Times" 1967 (Jessie). ¶TV: *Cheyenne*—"The Long Winter" 9-25-56 (Susan); *Gunsmoke*—"Mavis McCloud" 10-26-57 (Mavis McCloud), "A Man a Day" 12-30-61 (Bessie), "Wonder" 12-18-67 (Willy); *Have Gun Will Travel*—"High Wire" 11-2-57 (Rena); *Sugarfoot*—"Quicksilver" 11-26-57 (Susie); *Maverick*—"Naked Gallows" 12-15-57 (Ruth Overton), "The Goose-Drownder" 12-13-59 (Stella Legendre), "Bolt from the Blue" 11-27-60 (Angelica Garland), "The Cactus Switch" 1-15-61 (Lana Cane); *The Restless Gun*—"Pressing Engagement" 2-24-58 (Helen Rockwood), "A Very Special Investigation" 6-15-59 (Serena); *Tombstone Territory*—"Pick Up the Gun" 5-14-58 (Lisa); *The Texan*—"The Easterner" 12-15-58 (Ann Dowd); *Bat Masterson*—"The Tumbleweed Wagon" 3-25-59 (Julie Poe); *Stripe Playhouse*—"Ballad to Die By" 7-31-59 (Anna Carrick); *Wanted—Dead or Alive*—"The Matchmaker" 9-19-59 (Amy Williams), "Angela" 1-9-

60 (Angela Prior); *Rawhide*—"Incident of the Valley in Shadow" 11-20-59 (Winoka), "Incident in the Middle of Nowhere" 4-7-61 (Barbara Fraser), "Incident of the Lost Woman" 11-2-62 (Lissa Hobson); *Bonanza*—"The Sisters" 12-12-59 (Sue Ellen Terry); *Laramie*—"Duel at Alta Mesa" 2-23-60 (Gloria Patterson), "No Second Chance" 12-6-60 (Fran Erickson), "Vengeance" 1-8-63 (Gladys); *The Alaskans*—"Peril at Caribou Crossing" 2-28-60 (Janice Collier), "The Bride Wore Black" 4-10-60 (Ellen Hawley); *The Deputy*—"Lady for a Hanging" 12-3-60 (Sally Tornado); *Riverboat*—"Duel on the River" 12-12-60 (Laurie Rawlins); *Gunslinger*—"Border Incident" 2-9-61 (Martha); *Tales of Wells Fargo*—"The Angry Sky" 4-21-62 (Marie Jarnier); *Stoney Burke*—"Cat's Eyes" 2-11-63 (Libby Ferris); *Daniel Boone*—"The Sisters O'Hannrahan" 12-3-64 (Kathleen O'Hannrahan); *A Man Called Shenandoah*—"The Accused" 1-3-66 (Millie Turner); *Death Valley Days*—"A Calamity Called Jane" 2-11-67 (Calamity Jane); *Iron Horse*—"Six Hours to Sky High" 11-25-67 (Marian).

Spalding, Kim. Films: "The Gunfighter" 1950 (Clerk); "A Man Alone" 1955 (Sam Hall). ¶TV: *The Lone Ranger*—"Million Dollar Wallpaper" 9-14-50, "Backtrail" 1-25-51, "Tumblerock Law" 2-26-53; *The Deputy*—"Queen Bea" 2-20-60 (Briscoe).

Spalla, Ignazio. *see* Sanchez, Pedro.

Spang, Laurette (1951-). TV: *Alias Smith and Jones*—"Only Three to a Bed" 1-13-73 (Emma Sterling).

Spanier, Frances (-5/10/81). TV: *The Virginian*—"Stopover" 1-8-69 (Mrs. Perry); *Lancer*—"Splinter Group" 3-3-70 (Mrs. Wilkes).

Spano, Joe (1946-). Films: "Northern Lights" 1978 (John Sorenson).

Sparks, Ned (1883-4/3/57). Films: "Wide Open Spaces" 1932-short; "Secrets" 1933 (Sunshine).

Sparv, Camilla (1940-). Films: "MacKenna's Gold" 1969 (Inga).

Spaugh, Nell. Films: "Four Hearts" 1922 (Mary Reynolds).

Spell, George (1958-). Films: "Man and Boy" 1971 (Billy Revers). ¶TV: *Bonanza*—"The Wish" 3-9-69 (John O. Davis); *Daniel Boone*—"The Road to Freedom" 10-2-69 (Jimmy Hill); *Kung Fu*—"The Well" 9-27-73 (Daniel Brown), "The Last Raid" 4-26-75 (Daniel Brown).

Spelling, Aaron (1928-). Films: "Three Young Texans" 1954 (Catur); "Wyoming Renegades" 1955 (Petie Carver). ¶TV: *Gunsmoke*—"The Guitar" 7-21-56 (Weed Pindle).

Spence, Bruce (1945-). Films: "Bullseye!" 1986-Australia (Purdy).

Spencer, Bud (Carlo Pedersoli) (1931-). Films: "God Forgives—I Don't" 1966-Ital./Span. (Earp Hargitay); "Ace High" 1967-Ital./Span. (Hutch); "Beyond the Law" 1968-Ital.; "Today It's Me ... Tomorrow You!" 1968-Ital.; "Boot Hill" 1969-Ital.; "The Five Man Army" 1969-Ital. (Mesito); "They Call Me Trinity" 1970-Ital. (Bambino); "The Big and the Bad" 1971-Ital./Fr./Span.; "It Can be Done ... Amigo" 1971-Ital./Fr./Span. (Coburn); "Massacre at Fort Holman" 1972-Ital./Fr./Span./Ger. (Eli Sampson); "Trinity Is Still My Name" 1974-Ital. (Bambino); "Buddy Goes West" 1981-Ital.

Spencer, Dean. Films: "Across the Plains" 1939 (Rip); "Drifting Westward" 1939 (Red).

Spencer, Douglas (1910-10/6/60). Films: "Smoky" 1946 (Gambler); "The Redhead and the Cowboy" 1951 (Perry); "Untamed Frontier" 1952 (Clayton Vance); "Shane" 1953 (Shipstead); "River of No Return" 1954 (Sam Benson); "The Kentuckian" 1955 (Fromes Brother); "A Man Alone" 1955 (Henry Slocum); "Smoke Signal" 1955 (Garode); "Man from Del Rio" 1956 (Jack Tillman); "Pardners" 1956 (Smith); "Cole Younger, Gunfighter" 1958 (Woodruff); "Saddle the Wind" 1958 (Hamp Scribner). ¶TV: *Cheyenne*—"Hired Gun" 12-17-57 (Preacher); *The Rifleman*—"The Deadeye Kid" 2-10-59 (Jackson); *Bonanza*—"The Gunmen" 1-23-60 (Alonzo McFadden); *Tales of Wells Fargo*—"Doc Dawson" 9-19-60 (Sheriff); *The Rebel*—"Explosion" 11-27-60 (Joe).

Spencer, James P. (1877-7/28/43) Films: "Pueblo Terror" 1931 (Pedro).

Spencer, Sundown. Films: "Junior Bonner" 1972 (Nick Bonner). ¶TV: *Bonanza*—"The Medal" 10-26-69 (Boy); *Lancer*—"Welcome to Genesis" 11-18-69.

Spencer, Tim (Sons of the Pioneers) (1908-4/26/74). Films: "Gallant Defender" 1935; "The Mysterious Avenger" 1936; "Rhythm on the Range" 1936; "Song of the Saddle" 1936; "The Big Show" 1937; "The California Mail" 1937; "The Old Wyoming Trail" 1937; "Western Caravans" 1939; "Blazing Six Shooters"

1940 (Tim); "The Durango Kid" 1940 (Tim); "Texas Stagecoach" 1940; "Thundering Frontier" 1940 (Tim); "West of Abilene" 1940 (Tim).

Spencer, Walter (1882-9/8/27). Films: "The Assayer of Lone Gap" 1915; "A Question of Honor" 1915.

Sperber, Wendie Jo. Films: "Back to the Future, Part III" 1990 (Linda McFly).

Sperdakos, George (1931-). TV: *Hudson's Bay*—"Sally MacGregor" 2-15-58 (the Heavy); *Cimarron Strip*—"Without Honor" 2-29-68.

Spielberg, David (1939-). TV: *Barbary Coast*—"Jesse Who?" 9-22-75 (Jesse JAmes).

Spiker, Ray (1902-2/23/64). Films: "Riding High" 1943 (Cameron Troupe Member); "San Antonio" 1945 (Rebel White); "Rustler's Roundup" 1946 (Andy); "River Lady" 1948 (Logger); "The Man Behind the Gun" 1952; "Shane" 1953 (Johnson).

Spilsbury, Klinton. Films: "The Legend of the Lone Ranger" 1981 (the Lone Ranger).

Spindola, Robert. Films: "Ramona" 1936 (Paquito); "Henry Goes Arizona" 1939 (Pancho Garcia).

Spinell, Joseph (1938-1/13/89). Films: "Rancho Deluxe" 1975 (Colson).

Spingler, Harry (1890-4/22/53). Films: "The Plunderer" 1915 (Dick Townsend).

Spivy, Madame (1907-1/8/71). TV: *Wild Wild West*—"The Night of the Skulls" 12-16-66 (Axe Lady); *Daniel Boone*—"A Matter of Blood" 12-28-67 (Tatama).

Spooner, Cecil (1875-5/13/53). Films: "One Law for the Woman" 1924 (Phyllis Dair). TV: *The Lone Ranger*—"Never Say Die" 4-6-50.

Spooner, Franklyn E. (1860-1/14/43). Films: "As the Sun Went Down" 1919 (Gin Mill Jack).

Spradlin, G.D. (1926-). Films: "Will Penny" 1968 (Anse Howard); "Monte Walsh" 1970 (Hat Henderson); "The Hunting Party" 1971-Brit./Ital./Span. (Sam Bayard); "Sam Hill: Who Killed the Mysterious Mr. Foster?" TVM-1971 (Reverend Foster); "The Oregon Trail" TVM-1976 (Thomas Hern); "Dream West" TVM-1986 (General Steven Watts Kearny); "Houston: The Legend of Texas" TVM-1986 (Andy Jackson). TV: *The Rounders*—10-18-66 (Jed), 1-3-67 (Jed); *Pistols 'n' Petticoats*—11-12-66 (Marshal); *Bonanza*—"Differ-

ent Pines, Same Wind" 9-15-68 (Jenks), "The Trouble with trouble" 10-25-70 (Chip); *The Virginian*—"Home to Methuselah" 11-26-69 (Preacher); *Alias Smith and Jones*—"Witness to a Lynching" 12-16-72 (Simpson); *Kung Fu*—"The Ancient Warrior" 5-3-73 (Lucas Bass).

Spriggins, Deuce. Films: "Song of the Prairie" 1945; "Cowboy Blues" 1946; "That Texas Jamboree" 1946; "Cheyenne Cowboy" 1949-short; "Coyote Canyon" 1949-short; "The Girl from Gunsight" 1949-short; "The Pecos Pistol" 1949-short; "Silver Butte" 1949-short; "Six Gun Music" 1949-short; "South of Santa Fe" 1949-short; "West of Laramie" 1949-short; "Cactus Caravan" 1950-short; "The Fargo Phantom" 1950-short; "Gold Strike" 1950-short; "Prairie Pirates" 1950-short; "Ready to Ride" 1950-short.

Spring, Helen (-2/21/78). Films: "Strange Lady in Town" 1955 (Mrs. Harker). TV: *The Roy Rogers Show*—"Sheriff Missing" 3-17-56 (Mrs. Blodgett); *The Californians*—"Prince of Thieves" 11-11-58 (Mrs. Van Ness); *The Adventures of Rin Tin Tin*—"Grandpappy's Love Affair" 11-14-58 (Vera Appleton).

Springford, Ruth. Films: "Five Card Stud" 1968 (Mama Malone).

Sprotte, Berthold (1870-12/30/49). Films: "The Border Wireless" 1918 (Von Helm); "Selfish Yates" 1918 (Rocking Chair Riley); "Breed of Men" 1919 (Wesley Prentice); "Tempest Cody Backs the Trust" 1919; "Wagon Tracks" 1919 (Brick Muldoon); "The Golden Trail" 1920 (Jim Sykes); "Out of the Dust" 1920 (Dan Macklier); "Two Moons" 1920 (Sheriff Red Agnew); "Bob Hampton of Placer" 1921 (the Sheriff); "The Night Horsemen" 1921 (Mac Strann); "O'Malley of the Mounted" 1921 (Sheriff); "The Ropin' Fool" 1921; "Trailin'" 1921 (John Woodbury); "White Oak" 1921 (Eliphalet Moss); "Blue Blazes" 1922 (Black Lanning); "Fighting Streak" 1922 (Hal Dozier); "For Big Stakes" 1922 (Rowell Clark); "The Miracle Baby" 1923 (Sam Brodford); "Snowdrift" 1923 (Jean McLaire); "Wild Bill Hickok" 1923 (Bob Wright); "Singer Jim McKee" 1924 (Dan Gleason); "The Human Tornado" 1925 (Chet Marlow); "The Fighting Hombre" 1927 (Henry Martin).

Spruance, Don. TV: *Wrangler*—"Incident of the Wide Lop" 9-1-60 (Frank); *Two Faces West*—"The Avengers" 1-16-61 (J.C. Wilkes); *Gunsmoke*—"Old York" 5-4-63 (Jim);

Redigo—"Man in a Blackout" 11-5-63 (Al).

Squire, Katherine (1903-3/29/95). Films: "Ride in the Whirlwind" 1966 (Catherine). TV: *Tales of Wells Fargo*—"The Quiet Village" 11-2-59 (Louise); *The Texan*—"Thirty Hours to Kill" 2-1-60 (Mrs. Dawson); *The Virginian*—"The Devil's Children" 12-5-62 (Sophie McCallum); *The Road West*—"This Savage Land" 9-12-66 & 9-19-66 (Grandma).

Squire, Ronald (1886-11/16/58). Films: "The Sheriff of Fractured Jaw" 1958-Brit. (Toynbee).

Staccioli, Ivano. Films: "Cemetery Without Crosses" 1968-Ital./Fr.; "God Made Them ... I Kill Them" 1968-Ital.; "Nephews of Zorro" 1969-Ital. (Don Diego); "And the Crows Will Dig Your Grave" 1971-Ital./Span.; "Have a Good Funeral, My Friend ... Sartana Will Pay" 1971-Ital.; "Kill the Poker Player" 1972-Ital./Span.

Stack, Robert (1919-). Films: "Badlands of Dakota" 1941 (Jim Holliday); "Men of Texas" 1942 (Barry Conovan); "My Brother, the Outlaw" 1951 (Patrick O'More); "Conquest of Cochise" 1953 (Maj. Burke); "War Paint" 1953 (Lt. Billings); "Great Day in the Morning" 1956 (Owen Pentecost).

Stacy, James (1936-). Films: "Posse" 1975 (Hellman, the Editor). TV: *Have Gun Will Travel*—"Man in an Hourglass" 12-1-62 (Johnny Tully); *Gunsmoke*—"Aunt Thede" 12-19-64 (George Rider), "Vengeance" 10-2-67 & 10-9-67 (Bob Johnson), "Yankton" 2-7-72 (Yankton), "The Widow and the Rogue" 10-29-73 (J.J. Honegger); *The Monroes*—"Ride with Terror" 9-21-66 (Perry Hutchins); *Cimarron Strip*—"The Judgment" 1-4-68 (Joe Bravo); *Lancer*—Regular 1968-70 (Johnny Lancer).

Stacy, Michelle. Films: "The Awakening Land" TVM-1978 (Sulie Luckett); "Belle Starr" TVM-1980 (Pearl Younger). TV: *The Young Pioneers*—Regular 1978 (Flora Peters).

Stader, Paul. Films: "Surrender" 1950 (Gentleman Gambler); "Montana Belle" 1952 (Stunts); "Hell's Outpost" 1954; "Jubilee Trail" 1954 (Barbour); "The Outlaw's Daughter" 1954 (Stunts). TV: *Zane Grey Theater*—"The Man from Yesterday" 12-22-60 (Farmer); *Wagon Train*—"The Link Cheney Story" 4-13-64 (Rankin); *Daniel Boone*—"A Pinch of Salt" 5-1-69.

Stafford, Dan. TV: *Have Gun Will Travel*—"The Vigil" 9-16-61

(Reamer); *Gunsmoke*—"Harper's Blood" 10-21-61 (Kyle Cooley), "With a Smile" 3-30-63 (Kelly); *Rawhide*—"Deserter's Patrol" 2-9-62 (Henderson); *Temple Houston*—"Seventy Times Seven" 12-5-63 (Fritz Bergen); *Death Valley Days*—"After the O.K. Corral" 5-2-64 (Doc).

Stafford, Hanley (1898-9/9/68). TV: *Maverick*—"Easy Mark" 11-15-59 (Cornelius Van Rensselaer, Sr.); *Sugarfoot*—"Return to Boot Hill" 3-15-60 (Judge Lodge); *Cheyenne*—"The Beholden" 2-27-61 (Harvey Perkins).

Stafford, Harry B. (1874-9/16/50). Films: "Wells Fargo" 1937 (Dismore).

Stafford, Harvey. Films: "Ace of Cactus Range" 1924 (Randolph Truthers).

Stahl, Nick. Films: "Tall Tales: The Unbelievable Adventures of Pecos Bill" 1995 (Daniel Hackett).

Stahl, Richard (1928-). Films: "Dirty Little Billy" 1972 (Earl Lovitt); "Honky Tonk" TVM-1974. ¶TV: *Sheriff Who?*—Pilot 9-5-67 (Whittler); *Bonanza*—"The Big Jackpot" 1-18-70 (Fiber); *Nichols*—"Flight of the Century" 2-22-72.

Staley, Helen. TV: *Walt Disney Presents*—"Davy Crockett"—Regular 1954-55 (Polly Crockett).

Staley, James. Films: Gun Fight" 1961 (Nora Blaine); "Gunpoint" 1966 (Uvalde). ¶TV: *Bret Maverick*—"Faith, Hope and Clarity" 4-13-82 & 4-20-82 (Wertman); *Adventures of Brisco County, Jr.*—"Showdown" 10-29-93 (Mayor Dartly).

Staley, Joan (1940-). TV: *Bonanza*—"The Stranger" 2-27-60 (Dixie), "The Burma Rarity" 10-22-61; *Tales of Wells Fargo*—"To Kill a Town" 3-21-62 (Clarissa); *The Dick Powell Show*—"Colossus" 3-12-63 (Kathy Quire); *Stoney Burke*—"Kelly's Place" 4-15-63 (Gita); *Laredo*—"Anybody Here Seen Billy?" 10-21-65 (Laurie Martin); *The Virginian*—"Beyond the Border" 11-24-65 (Maggie); *Rango*—"Gunfight at the K.O. Saloon" 2-3-67 (Lilly); *Pistols 'n' Petticoats*—3-11-67 (Cynthia).

Stallone, Frank. Films: "Tombstone" 1993 (Ed Bailey).

Stalnaker, Charles. Films: "Custer of the West" 1967-U.S./Span. (Lt. Howells); "Shalako" 1968-Brit./Fr. (Marker); "Land Raiders" 1969-U.S./Span. (Willis); "El Condor" 1970 (Bandit); "Captain Apache" 1971-Brit./Span. (O'Rourke).

Stamp, Terence (1939-). Films: "Blue" 1968 (Blue/Azul); "Young Guns" 1988 (John Henry Tunstall).

Stander, Lionel (Red Carter) (1908-11/30/94). Films: "In Old Sacramento" 1946 (Eddie Dodge); "Beyond the Law" 1968-Ital.; "Once Upon a Time in the West" 1968-Ital. (Barman); "Boot Hill" 1969-Ital.; "Miss Dynamite" 1972-Ital./Fr.; "Sting of the West" 1972-Ital. (Stinky Manuel); "Anything for a Friend" 1973-Ital. (Jonas Dickerson); "Halleluja to Vera Cruz" 1973-Ital. (Sam the Bishop); "Red Coat" 1975-Ital.; "Who's Afraid of Zorro?" 1975-Ital./Span. (the Monk)

Standing, Gordon (1887-5/22/27). Films: "Skedaddle Gold" 1927 (John Martin).

Standing, Herbert (1846-12/5/23). Films: "Buckshot John" 1915 (John Mason); "Captain Courtesy" 1915 (Father Reinaldo); "Ben Blair" 1916 (James Winthrop); "Davy Crockett" 1916 (Col. Hector Royston); "The Hidden Spring" 1917 (Quartus Hembley); "The Man from Painted Post" 1917 (Warren Bronson); "The Squaw Man" 1918 (Dean of Trentham); "Wild Honey" 1918 (Rev. David Warwick); "While Satan Sleeps" 1922 (Bishop).

Standing, Jack (1886-10/26/17). Films: "The Accidental Outlaw" 1911; "Rescued in Time" 1911; "One Touch of Sin" 1917 (Richard Mallaby); "Hell's Hinges" 1919 (Reverend Robert Henly).

Standing, Jr., Jack. Films: "With Hoops of Steel" 1919 (Paul Delarue).

Standing, Joan (1903-2/3/79). Films: "The Branding Iron" 1920 (Maude Upper).

Standing, Wyndham (1881-2/1/63). Films: "The Bugle Call" 1916 (Captain Andrews); "The Reckless Sex" 1925 (Carter Trevor); "Billy the Kid" 1930 (Tunston); "Out West with the Peppers" 1940 (Specialist); The Sea of Grass" 1947 (Gambler).

Standing Bear, Chief (1860-2/20/39). Films: "Ramona" 1916; "White Oak" 1921 (Long Knife); "The Santa Fe Trail" 1930 (Chief Sutanek); "The Conquering Horde" 1931 (White Cloud); "Texas Pioneers" 1932 (Chief); "Circle of Death" 1935 (Indian Chief); "Cyclone of the Saddle" 1935 (Porcupine); "Fighting Pioneers" 1935 (Black Hawk); "The Miracle Rider" 1935-serial (Chief Last Elk).

Stang, Arnold (1927-). TV: *Wagon Train*—"The Ah Chong Story" 6-14-61 (Ah Chong); *Bonanza*—"The Many Faces of Gideon Flinch" 11-5-61 (Jake the Weasel).

Stanhope, Ted (1902-7/10/77). Films: "High Noon" 1952 (Station Master); "Terror in a Texas Town" 1958 (Sven Hansen). ¶TV: *Wild Bill Hickok*—"Masked Riders" 10-30-51; *The Rifleman*—"Tension" 10-27-59; *Rawhide*—"Incident of the Music Maker" 5-20-60, "Incident of the Painted Lady" 5-12-61, "Gold Fever" 5-4-62; *Zane Grey Theater*—"One Must Die" 1-12-61 (Minister).

Stanley, Barbara. Films: "Train to Tombstone" 1950 (Doris); "Valley of Fire" 1951 (Gail). ¶TV: *The Gene Autry Show*—"The Star Toter" 8-20-50, "Trouble at Silver Creek" 3-9-52; *The Range Rider*—"Sealed Justice" 12-6-52.

Stanley, Edwin (1880-12/24/44). Films: "Treason" 1933 (District Attorney); "Trailin' West" 1936 (Pinkerton); "Billy the Kid Returns" 1938 (Miller); "Union Pacific" 1939; "Arkansas Judge" 1941 (Judge Carruthers); "Buffalo Bill" 1944 (Doctor).

Stanley, Forrest (1889-8/27/69). Films: "Tiger Rose" 1923 (Michael Devlin); "Beauty and the Bad Man" 1925 (Madoc Bill); "Rider of Death Valley" 1932 (Doc Larribe). ¶TV: *Wild Bill Hickok*—"Marvins' Mix-Up" 5-19-53; *Gunsmoke*—"Overland Express" 5-31-58 (Griffin).

Stanley, George. Films: "Omens of the Desert" 1912; "The Angel of the Desert" 1913; "When the West Was Young" 1913; "Anne of the Mines" 1914; "The Little Angel of Canyon Creek" 1914 (Parson Bill); "The Little Sheriff" 1914; "Love and Law" 1915; "The Worthier Man" 1915; "Smashing Barriers" 1919-serial; "Fightin' Mad" 1921 (Col. Gates); "Where Men Are Men" 1921 (Frank Valone); "Crimson Gold" 1923 (Ike Slade).

Stanley, Helene. Films: "Bandit King of Texas" 1949 (Cynthia Turner); "Davy Crockett, King of the Wild Frontier" 1955 (Polly Crockett). ¶TV: *Have Gun Will Travel*—"Les Girls" 9-26-59 (Yvonne).

Stanley, Louise. Films: "Gun Lords of Stirrup Basin" 1937 (Gail Dawson); "Lawless Land" 1937 (Letty Winston); "Riders of the Rockies" 1937 (Louise Rogers); "Sing, Cowboy, Sing" 1937 (Madge Summers); "Durango Valley Raiders" 1938 (Betty McKay); "Gun Packer" 1938 (Ruth Adams); "Gunsmoke Trail" 1938 (Nola Day); "Land of Fighting Men" 1938 (Connie Mitchell); "Thunder in the Desert" 1938 (Betty Andrews); "The Oregon Trail" 1939-serial (Margaret Mason); "The

Cheyenne Kid" 1940 (Ruth Adams); "Land of the Six Guns" 1940 (Carol Howard); "Pinto Canyon" 1940 (Helen Jones); "Sky Bandits" 1940 (Madeleine Lewis); "Yukon Flight" 1940 (Louise Howard); "Wells Fargo Days" 1944-short.

Stanton, Ernie (1890-2/6/44). Films: "The Devil's Saddle Legion" 1937 (Reggie); "Desert Bandit" 1941 (Sheriff Warde).

Stanton, Fred (1881-5/27/25). Films: "Perils of the Yukon" 1922-serial; "The Son of the Wolf" 1922 (the Bear); "Canyon of the Fools" 1923 (Jim Harper/Polhill).

Stanton, Harry Dean (1926-). Films: "Revolt at Fort Laramie" 1957 (Rinty); "Tomahawk Trail" 1957 (Pvt. Miller); "The Proud Rebel" 1958 (Jeb Burleigh); "How the West Was Won" 1962 (Outlaw); "The Dangerous Days of Kiowa Jones" TVM-1966 (Jelly); "Ride in the Whirlwind" 1966 (Blind Dick); "A Time for Killing" 1967 (Sgt. Dan Way); "Day of the Evil Gun" 1968 (Sgt. Parker); "The Intruders" TVM-1970 (Whit Dykstra); "Count Your Bullets" 1972 (Luke Tod); "Pat Garrett and Billy the Kid" 1973 (Luke); "Zandy's Bride" 1974 (Songer); "Rancho Deluxe" 1975 (Curt); "The Missouri Breaks" 1976 (Calvin). ¶TV: *Gunsmoke*—"The Cabin" 2-22-58 (Alvie), "Love Thy Neighbor" 1-28-61 (Harley), "Old Yellow Boots" 10-7-61 (Leroy Parker), "The Boys" 5-26-62 (Nate), "Tobe" 10-19-63 (Young Man), "Comanches Is Safe" 3-7-64, "Take Her, She's Cheap" 10-31-64 (Rainey Carp), "Johnny Cross" 12-23-68 (Hodge); *Decision*—"The Tall Man" 7-27-58 (Simeon Dawson); *The Adventures of Rin Tin Tin*—"Escape to Danger" 9-26-58 (Clint Dirkson), "Decision of Rin Tin Tin" 10-3-58 (Clint Dirkson); *The Texan*—"The Troubled Town" 10-13-58 (Frank Kaler), "Blue Norther" 10-12-59 (Chad Bisbee); *Zane Grey Theater*—"To Sit in Judgment" 11-13-58 (Robert), "So Young the Savage Land" 11-20-60 (Roby), "Ambush" 1-5-61 (Private Brock), "Storm Over Eden" 5-4-61 (Fletcher); *Have Gun Will Travel*—"Treasure Trail" 1-24-59 (Stoneman), "The Waiting Room" 2-24-62 (Slim Wilder); *Bat Masterson*—"Deadline" 4-8-59 (Jay Simms); *The Rifleman*—"Tension" 10-27-59 (Clemmie Martin); *Rawhide*—"Incident at the Buffalo Smokehouse" 10-30-59, "Incident of the Lost Woman" 11-2-62 (Jess Hobson), "Incident of the Prophecy" 11-21-63 (Dexter); *Laramie*—"Dark Verdict" 11-24-59 (Vern

Cowan), "Cactus Lady" 2-21-61 (Virgil), "The Confederate Express" 1-30-62 (Amos Kerrigan), "The Betrayers" 1-22-63; *Man from Blackhawk*—"Diamond Cut Diamond" 3-18-60 (Sonny Blakey); *Johnny Ringo*—"The Gunslinger" 3-24-60 (Frank Broger); *Bonanza*—"The Dark Gate" 3-4-61 (Billy Todd), "The Way of Aaron" 3-10-63 (Stiles); *Stoney Burke*—"Point of Honor" 10-22-62 (Dell Tindall); *Empire*—"Breakout" 4-16-63 (Nick Crider); *Daniel Boone*—"A Short Walk to Salem" 11-19-64 (Jeb Girty); *A Man Called Shenandoah*—"The Debt" 10-18-65; *The Big Valley*—"By Force and Violence" 3-30-66; *Wild Wild West*—"The Night of the Hangman" 10-20-67 (Lucius Brand); *The Guns of Will Sonnett*—"Meeting at Devil's Fork" 10-27-67 (J.J. Kotes); *Cimarron Strip*—"Till the End of the Night" 11-16-67 (Luther Happ); *The High Chaparral*—"Gold Is Where You Leave It" 1-21-68 (John Faro); *The Virginian*—"Ride the Misadventure" 11-6-68 (Clint Daggert); *Young Maverick*—"Dead Man's Hand" 12-26-79 & 1-2-80.

Stanton, Paul (1884-10/9/55). Films: "Santa Fe" 1951.

Stanton, Richard. Films: "The Reckoning" 1912; "The Sergeant's Secret" 1913; "A Shadow of the Past" 1913; "The Wheels of Destiny" 1913; "The Golden Trail" 1915.

Stanton, Robert. Films: "Army Surgeon" 1912; "Mary of the Mines" 1912; "The Land of Dead Things" 1913; "The Tell Tale Hat Band" 1913.

Stanton, Robert. *see* Grant, Kirby.

Stanton, Will (1885-12/18/69). Films: "The Two Gun Man" 1931 (Kettle Belly); "The Last of the Mohicans" 1936 (Jenkins).

Stanwood, Michael. TV: *Laredo*—"Which Way Did They Go?" 11-18-65; *The Virginian*—"The Inchoworm's Got No Wings at All" 2-2-66 (Jennings), "A Bald-Faced Boy" 4-13-66 (Peck); *Here Come the Brides*—"The Road to the Cradle" 11-7-69.

Stanwood, Rita (1888-11/15/61). Films: "The Deserter" 1916 (Barbara Taylor); "The Gray Wolf's Ghost" 1919 (Senorita Maruja Saltonstall).

Stanwyck, Barbara (1907-1/20/90). Films: "Annie Oakley" 1935 (Annie Oakley); "Union Pacific" 1939 (Mollie Monahan); "The Great Man's Lady" 1942 (Hannah Sempler); "California" 1946 (Lily Bishop); "The Furies" 1950 (Vance Jeffords); "Blowing Wind" 1953 (Marina); "The Moon-

lighter" 1953 (Rela); "Cattle Queen of Montana" 1954 (Sierra Nevada Jones); "The Violent Men" 1955 (Martha Wilkison); "The Maverick Queen" 1956 (Kit Banion); "Forty Guns" 1957 (Jessica Drummond); "Trooper Hook" 1957 (Cora Sutliff). ¶TV: *Ford Theater*—"Sudden Silence" 10-10-56 (Irene Frazier); *Zane Grey Theater*—"The Freighter" 1-17-58 (Belle Garrison), "Trail to Nowhere" 10-2-58 (Julie Holman), "Hang the Heart High" 1-15-59 (Regan Moore), "Lone Woman" 10-8-59 (Leona Butler); *Western Theatre*—Host 1959; *Wagon Train*—"The Maud Frazer Story" 10-11-61 (Maud Frazer), "The Caroline Casteel Story" 9-26-62 (Caroline Casteel), "The Molly Kincaid Story" 9-16-63 (Molly Kincaid), "The Kate Crawley Story" 1-27-64 (Kate Crawley); *Rawhide*—"The Captain's Wife" 1-12-62 (Nora Holloway); *The Big Valley*—Regular 1965-69 (Victoria Barkley).

Staples, Frank. Films: "Under Northern Lights" 1920 (Henry Foucharde).

Stapleton, Joan (1923-). Films: "The Devil's Mistress" 1968 (Liah).

Stapp, Marjorie. Films: "The Blazing Trail" 1949 (Janet Masters); "Laramie" 1949; "Rimfire" 1949 (Dancehall Girl); "The Far Country" 1955 (Girl); "Gun for a Coward" 1957 (Rose); "Shoot-Out at Medicine Bend" 1957; "The Saga of Hemp Brown" 1958 (Mrs. Ford); "The Wild Westerners" 1962 (Lily). ¶TV: *Wyatt Earp*—"It Had to Happen" 4-1-58 (Daisy); *Tales of the Texas Rangers*—"Ambush" 12-26-58 (Stacey Walker); *The Rebel*—"In Memory of a Son" 5-8-60 (Blondie).

Starke, Pauline (1901-2/3/77). Films: "Madame Bo-Peep" 1917 (Juanita); "Until They Get Me" 1917 (Margy); "The Untamed" 1920 (Kate Cumberland); "Eyes of the Forest" 1923 (Ruth Melier); "War Paint" 1926 (Polly Hopkins).

Starkey, Bert (1880-6/10/39). Films: "Put 'Em Up" 1928 (Slim Hanson).

Starling, Patricia. Films: "San Fernando Valley" 1944; "The Singing Sheriff" 1944; "Rainbow Over the Rockies" 1947; "Deadline" 1948; "Fighting Mustang" 1948; "Sunset Carson Rides Again" 1948; "Battling Marshal" 1950.

Starr, Barbara. Films: "Let's Go Gallagher" 1925 (Dorothy Manning); "Blue Blazes" 1926 (Grace Macy); "The Escape" 1926 (Evelyn Grant); "The Ore Raiders" 1927; "Splitting the Breeze" 1927 (Lois Cortez); "Range Riders" 1934 (Elsie Waldron).

Starr, Frederick (1878-8/20/21). Films: "Riders of the Dawn" 1920 (Nash); "The Square Shooter" 1920 (Bill Morris); "The U.P. Trail" 1920 (Fresno); "Man of the Forest" 1921 (John Wilson); "The Mysterious Rider" 1921 (Ed Smith).

Starr, Ringo (1940-). Films: "Blindman" 1971-Ital. (Candy).

Starr, Ron. Films: "Ride the High Country" 1962 (Heck Longtree). ¶TV: *The Texan*—"Presentation Gun" 4-4-60 (Chris Calvin); *The Deputy*—"The Fatal Urge" 10-15-60 (Phil Jackson); *The Tall Man*—"The Great Western" 6-3-61 (Lt. Brian Riley); *Bonanza*—"The Dark Past" 5-3-64 (Jamey Boy Briggs).

Starr, Sally. Films: "Smashing Through" 1918 (Holly Brandon); "Pardon My Gun" 1930 (Mary); "The Outlaws Is Coming!" 1965 (Belle Starr).

Starr, Tex. Films: "Fangs of Fate" 1925 (Bill); "Cyclone Bob" 1926 (Spook Nelson).

Starrett, Charles (1904-3/22/86). Films: "Gallant Defender" 1935 (Johnny Flagg); "Undercover Men" 1935; "The Cowboy Star" 1936 (Spencer Yorke); "The Mysterious Avenger" 1936 (Ranny Maitland); "Secret Patrol" 1936 (Alan Craig); "Stampede" 1936 (Larry Carson); "Code of the Range" 1937 (Lee Jamison); "Dodge City Trail" 1937 (Steve Braddock); "The Old Wyoming Trail" 1937 (Bob Patterson); "One Man Justice" 1937 (Larry Clarke); "Outlaws of the Prairie" 1937 (Dart Collins); "Trapped" 1937 (Ted Haley); "Two-Fisted Sheriff" 1937 (Dick Houston); "Two Gun Law" 1937 (Bob Larson); "Westbound Mail" 1937 (Jim Bradley/Mule Skinner); "Call of the Rockies" 1938 (Clint Buckley); "Cattle Raiders" 1938 (Tom Reynolds); "Colorado Trail" 1938 (Grant Bradley); "Law of the Plains" 1938 (Chuck Saunders); "Rio Grande" 1938 (Cliff Houston); "South of Arizona" 1938 (Clay Travers); "West of Cheyenne" 1938 (Brad Buckner); "West of Santa Fe" 1938 (Steve Lawlor); "The Man from Sundown" 1939 (Larry Whalen); "North of the Yukon" 1939 (Jim Cameron); "Outpost of the Mounties" 1939 (Sgt. Neal Crawford); "Riders of the Black River" 1939 (Wade Patterson); "Spoilers of the Range" 1939 (Jeff Strong); "The Stranger from Texas" 1939 (Tom Murdock/Tom Morgan); "Texas Stampede" 1939 (Tom Randall);

"The Thundering West" 1939 (Jim Dale); "Western Caravans" 1939 (Jim Carson); "Blazing Six Shooters" 1940 (Jeff Douglas); "Bullets for Rustlers" 1940 (Steve Beaumont); "The Durango Kid" 1940 (Bill Lowery/the Durango Kid); "Texas Stagecoach" 1940 (Larry Kincaid); "Thundering Frontier" 1940 (Jim Filmore); "Two-Fisted Rangers" 1940 (Thad Lawson); "West of Abilene" 1940 (Tom Garfield); "The Medico of Painted Springs" 1941 (Steven Monroe); "Outlaws of the Panhandle" 1941 (Jim Endicott); "The Pinto Kid" 1941 (Jud Calvert); "Prairie Stranger" 1941 (Steven Monroe); "Riders of the Badlands" 1941 (Mac Collins/Steve Langdon); "The Royal Mounted Patrol" 1941 (Tom Jeffries); "Thunder Over the Prairie" 1941 (Dr. Steven Monroe); "Bad Men of the Hills" 1942 (Steve Carlton); "Down Rio Grande Way" 1942 (Steve Martin); "Lawless Plainsmen" 1942 (Steve Rideen); "Overland to Deadwood" 1942; "Pardon My Gun" 1942 (Steve Randall); "Riders of the Northland" 1942 (Steve Bowie); "Riding Through Nevada" 1942; "West of Tombstone" 1942 (Steve Langdon); "Cowboy in the Clouds" 1943 (Steve Kendall); "The Fighting Buckaroo" 1943 (Steve Harrison); "Frontier Fury" 1943 (Steve Langdon); "Hail to the Rangers" 1943 (Steve McKay); "Law of the Northwest" 1943 (Steve King); "Robin Hood of the Range" 1943 (Steve Marlowe); "Cowboy Canteen" 1944 (Steve Bradley); "Cowboy from Lonesome River" 1944; "Cyclone Prairie Rangers" 1944; "Riding West" 1944 (Steve Jordan); "Saddle Leather Law" 1944; "Sundown Valley" 1944 (Steve Denton); "Blazing the Western Trail" 1945 (the Durango Kid); "Both Barrels Blazing" 1945; "Outlaws of the Rockies" 1945 (Steve Williams); "Return of the Durango Kid" 1945; "Rough Ridin' Justice" 1945 (Steve Holden); "Rustlers of Badlands" 1945; "Texas Panhandle" 1945; "The Desert Horseman" 1946 (Capt. Steve Grant/Steve Godfrey/the Durango Kid); "The Fighting Frontiersman" 1946; "Frontier Gunlaw" 1946; "Galloping Thunder" 1946; "Gunning for Vengeance" 1946; "Heading West" 1946; Landrush" 1946 (Steve Harmon/the Durango Kid); "Lawless Empire" 1946 (Steve Random); "Roaring Rangers" 1946; "Terror Trail" 1946; "Two-Fisted Ranger" 1946; "Last Days of Boot Hill" 1947 (Steve Waring/the Durango Kid); "Law of the Canyon" 1947; "The Lone Hand Texan" 1947 (Steve Driscoll/the Durango Kid);

"Prairie Raiders" 1947; "Riders of the Lone Star" 1947; "South of the Chisholm Trail" 1947; "The Stranger from Ponca City" 1947; "West of Dodge City" 1947; "Blazing Across the Pecos" 1948; "Buckaroo from Powder River" 1948 (Steve Lacy/the Durango Kid); "Phantom Valley" 1948 (the Durango Kid); "Quick on the Trigger" 1948 (Steve Warren/the Durango Kid); "Six-Gun Law" 1948 (Steve Norris); "Trail to Laredo" 1948; "West of Sonora" 1948 (Steve Rollins/the Durango Kid); "Whirlwind Raiders" 1948 (Steve Lanning/the Durango Kid); "Laramie" 1949 (Steve Holden/the Durango Kid); "The Blazing Trail" 1949 (the Durango Kid/Steve Allan); "Challenge of the Range" 1949 (Steve Roper); "Desert Vigilante" 1949 (Steve Brooks); "El Dorado Pass" 1949 (the Durango Kid); "Renegades of the Sage" 1949 (Steve Duncan/the Durango Kid); "South of Death Valley" 1949 (Steve Downey/the Durango Kid); "Across the Badlands" 1950 (Steve Ransom/the Durango Kid); "Frontier Outpost" 1950 (Steve Lawton/the Durango Kid); "Horsemen of the Sierras" 1950 (Steve Saunders/the Durango Kid); "Lightning Guns" 1950 (Steve Brandon/the Durango Kid); "Outcast of Black Mesa" 1950 (Steve Norman/the Durango Kid); "Raiders of Tomahawk Creek" 1950 (Steve Blake/the Durango Kid); "Streets of Ghost Town" 1950 (Steve Woods/the Durango Kid); "Texas Dynamo" 1950 (Steve Drake/the Durango Kid); "Trail of the Rustlers" 1950; "Bandits of El Dorado" 1951 (Steve Carson); "Bonanza Town" 1951 (Steve Ramsey/the Durango Kid); "Cyclone Fury" 1951 (Steve Reynolds/the Durango Kid); "Fort Savage Raiders" 1951 (Steve Drake/the Durango Kid); "The Kid from Amarillo" 1951 (the Durango Kid); "Pecos River" 1951 (Steve Baldwin/the Durango Kid); "Prairie Roundup" 1951 (Steve Carson/the Durango Kid); "Ridin' the Outlaw Trail" 1951 (Steve Forsythe); "Snake River Desperadoes" 1951 (Steve Reynolds/the Durango Kid); "The Hawk of Wild River" 1952 (Steve Martin/the Durango Kid); "Junction City" 1952 (Steve Rollins/the Durango Kid); "The Kid from Broken Gun" 1952 (Steve Reynolds/the Durango Kid); "Laramie Mountains" 1952 (Steve Holden/the Durango Kid); "The Rough, Tough West" 1952 (Steve Holden); "Smoky Canyon" 1952 (Steve Brent/the Durango Kid). ¶TV: *Gunsmoke*—"The Lady Killer" 4-23-60 (Cowboy).

Starrett, Jack (1936-3/27/89).

Films: "Cry Blood, Apache" 1970 (Deacon); "Mr. Horn" TVM-1979 (Gen. George Crook). ¶TV: *Big Hawaii*—"Yesterdays" 1977; *Wildside*—3-2-85.

Starrett, Michael. Films: "The Night Rider" TVM-1979 (Chock Hollister/Young Thomas).

Starrett, Valerie (1934-). TV: *Death Valley Days*—"Dead Man's Tale" 3-8-61 (Bella Robbins).

Steadman, John (1909-1/28/93). Films: "Hot Lead and Cold Feet" 1978 (Old Codger). ¶TV: *Bonanza*—"The Younger Brothers' Younger Brother" 3-12-72 (Sam); *The Quest*—"Shanklin" 10-13-76 (W6).

Steadman, Vera (1900-12/14/66). Films: "The Texans" 1938 (Woman on Street).

Stedman, Lincoln (1907-3/22/48). Films: "The Freshie" 1922 (Tubby Tarpley).

Stedman, Marshall (1874-12/16/43). Films: "Jim's Vindication" 1912; "The Whiskey Runners" 1912; "Juggling with Fate" 1913; "Buckshot John" 1915 (Warden at State Prison).

Stedman, Myrtle (1885-1/8/38). Films: "The Bully of Bingo Gulch" 1911; "A New York Cowboy" 1911; "Romance of the Rio Grande" 1911; "The Telltale Knife" 1911; "Told in Colorado" 1911; "Western Hearts" 1911; "Why the Sheriff Is a Bachelor" 1911 (Alice Craig); "Between Love and the Law" 1912; "The Brand Blotter" 1912; "Buck's Romance" 1912; "The Cattle Rustlers" 1912; "The Cowboy's Best Girl" 1912 (Alice Marson); "Driftwood" 1912; "The Dynamiters" 1912; "An Equine Hero" 1912; "The Horseshoe" 1912; "The Ranger and His Horse" 1912; "Roped In" 1912; "A Rough Ride with Nitroglycerine" 1912; "The Scapegoat" 1912; "So-Jun-Wah and the Tribal Law" 1912; "Two Men and a Girl" 1912; "The Whiskey Runners" 1912; "Why Jim Reformed" 1912; "An Apache's Gratitude" 1913; "The Bank's Messenger" 1913; "Buster's Little Game" 1913; "The Capture of Bad Brown" 1913; "The Cattle Thief's Escape" 1913; "A Child of the Prairies" 1913; "The Cowboy Editor" 1913; "Cupid in the Cow Camp" 1913; "The Deputy's Sweetheart" 1913; "Dishwash Dick's Counterfeit" 1913; "The Escape of Jim Dolan" 1913; "The Galloping Romeo" 1913; "The Good Indian" 1913; "How Betty Made Good" 1913; "How It Happened" 1913; "Howlin' Jones" 1913; "The Law and the Outlaw" 1913; "The Life Timer" 1913; "The Lonely Heart" 1913;

"Made a Coward" 1913; "The Marshal's Capture" 1913; "Mother Love vs. Gold" 1913; "Physical Culture on the Quarter Circle V Bar" 1913; "The Range Law" 1913; "The Rejected Lover's Luck" 1913 (Sadie); "Religion and Gun Practice" 1913 (Winona); "Sallie's Sure Shot" 1913; "Saved from a Vigilantes" 1913 (Pearl); "The Schoolmarm's Shooting Match" 1913 (Mollie); "The Sheriff of Yawapai County" 1913; "The Shotgun Man and the Stage Driver" 1913; "The Silver Grindstone" 1913; "The Stolen Moccasins" 1913; "Taming a Tenderfoot" 1913; "The Taming of Texas Pete" 1913; "That Mail Order Suit" 1913; "Sagebrush Tom" 1915; "The World Apart" 1917 (Beth Hoover); "Crashin' Thru" 1923 (Celia Warren); "Klondike" 1932 (Miss Fielding); "Song of the Saddle" 1936 (Mrs. Coburn).

Steel, Alan (John Wyler, Sergio Ciani). Films: "Lost Treasure of the Incas" 1965-Ger./Ital./Fr./Span. (Samson); "Saguaro" 1968-Ital.; "Fasthand" 1972-Ital./Span. (Captain Jeff Madison).

Steel, Anthony (1920-). Films: "Valerie" 1957 (Rev. Blake); "Last of the Renegades" 1966-Fr./Ital./Ger./Yugo. (Bud Forrester).

Steele, Bob (1907-12/22/88). Films: "Bells of San Juan" 1922 (Kid Rickard); "Huntin' Trouble" 1924; "The Bandit's Son" 1927 (Bob McCall); "The Mojave Kid" 1927 (Bob Saunders); "Breed of the Sunsets" 1928 (Jim Collins); "Driftin Sands" 1928 (Driftin' Sands); "Man in the Rough" 1928 (Bruce Sherwood); "The Riding Renegade" 1928 (Bob Taylor); "The Trail of Courage" 1928 (Tex Reeves); "The Amazing Vagabond" 1929 (Jimmy Hobbs); "The Cowboy and the Outlaw" 1929 (George Hardcastle); "The Invaders" 1929; "A Texas Cowboy" 1929; "Breezy Bill" 1930 (Breezy Bill); "Headin' North" 1930 (Jim Curtis); "The Land of Missing Men" 1930 (Steve O'Neil); "The Man from Nowhere" 1930 (Terry Norton); "Near the Rainbow's End" 1930 (Jim Bledsoe); "Oklahoma Cyclone" 1930 (Jim Smith/Oklahoma Cyclone); "The Oklahoma Sheriff" 1930; "At the Ridge" 1931 (Jim Sullivan); "Near the Trail's End" 1931 (Johnny Day); "The Nevada Buckaroo" 1931 (Buck Hurley/the Nevada Kid); "The Ridin' Fool" 1931 (Steve Kendall); "Sunrise Trail" 1931 (Tex Texas); "Fighting Champ" 1932 (Brick Loring); "Hidden Valley" 1932 (Bob Harding); "Law of the West" 1932 (Bob Car-

ruthers); "Man from Hell's Edges" 1932 (Bob Williams/Flash "the Kid" Manning); "Riders of the Desert" 1932 (Bob Houston); "Son of Oklahoma" 1932 (Dan Clayton); "South of Sante Fe" 1932 (Tom Keene); "Texas Buddies" 1932 (Ted Garner); "Young Blood" 1932 (Nick the Kid); "Breed of the Border" 1933 (Speed Brent); "The California Trail" 1933 (Pedro); "The Gallant Fool" 1933 (Kit Denton); "Galloping Romeo" 1933 (Bob Rivers); "The Ranger's Code" 1933 (Bob Baxter); "Trailing North" 1933 (Lee Evans); "Brand of Hate" 1934 (Rod Kent); "A Demon for Trouble" 1934 (Bob Worth); "Alias John Law" 1935 (John Clark); "Big Calibre" 1935 (Bob Neal); "Kid Courageous" 1935 (Bob Bannister); "No Man's Range" 1935 (Jim Hale); "Powdersmoke Range" 1935 (Jeff Ferguson/Guadalupe Kid); "The Rider of the Law" 1935; "Smokey Smith" 1935 (Smokey Smith); "Tombstone Terror" 1935 (Duke Dixon/Jimmy Dixon); "Trail of Terror" 1935 (Spike Manning/Wilson); "Western Justice" 1935 (Jim/Ace); "Brand of the Outlaws" 1936 (Gary Gray); "Cavalry" 1936 (Ted Thorne); "The Kid Ranger" 1936 (Ray Burton); "The Last of the Warrens" 1936 (Ted Warren); "The Law Rides" 1936 (Bruce Conway); "Sundown Saunders" 1936 (Jim "Sundown" Saunders); "Arizona Gunfighter" 1937 (Colt Ferron); "Border Phantom" 1937 (Larry O'Day); "Doomed at Sundown" 1937 (Dave Austin); "Gun Lords of Stirrup Basin" 1937 (Dan Stockton); "The Gun Ranger" 1937 (Dan Larson); "Lightnin' Crandall" 1937 (Bob Crandall); "The Red Rope" 1937 (Tom Shaw); "Ridin' the Lone Trail" 1937 (Bob McArthur); "The Trusted Outlaw" 1937 (Dan Ward); "Colorado Kid" 1938 (the Colorado Kid/Robert Drake); "Desert Patrol" 1938 (Dave Austin); "Durango Valley Raiders" 1938 (Keene Cordner); "The Feud Maker" 1938 (Texas Ryan); "Paroled to Die" 1938 (Doug Redfern); "Thunder in the Desert" 1938 (Bob Radford); "El Diablo Rides" 1939; "Feud of the Range" 1939 (Bob Gray); "Mesquite Buckaroo" 1939 (Bob Allen); "The Pal from Texas" 1939 (Bob Barton); "Riders of the Sage" 1939 (Bob Burke); "Smoky Trails" 1939 (Bob Archer); "Billy the Kid in Texas" 1940 (Billy the Kid); "Billy the Kid Outlawed" 1940 (Billy the Kid); "Billy the Kid's Gun Justice" 1940 (Billy the Kid); "The Carson City Kid" 1940 (Lee Jessup); "Lone Star Raiders" 1940 (Tucson Smith); "Pinto Canyon" 1940 (Bob Hall); "The Trail Blazers" 1940 (Tucson Smith); "Under Texas Skies" 1940 (Tucson Smith); "Wild Horse Valley" 1940 (Bob Evans); "Billy the Kid in Santa Fe" 1941 (Billy the Kid); "Billy the Kid's Fighting Pals" 1941 (Billy the Kid); "Billy the Kid's Range War" 1941 (Billy the Kid); "Gangs of Sonora" 1941 (Tucson Smith); "Gauchos of El Dorado" 1941 (Tucson Smith); "Outlaws of the Cherokee Trail" 1941 (Tucson Smith); "Pals of the Pecos" 1941 (Tucson Smith); "Prairie Pioneers" 1941 (Tucson Smith); "Saddlemates" 1941 (Tucson Smith); "West of Cimarron" 1941; "Code of the Outlaw" 1942; "The Phantom Plainsmen" 1942 (Tucson Smith); "Raiders of the Range" 1942 (Tucson Smith); "Shadows on the Sage" 1942 (Tucson Smith); "Valley of Hunted Men" 1942 (Tucson Smith); "Westward Ho" 1942 (Tucson Smith); "The Blocked Trail" 1943; "Riders of the Rio Grande" 1943 (Tucson Smith); "Santa Fe Scouts" 1943 (Tucson Smith); "Thundering Trails" 1943; "Arizona Whirlwind" 1944 (Bob Steele); "Beneath Western Skies" 1944; "Cheyenne Wildcat" 1944; "Death Valley Rangers" 1944 (Bob); "Marked Trails" 1944 (Bob Stevens); "Outlaw Trail" 1944 (Bob); "Sonora Stagecoach" 1944 (Bob); "Trigger Law" 1944; "The Utah Kid" 1944; "Westward Bound" 1944 (Bob); "The Navajo Kid" 1945 (Navajo Kid); "Northwest Trail" 1945; "Wildfire" 1945 (Happy Hay); "Ambush Trail" 1946 (Curley Thompson); "Rio Grande Raiders" 1946; "Sheriff of Redwood Valley" 1946; "Six Gun Man" 1946 (Bob Storm); "Thunder Town" 1946 (Jim Brandon); "Bandits of Dark Canyon" 1947 (Ed Archer); "Cheyenne" 1947 (Lucky); "Twilight on the Rio Grande" 1947 (Dusty); "South of St. Louis" 1949 (Slim Hansen); "The Savage Horde" 1950 (Dancer); "Cattle Drive" 1951 (Careless); "Fort Worth" 1951 (Shorty); "Silver Canyon" 1951 (Walt Middler); "Bugles in the Afternoon" 1952 (Horseman); "The Lion and the Horse" 1952 (Mat Jennings); "Rose of Cimarron" 1952 (Rio); "Column South" 1953 (Sgt. McAfee); "San Antone" 1953 (Bob); "Savage Frontier" 1953 (Sam Webb); "Drums Across the River" 1954 (Billy Costa); "The Outcast" 1954 (Duke Rankin); "Last of the Desperadoes" 1955 (Bowdre); "The Spoilers" 1955 (Miner); "Pardners" 1956 (Shorty); "Duel at Apache Wells" 1957 (Joe Dunn); "Gun for a Coward" 1957 (Durkee); "The Par-

son and the Outlaw" 1957; "Once Upon a Horse" 1958 (Bob Steele); "Rio Bravo" 1959 (Matt Harris); "Hell Bent for Leather" 1960 (Jared); "The Comancheros" 1961 (Pa Schofield); "Six Black Horses" 1962 (Puncher); "The Wild Westerners" 1962 (Deputy Marshal Casey Banner); "McClintock" 1963 (Railroad Engineer); "Bullet for a Badman" 1964; "Four for Texas" 1964; "Taggart" 1964 (Cook); "The Bounty Killer" 1965 (Red); "Requiem for a Gunfighter" 1965 (Max); "Shenandoah" 1965 (Union Guard with Beard); "Town Tamer" 1965 (Vigilante); "Hang 'Em High" 1968 (Jenkins); "The Great Bank Robbery" 1969 (Guard); "Rio Lobo" 1970 (Deputy Sheriff); "Something Big" 1971 (Teamster). ¶TV: *Screen Director's Playhouse*—"Arroyo" 10-26-55 (Deputy Dodd); *Wyatt Earp*—"Trail's End for a Cowboy" 12-6-55, "Rich Man's Son" 12-13-55 (Deputy); *Cheyenne*—"Lone Gun" 12-4-56 (Dugan); *Maverick*—"The War of the Silver Kings" 9-22-57, "The Seventh Hand" 3-2-58 (Wells), "Holiday at Hollow Rock" 12-28-58 (Billy); *Have Gun Will Travel*—"The High Graders" 1-18-58 (Jockey); *The Californians*—"The Marshal" 3-11-58 (Griggs), "Gold-Tooth Charlie" 3-10-59; *Tales of Wells Fargo*—"The Happy Tree" 12-22-58 (Jake Kramer); *Rawhide*—"Incident of the Tumbleweed Wagon" 1-9-59, "Incident of Fear in the Streets" 5-8-59, "Incident of the Deserter" 4-29-60; *The Rebel*—"Judgment" 10-11-59 (Will Randall); *Hotel De Paree*—"The Man Who Believed in Law" 11-27-59 (Stage Driver), "Sundance and the Bare-Knuckled Fighters" 1-8-60 (Jepsen); *Wide Country*—"The Bravest Man in the World" 12-6-62 (Captain Ainslee); *Temple Houston*—"Gallows in Galilee" 10-31-63 (Yeager); *F Troop*—Regular 1965-67 (Duffy).

Steele, George. Films: "The Tall Texan" 1953 (Jaqui). ¶TV: *The Gene Autry Show*—"Lost Chance" 10-15-55, "The Peace Maker" 12-17-50.

Steele, Karen (1934-). Films: "Decision at Sundown" 1957 (Lucy Sumemrton); "Ride Lonesome" 1959 (Carrie Lane); "Westbound" 1959 (Jeannie Miller); "Trap on Cougar Mountain" 1972. ¶TV: *Maverick*—"Point Blank" 9-29-57 (Molly Gleason), "You Can't Beat the Percentage" 10-4-59 (Myra); *Wagon Train*—"The Riley Gratton Story" 12-4-57 (Sarah Dawson); *Jefferson Drum*—"Madame Faro" 6-6-58 (Madam Faro); *Northwest Passage*—"The Killers" 3-13-59 (Mary Clark); *Bat Masterson*—"The

Desert Ship" 7-15-59 (Elsa Dorn); *The Alaskans*—"The Trial of Reno McKee" 1-10-60 (Ellen Chambers), "Black Sand" 2-14-60 (Nora Weber), "Counterblow" 4-24-60 (Linda Fair); *The Deputy*—"Palace of Chance" 5-21-60 (Julie Grant); *Riverboat*—"Hang the Men High" 3-21-60 (Sue Parker); *Lawman*—"Man on a Wire" 5-22-60 (Laura Soldano); *Laramie*—"The Lost Dutchman" 2-14-61 (Mary Lake), "A Grave for Cully Brown" 2-13-62 (Linda James); *Bronco*—"One Came Back" 11-27-61 (Vicky); *Bonanza*—"The Tin Badge" 12-17-61 (Sylvia Ann); *Rawhide*—"Incident of the Woman Trap" 1-26-62 (Dolly); *Empire*—"Burnout" 3-19-63 (Kate Callahan); *Branded*—"I Killed Jason McCord" 10-3-65 (Lorrie Heller); *A Man Called Shenandoah*—"The Reward" 11-29-65 (Naomi).

Steele, Marjorie. Films: "Tough Assignment" 1949 (Margie Reilly); "Face to Face" 1952 ("The Bride Comes to Yellow Sky" segment—the Bride).

Steele, Mike. Films: "Station West" 1948 (Jerry); "Saddle Tramp" 1950. ¶TV: *Have Gun Will Travel*—"The Scorched Feather" 2-14-59 (Al); *Wanted—Dead or Alive*—"The Kovack Affair" 3-28-59.

Steele, Tom (1909-10/30/90). Films: "Riders of the Whistling Skull" 1937; "Call the Mesquiteers" 1938; "Flaming Frontier" 1938-serial; "Renegade Ranger" 1938 (Outlaw); "In Old Monterey" 1939; "The Oregon Trail" 1939-serial; "King of the Texas Rangers" 1941-serial; "King of the Mounties" 1942-serial (Jack/Spike #2); "Outlaws of Pine Ridge" 1942; "Raiders of the Range" 1942; "Texas to Bataan" 1942 (Lamac); "Beyond the Last Frontier" 1943; "Carson City Cyclone" 1943; "Daredevils of the West" 1943-serial (Marker/Cave Heavy); "The Lone Star Trail" 1943 (Mitchum's Double); "Overland Mail Robbery" 1943; "Wagon Tracks West" 1943; "Code of the Prairie" 1944 (Burley); "Hidden Valley Outlaws" 1944; "Marshal of Reno" 1944; "Mojave Firebrand" 1944; "The San Antonio Kid" 1944; "Silver City Kid" 1944; "Tucson Raiders" 1944; "Zorro's Black Whip" 1944-serial (Ed Hull/Ambusher #2/Attacker #3/Citizen #3/Mack); "Lone Texas Ranger" 1945; "Trail of Kit Carson" 1945; "King of the Forest Rangers" 1946-serial (Martin/Al/Baker/Wade)."Jesse James Rides Again" 1947-serial (Goff/Bates/Cole/Hood); "Son of Zorro" 1947-serial (Leach/Spike); "Vigilantes of Boomtown" 1947; "The Adventures of Frank and Jesse James" 1948-serial (Mike Steele/Barton/Gus); "Dangers of the Canadian Mounted" 1948-serial (Fagin/Durry/Driver/Lou/Sloan/Spike); "The Denver Kid" 1948; "Ghost of Zorro" 1949-serial (Brace/Spike); "Outcasts of the Trail" 1949; "Desperadoes of the West" 1950-serial (Gregg/Blake); "The James Brothers of Missouri" 1950-serial (Slim/Drake); "Don Daredevil Rides Again" 1951-serial (Black); "Montana Belle" 1952 (Stunts); "Canadian Mounties vs. Atomic Invaders" 1953-serial (Mack); "Cattle Queen of Montana" 1954; "Man with the Steel Whip" 1954-serial (Gage/Tom); "Blazing Saddles" 1974. ¶TV: *Wild Bill Hickok*—"Pony Express vs. Telegraph" 9-25-51, "Masked Riders" 10-30-51; *Have Gun Will Travel*—"The Taffeta Mayor" 1-10-59; *The Westerner*—"The Painting" 12-30-60; *Laramie*—"Deadly Is the Night" 11-7-61; *Hondo*—"Hondo and the Death Drive" 12-1-67 (Hudson).

Steele, Vernon (1882-7/23/55). Films: "North of the Yukon" 1939 (Inspector Wylie); "Riders of the Northwest Mounted" 1943.

Steele, William A. (William Gettinger) (1889-2/13/66). Films: "The Ring of Destiny" 1915; "A Knight of the Range" 1916 (Buck); "Bucking Broadway" 1917 (Foreman); "Cheyenne's Pal" 1917; "The Fighting Gringo" 1917 (Jim); "The Golden Bullet" 1917; "Hair-Trigger Burk" 1917; "A Marked Man" 1917 (Sheriff); "The Outlaw and the Lady" 1917; "The Secret Man" 1917 (Foreman); "Six-Shooter Justice" 1917; "Sure Shot Morgan" 1917; "The Texas Sphinx" 1917; "The Wrong Man" 1917; "The Phantom Riders" 1918 (Dave Bland); "Riding with Death" 1921 (Chick Dillon); "Riding with Death" 1921 (Garrity's Friend); "The Wallop" 1921 (Christopher Foy); "The Fast Mail" 1922 (Pierre LaFitte); "Pardon My Nerve!" 1922 (Nebraska Jones); "Dead Game" 1923 (Sam Antone); "Don Quickshot of the Rio Grande" 1923 (Bill Barton); "Shootin' for Love" 1923 (Dan Hobson); "Singled-Handed" 1923 (Windy Smith); "The Ridin' Kid from Powder River" 1924 (Lightnin' Bill Smith); "The Sunset Trail" 1924 (Brand Williams); "Don Dare Devil" 1925 (Benito Menocal); "The Hurricane Kid" 1925 (Lafe Baxter); "Let 'Er Buck" 1925 (Kent Crosby); "The Saddle Hawk" 1925 (Steve Kern); "The Sagebrush Lady" 1925 (Sheriff Martin); "Two-Fisted Jones" 1925 (Hank Gage); "The Fighting Peace-

maker" 1926 (Clell Danert); "Flaming Frontier" 1926 (Penfield); "The Ridin' Rascal" 1926; "A Six Shootin' Romance" 1926 (Currier King); "Wild Horse Stampede" 1926 (Charlie Champion); "The Battling Buckaroo" 1927 (Hoof Marks" 1927 (Sam Trapp); "Loco Luck" 1927 (Frank Lambert); "Range Courage" 1927 (Tex Lucas); "Rough and Ready" 1927 (Morris Manning); "The Valley of Hell" 1927 (James Brady); "Whispering Sage" 1927 (Tom Kildare); "The Black Ace" 1928; "Call of the Heart" 1928 (Dave Crenshaw); "The Fearless Rider" 1928 (Dr. Lucifer Blade); "Thunder Riders" 1928 (Lem Dawson); "The Lone Star Ranger" 1930 (1st Deputy); "Flaming Guns" 1932 (Rustler); "Gordon of Ghost City" 1933-serial (Bob); "King of the Arena" 1933; "The Red Rider" 1934-serial; "When a Man Sees Red" 1934 (Spike); "Romance Rides the Range" 1936 (Slick); "Destry Rides Again" 1939 (Cowboy); "The Westerner" 1940 (Tex Cole); "The Outlaw" 1943 (Deputy); "San Antonio" 1945 (Roper); "She Wore a Yellow Ribbon" 1949 (Noncommissioned Officer); "Colt .45" 1950; "The Showdown" 1950 (Terry); "The Searchers" 1956 (Nesby).

Steelman, Hosea (1876-7/4/53). Films: "The Virginian" 1914 (Lincoln McLean).

Steen, Mike (1928-5/9/83). Films: "The True Story of Jesse James" 1957 (Deputy Ed).

Steenburgen, Mary (1952-). Films: "Goin' South" 1978 (Julia Tate); "Back to the Future, Part III" 1990 (Clara Clayton).

Steers, Larry (1888-2/15/51). Films: "Ten Scars Make a Man" 1924-serial; "The Phantom Flyer" 1928 (Joe Calvert); "In Old California" 1929 (Ollie Radanell); "Redskin" 1929 (John Walton); "Riding the Wind" 1942 (Jackson); "Hands Across the Border" 1943 (Col. Carter); "Mojave Firebrand" 1944; "Saddle Pals" 1947.

Stefanelli, Benito. Films: "For a Few Dollars More" 1965-Ital./Ger./Span. (Indio's Gang Member); "The Big Gundown" 1966-Ital. (Jess); "The Good, the Bad, and the Ugly" 1966-Ital.; "The Hellbenders" 1966-U.S./Ital./Span. (Slim); "Day of Anger" 1967-Ital./Ger.; "Once Upon a Time in the West" 1968-Ital.; "Gentleman Killer" 1969-Span./Ital.

Stefani, Joseph. *see* DeStefani, Joseph.

Stefani, Michael. TV: *The*

Rifleman—"Nora" 5-24-60 (Chad Morgan); *Two Faces West*—"The Operation" 11-14-60 (Tom); *Bonanza*—"Big Shadow on the Land" 4-17-66 (Lorenzo Rossi), "The Deed and the Dilemma" 3-26-67 (Lorenzo Rossi), "The Sound of Drums" 11-17-68 (Lorenzo).

Steffen, Anthony (Antonio De Teffe) (1932-). Films: "Coffin for the Sheriff" 1965-Ital./Span. (Sheriff); "The Last Tomahawk" 1965-Ger./Ital./Span. (Strongheart); "Few Dollars for Django" 1966-Ital./Span. (Django); "Blood at Sundown" 1967-Span./Ital. (Steve McDougall); "Killer Kid" 1967-Ital. (Tom Morrison); "Train for Durango" 1967-Ital./Span. (Gringo); "Two Pistols and a Coward" 1967-Ital. (Gary McGuire); "Cry for Revenge" 1968-Ital./Span. (Fred); "Ringo: Face of Revenge" 1968-Ital./Span. (Tim); "Seven Dollars on the Red" 1968-Ital./Span. (Johnny); "Stranger in Paso Bravo" 1968-Ital. (Gary); "Blood at Sundown" 1969-Ital./Span. (Johnny); "Dead Are Countless" 1969-Ital./Span. (Lt. Garringo); "Django the Bastard" 1969-Ital./Span. (Django); "Gentleman Killer" 1969-Span./Ital. (Gentleman Jo); "Man Who Cried for Revenge" 1969-Ital./Span. (Drake); "No Room to Die" 1969-Ital. (Django/Brandon); "Shango" 1969-Ital. (Shango); "Arizona" 1970-Ital./Span. (Arizona Colt); "Apocalypse Joe" 1970-Ital./Span. (Apocalypse Joe); "Sabata the Killer" 1970-Ital./Span. (Sabata); "Man Called Django" 1971-Ital. (Django); "Dallas" 1972-Span./Ital. (Jake); "Tequila" 1974-Ital./Span.; "Too Much Gold for One Gringo" 1974-Ital./Span.

Stehli, Edgar (1884-7/25/73). Films: "Drum Beat" 1954 (Jesse Grant); "No Name on the Bullet" 1959 (Judge Benson). ¶TV: *Gunsmoke*—"Pucket's New Year" 1-5-57 (Ira Pucket); *The Texan*—"A Quart of Law" 1-12-59 (Winthrop Davis); *Buckskin*—"Charlie, My Boy" 4-6-59 (Steve); *The Restless Gun*—"Code for a Killer" 4-27-59; *Sugarfoot*—"The Avengers" 5-12-59; *Cheyenne*—"Reprieve" 10-5-59 (Harmon).

Steiger, Rod (1925-). Films: "Oklahoma!" 1955 (Jud Fry); "Jubal" 1956 (Pinky); "Run of the Arrow" 1957 (O'Meara); "Duck, You Sucker!" 1971-Ital. (Juan Miranda); "Cattle Annie and Little Britches" 1981 (Tilighman); "Desperado: Avalanche at Devil's Rider" TVM-1988 (Silas Slaten). ¶TV: *Wagon Train*—"The Saul Bevins Story" 4-12-61 (Sal Bevins).

Stein, Sammy (1906-3/30/66). Films: "Prairie Schooners" 1940 (Dude Getter); "Sierra Sue" 1941; "Wildcat of Tucson" 1941 (Logan).

Steiner, John (1941-). Films: "Blood and Guns" 1968-Ital./Span.; "Man Called Blade" 1977-Ital. (Theo Voller).

Stella, Luciano. *see* Kendall, Tony.

Stephens, Harvey (1901-12/22/86). Films: "Robin Hood of El Dorado" 1936 (Capt. Osborne); "Forlorn River" 1937 (Les Setter); "The Texans" 1938 (Lt. David Nichols); "The Oklahoma Kid" 1939 (Ned Kincaid); "Stagecoach War" 1940 (Neal Holt); "Texas Rangers Ride Again" 1940 (Ranger Blair); "When the Daltons Rode" 1940 (Rigby); "Tombstone, the Town Too Tough to Die" 1942 (Morgan Earp); "Three Young Texans" 1954 (Jim Colt); "Oregon Passage" 1958 (Capt. Boyson); "The Plunderers" 1960 (Doc Fuller); "Advance to the Rear" 1964 (Gen. Dunlap). ¶TV: *Tales of Wells Fargo*—"The Prisoner" 2-17-58 (Senator); *Colt .45*—"Circle of Fear" 3-7-58 (Maj. David Trevelen); *The Restless Gun*—"The Whip" 3-31-58 (Father); *Wagon Train*—"The Sacramento Story" 6-25-58 (Maxwell Revere); *Bat Masterson*—"The Treasure of Worry Hill" 12-3-58 (Isaac Parker), "Shakedown at St. Joe" 10-29-59 (Judge Thatcher); *Rough Riders*—"Witness Against the Judge" 2-26-59 (Judge Allison); *Tombstone Territory*—"Red Terror of Tombstone" 10-9-59; *Bonanza*—"The Thunder Man" 5-5-63 (Uncle Fred), "All Ye His Saints" 12-19-65 (Dr. Randall).

Stephens, James (1951-). Films: "True Grit" TVM-1978 (Joshua); "Houston: The Legend of Texas" TVM-1986 (Stephen Austin). ¶TV: *How the West Was Won*—Episode One 2-12-78 (C.I. Bradley).

Stephens, Laraine (1942-). Films: "40 Guns to Apache Pass" 1967 (Ellen). ¶TV: *Laramie*—"Badge of Glory" 5-7-63; *Laredo*—"Above the Law" 1-13-66 (Ruth Phelps), "Sound of Terror" 4-7-66 (Barbara Halsey); *The Quest*—"Prairie Woman" 11-10-76 (Seba Alcott).

Stephens, Rachel. Films: "The True Story of Jesse James" 1957 (Anne); "One Foot in Hell" 1960 (Ellie Barrett).

Stephenson, James (1889-7/29/41). Films: "Cowboy from Brooklyn" 1938 (Prof. Landis); "Heart of the North" 1938 (Inspector Stephen Gore); "River's End" 1940 (Inspector McDowell).

Stephenson, John. TV: *The Lone Ranger*—"Dan Reid's Fight for Life" 11-18-54 (Roy Barnett); *The Restless Gun*—"The Whip" 3-31-58 (Suitor); *Wichita Town*—"Day of Battle" 1-18-59 (Cavendish); *Bonanza*—"The Sisters" 12-12-59; *Tales of Wells Fargo*—"The Lat Mayor Brown" 3-7-60 (Miles Rogers); *Whispering Smith*—"The Idol" 9-18-61 (Eddie Royce); *F Troop*—"Old Ironpants" 11-2-65 (Custer).

Stephenson, Robert (1901-9/5/70). Films: "Silver River" 1948 (Soldier); "Copper Canyon" 1950 (Miner); "The Wild North" 1952 (Drunk); "Riding Shotgun" 1954; "Tall Man Riding" 1955. ¶TV: *Wanted—Dead or Alive*—"Tolliver Bender" 2-13-60.

Steppling, John (1870-4/6/32). Films: "The Promise" 1917 (Fallon); "Soft Shoes" 1925 (Markham).

Sterling, Edythe (1892-6/5/62). Films: "The Girl from Texas" 1914; "The Sheriff's Story" 1914; "Cattle Queen's Romance" 1915; "The Ghost Wagon" 1915 (Bara); "The Superior Claim" 1915; "When the Fiddler Came to Big Horn" 1915; "The Stain in the Blood" 1916 (Mary Thompson); "The Secret Man" 1917 (Molly); "The Arizona Catclaw" 1919 (Blossom Ruggles); "Call of the West" 1920; "The Cowboy's Sweetheart" 1920; "The Fiddler of the Little Big Horn" 1920; "The Girl Who Dared" 1920 (Barbara Hampton); "The One Way Trail" 1920 (Wanda Walker); "Ranch and Range" 1920; "Vulture of the West" 1920; "The Stranger in Canyon Valley" 1921; "Crimson Gold" 1923 (Grace Miller); "Danger" 1923 (Judy).

Sterling, Ford (1884-10/13/39). Films: "The Spoilers" 1923 (Slapjack Simms); "Drums of the Desert" 1927 (Perkins).

Sterling, Jan (1923-). Films: "Sky Full of Moon" 1952 (Dixie Delmar); "Pony Express" 1953 (Denny); "The Vanquished" 1953 (Rose Slater); "Man with the Gun" 1955 (Nelly Bain). ¶TV: *Wagon Train*—"The Annie Griffith Story" 2-25-59 (Annie Griffith), "The Selena Hartnell Story" 10-18-61 (Selena Hartnell); *Riverboat*—"Strange Request" 12-13-59 (Lorna Langton); *Bonanza*—"The Blood Line" 12-31-60 (Dianne Jordan); *The Road West*—"Eleven Miles to Eden" 3-13-67 (Sarah Meagen); *The Men from Shiloh*—"Jump-Up" 3-24-71 (Mary Beth); *Kung Fu*—"This Valley of Terror" 9-28-74 (Mary Jenkins).

Sterling, Richard (1880-4/15/

59). Films: "Ramona" 1916 (Angus Phail).

Sterling, Robert (1917-). Films: "The Gay Caballero" 1940 (Billy Brewster); "Roughshod" 1949 (Clay); "The Sundowners" 1950 (Tom Cloud); "Column South" 1953 (Capt. Lee Whitlock). ¶TV: *Wagon Train*—"The Julia Gage Story" 12-18-57.

Sterling, Tisha (1944-). Films: "Journey to Shiloh" 1968 (Airybelle Sumner); "Powderkeg" TVM-1971 (Beth Parkinson). ¶TV: *The Road West*—"Eleven Miles to Eden" 3-13-67 (Tassie); *Bonanza*—"Star Crossed" 3-10-68 (Laura Jean Pollard); *The Men from Shiloh*—"Flight from Memory" 2-17-71 (Melissa).

Stern, Daniel (1957-). Films: "City Slickers" 1991 (Phil Berquist); "City Slickers II: The Legend of Curly's Gold" 1994 (Phil Berquist).

Stern, George (1904-5/3/72). Films: "Barricade" 1950 (Tippy); "Rogue River" 1950 (H.P. Jackson).

Stern, Louis (1860-2/15/41). Films: "In Old California" 1929 (Ramon De Hermosa).

Stern, Tom (1934-). Films: "The Hallelujah Trail" 1965 (Kevin O'Flaherty). ¶TV: *The Loner*—"Flight of the Arctic Tern" 10-23-65 (Rob Clark); *Gunsmoke*—"The Hanging" 12-31-66 (Billy Boles), "Abelia" 11-18-68 (Tom Cole); *Rango*—"If You Can't Take It with You, Don't Go" 4-21-67 (Jay Larson).

Sterne, Morgan (1926-). TV: *Bonanza*—"Return Engagement" 3-1-70 (Stanhope).

Stevens, Andrew (1936-). Films: "The Oregon Trail" TVM-1976 (Andrew Thorpe); "Death Hunt" 1981 (Alvin). ¶TV: *The Quest*—"Portrait of a Gunfighter" 12-22-76 (Minter); *The Oregon Trail*—Regular 1977 (Andrew Thorpe).

Stevens, Angela. Films: "The Kid from Broken Gun" 1952 (Gail Kingston); "Jack McCall, Desperado" 1953 (Rose Griffith); "Blackjack Ketchum, Desperado" 1956 (Laurie Webster); "Utah Blaine" 1957 (Mary Blake). ¶TV: *Circus Boy*—"Joey's Wedding Day" 2-24-57 (Susie); *Death Valley Days*—"Valley of Danger" 5-12-59 (Anita); *Have Gun Will Travel*—"The Trial" 6-11-60.

Stevens, Byron (1904-12/15/64). Films: "Union Pacific" 1939.

Stevens, Charles (1893-8/22/64). Films: "The Good Bad Man" 1916; "The Man from Painted Post" 1917 (Tony Lopez); "Wild and Woolly" 1917 (Pedro); "Six-Shooter

Andy" 1918 (Mexican John); "Mark of Zorro" 1920; "The Mollycoddle" 1920 (Yellow Horse); "Captain Fly-By-Night" 1922 (Indian); "Don Q, Son of Zorro" 1925 (Robledo); "A Son of His Father" 1925 (Pablo); "The Vanishing American" 1925 (Shoie); "The Virginian" 1929 (Pedro); "The Big Trail" 1930 (Lopez); "Cisco Kid" 1931 (Lopez); "The Conquering Horde" 1931 (John); "The Broken Wing" 1932 (Chicken Thief); "The Golden West" 1932; "Heritage of the Desert" 1932; "Mystery Ranch" 1932 (Tonto); "South of the Rio Grande" 1932 (Pedro); "The California Trail" 1933 (Juan); "Drum Taps" 1933 (Indian Joe); "Call of the Wild" 1935 (Francois); "Under the Pampas Moon" 1935 (Groom); "Aces and Eights" 1936 (Capt. Felipe); "Bold Caballero" 1936 (Captan Vargas); "Robin Hood of El Dorado" 1936 (Bandit); "Rose of the Rancho" 1936 (Peon Spy); "The Three Godfathers" 1936 (Horse Thief); "Three on the Trail" 1936 (Pecos Kane); "Fair Warning" 1937; "Wild West Days" 1937-serial; "Flaming Frontier" 1938-serial (Breed); "Forbidden Valley" 1938 (Blackjack); "Renegade Ranger" 1938 (Manuel); "The Arizona Wildcat" 1939 (Carlos); "Desperate Trails" 1939 (Ortega); "Frontier Marshal" 1939 (Indian Charlie); "Man of Conquest" 1939 (Zavola); "The Oregon Trail" 1939-serial; "Union Pacific" 1939 (Indian); "Geronimo" 1940 (Indian); "The Girl and the Gambler" 1939 (Andres); "Kit Carson" 1940 (Ruiz); "Wagons Westward" 1940 (Pima); "Winners of the West" 1940-serial (Snakeye); "The Bad Man" 1941 (Venustiano); "Roaring Frontiers" 1941; "Overland Mail" 1942-serial (Puma); "Pierre of the Plains" 1942 (Crying Loon); "Marked Trails" 1944 (Denver); "Bad Men of the Border" 1945; "Bandits of the Badlands" 1945; "San Antonio" 1945 (Sojer Harris); "South of the Rio Grande" 1945 (Sebastian); "Border Bandits" 1946 (Jose); "My Darling Clementine" 1946 (Indian Charlie); "Buffalo Bill Rides Again" 1947 (White Mountain); "Fury at Furnace Creek" 1948 (Artego); "Return of the Badmen" 1948 (Grey Eagle); "Roll, Thunder, Roll" 1949 (Felipe); "Square Dance Jubilee" 1949 (Bert); "The Walking Hills" 1949 (Cleve); "Ambush" 1950 (Diablito); "California Passage" 1950 (Pedro); "Indian Territory" 1950 (Soma); "The Savage Horde" 1950; "The Showdown" 1950 (Indian Joe); "Ticket to Tomahawk" 1950 (Trancos); "Oh! Susanna" 1951 (Charlie Grass); "Warpath" 1951

(Courier); "The Lion and the Horse" 1952 (Deputy Britt); "Smoky Canyon" 1952 (Johnny Big Foot); "Wagons West" 1952 (Kaw Chief); "Escape from Fort Bravo" 1953 (Eliota); "Ride, Vaquero!" 1953 (Vaquero); "Jubilee Trail" 1954 (Pablo, the Peon); "Man with the Steel Whip" 1954-serial (Blackjack Sam); "The Vanishing American" 1955 (Quah-Tain); "Pardners" 1956 (Indian); "Last Train from Gun Hill" 1959 (Keno). ¶TV: The Lone Ranger— "White Man's Magic" 7-13-50, "White Brown Pony" 5-14-53, "White Hawk's Decision" 10-18-56, "Quarter Horse War" 11-8-56, "Ghost Canyon" 12-27-56; Sky King—"The Rainbird" 10-14-51; Wild Bill Hickok—"Mexican Gun Running Story" 1-8-52; The Adventures of Rin Tin Tin—"Rusty Meets Mr. Nobody" 5-4-56 (Wynoki), "O'Hara Gets Culture" 3-8-57, "Tomahawk Tubbs" 2-7-58 (Geronimo); Sergeant Preston of the Yukon—"Bad Medicine" 5-17-56 (Medicine Man), "Rebellion in the North" 7-12-56 (Atasuk), "King of Herschel Island" 10-25-56 (Atasuk); Wagon Train—"The Nels Stack Story" 10-23-57, "The Mark Hanford Story" 2-26-58 (Medicine Man); Broken Arrow—"The Teacher" 11-19-57 (Neche); Zorro—"Shadow of Doubt" 1-9-58 (Josofat); The Law of the Plainsman—"Cavern of the Wind" 4-21-60; The Alaskans—"Heart of Gold" 5-1-60 (Chinook), "The Silent Land" 5-15-60 (Chinook); Maverick—"Arizona Black Maria" 10-9-60 (Indian Chief); Rawhide—"Incident of the Buffalo Soldier" 1-1-61, "Incident of the Boomerang" 3-24-61.

Stevens, Charlotte. Films: "One Law for the Woman" 1924 (Nellie); "Flying Hoofs" 1925 (Emily Perdee); "Kit Carson Over the Great Divide" 1925 (Nancy Webb); "Thunder Riders" 1928 (Betty Barton).

Stevens, Clarke. Films: "Gangsters of the Frontier" 1944; "Buffalo Bill Rides Again" 1947 (Jeff); "Son of Billy the Kid" 1949 (2nd Outlaw); "The Daltons' Women" 1950; "The Thundering Trail" 1951 (Clarke); "The Vanishing Outpost" 1951 (Denton); "The Black Lash" 1952 (Johnson); "The Frontier Phantom" 1952.

Stevens, Connie (1938-). TV: Sugarfoot—"Misfire" 12-10-57 (Patience Preston), "The Wild Bunch" 9-29-59 (Jenny Markham); Maverick—"Two Tickets to Ten Strike" 3-15-59 (Frankie French); Cheyenne—"Reprieve" 10-5-59 (Clovis); Temple Houston—"The Town That Trespassed" 3-26-64 (Charity Simpson).

Stevens, Craig (1918-). Films: "Drums in the Deep South" 1951 (Braxton Summers); "The Lady from Texas" 1951 (Cyril Guthrie); "Buchanan Rides Alone" 1958 (Abe Carbo). ¶TV: The Lone Ranger— "Bullets for Ballots" 5-11-50; Alias Smith and Jones—"Miracle at Santa Marta" 12-30-71 (Rolf Hanley); The Men from Shiloh—"Tate, Ramrod" 2-24-71 (Joe Benson); Gunsmoke— "Trail of Bloodshed" 3-4-74 (Gambler).

Stevens, Edwin (1860-1/1/23). Films: "The Squaw Man" 1918 (Bud Hardy); "Sting of the Lash" 1921 (Daniel Keith); "Quicksands" 1923 (Ring Member); "The Spider and the Rose" 1923 (Bishop Oliveros).

Stevens, Inger (1931-4/30/70). Films: "A Time for Killing" 1967 (Emily Biddle); "Firecreek" 1968 (Evelyn); "Five Card Stud" 1968 (Lily Langford); "Hang 'Em High" 1968 (Rachel); "Run, Simon, Run" TVM-1970 (Carroll Reunard). ¶TV: Bonanza—"The Newcomers" 9-26-59 (Emily Pennington); Zane Grey Theater—"Calico Bait" 3-31-60 (Beth); Empire—"Duet for Eight Wheels" 4-30-63 (Ellen Thompson).

Stevens, Katharine (1919-6/13/94). Films: "The Great Man's Lady" 1942 (Girl Biographer).

Stevens, K.T. (1919-6/13/94). Films: "Tumbleweed" 1953 (Louella Buckley). ¶TV: Wagon Train—"The Zeke Thomas Story" 11-27-57; The Rifleman—"Heller" 2-23-60, "The Fourflusher" 5-3-60 (Molly Fenway), "Face of Yesterday" 1-31-61 (Nancy Clay), "Honest Abe" 11-20-61 (Emma), "End of the Hunt" 2-18-63 (Granny Mede); Rawhide—"Incident of the Slavemaster" 11-11-60 (Martha Bradley); The Rebel—"Berserk" 12-18-60 (Mrs. Dunsen); Zane Grey Theater—"The Broken Wing" 2-9-61 (Ada Kihlgren); The Big Valley— "Under a Dark Sea" 2-9-66 (Meg), "Image of Yesterday" 1-9-67; Iron Horse—"Through Ticket to Gunsight" 11-28-66 (Kate).

Stevens, Landers (1877-12/19/40). Films: "Shadows of Conscience" 1921 (Wade Curry); "Youth Must Have Love" 1922 (Frank Hibbard); "Rainbow Trail" 1932 (Presby); "The Country Beyond" 1936 (Party Guest); "The Cowboy Star" 1936 (Kinswell).

Stevens, Lenore (1943-). Films: "Scandalous John" 1971 (Girl). ¶TV: The High Chaparral—"The Glory Soldiers" 1-31-69 (Teresa); Bonanza— "The Law and Billy Burgess" 2-15-70 (Inez); The Men from Shiloh—"Last of the Comancheros" 12-9-70 (Laurita).

Stevens, Mark (1917-9/15/94). Films: "Jack Slade" 1953 (Jack Slade); "Gunsight Ridge" 1957 (Velvet); "Gun Fever" 1958 (Lucas); "Gunsmoke in Tucson" 1958 (Chip Coburn); "Sunscorched" 1966-Span./Ger. (Sheriff Jeff Kinley). ¶TV: *Zane Grey Theater*—"Dangerous Orders" 2-8-57 (Capt. Hunter), "The Stranger" 2-28-58 (Cort McConnell); *Wagon Train*—"The Nels Stack Story" 10-23-57 (Nels Stack); *Rawhide*—"Incident of the Hunter" 9-28-62 (John Shepard).

Stevens, Marya. TV: *Broken Arrow*—"Iron Maiden" 3-25-58 (Melana), "Old Enemy" 5-6-58 (Melana); *The Restless Gun*—"Thunder Valley" 10-13-58 (Elena Sandoval), "Melany" 3-2-59 (Melany); *Northwest Passage*—"The Vulture" 12-28-58 (Lady Kate Stanley); *Rawhide*—"Incident of the Haunted Hills" 11-6-59 (Indian Girl), "Incident of the Stargazer" 4-1-60 (Teela); *Bat Masterson*—"Dagger Dance" 4-20-61 (Nione); *Tales of Wells Fargo*—"Portrait of Teresa" 2-10-62 (Rosita).

Stevens, Naomi (1925-). TV: *Have Gun Will Travel*—"Helen of Abajinian" 12-28-57, "Cream of the Jest" 5-5-62 (Mrs. Kafka); *Rawhide*—"The Hostage Child" 3-9-62 (Maria); *Empire*—"Between Friday and Monday" 5-7-63 (Mrs. Quintero); *Wagon Train*—"The Last Circle Up" 4-27-64 (Hannah Moses); *The Big Valley*—"Winner Lose All" 10-27-65 (Anjelina); *Laredo*—"The Callico Kid" 1-6-66).

Stevens, Onslow (1902-1/5/77). Films: The Golden West" 1932 (Calvin Brown); "Heroes of the West" 1932-serial (Tom Crosby); "Yellow Dust" 1936 (Jack Hanway); "Go West, Young Lady" 1941 (Tom Hannegan); "Sunset Serenade" 1942 (Gregg Jackson); "Hands Across the Border" 1943 (Brock Danvers); "Idaho" 1943 (Chief Ranger); "Canyon Passage" 1946 (Lestrade); "Hills of Utah" 1951 (Jayde McQueen); "The San Francisco Story" 1952 (Jim Martin); "The Charge at Feather River" 1953 (Grover Johnson); "Fangs of the Wild" 1954 (Jim); "They Rode West" 1954 (Col. Ethan Walters); "Tribute to a Badman" 1956 (Hearn). ¶TV: *Cavalcade of America*—"A Matter of Honor" 2-18-53 (Sam Houston); *Cheyenne*—"The Outlander" 12-13-55 (Judge Culver); *Have Gun Will Travel*—"Strange Vendetta" 10-26-57; *Zane Grey Theater*—"A Gun for My Bride" 12-27-57 (Roger Morrow); *Wagon Train*—"The Mark Hanford Story" 2-26-58 (Jack

Hanford), "The Bije Wilcox Story" 11-19-58 (Francis Mason), "The Danny Benedict Story" 12-2-59 (Colonel Benedict), "The Sam Livingston Story" 6-15-60 (Cass Flemming); *Texas John Slaughter*—Regular 1958-61 (General Miles); *The Adventures of Rin Tin Tin*—"The Foot Soldier" 10-10-58 (Maj. Edward Karn); *Wanted—Dead or Alive*—"Ricochet" 11-22-58 (Sheriff Adler); *Black Saddle*—"Client: Travers" 1-10-59 (Pardee); *The Restless Gun*—"The Pawn" 4-6-59 (Mr. McGiven); *Gunsmoke*—"Murder Warrant" 4-18-59 (Sheriff Ben Goddard); *The Deputy*—"Powder Keg" 10-10-59 (Tom Deaver); *Bonanza*—"The Hanging Posse" 11-28-59 (Flint Johnson); *Overland Trail*—"The Most Dangerous Gentleman" 6-5-60 (President Ulysses S. Grant); *The Outlaws*—"Ballad for a Badman" 10-6-60 (John Kyle); *Laramie*—"Killer Without Cause" 1-24-61 (Gen. Taylor Roberts).

Stevens, Oren (1937-). TV: *Bonanza*—"Mrs. Wharton and the Lesser Breeds" 1-19-69 (Billy Buckman).

Stevens, Paul. see Gozlino, Paolo.

Stevens, Paul (1920-6/4/86). Films: "Law of the Land" TVM-1976 (Dwight Canaway). ¶TV: *Wild Wild West*—"The Night of the Samurai" 10-13-67 (Gideon Falconer); *Gunsmoke*—"Trafton" 10-25-71 (Reverend English), "The Golden Land" 3-5-73 (Moshe Gorofsky), "A Game of Death … An Act of Love" 11-5-73 & 11-12-73 (Cicero Wolfe); *Dirty Sally*—3-22-74 (the Rev. Lucius Collier).

Stevens, Robert (Robert Kellard) (1880-12/19/63). Films: "King of the Royal Mounted" 1940-serial (Corporal Tom Merritt, Jr.); "Prairie Pioneers" 1941 (Roberto Ortega); "Perils of the Royal Mounted" 1942-serial (Sergeant MacLane); "The Fighting Buckaroo" 1943 (Fletch Thacher); "Lone Star Moonlight" 1946; "That Texas Jamboree" 1946; "Throw a Saddle on a Star" 1946; "The Lone Hand Texan" 1947 (Boemer Kildea); "Tex Granger" 1948-serial (Tex Granger); "They Came to Cordura" 1959 (Col. Rogers). ¶TV: *The Lone Ranger*—"Barnaby Boggs, Esquire" 2-2-50, "Buried Treasure" 3-2-50, "Gold Train" 3-16-50, "Man Without a Gun" 6-15-50, "Bad Medicine" 12-7-50, "Mr. Trouble" 3-8-51; *Wagon Train*—"The Annie MacGregor Story" 2-5-58.

Stevens, Rory. TV: *Wagon Train*—"The Nancy Palmer Story" 3-8-61; *Bonanza*—"The Legacy" 12-15-

63; *The Legend of Jesse James*—"The Pursuers" 10-11-65 (Timmy); *The Virginian*—"The Laramie Road" 12-8-65; *Laredo*—"The Legend of Midas Mantee" 9-16-66 (David); *Daniel Boone*—"A Tall Tale of Prater Beasely" 1-16-69 (Joe).

Stevens, Stella (1936-). Films: "Advance to the Rear" 1964 (Martha Lou); "The Ballad of Cable Hogue" 1970 (Hildy); "A Town Called Hell" 1971-Span./Brit. (Alvira); "Honky Tonk" TVM-1974 (Gold Dust); "Wanted: The Sundance Woman" TVM-1976 (Lola Watkins); "Charlie Cobb: Nice Night for a Hanging" TVM-1977 (Martha McVea); "No Man's Land" TVM-1984 (sheriff Nellie Wilder). ¶TV: *Johnny Ringo*—"Uncertain Vengeance" 3-10-60 (Suzanne); *Bonanza*—"Silent Thunder" 12-10-60 (Ann Croft); *Riverboat*—"Zigzag" 12-26-60 (Sugie Walters); *Frontier Circus*—"The Balloon Girl" 1-11-62 (Katy Cogswell); *Hec Ramsey*—"Hangman's Wages" 10-29-72 (Ivy Tunwright); *The Oregon Trail*—"Hannah's Girls" 10-26-77 (Hannah Morgan).

Stevens, Steve. Films: "Sunset Pass" 1946 (Posse Man). ¶TV: *The Roy Rogers Show*—"His Weight in Wildcats" 11-11-56 (Petey Driggs); *Zorro*—"The Man with the Whip" 5-8-58 (Don Rodolfo Martinez), "The Cross of the Andes" 5-15-58 (Don Rodolfo Martinez); *Gunsmoke*—"Shona" 2-9-63.

Stevens, Warren (1919-). Films: "Shark River" 1953 (Clay Webley); "The Man from Bitter Ridge" 1955 (Linc Jackman); "Robbers' Roost" 1955 (Smokey); "Man or Gun" 1958 (Mike Ferris); "No Name on the Bullet" 1959 (Lou Fraden); "Stagecoach to Dancer's Rock" 1962 (Jess Dollard); "Gunpoint" 1966 (Nate Harlan). ¶TV: *Have Gun Will Travel*—"The Yuma Treasure" 12-14-57 (Major Wilson), "The Eve of St. Elmo" 3-23-63 (Colonel Draco), "The Mountebank" 8-3-63 (Costigan); *Gunsmoke*—"Kitty Lost" 12-21-57 (Rackmil), "Old Yellow Boots" 10-7-61 (Cassidy), "Anybody Can Kill a Marshal" 3-9-63 (Lucas); *Wagon Train*—"The Kate Parker Story" 5-6-59 (Jonas Parker), "The John Turnbull Story" 5-30-62 (Jack Thorne); *Tales of Wells Fargo*—"Clay Allison" 6-15-59 (Clay Allison); *Laramie*—"Dark Verdict" 11-24-59 (Jim Hedrick); *Lawman*—"To Capture the West" 2-7-60 (Frederick Jameson); *The Alaskans*—"Partners" 3-13-60 (Jim Hendricks); *The Rebel*—"The Road to Jericho" 2-19-61 (Christopher Portal); *The Dakotas*—"Crisis at High Banjo" 2-11-63 (Cain Manning); *Profiles in Courage*—"Sam Houston" 12-13-64 (Lt. Gov. Edward Clark); *Bonanza*—"The Ballerina" 1-24-65 (Paul Mandel), "The Prince" 4-2-67 (Count Alexis), "The Trackers" 1-7-68 (Sam Bragan), "El Jefe" 11-15-70 (Owen Driscoll); *Rawhide*—"Clash at Broken Bluff" 11-2-65 (Talbot); *The Loner*—"Westward the Shoemaker" 11-27-65 (Charlie Parker); *Daniel Boone*—"The Prisoners" 2-10-66 (Matthew Eliot/Edward Eliot), "The Williamsburg Cannon" 1-12-67 & 1-19-67 (Capt. Robert George); *The Legend of Jesse James*—"South Wind" 2-14-66 (Sheriff Boyd Stevens); *A Man Called Shenandoah*—"The Riley Brand 2-21-66 (Jared Abel); *The Big Valley*—"Tunnel of Gold" 4-20-66 (Bert Jason); *Death Valley Days*—"Doc Holliday's Gold Bard" 12-31-66 (Doc Holliday); *The Virginian*—"The Girl on the Pinto" 3-29-67 (Pierce); *The High Chaparral*—"Best Man for the Job" 9-24-67 (Captain Dabney); *Iron Horse*—"Four Guns to Scalplock" 11-11-67 (Morgan Kinlock); *The Men from Shiloh*—"Hannah" 12-30-70 (Paul Carson).

Stevens, William. Films: "Lone Texas Ranger" 1945; "Showdown at Boot Hill" 1958 (1st Cowhand). ¶TV: *Have Gun Will Travel*—"The Man Who Wouldn't Talk" 9-20-58 (Morely), "Alive" 3-17-62; *The Deputy*—"Tension Point" 4-8-61 (Whip); *The Virginian*—"Legend for a Lawman" 3-3-65 (Shagrue).

Stevenson, Charles A. (1851-7/2/29). Films: "Aflame in the Sky" 1927 (Grandfather Carillo).

Stevenson, George. Films: "Quintana: Dead or Alive" 1969-Ital./Span. (Quintana/Jose de Loma).

Stevenson, Hayden. Films: "The Great Divide" 1915 (Phil Jordan); "The Lone Hand" 1922 (Buck); "Lightning Warrior" 1931-serial (Carter); "Wells Fargo" 1937; "The Fargo Kid" 1940 (Hotel Clerk).

Stevenson, Houseley (1879-8/6/53). Films: "Dakota" 1945 (Railroad Clerk); "Four Faces West" 1948 (Anderson); "The Paleface" 1948 (Pioneer); "Calamity Jane and Sam Bass" 1949 (Dakota); "Colorado Territory" 1949 (Prospector); "Masked Raiders" 1949 (Uncle Henry); "The Walking Hills" 1949 (King); "The Gunfighter" 1950 (Barlow); "Sierra" 1950 (Sam Coulter); "Cave of Outlaws" 1951 (Cooley); "The Secret of Convict Lake" 1951 (Pawnee Sam); "Oklahoma Annie" 1952 (Blinky); "The Wild North" 1952 (Old Man).

Stevenson, Parker (1953-). TV: *Gunsmoke*—"To Ride a Yellow Horse" 3-18-74 (Steven).

Stevenson, Robert J. (1915-3/4/75). Films: "God's Country and the Woman" 1937 (Lars); "Wells Fargo" 1937 (Southerner); "Dodge City" 1939; "Union Pacific" 1939 (Irish Paddy); "Valley of Hunted Men" 1942 (Kruger); "Fangs of the Wild" 1954 (Deputy Sheriff); "Gun Fever" 1958 (Norris). ¶TV: *Have Gun Will Travel*—"The Colonel and the Lady" 11-23-57, "The Night the Town Died" 2-6-60 (Sheriff Howard), "The Last Judgment" 3-11-61, "Pandora's Box" 5-19-62 (Woody), "Be Not Forgetful to Strangers" 12-22-62 (Jake), "Sweet Lady of the Moon" 3-9-63 (Sheriff), "The Mountebank" 8-3-63 (Clemenceau); *Maverick*—"Diamond in the Rough" 1-26-58 (Sailor); *Tombstone Territory*—"Cave-In" 3-26-58 (Big Bill Hartley); *Jefferson Drum*—Regular 1958-59 (Big Ed); *Rough Riders*—"Killers at Chocktaw Valley" 12-4-58 (Carl Latham); *Bonanza*—"The Julia Bulette Story" 10-17-59 (George Romley), "The Frenchman" 12-10-61 (Proprietor), "The Wooing of Abigail Jones" 3-4-62, "The Return" 5-2-65, "Amigo" 2-12-67 (Benton); *Man from Blackhawk*—"The Hundred Thousand Dollar Policy" 1-22-60 (Speculator), "In His Steps" 5-20-60 (Lieutenant Ringer); *Bat Masterson*—"Incident at Fort Bowie" 4-31-60 (Ben Roper); *The Deputy*—"The Jason Harris Story" 10-8-60 (Morgan); *Laramie*—"Ride the Wild Wind" 10-11-60 (Sheriff Davis); *The Tall Man*—"A Bounty for Billy" 10-15-60 (Beldon); *Stagecoach West*—"Life Sentence" 12-6-60 (Marshal Strickland), "The Storm" 12-13-60 (Marshal Strickland), "House of Violence" 3-21-61 (Marshal Strickland); *Tales of Wells Fargo*—"Frightened Witness" 12-26-60 (Les Watkins), "End of a Minor God" 4-7-62 (Art Riddle); *Two Faces West*—"The Sure Thing" 7-3-61 (Fancher); *Gunsmoke*—"The Gallows" 3-3-62 (Ax Parsons), "The Summons" 4-21-62 (Cape); *The Virginian*—"The Brazen Bell" 10-17-62; *Rawhide*—"Incident of the Dogfaces" 11-9-62 (Beard), "Incident at Crooked Hat" 2-1-63 (Asa Carter), "Incident of the Gilded Goddess" 4-30-64 (A.J. Hogan); *Empire*—"65 Miles Is a Long, Long Way" 4-23-63 (Sam Tate).

Stevenson, Venetia. Films: "Day of the Outlaw" 1959 (Emine); "Seven Ways from Sundown" 1960 (Joy Karrington). ¶TV: *Sugarfoot*—"Trail's End" 11-12-57 (Kathy Larsen), "Price on His Head" 4-29-58 (Girl), "Brink

of Fear" 6-30-58 (Dodie Logan); *Colt .45*—"Mantrap" 2-14-58 (Valintine); *Lawman*—"The Badge" 11-23-58 (Molly Matson).

Stewart, Alexandra (1939-). Films: "Man Called Gringo" 1964-Ger./Span.

Stewart, Anita (1895-5/4/61). Films: "The Fighting Shepherdess" 1920 (Kate Prentice); "Baree, Son of Kazan" 1925 (Nepeese); "Morgan's Finish" 1926 (Barbara Wesley); "Rustlin' for Cupid" 1926 (Sybil Hamilton).

Stewart, Art. Films: "Gold of the Seven Saints" 1961 (Ricca). ¶TV: *Maverick*—"Arizona Black Maria" 10-9-60 (Lem), "The Ice Man" 1-29-61 (Gom Wales); *Bat Masterson*—"A Time to Die" 12-15-60 (Old Man); *Cheyenne*—"Cross Purpose" 10-9-61 (Morse); *Daniel Boone*—"The Witness" 1-25-68.

Stewart, Catherine Mary (1959-). Films: "Samurai Cowboy" 1993.

Stewart, Charlotte (1941-). Films: "The Cheyenne Social Club" 1970 (Mae). ¶TV: *Bonanza*—"The Stalker" 11-2-69 (Lisa Campbell), "The Grand Swing" 9-19-71 (Betsy); *The Virginian*—"Train of Darkness" 2-4-70 (Lotte); *Gunsmoke*—"Morgan" 3-2-70 (Jenny), "The Schoolmarm" 2-25-74; *Little House on the Prairie*—Regular 1974-77 (Miss Beadle); *The Texas Wheelers*—7-17-75 (Antique Dealer).

Stewart, David J. (1914-12/24/66). TV: *Have Gun Will Travel*—"The Siege" 4-1-61 (Kessler).

Stewart, Donald (1911-3/1/66). Films: "Where Trails End" 1942; "Wild Horse Stampede" 1943 (Donny); "Arizona Whirlwind" 1944 (Donny Davis). ¶TV: *Laredo*—"Rendezvous at Arillo" 10-7-65 (Aaron Jaison); *The Virginian*—"Letter of the Law" 12-22-65 (Lathrop).

Stewart, Elaine (1929-). Films: "Sky Full of Moon" 1952 (Change Girl); "Night Passage" 1957 (Verna Kimball); "Escort West" 1959 (Beth Drury). ¶TV: *Bat Masterson*—"The Rage of Princess Ann" 10-20-60 (Ann Eaton).

Stewart, Eleanor (1913-). Films: "Arizona Days" 1937 (Madge Workman); "The Gun Ranger" 1937 (Molly Pearson); "Headin' for the Rio Grande" 1937 (Laura); "Range Defenders" 1937 (Sylvia Ashton); "The Rangers Step In" 1937 (Terry Warren); "Santa Fe Rides" 1937; "Where Trails Divide" 1937 (Nora Hart); "Mexicali Kid" 1938 (Jean Carter);

"The Painted Trail" 1938 (Alice Banning); "Rolling Caravans" 1938 (Alice Rankin); "Stagecoach Days" 1938 (Mary Martin); "Flaming Lead" 1939 (Kay Burke); "Pirates on Horseback" 1941 (Trudy Pendleton); "Riders of the Timberline" 1941 (Elaine); "The Great Man's Lady" 1942 (Daughter); "Silver Queen" 1942 (Millicent Bailey); "Mystery Man" 1944 (Diane Newhall).

Stewart, Evelyn (Ida Galli). Films: "Adios Gringo" 1965-Ital./Fr./Span. (Lucy Tillson); "Blood for a Silver Dollar" 1965-Ital./Fr. (Judy O'Hara); "He Who Shoots First" 1966-Ital.; "Seven Guns for Timothy" 1966-Span./Ital.; "Blood at Sundown" 1967-Span./Ital.; "Machine Gun Killers" 1968-Ital./Span.; "No Graves on Boot Hill" 1968-Ital.; "Man Who Cried for Revenge" 1969-Ital./Span.; "Chuck Moll" 1970-Ital.; "Four Gunmen of the Holy Trinity" 1971-Ital. (Sarah).; "Man Called Invincible" 1973-Ital.

Stewart, George (1888-12/24/45). Films: "The Mollycoddle" 1920 (Ole Olsen); "Shod with Fire" 1920 (Benny Lynch).

Stewart, James (1908-). Films: "Rose Marie" 1936 (John Flower); "Destry Rides Again" 1939 (Tom Destry); "Broken Arrow" 1950 (Tom Jeffords); "Winchester '73" 1950 (Lin McAdam); "Bend of the River" 1952 (Glyn McLyntock); "The Naked Spur" 1953 (Howard Kemp); "The Far Country" 1955 (Jeff); "The Man from Laramie" 1955 (Will Lockhart); "Night Passage" 1957 (Grant McLaine); "Two Rode Together" 1961 (Guthrie McCabe); "How the West Was Won" 1962 (Linus Rawlings); "The Man Who Shot Liberty Valance" 1962 (Ransom Stoddard); "Cheyenne Autumn" 1964 (Wyatt Earp); "Shenandoah" 1965 (Charlie Anderson); "The Rare Breed" 1966 (Sam Burnett); "Bandolero!" 1968 (Mace Bishop); "Firecreek" 1968 (Johnny Cobb); "The Cheyenne Social Club" 1970 (John O'Hanlan); "Fools' Parade" 1971 (Mattie Appleyard); "The Shootist" 1976 (Dr. Hostetler); "An American Tail: Fievel Goes West" 1991 (voice of Wylie Burp).

Stewart, Johnny (1934-). Films: "Last of the Comanches" 1952 (Little Knife).

Stewart, Kay (1919-). Films: "40 Guns to Apache Pass" 1967 (Kate Malone). ¶TV: *Death Valley Days*— "The Rainbow Chaser" 5-26-54, "Tribute to the Dog" 12-27-64 (Mrs. Cody), "The Lone Grave" 10-28-67

(Millie); *Wagon Train*—"The Major Adams Story" 4-23-58 & 4-30-58 (Mary Bradley), "The Ben Courtney Story" 1-28-59 (Leona Ramsey), "The St. Nicholas Story" 12-23-59, "The Jane Hawkins Story" 11-30-60, "Swamp Devil" 4-4-62 (Mrs. Harris), "The Nancy Davis Story" 5-16-62 (Mrs. Davis), "The Eli Bancroft Story" 11-11-63, "The Santiago Quesada Story" 3-30-64, "The Last Circle Up" 4-27-64 (Priscilla Jameson); *The Restless Gun*—"The Manhunters" 6-2-58 (Laura Bascomb), "Multiply One Boy" 12-8-58 (Gloria Higgins); *Cimarron City*—"Twelve Guns" 11-1-58 (Susan Buckley); *Tales of Wells Fargo*—"The Happy Tree" 12-22-58 (Martha Benson); *Northwest Passage*—"The Witch" 2-13-59 (Ruth Gant); *Black Saddle*—"A Case of Slow" 4-15-60 (Mary Forrest); *Zane Grey Theater*—"The Ox" 11-3-60; *Whispering Smith*—"The Quest" 6-26-61 (Bella Laughlin); *Bonanza*—"Gift of Water" 2-11-62 (Mrs. Collins); *The Virginian*—"The Brazen Bell" 10-17-62; *The Big Valley*—"Judgement in Heaven" 12-22-65 (Helen Travis); *The Legend of Jesse James*—"Wanted: Dead and Only" 5-2-66 (Widow); *The Men from Shiloh*—"Hannah" 12-30-70 (Mrs. Crandall).

Stewart, Larry. Films: "Little Big Horn" 1951 (Bugle Stevie Williams); "Deserter" 1970-U.S./Ital./Yugo. (Robinson).

Stewart, Marianne. TV: *Gunsmoke*—"Gone Straight" 2-9-57 (Mrs. Timble); *Buckskin*—"Who Killed Pat Devlin?" 2-16-59 (Vanessa Devlin); *Man from Blackhawk*—"The Gypsy Story" 11-6-59 (Molly Davenant); *Bonanza*—"House Divided" 1-16-60 (Lily).

Stewart, Melvin (1928-). Films: "Kid Blue" 1973 (Blackman).

Stewart, Paul (1908-2/17/86). Films: "Bite the Bullet" 1975 (J.B. Parker). ¶TV: *Wagon Train*—"The Chottsie Gubenheimer Story" 1-10-65 (Jim Brannan); *Gunsmoke*—"The Cage" 3-23-70 (Sanders).

Stewart, Peggy (1923-). Films: "Wells Fargo" 1937 (Alice MacKay); "Cheyenne Wildcat" 1944; "Code of the Prairie" 1944 (Helen Matson); "Firebrands of Arizona" 1944 (Poppy Calhoun); "Sheriff of Las Vegas" 1944; "Silver City Kid" 1944; "Stagecoach to Monterey" 1944; "Tucson Raiders" 1944; "Bandits of the Badlands" 1945; "Marshal of Laredo" 1945; "Oregon Trail" 1945 (Jill Layton); "Rough Riders of Cheyenne" 1945; "Utah" 1945 (Jackie); "Alias Billy the Kid" 1946 (Ann Marshall);

"California Gold Rush" 1946; "Conquest of Cheyenne" 1946; "Days of Buffalo Bill" 1946; "The Phantom Rider" 1946-serial (Doris Hammond); "Red River Renegades" 1946; "Sheriff of Redwood Valley" 1946; "Stagecoach to Denver" 1946 (Beautiful); "Rustlers of Devil's Canyon" 1947 (Bess); "Son of Zorro" 1947-serial (Kate Wells); "Trail to San Antone" 1947 (Kit Barlow); "Vigilantes of Boomtown" 1947 (Molly McVey); "Dead Man's Gold" 1948 (June Thornton); "Frontier Revenge" 1948 (Joan De Lysa); "Tex Granger" 1948-serial (Helen Kent); "Desert Vigilante" 1949 (Betty Long); "Ride, Ryder, Ride" 1949 (Libby Brooks); "Cody of the Pony Express" 1950-serial (Linda Graham); "The Fighting Redhead" 1950 (Sheila); "The Black Lash" 1952 (Joan); "Kansas Territory" 1952 (Kay Collins); "Montana Incident" 1952; "Gun Street" 1961 (Mrs. Knudson); "The Way West" 1967 (Mrs. Turley); "The Animals" 1971 (Mrs. Emily Perkins); "Donner Pass: The Road to Survival" TVM-1978 (Mrs. Breen); "The Capture of Grizzly Adams" TVM-1982 (Widow Thompkins). ¶TV: *The Gene Autry Show*—"The Peace Maker" 12-17-50; *The Cisco Kid*—"Counterfeit Money" 1-27-51, "Oil Land" 2-24-51, "Cattle Quarantine" 3-31-51, "Lodestone" 4-26-52, "Gun Totin' Papa" 5-24-52; *Wild Bill Hickok*—"Pony Express vs. Telegraph" 9-25-51; *The Roy Rogers Show*—"Ghost Gulch" 3-30-52, "Doc Stevens' Traveling Store" 7-25-54; *Have Gun Will Travel*—"The Outlaw" 9-21-57, "The Brothers" 11-25-61 (Edna Raleigh); *Wyatt Earp*—"The Underdog" 4-22-58 (Etta Jackson), "How to Be a Sheriff" 3-24-59 (Elsa Jordan); *Yancy Derringer*—"Panic in Town" 2-12-59 (Karen Ogilvie); *Gunsmoke*—"Fawn" 4-4-59 (Mrs. Phillips), "Old Flame" 5-28-60 (Mary), "Long, Long Trail" 11-4-61 (Fan), "The Promoter" 4-25-64 (Daisy Huckaby), "Help Me, Kitty" 11-7-64 (Nettie Farmer); *Hotel De Paree*—"Hard Luck for Sundance" 2-19-60; *The Rebel*—"The Burying of Sammy Hart" 3-5-61 (Sarah Wallace); *Daniel Boone*—"A Rope for Mingo" 12-2-65 (Ida Morgan); *Hondo*—"Hondo and the Commancheros" 11-10-67 (Mr. Malcolm); *Paradise*—"The Bounty" 1-11-91 (Rae Miller).

Stewart, Roy (1883-4/26/33). Films: "The Exile of Bar-K Ranch" 1915; "The Greater Courage" 1915; "The Terror of Twin Mountains" 1915; "Liberty" 1916-serial; "Mixed Blood" 1916 (Big Jim); "The Bond of Fear" 1917; "The Devil Dodger" 1917

(Silent Scott); "Follow the Girl" 1917 (Larry O'Keefe); "The Learnin' of Jim Benton" 1917 (Jim Benton); "The Medicine Man" 1917 (Jim Walton); "One Shot Ross" 1917 (One Shot Ross); "Boss of the Lazy Y" 1918 (Calumet Marston); "By Proxy" 1918 (Red Saunders); "Cactus Crandall" 1918 (Cactus Bob Crandall); "Faith Endurin'" 1918 (Jeff Flagg); "The Fly God" 1918 (Red Saunders); "The Gun Woman" 1918; "Keith of the Border" 1918 (Jack Keith); "The Law's Outlaw" 1918 (Charles Easton); "Paying His Debt" 1918 (Frank Borden/Pete Morton); "The Red Haired Cupid" 1918 (Wiliam "Red" Saunders); "The Silent Rider" 1918 (Bob Gordon); "Untamed" 1918 (Jim Jason); "Wolves of the Border" 1918; "The Westerners" 1919 (Cheyenne Harry); "The Lone Hand" 1920 (Bob Benton); "Riders of the Dawn" 1920 (Kurt Dorn); "The Sagebrusher" 1920 (Dr. Barnes); "The U.P. Trail" 1920 (Warren Neale); "Heart of the North" 1921 (Sgt. John Whitley/Bad Maupome); "Back to Yellow Jacket" 1922 (Jim Ballantyne); "Blue Blood and Red" 1922; "Giants of the Open" 1922; "One-Eighth Apache" 1922 (Brant Murdock); "Rustlers of the Redwoods" 1922; "The Sagebrush Trail" 1922; "The Snowshoe Trail" 1922 (Bill Bronson); "Timberland Treachery" 1922; "Better Than Gold" 1923; "The Doomed Sentinels" 1923; "A Fight for a Mine" 1923; "God's Law" 1923; "The Guilty Hand" 1923; "Hard to Beat" 1923; "Hearts of Oak" 1923; "King of the Forest" 1923; "Knights of the Timber" 1923; "The Love Brand" 1923; "Pure Grit" 1923 (Bob Evans); "Sundown" 1924 (Hugh Brent); "Kit Carson Over the Great Divide" 1925 (Seaton Maurey); "Where the Worst Begins" 1925 (Cliff Ranger); "Buffalo Bill on the U.P. Trail" 1926 (Buffalo Bill Cody); "Daniel Boone Thru the Wilderness" 1926; "The Lady from Hell" 1926 (Sir Robin Carmichael); "General Custer at the Little Big Horn" 1927 (Lem Hawks); "Little Big Horn" 1927 (Lem Hawks); "The Great Divide" 1929 (Joe Morgan); "In Old Arizona" 1929 (Commandant); "The Lone Star Ranger" 1930 (Capt. McNally); "Rough Romance" 1930 (Sheriff Milt Powers); "Fighting Caravans" 1931 (Couch); "Three Rogues" 1931; "Come on, Danger!" 1932 (Insp. Clay); "Mystery Ranch" 1932 (Buck Johnson); "Come on Tarzan" 1933 (Butch Carson); "Fargo Express" 1933 (Sam Goss); "Rustlers' Roundup" 1933 (Dave Winters).

Stewart, Trish. Films: "Wild Times" TVM-1980 (Jeanette Fowler).

Stiers, David Ogden (1942-). Films: "The Alamo: 13 Days to Glory" TVM-1987 (Col. Black); "Iron Will" 1994 (J.P. Harper); "The Last of His Tribe" TVM-1994 (Pope).

Stine, Jan. Films: "The Horse Soldiers" 1959 (Dying Man). ¶TV: *Black Saddle*—"Client: Tagger" 2-14-59 (Floyd Britt); *Zane Grey Theater*—"Deadfall" 2-19-59 (Randy Kayler); *Wichita Town*—"Out of the Past" 12-9-59 (Gus Ritter, Jr.); *The Rifleman*—"Woman from Hog Ridge" 10-4-60 (Johnny Boyle), "The High Country" 12-18-61 (Gorwin); *Wanted-Dead or Alive*—"To the Victor" 11-9-60 (Ken Adams); *Klondike*—"Sure Thing, Men" 11-28-60 (Billy Gladson); *Lawman*—"Firehouse Lil" 1-8-61 (Bandit), "The Wanted Man" 4-8-62 (Ben Jesse); *Gunslinger*—"The Recruit" 3-23-61 (Trooper Williams); *The Virginian*—"Woman from White Ting" 9-26-62, "Riff-Raff" 11-7-62, "It Tolls for Thee" 11-21-62; *Temple Houston*—"Letter of the Law" 10-3-63 (Prue Harrod).

Stinson, Mortimer E. (1871-7/20/27). Films: "Loco Luck" 1927 (Mark Randell).

Stirling, Linda (1921-). Films: "The San Antonio Kid" 1944; "Sheriff of Sundown" 1944 (Lois Carpenter); "Vigilantes of Dodge City" 1944; "Zorro's Black Whip" 1944-serial (Barbara Meredith); "The Cherokee Flash" 1945; "Dakota" 1945 (Entertainer); "Santa Fe Saddlemates" 1945; "Sheriff of Cimarron" 1945 (Helen Burton); "The Topeka Terror" 1945 (Jane Hardy); "Wagon Wheels Westward" 1945; "Rio Grande Raiders" 1946; "Jesse James Rides Again" 1947-serial (Ann Bolton). ¶TV: *The Adventures of Kit Carson*—"The Teton Tornado" 12-8-51; *Wyatt Earp*—"The Suffragette" 3-27-56 (Joan Laramie).

Stock-Poynton, Amy. Films: "Gunsmoke: The Last Apache" TVM-1990 (Beth Yardner); "Gunsmoke: To the Last Man" TVM-1991 (Beth); "Gunsmoke: The Long Ride" TVM-1993 (Beth); "Gunsmoke: One Man's Justice" TVM-1994 (Beth).

Stockdale, Carl (1874-3/15/53). Films: "Days of the Pony Express" 1913; "The Atonement" 1914; "Broncho Billy and the Rattler" 1914; "Broncho Billy and the Sheriff" 1914; "Broncho Billy—Favorite" 1914; "Broncho Billy—Outlaw" 1914; "Broncho Billy Puts One Over" 1914; "The Calling of Jim Barton" 1914; "Dan Cupid, Assayer" 1914; "The Good for Nothing" 1914 (John Ster-

ling); "The Hills of Peace" 1914; "Single-Handed" 1914; "Broncho Billy's Sentence" 1915; "Broncho Billy's Teachings" 1915; "The Land of Long Shadows" 1917 (Constable McKenzie); "Men of the Desert" 1917 (Mason); "Open Places" 1917 (Dan Clark); "The Range Boss" 1917 (Willard Masten); "The Lady of the Dugout" 1918 (the Killer); "The Sundown Trail" 1919 (the Planter); "When a Man Rides Alone" 1919 (the Vulture); "Where the West Begins" 1919 (Gunner McCann); "The Coast of Opportunity" 1920 (Marr's Secretary); "The Half-Breed" 1922 (John Spavinaw); "Suzanna" 1922 (Ruiz); "The Grail" 1923 (Rev. Bledsoe); "Man's Size" 1923 (Whaley); "The Desert's Price" 1925 (Gitner); "A Son of His Father" 1925 (Zobester); "The Trail Rider" 1925 (Jim Mackey); "Somewhere in Sonora" 1927 (Bob Leadley); "The Shepherd of the Hills" 1928 (Jim Lane); "Get That Girl" 1932; "Battle of Greed" 1934 (Sawyer); "Rocky Rhodes" 1934 (Bowles); "The Crimson Trail" 1935 (Jim Bellaire); "Ivory-Handled Gun" 1935 (Bill Ward); "Outlawed Guns" 1935; "End of the Trail" 1936 (Simmons); "Oh, Susanna!" 1936 (Jeff Lee); "Courage of the West" 1937 (Rufe Lambert); "The Law Commands" 1937 (Jed Johnson); "Law for Tombstone" 1937 (Judge Hart); "Hawaiian Buckaroo" 1938 (Brady); "Lawless Valley" 1938; "The Lone Ranger" 1938-serial (Haskins); "Rawhide" 1938 (Bascomb); "The Singing Outlaw" 1938 (Sheriff Haight); "The Marshal of Mesa City" 1939 (Judge Wainwright); "Overland with Kit Carson" 1939-serial; "The Fargo Kid" 1940; "Konga, the Wild Stallion" 1940 (Mason); "Pioneers of the Frontier" 1940 (Jim Darcey); "Shooting High" 1940 (Ab); "Stage to Chino" 1940 (Charles Lait); "Texas Stagecoach" 1940; "Thundering Frontier" 1940 (Andrew Belknap); "Wagon Train" 1940 (Wilks); "Along the Rio Grande" 1941 (Turner); "The Bandit Trail" 1941; "The Return of Daniel Boone" 1941 (Jeb Brandon); "The Outlaw" 1943 (Minister).

Stockman, Boyd. Films: "Lawless Empire" 1946 (Skids); "'Neath Canadian Skies" 1946; "Sunset Pass" 1946 (Robber); "Code of the Saddle" 1947; "Gun Talk" 1947 (Diggs); "Prairie Express" 1947 (Perry); "Crossed Trails" 1948; "Frontier Agent" 1948; "Gunning for Justice" 1948; "Outlaw Brand" 1948; "Overland Trails" 1948; "Partners of the Sunset" 1948; "The Rangers Ride" 1948; "Across the Rio Grande" 1949

(Ed); "Brand of Fear" 1949; "Crashing Thru" 1949; "Hidden Danger" 1949 (Loop); "Riders in the Sky" 1949; "Rim of the Canyon" 1949; "Stampede" 1949 (Fred); "Trail's End" 1949 (Idaho); "West of El Dorado" 1949 (Joe); "Beyond the Purple Hills" 1950; "The Blazing Sun" 1950; "Indian Territory" 1950; "Law of the Panhandle" 1950; "Stage to Tucson" 1950 (Juan Lopez); "Gene Autry and the Mounties" 1951; "Hills of Utah" 1951; "Silver Canyon" 1951; "Whirlwind" 1951; "Night Raiders" 1952; "Night Stage to Galveston" 1952; "Gun Belt" 1953 (Turkey Creek); "The Man from Laramie" 1955 (Spud Oxton); "Wyoming Renegades" 1955 (Tom McCarthy); "Secret of Treasure Mountain" 1956 (Stub McCurdy); "Apache Warrior" 1957; "Night Passage" 1957 (Torgenson); "Frontier Gun" 1958 (Marshal Swain); "Lone Texan" 1959 (Indian); "Ride Lonesome" 1959 (Indian Chief); "Five Guns to Tombstone" 1961; "The Gambler Wore a Gun" 1961 (Dave); "Gun Fight" 1961 (Cadiz). ¶TV: *The Gene Autry Show*—"Twisted Trails" 11-12-50, "The Sheriff of Santa Rosa" 12-24-50, "The Raiders" 4-14-51; *Gunsmoke*—"Unmarked Grave" 8-18-56 (Stage Driver); *Tales of Wells Fargo*—"Dr. Alice" 2-23-58 (Driver), "Pearl Hart" 5-9-60 (Driver), "Portrait of Teresa" 2-10-62 (Cowboy), "Winter Storm" 3-3-62 (Tom); *Laramie*—"The Day of the Savage" 3-13-62; *The Guns of Will Sonnett*—"Join the Army" 1-3-69 (Barkeep).

Stockwell, Dean (1936-). Films: "Stars in My Crown" 1950 (John Kenyon); "Cattle Drive" 1951 (Chester Graham, Jr.); "Gun for a Coward" 1957 (Hade Keough); "The Gambler, Part III—The Legend Continues" TVM-1987; "Son of the Morning Star" TVM-1991 (Gen. Sheridan). ¶TV: *Wagon Train*—"The Ruth Owens Story" 10-9-57, "The Juan Ortega Story" 10-8-58 (Juan Ortega), "The Rodney Lawrence Story" 6-10-59 (Rodney Lawrence), "The Will Santee Story" 5-3-61 (Will Santee); *The Restless Gun*—"Mercyday" 10-6-58; *Cimarron City*—"Kid on a Calico Horse" 11-22-58 (Bud Tatum); *The Outlaws*—"Assassin" 2-9-61 (Billy Joe Minden); *Bonanza*—"The Medal" 10-26-69 (Matthew Rush).

Stockwell, Guy (1934-). Films: "Three Swords of Zorro" 1963-Ital./Span.; "...And Now Miguel" 1965 (Perez); "The Plainsman" 1966 (Buffalo Bill Cody); "The Gatling Gun" 1972 (Lt. Malcolm); "Bonanza: The Return" TVM-1993. ¶TV:

Rawhide—"Incident of Fear in the Streets" 5-8-59 (Gregg Mason); *Stagecoach West*—"Red Sand" 11-22-60 (Sergeant Williams); *Gunsmoke*—"No Chip" 12-3-60 (Lee Dolan), "The Cook" 12-17-60 (Sandy King); *Lawman*—"No Contest" 2-4-62 (Jib); *Bonanza*—"Invention of a Gunfighter" 9-20-64 (Johnny Chapman), "Anatomy of a Lynching" 10-12-69 (John Degnan); *Wagon Train*—"The Richard Bloodgood Story" 11-29-64 (Richard Bloodgood); *Wild Wild West*—"The Night of the Cossacks" 3-21-69 (Prince Gregor); *Lancer*—"The Man Without a Gun" 3-25-69 (Clay Criswell); *The Virginian*—"The Runaway Boy" 10-22-69 (Bayo); *How the West Was Won*—"The Rustler" 1-22-79 (Sheriff Andrews).

Stockwell, John. TV: *Young Riders*—"Dark Brother" 6-4-92 (Barlow).

Stokes, Ernest (1907-5/26/64). Films: "The Lone Hand Texan" 1947.

Stokes, Olive (1887-11/1/72). Films: "Dad's Girls" 1911; "Told in Colorado" 1911.

Stollery, David. Films: "Westward Ho the Wagons" 1956 (Dan Thompson); "Drango" 1957 (Burke); "Ten Who Dared" 1960 (Andrew Hall).

Stone, Arthur (1883-9/4/40). Films: "The Arizona Kid" 1930 (Snakebite Pete); "The Bad Man" 1930 (Pedro); "Girl of the Golden West" 1930 (Joe Castro); "The Lash" 1930 (Juan); "The Conquering Horde" 1931 (Lumpy Lorrigan); "Secret Menace" 1931; "The Broken Wing" 1932 (Justin Bailey); "Under the Pampas Moon" 1935 (Rosa's Father); "Westbound Mail" 1937 (Andy). ¶TV: *The Lone Ranger*—"Drink of Water" 10-26-50.

Stone, Carol. TV: *Wyatt Earp*—Regular 1957-58 (Kate Holliday).

Stone, Christopher (1942-10/29/95). TV: *The Outcasts*—"Three Ways to Die" 10-7-68 (Tom Jeremy); *Here Come the Brides*—"A Hard Card to Play" 10-23-68 (Corky), "Loggerheads" 3-26-69, "The Soldier" 10-10-69.

Stone, Fred (1873-3/6/59). Films: "Johnny, Get Your Gun" 1919 (Johnny Wiggins); "Duke of Chimney Butte" 1921 (Jeremeah Lambert); "Billy Jim" 1922 (Billy Jim); "Konga, the Wild Stallion" 1940 (Yance Calhoun); "The Westerner" 1940 (Caliphet Mathews).

Stone, George E. (1903-5/26/67). Films: "The Gunfighter" 1916 (Jimmy Wright); "The Patriot" 1916 (Little Bobs); "Six-Shooter Andy"

1918 (Susan's Brother); "Just Pals" 1920 (Bill); "Rio Grande" 1920 (Danny O'Neil); "Penny of Top Hill Trail" 1921 (Francis Kingdon); "Under a Texas Moon" 1930 (Pedro); "Cimarron" 1931 (Sol Levy); "Frontier Marshal" 1934 (Abe Ruskin); "Moonlight on the Prairie" 1935 (Small Change Turner); "Rhythm on the Range" 1936 (Shorty); "Cherokee Strip" 1940 (Abe Gabbert); "Northwest Mounted Police" 1940 (Johnny Pelang); "Last of the Duanes" 1941 (Euchre); "Lone Star Ranger" 1942 (Ecuhre); "The Untamed Breed" 1948 (Pablo); "Broken Lance" 1954 (Paymaster); "Sierra Stranger" 1957 (Dan); "Alias Jesse James" 1959 (Gibson Girl Fan). ¶TV: *Have Gun Will Travel*—"The Prize Fight Story" 4-5-58 (Friend).

Stone, Harold J. (1911-). Films: "Three Thousand Hills" 1959 (Ram Butler); "Showdown" 1963 (Lavalle). ¶TV: *Philco Television Playhouse*—"The Death of Billy the Kid" 7-24-55 (Saval Guiterrez); *Gunsmoke*—"Who Lives by the Sword" 5-18-57 (Joe Delk), "Letter of the Law" 10-11-58 (Judge Rambeau), "Buffalo Hunter" 5-2-59 (Jim Gatluf), "Miss Kitty" 10-14-61 (Horace), "Homecoming" 5-23-64 (Orval Bass), "Hung High" 11-14-64 (Jim Downey), "He Who Steals" 5-29-65 (Jeff Sutro); *Have Gun Will Travel*—"A Matter of Ethics" 10-12-57 (Bart Holgate), "The Bride" 10-19-57, "Helen of Abajinian" 12-28-57 (Samuel Abajinian), "The Last Judgment" 3-11-61 (Judge Elroy Greenleaf); *Cheyenne*—"The Last Comanchero" 1-14-58 (Rafe Larkin), "The Wedding Rings" 1-8-62 (Perez); *Zane Grey Theater*—"Trial by Fear" 1-20-58 (Tuphill); *Trackdown*—"The Witness" 1-24-58 (Aaron Yewcic), "The Schoolteacher" 11-7-58 (Quince Flanders), "Fear" 3-18-59 (Ambrose Hocker); *The Restless Gun*—"Sheriff Billy" 3-10-58 (Ben Reed); *Tales of Wells Fargo*—"The Sniper" 5-26-58 (Roy Dorcas), "Man for the Job" 5-30-60 (Phil), "Royal Maroon" 4-28-62 (Brian); *The Rifleman*—"Home Ranch" 10-7-58 (Oat Jackford), "Trail of Hate" 9-27-60 (Benjamin Stark), "The Bullet" 2-25-63 (Marshal); *Cimarron City*—"A Respectable Girl" 12-6-58 (Fred Barker); *Sugarfoot*—"Yampa Crossing" 12-9-58 (Galt Kimberly); *Zorro*—"The Iron Box" 1-15-59 (Salvio); *Texas John Slaughter*—"The Slaughter Trail" 3-20-59 (John Chisholm); *Bat Masterson*—"Man of Action" 4-22-59 (Jess Hobart); *The Alaskans*—"The Long Pursuit" 1-31-60 (Ed Bundy); *Overland Trail*—"The Reckoning" 5-

29-60 (Cash); *Wanted—Dead or Alive*—"The Cure" 9-28-60 (Harry Simmons); *The Tall Man*—"The Parson" 10-29-60 (Ben Myers); *Laramie*—"The Dark Trail" 11-1-60 (Sam Bronson); *Rawhide*—"Incident of the Night Visitor" 11-4-60 (Nick Mesa), "Incident at the Trail's End" 1-11-63 (Harry Maxton); *Stagecoach West*—"Red Sand" 11-22-60 (Tanner); *Wyatt Earp*—"The Fanatic" 11-22-60 (Hiram Grant); *Empire*—"The Tiger Inside" 2-12-63 (Gerald Wormser); *The Travels of Jaimie McPheeters*—"The Day of the Dark Deeds" 3-8-64 (Colonel Dolan); *Bonanza*—"The Hostage" 9-27-64 (Chad); *Daniel Boone*—"The Family Fluellen" 10-15-64 (Greenbriar); *The Virginian*—"The Laramie Road" 12-8-65 (Ev Clinchy), "The Hills of Man" 4-20-66 (Jake), "Ride to Delphi" 9-21-66 (Einar Carlson), "Death Wait" 1-15-69 (Grant Buchanan), "The Shiloh Years" 1-28-70(Adam Southcott); *The Big Valley*—"Teacher of Outlaws" 2-2-66 (Sam Beldon); *A Man Called Shenandoah*—"The Unfamiliar Tune" 4-11-66 (Jason Pruitt); *The Legend of Jesse James*—"A Field of Wild Flowers" 4-25-66 (Sergeant Foy); *Iron Horse*—"Steel Chain to a Music Box" 11-18-67 (Josh Wyatt); *Hec Ramsey*—"Only Birds and Fools" 4-7-74.

Stone, James F. (1898-1/9/69). Films: "Gunsmoke" 1953 (Shay); "Law and Order" 1953 (Martin); "Broken Lance" 1954 (Stable Owner); "Five Guns West" 1955 (Uncle Mime); "The Rainmaker" 1956 (Townsman). ¶TV: *The Restless Gun*—"The Battle of Tower Rock" 4-28-58 (Cal Curtis); *Have Gun Will Travel*—"The Lady on the Wall" 2-20-60 (Ezekiel Beckett).

Stone, Jeffrey. Films: "Money, Women and Guns" 1958 (Johnny Bee). ¶TV: *The Californians*—"The Duel" 2-18-58 (Claude Talbot), "The Golden Bride" 5-20-58 (Drake); *Death Valley Days*—"The Salt War" 1-25-61 (Dave Reid); *Bonanza*—"A Passion for Justice" 9-29-63.

Stone, Leonard (1923-). TV: *The Rifleman*—"Miss Bertie" 12-27-60, "Deadly Image" 2-26-62 (K.C. Peters); *Empire*—"Green, Green, Hills" 12-25-62 (Lawrence Rowan), "End of an Image" 1-15-63 (Raymond Carlisle); *Gunsmoke*—"Chief Joseph" 1-30-65 (Wiley), "Jessie" 2-19-73 (Abel Glass), "Kitty's Love Affair" 10-22-73 (Corley Deems), "The Fourth Victim" 11-4-74 (Ray Price); *Hondo*—"Hondo and the sudden Town" 11-17-67 (Kelso); *Cimarron*

Strip—"The Judgment" 1-4-68 (Judge Samuel Gilroy); *The High Chaparral*—"Ebenezer" 11-1-68 (Stoop); *Lancer*—"The Lorelei" 1-27-70 (Bertram Ames); *The Men from Shiloh*—"The Town Killer" 3-10-71 (Tom Wagner).

Stone, Lewis (1879-9/13/53). Films: "Nomads of the North" 1920 (Cpl. O'Conner); "The Three Godfathers" 1936 (James "Doc" Underwood); "The Bad Man of Brimstone" 1938 (Mr. Jack Douglas); "Out West with the Hardys" 1938 (Judge Hardy); "Stars in My Crown" 1950 (Dr. D.K. Harris, Sr.).

Stone, Milburn (1904-6/12/80). Films: "The Three Mesquiteers" 1936 (John); "California Frontier" 1938 (Hal Halstead); "Crashing Thru" 1939 (Herrington); "Fighting Mad" 1939 (Cardigan); "Colorado" 1940 (Don Burke); "The Phantom Cowboy" 1941 (Borden); "Death Valley Rangers" 1944 (Jeff); "Twilight on the Prairie" 1944; "The Daltons Ride Again" 1945 (Graham); "Royal Mounted Rides Again" 1945-serial (Taggart); "The Michigan Kid" 1947 (Lanny); "Calamity Jane and Sam Bass" 1949 (Abe Jones); "Snow Dog" 1950 (Dr. McKenzie); "Branded" 1951 (Dawson); "The Savage" 1952 (Cpl. Martin); "Arrowhead" 1953 (Sandy MacKinnon); "The Siege at Red River" 1954 (Benjy); "Smoke Signal" 1955 (Sgt. Miles); "White Feather" 1955 (Commissioner Trenton); "Drango" 1957 (Col. Bracken). ¶TV: *Wild Bill Hickok*—"The Silver Mine Protection Story" 7-24-51; *Gunsmoke*—Regular 1955-75 (Doc Galen Adams).

Stone, Paula. Films: "Hopalong Cassidy" 1935 (Mary Meeker); "Trailin' West" 1936 (Lucy Blake); "Treachery Rides the Range" 1936 (Ruth Drummond).

Stone, Sharon (1958-). Films: "The Quick and the Dead" 1995 (Ellen).

Stonehouse, Ruth (1892-5/12/41). Films: "Fighting for Love" 1917 (Sylvia); "Follow the Girl" 1917 (Hilda Swanson); "The Masked Rider" 1919-serial; "Rosalind at Red Gate" 1919; "Blood and Steel" 1925 (Vera); "The Fugitive" 1925 (the Girl); "Ridin' Through" 1925; "The Scarlet West" 1925 (Mrs. Custer); "A Two-Fisted Sheriff" 1925 (Midge Blair).

Stoner, Sherri. Films: "Little House on the Prairie: Look Back to Yesterday" TVM-1983 (Rache Brown); "Little House: The Last Farewell" TVM-1984 (Rachel Brown).

Stoney, Jack (1897-1/29/78). Films: "White Fang" 1936 (Posse Member); "Frontier Marshal" 1939 (Drunk); "The Gay Caballero" 1940 (Stage Guard); "Last of the Duanes" 1941 (Man); "The Sea of Grass" 1947 (Man); "Station West" 1948 (Bouncher).

Stoppa, Paolo (1906-5/1/88). Films: "Once Upon a Time in the West" 1968-Ital. (Sam).

Storch, Larry (1923-). Films: "Gun Fever" 1958 (Amigo); "The Great Bank Robbery" 1969 (Juan); "The Incredible Rocky Mountain Race" TVM-1977 (Eagle Feather). ¶TV: *F Troop*—Regular 1965-67 (Corporal Randolph Agarn), "El Diablo" 1-18-66 (El Diablo/Grandma Agarn/Gaylord Agarn/Carmen Agarnado), "The Singing Mountie" 9-8-66 (Lucky Pierre Agarniere); *Alias Smith and Jones*—"The Long Chase" 9-16-72 (Mugs McGeehu); *The Life and Times of Grizzly Adams*—"Gold Is Where You Find It" 11-23-77.

Storey, Edith (1892-9/23/55). Films: "Onawanda" 1909; "Billy the Kid" 1911; "A Spanish Love Song" 1911; "A Western Heroine" 1911; "Yellow Bird" 1912; "O'Garry of the Royal Mounted" 1915; "The Captain of the Gray Horse Troop" 1917 (Elsie); "The Claim" 1918 (Belle Jones); "Revenge" 1918 (Alva Leigh); "As the Sun Went Down" 1919 (Col Billy); "The Golden Hope" 1921.

Storey, June (1918-12/18/91). Films: "Blue Montana Skies" 1939 (Dorothy Hamilton); "Colorado Sunset" 1939 (Carol Haines); "Home on the Prairie" 1939 (Martha Wheeler); "In Old Monterey" 1939 (Jill Whittaker); "Mountain Rhythm" 1939 (Alice); "South of the Border" 1939 (Lola Martin); "Carolina Moon" 1940 (Caroline); "Gaucho Serenade" 1940 (Joyce Halloway); "Rancho Grande" 1940 (Kay Dodge); "Ride, Tenderfoot, Ride" 1940 (Ann Randolph); "Song of the Prairie" 1945.

Storm, Gale (1922-). Films: "Jesse James at Bay" 1941 (Jane Fillmore); "Red River Valley" 1941; "Saddlemates" 1941 (Susan Langley); "Man from Cheyenne" 1942 (Judy); "The Dude Goes West" 1948 (Liza Crockett); "Stampede" 1949 (Connie); "Curtain Call at Cactus Creek" 1950 (Julie Martin); "The Kid from Texas" 1950 (Irene Kain); "The Texas Rangers" 1951 (Helen Fenton); "Al Jennings of Oklahoma" 1951 (Margo St. Claire); "Woman of the North Country" 1952 (Cathy Nordlund).

Storm, Jerome (1890-7/10/58).

Films: "The Primal Lure" 1916 (Pierre); "Diamond Trail" 1933 (Muggs); "Rainbow Ranch" 1933 (Sam); "The Lone Cowboy" 1934 (Storekeeper); "Wells Fargo" 1937.

Storm, Wayne. Films: "Oklahoma Crude" 1973 (Hobo); "Hearts of the West" 1975 (Lyle, the Film Star). ¶TV: *Bonanza*—"The Witness" 9-21-69 (Bo); *The High Chaparral*—"The Guns of Johnny Rondo" 2-6-70; *Kung Fu*—"The Assassin" 10-4-73 (Carey).

Storrs, Suzanne. TV: *Maverick*—"Guatemala City" 1-31-60 (Ellen Johnson); *Lawman*—"Fast Trip to Cheyenne" 6-19-60 (Amy Saunders); *Wanted—Dead or Alive*—"To the Victor" 11-9-60 (Liz Strata); *Sugarfoot*—"Trouble at Sand Springs" 4-17-61 (Rhonda Rigsby).

Stossel, Ludwig (1883-1/29/73). TV: *Shotgun Slade*—"Flower for Jenny" 6-14-60 (Maximillian).

Stowe, Leslie (1886-7/16/49). Films: "Jamestown" 1923 (the Rev. Richard Buck); "Tongues of Flame" 1924 (Hornblower).

Stowe, Madeleine. Films: "The Deerslayer" TVM-1978 (Hetty Hut) (Cora); "Bad Girls" 1994 (Cody Zamora).

Stowell, William (1885-12/19). Films: "The Rose of Old St. Augustine" 1911; "The Horseshoe" 1912; "Sons of the Northwoods" 1912; "The Buzzard's Shadow" 1915 (Dr. Deschamps); "The Old Code" 1915; "Immediate Lee" 1916 (King); "Overalls" 1916 (Herbert Drew); "Fighting Mad" 1917 (Doctor Lambert); "Pay Me!" 1917 (Bill the Bass); "The Grand Passion" 1918 (Dick Evans); "When a Girl Loves" 1919 (Eagle Ryan).

Straight, Clarence. Films: "The Far Frontier" 1949 (Defendant); "The Golden Stallion" 1949 (Spud); "Mrs. Mike" 1949 (Cameron); "Pioneer Marshal" 1949 (Bartender); "Powder River Rustlers" 1949 (Telegraph Operator); "Colorado Sundown" 1952 (Postman); "Gunmen from Laredo" 1959 (Frank Bass); "The Hanging Tree" 1959 (Dealer). ¶TV: *The Lone Ranger*—"The Star Witness" 8-17-50, "Behind the Law" 2-1-51, "Outlaw's Trail" 10-21-54; *My Friend Flicka*—"The Unmasking" 4-13-56 (Styner); *Wagon Train*—"The Jessie Cowan Story" 1-8-58 (Troy Cowan); *Tales of Wells Fargo*—"The Prisoner" 2-17-58 (Carter); *The Texan*—"Reunion" 5-4-59 (Mr. Plummer); *Laramie*—"Hour After Dawn" 3-15-60 (Cruse); *Bonanza*—"The Hopefuls" 10-8-60.

Strang, Harry (1892-4/10/72). Films: "The Country Beyond" 1936 (Mountie); "Fair Warning" 1937 (O'Reilly); "Ranger Courage" 1937 (Snaky); "Wells Fargo" 1937; "Zorro Rides Again" 1937-serial (O'Brien); "Gunsmoke Trail" 1938 (Stub); "Phantom Ranger" 1938 (Jeff); "The Purple Vigilantes" 1938 (Murphy); "Rio Grande" 1938; "Two-Gun Justice" 1938 (Joe); "The Cisco Kid and the Lady" 1939 (Telegraph Operator); "Cowboys from Texas" 1939; "Frontier Marshal" 1939; "The Return of the Cisco Kid" 1939 (Deputy); "Stand Up and Fight" 1939 (Deputy Thomas); "The Dark Command" 1940; "Gaucho Serenade" 1940; "Kit Carson" 1940 (Sgt. Clanahan); "Lucky Cisco Kid" 1940 (Corporal); "Oklahoma Renegades" 1940; "Santa Fe Trail" 1940 (Sergeant); "The Trail Blazers" 1940; "They Died with Their Boots On" 1941 (Orderly); "Western Union" 1941 (Henchman); "Sin Town" 1942 (Jessup); "The Lone Star Trail" 1943 (Sheriff Waddell); "Death Valley Rangers" 1944; "The Old Texas Trail" 1944; "King of the Forest Rangers" 1946-serial (Harmon); "Roll on, Texas Moon" 1946 (Don Williams); "Silver River" 1948 (Soldier); "Sinister Journey" 1948; "Wagons West" 1952 (Territorial Marshal); "At Gunpoint" 1955 (Postmaster); "Toughest Gun in Tombstone" 1958 (Dr. MacAvoy). ¶TV: *Wild Bill Hickok*—"Chain of Events" 6-24-52; *The Cisco Kid*—"Battle of Bad Rock" 10-4-52; *The Roy Rogers Show*—"The Secret of Indian Gap" 1-24-54 (Jasper Riley), "The High-Graders of Paradise Valley" 2-28-54 (Mart Woodward), "Head for Cover" 10-21-56; *Tales of the Texas Rangers*—"Last Days of Boot Hill" 2-11-56 (Wells); *The Adventures of Rin Tin Tin*—"Homer the Great" 4-20-56, "The Silent Witness" 3-29-57 (Sheriff Porter), "A Look of Eagles" 10-11-57 (Sheriff Macomber), "The Cloudbusters" 10-31-58 (Sheriff), "Deadman's Valley" 11-7-58 (Sheriff), "The Epidemic" 11-21-58 (Sheriff), "The Ming Vase" 3-13-59, "The Failure" 5-8-59; *Circus Boy*—"Elmer the Aeronaut" 1-13-57 (Sheriff); *The Lone Ranger*—"A Message from Abe" 2-7-57, "Clover in the Dust" 3-7-57, "Journey to San Carlos" 5-9-57; *Sergeant Preston of the Yukon*—"Old Ben's Gold" 10-3-57 (Ben Taylor); *Maverick*—"Relic of Fort Tejon" 11-3-57 (Delivery Man); *Death Valley Days*—"Ten in Texas" 2-17-58; *Tales of Wells Fargo*—"The Killer" 12-1-58 (Pete Hampton).

Strange, Glenn (1899-9/20/73). Films: "Border Law" 1931; "Hard Hombre" 1931; "The Range Feud" 1931; "Wild Horse" 1931; "McKenna of the Mounted" 1932; "Ride Him, Cowboy" 1932; "The Law of the Wild" 1934-serial; "The Star Packer" 1934; "Border Vengeance" 1935; "Cyclone of the Saddle" 1935 (Townsman); "Gallant Defender" 1935; "His Fighting Blood" 1935; "Law of the 45's" 1935 (Monte); "Lawless Range" 1935; "Moonlight on the Prairie" 1935; "The New Frontier" 1935 (Norton); "Stormy" 1935 (Wrangler); "Westward Ho" 1935 (Carter); "Avenging Waters" 1936 (Jake); "The Cattle Thief" 1936; "The Fugitive Sheriff" 1936; "Song of the Gringo" 1936 (Blackie); "Sunset of Power" 1936; "Trailin' West" 1936; "Arizona Days" 1937 (Pete); "Blazing Sixes" 1937 (Peewee); "The California Mail" 1937 (Bud); "Cherokee Strip" 1937; "Danger Valley" 1937; "Courage of the West" 1937; "The Devil's Saddle Legion" 1937 (Peewee); "Empty Holsters" 1937 (Tex Roberts); "Guns of the Pecos" 1937; "Land Beyond the Law" 1937 (Bandy Malarkey); "A Tenderfoot Goes West" 1937; "Trouble in Texas" 1937; "Black Bandit" 1938 (Johnson); "Border Wolves" 1938 (Deputy); "California Frontier" 1938 (Blackie); "Call of the Rockies" 1938 (Kelso); "Forbidden Valley" 1938 (Corlox); "Ghost Town Riders" 1938 (Tex); "Guilty Trails" 1938 (Sheriff); "Gun Packer" 1938 (Sheriff); "Gunsmoke Trail" 1938; "In Old Mexico" 1938 (Burk); "The Last Stand" 1938 (Joe); "Mexicali Kid" 1938 (Jed); "The Mysterious Rider" 1938 (Cramer); "The Painted Trail" 1938 (Sheriff Ed); "Prairie Justice" 1938 (Haynes); "Pride of the West" 1938 (Saunders); "The Singing Outlaw" 1938 (Pete); "Six Shootin' Sheriff" 1938 (Andy); "Sunset Trail" 1938 (Bouncer); "Whirlwind Horseman" 1938 (Bull); "Across the Plains" 1939 (Jeff Masters); "Arizona Legion" 1939 (Kirby); "Blue Montana Skies" 1939 (Causer); "Cupid Rides the Range" 1939-short; "Days of Jesse James" 1939 (Cole Younger); "The Fighting Gringo" 1939 (Rance Potter); "Honor of the West" 1939 (Bat Grimes); "Law of the Pampas" 1939 (Slim); "The Llano Kid" 1939 (Henderson); "The Lone Ranger Rides Again" 1939-serial (Thorne); "The Night Riders" 1939; "Oklahoma Terror" 1939 (Haddon); "Overland Mail" 1939 (Dawson); "The Phantom Stage" 1939 (Sheriff); "Range War" 1939 (Sheriff); "Rough Riders' Round-Up" 1939 (Boggs); "Western Caravans" 1939 (Scanlon); "Bar Buckaroos" 1940-short; "Covered Wagon Trails"

1940 (Fletcher); "Cowboy from Sundown" 1940 (Bret Stockton); "The Dark Command" 1940 (Tough); "The Fargo Kid" 1940 (Sheriff); "Land of the Six Guns" 1940 (Manny); "Pals of the Silver Sage" 1940 (Vic Insley); "Pioneer Days" 1940 (Sheriff); "Rhythm of the Rio Grande" 1940 (Hayes); "Stage to Chino" 1940 (Bill Hoagland); "Three Men from Texas" 1940 (Stokes); "Triple Justice" 1940 (Frank Wiley); "Wagon Train" 1940 (Driver); "Wyoming" 1940 (Bill Smalley); "Arizona Cyclone" 1941 (Jessup); "The Bandit Trail" 1941 (Idaho); "Billy the Kid Wanted" 1941 (Matt); "Billy the Kid's Roundup" 1941 (Vic); "California or Bust" 1941-short; "The Driftin' Kid" 1941; "Dude Cowboy" 1941 (Krinkle); "Forbidden Trails" 1941 (Howard); "Fugitive Valley" 1941 (Gray); "In Old Colorado" 1941 (Blackie Reed); "The Kid's Last Ride" 1941 (Bart); "Lone Star Law Men" 1941 (Scott); "Riders of Death Valley" 1941-serial (Tex); "Saddlemates" 1941 (Little Bear); "Westward Ho-Hum" 1941-short; "Wide Open Town" 1941 (Ed Stark); "Bandit Ranger" 1942; "Billy the Kid Trapped" 1942 (Stanton); "Boot Hill Bandits" 1942 (Maverick); "Come on, Danger!" 1942 (Sloan); "Down Texas Way" 1942 (Sheriff); "Little Joe, the Wrangler" 1942 (Jeff Corey); "The Lone Rider and the Bandit" 1942; "Overland Stagecoach" 1942; "Prairie Gunsmoke" 1942; "Raiders of the West" 1942; "Rolling Down the Great Divide" 1942 (Joe); "Romance on the Range" 1942 (Stokes); "Stagecoach Buckaroo" 1942 (Braddock); "Sunset on the Desert" 1942 (Louie); "Texas Trouble Shooters" 1942 (Roger Danby); "Western Mail" 1942 (Collins); "Arizona Trail" 1943 (Matt Baker); "Black Market Rustlers" 1943 (Corbin); "Bullets and Saddles" 1943; "The Desperadoes" 1943 (Lem); "False Colors" 1943 (Sonora); "The Haunted Ranch" 1943; "The Kansan" 1943; "The Kid Rides Again" 1943 (Tom); "The Return of the Rangers" 1943; "Western Cyclone" 1943 (Dirk Randall); "Wild Horse Stampede" 1943 (Tip); "The Woman of the Town" 1943 (Walker); "Alaska" 1944; "Death Valley Rangers" 1944; "Forty Thieves" 1944 (Ike Simmons); "The San Antonio Kid" 1944; "Silver City Kid" 1944; "Sonora Stagecoach" 1944 (Paul Kenton); "Trail to Gunsight" 1944 (Duke Ellis); "Valley of Vengeance" 1944 (Marshal Baker); "Bad Men of the Border" 1945; "Renegades of the Rio Grande" 1945 (Bart Drummond); "Beauty and the Ban-

dit" 1946; "The Devil's Playground" 1946; "The Fabulous Texan" 1947; "The Sea of Grass" 1947 (Bill Roach); "White Stallion" 1947 (U.S. Marshal Taylor); "The Wistful Widow of Wagon Gap" 1947 (Lefty); "Wyoming" 1947 (Cowboy); "The Gallant Legion" 1948; "Red River" 1948 (Naylor); "Rimfire" 1949 (Stagecoach Driver); "Roll, Thunder, Roll" 1949 (Ace Hanlon); "Comanche Territory" 1950 (Big Joe); "Surrender" 1950 (Lon, the Deputy); "Callaway Went Thataway" 1951 (Black Norton); "Vengeance Valley" 1951 (Dave Allard); "The Lawless Breed" 1952 (Ben Hanley); "The Lusty Men" 1952 (Rig Ferris, the Foreman); "Montana Belle" 1952 (Deputy); "Wagons West" 1952 (Joplin Marshal); "Born to the Saddle" 1953; "Devil's Canyon" 1953 (Marshall, the Wagon Driver); "Escape from Fort Bravo" 1953 (Sgt. Compton); "The Great Sioux Uprising" 1953 (Stand Watie); "Jubilee Trail" 1954 (Tom Branders); "The Road to Denver" 1955 (Big George); "The Vanishing American" 1955 (Beleanth); "Fastest Gun Alive" 1956 (Sheriff); "Gunfire at Indian Gap" 1957 (Matt); "The Halliday Brand" 1957; "The Last Stagecoach West" 1957; "Quantrill's Raiders" 1958 (Todd); "Last Train from Gun Hill" 1959 (Saloon Bouncer). ¶TV: *The Lone Ranger*—"Enter the Lone Ranger" 9-15-49 (Butch Cavendish), "The Lone Ranger Fights On" 9-22-49 (Butch Cavendish), "The Lone Ranger's Triumph" 9-29-49 (Butch Cavendish), "Never Say Die" 4-6-50, "The Woman from Omaha" 7-2-53, "Ex-Marshal" 9-16-54; *The Cisco Kid*—"Cisco and the Giant" 10-31-53, "Dangerous Shoemaker" 5-15-54; *Fireside Theater*—"Man of the Comstock" 11-3-53 (Sam Brown); *Stories of the Century*—"Last Stagecoach West" 1954; *The Gene Autry Show*—"The Portrait of White Cloud" 10-15-55, "Dynamite" 12-24-55; *Judge Roy Bean*—"Ah Sid, Cowboy" 1-1-56 (Fallon), "The Hidden Truth" 1-1-56 (Sampson), "The Judge's Dilemma" 1-1-56 (Mason), "Border Raiders" 7-1-56 (Tom Holman), "The Cross-Draw Kid" 7-1-56 (King Lonagan), "The Refugee" 7-1-56 (Nolan); *Wyatt Earp*—"The Frontier Theatre" 2-7-56 (Jeff Pruitt), "Little Pistol" 11-5-57 (One-Eye Milburn), "Johnny Ringo's Girl" 12-13-60; *The Adventures of Rin Tin Tin*—"The Lieutenant's Lesson" 2-8-57 (Grey Fox); *Tales of Wells Fargo*—"The Hijackers" 6-17-57 (Tom), "Kelly's Clover Girls" 12-9-61 (Craiger); *The Restless Gun*—"Hornitas Town" 2-10-58 (Deputy Chuck);

Death Valley Days—"Cockeyed Charlie Parkhurst" 3-25-58; *26 Men*—"Chain Gang" 5-6-58; *Frontier Doctor*—"Queen of the Cimarron" 9-27-58; *MacKenzie's Raiders*—"Apache Indian Boy" 10-15-58; *The Rifleman*—"Duel of Honor" 11-11-58 (Stagecoach Driver), "The Deadeye Kid" 2-10-59, "The Woman" 5-5-59, "The Blowout" 10-13-59, "The Spiked Rifle" 11-24-59, "Miss Bertie" 12-27-60 (Stage Driver); *Rawhide*—"Incident of the Haunted Hills" 11-6-59 (Indian Chief); *Colt .45*—"Attack" 5-24-60; *Sugarfoot*—"Welcome Enemy" 12-26-60 (Chief Red Wing); *Gunsmoke*—"Melinda Miles" 6-3-61 (Man), Regular 1962-74 (Sam the Bartender).

Strange, Robert (1881-2/22/52). Films: "King of the Royal Mounted" 1940-serial (John Kettler); "Arizona Cyclone" 1941 (Draper); "Desert Bandit" 1941 (Hatfield); "Robin Hood of the Pecos" 1941 (Cravens); "South of Santa Fe" 1942; "Silver Trails" 1948 (Esteban); "The Far Frontier" 1949 (Willis Newcomb).

Strangis, Judy (1951-). Films: "Dragoon Wells Massacre" 1957 (Susan). ¶TV: *Barbary Coast*—"Mary Had More Than a Little" 1-2-76 (Mary Ellen).

Strano, Dino. see Stratford, Dean.

Strasberg, Susan (1938-). TV: *Our American Heritage*—"Destiny West" 1-24-60 (Jessie Fremont); *The Legend of Jesse James*—"Reunion" 1-10-66 (Ellen Bethard); *The Virginian*—"The Captive" 9-28-66 (Liliota); *The Big Valley*—"Night in a Small Town" 10-9-67 (Sally); *Bonanza*—"A Severe Case of Matrimony" 7-7-68 (Rosalita); *Lancer*—"Julie" 10-29-68 (Julie); *The Men from Shiloh*—"Crooked Corner" 10-28-70 (Clara Hansch); *Alias Smith and Jones*—"Escape from Wickenberg" 1-28-71 (Mary Cunningham).

Stratas, Teresa (1939-). Films: "The Canadians" 1961-Brit. (White Squaw).

Stratford, Dean (Dino Strano). Films: "Thompson 1880" 1966-Ital./Ger.; "Shadow of Sartana … Shadow of Your Death" 1968-Ital. (Nick Logan); "Finders Killers" 1969-Ital. (Dexter); "Chuck Moll" 1970-Ital.; "Brother Outlaw" 1971-Ital. (Donovan); "His Name Was Sam Walbash, But They Call Him Amen" 1971-Ital. (Mash Flanigan/Donovan); "One Damned Day at Dawn … Django Meets Sartana" 1971-Ital. (Bud Wheeler); "Reach You Bastard!" 1971-Ital. (Wild Bill Hickock); "The Dirty

Outlaws" 1971-Ital.; "Shoot the Living ... Pray for the Dead" 1971-Ital. (Reed); "Thirteenth Is a Judas" 1971-Ital.; "On the Third Day Arrive the Crow" 1972-Ital./Span.; "They Called Him Trinity" 1972-Ital./Span. (Chad Randall).

Stratford, Peggy. Films: "Trapped" 1937 (Adele Rogers); "Two Gun Law" 1937 (Mary Hammond).

Stratford, Tracy. Films: "The Miracle of the Hills" 1959 (Laurie Leonard); "The Second Time Around" 1961 (Cissie). ¶TV: *Bonanza*—"Blessed Are They" 4-22-62.

Stratton, Chet (1910-7/7/70). Films: "Journey to Shiloh" 1968 (Mr. Claiborne). ¶TV: *Broken Arrow*—"The Missionaries" 1-29-57 (Jason); *Wagon Train*—"The Annie MacGregor Story" 2-5-58 (Hamish), "Princess of a Lost Tribe" 11-2-60 (John Miller); *The Californians*—"Mutineers from Hell" 9-30-58 (Stratton); *Have Gun Will Travel*—"The Ballad of Oscar Wilde" 12-6-58 (Secretary), "The Gladiators" 3-19-60 (Harry), "The Gold Bar" 3-18-61 (Bank Examiner); *Maverick*—"The Rivals" 1-25-59 (Desk Clerk), "A Flock of Trouble" 2-14-60 (Mr. Crabill); *Destry*—"One Hundred Bibles" 5-8-64 (the Rev. Mr. Foote); *Wild Wild West*—"The Night of the Inferno" 9-17-65 (Bedford), "The Night of the Bars of Hell" 3-4-66 (Adams); *Bonanza*—"The Lady and the Mountain Lion" 2-23-69 (Clerk).

Strauch, Jr., Joe (1930-5/31/86). Films: "Under Fiesta Stars" 1941; "Bells of Capistrano" 1942 (Tadpole Millhouse); "Call of the Canyon" 1942 (Tadpole); "Heart of the Rio Grande" 1942 (Tadpole); "Home in Wyomin'" 1942 (Tadpole); "Beneath Western Skies" 1944 (Tadpole).

Strauss, Peter (1947-). Films: "Soldier Blue" 1970 (Pvt. Honus Gant); "Proud Men" TVM-1987 (Charley MacLeod, Jr.).

Strauss, Robert (1913-2/20/75). Films: "The Redhead from Wyoming" 1953 (Knuckles Hogan); "Frontier Gun" 1958 (Yubo); "Stage to Thunder Rock" 1964 (Judge Bates); "Fort Utah" 1967 (Ben Stokes). ¶TV: *Wanted—Dead or Alive*—"Rope Law" 1-3-59 (Brace Logan); *Wagon Train*—"The Elizabeth McQueeney Story" 10-28-59 (the Count), "The Cassie Vance Story" 12-23-63 (Lloyd); *Bat Masterson*—"A Time to Die" 12-15-60 (Howard C. Smith); *Stagecoach West*—"The Brass Lily" 1-17-61 (Vernon Mibbs); *Bonanza*—"Gallagher

Sons" 12-9-62 (Blake); *Rawhide*—"Incident of the Black Ace" 4-12-63 (Sam Lewellyn); *Rango*—"The Town Tamer" 1-27-67 (Blackie); *The Virginian*—"The Deadly Past" 9-20-67 (Ben Roper).

Strauss, William H. (1885-8/5/43). Films: "The Rawhide Kid" 1928 (Simon Silverberg); "The Texas Rangers" 1936 (Juror).

Strickland, Amzie. Films: "Man with the Gun" 1955 (Mary Atkins); "Drango" 1957 (Mrs. Randolph). ¶TV: *Gunsmoke*—"Night Incident" 10-29-55 (Mrs. Hinton), "Greater Love" 12-1-56 (Mrs. Brant), "The Violators" 10-17-64 (Mrs. Hewitt), "Sam McTavish, M.D." 10-5-70 (Minnie Carver); *Jim Bowie*—"Charivari" 11-15-57 (Denise); *The Restless Gun*—"The Crisis at Easter Creek" 4-7-58 (Elvira Peebles); *Trackdown*—"The Governor" 5-23-58 (Madge Roberts); *Wagon Train*—"The Millie Davis Story" 11-26-58 (Martha), "The C.L. Harding Story" 10-14-59 (Arletta), "The Hobie Redman Story" 1-17-62 (Agnes Montgomery), "The Kurt Davos Story" 11-28-62 (Minnie Hershey), "The Barnaby West Story" 6-5-63 (Mrs. West), "The Melanie Craig Story" 2-17-64; *Black Saddle*—"Client: Banke" 4-11-59 (Polly Banks); *Rawhide*—"Incident of Fear in the Streets" 5-8-59, "Incident of the Thirteenth Man" 10-23-59 (Grace Winston); *Bonanza*—"Blessed Are They" 4-22-62; *The Virginian*—"The Mountain of the Sun" 4-17-63 (Ruth Arlen); *Death Valley Days*—"The Lady and the Sourdough" 10-8-66 (Laticia Daigle); *The Big Valley*—"Down Shadow Street" 1-23-67 (Beanie); *F Troop*—"Is This Fort Really Necessary?" 4-6-67; *The Road West*—"Elizabeth's Odyssey" 5-1-67 (Anna Grimmer); *Cimarron Strip*—"The Search" 11-9-67 (Mrs. Andrews); *Alias Smith and Jones*—"Escape from Wickenberg" 1-28-71, "The Day They Hanged Kid Curry" 9-16-71; *Father Murphy*—"Graduation" 1-5-82 (Ruby Dobbins).

Strickland, Mabel (1897-1/3/76). Films: "Rough Riding Ranger" 1935 (Mrs. Francis); "Custer's Last Stand" 1936-serial (Mabel).

Stricklyn, Ray (1930-). Films: "The Last Wagon" 1956 (Clint); "The Plunderers" 1960 (Jeb); "Young Jesse James" 1960 (Jesse James); "Arizona Raiders" 1965 (Danny Bonner). ¶TV: *Jim Bowie*—"The General's Disgrace" 4-12-57 (Phillip Rogers); *Wagon Train*—"The Sam Elder Story" 1-18-61 (Perks), "The Lieutenant Burton Story" 2-28-62 (Danny Maitland);

Lawman—"Homecoming" 2-5-61 (Eddy); *Cheyenne*—"The Greater Glory" 5-15-61 (Billy the Kid); *Broken Arrow*—"The Captive" 10-23-56 (Nahilo), "Legacy of a Hero" 2-26-57 (Joey); *Bronco*—"The Soft Answer" 11-3-59 (Billy the Kid); *Bonanza*—"The Fear Merchants" 1-30-60 (Billy Wheeler), "Peace Officer" 2-6-66 (Cliff).

Stritch, Elaine (1925-). Films: "Three Violent People" 1956 (Ruby LaSalle). ¶TV: *Wagon Train*—"The Tracy Sadler Story" 3-9-60 (Tracy Sadler).

Strode, Woody (1914-12/31/94). Films: "The Gambler from Natchez" 1954 (Josh); "Sergeant Rutledge" 1960 (1st Sgt. Braxton Rutledge); "Two Rode Together" 1961 (Stone Calf); "The Man Who Shot Liberty Valance" 1962 (Pompey); "The Professionals" 1966 (Jacob Sharp); "Once Upon a Time in the West" 1968-Ital. (Stony); "Shalako" 1968-Brit./Fr. (Chato); "Boot Hill" 1969-Ital. (Thomas); "Chuck Moll" 1970-Ital. (Deserter" 1970-U.S./Ital./Yugo. (Jackson); "The Last Rebel" 1971-Ital./U.S./Span. (Duncan); "The Gatling Gun" 1972 (Runner); "The Revengers" 1972-U.S./Mex. (Job); "Keoma" 1975-Ital./Span.; "Winterhawk" 1975 (Big Rude); "Lust in the Dust" 1985 (Blackman); "Posse" 1993 (Storyteller); "The Quick and the Dead" 1995 (Charles Moonlight). ¶TV: *Man from Blackhawk*—"The Savage" 1-15-60 (Tego); *Rawhide*—"Incident of the Buffalo Soldier" 1-1-61 (Cpl. Gabe Washington), "Incident of the Boomerang" 3-24-61 (Binnaburra); *Daniel Boone*—"Goliath" 9-29-66 (Goliath); *The Quest*—"The Longest Drive" 12-1-76 & 12-8-76 (Tucker).

Stroll, Edson. Films: "The Wild and the Innocent" 1959 (Henchman). ¶TV: *Tombstone Territory*—2-5-60 (Vince Sanders).

Stromsoe, Fred (1930-9/30/94). Films: "Westbound" 1959; "Jesse James Meets Frankenstein's Daughter" 1966. ¶TV: *Wild Wild West*—"The Night of the Iron Fist" 12-8-67 (Cal), "The Night of the Doomsday Formula" 10-4-68 (Gunslinger), "The Night of Fire and Brimstone" 11-22-68 (Lefty); *Gunsmoke*—"Trafton" 10-25-71 (Prew).

Strong, Eugene (1893-6/25/62). Films: "The Trail of the Shadow" 1917 (Henry Hilliard); "The Border Legion" 1918 (Jim Cleeves); "Men of America" 1933 (Bugs Foster).

Strong, Leonard (1908-1/23/80). Films: "Shane" 1953 (Wright).

¶TV: *The Lone Ranger*—"Gold Fever" 4-13-50; *Walt Disney Presents*—"Elfego Baca" Regular 1958-60 (Zangano); *The Alaskans*—"The Silent Land" 5-15-60 (Shaman); *Rawhide*—"The Book" 1-8-65 (Leroy Means).

Strong, Michael (1925-1/23/80). TV: *Philco Television Playhouse*—"The Death of Billy the Kid" 7-24-55 (John Poe); *Gunsmoke*—"Snap Decision" 9-17-66 (Shaver), "Kimbro" 2-12-73 (Peak Stratton); *Cimarron Strip*—"Journey to a Hanging" 9-7-67 (Latch); *The Big Valley*—"Days of Wrath" 1-8-68 (Cass Hyatt).

Strongheart, Nipo (1891-12/30/66). Films: "Young Daniel Boone" 1950 (Walking Eagle); "Across the Wide Missouri" 1951; "Westward the Women" 1951; "Lone Star" 1952; "Pony Soldiers" 1952 (Medicine Man).

Stroud, Claude (1907-10/16/85). Films: "Border Rangers" 1950 (Randolph); "Gunfire" 1950 (Mundy); "I Shot Billy the Kid" 1950 (Wallace); "Train to Tombstone" 1950 (Brown); "The Man from Galveston" 1964 (Harvey Sprager); "J.W. Coop" 1971 (Rodeo Manager). ¶TV: *Maverick*—"Kiz" 12-4-60 (Henry); *Klondike*—"Bathhouse Justice" 12-26-60 (Bartender); *Temple Houston*—"The Man from Galveston" 1963 (Harvey Sprager), "Do Unto Others, Then Gallop" 3-19-64 (Murdock), "The Town That Trespassed" 3-26-64 (Murdock).

Stroud, Don (1937-). Films: "Ballad of Josie" 1968 Bratsch); "Journey to Shiloh" 1968 (Todo McLean); "Something for a Lonely Man" TVM-1968 (Eben Duren); "The Daughters of Joshua Cabe" TVM-1972 (Blue Wetherall); "Joe Kidd" 1972 (Lamarr). ¶TV: *The Virginian*—"Long Journey Home" 12-14-66 (Cate), "Paid in Full" 11-22-67 (Frank Hollis), "Image of an Outlaw" 10-23-68 (Rafe Judson/McCullough); *Hec Ramsey*—"The Mystery of the Yellow Rose" 1-28-73 (Brock McCabe); *Gunsmoke*—"Jessie" 2-19-73 (Pete Murphy), "A Town in Chains" 9-16-74 (Foss); *Kung Fu*—"Cry of the Night Beast" 10-19-74 (Neulin); *Paradise*—"A House Divided" 2-16-89 (Moses Henderson); *Ned Blessing: The Story of My Life and Times*—"Oscar" 9-8-93; *Adventures of Brisco County, Jr.*—"Riverboat" 10-1-93 (Randy Hatchett); *Dr. Quinn, Medicine Woman*—"Progress" 2-27-93 (Tate Rankin).

Strudwick, Sheppard (John Sheppard) (1907-1/15/83). Films: "Belle Starr" 1941 (Ed Shirley); "The

Kid from Texas" 1950 (Jameson). ¶TV: *Wagon Train*—"The Clara Beauchamp Story" 12-11-57 (Col. Beauchamp); *The Californians*—"The Marshal" 3-11-58 (Father Holzer); *Have Gun Will Travel*—"The Prophet" 1-2-60 (Colonel Nunez).

Struycken, Carel. Films: "Oblivion" 1994 (Mr. Gaunt).

Stuart, Barbara (1930-). TV: *Jefferson Drum*—"The Bounty Man" 5-2-58 (Ellie), "The Outlaw" 6-20-58 (Ellie); *Lawman*—"The Oath" 10-26-58 (Lola Bordeaux); *Colt .45*—"The Magic Box" 4-19-59 (Belle); *The Texan*—"The Taming of Rio Nada" 1-11-60 (Poker Alice), "Sixgun Street" 1-18-60 (Poker Alice), "The Terrified Town" 1-25-60 (Poker Alice); *Riverboat*—"The Sellout" 4-18-60 (Nanette); *Two Faces West*—"The Challenge" 10-7-60 (Millie Adams); *Tales of Wells Fargo*—"All That Glitters" 10-24-60 (Meg), "A Fistful of Pride" 11-18-61 (Lucy Croydon); *Frontier Circus*—"Karina" 11-9-61 (Melda); *The Outlaws*—"Roly" 11-23-61 (Juno); *Rawhide*—"Incident of the Wild Deuces" 12-12-63 (Lorelie Mears); *Destry*—"Destry Had a Little Lamb" 2-21-64 (Amy); *Iron Horse*—"Sister Death" 4-3-67 (Lil Kane); *Alias Smith and Jones*—"Smiler with a Gun" 10-7-71 (Lurene); *Kung Fu*—"The Third Man" 4-26-73 (Fay).

Stuart, Donald (1898-2/22/44). Films: "The Girl-Shy Cowboy" 1928 (Red Harden).

Stuart, Gilchrist (1919-6/8/77). Films: "Fancy Pants" 1950 (Wicket Keeper). ¶TV: *Cheyenne*—"The Dark Rider" 9-11-56 (Arthur Thurston Wells); *Maverick*—"Kiz" 12-4-60 (Poker Player).

Stuart, Jack. *see* Rossi-Stuart, Giacomo.

Stuart, Mary. Films: "Thunderhoof" 1948 (Margarita); "The Cariboo Trail" 1950 (Jane Winters).

Stuart, Maxine (1918-). TV: *Wanted—Dead or Alive*—"The Choice" 12-14-60 (Jane Koster); *Stoney Burke*—"Gold-Plated Maverick" 1-7-63 (Hilda Pollard); *The New Land*—"The Word Is: Mortal" 10-5-74.

Stuart, Nicholas (1910-). Films: "The Sheriff of Fractured Jaw" 1958-Brit. (Feeney).

Stuart, Nick (1903-4/7/73). Films: "Sundown Trail" 1931 (Flash Prescott); "A Demon for Trouble" 1934 (Buck Morton); "Rio Grande Romance" 1936 (George Bates); "Fighting Playboy" 1937 (Don); "Gunsmoke" 1947.

Stuart, Randy. Films: "Star in the Dust" 1956 (Nan Hogan); "Man from God's Country" 1958 (Nancy Dawson). ¶TV: *Cavalcade of America*—"A Matter of Honor" 2-18-53; *Colt .45*—"Blood Money" 1-17-58 (Julie); *Cheyenne*—"White Warrior" 3-11-58 (Pioneer Woman), "The Long Search" 4-22-58 (Peg Ellis), "Two Trails to Santa Fe" 10-28-60 (Amy Brandon), "Retaliation" 11-13-61 (Cora); *Wyatt Earp*—Regular 1959-60 (Nellie Cashman); *Bronco*—"Tangled Trail" 5-3-60 (Claire Russo); *Lawman*—"The Judge" 5-15-60 (Rose Grant), "The Frame-Up" 1-15-61 (Jessica Kindle); *Bonanza*—"The Duke" 3-11-61 (Marge); *Maverick*—"Benefit of Doubt" 4-9-61 (Mavis Todd).

Stubbs, Harry (1874-3/9/50). Films: "The Plainsman" 1936 (John F. Usher); "Sutter's Gold" 1936; "The Singing Hill" 1941.

Studi, Wes. Films: "The Last of the Mohicans" 1992 (Magua); "Geronimo: An American Legend" 1993 (Geronimo). ¶TV: *Ned Blessing: The Story of My Life and Times*—Regular 1993 (One Horse).

Study, Lomax (1924-). Films: "Station West" 1948 (Man). ¶TV: *Riverboat*—"The Two Faces of Grey Holden" 10-3-60 (Father Paul).

Sturgess, Olive. Films: "Requiem for a Gunfighter" 1965 (Bonnie Young). ¶TV: *Cheyenne*—"Renegades" 2-11-58 (Kathy Donovan); *Sugarfoot*—"Short Range" 5-13-58 (Olive Turner); *The Texan*—"The Ringer" 2-16-59 (Mary Lou Martin); *Rawhide*—"Incident at Chubasco" 4-3-59 (Sally Devereaux); *Have Gun Will Travel*—"The Chase" 4-11-59 (Helen Martin); *Lawman*—"The Huntress" 5-3-59 (Buckskin—"Mary MacNamara" 5-18-59 (Mary MacNamara); *The Rebel*—"The Scavengers" 11-8-59 (Jeannie), "The Pit" 3-12-61 (Charity); *Laramie*—"Company Man" 2-9-60 (Caroline); *Wagon Train*—"The Benjamin Burns Story" 2-17-60 (Kathy Burns), "Wagons Ho!" 9-28-60; *Maverick*—"Last Wire from Stop Gap" 10-16-60 (Phyllis), "The Golden Fleecing" 10-8-61 (Phoebe Albright); *The Tall Man*—"McBean Rides Again" 12-10-60 (May McBean), "The Reluctant Bridegroom" 2-18-61 (May McBean), "Millionaire McBean" 4-15-61 (May McBean); *The Outlaws*—"The Sisters" 2-15-62 (Ruth Durant); *Bonanza*—"A Hot Day for a Hanging" 10-14-62 (Mary Ann), "Lothario Larkin" 4-25-65 (Nancy); *Wide Country*—"The Girl from Nob Hill"

3-8-63 (Bibsy); *Destry*—"Deputy for a Day" 4-3-64 (Sally); *The Virginian*—"Big Image ... Little Man" 10-28-64 (Laura Carter).

Sturgess, Solomon (1941-). Films: "Charro!" 1969 (Billy Roy). ¶TV: *Cimarron Strip*—"The Judgment" 1-4-68 (Sandy); *The Guns of Will Sonnett*—"And He Shall Lead the Children" 1-19-68 (Billy); *The High Chaparral*—"Spokes" 9-25-70 (Bud Pierce).

Sturgis, Edward (1881-12/13/47). Films: "Hard-Boiled" 1926 (1st Crook); "Wanderer of the Wasteland" 1935 (Dealer).

Sturgis, Norman. TV: *Gunsmoke*—"False Witness" 12-12-59 (Jake); *Bat Masterson*—"Death by the Half Dozen" 2-4-60 (Slim Tobey).

Sturkie, Dan (-5/10/92). Films: "They Call Me Trinity" 1970-Ital. (Tobias).

Sturlin, Ross. TV: *The Rebel*—"You Steal My Eyes" 3-20-60 (Sculley), "The Bequest" 9-25-60 (Joe Redfern), "The Waiting" 10-9-60 (the Yellow Sky Kid), "The Scalp Hunter" 12-11-60 (Apache), "Miz Purdy" 4-2-61 (Mexican); *Have Gun Will Travel*— "Black Sheep" 4-30-60 (Joaquin Jim), "The Princess and the Gunfighter" 1-21-61 (Guide).

Stutenroth, Gene. *see* Roth, Gene.

Stuthman, Fred (1914-7/7/82). Films: "Another Man, Another Chance" 1977-Fr. (Mary's Father).

Styne, Jan. Films: "Sergeant Rutledge" 1960 (Chris Hubble).

Suarez, Jose (1919-). Films: "Jaguar" 1964-Span. (Llanos); "The Avengers" 1966-Ital.; "Texas, Adios" 1966-Ital./Span.; "Forgotten Pistolero" 1970-Ital./Span.; "Massacre at Fort Holman" 1972-Ital./Fr./Span./Ger.

Sues, Alan. TV: *Wild Wild West*—"The Night of the Fatal Trap" 12-24-65 (Matt Dawson).

Suhor, Yvonne. TV: *Young Riders*—Regular 1990-92 (Lou McCloud).

Sullivan, Barry (1912-6/6/94). Films: "The Woman of the Town" 1943 (King Kennedy); "Bad Men of Tombstone" 1949 (Tom); "The Outriders" 1950 (Jesse Wallace); "Inside Straight" 1951 (Johnny Sanderson); "Texas Lady" 1955 (Chris Mooney); "The Maverick Queen" 1956 (Jeff); "Dragoon Wells Massacre" 1957 (Link Ferris); "Forty Guns" 1957 (Griff Bonnell); "Seven Ways from Sundown" 1960 (Jim Flood); "Stage

to Thunder Rock" 1964 (Sheriff Horne); "Buckskin" 1968 (Chaddock); "Tell Them Willie Boy Is Here" 1969 (Ray Calvert); "Yuma" TVM-1971 (Nels Decker); "Kung Fu" TVM-1972 (Dillon); "Take a Hard Ride" 1974-Ital./Brit./Ger. (Sheriff Kane). ¶TV: *Zane Grey Theater*—"Shadow of a Dead Man" 4-11-58 (Raney Benson), "Bury Me Dead" 12-11-58 (Jed Lorimer), "The Lonely Gun" 10-22-59 (Clint Shannon); *Bonanza*—"The Sun Mountain Herd" 9-19-59 (Mark Burdette), "Judgment at Olympus" 10-8-67 (Fuller); *The Tall Man*—Regular 1960-62 (Deputy Sheriff Pat Garrett); *The Virginian*—"Woman from White Ting" 9-26-62 (Frank Dawson), "The Power Seekers" 10-8-69 (John Springfield); *The Loner*—"The Oath" 12-4-65 (Dr. Bohan); *The Road West*—Regular 1966-67 (Ben Pride); *The High Chaparral*—"A Matter of Survival" 10-16-70 (Dan Casement), "A Matter of Vengeance" 11-27-70 (Dan Casement); *Kung Fu*—"Cross-ties" 2-21-74 (Edwards).

Sullivan, Billy (1891-5/23/46). Films: "The Double X" 1924; "An Eyeful" 1924; "Her Rodeo Hero" 1924; "A Race for a Ranch" 1924; "The Red Rage" 1924; "The Fighting Terror" 1925; "Fighting Thorobreds" 1925; "The Loser Wins" 1925; "Ridin' Pretty" 1925 (Stringbean); "The Way of the West" 1925; "The Whip Hand" 1925; "Red Clay" 1927 (Bob Lee).

Sullivan, Brad (1931-). Films: "The Gambler Returns: The Luck of the Draw" TVM-1991. ¶TV: *Best of the West*—9-10-81 (Lance).

Sullivan, Brick (1899-9/4/59). TV: *Gunsmoke*—"Jesse" 10-19-57 (Sam), "Doc's Reward" 12-14-57 (Bartender).

Sullivan, Charles (1899-6/25/72). Films: "The Fourth Horseman" 1933; "The Old Corral" 1936 (Frank); "Fugitive from Sonora" 1937; "Wells Fargo" 1937 (Northerner); "Dead Man's Gulch" 1943; "Marshal of Reno" 1944; "Bells of Rosarita" 1945; "Bandits of the Badlands" 1945; "The El Paso Kid" 1946 (Lowery); "King of the Forest Rangers" 1946-serial (Turner); "River Lady" 1948 (Logger); "Calamity Jane and Sam Bass" 1949; "Hoedown" 1950 (Tiny); "Jubilee Trail" 1954 (Card Player); "Man with the Steel Whip" 1954-serial (Mike).

Sullivan, Donald E. Films: "Seven Guns to Mesa" 1958 (Louis Middleton). ¶TV: *Wild Bill Hickok*—"The Gatling Gun" 5-5-53.

Sullivan, Elliott (1907-6/2/74). Films: "Wells Fargo" 1937; "The Oklahoma Kid" 1939 (Henchman); "Wild Bill Hickok Rides" 1942 (Bart Hanna); "The Spikes Gang" 1974 (Billy).

Sullivan, Grant. TV: *Pony Express*—Regular 1960-61 (Brett Clark); *Tales of Wells Fargo*—"The Diamond Dude" 2-27-61 (Beam), "Death Raffle" 10-21-61 (Dutch).

Sullivan, Joseph. TV: *Tales of Wells Fargo*—"Double Reverse" 10-19-59 (Josh); *Zane Grey Theater*—"The Grubstake" 12-24-59 (Sheriff Winters).

Sullivan, John Maurice (1876-3/8/49). Films: "High, Wide and Handsome" 1937 (Old Gentleman); "Union Pacific" 1939; "Geronimo" 1940 (Ebenezer Hoar).

Sullivan, Liam (1923-). TV: *Death Valley Days*—"Nevada's Plymouth Rock" 3-10-56; *Gunsmoke*—"The Executioner" 2-2-57 (Tom Clegg), "Quaker Girl" 12-10-66 (Benjamin Ellis); *Cheyenne*—"Gold, Glory and Custer—Prelude" 1-4-60 (Major Reno), "Gold, Glory and Custer—Requiem" 1-11-60 (Major Reno); *Tombstone Territory*—1-29-60 (Jason Douglas); *Have Gun Will Travel*—"The Prisoner" 12-17-60 (Judge Bradford); *Bat Masterson*—"End of the Line" 1-26-61 (Dick Jeffers); *Wagon Train*—"The Bruce Saybrook Story" 11-22-61 (Tommy); *Rawhide*—"The Winter Soldier" 3-12-65 (Lieutenant Whitley); *Walt Disney Presents*—"Gallegher" 1965-67 (Charles Van Raalte); *Bonanza*—"A Dublin Lad" 1-2-66 (Terence O'Tooley); *The Legend of Jesse James*—"Benjamin Bates" 2-28-66 (Benjamin Bates); *The Virginian*—"That Saunders Woman" 3-30-66 (John Ballinger); *The Monroes*—Regular 1966-67 (Major Mapoy); *Daniel Boone*—"Love and Equity" 3-13-69 (Patrick Henry), "Perilous Passage" 1-15-70 (Colonel Trevelyan).

Sullivan, Ruth. Films: "Jaws of Justice" 1933 (Judy Dean); "The Ferocious Pal" 1934 (Patsy Boliver).

Sullivan, Tim. Films: "The Tin Star" 1957 (Virgil Hough); "Badman's Country" 1958; "The Wild Westerners" 1962 (Rev. Thomas). ¶TV: *Wild Bill Hickok*—"Blake's Kid" 12-23-52.

Sully, Frank (1908-12/17/75). Films: "High, Wide and Handsome" 1937 (Gabby Johnson); "The Return of Frank James" 1940 (Pappy, the Old Actor); "Along Came Jones" 1945 Cherry's Brother); "Renegades" 1946

(Link); "Throw a Saddle on a Star" 1946; "South of the Chisholm Trail" 1947; "Gun Smugglers" 1948 (Clancy); "Man in the Saddle" 1951 (Lee Repp); "Prairie Roundup" 1951 (Sheriff); "Night Stage to Galveston" 1952 (Kelly); "Northern Patrol" 1953 (Bartender); "Take Me to Town" 1953 (Sammy); "Battle of Rogue River" 1954 (Kohler); "The Law vs. Billy the Kid" 1954 (Jack Poe); "Silver Lode" 1954 (Paul Herbert); "The Spoilers" 1955 (Miner); "The Desperados Are in Town" 1956 (Branch); "Frontier Gambler" 1956; "The Buckskin Lady" 1957 (Jed). ¶TV: *The Lone Ranger*—"Dead Man's Chest" 9-28-50; *Wild Bill Hickok*—"Jingles Gets the Bird" 3-24-53; *Stage 7*—"Billy and the Bride" 5-8-55 (Pat Turner); *The Adventures of Rin Tin Tin*—"The Lonesome Road" 6-4-55 (Detective); *Schlitz Playhouse of the Stars*—"The Bitter Land" 4-13-56 (Coots Larkin); *The Restless Gun*—"The Gold Star" 5-19-58 (Man); *The Rifleman*—"The Wrong Man" 3-31-59; *Wanted—Dead or Alive*—"Vanishing Act" 12-26-59, "Tolliver Bender" 2-13-60; *Maverick*—"Dutchman's Gold" 1-22-61 (Bartender); *The Tall Man*—"An Item for Auction" 10-14-61 (Bar Patron); *Laramie*—"The Jailbreakers" 12-19-61; *The Virginian*—"Echo from Another Day" 3-27-63, "The Dark Challenge" 9-23-64 (Bartender); "Felicity's Springs" 10-14-64 (Danny), "Shadows of the Past" 2-24-65 (Bartender).

Sul-Te-Wan, Madame (1873-2/1/59). Films: "The Lightning Rider" 1924 (Mammy).

Summers, Ann (1920-1/15/74). Films: "The Avenging Rider" 1943 (Jean); "Fighting Frontier" 1943 (Jeannie).

Summers, Don. Films: "Jesse James Rides Again" 1947-serial; "The Three Godfathers" 1948 (Posse Member); "She Wore a Yellow Ribbon" 1949 (Jenkins); "Wagonmaster" 1950 (Sam Jenkins).

Summers, Hope (1901-7/22/79). Films: "The Hallelujah Trail" 1965 (Mrs. Hasselrad); "Five Card Stud" 1968 (Woman Customer); "The Shakiest Gun in the West" 1968 (Celia). ¶TV: *The Rifleman*—Regular 1958-63 (Hattie Denton); *Gunsmoke*—"The Gypsum Hills Feud" 12-27-58 (Ellen Cade), "Old Fool" 12-24-60 (Della Bass), "Legends Don't Sleep" 10-12-63 (Aunt Jen); *Maverick*—"The Brasada Spur" 2-22-59 (Martha Abbot); *The Law of the Plainsman*—"Passenger to Mescalero" 10-29-59 (Mrs. Dodge); *Fury*—"The

Wtich" 1-16-60; *The Travels of Jaimie McPheeters*—"The Day of the First Suitor" 9-29-63 (Mrs. Rutledge).

Summers, Jerry (1931-). Films: "Lone Texan" 1959 (Indian); "The Purple Hills" 1961 (Martin Beaumont); "The Firebrand" 1962 (Rafael Vasconcelos); "Law of the Lawless" 1964 (Johnson Brother); "Young Fury" 1965 (Gabbo); "Scalplock" TVM-1966. ¶TV: *Annie Oakley*—"Indian Justice" 7-29-56 (Desert Wind); *Tales of Wells Fargo*—"End of the Trail" 10-20-58 (Little Wolf); *The Adventures of Rin Tin Tin*—"The Epidemic" 11-21-58 (Johnny); *The Tall Man*—"The Grudge Fight" 1-21-61 (Indian); *Have Gun Will Travel*—"Fandango" 3-4-61 (James Horton), "The Eve of St. Elmo" 3-23-63 (Collie March), "The Sanctuary" 6-22-63; *The Virginian*—"Impasse" 11-14-62 (Eddie Milford), "The Accomplice" 12-19-62 (Eddie); *Laramie*—"The Renegade Brand" 2-26-63; *Bonanza*—"The Prince" 4-2-67 (Rivers), "The Wish" 3-9-69 (Johnson); *The High Chaparral*—"The High Chaparral" 9-10-67 (Ira), "Best Man for the Job" 9-24-67 (Ira), "Young Blood" 10-8-67 (Ira); *Gunsmoke*—"O'Quillian" 10-28-68 (Breed); *Nichols*—"The One Eyed Mule's Time Has Come" 11-23-71.

Summers, Neil. Films: "The Life and Times of Judge Roy Bean" 1972 (Snake River Rufus Krile); "My Name Is Nobody" 1973-Ital. (Westerner); "The Gambler" TVM-1980 (Polo). ¶TV: *Gunsmoke*—"Tatum" 11-13-72 (Joe Beel), "Matt's Love Story" 9-24-73 (Man), "A Town in Chains" 9-16-74 (Townsman).

Summerville, George "Slim" (1892-1/5/46). Films: "Wild West Love" 1914; "Ranch Romeos" 1922; "The Texas Streak" 1926 (Swede Sonberg); "The Denver Dude" 1927 (Slim Jones); "Hey! Hey! Cowboy" 1927 (Spike Doolin); "Painted Ponies" 1927 (Beanpole); "Riding for Fame" 1928 (High-Pockets); "King of the Rodeo" 1929 (Slim); "Tiger Rose" 1929 (Heine); "The Spoilers" 1930 (Slapjack Simms); "Under Montana Skies" 1930 (Sunshine); "Lasca of the Rio Grande" 1931 (Crabapple Thompson); "White Fang" 1936 (Slats Magee); "Henry Goes Arizona" 1939 (Sheriff Parton); "Jesse James" 1939 (Jailer); "Western Union" 1941 (Herman); "Valley of Vanishing Men" 1942-serial (Missouri Benson); "Swing in the Saddle" 1944; "Sing Me a Song of Texas" 1945.

Sun, Irene Yah-Ling. Films: "The Quest" TVM-1976 (China).

¶TV: *The Quest*—"Welcome to America, Jade Snow" 11-24-76.

Sundberg, Clinton (1919-12/14/87). Films: "The Kissing Bandit" 1948 (Colonel Gomez); "Big Jack" 1949 (C. Patronius Smith); "Annie Get Your Gun" 1950 (Foster Wilson); "How the West Was Won" 1962 (Hylan Seabury). ¶TV: *Have Gun Will Travel*—"The Englishman" 12-7-57; *Sugarfoot*—"Apollo with a Gun" 12-8-59 (David Pickering); *Lawman*—"The Man Behind the News" 5-13-62 (Luther Boardman); *Laredo*—"A Question of Discipline" 10-28-65 (Fatty Brown); *Pistols 'n' Petticoats*—"The Triangle" 10-22-66 (Loomis).

Sundholm, Bill (1898-2/28/71). Films: "Trail to Vengeance" 1945 (Clergyman); "Loaded Pistols" 1948; "Calamity Jane and Sam Bass" 1949.

Sundstrom, Florence (1918-). Films: "The Last Challenge" 1967 (Outdoors). ¶TV: *Bonanza*—"Rich Man, Poor Man" 5-12-63 (Daisy); *Wild Wild West*—"The Night of the Circus of Death" 11-3-67 (Mrs. Moore).

Sunshine Boys, The (M.H. Richman, J.O. Smith, A.L. Smith & Edward F. Wallace). Films: "Driftin' River" 1946; "Quick on the Trigger" 1948; "Challenge of the Range" 1949; "Prairie Roundup" 1951.

Supplee, Cuyler (1894-5/3/44). Films: "Lightning Romance" 1924 (Arnold Stewart); "Brand of Cowardice" 1925; "Fighting with Buffalo Bill" 1926-serial; "Danger Ahead" 1927; "On Special Duty" 1927; "One Glorious Scrap" 1927 (Carl Kramer); "The Two Outlaws" 1928 (the Other Man).

Suratt, Valeska (1882-7/2/62). Films: "The Siren" 1917 (Cherry Millard).

Surovy, Nicolas (1944-). TV: *The Big Valley*—"Judgement in Heaven" 12-22-65 (Billy Joe Gaines); *Paradise*—"Founder's Day" 11-10-88 (P.J. Brackenhouse), "Ghost Dance" 11-24-88 (P.J. Brackenhouse), "Devil's Canyon" 12-1-88 (P.J. Brackenhouse), "Stray Bullet" 12-8-88 (P.J. Brackenhouse), "A Private War" 1-5-89 (P.J. Brackenhouse); *Adventures of Brisco County, Jr.*—"Hard Rock" 2-4-94 (Roy Hondo).

Suss, Bernard. Films: "Wells Fargo" 1937 (Bearded Man); "Mountain Rhythm" 1939 (MacCauley).

Sutch, Herbert (1884-1/22/39). Films: "Scarlet Days" 1919 (Marshal).

Sutherland, Dick (1881-2/3/34). Films: "Hell's Hole" 1923 (Prisoner);

"The Mask of Lopez" 1923 (Mexican); "Quicksands" 1923 (Cupid); "Fighter's Paradise" 1924; "Riders of the Dark" 1928 (Rogers).

Sutherland, Donald (1934-). Films: "Dan Candy's Law" 1975-U.S./Can.; "Shadow of the Wolf" 1993-Can./Fr. (Henderson).

Sutherland, Edward (1895-12/31/73). Films: "The Round Up" 1920 (Bud Lane); "The Loaded Door" 1922 (Joe Grainger); "Girl from the West" 1923.

Sutherland, Hope. Films: "God's Country and the Law" 1922 (Oachi).

Sutherland, Hugh. Films: "Beyond the Shadows" 1918 (Santel); "Tongues of Flame" 1918 (Jack Brace); "Trimmed" 1922 (Lem Fyfer).

Sutherland, Keifer (1966-). Films: "Young Guns" 1988 (Josiah "Doc" Scurlock), "Young Guns II" 1990 (Doc Scurlock).

Sutherland, Victor (1889-8/29/68). Films: "The Sign Invisible" 1918 (Dr. Robert Winston); "Calibre 38" 1919 (Ford Benton); "The Love Bandit" 1924 (Jim Blazes); "Lone Star" 1952 (President Anson Jones); "Powder River" 1953 (Mayor Lowery). ¶TV: *Jim Bowie*—"A Grave for Jim Bowie" 2-28-58 (Col. Whitby).

Sutherlin, Wayne (1939-). Films: "Tell Them Willie Boy Is Here" 1969 (Harry); "Bounty Man" TVM-1972 (Tully); "The Culpepper Cattle Company" 1972 (Missoula); "The Great Northfield, Minnesota Raid" 1972 (Charley Pitts); "This Was the West That Was" TVM-1974. ¶TV: *Bonanza*—"A Place to Hide" 3-19-72 (Thibideaux).

Sutton, Dudley (1933-). Films: "A Town Called Hell" 1971-Span./Brit. (Spectre).

Sutton, Frank (1922-6/28/74). TV: *Maverick*—"The War of the Silver Kings" 9-22-57; *Gunsmoke*—"Miss Kitty" 10-14-61 (Charlie), "Catawomper" 2-10-62 (Olie), "Old Comrade" 12-29-62 (Billy Marston); *Have Gun Will Travel*—"The Trap" 3-3-62 (Davey Walsh); *Empire*—"Seven Days on Rough Street" 2-26-63 (Young Floyd); *Temple Houston*—"The Third Bullet" 10-24-63 (Logan Stocker); *Death Valley Days*—"Diamond Field Jack" 10-27-63 (Jack Davis).

Sutton, Grady (1908-9/17/95). Films: "Stone of Silver Creek" 1935 (Jimmy); "King of the Royal Mounted" 1936 (Slim Blandon); "Dudes Are Pretty People" 1942 (George); "A Lady Takes a Chance" 1943 (Malcolm); "Song of the Prairie" 1945; "Plainsman and the Lady" 1946 (Male Secretary); "Last of the Wild Horses" 1948 (Curly); "Grand Canyon" 1949 (Halfnote); "The Bounty Killer" 1965 (Minister); "Tickle Me" 1965 (Mr. Dabney); "Something for a Lonely Man" TVM-1968; "The Great Bank Robbery" 1969 (Reverend Sims); "Support Your Local Gunfighter" 1971 (Storekeeper). ¶TV: *Wyatt Earp*—"One of Jesse's Gang" 3-13-56; *Lawman*—"The Old War Horse" 10-9-60 (Stiles), "Trapped" 9-17-61 (Ben Toomey), "Owny O'Reilly, Esq." 10-15-61 (Ben Toomey), "The Appointment" 11-26-61 (Ben Toomey), "Incident of the Night on the Town" 6-2-61; *Sugarfoot*—"Welcome Enemy" 12-26-60 (Clerk).

Sutton, John (1908-7/10/63). Films: "Susannah of the Mounties" 1939 (Cpl. Piggot); "Hudson Bay" 1941 (Lord Edward Crew); "The Canadians" 1961-Brit. (Supt. Walker). ¶TV: *The Californians*—"Prince of Thieves" 11-11-58 (Sam Crawford); *Bat Masterson*—"Lottery of Death" 5-13-59 (Andrew Stafford), "The Canvas and the Cane" 12-17-59 (Orrin Thackery); *Tombstone Territory*—"Death Is to Write About" 5-29-59 (David Armbruster); *Man from Blackhawk*—"Contraband Cargo" 12-4-59 (Bart Mason); *The Rebel*—"Gold Seeker" 1-17-60 (Man), "The Earl of Durango" 6-12-60 (Spencer Scott); *Stagecoach West*—"Finn McColl" 1-24-61 (Robert Allison); *Rawhide*—"The Gentleman's Gentleman" 12-15-61 (Lord Ashton).

Sutton, Paul (1912-1/31/70). Films: "Rio Grande Ranger" 1936 (Jim Sayres); "Under Strange Flags" 1937 (George Barranca); "Bar 20 Justice" 1938 (Slade); "In Old Mexico" 1938 (the Fox); "The Cisco Kid and the Lady" 1939; "The Girl and the Gambler" 1939 (Manuelo); "Jesse James" 1939 (Lynch); "North of the Yukon" 1939 (Pierre Ldeoux); "Mark of Zorro" 1940 (Soldier); "Northwest Mounted Police" 1940 (Indian); "Viva Cisco Kid" 1940 (Joshua); "The Pinto Kid" 1941 (Vic Landreau); "Ride on, Vaquero" 1941 (Sleepy); "In Old California" 1942 (Chick); "Riders of the Northland" 1942 (Chris Larsen); "Sundown Jim" 1942 (Dale); "Tombstone, the Town Too Tough to Die" 1942 (Tom McLowery); "Silver City Raiders" 1943 (Dawson); "Wyoming Hurricane" 1944; "Along Came Jones" 1945 (Man at Bar).

Suzanne, Jacques. Films: "The Spell of the Yukon" 1916 (Billy Denny); "Out of the Snows" 1920 (Antoine Dufresne).

Svenson, Bo (1941-). Films: "The Bravos" TVM-1972 (Raeder); "Hitched" TVM-1973 (Jay Appleby); "Manhunt" 1984-Ital. ¶TV: *Lancer*—"The Wedding" 1-7-69 (Josh); *The High Chaparral*—"Trail to Nevermore" 10-31-69 (Bennett); *The Men from Shiloh*—"The Price of the Hanging" 11-11-70 (Lonnie); *Kung Fu*—"The Spirit Helper" 11-8-73 (Pike).

Swain, Mack (1876-8/25/35). Films: "Fatty and Minnie He-Haw" 1915; "Hands Up!" 1926 (Mine Owner); "A Texas Steer" 1927 (Bragg).

Swan, Robert C. (1921-). Films: "The Maverick Queen" 1956 (Card Player); "Thunder Over Arizona" 1956; "Gunfight at the O.K. Corral" 1957 (Shaugnessy Man); "The Lawless Eighties" 1958. ¶TV: *Sky King*—"Bounty Hunters" 7-27-52 (Max Wilson); *Wild Bill Hickok*—"Meteor Mesa" 6-16-53; *Judge Roy Bean*—"Checkmate" 1-1-56 (Hendron), "The Eyes of Texas" 1-1-56 (Big Elk), "The Travelers" 1-1-56 (Mulloy); *Sergeant Preston of the Yukon*—"Rebellion in the North" 7-12-56 (Cpl. Rogers), "Lost River Roundup" 12-12-57 (Mike Calico); *The Lone Ranger*—"White Hawk's Decision" 10-18-56, "Ghost Canyon" 12-27-56; *Tales of Wells Fargo*—"Barbara Coast" 11-25-57; *Wagon Train*—"The Clara Beauchamp Story" 12-11-57 (Corporal); *The Restless Gun*—"The Manhunters" 6-2-58 (Cyril Cotterman); *Bat Masterson*—"A Noose Fits Anybody" 11-19-58 (Ben Thompson), "The Pied Piper of Dodge City" 1-7-60 (Bill Harris), "The Reluctant Witness" 3-31-60 (Charlie Bassett), "Run for Your Money" 3-2-61 (Charlie Bassett); *Gunsmoke*—"Wind" 3-21-59 (John), "The Cage" 3-23-70 (Weden), "The Witness" 11-23-70 (Texan), "Milligan" 11-6-72 (Looter), "Cowtown Hustler" 3-11-74 (Cox); *Wyatt Earp*—"The Trail to Tombstone" 9-8-59 (Bartender), "Roscoe Turns Detective" 5-3-60; *Wichita Town*—"The Devil's Choice" 12-23-59 (Rev. Nichols); *The Rebel*—"The Bequest" 9-25-60 (Cleve Redfern); *Rawhide*—"Incident at Poco Tiempo" 12-9-60; *Branded*—"McCord's Way" 1-30-66 (Bud Lee); *Cimarron Strip*—"Big Jessie" 2-8-68.

Swan, William. TV: *Zane Grey Theater*—"Decision at Wilson's Creek" 5-17-57 (Lt. Grimes); *Have Gun Will Travel*—"Ella West" 1-4-58 (Tracey Calvert).

Swarthout, Gladys (1904-7/7/69). Films: "Rose of the Rancho" 1936 (Rosita Castro/Don Carlos).

Swartz, Tony. Films: "No Man's Land" TVM-1984 (Munroe).

Swayze, Don. Films: "The Tracker" TVM-1988 (Brewer). ¶TV: *Paradise*—"A House Divided" 2-16-89 (Langston).

Swayze, Patrick (1954-). Films: "Tall Tales: The Unbelievable Adventures of Pecos Bill" 1995 (Pecos Bill).

Sweeney, Bob (1919-6/7/92). TV: *The Rifleman*—"The Pitchman" 10-18-60 (Speedy Sullivan), "Assault" 3-21-61 (Speed Sullivan).

Sweeney, D.B. (1961-). Films: "Lonesome Dove" TVM-1989 (Dish Boggett).

Sweeney, Joseph (-11/25/63). Films: "Fastest Gun Alive" 1956 (Reverend).

Sweet, Blanche (1896-9/6/86). Films: "The Indian Brothers" 1911; "The Last Drop of Water" 1911; "Was He a Coward?" 1911; "The Chief's Blanket" 1912; "Goddess of Sagebrush Gulch" 1912 (the Girl); "Man's Lust for Gold" 1912; "The Massacre" 1912; "A Temporary Truce" 1912; "Three Friends" 1912; "Under Burning Skies" 1912; "The Battle at Elderbrush Gulch" 1913; "The Broken Ways" 1913; "A Chance Deception" 1913; "Two Men of the Desert" 1913; "Strongheart" 1914; "Fighting Cressy" 1920 (Cressy McKinstry); "That Girl Montana" 1921 (Montana Rivers); "The Lady from Hell" 1926 (Lady Margaret Darnely); "The Silver Horde" 1930 (Queenie).

Sweet, Katie. TV: *Wide Country*—"The Man Who Ran Away" 2-7-63 (Polly Lund); *Wagon Train*—"The Annie Duggan Story" 3-13-63 (Jennie); *The Travels of Jaimie McPheeters*—"The Day of the Long Night" 11-10-63 (Lucy Ann); *Bonanza*—"The Waiting Game" 12-8-63 (Peggy Dayton), "The Cheating Game" 2-9-64, "The Pressure Game" 5-10-64 (Peggy Dayton), "Triangle" 5-17-64 (Peggy Dayton); *Great Adventure*—"Teeth of the Lion" 1-17-64 (Melissa).

Swenson, Inga (1932-). Films: "Testimony of Two Men" TVM-1977 (Amelia Foster). ¶TV: *Bonanza*—"Inger, My Love" 4-15-62 (Inger), "Journey Remembered" 11-11-63 (Inger Cartwright); *Sara*—3-5-76 (Henrietta).

Swenson, Karl (1908-10/8/78). Films: "The Hanging Tree" 1959 (Tom Flaunce); "No Name on the Bullet" 1959 (Earl Sticker); "Flaming Star" 1960 (Dred Pierce); "North to Alaska" 1960 (Lars Nordquist); "One Foot in Hell" 1960 (Sheriff Olson); "How the West Was Won" 1962 (Train Conductor); "Lonely Are the Brave" 1962 (Rev. Hoskins); "The Man from Galveston" 1964 (Sheriff); "Major Dundee" 1965 (Capt. Waller); "The Sons of Katie Elder" 1965 (Doc Isdel/Bartender); "Hour of the Gun" 1967 (Dr. Goodfellow); "The Wild Country" 1971 (Jenson); "Ulzana's Raid" 1972 (Rukeyser); "The Gun and the Pulpit" TVM-1974 (Adams). ¶TV: *Circus Boy*—"The Magic Lantern" 11-7-57 (Lars Larsen); *Gunsmoke*—"Fingered" 11-23-57 (Hank Luz), "Kitty's Injury" 9-19-59 (Raff Judson), "Potshot" 3-11-61 (Hutch Dawkins), "Chester's Indian" 5-12-62 (Adam Dill), "Blue Heaven" 9-26-64 (Tabe), "Harvest" 3-26-66 (Ian McGovern), "The Newcomers" 12-3-66 (Lars Karlgren), "The Devil's Outpost" 9-22-69 (McGruder), "Lavery" 2-22-71 (Hubert); *Maverick*—"The Wrecker" 12-1-57 (Capt. Nares), "Shady Deal at Sunny Acres" 11-23-58 (Sheriff Griffin), "Family Pride" 1-8-61 (Gen. Josiah Warren); *Have Gun Will Travel*—"The Hanging Cross" 12-21-57, "Deliver the Body" 5-24-58 (Milo Culligan), "A Sense of Justice" 11-1-58 (Sheriff Grayson), "Alaska" 4-18-59 (Boris Tosheff), "Fandango" 3-4-61 (Lloyd Petty), "El Paso Stage" 4-15-61 (Sam DeWitt), "My Brother's Keeper" 5-6-61 (Sheriff); *Sugarfoot*—"Small War at Custer Junction" 1-7-58 (Andy Burke), "Price on His Head" 4-29-58 (Outlaw), "The Extra Hand" 1-20-59 (Sharlakov); *Jim Bowie*—"Curfew Cannon" 1-24-58 (Andre); *Zane Grey Theater*—"This Man Must Die" 1-24-58 (Lee Willis), "King of the Valley" 11-26-59 (Will Harmon), "The Sunrise Gun" 5-19-60 (Luis Greening); *Colt .45*—"Long Odds" 4-11-58 (Courtwright); *Jefferson Drum*—"The Lawless" 7-18-58 (Kiley); *The Texan*—"Law of the Gun" 9-29-58 (Sheriff), "Cowards Don't Die" 11-30-59 (Sam Maitland); *Bat Masterson*—"Cheyenne Club" 12-17-58 (Pate); *Trackdown*—"Terror" 2-4-59 (Monroe); *Bronco*—"The Silent Witness" 3-10-59 (Casey), "Red Water North" 6-16-59; *Bonanza*—"The Sun Mountain Herd" 9-19-59 (Carl Harris), "Day of Reckoning" 10-22-60 (Ike Daggett), "A Natural Wizard" 12-12-65 (Dr. Woods), "Showdown at Tahoe" 11-19-67 (Captain Larson); *Riverboat*—"The Fight Back" 10-18-59 (Ansel Torgin); *Man from Blackhawk*—"The New Semaria Story" 10-23-59; *The Rebel*—"Panic" 11-1-59 (Lew Bussey);

Black Saddle—"Four from Stillwater" 11-27-59 (Doc Wile); *Hotel De Paree*—"Sundance and the Marshal of Water's End" 3-18-60 (Jed Holmes); *The Rifleman*—"The Vision" 3-22-60 (Svenson), "The Jailbird" 5-10-60 (Chris Manse); *Johnny Ringo*—"Lobo Lawman" 6-23-60 (Marshal Kramer); *Klondike*—"Klondike Fever" 10-10-60 (Judge Frank Weinstock), "Swing Your Partner" 1-9-61 (Dr. Edwards); *The Westerner*—"Line Camp" 12-9-60; *Wagon Train*—"The Jim Bridger Story" 5-10-61 (Jim Bridger), "The Jed Whitmore Story" 1-13-64 (Harry Whitmore); *Laramie*—"A Grave for Cully Brown" 2-13-62 (Bryan James), "Trial by Fire" 4-10-62 (Lars Carlson), "The Stranger" 4-23-63 (Emil Viktor); *The Virginian*—"Riff-Raff" 11-7-62 (Col. Teddy Roosevelt), "Run Away Home" 4-24-63 (Karl Swenson), "Blaze of Glory" 12-29-65 (Ben Wallace), "The Heritage" 10-30-68 (Nelson), "The Substitute" 12-5-69 (Ezra Gates); *The Dakotas*—"Thunder in Pleasant Valley" 2-4-63 (Harry McNeill); *Temple Houston*—"The Man from Galveston" 1963 (Sheriff), "Seventy Times Seven" 12-5-63 (Sam Wade); *The Travels of Jaimie McPheeters*—"The Day of the First Suitor" 9-29-63 (Coley Bishop), "The Day of the Search" 1-19-64 (Bigger); *Death Valley Days*—"A Bargain Is for Keeping" 2-28-65; *The Big Valley*—"Winner Lose All" 10-27-65 (Hadley), "Last Train to the Fair" 4-27-66 (Aaron Moyers), "Wagonload of Dreams" 1-2-67 (Steve Minter); *A Man Called Shenandoah*—"End of a Legend" 2-7-66 (Sheriff Ben Garrett); *Cimarron Strip*—"Broken Wing" 9-21-67 (Dr. Kihlgren), "The Battle of Blood Stone" 10-12-67, "The Beast That Walks Like a Man" 11-30-67, "Nobody" 12-7-67, "The Assassin" 1-11-68, "Knife in the Darkness" 1-25-68; *The Guns of Will Sonnett*—"Stopover in a Troubled Town" 2-2-68 (Walden); *The Outcasts*—"Act of Faith" 2-10-69 (Tom Reed).

Swickard, Charles (1868-5/12/29). Films: "Shorty Escapes Marriage" 1914 (Bud Simms).

Swickard, Josef (1866-3/1/40). Films: "The Light of Western Stars" 1918 (Padre Marcos); "The Lady of Red Butte" 1919 (Delicate Hanson); "The Last of His People" 1919 (Baron Bonart); "The Storm" 1922 (Jacques Fachard); "The Eternal Struggle" 1923 (Pierre Grange); "North of Nevada" 1924 (Mark Ridgeway); "The Sign of the Cactus" 1925 (Old Man Hayes); "The Border Whirlwind" 1926 (Jose Cordova); "Desert Gold" 1926 (Sebastian Castanada); "Senor

Daredevil" 1926 (Juan Estrada); "The Unknown Cavalier" 1926 (Lingo); "Whispering Canyon" 1926 (Eben Beauregard); "The Golden Stallion" 1927-serial; "Phantom of the North" 1929 (Col. Bayburn); "The Lone Defender" 1930-serial (Juan Valdez); "Phantom of the Desert" 1930 (Benny Mack); "Song of the Caballero" 1930 (Manuel); "The Irish Gringo" 1935; "Boss Rider of Gun Creek" 1936 (Lafe Turner); "Caryl of the Mountains" 1936 (Jean Foray); "Custer's Last Stand" 1936-serial (Major Trent); "Sandflow" 1937 (Mr. Porter); "Zorro Rides Again" 1937-serial (Old Man); "Mexicali Rose" 1939; "The Pal from Texas" 1939 (Texas Malden).

Swift, Joan. Films: "Deadly Trackers" 1973. ¶TV: *Death Valley Days*—"Arsenic Springs" 11-18-57; *Laramie*—"Naked Steel" 1-1-63 (Saloon Girl).

Swift, Susan. Films: "The Chisholms" TVM-1979 (Annabel Chisholm). ¶TV: *The Chisholms*—Regular 1979-80 (Annabel Chisholm/ Mercy Howell).

Swit, Loretta (1937-). TV: *Gunsmoke*—"The Pack Rat" 1-12-70 (Belle Clark), "Snow Train" 10-19-70 & 10-26-70 (Donna); *Bonanza*—"A Visit to Upright" 3-26-72 (Ellen Sue).

Switzer, Carl (1927-1/21/59). Films: "Wild and Woolly" 1937 (Zero); "Gas House Kids Go West" 1947 (Alfalfa); "Redwood Forest Trail" 1950 (Alfalfa Donahue); "Track of the Cat" 1954 (Joe Sam); "Dig That Uranium" 1956 (Shifty Robertson). ¶TV: *The Roy Rogers Show*— "The Treasure of Howling Dog Canyon" 1-27-52 (Clyde Stockton), "Shoot to Kill" 4-27-52 (Elmer Kirby), "Ghost Town Gold" 5-25-52, "Go for Your Gun" 11-23-52 (Bob), "Dead End Trail" 2-20-55 (Timmy Horton), "Quick Draw" 3-20-55 (Duncan Wright), "And Sudden Death" 10-9-55.

Swofford, Ken (1933-). Films: "Cutter's Trail" TVM-1970 (Clay Wooten); "The Intruders" TVM-1970; "One Little Indian" 1973 (Pvt. Dixon); "Scott Free" TVM-1976 (Ed McGraw); "The Gambler, Part II— The Adventure Continues" TVM-1983 (Witchita Pike); "Gunsmoke: To the Last Man" TVM-1991 (Charlie Tewksbury). ¶TV: *The Big Valley*— "A Day of Terror" 12-12-66 (Wes); *Cimarron Strip*—"Nobody" 12-7-67 (Christie); *Wild Wild West*—"The Night of the Running Death" 12-15-67 (Sloane); *Gunsmoke*—"Wonder"

12-18-67 (Bo Warrick), "The Hide Cutters" 9-30-68 (Sugar John), "Lobo" 12-16-68 (Guffy), "The Devil's Outpost" 9-22-69 (Loomis), "Hackett" 3-16-70 (Alvin Bronk), "Lavery" 2-22-71 (Harry), "Waste" 9-27-71 & 10-4-71 (Speer), "Tara" 1-17-72 (Dirk), "Lynch Town" 11-19-73 (Jake Fielder), "I Have Promises to Keep" 3-3-75 (Dunbar); *The Virginian*—"The Death Wagon" 1-3-68 (Wrengel), "Jed" 1-10-68 (Seth Pettit), "Ride the Misadventure" 11-6-68 (Seth Petit), "The Girl in the Shadows" 3-26-69 (Seth); *Daniel Boone*— "Fort New Madrid" 2-15-68 (Mick O'Toole); *Here Come the Brides*— "The Wealthiest Man in Seattle" 10-3-69 (Gil), "Land Grant" 11-21-69; *Lancer*—"Splinter Group" 3-3-70 (Rufus); *Kung Fu*—"Night of the Owls, Day of the Doves" 2-14-74 (Max Frazer), "This Valley of Terror" 9-28-74 (Dr. Tracer); *Dirty Sally*— "Wimmen's Rights" 3-15-74 (Sheriff); *How the West Was Won*—"Luke" 4-2-79 (Dan Grimes).

Swoger, Harry (1919-6/14/70). Films: "Scalplock" TVM-1966. ¶TV: *The Texan*—"Outpost" 1-19-59 (Nate Woods); *The Law of the Plainsman*— "Prairie Incident" 10-1-59; *Gunsmoke*—"Tail to the Wind" 10-17-59 (Burke Reese), "Colleen So Green" 4-2-60 (Bull Reeger), "The Badge" 11-12-60 (Ike), "The Cook" 12-17-60 (Hank Green), "Milly" 11-25-61 (Lawson); *Rawhide*—"Incident at the Buffalo Smokehouse" 10-30-59; *Hotel De Paree*—"Sundance and the Hostiles" 12-11-59 (Big Huston), "Sundance and the Good-Luck Coat" 5-6-60 (Moose); *Bonanza*—"The Avenger" 3-19-60, "Silent Thunder" 12-10-60 (Tom), "The Man Faces of Gideon Flinch" 11-5-61 (Bullethead Burke), "The War Comes to Washoe" 11-4-62, "Song in the Dark" 1-13-63, "The Gentleman from New Orleans" 2-2-64 (Whittaker); *The Alaskans*— "The Silent Land" 5-15-60 (Morse); *Maverick*—"Arizona Black Maria" 10-9-60 (Rufus), "Destination Devil's Flat" 12-25-60 (Conductor); *The Westerner*—"Brown" 10-21-60 (Tom Lacette); *The Tall Man*—"An Hour to Die" 2-17-62 (Larker); *Stoney Burke*— "The Journey" 5-20-63 (Charlie); *Wagon Train*—"The Gus Morgan Story" 9-30-63 (Ben); *The Virginian*—"Farewell to Honesty" 3-24-65 (Killigrew); *The Big Valley*—"Heritage" 10-20-65 (Newton), "The Fallen Hawk" 3-2-66 (Harry, the Bartender), "The Stallion" 1-30-67 (Harry, the Bartender), "Explosion!" 11-20-67 & 11-27-67 (Harry, the Bartender), "Run of the Savage" 3-11-68

(Harry, the Bartender), "Lightfoot" 2-17-69; *The Legend of Jesse James*—"A Burying for Rosey" 5-9-66 (Stableman); *Iron Horse*—"Joy Unconfined" 9-12-66 (Jake Groat); *Laredo*—"The Sweet Gang" 11-4-66, "A Question of Guilt" 3-10-67; *Wild Wild West*— "The Night of the Cut Throats" 11-17-67 (Bartender); *The Guns of Will Sonnett*—"What's in a Name?" 1-5-68, "Reunion" 9-27-68, "The Man Who Killed James Sonnett" 3-21-69 (Bartender); *Lancer*—"The Last Train for Charlie Poe" 11-26-68 (Mick), "Shadow of a Dead Man" 1-6-70 (Liveryman).

Sydes, Anthony. Films: "Gunsmoke in Tucson" 1958 (Young Brazos). ¶TV: *Wild Bill Hickok*—"Lost Indian Mine" 12-11-51; *Hopalong Cassidy*—"Don't Believe in Ghosts" 6-28-52.

Sykes, Brenda (1948-). Films: "Skin Game" 1971 (Naomi).

Sykes, Eric (1923-). Films: "Shalako" 1968-Brit./Fr. (Mako).

Sylvester, Henry (1881-6/8/61). Films: "The Eagle's Brood" 1936 (Sheriff); "Riddle Ranch" 1936 (Sheriff); "Go West" 1940 (Conductor); "Twenty Mule Team" 1940; "The Sea of Grass" 1947 (Man).

Sylvester, William (1922-). TV: *The High Chaparral*—"No Bugles, No Women" 3-14-69 (Jack Simmons), "The Little Thieves" 12-26-69 (Croswell); *Bonanza*—"Danger Road" 1-11-70 (Cambeau), "The Bucket Dog" 12-19-72 (Horace Kingston).

Symon, Burk (1888-2/20/50). Films: "Fighting Man of the Plains" 1949 (Meeker).

Syms, Sylvia (1934-). Films: "The Desperados" 1969 (Laura).

Szabo, Sandor (1906-10/13/66). TV: *Bonanza*—"Queen High" 12-1-68 (Ludwig).

Szold, Bernard (1894-11/16/60). Films: "The Secret of Convict Lake" 1951 (Bartender). ¶TV: *The Gene Autry Show*—"The Old Prospector" 8-4-53, "Gypsy Woman" 8-25-53.

Taber, Anthony P. see Tabernero, Julio P.

Taber, Robert. Films: "Heart of the Sunset" 1918 (Ed Austin); "The Unbroken Promise" 1919 (Fadeaway).

Tabernero, Julio Perez (Anthony P. Taber). Films: "Seven Guns for the MacGregors" 1965-Ital./Span. (Mark MacGregor); "Two Thousand Dollars for Coyote" 1965-Span.; "Son of a Gunfighter" 1966-U.S./Span.; "Up the MacGregors!" 1967-Ital./ Span. (Mark MacGregor); "Five Dollars for Ringo" 1968-Ital./Span. (Lester Sands).

Tabler, P. Dempsey (1876-6/7/56). Films: "The Patriot" 1916 (Jordan Mason); "The Gamesters" 1920 (Brad Bascom); "Spawn of the Desert" 1923 (Silver Sleed).

Tabor, Joan (1933-12/18/68). TV: *Laramie*—"Men in Shadows" 5-30-61 (Julie); *Bat Masterson*—"Jeopardy at Jackson Hole" 6-1-61 (Kate); *Have Gun Will Travel*—"The Exiles" 1-27-62.

Tabori, Kristoffer (1952-). Films: "Journey Through Rosebud" 1972 (Danny). ¶TV: *Nichols*—"The One Eyed Mule's Time Has Come" 11-23-71 (Frankie).

Taeger, Ralph (1936-). Films: "Stage to Thunder Rock" 1964 (Reese Sawyer). ¶TV: *Bat Masterson*—"Welcome to Paradise" 5-5-60 (Frank Dexter); *Tombstone Territory*—7-1-60 (Horn); *Klondike*—Regular 1960-61 (Mike Halliday); *Hondo*—Regular 1967 (Hondo Lane).

Tafoya, Alfonso (1929-9/22/89). Films: "The Mark of Zorro" TVM-1974 (Miguel).

Taft, Sara (1893-9/24/73). Films: "Death of a Gunfighter" 1969 (Mexican Woman). ¶TV: *The Rifleman*—"Dead Cold Cash" 11-22-60 (Sara Carruthers), "Waste" 10-1-62 & 10-8-62 (Old Woman); *Gunsmoke*—"Tell Chester" 4-20-63 (Tao); *Wild Wild West*—"The Night of the Steel Assassin" 1-7-66 (Maria), "The Night of the Puppeteer" 2-25-66 (Mrs. Chayne).

Tafur, Robert (1915-). Films: "The Three Outlaws" 1956. ¶TV: *Death Valley Days*—"The Valencia Cake" 10-24-55, "The Bear Flag" 10-21-56; *Jim Bowie*—"Rezin Bowie, Gambler" 3-22-57 (Paul); *The Tall Man*—"The Great Western" 6-3-61 (Acca); *Branded*—"The Ghost of Murrieta" 3-20-66 (Ramirez); *Gunsmoke*—"The Mission" 10-8-66 (Colonel Romero); *Bearcats!*—"Dos Gringos" 9-30-71 (Ignacio Gomez).

Taggart, Ben (1889-5/17/47). Films: "Robin Hood of El Dorado" 1936 (Rancher); "The Overland Express" 1938 (Adams); "The Durango Kid" 1940; "Son of Roaring Dan" 1940 (Sheriff); "The Medico of Painted Springs" 1941 (John Richards); "Wildcat of Tucson" 1941 (Judge); "Overland Mail" 1942-serial.

Taggart, Hal (1882-12/12/71). Films: "The First Traveling Saleslady" 1956 (Man). ¶TV: *Circus Boy*—"Big Top Angel" 1-27-57 (Doctor), "The

Knife Thrower" 2-17-57 (Doc); *Rawhide*—"Incident of the Devil and His Due" 1-22-60.

Taka, Miiko. TV: *Wild Wild West*—"The Night of the Deadly Blossom" 3-17-67 (Haruko Ishuda).

Takei, George (1940-). Films: "Oblivion" 1994 (Doc Valentine). ¶TV: *Death Valley Days*—"The Boog" 1-15-66.

Talbot, Brud (1940-11/20/86). Films: "Finger on the Trigger" 1965-Span./Ital./U.S. (Fred).

Talbot, Helen. Films: "California Joe" 1943 (Judith Cartaret); "Canyon City" 1943 (Edith Gleason); "Outlaws of Santa Fe" 1944 (Ruth Gordon); "San Fernando Valley" 1944; "Song of Nevada" 1944; "Bells of Rosarita" 1945; "Corpus Christi Bandits" 1945 (Dorothy); "Don't Fence Me In" 1945; "Lone Texas Ranger" 1945; "Trail of Kit Carson" 1945; "King of the Forest Rangers" 1946-serial (Marion Brennan).

Talbot, Jay "Slim" (1896-1/25/73). Films: "The Texans" 1938 (Cowboy); "Dallas" 1950 (Stage Driver); "Giant" 1956 (Clay Hodgins); "The Big Country" 1958 (Terrill Cowboy); "The Hanging Tree" 1959 (Stage Driver); "The Man Who Shot Liberty Valance" 1962.

Talbot, Lyle (1902-). Films: "Klondike" 1932 (Dr. Robert Cromwell); "Call of the Yukon" 1938 (Hugo Henderson); "Trail to Gunsight" 1944 (Bill Hollister); "Gun Town" 1946 (Lucky Dorgan); "North of the Border" 1946; "Song of Arizona" 1946 (King Blaine); "The Vigilante" 1947-serial (George Pierce); "Quick on the Trigger" 1948 (Garvey Yager); "Thunder in the Pines" 1948 (Nick); "Border Rangers" 1950 (Capt. McLane); "Cherokee Uprising" 1950 (Marshall); "The Daltons' Women" 1950; "Abilene Trail" 1951 (Doctor); "Colorado Ambush" 1951 (Sheriff Ed Lowery); "Gold Raiders" 1951 (Ed Taggert); "Man from Sonora" 1951; "Oklahoma Justice" 1951; "Texas Lawmen" 1951; "Desperadoes' Outpost" 1952 (Walter Fleming); "Kansas Territory" 1952 (Collins); "Montana Incident" 1952; "The Old West" 1952 (Doc Lockwood); "Outlaw Women" 1952 (Judge Dixon); "Son of Geronimo" 1952-serial (Colonel Foster); "Texas City" 1952 (Hamilton); "Star of Texas" 1953 (Telegraph Operator); "Tumbleweed" 1953 (Weber); "Gunfighters of the Northwest" 1954-serial (Inspector Wheeler). ¶TV: *The Lone Ranger*—"Trouble for Tonto" 7-20-50, "Mrs. Banker" 3-26-53, "Two from Juan

Ringo" 12-23-54, "Code of the Pioneers" 2-17-55; *The Cisco Kid*—"Lynching Story" 4-28-51, "The Gramophone" 9-20-52, "Indian Uprising" 11-8-52, "Not Guilty" 12-20-52; *Wild Bill Hickok*—"The Border City Election" 9-15-51, "Wrestling Story" 4-8-52, "The Right of Way" 8-5-52, "Wild Bill's Odyssey" 3-31-53; *The Range Rider*—"The Holy Terror" 3-22-52; *Cowboy G-Men*—"Chippewa Indians" 10-11-52; *The Roy Rogers Show*—"Loaded Guns" 4-15-53; *The Gene Autry Show*—"Thunder Out West" 7-14-53, "The Old Prospector" 8-4-53, "Gypsy Woman" 8-25-53; *The Adventures of Rin Tin Tin*—"The Legacy of Sean O'Hara" 3-4-55 (Brad Shotman), "Witch of the Woods" 9-14-56 (Troy Bengham); *Buffalo Bill, Jr.*—"Rain Wagon" 9-17-55; *Annie Oakley*—"Flint and Steel" 10-14-56 (Pa Wiggins); *Tales of Wells Fargo*—"Stage to Nowhere" 6-24-57; *The Restless Gun*—"Quiet City" 2-3-58 (Doc Upton), "The Englishman" 6-8-59 (Mort Askins); *Wagon Train*—"The Dick Richardson Story" 12-31-58 (Ken Milford), "The Jonas Murdock Story" 4-13-60 (Jameson); *Cimarron City*—"Runaway Train" 1-31-59 (Frank Harvey); *Maverick*—"Two Tickets to Ten Strike" 3-15-59 (Martin Stone); *Buckskin*—"Act of Faith" 3-23-59 (Ernie Burk); *Rawhide*—"Incident of the Misplaced Indians" 5-1-59 (Dr. Otis Gray); *Colt .45*—"The Sanctuary" 5-10-59 (Sheriff Clyde Chadwick); *Bonanza*—"The Courtship" 1-7-61 (Sugar Daddy); *Stagecoach West*—"The Outcasts" 3-7-61 (Hal Franklin); *Lawman*—"By the Book" 12-24-61 (Orville Luster); *Wide Country*—"The Girl in the Sunshine Smile" 11-15-62 (Wilt Marlowe), "Don't Cry for Johnny Devlin" 1-24-63 (Harry Keating); *Laredo*—"Which Way Did They Go?" 11-18-65, "One Too Many Voices" 11-18-66; *The Legend of Jesse James*—"Vendetta" 10-25-67 (Warden).

Talbot, Nita (1930-). Films: "Montana" 1950 (Woman); "Once Upon a Horse" 1958 (Miss Dovey Barnes); "Buck and the Preacher" 1972 (Mme. Esther); "The Sweet Creek County War" 1979 (Firetop Alice Dewey). ¶TV: *Gunsmoke*—"Land Deal" 11-8-58 (Sidna), "Belle's Back" 5-14-60 (Belle Ainsley); *Maverick*—"Easy Mark" 11-15-59 (Jeannie), "The Resurrection of Joe November" 2-28-60 (Bessie Bison); *Man from Blackhawk*—"In His Steps" 5-20-60 (Kay); *Rawhide*—"Incident of the White Eyes" 5-3-63 (Delilah Butler); *The Virginian*—"Ride a Cock-Horse to Laramie Cross" 2-23-66

(Melinda); *Daniel Boone*—"The Search" 3-3-66 (Sylvie Du Marais); *Bonanza*—"Justice Deferred" 12-17-67 (Gladys).

Talbot, Stephen. TV: *Lawman*—"The Visitor" 3-15-59; *Sugarfoot*—"The Twister" 4-14-59 (Ab Martin); *Wanted—Dead or Alive*—"The Matchmaker" 9-19-59 (Rufe Meecham); *The Law of the Plainsman*—"Fear" 1-7-60 (Steve).

Talbott, Gloria (1931-). Films: "Desert Pursuit" 1952; "Northern Patrol" 1953 (Meg Stevens); "The Young Guns" 1956 (Nora); "The Oklahoman" 1957 (Maria Smith); "Cattle Empire" 1958 (Sandy); "Alias Jesse James" 1959 (Indian Maiden); "The Oregon Trail" 1959 (Shona Hastings); "Oklahoma Territory" 1960 (Ruth Red Hawk); "Arizona Raiders" 1965 (Martina); "An Eye for an Eye" 1966 (Bri Quince). ¶TV: *Wild Bill Hickok*—"Border City" 11-13-51; *The Cisco Kid*—"Pancho and the Wolf Dog" 9-13-52, "Faded General" 10-25-52; *The Gene Autry Show*—"Gypsy Woman" 8-25-53; *The Roy Rogers Show*—"The Land Swindle" 3-14-54 (Amy Woodruff); *Annie Oakley*—Semi-Regular 1954-57 (Priscilla Bishop); *Wyatt Earp*—"Mr. Earp Becomes a Marshal" 9-6-55 (Abbie Crandall), "Mr. Earp Meets a Lady" 9-13-55 (Abbie Crandall), "Hiding Behind a Star" 5-23-61 (Martha Connell); *Gunsmoke*—"Home Surgery" 10-8-55 (Holly Hawtree), "Cody's Code" 1-20-62 (Rose Loring), "The Cousin" 2-2-63 (Hallie); *Frontier*—"The Ten Days of John Leslie" 1-22-56 (Molly); *Zane Grey Theater*—"Stars Over Texas" 12-28-56 (Caroline); *The Restless Gun*—"Hang and Be Damned" 1-27-58 (Valya), "The Outlander" 4-21-58 (Sophie), "Mercyday" 10-6-58 (Mercyday); *Wanted—Dead or Alive*—"Fatal Memory" 9-13-58 (Jody Sykes), "Tolliver Bender" 2-13-60 (Adelaide Bender), "Three for One" 12-21-60 (Jennifer); *Bat Masterson*—"Trail Pirate" 12-31-58 (Ellen Parish), "Barbary Castle" 6-30-60 (Mary); *Tales of Wells Fargo*—"Showdown Trail" 1-5-59 (Fay Dooley), "Defiant at the Gate" 11-25-61 (Narcissa); *Zorro*—"The Man from Spain" 4-9-59 (Senorita Moneta Esperon), "Treasure for the King" 4-16-59 (Senorita Moenta Esperon), "Exposing the Tyrant" 4-23-59 (Senorita Moneta Esperon), "Zorro Takes a Dare" 4-30-59 (Senorita Moneta Esperon); *Cimarron City*—"Have Sword, Will Duel" 3-14-59 (Conchita Lolita); *Rawhide*—"Incident of the Calico Gun" 4-24-59 (Jenny Watson), "Incident of the Broken Word"

1-20-61 (Lucille Foley), "The Prairie Elephant" 11-17-61 (Jenny); *Riverboat*—"Landlubbers" 1-10-60 (Nora Lanyard), "Devil in Skirts" 11-21-60 (Lucinda); *Bonanza*—"Escape to the Ponderosa" 3-5-60 (Neda); *Laramie*—"Hour After Dawn" 3-15-60 (Maud), "The Passing of Kuba Smith" 1-3-61 (Jane), "Ladies' Day" 10-3-61 (Sally Malone), "Naked Steel" 1-1-63; *The Law of the Plainsman*—"Stella" 3-31-60 (Stella Meeker); *The Rebel*—"Absolution" 4-24-60 (Genevieve); *Whispering Smith*—"The Grudge" 5-15-61 (Cora Gates); *Death Valley Days*—"Queen of Spades" 10-11-61 (Mary Kileen), "The Bigger They Are" 4-4-64 (Gilda Benning), "Kate Melville and the Law" 6-20-65 (Kate Melville); *Bronco*—"Rendezvous with a Miracle" 2-12-62 (Valentine Ames); *Frontier Circus*—"Never Won Fair Lady" 4-12-62 (Pamela); *Wagon Train*—"The Frank Carter Story" 5-23-62 (Martha Chambers).

Talent, Jane. Films: "The Jaws of Justice" 1919; "The Last Straw" 1920 (Bobby Cole); "Double Crossers" 1921; "Dangerous Trails" 1923 (Beatrice Layton).

Taliaferro, Floyd. Films: "Crossing Trails" 1921 (Peter Marcus); "Western Hearts" 1921 (Pete Marcel).

Taliaferro, Hal. *see* Wales, Wally.

Talmadge, Constance (1898-11/23/73). Films: "Girl of the Timber Claims" 1917 (Jess).

Talmadge, Norma (1893-12/24/57). Films: "The Heart of Wetona" 1919 (Wetona).

Talmadge, Richard (1892-1/25/81). Films: "Lucky Dan" 1922 (Lucky Dan); "The Cavalier" 1928 (El Caballero/Taki); "Yankee Don" 1931 (Dick Carsey); "Get That Girl" 1932 (Dick); "The Phantom Empire" 1935-serial; "Black Eagle" 1948 (Mort).

Talman, William (1915-8/30/68). Films: "The Kid from Texas" 1950 (Minniger); "Smoke Signal" 1955 (Capt. Harper); "Two-Gun Lady" 1956 (Dan Corbin); "The Persuader" 1957 (Matt Bonham/Mark Bonham); "Ballad of Josie" 1968 (Charlie Lord). ¶TV: *Cavalcade Theatre*—"The Texas Rangers" 9-27-55; *DuPont Theater*—"The Texas Ranger" 4-9-57 (Hardin); *Tombstone Territory*—"The Return of the Outlaw" 3-12-58 (Logan Beatty); *Wagon Train*—"The Sarah Drummond Story" 4-2-58 (Walt Archer); *Cimarron City*—"To Become a Man" 10-25-58 (Mr. Conway); *Have Gun Will Travel*—"The Shooting of Jesse May"

10-20-60 (Jundill), "Long Way Home" 2-4-61 (Sheriff); *Gunsmoke*—"Legends Don't Sleep" 10-12-63 (Race Fallon); *Wild Wild West*—"The Night of the Man-Eating House" 12-2-66 (Sheriff).

Talton, Alix (1919-4/17/92). TV: *Have Gun Will Travel*—"The Englishman" 12-7-57 (Felicia Carson); *The Restless Gun*—"The Red Blood of Courage" 2-2-59 (Ann Langley).

Tamba, Tetsuro (1926-). Films: "The Five Man Army" 1969-Ital. (Samurai).

Tamberlani, Carlo (1899-8/5/80). Films: "Sign of Zorro" 1964-Ital./Span.

Tamblyn, Russ (1934-). Films: "Many Rivers to Cross" 1955 (Shields); "Fastest Gun Alive" 1956 (Eric Doolittle); "The Last Hunt" 1956 (Jimmy); "The Young Guns" 1956 (Tully); "Cimarron" 1960 (the Kid); "How the West Was Won" 1962 (Reb Soldier); "Son of a Gunfighter" 1966-U.S./Span. (Johnny); "The Female Bunch" 1971 (Russ). ¶TV: *Gunsmoke*—"He Who Steals" 5-19-65 (Billy Walters); *Iron Horse*—"Decision at Sundown" 2-27-67 (Kehoe); *The Quest*—"The Captive" 9-22-76 (Kelly); *The Life and Times of Grizzly Adams*—5-5-78.

Tambor, Jeffrey. Films: "City Slickers" 1991 (Lou).

Tamburrelli, Karla. Films: "City Slickers" 1991; "The Gambler V: Playing for Keeps" TVM-1994 (Marchette).

Tamiroff, Akim (1899-9/17/72). Films: "High, Wide and Handsome" 1937 (Joe Varese); "Union Pacific" 1939 (Fiesta); "Northwest Mounted Police" 1940 (Dan Duroc); "Texas Rangers Ride Again" 1940 (Mio Pio); "Relentless" 1948 (Joe Faringo); "The Great Bank Robbery" 1969 (Papa Pedro). ¶TV: *The Rifleman*—"New Orleans Menace" 12-2-58 (Tiffauges); *Johnny Ringo*—"The Assassins" 2-18-60 (Andrevich Baranov); *Wagon Train*—"The Joe Muharich Story" 4-19-61 (Joe Muharich).

Tandy, Jessica (1909-9/11/94). Films: "The Light in the Forest" 1958 (Myra Butler).

Tang, Frank (1905-6/29/68). Films: "The Great Divide" 1929 (Wong).

Tannen, Charles D. (1915-12/28/80). Films: "Blazing Justice" 1936; "Fair Warning" 1937 (Bellhop); "Drums Along the Mohawk" 1939 (Robert Johnson); "Jesse James" 1939 (Charles Ford); "The Return of the Cisco Kid" 1939 (Teller); "Lucky

Cisco Kid" 1940; "The Return of Frank James" 1940 (Charles Ford); "Sundown Jim" 1942 (Dan Barr); "Green Grass of Wyoming" 1948 (Veterinarian); "City of Badmen" 1953 (Cashier); "The First Traveling Saleslady" 1956 (Buyer); "The Proud Ones" 1956 (2nd Foreman); "Stagecoach to Dancer's Rock" 1962 (Sheriff). ¶TV: *The Roy Rogers Show*—"The Kid from Silver City" 1-17-54 (Rod Miner), "The Lady Killer" 9-12-54; *Maverick*—"Ghost Riders" 10-13-57; *Colt .45*—"Sign in the Sand" 1-3-58 (the Wrangler); *Zane Grey Theater*—"The Freighter" 1-17-58 (Ben); *Gunsmoke*—"Kitty Caught" 1-18-58 (Cashier); *Tales of Wells Fargo*—"The Reward" 4-21-58 (Gus), "The Has-Been" 1-16-61 (Roz Gilmore); *26 Men*—"The Glory Road" 10-7-58; *Have Gun Will Travel*—"The Protege" 10-18-58 (Floyd); *Tales of the Texas Rangers*—"Kickback" 12-12-58 (Vince); *Wagon Train*—"The Beauty Jamison Story" 12-17-58 (Ralph Jessop); *Rawhide*—"Incident of the Thirteenth Man" 10-23-59 (Jed Hodges), "Incident on the Road to Yesterday" 11-18-60, "Incident of the Big Blowout" 2-10-61, "The Sendoff" 10-6-61, "Gold Fever" 5-4-62 (Nelson); *The Rifleman*—"The Jailbird" 5-10-60, "Woman from Hog Ridge" 10-4-60, "Miss Milly" 11-15-60, "The Actress" 1-24-61; *Bonanza*—"The Ape" 12-17-60 (Bartender); *Klondike*—"Halliday's Club" 12-19-60 (Badger); *Gunslinger*—"The Hostage Fort" 2-16-61 (Royce); *Lawman*—"The Promise" 6-11-61 (Hardy Albrecht); *Daniel Boone*—"The Fallow Land" 4-13-67; *Gunsmoke*—"Nowhere to Run" 1-15-68 (John Hirschbeck), "The Devil's Outpost" 9-22-69 (Townsman).

Tannen, Julius (1881-1/3/65). Films: "Fair Warning" 1937 (Mr. Taylor).

Tannen, William (1911-12/2/76). Films: "Stand Up and Fight" 1939 (Lewis); "Wyoming" 1940 (Reynolds); "Lust for Gold" 1949 (Eager Fellow); "The Mysterious Desperado" 1949 (Barton); "South of Santa Fe" 1949-short; "Annie Get Your Gun" 1950 (Barker); "Riders of the Range" 1950 (Trump); "Sunset in the West" 1950 (John Kimball); "Best of the Badmen" 1951; "New Mexico" 1951 (Pvt. Cheever); "Santa Fe" 1951; "Road Agent" 1952 (Bill Collins); "El Paso Stampede" 1953 (Joe); "Jack McCall, Desperado" 1953 (Spargo); "Law and Order" 1953 (Stranger); "Jesse James Versus the Daltons" 1954 (Emmett Dalton); "The Law vs. Billy the Kid" 1954 (Dave Rudabaugh);

"Sitting Bull" 1954 (O'Connor); "Blackjack Ketchum, Desperado" 1956 (Dee Havalik); "Badlands of Montana" 1957 (2nd Outlaw); "Noose for a Gunman" 1960 (Willetts); "The Great Sioux Massacre" 1965 (Miner). ¶TV: *The Lone Ranger*—"Man of the House" 1-26-50, "Quarter Horse War" 11-8-56; *The Roy Rogers Show*—"The Outlaw's Girl" 2-17-52, "Outlaws' Town" 3-1-52, "Blind Justice" 12-14-52, "The Mingo Kid" 4-26-53 (Turk Black), "The Kid from Silver City" 1-17-54 (Bob Kelso), "The Lady Killer" 9-12-54, "Uncle Steve's Finish" 2-3-55 (Tom Everett), "And Sudden Death" 10-9-55; *Wild Bill Hickok*—"The Doctor Story" 7-1-52 (Rand), "The Maverick" 8-19-52; *The Cisco Kid*—"The Gramophone" 9-20-52, "Indian Uprising" 11-8-52, "New Evidence" 9-19-53; *Colt .45*—"Sign in the Sand" 1-3-58 (Dave); *Annie Oakley*—"Annie and the Chinese Puzzle" 2-13-55 Clint Scanlon); *Sergeant Preston of the Yukon*—"Dog Race" 1-19-56 (Nantee); *Tales of the Texas Rangers*—"Last Days of Boot Hill" 2-11-56 (Frenshaw); *The Adventures of Rin Tin Tin*—"Rin Tin Tin and the Second Chance" 6-1-56, "The Southern Colonel" 10-18-57 (Clay Cooper); *Wyatt Earp*—Regular 1957-58 (Deputy Harold Norton); *Wagon Train*—"The Ruttledge Munroe Story" 5-21-58 (Masters); *Tales of Wells Fargo*—"The Sniper" 5-26-58 (Acey-Deucie), "Captain Scoville" 1-9-61 (Keenan), "Don't Wake a Tiger" 5-12-62 (Ollie Cooper); *Bat Masterson*—"Cheyenne Club" 12-17-58 (John Conant), "Deadly Diamonds" 2-11-60, "A Time to Die" 12-15-60 (Sheriff Geary), "Dagger Dance" 4-20-61 (Doc); *The Californians*—"The Long Night" 12-23-58 (Sam); *The Texan*—"The Man Hater" 6-15-59 (Sheriff); *Rough Riders*—"Reluctant Hostage" 6-18-59; *Rawhide*—"Incident of the Roman Candles" 7-10-59, "Incident at Red River Station" 1-15-60 (Wiley), "Incident of the Deserter" 4-29-60 (Noah Detrick), "The Peddler" 1-19-62 (Sheriff); *Laramie*—"The Legend of Lily" 1-26-60 (Sheriff of Laramie); *Bonanza*—"The Stranger" 2-27-60 (Clerk), "The Boss" 5-19-63, "The Saga of Squaw Charlie" 12-27-64 (Lem), "Five Sundowns to Sunup" 12-5-65 (Albee), "A Dream to Dream" 4-14-68 (Bartender); *Wanted—Dead or Alive*—"Prison Trail" 5-14-60 (Hale Dane); *Gunslinger*—"Golden Circle" 4-13-61 (Ben Tracy); *Whispering Smith*—"Swift Justice" 9-11-61 (Angus Campbell); *Death Valley Days*—"After

the O.K. Corral" 5-2-64 (Ike Clanton); *The Virginian*—"Ride a Cock-Horse to Laramie Cross" 2-23-66 (Ely); *Daniel Boone*—"Grizzly" 10-6-66 (John), "The Enchanted Gun" 11-17-66 (Clark), "The Jasser Ledbedder Story" 2-2-67 (Ben Clark), "Bitter Mission" 3-30-67; *The High Chaparral*—"Shadows on the Land" 10-15-67 (Bartender), "Gold Is Where You Leave It" 1-21-68 (Bartender), "The Kinsman" 1-28-68 (Bartender), "No Irish Need Apply" 1-17-69; *Cimarron Strip*—"The Deputy" 12-21-67; *Cowboy in Africa*—"John Henry's Eden" 3-18-68 (Bill).

Tanner, Clay (1929-). Films: "Mr. Horn" TVM-1979 (Lt. Henry Lawton). ¶TV: *Bonanza*—"Ride the Wind" 1-16-66 & 1-23-66 (Herb), "The Last Mission" 5-8-66 (Wiggins), "The Pursued" 10-2-66 & 10-9-66 (Tex); *Laredo*—"The Other Cheek" 2-10-67 (Abe); *The Big Valley*—"Court Martial" 3-6-67; *Kung Fu*—"An Eye for an Eye" 1-25-73 (Barr), "The Ancient Warrior" 5-3-73 (Ty), "The Chalice" 10-11-73 (Marshal), "My Brother, My Executioner" 10-12-74 (Sheriff Talley); *Gunsmoke*—"The Town Tamers" 1-28-74 (Texan Leader).

Tansey, Emma (1884-3/23/42). Films: "Beyond the Rio Grande" 1930 (Mrs. Burke); "Gun Lords of Stirrup Basin" 1937; "The Red Rope" 1937; "Knight of the Plains" 1938 (Martha Lane).

Tansey, Sherry (James Sheridan) (1906-4/12/61). Films: "The Fighting Boob" 1926 (Timothy Raymond); "Code of the Cow Country" 1927 (Ted Calhoun); "The Obligin' Buckaroo" 1927; "Riders of the Rio" 1931 (Buck); "Carrying the Mail" 1934-short; "Desert Man" 1934; "The Lone Rider" 1934; "Pals of the Prairie" 1934-short; "Pals of the West" 1934-short; "The Sundown Trail" 1934; "The Way of the West" 1934 (Skippy); "West of the Law" 1934-short; "Between Men" 1935 (Tampas); "The Dawn Rider" 1935 (Townsman); "Courage of the North" 1935; "Law of the 45's" 1935 (Toral); "Lawless Range" 1935; "The New Frontier" 1935; "Paradise Canyon" 1935; "The Phantom Cowboy" 1935 (Jack Rogers); "The Rider of the Law" 1935; "Timber Terrors" 1935 (Bill Barton); "Custer's Last Stand" 1936-serial (Jim); "Guns and Guitars" 1936; "The Lawless Nineties" 1936; "Pinto Rustlers" 1936 (Outlaw); "Roamin' Wild" 1936; "Arizona Gunfighter" 1937; "Boothill Brigade" 1937; "Doomed at Sundown" 1937;

"The Fighting Deputy" 1937 (Buck); "The Gambling Terror" 1937 (Pete); "God's Country and the Man" 1937; "Gun Lords of Stirrup Basin" 1937 (Outlaw); "Guns in the Dark" 1937; "Headin' for the Rio Grande" 1937; "The Idaho Kid" 1937 (Henchman); "A Lawman Is Born" 1937; "Lightnin' Crandall" 1937; "Moonlight on the Range" 1937; "The Red Rope" 1937; "Riders of the Dawn" 1937; "The Silver Trail" 1937 (Tex); "Sing, Cowboy, Sing" 1937; "Stars Over Arizona" 1937; "The Trusted Outlaw" 1937; "Where Trails Divide" 1937 (Spade); "Whistling Bullets" 1937 (Sam); "The Feud Maker" 1938; "Gun Packer" 1938; "Gunsmoke Trail" 1938; "Heroes of the Alamo" 1938; "In Early Arizona" 1938; "Knight of the Plains" 1938; "Man's Country" 1938; "Mexicali Kid" 1938; "Paroled to Die" 1938 (Heavy Matson); "Rolling Caravans" 1938; "West of Rainbow's End" 1938; "Wild Horse Canyon" 1938; "Across the Plains" 1939; "Drifting Westward" 1939 (Piute); "Phantom Ranger" 1938; "The Rangers' Roundup" 1938; "Six-Gun Trail" 1938; "Songs and Bullets" 1938; "Starlight Over Texas" 1938; "Lure of the Wasteland" 1939; "Thunder in the Desert" 1938; "The Man from Texas" 1939; "Overland Mail" 1939 (Joe); "Silver on the Sage" 1939 (Baker); "Six-Gun Rhythm" 1939 (Pat); "Trigger Smith" 1939; "Arizona Frontier" 1940 (Outlaw); "Billy the Kid in Texas" 1940; "Billy the Kid Outlawed" 1940 (Outlaw); "Cowboy from Sundown" 1940; "Frontier Crusader" 1940; "The Golden Trail" 1940; "Phantom Rancher" 1940 (Joe); "Take Me Back to Oklahoma" 1940; "The Driftin' Kid" 1941; "The Lone Rider Crosses the Rio" 1941; "Lone Star Law Men" 1941 (Red); "Outlaws of the Rio Grande" 1941; "Riding the Sunset Trail" 1941 (Rip Carson); "Wanderers of the West" 1941 (Jeff Haines); "Arizona Roundup" 1942; "Western Mail" 1942 (Cheyenne); "Where Trails End" 1942.

Tapley, Colin (1911–). Films: "Arizona" 1940 (Bert Massey).

Tapley, Rose E. (1883-2/23/56). Films: "Britton of the Seventh" 1916 (Madge Eversly); "The Pony Express" 1925 (Aunt); "Morganson's Finish" 1926 (Mrs. Williams).

Tapscott, Mark. TV: *Maverick*— "The Long Hunt" 10-20-57 (Player #1), "Stampede" 11-17-57 (Deputy), "The Thirty-Ninth Star" 11-16-58 (Farfan), "The Spanish Dancer" 12-14-58 (Charlie), "The Strange Jour-

ney of Jenny Hill" 3-29-59 (Crowley), "Trooper Maverick" 11-29-59 (Sergeant Rogers), "The Devil's Necklace" 4-16-61 & 4-23-61 (Enlisted Man); *Tombstone Territory*— "The Outcast" 4-23-58 (Mace), "Surrender at Sunglow" 5-15-59 (Denver); *Rough Riders*—"The Maccabites" 10-16-58 (Tranko); *Have Gun Will Travel*—"The Man Who Lost" 2-7-59 (Semper); *Black Saddle*—"Client: Steele" 3-21-59 (Pete Hale); *Hotel De Paree*—"Vein of Ore" 10-16-59 (Arlington Rand); *The Deputy*—"Proof of Guilt" 10-24-59; *Rawhide*—"Incident on the Road Back" 2-24-61, "Incident of the Wager on Payday" 6-16-61 (Deputy); *The Tall Man*—"Hard Justice" 3-25-61 (Tom), "Shadow of the Past" 10-7-61 (Deputy), "Fool's Play" 12-2-61 (Deputy), "Legend of Billy" 12-9-61 (Deputy), "The Hunt" 1-27-62 (Andy), "Quarantine" 3-17-62 (Andy), "The Frame" 4-21-62 (Andy); *Wagon Train*—"The Sam Spicer Story" 10-28-63; *The Virginian*—"High Stakes" 11-16-66 (Sheriff Adams), "Seth" 3-20-68 (Stableman), "Nora" 12-11-68 (Lieutenant Jones), "Fox, Hound, and the Widow McCloud" 4-2-69 (Gambler); *The Big Valley*—"The Great Safe Robbery" 11-21-66 (Sheriff), "Rimfire" 2-19-68 (Miner), "Presumed Dead" 10-7-68 (Guard #1), "Hell Hath No Fury" 11-18-68 (Phil), "The Profit and the Lost" 12-2-68 (Bates), "Joshua Watson" 1-20-69 (Bert), "The Battle of Mineral Springs" 3-24-69; *Bonanza*—"The Sound of Drums" 11-17-68 (Sabin), "Long Way to Ogden" 2-22-70 (Steve Rance), "The Night Virginia City Died" 9-13-70 (Hamilton); *Death Valley Days*—"The Visitor" 12-27-69; *Lancer*—"Lamp in the Wilderness" 3-10-70 (Prospector); *The High Chaparral*—"Bad Day for Bad Men" 10-17-69, "Wind" 10-9-70.

Tarkington, Rockne (1932–). Films: "Savage Red—Outlaw White" 1974; "The Great Gundown" 1977 (Sutton); "Wyatt Earp" 1994 (Stable Hand); "The Desperate Trail" TVM-1995. ¶TV: *Cowboy in Africa*—"Lake Sinclair" 11-13-67 (Jacob); *The High Chaparral*—"Ride the Savage Land" 2-11-68 (Sergeant); *Bearcats!*—11-18-71 (Lukas).

Tarola, Mary Jo. *see* Douglas, Linda.

Tarron, Elsie (1903-10/24/90). Films: "Cyclone of the Range" 1927 (Mollie Butler); "An Exciting Day" 1927; "Sky-High Saunders" 1927 (Helen Leland).

Tartan, James. TV: *Bonanza*—

"Song in the Dark" 1-13-63, "Return to Honor" 3-22-64; *Cimarron Strip*—"The Deputy" 12-21-67 (Tullis).

Tashman, Lilyan (1900-3/21/34). Films: "Whispering Smith" 1926 (Marion Sinclair); "A Texas Steer" 1927 (Dixie Style).

Tate, Cullen (1896-10/12/47). Films: "Rose of the Golden West" 1927.

Tate, Kevin. Films: "Bullet for a Badman" 1964 (Sammy); "Firecreek" 1968 (Aaron). ¶TV: *The Legend of Jesse James*—"Dark Side of the Moon" 4-18-66 (Jamie Shepard).

Tate, Lincoln. Films: "Bastard, Go and Kill" 1971-Ital.; "Hero Called Allegria" 1971-Ital. (Lobo); "Holy Water Joe" 1971-Ital. (Acquasanta Joe); "On the Third Day Arrive the Crow" 1972-Ital./Span. (Link); "Return of Halleluja" 1972-Ital./Ger. (Archie); "For a Book of Dollars" 1973-Ital./Span. (Amen); "The Legend of the Lone Ranger" 1981 (General Custer). ¶TV: *Lancer*—"Julie" 10-29-68 (Jonas).

Tate, Patricia. Films: "Dangerous Venture" 1947 (Talu); "Unexpected Guest" 1947 (Ruth Baxter).

Tatro, Richard. TV: *Cheyenne*—"Cross Purpose" 10-9-61 (Lieutenant Cole); *Branded*—"Call to Glory" 2-27-66, 3-6-66 & 3-13-66 (Lt. Douglas Briggs).

Taurins, Ilze. TV: *The Virginian*—"The Golden Door" 3-13-63 (Maria Rilke); *Bonanza*—"The Deadliest Game" 2-21-65 (Petina); *Wild Wild West*—"The Night of the Dancing Death" 11-5-65 (Marianna).

Tavares, Arthur (1884-5/27/54). Films: "Ramona" 1916 (Lt. Francis Ortegna); "Hungry Eyes" 1918 (Scott).

Tayback, Vic (1929-5/25/90). TV: *Buckskin*—"The Ballad of Gabe Pruitt" 7-24-58 (Claude); *Rawhide*—"The Gray Rock Hotel" 5-21-65 (Monte); *Gunsmoke*—"Ladies from St. Louis" 3-25-67 (Gaines), "The Long Night" 2-17-69 (Rawlins), "The Convict" 2-1-71 (Dirks), "The Fugitives" 10-23-72 (Bill Hankins); *F Troop*—"Corporal Agarn's Farewell to the Troops" 10-5-65 (Bill Colton); *Cimarron Strip*—"The Hunted" 10-5-67 (Mulady); *Here Come the Brides*—"Here Come the Brides" 9-25-68, "Debt of Honor" 1-23-70; *Lancer*—"Devil's Blessing" 4-22-69 (Porter), "Cut the Wolf Loose" 11-4-69 (Durham); *Bonanza*—"Caution: Easter Bunny Crossing" 3-29-70 (Everett).

Taylor, Adam. Films: "The Return of Desperado" TVM-1988;

"Conagher" TVM-1991; "Wyatt Earp" 1994 (Texas Jack).

Taylor, Al (1882-10/10/47). Films: "The Bandit Buster" 1926; "The Bonanza Buckaroo" 1926 (Carney); "The Dangerous Dub" 1926 (Scar-Face Hanan); "The Fighting Cheat" 1926 (Cook); "Rawhide" 1926 (Jim Reep); "Between Dangers" 1927 (Charlie); "The Interferin' Gent" 1927 (Ben Douglas); "Soda Water Cowboy" 1927 (Joe); "The Ballyhoo Buster" 1928; "Desperate Courage" 1928; "The Avenger" 1931; "Branded Men" 1931; "The Nevada Buckaroo" 1931; "The Phantom of the West" 1931-serial; "Quick Trigger Lee" 1931; "The Vanishing Legion" 1931-serial (Sheriff of Clocum); "The Devil Horse" 1932-serial; "Ghost City" 1932; "Ghost Valley" 1932 (Henchman); "Law and Lawless" 1932; "The Saddle Buster" 1932 (Blackie); "Come on Tarzan" 1933; "The Law of the Wild" 1934-serial; "Nevada" 1935 (Hodge); "Westward Ho" 1935; "The Cattle Thief" 1936; "Comin' Round the Mountain" 1936; "The Fugitive Sheriff" 1936; "Guns and Guitars" 1936; "The Lawless Nineties" 1936 (Red); "Rio Grande Ranger" 1936; "Roarin' Guns" 1936; "The Traitor" 1936 (Outlaw); "The Unknown Ranger" 1936; "Vigilantes Are Coming" 1936-serial (Rancher); "Boots and Saddles" 1937; "Come on Cowboys" 1937; "Git Along, Little Dogies" 1937; "Law of the Ranger" 1937; "Range Defenders" 1937; "Ranger Courage" 1937; "Reckless Ranger" 1937; "The Trusted Outlaw" 1937; "Yodelin' Kid from Pine Ridge" 1937; "Zorro Rides Again" 1937-serial (Raider #2); "Billy the Kid Returns" 1938; "Call the Mesquiteers" 1938; "Gold Mine in the Sky" 1938; "Heroes of the Alamo" 1938; "The Lone Ranger" 1938-serial (Trooper); "Man from Music Mountain" 1938 (Hank); "Prairie Moon" 1938; "Red River Range" 1938; "Come on, Rangers" 1939; "The Lone Ranger Rides Again" 1939-serial (Colt); "Mexicali Rose" 1939; "Mountain Rhythm" 1939; "Union Pacific" 1939 (Irishman); "Wyoming Outlaw" 1939; "Zorro's Fighting Legion" 1939-serial (Rico); "Adventures of Red Ryder" 1940-serial (Slim); "Billy the Kid's Gun Justice" 1940; "The Carson City Kid" 1940; "Covered Wagon Days" 1940; "The Dark Command" 1940; "Ghost Valley Raiders" 1940; "Heroes of the Saddle" 1940 (Hendricks); "King of the Royal Mounted" 1940-serial (Red); "Oklahoma Renegades" 1940; "Gangs of Sonora" 1941; "King of the Texas Rangers" 1941-serial (Dude Ward); "Outlaws of the Cherokee Trail" 1941; "Along the Sundown Trail" 1942; "Call of the Canyon" 1942; "Code of the Outlaw" 1942; "The Cyclone Kid" 1942; "Man from Cheyenne" 1942; "Outlaws of Pine Ridge" 1942; "The Phantom Plainsmen" 1942 (Outlaw); "Prairie Pals" 1942 (Rancher); "Raiders of the Range" 1942; "Westward Ho" 1942; "Beyond the Last Frontier" 1943; "Black Hills Express" 1943 (Denver); "The Blocked Trail" 1943; "Daredevils of the West" 1943-serial (Citizen #6/Indian); "Dead Man's Gulch" 1943 (Buck Lathrop); "Death Valley Manhunt" 1943 (Lawson); "The Man from Thunder River" 1943; "Raiders of Sunset Pass" 1943 (Rustler); "Santa Fe Scouts" 1943; "Thundering Trails" 1943; "Marshal of Reno" 1944; "Duel in the Sun" 1946 (Man at Barbecue); "Rio Grande Raiders" 1946; "Dangers of the Canadian Mounted" 1948-serial (Track Heavy #1); "Desperadoes of the West" 1950-serial (Jensen).

Taylor, Beth (1889-3/1/51). Films: "The Prairie" 1947 (Annie Morris).

Taylor, Buck (1938-). Films: "…And Now Miguel" 1966 (Gabriel); "Pony Express Rider" 1976 (Bovey); "Kate Bliss and the Ticker Tape Kid" TVM-1978 (Joe); "Standing Tall" TVM-1978 (George Fewster); "The Sacketts" TVM-1979 (Reed Carney); "Wild Times" TVM-1980 (Joe McBride); "Cattle Annie and Little Britches" 1981 (Dynamite Dick); "The Legend of the Lone Ranger" 1981 (Gattlin); "No Man's Land" TVM-1984 (Fenny); "Triumphs of a Man Called Horse" 1984 (Sergeant Bridges); "Wild Horses" TVM-1985 (Cowboy); "Dream West" TVM-1986 (Egloffstein); "The Alamo: 13 Days to Glory" TVM-1987; "Down the Long Hill" TVM-1987 (Grey); "Gunsmoke: Return to Dodge" TVM-1987 (Newly O'Brien); "Proud Men" TVM-1987 (Homer); "Desperado: The Outlaw Wars" TVM-1989 (Porter); "Conagher" TVM-1991; "Tombstone" 1993 (Turkey Creek Jack Johnson). ¶TV: *Have Gun Will Travel*—"The Treasure" 12-29-62 (Eddie); *Stoney Burke*—"Gold-Plated Maverick" 1-7-63, "Kincaid" 4-22-63 (Mule); *The Virginian*—"Smile of a Dragon" 2-26-64 (Deputy Plumb), "A Gallows for Sam Horn" 12-2-64 (Scott Briscoe), "Men with Guns" 1-12-66 (Lem Bliss); *Bonanza*—"The Hostage" 9-27-64 (Billy); *Wagon Train*—"The Chottsie Gubenheimer Story" 1-10-65 (Skeeter Ames); *The Legend of Jesse James*—"The Dead Man's Hand" 9-20-65 (John Bedford); *The Big Valley*—"Young Marauders" 10-6-65 (Turk); *Branded*—"A Destiny Which Made Us Brothers" 1-23-66 (Corporal); *Daniel Boone*—"The Lost Colony" 12-8-66 (Jonathan Warren); *The Monroes*—"To Break a Colt" 1-11-67 (John "Brad" Bradford), "Race for the Rainbow" 1-18-67 (John "Brad" Bradford), "Ghosts of Paradox" 3-15-67; *Gunsmoke*—"Vengeance" 10-2-67 & 10-9-67 (Leonard Parker), Regular 1967-75 (Newly O'Brian); *Death Valley Days*—"The Taming of Trudy Bell" 12-6-69 (Will); *The Busters*—Pilot 5-28-78 (Billy Burnett); *The Cherokee Trail*—Pilot 11-28-81 (Laird); *Paradise*—"Squaring Off" 5-13-89 (Frank), "The Women" 1-25-91 (Slatter); *Young Riders*—"The Presence of Mine Enemies" 11-9-91 (Metcalfe).

Taylor, Cliff. Films: "Dead Man's Gold" 1948 (Miner); "Frontier Revenge" 1948 (Bartender); "Mark of the Lash" 1948; "The Dalton Gang" 1949 (Doctor); "Rimfire" 1949 (Bartender); "Son of Billy the Kid" 1949 (Jake); "Crooked River" 1950 (Doctor); "The Daltons' Women" 1950; "Fast on the Draw" 1950; "Hostile Country" 1950 (Dad); "King of the Bullwhip" 1950; "Marshal of Heldorado" 1950 (Doctor); "The Thundering Trail" 1951 (Moore); "The Vanishing Outpost" 1951 (Bartender); "The Frontier Phantom" 1952; "The Wild North" 1952 (Quartette Member).

Taylor, Delores (1932-). Films: "Billy Jack" 1971 (Jean Roberts); "The Trial of Billy Jack" 1974 (Jean Roberts).

Taylor, Don (1920-). Films: "Ambush" 1950 (Lt. Linus Delaney); "The Savage Guns" 1961-U.S./Span. (Mike Summers). ¶TV: *Telephone Time*—"Sam Houston's Decision" 12-10-57 (Sam Houston); *Zane Grey Theater*—"The Silent Sentry" 2-16-61 (Yankee).

Taylor, Dub "Cannonball" (1908-9/3/94). Films: "Across the Sierras" 1931 (Cannonball); "The Taming of the West" 1939 (Cannonball); "Beyond the Sacramento" 1940 (Cannonball); "The Man from Tumbleweeds" 1940 (Cannonball); "One Man's Law" 1940 (Nevady); "Pioneers of the Frontier" 1940 (Cannonball); "Prairie Schooners" 1940 (Cannonball); "The Return of Wild Bill" 1940 (Cannonball); "Hands Across the Rockies" 1941 (Cannonball); "King of Dodge City" 1941 (Cannonball); "North from the Lone Star" 1941 (Cannonball); "The

Return of Daniel Boone" 1941 (Cannonball); "The Son of Davy Crockett" 1941 (Cannonball); "Wildcat of Tucson" 1941 (Cannonball); "The Lone Prairie" 1942; "A Tornado in the Saddle" 1942; "Cowboy in the Clouds" 1943 (Cannonball); "Riders of the Northwest Mounted" 1943; "Saddles and Sagebrush" 1943; "Silver City Raiders" 1943 (Cannonball); "Cowboy Canteen" 1944 (Cannonball); "Cowboy from Lonesome River" 1944; "Cyclone Prairie Rangers" 1944; "The Last Horseman" 1944 (Cannonball); "Saddle Leather Law" 1944; "Sundown Valley" 1944 (Cannonball); "The Vigilantes Ride" 1944 (Cannonball); "Blazing the Western Trail" 1945; "Both Barrels Blazing" 1945; "Outlaws of the Rockies" 1945 (Cannonball); "Rough Ridin' Justice" 1945 (Cannonball); "Rustlers of the Badlands" 1945; "Texas Panhandle" 1945; "Wyoming Hurricane" 1944; "Frontier Gunlaw" 1946; "Lawless Empire" 1946 (Cannonball); "Ridin' Down the Trail" 1947; "Courtin' Trouble" 1948 (Cannonball); "Cowboy Cavalier" 1948; "Oklahoma Blues" 1948 (Cannonball); "Outlaw Brand" 1948; "Partners of the Sunset" 1948; "Range Renegades" 1948; "The Rangers Ride" 1948; "Silver Trails" 1948 (Cannonball); "Song of the Drifter" 1948; "Across the Rio Grande" 1949 (Cannonball); "Brand of Fear" 1949; "Gun Law Justice" 1949; "Gun Runner" 1949 (Cannonball); "Lawless Code" 1949; "Roaring Westward" 1949 (Cannonball); "The Charge at Feather River" 1953 (Canowicz); "The Bounty Hunter" 1954 (Danvers); "Riding Shotgun" 1954 (Eddie); "Tall Man Riding" 1955; "Fastest Gun Alive" 1956; "The Hallelujah Trail" 1965 (Clayton Howell); "Major Dundee" 1965 (Priam); "The Adventures of Bullwhip Griffin" 1967 (Timekeeper); "Bandolero!" 1968 (Attendant); "The Shakiest Gun in the West" 1968 (Pop McGovern); "Something for a Lonely Man" TVM-1968; "Death of a Gunfighter" 1969 (Doc Adams); "The Undefeated" 1969 (McCartney); "The Wild Bunch" 1969 (Mayor Wainscoat); "A Man Called Horse" 1970 (Joe); "Man and Boy" 1971 (Atkins); "Sam Hill: Who Killed the Mysterious Mr. Foster?" TVM-1971; "Support Your Local Gunfighter" 1971 (Doc Shultz); "The Wild Country" 1971 (Phil); "Junior Bonner" 1972 (Del, the Bartender); "Pat Garrett and Billy the Kid" 1973 (Josh); "Honky Tonk" TVM-1974; "Shootout in a One-Dog Town" TVM-1974

(Hall); "The Daughters of Joshua Cabe Return" TVM-1975 (Bitteroot); "Hearts of the West" 1975 (Nevada Ticket Agent); "Pony Express Rider" 1976 (Boomer); "The Winds of Autumn" 1976; "Once Upon a Texas Train" TVM-1988 (Charlie); "Back to the Future, Part III" 1990 (Saloon Old Timer); "Conagher" TVM-1991; "The Gambler Returns: The Luck of the Draw" TVM-1991; "My Heroes Have Always Been Cowboys" 1991; "Maverick" 1994 (Room Clerk). ¶TV: *The Roy Rogers Show*—"Money to Burn" 6-28-53 (Otis Cooper), "Gun Trouble" 11-22-53, "The Peddler from the Pecos" 12-13-53 (Peter G. Brady), "Little Dynamite" 1-3-54 (Phil Orrin), "Hidden Treasure" 12-19-54, "The Big Chance" 1-23-55; *The Adventures of Rin Tin Tin*—"The Courtship of Marshal Higgins" 9-27-57 (Hud); *26 Men*—"The Last Rebellion" 11-4-58; *Tales of the Texas Rangers*—"The Fifth Plague" 12-19-58 (Jack Geyer); *Casey Jones*—Regular 1958-59 (Willie Sims); *Wichita Town*—"Sidekicks" 4-6-60 (Newt); *Zane Grey Theater*—"A Gun for Willie" 10-6-60 (Yancie), "The Empty Shell" 3-30-61 (Harper); *The Westerner*—"School Days" 10-7-60; *Death Valley Days*—"Justice at Jackson Creek" 2-28-62 (Jake), "The Hat That Huldah Wore" 6-25-66 (Rupert), "The Hero of Apache Pass" 1-14-67 (Jesse), "Chicken Bill" 10-14-67 (Chicken Bill); *Temple Houston*—"Jubilee" 11-14-63 (Cliff Willard); *The Virginian*—"A Little Learning..." 9-29-65 (Walt Cooper), "Long Ride to Wind River" 1-19-66 (Runty Bojohn); *Laredo*—"Yahoo" 9-30-65 (Denny Moran), "Limit of the Law Larkin" 1-27-66 (Dude Meeker); *Wild Wild West*—"The Night of the Casual Killer" 10-15-65 (Guard), "The Night of the Running Death" 12-15-67 (Peter Carstairs); *The Loner*—"The Sheriff of Fetterman's Crossing" 11-13-65; *Gunsmoke*—"My Father's Guitar" 2-21-66 (Sonny Starr), "Saturday Night" 1-7-67 (Cook), "Mad Dog" 1-14-67 (Bartender), "Nitro!" 4-8-67 & 4-15-67 (Farnum), "Slocum" 10-21-68 (Noah Riker), "Kitowa!" 2-16-70 (the Rev. Finney Cox); *The Big Valley*—"Lost Treasure" 9-12-66 (Bartender), "Fall of a Hero" 2-5-68 (Doc Tulley); *The Monroes*—"War Arrow" 11-2-66, "Wild Bull" 2-15-67; *Bonanza*—"Ponderosa Explosion" 1-1-67 (Barlow), "The Gold Detector" 12-24-67 (Simon), "Meena" 11-16-69 (Luke), "The Horse Traders" 4-5-70 (Luke Calhoun), "An Earthquake Called Callahan" 4-11-71 (Otto), "Easy

Come, Easy Go" 12-12-71 (Luke); *Dundee and the Culhane*—"The 3:10 to a Lynching Brief" 11-8-67 (Conductor); *The Guns of Will Sonnett*—"Look for the Hound Dog" 1-26-68 (Henry Jackson); *Cimarron Strip*—"The Greeners" 3-7-68 (Owley); *The High Chaparral*—"Tornado Frances" 10-11-68, "Lady Fair" 11-14-69 (Fargo); *Lancer*—"The Last Train for Charlie Poe" 11-26-68 (Davey Horn), "Zee" 9-30-69 (Harker); *Alias Smith and Jones*—"Journey from San Juan" 4-8-71; *Bret Maverick*—"The Hidalgo Thing" 5-4-82 (Toothless Tim Teal); *Father Murphy*—"John Michael Murphy, R.I.P." 12-7-82 (Billy Bob).

Taylor, Duke. Films: "The Painted Stallion" 1937-serial (Bill); "Zorro Rides Again" 1937-serial (Raider #9); "The Lone Ranger" 1938-serial (Trooper); "The Lone Ranger Rides Again" 1939-serial (Posseman #6); "King of the Royal Mounted" 1940-serial (Smelter Heavy #1); "King of the Texas Rangers" 1941-serial; "King of the Mounties" 1942-serial (Becker/Mountie/Smnelter Heavy #1); "Outlaws of Pine Ridge" 1942; "Zorro's Black Whip" 1944-serial (Mine Heavy #2/Trail Heavy #1); "The Phantom Rider" 1946-serial (Schwartz); "Jesse James Rides Again" 1947-serial (Gil); "Son of Zorro" 1947-serial (John Dixon/Jarvis); "The Adventures of Frank and Jesse James" 1948-serial (Bull); "Desperadoes of the West" 1950-serial (Cody); "The James Brothers of Missouri" 1950-serial (Flint); "Canadian Mounties vs. Atomic Invaders" 1953-serial.

Taylor, Elizabeth (1932-). Films: "Giant" 1956 (Leslie Benedict); "Poker Alice" TVM-1987 (Poker Alice Moffit).

Taylor, Estelle (1899-4/15/58). Films: "A California Romance" 1923 (Donna Dolores); "Cimarron" 1931 (Dixie Lee).

Taylor, Ferris (1893-3/6/61). Films: "The Luck of Roaring Camp" 1937 (Judge Brandt); "Flaming Frontier" 1938-serial; "Forbidden Valley" 1938 (Sheriff Walcott); "Santa Fe Stampede" 1938 (Judge); "Chip of the Flying U" 1939 (Sheriff); "Frontier Marshal" 1939 (Doctor); "Man of Conquest" 1939 (Jonas Lea); "Mountain Rhythm" 1939 (Judge Worthington); "The Dark Command" 1940 (Banker); "Mexican Spitfire Out West" 1940 (Thorne); "Prairie Law" 1940; "Rancho Grande" 1940 (Emory Benson); "Ridin' on a Rainbow" 1941 (Capt. Bartlett); "The Man from Rainbow

Valley" 1946 (Col. Winthrop); "The Gallant Legion" 1948; "The Gunfighter" 1950 (Grocer); "Two Flags West" 1950 (Dr. Magowan); "Hannah Lee" 1953 (Station Master); "The Siege at Red River" 1954 (Anderson Smith). ¶TV: *The Cisco Kid*—"Newspaper Crusade" 5-5-51, "Freight Line Feud" 6-2-51; "Performance Bond" 6-30-51, "Talking Dog" 2-23-52, "Montezuma's Treasure" 11-7-53; *The Roy Rogers Show*—"Outlaws' Town" 3-1-52, "The Minister's Son" 3-23-52, "Doc Stevens' Traveling Store" 7-25-54 (Doc Stevens); *The Lone Ranger*—"The Devil's Bog" 2-5-53; *The Gene Autry Show*—"Prize Winner" 7-27-54; *Buckskin*—"The Gold Watch" 8-28-58 (Mr. Hagedorn).

Taylor, Forrest (1884-2/19/65). Films: "In the Sunset Country" 1915; "Man-Afraid-of-His-Wardrobe" 1915; "The Sheriff of Willow Creek" 1915; "The Terror of Twin Mountains" 1915; "There's Good in the Worst of Us" 1915; "The Trail of the Serpent" 1915; "Two Spot Joe" 1915; "The Valley Feud" 1915; "The Warning" 1915; "No Man's Gold" 1926 (Wat Lyman); "Riders of Destiny" 1933 (James Kincaid); "The Lone Bandit" 1934; "Between Men" 1935 (Wyndham); "Big Calibre" 1935 (Jack Bently); "The Courageous Avenger" 1935 (Marshal Taggart); "No Man's Range" 1935; "The Rider of the Law" 1935; "Trail of Terror" 1935 (Blake); "Men of the Plains" 1936 (James Travis); "The Phantom of the Range" 1936; "Rio Grande Romance" 1936 (Richard Shelby); "Rip Roarin' Buckaroo" 1936 (Luke Slater); "Rogue of the Range" 1936 (Pinky, the Prison Guard); "Song of the Gringo" 1936; "Too Much Beef" 1936 (Rocky Brown/Hugh Stanford); "Valley of the Lawless" 1936 (Gambler); "West of Nevada" 1936 (Steven Cutting); "Arizona Days" 1937 (Price); "Courage of the West" 1937; "Desert Phantom" 1937; "Headin' for the Rio Grande" 1937 (Sheriff Ed Saunders); "Lost Ranch" 1937 (Garson); "Moonlight on the Range" 1937; "The Mystery of the Hooded Horseman" 1937 (Norton); "Orphan of the Pecos" 1937 (Jess Brand); "The Red Rope" 1937 (Parson Pete); "Riders of the Dawn" 1937 (Brady); "The Roaming Cowboy" 1937 (Evans); "Stars Over Arizona" 1937; "Tex Rides with the Boy Scouts" 1937 (Dorman); "Where Trails Divide" 1937 (Mr. Grey); "Black Bandit" 1938 (Sheriff Robert Warner); "California Frontier" 1938 (Gen. Wyatt); "Cattle Raiders" 1938; "Desert Patrol" 1938 (Martin Rand); "Durango Valley Raiders" 1938

(Sheriff Devlin); "The Feud Maker" 1938 (Marshal John Kincaid); "Frontier Town" 1938 (Sheriff Lane); "Ghost Town Riders" 1938 (Gomer); "Guilty Trails" 1938 (Dan Lawson); "Gun Packer" 1938 (Express Manager); "Heroes of the Hills" 1938 (Sheriff); "The Last Stand" 1938 (Turner); "Law of the Texan" 1938 (Capt. Moore); "Lightning Carson Rides Again" 1938; "Man's Country" 1938 (Colonel Hay); "Outlaw Express" 1938 (Ferguson); "The Painted Trail" 1938 (Jackson); "Prairie Justice" 1938 (Sheriff Randall); "Rio Grande" 1938; "Western Trails" 1938 (Williams); "Chip of the Flying U" 1939 (J.G. Whitmore); "Code of the Cactus" 1939 (Blackton); "The Fighting Gringo" 1939 (Jury Foreman); "Fighting Renegade" 1939 (Prof. Lucius Lloyd); "Honor of the West" 1939 (Len Walker); "The Law Comes to Texas" 1939; "The Lone Ranger Rides Again" 1939-serial (Miller); "The Oregon Trail" 1939-serial; "Outlaw's Paradise" 1939 (Eddie); "The Phantom Stage" 1939 (Gabe Lawson); "Riders of the Black River" 1939 (Sheriff Dave Patterson); "Riders of the Frontier" 1939; "Rovin' Tumbleweeds" 1939; "Stand Up and Fight" 1939; "Straight Shooter" 1939 (Luke); "Texas Wildcats" 1939 (Jim Burrows); "Trigger Fingers" 1939 (Crane); "Trigger Smith" 1939; "Arizona Gangbusters" 1940 (Lambert); "Billy the Kid's Gun Justice" 1940 (Roberts); "The Cheyenne Kid" 1940 (Sheriff); "The Durango Kid" 1940 (Ben Winslow); "Frontier Crusader" 1940 (John Stoner); "The Golden Trail" 1940 (Rawls); "The Kid from Santa Fe" 1940 (Sheriff Holt); "Rhythm of the Rio Grande" 1940 (Crane); "The Sagebrush Family Trails West" 1940 (Len Gorman); "The Trail Blazers" 1940; "Trailing Double Trouble" 1940 (Sheriff); "West of Abilene" 1940 (Sheriff); "Wild Horse Range" 1940 (Harvey Mitchell); "Billy the Kid's Fighting Pals" 1941 (Hanson); "Kansas Cyclone" 1941 (Ben Brown); "King of the Texas Rangers" 1941-serial (Clerk); "The Lone Rider Rides On" 1941; "Pals of the Pecos" 1941; "Ridin' on a Rainbow" 1941 (Jeff Billings); "Ridin' the Cherokee Trail" 1941 (Craven); "Underground Rustlers" 1941 (Bently); "Wildcat of Tucson" 1941; "Wrangler's Roost" 1941 (the Deacon); "Arizona Stagecoach" 1942; "Bullets for Bandits" 1942; "Code of the Outlaw" 1942; "Cowboy Serenade" 1942; "Down Rio Grande Way" 1942; "Home in Wyomin'" 1942 (Pop); "In Old California" 1942;

"King of the Mounties" 1942-serial (Telegrapher); "King of the Stallions" 1942; "The Lone Star Vigilantes" 1942 (Dr. Banning); "Outlaws of Pine Ridge" 1942 (Sheriff Gibbons); "Perils of the Royal Mounted" 1942-serial (Hinsdale); "The Rangers Take Over" 1942 (Capt. Wyatt); "Ridin' Down the Canyon" 1942 (Jim Fllowes); "Sons of the Pioneers" 1942 (Bixby); "The Spoilers" 1942 (Bennett); "Sunset on the Desert" 1942 (Belknap); "Trail Riders" 1942 (Rand); "Bullets and Saddles" 1943; "The Fighting Buckaroo" 1943 (Mark Comstock); "King of the Cowboys" 1943 (Cowhand); "Land of Hunted Men" 1943; "Silver Spurs" 1943 (Judge Pebble); "Song of Texas" 1943; "Thundering Trails" 1943; "Wild Horse Stampede" 1943; "Boss of Boomtown" 1944; "Cheyenne Wildcat" 1944; "Cyclone Prairie Rangers" 1944; "Death Valley Rangers" 1944; "The Last Horseman" 1944 (Bert Saunders); "Mojave Firebrand" 1944; "Mystery Man" 1944 (Sheriff Sam Newhall); "Outlaws of Santa Fe" 1944; "Range Law" 1944; "Song of Nevada" 1944 (Col. Jack Thompson); "Sonora Stagecoach" 1944 (Judge Crandall); "Sundown Valley" 1944 (Gunsight Hawkins); "Trail to Gunsight" 1944 (Sheriff); "Zorro's Black Whip" 1944-serial (Becker); "Bandits of the Badlands" 1945; "Beyond the Pecos" 1945; "Blazing the Western Trail" 1945; "Rockin' in the Rockies" 1945 (Sam Clemens); "Rough Ridin' Justice" 1945 (Padgett); "Texas Panhandle" 1945; "The Caravan Trail" 1946 (Silas Black); "Colorado Serenade" 1946 (Judge Hilton); "Driftin' River" 1946 (Trigger); "Galloping Thunder" 1946; "Lawless Empire" 1946 (Doc Weston); "Renegades" 1946 (Frank Dembrow); "Romance of the West" 1946 (Father Sullivan); "Santa Fe Uprising" 1946; "Stagecoach to Denver" 1946 (Matt Disher); "Along the Oregon Trail" 1947; "Rustlers of Devil's Canyon" 1947 (Doc Glover); "The Sea of Grass" 1947 (Homesteader); "The Stranger from Ponca City" 1947; "Trail Street" 1947 (Dave); "Yankee Fakir" 1947 (Mason); "Buckaroo from Powder River" 1948 (Pop Ryland); "Coroner Creek" 1948 (McCune); "Four Faces West" 1948 (Conductor #2); "Return of the Badmen" 1948 (Farmer); "Death Valley Gunfighter" 1949 (Lester); "Deputy Marshal" 1949 (Sheriff Lance); "Navajo Trail Raiders" 1949 (Sam Byrnes); "The Pecos Pistol" 1949-short; "Stallion Canyon" 1949 (Larsen); "Cherokee Uprising" 1950

(Welch); "Code of the Silver Sage" 1950 (Sandy Wheeler); "Cowboy and the Prizefighter" 1950 (Stevenson); "The Fargo Phantom" 1950-short; "The Fighting Redhead" 1950 (O'-Connor); "The Fighting Stallion" 1950 (Martin Evans); "Montana" 1950 (Clark); "Rustlers on Horse-back" 1950 (Josh Taylor); "Winchester '73" 1950 (Target Clerk); "Blazing Bullets" 1951; "Don Daredevil Rides Again" 1951-serial (Taylor); "Prairie Roundup" 1951 (Dan Kelly); "Wells Fargo Gunmaster" 1951 (Doctor); "Border Saddlemates" 1952 (Mel Richards); "Night Raiders" 1952 (Chairman); "Smoky Canyon" 1952 (Wyler); "South Pacific Trail" 1952 (Conductor); "Iron Mountain Trail" 1953 (Sam Sawyer); "The Marshal's Daughter" 1953 (Uncle Jed); "Bitter Creek" 1954 (Harley Pruitt); "Dawn at Socorro" 1954 (Jebb Hayes). ¶TV: *The Cisco Kid*—"Counterfeit Money" 1-27-51, "Convict Story" 2-17-51, "Oil Land" 2-24-51, "Railroad Land Rush" 3-17-51, "The Will" 3-24-51, "Cattle Quarantine" 3-31-51, "False Marriage" 4-14-51, "Wedding Blackmail" 4-21-51, "Church in Town" 5-17-52, "Bandaged Badman" 10-11-52, "The Black Terror" 11-29-52; *The Roy Rogers Show*—"Dead Men's Hills" 3-15-52 (Sheriff), "Ride in the Death Wagon" 4-6-52, "The Hijackers" 10-24-54, "Bad Neighbors" 11-21-54 (Al Houston), "Outcasts of Paradise Valley" 1-9-55 (Joe Salem); *Wild Bill Hickok*—"Marriage Feud of Ponca City" 5-13-52; *The Gene Autry Show*—"The Hold-Up" 12-14-52, "The Hoodoo Canyon" 8-17-54; *Wyatt Earp*—"The War of the Colonels" 4-10-56 (Col. Frentress), "Siege at Little Alamo" 2-5-57 (Todd); *My Friend Flicka*—"The Unmasking" 4-13-56 (Judge Spencer), "Lost River" 6-15-56; *Zane Grey Theater*—"The Doctor Keeps a Promise" 3-21-58 (Dr. Caslin); *Maverick*—"Greenbacks Unlimited" 3-13-60 (Proprietor); *Tales of Wells Fargo*—"Run for the River" 11-7-60 (Pop Kyle); *Bonanza*—"The Tall Stranger" 1-7-62.

Taylor, George (1900-12/20/70). Films: "Buckaroo Sheriff of Texas" 1951; "The Treasure of Lost Canyon" 1952 (Clem); "The Redhead from Wyoming" 1953 (Doctor); "Badlands of Montana" 1957 (Bank Teller). ¶TV: *Laramie*—"The Fatal Step" 10-24-61; *Pistols 'n' Petticoats*—11-5-66 (Philip).

Taylor, Grant (1917-71). Films: "The Kangaroo Kid" 1950 (Phil Romero). ¶TV: *Whiplash*—"Barbed Wire" 3-18-61, "Storm River" 8-12-61.

Taylor, Henry (1908-3/1/69). Films: "Beyond the Rio Grande" 1930 (Doctor).

Taylor, Jack (1936-). Films: "Billy the Kid" 1962-Span.; "Last of the Mohicans" 1965-Ital./Span./Ger. (Duncan Heywood); "The Christmas Kid" 1966-Span./Ital. (John Novak); "Three from Colorado" 1967-Span.

Taylor, Joan. Films: "Fighting Man of the Plains" 1949 (Evelyn Slocum); "The Savage" 1952 (Luta); "War Paint" 1953 (Wanima); "Rose Marie" 1954 (Wanda); "Apache Woman" 1955 (Anne Libeau); "Fort Yuma" 1955 (Francesca); "War Drums" 1957 (Riva). ¶TV: *Wagon Train*—"A Man Called Horse" 3-26-58 (Bright Star); *Yancy Derringer*—"An Ace Called Spade" 10-30-58 (Lavinia Lake); *Gunsmoke*—"Young Love" 1-3-59 (Anna Wheat); *The Texan*—"Trouble on the Trail" 11-23-59; *Colt .45*—"Calamity" 12-13-59 (Dr. Ellen McGraw); *The Rifleman*—Regular 1960-62 (Millie Scott); *Rawhide*—"Incident Before Black Pass" 5-19-61 (Paibada); *Bronco*—"A Sure Thing" 1-22-62 (Lorain).

Taylor, Joyce (1932-). TV: *Lawman*—"The Runaway" 2-1-59 (Dora); *Rough Riders*—"The Promise" 4-2-59 (Jenny Kirby); *Bat Masterson*—"Cattle and Cane" 3-3-60 (Jane Taylor); *Tales of Wells Fargo*—"The Great Bullion Robbery" 3-21-60 (Ann), "Vignette of a Sinner" 6-2-62 (Rachel Whitman); *Whispering Smith*—"Stakeout" 5-29-61 (Edie); *Wagon Train*—"The Baylor Crowfoot Story" 3-21-62 (Ruth Creech); *Bonanza*—"The War Comes to Washoe" 11-4-62 (Morvath Terry).

Taylor, Kent (1907-4/9/87). Films: "The Mysterious Rider" 1933 (Wade Benton); "Sunset Pass" 1933 (Clink Peeples); "Under the Tonto Rim" 1933; "Ramona" 1936 (Felipe Moreno); "Tombstone, the Town Too Tough to Die" 1942 (Doc Holliday); "Alaska" 1944; "The Daltons Ride Again" 1945 (Bob Dalton); "Western Pacific Agent" 1950; "Frontier Gambler" 1956; "Ghost Town" 1956 (Anse Conroy); "The Iron Sheriff" 1957 (Quincy); "Fort Bowie" 1958 (Col. Garrett); "Walk Tall" 1960 (Ed Carter); "The Purple Hills" 1961 (Johnny Barnes); "The Broken Land" 1962 (Marshall); "The Firebrand" 1962 (Maj. Tim Bancroft); "Law of the Lawless" 1964 (Rand McDonald); "Fort Courageous" 1965. ¶TV: *Colt .45*—"Last Chance" 12-6-57 (Wallace Grant); *The Restless Gun*—"Imposter for a Day" 2-17-58 (Deiblery); *Tales of Wells Fargo*—"Alias Jim Hardie" 3-

10-58 (Quirt Johnson); *Zorro*—"The Man with the Whip" 5-8-58 (Carlos Murrieta), "The Cross of the Andes" 5-15-58 (Carlos Murrietta); *Rough Riders*—Regular 1958-59 (Captain Flagg); *Bronco*—"The Last Resort" 11-17-59 (Three Finger Jack); "Stage to the Sky" 4-24-61 (Billy Rawlins); *Laramie*—"The Legend of Lily" 1-26-60 (Ben Carson); *Riverboat*—"The Treasure of Hawk Hill" 2-8-60 (Murrell); *Bat Masterson*—"Three Bullets for Bat" 3-24-60 (John Martin); *Sugarfoot*—"Funeral at Forty Mile" 5-24-60 (Hank Farragut); *The Rifleman*—"The Wyoming Story" 2-7-61 & 2-14-61 (McKee); *Rango*—"The Daring Holdup of the Deadwood Stage" 1-20-67 (Bancroft).

Taylor, Larry (1918-). Films: "The Sheriff of Fractured Jaw" 1958-Brit. (Gun Guard).

Taylor, Libby. Films: "When a Man Sees Red" 1934 (Mandy); "Ruggles of Red Gap" 1935 (Servant); "Santa Fe Trail" 1940 (Black).

Taylor, Regina. Films: "Children of the Dust" TVM-1995 (Drusilla).

Taylor, Robert (1911-6/8/69). Films: "Stand Up and Fight" 1939 (Blake Cantrell); "Billy the Kid" 1941 (Billy Bonney); "Ambush" 1950 (Ward Kinsman); "The Devil's Doorway" 1950 (Lance Poole); "Westward the Women" 1951 (Buck Wyatt); "Ride, Vaquero!" 1953 (Rio); "Many Rivers to Cross" 1955 (Bushrod Gentry); "The Last Hunt" 1956 (Charles Gilson); "The Law and Jake Wade" 1958 (Jake Wade); "Saddle the Wind" 1958 (Steve Sinclair); "The Hangman" 1959 (Mackenzie Bovard); "Cattle King" 1963 (Sam Brassfield); "Savage Pampas" 1966-U.S./Span./Arg. (Capt. Martin); "Return of the Gunfighter" TVM-1967 (Ben Wyatt). ¶TV: *Death Valley Days*—Host 1966-68, "The Day All Marriages Were Cancelled" 12-3-66 (Mayor Charles Poston), "A Wrangler's Last Ride" 4-8-67 (Charles M. Russell), "Halo for a Badman" 4-15-67 (Porter Stockton), "Major Horace Bell" 5-20-67 (Major Horace Bell), "Shanghai Kelly's Birthday Party" 10-7-67 (Shanghai Kelly), "The Lone Grave" 10-28-67 (John Hall), "The Friend" 2-17-68, "Lady with a Past" 12-28-68 (Frank Johnson); *Hondo*—"Hondo and the Eagle Claw" 9-8-67 (Gallagher).

Taylor, Rod (1929-). Films: "Top Gun" 1955 (Sutter); "Giant" 1956 (Sir David Karfrey); "Chuka" 1967 (Chuka); "Powderkeg" TVM-1971 (Hank Bracket); "Deadly Trackers" 1973 (Brand); "The Train Robbers" 1973 (Grady); "The Oregon Trail" TVM-1976 (Evan Thorpe); "Outlaws" TVM-1986 (Sheriff Jon Grail). ¶TV: *Cheyenne*—"The Argonauts" 11-1-55 (Duncan); *Zane Grey Theater*—"Picture of Sal" 1-28-60 (Jed Harper); *Bearcats!*—Regular 1971 (Hank Brackett); *The Oregon Trail*—Regular 1977 (Evan Thorpe); *Outlaws*—Regular 1986-87 (Sheriff Jonathan Grail).

Taylor, Stanley (1900-11/27/80). Films: "Red Hot Hoofs" 1926 (Gerald Morris); "The Bandit's Son" 1927 (Rufe Bolton); "The War Horse" 1927 (Lt. Caldwell); "Code of Honor" 1930 (Tom Bradfield).

Taylor, Vaughn (1911-5/3/83). Films: "Decision at Sundown" 1957 (Barber); "Cowboy" 1958 (Mr. Fowler); "Gunsmoke in Tucson" 1958 (Ben Bodeen); "Warlock" 1959 (Richardson); "The Plunderers" 1960 (Jess Walters); "The Professionals" 1966 (Banker); "The Shakiest Gun in the West" 1968 (Rev. Longbaugh); "The Ballad of Cable Hogue" 1970 (Powell). ¶TV: *Trackdown*—"Law in Lampasas" 10-11-57 (Doc Rivers); *Wagon Train*—"The Mary Halstead Story" 11-20-57 (James Ferguson); *Gunsmoke*—"Claustrophobia" 1-25-58 (Olie Ridgers), "Box O'Rocks" 12-5-59 (Reverend Blouze), "O'Quillian" 10-28-68 (Judge Fletcher Anderson); *Cheyenne*—"Ghost of Cimarron" 3-25-58 (Doc Johnson), "The Vanishing Breed" 11-19-62 (Judge Kinkaid); *Wanted—Dead or Alive*—"The Martin Poster" 9-6-58 (Dr. Glen Leach), "The Tyrant" 10-31-59, "Criss Cross" 11-16-60 (Doc Adams); *The Texan*—"Jail for the Innocents" 11-3-58 (Sheriff Loomis); *Have Gun Will Travel*—"Something to Live For" 12-20-58 (Hugh Evans); *Bronco*—"The Belles of Silver Flat" 3-24-59 (Doc Moody), "Ride the Whirlwind" 1-15-62 (Dr. Miles Gillis); *Black Saddle*—"Client: Banke" 4-11-59 (Eli Banks); *Colt .45*—"The Magic Box" 4-19-59 (Oliver Pate), "Strange Encounter" 4-26-60 (Dr. Craig); *Man from Blackhawk*—"The Trouble with Tolliver" 10-16-59 (Jeremy Toliver); *Rawhide*—"Incident of the One Hundred Amulets" 5-6-60 (Perce Morgan), "Incident of the Phantom Burglar" 4-14-61 (Judge Brady), "Six Weeks to Bent Fork" 9-28-65; *Tales of Wells Fargo*—"The Wade Place" 11-28-60 (Seth Wade); *Gunslinger*—"The Hostage Fort" 2-16-61 (Matt Calvin); *Laramie*—"The Debt" 4-18-61 (Pettis); *Wide Country*—"To Cindy, with Love" 2-28-63 (Dr. Jones); *The Virginian*—"No Tears for Savannah" 10-2-63 (Judge Shelly), "A Small Taste of Justice" 12-20-67 (Doc Kane); *Temple Houston*—"Last Full Moon" 2-27-64 (Colonel Grove); *Death Valley Days*—"Raid on the San Francisco Mint" 5-23-65 (Harpending); *Walt Disney Presents*—"Gallegher" 1965-67 (Baildad); *Wild Wild West*—"The Night of the Double-Edged Knife" 11-12-65 (Benjamin Adamson); *The Legend of Jesse James*—"Things Don't Just Happen" 3-14-66 (Prosecutor Clayton); *Daniel Boone*—"The Accused" 3-24-66 (Justice Godwin), "The Cache" 12-4-69 (Judge Qualey); *Bonanza*—"A Real Nice, Friendly Little Town" 11-27-66 (C.R. Lively), "Judgment at Olympus" 10-8-78 (Eggers), "Is There Any Man Here?" 2-8-70 (Bert Taylor); *Laredo*—"A Question of Guilt" 3-10-67 (Judge Jacob Lamprey); *The High Chaparral*—"A Quiet Day in Tucson" 10-1-67 (Asa); *The Guns of Will Sonnett*—"Ride the Man Down" 11-17-67 (Evans); *Lancer*—"Chase a Wild Horse" 10-8-68, "Zee" 9-30-69 (Trask); *Alias Smith and Jones*—"Return to Devil's Hole" 2-25-71, "The Day They Hanged Kid Curry" 9-16-71.

Taylor, Wayne (1933-). Films: "The Charge at Feather River" 1953; "J.W. Coop" 1971 (Gas Station Attendant).

Taylor, Wilton (1869-1/24/25). Films: "Ridin' Wild" 1922 (Sheriff Nolan).

Taylor-Young, Leigh (1944-). TV: *Outlaws*—"Tintype" 1-3-87 (Diane); *Young Riders*—"Lessons Learned" 7-9-92 (Polly Hunter).

Tead, Phil (1894-6/9/74). Films: "The Westerner" 1940 (Prisoner); "Fangs of the Arctic" 1953; "Fangs of the Wild" 1954 (Mac). ¶TV: *The Lone Ranger*—"Bullets for Ballots" 5-11-50, "Damsels in Distress" 6-8-50, "Through the Wall" 10-9-52, "Death in the Forest" 6-4-53, "A Broken Match" 12-2-54, "Showdown at Sand Creek" 5-26-55; *Broken Arrow*—"Water Witch" 1-7-58 (Mr. Amos).

Teagarden, Jack (1906-1/15/64). Films: "Twilight on the Prairie" 1944.

Teague, Guy (-1/24/70). Films: "The Adventures of Frank and Jesse James" 1948-Serial (Dirk #2); "Desperadoes of the West" 1950-serial (Jack); "The Showdown" 1950 (Pickney); "Vigilante Hideout" 1950 (Blackie); "Don Daredevil Rides Again" 1951-serial (Deputy Sheriff); "The Kid from Amarillo" 1951 (Dirk); "The Battles of Chief Pontiac" 1952 (Von Weber's Aide); "Cattle Town" 1952 (Easy); "The Stranger Wore a Gun" 1953; "The Bounty Hunter" 1954; "Man with the Steel Whip" 1954-serial (Price); "The Outlaw Stallion" 1954 (Trimble); "A Lawless Street" 1955; "Wyoming Renegades" 1955 (Black Jack Ketchum); "Fury at Gunsight Pass" 1956 (Hammond); "Giant" 1956 (Harper); "The White Squaw" 1956 (Joe Hide). ¶TV: *Wild Bill Hickok*—"A Joke on Sir Antony" 4-1-52, "Grandpa and Genie" 5-20-52, "The Right of Way" 8-5-52, "Spurs for Johnny" 5-26-53; *Fury*—"Stolen Fury" 1-28-56 (Deputy Sheriff); *Zane Grey Theater*—"The Lariat" 11-2-56 (Charlie); *Maverick*—"The Thirty-Ninth Star" 11-16-58 (Stagecoach Driver); *Tales of the Texas Rangers*—"The Fifth Plague" 12-19-58 (Policeman); *Gunsmoke*—"Wind" 3-21-59 (Norman); *Wanted—Dead or Alive*—"No Trail Back" 11-28-59; *Rawhide*—"Incident of the Last Chance" 6-10-60, "The Sendoff" 10-6-61, "Abilene" 5-18-62, "Incident of the White Eyes" 5-3-63 (Indian).

Teal, Ray (1902-4/2/76). Films: "Zorro Rides Again" 1937-serial (Pete); "Western Jamboree" 1938 (McCall); "Adventures of Red Ryder" 1940-serial (Shark); "Cherokee Strip" 1940 (Smokey Morrell); "Northwest Passage" 1940 (Bradley McNeill); "Pony Post" 1940 (Claud Richards); "Prairie Schooners" 1940 (Wolf Tanner); "The Trail Blazers" 1940; "Trail of the Vigilantes" 1940 (Deputy Sheriff); "Viva Cisco Kid" 1940 (Josh); "Honky Tonk" 1941 (Poker Player); "Outlaws of the Panhandle" 1941 (Walt Burnett); "They Died with Their Boots On" 1941 (Barfly); "Wild Bill Hickok Rides" 1942 (Jack Henley); "Apache Trail" 1943 (Ed Cotton); "Gentle Annie" 1944 (Expressman); "Along Came Jones" 1945 (Kriendler); "Canyon Passage" 1946 (Neil Howlson); "The Harvey Girls" 1946 (Conductor); "Cheyenne" 1947 (Gambler); "Desert Fury" 1947 (Bus Driver); "The Fabulous Texan" 1947; "The Michigan Kid" 1947 (Sergeant); "Northwest Outpost" 1947 (Wounded Trapper); "Pursued" 1947 (Army Captain); "Ramrod" 1947 (Burma); "The Sea of Grass" 1947 (Cattleman); "Unconquered" 1947 (Soldier at Gilded Beaver); "Fury at Furnace Creek" 1948 (Sergeant); "Whispering Smith" 1948; "Streets of Laredo" 1949 (Cantrel); "Ambush" 1950 (Capt. J.R. Wolverson); "Davy Crockett, Indian Scout" 1950 (Capt. McHale); "The Kid from Texas" 1950 (Sheriff Rand); "Winchester '73" 1950 (Marshal Noonan); "Distant Drums" 1951 (Pvt. Mohair); "Along the Great Divide" 1951 (Lou Gray);

"Fort Worth" 1951 (Gabe Clevenger); "The Redhead and the Cowboy" 1951 (Brock); "The Secret of Convict Lake" 1951 (Sheriff); "Cattle Town" 1952 (Jud Hastings); "Flaming Feather" 1952; "Hangman's Knot" 1952 (Quincey); "The Lion and the Horse" 1952 (Dave Tracy); "Montana Belle" 1952 (Emmett Dalton); "The Wild North" 1952 (Ruger); "Ambush at Tomahawk Gap" 1953 (Doc); "The Command" 1953 (Dr. Trent); "Apache Ambush" 1955 (Sgt. O'Roarke); "The Indian Fighter" 1955 (Morgan); "The Man from Bitter Ridge" 1955 (Shep Bacom); "Rage at Dawn" 1955 (Constable Brant); "Run for Cover" 1955 (Sheriff); "The Burning Hills" 1956 (Joe Sutton); "Decision at Sundown" 1957 (Morley Chase); "The Guns of Fort Petticoat" 1957 (Salt Pork); "The Oklahoman" 1957 (Jason, the Stableman); "The Phantom Stagecoach" 1957 (Sheriff Ned Riorden); "The Tall Stranger" 1957 (Cap); "Utah Blaine" 1957 (Russ Nevers); "Gunman's Walk" 1958 (Jensen Steverts); "Saddle the Wind" 1958 (Brick Larson); "One-Eyed Jacks" 1961 (Bartender); "Posse from Hell" 1961 (Larson); "Cattle King" 1963 (Ed Winters); "Taggart" 1964 (Ralph Taggart); "Chisum" 1970 (Justice Wilson); "The Hanged Man" TVM-1974 (Judge Bayne). ¶TV: *The Lone Ranger*—"Never Say Die" 4-6-50, "Ex-Marshal" 9-16-54, "The TooPerfect Signature" 1-31-55; *Cheyenne*—"Julesburg" 10-11-55 (McCanles), "The Black Hawk War" 1-24-56 (Major Heffler), "Counterfeit Gun" 10-10-60 (Sheriff), "Showdown at Oxbend" 12-17-62 (Sheriff Ben Jethro); *Frontier*—"Cattle Drive to Casper" 11-27-55; *Broken Arrow*—"Hermano" 11-20-56 (Col. McBride), "The Bounty Hunters" 11-26-57 (Fenster); *Circus Boy*—"The Remarkable Ricardo" 1-20-57 (Sheriff Green); *Tales of Wells Fargo*—"Sam Bass" 6-10-57 (Capt. McNelly); *Wagon Train*—"The Les Rand Story" 10-16-57, "The Jess MacAbbee Story" 11-25-59 (Jed Culpepper); *Maverick*—"Stage West" 10-27-57 (Mart Fallon), "The Day They Hanged Bret Maverick" 9-21-58 (Sheriff Chick Tucker), "Two Beggars on Horseback" 1-18-59 (Stryker), "A Tale of Three Cities" 10-18-59 (Sheriff Murray), "Mr. Muldoon's Partner" 4-15-62 (Sheriff Bundy); *Trackdown*—"Look for the Woman" 12-6-57 (Sheriff Michael), "Three Legged Fox" 12-5-58 (Ward); *Zorro*—"Slaves of the Eagle" 1-23-58; *The Restless Gun*—"Hang and Be Damned" 1-27-58 (Sheriff), "The Hand Is Quicker"

3-17-58 (Sheriff Lander); *Gunsmoke*—"Carmen" 5-24-58 (Sgt. Jones); *The Californians*—"Hangtown" 11-18-58 (Yotts Meyer); *Wanted—Dead or Alive*—"Die by the Gun" 12-6-58 (Nebro); *The Texan*—"No Tears for the Dead" 12-8-58 (Dave Travers); *Bronco*—"Riding Solo" 2-10-59 (Tom Biggert), "The Devil's Spawn" 12-1-59 (Jeb Donner); *Laramie*—"Glory Road" 9-22-59; *Bat Masterson*—"No Funeral for Thorn" 10-22-59 (Vergil Gardiner), "Law of the Land" 10-6-60 (H.G. Cogswell); *The Rifleman*—"Eddie's Daughter" 11-3-59 (Albie Finley); *The Alaskans*—"The Abominable Snowman" 12-13-59 (Ezra Granit); *Walt Disney Presents*—"Elfego Baca: Friendly Enemies at Law" 3-18-60 (Frank Oxford); *Colt .45*—"The Trespasser" 6-21-60 (Mike O'Tara); *Klondike*—"Klondike Fever" 10-10-60 (Augie Teejen); *Riverboat*—"Zigzag" 12-26-60 (Sheriff Clay); *Lawman*—"The Trial" 5-7-61 (Judge Whitehall); *Bonanza*—Regular 1961-71 (Sheriff Roy Coffee); *Rawhide*—"Judgment at Hondo Seco" 10-20-61 (Hennegan); *Wide Country*—"Straightjacket for an Indian" 10-25-62 (Harry Kemper), "A Devil in the Chute" 11-8-62 (Frank Higgins), "Speckle Bird" 1-31-63 (Charlie); *Empire*—"The Tall Shadow" 11-20-62 (Mr. Todd); *Walt Disney Presents*—"Gallegher" 1965-67 (Sheriff Snead); *The Monroes*—"Silent Night, Deathly Night" 11-23-66 (Laif Goff); *World of Disney*—"Hacksaw" 9-26-71 & 10-3-71 (Rancher).

Tearle, Conway (1878-10/1/38). Films: "The Great Divide" 1925 (Stephen Ghent); "Smoke Bellew" 1929 (Kid "Smoke" Bellew); "The Judgement Book" 1935 (Steve Harper); "Trails End" 1935 (Jim "Trigger" Malloy); "Desert Guns" 1936 (Kirk Allenby/Bob Enright); "Senor Jim" 1936 (Senor Jim Stafford).

Tedd, Steven. Films: "Beast" 1970-Ital.; "Requiem for a Bounty Hunter" 1970-Ital.; "Reverend Colt" 1970-Ital./Span.; "Death Played the Flute" 1972-Ital./Span.

Tedrow, Irene (1907-3/10/95). Films: "Santa Fe Passage" 1955 (Ptewaquin); "Saddle the Wind" 1958; "A Thunder of Drums" 1961 (Mrs. Scarborough); "A Cry in the Wilderness" TVM-1974 (Old Woman). ¶TV: *The Restless Gun*—"Friend in Need" 1-13-58; *Jefferson Drum*—"Showdown" 9-26-58 (Mary Easton); *Northwest Passage*—"The Bound Women" 10-12-58 (Cora Klagg); *Maverick*—"Gun-Shy" 1-11-59 (Mrs. Adams), "Cruise of the

Cynthia B" 1-10-60 (Miss Tutwiler; *The Texan*—"The Peddler" 1-26-59, 9-12-60 (Mrs. Petrie); *Rawhide*—"Incident Below the Brazos" 5-15-59 (Minnie Lou); *Bonanza*—"The Outcast" 1-9-60, "Blessed Are They" 4-22-62 (Mrs. Mahan), "Different Pines, Same Wind" 9-25-68 (Carrie), "Abner Willoughby's Return" 12-21-69 (Minnie), "The Sound of Loneliness" 12-5-72 (Miss Gaines); *The Tall Man*—"Three for All" 3-10-62 (Maw Killgore); *Wagon Train*—"The Joshua Gilliam Story" 3-30-60 (Freda); *Death Valley Days*—"Magic Locket" 5-16-65 (Head Librarian), "Lady of the Plains" 7-23-66 (Mrs. Hemingway), "Pioneer Pluck" 4-4-70 (Granny Colvin); *The Virginian*—"The Mark of a Man" 4-20-66 (Gran McDevitt); *Dundee and the Culhane*—10-25-67 (Widow Hughes); *Kung Fu*—"The Centoph" 4-4-74 & 4-11-74 (Mrs. Stekel); *The Cowboys*—"Requiem for a Lost Son" 5-8-74 (Harriet Graff); *Centennial*—Regular 1978-79 (Mother Zendt).

Telaak, Bill (1898-12/21/63). Films: "Bells of Capistrano" 1942.

Tell, Olive (1896-6/6/51). Films: "Woman Hungry" 1931 (Betty Temple).

Tellegen, Lou (1881-11/1/34). Films: "The Long Trail" 1917 (Andre Dubois); "Three Bad Men" 1926 (Layne Hunter).

Teller, Francis Kee. Films: "Navajo" 1952 (Son of the Hunter).

Tello, Alfonso Sanchez (-4/18/79). Films: "Bandido" 1956 (G. Brucero).

Temoff, Serge. Films: "Tyrant of Red Gulch" 1928 (Boris Kosloff).

Temple, Brooks. Films: "Riders of the Dawn" 1945; "Six Gun Man" 1946 (Ed Slater).

Temple, Mary Jane. Films: "The Cowboy Kid" 1928 (Janet Grover).

Temple, Shirley (1929-). Films: "To the Last Man" 1933 (Mary Standing); "Susannah of the Mounties" 1939 (Susannah Sheldon); "Fort Apache" 1948 (Philadelphia Thursday).

Tenbrook, Harry (1887-9/14/60). Films: "A Frontier Providence" 1913; "Thieves' Gold" 1918 (Col. Betoski); "The Fightin' Terror" 1920; "Kindled Courage" 1923 (Sid Garrett); "The Measure of a Man" 1924 (Charley, the Bartender); "The Burning Trail" 1925 (Reginald Cholmondeley); "The Silent Guardian" 1926 (Jeb Stevens); "The Outlaw Dog" 1927 (Mike); "Thunderbolt's Tracks" 1927 (Cpl. Biff Flanagan)

"Come on, Danger!" 1932 (Bill); "Heroes of the West" 1932-serial (Butch Gole); "The Fourth Horseman" 1933; "Terror Trail" 1933 (Deputy Sheriff); "The Roaring West" 1935-serial; "Roarin' Lead" 1936; "Hit the Saddle" 1937 (Joe Harvey); "Rawhide" 1938 (Rusty); "Chip of the Flying U" 1939; "Destry Rides Again" 1939 (Stage Driver); "Oklahoma Frontier" 1939 (Grimes); "Stagecoach" 1939 (Telegraph Operator); "Ragtime Cowboy Joe" 1940 (Del Porter); "White Eagle" 1941-serial; "Fighting Bill Fargo" 1942; "Stagecoach Buckaroo" 1942; "Fort Apache" 1948 (Courier); "Santa Fe" 1951.

Ten Eyck, Lillian (1886-12/6/66). Films: "Defying the Law" 1935 (Mother Lane).

Tennant, Barbara. Films: "The Trail of the Hanging Rock" 1913; "The Devil Fox of the North" 1914; "The First Nugget" 1914; "M'Liss" 1915 (M'Liss); "Shadows of Conscience" 1921 (Alice); "Bulldog Courage" 1922 (Mary Allen); "The Love Gambler" 1922 (Kate); "The Old Fool" 1923 (Dora Steele).

Tennant, Bill. TV: *Tate*—"Stopover" 6-15-60 (Will Smith); *The Outlaws*—"The Daltons Must Die" 1-26-61 & 2-2-61 (Emmett Dalton); *Laramie*—"Strange Company" 6-6-61 (Bob Wilson).

Tennant, Dorothy (1865-7/3/42). Films: "The Rancher's Lottery" 1912; "Wells Fargo" 1937 (Mrs. Ward).

Tenney, Jon. Films: "Tombstone" 1993 (Behan).

Tenorio, Jr., John. TV: *Nakia*—Regular 1974 (Half Cub).

Ter, Angel. Films: "The Last Tomahawk" 1965-Ger./Ital./Span.; "Few Dollars for Django" 1966-Ital./Span.; "Sheriff Won't Shoot" 1967-Ital./Fr./Brit.

Terhune, Bob. Films: "Rio Bravo" 1959 (Charlie, the Bartender); "Smoky" 1966 (Cowboy); "Welcome to Hard Times" 1967 (1st Drinker); "The Gambler, Part II—The Adventure Continues" TVM-1983 (Thayer); "Silverado" 1985 (Guard Cowboy); "Grim Prairie Tales" 1990 (Stunts). TV: *The Texan*—"Friend of the Family" 1-4-60 (Wally); *Daniel Boone*—"The Deserter" 1-20-66 (Ab Varney), "The High Cumberland" 4-14-66 & 4-21-66 (Big John).

Terhune, Max (1891-6/5/73). Films: "Ride, Ranger, Ride" 1936 (Rufe); "Roarin' Lead" 1936 (Lullaby Joslin); "The Big Show" 1937 (Max);

"Boots and Saddles" 1937; "Come on Cowboys" 1937 (Lullaby Joslin); "Ghost Town Gold" 1937 (Lullaby Joslin); "Gunsmoke Ranch" 1937 (Lullaby Joslin); "Heart of the Rockies" 1937 (Lullaby Joslin); "Hit the Saddle" 1937 (Lullaby Joslin); "Range Defenders" 1937 (Lullaby Joslin); "Riders of the Whistling Skull" 1937 (Lullaby Joslin); "The Trigger Trio" 1937 (Lullaby Joslin); "Wild Horse Rodeo" 1937 (Lullaby Joslin); "Call the Mesquiteers" 1938 (Lullaby Joslin); "Heroes of the Hills" 1938 (Lullaby Joslin); "Outlaws of Sonora" 1938 (Lullaby Joslin); "Overland Stage Raiders" 1938 (Lullaby Joslin); "Pals of the Saddle" 1938 (Lullaby Joslin); "The Purple Vigilantes" 1938 (Lullaby Joslin); "Red River Range" 1938 (Lullaby Joslin); "Riders of the Black Hills" 1938 (Lullaby Joslin); "Santa Fe Stampede" 1938 (Lullaby Joslin); "Man of Conquest" 1939 (Deaf Smith); "The Night Riders" 1939 (Lullaby Joslin); "Three Texas Steers" 1939 (Lullaby Joslin); "The Range Busters" 1940 (Alibi); "Trailing Double Trouble" 1940 (Alibi); "West of Pinto Basin" 1940 (Alibi); "Fugitive Valley" 1941 (Alibi); "The Kid's Last Ride" 1941 (Alibi); "Saddle Mountain Roundup" 1941 (Alibi); "Tonto Basin Outlaws" 1941 (Alibi); "Trail of the Silver Spurs" 1941 (Alibi); "Tumbledown Ranch in Arizona" 1941 (Alibi); "Underground Rustlers" 1941 (Alibi); "Wrangler's Roost" 1941 (Alibi Joslin); "Arizona Stagecoach" 1942 (Alibi); "Boot Hill Bandits" 1942 (Alibi); "Rock River Renegades" 1942 (Lullaby Joslin); "Texas to Bataan" 1942 (Alibi); "Texas Trouble Shooters" 1942 (Alibi); "Thunder River Feud" 1942 (Alibi); "Trail Riders" 1942 (Alibi); "Black Market Rustlers" 1943 (Alibi); "Bullets and Saddles" 1943 (Alibi); "Cowboy Commandos" 1943 (Alibi); "The Haunted Ranch" 1943; "Land of Hunted Men" 1943; "Two Fisted Justice" 1943 (Alibi); "Cowboy Canteen" 1944; "Sheriff of Sundown" 1944 (Third Grade Simms); "Swing, Cowboy, Swing" 1944; "Along the Oregon Trail" 1947 (Max Terhune); "White Stallion" 1947 (Max Terhune); "Gunning for Justice" 1948; "The Sheriff of Medicine Bow" 1948; "Hidden Danger" 1949 (Alibi); "Law of the West" 1949 (Alibi); "Range Justice" 1949 (Alibi); "Square Dance Jubilee" 1949 (Sheriff); "Trail's End" 1949 (Alibi); "West of El Dorado" 1949 (Alibi); "Western Renegades" 1949 (Alibi); "Rawhide" 1951 (Miner); "Giant" 1956 (Dr. Walker). TV: *The Lone Ranger*—"Danger Ahead" 10-12-50;

Annie Oakley—"Sharpshooting Annie" 6-12-54.

Terlesky, John T. Films: "Longarm" TVM-1988 (Custis Long). TV: *Paradise*—Regular 1990-91 (Dakota).

Terrell, Kenneth (1904-3/8/66). Films: "Zorro's Fighting Legion" 1939-serial (Martin); "Adventures of Red Ryder" 1940-serial (Bart Wade); "Covered Wagon Days" 1940; "King of the Royal Mounted" 1940-serial (Al); "Oklahoma Renegades" 1940; "King of the Texas Rangers" 1941-serial (Oil Field Heavy); "Cowboy Serenade" 1942; "King of the Mounties" 1942-serial (Al); "Outlaws of Pine Ridge" 1942; "Raiders of the Range" 1942; "Bordertown Gunfighters" 1943; "Daredevils of the West" 1943-serial (Bartender); "The Man from the Rio Grande" 1943; "Code of the Prairie" 1944 (Outlaw in Brawl); "Girl Rush" 1944; "Marshal of Reno" 1944; "Song of the Range" 1944; "Zorro's Black Whip" 1944-serial (Mike/Mine Heavy #1); "In Old New Mexico" 1945 (Cliff); "Marshal of Laredo" 1945; "King of the Forest Rangers" 1946-serial (Naylor); "Jesse James Rides Again" 1947-serial (Price); "Robin Hood of Texas" 1947; "Son of Zorro" 1947-serial (George Thomas); "The Adventures of Frank and Jesse James" 1948-serial (Zeb); "The Bold Frontiersman" 1948 (Judd); "Dangers of the Canadian Mounted" 1948-serial (Art/Curry/Fenton/Grady/Guard/Masters/Tom); "The Gay Ranchero" 1948 (Roberts); "Grand Canyon Trail" 1948 (Make Delsing); "Ghost of Zorro" 1949-serial (Morley); "The James Brothers of Missouri" 1950-serial (Stark/Trent); "Pals of the Golden West" 1951 (Tony); "Drums Across the River" 1954 (Red Knife); "The Proud Ones" 1956 (the Weasel). TV: *The Cisco Kid*—"Gold Strike" 3-14-53, "The Hospital" 5-16-53, "Cisco and the Giant" 10-31-53; *Wagon Train*—"The Don Alvarado Story" 6-21-61 (Hayes).

Terrell, Steven. Films: "The Naked Hills" 1956 (Billy as a Young Man). TV: *Gunsmoke*—"Who Lives by the Sword" 5-18-57 (Billy Baxter), "Jailbait Janet" 2-27-60 (Jerry); *Have Gun Will Travel*—"A Matter of Ethics" 10-12-57 (Deputy); *Zane Grey Theater*—"The Open Cell" 11-22-57 (Jess Bolin); *Trackdown*—"The Judge" 3-14-58 (Malcolm Henry); *Tales of Wells Fargo*—"The Break" 5-19-58 (Bud Sawyer), "Reward for Gaine" 1-20-62 (Tribly); *Tombstone Territory*—"Thicker Than Water" 9-

10-58; *The Texan*—"The Man with the Solid Gold Star" 10-6-58, "Friend of the Family" 1-4-60 (Evan Randolph), "Town Divided" 3-21-60 (Ken Crowley); *The Restless Gun*—"The Nowhere Kid" 10-20-58 (Johnny Smith); *Man Without a Gun*—"Wire's End" 12-20-58 (Tod); *Bat Masterson*—"Dead Men Don't Pay Debts" 11-19-59 (Hal Clements); *Bonanza*—"The Last Hunt" 12-19-59 (Jason Kyle), "The Spitfire" 1-14-61 (Bud Harvey); *Maverick*—"Maverick and Juliet" 1-17-60 (Sonny Montgomery); *Death Valley Days*—"The Wind at Your Back" 12-7-60 (Johnny); *Stagecoach West*—"A Place of Still Waters" 4-11-61 (Julian Tibbs).

Terry, Al (1893-7/15/67). Films: "Man from Music Mountain" 1938 (Buddy); "Deadline" 1948; "Fighting Mustang" 1948; "Sunset Carson Rides Again" 1948; "Battling Marshal" 1950; "Bullwhip" 1958 (Lem).

Terry, Alice (1899-12/22/87). Films: "The Great Divide" 1925 (Ruth Jordan).

Terry, Bob. Films: "Renfrew of the Royal Mounted" 1937 (Duke); "Sandflow" 1937 (Lane Hallett); "Brothers of the West" 1938 (Ed Wade); "California Frontier" 1938; "Lightning Carson Rides Again" 1938 (Paul Smith); "Renfrew on the Great White Trail" 1938 (Sgt. Kelly); "Six-Gun Trail" 1938; "Six Shootin' Sheriff" 1938 (Kid); "Songs and Saddles" 1938 (Klinker); "Starlight Over Texas" 1938 (Farrell); "The Stranger from Arizona" 1938 (Talbot); "Where the Buffalo Roam" 1938 (Shifty); "Code of the Cactus" 1939 (Lefty); "Down the Wyoming Trail" 1939 (Blackie); "Flaming Lead" 1939 (Blackie); "Lure of the Wasteland" 1939; "Outlaw's Paradise" 1939 (Steve); "Rollin' Westward" 1939 (Jeff); "Smoky Trails" 1939 (Burke); "Song of the Buckaroo" 1939 (Neal); "Sundown on the Prairie" 1939; "Texas Wildcats" 1939 (Mort Burrows); "Danger Ahead" 1940 (Gimpy); "Lightning Strikes West" 1940 (Tad Grant); "Sky Bandits" 1940 (Hutchins); "Yukon Flight" 1940 (DeLong).

Terry, Don (1902-10/6/88). Films: "Border Romance" 1930 (Bob Hamlin); "Whistlin' Dan" 1932 (Bob); "Overland Mail" 1942-serial (Buckskin Billy Burke); "Valley of the Sun" 1942 (Lieutenant).

Terry, Edwin. Films: "California" 1927 (Brig. Gen. Stephen W. Kearny); "Wolf's Trail" 1927 (Simeon Kraft).

Terry, Ethel Grey (1891-1/6/31).

Films: "The Kick Back" 1922 (Nellie); "Travelin' On" 1922 (Susan Morton); "Wild Bill Hickok" 1923 (Calamity Jane); "Hard-Boiled" 1926 (Mrs. Sarah Morton).

Terry, Philip. Films: "Northwest Mounted Police" 1940 (Constable Judson); "The Parson of Panamint" 1941 (Rev. Phillip Pharo); "Man from God's Country" 1958 (Sheriff); "Money, Women and Guns" 1958 (Damion Bard). ¶TV: *Maverick*—"The Burning Sky" 2-23-58 (Chick Braus); *The Californians*—"Corpus Delicti" 2-3-59 (Mark Brank); *Lawman*—"The Grubstake" 4-16-61 (Clayton Rambeau).

Terry, Richard. *see* Perrin, Jack.

Terry, Ruth. Films: "Call of the Canyon" 1942 (Kit Carson); "Heart of the Golden West" 1942 (Mary Lou Popen); "Hands Across the Border" 1943 (Kim Adams); "Man from Music Mountain" 1943 (Laramie Winters); "Smoky River Serenade" 1947. ¶TV: *Maverick*—"The People's Friend" 2-7-60 (Librarian).

Terry, Sheila (1910-1/18/57). Films: "Haunted Gold" 1932 (Janet Carter); "The Lawless Frontier" 1934 (Ruby); "'Neath the Arizona Skies" 1934 (Clara Moore); "Rocky Rhodes" 1934 (Nan Street).

Terry, Tex (1903-5/18/85). Films: "Covered Wagon Trails" 1940 (Ogden); "Heroes of the Saddle" 1940; "Pioneers of the West" 1940; "Boss of Bullion City" 1941 (Cowboy); "Kansas Cyclone" 1941; "Rawhide Rangers" 1941; "Sunset in Wyoming" 1941; "Outlaws of Pine Ridge" 1942; "The San Antonio Kid" 1944; "Along the Navajo Trail" 1945; "Bandits of the Badlands" 1945; "The Man from Oklahoma" 1945; "Oregon Trail" 1945 (Moyer); "Rough Riders of Cheyenne" 1945; "Sunset in El Dorado" 1945; "Alias Billy the Kid" 1946 (Buckskin); "The El Paso Kid" 1946 (Kramer); "Plainsman and the Lady" 1946; "Red River Renegades" 1946; "Rio Grande Raiders" 1946; "Sioux City Sue" 1946; "Apache Rose" 1947 (Likens); "Jesse James Rides Again" 1947-serial (Blair); "Son of Zorro" 1947-serial (Cowman); "Twilight on the Rio Grande" 1947 (Joe); "Wyoming" 1947 (Morrison); "The Gallant Legion" 1948 (Sgt. Clint Mason); "The Last Bandit" 1949; "Beyond the Purple Hills" 1950; "Surrender" 1950 (Dealer); "Don Daredevil Rides Again" 1951-serial (Townsman #5); "The Old West" 1952; "Pack Train" 1953; "Jubilee Trail" 1954 (Penrose); "Man with the Steel Whip" 1954-serial

(Townsman #1); "The Road to Denver" 1955 (Passenger); "Timberjack" 1955 (Charley); "Toughest Gun in Tombstone" 1958 (Stage Driver); "The Oregon Trail" 1959 (Brizzard). ¶TV: *The Gene Autry Show*—"Sharpshooter" 8-3-54, "Outlaw of Blue Mesa" 9-7-54; *Gunsmoke*—"Robber and Bridegroom" 12-13-58 (Pete); *Have Gun Will Travel*—"Juliet" 1-31-59 (Driver).

Tesler, Jack (1898-9/8/76). TV: *Have Gun Will Travel*—"Bear Bait" 5-13-61.

Tessier, Robert (1934-10/11/90). Films: "Cry Blood, Apache" 1970 (Two Card); "Breakheart Pass" 1976 (Sepp Calhoun); "Last of the Mohicans" TVM-1977 (Magua); "The Villain" 1979 (Mashing Finger). ¶TV: *Kung Fu*—"The Demon God" 12-13-74 (Aztec Warrior); *Centennial*—Regular 1978-79 (Rude Water).

Testi, Fabio (1942-). Films: "Dead Men Ride" 1970-Ital./Span. (Roy Greenford); "One Damned Day at Dawn … Django Meets Sartana" 1971-Ital. (Jack Ronson/Sartana); "Blood River" 1974-Ital.; "Four Horsemen of the Apocalpyse" 1975-Ital. (Preston); "Red Coat" 1975-Ital.; "China 9, Liberty 37" 1978-Ital./Span./U.S. (Shaw).

Teters, Verne. Films: "Badman's Gold" 1951 (Sheriff); "Cattle Queen" 1951 (Trig); "Son of the Renegade" 1953 (Sheriff Masters).

Tetley, Walter (1915-9/4/75). Films: "Prairie Moon" 1938 (Clarence "Nails" Barton); "Under Texas Skies" 1940 (Theodore).

Tetrick, Robert. Films: "Noose for a Gunman" 1960 (Anders). ¶TV: *Have Gun Will Travel*—"The Gentleman" 9-27-58 (the Wrangler); *Trackdown*—"Tenner Smith" 10-24-58 (Michel Doolin); *Rough Riders*—"Gunpoint Persuasion" 4-30-59 (Deke Masters); *Rawhide*—"Incident at the Buffalo Smokehouse" 10-30-59; *Bonanza*—"Feet of Clay" 4-16-60 (Pike).

Tetzel, Joan (1921-10/31/77). Films: "Duel in the Sun" 1946 (Helen Langford). ¶TV: *Gunsmoke*—"Jealousy" 7-6-57 (Tilda); *Zane Grey Theater*—"Bury Me Dead" 12-11-58 (Kathy Lorimer); *The Outlaws*—"The Sooner" 4-27-61 (Jane).

Teuber, Andreas (1941-). TV: *The Big Valley*—"The Buffalo Man" 12-25-67 (Jaimy).

Texas Playboys, Bob Wills and His (Bob Wills, Johnny Lee Wills, Leon McAuliffe, Sonny Lansford, Wayne Johnson & Eldon Shamblin).

Texeira, Virgilio. Films: "Return of the Seven" 1966-Span. (Luis).

Thane, Dirk. Films: "Senor Jim" 1936 (Roxy Stone); "Zorro Rides Again" 1937-serial (John); "Overland Stage Raiders" 1938; "Trigger Pals" 1939 (Art); "Riders on Black Mountain" 1940 (Jim); "West of Pinto Basin" 1940 (Hank); "Two-Gun Sheriff" 1941 (Duke); "Texas Justice" 1942.

Thatcher, Evelyn "Eva" (1862-9/28/42). Films: "Not Guilty for Runnin'" 1924 (Martha Coberly); "Payable on Demand" 1924 (Mrs. Martin Selby); "Flash O'Lightning" 1925 (Aunt M'liss); "The Knockout Kid" 1925 (Widow Jenkins); "Ranchers and Rascals" 1925 (Mrs. Williams); "The Trouble Buster" 1925 (Mrs. Williams); "Blind Trail" 1926 (the Cook); "The Outlaw Express" 1926 (Ma Hemstetter); "Blazing Days" 1927 (Ma Bascomb).

Thatcher, Torin (1905-3/4/81). Films: "The Canadians" 1961-Brit. (Master Sgt. McGregor). ¶TV: *Zane Grey Theater*—"Welcome Home a Stranger" 1-15-59 (Ab Richards); *Wagon Train*—"The Steve Campden Story" 5-13-59 (Steve Camden); *Bonanza*—"Elizabeth, My Love" 5-27-61 (Captain Stoddard); *Tales of Wells Fargo*—"Casket 7.3" 9-30-61 (Grey Man); *Destry*—"One Hundred Bibles" 5-8-64 (James Fairhaven); *Gunsmoke*—"Fandango" 2-11-67 (John Tyson); *Daniel Boone*—"Take the Southbound Stage" 4-6-67 (President John Adams), "To Slay a Giant" 1-9-69 (Cyrus/Enoch Blake); *Cowboy in Africa*—"What's an Elephant Mother to Do?" 10-2-67 (Hawkins); *The Guns of Will Sonnett*—"The Sins of the Father" 2-23-68 (Simeon).

Thaxter, Phyllis (1921-). Films: "The Sea of Grass" 1947 (Sarah Beth Brewton); "Blood on the Moon" 1948 (Carol Lufton); "Fort Worth" 1951 (Flora Talbot); "Springfield Rifle" 1952 (Erin Kearney). ¶TV: *Wagon Train*—"The Vivian Carter Story" 3-11-59 (Vivian Carter), "The Christine Elliot Story" 3-23-60 (Christine Elliott); *The Outlaws*—"The Quiet Killer" 12-29-60 (Mae); *Rawhide*—"The Blue Sky" 12-8-61 (Pauline Wakefield); *Lancer*—"The Prodigal" 11-12-68 (Marcy Dane); *Bonanza*—"The Clarion" 2-9-69 (Ruth Manning).

Thayer, Brynn. Films: "The Tracker" TVM-1988 (Lottie).

Thayer, Julia. *see* Carmen, Jean.

Thayer, Lorna (1919-). Films: "The Lusty Men" 1952 (Grace Burgess); "Texas City" 1952 (Aunt Harriet); "Mrs. Sundance" TVM-1974 (Fanny Porter); "Smoke in the Wind" 1975 (Ma Mondier). ¶TV: *The Adventures of Rin Tin Tin*—"Rusty Goes to Town" 11-25-55 (Belle); *Jim Bowie*—"The Beggar of New Orleans" 1-11-57 (Celeste Durand), "Bowie's Baby" 5-2-58 (Christine); *Circus Boy*—"Uncle Cyrus" 11-28-57 (Zelda); *The Californians*—"The Foundling" 4-29-58 (Millicent); *Wyatt Earp*—"Dig a Grave for Ben Thompson" 5-20-58 (Girl); *Black Saddle*—"Client: Reynolds" 5-23-59; *Have Gun Will Travel*—"The Gold Toad" 11-21-59 (Doris Golemon), "The Prophet" 1-2-60 (Serafina), "Love's Young Dream" 9-17-60 (Augusta), "Pandora's Box" 5-19-62 (Hanna); *The Tall Man*—5-26-62 (Woman); *Bonanza*—"Peace Officer" 2-6-66 (Mrs. Roberts).

Thayer, Otis. Films: "Western Hearts" 1911; "Why the Sheriff Is a Bachelor" 1911; "Told in the Rockies" 1915; "The Desert Scorpion" 1920 (the Sheriff).

Thayler, Carl. Films: "Man from Del Rio" 1956 (the Kid); "The True Story of Jesse James" 1957 (Robby). ¶TV: *The Texan*—"Law of the Gun" 9-29-58 (Gunslinger).

Theby, Rosemary. Films: "Rio Grande" 1920 (Maria Inez); "Across the Divide" 1921 (Rosa); "Fightin' Mad" 1921 (Nita de Garma); "The Last Trail" 1921 (Chiquita); "I Am the Law" 1922 (Mrs. Georges Mardeaux); "The Girl of the Golden West" 1923 (Nina Micheltorena).

Theis, Manuela (1943-). TV: *Death Valley Days*—"The Other Cheek" 11-16-68 (Ann Elsworth).

Theiss, Ursula. Films: "The Americano" 1955 (Marianna Figuerido); "Bandido" 1956 (Lisa).

Thinnes, Roy (1938-). Films: "Black Noon" TVM-1971 (Rev. John Keyes); "Charley One-Eye" 1973-Brit. (Indian). ¶TV: *Gunsmoke*—"False Front" 12-22-62 (Harry), "Jeb" 5-25-63 (Ab Singleton).

Thomas, B.J. (1942-). Films: "Jory" 1972 (Jocko).

Thomas, Buckwheat (1931-10/10/80). Films: "Colorado Pioneers" 1945.

Thomas, Charles. Films: "The Lone Ranger" 1938-serial (Blake); "Adventures of Red Ryder" 1940-serial (Lon Walker); "King of the Royal Mounted" 1940-serial (Bayliss); "The Tulsa Kid" 1940; "King of the Texas Rangers" 1941-serial (Rancho Heavy #2); "Two-Gun Sheriff" 1941 (Tex).

Thomas, Danny (1914-2/6/91). TV: *Zane Grey Theater*—"A Thread of Respect" 2-12-59 (Gino Pelleti), "Honor Bright" 2-2-61 (Ed Dubro).

Thomas, Evan. Films: "Northwest Mounted Police" 1940 (Capt. Gower); "The Royal Mounted Patrol" 1941 (Commander).

Thomas, Frank M. (1889-11/25/89). Films: "The Last Outlaw" 1936 (Dr. Mason); "The Outcasts of Poker Flat" 1937 (Bedford); "Renegade Ranger" 1938 (Carsen); "Saga of Death Valley" 1939 (Ed Tasker); "Brigham Young—Frontiersman" 1940 (Hubert Crum); "Geronimo" 1940 (Politician); "The Man from Dakota" 1940 (Surgeon); "Shooting High" 1940 (Calvin Pritchard); "Arkansas Judge" 1941 (August Huston); "Sierra Sue" 1941 (Stacy Bromfield); "Wyoming Wildcat" 1941; "The Great Man's Lady" 1942 (Senator Knobbs); "Sunset on the Desert" 1942 (Judge Kirby); "Sunset Serenade" 1942 (Clifford Sheldon); "Apache Trail" 1943 (Major Lowden).

Thomas, Gretchen (1897-11/1/64). TV: *The Californians*—"The First Gold Brick" 1-6-59 (Kitty).

Thomas, Jameson (1889-1/10/39). Films: "Death Goes North" 1939 (Mr. Barlow).

Thomas, Lonnie. Films: "Return of the Texan" 1952 (Yo-Yo). ¶TV: *Wild Bill Hickok*—"Clem's Reformation" 7-7-53; *My Friend Flicka*—"The Settler" 1-27-56 (Billy Hunter).

Thomas, Lyn. Films: "Covered Wagon Raid" 1950 (Gail Warren); "The Missourians" 1950 (Peg); "Red River Shore" 1953 (Peggy Taylor); "Frontier Gun" 1958 (Kate Durand); "Noose for a Gunman" 1960 (Della Haines). ¶TV: *The Cisco Kid*—"Phony Heiress" 7-21-51, "Ghost Story" 9-1-51, "Water Well Oil" 10-13-51; *Death Valley Days*—"Which Side of the Fence?" 9-23-53, "The Sinbuster" 6-2-56; *Sergeant Preston of the Yukon*—"One Bear Too Many" 12-15-55, "Trapped" 2-2-56 (Eileen Mabry), "Skagway Secret" 2-16-56 (Madge Dayton); *Colt .45*—"The Gypsies" 12-27-57 (Nan Wilson); *Jefferson Drum*—"Law and Order" 5-9-58 (Nora); *26 Men*—"Tumbleweed Ranger" 6-2-59; *Man from Blackhawk*—"Gold Is Where You Find It" 6-24-60 (Bonnie Owen); *Wyatt Earp*—"Wyatt Takes the Primrose Path" 3-28-61 (Lola).

Thomas, Marlo (1937-). TV: *Zane Grey Theater*—"Honor Bright" 2-2-61 (Laurie Dubro); *Bonanza*—

"Pink Cloud Comes from Old Cathay" 4-12-64 (Tai Li).

Thomas, Melody (1956-). Films: "The Shootist" 1976 (Girl on Streetcar).

Thomas, Nona. Films: "The Darkening Trail" 1915 (Ruth Welles); "The Apostle of Vengeance" 1916 (Mary McCoy).

Thomas, Olive (188-9/10/20). Films: "Broadway, Arizona" 1917 (Fritzi Carlyle).

Thomas, Ralph. TV: *Johnny Ringo*—"Single Debt" 5-12-60 (Webb Scanlon); *Rawhide*—"Incident at Dragoon Crossing" 10-21-60 (Billy Bates); *Laramie*—"The Violent Ones" 3-5-63.

Thomas, Richard (1951-). TV: *Bonanza*—"The Weary Willies" 9-27-70 (Billy).

Thomas, Robert C. Films: "Ride, Ranger, Ride" 1936; "Ghost Town Gold" 1937 (Champ Thunderbolt O'Brien); "Saga of Death Valley" 1939.

Thomas, Scott (1940-). Films: "Guns of the Magnificent Seven" 1969 (P.J.). ¶TV: *Bonanza*—"Five Candles" 3-2-69 (Jonathan Pike); *The New Land*—Regular 1974 (Christian Larsen).

Thomas, Sharon. Films: "Young Guns" 1988 (Susan McSween).

Thomas, W.L. Films: "Clancy of the Mounted" 1933-serial (Black MacDougal).

Thomerson, Tim. Films: "The Cisco Kid" CTVM-1994 (Lundquist). ¶TV: *Gun Shy*—Regular 1983 (Theodore); *Legend*—Pilot 4-18-95 (John Wesley Coe).

Thompson, Bennett. Films: "When the Legends Die" 1972 (Albert Left Hand).

Thompson, Blackie (1877-5/17/36). Films: "Sky High Coral" 1926 (Gregg); "The Westerner" 1934 (Cowboy).

Thompson, Bob. Films: "Closin' In" 1918 (Sgt. Barry); "The Law's Outlaw" 1918 (Sancho Ramirez).

Thompson, Carlos (1916-10/10/90). Films: "The Last Rebel" 1961-Mex. (Joaquin Murrieta).

Thompson, Charles P. TV: *Gunsmoke*—"Sky" 2-14-59 (Clabe), "Johnny Cross" 12-23-68 (Mr. Cross); *Wanted—Dead or Alive*—"The Cure" 9-28-60; *Branded*—"The Vindicator" 1-31-65 (Telegrapher); *Bonanza*—"Emily" 3-23-69 (Storekeeper), "Speak No Evil" 4-20-69 (Claude), "The Gold Mine" 3-8-70 (Clerk).

Thompson, Dee J. Films: "Trooper Hook" 1957 (Tess). ¶TV: *Gunsmoke*—"The Big Broad" 4-28-56 (Lena Wave), "Eliab's Aim" 2-27-65 (Pearl); *Rawhide*—"Incident in No Man's Land" 6-12-59; *The Rifleman*—"Woman from Hog Ridge" 10-4-60 (Ma Boyle); *Stoney Burke*—"Child of Luxury" 10-15-62 (Lorraine); *The Big Valley*—"Down Shadow Street" 1-23-67 (Miss Alice).

Thompson, Duane (1908-8/15/70). Films: "The Desert Pirate" 1927 (Ann Farnham); "One Hour of Love" 1927 (Neely); "Beauty and Bullets" 1928 Mary Crawford); "The Fightin' Redhead" 1928 (Jane Anderson); "The Flying Buckaroo" 1928 (Sally Brown); "Phantom of the Range" 1928 (Patsy O'Brien); "Wizard of the Saddle" 1928 (Jenny Adams); "Born to the Saddle" 1929 (Helen Pearson).

Thompson, Elizabeth (1944-). Films: "The Magnificent Seven Ride" 1972 (Skinner's Woman). ¶TV: *Wide Country*—"Memory of a Filly" 1-3-63 (Nurse); *Bonanza*—"The Trouble with Amy" 1-25-70 (Sally).

Thompson, Hal (1894-3/3/66). Films: "Comin an' Going" 1926 (James Brice Brown). ¶TV: *Wyatt Earp*—"Caught by a Whisker" 10-7-58 (Mr. Cummings).

Thompson, Hillaire (1949-). TV: *The Outcasts*—"The Town That Wouldn't" 3-31-69 (Bonnie); *Gunsmoke*—"Hawk" 10-20-69 (Rachel Clifford); *Hec Ramsey*—"Scar Tissue" 3-10-74 (Betsy Alexander).

Thompson, Hugh. Films: "The Half-Breed" 1922 (Ross Kennion).

Thompson, Jack (1940-). Films: "Mad Dog Morgan" 1975-Australia (Detective Manwaring); "The Man from Snowy River" 1982-Australia (Clancy).

Thompson, Jeff (1928-). Films: "Davy Crockett, King of the Wild Frontier" 1955 (Charlie Two Shirts).

Thompson, Larry. Films: "Dakota" 1945 (Poli's Footman); "King of the Forest Rangers" 1946-serial (Steve King).

Thompson, Lea (1961-). Films: "Back to the Future, Part III" 1990 (Maggie/Lorriane McFly); "Montana" TVM-1990 (Peg); "Substitute Wife" TVM-1994 (Amy Hightower).

Thompson, Lotus (1906-5/19/63). Films: "The Yellow Back" 1926 (Anne Pendleton); "Desert Dust" 1927 (Helen Marsden); "A One Man Game" 1927 (Millicent Delacey); "The Crimson Canyon" 1928 (Daisy Lanning); "Cowboy Pluck" 1929; "The Freckled Rascal" 1929 (Sally);

"In Line of Duty" 1929; "The Lone Rider" 1929; "'Neath Western Skies" 1929 (Ann Givens); "The Phantom Rider" 1929 (Grace Darling); "The Thrill Hunter" 1929.

Thompson, Margaret (1889-12/26/69). Films: "The Sergeant's Secret" 1913; "The Grudge" 1915; "Keno Bates—Liar" 1915; "Satan McAllister's Heir" 1915; "The Flame of the Yukon" 1917 (Dolly).

Thompson, Marshall (1925-5/18/92). Films: "Bad Bascomb" 1946 (Jimmy Holden); "The Devil's Doorway" 1950 (Rod MacDougall); "Stars in My Crown" 1950 (Narrator). ¶TV: *Zane Grey Theater*—"The Open Cell" 11-22-57 (Eli Hendricks); *Gunsmoke*—"Widow's Mite" 5-10-58 (Leach Fields); *Bronco*—"The Last Resort" 11-17-59 (Billy Styles); *Wagon Train*—"Trial for Murder" 4-27-60 & 5-4-60 (Brad Mason), "The Grover Allen Story" 2-3-64 (Will Stebbins); *Death Valley Days*—"The Streets of El Paso" 5-16-64 (Mayor Ben Dowell); *Hec Ramsey*—"The Detroit Connection" 12-30-73 (Judd White); *Centennial*—Regular 1978-79 (Dennis).

Thompson, Mort. Films: "A Child of the Prairie" 1925 (Sam Jones); "Night Riders of Montana" 1951 (Jim Foster). ¶TV: *The Lone Ranger*—"The Hooded Men" 2-22-51.

Thompson, Myrna. Films: "West of the Law" 1926 (Phyllis Parker).

Thompson, Natalie. Films: "The Vanishing Virginian" 1941 (Margaret Yancey).

Thompson, Nick (1890-4/22/80). Films: "The Mohican's Daughter" 1922 (Chatanna); "Tongues of Flame" 1924 (Adam John); "The Riding Renegade" 1928 (Chief White Cloud); "The Storm" 1930; "Under the Pampas Moon" 1935 (Waiter); "Rose of the Rancho" 1936 (Vigilante); "The Girl of the Golden West" 1938 (Billy Jack Rabbit); "In Old Cheyenne" 1941; "The Phantom Cowboy" 1941 (Pancho); "The Son of Davy Crockett" 1941; "Tumbledown Ranch in Arizona" 1941; "Border Roundup" 1942; "Lawless Plainsmen" 1942 (Ochella); "Perils of the Royal Mounted" 1942-serial (Black Bear); "Black Arrow" 1944-serial; "Buffalo Bill" 1944 (Medicine Man); "The Last Horseman" 1944 (Karp); "Renegade Girl" 1946; "Singin' in the Corn" 1946 (Indian Chief); "Apache Warrior" 1957 (Horse Trader).

Thompson, Peter. Films: "The Wistful Widow of Wagon Gap" 1947 (Phil); "Fort Savage Raiders" 1951

(Lt. James Sutter); "Indian Uprising" 1951 (Lt. Baker); "Ridin' the Outlaw Trail" 1951 (Tom Chapman); "Santa Fe" 1951 (Tom Canfield); "Fury in Paradise" 1955-U.S./Mex. ¶TV: *The Lone Ranger*—"The Woman in the White Mask" 5-12-55; *Death Valley Days*—"The Sinbuster" 6-2-56, "The Rosebush of Tombstone" 3-3-57; *Wyatt Earp*—"The Clantons' Family Row" 12-8-59 (Johnny Ringo), "The Toughest Judge in Arizona" 5-24-60 (Johnny Ringo).

Thompson, Ray (1898-6/29/27). Films: "Horse Sense" 1924 (Bluff Harkins); "When a Man's a Man" 1924 (Curley Elson); "Go West" 1925 (Foreman); "The Enchanted Hill" 1926 (Tommy Scaife); "The Fighting Buckaroo" 1926 (2nd Cook).

Thompson, Shorty (and His Saddle Rockin' Rhythm). Films: "El Dorado Pass" 1949.

Thompson, Victoria (1952-). TV: *The Guns of Will Sonnett*—"Home Free" 11-22-68; *Alias Smith and Jones*—"The Root of It All" 4-1-71 (Margaret Chapman); *Bonanza*—"Bushwacked" 10-3-71 (Julia).

Thompson, William (1852-2/4/23). Films: "The Mohican's Daughter" 1922 (Amos Pentley).

Thomson, Amy. Films: "Death of a Gunfighter" 1969 (Angela). ¶TV: *The Virginian*—"Image of an Outlaw" 10-23-68 (Angie Becker); *The Big Valley*—"Lightfoot" 2-17-69 (Lil Bailey).

Thomson, Anna. Films: "Unforgiven" 1992 (Delilah Fitzgerald).

Thomson, Fred (1890-12/25/28). Films: "The Mask of Lopez" 1923 (Jack O'Neil); "The Dangerous Coward" 1924 (Bob Trent, the Lightning Kid); "The Fighting Sap" 1924 (Craig Richmond); "Galloping Gallagher" 1924 (Bill Gallagher); "North of Nevada" 1924 (Tom Taylor); "The Silent Stranger" 1924 (Jack Taylor); "Thundering Hoofs" 1924 (Dave Marshall); "Ridin' the Wind" 1925 (Jim Harkness); "All Around the Frying Pan" 1925 (Bart Andrews); "The Bandit's Baby" 1925 (Tom Bailey); "That Devil Quemado" 1925 (Quemado); "The Wild Bull's Lair" 1925 (Dan Allen); "Hands Across the Border" 1926 (Fred Drake); "Lone Hand Saunders" 1926 (Fred Saunders); "A Regular Scout" 1926 (Fred Blake); "The Tough Guy" 1926 (Fred Saunders); "The Two-Gun Man" 1926 (Dean Randall); "Arizona Nights" 1927 (Fred Coulter); "Don Mike" 1927 (Don Miguel Arguella); "Jesse James" 1927 (Jesse James); "Silver Comes Through" 1927 (Fred); "Kit Carson" 1928 (Kit Carson); "The Pioneer Scout" 1928 (Fred); "The Sunset Legion" 1928 (Black-Robed Stranger/Whittling Cowboy).

Thomson, Kenneth (1899-1/27/67). Films: "White Gold" 1927 (Alec Carson); "Woman Hungry" 1931 (Leonard Temple); "In Old Santa Fe" 1934 (Chandler); "Hopalong Cassidy" 1935 (Pecos Jack Anthony); "Whispering Smith Speaks" 1935 (J. Wesley Hunt).

Thor, Jerome (1915-8/12/93). TV: *The Deputy*—"Tension Point" 4-8-61 (Ben Meadows); *Daniel Boone*—"The Accused" 3-24-66 (Sam Thurston).

Thor, Larry (1917-3/15/76). Films: "Five Guns West" 1955 (Confederate Captain). ¶TV: *Wagon Train*—"The Sally Potter Story" 4-9-58 (Sergeant); *Rawhide*—"Incident of the Judas Trap" 6-5-59; *The Rifleman*—"The Tinhorn" 3-12-62 (Jesse); *A Man Called Shenandoah*—"Muted Fifes, Muffled Drums" 2-28-66 (Doctor); *Shane*—"The Great Invasion" 12-17-66 & 12-24-66 (Fretwell).

Thordsen, Kelly (1916-1/23/78). Films: "The Desperados Are in Town" 1956 (Tobe Lapman); "Money, Women and Guns" 1958 (Joe); "Shenandoah" 1965 (Carroll); "Gunpoint" 1966 (Ab); "Texas Across the River" 1966 (Turkey Shoot Boss). ¶TV: *Zane Grey Theater*—"Blood in the Dust" 10-11-57 (Bartender); *Gunsmoke*—"Mavis McCloud" 10-26-57 (Lin), "The Storm" 9-25-65 (Mel Woodley), "The Prodigal" 9-25-67 (Regal); *The Californians*—"The Barber's Boy" 11-19-57 (Tom Kemp), "Gold-Tooth Charlie" 3-10-59; *Tales of the Texas Rangers*—"Cattle Drive" 10-30-58 (Muncho); *Northwest Passage*—"The Hostage" 11-2-58 (Lt. Gordon); *Lawman*—"Wanted" 11-16-58 (Carver); *The Texan*—"A Race for Life" 3-16-59; *Yancy Derringer*—"Fire on the Frontier" 4-2-59 (Colorado Charlie), "Outlaw at Liberty" 5-7-59 (Colorado Charlie), "Gone But Not Forgotten" 5-28-59 (Colorado Charlie); *Bronco*—"Red Water North" 6-16-59; *Tales of Wells Fargo*—"Young Jim Hardie" 9-7-59 (Freight Car), "Death Raffle" 10-21-61 (Ben), "Don't Wake a Tiger" 5-12-62 (Sheriff); *Wyatt Earp*—"The Nugget and the Epitaph" 10-6-59; *Colt .45*—"The Reckoning" 10-11-59; *Maverick*—"Full House" 10-25-59 (Sam Bass), "The Resurrection of Joe November" 2-28-60 (Police Chief), "Dodge City or Bust" 12-11-60 (Customer), "Deadly Image" 3-12-61 (Hammett); *The Deputy*—"The Deal" 12-5-59 (Hamish); *Overland Trail*—"All the O'Mara's Horses" 3-13-60 (Chino); *The Alaskans*—"The Devil Made Five" 6-19-60 (Bartender); *The Rifleman*—"Closer Than a Brother" 2-21-61 (Truelove), "The Score Is Even" 4-11-61 (Andy); *Cheyenne*—"Retaliation" 11-13-61 (Brown); *Laramie*—"The Accusers" 11-14-61, "Vengeance" 1-8-63; *The Tall Man*—"The Girl from Paradise" 1-13-62 (Rafe Tollinger); *Bonanza*—"A Hot Day for a Hanging" 10-14-62 (Larsen), "Five into the Wind" 4-21-63 (Howard Benson), "Enter Thomas Towers" 4-26-64 (Sam), "The Search" 2-14-65 (Sheriff Conners), "The Dilemma" 9-19-65 (Drugan), "The Gold Detector" 12-24-67 (Vern Higgins); *Empire*—"The Fire Dancer" 11-13-62 (George); *Wagon Train*—"The Fenton Canaby Story" 12-30-63; *Rawhide*—"Incident of the Rusty Shotgun" 1-9-64 (Amos Claybank), "Incident at Zebulon" 3-5-64, "The Calf Women" 4-30-65 (Ryan); *Daniel Boone*—"Mountain of the Dead" 12-17-64 (Guthrie MacAnders), "The Necklace" 3-9-67 (Pa Grimes), "The Traitor" 11-2-67 (Sergeant Reynolds), "The Bait" 11-7-68 (Constable Blackstore); *A Man Called Shenandoah*—"Incident at Dry Creek" 11-15-65; *The Virginian*—"The Horse Fighter" 12-15-65 (Mace), "The Return of Golden Tom" 3-9-66 (Amos Coe), "Bitter Autumn" 11-1-67 (the Judge), "Execution at Triste" 12-13-67 (the Constable); *The Legend of Jesse James*—"Wanted: Dead and Only" 5-2-66 (McCoy); *The Road West*—"Ashes and Tallow and One True Love" 10-24-66 (Charlie); *The Big Valley*—"The Velvet Trap" 11-7-66 (Pierce); *Cimarron Strip*—"The Legend of Jud Starr" 9-14-67 (Moose O'Hare); *The High Chaparral*—"The Hair Hunter" 3-10-68 (Austin), "The Covey" 10-18-68 (Bruger); *Here Come the Brides*—"Hosanna's Way" 10-31-69; *Nichols*—2-29-72 (Jacob); *Hec Ramsey*—"The Detroit Connection" 12-30-73; *Kung Fu*—"The Nature of Evil" 3-21-74 (Mule Jesse).

Thornby, Robert (1889-3/6/53). Films: "Omens of the Desert" 1912; "When California Was Young" 1912.

Thorndike, Oliver (1918-4/14/54). Films: "Unconquered" 1947 (Lt. Billie).

Thorne, Frank (1881-5/28/53). Films: "The Feud" 1919 (Bob Lynch); "The Rose of Nome" 1920 (Joseph Boardman); "Billy Jim" 1922 (Roy Forsythe).

Thorne, Lizette. Films: "In the Sunset Country" 1915; "Penny of Top Hill Trail" 1921 (Mrs. Kingdon).

Thorne, William L. (1878-3/10/48). Films: "Fighting Thru" 1930 (Ace); "The Montana Kid" 1931 (Chuck Larson); "Law of the North" 1932; "Rainbow Trail" 1932 (Dyer); "Vanishing Men" 1932; "Clancy of the Mounted" 1933-serial; "Nevada" 1935 (Card Player); "The Roaring West" 1935-serial (Marco Brett); "The Man from Sundown" 1939 (Sam Cooper).

Thornton, Billy Bob. Films: "Tombstone" 1993 (Johnny Tyler); "Dead Man" 1995 (Big George Drakoulious).

Thornton, Evans. Films: "The Trial of Billy Jack" 1974 (Prosecuting Attorney). ¶TV: *The High Chaparral*—"Apache Trust" 11-7-69 (Willkmapf), "Sangre" 2-26-71 (Major Benson); *Bonanza*—"Bushwacked" 10-3-71 (Flanders); *Gunsmoke*—"The Sodbusters" 11-20-72 (Murphy).

Thornton, Sigrid. Films: "The Man from Snowy River" 1982-Australia (Jessica). ¶TV: *Paradise*—Regular 1988-91 (Amelia Lawson).

Thorpe, Jim (1886-3/28/53). Films: "Battling with Buffalo Bill" 1931-serial (Swift Arrow); "My Pal, the King" 1932 (Black Cloud); "White Eagle" 1932 (Indian Chief); "Wild Horse Mesa" 1932 (Indian Chief); "The Red Rider" 1934-serial (Bill Abel); "The Arizonian" 1935; "Code of the Mounted" 1935 (Eagle Feather); "Courage of the North" 1935; "Rustlers of Red Dog" 1935-serial (Chief Scarface); "Wanderer of the Wasteland" 1935 (Charlie Jim); "The Phantom Rider" 1936-serial; "Sutter's Gold" 1936; "Trailin' West" 1936 (Black Eagle); "Treachery Rides the Range" 1936 (Chief Red Smoke); "Wildcat Trooper" 1936 (Indian); "Cattle Raiders" 1938; "Henry Goes Arizona" 1939 (Indian); "The Man from Texas" 1939; "The Oregon Trail" 1939-serial; "Arizona Frontier" 1940 (Gray Cloud); "Prairie Schooners" 1940 (Chief Sanche); "Prairie Spooners" 1941-short; "Outlaw Trail" 1944 (Spike); "Beyond the Pecos" 1945; "Wagonmaster" 1950 (Navajo).

Thorpe, Ted (1917-12/18/70). Films: "Hang 'Em High" 1968.

Thorsen, Duane. see Grey, Duane.

Thorson, Russell (1906-82). Films: "Good Day for a Hanging" 1958 (Landers); "Gun Fever" 1958 (Thomas); "Gunfighters of Abilene" 1960 (Wilkinson); "Hang 'Em High" 1968 (Mr. Madow); "The Stalking Moon" 1969 (Ned). ¶TV: *The Cisco Kid*—"Cisco and the Giant" 10-31-53; *Gunsmoke*—"Helping Hand" 3-17-56 (Emmett Bowers), "Chester's Mail Order Bride" 7-14-56 (Brady), "Pa Hack's Brood" 12-28-63 (Pa Willis), "Song for Dying" 2-13-65 (Mace); *Tales of Wells Fargo*—"The Thin Rope" 3-18-57 (Jefferson), "Alder Gulch" 4-8-57 (John Carter), "The Wade Place" 11-28-60, "Incident at Crossbow" 2-3-62 (Jug Peery); *Wagon Train*—"The Les Rand Story" 10-16-57, "The Eleanor Culhane Story" 5-17-61 (Harris), "The Captain Dan Brady Story" 9-27-61 (the Major); *Zane Grey Theater*—"Ride a Lonely Trail" 11-2-57 (Judge); *Have Gun Will Travel*—"The Yuma Treasure" 12-14-57; *Cheyenne*—"Hired Gun" 12-17-57 (Sheriff Hardin); *Maverick*—"Day of Reckoning" 2-2-58 (Marshal Walt Hardie); *Jefferson Drum*—"The Hanging of Joe Lavetti" 8-1-58 (Bert Temple); *Wanted—Dead or Alive*—"Fatal Memory" 9-13-58 (Col. J.J. Sykes), "The Monsters" 1-16-60 (Sheriff); *The Adventures of Rin Tin Tin*—"Escape to Danger" 9-26-58 (John Burton); *Lawman*—"Wanted" 11-16-58 (Wilson), "The Brand Release" 1-25-59 (Sheriff Lang); *The Texan*— "The Widow of Paradise" 11-24-58 (Sheriff); *Tales of the Texas Rangers*—"Ambush" 12-26-58; *Trackdown*—"The Protector" 4-1-59 (Jesse Jackson); *Rawhide*—"Incident of the Thirteenth Man" 10-23-59 (Mort Billings), "The Gentleman's Gentleman" 12-15-61 (Mayor Thurman Osgood), "Incident of the Pale Rider" 3-15-63 (Sheriff); *The Rifleman*—"The Wyoming Story" 2-7-61 & 2-14-61 (Marshal Burk); *Laramie*—"Man from Kansas" 1-10-61 (Bates); *The Outlaws*—"The Verdict" 12-28-61 (Titus Holbrook); *Bonanza*—"The Tall Stranger" 1-7-62 (Owens), "The Real People of Muddy Creek" 10-6-68 (Simon), "The Hidden Enemy" 11-27-72; *The Tall Man*—"The Black Robe" 5-5-62 (Major Graves); *The Virginian*—"West" 11-20-62 (Sheriff Evans), "The Devil's Children" 12-5-62 (Sheriff Evans), "Duel at Shiloh" 1-2-63 (Sheriff Tybee), "The Golden Door" 3-13-63 (Sheriff Evans), "Echo from Another Day" 3-27-63, "Timberland" 3-10-65 (Ollie), "Rich Man, Poor Man" 3-11-70 (Josh); *Empire*—"A House in Order" 3-5-63 (Austin); *Temple Houston*—"The Siege at Thayer's Bluff" 11-7-63 (Red Gilman); *Death Valley Days*—"A Bell for Volcano" 1-24-65 (Dan Davidson); *A Man Called Shenandoah*—"Rope's End" 1-17-66 (Judge Harvey), "Trail by Combat" 5-27-60 (Perry); *Cimarron Strip*—"The Assassin" 1-11-68 (Hank Martin); *Lancer*—"Jelly" 11-19-68 (Doc Jenkins), "Blind Man's Bluff" 9-23-69 (Dr. Sam Poovy); *The Big Valley*—"Point and Counterpoint" 5-19-69 (Otis Clark).

Thourlby, William. Films: "Vengeance" 1964 (Capt. Lafe Todd). ¶TV: *Rawhide*—"Incident of the Silent Web" 6-3-60 (Morgan); *Wyatt Earp*—"Wyatt Takes the Primrose Path" 3-28-61 (Chief Natchez).

Threatt, Elizabeth. Films: "The Big Sky" 1952 (Teal Eye).

Thrett, Maggie. TV: *Wild Wild West*—"The Night of the Freebooters" 4-1-66 (Rita Leon), "The Night of the Running Death" 12-15-67 (Deidra/Topaz); *Dundee and the Culhane*—11-15-67 (Wimea).

Thring, Frank (1926-12/29/94). Films: "Ned Kelly" 1970-Brit. (Judge Barry); "Mad Dog Morgan" 1975-Australia (Superintendent Cobham).

Throne, Malachi (1927-). Films: "Longarm" TVM-1988 (Blalock). ¶TV: *Rawhide*—"El Hombre Bravo" 5-14-65 (Vallino), "The Vasquez Woman" 10-26-65; *The Big Valley*—"Palms of Glory" 9-15-65 (Charles Crown), "Tunnel of Gold" 4-20-66 (Frank Colder), "Pursuit" 10-10-66 (Father Andre); *Iron Horse*—"The Dynamite Driver" 9-19-66 (Royal McClintock); *Laredo*—"Finnegan" 10-21-66 (Sean Finnegan); *Wild Wild West*—"The Night of the Tartar" 2-3-67 (Kuprin); *The Virginian*—"To Bear Witness" 11-29-67 (Dr. Baldwin); *The High Chaparral*—"Bad Day for Bad Men" 10-17-69 (Matar).

Thunder, Alf. *see* Caltabiano, Alfio.

Thunderbird, Chief (1867-4/6/46). Films: "Battling with Buffalo Bill" 1931-serial (Chief Thunderbird); "Heroes of the West" 1932-serial; "Rustlers of Red Dog" 1935-serial (Chief); "The Country Beyond" 1936 (Indian); "For the Service" 1936 (Chief Big Bear); "Wild West Days" 1937-serial (Red Hatchet); "Susannah of the Mounties" 1939 (Indian); "Geronimo" 1940 (Chief Eskiminzu); "Northwest Mounted Police" 1940 (Indian).

Thundercloud, Chief (Scott T. Williams) (1898-1/31/67). Films: "99 Wounds" 1931 (Medicine Man).

Thunder Cloud, Chief (Victor Daniels) (1889-11/30/55). Films: "Annie Oakley" 1935 (Sitting Bull);

"Cyclone of the Saddle" 1935 (Yellow Wolf); "Fighting Pioneers" 1935 (Eagle Feathers); "Rustlers of Red Dog" 1935-serial; "Rustlers' Paradise" 1935; "Saddle Aces" 1935; "The Singing Vagabond" 1935 (Young Deer); "Wagon Trail" 1935; "Bold Caballero" 1936 (Servant); "Custer's Last Stand" 1936-serial (Young Wolf); "Gun Smoke" 1936; "Ramona" 1936 (Pablo); "Ride, Ranger, Ride" 1936 (Little Wolf); "Renfrew of the Royal Mounted" 1937 (Pierre); "Riders of the Whistling Skull" 1937 (High Priest); "Wild West Days" 1937-serial; "Flaming Frontier" 1938-serial (Thunder Cloud); "The Great Adventures of Wild Bill Hickok" 1938 (Gray Eagle); "The Lone Ranger" 1938-serial (Tonto); "Fighting Mad" 1939 (Indian); "The Lone Ranger Rides Again" 1939-serial (Tonto); "Union Pacific" 1939 (Indian Brave); "Geronimo" 1940 (Geronimo); "Murder on the Yukon" 1940 (Monti); "Northwest Mounted Police" 1940 (Wandering Spirit); "Wyoming" 1940 (Lightfoot); "Young Buffalo Bill" 1940 (Akuna); "Hudson Bay" 1941 (Grimha); "Silver Stallion" 1941 (Freshwater); "Western Union" 1941 (Indian Leader); "King of the Stallions" 1942; "Overland Mail" 1942-serial; "Shut My Big Mouth" 1942 (Indian Interpreter); "Valley of Vanishing Men" 1942-serial; "Daredevils of the West" 1943-serial (Indian Chief); "The Law Rides Again" 1943 (Indian); "Black Arrow" 1944-serial; "Buffalo Bill" 1944 (Crazy Horse); "Outlaw Trail" 1944 (Thundercloud); "Raiders of Ghost City" 1944-serial; "Sonora Stagecoach" 1944 (Thunder Cloud); "Badman's Territory" 1946 (Chief Tahlequah); "The Phantom Rider" 1946-serial (Yellow Wolf); "Renegade Girl" 1946; "Romance of the West" 1946 (Chief Eagle Feather); "The Prairie" 1947 (Eagle Feather); "Unconquered" 1947 (Chief Killbuck); "Blazing Across the Pecos" 1948; "Call of the Forest" 1949; "Ambush" 1950 (Tana); "Colt .45" 1950 (Walking Bear); "Davy Crockett, Indian Scout" 1950 (Sleeping Fox); "I Killed Geronimo" 1950 (Geronimo); "Indian Territory" 1950; "Ticket to Tomahawk" 1950 (Crooked Knife); "Santa Fe" 1951 (Chief Longfeather); "Buffalo Bill in Tomahawk Territory" 1952. ¶TV: *The Gene Autry Show*— "The Poisoned Waterhole" 10-8-50.

Thurman, Bill (1920-). Films: "Tom Horn" 1980 (Ora Haley); "Silverado" 1985 (Proprietor).

Thurman, Mary (1894-12/22/ 25). Films: "This Hero Stuff" 1919

(Teddy Craig); "Sand!" 1920 (Margaret Young); "The Primal Law" 1921 (Janice Webb).

Thursby, David (1888-4/20/ 77). Films: "Union Pacific" 1939 (Irishman). ¶TV: *Bat Masterson*—"To the Manner Born" 10-1-59 (Captain Larkin).

Thurston, Carol (1923-12/31/ 69). Films: "The Last Round-Up" 1947 (Lydia Henry); "Apache Chief" 1949 (Watona); "Flaming Feather" 1952 (Turquoise); "Conquest of Cochise" 1953 (Terua); "Yukon Vengeance" 1954; "Showdown" 1963 (Smithy's Wife). ¶TV: *The Lone Ranger*—"Finders Keepers" 12-8-49, "The Squire" 11-9-50; *Wild Bill Hickok*—"Mexican Rustlers Story" 10-23-51; *Death Valley Days*—"Sequoia" 12-6-54; *Frontier*—"Paper Gunman" 9-25-55 (Mrs. McGill), "Salt War" 4-22-56 (Annie Brayer); *Wyatt Earp*—"Old Jake" 4-9-57 (Mrs. McCafferty), "Indian Wife" 12-10-57 (Laura Melaney), "Death for a Stolen Horse" 1-13-59 (Helen Riva), Regular 1959-60 (Emma Clanton); *Have Gun Will Travel*—"Winchester Quarantine" 10-5-57, "Heritage of Anger" 6-6-59 (Nita); *Rough Riders*—"Blood Feud" 11-13-58 (Abby Pearce); *Rawhide*—"Incident of the Power and the Plow" 2-13-59 (Waneea).

Thurston, Charles (1869-3/5/ 40). Films: "The Pretender" 1918 (Harold Whiteside); "The Black Sheep" 1921 (Sheriff Summers); "Doubling for Romeo" 1922 (Duffy Saunders); "Ridgeway of Montana" 1924 (Rev. McNabb); "Between Dangers" 1927 (Sheriff); "The Fightin' Comeback" 1927 (Boulder City Sheriff); "Spoilers of the West" 1928; "When the Law Rides" 1928 (Joshua Ross); "Unknown Valley" 1933 (Younger).

Tibbett, Jr., Lawrence. Films: "El Paso" 1949 (Denton).

Tibbetts, Martha. Films: "The Unknown Ranger" 1936 (Ann Wright); "Ranger Courage" 1937 (Alice).

Tibbs, Casey (1929-1/20/90). Films: "Bronco Buster" 1952; "Wild Heritage" 1958 (Rusty); "A Thunder of Drums" 1961 (Trooper Baker); "Tomboy and the Champ" 1961; "The Rounders" 1965 (Rafe); "Junior Bonner" 1972; "Breakheart Pass" 1976 (Jackson); "More Wild Wild West" TVM-1980 (Brother). ¶TV: *Stoney Burke*—"Point of Honor" 10-22-62 (Rodeo Judge), "Kincaid" 4-22-63 (Himself); *Tales of Wells Fargo*—"Town Against a Man" 1-23-61 (Sheriff Jim Hogan); *Branded*—

"Romany Roundup" 12-5-65 & 12-12-65; *The Rounders*—11-15-66 (Folliat); *The Monroes*—"To Break a Colt" 1-11-67 (Cowboy).

Tichy, Gerard (1920-). Films: "Gunmen of the Rio Grande" 1964-Fr./Ital./Span. (Zack Williams); "Four Dollars for Vengeance" 1965-Span./Ital.; "Man from Canyon City" 1965-Span./Ital.; "One Hundred Thousand Dollars for Ringo" 1966-Ital./Span.; "A Place Called Glory" 1966-Span./Ger. (Jack Vallone); "The Texican" 1966-U.S./Span. (Thompson); "Sartana Does Not Forgive" 1968-Span./Ital.

Tidmarsh, Ferdinand (1883-11/22). Films: "The Long Trail" 1917 (Frank Farrington).

Tiernan, Patricia. Films: "Apache War Smoke" 1952 (Lorraine Sayburn). ¶TV: *The Cisco Kid*—"Cisco and the Giant" 10-31-53; *Cheyenne*—"Death Deals This Hand" 10-9-56 (Caroline).

Tierney, Gene (1920-11/6/91). Films: "The Return of Frank James" 1940 (Eleanor Stone); "Belle Starr" 1941 (Belle Starr); "Hudson Bay" 1941 (Barbara Hall); "The Secret of Convict Lake" 1951 (Marcia Stoddard); "Way of a Gaucho" 1952 (Teresa).

Tierney, Lawrence (1919-). Films: "Badman's Territory" 1946 (Jesse James); "Best of the Badmen" 1951 (Jesse James); "The Bushwackers" 1952 (Sam Tobin); "Custer of the West" 1967-U.S./Span. (Gen. Philip Sheridan).

Tiffin, Pamela (1942-). Films: "The Hallelujah Trail" 1965 (Louise Gearhart); "Deaf Smith and Johnny Ears" 1972-Ital. (Suzie).

Tigar, Kenneth. TV: *Adventures of Brisco County, Jr.*—"The Brooklyn Dodgers" 2-11-94 (Flint).

Tighe, Kevin (1944-). Films: "Geronimo: An American Legend" 1993 (Brig. Gen. Nelson Miles); "The Avenging Angel" TVM-1995. ¶TV: *Bonanza*—"The Weary Willies" 9-27-70 (Krulak).

Til, Roger. TV: *Jim Bowie*—"Monsieur Francois" 12-28-56 (Edouard Dubois); *Northwest Passage*—"The Red Coat" 9-21-58 (Gen. Calgrenne).

Tilbury, Zeffie (1863-7/22/50). Films: "Sheriff of Tombstone" 1941 (Granny Carson).

Tilghman, William (1854-12/1/ 24). Films: "Passing of the Oklahoma Outlaw" 1915.

Tilles, Ken (1912-1/31/70). TV:

Here Come the Brides—"Candy and the Kid" 2-13-70 (Drifter).

Tillis, Mel (1932-). Films: "The Villain" 1979 (Telegrapher).

Tilly, Jennifer. Films: "Shadow of the Wolf" 1993-Can./Fr. (Igiyook).

Tilton, Edwin Booth (1859-1/16/26). Films: "Cupid's Round Up" 1918 (James Kelly); "Riddle Gawne" 1918 (Colonel Harkless); "Forbidden Trails" 1920 (Judge Butterfield); "Just Pals" 1920 (Dr. Stone); "The Square Shooter" 1920 (Harold L. Montague, Sr.); "Sunset Sprague" 1920 (Calico Barnes); "Two Moons" 1920 (Strayhorn); "The Primal Law" 1921 (Peter Webb); "The Taming of the West" 1925 (John P. Carleton).

Tindall, Lorin (1921-5/10/73). TV: *Tales of Wells Fargo*—"Toll Road" 3-23-59 (Buff); *Overland Trail*—"Escort Detail" 5-22-60 (John Sumpter).

Tingley, Clyde (1884-12/24/60). Films: "The Texas Rangers" 1936.

Tingwell, Charles (1917-). Films: "Kangaroo" 1952 (Matt).

Tinney, Cal. Films: "The Missouri Traveler" 1958 (Clyde Hamilton). ¶TV: *Bat Masterson*—"Promised Land" 6-10-59 (U.S. Marshal).

Tinti, Gabriele (1932-). Films: "Son of Django" 1967-Ital. (Clint); "Cannon for Cordoba" 1970 (Lt. Antonio Gutierrez).

Tipton, Charles. Films: "The Telltale Knife" 1911; "The Brand Blotter" 1912; "Two Men and a Girl" 1912.

Titheradge, Dion (1889-11/16/34). Films: "The Crimson Dove" 1917 (Philip Burbank).

Tittle, Sam. Films: "Lightnin' Smith Returns" 1931 (Tom Parker); "The Riding Kid" 1931 (Tom Barton).

Titus, Lydia Yeamans (1866-12/30/29). Films: "Babbling Tongues" 1915; "Fatherhood" 1915; "Judge Not, or the Woman of Mona Diggings" 1915 (Housekeeper); "Davy Crockett" 1916 (Widow Crockett); "A Gun Fightin' Gentleman" 1919 (Helen's Aunt); "Partners Three" 1919 (Gossip); "The Freeze-Out" 1921 (Mrs. McGuire); "Two Kinds of Women" 1922 (Mrs. Simpson); "The Footlight Ranger" 1923 (Ms. Amelia); "The Arizona Romeo" 1925 (Martha); "The Water Hole" 1928 (Ma Bennett).

Tobey, Kenneth (1919-). Films: "The Gunfighter" 1950 (Swede); "Rawhide" 1951 (Wingate); "Davy Crockett, King of the Wild Frontier" 1955 (Col. Jim Bowie); "Rage at Dawn" 1955 (Monk Claxton); "Davy Crockett and the River Pirates" 1956 (Jocko); "The Great Locomotive Chase" 1956 (Anthony Murphy); "Gunfight at the O.K. Corral" 1957 (Bat Masterson); "Seven Ways from Sundown" 1960 (Lt. Herly); "40 Guns to Apache Pass" 1967 (Cpl. Bodine); "A Time for Killing" 1967 (Sgt. Cleehan); "Billy Jack" 1971 (Deputy); "Wild and Wooly" TVM-1978 (Mark Hannah). ¶TV: *The Lone Ranger*—"Spanish Gold" 6-1-50; *Walt Disney Presents*—"Davy Crockett"—Regular 1954-55 (Jim Bowie/Jocko); *Frontier*—"The Return of Jubal Dolan" 8-26-56 (Gabe Sharp), "The Hostage" 9-9-56; *Sheriff of Cochise*—"Bandit Chief" 2-15-57 (Jim Callahan); *Jefferson Drum*—"$50 for a Dead Man" 11-13-58 (John Wallach); *Wanted—Dead or Alive*—"The Legend" 3-7-59; *Bat Masterson*—"Deadly Diamonds" 2-11-60 (Meade Amhurst); *Lawman*—"The Parting" 5-29-60 (Tom Bishop), "The Trojan Horse" 12-31-61 (Duncan Clooney); *Bronco*—"The Mustangers" 10-17-60 (Campbell); *Gunsmoke*—"The Worm" 10-29-60 (Spadden), "Once a Haggen" 2-1-64 (Fickett), "The Prisoner" 3-17-69 (Bob Mathison), "Tatum" 11-13-72 (Ed Terrall); *Have Gun Will Travel*—"Broken Image" 4-29-61 (Tim Decker); *Frontier Circus*—"The Good Fight" 4-19-62 (Marshal Walden); *Stoney Burke*—"Forget Me More" 3-25-63 (Ryan); *Temple Houston*—"Sam's Boy" 1-23-64 (Dan Powers); *Daniel Boone*—"The Wolf Man" 1-26-67 (Taggart); *Iron Horse*—"T Is for Traitor" 12-2-67 (Patch); *Bonanza*—"The Thirteenth Man" 1-21-68 (Heath), "Search in Limbo" 2-20-72 (Notary); *The Virginian*—"The Decision" 3-13-68 (Sheriff Dan Porter), "Rich Man, Poor Man" 3-11-70 (Joe); *The Outcasts*—"The Man from Bennington" 12-16-68 (Sheriff Garrett); *The Men from Shiloh*—"Lady at the Bar" 11-4-70 (Sheriff Action); *Alias Smith and Jones*—"Jailbreak at Junction City" 9-30-71 (Sheriff Slocum), "Witness to a Lynching" 12-16-72 (Sheriff Kimball); *Kung Fu*—"Alethea" 3-15-73 (Sheriff Ingram).

Tobias, George (1901-2/27/80). Films: "River's End" 1940 (Andy Dijon); "Mark of the Renegade" 1951 (Bardosa); "Rawhide" 1951 (Gratz); "Desert Pursuit" 1952 (Ghazili); "Bullet for a Badman" 1964 (Diggs). ¶TV: *Hudson's Bay*—Regular 1958 (Pierre Falcon); *Laramie*—"The Legend of Lily" 1-26-60 (Shanghai Pierce); *Overland Trail*—"Lawyer in Petticoats" 3-27-60 (Hard Rock Sam

Jackson); *The Deputy*—"Lucifer Urge" 5-14-60 (Barney Wagner); *The Rebel*—"The Earl of Durango" 6-12-60 (Sheriff Boyd).

Tobin, Dan (1909-11/26/82). TV: *Maverick*—"Relic of Fort Tejon" 11-3-57 (Howard Harris), "The Rivals" 1-25-59 (Lucius Benson), "Diamond Flush" 2-5-61 (Ralph Ferguson); *Yancy Derringer*—"Fire on the Frontier" 4-2-59 (Alvin Watson); *Wagon Train*—"The Steele Family" 6-17-59, "The Allison Justis Story" 10-19-60; *Bonanza*—"Bank Run" 1-28-61 (Finch), "The Passing of a King" 10-13-68 (Judge Rideout), "The Luck of Pepper Shannon" 11-22-70 (Mills); *Gunsmoke*—"Panacea Sykes" 4-13-63 (Foote), "Champion of the World" 12-24-66 (the Professor); *Wild Wild West*—"The Night of the Burning Diamond" 4-8-66 (Thaddeus Baines); *The Outcasts*—"The Bounty Children" 12-23-68 (Coker).

Tobin, Michele (1961-). TV: *Wild Wild West*—"The Night of the Falcon" 11-10-67 (Bonnie); *Bonanza*—"A Dream to Dream" 4-14-68 (Sally Carter), "It's a Small World" 1-4-70 (Annie).

Toby, Doug. Films: "Calamity Jane" TVM-1984 (Jackie); "The Mystic Warrior" TVM-1984 (Young Ahbleza).

Tochi, Brian. TV: *Kung Fu*—"The Tide" 2-1-73 (Ho Gong), "The Demon God" 12-13-74 (Shen Ung).

Todd, Ann E. (1909-5/6/93). Films: "Destry Rides Again" 1939 (Claggett Girl); "Brigham Young—Frontiersman" 1940 (Mary Kent); "Bad Men of Missouri" 1941 (Amy Younger); "Homesteaders of Paradise Valley" 1947.

Todd, Beverly (1946-). TV: *Wild Wild West*—"The Night of the Diva" 3-7-69 (Angelique); *Father Murphy*—"The Matchmakers" 6-10-83.

Todd, Harry (1865-2/16/35). Films: "The Making of Broncho Billy" 1913; "The Naming of the Rawhide Queen" 1913; "Broncho Billy and the Red Man" 1914; "Broncho Billy—Outlaw" 1914; "Broncho Billy's Wild Ride" 1914; "The Cast of the Die" 1914; "A Gambler's Way" 1914; "Andy of the Royal Mounted" 1915; "Broncho Billy and the Card Sharp" 1915; "Broncho Billy and the Vigilante" 1915; "Broncho Billy's Cowardly Brother" 1915; "Broncho Billy's Protege" 1915; "A Christmas Revenge" 1915; "The Convict's Threat" 1915; "An Unexpected Romance" 1915; "Shootin' Mad" 1918

(Mary's Father); "The Face in the Watch" 1919; "The Flip of a Coin" 1919; "A Prisoner for Life" 1919; "The Son of a Gun" 1919 (Sheriff); "Tapering Fingers" 1919; "The Sky Pilot" 1921 (the Old Timer); "Bells of San Juan" 1922 (John Engel); "Three Jumps Ahead" 1923 (Cicero); "Horseshoe Luck" 1924; "Ride for Your Life" 1924 (Plug Hanks); "The Sawdust Trail" 1924 (Quid Jackson); "Thundering Romance" 1924 (Davey Jones); "Daring Days" 1925 (Hank Skinner); "The Desert Demon" 1925 (Snitz Doolittle); "The Hurricane Kid" 1925 (Hezekial Potts); "The Outlaw's Daughter" 1925 (Bookkeeper); "Quicker'n Lightnin'" 1925 (Al McNutt); "Saddle Cyclone" 1925 (Andy Simms); "Two-Fisted Jones" 1925 (Bart Wilson); "The Bonanza Buckaroo" 1926 (Chewin' Charlie); "The Buckaroo Kid" 1926 (Tom Darby); "Chip of the Flying U" 1926 (Weary); "Comin an' Going" 1926 (Andy Simms); "Flaming Frontier" 1926 (California Joe); "Rawhide" 1926 (Two Gun); "Under Western Skies" 1926; "The Bugle Call" 1927 (Corporal Jansen); "The Interferin' Gent" 1927 (Buddy); "The Obligin' Buckaroo" 1927; "A One Man Game" 1927 (Sam Baker); "The Ridin' Rowdy" 1927 (Deefy); "Roarin' Broncs" 1927; "Skedaddle Gold" 1927 (Rusty); "White Pebbles" 1927 (Tim); "The Flyin' Cowboys" 1928 (Tom Gordon); "The Rawhide Kid" 1928 (Comic); "Under the Tonto Rim" 1928 (Bert); "Courtin' Wildcats" 1929 (McKenzie); "King of the Rodeo" 1929 (J.G.); "The Fighting Legion" 1930 (Dad Williams); "Lucky Larkin" 1930 (Bill Parkinson); "Sons of the Saddle" 1930 (Pop Higgins); "Under Montana Skies" 1930 (Abner Jenkins); "Branded" 1931; "The Fighting Marshal" 1931 (Pop Caldwell); "In Old Cheyenne" 1931 (Ben); "Law of the Rio Grande" 1931 (Cookie); "Shotgun Pass" 1931; "The Sign of the Wolf" 1931-serial (Jed Farnum); "The Texas Ranger" 1931 (Lynn); "The Deadline" 1932 (Chloride); "The Fighting Fool" 1932 (Hoppy); "Fighting for Justice" 1932 (Cooky); "Gold" 1932; "One-Man Law" 1932 (Hank); "Wyoming Whirlwind" 1932; "Gun Law" 1933 (Black Jack); "The Sundown Rider" 1933; "The Thrill Hunter" 1933 (Baggage Man); "Trouble Busters" 1933 (Skinny Cassidy); "The Prescott Kid" 1934 (Dr. Haley); "The Westerner" 1934 (Uncle Ben); "Law Beyond the Range" 1935 (Judge Avery).

Todd, James (1908-2/8/68). Films: "Riders of the Purple Sage"

1931 (Venters); "Fighting Man of the Plains" 1949 (Hobson). ¶TV: *The Lone Ranger*—"Triple Cross" 5-21-53.

Todd, Lisa (1949-). Films: "Dirty Dingus Magee" 1970 (Belle's Girl). ¶TV: *Kung Fu*—"Barbary House" 2-15-75 (Lilly), "Flight to Orion" 2-22-75 (Lilly), "The Brothers Cain" 3-1-75 (Lilly), "Full Circle" 3-15-75 (Lilly).

Todd, Lola. Films: "The Rustlin' Buster" 1923; "Border Raid" 1924; "Down in Texas" 1924; "Flying Eagle" 1924; "The King's Command" 1924; "The Best Man" 1925; "The Demon" 1926 (Goldie Fleming); "The Fighting Peacemaker" 1926 (Jess Marshall); "The Tough Guy" 1926 (June Hardy); "Red Clay" 1927 (Betty Morgan); "The Return of the Riddle Rider" 1927-serial; "The War Horse" 1927 (Audrey Evans); "Taking a Chance" 1928 (Jessie Smith).

Todd, Sally. TV: *Johnny Ringo*—"Soft Cargo" 5-5-60 (Carol Carpenter).

Todd, Sean. *see* Rassimov, Ivan.

Todd, Thelma (1905-12/18/35). Films: "The Gay Defender" 1927 (Ruth Ainsworth); "Nevada" 1927 (Hettie Ide); "The Fighting Parson" 1930-short; "Klondike" 1932 (Klondike).

Todd, Tony Films: "Black Fox" TVM-1995 (Britt Johnson).

Tognazzi, Ugo (1922-10/27/90). Films: "Don't Touch White Women!" 1974-Ital. (Mitch).

Tolan, Lawrence. Films: "Fort Worth" 1951 (Mort); "The Savage" 1952 (Long Mane).

Tolan, Michael (1925-). Films: "Hiawatha" 1952 (Neyadji); "Hour of the Gun" 1967 (Pete Spence). ¶TV: *Nichols*—"The Indian Giver" 9-30-71 (Flying Fox).

Tolbert, R.L. Films: "The Legend of the Golden Gun" TVM-1979 (Buffalo Bill); "The Sacketts" TVM-1979; "The Quick and the Dead" CTVM-1987; "Conagher" TVM-1991; "Posse" 1993 (Stunts); "The Desperate Trail" TVM-1995.

Toler, Sidney (1874-2/12/47). Films: "Massacre" 1934 (Thomas Shanks); "Call of the Wild" 1935 (Groggin); "The Three Godfathers" 1936 (Prof. Snape); "Gold Is Where You Find It" 1938 (Harrison McCoy); "The Mysterious Rider" 1938 (Frosty Kilburn); "Heritage of the Desert" 1939 (Nosey); "Law of the Pampas" 1939 (Don Fernando Rameriez).

Tolkan, James (1931-). Films: "Back to the Future, Part III" 1990 (Marshal Strickland).

Tolo, Marilu (1943-). Films: "Django Kill" 1967-Ital./Span.; "Roy Colt and Winchester Jack" 1970-Ital.; "Don't Turn the Other Cheek" 1974-Ital./Ger./Span.

Tolsky, Susan (1943-). TV: *Here Comes the Brides*—Regular 1968-70 (Biddie Cloom).

Tomack, Sid (1907-11/12/62). Films: "Last Train from Gun Hill" 1959 (Roomer). ¶TV: *Fury*—"Wonder Horse" 3-24-56 (Smokey).

Tombes, Andrew (1891-76). Films: "The Country Beyond" 1936 (Sen. Rawlings); "Fair Warning" 1937 (J.C. Farnham); "Down Mexico Way" 1941 (Mayor Tubbs); "Last of the Duanes" 1941 (Sheriff); "Texas" 1941; "Riding High" 1943 (P.D. Smith); "San Fernando Valley" 1944 (John "Cyclone" Kenyon); "The Singing Sheriff" 1944 (Jonas); "Don't Fence Me In" 1945 (Cartwright); "Frontier Gal" 1945 (Judge Prescott); "Badman's Territory" 1946 (Doc Grant); "Hoppy's Holiday" 1947 (Mayor Patton); "Two Guys from Texas" 1948 (the Texan); "Oklahoma Annie" 1952 (Mayor).

Tomlin, Pinky (1908-12/12/87). Films: "Sing Me a Song of Texas" 1945.

Tompkins, Angel (1943-). TV: *Wild Wild West*—"The Night of the Death-Maker" 2-23-68 (Marcia); *Here Come the Brides*—"Man of the Family" 10-16-68; *Bonanza*—"The Night Virginia City Died" 9-13-70 (Janie); *The Buffalo Soldiers*—Pilot 5-26-79 (Townsperson).

Tompkins, Joan (1916-). Films: "The Awakening Land" TVM-1978 (Aunt Cornelia). ¶TV: *The Californians*—"Halfway House" 12-2-58 (Patience); *Maverick*—"A Bullet for the Teacher" 10-30-60 (Mary Buch); *The Travels of Jaimie McPheeters*—"The Day of the Wizard" 1-12-64 (Martha Pollux); *Bonanza*—"Erin" 1-26-69 (Mrs. Murray).

Toncray, Kate. Films: "The Lamb" 1915; "Hands Up!" 1917 (Mrs. Farley); "The Snowshoe Trail" 1922 (Mrs. Bronson).

Tone, Franchot (1905-9/18/68). Films: "Trail of the Vigilantes" 1940 (Kansas Tim Mason). ¶TV: *Bonanza*—"Denver McKee" 10-15-60 (Denver McKee); *Wagon Train*—"The Malachi Hobart Story" 1-24-62 (Malachi Hobart); *The Virginian*—"The Old Cowboy" 3-31-65 (Murdock).

Tone Loc (1966-). Films: "Posse" 1993 (Angel).

Toner, Tom (1928-). TV: *The*

High Chaparral—"Spokes" 9-25-70 (Doctor).

Toney, Jim (1884-9/19/73). Films: "The Red Rider" 1934-serial; "The Lonely Trail" 1936 (Jed); "Rhythm on the Range" 1936 (Oil Station Proprietor); "Left-Handed Law" 1937; "Bar 20 Justice" 1938; "Cassidy of Bar 20" 1938 (Cowhand; "Flaming Frontier" 1938-serial; "Pride of the West" 1938; "Sunset Trail" 1938; "The Oregon Trail" 1939-serial;"Wagon Train" 1940 (Station Agent); "The Harvey Girls" 1946 (Mule Skinner).

Tong, Kam (1907-11/8/69). Films: "King of the Mounties" 1942-serial (Jap Pilot). ¶TV: *Have Gun Will Travel*—Regular 1957-63 (Hey Boy); *The Californians*—"Death by Proxy" 3-18-58 (Lee Ying); *The Virginian*—"Smile of a Dragon" 2-26-64 (Ming Yang); *Bonanza*—"The Meredith Smith" 10-31-65 (Ching); *The Big Valley*—"Down Shadow Street" 1-23-67 (Wing Lee), "The Emperor of Rice" 2-12-68 (Key), "The Royal Road" 3-3-69 (House Boy).

Tong, Sammee (1901-10/27/64). TV: *Judge Roy Bean*—"Ah Sid, Cowboy" 1-1-56 (Ah Sid); *My Friend Flicka*—"Lost River" 6-15-56; *The Californians*—"Gold-Tooth Charlie" 3-10-59 (Quon Wei); *Bonanza*—"A Rose for Lotta" 9-12-59 (Hop Ling).

Tonge, Philip (1898-1/28/59). Films: "Ricochet Romance" 1954 (Mr. Webster); "Track of the Cat" 1954 (Pa Bridges); "Pardners" 1956 (Footman); "The Peacemaker" 1956 (Elijah Maddox). ¶TV: *My Friend Flicka*—"Mister Goblin" 3-23-56; *Northwest Passage*—Regular 1958-59 (General Amherst).

Tooker, William H. (1864-10/12/36) Films: "A Woman's Man" 1920 (C. Lambert Grey); "God's Country and the Law" 1922 (Jacques Dore).

Toomey, Regis (1902-10/12/91). Films: "The Light of the Western Stars" 1930 (Bob Drexel); "A Man from Wyoming" 1930 (Jersey); "Skull and Crown" 1935 (Bob Franklin/ Rocky Morgan); "Union Pacific" 1939 (Paddy O'Rourke); "Arizona" 1940 (Grant Oury); "Northwest Mounted Police" 1940 (Constable Jerry More); "Northwest Passage" 1940 (Webster); "They Died with Their Boots On" 1941 (Fitzhugh Lee); "Raiders of Ghost City" 1944-serial (Captain Clay Randolph); "Station West" 1948 (Goddard); "Dynamite Pass" 1950 (Dan); "Frenchie" 1950 (Carter); "Tomahawk" 1951 (Smith); "The Battle at Apache Pass" 1952

(Dr. Carter); "The Nebraskan" 1953 (Col. Markham); "Son of Belle Star" 1953 (Tom Wren, Editor); "Drums Across the River" 1954 (Sheriff Beal); "Top Gun" 1955 (O'Hara); "Dakota Incident" 1956 (Minstrel); "Great Day in the Morning" 1956 (Father Murphy); "Warlock" 1959 (Skinner); "Guns of the Timberland" 1960 (Sheriff Taylor); "The Last Sunset" 1961 (Milton Wing); "The Night of the Grizzly" 1966 (Cotton Benson). ¶TV: *Cheyenne*—"The Storm Riders" 2-7-56 (Dembo), "Hard Bargain" 5-21-57 (Pat), "The Vanishing Breed" 11-19-62 (Ray Masters); *Zane Grey Theater*—"Time of Decision" 1-18-57 (Will Jenkins); *Jim Bowie*—"The Pearls of Talimeco" 11-8-57; *Broken Arrow*—"Transfer" 6-24-58 (Bouchet); *Trackdown*—"Matter of Justice" 10-17-58 (Murdoch), "Guilt" 12-19-58 (Sheriff Waterman); *Wanted—Dead or Alive*—"Ricochet" 11-22-58; *Maverick*—"Shady Deal at Sunny Acres" 11-23-58 (Ben Granville); *The Restless Gun*—"The Hill of Death" 6-22-59 (Dr. Lem Shepherd); *Rawhide*—"Incident of the Stalking Death" 11-13-59 (Goldie), "Incident at Tinker's Dam" 2-5-60 (T.J. Wishbone); *Texas John Slaughter*—"Range War at Tombstone" 12-18-59 (Pa Howell), "Apache Friendship" 2-19-60 (Pa Howell); *Bronco*—"Volunteers from Aberdeen" 2-9-60; *Tombstone Territory*—2-19-60 (Feeny Spindler); *Lawman*—"Left Hand of the Law" 3-27-60 (Jubal Matthews); *The Deputy*—"Marked for Bounty" 4-2-60 (Warden Jess Martin); *Tales of Wells Fargo*—"Man for the Job" 5-30-60 (Hull); *Man from Blackhawk*—"The Lady in Yellow" 6-17-60 (Dickson); *The Tall Man*—"And the Beast" 11-26-60 (Doc Corbin); *Sugarfoot*—"Shepherd with a Gun" 2-6-61 (John Peel); *Death Valley Days*—"The Hold-Up Proof Safe" 10-4-61 (Gus Lammerson); *The Virginian*—"The Judgment" 1-16-63; *The Legend of Jesse James*—"Things Don't Just Happen" 3-14-66 (Defense Attorney Reed).

Toones, Fred "Snowflake" (1906-2/13/62). Films: "Human Targets" 1932 (Snowflake); "Single-Handed Sanders" 1932; "Robbers' Roost" 1933 (Ferryboat Driver); "Valley of Wanted Men" 1935 (Snowflake); "Desert Justice" 1936; "Frontier Justice" 1936 (Snowflake); "Hair-Trigger Casey" 1936 (Snowflake); "The Lawless Nineties" 1936 (Mose); "The Lonely Trail" 1936 (Snowflake); "Oh, Susanna!" 1936; "Riddle Ranch" 1936 (Snowflake); "The Singing Cowboy" 1936 (Entertainer); "Wildcat Saunders" 1936

(Snowflake); "Aces Wild" 1937 (Snowflake); "Dodge City Trail" 1937 (Snowflake); "Fair Warning" 1937 (Porter); "Gunsmoke Ranch" 1937; "Range Defenders" 1937 (Cook); "Way Out West" 1937 (Janitor); "Wild Horse Rodeo" 1937 (Snowflake); "Yodelin' Kid from Pine Ridge" 1937 (Sam); "Gold Mine in the Sky" 1938 (Snowflake); "Hawaiian Buckaroo" 1938 (Flash); "Heroes of the Alamo" 1938; "Red River Range" 1938 (Bellhop); "Riders of the Black Hills" 1938 (Snowflake); "Mexicali Rose" 1939; "Rovin' Tumbleweeds" 1939; "Frontier Vengeance" 1940 (Snowflake); "Gaucho Serenade" 1940; "One Man's Law" 1940 (Snowflake); "Ride, Tenderfoot, Ride" 1940; "Texas Terrors" 1940 (Snowflake); "The Tulsa Kid" 1940 (Snowball); "The Apache Kid" 1941 (Snowflake); "Back in the Saddle" 1941; "A Missouri Outlaw" 1941; "Two-Gun Sheriff" 1941 (Snowflake); "Arizona Terrors" 1942; "The Great Man's Lady" 1942 (Fogey); "Raiders of the West" 1942; "Silver Queen" 1942 (Butler); "The Haunted Ranch" 1943; "Land of Hunted Men" 1943; "Death Valley Rangers" 1944 (Snowflake); "Firebrands of Arizona" 1944 (Charlie); "Hidden Valley Outlaws" 1944; "Fool's Gold" 1946 (Speed); "Bells of San Angelo" 1947 (the Cook).

Toone, Geoffrey (1910-). TV: *The Westerner*—"Jeff" 9-30-60 (Denny Lipp).

Tootoosis, George. Films: "Dan Candy's Law" 1975-U.S./Can.; "Marie-Ann" 1978-Can. (Indian Chief).

Tootoosis, Gordon. Films: "Call of the Wild" TVM-1993 (Indian Charlie); "Blood River" TVM-1994. ¶TV: *Lonesome Dove*—Pilot 10-2-94, 10-9-94 & 10-16-94.

Topol (1935-). Films: "Talent for Loving" 1969-Brit./Span.

Topper, Burt (1934-). Films: "Plunderers of Painted Flats" 1959 (Bart).

Tordi, Pietro (Peter Tordy) (1906-). Films: "Man Called Gringo" 1964-Ger./Span. (Sam Martin); "Arizona Colt" 1965-Ital./Fr./Span. (Priest).

Tordy, Peter. *see* Tordi, Pietro.

Torena, Juan. Films: "The Gay Caballero" 1932 (Juan Rodrigues); "The Eagle's Brood" 1936 (Estaban).

Torey, Hal. TV: *Jim Bowie*—"Bowie's Baby" 5-2-58 (Sheriff); *Colt .45*—"Appointment in Agoura" 6-7-60 (Abel Sanger); *Sugarfoot*—"Welcome Enemy" 12-26-60 (General Watson); *Lawman*—"The Robbery" 1-1-61 (Sam Deever); *Zane Grey Theater*—"Blood Red" 1-29-61 (Sheriff); *Death Valley Days*—"The Battle of San Francisco Bay" 4-11-65 (Calhoun).

Torme, Mel (1923-). Films: "Walk Like a Dragon" 1960 (the Deacon). ¶TV: *The Virginian*—"The Handy Man" 3-6-68 (Jim).

Torn, Rip (1931-). Films: "Heartland" 1980 (Clyde); "Dream West" TVM-1986 (Kit Carson). ¶TV: *The Restless Gun*—"Jody" 11-4-57 (Jody); *Frontier Circus*—"The Hunter and the Hunted" 11-2-61 (Jess Evans); *Great Adventure*—"The Pathfinder" 3-6-64 (Lt. John C. Fremont); *Rawhide*—"Escape to Doom" 10-12-65 (Jacob); *Bonanza*—"Blind Hunch" 11-21-71 (Will Hewitt).

Torray, Nuria. Films: "Two Thousand Dollars for Coyote" 1965-Span.; "Fury of the Apaches" 1966-Span./Ital.; "Seven for Pancho Villa" 1966-Span.; "Django Does Not Forgive" 1967-Ital./Span.

Torrence, David (1864-12/26/51). Films: "The Sawdust Trail" 1924 (Jonathan Butts); "The Reckless Sex" 1925 (Robert Lanning); "The Unknown Cavalier" 1926 (Peter Gaunt); "The Wolf Hunters" 1926; "The Mysterious Rider" 1927 (Mark King); "The Cavalier" 1928 (Ramon Torreno); "Untamed Justice" 1929 (George Morrow); "River's End" 1930 (Col. McDowell).

Torrence, Ernest (1878-5/15/33). Films: "Broken Chains" 1922 (Boyan Boone); "The Covered Wagon" 1923 (Jackson); "Ruggles of Red Gap" 1923 (Cousin Egbert Floud); "Heritage of the Desert" 1924 (August Naab); "North of '36" 1924 (Jim Nabours); "The Pony Express" 1925 (Ascension Jones); "Fighting Caravans" 1931 (Bill Jackson).

Torres, Jose (1917-). Films: "The Big Gundown" 1966-Ital. (Nathan); "Deguello" 1966-Ital. (David Isaac); "Ramon the Mexican" 1966-Ital./Span.; "Blood at Sundown" 1967-Span./Ital.; "Death Rides a Horse" 1967-Ital. (Pedro); "Face to Face" 1967-Ital.; "Poker with Pistols" 1967-Ital.; "Run Man, Run" 1967-Ital./Fr.; "Thirty Winchesters for El Diablo" 1967-Ital.; "All Out" 1968-Ital./Span.; "Any Gun Can Play" 1968-Ital.; "Blood and Guns" 1968-Ital./Span.; "Get the Coffin Ready" 1968-Ital.; "The Five Man Army" 1969-Ital. (Mexican Spy); "God Will Forgive My Pistol" 1969-Ital. (Prescott); "I Am Sartana, Your

Angel of Death" 1969-Ital./Fr.; "Django Challenges Sartana" 1970-Ital.; "Durango Is Coming, Pay or Die" 1972-Ital./Span.; "Colt in the Hand of the Devil" 1972-Ital.; "Death Is Sweet from the Soldier of God" 1972-Ital.; "God in Heaven … Arizona on Earth" 1972-Span./Ital.; "Shoot Joe, and Shoot Again" 1972-Ital.; "Gunmen and the Holy Ghost" 1973-Ital.

Torres, Liz (1947-). Films: "More Wild Wild West" TVM-1980 (Juanita); "Sunset" 1988 (Rosa).

Torres, Raquel (1908-8/10/87). Films: "The Desert Rider" 1929 (Dolores); "Under a Texas Moon" 1930 (Raquella).

Torres, Tomas. Films: "Coffin for the Sheriff" 1965-Ital./Span.; "Four Dollars for Vengeance" 1965-Span./Ital.; "Yankee" 1967-Ital./Span.; "Sartana Does Not Forgive" 1968-Span./Ital.

Torrey, Roger. Films: "The Plunderers" 1960 (Jule); "Town Tamer" 1965 (Flon); "Scalplock" TVM-1966 (Nils Tovald); "Little House: The Last Farewell" TVM-1984 (Colonel Forbes). ¶TV: *Bonanza*—"A Woman Lost" 3-17-63 (Tiny); *Gunsmoke*—"May Blossoms" 2-15-64 (Feeder), "He Who Steals" 5-29-65, "The River" 9-11-72 & 9-18-72 (Finn MacCool); *Wagon Train*—"The Melanie Craig Story" 2-17-64 (Sonny); *The Virginian*—"Big Image … Little Man" 10-28-64 (Dolan), "Big Tiny" 12-18-68 (Tiny Morgan); *Iron Horse*—Regular 1966-68 (Nils Torvald); *Bret Maverick*—"Welcome to Sweetwater" 12-8-81 (Schroeder).

Torruco, Miguel (1920-4/22/56). Films: "Massacre" 1956 (Chavez).

Tortosa, Jose Luis. Films: "Law of the Texan" 1938 (Sanchez); "Doomed Caravan" 1941 (Don Pedro); "Vengeance of the West" 1942.

Torvay, Jose (-1973). Films: "The Treasure of the Sierra Madre" 1948 (Pablo); "My Brother, the Outlaw" 1951 (Ortiz); "Strange Lady in Town" 1955 (Bartolo Diaz); "From Hell to Texas" 1958 (Miguel); "The Last Sunset" 1961 (Rosario); "Two Mules for Sister Sara" 1970; "Kid Blue" 1973 (Old Coyote).

Totten, Robert (1937-1/27/95). Films: "Cutter's Trail" TVM-1970 (Thatcher); "The Apple Dumpling Gang Rides Again" 1979. ¶TV: *Gunsmoke*—"The Mark of Cain" 2-3-69 (Corley), "The Long Night" 2-17-69 (Ben Miller), "Hackett" 3-16-70

(Phelps Tully), "Gentry's Law" 10-12-70 (Abner), "Captain Sligo" 1-4-71 (Blacksmith), "Cleavus" 2-15-71 (Cleavus Lukens), "Alias Festus Haggen" 3-6-72 (Walker), "Talbot" 2-26-73 (Eli Snider); *Dirty Sally*—"My Fair Laddie" 3-29-74 (Cave).

Totter, Audrey (1918-). Films: "The Woman They Almost Lynched" 1953 (Kate Quantrill); "Massacre Canyon" 1954 (Flaxy); "The Vanishing American" 1955 (Marian Warner); "Man or Gun" 1958 (Fran Dare); "The Apple Dumpling Gang Rides Again" 1979 (Martha). ¶TV: *Zane Grey Theater*—"Return to Nowhere" 12-7-56 (Martha); *The Californians*—"Strange Quarantine" 12-10-57 (Dr. Louise Kendall); *Cheyenne*—"The Empty Gun" 2-25-58 (Martha); *Cimarron City*—Regular 1958-59 (Beth Purcell); *Wagon Train*—"The Tent City Story" 12-10-58 (Goldie); *Rawhide*—"Abilene" 5-18-62 (Vada); *Bonanza*—"A Time to Step Down" 9-25-66 (Beth Riley); *The Virginian*—"Yesterday's Timepiece" 1-18-67 (Mrs. Archer), "Home to Methuselah" 11-26-69 (Audry).

Tourneur, Andree. Films: "The Desert's Crucible" 1922 (Miss Benson); "Gaints of the Open" 1922; "Lights of the Desert" 1922 (Marie Curtis); "The Marshal of Moneymint" 1922 (Mollie Benton); "Rustlers of the Redwoods" 1922; "Trail of Hate" 1922 (Sunny Kerry); "Wolf Tracks" 1923 (Jean Meredith).

Tovar, Lupita. Films: "Border Law" 1931 (Tonita); "Yankee Don" 1931 (Juanita); "The Fighting Gringo" 1939 (Nita Del Campo); "South of the Border" 1939 (Dolores Mendoza); "The Westerner" 1940 (Teresita); "Two-Gun Sheriff" 1941 (Nita); "Gun to Gun" 1944-short.

Towers, Constance (1933-). Films: "The Horse Soldiers" 1959 (Hannah Hunter); "Sergeant Rutledge" 1960 (Mary Beecher). ¶TV: *Zane Grey Theater*—"Knight of the Sun" 3-9-61 (Beth Woodfield).

Towne, Aline (1929-). Films: "The Vanishing Westerner" 1950 (Barbara); "Don Daredevil Rides Again" 1951-serial (Patricia Doyle); "Rough Riders of Durango" 1951 (Janis). ¶TV: *The Lone Ranger*—"Trader Boggs" 1-15-53, "Christmas Story" 12-20-56; *Wyatt Earp*—"They Hired Some Guns" 2-26-57 (Amelia Woodruff); *Tales of Wells Fargo*—"Billy the Kid" 10-21-57; *Colt .45*—"Last Chance" 12-6-57 (Marion Whittier); *Maverick*—"Trail West to Fury" 2-16-58 (Laura Miller); *Rough Riders*—"Strand of Wire" 12-18-58

(Mollie Randolph), "The High-graders" 5-28-59 (Maggie Hill); *Wagon Train*—"The Dick Richardson Story" 12-31-58 (Laura Milford), "The Clayton Tucker Story" 2-10-60, "The Jose Morales Story" 10-19-60 (Patience Oliver), "The Hiram Winthrop Story" 6-6-62 (Meg), "The Tom O'Neal Story" 4-24-63 (Mrs. O'Neal), "The Pearlie Garnet Story" 2-24-64 (Lovey); *Whispering Smith*—"The Deadliest Weapon" 6-19-61 (Tina Miller).

Towne, Rosella. Films: "Cowboy from Brooklyn" 1938 (Panthea); "Rocky Mountain Rangers" 1940 (Doris Manners).

Townes, Harry (1918-). Films: "Heaven with a Gun" 1969 (Gus Sampson); "Santee" 1973; "Last Ride of the Dalton Gang" TVM-1979 (Reverend Johnson). ¶TV: *Gunsmoke*—"Spring Team" 12-15-56 (Bill Lee), "Monopoly" 10-4-58 (Ivy), "Tail to the Wind" 10-17-59 (Pezzy Neller), "Tobe" 10-19-63 (Tobe Hostader), "Two Tall Men" 5-8-65 (Abihu Howell), "Malachi" 11-13-65 (Malachi Harper), "Lijah" 11-8-71 (Hale Parker); *Have Gun Will Travel*—"The Bostonian" 2-1-58 (Henry Prince); *Zane Grey Theater*—"Deadfall" 2-19-59 (Hugh Perry), "Interrogation" 10-1-59 (Corporal Durbin); *Rawhide*—"Incident of the Town in Terror" 3-6-59 (Amos Stauffer), "Incident of the Night on the Town" 6-2-61 (Lewis Lewis), "Incident at Seven Fingers" 5-7-64 (Captain Jesse Coulter), "The Lost Herd" 10-16-64 (Dillman); *Desilu Playhouse*—"Six Guns for Donegan" 10-16-59 (Cowardly Citizen); *Wanted—Dead or Alive*—"Mental Lapse" 1-2-60 (Olin McDonald), "Vendetta" 4-9-60 (Capt. William Phelps); *The Rebel*—"The Death of Gray" 1-3-60 (Colonel); *Death Valley Days*—"His Brother's Keeper" 1-19-60 (Edwin Booth); *Laramie*—"Rope of Steel" 2-16-60 (Mace Stringer); *The Deputy*—"The Truly Yours" 4-9-60; *Johnny Ringo*—"Judgment Day" 4-14-60 (Judge Bentley); *Wrangler*—"Incident of the Wide Lop" 9-1-60 (Cole Barton); *Bonanza*—"The Mill" 10-1-60 (Tom Edwards), "The War Comes to Washoe" 11-4-62 (Judge Terry), "The Medal" 10-26-69 (Seth Nagel); *Stagecoach West*—"Life Sentence" 12-6-60 (Toby Reese); *The Outlaws*—"Masterpiece" 12-21-61 (Jerry Rome), "A Day to Kill" 2-22-62 (Frank Wagner); *The Tall Man*—"The Frame" 4-21-62 (Henry Stewart); *The Dakotas*—"Feud at Snake River" 4-29-63 (George Deus); *The Virginian*—"A Little Learning..." 9-29-65 (Cal Bee-

som); *A Man Called Shenandoah*—"The Verdict" 11-1-65 (Dr. Stanton); *Wild Wild West*—"The Night of the Double-Edged Knife" 11-12-65 (Penrose), "The Night of the Tottering Tontine" 1-6-67 (Prof. Raven); *Branded*—"The Golden Fleece" 1-2-66 (Kirby); *The Monroes*—"The Friendly Enemy" 11-9-66 (Joe Smith); *The Big Valley*—"The Emperor of Rice" 2-12-68 (Warren Masters); *Kung Fu*—"An Eye for an Eye" 1-25-73 (Amos Buchanan); *Sara*—2-27-76 (Doc Vaughn).

Townsend, Jill (1945-). TV: *Cimarron Strip*—Regular 1967-68 (Dulcey Coppersmith); *Wild Wild West*—"The Night of the Sabatini Death" 2-2-69 (Sylvia Nolan); *Bonanza*—"Another Windmill to Go" 9-14-69 (Abbey); *The Virginian*—"Black Jade" 12-31-69 (Roseanna).

Tozere, Frederic (1901-8/5/72). TV: *The Lone Ranger*—"Bullets for Ballots" 5-11-50.

Tozzi, Fausto (1921-12/10/78). Films: "Pyramid of the Sun God" 1965-Ger./Ital./Fr.; "The Man Who Killed Billy the Kid" 1967-Span./Ital. (Pat Garrett); "Deserter" 1970-U.S./Ital./Yugo. (Orozco); "Man Called Sledge" 1971-Ital./U.S.; "Chino" 1973-Ital./Span./Fr. (Cruz).

Trace, Al (and his Silly Symphonists). Films: "Rustlers of the Badlands" 1945; "Frontier Gunlaw" 1946.

Tracey, Doreen. Films: "Westward Ho the Wagons" 1956 (Bobo Stephen).

Tracey, Ray. Films: "Joe Panther" 1976 (Joe Panther). ¶TV: *How the West Was Won*—Episode Six 3-26-78 (Teel-O), Episode Seven 4-9-78 (Teel-O), Episode Eight 4-16-78 (Teel-O); *Centennial*—Regular 1978-79 (Young Lame Beaver); *Young Maverick*—"Makin' Tracks" 1-9-80 (Russell Two Eagles).

Tracy, Lee (1898-10/18/68). Films: "Sutter's Gold" 1936 (Pete Perkins). ¶TV: *Wagon Train*—"The George B. Hanrahan Story" 3-28-62 (George B. Hanrahan).

Tracy, Marlene. Films: "The Intruders" TVM-1970; "Lock, Stock and Barrel" TVM-1971 (Jean). ¶TV: *Wild Wild West*—"The Night of the Headless Woman" 1-5-68 (Joanne).

Tracy, Spencer (1900-6/10/67). Films: "Northwest Passage" 1940 (Maj. Robert Rogers); "The Sea of Grass" 1947 (Col. Jim Brewton); "Broken Lance" 1954 (Matt Devereaux); "Bad Day at Black Rock" 1955 (John J. Macreedy); "How the West Was Won" 1962 (Narrator).

Tracy, Steve (1952-11/27/86). TV: *Little House on the Prairie*—Regular 1980-81 (Percival Dalton).

Tracy, William (1917-6/18/67). TV: *The Westerner*—"School Days" 10-7-60 (Doug Ritchie); *Wyatt Earp*—"Wyatt Earp's Baby" 4-25-61 (Arnold Trask).

Traeger, Rick (1912-11/14/87). Films: "The Legend of the Lone Ranger" 1981 (German).

Trahey, Madalyn. Films: "The Parson and the Outlaw" 1957 (Elly McCloud); "Mustang" 1959 (Nancy).

Trainor, Leonard (1879-7/28/40). Films: "Tempest Cody Hits the Trail" 1919; "Galloping Jinx" 1925; "The Border Sheriff" 1926 (Sheriff); "Hi-Jacking Rustlers" 1926; "Terror Trail" 1933 (Jones); "Stagecoach" 1939; "Water Rustlers" 1939 (Jurgens).

Travanty, Dan (1940-). TV: *Here Come the Brides*—"A Jew Named Sullivan" 11-20-68 (Sullivan); *Lancer*—"The Escape" 12-31-68 (Dan Cassidy); *Gunsmoke*—"Like Old Times" 1-21-74 (Aaron Barker), "The Colonel" 12-16-74 (Carl).

Travers, Arthur. Films: "The Indian Uprising at Santa Fe" 1912; "The Savage" 1917 (Joe Bedotte).

Travers, Bill (1922-3/28/94). Films: "Duel at Diablo" 1966 (Lt. McAllister). ¶TV: *Rawhide*—"Incident at Two Graves" 11-7-63 (Jeremiah O'Neal).

Travers, Henry (1874-10/18/65). Films: "Dodge City" 1939 (Dr. Irving); "Wyoming" 1940 (Sheriff); "The Bad Man" 1941 (Mr. Hardy); "Pierre of the Plains" 1942 (Mr. Wellsby).

Travers, Richard (1890-4/20/35). Films: "Pierre of the North" 1914; "The Dangerous Dude" 1925.

Traverse, Madelaine (1876-1/7/64). Films: "Rose of the West" 1919 (Rose Labelle).

Travis, Charles W. (1861-8/12/17) Films: "Thou Shalt Not" 1914 (Peter Cooper).

Travis, Merle (and His Bronco Busters) (1918-10/20/83). Films: "The Old Texas Trail" 1944 (Jake); "Galloping Thunder" 1946; "Lone Star Moonlight" 1946; "Roaring Rangers" 1946; "Cyclone Fury" 1951; "Night Rider" 1962-short.

Travis, Randy (1959-). Films: "Young Guns" 1988 (Ring Member); "Dead Man's Revenge" TVM-1994 (Harriman); "Frank and Jesse" TVM-1995 (Cole Younger); "James A. Michener's Texas" TVM-1995 (Capt. Sam Garner).

Travis, Richard (1913-7/11/89). Films: "Riders of Death Valley" 1941-serial; "Passage West" 1951 (Ben Johnson). ¶TV: *The Gene Autry Show*—"Blazeaway" 2-22-52, "Six Gun Romeo" 3-16-52; *Fury*—"Joey Saves the Day" 12-10-55 (Ford); *The Lone Ranger*—"The Frightened Woman" 9-30-54, "Wanted … the Lone Ranger" 5-5-55; *Wyatt Earp*—"Mr. Earp Becomes a Marshal" 9-6-55, "Mr. Earp Meets a Lady" 9-13-55, "Bill Thompson Gives In" 9-22-55; *Tales of Wells Fargo*—"The Break" 5-19-58 (Frank Woodson); *Cimarron City*—"The Bitter Lesson" 1-3-59 (Paul Erskine); *The Texan*—"Image of Guilt" 9-21-59 (Jess Grady), "The Governor's Lady" 3-14-60 (Governor); *The Legend of Jesse James*—"The Dead Man's Hand" 9-20-65 (Al Hoyt).

Traylor, William (1929-9/23/89). Films: "The Last Frontier" 1955 (Soldier); "The Long Riders" 1980. ¶TV: *The Outcasts*—"Give Me Tomorrow" 4-21-69 (Todd Spencer); *Kung Fu*—"The Raiders" 1-24-74 (Maulpede).

Treacy, Emerson (1905-1/10/67). Films: "Wyoming Mail" 1950 (Ben); "Fort Worth" 1951 (Ben Garvin); "Run for Cover" 1955 (Bank Manager). ¶TV: *Buckskin*—"The Man Who Waited" 7-10-58 (Doc Harris), "Tree of Death" 8-21-58 (Doc Harris); *Lawman*—"The Posse" 3-8-59 (Blinker); *Tales of Wells Fargo*—"Hometown Doctor" 2-17-62 (Doc Quinney).

Treadwell, Laura (1879-11/22/60). "Hawaiian Buckaroo" 1938; "King of the Bandits" 1947 (Mrs. Mason); "The Sea of Grass" 1947 (Bit).

Tree, Dorothy (1909-2/12/92). Films: "The Three Godfathers" 1936 (Blackie Winters).

Tree, Marietta (1917-8/15/91). Films: "The Misfits" 1961 (Susan).

Treen, Mary (1907-7/20/89). Films: "Romance of the West" 1935-short; "God's Country and the Woman" 1937 (Miss Flint); "Rodeo Dough" 1940-short; "The Great Man's Lady" 1942 (Persis); "Hands Across the Border" 1943 (Sophie Lawrence); "Swing in the Saddle" 1944; "Young Daniel Boone" 1950 (Helen Bryan); "The Great Jesse James Raid" 1953 (Mrs. Angus); "Gun Duel in Durango" 1957 (Spinster). ¶TV: *The Gene Autry Show*—"Blazeaway" 2-22-52, "Six Gun Romeo" 3-16-52; *Stories of the Century*—"Last Stagecoach West" 1954 (Miss Feeney); *Stage 7*—"Billy and the

Bride" 5-8-55 (Louise); *Wagon Train*—"Trial for Murder" 4-27-60 & 5-4-60; *Bonanza*—"The Mountain Girl" 5-13-62 (Annie).

Tremayne, Les (1913-). Films: "Shoot Out at Big Sag" 1962 (Chan Bartholomew, Saloon Owner). ¶TV: *The Adventures of Rin Tin Tin*—Regular 1958-59 (Major Stone); *The Texan*—"Outpost" 1-19-59 (Dr. Neal Carter); *The Rifleman*—"The Challenge" 4-7-59 (Professor); *Wagon Train*—"The Maggie Hamilton Story" 4-6-60 (H.J. Hamilton), "The Tom O'Neal Story" 4-24-63 (Mr. Howard), "The Jed Whitmore Story" 1-13-64 (William Carr); *Rawhide*—"Incident at the Top of the World" 1-27-61 (Dr. Gardner); *Zane Grey Theater*—"Jericho" 5-18-61 (Attorney General); *Whispering Smith*—"Safety Value" 6-5-61 (Colonel Middleton); *Bonanza*—"The Law Maker" 3-11-62 (Judge Jackson), "The Law and Billy Burgess" 2-15-70 (Doc Lyman); *Wide Country*—"The Girl from Nob Hill" 3-8-63 (Mr. Never); *The Dakotas*—"Sanctuary at Crystal Springs" 5-6-63 (Mr. Barton); *The Virginian*—"A Slight Case of Charity" 2-10-65 (Lowell), "An Echo of Thunder" 10-5-66 (Troost).

Trenker, Luis (1893-4/13/90). Films: "Kaiser von Kalifornien" 1936-Ger. (J.A. Sutter).

Trent, Jack (1897-8/1/61). Films: "The Little Warrior" 1926; "The Spoilers" 1930 (Bronco Kid); "Mounted Fury" 1931 (Phil Grover); "Outlaw Justice" 1933; "Stick to Your Guns" 1941 (Red). ¶TV: *The Roy Rogers Show*—"Tossup" 12-2-56.

Trent, Jean. Films: "Sin Town" 1942 (Dance Hall Girl); "Western Mail" 1942 (Julia); "Frontier Gal" 1945 (Hostess); "Salome, Where She Danced" 1945 (Salome Girl).

Trent, Karen Sue. TV: *Wagon Train*—"The Vincent Eaglewood Story" 4-15-59 (Oma Jean); *The Rifleman*—"Old Tony" 4-8-63 (Lorrie).

Trent, Lee (1909-1/11/88). TV: *Circus Boy*—"General Pete" 4-28-57 (Capt. Stanforth).

Trent, Russell. TV: *The Lone Ranger*—"Lady Killer" 12-21-50, "Mr. Trouble" 3-8-51; *Rawhide*—"Incident of the Shambling Men" 10-9-59, "The Pitchwagon" 3-2-62; *The Big Valley*—"Night of the Wolf" 12-1-65.

Tretter, Richard. Films: "Cattle King" 1963 (Hobie). ¶TV: *Temple Houston*—"Sam's Boy" 1-23-64 (Jake Harvey); *Daniel Boone*—"The Renegade" 9-28-67.

Trevino, Jorge (George Trevino). Films: "The Beast of Hollow Mountain" 1956 (Shopkeeper); "Black Patch" 1957 (Pedoline); "The Ride Back" 1957 (Guard); "The Last of the Fast Guns" 1958 (Manuel); "Villa!" 1958 (Capt. Castillo). ¶TV: *Telephone Time*—"Elfego Baca" 4-18-57 (Naranjo).

Trevor, Claire (1909-). Films: "The Last Trail" 1933 (Patricia Carter); "Life in the Raw" 1933 (Judy Halloway); "Allegheny Uprising" 1939 (Janie MacDougle); "Stagecoach" 1939 (Dallas); "The Dark Command" 1940 (Mary McCloud); "Honky Tonk" 1941 (Gold Dust Nelson); "Texas" 1941 (Mike King); "The Desperadoes" 1943 (Countess Maletta); "The Woman of the Town" 1943 (Dora Hand); "Best of the Badmen" 1951 (Lily Fowler); "The Stranger Wore a Gun" 1953 (Josie Sullivan); "Man Without a Star" 1955 (Idonee). ¶TV: *Wagon Train*—"The C.L. Harding Story" 10-14-59 (C.L. Harding).

Trevor, Hugh (1903-11/10/33). Films: "The Pinto Kid" 1928 (Dan Logan).

Tricoli, Carlo (1889-4/11/66). Films: "Wagon Team" 1952 (Dr. Kunody).

Triesault, Ivan (1900-1/3/80). Films: "Home in San Antone" 1949; "Back to God's Country" 1953 (Reinhardt); "Border River" 1954 (Baron Von Hollden); "The Gambler from Natchez" 1954 (Raoul); "Cimarron" 1960 (Lewis Venable). ¶TV: *Jim Bowie*—"Jim Bowie and His Slave" 11-30-56 (Maurice Toulouse), "The Return of the Alciblade" 12-21-56, "Spanish Intrigue" 2-8-57 (Maurice Toulouse); *Northwest Passage*—"The Hostage" 11-2-58 (Father Ricard); *Wild Wild West*—"The Night of the Surreal McCoy" 3-3-67 (Ambassador of Hertzburg); *Bonanza*—"Commitment at Angelus" 4-7-68 (Thad).

Trikonis, Gus (1937-). TV: *The Virginian*—"The Captive" 9-28-66 (Running Elk); *Iron Horse*—"Decision at Sundown" 2-27-67 (Manolo); *Dundee and the Culhane*—11-15-67 (Tonoka).

Trinka, Paul. TV: *The Big Valley*—"Tunnel of Gold" 4-20-66 (Dave).

Trintignant, Jean-Louis (1930-). Films: "Great Silence" 1968-Ital./Fr. (Silence).

Tripp, Paul. TV: *Empire*—"The Day the Empire Stood Still" 9-25-62 (Thayer Wilson); *Have Gun Will*

Travel—"A Place for Abel Hix" 10-6-62 (Reverend Harber).

Tristan, Dorothy (1934-). TV: *Gunsmoke*—"The Guns of Cibola Blanca" 9-23-74 & 9-30-74 (Lyla).

Tritt, Travis. Films: "Rio Diablo" TVM-1993 (Benjamin Tabor).

Troughton, Patrick (1920-3/28/87). TV: *The Law of the Plainsman*—"The Matriarch" 2-18-60.

Troup, Bobby (1918-). TV: *Rawhide*—"Incident at Rojo Canyon" 9-30-60 (Nelson Hoyt).

Troupe, Tom (1928-). TV: *Rawhide*—"Incident at Rojo Canyon" 9-30-60 (Trooper); *Lawman*—"Cornered" 12-11-60 (Jim Barker); *Wild Wild West*—"The Night of the Egyptian Queen" 11-15-68 (Jason Starr); *Barbary Coast*—"The Day Cable Was Hanged" 12-26-75 (Carter).

Trout, Tom. Films: "The Kid from Texas" 1950 (Denby); "The Palomino" 1950 (Williams). ¶TV: *The Californians*—"Wolf's Head" 2-24-59 (Policeman); *The Texan*—"The Telegraph Story" 10-26-59 (Bill Ness).

Trowbridge, Charles (1882-10/30/67). Films: "Robin Hood of El Dorado" 1936 (Ramon de la Cuesta); "Cherokee Strip" 1940 (Senator Cross); "Trail of the Vigilantes" 1940 (John Thronton); "Virginia City" 1940 (Seddon); "Belle Starr" 1941 (Col. Bright); "King of the Texas Rangers" 1941-serial (Robert Crawford); "Hurricane Smith" 1942 (Mark Harris); "The Sea of Grass" 1947 (George Cameron); "The Paleface" 1948 (Gov. Johnson); "The Bushwackers" 1952 (Justin Stone).

Troy, Louise (1933-5/5/94). TV: *Iron Horse*—"Five Days to Washtiba" 10-7-67 (the Countess); *Dundee and the Culhane*—11-1-67 (Mrs. Amber).

Truax, John (-6/14/69). Films: "Riding with Buffalo Bill" 1954-serial; "Curse of the Undead" 1959 (Henchman). ¶TV: *Wild Bill Hickok*—"Town Without Law" 6-23-53; *The Roy Rogers Show*—"Money Is Dangerous" 1-29-56, "Horse Crazy" 2-26-56; *Cheyenne*—"Deadline" 2-26-57 (Murkle); *Tales of the Texas Rangers*—"Trail Herd" 11-10-57 (Tom Powers); *Maverick*—"The Ice Man" 1-29-61 (Brazos); *Laredo*—"The Legend of Midas Mantee" 9-16-66 (Val Verde Sheriff).

True, Bess (1899-7/9/47). Films: "Heartbound" 1925 (Beth).

Truesdell, Howard (1861-12/8/41). Films: "Out of Luck" 1923 (Ezra Day); "Ride for Your Life" 1924 (Dan Burke); "The Ridin 'Kid from Powder River" 1924 (Pop Watkins); "Go West" 1925 (Thompson); "The Wild West Wallop" 1925; "The Dude Cowboy" 1926 (Amos Wrigmint); "Fighting with Buffalo Bill" 1926-serial; "The Stolen Ranch" 1926 (Tom Marston); "The Denver Dude" 1927 (Colonel La Mar); "The Lawless Legion" 1929 (Sheriff Keiver); "The Long, Long Trail" 1929 (Uncle Josh).

Trueman, Paula (1907-3/23/94). Films: "The Outlaw Josey Wales" 1976 (Grandma Smith).

Truex, Barry. TV: *Wyatt Earp*—"The Desperate Half-Hour" 2-28-56 (Lonnie McVey); *Sergeant Preston of the Yukon*—"Fancy Dan" 4-5-56 (Tim Norton).

Truex, Ernest (1889-6/27/73). TV: *Bonanza*—"Square Deal Sam" 11-8-64 (Sam Washburn).

Trumbull, Brad (1924-11/25/94). Films: "Five Guns to Tombstone" 1961; "The Gambler Wore a Gun" 1961 (Deputy). ¶TV: *Tombstone Territory*—"The Youngest Gun" 1-1-58 (Jim Reno); *Have Gun Will Travel*—"The Haunted Trees" 6-13-59 (Brad); *Gunsmoke*—"False Witness" 12-12-59 (Sawyer), "The Cook" 12-17-60 (Pete), "Reprisal" 3-10-62 (Ives); *Hotel De Paree*—"Sundance and the Cattlemen" 5-13-60 (Roach); *Wild Wild West*—"The Night of the Turncoat" 12-1-67 (Doctor).

Trundy, Natalie (1942-). Films: "Walk Like a Dragon" 1960 (Susan). ¶TV: *Pony Express*—"The Pendant" 3-16-60 (Amber); *Bonanza*—"Denver McKee" 10-15-60 (Connie McKee); *The Dakotas*—"Return to Drydock" 1-7-63 (Betty Lou); *Wagon Train*—"The Naomi Kaylor Story" 1-30-63 (Grace Kaylor).

Trunnelle, Mabel (1879-4/29/81). Films: "A Perilous Ride" 1911; "The Disputed Claim" 1912; "The Man from the West" 1913; "The Ranch Owner's Love-Making" 1913; "A Tale of Old Tucson" 1914; "Ranson's Folly" 1915 (Mary Cahill).

Tryon, Glenn (1899-4/18/70). Films: "The Denver Dude" 1927 (Percy, the Dude); "Secret Menace" 1931.

Tryon, Tom (1926-9/4/91). Films: "Three Violent People" 1956 (Cinch Saunders); "The Glory Guys" 1965 (Demas Harrod); "Winchester '73" TVM-1967 (Lin McAdam). ¶TV: *Frontier*—"King of the Dakotas" 11-13-55 & 11-20-55; *Zane Grey Theater*—"Black Is for Grief" 4-12-57 (Jeff Anderson); *Wagon Train*—"The Mark Hanford Story" 2-26-58 (Mark Hanford); *The Restless Gun*—"Sheriff Billy" 3-10-58 (Sheriff Bill Riddle); *Texas John Slaughter*—Regular 1958-61 (Texas John Slaughter); *The Virginian*—"The Man from the Sea" 12-26-62 (Kevin Doyle), "Girl on the Glass Mountain" 12-28-66 (Howie Sheppard), "Star Crossed" 10-4-67 (Andrew Hiller); *The Big Valley*—"The Midas Man" 4-13-66 (Scott Breckenridge); *The Road West*—"Charade of Justice" 3-27-67 (Sheriff Platt); *The Men from Shiloh*—"The Price of the Hanging" 11-11-70 (Sheriff Tolliver).

Tsiang, H.T. (1899-7/16/71). Films: "In Old Sacramento" 1946. ¶TV: *Sugarfoot*—"The Highbinder" 1-19-60 (Yup Toy); *Wagon Train*—"The Widow O'Rourke Story" 10-7-63 (the Mandarin); *Bonanza*—"Found Child" 10-24-65 (Su Chin); *Gunsmoke*—"Gunfighter, R.I.P." 10-22-66 (Ching Fa).

Tsopei, Corinna (1944-). Films: "A Man Called Horse" 1970 (Running Deer). ¶TV: *Daniel Boone*—"The Flaming Rocks" 2-1-68.

Tsu, Irene (1943-). TV: *Laredo*—"The Bitter Yen of General Ti" 2-3-67 (Jem Sing); *Wild Wild West*—"The Night of the Samurai" 10-13-67 (Reiko O'Hara).

Tubb, Barry. Films: "Lonesome Dove" TVM-1989 (Jasper Fant); "Return to Lonesome Dove" TVM-1993 (Jasper Fant).

Tubb, Ernest (1914-9/6/84). Films: "The Fighting Buckaroo" 1943 (Ernie); "Riding West" 1944 (Ernie); "Hollywood Barn Dance" 1947 (Ernie).

Tucker, Forrest (1919-10/25/-86). Films: "The Westerner" 1940 (Wade Harper); "Shut My Big Mouth" 1942 (Red); "The Gunfighters" 1947 (Hen Orcutt); "Adventures in Silverado" 1948 (the Monk); "Coroner Creek" 1948 (Ernie Combs); "The Plunderers" 1948 (Whit Lacey); "Two Guys from Texas" 1948 (Tex Bennett); "Brimstone" 1949 (Sheriff Henry McIntyre); "Hellfire" 1949 (Bucky McLean); "The Last Bandit" 1949 (Jim Plummer); "California Passage" 1950 (Mike Prescott); "The Nevadan" 1950 (Tom Tanner); "Rock Island Trail" 1950 (Reed Loomis); "Oh! Susanna" 1951 (Lt. Col. Unger); "Warpath" 1951 (Sgt. O'Hara); "Bugles in the Afternoon" 1952 (Donavan); "Flaming Feather" 1952 (Lt. Tom Blaine); "Montana Belle" 1952 (Mac); "Ride the Man Down" 1952 (Sam Danfelser); "Pony Express" 1953 (Wild Bill Hickok); "San Antone" 1953 (Brian Culver); "Jubilee Trail" 1954

(John Ives); "Rage at Dawn" 1955 (Frank Reno); "The Vanishing American" 1955 (Morgan); "Stagecoach to Fury" 1956 (Frank Townsend); "Three Violent People" 1956 (Cable, the Deputy Commissioner); "The Deerslayer" 1957 (Harry Marsh); "The Quiet Gun" 1957 (Carl, the Sheriff); "Fort Massacre" 1958 (McGurney); "Gunsmoke in Tucson" 1958 (John Brazos); "Barquero" 1970 (Mountain Phil); "Chisum" 1970 (Lawrence Murphy); "Alias Smith and Jones" TVM-1971 (Deputy Harker); "The Wackiest Wagon Train in the West" 1976 (Mr. Callahan); "The Incredible Rocky Mountain Race" TVM-1977 (Mike Fink). ¶TV: *Wagon Train*—"The Rex Montana Story" 5-28-58 (Rex Montana); *Whispering Smith*—"The Trademark" 8-14-61 (Gunman Bardot); *Wide Country*—"Speckle Bird" 1-31-63 (Lynn Horn); *Rawhide*—"Incident of the Death Dancer" 12-5-63 (Dan Carloc); *Death Valley Days*—"Three Minutes to Eternity" 1-26-64 (Bob Dalton); *Gunsmoke*—"Double Entry" 1-2-65 (Brad McClain), "The Storm" 9-25-65 (Adam Benteen), "Cattle Barons" 9-18-67 (John Charron), "The War Priest" 1-5-70 (Sgt. Emmett Holly), "Sergeant Holly" 12-14-70 (Sergeant Holly), "Yankton" 2-7-72 (Will Donavan); *The Virginian*—"Hideout" 1-13-65 (Martin Evers); *F Troop*—Regular 1965-67 (Sergeant Morgan O'Rourke); *Daniel Boone*—"The Ballad of Sidewinder and Cherokee" 9-14-67 (Joe Snag), "The Return of Sidewinder" 12-12-68 (Joe Snag); *Hondo*—"Hondo and the Judas" 11-3-67 (Colonel); *Bonanza*—"Warbonnet" 12-26-71 (Ryan); *Dusty's Trail*—Regular 1973 (Callahan); *The Life and Times of Grizzly Adams*—"Gold Is Where You Find It" 11-23-77.

Tucker, Harland (1893-3/22/49). Films: "Desert Fury" 1947 (Chuck, The Crap Dealer).

Tucker, Richard (1884-12/5/42). Films: "Black Eagle" 1915; "Pardners" 1917 (Justus Morrow); "The Branding Iron" 1920 (Prosper Gael); "Forty-Horse Hawkins" 1924 (Rudolph Catalina); "The Lure of the Wild" 1925 (Gordon Daniels); "Border Patrol" 1928 (Earl Hanway); "A Holy Terror" 1931 (Tom Hedges); "The Girl of the Golden West" 1938 (Colonel); "Renfrew on the Great White Trail" 1938 (Inspector Newcomb); "The Texans" 1938 (Gen. Corbett).

Tucker, Wayne. TV: *The Law of the Plainsman*—"The Dude" 12-3-59,

"The Comet" 1-21-60 (Bunsing); *Johnny Ringo*—"Four Came Quietly" 1-28-60 (Grat Jethro); *The Westerner*—"Jeff" 9-30-60, "Hand on the Gun" 12-23-60.

Tudor, Pamela. Films: "Death at Owell Rock" 1967-Ital.; "Time of Vultures" 1967-Ital. (Steffi); "Dollars for a Fast Gun" 1968-Ital./Span. (Helen Ray); "One After Another" 1968-Span./Ital.; "Canadian Wilderness" 1969-Span./Ital.; "Sartana in the Valley of Death" 1970-Ital.

Tuerpe, Paul. Films: "Maverick" 1994 (Poker Player). ¶TV: *Paradise*—"Stray Bullet" 12-8-88 (Jake).

Tufts, Sonny (1912-6/5/70). Films: "The Virginian" 1946 (Steve); "The Untamed Breed" 1948 (Tom Kilpatrick); "The Parson and the Outlaw" 1957 (Jack Slade); "Town Tamer" 1965 (Carmichael). ¶TV: *The Virginian*—"Ride a Dark Trail" 9-18-63 (Frank Trampas); *Bob Hope Chrysler Theatre*—"Have Girls—Will Travel" 10-16-64 (Monk); *The Loner*—"The Ordeal of Bud Windom" 12-25-65 (Barney Windom).

Tulli, Marco (1922-). Films: "Shadow of Zorro" 1963-Span./Ital.

Tully, Phil. Films: "The Stranger Wore a Gun" 1953. ¶TV: *The Deputy*—Regular 1959-61 (Charlie, the Bartender); *Maverick*—"The Witch of Hound Dog" 11-6-60 (Cyrus), "Diamond Flush" 2-5-61 (Tim O'Rourke); *Riverboat*—"Zigzag" 12-26-60 (Bartender); *Tales of Wells Fargo*—"Return to Yesterday" 1-13-62 (McGuire).

Tully, Tom (1896-4/27/82). Films: "The Virginian" 1946 (Nebraska); "Blood on the Moon" 1948 (John Lufton); "Rachel and the Stranger" 1948 (Parson Jackson); "Branded" 1951 (Ransome); "Tomahawk" 1951 (Dan Costello); "Return of the Texan" 1952 (Stud Spiller); "Arrow in the Dust" 1954 (Crowshaw). ¶TV: *Zane Grey Theater*—"Black Is for Grief" 4-12-57 (Tom Roarke), "Badge of Honor" 5-3-57 (Jed Phillips); *Rawhide*—"Incident at Rio Salado" 9-29-61 (Jake Yates), "Blood Harvest" 2-12-65 (Williams); *Tales of Wells Fargo*—"Defiant at the Gate" 11-25-61 (Matt Blackner); *Empire*—"Long Past, Long Remembered" 10-23-62 (Tom Cole); *The Virginian*—"The Hour of the Tiger" 12-30-64 (Junius Antlow); *Bonanza*—"The Dilemma" 9-19-65 (Sundown), "The Sure Thing" 11-12-67 (Burt Loughlin); *The Loner*—"Hunt the Man Down" 12-11-65 (Shaftoe); *The Legend of Jesse James*—"The Man Who Killed Jesse" 12-27-65 (Doc

Pierson); *Shane*—Regular 1966 (Tom Starrett); *The Guns of Will Sonnett*—"The Favor" 11-10-67 (Corky Dobbs), "Join the Army" 1-3-69 (Pachen); *The High Chaparral*—"The Last Hundred Miles" 1-24-69 (General Tirrel).

Tupou, Manu (1939-). Films: "A Man Called Horse" 1970 (Yellow Hand); "The Castaway Cowboy" 1974 (Kimo). TV: *Young Dan'l Boone*—"The Salt Licks" 9-26-77 (Running Dear); *Born to the Wind* 1982 (Cold Maker).

Turich, Felipe (1898-3/9/92). Films: "The Lone Rider Crosses the Rio" 1941 (Lt. Mendoza); "Outlaws of the Rio Grande" 1941 (Pancho); "Beauty and the Bandit" 1946; "The Bells of San Fernando" 1947 (Mule Driver); "Robin Hood of Monterey" 1947; "Son of Billy the Kid" 1949 (Jose Gonzales); "Bandit Queen" 1950 (Ortiz); "The Capture" 1950 (Valdez); "Ready to Ride" 1950-short; "Short Grass" 1950 (Manuel); "Wyoming Mail" 1950 (Pete); "Jubilee Trail" 1954 (Pedro); "Three Hours to Kill" 1954 (Esteban); "Giant" 1956 (Gomez); "One-Eyed Jacks" 1961 (Card Sharp); "Jesse James Meets Frankenstein's Daughter" 1966 (Manuel). ¶TV: *Black Saddle*—"Client: Martinez" 3-7-59 (El Mudo); *Bonanza*—"The Gift" 4-1-61; *The High Chaparral*—"Fiesta" 11-20-70; *Kung Fu*—"The Brujo" 10-25-73 (Tadeo); *The Cowboys*—"The Accused" 3-13-74 (Adolfo).

Turich, Rosa. Films: "Zorro Rides Again" 1937-serial (Tia); "Rose of the Rio Grande" 1938 (Maria); "Starlight Over Texas" 1938 (Maria); "Drifting Westward" 1939; "Rangers of Fortune" 1940 (Caressa); "South of Monterey" 1946; "Bowery Buckaroos" 1947 (Ramona); "Riding the California Trail" 1947; "The Adventures of Frank and Jesse James" 1948-serial (Rosita); "Son of Billy the Kid" 1949 (Rosa Gonzalez); "Dakota Lil" 1950; "The Kid from Texas" 1950 (Marita); "Jubilee Trail" 1954 (Senora Silva); "Passion" 1954 (Maraquita); "The Phantom Stallion" 1954; "Jesse James Meets Frankenstein's Daughter" 1966 (Nina); "El Dorado" 1967 (Rosa). ¶TV: *The Lone Ranger*—"Mission Bells" 9-21-50; *Wild Bill Hickok*—"The Avenging Gunman" 7-29-52; *The Cisco Kid*—"The Gramophone" 9-20-52; *The Restless Gun*—"The Woman from Sacramento" 3-3-58 (Rosaria), "Dragon for a Day" 9-29-58 (Tio Paco); *Maverick*—"The Judas Mask" 11-2-58 (Mexican Woman); *The Rebel*—"Don Gringo" 11-20-60 (Dona Theresa); *Lancer*—

"Foley" 10-15-68; *The High Chaparral*—"A Way of Justice" 12-13-68 (Mamacita).

Turkel, Joseph (1927-). Films: "Friendly Persuasion" 1956 (Poor Loser); "Warlock" 1959 (Chet Haggin); "The Animals" 1971 (Peyote). ¶TV: *The Lone Ranger*—"The Sheriff's Wife" 8-18-55; *Wyatt Earp*—"So Long, Dora, So Long" 11-13-56 (Bob Rellance); *The Adventures of Rin Tin Tin*—"Higgins' Last Stand" 1-4-57 (Stubb Gull), "The Silent Witness" 3-29-57 (Walt Coles); *Broken Arrow*—"Legacy of a Hero" 2-26-57 (Marvin); *Jefferson Drum*—"The Keeney Gang" 10-3-58 (Tom); *Tales of the Texas Rangers*—"Deadfall" 11-6-58 (Chance Dembrow); *Bat Masterson*—"Dude's Folly" 11-26-58 (Woody Larkin), "Wanted—Alive Please" 5-26-60 (Fargo); *The Texan*—"No Way Out" 9-14-59 (Evan McBeem); *Two Faces West*—"The Accused" 2-27-61; *Bonanza*—"The Many Faces of Gideon Flinch" 11-5-61, "Alias Joe Cartwright" 1-26-64 (Private Peters), "Trouble Town" 3-17-68 (Lupe); *Wagon Train*—"The Jud Steele Story" 5-2-62 (Eddie).

Turman, Glynn (1946-). Films: "Thomasine and Bushrod" 1974 (Jomo). ¶TV: *Centennial*—Regular 1978-79 (Nate Person).

Turnbull, Glenn. TV: *Sergeant Preston of the Yukon*—"Storm the Pass" 10-24-57 (Tex Corey); *Tales of the Texas Rangers*—"A Texas Million" 10-27-57; *Wyatt Earp*—"Little Pistol" 11-5-57 (Rocky); *Rawhide*—"Incident at the Buffalo Smokehouse" 10-30-59; *Empire*—"Echo of a Man" 12-11-62 (Canaday).

Turner, Barbara (1933-). Films: "Two-Gun Lady" 1956 (Jenny Ivers); "Soldier Blue" 1970 (Mrs. Long); "Desperate Mission" TVM-1971. ¶TV: *The Virginian*—"Harvest of Strangers" 2-16-66 (Louise Devers).

Turner, Bowditch M. "Smoke" (1878-9/12/33). Films: "The Coming of the Law" 1919 (Potter); "Hell Roarin' Reform" 1919 (Minister); "The Ridin' Kid from Powder River" 1924 (Manuel).

Turner, Doreen. Films: "The Love Gambler" 1922 (Ricardo, Kate's Child); "Daring Chances" 1924 (Bebe Slavin); "Western Vengeance" 1924 (Helen Caldwell).

Turner, Emanuel (1884-12/13/41). Films: "The Three Godfathers" 1936 (Drunk Man at Bar).

Turner, Florence (1885-8/28/46). Films: "Ranson's Folly" 1910; "Indian Romeo and Juliet" 1912;

"Una of the Sierras" 1912; "The Deerslayer" 1913; "The Overland Stage" 1927 (Alice Gregg); "The Ridin' Fool" 1931 (Ma Warren).

Turner, Fred A. (1842-2/13/23). Films: "A Man and His Mate" 1915; "Girl of the Timber Claims" 1917 (Jess' Father); "Madame Bo-Peep" 1917 (Colonel Beaupree); "The Heart of Wetona" 1919 (Pastor David Wells).

Turner, George (1877-10/3/47). Films: "The Old Texas Trail" 1944; "Range Beyond the Blue" 1947 (Bragg); "Son of Zorro" 1947-serial (Jeff Stewart/Zorro); "Vigilantes of Boomtown" 1947 (James J. Corbett).

Turner, Lana (1920-6/29/95). Films: "Honky Tonk" 1941 (Elizabeth Cotton).

Turner, Martin (1882-5/14/57). Films: "Rainbow Rangers" 1924 (Barbecue Sam); "Sell 'Em Cowboy" 1924 (Romeo); "Western Vengeance" 1924 (Luke Mosby); "Double Fisted" 1925; "The Ghost Rider" 1925 (Felix); "The Knockout Kid" 1925 (Snowball); "A Ropin' Ridin' Fool" 1925 (Major); "Silent Sheldon" 1925 (Ivory); "Temporary Sheriff" 1926; "Smoking Guns" 1934 (Cinders); "Cavalry" 1936 (Mose); "Ghost Town Riders" 1938 (Rosebud).

Turner, Moira. TV: *Have Gun Will Travel*—"Lady with a Gun" 4-9-60; *Gunsmoke*—"Harper's Blood" 10-21-61 (Sarah Cooley).

Turner, Raymond. Films: "The No-Gun Man" 1925 (Obediah Abraham Lincoln Brown); "O.U. West" 1925 (Porter); "Kit Carson" 1928 (Smokey); "A Tenderfoot Goes West" 1937 (Gun Packer" 1938 (Pinky).

Turner, William H. (1861-9/27/42). Films: "Fast and Fearless" 1924 (Judge Brown); "The Measure of a Man" 1924 (Tom Hitch); "Gold and Grit" 1925 (Bill Mason); "The Pony Express" 1925 (William Russell); "White Thunder" 1925 (Charles Evans); "The Phantom Bullet" 1926 (Judge Terrill); "Red Hot Leather" 1926 (Morton Kane); "The Texas Streak" 1926 (Charles Logan); "Driftin' Sands" 1928 (Don Roberto Aliso).

Turpin, Ben (1869-7/1/40). Films: "Broncho Billy's Protege" 1915; "A Christmas Revenge" 1915; "Hogan Out West" 1915; "Too Much Turkey" 1915; "The Law of the Wild" 1934-serial (Henry).

Turpin, Carrie (1882-10/3/25). Films: "Too Much Turkey" 1915.

Tuttle, Lurene (1907-5/28/86). Films: "Heaven Only Knows" 1947

(Mrs. O'Donnell); "Mrs. Sundance" TVM-1974 (Mrs. Lee). ¶TV: *My Friend Flicka*—"The Settler" 1-27-56 (Martha Hunter); *Broken Arrow*—"Powder Keg" 2-19-57 (Kate Connor); *Jim Bowie*—"The Bound Girl" 5-10-57; *The Restless Gun*—"General Gilford's Widow" 11-11-57 (Hanah Gilford); *Colt .45*—"Young Gun" 12-13-57 (Frances Benedict), "Trial by Rope" 5-3-60 (Lottie Strong); *The Californians*—"Skeleton in the Closet" 4-8-58 (Belle Calhoun), "The Painted Lady" 1-13-59 (Maude Sorel); *Have Gun Will Travel*—"The Five Books of Owen Deaver" 4-26-58 (Ma Deaver); *Buckskin*—"Cash Robertson" 8-7-58 (Edith); *Trackdown*—"Outlaw's Wife" 9-12-58 (Emma Perkins); *Wanted—Dead or Alive*—"The Giveaway Gun" 10-11-58 (Mrs. Walker); *The Texan*—"A Tree for Planting" 11-10-58 (Amy Bofert); *Lawman*—"The Bandit" 5-31-59, "The Inheritance" 3-5-61 (Mrs. Pruitt); *Wagon Train*—"The Lita Foladaire Story" 1-6-60; *Johnny Ringo*—"Killer, Choose a Card" 6-9-60 (Mamie Murphy); *Gunsmoke*—"Brother Love" 12-31-60 (Mrs. Cumbers), "Homecoming" 1-8-73 (Anna Wilson); *Tales of Wells Fargo*—"Town Against a Man" 1-23-61; *Rawhide*—"Incident of the Wager on Payday" 6-16-61 (Mrs. Porter); *Wide Country*—"Good Old Uncle Walt" 12-13-62 (Mrs. Sturgis); *Pistols 'n' Petticoats*—12-10-66 (Adelaide Coulter); *Bonanza*—"Justice" 1-8-67 (Mrs. Cutler); *Iron Horse*—"Sister Death" 4-3-67 (Mrs. Emerson); *The Cowboys*—2-27-74 (Gradma Jesse).

Tuttle, Wesley. Films: "Riders of the Dawn" 1945; "Song of the Sierras" 1946; "Rainbow Over the Rockies" 1947; "Night Rider" 1962-short.

Tweddell, Frank (1895-12/20/71). TV: *Jim Bowie*—"The Quarantine" 10-11-57 (Dr. Beranger).

Tweed, Shannon (1957-). Films: "Longarm" TVM-1988 (Crazy Sally).

Twelvetrees, Helen (1908-2/14/58). Films: "The Painted Desert" 1931 (Mary Ellen Cameron); "Hollywood Roundup" 1938 (Carol Stevens).

Twitchell, Archie (1906-1/31/57). Films: "Wells Fargo" 1937 (Man with Paper); "The Texans" 1938 (Cpl. Thompson); "The Arizona Kid" 1939 (Lt. Fox); "Union Pacific" 1939 (Male Secretary); "Buck Benny Rides Again" 1940 (Attendant); "Geronimo" 1940 (General's Orderly); "Northwest Mounted Police" 1940; "Young Bill Hickok" 1940 (Phillip);

"Bad Man of Deadwood" 1941; "Prairie Stranger" 1941 (Barton); "Thundering Hoofs" 1942 (Farley); "Fort Apache" 1948 (Reporter); "The Daltons' Women" 1950; "I Shot Billy the Kid" 1950 (Grant); "The Thundering Trail" 1951 (Tom Emery); "The Vanishing Outpost" 1951 (Matt); "The Frontier Phantom" 1952; "The Bounty Hunter" 1954 (Harrison).

Tyburn, Gene. TV: *The Rifleman*—"The Bullet" 2-25-63 (Deputy); *Bonanza*—"Love Me Not" 3-1-64 (Tom), "The Fighters" 4-24-66 (Smitty), "Silence at Stillwater" 9-28-69 (Deputy); *Gunsmoke*—"Outlaw's Woman" 12-11-65 (Eddie), "Milligan" 11-6-72 (Logan); *Wild Wild West*—"The Night of the Ready-Made Corpse" 11-25-66 (Finley), "The Night of the Falcon" 11-10-67 (Felton), "The Night of the Egyptian Queen" 11-15-68 (Gambler), "The Night of Bleak Island" 3-14-69 (Mark Chambers); *Here Come the Brides*—"One Good Lie Deserves Another" 2-12-69 (Dewey); *Barbary Coast*—"Mary Had More Than a Little" 1-2-76; *Young Maverick*—"Hearts O'Gold" 12-12-79.

Tyke, Johnny (1894-2/23/40). Films: "Hell's Oasis" 1920 (Hawk Allen); "Circle Canyon" 1934.

Tyler, Beverly (1924-). Films: "The Palomino" 1950 (Maria Guevara); "The Cimarron Kid" 1951 (Carrie Roberts); "The Battle at Apache Pass" 1952 (Mary Kearny); "Toughest Gun in Tombstone" 1958 (Beverly Cooper). ¶TV: *Death Valley Days*—"Escape" 4-21-56 (Evelyn Neilson); *Bronco*—"Quest of the Thirty Dead" 10-7-58 (Irene Lang); *Tales of Wells Fargo*—"Wanted: Jim Hardie" 12-21-59 (Polly); *Shotgun Slade*—"Sudden Death" 7-5-60 (Peaches); *Bonanza*—"The Fugitive" 2-11-61 (Mary).

Tyler, Harry O. (1888-9/15/61). Films: "Arizona Mahoney" 1936 (Bidder on Horses); "Jesse James" 1939 (Farmer); "Go West" 1940 (Telegrapher); "Buffalo Bill" 1944 (Barker); "The Untamed Breed" 1948 (Elisha Jones); "Hellfire" 1949 (Bartender); "Rider from Tucson" 1950 (Hardrock Jones); "Santa Fe" 1951 (Rusty); "Texans Never Cry" 1951 (Dan Carter); "Wagons West" 1952 (Old Man); "A Perilous Journey" 1953 (Vagrant); "A Lawless Street" 1955 (Tony Cabillo); "Texas Lady" 1955 (Choate); "A Day of Fury" 1956. ¶TV: *Wild Bill Hickok*—"Daughter of Casey O'-Grady" 7-21-53; *Fury*—"Joey Saves the Day" 12-10-55 (Druggist), "Pete's

Folly" 12-15-56 (Alex Harrington); *Sergeant Preston of the Yukon*—"Scourge of the Wilderness" 1-11-57 (Lafe Wilson); *The Roy Rogers Show*—"High Stakes" 2-24-57, "Brady's Bonanza" 3-31-57 (L.M. Roberts); *Buckskin*—"A Man from the Mountains" 10-30-58 (Burton); *Maverick*—"Dodge City or Bust" 12-11-60 (Shopkeeper); *Laramie*—"The Passing of Kuba Smith" 1-3-61 (Farmer).

Tyler, Leon. Films: "Great Stagecoach Robbery" 1945; "Lay That Rifle Down" 1955 (Horace Speckleton). ¶TV: *The Restless Gun*—"Tomboy" 11-10-58 (George Belknap); *Maverick*—"Shady Deal at Sunny Acres" 11-23-58 (Henry Hibbs).

Tyler, T. Texas (1916-1/23/72). Films: "Horsemen of the Sierras" 1950 (Himself).

Tyler, Tom (1903-5/1/54). Films: "The Cowboy Musketeer" 1925 (Tom Latigo); "Let's Go Gallagher" 1925 (Tom Gallagher); "The Wyoming Wildcat" 1925 (Phil Stone); "The Arizona Streak" 1926 (Dandy Darrell); "Born to Battle" 1926 (Dennis Terhune); "The Cowboy Cop" 1926 (Jerry McGill); "The Masquerade Bandit" 1926 (Jeff Morton); "Out of the West" 1926 (Tom Hanley); "Red Hot Hoofs" 1926 (Tom Buckley); "Tom and His Pals" 1926 (Tom Duffy); "Wild to Go" 1926 (Tom Blake); "The Cherokee Kid" 1927 (Bill Duncan); "Cyclone of the Range" 1927 (Tom Mackay); "The Desert Pirate" 1927 (Tom Corrigan); "The Flying U Ranch" 1927 (Senor Miguel Garcia); "Lightning Lariats" 1927 (Tom Potter); "The Sonora Kid" 1927 (Tom MacReady); "Splitting the Breeze" 1927 (Death Valley Drake); "Tom's Gang" 1927 (Dave Collins); "Phantom of the Range" 1928 (Duke Carlton); "Terror Mountain" 1928 (Tom Tyler); "The Texas Tornado" 1928 (Tom King); "Tyrant of Red Gulch" 1928 (Tom Masters); "When the Law Rides" 1928 (Tom O'Malley); "Gun Law" 1929 (Tom O'Brien); "Idaho Red" 1929 (Andy Thornton); "Law of the Plains" 1929; "The Lone Horseman" 1929 (Jack Gardiner); "The Man from Nevada" 1929 (Jack Carter); "'Neath Western Skies" 1929 (Tex McCloud); "The Phantom Rider" 1929 (Dick Cartwright); "Pioneers of the West" 1929 (Phil Sampson); "The Pride of Pawnee" 1929 (Kirk Stockton); "The Trail of the Horse Thieves" 1929 (Vic Stanley); "Call of the Desert" 1930 (Rex Carson); "The Canyon of Missing Men" 1930 (Dave

Brandon); "Battling with Buffalo Bill" 1931-serial (Buffalo Bill); "God's Country and the Man" 1931 (Tex); "The Man from Death Valley" 1931 (Dave); "99 Wounds" 1931 (Hank Johnson); "Partners of the Trail" 1931 (Larry Condon); "The Phantom of the West" 1931-serial (Jim Lester); "Rider of the Plains" 1931 (Blackie); "Two-Fisted Justice" 1931 (Kentucky Carson); "West of Cheyenne" 1931 (Tom Langdon); "The Forty-Niners" 1932 (Tennessee Matthews); "Galloping Thru" 1932; "Honor of the Mounted" 1932; "The Man from New Mexico" 1932 (Jess Ryder); "Single-Handed Sanders" 1932 (Sanders); "Vanishing Men" 1932; "Clancy of the Mounted" 1933-serial (Sergeant Tom Clancy); "Deadwood Pass" 1933 (Tom Whitlock); "War on the Range" 1933 (the Cowboy); "When a Man Rides Alone" 1933 (Tom Harris/the Llano Kid); "Fighting Hero" 1934 (Tom Hall); "Mystery Ranch" 1934 (Robert Morris); "Terror of the Plains" 1934 (Tom Lansing); "Born to Battle" 1935 (Tom Saunders); "Coyote Trails" 1935 (Tom Riley); "The Laramie Kid" 1935 (Tom Talbot); "Powdersmoke Range" 1935 (Sundown Saunders); "Ridin' Thru" 1935 (Tom Saunders); "Rio Rattler" 1935 (Tom Denton); "Silent Valley" 1935 (Tom Hall); "The Silver Bullet" 1935 (Tom Henderson); "Tracy Rides" 1935 (Sheriff Tom Tracy); "Trigger Tom" 1935 (Trigger Tom Hunter); "The Unconquered Bandit" 1935 (Tom Morgan); "Fast Bullets" 1936 (Tom); "The Last Outlaw" 1936 (Al Goss); "The Phantom of the Range" 1936 (Jerry Lane); "Pinto Rustlers" 1936 (Tom Dawson); "Ridin' On" 1936 (Tom Roarke); "Rip Roarin' Buckaroo" 1936 (Scotty McWade); "Roamin' Wild" 1936 (Tom Barton); "Santa Fe Bound" 1936 (Tom Cranshaw); "Cheyenne Rides Again" 1937 (Cheyenne); "Lost Ranch" 1937 (Tom Wade); "Mystery Range" 1937 (Tom Wade); "Orphan of the Pecos" 1937 (Tom Rayburn); "Brothers of the West" 1938 (Tom Wade); "Feud of the Trail" 1938 (Tom Wade/Jack Granger); "Frontier Marshal" 1939 (Buck Newton); "The Night Riders" 1939 (Jackson); "Stagecoach" 1939 (Luke Plummer); "Cherokee Strip" 1940 (Frank Morrell); "The Light of Western Stars" 1940 (Sheriff Tom Hawes); "Texas Rangers Ride Again" 1940 (Ranger Gilpin); "The Westerner" 1940 (King Evans); "Border Vigilantes" 1941 (Jim Yager); "Gauchos of El Dorado" 1941 (Stony Brodie); "Outlaws of the Cherokee

Trail" 1941 (Stony Brook); "Riders of the Timberline" 1941 (Slade); "West of Cimarron" 1941; "Code of the Outlaw" 1942; "The Phantom Plainsmen" 1942 (Stony Brooke); "Raiders of the Range" 1942 (Stony Brooke); "Shadows on the Sage" 1942 (Stony Brooke); "Valley of Hunted Men" 1942 (Stony Brooke); "Valley of the Sun" 1942 (Geronimo); "Westward Ho" 1942 (Stony Brooke); "The Blocked Trail" 1943; "Riders of the Rio Grande" 1943 (Stony Brooke); "Santa Fe Scouts" 1943 (Stony Brooke); "Thundering Trails" 1943; "Wagon Tracks West" 1943 (Clawtooth); "Boss of Boomtown" 1944 (Jim); "Gun to Gun" 1944-short; "San Antonio" 1945 (Lafe McWilliams); "Sing Me a Song of Texas" 1945; "Badman's Territory" 1946 (Frank James); "Cheyenne" 1947 (Pecos); "Blood on the Moon" 1948 (Frank Reardan); "The Dude Goes West" 1948 (Spiggoty); "Red River" 1948 (Quitter); "Return of the Badmen" 1948 (Wild Bill Yeager); "I Shot Jesse James" 1949 (Frank James); "Lust for Gold" 1949 (Luke); "Masked Raiders" 1949 (Trig); "She Wore a Yellow Ribbon" 1949 (Cpl. Mike Quayne); "Square Dance Jubilee" 1949 (Buck); "The Younger Brothers" 1949 (Hatch); "Crooked River" 1950 (Weston); "The Daltons' Women" 1950; "Fast on the Draw" 1950 (Bandit Leader); "Hostile Country" 1950 (Tom); "Marshal of Heldorado" 1950 (Mike); "Riders of the Range" 1950 (Kid Ringo); "Rio Grande Patrol" 1950 (Vance); "Trail of Robin Hood" 1950; "West of the Brazos" 1950 (Sam); "Best of the Badmen" 1951 (Frank James); "The Great Missouri Raid" 1951 (Allen Parmer); "The Lion and the Horse" 1952 (Bud Sabin); "Road Agent" 1952 (Larkin); "Cow Country" 1953 (Pete). ¶TV: *The Lone Ranger*—"Damsels in Distress" 6-8-50; *The Cisco Kid*—"Haven for Heavies" 5-19-51, "Phony Sheriff" 6-16-51, "Uncle Disinherits Niece" 7-14-51; *Wild Bill Hickok*—"Mexican Gun Running Story" 1-8-52; *The Roy Rogers Show*—"The Outlaw's Girl" 2-17-52, "Outlaws' Town" 3-1-52, "End of the Trail" 1-27-57 (Jed Medford); *The Gene Autry Show*—"Trouble at Silver Creek" 3-9-52, "Trail of the Witch" 3-30-52, "Thunder Out West" 7-14-53, "Bandidos" 9-1-53.

Tylo, Michael. Films: "Lonesome Dove" TVM-1989.

Tynan, Brandon (1879-3/19/67). Films: "Wells Fargo" 1937 (Edwards, the Newspaper Publisher); "The Girl of the Golden West" 1938

(the Professor); "Rangers of Fortune" 1940 (Homer Granville Clayborn); "Virginia City" 1940 (Trenholm).

Tyne, George. Films: "Tell Them Willie Boy Is Here" 1969 (Le Marie); "Skin Game" 1971 (Bonner). ¶TV: *F Troop*—"How to Be F Troop Without Really Trying" 9-15-66 (Major Bradley).

Tyner, Charles (1925-). Films: "The Stalking Moon" 1969 (Dace); "The Cheyenne Social Club" 1970 (Charlie Bannister); "Monte Walsh" 1970 (Doctor); "Lawman" 1971 (Minister); "Bad Company" 1972 (Farmer); "The Cowboys" 1972 (Jenkins); "Jeremiah Johnson" 1972 (Robidoux); "Young Pioneers" TVM-1976 (Mr. Beaton); "Peter Lundy and the Medicine Hat Stallion" TVM-1977 (Lefty Slade); "The Awakening Land" TVM-1978 (Reverend Hutchins). ¶TV: *The Big Valley*—"Journey into Violence" 12-18-67 (Hemit); *The High Chaparral*—"No Irish Need Apply" 1-17-69 (Gregg); *Alias Smith and Jones*—"Miracle at Santa Marta" 12-30-71 (Turner); *Kung Fu*—"Alethea" 3-15-73 (Larrabee); *How the West Was Won*—"The Innocent" 2-12-79 (Eli Kelsay); *Father Murphy*—Regular 1981-82 (Howard Rodman); *Paradise*—"Founder's Day" 11-10-88 (Herb Applegate), "Ghost Dance" 11-24-88 (Herb Applegate).

Tyrrell, Ann. Films; "Take Me to Town" 1953 (Louise Pickett); "Seven Angry Men" 1955 (Mrs. Brown).

Tyrrell, John (1902-9/19/49). Films: "End of the Trail" 1936 (Bugler Joe); "Call of the Rockies" 1938 (Swale); "Law of the Plains" 1938 (Hotel Clerk); "Rio Grande" 1938 (Bartender); "South of Arizona" 1938; "West of Cheyenne" 1938 (Trigger); "West of Santa Fe" 1938 (Collins); "Overland with Kit Carson" 1939-serial; "The Taming of the West" 1939 (Coleman); "Blazing Six Shooters" 1940 (Savage); "The Durango Kid" 1940 (Banning); "Konga, the Wild Stallion" 1940 (Pilot); "The Man from Tumbleweeds" 1940 (Heavy); "Thundering Frontier" 1940 (Mac); "West of Abilene" 1940 (Vic); "The Son of Davy Crockett" 1941; "Bullets for Bandits" 1942; "Shut My Big Mouth" 1942 (Man); "Vengeance of the West" 1942; "Cowboy in the Clouds" 1943 (Mack Judd); "Silver City Raiders" 1943; "Cowboy from Lonesome River" 1944; "Cyclone Prairie Rangers" 1944; "Song of the Prairie" 1945; "Gunning for Vengeance" 1946.

Tyrell, Susan (1946-). Films:

"Shoot Out" 1971 (Alma); "Zandy's Bride" 1974 (Maria Cordova); "Another Man, Another Chance" 1977-Fr. (Debbie/Alice); "Poker Alice" TVM-1987 (Mad Mary). ¶TV: *Bonanza*—"Fallen Woman" 9-26-71 (Jill); *Nichols*—"The Marrying Fool" 12-28-71 (Caralee).

Tyson, Cicely (1933-). TV: *Cowboy in Africa*—"Tomorrow on the Wind" 11-20-67 (Julie Anderson); *Here Come the Brides*—"A Bride for Obie Brown" 1-9-70 (Lucenda); *Gunsmoke*—"The Scavengers" 11-16-70 (Rachel Biggs).

Udell, Peggy. Films: "The Ridin' Streak" 1925 (Ruth Howells).

Udy, Helen. TV: *Dr. Quinn, Medicine Woman*—Regular 1993-(Myra); *Lonesome Dove*—"Long Shot" 11-13-94.

Ugarte, Julian. Films: "The Man Called Noon" 1973-Brit./Span./Ital. (Cristobal); "Stranger and the Gunfighter" 1973-Ital./Span./Hong Kong (Yancy).

Ullman, Carl. Films: "The Flame of the Yukon" 1917 (2nd George Fowler); "The Medicine Man" 1917 (Luther Hill); "Wolf Lowry" 1917 (Owen Thorpe).

Ullmann, Liv (1939-). Films: "The New Land" 1973-Swed. (Kristina); "Zandy's Bride" 1974 (Hannah Lund).

Ulric, Lenore (1892-12/30/70). Films: "Her Own People" 1917; "Tiger Rose" 1923 (Tiger Rose Bocion); "Northwest Outpost" 1947 (Baroness Kruposny).

Ulrich, Florence. Films: "The Galloping Cowboy" 1926 (Mary Pinkleby).

Umeki, Miyoshi (1929-). TV: *Rawhide*—"Incident of the Geisha" 12-19-63 (Nami); *The Virginian*—"Smile of a Dragon" 2-26-64 (Kim Ho).

Undari, Claudio. *see* Hundar, Robert.

Underhill, John (1870-5/26/41). Films: "The Joyous Troublemaker" 1920 (Butler).

Underwood, Blair. Films: "Posse" 1993 (Carver).

Underwood, Lawrence (1871-2/2/39). Films: "Thundering Through" 1925 (John Richmond); "Twisted Triggers" 1926 (Sheriff); "The Phantom Buster" 1927 (Sheriff).

Underwood, Loyal (1893-9/30/66). Films: "Shootin' Irons" 1927 (Blinky); "The Paleface" 1948 (Bearded Character).

Ung, Tom. Films: "Empty Holsters" 1937 (Chinese Cook); "Forlorn River" 1937 (Barber); "Wells Fargo" 1937 (Chinese Brick Mason).

Upton, Julian. Films: "The Marshal's Daughter" 1953 (Brad). ¶TV: *The Gene Autry Show*—"Outlaw Stage" 7-21-53, "Border Justice" 8-18-53.

Ure, Mary (1933-4/3/75). Films: "Custer of the West" 1967-U.S./Span. (Elizabeth Custer).

Urecal, Minerva (1884-2/26/66). Films: "The Three Godfathers" 1936 (Parishioner); "God's Country and the Woman" 1937 (Maisie); "Destry Rides Again" 1939 (Mrs. DeWitt); "Frontier Scout" 1939; "The Sagebrush Family Trails West" 1940 (Widow Gail); "Arkansas Judge" 1941 (Miranda Wolfson); "The Cowboy and the Blonde" 1941 (Murphy); "They Died with Their Boots On" 1941 (Nurse); "In Old California" 1942 (Mrs. Carson); "Riding Through Nevada" 1942; "Sons of the Pioneers" 1942 (Mrs. Bixby); "Wagon Tracks West" 1943; "Moonlight and Cactus" 1944 (Abigail); "Wanderer of the Wasteland" 1945 (Mama Rafferty); "California" 1946 (Emma); "Rainbow Over Texas" 1946 (Mama Lolita); "Sioux City Sue" 1946; "Apache Rose" 1947 (Felicia); "Bowery Buckaroos" 1947 (Kate Barlow); "Saddle Pals" 1947; "Fury at Furnace Creek" 1948 (Mrs. Crum); "Marshal of Amarillo" 1948 (Mrs. Pettigrew); "Sundown in Santa Fe" 1948; "Outcasts of the Trail" 1949 (Mrs. Rysen); "The Arizona Cowboy" 1950 (Cactus Kate Millican); "Texans Never Cry" 1951 (Martha Carter); "Lost in Alaska" 1952 (Mrs. McGillicuddy); "Oklahoma Annie" 1952 (Mrs. Fling); "The Woman They Almost Lynched" 1953 (Mrs. Stewart); "A Man Alone" 1955 (Mrs. Maule). ¶TV: *The Lone Ranger*—"Billie the Great" 3-30-50, "Homer with a High Hat" 12-16-54; *The Gene Autry Show*—"The Doodle Bug" 8-13-50; *Wild Bill Hickok*—"The Slocum Family" 12-4-51; *The Roy Rogers Show*—"Badman's Brother" 2-10-52 (Geraldine O'Fallon), "Phantom Rustlers" 4-25-54 (Mrs. MacGuiness); *My Friend Flicka*—"The Runaways" 2-17-56; *Jim Bowie*—"Jim Bowie Comes Home" 10-26-56 (Maw Bowie), "Outlaw Kingdom" 12-7-56 (Maw Bowie), "Rezin Bowie, Gambler" 3-22-57 (Maw Bowie); *Wagon Train*—"The Don Alvarado Story" 6-21-61 (Maria); *Whispering Smith*—"Swift Justice" 9-11-61 (Flora MacDonald).

Urich, Robert (1947-). Films:

"Lonesome Dove" TVM-1989 (Jake Spoon). ¶TV: *Kung Fu*—"Blood Brother" 1-18-73 (Greg Dundee); *Nakia*—"A Beginning in the Wilderness" 10-26-74 (Tom); *Gunsmoke*—"Manolo" 3-17-75 (Manolo Etchahoun).

Urueta, Chano. Films: "Guns for San Sebastian" 1967-U.S./Fr./Mex./Ital. (Miguel); "The Wild Bunch" 1969 (Don Jose); "The Wrath of God" 1972 (Antonio).

Usher, Guy (1875-6/16/44). Films: "Justice of the Range" 1935 (Hadley Graves); "Law Beyond the Range" 1935 (Daniel Heston); "Boots and Saddles" 1937 (Colonel Allen); "The Old Wyoming Trail" 1937 (Lafe Kenney); "Renegade Ranger" 1938 (Maj. Jameson); "Under Western Stars" 1938 (John D. Fairbanks); "Arizona Legion" 1939; "Rough Riders' Round-Up" 1939 (Blair); "Rovin' Tumbleweeds" 1939 (Craig); "Timber Stampede" 1939 (Jay Jones); "Union Pacific" 1939 (Leland Stanford); "Wolf Call" 1939 (Michael Vance, Sr.); "Danger Ahead" 1940 (Inspector); "One Man's Law" 1940; "Queen of the Yukon" 1940 (Stake); "The Bandit Trail" 1941 (Mayor); "Kansas Cyclone" 1941; "The Kid from Kansas" 1941 (Maloney); "King of Dodge City" 1941 (Morgan King); "Ridin' on a Rainbow" 1941 (Sheriff); "West of Cimarron" 1941; "Bad Men of the Hills" 1942 (Doctor Mitchell); "Bells of Capistrano" 1942; "In Old California" 1942; "Pardon My Gun" 1942; "Sin Town" 1942 (Man on Train); "The Avenging Rider" 1943; "Lost Canyon" 1943 (Rogers).

Ustinov, Paula. Films: "The Wild Wild West Revisited" TVM-1979 (Nadia).

Vacarro, Brenda (1939-). Films: "Zorro, the Gay Blade" 1981 (Florinda). ¶TV: *Sara*—Regular 1976 (Sara Yarnell).

Vacio, Natividad (1912-). Films: "Giant" 1956 (Eusebio); "Escape from Red Rock" 1958 (Miguel Chavez); "The Gun Hawk" 1963. ¶TV: *The Lone Ranger*—"Dead Man's Chest" 9-28-50; *The Adventures of Rin Tin Tin*—"A Look of Eagles" 10-11-57 (Manuel); *The Texan*—"The Easterner" 12-15-58 (Huelo), "Border Incident" 12-7-59; *Colt .45*—"The Rival Gun" 10-25-59 (Senor Afilador); *The Rifleman*—"The Vision" 3-22-60 (Pedro); *The Tall Man*—"A Tombstone for Billy" 12-16-61 (Juan Gonzales); *Cimarron Strip*—"The Battleground" 9-28-67; *The High Chaparral*—"The Promised Land" 10-25-68 (Padre), "New Hostess in

Town" 3-20-70 (Major Domo); *Gunsmoke*—"The Noonday Devil" 12-7-70 (Diego); *Paradise*—"Founder's Day" 11-10-88 (Manuel).

Vadis, Dan (-6/11/87). Films: "Pirates of the Mississippi" 1963-Ger./Ital./Fr.; "Deguello" 1966-Ital. (Ramon); "Fort Yuma Gold" 1966-Ital./Fr./Span.; "The Scalphunters" 1968 (Yuma); "God Will Forgive My Pistol" 1969-Ital. (Martin); "The Stranger Returns" 1967-U.S./Ital./Ger./Span. (En Plein); "Cahill, United States Marshal" 1973 (Brownie); "High Plains Drifter" 1973 (Dan Carlin); "The White Buffalo" 1977 (Tall Man); "Mr. Horn" TVM-1979; "Bronco Billy" 1980 (Chief Big Eagle).

Vague, Vera. *see* Allen, Barbara Jo.

Vahanian, Marc (1956-). Films: "Ransom for Alice!" TVM-1977 (Nick Vithanian).

Vail, Lester (1899-11/28/59). TV: *Wyatt Earp*—"The Arizona Lottery" 2-16-60 (Milligan).

Val, William. Films: "Fighting Mustang" 1948; "Sunset Carson Rides Again" 1948; "The Kid from Gower Gulch" 1949; "Battling Marshal" 1950.

Valdemar, Thais. Films: "Against All Odds" 1924 (Olivetta); "The Range Terror" 1925 (Virginia Allen).

Valdez, Reina. Films: "Broncho Billy's Mexican Wife" 1912; "The Atonement" 1914; "Dan Cupid, Assayer" 1914; "A Gambler's Way" 1914; "The Night on the Road" 1914; "Single-Handed" 1914.

Valdis, Sigrid. TV: *Wild Wild West*—"The Night the Wizard Shook the Earth" 10-1-65 (Miss Piecemeal), "The Night of the Torture Chamber" 12-10-65 (Miss Piecemeal).

Vale, Virginia. Films: "The Marshal of Mesa City" 1939 (Virginia King); "Bullet Code" 1940 (Molly Mathews); "Corralling a School Marm" 1940-short; "Legion of the Lawless" 1940 (Ellen Ives); "Prairie Law" 1940 (Priscilla); "Stage to Chino" 1940 (Caroline Crinnie McKay); "Triple Justice" 1940 (Lorna Payson); "California or Bust" 1941-short; "The Musical Bandit" 1941-short; "Prairie Spooners" 1941-short; "Redskins and Redheads" 1941-short; "Robbers of the Range" 1941 (Alice); "Cactus Capers" 1942-short; "Keep Shooting" 1942-short; "Range Rhythm" 1942-short.

Vale, Vola. Films: "The Secret of Black Mountain" 1917 (Miriam Vale);

"The Silent Man" 1917 (Betty Bryce); "The Son of His Father" 1917 (Hazel Mallinsbee); "Wolves of the Rail" 1918 (Faith Lawson); "Six Feet Four" 1919 (Winifred Waverly); "The Iron Rider" 1920 (Mera Donovan); "Overland Red" 1920 (Louise Alacarme); "Duke of Chimney Butte" 1921 (Vesta Philbrook); "Singing River" 1921 (Alice Thornton); "White Oak" 1921 (Barbara); "Good Men and True" 1922 (Georgie Hibbler); "Crashin' Thru" 1923 (Diane Warren).

Valentine, Elizabeth (1887-7/23/71). Films: "Santa Fe Scouts" 1943 (Minerva Clay).

Valentine, Karen (1947-). Films: "The Daughters of Joshua Cabe" TVM-1972 (Charity); "Go West, Young Girl" TVM-1978 (Netty Booth); "Hot Lead and Cold Feet" 1978 (Jenny). ¶TV: *The Deputy*—"Lucifer Urge" 5-14-60 (Alva Wagner).

Valentine, Nancy. TV: *The Texan*—"The Gunfighter" 6-8-59 (Helen); *Have Gun Will Travel*—"The Gold Toad" 11-21-59; *Lawman*—"The Parting" 5-29-60 (Jennie); *Zane Grey Theater*—"A Gun for Willie" 10-6-60 (Lilly); *Whispering Smith*—"Stain of Justice" 6-12-61 (Stella Dean).

Valenty, Lili (1900-3/11/87). TV: *Maverick*—"Diamond in the Rough" 1-26-58 (Madame); *Bonanza*—"Dark Star" 4-23-60 (Bruja), "Marie, My Love" 2-10-63, "The Deadliest Game" 2-21-65 (Donna Luisa), "A Severe Case of Matrimony" 7-7-68 (Dolores).

Valkis, Helen. Films: "Blazing Sixes" 1937 (Barbara Morgan); "Cherokee Strip" 1937 (Molly Valley); "The Old Barn Dancer" 1938 (Sally Dawson).

Vallee, Rudy (1901-7/3/86). Films: "Ricochet Romance" 1954 (Worthington Higgenmacher). ¶TV: *Death Valley Days*—"The Friend" 2-17-68; *Alias Smith and Jones*—"Dreadful Sorry, Clementine" 11-18-71 (Winford Fletcher), "The Man Who Broke the Bank at Red Gap" 1-20-72 (Winford Fletcher).

Valli, Romolo (1925-2/1/80). Films: "Duck, You Sucker!" 1971-Ital. (Dr. Villega).

Valli, Virginia (1900-9/24/68). Films: "Ruggles of Red Gap" 1918 (Widow Judson); "His Back Against the Wall" 1922 (Mary Welling); "The Storm" 1922 (Manette Fachard); "Tracked to Earth" 1922 (Anna Jones).

Vallin, Rick (1920-8/31/77).

Films: "King of the Stallions" 1942; "Perils of the Royal Mounted" 1942-serial (Little Wolf); "Riders of the Rio Grande" 1943 (Tom Owens); "Wagon Tracks West" 1943 (Fleetwing); "Last of the Redmen" 1947 (Uncas); "Northwest Outpost" 1947 (Dovkin); "Cody of the Pony Express" 1950-serial (Denver); "Comanche Territory" 1950 (Pakanah); "Rio Grande Patrol" 1950 (Trevino); "Roar of the Iron Horse" 1950-serial; "Snow Dog" 1950 (Louis); "When the Redskins Rode" 1951 (Duprez); "Son of Geronimo" 1952-serial (Eadie); "The Fighting Lawman" 1953; "The Homesteaders" 1953 (Slim); "The Marksman" 1953; "Star of Texas" 1953 (William Vance); "Topeka" 1953 (Ray Hammond); "Riding with Buffalo Bill" 1954-serial (Reb Morgan); "Thunder Pass" 1954; "At Gunpoint" 1955 (Moore); "Treasure of Ruby Hills" 1955 (Vernon); "Frontier Gambler" 1956; "The Naked Gun" 1956; "Perils of the Wilderness" 1956-serial (Little Bear); "The Badge of Marshal Brennan" 1957 (Deputy); "Raiders of Old California" 1957; "The Storm Rider" 1957 (Jack Feylan); "Bullwhip" 1958 (Marshal); "Escape from Red Rock" 1958 (Judd). ¶TV: *Wild Bill Hickok*—"Civilian Clothes Story" 12-18-51, "Missing Diamonds" 3-17-53; *Hopalong Cassidy*—"The Renegade Press" 7-5-52; *Cowboy G-Men*—"Gypsy Traders" 2-28-53; *The Gene Autry Show*—"Narrow Escape" 8-11-53, "Prize Winner" 7-27-54, "Battle Axe" 8-31-54, "Boots and Ballots" 9-25-54; *The Roy Rogers Show*—"The Outlaws of Paradise Valley" 11-8-53, "Brady's Bonanza" 3-31-57; *Wyatt Earp*—"The Man Who Lied" 10-11-55 (Yancy), "Nineteen Notches on His Gun" 12-11-56 (Mort Newcomb), "Frontier Surgeon" 1-19-60 (Outlaw); *Brave Eagle*—"The Challenge" 12-21-55 (Black Raven); *Annie Oakley*—"Annie Finds Strange Treasure" 3-6-54, "The Saga of Clement O'Toole" 11-4-56 (Al); *Judge Roy Bean*—"Deliver the Body" 6-1-56 (Del), "The Hypnotist" 6-1-56 (Crazy George), "Terror Rides the Trail" 6-1-56 (Cherokee Joe); *The Adventures of Rin Tin Tin*—"The Indian Hater" 1-11-57 (Pacing Bear); *Circus Boy*—"The Knife Thrower" 2-17-57 (Firpo); *The Lone Ranger*—"Journey to San Carlos" 5-9-57; *Tales of Wells Fargo*—"Renegade Raiders" 5-20-57 (Broken Wrist); *Jefferson Drum*—"Madame Faro" 6-6-58 (Tanner); *Cimarron City*—"I, the People" 10-11-58 (Bandit Leader); *Daniel Boone*—"The Prisoners" 2-10-66 (Sentry); *Bat

Masterson—"The Marble Slab" 5-11-61.

Vallon, Michael (1897-11/13/73). Films: "Death Rides the Range" 1940 (Dr. Wahl); "Lightning Strikes West" 1940 (Butch Taggart); "Boss of Bullion City" 1941; "Boss of Hangtown Mesa" 1942 (Clint Rayner); "Little Joe, the Wrangler" 1942 (Clem); "Old Chisholm Trail" 1942 (Sheriff); "The Silver Bullet" 1942; "Valley of Vanishing Men" 1942-serial; "Bad Men of Thunder Gap" 1943; "Border Buckaroos" 1943 (Seth Higgins); "Frontier Law" 1943 (Ferrell); "The Lone Star Trail" 1943 (Jonathan Bentley); "Raiders of San Joaquin" 1943 (Clark); "Girl Rush" 1944 (Prospector); "Gunsmoke Mesa" 1944 (Judge Plymouth); "Marshal of Gunsmoke" 1944 (Ezra Peters); "Trigger Trail" 1944 (Bender); "Barbed Wire" 1952 (August Gormley); "Rebel City" 1953 (Sam); "Topeka" 1953; "Gun Battle at Monterey" 1957; "Snowfire" 1958 (Poco). ¶TV: *Wild Bill Hickok*—"Pony Express vs. Telegraph" 9-25-51, "Papa Antinelli" 11-27-51, "The Boy and the Bandit" 3-25-52, "Money Shines" 6-2-53; *The Cisco Kid*—"Robber Crow" 11-24-51, "Spanish Dagger" 1-5-52; *Annie Oakley*—"Annie Finds Strange Treasure" 3-6-54; *Death Valley Days*—"A Killing in Diamonds" 11-21-55; *Wyatt Earp*—"Vengeance Trail" 2-12-57 (Mathew Watkins), "The Actress" 4-14-59 (Hack); *The Adventures of Rin Tin Tin*—"Border Incident" 3-28-58 (Don Paulao Pedrosa); *Laramie*—"Duel at Parkison Town" 12-13-60 (Citizen).

Vallone, Raf (1918-). Films: "Nevada Smith" 1966 (Father Zaccardi); "Cannon for Cordoba" 1970 (Cordoba); "A Gunfight" 1971 (Francisco Alvarez).

Van, Connie (1909-7/16/61). Films: "The Far Country" 1955 (Molasses). ¶TV: *Maverick*—"Bolt from the Blue" 11-27-60 (Hotel Clerk).

Van Ark, Joan (1943-). Films: "Testimony of Two Men" TVM-1977 (Jane Robson). ¶TV: *Bonanza*—"Sweet Annie Laurie" 1-5-69 (Laurie Adams); *The Guns of Will Sonnett*—"The Man Who Killed James Sonnett" 3-21-69 (Laurie); *Gunsmoke*—"Stryker" 9-29-69 (Sara Jean Stryker); *Barbary Coast*—"Guns for a Queen" 10-6-75 (Eleanor).

Van Auker, Cecil K. (-2/18/38). Films: "Up and Going" 1922 (Albert Brandon); "Youth Must Have Love" 1922 (Marvin); "The Gunfighter" 1923 (William Camp).

Van Bergen, Lewis. Films: "Outlaws" TVM-1986 (D.J.).

Van Buren, Katherine. Films: "The Last of His People" 1919 (Yvonne Lacombe); "Two-Gun Betty" 1919 (Ethel Roberts); "Firebrand Trevison" 1920 (Hester Keyes).

Van Buren, Mabel (1878-11/4/47). Films: "The Charmed Arrow" 1914; "Bill Haywood, Producer" 1915; "The Girl of the Golden West" 1915 (the Girl); "Ramona" 1916 (Ramona in Prolog); "The Jaguar's Claws" 1917 (Marie); "The Squaw Man's Song" 1917 (Lady Stuckley); "The Winding Trail" 1918 (Lou); "While Satan Sleeps" 1922 (Sunflower Sadie); "The Meddlin' Stranger" 1927 (Mrs. Crawford); "The Flying Buckaroo" 1928 (Mrs. Brown).

Vance, Byron. Films: "The Sagebrush Family Trails West" 1940 (Seth); "The Lone Rider in Ghost Town" 1941; "The Texas Marshal" 1941 (Deputy).

Vance, Lucille (1893-5/10/74). Films: "Bad Men of Thunder Gap" 1943; "Boss of Rawhide" 1944 (Mrs. Periwinkle).

Vance, Vivian (1913-8/17/79). TV: *The Deputy*—"Land Greed" 12-12-59 (Emma Gant).

Van Cleef, Lee (1925-12/16/89). Films: "High Noon" 1952 (Jack Colby); "The Lawless Breed" 1952 (Dirk Hanley); "Untamed Frontier" 1952 (Dave Chittun); "Arena" 1953 (Smitty); "Jack Slade" 1953 (Toby Mackay); "The Nebraskan" 1953 (Reno); "Tumbleweed" 1953 (Mary); "Arrow in the Dust" 1954 (Crew Boss); "Dawn at Socorro" 1954 (Earl Ferris); "The Desperado" 1954 (Buck Creyton/Paul Creyton); "Gypsy Colt" 1954 (Hank); "Rails into Laramie" 1954 (Ace Winton); "The Yellow Tomahawk" 1954 (Fireknife); "A Man Alone" 1955 (Clantin); "The Road to Denver" 1955 (Pecos Larry); "Ten Wanted Men" 1955 (Al Drucker); "Treasure of Ruby Hills" 1955 (Emmett); "The Vanishing American" 1955 (Jay Lord); "Pardners" 1956 (Gus); "Tribute to a Badman" 1956 (Fat Jones); "The Badge of Marshal Brennan" 1957 (Shad Donaphin); "Gun Battle at Monterey" 1957 (Kirby); "Gunfight at the O.K. Corral" 1957 (Ed Bailey); "Joe Dakota" 1957 (Adam Grant); "The Last Stagecoach West" 1957; "The Lonely Man" 1957 (Faro); "The Quiet Gun" 1957 (Sadler, the Killer); "Raiders of Old California" 1957;"The Tin Star" 1957 (Ed McGaffrey); "The Bravados" 1958 (Alfonso Parral); "Day of the Bad Man" 1958 (Jake Hayes); "Ride Lonesome" 1959 (Frank); "Posse from Hell" 1961

(Leo); "How the West Was Won" 1962 (Marty); "The Man Who Shot Liberty Valance" 1962 (Reese); "For a Few Dollars More" 1965-Ital./Ger./Span. (Col. Douglas Mortimer); "The Big Gundown" 1966-Ital. (Jonathan Corbett); "The Good, the Bad, and the Ugly" 1966-Ital. (Setenza); "Day of Anger" 1967-Ital./Ger. (Frank Talby); "Death Rides a Horse" 1967-Ital. (Ryan); "Beyond the Law" 1968-Ital. (Cudilip); "Sabata" 1969-Ital. (Sabata); "Barquero" 1970 (Travis); "El Condor" 1970 (Jaroo); "Bad Man's River" 1971-Span./Ital./Fr. (King); "Captain Apache" 1971-Brit./Span. (Captain Apache); "Big Showdown" 1972-Ital./Fr. (Clayton); "The Magnificent Seven Ride" 1972 (Chris); "Return of Sabata" 1972-Ital./Fr./Ger. (Sabata); "Stranger and the Gunfighter" 1973-U.S./Hong Kong (Dakota); "Take a Hard Ride" 1974-Ital./Brit./Ger. (Kiefer); "God's Gun" 1976-Ital./Israel (Father John/Louis); "Kid Vengeance" 1976-Ital./U.S./Israel. ¶TV: *The Lone Ranger*—"Desperado at Large" 10-2-52, "The Brown Pony" 5-14-53, "Stage to Estacado" 7-23-53; *Four Star Playhouse*—"Trail's End" 1-29-53; *The Gene Autry Show*—"Rio Renegades" 9-29-53, "Outlaw Warning" 10-2-54; *Stories of the Century*—"Last Stagecoach West" 1954 (Steve Margolis), "Frank and Jesse James" 4-8-55; *Sheriff of Cochise*—"Fire on Chiricahua Mountains" 11-2-56 (Hackett); *Tales of Wells Fargo*—"Alder Gulch" 4-8-57 (Cherokee Bob); *Trackdown*—"The Town" 12-13-57 (Ben Fraser); *Colt .45*—"Dead Reckoning" 1-24-58 (Devery), "The Trespasser" 6-21-60 (Red Feather); *Lawman*—"The Deputy" 10-5-58 (Hawks Brother), "Conclave" 6-14-59, "Man on a Mountain" 6-12-60 (Clyde Wilson), "The Return of Owny O'Reilly" 10-16-60 (Jack Saunders); *Zorro*—"Welcome to Monterey" 10-9-58; *Frontier Doctor*—"Great Stagecoach Robbery" 12-6-58; *Northwest Passage*—"The Fourth Brother" 1-30-59 (Frank Wade); *The Rifleman*—"The Deadly Wait" 3-24-59 (Dan Mowry), "The Prodigal" 4-26-60, "The Clarence Bibbs Story" 4-4-61 (Wicks), "Death Never Rides Alone" 10-29-62 (Johnny Drako); *Cimarron City*—"The Town Is a Prisoner" 3-28-59 (Tom); *Tombstone Territory*—"Gun Hostage" 5-1-59 (Sam Carver); *Yancy Derringer*—"Outlaw at Liberty" 5-7-59 (Ike Melton); *Wanted—Dead or Alive*—"The Empty Cell" 10-17-59; *Riverboat*—"Strange Request" 12-13-59 (Luke Cragg); *The Law of the Plainsman*—"Clear Title"

12-17-59 (Killer); *Hotel De Paree*—"Sundance and the Man in Room Seven" 2-12-60; *The Alaskans*—"Peril at Caribou Crossing" 2-28-60 (Roc); *Black Saddle*—"The Cabin" 4-1-60 (Frank); *The Deputy*—"Palace of Chance" 5-21-60 (the Cherokee Kid); *Gunsmoke*—"Old Flame" 5-28-60 (Rad Meadows), "The Pariah" 4-17-65 (John Hooker), "My Father, My Son" 4-23-66 (Ike Jeffords); *Laramie*—".45 Calibre" 11-15-60 (Wes Torrey), "Killer's Odds" 4-25-61 (Dawson), "Vengeance" 1-8-63, "The Stranger" 4-23-63 (Caleb); *Bonanza*—"The Blood Line" 12-31-60 (Appling); *Maverick*—"Red Dog" 3-5-61 (Wolf McManus); *Bronco*—"Yankee Tornado" 3-13-61, "One Evening in Abilene" 3-19-62; *Stagecoach West*—"Never Walk Alone" 4-18-61 (Lin Hyatt); *Cheyenne*—"Trouble Street" 10-2-61 (Deputy Braden); *Death Valley Days*—"The Hat That Won the West" 10-31-62 (Brogger); *Have Gun Will Travel*—"The Treasure" 12-29-62 (Corbin), "Face of a Shadow" 4-20-63 (Golias); *The Dakotas*—"Thunder in Pleasant Valley" 2-4-63 (Slade Tucker); *The Slowest Gun in the West* 7-29-63 (Sam Bass); *The Travels of Jaimie McPheeters*—"The Day of the Misfits" 12-15-63 (Raoul Volta); *Destry*—"Destry Had a Little Lamb" 2-21-64 (Ace Slater); *Rawhide*—"The Enormous Fist" 10-2-64 (Fred Grant), "Piney" 10-9-64 (Deck); *Branded*—"The Richest Man in Boot Hill" 10-31-65 (Fred Slater), "Call to Glory" 2-27-66, 3-6-66 & 3-13-66 (Charlie Yates); *Laredo*—"Quarter Past Eleven" 3-24-66 (Big Mike Kelly).

Vandergrift, Monte (1893-7/29/39). Films: "Shotgun Pass" 1931 (Jake Mitchell); "Sunset of Power" 1936; "Wells Fargo" 1937 (Sailor); "Cowboy from Brooklyn" 1938 (Brakeman).

Vanders, Warren (1930-). Films: "Rough Night in Jericho" 1967 (Harvey); "The Price of Power" 1969-Ital./Span.; "The Revengers" 1972-U.S./Mex. (Tap); "Nevada Smith" TVM-1975 (Red Fickett); "Rooster Cogburn" 1975 (Bagby); "Hot Lead and Cold Feet" 1978 (Boss Snead). ¶TV: *Stagecoach West*—"Red Sand" 11-22-60 (Guard); *Gunsmoke*—"Catawomper" 2-10-62 (Pete), "The Brothers" 3-12-66 (Wat), "Stage Stop" 11-26-66 (Lingo), "Quaker Girl" 12-10-66 (John Thenley), "The Lure" 2-25-67 (Boles), "The Wreckers" 9-11-67 (Reb), "The Victim" 1-1-68 (Lefty), "Zavala" 10-7-68 (Densen), "The Night Riders" 2-24-69 (Williams), "The Devil's Outpost" 9-22-

69 (Bo Harper), "Roots of Fear" 12-15-69 (Ridge Sadler), "The Noonday Devil" 12-7-70 (Bones Cunningham), "The Boy and the Sinner" 10-1-73 (Otis Miller); *Empire*—Regular 1962-63 (Chuck Davis); *Destry*—"Blood Brother-in-Law" 4-17-64 (Lonzo Motley); *Bonanza*—"The Far, Far Better Thing" 1-10-65 (Tuck), "Ride the Wind" 1-16-66 & 1-23-66 (Hoke), "The Trackers" 1-7-68 (Buzz), "The Desperado" 2-7-71 (Cal); *The Legend of Jesse James*—"The Raiders" 10-18-65 (Jim Dancer); *Daniel Boone*—"The Gun" 2-3-66 (Pike), "Three Score and Ten" 2-6-69 (Ben), "The Road to Freedom" 10-2-69 (Ben); *Iron Horse*—"No Wedding Bells for Tony" 11-7-66 (Lou), "Consignment, Betsy the Boiler" 9-23-67 (Willard); *The Road West*—"No Sanctuary" 2-6-67 (Lew); *Cimarron Strip*—"The Legend of Jud Starr" 9-14-67, "Broken Wing" 9-21-67 (Thatch); *The Big Valley*—"Presumed Dead" 10-7-68 (Charley Slim); *Nichols*—"Eddie Joe" 1-4-72 (Pel De Carlo); *Alias Smith and Jones*—"The Day the Amnesty Came Through" 11-25-72 (Curly Red Johnson); *Kung Fu*—"Chains" 3-8-73 (Sgt. Bedford), "In Uncertain Bondage" 2-7-74 (Clifford Tait); *How the West Was Won*—Episode Seven 4-9-78 (Brant).

Vanderveen, Joyce. TV: *Jim Bowie*—"The Select Females" 11-23-56 (Angelique), "Monsieur Francois" 12-28-56 (Marie de Gravien), "The Beggar of New Orleans" 1-11-57 (Marie de Gravien), "Master at Arms" 1-25-57 (Marie de Gravien), "Thieves' Market" 3-29-57 (Marie de Gravien), "The Intruder" 4-26-57 (Marie de Gravien), "The Quarantine" 10-11-57 (Marie de Gravien); *Circus Boy*—"Alex the Great" 10-10-57 (Alice Freeman); *Death Valley Days*—"Pioneer Circus" 3-10-59 (Juliette Bonet).

Vandever, Michael. TV: *The Law of the Plainsman*—"Blood Trails" 11-5-59; *The Rebel*—"He's Only a Boy" 2-28-60 (Till), "The Calley Kid" 5-21-61 (Wood); *The Dakotas*—"Walk Through the Badlands" 3-18-63 (Private Tentress); *The Virginian*—"Run Away Home" 4-24-63 (Jody Swenson), "The Barren Ground" 12-6-67 (Chee Philips); *Gunsmoke*—"Seven Hours to Dawn" 9-18-65 (Raider), "Gold Mine" 12-25-65 (Ed Gibbijohn), "The Jackals" 2-12-68 (Poorly); *Laredo*--"The Seventh Day" 1-6-67 (Lacy Walsh); *Bonanza*—"Mark of Guilt" 12-15-68 (Davis).

Vandis, Titos (1918-). TV: *How*

the West Was Won—"L'Affaire Riel" 3-5-79 (Henri).

Van Doren, Mamie (1933-). Films: "Star in the Dust" 1956 (Ellen Ballard); "Born Reckless" 1959 (Jackie); "Sheriff Was a Lady" 1965-Ger.; "Arizona Kid" 1974-Ital./Phil.

Van Dreelen, John (1922-). TV: *Lawman*—"The Promoter" 2-19-61 (Malcolm Tyler De Vries); *Gunsmoke*—"Chester's Dilemma" 5-20-61 (Hans Gruber); *Rawhide*—"The Immigrants" 3-16-62 (Ulrich); *Wild Wild West*—"The Night of the Watery Death" 11-11-66 (Philippe de La Mer).

Van Dyke, Barry (1951-). TV: *Gun Shy*—Regular 1983 (Russell Donovan).

Van Dyke, Conny (1940-). TV: *Nakia*—"The Moving Target" 11-9-74 (Beth Streeter); *Barbary Coast*—"Irish Coffee" 10-13-75 (Rose).

Van Dyke, Jerry (1931-). Films: "McClintock" 1963 (Matt Douglas, Jr.).

Van Dyke, Truman (1898-5/6/84). Films: "Riders of the Pony Express" 1949.

Van Eyck, Peter (1913-7/15/69). Films: "The Rawhide Years" 1956 (Andre Boucher); "Duel at Sundown" 1965-Fr./Ger. (Don McGow); "Shalako" 1968-Brit./Fr. (Frederick von Hallstatt).

Van Fleet, Jo (1919-). Films: "King and Four Queens" 1956 (Ma McDade); "Gunfight at the O.K. Corral" 1957 (Kate Fisher). ¶TV: *Frontier Circus*—"The Courtship" 2-15-62 (Amelia Curtis); *The Virginian*—"Legacy of Hate" 9-14-66 (Lee Calder); *Wild Wild West*—"The Night of the Tycoons" 3-28-69 (Amelia Bronston); *Bonanza*—"The Trouble with Amy" 1-25-70 (Amy Wilder), "The Stillness Within" 3-14-71 (Ellen Dobbs).

Van Horn, Buddy. Films: "High Plains Drifter" 1973 (Marshal Jim Duncan); "Bite the Bullet" 1975. ¶TV: *Laredo*—"The Legend of Midas Mantee" 9-16-66 (Hutch).

Van Horn, James (1917-4/20/66). Films: "The Cherokee Kid" 1927 (Red Flynne); "Fast on the Draw" 1950; "Hostile Country" 1950 (Rancher); "Marshal of Heldorado" 1950 (Townsman); "Cave of Outlaws" 1951 (Jed Delancey); "Silver City" 1951 (Townsman); "Son of Paleface" 1952 (Posse); "Gunsmoke" 1953 (Clay); "Taza, Son of Cochise" 1954 (Skinya).

Van Husen, Dan. Films: "El Condor" 1970 (Bandit); "Doc" 1971

(Clanton Cowboy); "Don't Turn the Other Cheek" 1974-Ital./Ger./Span.

Van Lynn, Vincent. TV: *Laredo*—"A Question of Discipline" 10-28-65 (Louis Montaigne); *The Big Valley*—"The Haunted Gun" 2-6-67 (Verne Keller).

Van Meter, Harry (1871-6/2/56). Films: "The Belle of the Bar Z Ranch" 1912; "The Half-Breed's Way" 1912; "Redbird Wins" 1914; "Sir Galahad of Twilight" 1914; "The Buzzard's Shadow" 1915 (Unitah, the Half-Breed); "The Poet of the Peaks" 1915; "The Purple Hills" 1915; "Lone Star" 1916 (John Mattes); "The Challenge of Chance" 1919 (El Capitan); "A Gun Fightin' Gentleman" 1919 (Earl of Jollywell); "A Man's Fight" 1919 (Jarvis); "Dangerous Love" 1920 (Gerald Lorimer); "The Lone Hand" 1920 (Joe Rollins); "The Beautiful Gambler" 1921 (Lee Krik); "Heart of the North" 1921 (DeBrac); "When Romance Rides" 1922 (Bill Cordis); "Sagebrush Gospel" 1924 (Linyard Lawton); "The Texas Bearcat" 1925 (John Crawford); "Triple Action" 1925 (Eric Prang); "Border Romance" 1930 (Captain of Rurales).

Vann, Frankie (1906-7/19/79). Films: "Curse of the Undead" 1959 (Henchman).

Vanner, Louis. *see* Vanucchi, Luigi.

Vanni, Renata (1917-). Films: "Westward the Women" 1951 (Mrs. Moroni); "The Command" 1953 (Mrs. Pellegrini); "The Hard Man" 1957 (Juanita); "Frontier Uprising" 1961. ¶TV: *The Rebel*—"The Uncourageous" 5-7-61 (Rosa); *Wagon Train*—"The Eleanor Culhane Story" 5-17-61 (Inez); *Gunsmoke*—"The Cage" 3-23-70 (Mrs. Ramos).

Van Nutter, Rik (Clyde Rogers). Films: "Seven Hours of Gunfire" 1964-Span./Ital. (Buffalo Bill); "Dynamite Joe" 1966-Ital./Span. (Dynamite Joe).

Van Patten, Dick (1928-). Films: "Zachariah" 1971 (the Dude); "Dirty Little Billy" 1972 (Harry); "Hec Ramsey" TVM-1972 (Earl Enright); "Joe Kidd" 1972 (Hotel Manager); "Westworld" 1973 (Banker). ¶TV: *Rawhide*—"Incident of the Power and the Plow" 2-13-59 (Matt Reston).

Van Patten, Jimmy (1956-). Films: "Hot Lead and Cold Feet" 1978 (Jake); "The Apple Dumpling Gang Rides Again" 1979; "The Chisholms" TVM-1979 (Beau Chisholm). ¶TV: *Bonanza*—"The Initiation" 9-26-72 (Corky Sibley);

Gunsmoke—"The Hanging of Newly O'Brien" 11-26-73 (Tim); *The Chisholms*—Regular 1979-80 (Bo Chisholm).

Van Patten, Joyce (1934-). Films: "Something Big" 1971 (Polly Standall). ¶TV: *Wide Country*—"Who Killed Edde Gannon?" 10-11-62 (Nina Corbello); *Gunsmoke*—"Anybody Can Kill a Marshal" 3-9-63; *Stoney Burke*—"Joby" 3-18-63 (Laura); *The Virginian*—"Ring of Silence" 10-27-65 (Mary); *The Loner*—"The Mourners for Johnny Sharp" 2-5-66 & 2-12-66 (Peggy); *Iron Horse*—"Death Has Two Faces" 12-23-67 (Alice); *Nichols*—"The Paper Badge" 10-14-71 (Arletta McGreery).

Van Patten, Vincent (1957-). Films: "The Bravos" TVM-1972 (Peter Harkness); "Chino" 1973-Ital./Span./Fr. (Jamie Wagner). ¶TV: *Bonanza*—"A Matter of Circumstance" 4-19-70 (Tim), "Stallion" 11-14-72 (Tommy Brenner); *The High Chaparral*—"Spokes" 9-25-70 (Culley); *Nichols*—"About Jesse James" 2-15-72 (Grover); *Gunsmoke*—"Bohannan" 9-25-72 (Heck), "The Boy and the Sinner" 10-1-73 (Colby Eaton); *Dirty Sally*—1-18-74 (George); *How the West Was Won*—"The Rustler" 1-22-79 (Bob Cooper).

Van Peebles, Mario. Films: "Posse" 1993 (Jessie Lee).

Van Peebles, Melvin (1932-). Films: "Posse" 1993 (Papa Joe).

Van Pelt, Ernest. Films: "Broncho Billy's Brother" 1915; "Broncho Billy's Sentence" 1915; "Bring Him In" 1921 (Canby); "Montana Bill" 1921; "Lucky Dan" 1922; "Riders of the Whistling Skull" 1937 (Prof. Marsh).

Van Rooten, Luis (1906-6/17/73). TV: *Gunsmoke*—"Hanging Man" 4-19-58 (Mel Tucker); *The Californians*—"The Foundling" 4-29-58 (Alonzo Hicks); *Northwest Passage*—"Stab in the Back" 2-20-59 (Mr. Duren).

Van Sickel, Dale (1907-1/25/77). Films: "King of the Royal Mounted" 1940-serial (Radioman); "The Return of Frank James" 1940 (Reporter); "Girl Rush" 1944; "Zorro's Black Whip" 1944-serial (Danley/Karl/Camp Heavy); "Lone Texas Ranger" 1945; "King of the Forest Rangers" 1946-serial (Blaine/Hughes); "The Phantom Rider" 1946-serial (Bart/Lyons/Mack/Pete); "Bells of San Angelo" 1947; "Jesse James Rides Again" 1947-serial (Raider #2/Brock/Boyd/Gow); "The Last Round-Up" 1947; "Son of Zorro" 1947-serial (Murray/Dale/Forney/Kaw/Ted); "Carson City Raiders" 1948 (Brennon); "The Adventures of Frank and Jesse James" 1948-serial (Thomas Dale/Art Carvery/Jones); "Dangers of the Canadian Mounted" 1948-serial (Boyd/Bart/Pete/Scott/Steele); "Desperadoes of Dodge City" 1948 (Pete); "Oklahoma Badlands" 1948 (Sharkey); "Renegades of Sonora" 1948; "Ghost of Zorro" 1949-serial (Mike Hodge/Mead); "The Golden Stallion" 1949 (Ed Hart); "Desperadoes of the West" 1950-serial (Reed); "The James Brothers of Missouri" 1950-serial (Harry Sharkey); "Don Daredevil Rides Again" 1951-serial (Dan Farley); "Rough Riders of Durango" 1951; "Dead Man's Trail" 1952; "Canadian Mounties vs. Atomic Invaders" 1953-serial (Beck); "Northern Patrol" 1953 (Jason); "Topeka" 1953 (Jake Manning); "Man with the Steel Whip" 1954-serial (Crane); "The Searchers" 1956 (Stunts); "Shoot-Out at Medicine Bend" 1957; "Seven Ways from Sundown" 1960 (2nd Waggoner); "Six Black Horses" 1962 (Man); "Requiem for a Gunfighter" 1965 (Kelly); "Town Tamer" 1965; "Johnny Reno" 1966 (Ab Connors). ¶TV: *The Roy Rogers Show*—"The Unwilling Outlaw" 3-8-52, "Ghost Gulch" 3-30-52; *Sheriff of Cochise*—"Triangle" 2-22-57 (Doc Sheldon); *Wagon Train*—"The Nels Stack Story" 10-23-57; *Wanted—Dead or Alive*—"Call Your Shot" 2-7-59; *Bonanza*—"The Mission" 9-17-60 (Morgan); *Wyatt Earp*—"The Shooting Starts" 4-18-61 (Tough); *Wild Wild West*—"Night of the Deadly Bed" 9-24-65 (Guitar Player).

Van Sloan, Edward (1882-3/6/64). Films: "The Arizonian" 1935; "Valley of Hunted Men" 1942 (Dr. Henry Steiner); "Riders of the Rio Grande" 1943 (Pop Owens).

Van Slyke, Arthur. Films: "Black Aces" 1937 (Silver Tip Joe); "Law for Tombstone" 1937; "Sandflow" 1937 (Santone); "Black Bandit" 1938 (Ramsay); "Border Wolves" 1938 (John Benton); "Outlaw Express" 1938 (Postmaster).

Van Tassell, Marie (1874-1/46). Films: "The Only Road" 1918 (Rosa Lopez).

Van Trump, Jessalyn (1885-5/2/39). Films: "The Sheriff's Sisters" 1911; "The Smoke of the Forty-Five" 1911; "Driftwood" 1912; "The Eastern Girl" 1912; "End of the Feud" 1912; "The Intrusion of Compoc" 1912; "The Jealous Rage" 1912; "The Land of Death" 1912; "The Outlaw Cowboy" 1912; "The Pensioner" 1912; "The Power of Love" 1912; "The Promise" 1912; "Reformation of Sierra Smith" 1912; "Under False Pretenses" 1912; "The Angel of the Canyons" 1913; "Calamity Anne's Beauty" 1913; "Calamity Anne's Inheritance" 1913; "Women Left Alone" 1913.

Van Tuyl, Helen Marr (1892-8/22/64). TV: *Wild Bill Hickok*—"Widow Muldane" 8-14-51; *Wyatt Earp*—"She Almost Married Wyatt" 2-24-59.

Vanucchi, Luigi (Louis Vanner) (1930-). Films: "Johnny Yuma" 1966-Ital. (Pedro); "Days of Violence" 1967-Ital. (Butch).

Van Vleck, Bill (1886-5/19/66). Films: "The Sea of Grass" 1947 (Nestor).

Van Vleet, Richard. Films: "The Young Country" TVM-1970 (Randy Willis) ¶TV: *The Virginian*—"Eileen" 3-5-69 (Peter Bowder); *The Men from Shiloh*—"Last of the Comancheros" 12-9-70 (Mooney).

Van Zandt, Julie. TV: *Wyatt Earp*—"The Englishman" 2-21-56; *Gunsmoke*—"Kick Me" 1-26-57 (Jennifer Myers); *Zorro*—"Sweet Face of Death" 1-30-58 (Magdalena), "Zorro Fights His Father" 2-6-58 (Magdalena); *Tales of Wells Fargo*—"The Cleanup" 1-26-59 (Lucy Haney); *Lawman*—"The Locket" 1-7-62 (Marcia).

Van Zandt, Phil (1904-2/16/58). Films: "In Old Colorado" 1941 (Vender); "Deerslayer" 1943 (Briarthorn); "Outlaws of the Rockies" 1945 (Dan Chantry); "California" 1946 (Mr. Gunce); "Last Frontier Uprising" 1947 (Lyons); "Copper Canyon" 1950 (Sheriff Wattling); "Indian Territory" 1950 (Curt Raidler); "Viva Zapata!" 1952 (Commanding Officer); "Yukon Gold" 1952; "Captain John Smith and Pocahontas" 1953 (Davis); "A Perilous Journey" 1953 (Tout); "Ride, Vaquero!" 1953 (Dealer); "The Lonely Man" 1957 (Burnsey); "Shoot-Out at Medicine Bend" 1957. ¶TV: *Sky King*—"Triple Exposure" 5-11-52 (De Moines); *Wild Bill Hickok*—"The Hideout" 1-20-53; *The Adventures of Rin Tin Tin*—"Lost Treasure" 5-25-56 (Blake); *Fury*—"Pete's Folly" 12-15-56 (Smith); *Broken Arrow*—"The Trial" 1-22-57 (Walters); *Circus Boy*—"Counterfeit Clown" 4-7-57 (Gerald Van Dorne); *Death Valley Days*—"Rough and Ready" 12-23-57 (Joe Sweigart).

Vaquero, Rafael. Films: "Three

Swords of Zorro" 1963-Ital./Span.; "Two Thousand Dollars for Coyote" 1965-Span.; "Django" 1966-Ital./Span.; "The Hellbenders" 1966-U.S./Ital./Span.

Varconi, Victor (1891-6/16/76). Films: "Captain Thunder" 1931 (Captain Thunder); "The Plainsman" 1936 (Painted Horse); "Dakota" 1945 (Frenchman); "Pirates of Monterey" 1947 (Capt. Cordova); "Unconquered" 1947 (Capt. Simson Ecuyer).

Varden, Norma (1898-1/19/89). Films: "Fancy Pants" 1950 (Lady Maude). ¶TV: *Bonanza*—"The Wooing of Abigail Jones" 3-4-62 (Ma Nutley); *The Travels of Jaimie McPheeters*—"The Day of the Flying Dutchman" 12-1-63 (Sonia Van Creel).

Varela, Jay. Films: "Kid Blue" 1973 (Mendoza); "The Man Who Loved Cat Dancing" 1973 (Charlie); "Nakia" TVM-1974 (Indiana Johnny). ¶TV: *Nichols*—3-7-72.

Varela, Nina (1899-2/13/83). Films: "Viva Zapata!" 1952 (Aunt); "The Woman They Almost Lynched" 1953 (Mayor Delilah Courtney); "Jubilee Trail" 1954 (Dona Manuela). ¶TV: *Gunsmoke*—"Ma Tennis" 2-2-58 (Ma Tennis), "Hinka Do" 1-30-60 (Mamie); *The Deputy*—"Ma Mack" 7-9-60 (Ma Mack).

Varga, Billy. Films: "Oklahoma Crude" 1973 (Cook).

Vargas, Daniele. Films: "Deguello" 1966-Ital.; "Django, Last Killer" 1967-Ital.; "Son of Django" 1967-Ital.; "The Stranger Returns" 1967-U.S./Ital./Ger./Span. (God Jim); "Cemetery Without Crosses" 1968-Ital./Fr.; "Wanted" 1968-Ital./Fr.; "Shotgun" 1969-Ital.; "Zorro, the Navarra Marquis" 1969-Ital./Span. (Colonel Brizard); "Those Dirty Dogs!" 1973-U.S./Ital./Span. (Gen. Mueller).

Varno, Roland. Films: "Three Faces West" 1940 (Dr. Eric Von Scherer); "Valley of Hunted Men" 1942 (Carl Baum). ¶TV: *Wild Bill Hickok*—"Mexican Rustlers Story" 10-23-51, "Vigilante Story" 1-22-52.

Varron, Alegra. Films: "Riding Shotgun" 1954 (Mrs. Fritz); "The Rounders" 1965 (Mrs. Norson). ¶TV: *Maverick*—"The Judas Mask" 11-2-58 (Woman); *Rawhide*—"The Long Count" 1-5-62; *Wide Country*—"Yanqui, Go Home!" 4-4-63 (Tia Marguerita).

Varsi, Diane (1938-11/19/92). Films: "From Hell to Texas" 1958 (Juanita Bradley).

Vaughan, Dorothy (1889-3/15/

55). Films: "Cowboy from Brooklyn" 1938 (Fat Woman); "Bad Men of Missouri" 1941 (Mrs. Dalton); "Robin Hood of Texas" 1947 (Mrs. O'Brien); "The Sea of Grass" 1947 (Mrs. Hodges); "Trail to San Antone" 1947 (the Commodore); "Song of Idaho" 1948 (Sara Mom); "Home in San Antone" 1949; "Rider from Tucson" 1950 (Mrs. O'Reilly). ¶TV: *The Roy Rogers Show*—"The Double Crosser" 6-1-52 (Ma Colton).

Vaughn, Ada Mae (1906-9/1/43). Films: "The Arizona Streak" 1926 (Ruth Castleman).

Vaughn, Alberta (1904-4/26/92). Films: "Points West" 1929 (Dorothy); "Wild Horse" 1931 (Alice Hall); "Daring Danger" 1932 (Jerri Norris); "Randy Rides Alone" 1934 (Sally Rogers); "The Laramie Kid" 1935 (Peggy Bland).

Vaughn, Heidi. TV: *The High Chaparral*—"The Glory Soldiers" 1-31-69 (Mercy); *Gunsmoke*—"The Pack Rat" 1-12-70 (Martha Mason); *Death Valley Days*—"Amos and the Black Bull" 2-28-70 (Maggie).

Vaughn, Jean. TV: *Gunsmoke*—"Crackups" 9-14-57 (Girl); *Rough Riders*—"The Duelists" 10-23-58 (Monique); *Wyatt Earp*—"The Posse" 5-10-60 (Martha Smith); *Have Gun Will Travel*—"The Cure" 5-20-61 (Lucy Weyerhauser); *Lawman*—"Parphyrias Lover" 11-19-61 (Eve); *Wild Wild West*—"The Night of a Thousand Eyes" 10-22-65 (Glory).

Vaughn, Robert (1932-). Films: "Hell's Crossroads" 1957 (Bob Ford); "Good Day for a Hanging" 1958 (the Kid); "The Magnificent Seven" 1960 (Lee); "Desperado" TVM-1987 (Sheriff John Whaley). ¶TV: *Gunsmoke*—"Cooter" 5-19-56, "Romeo" 11-9-57 (Andy Bowers); *Frontier*—"The Return of Jubal Dolan" 8-26-56 (Cliff Dolan); *Zane Grey Theater*—"Courage Is a Gun" 12-14-56 (Johnny), "A Gun Is for Killing" 10-18-57 (Billy Jack); *Tales of Wells Fargo*—"Billy the Kid" 10-21-57 (Billy the Kid), "Treasure Coach" 10-14-61 (Billy Brigode); *Wagon Train*—"The John Wilbot Story" 6-11-58 (Roy Pelham), "The Roger Bigelow Story" 12-21-60 (Roger Bigelow); *Jefferson Drum*—"Return" 10-30-58 (Shelly Poe); *The Rifleman*—"The Apprentice Sheriff" 12-9-58 (Dan Willard); *Zorro*—"Spark of Revenge" 2-19-59 (Miguel Roverto); *Bronco*—"Borrowed Glory" 2-24-59 (Sheriff Lloyd Stover); *Frontier Doctor*—"A Twisted Road" 4-25-59; *Riverboat*—"About Roger Mowbray" 9-27-59 (Roger Mowbray); *Wichita Town*—"Passage

to the Enemy" 12-2-59 (Frank Warren); *The Law of the Plainsman*—"The Dude" 12-3-59 (Teddy Roosevelt), "The Innocents" 12-10-59 (Ross Drake); *The Rebel*—"Noblesse Oblige" 2-14-60 (Major); *Man from Blackhawk*—"Remember Me Not" 9-9-60 (Hayworth); *Laramie*—"The Dark Trail" 11-1-60 (Sandy Kayle); *Stagecoach West*—"Object: Patrimony" 1-3-61 (Beaumont Butler Buell); *Bonanza*—"The Way Station" 10-29-62 (Luke Martin); *Empire*—"No Small Wars" 2-5-63 (Capt. Paul Terman); *The Virginian*—"If You Have Tears" 2-13-63 (Simon Clain); *Centennial*—Regular 1978-79 (Morgan Wendell).

Vaughn, Skeeter (1922-3/8/89). Films: "Starbird and Sweet William" 1975; "Bridger" TVM-1976 (Paiute Chief). ¶TV: *The Cherokee Trail*—Pilot 11-28-81 (Indian).

Vaughn, William. see von Brincken, Wilhelm.

Vaughn, William. Films: "Ambush at Cimarron Pass" 1958 (Henry). ¶TV: *The Cisco Kid*—"Tangled Trails" 5-29-54; *Gunsmoke*—"Indian Scout" 3-31-56 (Twitchell); *Zane Grey Theater*—"Man Unforgiving" 1-3-58 (Chuck), "Man Alone" 3-5-59; *Tombstone Territory*—"Postmarked for Death" 2-12-58 (Pat Cormick); *Bat Masterson*—"Double Showdown" 10-8-58 (Nelson), "Death by the Half Dozen" 2-4-60 (Eddie Griswell); *The Texan*—"Blood Money" 4-20-59; *Have Gun Will Travel*—"Gold and Brimstone" 6-20-59 (Rudy); *Wyatt Earp*—"Roscoe Turns Detective" 5-3-60, "Woman of Tucson" 11-15-60 (Slim Bailey); *Wanted—Dead or Alive*—"The Showdown" 10-26-60; *Bat Masterson*—"The Last of the Night Raiders" 11-24-60 (Arkansas Tom); *Gunslinger*—"The New Savannah Story" 5-18-61 (Bart Myrick); *Laredo*—"Yahoo" 9-30-65 (Clyde), "Which Way Did They Go?" 11-18-65, "No Bugles, One Drum" 2-24-66; *Lancer*—"The Man Without a Gun" 3-25-69; *The High Chaparral*—"The Long Shadow" 1-2-70 (Matheny); *Kung Fu*—"Alethea" 3-15-73 (Sampler Harte).

Vavitch, Michael (1876-10/5/30). Films: "Wolf Song" 1929 (Don Solomon Salazar).

Vaz Dias, Selma (1911-9/77). Films: "The Singer Not the Song" 1961-Brit. (Chela).

Veazie, Carol (1895-7/19/84). Films: "Cat Ballou" 1965 (Mrs. Parker).

Vedder, William (1872-3/3/61). Films: "The Gunfighter" 1950 (Minister). ¶TV: *The Lone Ranger*—"The Star Witness" 8-17-50, "Dead Man's Chest" 9-28-50, "Black Gold" 4-9-53; *The Cisco Kid*—"Pot of Gold" 4-25-53.

Vega, Isela (1940-). Films: "Eye for an Eye" 1972-Ital./Span./Ital.; "Deadly Trackers" 1973 (Maria); "Joshua" 1977; "Barbarosa" 1982 (Josephina); "The Alamo: 13 Days to Glory" TVM-1987.

Vejar, Harry (1889-3/1/68). Films: "West to Glory" 1947 (Don Lopez); "The Treasure of the Sierra Madre" 1948 (Bartender).

Velasco, Jerry (1928-). Films: "Tell Them Willie Boy Is Here" 1969 (Chino).

Velazquez, Pilar. Films: "Awkward Hands" 1968-Span./Ital.; "Forgotten Pistolero" 1970-Ital./Span.; "Forewarned, Half-Killed ... The Word of the Holy Ghost" 1971-Ital./Span.; "Thunder Over El Paso" 1972-Ital./Span.; "Arizona Kid" 1974-Ital./Phil.

Velez, Lupe (1908-12/14/44). Films: "Tiger Rose" 1929 (Rose); "Wolf Song" 1929 (Lola Salazar); "The Storm" 1930 (Manette Fachard); "The Squaw Man" 1931 (Naturich); "The Broken Wing" 1932 (Lolita); "Mexican Spitfire Out West" 1940 (Carmelita Lindsay).

Veloz, Frank (1906-2/27/81) & **Yolanda** (1910-3/24/95). Films: "Under the Pampas Moon" 1935 (Dancers in Cafe).

Venable, Evelyn (1913-11/16/93). Films: "North of Nome" 1936 (Camilla Bridle); "The Frontiersman" 1938 (June Lake); "Heritage of the Desert" 1939 (Miriam Naab); "Lucky Cisco Kid" 1940 (Mrs. Emily Lawrence).

Venantini, Venantino (1933-). Films: "Bandidos" 1967-Ital.

Ventura, Clyde. TV: *The Big Valley*—"The Martyr" 10-17-66 (Julio); *Shane*—"The Day the Wolf Laughed" 11-19-66 (Jud); *Death Valley Days*—"Along Came Mariana" 5-27-67 (Pedro); *Dundee and the Culhane*—11-15-67 (Kawia); *The Virginian*—"Death Wait" 1-15-69 (Cass Buchanan).

Ventura, Viviane (1945-). TV: *The Loner*—"The Oath" 12-4-65 (Maria); *Wild Wild West*—"The Night of the Torture Chamber" 12-10-65 (Angelique Lousea).

Venture, Richard (1923-). TV: *Adventures of Brisco County, Jr.*—"Showdown" 10-29-93 (Mack Brackman).

Venus, Brenda. Films: "Against a Crooked Sky" 1975; "Joshua" 1977. ¶TV: *Kung Fu*—"The Demon God" 12-13-74 (Aztec Woman).

Venuta, Benay (1911-9/1/95). Films: "Annie Get Your Gun" 1950 (Dolly Tate); "Ricochet Romance" 1954 (Claire Renard). ¶TV: *Annie Get Your Gun* 3-19-67 (Dolly Tate).

Vera, Carlos. Films: "Ten Wanted Men" 1955. ¶TV: *The Lone Ranger*—"The Angel and the Outlaw" 5-23-57; *Tales of Wells Fargo*—"Laredo" 12-23-57 (Pepito); *Fury*—"Gaucho" 2-20-60.

Vera, Ricky. TV: *Broken Arrow*—"Cry Wolf" 12-11-56; *Circus Boy*—"Little Vagabond" 6-23-57 (Gene); *Have Gun Will Travel*—"Heritage of Anger" 6-6-59 (Joe); *Bonanza*—"Look to the Stars" 3-18-62; *Gunsmoke*—"Extradition" 12-7-63 & 12-14-63 (Boy).

Veras, Linda. Films: "Run Man, Run" 1967-Ital./Fr.; "God Made Them ... I Kill Them" 1968-Ital.; "Sabata" 1969-Ital. (Jane); "Gold of the Heroes" 1971-Ital./Fr. (Maria Shannon).

Verdugo, Elena (1926-). Films: "The Big Sombrero" 1949 (Estrellita Estrada); "El Dorado Pass" 1949 (Dolores); "Snow Dog" 1950 (Andree); "Gene Autry and the Mounties" 1951 (Marie Duval); "The Pathfinder" 1952 (Lokawa); "The Marksman" 1953. ¶TV: *The Law of the Plainsman*—"The Innocents" 12-10-59 (Connie); *Rawhide*—"Incident at Spanish Rock" 12-18-59 (Maria Carroyo); *Redigo*—Regular 1963 (Gerry); *Iron Horse*—"The Bride at Forty-Mile" 1-23-67 (Abigail Bennett); *Daniel Boone*—"Copperhead Izzy" 1-30-69 (Violet Morton).

Verebes, Erno (1902-6/13/71). Films: "Northwest Outpost" 1947 (Kyril, Balinin's Aide); "Copper Canyon" 1950 (Professor).

Verne, Karen (1918-12/23/67). TV: *Bronco*—"Flight from an Empire" 12-15-59 (Ilse Von Weldenheim).

Vernon, Agnes. Films: "A Ranch Romance" 1914; "Prayer of a Horse" 1915; "The Man Who Took a Chance" 1917 (Constance Lanning); "Bare-Fisted Gallagher" 1919 (Jem Mason).

Vernon, Dorothy (1875-10/28/70). Films: "Tricks" 1925 (Housekeeper); "Headin' Westward" 1928 (Lizzie); "Manhattan Cowboy" 1928; "Riders of the Storm" 1929; "Raw Timber" 1937; "Heroes of the Alamo" 1938; "Geronimo" 1940 (Im-

migrant); "My Little Chickadee" 1940 (Diner); "Riders from Nowhere" 1940 (Mrs. Gregory); "Prairie Rustlers" 1945.

Vernon, Harvey. Films: "Little House: Bless All the Dear Children" TVM-1984 (Dr. Baker).

Vernon, John (1932-). Films: "Tell Them Willie Boy Is Here" 1969 (Hacker); "One More Train to Rob" 1971 (Timothy X. Nolan); "The Barbary Coast" TVM-1975 (Robin Templar); "The Outlaw Josey Wales" 1976 (Fletcher); "The Sacketts" TVM-1979 (Jonathan Pritts). ¶TV: *Hawkeye and the Last of the Mohicans*—"Tolliver Gang" 9-4-57; *Bonanza*—"Yonder Man" 12-8-68 (Beaudry); *The High Chaparral*—"No Irish Need Apply" 1-17-69 (Sean McLaren); *Bearcats!*—9-16-71 (Jason Ryker); *Kung Fu*—"My Brother, My Executioner" 10-12-74 (Forbes), "Barbary House" 2-15-75 (Gen. Cantrell), "Flight to Orion" 2-22-75 (Gen. Cantrell), "The Brothers Cain" 3-1-75 (Gen. Cantrell), "Full Circle" 3-15-75 (Gen. Cantrell); *Gunsmoke*—"The First of Ignorance" 1-27-75 (Oliver Harker); *The Oregon Trail*—"Hard Ride Home"/"The Last Game" 9-21-77 (Charles Shrigley).

Vernon, Lou (1888-12/22/71). TV: *Gunsmoke*—"Night Incident" 10-29-55 (Cal Ross), "The Hunter" 11-26-55 (Cal Ross).

Vernon, Wally (1904-3/7/70). Films: "Fugitive from Sonora" 1937 (Jackpot Murphy); "Black Hills Express" 1943 (Deadeye); "California Joe" 1943 (Tumbleweed Smith); "Canyon City" 1943 (Beauty Bradshaw); "The Man from the Rio Grande" 1943 (Jimpson Simpson); "Outlaws of Santa Fe" 1944 (Buckshot); "Silver City Kid" 1944; "Stagecoach to Monterey" 1944; "Square Dance Jubilee" 1949 (Seldom); "Border Rangers" 1950 (Hungry); "Gunfire" 1950 (Clem); "I Shot Billy the Kid" 1950 (Vicenti); "Train to Tombstone" 1950 (Gulliver); "Fury at Gunsight Pass" 1956 (Okay, Okay); "The White Squaw" 1956 (Faro Bill). ¶TV: *Tales of the Texas Rangers*—"Both Barrels Blazing" 10-20-57 (Grubstake).

Versini, Marie. Films: "Apache Gold" 1965-Ger. (Nscho-tschi); "Bullets and the Flesh" 1965-Ital./Fr./Span.; "Thunder at the Border" 1967-Ger./Yugo.

Ve Sota, Bruno (1922-9/24/76). Films: "Gunslinger" 1956 (Zebelon Tabb); "The Oklahoma Woman" 1956; "Wild Rovers" 1971 (Cantina Bartender). ¶TV: *The Rebel*—"A

Grave for Johnny Yuma" 5-1-60 (Mason), "The Earl of Durango" 6-12-60 (Klemo), "Decision at Sweetwater" 4-23-61 (Jim), "Ben White" 5-28-61 (Basto); *The Tall Man*—"Hard Justice" 3-25-61 (Peddler); *Bonanza*—"The Brass Box" 9-26-65 (Bartender), "The Code" 2-13-66 (Tucker), "The Genius" 4-3-66 (Bartender), "Something Hurt, Something Wild" 9-11-66 (Bartender), "A Time to Step Down" 9-25-66 (Bartender), "Old Charlie" 11-6-66 (Bartender), "The Crime of Johnny Mule" 2-25-68 (Bartender), "Star Crossed" 3-10-68 (Bartender), "Stage Door Johnnies" 7-28-68 (Bartender), "The Last Vote" 10-20-68 (Bartender), "Yonder Man" 12-8-68 (Bartender); *Wild Wild West*—"The Night of the Steel Assassin" 1-7-66 (Bartender); *Branded*—"Headed for Doomsday" 4-10-66 (Laird Sawyer); *Daniel Boone*—"Requiem for Craw Green" 12-1-66 (Reuben); *Hondo*—"Hondo and the Commancheros" 11-10-67 (Biddle).

Vetri, Victoria (Angela Dorian) (1944-). Films: "Chuka" 1967 (Helena Chavez). ¶TV: *Cheyenne*—"Johnny Brassbuttons" 12-3-62 (White Bird); *Destry*—"Ride to Rio Verde" 4-10-64 (Maiya); *Wagon Train*—"The Zebedee Titus Story" 4-20-64 (Maria), "The Jarbo Pierce Story" 5-2-65 (Marie); *Bonanza*—"Devil on Her Shoulder" 10-17-65 (Essie); *The Big Valley*—"Legend of a General" 9-19-66 & 9-26-66 (Teresa); *Death Valley Days*—"The Girl Who Walked the West" 11-4-67 (Sacajawea); *Daniel Boone*—"Noblesse Oblige" 3-26-70.

Vianello, Raimondo. Films: "Terrible Sheriff" 1963-Span./Ital.; "Heroes of the West" 1964-Span./Ital. (Colorado); "Twins from Texas" 1964-Ital./Span.; "For a Few Dollars Less" 1966-Ital. (Frank); "Ringo and Gringo Against All" 1966-Ital./Span.

Vickers, Martha (1925-11/2/71) Films: "Daughter of the West" 1949 (Lolita Moreno); "Four Fast Guns" 1959 (Mary). ¶TV: *The Rebel*—"The Rattler" 3-13-60 (Bess), "Vindication" 12-4-60 (Agnes Boley).

Vickers, Yvette (1936-). Films: "The Saga of Hemp Brown" 1958 (Amelia Smedley); "Hud" 1963 (Lily Peters). ¶TV: *Rough Riders*—"The Imposters" 10-30-58 (Ellie Winters), "The Electioners" 1-1-59; *Bat Masterson*—"Double Trouble in Trinidad" 1-7-59 (Jessie Simmons); *The Rebel*—"Shriek of Silence" 3-19-61 (Nancy), "Decision at Sweetwater" 4-23-61 (Catherine); *Tales of Wells Fargo*—

"Return to Yesterday" 1-13-62 (Agnes Jenkins).

Vico, Antonio. Films: "Up the MacGregors!" 1967-Ital./Span. (Frank James); "I Came, I Saw, I Shot" 1968-Ital./Span.

Victor, Henry (1898-5/15/45). Films: "Braveheart" 1925 (Sam Harris).

Vida, Piero (1938-). Films: "Pecos Cleans Up" 1967-Ital.; "Dead for a Dollar" 1968-Ital.; "Execution" 1968-Ital./Fr.; "Payment in Blood" 1968-Ital.; "And They Smelled the Strange, Exciting, Dangerous Scent of Dollars" 1973-Ital. (Charity Jenkins).

Vidor, Florence (1895-11/3/77). Films: "The Virginian" 1923 (Molly Woods); "The Enchanted Hill" 1926 (Gail Ormsby).

Vigran, Herb (1910-11/28/86). Films: "Oklahoma Annie" 1952 (Croupier); "Gunsight Ridge" 1957 (Justice); "Plunderers of Painted Flats" 1959 (Mr. Perry); "Support Your Local Gunfighter" 1971 (Fat); "Hawmps!" 1976 (Smitty); "Testimony of Two Men" TVM-1977. ¶TV: *Tales of the Texas Rangers*—"Singing on the Trail" 12-24-55 (Warren Jamison); *The Adventures of Rin Tin Tin*—"The Cloudbusters" 10-31-58 (Prof. Wirt); *Wanted—Dead or Alive*—"Rope Law" 1-3-59; *Bonanza*—"San Francisco Holiday" 4-2-60 (Bartender), "A Real Nice, Friendly Little Town" 11-27-66 (Card Player), "Joe Cartwright, Detective" 3-5-67 (Charlie); *Maverick*—"Hadley's Hunters" 9-25-60 (Pender), "The Bold Fenian Men" 12-18-60 (Ed Cramer), "The Golden Fleecing" 10-8-61 (Mr. Butler), "Marshal Maverick" 3-11-62 (Elkins); *Lawman*—"The Catalog Woman" 11-5-61 (Perkins); *Laramie*—"Handful of Fire" 12-5-61; *Tales of Wells Fargo*—"A Killing in Calico" 12-16-61 (Shopkeeper); *The Virginian*—"The Exiles" 1-9-63; *The Dakotas*—"Requiem at Dancer's Hill" 2-18-63 (Olin Bates); *Temple Houston*—"Sam's Boy" 1-23-64 (Walt); *A Man Called Shenandoah*—"The Unfamiliar Tune" 4-11-66 (Judge); *Gunsmoke*—Regular 1970-75 (Judge Brooker).

Vignola, Robert (1882-10/25/53). Films: "The Kentuckian" 1908.

Viharo, Robert (1939-). Films: "Villa Rides" 1968 (Urbina). ¶TV: *Cimarron Strip*—"The Battle of Blood Stone" 10-12-67; *The High Chaparral*—"Alliance" 12-12-69 (Johnny Ringo); *Gunsmoke*—"The Sodbusters" 11-20-72 (Dick Shaw).

Villagio, Paolo. Films: "In the Name of the Father" 1968-Ital.; "What Am I Doing in the Middle of the Revolution?" 1973-Ital. (Guido Guidi); "Don't Touch White Women!" 1974-Ital. (CIA Man).

Villareal, Julio (1885-8/4/58). Films: "The Beast of Hollow Mountain" 1956 (Don Pedro).

Villarias, Carlos. Films: "The California Trail" 1933 (Governor); "When Love Laughs" 1933-Mex.; "California Frontier" 1938 (Don Pedro Cantova); "Rose of the Rio Grande" 1938; "Starlight Over Texas" 1938 (Gov. Ruiz); "Frontiers of '49" 1939 (Padre).

Villegas, Lucio (1883-7/20/68). Films: "Under the Pampas Moon" 1935 (Magistrate); "Renegade Ranger" 1938 (Juan Capillo); "The Fighting Gringo" 1939 (Don Aliso Del Campo); "The Light of Western Stars" 1940 (Marco); "Mark of Zorro" 1940 (Caballero); "Three Men from Texas" 1940; "Border Bandits" 1946 (Nogales); "Pirates of Monterey" 1947 (Padre).

Vincenot, Louis (1884-2/25/67). Films: "Big Boy Rides Again" 1935 (Sing Fat).

Vincent, Allen (1903-11/30/79). Films: "Sutter's Gold" 1936 (Alvarado, Jr.).

Vincent, Billy. Films: "The San Antonio Kid" 1944; "Santa Fe Saddlemates" 1945; "Trail Street" 1947 (Henchman); "Return of the Badmen" 1948 (Deputy); "Montana" 1950 (Baker); "The Man Behind the Gun" 1952. ¶TV: *The Lone Ranger*—"Sheriff of Gunstock" 7-27-50, "Lady Killer" 12-21-50, "Delayed Action" 11-6-52; *Wanted—Dead or Alive*—"Baa-Baa" 1-4-61.

Vincent, Jan-Michael (1944-). Films: "Journey to Shiloh" 1968 (Little Bit Lucket); "The Undefeated" 1969 (Bubba Wilkes); "Bite the Bullet" 1975 (Carbo); "Shadow of the Hawk" 1976 (Mike). ¶TV: *Bonanza*—"The Arrival of Eddie" 5-19-68 (Eddie Makay), "The Unwanted" 4-6-69 (Rick Miller); *Gunsmoke*—"The Legend" 10-18-71 (Travis Colter).

Vincent, June (1919-). Films: "Song of Idaho" 1948 (Eve Allen); "Colorado Sundown" 1952 (Carrie Hurley); "The Miracle of the Hills" 1959 (Mrs. Leonard). ¶TV: *Have Gun Will Travel*—"Strange Vendetta" 10-26-57 (Maria Rojas), "The Colonel and the Lady" 11-23-57 (Martha Lathrop), "Black Sheep" 4-30-60 (Mrs. Duvoisin), "Everyman" 3-25-

61 (Mme. Destin), "Broken Image" 4-29-61 (Mrs. Decker); *Zane Grey Theater*—"Wire" 1-31-58 (Abby Fraser); *Trackdown*—"The Wedding" 2-14-58 (Mary Howard); *Wanted—Dead or Alive*—"Double Fee" 3-21-59 (Stella Winter); *The Rifleman*—"The Visitors" 1-26-60 (Jenny Morgan); *Riverboat*—"End of a Dream" 9-19-60 (Countess de Madrigal); *Tales of Wells Fargo*—"The Wayfarers" 5-19-62 (Grace Adams); *Great Adventure*—"The Testing of Sam Houston" 1-31-64 (Mrs. Allen); *The Virginian*—"Dead Eye Dick" 11-9-66 (Lucille Hammond), "With Help from Ulysses" 1-17-68 (Mrs. Martin); *Kung Fu*—"The Raiders" 1-24-74 (Meg).

Vincent, Romo (1908-1/16/89). Films: "Law of the Lawless" 1964.

Vincent, Russ. Films: "Apache Rose" 1947 (Carlos Vega); "The Last Round-Up" 1947 (Jeff Henry); "The Prairie" 1947 (Abiram White); "Twilight in the Sierras" 1950 (Ricardo Chavez).

Vincent, Sailor (1896-7/12/66). Films: "The Gay Desperado" 1936; "King of the Forest Rangers" 1946-serial (Graham); "Escape from Red Rock" 1958; "Advance to the Rear" 1964 (Deckhand); "Young Fury" 1965. ¶TV: *Maverick*—"According to Hoyle" 10-6-57 (Man).

Vincent, Virginia (1924-). Films: "Navajo Run" 1966 (Sarah Grog). ¶TV: *Sheriff of Cochise*—"Mechanic" 10-11-57 (Lois Thorne); *The Virginian*—"The Captive" 9-28-66 (Louise Emory); *Gunsmoke*—"The Money Store" 12-30-68 (Louise Thorpe).

Vinson, Gary (1936-). Films: "Yellowstone Kelly" 1959 (Lieutenant). ¶TV: *Gunsmoke*—"Never Pester Chester" 11-16-57 (Jim); *Bronco*—"Four Guns and a Prayer" 11-4-58 (Jamie Ringgold), "The Devi's Spawn" 12-1-59 (Bud Donner); *Bat Masterson*—"A Noose Fits Anybody" 11-19-58 (Billy Thompson); *Lawman*—"The Badge" 11-23-58 (Bill Andrews), "Explosion" 6-3-62 (Jesse Billings); *Rough Riders*—"A Matter of Instinct" 2-19-59 (Clayton); *The Deputy*—"The Wild Wind" 9-19-59 (Hipockets); *Maverick*—"A Fellow's Brother" 11-22-59 (Smoky Vaughn); *Sugarfoot*—"Return to Boot Hill" 3-15-60 (Jack Guild); *The Alaskans*—"The Last Bullet" 3-27-60 (Larry Hoyt), "Heart of Gold" 5-1-60 (Frank Andrews); *Colt .45*—"Chain of Command" 4-5-60, "The Trespasser" 6-21-60 (Lieutenant Sims); *Bronco*—"The Invaders" 1-23-61;

Laramie—"The Day of the Savage" 3-13-62 (Lieutenant Taylor); *The Tall Man*—"The Runaway Groom" 4-28-62 (Charlie); *Wagon Train*—"The Levy-McGowan Story" 11-14-62 (Sean McGowan); *Pistols 'n' Petticoats*—Regular 1966-67 (Harold Sikes); *The Virginian*—"Crime Wave at Buffalo Spring" 1-29-69 (Sheriff Tom Wade).

Vint, Alan (1944-). Films: "The McMasters" 1970 (Hank); "Belle Starr" TVM-1980 (Grat Dalton); "The Ballad of Gregorio Cortez" 1983 (Sheriff Trimmell). ¶TV: *Bonanza*—"To Stop a War" 10-19-69 (Pete Hill); *The High Chaparral*—"The Little Thieves" 12-26-69; *Nichols*—"Where Did Everybody Go?" 11-30-71 (Fred); *Centennial*—Regular 1978-79 (Beeley Garrett as an Adult).

Vint, Bill (1942-). Films: "Hec Ramsey" TVM-1972. ¶TV: *Lancer*—"Goodbye, Lizzie" 4-28-70 (Mossy); *Nichols*—"Where Did Everybody Go?" 11-30-71 (Bob).

Vint, Jesse (1940-). Films: "Little Big Man" 1971 (Lieutenant); "The Godchild" TVM-1974 (Loftus); "Belle Starr" TVM-1980 (Bob Dalton). ¶TV: *Nichols*—"Where Did Everybody Go?" 11-30-71 (Charley); *Centennial*—Regular 1978-79 (Amos Calendar); *Bret Maverick*—"The Not So Magnificent Six" 3-2-82 (Willie Trueblood); *Young Riders*—"'Til Death Do Us Part" 7-22-92 (Pierson).

Vinton, Arthur (1898-2/26/63). Films: "The Man Trailer" 1934 (Jim Burk).

Vinton, Bobby (1935-). Films: "Big Jake" 1971 (Jeff McCandles); "The Train Robbers" 1973 (Ben Young).

Vinton, Victoria. Films: "Pals of the Prairie" 1934-short; "Cheyenne Tornado" 1935 (Jane Darnell); "Ambush Valley" 1936 (Ann Morgan); "Vengeance of Rannah" 1936 (Mary); "The Singing Buckaroo" 1937.

Visaroff, Michael (1892-2/27/51). Films: "The Adventurer" 1928 (Samaroff); "Ramona" 1928 (Juan Canito); "Arizona Terror" 1931 (Emilio Vasquez); "King of the Arena" 1933 (Baron Petroff); "Wagon Wheels" 1934 (Russian); "The Gay Desperado" 1936 (Theatre Manager); "Dakota" 1945 (Russian); "Don Ricardo Returns" 1946; "Northwest Outpost" 1947 (Capt. Tikhonoff).

Vischer, Blanca. Films: "Under the Pampas Moon" 1935 (Elena);

"Billy the Kid's Gun Justice" 1940 (Juanita).

Vismara, Wanda. *see* Glass, Uschi.

Vitale, Joseph A. (-6/5/94). Films: "The Paleface" 1948 (Indian Scout); "Fancy Pants" 1950 (Wampum); "The Stranger Wore a Gun" 1953 (Dutch Mueller); "The Deerslayer" 1957 (Huron Chief); "Alias Jesse James" 1959 (Sam Hiawatha); "Apache Rifles" 1964 (Victorio). ¶TV: *Wild Bill Hickok*—"Good Indian" 8-4-53; *The Lone Ranger*—"The Letter Bride" 11-15-56, "The Law and Miss Aggie" 4-11-57; *Circus Boy*—"Return of Casey Perkins" 10-17-57 (Broken Claw); *Wyatt Earp*—"The General's Lady" 1-14-58; *The Adventures of Rin Tin Tin*—"Bitter Bounty" 3-14-58 (Cortine), "Miracle of the Mission" 12-12-58 (Red Eagle); *Wagon Train*—"The Rex Montana Story" 5-28-58 (Shanwaukee); *The Restless Gun*—"Bonner's Squaw" 11-3-58 (Chief Tashuca); *Tales of Wells Fargo*—"A Matter of Honor" 11-3-58 (Black Antelope); *Northwest Passage*—"Vengeance Trail" 12-21-58 (Chief Akacita); *Rawhide*—"Incident at Sulphur Creek" 3-11-60, "Incident at Gila Flats" 1-30-64 (Nantanta); *Empire*—"The Four Thumbs Story" 1-8-63 (Quicker Than You).

Vitanza, A.G. TV: *The Virginian*—"Man of the People" 12-23-64 (Pelligrini); *Laredo*—"The Heroes of San Gill" 12-23-65 (Dork); *Bonanza*—"Trouble Town" 3-17-68 (Bartender).

Viterbo, Patricia (1943-11/10/66). Films: "Bullets and the Flesh" 1965-Ital./Fr./Span. (Mabel).

Viva (1942-). Films: "Lonesome Cowboys" 1968.

Vivyan, John (1916-12/20/83). Films: "Rider on a Dead Horse" 1962 (Hayden). ¶TV: *Wyatt Earp*—"Wichita Is Civilized" 8-18-56, "Dodge Is Civilized" 4-28-59 (Mike de Graff); *Tombstone Territory*—"Desert Survival" 12-4-57 (Glade Rafferty), "Red Terror of Tombstone" 10-9-59; *Maverick*—"The Quick and the Dead" 12-8-57 (John Stacey), "Black Fire" 3-16-58 (Cousin Millard), "The Judas Mask" 11-2-58 (Walter Osbourne), "A Cure for Johnny Rain" 12-20-59 (Tinhorn); *Colt .45*—"The Mirage" 1-10-58 (John F. Foley); *Sugarfoot*—"Deadlock" 2-4-58 (Victor Valla); *MacKenzie's Raiders*—"Little Bit of Courage" 10-29-58; *Rough Riders*—"The Counterfeiters" 12-11-58 (Brink Mantell); *Yancy Derringer*—"Duel at the Oaks" 4-9-59 (LeBow); *Rawhide*—"Incident of the Dog

Days" 4-17-59 (Toby Clark), "Incident of the White Eyes" 5-3-63 (Beaumont Butler); *Bat Masterson*—"A Matter of Honor" 4-29-59 (Chip Grimes), "The Hunter" 10-27-60 (Sir Edward Marion); *Texas John Slaughter*—"The Robber Stallion" 12-4-59 (Jason Hemp), "Wild Horse Revenge" 12-11-59 (Jason Hemp); *Death Valley Days*—"The Lady Was an M.D." 1-11-61 (Ed), "Showdown at Kamaaina Flats" 7-4-62 (Jeremy Whitlock); *Empire*—"Down There, the World" 3-12-63 (Shelly Hanson); *Daniel Boone*—"Not in Our Stars" 12-31-64 (Major Halpen).

Vize, Tom. TV: *Zane Grey Theater*—"This Man Must Die" 1-24-58 (Cochran); *Wanted—Dead or Alive*—"The Trial" 9-21-60.

Vlahos, Sam. Films: "Little House on the Prairie" TVM-1974 (1st Indian); "Gunsmoke: The Last Apache" TVM-1990 (Tomas). ¶TV: *Young Riders*—"Dark Brother" 6-4-92 (White Feather).

Vogan, Emmett (1893-11/13/69). Films: "Rhythm on the Range" 1936 (Clerk); "Two in Revolt" 1936 (Mason); "Empty Holsters" 1937 (Ace Cain); "Wells Fargo" 1937 (Merchant); "Cowboy from Brooklyn" 1938 (Loudspeaker Announcer); "Heart of the North" 1938 (Radio Operator); "Rhythm of the Saddle" 1938; "Geronimo" 1940 (Post Doctor); "Santa Fe Trail" 1940 (Lieutenant); "Shooting High" 1940 (McCormack); "Lady from Cheyenne" 1941 (Stanton); "Hurricane Smith" 1942 (Prosecuting Attorney); "Stardust on the Sage" 1942 (Pearson); "Canyon City" 1943 (Emerson Wheeler); "In Old Oklahoma" 1943 (Pres. Roosevelt's Aide); "King of the Cowboys" 1943 (Saboteur); "Raiders of Ghost City" 1944-serial (Carl Lawton); "Song of Nevada" 1944 (Master of Ceremonies); "The Yellow Rose of Tesas" 1944; "Along the Navajo Trail" 1945 (Roger Jerrold); "Colorado Pioneers" 1945; "Corpus Christi Bandits" 1945 (Governor); "Flame of the Barbary Coast" 1945 (Rita's Agent); "Senorita from the West" 1945; "Utah" 1945 (District Attorney); "Homesteaders of Paradise Valley" 1947; "Last of the Redmen" 1947 (Bob Wheelwright); "Smoky River Serenade" 1947; "The Denver Kid" 1948; "The Gallant Legion" 1948; "Brothers in the Saddle" 1949; "Down Dakota Way" 1949 (Dr. George Fredericks); "Riders of the Whistling Pines" 1949; "South of Rio" 1949 (Henry Waterman); "Pals of the Golden West" 1951 (Col.

Wells); "Red River Shore" 1953 (Benjamin Willoughby). ¶TV: *Fireside Theater*—"Man of the Comstock" 11-3-53 (Governor Nye); *Death Valley Days*—"A Killing in Diamonds" 11-21-55.

Vogeding, Frederick (1890-4/18/42). Films: "Cowboy and the Lady" 1938 (Captain); "Three Faces West" 1940 (Schmidt).

Vogel, Carol. TV: *Bonanza*—"New Man" 10-10-72 (Amy); *Gunsmoke*—"The Angry Land" 2-3-75 (Rachel); *How the West Was Won*—"The Scavengers" 3-12-79 (Chastity).

Vogel, Mitch (1956-). TV: *Dundee and the Culhane*—11-22-67 (Jeffrey Bennett); *The Virginian*—"The Storm Gate" 11-13-68 (Boy); *Death Valley Days*—"The Tenderfoot" 11-15-69 (Jerry); *Here Come the Brides*—"Absalom" 3-20-70 (Absalom); *Bonanza*—Regular 1970-72 (Jamie Hunter); *Gunsmoke*—"McCabe" 11-30-70 (Dobie), "Lynch Town" 11-19-73 (Rob Fielder), "The Hiders" 1-13-75 (Dink); *The Quest*—"Seventy-Two Hours" 11-3-76 (Jess).

Vohs, Joan (1931-). Films: "Fort Ti" 1953 (Fortune Mallory); "Fort Yuma" 1955 (Melanie Crowne). ¶TV: *Frontier*—"Romance of Poker Alice" 12-11-55; *Maverick*—"The Long Hunt" 10-20-57 (Martha Ferris); *Colt .45*—"Dead Reckoning" 1-24-58 (Katherine Norton); *The Rebel*—"The Liberators" 1-1-61 (Bless Stelling).

Voight, Jon (1938-). Films: "Hour of the Gun" 1967 (Curly Bill Brocius); "Return to Lonesome Dove" TVM-1993 (Capt. Woodrow F. Call); "The Last of His Tribe" TVM-1994 (Prof. Albert Kroeber). ¶TV: *Gunsmoke*—"The Newcomers" 12-3-66 (Petter Karlgren), "Prairie Wolfers" 11-13-67 (Cory), "The Prisoner" 3-17-69 (Steven Downing); *Cimarron Strip*—"Without Honor" 2-29-68 (Private Bill Mason).

Voland, Herbert (-4/26/81). Films: "Scalplock" TVM-1966; "The Shakiest Gun in the West" 1968 (Dr. Friedlander). ¶TV: *The Virginian*—"Farewell to Honesty" 3-24-65 (the Judge); *Iron Horse*—"Joy Unconfined" 9-12-66 (Buckeye); *Bonanza*—"Different Pines, Same Wind" 9-15-68 (Millburn).

Volante, Vicki. Films: "Five Blood Graves" 1969 (Nora Miller).

Volkie, Ralph (1910-3/6/87). Films: "New Mexico" 1951 (1st Rider); "Slaughter Trail" 1951 (Sentry); "The Lusty Men" 1952 (Slicker); "The Man Who Shot Liberty Valance" 1962 (Townsman); "McClin-

tock" 1963 (Loafer); "Four for Texas" 1964; "The Sons of Katie Elder" 1965 (Bit); "El Dorado" 1967; "Chisum" 1970 (Blacksmith).

Volonte, Gian Maria (John Wells) (1933-12/6/94). Films: "A Fistful of Dollars" 1964-Ital./Ger./Span. (Ramon Rojo); "For a Few Dollars More" 1965-Ital./Ger./Span. (Indio); "A Bullet for the General" 1966-Ital. (Chuncho); "Face to Face" 1967-Ital. (Brad Fletcher).

Voloshin, Alex (1886-11/23/60). Films: "Destry Rides Again" 1939 (Assistant Bartender).

Volz, Nedra (1908-). Films: "Lust in the Dust" 1985 (Big Ed).

Von Beltz, Brad. TV: *Have Gun Will Travel*—"The Return of Roy Carter" 5-2-59 (Eddie Clinton), "The Prophet" 1-2-60 (Brother), "The Campaign of Billy Banjo" 5-28-60 (Miner); *Lawman*—"The Friend" 6-28-59; *Fury*—"Trottin' Horse" 2-6-60 (Buck Noska).

von Brincken, William (William Vaughn) (1891-1/18/46). Films: "The Lonesome Tail" 1930 (Man in White Sombrero); "The Mystery Trooper" 1931-serial; "Mexicali Kid" 1938 (Fredric Gorson); "King of the Mounties" 1942-serial (Marshal Von Horst); "Where Trails End" 1942 .

Von Eltz, Theodore (1894-10/6/64). Films: "Tiger Rose" 1923 (Bruce Norton); "No Man's Law" 1927 (Spider O'Day); "The Arizona Kid" 1930 (Nick Hoyt); "Secrets" 1933 (Robert Carlton); "Trails of the Wild" 1935 (Kincaid); "The Great Man's Lady" 1942. ¶TV: *Wild Bill Hickok*—"The Right of Way" 8-5-52.

von Friedl, Loni. "The Moment to Kill" 1968-Ital./Ger. (Regina).

von Furstenberg, Betsy (1935-). TV: *Have Gun Will Travel*—"The Girl from Piccadilly" 2-22-58 (Isobella).

Von Holland, Mildred. TV: *The Adventures of Rin Tin Tin*—"Rin Tin Tin and the Printer's Devil" 4-15-55, "Rusty Goes to Town" 11-25-55 (Myra), "The Missing Heir" 1-13-56 (Mrs. Barrington), "Hubert Goes West" 5-18-56 (Mrs. Barrington), "Witch of the Woods" 9-14-56 (Mrs. Fitch), "The Southern Colonel" 10-18-57 (Myra Miller), "Decision of Rin Tin Tin" 10-3-58 (Mrs. Barrington); *Tales of the Texas Rangers*—"The Devil's Deputy" 1-7-56 (Martha); *Maverick*—"The Judas Mask" 11-2-58 (Adele); *Laramie*—"The Star Trail" 10-13-59 (Ma).

Von Homburg, Wilhelm. TV: *Gunsmoke*—"The Promoter" 4-25-64

(Otto Gunlach); *Wild Wild West*—"The Night of the Iron Fist" 12-8-67 (Abel Garrison), "The Night of the Big Blackmail" 9-27-68 (Herr Hess).

Von Leer, Hunter (1944-). Films: "Cahill, United States Marshal" 1973 (Deputy Jim Kane); "The Missouri Breaks" 1976 (Sandy). ¶TV: *Paradise*—"The Traveler" 2-2-89 (Aleck Varna).

Von Meter, Harry. *see* Van Meter, Harry.

Vonn, Viola. Films: "Ragtime Cowboy Joe" 1940 (Cabaret Singer); "The Big Sky" 1952.

von Ritzau, Erich (1877-2/28/36). Films: "The Prairie Wife" 1925 (Doctor).

Von Schiller, Carl (1890-4/15/62). Films: "Breed of the West" 1913; "Buckshot John" 1915 (Jimmy Dacey); "Captain Courtesy" 1915 (Jocoso); "Colorado" 1915 (Frank Austin); "A Law Unto Himself" 1916 (Bob Clayton).

von Seyffertitz, Gustav (1863-12/25/43). Films: "Rimrock Jones" 1918 (Stoddard); "Rose of the Golden West" 1927 (Gomez).

von Sydow, Max (1929-). Films: "The Reward" 1965 (Scott Swanson); "The New Land" 1973-Swed. (Karl Oskar).

Von Zell, Harry (1906-11/21/81). Films: "Two Flags West" 1950 (Ephraim Strong); "Son of Paleface" 1952 (Stoner). ¶TV: *Wagon Train*—"The Tobias Jones Story" 10-22-58 (Nathaniel Ferguson), "The Will Santee Story" 5-3-61 (Fred McDermott), "Clyde" 12-27-61 (John Sherman), "The Link Cheney Story" 4-13-64 (Henry Baffle); *The Tall Man*—"Full Payment" 9-9-61 (Murphy), "Petticoat Crusade" 11-18-61 (Murphy).

Vosburgh, Alfred. *see* Whitman, Gayne.

Voskovec, George (1905-7/1/81). Films: "The Iron Mistress" 1952 (James Audubon); "The Bravados" 1958 (Gus Steinmetz); "Barbarosa" 1982 (Herman).

Vosper, John (1902-4/6/54). Films: "Undercover Man" 1942 (Ed Carson); "Dead Man's Gulch" 1943 (Hobart Patterson); "The Sea of Grass" 1947 (Hotel Clerk); "Black Hills Ambush" 1952 (Gaines).

Votrian, Peter. "The Oklahoman" 1957 (Little Charlie). ¶TV: *Wild Bill Hickok*—"School Teacher Story" 1-15-52; *The Gene Autry Show*—"Battle Axe" 8-31-54, "The Million Dollar Fiddle" 10-1-55 (Reginald Redaldo), "Ride, Rancheros" 12-

10-55, "The Rangerette" 12-17-55; *The Roy Rogers Show*—"The Lady Killer" 9-12-54 (Jamie Jenkins); *Frontier*—"A Stillness in Wyoming" 10-16-55; *Gunsmoke*—"Night Incident" 10-29-55 (Timmy Wyatt), "Indian White" 10-27-56 (Dennis); *My Friend Flicka*—"The Little Visitor" 12-30-55 (Fredd Williams); *Fury*—"Joey Shows the Way" 1-26-57 (Tim), "Bad Medicine" 1-31-59; *Zane Grey Theater*—"A Fugitive" 3-22-57 (Joby Kimball); *Circus Boy*—"Royal Roustabout" 9-26-57 (Eric); *The Restless Gun*—"Rink" 10-14-57 (Rink); *Broken Arrow*—"Bad Boy" 1-21-58 (Willy); *Northwest Passage*—"War Sign" 11-30-58 (Johnny Martin).

Votrian, Ralph. Films: "Pillars of the Sky" 1956 (Music). ¶TV: *Black Saddle*—"Client: Robinson" 2-21-59 (Billy Griggs); *Rawhide*—"Incicdent of a Burst of Evil" 6-26-59; *The Tall Man*—"Bad Company" 9-24-60 (Johnny Nagel), "A Scheme of Hearts" 4-22-61 (Tammy).

Vroom, Frederick (1858-6/24/42). Films: "A Ticket to Red Horse Gulch" 1914; "Little Red Decides" 1918 (Col. Ferdinand Aliso); "Fighting Through" 1919 (Braxton Warren); "Where the West Begins" 1919 (Luther Caldwell).

Vye, Murvyn (1913-8/17/76). Films: "Whispering Smith" 1948 (Blake Barton); "Black Horse Canyon" 1954 (Jennings); "River of No Return" 1954 (Dave Colby). ¶TV: *Sergeant Preston of the Yukon*—"Turnabout" 8-22-56 (Len Bryce); *Sheriff of Cochise*—"The Relatives" 3-8-57 (Cravath); *Maverick*—"The Wrecker" 12-1-57 (Craven), "Day of Reckoning" 2-2-58, "The Cats of Paradise" 10-11-59 (Captain Puget); *Have Gun Will Travel*—"The Englishman" 12-7-57 (N.G. Smith); *Tales of Wells Fargo*—"Butch Cassidy" 10-13-58 (Virgie); *Bat Masterson*—"Two Graves for Swan Valley" 10-15-58 (Big Ed Bacon), "A Noose Fits Anybody" 11-19-58 (Big Ed Bacon); *The Texan*—"The Lord Will Provide" 12-29-58 (Pete Phillips); *Northwest Passage*—"Death Rides the Wind" 1-23-59 (Matt Stacey); *Lawman*—"Warpath" 2-8-59 (Tom Cardigan), "Reunion in Laramie" 3-13-60 (Vint Fell); *Buckskin*—"Mary MacNamara" 5-18-59 (Rev. Joe Carson); *Bonanza*—"San Francisco Holiday" 4-2-60 (Cut-Rate Joe); *Wagon Train*—"Trial for Murder" 4-27-60 & 5-4-60 (Miller), "The Madame Sagittarius Story" 10-3-62 (Jeb); *The Law of the Plainsman*—"Trojan Horse" 5-5-60 (Frank Seed); *The Rifleman*—"Nora" 5-24-60

(Jude Nichols); *The Virginian*—"The Final Hour" 5-1-63.

Wade, Bessie (1885-10/19/66). Films: "Wagon Train" 1940.

Wade, John (1876-7/14/49). Films: "Heroes of the Hills" 1938 (Board Chairman).

Wade, Russell. Films: "Bandit Ranger" 1942; "Pirates of the Prairie" 1942; "Fighting Frontier" 1943; "Red River Robin Hood" 1943; "Tall in the Saddle" 1944 (Clint Haroldan); "Renegade Girl" 1946; "Sundown Riders" 1948 (Sundown Rider).

Wade, Warren (1896-1/14/73). "Heller in Pink Tights" 1960 (Hodges).

Wadsworth, William (1873-6/6/50). Films: "The Daisy Cowboy" 1911; "The Story of the Indian Lodge" 1911; "How the Boys Fought the Indians" 1912; "Salt of the Earth" 1917 (Brandon P. Hyde); "Loaded Dice" 1925.

Wagenheim, Charles (1895-3/6/79). Films: "Sin Town" 1942 (Dry Hole); "Frontier Badman" 1943 (Melvin); "Raiders of Ghost City" 1944-serial (Abel Rackerby); "Salome, Where She Danced" 1945 (Telegrapher); "Pirates of Monterey" 1947 (Juan); "River Lady" 1948 (Man); "Canyon Crossroads" 1955 (Pete Barnwell); "Blackjack Ketchum, Desperado" 1956 (Jerry Carson); "Toughest Gun in Tombstone" 1958 (Bearsley); "Cat Ballou" 1965 (James); "The Missouri Breaks" 1976 (Freighter). ¶TV: *The Lone Ranger*—"The Breaking Point" 1-24-57; *Sergeant Preston of the Yukon*—"Ghost Mine" 11-14-57 (Jake Peavy); *The Restless Gun*—"Hang and Be Damned" 1-27-58 (Prospector); *Tales of Wells Fargo*—"The Manuscript" 9-15-58 (Quinn); *Bonanza*—"Mr. Henry Comstock" 11-7-59 (Pike), "Breed of Violence" 11-5-60, "The Code" 2-13-66 (Felger), "Riot!" 10-3-72 (Donovan); *Wyatt Earp*—"The Buntline Special" 3-8-60 (Spangenberg), "Hiding Behind a Star" 5-23-61 (Spangenberg); *The Big Valley*—"Tunnel of Gold" 4-20-66 (Clerk); *The Rounders*—9-20-66 (Charlie Brown); *Gunsmoke*—Regular 1967-75 (Halligan), "The Tycoon" 1-25-71 (Parson Mueller); *Wild Wild West*—"The Night of the Flaming Ghost" 2-4-66 (Shukie Summers); *Cimarron Strip*—"The Hunted" 10-5-67 (Prospector); *The Guns of Will Sonnett*—"Pariah" 10-18-68; *Lancer*—"Splinter Group" 3-3-70 (William); *Alias Smith and Jones*—"The McCreedy Bush" 1-21-71 (Bartender); *The New Land*—"The Word Is: Celebration" 10-19-74.

Waggner, George (1894-12/11/84). Films: "Desert Driven" 1923 (Craydon); "The Iron Horse" 1924 (Colonel Buffalo Bill Cody).

Waggoner, Lyle (1935-). TV: *Gunsmoke*—"Wishbone" 2-19-66 (Aiken); *Gun Shy*—3-29-83.

Wagner, Emmett (1892-4/25/77). Films: "Hard-Boiled" 1926 (3rd Crook).

Wagner, Fernando. Films: "Garden of Evil" 1954 (Captain); "Sierra Baron" 1958 (Grandall); "Viva Maria" 1965-Fr./Ital. (Maria O'-Mally's Father); "The Wild Bunch" 1969 (German Army Officer).

Wagner, Jack (1897-2/6/65). TV: *Bat Masterson*—"A Noose Fits Anybody" 11-19-58 (Deputy); *Rough Riders*—"The Electioners" 1-1-59 (Moss).

Wagner, Lou (1940-). TV: *The Men from Shiloh*—"Nan Allen" 1-6-71 (Aaron Hill); *Alias Smith and Jones*—"A Fistful of Diamonds" 3-4-71; *Nichols*—2-29-72 (McKeever).

Wagner, Max (1902-11/16/75). Films: "Renegades of the West" 1932 (Bob); "The Last Trail" 1933 (Duke); "The Miracle Rider" 1935-serial; "Under the Pampas Moon" 1935 (Big Jose); "Two in Revolt" 1936 (Davis); "Border Cafe" 1937 (Shaky); "God's Country and the Woman" 1937 (Gus); "The Painted Desert" 1938 (Kincaid); "The Return of the Cisco Kid" 1939; "Buck Benny Rides Again" 1940 (Cowboy); "Trail of the Vigilantes" 1940 (Joe); "Cyclone on Horseback" 1941; "Boss of Boomtown" 1944 (Dunne); "Smoky" 1946 (Bart); "Bandits of El Dorado" 1951 (Paul); "The Secret of Convict Lake" 1951 (Jack Purcell); "The Big Sky" 1952. ¶TV: *The Cisco Kid*—"Cisco Meets the Gorilla" 12-13-52, "The Powder Trail" 2-14-53, "Tangled Trails" 5-29-54; *The Rifleman*—"Brood Brothers" 5-26-59; *Destry*—"Destry Had a Little Lamb" 2-21-64 (Drunk).

Wagner, Mike. Films: "Dirty Dingus Magee" 1970 (Driver); "Support Your Local Gunfighter" 1971 (Bartender); "The Wild Wild West Revisited" TVM-1979. ¶TV: *Preview Tonight*—"Roaring Camp" 9-4-66 (Brady); *Laredo*—"Any Way the Wind Blows" 10-28-66 (Soames); *Death Valley Days*—"A Calamity Called Jane" 2-11-67 (Moose); *The Big Valley*—"Bounty on a Barkley" 2-26-68; *The High Chaparral*—"Stinky Flanagan" 2-21-69.

Wagner, Robert (1930-). Films: "The Silver Whip" 1953 (Jess Harker); "Broken Lance" 1954 (Joe Devereaux); "White Feather" 1955 (Josh Tanner); "The True Story of Jesse James" 1957 (Jesse James). ¶TV: *20th Century Fox Hour*—"The Ox-Bow Incident" 11-2-55 (Gil Carter), "Gun in His Hand" 4-4-56 (Wade Connors).

Wagner, Wende (1942-). Films: "Rio Conchos" 1964 (Sally); "Guns of the Magnificent Seven" 1969 (Tina). ¶TV: *Wagon Train*—"The Luke Grant Story" 6-1-60 (Fay).

Wagner, William (1885-3/11/64). Films: "Rustlers' Roundup" 1933 (Homer Jones); "White Fang" 1936 (Minister).

Wainwright, James (1938-). Films: "Joe Kidd" 1972 (Mingo); "Bridger" TVM-1976 (Jim Bridger). ¶TV: *Death Valley Days*—"Chicken Bill" 10-14-67 (Mulcahy); *Bonanza*—"Night of Reckoning" 10-15-67 (Webster); *The Guns of Will Sonnett*—"And a Killing Rode into Town" 12-1-67 (Stacey), "A Difference of Opinion" 11-15-68 (Crewes); *Cowboy in Africa*—"The Man Who Has Everything" 12-4-67; *Gunsmoke*—"Slocum" 10-21-68 (Mark Riker); *Lancer*—"Jelly" 11-19-68 (Logan); *The Virginian*—"Last Grave at Socorro Creek" 1-22-69 (Jack Witchers); *Daniel Boone*—"Three Score and Ten" 2-6-69 (Cully), "The Printing Press" 10-23-69, "The Traitor" 10-30-69 (Cully), "The Landlords" 3-5-70 (Cully), "Run for the Money" 2-19-70; *The Men from Shiloh*—"The Animal" 1-20-71 (Boyd Dewey); *Alias Smith and Jones*—"Jailbreak at Junction City" 9-30-71 (Ribs Johnson); *Kung Fu*—"My Brother, My Executioner" 10-12-74 (Danny Caine); *The Oregon Trail*—"Return from Death" 1977; *The Life and Times of Grizzly Adams*—10-12-77 (Sam Steele).

Waite, Malcolm (1892-4/25/49). Films: "Durand of the Bad Lands" 1925 (Clem Allison); "The Lucky Horseshoe" 1925 (Denman); "No Man's Gold" 1926 (Pete Krell); "Broncho Twister" 1927 (Dan Bell); "Blazing Sixes" 1937 (Jamison); "Jackass Mail" 1942 (Cooke).

Waite, Ralph (1928-). Films: "Lawman" 1971 (Jack Dekker); "Chato's Land" 1972 (Elias Hooker); "The Magnificent Seven Ride" 1972 (Jim MacKay); "Kid Blue" 1973 (Drummer). ¶TV: *Bonanza*—"The Lady and the Mark" 2-1-70 (Hoby); *Nichols*—"The Dirty Half Dozen Run Amuck" 10-28-71 (Sam Burton).

Wakely, Jimmy (1914-9/23/82). Films: "Saga of Death Valley" 1939; "Pony Post" 1940; "Texas Terrors" 1940; "Trailing Double Trouble" 1940; "The Tulsa Kid" 1940; "Bury Me Not on the Lone Prairie" 1941; "Redskins and Redheads" 1941-short; "Stick to Your Guns" 1941 (Pete); "Twilight on the Trail" 1941; "Deep in the Heart of Texas" 1942; "Heart of the Rio Grande" 1942; "Little Joe, the Wrangler" 1942; "Old Chisholm Trail" 1942; "Cheyenne Roundup" 1943; "Cowboy in the Clouds" 1943 (Glen Avery); "The Lone Star Trail" 1943; "Raiders of San Joaquin" 1943; "Robin Hood of the Range" 1943; "Tenting Tonight on the Old Camp Ground" 1943; "Cowboy Canteen" 1944; "Cowboy from Lonesome River" 1944; "Saddle Leather Law" 1944; "Song of the Range" 1944 (Jimmy); "Sundown Valley" 1944; "Swing in the Saddle" 1944; "Lonesome Trail" 1945; "Riders of the Dawn" 1945 (Jimmy Wakely); "Rough Ridin' Justice" 1945; "Saddle Serenade" 1945; "Springtime in Texas" 1945; "Moon Over Montana" 1946; "Song of the Sierras" 1946; "Trail to Mexico" 1946; "West of Alamo" 1946 (Jimmy); "Rainbow Over the Rockies" 1947; "Ridin' Down the Trail" 1947; "Six Gun Serenade" 1947; "Song of the Wasteland" 1947; "Cowboy Cavalier" 1948; "Oklahoma Blues" 1948 (Jimmy Wakely); "Outlaw Brand" 1948; "Partners of the Sunset" 1948; "Range Renegades" 1948; "The Rangers Ride" 1948; "Silver Trails" 1948 (Jimmy); "Song of the Drifter" 1948; "Across the Rio Grande" 1949 (Jimmy); "Brand of Fear" 1949; "Desert Vigilante" 1949; "Gun Law Justice" 1949; "Gun Runner" 1949 (Jimmy); "Lawless Code" 1949; "Roaring Westward" 1949 (Jimmy); "The Marshal's Daughter" 1953; "Arrow in the Dust" 1954 (Carqueville).

Walberg, Gary (1921-). Films: "Charro!" 1969 (Martin Tilford); "Tell Them Willie Boy Is Here" 1969 (Dr. Mills); "When the Legends Die" 1972 (Superintendent). ¶TV: *Rawhide*—"Incident of the Town in Terror" 3-6-59, "Incident of the Coyote Weed" 3-20-59, "Incident at Dragoon Crossing" 10-21-60 (Cory Bates); *Gunsmoke*—"Buffalo Hunter" 5-2-59 (Tobe), "The Imposter" 5-13-61 (Harve Peters), "Marry Me" 12-23-61 (Rob Cotter), "A Man a Day" 12-30-61 (Hatcher), "Chester's Indian" 5-12-62 (Simeon), "The Way It Is" 12-1-62 (Bent Dillard), "Two of a Kind" 3-16-63 (Anson), "The Violators" 10-17-64 (Willie Scroggs), "A Game of Death ... An Act of Love" 11-5-73 & 11-12-73 (Dekker), "Tarnished Badge" 11-11-74 (Toby); *The*

Law of the Plainsman—"Clear Title" 12-17-59; *The Outlaws*—"Thirty a Month" 9-29-60 (Brazos); *Tales of Wells Fargo*—"Frightened Witness" 12-26-60 (Chris Matson); *Two Faces West*—"The Sure Thing" 7-3-61 (Connelly); *Death Valley Days*—"Girl with a Gun" 6-6-62 (Metcalf); *Destry*—"One Hundred Bibles" 5-8-64 (Henderson); *The Virginian*—"One Spring Like Long Ago" 3-2-66 (Weatherby); *The Road West*—"Power of Fear" 12-26-66 (Witt); *The High Chaparral*—"No Irish Need Apply" 1-17-69 (O'Fierna), "The Lieutenant" 2-27-70, "It Takes a Smart Man" 10-23-70 (Bartender); *Lancer*—"Child of Rock and Sunlight" 4-1-69; *Bonanza*—"The Fence" 4-27-69 (Bower).

Walburn, Raymond (1887-7/26/69). Films: "High, Wide and Handsome" 1937 (Doc Watterson); "Let Freedom Ring" 1939 (Underwood); "The Dark Command" 1940 (Buckner); "The Desperadoes" 1943 (Judge Cameron); "Plainsman and the Lady" 1946 (Judge Winters); "Short Grass" 1950 (McKenna); "The Spoilers" 1955 (Mr. Skinner).

Walcamp, Marie (1893-11/17/36). Films: "The Law of the Range" 1914; "The Trail Breakers" 1914; "Custer's Last Scout" 1915; "Liberty" 1916-serial; "The Indian's Lament" 1917; "The Red Ace" 1917-serial; "Tongues of Flame" 1918 (Teresa); "The Whirlwind Finish" 1918; "Tempest Cody Backs the Trust" 1919 (Tempest Cody); "Tempest Cody Flirts with Death" 1919 (Tempest Cody); "Tempest Cody Gets Her Man" 1919 (Tempest Cody); "Tempest Cody Hits the Trail" 1919 (Tempest Cody); "Tempest Cody, Kidnapper" 1919 (Tempest Cody); "Tempest Cody Plays Detective" 1919 (Tempest Cody); "Tempest Cody Rides Wild" 1919 (Tempest Cody); "Tempest Cody Turns the Table" 1919 (Tempest Cody); "Tempest Cody's Man Hunt" 1919 (Tempest Cody); "A Desperate Adventure" 1924; "Treasure Canyon" 1924; "Western Vengeance" 1924 (Mary Sterling).

Walcott, Gregory (1928-). Films: "Strange Lady in Town" 1955 (Scanlon); "Texas Lady" 1955 (Jess Foley); "Thunder Over Arizona" 1956; "The Persuader" 1957 (Jim Cleery); "Badman's Country" 1958 (Bat Masterson); "Joe Kidd" 1972 (Sheriff Mitchell); "A Man from the East" 1974-Ital./Fr. (Bull); "The Quest" TVM-1976 (Blacksmith); "Donner Pass: The Road to Survival" TVM-1978 (Will McKutchwon).

¶TV: *Cavalcade of America*—"Mountain Man" 9-28-54; *Zane Grey Theater*—"The Necessary Breed" 2-15-57 (Rafe); *Wagon Train*—"The Riley Gratton Story" 12-4-57 (John Dawson), "The Cathy Eckhardt Story" 11-9-60 (Jeff Miller); *Sugarfoot*—"Bullet Proof" 1-21-58 (Duke McKlintock); *Frontier Doctor*—"Queen of the Cimarron" 9-27-58; *The Rifleman*—"The Angry Gun" 12-23-58 (Blade Kelly), "Tension" 10-27-59; *Tales of Wells Fargo*—"Desert Showdown" 9-14-59 (Tyler), "Tom Horn" 10-26-59 (Sergeant), "Escort to Santa Fe" 12-19-60 (Kyle Gentry); *Maverick*—"Full House" 10-25-59 (Cole Younger); *Wichita Town*—"Ruby Dawes" 1-6-60 (Willy Sparks); *Bat Masterson*—"Mr. Fourpaws" 2-18-60 (Sam Long), "Farmer with a Badge" 5-18-61 (Lou); *Rawhide*—"Incident in the Garden of Eden" 6-17-60 (Crane), "Incident at Poco Tiempo" 12-9-60 (Mara), "Incident of the Hunter" 9-28-62 (Girard), "Incident of the Gallows Tree" 2-22-63 (Roy Kane), "Incident of the Wanderer" 2-27-64 (Les Hunt); *The Tall Man*—"The Shawl" 10-1-60 (James Roberts); *Wyatt Earp*—"The Doctor" 10-4-60 (Odie Hewitt); *Riverboat*—"The Water of Gorgeous Springs" 11-7-60 (Salem Cox); *Laramie*—"Drifter's Gold" 11-29-60 (Duke), "Trigger Point" 5-16-61 (Shelly Stack), "The Sunday Shoot" 11-13-62 (Rafe Seton), "Protective Custody" 1-15-63 (Willard); *The Deputy*—"The Legend of Dixie" 5-20-61 (Gar Logan); *Bonanza*—"Death at Dawn" 4-30-60 (Farmer Perkins), "Song in the Dark" 1-13-63 (Danny Morgan), "Amigo" 2-12-67 (Cap Fenner), "My Friend, My Enemy" 1-12-69 (Sheriff Crowley), "A Darker Shadow" 11-23-69 (Wade Turner), "Thorton's Account" 11-1-70 (Thorton), "Riot!" 10-3-72 (Will Cooper); *The Dakotas*—"Thunder in Pleasant Valley" 2-4-63 (Tom Davis); *A Man Called Shenandoah*—"The Accused" 1-3-66 (Marshal), "The Death of Matthew Eldridge" 3-21-66 (Sheriff Healy); *Shane*—"Day of the Hawk" 10-22-66 (Harmon); *The Big Valley*—"The Man from Nowhere" 11-14-66 (Hoyt Vatcher); *Daniel Boone*—"The Renegade" 9-28-67 (Tom Jimson); *The High Chaparral*—"No Bugles, No Women" 3-14-69 (Truescott), "Auld Lang Syne" 4-10-70 (Winslow); *Alias Smith and Jones*—"Miracle at Santa Marta" 12-30-71 (Sam Bleeker); *The Cowboys*—"The Avenger" 3-6-74 (Culpeper).

Wald, Jerry (1912-7/13/62). Films: "Swing the Western Way" 1947.

Waldis, Otto (1906-3/25/74). Films: "Rebel City" 1953 (Spain); "Man from Del Rio" 1956 (Tom Jordan). ¶TV: *The Adventures of Rin Tin Tin*—"Rinty Finds a Bone" 4-27-56 (Prof. August Schimmel); *Circus Boy*—"The Proud Pagliacci" 11-18-56 (Fritz Phieffer); *Maverick*—"Diamond in the Rough" 1-26-58 (Scharf); *Tales of Wells Fargo*—"The Reward" 4-21-58; *Wagon Train*—"The Swift Cloud Story" 4-8-59 (Amos Peeks), "The Horace Best Story" 10-5-60 (Osterloh), "Swamp Devil" 4-4-62 (Otto Burger); *The Tall Man*—"Bad Company" 9-24-60 (Karl Nagel); *Lawman*—"Detweiler's Kid" 2-26-61 (Detweiler); *Have Gun Will Travel*—"My Brother's Keeper" 5-6-61; *Gunslinger*—"The New Savannah Story" 5-18-61 (Hans Kroeger); *Whispering Smith*—"The Devil's Share" 5-22-61 (Emil Dunker).

Waldo, Janet. Films: "One Man's Law" 1940 (Joyce Logan); "The Bandit Trail" 1941 (Ellen Grant); "Silver Stallion" 1941 (Jan); "Land of the Open Range" 1942 (Mary Cook).

Waldron, Andrew (1847-3/1/32). Films: "The Fighting Sheriff" 1919; "The Four-Bit Man" 1919; "Gun Magic" 1919; "The Kid and the Cowboy" 1919; "The Champion Liar" 1920; "Hair-Trigger Stuff" 1920; "Gun Shy" 1922 (Pop Benson); "Hills of Missing Men" 1922 (Buck Allis); "When East Comes West" 1922 (the Chinaman); "The Man Who Won" 1923 (Minkie); "Wolves of the Border" 1923; "Baffled" 1924; "Battlin' Buckaroo" 1924 (Judd Stevens); "The Cowboy and the Flapper" 1924 (Al Lyman); "Down by the Rio Grande" 1924; "Fighter's Paradise" 1924; "Flashing Spurs" 1924 (Flynn); "The Man from God's Country" 1924 (Judge Packard); "That Wild West" 1924; "The Whipping Boss" 1924 (Timkins); "Pals" 1925 (Molly's Grandpa); "The Wild Girl" 1925 (Grandpapa Tot); "The Ace of Clubs" 1926 (Sandy McGill); "The Grey Devil" 1926; "The Lost Trail" 1926; "Clearing the Trail" 1928 (Judge Price); "The Lariat Kid" 1929 (George Carson).

Waldron, Charles (1874-3/4/46). Films: "Wanderer of the Wasteland" 1935 (Mr. Virey); "Ramona" 1936 (Dr. Weaver); "Three Faces West" 1940 (Dr. Thorpe).

Waldron, Wendy. Films: "Over the Border" 1950 (Tess Malloy); "Trail Guide" 1952 (Mary). ¶TV: *The Gene Autry Show*—"The Posse" 9-17-50, "The Devil's Brand" 9-24-50,

"Ghost Town Raiders" 10-6-51, "Silver Dollars" 10-20-51, "Thunder Out West" 7-14-53, "Bandidos" 9-1-53; *Wild Bill Hickok*—"Indian Bureau Story" 7-31-51.

Wales, Ethel (1881-2/15/52). Films: "The Covered Wagon" 1923 (Mrs. Wingate); "Stepping Fast" 1923 (Miss Higgins); "The Dude Wrangler" 1930 (Mattie); "Under Montana Skies" 1930 (Martha Jenkins); "The Fighting Fool" 1932 (Aunt Jane); "Klondike" 1932 (Sadie Jones); "A Man's Land" 1932 (Flossie Doolittle); "The Fighting Parson" 1933 (Mrs. Bessie Larkin); "Desert Man" 1934; "The Laramie Kid" 1935 (Guard); "Bar 20 Rides Again" 1936 (Clarissa Peters); "The Eagle's Brood" 1936; "Days of Jesse James" 1939 (Mrs. Samuels); "Frontier Pony Express" 1939 (Mrs. Murphy); "In Old Caliente" 1939 (Felicia); "Hidden Gold" 1940 (Matilda Purdy); "Knights of the Range" 1940 (Myra Ripple); "Wyoming" 1940 (Mrs. Bronson); "Young Bill Hickok" 1940 (Mrs. Stout); "Border Vigilantes" 1941 (Aunt Jennifer Forbes); "Lumberjack" 1944 (Abbey); "In Old Sacramento" 1946; "Unconquered" 1947; "Fancy Pants" 1950 (Mrs. Wilkins).

Wales, Leslie. TV: *Bonanza*—"Blessed Are They" 4-22-62 (Peggy); *Rawhide*—"Incident of the Hostages" 4-19-63 (Yellow Sky), "Incident at Gila Flats" 1-30-64 (Lalota).

Wales, Wally (Hal Taliaferro, Walt Williams, Floyd T. Alderson) (1896-2/12/80). Films: "Galloping On" 1925 (Wally Moore); "Tearin' Loose" 1925 (Wally Blake); "Ace of Action" 1926 (Wally Rand); "Double Daring" 1926 (Wally Meeker); "The Fighting Cheat" 1926 (Wally Kenyon); "Hurricane Horseman" 1926 (Wally Marden); "Riding Rivals" 1926; "Roaring Rider" 1926; "Twisted Triggers" 1926 (Wally Weston); "Vanishing Hoofs" 1926 (Wally Marsh); "The Cyclone Cowboy" 1927 (Wally Baxter); "The Desert of the Lost" 1927 (Jim Drake); "The Meddlin' Stranger" 1927 (Wally Fraser); "Skedaddle Gold" 1927 (Kent Blake); "Soda Water Cowboy" 1927 (Wally); "Tearin' into Trouble" 1927 (Wally Tilland); "White Pebbles" 1927 (Zip Wallace); "Desperate Courage" 1928 (Jim Dane); "The Flying Buckaroo" 1928 (Bill Matthews); "Saddle Mates" 1928 (John Benson); "Overland Bound" 1929 (Buck Hawkins); "Bar L Ranch" 1930 (Frank Kellogg); "Breed of the West" 1930 (Wally Weldon); "Canyon Hawks" 1930 (Dick Carson); "Trails

of Danger" 1930 (Bob Bartlett); "Flying Lariats" 1931 (Wally Dunbar); "Hell's Valley" 1931 (Wally Madison); "99 Wounds" 1931 (Chief Slow Water); "Red Fork Range" 1931 (Wally Hamilton); "Riders of the Cactus" 1931 (Jack Convers); "Law and Lawless" 1932 (Buck Daggett); "Whistlin' Dan" 1932; "Deadwood Pass" 1933 (Pete Sorrenson); "The Fighting Texans" 1933; "Sagebrush Trail" 1933 (Deputy Sheriff); "The Trail Drive" 1933; "Arizona Cyclone" 1934; "The Cactus Kid" 1934 (Andy); "Carrying the Mail" 1934-short; "Fighting Through" 1934; "Honor of the Range" 1934; "The Law of the Wild" 1934-serial; "The Lone Bandit" 1934 (Sheriff Jim Mach); "The Lone Rider" 1934; "Mystery Mountain" 1934-serial; "Nevada Cyclone" 1934; "Pals of the West" 1934-short; "Potluck Pards" 1934; "Smoking Guns" 1934; "The Sundown Trail" 1934; "The Way of the West" 1934 (Inspector Wallace Gordon); "West of the Law" 1934-short; "Wheels of Destiny" 1934; "Between Men" 1935 (Blacksmith Pete); "Border Guns" 1935 (Sheriff Tom); "The Cowboy and the Bandit" 1935 (Chuck); "Danger Trails" 1935 (Desolation); "Fighting Caballero" 1935 (Wildcat); "Five Bad Men" 1935 (Bad Man); "Gun Play" 1935 (George Holt); "Heir to Trouble" 1935 (Spurs); "Lawless Riders" 1935 (Carl); "The Miracle Rider" 1935-serial (Burnett); "The Pecos Kid" 1935 (Eric Grayson); "The Phantom Empire" 1935-serial; "Powdersmoke Range" 1935 (Aloysius "Bud" Taggert); "Range Warfare" 1935; "Rustlers of Red Dog" 1935-serial (Wally); "Silent Valley" 1935 (Fred Jones); "The Silver Bullet" 1935 (Dick); "Six Gun Justice" 1935; "Swifty" 1935 (Price McNeill); "Trigger Tom" 1935 (Sam Slater); "The Unconquered Bandit" 1935; "The Vanishing Riders" 1935 (Wolf Lawson); "Western Courage" 1935; "Western Racketeers" 1935 (Sheriff Rawlins); "Ambush Valley" 1936 (Joel Potter); "Avenging Waters" 1936 (Slivers); "Cavalry" 1936 (Conspirator); "Hair-Trigger Casey" 1936 (Dave Casey); "Heroes of the Range" 1936; "Law and Lead" 1936 (Steve Bradley); "Lucky Terror" 1936 (Spike); "The Phantom Rider" 1936-serial; "Rio Grande Ranger" 1936 (Hal); "The Traitor" 1936 (Hunk); "The Unknown Ranger" 1936 (Chuckler); "The Gun Ranger" 1937; "Heart of the Rockies" 1937 (Charlie); "Law of the Ranger" 1937 (Wally Hood); "One Man Justice" 1937 (Neal King); "The Painted Stal-

lion" 1937-serial (Jim Bowie); "The Rangers Step In" 1937 (Breck Warren); "Rootin' Tootin' Rhythm" 1937 (Buffalo Bradley); "The Trigger Trio" 1937 (Luke); "Two Gun Law" 1937 (Cattle Buyer); "Wells Fargo" 1937; "Black Bandit" 1938 (Weepy); "The Great Adventures of Wild Bill Hickok" 1938; "Guilty Trails" 1938 (Sundown Adsel); "The Lone Ranger" 1938-serial (Bob Stuart); "Pioneer Trail" 1938 (Smokey); "Prairie Justice" 1938 (Alfalfa); "Rio Grande" 1938 (Bart Andrews); "South of Arizona" 1938 (Ranger Frank Madison); "Stagecoach Days" 1938 (Milt Dodds); "West of Santa Fe" 1938; "Frontiers of '49" 1939 (Kit); "North of the Yukon" 1939; "Outpost of the Mounties" 1939 (Evans); "Overland with Kit Carson" 1939-serial; "Riders of the Frontier" 1939 (Buck); "Saga of Death Valley" 1939 (Rex); "The Stranger from Texas" 1939 (Clay Billings); "The Thundering West" 1939 (Frank Kendall); "Western Caravans" 1939 (Jed Winters); "Adventures of Red Ryder" 1940-serial (Cherokee Sims); "The Border Legion" 1940 (the Sheriff); "Bullets for Rustlers" 1940 (Eb Smith); "The Carson City Kid" 1940 (Harmon); "Cherokee Strip" 1940 (Ben Blivens); "Colorado" 1940 (Weaver); "The Dark Command" 1940 (Vigilante); "Pioneers of the West" 1940 (Jed Clark); "Texas Terrors" 1940; "Two-Fisted Rangers" 1940 (Sheriff Jim Hanley); "Young Bill Hickok" 1940 (Morrell); "Along the Rio Grande" 1941 (Sheriff); "Bad Man of Deadwood" 1941 (Ripper); "Border Vigilantes" 1941 (Ed Stone); "In Old Cheyenne" 1941 (Pete); "Jesse James at Bay" 1941 (Sloane); "Law of the Range" 1941 (Tim O'Brien); "Red River Valley" 1941; "Riders of the Timberline" 1941 (Petrie); "Roaring Frontiers" 1941; "Sheriff of Tombstone" 1941 (Slade); "Under Fiesta Stars" 1941; "American Empire" 1942 (Malone); "Bullets for Bandits" 1942; "Heart of the Golden West" 1942; "King of the Mounties" 1942-serial (Ed Johnson); "Little Joe, the Wrangler" 1942 (Travis); "Ridin' Down the Canyon" 1942 (Pete); "Romance on the Range" 1942 (Sheriff Wilson); "Sons of the Pioneers" 1942 (Briggs); "Cowboy in the Clouds" 1943 (Dean); "Frontier Law" 1943 (Rogers); "Hoppy Serves a Writ" 1943 (Greg Jordan); "Idaho" 1943 (Bud); "The Leather Burners" 1943 (Lafe); "Man from Music Mountain" 1943 (Slade); "Silver Spurs" 1943 (Steve Corlan); "Song of Texas" 1943 (Pete); "The Woman of the Town"

1943 (Wagner); "Cowboy and the Senorita" 1944 (Ferguson); "Forty Thieves" 1944; "Lumberjack" 1944 (Taggart); "Vigilantes of Dodge City" 1944; "The Yellow Rose of Tesas" 1944 (Ferguson); "Zorro's Black Whip" 1944-serial (Baxter); "San antonio" 1945 (Cowboy); "Utah" 1945 (Steve Lacey); "Heading West" 1946; "In Old Sacramento" 1946; "The Phantom Rider" 1946-serial (Nugget); "Plainsman and the Lady" 1946 (Pete); "Ramrod" 1947 (Jess Moore); "The Gallant Legion" 1948 (Billy Smith); "Red River" 1948 (Old Leather); "West of Sonora" 1948 (Sandy Clinton); "Brimstone" 1949 (Dave Watts); "Colt .45" 1950; "The Savage Horde" 1950 (Sgt. Gowdy); "Junction City" 1952 (Sandy Clinton); "Law of the Lawless" 1964 (Rider).

Walken, Christopher (1943-). Films: "Heaven's Gate" 1980 (Nathan D. Champion).

Walker, Art. Films: "Scar Hanan" 1925 (Sheriff); "A Two-Fisted Sheriff" 1925 (Stranger).

Walker, Bill (1899-1/27/92). Films: "Rebel City" 1953 (William); "The Outcast" 1954 (Sam Allen); "The Far Horizons" 1955; "Ride a Crooked Trail" 1958 (Jackson); "The Last Challenge" 1967 (Servant). ¶TV: *Circus Boy*—"Farewell to the Circus" 1-6-57 (Cecil); *Yancy Derringer*—"Old Dixie" 12-25-58 (Obadiah), "V As in Voodoo" 5-14-59 (Obadiah); *Bat Masterson*—"Promised Land" 6-10-59 (Driver); *Maverick*—"The Resurrection of Joe November" 2-28-60 (Attendant); *Rawhide*—"The Captain's Wife" 1-12-62 (Sandy); *Bronco*—"Moment of Doubt" 4-2-62 (Dorso); *The Dakotas*—"The Chooser of the Slain" 4-22-63 (William); *Laredo*—"Yahoo" 9-30-65 (Ulmer Applin); *The Outcasts*—"The Candidates" 1-27-69 (Samuel); *Kung Fu*—"The Raiders" 1-24-74 (Miner).

Walker, Charlotte (1878-3/24/58). Films: "Pardners" 1917 (Olive Troop).

Walker, Cheryl (1922-10/24/71). Films: "Shadows on the Sage" 1942 (Doris Jackson); "Trial by Trigger" 1944-short; "Rhythm Round-Up" 1945.

Walker, Clint (1927-). Films: "Fort Dobbs" 1958 (Gar Davis); "Yellowstone Kelly" 1959 (Kelly); "Gold of the Seven Saints" 1961 (Jim Rainbolt); "The Night of the Grizzly" 1966 (Jim Cole); "More Dead Than Alive" 1968 (Killer Cain); "The Great Bank Robbery" 1969 (Ben Quick); "Sam Whiskey" 1969 (O.W. Brandy);

"Yuma" TVM-1971 (Marshal Dave Harmon); "Bounty Man" TVM-1972 (Kincaid); "Hardcase" TVM-1972 (Jack Rutherford); "Pancho Villa" 1975-Span. (Villa's Lieutenant); "Baker's Hawk" 1976 (Dan Baker); "The White Buffalo" 1977 (Whistling Jack Kileen); "The Gambler Returns: The Luck of the Draw" TVM-1991 (Cheyenne Bodie). ¶TV: *Cheyenne*—Regular 1955-63 (Cheyenne Bodie); *Maverick*—"Hadley's Hunters" 9-25-60 (Cheyenne Bodie); *Centennial*—Regular 1978-79 (Joe Bean).

Walker, Francis. Films: "Between Men" 1935 (Henchman); "Courageous Avenger" 1935; "Danger Trails" 1935; "Fighting Pioneers" 1935; "The Judgement Book" 1935; "The Last of the Clintons" 1935; "Law of the 45's" 1935 (Wrangler); "Lawless Range" 1935; "The Pecos Kid" 1935 (Chuck); "The Reckless Buckaroo" 1935; "The Vanishing Riders" 1935 (Slim); "Wagon Trail" 1935; "Wild Mustang" 1935; "Cavalcade of the West" 1936; "Everyman's Law" 1936 (Henchman); "Lightning Bill Carson" 1936; "The Lonely Trail" 1936; "Ridin' On" 1936; "The Riding Avenger" 1936 (Welch); "Valley of the Lawless" 1936; "Cheyenne Rides Again" 1937 (Joe); "Galloping Dynamite" 1937 (Dolson); "Guns in the Dark" 1937; "Law for Tombstone" 1937; "The Rangers Step In" 1937; "Trail of Vengeance" 1937 (Rancher); "Feud of the Trail" 1938; "Heroes of the Alamo" 1938; "Rolling Caravans" 1938; "The Singing Outlaw" 1938; "The Night Riders" 1939; "Texas Stampede" 1939; "Blazing Six Shooters" 1940 (Shorty); "Bullets for Rustlers" 1940 (Ellis); "The Durango Kid" 1940 (Steve); "The Man from Tumbleweeds" 1940 (Lightning Barlow); "Pioneers of the Frontier" 1940 (Joe); "The Return of Wild Bill" 1940 (Jake Kilgore); "Texas Stagecoach" 1940 (Jug Wilson); "Thundering Frontier" 1940 (Stub); "Two-Fisted Rangers" 1940 (Stub); "West of Abilene" 1940 (Bat); "King of Dodge City" 1941 (Carney); "The Pinto Kid" 1941 (Curt Harvey); "Prairie Stranger" 1941 (Craig); "The Return of Daniel Boone" 1941 (Bowers); "Riders of the Badlands" 1941; "Roaring Frontiers" 1941; "Wildcat of Tucson" 1941; "Overland to Deadwood" 1942; "Prairie Gunsmoke" 1942; "Riders of the Northland" 1942 (Dobie); "West of Tombstone" 1942; "Blazing the Western Trail" 1945.

Walker, Inez. Films: "The Man from the East" 1914; "The Ranger's Romance" 1914; "Saved by a Watch" 1914; "The Grizzly Gulch Chariot Race" 1915; "Roping a Bride" 1915.

Walker, Jack. Films: "Ridin' Wild" 1922 (George Berge); "South of Sonora" 1930.

Walker, Johnnie (1896-12/4/49). Films: "Captain Fly-By-Night" 1922 (First Stranger); "The Sagebrush Trail" 1922; "Galloping Hoofs" 1924-serial; "The Reckless Sex" 1925 (Robert Lanning, Jr.); "The Scarlet West" 1925 (Lt. Parkman); "Morganson's Finish" 1926 (Dick Gilbert); "Girl of the Golden West" 1930 (Nick).

Walker, June (1904-2/1/66). Films: "The Unforgiven" 1960 (Hagar Rawlins). ¶TV: *Whispering Smith*—"The Grudge" 5-15-61 (Ma Gates).

Walker, Lillian (1887-10/10/75). Films: "The White Man's Courage" 1919 (Dorothy Charlton).

Walker, Marcy. Films: "The Return of Desperado" TVM-1988 (Caitlin Jones).

Walker, Peter (1927-). Films: "Valerie" 1957 (Herb Garth). ¶TV: *The Adventures of Rin Tin Tin*—"The General's Daughter" 9-19-58 (Lieutenant Parke); *Jim Bowie*—"The Return of the Alciblade" 12-21-56; *Death Valley Days*—"The Big Rendezvous" 4-15-58.

Walker, Ray (1904-10/6/80). Films: "Outlaws of the Orient" 1937 (Lucky Phelps); "Robin Hood of Texas" 1947 (Lacey); "Black Bart" 1948 (MacFarland); "Pioneer Marshal" 1949 (Harvey Masters); "Hoedown" 1950 (Knoxie); "Under Mexicali Stars" 1950 (Handley); "Skipalong Rosenbloom" 1951; "The Homesteaders" 1953 (Col. Peterson); "Rebel City" 1953 (Col. Barnes); "Yaqui Drums" 1956; "The Iron Sheriff" 1957; "Ten Who Dared" 1960 (McSpadden). ¶TV: *Wild Bill Hickok*—"Treasure Trail" 12-30-52; *Fury*—"My Horse Ajax" 3-9-57 (Brighton); *Maverick*—"Royal Four-Flush" 9-20-59 (Hotel Clerk), "Greenbacks Unlimited" 3-13-60 (Bartender); *Sugarfoot*—"Man from Medora" 11-21-60 (Dan Moore).

Walker, Robert "Bob" (1888-3/4/54). Films: "The Double Hold-Up" 1919; "Isobel, or the Trail's End" 1920 (Private Thomas Pelliter); "Prairie Trails" 1920 (Winthrope Adams Endicott); "The Texan" 1920 (Winthrop Endicott); "White Oak" 1921 (Harry); "A Daughter of the Sioux" 1925 (Eagle Wing); "Drug Store Cowboy" 1925 (Gentleman Jack); "The Mystery Box" 1925-serial; "The Outlaw's Daughter" 1925 (Slim Cole); "Ridin' Comet" 1925 (Austin

Livingston); "The Rip Snorter" 1925 (Robert Willis); "Tonio, Son of the Sierras" 1925 (Lt. Willett); "Warrior Gap" 1925 (Major Burleigh); "Deuce High" 1926 (Ranger McLeod); "Western Courage" 1927; "Code of the Scarlet" 1928 (Frank Morgan); "The Cowboy Cavalier" 1928; "The Upland Rider" 1928 (Bent); "Bar L Ranch" 1930; "Breed of the West" 1930 (Longrope Wheeler); "Canyon Hawks" 1930 (Steve Knowles); "The Fighting Legion" 1930 (Tom Dawson); "Phantom of the Desert" 1930 (Steve); "Ridin' Law" 1930; "Westward Bound" 1930 (Steve); "Headin' for Trouble" 1931 (Butch Morgan); "The Kid from Arizona" 1931; "Pueblo Terror" 1931 (Bob Morgan); "The Sign of the Wolf" 1931-serial (Joe); "The Vanishing Legion" 1931-serial (Allen); "West of Cheyenne" 1931 (Nevada); "The Man from New Mexico" 1932 (Mort Snyder); "Scarlet Brand" 1932 (Bill Morse); "Come on Tarzan" 1933; "Jaws of Justice" 1933 (Boone Jackson); "King of the Arena" 1933; "The Lone Avenger" 1933; "The Phantom Thunderbolt" 1933; "Strawberry Roan" 1933 (Bart); "Loser's End" 1934 (Joe); "The Pecos Dandy" 1934; "Potluck Pards" 1934; "Rawhide Mail" 1934 (Brown); "Terror of the Plains" 1934 (Sheriff); "Born to Battle" 1935; "Coyote Trails" 1935; "The Crimson Trail" 1935 (Red); "Fighting Caballero" 1935 (Bull); "Outlawed Guns" 1935; "The Pecos Kid" 1935 (Sheriff); "Rough Riding Ranger" 1935 (Ram Hansen); "Skull and Crown" 1935 (Saunders); "Texas Jack" 1935 (Dan Corey); "The Throwback" 1935 (Sheriff Carey); "Tracy Rides" 1935; "Wolf Riders" 1935; "Caryl of the Mountains" 1936 (Enos Colvin); "Custer's Last Stand" 1936-serial (Pete); "Fast Bullets" 1936 (Frank); "Hair-Trigger Casey" 1936 (Colton); "Borderland" 1937; "Gunsmoke Ranch" 1937 (Williams); "Two-Fisted Sheriff" 1937 (Lyons); "Rollin' Plains" 1938; "El Diablo Rides" 1939; "The Pal from Texas" 1939; "Trigger Pals" 1939 (Clem); "Pioneer Days" 1940 (Trigger); "The Last Round-Up" 1947; "The Sea of Grass" 1947 (Brock Brewton); "Riders in the Sky" 1949; "Vengeance Valley" 1951 (Lee Strobie).

Walker, Jr., Robert (1940-). Films: "The War Wagon" 1967 (Billy Hyatt); "Young Billy Young" 1969 (Billy Young). ¶TV: *The Big Valley*—"My Son, My Son" 11-3-65 (Evan Miles); *The Road West*—"Ashes and Tallow and One True Love" 10-24-66 (Cpl. Marsh Courtney); *The Mon-*

roes—"Killer Cougar" 2-1-67 (Quint Gregger); *Time Tunnel*—"Billy the Kid" 2-10-67 (Billy the Kid); *Bonanza*—"The Gentle Ones" 10-29-67 (Mark).

Walker, Scott. Films: "Dirty Little Billy" 1972 (Stormy); "Cahill, United States Marshal" 1973 (Ben Tildy); "High Plains Drifter" 1973 (Bill Borders); "The White Buffalo" 1977 (Gyp Hook-Hand). ¶TV: *Bonanza*—"Thorton's Account" 11-1-70 (Blue), "The Rattlesnake Brigade" 12-5-71 (Amber), "Shanklin" 2-13-72 (Grange); *Gunsmoke*—"Milligan" 11-6-72 (Mattis), "The Schoolmarm" 2-25-74 (Jack Stokes).

Walker, Terry. Films: "Renfrew on the Great White Trail" 1938 (Kay Larkin); "Billy the Kid in Texas" 1940 (Mary Morgan); "Take Me Back to Oklahoma" 1940 (Jane Winters); "The Medico of Painted Springs" 1941 (Nancy Richards).

Walker, Walter "Wally" (1901-8/7/75). Films: "The Conquerors" 1932 (Mr. Ogden); "Cowboy and the Lady" 1938 (Ames); "Trail of the Yukon" 1949.

Walker, William (1897-1/27/92). Films: "Big Jake" 1971 (Moses Brown). ¶TV: *Hawkeye and the Last of the Mohicans*—"Delaware Hoax" 5-1-57, "Powder Keg" 7-3-57, "The Brute" 7-24-57; *Daniel Boone*—"The Landlords" 3-5-70, "Readin', Ritin', and Revolt" 3-12-70.

Wall, Geraldine (1913-6/22/70). Films: "Boy's Ranch" 1946 (Mrs. Harper); "Green Grass of Wyoming" 1948 (Neil McLaughlin); "Heller in Pink Tights" 1960 (Madam). ¶TV: *Here Come the Brides*—"Break the Bank of Tacoma" 1-16-70.

Wallace, Beryl (1910-6/17/48). Films: "The Woman of the Town" 1943 (Louella Parsons); "Romance of the Rockies" 1937 (Betty); "Rough Ridin' Rhythm" 1937 (Helen Hobart); "Sunset on the Desert" 1942 (Julie Craig); "The Kansan" 1943 (Soubret).

Wallace, Bill "Superfoot." Films: "Manchurian Avenger" 1985 (Kamikaze).

Wallace, George D. (1917-). Films: "The Big Sky" 1952; "The Lawless Breed" 1952 (Bully Brady); "Arena" 1953 (Buster Cole); "The Homesteaders" 1953 (Meade); "Star of Texas" 1953 (Clampett); "Vigilante Terror" 1953; "Border River" 1954 (Fletcher); "Destry" 1954 (Curley); "Drums Across the River" 1954 (Les Walker); "Man Without a Star" 1955 (Tom Carter); "Strange Lady in

Town" 1955 (Curley); "Six Black Horses" 1962 (Boone); "Texas Across the River" 1966 (Floyd Willet); "Skin Game" 1971 (Auctioneer). ¶TV: *Gunsmoke*—"Hack Prine" 5-12-56 (Dolph Trimble), "Easy Come" 10-26-63 (Tobin), "The Wedding" 3-13-72 (Sheriff Hennings); *Zane Grey Theater*—"Village of Fear" 3-1-57 (Brill), "The Accuser" 10-30-58, "Sundown Smith" 3-24-60 (Borkman); *Tales of Wells Fargo*—"The Thin Rope" 3-18-57 (Sheriff), "Desert Showdown" 9-14-59 (Bedell), "Hometown Doctor" 2-17-62 (Cross); *Bronco*—"Shadow of a Man" 5-19-59 (Sheriff Purdom); *Lawman*—"Red Ransom" 6-21-59 (Nat Gruber), "Hassayampa" 2-12-61 (Clyde Morton); *The Alaskans*—"Winter Song" 11-22-59 (Bill Adams); *Black Saddle*—"The Killer" 1-1-60 (Jim House); *Death Valley Days*—"Pirates of San Francisco" 4-26-60; *Maverick*—"A Flock of Trouble" 2-14-60 (Verne Scott), "Benefit of Doubt" 4-9-61 (Sheriff Joe Holly); *Rawhide*—"Incident of the Night Horse" 2-19-60 (Jed Carst), "Incident of the Fish Out of the Water" 2-17-61 (Carnival Boss), "The Blue Sky" 12-8-61 (Brady); *Overland Trail*—"High Bridge" 2-28-60 (Matt); *Sugarfoot*—"Blackwater Swamp" 3-1-60 (John Crain); *The Rifleman*—"Sins of the Father" 4-19-60 (Andy Moon); *Walt Disney Presents*—"Daniel Boone: ... And Chase the Buffalo" 12-11-60 (Mordecai Tompkins); *The Deputy*—"Second Cousin to the Czar" 12-24-60 (Dan Farrell); *The Tall Man*—"One of One Thousand" 12-31-60 (Jim Miles); *Wyatt Earp*—"Doc Holliday Faces Death" 2-28-61 (Frank McLowery), "The Law Must Be Fair" 5-2-61 (Frank McLowery), "Just Before the Battle" 6-13-61 (Frank McLowery), "Gunfight at the O.K. Corral" 6-21-61 (Frank McLowery); *The Rebel*—"The Burying of Sammy Hart" 3-5-61 (Aaron Wallace); *Laramie*—"Badge of the Outsider" 5-23-61 (Gip), "Deadly Is the Night" 11-7-61 (Alby), "Justice in a Hurry" 3-20-62, "Double Eagles" 11-20-62 (Sloan), "Badge of Glory" 5-7-63; *Cheyenne*—"The Brahma Bull" 12-11-61 (Blaney Hawker); *The Virginian*—"The Mountain of the Sun" 4-17-63 (Dixon), "Outcast" 10-26-66 (Portersville Sheriff); *The Road West*—"Lone Woman" 11-7-66 (Chad); *Daniel Boone*—"When a King Is a Pawn" 12-22-66; *Bonanza*—"Decision at Los Robles" 3-22-70 (Doctor); *How the West Was Won*—Episode One 2-12-78 (Davey Wordley).

Wallace, Helen. Films: "Sioux

City Sue" 1946 (Mrs. Price); "The Marshal of Cripple Creek" 1947 (Mrs. Lambert); "The Last Posse" 1953 (Mrs. White); "Three Young Texans" 1954 (Mrs. Colt); "The Far Horizons" 1955 (Mrs. Hancock); "Drango" 1957 (Mrs. Allen); "Ride a Violent Mile" 1957 (Mrs. Bartold). ¶TV: *Gunsmoke*—"Reward for Matt" 1-28-56 (Sarah Stoner), "Alarm at Pleasant Valley" 8-25-56 (Ma Fraser), "Coventry" 3-17-62; *Broken Arrow*—"Cry Wolf" 12-11-56; *The Texan*—"Law of the Gun" 9-29-58 (Mrs. Richards), "No Way Out" 9-14-59 (Sarah Partland), "The Guilty and the Innocent" 3-28-60 (Ma Lewis); *Rawhide*—"Incident of the Running Man" 5-5-61.

Wallace, John (1869–7/16/46). Films: "Border Law" 1931 (Pegleg Barnes); "The Fighting Ranger" 1934 (Capt. Wilkes); "The Three Godfathers" 1936 (Peg Leg Man); "The Luck of Roaring Camp" 1937; "Zorro's Fighting Legion" 1939-serial (Jailer).

Wallace, Katherine. Films: "Cupid, the Cowpuncher" 1920 (Rose); "Daring Chances" 1924 (Ethel Slavin).

Wallace, May (1877–12/11/38). Films: "Oh, You Tony!" 1924 (Etiquette Instructor); "Way Out West" 1937 (Cook).

Wallace, Morgan (1888–12/12/53). Films: "Smoke Lightning" 1933 (Sheriff Archie Kyle); "Thunder Mountain" 1935 (Rand Levitt); "Sutter's Gold" 1936; "The Californian" 1937 (Tod Barsto); "Billy the Kid Returns" 1938 (Morganson); "Timber Stampede" 1939 (Foss Dunlap); "Union Pacific" 1939 (Sen. Smith); "My Little Chickadee" 1940 (Gambler); "Three Men from Texas" 1940 (Andrews); "Honky Tonk" 1941 (Adams); "In Old Colorado" 1941 (Jack Collins).

Wallace, Regina (1892–2/13/78). Films: "Swing the Western Way" 1947; "Rachel and the Stranger" 1948 (Mrs. Green).

Wallach, Eli (1915–). Films: "The Magnificent Seven" 1960 (Calvera); "The Misfits" 1961 (Guido); "How the West Was Won" 1962 (Charlie Gant); "The Good, the Bad, and the Ugly" 1966-Ital. (Tuco); "Ace High" 1967-Ital./Span. (Cacopoulos); "MacKenna's Gold" 1969 (Ben Baker); "Don't Turn the Other Cheek" 1974-Ital./Ger./Span.; "The White, the Yellow, and the Black" 1974-Ital./Span./Fr. (Black). ¶TV: *The Outlaws*—"A Bit of Glory" 2-1-62 (Ned Danvers).

Waller, Eddy (1889–8/20/77). Films: "Rhythm on the Range" 1936 (Field Judge); "The Bad Man of Brimstone" 1937 (Cassius Bundy); "Wild and Woolly" 1937 (Fireman); "Call the Mesquiteers" 1938 (Hardy); "Flaming Frontier" 1938-serial; "The Great Adventures of Wild Bill Hickok" 1938 (Stone); "Out West with the Hardys" 1938 (Doc Hodge); "Allegheny Uprising" 1939 (Jailer); "The Cisco Kid and the Lady" 1939 (Stage Driver); "Jesse James" 1939 (Deputy); "New Frontier" 1939 (Maj. Braddock); "North of the Yukon" 1939 (LaRue); "The Return of the Cisco Kid" 1939 (Guard); "Rough Riders' Round-Up" 1939; "Stand Up and Fight" 1939 (Conductor); "Carolina Moon" 1940 (Stanhope); "Konga, the Wild Stallion" 1940 (Gloomy); "Legion of the Lawless" 1940 (Lafe Barton); "Man from Montreal" 1940 (Old Jacques); "Santa Fe Trail" 1940 (Man); "Stagecoach War" 1940 (Quince Cobalt); "Texas Terrors" 1940 (Judge Bennett); "Twenty Mule Team" 1940 (Horsecollar, the Bartender); "Viva Cisco Kid" 1940 (Stage Driver); "The Bandit Trail" 1941 (Tom Haggerty); "Hands Across the Rockies" 1941; "Honky Tonk" 1941 (Train Conductor); "In Old Colorado" 1941 (Jim Stark); "Six Gun Gold" 1941 (Ben Blanchard); "The Son of Davy Crockett" 1941 (Grandpa Mathews); "Western Union" 1941 (Stagecoach Driver); "Call of the Canyon" 1942; "Lone Star Ranger" 1942 (Mitchell); "Shut My Big Mouth" 1942 (Happy); "Sin Town" 1942 (Forager); "Sundown Jim" 1942 (Clem Black); "Frontier Badman" 1943 (Auctioneer); "The Kansan" 1943 (Ed Gilbert); "A Lady Takes a Chance" 1943 (Bus Station Attendant); "Silver Spurs" 1943; "Raiders of Ghost City" 1944-serial (Doc Blair); "Tall in the Saddle" 1944; "Dakota" 1945 (Stagecoach Driver); "Rough Riders of Cheyenne" 1945; "San Antonio" 1945 (Cattleman); "Under Western Skies" 1945 (Preacher); "Abilene Town" 1946 (Hannaberry); "In Old Sacramento" 1946; "Plainsman and the Lady" 1946 (Fred Willats); "Renegades" 1946 (Davy Lane); "Rustler's Roundup" 1946 (Tom Freemont); "Singing on the Trail" 1946; "Sun Valley Cyclone" 1946; "Bandits of Dark Canyon" 1947 (Nugget Clark); "The Michigan Kid" 1947 (Post Office Clerk); "Pursued" 1947; "The Sea of Grass" 1947 (Homesteader); "The Wild Frontier" 1947 (Nugget Clark); "Wyoming" 1947 (Grub Liner); "Black Bart" 1948 (Mason); "The Bold Frontiersman"

1948 (Nugget Clark); "Adventures in Silverado" 1948; "Carson City Raiders" 1948 (Nugget Clark); "The Denver Kid" 1948; "Desperadoes of Dodge City" 1948 (Nugget Clark); "Marshal of Amarillo" 1948 (Nugget Clark); "Oklahoma Badlands" 1948 (Nugget Clark); "Renegades of Sonora" 1948; "River Lady" 1948 (Hewitt); "The Strawberry Roan" 1948 (Steve); "Sundown in Santa Fe" 1948; "Whispering Smith" 1948 (Conductor); "Bandit King of Texas" 1949 (Nugget Clark); "Death Valley Gunfighter" 1949 (Nugget Clark); "Frontier Marshal" 1949 (Nugget Clark); "Lust for Gold" 1949 (Coroner); "Massacre River" 1949 (Joe); "Navajo Trail Raiders" 1949 (Nugget Clark); "Powder River Rustlers" 1949 (Nugget Clark); "Sheriff of Wichita" 1949 (Nugget Clark); "The Wyoming Bandit" 1949 (Nugget Clark); "California Passage" 1950 (Walter); "Code of the Silver Sage" 1950 (Nugget Clark); "Covered Wagon Raid" 1950 (Nugget Clark); "Curtain Call at Cactus Creek" 1950; "Frisco Tornado" 1950 (Nugget Clark); "The Furies" 1950 (Old Man); "Gunmen of Abilene" 1950 (Nugget Clark); "Rustlers on Horseback" 1950 (Nugget Clark); "Salt Lake Raiders" 1950 (Nugget Clark); "Vigilante Hideout" 1950 (Nugget Clark); "Cavalry Scout" 1951 (Gen. Sherman); "Indian Uprising" 1951 (Sagebrush); "Black Hills Ambush" 1952 (Nugget Clark); "Desperadoes' Outpost" 1952 (Nugget Clark); "Leadville Gunslinger" 1952 (Nuggel Clark); "Montana Territory" 1952 (Possum); "Thundering Caravans" 1952 (Nugget Clark); "Bandits of the West" 1953 (Nugget Clark); "El Paso Stampede" 1953 (Nugget Clark); "The Last Posse" 1953 (Dr. Pryor); "Marshal of Cedar Rock" 1953 (Nugget Clark); "Savage Frontier" 1953 (Nugget Clark); "The Far Country" 1955 (Yukon Sam); "The Man from Laramie" 1955 (Dr. Selden); "Man Without a Star" 1955 (Bill Cassidy); "The Phantom Stagecoach" 1957 (Sam); "The Restless Breed" 1957 (Caesar); "Day of the Bad Man" 1958 (Mr. Slocum). ¶TV: *The Cisco Kid*—"Gold Strike" 3-14-53, "The Hospital" 5-16-53; *The Lone Ranger*—"The Gentleman from Julesburg" 6-11-53; *Steve Donovan, Western Marshal*—Regular 1955-56 (Rusty Lee); *Fury*—"Tungsten Queen" 1-14-56 (Hank Enos); *Broken Arrow*—"The Rescue" 1-8-57 (Hank Thompson); *Jim Bowie*—"The Bounty Hunter" 5-17-57 (Press Harper); *Wagon Train*—"The Jennifer Churchill Story" 10-15-58 (Ned);

Wyatt Earp—"The Truth About Rawhide Geraghty" 2-17-59 (Rawhide Geraghty); *Tales of Wells Fargo*—"The Last Stand" 4-13-59 (Pat Rankin), "Moment of Glory" 5-1-61 (Grandpa Bridger); *Laramie*—Regular 1959-63 (Mose Shell); *The Texan*—"Blue Norther" 10-12-59 (Stage Driver); *Walt Disney Presents*—"Daniel Boone" 1960-61 (John Finley); *Bonanza*—"The First Born" 9-23-62 (Harry); *Empire*—"The Earth Mover" 11-27-62 (Abel Saunders).

Walley, Deborah (1941-). TV: *Wagon Train*—"The Nancy Styles Story" 11-22-64 (Nancy Styles); *The Men from Shiloh*—"With Love, Bullets, and Valentines" 10-7-70 (Corey).

Walling, William (1872-3/5/32). Films: "The Killer" 1921 (John Emory); "The Crimson Challenge" 1922 (Jim Last); "His Back Against the Wall" 1922 (Sheriff Lawrence); "North of the Rio Grande" 1922 (John Hannon); "The Siren Call" 1922 (Gore); "While Satan Sleeps" 1922 (Bud Deming); "Without Compromise" 1922 (Bill Murray); "The Iron Horse" 1924 (Thomas Marsh); "North of Hudson Bay" 1924 (Angus McKenzie); "Clash of the Wolves" 1925 (Sam Barstowe); "Ranger of the Big Pines" 1925 (Sam Gregg); "The Timber Wolf" 1925 (Sheriff); "The Trail Rider" 1925 (Malcolm Dunning); "The Canyon of Light" 1926; "The Gentle Cyclone" 1926 (Marshall Senior); "The Great K & A Train Robbery" 1926 (Eugene Cullen); "Whispering Smith" 1926 (Murray Sinclair); "The Devil's Saddle" 1927 (Sheriff Morrell); "Winners of the Wilderness" 1927 (General Edward Braddock); "Beyond the Law" 1930 (Reingold); "The Painted Desert" 1931 (Kirby); "The Range Feud" 1931 (Dad Turner); "Riders of the North" 1931 (Inspector Devlin); "Two-Fisted Justice" 1931 (Nick Slavin); "Ridin' for Justice" 1932 (Wilson).

Wallis, Shani (1938-). TV: *Gunsmoke*—"Women for Sale" 9-10-73 & 9-17-73 (Stella).

Wallock, Edwin N. (1878-2/4/51). Films: "The Old Code" 1915; "The Cold Deck" 1917 (Black Jack Hurley); "Fame and Fortune" 1918 (Kunseen); "The Whirlwind Finish" 1918; "The Sagebrusher" 1920 (Frederick Waldhorn); "Kazan" 1921 (Black McCready); "The Struggle" 1921 (Hayes Storm); "Eyes of the Forest" 1923 (Julius Duval).

Walmsley, Jon (1956-). TV: *Daniel Boone*—"The Witness" 1-25-68 (Pudge Farmingham).

Walsh, Edward (1935-). Films: "The Gambler" TVM-1980 (Charlie Rose). ¶TV: *Kung Fu*—"Arrogant Dragons" 3-14-74 (Jake).

Walsh, Frank (1860-7/19/32). Films: "On the Little Big Horn or Custer's Last Stand" 1909; "The Long Trail" 1910; "The Fifty Man" 1914.

Walsh, George (1889-6/13/81). Films: "Blue Blood and Red" 1916 (Algernon DuPont); "The Mediator" 1916 (Lish Henley); "Pinto Rustlers" 1936 (Nick Furnicky); "Rio Grande Romance" 1936 (Joe Bradley).

Walsh, Joey (1937-). TV: *Gunsmoke*—"The Miracle Man" 12-2-68 (Gerard).

Walsh, Kathryn. TV: *Daniel Boone*—"The Lost Colony" 12-8-66 (Elizabeth Corbett); *The Virginian*—"Without Mercy" 2-15-67 (Kathy Young).

Walsh, M. Emmet (1935-). Films: "Little Big Man" 1971 (Shotgun Guard); "Kid Blue" 1973 (Barber); "The Invasion of Johnson County" TVM-1976 (Irvine); "High Noon, Part II: The Return of Will Kane" TVM-1980 (Harold Patton); "Sunset" 1988 (Chief Dibner); "Four Eyes and Six-Guns" TVM-1992 (Mayor Thornbush). ¶TV: *Nichols*—Regular 1971-72 (Gabe McCutcheon); *Bonanza*—"Warbonnet" 12-26-71 (Mattheson).

Walsh, Raoul (1887-12/31/80). Films: "The Angel of Contention" 1914; "Sierra Jim's Reformation" 1914; "The Outlaw's Revenge" 1916 (the Outlaw).

Walsh, Sydney. Films: "Desperado" TVM-1987 (Sally). ¶TV: *Young Riders*—"Song of Isiah" 1-18-92 (Rosemary), "'Til Death Do Us Part" 7-22-92 (Rosemary).

Walsh, Tom (1863-4/25/25). Films: "The Trey O'Hearts" 1914-serial; "Rustling a Bride" 1919 (Dan).

Walsh, William (1879-11/8/21). Films: "Dangerous Love" 1920.

Walston, Ray (1918-). Films: "Paint Your Wagon" 1969 (Mad Dog Duncan). ¶TV: *The Outlaws*—"Beat the Drum Slowly" 10-20-60 (Judge), "The Cutups" 10-26-61 (Willie); *Wide Country*—"The Girl in the Sunshine Smile" 11-15-62 (Arthur Callan); *Wild Wild West*—"The Night of Montezuma's Hordes" 10-27-67 (Dr. Henry Johnson); *Custer*—"Breakout" 11-1-67 (Ned Quimbo); *Paradise*—"A Gather of Guns" 9-10-89 (Alexander R.R. Morgan).

Walter, Jessica (1940-). Films: "Wild and Wooly" TVM-1978 (Megan). ¶TV: *Alias Smith and Jones*—"Everything Else You Can Steal" 12-16-71 (Louise Carson).

Walter, Perla. Films: "The War Wagon" 1967 (Rosita).

Walter, Tracey (1952-). Films: "Goin' South" 1978 (Coogan); "High Noon, Part II: The Return of Will Kane" TVM-1980 (Harlan Tyler); "Timerider" 1983 (Carl Dorsett); "City Slickers" 1991 (Cookie); "Buffalo Girls" TVM-1995 (Jim Ragg). ¶TV: *Best of the West*—Regular 1981-82 (Frog); *Adventures of Brisco County, Jr.*—"No Man's Land" 9-10-93 (Phil Swill), "Mail Order Brides" 12-10-93 (Phil Swill).

Walters, Jack (1885-1/23/44). Films: "Ace High" 1919; "The Ace of the Saddle" 1919 (Inky O'Day); "The Gun Packer" 1919; "The Last Outlaw" 1919; "Neck and Noose" 1919; "Tempest Cody Plays Detective" 1919; "The Boss of Copperhead" 1920; "The Champion Liar" 1920; "The Great Round Up" 1920; "Marryin' Marion" 1920; "Tipped Off" 1920; "Two from Texas" 1920; "Sure Fire" 1921 (Overland Kid); "The Better Man Wins" 1922 (Dick Murray); "The Galloping Kid" 1922 (Steve Larabee); "Headin' North" 1922 (Arthur Stowell); "Never Let Go" 1922; "McGuire of the Mounted" 1923 (Sgt. Murphy); "Wild West Romance" 1928; "The Revenge Rider" 1935; "The Mysterious Avenger" 1936 (Ranger); "Frontiers of '49" 1939 (Pete).

Walters, Luana. Films: "End of the Trail" 1932 (Luanna); "The Fighting Texans" 1933 (Joan Carver); "Aces and Eights" 1936 (Juanita Hernandez); "Ride 'Em Cowboy" 1936 (Lillian Howard); "Under Strange Flags" 1937 (Dolores de Vargas); "Where the West Begins" 1938 (Lynne Reed); "Mexicali Rose" 1939 (Anita Loredo); "The Durango Kid" 1940 (Nancy Winslow); "The Range Busters" 1940 (Carol Thorpe); "The Return of Wild Bill" 1940 (Kate Kilgore); "The Tulsa Kid" 1940 (Mary Wallace); "Across the Sierras" 1941 (Alice); "Arizona Bound" 1941; "The Kid's Last Ride" 1941 (Sally Rall); "Law of the Wolf" 1941; "Road Agent" 1941 (Teresa); "Bad Men of the Hills" 1942 (Laurie Bishop); "Down Texas Way" 1942 (Mary); "Lawless Plainsmen" 1942 (Baltimore Bonnie); "The Lone Star Vigilantes" 1942 (Marcia Banning); "Thundering Hoofs" 1942 (Nancy).

Walters, Paul. Films: "Blood and Steel" 1925 (Tommy); "The Ridin' Streak" 1925 (Leete Gleed).

Walthall, Anna May (1896-4/17/50). Films: "Bare Fists" 1919

(Ruby); "With Hoops of Steel" 1919 (Amanda Garcia); "The Desert Flower" 1925 (Flozella).

Walthall, Henry B. (1878-6/17/36). Films: "The Honor of the Family" 1909; "The Gold Seekers" 1910; "In Old California" 1910; "In the Border States" 1910; "Ramona" 1910; "The Tenderfoot's Triumph" 1910; "The Thread of Destiny" 1910; "Western Justice" 1910; "In the Aisles of the Wild" 1912; "Iola's Promise" 1912; "My Hero" 1912; "Three Friends" 1912; "The Battle at Elderbrush Gulch" 1913; "The Broken Ways" 1913; "During the Round-Up" 1913; "The Sheriff's Baby" 1913; "The Tenderfoot's Money" 1913; "Two Men of the Desert" 1913; "His First Ride" 1914; "The Mountain Rat" 1914 (Douglas Williams); "Strongheart" 1914; "With Hoops of Steel" 1919 (Emerson Mead); "The Able-Minded Lady" 1922 (Breezy Bright); "The Kick Back" 1922 (Aaron Price); "The Long Chance" 1922 (Harley P. Hennage); "Kit Carson Over the Great Divide" 1925 (Dr. Samuel Webb); "In Old California" 1929 (Don Pedro DeLeon); "Klondike" 1932 (Mark Armstrong); "Ride Him, Cowboy" 1932 (John Gaunt); "Somewhere in Sonora" 1933 (Bob Leadly); "The Last Outlaw" 1936 (Calvin Yates); "The Mine with the Iron Door" 1936 (David Burton).

Walton, Douglas (1909-11/15/61). Films: "Bad Lands" 1939 (Mulford); "Northwest Passage" 1940 (Lt. Avery); "Jesse James, Jr." 1942 (Archie McDonald); "Calamity Jane and Sam Bass" 1949 (Bookmaker).

Walton, Fred (1865-12/28/36). Films: "The Country Beyond" 1936 (Station Agent).

Walton, Jess (1949-). TV: *The Guns of Will Sonnett*—"Robber's Roost" 1-17-69 (Abbey); *Gunsmoke*—"Patricia" 1-22-73 (Patricia Colby), "Manolo" 3-17-75 (Kattalin Larralde).

Waltz, Patrick (1924-8/13/72). TV: *Circus Boy*—"Alex the Great" 10-10-57 (Jim Freeman); *Death Valley Days*—"Fifty Years a Mystery" 11-11-57; *Sugarfoot*—"The Stallion Trail" 12-24-57 (Lon Tracy); *Tombstone Territory*—"The Tin Gunman" 4-16-58 (Johnny Pearce), 4-15-60 (Dan Jensen); *Rough Riders*—"The Duelists" 10-23-58 (Charles Des Ambres); *Bat Masterson*—"The Fighter" 11-5-58 (Jim Bemis), "Death by the Half Dozen" 2-4-60 (Buck Peters); *The Tall Man*—"McBean Rides Again" 12-10-60 (Baxter).

Walzman, Max. Films: "Adven-

tures of Red Ryder" 1940-serial (Cole); "The Gunman from Bodie" 1941; "King of the Texas Rangers" 1941-serial (Gus); "Raiders of the Range" 1942 (Coroner).

Wanamaker, Sam (1919-12/18/93). TV: *Wild Wild West*—"The Night of the Howling Light" 12-17-65 (Dr. Arcularis); *Gunsmoke*—"Parson Comes to Town" 4-30-66 (Asa Longworth).

Wang, George. Films: "Cisco" 1966-Ital.; "Taste for Killing" 1966-Ital./Span.; "Colt in the Hand of the Devil" 1967-Ital.; "Blood and Guns" 1968-Ital./Span.; "Have a Good Funeral, My Friend ... Sartana Will Pay" 1971-Ital.; "Kill Django ... Kill First" 1971-Ital. (Ramon); "Colt in the Hand of the Devil" 1972-Ital.; "Deadly Trackers" 1972-Ital.; "Jesse and Lester, Two Brothers in a Place Called Trinity" 1972-Ital.; "Fighting Fists of Shanghai Joe" 1973-Ital.; "Son of Zorro" 1973-Ital./Span.

Wang, James (1853-4/20/35). Films: "Hills of Missing Men" 1922 (Li Fung); "Desert Driven" 1923 (Cook); "The Eagle's Feather" 1923 (Wing Ling).

Wanzer, Arthur G. (1880-12/15/48). Films: "Law and Order" 1932 (George Dixon); "Unknown Valley" 1933 (Tim).

War Eagle, John (1901-77). Films: "The Golden West" 1932; "Broken Arrow" 1950 (Nahilzay); "Ticket to Tomahawk" 1950 (Lone Eagle); "Winchester '73" 1950 (Indian Interpreter); "The Last Outpost" 1951 (Geronimo); "Tomahawk" 1951 (Red Cloud); "Bugles in the Afternoon" 1952 (Red Owl); "Laramie Mountains" 1952 (Chief Lone Tree); "Last of the Comanches" 1952 (Black Cloud); "Pony Soldier" 1952 (Indian); "The Wild North" 1952 (Indian Chief); "The Great Sioux Uprising" 1953 (Red Cloud); "Saginaw Trail" 1953 (Red Bird); "The Black Dakotas" 1954 (War Cloud); "They Rode West" 1954 (Chief Quanah); "The Man from Laramie" 1955 (Frank Darrah); "Westward Ho the Wagons" 1956 (Wolf's Brother); "Dragoon Wells Massacre" 1957; "Tonka" 1958 (Sitting Bull); "Flap" 1970 (Luke Wolf); "When the Legends Die" 1972 (Blue Elk). TV: *The Adventures of Rin Tin Tin*—"The Burial Ground" 12-30-55 (Cheronini); *Loretta Young Show*—"The Wise One" 3-26-56 (Garage Man); *Annie Oakley*—"Annie and the First Phone" 7-22-56 (Thunder Cloud), "Indian Justice" 7-29-56 (Thunder Cloud); *The Roy Rogers Show*—"Paleface Justice" 11-18-56; *Disneyland*—"The

Saga of Andy Burnett"—Regular 1957-58 (Chief Matosuki); *Rawhide*—"Incident of the Tumbleweed Wagon" 1-9-59 (Virgo), "Incident of the Silent Web" 6-3-60; *Wagon Train*—"The Jeremy Dow Story" 12-28-60 (Iron Hand), "The John Turnbull Story" 5-30-62 (Nah-An-Kanay); *Tales of Wells Fargo*—"Reward for Gaine" 1-20-62 (Kill Eagle); *Branded*—"The Test" 2-7-65; *Gunsmoke*—"Kioga" 10-23-65 (Katawa); *Iron Horse*—"Hellcat" 12-26-66 (Sioux Chief); *The Outcasts*—"Alligator King" 1-20-69 (Shaman); *Kung Fu*—"An Eye for an Eye" 1-25-73 (Indian Chief), "Cry of the Night Beast" 10-19-74 (Tashaka); *The Life and Times of Grizzly Adams*—10-26-77 (Chief).

Warburton, John (1903-10/27/81). Films: "Partners of the Plains" 1938 (Ronald Harwood). TV: *Judge Roy Bean*—"Sunburnt Gold" 10-1-55 (Chuck Tilden), "Black Jack" 11-1-55 (Uncle Bart Rollins), "Judge Decarles a Holiday" 11-1-55 (Jim Connelly), "The Fugitive" 12-1-55 (Conley), "Letty Leaves Home" 12-1-55 (Carlson), "The Elopers" 4-11-56 (Bender), "Spirit of the Law" 4-11-56 (Thad Wells), "Luck O' the Irish" 7-1-56 (Pat O'Hara); *The Californians*—"The Painted Lady" 1-13-59 (Cyrus Draton); *Gunsmoke*—"Breckinridge" 3-13-65 (Judge Danby).

Ward, Amelita. Films: "Rim of the Canyon" 1949 (Lily Shannon).

Ward, Bill. Films: "Gold Raiders" 1951 (Red); "Son of the Renegade" 1953 (Baby Face Bill); "War Arrow" 1953 (Trooper); "The Black Whip" 1956 (Red Leg); "Hidden Guns" 1956 (Joe Miller); "The Naked Gun" 1956. TV: *The Lone Ranger*—"Rifles and Renegades" 5-4-50, "White Man's Magic" 7-13-50, "Trouble for Tonto" 7-20-50; *Zane Grey Theater*—"Man of Fear" 3-14-58.

Ward, Blackjack (Jerome Ward) (1891-8/29/54). Films: "The Avenger" 1931; "Branded" 1931; "The Fighting Marshal" 1931; "Range Law" 1931; "Outlaw Justice" 1933; "The Phantom Thunderbolt" 1933; "Sagebrush Trail" 1933; "Lightning Bill" 1934; "The Westerner" 1934 (Cowboy); "Wheels of Destiny" 1934; "Fighting Pioneers" 1935; "The Ghost Rider" 1935 (Chalky); "End of the Trail" 1936 (Mason's Man); "The Fugitive Sheriff" 1936; "Heroes of the Range" 1936; "The Mysterious Avenger" 1936 (Rustler); "O'Malley of the Mounted" 1936; "The Plainsman" 1936; "Toll of the Desert" 1936; "Vigilantes Are Coming" 1936-serial

(Rancher); "Dodge City Trail" 1937 (Dawson's Gang Member); "Hopalong Rides Again" 1937; "The Old Wyoming Trail" 1937; "Two-Fisted Sheriff" 1937; "Cattle Raiders" 1938 (Outlaw); "The Colorado Trail" 1938 (Henchman); "Flaming Frontier" 1938-serial; "The Frontiersman" 1938 (Rustler); "Gunsmoke Trail" 1938; "Outlaws of Sonora" 1938; "Panamint's Bad Man" 1938; "Santa Fe Stampede" 1938; "Stagecoach Days" 1938; "The Lone Ranger Rides Again" 1939-serial (Safe Heavy); "Texas Stampede" 1939 (Abe Avery); "Zorro's Fighting Legion" 1939-serial (Cave Heavy #2); "Beyond the Sacramento" 1940 (3rd Henchman); "Pioneers of the Frontier" 1940 (Shorty); "Texas Terrors" 1940; "The Westerner" 1940 (Buck Harrigan); "Riders of the Northland" 1942 (Henchman); "Shut My Big Mouth" 1942 (Bandit).

Ward, Carrie Clark (1862-2/6/26). Films: "One Touch of Sin" 1917 (the Widow); "The Orphan" 1920 (Aunt Cynthia); "Bob Hampton of Placer" 1921 (Housekeeper); "Thundering Hoofs" 1924 (Duenna).

Ward, Chance (1877-1/16/73). Films: "Medicine Bend" 1916 (George McCloud).

Ward, Dave (1890-12/31/45). Films: "The Arizona Streak" 1926 (Denver).

Ward, Dorothy. Films: "Cinders" 1920; "Walloping Kid" 1926 (Sally Carter); "The Golden West" 1932 (Mary Lynch).

Ward, Douglas Turner (1930-). Films: "Man and Boy" 1971 (Lee Christmas).

Ward, Fannie (1872-1/27/52). Films: "Tennessee's Pardner" 1916 (Tennessee); "On the Level" 1917 (Merlin Warner/Mexiicali Mae).

Ward, Fred (1943-). Films: "Belle Starr" TVM-1980 (Ned Christie); "Timerider" 1983 (Lyle Swann); "Four Eyes and Six-Guns" TVM-1992 (Wyatt Earp).

Ward, Jack. Films: "The One Way Trail" 1931; "The Pocatello Kid" 1931; "The Two Gun Man" 1931; "Between Fighting Men" 1932; "Hell Fire Austin" 1932; "Texas Gun Fighter" 1932; "Come on Tarzan" 1933; "The Lone Avenger" 1933; "Gun Justice" 1934; "Honor of the Range" 1934; "Rainbow Riders" 1934; "Smoking Guns" 1934; "Heir to Trouble" 1935.

Ward, Jerome. see Ward, Blackjack.

Ward, John. Films: "Boots and Saddles" 1937 (Wyndham); "Galloping Dynamite" 1937 (Wilkes); "Riders of the Whistling Skull" 1937 (Brewster); "Two-Gun Troubador" 1939; "Ridin' the Trail" 1940 (Pa Bailey).

Ward, John (1923-3/23/95). Films: "Gunsmoke in Tucson" 1958 (Slick Kirby).

Ward, Katherine Clare (1871-10/14/38). Films: "Call of the West" 1930 (Ma Dixon); "The Conquering Horde" 1931 (Mrs. Corley).

Ward, Larry (1915-2/16/85). Films: "A Distant Trumpet" 1964 (Sgt. Kroger); "Hombre" 1967 (Soldier); "God Does Not Pay on Saturday" 1968-Ital. (Lam); "Saguaro" 1968-Ital.; "The Gun and the Pulpit" TVM-1974 (Max). ¶TV: *Lawman*—"The Hold-Out" 2-18-62 (Blake Stevens); *Cheyenne*—"A Man Called Ragan" 4-23-62 (Ragan); *Have Gun Will Travel*—"Memories of Monica" 10-27-62 (Ben Turner); *Gunsmoke*—"Louie Pheeters" 1-5-63 (Bart Felder), "He Who Steals" 5-29-65 (Sid Perce), "Sanctuary" 2-26-66 (Ayres), "The Hanging" 12-31-66 (Preston); *The Dakotas*—Regular 1963 (Marshal Frank Ragan); *Temple Houston*—"Last Full Moon" 2-27-64 (Harry Cobb); *The Loner*—"The Flight of the Arctic Tern" 10-23-65 (Monte); *The Road West*—"Shaman" 11-14-66 (Curtin); *Bonanza*—"The Passing of a King" 10-13-68 (Carver), "Yonder Man" 12-8-68 (Stryker), "The Power of Life and Death" 10-11-70 (Sheriff), "Blind Hunch" 11-21-71 (Deputy), "Easy Come, Easy Go" 12-12-71 (Pete), "Second Sight" 1-9-72 (Harve); *The Virginian*—"Last Grave at Socorro Creek" 1-22-69 (Bill Burden); *Sara*—4-23-76 (Joe).

Ward, Sandy. Films: "Lacy and the Mississippi Queen" TVM-1978 (Mitchell Beacon). ¶TV: *Alias Smith and Jones*—"The Girl in Boxcar Number Three" 2-11-71 (Brakeman); *Big Hawaii*—"The Trouble with Tina" 1977.

Ward, Sela. Films: "Rustler's Rhapsody" 1985 (Colonel Ticonderoga's Daughter).

Ward, Skip (1930-). Films: "Hombre" 1967 (Steve Early). ¶TV: *Daniel Boone*—"The Bait" 11-7-68 (Davey).

Ward, Tony. see Warde, Anthony.

Ward, W. Bradley. Films: "The Fire Eater" 1921 (Marty Frame); "Shadows of Conscience" 1921 (Pedro, the Halfbreed).

Warde, Anthony (Tony Ward) (1909-1/8/75). Films: "Chip of the Flying U" 1939 (Duncan); "Oklahoma Frontier" 1939 (Wayne); "Ridin' on a Rainbow" 1941 (Morrison); "King of the Mounties" 1942-serial (Stark); "Riders of the Deadline" 1943 (Madigan); "The Cisco Kid Returns" 1945 (Conway); "Don Ricardo Returns" 1946; "King of the Forest Rangers" 1946-serial (Burt Spear); "North of the Border" 1946; "The Bells of San Fernando" 1947 (Mendoza); "King of the Bandits" 1947 (Smoke Kirby); "Where the North Begins" 1947; "Dangers of the Canadian Mounted" 1948-serial (Mort Fowler); "Trail of the Yukon" 1949 (Muskeg). ¶TV: *Jim Bowie*—"Jim Bowie and His Slave" 11-30-56 (Deshon); *The Texan*—"Return to Friendly" 2-2-59, "Badman" 6-20-60 (Clem Bodie); *Wyatt Earp*—"The Judge" 4-19-60 (Curt Dance).

Warde, Ernest C. (1874-9/9/23) Films: "The Midnight Stage" 1919 (Rat McGrough); "Ruth of the Range" 1923-serial.

Warde, Harlan (1917-3/13/80). Films: "Last of the Badmen" 1957 (Green); "Advance to the Rear" 1964 (Maj. Hayward). ¶TV: *Fury*—"Junior Rodeo" 12-24-55 (Charley Jones), "Second Chance" 3-29-58 (Sheriff); *Colt .45*—"The Three Thousand Dollar Bullet" 11-1-57 (Dan Crawford); *The Rifleman*—Regular 1958-62 (Banker John Hamilton); *Rough Riders*—"The Scavengers" 1-8-59 (Jared Spangler); *The Californians*—"Cat's Paw" 3-3-59 (Les Lane); *Wanted–Dead or Alive*—"Payoff at Pinto" 5-21-60; *Wyatt Earp*—"Clanton and Cupid" 3-21-61 (Tom Ware); *Bonanza*—"Inger, My Love" 4-15-62, "Justice Deferred" 12-17-67 (Monroe), "The Bottle Fighter" 5-12-68 (Ogleby), "The Law and Billy Burgess" 2-15-70 (Nicholson), "Thorton's Account" 11-1-70 (Boyle), "One Ace Too Many" 4-2-72 (Osgood), "The Twenty-Sixth Grave" 10-31-72 (Osgood); *Laramie*—"Naked Steel" 1-1-63 (Mat Christy); *The Dakotas*—"Feud at Snake River" 4-29-63 (Claude Deus); *Wagon Train*—"The Gus Morgan Story" 9-30-63 (Dr. Haynes); *The Virginian*—Regular 1964-66 (Sheriff Brannon); *Wild Wild West*—"The Night of the Sudden Death" 10-8-65 (Foxx); *The Big Valley*—"The Odyssey of Jubal Tanner" 10-13-65 (Finletter), "Into the Widow's Web" 3-23-66, "Target" 10-31-66, "Wagonload of Dreams" 1-2-67, "The Stallion" 1-30-67, "Guilty" 10-30-67 (Arthur Kleeber), "Point and Counterpoint" 5-19-69 (Mr. Bickers); *The Road West*—"Ashes and Tallow and One True Love" 10-24-66 (Captain Lindstrom); *Iron Horse*—

"The Prisoners" 12-30-67 (Marshal); *Daniel Boone*—"Before the Tall Man" 2-12-70 (Nicholas Burns).

Warden, Jack (1920-). Films: "Billy Two Hats" 1973-Brit. (Gifford); "The Man Who Loved Cat Dancing" 1973 (Dawes); "The Godchild" TVM-1974 (Dobbs); "The White Buffalo" 1977 (Charlie Zane). ¶TV: *Bonanza*—"The Paiute War" 10-3-59 (Mike Wilson); *Stagecoach West*—"A Fork in the Road" 11-1-60 (Stacey Gibbs); *The Outlaws*—"Starfall" 11-24-60 & 12-1-60 (Ollie); *Wagon Train*—"The Martin Onyx Story" 1-3-62 (Martin Onyx), "The Miss Mary Lee McIntosh Story" 2-28-65 (Daniel Delaney); *Tales of Wells Fargo*—"The Traveler" 2-24-62 (Brad Axton); *The Virginian*—"Throw a Long Rope" 10-3-62 (Jubal Tatum), "Shadows of the Past" 2-24-65 (John Conway); *Walt Disney Presents*—"Gallegher" 1965-67 (Lieutenant Fergus).

Ware, Helen (1877-1/25/39). Films: "Thieves' Gold" 1918 (Mrs. Savage); "Colorado Pluck" 1921 (Lady Featherstone); "The Virginian" 1929 (Ma Taylor).

Ware, Irene (1911-). Films: "Whispering Smith Speaks" 1935 (Nan Roberts); "O'Malley of the Mounted" 1936 (Edith Hyland).

Ware, Midge. TV: *The Rifleman*—"The Illustrator" 12-13-60 (Hanna); *Gunslinger*—Regular 1961 (Amber "Amby" Hollister).

Warfield, Chris. TV: *Colt .45*—"The Manbuster" 4-4-58 (Monty Chandler); *The Californians*—"The Long Night" 12-23-58 (Johnny Vonn); *Death Valley Days*—"The Invaders" 3-17-59 (Jim Preston).

Warfield, Emily. Films: "Bonanza: The Return" TVM-1993 (Sarah Cartwright); "Bonanza: Under Attack" TVM-1995 (Sarah Cartwright).

Warfield, Irene (1896-4/10/61). Films: "The Girl I Left Behind Me" 1915 (Fawn Afraid).

Waring, Joseph. Films: "Conquest of Cochise" 1953 (Running Cougar); "Kiss of Fire" 1955 (Victor). ¶TV: *Wyatt Earp*—"Bat Masterson for Sheriff" 3-3-57, "Little Brother" 12-23-58 (Greg Norton); *The Adventures of Rin Tin Tin*—"O'Hara Gets Amnesia" 5-17-57; *Zorro*—"Zorro Rides Alone" 10-16-58 (Lieutenant); *26 Men*—"Run No More" 12-9-58.

Warner, David (1941-). Films: "The Ballad of Cable Hogue" 1970 (Joshua); "Desperado" TVM-1987 (Gentleman Johnny Ballard). ¶TV:

Adventures of Brisco County, Jr.—"Deep in the Heart of Dixie" 11-5-93 (Winston Smiles).

Warner, H.B. (1876-12/24/58). Films: "The Gray Wolf's Ghost" 1919 (Dr. West/Harry West); "The Hellion" 1924; "Whispering Smith" 1926 (Whispering Smith); "Tiger Rose" 1929 (Dr. Cusick); "In Old Santa Fe" 1934 (Charlie Miller); "Rose of the Rancho" 1936 (Don Pascual Castro); "The Girl of the Golden West" 1938 (Father Sienna); "Let Freedom Ring" 1939 (Rutledge); "El Paso" 1949 (Judge Fletcher); "Hellfire" 1949 (Brother Joseph).

Warner, J.B. (1895-11/9/24). Films: "The Danger Trail" 1917 (John Howland); "Blazing the Way" 1920; "The Smoke Signal" 1920; "A Tough Tenderfoot" 1920; "Crossing Trails" 1921 (Bull Devine); "Big Stakes" 1922 (Jim Gregory); "Flaming Hearts" 1922; "Crimson Gold" 1923 (Larry Crawford); "Danger" 1923 (Dave Collins); "The Lone Fighter" 1923 (Ranger Certain Lee); "Behind Two Guns" 1924; "The Covered Trail" 1924 (Bill Keats); "Horseshoe Luck" 1924; "Treasure Canyon" 1924; "Wanted by the Law" 1924; "Westbound" 1924 (Bob Lanier); "Wolf Man" 1924.

Warner, Robert (1942-). Films: "Big Jake" 1971 (Will Fain).

Warner, Wes. Films: "The Devil Horse" 1932-serial; "Texas Tornado" 1932 (Pete); "Sagebrush Troubador" 1935; "Guns and Guitars" 1936 (Henchman); "The Singing Cowboy" 1936 (Jack); "Vigilantes Are Coming" 1936-serial (Rancher); "Gunsmoke Ranch" 1937 (Old Man).

Warno, Helen (1926-12/25/70). TV: *Wyatt Earp*—"The Vultures" 3-19-57 (Allie Younger).

Warren, Bruce. Films: "The Plainsman" 1936 (Captain of the Lizzie Gill); "Heroes of the Alamo" 1938 (Almerlan Dickinson); "Phantom Ranger" 1938 (Rogers); "Renfrew on the Great White Trail" 1938; "Renfrew on the Great White Trail" 1938.

Warren, E. Alyn (1875-1/22/40). Films: "Born to the West" 1926 (Sam Rudd); "The Trail of '98" 1929 (Engineer); "Fighting Caravans" 1931 (Barlow); "Smoke Lightning" 1933 (Carter Blake); "Wagon Wheels" 1934 (the Factor); "The Bad Man of Brimstone" 1937 (George Emerson); "The Girl of the Golden West" 1938 (Miner).

Warren, Frank. TV: *Bat Masterson*—"Cheyenne Club" 12-17-58

(Marshal), "Shakedown at St. Joe" 10-29-59 (Hoodlum), "The Elusive Baguette" 6-2-60 (Sheriff Simpson); *Riverboat*—"Landlubbers" 1-10-60 (Brady).

Warren, Fred (1880-12/5/40). Films: "The Girl of the Golden West" 1923 (Old Jed Hawkins); "The Desert Flower" 1925 (Dizzy); "California" 1927 (Kit Carson); "Sitting Bull at the Spirit Lake Massacre" 1927 (Happy Hartz); "In Old Arizona" 1929 (Piano Player); "Girl of the Golden West" 1930 (Jack Wallace); "The Phantom Rider" 1936-serial; "High, Wide and Handsome" 1937 (Piano Player); "Go West" 1940 (Pianist).

Warren, James. Films: "Wanderer of the Wasteland" 1945 (Adam Larey); "Badman's Territory" 1946 (John Rowley); "Sunset Pass" 1946 (Rocky); "Code of the West" 1947 (Bob Wade).

Warren, Jennifer (1941-). Films: "Banjo Hackett: Roamin' Free" TVM-1976 (Mollie Brannen); "Another Man, Another Chance" 1977-Fr. (Mary).

Warren, Katherine (1905-7/17/65). Films: "The Battles of Chief Pontiac" 1952 (Chia); "The Man Behind the Gun" 1952 (Phoebe Sheldon); "The Violent Men" 1955 (Mrs. Vail); "Fury at Gunsight Pass" 1956 (Mrs. Boggs); "Drango" 1957 (Mrs. Scott). ¶TV: *Laramie*—".45 Calibre" 11-15-60 (Mrs. Byrd), "Cactus Lady" 2-21-61 (Mrs. Thomson), "The Dispossessed" 2-19-63; *Bonanza*—"The Spitfire" 1-14-61 (Maud Hoad); *The Outlaws*—"Walk Tall" 11-16-61 (Mrs. McClure); *The Tall Man*—"Property of the Crown" 2-24-62 (Emma Wainwright).

Warren, Lesley Ann (1946-). Films: "The Daughters of Joshua Cabe" TVM-1972 (Mae). ¶TV: *Gunsmoke*—"Harvest" 3-26-66 (Betsy Payson).

Warren, Phil. Films: "Badman's Territory" 1946 (Grat Dalton); "Code of the West" 1947 (Wescott); "Dangers of the Canadian Mounted" 1948-serial (George Hale).

Warren, Richard. Films: "The Rawhide Trail" 1958 (Collier). ¶TV: *Sergeant Preston of the Yukon*—"Blind Justice" 1-17-57 (Otto Holst), "Boy Alone" 2-20-58 (Moose); *Wyatt Earp*—"The Scout" 3-1-60 (Mose); *Bonanza*—"Badge Without Honor" 9-24-60 (Gid Clevenger); *The Deputy*—"The Means and the End" 3-18-61 (Lon Spivak); *Tales of Wells Fargo*—"Portrait of Teresa" 2-10-62 (Blacksmith).

Warren, Ruth. Films: "Hello Trouble" 1932 (Emmy); "The Last Trail" 1933 (Sally Olsen); "Forlorn River" 1937 (Millie Moran); "Wells Fargo" 1937 (Mrs. Andrews); "The Cisco Kid and the Lady" 1939 (Ma Saunders); "Jackass Mail" 1942 (Doctor's Wife); "King of the Wild Horses" 1947; "Montana Territory" 1952 (Mrs. Nelson). ¶TV: *Maverick*—"Lonesome Reunion" 9-28-58 (Local Gossip).

Warren, Steve. Films: "Friendly Persuasion" 1956 (Haskell); "Gunfire at Indian Gap" 1957 (Ed Stewart). ¶TV: *Sergeant Preston of the Yukon*—"The Rookie" 9-20-56 (Dennis Burns); *Circus Boy*—"Corky's Big Parade" 3-24-57 (Cass); *Wagon Train*—"The Kitty Angel Story" 1-7-59 (Slim); *Bat Masterson*—"Come Out Fighting" 4-7-60 (Paddy Muldoon); *Gunsmoke*—"Big Man" 3-25-61 (Cowboy), "Long Hours, Short Pay" 4-29-61 (Sergeant); *The Tall Man*—"Hard Justice" 3-25-61 (Hank); *Have Gun Will Travel*—"The Uneasy Grave" 6-3-61; *Tales of Wells Fargo*—"Jeremiah" 11-11-61 (Donner); *The Rifleman*—"Honest Abe" 11-20-61 (Joe); *Laramie*—"The Perfect Gift" 1-2-62 (Lon Cady).

Warrenton, Lule (1863-5/14/32). Films: "When a Man Rides Alone" 1919 (Guadalupe Moreno); "The Wilderness Trail" 1919 (Old Mary); "The Rose of Nome" 1920 (Quita); "Blind Hearts" 1921 (Rita).

Warrick, Ruth (1915-). Films: "Ride Beyond Vengeance" 1966 (Aunt Gussie); "The Great Bank Robbery" 1969 (Mrs. Applebee). ¶TV: *Gunsmoke*—"The Storm" 9-25-65 (Clara Benteen); *Daniel Boone*—"How to Become a Goddess" 4-30-70 (the Wise Woman).

Warrington, Ann (1859-11/13/34). Films: "The Cyclone Cowboy" 1927 (Laura Tuttle).

Warwick, Richard (1945-). TV: *Masterpiece Theatre*—"The Last of the Mohicans" 1972 (Uncas).

Warwick, Robert (1878-6/4/64). Films: "All Man" 1916 (Jim Blake); "In Mizzoura" 1919 (Jim Radburn); "Told in the Hills" 1919 (Jack Stuart); "A Holy Terror" 1931 (Thomas Woodbury); "Three Rogues" 1931 (Layne Hunter); "Fighting with Kit Carson" 1933-serial; "Code of the Mounted" 1935 (Insp. Malloy); "Hopalong Cassidy" 1935 (Jim Meeker); "Timber War" 1935 (Ferguson); "Bold Caballero" 1936 (Governor Palma); "Sutter's Gold" 1936 (Gen. Rotscheff); "Vigilantes Are Coming" 1936-serial

(Count Ivan Raspinoff); "The Trigger Trio" 1937 (John Evans); "Law of the Plains" 1938 (Willard McGowan); "In Old Monterey" 1939 (Major Forbes); "Konga, the Wild Stallion" 1940 (Jordan Hadley); "Deerslayer" 1943 (Chief Uncas); "In Old Oklahoma" 1943 (Big Tree); "Pirates of Monterey" 1947 (Governor); "Unconquered" 1947 (Pontiac, Chief of the Ottawas); "Fury at Furnace Creek" 1948 (Gen. Blackwell); "Gun Smugglers" 1948 (Col. Davis); "Mark of the Renegade" 1951 (Col. Vega); "Sugarfoot" 1951 (J.C. Crane); "Passion" 1954 (Money Lender); "Silver Lode" 1954 (Judge Cranston); "Chief Crazy Horse" 1955 (Spotted Tail); "Walk the Proud Land" 1956 (Eskiminzin); "Shoot-Out at Medicine Bend" 1957 (Brother Abraham). ¶TV: *20th Century Fox Hour*—"Broken Arrow" 5-2-56 (General Howard); *Broken Arrow*—"Battle at Apache Pass" 10-2-56 (Gen. Howard), "Bear Trap" 4-29-58 (Gen. Howard); *The Adventures of Rin Tin Tin*—"The Old Man of the Mountain" 6-21-57 (Wind from the South), "The Last Navajo" 10-18-57 (Big Bear), "Rusty's Strategy" 11-15-57, "Star of India" 1-2-59 (Gen. Tyne-Ffyfe); *Circus Boy*—"Royal Roustabout" 9-26-57 (Count Brecht); *Colt .45*—"Rebellion" 12-20-57 (Judge Killian); *Jim Bowie*—"Choctaw Honor" 1-3-58 (Chief Minko); *Bronco*—"The Besieged" 9-23-58 (Jeremiah Cabot), "Payroll of the Dead" 1-27-59 (Pete), "Seminole War Pipe" 12-12-60 (Akacita); *Sugarfoot*—"Small Hostage" 5-26-59 (Col. Cyrus Craig); *The Deputy*—"Man of Peace" 12-19-59 (Chief Magnus); *The Law of the Plainsman*—"Amnesty" 4-7-60 (Gen. Lew Wallace); *Tate*—"The Bounty Hunter" 6-22-60 (Sean McConnell); *Maverick*—"Thunder from the North" 11-13-60 (Chief Standing Bull); *Zane Grey Theater*—"The Last Bugle" 11-24-60 (General Miles), "Honor Bright" 2-2-61 (Warden).

Warwick, Virginia. Films: "Hands Off" 1921 (Bonita); "Ace of Cactus Range" 1924 (Virginia Marsden); "The Vagabond Trail" 1924 (Nellie LeBrun); "Roped by Radio" 1925; "Wild West" 1925-serial; "The Desperate Game" 1926 (Belle Deane); "Moran of the Mounted" 1926 (Fleurette); "My Own Pal" 1926 (Molly).

Washbrook, Johnny (1944-). TV: *My Friend Flicka*—Regular 1955-56 (Ken McLaughlin); *Zane Grey Theater*—"To Sit in Judgment" 11-13-58 (Jamie MacPherson); *Wagon Train*—"The Swift Cloud Story" 4-8-

59 (Tommy Peeks), "The Beth Pearson Story" 2-22-61 (Ronald Pearson); *The Outlaws*—"The Quiet Killer" 12-29-60 (Vince Nickels).

Washburn, Beverly (1942-). Films: "The Lone Ranger" 1956 (Lila); "Old Yeller" 1957 (Lisbeth Searcy). ¶TV: *Fury*—"Joey Sees It Through" 1-21-56 (Betsy Parker); *Zane Grey Theater*—"Stars Over Texas" 12-28-56 (Annie); *Wagon Train*—"The Willy Moran Story" 9-18-57 (Susan), "The Tobias Jones Story" 10-22-58 (Midge), "The Cassie Vance Story" 12-23-63; *The Texan*—"No Tears for the Dead" 12-8-58 (Henrietta Tovers), "Badman" 6-20-60 (Greta Branden).

Washburn, Bryant (1889-4/30/63). Films: "The Ghost of the Rancho" 1918 (Jeffrey Wall); "That Girl Oklahoma" 1926; "Sitting Bull at the Spirit Lake Massacre" 1927 (Donald Keefe); "The Irish Gringo" 1935; "The Throwback" 1935 (Jack Thorne); "Sutter's Gold" 1936 (Capt. Petroff); "Stagecoach" 1939 (Capt. Simmons); "King of the Royal Mounted" 1940-serial (Matt Crandall); "Shadows on the Sage" 1942 (John Carson); "Sin Town" 1942 (Anderson); "Carson City Cyclone" 1943 (Dr. Andrews); "The Law Rides Again" 1943 (Commissioner Lee); "Nevada" 1944; "West of the Pecos" 1945 (Doc Howard); "Shane" 1953 (Ruth Lewis).

Washington, Dino (1942-). TV: *Daniel Boone*—"Run for the Money" 2-19-70 (Linus Hunter).

Washington, Edgar "Blue" (1898-9/15/70). Films: "Phantom City" 1928 (Blue); "Wyoming" 1928 (Mose); "Lucky Larkin" 1930 (Hambone); "Mountain Justice" 1930 (Sam); "Parade of the West" 1930 (Sambo); "Haunted Gold" 1932 (Clarence Washington Brown); "King of the Arena" 1933; "Smoking Guns" 1934; "Wells Fargo" 1937 (Coachman).

Wassil, Chuck. TV: *The Texan*—"No Place to Stop" 4-27-59 (Chick Bowdrie); *Maverick*—The Ghost Soldiers" 11-8-59 (Lieutenant Jennings); *Cheyenne*—"Prisoner of Moon Mesa" 11-16-59 (Clay Mason).

Wasson, Craig (1954-). TV: *Dr. Quinn, Medicine Woman*—"Luck of the Draw" 3-5-94 (Julius Hoffman).

Waterman, Albert. *see* Dell'Acqua, Alberto.

Waterman, Dennis (1948-). Films: "Man in the Wilderness" 1971-U.S./Span. (Lowrie).

Waterman, Willard (1914-2/2/

95). TV: *Jim Bowie*—"Land Jumpers" 11-16-56 (Judge Koford); *The Adventures of Rin Tin Tin*—"Major Mockingbird" 1-30-59 (Maj. Morton Mockingbird); *Bat Masterson*—"The Death of Bat Masterson" 5-20-59 (Bank Manager), "Death by th Half Dozen" 2-4-60 (Mayor Goodwin); *Lawman*—"The Hoax" 12-20-59 (Rev. Winters); *Riverboat*—"Trunk Full of Dreams" 10-31-60 (de Lesseps); *Wagon Train*—"The Jed Polke Story" 3-1-61 (Dr. Day), "The Saul Bevins Story" 4-12-61 (Andrew Harley), "The Clementine Jones Story" 10-25-61 (the Mayor); *Laramie*—"Trigger Point" 5-16-61 (Bender); *Cheyenne*—"Day's Pay" 10-30-61 (Purdie); *Maverick*—"Three Queens Full" 11-12-61 (Whittleseed), "Marshal Maverick" 3-11-62 (Mayor Oliver); *Bonanza*—"The Infernal Machine" 4-11-62 (Throckmorton).

Waters, Ethel (1896-9/1/77). TV: *Daniel Boone*—"Mamma Cooper" 2-5-70 (Rachael Cooper).

Waters, James (1926-12/12/85). Films: "Sergents 3" 1962 (Colonel's Aide). ¶TV: *Lawman*—"Mark of Cain" 3-26-61 (Bates); *The Dakotas*—"Walk Through the Badlands" 3-18-63 (Soldier).

Waters, Ozie (and his Colorado Rangers). Films: "Cowboy from Lonesome River" 1944 (Tex); "Mystery Man" 1944 (Tex); "Landrush" 1946; "Terror Trail" 1946; "Prairie Raiders" 1947; "Phantom Valley" 1948; "Outcast of Black Mesa" 1950; "Streets of Ghost Town" 1950.

Waters, Reba. Films: "Escort West" 1959 (Abbey Lassiter). ¶TV: *My Friend Flicka*—"Growing Pains" 6-8-56; *Wagon Train*—"The Luke O'Malley Story" 1-1-58 (Kate); *Sugarfoot*—"Small War at Custer Junction" 1-7-58 (Maggie); *Rawhide*—"Incident of the Silent Web" 6-3-60 (Jeanie Porter); *Stagecoach West*—"Come Home Again" 1-10-61 (Abigail).

Waters, Tom. Films: "The Apple Dumpling Gang" 1975 (Rowdy Joe Dover). ¶TV: *Gunsmoke*—"9:12 to Dodge" 11-11-68 (Fox), "Murdoch" 2-8-71 (Morris); *Alias Smith and Jones*—"Which Way to the O.K. Corral?" 2-10-72; *Kung Fu*—"The Hoots" 12-13-73 (Ferguson).

Waterston, Sam (1940-). Films: "Rancho Deluxe" 1975 (Cecil Colson); "Eagle's Wing" 1979-Brit./Span. (White Bull); "Heaven's Gate" 1980 (Frank Canton).

Watkin, Pierre (1887-2/3/60). Films: "The Californian" 1937

(Miller); "Wall Street Cowboy" 1939 (Roger Hammond); "Geronimo" 1940 (Col. White); "Out West with the Peppers" 1940 (King); "Jesse James at Bay" 1941 (Krager); "Nevada City" 1941; "Heart of the Rio Grande" 1942 (Mr. Lane); "Riding High" 1943 (Masters); "Song of the Range" 1944; "Dakota" 1945 (Wexton Geary); "Plainsman and the Lady" 1946 (Sen. Allen); "Sioux City Sue" 1946 (G.W. Rhodes); "The Fabulous Texan" 1947; "The Red Stallion" 1947 (Richard Moresby); "The Wild Frontier" 1947 (Marshal Frank Lane); "Frontier Outpost" 1950 (Col. Warick); "Over the Border" 1950 (Rand Malloy); "Redwood Forest Trail" 1950 (Arthur Cameron); "Rock Island Trail" 1950 (Major); "Sunset in the West" 1950 (MacKnight); "In Old Amarillo" 1951 (George B. Hills); "Thundering Caravans" 1952 (Head Marshal); "Canadian Mounties vs. Atomic Invaders" 1953-serial (Commander Morrison); "The Stranger Wore a Gun" 1953 (Jason Conroy); "Lay That Rifle Down" 1955 (Mr. Coswell); "The Maverick Queen" 1956 (McMillan). ¶TV: *The Lone Ranger*—"White Man's Magic" 7-13-50, "The Outcast" 1-18-51, "The Durango Kid" 4-16-53, "Gold Town" 10-7-54, "The Bounty Hunter" 5-19-55; *The Cisco Kid*—"Big Switch" 2-10-51, "Railroad Land Rush" 3-17-51, "Renegade Ranch" 4-7-51; *The Gene Autry Show*—"Blazeaway" 2-22-52, "Six Gun Romeo" 3-16-52; *The Roy Rogers Show*—"Peril from the Past" 4-13-52, "The Outlaws of Paradise Valley" 11-8-53; *Wild Bill Hickok*—"Grandpa and Genie" 5-20-52, "Missing Diamonds" 3-17-53; *The Adventures of Rin Tin Tin*—"The Wild Stallion" 9-23-55, "A Look of Eagles" 10-11-57 (Vet); *Fury*—"Joey and the Gypsies" 11-26-55 (Ellis); *Sergeant Preston of the Yukon*—"The Jailbreaker" 11-21-57 (Inspector); *Colt .45*—"Decoy" 1-31-58 (Col. Duncan); *The Restless Gun*—"Hiram Grover's Strike" 5-12-58 (Doc Nibble); *Tombstone Territory*—"The Black Diamond" 4-17-59 (Mr. Starr); *Bat Masterson*—"A Picture of Death" 1-14-60 (Judge Smith); *Wanted—Dead or Alive*—"Jason" 1-30-60.

Watkins, Charlene (1952-). TV: *Cliffhangers*—"The Secret Empire" 1979 (Miller); *Best of the West*—Regular 1981-82 (Elvira Best).

Watkins, Frank. Films: "Gun Fight" 1961 (Roark). ¶TV: *Bat Masterson*—"Trail Pirate" 12-31-58 (Man); *Tales of Wells Fargo*—"Showdown Trail" 1-5-59 (Sam Dooley); *Shotgun Slade*—"The Missing Train" 3-15-60;

The Tall Man—"The Leopard's Spots" 11-11-61 (Keeler); *Lawman*—"No Contest" 2-4-62 (Ames); *The Virginian*—"Echo from Another Day" 3-27-63.

Watkins, Linda (1909-10/31/76). Films: "The Gay Caballero" 1932 (Ann Grey). ¶TV: *Death Valley Days*—"One in a Hundred" 12-23-53 (Hannah Gaines); *Wagon Train*—"The Les Rand Story" 10-16-57; *Cheyenne*—"Border Affair" 11-5-57 (Baroness Entrade); *Jim Bowie*—"Bowie's Baby" 5-2-58 (Ellie); *Gunsmoke*—"Sky" 2-14-59 (Frog-Mouth Kate), "Old Fool" 12-24-60 (Elsie Hedgepeth), "Miss Kitty" 10-14-61 (Mattie), "The Hunger" 11-17-62 (Mrs. Dorf), "Take Her, She's Cheap" 10-31-64 (Ma Carp), "Shadler" 1-15-73 (Abby Shadler); *Bonanza*—"The Trouble with Amy" 1-25-70 (Margaret), "Shadow of a Hero" 2-21-71 (Bertha Cloninger).

Watson, Adele (1890-5/27/33). Films: "Good as Gold" 1927 (Timothea).

Watson, Ben (-1968). Films: "The Ox-Bow Incident" 1943 (Posse); "Across the Wide Missouri" 1951 (Markhead).

Watson, Bobs (1930-). Films: "Dodge City" 1939 (Harry Cole); "Wyoming" 1940 (Jimmy Kincaid). ¶TV: *Bonanza*—"The Jury" 12-30-62; *The Virginian*—"Vengeance Is the Spur" 2-27-63, "The Golden Door" 3-13-63, "A Distant Fury" 3-20-63 (Matt Lewis), "It Takes a Big Man" 10-23-63 (Hotel Clerk).

Watson, Bruce. TV: *Pistols 'n' Petticoats*—12-3-66 (Billy Blanton); *Gunsmoke*—"The Miracle Man" 12-2-68 (Howard); *Bonanza*—"Another Windmill to Go" 9-14-69 (Clay).

Watson, David (1941-). TV: *Rawhide*—Regular 1965-66 (Ian Cabot); *Daniel Boone*—"The Dandy" 10-10-68 (David Scott), "Noblesse Oblige" 3-26-70.

Watson, Debbie. TV: *The Virginian*—"Requiem for a Country Doctor" 1-25-67 (Lucy Marsh), "Eileen" 3-5-69 (Eileen Linden).

Watson, Delmar. Films: "The Lone Star Ranger" 1930 (Baby Jones); "The Fourth Horseman" 1933; "To the Last Man" 1933 (Ted Standing); "Annie Oakley" 1935 (Wesley Oakley); "Outlaws of the Prairie" 1937 (Dart Collins); "Legion of the Lawless" 1940 (Little Lafe); "My Little Chickadee" 1940 (Schoolboy).

Watson, Douglass (1921-5/1/89). Films: "Ulzana's Raid" 1972 (Maj. Cartwright).

Watson, Harry (1876-9/23/30). Films: "Zander the Great" 1925 (Good News); "Pardon My Gun" 1930.

Watson, Jr., James A. (1945-). TV: *The Virginian*—"Black Jade" 12-31-69 (Cobey Jade); *Kung Fu*—"The Spirit Helper" 11-8-73 (Diego).

Watson, Justice (1908-7/6/62). TV: *The Tall Man*—"Dark Moment" 2-11-61 (Doc); *The Deputy*—"The Means and the End" 3-18-61 (the Judge); *Tales of Wells Fargo*—"John Jones" 6-26-61 (John Jones).

Watson, Mills (1940-). Films: "Lock, Stock and Barrel" TVM-1971 (Plye); "The Wild Country" 1971 (Feathers); "Dirty Little Billy" 1972 (Ed); "The Invasion of Johnson County" TVM-1976 (Sheriff Angus); "Ransom for Alice!" TVM-1977 (Toby); "Gunsmoke: To the Last Man" TVM-1991 (Horse Trader); "Blood River" TVM-1994 (Jake). ¶TV: *Gunsmoke*—"Blood Money" 1-22-68 (Brent), "Lyle's Kid" 9-23-68 (Drover), "Slocum" 10-21-68 (Peter Riker), "Waco" 12-9-68 (Hood), "Stryker" 9-29-69 (Reager), "Morgan" 3-2-70 (Greer), "McCabe" 11-30-70 (Kipp), "The Bullet" 11-29-71, 12-6-71 & 12-13-71 (Pony), "The Predators" 1-31-72 (Currie), "Arizona Midnight" 1-1-73 (Fred), "A Family of Killers" 1-14-74 (Crazy Harley); *Here Come the Brides*—"Lovers and Wanderers" 11-6-68 (Steve), "The Wealthiest Man in Seattle" 10-3-69 (George), "Absalom" 3-20-70 (Beef); *The Guns of Will Sonnett*—"The Fearless Man" 12-13-68; *The High Chaparral*—"A Way of Justice" 12-13-68 (Cable), "New Hostess in Town" 3-20-70 (Greer); *The Virginian*—"Last Grave at Socorro Creek" 1-22-69 (Sam Blount); *Bonanza*—"Anatomy of a Lynching" 10-12-69 (Pete), "The Iron Butterfly" 11-28-71 (Fontaine); *Lancer*—"Chad" 1-20-70 (Buck); *Alias Smith and Jones*—"The Mc-Creedy Bush" 1-21-71 (Blake), "The Root of It All" 4-1-71 (Squint Simpson), "Bad Night in Big Butte" 3-2-72, "The Clementine Incident" 10-7-72; *Dirty Sally*—2-1-74 (Potts); *Kung Fu*—"King of the Mountain" 10-14-72 (Prospector); *The Quest*—"Day of Outrage" 10-27-76 (Buck); *The Oregon Trail*—"Hannah's Girls" 10-26-77 (Dixie Long); *How the West Was Won*—"Luke" 4-2-79 (Thomas Hutch).

Watson, Minor (1889-7/28/65). Films: "Rose of the Rancho" 1936 (Jonathon Hill); "The Llano Kid" 1939 (Sheriff McLane); "Stand Up and Fight" 1939 (Marshal Cole);

"Hidden Gold" 1940 (Ed Colby); "Rangers of Fortune" 1940 (Clem Bowdry); "Twenty Mule Team" 1940 (Marshal); "Viva Cisco Kid" 1940 (Jesse Allen); "The Parson of Panamint" 1941 (Sheriff Nickerson); "They Died with Their Boots On" 1941 (Sen. Smith); "Western Union" 1941 (Pat Grogan); "Boy's Ranch" 1946 (Mr. Harper); "The Virginian" 1946 (Judge Henry); "Face to Face" 1952 ("The Bride Comes to Yellow Sky" segment—the Bad Man); "Untamed Frontier" 1952 (Matt Denbow); "Ten Wanted Men" 1955 (Jason Carr); "The Rawhide Years" 1956 (Matt Comfort).

Watson, Robert "Bobby" (1888-5/22/65). Films: "The Paleface" 1948 (Toby Preston); "Copper Canyon" 1950 (Bixby). ¶TV: *The Adventures of Rin Tin Tin*—"The Legacy of Sean O'Hara" 3-4-55 (Harry).

Watson, Roy (1876-6/7/37). Films: "The Cowboy's Adopted Child" 1911; "A Frontier Girl's Courage" 1911; "In the Days of Gold" 1911; "John Oakhurst—Gambler" 1911; "The Night Herder" 1911; "Told in the Sierras" 1911; "The Bandit's Mask" 1912; "Big Rock's Last Stand" 1912; "A Broken Spur" 1912; "A Crucial Test" 1912; "Darkfeather's Strategy" 1912; "A Reconstructed Rebel" 1912; "Trapper Bill, King of the Scouts" 1912; "Jimmy Hayes and Muriel" 1914; "The Ranger's Romance" 1914; "The Sheriff's Reward" 1914; "The Way of the Redman" 1914; "Why the Sheriff Is a Bachelor" 1914; "Bill Haywood, Producer" 1915; "The Grizzly Gulch Chariot Race" 1915; "Roping a Bride" 1915; "Cupid's Round Up" 1918 (Bucklan); "Slim Higgins" 1919; "The Trail of the Hold-Up Man" 1919; "The Ranger and the Law" 1921 (Slim Dixon); "Blue Blazes" 1922 (Ranch Foreman); "The Loser's End" 1924 (Capt. Harris); "Luck and Sand" 1925 (Sheriff); "Win, Lose or Draw" 1925 (U.S. Marshal); "Chasing Trouble" 1926 (Judge Gregg); "Cactus Trails" 1927 (Sheriff Upshaw); "Wanderer of the West" 1927.

Watson, William (1938-). Films: "The Hunting Party" 1971-Brit./Ital./Span. (Loring); "Lawman" 1971 (Choctaw Lee); "Chato's Land" 1972 (Harvey Lansing). ¶TV: *Gunsmoke*—"Saturday Night" 1-7-67 (Carl Craddock), "The Pack Rat" 1-12-70 (Sam Danton), "Island in the Desert" 12-2-74 & 12-9-74 (Gard Dixon); *Cimarron Strip*—"Nobody" 12-7-67 (Burke Stegman); *The High Chaparral*—"The Kinsman" 1-28-68

(Mace), "No Trouble at All" 5-5-70 (Brady); *The Outcasts*—"The Heady Wine" 12-2-68 (Cart Munson); *Bonanza*—"He Was Only Seven" 3-5-72 (Zack); *Young Dan'l Boone*—"The Pirate" 9-19-77 (Fraker).

Watters, William. see Hall, Sr., Arch.

Watts, Charles (1902-12/13/66). Films: "Dallas" 1950 (Bill Walters); "The Silver Whip" 1953 (Doc Summers); "The Boy from Oklahoma" 1954 (Harry); "Ricochet Romance" 1954 (Mr. Harvey); "Tall Man Riding" 1955 (Al, the Bartender); "Giant" 1956 (Whiteside); "The Big Land" 1957 (McCullough); "Outlaw's Son" 1957 (Marshal Eric Blessingham); "The Lone Ranger and the Lost City of Gold" 1958 (Oscar Matthison); "No Name on the Bullet" 1959 (Sid); "Apache Rifles" 1964. ¶TV: *The Lone Ranger*—"The Star Witness" 8-17-50, "Thieves' Money" 11-2-50, "Paid in Full" 12-28-50; *The Cisco Kid*—"Phony Heiress" 7-21-51, "Ghost Story" 9-1-51, "Water Well Oil" 10-13-51, "Double Deal" 1-17-53; *Fury*—"The 4-H Story" 12-17-55 (Judge); *Jim Bowie*—"Outlaw Kingdom" 12-7-56 (Silas Ogleby); *The Rifleman*—"The Brother-in-Law" 10-28-58 (Alvah Kemper), "Panic" 11-10-59., "The Mescalero Curse" 4-18-61 (Joe Beaseley); *The Texan*—"The Widow of Paradise" 11-24-58 (Judge Whittaker); *Death Valley Days*—"RX—Slow Death" 4-28-59 (Prof. Peacock); *Maverick*—"Guatemala City" 1-31-60 (Spelvin); *Man from Blackhawk*—"Incident at Tupelo" 4-29-60 (Sheriff); *Wyatt Earp*—"Old Slanders Never Die" 1-31-61 (Dameron), "The Outlaws Cry Murder" 6-27-61 (Dameron); *Bonanza*—"Tax Collector" 2-18-61 (Ellery), "The Burma Rarity" 10-22-61, "A Knight to Remember" 12-20-64 (Sheriff Munsey); *The Tall Man*—"Rovin' Gambler" 3-18-61 (Judge), "A Time to Run" 4-7-62 (Hiram Sunday); *Rawhide*—"Incident of the Wager on Payday" 6-16-61 (Albert Porter); *Tales of Wells Fargo*—"Tanoa" 10-28-61 (Anderson); *Gunsmoke*—"Panacea Sykes" 4-13-63 (Little); *Temple Houston*—"A Slight Case of Larceny" 2-13-64 (Paul Hillings).

Watts, George (1877-7/1/42). Films: "Apache Trail" 1943 (Judge Keeley).

Watts, Twinkle. Films: "California Joe" 1943 (Twinkle); "Canyon City" 1943 (Twinkle Hardy); "The Man from the Rio Grande" 1943 (Twinkle); "Outlaws of Santa Fe" 1944 (Winky Gordon); "Sheriff of

Sundown" 1944 (Little Jo); "Silver City Kid" 1944; "Stagecoach to Monterey" 1944; "Corpus Christi Bandits" 1945 (Nancy); "The Topeka Terror" 1945 (Midge Hardy); "Trail of Kit Carson" 1945.

Waxman, Al (1935-). Films: "The Last Gunfighter" 1961-Can.

Wayland, Len. Films: "The Intruders" TVM-1970. ¶TV: *Gunsmoke*—"He Who Steals" 5-19-65 (Jim Donner), "The Lure" 2-25-67 (Stationmaster); *The Big Valley*—"Palms of Glory" 9-15-65 (Sheriff Lyman); *The Road West*—"Shaman" 11-14-66 (Gorse); *Wild Wild West*—"The Night of the Firebrand" 9-15-67 (Major Jason); *Daniel Boone*—"Israel and Love" 5-7-70; *Paradise*—"A House Divided" 2-16-89 (McMurtry).

Wayne, Aissa. Films: "The Alamo" 1960 (Angelina Dickinson); "The Comancheros" 1961 (Bessie); "McClintock" 1963 (Alice Warren).

Wayne, Billy. Films: "Cowboy and the Lady" 1938 (Rodeo Rider); "Heart of the North" 1938 (Mechanic); "Go West" 1940 (Fireman); "Belle Starr" 1941; "River Lady" 1948 (Dealer); "Lost in Alaska" 1952 (Croupier). ¶TV: *Fury*—"Wonder Horse" 3-24-56 (Meadows).

Wayne, David (1914-2/9/95). Films: "The Naked Hills" 1956 (Tracy Powell); "The Apple Dumpling Gang" 1975 (Col. T.T. Clydesdale); "Poker Alice" TVM-1987 (Amos). ¶TV: *Ruggles of Red Gap* 2-3-57 (Egbert Floud); *Overland Trail*—"Escort Detail" 5-22-60 (Lt. Adam King); *Wagon Train*—"The Shad Bennington Story" 6-22-60 (Shad Bennington); *The Outlaws*—"No More Pencils—No More Books" 3-16-61 (Darius Woodley), "Roly" 11-23-61 (Roly McDonough); *The Virginian*—"The Small Parade" 2-20-63 (Martin Reese); *Gunsmoke*—"Lynch Town" 11-19-73 (Judge Warfield), "I Have Promises to Keep" 3-3-75 (Reverend Byrne); *Big Hawaii*—"You Can't Lose 'Em All" 11-30-77 (Derby O'Brian).

Wayne, Frank. Films: "Lightning Carson Rides Again" 1938; "Six-Gun Trail" 1938; "Code of the Cactus" 1939 (Jake); "The Man from Texas" 1939 (Longhorn); "Smoky Trails" 1939 (Sloan); "King of the Royal Mounted" 1940-serial (Brant); "King of the Mounties" 1942-serial (Brant).

Wayne, Fredd (1923-). TV: *Gunsmoke*—"Young Man with a Gun" 10-20-56 (Sam Kertcher); *Maverick*—

"Relic of Fort Tejon" 11-3-57 (Honest Carl Jimson), "Diamond in the Rough" 1-26-58 (Van Buren Kingsley); *Sugarfoot*—"The Canary Kid, Inc." 11-10-59; *The Alaskans*—"The Trial of Reno McKee" 1-10-60 (Burton); *Man from Blackhawk*—"Trail by Combat" 5-27-60 (Garrison); *Have Gun Will Travel*—"A Quiet Night in Town" 1-7-61 & 1-14-61; *Rawhide*—"Incident of the Pale Rider" 3-15-63 (Calhoun); *The Monroes*—"To Break a Colt" 1-11-67 (Winton); *Daniel Boone*—"The Printing Press" 10-23-69 (Benjamin Franklin).

Wayne, John (1907-6/11/79). Films: "The Big Trail" 1930 (Breck Coleman); "Rough Romance" 1930; "The Range Feud" 1931 (Clint Turner); "The Big Stampede" 1932 (John Steele); "Haunted Gold" 1932 (John Mason); "Ride Him, Cowboy" 1932 (John Drury); "Texas Cyclone" 1932 (Steve Pickett); "Two-Fisted Law" 1932 (Duke); "The Man from Monterey" 1933 (Capt. John Holmes); "Riders of Destiny" 1933 (Singin' Sandy Saunders); "Sagebrush Trail" 1933 (John Brant); "Somewhere in Sonora" 1933 (John Bishop); "The Telegraph Trail" 1933 (John Trent); "Blue Steel" 1934 (John Carruthers); "The Lawless Frontier" 1934 (John Tobin); "The Lucky Texan" 1934 (Jerry Mason); "The Man from Utah" 1934 (John Weston); "'Neath the Arizona Skies" 1934 (Chris Morrell); "Randy Rides Alone" 1934 (Randy Bowers); "The Star Packer" 1934 (U.S. Marshal John Travers); "The Trail Beyond" 1934 (Rod Drew); "West of the Divide" 1934 (Ted Hayden/Gat Ganns); "Dawn Rider" 1935 (John Mason); "Desert Trail" 1935 (John Scott); "Lawless Range" 1935 (John Middleton/John Allen); "The New Frontier" 1935 (John Dawson); "Paradise Canyon" 1935 (John Wyatt); "Rainbow Valley" 1935 (John Martin); "Texas Terror" 1935 (Sheriff John Higgins); "Westward Ho" 1935 (John Wyatt); "King of the Pecos" 1936 (John Clayborn); "The Lawless Nineties" 1936 (John Tipton); "The Lonely Trail" 1936 (John Ashley); "The Oregon Trail" 1936 (Capt. John Delmont); "Winds of the Wasteland" 1936 (John Blair); "Born to the West" 1937 (Dare Rudd); "Overland Stage Raiders" 1938 (Stoney Brooke); "Pals of the Saddle" 1938 (Stony Brooke/Ezeckial Saunders); "Red River Range" 1938 (Stony Brooke); "Santa Fe Stampede" 1938 (Stony Brooke); "Allegheny Uprising" 1939 (Jim Smith); "New Frontier" 1939 (Stony Brooke); "The Night Riders" 1939

(Stony Brooke); "Stagecoach" 1939 (the Ringo Kid); "Three Texas Steers" 1939 (Stony Brooke); "Wyoming Outlaw" 1939 (Stony Brooke); "The Dark Command" 1940 (Bob Seton); "Three Faces West" 1940 (John Phillips); "The Shepherd of the Hills" 1941 (Young Matt Matthews); "In Old California" 1942 (Tom Craig); "The Spoilers" 1942 (Roy Glennister); "In Old Oklahoma" 1943 (Dan Somers); "A Lady Takes a Chance" 1943 (Duke Hudkins); "Tall in the Saddle" 1944 (Rocklin); "Dakota" 1945 (John Devlin); "Flame of the Barbary Coast" 1945 (Duke Fergus); "Angel and the Badman" 1947 (Quirt Evans); "Fort Apache" 1948 (Capt. Kirby York); "Red River" 1948 (Tom Dunson); "The Three Godfathers" 1948 (Robert Marmaduke Hightower); "The Fighting Kentuckian" 1949 (John Breen); "She Wore a Yellow Ribbon" 1949 (Capt. Nathan Brittles); "Rio Grande" 1950 (Lt. Col. Kirby Yorke); "Hondo" 1953 (Hondo Lane); "The Searchers" 1956 (Ethan Edwards); "The Horse Soldiers" 1959 (Col. John Marlowe); "Rio Bravo" 1959 (John T. Chance); "The Alamo" 1960 (Col. David Crockett); "North to Alaska" 1960 (Sam McCord); "The Comancheros" 1961 (Cutter); "How the West Was Won" 1962 (Gen. William T. Sherman); "The Man Who Shot Liberty Valance" 1962 (Tom Doniphon); "McClintock" 1963 (George Washington McLintock); "The Sons of Katie Elder" 1965 (John Elder); "El Dorado" 1967 (Cole Thornton); "The War Wagon" 1967 (Taw Jackson); "True Grit" 1969 (Reuben J. "Rooster" Cogburn); "The Undefeated" 1969 (Col. John Henry Thomas); "Chisum" 1970 (John Chisum); "Rio Lobo" 1970 (Col. Cord McNally); "Big Jake" 1971 (Jacob McCandles); "The Cowboys" 1972 (Will Anderson); "Cahill, United States Marshal" 1973 (J.D. Cahill); "The Train Robbers" 1973 (Lane); "Rooster Cogburn" 1975 (Rooster Cogburn); "The Shootist" 1976 (John Bernard Books). ¶TV: *Wagon Train*—"The Colter Craven Story" 11-23-60 (General Sherman).

Wayne, John Ethan (1961-). Films: "Big Jake" 1971 (Little Jake McCandless); "Manhunt" 1984-Ital.

Wayne, Marilyn. TV: *Wagon Train*—"The Nancy Styles Story" 11-22-64 (Jenny Phillips); *The Virginian*—"Dangerous Road" 3-17-65 (Kitty).

Wayne, Maude (1895-10/10/83). Films: "By Proxy" 1918 (Lindy);

"Closin' In" 1918 (Barbara Carlton); "The Fighting Shepherdess" 1920 (Beth); "The Mysterious Rider" 1921 (Madge Smith); "The Bachelor Daddy" 1922 (Ethel McVae).

Wayne, Patrick (1939-). Films: "Rio Grande" 1950; "The Searchers" 1956 (Lt. Greenhill); "The Young Land" 1959 (Jim Ellison); "The Alamo" 1960 (Capt. James Butler Bonham); "The Comancheros" 1961 (Tobe); "McClintock" 1963 (Devlin Warren); "Cheyenne Autumn" 1964 (2nd Lieutenant Scott); "Shenandoah" 1965 (James Anderson); "An Eye for an Eye" 1966 (Benny); "Deserter" 1970-U.S./Ital./Yugo. (Bill Robinson); "Big Jake" 1971 (James McCandles); "The Gatling Gun" 1972 (Jim Beland); "Mustang Country" 1976 (Tee Jay); "Rustler's Rhapsody" 1985 (Bob Barber); "Young Guns" 1988 (Pat Garrett). ¶TV: *Have Gun Will Travel*—"Black Sheep" 4-30-60 (Ben Huttner); *Branded*—"The Mission" 3-14-65, 3-21-65 & 3-28-65 (Corporal Dewey); *The Rounders*—Regular 1966-67 (Howdy Lewis); *The Life and Times of Grizzly Adams*—3-22-78 (Brad).

Wayne, Richard (-3/15/58). Films: "A Daughter of the Wolf" 1919 (Sgt. Tim Roper); "Two-Gun Betty" 1919 (Irish Dave).

Wayne, Robert (1864-9/26/46). Films: "King of the Royal Mounted" 1940-serial (Lieutenant).

Weathers, Carl (1948-). Films: "Death Hunt" 1981 (Sundog). ¶TV: *Kung Fu*—"Barbary House" 2-15-75 (Bad Sam), "Flight to Orion" 2-22-75 (Bad Sam), "The Brothers Cain" 3-1-75 (Bad Sam), "Full Circle" 3-15-75 (Bad Sam).

Weatherwax, Ruddel (1907-2/25/85). Films: "The Crow's Nest" 1922 (Estaban as a Boy).

Weatherwax, W.S. (1867-1/19/43). Films: "The Kingfisher's Roost" 1922 (Bill Jackson).

Weaver, Dennis (1924-). Films: "Horizons West" 1952 (Dandy Taylor); "The Lawless Breed" 1952 (Jim Clements); "The Raiders" 1952 (Dick Logan); "Column South" 1953 (Menguito); "Law and Order" 1953 (Frank Durling); "The Nebraskan" 1953 (Capt. DeWitt); "The Redhead from Wyoming" 1953 (Matt Jessup); "War Arrow" 1953 (Pino); "Chief Crazy Horse" 1955 (Maj. Carlisle); "Seven Angry Men" 1955 (John Jr.); "Ten Wanted Men" 1955 (Sheriff Clyde Gibbons); "Duel at Diablo" 1966 (Willard Grange); "Man Called Sledge" 1971-Ital./U.S. (Ward); "Female Artillery" TVM-1973 (Deke Chambers). ¶TV: *The Lone Ranger*—"The Tell-Tale Bullet" 4-14-55; *Gunsmoke*—Regular 1955-64 (Chester B. Goode); *The Virginian*—"Train of Darkness" 2-4-70 (Jed); *Centennial*—Regular 1978-79 (R.J. Poteet); *Lonesome Dove*—Pilot 10-2-94, 10-9-94 & 10-16-94 (Buffalo Bill), "Last Stand" 11-20-94 (Buffalo Bill).

Weaver, Doodles (1911-1/17/83). Films: "The Singing Sheriff" 1944 (Ivory); "San Antonio" 1945 (Square Dance Caller); "Frontier Gun" 1958 (Eph Loveman); "Mail Order Bride" 1964 (Charlie Mary); "The Rounders" 1965 (Arlee); "The Daughters of Joshua Cabe" TVM-1972 (Telegrapher); "Savage Red—Outlaw White" 1974; "Banjo Hackett: Roamin' Free" TVM-1976 (Old Turkey). ¶TV: *Fury*—"Packy's Dilemma" 2-13-50 (Jake); *Maverick*—"Gun-Shy" 1-11-59 (Lem); *Lawman*—"The Thimblerigger" 2-28-60 (Jack), "The Lady Belle" 5-1-60 (Jack Stiles), "The Parting" 5-29-60 (Hotel Clerk); *Wagon Train*—"The Joe Muharich Story" 4-19-61 (Efen); *Laramie*—"Handful of Fire" 12-5-61; *Bronco*—"Moment of Doubt" 4-2-62 (Grimes); *Have Gun Will Travel*—"Shootout at Hogtooth" 11-10-62 (Hildreth); *Wide Country*—"The Judas Goat" 2-21-63 (Jones); *The Travels of Jaimie McPheeters*—"The Day of the Tin Trumpet" 2-2-64 (Pettigrew); *Laredo*—"Which Way Did They Go?" 11-18-65, "The Heroes of San Gill" 12-23-65 (Wilbur); *Daniel Boone*—"Run a Crooked Mile" 10-20-66 (Horseman), "Take the Southbound Stage" 4-6-67 (Bartender); *Bonanza*—"Maestro Hoss" 5-7-67 (Barney), "Trouble Town" 3-17-68 (Stable Man).

Weaver, Frank "Cicero" (1891-10/29/67). Films: "Jeepers Creepers" 1939 (Cicero); "Arkansas Judge" 1941 (Cicero).

Weaver, Fritz (1926-). Films: "Dream West" TVM-1986 (Thomas Hart Benton). ¶TV: *Rawhide*—"Damon's Road" 11-13-64 & 11-20-64 (Jonathan Damon); *Gunsmoke*—"Old Friend" 2-4-67 (Marshal Burl Masters); *The Big Valley*—"Four Days to Furnace Hill" 12-4-67 (Burke Jordan), "A Passage of Saints" 3-10-69 (Hebron Grant); *The Outcasts*—"The Man from Bennington" 12-16-68 (Sam Croft); *Kung Fu*—"The Raiders" 1-24-74 (Hillquist).

Weaver, June "Elviry" (1891-11/27/77). Films: "Jeepers Creepers" 1939 (Elviry); "Arkansas Judge" 1941 (Elviry).

Weaver, Leon "Abner" (1883-5/27/50). Films: "Jeepers Creepers" 1939 (Abner); "Arkansas Judge" 1941 (Abner); "Loaded Pistols" 1948 (Jake Harper); "Riders of the Whistling Pines" 1949 (Abner Weaver).

Weaver, Loretta. Films: "Jeepers Creepers" 1939 (Violey); "Heroes of the Saddle" 1940 (Ruth Miller); "Arkansas Judge" 1941 (Violey).

Weaver, Marjorie (1913-). Films: "The Californian" 1937 (Rosalia Miller); "The Cisco Kid and the Lady" 1939 (Julie Lawson); "Shooting High" 1940 (Marjorie Pritchard).

Webb, Frank (1948-12/20/74). TV: *Bonanza*—"The Fence" 4-27-69 (Teddy); *The Virginian*—"Family Man" 10-15-69 (Obie); *The High Chaparral*—"Pale Warrior" 12-11-70 (Talbot).

Webb, George (1887-5/24/43). Films: "The Sheriff of Willow Creek" 1915; "The Trail of the Serpent" 1915; "The Bond of Fear" 1917; "The Fighting Gringo" 1917 (Arthur Saxon); "The Crusader" 1922 (James Symonds); "Romance Land" 1923 (Counterfeit Bill); "Dude Ranch" 1931 (Burson).

Webb, Richard (1915-6/11/93). Films: "American Empire" 1942 (Crane); "Distant Drums" 1951 (Richard Tufts); "Carson City" 1952 (Alan Kincaid); "The Nebraskan" 1953 (Ace Eliot); "The Black Dakotas" 1954 (Frank Gibbs); "Jubilee Trail" 1954 (Capt. Brown); "Three Hours to Kill" 1954 (Carter Mastin); "Count Three and Pray" 1955 (Big); "The Phantom Stagecoach" 1957 (Tom Bradley); "Town Tamer" 1965 (Kevin). ¶TV: *Stories of the Century*—"John Wesley Hardin" 6-10-55; *Maverick*—"The Long Hunt" 10-20-57 (Ben Maxwell), "The White Widow" 1-24-60 (George Manton); *Trackdown*—"Self-Defense" 11-22-57 (Sheriff Eden Lake), "The Farrand Story" 1-10-58 (Sheriff Eden Lake); *Colt .45*—"Dead Reckoning" 1-24-58 (Rocky Morton); *Jefferson Drum*—"Wheel of Fortune" 6-27-58 (Duane); *Rawhide*—"Incident of the Stargazer" 4-1-60 (Henry Walker), "The Little Fishes" 11-24-61 (Paul Morgan); *The Alaskans*—"Calico" 5-22-60 (Clay); *Cheyenne*—"Two Trails to Santa Fe" 10-28-60 (Jed Brandon), "The Bad Penny" 3-12-62 (Clay McConnell), "Wanted for the Murder of Cheyenne Bodie" 12-10-62 (Bill Walton); *Death Valley Days*—"The Peacemaker" 11-3-63, "Measure of a Man" 11-17-63; *Gunsmoke*—"Treasure of John Walking Fox" 4-16-66 (Aaron Tigue), "The Returning" 2-18-67 (Will Hayes); *Branded*—"Kellie" 4-

24-66 (Trask); *Daniel Boone*—"The Long Way Home" 2-16-67 (Murdock), "The Secret Code" 12-14-67; *The Guns of Will Sonnett*—"The Warriors" 3-1-68.

Webber, Peggy. TV: *Frontier*—"Mother of the Brave" 1-15-56 (Meg Horn); *Cheyenne*—"Quicksand" 4-3-56 (Ella McIntyre); *Zane Grey Theater*—"Badge of Honor" 5-3-57 (Nora); *Gunsmoke*—"Cheap Labor" 5-4-57 (Flora Stancil); *Wanted—Dead or Alive*—"Amos Carter" 5-9-59; *Trackdown*—"Back to Crawford" 9-9-59 (Sarah); *The Law of the Plainsman*—"Fear" 1-7-60 (Hattie Mullen); *The Rebel*—"Unsurrendered Sword" 4-3-60 (Juanita); *Laramie*—"The Confederate Express" 1-30-62 (Martha Grundy).

Webber, Robert (1928-5/17/89). Films: "No Man's Land" TVM-1984 (Will Blackfield). ¶TV: *The Rifleman*—"The Retired Gun" 1-20-59 (Wes Carney); *Stoney Burke*—"Spin a Golden Web" 11-26-62 (Roy Hazelton); *The Men from Shiloh*—"The Mysterious Mr. Tate" 10-14-70 (Jackson Reed); *Bret Maverick*—"Faith, Hope and Clarity" 4-13-82 & 4-20-82 (Everest Sinclair).

Webster, Byron (1933-12/1/91). Films: "The Barbary Coast" TVM-1975 (Mr. Speece). ¶TV: *Bonanza*—"Emily" 3-23-69 (Dr. Stebbins).

Webster, Chuck. Films: "Drango" 1957 (Scott). ¶TV: *Sergeant Preston of the Yukon*—"Skagway Secret" 2-16-56 (Mal Rebow); *Gunsmoke*—"Unmarked Grave" 8-18-56 (Sheriff Benson); *Klondike*—"Swing Your Partner" 1-9-61 (Buck Stubblefield); *The Tall Man*—"Dark Moment" 2-11-61 (Isaiah); *Bat Masterson*—"Dead Man's Claim" 5-4-61 (Judd Elkins); *Iron Horse*—"Broken Gun" 10-17-66 (Ticket Seller).

Webster, Hugh (1928-5/31/86). Films: "King of the Grizzlies" 1970 (Shorty).

Webster, Judith. Films: "Fast on the Draw" 1950; "Hostile Country" 1950 (Marie); "West of the Brazos" 1950 (Judy).

Webster, Mary. Films: "The Tin Star" 1957 (Millie Parker). ¶TV: *The Texan*—"Return to Friendly" 2-2-59 (Bess Wallen), "Johnny Tuvo" 5-30-60 (Carrie); *Buckskin*—"The Knight Who Owned Buckskin" 3-2-59 (Minnie); *The Restless Gun*—"Ricochet" 3-9-59 (Abigail Garrick); *Tombstone Territory*—"Warrant for Death" 5-8-59; *Colt .45*—"Don't Tell Joe" 6-14-59 (Martha); *Death Valley Days*—"Lady of the Press" 12-29-59 (Laura);

Tales of Wells Fargo—"The Town" 4-4-60 (Lucy Potter); *Shotgun Slade*—"The Golden Tunnel" 6-7-60; *The Tall Man*—"A Gun Is for Killing" 1-14-61 (Marion Swift).

Weddle, Vernon. TV: *Bonanza*—"The Stalker" 11-2-69 (South); *Young Maverick*—"Makin' Tracks" 1-9-80.

Weed, Frank. Films: "Dad's Girls" 1911; "The Rose of Old St. Augustine" 1911; "Driftwood" 1912; "The Horseshoe" 1912; "A Texas Steer" 1915 (Colonel Brassy Gall); "Three Gold Coins" 1920 (One-Legged Townsman); "Playing It Wild" 1923 (Bill Rucker).

Weeks, Barbara. Films: "Two-Fisted Justice" 1931 (Nancy Cameron); "Forbidden Trail" 1932 (Mary Middleton); "White Eagle" 1932 (Janet Rand); "Rusty Rides Alone" 1933 (Mollie Martin); "The Sundown Rider" 1933 (Molly McCall); "The Old Wyoming Trail" 1937 (Elsie Haliday); "One Man Justice" 1937 (Mary Crockett); "Two-Fisted Sheriff" 1937 (Molly Herrick).

Weeks, Ranny (1907-4/26/79). Films: "Heart of the Rockies" 1937.

Weidler, Virginia (1927-7/1/68). Films: "The Outcasts of Poker Flat" 1937 (Luck); "Out West with the Hardys" 1938 (Jake Holt); "Henry Goes Arizona" 1939 (Molly Cullison).

Weigel, Paul (1867-5/25/51). Films: "The Claim" 1918 (Mike Bryan); "The Only Road" 1918 (Manuel Lopez); "Evangeline" 1919 (Father Felicien); "Bring Him In" 1921 (Braganza); "Up and Going" 1922 (Father Le Clair); "Fighting for Justice" 1924 (Sam Culvert); "Soft Shoes" 1925 (Dummy O'Day); "The Wagon Show" 1928 (Joey); "The Vanishing Legion" 1931-serial (Laribee); "Sutter's Gold" 1936.

Weil, Elvira. Films: "Untamed" 1918 (Dolores); "Another Man's Boots" 1922 (Nell Hadley).

Weil, Harry (1878-1/23/43). Films: "Triple Justice" 1940 (Minister).

Weinrib, Lennie (1935-). TV: *The Rebel*—"The Hunted" 11-6-60 (Sheriff); *Laredo*—"The Sweet Gang" 11-4-66 (Bud Sweet).

Weismuller, Johnny (1904-1/20/84). Films: "Rodeo Dough" 1940-short.

Weisser, Norbert. Films: "Three Amigos" 1986 (German's Friend).

Welch, James (1869-4/6/49). Films: "The Marshal of Moneymint" 1922 (Jimsy MacTavish); "Two-Fisted Jefferson" 1922; "The Santa Fe

Trail" 1923-serial; "The Iron Horse" 1924 (Private Schultz); "The Little Buckaroo" 1928 (Jim Crawford); "Stormy" 1935 (Boy).

Welch, Nelson. TV: *Rawhide*—"Incident at Rojo Canyon" 9-30-60 (Purkey); *Wild Wild West*—"The Night of the Deadly Bubble" 2-24-67 (Prof. McClendon).

Welch, Niles (1895-11/21/76). Films: "A Yellow Streak" 1915 (Tom Austin); "Fear-Bound" 1925 (Tod Vane); "Border Devils" 1932 (Tom Hope); "Cornered" 1932 (Rudi Pearson); "McKenna of the Mounted" 1932 (Morgan); "Rainbow Trail" 1932 (Willets); "Come on Tarzan" 1933 (Steve Frazer); "The Lone Avenger" 1933 (Martin Carter); "The Mysterious Rider" 1933 (John Foster); "The Sundown Rider" 1933 (Houseman); "The Fighting Code" 1934 (Crosby); "Ivory-Handled Gun" 1935 (Young Pat Moore); "The Miracle Rider" 1935-serial; "Riding Wild" 1935 (Clay Stevens); "The Singing Vagabond" 1935 (Judge Forsythe Lane); "Stone of Silver Creek" 1935 (Timothy Tucker); "The Country Beyond" 1936 (Party Guest); "Empty Saddles" 1937 (Jasper Kade).

Welch, Raquel (1940-). Films: "Bandolero!" 1968 (Maria); "100 Rifles" 1969 (Sarita); "Hannie Calder" 1971-Brit./Span./Fr. (Hannie Calder); "The Legend of Walks Far Woman" TVM-1982.

Welch, William. see Welsh, William.

Weld, Tuesday (1943-). TV: *Zane Grey Theater*—"The Mormons" 12-15-60 (Beth Lawson); *Cimarron Strip*—"Heller" 1-18-68 (Heller).

Welden, Ben (1901-). Films: "Westbound Mail" 1937 (Steve Hickman); "Stand Up and Fight" 1939 (Foreman); "The Dude Goes West" 1948; "Riders in the Sky" 1949 (Dave); "Tough Assignment" 1949 (Sniffy); "Night Stage to Galveston" 1952; "Hidden Guns" 1956 (Peabody). ¶TV: *The Gene Autry Show*—"Head for Texas" 7-23-50, "Silver Arrow" 8-6-50, "Outlaw Escape" 12-1-51, "The Return of Maverick Dan" 12-15-51; *The Lone Ranger*—"Two Gold Lockets" 2-15-51, "Delayed Action" 11-6-52, "Right to Vote" 2-12-53, "Stage to Tishomingo" 10-28-54, "Trouble at Tylerville" 12-13-56; *Wild Bill Hickok*—"Jingles on Jail Road" 7-14-53; *Fury*—"A Fish Story" 3-8-58 (Mac); *Branded*—"The Ghost of Murrieta" 3-20-66 (Vega).

Weldon, Jasper (1895-2/4/68).

Films: "The Lone Hand Texan" 1947 (Coachman).

Weldon, Joan (1933-). Films: "The Command" 1953 (Martha); "The Stranger Wore a Gun" 1953 (Shelby Conroy); "Riding Shotgun" 1954 (Orissa Flynn); "Gunsight Ridge" 1957 (Molly); "Day of the Bad Man" 1958 (Myra Owens). ¶TV: *Cheyenne*—"The Conspirators" 10-8-57 (Nellie Marritt); *Have Gun Will Travel*—"The Singer" 2-8-58 (Faye Hollister); *Colt .45*—"Circle of Fear" 3-7-58 (Edith Murrow); *Maverick*—"Plunder of Paradise" 3-9-58 (Grace Wheeler).

Weldon, Marion. Films: "Desert Patrol" 1938 (Jean Drury); "Knight of the Plains" 1938 (Gale Rand).

Weldon, Mirian. Films: "Dodge City Trail" 1937 (Marian Phillips); "Colorado Kid" 1938 (Iram Toles); "The Feud Maker" 1938 (Sally Harbison).

Welker, Frank (1946-). Films: "Dirty Little Billy" 1972 (Young Punk); "Zorro, the Gay Blade" 1981 (Narrator). ¶TV: *The Kowboys*—Pilot 7-13-70 (Clem).

Weller, Peter (1947-). Films: "Butch and Sundance: The Early Days" 1979 (Joe LeFors); "Substitute Wife" TVM-1994 (Martin Hightower).

Welles, Mel (1930-). Films: "Gun Fury" 1953; "Massacre Canyon" 1954 (Gonzales); "Wyoming Renegades" 1955 (Whiskey Pearson). ¶TV: *Tales of the Texas Rangers*—"Blood Trail" 9-24-55 (Karl Henckel); *Sheriff of Cochise*—"Bandit Chief" 2-15-57 (Mora); *The Adventures of Rin Tin Tin*—"Border Incident" 3-28-58 (Gomez); *Have Gun Will Travel*—"The Protege" 10-18-58 (Red Harper); *Maverick*—"The Judas Mask" 11-2-58 (Carlos); *The Texan*—"The Ringer" 2-16-59; *The Deputy*—"The Deal" 12-5-59 (Jack Usher).

Welles, Orson (1915-10/10/85). Films: "Duel in the Sun" 1946 (Narrator); "Man in the Shadow" 1957 (Virgil Renchler); "Blood and Guns" 1968-Ital./Span.

Welles, Rebecca. TV: *Gunsmoke*—"Moon" 5-11-57 (Nan Mellors); *Boots and Saddles*—"The Treasure" 12-12-57 (Laurie); *Trackdown*—"The Brothers" 5-16-58 (Julie); *The Californians*—"Bridal Bouquet" 6-10-58 (Cora Sue Sommers), "The Fugitive" 4-28-59 (Clara Keel); *Northwest Passage*—"The Bound Women" 10-12-58 (Maureen Carver); *Wagon Train*—"The Flint McCullough Story" 1-14-59 (Jean Yates);

Zorro—"The Iron Box" 1-15-59 (Moneta); *Bat Masterson*—"Brunette Bombshell" 4-1-59 (Isabel Fowler); *Bronco*—"Shadow of a Man" 5-19-59 (Lynne Henderson); *Man from Blackhawk*—"The Harpoon Story" 5-6-60 (Janet).

Wellman, William (1896-12/9/75). Films: "The Knickerbocker Buckaroo" 1919 (Mercedes' Brother).

Wellman, Jr., William (1937-). Films: "The Horse Soldiers" 1959 (Bugler); "Gunfight at Comanche Creek" 1964; "Young Fury" 1965 (Peters). ¶TV: *Gunsmoke*—"There Never Was a Horse" 5-16-59 (Roy); *Have Gun Will Travel*—"Episode in Laredo" 9-19-59, "The Posse" 10-3-59 (Man), "The Gold Toad" 11-21-59 (Bob), "Never Help the Devil" 4-16-60, "Coming of the Tiger" 4-14-62 (Billy); *Rawhide*—"Incident at Rojo Canyon" 9-30-60 (Chatsworth), "The Reunion" 4-6-62 (Sergeant Bennett), "Incident of the Dogfaces" 11-9-62 (Harvey Dobkins), "Incident at Hourglass" 3-12-64; *Laramie*—"The High Country" 2-6-62 (Tim Bishop), "Naked Steel" 1-1-63, "The Violent Ones" 3-5-63.

Wells, Allan. Films: "Apache Chief" 1949 (Lame Bull); The Great Missouri Raid" 1951 (Dick Liddil); "Man with the Steel Whip" 1954-serial (Quivar); "Canyon Crossroads" 1955 (Charlie Rivers); "The Return of Jack Slade" 1955 (George Hagen). ¶TV: *Wild Bill Hickok*—"The Sheriff's Secret" 10-21-52, "Return of Chief Red Hawk" 2-10-53; *The Lone Ranger*—"The Red Mark" 9-3-53, "The Avenger" 1-10-57; *The Cisco Kid*—"Vendetta" 11-14-53; *The Roy Rogers Show*—"Bad Neighbors" 11-21-54 (Jeff Clark), "Outcasts of Paradise Valley" 1-9-55 (Lou Woodburn); *Death Valley Days*—"The Seventh Day" 3-14-55; *Tales of the Texas Rangers*—"Horseman on the Sierras" 1-14-56 (Bear McCord); *Wyatt Earp*—"Killing at Cowskin Creek" 2-14-56 (Jeff Burns), "It Had to Happen" 4-1-58 (George Hoyt), "Johnny Ringo's Girl" 12-13-60; *Zane Grey Theater*—"A Time to Live" 4-5-57; *The Adventures of Rin Tin Tin*—"The Old Man of the Mountain" 6-21-57 (Sun in the Sky); *Tales of Wells Fargo*—"Chips" 11-4-57; *Cheyenne*—"Town of Fear" 12-3-57 (Teddy Curtis); *The Texan*—"The Man with the Solid Gold Star" 10-6-58; *Trackdown*—"Matter of Justice" 10-17-58 (Dorcas); *Wanted—Dead or Alive*—"Drop to Drink" 12-27-58 (Sam Jarvis), "Reunion for Revenge" 1-24-59 (Cutler), "The Kovack Affair" 3-28-59 (Charlie), "Man on Horseback" 12-5-59.

Wells, Carole (1942-). Films: "A Thunder of Drums" 1961 (Camden Yates) ¶TV: *Maverick*—"The Lass with the Poisonous Air" 11-1-59 (Cathy), "Maverick and Juliet" 1-17-60 (Juliet Carteret); *Fury*—"Packy's Dream" 3-19-60 (Babs Nelson); *Wagon Train*—"The Mary Beckett Story" 5-9-62 (Ginny Beckett); *Wide Country*—"Tears on a Painted Face" 11-29-62 (Holly); *Laramie*—"Gun Duel" 12-25-62; *Pistols 'n' Petticoats*—Regular 1966-67 (Lucy Hanks); *The Virginian*—"The Welcoming Town" 3-22-67 (Kathy Atkins).

Wells, Dawn. Films: "Winterhawk" 1975 (Clayanna). ¶TV: *Maverick*—"Deadly Image" 3-12-61 (Caprice Rambeau); *Wagon Train*—"The Captain Dan Brady Story" 9-27-61 (Mrs. Murray); *Tales of Wells Fargo*—"Kelly's Clover Girls" 12-9-61 (Molly); *Lawman*—"No Contest" 2-4-62 (Elly Stratton); *Bonanza*—"The Way Station" 10-29-62 (Marty), "The Burning Sky" 1-28-68 (Moon Holt); *Laramie*—"The Violent Ones" 3-5-63 (Millie); *Wild Wild West*—"The Night of the Headless Woman" 1-5-68 (Betsy Jeffers).

Wells, Jacqueline. *see* Bishop, Julie.

Wells, John. *see* Volonte, Gian Maria.

Wells, L.M. (1862-1/1/23). Films: "Liberty" 1916-serial; "The Passing of Hell's Crown" 1916; "Bucking Broadway" 1917 (Molly's Father); "The Red Ace" 1917-serial; "Right-of-Way Casey" 1917; "The Flame of the West" 1918; "Thieves' Gold" 1918 (Mr. Savage); "The Forfeit" 1919 (Bud Tristam); "Runnin' Straight" 1920; "Vanishing Trails" 1920-serial.

Wells, Marie (1894-7/2/49). Films: "The Man from New York" 1923 (Ruth Crawford); "Song of the West" 1930 (Lotta); "Beyond the Rockies" 1932 (Ruby Sherman); "Call of the Wild" 1935 (Hilda).

Wells, Maurice (1903-6/26/78). TV: *Rough Riders*—"Strand of Wire" 12-18-58 (James Randolph); *The Big Valley*—"Rimfire" 2-19-68 (Mule Skinner).

Wells, Raymond (1881-8/9/41). Films: "Anything Once" 1917 (Horned Toad Smith); "Tony Runs Wild" 1926 (Sheriff); "The Unknown Cavalier" 1926 (Bad Man); "The Yankee Senor" 1926 (Ranch Foreman); "Death Valley" 1927 (the Man); "Burning Brides" 1928 (Slabs); "Trails of Adventure" 1935.

Wells, Roxene. Films: "The

Oregon Trail" 1959 (Flossie Shoemaker).

Wells, Sheilah. TV: *The Virginian*—"Six Graves at Cripple Creek" 1-27-65 (Lucille Carver); *Laredo*—"It's the End of the Road, Stanley" 3-10-66 (Marryann); *Wild Wild West*—"The Night of the Cadre" 3-24-67 (Josephine); *Bonanza*—"A Girl Named George" 1-14-68 (George), "Winter Kill" 3-28-71 (Landis).

Wells, Ted (Pawnee Bill, Jr.) (1899-6/7/48) Films: "Desert Dust" 1927 (Frank Fortune); "Shooting Straight" 1927 (Jack Roberts); "Straight Shootin'" 1927 (Jack Roberts); "Across the Plains" 1928 (Jim Blake); "Arizona Speed" 1928; "Beauty and Bullets" 1928 (Bill Allen); "The Border Wildcat" 1928 (Sheriff Bob Shaw); "Cheyenne Trails" 1928; "The Clean-Up Man" 1928 (Steve Banning/Johnny Parker); "The Crimson Canyon" 1928 (Phil "Six Gun" Lang); "Forbidden Trails" 1928; "Greased Lightning" 1928 (Johnny Parker); "Made-to-Order Hero" 1928 (Bert Lane); "Texas Flash" 1928; "The Thrill Chaser" 1928; "Thunder Riders" 1928 (Jack Duncan); "Where the West Begins" 1928; "Born to the Saddle" 1929 (Ted Dorgan); "Grit Wins" 1929 (Jack Deering); "The Ridin' Demon" 1929 (Dan Riordan/Pat Riordan); "The Smiling Terror" 1929 (Ted Wayne); "White Renegade" 1931; "Defying the Law" 1935 (Captain Bill Taylor); "The Phantom Cowboy" 1935 (Bill Collins/the Phantom Rider); "The Lone Ranger Rides Again" 1939-serial (Raider #4); "Geronimo" 1940 (Soldier Wall); "West of Carson City" 1940 (Slim); "The Westerner" 1940 (Joe Lawrence); "Border Vigilantes" 1941; "Undercover Man" 1942 (Jim, the Rancher); "Sundown Riders" 1948 (Bill).

Wells, Tiny. Films: "Hawmps!" 1976 (Higgins); "Wanda Nevada" 1979; "High Noon, Part II: The Return of Will Kane" TVM-1980 (Riley).

Wells, Vernon. Films: "Sunset" 1988 (Australian Houseman).

Welsh, James. Films: "The Broken Spur" 1921 (Bill Lambert); "Barb Wire" 1922 (Bob Lorne); "The Sheriff of Sun-Dog" 1922 (Scott Martin); "God's Law" 1923; "The Red Warning" 1923 (David Ainslee); "Wolf Tracks" 1923 (Bob Meredith); "Behind Two Guns" 1924; "Tonio, Son of the Sierras" 1925 (Col. Archer); "Warrior Gap" 1925 (Col. Stevens); "Blue Blazes" 1926 (McKeller); "The Desperate Game" 1926 (Jim's Father); "Speedy Spurs" 1926 (Luke Tuttle); "West of the Rainbow's End" 1926 (Abe Brandon); "The Pinto Kid" 1928 (Andy Bruce); "Rough Ridin' Red" 1928 (Pap Curtis); "A Son of the Desert" 1928 (Col. Dobson); "Wizard of the Saddle" 1928 (Pop Adams); "Headin' North" 1930 (Old Actor); "Ruggles of Red Gap" 1935 (Man in Saloon).

Welsh, Kenneth. TV: *Lonesome Dove*—"Duty Bound" 11-6-94 (Col. Paget).

Welsh, William (William Welch) (1870-7/16/46). Films: "Bull's Eye" 1918-serial; "Crossed Clues" 1921; "Roaring Waters" 1921; "The Lone Hand" 1922 (Al Sheridan); "Ridin' Wild" 1922 (John Henderson); "Dead Game" 1923 (Harris); "The Ramblin' Kid" 1923 (Lafe Dorsey); "The Red Warning" 1923 (George Ainslee); "Shadows of the North" 1923 (Jeffrey Neilson); "Shootin' em Up" 1923; "Shootin' for Love" 1923 (Bill Randolph); "The Man from Wyoming" 1924 (David Messiter); "The Western Wallop" 1924 (Italian Convict); "Don Dare Devil" 1925 (Jose Remado); "The Fighting Ranger" 1925-serial; "Flying Hoofs" 1925 (Banker Conner); "The Red Rider" 1925 (Ben Hanfer); "Two-Fisted Jones" 1925 (Henry Mortimer); "The White Outlaw" 1925 (Malcolm Gale); "The Demon" 1926 (Percival Wade); "The Man from the West" 1926 (Bill Hayes); "The Set-Up" 1926 (Sheriff Hayes); "Western Pluck" 1926 (Dynamite Dan Dyer); "Chain Lightning" 1927 (George Clearwater); "Hills of Peril" 1927 (Grimes); "The Western Rover" 1927 (Alexander Seaton); "Daredevil's Reward" 1928 (James Powell); "Sundown Trail" 1931 (Pa Stoddard); "Beyond the Rockies" 1932 (Frank Allen); "Freighters of Destiny" 1932 (Mercer); "Ruggles of Red Gap" 1935 (Eddie); "Stormy" 1935 (Old Miner); "Wanderer of the Wasteland" 1935 (1st Man); "Cavalry" 1936 (General John Harvey).

Wendell, Bruce. TV: *Gunsmoke*—"Doc's Reward" 12-14-57 (Joe); *Rawhide*—"Incident of the Shambling Men" 10-9-59; *Maverick*—"The Town That Wasn't Threre" 10-2-60 (Henry Pitkin).

Wendell, Howard (1908-8/11/75). Films: "The Black Dakotas" 1954 (Judge Baker); "A Day of Fury" 1956 (Vanryzin). TV: *Wyatt Earp*—"The Suffragette" 3-27-56 (Senator Teague), "They Hired Some Guns" 2-26-57 (Mike Teague), "Remittance Man" 11-4-58 (Henry Dart); *Jim Bowie*—"The Lottery" 4-19-57 (Col. Elmwood); *The Texan*—"A Time of the Year" 12-22-58 (Doc Morton); *Zorro*—"The Gay Caballero" 1-22-59 (Don Marcos); *The Restless Gun*—"One on the House" 4-20-59 (Taylor); *Bonanza*—"House Divided" 1-16-60 (Mine Owner), "Bank Run" 1-28-61, "Sam Hill" 6-3-61 (Willis), "The Last Haircut" 2-3-63, "The Flapjack Contest" 1-3-65 (Banker); *Rawhide*—"Incident at Sulphur Creek" 3-11-60 (Porteous); *The Deputy*—"The X Game" 5-28-60 (Webb); *Wagon Train*—"The Kitty Allbright Story" 10-4-61 (Father Allbright); *The Virginian*—"Say Goodbye to All That" 1-23-63; *Gunsmoke*—"Ex-Con" 11-30-63 (Judge), "Owney Tupper Had a Daughter" 4-4-64 (Judge), "Old Man" 10-10-64; *Laredo*—"Pride of the Rangers" 12-16-65, "That's Noway, Thataway" 1-20-66, "The Legend of Midas Mantee" 9-16-66 (Winston); *The Big Valley*—"The Man from Nowhere" 11-14-66 (Simon Blair).

Wengraf, John (1897-5/4/74). Films: "The Gambler from Natchez" 1954 (Cadiz); "Valerie" 1957 (Louis Horvat). TV: *Tombstone Territory*—"Death Is to Write About" 5-29-59; *Bat Masterson*—"The Desert Ship" 7-15-59 (Anders Dorn); *Bonanza*—"Desert Justice" 2-20-60 (Dr. Strasser); *Colt .45*—"The Gandy Dancers" 5-10-60 (Kozak).

Wenland, Burt. Films: "Trail of the Yukon" 1949. TV: *Wild Bill Hickok*—"A Close Shave for the Marshal" 4-29-52, "The Music Teacher" 12-2-52, "Ghost Town Lady" 1-27-53.

Wentworth, Martha (1889-3/8/74). Films: "Santa Fe Uprising" 1946; "Stagecoach to Denver" 1946 (the Duchess); "Homesteaders of Paradise Valley" 1947; "The Marshal of Cripple Creek" 1947 (the Duchess); "Oregon Trail Scouts" 1947 (the Duchess); "Rustlers of Devil's Canyon" 1947 (the Duchess); "Vigilantes of Boomtown" 1947 (the Duchess). TV: *Northwest Passage*—"The Witch" 2-13-59 (Mrs. Wilcox).

Wenzel, Arthur (1907-2/10/61). Films: "South of the Border" 1939; "Bad Men of Thunder Gap" 1943 (Cal Shrum's Rhythm Rangers); "Cowboy from Lonesome River" 1944.

Werle, Barbara (1934-). Films: "Tickle Me" 1965 (Barbara); "The Rare Breed" 1966 (Gert); "Gunfight in Abilene" 1967 (Leann); "Charro!" 1969 (Sara Ramsey). TV: *Laredo*—"A Question of Discipline" 10-28-65

(Rosalinda), "Leave It to Dixie" 12-30-66 (Molly), "Enemies and Brother" 2-17-67 (Liza Curtis); *The Virginian*—"An Echo of Thunder" 10-5-66 (Dolores), "Stacey" 2-28-68 (Mrs. Buell), "Ride the Misadventure" 11-6-68 (Clair), "Train of Darkness" 2-4-70 (Evangeline); *The Road West*—"Power of Fear" 12-26-66 (Ruth Burrus), "The Agreement" 4-24-67 (Laura Bishop).

Wertimer, Ned (1923-). Films: "Bad Company" 1972 (Bishop's Father). ¶TV: *Gunsmoke*—"MacGraw" 12-8-69 (Jed Douglas); *How the West Was Won*—Episode One 2-6-77 (Elias Kulp), Episode Two 2-7-77 (Elias Kulp), Episode Three 2-14-77 (Elias Kulp).

Wescoatt, Rusty (1911-9/3/87). Films: "Roar of the Iron Horse" 1950-serial (Scully); "When the Redskins Rode" 1951 (Znueau); "Brave Warrior" 1952 (Standish); "Snowfire" 1958 (Luke Stoner). ¶TV: *Wild Bill Hickok*—"The Doctor Story" 7-1-52 (Ben), "Counterfeit Ghost" 8-11-53; *The Lone Ranger*—"The Condemned Man" 12-11-52; *The Gene Autry Show*—"Steel Ribbon" 9-22-53, "Ransom Cross" 10-6-53; *The Roy Rogers Show*—"The Outlaws of Paradise Valley" 11-8-53, "The Peddler from the Pecos" 12-13-53 (Joe Burnside), "Little Dynamite" 1-3-54 (Fred Willow), "Hidden Treasure" 12-19-54, "The Big Chance" 1-23-55 (Lefty Young), "Junior Outlaw" 2-10-57, "Portrait of Murder" 3-17-57; *Sergeant Preston of the Yukon*—"Fancy Dan" 4-5-56 (Madigan); *The Adventures of Rin Tin Tin*—"Rinty Finds a Bone" 4-27-56; *Circus Boy*—"Hortense the Hippo" 6-2-57 (Deputy); *Gunsmoke*—"The Man Who Would Be Marshal" 6-15-57 (Gere); *Tales of the Texas Rangers*—"Riders of the Lone Star" 12-1-57 (Blackie); *Maverick*—"A Rage for Vengeance" 1-12-58 (2nd Passenger), "The Belcastle Brand" 10-12-58 (Outlaw Leader), "Bundle from Britain" 9-18-60 (Muldoon); *Trackdown*—"The Mistake" 4-18-58 (Bartender), "The Trick" 4-15-59; *Wanted—Dead or Alive*—"Call Your Shot" 2-7-59; *Lawman*—"Mountain Man" 3-25-62 (Blacksmith); *The Legend of Jesse James*—"The Judas Boot" 11-8-65 (Blacksmith).

Wescott, Gordon (1903-10/31/35). Films: "Heritage of the Desert" 1932 (Snap Nash).

Wescourt, Gordon (1936-). TV: *Redigo*—"The Black Rainbow" 12-24-63 (Bert Baker); *Temple Houston*—"The Case for William Gotch" 2-6-64 (Bryce); *Bonanza*—"The Code" 2-13-66 (Win); *The Monroes*—"Range War" 12-21-66.

Wessel, Max. Films: "Rangeland" 1922 (Bud Spaugh); "West of the Pecos" 1922 (Joe Madison).

Wessel, Richard (1913-4/20/65). Films: "Round-Up Time in Texas" 1937 (Craig Johnson); "The Border Legion" 1940 (Red); "Desert Bandit" 1941 (Hawk); "Red River Valley" 1941; "They Died with Their Boots On" 1941 (Staff Sgt. Brown); "Bells of Capistrano" 1942; "Romance on the Range" 1942; "Sunset Serenade" 1942; "King of the Cowboys" 1943 (Hershel); "Silver Spurs" 1943 (Buck Walters); "Dakota" 1945 (Roughneck); "California" 1946 (Blacksmith); "In Old Sacramento" 1946 (Oscar); "River Lady" 1948 (Logger); "Bad Men of Tombstone" 1949 (Bartender); "Canadian Pacific" 1949 (Bailey); "Frontier Outpost" 1950 (Sgt. Murphy); "Punchy Cowpunchers" 1950-short (Sgt. Mullins); "The Lawless Breed" 1952 (Marv, the Bartender); "Rancho Notorious" 1952 (Deputy); "Untamed Heiress" 1954 (Cruncher); "The Desperados Are in Town" 1956 (Hank). ¶TV: *Wild Bill Hickok*—"The Steam Wagon" 5-12-53; *The Lone Ranger*—"Gold Freight" 4-28-55; *Fury*—"Scorched Earth" 11-12-55 (Fred); *Broken Arrow*—"The Captive" 10-23-56 (Bartender); *Riverboat*—"Escape to Memphis" 10-25-59 (Carnel), "Strange Request" 12-13-59 (Carney); *Pony Express*—"The Wedding of Big Zack" 4-27-60 (Big Zack); *Rawhide*—"Judgment at Hondo Seco" 10-20-61 (Barker), "Incident at Confidence Creek" 11-28-63 (Jed); *Bonanza*—"Cut-Throat Junction" 3-18-61; *Laramie*—"Strange Company" 6-6-61 (Higgins); *Daniel Boone*—"Four-Leaf Clover" 3-25-65 (Moses Hennepin); *Gunsmoke*—"Honey Pot" 5-15-65 (Sol Durham).

Wesson, Dick (1919-1/27/79). Films: "The Man Behind the Gun" 1952 (Monk); "Calamity Jane" 1953 (Francis Fryer); "The Charge at Feather River" 1953 (Cullen).

Wesson, Eileen (1948-). Films: "Journey to Shiloh" 1968 (Ella Newsome). ¶TV: *Laredo*—"The Short, Happy Fatherhood of Reese Bennett" 1-27-67; *The Virginian*—"With Help from Ulysses" 1-17-68 (Betty Martin).

Wesson, Gene (1921-8/22/75). Films: "Wichita" 1955 (1st Robber).

West, Adam (1929-). Films: "Geronimo" 1962 (Delahay); "The Outlaws Is Coming!" 1965 (Kenneth Cabot); "Relentless Four" 1966-Span./Ital. (Marshal Garrett);

"Nevada Smith" TVM-1975 (Frank Hartlee). ¶TV: *Sugarfoot*—"The Mysterious Straner" 2-17-59 (Frederick Pulaski), "The Trial of the Canary Kid" 9-15-59 (Doc Holliday); *Maverick*—"Two Tickets to Ten Strike" 3-15-59 (Vic Nolan), "Pappy" 9-13-59 (Rudolph St. Cloud), "A Fellow's Brother" 11-22-59 (Henry Arnett); *Colt .45*—"The Escape" 4-5-59 (Sgt. Ed Kallen), "Don't Tell Joe" 6-14-59 (Marshal Joe Benjamin), "The Devil's Godson" 10-18-59 (Doc Holliday); *Lawman*—"The Wayfarer" 6-7-59 (Doc Holliday); *Cheyenne*—"Blind Spot" 9-21-59 (Ashley); *Bronco*—"The Burning Spring" 10-6-59 (Major Carter); *Laramie*—"Man from Kansas" 1-10-61 (Deputy), "The Betrayers" 1-22-63 (Kett Darby); *Tales of Wells Fargo*—"The Has-Been" 1-16-61 (Steve Daco); *Bonanza*—"The Bride" 1-21-61 (Frank Milton); *The Rifleman*—"Stopover" 4-25-61 (Rolf); *Gunsmoke*—"Ash" 2-16-63 (Emmett Hall); *The Virginian*—"Legend for a Lawman" 3-3-65 (Sam Loomis); *The Big Valley*—"In Silent Battle" 9-23-68 (Major Jonathan Elliot); *Alias Smith and Jones*—"The Man Who Corrupted Hadleyburg" 1-27-72 (Brubaker).

West, Billie (1891-6/7/67). Films: "The Angel of the Gulch" 1914; "Blue Peter's Escape" 1914; "The Arrow Maiden" 1915; "The Last Card" 1915; "The Hidden Spring" 1917.

West, Billy (1893-7/21/75). Films: "Diamond Trail" 1933 (Lefty).

West, Charles H. (1885-10/10/43). Films: "In Old California" 1910; "A Romance of the Western Hills" 1910; "That Chink at Golden Gulch" 1910; "The Last Drop of Water" 1911; "Black Sheep" 1912; "Fate's Interception" 1912; "The Female of the Species" 1912; "Goddess of Sagebrush Gulch" 1912 (Blue-Grass Pete); "Iola's Promise" 1912; "A Lodging for the Night" 1912; "The Massacre" 1912; "A Temporary Truce" 1912; "The Tourists" 1912; "Just Gold" 1913; "The Gambler of the West" 1914 (Dan Reardon); "The Indian" 1914; "The Battle of Frenchman's Run" 1915; "The Gambler's I.O.U." 1915; "The Heart of a Bandit" 1915; "Revenge" 1918 (Donald Jaffray); "Bob Hampton of Placer" 1921 (Maj. Brant); "In the North Woods" 1921; "Law of the West" 1932 (Clem Tracy); "The Man Trailer" 1934 (Gorman).

West, Christopher (1936-). Films: "El Dorado" 1967.

West, Ford (1873-1/3/36). Films: "The King of the Wild Horses" 1933 (Davidson).

West, Henry (1868-1/29/36). Films: "All Man" 1916 (McKin); "The Crimson Dove" 1917 (Jim Carewe).

West, Jennifer. TV: *Buckskin*—"A Permanent Juliet" 10-23-58 (Chrissie Miller); *Bronco*—"The Masquerade" 1-26-60 (Anne Davis); *Sugarfoot*—"The Long Dry" 4-10-60 (Anne Carmody); *The Outlaws*—"Assassin" 2-9-61 (Marcia Fremont); *Here Come the Brides*—"And Jason Makes Five" 10-9-68 (Holly Houston), "Debt of Honor" 1-23-70 (Holly); *Gunsmoke*—"Hackett" 3-16-70 (Geneva Sargent).

West, Josephine. Films: "A Cowboy's Mother" 1912; "The Curse of the Great Southwest" 1913; "Bringing in the Law" 1914; "The Pirates of the Plains" 1914; "The Great Barrier" 1915; "Told in the Rockies" 1915.

West, Judi (1939-). Films: "A Man Called Gannon" 1969 (Beth). ¶TV: *Gunsmoke*—"Lavery" 2-22-71 (April).

West, Lillian. Films: "Boots and Saddles" 1916 (Lucy Ward); "The Hidden Children" 1917 (Jeanne de Contrecoeur); "Barriers of Folly" 1922 (Madge Spencer).

West, Mae (1892-11/22/80). Films: "My Little Chickadee" 1940 (Flower Belle Lee).

West, Martin (1934-). Films: "The Man from Galveston" 1964 (Stonewall Grey); "Soldier Blue" 1970 (Lt. Spingarn). ¶TV: *Have Gun Will Travel*—"Bear Bait" 5-13-61 (Bunk), "Pandora's Box" 5-19-62 (Billy Joe); *Temple Houston*—"The Man from Galveston" 1963 (Stonewall Grey), "The Town That Trespassed" 3-26-64 (Lawson); *The Virginian*—"Man of the People" 12-23-64 (Lt. David O'Mara); *Gunsmoke*—"Prime of Life" 5-7-66 (Jack Brown); *Bonanza*—"Judgment at Red Creek" 2-26-67 (Hill); *Rango*—"If You Can't Take It with You, Don't Go" 4-21-67 (Kurt Larson).

West, Neva (1883-10/5/65). Films: "Broncho Billy and the Revenue Agent" 1916.

West, Pat (1889-4/10/44). Films: "Rose Marie" 1936 (Traveling Salesman); "Song of the Saddle" 1936 (Curley); "High, Wide and Handsome" 1937 (Razorback); "The Texans" 1938 (Real Estate Man); "Geronimo" 1940 (Soldier); "When the Daltons Rode" 1940 (Pete, the Restaurant Owner); "The Outlaw" 1943 (Bartender).

West, Red (1933-). Films: "Proud Men" TVM-1987 (Cookie); "Once Upon a Texas Train" TVM-1988. ¶TV: *Wild Wild West*—"The Night of the Circus of Death" 11-3-67, "The Night of the Cut Throats" 11-17-67, "The Night of the Iron Fist" 12-8-67 (Roy), "The Night of the Vipers" 1-12-68 (Jack Claxton), "The Night of the Underground Terror" 1-19-68 (Lt. Maverly), "The Night of the Doomsday Formula" 10-4-68 (Guard), "The Night of the Sedgewick Curse" 10-18-68 (Man), "The Night of the Gruesome Games" 10-25-68, "The Night of Fire and Brimstone" 11-22-68 (Chuck), "The Night of the Avaricious Actuary" 12-6-68, "The Night of the Sabatini Death" 2-2-69 (Heavy), "The Night of the Janus" 2-15-69 (Villain), "The Night of the Plague" 4-4-69 (Carl).

West, Tony (1867-6/25/23). Films: "Dead Game" 1923 (Hiram).

West, Wally (Tom Wynn) (1902-). Films: "Courageous Avenger" 1935; "Danger Trails" 1935; "Desert Mesa" 1935 (Jim Kirk); "Desert Trail" 1935; "Hopalong Cassidy" 1935; "Justice of the Range" 1935; "Riding Wild" 1935; "Thunderbolt" 1935; "Ambush Valley" 1936 (Nester); "Outlaws of the Range" 1936 (Deputy); "Pinto Rustlers" 1936; "Ridin' On" 1936; "Rip Roarin' Buckaroo" 1936; "Roamin' Wild" 1936 (Jim Barton); "Roarin' Guns" 1936; "Rogue of the Range" 1936 (Prison Guard); "Santa Fe Bound" 1936 (Deputy); "The Traitor" 1936 (Bud); "Vengeance of Rannah" 1936 (Stranger); "Vigilantes Are Coming" 1936-serial (Rancher); "Boots of Destiny" 1937; "Fighting Texan" 1937 (Henchman); "Ghost Town Gold" 1937; "Hit the Saddle" 1937 (Patron); "A Lawman Is Born" 1937; "The Red Rope" 1937; "Riders of the Whistling Skull" 1937; "Trail of Vengeance" 1937 (Rancher); "The Trusted Outlaw" 1937; "Two-Fisted Sheriff" 1937; "Where Trails Divide" 1937; "Cattle Raiders" 1938; "Colorado Kid" 1938; "The Feud Maker" 1938; "Gunsmoke Trail" 1938; "Phantom Ranger" 1938; "Renfrew on the Great White Trail" 1938; "Whirlwind Horseman" 1938; "Straight Shooter" 1939; "Sundown on the Prairie" 1939 (Slim); "Trigger Pals" 1939 (Jim); "Cowboy from Sundown" 1940; "Death Rides the Range" 1940; "Melody Ranch" 1940; "Phantom Rancher" 1940; "Rhythm of the Rio Grande" 1940; "The Sagebrush Family Trails West" 1940 (Hank); "Bad Man of Deadwood" 1941; "Billy the Kid Wanted" 1941; "Billy the Kid's Fighting Pals" 1941; "Billy the Kid's Roundup" 1941; "The Driftin' Kid" 1941; "Gangs of Sonora" 1941; "The Lone Rider in Frontier Fury" 1941; "The Lone Rider Rides On" 1941; "Billy the Kid Trapped" 1942; "Code of the Outlaw" 1942; "Black Market Rustlers" 1943; "Raiders of Red Gap" 1943; "The Renegade" 1943; "Death Valley Rangers" 1944; "Cowboy and the Senorita" 1944; "Death Valley Rangers" 1944; "The Drifter" 1944; "Bells of Rosarita" 1945; "Gangster's Den" 1945 (Deputy); "The Man from Oklahoma" 1945; "Gentleman from Texas" 1946; "Overland Riders" 1946; "Pioneer Justice" 1947; "Stage to Mesa City" 1947; "Check Your Guns" 1948; "Marshal of Heldorado" 1950 (Bagen); "Son of Geronimo" 1952-serial. ¶TV: *The Roy Rogers Show*—"The Knockout" 12-28-52 (Mack Fuller), "The Silver Fox Hunt" 4-19-53, "Bad Company" 12-27-53, "The Hijackers" 10-24-54, "Strangers" 12-5-54, "False Faces" 2-5-56, "His Weight in Wildcats" 11-11-56, "Tossup" 12-2-56, "End of the Trail" 1-27-57, "Accessory to Crime" 3-3-57; *Brave Eagle*—"The Spirit of Hidden Valley" 1-4-56.

West, William H. (1860-8/28/15). Films: "The Indian Uprising at Santa Fe" 1912; "Red Wing and the Paleface" 1912; "The Water Right War" 1912; "The Pride of Angry Bear" 1913; "The Skeleton in the Closet" 1913.

West, William Lyons. Films: "The Apache Renegade" 1912; "Driver of the Deadwood Coast" 1912; "The Peril of the Cliffs" 1912; "At Bear Track Gulch" 1913; "The Big Horn Massacre" 1913; "The Invaders" 1913; "The Last Blockhouse" 1913; "The Man from the West" 1913; "On the Brink of Ruin" 1913; "The Death Sign at High Noon" 1914; "The Man in Irons" 1915; "Dangerous Love" 1920 (Cafe Owner); "Heart of the North" 1921 (Mad Pierre Maupome); "Western Courage" 1935.

Westcott, Helen (1929-). Films: "Thunder Over Texas" 1934 (Tiny); "The Gunfighter" 1950 (Peggy Walsh); "The Secret of Convict Lake" 1951 (Susan Haggerty); "The Battles of Chief Pontiac" 1952 (Winifred Lancester); "Return of the Texan" 1952 (Averill); "The Charge at Feather River" 1953 (Ann McKeever); "Cow Country" 1953 (Linda Garnet); "Gun Belt" 1953 (Arlene Reach); "I Killed Wild Bill Hickok" 1956 (Bell Longtree); "Day of the Outlaw" 1959 (Vivian). ¶TV: *Jefferson Drum*—"Stagecoach Episode" 10-10-58 (Hilda); *Schlitz Playhouse of the Stars*—"A Tale of Wells Fargo" 12-14-58 (Bess); *Rawhide*—"Incident of the

Day of the Dead" 9-18-59; *Bonanza*—"The Fear Merchants" 1-30-60 (Amanda Ridley), "The Colonel" 1-6-63 (Emily); *Wanted—Dead or Alive*—"A House Divided" 2-20-60; *Pony Express*—"The Story of Julesburg" 3-9-60 (Lucy).

Westerfield, James (1913-9/20/71). Films: "Three Hours to Kill" 1954 (Sam Minor); "Chief Crazy Horse" 1955 (Caleb Mantz); "Man with the Gun" 1955 (Drummer); "The Violent Men" 1955 (Magruder); "Decision at Sundown" 1957 (Otis); "Cowboy" 1958 (Mike Adams); "The Proud Rebel" 1958 (Birm Bates, the Sheep Buyer); "The Gunfight at Dodge City" 1959 (Rev. Howard); "The Hangman" 1959 (Herb Loftus); "The Plunderers" 1960 ((Mike Baron, Saloon Owner); "The Sons of Katie Elder" 1965 (Banker Vannar); "Scalplock" TVM-1966 (Nehemiah); "Blue" 1968 (Abe); "Hang 'Em High" 1968 (Prisoner); "A Man Called Gannon" 1969 (Amos); "Smith" 1969 (Sheriff); "True Grit" 1969 (Judge Parker); "Lucky Johnny: Born in America" 1973-Ital./Mex. ¶TV: *The Lone Ranger*—"Texas Draw" 11-5-54 (Crane Dillon); *Gunsmoke*—"Hot Spell" 9-17-55 (Rance Bradley), "How to Kill a Friend" 11-22-58 (Harry Duggan), "Anybody Can Kill a Marshal" 3-9-63 (Cleed), "The Still" 11-10-69 (Franks); *Zane Grey Theater*—"Courage Is a Gun" 12-14-56 (Bert); *Telephone Time*—"Elfego Baca" 4-18-57 (Wilson), "Sam Houston's Decision" 12-10-57 (Edward Burleson); *Wagon Train*—"The Riley Gratton Story" 12-4-57 (McSorley); *Jim Bowie*—"Home Sweet Home" 1-31-58 (Joe Heacock), "Bowie's Baby" 5-2-58 (McQueen); *The Californians*—"The Man from Paris" 2-11-58 (Buck Carteret); *Trackdown*—"The Deal" 4-25-58 (Dingo Noble); *The Texan*—"A Tree for Planting" 11-10-58 (Sam Bofert); *Bat Masterson*—"Bear Bait" 11-12-58 (Shapley Howell); *Rawhide*—"Incident at the Curious Street" 4-10-59 (Matt Lucas); *The Rifleman*—"The Woman" 5-5-59, "The Fourflusher" 5-3-60 (Jake Preston); *Rough Riders*—"Forty-Five Calibre Law" 5-14-59 (Judge Tolt); *Wanted—Dead or Alive*—"The Healing Woman" 9-12-59 (Dr. Langland), "Vanishing Act" 12-26-59 (Frank Decker); *The Deputy*—"Like Father" 10-17-59 (Ches Vantage); *The Alaskans*—"Starvation Stampede" 11-1-59 (Jess Rodick); *Maverick*—The Ghost Soldiers" 11-8-59 (Sergeant Baines), "The Art Lovers" 10-1-61 (Paul Sutton); *The Rebel*—"The Scavengers" 11-8-59 (Siouxy); *Texas John*

Slaughter—"Range War at Tombstone" 12-18-59 (Ike Clanton); *Johnny Ringo*—"Bound Boy" 12-31-59 (Aben Burke); *Tombstone Territory*—2-19-60 (Big Jim Gerson); *Bonanza*—"The Trail Gang" 11-26-60 (Sheriff Logan), "The Lady and the Mark" 2-1-70 (Blackwell); *The Law of the Plainsman*—"Trojan Horse" 5-5-60 (Joshua); *They Went Thataway*—Pilot 8-15-60 (Black Ace Burton); *Laramie*—"Killer Without Cause" 1-24-61 (Carl Vail); *The Tall Man*—"Maria's Little Lamb" 2-25-61 (Maddock); *Lawman*—"The Son" 10-8-61 (Zachariah Herod); *Tales of Wells Fargo*—"Remember the Yazoo" 4-14-62 (Sam Heffridge); *Wide Country*—"What Are Friends For?" 10-18-62 (Sheriff Morse); *The Dakotas*—"Feud at Snake River" 4-29-63 (Simon Deus); *The Travels of Jaimie McPheeters*—Regular 1963-64 (John Murrel); *Daniel Boone*—"A Short Walk to Salem" 11-19-64 (Simon Girty); "The Scrimshaw Ivory Chart" 1-4-68 (Hand); *Walt Disney Presents*—"Gallegher" 1965-67 (Charles Mardis); *The Outcasts*—"The Heroes" 11-11-68 (Blackburn); *The Big Valley*—"The Long Ride" 11-25-68 (Jeb Lassiter); *Wild Wild West*—"The Night of Bleak Island" 3-14-69 (Ronald McAvity).

Westerman, Floyd Red Crow. Films: "Dances with Wolves" 1990 (Ten Bears); "Son of the Morning Star" TVM-1991; "Buffalo Girls" TVM-1995 (No Ears).

Western, Johnny. Films: "The Dalton Girls" 1957 (Joe); "Fort Bowie" 1958 (Sergeant); "Night Rider" 1962-short. ¶TV: *Boots and Saddles*—"The Obsession" 10-3-57, "The Treasure" 12-12-57 (Pvt. Ben Jordan); *Tales of Wells Fargo*—"The Prisoner" 2-17-58 (Young Outlaw); *Have Gun Will Travel*—"Twenty-Four Hours to North Fork" 5-17-58 (Steve).

Westman, Nydia (1902-5/23/70). Films: "The Bad Man" 1941 (Angela Hardy). ¶TV: *Bonanza*—"Square Deal Sam" 11-8-64 (Martha Washburn); *Lancer*—"The Black McGloins" 1-21-69 (Bridget McGloin).

Westmoreland, James (1935-). TV: *The Monroes*—Regular 1966-67 (Ruel); *Wild Wild West*—"The Night of the Golden Cobra" 9-23-66 (Chandra); *The Guns of Will Sonnett*—"First Love" 11-3-67 (Lafe Banning).

Weston, Brad (1928-). Films: "Savage Sam" 1963 (Ben Todd); "Stagecoach" 1966 (Matt Plummer); "Rough Night in Jericho" 1967 (Tor-

rey); "Barquero" 1970 (Driver); "Hot Lead and Cold Feet" 1978. ¶TV: *The Deputy*—"The Next Bullet" 11-28-59 (Tom Clements); *Have Gun Will Travel*—"The Pledge" 1-16-60 (Esteban), "Fight at Adobe Wells" 3-12-60 (Quanah Parker), "The Siege" 4-1-61 (Bobby Joe Brent), "The Gospel Singer" 10-21-61 (Will Durbin); *Riverboat*—"Fort Epitaph" 3-7-60 (Lt. Tom Henshaw), "Devil in Skirts" 11-21-60 (Tony); *Sugarfoot*—"Vinegaroom" 3-29-60 (Jemmy); *Laramie*—"Queen of Diamonds" 9-20-60 (Bart Reeves), "Ride into Darkness" 10-18-60 (Chuck), "Bad Blood" 12-4-62; *The Rifleman*—"The Silent Knife" 12-20-60 (Mark C.); *Maverick*—"The Cactus Switch" 1-15-61 (Mutt Craven); *Cheyenne*—"Lone Patrol" 4-10-61 (Lieutenant Patterson), "Wanted for the Murder of Cheyenne Bodie" 12-10-62 (Lar Walton); *Tales of Wells Fargo*—"Reward for Gaine" 1-20-62 (Prentiss); *The Virginian*—"The Exiles" 1-9-63 (Fred Daly), "The Brothers" 9-15-65 (Trooper), "Morgan Starr" 2-9-66 (Ben); *Wide Country*—"A Cry from the Mountain" 1-17-63 (Deputy Lyon); *Temple Houston*—"Thunder Gap" 11-21-63 (Lew Sykes); *Destry*—"Go Away, Little Sheba" 3-27-64 (Benedict Arnold Bedloe); *Branded*—"Elsie Brown" 2-14-65 (Vance); *Gunsmoke*—"The Goldtakers" 9-24-66 (Jenkins).

Weston, Cecile (1890-8/7/76). Films: "Dude Ranch" 1931 (Mrs. Merridew); "The Phantom Rider" 1936-serial; "Ramona" 1936 (Pablo's Wife); "Brigham Young—Frontiersman" 1940 (Woman); "Belle Starr" 1941 (Mother); "Two Fisted Justice" 1943 (Miss Adams); "Buffalo Bill" 1944 (Maid); "Bandit Queen" 1950 (Zara Montalve); "Noose for a Gunman" 1960 (Mrs. Franklyn).

Weston, Dick. *see* Rogers, Roy.

Weston, Don. Films: "Bad Men of Thunder Gap" 1943 (Cal Shrum's Rhythm Rangers); "Swing, Cowboy, Swing" 1944; "Ridin' Down the Trail" 1947; "Courtin' Trouble" 1948; "Cowboy Cavalier" 1948; "Oklahoma Blues" 1948 (Ray); "Partners of the Sunset" 1948; "Range Renegades" 1948; "The Rangers Ride" 1948.

Weston, Doris (1917-7/27/60). Films: "Chip of the Flying U" 1939 (Margaret Whitmore).

Weston, Ellen. TV: *Bonanza*—"Anatomy of a Lynching" 10-12-69 (Louise Thurston).

Weston, Jack (1924-). TV: *Gunsmoke*—"Sunday Supplement" 2-8-58 (Samuel Spring), "The New Society" 5-22-65 (Wesley); *Rawhide*—"Incident at the Buffalo Smokehouse" 10-30-59; *Have Gun Will Travel*—"Lady with a Gun" 4-9-60 (Rudy Rossback), "The Poker Friend" 11-12-60 (Neal); *Stoney Burke*—"A Matter of Percentage" 1-28-63 (Harry Marsh); *Laredo*—"It's the End of the Road, Stanley" 3-10-66 (Crazy John), "The Last of the Caesars—Absolutely" 12-2-66 (Hannibal Rex).

Westover, Winifred (Winifred Hart) (1899-3/19/78). Films: "Marked Men" 1919 (Ruby Merrill); "This Hero Stuff" 1919 (Nedra Joseph); "Firebrand Trevison" 1920 (Rosalind Benham); "Forbidden Trails" 1920 (Marion Harlan); "The Cowboy Star" 1936.

Westwood, Patrick. TV: *Buckskin*—"The Ghost of Balaclava" 9-4-58 (Harris); *Wagon Train*—"Around the Horn" 10-1-58 (Marks); *Riverboat*—"Forbidden Island" 1-24-60 (Pierre); *Maverick*—"Greenbacks Unlimited" 3-13-60 (London Latimer), "Destination Devil's Flat" 12-25-60 (Snake Randall), "The Money Machine" 4-8-62 (London Louis).

Wever, Ned. Films: "Ride a Crooked Trail" 1958 (Attorney Clark); "Three Thousand Hills" 1959 (Gorham). ¶TV: *Northwest Passage*—"The Vulture" 12-28-58 (Walter Van Horn); *The Texan*—"Blue Norther" 10-12-59 (John Camden); *Bonanza*—"The Spanish Grant" 2-6-60; *The Big Valley*—"Judgement in Heaven" 12-22-65 (Judge Parker).

Wexler, Paul (1929-11/21/79). Films: "The Silver Whip" 1953 (Homer); "Drum Beat" 1954 (William Brody); "The Kentuckian" 1955 (Fromes Brother); "Day of the Outlaw" 1959 (Vause); "The Miracle of the Hills" 1959 (Sam Jones); "The Way West" 1967 (Barber). ¶TV: *Death Valley Days*—"The Homeliest Man in Nevada" 11-7-55; *Gunsmoke*—"Sins of the Father" 1-19-57 (Rodin), "Uncle Oliver" 5-25-57 (Viney Stang), "The Gold Mine" 1-27-69 (Stone); *Wanted—Dead or Alive*—"Miracle at Pot Hole" 10-25-58 (Lester Bailey); *Pony Express*—"The Pendant" 3-16-60 (Big Dipper); *The Alaskans*—"The Devil Made Five" 6-19-60 (Bookkeeper); *The Rifleman*—"The Pitchman" 10-18-60, "The Queue" 5-16-61 (Les Foster), "Sheer Terror" 10-16-61, "Outlaw Shoes" 4-30-62 (Joe Weiden); *Wyatt Earp*—"Study of a Crooked Sheriff" 10-25-60 (Shakey Jenkins); *The Guns of Will Sonnett*—"A Bell for Jeff Sonnett" 9-15-67 (Cal Jessup).

Wexler, Yale. TV: *Wichita Town*—"The Hanging Judge" 3-9-60

(Jim Kling); *The Rebel*—"The Hunted" 11-6-60 (Keller).

Whalen, Michael (1902-4/14/74). Films: "White Fang" 1936 (Weedon Scott); "Thunder in the Pines" 1948 (Pete); "Son of a Badman" 1949 (Dr. Jarvis/El Sombre); "Tough Assignment" 1949 (Hutchinson); "King of the Bullwhip" 1950 (Henchman); "Waco" 1952 (Barnes); "Outlaw Treasure" 1955; "The Silver Star" 1955 (Brainey). ¶TV: *The Lone Ranger*—"High Heels" 11-17-49, "The Black Widow" 8-24-50, "False Accusations" 4-21-55; *The Cisco Kid*—"Jewelry Store Fence" 8-11-51, "Water Toll" 9-22-51, "The Iron Mask" 1-10-53; *Tombstone Territory*—"Reward for a Gunslinger" 10-23-57 (Mayor Fred Donolon); *Tales of Wells Fargo*—"Fraud" 3-13-61 (Abel Boyce).

Whaley, Bert (1909-1/17/73). TV: *The Big Valley*—"Under a Dark Sea" 2-9-66 (Warden).

Whalin, Justin. TV: *Young Riders*—"The Sacrifice" 6-25-92 (Dawkins).

Wheat, Laurence (1876-8/7/63). Films: "The Bachelor Daddy" 1922 (Charles Henley); "Nevada" 1944 (Ben Ide); "West of the Pecos" 1945 (Butler).

Wheatcroft, Stanhope (1888-2/12/66). Films: "Her Five-Foot Higness" 1920 (Lord Pomeroy); "West Is Best" 1920; "Two Kinds of Women" 1922 (Ferris); "Broadway or Bust" 1924 (Freddie); "The Iron Horse" 1924 (John Hay); "Ridin' Pretty" 1925 (Miller); "The Plainsman" 1936; "Union Pacific" 1939 (Secretary).

Wheeler, Bert (1895-1/18/68). Films: "Captain Fly-By-Night" 1922 (Governor). ¶TV: *Brave Eagle*—Regular 1955-56 (Smokey Joe).

Wheeler, John L. (1930-). Films: "Tell Them Willie Boy Is Here" 1969 (Newman); "Support Your Local Gunfighter" 1971 (Croupier); "The Apple Dumpling Gang Rides Again" 1979; "The Wild Wild West Revisited" TVM-1979. ¶TV: *Bonanza*—"Different Pines, Same Wind" 9-15-68 (Bartender), "Warbonnet" 12-26-71 (Hill); *Gunsmoke*—"I Have Promises to Keep" 3-3-75 (Waiter).

Wheeler-Nicholson, Dana. Films: "Tombstone" 1993 (Mattie Earp); "Frank and Jesse" TVM-1995 (Annie).

Wheelock, Charles (1875-5/25/48). Films: "A Mixup on the Plains" 1913; "The Moving Picture Cowboy" 1914; "Dead Shot Baker" 1917 (Postmaster); "The Tenderfoot" 1917

(Rogers' Partner); "One He Man" 1920.

Whelan, Arleen (1916-4/8/93). Films: "Sundown Jim" 1942 (Catherine Barr); "Ramrod" 1947 (Rose); "Passage West" 1951 (Rose Billings); "Flaming Feather" 1952 (Carolina); "San Antone" 1953 (Julia Allerby); "The Badge of Marshal Brennan" 1957 (Murdock); "Raiders of Old California" 1957.

Whelan, Ron (1905-12/8/65). Films: "Kangaroo" 1952 (Fenner); "The Gun Hawk" 1963 (Blackjack). ¶TV: *Wild Wild West*—"The Night of the Glowing Corpse" 10-29-65 (Consul General Potez).

Whelchel, Lisa. Films: "The Wild Women of Chastity Gulch" TVM-1982 (Amy Cole).

Whipper, Leigh (1877-7/26/75). Films: "Symbol of the Unconquered" 1921; "Robin Hood of the Pecos" 1941 (Kezeye); "The Vanishing Virginian" 1941 (Uncle Josh); "Heart of the Golden West" 1942 (Rango); "The Ox-Bow Incident" 1943 (Sparks).

Whitaker, Charles "Slim" (1893-7/27/60). Films: "When Thieves Fall Out" 1914; "The End of the Trail" 1916 (Trading-Post Inspector); "The Man from Bitter Roots" 1916 (Slim Naudain); "Galloping On" 1925 (Jack Bowers); "On the Go" 1925 (Tom Evans); "A Streak of Luck" 1925 (Black Pete); "Tearin' Loose" 1925 (Matt Harris); "Ace of Action" 1926; "The Ace of Clubs" 1926; "The Bandit Buster" 1926 (Steve); "The Bonanza Buckaroo" 1926 (Fraction Jack); "Bucking the Truth" 1926 (Red Sang); "Desperate Chance" 1926; "Double Daring" 1926 (Blackie Gorman); "The Fighting Cheat" 1926 (Jud Nolan); "Hurricane Horseman" 1926 (Mike Wesson); "The Lost Trail" 1926; "Rawhide" 1926 (Blackie Croont); "Speedy Spurs" 1926 (the Convict); "The Stolen Ranch" 1926 (Hank); "Trumpin' Trouble" 1926 (Red Star Dorgan); "Twin Triggers" 1926 (Kelly, the Garage Proprietor); "Vanishing Hoofs" 1926 (the Doctor); "The Desert of the Lost" 1927; "Gun Gospel" 1927 (Brogan's Henchman); "The Phantom Buster" 1927 (Cassidy); "The Ridin' Rowdy" 1927 (Miller); "Soda Water Cowboy" 1927 (Ross); "The Canyon of Adventure" 1928 (Slim Burke); "Desperate Courage" 1928; "The Flying Buckaroo" 1928 (Delno, the Bandit); "Headin' Westward" 1928 (Buck McGrath); "Manhattan Cowboy" 1928; "The Ranger Patrol" 1928; "Saddle

Mates" 1928 (Bob Grice); "Bad Man's Money" 1929; "Captain Cowboy" 1929; "Cheyenne" 1929 (Klaxton); "Riders of the Storm" 1929; "The Dawn Trail" 1930 (Steve); "The Fighting Legion" 1930 (Red Hook); "Oklahoma Cyclone" 1930 (Rawhide); "Shadow Ranch" 1930 (Curley); "The Avenger" 1931; "Branded Men" 1931; "Desert Vengeance" 1931 (Whiskey); "A Holy Terror" 1931 (Johnson); "In Old Cheyenne" 1931; "Lightnin' Smith Returns" 1931; "The One Way Trail" 1931; "Rider of the Plains" 1931 (Castor); "Between Fighting Men" 1932; "The Cheyenne Cyclone" 1932; "Flaming Guns" 1932; "Freighters of Destiny" 1932 (Toller); "Ghost Valley" 1932 (Henchman); "Guns for Hire" 1932; "Haunted Gold" 1932; "Hell Fire Austin" 1932; "The Man from New Mexico" 1932 (Russ); "A Man's Land" 1932; "The Saddle Buster" 1932 (Keno); "The Sunset Trail" 1932; "Come on Tarzan" 1933; "The Cowboy Counsellor" 1933; "Deadwood Pass" 1933 (Butch Cassidy); "Drum Taps" 1933 (Stubby Lane); "The Dude Bandit" 1933; "Fighting with Kit Carson" 1933-serial; "The Man from Monterey" 1933 (Jake Morgan); "Outlaw Justice" 1933; "Sagebrush Trail" 1933; "Somewhere in Sonora" 1933; "The Telegraph Trail" 1933; "The Trail Drive" 1933; "Trouble Busters" 1933 (Big Bill Jarvis); "War on the Range" 1933; "The Cactus Kid" 1934 (Killer Plug Perkins); "The Fiddlin' Buckaroo" 1934 (Swede); "Fighting Through" 1934 (Sheriff); "Gun Justice" 1934; "Honor of the Range" 1934; "The Law of the Wild" 1934-serial (Mack); "The Lone Bandit" 1934 (Buck Rawlins); "The Man from Hell" 1934 (Tom Hosford); "The Outlaw Tamer" 1934 (Bowie Harris); "The Prescott Kid" 1934 (Cowboy); "Ridin' Gent" 1934-short; "Smoking Guns" 1934 (Slim); "Terror of the Plains" 1934 (Nevada); "The Westerner" 1934 (Henchman); "Wheels of Destiny" 1934; "Arizona Bad Man" 1935 (Black Bart Dunstan); "Blazing Guns" 1935 (Deputy Carter); "Border Vengeance" 1935 (Sheriff); "Bulldog Courage" 1935; "Circle of Death" 1935 (Lane Merrill); "Coyote Trails" 1935 (Bert); "Gallant Defender" 1935; "Gunfire" 1935 (Henchman); "Heir to Trouble" 1935; "Horses' Collars" 1935-short (Cowboy); "The Last of the Clintons" 1935; "Law Beyond the Range" 1935 (Texas Ranger); "Lawless Range" 1935; "Lawless Riders" 1935 (Prod); "Range Warfare" 1935; "Rio Rattler" 1935 (Rattler); "The Roar-

ing West" 1935-serial; "Rustlers of Red Dog" 1935-serial; "Rustlers' Paradise" 1935; "Silent Valley" 1935 (Pete Childers); "The Silver Bullet" 1935 (Scurvy); "Sunset Range" 1935; "Tumbling Tumbleweeds" 1935 (Higgins); "The Unconquered Bandit" 1935; "Valley of Wanted Men" 1935; "Western Frontier" 1935; "Wolf Riders" 1935 (Butch's Henchman); "Bold Caballero" 1936; "Desert Guns" 1936; "Everyman's Law" 1936 (Pete); "Fast Bullets" 1936 (Pat); "The Fugitive Sheriff" 1936; "Ghost Patrol" 1936 (Frank); "Lightning Bill Carson" 1936 (Henchman); "The Phantom Rider" 1936-serial; "Pinto Rustlers" 1936 (Sheriff); "Ridin' On" 1936 (Black Mike Gonzado); "The Riding Avenger" 1936 (Slim); "Rio Grande Ranger" 1936 (Jack); "Roamin' Wild" 1936 (Marshal); "Roarin' Guns" 1936; "Rogue of the Range" 1936 (Henchman); "Santa Fe Bound" 1936 (Morgan); "Song of the Gringo" 1936; "The Traitor" 1936 (Plainview Man); "The Big Show" 1937; "Borderland" 1937; "Cheyenne Rides Again" 1937 (Sheriff Jed Martin); "Fugitive from Sonora" 1937; "Guns in the Dark" 1937; "Hollywood Round-Up" 1937; "Law for Tombstone" 1937; "Law of the Ranger" 1937 (Steve); "Lost Ranch" 1937 (Sheriff); "Melody of the Plains" 1937 (Cass); "Mystery Range" 1937; "The Old Wyoming Trail" 1937 (Guard); "Orphan of the Pecos" 1937 (Sheriff); "Prairie Thunder" 1937 (Blacky); "Raw Timber" 1937; "Reckless Ranger" 1937 (Steve); "The Roaming Cowboy" 1937; "Roaring Six Guns" 1937 (Skeeter); "Round-Up Time in Texas" 1937 (Police Captain); "Santa Fe Rides" 1937; "The Silver Trail" 1937 (Slug); "Smoke Tree Range" 1937; "Valley of Terror" 1937; "Black Bandit" 1938; "Feud of the Trail" 1938; "Flaming Frontier" 1938-serial; "The Great Adventures of Wild Bill Hickok" 1938; "Gunsmoke Trail" 1938; "Heroes of the Alamo" 1938; "In Early Arizona" 1938 (Sheriff); "The Lone Ranger" 1938-serial (Perkins); "Overland Stage Raiders" 1938 (Hawkins); "Phantom Gold" 1938 (Rattler); "Pioneer Trail" 1938 (Curley); "Prairie Justice" 1938; "Rawhide" 1938 (Biff); "Rolling Caravans" 1938 (Boots); "Stagecoach Days" 1938 (Butch Flint); "Under Western Stars" 1938 (Tremaine); "Code of the Cactus" 1939 (Sheriff); "Colorado Sunset" 1939; "The Fighting Gringo" 1939 (Monty); "Frontier Scout" 1939 (King); "Frontiers of '49" 1939 (Brad); "The Law Comes to Texas" 1939 (Barney); "The Lone

Ranger Rides Again" 1939-serial (Black); "Lone Star Pioneers" 1939 (Buck Barry); "The Marshal of Mesa City" 1939 (Jake Morse); "New Frontier" 1939 (Turner); "Oklahoma Terror" 1939; "Rollin' Westward" 1939 (Bart); "South of the Border" 1939; "Texas Wildcats" 1939 (Durkin); "The Thundering West" 1939 (Roper); "Trouble in Sundown" 1939; "Billy the Kid in Texas" 1940 (Windy); "Bullet Code" 1940 (Pop Norton); "Legion of the Lawless" 1940 (Ben Leighton); "Melody Ranch" 1940; "Prairie Law" 1940 (Silent); "Ragtime Cowboy Joe" 1940 (Foreman); "Rancho Grande" 1940; "Ride, Tenderfoot, Ride" 1940; "Young Bill Hickok" 1940; "Along the Rio Grande" 1941 (Pete); "Arizona Bound" 1941; "Billy the Kid Wanted" 1941 (Sheriff); "Billy the Kid's Roundup" 1941 (Sheriff); "Bury Me Not on the Lone Prairie" 1941; "Cyclone on Horseback" 1941; "Hands Across the Rockies" 1941; "King of the Texas Rangers" 1941-serial (Jake); "Law of the Range" 1941; "Riders of Death Valley" 1941-serial; "Saddle Mountain Roundup" 1941; "Six Gun Gold" 1941 (Miller); "Arizona Stagecoach" 1942; "Billy the Kid's Smoking Guns" 1942; "Come on, Danger!" 1942 (Sheriff); "In Old California" 1942; "Little Joe, the Wrangler" 1942 (Charlie); "The Lone Rider and the Bandit" 1942; "The Mysterious Rider" 1942; "Raiders of the West" 1942; "The Rangers Take Over" 1942 (Jake); "The Silver Bullet" 1942; "Texas Justice" 1942; "The Desperadoes" 1943 (Tolliver); "Fighting Frontier" 1943 (Sheriff Logan); "In Old Oklahoma" 1943 (Man on Train); "The Kid Rides Again" 1943 (Texas Sheriff); "Raiders of San Joaquin" 1943; "Silver Spurs" 1943; "Wolves of the Range" 1943; "Death Rides the Plains" 1944 (Sheriff); "The Drifter" 1944 (Marshal Hodges); "The Laramie Trail" 1944; "Marshal of Gunsmoke" 1944 (Nevada); "Oklahoma Raiders" 1944 (Sheriff Banning); "Outlaw of the Plains" 1946; "Overland Riders" 1946; "Law of the Lash" 1947 (Bart); "Pioneer Justice" 1947; "Return of the Lash" 1947; "The Westward Trail" 1948 (Bartender).

Whitaker, Jr., Charles. Films: "Speedy Spurs" 1926 (Buttons).

Whitaker, Johnnie (1959–). TV: *Gunsmoke*—"The Returning" 2-18-67 (Shem Todd), "Waste" 9-27-71 & 10-4-71 (Willie Hubbard); *Bonanza*—"A Dream to Dream" 4-14-68 (Timmy Carter); *Lancer*—"Child of Rock and Sunlight" 4-1-69 (Andy-Jack); *The*

Virginian—"The Runaway Boy" 10-22-69 (Hoot).

White, Betty (1922-). TV: *Best of the West*—"Mail Order Bride" 1-28-82.

White, Carol (1941-9/16/91). Films: "Something Big" 1971 (Dover MacBride).

White, Christine (1926-). TV: *Have Gun Will Travel*—"The O'Hare Story" 3-1-58 (Girl), "The Road to Wickenberg" 10-25-58 (Susan); *The Rifleman*—"The Visitors" 1-26-60 (Ann Dodd); *Bonanza*—"Badge Without Honor" 9-24-60 (Mariette); *The Outlaws*—"The Brothers" 5-11-61 (Persis); *Wide Country*—"The Judas Goat" 2-21-63 (Angel).

White, Daniel (-7/7/80). Films: "Prairie Moon" 1938; "In Old Monterey" 1939; "The Law Comes to Texas" 1939; "Rough Riders' Round-Up" 1939 (Patrolman); "Adventures of Red Ryder" 1940-serial (Masked Heavy #2); "The Lone Rider in Frontier Fury" 1941; "Arizona Trail" 1943 (Sheriff); "Blazing Guns" 1943; "False Colors" 1943 (Bar Spectator); "Fighting Valley" 1943; "Outlaws of Stampede Pass" 1943; "The Renegade" 1943; "Arizona Whirlwind" 1944 (Jim Lockwood); "The Big Bonanza" 1944; "Black Arrow" 1944-serial; "Boss of Rawhide" 1944 (Minstrel); "Death Rides the Plains" 1944; "Marshal of Gunsmoke" 1944; "Trail of Terror" 1944; "The Utah Kid" 1944; "Westward Bound" 1944; "Beyond the Pecos" 1945; "Both Barrels Blazing" 1945; "Flaming Bullets" 1945; "Frontier Feud" 1945; "Rough Ridin' Justice" 1945 (Mike); "San Antonio" 1945 (Joe Sims); "Trail to Vengeance" 1945 (1st Thug); "Duel in the Sun" 1946 (Ed); "Gun Town" 1946 (Joe); "Gunman's Code" 1946; "The Sea of Grass" 1947 (Ike Randall); "White Stallion" 1947 (Bronco); "Albuquerque" 1948 (Jackson); "Four Faces West" 1948 (Clint Waters); "Gunning for Justice" 1948; "Red River" 1948 (Laredo); "Silver River" 1948 (Miner); "Station West" 1948 (Pete); "Sunset Carson Rides Again" 1948; "Outlaw Country" 1949 (Jim McCord); "Drums in the Deep South" 1951 (Cpl. Jennings); "Rawhide" 1951 (Gilchrist); "Red Mountain" 1951 (Braden); "Sugarfoot" 1951; "Vengeance Valley" 1951 (Cowhand); "Horizons West" 1952 (Dennis); "The Lusty Men" 1952 (Announcer); "Born to the Saddle" 1953; "The Silver Whip" 1953 (Dodd Burdette); "Jubilee Trail" 1954 (Henry); "Taza, Son of Cochise" 1954 (Tiswin); "The Americano" 1955 (Barney Dent); "The Road to Denver" 1955 (Joslyn); "The First Traveling Saleslady" 1956 (Sheriff); "Great Day in the Morning" 1956 (Rogers); "The Last Hunt" 1956 (Deputy); "The Rainmaker" 1956 (Deputy); "Gunfire at Indian Gap" 1957 (Moran); "The Lonely Man" 1957; "Escape from Red Rock" 1958 (Farris); "Frontier Gun" 1958 (Sam Kilgore); "Quantrill's Raiders" 1958 (Fred Thomas); "The Bounty Killer" 1965 (Marshal Davis); "Jesse James Meets Frankenstein's Daughter" 1966; "Waco" 1966; "Red Tomahawk" 1967 (Ned Crone); "Smoke in the Wind" 1975 (Col. Cullen). ¶TV: *The Cisco Kid*—"The Iron Mask" 1-10-53, "Cisco Plays the Ghost" 2-21-53, "Gold, Death and Dynamite" 2-13-54; *Tales of the Texas Rangers*—"Last Days of Boot Hill" 2-11-56 (Sheriff); *Sheriff of Cochise*—"The Kidnaper" 1-18-57 (Charlie Desmond); *Circus Boy*—"The Pawnee Strip" 4-14-57 (Ben Otis); *Maverick*—"The Third Rider" 1-5-58 (Cowpoke), "Maverick at Law" 2-26-61 (Poe); *Tales of Wells Fargo*—"The Manuscript" 9-15-58 (Nedy West); *Wagon Train*—"The Dick Richardson Story" 12-31-58 (Joe Lassiter), "The Levi Hale Story" 4-18-62 (Driver); *The Californians*—"Wolf's Head" 2-24-59 (Roadhouse Proprietor); *Rawhide*—"Incident of the Town in Terror" 3-6-59, "Grandma's Money" 2-23-62 (Elkville Sheriff), "Incident of the Pale Rider" 3-15-63 (Gravedigger), "Incident of Iron Bull" 10-3-63 (Charlie), "Incident of the Wanderer" 2-27-64; *The Texan*—"The Ringer" 2-16-59 (Sheriff Winters), 9-12-60; *Bat Masterson*—"Cattle and Cane" 3-3-60 (Ben Taylor); "Episode in Eden" 3-16-61 (Sheriff Sloane); *Bonanza*—"The Avenger" 3-19-60 (Jackson), "Cut-Throat Junction" 3-18-61, "A Stranger Passed This Way" 3-3-63 (Stable Man), "The Boss" 5-19-63, "Five Sundowns to Sunup" 12-5-65 (Weems); *Gunsmoke*—"Belle's Back" 5-14-60 (Mr. Ainsley), "Hammerhead" 12-26-64 (Attendant), "Mirage" 1-11-71 (Stocker), "The Avenger" 11-27-72 (Oldtimer); *The Outlaws*—"Starfall" 11-24-60 & 12-1-60 (Clay Fisher); *The Deputy*—"Judas Town" 12-31-60 (Joab); *The Rebel*—"Paperback Hero" 1-29-61 (Corby); *Wyatt Earp*—"The Good Mule and the Bad Mule" 3-14-61 (Zack Burton); *Laramie*—"The Sunday Shoot" 11-13-62; *Have Gun Will Travel*—"Man in an Hourglass" 12-1-62; *The Virginian*—"The Devil's Children" 12-5-62; *The High Chaparral*—"Wind" 10-9-70; *The Men from Shiloh*—"Hannah" 12-30-70 (Conductor).

White, David (1916-11/26/90). TV: *Have Gun Will Travel*—"The Unforgiven" 11-7-59 (General Crommer), "The Gold Toad" 11-21-59 (Ben Webster), "Everyman" 3-25-61 (Cus Mincus), "Marshal of Sweetwater" 11-24-62 (Tom Carey); *Bonanza*—"San Francisco Holiday" 4-2-60 (Mr. Pendleton/Shanghai Pete); *Hotel De Paree*—"Sundance and the Cattlemen" 5-13-60 (Cotton); *The Outlaws*—"Chalk's Lot" 10-5-61 (Charlie Peal); *Tales of Wells Fargo*—"A Fistful of Pride" 11-18-61; *The Virginian*—"The Man Who Couldn't Die" 1-30-63; *The Rifleman*—"Hostages to Fortune" 2-4-63; *The Dakotas*—"One Day in Vermillion" 4-8-63; *Great Adventure*—"The Testing of Sam Houston" 1-31-64 (John C. Calhoun), "The Pathfinder" 3-6-64 (Benton); *Destry*—"Destry Had a Little Lamb" 2-21-64 (Austin Karnes).

White, Dean. Films: "Return of the Badmen" 1948 (Billy the Kid).

White, Jacqueline (-6/21/64). Films: "Return of the Badmen" 1948 (Madge Allen); "The Capture" 1950 (Luana); "Riders of the Range" 1950 (Dusty).

White, Jesse (1919-). Films: "Callaway Went Thataway" 1951 (George Markham); "Gunsmoke" 1953 (Professor); "Tomboy and the Champ" 1961 (Windy Skiles); "The Brothers O'Toole" 1973. ¶TV: *The Lone Ranger*—"Wanted … the Lone Ranger" 5-5-55; *The Texan*—"Private Account" 4-6-59 (Weeb Martin); *The Alaskans*—"Big Deal" 11-8-59; *Bonanza*—"The Saga of Muley Jones" 3-29-64 (Esky); *Wild Wild West*—"The Night of the Whirring Death" 2-18-66 (Governor Lewis); *Rango*—"My Teepee Runneth Over" 3-10-67 (Gus).

White, Johnstone (1892-4/7/69). Films: "Pardners" 1956 (Businessman). ¶TV: *Riverboat*—"Salvage Pirates" 1-31-60 (James Kincannon).

White, Lee "Lasses" (1888-12/16/49). Films: "Trailin' West" 1936 (Card Dealer); "The Painted Stallion" 1937-serial (Peters); "Rovin' Tumbleweeds" 1939 (Storekeeper); "Corralling a School Marm" 1940-short; "Molly Cures a Cowboy" 1940-short; "Oklahoma Renegades" 1940 (Jim Keith); "The Bandit Trail" 1941 (Whopper); "Cyclone on Horseback" 1941 (Whopper); "Dude Cowboy" 1941 (Whopper); "The Round Up" 1941; "Six Gun Gold" 1941 (Whopper); "Come on, Danger!" 1942 (Whopper); "Land of the Open Range" 1942 (Whopper); "Range Rhythm" 1942-short; "Riding the Wind" 1942

(Whopper); "Thundering Hoofs" 1942 (Whopper); "The Outlaw" 1943 (Coach Driver); "Alaska" 1944; "Song of the Range" 1944 (Lasses); "In Old New Mexico" 1945 (Sheriff); "Lonesome Trail" 1945; "Riders of the Dawn" 1945 (Lasses); "Saddle Serenade" 1945; "Springtime in Texas" 1945; "Moon Over Montana" 1946; "Song of the Sierras" 1946; "Trail to Mexico" 1946; "West of Alamo" 1946 (Lasses); "Cheyenne" 1947 (Charlie, the Hotelkeeper); "My Pal Ringeye" 1947-short; "Rainbow Over the Rockies" 1947; "Six Gun Serenade" 1947; "Song of the Wasteland" 1947; "The Wistful Widow of Wagon Gap" 1947 (Shot Gun Rider); "The Dude Goes West" 1948 (Baggage Master); "Indian Agent" 1948 (Inky); "The Valiant Hombre" 1948 (Old Prospector); "Red Rock Outlaw" 1950; "The Texan Meets Calamity Jane" 1950 (Colorado Charley).

White, Leo (1880-9/21/48). Films: "Headin' West" 1922 (Honey Giroux); "Breed of the Sunsets" 1928 (Senor Diego Valdez); "Thunder Riders" 1928 (Prof. Wilfred Winkle); "Born to the Saddle" 1929 (Clyde Montgomery Wilpenny); "Smilin' Guns" 1929 (Count Baretti); "Roaring Ranch" 1930 (Reginald Sobuski); "River's End" 1940 (Barber); "Silver River" 1948 (Barber).

White, Patricia. Films: "Blazing Across the Pecos" 1948; "Riders of the Whistling Pines" 1949 (Helen Carter).

White, Pearl (1889-8/4/38). Films: "The Girl from Arizona" 1910; "The Maid of Niagara" 1910; "The Arrowmaker's Daughter" 1912; "The Perils of Pauline" 1914-serial.

White, Peter. Films: "Colt Is the Law" 1965-Ital./Span.; "If You Want to Live ... Shoot!" 1967-Ital./Span.; "No Graves on Boot Hill" 1968-Ital. (Priest); "Kill Django ... Kill First" 1971-Ital.

White, Ruth (1914-12/3/69). Films: "Hang 'Em High" 1968 (Madam Peaches Sophie).

White, Sam. Films: "Honeymoon Ranch" 1920 (Shorty); "West of the Rio Grande" 1921 (Shorty).

White, Sammy (1896-3/3/60). Films: "The Half-Breed" 1952 (Willy Wayne).

White, Ted. Films: "Rio Bravo" 1959 (Bart); "Cat Ballou" 1965 (Gunslinger); "Smoky" 1966 (Abbott); "Conagher" TVM-1991. ¶TV: *Maverick*—"Alias Bart Maverick" 10-5-58 (Sioux Indian #2); *The Alaskans*—"The Ballad of Whitehorse" 6-12-60

(Brown); *Wagon Train*—"The Hide Hunters" 9-27-64 (Cougar); *Daniel Boone*—"A Place of 1000 Spirits" 2-4-65 (Carata), "The Trek" 10-21-65 (Hawks), "The Peace Tree" 11-11-65 (Pushta), "The Thanksgiving Story" 11-25-65, "The Deserter" 1-20-66 (Sgt. Judd Blake), "Thirty Pieces of Silver" 3-28-68, "The Plague That Came to Ford's Run" 10-31-68, "Hannah Comes Home" 12-25-69 (Aweelok), "Noblesse Oblige" 3-26-70; *Kung Fu*—"Night of the Owls, Day of the Doves" 2-14-74 (Ernie Greene).

White, Will J. (-4/23/92). Films: "The Lawless Eighties" 1958; "Westworld" 1973 (Workman). ¶TV: *Sergeant Preston of the Yukon*—"Underground Ambush" 4-25-57; *Death Valley Days*—"Thorn of the Rose" 6-16-57 (Matt Smart); *Maverick*—"The Long Hunt" 10-20-57 (1st Holdup Man), "The Troubled Heir" 4-1-62 (Hub); *Tales of Wells Fargo*—"The Inscrutable Man" 12-9-57 (Jeff McKay), "Toll Road" 3-23-59; *Wagon Train*—"The Clara Beauchamp Story" 12-11-57 (Soldier); *Wyatt Earp*—"Wyatt Earp Rides Shotgun" 2-18-58; *Riverboat*—"Three Graves" 3-14-60 (Man); *The Tall Man*—"The Shawl" 10-1-60 (Ed Peters); *Bonanza*—"The Decision" 12-16-62, "The Legacy" 12-15-63, "Ballad of the Ponderosa" 11-13-66 (Hank), "The Wormwood Cup" 4-23-67; *The Big Valley*—"Top of the Stairs" 1-6-69.

White, William "Bill" (1857-8/21/33). Films: "The Sheriff of Sun-Dog" 1922 (Jeff Sedley); "Two-Fisted Jefferson" 1922; "At Devil's Gorge" 1923 (Pop Morgan); "The Devil's Dooryard" 1923 (Sheriff Allen); "Western Feuds" 1924 (Bill Warner); "Western Yesterdays" 1924 (Sheriff Bill Hickson).

White Eagle, Chief (1873-1/18/46). Films: "The Heart of Wetona" 1919 (Nipo); "Oklahoma Jim" 1931; "Trails of the Golden West" 1931; "End of the Trail" 1932 (Indian Eagle).

White Feather, Felix. Films: "Buffalo Bill on the U.P. Trail" 1926 (White Spear); "Red Clay" 1927 (Indian Chief)."Courage of the North" 1935.

Whiteford, J.P. "Blackie" (1873-3/21/62). Films: "Cyclone Kid" 1931 (Pete); "The Fighting Marshal" 1931; "The Texas Ranger" 1931; "Cornered" 1932; "Man from Hell's Edges" 1932; "The Man from New Mexico" 1932 (Bat Murchison); "Mark of the Spur" 1932 (Butch); "Mason of the Mounted" 1932; "Scarlet Brand"

1932 (Cactus); "Breed of the Border" 1933; "Crashing Broadway" 1933 (Blackie); "Deadwood Pass" 1933 (Bull); "The Dude Bandit" 1933; "The Fighting Parson" 1933; "Somewhere in Sonora" 1933; "Brand of Hate" 1934; "A Demon for Trouble" 1934 (Killer); "Gun Justice" 1934; "Rawhide Mail" 1934; "West of the Divide" 1934 (Hutch); "Big Calibre" 1935; "Born to Battle" 1935; "The Ghost Rider" 1935 (Bull); "The Judgement Book" 1935 (Bernie Cummins); "North of Arizona" 1935 (Barfly); "Pals of the Range" 1935 (Joe); "Rio Rattler" 1935; "The Silver Bullet" 1935 (Henchman); "Six Gun Justice" 1935; "Texas Jack" 1935 (Cal Kramer); "Thunderbolt" 1935; "Wolf Riders" 1935; "Cavalcade of the West" 1936 (Outlaw); "End of the Trail" 1936 (Mason's Man); "The Last of the Warrens" 1936 (Slip); "The Law Rides" 1936; "The Mysterious Avenger" 1936 (Rustler); "The Riding Avenger" 1936 (Henchman); "Rogue of the Range" 1936 (Henchman); "Toll of the Desert" 1936; "Valley of the Lawless" 1936; "Dodge City Trail" 1937 (Dawson's Gang Member); "Fighting Texan" 1937 (Bartender); "The Old Wyoming Trail" 1937; "Outlaws of the Prairie" 1937; "Romance of the Rockies" 1937; "Two-Fisted Sheriff" 1937; "Cattle Raiders" 1938 (Rustler); "The Colorado Trail" 1938 (Henchman); "The Great Adventures of Wild Bill Hickok" 1938; "The Lone Ranger" 1938-serial (Trooper); "The Overland Express" 1938; "West of Santa Fe" 1938 (Cane); "Where the Buffalo Roam" 1938; "Oklahoma Frontier" 1939; "Texas Stampede" 1939; "The Thundering West" 1939 (Trigger); "Brigham Young—Frontiersman" 1940 (Court Spectator); "Texas Stagecoach" 1940; "Thundering Frontier" 1940; "Outlaws of the Panhandle" 1941; "Fighting Bill Fargo" 1942; "Stagecoach Buckaroo" 1942; "A Tornado in the Saddle" 1942; "Valley of Vanishing Men" 1942-serial; "Saddles and Sagebrush" 1943; "The Last Horseman" 1944 (Slade); "Riding West" 1944 (Sgt. Dobbs); "The Vigilantes Ride" 1944 (Hench); "Rio Grande Raiders" 1946; "The Last Round-Up" 1947; "Quick on the Trigger" 1948; "El Dorado Pass" 1949; "Cow Town" 1950; "Trail of the Rustlers" 1950; "Santa Fe" 1951.

Whitehead, James. Films: "Mesquite Buckaroo" 1939 (Mort); "Riders of the Sage" 1939 (Steve Reynolds); "My Little Chickadee" 1940.

Whitehead, Joe. Films: "Gold Mine in the Sky" 1938; "Law of the

Texan" 1938 (Flaherty); "Shine on Harvest Moon" 1938 (Sheriff Clay); "Henry Goes Arizona" 1939 (Mike); "Mesquite Buckaroo" 1939; "Stick to Your Guns" 1941 (Buck); "Copper Canyon" 1950 (Proprietor).

Whitehead, O.Z. (1913-). Films: "Dallas" 1950 (Settler); "The San Francisco Story" 1952 (Alfey); "The Horse Soldiers" 1959 (Hoppy Hopkins); "Two Rode Together" 1961 (Lt. Chase); "The Man Who Shot Liberty Valance" 1962 (Ben Carruthers). ¶TV: *Gunsmoke*—"Lynching Man" 11-15-58 (Hank Blenis); *Man from Blackhawk*—"Diamond Cut Diamond" 3-18-60 (Charley Welsh); *Bonanza*—"San Francisco Holiday" 4-2-60 (Hamp); *Hotel De Paree*—"Sundance and the Good-Luck Coat" 5-6-60 (Hardcastle).

Whitehorse. Films: "Leatherstocking" 1924-serial; "The Loser's End" 1924 (John Kincaid); "Not Guilty for Runnin'" 1924 (Grizzly Dobbs); "Way of a Man" 1924-serial; "Flash O'Lightning" 1925 (Caleb Flint); "Ranchers and Rascals" 1925 (Indian); "The Shield of Silence" 1925; "Silent Sheldon" 1925 (Mary's Father); "The Trouble Buster" 1925 (Rawhide Williams); "Win, Lose or Draw" 1925 (Pierre Fayette); "Blind Trail" 1926 (Sheriff); "The High Hand" 1926 (John Oaks); "War Paint" 1926 (White Hawk); "West of the Rainbow's End" 1926 (Tom Palmer); "Without Orders" 1926 (Harvey Wells); "The Devil's Twin" 1927 (Solon Kemper); "Don Desperado" 1927 (Ables); "Hawk of the Hills" 1927-serial; "Two-Gun of the Tumbleweed" 1927; "The Apache Raider" 1928 (Ed Stillwell); "The Bronc Stomper" 1928 (Marshal); "The Three Outcasts" 1929 (Nels Nolan); "Stagecoach" 1939 (Geronimo).

Whiteman, Russ. Films: "Alias Billy the Kid" 1946 (Peewee); "Rough Riders of Durango" 1951; "Canyon Ambush" 1952; "The Gunman" 1952; "Montana Incident" 1952; "Waco" 1952 (Sheriff of Pecos); "The Marksman" 1953. ¶TV: *Wild Bill Hickok*—"A Joke on Sir Antony" 4-1-52; *Fury*—"Gymkhana" 1-23-60 (Ed Connor); *The Virginian*—"The Man from the Sea" 12-26-62; *Laramie*—"The Renegade Brand" 2-26-63.

Whiteside, Ray. TV: *Walt Disney Presents*—"Davy Crockett"—Regular 1954-55 (Johnny Crockett); *Sergeant Preston of the Yukon*—"The Devil's Roost" 4-11-57 (Gil).

Whitespear, Gregg Star (1897-2/20/56). Films: "The Iron Horse"

1924 (Sioux Chief); "Painted Ponies" 1927; "The Water Hole" 1928 (Indian); "Riders of the Desert" 1932 (Apache Joe); "Ride, Ranger, Ride" 1936; "The Painted Stallion" 1937-serial (Topek); "Union Pacific" 1939 (Indian Brave).

Whitfield, Ann. Films: "The Gunfighter" 1950 (Carrie Lou). ¶TV: *Cheyenne*—"The Storm Riders" 2-7-56 (Johnny), "The Young Fugitives" 10-23-61 (Nita); *Bonanza*—"Enter Mark Twain" 10-10-59 (Rosemary); *Tate*—"Comanche Scalps" 8-10-60 (Lucy); *Gunsmoke*—"Don Mateo" 10-22-60 (Trudy), "Stage Stop" 11-26-66 (Lori Coombs); *Tales of Wells Fargo*—"That Washburn Girl" 2-13-61 (Ruby Coe); *Rawhide*—"Incident of the Night on the Town" 6-2-61 (Carol North), "Judgment at Hondo Seco" 10-20-61 (Joanna Quince); *Laramie*—"Time of the Traitor" 12-11-62 (Miller); *The Dakotas*—"Requiem at Dancer's Hill" 2-18-63 (Virginia Kendrick).

Whitfield, Jordan "Smoki" (1917-11/11/67). Films: "Seven Angry Men" 1955 (Newby). ¶TV: *Laredo*—"The Heroes of San Gill" 12-23-65, "That's Noway, Thataway" 1-20-66; *The Virginian*—"Requiem for a Country Doctor" 1-25-67 (Carpenter).

Whiting, A.E. Films: "Two Men of Sandy Bar" 1916 (Concho); "The Son of a Gun" 1919 (W.L. "Old Man" Brown).

Whiting, Margaret (1924-). TV: *Colt .45*—"Martial Law" 5-17-60 (Vinnie Berkeley).

Whiting, Napoleon (1909-10/22/84). Films: "Riding High" 1943 (Red Cap); "Giant" 1956 (Swaey); "Skin Game" 1971 (Ned). ¶TV: *The Big Valley*—Regular 1965-69 (Silas); *Nichols*—"Eddie Joe" 1-4-72; *Bonanza*—"He Was Only Seven" 3-5-72 (Bert).

Whitley, Crane (1899-2/28/58). Films: "Daredevils of the West" 1943-serial (Maxwell); "California" 1946 (Abe Clinton); "The Fabulous Texan" 1947; "Pursued" 1947; "The Savage Horde" 1950; "Red Mountain" 1951 (Cavalry Major); "Hannah Lee" 1953 (Loafer).

Whitley, Ray (1902-2/21/79). Films: "Hopalong Cassidy Returns" 1936 (Davis); "Hittin' the Trail" 1937; "The Mystery of the Hooded Horseman" 1937; "The Old Wyoming Trail" 1937; "Rhythm Wranglers" 1937-short; "Border G-Man" 1938 (Luke); "A Buckaroo Broadcast" 1938-short; "Gun Law" 1938

(Singing Sam McGee); "The Painted Desert" 1938 (Steve); "Prairie Papas" 1938-short; "Renegade Ranger" 1938 (Happy); "A Western Welcome" 1938-short; "Where the West Begins" 1938; "Bandits and Ballads" 1939-short; "Cupid Rides the Range" 1939-short; "Racketeers of the Range" 1939 (Ray); "Ranch House Romeo" 1939-short; "Sagebrush Serenade" 1939-short; "Trouble in Sundown" 1939 (Ray); "Bar Buckaroos" 1940-short; "Corralling a School Marm" 1940-short; "The Fargo Kid" 1940 (Johnny); "Molly Cures a Cowboy" 1940-short; "Wagon Train" 1940 (Ned); "Along the Rio Grande" 1941 (Smokey); "The Bandit Trail" 1941 (Smokey); "California or Bust" 1941-short; "Cyclone on Horseback" 1941; "Dude Cowboy" 1941 (Smokes); "The Musical Bandit" 1941-short; "Prairie Spooners" 1941-short; "Redskins and Redheads" 1941-short; "Robbers of the Range" 1941 (Smokey); "Six Gun Gold" 1941 (Smokey); "Cactus Capers" 1942-short; "Come on, Danger!" 1942 (Smokey); "Keep Shooting" 1942-short; "Land of the Open Range" 1942 (Smokey); "Range Rhythm" 1942-short; "Riding the Wind" 1942 (Smokey); "Thundering Hoofs" 1942 (Smokey); "Boss of Boomtown" 1944 (Clark); "The Old Texas Trail" 1944 (Amarillo); "Riders of the Santa Fe" 1944 (Hank); "Trail to Gunsight" 1944 (Barton); "Trigger Trail" 1944; "Beyond the Pecos" 1945; "Renegades of the Rio Grande" 1945 (Tex Henry); "Renegades of the Rio Grande" 1945; "West of Alamo" 1946; "Outlaw Brand" 1948; "Partners of the Sunset" 1948; "Brand of Fear" 1949; "Gun Law Justice" 1949; "Gun Runner" 1949; "Giant" 1956 (Watts). ¶TV: *The Roy Rogers Show*—"The Peddler from the Pecos" 12-13-53 (John Wilkins), "Little Dynamite" 1-3-54 (Jim Sprague), "The Kid from Silver City" 1-17-54 (Bill Culver).

Whitlock, Lloyd (1891-1/8/66). Films: "The Man Who Took a Chance" 1917 (Wilbur Mason); "The Gray Wolf's Ghost" 1919 (Jim Prince); "Lasca" 1919 (John Davis); "The Love Call" 1919 (Joe Emery); "Cupid, the Cowpuncher" 1920 (Dr. Leroy Simpson); "The Girl Who Ran Wild" 1922 (Jack Velvet); "The Snowshoe Trail" 1922 (Harold Lounsbury); "The Man Who Won" 1923 (Lord James); "The Thrill Chaser" 1923; "The Prairie Pirate" 1925 (Howard Steele); "The Fighting Buckaroo" 1926 (Glenmore Bradley); "The Man in the Saddle" 1926 (Lawrence); "The War Horse" 1927

(Capt. Collins); "Mounted Fury" 1931 (Dick Simpson); "Diamond Trail" 1933 (Flash Barret); "The Whirlwind" 1933 (Blackton); "The Lawless Frontier" 1934; "The Lucky Texan" 1934 (Harris); "West of the Divide" 1934 (Gentry); "Ride, Ranger, Ride" 1936 (Maj. Crosby); "Sunset in Wyoming" 1941; "White Eagle" 1941-serial.

Whitman, Alfred. *see* Whitman, Gayne.

Whitman, Ernest (1893-8/5/54). Films: "Jesse James" 1939 (Pinky); "Buck Benny Rides Again" 1940; "The Return of Frank James" 1940 (Pinky Washington); "Santa Fe Trail" 1940 (Black).

Whitman, Frank. Films: "Bulldog Courage" 1922 (Big Bog Phillips).

Whitman, Gayne (Alfred Whitman, Alfred Vosburgh) (1890-8/31/58). Films: "Anne of the Mines" 1914; "The Horse Thief" 1914; "The Legend of the Lone Tree" 1915; "The Divorcee" 1917 (Rev. Jerry Ferguson); "Sunlight's Last Raid" 1917 (Jack Conway); "Baree, Son of Kazan" 1918 (Jim Carvel); "Cavanaugh of the Forest Rangers" 1918 (Ranger Ross Cavanaugh); "Desert Law" 1918 (Donald McLane); "The Home Trail" 1918 (Tom Evans); "Tongues of Flame" 1918 (L'Eau Dormant); "The End of the Game" 1919 (Frank Miller); "Night Cry" 1926 (Miguel Hernandez); "The Adventurer" 1928 (the Tornado); "Yankee Don" 1931; "The Texas Rangers" 1936 (Announcer); "Adventures of Red Ryder" 1940-Serial (Harrison).

Whitman, Kip. TV: *Bonanza*—"Sense of Duty" 9-24-67 (Tim Kelly); *Hondo*—"Hondo and the Judas" 11-3-67 (Jim Younger); *Cimarron Strip*—"The Judgment" 1-4-68 (Jerry); *Gunsmoke*—"Time of the Jackals" 1-13-69 (Daggett), "Charlie Noon" 11-3-69 (Takawa); *Kung Fu*—"The Soldier" 11-29-73 (1st Cavalryman); *Nakia*—"A Matter of Choice" 12-7-74 (Richie).

Whitman, Stuart (1926-). Films: "Barbed Wire" 1952; "Passion" 1954 (Bernal Vaquaro); "Silver Lode" 1954 (Wickers); "Seven Men from Now" 1956 (Cavalry Lieutenant); "War Drums" 1957 (Johnny Smith); "Three Thousand Hills" 1959 (Tom Ping); "The Comancheros" 1961 (Regret); "Rio Conchos" 1964 (Capt. Haven); "Captain Apache" 1971-Brit./Span. (Griffin); "The White Buffalo" 1977 (Winifred Coxy); "Go West, Young Girl" TVM-1978 (Deputy Shreeve); "Once Upon a Texas

Train" TVM-1988 (George). ¶TV: *The Roy Rogers Show*—"Dead Men's Hills" 3-15-52, "The Feud" 11-16-52, "The Run-A-Round" 2-22-53 (Ted Willis); *Gunsmoke*—"Cholera" 12-29-56 (Bart); *Zane Grey Theater*—"Until the Man Dies" 1-25-57 (Dave Jordan); *Trackdown*—"The Town" 12-13-57 (Cal Fraser); *Have Gun Will Travel*—"The Last Laugh" 1-25-58 (Gil Borden); *Cimarron Strip*—Regular 1967-68 (Marshal Jim Crown); *Hec Ramsey*—"A Hard Road to Vengeance" 11-25-73 (Bassett); *Adventures of Brisco County, Jr.*—Pilot 8-27-93 (Granville Thorgood).

Whitman, Walt (1868-3/27/28). Films: "The Firefly of Tough Luck" 1917 (Tough Luck Baxter); "The Desert Man" 1917 (Old Burns); "Boss of the Lazy Y" 1918 (Malcolm Clayton); "Desert Law" 1918; "His Enemy, the Law" 1918 (Mr. Catherwood); "Two Men of Tainted Butte" 1919; "Mark of Zorro" 1920 (Fra Felipe); "The Mysterious Rider" 1921 (Bellounds).

Whitmore, James (1921-). Films: "The Outriders" 1950 (Clint Priest); "The Command" 1953 (Sgt. Elliott); "The Last Frontier" 1955 (Gus); "Oklahoma!" 1955 (Carnes); "Chuka" 1967 (Trent); "Waterhole No. 3" 1967 (Capt. Shipley); "Guns of the Magnificent Seven" 1969 (Levi Morgan); "Chato's Land" 1972 (Joshua Everette); "I Will Fight No More Forever" TVM-1975 (Gen. Oliver O. Howard). ¶TV: *Zane Grey Theater*—"The Fearful Courage" 10-12-56 (Jeb), "Debt of Gratitude" 4-18-58 (Ben Kincaid), "Checkmate" 4-30-59 (Joel Begley), "Wayfarers" 1-21-60 (Jonas); *Wagon Train*—"The Gabe Carswell Story" 1-15-58 (Gabe Carswell); *Western Theatre*—Host 1959; *Desilu Playhouse*—"The Hanging Judge" 12-4-59 (Lee Anderson); *Rawhide*—"Incident of the Dogfaces" 11-9-62 (Sergeant Duclos), "Incident of Iron Bull" 10-3-63 (Colonel John Macklin); *The Travels of Jaimie McPheeters*—"The Day of the Golden Fleece" 10-6-63 (Foxy Smith); *Gunsmoke*—"Dry Road to Nowhere" 4-3-65 (Amos Campbell), "The Reward" 11-6-65 (Jim Forbes), "Women for Sale" 9-10-73 & 9-17-73 (Timothy Fitzpatrick); *The Virginian*—"Nobody Said Hello" 1-5-66 (Piper Pritikin), "Paid in Full" 11-22-67 (Ezra Hollis), "A Flash of Darkness" 9-24-69 (Carl Kabe); *The Loner*—"The Mourners for Johnny Sharp" 2-5-66 & 2-12-66 (Doc Fritchman); *The Big Valley*—"The Death Merchant" 2-23-66 (Handy Random), "Target" 10-31-66 (Josh Hawks), "Night in a Small

Town" 10-9-67 (Tom Wills), "Shadow of a Giant" 1-29-68 (Marshal Seth Campbell); *Shane*—"Day of the Hawk" 10-22-66 (Harry Himber); *The Monroes*—"The Hunter" 10-26-66 (Blaikner); *Custer*—"Spirit Woman" 12-13-67 (Eldo); *Cowboy in Africa*—"First to Capture" 1-29-68 (Ryan Crose); *Bonanza*—"To Die in Darkness" 5-5-68 (Ben Postley); *The Men from Shiloh*—"Lady at the Bar" 11-4-70 (Marshal Krug).

Whitmore, Jr., James. Films: "The Long Riders" 1980 (Mr. Rixley). ¶TV: *Bret Maverick*—"The Ballad of Bret Maverick" 2-16-82 (Justice Smith).

Whitney, CeCe (1932-). Films: "Bullet for a Badman" 1964 (Goldie). ¶TV: *Tombstone Territory*—"The Assassin" 5-21-58 (Katie Doolin); *Bonanza*—"The Dark Gate" 3-4-61 (Mrs. Marquett); *Gunsmoke*—"The Dreamers" 4-28-62 (Julia), "The Sisters" 12-29-69 (Ivy Landers).

Whitney, Claire (1890-8/27/69). Films: "The Girl I Left Behind Me" 1915 (General's Daughter); "The Plunderer" 1915 (Joan Presby); "Chip of the Flying U" 1939 (Miss Robinson); "The Silver Bullet" 1942; "The Woman of the Town" 1943 (Mrs. Wright); "Under Western Skies" 1945 (Mrs. Simms); "The Haunted Mine" 1946; "Cowboy Cavalier" 1948; "Oklahoma Badlands" 1948 (Agatha Scragg); "Frontier Marshal" 1949 (Molly Bright); "Roaring Westward" 1949 (Aunt Jessica).

Whitney, Grace Lee (1930-). Films: "The Man from Galveston" 1964 (Texas Rose). ¶TV: *Zane Grey Theater*—"Honor Bright" 2-2-61 (Ellen); *Bat Masterson*—"The Good and the Bad" 3-23-61 (Louise Talbot); *Gunsmoke*—"Reprisal" 3-10-62 (Pearl); *The Rifleman*—"The Tinhorn" 3-12-62 (Rose); *Death Valley Days*—"The Last Shot" 12-12-62 (Della), "Out of the Valley of Death" 5-25-68 (Angela); *The Virginian*—"Echo from Another Day" 3-27-63, "The Mustangers" 12-4-68 (Heather); *Temple Houston*—"The Man from Galveston" 1963 (Texas Rose), "Do Unto Others, Then Gallop" 3-19-64 (Tangerine O'Shea); *Wagon Train*—"The Andrew Elliott Story" 2-10-64; *Rango*—"My Teepee Runneth Over" 3-10-67 (Girl); *Cimarron Strip*—"Knife in the Darkness" 1-25-68; *The Big Valley*—"Run of the Savage" 3-11-68 (Maggie).

Whitney, Michael (-1983). TV: *Bonanza*—"Mighty Is the Word" 11-7-65 (Cliff Rexford), "Tommy" 12-18-66 (Jess Miler), "The Stronghold"

5-26-68 (Josh Farrell), "The Prisoners" 10-17-71 (Hank Simmons); *Gunsmoke*—"South Wind" 11-27-65 (Cavalry Captain); *Iron Horse*—"The Execution" 3-13-67 (Jared Hobson).

Whitney, Peter (1916-3/30/72). Films: "Valley of the Sun" 1942 (Willie, the Idiot); "Canyon Passage" 1946 (Van Houten); "Northwest Outpost" 1947 (Volkoff, the Overseer); "The Great Sioux Uprising" 1953 (Ahab Jones); "The Black Dakotas" 1954 (Grimes); "The Last Frontier" 1955 (Sgt. Maj. Decker); "Great Day in the Morning" 1956 (Phil the Cannibal); "Man from Del Rio" 1956 (Ed Bannister); "Domino Kid" 1957 (Lafe Prentiss); "Buchanan Rides Alone" 1958 (Amos Agry); "The Great Bank Robbery" 1969 (Brother Jordan); "The Ballad of Cable Hogue" 1970 (Cushing). ¶TV: *The Lone Ranger*—"Heritage of Treason" 2-3-55; *My Friend Flicka*—"A Case of Honor" 10-14-55 (Crothers); *Gunsmoke*—"The Hunter" 11-26-55 (Jase Murdock), "Sins of the Father" 1-19-57 (Dan Daggit), "Kangaroo" 10-10-59 (Ira Scurlock), "Harper's Blood" 10-21-61 (Gip Cooley), "Run, Sheep, Run" 1-9-65 (Dan Braden), "The Reward" 11-6-65 (Jason Holt); *Zane Grey Theater*—"No Man Living" 1-11-57 (Chub), "License to Kill" 2-7-58 (Growler), "The Bible Man" 2-23-61 (Matt), "Man from Everywhere" 4-13-61 (Moose); *Sheriff of Cochise*—"The Relatives" 3-8-57 (Saul); *Jim Bowie*—"Epitaph for an Indian" 9-6-57 (1st Gunman); *Tombstone Territory*—"Apache Vendetta" 12-11-57 (Karl Rank); *The Californians*—"Truce of the Tree" 12-17-57, "Shanghai Queen" 6-3-58 (Capt. Rutland); *Have Gun Will Travel*—"The Last Laugh" 1-25-58 (Judd Calhoun), "Fogg Bound" 12-3-60 (Major Proctor); *Maverick*—"The Savage Hills" 2-9-58 (Agent Gunnerson), "Dodge City or Bust" 12-11-60 (Brock); *Colt .45*—"Mantrap" 2-14-58 (Ralph); *Cheyenne*—"White Warrior" 3-11-58 (Eli Henderson), "The Imposter" 11-2-59 (Sam Magruder), "The Long Rope" 10-3-60 (Hugo Parma), "Legacy of the Lost" 12-4-61 (Lionel Abbott); *Wagon Train*—"The Rex Montana Story" 5-28-58 (Rodney), "The Lizabeth Ann Calhoun Story" 12-6-61 (El Ladron), "The Shiloh Degnan Story" 11-7-62 (Galloway), "The Hollister John Garrison Story" 2-6-63 (Kempton), "The David Garner Story" 5-8-63 (Judd), "The Stark Bluff Story" 4-6-64 (Sheriff Pincus), "The Betsy Blee Smith Story" 3-28-65 (Buter Blee); *Rough Riders*—Regular 1958-59 (Sergeant Sinclair);

Northwest Passage—"Trial by Fire" 3-6-59 (Daumier); *The Texan*—"The Dishonest Posse" 10-5-59 (Nate Jeeter); *The Law of the Plainsman*—"The Hostiles" 10-22-59, "The Dude" 12-3-59 (Sterling), "The Rawhiders" 1-28-60 (John Wesley); *The Rifleman*—"Eddie's Daughter" 11-3-59 (Tracey Blanch), "Mail Order Groom" 1-12-60 (John Jupiter), "Heller" 2-23-60 (Andrew Bechtol), "Strange Town" 10-25-60 (Ott Droshek), "The Queue" 5-16-61 (Vince Fergus), "Long Gun from Tucson" 12-11-61 (John Holliver), "Lou Mallory" 10-15-62 (Neb), "Gun Shy" 12-10-62 (Vantine), "Which Way'd They Go?" 4-1-63 (Neb Jackman); *Hotel De Paree*—"A Rope Is for Hanging" 11-6-59 (Coley); *Riverboat*—"A Night at Trapper's Landing" 11-8-59 (Noah Woodley); *Johnny Ringo*—"Dead Wait" 11-19-59 (Arnold Riker); *Fury*—"The Vanishing Blacksmith" 12-19-59 (Eli Kane); *The Alaskans*—"The Seal Skin-Game" 2-21-60 (Bear River Blewett), "White Vengeance" 6-5-60 (Jobka); *Tales of Wells Fargo*—"Forty-Four Forty" 2-29-60 (Big Duggin), "Something Pretty" 4-17-61 (Moose Gilliam); *Lawman*—"The Surface of Truth" 4-17-60 (Lucas Beyer), "The Stalker" 10-29-61 (Alteeka McClintoch); *Overland Trail*—"First Stage to Denver" 5-1-60 (Governor Sutcliff); *Rawhide*—"Incident of the One Hundred Amulets" 5-6-60, "Incident of the Music Maker" 5-20-60 (Anton Zwahlen); *Tate*—"Before Sunup" 8-17-60 (Clay Sedon); *Bonanza*—"The Mission" 9-17-60 (Lewt Cutter), "Commitment at Angelus" 4-7-68 (Hudson); *The Rebel*—"The Promise" 1-15-61 (Hobie Kincaid); *Death Valley Days*—"Who's for Divide?" 3-1-61 (Joe Meek), "From the Earth, a Heritage" 12-13-64 (Nat Halper), "Peter the Hunter" 2-14-65 (Peter the Hunter), "A Picture of a Lady" 3-19-66 (Judge Roy Bean), "Crullers at Sundown!" 5-21-66 (Joe Fuller); *Laramie*—"The Fortune Hunter" 10-9-62 (Fred McAllen); *Wide Country*—"The Quest for Jacob Blaufus" 3-7-63 (Amos Blaufus); *The Travels of Jaimie McPheeters*—"The Day of the Skinners" 10-20-63 (Daddy Scoggins); *Temple Houston*—"Jubilee" 11-14-63 (Cletus Emory); *The Virginian*—"A Bride for Lars" 4-15-64 (Lars Holstrum), "The Showdown" 4-14-65 (Jake Landers), "Nobody Said Hello" 1-5-66 (Ansel Miller), "The Runaway Boy" 10-22-69 (McPhearson); *Daniel Boone*—"Pompey" 12-10-64 (Caleb Calhoun); *The Legend of Jesse James*—"The Raiders" 10-18-65 (Quantrill); *The

Guns of Will Sonnett—"Of Lasting Summers and Jim Sonnett" 10-6-67 (Lastings Summers); *Iron Horse*—"T Is for Traitor" 12-2-67 (Matthew Kelsoe); *The Big Valley*—"Night of the Executioners" 12-11-67 (Sheriff Dan Kincaide); *Here Come the Brides*—"The Eyes of London Bob" 11-28-69 (London Bob).

Whitney, Ruth. Films: "The Texan Meets Calamity Jane" 1950 (Cecelia Mullen); "Hannah Lee" 1953 (Mrs. Stiver).

Whitney, Susan. Films: "Passage West" 1951 (Lea Johnson). ¶TV: *Bat Masterson*—"One Bullet from Broken Bow" 1-21-59 (Lori Rafferty).

Whitson, Frank (1876-3/19/46). Films: "Gold and the Woman" 1916; "A Daughter of the West" 1918 (Ralph Gordon); "The Dead Shot" 1918; "The Love Call" 1919 (O'-Keefe); "The Son of a Gun" 1919 (Double-Deck Harry); "Square Deal Sanderson" 1919 (Alva Dale); "Three Gold Coins" 1920 (Luther M. Reed); "Headin' West" 1922 (Stub Allen); "The Man from Hell's River" 1922 (Sgt. McKenna); "The White Messenger" 1922; "$50,000 Reward" 1924 (Asa Holman); "Her Man" 1924; "Fighting Courage" 1925 (Mark Crenshaw); "Bad Man's Bluff" 1926 (Dave Hardy); "The Fighting Boob" 1926 (Clayton); "Walloping Kid" 1926 (Mr. Carter); "The Texas Tornado" 1928 (Tim Briscoe); "Call of the Wild" 1935 (5th Poker Player).

Whitten, Margaret. Films: "Two Gun Man from Harlem" 1938 (Sally Thompson).

Whitworth, James. Films: "Fandango" 1970 (Dan Murphy).

Whorf, David. TV: *Gunsmoke*—"Sunday Supplement" 2-8-58 (Jack); *Tombstone Territory*—"The Black Marshal from Deadwood" 9-3-58 (Jackie); *Have Gun Will Travel*—"In an Evil Time" 9-13-58 (Jimmy Dawes); *Wanted—Dead or Alive*—"Rope Law" 1-3-59; *Rawhide*—"Incident of the Tumbleweed Wagon" 1-9-59; *Wichita Town*—"Brothers of the Knife" 2-10-60 (Joe); *Bonanza*—"The War Comes to Washoe" 11-4-62.

Whorf, Richard (1906-12/14/66). TV: *The Rifleman*—"The Illustrator" 12-13-60 (Jeremiah Crownley).

Whyte, Patrick. Films: "Fort Vengeance" 1953 (Harrington). ¶TV: *Wild Bill Hickok*—"Sheriff of Buckeye" 6-30-53; *Sergeant Preston of the Yukon*—"Lost Patrol" 10-18-56 (Insp. Fitzwilliam); *The Adventures of Rin Tin Tin*—"The White Wolf" 10-19-

56 (McKenzie), "Return of Rin Tin Tin" 10-26-56 (McKenzie), "The White Chief" 12-13-57 (Inspector McKenzie), "Star of India" 1-2-59 (Maj. Hollis); *Tales of the Texas Rangers*—"Warpath" 10-9-58 (Sgt. Reagan); *The Californians*—"The First Gold Brick" 1-6-59 (Minister); *Bat Masterson*—"The Canvas and the Cane" 12-17-59.

Wickes, Mary (1912-10/22/95). Films: "Destry" 1954 (Bessie Mae Curtis); "Cimarron" 1960 (Mrs. Hefner). ¶TV: *Zorro*—"The Deadly Bolas" 5-22-58, "The Well of Death" 5-29-58; *Bonanza*—"The Colonel" 1-6-63 (Martha), "A Christmas Story" 12-25-66 (Hattie); *Temple Houston*—Regular 1963-64 (Ida Goff); *F Troop*—"Marriage, Fort Courage Style" 3-9-67 (Samantha Oglesby).

Wickwire, Nancy (1926-7/10/74). TV: *Gunsmoke*—"My Sisters' Keeper" 11-2-63 (Nell Shuler).

Widdoes, Kathleen (1939-). TV: *Here Comes the Brides*—"A Crying Need" 10-2-68 (Dr. Allyn Wright); *Bonanza*—"Frenzy" 1-30-72 (Anna).

Widmark, Richard (1914-). Films: "Yellow Sky" 1948 (Dude); "Broken Lance" 1954 (Ben); "Garden of Evil" 1954 (Fiske); "Backlash" 1956 (Jim Slater); "The Last Wagon" 1956 (Todd); "The Law and Jake Wade" 1958 (Clint Hollister); "Warlock" 1959 (Johnny Gannon); "The Alamo" 1960 (Col. James Bowie); "Two Rode Together" 1961 (Lt. Jim Gary); "How the West Was Won" 1962 (Mike King); "Cheyenne Autumn" 1964 (Capt. Thomas Archer); "Alvarez Kelly" 1966 (Col. Tom Rossiter); "The Way West" 1967 (Lije Evans); "Death of a Gunfighter" 1969 (Marshal Frank Patch); "Talent for Loving" 1969-Brit./Span. (Nevada); "Halleluja and Sartana Strikes Again" 1972-Ger./Ital. (Sartana); "When the Legends Die" 1972 (Red Dillon); "Mr. Horn" TVM-1979 (Al Sieber); "Once Upon a Texas Train" TVM-1988 (Oren Hayes).

Widmark, Robert. *see* Dell'Acqua, Alberto.

Wiensko, Bob. TV: *Gunsmoke*—"Unwanted Deputy" 3-5-60 (Bob); *Sugarfoot*—"Blue Bonnet Stray" 4-26-60 (Ben Tracy), "Welcome Enemy" 12-26-60 (Long Knife); *Bronco*—"Tangled Trail" 5-3-60 (Dove); *Bonanza*—"The Savage" 12-3-60 (Kaska); *Maverick*—"Triple Indemnity" 3-19-61 (Jones).

Wiere, Harry (1908-). Films: "Hands Across the Border" 1943.

Wiere, Herbert (1908-). Films: "Hands Across the Border" 1943.

Wiere, Sylvester (1910-7/7/70). Films: "Hands Across the Border" 1943.

Wiggins, Chris. Films: "King of the Grizzlies" 1970 (Col. Pierson); "Welcome to Blood City" 1977-Brit./Can. (Gellor); "Black Fox" TVM-1995 (Ralph Holtz).

Wiggins, Russell. TV: *Alias Smith and Jones*—"The Posse That Wouldn't Quit" 10-14-71 (Hank Smithers); *Gunsmoke*—"The Deadly Innocent" 12-17-73 (Billy), "A Town in Chains" 9-16-74 (Pryor); *Hec Ramsey*—"Dead Heat" 2-3-74 (Neil Munson); *How the West Was Won*—"Luke" 4-2-79 (Alan).

Wilbanks, Don. Films: "Stagecoach to Dancer's Rock" 1962 (Maj. John Southern); "The Over-the-Hill Gang Rides Again" TVM-1970 (Cowboy); "Count Your Bullets" 1972 (Sergeant); "Zandy's Bride" 1974 (Farraday). ¶TV: *Death Valley Days*—"Vlley of Danger" 5-12-59 (William Marshall); *Rawhide*—"Incident of the Roman Candles" 7-10-59; *Laramie*—"Ride the Wild Wind" 10-11-60 (Deputy Morgan); *Tate*—"Home Town" 6-8-60 (Ike), "Voices of the Town" 7-6-60 (Billy Such), "Quiet After the Storm" 9-7-60 (Rupe); *Bronco*—"Seminole War Pipe" 12-12-60 (Corporal Tyrone); *Bat Masterson*—"Ledger of Guilt" 4-6-61 (Leith Windsor); *Wyatt Earp*—"Wyatt's Brothers Join Up" 6-6-61 (Breakenridge); *Bonanza*—"Land Grab" 12-31-61 (Jacks), "The Lila Conrad Story" 1-5-64; *Cheyenne*—"The Idol" 1-29-62 (Gene Kirby); *Empire*—"Duet for Eight Wheels" 4-30-63 (Corley); *The Virginian*—"No Tears for Savannah" 10-2-63 (Deputy), "Lost Yesterday" 2-3-65 (Feeney); *Destry*—"Go Away, Little Sheba" 3-27-64 (Jeff Wade); *Rango*—"It Ain't the Principle, It's the Money" 3-31-67 (Butch Dawson); *The Guns of Will Sonnett*—"Guilt" 11-29-68 (Don), "A Town in Terror" 2-7-69 & 2-14-69 (Fargo); *Lancer*—"The Kid" 10-7-69 (Foreman), "The Gifts" 10-28-69 (Hart), "Dream of Falcons" 4-7-70 (1st Cowboy).

Wilbur, Crane (1889-10/18/73). Films: "The Girl from Arizona" 1910; "Anona's Baptism" 1912; "On the Brink of the Chasm" 1912; "The Texas Twins" 1912; "The Perils of Pauline" 1914-serial; "A Law Unto Himself" 1916 (Jean Belleau/Allan Dwight); "Breezy Jim" 1919 (Breezy Jim).

Wilcox, Art (and his Arizona Rangers). Films: "Arizona Frontier" 1940; "Rainbow Over the Range" 1940.

Wilcox, Claire. TV: *The Virginian*—"First to Thine Own Self" 2-12-64 (Melanie), "The Barren Ground" 12-6-67 (Sarah Keogh); *Gunsmoke*—"Which Doctor" 3-19-66 (Piney); *Shane*—"Poor Tom's A-Cold" 11-5-66 (Louisa); *Laredo*—"Road to San Remo" 11-25-66 (Gussie Smith); *Daniel Boone*—"The Young Ones" 2-23-67 (Martha); *The High Chaparral*—"Ride the Savage Land" 2-11-68 (Olive).

Wilcox, Collin (1937-). Films: "A Cry in the Wilderness" TVM-1974 (Bess Millard). ¶TV: *Temple Houston*—"The Twisted Rope" 9-19-63 (Dorrie Chevenix); *The Travels of Jaimie McPheeters*—"The Day of the Long Night" 11-10-63 (Emmy); *Great Adventure*—"Teeth of the Lion" 1-17-64 (Elizabeth Cross); *The Road West*—"The Insider" 2-13-67 (Frances); *Death Valley Days*—"The Sage Hen" 10-12-68; *Gunsmoke*—"Horse Fever" 12-18-72 (Bess Frye).

Wilcox, Frank (1907-3/3/74). Films: "Pony Express Days" 1940-short; "River's End" 1940 (Constable Kentish); "Santa Fe Trail" 1940 (James Longstreet); "Virginia City" 1940 (Officer); "They Died with Their Boots On" 1941 (Capt. Webb); "Wild Bill Hickok Rides" 1942 (Martin); "Masked Raiders" 1949 (Corthell); "The Mysterious Desperado" 1949 (Stevens); "Annie Get Your Gun" 1950 (Mrs. Clay); "The Kid from Texas" 1950 (Sheriff Pat Garrett); "Cavalry Scout" 1951 (Matson); "The Half-Breed" 1952 (Sands); "Trail Guide" 1952 (Regan); "The Treasure of Lost Canyon" 1952 (Stranger); "Pony Express" 1953 (Walstrom); "Those Redheads from Seattle" 1953 (Vance Edmonds); "The Black Dakotas" 1954 (Zanchary Paige); "Three Young Texans" 1954 (Bill McAdoo); "Carolina Cannonball" 1955 (Professor); "The First Traveling Saleslady" 1956 (Marshal Duncan); "Seventh Cavalry" 1956 (Maj. Reno); "Hell's Crossroads" 1957 (Governor Crittenden); "Man from God's Country" 1958 (Beau Santee). ¶TV: *The Cisco Kid*—"Freedom of the Press" 9-27-52, "The Racoon Story" 11-15-52; *The Lone Ranger*—"Stage for Mademoiselle" 3-12-53, "Prisoner in Jeopardy" 8-20-53; *Jim Bowie*—"The Pearl and the Crown" 4-5-57 (Comm. Devereau); *Sugarfoot*—"Quicksilver" 11-26-57 (George Beaumont); *Broken Arrow*—"Smoke Signal" 12-10-57 (Col. Bradford), "Son of Cochise" 12-17-57 (Col. Cordell); *Wyatt Earp*—"Ballad and Truth" 3-4-58 (Les Piersall), "The Trail to Tombstone" 9-8-59 (Bywater); *The Restless Gun*—"The Crisis at Easter Creek" 4-7-58 (Sheriff Abner), "The Sweet Sisters" 3-23-59 (Sheriff Conroy); *Trackdown*—"The Governor" 5-23-58 (Gov. Henricks); *Zorro*—"An Eye for an Eye" 11-20-58, "Zorro and the Flag of Truce" 11-27-58, "Ambush" 12-4-58; *Rawhide*—"Incident of the Tumbleweed Wagon" 1-9-59 (Marshal Wilt Jackson), "Incident Near the Promised Land" 2-3-61 (Mr. Draper), "Incident of the Running Iron" 3-10-61 (Marshal Cox), "Grandma's Money" 2-23-62 (Colonel Agee), "Incident of the Prodigal Son" 10-19-62 (Mr. Whitney); *The Rifleman*—"The Sheridan Story" 1-13-59 (Col. Cass); *Bat Masterson*—"Shakedown at St. Joe" 10-29-59 (Haberdasher); *Wagon Train*—"The Tom Tuckett Story" 3-2-60, "The Clementine Jones Story" 10-25-61 (Nolan); *The Texan*—"Johnny Tuvo" 5-30-60 (Kincade); *Stagecoach West*—"Dark Return" 10-18-60 (Mr. Jessup); *Maverick*—"Mano Nera" 10-23-60 (Chief Rawlins); *Bronco*—"Moment of Doubt" 4-2-62 (Colonel); *Death Valley Days*—"Way Station" 5-2-62 (Mr. Waterfield); *Wide Country*—"Our Ernie Kills People" 11-1-62 (Larry Stannard); *Laredo*—"Pride of the Rangers" 12-16-65; *Wild Wild West*—"The Night of the Flying Pie Plate" 10-21-66 (Judge Bill Mott); *Pistols 'n' Petticoats*—12-17-66 (Arthur Grenoble); *Kung Fu*—"Alethea" 3-15-73 (Judge Moon).

Wilcox, Larry. Films: "The Last Hard Men" 1976 (Mike Shelby); "Last Ride of the Dalton Gang" TVM-1979 (Emmet Dalton).

Wilcox, Mary (1944-). TV: *Cimarron Strip*—"The Last Wolf" 12-14-67; *Here Come the Brides*—"A Jew Named Sullivan" 11-20-68.

Wilcox, Ralph (1951-). TV: *The Buffalo Soldiers*—Pilot 5-26-79 (Oakley).

Wilcox, Robert (1910-6/11/55). Films: "Wild and Woolly" 1937 (Editor Frank Bailey); "The Kid from Texas" 1939 (Duke Hastings); "Wild Beauty" 1946 (Gordon Madison); "The Vigilantes Return" 1947 (Clay Curtwright).

Wilcox, S.D. (1863-2/11/45). Films: "The Jack Rider" 1921 (John Welsh); "Danger Patrol" 1928 (Andre).

Wilcoxon, Henry (1905-3/6/84). Films: "The Last of the Mohicans" 1936 (Maj. Duncan Heyward); "Arizona Wildcat" 1938 (Richard Baldwin); "Unconquered" 1947 (Capt. Steele); "Man in the Wilderness" 1971-U.S./Span. (Indian Chief); "Against a Crooked Sky" 1975 (Cut Tongue); "Pony Express Rider" 1976 (Trevor). ¶TV: *The Big Valley*—"Winner Lose All" 10-27-65 (Don Alfredo Montero); *Daniel Boone*—"Forty Rifles" 3-10-66 (William Blunt); *The Road West*—"Shaman" 11-14-66 (Wills); *Cimarron Strip*—"The Battle of Blood Stone" 10-12-67 (Ghost Wolf); *Wild Wild West*—"The Night of the Pistoleros" 2-21-69 (Armando Gallando); *Gunsmoke*—"Stark" 9-28-70 (John Bramley).

Wild, John (-5/2/21). Films: "The Learnin' of Jim Benton" 1917; "Beyond the Shadows" 1918 (Father Wyatt); "The Law of the Great Northwest" 1918 (Priest).

Wilde, Cornel (1915-10/15/89). Films: "Two Flags West" 1950 (Capt. Mark Bradford); "California Conquest" 1952 (Con Arturo Bordega); "Passion" 1954 (Juan Obregon).

Wilde, Lois. Films: "Caryl of the Mountains" 1936 (Caryl Foray); "The Singing Cowboy" 1936 (Helen); "Stormy Trails" 1936 (Connie Curlew); "Wildcat Trooper" 1936 (Ruth); "Danger Valley" 1937 (Mickey Temple); "Hopalong Rides Again" 1937 (Laura Peters); "Brothers of the West" 1938 (Celia Chandler).

Wilde, Lyn. Films: "Sheriff of Wichita" 1949 (Nancy Bishop); "Tucson" 1949 (Gertie Peck).

Wilde, Sonja. TV: *Death Valley Days*—"The Man Everyone Hated" 4-12-60; *Cheyenne*—"Two Trails to Santa Fe" 10-28-60 (Aleeah); *Bonanza*—"The Last Viking" 11-12-60 (Carrie McClane); *Gunslinger*—"Johnny Sergeant" 5-4-61 (Tani); *Rawhide*—"The Lost Tribe" 10-27-61 (White Deer).

Wilder, Gene (1935-). Films: "Blazing Saddles" 1974 (Jim); "The Frisco Kid" 1979 (Avram Belinsky).

Wilder, Glenn (1938-). Films: "Bounty Man" TVM-1972 (Gault).

Wilder, John. Films: "Five Guns to Tombstone" 1961 (Ted Wade). ¶TV: *Circus Boy*—"The Great Gambino's Son" 3-10-57 (Tony); *The Adventures of Rin Tin Tin*—"Stagecoach Sally" 4-19-57 (Pete Benton); *Zane Grey Theater*—"Decision at Wilson's Creek" 5-17-57 (Sanborn), "Wire" 1-31-58 (Ben Fraser); *Broken Arrow*—"Duel" 3-18-58 (Ben); *Wanted—Dead or Alive*—"Die by the Gun" 12-6-58

(Joe); *Wagon Train*—"The Elizabeth McQueeney Story" 10-28-59.

Wiley, J.A. (1884-9/30/62). Films: "Chasing Trouble" 1926 (Stech).

Wiley, Jan (1916-6/3/93). Films: "Tonto Basin Outlaws" 1941 (Jane); "Dawn on the Great Divide" 1942 (Martha); "Thunder River Feud" 1942 (Maybelle); "Law Men" 1944 (Phyllis); "The Cisco Kid Returns" 1945 (Jeanette); "Frontier Gal" 1945 (Sheila Winthrop).

Wilke, Robert J. (1911-3/28/89). Films: "Come on, Rangers" 1939; "In Old Monterey" 1939; "Adventures of Red Ryder" 1940-serial (Street Heavy); "California Joe" 1943; "Beneath Western Skies" 1944; "The Big Bonanza" 1944; "Bordertown Trail" 1944; "Cheyenne Wildcat" 1944; "Code of the Prairie" 1944 (Outlaw in Office); "Cowboy and the Senorita" 1944; "Firebrands of Arizona" 1944 (Deputy Sheriff); "Hidden Valley Outlaws" 1944; "Marshal of Reno" 1944; "The San Antonio Kid" 1944; "Sheriff of Sundown" 1944 (Bradley); "Vigilantes of Dodge City" 1944; "The Yellow Rose of Tesas" 1944; "Zorro's Black Whip" 1944-serial (Bill Slocum); "Bandits of the Badlands" 1945; "Bells of Rosarita" 1945; "Corpus Christi Bandits" 1945 (Steve); "Great Stagecoach Robbery" 1945; "Lone Texas Ranger" 1945; "The Man from Oklahoma" 1945; "Rough Riders of Cheyenne" 1945; "Santa Fe Saddlemates" 1945; "Sheriff of Cimarron" 1945 (Shad); "Sunset in El Dorado" 1945 (Curley Roberts); "The Topeka Terror" 1945 (Townsman); "Trail of Kit Carson" 1945; "The El Paso Kid" 1946; "King of the Forest Rangers" 1946-serial (Carleton); "Out California Way" 1946 (Assistant Director); "The Phantom Rider" 1946-serial (Indian Rebel #1); "Roaring Rangers" 1946; "Last Days of Boot Hill" 1947 (Bronc Peters); "Law of the Canyon" 1947; "The Michigan Kid" 1947; "The Vigilantes Return" 1947 (Henchman); "Twilight on the Rio Grande" 1947; "West of Dodge City" 1947; "Carson City Raiders" 1948 (Ed Noble); "Dangers of the Canadian Mounted" 1948-serial (Baxter); "River Lady" 1948 (Man); "Six-Gun Law" 1948 (Larson); "Sundown in Santa Fe" 1948; "West of Sonora" 1948 (Brock); "Coyote Canyon" 1949-short; "Ghost of Zorro" 1949-serial (Townsman #1); "Laramie" 1949 (Cronin); "The Wyoming Bandit" 1949 (Sam); "Across the Badlands" 1950 (Duke Jackson/Keeno Jackson); "Beyond the

Purple Hills" 1950 (Jim Connors); "Frontier Outpost" 1950 (Krag Benson); "The James Brothers of Missouri" 1950-serial (Townsman #2); "Mule Train" 1950 (Bradshaw); "Outcast of Black Mesa" 1950 (Curt); "Twilight in the Sierras" 1950; "Best of the Badmen" 1951 (Jim Younger); "Cyclone Fury" 1951 (Bunco); "Gunplay" 1951 (Winslow); "Hot Lead" 1951 (Stoney Dawson); "Overland Telegraph" 1951 (Bellew); "Pistol Harvest" 1951 (Baylor); "Saddle Legion" 1951 (Hooker); "Vengeance Valley" 1951 (Cowhand); "Cattle Town" 1952 (Keeno); "Fargo" 1952; "Hellgate" 1952 (Sgt. Maj. Kearn); "High Noon" 1952 (James Pierce); "Laramie Mountains" 1952 (Mandel); "The Maverick" 1952 (William Massey); "Road Agent" 1952 (Slab); "Wyoming Roundup" 1952 (Wyatt); "Arrowhead" 1953 (Sgt. Stone); "Cow Country" 1953 (Sledge); "Powder River" 1953 (Will Horn); "War Paint" 1953 (Sgt. Grady); "The Lone Gun" 1954 (Hort Moran); "Two Guns and a Badge" 1954 (Moore); "The Far Country" 1955 (Madden); "Shotgun" 1955 (Bentley); "Smoke Signal" 1955 (1st Sgt. Daly); "Strange Lady in Town" 1955 (Karg); "Wichita" 1955 (Ben Thompson); "Backlash" 1956 (Jeff Welker); "Canyon River" 1956 (Graycoe); "The Lone Ranger" 1956 (Cassidy); "Raw Edge" 1956 (Sile Doty); "The Rawhide Years" 1956 (Neal); "Gun the Man Down" 1957 (Matt Rankin); "Night Passage" 1957 (Concho); "Man of the West" 1958 (Ponch); "Return to Warbow" 1958 (Red); "The Magnificent Seven" 1960 (Wallace); "The Long Rope" 1961 (Ben Matthews); "The Gun Hawk" 1963 (Johnny Flanders); "The Hallelujah Trail" 1965 (Chief Five Barrels); "Smoky" 1966 (Jeff); "The Cheyenne Social Club" 1970 (Corey Bannister); "Desperate Mission" TVM-1971 (Gant); "A Gunfight" 1971 (Marshal Cater); "Santee" 1973; "Wild and Wooly" TVM-1978 (Demas Scott); "The Sweet Creek County War" 1979 (Lucas K. Deering). ¶TV: *The Lone Ranger*—"The Man Who Came Back" 1-5-50; *The Gene Autry Show*—"The Posse" 9-17-50, "The Devil's Brand" 9-24-50, "The Western Way" 2-1-52, "Hot Lead and Old Lace" 2-15-52; *The Roy Rogers Show*—"The Train Robbery" 2-3-52, "Go for Your Gun" 11-23-52, "The Long Chance" 5-24-53, "M Stands for Murder" 12-6-53; *The Cisco Kid*—"The Kid Brother" 2-9-52, "Dutchman's Flat" 3-15-52, "Commodore Goes West" 7-12-52; *Cheyenne*—"Mountain Fortress" 9-20-55, "The Long Winter" 9-25-56 (Kelso), "The Mustang Trail" 11-20-56 (Begert), "The Mutton Puncher" 10-22-57 (Ben Creed), "Outcast of Cripple Creek" 2-29-60 (Carl Banner); *Jim Bowie*—"The Bound Girl" 5-10-57; *Disneyland*—"The Saga of Andy Burnett"—Regular 1957-58 (Ben Tilton); *Tombstone Territory*—"Revenge Town" 11-6-57 (Jess Caulfield), "Grave Near Tombstone" 5-22-59 (Burt Foster), 12-11-59 (Todd Gantry); *Colt .45*—"Long Odds" 4-11-58; *Gunsmoke*—"Matt for Murder" 9-13-58 (Wild Bill Hickok), "Saludos" 10-31-59 (Pegger), "Big Tom" 1-9-60 (Tom Burr), "The Ex-Urbanites" 4-9-60 (Pitt), "He Learned About Women" 2-24-62 (Ab Rankin), "The Basshops" 2-22-64 (Wayne Kelby), "Cattle Barons" 9-18-67 (Luke Cumberledge); *Tales of Wells Fargo*—"Faster Gun" 10-6-58, "The Wade Place" 11-28-60 (Mike Ross); *The Rifleman*—"The Marshal" 10-21-58 (Flory Sheltin), "The Pet" 1-6-59 (Ward Haskins); *Bat Masterson*—"The Fighter" 11-5-58 (Bull Kirby), "Dead Men Don't Pay Debts" 11-19-59 (Rod Clements); *Lawman*—"Wanted" 11-16-58 (Fallon), "The Journey" 4-26-59 (Sheriff Tom Haddon), "The Press" 11-29-59 (Lal Hoard); *Have Gun Will Travel*—"The Man Who Lost" 2-7-59 (Walt DeVries), "The Naked Gun" 12-19-59 (Rook), "Return to Fort Benjamin" 1-30-60 (Major Blake), "American Primitive" 2-2-63 (Will Tybee); *The Texan*—"The Marshal of Yellow Jacket" 3-2-59 (Marshal Bart Pennock), "Blood Money" 4-20-59, "Cowards Don't Die" 11-30-59 (Pete Torrey), "Killer's Road" 4-25-60 (Asa Kirby); *U.S. Marshal*—"A Matter of Friendship" 3-14-59 (Henry Brandon); *Man Without a Gun*—"Buried Treasure" 4-4-59; *Zorro*—"The Man from Spain" 4-9-59 (Captain Mendoza), "Treasure for the King" 4-16-59 (Captain Mendoza), "Exposing the Tyrant" 4-23-59 (Captain Mendoza), "Zorro Takes a Dare" 4-30-59 (Captain Mendoza); *Wanted—Dead or Alive*—"Littlest Giant" 4-25-59, "Estrelita" 10-3-59 (Jack Radovitch), "No Trail Back" 11-28-59 (Ben Hooker); *The Deputy*—"The Deputy" 9-12-59 (Ace Gentry); *Wichita Town*—"Bullet for a Friend" 10-14-59 (Johnny Burke); *The Law of the Plainsman*—"Desperate Decision" 11-12-59 (Amos); *Maverick*—"Hadley's Hunters" 9-25-60 (McCabe), "Epitaph of a Gambler" 2-11-62 (Diamond Jim Malone); *Overland Trail*—"Perilous Passage" 2-7-60 (Cole Younger); *Riverboat*—"End of a Dream" 9-19-60 (Red Dog Hanlon); *Laramie*—"The Track of the Jackal" 9-27-60 (Sumner Campbell), "A Sound of Bells" 12-27-60 (Slate), "The Fatal Step" 10-24-61 (Marshal Fletcher), "Justice in a Hurry" 3-20-62 (Sheriff), "Fall into Darkness" 4-17-62 (Bob Laird), "The Marshals" 4-30-63 (Clint Buckner); *The Westerner*—"The Old Man" 11-25-60; *Bonanza*—"The Trail Gang" 11-26-60 (Brazos), "Return to Honor" 3-22-64 (Marshall), "The Flannel-Mouth Gun" 1-31-65 (Simmons), "Trouble Town" 3-17-68 (Sheriff Booker), "Old Friends" 12-14-69 (Charlie Sheppard); *Wagon Train*—"The River Crossing" 12-14-60 (Jabez Moore), "The Jud Steele Story" 5-2-62 (Wesley Thomas), "The Johnny Masters Story" 1-16-63 (Colonel Stone), "The Fort Pierce Story" 9-23-63 (Sergeant Wick); *Stagecoach West*—"The Brass Lily" 1-17-61 (Taylor Norman); *The Tall Man*—"The Last Resource" 3-11-61 (Marshal Ben Hartley); *Rawhide*—"Incident of the Running Man" 5-5-61 (Sheriff McVey), "Incident of the Four Horsemen" 10-26-62 (Tom Gault), "Incident of the Mountain Man" 1-25-63 (Lafe Thomas); *The Outlaws*—"Night Riders" 11-2-61 (Meder); *Frontier Circus*—"Winter Quarters" 11-23-61 (Jack Gance); *Bronco*—"The Last Letter" 3-5-62 (Buckin); *The Dakotas*—"Crisis at High Banjo" 2-11-63 (Judge Markham); *The Slowest Gun in the West* 7-29-63 (Butcher Blake); *Death Valley Days*—"The Man Who Died Twice" 12-22-63 (Ben Holladay), "The Journey" 6-13-65 (Sergeant Wilks), "Brute Angel" 10-15-66 (Sheriff McBain); *The Virginian*—"Dark Destiny" 4-29-64 (Conrad); *The Legend of Jesse James*—Regular 1965-66 (Marshal Sam Corbett); *Daniel Boone*—"The Enchanted Gun" 11-17-66 (Jake Manning), "Heroes Welcome" 2-22-68; *The Monroes*—"Killer Cougar" 2-1-67 (Len Gregger); *Rango*—"It Ain't the Principle, It's the Money" 3-31-67 (Walker); *Cimarron Strip*—"The Battleground" 9-28-67 (Hardy Miller), "The Last Wolf" 12-14-67 (Hardy Miller); *The Guns of Will Sonnett*—"The Hero" 12-29-67 (Sheriff Dan Butler), "Meeting in a Small Town" 12-6-68 (Judd); *Wild Wild West*—"The Night of the Arrow" 12-29-67 (Gen. Titus Ord Baldwin); *Lancer*—"Chase a Wild Horse" 10-8-68 (Stryker); *The Outcasts*—"Gideon" 2-24-69 (Sheriff Gus); *Kung Fu*—"An Eye for an Eye" 1-25-73 (Bridgers); *The Quest*—"Dynasty of Evil" 1976; *How the West Was Won*—Episode Six 3-26-78 (Appleton).

Wilkerson, Guy (1898-7/15/71). Films: "Heart of the Rockies" 1937; "Yodelin' Kid from Pine Ridge" 1937 (Clem); "Gold Is Where You Find It" 1938 (Rancher); "Dodge City" 1939; "The Mysterious Rider" 1942; "The Rangers Take Over" 1942 (Panhandle Perkins); "Vengeance of the West" 1942; "Bad Men of Thunder Gap" 1943; "Border Buckaroos" 1943 (Panhandle Perkins); "The Return of the Rangers" 1943; "Fighting Valley" 1943 (Panhandle Perkins); "West of Texas" 1943 (Panhandle Perkins); "Boss of Rawhide" 1944 (Panhandle Perkins); "Brand of the Devil" 1944 (Panhandle Perkins); "Dead or Alive" 1944 (Panhandle Perkins); "Gangsters of the Frontier" 1944; "Guns of the Law" 1944; "Gunsmoke Mesa" 1944 (Panhandle Preston); "Outlaw Roundup" 1944; "The Pinto Bandit" 1944; "Spook Town" 1944; "Trail of Terror" 1944 (Panhandle Perkins); "The Whispering Skull" 1944; "Enemy of the Law" 1945 (Panhandle Perkins); "Flaming Bullets" 1945; "Frontier Fugitives" 1945; "Marked for Murder" 1945; "Three in the Saddle" 1945; "Duel in the Sun" 1946 (Barfly); "The Michigan Kid" 1947 (Shotgun Messenger); "The Sea of Grass" 1947 (Wake); "Fury at Furnace Creek" 1948 (Court Clerk); "Ticket to Tomahawk" 1950 (Dr. Brink); "Winchester '73" 1950 (Virgil); "Along the Great Divide" 1951 (Jury Foreman); "The Great Missouri Raid" 1951 (Clell Miller); "Santa Fe" 1951; "The Big Sky" 1952 (Longface); "The Last Posse" 1953 (George Romer); "The Stranger Wore a Gun" 1953 (Ike); "The Far Country" 1955 (Tanana Pete); "Jubal" 1956 (Cookie); "Decision at Sundown" 1957 (Abe); "Shoot-Out at Medicine Bend" 1957; "Cowboy" 1958 (Peggy); "Man of the West" 1958 (Conductor); "Wild Heritage" 1958 (Chaco); "The Hanging Tree" 1959 (Home Owner); "Black Spurs" 1965; "War Party" 1965; "The Great Bank Robbery" 1969 (Glazier); "True Grit" 1969 (the Hangman); "Monte Walsh" 1970 (Old Man). ¶TV: *Wild Bill Hickok*—"Rustling Stallion" 3-4-52; *The Cisco Kid*—"Laughing Badman" 3-8-52; *Tales of Wells Fargo*—"Hide Jumpers" 1-27-58 (Fresno Keeley); *Maverick*—"Seed of Deception" 4-13-58 (Cecil Mason), "The Thirty-Ninth Star" 11-16-58 (Desk Clerk), "Holiday at Hollow Rock" 12-28-58 (Sam), "Dade City Dodge" 9-18-61 (Herns), "The Money Machine" 4-8-62 (Mark Conway); *Gunsmoke*—"The Bear" 2-28-59 (Pete Wilkins); *The Tall Man*—"Bad Company" 9-24-60 (Jake Marlow); *Stagecoach*

West—"A Time to Run" 11-15-60 (Haddlebird); *Wanted—Dead or Alive*—"Criss Cross" 11-16-60; *Lawman*—"Cornered" 12-11-60 (Phillips); *The Virginian*—"If You Have Tears" 2-13-63, "Ring of Silence" 10-27-65 (Sheriff); *The Legend of Jesse James*—"The Celebrity" 12-6-65 (Bartender); *Death Valley Days*—"Crullers at Sundown!" 5-21-66 (Dokerson), "The Man Who Didn't Want Gold" 3-25-67 (Jack Winters); *Bonanza*—"Dead Wrong" 12-7-69 (Sheriff), "A Deck of Aces" 1-31-71 (Milt Jarvis).

Wilkerson, William C. "Bill" (1903-3/3/66). Films: "Susannah of the Mounties" 1939 (Indian); "King of the Stallions" 1942; "Frontier Fury" 1943 (Chief Eagle Feather); "Riding West" 1944 (Red Eagle); "Bowery Buckaroos" 1947 (Moose); "Robin Hood of Texas" 1947; "Apache Chief" 1949 (Grey Cloud); "Broken Arrow" 1950 (Juan); "Davy Crockett, Indian Scout" 1950 (High Tree); "Rock Island Trail" 1950 (Lakin); "Blue Canadian Rockies" 1952 (Dusty); "Brave Warrior" 1952 (Chief Little Cloud); "California Conquest" 1952 (Fernando); "Desert Pursuit" 1952; "Saginaw Trail" 1953 (the Fox); "Yukon Vengeance" 1954. ¶TV: *Wild Bill Hickok*—"Indians and the Delegates" 7-8-52.

Wilkes, Donna. TV: *Father Murphy*—"The First Miracle" 4-4-82 & 4-11-82 (Emma).

Wilkins, Barbara. Films: "Stagecoach" 1966 (Susan). ¶TV: *Bonanza*—"Thanks for Everything, Friend" 10-11-64 (Matilda); *The Big Valley*—"The Good Thieves" 1-1-68 (Olga).

Wilkins, June. Films: "Pioneer Days" 1940 (Mary Leeds); "When the Daltons Rode" 1940 (Suzy); "Lady from Cheyenne" 1941 (Chorus Girl).

Wilks, Darrell. Films: "The Last Days of Frank and Jesse James" TVM-1986 (Bob Ford).

Wilkus, Bill. Films: "Adventures of Red Ryder" 1940-serial (Water Heavy #3); "King of the Royal Mounted" 1940-serial (Bill); "King of the Texas Rangers" 1941-serial.

Willard, Ellen. TV: *The Outlaws*—"Last Chance" 11-10-60 (Sue Ellen McKim); *Wagon Train*—"The Bleymier Story" 11-16-60 (Belle); *The Tall Man*—"And the Beast" 11-26-60 (Agatha Evans); *Whispering Smith*—"The Quest" 6-26-61 (Charlotte Laughlin); *Lawman*—"The Lords of Darkness" 12-3-61 (Caroline); *Have Gun Will Travel*—"The Predators" 11-3-62, "The Walking Years" 3-2-63

(Mollie Dean); *Gunsmoke*—"The Hunger" 11-17-62 (Althea Dorf).

Willard, Jess (1881-12/15/68). Films: "The Challenge of Chance" 1919 (Joe Bates).

Willard, Lee. Films: "Bonnie of the Hills" 1913; "The Atonement" 1914; "Broncho Billy and the Greaser" 1914; "Broncho Billy and the Red Man" 1914; "Broncho Billy and the Sheriff's Office" 1914; "Broncho Billy—Favorite" 1914; "Broncho Billy's Indian Romance" 1914; "The Calling of Jim Barton" 1914; "The Good for Nothing" 1914 (Ralph Sterling); "Andy of the Royal Mounted" 1915; "Broncho Billy and the Card Sharp" 1915; "Broncho Billy and the Lumber King" 1915; "Broncho Billy and the Vigilante" 1915; "Broncho Billy Begins Life Anew" 1915; "Broncho Billy Misled" 1915; "Broncho Billy, Sheepman" 1915; "Broncho Billy Well Repaid" 1915; "Broncho Billy's Cowardly Brother" 1915; "The Burglar's Godfather" 1915; "The Convict's Threat" 1915; "The Escape of Broncho Billy" 1915; "The Face at the Curtain" 1915; "His Regeneration" 1915; "His Wife's Secret" 1915; "The Other Girl" 1915; "The Revenue Agent" 1915; "An Unexpected Romance" 1915; "The Book Agent's Romance" 1916; "The Mediator" 1916 (Bill Higgins).

Willes, Jean (1923-1/3/89). Films: "Son of Paleface" 1952 (Penelope); "Masterson of Kansas" 1954 (Dallas Corey); "Count Three and Pray" 1955 (Selma); "King and Four Queens" 1956 (Ruby); "Three Thousand Hills" 1959 (Jen); "Gun Street" 1961 (Joan Brady); "The Cheyenne Social Club" 1970 (Alice); "Bite the Bullet" 1975 (Rosie). ¶TV: *The Range Rider*—"The Border City Affair" 4-26-52; *Tales of the Texas Rangers*—"Carnival Criss-Cross" 9-3-55 (Belle Bishop); *Wyatt Earp*—"Bat Masterson Again" 4-17-56 (Amy Pelton); *Frontier*—"The Return of Jubal Dolan" 8-26-56 (Ruth); *Zane Grey Theater*—"The Long Road Home" 10-19-56 (Jenny Gracie), "The Necessary Breed" 2-15-57 (Kate), "Gift from a Gunman" 12-13-57 (Marcy); *Tales of Wells Fargo*—"Barbara Coast" 11-25-57; *The Californians*—"The Coward" 1-7-58 (Susan Jones); *Maverick*—"Day of Reckoning" 2-2-58 (Lil), "Full House" 10-25-59 (Belle Starr); *Colt .45*—"Circle of Fear" 3-7-58 (Blanche Waymer); *Trackdown*—"The Bounty Hunter" 3-7-58 (Janette York); *Tombstone Territory*—"Strange Vengeance" 4-9-58 (Libby), "The Black Diamond" 4-17-59 (Mrs.

Sarah Curtize); *Decision*—"The Tall Man" 7-27-58 (Laura Dawson); *Frontier Doctor*—"Queen of the Cimarron" 9-27-58; *Bat Masterson*—"Double Showdown" 10-8-58 (Lucy Slater), "The Inner Circle" 12-31-59 (Grace Williams); *Lawman*—"The Jury" 11-9-58 (Kate Wilson), "The Persecuted" 4-9-61 (Annie); *Wanted Dead or Alive*—"Ricochet" 11-22-58 (Dora Gaines), "Eager Man" 2-28-59, "The Kovack Affair" 3-28-59 (Meghan Francis), "Montana Kid" 9-5-59 (Manila Jones); *Wichita Town*—"Day of Battle" 1-18-59 (Myra Dudley); *Rough Riders*—"Double Cross" 1-22-59 (Belle Starr); *The Texan*—"The Man Behind the Star" 2-9-59 (Martha Driscoll); *Zorro*—"The Mountain Man" 3-19-59 (Carlotta), "The Hound of the Sierras" 3-26-59 (Carlotta), "Manhunt" 4-2-59 (Carlotta); *Yancy Derringer*—"The Quiet Firecracker" 5-21-59 (Jessie Bell); *Man from Blackhawk*—"The Man Who Stole Happiness" 10-30-59 (Belle Dawson), "The Money Machine" 6-10-60 (Lee Talman); *Bonanza*—"The Sisters" 12-12-59, "The Gentleman from New Orleans" 2-2-64 (Molly), "A Good Night's Rest" 4-11-65 (Mrs. Jenkins), "Star Crossed" 3-10-68 (Mrs. O'Brien); *The Deputy*—"Dark Reward" 3-26-60 (Rosie); *Wagon Train*—"The Charlene Brenton Story" 6-8-60 (Flo); *The Westerner*—"Dos Pinos" 11-4-60 (Sal); *Bronco*—"Beginner's Luck" 1-1-62 (Dolly); *Cheyenne*—"Vengeance Is Mine" 11-26-62 (Meg Stevens); *Empire*—"The Convention" 5-14-63 (Claire Hagen); *The Slowest Gun in the West* 7-29-63 (Kathy McQueen); *Temple Houston*—"Fracas at Kiowa Flats" 12-12-63 (Doll Lucas); *Death Valley Days*—"A Bell for Volcano" 1-24-65 (Maggie); *The Virginian*—"The Mark of a Man" 4-20-66 (Lily); *The Guns of Will Sonnett*—"The Secret of Hangtown Mine" 12-22-67 (Ellie).

William, Warren (1895-9/24/48). Films: "Arizona" 1940 (Jefferson Carteret); "Trail of the Vigilantes" 1940 (Mark Dawson); "Wild Bill Hickok Rides" 1942 (Harry Farrel).

Williams, Adam (1929-). Films: "The Yellow Tomahawk" 1954 (Cpl. Maddock); "The Lonely Man" 1957 (Lon); "The Oklahoman" 1957 (Bob Randell); "The Badlanders" 1958 (Leslie); "The Last Sunset" 1961 (Calverton); "Gunfight at Comanche Creek" 1964; "The Glory Guys" 1965 (Crain); "The Girl Called Hatter Fox" TVM-1977; "Last Ride of the Dalton Gang" TVM-1979 (Preacher). ¶TV: *Northwest Passage*—"Break

Out" 10-19-58 (Corporal Quill); *The Texan*—"The Ringer" 2-16-59 (Jebb Kilmer); *The Rifleman*—"The Challenge" 4-7-59 (Jake Pardee), "The Prisoner" 3-14-61 (Captain Trock), "The Score Is Even" 4-11-61 (Jax), "The Executioner" 5-7-62 (Russell Gannaway), "The Wanted Man" 9-25-62 (Mal Sherman), "The Anvil Chorus" 12-17-62; *Have Gun Will Travel*—"The Chase" 4-11-59 (Beckett), "Full Circle" 5-14-60 (Simon Quill); *Black Saddle*—"Client: Frome" 4-25-59 (Clint Frome), "Letter of Death" 1-8-60 (Brad Pickard); *Rawhide*—"Incident in No Man's Land" 6-12-59 (Kellino), "Gold Fever" 5-4-62 (Hank Kale); *Bonanza*—"The Hanging Posse" 11-28-59 (Blackie Marks), "Vengeance" 2-11-61 (Red Twilight), "The Brass Box" 9-26-65 (Muller); "The Prince" 4-2-67 (Hardesty); *Zane Grey Theater*—"Miss Jenny" 1-7-60 (Harlan Breckenridge); *The Westerner*—"Dos Pinos" 11-4-60 (Paul); *The Outlaws*—"Starfall" 11-24-60 & 12-1-60 (Burt); *Lawman*—"The Persecuted" 4-9-61 (Burley Keller); *Whispering Smith*—"Dark Circle" 9-4-61; *Gunsmoke*—"The Do-Badder" 1-6-62; *Maverick*—"Epitaph of a Gambler" 2-11-62 (Sam Elkins); *Cheyenne*—"Johnny Brassbuttons" 12-3-62 (Jeb Quinn); *Temple Houston*—"Do Unto Others, Then Gallop" 3-19-64 (Harmony Brown); *Daniel Boone*—"My Brother's Keeper" 10-8-64 (Mose); *The Virginian*—"The Old Cowboy" 3-31-65 (Roper); *A Man Called Shenandoah*—"Survival" 9-20-65 (Tate); *Custer*—"Blazing Arrows" 11-29-67 (Sergeant Carhew); *The High Chaparral*—"Bad Day for a Thirst" 2-18-68 (Burton).

Williams, Bert (1922-). Films: "From Noon to Three" 1976 (Sheriff); "The White Buffalo" 1977 (Paddy Welch); "Wanda Nevada" 1979 (Sherman Krupp); "Tom Horn" 1980 (Judge).

Williams, Bill (1917-9/21/92). Films: "Two-Fisted Sheriff" 1937 (Dunne); "West of the Pecos" 1945 (Tex Evans); "Smoky River Serenade" 1947; "Fighting Man of the Plains" 1949 (Johnny Tancred); "Range Justice" 1949 (Chuck); "California Passage" 1950 (Bob Martin); "The Cariboo Trail" 1950 (Mike Evans); "The Great Missouri Raid" 1951 (Jim Younger); "The Last Outpost" 1951 (Sgt. Tucker); "Bronco Buster" 1952; "Rose of Cimarron" 1952 (George Newcomb); "Son of Paleface" 1952 (Kirk); "The Outlaw's Daughter" 1954 (Jess); "Apache Ambush" 1955 (James Kingston); "The Broken Star" 1956 (Bill Gentry); "The Wild Dako-

tas" 1956; "Gunfight at the O.K. Corral" 1957 (Stunts); "The Halliday Brand" 1957 (Clay); "Pawnee" 1957 (Matt); "Slim Carter" 1957 (Frank Hannemann); "The Storm Rider" 1957 (Coulton); "Oklahoma Territory" 1960 (Temple Houston); "Law of the Lawless" 1964 (Silas Miller); "The Hallelujah Trail" 1965 (Brady); "Tickle Me" 1965 (Deputy Sturdivant); "Buckskin" 1968 (Frank Cody); "Rio Lobo" 1970 (Sheriff Pat Cronin); "Scandalous John" 1971 (Sheriff Hart). ¶TV: *The Adventures of Kit Carson*—Regular 1951-55 (Kit Carson); *Yancy Derringer*—"Ticket to Natchez" 10-23-58 (Winslow); *Texas John Slaughter*—"The Man from Bitter Creek" 3-6-59 (Paul Forbes), "The Slaughter Trail" 3-20-59 (Paul Forbes); *Laramie*—"Man of God" 12-1-59 (Root); *Lawman*—"Get Out of Town" 5-20-62 (Jim Bushrod); *Rawhide*—"The Lost Herd" 10-16-64 (Bickle); *Wild Wild West*—"The Night of the Casual Killer" 10-15-65 (Marshal Kirby); *Daniel Boone*—"The Spanish Horse" 11-23-67; *Gunsmoke*—"Talbot" 2-26-73 (Red Yeager); *The Quest*—"The Seminole Negro Indian Scouts" 1976.

Williams, Billy Dee (1937-). Films: "The Return of Desperado" TVM-1988 (Daniel Lancaster). ¶TV: *Lonesome Dove*—Pilot 10-2-94, 10-9-94 & 10-16-94 (Aaron Grayson).

Williams, Cara (1925-). Films: "The White Buffalo" 1977 (Cassie Ollinger). ¶TV: *Zane Grey Theater*—"Seed of Evil" 4-7-60 (Irene).

Williams, Charles B. (1898-1/3/58). Films: "Action Galore" 1925 (Luke McLean); "Arizona Mahoney" 1936 (Tim); "Rhythm on the Range" 1936 (Gopher); "Fair Warning" 1937 (Hotel Clerk); "The Lone Ranger" 1938-serial (Rancher); "Lady from Cheyenne" 1941 (Clerk); "Call of the Canyon" 1942; "The Great Man's Lady" 1942; "Call of the Rockies" 1944; "Gentle Annie" 1944 (Candy Butcher); "Heldorado" 1946 (Judge); "Saddle Pals" 1947 (Leslie); "The Dude Goes West" 1948 (Harris); "Marshal of Amarillo" 1948 (Hiram Short); "Grand Canyon" 1949 (Bert); "The Missourians" 1950 (Postmaster); "A Lawless Street" 1955 (Willis). ¶TV: *The Cisco Kid*—"Water Rights" 7-7-51, "The Photo Studio" 7-5-52.

Williams, Chili. Films: "Girl Rush" 1944 (Girl); "Gas House Kids Go West" 1947 (Nan Crowley); "The Lusty Men" 1952 (Woman).

Williams, Clara (1891-5/8/28). Films: "The Cowboy and the Squaw" 1910; "The Minister and the Outlaw"

1912; "Over the Divide" 1912; "Ranch-Mates" 1912; "Days of '49" 1913; "The Girl from Sunset Pass" 1913; "On the Mountain Ranch" 1913; "The Bargain" 1914 (Nell Brent); "Desert Gold" 1914 (Mary); "His Hour of Manhood" 1914; "Jim Cameron's Wife" 1914; "The Man from Oregon" 1915 (Harriet Lane); "The Ruse" 1915; "Carmen of the Klondike" 1918 (Dorothy Harlan); "Hell's Hinges" 1919 (Faith Henly).

Williams, III, Clarence (1946-). Films: "My Heroes Have Always Been Cowboys" 1991.

Williams, Curley. Films: "Riders of the Lone Star" 1947; "Echo Ranch" 1948-short; "Hidden Valley Days" 1948-short.

Williams, Earle (1880-4/25/27). Films: "When California Was Young" 1912; "Bring Him In" 1921 (Dr. John Hood); "The Eternal Struggle" 1923 (Sgt. Neil Tempest).

Williams, Elaine (1924-). TV: *Sergeant Preston of the Yukon*—"Emergency on Scarface Flat" 12-13-56 (Olivetta Godfrey).

Williams, Esther (1923-). TV: *Zane Grey Theater*—"The Black Wagon" 12-1-60 (Sarah Harmon).

Williams, Ezekial. TV: *Daniel Boone*—"The Far Side of Fury" 3-7-68 (Little Dan'l), "Big, Black and Out There" 11-14-68 (Little Dan'l), "To Slay a Giant" 1-9-69 (Little Dan'l); *The Outcasts*—"The Glory Wagon" 2-3-69 (Hickory).

Williams, George A. (1854-2/21/36) Films: "The Battle at Fort Laramie" 1913; "Buck Richard's Bride" 1913; "The Perilous Leap" 1917; "The Dawn of Understanding" 1918 (Silas Prescott); "The Black Sheep" 1921; "The Fire Eater" 1921 (Mort Frame); "The Girl in the Saddle" 1921; "Headin' West" 1922 (Barnaby Forest); "In the Days of Buffalo Bill" 1922-serial (Calvert Carter); "Jaws of Steel" 1922; "The Long Chance" 1922 (Dr. Taylor); "Lucky Dan" 1922 (the Girl's Father); "Never Let Go" 1922; "Perils of the Yukon" 1922-serial; "The Siren Call" 1922 (Judge Green); "The Fighting Sap" 1924 (Walter Stoddard); "The Phantom Horseman" 1924 (Judge); "The Silent Stranger" 1924 (Dad Warner); "Thundering Romance" 1924 (Oil Representative); "The Rattler" 1925 (Pop Warner); "Three Rogues" 1931 (Teamster).

Williams, Grant (1930-7/28/85). Films: "Red Sundown" 1956 (Chet Swann); "Showdown at Abilene" 1956 (Chip Tomlin); "Lone Texan" 1959 (Greg Banister); "Thirteen Fighting Men" 1960 (Forrest). ¶TV: *Gunsmoke*—"The Bear" 2-28-59 (Joe Plummer); *Yancy Derringer*—"Longhair" 3-5-59 (Gen. George Custer); *Texas John Slaughter*—"The Man from Bitter Creek" 3-6-59 (Mike Forbes); *Bonanza*—"Escape to the Ponderosa" 3-5-60 (Tyler), "Patchwork Man" 5-23-65 (Patch); *The Outcasts*—"The Candidates" 1-27-69 (John Mason).

Williams, Guinn "Big Boy" (1899-6/6/62). Films: "Cupid, the Cowpuncher" 1920 (Hairoil Johnson); "The Jack Rider" 1921 (Frank Stevens); "The Ropin' Fool" 1921; "The Vengeance Trail" 1921 (Big Boy Bronson); "Western Firebrands" 1921 (Billy Fargo); "Across the Border" 1922 (Andy Fowler); "Blaze Away" 1922 (Big Boy); "The Cowboy King" 1922 (Dud Smiley); "The Freshie" 1922 (Charles Taylor); "Cyclone Jones" 1923 (Cyclone Jones); "Rounding Up the Law" 1922 (Larry Connell); "Trail of Hate" 1922 (Silent Kerry); "End of the Rope" 1923; "$1,000 Reward" 1923; "Riders at Night" 1923; "The Avenger" 1924 (Nat Sherwood); "The Eagle's Claw" 1924; "Bad Man from Bodie" 1925; "Big Stunt" 1925; "Black Cyclone" 1925 (Jim Lawson); "Courage of Wolfheart" 1925; "Fangs of Wolfheart" 1925; "Red Blood and Blue" 1925 (Tom Butler); "Riders of the Sand Storm" 1925; "Rose of the Desert" 1925; "Sporting West" 1925; "Whistling Jim" 1925 (Whistling Jim); "The Desert's Toll" 1926; "Arizona Bound" 1927; "Lightning" 1927 (Cuth Stewart); "The Bad Man" 1930 (Red Giddings); "The Great Meadow" 1931 (Reuben Hall); "Heritage of the Desert" 1932 (Lefty); "Man of the Forest" 1933 (Big Casino); "Cowboy Holiday" 1934 (Buck Sawyer); "Thunder Over Texas" 1934 (Ted Wright); "Big Boy Rides Again" 1935 (Tom Duncan); "Danger Trails" 1935 (Bob Wilson); "Gun Play" 1935 (Bill Williams); "Law of the 45's" 1935 (Tucson Smith); "Powdersmoke Range" 1935 (Lullaby Joslin); "End of the Trail" 1936 (Bob Hildreth); "North of Nome" 1936 (Haage); "Vigilantes Are Coming" 1936-serial (Salvation); "The Bad Man of Brimstone" 1938 (Vulch McCreedy); "Bad Lands" 1939 (Billy Sweet); "Dodge City" 1939 (Tex Baird); "Santa Fe Trail" 1940 (Tex Bell); "Virginia City" 1940 (Marblehead); "Wagons Westward" 1940 (Jake Hardman); "Billy the Kid" 1941 (Ed Bronson); "Riders of Death Valley" 1941-serial (Borax Bill); "American Empire" 1942 (Sallaway); "Silver Queen" 1942 (Blackie); "The Desperadoes" 1943 (Nitro Rankin); "Hands Across the Border" 1943 (Teddy Bear); "Belle of the Yukon" 1944 (Marshall Maitland); "Cowboy and the Senorita" 1944 (Teddy Bear); "Cowboy Canteen" 1944 (Spud Marrigan); "Nevada" 1944 (Dusty); "Swing in the Saddle" 1944; "Rhythm Round-Up" 1945; "Sing Me a Song of Texas" 1945; "Song of the Prairie" 1945; "Cowboy Blues" 1946; "Singin' in the Corn" 1946 (Hank); "Singing on the Trail" 1946; "That Texas Jamboree" 1946; "Throw a Saddle on a Star" 1946; "King of the Wild Horses" 1947; "Over the Santa Fe Trail" 1947; "Smoky Mountain Melody" 1948 (Saddle Grease); "Station West" 1948 (Mick); "Bad Men of Tombstone" 1949 (Red); "Brimstone" 1949 (Art Benson); "Hoedown" 1950 (Small Potatoes Guinn); "Rocky Mountain" 1950 (Pap Dennison); "Al Jennings of Oklahoma" 1951 (Lon Tuttle); "Man in the Saddle" 1951 (Bourke Prine); "Hangman's Knot" 1952 (Smitty); "Springfield Rifle" 1952 (Sgt. Snow); "Massacre Canyon" 1954 (Peaceful); "The Outlaw's Daughter" 1954 (Moose); "Southwest Passage" 1954 (Tall Tale); "Hidden Guns" 1956 (Fiddler); "Man from Del Rio" 1956 (Fred Jasper); "The Hired Gun" 1957 (Elby Kirby); "The Alamo" 1960 (Lt. Finn); "Five Bold Women" 1960 (Big Foot); "The Comancheros" 1961 (Ed McBain). ¶TV: *Wild Bill Hickok*—"Blake's Kid" 12-23-52; *My Friend Flicka*—"The Wild Horse" 11-18-55, "The Royal Carriage" 3-16-56, "The Foundlings" 6-1-56 (Jeb Taylor); *Circus Boy*—Regular 1956-58 (Pete); *Gunsmoke*—"Skid Row" 2-23-57 (Hank Groet); *Cheyenne*—"The Conspirators" 10-8-57 (Prairie Dog); *Sugarfoot*—"Bullet Proof" 1-21-58 (Moose McKlintock); *The Adventures of Rin Tin Tin*—"The New C.O." 2-14-58 (Sgt. Muldoon); *Tales of Wells Fargo*—"Cow Town" 12-15-58 (Mike Forbes); *Wagon Train*—"The Vincent Eaglewood Story" 4-15-59 (Bryngelson); *The Restless Gun*—"A Trial for Jenny May" 5-25-59 (Jeff Bonsell).

Williams, Guy (1924-5/6/89). Films: "The Man from the Alamo" 1953 (Sergeant); "Take Me to Town" 1953 (Hero); "The Last Frontier" 1955 (Lt. Benton); "Seven Angry Men" 1955 (Salmon). ¶TV: *Zorro*—Regular 1957-59 (Don Diego de la Vega/Zorro); *Sergeant Preston of the Yukon*—"The Generous Hobo" 1-2-58 (Jim Lorane); *Bonanza*—"Return to Honor" 3-22-64 (Will Cartwright), "The Roper" 4-5-64 (Will Cartwright), "The Campaneros" 4-19-64 (Will Cartwright), "Triangle" 5-17-64 (Will Cartwright).

Williams, Hal. Films: "Sidekicks" TVM-1974 (Max). ¶TV: *Kung Fu*—"The Well" 9-27-73 (Caleb Brown), "The Last Raid" 4-26-75 (Caleb Brown); *Gunsmoke*—"Hard Labor" 2-24-75 (Widge).

Williams, Herb (1874-10/1/36). Films: "Rose of the Rancho" 1936 (Phineas P. Jones).

Williams, Jack (1920-). Films: "The Lion and the Horse" 1952 (Steve Collier); "Hondo" 1953; "The Far Country" 1955 (Shep); "Strange Lady in Town" 1955 (Rebstock); "Night Passage" 1957 (Dusty); "Man of the West" 1958 (Alcutt); "Westbound" 1959; "Gold of the Seven Saints" 1961 (Ames); "The Man Who Shot Liberty Valance" 1962 (Henchman); "The Sons of Katie Elder" 1965 (Andy Sharp); "Billy the Kid vs. Dracula" 1966; "Smoky" 1966 (Cowboy); "The Scalphunters" 1968 (Scalphunter); "Mrs. Sundance" TVM-1974 (Davis). ¶TV: *Maverick*—"The Thirty-Ninth Star" 11-16-58 (2nd Thug); *Rawhide*—"Incident of the Power and the Plow" 2-13-59 (Bannion), "The Greedy Town" 2-16-62 (Billy); *Laredo*—"Three's Company" 10-14-65, "Limit of the Law Larkin" 1-27-66 (Eusebio); *The Monroes*—"Ordeal by Hope" 10-19-66 (Corporal); *The Guns of Will Sonnett*—"And a Killing Rode into Town" 12-1-67 (Matt Claymore); *Lancer*—"The High Riders" 9-24-68, "The Knot" 3-18-69; *Bonanza*—"Caution: Easter Bunny Crossing" 3-29-70 (Stage Driver).

Williams, Jeff (1860-12/27/38). Films: "Just Squaw" 1919; "The Flame of Hellgate" 1920 (Old Man Dowell).

Williams, JoBeth (1953-). Films: "Wyatt Earp" 1994 (Bessie Earp).

Williams, John (1903-5/5/83). Films: "Hot Lead and Cold Feet" 1978 (Mansfield). ¶TV: *The Travels of Jaimie McPheeters*—"The Day of the Homeless" 12-8-63 (Stephen Runciman); *Wild Wild West*—"The Night of Bleak Island" 3-14-69 (Sir Nigel Scott).

Williams, Kathlyn (1872-9/23/60). Films: "A Romance of the Western Hills" 1910; "The Curse of the Red Man" 1911; "Dad's Girls" 1911; "In Old California When the Gringos Came" 1911; "The Rose of Old St. Augustine" 1911 (Dolores); "The

Totem Mark" 1911; "Wheels of Justice" 1911; "Driftwood" 1912; "The Horseshoe" 1912; "Sons of the Northwoods" 1912; "Chip of the Flying U" 1914; "The Flower of Faith" 1914; "His Fight" 1914; "The Lonesome Trail" 1914; "The Spoilers" 1914 (Cherry Malotte); "The Cost of Hatred" 1917 (Elsie Graves/Sarita Graves); "The Highway of Hope" 1917 (Lonely Lou); "The U.P. Trail" 1920 (Beauty Stanton); "The Wanderer of the Wasteland" 1924 (Magdalene Virey).

Williams, Lottie (1874-11/16/62). Films: "Arizona Nights" 1927 (Aunt Agatha); "The Cherokee Strip" 1937; "Empty Holsters" 1937 (Mrs. Allen).

Williams, Mack (1907-7/29/65). Films: "Rollin' Home to Texas" 1941; "Westbound" 1959 (Col. Vance). ¶TV: *Death Valley Days*—"Pat Garrett's Side of It" 11-18-56; *Sheriff of Cochise*—"Triangle" 2-22-57 (Dr. Greenwald); *Wagon Train*—"The Charles Avery Story" 12-13-57 (Major Forbes); *The Texan*—"The Eyes of Captain Wylie" 2-23-59 (Doctor).

Williams, Maston. Films: "Cavalier of the West" 1931 (Deputy Red Greeley); "Clearing the Range" 1931 (George Allen); "Border Devils" 1932 (the Hawk); "Without Honor" 1932 (Gambler); "Fighting with Kit Carson" 1933-serial; "Heart of the Rockies" 1937; "One Man Justice" 1937 (Lefty Gates); "The Painted Stallion" 1937-serial (Macklin); "Public Cowboy No. 1" 1937 (Thad Slaughter); "Two-Fisted Sheriff" 1937; "Whistling Bullets" 1937 (Ace Beldon); "Call the Mesquiteers" 1938 (Phillips); "Heroes of the Hills" 1938 (Nick); "The Lone Ranger" 1938-serial (Snead); "The Overland Express" 1938 (William Hawley); "Riders of the Black River" 1939 (Ed Gillis).

Williams, Oscar (1908-3/13/76). Films: "Dallas" 1950 (Prisoner).

Williams, Paul (1940-). Films: "The Wild Wild West Revisited" TVM-1979 (Michelito Loveless, Jr.).

Williams, Rhoda. Films: "The Persuader" 1957 (Nell Landis). ¶TV: *Zane Grey Theater*—"Blood Red" 1-29-61 (Woman); *The Big Valley*—"A Time to Kill" 1-19-66 (Esther), "Guilty" 10-30-67 (Mrs. Kleeber), "Alias Nellie Handley" 2-24-69 (Maud Elliot); *Laredo*—"That's Noway, Thataway" 1-20-66.

Williams, Rhys (1892-5/28/69). Films: "Fighting Man of the Plains" 1949 (Chandler Leach); "California Passage" 1950 (Norris); "The Devil's

Doorway" 1950 (Scott MacDougall); "The Showdown" 1950 (Cokecherry); "Johnny Guitar" 1954 (Mr. Andrews); "The Kentuckian" 1955 (Constable); "Many Rivers to Cross" 1955 (Lige Blake); "The Desperados Are in Town" 1956 (Jud Collins); "Fastest Gun Alive" 1956 (Brian Tibbs); "Mohawk" 1956 (Clem Jones); "The Restless Breed" 1957 (Ed Newton); "The Sons of Katie Elder" 1965 (Charlie Bob Striker). ¶TV: *Wagon Train*—"The Liam Fitzmorgan Story" 10-28-58 (James Grady); *Trackdown*—"The Unwanted" 5-13-59 (Jebediah); *The Rifleman*—"Brood Brothers" 5-26-59 (Doc), "Bloodlines" 10-6-59, "Letter of the Law" 12-1-59, "A Case of Identity" 1-19-60, "Sins of the Father" 4-19-60, "The Prodigal" 4-26-60 (Doc Burrage); *Riverboat*—"Strange Request" 12-13-59 (Josiah Cragg); *Maverick*—"Maverick and Juliet" 1-17-60 (Mr. Montgomery); *Wanted—Dead or Alive*—"The Parish" 3-26-60 (Dr. Horton), "Bounty on Josh" 1-25-61; *Tales of Wells Fargo*—"The Town" 4-4-60 (Jim Crook); *Bat Masterson*—"Come Out Fighting" 4-7-60 (Malachi Brody); *Temple Houston*—"Billy Hart" 11-28-63 (Judge Curry); *Wild Wild West*—"The Night of the Druid's Blood" 3-25-66 (Dr. Tristram), "The Night of the Undead" 2-2-68 (Gilly); *Here Come the Brides*—"A Kiss Just for You" 1-29-69 (Bishop Newkirk).

Williams, Robert B. (1904-6/17/78). Films: "Black Arrow" 1944-serial (Buck Sherman); "Song of the Prairie" 1945; "Gunning for Vengeance" 1946; "Unexpected Guest" 1947 (Ogden); "Fury at Furnace Creek" 1948 (Stranger); "Strange Gamble" 1948; "The Mysterious Desperado" 1949 (Whittaker); "Roughshod" 1949 (McCall); "Pioneer Marshal" 1949 (Rodney); "Stagecoach Kid" 1949 (Parnell); "The Hard Man" 1957 (Herb Thompson); "The Iron Sheriff" 1957 (Tilyou); "Apache Rifles" 1964; "Hang 'Em High" 1968. ¶TV: *The Lone Ranger*—"Frame for Two" 10-23-52, "Showdown at Sand Creek" 5-26-55; *Fury*—"The 4-H Story" 12-17-55 (Frankie Watts), "Junior Rodeo" 12-24-55 (Lem Wade); *Sheriff of Cochise*—"Escape from Train" 11-1-57; *Tales of Wells Fargo*—"The Sniper" 5-26-58 (Bob Benson), "Incident at Crossbow" 2-3-62 (Dodger); *Lawman*—"The Big Hat" 2-22-59 (Big Hat Anderson); *Bonanza*—"The Julia Bulette Story" 10-17-59, "To Bloom for Thee" 10-16-66 (Hotel Clerk), "The Wormwood Cup" 4-23-67

(Clerk); *Wyatt Earp*—"Wells Fargo Calling Marshal Earp" 12-29-59 (Burt); *Zane Grey Theater*—"Wayfarers" 1-21-60 (Joe); *The Alaskans*—"The Seal Skin-Game" 2-21-60 (Donlon); *Bronco*—"Legacy of Twisted Creed" 4-19-60 (Howsy McNellis); *The Rifleman*—"The Silent Knife" 12-20-60; *Rawhide*—"Incident of the New Start" 3-3-61, "A Woman's Place" 3-30-62 (Robert James), "Incident of the Wild Deuces" 12-12-63 (Joe), "Incident at the Odyssey" 3-26-64; *Cheyenne*—"The Idol" 1-29-62 (Clem Peters); *The Virginian*—"The Golden Door" 3-13-63, "Run Away Home" 4-24-63, "You Take the High Road" 2-17-65 (Dade), "The Gauntlet" 2-8-67 (Hardy); *The Big Valley*—"Earthquake!" 11-10-65 (Joel), "Under a Dark Sea" 2-9-66; *The Rounders*—9-13-66 (Doctor), 10-18-66 (Doctor); *Laredo*—"A Double Shot of Nepenthe" 9-30-66 (Mapes); *Bonanza*—"Shining in Spain" 3-27-66 (Hotel Clerk), "Ballad of the Ponderosa" 11-13-66 (Simpson), "A Bride for Buford" 1-15-67 (Searcy), "Joe Cartwright, Detective" 3-5-67 (Clerk); *Gunsmoke*—"Old Friend" 2-4-67 (Charley), "Noose of Gold" 3-4-67 (Sheriff Porter), "The Innocent" 11-24-69 (Phelps), "Cleavus" 2-15-71 (Woody); *The Road West*—"Charade of Justice" 3-27-67 (Telegrapher); *Cimarron Strip*—"Whitey" 10-19-67 (Sheriff Becker), "The Deputy" 12-21-67 (Gravedigger); *Alias Smith and Jones*—"Return to Devil's Hole" 2-25-71.

Williams, Roger. Films: "Trouble Busters" 1933 (Sheriff); "Alias John Law" 1935 (Sheriff); "Branded a Coward" 1935; "Cheyenne Tornado" 1935 (Clem); "Code of the Mounted" 1935 (Raoul Marlin); "Coyote Trails" 1935; "Fighting Pioneers" 1935 (Captain Burton); "The Ghost Rider" 1935; "Gun Play" 1935 (Cal); "Gunsmoke on the Guadalupe" 1935; "Lawless Borders" 1935; "No Man's Range" 1935 (Pete); "The Pecos Kid" 1935 (James Grayson); "Range Warfare" 1935; "The Reckless Buckaroo" 1935; "Rustlers' Paradise" 1935; "Saddle Aces" 1935; "Six Gun Justice" 1935; "The Texas Rambler" 1935; "Timber War" 1935 (Bowan); "Trails of the Wild" 1935 (Hammond); "The Vanishing Riders" 1935 (Joe Lang); "Wagon Trail" 1935 (Deputy Sheriff Joe); "Wild Mustang" 1935; "Ambush Valley" 1936; "The Cattle Thief" 1936 (Hutch); "The Crooked Trail" 1936 (Henchman); "Desert Justice" 1936; "Feud of the West" 1936 (Johnnie); "Fron-

tier Justice" 1936 (John Wilton); "Ghost Town" 1936 (Ed Gannon); "Gun Grit" 1936 (Mack); "Gun Smoke" 1936 (Sam Parsons); "Law and Lead" 1936 (Jeff); "Lightning Bill Carson" 1936; "Men of the Plains" 1936 (Cole); "Phantom Patrol" 1936 (Gustaf); "Pinto Rustlers" 1936 (Lugo); "Ridin' On" 1936 (Lou Bolton); "The Riding Avenger" 1936 (the Marshal); "Roarin' Guns" 1936; "Song of the Trail" 1936 (Miller); "Stormy Trails" 1936 (Daniels); "Toll of the Desert" 1936 (Tom Collins); "Vengeance of Rannah" 1936 (Norcross); "Wildcat Saunders" 1936 (Larime); "Wildcat Trooper" 1936 (Slim); "Aces Wild" 1937 (Slim); "Cheyenne Rides Again" 1937 (Mark); "Come on Cowboys" 1937 (Lou); "Guns in the Dark" 1937 (Ranger Adams); "Lawless Land" 1937; "Lost Ranch" 1937 (Terry); "Mystery Range" 1937; "Orphan of the Pecos" 1937 (Slim); "Reckless Ranger" 1937 (Snagger); "The Roaming Cowboy" 1937 (Walton); "Riders of the Whistling Skull" 1937 (Rutledge); "Santa Fe Rides" 1937; "The Silver Trail" 1937 (Sam Dunn); "The Singing Buckaroo" 1937; "Trailing Trouble" 1937 (Tom Crocker); "Valley of Terror" 1937 (Slim Jenkins); "Wild Horse Round-Up" 1937 (Pete); "Zorro Rides Again" 1937-serial (Manning); "Brothers of the West" 1938 (Jeff Tracy); "Call the Mesquiteers" 1938 (Frank); "Code of the Rangers" 1938 (Lawson); "The Feud Maker" 1938 (Sheriff Manton); "Feud of the Trail" 1938; "Heroes of the Alamo" 1938 (James Bowie); "Heroes of the Hills" 1938 (Warden); "Renfrew on the Great White Trail" 1938; "Red River Range" 1938 (Sheriff); "Rhythm of the Saddle" 1938; "Six Shootin' Sheriff" 1938 (Bart); "Whirlwind Horseman" 1938 (Ritter); "Code of the Fearless" 1939; "Frontier Scout" 1939 (Jessup); "The Lone Ranger Rides Again" 1939-serial (Sheriff); "Mountain Rhythm" 1939 (Kimball); "The Night Riders" 1939; "Wolf Call" 1939 (Tom Blake); "Colorado Pioneers" 1945.

Williams, Rush. Films: "Rocky Mountain" 1950 (Jonas Weatherby); "The Redhead from Wyoming" 1953 (Ned); "The Black Whip" 1956 (Jailer Garner); "Giant" 1956 (Waiter); "Copper Sky" 1957 (Corporal); "Ride a Violent Mile" 1957 (Edwards); "Trooper Hook" 1957 (Cpl. Stoner); "Bullwhip" 1958 (Judd); "Seven Guns to Mesa" 1958 (Duncan); "Curse of the Undead" 1959 (Henchman). ¶TV: *Wild Bill Hickok*—"Good Indian" 8-4-53; *Tales*

of the Texas Rangers—"Buckaroo from Powder River" 2-4-56 (Clint); *The Adventures of Rin Tin Tin*—"Rusty Meets Mr. Nobody" 5-4-56 (Sundown Kid); *Maverick*—"Relic of Fort Tejon" 11-3-57 (Deputy); *Tales of Wells Fargo*—"Alias Jim Hardie" 3-10-58 (Lee Shirley), "Royal Maroon" 4-28-62 (Shotgun); *Rawhide*—"Incident of the Judas Trap" 6-5-59, "Incident of the Thirteenth Man" 10-23-59 (Arthur Hennig), "Incident of the Deserter" 4-29-60; *Wyatt Earp*—"The Trail to Tombstone" 9-8-59 (Leader); *Bonanza*—"The Julia Bulette Story" 10-17-59, "The Dark Gate" 3-4-61, "No Less a Man" 3-15-64; *Laramie*—"The Renegade Brand" 2-26-63; *Destry*—"Big Deal at Little River" 3-20-64 (Jim); *Iron Horse*—"A Dozen Ways to Kill a Man" 12-19-66 (Jonas); *The High Chaparral*—"Best Man for the Job" 9-24-67 (2nd Cowboy); *Gunsmoke*—"9:12 to Dodge" 11-11-68 (Williams), "The Innocent" 11-24-69 (Stage Driver).

Williams, S.W. Films: "The White Rider" 1920 (Joel Brand); "Wolf Pack" 1922 (Henry Lamont/ Stephen Lamont).

Williams, Spencer (1893-12/13/69). Films: "Two Gun Man from Harlem" 1938 (Butch Carter); "The Bronze Buckaroo" 1939 (Pete); "Harlem Rides the Range" 1939 (Watson).

Williams, Tex (1917-10/11/85). Films: "Tex Williams and His Western Caravan" 1947-short; "Western Whoopee" 1948-short; "Cheyenne Cowboy" 1949-short; "Coyote Canyon" 1949-short; "The Girl from Gunsight" 1949-short; "The Pecos Pistol" 1949-short; "Silver Butte" 1949-short; "Six Gun Music" 1949-short; "South of Santa Fe" 1949-short; "West of Laramie" 1949-short; "Cactus Caravan" 1950-short; "The Fargo Phantom" 1950-short; "Gold Strike" 1950-short; "Priairie Pirates" 1950-short; "Ready to Ride" 1950-short; "Born Reckless" 1959 (Tex Williams).

Williams, Thad (1940-). Films: "Barquero" 1970 (Gibson).

Williams, Tiger (1963-). Films: "Mr. Horn" TVM-1979. ¶TV: *Cliffhangers*—"The Secret Empire" 1979 (Billy).

Williams, Van (1934-). Films: "The Night Rider" TVM-1979 (Jim Hollister). ¶TV: *Lawman*—"The Young Toughs" 4-12-59 (Zachary Morgan); *Colt .45*—"The Sanctuary" 5-10-59 (Tom Rucker); *Cheyenne*—"Vengeance Is Mine" 11-26-62 (Ray Masters); *Temple Houston*—"Ten Rounds for Baby" 1-30-64 (Joey

Baker); *The Big Valley*—"Rimfire" 2-19-68 (Sheriff Dave Barrett); *Gunsmoke*—"Thirty a Month a Found" 10-7-74 (Quincy); *How the West Was Won*—Episode One 2-12-78 (Captain MacAllister).

Williams, Walt. *see* Wales, Wally.

Williams, William A. (1870-5/4/42). Films: "The Sign Invisible" 1918 (Rev. Rene Mercier); "Calibre 38" 1919 (Barton).

Williams, William J. (1921-11/13/64). Films: "Black Horse Canyon" 1954 (Graves); "The Far Country" 1955 (Gant).

Williams, Zack (1885-5/25/58). Films: "The Killer" 1921 (Aloysius Jackson).

Williamson, Fred (1938-). Films: "The Legend of Nigger Charley" 1972 (Nigger Charley); "The Soul of Nigger Charley" 1973 (Charley); "Boss Nigger" 1974 (Boss Nigger); "Take a Hard Ride" 1974-Ital./Brit./Ger. (Tyree); "Adios Amigo" 1975 (Ben); "Joshua" 1977.

Williamson, Robert (1885-3/13/49). Films: "The Fighting Sap" 1924 (Chicago Kid); "Headin' Through" 1924 (the Duke); "Don X" 1925 (Red); "The Haunted Range" 1926 (Ralph Kellerd); "Lawless Trails" 1926 (Shorty Hill); "Circle Canyon" 1934 (Jim Moore).

Williamson, Robin (1889-2/21/35). Films: "The Valley of Lost Hope" 1915 (Dick Flint); "The Apache Raider" 1928.

Willing, Foy (and the Riders of the Purple Sage) (1915-7/24/78). Films: "Cowboy from Lonesome River" 1944; "Cyclone Prairie Rangers" 1944; "Twilight on the Prairie" 1944; "Saddle Serenade" 1945; "Sing Me a Song of Texas" 1945; "Out California Way" 1946; "Throw a Saddle on a Star" 1946; "Along the Oregon Trail" 1947; "Last Frontier Uprising" 1947; "Under Colorado Skies" 1947; "California Firebrand" 1948; "Grand Canyon Trail" 1948; "The Timber Trail" 1948; "Down Dakota Way" 1949; "The Far Frontier" 1949; "The Golden Stallion" 1949; "Susanna Pass" 1949; "Bells of Coronado" 1950; "North of the Great Divide" 1950; "Sunset in the West" 1950; "Trail of Robin Hood" 1950; "Trigger, Jr." 1950; "Twilight in the Sierras" 1950; "Heart of the Rockies" 1951; "Spoilers of the Plains" 1951.

Willingham, Noble (1931-). Films: "Butch and Sundance: The Early Days" 1979 (Capt. Prewitt);

"The Gambler" TVM-1980 (Conductor); "Dream West" TVM-1986 (President James Polk); "The Alamo: 13 Days to Glory" TVM-1987 (Dr. Pollard); "Longarm" TVM-1988; "City Slickers" 1991 (Clay Stone); "City Slickers II: The Legend of Curly's Gold" 1994 (Clay Stone). ¶TV: *Bonanza*—"Riot!" 10-3-72 (Mr. Kirby); *Gunsmoke*—"Whelan's Men" 2-5-73 (Tuck); *Black Bart*—Pilot 4-4-75 (Mayor Fern B. Malaga); *Young Maverick*—"A Fistful of Oats" 12-5-79.

Willingham, Willard. Films: "Law Comes to Gunsight" 1947; "Red Canyon" 1949 (Van); "Son of Paleface" 1952 (Jeb); "Pony Express" 1953 (Cavalryman); "Night Passage" 1957 (Click); "Arizona Raiders" 1965 (Eddie); "Deadwood '76" 1965 (Deputy Harding); "40 Guns to Apache Pass" 1967 (Fuller).

Willis, Austin (1917-). Films: "Wolf Dog" 1958-Can. (Krivak); "Hour of the Gun" 1967 (Anson Safford).

Willis, Bruce (1955-). Films: "Sunset" 1988 (Tom Mix).

Willis, Leo (1890-4/10/52). Films: "One Shot Ross" 1917 (Briggs); "The Law of the Great Northwest" 1918 (Manager); "The Silent Rider" 1918 (Dave Merrill); "The Toll Gate' 1920; "O'Malley of the Mounted" 1921 (Red Raeger); "Three Word Brand" 1921 (McCabe); "Broken Chains" 1922 (Gus); "The Timber Queen" 1922-serial; "Wild Bill Hickok" 1923 (Joe McCord); "The Tough Guy" 1926 (Sam Jacks); "The Fighting Parson" 1930-short; "The Tabasco Kid" 1932-short; "Drum Taps" 1933; "The Gold Ghost" 1934-short; "Horses' Collars" 1935-short (Lobo).

Willis, Marlene. TV: *Wagon Train*—"The Luke Grant Story" 6-1-60 (Angie); *Maverick*—"Flood's Folly" 2-19-61 (Sally Flood); *Laramie*—"Deadly Is the Night" 11-7-61 (Sue).

Willis, Matt (1914-3/30/89). Films: "Overland to Deadwood" 1942; "Singing on the Trail" 1946; "Fighting Man of the Plains" 1949 (Ferryman); "Home in San Antone" 1949.

Willis, Nolan. Films: "Oklahoma Terror" 1939 (Yucca); "Riders of the Frontier" 1939 (Gus); "Westbound Stage" 1939 (Lane); "Roll, Wagons, Roll" 1940 (Slade); "San Antonio" 1945 (Jay Witherspoon).

Willis, Norman (Jack Norman). Films: "Outlaws of the Prairie" 1937

(William Lupton); "Secret Valley" 1937 (Slick Collins); "Bad Man from Red Butte" 1940; "Beyond the Sacramento" 1940 (Nelson); "King of the Royal Mounted" 1940-serial (Captain Tarner); "Legion of the Lawless" 1940 (Leo Harper); "Belle Starr" 1941; "Gauchos of El Dorado" 1941 (Bart); "Outlaws of the Panhandle" 1941 (Faro Jack Vaughn); "Twilight on the Trail" 1941 (Kerry); "Down Rio Grande Way" 1942 (Vandall); "Overland to Deadwood" 1942; "The Avenging Rider" 1943 (Red); "Frontier Badman" 1943 (Randall); "Hail to the Rangers" 1943 (Monte Kerlin); "Gentle Annie" 1944 (Cowboy); "Roaring Guns" 1944-short; "In Old New Mexico" 1945 (Hastings); "Law of the Badlands" 1945-short; "Heading West" 1946; "Plainsman and the Lady" 1946 (Deputy); "Bandits of Dark Canyon" 1947 (Sheriff); "Bowery Buckaroos" 1947 (Blackjack); "Cheyenne" 1947 (Gambler); "Out West" 1947-short (Doc Barker); "Silver River" 1948 (Honest Harry); "Pals and Gals" 1954-short (Doc Barker); "The Bounty Killer" 1965 (Hank Willis). ¶TV: *The Lone Ranger*—"Legion of Old Timers" 10-6-49, "The Whimsical Bandit" 8-31-50; *Sergeant Preston of the Yukon*—"Father of the Crime" 4-19-56 (Carson); *Wagon Train*—"The Gabe Carswell Story" 1-15-58 (Wilkes); *Tales of Wells Fargo*—"The Prisoner" 2-17-58 (Terrill); *The Deputy*—"Brand of Honesty" 6-10-61 (Brandon Clark).

Willock, Dave (1909-11/12/90). Films: "Three Texas Steers" 1939 (Hotel Clerk); "Rodeo" 1952; "The Adventures of Bullwhip Griffin" 1967. ¶TV: *The Lone Ranger*—"The Squire" 11-9-50; *Boots and Saddles*—Regular 1957-59 (Lieutenant Binning); *Buckskin*—"Mail-Order Groom" 4-20-59 (Fred Corkle); *Wichita Town*—"They Won't Hang Jimmy Relson" 10-21-59 (Quincy), "The Devil's Choice" 12-23-59 (Quinch); *Wanted—Dead or Alive*—"Chain Gang" 12-12-59 (Jethro Dane), "The Looters" 10-12-60, "Baa-Baa" 1-4-61 (George Goode); *Bonanza*—"The Burma Rarity" 10-22-61 (Phil Axe), "Alias Joe Cartwright" 1-26-64 (Weems), "A Man to Admire" 12-6-64; *Gunsmoke*—"Easy Come" 10-26-63 (Clerk), "Chicken" 12-5-64; *Temple Houston*—"Ten Rounds for Baby" 1-30-64 (Speedy Jackson), "The Town That Trespassed" 3-26-64 (Seedy Jackson); *Alias Smith and Jones*—"Bad Night in Big Butte" 3-2-72.

Willow Bird, Chris. Films: "King of the Stallions" 1942; "Valley of the Sun" 1942 (Apache Indian); "Arizona Whirlwind" 1944; "Trail Street" 1947 (Indian); "Where the North Begins" 1947; "Daughter of the West" 1949 (Medicine Man); "Broken Arrow" 1950 (Nochalo).

Wills, Beverly (1934-10/24/63). TV: *Buckskin*—"Lament for Durango" 8-14-58 (Cassie); *The Tall Man*—"The Impatient Brides" 2-3-62 (Caroline).

Wills, Bob (and His Texas Playboys) (1905-5/13/75). Films: "Melody Ranch" 1940; "Take Me Back to Oklahoma" 1940; "Go West, Young Lady" 1941 (Bob); "The Lone Prairie" 1942; "A Tornado in the Saddle" 1942; "Riders of the Northwest Mounted" 1943; "Saddles and Sagebrush" 1943; "Silver City Raiders" 1943 (Bob Wills); "Bob Wills and His Texas Playboys" 1944-short; "The Last Horseman" 1944 (Bob); "The Vigilantes Ride" 1944 (Bob Allen); "Wyoming Hurricane" 1944; "Blazing the Western Trail" 1945; "Rhythm Round-Up" 1945; "Frontier Frolic" 1946-short; "Lawless Empire" 1946.

Wills, Chill (1903-12/15/78). Films: "Bar 20 Rides Again" 1936; "Call of the Prairie" 1936; "Way Out West" 1937 (Avalon Boy); "Lawless Valley" 1938 (Speedy McGow); "Arizona Legion" 1939 (Whopper Hatch); "Allegheny Uprising" 1939 (M'Cammon); "Racketeers of the Range" 1939 (Whopper); "Timber Stampede" 1939 (Whopper Hatch); "Trouble in Sundown" 1939 (Whopper); "The Westerner" 1940 (Southeast); "Wyoming" 1940 (Lafe); "The Bad Man" 1941 (Red Giddings); "Belle Starr" 1941 (Blue Duck); "Billy the Kid" 1941 (Tom Patterson); "Honky Tonk" 1941 (the Sniper); "Western Union" 1941 (Homer); "The Omaha Trail" 1942 (Henry); "Apache Trail" 1943 (Pike Skelton); "Barbary Coast Gent" 1944 (Sheriff Hightower); "The Harvey Girls" 1946 (H.H. Hartsey); "Loaded Pistols" 1948 (Sheriff Craner); "Northwest Stampede" 1948 (Mileaway); "Red Canyon" 1949 (Brackton); "Trailin' West" 1949; "High Lonesome" 1950 (Boatwhistle); "Rio Grande" 1950 (Dr. Wilkins); "Rock Island Trail" 1950 (Hogger); "The Sundowners" 1950 (Sam Beard); "Cattle Drive" 1951 (Dallas); "Oh! Susanna" 1951 (Sgt. Barhydt); "Bronco Buster" 1952 (Dan Bream); "Ride the Man Down" 1952 (Ike Adams); "The Man from the Alamo" 1953 (John Gage); "Tumbleweed" 1953 (Sheriff Murchoree); "Hell's

Outpost" 1954 (Kevin Russell); "Ricochet Romance" 1954 (Tom Williams); "Timberjack" 1955 (Steve Rilka); "Giant" 1956 (Uncle Bawley); "Kentucky Rifle" 1956; "Gun for a Coward" 1957 (Loving); "Gun Glory" 1957 (Preacher); "From Hell to Texas" 1958 (Amos Bradley); "The Sad Horse" 1959 (Capt. Connors); "The Alamo" 1960 (Beekeeper); "The Deadly Companions" 1961 (Turk); "Gold of the Seven Saints" 1961 (Doc Gates); "McClintock" 1963 (Drago); "Young Guns of Texas" 1963 (Preacher Sam Shelby); "The Rounders" 1965 (Jim Ed Love); "The Over-the-Hill Gang" TVM-1969 (Gentleman George); "The Over-the-Hill Gang Rides Again" TVM-1970 (George Agnew); "Guns of a Stranger" 1973; "Pat Garrett and Billy the Kid" 1973 (Lemuel). ¶TV: *The Gene Autry Show*—"Gray Dude" 12-3-50, "The Peace Maker" 12-17-50; *Wagon Train*—"The Bije Wilcox Story" 11-19-58 (Bije Wilcox); *Trackdown*—"The Samaritan" 2-18-59 (Sebulen Hunt); *The Texan*—"The Eyes of Captain Wylie" 2-23-59 (Capt. Wylie); *Frontier Circus*—Regular 1961-62 (Colonel Casey Thompson); *Gunsmoke*—"Abe Blocker" 11-24-62 (Abe Blocker), "A Hat" 10-16-67 (Red Conniston), "A Noose for Dobie Price" 3-4-68 (Eliha Gorman); *Rawhide*—"Incident at Dead Horse" 4-16-64 & 4-23-64 (Sheriff Asa Tanner); *The Rounders*—Regular 1966-67 (Jim Ed Love); *The Men from Shiloh*—"The Angus Killer" 2-10-71 (Reedy); *Alias Smith and Jones*—"The Biggest Game in the West" 2-3-72 (Bixby); *Hec Ramsey*—"Scar Tissue" 3-10-74 (Sam McDade).

Wills, Henry (1921-9/15/94). Films: "Zorro's Fighting Legion" 1939-serial; "Legion of the Lawless" 1940; "Young Bill Hickok" 1940; "In Old Colorado" 1941; "Nevada City" 1941; "Outlaws of the Cherokee Trail" 1941; "Saddlemates" 1941; "South of Santa Fe" 1942; "Sunset on the Desert" 1942 (Eddie); "Beyond the Last Frontier" 1943; "Silver Spurs" 1943; "The Big Bonanza" 1944; "Bordertown Trail" 1944; "Code of the Prairie" 1944 (Outlaw on Trail); "Lumberjack" 1944 (Slade); "The Old Texas Trail" 1944; "Riders of the Santa Fe" 1944; "The San Antonio Kid" 1944; "Song of Nevada" 1944; "Stagecoach to Monterey" 1944; "Trail to Gunsight" 1944 (Bar-6 Cowboy); "Bandits of the Badlands" 1945; "Beyond the Pecos" 1945; "Corpus Christi Bandits" 1945; "Great Stagecoach Robbery" 1945; "Rough Riders of Cheyenne" 1945;

"Santa Fe Saddlemates" 1945; "Sheriff of Cimarron" 1945 (Prisoner); "Trail of Kit Carson" 1945; "The Phantom Rider" 1946-serial; "Plainsman and the Lady" 1946 (Indian); "Sundown Riders" 1948 (Curly); "Shane" 1953 (Ryker Man); "Black Horse Canyon" 1954; "Saskatchewan" 1954 (Merrill); "Chief Crazy Horse" 1955 (He Dog); "Run for Cover" 1955 (Townsman); "Red Sundown" 1956; "The Searchers" 1956 (Stunts); "Gunfight at the O.K. Corral" 1957 (Alby); "Night Passage" 1957 (Pache); "Last Train from Gun Hill" 1959 (Jake); "One-Eyed Jacks" 1961 (Posseman); "Posse from Hell" 1961 (Chunk); "Six Black Horses" 1962 (Indian Leader); "Showdown" 1963 (Chaca); "Shenandoah" 1965 (Rider); "The Sons of Katie Elder" 1965 (Gus Dolly); "An Eye for an Eye" 1966 (Charles); "Red Tomahawk" 1967 (Samuels); "Return of the Gunfighter" TVM-1967 (Sam Boone); "The Cowboys" 1972 (Rustler); "Oklahoma Crude" 1973 (Walker); "The Soul of Nigger Charley" 1973 (Mexican); "Shootout in a One-Dog Town" TVM-1974. ¶TV: *The Roy Rogers Show*—"The Hermit's Secret" 5-1-52, "Haunted Mine of Paradise Valley" 5-18-52; *Wagon Train*—"The John Cameron Story" 10-2-57 (Tacker Brothers); *Zorro*—"Garcia Stands Accused" 1-16-58 (Colonel Melendez), "Sweet Face of Death" 1-30-58 (Castro); *Rawhide*—"Incident of the Widowed Dove" 1-30-59, "Incident at Poco Tiempo" 12-9-60, "Incident of the New Start" 3-3-61, "Incident of the Wager on Payday" 6-16-61, "Judgment at Hondo Seco" 10-20-61, "Incident at Cactus Wells" 10-12-62 (Kilroy), "Incident at Confidence Creek" 11-28-63 (Tom); *Bonanza*—"The Savage" 12-3-60 (McGregor), "The Tall Stranger" 1-7-62, "A Lonely Man" 1-2-72 (Sand), "Saddle Stiff" 1-16-72 (Yokum); *Laramie*—"Badge of Glory" 5-7-63; *Laredo*—"Lazyfoot, Where Are You?" 9-16-65; *The High Chaparral*—"The High Chaparral" 9-10-67, "Jelks" 1-23-70 (Murph), "Wind" 10-9-70, "Pale Warrior" 12-11-70 (Tommy), "The Badge" 12-18-70; *Lancer*—"The Man Without a Gun" 3-25-69; *Here Come the Brides*—"The Road to the Cradle" 11-7-69; *Kung Fu*—"The Elixir" 12-20-73 (Joe).

Wills, Norma. Films: "The Deadwood Coach" 1924 (Mrs. Shields); "The Golden Princess" 1925 (Indian Squaw).

Wills, Walter (1881-1/18/67). Films: "The Great Adventures of Wild Bill Hickok" 1938 (Bruce);

"Santa Fe Stampede" 1938 (Harris); "Songs and Saddles" 1938 (Pop Turner); "Cowboys from Texas" 1939 (Jefferson Morgan); "Honor of the West" 1939 (Farmer); "The Lone Ranger Rides Again" 1939-serial (Jones); "The Night Riders" 1939 (Hazelton).

Wilsey, Jay. *see* Bill, Jr., Buffalo.

Wilson, Al (-3/6/36). Films: "Ghost City" 1923-serial; "The Fighting Ranger" 1925-serial; "Sky-High Saunders" 1927 (Sky-High Saunders/Michael Saunders); "The Phantom Flyer" 1928 (Dick Stanton).

Wilson, Ben (1876-8/25/30). Films: "The Red Man's Burden" 1912; "The El Dorado Lode" 1913; "When the Cartridges Failed" 1914; "The Trail of the Upper Yukon" 1915; "The Valley of Silent Men" 1915; "The Desert Hawk" 1924 (Hollister); "His Majesty the Outlaw" 1924 (King Carson); "Notch Number One" 1924; "A Daughter of the Sioux" 1925 (John Field); "Fort Frayne" 1925 (Captain Malcolm Teale); "The Fugitive" 1925 (the Man); "The Man from Lone Mountain" 1925; "The Mystery Box" 1925-serial; "Renegade Holmes, M.D." 1925 (Renegade Holmes); "Sand Blind" 1925; "Tonio, Son of the Sierras" 1925 (Lt. Richard Harris); "Vic Dyson Pays" 1925 (Vic Dyson); "Warrior Gap" 1925 (Captain Deane); "Baited Trap" 1926 (Jim Banning); "The Sheriff's Girl" 1926; "West of the Law" 1926 (John Adams); "Wolves of the Desert" 1926; "The Mystery Brand" 1927; "The Range Riders" 1927 (Senora Shannon); "Riders of the West" 1927; "A Yellow Streak" 1927; "Shadow Ranch" 1930 (Tex).

Wilson, Bert (1871-10/14/56). Films: "Western Hearts" 1921 (Robert Caldwell); "Winners of the West" 1921-serial (Dr. Edwards); "Ridin' Wild" 1922 (Alfred Clark); "The Fighting Strain" 1923 (John Canfield).

Wilson, Charles (1894-1/7/48). Films: "The Mine with the Iron Door" 1936 (J. Horace Pitkins); "Roaring Timber" 1937 (Sam Garvin); "Silver Spurs" 1943 (Mr. Hawkins); "Blazing Across the Pecos" 1948.

Wilson, Clarence H. (1877-10/5/41). Films: "Flaming Guns" 1932 (Uncle Mulford); "The Mysterious Rider" 1933 (Hezekiah Gentry); "Smoke Lightning" 1933 (Jake Tully); "Ruggles of Red Gap" 1935 (Jake Henshaw); "When a Man's a Man" 1935 (Garby); "The Texans" 1938 (Sam Ross); "Desperate Trails" 1939 (Mal Culp); "Drums Along the Mohawk" 1939 (Paymaster); "Melody

Ranch" 1940 (Judge Skinny Henderson).

Wilson, Dick (1916-). Films: "The Shakiest Gun in the West" 1968 (Indian Chief). ¶TV: *Sergeant Preston of the Yukon*—"Follow the Leader" 3-15-56 (Beaver Louie), "Tobacco Smugglers" 11-29-56 (Skeeter), "The Jailbreaker" 11-21-57 (Jake Lucas); *Wagon Train*—"The Doctor Willoughby Story" 11-5-58 (Bartender); *Wyatt Earp*—"The Big Fight at Total Wreck" 1-12-60; *Maverick*—"The People's Friend" 2-7-60 (Crenshaw); *The Rifleman*—"Sins of the Father" 4-19-60; *Bat Masterson*—"The Court Martial of Major Mars" 1-12-61 (Tobias Tinker); *The Virginian*—"The Man from the Sea" 12-26-62; *Great Adventure*—"The Testing of Sam Houston" 1-31-64 (Mr. Metcalfe); *The Loner*—"The House Rules at Mrs. Wayne's" 11-6-65 (Bartender).

Wilson, Don (1900-4/25/82). Films: "Flying Lariats" 1931 (Mr. Appleby); "Riders of the Cactus" 1931 (Peon); "Buck Benny Rides Again" 1940 (Announcer); "The Round Up" 1941 (Slim). ¶TV: *Death Valley Days*—"Gates Ajar Morgan" 10-20-59 (Morgan).

Wilson, Dooley (1894-5/30/53). Films: "Passage West" 1951 (Rainbow).

Wilson, Dorothy (1909-). Films: "Men of America" 1933 (Annabelle); "Scarlet River" 1933 (Judy Blake); "When a Man's a Man" 1935 (Kitty Baldwin).

Wilson, Ed (1916-2/6/75). Films: "Flaming Frontier" 1926 (Grant's Secretary).

Wilson, Edna May (1880-7/23/60). Films: "Who Knows?" 1918 (Dusk Weaver); "A Man's Country" 1919 (Ruth Kemp).

Wilson, Ernest. Films: "The Drifter" 1929 (Uncle Abe); "The Phantom Cowboy" 1941 (Memphis).

Wilson, Hal (1887-5/22/33). Films: "Grease Paint Indians" 1913; "The Caballero's Wife" 1914; "Cavanaugh of the Forest Rangers" 1918 (Mr. Redfield); "The Home Trail" 1918 (Higgins); "Captive Bride" 1919; "The Hidden Badge" 1919; "Kingdom Come" 1919; "To the Tune of Bullets" 1919; "Hell's Oasis" 1920 (James Hardy); "Blaze Away" 1922 (Pop Melody); "Nan of the North" 1922-serial.

Wilson, Harry (1898-9/6/78). Films: "The Gay Desperado" 1936; "The Bad Man of Brimstone" 1937 (Bargee LaFarge); "The Lawless Breed" 1946.

Wilson, Howard. Films: "Wagon Wheels" 1934 (Permit Officer); "Home on the Range" 1935 (Bill Morris); "Rocky Mountain Mystery" 1935 (Fritz Ballard).

Wilson, Lois (1896-3/3/88). Films: "The Beckoning Trail" 1916 (Mary Helton); "Prisoner of the Pines" 1918 (Rosalie Dufrense); "The End of the Game" 1919 (Mary Miller); "A Man's Fight" 1919 (Mary Tompkins); "Without Compromise" 1922 (Jean Ainsworth); "The Call of the Canyon" 1923 (Carley Burch); "The Covered Wagon" 1923 (Molly Wingate); "Ruggles of Red Gap" 1923 (Kate Kenner); "To the Last Man" 1923 (Ellen Jorth); "North of '36" 1924 (Taisie Lockheart); "The Thundering Herd" 1925 (Milly Fayre); "The Vanishing American" 1925 (Marion Warner); "Law and Order" 1932 (Girl); "Rider of Death Valley" 1932 (Helen Joyce).

Wilson, Margery (1896-1/21/86). Films: "The Gunfighter" 1916 (Norma Wright); "The Primal Lure" 1916 (Lois Le Moyne); "The Return of Draw Egan" 1916 (Myrtle Buckton); "The Desert Man" 1917 (Jennie); "Wild Sumac" 1917 (Wild Sumac); "Wolf Lowry" 1917 (Mary Davis); "The Law of the Great Northwest" 1918 (Marie Monest); "Desert Gold" 1919 (Mercedes).

Wilson, Millard K. (1890-10/9/33). Films: "The Superior Claim" 1915; "The Stain in the Blood" 1916 (the Inventor); "Fighting Mad" 1917 (Frank Baxter); "The Branded Man" 1918; "Danger Ahead" 1918; "The Human Target" 1918; "Play Straight or Fight" 1918; "The Scarlet Drop" 1918 (Graham Lyons); "Smashing Through" 1918 (Ralph Brandon); "Under False Pretenses" 1918; "A Woman's Fool" 1918 (the Virginian); "Riders of Vengeance" 1919; "The Secret Peril" 1919; "Range Rivals" 1921.

Wilson, Rebecca. Films: "Chato's Land" 1972 (Edna Malechie).

Wilson, Scout. Films: "The Tracker" TVM-1988 (John "Red Jack" Stillwell); "Geronimo: An American Legend" 1993 (Redondo); "Tall Tales: The Unbelievable Adventures of Pecos Bill" 1995 (Zeb).

Wilson, Terry (1923-). Films: "The Last Hunt" 1956 (Buffalo Hunter); "Pillars of the Sky" 1956 (Capt. Fanning); "The Searchers" 1956 (Stunts); "The Plainsman" 1966 (Sgt. Womack); "The War Wagon" 1967 (Sheriff Strike); "The Shakiest Gun in the West" 1968 (Welsh); "A Man Called Gannon" 1969 (Cass);

"Dirty Dingus Magee" 1970 (Trooper); "Support Your Local Gunfighter" 1971 (Thug); "One Little Indian" 1973; "Westworld" 1973 (Sheriff); "The Daughters of Joshua Cabe Return" TVM-1975 (Sergeant Maxwell). ¶TV: *Wagon Train*—Regular 1957-65 (Bill Hawks); *Hondo*— "Hondo and the Death Drive" 12-1-67 (Dakota); *The Virginian*—"The Sins of the Father" 3-4-70 (Shaker); *The Men from Shiloh*—"The Regimental Line" 3-3-71 (Turner); *Gunsmoke*—"The Avenger" 11-27-72 (Liveryman).

Wilson, Tom (1880-2/19/65). Films: "The Martyrs of the Alamo" 1915 (Sam Houston); "A Yankee from the West" 1915 (Jim Dorsey); "Pay Me!" 1917 (Mae Jepson); "Wild and Woolly" 1917 (Engineer); "Isobel, or the Trail's End" 1920 (Corporal Bucky Smith); "Where Men Are Men" 1921 (Dutch Monahan); "Quicksands" 1923 (Sgt. Johnson); "Soft Boiled" 1923 (Butler); "The Heart Buster" 1924 (George); "The Best Bad Man" 1925 (Sam, the Butler); "The Pioneer Scout" 1928 (Handy Anderson); "Moonlight on the Prairie" 1935 (Cowboy); "Trailin' West" 1936 (Livery Stable Owner); "Treachery Rides the Range" 1936 (Denver); "Blazing Sixes" 1937 (Bartender); "The Cherokee Strip" 1937 (Hellman); "Heart of the North" 1938 (Miner); "River's End" 1940 (Dance Caller); "The Tall Men" 1955 (Miner).

Wilson, Whip (1915-10/23/64). Films: "Silver Trails" 1948 (Whip); "Crashing Thru" 1949; "Haunted Trails" 1949 (Whip); "Range Land" 1949 (Whip); "Riders of the Dusk" 1949 (Whip); "Shadows of the West" 1949 (Whip); "Arizona Territory" 1950 (Jeff); "Cherokee Uprising" 1950 (Bob); "Fence Riders" 1950; "Gunslingers" 1950 (Whip); "Outlaws of Texas" 1950 (Tom); "Silver Raiders" 1950 (Larry); "Abilene Trail" 1951 (Kansas Kid); "Canyon Raiders" 1951; "Lawless Cowboys" 1951 (Whip); "Nevada Badmen" 1951; "Stage to Blue River" 1951 (Whip); "Stagecoach Driver" 1951; "Wanted Dead or Alive" 1951; "The Gunman" 1952; "Montana Incident" 1952; "Night Raiders" 1952 (Whip); "Wyoming Roundup" 1952 (Whip Wilson); "The Kentuckian" 1955.

Wilton, Eric (1883-2/23/57). Films: "Gold Is Where You Find It" 1938 (Butler); "Hudson Bay" 1941 (Concillor).

Winchell, Paul (1923-). TV: *The Virginian*—"Dark Corridor" 11-27-68 (Jingo).

Windish, Ilka. TV: *Empire*—"Arrow in the Sky" 4-9-63 (Eva); *Bonanza*—"A Question of Strength" 10-27-63 (Mother Veronica); *Gunsmoke*—"The Pariah" 4-17-65 (Rosita Scanzano), "Nowhere to Run" 1-15-68 (Vera Stonecipher).

Windom, William (1923-). Films: "Cattle King" 1963 (Harry Travers); "Hour of the Gun" 1967 (Texas Jack Vermillion); "Fools' Parade" 1971 (Roy K. Sizemore); "Bridger" TVM-1976 (Daniel Webster); "Sommersby" 1993 (Reverend Powell). ¶TV: *Cheyenne*—"Legacy of the Lost" 12-4-61 (Carter); *Empire*—"Hidden Asset" 3-26-63 (Lawrence Rowan); *Gunsmoke*—"Nina's Revenge" 12-16-61 (Lee Sharky), "False Front" 12-22-62 (Paul Hill), "Spratt" 10-2-72 (Ira Spratt); *Stoney Burke*—"A Matter of Pride" 11-5-62 (Reese Ludlow); *Iron Horse*—"Town Full of Fear" 12-5-66 (Colin McCrory); *Custer*—"Under Fire" 11-15-67 (Samson); *Dundee and the Culhane*—11-22-67 (Robert Campbell); *The Virginian*—"To Bear Witness" 11-29-67 (Arthur Blanton), "The Orchard" 10-2-68 (Chick Mead), "Halfway Back from Hell" 10-1-69; *Bonanza*—"Star Crossed" 3-10-68 (Marshal Passmore); *Lancer*—"The Great Humbug" 3-4-69 (Claude Buttermere); *The Outcasts*—"The Stalking Devil" 4-7-69 (Lafe Partman); *The Men from Shiloh*—"The Politician" 1-13-71 (Foster Bonham); *Alias Smith and Jones*—"The Wrong Train to Brimstone" 2-4-71 (Jeremiah Daley).

Windsor, Claire (1897-10/24/72). Films: "Broken Chains" 1922 (Hortense Allen); "The Bugle Call" 1927 (Alice Tremayne); "The Frontiersman" 1927 (Lucy).

Windsor, Marie (1921-). Films: "The Fighting Kentuckian" 1949 (Ann Logan); "Hellfire" 1949 (Doll Brown); "Dakota Lil" 1950 (Lil); "Frenchie" 1950 (Diane); "The Showdown" 1950 (Adelaide); "Little Big Horn" 1951 (Celia Donlin); "Outlaw Women" 1952 (Iron Mae McLeod); "The Tall Texan" 1953 (Laura Niblett); "The Bounty Hunter" 1954 (Alice); "The Silver Star" 1955 (Karen); "Two-Gun Lady" 1956 (Bess); "The Parson and the Outlaw" 1957 (Tonya); "Day of the Bad Man" 1958 (Cora Johnson); "Mail Order Bride" 1964 (Hanna); "The Good Guys and the Bad Guys" 1969 (Polly); "Wild Women" TVM-1970 (Lottie Clampett); "One More Train to Rob" 1971 (Louella); "Support Your Local Gunfighter" 1971 (Goldie); "Cahill, United States Mar-

shal" 1973 (Mrs. Green); "Hearts of the West" 1975 (Woman in Nevada). ¶TV: *Stories of the Century*—"Belle Starr" 3-25-55; *Cheyenne*—"Decision at Gunsight" 4-23-57 (Leda Brandt), "The Mutton Puncher" 10-22-57 (Thora Flagg); *The Californians*—"The Regulators" 11-5-57 (Dolly); *Maverick*—"The Quick and the Dead" 12-8-57 (Cora), "Epitaph of a Gambler" 2-11-62 (Kit Williams); *Yancy Derringer*—"Ticket to Natchez" 10-23-58 (Billie Joe); *Bat Masterson*—"The Fighter" 11-5-58 (Polly Landers); *Rawhide*—"Incident at the Edge of Madness" 2-6-59 (Narcie), "Incident of the Painted Lady" 5-12-61 (Miss Kate), "Incident of the Rusty Shotgun" 1-9-64 (Amie Claybank); *Tales of Wells Fargo*—"The Warrior's Return" 9-21-59 (Dolly); *The Deputy*—"Back to Glory" 9-26-59 (Angela); *The Alaskans*—"Winter Song" 11-22-59 (Maria Julien); *The Rebel*—"Glory" 1-24-60 (Emma); *Wyatt Earp*—"Wyatt Earp's Baby" 4-25-61 (Lily Henry); *Whispering Smith*—"The Trademark" 8-14-61 (Maple Gray); *Bronco*—"The Equalizer" 12-18-61; *Lawman*—"The Wanted Man" 4-8-62 (Ann Jesse); *Destry*—"The Nicest Girl in Gomorrah" 3-13-64 (Jewel Scrogg); *Branded*—"That the Brave Endure" 4-25-65 (Carrie Milligan); *The Legend of Jesse James*—"The Quest" 11-1-65 (Queenie); *Bonanza*—"Five Sundowns to Sunup" 12-5-65 (Ma Lassiter); *Gunsmoke*—"Trafton" 10-25-71 (Mary K); *Alias Smith and Jones*—"High Lonesome Country" 9-23-72 (Helen Archer); *Hec Ramsey*—"The Green Feather Mystery" 12-17-72.

Windust, Irene. TV: *Wagon Train*—"The Clara Beauchamp Story" 12-11-57 (Mrs. Hawks), "The Julia Gage Story" 12-18-57, "The Major Adams Story" 4-23-58 & 4-30-58 (Mrs. Hawks), "The Colonel Harris Story" 1-13-60.

Windust, Penelope. Films: "The Call of the Wild" TVM-1976 (Rosemary); "Ghost Town" 1988 (Grace); "Iron Will" 1994 (Maggie Stoneman).

Winfield, Paul (1940-). TV: *Cowboy in Africa*—"What's an Elephant Mother to Do?" 10-2-67 (Kahutu); *The High Chaparral*—"Sea of Enemies" 1-3-69 (Graham Jessup); *Nichols*—"Eddie Joe" 1-4-72 (Eddie Joe).

Wing, Ah (1851-2/27/41). Films: "The She Wolf" 1919 (Mui Fing); "West Is Best" 1920; "The Masked Avenger" 1922 (Quong Lee).

Wing, Toby (1913-). Films: "Double Daring" 1926 (Nan).

Wing, Ward (1894-6/5/45). Films: "The Eagle" 1918 (Bob); "Twenty Mule Team" 1940.

Wingreen, Jason (1920-). Films: "The True Story of Jesse James" 1957 (Peter); "The Bravados" 1958; "The Cheyenne Social Club" 1970 (Dr. Carter); "Skin Game" 1971 (2nd Speaker); "The Magnificent Seven Ride" 1972 (Warden). ¶TV: *Rough Riders*—"The Duelists" 10-23-58 (Degnan); *Wanted—Dead or Alive*—"Journey for Josh" 10-5-60 (Nick); *Bonanza*—"The Way of Aaron" 3-10-63 (Hank), "Enter Thomas Bowers" 4-26-64 (Luke), "The Hidden Enemy" 11-28-72; *The Loner*—"Hunt the Man Down" 12-11-65 (Lucas); *The Big Valley*—"A Time to Kill" 1-19-66 (Ketchie); *Wild Wild West*—"The Night of the Whirring Death" 2-18-66 (Policeman); *A Man Called Shenandoah*—"Requiem for the Second" 5-2-66 (Hotel Clerk); *The Rounders*—Regular 1966-67 (Shorty); *Shane*—"Day of the Hawk" 10-22-66 (Ira Jackson); *The Road West*—"The Agreement" 4-24-67; *The Guns of Will Sonnett*—"Stopover in a Troubled Town" 2-2-68; *Cowboy in Africa*—"Search and Destroy" 3-4-68 (Sid); *Lancer*—"The Prodigal" 11-12-68, "Legacy" 12-9-69, "Splinter Group" 3-3-70 (Wilkes); *Gunsmoke*—"The Wedding" 3-13-72 (Dr. Cleery); *Kung Fu*—"A Praying Mantis Kills" 3-22-73 (Kennamer); *The Quest*—"Welcome to America, Jade Snow" 11-24-76.

Winkler, Robert. Films: "Blue Montana Skies" 1939 (Wilbur Potter); "Cherokee Strip" 1940 (Barrett Kid); "Gun Code" 1940 (Jerry Garrett); "Riders of Pasco Basin" 1940 (Tommy Scott); "Bad Men of Missouri" 1941 (Willie Younger); "Pals of the Pecos" 1941 (Tim Burke); "Wildcat of Tucson" 1941; "Prairie Express" 1947 (Dave Porter).

Winn, Charlotte. Films: "The Lone Horseman" 1929; "Pioneers of the West" 1929 (Dorothy McClure).

Winninger, Charles (1884-1/27/69). Films: "Fighting Caravans" 1931 (Marshal); "Gun Smoke" 1931 (Tack Gillup); "White Fang" 1936 (Doc McFane); "Destry Rides Again" 1939 (Wash Dimsdale); "A Lady Takes a Chance" 1943 (Waco); "Belle of the Yukon" 1944 (Pop Candless); "A Perilous Journey" 1953 (Capt. Eph Allan).

Winningham, Mare (1959-). Films: "Wyatt Earp" 1994 (Mattie Blaylock). ¶TV: *The Young Pioneers*—Regular 1978 (Nettie Peters).

Winona, Kim. TV: *Brave Eagle*—Regular 1955-56 (Morning Star).

Winslow, Dick (1915-2/7/91). Films: "Trumpin' Trouble" 1926 (Jimmie Dyson); "Range Courage" 1927 (Jimmy Blake); "Avalanche" 1928 (Jack at age 12); "The Apple Dumpling Gang" 1975 (Slippery Kid); "The Shootist" 1976 (Streetcar Driver). ¶TV: *Rawhide*—"Incident of His Brother's Keeper" 3-31-61, "The Child Woman" 3-23-62, "Abilene" 5-18-62; *Wagon Train*—"The Ben Engel Story" 3-16-64; *Wild Wild West*—"The Night of the Human Trigger" 12-3-65 (Piano Player); *Bonanza*—"Old Charlie" 11-6-66 (Heckler); *Daniel Boone*—"A Pinch of Salt" 5-1-69, "The Kidnaping" 1-22-70.

Winslow, George "Foghorn" (1946-). Films: "Wild Heritage" 1958 (Talbot Breslin).

Winslow, James. TV: *Gunsmoke*—"Claustrophobia" 1-25-58 (Giles); *Tombstone Territory*—"Johnny Ringo's Last Ride" 2-19-58 (Schmidt); *Bat Masterson*—"License to Cheat" 2-4-59 (Stan Larson).

Winslowe, Paula. TV: *Rawhide*—"Incident of the Dry Drive" 5-22-59 (Edythea Walker); *Wyatt Earp*—"Loyalty" 2-7-61 (Mrs. Stoney).

Winston, Ellen. Films: "Whispering Sage" 1927 (Mrs. Kildare).

Winter, Edward. Films: "The Invasion of Johnson County" TVM-1976 (Maj. Edward Fershay).

Winters, Gloria. Films: "Stagecoach Driver" 1951. ¶TV: *The Lone Ranger*—"Damsels in Distress" 6-8-50; *Sky King*—Regular 1951-53 (Penny); *The Gene Autry Show*—"Warning! Danger!" 11-10-51; *The Roy Rogers Show*—"The Hermit's Secret" 5-1-52; *Wild Bill Hickok*—"Chain of Events" 6-24-52; *Stories of the Century*—"Little Britches" 8-19-55; *Judge Roy Bean*—"Four Ladies from Laredo" 7-1-56 (Beth); *Sheriff of Cochise*—"The Kidnaper" 1-18-57 (Nancy); *Frontier Doctor*—"Flaming Gold" 6-27-59; *Wyatt Earp*—"Winning Streak" 12-27-60 (Ruthie Jensen).

Winters, Jonathan (1925-). Films: "More Wild Wild West" TVM-1980 (Albert Paradine II).

Winters, Linda. *see* Comingore, Dorothy.

Winters, Roland (1904-9/22/89). Films: "Inside Straight" 1951 (Alexander Tomson); "Raton Pass" 1951 (Sheriff Perigord); "Sierra Passage" 1951 (Sam). ¶TV: *Broken Arrow*—"Powder Keg" 2-19-57 (Perry); *DuPont Show of the Week*—"Big Deal in Laredo" 10-7-62 (Drummond).

Winters, Shelley (1922-). Films: "Red River" 1948 (Dance-Hall Girl); "Frenchie" 1950 (Frenchie Fontaine); "Winchester '73" 1950 (Lola Manners); "Untamed Frontier" 1952 (Jane Stevens); "Saskatchewan" 1954 (Grace Markey); "The Treasure of Pancho Villa" 1955 (Ruth Harris); "The Scalphunters" 1968 (Kate); "Flap" 1970 (Dorothy Bluebell). ¶TV: *Wagon Train*—"The Ruth Owens Story" 10-9-57 (Ruth Owens).

Wintersole, William (1931-). Films: "Squares" 1972 (State Policeman). ¶TV: *Wild Wild West*—"The Night of the Tottering Tontine" 1-6-67 (Baring); *The Outcasts*—"Alligator King" 1-20-69 (Krause); *Lancer*—"The Great Humbug" 3-4-69 (Timothy), "Blue Skies for Willie Sharpe" 1-13-70 (Businessman); *Here Come the Brides*—"Land Grant" 11-21-69; *Gunsmoke*—"Lijah" 11-8-71 (Will Standish); *Bonanza*—"The Witness" 1-2-73 (Schulte); *Sara*—Regular 1976 (George Bailey).

Winwood, Estelle (1883-6/20/84). Films: "Sergeant Rutledge" 1960 (Spectator); "The Misfits" 1961 (Church Lady).

Wirth, Billy. Films: "Children of the Dust" TVM-1995 (Corby/White Wolf).

Wise, Jack (1893-3/6/54). Films: "Smilin' Guns" 1929 (Professor); "Cowboy from Brooklyn" 1938 (Reporter).

Wiseman, Joseph (1918-). Films: "Viva Zapata!" 1952 (Fernando Aguirre); "The Unforgiven" 1960 (Abe Kelsey); "Lawman" 1971 (Lucas). ¶TV: *The Westerner*—"Ghost of a Chance" 12-2-60; *Wagon Train*—"The Santiago Quesada Story" 3-30-64 (James Case); *The Legend of Jesse James*—"The Last Stand of Captain Hammel" 4-4-66 (Captain Hammel).

Withers, Bernadette. TV: *Wild Bill Hickok*—"The Outlaw's Portrait" 11-18-52; *Wagon Train*—"The Old Man Charvanaugh Story" 2-18-59 (Sybil Lerner), "The Jonas Murdock Story" 4-13-60 (Alma Hardy).

Withers, Grant (1904-3/27/59). Films: "The Gentle Cyclone" 1926 (Wilkes Junior); "Tiger Rose" 1929 (Bruce); "The Red Rider" 1934-serial (Silent Slade); "Valley of Wanted Men" 1935 (Ranger); "The Arizona Raiders" 1936 (Monroe Adams); "Hollywood Roundup" 1938 (Grant Drexel); "Lure of the Wasteland" 1939 (Smitty); "Mexican Spitfire Out West" 1940 (Withers); "Billy the Kid"

1941 (Ed Shanahan); "The Masked Rider" 1941 (Douglas); "Northwest Rangers" 1942 (Fowler); "Apache Trail" 1943 (Lestrade); "In Old Oklahoma" 1943 (Richardson); "A Lady Takes a Chance" 1943 (Bob); "Bells of Rosarita" 1945 (William Ripley); "Dakota" 1945 (Slagin); "Utah" 1945 (Ben Bowman); "In Old Sacramento" 1946 (Capt. Marc Slayer); "My Darling Clementine" 1946 (Ike Clanton); "The Gunfighters" 1947 (Deputy Bill Yount); "Wyoming" 1947 (Joe Sublette); "Fort Apache" 1948 (Silas Meacham); "The Gallant Legion" 1948 (Wesley Hardin); "Night Time in Nevada" 1948 (Ran Farrell); "Old Los Angeles" 1948 (Marshal Luckner); "The Plunderers" 1948 (Tap Lawrence); "Sons of Adventure" 1948 (Sterling); "The Fighting Kentuckian" 1949 (George Hayden); "Hellfire" 1949 (Sheriff Martin); "The Last Bandit" 1949 (Ed Bagley); "Bells of Coronado" 1950 (Craig Bennett); "Rio Grande" 1950 (Deputy Marshal); "Rock Island Trail" 1950 (David Strong); "The Savage Horde" 1950 (Proctor); "Trigger, Jr." 1950 (Monty Manson); "Belle Le Grand" 1951 (Shannon); "Spoilers of the Plains" 1951 (Gregory Camwell); "Utah Wagon Train" 1951 (Bancroft); "Captive of Billy the Kid" 1952 (Van Stanley); "Leadville Gunslinger" 1952 (Jonathan Graves); "Oklahoma Annie" 1952 (Bull McCready); "Woman of the North Country" 1952 (Chapman); "Iron Mountain Trail" 1953 (Roger McCall); "Jubilee Trail" 1954 (Maj. Lynden); "Run for Cover" 1955 (Gentry); "The White Squaw" 1956 (Sheriff); "Hell's Crossroads" 1957 (Sheriff Steve Oliver); "The Last Stagecoach West" 1957. ¶TV: *Stories of the Century*—"Last Stagecoach West" 1954 (Ben Gibson); *Cheyenne*—"The Law Man" 11-6-56 (Matt Ellis); *Circus Boy*—"The Proud Pagliacci" 11-18-56 (Mr. Middleton), "Royal Roustabout" 9-26-57 (Keogh); *Gunsmoke*—"Pucket's New Year" 1-5-57 (Jed Larner); *Zane Grey Theater*—"They Were Four" 3-15-57 (Sheriff Metz), "Deadfall" 2-19-59 (Sheriff Roy Lamont); *Wyatt Earp*—"The Time for All Good Men" 6-4-57 (Gus Andrews), "King of the Frontier" 11-11-58 (Miles Breck); *Have Gun Will Travel*—"The Outlaw" 9-21-57 (Sheriff), "No Visitors" 11-30-57 (Mulrooney), "Twenty-Four Hours to North Fork" 5-17-58 (Sam Barton); *Wagon Train*—"The Jean LeBec Story" 9-25-57 (Mark Hammond); *Tales of the Texas Rangers*—"Cattle Drive" 10-30-58 (Ramrod Johnson); *26 Men*—"The Torch" 1-6-

59, "Fighting Man" 5-26-59; *Northwest Passage*—"The Fourth Brother" 1-30-59 (Fred Paget); *The Texan*—"The Ringer" 2-16-59 (Ed Martin).

Withers, Isabel (1896-9/3/68). Films: "Law Men" 1944 (Auntie Mac); "Wild Beauty" 1946 (Mrs. Anderson); "Riders in the Sky" 1949.

Withers, Jane (1927-). Films: "Wild and Woolly" 1937 (Arnette Flynn); "Arizona Wildcat" 1938 (Mary Jane Patterson); "Shooting High" 1940 (Jane Pritchard); "Giant" 1956 (Vashti Snythe).

Witherspoon, Cora (1890-11/17/57). Films: "Dodge City" 1939 (Mrs. McCoy).

Witney, Michael. Films: "The Way West" 1967 (Johnnie Mack); "Doc" 1971 (Ike Clanton). ¶TV: *The Travels of Jaimie McPheeters*—Regular 1963-64 (Buck Coulter); *Death Valley Days*—"No Gun Behind His Badge" 3-28-65 (Stranger); *A Man Called Shenandoah*—"Muted Fifes, Muffled Drums" 2-28-66 (Sergeant MacDonald); *Daniel Boone*—"The Flaming Rocks" 2-1-68 (Orville).

Witting, Arthur (1868-2/1/41). Films: "Gun-Hand Garrison" 1927; "Wild Born" 1927.

Witzel, Curley. Films: "The Fighting Strain" 1926; "When Bonita Rides" 1926; "The Whirlwind Driver" 1926; "Double Trouble" 1927.

Wix, Florence (1883-11/23/56). Films: "Wells Fargo" 1937.

Wixted, Michael-James (1961-). TV: *Gunsmoke*—"Hawk" 10-20-69 (Amos Clifford); *Lancer*—"Shadow of a Dead Man" 1-6-70 (Grady); *Daniel Boone*—"Mamma Cooper" 2-5-70 (Emmanuel); *Bonanza*—"The Love Child" 11-8-70 (Scott).

Wolbert, Dorothea (1874-9/16/58). Films: "Action" 1921 (Mirandy Meekin); "The Ruse of the Rattlesnake" 1921 (Mrs. Bludgeon); "The Galloping Ace" 1924 (Susie Williams); "Heir to Trouble" 1935 (Tillie).

Wolcott, Helen. Films: "Buckshot John" 1915 (Ruth Mason); "Fatherhood" 1915 (Lizzie).

Wolders, Robert (1937-). TV: *Laredo*—Regular 1966-67 (Erik Hunter); *Daniel Boone*—"Beaumarchais" 10-12-67 (Almaviva).

Wolfe, Bill (1894-2/16/75). Films: "Left-Handed Law" 1937; "Way Out West" 1937 (Man in Audience); "Man from Music Mountain" 1938; "Overland Stage Raiders" 1938; "Santa Fe Stampede" 1938; "Under Western Stars" 1938; "New

Frontier" 1939; "Teacher's Pest" 1939-short; "My Little Chickadee" 1940 (Barfly); "Young Bill Hickok" 1940; "Jesse James at Bay" 1941; "Arizona Trail" 1943; "Bordertown Gunfighters" 1943; "The Desperadoes" 1943; "Outlaws of Stampede Pass" 1943; "The Cherokee Flash" 1945; "Colorado Pioneers" 1945; "Gentleman from Texas" 1946.

Wolfe, Bud (1910-4/13/60). Films: "The Lone Ranger Rides Again" 1939-serial (Posseman #4); "King of the Texas Rangers" 1941-serial (Derrick Heavy #2); "Cowboy Serenade" 1942; "King of the Forest Rangers" 1946-serial (Pilot); "Jesse James Rides Again" 1947-serial (Stock); "Son of Zorro" 1947-serial (Hart/Haskill); "The Adventures of Frank and Jesse James" 1948-serial (Moody); "Dangers of the Canadian Mounted" 1948-serial (Vance/Zeke); "The James Brothers of Missouri" 1950-serial; "Jubilee Trail" 1954 (Blandy).

Wolfe, David. Films: "Kansas Raiders" 1950 (Tate); "The Cimarron Kid" 1951 (Swanson); "Mark of the Renegade" 1951 (Landlord); "The Iron Mistress" 1952 (James Black).

Wolfe, Ian (1896-1/23/92). Films: "Bold Caballero" 1936 (Priest); "Allegheny Uprising" 1939 (Poole); "Hudson Bay" 1941 (Mayor); "The Marauders" 1947 (Black); "Pursued" 1947 (Coroner); "Unexpected Guest" 1947; "Silver River" 1948 (Deputy); "Colorado Territory" 1949 (Wallace); "The Younger Brothers" 1949 (Chairman); "Copper Canyon" 1950 (Mr. Henderson). ¶TV: *The Lone Ranger*—"Six Gun Legacy" 11-24-49; *Jim Bowie*—"A Horse for Old Hickory" 1-4-57 (Judge Newhall); *Lawman*—"The Stranger" 1-17-60 (Jason Smith); *Bonanza*—"The Avenger" 3-19-60, "Bank Run" 1-28-61 (Harrison), "The Man Faces of Gideon Flinch" 11-5-61 (Gideon Flinch), "Bank Run" 1-28-61, "The Spotlight" 5-16-65; *Stoney Burke*—"Point of Honor" 10-22-62 (Judge Hewitt); *Gunsmoke*—"The New Society" 5-22-65; *Temple Houston*—"Jubilee" 11-14-63 (Judge Farnley); *Branded*—"Seward's Folly" 10-17-65 (William Henry Seward); *Lancer*—"The Last Train for Charlie Poe" 11-26-68, "Zee" 9-30-69 (Judge), "A Scarecrow at Hacket's" 12-16-69; *Hec Ramsey*—"The Mystery of the Yellow Rose" 1-28-73 (Judge); *The Cowboys*—"The Accused" 3-13-74 (Padre); *Barbary Coast*—"Crazy Cats" 9-15-75 (Larch).

Wolfe, Jane (1875-3/29/58).

Films: "Driver of the Deadwood Coast" 1912; "The Peril of the Cliffs" 1912; "Red Wing and the Paleface" 1912; "The Secret of the Miner's Cave" 1912; "The Tragedy of Big Eagle Mine" 1912; "The Fight at Grizzly Gulch" 1913; "The Invaders" 1913; "The Death Sign at High Noon" 1914; "On the Level" 1917 (Sontag's Wife); "The Round Up" 1920 (Josephine); "Under Strange Flags" 1937 (Mrs. Kenyon).

Wolff, Frank (1928-12/12/71). Films: "The Wild and the Innocent" 1959 (Henchman); "Few Dollars for Django" 1966-Ital./Span. (George Norton); "God Forgives—I Don't" 1966-Ital./Span. (Bill San Antonio); "A Stranger in Town" 1966-U.S./Ital. (Aguila); "Kill Them All and Come Back Alone" 1967-Ital./Span. (Captain Lynch); "Time of Vultures" 1967-Ital. (the Black One); "Five Dollars for Ringo" 1968-Ital./Span.; "Great Silence" 1968-Ital./Fr.; "I Came, I Saw, I Shot" 1968-Ital./Span. (Edwin); "Once Upon a Time in the West" 1968-Ital. (Brett McBain); "Ringo: Face of Revenge" 1968-Ital./Span. (Tricky); "Villa Rides" 1968 (Capt. Francisco Ramirez); "I Am Sartana, Your Angel of Death" 1969-Ital./Fr. ¶TV: *Jefferson Drum*—"Pete Henke" 11-20-58 (Sam Creighton); *Rawhide*—"Incident of the Wanted Painter" 1-29-60 (Holzman); *Wagon Train*—"The Maggie Hamilton Story" 4-6-60 (Sam Bass).

Wolfington, Iggie (1920-). TV: *Gunsmoke*—"Mad Dog" 1-14-67 (Mayor Wheeler).

Wolheim, Dan. Films: "Trail Dust" 1936 (Borden); "Hollywood Cowboy" 1937 (Morey); "The Oklahoma Kid" 1939 (Deputy).

Wolheim, Louis (1880-2/18/31). Films: "Wolf Song" 1929 (Gullion); "The Silver Horde" 1930 (George Balt).

Wolter, Ralf (1926-). Films: "Treasure of Silver Lake" 1963-Fr./Ger./Yugo. (Sam Hawkins); "Massacre at Marble City" 1964-Ger./Ital./Fr.; "Apache Gold" 1965-Ger. (Sam Hawkins); "The Desperado Trail" 1965-Ger./Yugo. (Sam Hawkins); "Pyramid of the Sun God" 1965-Ger./Ital./Fr.; "Half Breed" 1966-Ger./Yugo./Ital.; "Who Killed Johnny R.?" 1966-Ital./Span.; "Old Shatterhand" 1968-Ger./Yugo./Fr./Ital. (Sam Hawkens); "Winnetou and Shatterhand in the Valley of Death" 1968-Ger./Yugo./Ital.

Wong, Anna May (1907-2/3/61). Films: "The Desert's Toll" 1926

(Oneta). ¶TV: *Wyatt Earp*—"China Mary" 3-15-60 (China Mary).

Wong, Joe (1903-11/9/78). Films: "Fancy Pants" 1950 (Wong).

Wong, Victor (1906-4/7/72). Films: "Hair-Trigger Casey" 1936 (Lee Fix); "Ranch House Romeo" 1939-short; "The Taming of the West" 1939 (Cholly Wong).

Wong, W. Beal (1906-2/6/62). TV: *Have Gun Will Travel*—"Gun Shy" 3-29-58, "The Hatchet Man" 3-5-60.

Wood, Allan (1892-3/26/47). Films: "Home on the Range" 1935 (Flash Roberts); "Buck Bunny Rides Again" 1940 (Bellboy); "Heart of the Rio Grande" 1942.

Wood, Britt (1885-4/13/65). Films: "Trail Dust" 1936 (Lanky); "Range War" 1939 (Speedy MacGinnis); "Hidden Gold" 1940 (Speedy); "Knights of the Range" 1940 (Laigs); "Santa Fe Marshal" 1940 (Axel); "The Showdown" 1940 (Speedy McGinnis); "Stagecoach War" 1940 (Speedy); "Border Vigilantes" 1941 (Lafe Willis); "Pirates on Horseback" 1941 (Ben Pendleton)."Down Rio Grande Way" 1942 (Britt Haines); "Return of the Durango Kid" 1945; "Stagecoach to Denver" 1946; "Cheyenne" 1947 (Swamper); "Trail of the Mounties" 1947; "Dead Man's Gold" 1948 (Bartender); "Mark of the Lash" 1948; "Tex Granger" 1948-serial (Sandy); "Riders of the Whistling Pines" 1949 (Smith); "Square Dance Jubilee" 1949 (Grubby); "Return of the Frontiersman" 1950 (Barney); "Law and Order" 1953 (Drunk); "The Stranger Wore a Gun" 1953; "The Storm Rider" 1957 (Jake). ¶TV: *The Lone Ranger*—"Treason at Dry Creek" 12-4-52; *The Cisco Kid*—"Arroyo Millionaire's Castle" 12-12-53; *The Roy Rogers Show*—"The Scavenger" 11-27-55 (Old Mose), "Treasure of Paradise Valley" 12-11-55 (Bill York); *The Restless Gun*—"The Battle of Tower Rock" 4-28-58 (Gravy Gus).

Wood, Dorothy. Films: "The Big Catch" 1920; "The Champion Liar" 1920; "Double Danger" 1920; "Fight It Out" 1920; "Finger Prints" 1920; "A Gamblin' Fool" 1920; "The Grinning Granger" 1920; "In Wrong" Wright" 1920; "The Man with the Punch" 1920; "One Law for All" 1920; "A Pair of Twins" 1920; "The Shootin' Fool" 1920; "The Smilin' Kid" 1920; "Some Shooter" 1920; "Superstition" 1920; "Teacher's Pet" 1920; "The Trail of the Hound" 1920; "The Two-Fisted Lover" 1920; "The Grip of the Law" 1921; "The Saddle

King" 1921; "The Better Man Wins" 1922 (Nell Thompson); "Lucky Dan" 1922 (the Girl); "Trickery" 1922; "The Verdict" 1922; "West vs. East" 1922 (Betsy Macon); "Calibre 45" 1924; "Courage" 1924; "Rarin' to Go" 1924 (Miss Morton); "Wanted by the Law" 1924; "Border Intrigue" 1925 (Edith Harding); "Ranger Bill" 1925; "Ridin' Comet" 1925 (Bess Livingston); "Romance and Rustlers" 1925 (Ruth Larrabee); "Scar Hanan" 1925 (Marion Fleming); "A Streak of Luck" 1925 (Francie Oliver); "The Golden Trail" 1927; "The Idaho Kid" 1937 (Ma Endicott).

Wood, Douglas (1880-1/13/66). Films: "Guns of the Pecos" 1937 (Governor); "Honky Tonk" 1941 (Governor Wilson); "Border Outlaws" 1950 (Kimball); "Cattle Queen" 1951 (Judge Whipple). ¶TV: *The Lone Ranger*—"Double Jeopardy" 9-7-50, "Letter of the Law" 1-4-51.

Wood, Ernest (1892-7/13/42). Films: "High, Wide and Handsome" 1937 (Hotel Clerk); "Roaring Timber" 1937 (Slim Bagnell).

Wood, Freeman (1897-2/19/56). Films: "Out of Luck" 1923 (Cyril LaMount); "Hearts and Spurs" 1925 (Oscar Estabrook); "Wells Fargo" 1937.

Wood, Gordon D. *see* DeMain, Gordon.

Wood, Grace (1884-5/30/52). Films: "The Ferocious Pal" 1934 (Martha).

Wood, Harley. Films: "Law and Lead" 1936 (Hope Hawley); "The Law Rides" 1936 (Arline Lewis); "Border Phantom" 1937 (Barbara); "Valley of Terror" 1937 (Mary Scott); "Whistling Bullets" 1937 (Anita Saunders).

Wood, Jeanne. Films: "Canadian Mounties vs. Atomic Invaders" 1953-serial (Mrs. Anderson); "Joe Dakota" 1957 (Bertha Jensen). ¶TV: *Sergeant Preston of the Yukon*—"The Boy Nobody Wanted" 8-9-56 (Flora Coats); *The Law of the Plainsman*—"Toll Road" 12-24-59 (Mrs. Dawson); *The Rifleman*—"The Vision" 3-22-60 (Mrs. Svensen); *The Virginian*—"The Executioners" 9-19-62 (Woman).

Wood, John (1931-). Films: "Bullseye!" 1986-Australia (Blue McGurk).

Wood, John Lisbon. TV: *How the West Was Won*—Episode One 2-6-77 (Willy Judson), Episode Two 2-7-77 (Willy Judson), Episode Three 2-14-77 Willy Judson).

Wood, Ken. *see* Cianfriglia, Giovanni.

Wood, Lana (1944-). Films: "The Searchers" 1956 (Debbie as a Child); "The Over-the-Hill Gang Rides Again" TVM-1970 (Katie); "Grayeagle" 1977 (Beth Collier). ¶TV: *Wild Wild West*—"The Night of the Firebrand" 9-15-67 (Sheila "Vixen" O'Shaughnessy), "The Night of the Plague" 4-4-69 (Avri Trent); *Bonanza*—"The Gentle Ones" 10-29-67 (Dana).

Wood, Lynn. Films: "The Wackiest Wagon Train in the West" 1976 (Daphne Brookhaven). ¶TV: *Wild Wild West*—"The Night of the Falcon" 11-10-67 (Mother); *Dusty's Trail*—Regular 1973 (Mrs. Brookhaven).

Wood, Marjorie (1888-11/8/55). Films: "Annie Get Your Gun" 1950 (Constance).

Wood, Montgomery. *see* Gemma, Giuliano.

Wood, Natalie (1938-11/29/81). Films: "The Burning Hills" 1956 (Maria Colton); "The Searchers" 1956 (Debbie Edwards).

Wood, Peggy (1892-3/18/78). TV: *Zane Grey Theater*—"The Bitter Land" 12-6-57.

Wood, Robert. Films: "Whispering Smith" 1948 (Leroy Barton); "Redwood Forest Trail" 1950 (Luna Mason). ¶TV: *The Cisco Kid*—"Jewelry Store Fence" 8-11-51, "Water Toll" 9-22-51.

Wood, Sam (1883-9/22/49). Films: "Who Knows?" 1918 (Shed Applegate).

Wood, Ward. Films: "Ramrod" 1947 (Link Thomas); "Shotgun" 1955 (Ed). ¶TV: *My Friend Flicka*—"The Medicine Man" 5-11-56; *The Adventures of Rin Tin Tin*—"The Warrior's Promise" 1-25-57 (Otonah); *Gunsmoke*—"Gone Straight" 2-9-57 (Parker), "The Jackals" 2-12-68 (Bates); *Tales of the Texas Rangers*—"The Kid from Amarillo" 11-17-57 (Rackim); *Telephone Time*—"Sam Houston's Decision" 12-10-57 (Wiley Martin); *Have Gun Will Travel*—"Lady on the Stagecoach" 1-17-59 (Hank Slade), "The Fifth Man" 5-30-59 (Tom Bland); *Tales of Wells Fargo*—"End of a Legend" 11-23-59 (Bob Caine).

Woodbury, Joan (Nana Martinez) (1915-2/22/89). Films: "Bulldog Courage" 1935 (Helen Brennan); "Call of the Wild" 1935 (Girl Crossing Street); "The Eagle's Brood" 1936 (Dolores); "The Lion's Den" 1936 (Ann Merwin); "Song of the Gringo" 1936 (Dolores Del Valle/Lolita Valle); "God's Country and the Woman" 1937 (Frenchwoman); "The Luck of Roaring Camp" 1937 (Elsie); "Go West" 1940 (Melody); "In Old Cheyenne" 1941 (Dolores Casino); "Ride on, Vaquero" 1941 (Dolores); "Shut My Big Mouth" 1942 (Maria); "Sunset Serenade" 1942 (Vera Martin); "The Desperadoes" 1943 (Sundown); "Flame of the West" 1945 (Poppy); "Northwest Trail" 1945.

Woodell, Barbara. Films: "I Shot Jesse James" 1949 (Mrs. Zee James); "The Baron of Arizona" 1950 (Carry Lansing); "Gunfire" 1950 (Mrs. James); "I Shot Billy the Kid" 1950; "The Return of Jesse James" 1950; "Canyon Raiders" 1951; "Little Big Horn" 1951 (Mrs. Owens); "Fort Osage" 1952 (Martha Woodling); "Montana Incident" 1952; "Wild Stallion" 1952 (Mrs. Light); "The Great Jesse James Raid" 1953 (Zee); "The Homesteaders" 1953; "Silver Lode" 1954 (Townswoman); "At Gunpoint" 1955 (Mrs. Canfield); "Westward Ho the Wagons" 1956 (Mrs. Stephen); "Bullwhip" 1958 (Mrs. Mason); "Showdown at Boot Hill" 1958 (Mrs. Maynor). ¶TV: *The Lone Ranger*—"The New Neighbor" 12-18-52, "The Devil's Bog" 2-5-53; *Wild Bill Hickok*—"Blake's Kid" 12-23-52, "Wild Bill's Odyssey" 3-31-53; *Tales of the Texas Rangers*—"Double Edge" 10-8-55 (Liz Dawson); *Sergeant Preston of the Yukon*—"Mark of Crime" 7-10-58 (Amy Thatcher); *Rough Riders*—"The Plot to Assassinate President Johnson" 2-5-59 (Elizabeth Quantrill), "The Promise" 4-2-59 (Ida Kirby); *Overland Trail*—"Westbound Stage" 3-6-60 (Maude Akins); *Wagon Train*—"The Jim Bridger Story" 5-10-61 (Millie), "The Hiram Winthrop Story" 6-6-62 (Jessica); *The Dakotas*—"Trial at Grand Forks" 3-25-63 (Mary Kimberly).

Woodruff, Bert (1856-6/14/34). Films: "Hands Up!" 1917 (Tim Farley); "Six-Shooter Andy" 1918 (William Crawford); "The Mine with the Iron Door" 1924 (Bob Hill); "The Vanishing American" 1925 (Bart Wilson); "Driftin' Thru" 1926 (Joshua Reynolds); "The Texas Ranger" 1931 (Mr. Clayton).

Woodruff, Eleanor (1891-10/7/80). Films: "The Perils of Pauline" 1914-serial; "West Wind" 1915; "Britton of the Seventh" 1916 (Barbra Manning).

Woodruff, Henry (1870-10/6/16). Films: "A Man and His Mate" 1915 (Harry Ogden).

Woods, Craig. Films: "Cowboy from Lonesome River" 1944; "Partners of the Trail" 1944 (Joel); "Raiders of the Border" 1944 (Joe); "Angel and the Badman" 1947 (Ward Withers); "Fort Defiance" 1951 (Dave Parker). ¶TV: *The Cisco Kid*—"Romany Caravan" 11-17-51, "Buried Treasure" 12-29-51; *The Gene Autry Show*—"The Kid Comes West" 12-8-51, "Rocky River Feud" 1-18-52, "Trouble at Silver Creek" 3—52, "Trail of the Witch" 3-30-52; *Annie Oakley*—"Annie and the Chinese Puzzle" 2-13-55 (Nick Scanlon).

Woods, Donald (1909-). Films: "Heritage of the Desert" 1939 (John Abbott); "Mexican Spitfire Out West" 1940 (Dennis Lindsay); "The Bells of San Fernando" 1947 (Michael); "Daughter of the West" 1949 (Ralph Connors); "Born to the Saddle" 1953; "True Grit" 1969 (Barlow). ¶TV: *Bat Masterson*—"A Picture of Death" 1-14-60 (Roger Purcell); *The Rebel*—"He's Only a Boy" 2-28-60 (Sam Morse); *Wagon Train*—"The Christine Elliot Story" 3-23-60 (Phillip Ayers), "The Luke Grant Story" 6-1-60 (Luke Grant); *The Deputy*—"Trail of Darkness" 6-18-60 (Douglas Brainard); *Laramie*—"Two for the Gallows" 4-11-61 (Morgan Bennett); *Stoney Burke*—"A Girl Named Amy" 4-29-63 (Dave Jenson); *Wild Wild West*—"The Night of the Skulls" 12-16-66 (Senator Stephen Fenlow), "The Night of the Assassin" 9-22-67 (Griswold); *Bonanza*—"The Deed and the Dilemma" 3-26-67 (Gurney); *Hondo*—"Hondo and the Singing Wire" 9-22-67 (Doc Stanton); *Alias Smith and Jones*—"The Biggest Game in the West" 2-3-72 (Halberstam).

Woods, Gordon D. *see* DeMain, Gordon.

Woods, Grace. Films: "The Silent Guardian" 1926 (Sheriff's Wife); "The Flying U Ranch" 1927 (Little Doctor); "Rainbow Riders" 1934; "Trailing Trouble" 1937 (Mrs. Dunn).

Woods, Grant (-10/31/68). TV: *The Virginian*—"The Challenge" 10-19-66 (Walt Sturgess); *Pistols 'n' Petticoats*—11-19-66 (Matt Dexter); *Custer*—Regular 1967 (Captain Myles Keogh).

Woods, Harry (1880-12/28/68). Films: "Don Quickshot of the Rio Grande" 1923 (Knight); "The Steel Trail" 1923-serial; "The College Cowboy" 1924; "Ten Scars Make a Man" 1924-serial; "Wolves of the North" 1924-serial; "The Bandit's Baby" 1925 (Matt Hartigan); "A Man Four-Square" 1926 (Ben Taylor); "A Regular Scout" 1926 (Scar Stevens); "Cyclone of the Range" 1927 (the

Black Rider/Don Alvaro); "Jesse James" 1927 (Bob Ford); "Silver Comes Through" 1927 (Stanton); "Splitting the Breeze" 1927 (Dave Matlock); "Tom's Gang" 1927 (Bart Haywood); "Red Riders of Canada" 1928 (Monsieur LeBusard); "The Sunset Legion" 1928 (Honest John); "Tyrant of Red Gulch" 1928 (Ivan Petrovitch); "When the Law Rides" 1928 (the Raven); "The Desert Rider" 1929 (Williams); "Gun Law" 1929 (Bull Driscoll); "'Neath Western Skies" 1929 (Jim Canfield); "The Phantom Rider" 1929; "The Lone Rider" 1930 (Farrell); "Men Without Law" 1930 (Murdock); "Pardon My Gun" 1930 (Copper); "In Old Cheyenne" 1931 (Winslow); "The Range Feud" 1931 (Vandall); "The Texas Ranger" 1931 (Matt Taylor); "West of Cheyenne" 1931 (Kurt Raymer/the Laramie Kid); "Haunted Gold" 1932 (Joe Ryan); "Law and Order" 1932 (Walt Northrup); "Texas Gun Fighter" 1932 (Mason); "Call of the Wild" 1935 (Soapy Smith); "Gallant Defender" 1935 (Bart Munro); "Heir to Trouble" 1935 (John Motley); "Lawless Riders" 1935 (Bart); "Rustlers of Red Dog" 1935-serial (Rocky); "When a Man's a Man" 1935 (Nick Cambert); "Heroes of the Range" 1936 (Bull Lanson); "The Lawless Nineties" 1936 (Charles K. Plummer); "The Phantom Rider" 1936-serial (Harvey Delaney); "The Plainsman" 1936 (Quartermaster Sergeant); "Robin Hood of El Dorado" 1936 (Pete); "Rose of the Rancho" 1936; "The Unknown Ranger" 1936 (Van); "Courage of the West" 1937 (Al Wilkins); "Land Beyond the Law" 1937 (Tacosa); "Range Defenders" 1937 (Harvey); "Reckless Ranger" 1937 (Barlow); "Wells Fargo" 1937 (Timekeeper); "Arizona Wildcat" 1938 (Ross Harper); "Hawaiian Buckaroo" 1938 (M'-Tigue); "In Early Arizona" 1938 (Bull); "Panamint's Bad Man" 1938 (Todd Craven); "Rolling Caravans" 1938 (Thad Dalton); "The Singing Outlaw" 1938 (Cueball Qualey); "Stagecoach Days" 1938 (Moose Ringo); "The Texans" 1938 (Cavalry Officer); "Blue Montana Skies" 1939 (Hendricks); "Come on, Rangers" 1939 (Burke); "Days of Jesse James" 1939 (Capt. Worthington); "Frontier Marshal" 1939 (Curly Bill's Man); "In Old Caliente" 1939 (Calkins); "Union Pacific" 1939 (Al Brett); "Bullet Code" 1940 (Cass Barton); "The Dark Command" 1940 (Dental Patient); "The Ranger and the Lady" 1940 (Kincaid); "Triple Justice" 1940 (Al Reeves); "West of Car-

son City" 1940 (Mack Gorman); "Winners of the West" 1940-serial (King Carter); "Boss of Bullion City" 1941 (Sheriff); "Last of the Duanes" 1941 (Red Morgan); "Sheriff of Tombstone" 1941 (Shotgun Cassidy); "Dawn on the Great Divide" 1942 (Jim Corkle); "Deep in the Heart of Texas" 1942 (Idaho); "Down Texas Way" 1942 (Burt); "Jackass Mail" 1942 (Ranch Owner); "Riders of the West" 1942 (Duke Mason); "Romance on the Range" 1942 (Steve); "The Spoilers" 1942 (Complaining Miner); "West of the Law" 1942; "Beyond the Last Frontier" 1943 (Big Bill Hadley); "Bordertown Gunfighters" 1943 (Dave Strickland); "Cheyenne Roundup" 1943 (Blackie Dawson); "The Ghost Rider" 1943; "In Old Oklahoma" 1943 (Al Dalton); "Outlaws of Stampede Pass" 1943; "Call of the Rockies" 1944; "Gun to Gun" 1944-short; "Marshal of Gunsmoke" 1944 (Curtis); "Nevada" 1944 (Joe Powell); "Silver City Kid" 1944; "Tall in the Saddle" 1944 (George Clews); "Westward Bound" 1944 (Roger Caldwell); "Wanderer of the Wasteland" 1945 (Guerd Elliott); "West of the Pecos" 1945 (Brad Sawtelle); "My Darling Clementine" 1946 (Marshal); "South of Monterey" 1946; "Sunset Pass" 1946 (Cinnabar); "Code of the West" 1947 (Hatfield); "The Fabulous Texan" 1947; "Thunder Mountain" 1947 (Trimble Carson); "Trail Street" 1947 (Lance Larkin); "Wild Horse Mesa" 1947 (Jay Olmstead); "Wyoming" 1947 (Ben Jackson); "The Gallant Legion" 1948 (Lang); "Indian Agent" 1948 (Carter); "Silver River" 1948 (Card Player); "Western Heritage" 1948 (Arnold); "Colorado Territory" 1949 (Pluthner); "Hellfire" 1949 (Lew Stoner); "Masked Raiders" 1949 (Marshal Barlow); "She Wore a Yellow Ribbon" 1949 (Karl Rynders); "Short Grass" 1950 (Dreen); "Best of the Badmen" 1951; "Law of the Badlands" 1951 (Conroy); "Lone Star" 1952 (Dellman); "Hell's Outpost" 1954; "The Sheepman" 1958. ¶TV: *Gunsmoke*—"Who Lives by the Sword" 5-18-57 (Snyder), "The Tragedian" 1-23-60 (Ben); *Broken Arrow*—"Indian Medicine" 12-31-57; *Tombstone Territory*—"Postmarked for Death" 2-12-58 (Dr. Cunningham); *Frontier Doctor*—"Law of the Badlands" 2-28-59; *Bat Masterson*—"Run for Your Money" 3-2-61 (Dr. Fleming).

Woods, Jack. Films: "Blue Blood and Red" 1916; "The Fighting Brothers" 1919; "Gun Law" 1919; "The Gun Packer" 1919; "The Rider of the Law" 1919 (Jack West); "The

Rustlers" 1919; "Two from Texas" 1920; "Sure Fire" 1921 (Brazos Bart); "Under Pressure" 1922; "A Two-Fisted Sheriff" 1925 (Stranger).

Woods, James (1947-). TV: *Young Maverick*—"Dead Man's Hand" 12-26-79 & 1-2-80 (Lem Franker).

Woods, Leslie. TV: *Daniel Boone*—"A Matter of Blood" 12-28-67 (Elizabeth Creighton); *Bonanza*—"The Survivors" 11-10-68 (Agnes Smith); *Brett Maverick*—"Welcome to Sweetwater" 12-8-81 (Miss Rose).

Woods, N.S. (1858-3/21/36). Films: "Medicine Bend" 1916 (J.S. Bucks).

Woods, Robert. Films: "Five Thousand Dollars on One Ace" 1965-Span./Ital. (Jeff Clayton); "Four Dollars for Vengeance" 1965-Span./Ital. (Roy Dexter); "Man from Canyon City" 1965-Span./Ital. (Jeff Clayton); "Seven Guns for the MacGregors" 1965-Ital./Span. (Gregor MacGregor); "Johnny Colt" 1966-Ital. (Starblack); "My Name Is Pecos" 1966-Ital. (Pecos); "Pecos Cleans Up" 1967-Ital.; "Belle Starr Story" 1968-Ital.; "Black Jack" 1968-Ital. (Black Jack); "Machine Gun Killers" 1968-Ital./Span. (Chris Tanner); "Challenge of the Mackennas" 1969-Ital./Span.; "The Reward's Yours, the Man's Mine" 1970-Ital.; "His Name Was Sam Walbash, But They Call Him Amen" 1971-Ital. (Sam Walbash); "Mallory Must Not Die" 1971-Ital. (Mallory); "Colt in the Hand of the Devil" 1972-Ital. (Texas Ranger Wilton); "Kill the Poker Player" 1972-Ital./Span. (Ace); "My Colt, Not Yours" 1972-Span./Fr./Ital. (Sheriff Garingo).

Woods, William. Films: "Headin' for the Rio Grande" 1937; "Code of the Fearless" 1939 (Li Hung Lo); "Two-Gun Troubador" 1939 (Sheriff).

Woodson, William. *see* Hudson, William.

Woodthorpe, Georgia (1859-8/25/57). Films: "The Rose of Nome" 1920 (Madam Chartreau).

Woodville, Katherine (1939-). Films: "Posse" 1975 (Mrs. Cooper). ¶TV: *The Men from Shiloh*—"Follow the Leader" 12-2-70 (Vanessa MacKenzie); *Kung Fu*—"The Gunman" 1-3-74 (Nedra Chamberlain).

Woodward, Bob (1909-2/7/72). Films: "West of Nevada" 1936; "The California Mail" 1937 (Wyatt); "Fighting Texan" 1937; "Guns of the Pecos" 1937; "Flaming Frontier" 1938-serial; "Hollywood Roundup"

1938; "The Overland Express" 1938; "Santa Fe Stampede" 1938; "Frontier Scout" 1939 (Shorty); "Home on the Prairie" 1939 (Madden); "The Taming of the West" 1939 (Shifty); "Billy the Kid in Texas" 1940; "Two-Fisted Rangers" 1940 (Tom); "Bad Man of Deadwood" 1941; "Gauchos of El Dorado" 1941; "In Old Cheyenne" 1941 (Outlaw); "Jesse James at Bay" 1941; "Kansas Cyclone" 1941; "Nevada City" 1941; "White Eagle" 1941-serial; "The Cyclone Kid" 1942; "Raiders of the Range" 1942; "Sons of the Pioneers" 1942; "Sunset on the Desert" 1942; "Firebrands of Arizona" 1944 (Townsman); "The San Antonio Kid" 1944; "Cheyenne Takes Over" 1947 (Anderson); "Flashing Guns" 1947; "Pioneer Justice" 1947 (Jackson); "Return of the Lash" 1947; "Springtime in the Sierras" 1947; "Stage to Mesa City" 1947 (Pete); "Back Trail" 1948; "Courtin' Trouble" 1948 (Gill); "Cowboy Cavalier" 1948; "Crossed Trails" 1948 (Wright); "Dead Man's Gold" 1948; "The Fighting Ranger" 1948; "Frontier Agent" 1948; "Gunning for Justice" 1948; "Oklahoma Badlands" 1948; "Oklahoma Blues" 1948; "Overland Trails" 1948; "Partners of the Sunset" 1948; "Range Renegades" 1948; "The Rangers Ride" 1948; "The Sheriff of Medicine Bow" 1948; "Silver Trails" 1948 (Dirk); "Song of the Drifter" 1948; "The Tioga Kid" 1948 (Trigger); "Triggerman" 1948; "The Westward Trail" 1948 (Stage Driver); "Across the Rio Grande" 1949; "Brand of Fear" 1949; "Crashing Thru" 1949; "Gun Runner" 1949 (Sam); "Hidden Danger" 1949 (Joe); "Law of the West" 1949 (Spencer); "Range Justice" 1949 (Bob); "Roaring Westward" 1949 (Bob); "Shadows of the West" 1949 (Gus); "Stampede" 1949 (Whiskey); "West of El Dorado" 1949; "The Blazing Sun" 1950; "Outlaw Gold" 1950; "Over the Border" 1950; "Vigilante Hideout" 1950; "Hills of Utah" 1951; "Barbed Wire" 1952; "Blue Canadian Rockies" 1952 (Sergeant Midler); "Junction City" 1952 (Keely); "Night Stage to Galveston" 1952; "The Old West" 1952; "Winning of the West" 1953; "Cattle Queen of Montana" 1954; "Wyoming Renegades" 1955 (Matt Garner); "Apache Territory" 1958 (Graves); "Five Guns to Tombstone" 1961; "Gun Fight" 1961 (Mantz). ¶TV: *The Lone Ranger*—"Gold Train" 3-16-50, "Billie the Great" 3-30-50; *The Gene Autry Show*—"Gold Dust Charlie" 7-30-50, "The Posse" 9-17-50, "The Black Rider" 10-22-50, "The Breakup" 11-5-50, "Killer Horse" 12-

10-50, "Ghost Town Raiders" 10-6-51, "Killer's Trail" 10-27-51, "Revenge Trail" 11-17-51, "Horse Sense" 1-11-52, "Hot Lead and Old Lace" 2-15-52, "Blazeaway" 2-22-52, "Bullets and Bows" 3-2-52, "Trail of the Witch" 3-30-52, "Thunder Out West" 7-14-53, "Cold Decked" 9-15-53, "Steel Ribbon" 9-22-53, "Ransom Cross" 10-6-53, "Santa Fe Raiders" 7-6-54, "Prize Winner" 7-27-54, "Boots and Ballots" 9-25-54, "Outlaw Warning" 10-2-54, "The Golden Chariot" 10-29-55, "Ghost Ranch" 11-12-55, "Ride, Rancheros" 12-10-55, "Dynamite" 12-24-55; *Wild Bill Hickok*—"Mexican Gun Running Story" 1-8-52; *The Cisco Kid*—"The Fugitive" 11-1-52, "Pot of Gold" 4-25-53; *Annie Oakley*—"The Dude Stagecoach" 1-30-54, "Annie and the Silver Ace" 2-27-54, "Annie Finds Strange Treasure" 3-6-54, "The Tomboy" 7-17-54 (Jim), "Annie and the Bicycle Riders" 7-8-56 (Andy), "Annie and the First Phone" 7-22-56 (Hank), "The Saga of Clement O'-Toole" 11-4-56 (Stage Driver), "The Dutch Gunmaker" 2-17-57 (Stage Driver); *Tales of Wells Fargo*—"Ride with the Killer" 12-2-57 (Ben); *Wyatt Earp*—"Arizona Comes to Dodge" 5-26-59 (Driver); *Have Gun Will Travel*—"The Tax Gatherer" 2-11-61, "Broken Image" 4-29-61 (Sheriff), "Bandit" 5-12-62 (Floyd), "The Treasure" 12-29-62 (Gruber).

Woodward, Edward (1930-). Films: "Charley One-Eye" 1973-Brit. (Holstrom).

Woodward, Henry. Films: "Nan of Music Mountain" 1917 (Jeffries); "On the Level" 1917 (Judge Wilton); "Lawless Love" 1918 (Black Jim); "The Last of the Mohicans" 1920 (Major Duncan Hayward).

Woodward, Joanne (1930-). Films: "Yankee Fakir" 1947 (Mary Mason); "Count Three and Pray" 1955 (Lissy); "A Big Hand for the Little Lady" 1966 (Mary).

Woodward, Morgan (1926-). Films: "The Great Locomotive Chase" 1956 (Alex); "Westward Ho the Wagons" 1956 (Obie Foster); "The Gun Hawk" 1963 (Mitchell); "Gunpoint" 1966 (Drago); "Firecreek" 1968 (Willard); "Death of a Gunfighter" 1969 (Ivan Stanek); "The Wild Country" 1971 (Ab Cross); "Yuma" TVM-1971 (Arch King); "One Little Indian" 1973 (Sgt. Raines); "Running Wild" 1973; "The Quest" TVM-1976 (Sheriff Moses); "Gunsmoke: To the Last Man" TVM-1991 (Sheriff Abel Rose). ¶TV: *The Range Rider*—"Feud at Friend-

ship City" 3-1-52; *Zane Grey Theater*—"A Quiet Sunda in San Ardo" 11-23-56 (Pete); *Tales of Wells Fargo*—"Renegade Raiders" 5-20-57 (Phil Slavin), "Trackback" 12-30-61 (Steve Taggart); *Wyatt Earp*—"The Manly Art" 1-21-58 (Champ Starbuck), "Three" 5-13-58 (Captain Langley), Regular 1958-61 (Shotgun Gibbs); *Wagon Train*—"The Bill Tawnee Story" 2-12-58 (Laverty), "The Jeremy Dow Story" 12-28-60 (Jubal), "The Patience Miller Story" 1-11-61 (Spotted Horse), "The Jed Polke Story" 3-1-61 (Keene), "The Kitty Allbright Story" 10-4-61 (Barney), "The Martin Onyx Story" 1-3-62 (2nd Killer), "Charlie Wooster—Outlaw" 2-20-63 (Clel), "The Santiago Quesada Story" 3-30-64 (Jute), "The Hide Hunters" 9-27-64 (Zach Ryker), "The Jarbo Pierce Story" 5-2-65 (Clyde); *The Restless Gun*—"The Manhunters" 6-2-58 (Ben Cotterman), "Take Me Home" 12-29-58, "Incident at Bluefield" 3-30-59 (J.B. Cauter), "The Way Back" 7-13-59 (Jubal Carney); *Broken Arrow*—"The Outlaw" 6-10-58 (Blue); *Frontier Doctor*—"Strange Cargo" 5-23-59; *The Texan*—"Town Divided" 3-21-60 (Mark Jordan); *Bonanza*—"Death at Dawn" 4-30-60 (Sheriff Biggs), "The Secret" 5-6-61 (Deputy Conlee), "The Toy Soldier" 10-20-63 (McDermott), "Lothario Larkin" 4-25-65 (Gillis), "Four Sisters from Boston" 10-30-66 (Catlin), "Pride of a Man" 6-2-68 (Will McNab), "Old Friends" 12-14-69 (Jess Waddell), "The Prisoners" 10-17-71 (Moorehouse); *Bat Masterson*—"The Big Gamble" 6-16-60 (Kana); *Have Gun Will Travel*—"Man in an Hourglass" 12-1-62 (Canute); *The Virginian*—"The Small Parade" 2-20-63, "Requiem for a Country Doctor" 1-25-67 (Randall), "The Bugler" 11-19-69 (Mr. Hamilton); *Temple Houston*—"Jubilee" 11-14-63 (Sheriff Ivers); *Rawhide*—"The Photographer" 12-11-64 (Kale); *Daniel Boone*—"The First Stone" 1-28-65 (Tom Sutton), "The Christmas Story" 12-23-65 (Elisha Tully); *Gunsmoke*—"Seven Hours to Dawn" 9-18-65 (Deeks), "Taps for Old Jeb" 10-16-65 (Sholo), "The Good People" 10-15-66 (Ben Rucker), "The Whispering Tree" 11-12-66 (Earl Miller), "The Hanging" 12-31-66 (Beaumont), "Vengeance" 10-2-67 & 10-9-67 (Zack Johnson), "Death Train" 11-27-67 (Harl Townsend), "Lyle's Kid" 9-23-68 (Grant Lyle), "Lobo" 12-16-68 (Luke Brazo), "Stryker" 9-29-69 (Josh Stryker), "Hackett" 3-16-70 (Quent Sargent), "Luke" 11-2-70 (Luke Dangerfield), "The Wedding"

3-13-72 (Walt Clayton), "The Sodbusters" 11-20-72 (Lamoor Underwood), "A Game of Death … An Act of Love" 11-5-73 & 11-12-73 (Bear Sanderson), "Matt Dillon Must Die!" 9-9-74 (Abraham Wakefield); *The Big Valley*—"The Guilt of Matt Bentell" 12-8-65 (Aaron Condon); *Branded*—"The Wolfers" 1-9-66 (Clyde); *Death Valley Days*—"Hugh Glass Meets the Bear" 6-11-66 (Fitzpatrick), "An Organ for Brother Brigham" 7-16-66 (Luke); *Pistols 'n' Petticoats*—"No Sale" 9-24-66 (Hangman); *Iron Horse*—"Cougar Man" 10-24-66; *The Monroes*—"War Arrow" 11-2-66 (Crocker); *Cimarron Strip*—"The Roarer" 11-2-67 (Walter Forcey), "The Last Wolf" 12-14-67 (Bill Henderson), "Heller" 1-18-68 (Logan Purcell); *Hondo*—"Hondo and the Hanging Town" 12-8-67 (Colonel Spinner); *The High Chaparral*—"The Buffalo Soldiers" 11-22-68 (Hilliard), "The Journal of Death" 1-9-70 (Garnet), "The Badge" 12-18-70 (Billings); *The Guns of Will Sonnett*—"Trail's End" 11-31-69 (Wilk); *Lancer*—"The Great Humbug" 3-4-69 (Jay McKillen); *Bearcats!*—11-25-71 (Tiger Thompson); *Hec Ramsey*—"The Green Feather Mystery" 12-17-72 (Ben Buckley); *Kung Fu*—"Sun and Cloud Shadow" 2-22-73 (Colonel Binns), "The Nature of Evil" 3-21-74 (Adversary); *The Quest*—"Incident at Drucker's Tavern" 1976; *Centennial*—Regular 1978-79 (General Wade); *How the West Was Won*—Episode One 2-12-78 (the Stranger), "The Gunfighter" 1-15-79 (Coe); *Young Maverick*—"Clancy" 11-28-79 (Dalton); *Adventures of Brisco County, Jr.*—"Bounty Hunter's Convention" 1-7-94 (Sam Travis).

Woody, Jack. Films: "Carson City" 1952; "Last of the Comanches" 1952 (Cpl. Floyd); "Springfield Rifle" 1952 (Sims); "The Stranger Wore a Gun" 1953; "Thunder Over the Plains" 1953 (Henley); "Riding Shotgun" 1954 (Hardpan); "Day of the Outlaw" 1959 (Shorty). ¶TV: *Sergeant Preston of the Yukon*—"Justice at Goneaway Creek" 2-9-56 (Miner).

Wooley, Sheb (1921-). Films: "Trooper Hook" 1957 (Cooter Brown); "Rocky Mountain" 1950 (Kay Rawlins); "Distant Drums" 1951 (Pvt. Jessup); "Little Big Horn" 1951 (Quince); "Bugles in the Afternoon" 1952 (Gen. Custer); "Cattle Town" 1952 (Miller); "Hellgate" 1952 (Neill Price); "High Noon" 1952 (Ben Miller); "The Lusty Men" 1952 (Slim); "Sky Full of Moon" 1952 (Balladeer); "Texas Bad Man" 1953 (Mack); "The Boy from Oklahoma"

1954 (Pete Martin); "Johnny Guitar" 1954 (Posse); "Rose Marie" 1954 (Corporal); "Man Without a Star" 1955; "The Black Whip" 1956 (Lasater); "Giant" 1956 (Gabe Target); "The Oklahoman" 1957 (Henchman); "Ride a Violent Mile" 1957 (Jonathan Long); "Terror in a Texas Town" 1958 (Baxter); "The War Wagon" 1967 (Dan Snyder); "The Outlaw Josey Wales" 1976 (Cobb); "Silverado" 1985 (Cavalry Sergeant). ¶TV: *The Cisco Kid*—"Pancho and the Pachyderm" 2-2-52, "Laughing Badman" 3-8-52; *The Range Rider*—"Outlaw Pistols" 4-5-52, "Two-Fisted Justice" 9-6-52; *The Lone Ranger*—"Stage to Estacado" 7-23-53, "Message to Fort Apache" 9-23-54, "Wanted … the Lone Ranger" 5-5-55; *Stories of the Century*—"The Younger Brothers" 6-3-55; *The Adventures of Rin Tin Tin*—"The Star Witness" 12-9-55; *My Friend Flicka*—"The Unmasking" 4-13-56 (Harry Runyon); *Cavalry Patrol*—Pilot 1956 (Lank Clee); *Zane Grey Theater*—"Vengeance Canyon" 11-30-56 (Brock); *Cheyenne*—"The Iron Trail" 1-1-57 (Chev Jones); *Maverick*—"Relic of Fort Tejon" 11-3-57 (Sheriff); *Tales of Wells Fargo*—"Man in the Box" 11-11-57 (Lenny); *Wyatt Earp*—"Indian Wife" 12-10-57 (Rex Jones); *Rawhide*—Regular 1961-65 (Pete Nolan); *Death Valley Days*—"The Trouble with Taxes" 4-18-65 (Jeb Slade).

Woolley, Monty (1888-5/6/63). Films: "The Girl of the Golden West" 1938 (Governor).

Woolman, Claude (1933-). Films: "Heaven with a Gun" 1969 (Gilcher). ¶TV: *Laredo*—"A Question of Guilt" 3-10-67 (John Bright Star); *Daniel Boone*—"Faith's Way" 4-4-68 (Tahchee).

Woolvett, Jaimz. Films: "Unforgiven" 1992 (the Schofield Kid).

Wooters, Norman Jean. Films: "Bad Men of the Hills" 1942 (Buckshot); "The Fighting Buckaroo" 1943 (Buckshot).

Wootton, Stephen. Films: "At Gunpoint" 1955 (Joey Clark); "Red Sundown" 1956 (Chuck); "Stranger at My Door" 1956 (Dodie Jarret). ¶TV: *My Friend Flicka*—"Wind from Heaven" 2-3-56; *Have Gun Will Travel*—"Gun Shy" 3-29-58; *The Californians*—"The Foundling" 4-29-58 (Martin Van Buren Hicks); *Buckskin*—"Mary MacNamara" 5-18-59 (Buford); *Wyatt Earp*—"The Good Mule and the Bad Mule" 3-14-61 (Ollie Burton); *The Rifleman*—"The Tinhorn" 3-12-62 (Willie).

Worden, Hank (Heber Snow) (1901-11/6/92). Films: "Ghost Town Gold" 1937 (Mr. Crabtree); "Hittin' the Trail" 1937 (Hank); "Moonlight on the Range" 1937; "The Mystery of the Hooded Horseman" 1937 (Deputy); "Riders of the Rockies" 1937 (Henchman); "Sing, Cowboy, Sing" 1937 (Henchman); "Tex Rides with the Boy Scouts" 1937; "Frontier Town" 1938; "Ghost Town Riders" 1938 (Tom); "Rollin' Plains" 1938 (Squint); "The Singing Outlaw" 1938; "The Stranger from Arizona" 1938 (Skeeter); "Western Trails" 1938; "Where the Buffalo Roam" 1938 (Man at Barn Dance); "Chip of the Flying U" 1939; "Cupid Rides the Range" 1939-short; "The Night Riders" 1939; "Oklahoma Frontier" 1939; "Rollin' Westward" 1939 (Slim); "Sundown on the Prairie" 1939 (Hank); "Timber Stampede" 1939 (Photographer); "Gaucho Serenade" 1940; "Molly Cures a Cowboy" 1940-short; "Northwest Passage" 1940 (Ranger); "Prairie Law" 1940; "Triple Justice" 1940; "Viva Cisco Kid" 1940 (Deputy); "Border Vigilantes" 1941 (Wagon Driver); "Code of the Outlaw" 1942; "Cowboy Serenade" 1942; "Riding the Wind" 1942; "Black Market Rustlers" 1943 (Slim); "Canyon City" 1943; "Tenting Tonight on the Old Camp Ground" 1943 (Sleepy Martin); "Lumberjack" 1944; "Duel in the Sun" 1946 (Dancer); "The Lawless Breed" 1946; "Angel and the Badman" 1947 (Townsman); "Prairie Express" 1947 (Deputy); "The Sea of Grass" 1947 (Cowboy); "Fort Apache" 1948 (Bald-Headed Southern Recruit); "Red River" 1948 (Simms); "The Three Godfathers" 1948 (Deputy Sheriff); "Yellow Sky" 1948 (Rancher); "Hellfire" 1949; "Red Canyon" 1949 (Charley); "Wagonmaster" 1950 (Luke Clegg); "Sugarfoot" 1951 (Johnny-Behind-the-Stove); "Apache War Smoke" 1952 (Amber); "The Big Sky" 1952 (Poordevil); "Woman of the North Country" 1952 (Tom Gordon); "The Indian Fighter" 1955 (Crazy Bear); "Davy Crockett and the River Pirates" 1956; "The Searchers" 1956 (Mose Harper); "The Buckskin Lady" 1957 (Lon); "Dragoon Wells Massacre" 1957 (Hopi Charlie); "Forty Guns" 1957 (John Chisum); "The Quiet Gun" 1957 (Sampson, the Deputy); "Bullwhip" 1958 (Tex); "Toughest Gun in Tombstone" 1958 (Liveryman); "The Horse Soldiers" 1959 (Deacon); "The Alamo" 1960 (Parson); "Sergeant Rutledge" 1960 (Laredo); "One-Eyed Jacks" 1961

(Doc); "McClintock" 1963 (Jeth); "True Grit" 1969 (Undertaker); "Chisum" 1970 (Stage Depot Clerk); "Rio Lobo" 1970 (Hank); "Big Jake" 1971 (Hank); "Black Noon" TVM-1971 (Joseph); "Cahill, United States Marshal" 1973 (Undertaker); "The Hanged Man" TVM-1974 (Ab Wilkes); "Bronco Billy" 1980 (Mechanic); "Once Upon a Texas Train" TVM-1988. ¶TV: *The Lone Ranger*—"The Tenderfeet" 11-10-49, "Stage to Tishomingo" 10-28-54; *Sheriff of Cochise*—"Cain and Abel" 11-16-56; *Tales of Wells Fargo*—"The Reward" 4-21-58 (Sam); *Rawhide*—"Incident of the Devil and His Due" 1-22-60 (Wendell), "Incident of the Captive" 12-16-60; *Bonanza*—"The Stranger" 2-27-60; *Wagon Train*—"The Colter Craven Story" 11-23-60; *The Travels of Jaimie McPheeters*—"The Day of the Pawnees" 12-22-63 & 12-29-63 (Chief Hunting Hawk); *Daniel Boone*—"The Prophet" 1-21-65 (Blue Belly); *Iron Horse*—"T Is for Traitor" 12-2-67 (Ed); *Lancer*—"The Last Train for Charlie Poe" 11-26-68.

Workman, Lindsay (1924-). Films: "Westworld" 1973 (Supervisor). ¶TV: *Wanted—Dead or Alive*—"Competition" 1-31-59; *Have Gun Will Travel*—"Shot by Request" 10-10-59, "The Unforgiven" 11-7-59; *Hotel De Paree*—"A Rope Is for Hanging" 11-6-59 (Fleethill); *Colt .45*—"A Legend of Buffalo Bill" 11-8-59 (Ned Buntline); *Rawhide*—"Incident of the Devil and His Due" 1-22-60 (Hooper); *Bonanza*—"The Colonel" 1-6-63, "The Lila Conrad Story" 1-5-64, "The Search" 2-14-65, "Destiny's Child" 1-30-66 (Badgett), "Journey to Terror" 2-5-67 (Doc Jensen), "Cassie" 10-24-71 (Kendall); *Gunsmoke*—"Panacea Sykes" 4-13-63 (Station Agent); *Wild Wild West*—"The Night of the Human Trigger" 12-3-65 (Bartender), "The Night of the Two-Legged Buffalo" 3-11-66 (Manager); *Cimarron Strip*—"The Roarer" 11-2-67; *Here Come the Brides*—Regular 1968-70 (Reverend Adams); *Alias Smith and Jones*—"The Fifth Victim" 3-25-71 (Minister); *Bearcats!*—"Blood Knot" 11-4-71 (Mayor Cobb); *Father Murphy*—"Matthew and Elizabeth" 3-28-82 (Nate Hawkins).

Worlock, Frederic (1886-8/1/73). Films: "Northwest Passage" 1940 (Sir William Johnson); "Pierre of the Plains" 1942 (Inspector Cannody); "Last of the Redmen" 1947 (Gen. Webb).

Worne, Duke (1885-10/13/33). Films: "Just Jim" 1915; "John Ermine of the Yellowstone" 1917 (Lt. Butler);

"The Scrapper" 1917; "The Tornado" 1917; "The Trail of Hate" 1917 (Captain Holden).

Worth, Barbara. Films: "The Prairie King" 1927 (Edna Jordan); "The Fearless Rider" 1928 (Kate Lane); "Plunging Hoofs" 1928 (Nanette); "Lightnin' Smith Returns" 1931 (Helen Parker); "The Fighting Trooper" 1934 (Diane La Farge).

Worth, Constance (1915-10/18/63). Films: "Klondike Kate" 1942 (Lita); "Cyclone Prairie angers" 1944; "Western Renegades" 1949 (Annie).

Worth, David. Films: "Three Rogues" 1931 (Bruce Randall); "Riddle Ranch" 1936 (Bob Horton).

Worth, Harry. Films: "Bar 20 Rides Again" 1936 (Nevada); "The Cowboy and the Kid" 1936 (Jess Watson); "Lightning Bill Carson" 1936 (Silent Tom Rand); "Phantom Patrol" 1936 (Dapper Dan Geary/Stephen Norris); "The Big Show" 1937 (Rico); "Hopalong Rides Again" 1937 (Prof. Hepburn); "Outlaws of the Orient" 1937 (Sheldon); "The Llano Kid" 1939 (Dissipated Mexican); "Adventures of Red Ryder" 1940-serial (Calvin Drake); "Mark of Zorro" 1940 (Caballero); "Cyclone on Horseback" 1941; "Honky Tonk" 1941 (Harry Gates); "Kansas Cyclone" 1941 (Jud Parker); "Riders of the Rio Grande" 1943 (Sam Skelly).

Worth, Lillian. Films: "Rustlers' Ranch" 1926 (Tessie); "Stairs of Sand" 1929 (Babe); "The Fighting Sheriff" 1931 (Florabel).

Worth, Michael. Films: "Days of Jesse James" 1939 (Frank James).

Worth, Nancy. Films: "Raiders of Sunset Pass" 1943 (Janice Clark).

Worthington, Cathy. Films: "The Gambler" TVM-1980 (Lilly); "The Gambler, Part II—The Adventure Continues" TVM-1983 (Lilly); "Wild Horses" TVM-1985 (Lynda).

Worthington, William (1872-4/9/41). Films: "Battle of Greed" 1934 (Judge Avery); "The Gold Ghost" 1934-short; "The Oklahoma Kid" 1939 (Homesteader); "Union Pacific" 1939 (Oliver Ames); "Law and Order" 1940 (Judge Williams).

Wrather, Jr., Jack. Films: "The Big Land" 1957 (Olaf Johnson).

Wray, Fay (1907-). Films: "Don't Shoot" 1926; "Lazy Lightning" 1926 (Lila Rogers); "The Man in the Saddle" 1926 (Pauline Stewart); "One Wild Time" 1926; "The Saddle Tramp" 1926; "Wild Horse Stampede" 1926 (Jessie Hayen); "Loco Luck" 1927 (Molly Vernon); "Spurs and Saddles" 1927 (Mildred

Orth); "A One Man Game" 1927 (Roberts); "The Border Legion" 1930 (Joan Randall); "The Texan" 1930 (Consuelo); "Captain Thunder" 1931 (Ynez Dominguez); "The Conquering Horde" 1931 (Taisie Lockhart); "Three Rogues" 1931 (Lee Carlton). ¶TV: *Wagon Train*—"The Cole Crawford Story" 4-11-62.

Wray, John (1888-4/5/40). Films: "The Lone Cowboy" 1934 (Bill O'Neal); "The Bad Man of Brimstone" 1937 (Mr. Grant); "The Man from Dakota" 1940 (Carpenter).

Wren, Clare. TV: *Young Riders*—Regular 1990-92 (Rachel); *Adventures of Brisco County, Jr.*—"Bounty Hunter's Convention" 1-7-94 (Rosalind Peters).

Wren, Michael. Films: "Three Amigos" 1986 (Cowboy); "The Alamo: 13 Days to Glory" TVM-1987 (Seguin); "Down the Long Hill" TVM-1987 (Cal); "Where the Hell's That Gold?!!!" TVM-1988 (Lieutenant).

Wright, Armand "Curley" (1896-3/28/65). Films: "The Girl of the Golden West" 1938 (Renegade); "Panamint's Bad Man" 1938 (Nicola); "The Bandit Trail" 1941.

Wright, Ben (1915-7/2/89). Films: "The Lone Ranger" 1938-serial (Rancher); "Pride of the West" 1938 (Townsman); "Johnny Concho" 1956 (Benson); "Villa!" 1958 (Francisco Madero); "Three Thousand Hills" 1959 (Frenchy). ¶TV: *Gunsmoke*—"Dooley Surrenders" 3-8-58 (Mr. Ross), "Kitty's Rebellion" 2-7-59 (Whisky Drummer), "Groat's Grudge" 1-2-60, "Don Mateo" 10-22-60 (Chalmers), "The Renegades" 1-12-63 (Colonel Pate), "Two of a Kind" 3-16-63 (Harris), "Friend" 1-25-64 (Father Thom), "Father Love" 3-14-64 (Ross), "The Newcomers" 12-3-66 (Birger Engdahl); *Have Gun Will Travel*—"The Prize Fight Story" 4-5-58, "Incident at Borasca Bend" 3-21-59 (Jackson), "The Fifth Man" 5-30-59 (Whisky Drummer), "The Princess and the Gunfighter" 1-21-61 (Count di Cassals), "My Brother's Keeper" 5-6-61 (Boggs), "The Road" 5-27-61 (Beaman); *Northwest Passage*—"Dead Reckoning" 1-16-59; *Black Saddle*—"The Freight Line" 11-6-59, "The Apprentice" 3-11-60 (Everetts); *The Rebel*—"The Scavengers" 11-8-59 (Tom), "Grant of Land" 5-22-60 (Wicks), "The Threat" 2-12-61 (Eberhart); *Riverboat*—"End of a Dream" 9-19-60 (Mr. Shaftoe); *Zane Grey Theater*—"One Must Die" 1-12-61 (Paul Overland); *Lawman*—"The Promise" 6-11-

61; *The Virginian*—"The Exiles" 1-9-63, "The Orchard" 10-2-68 (McCabe); *Stoney Burke*—"Point of Entry" 3-4-63 (Manolo); *Wild Wild West*—"The Night the Dragon Screamed" 1-14-66 (Clive Allenby-Smythe), "The Night of the Sabatini Death" 2-2-69 (Clarence); *Bonanza*—"Ride the Wind" 1-16-66 & 1-23-66 (Spires); *Hondo*—"Hondo and the Mad Dog" 10-27-67 (Dr. Paul), "Hondo and the Ghost of Ed Dow" 11-24-67 (Dr. Paul); *The Guns of Will Sonnett*—"One Angry Juror" 3-7-69 (Doctor).

Wright, Ed (-3/31/75). Films: "Showdown at Boot Hill" 1958 (Brent); "The Oregon Trail" 1959 (Jessie).

Wright, Francis. *see* Wright, Frances.

Wright, Helen. Films: "Spurs" 1930 (Peggy Bradley).

Wright, Howard (1896-). Films: "Last of the Pony Riders" 1953 (Clyde Vesey); "The Gun That Won the West" 1955 (General Pope); "Seminole Uprising" 1955 (Col. Hannah); "Stranger at My Door" 1956 (Doc Parks); "The Legend of Tom Dooley" 1959 (Sheriff); "Apache Rifles" 1964. ¶TV: *Wyatt Earp*—"Mr. Earp Becomes a Marshal" 9-6-55; *Schlitz Playhouse of the Stars*—"Flowers for Jenny" 8-3-56 (Ned Hayes); *The Texan*—"Law of the Gun" 9-29-58 (Doctor); *Bat Masterson*—"Trail Pirate" 12-31-58 (Trail Outfitter); *Wagon Train*—"The Jenny Tannen Story" 6-24-59 (Doctor); *The Deputy*—"Silent Gun" 1-23-60 (Stoner); *Zane Grey Theater*—"The Sunday Man" 2-25-60; *Laramie*—"Ride or Die" 3-8-60 (Doctor), "Deadly Is the Night" 11-7-61 (Charlie); *Bonanza*—"The Burma Rarity" 10-22-61, "The Auld Sod" 2-4-62 (Howie), "The Hayburner" 2-17-63 (Sam), "The Search" 2-14-65; "The Meredith Smith" 10-31-65 (Cal), "The Oath" 11-20-66 (Sam); *Tales of Wells Fargo*—"Who Lives by the Gun" 3-24-62 (Doc Finley); *Gunsmoke*—"Us Haggens" 12-8-62 (Dietzer); *Death Valley Days*—"Lady of the Plains" 7-23-66 (Henry Otis); *Pistols 'n' Petticoats*—"A Crooked Line" 9-17-66 (Sanders); *Laredo*—"One Too Many Voices" 11-18-66.

Wright, Jean. Films: "Canadian Mounties vs. Atomic Invaders" 1953-serial (Betty Warner).

Wright, Mack V. (1895-8/14/65). Films: "The Brand of Courage" 1921; "Red Courage" 1921 (Sam Waters); "Perils of the Yukon" 1922-serial; "The Trail of the Wolf" 1922; "The Guilty Hand" 1923; "Singled-Handed" 1923 (Milo); "Crossed Trail" 1924 (Buck Sloman); "Huntin' Trouble" 1924; "Western Vengeance" 1924 (Dick Sterling); "Blood and Steel" 1925 (Devore Palmer); "Border Intrigue" 1925 (Juan Verdugo); "Border Justice" 1925 (Angus Bland); "Moccasins" 1925 (Robert Barlow); "Riders of Mystery" 1925 (Dan Blair); "Pioneers of the West" 1929 (Spike Harkness); "Arizona Days" 1928 (Villain); "Headin' Westward" 1928 (Slim McGee); "Manhattan Cowboy" 1928; "The Silent Trail" 1928; "West of Santa Fe" 1928; "The Lone Horseman" 1929; "The Oklahoma Sheriff" 1930; "Rainbow Riders" 1934; "Randy Rides Alone" 1934 (Posse Member).

Wright, Patrick (1939-). TV: *The Life and Times of Grizzly Adams*—"The Fugitive" 2-23-77 (Deputy); *Paradise*—"Twenty-Four Hours" 5-3-91 (Theodore).

Wright, Richard. Films: "Hot Lead and Cold Feet" 1978 (Pete). ¶TV: *Alias Smith and Jones*—"Twenty-One Days to Tenstrike" 1-6-72 (Hank), "The Man Who Broke the Bank at Red Gap" 1-20-72; *How the West Was Won*—"The Gunfighter" 1-15-79 (Glen Nealson).

Wright, Roy. TV: *Tales of Wells Fargo*—"Gunman's Revenge" 5-22-61 (Neil Brand); *The Deputy*—"Lawman's Conscience" 7-1-61 (Phil Briggs); *Bonanza*—"The Friendship" 11-12-61; *Gunsmoke*—"A Man a Day" 12-30-61 (Carver), "Catawomper" 2-10-62 (Bert Tassel); *Rawhide*—"Grandma's Money" 2-23-62 (Bartender).

Wright, Teresa (1918-). Films: "Pursued" 1947 (Thorley Callum); "The Capture" 1950 (Ellen); "California Conquest" 1952 (Julia Lawrence); "Track of the Cat" 1954 (Grace Bridges). ¶TV: *DuPont Show of the Week*—"Big Deal in Laredo" 10-7-62 (Mary); *Bonanza*—"My Son, My Son" 1-19-64 (Katherine Saunders); *Lancer*—"Yesterday's Vendetta" 1-28-69 (Ellen Haney).

Wright, Wen (1916-6/17/54). Films: "Silver on the Sage" 1939 (Lane); "The Whispering Skull" 1944; "Gun Smoke" 1945; "Marked for Murder" 1945; "California Gold Rush" 1946; "Dallas" 1950 (Cowpuncher).

Wright, Will (1891-6/19/62). Films: "Honky Tonk" 1941 (Man in Meeting House); "Shut My Big Mouth" 1942 (Long); "In Old Oklahoma" 1943 (Doctor); "Saddles and Sagebrush" 1943; "Salome, Where She Danced" 1945 (Sheriff); "California" 1946 (Chairman); "Along the Oregon Trail" 1947 (Jim Bridger); "Black Eagle" 1948 (Clancy); "Green Grass of Wyoming" 1948 (Jake); "Relentless" 1948 (Horse Dealer); "Whispering Smith" 1948 (Sheriff McSwiggens); "Big Jack" 1949 (Will Farnsworth); "Brimstone" 1949 (Martin Treadwell); "Lust for Gold" 1949 (Parsons); "Mrs. Mike" 1949 (Dr. McIntosh); "Dallas" 1950 (Judge Harper); "The Savage Horde" 1950 (Judge Cole); "Sunset in the West" 1950 (Sheriff Osborne); "Ticket to Tomahawk" 1950 (U.S. Marshal Dodge); "Vengeance Valley" 1951 (Mr. Willoughby); "The Last Posse" 1953 (Todd Mitchell); "Johnny Guitar" 1954 (Ned); "River of No Return" 1954 (Merchant); "The Tall Men" 1955 (Gus, the Bartender); "The Iron Sheriff" 1957 (Judge); "The Missouri Traveler" 1958 (Sheriff Peavy); "Quantrill's Raiders" 1958 (Judge Wood); "Alias Jesse James" 1959 (Titus Queasley); "The Deadly Companions" 1961 (Doctor). ¶TV: *Wild Bill Hickok*—"Grandpa and Genie" 5-20-52; *The Lone Ranger*—"Uncle Ed" 3-3-55; *Gunsmoke*—"Word of Honor" 10-1-55 (Ed Worth); *Fury*—"Ghost Town" 12-31-55 (Windy), "The Meanest Man" 3-1-58 (Malakey); *Circus Boy*—"Return of Casey Perkins" 10-17-57 (Sourdough Harry); *Zane Grey Theater*—"A Man to Look Up To" 11-29-57 (King); *Sugarfoot*—"The Stallion Trail" 12-24-57 (John Chamberlain), "Ring of Sand" 9-16-58 (Job Turner); *Maverick*—"Rope of Cards" 1-19-58 (Jabe Hallock), "Black Fire" 3-16-58 (Gen. Eakins), "Two Beggars on Horseback" 1-18-59 (Gen. Hoyt Bosco), "The Goose-Drownder" 12-13-59 (Boon Gillis), "The Maverick Line" 10-20-60 (Atherton Flayger), "The Troubled Heir" 4-1-62 (Sheriff Chester Bentley); *Trackdown*—"The Toll Road" 1-31-58 (Luke Monroe), "Gift Horse" 4-29-59 (Zack); *The Adventures of Rin Tin Tin*—"Sorrowful Joe's Policy" 3-21-58 (Herp Huntington); *Lawman*—"Bloodline" 11-30-58 (Luke Saint), "The Inheritance" 3-5-61 (Tecumsah Pruitt); *The Restless Gun*—"The Woman from Sacramento" 3-3-58 (Jim Blackwell), "Hiram Grover's Strike" 5-12-58 (Hiram Grover); *Tales of Wells Fargo*—"Showdown Trail" 1-5-59 (Joe Dooley), "The Legacy" 3-9-59 (Jeff Parris); *Bronco*—"Riding Solo" 2-10-59 (Doc Winkler); *Bat Masterson*—"Battle of the Pass" 2-25-59 (Billy Willow), "Incident at Fort Bowie" 3-31-60, "Bullwhacker's Bounty" 2-16-61

(Billy Willow); *Rough Riders*—"Deadfall" 5-21-59 (Adam Bunch); *Rawhide*—"Incident of the Roman Candles" 7-10-59 (Grandpa), "The Black Sheep" 11-10-61 (Grandfather); *Bonanza*—"Desert Justice" 2-20-60 (Bailey), "The Fugitive" 2-4-61 (Will Reagan), "The Mountain Girl" 5-13-62 (Seth); *The Tall Man*—"Death or Taxes" 5-27-61 (Hackett); *Laramie*—"The Jailbreakers" 12-19-61, "The Runaway" 1-23-62 (Dr. Lindley), "A Grave for Cully Brown" 2-13-62 (Doc Bigelow).

Wright, William (1912-1/19/49). Films: "Gas House Kids Go West" 1947 (Jim Kingsley).

Wrixon, Maris (1917-). Films: "Jeepers Creepers" 1939 (Connie Durant); "Ride, Cowboy, Ride" 1939-short; "Santa Fe Trail" 1940 (Girl); "Sons of the Pioneers" 1942 (Louis Harper); "Trail to Gunsight" 1944 (Mary Wagner). ¶TV: *The Cisco Kid*—"Postal Inspector" 8-4-51, "Kid Sister Trouble" 9-15-51.

Wulff, Kai. Films: "Heaven's Gate" 1980; "Barbarosa" 1982 (Otto).

Wurlitzer, Rudolph (1938-). Films: "Pat Garrett and Billy the Kid" 1973 (Tom O'Folliard).

Wyatt, Al (1920-8/12/92). Films: "Last of the Redmen" 1946; "Deadline" 1948; "Bonanza Town" 1951 (Bill Trotter); "Prairie Roundup" 1951 (Masked Man); "Whirlwind" 1951 (Bert); "Sitting Bull" 1954 (Swain); "The Far Horizons" 1955; "Robbers' Roost" 1955 (Slocum); "Shotgun" 1955 (Greybar); "Seventh Cavalry" 1956; "The Dalton Girls" 1957 (Sheriff St. Ives); "Gun Duel in Durango" 1957 (Jones); "Badman's Country" 1958; "Buchanan Rides Alone" 1958; "Man from God's Country" 1958 (Henchman); "The Rawhide Trail" 1958 (Stagecoach Driver); "Toughest Gun in Tombstone" 1958 (Olmstead); "Five Guns to Tombstone" 1961; "Duel at Diablo" 1966 (Miner); "Heaven with a Gun" 1969 (Indian); "Valdez Is Coming" 1971. ¶TV: *The Gene Autry Show*—"The Sheriff of Santa Rosa" 12-24-50; *Tales of Wells Fargo*—"Desert Showdown" 9-14-59 (Keyhole), "The Train Robbery" 10-12-59 (Jed), "Man for the Job" 5-30-60 (Garrett); *Wyatt Earp*—"Wyatt Takes the Primrose Path" 3-28-61; *Wild Wild West*—"The Night of the Two-Legged Buffalo" 3-11-66 (Coach Driver); *Cimarron Strip*—"The Legend of Jud Starr" 9-14-67, "Broken Wing" 9-21-67, "Nobody" 12-7-67; *Gunsmoke*—"The Fourth Victim" 11-4-74 (Earl Haines).

Wyatt, Charlene. Films: "Borderland" 1937 (Molly Rand).

Wyatt, Jane (1912-). Films: "The Kansan" 1943 (Eleanor Sager); "Canadian Pacific" 1949 (Dr. Edith Cabott); "Hurricane Smith" 1942 (Joan Wyatt); "Buckskin Frontier" 1943 (Vinnie Mar). ¶TV: *Wagon Train*—"The Heather Mahoney Story" 6-13-62 (Heather Mahoney); *The Virginian*—"The Secret of Brynmar Hall" 4-1-64 (Sarah Brynmar); *Here Come the Brides*—"Two Women" 4-3-70 (Emma Peak); *The Men from Shiloh*—"The Price of the Hanging" 11-11-70 (Lori Kinkaid); *Alias Smith and Jones*—"The Reformation of Harry Briscoe" 11-11-71 (Sister Julia).

Wyenn, Than (1919-). TV: *Gunsmoke*—"Magnus" 12-24-55 (Dealer), "Unmarked Grave" 8-18-56 (Sheriff Darcy), "Jealousy" 7-6-57 (Lonnie Pike); *Zorro*—"The Fall of Monastario" 1-2-58 (Licenciado Pina); *Zane Grey Theater*—"This Man Must Die" 1-24-58 (Dick Braus); *Jefferson Drum*—"Bandidos" 6-13-58 (Casey); *Trackdown*—"Deadly Decoy" 11-14-58 (Ed Teller); *U.S. Marshal*—"The Stool Pigeon" 12-6-58; *Death Valley Days*—"A Town Is Born" 1-20-59 (Isaacs), "Goodbye Five Hundred Pesos" 3-8-60; *Wanted—Dead or Alive*—"Bounty for a Bride" 4-4-59 (Yanqui Jones), "The Conquerers" 5-2-59 (Gregg Hagerty), "Payoff at Pinto" 5-21-60; *The Texan*—"Blood Money" 4-20-59; *Stagecoach West*—"A Time to Run" 11-15-60 (Nacho); *The Rifleman*—"The Vaqueros" 10-2-61 (Ramos); *Rawhide*—"Incident of the Comanchero" 3-22-63 (Malvado); *Wide Country*—"Yanqui, Go Home!" 4-4-63 (Father Lugarte); *The Virginian*—"The Dark Challenge" 9-23-64 (Coroner), "The Captive" 9-28-66 (Grey Horn), "The Decision" 3-13-68 (Morgan); *A Man Called Shenandoah*—"The Lost Diablo" 1-24-66 (Nacho); *The Big Valley*—"Legend of a General" 9-19-66 & 9-26-66 (Mateo), "Image of Yesterday" 1-9-67; *The High Chaparral*—"Only the Bad Come to Sonora" 10-2-70.

Wyler, Josie. TV: *Jim Bowie*—"Deputy Sheriff" 9-28-56 (Justine), "Osceola" 1-18-57 (Morning Dew); *Sheriff of Cochise*—"Question of Honor" 10-26-56; *Wagon Train*—"A Man Called Horse" 3-26-58 (Rising Sun).

Wyler, Link. TV: *Cimarron Strip*—"The Battleground" 9-28-67; *Gunsmoke*—"Major Glory" 10-30-67 (Doak), "9:12 to Dodge" 11-11-68 (Peter Frye), "The War Priest" 1-5-70

(1st Sentry), "The Scavengers" 11-16-70 (Logan), "The Lost" 9-13-71 (Lamond Mather); *Kung Fu*—"The Hoots" 12-13-73 (Tate).

Wyler, Richard (1923-). Films: "The Ugly Ones" 1966-Ital./Span. (Luke Chilson); "Two Pistols and a Coward" 1967-Ital. (Owl Roy); "Rattler Kid" 1968-Ital./Span. (Lt. Tony Garnett); "If One Is Born a Swine" 1972-Ital./Span. (Billy Walsh).

Wylie, Adam. TV: *Adventures of Brisco County, Jr.*—"Pirates" 10-8-93 (Charlie).

Wyllie, Meg (1919-). TV: *Have Gun Will Travel*—"Young Gun" 11-8-58 (Mrs. Wellman); *Zane Grey Theater*—"Make It Look Good" 2-5-59 (Mrs. Cole); *Wagon Train*—"The Elizabeth McQueeney Story" 10-28-59, "The John Augustus Story" 10-17-62 (Matilda), "Heather and Hamish" 4-10-63 (Sara MacIntosh), "The Betsy Blee Smith Story" 3-28-65; *Death Valley Days*—"Indian Emily" 12-8-59 (Mrs. Easton); *The Virginian*—"Say Goodbye to All That" 1-23-63; *The Travels of Jaimie McPheeters*—Regular 1963-64 (Mrs. Kissel); *A Man Called Shenandoah*—"The Bell" 12-20-65 (Mrs. Clay); *The Rounders*—9-27-66 (Irene); *Cimarron Strip*—"Whitey" 10-19-67 (Miss Becker); *Alias Smith and Jones*—"The Root of It All" 4-1-71 (Prudence Palmer); *Gunsmoke*—"Shadler" 1-15-73 (Mrs. Evans).

Wyman, Jane (1914-). Films: "Cheyenne" 1947 (Ann Kincaid); "Bad Men of Missouri" 1941 (Mary Hathaway). ¶TV: *Wagon Train*—"The Doctor Willoughby Story" 11-5-58 (Dr. Carol Willoughby), "The Wagon Train Mutiny" 9-19-62 (Hannah); *Dr. Quinn, Medicine Woman*—"The Visitor" 1-9-93 (Elizabeth Quinn).

Wymore, Patrice (1926-). Films: "Rocky Mountain" 1950 (Johanna Carter); "The Big Trees" 1952 (Daisy Fisher); "The Man Behind the Gun" 1952 (Lora Roberts); "The Sad Horse" 1959 (Leslie MacDonald). ¶TV: *Jefferson Drum*—"Simon Pitt" 12-11-58 (Goldie); *The Deputy*—"Passage to New Orleans" 11-19-60 (Lucy Ballance); *Cheyenne*—"The Beholden" 2-27-61 (Harriet Miller); *Tales of Wells Fargo*—"A Show from Silver Lode" 3-6-61 (Pearl Harvey); *F Troop*—"She's Only a Built in a Girdled Cage" 11-16-65 (Laura Lee), "Is This Fort Really Necessary?" 4-6-67 (Peggy Gray).

Wynant, H.M. (1927-). Films: "Decision at Sundown" 1957 (Spanish); "Run of the Arrow" 1957 (Crazy

Wolf); "Oregon Passage" 1958 (Black Eagle); "Tonka" 1958 (Yello Bull); "Last Ride of the Dalton Gang" TVM-1979 (Poker Player). ¶TV: *Gunsmoke*—"Spring Team" 12-15-56 (Barker), "The Worm" 10-29-60 (Cornet), "The Do-Badder" 1-6-62 (Sam Smith), "Old York" 5-4-63 (Sage), "Trip West" 5-2-64 (Meade Agate), "Winner Take All" 2-20-65 (Relko), "A Hat" 10-16-67 (Martin Brewster), "No Tomorrow" 1-3-72 (Morris Cragin); *The Restless Gun*— "The Woman from Sacramento" 3-3-58 (Steve Colby); *Broken Arrow*— "Turncoat" 4-15-58 (Joselito); *Cheyenne*—"Standoff" 5-6-58 (Ortega), "Indian Gold" 10-29-62 (White Crow); *Sugarfoot*—"Devil to Pay" 12-23-58 (Grey Hawk); *Bat Masterson*—"One Bullet from Broken Bow" 1-21-59 (Stone Calf), "Wanted—Alive Please" 5-26-60 (Benton Foster); *Rawhide*—"Incident of a Burst of Evil" 6-26-59 (Jonas); *Maverick*—"The Goose-Drownder" 12-13-59 (Rance, the Arapaho Kid); *Death Valley Days*—"The Battle of Mokelumne Hill" 3-1-60 (Paul Martain), "Pirates of San Francisco" 4-26-60, "The Red Petticoat" 3-29-61; *The Deputy*—"The Higher Law" 11-12-60 (Blackwing); *Hotel De Paree*—"Vengeance for Sundance" 4-8-60 (Gil); *Wagon Train*—"The Nellie Jefferson Story" 4-5-61 (Bart Haskell), "The Pearlie Garnet Story" 2-24-64 (Clay Boudreau); *Frontier Circus*—"Lippizan" 10-19-61 (Talby); *The Virginian*—"Fifty Days to Moose Jaw" 12-12-62 (Dalton Lacey), "The Fortress" 12-27-67 (Man); *Temple Houston*—"Letter of the Law" 10-3-63 (Jered Mallory); *Branded*—"The Mission" 3-14-65, 3-21-65 & 3-28-65 (Brissac), "Call to Glory" 2-27-66, 3-6-66 & 3-13-66 (Lionel MacAllister); *Wild Wild West*—"The Night of the Torture Chamber" 12-10-65 (Durand), "The Night of the Sudden Plague" 4-22-66 (Coley Rodman), "The Night of the Poisonous Posey" 10-28-66 (Little Pinto), "The Night of the Simian Terror" 2-16-68 (Aaron); *Daniel Boone*—"Flag of Truce" 11-21-68 (Major Howerton); *The Big Valley*—"Flight from San Miguel" 4-28-69 (Captain Chavez); *The Outcasts*—"How Tall Is Blood?" 5-5-69 (Bear Hunter); *Bearcats!*— "Blood Knot" 11-4-71 (Ben Shamrock).

Wyngarde, Peter. TV: *Walt Disney Presents*—"Gallegher" 1965-67 (Sir Richard Westerby).

Wynn, Ed (1886-6/19/66). TV: *Wagon Train*—"The Cappy Darrin Story" 11-11-59 (Cappy Darrin);

Rawhide—"Twenty-Five Santa Clauses" 12-22-61 (Bateman); *Bonanza*—"Ponderosa Birdman" 2-7-65 (Prof. Phineas T. Klump).

Wynn, Keenan (1916-10/14/86). Films: "Northwest Rangers" 1942 (Slip O'Mara); "Annie Get Your Gun" 1950 (Charlie Davenport); "Sky Full of Moon" 1952 (Al); "The Marauders" 1955 (Hook); "Johnny Concho" 1956 (Barney Clark); "The Naked Hills" 1956 (Sam Wilkins); "Stage to Thunder Rock" 1964 (Ross Sawyer); "The Night of the Grizzly" 1966 (Jed Curry); "Stagecoach" 1966 (Luke Plummer); "The War Wagon" 1967 (Wes Catlin); "Welcome to Hard Times" 1967 (Zar); "Once Upon a Time in the West" 1968-Ital. (Sheriff); "Shoot, Gringo ... Shoot!" 1968-Ital./Fr. (the Major); "MacKenna's Gold" 1969 (Sanchez); "Smith" 1969 (Vince Heber); "The Animals" 1971 (Pudge Elliot); "Calibre .38" 1971-Ital. (Kile Richards); "The Legend of Earl Durand" 1974; "The Quest" TVM-1976 (H.H. Small); "Kino, the Padre on Horseback" 1977; "The Capture of Grizzly Adams" TVM-1982 (Bert Woolman). ¶TV: *Wagon Train*—"The Luke O'-Malley Story" 1-1-58 (Luke O'Malley); *Rawhide*—"Incident at Cactus Wells" 10-12-62 (Simon Royce); *Death Valley Days*—"The Grass Man" 11-21-62 (David Douglas); *The Travels of Jaimie McPheeters*—"The Day of the Search" 1-19-64 (Sam Parks); *Bonanza*—"Alias Joe Cartwright" 1-26-64 (Sergeant O'Rourke); *Wild Wild West*—"The Night of the Freebooters" 4-1-66 (Thorwald Wolfe); *The Westerners*—Host 1966-67; *The Road West*—"No Sanctuary" 2-6-67 (Sam Brewster); *Lancer*—"Blue Skies for Willie Sharpe" 1-13-70 (Kansas Bill Sharpe); *Alias Smith and Jones*— "Stagecoach Seven" 3-11-71 (Charlie Utley), "Dreadful Sorry, Clementine" 11-18-71 (Wingate), "What Happened at the XST?" 10-28-72 (Artie Gorman); *Bearcats!*—11-18-71 (Mason Latimer); *Hec Ramsey*— "A Hard Road to Vengeance" 11-25-73 (Bullard); *The Quest*—"The Longest Drive" 12-1-76 & 12-8-76 (Cooler); *The Life and Times of Grizzly Adams*—"The Seekers" 1-25-78.

Wynn, Mary. Films: "Danger" 1923 (Phyllis Baxter); "The Range Patrol" 1923.

Wynn, May (1931-). Films: "They Rode West" 1954 (Manyi-ten); "The Violent Men" 1955 (Caroline Vail); "The White Squaw" 1956 (Ectay-O-Waynee).

Wynn, Ned. Films: "Stagecoach" 1966 (Ike Plummer).

Wynne, Gordon (-1967). Films: "Little Big Horn" 1951 (Pvt. Arndst Hofstetter); "The Bushwackers" 1952 (Quigley); "Thunder Pass" 1954; "Vengeance" 1964 (Col. Carl Dorsett). ¶TV: *Wild Bill Hickok*—"The Maverick" 8-19-52; *The Lone Ranger*—"Delayed Action" 11-6-52; *Wyatt Earp*—"The Cyclone" 5-12-59 (Mr. Kirby), "Wyatt Takes the Primrose Path" 3-28-61 (Colonel Warren), "Requiem for Old Man Clanton" 5-30-61 (Colonel Warren).

Wynne, Peggy. Films: "Trailing Danger" 1947; "The Denver Kid" 1948; "Desperadoes of Dodge City" 1948 (Mary).

Wynter, Dana (1927-). Films: "Santee" 1973 (Valerie). ¶TV: *Wagon Train*—"The Lizabeth Ann Calhoun Story" 12-6-61 (Lizabeth Ann Calhoun), "The Lisa Raincloud Story" 10-31-62 (Lisa Raincloud), "The Barbara Lindquist Story" 10-18-64 (Barbara Lindquist); *The Virginian*—"If You Have Tears" 2-13-63 (Leona Kelland); *Wild Wild West*—"The Night of the Two-Legged Buffalo" 3-11-66 (Lady Beatrice Marquand-Gaynesford); *Gunsmoke*—"Death Train" 11-27-67 (Isabel Townsend); *Dundee and the Culhane*—"The Widow's Weeds Brief" 11-29-67 (Martha).

Wynters, Charlotte. Films: "Ivory-Handled Gun" 1935 (Paddy Moore); "Sunset Trail" 1938 (Ann Marsh); "Renegade Trail" 1939 (Mary Joyce).

Wyss, Amanda. Films: "Silverado" 1985 (Phoebe); "Independence" TVM-1987 (Chastity); "Gunsmoke: To the Last Man" TVM-1991 (Lizzie Tewksbury).

Yaconelli, Frank (1898-11/19/65). Films: "Senor Americano" 1929 (Manana); "Firebrand Jordan" 1930 (Tony); "Parade of the West" 1930 (Sicily Joe); "Strawberry Roan" 1933 (Shanty); "Five Bad Men" 1935 (Tony); "Gun Play" 1935 (Frank Gorman); "Heir to Trouble" 1935; "Lawless Riders" 1935 (Pedro); "Western Frontier" 1935 (Haw Haw); "Blazing Justice" 1936 (Sheriff); "Lucky Terror" 1936 (Tony); "Robin Hood of El Dorado" 1936 (Peon); "Romance Rides the Range" 1936 (Tony); "The Three Mesquiteers" 1936 (Pete); "Wild West Days" 1937-serial (Mike); "Wild Horse Canyon" 1938 (Lopez); "Across the Plains" 1939 (Lopez); "Drifting Westward" 1939 (Lopez); "Trigger Smith" 1939 (Lopez); "Union Pacific" 1939 (Accordion Player/Card Player); "The

Cheyenne Kid" 1940 (Manuel); "Mark of Zorro" 1940 (Servant); "Pioneer Days" 1940 (Manuel); "Wild Horse Range" 1940 (Manny); "The Driftin' Kid" 1941; "Lone Star Law Men" 1941 (Lopez); "Riding the Sunset Trail" 1941 (Lopez Mendoza); "Arizona Roundup" 1942; "Western Mail" 1942 (Lopez); "Where Trails End" 1942; "Beauty and the Bandit" 1946; "South of Monterey" 1946; "Riding the California Trail" 1947; "Wild Horse Mesa" 1947; "The Dude Goes West" 1948; "Madonna of the Desert" 1948 (Peppo); "Hangman's Knot" 1952. ¶TV: *Jim Bowie*—"A Horse for Old Hickory" 1-4-57 (Pirate Guard).

Yaconelli, Zachary. Films: "The Baron of Arizona" 1950 (Greco); "The Command" 1953 (Mr. Pellegrini).

Yamamoto, Harry. Films: "The Son of His Father" 1917 (Hip Lee); "By Proxy" 1918 (Ah Sing); "Paying His Debt" 1918 (Ching).

Yang, C.K. (1934-). Films: "There Was a Crooked Man" 1970 (Ah-Ping Woo); "One More Train to Rob" 1971 (Wong).

Yanni, Rossana. Films: "White Comanche" 1967-Ital./Span./U.S. (Kelly); "What Am I Doing in the Middle of the Revolution?" 1973-Ital.

Yarbo, Lillian. Films: "Destry Rides Again" 1939 (Clara); "Lucky Cisco Kid" 1940 (Queenie); "The Return of Frank James" 1940 (Maid); "The Great Man's Lady" 1942 (Mandy); "Wild Bill Hickok Rides" 1942 (Daisy).

Yarbrough, Glenn (1930-). TV: *Wagon Train*—"The Richard Bloodgood Story" 11-29-64 (Guitarist).

Yarnell, Bruce (1938-11/30/73). TV: *The Outlaws*—Regular 1961-62 (Deputy Chalk Breeson); *Wide Country*—"The Lucky Punch" 4-18-63 (Tom Kidwell); *Bonanza*—"The Saga of Muley Jones" 3-29-64 (Muley Jones), "Hound Dog" 3-21-65 (Muley Jones); *Annie Get Your Gun* 3-19-67 (Frank Butler).

Yarnell, Celeste (1946-). TV: *Wild Wild West*—"The Night of a Thousand Eyes" 10-22-65 (Miss Purviance); *Bonanza*—"Queen High" 12-1-68 (Kate Kelly).

Yarnell, Lorene. Films: "The Wild Wild West Revisited" TVM-1979 (Sonya).

Yarnell, Sally. Films: "The Lusty Men" 1952 (Girl); "Rose Marie" 1954 (Hostess).

Ybarra, Roque (1900-12/12/65). Films: "Wyoming" 1947 (Indian

Boy); "Callaway Went Thataway" 1951 (Native Fisherman); "The Reward" 1965. ¶TV: *The Rebel*—"Deathwatch" 10-23-60 (Ignacio).

Yeager, Biff. Films: "Jessi's Girls" 1976 (Link); "The Girl Called Hatter Fox" TVM-1977.

Yeamans, Lydia. *see* Titus, Lydia Yeamans

Yearsley, Ralph (1897-12/4/28). Films: "Arabia" 1922 (Waldmar Terhune); "The Call of the Canyon" 1923 (Charlie Oatmeal); "The Fighting Sap" 1924 (Twister); "The Gambling Fool" 1925 (George Morgan); "Desert Gold" 1926 (Half Wit).

Yeoman, George (1869-11/2/36). Films: "Frontier Justice" 1936 (Sheriff).

Yip, William (1895-10/18/68). Films: "Bad Men of Tombstone" 1949; "The Sad Horse" 1959 (Ben). ¶TV: *Maverick*—"Prey of the Cat" 12-7-58 (Chan); *Stripe Playhouse*—"Ballad to Die By" 7-31-59; *Sugarfoot*—"The Highbinder" 1-19-60 (Yat Soong); *Gunsmoke*—"Harper's Blood" 10-21-61 (Ah Wong).

Yniquez, Richard (1946-). Films: "Houston: The Legend of Texas" TVM-1986 (General Santa Anna); "Rio Diablo" TVM-1993 (Chuy). ¶TV: *Bonanza*—"The Rattlesnake Brigade" 12-5-71 (Ricardo); *Nichols*—"Away the Rolling River" 12-7-71; *Kung Fu*—"A Lamb to the Slaughter" 1-11-75 (Jaibo); *Sara*—4-23-76 (Puma).

York, Dick (1928-2/20/92). Films: "They Came to Cordura" 1959 (Pvt. Renziehausen). ¶TV: *Stagecoach West*—"Three Wise Men" 12-20-60 (Webb Crawford); *Rawhide*—"Incident of the Broken Word" 1-20-61 (Frank Price), "Incident at Confidence Creek" 11-28-63 (Elwood P. Gilroy); *Wagon Train*—"The Clementine Jones Story" 10-25-61 (Willie Pettigrew), "The Charley Shutup Story" 3-7-62 (Charley Shutup), "The Michael Malone Story" 1-6-64 (Ben Mitchell); *The Outlaws*—"Night Riders" 11-2-61 (Sam Nichols); *The Virginian*—"Stopover in a Western Town" 11-27-63 (Jeff Tolliver).

York, Duke (1902-1/24/52). Films: "Rhythm on the Range" 1936 (Officer); "The Three Mesquiteers" 1936 (Chuck); "Union Pacific" 1939 (Engineer); "Trail of the Vigilantes" 1940 (Deputy Sheriff); "Riders of Death Valley" 1941-serial; "Texas" 1941 (Wise Guy); "Jackass Mail" 1942 (Rancher); "California Firebrand" 1948 (Zeke Mason); "The Paleface" 1948 (Henchman); "Stampede" 1949

(Maxie); "Call of the Klondike" 1950 (Luke); "Rogue River" 1950 (Bowers); "Snow Dog" 1950 (Duprez); "Winchester '73" 1950 (1st Man); "Fort Defiance" 1951 (Doniger); "Northwest Territory" 1951 (Dawson); "Silver Canyon" 1951 (Sgt. Laughlin); "Snake River Desperadoes" 1951 (Pete); "Texans Never Cry" 1951 (Baker); "Valley of Fire" 1951 (Piano); "Barbed Wire" 1952; "Cowboy" 1958 (Charlie). ¶TV: *The Lone Ranger*—"Greed for Gold" 1-19-50, "Million Dollar Wallpaper" 9-14-50, "Two Gold Lockets" 2-15-51; *Wild Bill Hickok*—"The Silver Mine Protection Story" 7-24-51; *Frontier Circus*—"The Shaggy Kings" 12-7-61 (Jeb Randall).

York, Francine (1938-). Films: "Tickle Me" 1965 (Mildred); "Cannon for Cordoba" 1970 (Sophia). ¶TV: *Death Valley Days*—"A Picture of a Lady" 3-19-66; *Wild Wild West*—"The Night of the Pelican" 12-27-68 (Dr. Sara Gibson); *Hec Ramsey*—"The Mystery of the Yellow Rose" 1-28-73 (Kate); *Dirty Sally*—"The Old Soldier" 1-25-74 (Lauraleen); *The Quest*—"Prairie Woman" 11-10-76.

York, Jeff (1912-). Films: "Unconquered" 1947 (Wide-Shouldered Youth); "The Paleface" 1948 (Joe); "Panhandle" 1948 (Jack); "Short Grass" 1950 (Curley); "Surrender" 1950 (Canning); "Davy Crockett and the River Pirates" 1956 (Mike Fink); "The Great Locomotive Chase" 1956 (William Campbell); "Westward Ho the Wagons" 1956 (Hank Breckenridge); "Old Yeller" 1957 (Bud Searcy); "Savage Sam" 1963 (Bud Searcy). ¶TV: *The Lone Ranger*—"Death Trap" 4-20-50, "The Black Hat" 5-18-50; *Walt Disney Presents*—"Davy Crockett"—Regular 1954-55 (Mike Fink); *Disneyland*—"The Saga of Andy Burnett"—Regular 1957-58 (Joe Crane); *Lawman*—"The Joker" 10-19-58 (Barney Tremain), "The Wayfarer" 6-7-59 (Sam Cates); *The Californians*—"Hangtown" 11-18-58 (Biggo Jessup); *Zorro*—"The Mountain Man" 3-19-59 (Joe Crane), "The Hound of the Sierras" 3-26-59 (Joe Crane), "Manhunt" 4-2-59 (Joe Crane); *Bronco*—"Backfire" 4-7-59 (Wide Stanton); *The Alaskans*—Regular 1959-60 (Reno McKee); *Cheyenne*—"Trial by Conscience" 10-26-59 (Nick Avalon); *The Rifleman*—"None So Blind" 3-19-62 (Mack); *Daniel Boone*—"Grizzly" 10-6-66 (Big Zack); *Iron Horse*—"Banner with a Strange Device" 2-6-67 (Big Jim Banner).

Yorke, Edith (1867-7/28/34).

Films: "Step on It!" 1922 (Mrs. Collins); "Silent Sanderson" 1925 (Mrs. Parsons); "Wild Horse Mesa" 1925 (Grandma Melberne); "Born to the West" 1926 (Mrs. Rudd); "Rustlers' Ranch" 1926 (Mary Shawn); "Rustlin' for Cupid" 1926 (Mrs. Blatchford); "The Western Whirlwind" 1927 (Mrs. Martha Howard).

Yothers, Tina (1973-). TV: *The Cherokee Trail*—Pilot 11-28-81 (Peggy Breydon); *Father Murphy*—"The Dream Day" 3-14-82 (Beatrice).

Young, Alan (1919-). Films: "Baker's Hawk" 1976 (Mr. Carson). ¶TV: *Death Valley Days*—"The Hat That Won the West" 10-31-62 (John Stetson).

Young, Bert. Films: "Six Gun Justice" 1935; "The Vanishing Riders" 1935 (Jed Stanley); "Back to the Woods" 1937 (Indian); "Rockin' Through the Rockies" 1940-short (Indian); "Wildcat of Tucson" 1941.

Young, Buck (1921-). TV: *Wyatt Earp*—"The Judas Goat" 3-31-59 (Rocky Griswold); *Bat Masterson*—"Dead Men Don't Pay Debts" 11-19-59 (Bill Bassett); *The Rebel*—"The Unwanted" 1-31-60 (Savage); *Hotel De Paree*—"Sundance and the Marshal of Water's End" 3-18-60 (Avery); *Gunsmoke*—"The Bobsy Twins" 5-21-60 (Bud Grant), "Stolen Horses" 4-8-61 (Jim Redigo), "Jeb" 5-25-63 (Andy), "Doctor's Wife" 10-24-64 (Carney), "Hung High" 11-14-64 (Cowboy); *The Virginian*—"Morgan Starr" 2-9-66 (Walker); *Daniel Boone*—"The Accused" 3-24-66 (Henry Foxx); *Lancer*—"Warburton's Edge" 2-4-69 (Santee), "The Man Without a Gun" 3-25-69.

Young, Carleton (Gordon Roberts) (1907-7/11/71). Films: "Come on Cowboys" 1937; "Git Along, Little Dogies" 1937 (Man); "Round-Up Time in Texas" 1937; "Black Bandit" 1938; "Cassidy of Bar 20" 1938 (Jeff Caffrey); "Guilty Trails" 1938 (Steve Yates); "Gunsmoke Trail" 1938; "Heroes of the Hills" 1938 (Jim Connors); "The Old Barn Dancer" 1938 (Peabody); "Outlaw Express" 1938 (Ramon); "Prairie Justice" 1938 (Dry Gulch); "El Diablo Rides" 1939; "Flaming Lead" 1939 (Hank); "Honor of the West" 1939 (Russ Whitely); "The Lone Ranger Rides Again" 1939-serial (Logan); "Mesquite Buckaroo" 1939 (Sands); "The Pal from Texas" 1939 (Joe Fox); "Riders of the Sage" 1939 (Luke Halsey); "Smoky Trails" 1939 (Mort); "Trigger Fingers" 1939 (Lee); "Zorro's Fighting Legion" 1939-serial (Benito

Juarez); "Adventures of Red Ryder" 1940-serial (Sheriff Dade); "Billy the Kid in Texas" 1940 (Gil Cooper); "Billy the Kid Outlawed" 1940 (Jeff Travis); "Billy the Kid's Gun Justice" 1940 (Jeff Blanchard); "Cowboy from Sundown" 1940 (Nick Cuttler); "Gun Code" 1940 (Slim Doyle); "One Man's Law" 1940; "Pals of the Silver Sage" 1940 (Jeff); "Take Me Back to Oklahoma" 1940; "Billy the Kid's Fighting Pals" 1941 (Jeff); "Billy the Kid's Range War" 1941 (Jeff); "Billy the Kid's Roundup" 1941 (Jeff); "A Missouri Outlaw" 1941 (Allen); "Prairie Pioneers" 1941; "Texas" 1941 (Henchman); "Two-Gun Sheriff" 1941; "Code of the Outlaw" 1942; "King of the Mounties" 1942-serial (Gus); "Overland Mail" 1942-serial; "South of Santa Fe" 1942; "Thunder River Feud" 1942 (Grover); "Valley of the Sun" 1942 (Nolte); "The Kissing Bandit" 1948 (Count Belmonte); "Best of the Badmen" 1951 (Wilson); "Gene Autry and the Mounties" 1951 (Pierre LaBlond); "Red Mountain" 1951 (Morgan); "Last of the Comanches" 1952 (Maj. Lanning); "Goldtown Ghost Raiders" 1953 (Jim Granby); "Arrow in the Dust" 1954 (Pepperis); "Bitter Creek" 1954 (Quentin Allen); "Great Day in the Morning" 1956 (Col. Gibson); "Run of the Arrow" 1957 (Doctor); "The Horse Soldiers" 1959 (Col. Jonathan Miles); "Sergeant Rutledge" 1960 (Capt. Shattuck); "How the West Was Won" 1962 (Union Soldier); "The Man Who Shot Liberty Valance" 1962 (Maxwell Scott); "Cheyenne Autumn" 1964 (Secretary to Schurz). ¶TV: *Wild Bill Hickok*—"The Sheriff's Secret" 10-21-52; *Wyatt Earp*—"The Big Baby Contest" 11-22-55 (Denver Jones), "Hunt the Man Down" 5-3-56, "Hang 'Em High" 3-12-57 (Judge Smith), "Frontier Woman" 11-25-58 (Olson), "A Murderer's Return" 1-5-60 (George McKean); *Annie Oakley*—"The Dutch Gunmaker" 2-17-57 (Colonel Jackson); *Frontier Doctor*—"The Confidence Gang" 6-6-59; *The Rebel*—"The Unwanted" 1-31-60 (Sheriff Peeples); *The Deputy*—"Lady with a Mission" 3-5-60 (Sam Hodges); *Bronco*—"Legacy of Twisted Creed" 4-19-60 (Pedrow); *Wagon Train*—"The Colter Craven Story" 11-23-60 (Cr. Colter), "The Clarence Mullins Story" 5-1-63 (Major Gaston); *The Outlaws*—"The Quiet Killer" 12-29-60 (Tobey), "The Verdict" 12-28-61 (Nathan Danbury); *Tales of Wells Fargo*—"Rifles for Red Hand" 5-15-61 (Captain Rawlings); *Whispering Smith*—"Dark Circle" 9-4-61 (Fender).

Young, Clara Kimball (1890-10/15/60). Films: "Oh, Susanna!" 1936 (Mrs. Lee); "Three on the Trail" 1936 (Rose Peters); "Hills of Old Wyoming" 1937 (Ma Hutchins); "The Frontiersman" 1938 (Amanda Peters); "The Round Up" 1941 (Mrs. Wilson).

Young, Clifton (1917-9/10/51). Films: "The Lonely Trail" 1936; "Pursued" 1947 (the Sergeant); "Blood on the Moon" 1948 (Joe Shotten); "The Treasure of the Sierra Madre" 1948 (Flophouse Man); "Calamity Jane and Sam Bass" 1949 (Link); "Bells of Coronado" 1950 (Ross); "The Return of Jesse James" 1950 (Bob Ford); "Salt Lake Raiders" 1950 (Luke Condor); "Trail of Robin Hood" 1950 (Mitch McCall, the Foreman).

Young, Evelyn. Films: "Prairie Schooners" 1940 (Virginia Bemton); "Wildcat of Tucson" 1941 (Vivian).

Young, Faron (1932-). Films: "Hidden Guns" 1956 (Faron); "Daniel Boone, Trail Blazer" 1957 (Faron Callaway); "Raiders of Old California" 1957.

Young, Gig (1913-10/19/78). Films: "They Died with Their Boots On" 1941 (Lt. Roberts); "Lust for Gold" 1949 (Pete Thomas); "Only the Valiant" 1951 (Lt. William Holloway); "Slaughter Trail" 1951 (Vaughn); "Arena" 1953 (Bob Danvers).

Young, Loretta (1913-). Films: "Call of the Wild" 1935 (Claire Blake); "Ramona" 1936 (Ramona); "Lady from Cheyenne" 1941 (Annie); "Along Came Jones" 1945 (Cherry de Longpre); "Rachel and the Stranger" 1948 (Rachel).

Young, Lucille (1892-8/2/34). Films: "Fighting for Gold" 1919 (Pansy); "Quicker'n Lightnin'" 1925 (Morella).

Young, Mary (1879-6/23/71). Films: "Alias Jesse James" 1959 (Ma James). ¶TV: *Annie Oakley*—"Annie and the Silver Ace" 2-27-54; *Circus Boy*—"The Fortune Teller" 6-9-57 (Mrs. Lilly); *The Virginian*—"Vengeance Is the Spur" 2-27-63; *F Troop*—"Reach for the Sky, Pardner" 9-29-66 (Widow O'Brien).

Young, Nedrick (1914-9/16/68). Films: "The Devil's Playground" 1946 (Curly); "Unexpected Guest" 1947 (Ralph Baxter); "Calamity Jane and Sam Bass" 1949 (Parsons); "The Iron Mistress" 1952 (Henri Contrecourt); "Springfield Rifle" 1952 (Sgt. Poole); "Riding Shotgun" 1954 (Maning); "Terror in a Texas Town" 1958 (Johnny Crale).

Young, Noah (1887-4/18/58). Films: "Don Mike" 1927 (Rueben Pettingill); "Gun Gospel" 1927 (Jack Goodshot); "The Land Beyond the Law" 1927 (Hanzup Harry).

Young, Olive (1907-10/4/40). Films: "Ridin' Law" 1930; "Trailin' Trouble" 1930 (Ming Toy).

Young, Otis (1932-). TV: *The Outcasts*—Regular 1968-69 (Jemal David).

Young, Paul (1944-). Films: "Chato's Land" 1972 (Brady Logan).

Young, Polly Ann (1908-). Films: "The One Way Trail" 1931 (Mollie); "The Man from Utah" 1934 (Marjorie Carter); "The Crimson Trail" 1935 (Kitty Bellaire); "His Fighting Blood" 1935 (Doris); "The Border Patrolman" 1936 (Patricia Huntley); "Wolf Call" 1939 (Natalie); "Murder on the Yukon" 1940 (Joan Manning).

Young, Ray. Films: "Border Fence" 1951. ¶TV: *Bonanza*—"The Trouble with Trouble" 10-25-70 (Rev); *Nichols*—"Flight of the Century" 2-22-72 (Ernest); *The Quest*—"The Buffalo Hunters" 9-29-76 (Meeker).

Young, Richard (1951-). Films: "Banjo Hackett: Roamin' Free" TVM-1976 (Luke Mintore). ¶TV: *Kung Fu*—"The Ancient Warrior" 5-3-73 (Vern); *Nakia*—"Roots of Anger" 11-30-74 (Arnold Haywood).

Young, Robert (1907-). Films: "Northwest Passage" 1940 (Langdon Towne); "Western Union" 1941 (Richard Blake); "Relentless" 1948 (Nick Buckley); "The Half-Breed" 1952 (Dan Craig).

Young, Roland (1887-6/5/53). Films: "The Squaw Man" 1931 (Sir John Applegate); "Ruggles of Red Gap" 1935 (George Van Bassingwell).

Young, Skip (1929-3/17/93). Films: "The Young Country" TVM-1970 (Hotel Manager).

Young, Tammany (1887-4/26/36). Films: "Wanderer of the Wasteland" 1935 (Paducah).

Young, Tex "Shorty." Films: "The Calgary Stampede" 1925 (Cook); "Ridin' Pretty" 1925 (Shorty); "The Escape" 1926 (Manuel Estrada); "The Water Hole" 1928 (Shorty); "The Virginian" 1929 (Shorty); "The Oregon Trail" 1939-serial.

Young, Tony (1932-). Films: "He Rides Tall" 1964 (Marshal Morg Rocklin); "Taggart" 1964 (Kent Taggart); "Charro!" 1969 (Lt. Rivera); "Man Called Sledge" 1971-Ital./U.S.

(Mallory). ¶TV: *Fury*—"The Timber Walkers" 11-14-59; *Lawman*—"The Prodigal" 11-22-59 (Mark McQueen); *Maverick*—"Trooper Maverick" 11-29-59 (Okando); *Laramie*—"Queen of Diamonds" 9-20-60 (Clem Reeves); *The Deputy*—"The Fatal Urge" 10-15-60 (Tweed); *Gunslinger*—Regular 1961 (Cord); *Bronco*—"One Evening in Abilene" 3-19-62 (Tod Chapman); *Cheyenne*—"Johnny Brassbuttons" 12-3-62 (Johnny Brassbuttons); *Death Valley Days*—"Phantom Procession" 6-16-63; *Wagon Train*—"The Melanie Craig Story" 2-17-64 (Quent); *Bonanza*—"The Return" 5-2-65 (Trace Cordell); *Iron Horse*—"Hellcat" 12-26-66 (Red Shirt); *The Virginian*—"The Gauntlet" 2-8-67 (Shoop).

Young, Walter (1878-4/18/57). Films: "The Devil's Saddle Legion" 1937 (John Logan).

Young Deer, James (-4/46). Films: "The Mended Lute" 1909; "A Cheyenne Brave" 1910; "Back to the Prairie" 1911; "Little Dove's Romance" 1911; "Under Handicap" 1917 (Lonesome Pete); "Man of Courage" 1922 (Aquila).

Younge, Lucille (1892-8/2/34). Films: "The Daredevil" 1920 (Mazie); "The Terror" 1920 (Fay LaCrosse).

Yowlachie, Chief (1891-3/7/66). Films: "Tonio, Son of the Sierras" 1925 (Tonio); "Forlorn River" 1926 (Modoc Joe); "Moran of the Mounted" 1926 (Biting Wolf); "War Paint" 1926 (Iron Eyes); "Hawk of the Hills" 1927-serial (Chief Long Hand); "Red Raiders" 1927 (Scar Face Charlie); "Sitting Bull at the Spirit Lake Massacre" 1927 (Sitting Bull); "The Glorious Trail" 1928 (High Wolf); "The Invaders" 1929; "Girl of the Golden West" 1930 (Bill Jackrabbit); "The Santa Fe Trail" 1930 (Brown Beaver); "Northwest Mounted Police" 1940 (Indian); "Winners of the West" 1940-serial (Chief War Eagle); "Outlaws of the Cherokee Trail" 1941; "Saddlemates" 1941; "White Eagle" 1941-serial (Running Deer); "King of the Stallions" 1942; "Ride 'Em, Cowboy" 1942 (Chief Tomahawk); "Frontier Fury" 1943; "Canyon Passage" 1946 (Indian Sppokesman); "Wild West" 1946 (Chief Black Fox); "Bowery Buckaroos" 1947 (Chief Hi-Octane); "Oregon Trail Scouts" 1947; "The Prairie" 1947 (Matoreeh); "The Dude Goes West" 1948 (Running Wolfe); "The Paleface" 1948 (Chief Yellow Feather); "Prairie Outlaws" 1948; "Red River" 1948 (Quo); "Yellow Sky" 1948 (Colorado); "The Cowboy

and the Indians" 1949 (Chief Long Arrow); "El Paso" 1949 (Piute Pete); "Mrs. Mike" 1949 (Atenou); "Annie Get Your Gun" 1950 (Little Horse); "Cherokee Uprising" 1950 (Gray Eagle); "Indian Territory" 1950; "Ticket to Tomahawk" 1950 (Pawnee); "Winchester '73" 1950 (Indian); "The Painted Hills" 1951 (Bald Eagle); "Warpath" 1951 (Chief); "Buffalo Bill in Tomahawk Territory" 1952; "Lone Star" 1952 (Indian Chief); "The Pathfinder" 1952 (Eagle Feather); "Son of Geronimo" 1952-serial (Geronimo); "Gunfighters of the Northwest" 1954-serial (Running Elk); "Rose Marie" 1954 (Black Eagle); "Heller in Pink Tights" 1960 (Indian). ¶TV: *The Lone Ranger*—"War Horse" 10-20-49; *The Roy Rogers Show*—"The Treasure of Howling Dog Canyon" 1-27-52; *The Cisco Kid*—"Choctaw Justice" 12-26-53; *The Adventures of Rin Tin Tin*—"Lost Treasure" 5-25-56 (Kipooki), "Boone's Grandpappy" 11-2-56 (Takima); *Zane Grey Theater*—"Blood Red" 1-29-61 (Comanche); *The Tall Man*—"The Black Robe" 5-5-62.

Yrigoyen, Bill. Films: "Two-Fisted Sheriff" 1937 (Pete); "The Lone Ranger" 1938-serial (Trooper); "The Lone Ranger Rides Again" 1939-serial (Posseman #2); "Zorro's Fighting Legion" 1939-serial (Stage Driver); "Adventures of Red Ryder" 1940-serial (Trail Heavy); "Daredevils of the West" 1943-serial (Blackie/Indian #1/Indian Rustler #2/Trail Heavy #1); "Zorro's Black Whip" 1944-serial (Attacker #2/Burke); "The Phantom Rider" 1946-serial (Indian Renegade/Lookout).

Yrigoyen, Joe. Films: "Square Shooter" 1935; "Winds of the Wasteland" 1936 (Pike); "The Old Wyoming Trail" 1937; "Outlaws of the Prairie" 1937 (Outlaw); "The Painted Stallion" 1937-serial (Rancher); "The Lone Ranger" 1938-serial (Trooper); "Man from Music Mountain" 1938 (Pete); "The Lone Ranger Rides Again" 1939-serial (Posseman #5); "Zorro's Fighting Legion" 1939-serial; "Adventures of Red Ryder" 1940-serial (Ambusher); "Melody Ranch" 1940; "King of the Texas Rangers" 1941-serial; "Daredevils of the West" 1943-serial (Barn Heavy #3/Bill/Guard/Indian Rustler #3); "King of the Forest Rangers" 1946-serial (Harbin); "The Phantom Rider" 1946-serial (Blackie/Logan/Ambusher #1/Attacker #1); "Robin Hood of Texas" 1947; "Saddle Pals" 1947; "The Adventures of Frank and Jesse James" 1948-serial (Grady); "Ghost of Zorro" 1949-serial (Indian Dynamiter);

"Montana Belle" 1952 (Stunts); "Canadian Mounties vs. Atomic Invaders" 1953-serial (Launch Heavy #1); "The Woman They Almost Lynched" 1953 (Guard); "Gun Duel in Durango" 1957 (Stacey); "The Legend of Tom Dooley" 1959 (Bix); "The Second Time Around" 1961 (Bonner's Pal); "Shenandoah" 1965 (Marshal); "The Sons of Katie Elder" 1965 (Buck Mason); "The Cowboys" 1972 (Rustler). ¶TV: *Wanted—Dead or Alive*—"Reunion for Revenge" 1-24-59; *The Deputy*—"Mother and Son" 10-29-60 (Driver), "Duty Bound" 1-7-61 (Stage Driver); *The Tall Man*—"Tiger Eye" 12-17-60 (Johnson); *Bonanza*—"The Gift" 4-1-61 (Cayetano), "The Campaneros" 4-19-64 (Santos); *Gunsmoke*—"The Wreckers" 9-11-67 (Stage Driver).

Yule, Joe (1894-3/30/50). Films: "Go West" 1940 (Bartender); "Billy the Kid" 1941 (Milton); "Jackass Mail" 1942 (Barky); "Jiggs and Maggie Out West" 1950 (Jiggs).

Yulin, Harris (1937-). Films: "Doc" 1971 (Wyatt Earp); "Ransom for Alice!" TVM-1977 (Isaac Pratt); "The Night Rider" TVM-1979 (Billy "Bowlegs" Baines); "Last Ride of the Dalton Gang" TVM-1979 (Jesse James). ¶TV: *How the West Was Won*—Regular 1978 (Deek Peasley).

Yung, Victor Sen (1915-11/9/80). Films: "Ticket to Tomahawk" 1950 (Long Time, the Laundryman); "Valley of Fire" 1951 (Ching Moon); "Jubilee Trail" 1954 (Mickey, the Chinese Man); "The Saga of Hemp Brown" 1958 (Chang); "Kung Fu" TVM-1972 (Chuen). ¶TV: *The Lone Ranger*—"The Letter Bride" 11-15-56; *Death Valley Days*—"Quong Kee" 12-9-57; *Broken Arrow*—"The Courage of Ling Tang" 5-20-58 (Ling Tang); *Bonanza*—Regular 1959-73 (Hop Sing); *The Rifleman*—"The Queue" 5-16-61 (Wang Chi); *Wild Wild West*—"The Night of the Camera" 11-29-68 (Baron Kyosai); *Kung Fu*—"A Praying Mantis Kills" 3-22-73 (Master Ling), "The Squaw Man" 11-1-73 (Farmer), "The Raiders" 1-24-74 (Chu), "Besieged: Death on Cold Mountain" 11-15-74 (Tamo), "Besieged: Cannon at the Gate" 11-22-74 (Tamo), "The Demon God" 12-13-74 (Mandarin); *How the West Was Won*—"China Girl" 4-16-79 (Hospital Attendant).

Yunkermann, Kelly. Films: "Wild Horses" TVM-1985 (Ted Holmes); "Dream West" TVM-1986 (1st Man on Trek 5); "The Gambler Returns: The Luck of the Draw" TVM-1991 (Smiling Charlie Adams).

Yurka, Blanche (1887-6/6/74). Films: "The Furies" 1950 (Herrera's Mother); "Thunder in the Sun" 1959 (Louise Dauphin).

Yuro, Robert (1932-). Films: "The Ride to Hangman's Tree" 1967 (Jeff Scott); "The Shakiest Gun in the West" 1968 (Arnold the Kid). ¶TV: *Rawhide*—"The Backshooter" 11-27-64 (Jack Cleet); *Death Valley Days*—"Traveling Trees" 11-13-65, "The King of Uvalde Road" 4-25-70 (King Fisher); *The Legend of Jesse James*—"The Cave" 2-7-66 (Pete Hicks); *Laredo*—"Meanwhile, Back at the Reservation" 2-10-66 (Jug Herriot), "A Taste of Money" 4-28-66 (Sab Melendez), "Scourge of San Rosa" 1-20-67 (Johnny Rhodes); *The Big Valley*—"Hazard" 3-9-66 (Gil Anders); *The Virginian*—"Paid in Full" 11-22-67 (Aiken); *The High Chaparral*—"A Joyful Noise" 3-24-68 (Ramon), "Bad Day for Bad Men" 10-17-69 (Kyle); *Bonanza*—"Catch as Catch Can" 10-27-68 (Rice), "The Marriage of Theodora Duffy" 1-9-73 (Dody Hendrickson).

Zabriskie, Grace. Films: "Children of the Dust" TVM-1995.

Zaccaro, John. TV: *Maverick*—"Easy Mark" 11-15-59 (Engineer), "Maverick and Juliet" 1-17-60 (Nat Carteret), "The Iron Hand" 2-21-60 (Slim), "Thunder from the North" 11-13-60 (Judd Marsh); *The Law of the Plainsman*—"Dangerous Barriers" 3-10-60 (Ty Loomis); *Gunsmoke*—"The Peace Officer" 10-15-60 (Ponce).

Zacha, W.T. Films: "Bridger" TVM-1976 (Army Lieutenant). ¶TV: *Bret Maverick*—"The Eight Swords of Cyrus and Other Illusions of Grandeur" 3-23-83 (Cutler).

Zacharias, Steffen (1927-). Films: "Ace HIgh" 1967-Ital./Span. (Harold); "They Call Me Trinity" 1970-Ital. (Jonathan); "Man Called Sledge" 1971-Ital./U.S.; "Vengeance Is a Dish Served Cold" 1971-Ital./Span. (Boone).

Zalewska, Halina. Films: "Dynamite Joe" 1966-Ital./Span.; "Seven Dollars on the Red" 1968-Ital./Span.

Zamperla, Nazareno (Nick Anderson). Films: "A Pistol for Ringo" 1965-Ital./Span.; Seven Guns for the MacGregors" 1965-Ital./Span. (Peter MacGregor); "Up the MacGregors!" 1967-Ital./Span. (Peter MacGregor).

Zane, Billy. Films: "Posse" 1993 (Colonel Graham); "Tombstone" 1993 (Mr. Fabian).

Zany, King (1889-2/19/39). Films: "Broadway or Bust" 1924 (Jeff Peters); "The Danger Rider" 1928

(Blinky Ben); "The Rainbow" 1929 (Dummy).

Zapata, Carmen (1927-). TV: *Bonanza*—"Gideon the Good" 10-18-70 (Maria); *Nakia*—"Pete" 12-21-74 (Emma Ironwood).

Zapien, Danny. Films: "The Purple Hills" 1961 (Chito); "Peace for a Gunfighter" 1967 (Igmagio); "The Hanged Man" TVM-1974; "Kino, the Padre on Horseback" 1977; "Wanda Nevada" 1979; "The Mountain Men" 1980. ¶TV: *Young Dan'l Boone*—"The Salt Licks" 9-26-77.

Zaremba, John (1908-12/15/86). Films: "Cowboy in the Clouds" 1943; "Cyclone Prairie Rangers" 1944; "Reprisal!" 1956 (Mister Willard); "Scandalous John" 1971 (Wales). ¶TV: *Zane Grey Theater*—"Ride a Lonely Trail" 11-2-57 (Banker), "Deadfall" 2-19-59 (Judge); *Maverick*—"The People's Friend" 2-7-60 (Gantry); *Tales of Wells Fargo*—"The Jealous Man" 4-10-61 (Henry Thorpe); *The Virginian*—"It Tolls for Thee" 11-21-62, "Vengeance Trail" 1-4-67 (Polk); *Time Tunnel*—Regular 1966-67 (Dr. Raymond Swain); *Bonanza*—"The Thirteenth Man" 1-21-68 (Charles), "Silence at Stillwater" 9-28-69 (Doctor), "The Initiation" 9-26-72 (Judge), "The Bucket Dog" 12-19-72 (Judge Wilcox); *Wild Wild West*—"The Night of the Undead" 2-2-68 (Dr. Paul Eddington); *Lancer*—"The Escape" 12-31-68 (Hotel Clerk), "The Wedding" 1-7-69; *The Outcasts*—"Hung for a Lamb" 3-10-69 (Remsen); *The High Chaparral*—"A Piece of Land" 10-10-69 (Price).

Zarzo, Manolo (1930-). Films: "Bullets and the Flesh" 1965-Ital./Fr./Span.; "Seven Guns for the MacGregors" 1965-Ital./Span. (David MacGregor); "The Ugly Ones" 1966-Ital./Span.; "Train for Durango" 1967-Ital./Span.

Zeliff, Seymour (1886-1/17/53). Films: "Shadows of the West" 1921 (Frank Akuri).

Zeller, Ben (1933-). Films: "Santee" 1973; "Showdown" 1973 (Perry Williams); "Boss Nigger" 1974; "Timerider" 1983 (Jack Peoples); "Silverado" 1985 (Townsman).

Zerbe, Anthony (1936-). Films: "Will Penny" 1968 (Dutchy); "The Life and Times of Judge Roy Bean" 1972 (Hustler); "Rooster Cogburn" 1975 (Breed); "The Chisholms" TVM-1979 (Jimmy Jackson); "Dream West" TVM-1986 (Bill Williams); "Independence" TVM-1987 (General Grey). ¶TV: *The Big Valley*—"The Guilt of Matt Bentell"

12-8-65 (Gil Condon); *Iron Horse*—"Banner with a Strange Device" 2-6-67; *Wild Wild West*—"The Night of the Legion of Death" 11-24-67 (Deke Montgomery); *Gunsmoke*—"Blood Money" 1-22-68 (Nick Skouras), "The Noonday Devil" 12-7-70 (Heraclio Cantrell/Father Hernando Cantrell), "Talbot" 2-26-73 (Talbot); *The Virginian*—"The Good-Hearted Badman" 2-7-68 (Powell); *Bonanza*—"A Ride in the Sun" 5-11-69 (John Spain); *Nichols*—3-14-72 (Quinn); *Kung Fu*—"The Hoots" 12-13-73 (Paul Klempt), "The Predators" 10-5-74 (Rafe); *How the West Was Won*—Episode One 2-6-77 (Captain Grey); *Hallmark Hall of Fame*—"The Court-Martial of General George Armstrong Carter" 12-1-77 (Jefferson Quinton); *Centennial*—Regular 1978-79 (Marvin Wendell); *The Chisholms*—3-29-79 (Jimmy Jackson); *Young Riders*—Regular 1990-92 (Teaspone Hunter).

Zier, Marjorie. Films: "Cactus Trails" 1927 (Sally Crater); "Phantom of the Range" 1928 (Vera Van Swank).

Zimbalist, Jr., Efrem (1923-). Films: "The Reward" 1965 (Frank Bryant). ¶TV: *Maverick*—"Stampede" 11-17-57 (Dandy Jim Buckley), "Trail West to Fury" 2-16-58 (Dandy Jim Buckley), "High Card Hangs" 10-19-58 (Dandy Jim Buckley), "The Jail at Junction Flats" 11-9-58 (Dandy Jim Buckley), "Shady Deal at Sunny Acres" 11-23-58 (Dandy Jim Buckley); *Sugarfoot*—"The Wizard" 10-14-58 (Kerrigan); *The Alaskans*—"The Trial of Reno McKee" 1-10-60 (John Conrad); *Bronco*—"The Prince of Darkness" 11-6-61 (Edwin Booth); *Rawhide*—"The Diehard" 4-9-65 (Jeff McKeever); *Zorro*—Regular 1990 (Don Alejandro de le Vega).

Zimbalist, Stephanie (1956-). TV: *Centennial*—Regular 1978-79 (Elly Zendt).

Zito, Louis. Films: "The True Story of Jesse James" 1957(Clell Miller) ¶TV: *Death Valley Days*—"Arsenic Springs" 11-18-57; *Tales of Wells Fargo*—"Laredo" 12-23-57 (Ed Flavin).

Zorich, Louis (1924-). TV: *Hudson's Bay*—"Civilization" 4-12-58 (Jack Cherry), "The Executioner" 5-3-58 (Jamie McKenzie).

Zsigmond, Vilmos (1930-). Films: "Maverick" 1994 (Albert Bierstadt).

Zuanelli, Marco. Films: "Once Upon a Time in the West" 1968-Ital. (Wobbles); "Sabata" 1969-Ital. (Sharky).

Zuckert, William (1915-). Films: "Hang 'Em High" 1968; "The Great Bank Robbery" 1969 (Ranger Commander); "Scandalous John" 1971 (Abernathy); "Hitched" TVM-1973; "The Incredible Rocky Mountain Race" TVM-1977 (Mayor Calvin Mercer); "California Gold Rush" TVM-1981 (Parson). ¶TV: *Bonanza*—"The Smiler" 9-24-61 (Gilbert), "Elegy for a Hangman" 1-20-63 (Cal Prince), "No Less a Man" 3-15-64 (Browning), "A Darker Shadow" 11-23-69 (Barker), "One Ace Too Many" 4-2-72 (Mack Fowler); *The Rifleman*—"The Long Goodbye" 11-27-61 (Debo); *Lawman*—"Tarot" 12-10-61 (Luther); *Gunsmoke*—"Quint Asper Comes Home" 9-29-62 (John Asper), "I Call Him Wonder" 3-23-63 (Enock), "The Magician" 12-21-63 (Ned), "Deputy Festus" 1-16-65 (Jacobsen), "Mirage" 1-11-71 (Hotel Clerk); *Cheyenne*—"Satonka" 10-1-62 (Ed Parker); *Stoney Burke*—"Fight Night" 10-8-62 (Coates); *The Virginian*—"The Big Deal" 10-10-62 (Bernie), "A Time Remembered" 12-11-63 (George); *Laramie*—"The Renegade Brand" 2-26-63; *The Dakotas*—"The Chooser of the Slain" 4-22-63 (Jim Clarke); *Death Valley Days*—"Kingdom for a Horse" 12-1-63 (Sheriff), "Tribute to the Dog" 12-27-64 (Sheriff), "There Was Another Dalton Brother" 6-6-65 (George Johnson), "Brute Angel" 10-15-66 (Ed Billings), "The Wizard of Aberdeen" 1-17-70, "Pioneer Pluck" 4-4-70; *The Loner*—"Widow on the Evening Stage" 10-30-65 (Stinnet); *A Man Called Shenandoah*—"The Verdict" 11-1-65 (Williams); *Wild Wild West*—"The Night of the Infernal Machine" 12-23-66 (Chief of Police Bulvon), "The Night of the Plague" 4-4-69 (Sheriff Dan Case); *The Road West*—"Elizabeth's Odyssey" 5-1-67 (Shuler); *Iron Horse*—"Gallows for Bill Pardew" 9-30-67 (Jess); *Cimarron Strip*—"Nobody" 12-7-67; *Here Come the Brides*—"And Jason Makes Five" 10-9-68 (Judge), "Loggerheads" 3-26-69, "Land Grant" 11-21-69, "The Last Winter" 3-27-70 (Magistrate); *The Guns of Will Sonnett*—"A Town in Terror" 2-7-69 & 2-14-69 (Ira Tucker); *Lancer*—"Welcome to Genesis" 11-18-69; *The Men from Shiloh*—"Lady at the Bar" 11-4-70 (Judge Conrad).

Zuniga, Daphne. Films: "Mad at the Moon" 1992 (Young Mrs. Miller).

Zurakowska, Dianik (Diane Zura). Films: "The Man Who Killed Billy the Kid" 1967-Span./Ital. (Helen Tunstill); "Ringo, the Lone Rider" 1967-Ital./Span.; "The Bang Bang Kid" 1968-U.S./Span./Ital. (Betsy Skaggel); "Cry for Revenge" 1968-Ital./Span.; "One Against One ... No Mercy" 1968-Span./Ital.; "Two Crosses at Danger Pass" 1968-Ital./Span.; "Adios Cjamango" 1969-Ital./Span.; "Rebels of Arizona" 1969-Span.

Zwerling, Darrell (1928-). TV: *Best of the West*—6-21-82 (Fredericks); *Father Murphy*—"Stopover in a One-Way Horse Town" 10-26-82 (Standish).

ZZ Top. Films: "Back to the Future, Part III" 1990 (Festival Band).

Section II

DIRECTORS, PRODUCERS AND WRITERS

Abbe, Derwin. Director. TV: *Judge Roy Bean*—"Family Ties" 10-1-55, "The Horse Thief" 10-1-55, "Sunburnt Gold" 10-1-55, "The Wedding of Old Sam" 10-1-55, "The Runaway" 10-15-55, "Slightly Prodigal": 10-15-55, "Black Jack" 11-1-55, "Judge Declares a Holiday" 11-1-55, "Connie Comes to Town" 12-1-55, "The Fugitive" 12-1-55, "Letty Leaves Home" 12-1-55, "Vinegarone" 12-1-55.

Abbey, Edward (1926-3/14/89). Writer. Films: "Lonely Are the Brave" 1962 (story).

Abbott, Charles. Director. Films: "Fighting Texan" 1937; "The Adventures of the Masked Phantom" 1939.

Abbott-Fish, Chris. Screenwriter. Films: "Little House: Bless All the Dear Children" TVM-1984.

Abrahams, Derwin. Director. Films: "Border Vigilantes" 1941; "Secrets of the Wastelands" 1941; "Both Barrels Blazing" 1945; "Northwest Trail" 1945; "Return of the Durango Kid" 1945; "Rough Ridin' Justice" 1945; "Rustlers of the Badlands" 1945; "Drifting Along" 1946; "The Fighting Frontiersman" 1946; "Frontier Gunlaw" 1946; "The Haunted Mine" 1946; "Prairie Raiders" 1947; "Riders of the Lone Star" 1947; "Smoky River Serenade" 1947; "South of the Chisholm Trail" 1947; "The Stranger from Ponca City" 1947; "Swing the Western Way" 1947; "Cowboy Cavalier" 1948; "The Rangers Ride" 1948; "Tex Granger" 1948-serial; "The Girl from San Lorenzo" 1950; "Whistling Hills" 1951. ¶TV: *The Cisco Kid* 1951-55.

Abrahamson, Jerry. Writer. Films: "Wagons East!" 1994 (story).

Abrams, Leon. Writer. Films: "Sunset in El Dorado" 1945 (story).

Abroms, Edward. Director. TV: *The Chisholms* 1980.

Abroms, Howard. Director. TV: *Alias Smith and Jones*—"The Ten Days That Shook Kid Curry" 11-4-72.

Ackerman, Harry (1912-2/3/91). Producer. TV: *Tales of the Texas Rangers* 1955-57.

Adams, Clifton (1919-). Screenwriter. Films: "The Desperado" 1954; "Outlaw's Son" 1957 (story only); "Cole Younger, Gunfighter" 1958 (story only); "The Dangerous Days of Kiowa Jones" TVM-1966 (story only).

Adams, Fred R. Writer. Films: "Cowboy and the Lady" 1938 (story).

Adams, Gerald Drayton (1904-). Screenwriter. Films: "The Gallant Legion" 1948; "Old Los Angeles" 1948; "The Plunderers" 1948; "The Lady from Texas" 1951; "The Battle at Apache Pass" 1952; "The Duel at Silver Creek" 1952; "Flaming Feather" 1952; "Untamed Frontier 1952; "Wings of the Hawk" 1953 (story only); "The Gambler from Natchez" 1954; "Taza, Son of Cochise" 1954 (& story); "Three Young Texans" 1954; "Chief Crazy Horse" 1955; "Gun Brothers" 1956; "War Drums" 1957; "Gun Fight" 1961; "The Wild Westerners" 1962.

Adams, Richard L. Screenwriter. Films: "Winchester '73" TVM-1967.

Adams, Samuel Hopkins. Writer. Films: "The Harvey Girls" 1946 (story).

Adamson, Al (1929-6/19/95). Director. Films: "Five Bloody Graves" 1969 (& prod.); "The Female Bunch" 1971; "Jessi's Girls" 1976 (& prod.).

Adamson, Ed. Producer. TV: *Wanted—Dead or Alive* 1958-61; *The Rounders* 1966-67.

Adamson, Ewart (1882-11/28/45). Screenwriter. Films: "The Man Who Won" 1923; "Night Cry" 1926; "The Silent Guardian" 1926; "Aflame

in the Sky" 1927; "The Outlaw Dog" 1927 (story only); "The Cow-Catcher's Daughter" 1931-short; "The Gold Ghost" 1934-short; "Annie Oakley" 1935 (story only); "Rhythm Wranglers" 1937-short.

Adamson, Victor. *see* Dixon, Denver.

Adcock, W. Director. Films: "Fighting Jim Grant" 1923 (& sp.); "Lone Hand Texas" 1924.

Addis, Justus (1917-10/26/79). Director. TV: *Wagon Train*—"The Mary Halstead Story" 11-20-57; *Rawhide*—"Incident of the New Start" 3-3-61, "Incident of the Running Man" 5-5-61, "The Long Shakedown" 10-13-61, "The Little Fishes" 11-24-61, "A Woman's Place" 3-30-62, "Blood Harvest" 2-12-65, "The Winter Soldier" 3-12-65, "The Empty Sleeve" 4-2-65, "Ride a Crooked Mile" 9-21-65, "The Prusuit" 11-9-65; *Wild Wild West*—"The Night of the Human Trigger" 12-3-65; *The High Chaparral*—"The Assassins" 1-7-68.

Addison, Thomas. Writer. Films: "The Grand Passion" 1918 (story).

Adler, Buddy (1909-7/12/60). Producer. Films: "Last of the Comanches" 1952.

Adler, Felix. Screenwriter. Films: "Horses' Collars" 1935-short; "Goofs and Saddles" 1937-short; "Way Out West" 1937; "Cowboy Canteen" 1944; "Shot in the Frontier" 1954-short.

Adolfi, John (1888-5/11/33). Director. Films: "The Horse Wrangler" 1914; "A Man and His Mate" 1915; "The Scarlet West" 1925.

Adreon, Franklyn (1902-). Director. Films: "Zorro Rides Again" 1937-serial (sp. only); "The Lone Ranger" 1938-serial (sp. only); "Sons of Adventure" 1938 (prod./sp. only);

"The Lone Ranger Rides Again" 1939-serial (sp. only); "Zorro's Fighting Legion" 1939-serial (sp. only); "Adventures of Red Ryder" 1940-serial (sp. only); "King of the Royal Mounted" 1940-serial; "Jesse James Rides Again" 1947-serial (sp. only); "Son of Zorro" 1947-serial (sp. only); "The Adventures of Frank and Jesse James" 1948-serial (prod./sp. only); "Dangerous of the Canadian Mounted" 1948-serial (sp. only); "Ghost of Zorro" 1949-serial (prod. only); "The Arizona Cowboy" 1950 (prod. only); "Desperadoes of the West" 1950-serial (prod. only); "Hills of Oklahoma" 1950 (prod. only); "The James Brothers of Missouri" 1950 (prod. only); "Redwood Forest Trail" 1950; "Don Daredevil Rides Again" 1951-serial (prod. only); "Canadian Mounties vs. Atomic Invaders" 1953-serial (& prod.); "Man with the Steel Whip" 1954-serial (& prod.); "Hell's Crossroads" 1957. ¶TV: *Cheyenne* 1955; *Colt .45* 1957; *Sugarfoot* 1957; *Maverick*—"The Wrecker" 12-1-57, "The Third Rider" 1-5-58; *Gunsmoke*—"Brother Love" 12-31-60.

Agee, James (1910-5/16/55). Screenwriter. Films: "Face to Face" 1952 ("The Bride Comes to Yellow Sky" segment).

Agnew, Frances. Screenwriter. Films: "The Golden Princess" 1925.

Agraz, Carlos Garcia. Director. Films: "My Dear Tom Mix" 1992-Mex.

Agrin, Roberto. Screenwriter. Films: "Roy Colt and Winchester Jack" 1970-Ital.

Ainsworth, Helen. Producer. Films: "The Hard Man" 1957; "Bullwhip" 1958.

Ainsworth, James. Director. TV: *Maverick*—"Family Pride" 1-8-61, "Last Stop: Oblivion" 2-12-61, "Maverick at Law" 2-26-61, "Deadly Image" 3-12-61,

Albert, Al. *see* Albertini, Adalberto.

Albert, Marvin H. (1924-). Screenwriter. Films: "The Law and Jake Wade" 1958 (story only); "Bullet for a Badman" 1964 (story only); "Duel at Diablo" 1966; "The Ugly Ones" 1966-Ital./Span. (story only); "Rough Night in Jericho" 1967 (& story).

Albertini, Adalberto (Al Albert, Bitto Albertini). Director. Films: "Fighters from Ave Maria" 1970-Ital./Ger. (& sp.); "Return of Shanghai Joe" 1974-Ger./Ital. (& sp.).

Albertini, Bitto. *see* Albertini, Adalberto.

Alcala, Felix Enriquez. Director. TV: *Adventures of Brisco County, Jr.*—"Stagecoach" 4-1-94.

Aldrich, Robert (1902-3/31/86). Director. Films: "Apache" 1954; "Vera Cruz" 1954; "The Last Sunset" 1961; "Ulzana's Raid" 1972; "The Frisco Kid" 1979.

Aldridge, Charles W. Screenwriter. Films: "Guns of a Stranger" 1973.

Alexander, Arthur (1909-4/3/89). Producer. Films: "Cowboy Holiday" 1934; "Thunder Over Texas" 1934; "Big Boy Rides Again" 1935; "Danger Trails" 1935; "Gun Play" 1935; "Law of the 45's" 1935; "Law and Lead" 1936; "Men of the Plains" 1936; "Too Much Beef" 1936; "West of Nevada" 1936; "The Idaho Kid" 1937; "Six Shootin' Sheriff" 1938; "Songs and Saddles" 1938; "Whirlwind Horseman" 1938; "Flaming Lead" 1939; "Death Rides the Range" 1940; "Lightning Strikes West" 1940; "Phantom Rancher" 1940; "The Rangers Take Over" 1942; "Bad Men of Thunder Gap" 1943; "Border Buckaroos" 1943; "Fighting Valley" 1943; "The Return of the Rangers" 1943; "West of Texas" 1943; "Brand of the Devil" 1944; "Dead or Alive" 1944; "Gangsters of the Frontier" 1944; "Guns of the Law" 1944; "Gunsmoke Mesa" 1944; "Spook Town" 1944; "Trail of Terror" 1944; "The Whispering Skull" 1944; "Enemy of the Law" 1945; "Flaming Bullets" 1945; "Frontier Fugitives" 1945; "Marked for Murder" 1945; "The Navajo Kid" 1945; "Three in the Saddle" 1945; "Ambush Trail" 1946; "Six Gun Man" 1946; "Thunder Town" 1946.

Alexander, David (1915-3/6/83). Director. TV: *F Troop* 1965; *Gunsmoke*—"Rope Fever" 12-4-67.

Alexander, Gilbert. Screenwriter. Films: "The Hunting Party" 1971-Brit./Ital./Span. (& story).

Alexander, J. Grubb. Screenwriter. Films: "Mixed Blood" 1916; "Fighting Mad" 1917 (story); "The Plow Woman" 1917; "The Third Woman" 1920; "Back to Yellow Jacket" 1922; "Belle of Alaska" 1922; "One-Eighty Apache" 1922; "The Lady from Hell" 1926.

Alexander, Jane (1939-). Producer. Films: "Calamity Jane" TVM-1984.

Alexander, Max. Producer. Films: "Cowboy Holiday" 1934; "Thunder Over Texas" 1934; "Big Boy Rides Again" 1935; "Danger Trails" 1935; "Law and Lead" 1936; "Men of the Plains" 1936; "Too Much Beef" 1936; "Six Shootin' Sheriff" 1938; "Songs and Saddles" 1938; "Whirlwind Horseman" 1938; "Flaming Lead" 1939; "Death Rides the Range" 1940; "Lightning Strikes West" 1940; "Phantom Rancher" 1940.

Alexander, W.R. Screenwriter. Films: "The Bounty Killer" 1965; "Requiem for a Gunfighter" 1965.

Alfaro, Italo. *see* Regnoli, Piero.

Alfiero, Carlo Alberto. Screenwriter. Films: "Fighting Fists of Shanghai Joe" 1973-Ital.; "Return of Shanghai Joe" 1974-Ger./Ital.

Algar, James. Director. Films: "Legend of Lobo" 1962 (& sp.).

Algier, Sidney (1885-4/25/45). Director. Films: "Wild Horse" 1931.

Allah, Ben. Screenwriter. Films: "Sitting Bull at the Spirit Lake Massacre" 1927.

Alland, William (1916-). Producer. Films: "The Lawless Breed" 1952 (& story); "The Raiders" 1952; "The Stand at Apache River" 1953; "Dawn at Socorro" 1954; "Four Guns to the Border" 1954; "Chief Crazy Horse" 1955; "Gun for a Coward" 1957; "The Rare Breed" 1966.

Allen, Corey (1934-). Director. TV: *Lancer*—"Child of Rock and Sunlight" 4-1-69; *The High Chaparral*—"A Good, Sound Profit" 10-30-70; *The Quest*—"Shanklin" 10-13-76.

Allen, Eric. Screenwriter. Films: "Smoke in the Wind" 1975.

Allen, Eugene. Screenwriter. Films: "Rodeo Rhythm" 1942.

Allen, Fred (1894-3/17/56). Director. Films: "The Lawless Legion" 1929 (sp. only); "Sundown Trail" 1931 (prod. only); "Beyond the Rockies" 1932; "Freighters of Destiny" 1932; "Ghost Valley" 1932; "Partners" 1932; "Ride Him, Cowboy" 1932; "The Saddle Buster" 1932; "The Mysterious Rider" 1933.

Allen, Gary. Screenwriter. Films: "The Wicked Die Slow" 1968.

Allen, Irving (1905-12/17/87). Producer. Films: "New Mexico" 1951; "Slaughter Trail" 1951 (& dir.); "The Desperados" 1969.

Allen, J.T. Screenwriter. Films: "Geronimo" TVM-1993; "The Good Old Boys" TVM-1995.

Allen, Lewis (1905-). Director. Films: "Desert Fury" 1947. ¶TV: *Ford Theater*—"Sudden Silence" 10-10-56; *The Rifleman*—"The Second Witness" 3-3-59, "One Went to Denver" 3-17-

59, "The Challenge" 4-7-59, "A Matter of Faith" 5-19-59, "Stranger at Night" 6-2-59, "The Grasshopper" 3-1-60; *Bonanza*—"The Outcast" 1-9-60, "House Divided" 1-16-60, "The Fear Merchants" 1-30-60, "Desert Justice" 2-20-60, "Dark Star" 4-23-60, "Showdown" 9-10-60, "The Blood Line" 12-31-60, "The Fugitive" 2-4-61, "Elizabeth, My Love" 5-27-61, "The Tin Badge" 12-17-61, "The Guilty" 2-25-62, "Inger, My Love" 4-15-62, "The Way Station" 10-29-62, "The Colonel" 1-6-63, "Marie, My Love" 2-10-63, "A Stranger Passed This Way" 3-3-63, "Mirror of a Man" 3-31-63, "The Thunder Man" 5-5-63, "Little Man—Ten Feet Tall" 5-26-63, "Rain from Heaven" 10-6-63, "Alias Joe Cartwright" 1-26-64, "Something Hurt, Something Wild" 9-11-66, "Justice" 1-8-67, "Journey to Terror" 2-5-67, "Clarissa" 4-30-67, "A Severe Case of Matrimony" 7-7-68, "The Clarion" 2-9-69, "Five Candles" 3-2-69, "The Fence" 4-27-69, "The Medal" 10-26-69, "Long Way to Ogden" 2-22-70, "The Imposters" 12-13-70, "Honest John" 12-20-70, "A Deck of Aces" 1-31-71, "Blind Hunch" 11-21-71, "Frenzy" 1-30-72, "One Ace Too Many" 4-2-72, "Riot!" 10-3-72; *Branded*—"The First Kill" 4-4-65; *The Big Valley*—"The Guilt of Matt Bentell" 12-8-65; *The Guns of Will Sonnett*—"The Man Who Killed James Sonnett" 3-21-69; *Little House on the Prairie* 1974.

Allen, Madeline. Writer. Films: "Yankee Don" 1931 (story).

Allen, W.H. Screenwriter. Films: "Rounding Up the Law" 1922.

Allman, Roger. Screenwriter. Films: "Swifty" 1935; "Lucky Terror" 1936 (& story).

Alonzo, John A. Director. Films: "Belle Starr" TVM-1980.

Aloza, Jerez. Screenwriter. Films: "Left Handed Johnny West" 1965-Span./Ital.

Alperson, Edward L. (1896-7/3/69). Producer. Films: "Belle Starr's Daughter" 1947; "Dakota Lil" 1950; "Rose of Cimarron" 1952; "Mohawk" 1956; "The Restless Breed" 1957.

Alsberg, Arthur. Screenwriter. Films: "Hot Lead and Cold Feet" 1978.

Alt, Al. *see* Kirkwood, Ray.

Altman, Robert (1925-). Director. Films: "McCabe and Mrs. Miller" 1971 (& sp.); "Buffalo Bill and the Indians, or Sitting Bull's History Lesson" 1976 (& prod.). ¶TV: *Sugarfoot* 1957; *Bronco* 1958; *Lawman* 1959; *Maverick*—"Bolt from the

Blue" 11-27-60; *Bonanza*—"Silent Thunder" 12-10-60, "Bank Run" 1-28-61, "The Rival" 4-15-61, "The Secret" 5-6-61, "Sam Hill" 6-3-61, "The Many Faces of Gideon Flinch" 11-5-61.

Amacker, Howard. Writer. Films: "No Name on the Bullet" 1959 (story).

Amateau, Rod (1923-). Director. Films: "The Bushwackers" 1952; "Sunset" 1988 (story only).

Amati, Edmondo. Producer. Films: "Fort Yuma Gold" 1966-Ital./Fr./Span.; "He Who Shoots First" 1966-Ital.; "Kill Them All and Come Back Alone" 1967-Ital./Span.

Amendola, Mario (Irving Jacobs). Screenwriter. Films: "Terror of Oklahoma" 1961-Ital. (& dir.); "Three Swords of Zorro" 1963-Ital./Span.; "Behind the Mask of Zorro" 1965-Ital./Span.; "Kill or Be Killed" 1966-Ital.; "Bad Kids of the West" 1967-Ital.; "Days of Violence" 1967-Ital.; "Great Silence" 1968-Ital./Fr.; "Shoot, Gringo ... Shoot!" 1968-Ital./Fr.; "Three Silver Dollars" 1968-Ital. (& dir.); "Killer Goodbye" 1969-Ital./Span.; "Calibre .38" 1971-Ital.; "Bandera Bandits" 1973-Ital./Span./Ger.; "The White, the Yellow, and the Black" 1974-Ital./Span./Fr.

Ambrosini, Luigi. Screenwriter. Films: "Black Jack" 1968-Ital.

Amiel, Jon (1948-). Director. Films: "Sommersby" 1993.

Amy, George (1903-12/18/86). Director. Films: "Ride, Cowboy, Ride" 1939-short; "The Royal Rodeo" 1939-short.

Anchisi, Piero. Screenwriter. Films: "Forgotten Pistolero" 1970-Ital./Span.; "Blindman" 1971-Ital.

Anderson, Bill. Producer. Films: "Savage Sam" 1963; "The Adventures of Bullwhip Griffin" 1967; "Smith" 1969; "The Apple Dumpling Gang" 1975.

Anderson, Charles. Screenwriter. Films: "The Pioneers" 1941.

Anderson, Doris. Screenwriter. Films: "Three Faces West" 1940.

Anderson, Jr., Edgar C. Screenwriter. Films: "Gold Fever" 1952.

Anderson, Gilbert M. "Broncho Billy" (1884-1/20/71). Director. Films: "Life of an American Cowboy" 1906; "The Bandit King" 1907; "The Bandit Makes Good" 1907; "Girl from Montana" 1907; "His First Ride" 1907; "The Life of Franks Jenks" 1907; "Western Justice" 1907; "The Heart of a Cowboy" 1909; "The

Indian Trailer" 1909; "A Mexican's Gratitude" 1909; "Broncho Billy's Christmas Dinner" 1911; "The Sheriff" 1911 (sp. only); "The Sheriff's Decision" 1911 (sp. only); "Shootin' Mad" 1911 (& story); "The Loafer's Mother" 1912; "Love on Tough Luck Ranch" 1912; "The Tomboy on Bar Z" 1912; "Broncho Billy and the Sheriff's Kid" 1913; "Broncho Billy's Capture" 1913; "Broncho Billy's Oath" 1913; "The Making of Broncho Billy" 1913; "Broncho Billy a Friend in Need" 1914; "Broncho Billy Butts In" 1914; "Broncho Billy's Indian Romance" 1914; "The Good for Nothing" 1914; "Red Riding Hood of the Hills" 1914; "Broncho Billy's Love Affair" 1915; "His Regeneration" 1915; "Too Much Turkey" 1915; "Naked Hands" 1918; "The Son of a Gun" 1919 (sp. only).

Andrei, Marcello (Mark Andrews). Director. Films: "Macho Killers" 1977-Ital. (& sp.).

Andrew, Mark. *see* Andrei, Marcello.

Andrews, Del (1894-10/27/42). Director. Films: "No Man's Law" 1925; "The Ridin' Streak" 1925; "Ridin' the Wind" 1925; "That Devil Quemado" 1925; "The Wild Bull's Lair" 1925; "Man Rustlin'" 1926; "Lone Hand Saunders" 1926 (sp. only); "The Yellow Back" 1926 (& sp.); "A Hero on Horseback" 1927; "The Rawhide" 1928; "The Wild West Show" 1928; "The Outlaw Deputy" 1935.

Andrews, Robert D. Screenwriter. Films: "The Man from Colorado" 1948.

Andrews, Robert Hardy (1903-11/11/76). Screenwriter. Films: "The Kid from Texas" 1950 (& story); "Wyoming Mail" 1950 (story only); "Best of the Badmen" 1951; "Mark of the Renegade" 1951; "The Half-Breed" 1952 (story only); "Great Day in the Morning" 1956 (story only).

Andrus, Jeff. Screenwriter. Films: "Proud Men" TVM-1987.

Andrus, Malon. Director. Films: "Ace of Cactus Range" 1924.

Angell, Buckley. Screenwriter. Films: "The Hired Gun" 1957.

Angelo, Luigi. Screenwriter. Films: "Black Tigress" 1967-Ital.; "Hate Thy Neighbor" 1969-Ital.

Anhalt, Edna. Screenwriter. Films: "The Younger Brothers" 1949; "Return of the Frontiersman" 1950; "Sierra" 1950.

Anhalt, Edward (1914-). Screenwriter. Films: "Hour of the

Gun" 1967; "Jeremiah Johnson" 1972.

Anies, Marie-Ange. Screenwriter. Films: "The Legend of Frenchie King" 1971-Fr./Ital./Span./Brit.

Annakin, Ken (1914-). Director. TV: *Hunter's Moon*—Pilot 12-1-79.

Annitzer, Paul. Screenwriter. Films: "The Sheriff's Oath" 1920.

Anthony, Joseph. Director. Films: "The Rainmaker" 1956.

Anthony, Scott. Screenwriter. Films: "Frontier Marshal" 1934.

Anthony, Stuart (1886-4/28/42). Screenwriter. Films: "Border Law" 1931; "Desert Vengeance" 1931; "The Fighting Sheriff" 1931; "End of the Trail" 1932; "McKenna of the Mounted" 1932; "The Vanishing Frontier" 1932; "Whistlin' Dan" 1932; "The Last Trail" 1933; "Life in the Raw" 1933; "Silent Men" 1933; "Smoky" 1933; "The Whirlwind" 1933; "Border Brigands" 1935; "Nevada" 1935; "Wanderer of the Wasteland" 1935; "Arizona Mahoney" 1936; "Desert Gold" 1936; "Drift Fence" 1936; "Born to the West" 1937; "Forlorn River" 1937; "Thunder Trail" 1937; "Saga of Death Valley" 1939; "The Ranger and the Lady" 1940; "When the Daltons Rode" 1940; "Along the Rio Grande" 1941 (story only); "The Shepherd of the Hills" 1941.

Anthony, Tony (1937-). Screenwriter. Films: "The Stranger Returns" 1967-U.S./Ital./Ger./Span. (story only); "Blindman" 1971-Ital. (& prod.); "Get Mean" 1975-Ital.; "Comin' at Ya" 1981-Ital. (prod. only).

Anthony, Walter. Screenwriter. Films: "When a Man's a Man" 1924.

Anton, Amerigo. *see* Boccia, Tanio.

Antonelli, Lamberto. Screenwriter. Films: "Black Tigress" 1967-Ital.

Antonini, Alfredo. *see* Band, Albert.

Antonio, Louis. Director. TV: *Here Come the Brides*—"Another Game in Town" 2-6-70; "Two Worlds" 2-20-70.

Apfel, Oscar C. (1879-3/21/38). Director. Films: "Rose of the Rancho" 1914; "The Squaw Man" 1914 (& sp.); "The End of the Trail" 1916 (& sp.); "Fighting Blood" 1916 (& sp.); "The Man from Bitter Roots" 1916 (& sp.); "The Hidden Children" 1917 (& sp.); "The Man Who Paid"

1922; "Call of the Klondike" 1926; "Code of the Cow Country" 1927.

Appel, David. Writer. Films: "Tonka" 1958 (story).

Arabia, Carlos. Screenwriter. Films: "I Want Him Dead" 1968-Ital./Span.

Arbeid, Ben (1924-). Producer. Films: "Eagle's Wing" 1979-Brit./Span.

Arbuckle, Roscoe "Fatty" (1887-6/29/33). Director. Films: "Fatty and Minnie He-Haw" 1915; "Out West" 1918.

Arcalli, Franco. Screenwriter. Films: "Django Kill" 1967-Ital./Span.

Arch, Jeff. Screenwriter. Films: "Iron Will" 1994.

Archainbaud, George (1890-2/20/59). Director. Films: "The Plunderer" 1924; "The Silver Horde" 1930; "False Colors" 1943; "Hoppy Serves a Writ" 1943; "The Kansan" 1943; "The Woman of the Town" 1943; "Alaska" 1944; "The Big Bonanza" 1944; "Mystery Man" 1944; "Texas Masquerade" 1944; "The Devil's Playground" 1946; "Fool's Gold" 1946; "Dangerous Venture" 1947; "King of the Wild Horses" 1947; "The Marauders" 1947; "Unexpected Guest" 1947; "Borrowed Trouble" 1948; "The Dead Don't Dream" 1948; "False Paradise" 1948; "Silent Conflict" 1948; "Sinister Journey" 1948; "Strange Gamble" 1948; "Border Treasure" 1950; "Apache Country" 1952; "Barbed Wire" 1952; "Blue Canadian Rockies" 1952; "Night Stage to Galveston" 1952; "The Old West" 1952; "Wagon Team" 1952; "Goldtown Ghost Raiders" 1953; "Last of the Pony Riders" 1953; "On Top of Old Smoky" 1953; "Pack Train" 1953; "Saginaw Trail" 1953; "Winning of the West" 1953. ¶TV: *The Lone Ranger*—"High Heels" 11-17-49, "Six Gun Legacy" 11-24-49, "Finders Keepers" 12-8-49, "The Man Who Came Back" 1-5-50, "Outlaw Town" 1-12-50, "Sheep Thieves" 2-9-50, "Jim Tyler's Luck" 2-16-50, "The Man with Two Faces" 2-23-50, "Buried Treasure" 3-2-50, "Trouble Waters" 3-9-50, "Never Say Die" 4-6-50, "Gold Fever" 4-13-50, "Death Trap" 4-20-50; *The Gene Autry Show*—"Blackwater Valley Feud" 9-3-50, "Doublecross Valley" 9-10-50, "The Posse" 9-17-50, "The Devil's Brand" 9-24-50, "Gun Powder Range" 10-29-50, "The Breakup" 11-5-50, "Twisted Trails" 11-12-50, "Fight at Peaceful Mesa" 11-19-50, "Hot Lead" 11-26-50, "Killer Horse" 12-10-50, "The Sheriff of Santa Rosa"

12-24-50, "T.N.T." 12-31-50, "Frontier Guard" 10-13-51, "Killer's Trail" 10-27-51, "Warning! Danger!" 11-10-51, "Bandits of Boulder Bluff" 11-24-51, "Outlaw Escape" 12-1-51, "The Kid Comes West" 12-8-51, "The Return of Maverick Dan" 12-15-51, "Galloping Hoofs" 12-22-51, "Melody Mesa" 1-4-52, "Rocky River Feud" 1-18-52, "The Lawless Press" 1-25-52, "The Western Way" 2-1-52, "Ruthless Renegade" 2-8-52, "Hot Lead and Old Lace" 2-15-52, "Trouble at Silver Creek" 3-9-52, "Trail of the Witch" 3-30-52, "Thunder Out West" 7-14-53, "Ghost Mountain" 7-28-53, "The Old Prospector" 8-4-53, "Gypsy Wagon" 8-25-53, "Bandidos" 9-1-53, "Dry Gulch at Devil's Elbow" 9-8-53, "Rio Renegades" 9-29-53, "Battle Axe" 8-31-54, "Boots and Ballots" 9-25-54, "Outlaw Warning" 10-2-54, "Stage to San Dimas" 10-8-55, "Law Comes to Scorpion" 10-22-55, "Guns Below the Border" 11-5-55, "Ghost Ranch" 11-12-55, "Feuding Friends" 11-26-55, "Saddle Up" 12-3-55, "Ride, Rancheros" 12-10-55, "The Rangerette" 12-17-55, "Dynamite" 12-24-55; *The Range Rider* 1951; *Annie Oakley*—"Sharpshooting Annie" 6-12-54, "The Tomboy" 7-17-54, "Dead Man's Bluff" 3-20-55, "Annie and the Bicycle Riders" 7-8-56, "Annie and the First Phone" 7-22-56, "Indian Justice" 7-29-56, "Western Privateer" 9-30-56, "Dude's Decision" 2-10-57, "Desperate Men" 2-24-57; *The Adventures of Champion* 1955; *Buffalo Bill, Jr.* 1955.

Archer, Ted. *see* Rossati, Nello.

Archer, Walter. Writer. Films: "Deputy Sheriff's Star" 1914 (story).

Arden, Edwin. Writer. Films: "The Eagle's Nest" 1915 (story).

Ardrey, Robert (1908-1/14/80). Screenwriter. Films: "A Lady Takes a Chance" 1943; "The Wonderful Country" 1959.

Areal, Alberto. Screenwriter. Films: "A Sky Full of Stars for a Roof" 1968-Ital.

Argento, Dario (1943-). Screenwriter. Films: "Cemetery Without Crosses" 1968-Ital./Fr.; "Once Upon a Time in the West" 1968-Ital. (story only); "Today It's Me ... Tomorrow You!" 1968-Ital.; "The Five Man Army" 1969-Ital.

Arlorio, Giorgio. Screenwriter. Films: "The Mercenary" 1968-Ital./Span. (story only); "Zorro" 1974-Ital./Fr.

Armer, Alan A. Producer. TV: *My Friend Flicka* 1955-56; *Man With-*

out a Gun 1958-59; *Lancer* 1968-71, "Chad" 1-20-70 (dir.).

Armstrong, Burt. Screenwriter. Films: "The Man with the Punch" 1920.

Armstrong, Paul. Writer. Films: "Salomy Jane" 1914 (story).

Arner, Gwen. Director. TV: *Dr. Quinn, Medicine Woman*—"The Healing" 1-23-93.

Arnold, Danny (1925-). Screenwriter. Films: "Fort Yuma" 1955; "Rebel in Town" 1956.

Arnold, Elliott (1913-5/13/80). Screenwriter. Films: "Broken Arrow" 1950 (story only); "Alvarez Kelly" 1966.

Arnold, Jack (1916-3/17/92). Director. Films: "The Man from Bitter Ridge" 1955; "Red Sundown" 1956; "Man in the Shadow" 1957; "No Name on the Bullet" 1959 (& prod.); "Boss Nigger" 1974 & prod.). ¶TV: *Wagon Train*—"The Matthew Lowry Story" 4-1-59; *Rawhide*—"Incident Below the Brazos" 5-15-59, "Incident in No Man's Land" 6-12-59, "Incident at Jacob's Well" 10-16-59, "Canliss 10-30-64; *The Guns of Will Sonnett*—"The Trap" 10-4-68; *The Men from Shiloh* 1970; *Alias Smith and Jones*—"Something to Get Hung About" 10-21-71, "Which Way to the O.K. Corral?" 2-10-72, "Bushwack!" 10-21-72, "What Happened at the XST?" 10-28-72.

Arnold, Jess. Writer. Films: "The Eagle and the Hawk" 1950 (story); "The Brass Legend" 1956 (story).

Arrigo, Frank. TV: *Wagon Train*—"The Odyssey of Flint McCullough" 2-15-61.

Arthur, Art (1911-4/23/85). Screenwriter. Films: "Riding High" 1943; "Heaven Only Knows" 1947; "Northwest Stampede" 1948.

Arthur, Robert (1909-10/28/86). Producer. Films: "The Wistful Widow of Wagon Gap" 1947; "Curtain Call at Cactus Creek" 1950; "Ricochet Romance" 1954; "A Day of Fury" 1956; "Pillars of the Sky" 1956; "Shenandoah" 1965; "One More Train to Rob" 1971.

Arthur, Victor. Screenwriter. Films: "Hills of Oklahoma" 1950; "Lightning Guns" 1950; "Trail of the Rustlers" 1950; "Ridin' the Outlaw Trail" 1951.

Arzner, Dorothy (1897-10/1/79). Screenwriter. Films: "The Breed of the Border" 1924; "The No-Gun Man" 1925.

Ascott, Anthony. *see* Carmineo, Giuliano.

Ashcroft, Ronnie (1923-12/14/88). Producer. Films: "Outlaw Queen" 1957.

Asher, Irving (1903-3/17/85). Producer. Films: "Billy the Kid" 1941; "The Redhead and the Cowboy" 1951.

Ashfield, Fred A. Screenwriter. Films: "The Navajo Ring" 1914.

Ashley, A. Screenwriter. Films: "Forbidden Grass" 1928.

Ashley, Luke. Screenwriter. Films: "God Does Not Pay on Saturday" 1968-Ital.

Ashley, Mike. Writer. Films: "The Tall Women" 1966-Austria/Ital./Span. (story).

Ashton, Rosalie. Screenwriter. Films: "Who Knows?" 1918.

Assed, Rene. Screenwriter. Films: "The White, the Yellow, and the Black" 1974-Ital./Span./Fr.

Athanas, Verne. Writer. Films: "The Proud Ones" 1956 (story).

Atkins, Thomas. Director. Films: "Hi Gaucho!" 1936.

Atkins, Zoe. Writer. Films: "The Sad Horse" 1959 (story).

Atkinson, Owen. Writer. Films: "Twenty Mule Team" 1940 (story).

Attias, Daniel. Director. TV: *Dr. Quinn, Medicine Woman*—"Sanctuary" 10-2-93; *Adventures of Brisco County, Jr.*—"Pirates" 10-8-93.

Atwater, Gladys. Screenwriter. Films: "American Empire" 1942; "In Old California" 1942 (story only); "El Paso" 1949 (story only); "The Great Sioux Uprising" 1953; "Overland Pacific" 1954; "The Seige at Red River" 1954 (story only); "The Treasure of Pancho Villa" 1955 (story only).

Aubrey, James A. Screenwriter. Films: "Under Montana Skies" 1930.

Aubrey, Richard. Screenwriter. Films: "A Town Called Hell" 1971-Span./Brit.

Aubrey, Robert S. Writer. Films: "Alias Jesse James" 1959 (story).

Auer, John H. (1906-3/15/75). Producer. Films: "Under Strange Flags" 1937 (story only); "Girl Rush" 1944. ¶TV: *U.S. Marshal* 1958-60.

Auer, Stephen. Producer. Films: "The San Antonio Kid" 1944; "Sheriff of Las Vegas" 1944; "Sheriff of Sundown" 1944; "Silver City Kid" 1944; "Stagecoach to Monterey" 1944; "Vigilantes of Dodge City" 1944; "The Topeka Terror" 1945; "Trail of Kit Carson" 1945; "Madonna of the Desert" 1948.

August, Edwin (1883-3/4/64).

Director. Films: "The Two-Gun Man" 1914.

Aured, Carlos. Screenwriter. Films: "Triumphs of a Man Called Horse" 1984.

Aurthur, Robert Alan (1922-11/20/78). Screenwriter. Films: "Warlock" 1959.

Austin, Edward R. Screenwriter. Films: "Death Goes North" 1939.

Autel, Franz (Francois Legrand). Films: "Trinity Plus the Clown and a Guitar" 1975-Ital./Austria/Fr.

Autry, Gene (1907-). Producer. TV: *Buffalo Bill, Jr.* 1955-56; *The Adventures of Champion* 1955-56.

Aux, Victor. Screenwriter. Films: "Taste for Killing" 1966-Ital./Span.; "I Do Not Forgive ... I Kill!" 1968-Span./Ital.

Averback, Hy (1925-). Director. Films: "The Great Bank Robbery" 1969; "The New Maverick" TVM-1978; "The Night Rider" TVM-1979. ¶TV: *F Troop* 1965-67 (exec. prod.); *Young Maverick*—"Dead Man's Hand" 12-26-79 & 1-2-80.

Avery, Charles (1873-7/23/26). Director. "Hogan Out West" 1915.

Avildsen, John G. (1936-). Director. Films: "8 Seconds" 1994.

Ayres, Sydney (-9/16). Director. Films: "Cameo of Yellowstone" 1914; "A Child of the Desert" 1914 (sp. only).

Azcona, Rafael. Screenwriter. Films: "The Big and the Bad" 1971-Ital./Fr./Span.; "It Can Be Done ... Amigo" 1971-Ital./Fr./Span.; "Don't Touch White Women!" 1974-Ital.

Azro, Natividad. Screenwriter. Films: "Gunmen of the Rio Grande" 1964-Fr./Ital./Span.

Azzella, Will. Screenwriter. Films: "Djurado" 1966-Ital./Span.

Babcock, Dwight. Screenwriter. Films: "Savage Frontier" 1953.

Bach, Steven. Producer. Films: "Butch and Sundance: The Early Days" 1979.

Bacher, William A. Producer. Films: "The Tall Men" 1955.

Bacon, Lloyd (1890-11/15/55). Director. Films: "Cowboy from Brooklyn" 1938; "The Oklahoma Kid" 1939; "Silver Queen" 1942; "The Great Sioux Uprising" 1953.

Bada, Astrain. Screenwriter. Films: "Dollar of Fire" 1967-Ital./Span.

Badger, Clarence (1880-6/17/64). Director. Films: "Jubilo" 1919;

"Leave It to Susan" 1919; "Cupid, the Cowpuncher" 1920; "Honest Hutch" 1920; "The Ropin' Fool" 1921; "Doubling for Romeo" 1922; "The Golden Princess" 1925; "Hands Up!" 1926; "The Bad Man" 1930; "Woman Hungry" 1931; "Rangle River" 1939-Australia (& prod.).

Badham, John (1939-). Director. Films: "The Godchild" TVM-1974. ¶TV: *Kung Fu*—"Alethea" 3-15-73.

Badiyi, Reza S. (1936-). Director. TV: *Dr. Quinn, Medicine Woman*—"Heroes" 5-1-93.

Baehr, Nicholas E. (1925-5/31/86). Screenwriter. Films: "The Invasion of Johnson County" TVM-1976.

Baggott, King (1879-7/11/48). Director. Films: "Tumbleweeds" 1925.

Bagni, Gwen. Screenwriter. Films: "Untamed Frontier" 1952; "The Last Wagon" 1956.

Bagni, John (1910-2/13/54). Screenwriter. Films: "Untamed Frontier" 1952; "Law and Order" 1953.

Bagni, Owen. Screenwriter. Films: "Law and Order" 1953.

Bagrain, Al. *see* Balcazar, Alfonso.

Bailey, Rex. Director. Films: "Fangs of the Arctic" 1953; "Northern Patrol" 1953.

Bain, Fred. Director. Films: "Thundering Through" 1925; "The Ramblin' Galoot" 1926.

Bakalyan, Richard (1931-). Producer. Films: "The Animals" 1971.

Baker, C. Graham (1888-5/15/50). Screenwriter. Films: "A Fight for Millions" 1918-serial; "The Perils of Thunder Mountain" 1919-serial; "Breaking Through" 1921-serial; "The Purple Riders" 1921-serial; "Pioneer Trails" 1923; "Playing It Wild" 1923; "Ramrod" 1947; "Four Faces West" 1948.

Baker, George B. Screenwriter. Films: "The Only Road" 1918; "As the Sun Went Down" 1919.

Baker, George D. Director. Films: "Some Duel" 1915.

Baker, Graham. Screenwriter. Films: "Smashing Barriers" 1919-serial; "Valley of the Sun" 1942 (prod. only); "Tennessee's Partner" 1955.

Baker, Hettie Gray. Writer. Films: "The Real Thing in Cowboys" 1914 (story).

Baker, Roy Ward (1916-). Director. Films: "The Singer Not the Song" 1961-Brit. (& prod.).

Baker, Tarkington. Writer.

Films: "Her Five-Foot Highness" 1920 (story); Human Stuff" 1920 (story).

Balaban, Bruce. Producer. Films: "A Place Called Glory" 1965-Span./Ger.; "The Texican" 1966-U.S./Span.

Balanos, Jose Antonio. Director. Films: "Lucky Johnny: Born in America" 1973-Ital./Mex. (& sp.).

Balcazar, Alfonso (Al Bagrain). Director. Films: "Five Thousand Dollars on One Ace" 1965-Span./Ital. (& sp.); "Four Dollars for Vengeance" 1965-Span./Ital.; "Man from Canyon City" 1965-Span./Ital.; "A Pistol for Ringo" 1965-Ital./Span.; "Dynamite Jim" 1966-Span./Ital. (& sp.); "Man with the Golden Pistol" 1966-Span./Ital. (& sp.); "Seven Guns for Timothy" 1966-Span./Ital. (sp. only); "Sunscorched" 1966-Span./Ger. (sp. only); "Thompson 1880" 1966-Ital./Ger. (sp. only); "Yankee" 1967-Ital./Span. (sp. only); "Clint the Stranger" 1968-Ital./Span./Ger. (& prod./sp.); "Five Giants from Texas" 1968-Ital./Span.; "Sartana Does Not Forgive" 1968-Span./Ital.; "Law of Violence" 1969-Span./Ital. (sp. only); "Desperado" 1972-Span./Ital. (& sp.); "Watch Out Gringo! Sabata Will Return" 1972-Ital./Span. (& sp.).

Balcazar, Jaime Jesus. (Robert M. White). Screenwriter. Films: "Man from Oklahoma" 1965-Ital./Span./Ger.; "Sunscorched" 1966-Span./Ger. (dir. only); "Sartana Does Not Forgive" 1968-Span./Ital.; "Red Blood, Yellow Gold" 1968-Ital./Span.; "Twice a Judas" 1968-Span./Ital.; "Gentleman Killer" 1969-Span./Ital.

Balchin, Nigel (1908-5/17/70). Screenwriter. Films: "The Singer Not the Song" 1961-Brit.

Baldanello, Gianfranco (Frank G. Carrol). Director. Films: "Kill Johnny Ringo" 1966-Ital. (& sp.); "Thirty Winchesters for El Diablo" 1967-Ital. (& sp.); "Black Jack" 1968-Ital. (& sp.); "This Man Can't Die" 1968-Ital.; "Colt in the Hand of the Devil" 1972-Ital. (& sp.); "Son of Zorro" 1973-Ital./Span. (& sp.); "Blood River" 1974-Ital.

Balderston, John (1889-3/8/54). Screenwriter. Films: "The Last of the Mohicans" 1936.

Baldi, Ferdinando. Director. Films: "The Avengers" 1966-Ital. (& sp.); "Texas, Adios" 1966-Ital./Span. (& sp.); "Rita of the West" 1967-Ital. (& sp.); "Get the Coffin Ready" 1968-Ital. (& sp.); "Hate Thy Neighbor" 1969-Ital. (& sp.); "Forgotten

Pistolero" 1970-Ital./Span. (& sp.); "Blindman" 1971-Ital.; "Carambla" 1974-Ital. (& sp.); "Carambola's Philosophy: In the Right Pocket" 1975-Ital. (& sp.); "Get Mean" 1975-Ital.; "Comin' at Ya" 1981-Ital.

Balducci, Richard. Director. Films: "Dust in the Sun" 1971-Fr. (& sp.).

Baldwin, Earl (1901-10/9/70). Screenwriter. Films: "Cowboy from Brooklyn" 1938.

Baldwin, Peter (1931-). Director. TV: *Gun Shy* 1983; *Zorro and Son* 1983.

Baldwin, Ruth Ann. Screenwriter. Films: "'49-'17" 1917 (& sp.); "Chasing Rainbows" 1919.

Baledon, Rafael. Director. Films: "Bullet for Billy the Kid" 1963.

Ball, Zachary. Writer. Films: "Joe Panther" 1976 (story).

Ballard, Todhunter (1903-80). Writer. Films: "The Outcast" 1954 (story).

Ballin, Hugo (1880-11/27/56). Director. Films: "The Prairie Wife" 1925 (& sp.).

Balluck, Don. Screenwriter. Films: "Four Rode Out" 1969-Ital./Span./U.S.; "Wild Times" TVM-1980.

Balshofer, Fred J. Director. Films: "Davy Crockett in Hearts United" 1909; "A True Indian's Heart" 1909; "His Better Self" 1912 (& sp.); "Mary of the Mines" 1912; "The Hidden Spring" 1917 (sp. only); "The Promise" 1917; "Under Handicap" 1917 (& sp.); "The Three Buckaroos" 1922 (& sp.).

Baltieri, Carlo. Screenwriter. Films: "Once Upon a Time in the Wild, Wild West" 1969-Ital.

Band, Albert (Alfredo Antonini) (1924-). Director. Films: "The Young Guns" 1956; "Gringo" 1963-Span./Ital. (prod./sp. only); "Massacre at Grant Canyon" 1963-Ital. (& prod./sp.); "The Tramplers" 1965-Ital. (& prod./sp.); "The Hellbenders" 1966-U.S./Ital./Span. (prod./sp. only); "A Minute to Pray, a Second to Die" 1967-Ital. (story only).

Banks, Charles. Screenwriter. Films: "A California Romance" 1923.

Bankson, Russell A. Writer. Films: "Feud of the West" 1936 (story).

Bar, Jacques (1921-). Producer. Films: "Guns for San Sebastian" 1967-U.S./Fr./Mex./Ital.

Barbash, Bob (1919-12/4/95). Screenwriter. Films: "The Plunderers" 1960.

Barboni, Enzo (E.B. Clucher). Director. Films: "Chuck Moll" 1970-Ital.; "They Call Me Trinity" 1970-Ital. (& sp.); "They Call Him Cemetery" 1971-Ital./Span. (sp. only); "A Man from the East" 1974-Ital./Fr. (& sp.); "Trinity Is Still My Name" 1974-Ital. (& sp.).

Bare, Richard L. (1909-). Director. Films: "Two-Gun Troubador" 1939 (sp. only); "Return of the Frontiersman" 1950; "So You Want to Be a Cowboy" 1951-short; "Shoot-Out at Medicine Bend" 1957. ¶TV: *Cheyenne* 1955; *Broken Arrow* 1956; *Colt .45* 1957; *Sugarfoot* 1957; *Maverick*—"Hostage!" 11-10-57, "Rope of Cards" 1-19-58, "The Seventh Hand" 3-2-58, "Seed of Deception" 4-13-58, "Lonesome Reunion" 9-28-58, "High Card Hangs" 10-19-58, "The Judas Mask" 11-2-58, "The Thirty-Ninth Star" 11-16-58, "Holiday at Hollow Rock" 12-28-58, "The Lass with the Poisonous Air" 11-1-59, "Trooper Maverick" 11-29-59; *Lawman* 1958; *The Dakotas* 1963; *The Virginian*—"If You Have Tears" 2-13-63, "Run Away Home" 4-24-63, "Felicity's Springs" 10-14-64; *Alias Smith and Jones*—Bad Night in Big Butte" 3-2-72.

Baretti, Bruno. Screenwriter. Films: "Fury of Johnny Kid" 1967-Span./Ital.

Barker, Buddy. Writer. Films: "Biff Bang Buddy" 1924 (story).

Barker, Reginald (1886-2/23/45). Director. Films: "Broncho Billy's Adventure" 1911; "The Indian Maiden's Lesson" 1911; "Broncho Billy's Bible" 1912; "For the Honor of the 7th" 1912; "The Sergeant's Boy" 1912; "The Bargain" 1914; "His Hour of Manhood" 1914; "Jim Cameron's Wife" 1914; "The Man from Oregon" 1915; "On the Night Stage" 1915; "The Bugle Call" 1916; "Jim Grimsby's Boy" 1916; "Golden Rule Kate" 1917; "Carmen of the Klondike" 1918; "The Hell Cat" 1918; "The Rustlers" 1919; "The Branding Iron" 1920; "The Storm" 1922; "The Eternal Struggle" 1923; "The Great Divide" 1925; "Quicker'n Lightnin'" 1925 (story only); "The Flaming Forest" 1926; "The Frontiersman" 1927; "The Great Divide" 1929; "The Rainbow" 1929.

Barker, Ron. Writer. Films: "Day of Anger" 1967-Ital./Ger. (story).

Barnes, Charles E. Writer. Films: "Ivory-Handled Gun" 1935 (story).

Barnes, Forrest. Screenwriter. Films: "Valley of Wanted Men" 1935; "Western Gold" 1937.

Barni, Aldo. Screenwriter. Films: "In a Colt's Shadow" 1965-Ital./Span.

Baron, Alexander. Screenwriter. Films: "Robbery Under Arms" 1958-Brit.

Barrett, James Lee (1929-10/15/89). Screenwriter. Films: "Shenandoah" 1965; "Bandolero!" 1968; "The Undefeated" 1969; "The Cheyenne Social Club" 1970; "Fools' Parade" 1971; "Something Big" 1971; "The Awakening Land" TVM-1978; "Belle Starr" TVM-1980; "Stagecoach" TVM-1986; "Poker Alice" TVM-1987; "The Quick and the Dead" CTVM-1987.

Barrett, Michael. Writer. Films: "The Reward" 1965 (story).

Barringer, Barry (1889-5/21/38). Screenwriter. Films: "Dynamite Ranch" 1932; "The Dude Ranger" 1934; "The Way of the West" 1934 (story only); "Northern Frontier" 1935; "Red Blood of Courage" 1935; "Valley of Wanted Men" 1935; "Song of the Trail" 1936.

Barringer, R.E. Screenwriter. Films: "Riders of the Rio" 1931.

Barron, Joseph. Director. TV: *The Big Valley*—"The Way to Kill a Killer" 11-24-65.

Barrows, Nicholas T. Screenwriter. Films: "The Gold Ghost" 1934-short; "I'm from the City" 1938.

Barry, Don "Red" (1912-7/17/80). Director. Films: "Train to Tombstone" 1950 (story only); "Jesse James' Women" 1954; "Convict Stage" 1954 (story only).

Barry, Philip (1896-1949). Writer. Films: "Ten Scars Make a Man" 1924-serial (story).

Barry, Tom (1884-11/7/31). Screenwriter. Films: "In Old Arizona" 1929.

Barry, Wesley (1906-4/11/94). Director. Films: "The Outlaw's Daughter" 1954 (& prod.). ¶TV: *Wild Bill Hickok* 1951-53 (assoc. prod.).

Barsha, Leon. Producer. Films: "One Man Justice" 1937 (dir. only); "Trapped" 1937; "Two-Fisted Sheriff" 1937; "Two Gun Law" 1937; "The Taming of the West" 1939; "Beyond the Sacramento" 1940; "The Man from Tumbleweeds" 1940; "Pioneers of the Frontier" 1940; "The Return of Wild Bill" 1940; "Texas Stagecoach" 1940; "Two-Fisted Rangers" 1940; "West of Abilene" 1940; "King of Dodge City" 1941; "North from the Lone Star" 1941; "The Return of Daniel Boone" 1941;

"Roaring Frontiers" 1941; "The Son of Davy Crockett" 1941; "Wildcat of Tucson" 1941; "Bullets for Bandits" 1942; "The Devil's Trail" 1942; "The Lone Prairie" 1942; "The Lone Star Vigilantes" 1942; "North of the Rockies" 1942; "Prairie Gunsmoke" 1942; "A Tornado in the Saddle" 1942; "Vengeance of the West" 1942; "Riders of the Northwest Mounted" 1943; "Saddles and Sagebrush" 1943; "Silver City Raiders" 1943; "The Last Horseman" 1944; "The Vigilantes Ride" 1944; "Wyoming Hurricane" 1944.

Bartel, Paul (1938-). Director. Films: "Lust in the Dust" 1985.

Bartlett, Charles. Director. Films: "Dangerous Love" 1920; "Tangled Trails" 1921 (& story); "Headin' North" 1922.

Bartlett, Hall (1922-9/8/93). Director. Films: "Navajo" 1952 (prod. only); "Drango" 1957 (& prod./sp.).

Bartlett, Juanita. Screenwriter. Films: "The New Maverick" TVM-1978; "No Man's Land" TVM-1984.

Bartlett, Lanier. Screenwriter. Films: "On the Little Big Horn or Custer's Last Stand" 1909; "The Trimming of Paradise Gulch" 1910 (story only); "The Curse of the Red Man" 1911; "In Old California When the Gringos Came" 1911 (story only); "Kit Carson's Wooing" 1911; "Romance of the Rio Grande" 1911 (story only); "The Schoolmaster of Mariposa" 1911 (story only); "The Bandit's Mask" 1912; "The Little Indian Martyr" 1912; "A Reconstructed Rebel" 1912 (story only); "Sergeant Byrne of the N.W.M.P." 1912 (story only); "The Shrinking Rawhide" 1912; "In the Long Ago" 1913; "Vengeance Is Mine" 1913; "Jim Grimsby's Boy" 1916; "Man Above the Law" 1918 (story only); "Tongues of Flame" 1918; "The Arizona Streak" 1926; "The Lash" 1930 (story only).

Bartlett, Richard H. Director. Films: "The Lonesome Trail" 1955 (& sp.); "The Silver Star" 1955 (& sp.); "Two-Gun Lady" 1956 (& prod./story); "Joe Dakota" 1957; "Slim Carter" 1957; "Money, Women and Guns" 1958. ¶TV: *Wagon Train*—"The Sarah Drummond Story" 4-2-58, "The Daniel Barrister Story" 4-16-58, "The Dan Hogan Story" 5-14-58, "The Ruttledge Munroe Story" 5-21-58, "The Sacramento Story" 6-25-58, "The Tent City Story" 12-10-58, "The Beauty Jamison Story" 12-17-58, "The Ruth Marshall Story" 12-30-59; *Cimarron City* 1958-59 (prod.); *Riverboat* 1959-61 (prod.); *Bonanza*—"Day of Reckoning" 10-22-60; *Laredo*—"The Small Chance Ghost" 3-3-67.

Bartlett, Sy (1900-5/29/78). Screenwriter. Films: "The Last Command" 1955 (story only); "The Big Country" 1958.

Bartlett, Virginia Stivers. Writer. Films: "The Lash" 1930 (story).

Bartlett, William. Screenwriter. Films: "Call of the Yukon" 1938.

Barton, Charles (1902-12/5/81). Director. Films: "Wagon Wheels" 1934; "Nevada" 1935; "Rocky Mountain Mystery" 1935; "Born to the West" 1937; "Forlorn River" 1937; "Thunder Trail" 1937; "Out West with the Peppers" 1940; "Shut My Big Mouth" 1942; "The Wistful Widow of Wagon Gap" 1947. ¶TV: *Zorro*—"Agent of the Eagle" 2-20-58, "Zorro Springs a Trap" 2-27-58, "The Unmasking of Zorro" 3-6-58, "Adios, Senor Magistrado" 4-3-58, "The Eagle's Brood" 4-10-58, "Zorro by Proxy" 4-17-58, "Quintana Makes a Choice" 4-24-58, "Zorro Lights a Fuse" 5-1-58, "The Tightening Noose" 6-5-58, "The Sergeant Regrets" 6-12-58, "The Eagle Leaves the Nest" 6-19-58, "Bernardo Faces Death" 6-26-58, "Day of Decision" 7-3-58, "An Eye for an Eye" 11-20-58, "Zorro and the Flag of Truce" 11-27-58, "Ambush" 12-4-58, "The Mountain Man" 3-19-59.

Bartsch, Joachim. Screenwriter. Films: "The Desperado Trail" 1965-Ger./Yugo.; "The Last Tomahawk" 1965-Ger./Ital./Span.

Bass, Milton R. (1923-). Writer. Films: "Jory" 1972 (story).

Bassler, Robert (1903-). Producer. Films: "Smoky" 1946; "Green Grass of Wyoming" 1948; "Ticket to Tomahawk" 1950; "Kangaroo" 1952; "The Silver Whip" 1953; "Gunsight Ridge" 1957. ¶TV: *The Californians* 1957-59; *Buckskin* 1958-59.

Bast, William E. Screenwriter. Films: "The Valley of Gwangi" 1969.

Bastia, Jean. Director. Films: "Dynamite Jack" 1963-Fr. (& sp).

Battaglia, Enzo. Screenwriter. Films: "Two Crosses at Danger Pass" 1968-Ital./Span.

Battista, Lloyd. Screenwriter. Films: "Get Mean" 1975-Ital.; "Comin' at Ya" 1981-Ital.

Battistrada, Lucio. Screenwriter. Films: "Stranger in Paso Bravo" 1968-Ital.

Battle, Gordon. Screenwriter. Films: "Treason" 1933.

Battle, John Tucker (1902-10/31/62). Screenwriter. Films: "A Man Alone" 1955; "Shoot-Out at Medicine Bend" 1957.

Batzella, Luigi (Paolo Solvay, Dean Jones, Arpad De Riso, Fred Lynn Morris). Director. Films: "Lost Treasure of the Incas" 1965-Ger./Ital./Fr./Span.; "Evan Django Has His Price" 1971-Ital./Span. (& sp.); "God Is My Colt .45" 1972-Ital. (& sp.); "In the Name of the Father, the Son and the Colt" 1972-Fr./Ital.; "Paid in Blood" 1972-Ital. (& sp.); "They Called Him Trinity" 1972-Ital./Span.; "Thunder Over El Paso" 1972-Ital./Span. (sp. only).

Baudry, Alain. Screenwriter. Films: "Last of the Mohicans" 1965-Ital./Span./Ger.

Bauman, W.J. Director. Films: "When the West Was Young" 1913; "The Perils of Thunder Mountain" 1919-serial.

Baur, Frank. Director. TV: *Black Saddle* 1959; *Johnny Ringo* 1959; *Wichita Town* 1959-60 (& exec. prod.).

Bava, Mario (John M. Olds) (1914-4/27/80). Director. Films: "The Road to Fort Alamo" 1966-Fr./Ital.; "Savage Gringo" 1966-Ital.; "Roy Colt and Winchester Jack" 1970-Ital.

Baxley, Craig R. Director. Films: "The Avenging Angel" TVM-1995.

Baxter, George Owen. *see* Brand, Max.

Bayer, T.P. Screenwriter. Films: "The Broken Ways" 1913.

Bayley, Wilson. Screenwriter. Films: "Oh, Johnny!" 1918.

Bayonas, J. Luis. Screenwriter. Films: "Fifteen Scaffolds for the Killer" 1968-Ital./Span.

Bazzoni, Camillo (Alex Burks). Director. Films: "A Long Ride from Hell" 1968-Ital.

Bazzoni, Luigi (Marc Meyer). Director. Films: "Man: His Pride and His Vengeance" 1967-Ital./Ger. (& sp.); "Brothers Blue" 1973-Ital./Fr.

Beach, Rex. Writer. Films: "The Spoilers" 1914 (story); "Pardners" 1917 (story); "Heart of the Sunset" 1918 (story); "Laughing Bill Hyde" 1918 (story); "The Spoilers" 1923 (story); "The Silver Horde" 1930 (story); "The Spoilers" 1930 (story); "The Barrier" 1937 (story); "The Spoilers" 1942 (story); "The Michigan Kid" 1947 (story); "The Spoilers" 1955 (story).

Beal, Frank (1862-12/20/34). Director. Films: "The Law of the North" 1912; "Chasing Rainbows" 1919.

Beale, Will. Writer. Films: "Partners of the Trail" 1931.

Beaton, Alex. Director. Films: "Scott Free" TVM-1976. ¶TV: *Kung Fu* 1972-75 (prod.), "Ambush" 4-5-75, "The Last Raid" 4-26-75.

Beauchamp, Clem. Director. Films: "Westward Ho-Hum" 1941-short.

Beauchamp, Daniel D. (1909-3/20/69). Screenwriter. Films: "The Wistful Widow of Wagon Gap" 1947 (story only); "River Lady" 1948; "Belle Le Grand" 1951; "The San Francisco Story" 1952; "Gunsmoke" 1953; "Law and Order" 1953; "The Man from the Alamo" 1953; "Son of Belle Star" 1953; "Destry" 1954; "Jesse James' Women" 1954; "Rails into Laramie" 1954; "Man Without a Star" 1955; "Tennessee's Partner" 1955; "Massacre" 1956; "The Rawhide Years" 1956; "Yaqui Drums" 1956; "Shoot-Out at Medicine Bend" 1957; "Alias Jesse James" 1959; "For the Love of Mike" 1960; "Natchez Trace" 1960; "A Man Called Gannon" 1969.

Beaudine, William (1892-3/18/70). Director. Films: "Catch My Smoke" 1922; "Bowery Buckaroos" 1947; "Gas House Kids Go West" 1947; "Tough Assignment" 1949; "Jiggs and Maggie Out West" 1950; "Rodeo" 1952; "Born to the Saddle" 1953; "Yukon Vengeance" 1954; "Westward Ho the Wagons" 1956; "Ten Who Dared" 1960; "Billy the Kid vs. Dracula" 1966; "Jesse James Meets Frankenstein's Daughter" 1966. ¶TV: *Broken Arrow* 1956.

Beaumont, Gabrielle. Director. TV: *Zorro and Son* 1983.

Beaumont, Gerald. Writer. Films: "Outlaws of Red River" 1927 (story).

Beaumont, Harry (1888-12/22/66). Director. Films: "Go West, Young Man" 1918; "Getting Some" 1920; "Lights of the Desert" 1922.

Beaver, Lee W. *see* Lizzani, Carlo.

Bechdolt, Frederick R. Writer. Films: "Thieves' Gold" 1918 (story).

Beche, Robert. Screenwriter. Films: "The Lone Ranger Rides Again" 1939-serial (& prod.).

Beck, John (1910-7/18/93). Producer. Films: "Fury at Showdown" 1957.

Beebe, Dick. Screenwriter. Films: "Into the Badlands" TVM-1991.

Beebe, Ford I. (1888-1978). Director. Films: "The Big Catch" 1920 (sp. only); "Double Danger" 1920 (sp. only); "A Gamblin' Fool" 1920; "The Grinning Granger" 1920 (sp. only); "'In Wrong' Wright" 1920 (sp. only); "Marryin' Marion" 1920 (sp. only); "One Law for All" 1920 (sp. only); "A Pair of Twins" 1920 (story only); "Teacher's Pet" 1920 (sp. only); "Tipped Off" 1920 (sp. only); "The Trail of the Hound" 1920 (sp. only); "The Two-Fisted Lover" 1920 (sp. only); "The Driftin' Kid" 1921 (sp. only); "Kickaroo" 1921 (sp. only); "No Man's Woman" 1921 (sp. only); "The Saddle King" 1921 (sp. only); "Sweet Revenge" 1921 (sp. only); "The White Horseman" 1921-serial (sp. only); "Winners of the West" 1921-serial (sp. only); "The Bar Cross War" 1922 (sp. only); "Deputized" 1922 (sp. only); "Here's Your Man" 1922 (sp. only); "His Enemy's Friend" 1922 (& sp.); "His Own Law" 1922 (sp. only); "Nine Points of the Law" 1922 (sp. only); "One Jump Ahead" 1922 (sp. only); "Rough Going" 1922; "Under Suspicion" 1922 (sp. only); "The Extra Seven" 1923 (sp. only); "Hyde and Zeke" 1923; "In Wrong Right" 1923 (sp. only); "King's Creek Law" 1923 (sp. only); "Lost, Strayed or Stolen" 1923 (sp. only); "100% Nerve" 1923 (sp. only); "Partners Three" 1923 (sp. only); "Smoked Out" 1923 (story only); "Steel Shod Evidence" 1923 (sp. only); "Tom, Dick and Harry" 1923 (sp. only); "The Unsuspecting Stranger" 1923 (sp. only); "Warned in Advance" 1923 (sp. only); "When Fighting's Necessary" 1923 (sp. only); "Wings of the Storm" 1923 (sp. only); "Yellow Gold and Men" 1923 (sp. only); "Headin' Through" 1924 (sp. only); "Huntin' Trouble" 1924 (sp. only); "The Loser's End" 1924; "Not Guilty for Runnin'" 1924 (sp. only); "Payable on Demand" 1924 (sp. only); "The Perfect Alibi" 1924 (sp. only); "Riding Double" 1924 (sp. only); "Across the Deadline" 1925 (story only); "The Blood Bond" 1925 (sp. only); "Flash O'Lightning" 1925 (sp. only); "Luck and Sand" 1925 (sp. only); "Ranchers and Rascals 1925 (sp. only); "The Shield of Silence" 1925 (sp. only); "The Trouble Buster" 1925 (sp. only); "Win, Lose or Draw" 1925 (story only); "The High Hand" 1926 (sp. only); "The Outlaw Express" 1926 (sp. only); "Without Orders" 1926 (sp. only); "Border Blackbirds" 1927 (sp. only); "The Devi's Twin" 1927 (sp. only); "Don Desperado" 1927 (sp. only); "The Long Loop on the Pecos" 1927; "The Man

from Hardpan" 1927 (sp. only); "Two-Gun of the Tumbleweed" 1927 (sp. only); "The Apache Raider" 1928 (sp. only); "The Black Ace" 1928 (sp. only); "The Boss of Rustler's Roost" 1928 (sp. only); "The Bronc Stomper" 1928 (sp. only); "Code of the Scarlet" 1928 (sp. only); "The Wagon Show" 1928 (sp. only); "45 Calibre War" 1929 (sp. only); "Overland Bound" 1929 (sp./story only); "The Indians Are Coming" 1930-serial (sp. only); "Oklahoma Cyclone" 1930 (sp. only); "Lightning Warrior" 1931-serial (sp. only); "Alias the Bad Man" 1931 (story only); "The Vanishing Legion" 1931-serial (& sp); "The Last of the Mohicans" 1932-serial (& sp.); "The Law of the Wild" 1934-serial (story only); "The Prescott Kid" 1934 (sp. only); "Fighting Shadows" 1935 (sp. only); "Gallant Defender" 1935 (sp. only); "Justice of the Range" 1935 (sp. only); "Law Beyond the Range" 1935; "The Man from Guntown" 1935 (& sp.); "The Outlaw Deputy" 1935 (sp. only); "The Revenge Rider" 1935 (sp. only); "Riding Wild" 1935 (sp. only); "Tumbling Tumbleweeds" 1935 (sp. only); "The Mysterious Avenger" 1936 (sp. only); "Stampede" 1936; "Code of the Range 1937 (sp. only); "Wild West Days" 1937-serial; "Oklahoma Frontier" 1939 (& sp.); "The Oregon Trail" 1939-serial; "Riders of the Black River" 1939 (story only); "The Stranger from Texas" 1939 (story only); "Riders of Pasco Basin" 1940 (sp. only); "Son of Roaring Dan" 1940; "Winners of the West" 1940-serial; "The Masked Rider" 1941; "Riders of Death Valley" 1941-serial; "Overland Mail" 1942-serial; "Frontier Badman" 1943 (& sp.); "Six Gun Serenade" 1947; "Courtin' Trouble" 1948; "The Dalton Gang" 1949 (& sp.); "Red Desert" 1949; "Satan's Cradle" 1949; "Davy Crockett, Indian Scout" 1950 (story only); "The Girl from San Lorenzo" 1950 (sp. only); "I Shot Billy the Kid" 1950 (sp. only); "Wagons West" 1952; "King of the Wild Stallions" 1959 (sp. only). ¶TV: *The Adventures of Champion* 1955.

Beebe, Francis. Screenwriter. Films: "King's Creek Law" 1923; "Headin' Through" 1924; "Huntin' Trouble" 1924; "Payable on Demand" 1924; "The Perfect Alibi" 1924; "Riding Double" 1924.

Beecher, Elizabeth. Screenwriter. Films: "Underground Rustlers" 1941; "Little Joe, the Wrangler" 1942; "The Silver Bullet" 1942; "Texas Trouble Shooters" 1942; "Bullets and Saddles" 1943; "Cowboy Commandos" 1943; "Cowboy in the

Clouds" 1943; "The Haunted Ranch" 1943; "Land of Hunted Men" 1943; "Tenting Tonight on the Old Camp Ground" 1943; "Wild Horse Stampede" 1943; "Cyclone Prairie Rangers" 1944; "Death Valley Rangers" 1944; "Saddle Leather Law" 1944; "Swing in the Saddle" 1944; "Rough Riders of Cheyenne" 1945; "Rough Ridin' Justice" 1945; "Sing Me a Song of Texas" 1945; "Lawless Empire" 1946 (story only).

Beeman, Greg. Director. TV: *Adventures of Brisco County, Jr.*— "Socrates' Sister" 9-24-93.

Behrman, S.N. (1893-9/9/73). Screenwriter. Films: "Cowboy and the Lady" 1938.

Beich, Albert (1919-). Writer. Films: "A Distant Trumpet" 1964 (adapt.).

Belasco, David (1853-5/14/31). Writer. Films: "Rose of the Rancho" 1914 (story); "The Girl I Left Behind Me" 1915 (story); "The Girl of the Golden West" 1915 (story); "The Girl of the Golden West" 1923 (story); "Tiger Rose" 1923 (story); "Tiger Rose" 1929 (story); "Girl of the Golden West" 1930 (story); "Rose of the Rancho" 1936 (story); "The Girl of the Golden West" 1938 (story); "The Girl of the Golden West" 1942-Ital. (story).

Belden, Charles S. (1903-11/3/54). Screenwriter. Films: "God's Country and the Woman" 1937 (story only); "Beauty and the Bandit" 1946; "The Gay Cavalier" 1946; "South of Monterey" 1946; "The Marauders" 1947; "Borrowed Trouble" 1948; "Silent Conflict" 1948.

Belgard, Arnold (1908-7/1/67). Screenwriter. Films: "Bar 20 Justice" 1938; "Triple Justice" 1940 (story only); "Calaboose" 1943; "Prairie Chickens" 1943; "Tucson" 1949.

Bell, Brand. Writer. Films: "Santee" 1973 (story).

Bell, Edward. Screenwriter. Films: "The Sheriff's Baby" 1913.

Bell, Emma. Screenwriter. Films: "The Conversion of Smiling Tom" 1915; "The Taking of Mustang Pete" 1915 (story only).

Bellah, James Warner (1899-9/22/76). Screenwriter. Films: "Fort Apache" 1948 (story only); "She wore a Yellow Ribbon" 1949 (story only); "Rio Grande" 1950 (story only); "The Command" 1953 (story only); "Sergeant Rutledge" 1960 (& story); "A Thunder of Drums" 1961; "The Man Who Shot Liberty Valance" 1962; "The Legend of Nigger Charley" 1972 (story only).

Bellamy, Earl (1917-). Director. Films: "Seminole Uprising" 1955; "Blackjack Ketchum, Desperado" 1956; "Toughest Gun in Tombstone" 1958; "Stagecoach to Dancer's Rock" 1962 (& prod.); "Gunpoint" 1966; "Incident at Phantom Hill" 1966; "Desperate Mission" TVM-1971; "The Trackers" TVM-1971; "Seven Alone" 1974; "Against a Crooked Sky" 1975. ¶TV: *The Adventures of Rin Tin Tin* 1954; *Sergeant Preston of the Yukon* 1955; *Sheriff of Cochise* 1956; *The Lone Ranger*—"White Hawk's Decision" 10-18-56, "Hot Spell in Panamint" 11-22-56, "Christmas Story" 12-20-56, "The Courage of Tonto" 1-17-57, "The Breaking Point" 1-24-57, "Outlaws in Grease Paint" 6-6-57; *Wagon Train*—"The Clara Beauchamp Story" 12-11-57, "The Gabe Carswell Story" 1-15-58; *U.S. Marshal* 1958; *Laramie* 1959; *The Virginian*—"The Big Deal" 10-10-62, "The Judgment" 1-16-63, "We've Lost a Train" 4-21-65; *Rawhide*—"Incident at El Crucero" 10-10-63; *Laredo*—"The Golden Trail" 11-4-65, "No Bugles, One Drum" 2-24-66, "The Would-Be Gentleman of Laredo" 4-14-66; *The Monroes*—"Ride with Terror" 9-21-66; *The Quest*—"The Buffalo Hunters" 9-29-76; *Young Dan'l Boone* 1977.

Belmore, Lionel (1868-1/30/53). Director. Films: "Britton of the Seventh" 1916.

Beloin, Edmund (1910-5/26/92). Screenwriter. Films: "Buck Benny Rides Again" 1940; "The Harvey Girls" 1946.

Belson, Jerry. Screenwriter. Films: "Evil Roy Slade" TVM-1972 (& prod.).

Bender, Jack. Director. Films: "The Gambler V: Playing for Keeps" TVM-1994. ¶TV: *Ned Blessing: The Story of My Life and Times*—"Return to Plum Creek" 8-18-93, "A Ghost Story" 8-25-93.

Bender, Russ (1910-8/16/69). Screenwriter. Films: "The Purple Hills" 1961; "The Broken Land" 1962.

Benedek, Laslo (1907-3/11/92). Director. Films: "The Kissing Bandit" 1948. ¶TV: *Rawhide*—"The Peddler" 1-19-62.

Benedict, Kingsley (1878-11/27/51). Screenwriter. Films: "The Stampede" 1921; "White Thunder" 1925.

Benedict, Richard (1916-5/25/84). Director. TV: *Lawman* 1958; *Laredo*—"Above the Law" 1-13-66; *The High Chaparral*—"The Doctor from Dodge" 10-29-67, "Ride the

Savage Land" 2-11-68, "The Peacemaker" 3-3-68, "A Joyful Noise" 3-24-68; *The Men from Shiloh* 1970; *Alias Smith and Jones*—The Great Shell Game" 2-18-71, "Stagecoach Seven" 3-11-71, "The Man Who Broke the Bank at Red Gap" 1-20-72.

Bennet, Spencer Gordon (1893-10/8/87). Director. Films: "Hawk of the Hills" 1927-serial; "The Yellow Cameo" 1928-serial; "Queen of the Northwoods" 1929-serial; "Rogue of the Rio Grande" 1930; "99 Wounds" 1931; "The Last Frontier" 1932-serial; "Jaws of Justice" 1933; "The Ferocious Pal" 1934; "Heir to Trouble" 1935; "Lawless Riders" 1935; "Western Courage" 1935; "Avenging Waters" 1936; "The Cattle Thief" 1936; "The Fugitive Sheriff" 1936; "Heroes of the Range" 1936; "The Phantom Rider" 1936-serial; "Rio Grande Ranger" 1936; "The Unknown Ranger" 1936; "Law of the Ranger" 1937; "Ranger Courage" 1937; "The Rangers Step In" 1937; "Reckless Ranger" 1937; "Across the Plains" 1939; "Oklahoma Terror" 1939; "Riders of the Frontier" 1939; "Westbound Stage" 1939; "Cowboy from Sundown" 1940; "Arizona Bound" 1941; "The Gunman from Bodie" 1941; "Ridin' the Cherokee Trail" 1941; "Valley of Vanishing Men" 1942-serial; "California Joe" 1943; "Calling Wild Bill Elliott" 1943; "Canyon City" 1943; "Beneath Western Skies" 1944; "Code of the Prairie" 1944; "Mojave Firebrand" 1944; "Tucson Raiders" 1944; "Zorro's Black Whip" 1944-serial; "Lone Texas Ranger" 1945; "King of the Forest Rangers" 1946-serial; "Son of Zorro" 1947-serial; "Cody of the Pony Express" 1950-serial; "Roar of the Iron Horse" 1950-serial; "Brave Warrior" 1952; "Son of Geronimo" 1952-serial; "Gunfighters of the Northwest" 1954-serial; "Riding with Buffalo Bill" 1954-serial; "Blazing the Overland Trail" 1956-serial; "Perils of the Wilderness" 1956-serial; "The Bounty Killer" 1965; "Requiem for a Gunfighter" 1965.

Bennett, Charles. Director. Films: "The Snowshoe Trail" 1922

Bennett, Charles (1900-6/15/95). Screenwriter. Films: "Unconquered" 1947.

Bennett, Chester. Director. Films: "Belle of Alaska" 1922.

Bennett, Connie Lee. Screenwriter. Films: "The Lady from Texas" 1951; "The Last Posse" 1953.

Bennett, Emerson. Writer. Films: "The Forest Rose" 1912 (& story).

Bennett, Richard. TV: *Alias Smith and Jones*—"The Strange Fate of Conrad Meyer Zulick" 12-2-72, "Witness to a Lynching" 12-16-72.

Bennett, Seymour. Screenwriter. Films: "The Last Posse" 1953.

Bennett-Thompson, Lillian. Writer. Films: "The Love Gambler" 1922 (story); "Without Compromise" 1922 (story).

Bennison, Andrew (1887-1/7/42). Screenwriter. Films: "Undercover Man" 1936; "Back to the Woods" 1937-short; "Lawless Land" 1937; "Chip of the Flying U" 1939; "Desperate Trails" 1939.

Benson, Hugh. Producer. Films: "The Castaway Cowboy" 1974 (story only); "Honky Tonk" TVM-1974. ¶TV: *The Outcasts* 1968-69.

Benson, Leon. Director. TV: *The Virginian*—"The Awakening" 10-13-65, "Show Me a Hero" 11-17-65, "Men with Guns" 1-12-66; *Laredo*—"Which Way Did They Go?" 11-18-65, "The Deadliest Kid in the West" 3-31-66; *Wild Wild West*—"The Night of the Cadre" 3-24-67; *Bonanza*—"Second Chance" 9-17-67, "Night of Reckoning" 10-15-67, "Desperate Passage" 11-5-67, "Check Rein" 12-3-67, "A Girl Named George" 1-14-68, "The Thirteenth Man" 1-21-68, "The Price of Salt" 2-4-68, "The Crime of Johnny Mule" 2-25-68, "The Late Ben Cartwright" 3-3-68, "Trouble Town" 3-17-68, "Commitment at Angelus" 4-7-68, "The Bottle Fighter" 5-12-68, "The Stronghold" 5-26-68, "Different Pines, Same Wind" 9-15-68, "Child" 9-22-68, "Salute to Yesterday" 9-29-68, "The Real People of Muddy Creek" 10-6-68, "The Passing of a King" 10-13-68, "The Survivors" 11-10-68, "Queen High" 12-1-68, "Mark of Guilt" 12-15-68, "My Friend, My Enemy" 1-12-69, "Mrs. Wharton and the Lesser Breeds" 1-19-69, "The Deserter" 3-16-69, "Emily" 3-23-69, "The Running Man" 3-30-69, "Speak No Evil" 4-20-69, "A Ride in the Sun" 5-11-69, "To Stop a War" 10-19-69, "The Trouble with Amy" 1-25-70, "The Lady and the Mark" 2-1-70, "The Gold Mine" 3-8-70; *The High Chaparral*—"The Ghost of Chaparral" 9-17-67, "A Hanging Offense" 11-12-67, "Time of Your Life" 9-19-69, "A Time to Laugh, a Time to Cry" 9-26-69, "The Brothers Cannon" 10-3-69, "A Piece of Land" 10-10-69, "The Journal of Death" 1-9-70, "It Takes a Smart Man" 10-23-70, "The Hostage" 3-5-71.

Benton, Curtis. Screenwriter. Films: "The Phantom Bullet" 1926.

Benton, Douglas. Writer. Films: "The Bravos" TVM-1972 (story). ¶TV: *Hec Ramsey* 1972-74 (prod.).

Benton, Robert (1932-). Director. Films: "There Was a Crooked Man" 1970 (sp. only); "Bad Company" 1972 (& sp.).

Benvenuti, Leo. Screenwriter. Films: "Find a Place to Die" 1968-Ital.

Beranger, George Andre (1893-3/8/73). Director. Films: "Western Luck" 1924.

Bercovici, Eric. Screenwriter. Films: "Day of the Evil Gun" 1968; "The Culpepper Cattle Company" 1972; "Take a Hard Ride" 1974-Ital./ Brit./Ger.; "Cowboy" TVM-1983 (prod. only).

Bercutt, Max. Screenwriter. Films: "Cactus Capers" 1942-short; "Range Rhythm" 1942-short (story only).

Berenges, Barry. Screenwriter. Films: "Timber War" 1935.

Beresford, Bruce (1940-). Director. Films: "Black Robe" 1991-Can./Australia.

Beresford, Frank. Screenwriter. Films: "The Border Raiders" 1918; "The Devil's Trail" 1919 (story only); "The Millionaire Cowboy" 1924; "Blue Blazes" 1926; "Chasing Trouble" 1926; "The Escape" 1926; "Painted Ponies" 1927.

Berg, Alex. Screenwriter. Films: "Massacre at Marble City" 1964-Ger./Ital./Fr.

Berger, Hal. Writer. Films: "King of the Arena" 1933 (story).

Berger, Rea. Director. Films: "Three Pals" 1916.

Berger, Richard H. Producer. Films: "Rachel and the Stranger" 1948; "Roughshod" 1949.

Berger, Thomas (1924-). Writer. Films: "Little Big Man" 1971 (story).

Bergerman, Stanley. Producer. Films: "Destry Rides Again" 1932; "Rider of Death Valley" 1932 (story only).

Bergman, Andrew (1945-). Screenwriter. Films: "Blazing Saddles" 1974.

Bergman, Helmer. Screenwriter. Films: "Senor Americano" 1929 (story only); "The Vanishing Legion" 1931-serial.

Bergonzelli, Sergio. Director. Films: "Last Gun" 1964-Ital.; "Stranger in Sacramento" 1964-Ital. (& sp.); "Cisco" 1966-Ital. (& sp.); "Colt in the Hand of the Devil" 1967-Ital. (&

sp.); "Raise Your Hands, Dead Man ... You're Under Arrest" 1971-Ital./Span. (sp. only).

Berk, Howard. Screenwriter. Films: "The Bang Bang Kid" 1968-U.S./Span./Ital.

Berke, William (Lester Williams) (1903-2/15/58). Director. Films: "The Last of the Clintons" 1935 (prod. only); "The Pecos Kid" 1935 (& prod.); "Rustlers' Paradise" 1935 (prod. only); "Wagon Trail" 1935 (prod. only); "Wild Mustang" 1935 (prod. only); "Desert Justice" 1936 (& prod.); "Ghost Town" 1936 (prod. only); "Gun Grit" 1936 (& prod.); "Hair-Trigger Casey" 1936 (prod. only); "Toll of the Desert" 1936 (& prod.); "Wildcat Saunders" 1936 (prod. only); "Aces Wild" 1937 (prod. only); "Ghost Town Gold" 1937 (prod. only); "Call the Mesquiteers" 1938 (prod. only); "Heroes of the Hills" 1938 (prod. only); "Outlaws of Sonora" 1938 (prod. only); "Overland Stage Raiders" 1938 (prod. only); "Pals of the Saddle" 1938 (prod. only); "Red River Range" 1938 (prod. only); "Riders of the Black Hills" 1938 (prod. only); "Santa Fe Stampede" 1938; "Three Texas Steers" 1938; "Colorado Sunset" 1939 (prod. only); "New Frontier" 1939 (prod. only); "The Night Riders" 1939 (prod. only); "Rovin' Tumbleweeds" 1939; "South of the Border" 1939; "Wyoming Outlaw" 1939 (prod. only); "Carolina Moon" 1940 (prod. only); "Gaucho Serenade" 1940; "Ride, Tenderfoot, Ride" 1940 (prod. only); "Prairie Stranger" 1941 (prod. only); "Riders of the Badlands" 1941 (prod. only); "The Royal Mounted Patrol" 1941 (prod. only); "Thunder Over the Prairie" 1941 (prod. only); "Bad Men of the Hills" 1942; "Down Rio Grande Way" 1942; "Lawless Plainsmen" 1942; "The Lone Prairie" 1942; "Overland to Deadwood" 1942; "Pardon My Gun" 1942; "Riders of the Northland" 1942; "Riding Through Nevada" 1942; "A Tornado in the Saddle" 1942; "West of Tombstone" 1942 (prod. only); "The Fighting Buckaroo" 1943; "Frontier Fury" 1943; "Hail to the Rangers" 1943; "Law of the Northwest" 1943; "Riders of the Northwest Mounted" 1943; "Robin Hood of the Range" 1943; "Saddles and Sagebrush" 1943; "Silver City Raiders" 1943; "The Last Horseman 1944; "Riding West" 1944; "The Vigilantes Ride" 1944; "Wyoming Hurricane" 1944; "Renegade Girl" 1946 (& prod.); "Sunset Pass" 1946; "Code of the West" 1947; "Deputy Marshal" 1949 (& sp.); "Bandit Queen" 1950

(& prod.); "Border Rangers" 1950 (& prod.); "Gunfire" 1950 (& prod./sp.); "I Shot Billy the Kid" 1950 (& prod.); "Train to Tombstone" 1950 (& prod.); "The Marshal's Daughter" 1953. ¶TV: *The Gene Autry Show*—"Steel Ribbon" 9-22-53, "Ransom Cross" 10-6-53; *Judge Roy Bean*—"The Judge of Pecos Valley" 9-10-55.

Berkeley, Martin. Screenwriter. Films: "Green Grass of Wyoming" 1948; "Kangaroo" 1952 (story only); "The Nebraskan" 1953; "War Paint" 1953; "Gypsy Colt" 1954; "Red Sundown" 1956; "Trooper Hook" 1957.

Berlin, Irving (1888-9/22/89). Writer. Films: "Annie Get Your Gun" 1950 (story).

Berloshan, Jerry. Screenwriter. Films: "The Legend of the Lone Ranger" 1981.

Berman, Pandro S. (1905-). Producer. Films: "Honky Tonk" 1941; "The Sea of Grass" 1947.

Bernabei, Claudio. Screenwriter. Films: "Red Coat" 1975-Ital.

Bernard, Ray. *see* Bernard B. Ray.

Bernardi, Massimo. Producer. Films: "Go Away! Trinity Has Arrived in Eldorado" 1972-Ital.; "Showdown for a Badman" 1972-Ital.

Bernds, Edward (1905-). Films: "Three Troubledoers" 1946-short; "Out West" 1947-short; "Punchy Cowpunchers" 1950-short (& sp.); "Gold Raiders" 1951; "Merry Mavericks" 1951-short (& sp.); "Dig That Uranium" 1956; "Escape from Red Rock" 1958 (& sp.); "Quantrill's Raiders" 1958; "Gunfight at Comanche Creek" 1964; "Tickle Me" 1965 (sp. only). ¶TV: *Colt .45* 1957; *Sugarfoot* 1957.

Berne, Josef (1904-12/19/64). Director. Films: "Lucky Cowboy" 1944-short.

Bernhard, Jack. Screenwriter. Films: "West of Carson City" 1940.

Berns, Seymour. Director. TV: *Gunsmoke*—"Overland Express" 5-31-58, "Monopoly" 10-4-58, "Young Love" 1-3-59.

Bernstein, Isadore. Screenwriter. Films: "The Miracle Baby" 1923; "Pure Grit" 1923; "The Red Warning" 1923; "The Back Trail" 1924; "Daring Chances" 1924; "Fighting Fury" 1924; "The Galloping Ace" 1924; "The Man from Wyoming" 1924; "The Phantom Horseman" 1924; "Ridgeway of Montana" 1924; "The Sunset Trail" 1924; "The Western Wallop" 1924; "Ace of Spades" 1925-serial (story only); "The

Burning Trail" 1925; "The Red Rider" 1925 (story only); "Ridin' Pretty" 1925; "Ridin' Thunder" 1925; "A Roaring Adventure" 1925; "The Sign of the Cactus" 1925; "The White Outlaw" 1925; "Arizona Sweepstakes" 1926; "The Valley of Hell" 1927; "The Rawhide Kid" 1928; "Destry Rides Again" 1932; "For the Service" 1936.

Bernstein, Jerry. Director. TV: *Here Come the Brides*—"Lovers and Wanderers" 11-6-68, "A Jew Named Sullivan" 11-6-68, "A Kiss Just for You" 1-29-69, "None to a Customer" 2-19-69, "A Man's Errand" 3-19-69, "His Sister's Keeper" 12-12-69, "Lorenzo Bush" 12-19-69, "Break the Bank of Tacoma" 1-16-70, "Candy and the Kid" 2-13-70.

Bernstein, Walter (1919-). Screenwriter. Films: "Heller in Pink Tights" 1960; "The Magnificent Seven" 1960.

Berrier, Thomas. Screenwriter. Films: "Barriers of Folly" 1922.

Berthelet, Arthur (1879-9/16/49). Director. Films: "Penny of Top Hill Trail" 1921.

Bertolucci, Bernardo (1941-). Director. Films: "Once Upon a Time in the West" 1968-Ital. (story only).

Bertram, William (1880-5/1/33). Director. Films: "Buck's Lady Friend" 1915; "Film Tempo" 1915; "Man-Afraid-of-His-Wardrobe" 1915; "The Terror of Twin Mountains" 1915; "This Is the Life" 1915; "Bond of Blood" 1916; "A Man's Friend" 1916; "Margy of the Foothills" 1916; "A Daughter of the West" 1918; "The Arizona Catclaw" 1919; "Ghost City" 1921; "The Purple Riders" 1921-serial; "The Wolverine" 1921; "Texas" 1922; "The Western Musketeer" 1922 (& sp.); "Ace of Action" 1926; "Hoodoo Ranch" 1926; "Tangled Herds" 1926; "Gold from Weepah" 1927; "The Phantom Buster" 1927.

Bertsch, Margaret. Screenwriter. Films: "Una of the Sierras" 1912.

Besier, Rudolf. Writer. Films: "Secrets" 1933 (story).

Bessi, Roberto. Director. Films: "Fighting Fists of Shanghai Joe" 1973-Ital.

Bettinson, Ralph. Screenwriter. Films: "Rose of the Rio Grande" 1938; "South of the Rio Grande" 1945.

Beyfuss, Alex E. Director. Films: "Salomy Jane" 1914.

Bezzerides, A.I. (1908-). Screenwriter. Films: "Track of the Cat" 1954; "The Jayhawkers" 1959.

Bianchi, Mario Adelchi (Frank Bronston, Renzo Spaziani). Director. Films: "Black Tigress" 1967-Ital.; "Winchester Does Not Forgive" 1968-Ital. (& sp.); "Fasthand" 1972-Ital./Span.; "Kill the Poker Player" 1972-Ital./Span. (& sp.); "In the Name of the Father, the Son and the Colt" 1972-Fr./Ital.; "For a Book of Dollars" 1973-Ital./Span.

Bianchi, Paolo (Paolo Bianchini, Paul Maxwell). Director. Films: "God Made Them ... I Kill Them" 1968-Ital.; "I Want Him Dead" 1968-Ital./Span.; "Machine Gun Killers" 1968-Ital./Span. (& sp.); "Hey Amigo! A Toast to Your Death!" 1971-Ital. (& sp.).

Bianchini, Paolo. *see* Bianchi, Paolo.

Bianco, Solly V. Producer. Films: "Buffalo Bill, Hero of the Far West" 1964-Ital./Ger./Fr.; "Bandidos" 1967-Ital.; "Django Challenges Sartana" 1970-Ital.; "Vengeance Is a Dish Served Cold" 1971-Ital./Span.

Biberman, Abner (1909-6/20/77). Director. Films: "Gun for a Coward" 1957. ¶TV: *Colt .45* 1957; *Maverick*—"Stapede" 11-17-57, "Naked Gallows" 12-15-57; *Wagon Train*—"The Bije Wilcox Story" 11-19-58, "The Ben Courtney Story" 1-28-59; *Empire*—"Ride to a Fall" 10-16-62; *Temple Houston* 1963; *Gunsmoke*—"Gold Mine" 12-25-65; *Laredo*—"A Double Shot of Nepenthe" 9-30-66, "Leave It to Dixie" 12-30-66; *The Men from Shiloh* 1970.

Bichanan, Donald I. Screenwriter. Films: "The Siren" 1917.

Bickham, Jack M. (1930-). Writer. Films: "The Apple Dumpling Gang" 1975 (story); "Baker's Hawk" 1976 (story).

Bickley, William. Screenwriter. Films: "Hawmps!" 1976.

Bigelow, Charles E. Producer. Films: "Ghost Guns" 1944; "Land of the Outlaws" 1944; "Law Men" 1944; "Law of the Valley" 1944; "Range Law" 1944; "Trigger Law" 1944; "West of the Rio Grande" 1944; "Frontier Feud" 1945; "Gun Smoke" 1945; "The Lost Trail" 1945; "The Navajo Trail" 1945; "Stranger from Santa Fe" 1945; "The Haunted Mine" 1946; "Silver Range" 1946; "Trigger Fingers" 1946; "Valley of Fear" 1947.

Biggons, Eliot. Screenwriter. Films: "Code of the Saddle" 1947.

Bigson, Tom. Screenwriter. Films: "Land of the Six Guns" 1940.

Bilkie, Helen S. Writer. Films: "The Naked Hills" 1956 (story).

Bill, Jr., Buffalo (Jay Wilsey) (1896-10/25/61). Director. Films: "Riding Speed" 1934; "Trails of Adventure" 1935.

Bill, Tony (1940-). Producer. Films: "Hearts of the West" 1975.

Biller, Hal. Screenwriter. Films: "Domino Kid" 1957.

Billian, Hans. Screenwriter. Films: "Massacre at Marble City" 1964-Ger./Ital./Fr.

Bilson, Bruce (1928-). Director. Films: "The New Daughters of Joshua Cabe" TVM-1976. ¶TV: *Bonanza*—"Caution: Easter Bunny Crossing" (3-29-70; *Alias Smith and Jones*—"Don't Get Mad, Get Even" 2-17-72; Barbary Coast—"Sharks Eat Sharks" 11-21-75.

Binder, John. Screenwriter. Films: "Houston: The Legend of Texas" TVM-1986; "Black Fox" TVM-1995.

Bingham, Edfrid A. Screenwriter. Films: "Cupid, the Cowpuncher" 1920; "The Call of the Canyon" 1923; "Riders of the Purple Sage" 1925; "Tony Runs Wild" 1926.

Binyon, Claude (1905-2/14/78). Screenwriter. Films: "Arizona" 1940; "North to Alaska" 1960.

Bischoff, Sam (1890-5/21/75). Producer. Films: "Between Fighting Men" 1932; "Dynamite Ranch" 1932; "Come On Tarzan" 1933; "Drum Taps" 1933; "Fargo Express" 1933; "The Lone Avenger" 1933; "The Phantom Thunderbolt" 1933; "The Oklahoma Kid" 1939; "Texas" 1941; "Mrs. Mike" 1949; "The Bounty Hunter" 1954.

Bishop, Curtis (Curt Carroll) (1912-67). Writer. Films: "Cow Country" 1953 (story); "San Antone" 1953 (story).

Bishop, Kenneth J. Producer. Films: "Fighting Playboy" 1937; "Death Goes North" 1939.

Bishop, Ron (1921-1/31/88). Screenwriter. Films: "The Godchild" TVM-1974.

Bistolfi, Emo. Producer. Films: "Terrible Sheriff" 1963-Span./Ital.; "Charge of the Seventh Cavalry" 1964-Ital./Span./Fr.; "Heroes of the West" 1964-Span./Ital.

Bixby, Bill (1935-11/21/93). Director. Films: "The Barbary Coast" TVM-1975. ¶TV: *Barbary Coast*—"Jesse Who?" 9-22-75; *The Oregon Trail* 1977.

Blache, Herbert (-10/23/53). Director. Films: "The Shooting of Dan McGrew" 1915; "The Calgary Stampede" 1925.

Black, John D.F. Screenwriter. Films: "Gunfight in Abilene" 1967.

Black, Noel (1937-). Director. TV: *Big Hawaii* 1977.

Black, Preston. Director. Films: "Back to the Woods" 1937-short.

Black, Ralph E. Director. TV: *Bonanza*—"Walter and the Outlaws" 5-24-64, "Found Child" 10-24-65, "Three Brides for Hoss" 2-20-66.

Blackburn, Thomas. Screenwriter. Films: "Colt .45" 1950; "Short Grass" 1950; "Cavalry Scout" 1951; "Raton Pass" 1951 (story only); "Sierra Passage" 1951; "Cattle Town" 1952; "Cattle Queen of Montana" 1954 (story only); "Riding Shotgun" 1954; "Davy Crockett, King of the Wild Frontier" 1955; "Davy Crockett and the River Pirates" 1956; "Westward Ho the Wagons" 1956; "The Wild Dakotas" 1956; "Sierra Baron" 1958 (story only); "Santee" 1973.

Blackton, J. Stuart (1875-8/13/41). Director. Films: "Onawanda" 1909; "Western Courtship" 1908.

Blackwell, E.E. Director. Films: "Neola, the Sioux" 1915.

Blackwell, Ken. Screenwriter. Films: "Triumphs of a Man Called Horse" 1984.

Blain, Luis. Screenwriter. Films: "The White, the Yellow, and the Black" 1974-Ital./Span./Fr.

Blair, George (1906-1/20/70). Director. Films: "Madonna of the Desert" 1948; "The Missourians" 1950; "Under Mexicali Stars" 1950; "Silver City Bonanza" 1951; "Thunder in God's Country" 1951; "Desert Pursuit" 1952; "The Twinkle in God's Eye" 1955. ¶TV: *The Gene Autry Show*—"Blazeaway" 2-22-52, "Bullets and Bows" 3-2-52, "Six Gun Romeo" 3-16-52, "The Sheriff Is a Lady" 3-23-52; *The Roy Rogers Show*—"The Brothers O'Dell" 11-20-55, "Three Masked Men" 12-18-55, "Ambush" 1-15-56, "Money Is Dangerous" 1-29-56, "False Faces" 2-5-56, "Horse Crazy" 2-26-56, "Smoking Guns" 3-3-56, "Empty Saddles" 3-10-56, "Sheriff Missing" 3-17-56, "The Morse Mixup" 3-24-56, "Johnny Rover" 6-9-57; *Wanted—Dead or Alive*—"Jason" 1-30-60, "Tolliver Bender" 2-13-60., "A House Divided" 2-20-60, "Triple Vise" 2-27-60, "Black Belt" 3-19-60, "Vendetta" 4-9-60, "Death, Divided by Three" 4-23-60; *Bonanza*—"Bitter Water" 4-9-60.

Blair, Joe. Writer. Films: "Sunset in Wyoming" 1941 (story).

Blake, Michael. Screenwriter. Films: "Dances With Wolves" 1990.

Blake, Norbert. Screenwriter. Films: "Pistol Packin' Preacher" 1972-Ital./Fr.

Blangsted, Folmer (1904-8/11/82). Director. Films: "The Old Wyoming Trail" 1937; "Westbound Mail" 1937; "Cattle Raiders" 1938 (story only).

Blanke, Henry (1901-5/28/81). Producer. Films: "The Treasure of the Sierra Madre" 1948; "The Iron Mistress" 1952; "Westbound" 1959.

Blankfort, Henry. Screenwriter. Films: "The Singing Sheriff" 1944; "The Daltons Ride Again" 1945.

Blankfort, Michael (1907-7/13/82). Screenwriter. Films: "Texas" 1941 (& story); "Broken Arrow" 1950; "Tribute to a Badman" 1956; "The Plainsman" 1966.

Blasco, Ricardo. Director. Films: "Gringo" 1963-Span./Ital. (& sp.); "Three Swoards of Zorro" 1963-Ital./Span. (& sp.); "Behind the Mask of Zorro" 1965-Ital./Span. (& sp.).

Blasdale, Evanne. Screenwriter. Films: "Bulldog Pluck" 1927; "The Fighting Hombre" 1927.

Blatty, William Peter (1928-). Screenwriter. Films: "The Great Bank Robbery" 1969.

Blaustein, Julian (1913-6/20/95). Producer. Films: "Broken Arrow" 1950; "The Outcasts of Poker Flat" 1952; "Cowboy" 1958.

Bleckner, Jeff. Director. TV: *Bret Maverick*—"The Ballad of Bret Maverick" 2-16-82.

Blees, Robert. Screenwriter. Films: "Cattle Queen of Montana" 1954; "The Yellow Mountain" 1954. ¶TV: *Bonanza* 1959-73 (prod.).

Bletcher, William (1894-1/5/79). Director. Films: "The Wild Girl" 1925; "The Silent Guardian" 1926.

Blighton, Frank. Screenwriter. Films: "Broncho Billy and the Sheriff's Office" 1914; "The Tell-Tale Hand" 1914 (story only).

Block, Alfred. Screenwriter. Films: "Way Out West" 1930 (& story).

Block, Ralph. Screenwriter. Films: "The Arizona Kid" 1930; "A Holy Terror" 1931; "Massacre" 1934 (& story).

Blodgett, Isobel. Screenwriter. Films: "Western Feuds" 1924.

Bloom, George Arthur. Screenwriter. Films: "A Knife for the Ladies" 1973.

Bloom, Harold Jack. Screenwriter. Films: "Arena" 1953; "The Naked Spur" 1953; "A Gunfight" 1971 (& prod.); "Hardcase" TVM-1972; "Hec Ramsey" TVM-1972. ¶TV: *Hec Ramsey* 1972-74 (prod.).

Bloom, Stephen. Screenwriter. Films: "Tall Tales: The Unbelievable Adventures of Pecos Bill" 1995.

Bluel, Richard. Producer. Films: "The Castaway Cowboy" 1974 (story only). ¶TV: *Temple Houston* 1963-64.

Blystone, John G. (1893-8/6/38). Director. Films: "Soft Boiled" 1923 (& sp.); "Oh, You Tony!" 1924; "Teeth" 1924; "The Best Bad Man" 1925; "The Everlasting Whisper" 1925; "The Lucky Horseshoe" 1925; "Hard-Boiled" 1926; "My Own Pal" 1926; "Wings of the Storm" 1926.

Boardman, True (1882-9/28/18). Screenwriter. Films: "Ride 'Em, Cowboy" 1942; "The Painted Hills" 1951.

Boccacci, Antonio. Screenwriter. Films: "Days of Violence" 1967-Ital.

Boccia, Tanio (Amerigo Anton). Director. Films: "Kill or Be Killed" 1966-Ital.; "God Does Not Pay on Saturday" 1968-Ital. (& sp.); "Saguaro" 1968-Ital. (& prod./sp.); "Deadly Trackers" 1972-Ital. (& sp.).

Bodeen, DeWitt (1908-3/12/88). Screenwriter. Films: "Mrs. Mike" 1949.

Boehm, Sydney (1908-6/25/90). Screenwriter. Films: "Branded" 1951; "The Savage" 1952; "The Siege at Red River" 1954; "The Tall Men" 1955; "One Foot in Hell" 1960 (& prod.); "Rough Night in Jericho" 1967.

Boetticher, Budd (1916-). Director. Films: "The Wolf Hunters" 1949; "The Cimarron Kid" 1951; "Bronco Buster" 1952; "Horizons West" 1952; "The Man from the Alamo" 1953; "Seminole" 1953; "Wings of the Hawk" 1953; "Seven Men from Now" 1956; "Decision at Sundown" 1957; "The Tall T" 1957; "Buchanan Rides Alone" 1958; "Ride Lonesome" 1959 (& prod.); "Westbound" 1959; "Comanche Station" 1960 (& prod.); "Two Mules for Sister Sara" 1970 (story only); "A Time for Dying" 1971 (& sp.). ¶TV: *Zane Grey Theater* 1956; *Maverick*—"The War of the Silver Kings" 9-22-57, "Point Blank" 9-29-57, "According to Hoyle" 10-6-57; *The Rifleman*—"Stopover" 4-25-61.

Bogart, Paul (1925-). Director. Films: "Skin Game" 1971. ¶TV: *Nichols* 1971.

Bogeaus, Benedict (1904-8/23/68). Producer. Films: "My Brother, the Outlaw" 1951; "Cattle Queen of Montana" 1954; "Passion" 1954; "Silver Lode" 1954; "Tennessee's Partner" 1955.

Boggs, Frank. Director. Films: "In the Bad Lands" 1909; "On the Border" 1909; "On the Little Big Horn or Custer's Last Stand" 1909; "The Pine Ridge Feud" 1909; "Ranch Life in the Great Southwest" 1909; "The Stampede" 1909; "The Tenderfoot" 1909; "Across the Plains" 1910; "Davy Crockett" 1910; "The Long Trail" 1910; "Pride of the Range" 1910; "The Trimming of Paradise Gulch" 1910; "The Curse of the Red Man" 1911; "Heart of John Barlow" 1911; "How Algy Captured a Wild Man" 1911; "In Old California When the Gringos Came" 1911; "Kit Carson's Wooing" 1911; "A New York Cowboy" 1911; "On Seperate Paths" 1911; "One of Nature's Noblemen" 1911; "Range Pals" 1911; "The Regeneration of Apache Kid" 1911 (& sp.); "The Rival Stage Lines" 1911; "The Schoolmaster of Mariposa" 1911; "Told in the Sierras" 1911; "The Totem Mark" 1911; "Wheels of Justice" 1911; "The White Medicine Man" 1911; "The Peacemaker" 1912.

Bohem, Endre (1900-5/5/90). Screenwriter. Films: "Pawnee 1957; "Cattle Empire" 1958. ¶TV: *Rawhide* 1959-66 (prod.).

Bohem, Leslie. Screenwriter. Films: "Desperado: Badlands Justice" TVM-1989 (& story).

Bohm, Mark. Director. Films: "Chetan, Indian Boy" 1972-Ger. (& sp.).

Bole, Cliff. Director. TV: *Paradise*—"Hard Choices" 1-12-89, "The Secret" 2-8-89, "Vengeance" 3-16-89, "A Matter of Honor" Part Two 4-15-89, "A Gather of Guns" 9-10-89, "All the Pretty Little Horses" 10-14-89, "A Proper Stranger" 11-11-89, "Till Death Do Us Part" 2-3-90, "Shadow of a Doubt" 3-3-90, "Out of Ashes" 1-4-91, "The Women" 1-25-91, "See No Evil" 2-22-91, "Shield of Gold" 4-12-91; *Young Riders*—"Mask of Fear" 5-28-92.

Boleslawski, Richard (1889-1/17/37). Director. Films: "The Three Godfathers" 1936.

Boley, Raymond. Director. Films: "Peace for a Gunfighter" 1967.

Bologna, Carmine. Screenwriter. Films: "Death Walks in Laredo" 1966-Ital./Span. (& prod.).

Bolognini, Manolo. Producer. Films: "Django" 1966-Ital./Span.; "Texas, Adios" 1966-Ital./Span.; "Rita of the West" 1967- Ital.;

"Chuck Moll" 1970-Ital.; "California" 1976-Ital./Span.

Bolzoni, Adriano. Screenwriter. Films: "Minnesota Clay" 1964-Ital./Fr./Span. (& story); "Man from Canyon City" 1965-Span./Ital.; "Ringo and His Golden Pistol" 1966-Ital.; "Let Them Rest" 1967-Ital./Ger.; "Pecos Cleans Up" 1967-Ital.; "Hole in the Forehead" 1968-Ital./Span.; "Thirteenth Is a Judas" 1971-Ital.; "Halleluja and Sartana Strikes Again" 1972-Ger./Ital.; "Man Called Amen" 1972-Ital.; "Trinity and Sartana Are Coming" 1972-Ital.; "Bandera Bandits" 1973-Ital./Span./Ger.

Bond, Lee. Writer. Films: "Land of the Open Range" 1942 (story).

Bondarchuk, Sergei (1922-10/20/94). Director. Films: "Mexico in Flames" 1982-Rus./Mex./Ital. (& sp.).

Bondelli, Phil. Director. TV: *Outlaws*—"Orleans" 1-17-87, "Hymn" 1-31-87, "Pursued" 3-7-87, "Jackpot" 4-4-87.

Bonelli, Gianfranco Luigi. Screenwriter. Films: "Tex and the Lord of the Deep" 1985-Ital.

Bonham, Frank. Writer. Films: "Stage to Tucson" 1950 (story).

Boone, Richard (1917-1/10/81). Director. TV: *Have Gun Will Travel*—"The Night the Town Died" 2-6-60, "Fight at Adobe Wells" 3-12-60, "Ambush" 4-23-60, "Black Sheep" 4-30-60, "The Campaign of Billy Banjo" 5-28-60, "Ransom" 6-4-60, "The Search" 6-18-60.

Booth, Charles G. (1896-5/22/49). Screenwriter. Films: "Hurricane Smith" 1942 (story only); "Fury at Furnace Creek" 1948.

Booth, Christopher. Screenwriter. Films: "The Meddlin' Stranger" 1927; "Tonto Kid" 1935 (story only).

Booth, Dolores. Screenwriter. Films: "Riding Speed" 1934.

Booth, John Hunter. Screenwriter. Films: "The Lone Star Ranger" 1930.

Borau, Jose Luis (J.L. Boraw). Director. Films: "Ride and Kill" 1964-Ital./Span.

Boraw, J.L. *see* Borau, Jose Luis.

Borden, Lon. Screenwriter. Films: "The Unconquered Bandit" 1935.

Boretz, Allen. Screenwriter. Films: "Two Guys from Texas" 1948.

Boris, Robert. Director. Films: "Frank and Jesse" TVM-1995 (& sp.).

Borland, Hal (1900-8/22/78).

Writer. Films: "When the Legends Die" 1972 (story).

Borowsky, Marvin. Screenwriter. Films: "Big Jack" 1949.

Borsos, Philip (1953-2/2/95). Director. Films: "The Grey Fox" 1983-Can.

Bortnik, Aida. Screenwriter. Films: "Old Gringo" 1989.

Borzage, Frank (1893-6/19/62). Director. Films: "Immediate Lee" 1916; "The Land O'Lizards" 1916; "Until They Get Me" 1917; "The Gun Woman" 1918; "The Duke of Chimney Butte" 1921; "Billy Jim" 1922; "The Valley of Silent Men" 1922; "Secrets" 1933; "The Vanishing Virginian" 1941.

Bosch, Juan. *see* Iquino, Ignacio.

Bosworth, Hobart (1867-12/30/43). Director. Films: "The Chief's Daughter" 1911 (& sp.); "The Convert of San Clemente" 1911 (& sp.); "Evangeline" 1911 (& sp.); "A Frontier Gal's Courage" 1911; "In the Days of Gold" 1911 (& story); "An Indian Vestal" 1911 (& sp.); "It Happened in the West" 1911; "Little Injin" 1911 (& sp.); "McKee Rankin's '49" 1911 (& sp.); "A Child of the Wilderness" 1912 (& sp.); "The Legend of the Lost Arrow" 1912; "The Trade Gun Bullet" 1912; "Buckshot John" 1915; "Captain Courtesy" 1915; "Fatherhood" 1915 (& story).

Boteler, Bruce. Screenwriter. Films: "Blaze Away" 1922.

Botsford, A.M. Producer. Films: "The Arizona Raiders" 1936; "Arizona Mahoney" 1936.

Boucicault, Dion. Writer. Films: "Onawanda" 1909 (story).

Boulanger, Daniel (1922-). Screenwriter. Films: "The Legend of Frenchie King" 1971-Fr./Ital./Span./Brit.

Bourguignon, Serge (1928-). Director. Films: "The Reward" 1965 (& sp.).

Bower, Bertha M. Screenwriter. Films: "The Last of Her Tribe" 1912; "Chip of the Flying U" 1914; "The Lonesome Trail" 1914; "Shotgun Jones" 1914 (prod. only); "When the Cook Fell Ill" 1914; "How Weary Went Wooing" 1915; "The Galloping Devil" 1920 (story only); "The Wolverine" 1921; "Ridin' Thunder" 1925 (story only); "Chip of the Flying U" 1926 (story only); "King of the Rodeo" 1929; "Points West" 1929 (story only); "Chip of the Flying U" 1939 (story only).

Bowers, Jess. *see* Buffington, Adele.

Bowers, William (1916-3/27/87). Screenwriter. Films: "The Wistful Widow of Wagon Gap" 1947 (story only); "Black Bart" 1948; "River Lady" 1948; "The Gunfighter" 1950 (& story); "The Law and Jake Wade" 1958; "The Sheepman" 1958; "Alias Jesse James" 1959; "Advance to the Rear" 1964; "Support Your Local Sheriff" 1969 (& prod.); "The Gun and the Pulpit" TVM-1974; "The Ride to Hangman's Tree" 1967; "Sidekicks" TVM-1974; "Kate Bliss and the Ticker Tape Kid" TVM-1978; "The Wild Wild West Revisited" TVM-1979; "More Wild Wild West" TVM-1980.

Bowman, Chuck. Director. TV: *Young Maverick* 1979-80 (prod.); *Dr. Quinn, Medicine Woman*—"Epidemic" 1-2-93, "Bad Water" 2-6-93, "A Cowboy's Lullaby" 2-20-93, "The Prisoner" 3-13-93, "Happy Birthday" 3-27-93, "Rite of Passage" 4-10-93, "The Race" 9-25-93, "Halloween" 10-30-93, "The Incident" 11-6-93, "Where the Heart Is" 11-20-93, "Sully's Choice" 12-11-93, "Crossing the Line" 1-1-94, "Another Woman" 1-22-94, "The First Circle" 3-26-94, "Just One Lullaby" 4-9-94.

Bowman, Earl Wayland. Writer. Films: "The Ramblin' Kid" 1923 (story); "The Long, Long Trail" 1929 (story).

Bowman, Rob. Director. TV: *Adventures of Brisco County, Jr.*—"AKA Kansas" 12-17-93.

Bowman, William J. (1877-1/1/60). Director. Films: "The Avenging Arrow" 1921-serial.

Boxer, Herman. Writer. Films: "Whoops, I'm an Indian" 1936-short (story).

Boyd, Jerold Hayden. Screenwriter. Films: "A Placed Called Glory" 1966-Span./Ger. (& story).

Boyd, William (1898-9/12/72). Producer. TV: *Hopalong Cassidy* 1952.

Boylan, Malcolm Stuart (1897-4/3/67). Screenwriter. Films: "Red River Valley" 1941; "Alaska" 1944.

Boyle, E.G. Director. Films: "The Fighting Failure" 1926.

Boyle, Marie. Screenwriter. Films: "The Big Trail" 1930.

Brabin, Charles (1883-11/3/57). Director. Films: "The Great Meadow" 1931 (& sp.).

Bracken, Bertram (1880-11/1/52). Director. Films: "The Primitive Call" 1917 (& sp.); "Code of the Yukon" 1918 (& sp.); "Kazan" 1921.

Brackett, Charles (1892-3/9/69). Screenwriter. Films: "Rose of the Rancho" 1936; "Garden of Evil" 1954 (prod. only).

Brackett, Leigh (1915-3/18/78). Screenwriter. Films: "Rio Bravo" 1959; "Gold of the Seven Saints" 1961; "El Dorado" 1967; "Rio Lobo" 1970.

Bradbury, Robert North. Director. Films: "The Canyon Holdup" 1919; "Jacques of the Silver North" 1919; "The Last of His People" 1919; "The Perils of Thunder Mountain" 1919-serial; "Beyond the Trail" 1921; "The Death Trap" 1921; "The Desert Wolf" 1921; "The Impostor" 1921; "Larue of Phantom Valley" 1921; "Lorraine of the Timberlands" 1921; "The Sagebrush Musketeers" 1921 (& sp.); "The Secret of Butte Ridge" 1921; "The Sheriff of Mojave" 1921; "The Tempest" 1921; "At Large" 1922; "Come Clean" 1922; "Daring Dangers" 1922; "A Guilty Cause" 1922; "The Hour of Doom" 1922; "It Is the Law" 1922; "Riders of the Law" 1922 (& sp.); "Ridin' Through" 1922; "Seeing Red" 1922; "Two Men" 1922; "The Desert Rider" 1923; "Face to Face" 1923; "The Forbidden Trail" 1923 (& sp.); "Galloping Thru" 1923; "No Tenderfoot" 1923; "The Red Warning" 1923; "Wolf Tracks" 1923; "The Wolf Trapper" 1923; "Behind Two Guns" 1924 (& sp.); "The Galloping Ace" 1924; "The Man from Wyoming" 1924; "The Phantom Horseman" 1924; "Wanted By the Law" 1924 (& sp); "Yankee Speed" 1924 (& sp.); "Hidden Loot" 1925; "Moccasins" 1925; "Riders of Mystery" 1925; "The Border Sheriff" 1926 (& sp.); "Daniel Boone Thru the Wilderness" 1926; "Davy Crockett at the Fall of the Alamo" 1926; "Looking for Trouble" 1926; "The Mojave Kid" 1927; "Sitting Bull at the Spirit Lake Massacre" 1927; "The Bantam Cowboy" 1928 (story only); "Dugan of the Badlands" 1931 (& sp.); "Son of the Plains" 1931; "Hidden Valley" 1932; "Law of the West" 1932 (& sp.); "Man from Hell's Edges" 1932 (& sp.); "Riders of the Desert" 1932; "Son of Oklahoma" 1932; "Breed of the Border" 1933; "The Gallant Fool" 1933 (& sp.); "Galloping Romeo" 1933 (& story); "The Ranger's Code" 1933; "Riders of Destiny" 1933 (& sp.); "Blue Steel" 1934 (& sp.); "The Lawless Frontier" 1934 (& sp.); "The Lucky Texan" 1934 (& sp.); "The Man from Utah" 1934; "The Star Packer" 1934 (& sp.); "The Trail Beyond" 1934; "West of the Divide" 1934 (& sp.); "Alias John Law" 1935; "Between Men" 1935 (& sp.); "Big Calibre" 1935; "The Coura-geous Avenger" 1935; "Dawn Rider" 1935 (& sp.); "Kid Courageous" 1935 (& sp.); "Lawless Range" 1935; "No Man's Range" 1935 (& story); "Rainbow Valley" 1935; "The Rider of the Law" 1935; "Smokey Smith" 1935 (& sp.); "Texas Terror" 1935 (& sp.); "Tombstone Terror" 1935 (& sp.); "Trail of Terror" 1935 (& sp.); "Westward Ho" 1935; "Western Justice" 1935 (& sp.); "Brand of the Outlaws" 1936; "Cavalry" 1936 (& story); "The Kid Ranger" 1936 (& sp.); "The Last of the Warrens" 1936 (& sp.); "The Law Rides" 1936; "Sundown Saunders" 1936 (& sp.); "Valley of the Lawless" 1936 (& sp.); "Danger Valley" 1937 (& prod.); "God's Country and the Man" 1937 (& prod.); "The Gun Ranger" 1937; "Headin' for the Rio Grande" 1937; "Hittin' the Trail" 1937; "Riders of the Dawn" 1937 (& prod.); "Riders of the Rockies" 1937; "Romance of the Rockies" 1937 (& prod.); "Sing, Cowboy, Sing" 1937; "Stars Over Arizona" 1937 (& prod.); "Trouble in Texas" 1937; "The Trusted Outlaw" 1937; "Where Trails Divide" 1937 (& prod.); "Forbidden Trails" 1941; "Texas Buddies" 1942 (& sp.).

Bradford, Gardner. Screenwriter. Films: "The Desert's Toll" 1926.

Bradshaw, Randy. Director. TV: *Lonesome Dove*—"High Lonesome" 2-12-95.

Brady, Al. *see* Brescia, Alfonso.

Brady, Cyrus Townsend. Screenwriter. Films: "The Little Angel of Canyon Creek" 1914 (story only); "When the West Was Young" 1914 (story only); "Britton of the Seventh" 1916.

Brady, Hal. *see* Miraglia, Emilio P.

Brady, James E. Writer. Films: "The Man She Brought Back" 1922 (story).

Brahm, John (1893-10/11/82). Director. TV: *Wagon Train*—"The Zeke Thomas Story" 11-17-57, "The Riley Gratton Story" 12-4-57; *Bonanza*—"Mr. Henry Comstock" 11-7-59; *The Virginian*—"The Golden Door" 3-13-63; *Gunsmoke*—"Kitty Cornered" 4-18-64; *Shane* 1966.

Bramson, David. Writer. Films: "Slim Carter" 1957 (story).

Branch, Houston. Screenwriter. Films: "Sioux Blood" 1929; "North of Nome" 1936 (story only); "The Trigger Trio" 1937 (story only); "River Lady" 1948 (story only); "Klondike Kate" 1943 (story only); "Belle of the Yukon" 1944 (story only); "Untamed Frontier" 1952 (story only); "Sierra Baron" 1958.

Brand, Max (Evan Evans, Frederick Faust, George Owen Baxter)(1892-1944). Writer. Films: "Lawless Love" 1918 (story); "The Night Horsemen" 1921 (story); "Trailin'" 1921 (story); "Just Tony" 1922 (story); "The Gunfighter" 1923 (story); "Against All Odds" 1924 (story); "Mile-a-Minute Romeo" 1924 (story); "The Vagabond Trail" 1924 (story); "The Best Bad Man" 1925 (story); "The Cavalier" 1928 (story); "Fair Warning" 1931 (story); "A Holy Terror" 1931 (story); "Destry Rides Again" 1932 (story); "Destry Rides Again" 1939 (story); "The Desperadoes" 1943 (story); "Rainbow Over Texas" 1946 (story); "Singing Guns" 1950 (story); "My Brother, the Outlaw" 1951 (story); "Branded" 1951 (story); "Destry" 1954.

Brando, Marlon (1924-). Director. Films: "One-Eyed Jacks" 1961.

Brandon, Curt (1912-67). Writer. Films: "Seminoole Uprising" 1955 (story).

Brannon, Fred C. (1902-4/6/53). Director. Films: "King of the Forest Rangers" 1946-serial; "The Phantom Rider" 1946-serial; "Jesse James Rides Again" 1947-serial; "Son of Zorro" 1947-serial; "The Adventures of Frank and Jesse James" 1948-serial; "Dangers of the Canadian Mounted" 1948-serial; "Bandit King of Texas" 1949; "Frontier Marshal" 1949; "Ghost of Zorro" 1949-serial; "Code of the Silver Sage" 1950; "Desperadoes of the West" 1950-serial; "Gunmen of Abilene" 1950; "The James Brothers of Missouri" 1950-serial; "Rustlers on Horseback" 1950; "Salt Lake Raiders" 1950; "Vigilante Hideout" 1950; "Arizona Manhunt" 1951; "Don Daredevil Rides Again" 1951-serial; "Night Riders of Montana" 1951; "Rough Riders of Durango" 1951; "Captive of Billy the Kid" 1952; "Wild Horse Ambush" 1952.

Brass, Tinto (1933-). Director. Films: "Yankee" 1967-Ital./Span. (& sp.).

Braus, Mortimer. Screenwriter. Films: "Five Bold Women" 1960.

Braxton, Harry. Screenwriter. Films: "Morgan's Last Raid" 1929.

Braxton, Steve. *see* Robins, Sam.

Brecher, Irving. Screenwriter. Films: "Go West" 1940.

Bredecka, Jiri. Screenwriter. Films: "Lemonade Joe" 1966-Czech.

Bren, J. Robert. Screenwriter. Films: "American Empire" 1942; "El Paso" 1949 (story only); "In Old California" 1942 (story only); "The Great Sioux Uprising" 1953; "Overland Pacific" 1954; "The Siege at Red River" 1954 (story); "The Treasure of Pancho Villa" 1955 (story).

Bren, Milton. Producer. Films: "The Desert Rider" 1929 (story only); "Wyoming" 1940.

Brennan, Andrew. Director. TV: *The Guns of Will Sonnett*—"Robber's Roost" 1-17-69.

Brennan, Frederick Hazlitt (1902-6/30/62). Screenwriter. Films: "Devil's Canyon" 1953.

Brenon, Herbert (1880-6/21/58). Director. Films: "Moonshine Valley" 1922 (& sp.).

Brent, Lynton W. Writer. Films: "The Texas Kid" 1943 (story).

Brent, William. Writer. Films: "The Cowboy and the Blonde" 1941 (story).

Brescia, Alfonso (Al Brady). Director. Films: "Colt Is the Law" 1965-Ital./Span. (& sp.); "Days of Violence" 1967-Ital.; "Killer Caliber .32" 1967-Ital.; "Thirty Winchesters for El Diablo" 1967-Ital. (sp. only); "If One Is Born a Swine … Kill Him" 1968-Ital.; "Colt in the Hand of the Devil" 1972-Ital. (sp. only); "If One Is Born a Swine" 1972-Ital./Span.

Bresler, Jerry (1912-8/23/77). Producer. Films: "Major Dundee" 1965.

Breslin, Howard (1912-5/30/64). Writer. Films: "Bad Day at Black Rock" 1955 (story).

Breslow, Lou (1900-11/10/87). Screenwriter. Films: "Shooting High" 1940.

Bretherton, Howard (1896-4/12/69). Director. Films: "Hopalong Cassidy" 1935; "Bar 20 Rides Again" 1936; "Call of the Prairie" 1936; "The Eagle's Brood" 1936; "King of the Royal Mounted" 1936; "Three on the Trail" 1936; "Wild Brian Kent" 1936; "Fugitive from Sonora" 1937; "Heart of the West" 1937; "It Happened Out West" 1937; "Secret Valley" 1937; "Western Gold" 1937; "The Showdown" 1940; "In Old Colorado" 1941; "Outlaws of the Desert" 1941; "Riders of the Badlands" 1941; "Twilight on the Trail" 1941; "Below the Border" 1942; "Dawn on the Great Divide" 1942; "Down Texas Way" 1942; "Ghost Town Law" 1942; "Pirates of the Prairie" 1942; "Riders of the West" 1942; "West of the Law" 1942; "West of Tombstone" 1942; "Beyond the Last Frontier" 1943; "Bordertown Gunfighters" 1943; "Carson City Cyclone" 1943; "The Man from the Rio Grande" 1943; "Riders of the Rio Grande" 1943; "Santa Fe Scouts" 1943; "Wagon Tracks West" 1943; "Hidden Valley Outlaws" 1944; "Law of the Valley" 1944; "Outlaws of Santa Fe" 1944; "The San Antonio Kid" 1944; "Gun Smoke" 1945; "The Navajo Trail" 1945; "Renegades of the Rio Grande" 1945; "The Topeka Terror" 1945; "Ridin' Down the Trail" 1947; "Trail of the Mounties" 1947; "Where the North Begins" 1947; "Triggerman" 1948; "Carson City" 1952; "Night Raiders" 1952.

Brewer, Jameson. Screenwriter. Films: "Ghost Town" 1956; "The Over-the-Hill Gang" TVM-1969.

Brice, Monte (1891-11/8/62). Screenwriter. Films: "Hands Up!" 1926; "Singin' in the Corn" 1946.

Bricken, Jules. Director. Films: "Drango" 1957. ¶TV: *Riverboat* 1959-61 (prod.).

Bricker, George (1899-1/22/55). Screenwriter. Films: "North to the Klondike" 1942; "Al Jennings of Oklahoma" 1951.

Bridges, James (1928-6/6/93). Screenwriter. Films: "The Appaloosa" 1966.

Bridson, T.H. Screenwriter. Films: "Hidden Treasure Rance" 1913.

Bright, Kevin S. Director. TV: *Adventures of Brisco County, Jr.*—"And Baby Makes Three" 4-22-94.

Bright, Maurice A. *see* Lucidi, Maurizio.

Briley, John. Screenwriter. Films: "Eagle's Wing" 1979-Brit./Span.

Brill, Leighton. Screenwriter. Films: "Black Arrow" 1944-serial.

Brisbane, Jane. Screenwriter. Films: "The Road to Fort Alamo" 1966-Fr./Ital.

Briskin, Fred. Producer. TV: *The Adventures of Rin Tin Tin* 1954-59; *Tales of the Texas Rangers* 1955-57 (exec. prod.).

Briskin, Irving. Producer. Films: "Border Law" 1931; "The One Way Trail" 1931; "The Range Feud" 1931; "Daring Danger" 1932; "End of the Trail" 1932; "Ridin' for Justice" 1932; "The Riding Tornado" 1932; "South of the Rio Grande" 1932; "Texas Cyclone" 1932; "Two-Fisted Law" 1932; "The Thrill Hunter" 1933; "The Fighting Ranger" 1934; "The Man Trailer" 1934; "Justice of the Range" 1935; "End of the Trail" 1936; "Klondike" 1943.

Briskin, Mort. Producer. Films: "A Man Alone" 1955 (story only).

¶TV: *Sheriff of Cochise* 1956-57; *U.S. Marshal* 1958-60.

Bristow, Gwen (1903-8/17/80). Writer. Films: "Jubilee Trail" 1954 (story).

Broadhurst, George. Writer. "The Call of the North" 1914 (story).

Broadwell, Robert. Director. Films: "A Law Unto Himself" 1916.

Brochero, Eduardo Maria. Screenwriter. Films: "Charge of the Seventh Cavalry" 1964-Ital./Span./Fr.; "For a Fist in the Eye" 1965-Ital./Span.; "Adios Hombre" 1966-Ital./Span.; "Outlaw of Red River" 1966-Ital.; "Ringo: Face of Revenge" 1966-Ital./Span.; "Ringo, the Lone Rider" 1967-Ital./Span.; "All Out" 1968-Ital./Span.; "Cowards Don't Pray" 1968-Ital./Span.; "One Against One ... No Mercy" 1968-Span./Ital.; "Stranger in Paso Bravo" 1968-Ital.; "Two Crosses at Danger Pass" 1968-Ital./Span.; "Apocalypse Joe" 1970-Ital./Span.; "Dead Men Ride" 1970-Ital./Span.; "Light the Fuse ... Sartana Is Coming" 1971-Ital./Fr.; "Matalo!" 1971-Ital./Span.; "Fasthand" 1972-Ital./Span. (story only).

Brock, Lou. Director. Films: "Bandits and Ballads" 1939-short (& sp.); "Cupid Rides the Range" 1939-short (& sp); "Ranch House Romeo" 1939-short.

Brocks, Lino. Screenwriter. Films: "Arizona Kid" 1974-Ital./Phil.

Brockwell, Lillian V. Screenwriter. Films: "A Law Unto Himself" 1916.

Brodkin, Herbert (1913-10/29/90). Producer. TV: *Shane* 1966.

Brodney, Oscar (1905-). Screenwriter. Films: "Comanche Territory" 1950; "Frenchie" 1950; "The Spoilers" 1955; "A Day of Fury" 1956; "Star in the Dust" 1956.

Broidy, William F. Producer. Films: "Call of the Klondike" 1950; "Yukon Gold" 1952; "Yukon Vengeance" 1954; "Treasure of Ruby Hills" 1955; "Yaqui Drums" 1956; "Seven Guns to Mesa" 1958. ¶TV: *Wild Bill Hickok* 1951-53.

Brolin, James (1942-). TV: *Young Riders*—"Shadowmen" 5-21-92.

Bromfield, Louis (1896-1956). Writer. Films: "Brigham Young—Frontiersman" 1940 (story).

Broneau, Helen. Screenwriter. Films: "O.U. West" 1925.

Bronston, Douglas. Screenwriter. Films: "The Oregon Trail" 1923-serial; "The Girl in the Garrett" 1927.

Bronston, Frank. *see* Bianchi, Mario.

Brooks, Marion. Screenwriter. Films: "The Man Who Paid" 1922 (& story).

Brooks, Mel (1926-). Director. Films: "Blazing Saddles" 1974 (& sp.).

Brooks, Richard (1912-3/11/92). Director. Films: "Men of Texas" 1942 (sp. only); "Sin Town" 1942 (sp. only); "The Last Hunt" 1956 (& sp.); "The Professionals" 1966 (& prod./sp.); "Bite the Bullet" 1975 (& prod./sp.).

Brooks, Van Dyke. Screenwriter. Films: "Bond of Blood" 1916.

Brooks, Virginia. Writer. Films: "Reformation" 1915 (story).

Brough, Walter. Screenwriter. Films: "The Desperados" 1969.

Brower, Otto (1891-1/25/46). Director. Films: "Avalanche" 1928; "Stairs of Sand" 1929; "Sunset Pass" 1929; "The Border Legion" 1930; "The Light of the Western Stars" 1930; "The Santa Fe Trail" 1930; "Clearing the Range" 1931; "Fighting Caravans" 1931; "Hard Hombre" 1931; "The Devil Horse" 1932-serial; "Fighting for Justice" 1932; "Gold" 1932; "Local Bad Man" 1932; "Spirit of the West" 1932; "Crossfire" 1933; "Scarlet River" 1933; "Mystery Mountain" 1934-serial; "Speed Wings" 1934; "The Outlaw Deputy" 1935; "The Phantom Empire" 1935-serial; "The Gay Caballero" 1940.

Brown, Clarence (1890-8/17/87). Director. Films: "The Great Redeemer" 1920; "The Last of the Mohicans" 1920; "The Trail of '98" 1929.

Brown, Donald H. Producer. Films: "Don't Fence Me In" 1945; "Utah" 1945.

Brown, Forrest. Writer. Films: "Boss of Lonely Valley" 1937 (story).

Brown, Harry (1917-11/2/86). Writer. Films: "El Dorado" 1967 (story only).

Brown, Harry Joe (1893-4/28/72). Director. Films: "North of Nevada" 1924 (prod. only); "The Dangerous Dude" 1925; "The Fighting Smile" 1925 (sp. only); "Fighting Thorobreds" 1925; "Moran of the Mounted" 1926; "Gun Gospel" 1927; "The Land Beyond the Law" 1927; "Code of the Scarlet" 1928; "The Wagon Show" 1928; "The Lawless Legion" 1929; "The Royal Rider" 1929; "Senor Americano" 1929; "The Wagon Master" 1929; "The Fighting Legion" 1930; "Lucky Larkin" 1930 (& prod.); "Mountain Justice" 1930 (& prod.); "Parade of the West" 1930; "Song of the Cabellero" 1930; "Sons of the Saddle" 1930; "Beyond the Rockies" 1932 (prod. only); "The Desperadoes" 1943; "The Gunfighter" 1947 (prod. only); "Coroner Creek" 1948 (prod. only); "The Untamed Breed" 1948 (prod. only); "The Doolins of Oklahoma" 1949 (prod. only); "The Walking Hills" 1949 (prod. only); "The Nevadan" 1950 (prod. only); "Stage to Tucson" 1950; "Apache Drums" 1951 (story only); "Man in the Saddle" 1951 (prod. only); "Only the Valiant" 1951 (sp. only); "Santa Fe" 1951 (prod. only); "Bugles in the Afternoon" 1952 (sp. only); "Hangman's Knot" 1952 (prod. only); "The Last Posse" 1953 (prod. only); "The Stranger Wore a Gun" 1953 (prod. only); "Three Hours to Kill" 1954 (prod. only); "A Lawless Street" 1955 (prod. only); "May Rivers to Cross" 1955 (sp. only); "Ten Wanted Men" 1955 (prod. only); "Seventh Cavalry" 1956 (prod. only); "Decision at Sundown" 1957 (prod. only); "The Guns of Fort Petticoat" 1957 (prod. only); "The Tall T" 1957; "Buchanan Rides Alone" 1958 (prod. only); "The Fiend Who Walked the West" 1958 (sp. only); "Comanche Station" 1960 (prod. only); "A Time for Killing" 1967 (prod. only).

Brown, Jr., Hiram S. Producer. Films: "Zorro's Fighting Legion" 1939-serial; "Adventures of Red Ryder" 1940-serial; "King of the Royal Mounted" 1940-serial; "King of the Texas Rangers" 1941.

Brown, J.P.S. (1930-). Writer. Films: "Pocket Money" 1972 (story).

Brown, Joe David (1916-4/22/76). Writer. Films: "Stars in My Crown" 1950 (story).

Brown, Karl (1897-3/25/90). Screenwriter. Films: "Prairie Pioneers" 1941 (story only); "Under Fiesta Stars" 1941 (& story); "The Vanquished" 1953 (story only).

Brown, Lee R. Writer. Films: "The Gay Buckaroo" 1932 (story).

Brown, Leete Renick. Writer. Films: "Kindled Courage" 1923 (story).

Brown, Reg. Director. Films: "Son of the Renegade" 1953.

Brown, Rowland (1900-5/6/63). Screenwriter. Films: "Points West" 1929; "The Nevadan" 1950.

Brown, Will C. Writer. Films: "Man of the West" 1958 (story).

Browne, Lewis Allen. Screenwriter. Films: "The Love Bandit" 1924.

Browne, Porter Emerson. Writer. Films: "The Bad Man" 1930 (story); "The Bad Man" 1941 (story).

Browne, Reg. Director. Films: "Gunsmoke" 1947 (sp. Only). ¶TV *Judge Roy Bean*—"Citizen Romeo" 12-1-55, "Murder in Langtry" 12-1-55, "Checkmate" 1-1-56, "The Eyes of Texas" 1-1-56, "The Travelers" 1-1-56, "Bad Medicine" 6-1-56, "The Defense Rests" 6-1-56, "The Cross-Draw Kid" 7-1-56.

Browning, Tod (1882-10/6/62). Director. Films: "Hands Up!" 1917; "Revenge" 1918.

Bruce, George (1898-). Director. Films: "Kit Carson" 1940 (sp. only); "Fury in Paradise" 1955-U.S./Mex. (& sp.); "Ride a Crooked Trail" 1958 (story); "Frontier Uprising" 1961 (story only).

Bruckman, Clyde (1895-1/4/55). Director. Films: "Horses' Collars" 1935-short; "Whoops, I'm an Indian" 1936-short; "Pest from the West" 1939-short; "Rockin' Through the Rockies" 1940-short; "Twilight on the Prairie" 1944; "Under Western Skies" 1945; "Out West" 1947-short; "Pals and Gals" 1954-short (story only).

Bruckner, William. Screenwriter. Films: "Riders of the Purple Sage" 1941; "Sundown Jim" 1942.

Brummell, Beau. Screenwriter. Films: "Three Bullets for a Long Gun" 1970-Ger./S.Afr. (& prod.).

Bruning, Mary C. Writer. Films: "Tricks" 1925 (story).

Bryan, Jay J. Screenwriter. Films: "Fast Bullets" 1936.

Bryan, Paul M. Screenwriter. Films: "The Steel Trail" 1923-serial; "The Dude Cowboy" 1926; "Hair Trigger Baxter" 1926; "The Four-Footed Ranger" 1928.

Bryden, Bill. Screenwriter. Films: "The Long Riders" 1980.

Bucceri, Franco. Screenwriter. Films: "Let Them Rest" 1967-Ital./Ger.; "California" 1976-Ital./Span.

Buchanan, William. Screenwriter. Films: "Rip Roarin' Buckaroo" 1936.

Buchman, Harold (1913-6/22/90). Screenwriter. Films: "Romance of the Rio Grande" 1941.

Buchs, Julio (Julio Garcia) (1926-1/19/73). Director. Films: "Django Does Not Forgive" 1967-Ital./Span. (& sp.); "The Man Who Killed Billy the Kid" 1967-Span./Ital. (& sp./story); "A Bullet for Sandoval" 1970-Ital./Span.

Buck, Jules (1917-). Producer.

Films: "The Great Scout and Cathouse Thursday" 1976.

Buckingham, Thomas (1895-9/7/34). Director. Films: "Tony Runs Wild" 1926; "Land of the Lawless" 1927; "Crashing Through" 1928; "The Painted Desert" 1931.

Buckley, Frank R. Writer. Films: "The Gentle Cyclone" 1926 (story).

Buckley, Harold. Screenwriter. Films: "The California Mail" 1937; "Guns of the Pecos" 1937.

Buckner, Robert (1903-1/24/61). Screenwriter. Films: "Gold Is Where You Find It" 1938; "Dodge City" 1939; "The Oklahoma Kid" 1939; "Santa Fe Trail" 1940; "Virginia City" 1940; "San Antonio" 1945 (prod. only); "Cheyenne" 1947 (prod. only); "The Man Behind the Gun" 1952 (story only); "Love Me Tender" 1956; "From Hell to Texas" 1958 (& prod.); "Return of the Gunfighter" TVM-1967 (& story).

Buell, Jed. Producer. Films: "Romance Rides the Range" 1936; "The Fighting Deputy" 1937; "Melody of the Plains" 1937; "Moonlight on the Range" 1937; "The Roaming Cowboy" 1937; "The Singing Buckaroo" 1937; "Knight of the Plains" 1938; "The Rangers' Roundup" 1938; "Songs and the Bullets" 1938; "The Terror of Tiny Town" 1938.

Buffington, Adele (Jess Bowers) (1900-11/23/73). Screenwriter. Films: "The Bloodhound" 1925; "Love on the Rio Grande" 1925; "The Galloping Cowboy" 1926; "The Avenging Rider" 1928 (story only); "Phantom City" 1928 (story only); "Freighters of Destiny" 1932; "Ghost Valley" 1932; "Haunted Gold" 1932; "A Man's Land" 1932; "Single-Handed Sanders" 1932 (story only); "Powdersmoke Range" 1935; "Hi Gaucho!" 1936; "Arizona Bound" 1941; "Forbidden Tails" 1941; "The Gunman from Bodie" 1941; "Below the Border" 1942; "Dawn on the Great Divide" 1942; "Down Texas Way" 1942; "Ghost Town Law" 1942; "Riders of the West" 1942; "West of the Law" 1942; "The Ghost Rider" 1943; "Outlaws of Stampede Pass" 1943; "Six Gun Gospel" 1943; "The Stranger from Pecos" 1943; "The Texas Kid" 1943; "Raiders of the Border" 1944; "Bad Men of the Border" 1945; "Flame of the West" 1945; "Frontier Feud" 1945; "The Lost Trail" 1945; "The Navajo Trail" 1945; "The Navajo Trail" 1945; "Drifting Along" 1946; "Shadows on the Range" 1946; "Wild Beauty" 1946; "Overland Trails" 1948; "The Valiant Hombre" 1948; "Crashing Thru" 1949;

"Haunted Trails" 1949; "Range Land" 1949; "Riders of the Dusk" 1949; "Shadows of the West" 1949; "West of El Dorado" 1949; "Western Renegades" 1949; "Arizona Territory" 1950; "Gunslingers" 1950; "Jiggs and Maggie Out West" 1950; "Six Gun Mesa" 1950; "West of Wyoming" 1950; "Overland Telegraph" 1951; "Born to the Saddle" 1953; "Cow Country" 1953; "Bullwhip" 1958.

Buffum, Ray (1904-12/13/80). Screenwriter. Films: "The Black Dakotas" 1954.

Bullock, Walter. Screenwriter. Films: "The Gay Caballero" 1940 (story only); "The Cowboy and the Blonde" 1941 (& story).

Bungerford, J. Edward. Writer. Films: "The Law and the Outlaw" 1913 (story).

Bunker, Robert. Writer. Films: "Jeremiah Johnson" 1972 (story).

Burbridge, Betty. Screenwriter. Films: "Battling Buddy" 1924; "Double Action Daniels" 1925; "Galloping Jinx" 1925; "Quicker'n Lightnin'" 1925; "Reckless Courage" 1925; "Saddle Cyclone" 1925; "Ace of Action" 1926; "Bad Man's Bluff" 1926; "The Bonanza Buckaroo" 1926; "Double Daring" 1926 (story only); "The Fighting Cheat" 1926; "Riding Rivals" 1926; "Trumpin' Trouble" 1926; "Twin Triggers" 1926; "Twisted Triggers" 1926; "Vanishing Hoofs" 1926; "Code of the Cow Country" 1927; "The Interferin' Gent" 1927; "The Phantom Buster" 1927; "Soda Water Cowboy" 1927; "Tearin' into Trouble" 1927; "White Pebbles" 1927; "The Flying Buckaroo" 1928; "In Old Cheyenne" 1931; "Law of the Rio Grande" 1931; "Mounted Fury" 1931; "The Sign of the Wolf" 1931-serial; "Between Fighting Men" 1932; "Hell Fire Austin" 1932; "The Lone Avenger" 1933 (& story); "The Phantom Thunderbolt" 1933; "Boss Cowboy" 1934; "Rawhide Mail" 1934; "Melody Trail" 1935; "The Singing Vagabond" 1935; "Tracy Rides" 1935; "Come On, Cowboys" 1937; "Springtime in the Rockies" 1937; "Wild Horse Rodeo" 1937; "Gold Mine in the Sky" 1938; "Heroes of the Hills" 1938; "Man from Music Mountain" 1938; "Outlaws of Sonora" 1938; "Pals of the Saddle" 1938; "Prairie Moon" 1938; "The Purple Vigilantes" 1938; "Red River Range" 1938; "Riders of the Black Hills" 1938 (& story); "Under Western Stars" 1938; "Colorado Sunset" 1939; "The Kansas Terrors" 1939; "New Frontier" 1939; "The Night Riders" 1939; "Robin' Tumbleweeds" 1939; "South of the

Border" 1939; "Three Texas Steers" 1939; "Wyoming Outlaw" 1939; "Gaucho Serenade" 1940; "Rancho Grande" 1940; "Ride, Tenderfoot, Ride" 1940 (story only); "Under Texas Skies" 1940; "Riders of the Badlands" 1941; "Thunder Over the Prairie" 1941; "Stardust on the Sage" 1942; "Frontier Fury" 1943; "Robin Hood of the Range" 1943; "Santa Fe Scouts" 1943; "Oklahoma Raiders" 1944; "Song of the Range" 1944; "West of the Rio Grande" 1944; "The Cherokee Flash" 1945; "The Cisco Kid Returns" 1945; "In Old New Mexico" 1945; "Oregon Trail" 1945; "Utah" 1945 (story only); "Alias Billy the Kid" 1946; "Home on the Range" 1946 (& story); "The Man from Rainbow Valley" 1946; "Out California Way" 1946; "Trail of the Mounties" 1947; "Where the North Begins" 1947; "The Return of Wildfire" 1948; "The Daring Caballero" 1949.

Burch, John (1896-7/29/69). Director. Films: "Gun Law" 1929.

Burkett, James S. Producer. Films: "Don Ricardo Returns" 1946; "Young Daniel Boone" 1950.

Burks, Alex. *see* Bazzoni, Camillo.

Burnett, W.R. (1899-4/25/82). Writer. Films: "Law and Order" 1932 (story); "Wild West Days" 1937 (story); "The Dark Command" 1940 (story); "Law and Order" 1940 (story); "San Antonio" 1945 (sp.); "Belle Starr's Daughter" 1947 (sp.); "Yellow Sky" 1948 (story); "Arrowhead" 1953 (story); "Law and Order" 1953 (story); "The Badlanders" 1958 (story); "Sergeants 3" 1962 (sp.).

Burns, Allan. Screenwriter. Films: "Butch and Sundance: The Early Days" 1979.

Burns, Fred (1878-7/18/55). Screenwriter. Films: "An Indian's Loyalty" 1913 (story only); "Mountain Blood" 1916.

Burns, Walter Noble. Writer. Films: "Billy the Kid" 1930 (story); "Robin Hood of El Dorado" 1936 (story); "Tombstone, the Town Too Tough to Die" 1942 (story).

Burr, C.C. Producer. Films: "Code of the Fearless" 1939; "In Old Montana" 1939; "Two-Gun Troubador" 1939; "Ridin' the Trail" 1940.

Burri, Emil. Screenwriter. Films: "Water for Canitoga" 1939-Ger.

Burt, Frank. Screenwriter. Films: "Law of the Barbary Coast" 1949; "Stage to Tucson" 1950; "The Man from Laramie" 1955.

Burt, Katherine Newlin. Writer. Films: "The Branding Iron" 1920 (story); "The Eagle's Feather" 1923 (story).

Burtis, Thomson. Screenwriter. Films: "In Old Oklahoma" 1943 (& story).

Burton, David (1877-12/30/63). Director. Films: "Fighting Caravans" 1931.

Burton, Shelly. Writer. Films: "The Electric Horseman" 1979 (story).

Burton, William A. Screenwriter. Films: "The Fighting Smile" 1925.

Busch, Melvin. Screenwriter. Films: "Her Perilous Ride" 1917.

Busch, Niven (1903-8/25/91). Screenwriter. Film: "The Westerner" 1940; "Belle Starr" 1941 (story only); "Duel in the Sun" 1946 (story only); "Pursued" 1947; "The Capture" 1950 (& prod.); "The Furies" 1950 (story only); "Distant Drums" 1951 (& story); "The Man from the Alamo" 1953 (story); "The Moonlighter" 1953; "The Treasure of Pancho Villa" 1955.

Bushelman, John. Director. Films: "The Broken Land" 1962.

Buss, Carl A. Screenwriter. Films: "Wagon Wheels" 1934.

Butler, Alexander. Director. Films: "The Night Rider" 1920 (& sp.).

Butler, David (1894-6/15/79). Director. Films: "White Fang" 1936; "Whispering Smith" 1938; "San Antoino" 1945; "Two Guys from Texas" 1948; "Calamity Jane" 1953; "The Command" 1953; "Strange Lady in Town" 1955. ¶TV: *Wagon Train*—"The Honorable Don Charlie Story" 1-22-58, "The Bill Tawnee Story" 2-12-58, "The Bernal Sierra Story" 3-12-58, "The Sally Potter Story" 4-9-58, "The Dick Richardson Story" 12-31-58, "The Jim Bridger Story" 5-10-61, "The Don Alvarado Story" 6-21-61; *Schlitz Playhouse of the Stars*—"Way of the West" 6-6-58; *The Deputy* 1959.

Butler, Frank (1890-6/10/67). Screenwriter. Films: "No Man's Law" 1927; "Montana Moon" 1930 (& story); "Rangers of Fortune" 1940; "California" 1946.

Butler, Hugh. Screenwriter. Films: "The Omaha Trail" 1942.

Butler, Hugo (1914-1/7/68). Screenwriter. Films: "Wyoming" 1940; "Roughshod" 1949.

Butler, John K. (1892-9/18/64). Screenwriter. Films: "Beyond the Last Frontier" 1943; "The Blocked Trail" 1943; "Raiders of Sunset Pass" 1943; "Silver Spurs" 1943; "Hidden Valley Outlaws" 1944; "Pride of the Plains" 1944; "Don't Fence Me In" 1945; "The Man from Oklahoma" 1945; "Sunset in El Dorado" 1945; "Utah" 1945; "My Pal Trigger" 1946; "Robin Hood of Texas" 1947; "California Firebrand" 1948; "The Gallant Legion" 1948 (story only); "Down Dakota Way" 1949; "Rim of the Canyon" 1949; "Susanna Pass" 1949; "Rodeo King and the Senorita" 1951; "Utah Wagon Train" 1951; "Toughest Man in Arizona" 1952; "Drums Across the River" 1954; "The Outcast" 1954; "Hell's Crossroads" 1957 (& story); "Ambush at Cimarron Pass" 1958.

Butler, Michael. Screenwriter. Films: "Nakia" TVM-1974 (& story); "Pale Rider" 1985.

Butler, Robert. Director. Films: "Scandalous John" 1971; "Hot Lead and Cold Feet" 1978; "Lacy and the Mississippi Queen" TVM-1978. ¶TV: *Bonanza*—"Broken Ballad" 10-29-61; *The Rifleman*—"The Princess" 1-8-62; *The Virginian*—"Day of the Scorpion" 9-22-65; *Shane* 1966; *Gunsmoke*—"Prairie Wolfer" 11-13-67, "Mannon" 1-20-69, "The Sodbusters" 11-20-72; *Cimarron Strip*—"The Judgment" 1-4-68, "Without Honor" 2-29-68; *Lancer*—"Death Bait" 1-14-69, "Shadow of a Dead Man" 1-6-70, "The Lion and the Lamb" 2-3-70, "Lifeline" 5-19-70; *Kung Fu*—"Sun and Cloud Shadow" 2-22-73, "Chains" 3-8-73, "The Stone" 4-12-73, "The Ancient Warrior" 5-3-73.

Butragueno, Fernando. Screenwriter. Films: "Shoot to Kill" 1963-Span.

Buzzell, Edward (1895-1/11/85). Director. Films: "Go West" 1940; "The Omaha Trail" 1942.

Buzzi, Gian Luigi. Screenwriter. Films: "Days of Violence" 1967-Ital.

Byrd, John. *see* Moffa, Paolo.

Byrnes, Jim. Screenwriter. Films: "Bounty Man" TVM-1972; "The Macahans" TVM-1976 (& prod.); "Ransom for Alice!" TVM-1977; "The Sacketts" TVM-1979 (& prod.); "The Gambler" TVM-1980 (& prod./story); "The Shadow Riders" TVM-1982; "The Gambler, Part II—The Adventure Continues" TVM-1983; "Gunsmoke: Return to Dodge" TVM-1987; "Miracle in the Wilderness" TVM-1991; "Dead Man's Revenge" TVM-1994. ¶TV: *Lancer*—"The Buscaderos" 3-17-70 (dir.).

Bywood, Clement. Screenwriter. Films: "The Legend of Frenchie King" 1971-Fr./Ital./Span./Brit.

Cabanne, W. Christy (1888-10/15/50). Director. Films: "A Chance Deception" 1913 (sp. only); "During the Round-Up" 1913; "A Misunderstood Boy" 1913 (story only); "Arms and the Gringo" 1914; "The Gunman" 1914; "The Lamb" 1915; "The Martyrs of the Alamo" 1915 (& sp.); "The Outlaw's Revenge" 1916; "Fighting Through" 1919 (& story); "God's Outlaw" 1919 (& sp.); "The Dawn Trail" 1930; "The Last Outlaw" 1936; "The Outcasts of Poker Flat" 1937; "Back Trail" 1938; "Man from Montreal" 1940; "King of the Bandits" 1947 (& story); "Robin Hood of Monterey" 1947; "Silver Trails" 1948.

Cady, Jerry (1908-11/8/48). Screenwriter. Films: "Arizona Wildcat" 1938.

Caesar, Arthur (1892-6/20/53). Writer. Films: "Northwest Rangers" 1942 (story).

Caffey, Michael. Director. Films: "The Silent Gun" TVM-1969; "The Devil and Miss Sarah" TVM-1971; "The Hanged Man" TVM-1974. ¶TV: *Wild Wild West*—"The Night of the Firebrand" 9-15-67, "The Night of the Simian Terror" 2-16-68, "The Night of the Kraken" 11-1-68; *Hondo*—"Hondo and the Apache Trail" 12-22-67; *Lancer*—"Lamp in the Wilderness" 3-10-70; *Paradise*—"Stray Bullet" 12-8-88, "The Traveler" 2-2-89, "Dead Run" 10-7-89, "Dangerous Cargo" 1-20-90, "The Bounty" 1-11-91, "The Valley of Death" 2-8-91; *Adventures of Brisco County, Jr.*—"Fountain of Youth" 1-14-94; *Hawkeye*—"The Plague" 3-2-95.

Cagney, William (1902-1/4/88). Producer. Films: "Only the Valiant" 1951; "Bugles in the Afternoon" 1952.

Cahan, George M. Director. TV: *Cowboy G-Men* 1952-53; *Union Pacific* 1958-60 (prod.); *Cowboy in Africa* 1967-68 (prod.).

Cahn, Edward L. (1899-8/25/63). Director. Films: "Law and Order" 1932; "Flesh and the Spur" 1957; "Gunfighters of Abilene" 1960; "Noose for a Gunman" 1960; "Oklahoma Territory" 1960; "Five Guns to Tombstone" 1961; "Frontier Uprising" 1961; "The Gambler Wore a Gun" 1961; "Gun Fight" 1961; "Gun Street" 1961.

Caiano, Mario (William Hawkins). Director. Films: "Ride and Kill" 1964-Ital./Span. (& sp.); "Sign of Coyote" 1964-Ital./Span.; "Sign of Zorro" 1964-Ital./Span.; "Coffin for the Sheriff" 1965-Ital./Span.; "Adios Hombre" 1966-Ital./Span. (& sp.); "Ringo: Face of Revenge" 1966-Ital./Span. (& sp.); "Ringo, the Lone Rider" 1967-Ital./Span. (& sp. only); "Train for Durango" 1967-Ital./Span. (& sp.); "Man Who Cried for Revenge" 1969-Ital./Span. (& sp.); "Fighting Fists of Shanghai Joe" 1973-Ital. (& sp.).

Cain, Christopher. Director. Films: "Young Guns" 1988 (& prod.).

Cain, James M. (1906-10/27/79). Screenwriter. Films: "Stand Up and Fight" 1939.

Calabrese, Franco. Screenwriter. Films: "Beast" 1970-Ital.

Caldwell, Fred. Director. Films: "The Lone Rider" 1922 (& sp.); "Western Justice" 1923 (& sp.); "The Lone Horseman" 1929 (& sp.).

Caldwell, Taylor (1900-8/30/85). Writer. Films: "Testimony of Two Men" TVM-1977 (story).

Calhoun, Rory (1922-). Producer. Films: "Shotgun" 1955 (sp. only); "Domino Kid" 1957 (& story); "The Hired Gun" 1957; "Apache Territory" 1958. ¶TV: *The Texan* 1958-60.

Callaghan, George H. Producer. Films: "Romance Rides the Range" 1936; "Moonlight on the Range" 1937; "The Singing Buckaroo" 1937.

Callahan, Robert E. Writer. Films: "Daughter of the West" 1949 (story).

Calleia, Joseph (1897-10/31/75). Screenwriter. Films: "Robin Hood of El Dorado" 1936.

Calloway, Ray. *see* Colucci, Mario.

Caltabiano, Alfio. Director. Films: "Ballad of a Gunman" 1967-Ital./Ger. (& sp.); "Man Called Amen" 1972-Ital. (& sp.); "They Still Call Me Amen" 1972-Ital. (& sp.).

Calvelli, Joseph. Screenwriter. Films: "Death of a Gunfighter" 1969.

Calvert, John. Producer. Films: "Gold Fever" 1952 (& story).

Camden, Tom. Screenwriter. Films: "Arizona Trails" 1935.

Caminito, Augusto. Screenwriter. Films: "Django, Last Killer" 1967-Ital.; "Pecos Cleans up" 1967-Ital.; "Poker with Pistols" 1967-Ital.; "Death Rides Alone" 1968-Ital./Span.; "Greatest Robbery in the West" 1968-Ital.; "Brothers Blue" 1973-Ital./Fr.

Camp, Joe (1939-). Director. Films: "Hawmps!" 1976 (& prod.).

Campbell, A. Bruce (1881-19??). Writer. Films: "The End of Black Bart" 1913 (story).

Campbell, Colin (1859-8/26/28). Director. Films: "Romance of the Rio Grande" 1911; "The God of Gold" 1912 (& sp.); "The Last of Her Tribe" 1912; "The Little Indian Martyr" 1912; "Opitsah" 1912; "A Reconstructed Rebel" 1912; "Sergeant Byrne of the N.W.M.P." 1912 (& story); "The Escape of Jim Dolan" 1913; "In the Long Ago" 1913; "The Noisy Six" 1913; "Vengeance Is Mine" 1913; "A Wild Ride" 1913 (& sp.); "Chip of the Flying U" 1914; "His Fight" 1914 (& story); "In Defiance of the Law" 1914 (& sp.); "In the Days of the Thundering Herd" 1914; "The Lonesome Trail" 1914; "Me an' Bill" 1914 (& sp.); "Shotgun Jones" 1914; "The Spoilers" 1914; "When the Cook Fell Ill" 1914; "When the West Was Young" 1914; "The Wilderness Mail" 1914; "Man's Law" 1915 (& sp.); "The Regeneration of Jim Halsey" 1916 (& sp.); "Her Perilous Ride" 1917; "Tongues of Flame" 1918; "Two Kinds of Women" 1922; "Bucking the Barrier" 1923; "The Buster" 1923; "The Grail" 1923; "Three Who Paid" 1923.

Campbell, E. Murray. Screenwriter. Films: "The Last Outlaw" 1936 (& story).

Campbell, R. Wright (1927-). Screenwriter. Films: "Five Guns West" 1955; "Gun for a Coward" 1957; "Quantez" 1957 (& story).

Camus, Mario. Director. Films: "Trinity Sees Red" 1971-Ital./Span. (& sp.).

Canavari, Cesare. Director. Films: "Matalo!" 1971-Ital./Span.

Cannell, Stephen J. (1943-). Screenwriter. Films: "Scott Free" TVM-1976; "The Night Rider" TVM-1979.

Cannon, Raymond (1892-7/7/77). Screenwriter. Films: "Go West" 1925.

Cano, Matteo. Director. Films: "Last of the Mohicans" 1965-Ital./Span./Ger.

Canutt, Yakima (1895-5/24/86). Director. Films: "The Iron Rider" 1926 (prod. only); "The Cheyenne Kid" 1930 (sp. only); "Riders of the Golden Gulch" 1932 (story only); "Sheriff of Cimarron" 1945; "The Adventures of Frank and Jesse James" 1948-serial; "Carson City Raiders" 1948; "Dangers of the Canadian Mounted" 1948-serial; "Oklahoma Badlands" 1948; "Sons of Adventure" 1948; "The Lawless Rider" 1954.

Capellani, Albert. Director. Films: "American Maid" 1917.

Capitani, Giorgio. Director. Films: "The Ruthless Four" 1968-Ital./Fr.

Capps, Dennis D. Screenwriter. Films: "Cowboy" TVM-1983.

Capra, Frank (1897-9/3/91). Director. Films: "Westward the Women" 1951 (story only).

Capri, Tito. Screenwriter. Films: "Payment in Blood" 1968-Ital.

Capriccoli, Massimilliano. Screenwriter. Films: "Fort Yuma Gold" 1966-Ital./Fr./Span.; "He Who Shoots First" 1966-Ital.

Capuano, Luigi (Lewis King, Francesco De Masi). Director. Films: "Magnificent Texan" 1967-Ital./Span.; "Blood Calls to Blood" 1968-Ital.

Carabatsos, Steven. Screenwriter. Films: "El Condor" 1970; "The Revengers" 1972-U.S./Mex. (story only).

Caravaglia, Giuliana. Screenwriter. Films: "Duel in the Eclipse" 1967-Span.

Carboni, Fabio. Screenwriter. Films: "Patience Has a Limit, We Don't" 1974-Span./Ital.

Cardiff, Albert. *see* Cardone, Albert.

Cardone, Albert (Albert Cardiff). Director. Films: "Long Day of the Massacre" 1968-Ital. (& sp.); "Seven Dollars on the Red" 1968-Ital./Span. (& sp.); "Twenty Thousand Dollars for Seven" 1968-Ital. (& sp.); "Wrath of God" 1968-Ital./Span. (& sp.); "Blood at Sundown" 1969-Ital./Ger.

Cardos, John (1928-). Director. Films: "The Red, White and Black" 1970; "The Female Bunch" 1971.

Carewe, Edwin (1881-1/22/40). Director. Films: "The Cowboy and the Lady" 1915; "Their Compact" 1917; "The Trail of the Shadow" 1917; "The Trail to Yesterday" 1918; "Isobel, or the Trail's End" 1920; "Rio Grande" 1920 (& sp.); "I Am the Law" 1922; "The Bad Man" 1923; "The Girl of the Golden West" 1923; "Ramona" 1928; "The Spoilers" 1930 (& prod.).

Carey, Harry (1878-9/21/47). Screenwriter. Films: "A Gambler's Honor" 1913 (story only); "A Knight of the Range" 1916; "Hell Bent" 1918; "Riders of Vengeance" 1919 (story only); "Human Stuff" 1920; "The Kick Back" 1922 (story only).

Carhart, Arthur (1892-). Writer. Films: "Ridin' On" 1936 (story).

Carlile, Clancy (1930-). Writer. Films: "Children of the Dust" TVM-1995 (story).

Carlos, Luciano B. Director. Films: "Arizona Kid" 1974-Ital./Phil. (& sp.).

Carleton, Lloyd B. Director. Films: "The Girl I Left Behind Me" 1915; "The Golden Spurs" 1915; "Two Men of Sandy Bar" 1916; "The Yaqui" 1916; "A Yoke of Gold" 1916; "Nine and Three-Fifths Seconds" 1925.

Carlson, Matthew. Screenwriter. Films: "Wagons East!" 1994.

Carlson, Richard (1912-11/25/77). Director. Films: "Four Guns to the Border" 1954; "The Saga of Hemp Brown" 1958; "Kid Rodelo" 1966-U.S./Span.

Carmineo, Giuliano (Anthony Ascott). Director. Films: "Find a Place to Die" 1968-Ital. (& sp.); "The Moment to Kill" 1968-Ital./Ger.; "I Am Sartana, Your Angel of Death" 1969-Ital./Fr.; "His Name Was Holy Ghost" 1970-Ital./Span.; "Forewarned, Half-Killed ... The Word of the Holy Ghost" 1971-Ital./Span. (& sp.); "Heads You Die ... Tails I Kill You" 1971-Ital. (& sp.); "Light the Fuse ... Sartana Is Coming" 1971-Ital./Fr. (& sp.); "They Call Him Cemetery" 1971-Ital./Span.; "Have a Good Funeral, My Friend ... Sartana Will Pay" 1972-Ital. (& sp.); "I Am Sartana, Trade Your Guns for a Coffin" 1972-Ital. (& sp.); "Return of Halleluja" 1972-Ital./Ger.; "Man Called Invincible" 1973-Ital.; "Dick Luft in Sacramento" 1974-Ital. (& sp.).

Carminito, Augusto. Screenwriter. Films: "Long Days of Vengeance" 1967-Ital./Span.

Carpenter, Edward Childs. Screenwriter. Films: "Captain Courtesy" 1915.

Carpenter, Horace B. (1875-5/21/45). Director. Films: "Wild and Woolly" 1917 (story only); "The Riding Fool" 1924; "Desperate Odds" 1925; "Fangs of Fate" 1925 (& sp.); "Flashing Steeds" 1925; "The Sagebrush Lady" 1925; "The Last Chance" 1926; "Western Trails" 1926; "Just Travelin'" 1927; "The Arizona Kid" 1929 (& sp.); "False Feathers" 1929; "West of the Rockies" 1929; "The Pecos Dandy" 1934.

Carpenter, John. Screenwriter. Films: "Son of the Renegade" 1953 (& prod.); "The Lawless Rider" 1954

(& prod.); "Outlaw Treasure" 1955 (& prod.); "I Killed Wild Bill Hickok" 1956 (& prod.); "El Diablo" CTVM-1990; "Blood River" TVM-1994.

Carpenter, Joseph. Screenwriter. Films: "Shark River" 1953.

Carpentieri, Luigi. Producer. Films: "The Hills Run Red" 1966-Ital.; "Navajo Joe" 1966-Ital./Span.

Carpi, Florenzo. Screenwriter. Films: "He Who Shoots First" 1966-Ital.

Carpi, Tito. Screenwriter. Films: "Few Dollars for Django" 1966-Ital./Span.; "Johnny Hamlet" 1966-Ital.; "Kill Them All and Come Back Alone" 1967-Ital./Span.; "Rick and John, Conquerors of the West" 1967-Ital.; "Son of Django" 1967-Ital.; "Between God, the Devil and a Winchester" 1968-Ital./Span.; "Dead for a Dollar" 1968-Ital.; "The Moment to Kill" 1968-Ital./Ger.; "On Against One ... No Mercy" 1968-Span./Ital.; "I Am Sartana, Your Angel of Death" 1969-Ital./Fr.; "His Name Was Holy Ghost" 1970-Ital./Span.; "Reverend Colt" 1970-Ital./Span.; "Forewarned, Half-Killed. .. The Word of the Holy Ghost" 1971-Ital./Span.; "Heads You Die ... Tails I Kill You" 1971-Ital.; "Light the Fuse ... Sartana Is Coming" 1971-Ital./Fr.; "Return of Halleluja" 1972-Ital./Ger.; "Sting of the West" 1972-Ital.; "Three Musketeers of the West" 1972-Ital.; "Man Called Invincible" 1973-Ital.

Carr, Harry. Screenwriter. Films: "When a Man's a Man" 1924.

Carr, John. Director. Films: "The Talisman" 1966 (& prod./sp.).

Carr, June. Screenwriter. Films: "The Frontier Phantom" 1952.

Carr, Mary Jane (1895-4/23/88). Writer. Films: "Westward Ho the Wagons" 1956 (story).

Carr, Richard (1928-6/13/88). Screenwriter. Films: "Man from Del Rio" 1956; "Heaven with a Gun" 1969; "Macho Callahan" 1970 (story only); "The Over-the-Hill Gang Rides Again" TVM-1970; "Wild Women" TVM-1970.

Carr, Thomas (1907-). Director. Films: "Bandits of the Badlands" 1945; "The Cherokee Flash" 1945; "Oregon Trail" 1945; "Rough Riders of Cheyenne" 1945; "Santa Fe Saddlemates" 1945 (& prod.); "Sheriff of Cimarron" 1945 (prod. only); "Alias Billy the Kid" 1946; "Days of Buffalo Bill" 1946; "The El Paso Kid" 1946; "Red River Renegades" 1946; "Rio Grande Raiders" 1946; "Code of the

Saddle" 1947; "Jesse James Rides Again" 1947-serial; "Song of the Wasteland" 1947; "Colorado Ranger" 1950; "Crooked River" 1950; "The Daltons' Women" 1950; "Fast on the Draw" 1950; "Hostile Country" 1950; "Marshal of Heldorado" 1950; "Outlaws of Texas" 1950; "Roar of the Iron Horse" 1950-serial; "West of the Brazos" 1950; "Wanted Dead or Alive" 1951; "The Man from Black Hills" 1952; "The Maverick" 1952; "Wyoming Roundup" 1952; "The Fighting Lawman" 1953; "Rebel City" 1953; "Star of Texas" 1953; "Topeka" 1953; "Bitter Creek" 1954; "The Desperado" 1954; "The Forty-Niners" 1954; "The Tall Stranger" 1957; "Gunsmoke in Tucson" 1958; "Cast a Long Shadow" 1959. ¶TV: *The Range Rider* 1951; *The Adventures of Champion* 1955; *Buffalo Bill, Jr.* 1955; *Cheyenne* 1955; *Wanted—Dead or Alive*—"The Martin Poster" 9-6-58, "Dead End" 9-27-58, "Eight Cent Record" 12-20-58, "The Legend" 3-7-59, "Railroaded" 3-14-59, "The Kovack Affair" 3-28-59, "Littlest Giant" 4-25-59, "Montana Kid" 9-5-59, "Twelve Hours to Crazy Horse" 11-21-59, "The Monsters" 1-16-60, "Prison Trail" 5-14-60; *Northwest Passage*—"The Witch" 2-13-59; *Stagecoach West* 1960; *Bonanza*—"Gabrielle" 12-24-61; *Rawhide*—"Incident of the Hunter" 9-28-62, "Incident of the Four Horsemen" 10-26-62, "Incident of the Lost Woman" 11-2-62, "Incident of the Wolvers" 11-16-62, "Incident of the Querencias" 12-7-62, "Incident of the Buryin' Man" 1-4-63, "Incident at Spider Rock" 1-18-63, "Incident of Judgment Day" 2-8-63, "Incident of the Married Widow" 3-1-63, "Incident of the Comanchero" 3-22-63, "Incident of the Black Ace" 4-12-63, "Incident at Rio Doloroso" 5-10-63, "Incident of the Red Wind" 9-26-63, "Incident at Paradise" 10-24-63, "Incident at Farragut Pass" 10-31-63, "Incident of the Prophecy" 11-21-63, "Incident of the Death Dancer" 12-5-63, "Incident of the Midnight Cave" 1-16-64, "Incident at Gila Flats" 1-30-64, "Incident of the Swinder" 2-20-64, "Incident at the Odyssey" 3-26-64, "Incident at El Toro" 4-9-64, "Incident at Deat Horse" 4-16-64 & 4-23-64, "Incident of the Peyote Cup" 5-14-64, "Six Weeks to Bent Fork" 9-28-65, "Walk into Terror" 10-5-65, "Brush War at Buford" 11-23-65; *Laramie*—"Gun Duel" 12-25-62; *Gunsmoke*—"Ex-Con" 11-30-63; *The Guns of Will Sonnett*—"The Natural Way" 9-29-67, "The Turkey Shoot" 11-24-67, "The Hero" 12-29-

67, "Stopover in a Troubled Town" 2-2-68.

Carr, Trem (1892-8/18/46). Producer. Films: "Bride of the Desert" 1929; "Headin' North" 1930; "The Land of Missing Men" 1930; "Near the Rainbow's End" 1930; "Oklahoma Cyclone" 1930; "At the Ridge" 1931; "Dugan of the Badlands" 1931; "The Montana Kid" 1931; "Near the Trail's End" 1931; "The Nevada Buckaroo" 1931; "Oklahoma Jim" 1931; "The Ridin' Fool" 1931; "Sunrise Trail" 1931; "Two-Fisted Justice" 1931; "Broadway to Cheyene" 1932; "Fighting Champ" 1932; "Galloping Thru" 1932; "Hidden Valley" 1932; "Honor of the Mounted" 1932; "Land of Wanted Men" 1932; "Law of the North" 1932; "Law of the West" 1932; "The Man from Arizona" 1932; "Man from Hell's Edges" 1932; "The Man from New Mexico" 1932; "Mason of the Mounted" 1932; "Riders of the Desert" 1932; "Single-Handed Sanders" 1932; "Son of Oklahoma" 1932; "South of Santa Fe" 1932; "Texas Buddies" 1932; "Texas Pioneers" 1932; "Vanishing Men" 1932; "Young Blood" 1932; "Diamond Trail" 1933; "The Fighting Texans" 1933; "The Fugitive" 1933; "The Gallant Fool" 1933; "Galloping Romeo" 1933; "Lucky Larrigan" 1933; "Rainbow Ranch" 1933; "The Ranger's Code" 1933; "Black Bandit" 1938; "Ghost Town Riders" 1938; "The Last Stand" 1938; "Outlaw Express" 1938; "Honor of the West" 1939.

Carradine, David (1945-). Director. TV: *Kung Fu*—"Besieged: Death on Cold Mountain" 11-15-74, "Besieged: Cannon at the Gate" 11-22-74, "The Demon God" 12-13-74.

Carre, Bartlett (1897-4/26/71). Director. Films: "Gunsmoke on the Guadalupe" 1935; "Gun Smoke" 1936.

Carreras, Michael (1927-4/19/94). Director. Films: "The Savage Guns" 1961-U.S./Span.

Carriere, Jean-Claude (1931-). Screenwriter. Films: "Viva Maria" 1965-Fr./Ital.; "Sommersby" 1993 (story only).

Carrol, Frank G. *see* Baldanello, Gianfranco.

Carroll, Curt. *see* Bishop, Curtis.

Carroll, Sidney (1913-11/3/88). Screenwriter. Films: "A Big Hand for the Little Lady" 1966.

Carruth, Clyde. Director. Films: "The Cowboys" 1924; "The Cowboy Kid" 1928.

Carson, Robert. Screenwriter. Films: "Western Union" 1941; "The Desperadoes" 1943.

Carter, Forrest (1927-79). Screenwriter. Films: "The Outlaw Josey Wales" 1976 (story only); "The Return of Josey Wales" 1987 (& story);

Carter, Lincoln J. Writer. Films: "The Fast Mail" 1922 (story).

Carter, Thomas. Director. TV: *Bret Maverick*—"The Hidalgo Thing" 5-4-82.

Cartray, Ricardo. Screenwriter. Films: "Eye for an Eye" 1972-Ital./Span./Mex.

Cartwright, Gary. Screenwriter. Films: "J.W. Coop" 1971.

Casacci, Mario. Screenwriter. Films: "Rojo" 1966-Ital./Span.

Casady, Cort (1947-). Writer. Films: "The Gambler" TVM-1980 (story).

Casaril, Guy. Director. Films: "The Legend of Frenchie King" 1971-Fr./Ital./Span./Brit. (& story).

Cascape, Marcello. Screenwriter. Films: "Seven Nuns in Kansas City" 1973-Ital.

Case, Carroll. Producer. Films: "Billy the Kid vs. Dracula" 1966; "An Eye for an Eye" 1966; "Jesse James Meets Frankenstein's Daughter" 1966; "Two Mules for Sister Sara" 1970. ¶TV: *Frontier* 1955-56.

Case, Robert Ormond. Screenwriter. Films: "Girl from Alsaska" 1942.

Cass, Dave. Screenwriter. Films: "Rio Diablo" TVM-1993; "The Gambler V: Playing for Keeps" TVM-1994 (story only).

Cassity, James C. Screenwriter. Films: "Man or Gun" 1958.

Castellari, Enzo G. (Enzo Girolami, E.G. Rowland). Director. Films: "Magnificent Brutes of the West" 1965-Ital./Span./Fr. (sp. only); "Johnny Hamlet" 1966-Ital. (& sp.); "Kill Them All and Come Back Alone" 1967-Ital./Span. (& sp.); "Two R-R-Ringos from Texas" 1967-Ital. (sp. only); "Any Gun Can Play" 1968-Ital./Span. (& sp.); "I Came, I Saw, I Shot" 1968-Ital./Span. (& sp.); "The Moment to Kill" 1968-Ital./Ger.; "Payment in Blood" 1968-Ital. (& sp.); "Sting of the West" 1972-Ital. (& sp.); "Cipolla Colt" 1975-Ital./Ger.; "Keoma" 1975-Ital./Span.; "Jonathan of the Bears" 1994-Ital./Rus. (& sp.).

Castillo, Arturo Ruiz. Director. Films: "Secret of Captain O'Hara" 1965-Span. (& sp.).

Castle, Sherle. Writer. Films: "Thunder Over Texas" 1934 (story).

Castle, William (1914-5/31/77). Director. Films: "North to the Klondike" 1942 (story only); "Klondike Kate" 1943; "Cave of Outlaws" 1951; "Conquest of Cochise" 1953; "Fort Ti" 1953; "Battle of Rogue River" 1954; "Jesse James Versus the Daltons" 1954; "The Law vs. Billy the Kid" 1954; "Masterson of Kansas" 1954; "The Americano" 1955; "The Gun That Won the West" 1955.

Catena, Victor A. Screenwriter. Films: "A Fistful of Dollars" 1964-Ital./Ger./Span.

Caterini, Lina. Screenwriter. Films: "Django Kills Softly" 1968-Ital.

Cates, Philip. Producer. Films: "The Last Days of Frank of Jesse James" TVM-1986; "The Quick and the Dead" CTVM-1987.

Cavara, Paola. Director. Films: "Deaf Smith and Johnny Ears" 1972 (& sp.).

Caven, Taylor. Screenwriter. Films: "Arizona Terrors" 1942; "Jesse James, Jr." 1942; "King of the Mounties" 1942-serial; "Marshal of Reno" 1944 (story only); "Silver City Kid" 1944.

Cavett, Frank. Writer. Films: "Across the Wide Missouri" 1951 (story).

Cayet, Marie. Writer. Films: "The Poet of the Peaks" 1915 (story).

Cazeneuve, Paul (-6/22/25). Director. Films: "The Square Shooter" 1920; "Sunset Sprague" 1920.

Ceballos, Larry. Director. Films: "Bullets and Ballads" 1940-short; "Swingin' in the Barn" 1940-short.

Cecchi D'Amico, Suso. Screenwriter. Films: "Man: His Pride and His Vengeance" 1967-Ital./Ger.

Cedar, Ralph (1898-11/29/51). Director. Films: "West of Abilene" 1940.

Celano, Guido. Director. Films: "Piluk, the Timid One" 1968-Ital.

Cendrars, Blaise (1887-1/21/61). Writer. Films: "Sutter's Gold" 1936 (story).

Cerami, Vicenzo. Screenwriter. Films: "Big Ripoff" 1967-Span./Ital.; "Stranger in Japan" 1969-Ital./U.S./Jap.; "Forgotten Pistolero" 1970-Ital./Span.; "Blindman" 1971-Ital.; "The Dirty Outlaws" 1971-Ital.

Cerchio, Fernando (Fred Ringoold). Director. Films: "Mutiny at

Fort Sharp" 1966-Ital. (& sp.); "Death on High Mountain" 1969-Ital./Span.

Cervi, Tonino. Director. Films: "Today It's Me ... Tomorrow You!" 1968-Ital. (& sp.).

Chadwick, Joseph. Writer. Films: "Rim of the Canyon" 1949 (story).

Chaffey, Don (1917-11/13/90). Director. Films: "Charley One-Eye" 1973-Brit. ¶TV: *Riding for the Pony Express*—Pilot 9-3-80; *Outlaws*—"Tintype" 1-3-87.

Chalmers, Steven. Writer. Films: "Looking for Trouble" 1926 (story).

Chamberlain, Lucia. Screenwriter. Films: "The Passing of Hell's Crown" 1916.

Champion, John C. (1924-10/94). Director. Films: "Panhandle" 1948 (prod./sp. only); "Stampede" 1949 (prod./sp. only); "Hellgate" 1952 (prod./story only); "Shotgun" 1955 (prod./sp. only); "The Texican" 1966-U.S./Span. (prod./sp. only); "Mustang Country" 1976 (& prod./sp.). ¶TV: *Laramie* 1959-63 (prod.).

Chandlee, Harry (1882-8/3/56). Screenwriter. Films: "The Eagle's Nest" 1915; "The Law of the Yukon" 1920; "False Brands" 1922; "One Law for the Woman" 1924.

Chandler, David (1912-10/19/90). Screenwriter. Films: "Apache Drums" 1951; "Jack McCall, Desperado" 1953 (story only); "Last of the Badmen" 1957; "Tomahawk Trail" 1957.

Chandler, Harry. Screenwriter. Films: "It Happened Out West" 1937.

Chaney, Lon (1883-8/26/30). Writer. Films: "The Tragedy of Whispering Creek" 1914 (story).

Chanslor, Roy (1899-4/16/64). Screenwriter. Films: "Idaho" 1943; "The Daltons Ride Again" 1945; "The Michigan Kid" 1947; "The Vigilantes Return" 1947; "Johnny Guitar" 1954 (story only); "Cat Ballou" 1965 (story only).

Chantler, David T. Screenwriter. Films: "Face of a Fugitive" 1959.

Chapin, Anne Morrison (-4/7/67). Screenwriter. Films: "Sunset in Wyoming" 1941.

Chapin, Frederic. Screenwriter. Films: "A Child of the North" 1915; "Heart of the Sunset" 1918; "Against All Odds" 1924; "Mark of the Spur" 1932.

Chapin, Martha. Screenwriter. Films: "Lightning Strikes West" 1940.

Chaplin, Prescott. Writer. Films: "Flame of the Barbary Coast" 1945 (story).

Chapman, Jay. Screenwriter. Films: "Man Rustlin'" 1926.

Chapman, Tom. Screenwriter. Films: "The Incredible Rocky Mountain Race" TVM-1977; "California Gold Rush" TVM-1981.

Chappell, Edward. Screenwriter. Films: "Madron" 1970-U.S./Israel.

Chase, Borden (1900-3/8/71). Screenwriter. Films: "Flame of the Barbary Coast" 1945; "The Man from Colorado" 1948 (story only); "Red River" 1948 (& story); "Montana" 1950; "Winchester '73" 1950; "Bend of the River" 1952; "Lone Star" 1952 (& story); "Vera Cruz" 1954 (story only); "The Far Country" 1955; "Man Without a Star" 1955; "Backlash" 1956; "Night Passage" 1957; "Ride a Crooked Trail" 1958; "Gunfighters of Casa Grande" 1965-U.S./Span.; "A Man Called Gannon" 1969.

Chase, Carroll. Producer. TV: *Sugarfoot* 1957-60; *The Texan* 1958-60.

Chase, Jr., Francis S. Writer. Films: "The Buckskin Lady" 1957 (story).

Chase, Patricia. Screenwriter. Films: "Gunfighters of Casa Grande" 1965-U.S./Span.

Chatterton, Tom (1881-8/17/52). Director. Films: "His Hour of Manhood" 1914 (sp. only); "The Cactus Blossom" 1915.

Chaudet, Louis (1884-5/10/65). Director. Films: "Follow the Girl" 1917; "The Love Call" 1919; "The Kingfisher's Roost" 1922 (& sp.); "Fools of Fortune" 1922; "A Man of Nerve" 1925; "Fighting Jack" 1926; "Lightning Bill" 1926; "Speeding Hoofs" 1927.

Chautard, Emile (1865-4/24/34). Director. Films: "All Man" 1916.

Chayefsky, Paddy (1923-8/1/81). Screenwriter. Films: "Paint Your Wagon" 1969.

Chechik, Jeremiah. Director. Films: "Tall Tales: The Unbelievable Adventures of Pecos Bill" 1995.

Chehak, Tom. Director. TV: *Adventures of Brisco County, Jr.*—"Mail Order Brides" 12-10-93.

Cheney, J. Benton. Screenwriter. Films: "The Old Wyoming Trail" 1937 (story only); "Rocky Mountain Rangers" 1940 (story only); "Border Vigilantes" 1941; "Doomed Caravan" 1941; "In Old

Colorado" 1941; "Outlaws of the Desert" 1941; "Pirates on Horseback" 1941; "Riders of the Timberline" 1941; "Stick to Your Guns" 1941; "Twilight on the Trail" 1941; "Wide Open Town" 1941; "The Lone Prairie" 1942 (story only); "Pirates of the Prairie" 1942; "Romance on the Range" 1942; "Shadows on the Sage" 1942; "Undercover Man" 1942; "Fighting Frontier" 1943; "Hands Across the Border" 1943; "King of the Cowboys" 1943; "Man from Music Mountain" 1943; "The Man from Thunder River" 1943; "Silver Spurs" 1943; "The Laramie Trail" 1944; "Mystery Man" 1944; "Blazing the Western Trail" 1945; "Outlaws of the Rockies" 1945; "Return of the Durango Kid" 1945; "Rockin' in the Rockies" 1945; "Rustlers of the Badlands" 1945; "Sing Me a Song of Texas" 1945; "Song of the Prairie" 1945; "Cowboy Blues" 1946; "Gentleman from Texas" 1946; "Silver Range" 1946; "Singing on the Trail" 1946; "That Texas Jamboree" 1946; "Throw a Saddle on a Star" 1946; "Under Arizona Skies" 1946; "Under Nevada Skies" 1946; "Gun Talk" 1947; "Hoppy's Holiday" 1947; "Land of the Lawless" 1947; "Law Comes to Gunsight" 1947; "Raiders of the South" 1947; "Song of the Wasteland" 1947; "Trailing Danger" 1947; "Valley of Fear" 1947; "Back Trail" 1948; "California Firebrand" 1948; "Cowboy Cavalier" 1948; "Frontier Agent" 1948; "Gunning for Justice" 1948; "Outlaw Brand" 1948; "Partners of the Sunset" 1948; "Phantom Valley" 1948; "The Sheriff of Medicine Bow" 1948; "Silver Trails" 1948; "Gun Runner" 1949; "Hidden Danger" 1949; "Law of the West" 1949; "Satan's Cradle" 1949; "Trail's End" 1949; "Over the Border" 1950.

Chermak, Cy (1929-). Producer. TV: *The Barbara Coast* 1975-76 (exec.prod.).

Chernus, Sonia. Screenwriter. Films: "The Outlaw Josey Wales" 1976.

Cherry, Carole S. Screenwriter. Films: "Cowboy" TVM-1983.

Cherry, Stanley Z. Screenwriter. Films: "Cowboy" TVM-1983.

Chertok, Jack. Producer. Films: "The Omaha Trail" 1942. ¶TV: *The Lone Ranger* 1949-57; *Sky King* 1951-53; *Steve Donovan, Western Marshal* 1955-56.

Chester, George R. (1869-1924). Writer. Films: "Blue Peter's Escape" 1914 (writer).

Chianetta, Oscar. Screenwriter.

Films: "Cowards Don't Pray" 1968-Ital./Span.

Childs, Herbert. Writer. Films: "Way of a Gaucho" 1952 (story).

Chiro, Alessandor. Screenwriter. Films: "Brother Outlaw" 1971-Ital.

Chisholm, David. Screenwriter. Films: "Longarm" TVM-1988; "Dead Man's Revenge" TVM-1994.

Chodorov, Edward (1904-10/9/88). Producer. Films: "The Man from Dakota" 1940.

Chodorov, Jerome (1911-). Screenwriter. Films: "The Man from Texas" 1947.

Chomsky, Marvin J. (1929-). Director. Films: "Female Artillery" TVM-1973; "Mrs. Sundance" TVM-1974; "Mackintosh & T.J." 1975. ¶TV: *Wild Wild West*—"The Night of the Falcon" 11-10-67, "The Night of the Iron Fist" 12-8-67, "The Night of the Vipers" 1-12-68, "The Night of the Undead" 2-2-68, "The Night of the Sedgewick Curse" 10-18-68, "The Night of the Gruesome Games" 10-25-68, "The Night of the Egyptian Queen" 11-15-68, "The Night of the Camera" 11-29-68, "The Night of the Winged Terror" 1-17-68 & 1-24-68, "The Night of Bleak Island" 3-14-69; *Gunsmoke*—"9:12 to Dodge" 11-11-68, "Railroad" 11-25-68, "The Innocent" 11-24-69; *Big Hawaii* 1977.

Christ, Harry C. see Fraser, Harry.

Christian-Jaque (1904-7/8/94). Director. Films: "The Legend of Frenchie King" 1971-Fr./Ital./Span./Brit.

Christie, Alfred E. (1882-4/14/51). Director. Films: "The Girl and the Sheriff" 1912; "Under Western Skies" 1913.

Christie, Howard (1912-3/25/92). Producer. Films: "Lost in Alaska" 1952; "Back to God's Country" 1953; "The Lone Hand" 1953; "Seminole" 1953; "Smoke Signal" 1955; "Showdown at Abilene" 1956; "Joe Dakota" 1957; "The Last of the Fast Guns" 1958; "No Name on the Bullet" 1959; "The Raiders" 1964; "Gunfight in Abilene" 1967; "The Ride to Hangman's Tree" 1967; "Journey to Shiloh" 1968; "A Man Called Gannon" 1969. ¶TV: *Wagon Train* 1957-65; *The Virginian* 1962-70.

Christina, Frank. Screenwriter. Films: "Billy Jack" 1971; "The Trial of Billy Jack" 1974.

Christina, Teresa. Screenwriter. Films: "Billy Jack" 1971; "The Trial of Billy Jack" 1974.

Chroscicki, Enrico. Producer. Films: "Day of Anger" 1967-Ital./Ger.; "Death Rides a Horse" 1967-Ital.; "Beyond the Law" 1968-Ital.; "The Big and the Bad" 1971-Ital./Fr./Span.; "It Can Be Done.. Amigo" 1971-Ital./Fr./Span.

Church, C.C. Writer. Films: "The Laramie Kid" 1935 (story).

Church, Fred. Screenwriter. Films: "The Unknown Rider" 1929.

Churchill, Edward. Screenwriter. Films: "Rocky Rhodes" 1934.

Churchill, Robert B. Screenwriter. Films: "The Fighting Vigilantes" 1947; "West to Glory" 1947.

Ciani, Sergio (Alan Steel, John Wyler). Producer. Films: "Fasthand" 1972-Ital./Span. (& story); "In the Name of the Father, the Son and the Colt" 1972-Fr./Ital.; "For a Book of Dollars" 1973-Ital./Span.

Cicero, Fernando. Screenwriter. Films: "Twice a Judas" 1968-Span./Ital.

Cicero, Nando. Director. Films: "Time of Vultures" 1967-Ital.; "Red Blood, Yellow Gold" 1968-Ital./Span. (& sp.); "Twice a Judas" 1968-Span./Ital.

Cimino, Michael (1943-). Director. Films: "Heaven's Gate" 1980 (& sp.).

Ciorciolini, Marcello (Frank Reed). Director. Films: "Two Gangsters in the Wild West" 1965-Ital./Span. (sp. only); "Two Sergeants of General Custer" 1965-Ital./Span. (sp. only); "Two Sons of Ringo" 1966-Ital. (sp. only); "Ciccio Forgives, I Don't" 1968-Ital. (& sp.); "Nephews of Zorro" 1969-Ital. (& sp.).

Ciuffini, Sabattino. Screenwriter. Films: "Drop Them or I'll Shoot" 1969-Fr./Ger./Span.; "Bandera Bandits" 1973-Ital./Span./Ger.

Civirani, Osvaldo (Glenn Eastman, Richard Kean). Director. Films: "Sheriff with the Gold" 1966-Ital./Span.; "Rick and John, Conquerors of the West" 1967-Ital (& sp.); "Son of Django" 1967-Ital.; "Dead for a Dollar" 1968-Ital. (& sp.); "Two Sons of Trinity" 1972-Ital. (& sp.).

Clair, Robert S. Screenwriter. Films: "I'm from the City" 1938.

Claire, Roy. Screenwriter. Films: "Circle of Death" 1935.

Clancy, Eugene. Writer. Films: "A Tale of Old Tucson" 1914 (story).

Clark, C.M. Writer. Films: "The Silent Rider" 1918 (story).

Clark, Colbert. Producer.

Films: "Lightning Warrior" 1931-serial; "The Last of the Mohicans" 1932-serial; "Fighting with Kit Carson" 1933-serial (& sp.); "In Old Santa Fe" 1934 (sp. only); "Blazing the Western Trail" 1945; "Both Barrels Blazing" 1945; "Outlaws of the Rockies" 1945; "Return of the Durango Kid" 1945; "Rhythm Round-Up" 1945; "Rockin' in the Rockies" 1945; "Rustlers of the Badlands" 1945; "Sing Me a Song of Texas" 1945; "Song of the Prairie" 1945; "Texas Panhandle" 1945; "Cowboy Blues" 1946; "The Desert Horseman" 1946; "The Fighting Frontiersman" 1946; "Frontier Gunlaw" 1946; "Galloping Thunder" 1946; "Gunning for Vengeance" 1946; "Heading West" 1946; "Landrush" 1946; "Lawless Empire" 1946; "Lone Star Moonlight" 1946; "Roaring Rangers" 1946; "Singing on the Trail" 1946; "Terror Trail" 1946; "That Texas Jamboree" 1946; "Throw a Saddle on a Star" 1946; "Two-Fisted Stranger" 1946; "Last Days of Boot Hill" 1947; "Law of the Canyon" 1947; "The Lone Hand Texan" 1947; "Over the Santa Fe Trail" 1947; "Prairie Raiders" 1947; "Riders of the Lone Star" 1947; "Smoky River Serenade" 1947; "South of the Chisholm Trail" 1947; "The Stranger from Ponca City" 1947; "Swing the Western Way" 1947; "West of Dodge City" 1947; "Blazing Across the Pecos" 1948; "Buckaroo from Powder River" 1948; "Phantom Valley" 1948; "Quick on the Trigger" 1948; "Singing Spurs" 1948; "Six-Gun Law" 1948; "Smoky Mountain Melody" 1948; "Song of Idaho" 1948; "Trail to Laredo" 1948; "West of Sonora" 1948; "Whirlwind Raiders" 1948; "Whirlwind Raiders" 1948; "The Blazing Trail" 1949; "Challenge of the Range" 1949; "Desert Vigilante" 1949; "El Dorado Pass" 1949; "Home in San Antone" 1949; "Laramie" 1949; "Renegades of the Sage" 1949; "South of Death Valley" 1949; "Across the Badlands" 1950; "Frontier Outpost" 1950; "Hoedown" 1950; "Horsemen of the Sierras" 1950; "Outcast of Black Mesa" 1950; "Raiders of Tomahawk Creek" 1950; "Lightning Guns" 1950; "Streets of Ghost Town" 1950; "Texas Dynamo" 1950; "Trail of the Rustlers" 1950; "Bandits of El Dorado" 1951; "Bonanza Town" 1951; "Cyclone Fury" 1951; "Fort Savage Raiders" 1951; "The Kid from Amarillo" 1951; "Pecos River" 1951; "Prairie Roundup" 1951; "Ridin' the Outlaw Trail" 1951; "Snake River Desperadoes" 1951; "The Hawk of Wild River" 1952; "Junction City" 1952; "The Kid from Broken Gun" 1952;

"Laramie Mountains" 1952; "Montana Territory" 1952; "The Rough, Tough West" 1952; "Smoky Canyon" 1952. ¶TV: *Annie Oakley* 1954-57; *Tales of the Texas Rangers* 1955-57.

Clark, Dennis Lynton. Screenwriter. Films: "Comes a Horseman" 1978.

Clark, Frank Howard. Screenwriter. Films: "Bull's Eye" 1918-serial; "Jacques of the Silver North" 1919; "The Last of His People" 1919; "Prairie Trails" 1920; "Hands Off" 1921; "Big Stakes" 1922; "Billy Jim" 1922; "Flaming Hearts" 1922; "Crimson Gold" 1923 (story only); "Danger" 1923 (story only); "The Desert Rider" 1923; "$50,000 Reward" 1924; "Wolves of the North" 1924-serial; "Fighting Courage" 1925; "The Haunted Range" 1926; "Under Fire" 1926; "The Bandit's Son" 1927; "The Boy Rider" 1927; "The Desert Pirate" 1927; "The Prairie King" 1927; "Splitting the Breeze" 1927; "Tom's Gang" 1927; "The Avenging Writer" 1928; "The Bantam Cowboy" 1928; "The Fightin' Redhead" 1928; "King Cowboy" 1928; "The Little Buckaroo" 1928; "Man in the Rough" 1928; "Phantom of the Range" 1928; "The Riding Renegade" 1928; "Rough Ridin' Red" 1928; "Terror Mountain" 1928; "The Texas Tornado" 1928 (& dir.); "Tracked" 1928; "The Trail of Courage" 1928; "Wizard of the Saddle" 1928 (& sp.); "The Amazing Vagabond" 1929; "The Freckled Rascal" 1929; "Idaho Red" 1929; "The Little Savage" 1929; "The One Man Dog" 1929; "Pals of the Prairie 1929 (story only); "The Pride of Pawnee" 1929; "The Trail of the Horse Thieves" 1929; "The Lone Rider" 1930 (story only); "Shadow Ranch" 1930; "The Utah Kid" 1930; "The Fighting Marshal" 1931; "The Fighting Fool" 1932; "Wild Horse Mesa" 1932; "Rustlers' Roundup" 1933; "O'Malley of the Mounted" 1936; "Two in Revolt" 1936.

Clark, James B. (1908-). Director. Films: "Sierra Baron" 1958; "Villa!" 1958; "The Sad Horse" 1959; "One Foot in Hell" 1960; "...And Now Miguel" 1966. ¶TV: *My Friend Flicka* 1955; *The Monroes*—"The Forest Devil" 9-28-66, "Wild Dog of the Tetons" 10-5-66, "Ordeal by Hope" 10-19-66, "The Friendly Enemy" 11-9-66, "Mark of Death" 1-4-67; *Wild Wild West*—"The Night of the Hangman" 10-20-67, "The Night of the Turncoat" 12-1-67, "The Night of the Underground Terror" 1-19-68, "The Night of Miguelito's Revenge" 12-13-68; *Here Come the Brides*—"Stand

Off" 11-27-68; *Bonanza*—"Another Windmill to Go" 9-14-69; *The High Chaparral*—"To Stand for Something More" 10-24-69, "Generation" 4-17-70.

Clark, Walter Van Tilburg (1909-11/20/71). Writer. Films: "The Ox-Bow Incident" 1943 (story); "Track of the Cat" 1954 (story).

Clarke, Kenneth. Screenwriter. Films: "The Buzzard's Shadow" 1915; "Immediate Lee" 1916; "The Land O'Lizards" 1916; "Lone Star" 1916; "Until They Get Me" 1917; "Prisoner of the Pines" 1918 (story only); "Untamed" 1918; "Sundown" 1924; "Rough Romance" 1930 (story only).

Claughter, Frank G. Screenwriter. Films: "Naked in the Sun" 1957.

Clauser, Suzanne. Screenwriter. Films: "Pioneer Woman" TVM-1973; "Calamity Jane" TVM-1984.

Clavell, James (1923-9/6/94). Director. Films: "Walk Like a Dragon" 1960 (& prod./sp.). ¶TV: *The Rifleman*—"Miss Bertie" 12-27-60, "The Queue" 5-16-61.

Claver, Bob. Director. TV: *Here Come the Brides* 1968-70 (exec. prod.), "A Crying Need" 10-2-68, "A Hard Card to Play" 10-23-68; *The Texas Wheelers* 1974; *Young Maverick*—"Have I Got a Girl for You" 1-16-80.

Clawson, Elliott J. (1891-7/21/42). Screenwriter. Films: "Davy Crockett" 1916 (story only); "The Desire of the Moth" 1917; "The Savage" 1917; "Hands Down" 1918 (story); "The Sleeping Lion" 1919; "Desperate Trails" 1921; "The Spoilers" 1923; "The Man from Red Gulch" 1925; "Whispering Smith" 1926.

Claxton, William F. Director. Films: "Tucson" 1949; "Fangs of the Wild" 1954 (& sp.); "Stagecoach to Fury" 1956; "The Quiet Gun" 1957; "Young Jesse James" 1960; "Law of the Lawless" 1964; "Stage to Thunder Rock" 1964; "Bonanza: The Next Generation" TVM-1988. ¶TV: *Black Saddle* 1959; *Law of the Plainsman* 1959; *The Rifleman*—"The Horse Traders" 2-9-60, "Woman from Hog Ridge" 10-4-60, "The Score Is Even" 4-11-61, "Skull" 1-1-62; *Rawhide*—"Incident of the Dancing Death" 4-8-60; *Bonanza*—"A Hot Day for a Hanging" 10-14-62, "Knight Errant" 11-18-62, "The Decision" 12-16-62, "The Last Haircut" 2-3-63, "The Hayburner" 2-17-63, "Five into the Wind" 4-21-63, "The Campaneros" 4-19-64, "A Dime's Worth of Glory"

11-1-64, "The Debt" 9-12-65, "The Dilemma" 9-19-65, "The Brass Box" 9-26-65, "The Other Son" 10-3-65, "Mighty Is the Word" 11-7-65, "All Ye His Saints" 12-19-65, "A Dublin Lad" 1-2-66, "To Kill a Buffalo" 1-9-66, "The Code" 2-13-66, "The Emperor Norton" 2-27-66, "Big Shadow on the Land" 4-17-66, "Credit for a Kill" 10-23-66, "The Bridegroom" 12-4-66, "Old Charlie" 11-6-66, "Ballad of the Ponderosa" 11-13-66, "Ponderosa Explosion" 1-1-67, "A Bride for Buford" 1-15-67, "Black Friday" 1-22-67, "Amigo" 2-12-67, "Judgment at Red Creek" 2-26-67, "Joe Cartwright, Detective" 3-5-67, "The Deed and the Dilemma" 3-26-67, "The Prince" 4-2-67, "The Wormwood Cup" 4-23-67, "Maestro Hoss" 5-7-67, "Star Crossed" 3-10-68, "A Dream to Dream" 4-14-68, "Pride of a Man" 6-2-68, "Stage Door Johnnies" 7-28-68, "Danger Road" 1-11-70, "The Law and Billy Burgess" 2-15-70, "What Are Pardners For?" 4-12-70, "A Matter of Circumstance" 4-19-70, "Thorton's Account" 11-1-70, "El Jefe" 11-15-70, "Top Hand" 1-17-71, "The Grand Swing" 9-19-71, "The Prisoners" 10-17-71, "A Lonely Man" 1-2-72; *Gunsmoke*—"Circus Trick" 2-6-65; *The High Chaparral* 1967-71 (prod.), "The High Chaparral" 9-10-67, "Best Man for the Job" 9-24-67, "Young Blood" 10-8-67, "Shadows on the Land" 10-15-67, "The Widow from Red Rock" 11-26-67, "Mark of the Turtle" 12-10-67, "The Champion of the Western World" 2-4-68, "Bad Day for a Thirst" 2-18-68, "Threshold of Courage" 3-31-68, "Ten Little Indians" 9-27-68, "Follow Your Heart" 10-4-68, "The Covey" 10-18-68, "For What We Are About to Receive" 11-29-68, "Stinky Flanagan" 2-21-69, "Surtee" 2-28-69, "A Fella Named Kilroy" 3-7-69, "The Lion Sleeps" 3-28-69, "For the Love of Carlos" 4-4-69; *Here Come the Brides*—"The Road to the Cradle" 11-7-69, "The She-Bear" 1-30-70; *Little House on the Prairie* 1974-82 (& prod.); *Sara* 1976; *Father Murphy*—"Will's Surprise" 1-12-82, "Knights of the White Camelia" 2-2-82, "Matthew and Elizabeth" 3-28-82, "The First Miracle" 4-4-82 & 4-11-82, "The Reluctant Runaway" 11-16-82 & 11-23-82, "Buttons and Beaux" 11-30-82, "Blood Right" 12-21-82.

Clay, Lewis. Screenwriter. Films: "Valley of Vanishing Men" 1942-serial; "The Vigilante" 1947-serial; "Tex Granger" 1948-serial; "Cody of the Pony Express" 1950-serial.

Clegg, Valce V. (1888-7/29/47). Director. Films: "Lucky Spurs" 1927.

Clements, Jr., Calvin. Screenwriter. Films: "Firecreek" 1968; "The Devil and Miss Sarah" TVM-1971; "The Wild Country" 1971.

Clements, Colin. Screenwriter. Films: "Call of the West" 1930.

Clements, Roy (1877-7/15/48). Director. Films: "The Double O" 1921 (& sp.); "Sparks of Flint" 1921 (& sp.); "A Desert Bridegroom" 1922 (& sp.); "The Desert's Crucible" 1922 (& sp.); "The Marshal of Moneymint" 1922 (& sp.); "Two-Fisted Jefferson" 1922 (& sp.); "Nine and Three-Fifths Seconds" 1925 (sp. only).

Cleveland, Val. Screenwriter. Films: "The Timber Queen" 1922-serial (story only); "White Eagle" 1922-serial (story only); "The Vanishing Rider" 1928-serial.

Clifford, William H. (1874-10/9/38). Director. Films: "An Indian's Honor" 1913 (sp. only); "Love's Sacrifice" 1914; "Shorty Escapes Marriage" 1914 (sp. only); "The Ranger" 1918 (story only); "Riders of the Dawn" 1920 (sp. only); "The Sagebrusher" 1920 (sp. only); "The U.P. Trail" 1920 (prod. only); "Man of the Forest" 1921 (sp. only).

Clift, Denison (1885-12/17/61). Screenwriter. Films: "Wolves of the Rail" 1918; "The Coming of the Law" 1919; "Rose of the West" 1919; "The Challenge of the Law" 1920; "Firebrand Trevison" 1920; "The Last Straw" 1920 (dir. only); "The Square Shooter" 1920.

Clifton, Elmer P. (Elmer S. Pond) (1890-10/15/49). Director. Films: "The Eagle" 1918; "Smashing Through" 1918; "Winner Takes All" 1918; "Nugget Nell" 1919; "The Sunset Legion" 1928 (sp. only); "Cyclone of the Saddle" 1935 (& sp.); "Fighting Caballero" 1935 (& sp.); "Pals of the Range" 1935 (& sp.); "Rough Riding Ranger" 1935 (& sp.); "Skull and Crown" 1935; "Custer's Last Stand" 1936-serial; "Wildcat Trooper" 1936; "California Frontier" 1938; "Law of the Texan" 1938; "The Stranger from Arizona" 1938; "Crashing Thru" 1939; "West of Pinto Basin" 1940 (story only); "Trail of the Silver Spurs" 1941 (story only); "Deep in the Heart of Texas" 1942; "Old Chisholm Trail" 1942 (& sp.); "The Rangers Take Over" 1942 (sp. only); "The Sundown Kid" 1942; "Bad Men of Thunder Gap" 1943 (sp. only); "The Blocked Trail" 1943; "Cheyenne Roundup" 1943 (sp. only);

"Days of Old Cheyenne" 1943; "Frontier Law" 1943 (& sp.); "Raiders of San Joaquin" 1943 (sp. only); "The Return of the Rangers" 1943 (& sp.); "Boss of Rawhide" 1944 (& sp.); "Brand of the Devil" 1944 (sp. only); "Dead or Alive" 1944; "Gangsters of the Frontier" 1944 (& sp.); "Guns of the Law" 1944 (& sp.); "Gunsmoke Mesa" 1944; "Outlaw Roundup" 1944 (sp. only); "The Pinto Bandit" 1944 (& sp.); "Spook Town" 1944 (& sp.); "Swing, Cowboy, Swing" 1944 (& sp.); "The Whispering Skull" 1944; "Frontier Fugitives" 1945 (sp. only); "Marked for Murder" 1945 (& sp.); "Three in the Saddle" 1945 (sp. only); "Ambush Trail" 1946 (sp. only); "Lightning Raiders" 1946 (sp. only); "Outlaw of the Plains" 1946 (story only); "Song of the Sierras" 1946 (sp. only); "Rainbow Over the Rockies" 1947 (sp. only); "West to Glory" 1947; "Quick on the Trigger" 1948; "Sunset Carson Rides Again" 1948 (sp. only); "The Kid from Gower Gulch" 1949 (sp. only); "Outcast of Black Mesa" 1950 (story only); "Red Rock Outlaw" 1950 (& prod.); "The Silver Bandit" 1950 (& sp.).

Clifton, Frank M. Screenwriter. Films: "Ridin' the Wind" 1925 (story only); "Hands Across the Border" 1926 (story only); "Don Mike" 1927; "Jesse James" 1927; "Silver Comes Through" 1927 (story only); "Kit Carson" 1928 (story only); "The Pioneer Scout" 1928.

Clifton, Wallace C. Screenwriter. Films: "The Face at the Window" 1915 (story only); "The Foreman of the Bar-Z Ranch" 1915 (story only); "Heart's Desire" 1915 (story only); "The Spell of the Yukon" 1916; "Tracked to Earth" 1922; "Trimmed" 1922; "Out of the Silent North" 1922.

Cline, Edward F. (1892-5/22/61). Director. Films: "The Paleface" 1922 (& sp.); "When a Man's a Man" 1924; "The Dude Ranger" 1934; "Fighting to Live" 1934; "Cowboy Millionaire" 1935; "My Little Chickadee" 1940; "Moonlight and Cactus" 1944.

Clucher, E.B. see Barboni, Enzo.

Clum, Woodworth. Writer. Films: "Walk the Proud Land" 1956 (story).

Clymer, John B. (1887-5/24/37). Writer. Films: "What Am I Bid?" 1919 (story only); "Hills of Missing Men" 1922 (story only); "When Danger Smiles" 1922; "The Wild West Show" 1928.

Coates, Franklin B. Director.

Films: "Jesse James As the Outlaw" 1921 (& sp.); "Jesse James Under the Black Flag" 1921 (& sp.).

Cobianchi, Luigi. Screenwriter. Films: "No Graves on Boot Hill" 1968-Ital.

Coblenz, Walter. Producer. Films: "The Legend of the Lone Ranger" 1981.

Cobos, Juan. Screenwriter. Films: "Bandidos" 1967-Ital.; "Seven Dollars on the Red" 1968-Ital./Span.

Coburn, Wallace G. Writer. Films: "The Sunset Princess" 1918 (story).

Coburn, Walter (1889-19??). Screenwriter. Films: "The Back Trail" 1924 (story only); "Deuce High" 1926; "Rusty Rides Alone" 1933 (story only); "Silent Men" 1933 (story only); "The Westerner" 1934 (story only); "The Return of Wild Bill" 1940 (story only); "Shoot Out at Big Sag" 1972 (story only).

Cochran, Dorcas. Screenwriter. Films: "Fighting Bill Fargo" 1942.

Cochrane, George. Director. Films: "Mountain Blood" 1916; "The Red Stain" 1916; "The Timber Wolf" 1916; "The Getaway" 1917; "The Girl in the Garrett" 1927.

Coe, Fred (1914-4/29/79). Producer. Films: "The Left-Handed Gun" 1958.

Coe, Wayne. Director. Films: "Grim Prairie Tales" 1990 (& sp.).

Coen, Franklin. Screenwriter. Films: "Four Guns to the Border" 1954; "Chief Crazy Horse" 1955; "Kiss of Fire" 1955; "Alvarez Kelly" 1966 (& story).

Coffee, Lenore (1897-7/2/84). Screenwriter. Films: "The Squaw Man" 1931.

Coffin, Edwin Ray. Writer. Films: "Physical Culture on the Quarter Circle V Bar" 1913 (story); "Cactus Jake, Heart-Breaker" 1914 (story); "A Militant School Ma'am" 1914 (story); "Bad Man Bobbs" 1915 (story); "Cactus Jim's Shopgirl" 1915 (story); "The Chef at Circle G" 1915 (story); "Harold's Bad Man" 1915 (story); "An Angelic Attitude" 1916 (story); "Twisted Trails" 1916.

Cohen, Albert J. Producer. Films: "Horizons West" 1952; "The Great Sioux Uprising" 1953; "Border River" 1954.

Cohen, Bennett R. Screenwriter. Films: "The Dawn Road" 1915; "From Out of the Big Snows" 1915 (story only); "The Superior Claim" 1915; "The Man Who Took a Chance" 1917 (story only); "Fame and Fortune" 1918; "The Avenging Arrow" 1921-serial (story only); "Sell 'Em Cowboy" 1924; "Two Fisted Justice" 1924 (story only); "Fightin' Odds" 1925 (& dir.); "The Grey Devil" 1926 (dir. only); "Hi-Jacking Rustlers" 1926 (dir. only); "A Ridin' Gent" 1926 (& dir.); "Roaring Bill Atwood" 1926 (dir. only); "West of the Rainbow's End" 1926 (prod. only); "The Laffin' Fool" 1927 (dir. only); "Thunderbolt's Tracks" 1927; "Where the North Holds Sway" 1927 (dir. only); "Laddie Be Good" 1928 (dir. only); "The Lawless Legion" 1929 (& story); "The Saddle King" 1929 (story only); "Senor Americano" 1929; "Bar L Ranch" 1930 (& story); "The Fighting Legion" 1930; "Mountain Justice" 1930; "Parade of the West" 1930 (story only); "Song of the Cabellero" 1930; "Sons of the Saddle" 1930; "In Old Cheyenne" 1931 (story only); "Law of the Rio Grande" 1931 (& dir.); "The Sign of the Wolf" 1931-serial; "West of Cheyenne" 1931; "Come On, Danger!" 1932; "The Sunset Trail" 1932; "Texas Gun Fighter" 1932; "Girl Trouble" 1933; "Arizona Nights" 1934; "Mystery Mountain" 1934-serial; "Nevada Cyclone" 1934; "Potluck Pards" 1934; "Rainbow Riders" 1934 (& dir.); "Rawhide Mail" 1934 (story only); "Ridin' Gent" 1934-short (& dir.); "West on Parade" 1934; "Rio Rattler" 1935 (story only); "Skull and Crown" 1935; "Swifty" 1935; "Wilderness Mail" 1935; "Ambush Valley" 1936; "The Border Patrolman" 1936; "The Fighting Deputy" 1937 (story only); "The Law Commands" 1937; "Melody of the Plains" 1937; "Raw Timber" 1937 (& story); "Renegade Range" 1938 (story only); "South of Arizona" 1938; "West of Santa Fe" 1938; "North of the Yukon" 1939; "Riders of the Black River" 1939; "The Thundering West" 1939; "Western Caravans" 1939; "Frontier Vengeance" 1940; "Ghost Town Raiders" 1940; "One Man's Law" 1940; "Pioneer Days" 1940; "Desert Bandit" 1941; "Man from Montana" 1941; "Two-Gun Sheriff" 1941 (& story); "Wyoming Wildcat" 1941 (& story); "Bandit Ranger" 1942 (& story); "Come On, Danger!" 1942 (story only); "False Colors" 1943; "Red River Robin Hood" 1943; "Riders of the Deadline" 1943; "Sagebrush Law" 1943; "Ghost Guns" 1944; "Silver City Kid" 1944 (story only); "Trail to Gunsight" 1944; "Bandits of the Badlands" 1945; "Beyond the Pecos" 1945; "The Cherokee Flash" 1945 (& prod.); "Oregon Trail" 1945; "Rough Riders of Cheyenne" 1945 (prod. only); "Santa Fe Saddlemates" 1945; "Sheriff of Cimarron" 1945; "Alias Billy the Kid" 1946 (prod. only); "Days of Buffalo Bill" 1946 (prod. only); "The El Paso Kid" 1946; "Frontier Gunlaw" 1946; "Lawless Empire" 1946; "Red River Renegades" 1946 (prod. only); "Rio Grande Raiders" 1946 (prod. only); "Hoppy's Holiday" 1947; "King of the Bandits" 1947; "Ridin' Down the Trail" 1947 (& prod.); "Robin Hood of Monterey" 1947; "Oklahoma Blues" 1948; "Devil's Canyon" 1953 (story only).

Cohen, Herman (1928-). Producer. Films: "The Brass Legend" 1956; "Django the Bastard" 1969-Ital./Span.

Cohen, Larry (1947-). Screenwriter. Films: "Return of the Seven" 1966-Span.; "El Condor" 1970; "Shootout in a One-Dog Town" TVM-1974 (& story); "Desperado: Avalanche at Devil's Ridge" TVM-1988.

Cohen, Ronald M. Screenwriter. Films: "Blue" 1968; "The Good Guys and the Bad Guys" 1969 (& prod.); "Draw" CTVM-1984 (prod. only).

Cohn, Alfred (1880-2/3/51). Screenwriter. Films: "Cisco Kid" 1931; "A Holy Terror" 1931; "Mystery Ranch" 1932.

Cohn, Ben. Director. Films: "Code of the Range" 1927.

Cohn, Harry (1891-2/27/58). Producer. Films: "The Lure of the Wild" 1925; "The Dawn Trail" 1930; "Shadow Ranch" 1930.

Cohn, J.J. Producer. Films: "Out West with the Hardys" 1938.

Cohn, Maurice. Producer. Films: "Red Blood of Courage" 1935.

Colasanto, Nicholas (1923-2/12/85). Director. TV: *Here Come the Brides*—"How Dry We Are" 3-6-70, "Bolt of Kilmaren" 3-13-70; *Alias Smith and Jones*—Six Strangers at Apache Springs" 10-28-71; *Bonanza*—"Ambush at Rio Lobo" 10-24-72.

Coldeway, Anthony. Screenwriter. Films: "The Girl from Arizona" 1910; "Flaming Arrow" 1911; "The Frame-Up" 1915; "The Jack of Hearts" 1919; "The Ruse of the Rattlesnake" 1921; "When East Comes West" 1922; "The Oregon Trail" 1923-serial; "Ruggles of Red Gap" 1923; "A Son of His Father" 1925; "Trailin' West" 1936; "Blazing Sixes" 1937 (story only); "Guns of the Pecos" 1937 (story only); "Texas Terrors" 1940; "The Tulsa Kid" 1940; "Under Texas Skies" 1940; "Wyoming

Wildcat" 1941; "Calling Wild Bill Elliott" 1943; "Death Valley Manhunt" 1943; "Code of the Prairie" 1944; "Marshal of Reno" 1944 (& story); "Tucson Raiders" 1944; "Vigilantes of Dodge City" 1944; "Prairie Express" 1947.

Cole, Lester (1904-8/15/85). Screenwriter. Films: "When the Daltons Rode" 1940.

Cole, Royal K. Screenwriter. Films: "Black Arrow" 1944-serial; "California Firebrand" 1948 (adapt. only); "Tex Granger" 1948-serial; "Ghost of Zorro" 1949-serial; "The James Brothers of Missouri" 1950-serial; "Roar of the Iron Horse" 1950-serial; "Son of Geronimo" 1952-serial; "Gunfighters of the Northwest" 1954-serial.

Coleman, Brysis. Screenwriter. Films: "Arizona Days" 1928 (story only); "The Silent Trail" 1928; "West of Santa Fe" 1928 (story only).

Coleman, Jr., C.C. Director. Films: "Code of the Range" 1937; "Dodge City Trail" 1937; "Outpost of the Mounties" 1939; "Spoilers of the Range" 1939.

Coleman, Herbert. Director. Films: "Posse from Hell" 1961. ¶TV: *Whispering Smith* 1961 (& prod.).

Coleman, Leo. *see* Savona, Leopoldo.

Coles, Ben. Screenwriter. Films: "Six Gun Serenade" 1947.

Coletti, Melchi. Screenwriter. Films: "Seven Dollars on the Red" 1968-Ital./Span.

Colizzi, Giuseppe. Director. Films: "God Forgives—I Don't" 1966-Ital./Span. (& sp.); "Ace High" 1967-Ital./Span.; "Boot Hill" 1969-Ital. (& sp.).

Colla, Richard (1918-). Director. TV: *Gunsmoke*—"The Moonstone" 12-17-66.

Collins, Boon. Director. Films: "Sally Fieldgood & Co." 1975-Can. (& sp.).

Collins, John H. Director. Films: "Flower of No Man's Land" 1916 (& sp.); "The Winding Trail" 1918.

Collins, Lewis D. (1899-8/24/54). Director. Films: "The Fighting Strain" 1926; "The Lone Prairie" 1926; "When Bonita Rides" 1926; "The Whirlwind Driver" 1926; "Clearing the Trail" 1927; "Double Trouble" 1927; "The Galloping Gobs" 1927 (story only); "The Racing Wizard" 1927; "The Red Warning" 1927; "The Riding Whirlwind" 1927; "Riding Gold" 1928; "The Un-

tamed" 1928; "Winged Hoofs" 1928; "Guns for Hire" 1932; "Gun Law" 1933 (& sp.); "Trouble Busters" 1933 (& sp.); "Via Pony Express" 1933 (& sp.); "Brand of Hate" 1934; "The Man from Hell" 1934; "Little Joe, the Wrangler" 1942; "Raiders of San Joaqin" 1943; "Tenting Tonight on the Old Camp Ground" 1943; "Oklahoma Raiders" 1944; "The Old Texas Trail" 1944; "Raiders of Ghost City" 1944-serial; "Trigger Trail" 1944; "Royal Mounted Rides Again" 1945-serial; "Frontier Frolic" 1946-short; "The Scarlet Horseman" 1946-serial; "Ride, Ryder, Ride" 1949; "Roll, Thunder, Rull" 1949; "Cherokee Uprising" 1950; "Cowboy and the Prizefighter" 1950; "The Fighting Redhead" 1950; "Law of the Panhandle" 1950; "Abilene Trail" 1951; "Canyon Raiders" 1951; "Colorado Ambush" 1951; "The Longhorn" 1951; "Man from Sonora" 1951; "Lawless Cowboys" 1951; "Nevada Badmen" 1951; "Oklahoma Justice" 1951; "Stage to Blue River" 1951; "Stagecoach Driver" 1951; "Texas Lawmen" 1951; "Canyon Ambush" 1952; "Dead Man's Trail" 1952; "Fargo" 1952; "The Gunman" 1952; "Kansas Territory" 1952; "Montana Incident" 1952; "Texas City" 1952; "Waco" 1952; "Wild Stallion" 1952; "The Homesteaders" 1953; "The Marksman" 1953; "Texas Bad Man" 1953; "Vigilante Terror" 1953; "Two Guns and a Badge" 1954.

Collins, Monty (1898-6/1/51). Screenwriter. Films: "Phony Express" 1943-short.

Collins, Richard. Screenwriter. Films: "Kiss of Fire" 1955; "The Badlanders" 1958; "Desperate Mission" TVM-1971; "The Godchild" TVM-1974 (prod. only). ¶TV: *Bonanza* 1959-73 (prod.); *Sara* 1976 (prod.).

Collinson, Peter (1938-12/16/80). Director. Films: "The Man Called Noon" 1973-Brit./Span./Ital.

Colombo, Arrigo. Screenwriter. Films: "A Fistful of Dollars" 1964-Ital./Ger./Span.; "Duel in the Eclipse" 1967-Span.; "More Dollars for the MacGregors" 1970-Ital./Span.

Coltellacci, Oreste. Producer. Films: "Red Blood, Yellow Gold" 1968-Ital./Span.; "They Call Him Veritas" 1972-Ital./Span. (sp. only); "Trinity Plus the Clown and a Guitar" 1975-Ital./Austria/Fr.

Colter, Eli. Writer. Films: "The Untamed Breed" 1948 (story).

Colucci, Mario (Ray Calloway). Director. Films: "Revenge for Revenge" 1968-Ital. (& sp.).

Comford, Will Levington. Writer. Films: "The Angel of Contention" 1914 (story); "Somewhere in Sonora" 1927 (story); "Somewhere in Sonora" 1933 (story).

Commandini, Adele. Screenwriter. Films: "The Country Beyond" 1936.

Compton, Frank. Director. Films: "Lone Hand Wilson" 1920.

Compton, J.C. Director. Films: "Buckeye and Blue" 1988 (& sp.); "Desperado: Avalanche at Devil's Ridge" TVM-1988.

Compton, Richard. Director. Films: "Wild Times" TVM-1980. ¶TV: *Young Riders*—"Survivors" 11-16-91; *Hawkeye*—"The Bear" 9-28-94.

Comstock, Harriet T. Writer. Films: "Joyce of the North Woods" 1913 (story).

Condon, Charles. Screenwriter. Films: "Jaws of Steel" 1927; "Land of the Silver Fox" 1928 (story only); "Get That Girl" 1932; "The Three Mesquiteers" 1936 (story only); "Galloping Dynamite" 1937; "Oklahoma Renegades" 1940 (story only); "Winners of the West" 1940-serial; "Cody of the Pony Express" 1950-serial.

Condon, Richard (1915-). Screenwriter. Films: "Talent for Loving" 1969-Brit./Span.

Conklin, Hal. Screenwriter. Films: "Arizona Nights" 1927.

Conlon, Casey. Screenwriter. Films: "Guardian of the Wilderness" 1976.

Conn, Maurice. Producer. Films: "The Fighting Trooper" 1934; "Code of the Mounted" 1935; "His Fighting Blood" 1935; "Northern Frontier" 1935; "Timber War" 1935; "Trails of the Wild" 1935; "Valley of Wanted Men" 1935; "Wilderness Mail" 1935; "Phantom Patrol" 1936; "Song of the Trail" 1936; "Wildcat Trooper" 1936; "Fighting Texan" 1937; "Galloping Dynamite" 1937; "Roaring Six Guns" 1937; "Rough Ridin' Rhythm" 1937; "Valley of Terror" 1937; "Whistling Bullets" 1937; "Wild Horse Round-Up" 1937; "Gunsmoke Trail" 1938; "Land of Fighting Men" 1938; "Phantom Ranger" 1938; "Two-Gun Justice" 1938; "West of Rainbow's End" 1938; "Where the West Begins" 1938; "Frontier Scout" 1939.

Connell, Charles. Producer. Films: "Riders of the Cactus" 1931 (& story).

Connell, Evan S. (1924-). Writer. Films: "Son of the Morning Star" TVM-1991 (story).

Connell, Jack. Screenwriter. Films: "Riders of Death Valley" 1941-serial.

Connell, W.M. Director. Films: "Trouble at Melody Mesa" 1944.

Conner, Ralph. Writer. Films: "The Sky Pilot" 1921 (story).

Connolly, Bobby. Director. Films: "The Devil's Saddle Legion" 1937; "West of the Rockies" 1941-short.

Connors, Barry. Screenwriter. Films: "Riders of the Purple Sage" 1931; "The Gay Caballero" 1932; "Rainbow Trail" 1932.

Conrad, Eugene (1895-1/28/64). Screenwriter. Films: "Moonlight and Cactus" 1944; "The Singing Sheriff" 1944; "Gas House Kids Go West" 1947.

Conrad, William (1923-2/11/93). Director. Films: "The Ride Back" 1957; "The Man from Galveston" 1964. ¶TV: *The Rifleman*—"Three-Legged Terror" 4-21-59; *Klondike* 1960-61 (& prod.); *Gunsmoke*—"Panacea Sykes" 4-13-63, "Captain Sligo" 1-4-71; *Temple Houston*—"The Man from Galveston" 1963.

Conselman, William (1896-5/25/40). Screenwriter. Films: "Three Rogues" 1931; "Frontier Marshal" 1934; "Last of the Duanes" 1941; "Lone Star Ranger" 1942.

Considine, Jr., John W. Producer. Films: "Robin Hood of El Dorado" 1936; "Jackass Mail" 1942.

Consumana, Ralph. Screenwriter. Films: "The Lone Bandit" 1934.

Continenza, Alessandro. Screenwriter. Films: "Heroes of the West" 1964-Span./Ital.; "Five Thousand Dollars on One Ace" 1965-Span./Ital.; "He Who Shoots First" 1966-Ital.; "Sugar Colt" 1966-Ital./Span.; "They Still Call Me Amen" 1972-Ital.

Contner, James A. Director. TV: *Adventures of Brisco County, Jr.*—"Brisco in Jalisco" 9-17-93.

Conway, Jack (1887-10/11/52). Director. Films: "An Indian's Honor" 1913; "The Beckoning Trail" 1916; "The Bond of Fear" 1917; "Desert Law" 1918; "Little Red Decides" 1918; "Riders of the Dawn" 1920; "The U.P. Trail" 1920; "The Long Chance" 1922; "Step on It!" 1922; "Quicksands" 1923; "The Heart Buster" 1924; "Let Freedom Ring" 1939; "Northwest Passage" 1940; "Honky Tonk" 1941.

Conway, James L. (1950-). Producer. Films: "The Incredible Rocky Mountain Race" TVM-1977; "Last of the Mohicans" TVM-1977; "Donner Pass: The Road to Survival" TVM-1978; "California Gold Rush" TVM-1981; "The Capture of Grizzly Adams" TVM-1982. ¶TV: *The Life and Times of Grizzly Adams* 1977; *Paradise*—"Long Lost Lawson" 5-20-89, "Avenging Angel" 2-10-90, "Dust on the Wind" 4-28-90.

Conway, Richard S. Screenwriter. Films: "Yankee Fakir" 1947.

Cook, Ad. Director. Films: "Western Grit" 1924 (& sp.).

Cook, Ella May. Writer. Films: "Riding Speed" 1934 (story).

Cook, Fielder (1923-). Director. Films: "A Big Hand for the Little Lady" 1966 (& prod.); "Sam Hill: Who Killed the Mysterious Mr. Foster?" TVM-1971; "This Was the West That Was" TVM-1974.

Cook, Will. Writer. Films: "The Tramplers" 1965-Ital. (story).

Cook, William Wallace (1867-1933). Writer. Films: "The Gold Grabbers" 1922 (story); "The Sunshine Trail" 1923 (story); "The Sonora Kid" 1927 (story); "Two Rode Together" 1961 (story).

Cooke, Virginia M. Screenwriter. Films: "Tomboy and the Champ" 1961.

Cooley, Frank (1870-7/6/41). Director. Films: "Broadcloth and Buckskin" 1915; "In the Sunset Country" 1915; "The Sheriff of Willow Creek" 1915; "The Trail of the Serpent" 1915; "The Valley Feud" 1915; "The Warning" 1915.

Coolidge, Dane. Writer. Films: "The Yaqui" 1916 (story); "Rimrock Jones" 1918 (story).

Coolidge, Karl. Screenwriter. Films: "The Gun Men of Plumas" 1914 (story only); "The Mysterious Outlaw" 1917; "Ace High" 1919; "The Crow" 1919; "The Gun Packer" 1919; "Nan of the North" 1922-serial; "Ghost City" 1923-serial; "The Steel Trail" 1923-serial; "Days of '49" 1924-serial (story only); "Riders of the Plains" 1924-serial; "Sagebrush Gospel" 1924.

Cooly, Carle. Screenwriter. Films: "The Sagebrush Lady" 1925.

Coon, Gene (1925-7/8/73). Director. Films: "Man in the Shadow" 1957 (sp. only); "No Name on the Bullet" 1959 (sp. only); "The Raiders" 1964 (sp. only); "Journey to Shiloh" 1968 (sp. only). ¶TV: *Wild Wild West* 1965-69 (prod.); *Laredo*—"It's the End of the Road, Stanley" 3-10-66; *The Men from Shiloh* 1970.

Cooper, Courtney Riley. Writer. Films: "Step on It!" 1922 (story); "The Last Frontier" 1926 (story); "The Last Frontier" 1932-serial (story); "The Plainsman" 1936 (story); "Desperate Trails" 1939 (story).

Cooper, Gary (1901-5/13/61). Producer. Films: "Along Came Jones" 1945.

Cooper, J. Gordon. Director. Films: "Sin Town" 1929 (& sp.).

Cooper, Jackie (1922-). Director. Films: "Rodeo Girl" TVM-1980. ¶TV: *The Texas Wheelers* 1974.

Cooper, James Fenimore (1779-1851). Writer. Films: "Leather Stocking" 1909 (story); "The Deerslayer" 1911 (story); "The Last of Mohicans" 1911 (story); "The Deerslayer" 1913 (story); "The Last of the Mohicans" 1920 (story); "Leatherstocking" 1924-serial (story); "The Last of the Mohicans" 1932-serial (story); "The Last of the Mohicans" 1936 (story); "The Pioneers" 1941 (story); "Deerslayer" 1943 (story); "Last of the Redmen" 1947 (story); "The Prairie" 1947 (story); "The Iroquois Trail" 1950 (story); "The Pathfinder" 1952 (story); "The Deerslayer" 1957 (story); "Last of the Mohicans" 1965-Ital./Span./Ger. (story); "Last of the Mohicans" TVM-1977 (story); "The Deerslayer" TVM-1978 (story); "The Last of the Mohicans" 1992 (story).

Cooper, Merian C. (1894-4/21/73). Producer. Films: "Fort Apache" 1948; "The Three Godfathers" 1948; "She Wore a Yellow Ribbon" 1949; "Rio Grande" 1950; "Wagonmaster" 1950; "The Searchers" 1956.

Cooper, Olive (1893-6/12/87). Screenwriter. Films: "The Border Legion" 1940; "Young Bill Hickok" 1940; "Down Mexico Way" 1941; "In Old Cheyenne" 1941; "Robin Hood of the Pecos" 1941; "Sheriff of Tombstone" 1941; "The Singing Hill" 1941; "Call of the Canyon" 1942 (& story); "Cowboy Serenade" 1942; "Idaho" 1943; "King of the Cowboys" 1943; "Song of Nevada" 1944; "Sioux City Sue" 1946; "Bandit King of Texas" 1949; "The Big Sombrero" 1949; "Outcasts of the Trail" 1949; "Hills of Oklahoma" 1950.

Cooper, Peter. Writer. Films: "Hannie Calder" 1971-Brit./Span./Fr. (story).

Cooper, William. Director. Films: "The Sunset Princess" 1918.

Copeland, Jodie. Director. Films: "Ambush at Cimarron Pass" 1958. ¶TV: *Sky King* 1951.

Corarito, Greg. Director. Films: "Hard Trail" 1969 (& sp.).

Corbett, Stanley. *see* Corbucci, Sergio.

Corbucci, Bruno (Tony Good, Frank B. Corlish, Dean Whitcomb). Director. Films: "Four Dollars for Vengeance" 1965-Span./Ital. (sp. only); "Django" 1966-Ital./Sp. (sp. only); "For a Few Dollars Less" 1966-Ital. (sp. only); "Ringo and Gringo Against All" 1966-Ital./Span.; "Bad Kids of the West" 1967-Ital. (& sp.); "Hate for Hate" 1967-Ital. (sp. only); "Great Silence" 1968-Ital./Fr. (sp. only); "Shoot, Gringo … Shoot!" 1968-Ital./Fr. (& sp.); "Three Silver Dollars" 1968-Ital. (sp. only); "Three Musketeers of the West" 1972-Ital. (& sp.); "Bandera Bandita" 1973-Ital./Span./Ger. (& sp.).

Corbucci, Sergio (Stanley Corbett) (1927-12/2/90). Director. Films: "Massacre at Grand Canyon" 1963-Ital. (& sp.); "Minnesota Clay" 1964-Ital./Fr./Span.   (&   sp.); "Django" 1966-Ital./Span. (& sp.); "For a Few Dollars Less" 1966-Ital. (sp. only); "The Hellbenders" 1966-U.S./Ital./Span.; "Johnny Hamlet" 1966-Ital. (story only); "Ringo and His Golden Pistol" 1966-Ital.; "Navajo Joe" 1966-Ital./Span.; "Great Silence" 1968-Ital./Fr. (& sp.); "The Mercenary" 1968-Ital./Span. (& sp.); "Drop Them or I'll Shoot" 1969-Fr./Ger./Span. (& prod./sp.); "Companeros" 1970-Ital./Span./Ger. (& sp.); "What Am I Doing in the Middle of the Revolution?" 1973-Ital. (& sp.); "The White, the Yellow, and the Black" 1974-Ital./Span./Fr. (& sp.).

Corby, Ellen (1913-). Screenwriter. Films: "Twilight on the Trail" 1941; "Hoppy's Holiday" 1947 (story only).

Corcoran, William. Writer. Films: "Trail Street" 1947 (story).

Corea, Nicholas. Director. Films: "Outlaws" TVM-1986 (& prod.). ¶TV: *Outlaws*—"Birthday" 5-2-87.

Corey, Jeff (1914-). Director. TV: *Alias Smith and Jones*—The Men That Corrupted Hadleyburg" 1-27-72, "The Day the Amnesty Came Through" 11-25-72.

Corey, William A. Writer. Films: "Religion and Gun Practice" 1913 (story); "The Senorita's Repentance" 1913 (story); "The Servant Question Out West" 1914 (story).

Corlish, Frank B. *see* Corbucci, Bruno.

Cormack, Bartlett (1898-9/16/42). Screenwriter. Films: "The Spoilers" 1930.

Corman, Roger (1926-). Director. Films: "Apache Woman" 1955 (& prod.); "Five Guns West" 1955 (& prod.); "Gunslinger" 1956 (& prod.); "The Oklahoma Woman" 1956 (& prod.).

Cornell, Evans W. Writer. Films: "Requiem for a Gunfighter" 1965 (story).

Correll, Charles. Director. Films: "Gunsmoke: The Last Apache" TVM-1990. ¶TV: *Legend*—Pilot 4-18-95, "Bone of Contention" 6-20-95.

Corrigan, Lloyd (1900-11/5/69). Director. Films: "Hands Up!" 1926; "Dude Ranch" 1931 (sp. only); "The Broken Wing" 1932.

Cort, Van. Writer. Films: "Mail Order Bride" 1964 (story).

Corvin, Anya. Screenwriter. Films: "Duel at Sundown" 1965-Fr./Ger.

Coscia, Cello. Screenwriter. Films: "The White, the Yellow, and the Black" 1974-Ital./Span./Fr.

Cosgriff, Robert James. Screenwriter. Films: "Roaring Timber" 1937 (& story).

Costa, Mario (John W. Fordson) (1904-10/22/95). Director. Films: "Buffalo Bill, Hero of the Far West" 1964-Ital./Ger./Fr.: "Beast" 1970-Ital. (& sp.).

Costner, Kevin (1955-). Director. Films: "Dances With Wolves" 1990 (& prod.); "Wyatt Earp" 1994 (prod. only).

Cottrel, H.D. Writer. Films: "The Half-Breed" 1922 (story).

Couderc, Pierre. Screenwriter. Films: "Silent Sheldon" 1925; "Captain Thunder" 1931 (story only).

Couffer, Jack. Director. Films: "Running Target" 1956 (prod./sp. only); "Nikki, Wild Dog of the North" 1961-U.S./Can.

Courtney, William B. Screenwriter. Films: "The Purple Riders" 1921-serial.

Cowan, Lester (1905-10/21/90). Producer. Films: "My Little Chickadee" 1940.

Cowan, Will (1911-1/4/94). Director. Films: "Arizona Cyclone" 1941 (prod. only); "Law of the Range" 1941; "Man from Montana" 1941; "The Masked Rider" 1941 (prod. only); "Rawhide Rangers" 1941 (prod. only); "Fighting Bill Fargo" 1942; "The Silver Bullet" 1942 (prod. only); "Stagecoach Buckaroo" 1942 (prod. only); "Frontier Frolic" 1946-short (prod. only); "Tumbleweed Tempos" 1946-short (& prod.); "Tex Williams and His Western Caravan" 1947-short (& prod.); "Western

Whoopee" 1948-short; "Cheyenne Cowboy" 1949-short (prod. only); "Coyote Canyon" 1949 (& prod.); "The Girl from Gunsight" 1949-short (& prod.); "The Pecos Pistol" 1949-short (& prod.); "Silver Butte 1949-short (prod. only); "Six Gun Music" 1949-short (prod. only); "South of Santa Fe" 1949-short (& prod.); "Spade Cooley and His Orchestra" 1949-short (& prod.); "West of Laramie" 1949-short (& prod.); "Cactus Caravan" 1950-short (& prod.); "The Fargo Phantom" 1950-short (& prod.); "Gold Strike" 1950-short (& prod.); "Prairie Pirates" 1950-short (& prod.); "Ready to Ride" 1950-short (& prod.); "Corral Cuties" 1954-short (& prod.); "Webb Pierce and His Wanderin' Boys" 1955-short (& prod.).

Cox, Alex (1954-). Director. Films: "Straight to Hell" 1987-Brit. (& sp.).

Cox, Doran. Director. Films: "Just in Time" 1929.

Cox, George L. Director. Films: "The Law of the North" 1912; "The Gamesters" 1920; "Sunset Jones" 1921.

Cox, Morgan B. Screenwriter. Films: "The Painted Stallion" 1937-serial (story only); "Zorro Rides Again" 1937-serial; "Overland with Kit Carson" 1939-serial; "Zorro's Fighting Legion" 1939-serial; "Deadwood Dick" 1940-serial; "Road Agent" 1941; "White Eagle" 1941-serial; "Frontier Badman" 1943; "Raiders of San Joaquin" 1943; "Raiders of Ghost City" 1944-serial (& prod.); "Royal Mounted Rides Again" 1945-serial (prod. only); "The Scarlet Horseman" 1946-serial (prod. only).

Cox, William R. (1901-8/7/88). Screenwriter. Films: "Natchez Trace" 1960.

Coyle, Ellen. Screenwriter. Films: "Ghost of Hidden Valley" 1946; "Overland Rider" 1946.

Craddock, Andrew. Writer. Films: "Johnny Reno" 1966 (story only); "Fort Utah" 1967; "Red Tomahawk" 1967 (story only); "Arizona Bushwhackers" 1968 (story only).

Craft, William J. (1890-6/30/31). Director. Films: "The White Rider" 1920 (& story); "Crossed Clues" 1921; "The Fightin' Actor" 1921 (& sp.); "The Showdown" 1921; "Another Man's Boots" 1922; "False Brands" 1922 (& story); "Headin' West" 1922; "Wolf Pack" 1922 (& sp.); "Forgettin' the Law" 1923; "In the Days of Daniel Boone" 1923-serial; "Lonesome Luck" 1923; "Smilin' On" 1923; "Between Fires" 1924; "Blue Wing's Revenge" 1924; "Border Raid" 1924; "The College Cowboy" 1924; "Flying Eagle" 1924; "The King's Command" 1924; "The Powerful Eye" 1924; "The Riddle Rider" 1924-serial; "A Sagebrush Vagabond" 1924; "The Bloodhound" 1925; "Galloping Vengeance" 1925; "The Range Terror" 1925; "The Galloping Cowboy" 1926; "King of the Saddle" 1926; "The Power of the Weak" 1926 (& sp.); "The Arizona Whirlwind" 1927.

Craig, Charles Grant. Screenwriter. Films: "The Return of Desperado" TVM-1988.

Craig, Dean (Mario Pierotti). Screenwriter. Films: "Death Walks in Laredo" 1966-Ital./Span.; "The Hills Run Red" 1966-Ital.; "The Hills Run Red" 1966-Ital.; "Navajo Joe" 1966-Ital./Span.; "Law of Violence" 1969-Span./Ital.; "Sometimes Life Is Hard, Right Providence?" 1972-Ital./Fr./Ger.

Crane, Barry (1928-85). Director. ¶TV: *Kung Fu*—"The Vanishing Image" 12-20-74, "Battle Hymn" 2-8-75; *The Quest*—"The Last of the Mountain Men" 1976; *How the West Was Won*—"The Rustlers" 5-21-78, "The Forgotten" 3-19-79.

Crane, Peter. Director. TV: *Paradise*—"Crossroads" 1-26-89, "The Last Warrior" 2-23-89.

Crane, Stephen (1871-1900). Writer. Films: "Face to Face" 1952 ("The Bride Comes to Yellow Sky" segment) (story only).

Crawford, Jack. Writer. Films: "The Colonel's Daughter" 1915 (story).

Crawford, John. Screenwriter. Films: "The Ballad of Cable Hogue" 1970.

Crawford, Julia. Screenwriter. Films: "Ben Blair" 1916.

Crays, Durrell Royce. Screenwriter. Films: "Kung Fu: The Movie" TVM-1986.

Crea, Gianni. Director. Films: "Finders Killers" 1969-Ital.; "Law of Violence" 1969-Span./Ital. (& sp.); "Magnificent West" 1972-Ital. (& sp.); "On the Third Day Arrived the Crow" 1972-Ital./Span.

Cresse, R.W. Producer. Films: "Hot Spur" 1968 (& story); "The Scavengers" 1969 (& sp.).

Crichton, Michael (1942-). Director. Films: "Westworld" 1973 (& sp.).

Crimmins, Robert. Writer.

Films: "The Lone Hand" 1922 (story).

Crinley, William (-1/1/27). Director. Films: "The Boundary Line" 1925; "The Gold Trap" 1925; "Range Law" 1925; "The Rider of the Pass" 1925; "The Rustlers of Boulder Canyon" 1925; "The Rustlin' Kid" 1925; "Taking Chances" 1925; "The Call of Hazard" 1926; "Coming Back" 1926; "The Frame-Up" 1926; "Grinning Fists" 1926; "The Man with a Scar" 1926; "Quick on the Draw" 1926; "Rustler by Proxy" 1926; "Trapped" 1926; "Under Desert Skies" 1926.

Crisp, Donald (1882-5/25/74). Director. Films: "Ramona" 1916; "Rimrock Jones" 1918; "Johnny, Get Your Gun" 1919; "Don Q, Son of Zorro" 1925.

Crispino, Armando. Director. Director: "John the Bastard" 1967-Ital. (& sp.); "Let Them Rest" 1967-Ital./Ger. (sp. only).

Crispo, Ramon. Screenwriter. Films: "Finger on the Trigger" 1965-Span./Ital./U.S.

Cristallini, Giorgio. Director. Films: "You're Jinxed, Friend, You Just Met Sacramento" 1970-Ital./Span. (& sp.); "Four Gunmen of the Holy Trinity" 1971-Ital. (& sp.).

Crizer, Tom. Screenwriter. Films: "My Pal, the King" 1932.

Croccolo, Carlo (Lucky Moore). Director. Films: "Sheriff Was a Lady" 1965-Ger.; "Gunman of One Hundred Crosses" 1971-Ger./Ital. (& sp.).

Crocker, Emerson. Screenwriter. Films: "The Treasure of Lost Canyon" 1952.

Cromwell, John (1887-9/26/79). Director. Films: "The Texan" 1930.

Crone, George. Director. Films: "Get That Girl" 1932.

Crosland, Alan (1894-7/16/36). Director. Films: "Captain Thunder" 1931; "Massacre" 1934.

Crosland, Jr., Alan. Director. Films: "Natchez Trace" 1960. ¶TV: *Cheyenne* 1955; *Sergeant Preston of the Yukon* 1955; *Colt .45* 1957; *Maverick*—"Trail West to Fury" 2-16-58; *Lawman* 1958; *Northwest Passage*—"The Long Rifle" 11-23-58, "The Fourth Brother" 1-30-59, "Stab in the Back" 2-20-49, "The Deserter" 2-27-59; *Gunsmoke*—"About Chester" 2-25-61; *The Virginian*—"The Money Cage" 3-6-63, "A Father for Toby" 11-4-64; *Rawhide*—"Escape to Doom" 10-12-65; *Wild Wild West*—"The Night of the Torture Chamber" 12-

10-65, "The Night of the Poisonous Posey" 10-28-66, "The Night of the Man-Eating House" 12-2-66, "The Night of the Skulls" 12-16-66, "The Night of the Gypsy Peril" 1-20-67, "The Night of the Surreal McCoy" 3-3-67, "The Night of the Deadly Blossom" 3-17-67, "The Night of the Assassin" 9-22-67, "The Night Dr. Loveless Died" 9-29-67, "The Night of the Cut Throats" 11-17-67, "The Night of the Headless Woman" 1-5-68; *Bonanza*—"Four Sisters from Boston" 10-30-66; *Hondo*—"Hondo and the Hanging Town" 12-8-67.

Cross, Barr. Screenwriter. Films: "Thundering Through" 1925; "The Dead Line" 1926; "The Devil's Gulch" 1926; "The Ramblin' Galoot" 1926 (story only).

Cross, Henry. *see* Spalding, Harry.

Crouch, William Forest. Director. Films: "Echo Ranch" 1948-short (& prod.); "Hidden Valley Days" 1948-short (& prod.).

Crowe, Christopher. Screenwriter. Films: "The Last of the Mohicans" 1992.

Crowley, William X. Director. Films: "Trail of the Yukon" 1949.

Croy, Homer. Writer. Films: "I Shot Jesse James" 1949 (story).

Crump, Owen. Screenwriter. Films: "Here Comes the Cavalry" 1941-short; "Silver River" 1948.

Crutchfield, Les. Writer. Films: "Last Train from Gun Hill" 1959 (story).

Cruze, James (1894-8/3/42). Director. Films: "The Covered Wagon" 1923 (& prod.); "Ruggles of Red Gap" 1923; "The Pony Express" 1925; "Sutter's Gold" 1936.

Crystal, Billy (1947-). Screenwriter. Films: "City Slickers II: The Legend of Curly's Gold" 1994 (& sp.).

Cukor, George (1899-1/24/83). Director. Films: "Heller in Pink Tights" 1960.

Cullison, Webster. Director. Films: "The Girl Stage Driver" 1914; "The Fighting Stranger" 1921; "The Last Chance" 1921; "Battling Bates" 1923.

Cullum, Ridgwell. Screenwriter. Films: "The Son of His Father" 1917 (story only); "The Trail of the Axe" 1922; "The Yosemite Trail" 1922 (story only).

Cummings, Dwight. Screenwriter. Films: "Smoky" 1946; "Loaded Pistols" 1948; "The Strawberry Roan" 1948; "The Cowboy and the Indians" 1949; "Saginaw Trail" 1953.

Cummings, Hugh. Screenwriter. Films: "Pardon My Gun" 1930.

Cummings, Irving (1888-4/18/59). Director. Films: "The Man from Hell's River" 1922 (& sp.); "The Desert Flower" 1925; "Rustlin' for Cupid" 1926; "The Brute" 1927; "In Old Arizona" 1929; "Cisco Kid" 1931; "A Holy Terror" 1931; "Belle Starr" 1941; "Last of the Duanes" 1941. ¶TV: *Fury* 1955-60 (prod.).

Cummings, Jr., Irving. Screenwriter. Films: "Lone Star Ranger" 1942.

Cummings, Jack. Producer. Films: "Go West" 1940; "Many Rivers to Cross" 1955; "The Second Time Around" 1961.

Cummins, Ralph. Writer. Films: "Where Men Are Men" 1921 (story); "The Loaded Door" 1922 (story); "Sky High Coral" 1926 (story).

Cunard, Grace (1893-1/18/67). Screenwriter. Films: "The Call of the Tribe" 1914 (story only); "The Curse of the Desert" 1915; "Three Bad Men and a Girl" 1915 (story only); "The Bandit's Wager" 1916.

Cunliff, Don. Director. Films: "Scar Hanan" 1925.

Cunningham, Jack (1882-10/4/41). Screenwriter. Films: "Wynona's Vengeance" 1913; "In the Sage Brush Country" 1915; "Wild Sumac" 1917; "The Wrong Man" 1917; "The Border Raiders" 1918; "The Ghost of the Rancho" 1918; "The Goddess of Lost Lake" 1918; "Little Red Decides" 1918; "The Midnight Stage" 1919; "Two-Gun Betty" 1919; "The Call of the North" 1921; "The Covered Wagon" 1923; "Don Q, Son of Zorro" 1925; "The Adventurer" 1928; "Wild West Romance" 1928; "Clearing the Range" 1931; "Flaming Guns" 1932; "Rider of Death Valley" 1932 (& story); "Texas Bad Man" 1932; "The Fourth Horseman" 1933; "Man of the Forest" 1933; "Rustlers' Roundup" 1933; "Silent Men" 1933; "Sunset Pass" 1933; "Terror Trail" 1933; "To the Last Man" 1933; "Under the Tonto Rim" 1933; "The Last Round-Up" 1934; "The Thundering Herd" 1934; "Wagon Wheels" 1934; "The Painted Desert" 1938 (story only); "Union Pacific" 1939.

Cunningham, John M. Writer. Films: "High Noon" 1952 (story); "The Stranger Wore a Gun" 1953 (story); "Day of the Bad Man" 1958 (story).

Curran, Charles W. Screenwriter. Films: "Echo Ranch" 1948-short; "Hidden Valley Days" 1948-short.

Curran, William Hughes. Director. Films: "Blaze Away" 1922; "The Freshie" 1922 (& story); "Lucky Dan" 1922; "Trail of Hate" 1922; "Westbound" 1924.

Curtis, Allen. Director. Films: "The Lady Doctor of Grizzly Gulch" 1915.

Curtis, Dan (1928-). Director. Films: "Last Ride of the Dalton Gang" TVM-1979.

Curtis, Jack (1880-3/16/56). Screenwriter. Films: "The Cheyenne Kid" 1933.

Curtis, Leslie. Screenwriter. Films: "Western Courage" 1927.

Curtis, Nathaniel. Screenwriter. Films: "The Harvey Girls" 1946.

Curtiz, Michael (1888-4/10/62). Director. Films: "River's End" 1930; "Under a Texas Moon" 1930; "Gold Is Where You Find It" 1938; "Dodge City" 1939; "Santa Fe Trail" 1940; "Virginia City" 1940; "The Boy from Oklahoma" 1954; "The Proud Rebel" 1958; "The Hangman" 1959; "The Comancheros" 1961.

Curwood, James Oliver. Writer. Films: "In Defiance of the Law" 1914 (story); "The Test" 1914 (story); "The Coyote" 1915 (story); "Getting a Start in Life" 1915 (story); "Man's Law" 1915 (story); "The Old Code" 1915 (story); "The Danger Trail" 1917 (story); "Baree, Son of Kazan" 1918 (story); "The Girl Who Wouldn't Quit" 1918 (story); "Isobel, or the Trail's End" 1920 (story); "Nomads of the North" 1920 (sp./story); "Kazan" 1921 (story); "The Girl from Porcupine" 1922 (story); "God's Country and the Law" 1922 (story); "The Man from Hell's River" 1922 (story); "The Valley of Silent Men" 1922; "Baree, Son of Kazan" 1925 (story); "The Gold Hunters" 1925 (story); "Steele of the Royal Mounted" 1925 (story); "The Flaming Forest" 1926 (story); "The Wolf Hunters" 1926 (story); "The Yellowback" 1929; "River's End" 1930 (story); "The Fighting Trooper" 1934 (story); "The Trail Beyond" 1934 (story); "Code of the Mounted" 1935 (story); "His Fighting Blood" 1935 (story); "Northern Frontier" 1935 (story); "Red Blood of Courage" 1935 (story); "Skull and Crown" 1935 (story); "Timber War" 1935 (story); "Trails End" 1935 (story); "Trails of the Wild" 1935 (story); "Wilderness Mail" 1935 (story); "Caryl of the

Mountains" 1936 (story); "The Country Beyond" 1936 (story); "Phantom Patrol" 1936 (story); "Song of the Trail" 1936 (story); "Vengeance of Rannah" 1936 (story); "Wildcat Trooper" 1936 (story); "Fighting Texan" 1937 (story); "Galloping Dynamite" 1937 (story); "God's Country and the Woman" 1937 (story); "Roaring Six Guns" 1937 (story); "Rough Ridin' Rhythm" 1937 (story); "The Silver Trail" 1937 (sp.); "Valley of Terror" 1937 (story); "Whistling Bullets" 1937 (story); "Wild Horse Round-Up" 1937 (story); "Call of the Yukon" 1938 (story); "River's End" 1940 (story); "Dawn on the Great Divide" 1942 (story); "God's Country" 1946 (story); "'Neath Canadian Skies" 1946 (story); "North of the Border" 1946 (story); "Trail of the Yukon" 1949 (story); "The Wolf Hunters" 1949 (story); "Call of the Klondike" 1950 (story); "Snow Dog" 1950 (story); "Northwest Territory" 1951 (story); "Yukon Manhunt" 1951 (story); "Yukon Gold" 1952 (story); "Back to God's Country" 1953 (story); "Fangs of the Arctic" 1953 (story); "Northern Patrol" 1953 (story); "Yukon Vengance" 1954 (story); "Nikki, Wild Dog of the North" 1961-U.S./Can. (story).

Cushman, Dan (1909-). Writer. Films: "Timberjack" 1955 (story).

Cusso, Miguel. Screenwriter. Films: "Death Knows No Time" 1968-Span./Ital.

Cutting, John. Screenwriter. Films: "Deadwood Dick" 1940-serial; "White Eagle" 1941-serial.

Dackow, Joseph. Producer. Films: *The Outlaws* 1960-62; *Temple Houston* 1963-64.

DaGradi, Don. Screenwriter. Films: "Scandalous John" 1971.

Dague, Roswell. Screenwriter. Films: "Jamestown" 1923.

Dakin, Raymond E. Screenwriter. Films: "Salt of the Earth" 1917.

Dales, Arthur. Screenwriter. Films: "The Sheriff of Fractured Jaw" 1958-Brit.

Daley, Robert. Producer. Films: "High Plains Drifter" 1972; "The Outlaw Josey Wales" 1976.

Dallamano, Massimo (Max Dillmann) (1917-11/76). Director. Films: "Bandidos" 1967-Ital.

Dalmas, Herbert. Screenwriter. Films: "Saddlemates" 1941; "North of the Rockies" 1942; "Last of the Redmen" 1947.

Dalton, Emmett. Writer. Films:

"When the Daltons Rode" 1940 (story).

Dalton, James. Screenwriter. Films: "The Vengeance of the Sky Stone" 1913.

Daly, William Robert. Director. Films: "When California Was Wild" 1915.

D'Amato, Jo. *see* Massaccesi, Aristide.

Damiani, Damiano (1922-). Director. Films: "A Bullet for the General" 1966-Ital.; "Genius" 1975-Ital./Fr./Ger. (& sp.).

Damski, Mel. Director. Films: "The Legend of Walks Far Woman" TVM-1982; "Blood River" TVM-1994.

Dandy, Ned (1888-8/8/48). Screenwriter. Films: "Overland with Kit Carson" 1939-serial; "Trouble at Melody Mesa" 1944.

Daniels, George. Screenwriter. Films: "Blazing Bullets" 1951.

Daniels, Harold (1903-12/27/71). Director. Films: "Daughter of the West" 1949.

Daniels, Marc (1911-4/23/89). Director. TV: *Colt .45* 1957; *Gunsmoke*—"The Reward" 11-6-65, "Killer at Large" 2-5-66, "Wishbone" 2-19-66, "Treasure of John Walking Fox" 4-16-66, "Parson Comes to Town" 4-30-66, "The Well" 11-19-66, "Champion of the World" 12-24-66, "The Returning" 2-18-67, "The Lure" 2-25-67, "The Favor" 3-11-67; *Branded*—"Kellie" 4-24-66; *Shane* 1966; *Bonanza*—"The Trackers" 1-7-68, "In Defense of Honor" 4-28-68, "The Arrival of Eddie" 5-19-68; *Prudence and the Chief*—Pilot 8-26-70; *The Men from Shiloh* 1970; *Kung Fu*—"The Garments of Rage" 11-8-74, "One Step to Darkness" 1-25-75, "Barbary House" 2-15-75, "Flight to Orion" 2-22-75, "Full Circle" 3-15-75; *Gun Shy* 1983.

Daniels, Stan. Screenwriter. Films: "Substitute Wife" TVM-1994.

D'Arcy, Harry. Director. Films: "Prairie Spooners" 1941-short (& sp.); "Redskins and Redheads" 1941-short (& sp.); "Keep Shooting" 1942-short (& sp.).

Dark Cloud. Screenwriter. Films: "The Boundary Line" 1915.

Darling, Kenneth. Screenwriter. Films: "Stagecoach to Dancer's Rock" 1962.

Darling, W. Scott (1898-10/29/51). Screenwriter. Films: "The Meddler" 1925; "Sporting West" 1925 (story only); "Two-Fisted Jones" 1925; "The Pocatello Kid" 1931;

"Gold" 1932; "Outlaw Justice" 1933 (story only); "Frontier Justice" 1936; "King of the Sierras" 1938; "Sin Town" 1942; "The Wolf Hunters" 1949; "Desert Pursuit" 1952.

Darmour, Larry (1895-3/11/42). Producer. Films: "Gold" 1932; "Law and Lawless" 1932; "Gun Law" 1933; "Outlaw Justice" 1933; "Trouble Busters" 1933; "Via Pony Express" 1933; "Heir to Trouble" 1935; "Lawless Riders" 1935; "Western Courage" 1935; "Western Frontier" 1935; "Avenging Waters" 1936; "The Cattle Thief" 1936; "The Fugitive Sheriff" 1936; "Heroes of the Range" 1936; "North of Nome" 1936; "Rio Grande Ranger" 1936; "The Unknown Ranger" 1936; "Law of the Ranger" 1937; "Ranger Courage" 1937; "The Rangers Step In" 1937; "Reckless Ranger" 1937; "Roaring Timber" 1937; "In Early Arizona" 1938; "Phantom Gold" 1938; "Pioneer Trail" 1938; "Rolling Caravans" 1938; "Stagecoach Days" 1938; "Frontiers of '49" 1939; "The Law Comes to Texas" 1939; "Lone Star Pioneers" 1939; "Deadwood Dick" 1940-serial; "White Eagle" 1941-serial; "Perils of the Royal Mounted" 1942-serial; "Valley of Vanishing Men" 1942-serial.

Darnton, Charles. Screenwriter. Films: "The Cowboy and the Countess" 1926; "The Fighting Buckaroo" 1926; "Hard-Boiled" 1926.

Dattlebaum, Myron. Screenwriter. Films: "Outlaws' Highway" 1934.

Daugherty, Herschel (1910-3/5/93). Director. Films: "The Light in the Forest" 1958; "The Raiders" 1964; "Winchester '73" TVM-1967. ¶TV: *Wagon Train*—"The Willy Moran Story" 9-18-57, "Around the Horn" 10-1-58, "The Tobias Jones Story" 10-22-58, "The Liam Fitzmogran Story" 10-28-58, "The Sakae Ito Story" 12-3-58, "The Tom Tuckett Story" 3-2-60, "The Christine Elliot Story" 3-23-60, "Wagons Ho!" 9-28-60, "The Albert Farnsworth Story" 10-12-60, "The Christopher Hale Story" 3-15-61, "The Andrew Elliott Story" 2-10-64, "The Pearlie Garnet Story" 2-24-64, "The Duncan McIvor Story" 3-9-64; *The Deputy* 1959; *The Virginian*—"The Man from the Sea" 12-26-62; *The Slowest Gun in the West* 7-29-63; *Rawhide*—"The Backshooter" 11-27-64, "Josh" 1-15-65; *Shane* 1966; *Cimarron Strip*—"Whitey" 10-19-67, "The Assassin" 1-11-68, "Big Jessie" 2-8-68; *Gunsmoke*—"Johnny Cross" 12-23-68, "Exodus 21:22" 3-24-69; *Bonanza*—

"The Unwanted" 4-6-69, "Meena" 11-16-69, "Abner Willoughby's Return" 12-21-69, "The Big Jackpot" 1-18-70, "The Horse Traders" 4-5-70, "Gideon the Good" 10-18-70, "The Trouble with Trouble" 10-25-70, "An Earthquake Called Callahan" 4-11-71, "Rock-a-Bye, Hoss" 10-10-71, "Cassie" 10-24-71, "A Place to Hide" 3-19-72; *The High Chaparral*—"Apache Trust" 11-7-69, "Auld Lang Syne" 4-10-70; *Here Come the Brides*—"Debt of Honor" 1-23-70; *The Texas Wheelers* 1974.

Daumery, John. Director. Films: "Rough Waters" 1930.

Davenport, Gail. Writer. Films: "Rockin' in the Rockies" 1945 (story).

Daves, Delmer (1904-8/17/77). Director. Films: "Broken Arrow" 1950; "Return of the Texan" 1952; "Drum Beat" 1954 (& sp.); "White Feather" 1955; "Jubal" 1956 (& sp.); "The Last Wagon" 1956 (& sp.); "3:10 to Yuma" 1957; "The Badlanders" 1958; "Cowboy" 1958; "The Hanging Tree" 1959.

Daves, Don. Director. TV: *Bonanza*—"A Dollar's Worth of Trouble" 5-15-66, "Dark Enough to See the Stars" 3-12-67, "A Man Without Land" 4-9-67, "The Greedy Ones" 5-14-67, "Six Black Horses" 11-26-67, "The Gold Detector" 12-24-67.

Davey, Horace. Director. Films: "The Sagebrush Lady" 1925.

David, Marjorie. Screenwriter. Films: "Into the Badlands" TVM-1991.

David, Peter (1956-). Screenwriter. Films: "Oblivion" 1994.

David, William B. Producer. Films: "Northwest Trail" 1945; "God's Country" 1946; "'Neath Canadian Skies" 1946; "North of the Border" 1946.

Davidson, Ronald (1899-7/28/65). Screenwriter. Films: "The Painted Stallion" 1937-serial (story only); "Zorro Rides Again" 1937-serial; "The Lone Ranger" 1938-serial; "The Lone Ranger Rides Again" 1939-serial; "Zorro's Fighting Legion" 1939-serial; "Adventures of Red Ryder" 1940-serial; "King of the Texas Rangers" 1941-serial; "King of the Mounties" 1942-serial; "Daredevils of the West" 1943-serial; "Zorro's Black Whip" 1944-serial (prod. only); "King of the Forest Rangers" 1946-serial (prod. only); "The Phantom Rider" 1946-serial (prod. only); "Son of Zorro" 1947-serial (prod. only); "Courtin' Trouble" 1948; "Cowboy Cavalier" 1948; "The Fighting Ranger" 1948; "Range Renegades" 1948; "Triggerman" 1948; "Across the Rio Grande" 1949; "Range Justice" 1949; "Roaring Westward" 1949; "Desperadoes of the West" 1950-serial; "Don Daredevil Rides Again" 1951-serial; "Black Hills Ambush" 1952; "Canadian Mounties vs. Atomic Invaders" 1953-serial; "Man with the Steel Whip" 1954-serial.

Davis, A. Byron. Director. Films: "Fools of Fortune" 1922.

Davis, Donald. Screenwriter. Films: "Rough Romance" 1930.

Davis, Eddie. Producer. Films: "Racketeer Round-Up" 1934 (story only); "Haunted Trails" 1949; "Range Land" 1949; "Riders of the Dusk" 1949; "Western Renegades" 1949; "Six Gun Mesa" 1950; "West of Wyoming" 1950. ¶TV: *The Cisco Kid* 1951-55 (dir.).

Davis, Frank. Screenwriter. Films: "California" 1927; "Springfield Rifle" 1952; "The Indian Fighter" 1955; "The Boy from Oklahoma" 1954.

Davis, Frank Foster. Writer. Films: "Silent Pal" 1925 (story).

Davis, Glen Vincent. *see* Musolino, Vincenzo.

Davis, J. Charles. Producer. Films: "West of the Rockies" 1929.

Davis, James. Director. Films: "The Perilous Leap" 1917; "Danger Ahead" 1918; "Under False Pretenses" 1918.

Davis, Jerry. Screenwriter. Films: "Apache War Smoke" 1952; "Pardners" 1956.

Davis, Norbert. Writer. Films: "Hands Across the Rockies" 1941 (story).

Davis, Owen. Writer. Films: "The Gambler of the West" 1914 (writer).

Davis, Richard Harding (1864-1916). Writer. Films: "Ranson's Folly" 1910 (story); "Ranson's Folly" 1915 (story); "Ranson's Folly" 1926 (story).

Davis, Jr., Sammy (1925-5/16/90). Producer. Films: "The Trackers" TVM-1971 (& story).

Davis, Ulysses. Director. Films: "Anne of the Mines" 1914; "The Horse Thief" 1914; "Mareea, the Half-Breed" 1914; "The Navajo Ring" 1914; "Wards Claim" 1914; "The Legend of the Lone Tree" 1915; "The Man from the Desert" 1915; "The Worthier Man" 1915.

Davis, Will H. Director. Films: "Thou Shalt Not" 1914 (& sp.).

Davis, William B. Producer.

Films: "Wildfire" 1945; "Death Valley" 1946.

Davitt, Hal. Writer. Films: "Captain Thunder" 1931 (story).

Dawley, J. Searle (1878-3/29/49). Director. Films: "A Perilous Ride" 1911; "Salomy Jane" 1914.

Dawn, Isabel (1904-6/29/66). Screenwriter. Films: "The Girl of the Golden West" 1938; "Singin' in the Corn" 1946.

Dawn, Norman (1884-2/2/75). Director. Films: "Lasca" 1919; "Two Men of Tainted Butte" 1919; "The Line Runners" 1920; "The Son of the Wolf" 1922; "Lure of the Yukon" 1924 (& sp.).

Dawn, Vincent. *see* Mattei, Bruno.

Dawson, Anthony. *see* Margheriti, Antonio.

Dawson, Bordon. Screenwriter. Films: "Bret Maverick" TVM-1981

Dawson, Douglas. Writer. Films: "Hurrican Horseman" 1931 (story).

Dawson, Gordon. Screenwriter. Films: "Independence" TVM-1987; "Into the Badlands" TVM-1991.

Dawson, Peter. Writer. Films: "Face of a Fugitive" 1959 (story).

Day, Edmund. Writer. Films: "The Round Up" 1920 (story); "The Round Up" 1941 (story).

Day, Richard. Director. Films: "The Quick and the Dead" CTVM-1987.

Dayton, James. Screenwriter. Films: "The Sheriff of Red Rock Gulch" 1915; "Shadows of the West" 1921.

Dayton, Lyman D. Director. Films: "Pony Express Rider" 1972 (sp. only); "Seven Alone" 1974 (prod. only); "Against a Crooked Sky" 1975 (prod. only); "Baker's Hawk" 1976 (& prod.).

Dazey, Charles Turner. Screenwriter. Films: "Wolf Lowry" 1917.

Dazey, Frank M. Screenwriter. Films: "The Fighting Shepherdess" 1920; "When a Man's a Man" 1935.

Dean, Harry O. Screenwriter. Films: "Breed of the Border" 1933.

Dean, Margia. Producer. Films: "The Long Rope" 1961.

Dean, W. Screenwriter. Films: "The Silent Signal" 1912.

De Angelis, Fabrizio (Larry Ludman). Director. Films: "Run Man, Run" 1967-Ital./Fr. (sp. only); "Manhunt" 1984-Ital. (& sp.).

Dear, William. Director. Films: "Timerider" 1983 (& sp.).

Dearholt, Ashton (1894-4/27/42). Director. Films: "At Devil's Gorge" 1923; "The Santa Fe Trail" 1923-serial; "Western Feuds" 1924.

De Balboa, Nunez. Producer. Films: "One After Another" 1968-Span./Ital.

Decker, Harry L. Producer. Films: "Gallant Defender" 1935; "The Revenge Rider" 1935; "The Mysterious Avenger" 1936; "The Old Wyoming Trail" 1937; "Outlaws of the Prairie" 1937; "Trapped" 1937; "Two-Fisted Sheriff" 1937; "Call of the Rockies" 1938; "Cattle Raiders" 1938; "Colorado Trail" 1938; "Law of the Plains" 1938; "Rio Grande" 1938; "South of Arizona" 1938; "North of the Yukon" 1939; "Spoilers of the Range" 1939; "The Stranger from Texas" 1939; "Texas Stampede" 1939.

De Concini, Ennio. Screenwriter. Films: "Guns for San Sebastian" 1967-U.S./Fr./Mex./Ital.; "Four Horsemen of the Apocalypse" 1975-Ital.

De Cordova, Frederick (1910-). Director. Films: "Column South" 1953.

De Cordova, Leander (1878-9/19/69). Director. Films: "Trails of the Golden West" 1931.

de Courcey, Walter. Director. Films: "Fighting for Justice" 1924.

Deem, Miles. *see* Fidani, Demofilo.

De Grasse, Joseph (1873-5/24/40). Director. Films: "The Desert Breed" 1915; "Anything Once" 1917; "The Empty Gun" 1917; "Pay Me!" 1917; "The Fighting Grin" 1918.

De Haven, Carter (1886-7/20/77). Producer. Films: "Girl from the West" 1923 (story only); "Ulzana's Raid" 1972.

Dein, Edward. Director. Films: "Seven Guns to Mesa" 1958 (& sp.); "Curse of the Undead" 1959 (& sp.). ¶TV: *Bronco* 1958; *Wild Wild West*— "The Night of the Two-Legged Buffalo" 3-11-66, "The Night of the Freebooters" 4-1-66.

Dein, Mildred. Screenwriter. Films: "Seven Guns to Mesa" 1958; "Curse of the Undead" 1959.

Dejeans, Elizabeth. Writer. Films: "Crashin' Thru" 1923 (story).

De Lacey, Robert. Director. Films: "The Cowboy Musketeer" 1925; "Let's Go Gallagher" 1925; "The Wyoming Wildcat" 1925; "The Arizona Streak" 1926; "Born to Battle" 1926; "The Cowboy Cop" 1926; "The Masquerade Bandit" 1926; "Out of the West" 1926; "Red Hot

Hoofs" 1926; "Tom and His Pals" 1926; "Wild to Go" 1926; "The Cherokee Kid" 1927; "Cyclone of the Range" 1927; "The Flying U Ranch" 1927; "Lightning Lariats" 1927; "The Sonora Kid" 1927; "Splitting the Breeze" 1927; "Tom's Gang" 1927; "King Cowboy" 1928; "Red Riders of Canada" 1928; "Tyrant of Red Gulch" 1928; "When the Law Rides" 1928; "The Drifter" 1929; "Idaho Red" 1929; "The Pride of Pawnee" 1929; "The Trail of the Horse Thieves" 1929; "Pardon My Gun" 1930.

Delacour, A.C. Writer. Films: "The Midnight Stage" 1919 (story).

Delacour, Giraoudin. Writer. Films: "The Midnight Stage" 1919 (story).

De La Fuente, Julio. Producer. Films: "My Colt, Not Yours" 1972-Span./Fr./Ital.; "None of the Three Were Called Trinity" 1974-Span.

de la Loma, Jose Antonio. Director. Films: "Five Thousand Dollars on One Ace" 1965-Span./Ital. (sp. only); "Man from Canyon City" 1965-Span./Ital. (sp. only): "Dynamite Jim" 1966-Span./Ital. (sp. only); "Man with the Golden Pistol" 1966-Span./Ital. (sp. only); "Seven Guns for Timothy" 1966-Span./Ital. (sp. only); "Sunscorched" 1966-Span./Ger. (sp. only); "The Texicans" 1966-U.S./Span. (sp. only); "Blood at Sundown" 1967-Span./Ital.; "Clint the Stranger" 1968-Ital./Span./Ger. (sp. only); "Red Blood, Yellow Gold" 1968-Ital./Span. (sp. only); "The Boldest Job in the West" 1969-Ital. (& sp.).

Del Amo, Antonio. *see* Hoven, Adrien.

De La Mothe, Leon (1880-6/12/43). Director. Films: "Buck Simmons, Puncher" 1916 (& sp.); "Play Straight or Fight" 1918 (story only); "Vanishing Trails" 1920-serial; "Vengeance and the Girl" 1920; "The Desert Hawk" 1924; "Ridin' Wild" 1925.

De Laurentiis, Dino (1919-). Producer. Films: "Man Called Sledge" 1971-Ital./U.S.

De Lay, Melville. Director. Films: "Law of the Saddle" 1943.

Del Castillo, Angel. Screenwriter. Films: "Billy the Kid" 1962-Span.

DeLeon, Walter (1884-8/1/47). Screenwriter. Films: "Ruggles of Red Gap" 1935; "Rhythm on the Range" 1936; "Union Pacific" 1939; "Riding High" 1943.

Della Mea, Ivan. Screenwriter.

Films: "Blood and Guns" 1968-Ital./Span.

Dell'Aquila, Enzo (Vincent Eagle). Screenwriter. Films: "Seven Guns for the MacGregors" 1965-Ital./Span.; "Sheriff with the Gold" 1966-Ital./Span.; "Up the MacGregors!" 1967-Ital./Span.; "Bury Them Deep" 1968-Ital.; "Red Blood, Yellow Gold" 1968-Ital./Span.; "Time and Place for Killing" 1968-Ital. (& sp.); "I Am Sartana, Your Angel of Death" 1969-Ital./Fr.

Delmar, Vina (1903-1/19/90). Writer. Films: "The Great Man's Lady" 1942 (story).

Delmas, Herbert. Screenwriter. Films: "Pals of the Pecos" 1941.

de los Arcos, Luis. Screenwriter. Films: "Finger on the Trigger" 1965-Span./Ital./U.S.

Del Ruth, Roy (1895-4/27/61). Director. Films: "Barbary Coast Gent" 1944.

De Luca, Lorenzo. Screenwriter. Films: "Jonathan of the Bears" 1994-Ital./Rus. (& story).

De Martino, Alberto (Herbert Martin). Director. Films: "Charge of the Seventh Cavalry" 1964-Ital./Span./Fr.; "He Who Shoots First" 1966-Ital. (& sp.); "One Hundred Thousand Dollars for Ringo" 1966-Ital./Span. (& sp.); "Here We Go Again, Eh Providence?" 1973-Ital./Fr./Span.

De Masi, Francesco. *see* Capuano, Luigi.

Demichelli, Tulio. Director. Films: "Gunmen of the Rio Grande" 1964-Fr./Ital./Span. (& sp.); "Man and a Colt" 1967-Span./Ital. (& sp.); "Sabata the Killer" 1970-Ital./Span. (& sp.); "Tequila" 1974-Ital./Span. (& sp.).

De Mille, Beatrice. Screenwriter. Films: "The Jaguar's Claws" 1917.

DeMille, Cecil B. (1881-1/21/59). Director. Films: "The Call of the North" 1914 (& sp.); "Rose of the Rancho" 1914 (& sp.); "The Virginian" 1914 (& prod./sp.); "Chimmie Fadden Out West" 1915 (& sp.); "The Girl of the Golden West" 1915 (& prod./sp.); "The Love Mask" 1916 (sp. only); "A Romance of the Redwoods" 1917 (& sp.); "The Squaw Man" 1917 (& sp.); "The Squaw Man" 1918 (& prod.); "The Squaw Man" 1931 (& prod.); "The Plainsman" 1936 (& prod.); "Union Pacific" 1939 (& prod.); "Northwest Mounted Police" 1940 (& prod.); "Unconquered" 1947 (& prod.).

DeMille, William Churchill (1878-3/8/55). Writer. Films: "Braveheart" 1925 (story).

Deming, Norman. Director. Films: "Overland with Kit Carson" 1939-serial; "Riders of the Black River" 1939; "The Taming of the West" 1939.

DeMond, Albert. Screenwriter. Films: "North of Nome" 1936; "Gangs of Sonora" 1941; "Gauchos of El Dorado" 1941; "Outlaws of the Cherokee Trail" 1941; "Saddlemates" 1941; "West of Cimarron" 1941; "Raiders of the Range" 1942; "Ridin' Down the Canyon" 1942; "Valley of Hunted Men" 1942; "Riders of the Rio Grande" 1943; "Beneath Western Skies" 1944 (& story); "Code of the Prairie" 1944; "Trail of Kit Carson" 1945; "King of the Forest Rangers" 1946-serial; "The Phantom Rider" 1946-serial; "Code of the Saddle" 1947 (story only); "The Wild Frontier" 1947; "Madonna of the Desert" 1948; "Prince of the Plains" 1949; "Pals of the Golden West" 1951; "Border Saddlemates" 1952; "Desperadoes' Outpost" 1952; "Old Oklahoma Plains" 1952; "Marshal of Cedar Rock" 1953.

De Nardo, Mario. Screenwriter. Films: "Fifteen Scaffolds for the Killer" 1968-Ital./Span.

de Navarro, Carlos. Writer. Films: "Mareea, the Half-Breed" 1914 (story).

De Nesle, Robert. Screenwriter. Films: "Left Handed Johnny West" 1965-Span./Ital.

Denger, Fred. Screenwriter. Films: "Flaming Frontier" 1965-Ger./Yugo.; "Rampage at Apache Wells" 1965-Ger./Yugo. (& sp.); "Half Breed" 1966-Ger./Yugo./Ital.

Denison, Muriel. Writer. Films: "Susannah of the Mounties" 1939 (story).

Denmark, Wilton. Screenwriter. Films: "Cain's Way" 1969.

Dennis, Irving. Screenwriter. Films: "Sunscorched" 1966-Span./Ger.

Dennis, Robert C. (1916-9/14/83). Screenwriter. Films: "Revolt at Fort Laramie" 1957.

Denton, Charles. Screenwriter. Films: "A Man Four-Square" 1926.

Deodato, Ruggero. Director. Films: "In The Name of the Father" 1968-Ital.

De Ossorio, Armando. Director. Films: "Three from Colorado" 1967-Span. (& sp.); "Canadian Wilderness" 1969-Span./Ital. (& sp.);

"Patience Has a Limit, We Don't" 1974-Span./Ital. (sp. only).

Dereszke, David. Screenwriter. Films: "Thunder at the Border" 1967-Ger./Yugo.

De Riso, Arpad. *see* Batzella, Luigi.

De Rita, Massimo. Screenwriter. Films: "Companeros" 1970-Ital./Span./Ger.; "Chino" 1973-Ital./Span./Fr.; "Don't Turn the Other Cheek" 1974-Ital./Ger./Span.

De Rosa, Mario. Screenwriter. Films: "Evan Django Has His Price" 1971-Ital./Span.; Son of Zorro" 1973-Ital./Span.

Derr, E.B. Producer. Films: "Pardon My Gun" 1930; "The Painted Desert" 1931; "Battle of Greed" 1934; "Rebellion" 1936; "Drums of Destiny" 1937; "The Glory Trail" 1937; "The Law Commands" 1937; "Old Louisiana" 1937; "Raw Timber" 1937; "Under Strange Flags" 1937; "Deerslayer" 1943 (& sp.).

DeSailly, Claude. Screenwriter. Films: "Cemetery Without Crosses" 1968-Ital./Fr.

De Teffe, Antonio. Screenwriter. Films: "Django the Bastard" 1969-Ital./Span. (& prod.); "Shango" 1969-Ital.

Detiege, David. Director. Films: "The Man from Button Willow" 1965 (& sp.).

De Toth, Andre (1900-). Director. Films: "Ramrod" 1947; "The Gunfighter" 1950 (story only); "Man in the Saddle" 1951; "Last of the Comanches" 1952; "Springfield Rifle" 1952; "The Stranger Wore a Gun" 1953; "Thunder Over the Plains" 1953; "The Bounty Hunter" 1954; "Riding Shotgun" 1954; "The Indian Fighter" 1955; "Day of the Outlaw" 1959; "El Condor" 1970 (prod. only). ¶TV: *Bronco* 1958; *Maverick*—"Cruise of the Cynthia B" 1-10-60; *The Westerner*—"School Days" 10-7-60, "The Old Man" 11-25-60.

De Urrutia, Frederico. Screenwriter. Films: "Two Thousand Dollars for Coyote" 1965-Span.; "Django, A Bullet for You" 1966-Span./Ital.; "Djurado" 1966-Ital./Span.; "Relentless Four" 1966-Span./Ital.; "The Man Who Killed Billy the Kid" 1967-Span./Ital. (& story); "Hour of Death" 1968-Span./Ital.; "Stranger in Paso Bravo" 1968-Ital.; "A Bullet for Sandoval" 1970-Ital./Span.; "Forgotten Pistolero" 1970-Ital./Span.; "His Name Was Holy Ghost" 1970-Ital./Span.; "Forewarned, Half-Killed ... The Word of the Holy Ghost" 1971-Ital./Span.

Deutsch, Armand. Producer. Films: "Ambush" 1950; "Saddle the Wind" 1958.

de Viliers, Victor. Screenwriter. Films: "The Border Legion" 1918.

De Voto, Bernard (1897-1955). Writer. Films: "Across the Wide Missouri" 1951 (orig. story).

Dewitt, Jack. Director. Films: "Lone Hand Wilson" 1920.

DeWitt, Jack. Screenwriter. Films: "Don Ricardo Returns" 1946; "The Bells of San Fernando" 1947; "Canadian Pacific" 1949; "The Battles of Chief Pontiac" 1952; "Fargo" 1952; "Gun Belt" 1953; "Son of Belle Star" 1953 (story only); "Sitting Bull" 1954; "The Beast of Hollow Mountain" 1956; "Oregon Passage" 1958; "Five Guns to Tombstone" 1961; "A Man Called Horse" 1970; "Man in the Wilderness" 1971-U.S./Span.; "The Return of a Man Called Horse" 1976; "Triumphs of a Man Called Horse" 1984 (story only).

Dewlin, Al (1921-). Writer. Films: "Ride Beyond Vengeance" 1966 (story).

DeWolf, Karen. Screenwriter. Films: "Saga of Death Valley" 1939; "Pioneers of the West" 1940; "Go West, Young Lady" 1941; "Saddlemates" 1941 (story only); "Shut My Big Mouth" 1942; "Silver Lode" 1954.

Dexter, Maury (1927-). Director. Films: "Walk Tall" 1960 (& prod.); "The Purple Hills" 1961 (& prod.); "The Firebrand" 1962 (& prod.); "Young Guns of Texas" 1963 (& prod.); "Outlaw of Red River" 1966-Ital. ¶TV: *Little House on the Prairie* 1974; *Father Murphy*—"The Dream Day" 3-14-82; *Little House: A New Beginning* 1982.

Diamond, I.A.L. (1915-4/21/88). Screenwriter. Films: "Two Guys from Texas" 1948.

Dickerson, Lucky. *see* Fidani, Demofilo.

Dickey, Basil (1881-6/7/58). Screenwriter. Films: "The Frontier Trail" 1926; "Wolf's Trail" 1927; "Border Cavalier" 1927; "Call of the Heart" 1928; "The Fearless Rider" 1928; "Guardians of the Wild" 1928; "Plunging Hoofs" 1928 (story only); "Quick Triggers" 1928; "The Ridin' Demon" 1929; "Heroes of the West" 1932-serial; "Clancy of the Mounted" 1933-serial; "Gordon of Ghost City" 1933-serial; "When a Man Sees Red" 1934; "The Roaring West 1935-serial; "Rustlers of Red Dog" 1935-serial; "Law and Lead" 1936; "The Phantom of the Range" 1936; "The

Phantom Rider" 1936-serial; "Cheyenne Rides Again" 1937; "Lost Ranch" 1937; "Mystery Range" 1937; "Orphan of the Pecos" 1937; "Brothers of the West" 1938; "Feud of the Trail" 1938; "Flaming Frontier" 1938-serial; "The Oregon Trail" 1939-serial; "Outlaw's Paradise" 1939; "Straight Shooter" 1939 (& story); "Trigger Fingers" 1939; "Winners of the West" 1940-serial; "Riders of Death Valley" 1941-serial; "Perils of the Royal Mounted" 1942-serial; "Daredevils of the West" 1943-serial; "Zorro's Black Whip" 1944-serial; "King of the Forest Rangers" 1946-serial; "The Phantom Rider" 1946-serial; "Jesse James Rides Again" 1947-serial; "Son of Zorro" 1947-serial; "The Adventures of Frank and Jesse James" 1948-serial; "Dangers of the Canadian Mounted" 1948-serial; "The Rangers Ride" 1948; "Brand of Fear" 1949; "Gun Law Justice" 1949; "Lawless Code" 1949.

Dickey, James (1923-). Screenwriter. Films: "The Call of the Wild" TVM-1976.

Dickey, Paul. Writer. Films: "The Broken Wing" 1932 (story).

Diege, Samuel. Director. Films: "King of the Sierras" 1938; "Ride 'Em, Cowgirl" 1939; "The Singing Cowgirl" 1939; "Water Rustlers" 1939.

Dieterle, William (1893-12/8/72). Director. Films: "Red Mountain" 1951.

Dietrich, Ralph. Producer. Films: "The Gay Caballero" 1940; "The Cowboy and the Blonde" 1941; "My Friend Flicka" 1943.

Di Girolamo, Roberto. Screenwriter. Films: "White Apache" 1984-Ital./Span. (story only); "Scalps" 1986-Ital./Ger.

Di Geronimo, Bruno. Screenwriter. Films: "Dead Men Ride" 1970-Ital./Span.

DiLeo, Fernando (Fernando Lion). Screenwriter. Films: "Seven Guns for the MacGregors" 1965-Ital./Span.; "Johnny Yuma" 1966-Ital.; "Massacre Time" 1966-Ital./Span./Ger.; "Navajo Joe" 1966-Ital./Span.; "The Return of Ringo" 1966-Ital./Span.; "Sugar Colt" 1966-Ital./Span.; "Hate for Hate" 1967-Ital.; "Long Days of Vengeance" 1967-Ital./Span.; "Pecos Cleans Up" 1967-Ital.; "Poker with Pistols" 1967-Ital.; "Up the MacGregors!" 1967-Ital./Span.; "Beyond the Law" 1968-Ital./Span.; "Death Rides Alone" 1968-Ital./Span.; "God Made Them ... I Kill Them" 1968-Ital.; "The Ruthless

Four" 1968-Ital./Ger.; "Time and Place for Killing" 1968-Ital.; "Wanted" 1968-Ital./Fr.

Dille, Flint. Screenwriter. Films: "An American Tail: Fievel Goes West" 1991.

Diller, Helen. Screenwriter. Films: "Night Rider" 1962-short.

Dillmann, Max. *see* Dallamano, Massimo.

Dillon, Anthony. Screenwriter. Films: "The Prairie Pirate" 1925.

Dillon, Ed (1879-7/11/33). Director. Films: "Fatty and Minnie He-Haw" 1915.

Dillon, Jack. Director. Films: "The Flip of a Coin" 1919; "A Prisoner for Life" 1919; "Tapering Fingers" 1919.

Dillon, James Francis (1883-4/4/34). Director. Films: "Girl of the Golden West" 1930.

Dillon, Robert. Screenwriter. Films: "The Stain in the Blood" 1916; "The Last of the Mohicans" 1920; "Beating the Game" 1921; "The Man Who Woke Up" 1921; "Winners of the West" 1921-serial; "In the Days of Buffalo Bill" 1922-serial; "The Oregon Trail" 1923-serial; "The Santa Fe Trail" 1923-serial (& dir.); "Leatherstocking" 1924-serial; "The Range Riders" 1927; "Riders of the West" 1927; "Thundering Thompson" 1929 (story only); "Wilderness Mail" 1935.

Di Lorenzo, Edward. Screenwriter. Films: "A Place Called Glory" 1966-Span./Ger.

DiMaggio-Wagner, Madeline. Screenwriter. Films: "Lacy and the Mississippi Queen" TVM-1978.

Dimsdale, Howard. Screenwriter. Films: "Senorita from the West" 1945; "Curtain Call at Cactus Creek" 1950 (& story).

Di Nardo, Mario. Screenwriter. Films: "Chuck Moll" 1970-Ital.; "Roy Colt and Winchester Jack" 1970-Ital.

Disney, Walt (1901-12/15/66). Producer. Films: "Melody Time" 1948; "Old Yeller" 1957; "The Light in the Forest" 1958; "Ten Who Dared" 1960; "Nikki, Wild Dog of the North" 1961-U.S./Can.; "Legend of Lobo" 1962; "The Adventures of Bullwhip Griffin" 1967. ¶TV: *Zorro* 1957-59; *Texas John Slaughter* 1958-61 (exec. prod.).

Dittmar, Harry. Screenwriter. Films: "Hidden Loot" 1925; "Chip of the Flying U" 1926.

Dix, Beulah Marie (1876-9/25/70). Screenwriter. Films: "The Cost of Hatred" 1917; "Nan of Music Mountain" 1917; "The Sunset Trail" 1917; "The Squaw Man" 1918; "In Mizzoura" 1919; "The Crimson Challenge" 1922.

Dix, Robert. Screenwriter. Films: "Five Bloody Graves" 1969.

Dixon, Denver (Victor Adamson) (1890-11/9/72). Director. Films: "The Lone Rider" 1922 (& sp.); "Ace of Cactus Range" 1924; "The Man from the Rio Grande" 1926; "Sagebrush Politics" 1930 (& prod.); "Fighting Cowboy" 1933 (& prod.); "Boss Cowboy" 1934 (& prod.); "Circle Canyon" 1934 (& prod.); "Lightning Bill" 1934 (& prod.); "Lightning Range" 1934 (& prod.); "The Pecos Dandy" 1934 (prod. only); "Range Riders" 1934 (& prod.); "Rawhide Romance" 1934 (& prod.); "Rawhide Terror" 1934 (& prod.); "Riding Speed" 1934 (prod. only); "Arizona Trails" 1935 (prod. only); "Desert Mesa" 1935 (prod. only); "Roll, Wagons, Roll" 1940 (sp. only).

Dixon, Ivan (1931-). Director. TV: *Nichols*—"Away the Rolling River" 12-7-71; *Bret Maverick*—"Anything for a Friend" 12-15-81, "The Mayflower Women's Historical Society" 2-2-82.

Dixon, Peter. Screenwriter. Films: "Down the Wyoming Trail" 1939.

Dixon, Jr., Thomas. Screenwriter. Films: "Bring Him In" 1921; "Where Men Are Men" 1921; "The Trail Rider" 1925; "The Gentle Cyclone" 1926.

Dmytryk, Edward (1908-). Director. Films: "Trail of the Hawk" 1935; "Broken Lance" 1954; "Warlock" 1959 (& prod.); "Alvarez Kelly" 1966; "Shalako" 1968-Brit./Fr.

Dobbs, Frank Q. Screenwriter. Films: "Houston: The Legend of Texas" TVM-1986 (prod. only); "Rio Diablo" TVM-1993; "The Gambler V: Playing for Keeps" TVM-1994 (& story).

Dobbs, Fred C. Screenwriter. Films: "The Great Sioux Massacre" 1965.

Dobkin, Lawrence (1920-). Director. Films: "The Cowboy" 1954 (prod. only); "The Life and Times of Grizzly Adams" 1975 (sp. only). ¶TV: *The Rifleman*—"The Man from Salinas" 2-12-62, "The tinhorn" 3-12-62, "Jealous Man" 3-26-62, "Day of Reckoning" 4-9-62, "The Executioner" 5-7-62; *Temple Houston* 1963-64 (prod.); *Laredo*—"Anybody Here Seen Billy?" 10-21-65, "A Medal of Reese" 12-30-65, "The Callico Kid" 1-6-66; *Wild Wild West*—"The Night of the Amnesiac" 2-9-68; *The Big Valley*—"Lightfoot" 2-17-69, "Flight from San Miguel" 4-28-69.

Dobson, Kevin James. Director. Films: "Miracle in the Wilderness" TVM-1991.

Doctorow, E.L. (1931-). Writer. Films: "Welcome to Hard Times" 1967 (story).

Doheny, Lawrence (1925-9/7/82). Director. TV: *Big Hawaii* 1977.

Doherty, Ethel. Screenwriter. Films: "The Vanishing American" 1925; "Home on the Range" 1935; "Rocky Mountain Mystery" 1935.

Dolman, Bob. Screenwriter. Films: "Far and Away" 1992 (& story).

Donaldson, Dick. Director. Films: "The Good Loser" 1918.

Donati, Ermanno. Producer. Films: "The Hills Run Red" 1966-Ital.; "Navajo Joe" 1966-Ital./Span.

Donati, Sergio. Screenwriter. Films: "The Big Gundown" 1966-Ital.; "Dollars for a Fast Gun" 1968-Ital./Span.; "Once Upon a Time in the West" 1968-Ital.; "Ben and Charlie" 1970-Ital.; "Duck, You Sucker!" 1971-Ital.; "Cipolla Colt" 1975-Ital./Ger.; "Buddy Goes West" 1981-Ital.

Doniger, Walter (1917-). Screenwriter. Films: "Along the Great Divide" 1951; "The Guns of Fort Petticoat" 1957. ¶TV: *Maverick*—"The Jail at Junction Flats" 11-9-58; *Kung Fu*—"The Tide" 2-1-73, "The SPirit Helper" 11-8-73, "The Elixir" 12-20-73.

Donnell, Kathy. Screenwriter. Films: "Lacy and the Mississippi Queen" TVM-1978.

Donnelly, Budd. Screenwriter. Films: "Jessi's Girls" 1976.

Donner, Richard (1939-). Director. Films: "Maverick" 1994 (& prod.). ¶TV: *Wanted—Dead or Alive*—"The Twain Shall Meet" 10-19-60, "The Medicine Man" 11-23-60, "The Last Retreat" 1-11-61, "Bounty on Josh" 1-25-61, "The Voice of Silence" 2-15-61, "Barney's Bounty" 3-29-61; *The Rifleman*—"Gunfire" 1-15-62, "Deadly Image" 2-26-62, "The Debit" 3-5-62, "Guilty Conscience" 4-2-62, "The Day a Town Slept" 4-16-62, "Milly's Brother" 4-23-62, "Outlaw Shoes" 4-30-62; *Wild Wild West*—"The Night of the Bars of Hell" 3-4-66, "The Night of the Murderous Spring" 4-15-66, "The Night of the Returning Dead" 10-14-66.

Donovan, Martin. Director.

Films: "Mad at the Moon" 1992 (& sp.).

Dorfmann, Jacques. Director. Films: "Shadow of the Wolf" 1993-Can./Fr.

Dorn, Doris. Screenwriter. Films: "The Lightning Rider" 1924.

Dorso, Richard J. Screenwriter. Films: "Sierra Stranger" 1957.

Dortort, David. Screenwriter. Films: "The Lusty Men" 1952; "Reprisal!" 1956; "The Big Land" 1957; "The Chisholms" TVM-1979 (exec. prod. only); "Bonanza: The Next Generation" TVM-1988 (prod. only). ¶TV: *The Restles Gun* 1957-59 (prod.); *Bonanza* 1959-73 (prod.); *The High Chaparral* 1967-71 (exec. prod.); *The Cowboys* 1974 (exec. prod.).

Doud, Gil. Screenwriter. Films: "Saskatchewan" 1954; "Walk the Proud Land" 1956.

Douglas, Flora E. Producer. Films: "Phantom of the North" 1929 (story only); "Bar L Ranch" 1930; "Beyond the Rio Grande" 1930; "Breed of the West" 1930; "Canyon Hawks" 1930; "Firebrand Jordan" 1930; "Phantom of the Desert" 1930; "Ridin' Law" 1930; "Trails of Danger" 1930; "Westward Bound" 1930; "Hell's Valley" 1931; "Law of the Rio Grande" 1931; "The Mystery Trooper" 1931-serial (& story).

Douglas, Gordon (1909-9/29/93). Director. Films: "Girl Rush" 1944; "The Doolins of Oklahoma" 1949; "The Nevadan" 1950; "The Great Missouri Raid" 1951; "Only the Valiant" 1951; "The Iron Mistress" 1952; "The Charge at Feather River" 1953; "The Big Land" 1957; "The Fiend Who Walked the West" 1958; "Fort Dobbs" 1958; "Yellowstone Kelly" 1959; "Gold of the Seven Saints" 1961; "Rio Conchos" 1964; "Stagecoach" 1966; "Chuka" 1967; "Barquero" 1970; "Nevada Smith" TVM-1975. ¶TV: *Maverick*—"The Burning Sky" 2-23-58.

Douglas, J.S. Writer. Films: "Calamity Anne's Love Affair" 1914 (story).

Douglas, Kirk (1916-). Director. Films: "Posse" 1975 (& prod.).

Douglas, Malcolm. Writer. Films: "Saved from the Vigilantes" 1913 (story); "The Parson Who Fled West" 1915 (story).

Douglas, Robert. TV: *Maverick*—"Kiz" 12-4-60; "Dutchman's Gold" 1-22-61; *The Virginian*—"The Final Hour" 5-1-63; *The Monroes*—"Wild Bull" 2-15-67, "Manhunt" 3-1-67; *Big Hawaii* 1977.

Douglas, Warren. Screenwriter. Films: "Fangs of the Arctic" 1953; "Jack Slade" 1953; "Northern Patrol" 1953; "The Return of Jack Slade" 1955; "Dragoon Wells Massacre" 1957; "The Night of the Grizzly" 1966.

Dowd, Homer F. Screenwriter. Films: "Battle-Ground" 1912 (story only); "The Fall of Black Hawk" 1912.

Dowling, Edward. Writer. Films: "Heart of the North" 1921 (story).

Dox, Doran. Director. Films: "Dodging Danger" 1929.

Doyle, Laird. Screenwriter. Films: "Northwest Outpost" 1947.

Dozier, Robert. Screenwriter. Films: "When the Legends Die" 1972.

Dozier, William (1908-4/23/91). Producer. TV: *The Loner* 1965-66 (exec. prod.).

Drago, Harry Sinclair (Bliss Lomax) (1888-1979). Writer. Films: "Silver Valley" 1927 (story); "Whispering Sage" 1927 (story); "Sioux Blood" 1929 (story); "Secrets of the Wastelands" 1941 (story); "Buckskin Frontier" 1943 (story); "The Leather Burners" 1943 (story).

Dragoti, Stan (1932-). Director. Films: "Dirty Little Billy" 1972 (& sp.).

Drake, Oliver (1903-8/5/91). Director. Films: "The Cherokee Kid" 1927 (sp. only); "Cyclone of the Range" 1927 (story only); "The Desert Pirate" 1927 (sp. only); "The Flying U Ranch" 1927 (sp. only); "The Mojave Kid" 1927 (sp. only); "The Slingshot Kid" 1927 (sp. only); "Breed of the Sunsets" 1928 (sp. only); "Driftin' Sands" 1928 (sp. only); "Orphan of the Sage" 1928 (sp. only); "Phantom of the Range" 1928 (story only); "The Pinto Kid" 1928 (story only); "Red Riders of Canada" 1928 (sp. only); "Tyrant of Red Gulch" 1928 (sp. only); "When the Law Rides" 1928 (sp. only); "The Desert Rider" 1929 (sp. only); "Gun Law" 1929 (sp. only); "Pals of the Prairie" 1929 (sp. only); "The Vagabond Cub" 1929 (sp. only); "Rogue of the Rio Grande" 1930 (sp. only); "Hurricane Horseman" 1931 (sp. only); "West of Cheyenne" 1931 (sp. only); "Battling Buckaroo" 1932 (sp. only); "The Cheyenne Cyclone" 1932 (sp. only); "Guns for Hire" 1932 (sp. only); "Law and Lawless" 1932 (sp. only); "Lawless Valley" 1932 (sp. only); "The Reckless Rider" 1932 (sp. only); "The Saddle Buster" 1932 (sp.

only); "Texas Tornado" 1932 (& prod./sp.); "Deadwood Pass" 1933 (sp. only); "Gun Law" 1933 (sp. only); "Outlaw Justice" 1933 (prod. only); "Trouble Busters" 1933 (sp./story only); "Via Pony Express" 1933 (sp./story only); "War on the Range" 1933 (sp. only); "When a Man Rides Alone" 1933 (sp. only); "Born to Battle" 1935 (story only); "Cyclone Ranger" 1935 (story only); "Sagebrush Troubador" 1935 (sp./story only); "The Singing Vagabond" 1935 (sp./story only); "Six Gun Justice" 1935 (sp. only); "The Texas Rambler" 1935; "The Vanishing Riders" 1935 (sp. only); "Comin' Round the Mountain" 1936 (sp. only); "Oh, Susanna!" 1936 (sp. only); "Roarin' Lead" 1936 (sp. only); "Boots and Saddles" 1937 (sp. only); "Ghost Town Gold" 1937 (sp. only); "Gunsmoke Ranch" 1937 (sp. only); "Heart of the Rockies" 1937 (sp. only); "Hit the Saddle" 1937; "Public Cowboy No. 1" 1937 (sp. only); "Riders of the Whistling Skull" 1937 (sp./story only); "Round-Up Time in Texas" 1937 (sp. only); "The Trigger Trio" 1937 (sp. only); "Wild Horse Rodeo" 1937 (story only); "Border G-Man" 1938 (sp. only); "Gun Law" 1938 (sp. only); "Lawless Valley" 1938 (sp. only); "The Painted Desert" 1938 (sp. only); "The Purple Vigilantes" 1938 (sp. only); "Renegde Ranger" 1938 (sp. only); "Arizona Legion" 1939 (sp. only); "Cowboys from Texas" 1939 (sp. only); "The Fighting Gringo" 1939 (sp. only); "Racketeers of the Range" 1939 (sp. only); "Trouble in Sundown" 1939 (sp. only); "Billy the Kid Outlawed" 1940 (sp. only); "Billy the Kid's Gun Justice" 1940 (sp. only); "Molly Cures a Cowboy" 1940-short (sp. only); "Trailing Double Trouble" 1940 (sp. only); "The Tulsa Kid" 1940 (sp. only); "Forbidden Trails" 1941 (story only); "Fugitive Valley" 1941 (sp. only); "Kansas Cyclone" 1941 (sp. only); "The Lone Rider Ambushed" 1941 (sp. only); "Pals of the Pecos" 1941 (& story); "Riders of Death Valley" 1941-serial (story only); "Robbers of the Range" 1941 (story only); "Billy the Kid Trapped" 1942 (sp. only); "Boss of Hangtown Mesa" 1942 (prod./sp. only); "Deep in the Heart of Texas" 1942 (prod./sp. only); "Little Joe, the Wrangler" 1942 (prod. only); "The Lone Rider in Cheyenne" 1942 (sp. only); "Old Chisholm Trail" 1942 (prod. only); "Raiders of the West" 1942 (sp. only); "Shut My Big Mouth" 1942 (sp./story only); "The Silver Bullet" 1942 (story only); "Arizona Trail" 1943 (prod. only); "Burder Buckaroos" 1943 (& sp.); "Cheyenne Roundup" 1943 (prod. only); "Fighting Valley" 1943 (& sp.); "Frontier Law" 1943 (prod. only); "The Lone Star Trail" 1943 (prod./sp. only); "Raiders of San Joaquin" 1943 (prod. only); "Tenting Tonight on the Old Camp Ground" 1943; "West of Texas" 1943 (& sp.); "Boss of Boomtown" 1944 (prod. only); "Marshal of Gunsmoke" 1944 (prod. only); "Oklahoma Raiders" 1944 (prod. only); "The Old Texas Trail" 1944 (prod. only); "Pride of the Plains" 1944 (story only); "Riders of the Santa Fe" 1944; "Trail of Terror" 1944 (& sp.); "Trail to Gunsight" 1944 (prod. only); "Trigger Trail" 1944 (prod. only); "Beyond the Pecos" 1945; "Lonesome Trail" 1945 (& prod./story); "Renegades of the Rio Grande" 1945 (prod. only); "Riders of the Dawn" 1945 (& prod.); "Saddle Serenade" 1945 (& prod.); "Springtime in Texas" 1945 (& prod.); "Moon Over Montana" 1946 (& prod./story); "Song of the Sierras" 1946 (& prod./story); "Trail to Mexico" 1946 (& prod./sp.); "West of the Alamo" 1946 (& prod.); "Rainbow Over the Rockies" 1947 (& prod./story); "Deadline" 1948 (& prod./sp.); "Fighting Mustang" 1948; "Sunset Carson Rides Again" 1948; "Across the Rio Grande" 1949; "Brand of Fear" 1949; "The Kid from Gower Gulch" 1949; "Lawless Code" 1949; "Roaring Westward" 1949; "Trail of the Yukon" 1949 (sp. only); "Battling Marshal" 1950; "Outlaw Treasure" 1955; "Dragoon Wells Massacre" 1957 (story only); "The Parson and the Outlaw" 1957 (& sp.). ¶TV: *Sky King* 1951; *Colt .45* 1957.

Dreifuss, Arthur (1908-12/31/93). Producer. Films: "Ride 'Em, Cowgirl" 1939.

Dresher, Beatrice A. Screenwriter. Films: "Passion" 1954 (& story).

Dresner, Hal. Screenwriter. Films: "Zorro, the Gay Blade" 1981 (& story).

Drew, Edward. Director. Films: "The Naked Gun" 1956.

Drew, Sidney. Director. Films: "The Red Devils" 1911 (& sp.).

Drudi, Lucia. Screenwriter. Films: "Deaf Smith and Johnny Ears" 1972-Ital.

Druxman, Michael B. Screenwriter. Films: "Cheyenne Warrior" 1994.

Dry, Tony. *see* Secchi, Toni.

Dubin, Charles S. (1919-). Director. TV: *The Virginian* —"The

Laramie Road" 12-8-65; *The Big Valley*—"The Time After Midnight" 10-2-67, "Rimfire" 2-19-68, "In Silent Battle" 9-23-68; *Kung Fu*—"A Praying Mantis Kills" 3-22-73, "Superstition" 4-5-73, "The Third Man" 4-26-73.

Ducci, Nico. Screenwriter. Films: "Matalo!" 1971-Ital./Span.; "Carambola" 1974-Ital.; "Carambola's Philosophy: In the Right Pocket" 1975-Ital.

Duff, Nellie Browne. Writer. Films: "Her Fighting Chance" 1914 (story).

Duff, Warren (1904-8/5/73). Screenwriter. Films: "Gold Is Where You Find It" 1938; "The Oklahoma Kid" 1939; "Lady from Cheyenne" 1941; "The Last Command" 1955.

Duffy, Albert (1903-9/15/76). Screenwriter. Films: "The Gay Caballero" 1940 (story only); "Down Mexico Way" 1941.

Duffy, Gerald C. Screenwriter. Films: "The Spider and the Rose" 1923.

Duffy, Jesse. Screenwriter. Films: "Law of the Ranger" 1937 (story only); "The Rangers Step In" 1937; "Reckless Ranger" 1937 (story only); "Riders of the Frontier" 1939; "Perils of the Royal Mounted" 1942-serial; "Bordertown Trail" 1944; "Zorro's Black Whip" 1944-serial; "King of the Forest Rangers" 1946-serial; "The Phantom Rider" 1946-serial; "Jesse James Rides Again" 1947-serial; "Son of Zorro" 1947-serial.

Dugan, James. Director. Films: "The Desert Pirate" 1927; "Phantom of the Range" 1928.

Duggan, Pat. Producer. Films: "Red Garters" 1954; "The Lonely Man" 1957.

Dull, Orville O. Director. Films: "The Flying Horseman" 1926; "Black Jack" 1927; "Broncho Twister" 1927; "Barbary Coast Gent" 1944 (prod. only); "Bad Bascomb" 1946 (prod. only).

Dullfield, Brainerd. Screenwriter. Films: "The Treasure of Lost Canyon" 1952.

Dumas, Jacques. Screenwriter. Films: "Three Swords of Zorro" 1963-Ital./Span.

Dumas, John. Director. TV: *Alias Smith and Jones*—"What's in It for Mia?" 2-24-72.

Dunbar, J. Francis. Writer. Films: "Breezy Jim" 1919 (story).

Duncan, Renault. *see* Renaldo, Duncan.

Duncan, Bob. Screenwriter.

Films: "The Marshal's Daughter" 1953.

Duncan, Norman (1871-1916). Writer. Films: "The Measure of a Man" 1924 (story).

Duncan, Sam G. Screenwriter. Films: "White Fang" 1936.

Duncan, William (1879-2/7/61). Director. Films: "Buck's Romance" 1912 (& sp.); "The Dynamiters" 1912 (& sp.); "Jim's Vindication" 1912 (& sp.); "The Ranger and His Horse" 1912; "A Rough Ride with Nitroglycerine" 1912 (& sp.); "Why Jim Reformed" 1912 (& sp.); "An Apache's Gratitude" 1913 (& story); "The Bank's Messenger" 1913 (& sp.); "Buster's Little Game" 1913; "The Capture of Bad Brown" 1913; "The Cattle Thief's Escape" 1913; "A Child of the Prairies" 1913; "The Cowboy Editor" 1913 (& sp.); "Cupid in the Cow Camp" 1913; "The Deputy's Sweetheart" 1913; "Dishwash Dick's Counterfeit" 1913; "The Galloping Romeo" 1913; "The Good Indian" 1913; "His Father's Deputy" 1913 (& story); "How Betty Made Good" 1913; "How It Happened" 1913 (& story); "Howlin' Jones" 1913; "Juggling with Fate" 1913; "The Law and the Outlaw" 1913; "The Life Timer" 1913 (& story); "Made a Coward" 1913; "The Marshal's Capture" 1913; "A Mixup on the Plains" 1913; "Mother Love vs. Gold" 1913; "Physical Culture on the Quarter Circle V Bar" 1913; "The Range Law" 1913; "The Rejected Lover's Luck" 1913; "Religion and Gun Practice" 1913; "The Rustler's Reformation" 1913; "Sallie's Sure Shot" 1913; "Saved from the Vigilantes" 1913; "The Schoolmarm's Shooting Match" 1913; "The Senorita's Repentance" 1913; "The Sheriff and the Rustler" 1913; "The Sheriff of Yawapai County" 1913 (& story); "The Shotgun Man and the Stage Driver" 1913 (& story); "The Silver Grindstone" 1913; "The Stolen Moccasins" 1913; "Taming a Tenderfoot" 1913; "The Taming of Texas Pete" 1913; "Two Sacks of Potatoes" 1913; "A Friend in Need" 1914; "The Servant Question Out West" 1914; "Love and Law" 1915 (sp. only); "Dead Shot Baker" 1917; "The Fighting Trail" 1917-serial; "The Tenderfoot" 1917; "Vengeance and the Woman" 1917-serial; "A Fight for Millions" 1918-serial; "Smashing Barriers" 1919-serial; "Steelheart" 1921; "Where Men Are Men" 1921; "The Fighting Guide" 1922; "When Danger Smiles" 1922; "Playing It Wild" 1923; "The Steel Trail" 1923-serial; "Wolves of the North" 1924-serial.

Dunham, Phil (1885-9/5/72). Screenwriter. Films: "Rainbow Ranch" 1933; "Feud of the West" 1936; "Ridin' the Trail" 1940.

Dunlap, Scott R. (1892-3/30/70). Director. Films: "The Challenge of the Law" 1920; "Forbidden Trails" 1920 (& sp.); "The Iron Rider" 1920; "Twins of Suffering Creek" 1920; "Bells of San Juan" 1922; "Trooper O'Neil" 1922; "West of Chicago" 1922; "Western Speed" 1922 (& sp.); "The Footlight Ranger" 1923; "Snowdrift" 1923; "Beyond the Border" 1925; "Silent Sanderson" 1925; "The Texas Trail" 1925; "Desert Valley" 1926; "Driftin' Thru" 1926; "The Frontier Trail" 1926; "The Seventh Bandit" 1926; "Good As Gold" 1927; "Whispering Sage" 1927; "Smoke Bellew" 1929; "The Luck of Roaring Camp" 1937 (prod. only); "Drifting Westward" 1939 (prod. only): "Queen of the Yukon" 1940 (prod. only); "Arizona Bound" 1941 (prod. only); "Forbidden Trails" 1941 (prod. only); "The Gunman from Bodie" 1941; "Below the Border" 1942 (prod. only); "Dawn on the Great Divide" 1942 (prod. only); "Down Texas Way" 1942 (prod. only); "Ghost Town Law" 1942 (prod. only); "Riders of the West" 1942 (prod. only); "West of the Law" 1942; "The Ghost Rider" 1943; "Outlaws of Stampede Pass" 1943 (prod. only); "Six Gun Gospel" 1943 (prod. only); "The Stranger from Pecos" 1943 (prod. only); "The Texas Kid" 1943 (prod. only); "Partners of the Trail" 1944 (prod. only); "Raiders of the Border" 1944 (prod. only); "Flame of the West" 1945 (prod. only); "Beauty and the Bandit" 1946 (prod. only); "Border Bandits" 1946 (prod. only); "Drifting Along" 1946 (prod. only); "The Gay Cavalier" 1946 (prod. only); "Gentleman from Texas" 1946 (prod. only); "Shadows on the Range" 1946 (prod. only); "South of Monterey" 1946 (prod. only); "Under Arizona Skies" 1946 (prod. only); "Raiders of the South" 1947 (prod. only); "Riding the California Trail" 1947 (prod. only); "Stampede" 1949 (prod. only); "Short Grass" 1950 (prod. only); "Cow Country 1953 (prod. only); "Man from God's Country" 1958.

Dunn, J. Allen. Writer. Films: "Cupid in the Cow Camp" 1913 (story); "Sandy Burke of the U-Bar-U" 1919 (story); "No Man's Gold" 1926 (story).

Dunn, Winifred. Screenwriter. Films: "Two Kinds of Women" 1922; "The Eagle's Feather" 1923.

Dunne, Philip (1908-6/2/92). Screenwriter. Films: "The Last of the Mohicans" 1936; "Way of a Gaucho" 1952 (& prod.).

Durant, E. Mason. Screenwriter. Films: "The Red Woman" 1917.

Durham, Marilyn (1930-). Writer. Films: "The Man Who Loved Cat Dancing" 1973 (story).

Durham, W. Hanson. Writer. Films: "The Outlaw" 1913 (story); "When the West Was Young" 1913 (story).

Durlam, George Arthur. Screenwriter. Films: "The Ace of Clubs" 1926 (story only); "Red Blood" 1926 (story only); "Riding Romance" 1926; "Beyond the Law" 1930 (story only); "Code of Honor" 1930; "The Lonesome Trail" 1930; "Under Texas Skies" 1930; "The Man from Death Valley" 1931; "The Montana Kid" 1931; "Near the Trail's End" 1931; "Oklahoma Jim" 1931; "Partners of the Trail" 1931; "Riders of the North" 1931 (& prod.); "Two-Fisted Justice" 1931 (& dir.); "South of Santa Fe" 1932; "Custer's Last Stand" 1936-serial; "Lightning Bill Carson" 1936 (story only); "The Great Adventures of Wild Bill Hickok" 1938-serial; "Frontier Crusader" 1940 (story only); "Boot Hill Bandits" 1942.

Durney, Dennis (1933-4/6/94). Producer. Films: "Molly and Lawless John" 1972; "The Shadow Riders" TVM-1982.

Durning, Bernard J. (1893-8/29/23). Director. Films: "The One-Man Trail" 1921; "The Primal Law" 1921; "Straight from the Shoulder" 1921; "To a Finish" 1921; "The Fast Mail" 1922; "Iron to Gold" 1922; "While Justice Waits" 1922; "The Yosemite Trail" 1922.

DuSoe, Robert C. (1892-1958). Writer. Films: "Twenty Mule Team" 1940 (story).

D'Usseau, Leon (1996-6/6/63). Director. Films: "The One Man Dog" 1929.

Duvane, Jean. Screenwriter. Films: "Marry in Haste" 1924.

Dwan, Allan (1885-12/21/81). Director. Films: "The Angel of Paradise Rance" 1911; "The Actress and the Cowboys" 1911; "Auntie and the Cowboys" 1911; "The Blotted Brand" 1911; "The Broncho Buster's Bride" 1911; "The Call of the Open Range" 1911; "Cattle, Gold and Oil" 1911; "The Cattle Rustler's End" 1911; "The Cattle Thief's Brand" 1911; "The Circular Fence" 1911; "The

Claim Jumpers" 1911; "The Cowboy and the Artist" 1911 (& sp.); "The Cowboy and the Outlaw" 1911; "The Cowboy's Mother-in-Law" 1911; "Cupid in Chaps" 1911; "The Eastern Cowboy" 1911; "The Elopements on Double L Ranch" 1911; "$5,000 Reward, Dead or Alive" 1911; "The Gold Lust" 1911; "The Gun Man" 1911; "The Hermit's Gold" 1911; "The Horse Thief's Bigamy" 1911; "The Land Thieves" 1911; "The Last Notch" 1911; "Law and Order on the Bar L Ranch" 1911; "The Lonely Range" 1911; "The Love of the West" 1911; "The Man Hunt" 1911; "The Miner's Wife" 1911; "The Outlaw's Trail" 1911; "The Parting Trails" 1911; "The Poinsoned Flame" 1911; "The Ranch Chicken" 1911; "The Ranch Girl" 1911; "The Ranch Tenor" 1911; "The Ranchman's Nerve" 1911; "The Rustler Sheriff" 1911; "The Sage-Brush Phrenologist" 1911; "The Schoolma'am of Snake" 1911; "The Sheepman's Daughter" 1911; "The Sheriff's Sisters" 1911; "The Sky Pilot's Intemperance" 1911; "The Stage Robbers of San Juan" 1911; "The Stranger at Coyote" 1911; "The Test" 1911; "Three Daughters of the West" 1911; "Three Million Dollars" 1911; "The Trail of the Eucalyptus" 1911; "A Trooper's Heart" 1911; "The Water War" 1911; "The Way of the West" 1911; "The Western Doctor's Peril" 1911; "A Western Dream" 1911; "A Western Waif" 1911; "The Witch of the Range" 1911; "The Agitator" 1912; "A Bad Investment" 1912; "Bad Man and the Ranger" 1912; "The Bandit of Point Loma" 1912; "Battle-Ground" 1912; "Blackened Hills" 1912; "The Brand" 1912; "Calamity Anne's Ward" 1912; "The Canyon Dweller" 1912; "The Coward" 1912; "The Daughters of Senor Lopez" 1912; "Driftwood" 1912; "The Eastern Girl" 1912; "End of the Feud" 1912; "The Evil Inheritance" 1912; "The Fear" 1912; "For the Good of Her Men" 1912; "From the Four Hundred to the Herd" 1912; "The Full Value" 1912; "The Girl and the Gun" 1912; "God's Unfortunate" 1912; "The Intrusion of Compoc" 1912; "The Jack of Diamonds" 1912; "The Jealous Rage" 1912; "Justice of the Sage" 1912; "The Land Baron of San Tee" 1912; "The Land of Death" 1912; "The Law of God" 1912; "Maiden and Men" 1912; "A Man's Calling" 1912; "The Marauders" 1912; "The Mormon" 1912; "Nell of the Pampas" 1912; "The New Cowpuncher" 1912; "Objections Overruled" 1912; "The Outlaw Cowboy" 1912; "The Pensioners" 1912; "The

Power of Love" 1912; "The Promise" 1912; "The Ranchman's Marathon" 1912; "The Range Detective" 1912; "The Real Estate Fraud" 1912; "Reformation of Sierra Smith" 1912; "The Relentless Law" 1912; "The Reward of Valor" 1912; "Society and Chaps" 1912; "The Telltale Shells" 1912; "Their Hero Son" 1912; "The Thief's Wife" 1912; "The Thread of Life" 1912; "The Tramp's Gratitude" 1912; "Under False Pretenses" 1912; "The Vanishing Race" 1912; "Vengeance That Failed" 1912; "The Wanderer" 1912; "The Weaker Brother" 1912; "Where Broadway Meets the Mountains" 1912; "The Wining of La Mesa" 1912; "The Wooers of Mountain Kate" 1912; "Calamity Anne, Detective" 1913; "Calamity Anne Parcel Post" 1913; "Calamity Anne's Beauty" 1913; "Calamity Anne's Inheritance" 1913; "Calamity Anne's Trust" 1913; "Calamity Anne's Vanity" 1913; "The Angel of the Canyons" 1913; "Bloodhounds of the North" 1913; "An Eastern Flower" 1913; "The Fugitive" 1913; "Hearts and Horses" 1913; "High and Low" 1913; "Oil on Troubled Waters" 1913; "On the Border" 1913; "The Orphan's Mine" 1913; "The Renegade's Heart" 1913; "The Reward of Courage" 1913; "The Romance" 1913; "A Rose of Old Mexico" 1913; "The Silver-Plated Gun" 1913; "The Transgression of Manuel" 1913; "When the Light Fades" 1913; "Where Destiny Guides" 1913; "Woman's Honor" 1913; "The Honor of the Mounted" 1914; "The Tragedy of Whispering Creek" 1914; "The Unlawful Trade" 1914; "Jordan Is a Hard Road" 1915; "The Love Route" 1915; "The Accusing Evidence" 1916; "The Good Bad Man" 1916; "The Half Breed" 1916; "A Modern Musketeer" 1917 (& sp.); "Headin' South" 1918 (sp. only); "The Cowboy's Deliverance" 1919; "Tide of Empire" 1929; "Frontier Marshal" 1939; "Trail of the Vigilantes" 1940 (& prod.); "Northwest Outpost" 1947; "Surrender" 1950; "Belle Le Grand" 1951; "Montana Belle" 1952; "The Woman They Almost Lynched" 1953 (& prod.); "Cattle Queen of Montana" 1954; "Passion" 1954; "Silver Lode" 1954; "Tennessee's Partner" 1955; "The Restless Breed" 1957.

Eagle, Vincent. *see* Dell'Aquila, Enzo.

Eagleshirt, William. Screenwriter. Films: "War on the Plains" 1912.

Earl, Kenneth. Writer. Films: "The Big Trees" 1952 (story).

Earle, Edward (1882-12/15/72).

Screenwriter. Films: "Wide Open Spaces" 1932-short.

Eason, B. Reeves (1886-6/9/56). Director. Films: "Redbird Wins" 1914 (story only); "The Assayer of Lone Gap" 1915; "The Exile of Bar-K Ranch" 1915; "The Poet of the Peaks" 1915; "A Question of Honor" 1915; "The Crow" 1919; "The Fighting Heart" 1919; "The Fighting Line" 1919; "The Four-Bit Man" 1919; "The Hidden Badge" 1919; "The Jack of Hearts" 1919; "The Kid and the Cowboy" 1919; "The Tell Tale Wire" 1919; "Blue Streak McCoy" 1920; "Held Up for the Makin's 1920; "Human Stuff" 1920 (& sp.); "Hair-Trigger Stuff" 1920; "The Moon Riders" 1920-serial; "The Prospector's Vengeance" 1920; "The Rattler's Hiss" 1920; "The Texas Kid" 1920 (& sp.); "The Fire Eater" 1921; "Red Courage" 1921; "The Lone Hand" 1922; "Pardon My Nerve!" 1922; "Rough Shod" 1922; "When East Comes West" 1922; "Flashing Spurs" 1924; "Tiger Thompson" 1924; "Trigger Finger" 1924; "Border Justice" 1925; "The Texas Bearcat" 1925; "Lone Hand Saunders" 1926; "The Denver Dude" 1927; "Galloping Fury" 1927; "Painted Ponies" 1927; "The Prairie King" 1927; "Clearing the Trail" 1928; "The Flyin' Cowboys" 1928; "Riding for Fame" 1928 (& sp.); "A Trick of Hearts" 1928; "The Lariat Kid" 1929; "Roaring Ranch" 1930 (& sp.); "Spurs" 1930 (& sp.); "Trigger Tricks" 1930 (& sp.); "The Vanishing Legion" 1931-serial; "Cornered" 1932; "The Last of the Mohicans" 1932-serial; "The Sunset Trail" 1932; "The Law of the Wild" 1934-serial (& sp.); "Mystery Mountain" 1934-serial (& story); "The Miracle Rider" 1935-serial; "The Phantom Empire" 1935-serial; "Red River Valley" 1936 (& prod.); "Empty Holsters" 1937; "Land Beyond the Law" 1937; "Law for Tombstone" 1937; "Prairie Thunder" 1937; "Call of the Yukon" 1938; "Blue Montana Skies" 1939; "Mountain Rhythm" 1939; "Pony Express Days" 1940-short; "Oklahoma Outlaws" 1943-short; "Wagon Wheels West" 1943-short; "'Neath Canadian Skies" 1946; "North of the Border" 1946; "Rimfire" 1949.

Eastman, George. *see* Montefiori, Luigi.

Eastman, Glenn. *see* Civirani, Osvaldo.

Easton, H.C. Director. Films: "The Trail of the Upper Yukon" 1915; "The Valley of Silent Men" 1915.

Easton, Miller. Screenwriter.

Films: "Toll of the Desert" 1936; "Wildcat Saunders" 1936.

Eastwood, Clint (1930-). Director. Films: "High Plains Drifter" 1973; "The Outlaw Josey Wales" 1976; "Bronco Billy" 1980; "Pale Rider" 1985 (& prod.); "Unforgiven" 1992 (& prod.).

Eber, Gunter. Screenwriter. Films: "Don't Turn the Other Cheek" 1974-Ital./Ger./Span.

Eberson, Drew. Director. Films: "The Overland Express" 1938.

Ebert, Fritz. Screenwriter. Films: "Companeros" 1970-Ital./Span./Ger.

Eby, Lois. Screenwriter. Films: "The Lone Ranger" 1938-serial.

Eddy, Nathaniel. Writer. Films: "The Rustlers of Red Dog" 1935-serial (story).

Eddy, Robert. Director. Films: "Hearts and Saddles" 1917; "Action Galore" 1925; "Galloping Jinx" 1925; "Hurricane Horseman" 1926.

Edelman, Louis F. (1900-1/6/76). Producer. Films: "The Big Trees" 1952; "Springfield Rifle" 1952. ¶TV: *Wyatt Earp* 1955-61 (exec. prod.); *Jim Bowie* 1956-58; *The Californians* 1957-59 (exec. prod.).

Edgeworth, Patrick. Screenwriter. Films: "Raw Deal" 1977-Australia (& prod.).

Edington, May. Writer. Films: "Secrets" 1933 (story).

Edmiston, James. Screenwriter. Films: "A Day of Fury" 1956; "Four Fast Guns" 1959; "Rider on a Dead Horse" 1962 (story only).

Edmonds, Walter D. (1903-). Writer. Films: "Drums Along the Mohawk" 1939 (story).

Edwardes-Hall, George. Screenwriter. Films: "The Kick Back" 1922.

Edwards, Anne (1927-). Writer. Films: "Quantez" 1957 (story).

Edwards, Blake (1922-). Director. Films: "Panhandle" 1948 (prod./sp. only); "Stampede 1949 (prod./sp. only); "Wild Rovers" 1971 (& prod./sp.); "Sunset" 1988 (& sp.).

Edwards, Enos. Screenwriter. Films: "The Three Outcasts" 1929.

Edwards, Harry (1889-5/26/52). Director. Films: "Pistol Packin' Nitwits" 1945-short.

Edwards, J. Gordon (1867-12/31/25). Director. Films: "Last of the Duanes" 1919; "The Lone Star Ranger" 1919; "Drag Harlan" 1920; "The Joyous Troublemaker" 1920; "The Orphan" 1920.

Edwards, P.F. Screenwriter.

Films: "Tecumseh: The Last Warrior" TVM-1995.

Edwards, Paul. Director. TV: *Gunsmoke*—"Whelan's Men" 2-5-73.

Edwards, Ralph (1913-). Producer. TV: *Wide Country* 1962-63 (exec. prod.).

Edwards, Robert. Director. Films: "Thunder in the Pines" 1948.

Edwards, Walter. Director. Films: "The Panther" 1914; "Ashes of Hope" 1917; "Lieutenant Danny, U.S.A." 1916; "The Man from Funeral Range" 1918.

Edwards, Weston. *see* Fraser, Harry.

Edwin, Walter. Director. Films: "The Ranch Owner's Love-Making" 1913; "When East Met West in Boston" 1914; "Gloria's Romance" 1916-serial.

Eggers, Fred. Screenwriter. Films: "Thunder Pass" 1954; "Treasure of Ruby Hills" 1955.

Eldridge, E.M. Director. Films: "Forbidden Grass" 1928.

Elfelt, Clifford S. Director. Films: "Big Stakes" 1922; "Flaming Hearts" 1922; "Crimson Gold" 1923; "Danger" 1923; "50,000 Reward" 1924; "Fighting Courage" 1925; "Under Fire" 1926.

Elias, Michael. Screenwriter. Films: "The Frisco Kid" 1979.

Eliason, Joyce. Screenwriter. Films: "Children of the Dust" TVM-1995.

Elikann, Larry. Director. Films: "Tecumseh: The Last Warrior" TVM-1995.

Eliott, Jr., George. Writer. Films: "Miss Arizona" 1919 (story).

Elkins, Saul. Producer. Films: "The Younger Brothers" 1949; "Barricade" 1950; "Colt .45" 1950; "Return of the Frontiersman" 1950; "Raton Pass" 1951; "Sugarfoot" 1951.

Ellis, Antony. Screenwriter. Films: "The Ride Back" 1957. ¶TV: *Black Saddle* 1959 (prod.).

Ellis, Bob. Screenwriter. Films: "Bullseye!" 1986-Australia.

Ellis, Edith (1874-12/27/60). Screenwriter. Films: "The Great Meadow" 1931.

Ellis, John Breckenridge. Writer. Films: "Lahoma" 1920 (story).

Ellis, Robert (1892-12/29/74). Screenwriter. Films: "Susannah of the Mounties" 1939; "Lucky Cisco Kid" 1940.

Ellis, Will. Writer. Films: "The Last Card" 1915 (story).

Elorrieta, Jose M. (Joe Lacy). Director. Films: "Massacre at Fort Grant" 1963-Span. (& sp.)."Secret of Captain O'Hara" 1965-Span. (sp. only); "Fury of the Apaches" 1966-Span./Ital. (& sp.); "Seven for Pancho Villa" 1966-Span.; "If You Want to Live ... Shoot!" 1967-Ital./Span. (sp. only); "If You Shoot ... You Live!" 1974-Span. (& sp.).

Emanuelle, Luigi. Screenwriter. Films: "Damned Pistols of Dallas" 1964-Span./Ital./Fr.; "This Man Can't Die" 1968-Ital.

Emerson, John (1871-3/7/56). Director. Films: "The Agitator" 1912 (sp. only); "Geronimo's Last Raid" 1912 (sp. only); "Wild and Woolly" 1917.

Emmanuel, Jacques. Screenwriter. Films: "Dynamite Jack" 1963-Fr.

Emmett, Robert. see Tansey, Robert Emmett.

Emmons, Della Gould (1890-83). Writer. Films: "The Far Horizons" 1955 (story).

Engel, Fred. Producer. Films: "Duel at Diablo" 1966; "Will Penny" 1968.

Engel, Samuel G. (1904-4/7/84). Screenwriter. Films: "Viva Cisco Kid" 1940; "Ride On, Vaquero" 1941; "Romance of the Rio Grande" 1941; "My Darling Clementine" 1946 (& prod.); "Rawhide" 1951 (prod. only); "Pony Soldier" 1952 (prod. only).

English, John (1903-10/11/69). Director. Films: "His Fighting Blood" 1935; "Red Blood of Courage" 1935; "Arizona Days" 1937; "Whistling Bullets" 1937; "Zorro Rides Again" 1937-serial; "Call the Mesquiteers" 1938; "The Lone Ranger" 1938-serial; "The Lone Ranger Rides Again" 1939-serial; "Zorro's Fighting Legion" 1939-serial; "Adventures of Red Ryder" 1940-serial; "King of the Royal Mounted" 1940-serial; "Gangs of Sonora" 1941; "King of the Texas Rangers" 1941-serial; "Code of the Outlaw" 1942; "The Phantom Plainsmen" 1942; "Raiders of the Range" 1942; "Valley of Hunted Men" 1942; "Westward Ho" 1942; "Black Hills Express" 1943; "Daredevils of the West" 1943-serial; "Dead Man's Gulch" 1943; "Death Valley Manhunt" 1943; "The Man from Thunder River" 1943; "Overland Mail Robbery" 1943; "Raiders of Sunset Pass" 1943; "Thundering Trail" 1943; "The Laramie Trail" 1944; "San Fernando Valley" 1944; "Silver City Kid" 1944;

"Don't Fence Me In" 1945; "Utah" 1945; "The Last Round-Up" 1947; "Trail to San Antone" 1947; "Loaded Pistols" 1948; "The Strawberry Roan" 1948; "The Cowboy and the Indians" 1949; "Riders in the Sky" 1949; "Riders of the Whistling Pines" 1949; "Rim of the Canyon" 1949; "Sons of New Mexico" 1949; "Beyond the Purple Hills" 1950; "The Blazing Sun" 1950; "Copper Canyon" 1950 (story only); "Cow Town" 1950; "Indian Territory" 1950; "Mule Train" 1950; "Gene Autry and the Mounties" 1951; "Hills of Utah" 1951; "Silver Canyon" 1951; "Valley of Fire" 1951; "Whirlwind" 1951. ¶TV: *The Gene Autry Show*—"The Raiders" 4-14-51, "Double Barrelled Vengeance" 4-21-51; *The Roy Rogers Show*—"Jailbreak" 12-30-51, "The Desert Fugitive" 2-24-52, "The Minister's Son" 3-23-52, "Bullets and a Burro" 11-15-53; *The Adventures of Champion* 1955; *Buffalo Bill, Jr.* 1955; *My Friend Flicka* 1955; *Zane Grey Theater* 1956; *Black Saddle* 1959; *Johnny Ringo* 1959; *The Rifleman*—"The Spiked Rifle" 11-24-59; *Wagon Train*—"The Nancy Palmer Story" 3-8-61; *The Virginian*—"A Distant Fury" 3-20-63; *Gunsmoke*—"Tobe" 10-19-63, "Extradition" 12-7-63 & 12-14-63; *Laredo*—"Any Way the Wind Blows" 10-28-66.

English, Richard (1910-10/2/57). Screenwriter. Films: "Lust for Gold" 1949.

Englund, George. Director. Films: "Zachariah" 1971 (& prod.).

Enright, Ray (1896-4/3/65). Director. Films: "Jaws of Steel" 1927; "Tracked by the Police" 1927; "Land of the Silver Fox" 1928; "Song of the West" 1930; "River's End" 1940; "Bad Men of Missouri" 1941; "Men of Texas" 1942; "Sin Town" 1942; "The Spoilers" 1942; "Wild Bill Hickok Rides" 1942; "Trail Street" 1947; "Albuquerque" 1948; "Coroner Creek" 1948; "Return of the Badmen" 1948; "South of St. Louis" 1949; "Kansas Raiders" 1950; "Montana" 1950; "Flaming Feather" 1952.

Ensescalle, Jr., Bob. Screenwriter. Films: "The Stranger Returns" 1967-U.S./Ital./Ger./Span.

Ensminger, Robert. Director. Films: "Whatever the Cost" 1918; "Breaking Through" 1921-serial; "Bring Him In" 1921.

Epstein, Mel. Producer. Films: "Whispering Smith" 1948; "Copper Canyon" 1950; "Branded" 1951; "The Savage" 1952. ¶TV: *Broken Arrow* 1956-58; *Man Without a Gun* 1958-59.

Ercoli, Luciano. Producer. Films: "A Pistol for Ringo" 1965-Ital./Span.; "The Return of Ringo" 1966-Ital./Span.; "The Ruthless Four" 1968-Ital./Ger.

Erdman, Richard (1925-). Director. Films: "The Brothers O'Toole" 1973.

Erickson, A.F. Director. Films: "The Lone Star Ranger" 1930 (& prod.); "Rough Romance" 1930.

Erskine, Chester (1905-4/7/86). Producer. Films: "The Wonderful Country" 1959.

Erskine, Laurie York (1894-1976). Writer. Films: "Renfrew of the Royal Mounted" 1937 (story); "Renfrew on the Great White Trail" 1938 (story); "Crashing Thru" 1939 (story); "Fighting Mad" 1939 (story); "Danger Ahead" 1940 (story); "Murder on the Yukon" 1940 (story); "Sky Bandits" 1940 (story); "Yukon Flight" 1940 (story).

Erwin, E.L. Screenwriter. Films: "Dalton That Got Away" 1960; "Vengeance" 1964.

Escribano, Antonio. Screenwriter. Films: "Shoot to Kill" 1963-Span.

Espinosa, Jose L. Director. Films: "The Texican" 1966-U.S./Span.

Essex, Harry (1910-). Screenwriter. Films: "Wyoming Mail" 1950; "Devil's Canyon" 1953; "Southwest Passage" 1954 (& story); "Raw Edge" 1956; "The Lonely Man" 1957; "The Sons of Katie Elder" 1965; "Man and Boy" 1971; "Deaf Smith and Johnny Ears" 1972-Ital. (& story).

Estabrook, Howard (1884-7/16/78). Screenwriter. Films: "The Highway of Hope" 1917; "The Virginian" 1929; "The Bad Man" 1930; "Cimarron" 1931; "Woman Hungry" 1931; "The Conquerors" 1932; "Dakota" 1945; "The Virginian" 1946; "Lone Star" 1952; "Cattle Queen of Montana" 1954; "Passion" 1954.

Esteba, Manuel (Ted Mulligan). Director. Films: "Twenty Paces to Death" 1970-Ital./Span.

Estrada, Luis. Director. Films: "Bandidos" 1991-Mex. (& sp.).

Eunson, Dale. Screenwriter. Films: "Joe Panther" 1976.

Evans, A. Frederic. Screenwriter. Films: "Outlaw of the Plains" 1946.

Evans, Evan. *see* Brand, Max.

Evans, Julius. Writer. Films: "Gun Fever" 1958 (story).

Evans, Max (1925-). Writer. Films: "The Rounders" 1965 (story).

Evarts, Hal G. (1887-1934). Writer. Films: "The Silent Call" 1921 (story); "Tumbleweeds" 1925 (story); "The Big Trail" 1930 (story); "The Santa Fe Trail" 1930 (story).

Everett, Arthur. Screenwriter. Films: "Roaring Six Guns" 1937; "Rough Ridin' Rhythm" 1937.

Eyre, David. Screenwriter. Films: "Cattle Annie and Little Britches" 1981.

Fabian, Walter. Director. Films: "Battling Justice" 1927; "The Lone Ranger" 1927; "The Law Rider" 1927; "On Special Duty" 1927; "The Smiling Wolf" 1927; "Buckskin Days" 1928; "The Card of Destiny" 1928; "A Clean Sweep" 1928; "The Death's Head" 1928; Films: "Fighting Destiny" 1928; "The Fighting Forester" 1928; "A Fighting Tederfoot" 1928; "The Gauge of Battle" 1928; "The Ride for Help" 1928; "The Ranger Patrol" 1928; "A Romeo of the Range" 1928; "Ropin' Romance" 1928; "Saps and Saddles" 1928; "The Secret Outlaw" 1928; "A Son of the Frontier" 1928; "Speed and Spurs" 1928; "A Tenderfoot Hero" 1928; "An Unexpected Hero" 1928; "Wolves of the Ragne" 1928; "A Close Call" 1929; "Cowboy Pluck" 1929; "A Daring Dude" 1929; "Days of Daring" 1929; "The Go Get 'Em Kid" 1929; "Kidnapped" 1929; "The Lone Rider" 1929; "Playing False" 1929; "The Range of Fear" 1929; "The Range Wolf" 1929; "Red Romance" 1929; "Ridin' Leather" 1929; "Riding for Life" 1929; "A Tenderfoot Terror" 1929; "The Thrill Hunter" 1933.

Fabrini, J.C. Screenwriter. Films: "The Old Fool" 1923.

Fadiman, William. Producer. Films: "The Last Frontier" 1955; "Jubal" 1956.

Fagan, Myron. Screenwriter. Films: "A Holy Terror" 1931.

Fago, Giovanni (Sidney Lean). Director. Films: "For One Hundred Thousand Dollars Per Killing" 1967-Ital.; "To Hell and Back" 1968-Ital./Span. (& sp.); "The Magnificent Bandits" 1969-Ital./Span. (& sp).

Fahrney, Milton H. (1872-3/26/41) Director. Films: "The Law of the Range" 1911; "A True Westerner" 1911; "The White Medicine Man" 1911; "The Squatter's Child" 1912.

Fairbanks, Douglas (Elton Thomas) (1883-12/12/39). Director. Films: "The Good Bad Man" 1916 (sp. only); "The Man from Painted Post" 1917 (sp. only); "Arizona" 1918 (& sp.); "The Knickerbocker Buckaroo" 1919 (sp. only); "Mark of Zorro" 1920 (& prod.); "The Mollycoddle" 1920.

Fairfax, Marion (1875-10/2/70). Screenwriter. Films: "Tennessee's Pardner" 1916; "On the Level" 1917; "A Daughter of the Wolf" 1919; "Bob Hampton of Placer" 1921; "The Snowshoe Trail" 1922.

Falk, Harry. Director. TV: *Alias Smith and Jones*—"The Posse That Wouldn't Quit" 10-14-71; *Big Hawaii* 1977; *How the West Was Won*—"L'Affaire Riel" 3-5-79.

Fallon, David. Screenwriter. Films: "White Fang" 1991; "White Fang 2: Myth of the White Wolf" 1994.

Fallon, Thomas F. Screenwriter. Films: "Sacred Silence" 1919.

Fanning, Frank (1879-3/1/34). Director. Films: "The Masked Avenger" 1922.

Fante, John. Screenwriter. Films: "Something for a Lonely Man" TVM-1968.

Faradine, Oskar. Director. Films: "Bounty Hunter in Trinity" 1972-Ital.

Faragoh, Frances Edwards (1895-7/25/66). Screenwriter. Films: "My Friend Flicka" 1943; "Renegades" 1946.

Faralla, William Dario. Director. Films: "The Ballad of Cable Hogue" 1970 (prod. only). ¶TV: *Black Saddle* 1959; *Johnny Ringo* 1959; *Zane Grey Theater*—"The Sunday Man" 2-25-60; *Maverick*—"Thunder from the North" 11-13-60; *Bonanza*—"The Rescue" 2-25-61; *Gunsmoke*—"Melinda Miles" 6-3-61.

Farley, Dot (1881-5/21/71). Screenwriter. Films: "The Lust of the Red Man" 1914 (story only); "The Toll of the War-Path" 1914.

Farney, Charles. Director. Films: "The Romance of the Utah Pioneers" 1913.

Farnham, Joe. Screenwriter. Films: "Montana Moon" 1930; "Way Out West" 1930.

Farnum, Dustin (1874-7/3/29). Director. Films: "When We Were Young" 1914.

Farnum, Martin. Director. Films: "The Arrow's Tongue" 1914.

Farrar, Walter. Screenwriter. Films: "Swifty" 1935.

Farrell, Cliff (1899-1977). Writer. Films: "Outlawed Guns" 1935 (story).

Farrow, John (1904-1/27/63). Director. Films: "Wolf Song" 1929 (sp. only); "Reno" 1939; "California" 1946; "Copper Canyon" 1950; "Hondo" 1953; "Ride, Vaquero!" 1953; "A Bullet Is Waiting" 1954. ¶TV: *Empire*—"The Tall Shadow" 11-20-62.

Fast, Howard (1914-). Writer. Films: "Rachel and the Stranger" 1948 (story).

Faye, Randall. Screenwriter. Films: "Desert Valley" 1926; "Branded" 1931; "Lasca of the Rio Grande" 1931; "McKenna of the Mounted" 1932 (story only); "Texas Cyclone" 1932; "Cheyenne Wildcat" 1944; "Firebrands of Arizona" 1944.

Fearnley, Neill. Director. TV: *Hawkeye*—"Out of the Past" 11-9-94.

Feeney, Edward. Director. Films: "The Boss of Copperhead" 1920; "Fighting Pals" 1920; "Two from Texas" 1920; "Under Pressure" 1922.

Feist, Felix (1906-9/2/65). Director. Films: "The Battles of Chief Pontiac" 1952; "The Big Trees" 1952; "The Man Behind the Gun" 1952. ¶TV: *Zane Grey Theater* 1956; *The Californians* 1957-59 (prod.): *Bonanza*—"Blood on the Land" 2-13-60.

Fejos, Paul (1897-4/23/63). Screenwriter. Films: "Land of the Lawless" 1927.

Feldman, Phil. Producer. Films: "The Wild Bunch" 1969; "The Ballad of Cable Hogue" 1970.

Fellows, Robert. Producer. Films: "Virginia City" 1940; "Tall in the Saddle" 1944; "Streets of Laredo" 1949; "Hondo" 1953; "Track of the Cat" 1954.

Felsen, Henry Gregor (1916-). Writer. Films: "Once Upon a Horse" 1958 (story).

Feltini, Monica. Screenwriter. Films: "Vengeance Is a Dish Served Cold" 1971-Ital./Span.

Felton, Earl (1910-5/2/72). Screenwriter. Films: "Sierra Sue" 1941; "Heart of the Golden West" 1942; "Sunset Serenade" 1942; "The Marauders" 1955; "Bandido" 1956; "The Rawhide Years" 1956.

Fenady, Andrew J. Screenwriter. Films: "Ride Beyond Vengeance" 1966 (& prod.); "Chisum" 1970 (& prod.); "Black Noon" TVM-1971 (& prod.); "The Hanged Man" TVM-1974 (prod. only). ¶TV: *The Rebel* 1959-61 (prod.); *Branded* 1965-66 (prod.); *Hondo* 1967 (prod.).

Fencroft, George. Writer. Films: "99 Wounds" 1931 (story).

Fennelly, Vincent M. Producer.

Films: "Arizona Territory" 1950; "Cherokee Uprising" 1950; "Outlaw Gold" 1950; "Outlaws of Texas" 1950; "Silver Raiders" 1950; "Abilene Trail" 1951; "Blazing Bullets" 1951; "Canyon Raiders" 1951; "Colorado Ambush" 1951; "Lawless Cowboys" 1951; "The Longhorn" 1951; "Man from Sonora" 1951; "Montana Desperado" 1951; "Nevada Badmen" 1951; "Oklahoma Justice" 1951; "Stage to Blue River" 1951; "Stagecoach Driver" 1951; "Texas Lawmen" 1951; "Wanted Dead or Alive" 1951; "Whistling Hills" 1951; "Canyon Ambush" 1952; "Dead Man's Trail" 1952; "Fargo" 1952; "The Gunman" 1952; "Kansas Territory" 1952; "The Man from Black Hills" 1952; "The Maverick" 1952; "Montana Incident" 1952; "Night Raiders" 1952; "Texas City" 1952; "Waco" 1952; "Wagons West" 1952; "Wyoming Roundup" 1952; "The Fighting Lawman" 1953; "The Homesteaders" 1953; "The Marksman" 1953; "Rebel City" 1953; "Star of Texas" 1953; "Texas Bad Man" 1953; "Topeka" 1953; "Vigilante Terror" 1953; "Bitter Creek" 1954; "The Desperado" 1954; "The Forty-Niners" 1954; "Two Guns and a Badge" 1954; "At Gunpoint" 1955; "Seven Angry Men" 1955; "Last of the Badmen" 1957; "Guns of the Magnificent Seven" 1969; "Cannon for Cordoba" 1970. ¶TV: *Trackdown* 1957-59; *Rawhide* 1959-66; *Stagecoach West* 1960-61.

Fenton, Frank (1906-8/23/71). Screenwriter. Films: "Wild and Woolly" 1937; "Station West" 1948; "Whispering Smith" 1948 (dir. only); "The Wild North" 1952; "Escape from Fort Brave" 1953; "Garden of Evil" 1954; "River of No Return" 1954; "The Jayhawkers" 1959; "The Dangerous Days of Kiowa Jones" TVM-1966; "Something for a Lonely Man" TVM-1968.

Fenton, Leslie (1903-3/25/78). Director. Films: "The Man from Dakota" 1940; "Streets of Laredo" 1949; "The Redhead and the Cowboy" 1951; "Ride, Vaquero!" 1953 (sp. only).

Ferber, Edna (1885-4/16/68). Writer. Films: "Cimarron" 1931 (story); "Giant" 1956 (story); "Cimarron" 1960 (story).

Ferber, Mel (1917-). Director. TV: *Alias Smith and Jones*—"Twenty-One Days to Tenstrike" 1-6-72.

Ferguson, Al (1888-12/4/71). Director. Films: "The Fighting Romeo" 1925.

Ferguson, Harvey. Screenwriter. Films: "Wolf Song" 1929 (story only); "Stand Up and Fight" 1939.

Ferrando, Giancarlo. Screenwriter. Films: "Stranger in Japan" 1969-Ital./U.S./Jap.

Ferrau, Antonio. Screenwriter. Films: "Rick and John, Conquerors of the West" 1967-Ital.

Ferreri, Marco. Director. Films: "Don't Touch White Women!" 1974-Ital. (& sp.).

Ferris, Beth. Screenwriter. Films: "Heartland" 1980 (& prod.).

Ferris, Walter. Writer. Films: "Susannah of the Mounties" 1939 (story).

Ferroni, Giorgio (Calvin J. Padget). Director. Films: "Blood for a Silver Dollar" 1965-Ital./Fr. (& sp.); "Fort Yuma Gold" 1966-Ital./Fr./Span.; "Two Pistols and a Coward" 1967-Ital. (& sp.); "Wanted" 1968-Ital./Fr.

Fessier, Michael (1906-9/19/88). Screenwriter. Films: "Frontier Gal" 1945 (& prod.); "The Woman They Almost Lynched" 1953 (story only); "The Boy from Oklahoma" 1954 (story only); "Red Garters" 1954.

Fidani, Demofilo (Miles Deem, Dennis Ford, Lucky Dickerson, Sean O'Neal). Director. Films: "Shadow of Sartana … Shadow of Your Death" 1968-Ital. (& sp.); "Four Came to Kill Sartnaa" 1969-Ital. (& sp.); "Django and Sartana Are Coming … It's the End" 1970-Ital. (& sp.); "Hero Called Allegria" 1971-Ital.; "Fistful of Death" 1971-Ital. (& prod./sp.); "His Name Was Sam Walbash, But They Call Him Amen" 1971-Ital. (& sp.); "One Damned Day at Dawn … Django Meets Sartana" 1971-Ital. (& prod./sp.); "Rach You Bastard!" 1971-Ital. (& sp.); "Stranger That Kneels Beside the Shadow of a Corpse" 1971-Ital. (& sp.); "Go Away! Trinity Has Arrived in Eldorado" 1972-Ital.; "Showdown for a Badman" 1972-Ital. (& sp.); "Anything for a Friend" 1973-Ital. (& sp.).

Field, Edward Salisbury. Writer. Films: "Zander the Great" 1925 (story).

Field, Salisbury. Screenwriter. Films: "Secrets" 1933.

Fielder, Pat. Screenwriter. Films: "Geronimo" 1962 (& story).

Fielder, Richard. Screenwriter. Films: "A Distant Trumpet" 1964 (adapt only); "Wanted: The Sundance Woman" TVM-1976.

Fielding, Romaine (1879-12/15/27). Director. Films: "Chief White Eagle" 1912 (& sp.); "The Cringer"

1912; "The Deputy's Peril" 1912; "The Forest Ranger" 1912; "A Soldier's Furlough" 1912 (& sp.); "An Adventure on the Mexican Border" 1913 (& sp.); "The Reformed Outlaw" 1913; "A Cowboy Pastime" 1914 (& sp.); "The Man from the West" 1914 (story only); "The Eagle's Nest" 1915 (& sp.); "The Trapper's Revenge" 1915; "The Valley of Lost Hope" 1915; "A Western Governor's Humanity" 1915 (& sp.); "The Desert Rat" 1916; "The Crimson Dove" 1917.

Fielding, Sol Baer (1909-9/2/92). Producer. Films: "Trooper Hook" 1957.

Fields, Dorothy (1905-74). Writer. Films: "Annie Get Your Gun" 1950 (story).

Fields, Herbert. Writer. Films: "Annie Get Your Gun" 1950 (story).

Fields, Joseph A. Screenwriter. Films: "Annie Oakley" 1935 (story only); "The Girl and the Gambler" 1939; "The Man from Texas" 1947 (& prod.).

Fields, W.C. (1879-12/25/46). Screenwriter. Films: "My Little Chickadee" 1940.

Fier, Jack. Producer. Films: "The Durango Kid" 1940; "The Medico of Painted Springs" 1941; "Outlaws of the Panhandle" 1941; "The Pinto Kid" 1941; "Bad Men of the Hills" 1942; "Down Rio Grande Way" 1942; "Lawless Plainsmen" 1942; "Overland to Deadwood" 1942; "Pardon My Gun" 1942; "Riders of the Northland" 1942; "Riding Through Nevada" 1942; "Cowboy in the Clouds" 1943; "The Fighting Buckaroo" 1943; "Frontier Fury" 1943; "Hail to the Rangers" 1943; "Law of the Northwest" 1943; "Robin Hood of the Range" 1943; "Cowboy Canteen" 1944; "Cowboy from Lonesome River" 1944; "Cyclone Prairie Rangers" 1944; "Riding West" 1944; "Saddle Leather Law" 1944; "Sundown Valley" 1944; "Swing in the Saddle" 1944; "Rough Ridin' Justice" 1945.

Fife, Shannon. Screenwriter. Films: "The Valley of Lost Hope" 1915.

Figuerola, Mallorqui. Screenwriter. Films: "Killer Goodbye" 1969-Ital./Span.

Finch, Scot. Screenwriter. Films: "Shalako" 1968-Brit./Fr.; "Catlow" 1971-Span.; "The Man Called Noon" 1973-Brit./Span./Ital.

Finch, Yolande. Screenwriter. Films: "Bad Girls" 1994.

Fine, Hank. Writer. Films: "Showdown" 1973 (story).

Fine, Mort (1916-3/7/91). Producer. TV: *Bearcats!* 1971.

Fink, Harry Julian. Screenwriter. Films: "Major Dundee" 1965 (& story); "Big Jake" 1971; "Cahill, United States Marshal" 1973.

Fink, Rita M. Screenwriter. Films: "Big Jake" 1971; "Cahill, United States Marshal" 1973.

Finkel, R. Director. Films: "Fugitive Valley" 1941.

Finkle, Robert. Screenwriter. Films: "Wrangler's Roost" 1941.

Finlay, George. *see* Stegani, Giorgio.

Finley, Ned (-9/27/20). Director. Films: "O'Garry of the Royal Mounted" 1915 (& sp.).

Finn, Jonathan (1884-1971). Writer. Films: "Lady from Cheyenne" 1941 (story).

Finnegan, Bill. Producer. Films: "Support Your Local Gunfighter" 1971; "The Alamo: 13 Days to Glory" TVM-1987; "Down the Long Hill" TVM-1987. ¶TV: *Big Hawaii* 1977.

Finnegan, Frank X. Screenwriter. Films: "Rimrock Jones" 1918.

Finney, Edward F. Producer. Films: "Song of the Gringo" 1936; "Arizona Days" 1937; "Headin' for the Rio Grande" 1937; "Hittin' the Trail" 1937; "The Mystery of the Hooded Horsemen" 1937; "Riders of the Rockies" 1937; "Sing, Cowboy, Sing" 1937; "Tex Rides with the Boy Scouts" 1937; "Trouble in Texas" 1937; "Frontier Town" 1938; "Rollin' Plains" 1938; "Starlight Over Texas" 1938; "Utah Trail" 1938; "Where the Buffalo Roam" 1938; "Down the Wyoming Trail" 1939; "The Man from Texas" 1939; "Riders of the Frontier" 1939; "Rollin' Westward" 1939; "Song of the Buckaroo" 1939; "Sundown on the Prairie" 1939; "Westbound Stage" 1939; "Arizona Frontier" 1940; "Cowboy from Sundown" 1940; "The Golden Trail" 1940; "Pals of the Silver Sage" 1940; "Rainbow Over the Range" 1940; "Rhythm of the Rio Grande" 1940; "Roll, Wagons, Roll" 1940; "Take Me Back to Oklahoma" 1940; "The Pioneers" 1941; "Ridin' the Cherokee Trail" 1941; "Rollin' Home to Texas" 1941; "Silver Stallion" 1941 (& dir); "King of the Stallions" 1942 (& dir.); "The Prairie" 1947; "Call of the Forest" 1949; "Buffalo Bill in Tomahawk Territory" 1952.

Finocchi, Augusto. Screenwriter. Films: "Fort Yuma Gold" 1966-Ital./Fr./Span.; "Sugar Colt" 1966-Ital./Span.; "Two Pistols and a Coward" 1967-Ital.; "Black Jack"

1968-Ital.; "Greatest Robbery in the West" 1968-Ital.; "I Came, I Saw, I Shot" 1968-Ital./Span.; "Wanted" 1968-Ital./Fr.; "Deaf Smith and Johnny Ears" 1972-Ital.; "Who's Afraid of Zorro?" 1975-Ital./Span.

Fior, Odardo. Screenwriter. Films: "Death Knows No Time" 1968-Span./Ital.

Fischer, Jeffrey. Producer. Films: "Charlie Cobb: Nice Night for a Hanging" TVM-1977 (& sp.); "Bret Maverick" TVM-1981. ¶TV: *Bret Maverick* 1981-82.

Fisher, Clay (1912-). Writer. Films: "Santa Fe Passage" 1955 (story); "The Tall Men" 1955 (story); "Yellowtone Kelly" 1959 (story).

Fisher, Michael. Screenwriter. Films: "Buckskin" 1968.

Fisher, Steve (1913-3/27/80). Screenwriter. Films: "The Man from the Alamo" 1953; "San Antone" 1953; "The Woman They Almost Lynched" 1953; "Top Gun" 1955 (& story); "The Restless Breed" 1957; "Noose for a Gunman" 1960 (story only); "Law of the Lawless" 1964; "The Quick Gun" 1964 (story only); "Black Spurs" 1965; "Young Fury" 1965 (& story); "Johnny Reno" 1966 (& story); "Waco" 1966; "Fort Utah" 1967; "Hostile Guns" 1967; "Red Tomahawk" 1967 (& story); "Arizona Bushwhackers" 1968 (& story); "Savage Red—Outlaw White" 1974; "The Great Gundown" 1977.

Fisher, Vardis (1895-7/9/68). Writer. Films: "Jeremiah Johnson" 1972 (story).

Fisz, S. Benjamin (1922-11/17/89). Producer. Films: "A Town Called Hell" 1971-Span./Brit.

Fitch, Clyde (1865-1909). Writer. Films: "The Cowboy and the Lady" 1922 (story).

Fitch, Donald. Screenwriter. Films: "Down by the Rio Grande" 1924.

Fitts, Margaret. Screenwriter. Films: "Stars in My Crown" 1950; "King and Four Queens" 1956 (& story).

Fitzmaurice, George (1895-6/13/40). Director. Films: "Rose of the Golden West" 1927; "Tiger Rose" 1929.

Fitzroy, Louis (1870-1/26/47). Writer. Films: "The Silent Way" 1914 (story).

Fix, Paul (1902-10/14/83). Screenwriter. Films: "Tall in the Saddle" 1944.

Fizarotti, Ettore. Director. Films: "I'll Sell My Skin Dearly" 1968-Ital. (& sp.).

Flaherty, William Barby. Writer. Films: "Guns for San Sebastian" 1967-U.S./Fr./Mex./Ital. (story).

Flamini, Vincenzo. Screenwriter. Films: "He Who Shoots First" 1966-Ital.

Flannery, Mary. Screenwriter. Films: "The Thundering Herd" 1934.

Flaven, Arthur J. Director. Films: "The Gun Game" 1920; "Runnin' Straight" 1920; "When the Cougar Called" 1920; "Go Get 'Em Yates" 1922.

Fleischer, Richard (1916-). Director. Films: "Arena" 1953; "Bandido" 1956; "These Thousand Hills" 1959; "The Spikes Gang" 1974.

Fleischman, A.S. Screenwriter. Films: "The Deadly Companions" 1961.

Fleischmann, Sid (1920-). Writer. Films: "The Adventures of Bullwhip Griffin" 1967 (story).

Fleming, Caryl. Director. Films: "Beating Back" 1914 (& sp.).

Fleming, J.J. Writer. Films: "The Fighting Romeo" 1925 (story).

Fleming, Victor (1883-1/6/49). Director. Films: "The Mollycoddle" 1920; "The Call of the Canyon" 1923; "To the Last Man" 1923; "A Son of His Father" 1925; "Wolf Song" 1928 (& prod.).

Flocker, James T. Director. Films: "Grizzly and the Treasure" 1975 (& prod.); "Secret of Navajo Cave" 1977 (& prod./sp.).

Florea, John. Director. TV: *Bonanza*—"Breed of Violence" 11-5-60, "The Last Viking" 11-12-60, "Any Friend of Walter's" 3-24-63, "Rich Man, Poor Man" 5-12-63, "Twilight Town" 10-13-63, "Hoss and the Leprechauns" 12-22-63, "The Saga of Muley Jones" 3-29-64, "The Roper" 4-5-64, "Invention of a Gunfighter" 9-20-64, "Old Sheba" 11-22-64, "The Meredith Smith" 10-31-65; *The Outlaws*—"Charge!" 3-22-62; *Temple Houston* 1963; *The High Chaparral*—"Fiesta" 11-20-70; *Barbary Coast*—"The Ballad of Redwing Jail" 9-29-75.

Florey, Robert (1900-5/16/79). Director. Films: "One Hour of Love" 1927. ¶TV: *Schlitz Playhouse of the Stars*—"The Restless Gun" 3-29-57; *Wagon Train*—"The Ruth Owens Story" 10-9-57, "The Les Rand Story" 10-16-57.

Florio, Aldo. Director. Films: "Five Giants from Texas" 1968-Ital./Span.; "Dead Men Ride" 1970-Ital./Span. (& sp.).

Flothow, Rudolph C. Producer.

Films: "Black Arrow" 1944-serial; "Al Jennings of Oklahoma" 1951.

Flournoy, Richard. Screenwriter. Films: "Go West, Young Lady" 1941.

Fluharty, Vernon L. Writer. Films: "Decision at Sundown" 1957 (story).

Flynn, Emmett J. (1892-6/4/37). Director. Films: "Eastward Ho!" 1919; "Shod with Fire" 1920; "The Untamed" 1920; "The Last Trail" 1921; "Without Compromise" 1922; "Hell's Hole" 1923; "The Yankee Senor" 1925; "Three Rogues" 1931 (sp. only).

Flynn, Ray. Director. Films: "Blood WIll Tell" 1928.

Flynn, Thomas T. Writer. Films: "The Man from Laramie" 1955 (story).

Fodor, Ladislas. Screenwriter. Films: "Pyramid of the Sun God" 1965-Ger./Ital./Fr.; "Who Killed Johnny R.?" 1966-Ital./Span.; "Old Shatterhand" 1968-Ger./Yugo./Fr./Ital.

Fodor, Laszlo. Writer. Films: "North to Alaska" 1960 (story).

Fogagnolo, Franco. Screenwriter. Films: "10,000 Dollars Blood Money" 1966-Ital.

Folsey, Jr., George. Producer. Films: "Three Amigos" 1986.

Fonda, Peter (1939-). Director. Films: "The Hired Hand" 1971; "Wanda Nevada" 1979.

Fondato, Marc. Screenwriter. Films: "Two Gunmen" 1964-Span./Ital.

Fons, Jorge. Director. Films: "Jory" 1972.

Fonseca, John. Screenwriter. Films: "God's Gun" 1976-Ital./Israel.

Foote, Bradbury. Writer. Films: "Billy the Kid" 1941 (story).

Foote, John Tainton (1881-1/28/50). Screenwriter. Films: "Mark of Zorro" 1940.

Ford, Charles E. Producer. Films: "Billy the Kid Returns" 1938; "Man from Music Mountain" 1938; "Shine on Harvest Moon" 1938; "Come On, Rangers" 1939.

Ford, Dennis. *see* Fidani, Demofilo.

Ford, Francis (1882-9/5/53). Director. Films: "Army Surgeon" 1912; "The Ball Player and the Bandit" 1912; "Custer's Last Fight" 1912; "The Invaders" 1912; "A Frontier Wife" 1913; "Texas Kelly at Bay" 1913; "Wynona's Vengeance" 1913; "Shorty Turns Judge" 1914; "Shorty's

Sacrifice" 1914; "Shorty's Strategy" 1914; "Shorty's Trip to Mexico" 1914; "Three Bad Men and a Girl" 1915; "The Bandit's Wager" 1916 (& sp.); "The Dumb Bandit" 1916; "The Unexpected" 1916; "John Ermine of the Yellowstone" 1917; "The Man from Nowhere" 1920; "Cyclone Bliss" 1921; "I Am the Woman" 1921; "The Stampede" 1921; "Angel Citizens" 1922; "Cross Roads" 1922; "The Gold Grabbers" 1922; "So This Is Arizona" 1922; "Trail's End" 1922; "The Cowboy Prince" 1924; "Cupid's Rustler" 1924 (& sp.); "Lash of the Whip" 1924 (& sp.); "Midnight Shadows" 1924 (& sp.); "Range Blood" 1924 (& sp.); "A Rodeo Mixup" 1924 (& sp.); "Western Feuds" 1924; "Western Yesterdays" 1924 (& sp.); "Wolf's Trail" 1927; "Call of the Heart" 1928; "The Tell Tale Hat Band" 1933.

Ford, Hugh. Director. Films: "In Mizzoura" 1919.

Ford, John (1894-8/31/73). Director. Films: "Bucking Broadway" 1917; "Cheyenne's Pal" 1917; "A Marked Man" 1917; "The Scrapper" 1917 (& sp.); "The Secret Man" 1917 (& sp.); "The Soul Herder" 1917; "Straight Shooting" 1917; "The Tornado" 1917 (& sp.); "The Trail of Hate" 1917 (& sp.); "Hell Bent" 1918 (& sp.); "The Phantom Riders" 1918; "The Scarlet Drop" 1918; "Thieves' Gold" 1918; "Three Mounted Men" 1918; "Wild Women" 1918; "A Woman's Fool" 1918; "The Ace of the Saddle" 1919; "Bare Fists" 1919; "By Indian Post" 1919; "A Fight for Love" 1919; "The Fighting Brothers" 1919; "A Gun Fightin' Gentleman" 1919; "Gun Law" 1919; "The Gun Packer" 1919; "The Last Outlaw" 1919; "Marked Men" 1919; "The Outcasts of Poker Flat" 1919; "The Rider of the Law" 1919; "Riders of Vengeance" 1919 (& story); "Roped" 1919; "Hitchin's Posts" 1920; "Just Pals" 1920; "Action" 1921; "The Big Punch" 1921; "Desperate Trails" 1921; "The Freeze-Out" 1921; "The Wallop" 1921; "Sure Fire" 1921; "Three Jumps Ahead" 1923 (& story); "The Iron Horse" 1924; "North of Hudson Bay" 1924; "Three Bad Men" 1926; "The Last Outlaw" 1936 (story only); "Drums Along the Mohawk" 1939; "Stagecoach" 1939; "My Darling Clementine" 1946; "Fort Apache" 1948 (& prod.); "The Three Godfathers" 1948 (& prod.); "She Wore a Yellow Ribbon" 1949 (& prod.); "Rio Grande" 1950 (& prod.); "Wagonmaster" 1950 (& prod. & story); "The Searchers" 1956; "The Horse Soldiers" 1959; "Sergeant Rutledge" 1960; "Two Rode Together" 1961;

"How the West Was Won" 1962; "The Man Who Shot Liberty Valance" 1962; "Cheyenne Autumn" 1964. ¶TV: *Wagon Train*—"The Colter Craven Story" 11-23-60.

Ford, Luci. Screenwriter. Films: "Trail to San Antone" 1947.

Ford, Patrick. Producer. Films: "Wagonmaster" 1940 (sp. only): "The Missouri Traveler" 1958; "The Young Land" 1959; "Sergeant Rutledge" 1960.

Ford, Paul Leicester. Writer. Films: "The Great K & A Train Robbery" 1926 (story).

Ford, Philip (1900-1/12/76). Director. Films: "Bandits of Dark Canyon" 1947; "The Wild Frontier" 1947; "The Bold Frontiersman" 1948; "California Firebrand" 1948; "The Denver Kid" 1948; "Desperadoes of Dodge City" 1948; "Marshal of Amarillo" 1948; "The Timber Trail" 1948; "Law of the Golden West" 1949; "Outcasts of the Trail" 1949; "Pioneer Marshal" 1949; "Powder River Rustlers" 1949; "Prince of the Plains" 1949; "Ranger of Cherokee Strip" 1949; "San Antone Ambush" 1949; "South of Rio" 1949; "The Wyoming Bandit" 1949; "The Old Frontier" 1950; "Redwood Forest Trail" 1950; "The Vanishing Westerner" 1950; "Buckaroo Sheriff of Texas" 1951; "The Dakota Kid" 1951; "Rodeo King and the Senorita" 1951; "Utah Wagon Train" 1951; "Wells Fargo Gunmaster" 1951; "Desperadoes' Outpost" 1952.

Ford, Wallace W. (1898-6/11/66). Director. Films: "Trail to Vengeance" 1945 (& prod.).

Forde, Eugene (1898-1986). Director. Films: "Daredevil's Reward" 1928; "Hello Cheyenne" 1928; "Painted Post" 1928; "Son of the Golden West" 1928; "The Big Diamond Robbery" 1929; "Outlawed" 1929; "Smoky" 1933; "The Country Beyond" 1936.

Forde, Victoria (1896-7/24/64). Writer. Films: "An Eventful Evening" 1916 (story).

Fordson, John W. *see* Costa, Mario.

Foreman, Carl (1915-6/26/84). Screenwriter. Films: "Dakota" 1945 (story only); "High Noon" 1952.

Foreman, Carol. Screenwriter. Films: "Mackenna's Gold" 1969 (& prod.).

Foreman, John (1925-11/20/92). Producer. Films: "Butch Cassidy and the Sundance Kid" 1969; "The Life and Times of Judge Roy Bean" 1972; "Pocket Money" 1972.

Foreman, L.L. (1901-). Writer. Films: "The Savage" 1952 (story); "Arrow in the Dust" 1954 (story); "The Gambler Wore a Gun" 1961 (story).

Forester, Frank (Donal Mooch). Screenwriter. Films: "Bullets Don't Argue" 1964-Ital./Ger./Span.

Forman, Eddie. Screenwriter. Films: "Skipalong Rosenbloom" 1951.

Forman, Henry James (1879-1966). Writer. Film: "The Pony Express" 1925 (story).

Forman, Tom (1892-11/7/26). Director. Films: "The Desert Breed" 1915 (sp. only); "The Round Up" 1920 (sp. only); "The Virginian" 1923; "The Flaming Forties" 1925; "Whispering Canyon" 1926.

Forrester, Izola. Writer. Films: "The Quitter" 1916 (story).

Forslund, Bengi. Screenwriter. Films: "The New Land" 1973-Swed. (& prod.).

Forst, Emil. Screenwriter. Films: "Prowlers of the Night" 1926.

Fort, Garrett (1898-10/26/45). Screenwriter. Films: "White Gold" 1927; "Mark of Zorro" 1940 (adapt. only).

Forte, Vincent. Writer. Films: "Wild Women" TVM-1970 (story).

Fortune, Jan. Screenwriter. Films: "The Dark Command" 1940; "The Vanishing Virginian" 1941.

Foster, Bennett. Writer. Films: "The Desperados Are in Town" 1956 (story).

Foster, Harry (1906-7/13/85). Producer. TV: *Cheyenne* 1955-63.

Foster, John. Writer. Films: "Westbound Stage" 1939 (story only).

Foster, Lewis R. (1899-6/10/74). Director. Films: "El Paso" 1949 (& sp.); "The Eagle and the Hawk" 1950 (& sp.); "The Last Outpost" 1951; "Passage West" 1951 (& sp.); "Those Redheads from Seattle" 1953 (& sp.); "The Vanquished" 1953 (sp. only); "Dakota Incident" 1956; "Tonka" 1958 (& sp.). ¶TV: *Jim Bowie* 1956-58 (prod.); *Zorro*—"Zorro's Romance" 11-7-57, "Zorro Saves a Friend" 11-14-57, "Monastario Sets a Trap" 11-21-57, "Zorro's Ride into Terror" 11-28-57; *Walt Disney Presents*—"Daniel Boone" 1960-61.

Foster, Norman (1900-7/7/76). Director. Films: "Fair Warning" 1937 (& sp.); "Viva Cisco Kid" 1940; "Rachel and the Stranger" 1948; "Navajo" 1952 (& sp.); "Sky Full of Moon" 1952 (& sp.); "Davy Crockett, King of the Wild Frontier" 1955; "Davy Crockett and the River Pi-

rates" 1956 (& sp.); "Indian Paint" 1965 (& sp.). ¶TV: *Walt Disney Presents*—"Davy Crockett" 1954-55, "Elfego Baca" 1958-60; *Zorro*—"Presenting Senor Zorro" 10-10-57, "Zorro's Secret Passage" 10-17-57, "Zorro Rides to the Mission" 10-24-57, "The Ghost of the Mission" 10-31-57, "A Fair Trial" 12-5-57, "Garcia's Sweet Mission" 12-12-57, "Double Trouble for Zorro" 12-19-57, "The Luckiest Swordsman Alive" 12-26-57, "The Fall of Monastario" 1-2-58, "The Secret of the Sierra" 3-13-58, "The New Commandante" 3-20-58, "The Fox and the Coyote" 3-26-58; *The Monroes*—"To Break a Colt" 1-11-67, "Race for the Rainbow" 1-18-67, "Trapped" 2-22-67, "Teach the Tigers to Purr" 3-8-67.

Foster, W. Bert. Writer. Films: "Bulldog Pluck" 1927 (story).

Fournier, Claude. Director. Films: "Dan Candy's Law" 1975-U.S./Can.

Fowler, Gene (1890-7/2/60). Screenwriter. Films: "Call of the Wild" 1935; "Billy the Kid" 1941; "White Fang" 1936; "Big Jack" 1949.

Fowler, Jr., Gene. Director. Films: "My Brother, the Outlaw" 1951 (sp. only); "Showdown at Boot Hill" 1958; "The Oregon Trail" 1959 (& sp.). ¶TV: *Rawhide*—"Incident at Red River Station" 1-15-60, "Incident at Tinker's Dam" 2-5-60; *Gunsmoke*—"Harriet" 3-4-61.

Fox, Finis (1884-11/7/49). Screenwriter. Films: "Isobel, or the Trail's End" 1920; "Penny of Top Hill Trail" 1921; "Border Patrol" 1928; "Ramona" 1928.

Fox, Frederic Louis. Screenwriter. Films: "Dakota Incident" 1956; "Charro!" 1969 (story only).

Fox, Norman A. (1911-60). Writer. Films: "Gunsmoke" 1953 (story); "Overland Pacific" 1954 (story); "Tall Man Riding" 1955 (story); "The Rawhide Years" 1956 (story); "Night Passage" 1957 (story).

Fox, Stephen. Screenwriter. Films: "Six Feet Four" 1919; "Some Liar" 1919; "This Hero Stuff" 1919; "When a Man Rides Alone" 1919; "Where the West Begins" 1919.

Fox, Wallace W. (1895-6/30/58). Director. Films: "The Bandit's Son" 1927; "The Avenging Rider" 1928; "Breed of the Sunsets" 1928; "Driftin' Sands" 1928; "Man in the Rough" 1928; "The Riding Renegade" 1928; "The Trail of Courage" 1928; "The Amazing Vagabond" 1929; "Near the Trail's End" 1931; "Partners of the Trail" 1931; "Powdersmoke Range" 1935; "Yellow Dust" 1936; "Gun Packer" 1938; "Mexicali Kid" 1938; "Blazing Bullets" 1941; "Bullets for Bandits" 1942; "The Lone Star Vigilantes" 1942; "The Ghost Rider" 1943; "Outlaws of Stampede Pass" 1943; "Pride of the Plains" 1944; "Riders of the Santa Fe" 1944; "Song of the Range" 1944; "Bad Men of the Border" 1945 (& prod.); "Code of the Lawles" 1945 (& prod.); "Rustler's Roundup" 1946 (& prod.); "Gun Town" 1946 (& prod.); "Gunman's Code" 1946 (& prod.); "The Lawless Breed" 1946 (& prod.); "Wild Beauty" 1946 (& prod.); "The Vigilante" 1947-serial; "The Valiant Hombre" 1948; "The Daring Caballero" 1949; "The Gay Amigo" 1949; "Western Renegades" 1949; "Arizona Territory" 1950; "Fence Riders" 1950 (& prod.); "Outlaw Gold" 1950; "Over the Border" 1950 (& prod.); "Silver Raiders" 1950; "Six Gun Mesa" 1950; "Gunslingers" 1950 (& prod.); "West of Wyoming" 1950; "Montana Desperado" 1951. ¶TV: *The Gene Autry Show*—"Heir to the Lazy L" 12-29-51, "Horse Sense" 1-11-52, "Outlaw Stage" 7-21-53, "Border Justice" 8-18-53, "Cold Decked" 9-15-53.

Fox, William (1879-5/8/52). Producer. Films: "Just Tony" 1922; "The Iron Horse" 1924; "The Last of the Duanes" 1924; "The Rainbow Trail" 1925; "The Great K & A Train Robbery" 1926.

Foy, Bryan (1897-4/20/77). Producer. Films: "Moonlight on the Prairie" 1935; "Song of the Saddle" 1936; "Trailin' West" 1936; "Treachery Rides the Range" 1936; "The California Mail" 1937; "Cherokee Strip" 1937; "The Devil's Saddle Legion" 1937; "Empty Holsters" 1937; "Guns of the Pecos" 1937; "Land Beyond the Law" 1937; "Prairie Thunder" 1937; "Heart of the North" 1938; "Cattle Town" 1952; "The Lion and the Horse" 1952.

Fraker, William A. (1923-). Director. Films: "Monte Walsh" 1970; "The Legend of the Lone Ranger" 1981.

Frame, Park. Director. Films: "The Gray Wolf's Ghost" 1919; "The Mints of Hell" 1919; "Looped for Life" 1924; "Drug Store Cowboy" 1925.

Franchi, Fernando. Screenwriter. Films: "Execution" 1968-Ital./Fr. (& prod.).

Franchon, Leonard. Director. Films: "Cotton and Cattle" 1921; "A Cowboy Ace" 1921; "Flowing Gold" 1921; "Out of the Clouds 1921; "The

Range Pirate" 1921; "Rustlers of the Night" 1921; "The Trail to Red Dog" 1921.

Franciosa, Massimo. Screenwriter. Films: "Calibre .38" 1971-Ital.

Francis, Owen. Screenwriter. Films: "Man from Montreal" 1940; "Shooting High" 1940.

Franco, Jess. Director. Films: "Jaguar" 1964-Span. (& sp.).

Frank, Bruno. Writer. Films: "Sutter's Gold" 1936 (story).

Frank, Frederic M. Screenwriter. Films: "Unconquered" 1947.

Frank, Jr., Harriett. Screenwriter. Films: "Silver River" 1948; "Run for Cover" 1955 (story only); "Ten Wanted Men" 1955 (story only); "Hombre" 1967; "The Cowboys" 1972; "The Spikes Gang" 1974.

Frank, Jacqun. Screenwriter. Films: "The Block Trail" 1943.

Frank, Melvin (1913-10/13/88). Director. Films: "Callaway Went Thataway" 1951 (& prod./sp.); "The Jayhawkers" 1959 (& prod./sp.); "The Duchess and the Dirtwater Fox" 1976 (& prod./sp.).

Frank, T.C. *see* Laughlin, Tom

Frankenberg, Julius. Director. Films: "Humanizing Mr. Winsby" 1916; "The Land Just Over Yonder" 1916.

Franklin, Chester M. (1890-3/12/54). Director. Films: "Six-Shooter Andy" 1918; "The Painted Hills" 1951 (prod. only).

Franklin, George Cory. Writer. Films: "Trigger Tom" 1935 (story); "Prairie Schooners" 1940 (story).

Franklin, Harry L. (1880-7/3/27) Director. Films: "Her Five-Foot Highness" 1920.

Franklin, Harry S. Writer. Films: "Gun Fever" 1958 (story).

Franklin, Paul. Screenwriter. Films: "Headin' East" 1937; "Outlaws of the Orient" 1937; "Roaring Timber" 1937; "Secret Valley" 1937; "Rhythm of the Saddle" 1938; "The Man from Sundown" 1939; "Spoilers of the Range" 1939; "The Stranger from Texas" 1939; "Timber Stampede" 1939 (story only); "Blazing Six Shooters" 1940; "The Durango Kid" 1940; "Thundering Frontier" 1940; "West of Abilene" 1940; "Across the Sierras" 1941; "Hands Across the Rockies" 1941; "Outlaws of the Panhandle" 1941; "The Return of Daniel Boone" 1941 (& story); "Down Rio Grande Way" 1942; "Overland to Deadwood" 1942; "Riders of the Northland" 1942; "Thundering Hoofs" 1942; "Ride, Ryder, Ride"

1949; "Roll, Thunder, Roll" 1949; "The Fighting Redhead" 1950; "Fighting Bill Fargo" 1952.

Franklin, Sidney (1893-5/18/72). Director. Films: "Six-Shooter Andy" 1918; "The Heart of Wetona" 1919; "Tiger Rose" 1923; "Gypsy Colt" 1954 (prod. only).

Franklin, Jr., Sidney A. Director. Films: "Sky Full of Moon" 1952 (prod. only); "Gun Battle at Monterey" 1957.

Franklyn, Irwin. Screenwriter. Films: "Daughter of the West" 1949.

Frankovitch, Mike J. (1910-1/1/92). Producer. Films: "Jesse James Rides Again" 1947-serial; "Dangers of the Canadian Mounted" 1948-serial; "From Noon to Three" 1976; "The Shootist" 1976.

Frant, Morton. Screenwriter. Films: "Riding the Wind" 1942.

Franz, Joseph J. (1884-9/9/70). Director. Films: "The Gun Men of Plumas" 1914; "The Dawn Road" 1915 (& sp.); "The Ghost Wagon" 1915; "The Superior Claim" 1915; "Bare-Fisted Gallagher" 1919; "The Blue Bandanna" 1919; "A Sage Brush Hamlet" 1919; "A Broadway Cowboy" 1920; "The Love Gambler" 1922; "Smiling Jim" 1922; "Tracks" 1922; "Youth Must Have Love" 1922; "Stepping Fast" 1923; "Horseshoe Luck" 1924; "Blue Blazes" 1926; "The Desperate Game" 1926.

Fraser, Harry (Harry C. Christ, Harry O. Jones, Weston Edwards) (1889-4/8/74). Director. Films: "The Wildcat" 1919; "Queen of Spades" 1925; "West of Mojave" 1925; "Sheep Trail" 1926; "Cactus Trails" 1927 (sp. only); "General Custer at Little Big Horn" 1927; "Wings of Adventure" 1930 (sp./story only); "Cavalier of the West" 1931 (sp. only); "The Montana Kid" 1931 (& story); "Oklahoma Jim" 1931 (& story); "Border Devils" 1932; "Broadway to Cheyenne" 1932 (& sp.); "Ghost City" 1932 (& sp.); "Honor of the Mounted" 1932; "Land of Wanted Men" 1932 (& sp.); "Law of the North" 1932 (& sp.); "The Man from Arizona" 1932; "Mason of the Mounted" 1932 (& sp.); "The Night Rider" 1932 (sp. only); "Texas Pioneers" 1932 (& story); "Vanishing Men" 1932; "Without Honor" 1932 (sp. only); "Diamond Trail" 1933 (& sp.); "The Fighting Parson" 1933 (& sp.); "The Fugitive" 1933 (& sp.); "The Gallant Fool" 1933 (sp. only); "Galloping Romero" 1933 (sp. only); "Rainbow Ranch" 1933 (& story); "The Ranger's Code" 1933; "Trailing

North" 1933 (story only); "Fighting Through" 1934 (& sp.); "'Neath the Arizona Skies" 1934; "Randy Rides Alone" 1934; "Fighting Pioneers" 1935 (& sp.); "Gunfire" 1935 (& sp.).; "The Last of the Clintons" 1935 (& sp.); "The Reckless Buckaroo" 1935; "Rustlers' Paradise" 1935 (& sp.); "Saddle Aces" 1935 (& sp.); "Tonto Kid" 1935 (& sp.); "Wagon Trail" 1935; "Wild Mustang" 1935 (& sp.); "Cavalcade of the West" 1936; "Feud of the West" 1936; "Ghost Town" 1936 (& sp.); "Hair-Trigger Casey" 1936; "The Riding Avenger" 1936; "Romance Rides the Range" 1936; "Wildcat Saunders" 1936; "Aces Wild" 1937; "Galloping Dynamite" 1937; "Heroes of the Alamo" 1938; "Six Shootin' Sheriff" 1938 (& sp.); "Songs and Saddles" 1938 (& sp.); "Lure of the Wasteland" 1939; "Lightning Strikes West" 1940; "Phantom Rancher" 1940; "Old Chisholm Trail" 1942 (story only); "Valley of Vanishing Men" 1942-serial (sp. only); "Tenting Tonight on the Old Camp Ground" 1943 (story only); "Brand of the Devil" 1944; "Dead or Alive" 1944 (sp. only); "Gunsmoke Mesa" 1944; "Outlaw Roundup" 1944; "The Whispering Skull" 1944 (sp. only); "Enemy of the Law" 1945 (& sp.); "Flaming Bullets" 1945 (& sp.); "Frontier Fugitives" 1945; "The Navajo Kid" 1945 (& sp.); "Three in the Saddle" 1945; "Ambush Trail" 1946; "Six Gun Man" 1946 (& sp.); "Thunder Town" 1946; "Tex Granger" 1948-serial (sp. only); "Stallion Canyon" 1949; "Abilene Trail" 1951 (sp. only).

Frasier, Harry L. Director. Films: "Little Big Horn" 1927.

Frawley, James (1937-). Director. Films: "Kid Blue" 1973. ¶TV: *The Texas Wheelers* 1974.

Frazee, Steve (1909-). Writer. Films: "Running Target" 1956 (story); "Wild Heritage" 1958 (story); "Gold of the Seven Saints" 1961 (story).

Frazer, Elizabeth. Writer. Films: "The Marshal's Capture" 1913 (story); "A Muddle in Horse Thieves" 1913 (story).

Freda, Riccardo (George Lincoln). Director. Films: "Death at Owell Rock" 1967-Ital. (& sp.).

Frederick, Beatrice. Screenwriter. Films: "Across the Divide" 1921.

Frederickson, Gray. Writer. Films: "Bad Girls" 1994 (story).

Freed, Arthur (1894-4/12/73). Producer. Films: "The Harvey Girls" 1946; "Annie Get Your Gun" 1950.

Freedle, Sam C. Screenwriter. Films: "Gun the Man Down" 1957 (story only); "Gun Street" 1961.

Freedman, Benedict (1919-). Writer. Films: "Mrs. Mike" 1949 (story).

Freedman, Hy. Screenwriter. Films: "The Phantom Empire" 1935-serial (story only).

Freedman, Nancy (1920-). Writer. Films: "Mrs. Mike" 1949 (story).

Freeman, Bud. Screenwriter. Films: "Female Artillery" TVM-1973 (& story).

Freeman, Devery. Screenwriter. Films: "The First Traveling Saleslady" 1956 (& prod.).

Freeman, Harry. *see* Zabalza, Jose Maria

Freeman, Leonard (1921-1/20/74). Screenwriter. Films: "Gold of the Seven Saints" 1961 (& prod.); "Hang 'Em High" 1968 (& prod.).

Freeman, Paul. Producer. Films: "The Chisholms" TVM-1979; "The Mystic Warrior" TVM-1984. ¶TV: *The Chisholms* 1980.

Freers, Rick. Director. Films: "Scorching Fury" 1952.

Fregonese, Hugo (1908-1/17/87). Director. Films: "Saddle Tramp" 1950; "Apache Drums" 1951; "Mark of the Renegade" 1951; "Untamed Frontier" 1952; "Blowing Wild" 1953; "Savage Pampas" 1966-U.S./Span./Arg. (& sp.); "Find a Place to Die" 1968-Ital.; "Old Shatterhand" 1968-Ger./Yugo./Fr./Ital.

Freiberger, Fred. Writer. Films: "War Paint" 1953 (story); "Garden of Evil" 1954 (story); "Massacre" 1956 (story); "Blood Arrow" 1958 (sp.). ¶TV: *A Man Called Shenandoah* 1965-66 (prod.); *Wild Wild West* 1965-69 (prod.).

Freiwald, Eric. Screenwriter. Films: "Raiders of Tomahawk Creek" 1950 (story only); "The Lone Ranger and the Lost City of Gold" 1958.

French, Charles K. (1860-8/2/52). Screenwriter. Films: "Davy Crockett in Hearts United" 1909; "A True Indian's Heart" 1909; "His Punishment" 1912; "His Partner's Sacrifice" 1915.

French, Lloyd (1900-5/24/50). Director. Films: "Bar Buckaroos" 1940-short (& sp.); "California or Bust" 1941-short (& sp.).

French, Victor (1934-6/15/89). Director. Films: "Little House on the Prairie: Look Back to Yesterday" TVM-1983; "Little House: Bless All the Dear Children" TVM-1984.

¶TV: *Gunsmoke*—"Matt Dillon Must Die" 9-9-74, "The Wiving" 10-14-74, "The Hiders" 1-13-75, "The Fires of Ignorance" 1-27-75, "Brides and Grooms" 2-10-75; *Little House on the Prairie* 1974-82; *Little House: A New Beginning* 1982.

Friedenberg, Richard. Director. Films: "The Life and Times of Grizzly Adams" 1975; "The Adventures of Frontier Fremont" 1976; "The Deerslayer" TVM-1978.

Friedkin, David. TV: *The Rifleman*—"The Clarence Bibbs Story" 4-4-61; *The Virginian*—"The Executioners" 9-19-62, "The Man Who Couldn't Die" 1-30-63; *Bearcats!* 1971 (prod.).

Friedlander, Howard. Screenwriter. Films: "Kung Fu" TVM-1972.

Friedlander, Louis. *see* Landers, Lew.

Friedman, I.K. Writer. Films: "How Callahan Cleaned Up Little Hell" 1915 (story).

Friedman, Harry. Screenwriter. Films: "Westward Ho" 1935.

Friedman, Ken. Screenwriter. Films: "Bad Girls" 1994.

Friedman, Seymour. Director. Films: "Secret of Treasure Mountain" 1956.

Friedman, Sherwood. Screenwriter. Films: "The Wackiest Wagon Train in the West" 1976.

Friedman, Stephen. Screenwriter. Films: "Lovin' Molly" 1974 (& prod.).

Friend, Oscar J. Writer. Films: "The Phantom Bullet" 1926 (story).

Friend, Robert L. Director. TV: *They Went Thataway*—Pilot 8-15-60; *Rawhide*—"The Prairie Elephant" 11-17-61, "Twenty-five Santa Clauses" 12-22-61, "The Diehard" 4-9-65; *The Monroes*—"Court Martial" 11-16-66, "Silent Night, Deathly Night" 11-23-66; *Bonanza*—"Catch as Catch Can" 10-27-68, "The Sound of Drums" 11-17-68; *The High Chaparral*—"Sea of Enemies" 1-3-69, "Bad Day for Bad Men" 10-17-69.

Friendly, Ed. Producer. Films: "Young Pioneers" TVM-1976; "Young Pioneers' Christmas" TVM-1976; "Peter Lundy and the Medicine Hat Stallion" TVM-1977. ¶TV: *The Young Pioneers* 1978 (exec. prod.).

Friml, Rudolf (1879-11/12/72). Writer. Films: "Rose Marie" 1936 (story); "Rose Marie" 1954 (story).

Fritsch, George. Director. TV: *Bronco* 1958; *Lawman* 1958.

Fritz, Joseph. Screenwriter. Films: "Walk Tall" 1960.

Fritzell, Jim. Screenwriter. Films: "The Shakiest Gun in the West" 1968.

Froeschel, George (1891-11/22/79). Screenwriter. Films: "Rose Marie" 1954.

Fromkess, Leon. Producer. Films: "Blood on the Arrow" 1964; "The Great Sioux Massacre" 1965. ¶TV: *Fury* 1955-60.

Frost, R.L. Director. Films: "Hot Spur" 1968 (& sp.); "The Scavengers" 1969.

Fuentes, Carlos (1928-). Writer. Films: "Old Gringo" 1989 (story).

Fulci, Lucio (1927-). Director. Films: "Massacre Time" 1966-Ital./Span./Ger.; "Four Horsemen of the Apocalypse" 1975-Ital. (& sp.); "Silver Saddle" 1978-Ital. (& sp.).

Fulgozzi, Niska. Director. Films: "Deserter" 1970-U.S./Ital./Yugo.

Fuller, Michael W. Screenwriter. Films: "Peace for a Gunfighter" 1967.

Fuller, Samuel (1911-). Director. Films: "I Shot Jesse James" 1949 (& sp.); "The Baron of Arizona" 1950 (& sp.); "The Command" 1953 (sp. only); "Forty Guns" 1957 (& prod./sp.); "Run of the Arrow" 1957 (& prod./sp.); "Deadly Trackers" 1973 (story only).

Furey, Bernard. Writer. Films: "Headin' North" 1922 (story).

Furie, Sidney J. (1933-) Director. Films: "The Appaloosa" 1966. ¶TV: *Hudson's Bay*—"Sally MacGregor" 2-15-58, "His Name Was Choctaw" 2-22-58, "The Accounting" 3-1-58, "Batiste LeGrande" 3-8-58, "Montgomery Velvet" 3-15-58, "The Drummer Boy" 3-22-58, "Warrant's Depot" 3-29-58, "Civilization" 4-12-58, "Fort Caribou" 4-19-58, "The Northern Cheyenne" 4-26-59, "The Executioner" 5-3-58.

Furthman, Jules G. (1888-9/22/66). Screenwriter. Films: "The Iron Rider" 1920; "Twins of Suffering Creek" 1920; "The Big Punch" 1921; "Colorado Pluck" 1921 (& sp.); "The Last Trail" 1921; "Singing River" 1921; "The Love Gambler" 1922; "North of Hudson Bay" 1924; "Call of the Mate" 1934; "The Outlaw" 1943; "Rio Bravo" 1959.

Fusco, John. Screenwriter. Films: "Young Guns" 1988; "Young Guns II" 1990.

Futter, Walter. Producer. Films: "Swifty" 1935; "Cavalcade of the West" 1936; "Feud of the West" 1936; "Frontier Justice" 1936; "Lucky Terror" 1936; "The Riding Avenger" 1936.

Fyles, Franklyn. Writer. Films: "The Girl I Left Behind Me" 1915 (story).

Gaddis, Pearl. Writer. Films: "The Ghost of the Hacienda" 1913 (story).

Gaiser, Gerald. Screenwriter. Films: "The Trackers" TVM-1971.

Gale, Bob. Screenwriter. Films: "Back to the Future, Part III" 1990 (& prod.).

Galiano, Vittorio. Producer. Films: "Arizona" 1970-Ital./Span.; "God in Heaven ... Arizona on Earth" 1972-Span./Ital.

Gallico, Paul (1897-7/15/76). Writer. Films: "Miracle in the Wilderness" TVM-1991 (story).

Gamet, Kenneth (1904-10/13/71). Screenwriter. Films: "Adventures in Silverado" 1948; "Coroner Creek" 1948; "Thunderhoof" 1948; "The Doolins of Oklahoma" 1949; "The Savage Horde" 1950; "Indian Uprising" 1951; "Man in the Saddle" 1951; "Santa Fe" 1951; "Last of the Comanches" 1952; "The Last Posse" 1953; "The Stranger Wore a Gun" 1953; "Hell's Outpost" 1954; "A Lawless Street" 1955; "Ten Wanted Men" 1955; "The Maverick Queen" 1956; "Domino Kid" 1957; "The Lawless Eighties" 1958.

Gamon, Marshall E. Writer. Films: "With the Aid of the Law" 1915 (story).

Gangelin, Paul (1897-9/25/61). Screenwriter. Films: "The Breed of the Border" 1924; "The No-Gun Man" 1925; "Arizona Bound" 1927; "Blood Will Tell" 1928; "Cowboy Canteen" 1944; "The Daltons Ride Again" 1945; "My Pal Trigger" 1946 (story only); "Roll on, Texas Moon" 1946; "Under Nevada Skies" 1946; "Son of God's Country" 1948; "Under California Stars" 1948 (& story); "Sons of New Mexico" 1949.

Gannaway, Albert C. Director. Films: "Hidden Guns" 1956 (& prod./sp.); "The Badge of Marshal Brennan" 1957 (& prod.); "Daniel Boone, Trail Blazer" 1957 (& prod.); "Raiders of Old California" 1957 (& prod.); "Man or Gun" 1958; "Plunderers of Painted Flats" 1959 (& prod.); "Buffalo Gun" 1961.

Ganz, Lowell. Screenwriter. Films: "City Slickers" 1991; "City Slickers II: The Legend of Curly's Gold" 1994.

Ganz, Serge. Screenwriter. Films: "Guns for San Sebastian" 1967-U.S./Fr./Mex./Ital.

Ganzer, Alvin. Director. TV: *Broken Arrow* 1956; *Laramie* 1959; *Have Gun Will Travel*—"The Gladiators" 3-19-60; *Temple Houston* 1963; *Wild Wild West*—"The Night That Terror Stalked the Town" 11-19-65; *Gunsmoke*—"Sweet Billy, Singer of Songs" 1-15-66, "The Jackals" 2-12-68; *Cimarron Strip*—"The Hunted" 10-5-67, "Till the End of the Night" 11-16-67, "The Deputy" 12-21-67.

Ganzhorn, Jack. Writer. Films: "Prairie Gunsmoke" 1942 (story).

Garcia, Ronald V. Screenwriter. Films: "Machismo—40 Graves for 40 Guns" 1970 (& prod.).

Gardner, Arthur. Producer. Films: "The Glory Guys" 1965; "The Scalphunters" 1968; "Sam Whiskey" 1969; "The Honkers" 1972. ¶TV: *The Rifleman* 1958-63; *Law of the Plainsman* 1959-60 (exec. prod.); *The Big Valley* 1965-69 (exec. prod.).

Gardner, Richard (1931-). Writer. Films: "Scandalous John" 1971 (story).

Garfield, Brian (1939-). Writer. Films: "The Last Hard Men" 1976 (story); "Wild Times" TVM-1980 (story).

Garfield, Frank. *see* Giraldi, Franco.

Garfield, Warren. Screenwriter. Films: "A Stranger in Town" 1966-U.S./Ital.

Garfinkle, Louis. Screenwriter. Films: "The Young Guns" 1956; "The Hellbenders" 1966-U.S./Ital./Span.; "A Minute to Pray, a Second to Die" 1967-Ital.

Gariazzo, Mario (Robert Paget). Director. Films: "God Will Forgive My Pistol" 1969-Ital. (& sp.); "Holy Water Joe" 1971-Ital. (& sp.); "In the Name of the Father, the Son and the Colt" 1972-Fr./Ital. (sp. only); "Drummer of Vengeance" 1974-Brit./Ital. (& prod./sp.).

Garland, Hamlin (1860-3/4/40). Writer. Films: "The Captain of the Gray Horse Troop" 1917 (story); "Cavanaugh of the Forest Rangers" 1918; (story); "Ranger of the Big Pines" 1925 (story).

Garland, Robert. Screenwriter. Films: "The Electric Horseman" 1979.

Garmes, Lee (1898-8/31/78). Director. Films: "Hannah Lee" 1953 (& prod.).

Garnet, Kenneth. Screenwriter. Films: "Canadian Pacific" 1949.

Garnett, Tay (1898-10/3/77). Director. Films: "White Gold" 1927 (sp. only); "Cattle King" 1963. ¶TV: *Wagon Train*—"The Kate Parker Story" 5-6-59, "The Jose Maria Moran Story" 5-27-59, "The Candy O'Hara Story" 12-7-60; *The Deputy* 1959; *Laramie* 1959; *Gunsmoke*— "Nina's Revenge" 12-16-61, "He Learned About Women" 2-24-62, "The Brothers" 3-12-66; *Rawhide*— "The Captain's Wife" 1-12-62, "The Immigrants" 3-16-62, "The House of the Hunter" 4-20-62; *Bonanza*— "The Toy Soldier" 10-20-63, "The Lila Conrad Story" 1-5-64, "Bullet for a Bride" 2-16-64, "Love Me Not" 3-1-64, "The Pressure Game" 5-10-64, "Triangle" 5-17-64.

Garraway, Tom. Producer. Films: "Jesse James' Women" 1954; "Frontier Woman" 1956.

Garrett, Grant. Screenwriter. Films: "Home on the Range" 1935; "Barbary Coast Gent" 1944; "Bad Bascomb" 1946.

Garrett, Oliver H.P. (1894-2/22/52). Screenwriter. Films: "The Texan" 1930; "Duel in the Sun" 1946.

Garrido, Consuelo. Screenwriter. Films: "My Dear Tom Mix" 1992-Mex.

Garrison, Michael (1923-8/17/66). Producer. TV: *Wild Wild West* 1965-66 (exec. prod.).

Garrone, Sergio (Willy S. Regan). Director. Films: "Deguello" 1966-Ital. (sp. only); "If You Want to Live ... Shoot!" 1967-Ital./Span. (& sp.); "Killer Kid" 1967-Ital.; "No Graves on Boot Hill" 1968-Ital. (& sp.); "Django the Bastard" 1969-Ital./Span. (& sp.); "No Room to Die" 1969-Ital. (& sp.); "Bastard, Go and Kill" 1971-Ital. (sp. only); "Kill Django ... Kill First" 1971-Ital. (& sp.); "Vendetta at Dawn" 1971-Ital. (& sp.).

Garson, Harry (1882-9/21/38). Director. Films: "The Breed of the Border" 1924; "The Millionaire Cowboy" 1924; "The No-Gun Man" 1925; "O.U. West" 1925.

Garth, David. Writer. Films: "Fury at Furnace Creek" 1948 (story).

Garwood, William (1884-12/28/50). Director. Films: "A Proxy Husband" 1919.

Gary, Eileen. Screenwriter. Films: "Law of the Canyon" 1947; "Over the Santa Fe Trail" 1947 (story only).

Gasnier, Louis (1875-2/15/63). Director. Films: "The Perils of Pauline" 1914-serial; "Murder on the Yukon" 1940.

Gaspar, Luis. Screenwriter. Films: "Shoot to Kill" 1963-Span.; "Prey of Vultures" 1973-Span./Ital.

Gasperini, Italo. Screenwriter. Films: "Wrath of God" 1968-Ital./Span.; "Scalps" 1986-Ital./Ger.

Gastaldi, Ernesto. Screenwriter. Films: "Arizona Colt" 1965-Ital./Fr./Span.; "10,000 Dollars Blood Money" 1966-Ital.; "Day of Anger" 1967-Ital./Ger.; "Cowards Don't Pray" 1968-Ital./Span.; "To Hell and Back" 1968-Ital./Span.; "Blood at Sundown" 1969-Ital./Ger.; "Arizona" 1970-Ital./Span.; "Big Showdown" 1972-Ital./Fr.; "Massacre at Fort Holman" 1972-Ital./Fr./Span./Ger.; "My Name Is Nobody" 1973-Ital. (& story); "Genius" 1975-Ital./Fr./Ger.

Gates, Eleanor. Writer. Films: "The Plow Woman" 1917 (story).

Gates, Harvey. Screenwriter. Films: "Colorado" 1915; "Judge Not, or the Woman of Mona Diggings" 1915; "The Long Chancer" 1915; "For the Love of a Girl" 1916; "The Red Stain" 1916; "The Three Godfathers" 1916; "The Highway of Hope" 1917; "The Man from Montana" 1917; "Bull's Eye" 1918-serial; "Lightning Bryce" 1919-serial; "Smashing Barriers" 1919-serial; "Blue Streak McCoy" 1920; "The Fightin' Terror" 1920; "Ransom" 1920 (story only); "Action" 1921; "The Fire Eater" 1921; "Red Courage" 1921; "Belle of Alaska" 1922; "Headin' West" 1922; "The Bad Lands" 1925; "Beyond the Border" 1925; "The Flaming Forties" 1925; "Silent Sanderson" 1925; "Soft Shoes" 1925; "Driftin' Thru" 1926; "The Brute" 1927; "The Mysterious Rider" 1933; "The Luck of Roaring Camp" 1937; "Northwest Trail" 1945; "Last Frontier Uprising" 1947.

Gates, Richard Allen. Writer. Films: "Shoootin' Irons" 1927 (story).

Gates, Robert Allen. Writer. Films: "Arizona Bound" 1927 (story).

Gatzert, Nate (1890-9/1/59). Screenwriter. Films: "The Royal Rider" 1929; "Strawberry Roan" 1933; "The Fiddlin' Buckaroo" 1934; "Honor of the Range" 1934; "Smoking Guns" 1934; "Wheels of Destiny" 1934; "Heir to Trouble" 1935; "Lawless Riders" 1935; "The Roaring West" 1935-serial; "Rustlers of Red Dog" 1935-serial; "Western Courage" 1935; "Western Frontier" 1935; "Avenging Waters" 1936; "The Cattle Thief" 1936; "The Fugitive Sheriff" 1936; "Heroes of the Range" 1936; "Rio Grande Ranger" 1936; "The Unknown Ranger" 1936; "Law of the Ranger" 1937; "Ranger Courage"

1937; "The Rangers Step In" 1937; "Reckless Ranger 1937; "In Early Arizona" 1938; "Phantom Gold" 1938; "Pioneer Trail" 1938 (& story); "Rolling Caravans" 1938; "Stagecoach Days" 1938; "Frontiers of '49" 1939; "The Law Comes to Texas" 1939; "Lone Star Pioneers" 1939.

Gaulden, Ray (1914-). Writer. Films: "Five Card Stud" 1968 (story).

Gaultois, Dallas. Screenwriter. Films: "Four Fast Guns" 1959.

Gaunthier, Gene (-12/18/66). Screenwriter. Films: "Wolfe, or the Conquest of Quebec" 1914.

Gay, Frank. Writer. Films: "King of the Sierras" 1938 (story).

Gay, John. Screenwriter. Films: "The Hallelujah Trail" 1965; "Texas Across the Riveer" 1966; "Soldier Blue" 1970; "Pocket Money" 1972.

Geller, Bruce (1930-5/21/78). Director. TV: *Rawhide* 1959-66 (prod.); *The Westerner*—"Ghost of a Chance" 12-2-60.

Genez, L. Writer. Films: "One Touch of Sin" 1917 (story).

Gengelin, Paul. Screenwriter. Films: "The Big Bonanza" 1944.

Genta, Renzo. Screenwriter. Films: "Days of Anger" 1967-Ital./Ger.; "Jesse and Lester, Two Brothers in a Place Called Trinity" 1972-Ital.

Gentili, Giorgio. Director. Films: "Man Called Sledge" 1971-Ital./U.S.

George, Burton. Director. Films: "The Valley of Doubt" 1920.

George, George W. Screenwriter. Films: "The Nevadan" 1950; "Red Mountain" 1951 (& story); "City of Badmen" 1953; "Smoke Signal" 1955; "The Halliday Brand" 1957; "Apache Territory" 1958; "Fort Dobbs" 1958.

George, Kathleen B. Writer. Films: "Gun Fury" 1953 (story).

Geraghty, Gerald (1906-7/8/54). Screenwriter. Films: "Silent Men" 1933; "Sunset Pass" 1933; "Under the Tonto Rim" 1933; "The Miracle Rider" 1935-serial; "The Phantom Empire" 1935-serial (story only); "Bar 20 Rides Again" 1936; "Wells Fargo" 1937; "Western Jamboree" 1938; "The Arizona Kid" 1939; "Blue Montana Skies" 1939; "Come On Rangers" 1939; "In Old Caliente" 1939; "In Old Monterey" 1939 (& story); "Mexicali Rose" 1939; "Mountain Rhythm" 1939; "South of the Border" 1939; "Southward Ho!" 1939; "Wall Street Cowboy" 1939; "Young Buffalo Bill" 1940; "Carson City Kid" 1940; "Hidden Gold" 1940; "Pioneers of the West" 1940; "The Ranger and the Lady" 1940; "Badlands of Dakota" 1941; "King of Dodge City" 1941; "Secrets of the Wastelands" 1941; "Riding Through Nevada" 1942; "Sin Town" 1942; "Sunset on the Desert" 1942; "Frontier Badman" 1943; "Hail to the Rangers" 1943; "Hoppy Serves a Writ" 1943; "Along the Navajo Trail" 1945; "Frisco Sal" 1945; "Wagon Wheels Westward" 1945 (story only); "Heldorado" 1946; "Home in Oklahoma" 1946; "Rainbow Over Texas" 1946; "Apache Rose" 1947; "On the Old Spanish Trail" 1947 (story only); "Wyoming" 1947; "The Gallant Legion" 1948 (story only); "Grand Canyon Trail" 1948; "The Plunderers" 1948; "Riders in the Sky" 1949; "Cow Town" 1950; "Mule Train" 1950; "The Savage Horde" 1950 (story only); "Sunset in the West" 1950; "Trail of Robin Hood" 1950; "Trigger, Jr." 1950; "Hills of Utah" 1951; "Silver Canyon" 1951; "Valley of Fire" 1951; "Barbed Wire" 1952; "Blue Canadian Rockies" 1952; "The Old West" 1952; "Rose of Cimarron" 1952; "Wagon Team" 1952; "Bandits of the West" 1953; "Down Laredo Way" 1953; "Goldtown Ghost Raiders" 1953; "Iron Mountain Trail" 1953; "On Top of Old Smoky" 1953; "Red River Shore" 1953; "Savage Frontier" 1953; "Shadows of Tombstone" 1953; "The Phantom Stallion" 1954.

Geraghty, Maurice (1908-6/30/87). Screenwriter. Films: "The Phantom Empire" 1935-serial (story only); "Vigilantes Are Coming" 1936-serial (& story); "Hills of Old Wyoming" 1937; "Law of the Plains" 1938; "The Mysterious Rider" 1938; "Silver on the Sage" 1939; "West of Tombstone" 1942; "Apache Trail" 1943; "Calamity Jane and Sam Bass" 1949; "Red Canyon" 1949; "Dakota Lil" 1950; "Tomahawk" 1951; "Robbers' Roost" 1955; "Love Me Tender" 1956 (story only); "Mohawk" 1956. ¶TV: The Virginian—"Impasse" 11-14-62, "The Accomplice" 12-19-62, "Return a Stranger" 11-18-64 (dir.); Bonanza—"Shining in Spain" 3-27-66 (dir.).

Geraghty, Tom (1883-6/5/45). Screenwriter. Films: "A Man's Fight" 1919; "With Hoops of Steel" 1919; "The Mollycoddle" 1920.

Gerard, Barney. Screenwriter. Films: "Jiggs and Maggie Out West" 1950 (& prod.).

Gerard, Merwin. Screenwriter. Films: "Bridger" TVM-1976.

Gerber, Fred. Director. TV: Ad-ventures of Brisco County, Jr.—"Riverboat" 10-1-93.

Gereghty, William. Director. TV: Legend—"Mr. Pratt Goes to Sheridan" 2-25-95, "Custer's Next to Last Stand" 5-9-95.

Gering, Marion. Director (1904-4/19/77). Films: "Rose of the Rancho" 1936.

Geronimi, Clyde (1900-4/24/89). Director. Films: "Melody Time" 1948.

Gerould, Katherine Fullerton (1879-1944). Writer. Films: "The Yankee Senor" 1926 (story); "Romance of the Rio Grande" 1929 (story); "Romance of the Rio Grande" 1941 (story).

Gershenson, Joseph (1904-). Producer. Films: "Curse of the Undead" 1959.

Gerstad, Harry. Director. Films: "Thirteen Fighting Men" 1960.

Gertsman, Maury (1910-). Screenwriter. Films: "Gun Town" 1946.

Gessner, Robert. Writer. Films: "Massacre" 1934 (story).

Gevne, Jack T.O. see Jevne, Jack.

Giambriccio, Antonio. Screenwriter. Films: "Rojo" 1966-Ital./Span.

Gianviti, Roberto. Screenwriter. Films: "Rojo" 1966-Ital./Span.; "Sheriff with the Gold" 1966-Ital./Span.; "Two Sons of Ringo" 1966-Ital.; "Two R-R-Ringos from Texas" 1967-Ital.; "Red Blood, Yellow Gold" 1968-Ital./Span.; "Nephews of Zorro" 1969-Ital.; "And the Crows Will Dig Your Grave" 1971-Ital./Span.; "Have a Good Funeral, My Friend ... Sartana Will Pay" 1972-Ital.

Gibbons, Eliot. Screenwriter. Films: "The Apache Kid" 1941; "Desert Bandit" 1941; "Under Fiesta Stars" 1941; "Hidden Danger" 1949; "Fence Riders" 1950.

Giblyn, Charles (1871-3/14/34). Director. Films: "His Squaw" 1912; "An Indian Legend" 1912; "The Vengeance of Fate" 1912; "The Green Shadow" 1913; "A Slave's Devotion" 1913; "Singing River" 1921.

Gibney, Sheridan (1893-4/11/88). Screenwriter. Films: "Massacre" 1934.

Gibson, Hoot (1892-8/23/62). Director. Films: "The Champion Liar" 1920; "The Fightin' Terror" 1920; "The Shootin' Kid" 1920; "The Smilin' Kid" 1920; "Some Shooter" 1920; "The Cactus Kid" 1921; "Out O' Luck" 1921; "The Shoot 'Em Up Kid" 1926; "Courtin' Wildcats" 1929 (prod. only); "King of the Rodeo" 1929 (prod. only); "The Long, Long Trail" 1929 (prod. only); "The Concentratin' Kid" 1930 (prod. only); "The Mounted Stranger" 1930 (prod. only); "Roaring Ranch" 1930 (prod. only); "Spurs" 1930 (prod. only); "Trailin' Trouble" 1930; "Trigger Tricks" 1930.

Gibson, Tom. Director. Films: "Bull's Eye" 1918-serial (sp. only); "The Web of the Law" 1923; "A Game Fighter" 1924; "The Mystery of Lost Ranch" 1925; "Range Buzzards" 1925; "Reckless Courage" 1925; "Stampede Thunder" 1925; "Triple Action" 1925 (& sp.); "West of Arizona" 1925; "Tex" 1926; "Trigger Tom" 1935 (sp. only); "Caryl of the Mountains" 1936 (sp. only); "Romance Rides the Range" 1936 (sp. only); "The Singing Cowboy" 1936 (story only); "Santa Fe Rides" 1937 (story only); "The Singing Buckaroo" 1937 (& sp.); "The Cheyenne Kid" 1940 (sp. only); "Covered Wagon Trails" 1940 (sp. only); "Cyclone on Horseback" 1941 (story only); "Law of the Wolf" 1941 (story only); "Six Gun Gold" 1941 (story only); "The Scarlet Horseman" 1946-serial (sp. only).

Gibson, Victor. Screenwriter. Films: "Heart O' the Range" 1921; "The Web of the Law" 1923.

Gicca, Fulvio. Screenwriter. Films: "Time of Vultures" 1967-Ital.

Gicca Palli, Enzo (Vincent Thomas). Director. Films: "The Road to Fort Alamo" 1966-Fr./Ital. (& story); "Killer Caliber .32" 1967-Ital. (sp. only); "Night of the Serpent" 1969-Ital. (sp. only); "The Price of Death" 1972-Ital. (& sp.).

Gideon, Ralph. see Reynolds, Sheldon.

Giebler, A.M. Writer. Films: "The Ranch Owner's Love-Making" 1913 (story).

Gielgud, Gwen Bagni. see Bagni, Gwen.

Gilbert, Fran. Screenwriter. Films: "Buffalo Bill Rides Again" 1947.

Gilbert, Rod. see Guerrieri, Romolo.

Giler, Berne (1908-7/24/67). Screenwriter. Films: "Legion of the Lawless" 1940 (story only); "Pirates of the Prairie" 1942 (story only); "Showdown at Abilene" 1956; "Westbound" 1959 (& story); "Guns of Diablo" 1964; "Gunfight in Abilene" 1967.

Gilgore, Jay. Screenwriter. Films: "Canyon Raiders" 1951.

Gill, Jr., Frank. Writer. Films: "Carolina Cannonball" 1955 (story).

Gill, Thomas. Screenwriter. Films: "The Gay Caballero" 1932 (story only); "Border Cafe" 1937.

Gilmore, Stuart (1913-11/19/71). Director. Films: "The Virginian" 1946; "Hot Lead" 1951; "The Half-Breed" 1952; "Target" 1952.

Gilroy, Bert. Producer. Films: "Rhythm Wranglers" 1937-short; "Border G-Man" 1938; "Gun Law" 1938; "Lawless Valley" 1938; "The Painted Desert" 1938; "Renegade Ranger" 1938; "Arizona Legion" 1939; "The Fighting Gringo" 1939; "The Marshal of Mesa City" 1939; "Racketeers of the Range" 1939; "Timber Stampede" 1939; "Trouble in Sundown" 1939; "Bullet Code" 1940; "The Fargo Kid" 1940; "Legion of the Lawless" 1940; "Prairie Law" 1940; "Stage to Chino" 1940; "Triple Justice" 1940; "Wagon Trin" 1940; "Along the Rio Grande" 1941; "The Bandit Trail" 1941; "Cyclone on Horseback" 1941; "Dude Cowboy" 1941; "Robbers of the Range" 1941; "Six Gun Gold" 1941; "Bandit Ranger" 1942; "Come On, Danger!" 1942; "Land of the Open Range" 1942; "Pirates of the Prairie" 1942; "Riding the Wind" 1942; "Thundering Hoffs" 1942; "The Avenging Rider" 1943; "Fighting Frontier" 1943; "Red River Robin Hood" 1943; "Sagebrush Law" 1943.

Gilroy, Frank D. (1925-). Director. Films: "Fastest Gun Alive" 1956 (sp. only); "From Noon to Three" 1976 (& sp.).

Ginna, Robert Emmett. Screenwriter. Films: "The Last Challenge" 1967.

Gipson, Fred (1908-8/14/73). Screenwriter. Films: "Return of the Texan" 1952; "Old Yeller" 1957 (& story); "Savage Sam" 1963 (& story).

Giraldi, Franco (Frank Garfield). Director. Films: "Seven Guns for the MacGregors" 1965-Ital./Span.; "Sugar Colt" 1966-Ital./Span.; "A Minute to Pray, a Second to Die" 1967-Ital.; "Up the MacGregors!" 1967-Ital./Span.

Girard, Bernard (1929-). Director. Films: "Ride Out for Revenge" 1957; "The Saga of Hemp Brown" 1958 (story only). ¶TV: *Wagon Train*—"The Charles Avery Story" 12-13-57; *The Virginian*—"Riff-Raff" 11-7-62, "The Exiles" 1-9-63; *Rawhide*—"Moment in the Sun" 1-29-65.

Girault, Jean. Screenwriter. Films: "Judge Roy Bean" 1970-Fr.

Girolami, Enzo. *see* Castellari, Enzo G.

Girolami, Marino (Dario Silvestre, Frank Martin, Fred Wilson). Director. Films: "Bullets and the Flesh" 1965-Ital./Fr./Span.; "Magnificent Brutes of the West" 1965-Ital./Span./Fr.; "Two R-R-Ringos from Texas" 1967-Ital.; "Two Sides of the Dollar" 1967-Fr./Ital. (sp. only); "Between God, the Devil and a Winchester" 1968-Ital./Span. (& sp.).

Girotti, Ken. Director. TV: *Hawkeye*—"The Vision" 11-2-94, "Warrior" 11-16-94.

Gist, Robert. Director. TV: *Laredo*—"Like One of the Family" 3-24-67; *The High Chaparral*—"The Hair Hunter" 3-10-68.

Gittens, Wyndham. Screenwriter. Films: "Desert Driven" 1923; "The Measure of a Man" 1924; "Don Dare Devil" 1925; "The Everlasting Whisper" 1925; "Out of the West" 1926; "The Power of the Weak" 1926; "Western Pluck" 1926; "Crashing Through" 1928; "Lightning Warrior" 1931-serial; "The Vanishing Legion" 1931-serial; "The Devil Horse" 1932-serial; "The Last of the Mohicans" 1932-serial; "Fighting with Kit Carson" 1933-serial; "Ghost Patrol" 1936; "Wild West Days" 1937-serial; "Flaming Frontier" 1938-serial; "Forbidden Valley" 1938 (& dir.); "Deadwood Dick" 1940-serial; "The Medico of Painted Springs" 1941; "Pardon My Gun" 1942.

Glachin, Luigi. Screenwriter. Films: "Four Came to Kill Sartnaa" 1969-Ital.; "Hero Called Allegria" 1971-Ital.

Glandbard, Max. Screenwriter. Films: "Hell Canyon Outlaws" 1957.

Glaser, Allan. Producer. Films: "Lust in the Dust" 1985.

Glasser, Bernard. Producer. Films: "Escape from Red Rock" 1958.

Glazer, Benjamin (1887-3/18/56). Screenwriter. Films: "The Great Divide" 1925; "The Trail of '98" 1929; "Rhythm on the Range" 1936 (prod. only).

Gleason, Michael. Screenwriter. Films: "The Oregon Trail" TVM-1976 (& prod.). ¶TV: *The Oregon Trail* (exec. dir.).

Glendon, Frank (1886-3/17/37). Director. Films: "Circle of Death" 1935.

Glennon, Bert (1893-6/29/67). Director. Films: "South of Santa Fe" 1932.

Glickman, Joel (1930-12/1/89).

Producer. Films: "Buck and the Preacher" 1972.

Globus, Yoram. Producer. Films: "God's Gun" 1976-Ital./Israel.

Gluck, Marvin. Writer. Films: "The Great Sioux Massacre" 1965 (story).

Gniazdowski, Tom. Director. Films: "Tin Star Void" 1988 (& prod./sp.).

Goddard, Charles W. Writer. Films: "The Perils of Pauline" 1914-serial (story); "The Broken Wing" 1932 (story).

Godfrey, Peter (1899-3/4/70). Director. Films: "Barricade" 1950.

Goetz, William (1903-8/15/69). Producer. Films: "The Man from Laramie" 1955; "They Came to Cordura" 1959.

Goff, Ivan (1910-). Screenwriter. Films: "Sunset in Wyoming" 1941; "The Legend of the Lone Ranger" 1981.

Golan, Menachem (1929-). Producer. Films: "God's Gun" 1976-Ital./Israel; "Kid Vengeance" 1976-Ital./U.S./Israel.

Gold, Zachary. Screenwriter. Films: "South of St. Louis" 1949.

Goldaine, Mark. Writer. Films: "The Rip Snorter" 1925 (story).

Goldbeck, Willis (1899-9/17/79). Screenwriter. Films: "The Lone Ranger" 1956 (prod. only); "Sergeant Rutledge" 1960 (& prod.); "The Man Who Shot Liberty Valance" 1962 (& prod.).

Goldberg, Mel. Screenwriter. Films: "Hang 'Em High" 1968.

Goldburg, Jesse J. Producer. Films: "The Fighting Smile" 1925; "Hair Trigger Baxter" 1926; "The Valley of Bravery" 1926.

Golden, Joseph A. Director. Films: "The Girl from Arizona" 1910; "The Maid of Niagara" 1910; "Flaming Arrow" 1911; "Told in Colorado" 1911 (& story); "Western Hearts" 1911 (& sp.); "Why the Sheriff Is a Bachelor" 1911 (& story).

Golden, Murray (1912-8/5/91). Director. TV: *The Rifleman*—"Smoke Screen" 4-5-60; *Wanted—Dead or Alive*—"The Showdown" 10-26-60, "Surprise Witness" 11-2-60, "To the Victor" 11-9-60, "Criss Cross" 11-16-60, "Detour" 3-1-61, "Monday Morning" 3-8-61, "Dead Reckoning" 3-22-61; *Rawhide*—"The Greedy Town" 2-16-62, "The Child Woman" 3-23-62; *Bonanza*—"The Way of Aaron" 3-10-63, "A Passion for Justice" 9-29-63, "Enter Thomas Bowers" 4-26-64, "The Dark Past" 5-3-

64; *The Big Valley*—"Judgement in Heaven" 12-22-65; *The Men from Shiloh* 1970-71.

Goldman, Martin. Director. Films: "The Legend of Nigger Charley" 1972 (& sp.).

Goldman, William (1931-). Screenwriter. Films: "Butch Cassidy and the Sundance Kid" 1969; "Mr. Horn" TVM-1979; "Maverick" 1994.

Goldrup, Ray. Screenwriter. Films: "Windwalker" 1980.

Goldsmith, Martin G. Screenwriter. Films: "Overland Pacific" 1954; "Fort Massacre" 1958; "Cast a Long Shadow" 1959; "The Gunfight at Dodge City" 1959.

Goldstein, Leonard. Producer. Films: "Black Bart" 1948; "River Lady" 1948; "Calamity Jane and Sam Bass" 1949; "Red Canyon" 1949; "Comanche Territory" 1950; "Saddle Tramp" 1950; "Cave of Outlaws" 1951; "The Lady from Texas" 1951; "Tomahawk" 1951; "The Battle at Apache Pass" 1952; "The Duel at Silver Creek" 1952; "The Treasure of Lost Canyon" 1952; "Untamed Frontier" 1952; "City of Badmen" 1953; "The Redhead from Wyoming" 1953; "Take Me to Town" 1953; "The Gambler from Natchez" 1954; "The Siege at Red River" 1954; "Three Young Texans" 1954; "Robbers' Roost" 1955.

Goldstein, Robert (1903-4/6/74). Producer. Films: "Robbers' Roost" 1955; "Stranger on Horseback" 1955.

Goldstone, James (1931-). Director. Films: "Scalplock" TVM-1966 (& story); "A Man Called Gannon" 1969; "Calamity Jane" TVM-1984. ¶TV: *Rawhide*—"The Retreat" 3-26-65.

Goldstone, Phil. Producer. Films: "Montana Bill" 1921; "Her Man" 1924; "Fighting Thru" 1930; "Alias the Bad Man" 1931; "Arizona Terror" 1931; "Branded Men" 1931; "The Pocatello Kid" 1931; "Range Law" 1931; "The Two Gun Man" 1931; "Hell Fire Austin" 1932; "The Sunset Trail" 1932; "Texas Gun Fighter" 1932; "Whistlin' Dan" 1932; "Renfrew on the Great White Trail" 1938; "Sky Bandits" 1940.

Goldstone, Richard (1912-). Producer. Films: "The Outriders" 1950; "Inside Straight" 1951.

Goldwyn, Samuel (1882-1/31/74). Producer. Films: "The Winning of Barbara Worth" 1926; "Cowboy and the Lady" 1938; "The Westerner" 1940.

Goldwyn, Jr., Samuel (1926-). Producer. Films: "Man with the Gun" 1955; "The Proud Rebel" 1958.

Golitzen, Alexander (1907-). Producer. Films: "Salome, Where She Danced" 1945.

Gonzalez, Jr., Rogelio A. Director. Films: "The Naked Man" 1987-Mex. (& sp.).

Good, Tony. *see* Corbucci, Bruno.

Gooden, Arthur Henry. Screenwriter. Films: "The Double Hold-Up" 1919; "The Face in the Watch" 1919; "The Lone Hand" 1919 (story only); "The Broncho Kid" 1920; "Roarin' Dan" 1920; "Superstition" 1920; "Lawless Men" 1924; "The Riddle Rider" 1924-serial; "The Verdict of the Desert" 1925 (story only); "The Scarlet Brand" 1927-serial; "Whispering Smith Rides" 1927-serial; "The Scarlet Arrow" 1928-serial; "Smoke Tree Range" 1937 (story only).

Goodfriend, Pliny. Screenwriter. Films: "Santa Fe Rides" 1937.

Goodking, Saul A. Director. Films: "The Oregon Trail" 1939-serial.

Goodman, David Z. Screenwriter. Films: "Monte Walsh" 1970.

Goodman, Hal. Writer. Films: "Invitation to a Gunfighter" 1964 (story).

Goodrich, Frances (1901-1/29/84). Screenwriter. Films: "The Virginian" 1946.

Goodrich, John F. Screenwriter. Films: "Riders of the Purple Sage" 1931.

Goodwins, Leslie (1899-1/8/69). Director. Films: "A Western Welcome" 1938-short (& sp.); "Mexican Spitfire Out West" 1940; "The Singing Sheriff" 1944; "Gold Fever" 1952. ¶TV: *The Cisco Kid* 1951-55; *Sugarfoot* 1957; *Bronco* 1958; *The Alaskans* 1959; *Maverick*—"A Fellow's Brother" 11-22-59, "The White Widow" 1-24-60, "The People's Friend" 2-7-60, "The Iron Hand" 2-21-60, "The Resurrection of Joe November" 2-28-60, "The Witch of Hound Dog" 11-6-60, "The Maverick Line" 11-20-60; *F Troop* 1965.

Gora, Claudio. Director. Films: "Hatred of God" 1967-Ital./Ger. (& sp.).

Gordon, Alex (1922-). Producer. Films: "The Lawless Rider" 1954; "Flesh and the Spur" 1957; "The Bounty Killer" 1965; "Requiem for a Gunfighter" 1965.

Gordon, Arthur (1912-). Writer. Films: "Reprisal!" 1956 (story).

Gordon, Bernard. Screenwriter. Films: "The Lawless Breed" 1952; "Custer of the West" 1967-U.S./Span.; "Bad Man's River" 1971-Span./Ital./Fr. (prod. only); "Pancho Villa" 1975-Span.

Gordon, Dan. Screenwriter. Films: "Wyatt Earp" 1994.

Gordon, Edward R. Director. Films: "Gun-Hand Garrison" 1927; "Wild Born" 1927; "Ridin' Leather" 1929.

Gordon, Harry. Writer. Films: "El Diablo Rides" 1939 (story); "Wild Horse Valley" 1940 (story).

Gordon, Homer King. Screenwriter. Films: "The Judgement Book" 1935 (story only); "The Gun Ranger" 1937 (story only); "In Old Montana" 1939.

Gordon, James B. Screenwriter. Films: "The Gun That Won the West" 1955; "Utah Blaine" 1957; "Noose for a Gunman" 1960.

Gordon, Leo (1922-). Screenwriter. Films: "Black Patch" 1957; "Escort West" 1959; "The Bounty Killer" 1965.

Gordon, Michael (1909-4/29/93). Director. Films: "The Secret of Convict Lake" 1951; "Texas Across the River" 1966.

Gordon, Richard. Director. TV: *The Alaskans* 1959-60.

Gordon, Robert. Director. Films: "Black Eagle" 1948; "The Rawhide Trail" 1958; "The Gatling Gun" 1972. ¶TV: *My Friend Flicka* 1955; *Law of the Plainsman* 1959; *Maverick*—"Full House" 10-25-59; *Bonanza*—"The Dark Gate" 3-4-61.

Gordon, Rose. Screenwriter. Films: "Fighting Hero" 1934; "Loser's End" 1934; "Mystery Ranch" 1934; "Rawhide Mail" 1934; "Terror of the Plains" 1934 (story only); "Born to Battle" 1935; "Coyote Trails" 1935; "Ridin' Thru" 1935; "Silent Valley" 1935; "The Silver Bullet" 1935; "Tracy Rides" 1935; "The Unconquered Bandit" 1935; "Fast Bullets" 1936; "Santa Fe Bound" 1936.

Gordon, Warren. Director. Films: "A Woman's Man" 1920.

Gorshin, Frank (1935-). Director. TV: *Have Gun Will Travel*—"The Sons of Aaron Murdock" 5-9-59.

Goscinny, Rene (1926-11/5/77). Director. Films: "Lucky Luke" 1971-Fr./Belg. (& prod./sp.).

Gottlieb, Alex (1906-10/9/88). Screenwriter. Films: "Ride 'Em, Cowboy" 1942; "Two Guys from Texas" 1948 (prod. only); "The Fighter" 1952 (prod. only); "Three

Hours to Kill" 1954 (story only); "Arizona Raiders" 1965.

Gottlieb, Franz J. Director. Films: "Massacre at Marble City" 1964-Ger./Ital./Fr.

Gould, Clifford Newton. Screenwriter. Films: "Macho Callahan" 1970.

Goulding, Edmund (1891-12/24/59). Screenwriter. Films: "Tiger Rose" 1923.

Governor, Richard. Director. Films: "Ghost Town" 1988.

Graham, James. Writer. Films: "The Wrath of God" 1972 (story).

Graham, Rodney J. Screenwriter. Films: "Sundown Riders" 1948.

Graham, William A. (1930-). Director. Films: "Waterhole No. 3" 1967; "The Intruders" TVM-1970; "Count Your Bullets" 1972; "Orphan Train" TVM-1979; "Harry Tracy-Desperado" 1982; "The Last Days of Frank of Jesse James" TVM-1986; "Proud Men" TVM-1987; "Montana" TVM-1990. ¶TV: *The Virginian*—"Echo from Another Day" 3-27-63; *The Big Valley*—"Palms of Glory" 9-15-65.

Grainger, Edmund (1906-7/6/81). Producer. Films: "A Holy Terror" 1931; "The Gay Caballero" 1932; "Sutter's Gold" 1936; "Wild Bill Hickok Rides" 1942; "The Fabulous Texan" 1947; "Devil's Canyon" 1953; "The Treasure of Pancho Villa" 1955; "Great Day in the Morning" 1956; "The Sheepman" 1958.

Grais, Michael. Screenwriter. Films: "Death Hunt" 1981.

Grandon, Frank J. Director. Films: "The New Ranch Foreman" 1912 (& sp.); "Over the Divide" 1912 (story only); "Ranch-Mates" 1912; "On the Mountain Ranch" 1913; "Buffalo Hunting" 1914; "The Fifty Man" 1914; "The Flower of Faith" 1914; "The Lure O' the Windigo" 1914; "Wade Brent Pays" 1914 (& story); "The Face at the Window" 1915; "Heart's Desire" 1915; "Jack's Pals" 1915; "The Puny Soul of Peter Rand" 1915; "Wild Honey" 1918; "Barb Wire" 1922; "Rustlin'" 1923; "True Gold" 1923.

Graneman, Eddy. Screenwriter. Films: "Thunder Over Texas" 1934; "Custer's Last Stand" 1936-serial.

Grange, Maude. Screenwriter. Films: "The Fighting Gringo" 1917; "John Ermine of the Yellowstone" 1917.

Granger, Edward. Producer. Films: "Cimarron" 1960.

Granger, Robert A. Writer. Films: "Gun Fury" 1953 (story).

Grant, James Edward (1905-2/19/66). Screenwriter. Films: "Belle of the Yukon" 1944; "Angel and the Badman" 1947 (& dir.); "The Plunderers" 1948 (story only); "California Passage" 1950; "Rock Island Trail" 1950; "Surrender" 1950 (& story); "Hondo" 1953; "The Last Wagon" 1956; "Three Violent People" 1956; "The Proud Rebel" 1958 (story only); "The Sheepman" 1958 (story only); "The Alamo" 1960; "The Comancheros" 1961; "McLintock" 1963; "Hostile Guns" 1967; "Support Your Local Gunfighter" 1971.

Grant, John. Screenwriter. Films: "Ride 'Em, Cowboy" 1942; "The Wistful Widow of Wagon Gap" 1947.

Grant, Morton (1904-7/25/80). Screenwriter. Films: "Timber Stampede" 1939; "The Fargo Kid" 1940; "Stage to Chino" 1940; "Triple Justice" 1940; "Wagon Train" 1940; "Along the Rio Grande" 1941; "Dude Cowboy" 1941; "Robbers of the Range" 1941; "Bandit Ranger" 1942; "Land of the Open Range" 1942; "Valley of Hunted Men" 1942; "Westward Ho" 1942 (& story); "The Avenging Rider" 1943; "Bar 20" 1943; "Beyond the Last Frontier" 1943; "Santa Fe Scouts" 1943; "Swing in the Saddle" 1944; "The Younger Brothers" 1949 (story only).

Grashin, Mauri. Screenwriter. Films: "Sons of the Pioneers" 1942 (& story); "Roll on, Texas Moon" 1946.

Grasshoff, Alex (1930-). Director. TV: *Barbary Coast*—"Irish Coffee" 10-13-75, "Arson and Old Lace" 11-14-75, "The Day Cable Was Hanged" 12-26-75, "The Dawson Marker" 1-9-76.

Grauman, Walter (1922-). Director. TV: *Colt .45* 1957; *Lancer*—"Chase a Wild Horse" 10-8-68.

Graves, Peter (1926-). Director. TV: *Gunsmoke*—"Which Doctor" 3-19-66,

Graves, Ralph (1900-2/18/77). Writer. Films: "Outlaws of the Orient" 1937 (story).

Gray, Bob. Director. Films: "The Ranger" 1918.

Gray, George Arthur. Screenwriter. Films: "Hawk of the Hills" 1927-serial; "The Yellow Cameo" 1928-serial; "Queen of the Northwoods" 1929-serial; "Valley of Vanishing Men" 1942-serial.

Gray, Harry. Producer. Films: "Covered Wagon Days" 1940; "Ridin' Down the Canyon" 1942.

Gray, John W. Screenwriter. Films: "Canyon of the Fools" 1923; "Rockin' in the Rockies" 1945.

Gray, Louis. Producer. Films: "Lone Star Raiders" 1940; "Gangs of Sonora" 1941; "Outlaws of the Cherokee Trail" 1941; "Pals of the Pecos" 1941; "Prairie Pioneers" 1941; "Saddlemates" 1941; "West of Cimarron" 1941; "Code of the Outlaw" 1942; "The Phantom Plainsmen" 1942; "Raiders of the Range" 1942; "Shadows on the Sage" 1942; "Valley of Hunted Men" 1942; "Westward Ho" 1942; "Beyond the Last Frontier" 1943; "The Blocked Trail" 1943; "Overland Mail Robbery" 1943; "Raiders of Sunset Pass" 1943; "Riders of the Rio Grande" 1943; "Santa Fe Scouts" 1943; "Thundering Trails" 1943; "Wagon Tracks West" 1943; "Beneath Western Skies" 1944; "Bordertown Trail" 1944; "Call of the Rockies" 1944; "Cheyenne Wildcat" 1944; "Firebrands of Arizona" 1944; "Hidden Valley Outlaws" 1944; "The Laramie Trail" 1944; "Marshal of Reno" 1944; "Pride of the Plains" 1944; "Great Stagecoach Robbery" 1945; "Lone Texas Ranger" 1945; "The Man from Oklahoma" 1945; "Sunset in El Dorado" 1945; "Home on the Range" 1946; "The Man from Rainbow Valley" 1946; "Out California Way" 1946; "Last Frontier Uprising" 1947; "Courtin' Trouble" 1948; "Cowboy Cavalier" 1948; "Crossed Trails" 1948; "Oklahoma Blues" 1948; "Outlaw Brand" 1948; "Partners of the Sunset" 1948; "Range Renegades" 1948; "The Rangers Ride" 1948; "Silver Trails" 1948; "Song of the Drifter" 1948; "Across the Rio Grande" 1949; "Brand of Fear" 1949; "Gun Law Justice" 1949; "Gun Runner" 1949; "Lawless Code" 1949; "Roaring Westward" 1949. ¶TV: *The Gene Autry Show* 1950-55; *The Range Rider* 1951-53; *Annie Oakley* 1954-57; *Buffalo Bill, Jr.* 1955-56; *The Adventures of Champion* 1955-56.

Gray, Tommy. Writer. Films: "The Cyclone Cowboy" 1927 (story).

Grayson, Charles (1904-5/4/73). Screenwriter. Films: "Bad Men of Missouri" 1941; "Will Bill Hickok Rides" 1942.

Greci, Aldo. Screenwriter. Films: "Cisco" 1966-Ital.

Green, Alfred E. (1889-9/4/60). Director. Films: "The Bachelor Daddy" 1922; "Shooting High" 1940; "Badlands of Dakota" 1941; "Four Faces West" 1948; "Sierra" 1950.

Green, Anthony. *see* Zeglio, Primo.

Green, George D. Screenwriter. Films: "Apache Chief" 1949 (& story).

Green, Howard J. Screenwriter. Films: "The Long, Long Trail" 1929; "The Hawk of Wild River" 1952.

Green, John. Screenwriter. Films: "Law of the Range" 1941.

Green, Walon (1936-). Screenwriter. Films: "The Wild Bunch" 1969 (& story).

Greenbaum, Everett. Screenwriter. Films: "The Shakiest Gun in the West" 1968.

Greene, Clarence (1918-). Producer. Films: "Fastest Gun Alive" 1956; "Thunder in the Sun" 1959.

Greene, David. Director. Films: "Children of the Dust" TVM-1995.

Greene, Harold. Screenwriter. Films: "Texas Across the River" 1966.

Greene, Herbert. Director. Films: "Outlaw Queen" 1957.

Greene, John (1913-10/4/95). Screenwriter. Films: "Plunderers of Painted Flats" 1959.

Greenwald, Maggie. Director. Films: "The Ballad of Little Jo" 1993 (& sp.).

Greepy, Anthony. *see* Zeglio, Primo.

Greer, Dan. Screenwriter. Films: "Baker's Hawk" 1976; "Pony Express Rider" 1976 (& sp.).

Gregoretti, Luciano. Screenwriter. Films: "Dead for a Dollar" 1968-Ital.

Gregory, Jackson. Writer. Films: "The Man from Painted Post" 1917 (story); "The Secret of Black Mountain" 1917 (story); "The Joyous Troublemaker" 1920 (story); "Bells of San Juan" 1922 (story); "Billy Jim" 1922 (story); "Man to Man" 1922 (story); "Two Kinds of Women" 1922 (story); "Desert Valley" 1926 (story); "Sudden Bill Dorn" 1937 (story); "The Laramie Trail" 1944 (story).

Grey, Harry. Producer. Films: "Prairie Moon" 1938; "Rhythm of the Saddle" 1938; "Western Jamboree" 1938; "Blue Montana Skies" 1939; "Cowboys from Texas" 1939; "Home on the Prairie" 1939; "The Kansas Terrors" 1939; "Mexicali Rose" 1939; "Mountain Rhythm" 1939; "Heroes of the Saddle" 1940; "Oklahoma Renegades" 1940; "Pioneers of the West" 1940; "Rocky Mountain Rangers" 1940; "The Trail Blazers" 1940; "Under Texas Skies" 1940; "Back in the Saddle" 1941; "Down Mexico Way" 1941; "Ridin' on a Rainbow" 1941; "Sierra Sue" 1941; "The Singing Hill" 1941; "Sunset in

Wyoming" 1941; "Under Fiesta Stars" 1941; "Bells of Capistrano" 1942; "Call of the Canyon" 1942; "Cowboy Serenade" 1942; "Heart of the Rio Grande" 1942; "Home in Wyomin'" 1942; "Stardust on the Sage" 1942; "Calling Wild Bill Elliott" 1943; "Hands Across the Border" 1943; "King of the Cowboys" 1943; "Man from Music Mountain" 1943; "The Man from Thunder River" 1943; "Silver Spurs" 1943; "Song of Texas" 1943; "Cowboy and the Senorita" 1944; "The Lights of Old Santa Fe" 1944; "Song of Nevada" 1944; "The Yellow Rose of Texas" 1944.

Grey, John. Screenwriter. Films: "Tracked by the Police" 1927; "I'm from the City" 1938; "The Singing Sheriff" 1944 (story only).

Grey, Zane (1872-10/23/39). Writer. Films: "The Border Legion" 1918 (story); "The Light of Western Stars" 1918 (story); "The Rainbow Trail" 1918 (story); "Riders of the Purple Sage" 1918 (story); "Desert Gold" 1919 (story); "Last of the Duanes" 1919 (story); "Riders of the Dawn" 1920 (story); "The U.P. Trail" 1920 (story); "The Last Trail" 1921 (story); "Man of the Forest" 1921 (story); "The Mysterious Rider" 1921 (story); "When Romance Rides" 1922 (story); "The Call of the Canyon" 1923 (story); "The Lone Star Ranger" 1923 (story); "To the Last Man" 1923 (story); "The Border Legion" 1924 (story); "Heritage of the Desert" 1924 (story); "The Last of the Duanes" 1924 (story); "The Wanderer of the Wasteland" 1924 (story); "Code of the West" 1925 (story); "The Light of Western Stars" 1925 (story); "The Rainbow Trail" 1925 (story); "Riders of the Purple Sage" 1925 (story); "The Vanishing American" 1925 (story); "Wild Horse Mesa" 1925 (story); "Born to the West" 1926 (story); "Desert Gold" 1926 (story); "Forlorn River" 1926 (story); "Man of the Forest" 1926 (story); "Drums of the Desert" 1927 (story); "The Last Trail" 1927 (story); "The Mysterious Rider" 1927 (story); "Nevada" 1927 (story); "Open Range" 1927 (story); "Avalanche" 1928 (story); "Under the Tonto Rim" 1928 (story); "The Water Hole" 1928 (story); "Stairs of Sand" 1929 (story); "Sunset Pass" 1929 (story); "The Border Legion" 1930 (story); "Last of the Duanes" 1930 (story); "The Light of the Western Stars" 1930 (story): "The Lone Star Ranger" 1930 (story); "Fighting Caravans" 1931 (story); "Riders of the Purple Sage" 1931 (story); "The Golden West" 1932 (story); "Heritage of the Desert" 1932 (story); "Rain-

bow Trail" 1932 (story); "Wild Horse Mesa" 1932 (story); "The Last Trail" 1933 (story); "Life in the Raw" 1933 (story); "Man of the Forest" 1933 (story); "The Mysterious Rider" 1933 (story); "Robbers' Roost" 1933 (story); "Smoke Lightning" 1933 (story); "Sunset Pass" 1933 (story); "To the Last Man" 1933 (story); "Under the Tonto Rim" 1933 (story); "The Dude Ranger" 1934 (story); "The Last Round-Up" 1934 (story); "The Thundering Herd" 1934 (story); "Wagon Wheels" 1934 (story); "West of the Pecos" 1934 (story); "Home on the Range" 1935 (story); "Nevada" 1935; "Rocky Mountain Mystery" 1935 (story); "Thunder Mountain" 1935 (story); "Wanderer of the Wasteland" 1935; "West of the Pecos" 1935 (story); "The Arizona Raiders" 1936 (story); "Arizona Mahoney" 1936 (story); "Desert Gold" 1936 (story); "Drift Fence" 1936 (story); "End of the Trail" 1936 (story); "King of the Royal Mounted" 1936 (story); "Born to the West" 1937 (story); "Forlorn River" 1937 (story); "Roll Along, Cowboy" 1937 (story); "Thunder Mountain" 1937 (story); "Thunder Trail" 1937 (story); "Under the Tonto Rim" 1937 (story); "The Mysterious Rider" 1938 (story); "Heritage of the Desert" 1939 (story); "Rangle River" 1939-Australia (story); "The Border Legion" 1940 (story); "Knights of the Range" 1940 (story); "The Light of Western Stars" 1940 (story); "Last of the Duanes" 1941 (story); "Riders of the Purple Sage" 1941 (story); "Western Union" 1941 (story); "King of the Mounties" 1942-serial (story); "The Lone Star Ranger" 1942 (story); "Nevada" 1944 (story); "Wanderer of the Wasteland" 1945 (story); "Sunset Pass" 1946; "Code of the West" 1947 (story); "The Gunfighters" 1947 (story); "Wild Horse Mesa" 1947 (story); "Red Canyon" 1949 (story); "Robbers' Roost" 1955 (story); "The Vanishing American" 1955 (story); "The Maverick Queen" 1956 (story).

Grieco, Sergio. Director. Films: "Miss Dynamite" 1972-Ital./Fr. (& sp.).

Gries, Tom (1922-1/3/77). Director. Films: "The Bushwackers" 1952; "Mustang" 1959 (sp. only); "Will Penny" 1968 (& sp.); "100 Rifles" 1969 (& sp.); "Journey Through Rosebud" 1972; "Breakheart Pass" 1976. ¶TV: *The Westerner*—"Line Camp" 12-9-60; *The Monroes*—"Night of the Wolf" 9-14-66, "The Hunter" 10-26-66.

Griffin, Eleanore (1903-7/26/

95). Screenwriter. Films: "In Old Oklahoma" 1943; "The Harvey Girls" 1946 (story only).

Griffin, Walter. Writer. Films: "Calibre 38" 1919 (story).

Griffith, Charles B. Screenwriter. Films: "Gunslinger" 1956; "Flesh and the Spur" 1957.

Griffith, D.W. (1875-7/23/48). Director. Films: "The Call of the Wild" 1908 (& sp.); "The Fight for Freedom" 1908; "The Girl and the Outlaw" 1908 (& sp.); "The Greaser's Gauntlet" 1908 (& sp.); "The Red Girl" 1908 (& sp.); "The Redman and the Child" 1908 (& sp.); "The Stage Rustler" 1908 (sp. only); "The Tavern-Keeper's Daughter" 1908; "The Vaquero's Vow" 1908 (& sp.); "Comata, the Sioux" 1909; "The Dancing Girl of Butte" 1909 (& sp.); "Fools of Fate" 1909; "The Honor of the Family" 1909; "The Indian Runner's Romance" 1909; "Leather Stocking" 1909; "The Mended Lute" 1909; "Mexican Sweethearts" 1909 (& sp.); "The Mountaineer's Honor" 1909 (& sp.); "The Redman's View" 1909; "The Reununciation" 1909 (& sp.); "The Broken Doll" 1910; "The Fugitive" 1910; "The Gold Seekers" 1910; "In Old California" 1910; "In the Border States" 1910; "The Man" 1910; "A Mohawk's Way" 1910; "Over Silent Paths" 1910; "Ramona" 1910 (& sp.); "A Romance of the Western Hills" 1910; "The Song of the Wildwood Flute" 1910; "That Chink at Golden Gulch" 1910; "The Thread of Destiny" 1910; "The Twisted Trails" 1910; "Two Brothers" 1910; "Unexpected Help" 1910; "Billy's Stratagem" 1911; "Fighting Blood" 1911; "The Heart of a Savage" 1911; "In the Days of '49" 1911; "The Indian Brothers" 1911; "The Last Drop of Water" 1911 (& sp.); "The Squaw's Love" 1911; "Was He a Coward?" 1911; "Black Sheep" 1912 (& sp.); "The Chief's Blanket" 1912; "Fate's Interception" 1912; "The Female of the Species" 1912; "Goddess of Sagebrush Gulch" 1912 (& sp.); "Heredity" 1912; "In the Aisles of the Wild" 1912; "Iola's Promise" 1912; "A Lodging for the Night" 1912; "Man's Lust for Gold" 1912; "The Massacre" 1912 (& sp.); "My Hero" 1912 (& sp.); "A Pueblo Legend" 1912 (& sp.); "A Tale of the Wilderness" 1912; "A Temporary Truce" 1912; "Three Friends" 1912; "Under Burning Skies" 1912; "The Battle at Elderbrush Gulch" 1913 (& sp.); "The Broken Ways" 1913; "A Chance Deception" 1913; "Just Gold" 1913; "A Misunderstood Boy" 1913; "The Sheriff's Baby" 1913;

"Two Men of the Desert" 1913 (& sp); "The Yaqui Cur" 1913; "The Lamb" 1915 (story only); "Scarlet Days" 1919; "In the North Woods" 1921.

Griffith, J.J. Screenwriter. Films: "Shalako" 1968-Brit./Fr.; "Catlow" 1971-Span.

Griffith, Raymond (1887-11/25/57). Producer. Films: "Drums Along the Mohawk" 1939; "Mark of Zorro" 1940.

Griffiths, Mark. Director. Films: "Cheyenne Warrior" 1994.

Grifton, Wallace. Writer. Films: "On the Mountain Ranch" 1913 (story).

Grilikhes, Michael M. Screenwriter. Films: "Duel at Diablo" 1966.

Grimaldi, Alberto (1926-). Producer. Films: "For a Few Dollars More" 1965-Ital./Ger./Span.; "Four Dollars for Vengeance" 1965-Span./Ital.; "The Big Gundown" 1966-Ital.; "The Good, the Bad, and the Ugly" 1966-Ital.; "Face to Face" 1967-Ital.; "The Mercenary" 1968-Ital./Span.; "Sabata" 1969-Ital.; "Adios, Sabata" 1970-Ital./Span.; "The Bounty Hunters" 1970-Ital.; "Companeros" 1970-Ital./Span./Ger.; "Return of Sabata" 1972-Ital./Fr./Ger.; "A Man from the East" 1974-Ital./Fr.

Grimaldi, Giovanni. Director. Films: "In a Colt's Shadow" 1965-Ital./Span. (& sp.); "Johnny Colt" 1966-Ital. (& sp.); "The Handsome, the Ugly, and the Stupid" 1967-Ital. (& sp.); "Paths of War" 1969-Ital. (& sp.).

Grinde, Nick (1894-6/19/79). Director. Films: "Beyond the Sierras" 1928; "Riders of the Dark" 1928; "The Desert Rider" 1929; "Morgan's Last Raid" 1929; "Border Brigands" 1935; "Stone of Silver Creek" 1935; "Girl from Alaska" 1942.

Grinstead, Jesse Edward. Writer. Films: "Tumbling River" 1927 (story); "Sunset of Power" 1936 (story).

Grippo, Jan. Producer. Films: "Bowery Buckaroos" 1947.

Grissell, Wallace A. (1904-4/5/54). Director. Films: "Marshal of Reno" 1944; "Vigilantes of Dodge City" 1944; "Zorro's Black Whip" 1944-serial; "Corpus Christi Bandits" 1945; "Wanderer of the Wasteland" 1945; "Wild Horse Mesa" 1947; "Western Heritage" 1948.

Gross, Jack J. Producer. Films: "Return of the Badmen" 1948; "Pawnee" 1957.

Gross, Larry. Screenwriter.

Films: "Geronimo: An American Legend" 1993.

Groves, Herman. Screenwriter. Films: "Ride a Northbound Horse" 1969.

Grubb, Davis (1919-7/24/80). Writer. Films: "Fools' Parade" 1971 (story).

Gruber, Frank (1904-12/9/69). Screenwriter. Films: "The Kansan" 1943 (story only); "Oregon Trail" 1945 (story only); "In Old Sacramento" 1946 (story only); "Fighting Man of the Plains" 1949 (story only); "The Cariboo Trail" 1950; "Dakota Lil" 1950 (story only); "The Great Missouri Raid" 1951 (story only); "Silver City" 1951 (story only); "The Texas Rangers" 1951 (story only); "Warpath" 1951; "Denver and the Rio Grande" 1952 (story only); "Flaming Feather" 1952 (story only); "Pony Express" 1953 (story only); "Rage at Dawn" 1955 (story only); "Backlash" 1956 (story only); "Tension at Table Rock" 1956 (story only); "The Big Land" 1957 (story only); "Arizona Raiders" 1965 (story only); "Town Tamer" 1965. ¶TV: *Shotgun Slade* 1959 (prod.).

Gruen, James. Director. Films: "Let's Go Gallagher" 1925 (& sp.)."In Old Santa Fe" 1934 (sp. only); "Wild Brian Kent" 1936 (sp. only); "South of Death Valley" 1949 (story only).

Gruenberg, Axel. Screenwriter. Films: "Starbird and Sweet William" 1975.

Guerra, Mario. Screenwriter. Films: "Terrible Sheriff" 1963-Span./Ital.; "Shots Ring Out!" 1965-Ital./Span.

Guerra, Ugo. Screenwriter. Films "Johnny Hamlet" 1966-Ital. (prod. only); "Ringo and Gringo Against All" 1966-Ital./Span.; "Big Ripoff" 1967-Span./Ital.; "Django Does Not Forgive" 1967-Ital./Span.; "Wrath of God" 1968-Ital./Span.; "A Bullet for Sandoval" 1970-Ital./Span. (& prod.); "The Dirty Outlaws" 1971-Ital. (& prod.).

Guerrieri, Romolo (Rod Gilbert). Director. Films: "Johnny Yuma" 1966-Ital. (& sp.); "Seven Guns for Timothy" 1966-Span./Ital.; "10,000 Dollars Blood Money" 1966-Ital.; "Any Gun Can Play" 1968-Ital./Span. (sp. only).

Guihan, Frances. Screenwriter. Films: "The Mainspring" 1917; "Bulldog Courage" 1935; "The Throwback" 1935; "Boss Rider of Gun Creek" 1936; "The Cowboy and the Kid" 1936; "The Cowboy Star" 1936; "Ride 'Em Cowboy" 1936; "Black

Aces" 1937; "Boss of Lonely Valley" 1937; "Empty Saddles" 1937; "Law for Tombstone" 1937; "Left-Handed Law" 1937; "Sandflow" 1937; "Smoke Tree Range" 1937; "Sudden Bill Dorn" 1937; "Westbound Mail" 1937; "Frontier Scout" 1939.

Guilfoyle, Paul (1902-6/27/61). Director. TV: *Colt .45* 1957; *Sugarfoot* 1957; *Lawman* 1958.

Guillerman, John (1925-). Director. Films: "El Condor" 1970; "The Tracked" TVM-1988.

Guiol, Fred (1898-5/23/64). Director. Films: "The Fighting Parson" 1930-short; "Prairie Chickens" 1943 (prod. only); "Giant" 1956 (sp. only).

Gulick, Bill (1916-). Writer. Films: "Bend of the River" 1952 (story); "The Road to Denver" 1955 (story); "The Hallelujah Trail" 1965 (story).

Gunzburg, Milton. Screenwriter. Films: "Sierra" 1950.

Guss, Jack. Screenwriter. Films: "Desperate Mission" TVM-1971.

Guthrie, Jr., A.B. (1901-4/26/91). Screenwriter. Films: "The Big Sky" 1952 (story only); "Shane" 1953; "The Kentuckian" 1955; "The Way West" 1967 (story only); "These Thousand Hills" 1959 (story only).

Gutierrez, Vincent. Screenwriter. Films: "Little House on the Prairie: Look Back to Yesterday" TVM-1983.

Guylder, Van. Director. Films: "The Ramrodder" 1969 (& sp.).

Haas, Charles F. (1913-). Director. Films: "Showdown at Abilene" 1956; "Star in the Dust" 1956; "Wild Heritage" 1958. ¶TV: *Broken Arrow* 1956; *The Alaskans* 1959-60; *Bonanza*—"Escape to the Ponderosa" 3-5-60, "Death at Dawn" 4-30-60, "The Abduction" 10-29-60; *Maverick*—"The Ice Man" 1-29-61; *Rawhide*—"Clash at Broken Bluff" 11-2-65.

Hackel, A.W. Producer. Films: "Brand of Hate" 1934; "A Demon for Trouble" 1934; "Alias John Law" 1935; "Between Men" 1935; "Big Calibre" 1935; "Branded a Coward" 1935; "The Courageous Avenger" 1935; "Kid Courageous" 1935; "No Man's Range" 1935; "The Rider of the Law" 1935; "Smokey Smith" 1935; "Tombstone Terror" 1935; "Trail of Terror" 1935; "Western Justice" 1935; "Brand of the Outlaws" 1936; "Cavalry" 1936; "The Crooked Trail" 1936; "Everyman's Law" 1936; "The Kid Ranger" 1936; "The Last of the Warrens" 1936; "The Law Rides" 1936; "Rogue of the Range"

1936; "Sundown Saunders" 1936; "Undercover Man" 1936; "Valley of the Lawless" 1936; "Bar Z Bad Men" 1937; "Arizona Gunfighter" 1937; "Boothill Brigade" 1937; "Border Phantom" 1937; "Desert Phantom" 1937; "Doomed at Sundown" 1937; "The Gambling Terror" 1937; "Gun Lords of Stirrup Basin" 1937; "The Gun Ranger" 1937; "Guns in the Dark" 1937; "Lawless Land" 1937; "A Lawman Is Born" 1937; "Lightnin' Crandall" 1937; "The Red Rope" 1937; "Ridin' the Lone Trail" 1937; "Trail of Vengeance" 1937; "The Trusted Outlaw" 1937; "Colorado Kid" 1938; "Desert Patrol" 1938; "Durango Valley Raiders" 1938; "The Feud Maker" 1938; "Paroled to Die" 1938; "Thunder in the Desert" 1938.

Hackett, Albert (1900-3/16/95). Screenwriter. Films: "Rose Marie" 1936; "The Virginian" 1946.

Hackin, Dennis. Screenwriter. Films: "Wanda Nevada" 1979 (& prod.); "Bronco Billy" 1980 (& prod.).

Haddock, William (1877-6/30/69). Director. Films: "Grease Paint Indians" 1913.

Haft, David. Screenwriter. Films: "Hannie Calder" 1971-Brit./Span./Fr.

Hagg, Russell. Director. Films: "Raw Deal" 1977-Australia (& prod.).

Haggard, Piers (1939-). Director. Films: "Four Eyes and Six-Guns" TVM-1992.

Haid, Charles (1943-). Director. Films: "Iron Will" 1994.

Haines, William Wister. Screenwriter. Films: "The Texans" 1938.

Hakim, Andre (1915-). Producer. Films: "Powder River" 1953.

Haldane, Donald. Director. Films: "Nikki, Wild Dog of the North" 1961-U.S./Can.

Hale, Alan (1892-1/22/50). Director. Films: "Braveheart" 1925.

Hale, Albert W. Director. Films: "The Trials of Texas Thompson" 1919.

Hale, Earl. Director. Films: "The Gentleman from Arizona" 1939 (& sp.).

Hale, Scott. Screenwriter. Films: "The Shootist" 1976.

Hale, William (1928-). Director. Films: "Gunfight in Abilene" 1967; "Journey to Shiloh" 1968. ¶TV: *Cheyenne* 1955; *Colt .45* 1957; *Sugarfoot* 1957; *Bronco* 1958; *Lancer*—"Julie" 10-29-68, "The Escape" 12-31-68, "The Fix-It Man" 2-11-69, "Juniper's Camp" 3-11-69.

Halevy, Julian. Screenwriter. Films: "Custer of the West" 1967-U.S./Span.; "Pancho Villa" 1975-Span.

Haley, Earl. Director. Films: "The King of the Wild Horses" 1933 (& story).

Hall, Allan. Screenwriter. Films: "Desert Justice" 1936 (story only); "Gun Grit" 1936; "Toll of the Desert" 1936 (story only).

Hall, Jr., Arch. Screenwriter. Films: "Deadwood '76" 1965.

Hall, Sr., Arch (Nicholas Merriwether) (1909-4/28/78). Producer. Films: "Deadwood '76" 1965 (& sp.).

Hall, Cliff (1894-10/6/72). Screenwriter. Films: "The Human Tornado" 1925.

Hall, Conrad. Screenwriter. Films: "Running Target" 1956.

Hall, Douglas Kent. Screenwriter. Films: "The Great American Cowboy" 1974.

Hall, Emmett Campbell. Screenwriter. Films: "That Chink at Golden Gulch" 1910; "Was He a Coward?" 1911; "The Bugler of Battery B" 1912; "The End of the Romance" 1912; "The Mexican Spy" 1913; "The Taking of Rattlesnake Bill" 1913 (story only); "On Bitter Creek" 1915.

Hall, George C. Screenwriter. Films: "Forlorn River" 1926.

Hall, George Edward. Screenwriter. Films: "Babbling Tongues" 1915; "Judge Her Not" 1921 (& dir.); "Good Men and True" 1922; "The Prairie Mystery" 1922.

Hall, Norman S. (1896-12/12/64). Screenwriter. Films: "Border Caballero" 1936 (story only); "Fugitive from Sonora" 1937; "Wild West Days" 1937-serial; "Frontier Pony Express" 1939; "Wall Street Cowboy" 1939; "Adventures of Red Ryder" 1940-serial; "King of the Royal Mounted" 1940-serial; "King of the Texas Rangers" 1941-serial; "Outlaws of Pine Ridge" 1942; "The Sombrero Kid" 1942; "The Sundown Kid" 1942; "Black Hills Express" 1943; "Bordertown Gunfighters" 1943; "California Joe" 1943; "Carson City Cyclone" 1943; "Days of Old Cheyenne" 1943; "Dead Man's Gulch" 1943; "Death Valley Manhunt" 1943; "The Man from the Rio Grande" 1943; "Thundering Trails" 1943; "Mojave Firebrand" 1944; "Outlaws of Santa Fe" 1944; "The San Antonio Kid" 1944; "Sheriff of Las Vegas" 1944; "Sheriff of Sundown" 1944; "Stagecoach to Monterey" 1944; "Vigilantes of Dodge City" 1944 (&

story); "Corpus Christi Bandits" 1945; "The Topeka Terror" 1945; "Red River Renegades" 1946; "Rio Grande Raiders" 1946; "Last Days of Boot Hill" 1947; "Blazing Across the Pecos" 1948; "Buckaroo from Powder River" 1948; "Sundown in Santa Fe" 1948; "Whirlwind Raiders" 1948; "Brimstone" 1949 (story only); "Law of the Golden West" 1949; "San Antone Ambush" 1949; "South of Rio" 1949; "Beyond the Purple Hills" 1950; "Indian Territory" 1950; "Gene Autry and the Mounties" 1951; "Texans Never Cry" 1951; "Whirlwind" 1951; "Apache Country" 1952; "Carson City" 1952; "Montana Belle" 1952; "Night Stage to Galveston" 1952; "Pack Train" 1953; "Winning of the West" 1953; "The Missouri Traveler" 1958; "The Young Land" 1959.

Hall, Oakley (1920-). Writer. Films: "Warlock" 1959 (story).

Hall, Walter Richard. Writer. Films: "Partners of the Sunset" 1922 (story).

Hallenbeck, E. Daryl (1922-1/31/87). Director. TV: *Gunsmoke*—"Stranger in Town" 11-20-67.

Haller, Daniel (1926-). Director. TV: *Sara* 1976.

Hallet, Richard Matthews. Writer. Films: "Canyon of the Fools" 1923 (story).

Halligan, George. Director. Films: "Thorobred" 1922 (& sp.).

Halloway, Jack. Director. Films: "Overalls" 1916.

Halperin, Edward. Screenwriter. Films: "Code of the Cactus" 1939; "Danger Ahead" 1940; "Sky Bandits" 1940; "Yukon Flight" 1940.

Halperin, Victor (1895-1983). Writer. Films: "The Lone Star Trail" 1943 (story).

Halprin, A.H. Screenwriter. Films: "Taking a Chance" 1928.

Halsey, Forrest. Writer. Films: "Silver Queen" 1942 (story).

Hamby, William Henry. Writer. Films: "The Challenge of Chance" 1919 (story); "The Galloping Kid" 1922 (story).

Hamill, Pete (1935-). Screenwriter. Films: "Doc" 1971.

Hamilton, Donald (1916-). Writer. Films: "The Violent Men" 1955 (story); "The Big Country" 1958 (story).

Hamilton, George (1939-). Producer. Films: "Zorro, the Gay Blade" 1981.

Hamilton, Gilbert P. Director.

Films: "The Sheriff's Sacrifice" 1910; "The Sheriff" 1911; "The Sheriff's Decision" 1911; "Geronimo's Last Raid" 1912; "Their Hero Son" 1912 (sp. only); "The Lust of the Red Man" 1914; "The Pote Lariat of the Flying A" 1914; "The Toll of the War-Path" 1914.

Hamilton, James Shelley. Screenwriter. Films: "North of '36" 1924; "The Enchanted Hill" 1926.

Hamilton, Pat. Screenwriter. Films: "Manchurian Avenger" 1985.

Hamlin, John Harold. Writer. Films: "A Man of Nerve" 1925 (story); "Painted Ponies" 1927 (story).

Hammerstein, II, Oscar (1895-8/23/60). Screenwriter. Films: "Song of the West" 1930 (story only); "Rose Marie" 1936 (story only); "High, Wide and Handsome" 1937; "Rose Marie" 1954 (story only)."Oklahoma!" 1955 (story only).

Hammond, Victor. Screenwriter. Films: "Marked Trails" 1944; "Trigger Law" 1944; "The Utah Kid" 1944; "South of the Rio Grande" 1945.

Hamner, Robert. Screenwriter. Films: "Thirteen Fighting Men" 1960; "The Long Rope" 1961 (sp. only). ¶TV: *Maverick*—"Three Queens Full" 11-12-61 (dir.).

Hampton, Benjamin B. Director. Films: "Desert Gold" 1919 (prod. only); "Man of the Forest" 1921; "The Mysterious Rider" 1921; "When Romance Rides" 1922 (sp. only).

Hampton, Jesse D. Director. Films: "The End of the Game" 1919.

Hampton, Orville H. Screenwriter. Films: "I Shot Billy the Kid" 1950; "Train to Tombstone" 1950; "Three Desperate Men" 1951; "Outlaw Women" 1952; "Fangs of the Wild" 1954; "Last of the Desperadoes" 1955; "The Black Whip" 1956; "Frontier Gambler" 1956; "The Three Outlaws" 1956; "Badman's Country" 1958; "Toughest Gun in Tombstone" 1958; "Gunfighters of Abilene" 1960; "Oklahoma Territory" 1960; "Young Jesse James" 1960.

Hanalis, Blanche. Screenwriter. Films: "Little House on the Prairie" TVM-1974; "Young Pioneers" TVM-1976; "Young Pioneers' Christmas" TVM-1976.

Hanks, Arthur P. Screenwriter. Films: "The Rancher's Failing" 1913.

Hanley, William. Screenwriter. Films: "Testimony of Two Men" TVM-1977.

Hanna, Mark. Screenwriter. Films: "Gunslinger" 1956; "Flesh and

the Spur" 1957; "The Gatling Gun" 1972.

Hansell, Howard. Director. Films: "The Long Trail" 1917.

Hansen, Cecil Dan. Screenwriter. Films: "The Second Time Around" 1961.

Hanson, John. Director. Films: "Northern Lights" 1978 (& prod./sp.).

Harbach, Ottoa A. (1873-1/24/63). Writer. Films: "Rose Marie" 1936 (story); "Rose Marie" 1954 (story).

Harbringer, Mason. Writer. Films: "The Devil's Masterpiece" 1927 (story).

Harding, John Briard. Screenwriter. Films: "The Kissing Bandit" 1948.

Hardman, Rick. Screenwriter. Films: "Gunman's Walk" 1958 (story only); "The Rare Breed" 1966.

Hardy, Rod. Director. Films: "Rio Diablo" TVM-1993; "Buffalo Girls" TVM-1995.

Hardy, Stuart (1901-84). Writer. Films: "Forbidden Valley" 1938 (story); "Sierra" 1950 (story).

Hareson, Herta. Screenwriter. Films: "Last Ride to Santa Cruz" 1969-Ger./Fr.

Harmon, David P. Screenwriter. Films: "Johnny Concho" 1956 (& story); "Reprisal!" 1956; "The Last of the Fast Guns" 1958.

Harmon, Sidney (1907-2/29/88). Producer. Films: "Drums in the Deep South" 1951 (sp. only); "Day of the Outlaw" 1959.

Harper, Patricia. Screenwriter. Films: "Western Jamboree" 1938 (story only); "Prairie Pals" 1942; "Black Market Rustlers" 1943; "Raiders of San Joaquin" 1943 (story only); "Western Cyclone" 1943; "Blazing Frontier" 1944; "Death Rides the Plains" 1944 (story only); "The Drifter" 1944; "Trail to Gunsight" 1944; "Code of the Lawless" 1945; "The Topeka Terror" 1945 (& story); "The Scarlet Horseman" 1946-serial; "Border Feud" 1947; "Ghost Town Renegades" 1947; "Range Beyond the Blue" 1947.

Harrigan, Stephen. Screenwriter. Films: "The Last of His Tribe" TVM-1994.

Harriman, Karl. Writer. Films: "Chasing Rainbows" 1919 (story).

Harris, Frank. Writer. Films: "Cowboy" 1958 (story).

Harris, H.K. Writer. Films: "The Attack at Rocky Pass" 1913 (story).

Harris, Jr., Harry (1922-). Director. TV: *Stagecoach West* 1960; *Wanted—Dead or Alive*—1960-61 (prod.), "Journey for Josh" 10-5-60, "The Looters" 10-12-60, "The Choice" 12-14-60, "Witch Woman" 12-28-60, "Epitaph" 2-8-61; *Gunsmoke*—"Tall Trapper" 1-21-61, "Bad Seed" 2-4-61, "Potshot" 3-11-61, "Old Faces" 3-18-61, "Minnie" 4-15-61, "Perce" 9-30-61, "Miss Kitty" 10-14-61, "All That" 10-28-61, "Apprentice Doc" 12-9-61, "A Man a Day" 12-30-61, "Lacey" 1-13-62, "Catawomper" 2-10-62, "Reprisal" 3-10-62, "Durham Bull" 3-31-62, "The Dealer" 4-14-62, "Cale" 5-5-62, "The Boys" 5-26-62, "The Search" 9-15-62, "Call Me Dodie" 9-22-62, "Collie's Free" 10-20-62, "The Ditch" 10-27-62, "The Hunger" 11-17-62, "The Way It Is" 12-1-62, "Old Comrade" 12-29-62, "Louie Pheeters" 1-5-63, "Cotter's Girl" 1-19-63, "The Cousin" 2-2-63, "Ash" 2-16-63, "Anybody Can Kill a Marshal" 3-9-63, "I Call Him Wonder" 3-23-63, "The Far Places" 4-6-63, "Old York" 5-4-63, "Jeb" 5-25-63, "Kate Heller" 9-28-63, "Legends Don't Sleep" 10-12-63, "My Sister" 11-2-63, "Quint's Trail" 11-9-63, "The Magician" 12-21-63, "Dry Well" 1-11-64, "Friend" 1-25-64, "Comanches Is Safe" 3-7-64, "Father's Love" 3-14-64, "Caleb" 3-28-64, "Bently" 4-11-64, "Trip West" 5-2-64, "Scot-Free" 5-9-64, "Homecoming" 5-23-64, "Journey for Three" 6-6-64, "Old Man" 10-10-64, "The Violators" 10-17-64, "Doctor's Wife" 10-24-64, "Take Her, She's Cheap" 10-31-64, "Help Me Kitty" 11-7-64, "Jonah Hutchinson" 11-21-64, "Innocence" 12-12-64, "Run, Sheep, Run" 1-9-65, "Deputy Festus" 1-16-65, "The Pariah" 4-17-65, "Gilt Guilt" 4-24-65, "He Who Steals" 5-29-65, "Kioga" 10-23-65, "The Bounty Hunter" 10-30-65, "Sanctuary" 2-26-66, "Honor Before Justice" 3-5-66, "Harvest" 3-26-66; *Branded*—"The Bounty" 2-21-65, "Coward Step Aside" 3-7-65, "Now Join the Human Race" 9-19-65, "Barbed Wire" 2-13-66, "Yellow for Courage" 2-20-66; *Rawhide*—"Incident at Two Graves" 11-7-63, "Incident at Confidence Creek" 11-28-63, "Incident of the Wild Deuces" 12-12-63, "Incident of the Pied Pipder" 2-6-64; *Bonanza*—"The Gentle Ones" 10-29-67; *Hondo*—"Hondo and the Sudden Town" 11-17-67, "Hondo and the Ghost of Ed Dow" 11-24-67; *The High Chaparral*—"Ebenezer" 11-1-68, "North to Tucson" 11-8-68, "Our Lady of Guadalupe" 12-20-68, "No Irish Need Apply" 1-17-69, "The Glory Soldiers" 1-31-69, "Feather of an Eagle" 2-7-69; *The Man from Shiloh* 1970; *Kung Fu*—"This Valley of Terror" 9-28-74, "The Predators" 10-5-74, "A Lamb to the Slaughter" 1-11-75, "Forbidden Kingdom" 1-18-75, "The Brothers Caine" 3-1-75, "The Thief of Chendo" 3-29-75; *The Young Pioneers*—4-2-78; *Paradise*—"The Burial Ground" 11-4-89, "Boomtown" 11-18-89, "A Gathering of Guns" 2-17-90, "The Chase" 4-14-90, "Bad Blood" 2-1-91, "A Bullet Through the Heart" 2-15-91, "Birthright" 3-8-91, "The Search for K.C. Cavanaugh" 4-5-91, "Unfinished Business" 5-10-91; *Dr. Quinn, Medicine Woman*—"Life and Death" 3-12-94.

Harris, Margaret M. Screenwriter. Films: "Rough Ridin'" 1924.

Harris, Marilyn (1952-). Writer. Films: "The Girl Called Hatter Fox" TVM-1977 (story).

Harris, Owen. Screenwriter. Films: "Frontier Uprising" 1961; "The Gambler Wore a Gun" 1961.

Harris, R.R. Writer. Films: "Stone of Silver Creek" 1935 (story).

Harris, Ray. Screenwriter. Films: "Sunset Pass" 1929.

Harris, Roy. Screenwriter. Films: "The Gay Defender" 1927.

Harris, Sherman A. Producer. Films: "The Lone Ranger and the Lost City of Gold" 1958. ¶TV: *The Lone Ranger* 1949-57.

Harris, Theodosia. Screenwriter. Films: "The Martyrs of the Alamo" 1915 (story only); "The Hidden Law" 1916.

Harrison, C. Stanford. Writer. Films: "The Vigilantes" 1918 (story).

Harrison, C. William. Writer. Films: "The Guns of Fort Petticoat" 1957 (story).

Harrison, Jr., Hal. Director. Films: "Pony Express Rider" 1972 (& prod./sp.); "Baker's Hawk" 1976 (sp. only).

Harrison, Kay. Screenwriter. Films: "The Girl and the Law" 1920; "A Son of the North" 1920; "Under Northern Lights" 1920.

Harrison, P.S. Screenwriter. Films: "Deerslayer" 1943.

Harrison, Richard (James London). Director. Films: "Jesse and Lester, Two Brothers in a Place Called Trinity" 1972-Ital. (& prod./sp.); "Scalps" 1986-Ital./Ger. (sp. only).

Harrison, Saul. Director. Films: "Salt of the Earth" 1917.

Hart, Fred. Writer. Films: "In Old California" 1929 (story).

Hart, Harvey (1918-11/21/89). Director. Films: "Standing Tall" TVM-1978. ¶TV: *Laredo*—"I See By Your Outfit" 9-23-65, "Rendezvous at Arillo" 10-7-65; *Wild Wild West*—"The Night of the Dancing Death" 11-5-65; *Here Come the Brides*—"A Man and His Magic" 12-4-68.

Hart, Neal (1879-4/2/49). Director. Films: "Hell's Oasis" 1920; "Skyfire" 1920; "Butterfly Range" 1922 (& sp.); "Lure of Gold" 1922 (& sp.); "Rangeland" 1922 (& sp.); "South of the Northern Lights" 1922 (& sp.); "West of the Pecos" 1922 (& sp.); "Below the Rio Grande" 1923 (& sp.); "The Devil's Bowl" 1923 (& sp.); "The Fighting Strain" 1923 (& sp.); "The Forbidden Range" 1923 (& sp.); "Salty Saunders" 1923; "The Secret of the Pueblo" 1923; "Lawless Men" 1924; "The Left-Hand Brand" 1924 (& sp.); "Tucker's Top Hand" 1924 (& sp.); "The Valley of Vanishing Men" 1924; "The Verdict of the Desert" 1925; "The Scarlet Brand" 1927-serial; "Branded a Thief" 1935 (sp. only).

Hart, William S. (1864-6/23/46). Director. Films: "The Gringo" 1914; "The Passing of Two-Gun Hicks" 1914; "The Bad Buck of Santa Ynez" 1915; "Cash Parrish's Pal" 1915; "The Conversion of Frosty Blake" 1915; "The Darkening Trail" 1915; "The Grudge" 1915; "Keno Bates—Liar" 1915; "Mr. Silent Haskins" 1915; "Pinto Ben" 1915; "The Roughneck" 1915; "The Ruse" 1915; "The Scourge of the Desert" 1915; "The Taking of Luke McVane" 1915; "The Apostle of Vengeance" 1916; "The Aryan" 1916; "The Dawn Maker" 1916; "The Devil's Double" 1916; "The Gunfighter" 1916; "The Patriot" 1916; "The Primal Lure" 1916; "The Return of Draw Egan" 1916; "The Cold Deck" 1917; "The Desert Man" 1917; "The Silent Man" 1917; "The Square Deal Man" 1917; "Truthful Tulliver" 1917; "Wolf Lwory" 1917; "Blue Blazes Rawden" 1918; "The Border Wireless" 1918; "Branding Broadway" 1918; "The Narrow Trail" 1918 (prod./sp. only); "Riddle Gawne" 1918 (& prod.); "Selfish Yates" 1918; "The Tiger Man" 1918; "Wolves of the Rail" 1918; "Breed of Men" 1919; "Hell's Hinges" 1919; "The Money Corral" 1919 (& sp./story); "Square Deal Sanderson" 1919 (& prod.); "Sand!" 1920 (sp. only); "The Testing Blood" 1920 (story only); "The Toll Gate" 1920 (story only); "O'Malley of the Mounted

1921 (sp. only); "O'Malley of the Mounted" 1921 (story only); "White Oak" 1921 (story only); "Wild Bill Hickok" 1923 (prod./story only); "Singer Jim McKee" 1924 (story only); "Tumbleweeds" 1925 (prod. only).

Harte, Bret (1836-5/5/02). Writer. Films: "The Redman and the Child" 1908 (story); "The Luck of Roaring Camp" 1910 (story); "Goddess of Sagebrush Gulch" 1912 (story); "Salome Jane" 1914 (story); "The Bad Buck of Santa Ynez" 1915 (story); "The Lily of Poverty Flat" 1915 (story); "M'Liss" 1915 (story); "The Half Breed" 1916 (story); "Tennessee's Pardner" 1916 (story); "Two Men of Sandy Bar" 1916 (story); "The Dawn of Understanding" 1918 (story); "M'Liss" 1918 (story); "The Outcasts of Poker Flat" 1919 (story); "Fighting Cressy" 1920 (story); "The Girl Who Ran Wild" 1922 (story); "Salomy Jane" 1923 (story); "The Flaming Forties" 1925 (story); "The Golden Princess" 1925 (story); "The Man from Red Gulch" 1925 (story); "Taking a Chance" 1928 (story); "The Luck of Roaring Camp" 1937 (story); "The Outcasts of Poker Flat" 1937 (story); "The Outcasts of Poker Flat" 1952 (story); "Tennessee's Partner" 1955 (story); "California Gold Rush" TVM-1981 (story).

Hartford, David M. Director. Films: "Nomads of the North" 1920 (& sp.).

Hartford, Huntington. Producer. Films: "Face to Face" 1952 ("The Bride Comes to Yellow Sky" segment).

Hartigan, Pat (1881-5/8/51). Director. Films: "A Chance Shot" 1911.

Hartman, Edmund. Screenwriter. Films: "Ride 'Em, Cowboy" 1942 (story only); "The Paleface" 1948; "Fancy Pants" 1950; "The Shakiest Gun in the West" 1968 (story only).

Hartsook, Fred. Screenwriter. Films: "Escort West" 1959.

Hartung, Raymond. Director. TV: *Young Riders*—"The Road Not Taken" 6-11-92.

Harun, Helmut. Screenwriter. Films: "Man Called Gringo" 1964-Ger./Span.; "Five Thousand Dollars on One Ace" 1965-Span./Ital.; "Man from Oklahoma" 1965-Ital./Span./Ger.; "Clint the Stranger" 1968-Ital./Span./Ger.

Harvey, Anthony (1931-). Director. Films: "Eagle's Wing" 1979-Brit./Span.

Harvey, Harry. Director. Films:

"The Caballero's Wife" 1914; "The Folly of a Life of Crime" 1915; "The Yellow Bullet" 1917; "Captured Alive" 1918; "The Dead Shot" 1918; "The Robber" 1918; "Riding Wild" 1919; "The Silent Sentinel" 1918; "The Trail of No Return" 1918; "Wolves of the Range" 1918; "The Black Horse Bandit" 1919; "The Border Terror" 1919; "The Canyon Mystery" 1919.

Harvey, Jack. Screenwriter. Films: "Last of the Wild Horses" 1948; "Grand Canyon" 1949.

Harvey, Jerry. Screenwriter. Films: "China 9, Liberty 37" 1978-Ital./Span./U.S.

Haskin, Byron (1899-4/16/84). Director. Films: "Silver City" 1951; "Warpath" 1951; "Denver and Rio Grande" 1952; "The First Texan" 1956.

Hatch, Marian. Screenwriter. Films: "The White Masks" 1921.

Hathaway, Henry (1898-2/11/85). Director. Films: "Heritage of the Desert" 1932; "Wild Horse Mesa" 1932; "Man of the Forest" 1933; "To the Last Man" 1933; "Under the Tonto Rim" 1933; "The Last Round-Up" 1934; "The Thundering Herd" 1934; "Brigham Young—Frontiersman" 1940; "The Shepherd of the Hills" 1941; "Rawhide" 1951; "Garden of Evil" 1954; "From Hell to Texas" 1958; "North to Alaska" 1960 (& prod.); "How the West Was Won" 1962; "The Sons of Katie Elder" 1965; "Nevada Smith" 1966 (& prod.); "Five Card Stud" 1968; "True Grit" 1969; "Shoot Out" 1971.

Hatton, Dick (1891-7/9/31). Director. Films: "Four Hearts" 1922 (sp. only); "The Seventh Sheriff" 1923 (& sp.); "The Sting of the Scorpion" 1923; "Sagebrush Gospel" 1924; "Two Fisted Justice" 1924; "The Whirlwind Ranger" 1924; "A He-Man's Country" 1926; "Temporary Sheriff" 1926.

Hauff, Werner. Screenwriter. Films: "Hatred of God" 1967-Ital./Ger.

Hauser, Dwight. Screenwriter. Films: "Legend of Lobo" 1962.

Hauser, Lionel. Screenwriter. Films: "The Dark Comman" 1940.

Havey, M.B. Screenwriter. Films: "In the Days of '49" 1911.

Havinga, Nick. Director. TV: *Paradise*—"Squaring Off" 5-13-89, "A Study in Fear" 3-29-91.

Hawkins, William. *see* Caiano, Mario.

Hawks, Howard (1896-12/26/77). Director. Films: "Quicksands"

1923 (sp. only); "The Outlaw" 1943; "Red River" 1948 (& prod.); "The Big Sky" 1952 (& prod.); "Rio Bravo" 1959 (& prod.); "El Dorado" 1967 (& prod.); "Rio Lobo" 1970 (& prod.).

Hawks, J.G. Screenwriter. Films: "The Quakeress" 1913; "Jim Cameron's Wife" 1914; "The Bad Buck of Santa Ynez" 1915; "Cash Parrish's Pal" 1915; "The Conversion of Frosty Blake" 1915; "The Darkening Trail" 1915; "The Grudge" 1915; "Keno Bates—Liar" 1915; "The Man from Nowhere" 1915; "Mr. Silent Haskins" 1915; "The Ruse" 1915; "The Scourge of the Desert" 1915; "The Devil's Double" 1916; "Lieutenant Danny, U.S.A." 1916; "The Primal Lure" 1916; "The Cold Deck" 1917; "The Devil Dodger" 1917; "The Firefly of Tough Luck" 1917; "The Square Deal Man" 1917; "Truthful Tulliver" 1917; "Blue Blazes Rawden" 1918; "A Desert Wooing" 1918; "Flare-Up Sal" 1918; "Staking His Life" 1918; "The Tiger Man" 1918; "Breed of Men" 1919; "Partners Three" 1919; "The Sheriff's Son" 1919; "The Branding Iron" 1920; "The Storm" 1922; "The Eternal Struggle" 1923; "Wild Bill Hickok" 1923; "Singer Jim McKee" 1924; "The Splendid" 1925; "The Sonora Kid" 1927.

Hawks, William B. Producer. Films: "The Tall Men" 1955; "The Last Wagon" 1956; "The Law and Jake Wade" 1958.

Hawley, Lowell S. Screenwriter. Films: "The Adventures of Bullwhip Griffin" 1967.

Hawley, Rock. *see* Hill, Robert F.

Hay, Jacob (1920-). Writer. Films: "The Sheriff of Fractured Jaw" 1958-Brit. (story).

Haycox, Ernest. Writer. Films: "Stagecoach" 1939 (story); "Sundown Jim" 1942 (story); "Apache Trail" 1943 (story); "Abilene Town" 1946 (story); "Canyon Passage" 1946 (story); "Heaven Only Knows" 1947 (sp.); "Montana" 1950 (story); "Man in the Saddle" 1951 (story); "Bugles in the Afternoon" 1952 (story); "Apache War Smoke" 1952 (story); "Stagecoach" 1966 (story); "Stagecoach" TVM-1986 (story).

Hayden, Jeffrey. Director. TV: *Shane* 1966; *Alias Smith and Jones*—"A Fistful of Diamonds" 3-4-71, "The Man Who Murdered Himself" 3-18-71, "Journey from San Juan" 4-8-71, "The Legacy of Charlie O'Rourke" 4-22-71, "Jailbreak at Junction City"

9-30-71, "Shootout at Diablo Station" 12-2-71, "Only Three to a Bed" 1-13-7; *How the West Was Won* 1977-79 (prod.).

Hayden, Russell (1912-6/9/81). Screenwriter. Films: "In Old Colorado" 1941. ¶TV: *Judge Roy Bean* 1955-56 (prod.); *26 Men* 1958-59 (prod.).

Hayes, Alfred (1911-8/14/85). Screenwriter. Films: "These Thousand Hills" 1959.

Hayes, John. Director. Films: "Fandango" 1970 (& sp.).

Hayes, John Michael (1919-). Screenwriter. Films: "War Arrow" 1953; "Nevada Smith" 1966; "Nevada Smith" TVM-1975 (& prod.); "Iron Wills" 1994.

Hayes, Raphael. Screenwriter. Films: "Reprisal!" 1956.

Hayes, Steven. Writer. Films: "Escort West" 1959 (story).

Hayes, Ward. Director. Films: "Come On Cowboys!" 1924 (& sp.); "Horse Sense" 1924; "Sell 'Em Cowboy" 1924; "The Cactus Cure" 1925; "My Pal" 1925 (& story); "Range Justice" 1925; "Ridin' Easy" 1925; "The Rip Snorter" 1925; "The Secret of Black Canyon" 1925; "The Strange Rider" 1925; "A Two-Fisted Sheriff" 1925; "Where Romance Rides" 1925; "Wolves of the Road" 1925.

Hayward, Lillie (1891-6/29/77). Screenwriter. Films: "The Best Bad Man" 1925; "My Own Pal" 1926; "Ranson's Folly" 1926; "Heart of the Rio Grande" 1942; "My Friend Flicka" 1943; "Smoky" 1946; "Northwest Stampede" 1948; "Cattle Drive" 1951; "Bronco Buster" 1952; "The Raiders" 1952; "Santa Fe Passage" 1955; "The Proud Rebel" 1958; "Tonka" 1958.

Hayward, Willie. Screenwriter. Films: "Blood on the Moon" 1948.

Hazard, Lawrence. Screenwriter. Films: "Jackass Mail" 1942; "The Spoilers" 1942; "Gentle Annie" 1944; "Dakota" 1945; "The Fabulous Texan" 1947; "Wyoming" 1947.

Healey, Myron (1922-). Screenwriter. Films: "Colorado Ambush" 1951; "Texas Lawmen" 1951 (story only).

Heath, A.B. Writer. Films: "The Scarlet West" 1925 (story).

Heath, Arch. Screenwriter. Films: "White Eagle" 1941-serial.

Heath, Hy. Screenwriter. Films: "Stallion Canyon" 1949.

Heath, Percy (1886-2/9/33). Screenwriter. Films: "The Huntress" 1923; "Let's Go Gallagher" 1925;

"The Wyoming Wildcat" 1925 (story only); "The Sonora Kid" 1927; "The Border Legion" 1930; "Dude Ranch" 1931.

Heazlit, Eva B. Writer. Films: "A Knight of the West" 1921 (story).

Hecht, Ben (1894-4/18/64). Screenwriter. Films: "Let Freedom Ring" 1939; "The Indian Fighter" 1955.

Hecht, Harold (1907-5/26/85). Producer. Films: "Apache" 1954; "The Kentuckian" 1955; "Cat Ballou" 1965; "The Way West" 1967.

Hecklemann, Charles N. (1913-). Writer. Films: "Frontier Feud" 1945 (story); "Deputy Marshal" 1949 (story).

Heermance, Richard. Producer. Films: "Canyon River" 1946; "Wichita" 1955; "The Young Guns" 1956.

Heffron, Richard T. (1930-). Director. Films: "I Will Fight No More Forever" TVM-1975; "True Grit" TVM-1978; "The Mystic Warrior" TVM-1984. ¶TV: *Dr. Quinn, Medicine Woman*—"Great American Medicine Show" 2-13-93.

Heffron, Thomas N. Director. Films: "The Return" 1916; "A Man's Fight" 1919; "Deuce Duncan" 1918; "The Prodigal Liar" 1919; "Firebrand Trevison" 1920; "Sunset Sprague" 1920.

Heideman, Leonard. Screenwriter. Films: "Canyon Crossroads" 1955; "Valerie" 1957.

Heifetz, Louis. Screenwriter. Films: "Perils of the Royal Mounted" 1942.

Heilbron, Adelaide. Screenwriter. Films: "The Girl of the Golden West" 1923.

Heilweil, David (1917-2/15/89). Producer. Films: "3:10 to Yuma" 1957; "Face of a Fugitive" 1959.

Heims, Jo. Screenwriter. Films: "The Gun Hawk" 1963; "Navajo Run" 1966.

Heinemann, Arthur (1910-9/22/87). Screenwriter. Films: "The Capture of Grizzly Adams" TVM-1982.

Heinz, Ray. Director. Films: "Blazing Guns" 1935; "Border Vengeance" 1935.

Heisler, Stuart (1897-8/21/79). Director. Films: "Along Came Jones" 1945; "The Lone Ranger" 1956; "Dallas" 1950; "The Burning Hills" 1956. ¶TV: *Cheyenne* 1955; *Lawman* 1958; *Rawhide*—"Incident of the Roman Candles" 7-10-59, "Incident of the Day of the Dead" 9-18-59, "Incident at the Buffalo Smokehouse"

10-30-59, "Incident of the One Hundred Amulets" 5-6-60, "Incident at Superstition Prairie" 12-2-60, "Incident of the Captive" 12-16-60; *Gunsmoke*—"Thick 'n' Thin" 12-26-59; *The Dakotas* 1963.

Heller, Joseph (1923-). Screenwriter. Films: "Dirty Dingus Magee" 1970.

Heller, Lukas (1930-11/2/88). Screenwriter. Films: "Monte Walsh" 1970; "Deadly Trackers" 1973.

Hellman, Monte (1931-). Director. Films: "Ride in the Whirlwind" 1966 (& prod.); "The Shooting" 1966 (& prod.); "China 9, Liberty 37" 1978-Ital./Span./U.S.

Hellman, Sam (1885-8/11/50). Screenwriter. Films: "Frontier Marshal" 1939; "The Return of Frank James" 1940; "My Darling Clementine" 1946 (story only); "Pirates of Monterey" 1947; "Powder River" 1953 (story only).

Hellstrom, Gunnar. Director. TV: *Gunsmoke*—"Cattle Barons" 9-18-67, "Death Train" 11-27-67, "Mr. Sam'l" 2-26-68, "Gold Town" 1-27-69, "Hawk" 10-20-69, "The Still" 11-10-69, "Snow Train" 10-19-70 & 10-26-70, "Lynott" 11-1-71, "Sarah" 10-16-72, "Tatum" 11-13-72, "The Avenger" 11-27-72, "The Gang" 12-11-72, "Homecoming" 1-8-73, "Kimbro" 2-12-73, "This Golden Land" 3-5-73, "Matt's Love Story" 9-24-73, "A Game of Death … An Act of Love" 11-5-73 & 11-12-73, "A Family of Killers" 1-14-74, "The Town Tamers" 1-28-74, "The Iron Blood of Courage" 2-18-74, "Cowtown Hustler" 3-11-74, "Disciple" 4-1-74, "The Guns of Cibola Blanca" 9-23-74 & 9-30-74, "The Iron Man" 10-21-74, "In Performance of Duty" 11-18-74, "Island in the Desert" 12-2-74 & 12-9-74, "The Squaw" 1-6-75, "Larkin" 1-20-75, "Manolo" 3-17-75; *Wild Wild West*—"The Night of the Samurai" 10-13-67, "The Night of the Running Death" 12-15-67, "The Night of the Fugitives" 11-8-68; *Cimarron Strip*—"Heller" 1-18-68; *How the West Was Won*—"The Enemy" 2-5-79.

Hemmings, David (1941-). Director. Films: "Davy Crockett: Rainbow in the Thunder" TVM-1988. ¶TV: *Ned Blessing: The Story of My Life and Times*—"Oscar" 9-8-93.

Henabery, Joseph E. (1888-2/18/76). Director. Films: "The Man from Painted Post" 1917; "Tongues of Flame" 1924; "The Call of the North" 1921; "North of the Rio Grande" 1922; "While Satan Sleeps" 1922; "The Leather Burners" 1943.

Henaghan, James. Screenwriter. Films: "The Christmas Kid" 1966-Span./Ital.; "The Tall Women" 1966-Austria/Ital./Span.

Henderson, Dell (1877-12/2/56). Director. Films: "The Under-Sheriff" 1914; "Dead or Alive" 1921; "The Girl from Porcupine" 1922; "The Love Bandit" 1924; "One Law for the Woman" 1924; "The Bad Lands" 1925; "The Rambling Ranger" 1927.

Hendryx, James B. Writer. Films: "The Promise" 1917 (story); "The Texan" 1920 (story); "Snowdrift" 1923 (story).

Hengge, Paul. Screenwriter. Films: "Montana Trap" 1976-Ger.

Henkel, Peter. Director. Films: "Three Bullets for a Long Gun" 1970-Ger./S.Afr. (& prod.).

Henley, Hobart (1887-5/22/64). Director. Films" "Laughing Bill Hyde" 1918.

Hennessy, George. Screenwriter. Films: "Billy's Stratagem" 1911; "Heredity" 1912; "Man's Lust for Gold" 1912; "A Temporary Truce" 1912; "Just Gold" 1913.

Hennigar, William K. Director. Films: "The Wicked Die Slow" 1968.

Henreid, Paul (1907-3/29/92). Director. TV: *Sugarfoot* 1957; *Maverick*—"The Brasada Spur" 2-22-59, "Passage to Fort Doom" 3-8-59; *Johnny Ringo* 1959; *The Big Valley*—"My Son, My Son" 11-3-65, "Earthquake!" 11-10-65, "The Fallen Hawk" 3-2-66, "Boy into Man" 1-16-67, "The Stallion" 1-30-67, "Guilty" 10-30-67, "Miranda" 1-15-68, "The Devil's Masquerade" 3-4-68, "A Stranger Everywhere" 12-9-68; *Bonanza*—"A Time to Step Down" 9-25-66.

Henry, David Lee. Screenwriter. Films: "Harry Tracy—Desperado" 1982.

Henry, J.K. Writer. Films: "Mystery Ranch" 1934 (story).

Henry, Marguerite (1902-). Writer. Films: "Peter Lundy and the Medicine Hat Stallion" TVM-1977 (story).

Henry, O. (William Sydney Porter) (1862-6/5/10). Writer. Films: "A Western Prince Charming" 1912 (story); "The Caballero's Wife" 1914 (story); "The Stirrup Brother" 1914 (story); "Madame Bo-Peep" 1917 (story); "In Old Arizona" 1929 (story); "The Texan" 1930 (story); "Cisco Kid" 1931 (story); "The Llano Kid" 1939 (story); "Black Eagle" 1948 (story).

Henry, Will (1912-). Writer. Films: "Pillars of the Sky" 1956 (story); "Journey to Shiloh" 1968 (story); "Mackenna's Gold" 1969 (story); "Young Billy Young" 1969 (story).

Herbert, F. Hugh. Screenwriter. Films: "The Dark Command" 1940; "Three Faces West" 1940.

Herman, Al (1887-7/2/67). Director. Films: "Beyond the Trail" 1926; "Big Boy Rides Again" 1935; "The Cowboy and the Bandit" 1935; "Gun Play" 1935; "Trails End" 1935; "Western Frontier" 1935; "Blazing Justice" 1936; "Outlaws of the Range" 1936; "Renfrew of the Royal Mounted" 1937 (& prod.); "Valley of Terror" 1937; "Renfrew on the Great White Trail" 1938 (& prod.); "Rollin' Plains" 1938; "Starlight Over Texas" 1938; "Utah Trail" 1938; "Where the Buffalo Roam" 1938; "Down the Wyoming Trail" 1939; "The Man from Texas" 1939; "Rollin' Westward" 1939; "Song of the Buckaroo" 1939; "Sundown on the Prairie" 1939; "Arizona Frontier" 1940; "The Golden Trail" 1940; "Pals of the Silver Sage" 1940; "Rainbow Over the Range" 1940; "Rhythm of the Rio Grande" 1940; "Roll, Wagons, Roll" 1940; "Take Me Back to Oklahoma" 1940; "The Pioneers" 1941; "Rollin' Home to Texas" 1941; "The Rangers Take Over" 1942; "Bad Men of Thunder Gap" 1943.

Herman, Gerald. Screenwriter. Films "Jory" 1972.

Hermont, Robert. Director. TV: *Zorro*—"The Sergeant Sees Red" 5-14-59.

Hernandez, Joaquin Romero. *see* Romero Marchent, Joaquin L.

Herring, Moree. Screenwriter. Films: "Dead Man's Gold" 1948.

Hersholt, Jean (1886-6/2/56). Director. Films: "The Golden Trail" 1920; "When Romance Rides" 1922.

Hess, Henry. Screenwriter. Films: "The Pecos Kid" 1935.

Hessler, Gordon (1930-). Director. Films: "A Cry in the Wilderness" TVM-1974. ¶TV: *Sara* 1976.

Heston, Fraser Clarke. Screenwriter. Films: "The Mountain Men" 1980.

Hewitt, Lee J. Screenwriter. Films: "Kentucky Rifle" 1956.

Heyes, Douglas (1923-2/8/93). Director. Films: "Battle of Rogue River" 1954 (sp. only); "Masterson of Kansas" 1954 (sp. only); "Powderkeg" TVM-1971 (& prod./sp.); "Honky Tonk" TVM-1974; "The Barbary Coast" TVM-1975 (prod./sp. only). ¶TV: *The Adventures of Rin Tin Tin* 1954; *Cheyenne* 1955; *Circus Boy* 1956-58 (assoc. prod.); *Colt .45* 1957; *Maverick*—"The Long Hunt" 10-20-57, "The Quick and the Dead" 12-8-57, "Diamond in the Rough" 1-26-58, "The Savage Hills" 2-9-58, "Plunder of Paradise" 3-9-58; "Buriel Ground of the Gods" 3-30-58, "The Day They Hanged Bret Maverick" 9-21-58, "Alias Bart Maverick" 10-5-58, "Escape to Tampico" 10-26-58, "Prey of the Cat" 12-7-58, "Two Beggars on Horseback" 1-18-59, "Two Tickets to Ten Strike" 3-15-59, "The Strange Journey of Jenny Hill" 3-29-59; *Laramie* 1959; *Desilu Playhouse*—"Six Guns for Donegan" 10-16-59; *Alias Smith and Jones*—"Never Trust an Honest Man" 4-15-71; *Bearcats!* 1971 (exec. prod.); *The Barbary Coast* 1975-76 (prod.).

Heywood, W. Screenwriter. Films: "The Son of the Wolf" 1922.

Hibbard, Enid. Screenwriter. "The Border Whirlwind" 1926.

Hibbs, Jesse (1906-2/4/85). Director. Films: "Ride Clear of Diablo" 1953; "Black Horse Canyon" 1954; "Rails into Laramie" 1954; "The Yellow Mountain" 1954; "The Spoilers" 1955; "Walk the Proud Land" 1956; "Ride a Crooked Trail" 1958. ¶TV: *Wagon Train*—"The Rex Montana Story" 5-28-58, "The River Crossing" 12-14-60; *Bronco* 1958; *Gunsmoke*—"The Cast" 12-6-58, "Marshal Proudfoot" 1-10-59, "Kitty's Rebellion" 2-7-59, "The Bear" 2-28-59, "The Coward" 3-7-59, "Annie Oakley" 10-24-59, "The Boots" 11-14-59, "Tag, You're It" 12-19-59, "Jailbait Janet" 2-27-60, "Where'd They Go" 3-12-60, "I Thee Wed" 4-16-60, "Gentleman's Disagreement" 4-30-60, "Belle's Back" 5-14-60, "The Bobsy Twins" 5-21-60, "Old Flame" 5-28-60, "Friend's Pay-Off" 9-3-60, "The Peace Officer" 10-15-60, "Don Matteo" 10-22-60, "Unloaded Gun" 1-14-61, "Colorado Sheriff" 6-17-61; *Rawhide*—"Incident of the Coyote Weed" 3-20-59, "Incident of the Calico Gun" 4-24-59, "Incident of the Misplaced Indians" 5-1-59, "Incident of the Judas Trap" 6-5-59, "Incident of the Thirteenth Man" 10-23-59, "Incident of the Haunted Hills" 11-6-59, "Incident of the Druid's Curse" 1-8-60, "Incident of the Sharpshooter" 2-16-60, "The Lost Count" 1-5-62, "Prairie Fire" 3-19-65; *The Alaskans* 1959; *The Rifleman*—"The Mescalero Curse" 4-18-61; *Bonanza*—"Gift of Water" 2-11-62; *Laramie*—"The Betrayers"

1-22-63, "The Wedding Party" 1-29-63, "The Dispossessed" 2-19-63, "The Stranger" 4-23-63; *Wild Wild West*—"The Night of the Lord of Limbo" 12-30-66.

Hibler, Winston (1911-8/8/76). Producer. Films: "Melody Time" 1948 (sp. only); "Nikki, Wild Dog of the North" 1961-U.S./Can. (& sp.); "King of the Grizzlies" 1970; "One Little Indian" 1973; "The Castaway Cowboy" 1974.

Hickman, Howard (1880-12/30/49). Director. Films: "Two-Gun Betty" 1919; "The Killer" 1921; "Man of the Forest" 1921 (sp. only).

Hicks, Elinore. Screenwriter. Films: "Two Brothers" 1910.

Hicks, R.E. Writer. Films: "The Cattle Thief's Escape" 1913 (story).

Hickson, Russell. Writer. Films: "Buffalo Bill's Last Fight" 1927 (story).

Higgins, Howard (1891-12/16/38). Director. Films: "The Painted Desert" 1931 (& sp.); "Battle of Greed" 1934.

Higgins, John C. Screenwriter. Films: "Pony Soldier" 1952; "The Broken Star" 1956; "Quincannon, Frontier Scout" 1956.

Hiken, Nat. Screenwriter. Films: "Cliff Edwards and His Buckaroos" 1941-short.

Hill, Elizabeth. Writer. Films: "Streets of Laredo" 1949 (story).

Hill, Ethel (1898-5/17/54). Screenwriter. Films: "The Eagle" 1918; "The Law of Fear" 1928; "Young Whirlwind" 1928; "Scarlet Brand" 1932; "In Old Oklahoma" 1943.

Hill, George (1894-8/10/34). Director. Films: "Get Your Man" 1921; "The Man from God's Country" 1924 (sp. only); "Daring Days" 1925 (story only); "Zander the Great" 1925.

Hill, George Roy (1923-). Director. Films: "Butch Cassidy and the Sundance Kid" 1959.

Hill, Jack. Screenwriter. Films: "The Beast of Hollow Mountain" 1956.

Hill, James. Producer. Films: "Vera Cruz" 1954; "Thunder in the Sun" 1959 (story only); "The Unforgiven" 1960.

Hill, John. Screenwriter. Films: "Quigley Down Under" 1990.

Hill, Josephine. Screenwriter. Films: "The Drifter" 1922.

Hill, Robert F. (Rock Hawley) (1886-3/18/66). Director. Films: "Ju-

bilo" 1919 (sp. only); "The Alarm" 1921; "The Brand of Courage" 1921; "The Deputy's Double Cross" 1921; "Old Dynamite" 1921; "The Big Ranger" 1922; "Desperation" 1922; "Fighting Back" 1922; "The Trail of the Wolf" 1922; "Shadows of the North" 1923; "Idaho" 1925-serial; "Wild West" 1925-serial; "The Bar C Mystery" 1926-serial; "Blazing Days" 1927; "Range Courage" 1927 (sp. only); "The Return of the Riddle Rider" 1927-serial; "Sundown Trail" 1931 (& sp.); "Come On, Danger!" 1932; "The Last Frontier" 1932-serial; "The Cheyenne Kid" 1933; "Cowboy Holiday" 1934; "A Demon for Trouble" 1934; "Cowboy Holiday" 1934 (sp. only); "Frontier Days" 1934; "Outlaws' Highway" 1934; "Cyclone Ranger" 1935; "Danger Trail" 1935; "Six Gun Justice" 1935; "The Texas Rambler" 1935; "The Vanishing Riders" 1935; "Law and Lead" 1936 (& sp.); "Men of the Plains" 1936; "The Phantom of the Range" 1936; "Rio Grande Romance" 1936; "Rip Roarin' Buckaroo" 1936; "Too Much Beef" 1936 (& sp.); "West of Nevada" 1936 (& sp.); "Cheyenne Rides Again" 1937; "Fighting Playboy" 1937; "The Idaho Kid" 1937; "Mystery Range" 1937; "The Roaming Cowboy" 1937; "Feud of the Trail" 1938; "Man's Country" 1938; "The Painted Trail" 1938; "Whirlwind Horseman" 1938; "Wild Horse Canyon" 1938; "Drifting Westward" 1939; "Overland Mail" 1939; "Wanderers of the West" 1941; "Raw Edge" 1956 (sp. only).

Hill, Ruth Beebe. Writer. Films: "The Mystic Warrior" TVM-1984 (story).

Hill, Walter (1942-). Director. Films: "The Long Riders" 1980; "Geronimo: An American Legend" 1993 (& prod.).

Hiller, Arthur (1923-). Director. TV: *The Rifleman*—"The Apprentice Sheriff" 12-9-58, "Bloodlines" 10-6-59, "Mail Order Groom" 1-12-60, "The Schoolmaster" 11-29-60; *Gunsmoke*—"Love of a Good Woman" 1-24-59, "Wind" 3-21-59, "The Constable" 5-30-59, "Doc Judge" 2-6-60, "Kitty's Killing" 2-20-60, "The Deserter" 6-4-60, "The Worm" 10-29-60, "Distant Drummer" 11-19-60; *Wagon Train*—"The Jasper Cato Story" 3-4-59.

Hillyer, Lambert (1893-7/5/69). Director. Films: "The Desert Man" 1917 (sp. only); "One Shot Ross" 1917 (sp. only); "The Narrow Trail" 1918; "Breed of Men" 1919; "The Money Corral" 1919 (& sp.); "Square Deal Sanderson" 1919 (&

sp.); "Wagon Tracks" 1919; "Sand!" 1920 (& sp.); "The Testing Block" 1920 (& sp.); "The Toll Gate" 1920 (& sp./story); "O'Malley of the Mounted" 1921; "Three Word Brand" 1921 (& sp.); "White Oak" 1921; "Travelin' On" 1922 (& sp.); "Eyes of the Forst" 1923; "The Lone Star Ranger" 1923 (& sp.); "The Spoilers" 1923; "Mile-a-Minute Romeo" 1924; "Chain Lightning" 1927 (& sp.); "Hills of Peril" 1927; "The War Horse" 1927 (& sp.); "The Branded Sombrero" 1928 (& sp.); "Beau Bandit" 1930; "The Deadline" 1932 (& sp.); "The Fighting Fool" 1932; "Forbidden Trail" 1932; "Hello Trouble" 1932 (& sp.); "One-Man Law" 1932 (& sp.); "South of the Rio Grande" 1932; "White Eagle" 1932; "The California Trail" 1933 (& sp.); "The Sundown Rider" 1933 (& sp.); "Unknown Valley" 1933 (& sp.); "The Fighting Code" 1934 (& sp.); "The Man Trailer" 1934 (& sp.); "Law Beyond the Range" 1935 (sp. only); "Beyond the Sacramento" 1940; "The Durango Kid" 1940; "Hands Across the Rockies" 1941; "King of Dodge City" 1941; "The Medico of Painted Springs" 1941; "North from the Lone Star" 1941; "The Pinto Kid" 1941; "Prairie Stranger" 1941; "The Return of Daniel Boone" 1941; "Roaring Frontiers" 1941; "The Royal Mounted Patrol" 1941; "The Son of Davy Crockett" 1941 (& sp.); "Thunder Over the Prairie" 1941; "Wildcat of Tucson" 1941; "The Devil's Trail" 1942; "North of the Rockies" 1942; "Prairie Gunsmoke" 1942; "Vengeance of the West" 1942; "Fighting Frontier" 1943; "Six Gun Gospel" 1943; "The Stranger from Pecos" 1943; "The Texas Kid" 1943; "Ghost Guns" 1944; "Land of the Outlaws" 1944; "Law Men" 1944; "Partners of the Trail" 1944; "Range Law" 1944; "West of the Rio Grande" 1944; "Beyond the Pecos" 1945; "Flame of the West" 1945; "Frontier Feud" 1945; "The Lost Trail" 1945; "South of the Rio Grande" 1945; "Stranger from Santa Fe" 1945; "Border Bandits" 1946; "Gentleman from Texas" 1946; "Shadows on the Range" 1946; "Silver Range" 1946; "Trigger Fingers" 1946; "Under Arizona Skies" 1946; "Flashing Guns" 1947; "Gun Talk" 1947; "Land of the Lawless" 1947; "Law Comes to Gunsight" 1947; "Prairie Express" 1947; "Raiders of the South" 1947; "Trailing Danger" 1947; "Valley of Fear" 1947; "Crossed Trails" 1948; "The Fighting Ranger" 1948; "Frontier Agent" 1948; "Oklahoma Blues" 1948; "Outlaw Brand"

1948; "Overland Trails" 1948; "Partners of the Sunset" 1948; "Range Renegades" 1948; "The Sheriff of Medicine Bow" 1948; "Song of the Drifter" 1948; "Sundown Riders" 1948; "Gun Law Justice" 1949; "Gun Runner" 1949; "Haunted Trails" 1949; "Range Land" 1949; "Riders of the Dusk" 1949; "Trail's End" 1949. ¶TV: *The Cisco Kid* 1951-55.

Hilton, Arthur David. Director. Films: "The Return of Jesse James" 1950. ¶TV: *Law of the Plainsman* 1959; *Wanted—Dead or Alive*—"The Most Beautiful Woman" 1-23-60, "The Inheritance" 4-30-60.

Hilyard, Dene. Director. Films: "Vengeance" 1964.

Himm, Carl. Screenwriter. Films: "The King of the Wild Horses" 1924.

Hines, Gordon. Director. Films: "Trail Dust" 1924.

Hinkle, Robert. Director. Films: "Ole Rex" 1961 (& prod./sp.); "Guns of a Stranger" 1973 (& prod.).

Hinn, Michael. Director. Films: "Night Rider" 1962-short (& prod.).

Hirliman, George A. Producer. Films: "Daniel Boone" 1936; "Hollywood Cowboy" 1937; "Park Avenue Logger" 1937; "King of the Sierras" 1938; "The Singing Cowgirl" 1939.

Hirschman, Herbert (1914-7/3/85). Producer. Films: "Scalplock" TVM-1966; "Calamity Jane" TVM-1984. ¶TV: *The Virginian* 1962-70 (exec. prod.); *The Men from Shiloh* 1970-71 (& dir.).

Hirsh, Nathan. Producer. Films: "Border Guns" 1934; "The Border Menace" 1934; "The Lone Bandit" 1934; "The Outlaw Tamer" 1934; "Western Racketeers" 1935.

Hitchcock, Charles W. Director. Films: "The Sunset Princess" 1918.

Hite, Kathleen. Screenwriter. Films: "The Daughters of Hoshua Cabe Return" TVM-1975.

Hittleman, Carl K. Producer. Films: "Trail of the Mounties" 1947; "Where the North Begins" 1947 (& story); "Last of the Wild Horses" 1948; "The Return of Wildfire" 1948 (& sp.); "Grand Canyon" 1949; "I Shot Jesse James" 1949; "Tough Assignment" 1949 (& story); "The Baron of Arizona" 1950; "The Return of Jesse James" 1950 (& story); "Little Big Horn" 1951; "Kentucky Rifle" 1956 (& prod./sp.); "The Buckskin Lady" 1957 (& sp.); "Gun Battle at Monterey" 1957 (& dir.); "Billy the Kid vs. Dracula" 1966 (sp. only);

"Jesse James Meets Frankenstein's Daughter" 1966 (sp. only).

Hively, George. Screenwriter. Films: "A Western Romance" 1913; "Bucking Broadway" 1917; "A Marked Man" 1917 (story only); "Number 10, Westbound" 1917; "The Soul Herder" 1917; "Straight Shooting" 1917; "The Texas Sphinx" 1917; "Deuce Duncan" 1918; "The Phantom Riders" 1918; "The Scarlet Drop" 1918; "Thieves' Gold" 1918; "Wild Women" 1918; "A Woman's Fool" 1918; "The Ace of the Saddle" 1919; "The Black Horse Bandit" 1919; "The Fighting Brothers" 1919; "The Rustlers" 1919; "Cinders" 1920; "The Moon Riders" 1920-serial; "The Rattler's Hiss" 1920; "The Bearcat" 1922; "The Loaded Door" 1922; "Don Quickshot of the Rio Grande" 1923; "McGuire of the Mounted" 1923; "Men in the Raw" 1923; "Where Is This West?" 1923; "The Broken Law" 1924; "His Own Law" 1924 (story only); "The Passing of Wolf MacLean" 1924; "A Man of Nerve" 1925; "Pals" 1925; "The Rattler" 1925; "Three in Exile" 1925; "The Grey Vulture" 1926; "Looking for Trouble" 1926; "The Rambling Ranger" 1927; "The Western Rover" 1927.

Hively, Jack B. (1907-). Director. Films: "Starbird and Sweet William" 1975; "California Gold Rush" TVM-1981. ¶TV: *The Life and Times of Grizzly Adams* 1977.

Hoadley, Hal. Screenwriter. Films: "A Gun Fightin' Gentleman" 1919; "Dangerous Love" 1920; "Her Five-Foot Highness" 1920.

Hobart, Doty. Screenwriter. Films: "Circus Cowboy" 1924; "Not a Drum Was Heard" 1924; "The Plunderer" 1924; "The Vagabond Trail" 1924.

Hochberg, Victoria. Director. TV: *Dr. Quinn, Medicine Woman*—"The Visitor" 1-9-93.

Hoerl, Arthur (1892-2/6/68). Screenwriter. Films: "Gun-Hand Garrison" 1927; "Prince of the Plains" 1927; "Ridin' Luck" 1927; "Wanderer of the West" 1927; "Wild Born" 1927; "Danger Patrol" 1928; "Gypsy of the North" 1928; "Bride of the Desert" 1929; "In Old California" 1929; "Fighting Playboy" 1937; "California Frontier" 1938; "Law of the Texan" 1938; "Ride 'Em, Cowgirl" 1939; "The Singing Cowgirl" 1939; "Water Rustlers" 1939; "Arizona Stagecoach" 1942; "Texas to Bataan" 1942; "Texas Trouble Shooters" 1942; "Bullets and Saddles" 1943 (story only); "The Haunted Ranch" 1943 (story only); "The Vigilante" 1947-serial; "Tex

Granger" 1948-serial; "Border Outlaws" 1950; "Son of Geronimo" 1952-serial; "Gunfighters of the Northwest" 1954-serial.

Hofbauer, Ernst. Director. Films: "Black Eagle of Santa Fe" 1964-Ger./Ital./Fr.

Hoffman, Charles (1911-4/8/72). Screenwriter. Films: "The Spoilers" 1955; "The Miracle of the Hills" 1959; "The Sad Horse" 1959. ¶TV: *Bronco* 1958-60 (prod.).

Hoffman, Herman (1909-3/26/89). Director. Films: "Guns of the Magnificent Seven" 1969 (sp. only). ¶TV: *Laramie*—"Shadow of the Past" 10-16-62, "The Road to Helena" 5-21-63; *Temple Houston* 1963; *Rawhide*—"Hostage for Hanging" 10-19-65; *Bonanza*—"A Real Nice, Friendly Little Town" 11-27-66.

Hoffman, Hugh. Director. Films: "The Gypsy Trail" 1922.

Hoffman, Jerome. Screenwriter. Films: "The Duel at Silver Creek" 1952.

Hoffman, John. Director. Films: "I Killed Geronimo" 1950.

Hoffman, Joseph. Screenwriter. Films: "Headin' East" 1937 (story only); "Hollywood Roundup" 1938; "The Return of Daniel Boone" 1941; "The Lone Hand" 1953; "Rails into Laramie" 1954; "Tall Man Riding" 1955. ¶TV: *Colt .45* 1957-62 (prod.).

Hoffman, Lee. Writer. Films: "Chino" 1973-Ital./Span./Fr. (story).

Hoffman, Jr., M.H. (1881-3/6/44). Producer. Films: "Clearing the Range" 1931; "Hard Hombre" 1931; "Wild Horse" 1931; "The Boiling Point" 1932; "The Gay Buckaroo" 1932; "Local Bad Man" 1932; "A Man's Land" 1932; "Spirit of the West" 1932; "Cowboy Counsellor" 1933; "Boots of Destiny" 1937; "Trailing Trouble" 1937.

Hoffman, Otto (1879-6/23/44). Director. Films: "The Secret of Black Mountain" 1917.

Hoffman, William Dawson. Writer. Films: "Gun Gospel" 1927 (story).

Hogan, James P. (1891-11/6/43). Director. Films: "The Bandit's Baby" 1925; "Border Patrol" 1928; "Burning Brides" 1928; "The Sheriff's Secret" 1931 (& sp.); "The Arizona Raiders" 1936; "Arizona Mahoney" 1936; "Desert Gold" 1936; "Westbound Mail" 1937 (story only); "The Texans" 1938; "Texas Rangers Ride Again" 1940.

Hogan, Michael. Screenwriter. Films: "Tall in the Saddle" 1944.

Hogan, Paul (1940-). Producer. Films: "Lightning Jack" 1994-Australia (& sp.).

Hogan, Ray. Writer. Films: "Hell Bent for Leather" 1960 (story).

Hogan, Robert J. Writer. Films: "The Stand at Apache River" 1953.

Holcomb, Rod. Director. Films: "No Man's Land" TVM-1984 (& prod.). ¶TV: *Bret Maverick*—"Welcome to Sweetwater" 12-8-81.

Hole, Jr., William J. Director. Films: "Four Fast Guns" 1959 (& prod.).

Hollingshead, Gordon (1892-7/8/52). Producer. Films: "Oklahoma Outlaws" 1943-short; "Wagon Wheels West" 1943-short (prod. only); "Roaring Guns" 1944-short; "Trial by Trigger" 1944-short (& prod.); "Law of the Balands" 1945-short; "Spade Cooley, King of Western Swing" 1945-short.

Holloway, John. Director. Films: "Across the Divide" 1921.

Hollywood, Edwin L. Director. Films: "Jamestown" 1923.

Holmes, Ben (1890-12/2/43). Director. Films: "I'm from the City" 1938 (& story).

Holmes, Helen. Writer. Films: "A Desperate Leap" 1915 (story).

Holt, Felix. Writer. Films: "The Kentuckian" 1955 (story).

Holt, George. Director. Films: "Captive Bride" 1919; "The Four Gun Bandit" 1919; "Gun Magic" 1919; "The Hidden Badge" 1919; "The Jaws of Justice" 1919; "Kingdom Come" 1919; "The Lone Hand" 1919; "Neck and Noose" 1919; "A Pistol Point Proposal" 1919; "Tempest Cody Backs the Trust" 1919; "Tempest Cody Gets Her Man" 1919; "Tempest Cody Plays Detective" 1919; "Tempest Cody Turns the Table" 1919; "The Trail of the Hold-Up Man" 1919; "A Western Wooing" 1919; "The Wild Westerner" 1919; "The White Masks" 1921; "In the West" 1924 (& sp.); "Western Fate" 1924.

Holt, Nat (1894-8/3/71). Producer. Films: "Badman's Territory" 1946; "Trail Street" 1947; "Return of the Badmen" 1948; "Canadian Pacific" 1949; "Fighting Man of the Plains" 1949; "The Cariboo Trail" 1950; "The Great Missouri Raid" 1951; "Silver City" 1951; "Warpath" 1951; "Denver and Rio Grande" 1952; "Flaming Feather" 1952; "Arrowhead" 1953; "Pony Express" 1953; "Rage at Dawn" 1955; "Texas Lady" 1955; "Cattle King" 1963. ¶TV: *Shotgun Slade* 1959 (exec. prod.); *Over-*

land Trail 1960 (exec. prod.); *The Tall Man* 1960-62 (exec. prod.).

Holubar, Allen (1889-11/20/23). Director. Films: "Broken Chains" 1922.

Homes, Geoffrey (1902-1/31/77). Screenwriter. Films: "Roughshod" 1949; "The Eagle and the Hawk" 1950; "The Last Outpost" 1951; "Bugles in the Afternoon" 1952; "Powder River" 1953; "Those Redheads from Seattle" 1953; "Black Horse Canyon" 1954; "The Desperado" 1954; "Southwest Passage" 1954.

Hook, Harry. Director. Films: "The Last of His Tribe" TVM-1994.

Hooker, Brian. Screenwriter. Films: "Rose of the Rancho" 1936.

Hool, Lance (1948-). Producer. Films: "The Tracker" TVM-1988.

Hopkins, Omar. *see* Zeglio, Primo.

Hopkins, Seward W. Writer. Films: "The Gray Towers Mystery" 1919 (story).

Hopkins, Tom J. Screenwriter. Films: "The Lure of the Wild" 1925.

Hoplt, George. Director. Films: "Ace High" 1919.

Hopper, E. Mason (1885-1/3/67). Director. Films: "The Firefly of Tough Luck" 1917; "The Hidden Spring" 1917; "The Red Woman" 1917; "As the Sun Went Down" 1919.

Hopper, Hal. Screenwriter. Films: "Shalako" 1968-Brit./Fr.

Hopper, Jerry (1908-12/17/88). Director. Films: "Pony Express" 1953; "Smoke Signal" 1955; "The Missouri Traveler" 1958; "Madron" 1970-U.S./Israel. ¶TV: *Cheyenne* 1955; *Wagon Train*—"The Mark Hanford Story" 2-26-58, "The Jennifer Churchill Story" 10-15-58, "The Millie Davis Story" 11-26-58, "The Annie Griffith Story" 2-25-59, "The Vincent Englewood Story" 4-15-59, "The Clara Duncan Story" 4-22-59, "The Vittorio Bottecelli Story" 12-16-59, "The Lita Foladaire Story" 1-6-60, "The Dick Jarvis Story" 5-18-60, "The Horace Best Story" 10-5-60; *The Rifleman*—"End of a Young Gun" 10-14-58, "The Gaucho" 12-30-58, "The Deadeye Kid" 2-10-59, "The Angry Man" 4-28-59; *The Virginian*—"Duel at Shiloh" 1-2-63; *Gunsmoke*—"Carter Caper" 11-16-63, "Pa Hack's Brood" 12-28-63, "The Glory and the Mud" 1-4-64, "Owney Tupper Had a Daughter" 4-4-64; *Laredo*—"The Dance of the Laughing Death" 9-23-66.

Hopton, Russell (1900-4/7/45).

Director. Films: "Song of the Trail" 1936.

Horan, Charles. Director. Films: "The Quitter" 1916.

Horgan, Paul (1903-3/8/95). Writer. Films: "A Distant Trumpet" 1964 (story).

Horman, Arthur T. Writer. Films: "The Bandit Trail" 1941 (story).

Horn, Leonard J. (1926-5/25/75). Director. Films: "Nakia" TVM-1974. ¶TV: *Branded*—"The Test" 2-7-65, "Price of a Name" 5-23-65.

Hornblow, Jr., Arthur (1893-7/17/76). Producer. Films: "Ruggles of Red Gap" 1935; "High, Wide and Handsome" 1937; "Oklahoma!" 1955.

Horne, James W. (1881-6/29/42). Director. Films: "The Man in Irons" 1915; "The Pitfall" 1915; "Man from Tiajuana" 1917; "The Secret of Lost Valley" 1917; "Bull's Eye" 1918-serial; "Hands Up" 1918-serial; "The Sunshine Trail" 1923; "The Big Hop" 1928; "The Tabasco Kid" 1932-short; "Way Out West" 1937; "Deadwood Dick" 1940-serial; "White Eagle" 1941-serial; "Perils of the Royal Mounted" 1942-serial.

Horner, Harry (1910-12/5/94). Director. Films: "Man from Del Rio" 1956. ¶TV: *Gunsmoke*—"The Guitar" 7-21-56.

Horner, Robert J. Director. Films: "The Champion Liar" 1920 (sp. only); "The Smilin' Kid" 1920 (sp. only); "The Fighting Kid" 1922; "Cowboy Courage" 1925; "His Greatest Battle" 1925; "Ridin' Wild" 1925; "Pony Express Rider" 1926; "Twin Six O'Brien" 1926; "Walloping Kid" 1926 (& sp.); "Arizona Speed" 1928; "Across the Plains" 1928; "Cheyenne Trails" 1928 (& sp.); "Forbidden Trails" 1928; "The Ranger's Oath" 1928; "Riders of Vengeance" 1928 (& sp.); "Rip Roaring Logan" 1928; "Secrets of the Range" 1928 (& sp.); "Texas Flash" 1928 (& sp.); "The Thrill Chaser" 1928 (& sp.); "Throwing Lead" 1928; "Trails of Treachery" 1928 (& sp.); "Where the West Begins" 1928 (& sp.); "Far Western Trails" 1929 (& sp.); "The White Outlaw" 1929; "The Kid from Arizona" 1931 (& prod./story); "Pueblo Terror" 1931 (prod. only); "Wild West Whoopee" 1931 (& prod./sp.); "Forty-Five Calibre Echo" 1932; "The Border Menace" 1934; "Defying the Law" 1935 (& prod.); "The Phantom Cowboy" 1935 (& prod.); "Trails of Adventure" 1935 (prod. only); "Western Racketeers" 1935; "The Whirlwind Rider" 1935 (& prod.).

Horswell, Bert. Screenwriter. Films: "Conquest of Cheyenne" 1946; "Swing the Western Way" 1947 (story only); "West of Dodge City" 1947; "Bonanza Town" 1951.

Horton, Robert J. Writer. Films: "Singing River" (story); "Rip Roarin' Roberts" 1924 (story); "Walloping Wallace" 1924 (story).

Horwitz, Howie. Producer. Films: "Slim Carter" 1957; "Money, Women and Guns" 1958. ¶TV: *Maverick* 1960-61; *Redigo* 1963.

Hossein, Robert (1927-). Director. Films: "Taste of Violence" 1961-Fr. (& sp.); "Cemetery Without Crosses" 1968-Ital./Fr. (& sp.); "Judge Roy Bean" 1970-Fr.

Hotaling, Arthur (1873-7/13/38). Director. Films: "A Gentleman Preferred" 1928.

Hough, Donald. Writer. Films: "Dudes Are Pretty People" 1942 (story); "Prairie Chickens" 1943 (story); "Calaboose" 1943 (story).

Hough, Emerson Morton (1857-1923). Writer. Films: "The Sagebrusher" 1920 (story); "The Covered Wagon" 1923 (story); "North of '36" 1924 (story); "Way of a Man" 1924-serial (story); "The Conquering Horde" 1931 (story); "Boots of Destiny" 1937 (story); "The Texans" 1938 (story).

Hough, John (1941-). Director. Films: "Triumphs of a Man Called Horse" 1984.

Hough, R. John. Director. Films: "Yellowneck" 1955 (& story).

Hough, R. Lee. Director. Films: "The Girl-Shy Cowboy" 1928; "Wild West Romance" 1928.

Hough, Stanley L. Producer. Films: "Bandolero!" 1968 (story only); "The Undefeated" 1969 (story); "Mrs. Sundance" TVM-1974; "Gunsmoke: The Last Apache" TVM-1990.

Hough, Will M. Writer. Films: "The Flower of Faith" 1914 (story).

Houser, Lionel (1908-11/12/49). Screenwriter. Films: "Border Cafe" 1937.

Houser, Mervin J. Writer. Films: "Rhythm on the Range" 1936 (story); "Pardners" 1956 (story).

Houston, Norman. Screenwriter. Films: "The Law of the Range" 1928 (story only); "Cavalcade of the West" 1936; "Hopalong Rides Again" 1937; "Cassidy of Bar 20" 1938; "The Frontiersman" 1938;

"Heart of Arizona" 1938; "Sunset Trail" 1938; "Heritage of the Desert" 1939; "In Old Caliente" 1939; "Cherokee Strip" 1940; "Knights of the Range" 1940; "The Light of Western Stars" 1940; "Stagecoach War" 1940; "Young Buffalo Bill" 1940 (story only); "Ridin' Down the Canyon" 1942 (story only); "Bar 20" 1943; "Buckskin Frontier" 1943; "The Woman of the Town" 1943 (story only); "Lumberjack" 1944; "Nevada" 1944; "Texas Masquerade" 1944; "Wanderer of the Wasteland" 1945; "West of the Pecos" 1945; "The Riding Avenger" 1946; "Sunset Pass" 1946; "Code of the West" 1947; "Thunder Mountain" 1947; "Trail Street" 1947; "Under the Tonto Rim" 1947; "Wild Horse Mesa" 1947; "The Arizona Ranger" 1948; "Gun Smugglers" 1948; "Indian Agent" 1948; "Western Heritage" 1948; "Brothers in the Saddle" 1949; "Masked Raiders" 1949; "The Mysterious Desperado" 1949; "Stagecoach Kid" 1949; "Border Treasure" 1950; "Dynamite Pass" 1950; "Riders of the Range" 1950; "Rio Grande Patrol" 1950; "Pistol Harvest" 1951; "Desert Passage" 1952; "Road Agent" 1952; "Target" 1952.

Hoven, Adrien (Antonio Del Amo) (1924-4/28/81). Director. Films: "Jesse James' Kid" 1966-Span./Ital. (& sp.).

Howard, Clifford. Screenwriter. Films: "Lasca" 1919; "A White Man's Chance" 1919.

Howard, David (1896-12/21/41). Director. Films: "Lawless Valley" 1932; "The Golden West" 1932; "Mystery Ranch" 1932; "Rainbow Trail" 1932; "Smoke Lightning" 1933; "When Love Laughs" 1933-Mex.; "In Old Santa Fe" 1934; "Thunder Mountain" 1935; "Whispering Smith Speaks" 1935; "The Border Patrolman" 1936; "Daniel Boone" 1936; "The Mine with the Iron Door" 1936; "O'Malley of the Mounted" 1936; "Park Avenue Logger" 1937; "Border G-Man" 1938; "Gun Law" 1938; "The Painted Desert" 1938; "Renegade Ranger" 1938; "Arizona Legion" 1939; "The Fighting Gringo" 1939; "The Marshal of Mesa City" 1939; "Timber Stampede" 1939; "Trouble in Sundown" 1939; "Bullet Code" 1940; "Prairie Law" 1940; "Legion of the Lawless" 1940; "Triple Justice" 1940; "Dude Cowboy" 1941; "Six Gun Gold" 1941.

Howard, Eric. Writer. Films: "Gunfire" 1935 (story).

Howard, Matthew. Screen-

writer. Films: "Alias Smith and Jones" TVM-1971.

Howard, Nick. see Nostro, Nick.

Howard, Ron (1953-). Director. Films: "Far and Away" 1992 (& prod./story).

Howard, Sandford "Sandy". Producer. Films: "A Man Called Horse" 1970; "Man in the Wilderness" 1971-U.S./Span.

Howard, William K. (1899-2/21/54). Director. Films: "Get Your Man" 1921; "The One-Man Trail" 1921 (sp. only); "Captain Fly-By-Night" 1922; "The Crusader" 1922; "Trooper O'Neil" 1922 (sp. only); "The Border Legion" 1924; "Code of the West" 1925; "The Light of Western Stars" 1925; "The Thundering Herd" 1925; "White Gold" 1927; "Sin Town" 1929 (sp. only).

Howe, Eliot (1886-12/18/21). Director. Films: "With Hoops of Steel" 1919; "When Romance Rides" 1922.

Howell, Dorothy. Screenwriter. Films: "Men Without Law" 1930.

Howitzer, Bronson. Screenwriter. Films: "Showdown" 1963.

Hoyt, Charles Hale. Writer. Films: "A Texas Steer" 1915 (story); "A Texas Steer" 1927 (story).

Hoyt, Harry O. (1891-1961). Screenwriter. Films: "God's Country and the Law" 1922; "Fangs of the Wolf" 1924 (& dir.); "Sundown" 1924 (dir. only); "The Man from New Mexico" 1932; "Clancy of the Mounted" 1933-serial; "Gordon of Ghost City" 1933-serial; "The Thrill Hunter" 1933; "The Fighting Ranger" 1934; "Rustler's Valley" 1937; "The Last Stand" 1938; "The Singing Outlaw" 1938; "The Avenging Rider" 1943; "Lost Canyon" 1943.

Hoyt, Robert. Director. Films: "Racketeer Round-Up" 1934.

Hubbard, George. Writer. Films: "The Love Gambler" 1922 (story); "Without Compromise" 1922 (story).

Hubbard, Lucien (1889-12/31/71). Screenwriter. Films: "The Terror of the Range" 1919-serial (story only); "The Fox" 1921; "Code of the West" 1925; "The Thundering Herd" 1925; "Wild Horse Mesa" 1925; "The Light of Western Stars" 1925; "Born to the West" 1926; "Desert Gold" 1926; "The Squaw Man" 1931; "The Texans" 1938 (prod. only).

Hubbard, Philip. Screenwriter.

Films: "Hair-Trigger Stuff" 1920; "Held Up for the Makin's" 1920; "Runnin' Straight" 1920; "West Is Best" 1920.

Hubbard, Thomas G. (1919-6/4/74). Screenwriter. Films: "Thunder Pass" 1954; "Treasure of Ruby Hills" 1955; "The Badge of Marshal Brennan" 1957; "Daniel Boon, Trail Blazer" 1957; "Raiders of Old California" 1957.

Hudson, Hal. Producer. TV: *Zane Grey Theater* 1956-61; *Black Saddle* 1959; *The Westerner* 1960 (exec. prod.).

Huebsch, Edward. Screenwriter. Films: "Black Eagle" 1948.

Huffaker, Clair (1927-4/2/90). Screenwriter. Films: "Flaming Star" 1960; "Seven Ways from Sundown" 1960; "The Comancheros" 1961; "Posse from Hell" 1961; "Rio Conchos" 1964 (& story); "The War Wagon" 1967; "100 Rifles" 1969; "Deserter" 1970-U.S./Ital./Yugo.; "Flap" 1970; "Chino" 1973-Ital./Span./Fr.

Huggins, Roy (1914-). Director. Films: "Hangman's Knot" 1952 (& sp.); "Gun Fury" 1953 (sp. only); "Three Hours to Kill" 1954 (sp. only); "The Young Country" TVM-1970 (& prod./sp.); "The Invasion of Johnson County" TVM-1976 (prod. only). ¶TV: *Cheyenne* 1955; *Colt .45* 1957-62; *Maverick* 1957-59; *The Virginian* 1962-70 (prod.).

Hugh, R. John (1924-12/16/85). Director. Films: "Naked in the Sun" 1957 (& prod.).

Hughes, Howard (1905-4/5/76). Director. Films: "The Outlaw" 1943 (& prod.).

Hughes, Norman. Writer. Films: "Tracy Rides" 1935 (story).

Hughes, Roy M. (1894-1/12/28). Director. Films: "Fightin' Thru" 1924.

Hughes, Rupert (1872-9/9/56). Writer. Films: "Gloria's Romance" 1916-serial (story).

Hughes, Russell S. Screenwriter. Films: "Sugarfoot" 1951; "The Command" 1953; "Thunder Over the Plains" 1953; "The Yellow Mountain" 1954; "The Last Frontier" 1955; "Jubal" 1956.

Hughes, Unie. Writer. Films: "Border Wolves" 1938 (story).

Hull, Alexander. Writer. Films: "The Painted Hills" 1951 (story).

Hull, George C. Screenwriter. Films: "Hitchin's Posts 1920; "West Is West" 1920; "The Conflict" 1921; "The Freeze-Out" 1921; "Sure Fire"

1921; "The Wallop" 1921; "The Girl Who Ran Wild" 1922; "Man to Man" 1922; "Out of the Silent North" 1922; "The Border Legion" 1924; "The Wanderer of the Wasteland" 1924; "The Light of Western Stars" 1925; "The Mystery of Lost Ranch" 1925; "The Overland Telegraph" 1929; "Sioux Blood" 1929; "Son of Oklahoma" 1932.

Hull, Shelly. Producer. Films: "The Over-the-Hill Gang" TVM-1969; "The Over-the-Hill Gang Rides Again" TVM-1970; "The Wild Women of Chastity Gulch" TVM-1982. ¶TV: *Tate* 1960.

Hull, William C. Screenwriter. Films: "If Only Jim" 1921.

Humberstone, H. Bruce (1903-10/11/84). Director. Films: "Lucky Cisco Kid" 1940; "Fury at Furnace Creek" 1948; "Ten Wanted Men" 1955.

Hume, Cyril (1900-3/26/66). Screenwriter. Films: "Yellow Dust" 1936; "The Bad Man of Brimstone" 1938; "Twenty Mule Team" 1940; "Branded" 1951.

Humphreys, Joel Don. Screenwriter. Films: "My Heroes Have Always Been Cowboys" 1991.

Hunger, Ann. Writer. Films: "The Secret of Convict Lake" 1951 (story).

Hunsaker, Dave. Screenwriter. Films: "Samurai Cowboy" 1993 (& story).

Hunt, Helen Jackson. Writer. Films: "Ramana" 1910 (story); "Ramona" 1916 (story); "Ramona" 1928 (story); "Ramona" 1936 (story).

Hunt, Paul. Director. Films: "Machismo—40 Graves for 40 Guns" 1970 (& sp.); "Savage Red—Outlaw White" 1974; "The Great Gundown" 1977.

Hunt, Peter. Director. Films: "Death Hunt" 1981.

Hunter, Evan (1926-). Screenwriter. Films: "The Chisholms" TVM-1979; "The Legend of Walks Far Woman" TVM-1982; "Dream West" TVM-1986.

Hunter, George. Director. Films: "Law of the North" 1926; "Pioneer Blood" 1926; "The Dude Desperado" 1927; "The Peace Deputy" 1927; "Phantom of the North" 1929 (sp. only).

Hunter, John. Screenwriter. Films: "The Grey Fox" 1983-Can.

Hunter, Max. *see* Pupillo, Massimo.

Hunter, Robert. Director. Films: "Western Blood" 1923.

Hunter, Ross (1924-). Producer. Films: "Take Me to Town" 1953; "Tumbleweed" 1953; "Taza, Son of Cochise" 1954; "The Yellow Mountain" 1954; "The Spoilers" 1955.

Hunter, T. Hayes (1882-4/14/44). Director. Films: "The Border Legion" 1918; "Desert Gold" 1919.

Hunter, Tab (1931-). Producer. Films: "Lust in the Dust" 1985.

Hunting, Gardner. Screenwrier. Films: "Jack and Jill" 1917; "North of '53" 1917; "Unclaimed Goods" 1918; "Johnny, Get Your Gun" 1919.

Huntley, Fred (1964-11/1/31). Director. Films: "A Message to Kearney" 1912; "The Old Stage Coach" 1912; "The Rancher's Failing" 1913; "The Charmed Arrow" 1914; "When Thieves Fall Out" 1914.

Hurley, Harold. Producer. Films: "Heritage of the Desert" 1932; "Wild Horse Mesa" 1932; "Man of the Forest" 1933; "The Mysterious Rider" 1933; "To the Last Man" 1933; "The Last Round-Up" 1934; "The Thundering Herd" 1934; "Wagon Wheels" 1934; "Home on the Range" 1935; "Nevada" 1935; "Rocky Mountain Mystery" 1935; "Wanderer of the Wasteland" 1935; "Golden Gold" 1936; "Drift Fence" 1936; "Forlorn River" 1937.

Hurn, P.J. Screenwriter. Films: "The Whipping Boss" 1924.

Hurn, Philip Dutton. Screenwriter. Films: "The Siren Call" 1922; "Strings of Steel" 1926-serial.

Hurst, Paul (1888-2/27/53). Director. Films: "The Big Horn Massacre" 1913; "Lass of the Lumberlands" 1916-serial; "Play Straight or Fight" 1918; "Lightning Bryce" 1919-serial; "The Black Sheep" 1921; "Shadows of the West" 1921; "The Crow's Nest" 1922; "The Heart of a Texan" 1922 (& sp.); "The Kingfisher's Roost" 1922 (& sp.); "Rangeland" 1922 (sp. only); "Table Top Ranch" 1922 (& sp.); "Golden Silence" 1923; "Branded a Bandit" 1924; "The Passing of Wolf MacLean" 1924; "The White Man Who Turned Indian" 1924 (& sp.); "Branded a Thief" 1925; "The Demon Rider" 1925; "The Gold Hunters" 1925; "The Rattler" 1925; "The Son of Sontag" 1925; "A Western Engagement" 1925; "Battling Kid" 1926; "The Fighting Ranger" 1926; "The Haunted Range" 1926; "The Range Raiders" 1927; "Rider of the Law" 1927; "Blue Streak O'Neail" 1928.

Hust, Stephen G. Writer. Films: "Mark of the Spur" 1932 (story).

Huston, John (1906-8/28/87). Director. Films: "Law and Order 1932 (sp. only); "The Treasure of the Sierra Madre" 1948 (& sp.); "The Unforgiven" 1960; "The Misfits" 1961; "The Life and Times of Judge Roy Bean" 1972.

Huston, Paul. Screenwriter. Films: "Overland Mail" 1942-serial.

Hutchinson, Bruce. Writer. Films: "Park Avenue Logger" 1937 (story).

Hutchinson, James C. Director. Films: "Red Blood and Blue" 1925.

Hutchinson, Jerry. Screenwriter. Films: "Two in Revolt" 1936.

Hutchison, Charles (1879-5/30/49). Director. Films: "Pals of the Prairie" 1934-short; "The Judgement Book" 1935; "Desert Guns" 1936; "Phantom Patrol" 1936; "Riddle Ranch" 1936.

Hyland, Frances. Screenwriter. Films: "Arizona Wildcat" 1938 (story only); "The Cisco Kid and the Lady" 1939; "In Old California" 1942.

Iglesias, Miguel. Screenwriter. Films: "Tequila" 1974-Ital./Span.

Ihnat, Steve (1934-5/12/72). Director. Films: "The Honkers" 1972 (& sp.).

Ince, John (1878-4/10/47). Director. Films: "The Taking of Rattlesnake Bill" 1913.

Ince, Ralph (1882-4/11/37). Director. Films: "Una of the Sierras" 1912; "Out of the Snows" 1920; "Channing of the Northwest" 1922; "Men of America" 1933.

Ince, Thomas H. (1882-11/19/24). Director. Films: "Behind the Stockade" 1911; "An Indian Martyr" 1911; "Little Dove's Romance" 1911; "The Battle of the Red Man" 1912; "The Colonel's Peril" 1912; "The Colonel's War" 1912; "The Crisis" 1912; "Custer's Last Fight" 1912; "The Deserter" 1912; "A Double Reward" 1912; "The Hidden Trail" 1912; "The Indian Massacre" 1912; "The Law of the West" 1912; "The Invaders" 1912; "The Lieutenant's Last Flight" 1912; "The Prospector's Daughter" 1912; "War on the Plains" 1912 (& sp.); "Days of '49" 1913; "A Shadow of the Past" 1913; "The Bargain" 1914 (sp. only); "Desert Gold" 1914; "The Gringo" 1914 (sp. only); "In the Cow Country" 1914 (sp. only); "Last of the Line" 1914 (& sp.); "Love's Sacrifice" 1914; "The Passing of Two-Gun Hicks" 1914 (sp. only); "Shorty and the Fortune Teller" 1914; "Shorty Escapes Marriage" 1914 (sp. only); "The Word of His People" 1914; "The Conversion of Frosty Blake" 1915; "The

Disciple" 1915 (& prod./sp.); "Keno Bates—Liar" 1915; "The Man from Oregon" 1915 (prod. only); "On the Night Stage" 1915 (prod. only); "The Roughneck" 1915 (story only); "The Deserter" 1916 (story only); "The Gunfighter" 1916 (prod. only); "The Return of Draw Egan" 1916 (prod. only); "Ashes of Hope" 1917 (story only); "Hell's Hinges" 1919 (prod. only).

Ince, Jr., Thomas H. Screenwriter. Films: "The Man from Guntown" 1935.

Ingalls, Don. Producer. TV: *Have Gun Will Travel* 1957-63; *The Travels of Jaimie McPheeters* 1963-64.

Inghram, Frank L. Screenwriter. Films: "Biff Bang Buddy" 1924 (dir. only); "Galloping On" 1925; "On the Go" 1925; "A Streak of Luck" 1925; "Tearin' Loose" 1925; "Comin an' Going" 1926; "The Dangerous Dub" 1926; "Double Daring" 1926; "Rawhide" 1926; "Speedy Spurs" 1926; "The Desert of the Lost" 1927; "The Fightin' Comeback" 1927; "The Galloping Gobs" 1927; "The Obligin' Buckaroo" 1927; "Pals in Peril" 1927; "Red Clay" 1927; "Ride 'Em High" 1927; "The Ridin' Rowdy" 1927; "Roarin' Broncs" 1927; "Skedaddle Gold" 1927; "The Cowboy Cavalier" 1928; "Desperate Courage" 1928; "Saddle Mates" 1928; "The Valley of Hunted Men" 1928.

Ingleton, E. Magnus. Screenwriter. Films: "The Love Call" 1919.

Ingraham, Lloyd (1874-4/4/56). Director. Films: "Broncho Billy's Reason" 1913; "The Last Card" 1915; "The Lightning Rider" 1924; "Soft Shoes" 1925; "Arizona Nights" 1927; "Don Mike" 1927; "Jesse James" 1927; "Silver Comes Through" 1927 (& sp.); "The Ballyhoo Buster" 1928; "Kit Carson" 1928; "The Pioneer Scout" 1928; "The Sunset Legion" 1928.

Ingram, Jay. Screenwriter. Films: "The Peacemaker" 1956.

Ingster, Boris (1913-7/2/78). Producer. Films: "Guns of Diablo" 1964. ¶TV: *Cimarron City* 1958-59; *The Alaskans* 1959-60.

Inslee, Charles E. Writer. Films: "The Ranchero's Revenge" 1913 (story).

Iquino, Ignacio (John Wood, Juan Bosch, Steve MacCohy, Nick Nostro, Juan Xiol Marchel, Nick Howard). Director. Films: "Joe Dexter" 1965-Span./Ital.; "Dollar of Fire" 1967-Ital./Span. (& sp.); "Seven Pistols for a Gringo" 1967-Ital./Span. (& sp.); "Five Dollars for Ringo" 1968-

Ital./Span. (& sp.); "One After Another" 1968-Span./Ital. (& sp.); "Dig Your Grave, Friend … Sabata's Coming" 1970-Ital./Span./Fr. (& sp.); "The Reward's Yours, the Man's Mine" 1970-Ital.; "Twenty Paces to Death" 1970-Ital./Span. (sp. only); "And the Crows Will Dig Your Grave" 1971-Ital./Span. (& sp.); "With Friends, Nothing Is Easy" 1971-Span./Ital. (& sp.); "Dallas" 1972-Span./Ital (& sp.); "God in Heaven … Arizona on Earth" 1972-Span./Ital. (sp. only); "God in Heaven … Arizona on Earth" 1972-Span./Ital.; "My Colt, Not Yours" 1972-Span./Fr./Ital. (& sp.); "My Horse, My Gun, Your Widow" 1972-Ital./Span. (& sp.); "None of the Three Were Called Trinity" 1974-Span. (sp. only); "Too Much Gold for One Gringo" 1974-Ital./Span. (& sp.).

Ireland, John (1915-3/21/92). Director. Films: "Hannah Lee" 1953 (& prod.).

Ireland, Mary. Screenwriter. Films: "Old Louisiana" 1937; "Under Strange Flags" 1937.

Irvin, Sam. Director. Films: "Oblivion" 1994.

Irvin, Victor. Screenwriter. Films: "The Wanderer of the Wasteland" 1924; "The Cavalier" 1928.

Irving, Richard (1917-). Producer. TV: *Frontier Circus* 1961-62; *The Virginian* 1962-70.

Irving, Robert. Screenwriter. Films: "Jory" 1972.

Irwin, Charles W. Screenwriter. Films: "He Rides Tall" 1964.

Irwin, Jack. Director. Films: "Lightnin' Smith Returns" 1931 (& prod./sp.); "The Riding Kid" 1931 (& sp.); "White Renegade" 1931 (& prod./sp.).

Irwin, Will. Screenwriter. Films: "Beating Back" 1914.

Ivers, Julia Crawford (1871-5/7/30). Screenwriter. Films: "The World Apart" 1917.

Ives, Robert. Screenwriter. Films: "Fighting to Live" 1934.

Izzo, Renato. Screenwriter. Films: "Sartana" 1968-Ital./Ger.; "Sabata" 1969-Ital.; "Adios, Sabata" 1970-Ital./Span.; "The Bounty Hunters" 1970-Ital.; "Return of Sabata" 1972-Ital./Fr./Ger.; "Too Much Gold for One Gringo" 1974-Ital./Span.

Jaccard, Celia. Screenwriter. Films: "Rio Grande Ranger" 1936; "Senor Jim" 1936; "Rollin' Plains" 1938.

Jaccard, Jacques (1886-7/24/60). Director. Films: "A Bogus Bandit" 1915; "Across the Rio Grande" 1916; "The Code of the Mounted" 1916 (& sp.); "A Knight of the Range" 1916; "Liberty" 1916-serial (& sp.); "The Night Riders" 1916 (& sp.); "The Passing of Hell's Crown" 1916; "The Stampede in the Night" 1916 (& sp.); "The Red Ace" 1917-serial (& story); "Cyclone Smith Plays Trumps" 1919; "Cyclone Smith's Comeback" 1919; "Cyclone Smith's Partner" 1919; "Down But Not Out" 1919; "The Phantom Fugitive" 1919; "Tempest Cody Flirts with Death" 1919; "Tempest Cody Hits the Trail" 1919; "Tempest Cody Rides Wild" 1919; "Tempest Cody's Man Hunt" 1919; "The Wild Rider" 1919; "Big Stakes" 1920; "Desert Love" 1920 (& sp.); "The Forest Runners" 1920; "The Girl and the Law" 1920; "A Son of the North" 1920; "The Terror" 1920 (& sp.); "The Timber Wolf" 1920; "Under Northern Lights" 1920; "When the Devil Laughed" 1920; "Cyclone Smith's Vow" 1921; "If Only Jim" 1921; "The Pony Express Rider" 1921; "Riding with Death" 1921 (& story); "The Yellow Streak" 1921; "The Fast Mail" 1922 (sp. only); "The Miracle Baby" 1923 (sp. only); "Days of '49" 1924-serial; "The Galloping Ace" 1924 (story only); "His Majesty the Outlaw" 1924 (& sp.); "Riders of the Plains" 1924-serial (& story); "Ridin' Mad" 1924 (& sp.); "The Fugitive" 1925; "Sand Blind" 1925; "Vic Dyson Pays" 1925; "Desert Greed" 1926; "The Iron Rider" 1926 (& sp.); "The Lariat Kid" 1929; "The Apache Kid's Escape" 1930; "The Cheyenne Kid" 1930 (& sp.); "O'Malley Rides Alone" 1930; "Desert Guns" 1936 (sp. only); "Rio Grande Ranger" 1936 (story only); "Senor Jim" 1936; "Phantom of Santa Fe" 1937; "Rollin' Plains" 1938 (story only).

Jackman, Fred H. (1881-8/27/59). Director. Films: "The Timber Queen" 1922-serial; "White Eagle" 1922-serial; "Call of the Wild" 1923; "The King of the Wild Horses" 1924; "Black Cyclone" 1925; "The Devil Horse" 1926; "No Man's Law" 1927. ¶TV: *The Adventures of Rin Tin Tin* 1955; *Empire*—"The Fire Dancer" 11-13-62; *Gunsmoke*—"Quint's Indian" 3-2-63.

Jacks, Robert L. (1927-8/26/87). Producer. Films: "White Feather" 1955; "Bandido" 1956; "Man from Del Rio" 1956; "The Proud Ones" 1956; "Bandolero!" 1968; "The Undefeated" 1969; "Mr. Horn" TVM-1979; "The Wild Wild West Revisited" TVM-1979. ¶TV: *The Young Pioneers* 1978.

Jackson, Charles Tenney. Writer. Films: "The Golden Fetter" 1917 (writer).

Jackson, Felix (1902-12/4/92). Screenwriter. Films: "Destry Rides Again" 1939. ¶TV: *Cimarron City* 1958-59 (prod.).

Jackson, Frances. Screenwriter. Films: "Yankee Don" 1931.

Jackson, Frederick (1886-5/22/53). Screenwriter. "Wells Fargo" 1937.

Jackson, Henry. Screenwriter. Films: "Under the Pampas Moon" 1935.

Jackson, Joseph. Screenwriter. Films: "Land of the Silver Fox" 1928.

Jackson, Marion. Screenwriter. Films: "Galloping Gallagher" 1921; "The Mask of Lopez" 1923; "The Dangerous Coward" 1924; "The Fighting Sap" 1924 (story only); "Lightning Romance" 1924 (story only); "North of Nevada" 1924; "The Silent Stranger" 1924; "Thundering Hoofs" 1924; "The Bandit's Baby" 1925; "Ridin' the Wind" 1925; "The Wild Bull's Lair" 1925; "Satan Town" 1926; "Senor Daredevil" 1926; "The Unknown Cavalier" 1926; "Arizona Bound" 1927; "The Devil's Saddle" 1927; "Gun Gospel" 1927; "The Land Beyond the Law" 1927; "Men of Daring" 1927; "The Overland Stage" 1927; "Red Raiders" 1927; "Somewhere in Sonora" 1927; "The Canyon of Adventure" 1928; "The Glorious Trail" 1928; "The Shepherd of the Hills" 1928; "The Upland Rider" 1928 (story only); "The California Mail" 1929; "Cheyenne" 1929; "The Wagon Master" 1929; "Lucky Larkin" 1930; "The Big Stampede" 1932 (story only); "Land Beyond the Law" 1937 (story only).

Jackson, Wilfred. Director. Films: "Melody Time" 1948.

Jacobs, David. Director. TV: *Paradise*—"The News from St. Louis" 10-27-88, "The Gates of Paradise" 1-6-90.

Jacobs, Harrison (1883-4/9/68). Screenwriter. Films: "The Fighting Peacemaker" 1926; "Lazy Lightning" 1926; "Red Hot Leather" 1926; "The Man from the West" 1926; "The Ridin' Rascal" 1926; "Rustlers' Ranch" 1926; "The Set-Up" 1926; "Set Free" 1927; "Spurs and Saddles" 1927; "The Western Whirlwind" 1927; "Hopalong Cassidy" 1935; "The Eagle's Brood" 1936; "Hopalong Cassidy Returns" 1936; "The Barrier" 1937; "Borderland" 1937; "Texas Trail" 1937; "Bar 20 Justice" 1938; "The Frontiersman" 1938; "In Old Mexico" 1938; "Partners of the Plains" 1938; "Heritage of the Desert" 1939; "Law of the Pampas" 1939; "Renegade Trail" 1939; "Colorado" 1940; "Santa Fe Marshal" 1940; "Wagons Westward" 1940; "Young Buffalo Bill" 1940; "Jesse James at Bay" 1941 (story only); "Wide Open Town" 1941; "False Paradise" 1948.

Jacobs, William. Producer. Films: "Moonlight on the Prairie" 1935 (sp. only); "Song of the Saddle" 1936; "Treachery Rides the Range" 1936; "River's End" 1940; "Montana" 1950; "Rocky Mountain" 1950; "Calamity Jane" 1953.

Jacobsen, Norman. Screenwriter. Films: "It's a Bear" 1919.

Jacobson, Arthur. Director. Films: "Home on the Range" 1935.

Jacobson, Leigh. Writer. Films: "One Glorious Scrap" 1927 (story).

Jaffe, Sam (1897-3/24/84). Producer. Films: "The Vanishing Frontier" 1932.

Jaffe, Stanley R. (1940-). Producer. Films: "Bad Company" 1972.

James, Alan. *see* Neitz, Alvin J.

James, J. Frank. Director. Films: "The Legend of Earl Durand" 1974 (sp. only); "The Sweet Creek County War" 1979 (& prod./sp.).

James, Jason. Screenwriter. Films: "Fury at Showdown" 1957.

James, Jo Frances. Writer. Films: "Jesse James" 1939 (story).

James, Polly. Screenwriter. Films: "The Raiders" 1952; "Untamed Frontier" 1952; "The Redhead from Wyoming" 1953 (& story); "Quantrill's Raiders" 1958.

James, Wharton. Director. Films: "The Call from the Wild" 1921 (& prod./sp.).

James, Will (1892-1942). Writer. Films: "Smoky" 1933 (story); "The Lone Cowboy" 1934 (story); "Smoky" 1946 (story); "Smoky" 1966 (story); "Shoot Out" 1971 (story).

Jameson, Jerry. Director. Films: "The Call of the Wild" TVM-1976; "The Invasion of Johnson County" TVM-1976; "High Noon, Part II: The Return of Will Kane" TVM-1980; "Cowboy" TVM-1983; "Gunsmoke: To the Last Man" TVM-1991; "Bonanza: The Return" TVM-1993; "Gunsmoke: The Long Ride" TVM-1993; "Gunsmoke: One Man's Justice" TVM-1994 (& prod.).

Janis, Elsie (1889-2/27/56). Screenwriter. Films: "The Squaw Man" 1931.

Jannette, R.P. Screenwriter. Films: "Tenderfoot Bob's Resignation" 1912.

Janni, Joseph. Producer. Films: "Robbery Under Arms" 1958-Brit.; "Deaf Smith and Johnny Ears" 1972-Ital.

Jarmusch, Jim. Director. Films: "Dead Man" 1995 (& sp.).

Jarre, Kevin. Screenwriter. Films: "The Tracked" TVM-1988; "Tombstone" 1993.

Jarrett, Daniel (1894-3/13/38). Screenwriter. Films: "Cowboy Millionaire" 1935; "Thunder Mountain" 1935; "When a Man's a Man" 1935; "Whispering Smith Speaks" 1935; "The Border Patrolman" 1936; "Daniel Boone" 1936; "The Mine with the Iron Door" 1936; "O'Malley of the Mounted" 1936; "Hollywood Cowboy" 1937; "Park Avenue Logger" 1937; "Roll Along, Cowboy" 1937; "Secret Valley" 1937; "Hawaiian Buckaroo" 1938; "Rawhide" 1938 (& story); "Tomahawk" 1951 (story only).

Jarrico, Paul. Screenwriter. Films: "Men of the Timberland" 1941 (story only); "Who Killed Johnny R.?" 1966-Ital./Span.

Jason, Leigh (1904-2/19/79). Director. Films: "The Man from Texas" 1947.

Jay, Griffin (1905-3/30/54). Screenwriter. Films: "Trail of the Hawk" 1935; "The Kid from Kansas" 1941 (& story); "Men of the Timberland" 1941.

Jefferson, L.V. Screenwriter. Films: "Overalls" 1916 (story only); "Petticoats and Politics" 1918; "Put Up Your Hands" 1919; "The Desert Scorpion" 1920 (story); "Riders of the Dawn" 1920; "Crossing Trails" 1921; "No Man's Woman" 1921 (story only); "Daring Danger" 1922; "Nine Points of the Law" 1922 (story only); "Tracks" 1922; "Vanishing Hoofs" 1926; "Born to Battle" 1927; "Gold from Weepah" 1927; "A Gentleman Preferred" 1928; "Laddie Be Good" 1928; "Rip Roaring Logan" 1928; "The Ranger's Oath" 1928; "Throwing Lead" 1928; "Pueblo Terror" 1931; "Trails of the Golden West" 1931; "Fighting Cowboy" 1933; "Lighting Bill" 1934 (story only); "Lighting Range" 1934; "The Pecos Dandy" 1934; "Range Riders" 1934; "Rawhide Romance" 1934; "The Lion's Den" 1936 (story only); "Riddle Ranch" 1936.

Jenkins, Burke. Screenwriter. Films: "Cyclone Cavalier" 1925.

Jenks, George Elwood. Screen-

writer. Films: "Cactus Crandall" 1918; "Closin' In" 1918; "Desert Law" 1918; "The Good Loser" 1918; "His Enemy, the Law" 1918; "The End of the Game" 1919 (story only); "The Mints of Hell" 1919; "The Prodigal Liar" 1919; "A Sage Brush Hamlet" 1919; "The Desperate Game" 1926 (story only).

Jennings, Al (1863-12/26/61). Writer. Films: "Beating Back" 1914 (story); "Hands Up!" 1917 (story).

Jennings, Elizabeth. Screenwriter. Films: "Gunsight Ridge" 1957; "Gunsight Ridge" 1957.

Jennings, Talbot (1895-5/30/85). Screenwriter. Films: "Northwest Passage" 1940; "Across the Wide Missouri" 1951 (& story); "The Sons of Katie Elder" 1965 (story only).

Jennings, William Dale. Screenwriter. Films: "The Cowboys" 1972 (& story).

Jerez, Jose Luis. Screenwriter. Films: "Adios Gringo" 1965-Ital./Fr./Span.; "The Magnificent Bandits" 1969-Ital./Span.

Jeske, George (1891-10/28/51). Screenwriter. Films: "A Buckaroo Broadcast" 1938-short; "Sagebrush Serenade" 1939-short; "Corralling a School Marm" 1940-short.

Jessup, Richard. Screenwriter. Films: "Chuka" 1967.

Jevne, Jack (Jack T.O. Gevne, Jack Levine, John West). Director. Films: "The Trail of the Hold-Up Man" 1919 (sp. only); "The Jay Bird" 1920 (sp. only); "The Cowboy and the Bandit" 1935 (sp. only); "The Ghost Rider" 1935 (& sp.); "Thunderbolt" 1935 (sp. only); "Trails End" 1935 (sp. only); "Way Out West" 1937 (story only); "Wyoming" 1940 (sp./story only).

Jewison, Norman (1927-). Producer. Films: "Billy Two Hats" 1973-Brit.; "Geronimo" TVM-1993.

Jodorowsky, Alexandro. Director. Films: "El Topo" 1971-Mex. (& sp.).

Johnson, Adrian. Screenwriter. Films: "The Love Brand" 1923.

Johnson, Agnes Christine. Screenwriter. Films: "When a Man's a Man" 1935.

Johnson, Clint. Screenwriter. Films: "Young Daniel Boone" 1950 (& story); "Wanted Dead or Alive" 1951.

Johnson, Dorothy M. (1906-11/11/84). Writer. Films: "The Hanging Tree" 1959 (story); "The Man Who Shot Liberty Valance" 1962 (story); "A Man Called Horse" 1970

(story); "The Return of a Man Called Horse" 1976 (story).

Johnson, Earl. Writer. Films: "Two in Revolt" 1936 (story).

Johnson, Emilie. Writer. Films: "Blind Hearts" 1921 (story).

Johnson, George M. Writer. Films: "The Terror of Bar X" 1927 (story); "Shadow Ranch" 1930 (story).

Johnson, Gladys E. Writer. Films: "Lights of the Desert" 1922.

Johnson, Julian. Writer. Films: "Lucky Cisco Kid" 1940 (story).

Johnson, Krag. Screenwriter. Films: "Cyclone Cavalier" 1925.

Johnson, Lamont (1920-). Director. Films: "A Gunfight" 1971; "Cattle Annie and Little Britches" 1981. ¶TV: *Have Gun Will Travel*—"Gun Shy" 3-29-58, "The Five Books of Owen Deaver" 4-26-58, "The Silver Queen" 5-3-58, "Silver Convoy" 5-31-58, "A Sense of Justice" 11-1-58, "Young Gun" 11-8-58, "The Chase" 4-11-59; *The Rifleman*—"The Hawk" 4-14-59, "Long Trek" 1-17-61; *Johnny Ringo* 1959; *Cimarron Strip*—"The Roarer" 11-2-67.

Johnson, Lorimer. Director. Films: "Truth in the Wilderness" 1913; "Breezy Jim" 1919.

Johnson, Nunnally (1897-3/25/77). Screenwriter. Films: "Jesse James" 1939 (& prod.); "Along Came Jones" 1945; "The Gunfighter" 1950 (prod. only); "The True Story of Jesse James" 1957 (story only); "Flaming Star" 1960.

Johnson, Raymond K. Director. Films: "Code of the Fearless" 1939; "In Old Montana" 1939 (& sp.); "Two-Gun Troubador" 1939; "The Cheyenne Kid" 1940; "Covered Wagon Trails" 1940; "The Kid from Santa Fe" 1940; "Land of the Six Guns" 1940; "Pinto Canyon" 1940; "Riders from Nowhere" 1940; "Ridin' the Trail" 1940; "Wild Horse Range" 1940; "Law of the Wolf" 1941.

Johnson, Robert. see Mauri, Roberto.

Johnson, Robert Lee. Screenwriter. Films: "The Dude Wrangler" 1930; "The Taming of the West" 1939 (& story); "Prairie Schooners" 1940; "The Return of Wild Bill" 1940; "Roaring Frontiers" 1941; "Bullets for Bandits" 1942; "The Devil's Trail" 1942 (story only); "Two-Fisted Stranger" 1946.

Johnson, Van (1916-). Screenwriter. Films: "Desert Mesa" 1935.

Johnson, W. Ray. Producer. Films: "Under Texas Skies" 1930; "Son of the Plains" 1931.

Johnston, Agnes Christine (1896-7/19/78). Screenwriter. Films: "Out West with the Hardys" 1938.

Johnston, Calder. Screenwriter. Films: "The Desperado" 1916; "The Timber Wolf" 1916; "A Yoke of Gold" 1916; "The Purple Riders" 1921-serial.

Johnston, Ray. Director. Films: "Call of the Rockies" 1931.

Johnston, William Allen. Writer. Films: "Silver Queen" 1942 (story).

Jolley, Norman. Screenwriter. Films: "Two-Gun Lady" 1956 (& story); "Joe Dakota" 1957. ¶TV: *Cimarron City* 1958-59 (prod.); *Riverboat* 1959-61 (prod.).

Jolley, Stan. Producer. Films: "A Knife for the Ladies" 1973.

Jones, Arthur V. Screenwriter. Films: "The Fargo Kid" 1940; "Prairie Law" 1940; "Stage to Chino" 1940; "Triple Justice" 1940; "Along the Rio Grande" 1941; "Robbers of the Range" 1941; "Fighting Bill Fargo" 1942; "Stagecoach Express" 1942; "'Neath Canadian Skies" 1946; "North of the Border" 1946.

Jones, Buck (1889-11/30/42). Director. Films: "The Big Hop" 1928 (prod. only); "Rocky Rhodes" 1934 (prod. only); "When a Man Sees Red" 1934 (prod. only); "The Crimson Trail" 1935 (prod. only); "Ivory-Handled Gun" 1935 (prod. only); "Outlawed Guns" 1935 (prod. only); "The Throwback" 1935 (prod. only); "Boss Rider of Gun Creek" 1936 (prod. only); "The Cowboy and the Kid" 1936 (prod./story only); "For the Service" 1936 (& prod.); "Ride 'Em Cowboy" 1936 (prod./story only); "Sunset of Power" 1936 (prod. only); "Black Aces" 1937 (& prod.); "Boss of Lonely Valley" 1937 (prod. only); "Empty Saddles" 1937 (prod. only); "Law for Tombstone" 1937 (& prod.); "Left-Handed Law" 1937 (prod. only); "Sandflow" 1937 (prod. only); "Smoke Tree Range" 1937 (prod. only); "Sudden Bill Dorn" 1937 (prod. only).

Jones, Clark. Director. TV: *Ruggles of Red Gap* 2-3-57; *Annie Oakley* 3-19-67.

Jones, Dean. *see* Batzella, Luigi.

Jones, Edgar. Director. Films: "Men of the Mountain" 1915; "On Bitter Creek" 1915; "The Girl Angle" 1917; "The Girl Who Wouldn't Quit" 1918.

Jones, F. Richard (1893-12/14/30). Director. Films: "Suzanna" 1922; "No Man's Law" 1927 (story only); "The Water Hole" 1928.

Jones, Grover (1888-9/24/40). Screenwriter. Films: "Grinning Guns" 1927; "The Virginian" 1929; "The Light of the Western Stars" 1930; "The Conquering Horde" 1931; "Dude Ranch" 1931; "Gun Smoke" 1931."The Broken Wing" 1932; "The Plainsman" 1936 (story only); "The Dark Command" 1940; "The Shepherd of the Hills" 1941.

Jones, Harmon (1911-7/10/72). Director. Films: "City of Badmen" 1953; "The Silver Whip" 1953; "Canyon River" 1956; "A Day of Fury" 1956; "Bullwhip" 1958. ¶TV: *Rawhide*—"Incident of the Stalking Death" 11-13-59, "Incident of the Valley in Shadow" 11-20-59, "Incident at Spanish Rock" 12-18-59, "Incident of the Devil and his Due" 1-22-60, "Incident at Sulphur Creek" 3-11-60, "Incident of the Stargazer" 4-1-60, "Incident of the Running Iron" 3-10-61, "Incident of the Painted Lady" 5-12-61, "The Hostage Child" 3-9-62, "Texas Fever" 2-5-65, "The Violent Land" 3-5-65, "The Spanish Camp" 5-7-65; *Laramie*—"Naked Steel" 1-1-63; *The Monroes*—"Pawnee Warrior" 12-28-66.

Jones, Ian. Screenwriter. Films: "Ned Kelly" 1970-Brit.

Jones, Norman (1928-3/26/63). Director. TV: *Zorro*—"The Fortune Teller" 6-18-59.

Jones, Paul (1909-2/24/87). Producer. Films: "The Virginian" 1946; "Pardners" 1956.

Jones, Tommy Lee (1946-). Director. Films: "The Good Old Boys" TVM-1995 (& sp.).

Jones, X.Z. *see* Kennedy, Burt & Haft, David.

Jose, Edward (-12/18/30). Director. Films: "The Fighting Shepherdess" 1920.

Joseph, Robert. Screenwriter. Films: "Gunsmoke in Tucson" 1958.

Josephson, Julien (1883-4/13/59). Screenwriter. Films: "Playing the Game" 1918 (story only); "The Cowboy and the Lady" 1922; "His Back Against the Wall" 1922.

Josey, William Johnson. Director. Films: "The Cowpuncher" 1915 (& sp.).

Joy, Ron. Director. Films: "The Animals" 1971.

Joyce, Adrien. Screenwriter. Films: "The Shooting" 1966.

Jugo, William J. Director. Films: "Gavilan" 1968 (& prod./sp.).

Julian, Rupert (1879-12/27/43). Director. Films: "The Desperado" 1916; "The Desire of the Moth" 1917; "The Savage" 1917; "Hands Down" 1918; "Hungry Eyes" 1918; "The Sleeping Lion" 1919; "The Girl Who Ran Wild" 1922 (& sp.).

Julien, Martin. Screenwriter. Films: "Rooster Cogburn" 1975.

Julien, Max. Screenwriter. Films: "Thomasine and Bushrod" 1974 (& prod.).

Jungmeyer, Jack. Screenwriter. Films: "The Circus Ace" 1927; "Good As Gold" 1927; "Hills of Peril" 1927; "Tumbling River" 1927; "Men of America" 1933; "The Showdown" 1940 (story only); "When the Daltons Rode" 1940 (story only).

Junkermann, Kelly. Producer. Films: "Rio Diablo" TVM-1993; "The Gambler V: Playing for Keeps" TVM-1994 (& story).

Juran, Nathan (1907-). Director. Films: "Gunsmoke" 1953; "Law and Order" 1953; "Tumbleweed" 1953; "Drums Across the River" 1954; "Good Day for a Hanging" 1958; "Land Raiders" 1969-U.S./Span. ¶TV: *My Friend Flicka* 1955; *Daniel Boone*—"The Desperate Raid" 11-16-67, "A Matter of Blood" 12-28-67, "Heroes Welcome" 2-22-68, "Thirty Pieces of Silver" 3-28-68, "The Terrible Tarbots" 12-11-69, "Perilous Passage" 1-15-70, "Noblesse Oblige" 3-26-70, "The Homecoming" 4-9-70, "Israel and Love" (5-7-70.

Justice, Maibelle Heikes. Screenwriter. Films: "The Lure O' the Windigo" 1914 (story only); "The End of the Trail" 1916 (story only); "Durand of the Bad Lands" 1917.

Kabierske, Henry. Director. Films: "The Vigilantes" 1918.

Kadish, Ben. Writer. Films: "The Indian Fighter" 1955 (story).

Kagan, Jeremy (1945-). Director. TV: *Nichols* 1971; *Dr. Quinn, Medicine Woman*—Pilot 1-1-93.

Kahn, Gordon. Screenwriter. Films: "Northwest Rangers" 1942; "Cowboy and the Senorita" 1944; "The Lights of Old Santa Fe" 1944; "The Lights of Old Santa Fe" 1944; "Song of Nevada" 1944.

Kahn, Richard C. Director. Films: "Secret Menace" 1931 (& story); "Two Gun Man from Harlem" 1938 (& sp.); "The Bronze Buckaroo" 1939 (& prod./sp.); "Harlem Rides the Range" 1939 (& prod.); "Buzzy Rides the Range" 1940; "Buzzy and the Phantom Pinto" 1941. ¶TV: *Sky King* 1951.

Kamb, Karl. Screenwriter. Films: "Whispering Smith" 1948; "The Kid from Texas" 1950.

Kamins, Bernie. Screenwriter. Films: "Forty Thieves" 1944.

Kampendonk, Gustav. Screenwriter. Films: "Sheriff Was a Lady" 1965-Ger.

Kandel, Aben (1896-1/28/93). Screenwriter. Films: "The Fighter" 1952.

Kandel, Stephen. Screenwriter. Films: "Frontier Gun" 1958; "Scalplock" TVM-1966 (& story); "Winchester '73" TVM-1967; "Cannon for Cordoba" 1970.

Kane, George. Screenwriter. Films: "Lone Star Ranger" 1942.

Kane, Jay I. Director. Films: "The Demon Rider" 1925 (sp. only); "A Ropin' Ridin' Fool" 1925; "Bucking the Truth" 1926 (sp. only).

Kane, Joel. Writer. Films: "The Tin Star" 1957 (story).

Kane, Joseph (1894-8/25/75). Director. Films: "Riding for Life" 1926 (story only); "Overland Bound" 1929 (story only); "Melody Trail" 1935; "Sagebrush Troubador" 1935; "Tumbling Tumbleweeds" 1935; "Gun and Guitars" 1936; "King of the Pecos" 1936; "The Lawless Nineties" 1936; "The Lonely Trail" 1936; "Oh, Susanna!" 1936; "The Old Corral" 1936; "Ride, Ranger, Ride" 1936; "Boots and Saddles" 1937; "Come On, Cowboys" 1937; "Ghost Town Gold" 1937; "Git Along, Little Dogies" 1937; "Gunsmoke Ranch" 1937; "Heart of the Rockies" 1937; "Public Cowboy No. 1" 1937; "Round-Up Time in Texas" 1937; "Springtime in the Rockies" 1937; "Yodelin' Kid from Pine Ridge" 1937; "Billy the Kid Returns" 1938; "Gold Mine in the Sky" 1938; "Man from Music Mountain" 1938; "The Old Barn Dance" 1938; "Shine on Harvest Moon" 1938; "Under Western Stars" 1938; "The Arizona Kid" 1939 (& prod.); "Come On, Rangers" 1939; "Days of Jesse James" 1939 (& prod.); "Frontier Pony Express" 1939 (& prod.); "In Old Caliente" 1939 (& prod.); "In Old Monterey" 1939; "Rough Riders' Round-Up" 1939 (& prod.); "Saga of Death Valley" 1939 (& prod.); "Southward Ho!" 1939 (& prod.); "Wall Street Cowboy" 1939 (& prod.); "The Border Legion" 1940 (& prod.); "Carson City Kid" 1940 (& prod./story); "Colorado" 1940 (& prod.); "The Ranger and the Lady" 1940 (& prod.); "Young Bill Hickok" 1940 (& prod.); "Young Buffalo Bill" 1940 (& prod.); "Bad Man of Deadwood" 1941 (& prod.); "In Old Cheyenne" 1941 (& prod.); "Jesse James at Bay" 1941 (& prod.); "Nevada City" 1941 (& prod.); "Red River Valley" 1941 (& prod.); "Robin Hood of the Pecos 1941; "Sheriff of Tombstone" 1941 (& prod.); "Heart of the Golden West" 1942 (& prod.); "Man from Cheyenne" 1942 (& prod.); "Ridin' Down the Canyon" 1942; "Romance on the Range" 1942 (& prod.); "Sons of the Pioneers" 1942 (& prod.); "South of Santa Fe" 1942 (& prod.); "Sunset on the Desert" 1942 (& prod.); "Sunset Serenade" 1942 (& prod.); "Hands Across the Border" 1943; "Idaho" 1943; "King of the Cowboys" 1943; "Man from Music Mountain" 1943; "Silver Spurs" 1943; "Song of Texas" 1943; "Cowboy and the Senorita" 1944; "Song of Nevada" 1944; "The Yellow Rose of Texas" 1944; "Dakota" 1945 (& prod.); "Flame of the Barbary Coast" 1945 (& prod.); "In Old Sacramento" 1946 (& prod./story); "Plainsman and the Lady" 1946 (& prod.); "Wyoming" 1947 (& prod.); "The Gallant Legion" 1948 (& prod.); "Old Los Angeles" 1948 (& prod.); "The Plunderers" 1948 (& prod.); "Brimstone" 1949 (& prod.); "The Last Bandit" 1949 (& prod.); "California Passage" 1950 (& prod.); "Rock Island Trail" 1950; "The Savage Horde" 1950 (& prod.); "Oh! Susanna" 1951 (& prod.); "Ride the Man Down" 1952 (& prod.); "Woman of the North Country" 1952 (& prod.); "Joseph Kane" 1953 (& prod.); "Hell's Outpost" 1954 (& prod.); "Jubilee Trail" 1954; "The Road to Denver" 1955; "Timberjack" 1955; "The Vanishing American" 1955; "The Maverick Queen" 1956; "Thunder Over Arizona" 1956 (& prod.); "Duel at Apache Wells" 1957 (& prod.); "Gunfire at Indian Gap" 1957; "The Last Stagecoach West" 1957; "The Lawless Eighties" 1958; "Smoke in the Wind" 1975. ¶TV: *Stories of the Century*—"Last Stagecoach West" 1954; *Broken Arrow* 1956; *Bonanza*—"The Saga of Annie O'Toole" 10-24-59; *Rawhide*—"Incident of the Night Horse" 2-19-60, "Incident of the Champagn Bottles" 3-18-60, "Incident of the Arana Sacar" 4-22-60, "Incident of the Murder Steer" 5-13-60, "Incident of the Silent Web" 6-3-60, "Incident in the Garden of Eden" 6-17-60; *Laramie*—"The Mountain Men" 10-17-61, "The Fatal Step" 10-24-61, "The Last Journey" 10-31-61, "Handful of Fire" 12-5-61, "The Jailbreakers" 12-19-61, "The Barefoot Kid" 1-9-62, "Shadows in the Dust" 1-16-62, "The High Country" 2-6-62, "A Grave for Cully Brown" 2-13-62, "The Day of the Savage" 3-13-62, "Justice in a Hurry" 3-20-62, "Trial by Fire" 4-10-62, "Among the Missing" 9-25-62, "The Fortune Hunter" 10-9-62, "Lost Allegiance" 10-30-62, "Double Eagles" 11-20-62, "Bad Blood" 12-4-62, "Time of the Traitor" 12-11-62, "Vengeance" 1-8-63, "Protective Custody" 1-15-63, "The Fugitives" 2-12-63, "Badge of Glory" 5-7-63, "Trapped" 5-14-63.

Kane, Michael. Screenwriter. Films: "The Legend of the Lone Ranger" 1981; "The Cisco Kid" TVM-1994.

Kane, Robert G. Screenwriter. Films: "The Villain" 1979.

Kanew, Jeff. Screenwriter. Films: "The Wicked Die Slow" 1968.

Kanin, Fay. Screenwriter. Films: "The Outrage" 1964 (story only).

Kanin, Michael (1910-3/12/93). Screenwriter. Films: "The Outrage" 1964 (& story).

Kanter, Hal (1918-). Director. Films: "Once Upon a Horse" 1958 (& prod./sp.). ¶TV: *Bob Hope Chrysler Theatre*—"The Reason Nobody Hardly Ever Seen a Fat Outlaw in the Old West Is As Follows" 3-8-67.

Kantor, MacKinlay (1904-10/11/77). Screenwriter. Films: "The Man from Dakota" 1940 (story only); "Gentle Annie" 1944 (story only); "Hannah Lee" 1953 (& story).

Kaplan, Jonathan (1947-). Director. Films: "Bad Girls" 1994.

Karl, Gunter. Screenwriter. Films: "Trail of the Falcon" 1968-Ger./Sov.

Karlson, Phil (1908-12/12/85). Director. Films: "Adventures in Silverado" 1948; "Thunderhoof" 1948; "The Iroquois Trail" 1950; "The Texas Rangers" 1951; "They Rode West" 1954; "Gunman's Walk" 1958; "A Time for Killing" 1967.

Karr, David. Producer. Films: "The Dangerous Days of Kiowa Jones" TVM-1966; "Welcome to Hard Times" 1967.

Karth, Jay. Writer. Films: "Trail to Gunsight" 1944 (story); "Beyond the Pecos" 1945 (story).

Kas, Johannes. Screenwriter. Films: "Pirates of the Mississippi" 1963-Ger./Ital./Fr.

Kasdan, Lawrence (1949-). Director. Films: "Silverado" 1985 (& prod./sp.); "Wyatt Earp" 1994 (& prod./sp.).

Kasdan, Mark. Screenwriter. Films: "Silverado" 1985.

Kastner, Elliot (1930-). Producer. Films: "Count Your Bullets" 1972; "Rancho Deluxe" 1975; "The Missouri Breaks" 1976; "Frank and Jesse" TVM-1995.

Katcher, Leo (1911-2/27/91). Screenwriter. Films: "They Rode West" 1954 (story only); "The Hard Man" 1957.

Katterjohn, Monte M. (1891-9/8/49). Screenwriter. Films: "His Squaw" 1912; "The Apostle of Vengeance" 1916; "The Gunfighter" 1916; "The Patriot" 1916; "The Flame of the Yukon" 1917 (story); "Golden Rule Kate" 1917; "Carmen of the Klondike" 1918; "The Man from Funeral Range" 1918; "The Eternal Struggle" 1923; "The Flame of the Yukon" 1926 (story).

Katz, Lee. Screenwriter. Films: "Heart of the North" 1938.

Katzin, Lee H. (1935-). Director. Films: "Heaven with a Gun" 1969; "The Quest" TVM-1976. ¶TV: *Branded*—"Salute the Soldier Briefly" 10-24-65, "The Greatest Coward on Earth" 11-21-65, "Romany Roundup" 12-5-65 & 12-12-65, "The Golden Fleece" 1-2-66; *Wild Wild West*—"The Night of the Steel Assassin" 1-7-66, "The Night of the Flaming Ghost" 2-4-55; *Hondo*—"Hondo and the Eagle Claw" 9-8-67, "Hondo and the War Cry" 9-15-67, "Hondo and the Superstition Massacre" 9-29-67, "Hondo and the Judas" 11-3-67; *Young Riders*—"Just Like Old Times" 11-30-91, "The Sacrifice" 6-25-92, "The Debt" 7-16-92.

Katzman, Leonard. Director. TV: *Wild Wild West* 1965-69 (prod.); *Gunsmoke* 1970-75 (prod.), "The Sharecroppers" 3-31-75; Dirty Sally 1974 (& prod.).

Katzman, Sam (1901-8/4/73). Producer. Films: "The Phantom of the Range" 1936; "Rio Grande Romance" 1936; "Rip Roarin' Buckaroo" 1936; "Cheyenne Rides Again" 1937; "Lost Ranch" 1937 (& dir.); "Mystery Range" 1937; "Orphan of the Pecos" 1937 (& dir.); "Brothers of the West" 1938; "Feud of the Trail" 1938; "Lightning Carson Rides Again" 1938; "Six-Gun Trail" 1938; "Code of the Cactus" 1939; "Fighting Renegade" 1939; "Outlaw's Paradise" 1939; "Straight Shooter" 1939; "Texas Wildcats" 1939; "Trigger Fingers" 1939; "Last of the Redmen" 1947; "The Vigilante" 1947-serial; "Tex Granger" 1948-serial; "Cody of the Pony Express" 1950-serial; "Roar of the Iron Horse" 1950-serial; "When the Redskins Rode" 1951; "Brave Warrior" 1952; "California Con-

quest" 1952; "The Pathfinder" 1952; "Son of Geronimo" 1952-serial; "Conquest of Cochise" 1953; "Fort Ti" 1953; "Jack McCall, Desperado" 1953; "Battle of Rogue River" 1954; "Gunfighters of the Northwest" 1954-serial; "Jesse James Versus the Daltons" 1954; "The Law vs. Billy the Kid" 1954; "Masterson of Kansas" 1954; "Riding with Buffalo Bill" 1954-serial; "The Gun That Won the West" 1955; "Seminole Uprising" 1955; "Blackjack Ketchum, Desperado" 1956; "Blazing the Overland Trail" 1956-serial; "Perils of the Wilderness" 1956-serial; "Utah Blaine" 1957; "The Wild Westerners" 1962; "The Fastest Guitar Alive" 1967.

Kaufman, Allan. Screenwriter. Films: "Hell Canyon Outlaws" 1957.

Kaufman, Herbert. Producer. Films: "Gunsmoke in Tucson" 1958.

Kaufman, Joseph. Director. Films: "Nanette of the Wilds" 1916.

Kaufman, Millard (1917-). Screenwriter. Films: "Bad Day at Black Rock" 1955.

Kaufman, Philip (1936-). Director. Films: "The Great Northfield, Minnesota Raid" 1972 (& sp.); "The Outlaw Josey Wales" 1976 (sp. only).

Kavanaugh, Frances. Screenwriter. Films: "The Driftin' Kid" 1941; "Dynamite Canyon" 1941; "Lone Star Law Men" 1941; "Riding the Sunset Trail" 1941; "Arizona Roundup" 1942; "Trail Riders" 1942; "Where Trails End" 1942; "Blazing Guns" 1943; "The Law Rides Again" 1943; "Wild Horse Stampede" 1943 (story only); "Arizona Whirlwind" 1944; "Death Valley Rangers" 1944; "Outlaw Trail" 1944; "Sonora Stagecoach" 1944; "Westward Bound" 1944; "Saddle Serenade" 1945; "Song of Old Wyoming" 1945; "Springtime in Texas" 1945; "Wildfire" 1945; "The Caravan Trail" 1946; "Colorado Serenade" 1946; "Driftin' River" 1946; "God's Country" 1946; "Romance of the West" 1946; "Stars Over Texas" 1946; "Tumbleweed Trail" 1946; "Wild West" 1946; "White Stallion" 1947; "Prairie Outlaws" 1948; "The Daring Caballero" 1949; "The Fighting Stallion" 1950; "Cattle Queen" 1951.

Kay, Gilbert Lee. *see* Mendez, Jose Briz.

Kay, Gordon. Producer. Films: "Bandits of Dark Canyon" 1947; "The Wild Frontier" 1947; "The Bold Frontiersman" 1948; "Carson City Raiders" 1948; "The Denver Kid" 1948; "Desperadoes of Dodge City"

1948; "Marshal of Amarillo" 1948; "Oklahoma Badlands" 1948; "Renegades of Sonora" 1948; "Bandit King of Texas" 1949; "Death Valley Gunfighter" 1949; "Frontier Marshal" 1949; "Powder River Rustlers" 1949; "Sheriff of Wichita" 1949; "The Wyoming Bandit" 1949; "Code of the Silver Sage" 1950; "Covered Wagon Raid" 1950; "Frisco Tornado" 1950; "Gunmen of Abilene" 1950; "Rustlers on Horseback" 1950; "Salt Lake Raiders" 1950; "Vigilante Hideout" 1950; "Night Riders of Montana" 1951; "Rough Riders of Durango" 1951; "Wells Fargo Gunmaster" 1951; "Quantez" 1957; "Day of the Bad Man" 1958; "The Saga of Hemp Brown" 1958; "Hell Bent for Leather" 1960; "Seven Ways from Sundown" 1960; "Posse from Hell" 1961; "Six Black Horses" 1962; "Showdown" 1963; "Bullet for a Badman" 1964; "He Rides Tall" 1964; "Taggart" 1964; "Gunpoint" 1966.

Kay, Richard. Producer. Films: "Riders of the Pony Express" 1949.

Kay, Roger. Director. Films: "Shoot Out at Big Sag" 1962 (& sp.).

Kayden, Tony. Screenwriter. Films: "More Wild Wild West" TVM-1980.

Kaye, Louis S. Screenwriter. Films: "Dudes Are Pretty People" 1942.

Kazan, Elia (1909-). Director. Films: "The Sea of Grass" 1947; "Viva Zapata!" 1952.

Keach, James. Director. Films: *Young Riders*—"A House Divided" 9-28-91, "Jesse" 10-5-91, "Spirits" 12-7-91, "Spies" 1-25-92, "'Til Death Do Us Part" 7-22-92; *Dr. Quinn, Medicine Woman*—"Law of the Land" 1-16-93, "Progress" 2-27-93, "The Operation" 5-8-93, "Saving Souls" 11-13-93, "Best Friends" 12-4-93, "Mike's Dream—A Christmas Tale" 12-18-93, "The Offering" 1-8-94, "Buffalo Soldiers" 2-5-94.

Keach, Stacy (1941-). Screenwriter. Films: "The Long Rider" 1980.

Kean, Richard. *see* Civirani, Osvaldo.

Kearney, Gene (1930-11/4/79). Screenwriter. Films: "A Man Called Gannon" 1969.

Keaton, Buster (1895-2/1/66). Director. Films: "The Paleface" 1922 (& sp.); "Go West" 1925 (& story).

Keaton, Robert. Screenwriter. Films: "Magnificent Texan" 1967-Ital./Span.

Keays, Vernon. Director. Films:

"Arizona Trail" 1943; "Marshal of Gunsmoke" 1944; "Trail to Gunsight" 1944; "Trigger Law" 1944; "The Utah Kid" 1944; "Blazing the Western Trail" 1945; "Rhythm Round-Up" 1945; "Rockin' in the Rockies" 1945; "Sing Me a Song of Texas" 1945; "Landrush" 1946; "Lawless Empire" 1946; "Whirlwind Raiders" 1948.

Keeler, H.P. Screenwriter. Films: "Revenge" 1918; "The Winding rail" 1918; "Drag Harlan" 1920; "The Untamed" 1920.

Keighley, William (1894-6/24/84). Director. Films: "God's Country and the Woman" 1937; "Rocky Mountain" 1950.

Keith, Robert (1898-12/23/66). Screenwriter. Films: "Destry Rides Again" 1932.

Kelland, Clarence Budington (1881-2/18/64). Writer. Films: "The Conflict" 1921; "Arizona" 1940 (story); "Valley of the Sun" 1942 (story); "Sugarfoot" 1951 (story).

Keller, Harry (1913-1/19/87). Director. Films: "Desert of Lost Men" 1951 (& prod.); "Fort Dodge Stempede" 1951 (& prod.); "Black Hills Ambush" 1952; "Captive of Billy the Kid" 1952; "Leadville Gunslinger" 1952 (& prod.); "Rose of Cimarron" 1952; "Thundering Caravans" 1952; "Bandits of the West" 1953; "El Paso Stampede" 1953; "Marshal of Cedar Rock" 1953; "Red River Shore" 1953; "Savage Frontier" 1953; "The Phantom Stallion" 1954; "Quantez" 1957; "Day of the Bad Man" 1958; "Seven Ways from Sundown" 1960; "Six Black Horses" 1962; "Texas Across the River" 1966 (prod. only); "Skin Game" 1972 (prod. only). ¶TV: *Texas John Slaughter* 1958-61; *Empire*—"The Earth Mover" 11-27-62.

Kellogg, Ray (1906-7/5/76). TV: *The Monroes*—"Lost in the Wilderness" 11-30-66.

Kelly, Anthony P. (1897-9/26/32) Screenwriter. Films: "The Great Divide" 1915; "The Valley of Silent Men" 1915; "The Scarlet West" 1925.

Kelly, Burt. Producer. Films: "Between Fighting Men" 1932; "Dynamite Ranch" 1932; "Come On Tarzan" 1933; "Drum Taps" 1933; "Fargo Express" 1933; "The Phantom Thunderbolt" 1933.

Kelly, Duke. Director. Films: "My Name Is Legend" 1975 (& prod./sp.).

Kelly, Edward. Director. Films: "Wanderer of the Wasteland" 1945.

Kelly, Florence Finch. Writer.

Films: "With Hoops of Steel" 1919 (story).

Kelly, Jackie. Screenwriter. Films: "Dig Your Grave, Friend ... Sabata's Coming" 1970-Ital./Span./Fr.; "With Friends, Nothing Is Easy" 1971-Span./Ital.; "My Colt, Not Yours" 1972-Span./Fr./Ital.; "None of the Three Were Called Trinity" 1974-Span.

Kelly, Robert. Director. Films: "The Ranger and the Law" 1921.

Kelly, Ron. Director. Films: "King of the Grizzlies" 1970.

Kelsey, Fred A. (1884-9/2/61). Director. Films: "The Bad Man of Cheyenne" 1916 (& sp.); "The Almost Good Man" 1917; "Blood Money" 1917; "The Drifter" 1917; "The Fighting Gringo" 1917; "A 45 Calibre Mystery" 1917; "Goin' Straight" 1917; "The Golden Bullet" 1917; "Hair-Trigger Burk" 1917; "The Honor of an Outlaw" 1917 (& sp.); "The Mysterious Otulaw" 1917; "The Outlaw and the Lady" 1917; "Six-Shooter Justice" 1917; "Sure Shot Morgan" 1917; "The Texas Sphinx" 1917; "The Wrong Man" 1917; "The One Way Trail" 1920.

Kelly, Gene (1912-). Director. Films: "The Cheyenne Social Club" 1970 (& prod.).

Kelso, Edmund. Screenwriter. Films: "The Mystery of the Hooded Horsemen" 1937; "Tex Rides with the Boy Scouts" 1937 (& story); "Outlaws of Sonora" 1938; "Overland Stage Raiders" 1938 (story only); "Panamint's Bad Man" 1938 (story only); "Rollin' Plains" 1938; "Utah Trail" 1938 (& story); "The Oregon Trail" 1939-serial; "Sundown on the Prairie" 1939; "Roll, Wagons, Roll" 1940; "Ridin' the Cherokee Trail" 1941.

Kempler, Kurt. Screenwriter. Films: "The Big Stampede" 1932; "The Riding Tornado" 1932; "Two-Fisted Law" 1932; "The Telegraph Trail" 1933.

Kennedy, Aubrey M. Director. Films: "The Masked Rider" 1919-serial (& sp.); "The Desert Ruby" 1929 (& sp.).

Kennedy, Burt (1923-). Director. Films: "Seven Men from Now" 1956 (sp. only); "Gun the Man Down" 1957; "The Tall T" 1957 (sp. only); "Fort Dobbs" 1958; "Ride Lonesome" 1959 (sp. only); "Yellowstone Kelly" 1959 (prod. only); "Comanche Station" 1960 (sp. only); "The Canadians" 1961-Brit. (& sp.); "Six Black Horses" 1962 (sp. only); "Mail Order Bride" 1964 (& sp.);

"The Rounders" 1965 (& sp.); "Return of the Seven" 1966-Span.; "Return of the Gunfighter" TVM-1967 (story only); "The War Wagon" 1967; "Welcome to Hard Times" 1967 (& sp.); "The Good Guys and the Bad Guys" 1969; "Young Billy Young" 1969 (& sp.); "Deserter" 1970-U.S./Ital./Yugo.; "Support Your Local Sheriff" 1969; "Dirty Dingus Magee" 1970 (& prod.); "Hannie Calder" 1971-Brit./Span./Fr. (& dir.); "Support Your Local Gunfighter" 1971; "The Train Robbers" 1973 (& sp.); "Shootout in a One-Dog Town" TVM-1974; "Sidekicks" TVM-1974 (& prod.); "Kate Bliss and the Ticker Tape Kid" TVM-1978; "The Wild Wild West Revisited" TVM-1979; "More Wild Wild West" TVM-1980; "The Alamo: 13 Days to Glory" TVM-1987; "Down the Long Hill" TVM-1987; "Once Upon a Texa Train" TVM-1988 (& prod./sp.); "Where the Hell's That Gold?!!!" TVM-1988 (& prod./sp.). ¶TV: *Lawman* 1958; *The Virginian*—"Woman from White Wing" 9-26-62; *The Rounders* 1966-67 (exec. prod); *How the West Was Won*—Season One 1977.

Kennedy, Edith. Screenwriter. Films: "The Bond of Fear" 1917; "Rustling a Bride" 1919.

Kennedy, Joseph P. (1888-11/18/69). Producer. Films: "Cactus Trails" 1927.

Kennedy, Ken. Director. Films: "Kino, the Padre on Horseback" 1977 (& sp.).

Kennedy, Lyn Crost. Writer. Films: "The Raiders" 1952 (story).

Kent, Daisy. Screenwriter. Films: "West of the Rainbow's End" 1926.

Kent, Donald. Screenwriter. Films: "Trails of Adventure" 1935.

Kent, Leon. see De La Mothe, Leon.

Kent, Robert E. Screenwriter. Films: "Bad Men of Missouri" 1941 (story only); "Girl Rush" 1944; "Gas House Kids Go West" 1947; "The Red Stallion" 1947; "When the Redskins Rode" 1951; "Brave Warrior" 1952; "California Conquest" 1952; "The Pathfinder" 1952; "Fort Ti" 1953; "Jesse James Versus the Daltons" 1954; "Seminole Uprising" 1955; "Gun Duel in Durango" 1957 (prod. only); "Utah Blaine" 1957; "Badman's Country" 1958 (prod. only); "Toughest Gun in Tombstone" 1958 (prod. only); "Gunfighters of Abilene" 1960 (prod. only); "Noose for a Gunman" 1960 (prod. only);

"Oklahoma Territory" 1960 (prod. only); "Five Guns to Tombstone" 1961 (prod. only); "Frontier Uprising" 1961 (prod. only); "The Gambler Wore a Gun" 1961 (prod. only); ; "Gun Fight" 1961 (prod. only); "Gun Street" 1961 (prod. only); "Blood on the Arrow" 1964; "The Quick Gun" 1964; "The Fastest Guitar Alive" 1967.

Kent, William. Producer. Films: "Battling Buckaroo" 1932; "Arizona Bad Man" 1935.

Kent, Willis. Producer Films: "Hurricane Horseman" 1931; "The Cheyenne Cyclone" 1932; "Guns for Hire" 1932; "Lawless Valley" 1932; "The Reckless Rider" 1932; "Wyoming Whirlwind" 1932; "Fighting Through" 1934; "The Man from Hell" 1934; "Blazing Guns" 1935; "Cheyenne Tornado" 1935; "Border Vengeance" 1935; "Circle of Death" 1935; "Gunsmoke on the Guadalupe" 1935; "Lightning Triggers" 1935; "Outlaw Rule" 1935; "Range Warfare" 1935.

Kenton, Erle C. (1896-1/28/80). Director. Films: "End of the Trail" 1936; "North to the Klondike" 1942.

Kenyon, Albert. Screenwriter. Films: "Shootin' for Love" 1923.

Kenyon, Charles (1880-6/27/61). Screenwriter. Films: "The Lily of Poverty Flat" 1915; "The Silent Man" 1917; "The Claim" 1918 (story only); "Cupid's Round Up" 1918; "The Fighting Grin" 1918; "Nobody's Wife" 1918; "The Feud" 1919; "Fighting for Gold" 1919; "Hell Roarin' Reform" 1919; "Last of the Duanes" 1919; "The Lone Star Ranger" 1919; "Rough-Riding Romance" 1919; "The Wilderness Trail" 1919; "The Joyous Troublemaker" 1920; "Brass Commandments" 1923; "The Grail" 1923; "The Desert Outlaw" 1924; "The Iron Horse" 1924 (& story); "The Arizona Romeo" 1925; "River's End" 1930; "Phantom of the Plains" 1945; "Two Flags West" 1950 (story only).

Kenyon, Curtis. Screenwriter. Films: "The Persuader" 1957.

Kenyon, Jack. Director. Films: "The Last Stand of the Dalton Boys" 1912.

Kern, James V. (1909-11/9/66). Director. TV: *Sugarfoot* 1957; *Maverick*—"The Spanish Dancer" 12-14-58, "Game of Chance" 1-4-59, "Destination Devil's Flat" 12-25-60.

Kernochan, Sarah. Screenwriter. Films: "Sommersby" 1993.

Kerr, Alvah Milton. Writer. Films: "By Right of Possession" 1917 (story).

Kerrigan, J. Warren (1879-6/9/47). Director. Films: "Jack Meets His Waterloo" 1913.

Kershner, Irvin (1923-). Director. Films: "The Return of a Man Called Horse" 1976.

Kessler, Bruce. Director. TV: *Alias Smith and Jones*—"Return to Devil's Hole" 2-25-71.

Kessler, Don. Director. Films: "The Caputure of Grizzly Adams" TVM-1982.

Ketchum, Philip. Screenwriter. Films: "The Devil's Trail" 1942.

Keusch, Michael. Director. Films: "Samurai Cowboy" 1993 (& sp.).

Kibbee, Roland (1914-8/5/84). Screenwriter. Films: "Vera Cruz" 1954; "The Appaloosa" 1966; "Valdez Is Coming" 1971. ¶TV: *The Deputy* 1959-61 (prod.).

Kiefer, Warren. Screenwriter. Films: "Beyond the Law" 1968-Ital.; "The Last Rebel" 1971-Ital./U.S./Span.

Kiel, Richard (1939-). Screenwriter. Films: "The Giant of Thunder Mountain" 1991.

Kier, H.W. Director. Films: "Border Fence" 1951 (& prod.).

Killy, Edward. Director. Films: "The Fargo Kid" 1940; "Stage to Chino" 1940; "Wagon Train" 1940; "Along the Rio Grande" 1941; "The Bandit Trail" 1941; "Cyclone on Horseback" 1941; "Robbers of the Range" 1941; "Come On, Danger!" 1942; "Land of the Open Range" 1942; "Riding the Wind" 1942; "Nevada" 1944; "West of the Pecos" 1945.

Kilpatrick, Tom (1898-3/11/62). Screenwriter. Films: "Adventures in Silverado" 1948; "The Palomino" 1950.

Kimble, Lawrence. Screenwriter. Films: "Bells of Capistrano" 1942; "Pierre of the Plains" 1942.

King, Allan Winston. Director. Films: "Silence of the North" 1981.

King, Bradley. Producer. Films: "The Sunshine Trail" 1923; "Morgan's Last Raid" 1929; "The Lash" 1930; "Under the Pampas Moon" 1935.

King, Burton (1877-5/4/44). Director. Films: "Across the Desert" 1915; "In the Sunset Country" 1915; "The Parson Who Fled West" 1915; "The Valley of Regeneration" 1915; "The Spell of the Yukon" 1916; "In Old California" 1929; "Quick Trigger Lee" 1931 (prod. only); "The Forty-Niners" 1932 (prod. only);

"Mark of the Spur" 1932 (prod. only); "Scarlet Brand" 1932 (prod. only); "Deadwood Pass" 1933 (prod. only); "War on the Range" 1933 (prod. only); "When a Man Rides Alone" 1933.

King, Carlton S. (1881-7/6//32). Screenwriter. Films: "Lo, the Poor Indian" 1914.

King, Gen. Charles (1844-1933). Writer. Films: "The Adventures of Buffalo Bill" 1914 (sp.); "A Daughter of the Sioux" 1925 (story); "Fort Frayne" 1925 (story); "Tonio, Son of the Sierras" 1925 (story); "Warrior Gap" 1925 (story); "Under Fire" 1926 (story).

King, Frank (1913-2/12/89). Producer. Films: "The Dude Goes West" 1948; "Drums in the Deep South" 1951; "Return of the Gunfighter" TVM-1967; "Heaven with a Gun" 1969.

King, Fred. Director. Films: "Gunsmoke" 1947.

King, Henry (1896-6/29/82). Director. Films: "The Mainspring" 1917; "Six Feet Four" 1919; "Some Liar" 1919; "This Hero Stuff" 1919; "When a Man Rides Alone" 1919; "Where the West Begins" 1919; "Sting of the Lash" 1921; "The Winning of Barbara Worth" 1926; "Ramona" 1936; "Jesse James" 1939; "The Gunfighter" 1950; "The Bravados" 1958.

King, Lewis. *see* Capuano, Luigi.

King, Louis (1898-9/7/62). Director. Films: "Peaceful Peters" 1922; "The Sheriff of Sun-Dog" 1922; "The Devil's Dooryard" 1923; "The Law Rustlers" 1923; "Sun Dog Trails" 1923; "The Boy Rider" 1927; "The Slingshot Kid" 1927; "The Bantam Cowboy" 1928; "The Fightin' Redhead" 1928; "The Little Buckaroo" 1928; "Orphan of the Sage" 1928; "The Pinto Kid" 1928; "Rough Ridin' Red" 1928; "Terror Mountain" 1928; "Young Whirlwind" 1928; "The Freckled Rascal" 1929; "The Little Savage" 1929; "Pals of the Prairie" 1929; "The Vagabond Club" 1929; "The Lone Rider" 1930; "Men Without Law" 1930; "Shadow Ranch" 1930; "Border Law" 1931; "Desert Vengeance" 1931; "The Fighting Sheriff" 1931; "Life in the Raw" 1933; "Robbers' Roost" 1933; "Song of the Saddle" 1936; "Smoky" 1946; "Green Grass of Wyoming" 1948; "Mrs. Mike" 1949; "Frenchie" 1950; "The Lion and the Horse" 1952; "Powder River" 1953; "Massacre" 1956. ¶TV: *Gunsmoke*—"Gun for Chester" 9-21-57, "Blood Money" 9-28-57.

King, Maurice (1915-9/2/77). Producer. Films: "The Dude Goes West" 1948; "Drums in the Deep South" 1951; "Return of the Gunfighter" TVM-1967; "Heaven with a Gun" 1969.

King, Paul. Screenwriter. Films: "Wild Heritage" 1958.

Kingdom, Lewis. Screenwriter. Films: "Desert Justice" 1936.

Kingsley, Pierce. Screenwriter. Films: "The Maid of Niagara" 1910; "Tracy the Outlaw" 1928 (story only).

Kingsley-Smith, Terry. Screenwriter. Films: "Molly and Lawless John" 1972.

Kinney, Jack (1909-2/9/92). Director. Films: "Melody Time" 1948.

Kinon, Richard. Director. TV: *Here Come the Brides*—"A Christmas Place" 12-18-68, "The Firemaker" 1-15-69, "Wives for Wakando" 1-22-69, "Mr. and Mrs. J. Bolt" 3-12-69, "Loggerheads" 3-26-69, "Marriage Chinese Style" 4-9-69, "A Bride for Obie Brown" 1-9-70.

Kinoy, Ernest. Screenwriter. Films: "Buck and the Preacher" 1972 (& story).

Kirkland, David (1878-10/27/64). Director. Films: "Children of the Forest" 1913; "All Around the Frying Pan" 1925 (& sp.); "Hands Across the Border" 1926; "A Regular Scout" 1926 (& sp.); "The Tough Guy" 1926; "The Two-Gun Man" 1926; "Riders of the Cactus" 1931 (& prod./sp.).

Kirkland, Jack (1903-2/22/69). Screenwriter. Films: "Sutter's Gold" 1936.

Kirkwood, James (1875-8/24/63). Director. Films: "The Mountain Rat" 1914; "Strongheart" 1914.

Kirkwood, Ray (Al Alt). Producer. Films: "Frontier Days" 1934; "Cyclone Ranger" 1935; "Lawless Border" 1935; "The Reckless Buckaroo" 1935; "Six Gun Justice" 1935; "The Texas Rambler" 1935; "The Vanishing Riders" 1935; "Blazing Justice" 1936; "Outlaws of the Range" 1936.

Kjellin, Alf (1920-4/5/88). Director. Films: "The McMasters" 1970. ¶TV: *Gunsmoke*—"Bohannan" 9-25-72, "Patricia" 1-22-73, "A Quiet Day in Dodge" 1-29-73, "The Hanging of Newly O'Brien" 11-26-73; *Bonanza*—"The Initiation" 9-26-72; *Little House on the Prairie* 1974; *The Quest*—"Seventy-Two Hours" 11-3-76; *The Young Pioneers*—4-9-78; *How*

the West Was Won—"The Innocent" 2-12-79.

Klein, Hal. Producer. Films: "Convict Stage" 1965; "Fort Courageous" 1965; "War Party" 1965; "More Dead Than Alive" 1968; "Barquero" 1970.

Klein, Larry (1920-). Writer. Films: "Invitation to a Gunfighter" 1964 (story).

Klein, Paul. Writer. Films: "Night Cry" 1926 (story).

Klein, Philip. Screenwriter. Films: "Riders of the Purple Sage" 1931; "The Gay Caballero" 1932; "Rainbow Trail" 1932.

Klein, Wally. Screenwriter. Films: "The Oklahoma Kid" 1939 (story only); "They Died with Their Boots On" 1941.

Kleindorff, Eberhard. Screenwriter. Films: "Among Vultures" 1964-Ger./Ital./Fr./Yugo.

Kleiner, Harry (1916-). Screenwriter. Films: "Kangaroo" 1952; "The Violent Men" 1955.

Kleiser, Randal (1946-). Director. Films: "White Fang" 1991.

Klick, Roland. Director. Films: "Deadlock" 1970-Ital./Ger./Isr. (& prod./sp.).

Klimovsky, Leon. Director. Films: "Torrejon City" 1961-Span.; "Billy the Kid" 1962-Span.; "Two Thousand Dollars for Coyote" 1965-Span.; "Django, A Bullet for You" 1966-Span./Ital.; "Few Dollars for Django" 1966-Ital./Span.; "Death Knows No Time" 1968-Span./Ital. (& sp.); "Rattler Kid" 1968-Ital./Span.; "Challenge of the Mackennas" 1969-Ital./Span.; "Quinta: Fighting Proud" 1969-Ital./Span.; "Reverend Colt" 1970-Ital./Span.; "Raise Your Hands, Dead Man … You're Under Arrest" 1971-Ital./Span.

Kline, Benjamin (1894-1/7/74). Director. Films: "Lightning Warrior" 1931-serial; "Cowboy in the Clouds" 1943; "Cowboy from Lonesome River" 1944; "Cyclone Prairie Rangers" 1944; "Saddle Leather Law" 1944; "Sundown Valley" 1944.

Kline, Edward F. Director. Films: "When a Man's a Man" 1935.

Kline, Harold. Writer. Films: "Where the North Begins" 1947 (story).

Kline, Herbert. Director. Films: "The Fighter" 1952 (& sp.).

Klove, Jane. Screenwriter. Films: "…And Now Miguel" 1966.

Knarpf, Elinor. Screenwriter. Films: "A Cry in the Wilderness" TVM-1974.

Knarpf, Stephen. Screenwriter. Films: "A Cry in the Wilderness" TVM-1974.

Knibbs, Henry Herbert. Writer. Films: "Overland Red" 1920 (story); "The Sunset Trail" 1924 (story); "Tony Runs Wild" 1926 (story); "The Mounted Stranger" 1930 (story).

Knight, Eric. Writer. Films: "Gypsy Colt" 1954 (story).

Knoles, Harley (-6/6/36). Director. Films: "The Price of Pride" 1917.

Knop, Patricia Louisiana. Screenwriter. Films: "Silence of the North" 1981.

Knopf, Christopher. Screenwriter. Films: "The Tall Stranger" 1957; "Hell Bent for Leather" 1960; "The Bravos" TVM-1972 (& story); "Posse" 1975 (& story); "Mrs. Sundance" TVM-1994.

Knopf, Edwin H. Director. Films: "The Border Legion" 1930; "The Light of the Western Stars" 1930; "The Santa Fe Trail" 1930; "The Vanishing Virginian" 1941.

Knox, Werner. *see* Mattei, Bruno.

Koch, Carlo. Director. Films: "The Girl of the Golden West" 1942-Ital. (& sp.).

Koch, Howard W. (1916-). Producer. Films: "Virginia City" 1940 (sp. only); "War Paint" 1953; "The Yellow Tomahawk" 1954; "Fort Yuma" 1955; "The Broken Star" 1956; "Ghost Town" 1956; "Quincannon, Frontier Scout" 1956; "Rebel in Town" 1956; "The Dalton Girls" 1957; "Revolt at Fort Laramie" 1957; "Tomahawk Trail" 1957; "War Drums" 1957; "Fort Bowie" 1958 (dir. only); "Born Reckless" 1959 (dir. only). ¶TV: *Maverick*—"Comstock Conspiracy" 12-29-57 (dir.); *Johnny Ringo* 1959 (dir.).

Koenig, Laird. Screenwriter. Films: "Red Sun" 1971-Fr./Ital./Span. (& story).

Kohlmar, Fred (1905-10/13/69). Producer. Films: "Riding High" 1943; "Fury at Furance Creek" 1948; "Gunman's Walk" 1958.

Kohlmar, Lee (1873-5/14/46). Director. Films: "Bandits Beware" 1921; "Beating the Game" 1921; "Double Crossers" 1921; "Fighting Blood" 1921; "Too-Tired Jones" 1921; "Who Was That Man?" 1921; "The Wild Wild West" 1921; "The Man Who Woke Up" 1921.

Kohn, Ben Grauman. Screenwriter. Films: "American Empire" 1942.

Kolditz, Gottfried. Director. Films: "Trail of the Falcon" 1968-Ger./Sov. (& prod.).

Kolker, Henry (1870-7/15/47). Director. Films: "A Man's Country" 1919.

Kopit, Arthur (1937-). Writer. Films: "Buffalo Bill and the Indians, or Sitting Bull's History Lesson" 1976 (story).

Kotcheff, Ted (1931-). Director. Films: "Billy Two Hats" 1973-Brit.

Kowalski, Bernard (1929-). Director. Films: "Macho Callahan" 1970 (& prod.); "Black Noon" TVM-1971. ¶TV: *Broken Arrow* 1956; *The Rifleman*—"The Legacy" 12-8-59; *Rawhide*—1959-66 (prod.), "The Enormous Fist" 10-2-64, "Corporal Dasovik" 12-4-64, "The Book" 1-8-65; *The Westerner*—"Mrs. Kennedy" 10-28-60; *Wild Wild West*—"The Night the Wizard Shook the Earth" 10-1-65; *The Virginian*—"The Claim" 10-6-65; *The Monroes*—"The Intruders" 9-7-66; *Gunsmoke*—"Quaker Girl" 12-10-66, "The Hanging" 12-31-66.

Kowalski, Frank. Screenwriter. Films: "Man Called Sledge" 1971-Ital./U.S.

Kozlenka, William. Writer. Films: "Raw Edge" 1956 (story).

Krafft, John. Screenwriter. Films: "The Arizona Raiders" 1936; "In Old Cheyenne" 1941 (story only).

Kraike, Michael. Producer. Films: "Renegades" 1946; "Frenchie" 1950; "Sierra" 1950. ¶TV: *The Deputy* 1959-61.

Kramer, Cecile. Screenwriter. Films: "Twilight on the Trail" 1941; "Silver Queen" 1942; "Buffalo Bill" 1944; "Hoppy's Holiday" 1947 (story only); "Ramrod" 1947.

Kramer, Frank. *see* Parolini, Gianfranco.

Kramer, Robert. Director. Films: "Guns" 1980-Fr. (& sp.).

Kramer, Searle. Screenwriter. Films: "Whoops, I'm an Indian" 1936-short; "Back to the Woods" 1937-short (story only); "Teacher's Pest" 1939-short; "Yes, We Have No Bonanza" 1939-short.

Kramer, Stanley (1913-). Director. Films: "High Noon" 1952 (prod. only); "Oklahoma Crude" 1973 (& prod.).

Krasna, Norman (1910-11/1/84). Producer. Films: "The Lusty Men" 1952.

Krasna, Philip N. Producer. Films: "Crashing Thru" 1939; "Fighting Mad" 1939; "Trigger Pals" 1939;

"Danger Ahead" 1940; "Murder on the Yukon" 1940; "Song of the Range" 1944; "The Cisco Kid Returns" 1945; "In Old New Mexico" 1945; "South of the Rio Grande" 1945; "The Valiant Hombre" 1948; "The Daring Caballero" 1949; "The Gay Amigo" 1949; "Satan's Cradle" 1949; "The Girl from San Lorenzo" 1950; "Pawnee" 1957.

Krasny, Paul (1935-). Director. Films: "Joe Panther" 1976.

Kress, Harold F. Director. Films: "The Painted Hills" 1951; "Apache War Smoke" 1952.

Kreves, Rose. Screenwriter. Films: "Battling Marshal" 1950.

Krims, Milton (1904-7/11/88). Screenwriter. Films: "Dude Ranch" 1931 (story only); "The Range Feud" 1931; "Forbidden Trail" 1932; "South of the Rio Grande" 1932; "The Western Code" 1932; "West of the Pecos" 1934; "Tennessee's Partner" 1955; "Mohawk" 1956.

Krueger, Carl. Screenwriter. Films: "Comanche" 1956 (& sp.).

Krumgold, Joseph (1908-7/10/80). Writer. Films: "...And Now Miguel" 1966 (story).

Krusada, Carl. Screenwriter. Films: "King of the Saddle" 1926; "The Valley of Bravery" 1926; "The Arizona Whirlwind" 1927; "The Denver Dude" 1927; "Beauty and Bullets" 1928; "The Border Wildcat" 1928; "Thunder Riders" 1928; "Phantom of the North" 1929; "Bar L Ranch" 1930; "Beyond the Rio Grande" 1930; "Firebrand Jordan" 1930; "Phantom of the Desert" 1930; "Ridin' Law" 1930; "Westward Bound" 1930; "The Mystery Trooper" 1931-serial; "Forty-Five Calbire Echo" 1932; "Lariats and Sixshooters" 1933; "The Cactus Kid" 1934; "Fighting Hero" 1934; "Loser's End" 1934; "Mystery Ranch" 1934; "Terror of the Plains" 1934; "Born to Battle" 1935; "Coyote Trails" 1935; "Defying the Law" 1935; "The Laramie Kid" 1935; "North of Arizona" 1935; "The Phantom Cowboy" 1935; "Ridin' Thru" 1935 (story only); "Rio Rattler" 1935; "Silent Valley" 1935; "The Silver Bullet" 1935; "Skull and Crown" 1935; "Texas Jack" 1935; "The Unconquered Bandit" 1935 (story only); "Wolf Riders" 1935; "Fast Bullets" 1936; "Santa Fe Bound" 1936 (story only); "El Diablo Rides" 1939; "Feud of the Range" 1939; "The Pal from Texas" 1939; "Riders of the Sage" 1939; "The Kid from Santa Fe" 1940; "Pinto Canyon" 1940; "Riders from Nowhere" 1940;

"Wild Horse Range" 1940; "Wild Horse Valley" 1940.

Kulik, Buzz (1923-). Director. Films: "Villa Rides" 1968; "Pioneer Woman" TVM-1973. ¶TV: *Gunsmoke*—"Mavis McCloud" 10-26-57, "Born to Hang" 11-2-57, "Ma Tennis" 2-1-58, "Kitty's Injury" 9-19-59, "Johnny Red" 10-3-59; *Have Gun Will Travel*—"The Manhunter" 6-7-58, "A Score for Murder" 11-22-58, "Shot by Request" 10-10-59; *Rawhide*—"Incident at Chubasco" 4-3-59.

Kull, Edward. Director. Films: "At the Point of the Gun" 1919; "The Best Bad Man" 1919; "The Counterfeit Trail" 1919; "Dynamite" 1919; "The Face in the Watch" 1919; "The Fighting Sheriff" 1919; "Blind Chance" 1920; "Kaintuck's Ward" 1920; "A Battle of Wits" 1921; "Beauty and the Bandit" 1921; "The Call of Duty" 1921; "The Dream Girl" 1921; "Fair Fighting" 1921; "The Fight Within" 1921; "The Girl in the Saddle" 1921; "The Heart of Arizona" 1921; "The Honor of the Mounted" 1921; "The Man Trackers" 1921; "The Raiders of the North" 1921; "Roaring Waters" 1921; "The Shadow of Suspicion" 1921; "A Woman's Wits" 1921; "Barriers of Folly" 1922; "Bulldog Courage" 1922; "The Night Attack" 1922; "The Open Wire" 1922.

Kuller, Sid. Screenwriter. Films: "Slaughter Trail" 1951.

Kusel, Daniel. Screenwriter. Films: "The Showdown" 1940.

Kusel, Harold. Screenwriter. Films: "The Showdown" 1940.

Kyne, Peter B. (1880-1957). Writer. Films: "The Long Chance" 1915 (story); "The Parson of Panamint" 1916 (story); "The Three Godfathers" 1916 (story); "Salt of the Earth" 1917 (story); "Marked Men" 1919 (story); "The Beautiful Gambler" 1921 (story); "Red Courage" 1921 (story); "Back to Yellow Jacket" 1922 (story); "The Long Chance" 1922 (story); "One-Eighth Apache" 1922 (story); "While Satan Sleeps" 1922 (story); "Beauty and the Bad Man" 1925 (story); "The Golden Strain" 1925 (story); "The Buckaroo Kid" 1926 (story); "The Enchanted Hill" 1926 (story); "Rustlin' for Cupid" 1926 (story); "War Paint" 1926 (story); "California" 1927 (story); "Galloping Fury" 1927 (story); "A Hero on Horseback" 1927 (story); "Jim the Conqueror" 1927 (story); "The Rawhide Kid" 1928 (story); "Tide of Empire" 1929 (story); "Hell's Heroes" 1930 (story); "Wild Horse" 1931 (story); "Flaming

Guns" 1932 (story); "Heroes of the West" 1932-serial (story); "Local Bad Man" 1932 (story); "Gordon of Ghost City" 1933-serial (story); "Gallant Defender" 1935 (story); "Valley of Wanted Men" 1935 (story); "The Mysterious Avenger" 1936 (story); "Rio Grande Romance" 1936 (story); "Secret Patrol" 1936 (story); "Stampede" 1936 (story); "The Three Godfathers" 1936 (story); "One Man Justice" 1937 (prod. only); "Flaming Frontier" 1938-serial (story); "The Parson of Panamint" 1941 (story); "The Three Godfathers" 1948 (story); "Belle Le Grand" 1951 (story); "Bronco Buster" 1952 (story); "The Godchild" TVM-1974 (story).

Kyson, Charles. Writer. Films: "West of Nevada" 1936 (story).

La Barba, Fidel. Writer. Films: "Susannah of the Mounties" 1939 (story).

LaBlanche, Ethel. Screenwriter. Films: "Headin' East" 1937; "Hollywood Roundup" 1938; "Pirates on Horseback" 1941.

La Cava, Gregory (1892-3/1/52). Director. Films: "The Gay Defender" 1927.

Lacy, J.A. Films: "The Golden Thought" 1916.

Lacy, Joe. *see* Elorrieta, Jose M.

Ladd, Alan (1913-1/29/64). Producer. Films: "Drum Beat" 1954.

Lado, Aldo. Screenwriter. Films: "If One Is Born a Swine … Kill Him" 1968-Ital.

Laemmle, Carl (1867-9/24/39). Producer. Films: "The Phantom Bullet" 1926; "Hell's Heroes" 1930; "The Storm" 1930.

Laemmle, Jr., Carl (1908-9/24/79). Producer. Films: "My Pal, the King" 1932; "Rider of Death Valley" 1932; "Texas Bad Man" 1932; "Hidden Gold" 1933.

Laemmle, Edward (1887-4/2/37). Director. Films: "Cinders" 1920; "The Man with the Punch" 1920; "Superstition" 1920; "The Two-Fisted Lover" 1920; "Bib Bob" 1921; "Both Barrels" 1921; "The Call of the Blood" 1921; "The Cowpuncher's Comeback" 1921; "The Danger Man" 1921; "The Grip of the Law" 1921; "The Guilty Trail" 1921; "In the Nick of Time" 1921; "The Knockout Man" 1921; "The Midnight Raiders" 1921; "The Outlaw" 1921; "A Ranch Romeo" 1921; "Range Rivals" 1921; "The Rim of the Desert" 1921; "The Saddle King" 1921; "Stand Up and Fight" 1921; "Sweet Revenge" 1921; "The Valley of the Rogues" 1921; "Winners of the West" 1921-serial;

"In the Days of Buffalo Bill" 1922-serial; "The Ranger's Reward" 1922; "The Oregon Trail" 1923-serial; "The Traitor" 1924; "Spook Ranch" 1925; "The Top Hand" 1925; "Tricked" 1925; "The Way of the West" 1925; "The Whip Hand" 1925; "The Wild West Wallop" 1925; "The Tin Bronc" 1926; "The Winged Rider 1926; "Lasca of the Rio Grande" 1931; "Texas Bad Man" 1932.

Laemmle, Ernst. Director. Films: "The Boss of Bar 20" 1924; "The Double X" 1924; "An Eyeful" 1924; "Her Rodeo Hero" 1924; "The Little Savage" 1924; "The Lone Round-Up" 1924; "A Race for a Ranch" 1924; "The Red Rage" 1924; "Red Raymond's Girl" 1924; "The Sunset Trail" 1924; "The Bashful Whirlwind" 1925; "A Battle of Wits" 1925; "The Best Man" 1925; "Dynamite's Daughter" 1925; "The Fighting Schoolmarm" 1925; "The Fighting Terror" 1925; "Loaded Dice" 1925; "The Loser Wins" 1925; "One Glorious Scrap" 1925; "The Pronto Kid" 1925; "Queen of the Roundup" 1925; "The Road from Latigo" 1925; "The Ropin' Venus" 1925; "The Storm King" 1925; "The Emergency Man" 1926; "Four Square Steve" 1926; "Hearts of the West" 1926; "Prowlers of the Night" 1926 (& story); "The Rustler's Secret" 1926; "The Broncho Buster" 1927; "A Close Call" 1925; "The Cowboy Chaperone" 1927; "Hands Off" 1927; "The Man Tamer" 1927; "A One Man Game" 1927; "Pawns and Queens" 1927; "Range Courage" 1927; "Red Clay" 1927; "The Roaring Gulch 1927.

Lafferty, Perry. Director. TV: *Rawhide*—"Judgment at Honodo Seco" 10-20-61; *Big Hawaii* 1977 (exec. prod.).

Lahola, Leopoldo. Director. Films: "Duel at Sundown" 1965-Fr./Ger. (& prod./sp.).

Laird, Jack (1923-12/3/91). Director. Films: "Testimony of Two Men" TVM-1977 (prod. only). ¶TV: *Bronco* 1958.

Lait, Jr., Jack (1909-8/18/61). Screenwriter. Films: "The Marshal of Mesa City" 1939; "Death Valley Outlaws" 1941; "Texas Masquerade" 1944.

Lake, Stuart N. (1890-1/27/64). Writer. Films: "Frontier Marshal" 1934 (story); "Wells Fargo" 1937 (story); "Frontier Marshal" 1939 (story); "The Westerner" 1940 (story); "Wells Fargo Days" 1944-short (sp.); "Winchester '73" 1950 (story only); "Powder River" 1953 (story); "Winchester '73" TVM-1967 (story).

Lamas, Fernando (1915-10/8/82). Director. Films: "A Place Called Glory" 1966-Span./Ger. ¶TV: *Alias Smith and Jones*—"The Fifth Victim" 3-25-71, "Smiler with a Gun" 10-7-71; *Bret Maverick*—"The Rattlesnake Brigade" 4-27-82.

Lamb, Andre. Screenwriter. Films: "Riders of the Santa Fe" 1944; "Renegades of the Rio Grande" 1945; "Moon Over Montana" 1946; "Hoppy's Holiday" 1947; "Unexpected Guest" 1947; "The Texan Meets Calamity Jane" 1950 (& dir./prod.).

Lamb, Eleanor. Screenwriter. Films: "Seven Alone" 1974; "Against a Crooked Sky" 1975.

Lamb, Harold. Screenwriter. Films: "The Plainsman" 1936.

Lamb, Max. Screenwriter. Films: "Apache Uprising" 1966; "Waco" 1966 (story only).

Lambert, Glen. Director. Films: "Heartbound" 1925.

Lambert, Will. Writer. Films: "The Hurricane Kid" 1925 (story).

Lamont, B. Wayne. Screenwriter. Films: "Secret Menace" 1931; "Two Gun Caballero" 1931 (story only).

Lamont, Charles (1898-9/11/93). Director. Films: "The Gold Ghost" 1934-short; "Road Agent" 1941; "Frontier Gal" 1945; "Salome, Where She Danced" 1945; "The Untamed Breed" 1948; "Curtain Call at Cactus Creek" 1950; "Ricochet Romance" 1954; "Untamed Heiress" 1954; "Carolina Cannonball" 1955; "Lay That Rifle Down" 1955. ¶TV: *Zorro*—"The Man with the Whip" 5-8-58, "The Cross of the Andes" 5-15-58, "The Deadly Bolas" 5-22-58, "The Well of Death" 5-29-58, "The Practical Joker" 12-11-58, "The Flaming Arrow" 12-18-58, "Zorro Fights a Duel" 12-25-58, "Amnesty for Zorro" 1-1-59, "Senor China Boy" 6-25-59.

La Mothe, Julian. Screenwriter. Films: "The Legend of the Poisoned Pool" 1915; "The Worthier Man" 1915 (story only); "The Girl Angle" 1917.

L'Amour, Louis (1908-6/10/88). Writer. Films: "Hondo" 1953 (story); "Four Guns to the Border" 1954 (story); "Stranger on Horseback" 1955 (story); "Treasure of Ruby Hills" 1955 (story); "Blackjack Ketchum, Desperado" 1956 (story); "The Burning Hills" 1956 (story); "The Tall Stranger" 1957 (story); "Utah Blaine" 1957 (story); "Apache Territory" 1958 (story); "Guns of the Timberland" 1960 (story); "Heller in Pink Tights"

1960 (story); "Taggart" 1964 (story); "Kid Rodelo" 1966-U.S./Span. (story); "Shalako" 1968-Brit./Fr. (story); "Catlow" 1971-Span. (story); "The Man Called Noon" 1973-Brit./Span./Ital. (story); "The Sacketts" TVM-1979 (story); "The Shadow Riders" TVM-1982 (story); "Down the Long Hill" TVM-1987 (story); "The Quick and the Dead" CTVM-1987 (story); "Conagher" TVM-1991 (story).

Lampell, Millard. Screenwriter. Films: "Orphan Train" TVM-1979.

Lancaster, Burt (1913-10/20/94). Director. Films: "The Kentuckian" 1955.

Lancaster, Cliff. Screenwriter. Films: "Gold Fever" 1952.

Lancaster, G.B. Writer. Films: "The Eternal Struggle" 1923 (story).

Land, Charles. Screenwriter. Films: "Buchanan Rides Alone" 1958.

Landau, Richard (1914-9/18/93). Screenwriter. Films: "The Great Jesse James Raid" 1953; "Born Reckless" 1959 (& story); "Fort Courageous" 1965. ¶TV: *Wild Wild West* 1965-69 (prod.).

Landers, Lew (Louis Friedlander) (1901-12/16/62). Director. Films: "The Red Rider" 1934-serial; "Rustlers of Red Dog" 1935-serial; "Border Cafe" 1937; "Bad Lands" 1939; "The Girl and the Gambler" 1939; "Wagons Westward" 1940; "Back in the Saddle" 1941; "Ridin' on a Rainbow" 1941; "The Singing Hill" 1941; "Deerslayer" 1943; "Black Arrow" 1944-serial; "Cowboy Canteen" 1944; "Swing in the Saddle" 1944; "Death Valley" 1946; "Thunder Mountain" 1947; "Under the Tonto Rim" 1947; "The Adventures of Gallant Bess" 1948; "Law of the Barbary Coast" 1949; "Stagecoach Kid" 1949; "Davy Crockett, Indian Scout" 1950; "Dynamite Pass" 1950; "When the Redskins Rode" 1951; "California Conquest" 1952; "Captain John Smith and Pocahontas" 1953; "Apache Ambush" 1955. ¶TV: *The Adventures of Rin Tin Tin* 1954; *Cheyenne* 1955; *Colt .45* 1957; *Bronco* 1958; *Maverick*—"Easy Mark" 11-15-59, "Arizona Black Maria" 10-9-60.

Landis, James (1926-12/17/91). Director. Films: "Lone Texan" 1959 (sp./story only); "Deadwood '76" 1965. ¶TV: *Gunsmoke*—"Fandango" 2-11-67.

Landis, John (1950-). Director. Films: "Three Amigos" 1986.

Landon, Joseph. Screenwriter. Films: "Rio Conchos" 1964; "Stagecoach" 1966.

Landon, Michael (1937-7/1/91). Director. Films: "Little House on the Prairie" TVM-1974 (& prod.); "Little House: The Last Farewell" TVM-1984 (& sp.). ¶TV: *Bonanza*—"To Die in Darkness" 5-5-68, "The Wish" 3-9-69, "Dead Wrong" 12-7-69, "It's a Small World" 1-4-70, "Decision at Los Robles" 3-22-70, "The Love Child" 11-8-70, "Terror at 2:00" 3-7-71, "The Stillness Within" 3-14-71, "Don't Cry, My Son" 10-31-71, "He was Only Seven" 3-5-72, "The Younger Brothers' Younger Brother" 3-12-72, "Forever" 9-12-72, "The Sound of Loneliness" 12-5-72, "The Hunter" 1-16-73; *Little House on the Prairie* 1974-82 (& exec. prod.); *Father Murphy* 1981-82 (exec. prod.), Pilot 11-3-81; *Little House: A New Beginning* 1982-83 (& exec. prod.).

Landon, Jr., Michael. Screenwriter. Films: "Bonanza: The Return" TVM-1993 (story only).

Landres, Paul (1912-). Director. Films: "Grand Canyon" 1949; "Square Dance Jubilee" 1949; "Hell Canyon Outlaws" 1957; "Last of the Badmen" 1957; "Frontier Gun" 1958; "Man from God's Country" 1958; "Oregon Passage" 1958; "Lone Texan" 1959; "The Miracle of the Hills" 1959; "Son of a Gunfighter" 1966-U.S./Span. ¶TV: *The Lone Ranger* 1949-57 (prod.), "Treason at Dry Creek" 12-4-52, "The Condemned Man" 12-11-52, "The New Neighbor" 12-18-52, "Trader Boggs" 1-15-53, "The Godless Men" 1-29-53, "Right to Vote" 2-12-53, "Tumblerock Law" 2-26-53, "Son of Adoption" 3-19-53, "Mrs. Banker" 3-26-53, "Embezzler's Harvest" 4-30-53, "El Toro" 5-7-53, "The Brown Pony" 5-14-53, "Hidden Fortune" 6-18-53, "The Old Cowboy" 6-25-53, "The Perfect Crime" 7-30-53; *The Cisco Kid* 1951-55; *Sky King* 1951; *Cheyenne* 1955; *Sugarfoot* 1957; *Bronco* 1958; *The Rifleman*—"The Raid" 6-9-59, "Ordeal" 11-17-59, "Dark Day at North Fork" 3-7-61, "Short Rope for a Tall Man" 3-28-61; *Bonanza*—"The Sun Mountain Herd" 9-19-59, "The Paiute War" 10-3-59; *Maverick*—"Substitute Gun" 4-2-61, "Benefit of Doubt" 4-9-61, "The Devil's Necklace" 4-16-61 & 4-23-61; *The Dakotas* 1963.

Lane, Al. Screenwriter. Films: "Carrying the Mail" 1934-short; "The Lone Rider" 1934; "The Sundown Trail" 1934; "The Way of the West" 1934; "West of the Law" 1934-short; "Lure of the Wasteland" 1939 (prod. only).

Lane, Rose Wilder (1887-10/30/68). Writer. Films: "Young Pioneers" TVM-1976 (story).

Lanfield, Sidney (1900-6/30/72). Director. Films: "Station West" 1948. ¶TV: *Wagon Train*—"The Jean LeBec Story" 9-25-57, "The Emily Rossiter Story" 10-30-57, "The Julia Gage Story" 12-18-57, "A Man Called Horse" 3-26-58; *The Deputy* 1959.

Lanfranchi, Mario. Director. Films: "Death Sentence" 1967-Ital. (& prod./sp.).

Lang, Jr., Charles (1902-). Screenwriter. Films: "Call of the Klondike" 1950; "Decision at Sundown" 1957.

Lang, David. Screenwriter. Films: "Northwest Rangers" 1942; "Ambush at Tomahawk Gap" 1953; "The Nebraskan" 1953 (& story); "Black Horse Canyon" 1954 (adapt. only); "Massacre Canyon" 1954; "The Outlaw Stallion" 1954; "Wyoming Renegades" 1955; "Fury at Gunsight Pass" 1956; "Secret of Treasure Mountain" 1956; "The Buckskin Lady" 1957; "The Hired Gun" 1957; "The Phantom Stagecoach" 1957.

Lang, Fritz (1890-8/2/76). Director. Films: "The Return of Frank James" 1940; "Western Union" 1941; "Rancho Notorious" 1952.

Lang, Jennings (1915-). Producer. Films: "The Great Northfield, Minnesota Raid" 1972.

Lang, Otto (1908-). Director. TV: *The Rifleman*—"The Lonesome Ride" 5-2-61; *Lancer*—"Yesterday's Vendetta" 1-28-69.

Lang, Richard. Director. Films: "The Mountain Men" 1980; "Kung Fu: The Movie" TVM-1986; "James A. Michener's Texas" TVM-1995. ¶TV: *Kung Fu*—"The Soul Is The Warrior" 2-8-73, "The Assassin" 10-4-73, "The Brujo" 10-25-73, "The Soldier" 11-29-73, "The Salamander" 12-6-73, "The Gunman" 1-3-74, "A Dream Within a Dream" 1-17-74, "In Uncertain Bondage" 2-7-74, "Crossties" 2-21-74, "Arrogant Dragons" 3-14-74, "The Centoph" 4-4-74 & 4-11-74, "Blood of the Dragon" 9-14-74, "A Small Beheading" 9-21-74, "Cry of the Night Beast" 10-19-74.

Lange, Michael. TV: *Paradise*—"A Gather of Guns" 9-10-89, "Common Good" 9-23-89, "Devil's Escort" 1-13-90, "The Coward" 4-7-90; *Adventures of Brisco County, Jr.*—"Senior Spirit" 10-15-93.

Lansbury, Bruce. Producer. Films: "The Silent Gun" TVM-1969;

"Banjo Hackett: Roamin' Free" TVM-1976. ¶TV: *The Loner* 1965-66; *Wild Wild West* 1965-69.

Lansford, William Douglas. Writer. Films: "Villa Rides" 1968 (story); "The Intruders" TVM-1970 (story).

Lantz, Louis. Screenwriter. Films: "Rogue River" 1950; "Fort Defiance" 1951; "River of No Return" 1954 (story only).

Lapland, Harold. Screenwriter. Films: "The Master Gunfighter" 1975.

Larkin, John (-1/6/65). Screenwriter. Films: "The Gay Caballero" 1940.

La Roche, Pete. Screenwriter. Films: "Outlaw Queen" 1957.

Larraz, Jose Ramon. Screenwriter. "Watch Out Gringo! Sabata Will Return" 1972-Ital./Span.

Larsen, Keith (1925-). Director. Films: "Trap on Cougar Mountain" 1972 (& prod./sp.).

Larson, Glen A. Producer. Films: "Alias Smith and Jones" TVM-1971 (& sp./story). ¶TV: *Alias Smith and Jones* 1971-73.

La Shelle, Kirk. Writer. Films: "The Virginian" 1923 (story); "The Virginian" 1929; "The Virginian" 1946 (story).

Lasko, Edward. Screenwriter. Films: "The Broken Land" 1962.

Lasky, Jesse L. (1880-1/13/58). Producer. Films: "While Satan Sleeps" 1922; "Ruggles of Red Gap" 1923; "To the Last Man" 1923; "The Wanderer of the Wasteland" 1924; "The Light of Western Stars" 1925; "The Pony Express" 1925; "The Vanishing American" 1925; "Desert Gold" 1926; "Man of the Forest" 1926; "Jesse James" 1927; "Nevada" 1927; "Open Range" 1927; "Under the Tonto Rim" 1928; "The Gay Desperado" 1936.

Lasky, Jr., Jesse L. (1908-4/11/88). Screenwriter. Films: "Union Pacific" 1939; "Northwest Mounted Police" 1940; "Back in the Saddle" 1941; "The Singing Hill" 1941 (story only); "The Omaha Trail" 1942 (& story); "Unconquered" 1947; "The Silver Whip" 1953; "Land Raiders" 1969-U.S./Span. (story only).

Laszlo, Aladar. Writer. Films: "Girl Rush" 1944 (story).

Lathan, Arnold. Director. TV: *Gunsmoke*—"Shadler" 1-15-73.

Lathrop, William Addison. Writer. Films: "Some Duel" 1915; "The Sheriff of Pine Mountain" 1916 (story only); "Beyond the Law" 1918

(story); "His Pal's Gal" 1920 (story); "The Hobo of Pizen City" 1920 (story); "The Hold-Up Man" 1920 (story); "The Law of the Border" 1920 (story); "Tex of the Timberlands" 1920 (story only).

Latimer, Jonathan. Screenwriter. Films: "Copper Canyon" 1950; "The Redhead and the Cowboy" 1951.

Laub, William B. Screenwriter. Films: "False Brands" 1922.

Laughlin, Frank. Director. Films: "The Trial of Billy Jack" 1974.

Laughlin, Tom (T.C. Frank) (1931-). Director. Films: "Billy Jack" 1971; "The Master Gunfighter" 1975.

Laurani, Salvatore. Screenwriter. Films: "A Bullet for the General" 1966-Ital.

Laurel, Stan (1890-2/23/65). Producer. Films: "Way Out West" 1937; "Knight of the Plains" 1938.

Laurenti, Mariano. Director. Films: "Grandsons of Zorro" 1968-Ital. (& sp.).

Lauritzen, Jonreed. Writer. Films: "Kiss of Fire" 1955 (story).

Laven, Arnold (1922-). Director. Films: "Geronimo" 1962 (& prod./story); "The Glory Guys" 1965 (& prod.); "Rough Night in Jericho" 1967; "The Scalphunters" 1968 (prod. only); "Sam Whiskey" 1969 (& prod.). ¶TV: *Wagon Train*—"The Dora Gray Stoary" 1-29-58; *Zane Grey Theater*—"The Sharpshooter" 3-7-58; *The Rifleman*—1958-63 (prod.), "The Sharpshooter" 9-30-58, "Home Rance" 10-7-58, "The Brother-in-Law" 10-28-58, "Eight Hours to Die" 11-4-58, "New Orleans Menace" 12-2-58, "Young Englishman" 12-16-58, "The Sheridan Story" 1-13-59, "The Retired Gun" 1-20-59, "The Photographer" 1-27-59, "The Indian" 2-17-59, "The Wrong Man" 3-31-59, "The Woman" 5-5-59, "Blood Brothers" 5-26-59, "Trail of Hate" 9-27-60, "Death Trap" 5-9-61, "Two Ounces of Tin" 2-19-62, "Lou Mallory" 10-15-62, "Quiet Night, Deadly Night" 10-22-62, "Mark's Rifle" 11-19-62, "The Anvil Chorus" 12-17-62, "Incident at Line Shack Six" 1-7-63, "Which Way'd They Go?" 4-1-63; *Law of the Plainsman* 1959-60 (exec. prod.); *The Big Valley*—1965-69 (exec. prod.), "The Odyssey of Jubal Tanner" 10-13-65, "The Invaders" 12-29-65, "Hazard" 3-9-66, "The Midas Man" 4-13-66, "Journey into Violence" 12-18-67, "Bounty on a Barkley" 2-26-68.

Lawrence, Bert. Writer. Films:

"Dig That Uranium" 1956 (story); "Alias Jesse James" 1959 (story).

Lawrence, Marc (1910-). TV: *Bronco* 1958; *Lawman* 1958; *Maverick*—"A Techinical Error" 11-26-61, "Mr. Muldoon's Partner" 4-15-62.

Lawrence, Vincent (1890-11/24/46). Screenwriter. Films: "The Sea of Grass" 1947.

Lawton, Harry (1927-). Writer. Films: "Tell Them Willy Boy Is Here" 1969 (story).

Layet, Marie. Writer. Films: "Sir Galahad of Twilight" 1914 (story).

Lea, Tom (1907-). Writer. Films: "The Wonderful Country" 1959 (story).

Leacock, Philip (1917-7/14/90). Director. Films: "Firecreek" 1968; "The Daughters of Joshua Cabe" TVM-1972; "Wild and Wooly" TVM-1978; "The Wild Women of Chastity Gulch" TVM-1982. ¶TV: *Gunsmoke*—1964-67 (prod.), "The Devil's Outpost" 9-22-69, "MacGraw" 12-8-69, "Roots of Fear" 12-15-69, "The Sisters" 12-29-69, "The Pack Rat" 1-12-70, "Celia" 2-23-70, "The Thieves" 3-9-70, "The Witness" 11-12-70, "The Noon Day Devil" 12-7-70, "New Doctor in Town" 10-11-71, "The Legend" 10-18-71, "Spratt" 10-2-72,; *Rawhide*—"Piney" 10-9-64, "El Hombre Bravo" 5-14-65; *Wild Wild West*—1965-69 (exec. prod.); *Cimarron Strip* 1967-68 (exec. prod.); *The Men from Shiloh*—"With Love, Bullets, and Valentines" 10-7-70; *Bonanza*—"The Desperado" 2-7-71, "The Reluctant American" 2-14-71; *Dirty Sally* 1974; *The New Land* 1974 (& prod.).

Leader, Tony (1914-7/1/88). Director. Films: "The Cockeyed Cowboys of Calico County" 1970. ¶TV: *Sugarfoot* 1957; *Lawman* 1958; *Rawhide*—"Incident of the Night on the Town" 6-2-61, "The Black Sheep" 11-10-61, "Abilene" 5-18-62, "The Calf Women" 4-30-65; *The Virginian*—"The Brothers" 9-15-65; *Laredo*—"Pride of the Rangers" 12-16-65; *Nichols* 1971.

Leahman, Paul Evan. Screenwriter. Films: "Gunsmoke on the Guadalupe" 1935.

Leahy, Agnes Brand. Screenwriter. Films: "Stairs of Sand" 1929; "The Spoilers" 1930; "Caught" 1931; "Fighting Caravans" 1931; "The Lone Cowboy" 1934.

Lean, Sidney. see Fago, Giovanni.

LeBaron, William (1883-2/9/58). Producer. Films: "Young Whirlwind" 1928; "Beau Bandit" 1930;

"Cimarron" 1931; "Rose of the Rancho" 1936.

LeBorg, Reginald (1902-3/25/89). Director. Films: "Adventures of Don Coyote" 1947; "Wyoming Mail" 1950; "Young Daniel Boone" 1950 (& sp.); "The Great Jesse James Raid" 1953; "The Dalton Girls" 1957; "War Drums" 1957. ¶TV: *Maverick*—"Mano Nera" 10-23-60.

Leder, Bruno. Screenwriter. Films: "The Moment to Kill" 1968-Ital./Ger.

Lederer, Otto (1886-9/3/65). Director. Films: "The Struggle" 1921.

Lederman, D. Ross (1894-8/24/72). Director. Films: "Branded" 1931; "The Fighting Marshal" 1931; "The Phantom of the West" 1931-serial; "The Range Feud" 1931; "The Texas Ranger" 1931; "Daring Danger" 1932; "End of the Trail" 1932; "McKenna of the Mounted" 1932; "Ridin' for Justice" 1932; "The Riding Tornado" 1932; "Texas Cyclone" 1932; "Two-Fisted Law" 1932; "Rusty Rides Alone" 1933; "Silent Men" 1933; "The Whirlwind" 1933; "Moonlight on the Prairie" 1935; "Racketeers of the Range" 1939; "Thundering Frontier" 1940; "Across the Sierras" 1941; "Here Comes the Cavalry" 1941-short; "Gun to Gun" 1944-short. ¶TV: *The Gene Autry Show*—"Frame for Trouble" 11-3-51, "Narrow Escape" 8-11-53, "Santa Fe Raiders" 7-6-54, "Johnny Jackaroo" 7-13-54, "The Hold-Up" 12-14-52, "Prize Winner" 7-27-54, "Talking Guns" 8-10-54, "The Hoodoo Canyon" 8-17-54, "The Carnival Comes West" 8-24-54, "Civil War at Deadwood" 9-14-54; *Annie Oakley*—"Flint and Steel" 10-14-56, "Annie Rides the Navajo Trail" 11-18-56.

Lee, Connie. Writer. Films: "Mexicali Rose" 1939 (story); "Mountain Rhythm" 1939 (story); "Carolina Moon" 1940 (story); "Ghost Valley Raiders" 1940 (story); "Rancho Grande" 1940 (story); "Ride, Tenderfoot, Ride" 1940 (story).

Lee, DeWitt. Screenwriter. Films: "Pursuit" 1975.

Lee, Donald W. Screenwriter. Films: "Oh, You Tony!" 1924; "Teeth" 1924; "The Calgary Stampede" 1925 (story); "The Boiling Point" 1932; "Partners" 1932; "Unknown Valley" 1933 (story).

Lee, Jack (1913-). Director. Films: "Robbery Under Arms" 1958-Brit.

Lee, Jack. Screenwriter. Films: "Pursuit" 1975.

Lee, Leonard (1903-8/24/64). Screenwriter. Films: "Wyoming Mail" 1950.

Lee, Michele (1942-). Director. TV: *Dr. Quinn, Medicine Woman*—"Giving Thanks" 11-27-93.

Lee, Robert. *see* Johnson, Robert Lee.

Lee, Robert N. Screenwriter. Films: "Mile-a-Minute Romeo" 1924; "Western Luck" 1924; "The Mysterious Rider" 1933.

Lee, Rowland V. (1891-12/21/75). Director. Films: "Blind Hearts" 1921; "Cupid's Brand" 1921; "His Back Against the Wall" 1922; "A Man from Wyoming" 1930.

Lee, Sammy (1890-3/30/68). Director. Films: "Rodeo Dough" 1940-short.

Lee, William. Films: "The Fall of Black Hawk" 1912.

Leeds, Herbert I. (1912-5/16/54). Director. Films: "Arizona Wildcat" 1938; "The Cisco Kid and the Lady" 1939; "The Return of the Cisco Kid" 1939; "Ride On, Vaquero" 1941; "Romance of the Rio Grande" 1941.

Leewood, Jack. Producer. Films: "Lone Texan" 1959; "Thirteen Fighting Men" 1960; "Young Jesse James" 1960.

Legrand, Francois. *see* Autel, Franz.

Lehman, Paul Evan. Writer. Films: "The Idaho Kid" 1937 (story).

Lehrman, Henry (1886-11/7/46). Director. Films: "Double Dealing" 1923.

Leichter, Mitchell. Producer. Films: "The Judgement Book" 1935; "Trails End" 1935; "Desert Guns" 1936; "Riddle Ranch" 1936.

Leigh, Rowland (1902-10/8/63). Screenwriter. Films: "Heaven Only Knows" 1947.

Leighton, Lee. *see* Overholser, Wayne D.

Leinster, Murray (1896-6/8/75). Writer. Films: "Border Devils" 1932 (story).

Leisen, Mitchell (1898-10/29/72). TV: *Wagon Train*—"The Patience Miller Story" 1-11-61, "The Prairie Story" 2-1-61.

Leitch, Christopher. Director. TV: *Hawkeye*—"The Furlough" 10-5-94.

Lelouch, Claude (1937-). Director. Films: "Another Man, Another Chance" 1977-Fr. (& sp.).

Le May, Alan (1899-4/27/64). Screenwriter. Films: "Northwest

Mounted Police" 1940; "Along Came Jones" 1945 (story only); "San Antonio" 1945; "Cheyenne" 1947; "The Gunfighters" 1947; "Trailin' West" 1949 (& prod.); "The Walking Hills" 1949; "High Lonesome" 1950 (& story); "Rock Mountain" 1950 (& story); "The Sundowners" 1950 (& prod.); "The Vanishing American" 1955; "The Searchers" 1956 (story only); "The Unforgiven" 1960 (story only).

Lennard, Kay. Screenwriter. Films: "The Cimarron Kid" 1951 (story only); "Wings of the Hawk" 1953; "Ricochet Romance" 1954.

Lennart, Isobel (1916-1/25/71). Screenwriter. Films: "The Kissing Bandit" 1948.

Lenzi, Umberto. Director. Films: "All Out" 1968-Ital./Span.; "Pistol for a Hundred Coffins" 1968-Ital./Span. (& sp.).

Leo, Maurice. Writer. Films: "Swing of the Saddle" 1944 (story).

Leonard, Elmore (1925-). Screenwriter. Films: "The Tall T" 1957 (story only); "3:10 to Yuma" 1957 (story only); "Hombre" 1967 (story only); "Valdez Is Coming" 1971 (story only); "Joe Kidd" 1972; "High Noon, Part II: The Return of Will Kane" TVM-1980; "Desperado" TVM-1987.

Leonard, Herbert B. (1922-). Producer. TV: *The Adventures of Rin Tin Tin* 1954-59; *Circus Boy* 1956-58.

Leonard, Jack. Screenwriter. Films: "The Marauders" 1955; "Gun Battle at Monterey" 1957.

Leonard, Keith. Screenwriter. Films: "Charley One-Eye" 1973-Brit.

Leonard, L.G. Producer. Films: "Headin' East" 1937; "The Overland Express" 1938.

Leonard, Robert Z. (1889-8/27/68). Director. Films: "What Am I Bid?" 1919; "The Girl of the Golden West" 1938.

Leone, Sergio (1929-4/30/89). Director. Films: "A Fistful of Dollars" 1964-Ital./Ger./Span. (& sp.); "For a Few Dollars More" 1965-Ital./Ger./Span. (& story/sp.); "The Good, the Bad, and the Ugly" 1966-Ital. (& sp.); "Once Upon a Time in the West" 1968-Ital. (& sp./story); "Duck, You Sucker!" 1971-Ital. (& sp.); "My Name Is Nobody" 1973-Ital. (prod. only).

Leonio, Preston. Screenwriter. Films: "If One Is Born a Swine" 1972-Ital./Span.

Lerner, Alan Jay (1918-6/14/86).

Producer. Films: "Paint Your Wagon" 1969.

Lerner, Dan. Director. TV: *Ned Blessing: The Story of My Life and Times*—"The Smink Brothers" 9-1-93.

Lerner, Irving (1909-12/25/76). Director. Films: "Custer of the West" 1967-U.S./Span.

Lerner, Murray. Producer. Films: "Marshal of Heldorado" 1950; "West of the Brazos" 1950.

LeRoy, Mervyn (1900-9/13/87). Director. Films: "Stand Up and Fight" 1939 (prod. only); "Rose Marie" 1954 (& prod.); "Strange Lady in Town" 1955 (& prod.).

LeSaint, Edward J. (1870-9/10/40). Director. Films: "Spell of the Primeval" 1913; "His Father's Rifle" 1915; "The Long Chance" 1915; "The Three Godathers" 1916 (& sp.); "Fighting Mad" 1917; "The Golden Fetter" 1917; "The Squaw Man's Son" 1917; "The Wolf and His Mate" 1917; "Cupid's Round Up" 1918; "Nobody's Wife" 1918; "The Feud" 1919; "Fighting for Gold" 1919; "Hell Roarin' Reform" 1919; "The Wilderness Trail" 1919; "The Rose of Nome" 1920; "Two Moons" 1920 (& sp.).

Lesser, Julian. Producer. Films: "Massacre River" 1949.

Lesser, Sol (1890-9/19/80). Producer. Films: "The Lone Rider" 1930; "Men Without Law" 1930; "The Avenger" 1931; "Desert Vengeance" 1931; "The Fighting Sheriff" 1931; "The Texas Ranger" 1931; "Jaws of Justice" 1933; "Robbers' Roost" 1933; "The Dude Ranger" 1934; "The Ferocious Pal" 1934; "Fighting to Live" 1934; "Frontier Marshal" 1934; "Cowboy Millionaire" 1935; "Thunder Mountain" 1935; "When a Man's a Man" 1935; "Whispering Smith Rides" 1935; "The Border Patrolman" 1936; "King of the Royal Mounted" 1936; "The Mine with the Iron Door" 1936; "O'Malley of the Mounted" 1936; "Wild Brian Kent" 1936; "The Californian" 1937; "It Happened Out West" 1937; "Roll Along, Cowboy" 1937; "Secret Valley" 1937; "Western Gold" 1937; "Hawaiian Buckaroo" 1938; "Panamint's Bad Man" 1938; "Rawhide" 1938.

Lester, Budd. Screenwriter. Films: "Bandit Queen" 1950.

Lester, Elliott. Screenwriter. Films: "Rough Romance" 1930.

Lester, Louise. Screenwriter. Films: "Calamity Anne, Heronie" 1913; "Calamity Anne's Sacrifice" 1913; "Calamity Anne in Society" 1914.

Lester, Richard (1932-). Director. Films: "Butch and Sundance: The Early Days" 1979.

Lester, Seelag. Screenwriter. Films: "The Iron Sheriff" 1957.

Lester, William B. Screenwriter. Films: "Barb Wire" 1922 (story); "The Crow's Nest" 1922 (story only); "Good Men and Bad" 1923; "Wolf Tracks" 1923; "Flashing Spurs" 1924; "Trigger Finger" 1924; "Border Justice" 1925; "Cold Nerve" 1925; "The Fighting Boob" 1926 (story only); "The Shoot 'Em Up Kid" 1926; "The Broncho Buster" 1927; "The Denver Dude" 1927; "Desert Dust" 1927; "The Fighting Three" 1927; "Hands Off" 1927; "Hard Fists" 1927; "A One Man Game" 1927; "Rough and Ready" 1927; "Shooting Straight" 1927; "Straight Shootin'" 1927; "Arizona Cyclone" 1928; "Greased Lightning" 1928; "A Made-to-Order Hero" 1928; "Put 'Em Up" 1928.

L'Estrange, Dick (1889-11/19/63). Producer. Films: "Buzzy Rides the Range" 1940; "Buzzy and the Phantom Pinto" 1941.

Leto, Marco. Screenwriter. Films: "Cry for Revenge" 1968-Ital./Span.; "Pistol for a Hundred Coffins" 1968-Ital./Span.

Levering, Joseph. Director. Films: "Law of the Ranger" 1937 (story only); "The Rangers Step In" 1937; "Reckless Ranger" 1937 (story only); "In Early Arizona" 1938; "Phantom Gold" 1938; "Pioneer Trail" 1938; "Rolling Caravans 1938; "Stagecoach Days" 1938; "Frontiers of '49" 1939; "The Law Comes to Texas" 1939; "Lone Star Pioneers" 1939; "Riders of the Frontier" 1939 (sp. only).

Levey, A.M. Screenwriter. Films: "Montana Bill" 1921.

Levey, W.A. Screenwriter. Films: "Lucky Dan" 1922.

Levi, Alan J. Director. Films: "Go West, Young Girl" TVM-1978; "The Legend of the Golden Gun" TVM-1979; "Dead Man's Revenge" TVM-1994. ¶TV: *Outlaws*—"Madrid" 2-7-87.

Levien, Sonya (1888-3/19/60). Screenwriter. Films: "Cowboy and the Lady" 1938; "Drums Along the Mohawk" 1939; "Oklahoma!" 1955.

Levigard, Josef. Director. Films: "The Fighting Texan" 1927; "King of Hearts" 1927; "South of the Northern Lights" 1927; "The Ambuscade" 1928; "Bare Fists" 1928; "The Boundary Battle" 1928; "Code of the Mounted" 1928; "The Danger Trail" 1928; "A Dangerous Trail" 1928;

"The Fighting Kid" 1928; "The Iron Code" 1928; "Madden of the Mounted" 1928; "Riders of the Woods" 1928; "The Ring Leader" 1928; "The Ruse" 1928; "The Scrappin' Ranger" 1928; "Sealed Orders" 1928; "Yukon Gold" 1928; "The Border Wolf" 1929; "Born to the Saddle" 1929; "The Claim Jumpers" 1929; "Grit Wins" 1929; "Man of Daring" 1929; "The Red Coat's Code" 1929; "The Red Rider" 1929; "The Smiling Terror" 1929; "The Badge of Bravery" 1930; "Crimson Courage" 1930; "Crooked Trails" 1930; "Law in the Saddle" 1930; "The Lightning Rider" 1930; "The Man Hunter" 1930; "The Redcoat's Romance" 1930; "Trail of the Pack" 1930; "Wolf's Fangs" 1930.

Levin, Henry (1909-5/1/80). Director. Films: "The Man from Colorado" 1948; "The Gambler from Natchez" 1954; "Three Young Texans" 1954; "The Lonely Man" 1957; "The Desperados" 1969.

Levin, Peter. Director. Films: "Houston: The Legend of Texas" TVM-1986.

Levine, Jack. *see* Jevne, Jack.

Levine, Nat (1899-8/6/89). Producer. Films: "The Lone Defender" 1930-serial; "Lightning Warrior" 1931-serial; "The Phantom of the West" 1931-serial; "The Vanishing Legion" 1931-serial; "The Devil Horse" 1932-serial; "The Last of the Mohicans" 1932-serial; "Fighting with Kit Carson" 1933-serial; "In Old Santa Fe" 1934; "The Law of the Wild" 1934-serial; "Mystery Mountain" 1934-serial; "Melody Trail" 1935; "The Miracle Rider" 1935-serial; "The Phantom Empire" 1935-serial; "Sagebrush Troubador" 1935; "Tumbling Tumbleweeds" 1935; "Bold Caballero" 1936; "Comin' Round the Mountain" 1936; "Guns and Guitars" 1936; "The Lonely Trail" 1936; "Oh, Susanna!" 1936; "Ride, Ranger, Ride" 1936; "Roarin' Lead" 1936; "The Singing Cowboy" 1936; "The Three Mesquiteers" 1936; "Vigilantes Are Coming" 1936-serial; "Winds of the Wasteland" 1936; "The Big Show" 1937; "Ghost Town Gold" 1937; "Hit the Saddle 1937; "Riders of the Whistling Skull" 1937; "Round-Up Time in Texas" 1937.

Le Vino, Albert Shelby. Screenwriter. Films: "Their Compact" 1917; "Over the Border" 1922; "While Satan Sleeps" 1922; "Heritage of the Desert" 1924; "A Man from Wyoming" 1930; "Renegades of the West" 1932; "Tombstone, the Town Too Tough to Die" 1942; "Westbound" 1959 (story only).

Levinson, Richard (1934-3/12/87). Screenwriter. Films: "Sam Hill: Who Killed the Mysterious Mr. Foster?" TVM-1971.

Levitt, Gene (1920-). Director. Films: "Alias Smith and Jones" TVM-1971. ¶TV: *Alias Smith and Jones*—"The McCreedy Bust" 1-21-71.

Levy, Jules (1923-). Producer. Films: "The Glory Guys" 1965; "The Scalphunters" 1968; "Sam Whiskey" 1969; "The Honkers" 1972. ¶TV: *The Rifleman* 1958-63; *Law of the Plainsman* 1959-60 (exec. prod.); *The Big Valley* 1965-69 (exec. prod.).

Levy, Melvin (1902-12/1/80). Screenwriter. Films: "Robin Hood of El Dorado" 1936; "Renegades" 1946; "Calamity Jane and Sam Bass" 1949; "The Great Sioux Uprising" 1953.

Levy, Paul. Screenwriter. Films: "Up the MacGregors!" 1967-Ital./Span.

Lewis, Alfred Henry. Screenwriter. Films: "Dead Shot Baker" 1917 (story only)."The Tenderfoot" 1917 (story only); "Mrs. Mike" 1949.

Lewis, Arthur. Screenwriter. Films: "Conquest of Cochise" 1953.

Lewis, Cullin. Director. Films: "Desert Trail" 1935.

Lewis, David (1903-3/13/87). Producer. Films: "Son of the Border" 1933.

Lewis, Edgar (1875-5/21/38). Director. Films: "The Great Divide" 1915; "The Plunderer" 1915 (& sp.); "The Sign Invisible" 1918; "Calibre 38" 1919; "Lahoma" 1920; "The Sage Hen" 1921; "Red Love" 1925; "One Glorious Scrap" 1927; "Arizona Cyclone" 1928; "The Fearless Rider" 1928; "A Made-to-Order Hero" 1928; "Put 'Em Up" 1928.

Lewis, Edward. Producer. Films: "The Last Sunset" 1961; "Lonely Are the Brave" 1962.

Lewis, Eugene B. Screenwriter. Films: "Three Mounted Men" 1918; "Bare Fists" 1919; "The Blue Bandanna" 1919; "A Fight for Love" 1919; "Riders of Vengeance" 1919; "Roped" 1919.

Lewis, Gene (1888-3/27/79). Screenwriter. Films: "Trail Street" 1947; "Albuquerque" 1948.

Lewis, Jack. Screenwriter. Films: "King of the Bullwhip" 1950; "Outlaw Gold" 1950; "Whistling Hills" 1951 (story only); "The Naked Gun" 1956; "Black Eagle of Santa Fe" 1964-Ger./Ital./Fr.

Lewis, Joseph H. (1900-). Director. Films: "Courage of the West" 1937; "Border Wolves" 1938; "The Last Stand" 1938; "The Singing Outlaw" 1938; "Blazing Six Shooters" 1940; "The Man from Tumbleweeds" 1940; "The Return of Wild Bill" 1940; "Texas Stagecoach" 1940; "Two-Fisted Rangers" 1940; "Arizona Cyclone" 1941; "Boss of Hangtown Mesa" 1942; "The Silver Bullet" 1942; "A Lawless Street" 1955; "Seventh Cavalry" 1956; "The Halliday Brand" 1957; "Terror in a Texas Town" 1958. ¶TV: *The Rifleman*—"Duel of Honor" 11-11-58, "The Safe Guard" 11-18-58, "The Pet" 1-6-59, "Shivaree" 2-3-59, "The Trade" 3-10-59, "The Deadly Wait" 3-24-59, "The Patsy" 9-29-59, "Eddie's Daughter" 11-3-59, "Panic" 11-10-59, "Letter of the Law" 12-1-59, "Surveyors" 12-29-59, "Day of the Hunter" 1-5-60, "The Visitors" 1-26-60, "The Hero" 2-2-60, "The Spiler" 2-16-60, "Heller" 2-23-60, "The Deserter" 3-15-60, "Shotgun Man" 4-12-60, "The Fourflusher" 5-3-60, "The Hangman" 5-31-60, "Strange Town" 10-25-60, "Baranca" 11-1-60, "The Martinet" 11-8-60, "Miss Milly" 11-15-60, "Flowers by the Door" 1-10-61, "The Actress" 1-24-61, "Face of Yesterday" 1-31-61, "The Wyoming Story" 2-7-61 & 2-14-61, "Closer Than a Brother" 2-21-61, "The Prisoner" 3-14-61, "The Vaqueros" 10-2-61, "Sheer Terror" 10-16-61, "The Stand-In" 10-23-61, "The Journey Back" 10-30-61, "Honest Abe" 11-20-61, "The Shattered Idol" 12-4-61, "Long Gun from Tucson" 12-11-61, "The High Country" 12-18-61, "A Young Man's Fancy" 2-5-62, "Waste" 10-1-62 & 10-8-62, "Death Never Rides Alone" 10-29-62, "I Take This Woman" 11-5-62, "Squeeze Play" 12-3-62, "Suspicion" 1-14-63, "The Sidewinder" 1-21-63, "And the Devil Makes Five" 2-11-63, "The Guest" 3-11-63, "Old Tony" 4-8-63; *Bonanza*—"The Quality of Mercy" 11-17-63; *Gunsmoke*—"One Killer on Ice" 1-23-65, "Thursday's Child" 3-6-65; *The Big Valley*—"Boots with My Father's Name" 9-29-65, "Night of the Wolf" 12-1-65, "The Man from Nowhere" 11-14-66.

Lewis, Richard. Producer. TV: *Wagon Train* 1957-65; *Cimarron City* 1958-59; *Laramie* 1959-63; *Riverboat* 1959-61; *Whispering Smith* 1961 (exec. prod.).

Lewis, Robert M. (1934-). Director. TV: *Kung Fu*—"The Nature of Evil" 3-21-74, "The Devil's Champion" 11-29-74.

Lewis, Vance. *see* Vanzi, Luigi.

Lewton, Val (1904-3/14/51). Producer. Films: "Apache Drums" 1951.

Lewyn, Louis. Producer. Films: "Rodeo Dough" 1940-short.

Leytes, Josef (1902-5/27/83). Director. Films: "Passion" 1954 (sp./story only). ¶TV: *Bonanza*—"Silence at Stillwater" 9-28-69.

Liberatore, Ugo. Screenwriter. Films: "The Tramplers" 1965-Ital.; "The Hellbenders" 1966-U.S./Ital./Span.; "Mutiny at Fort Sharp" 1966-Ital.; "A Minute to Pray, a Second to Die" 1967-Ital. (& story).

Libott, Robert. Screenwriter. Films: "Law of the Barbary Coast" 1949; "Stage to Tucson" 1950.

Lichtman, James E. Director. TV: *The Big Valley*—"Point and Counterpoint" 5-19-69.

Lighton, Louis D. (1892-2/1/63). Screenwriter. Films: "The Virginian" 1923; "The Mine with the Iron Door" 1924; "Ranger of the Big Pines" 1925; "The Virginian" 1929 (prod. only).

Lillibridge, W. Writer. Films: "Where the Trail Divides" 1914 (story).

Lincoln, George. *see* Freda, Riccardo.

Lindemann, Mitch. Screenwriter. Films: "The Way West" 1967.

Linden, Eddie. Director. Films: "Scar Hanan" 1925.

Linden, Nat S. Screenwriter. Films: "Yellowneck" 1955.

Lindop, Audrey Erskine. Writer. Films: "The Singer Not the Song" 1961-Brit. (story).

Linford, Dee. Writer. Films: "Man Without a Star" 1955 (story); "A Man Called Gannon" 1969 (story).

Link, John. Director. Films: "Call of the Forest" 1949.

Link, William. Screenwriter. Films: "Sam Hill: Who Killed the Mysterious Mr. Foster?" TVM-1971.

Lion, Fernando. *see* DiLeo, Fernando.

Lionel, Guy. Screenwriter. Films: "Gunmen of the Rio Grande" 1964-Fr./Ital./Span.

Lipman, William. Screenwriter. Films: "Texas Rangers Ride Again" 1940; "Barbary Coast Gent" 1944; "Bad Bascomb" 1946.

Lippert, Jr., Robert L. (1928-). Producer. Films: "Last of the Wild Horses" 1948 (& dir.); "The Great Jesse James Raid" 1953; "The Tall Texan" 1953; "Fangs of the Wild" 1954; "Massacre" 1956.

Lippert, William H. Screenwriter. Films: "The Yelllow Bullet" 1917.

Lipscomb, W.P. Screenwriter. Films: "Robbery Under Arms" 1958-Brit.

Lipsitz, Harold B. Producer. Films: "Silver Valley" 1927; "Last of the Duanes" 1930.

Lipsky, Eleazar (1911-2/14/93). Writer. Films: "The Fiend Who Walked the West" 1958 (story).

Lipsky, Oldrich (1924-10/20/86). Director. Films: "Lemonade Joe" 1966-Czech. (& sp.).

Lipstadt, Aaron (1952-). TV: *Young Riders*—"The Blood of Others" 10-12-91, "Dark Brother" 6-4-92.

Lipton, Lew. Writer. Films: "A Man from Wyoming" 1930 (story).

Little, Jr., Herbert. Screenwriter. Films: "Trooper Hook" 1957.

Littleton, Scott. Screenwriter. Films: "Perils of the Royal Mounted" 1942-serial.

Lively, Bob. Screenwriter. Films: "Custer's Last Stand" 1936-serial.

Lively, William (1907-9/29/73). Screenwriter. Films: "The Fighting Deputy" 1937; "Fighting Renegade" 1939; "Death Rides the Range" 1940; "Frontier Crusader" 1940; "Phantom Rancher" 1940; "The Sagebrush Family Trails West" 1940; "Billy the Kid's Range War" 1941; "King of the Texas Rangers" 1941-serial; "The Lone Rider Crosses the Rio" 1941; "The Texas Marshal" 1941; "King of the Mounties" 1942-serial; "Texas Man Hunt" 1942; "Arizona Trail" 1943; "Daredevils of the West" 1943-serial; "Wagon Tracks West" 1943; "Boss of Boomtown" 1944; "Marshal of Gunsmoke" 1944; "The Old Texas Trail" 1944; "Both Barrels Blazing" 1945; "Days of Buffalo Bill" 1946; "Gunman's Code" 1946; "Range Renegades" 1948; "Tornado Range" 1948; "Ghost of Zorro" 1949-serial; "The James Brothers of Missouri" 1950-serial; "Arizona Manhunt" 1951; "The Dakota Kid" 1951; "Gold Raiders" 1951; "Hot Lead" 1951; "Colorado Sundown" 1952; "Trail Guide" 1952 (story only); "Wild Horse Ambush" 1952; "Iron Mountain Trail" 1953 (story only).

Lizzani, Carlo (Lee W. Beaver). Director. Films: "The Hills Run Red" 1966-Ital.; "Let Them Rest" 1967-Ital./Ger.

Lloyd, Archie R. Writer. Films: "The Legend of the Lone Tree" 1915 (story).

Lloyd, Euan (1923-). Producer. Films: "Shalako" 1968-Brit./Fr.; "Catlow" 1971-Span.; "The Man Called Noon" 1973-Brit./Span./Ital.

Lloyd, Frank (1888-8/10/60). Director. Films: "The Rainbow Trail" 1918 (& sp.); "Riders of the Purple Sage" 1918 (& sp.); "True Blue" 1918 (& sp.); "The Splendid Road" 1925; "The Lash" 1930; "Wells Fargo" 1937 (& prod.); "Lady from Cheyenne" 1941 (& sp.); "The Spoilers" 1942 (prod. only); "The Last Command" 1955 (& prod.).

Lloyd, John. Writer. Films: "The Invaders" 1913 (story).

Lloyd, Norman (1914-). Producer. Films: "The Bravos" TVM-1972.

Lobl, Victor. Director. TV: *Dr. Quinn, Medicine Woman*—"The Campaign" 5-7-94.

Lo Cascio, Franco. Director. Films: "Who's Afraid of Zorro?" 1975-Ital./Span.

Locke, Charles O. (1896-1977). Writer. Films: "From Hell to Texas" 1958 (story).

Lockhart, Caroline. Writer. Films: "The Man from Bitter Roots" 1916 (story); "The Dude Wrangler" 1930 (story).

Lockwood, Alyn. Screenwriter. Films: "Badman's Gold" 1951.

Lockwood, Jale. Screenwriter. Films: "The Female Bunch" 1971.

Lodge, Stephen. Screenwriter. Films:"The Honkers" 1972; "Rio Diablo" TVM-1993.

Loew, Jr., Arthur M. (1926-11/10/95). Producer Films: "Arena" 1953 (& story); "The Marauders" 1955.

Loew, Sherman. Writer. Films: "Road Agent" 1941 (story).

Lofton, Christopher. Screenwriter. Films: "Call of the Wild" TVM-1993.

Logan, Helen. Screenwriter. Films: "Susannah of the Mounties" 1939; "Lucky Cisco Kid" 1940.

Logan, Joshua (1908-7/12/88). Director. Films: "Paint Your Wagon" 1969.

Logue, Charles A. (1889-8/2/38). Screenwriter. Films: "Clash of the Wolves" 1925; "Ridin' Through" 1925; "Arizona Sweepstakes" 1926 (story only); "Red Clay" 1927; "Wagon Wheels" 1934; "Home on the Range 1935; "Renfrew of the Royal Mounted" 1937; "On the Great White Trail" 1938; "Renfrew on the Great White Trail" 1938.

Lomax, Bliss. *see* Drago, Harry Sinclair.

Lombardo, Paolo. Screenwriter. Films: "Cisco" 1966-Ital.; "Days of Violence" 1967-Ital.

London, Jack (1876-11/22/16). Writer. Films: "The Mohican's Daughter" 1922 (story); "The Son of the Wolf" 1922 (story); "Call of the Wild" 1923 (story); "Morganson's Finish" 1926 (story); "Smoke Bellew" 1929 (story); "Call of the Wild" 1935 (story); "White Fang" 1936 (story); "Wolf Call" 1939 (story); "Queen of the Yukon" 1940 (story); "North to the Klondike" 1942 (story); "The Call of the Wild" TVM-1976; "White Fang" 1991 (story); "Call of the Wild" TVM-1993.

London, Jerome R. (1937-). Director. TV: *The Quest*—"Portrait of a Gunfighter" 12-22-76; *Dr. Quinn, Medicine Woman*—"Father's Day" 1-30-93, "The Secret" 5-15-93, "Portraits" 5-22-93, "Orphan Train" 1-29-94, "Luck of the Draw" 3-5-94, "The Abduction" 4-30-94.

London, Roy (1943-8/8/93). Screenwriter. Films: "California Gold Rush" TVM-1981.

Lonergan, Philip. Writer. Films: "The Man from Galveston" 1964 (story).

Long, Hal. Screenwriter. Films: "White Fang" 1936; "Viva Cisco Kid" 1940; "Robin Hood of the Pecos" 1941 (story only); "King of the Cowboys" 1943 (story only); "The Fabulous Texan" 1947 (story only).

Long, Richard. Director. TV: *The Big Valley*—"Plunder at Hawk's Grove" 3-13-67, "The Twenty-five Graves of Midas" 2-3-69.

Longfellow, Henry Wadsworth (1807-1882). Writer. Films: "Hiawatha" 1909 (story); Hiawatha" 1952 (story).

Longstreet, Harry. Screenwriter. Films: "Gunsmoke: One Man's Justice" TVM-1994.

Longstreet, Renee. Screenwriter. Films: "Gunsmoke: One Man's Justice" TVM-1994.

Longstreet, Stephen. Screenwriter. Films: "Silver River" 1948 (& story); "The First Traveling Saleslady" 1956 (& prod.); "Rider on a Dead Horse" 1962.

Loos, Anita (1893-8/18/81). Screenwriter. Films: "Wild and Woolly" 1917.

Loos, Mary. Screenwriter. Films: "The Dude Goes West" 1948; "Ticket to Tomahawk" 1950. ¶TV: *Yancy Derringer* 1958-59 (& prod.).

Lopez-Portillo, Jorge. Director. Films: "Five Bold Women" 1960.

Lord, Del (1895-3/23/70). Director. Films: "Whoops, I'm an Indian" 1936-short; "Goofs and Saddles" 1937; "Pest from the West" 1939-short; "Teacher's Pest" 1939-short; "Yes, We Have No Bonanza" 1939-short; "Cactus Makes Perfect" 1942-short; "Phony Express" 1943-short (& prod.); "Singin' in the Corn" 1946.

Lord, Mindret. Writer. Films: "Yankee Fakir" 1947 (story).

Lord, Robert (1900-4/5/76). Screenwriter. Films: "The Lucky Horseshoe" 1925 (story only); "Tony Runs Wild" 1926; "Beyond the Sierras" 1928; "The Conquerors" 1932; "Dodge City" 1939 (prod. only).

Lord, Stephen. Screenwriter. Films: "Last of the Mohicans" TVM-1977. ¶TV: *Zane Grey Theater* 1956-61 (prod.).

Loring, Hope. Screenwriter. Films: "Masked" 1920; "Thieves' Clothes" 1920; "Wolf Tracks" 1920; "The Beautiful Gambler" 1921; "The Blue Fox" 1921-serial; "The Spoilers" 1923; "The Mine with the Iron Door" 1924; "Ranger of the Big Pines" 1925.

Lott, Milton (1919-). Writer. Films: "The Last Hunt" 1956 (story).

Louis, Will. Director. Films: "Capturing Bad Bill" 1915.

Love, Sherman. Screenwriter. Films: "The Old Corral" 1936.

Lovell, Dyson. Producer. Films: "Lonesome Dove" TVM-1989; "Return to Lonesome Dove" TVM-1993.

Lovering, Otto (1889-10/25/68). Films: "Wanderer of the Wasteland" 1935; "Drift Fence" 1936.

Lovet, Henry. Screenwriter. Films: "Those Dirty Dogs!" 1973-U.S./Ital./Span.

Lovett, Joseph. Screenwriter. Films: "The Bugle Call" 1927.

Lowe, Edward T. (1890-4/17/73). Screenwriter. Films: "Texas Rangers Ride Again" 1940 (prod. only); "Girl from Alaska" 1942; "Pirates of Monterey" 1947 (story only).

Lowe, Sherman (1894-1/23/68). Screenwriter. Films: "Diamond Trail" 1933; "The Law of the Wild" 1934-serial; "Mystery Mountain" 1934-serial (story only); "Melody Trail" 1935 (& story); "Arizona Days" 1937; "Galloping Dynamite" 1937; "Crashing Thru" 1939; "Law and Order" 1940; "Pony Post" 1940; "Ragtime Cowboy Joe" 1940; "West of Carson City" 1940; "Arizona Cyclone" 1941; "Bury Me Not on the Lone Prairie" 1941; "The Masked Rider" 1941; "Riders of Death Valley" 1941-serial; "King of the Stallions" 1942; "Little Joe, the Wrangler" 1942 (& story);

"Black Arrow" 1944-serial; "The Desert Horseman" 1946; "Gunman's Code" 1946; "Rustler's Roundup" 1946 (story only); "Silver Butte" 1949-short; "The Kangaroo Kid" 1950; "Prairie Pirates" 1950-short; "Roar of the Iron Horse" 1950-serial.

Lowry, Dick. Director. Films: "The Gambler" TVM-1980; "The Gambler, Part II—The Adventure Continues" TVM-1983 (& prod.); "Wild Horses" TVM-1985; "Dream West" TVM-1986; "The Gambler, Part III—The Legend Continues" TVM-1987.

Lowry, Hunt. Producer. Films: "Wild Horses" TVM-1985; "Dream West" TVM-1986; "The Last of the Mohicans" 1992.

Lowry, Ira M. Director. Films: "Oh, Johnny!" 1918; "High Pockets" 1919; "Sandy Burke of the U-Bar-U" 1919; "Speedy Meade" 1919 (& sp.).

Loxley, D.A. Writer. Films: "Bad Bascomb" 1946 (story).

Loy, Mino. Producer. Films: "10,000 Dollars Blood Money" 1966-Ital.; "For One Hundred Thousand Dollars Per Killing" 1967-Ital. (sp. only); "They Call Him Cemetery" 1971-Ital./Span.; "Man Called Invincible" 1973-Ital.; "Dick Luft in Sacramento" 1974-Ital.

Lozito, Tony. Screenwriter. Films: "The Giant of Thunder Mountain" 1991.

Luban, Milton. Screenwriter. Films: "Grand Canyon" 1949; "Tough Assignment" 1949.

Lubin, A. Ronald. Producer. Films: "The Outrage" 1964; "A Gunfight" 1971.

Lubin, Arthur (1901-5/11/95). Director. Films: "Ride 'Em, Cowboy" 1942; "The First Traveling Saleslady" 1956 (& prod.). ¶TV: *Cheyenne* 1955; *Bronco* 1958; *Maverick*—"Duel at Sundown" 2-1-59, "Royal Four-Flush" 9-20-59, "The Cats of Paradise" 10-11-59, "Maverick Springs" 12-6-59, "The Goose-Drowner" 12-13-59, "The Marquesa" 1-3-60, "Maverick and Juliet" 1-17-60, "Guatemala City" 1-31-60, "A Flock of Trouble" 2-14-60, "The Misfortune Teller" 3-6-60, "Greenbacks Unlimited" 3-13-60; *The Deputy* 1959; *Bonanza*—"San Francisco Holiday" 4-2-60, "Feet of Clay" 4-16-60, "Badge Without Honor" 9-24-60.

Luby, S. Roy. Director. Films: "Arizona Bad Man" 1935; "Lightning Triggers" 1935; "Outlaw Rule" 1935; "Range Warfare" 1935; "The Crooked Trail" 1936; "Rogue of the

Range" 1936; "Border Phantom" 1937; "Desert Phantom" 1937; "The Red Rope" 1937; "The Range Busters" 1940; "Trailing Double Trouble" 1940; "West of Pinto Basin" 1940; "Fugitive Valley" 1941; "The Kid's Last Ride" 1941; "Saddle Mountain Roundup" 1941; "Tonto Basin Outlaws" 1941; "Trail of the Silver Spurs" 1941; "Tumbledown Ranch in Arizona" 1941; "Underground Rustlers" 1941; "Wrangler's Roost" 1941; "Arizona Stagecoach" 1942; "Boot Hill Bandits" 1942; "Rock River Renegades" 1942; "Texas Trouble Shooters" 1942 (& prod.); "Thunder River Feud" 1942; "Black Market Rustlers" 1943; "Cowboy Commandos" 1943; "Land of Hunted Men" 1943.

Lucas, John Meredyth. Screenwriter. Films: "Red Mountain" 1951; "Tumbleweed" 1953. ¶TV: *Zorro*—"Sweet Face of Danger" 1-30-58, "Zorro Fights His Father" 2-6-58, "Death Stacks the Deck" 2-13-58.

Lucas, Luis. Screenwriter. Films: "Three Swords of Zorro" 1963-Ital./Span.

Lucas, Wilfred (1871-12/13/40). Director. Films: "The Chief's Blanket" 1912; "Bred in the Bone" 1913; "The Horse Thief" 1913; "The Desert's Sting" 1914; "The Trey O'-Hearts" 1914-serial; "Hands Up!" 1917 (& sp.); "The Red, Red Heart" 1918; "The Fighting Breed" 1921.

Lucidi, Maurizio (Maurice A. Bright). Director. Films: "My Name Is Pecos" 1966-Ital. (& sp.); "Pecos Cleans Up" 1967-Ital. (& sp.); "Greatest Robbery in the West" 1968-Ital.; "The Big and the Bad" 1971-Ital./Fr./Span.; "It Can Be Done ... Amigo" 1971-Ital./Fr./Span.

Luddy, Edward I. Director. Films: "The Man Who Waited" 1922 (& sp.).

Ludlum, Edward. TV: *Gunsmoke*—"Doc Quits" 2-21-59.

Ludman, Larry. *see* De Angelis, Fabrizio.

Ludwig, Alan. Writer. Films: "Wyoming Whirlwind" 1932 (story); "Tumbling Tumbleweeds" 1935 (story).

Ludwig, Edward (1895-8/20/82). Director. Films: "The Fabulous Texan" 1947; "The Vanquished" 1953; "The Gun Hawk" 1963. ¶TV: *Bonanza*—"A Rose for Lotta" 9-12-59; *Branded*—"Headed for Doomsday" 4-10-66.

Ludwig, Jerry. Screenwriter. Films: "Take a Hard Ride" 1974-Ital./Brit./Ger.

Ludwig, William (1912-). Screenwriter. Films: "Out West with the Hardys" 1938; "Boy's Ranch" 1946; "Oklahoma!" 1955; "Gun Glory" 1957.

Luigi, Gianni. Screenwriter. Films: "Sheriff of Rock Spring" 1971-Ital.

Lumet, Sidney (1924-). Director. Films: "Lovin' Molly" 1974.

Lund, Oscar A.C. Director. Films: "The Trail of the Hanging Rock" 1913; "The Devil Fox of the North" 1914; "Just Jim" 1915 (& sp.); "M'Liss" 1915; "The Trail of the Shadow" 1917 (story only); "Strings of Steel" 1926-serial (sp. only).

Luotto, Gene. Screenwriter. Films: "Gunmen of the Rio Grande" 1964-Fr./Ital./Span.

Lupino, Ida (1918-8/3/95). Director. TV: *Have Gun Will Travel*— "Hunt the Man Down" 4-25-59, "Charley Red Dog" 12-12-59, "The Lady on the Wall" 2-20-60, "Lady with a Gun" 4-9-60, "The Trial" 6-11-60; *The Rifleman*—"Assault" 3-21-61.

Lupo, Michele (1932-6/27/89). Director. Films: "Arizona Colt" 1965-Ital./Fr./Span. (& sp.); "For a Fist in the Eye" 1965-Ital./Span.; "Ben and Charlie" 1970-Ital.; "California" 1976-Ital./Span. (& sp.); "Buddy Goes West" 1981-Ital.

Luske, Hamilton. Director. Films: "Melody Time" 1948.

Lyland, Frances. Screenwriter. Films: "In Old Sacramento" 1946.

Lyle, Eugene P. Writer. Films: "The Silver Grindstone" 1913 (story); "A Modern Musketeer" 1917 (story).

Lyles, A.C. (1918-). Producer. Films: "Law of the Lawless" 1964; "Stage to Thunder Rock" 1964; "Black Spurs" 1965; "Town Tamer" 1965; "Young Fury" 1965 (& story); "Apache Uprising" 1966; "Johnny Reno" 1966 (& story); "Waco" 1966; "Fort Utah" 1967; "Hostile Guns" 1967; "Red Tomahawk" 1967; "Arizona Bushwhackers" 1968; "Buckskin" 1968.

Lyman, Abe. Producer. Films: "Singing Guns" 1950.

Lynch, John. Screenwriter. Films: "The Valley of Silent Men" 1922; "Kentucky Days" 1923 (story only).

Lynch, Roland. Screenwriter. Films: "Cowboy from Sundown" 1940; "The Golden Trail" 1940; "Rainbow Over the Range" 1940.

Lyon, Earle. Producer. Films: "The Lonesome Trail" 1955; "The Silver Star" 1955; "Stagecoach to Fury" 1956 (& story); "The Quiet Gun" 1957; "The Rawhide Trail" 1958.

Lyon, Francis D. (1905-73). Director. Films: "The Great Locomotive Chase" 1956; "Gunsight Ridge" 1957; "The Oklahoman" 1957; "Escort West" 1959; "Tomboy and the Champ" 1961.

Lyons, Richard E. (1921-3/18/89). Producer. Films: "Frontier Gun" 1958; "The Miracle of the Hills" 1959; "The Sad Horse" 1959; "Ride the High Country" 1962; "Mail Order Bride" 1964; "The Rounders" 1965; "The Plainsman" 1966; "Stranger on the Run" TVM-1967; "Winchester '73" TVM-1967; "Something for a Lonely Man" TVM-1968; "Death of a Gunfighter" 1969; "The Daughters of Joshua Cabe" TVM-1972; "Shootout in a One-Dog Town" TVM-1974; "The Daughters of Joshua Cabe Return" TVM-1975; "Kate Bliss and the Ticker Tape Kid" TVM-1978; "I Married Wyatt Earp" TVM-1983.

McAdams, James Duff. Producer. Films: "The Intruders" TVM-1970. ¶TV: *The Virginian* 1962-70; *The Road West* 1966-67.

MacArthur, Charles (1895-4/21/56). Screenwriter. Films: "Billy the Kid" 1930.

McCahon, Robert. Director. Films: "Running Wild" 1973 (& prod./sp.).

McCall, Jr., Mary (1904-4/3/86). Screenwriter. Films: "Ride the Man Down" 1952; "Slim Carter" 1957 (story only).

McCampbell, Barbara Hawks. Writer. Films: "Rio Bravo" 1959 (story).

McCarey, Leo (1898-7/5/69). Director. Films: "Ruggles of Red Gap" 1935; "Cowboy and the Lady" 1938 (story only).

McCarey, Ray (1898-12/1/48). Director. Films: "Sunset Range" 1935; "The Cowboy and the Blonde" 1941.

McCarthy, Henry. Screenwriter. Films: "The Ranger and the Law" 1921; "The Masked Avenger" 1922; "Senor Americano" 1929 (story only); "Men of America" 1933.

McCarthy, John P. (1885-9/4/62). Director. Films: "Out of the Dust" 1920 (& sp.); "Shadows of Conscience" 1921 (& sp.); "Brand of Cowardice" 1925 (& story); "Pals" 1925; "The Border Whirlwind" 1926; "Vanishing Hoofs" 1926; "The Devil's Masterpiece" 1927; "Headin' North" 1930 (& sp.); "The Land of Missing Men" 1930 (& sp.); "Oklahoma Cyclone" 1930 (& story); "At the Ridge" 1931; "Cavalier of the West" 1931 (& sp.); "God's Country and the Man" 1931 (& prod.); "The Nevada Buckaroo" 1931; "Rider of the Plains" 1931; "The Ridin' Fool" 1931; "Sunrise Trail" 1931; "Beyond the Rockies" 1932 (sp. only); "Fighting Champ" 1932; "The Forty-Niners" 1932; "The Western Code" 1932; "Crashing Broadway" 1933; "Lucky Larrigan" 1933; "Trailing North" 1933; "Lawless Borders" 1935; "Song of the Gringo" 1936 (& sp.); "Marked Trails" 1944 (& sp.); "Raiders of the Border" 1944; "The Cisco Kid Returns" 1945; "Law of the 45's" 1945; "Under Arizona Skies" 1946 (story only).

McCarthy, Leo J. Producer. Films: "Rodeo Rhythm" 1942 (& story).

McCarthy, Mary E. Writer. Films: "The Fighting Failure" 1926 (story).

McCarthy, William. Director. TV: *The Adventures of Champion* 1955; *Buffalo Bill, Jr.* 1955.

McCarty, Henry. Director. Films: "Blazing Arrows" 1922 (& sp.); "Silver Spurs" 1922; "Silent Pal" 1925.

MacCohy, Steve. see Iquino, Ignacio.

McCollum, Hugh. Producer. Films: "Phony Express" 1943-short; "Three Troubledoers" 1946-short; "Out West" 1947-short; "Punchy Cowpunchers" 1950-short; "Merry Mavericks" 1951-short.

McCollough, Andrew. Director. TV: *Maverick*—"Diamond Flush" 2-5-61.

McConnell, Fred J. Producer. Films: "The Fighting Raner" 1925-serial (story only); "The Return of the Riddle Rider" 1927-serial (story only); "The Last Frontier" 1932-serial; "The Lone Rider Fights Back" 1941 (story only).

McConville, Bernard. Screenwriter. Films: "Six-Shooter Andy" 1918; "Doubling for Romeo" 1922; "Without Compromise" 1922; "Hell's Hole" 1923 (story only); "Stepping Fast" 1923; "A Texas Steer" 1927; "King of the Pecos" 1936 (& story); "The Lonely Trail" 1936 (& story); "The Old Corral" 1936 (story only); "Ride, Ranger, Ride" 1936 (story only); "Ghost Town Gold" 1937 (story only); "Heart of the Rockies" 1937 (story only); "Public Cowboy No. 1" 1937 (story only); "Riders of the Whistling Skull" 1937 (story only); "Border G-Man" 1938 (story only); "Call the Mesquiters" 1938; "Man from Music Mountain" 1938 (story only); "The Old Barn Dance" 1938; "Overland Stage Raiders" 1938 (story only); "Riders of the Black Hills" 1938 (story only); "Arizona Legion" 1939 (story only); "Racketeers of the Range" 1939 (story only); "Timber Stampede" 1939 (story only); "Cherokee Strip" 1940; "Prairie Law" 1940 (story only); "The Ranger and the Lady" 1940 (story only); "Wagon Train" 1940 (story only); "Outlaws of the Desert" 1941; "Saddlemates" 1941 (story only); "Riding the Wind" 1942 (story only); "Cheyenne Roundup" 1943; "Fighting Frontier" 1943 (story only); "Home on the Range" 1946 (story only).

McCormack, Barrett. Screenwriter. Films: "The Disciple" 1915.

McCormick, Langdon. Writer. Films: "The Storm" 1922 (story).

McCormick, William Merrill (1892-8/19/53). Director. Films: "Good Men and Bad" 1923; "The Secret of Black Canyon" 1925 (story only); "A Son of the Desert" 1928 (& sp.).

McCowan, George (1931-11/1/95). Director. Films: "The Over-the-Hill Gang Rides Again" TVM-1970.

McCoy, Denys. Director. Films: "The Last Rebel" 1971-Ital./U.S./Span.

McCoy, Harry. Screenwriter. Films: "The Cow-Catcher's Daughter" 1931-short.

McCoy, Horace (1897-12/16/55). Screenwriter. Films: "Speed Wings" 1934; "Texas Rangers Ride Again" 1940; "Texas" 1941; "Valley of the Sun" 1942; "The Fabulous Texan" 1947; "Bronco Buster" 1952; "The Lusty Men" 1952; "Montana Belle" 1952; "Rage at Dawn" 1955; "The Road to Denver" 1955; "Texas Lady" 1955.

McCray, Kent. Producer. Films: "Little House on the Prairie: Look Back to Yesterday" TVM-1983; "Little House: The Last Farewell" TVM-1984; "Little House: Bless All the Dear Children" TVM-1984; "Bonanza: The Return" 1993. ¶TV: *Little House on the Prairie* 1974-82; *Little House: A New Beginning* 1982-83.

McCrea, Jody (1934-). Producer. Films: "Cry Blood, Apache" 1970.

McCulley, Johnston (1883-1958). Writer. Films: "Unclaimed Goods" 1918 (story); "Mark of Zorro" 1920 (story); "Ruth of the Rockies"

1920-serial (story); "Captain Fly-By-Night" 1922 (story); "Ride for Your Life" 1924 (story); "The Outlaw Deputy" 1935 (story); "The Red Rope" 1937 (story); "Rootin' Tootin' Rhythm" 1937 (story); "The Trusted Outlaw" 1937 (story); "Rose of the Rio Grande" 1938 (story); "Mark of Zorro" 1940 (story); "Doomed Caravan" 1941 (story); "Overland Mail" 1942-serial (story); "Outlaws of Stampede Pass" 1943 (story); "Raiders of the Border" 1944 (story); "Don Ricardo Returns" 1946 (story); "Mark of the Renegade" 1951 (story); "The Mark of Zorro" TVM-1974 (story).

MacCulloch, Campbel. Writer. Films: "The Child, the Dog, and the Villain" 1915 (story).

McCutcheon, Wallace (1894-1/27/28). Director. Films: "Daniel Boone" 1907; "The Kentuckian" 1908; "The Stage Rustler" 1908.

McDermid, Finlay. Writer. Films: "The Bounty Hunter" 1954 (story).

McDermott, John (1893-7/22/46). Director. Films: "The Sky Pilot" 1921 (sp. only); "The Spider and the Rose" 1923; "Where the Worst Begins" 1925.

McDonald, Colt. Writer. Films: "Daring Danger" 1932 (story).

MacDonald, Donald. Director. Films: "Two Spot Joe" 1915.

McDonald, Frank (1899-3/8/80). Director. Films: "Treachery Rides the Range" 1936; "Death Goes North" 1939; "Jeepers Creepers" 1939; "Carolina Moon" 1940; "Gaucho Serenade" 1940; "Rancho Grande" 1940; "Ride, Tenderfoot, Ride" 1940; "Arkansas Judge" 1941; "Under Fiesta Stars" 1941; "The Lights of Old Santa Fe" 1944; "Along the Navajo Trail" 1945; "Bells of Rosarita" 1945; "The Man from Oklahoma" 1945; "Sunset in El Dorado" 1945; "My Pal Trigger" 1946; "Rainbow Over Texas" 1946; "Sioux City Sue" 1946; "Song of Arizona" 1946; "Under Nevada Skies" 1946; "Twilight on the Rio Grande" 1947; "Gun Smugglers" 1948; "Apache Chief" 1949; "The Big Sombrero" 1949; "Call of the Klondike" 1950; "Snow Dog" 1950; "Northwest Territory" 1951; "Sierra Passage" 1951; "Texands Never Cry" 1951; "Yukon Manhunt" 1951; "Yukon Gold" 1952; "Son of Belle Star" 1953; "Thunder Pass" 1954; "Treasure of Ruby Hills" 1955; "Gunfight at Comanche Creek" 1964. ¶TV: *The Gene Autry Show*— "Head for Texas" 7-23-50, "Gold

Dust Charlie" 7-30-50, "Silver Arrow" 8-6-50, "The Doodle Bug" 8-13-50, "The Star Toter" 8-20-50, "Double Switch" 8-27-50, "Six Shooter Sweepstakes" 10-1-50, "Lost Chance" 10-15-50, "The Black Rider" 10-22-50, "Gray Dude" 12-3-50, "The Peace Maker" 12-17-50, "Ghost Town Raiders" 10-6-51, "Silver Dollars" 10-20-51, "Sharpshooter" 8-3-54, "Outlaw of Blue Mesa" 9-7-54; *The Range Rider* 1951; *Annie Oakley*— "The Dude Stagecoach" 1-30-54, "Annie and the Silver Ace" 2-27-54, "Annie Finds Strange Treasure" 3-6-54, "Annie and the Leprechauns" 9-2-56, "The Dutch Gunmaker" 2-17-57; *The Adventures of Champion* 1955; *Buffalo Bill, Jr.* 1955; *Broken Arrow* 1956; *Pony Express* 1960-61.

MacDonald, Ian. Screenwriter. Films: "The Lonesome Trail" 1955; "The Silver Star" 1955.

MacDonald, J.F. (1875-8/2/52). Director. Films: "On Burning Sands" 1913.

MacDonald, Wallace (1891-10/30/78). Producer. Films: "Girl from the West" 1923 (dir. only); "Cornered" 1932 (sp. only); "The Riding Tornado" 1932 (story only); "Wyoming Whirlwind" 1932; "In Old Santa Fe" 1934 (story only); "The Phantom Empire" 1935-serial (story only); "Konga, the Wild Stallion" 1940; "Law of the Barbary Coast" 1949; "Ambush at Tomahawk Gap" 1953; "The Nebraskan" 1953; "The Black Dakotas" 1954; "Massacre Canyon" 1954; "The Outlaw Stallion" 1954; "Apache Ambush" 1955; "Wyoming Renegades" 1955; "Fury at Gunsight Pass" 1956; "Secret of Treasure Mountain" 1956; "The White Squaw" 1956; "The Phantom Stagecoach" 1957; "Return to Warbow" 1958; "Gunmen from Laredo" 1959 (& dir.).

MacDonald, William Colt. Writer. Films: "Texas Cyclone" 1932 (story); "Two-Fisted Law" 1932 (story); "The Western Code" 1932 (story); "Man of Action" 1933 (story); "Law of the 45's" 1935 (story); "Powdersmoke Range" 1935 (story); "Too Much Beef" 1936 (story); "One Man Justice" 1937 (story); "Riders of the Whistling Skull" 1937 (story); "Two-Fisted Sheriff" 1937 (story); "The Trail Blazers" 1940 (story); "Gangs of Sonora" 1941 (story); "West of Cimarron" 1941 (story); "Along the Navajo Trail" 1945 (story).

McDonagh, J. Screenwriter. Films: "The Fugitive" 1910.

MacDonnell, Norman. Producer. Films: "Ballad of Josie" 1968.

¶TV: *Gunsmoke*—1959-64; *The Virginian* 1962-70 (exec. prod.).

McDonough, Dan. Director. TV: *The Virginian*—"Beyond the Border" 11-24-65.

McDougall, Don. Director. Films: "The Mark of Zorro" TVM-1974. ¶TV: *The Range Rider* 1951; *The Roy Rogers Show*—"Born Fugitive" 11-29-53, "The Young Defenders" 10-3-54, "Backfire" 10-10-54, "The Last of the Larrabee Kid" 10-17-54, "Hard Luck Story" 10-31-51, "Boys' Day in Paradise Valley" 11-7-54, "Bad Neighbors" 11-21-54, "Strangers" 12-5-54, "Hidden Treasure" 12-19-54, "Outcasts of Paradise Valley" 1-9-55, "The Big Chance" 1-23-55, "Uncle Steve's Finish" 2-3-55, "Dead End Trail" 2-20-55, "Quick Draw" 3-20-55, "The Ginger Horse" 3-20-55, "The Showdown" 5-22-55, "And Sudden Death" 10-9-55, "Ranch War" 10-23-55, "The Scavenger" 11-27-55, "Treasure of Paradise Valley" 12-11-55, "End of the Trail" 1-27-57, "Junior Outlaw" 2-10-57, "High Stakes" 2-24-57, "Accessory to Crime" 3-3-57, "Portrait of Murder" 3-17-57, "Brady's Bonanza" 3-31-57; *Buffalo Bill, Jr.* 1955; *Wanted—Dead or Alive*—"The Giveaway Gun" 10-11-58, "The Fourth Headstone" 11-1-58, "Drop to Drink" 12-27-58, "Rope Law" 1-3-59, "Call Your Shot" 2-7-59, "Secret Ballot" 2-14-59, "Eager Man" 2-28-59, "Double Fee" 3-21-59, "Crossroads" 4-11-59, "Vanishing Act" 12-26-59, "Payoff at Pinto" 5-21-60; *The Rifleman*—"The Prodigal" 4-26-60; *Stagecoach West* 1960; *The Westerner*—"Dos Pinos" 11-4-60; *Rawhide*—"Incident of the Dogfaces" 11-9-62, "Incident of the Reluctant Bridegroom" 11-30-62, "Incident of Decision" 12-28-62, "Incident at the Trail's End" 1-11-63, "Incident of the Mountain Man" 1-25-63, "Incident at Crooked Hat" 2-1-63, "Incident of the Clown" 3-29-63, "Incident of the Hostages" 4-19-63, "Incident at Alkali Sink" 5-24-63; *Bonanza*—"The Friendship" 11-12-61, "The Horse Breaker" 11-26-61, "The Tall Stranger" 1-7-62, "The Ride" 1-21-62, "Look to the Stars" 3-18-62, "Blessed Are They" 4-22-62, "The Mountain Girl" 5-13-62, "The Miracle Worker" 5-20-62, "The First Born" 9-23-62, "The Artist" 10-7-62, "The War Comes to Washoe" 11-4-62, "The Good Samaritan" 12-23-62, "Song in the Dark" 1-13-63, "Half a Rogue" 1-27-63, "A Woman Lost" 3-17-63, "King of the Mountain" 2-23-64, "She Walks in Beauty" 9-22-63, "A Question of Strength" 10-27-63, "Ponderosa Matador" 1-12-64, "The

Gentleman from New Orleans" 2-2-64, "The Pure Truth" 3-8-64, "No Less a Man" 3-15-64, "Return to Honor" 3-22-64, "Pink Cloud Comes from Old Cathay" 4-12-64, "The Hostage" 9-27-64, "Logan's Treasure" 10-18-64; *The Virginian*—"Dark Destiny" 4-29-64, "All Nice and Legal" 11-25-64, "Portrait of a Widow" 12-9-64; *The High Chaparral*—"A Man to Match the Land" 3-12-71; *The Men from Shiloh* 1970-71; *Barbary Coast*—"Guns for a Queen" 10-6-75, "Sauce for the Goose" 10-20-75; *Young Dan'l Boone* 1977; *Young Maverick*—"A Fistful of Oats" 12-5-79.

MacDougall, Ranald (1915-12/12/73). Screenwriter. Films: "The Cockeyed Cowboys of Calico County" 1970 (& prod.).

McEveety, Bernard. Director. Films: "Ride Beyond Vengeance" 1966; "One Little Indian" 1973; "The Macahans" TVM-1976. ¶TV: *The Virginian*—"The Mountain of the Sun" 4-17-63, "The Fatal Journey" 12-4-63, "The Black Stallion" 9-30-64; *Bonanza*—"The Legacy" 12-15-63; *Rawhide*—"The Race" 9-25-64, "The Vasquez Woman" 10-26-65; *Branded*—"The Mission" 3-14-65, 3-21-65 & 3-28-65, "One Way Out" 4-18-65, "Cowards Die Many Times" 4-17-66; *The Big Valley*—"Forty Rifles" 9-22-65, "A Time to Kill" 1-19-66, "The Death Merchant" 2-23-66, "The Iron Box" 11-28-66, "Last Stage to Salt Flats" 12-5-66, "The Haunted Gun" 2-6-67, "Price of Victory" 2-13-67, "Showdown in Limbo" 3-27-67, "The Day of Grace" 4-17-67, "Run of the Cat" 10-21-68, "The Profit and the Lost" 12-2-68, "Hunter's Moon" 12-30-68; *Laredo*—"Three's Company" 10-14-65, "Meanwhile, Back at the Reservation" 2-10-66, "Miracle at Massacre Mission" 3-3-66; *Gunsmoke*—"The Prodigal" 9-25-67, "Lyle's Kid" 9-23-68, "The Hide Cutters" 9-30-68, "Uncle Finney" 10-14-68, "The Miracle Man" 12-2-68, "Lobo" 12-16-68, "The Twisted Heritage" 1-6-69, "The Reprisal" 2-10-69, "The Good Samaritans" 3-10-69, "Coreyville" 10-6-69, "Danny" 10-13-69, "Ring of Darkness" 12-1-69, "The War Priest" 1-5-70, "Doctor Herman Schultz, M.D." 1-26-70, "Kiowa" 2-16-70, "Morgan" 3-2-70, "The Cage" 3-23-70, "Sam McTavish, M.D." 10-5-70, "Luke" 11-2-70, "The Gun" 11-9-70, "The Scavengers" 11-16-70, "McCabe" 11-30-70, "Sergeant Holly" 12-14-70, "The Tycoon" 1-25-71, "The Convict" 2-1-71, "Pike" 3-1-71 & 3-8-71, "Trafton" 10-25-71, "The Bul-

let" 11-29-71, 12-6-71 & 12-13-71, "Tara" 1-17-72, "One for the Road" 1-24-72, "The Predators" 1-31-72, "The Wedding" 3-13-72, "The Drummer" 10-9-72, "Milligan" 11-6-72, "Jesse" 2-19-73, "The Boy and the Sinner" 10-1-73, "The Widow Maker" 10-8-73, "The Widow and the Rogue" 10-29-73, "Lynch Town" 11-19-73, "Susan Was Evil" 12-3-73, "The Deadly Innocent" 12-17-73, "The Foundling" 2-11-74, "The Schoolmarm" 2-25-74, "Trail of Bloodshed" 3-4-74, "A Town in Chains" 9-16-74, "Thirty a Month and Found" 10-7-74, "The Fourth Victim" 11-4-74, "The Colonel" 12-16-74, "The Angry Land" 2-3-75, "Hard Labor" 2-24-75, "The Busters" 3-10-75; *Cimarron Strip*—1967-68 (prod.), "The Battle of Blood Stone" 10-12-67, "The Search" 11-9-67, "The Beast That Walked Like a Man" 11-30-67, "The Last Wolf" 12-14-67; *Wild Wild West*—"The Night of Fire and Brimstone" 11-22-68, "The Night of the Pistoleros" 2-21-69; *The Quest*—"Day of Outrage" 10-27-76, "Prairie Woman" 11-10-76, "Welcome to America, Jade Snow" 11-24-76, "The Longest Drive" 12-1-76 & 12-8-76, "Dynasty of Evil" 1976, "Incident at Drucker's Tavern" 1976; *How the West Was Won*—Season Two 1978; *Young Maverick*—"Clancy" 11-28-79; *Outlaws*—"Independents" 3-21-87.

McEveety, Joe. Screenwriter. Films: "Hot Lead and Cold Feet" 1978.

McEveety, Vincent. Director. Films: "Firecreek" 1968; "Cutter's Trail" TVM-1970; "The Castaway Cowboy" 1974; "The Apple Dumpling Gang Rides Again" 1979; "Gunsmoke: Return to Dodge" TVM-1987. ¶TV: *Rawhide*—"The Lost Herd" 10-16-64, "The Photographer" 12-11-64, "No Dogs or Drovers" 12-18-64; *Gunsmoke*—"Winner Take All" 2-20-65, "Breckinridge" 3-13-65, "Dry Road to Nowhere" 4-3-65, "Two Tall Men" 5-8-65, "Honey Pot" 5-15-65, "Seven Hours to Dawn" 9-18-65, "The Pretender" 11-20-65, "The Hostage" 12-4-65, "Judge Calvin Strom" 12-18-65, "The Raid" 1-22-66 & 1-29-66, "The Goldtakers" 9-24-66, "The Jailer" 10-1-66, "The Whispering Tree" 11-12-66, "The Pillagers" 11-6-67, "The Victim" 1-1-68, "Nowhere to Run" 1-15-68, "Zavala" 10-7-68, "Abelia" 11-18-68, "The Money Store" 12-30-68, "Time of the Jackals" 1-13-69, "The Mark of Cain" 2-3-69, "The Intruders" 3-3-69, "A Man Called Smith" 10-27-69, "Charlie Noon" 11-3-69, "The Judas Gun" 1-19-70, "The Badge" 2-2-70,

"Albert" 2-9-70, "Hackett" 3-16-70, "Chato" 9-14-70, "The Noose" 9-21-70, "Gentry's Law" 10-12-70, "Mirage" 1-11-71, "Cleavus" 2-15-71, "Lavery" 2-22-71, "Waste" 9-27-71 & 10-4-71, "Yankton" 2-7-72, "Alias Festus Haggin" 3-6-72, "Talbot" 2-26-73, "Women for Sale" 9-10-73 & 9-17-73, "Kitty's Love Affair" 10-22-73, "To Ride a Yellow Horse" 3-18-74, "I Have Promises to Keep" 3-3-75; *Branded*—"Judge Not" 9-12-65, "Mightier Than the Sword" 9-26-65, "Fill No Glass for Me" 11-7-65 & 11-14-65; *Cimarron Strip*—"Journey to a Hanging" 9-7-67, "The Legend of Jud Starr" 9-14-67, "The Greeners" 3-7-68; *Dirty Sally* 1974; *How the West Was Won*—Season Two 1978, "The Gunfighter" 1-15-79, "Luke" 4-2-79; *The Busters*—Pilot 5-28-78; *The Buffalo Soldiers*—Pilot 5-26-79.

MacFadden, Hamilton. Director. Films: "Riders of the Purple Sage" 1931; "The Fourth Horseman" 1933.

MacFarlane, Peter Clark. Writer. Films: "A Pair of Hellions" 1924 (story); "Tongues of Flame" 1924 (story).

McGann, William (1895-1977). Director. Films: "The Parson of Panamint" 1941; "American Empire" 1942; "In Old California" 1942; "Tombstone, the Town Too Tough to Die" 1942; "Frontier Badman" 1943; "Trial by Trigger" 1944-short.

McGaugh, Wilbur (1895-1/31/65). Director. Films: "Whistling Hills" 1925.

McGill, Lawrence. Director. Films: "The Sealed Valley" 1915.

McGinty, E.B. Writer. Films: "The Man from Texas" 1947 (story).

McGlynn, Frank (1866-5/18/51). Director. Films: "The Girl and the Outlaw" 1913.

McGowan, Dorrel. Screenwriter. Films: "Comin' Round the Mountain" 1936; "Guns and Guitars" 1936; "King of the Pecos" 1936; "Red River Valley" 1936; "Ride, Ranger, Ride" 1936; "The Singing Cowboy" 1936; "The Big Show" 1937; "Get Along, Little Dogies" 1937; "Yodelin' Kid from Pine Ridge" 1937; "Under Western Stars" 1938 (& story); "In Old Monterey" 1939; "Jeepers Creepers" 1939; "Rovin' Tumbleweeds" 1939; "South of the Border" 1939; "Trouble in Sundown" 1939; "Arkansas Judge" 1941; "Down Mexico Way" 1941 (story): "Stardust on the Sage" 1942; "The Big Bonanza" 1944; "San Fernando Valley" 1944; "Don't Fence Me In" 1945; "Saddle Pals"

1947 (story only); "Twilight on the Rio Grande" 1947; "The Showdown" 1950 (& dir.); "Singing Guns" 1950; "Snowfire" 1958 (& prod./dir.). ¶TV: *Sky King* 1951-53 (exec. prod.); *Death Valley Days* 1952-70 (prod.).

McGowan, George. Director. Films: "Run, Simon, Run" TVM-1970; "The Magnificent Seven Ride" 1972; "Shadow of the Hawk" 1976.

McGowan, J.P. (1880-3/26/52). Director. Films: "The Battle at Fort Laramie" 1913; "Brought to Bay" 1913; "The Identification" 1914; "A Desperate Leap" 1915; "The Girl and the Game" 1915-serial; "The Mettle of Jerry McGuire" 1915; "The Operator of Black Rock" 1915; "Lass of the Lumberlands" 1916-serial; "Medicine Bend" 1916; "Whispering Smith" 1916; "The Lost Express" 1917-serial (& sp.); "The Railroad Raiders" 1917-serial; "The Missing Bullet" 1919; "The Ruse of the Rattlesnake" 1921; "Hills of Missing Men" 1922; "Perils of the Yukon" 1922-serial; "Baffled" 1924; "Calibre 45" 1924; "Courage" 1924; "Crossed Trail" 1924; "A Desperate Adventure" 1924; "A Two Fisted Tenderfoot" 1924; "Western Vengeance" 1924; "The Whipping Boss" 1924; "Blood and Steel" 1925; "Border Intrigue" 1925; "Cold Nerve" 1925; "The Fighting Sheriff" 1925; "The Gambling Fool" 1925; "The Ace of Clubs" 1926; "Buried Gold" 1926; "Cyclone Bob" 1926; "Desperate Chance" 1926; "Fighting Luck" 1926; "Iron Fist" 1926; "The Lost Trail" 1926; "Red Blood" 1926; "Riding for Life" 1926; "Riding Romance" 1926; "Road Agent" 1926; "The Texas Terror" 1926; "Unseen Enemies" 1926; "Aflame in the Sky" 1927; "Thunderbolt's Tracks" 1927; "Arizona Days" 1928; "The Devil's Tower" 1928 (& sp.); "Headin' Westward" 1928; "Law of the Mounted" 1928; "Lightnin' Shot" 1928 (& sp.); "The Outlaw Dog" 1927; "Manhattan Cowboy" 1928; "Mystery Valley" 1928 (& sp.); "On the Divide" 1928; "The Painted Trail" 1928; "The Silent Trail" 1928; "The Trail Riders" 1928 (& sp.); "Trailin' Back" 1928 (& sp.); "West of Santa Fe" 1929; "Bad Man's Money" 1929 (& sp.); "Captain Cowboy" 1929 (& story); "Code of the West" 1929; "The Cowboy and the Outlaw" 1929; "The Fighting Terror" 1929; "The Invaders" 1929; "The Last Roundup" 1929; "Law of the Plains" 1929; "The Lone Horseman" 1929; "The Man from Nevada" 1929; "'Neath Western Skies" 1929; "The Oklahoma Kid" 1929 (& prod.); "The Phantom Rider" 1929; "Pioneers of the West" 1929; "Riders of

the Rio Grande" 1929; "Riders of the Storm" 1929 (& sp.); "A Texas Cowboy" 1929; "Beyond the Law" 1930; "Breezy Bill" 1930; "Call of the Desert" 1930; "Canyon Hawks" 1930; "The Canyon of Missing Men" 1930; "Code of Honor" 1930; "Covered Wagon Trails" 1930; "Hunted Men" 1930; "The Man from Nowhere" 1930; "Near the Rainbow's End" 1930; "The Oklahoma Sheriff" 1930; "O'Malley Rides Alone" 1930; "The Parting of the Trails" 1930 (& prod.); "Under Texas Skies" 1930; "Cyclone Kid" 1931; "Headin' for Trouble" 1931; "Riders of the North" 1931; "Shotgun Pass" 1931; "Human Targets" 1932; "Lawless Valley" 1932; "The Man from New Mexico" 1932; "Mark of the Spur" 1932; "Scarlet Brand" 1932; "Deadwood Pass" 1933; "Drum Taps" 1933 (& story); "War on the Range" 1933; "When a Man Rides Alone" 1933; "The Lone Bandit" 1934; "The Outlaw Tamer" 1934; "Secret Patrol" 1936; "Roaring Six Guns" 1937; "Rough Ridin' Rhythm" 1937; "Where the West Begins" 1938.

MacGowan, Kenneth (1888-4/27/63). Producer. Films: "The Return of the Cisco Kid" 1939; "Susannah of the Mounties" 1939; "Brigham Young—Frontiersman" 1940; "Belle Starr" 1941; "Hudson Bay" 1941.

McGowan, Robert (1873-1/27/55). Director. Films: "Frontier Justice" 1936; "Gass House Kids Go West" 1947 (sp. only).

McGowan, Stuart. Screenwriter. Films: "Comin' Round the Mountain" 1936; "Guns and Guitars" 1936; "King of the Pecos" 1936; "Red River Valley" 1936; "Ride, Ranger, Ride" 1936; "The Singing Cowboy" 1936; "The Big Show" 1937; "Get Along, Little Dogies" 1937; "Yodelin' Kid from Pine Ridge" 1937; "Under Western Stars" 1938 (& story); "In Old Monterey" 1939; "Jeeper Creepers" 1939; "Rovin' Tumbleweeds" 1939; "South of the Border" 1939; "Trouble in Sundown" 1939; "Arkansas Judge" 1941; "Down Mexico Way" 1941 (story); "Stardust on the Sage" 1942; "The Big Bonanza" 1944; "San Fernando Valley" 1944; "Don't Fence Me In" 1945; "Saddle Pals" 1947 (story only); "Twilight on the Rio Grande" 1947; "Hellfire" 1949; "The Showdown" 1950 (& dir.); "Singing Guns" 1950; "Snowfire" 1958 (& prod./dir.). ¶TV: *Sky King* 1951 (dir.).

McGrath, Harold. Screenwriter. Films: "Vengeance That Failed" 1912; "The Mollycoddle" 1920 (story only).

McGreevey, John. Director.

Films: "Cast a Long Shadow" 1959 (sp. only). ¶TV: *Wagon Train*—"The Fort Pierce Story" 9-23-63.

McGreevey, Michael. Screenwriter. Films: "Bonanza: The Return" 1993 (& story).

MacGregor, Norval. Director. Films: "Colorado" 1915; "Jacques of the Silver North" 1919.

MacGregor, Sean. Screenwriter. Films: "Cry Blood, Apache" 1970.

McGuane, Thomas (1939-). Screenwriter. Films: "Rancho Deluxe" 1975; "The Missouri Breaks" 1976; "Tom Horn" 1980.

McGuinness, James Kevin. Screenwriter. Films: "Rio Grande" 1950.

McGuire, Don (1919-79). Director. Films: "Johnny Concho" 1956 (& sp.).

McGuirk, Charles J. (1889-12/4/43). Screenwriter. Films: "Ruggles of Red Gap" 1918.

Mack, Charles W. (1878-11/29/56) Director. Films: "The Devil's Ghost" 1921; "Blue Blazes" 1922.

Mack, J.B. Writer. Films: "The Big Hop" 1928 (story).

Mack, Marion (1902-5/1/89). Screenwriter. Films: "Rodeo Dough" 1940-short.

Mack, Wayne. Director. Films: "No Man's Woman" 1921.

Mack, Willard (1873-11/18/34). Screenwriter. Films: "All Man" 1916 (story only); "Nanette of the Wilds" 1916 (story only); "Go West, Young Man" 1918; "The Hell Cat" 1918; "Laughing Bill Hyde" 1918; "Nine Points of the Law" 1922; "Tiger Rose" 1923 (story); "Tiger Rose" 1929 (story); "Men of the North" 1930; "The Girl and the Gambler" 1939 (story only).

McKay, Brian. Screenwriter. Films: "McCabe and Mrs. Miller" 1971.

McKay, James C. Director. Films: "Lightning" 1927.

McKee, Lafe S. (1872-8/10/59). Director. Films: "Lone Hand Wilson" 1920.

McKeel, Kathy. Screenwriter. Films: "The Black Lash" 1952.

McKenna, Dudley. Screenwriter. Films: "Courtin' Wildcats" 1929.

MacKenzie, Aeneas (1890-6/2/62). Screenwriter. Films: "They Died with Their Boots On" 1941; "The Woman of the Town" 1943; "Buffalo Bill" 1944.

MacKenzie, Donald (1879-

7/21/72). Director. Films: "The Perils of Pauline" 1914-serial; "The Challenge" 1916.

McKenzie, Robert (1880-7/8/49). Director. Films: "A Knight of the West" 1921; "Fightin' Devil" 1922; "A Western Demon" 1922; "The White Outlaw" 1929 (sp. only).

McKinstry, Reginald. Screenwriter. Films: "The Stranger at Coyote" 1911; "The Intrusion of Compoc" 1912; "Cameo of Yellowstone" 1914.

Mackley, Arthur. Director. Films: "The Sheriff's Wife" 1913; "Deputy Sheriff's Star" 1914; "The Sheriff's Choice" 1914; "The Boundary Line" 1915; "The Deputy's Chance That Won" 1915; "The Race War" 1915.

McLaglen, Andrew V. (1925-). Director. Films: "Seven Men from Now" 1956 (prod. only); "Gun the Man Down" 1957; "McLintock" 1963; "Shenandoah" 1965; "The Rare Breed" 1966; "The Way West" 1967; "Ballad of Josie" 1968; "Bandolero!" 1968; "The Undefeated" 1969; "Chisum" 1970; "Fools' Parade" 1971 (& prod.); "One More Train to Rob" 1971; "Something Big" 1971 (& prod.); "Cahill, United States Marshal" 1973; "Banjo Hackett: Roamin' Free" TVM-1976; "The Last Hard Men" 1976; "The Shadow Riders" TVM-1982. ¶TV: *Gunsmoke*—"Cow Doctor" 9-8-56, "Legal Revenge" 11-17-56, "The Mistake" 11-24-56, "Poor Pearl" 12-22-56, "Cholera" 12-29-56, "Pucket's New Year" 1-5-57, "Sins of the Father" 1-19-57, "Kick Me" 1-26-57, "The Executioner" 2-2-57, "Bloody Hands" 2-17-57, "Sweet and Sour" 3-2-57, "The Last Fling" 3-23-57, "Wrong Man" 4-13-57, "What the Whiskey Drummer Heard" 4-27-57, "Cheap Labor" 5-4-57, "Who Lives by the Sword" 5-18-57, "Uncle Oliver" 5-25-57, "Daddy-O" 6-1-57, "Liar from Blackhawk" 6-22-57, "Jealousy" 7-6-57, "Kitty's Outlaw" 10-5-57, "Jesse" 10-19-57, "Jayhawkers" 1-31-59, "The F.U." 3-14-59, "Fawn" 4-4-59, "Renegade White" 4-11-59, "Murder Warrant" 4-18-59, "Change of Heart" 4-25-59, "There Never Was a Horse" 5-16-59, "Blue Horse" 6-6-59, "Target" 9-5-59, "Horse Deal" 9-26-59, "Kangaroo" 10-10-59, "Saludos" 10-31-59, "Odd Man Out" 11-21-59, "Miguel's Daughter" 11-28-59, "Groat's Grudge" 1-2-60, "Big Tom" 1-9-60, "Hinka Do" 1-30-60, "Moo Moo Raid" 2-13-60, "Unwanted Deputy" 3-5-60, "Crowbait Bob" 3-26-60, "The Ex-Urbanites" 4-9-60, "The

Lady Killer" 4-23-60, "Speak Me Fair" 5-7-60, "Cherry Red" 6-11-60, "The Blacksmith" 9-17-60, "Small Water" 9-24-60, "Say Uncle" 10-1-60, "Shooting Stopover" 10-8-60, "The Badge" 11-12-60, "Ben Tolliver's Stud" 11-26-60, "Bad Sheriff" 1-7-61, "Kitty Shot" 2-11-61, "Stolen Horses" 4-8-61, "Long Hours, Short Pay" 4-19-61, "Harper's Blood" 10-21-61, "Long, Long Trail" 11-4-61, "Indian Ford" 12-2-61, "The Do-Badder" 1-6-62, "Cody's Code 1-20-62, "Old Dan" 1-27-62, "The Gallows" 3-3-62, "Wagon Girls" 4-7-62, "The Summons" 4-21-62, "The Dreamers" 4-28-62, "The Prisoner" 5-19-62, "Quint Asper Comes Home" 9-29-62, "Jenny" 10-13-62, "The Trappers" 11-3-62, "Phoebe Strunk" 11-10-62, "Abe Blocker" 11-24-62, "Us Haggens" 12-8-62, "False Front" 12-22-62, "The Renegades" 1-12-63, "Two of a Kind" 3-16-63, "With a Smile" 3-30-63, "Quint-Cident" 4-27-63, "The Odyssey of Jubal Tanner" 5-18-63, "The Quest for Asa Janin" 6-1-63, "Lover Boy" 10-5-63, "Easy Come" 10-26-63, "Prairie Wolfer" 1-18-64, "Once a Haggen" 2-1-64, "No Hands" 2-8-64, "May Blossoms" 2-15-64, "The Bassops" 2-22-64, "The Kite" 2-29-64, "Now That April's Here" 3-21-64, "The Promoter" 4-25-64, "The Warden" 5-16-64, "The Other Half" 5-30-64, "Crooked Mile" 10-3-64, "Chicken" 12-5-64, "Bank Baby" 3-20-65; *Have Gun Will Travel*—"Three Bells to Perdido" 9-14-57, "The Outlaw" 9-21-57, "The Great Mojave Chase" 9-28-57, "Winchester Quarantine" 10-5-57, "A Matter of Ethics" 10-12-57, "The Bride" 10-19-57, "Strange Vendetta" 10-26-57, "High Wire" 11-2-57, "Show of Force" 11-9-57, "The Long Night" 11-16-57, "The Colonel and the Lady" 11-23-57, "No Visitors" 11-30-57, "The Englishman" 12-7-57, "The Yuma Treasure" 12-14-57, "The Hanging Cross" 12-21-57, "Killer's Widow" 3-22-58, "The Prize Fight Story" 4-5-58, "Three Sons" 5-10-58, "Twenty-Four Hours to North Fork" 5-17-58, "The Statue of San Sebastian" 6-14-58, "In an Evil Time" 9-13-58, "The Man Who Wouldn't Talk" 9-20-58, "The Gentleman" 9-27-58, "The Hanging of Roy Carter" 10-4-58, "Duel at Florence" 10-11-58, "The Protege" 10-18-58, "The Road to Wickenberg" 10-25-58, "The Lady" 11-15-58, "The Solid Gold Patrol" 12-13-58, "Something to Live For" 12-20-58, "The Moor's Revenge" 12-27-58, "The Wager" 1-3-59, "The Taffeta Mayor" 1-10-59, "Juliet" 1-31-59, "The Scorched Feather" 2-14-59,

"The Return of the Lady" 2-21-59, "The Long Hunt" 3-7-59, "Incident at Borasca Bend" 3-21-59, "Alaska" 4-18-59, "The Return of Roy Carter" 5-2-59, "Commanche" 5-16-59, "The Haunted Trees" 6-13-59, "Episode in Laredo" 9-19-59, "Fragile" 10-31-59, "The Unforgiven" 11-7-59, "The Black Handkerchief" 11-14-59, "The Gold Toad" 11-21-59, "Champagne Safari" 12-5-59, "The Pledge" 1-16-60, "Jenny" 1-23-60, "Return to Fort Benjamin" 1-30-60, "The Ledge" 2-13-60, "The Hatchet Man" 3-5-60, "Never Help the Devil" 4-16-60, "The Twins" 5-21-60, "Shadow of a Man" 1-28-61, "The Revenger" 9-30-61; *Rawhide*—"Incident on the Edge of Madness" 2-6-59, "Incident of the Power and the Plow" 2-13-59, "Incident of Fear in the Streets" 5-8-59, "Incident of the Dry Drive" 5-22-59, "Incident of the Shambling Man" 10-9-59, "Deserter's Patrol" 2-9-62; *Royce*—Pilot 5-21-76.

McLaren, Alex. Screenwriter. Films: "The Desert Demon" 1925.

McLaughlin, J.B. Director. Films: "Beyond the Shadows" 1918.

McLaughlin, J.W. Director. Films: "Closin' In" 1918.

MacLean, Alistair (1922-2/2/87). Screenwriter. Films: "Breakheart Pass" 1976.

McLeod, Norman Z. (1895-1/26/64). Director. Films: "Taking a Chance" 1928; "Jackass Mail" 1942; "The Paleface" 1948; "Alias Jesse James" 1959.

MacLeod, Robert (1917-). Writer. Films: "The Appaloosa" 1966 (story); "100 Rifles" 1969 (story).

McLeod, Victor. Screenwriter. Films: "Law and Order" 1940; "Boss of Bullion City" 1941; "Bury Me Not on the Lone Prairie" 1941; "The Masked Rider" 1941; "Frontier Gunlaw" 1946 (story only); "Rustler's Roundup" 1946 (story only); "Silver Butte" 1949-short.

MacMacklin, Arthur. Director. Films: "The Purple Hills" 1915.

McMahon, Leo. Screenwriter. Films: "Madron" 1970-U.S./Israel (& story).

McMurtry, Larry (1936-). Writer. Films: "Hud" 1963 (story); "Lovin' Molly" 1974 (story); "Lonesome Dove" TVM-1989 (story); "Montana" TVM-1990 (story); "Buffalo Girls" TVM-1995 (story).

McNamara, Tom (1886-5/19/64). Screenwriter. Films: "Crossfire" 1933.

McNeill, Evrett. Screenwriter.

Films: "The Cowboy's Best Girl" 1912; "A Message to Kearney" 1912; "The Beaded Buckskin Bag" 1913.

McNutt, William Slavens (1885-1/25/38). Screenwriter. Films: "The Light of the Western Stars" 1930; "The Conquering Horde" 1931; "The Broken Wing" 1932.

MacPherson, Harry. Writer. Films: "Starlight Over Texas" 1938 (story).

Macpherson, Jeanie (1887-8/26/46). Screenwriter. Films: "The Desert's Sting" 1914; "Chimmie Fadden Out West" 1915; "The Love Mask" 1916; "A Romance of the Redwoods" 1917; "The Plainsman" 1936.

MacQuarrie, Murdock (1878-8/20/42). Director. Films: "Babbling Tongues" 1915; "The Flag of Fortune" 1915; "The Sacrifice of Jonathan Gray" 1915; "The Sheriff of Red Gulch" 1915; "The Trap That Failed" 1915; "The Stain in the Blood" 1916; "Thunderbolt Jack" 1921.

MacRae, Henry (1876-10/2/44). Director. Films: "The Iron Trail" 1913; "Pierre of the North" 1913; "The Return of Thunder Cloud's Spirit" 1913; "The Vengeance of the Sky Stone" 1913; "The Water War" 1913; "The Law of the Range" 1914; "The Trail Breakers" 1914; "The Vagabond Soldier" 1914; "Custer's Last Scout" 1915; "Ridgeway of Montana" 1915; "The War of the Wild" 1915 (& sp.); "The Conspiracy" 1916; "Giant Powder" 1916; "Guilty" 1916; "Liberty" 1916-serial; "The Railroad Bandit" 1916; "Dropped from the Clouds" 1917; "The Indian's Lament" 1917; "Lone Larry" 1917; "Number 10, Westbound" 1917; "The Whirlwind Finish" 1918; "Tempest Cody, Kidnapper" 1919; "Cameron of the Royal Mounted" 1922; "Ace of Spades" 1925-serial; "Strings of Steel" 1926-serial; "Burning the Wind" 1928; "The Danger Rider" 1928; "Guardians of the Wild" 1928; "Plunging Hoofs" 1928; "The Two Outlaws" 1928; "Harvest of Hate" 1929; "Hoofbeats of Vengeance" 1929; "King of the Rodeo" 1929; "Smilin' Guns" 1929; "Wild Blood" 1929; "The Indians Are Coming" 1930-serial (& prod.); "Battling with Buffalo Bill" 1931-serial (prod. only); "Heroes of the West" 1932-serial (prod. only); "Clancy of the Mounted" 1933-serial (prod. only); "Gordon of Ghost City" 1933-serial (prod. only); "Rustlers' Roundup" 1933; "The Red Rider" 1934-serial; "The Roaring West" 1935-serial (prod. only): "The Phantom Rider" 1936 (prod. only); "Wild West Days"

1937-serial (prod. only); "Flaming Frontier" 1938-serial (prod. only); "Forbidden Valley" 1938 (prod. only); "The Oregon Trail" 1939-serial (prod. only); "Winners of the West" 1940-serial (prod. only); "Riders of Death Valley" 1941-serial (prod. only); "Overland Mail" 1942-serial (prod. only).

McRoots, George. *see* Maruizzo, Giorgio.

McWade, Edward (1865-5/17/43). Screenwriter. Films: "The Totem Mark" 1911; "Wheels of Justice" 1911; "Juggling with Fate" 1913 (story only).

Maddow, Ben (1909-10/9/92). Screenwriter. Films: "The Man from Colorado" 1948; "The Unforgiven" 1960; "The Way West" 1967.

Madison, Cleo (1883-3/11/64). Director. Films: "The Ring of Destiny" 1915.

Madrid, Jose Luis. Director. Films: "Who Killed Johnny R.?" 1966-Ital./Span.; "Ruthless Colt of the Gringo" 1967-Ital./Span.

Maesso, Jose G. Screenwriter. Films: "The Savage Guns" 1961-U.S./Span.; "The Hellbenders" 1966-U.S./Ital./Span.; "The Ugly Ones" 1966-Ital./Span.; "Sting of the West" 1972-Ital.

Maffei, Mario. Director. Films: "Ringo's Big Night" 1966-Ital./Span.; "Garter Colt" 1967-Ital./Span./Ger. (sp. only); "Black Jack" 1968-Ital. (sp. only).

Magan, Guy. TV: *Young Riders*—"Lessons Learned" 7-9-92.

Magli, Franco. Producer. Films: "The Girl of the Golden West" 1942-Ital.

Mahin, John Lee (1902-4/18/84). Screenwriter. Films: "The Horse Soldiers" 1959 (& prod.); "North to Alaska" 1960.

Mahoney, Elizabeth. Screenwriter. Films: "The Golden Trail" 1920.

Maibaum, Richard (1909-1/4/91). Screenwriter. Films: "The Bad Man of Brimstone" 1938; "Twenty Mule Team" 1940.

Maigne, Charles (1881-11/28/29). Director. Films: "The Golden Fetter" 1917; "The Squaw Man's Son" 1917; "Heart of the Wilds" 1918; "The Cowboy and the Lady" 1922; "War Paint" 1926; "Clearing the Trail" 1928 (story only).

Mailo, Roberto. Screenwriter. Films: "Twenty Thousand Dollars for Seven" 1968-Ital.

Mainwaring, Daniel (1903-

1/31/77). Screenwriter. Films: "Cole Younger, Gunfighter" 1958; "Walk Like a Dragon" 1960; "Convict Stage" 1965.

Maiuri, Dino. Screenwriter. Films: "Companeros" 1970-Ital./Span./Ger.; "Chino" 1973-Ital./Span./Fr.; "Don't Turn the Other Cheek" 1974-Ital./Ger./Span.

Makelim, Hal R. Producer. Films: "The Peacemaker" 1956; "Valerie" 1957.

Malasomma, Nunzio. Director. Films: "Fifteen Scaffolds for the Killer" 1968-Ital./Span.

Malatesta, Guido (James Reed). Screenwriter. Films: "Sign of Zorro" 1964-Ital./Span.; "Coffin for the Sheriff" 1965-Ital./Span.

Malko, George. Screenwriter. Films: "Dan Candy's Law" 1975-U.S./Can.

Malle, Louis (1932-11/23/95). Director. Films: "Viva Maria" 1965-Fr./Ital. (& prod./sp.).

Mallick, Terry. Screenwriter. Films: "Pocket Money" 1972.

Mallock, Douglass. Writer. Films: "Jim" 1914 (story).

Mallorqui, Jose. Screenwriter. Films: "Magnificent Three" 1963-Span./Ital.; "Terrible Sheriff" 1963-Span./Ital.; "Heroes of the West" 1964-Span./Ital.; "Ride and Kill" 1964-Ital./Span.; "Sign of Coyote" 1964-Ital./Span.; "Shots Ring Out!" 1965-Ital./Span.

Malloy, Doris. Screenwriter. Films: "Wild Horse Stampede" 1926; "Ridin' on a Rainbow" 1941.

Maloney, Leo (1888-11/2/29). Director. Films: "The Big Catch" 1920; "A Gamblin' Fool" 1920; "The Grinning Granger" 1920; "The Honor of the Range" 1920; "One Law for All" 1920; "No Man's Woman" 1921; "The Bar Cross War" 1922 (& sp.); "Come and Get Me" 1922 (& sp.); "Deputized" 1922 (& sp.); "The Drifter" 1922 (& sp.); "Here's Your Man" 1922 (& sp.); "His Enemy's Friend" 1922 (& sp.); "His Own Law" 1922 (& sp.); "One Jump Ahead" 1922 (& sp.); "Rough Going" 1922; "Under Suspicion" 1922; "Under Suspicion" 1922 (sp. only); "The Extra Seven" 1923 (& sp.); "Hyde and Zeke" 1923 (& sp.); "In Wrong Right" 1923 (& sp.); "King's Creek Law" 1923; "Lost, Strayed or Stolen" 1923; "100% Nerve" 1923 (& sp.); "Partners Three" 1923 (& sp.); "Smoked Out" 1923; "Steel Shod Evidence" 1923 (& sp.); "Tom, Dick and Harry" 1923 (& sp.); "The Unsuspecting Stranger" 1923; "Warned in Advance" 1923 (& sp.); "When Fighting's Necessary" 1923 (& sp.); "Wings of the Storm" 1923 (& sp.); "Yellow Gold and Men" 1923 (& sp.); "Headin' Through" 1924; "Huntin' Trouble" 1924; "Not Guilty for Runnin'" 1924; "Payable on Demand" 1924; "Riding Double" 1924; "Across the Deadline" 1925; "Flash O'Lightning" 1925; "Luck and Sand" 1925; "Ranchers and Rascals" 1925; "The Shield of Silence" 1925; "The Trouble Buster" 1925; "Win, Lose or Draw" 1925; "Blind Trail" 1926; "The High Hand" 1926; "The Outlaw Express" 1926; "Without Orders" 1926; "Border Blackbirds" 1927; "The Devil's Twin" 1927; "Don Desperado" 1927; "The Long Loop on the Pecos" 1927; "The Man from Hardpan" 1927; "Two-Gun of the Tumbleweed" 1927; "The Apache Raider" 1928; "The Black Ace" 1928; "The Boss of Rustler's Roost" 1928; "The Bronc Stomper" 1928; "45 Calibre War" 1929; "Overland Bound" 1929 (& prod.).

Maltz, Albert (1908-4/26/85). Screenwriter. Films: "Two Mules for Sister Sara" 1970.

Malvern, Paul (1902-5/29/93). Producer. Films: "Crashing Broadway" 1933; "The Fugitive" 1933; "Riders of Destiny" 1933; "Sagebrush Trail" 1933; "Trailing North" 1933; "Breed of the Border" 1934; "Blue Steel" 1934; "The Lawless Frontier" 1934; "The Lucky Texan" 1934; "The Man from Utah" 1934; "'Neath the Arizona Skies" 1934; "Randy Rides Alone" 1934; "The Star Packer" 1934; "The Trail Beyond" 1934; "West of the Divide" 1934; "Dawn Rider" 1935; "Desert Trail" 1935; "Lawless Range" 1935; "The New Frontier" 1935; "Paradise Canyon" 1935; "Rainbow Valley" 1935; "Texas Terror" 1935; "Westward Ho" 1935; "King of the Pecos" 1936; "The Lawless Nineties" 1936; "The Oregon Trail" 1936; "Courage of the West" 1937; "Border Wolves" 1938; "Guilty Trails" 1938; "Prairie Justice" 1938; "The Singing Outlaw" 1938; "Western Trails" 1938; "The Phantom Stage" 1939; "Wolf Call" 1939; "Queen of the Yukon" 1940; "North to the Klondike" 1942; "Pirates of Monterey" 1947; "Rock Island Trail" 1950.

Malvestiti, Marcello. Screenwriter. Films: "Djano Kills Softly" 1968-Ital.

Mamoulian, Rouben (1897-12/4/87). Director. Films: "The Gay Desperado" 1936; "High, Wide and Handsome" 1937; "Mark of Zorro" 1940.

Mancini, Claudio. Producer. Films: "My Name Is Nobody" 1973-Ital.; "Genius" 1975-Ital./Fr./Ger.

Mancori, Carlo. Screenwriter. Films: "Kung Fu Brothers in the Wild West" 1973-Ital./Hong Kong.

Mandel, Alan. Screenwriter. Films: "Goin' South" 1978.

Mandel, Babaloo. Screenwriter. Films: "City Slickers" 1991; "City Slickers II: The Legend of Curly's Gold" 1994.

Manduke, Joe. Director. Films: "Kid Vengeance" 1976-Ital./U.S./Israel.

Manera, John. Screenwriter. Films: "Chrysanthemums for a Bunch of Swine" 1968-Ital.

Mang, Jone. *see* Mangione, Giuseppe.

Mangini, Gino. Director. Films: "This Man Can't Die" 1968-Ital. (sp. only); "Bastard, Go and Kill" 1971-Ital. (& sp.).

Mangini, Luigi. Screenwriter. Films: "Vendetta at Dawn" 1971-Ital.

Mangione, Giuseppe (Jone Mang). Screenwriter. Films: "A Stranger in Town" 1966-U.S./Ital.; "Sugar Colt" 1966-Ital./Span.; "The Stranger Returns" 1967-U.S./Ital./Ger./Span.

Maniates, Belle Kanaris. Writer. Films: "Penny of Top Hill Trail" 1921 (story).

Manini, Bianco. Screenwriter Films: "A Bullet for the General" 1966-Ital. (prod. only); "Taste for Killing" 1966-Ital./Span. (prod. only); "Train for Durango" 1967-Ital./Span. (prod. only); "The Price of Power" 1969-Ital./Span.; "Halleluja to Vera Cruz" 1973-Ital.

Mankiewicz, Herman (1897-3/5/53). Screenwriter. Films: "Avalanche" 1928.

Mankiewicz, John. Screenwriter. Films: "The Return of Desperado" TVM-1988.

Mankiewicz, Joseph L. (1909-2/5/93). Director. Films: "The Three Godfathers" 1936 (prod. only); "There Was a Crooked Man" 1970 (& prod.).

Mann, Anthony (1906-4/29/67). Director. Films: "The Devil's Doorway" 1950; "The Furies" 1950; "Winchester '73" 1950; "Bend of the River" 1952; "The Naked Spur" 1953; "The Far Country" 1955; "The Last Frontier" 1955; "The Man from Laramie" 1955; "The Tin Star" 1957; "Man of the West" 1958; "Cimarron" 1960.

Mann, Daniel (1912-1!/21/91). Director. Films: "The Revengers" 1972-U.S./Mex. ¶TV: *How the West Was Won*—Season One 1977.

Mann, Edward Beverly. Writer. Films: "Guns for Hire" 1932 (story); "Boss Rider of Gun Creek" 1936 (story); "Desert Phantom" 1937 (story); "Guns in the Dark" 1937 (story); "Lightnin' Crandall" 1937 (story); "Ridin' the Lone Trail" 1937 (story); "Trail of Vengeance" 1937 (story); "Stampede" 1949 (story).

Mann, Michael (1943-). Director. Films: "The Last of the Mohicans" 1992 (& prod./sp.).

Mann, Stanley (1928-). Screenwriter. Films: "Draw" CTVM-1984.

Manners, Kim. Director. TV: *Paradise*—"The Promise" 12-15-88, "Childhood's End" 12-29-88; *Adventures of Brisco County, Jr.*—"No Man's Land" 9-10-93, "Showdown" 10-29-93, "Iron Horses" 11-19-93, "Bounty Hunter's Convention" 1-7-94, "The Brooklyn Dodgers" 2-11-94, "Bye Bly" 2-18-94, "High Treason" Part One 5-13-94.

Mannheimer, Albert. Screenwriter. Films: "The Kid from Texas" 1939.

Manning, Bruce. Screenwriter. Films: "Jubilee Trail" 1954.

Mannon, Alfred T. Producer. Films: "Fighting Pioneers" 1935; "Gunfire" 1935; "Saddle Aces" 1935; "Tonto Kid" 1935.

Manse, Jean. Screenwriter. Films: "Dynamite Jack" 1963-Fr.

Mantley, John (1920-). Producer. Films: "The Parson and the Outlaw" 1957; "Firecreek" 1968; "Cutter's Trail" TVM-1970; "Gunsmoke: Return to Dodge" TVM-1987. ¶TV: *Wild Wild West* 1965-69; *Gunsmoke* 1967-75; *Dirty Sally* 1974 (exec. prod.); *How the West Was Won* 1977-79 (exec. prod.).

Manzanos, Eduardo. Screenwriter. Films: "Charge of the Seventh Cavalry" 1964-Ital./Span./Fr.; "Outlaw of Red River" 1966-Ital.; "Prey of Vultures" 1973-Span./Ital.

Maple, John E. Director. Films: "Before the White Man Came" 1920.

Marble, Scott. Writer. Films: "The Great Train Robbery" 1903 (story); "Tennessee's Pardner" 1916 (story).

Marcellini, Siro. Director. Films: "Black Tigress" 1967-Ital.

March, Alex (1921-6/11/89). Director. Films: "The Dangerous Days of Kiowa Jones" TVM-1966. ¶TV: *Empire*—"Walk Like a King" 10-30-62; *Shane* 1966.

March, Joseph Moncure (1899-2/14/77). Screenwriter. Films: "A Man from Wyoming" 1930 (story only); "Lone Star Raiders" 1940; "Three Faces West" 1940; "Wagons Westward" 1940.

Marchant, Jay. Director. Films: "Heritage of Hate" 1921; "A Race for a Rancho" 1921; "Square Deal" 1921; "Perils of the Yukon" 1922-serial; "False Play" 1923; "Gentlemen of the West" 1923; "Ghost City" 1923-serial; "Hard Luck Jack" 1923; "The Homeward Trail" 1923; "Shootin' em Up" 1923; "The Strike of the Rattler" 1923; "The Twilight Trail" 1923; "Hats Off" 1924; "Miscarried Plans" 1924; "The Fighting Ranger" 1925-serial; "The Fighting Smile" 1925.

Marchel, Juan Xiol. *see* Iquino, Ignacio F.

Marchent, Joaquin L. Romero. *see* Hernandez, Joaquin Romero

Marchent, Rafael Romero. *see* Romero Marchent, Rafael.

Marchenti, Paul. *see* Hernandez, Joaquin Romero.

Marcus, Alan. Writer. Films: "The Marauders" 1955 (story).

Margheriti, Antonio (Anthony Dawson) (1930-). Director. Films: "Dynamite Joe" 1966-Ital./Span.; "Vengeance" 1968-Ital./Ger. (& sp.); "And God Said to Cain" 1969-Ital. (& sp.); "Stranger and the Gunfighter" 1973-U.S./Span./Hong Kong; "Take a Hard Ride" 1974-Ital./ Brit./Ger.

Margolin, Stuart (1940-). Director. Films: "Bret Maverick" TVM-1981. ¶TV: *The Texas Wheelers* 1974; *Sara* 1976.

Marigold, Tod Hunter. Writer. Films: "The Cyclone" 1920 (story).

Marin, Edwin L. (1901-5/2/51). Director. Films: "Henry Goes Arizona" 1939; "Tall in the Saddle" 1944; "Abilene Town" 1946; "Canadian Pacific" 1949; "Fighting Man of the Plains" 1949; "The Younger Brothers" 1949; "The Cariboo Trail" 1950; "Colt .45" 1950; "Fort Worth" 1951; "Raton Pass" 1951; "Sugarfoot" 1951.

Marina, Craig. Screenwriter. Films: "Death Played the Flute" 1972-Ital./Span.

Marina, Rafael. Screenwriter. Films: "Secret of Captain O'Hara" 1965-Span. (prod. only); "Let's Go and Kill Sartana" 1972-Ital./Span.

Marinero, Manuel. Screenwriter. Films: "Trinity Sees Red" 1971-Ital./Span.

Marino, Antonio. Screenwriter. Films: "Sometimes Life Is Hard, Right Providence?" 1972-Ital./Fr./ Ger.

Marion, Charles R. (1915-9/29/80). Screenwriter. Films: "Rhythm Round-Up" 1945; "Rodeo" 1952; "Apache Territory" 1958.

Marion, Frances (1888-5/12/73). Screenwriter. Films: "All Man" 1916; "The Crimson Dove" 1917; "M'Liss" 1918; "Sundown" 1924; "Zander the Great" 1925; "The Winning of Barbara Worth" 1926; "The Wind" 1928; "Secrets" 1933.

Marion, Louise. Writer. Films: "Rhythm Round-Up" 1945 (story).

Mariscal, Alberto. *see* Marshall, Albert.

Marischka, Franz. Screenwriter. Films: "Legacy of the Incas" 1965-Ger./Ital. (& prod.).

Marischka, Georg. Director. Films: "Legacy of the Incas" 1965-Ger./Ital. (& prod./sp.); "Pyramid of the Sun God" 1965-Ger./Ital./Fr. (sp. only).

Markey, Gene (1894-5/1/80). Writer. Films: "Blinky" 1923 (story); "Range Courage" 1927 (story).

Markle, Peter. Director. Films: "El Diablo" CTVM-1990; "Wagons East!" 1994.

Marks, Clarence. Screenwriter. Films: "The Terror of Tiny Town" 1938.

Marks, Sherman (-3/4/75). Director. TV: *Wild Wild West*—"The Night of the Infernal Machine" 12-23-66.

Marks, William. Screenwriter. Films: "War Party" 1965; "Barquero" 1970.

Markson, David (1927-). Screenwriter. Films: "Dirty Dingus Magee" 1970 (story only); "Count Your Bullets" 1972.

Marquis, Don. Director. Films: "Blood Test" 1923.

Marshall, Albert (Alberto Mariscal). Director. Films: "Eye for an Eye" 1972-Ital./Span./Mex.; "Outlaws in the Viewfinder" 1987-Mex. (& sp.).

Marshall, Anthony. Director. Films: "Bullets and Saddles" 1943.

Marshall, Edison (1894-10/29/67). Writer. Films: "Shadows of the North" 1923 (story).

Marshall, Garry (1934-). Screenwriter. Films: "Evil Roy Slade" TVM-1972 (& prod.).

Marshall, George E. (1891-2/17/75). Director. Films: "Across the

Rio Grande" 1916 (sp. only); "The Committee on Credentials" 1916; "The Devil's Own" 1916 (& sp.); "Love's Lariat" 1916 (& sp.); "Bill Brennan's Claim" 1917; "Casey's Border Raid" 1917; "Double Suspicion" 1917; "The Honor of Men" 1917; "The Man from Montana" 1917 (& story); "The Raid" 1917; "Right-of-Way Casey" 1917; "Roped In" 1917; "Squaring It" 1917; "Swede Hearts" 1917; "Beating the Limited" 1918; "The Fast Mail" 1918; "The Husband Hunter" 1918; "The Midnight Flyer" 1918; "The Gun Runners" 1919; "Prairie Trails" 1920; "Ruth of the Rockies" 1920-serial; "Hands Off" 1921; "A Ridin' Romeo" 1921 (& sp.); "Don Quickshot of the Rio Grande" 1923; "Men in the Raw" 1923; "Where Is This West?" 1923; "Destry Rides Again" 1939; "When the Daltons Rode" 1940; "Texas" 1941; "Valley of the Sun" 1942; "Riding High" 1943; "Fancy Pants" 1950; "The Savage" 1952; "Destry" 1954; "Red Garters" 1954; "Pillars of the Sky" 1956; "The Guns of Fort Petticoat" 1957; "The Sheepman" 1958; "How the West Was Won" 1962; "Advance to the Rear" 1964. ¶TV: *Daniel Boone*—"The Scrimshaw Ivory Chart" 1-4-68, "Nightmare" 3-14-68, "Before the Tall Man" 2-12-70.

Marshall, James. Writer. Films: "Santa Fe" 1951 (story).

Marston, Laurence. Screenwriter. Films: "The Border Legion" 1918.

Marston, Theodore. Director. Films: "The Last of the Mohicans" 1911 (& sp.); "The Forest Rose" 1912 (& sp.); "The Battle of Frenchman's Run" 1915 (& sp.); "From Out of the Big Snows" 1915; "Beyond the Law" 1918.

Martin, Al (1896-10/10/71). Screenwriter. Films: "Rider of Death Valley" 1932; "The Law of the Wild" 1934-serial (story only); "The Law Rides" 1936; "Rio Grande Romance" 1936; "Trail Dust" 1936; "Stagecoach Buckaroo" 1942.

Martin, Allen A. Writer. Films: "The Rival Stage Lines" 1914 (story).

Martin, Charles. Director. TV: *Gunsmoke*—"Root Down" 10-6-62, "The Bad One" 1-26-63.

Martin, Charles M. Writer. Films: "Law for Tombstone" 1937 (story); "Left-Handed Law" 1937 (story).

Martin, Don (1911-12/24/85). Screenwriter. Films: "Arrow in the Dust" 1954; "The Lone Gun" 1954; "Stranger on Horseback" 1955; "The

Brass Legend" 1956; "Quincannon, Frontier Scout" 1956.

Martin, Dorothea Knox. Screenwriter. "Hollywood Barn Dance" 1947.

Martin, E.A. Director. Films: "The Rival Stage Lines" 1911 (sp. only); "The Beaded Buckskin Bag" 1913; "The Redemption of Railroad Jack" 1913 (& sp.); "The Trail of Cards" 1913; "The Old Code" 1915; "The Heart of Texas Ryan" 1917.

Martin, Eugenio. Director. Films: "The Ugly Ones" 1966-Ital./Span. (& sp.); "Duel in the Eclipse" 1967-Span.; "Bad Man's River" 1971-Span./Ital./Fr. (& sp.); "Pancho Villa" 1975-Span.

Martin, Francis. Screenwriter. Films: "Rhythm on the Range" 1936; "Shut My Big Mouth" 1942.

Martin, Frank. *see* Girolami, Marino.

Martin, George. Director. Films: "Under Western Skies" 1921; "Pals of the Silver Sage" 1940 (sp. only).

Martin, George. Director. Films: "Return of Clint the Strange" 1971-Ital./Span.

Martin, Herbert. *see* De Martino, Alberto

Martin, Irvin J. Screenwriter. Films: "Out of the Snows" 1920.

Martin, Louis. Screenwriter. Films: "Taste of Violence" 1961-Fr.

Martin, Sobey (1909-7/27/78). Director. TV: *The Cisco Kid* 1951-55; *Rawhide*—"The Blue Sky" 12-8-61, "The Gentleman's Gentleman" 12-15-61, "The Bosses' Daughter" 2-2-62, "Grandma's Money" 2-23-62, "The Pitchwagon" 3-2-62, "The Reunion" 4-6-62; *Lancer*—"The Prodigal" 11-12-68, "The Heart of Pony Alice" 12-17-68, "The Wedding" 1-7-69.

Martin, Steve (1945-). Screenwriter. Films: "Three Amigos" 1986.

Martin, Townsend (1896-11/22/51). Screenwriter. Films: "Tongues of Flame" 1924.

Martinenghi, Italo. Director. Films: "Three Supermen of the West" 1974-Ital./Span. (& sp.).

Martinez, Maria Del Carmin. Screenwriter. Films: "Dynamite Joe" 1966-Ital./Span.; "Fury of Johnny Kid" 1967-Span./Ital.

Martino, Francesco. Screenwriter. Films: "A Sky Full of Stars for a Roof" 1968-Ital.

Martino, Leonardo. Screenwriter. Films: "Three Musketeers of the West" 1972-Ital.

Martino, Luciano. Screenwriter. Films: "Buffalo Bill, Hero of the Far West" 1964-Ital./Ger./Fr.: "10,000 Dollars Blood Money" 1966-Ital. (& story); "Beast" 1970-Ital. (& sp.); "Arizona Colt" 1965-Ital./Fr./Span.; "For One Hundred Thousand Dollars Per Killing" 1967-Ital.; "Man Called Blade" 1977-Ital. (prod. only).

Martino, Sergio. Director. Films: "For One Hundred Thousand Dollars Per Killing" 1967-Ital. (sp. only); "Arizona" 1970-Ital./Span.; "Man Called Blade" 1977-Ital. (& sp.).

Martinson, Leslie H. Director. TV: *The Roy Rogers Show*—1951-57 (prod.), "Pat's Inheritance" 11-11-53, "The Peddler from the Pecos" 12-13-53, "Bad Company" 12-27-53, "Little Dynamite" 1-3-54, "The Kid from Silver City" 1-17-54, "The Secret of Indian Gap" 1-24-54, "The Deputy Sheriff" 2-7-54, "The High-Graders of Paradise Valley" 2-28-54, "The Land Swindle" 3-14-54, "Head for Cover" 10-21-56, "Paleface Justice" 11-18-56, "Fighting Sire" 12-16-56; *Cheyenne* 1955; *Colt .45* 1957; *Sugarfoot* 1957; *Maverick*—"Ghost Riders" 10-13-57, "Stage West" 10-27-57, "Relic of Fort Tejon" 11-3-57, "The Jeweled Gun" 11-24-57, "A Rage for Vengeance" 1-12-58, "Day of Reckoning" 2-2-58, "Black Fire" 3-16-58, "The Belcastle Brand" 10-12-58, "Shady Deal at Sunny Acres" 11-23-58, "Gun-Shy" 1-11-59, "The Rivals" 1-25-59, "The Saga of Waco Williams" 2-15-59, "Betrayal" 3-22-59, "A Tale of Three Cities" 10-18-59, "The Ghost Soldiers" 11-8-59, "Bundle from Britain" 9-18-60, "Hadley's Hunters" 9-25-60, "Triple Indemnity" 3-19-61; *Bronco* 1958; *Lawman* 1958; *The Alaskans* 1959; *Temple Houston* 1963; *Alias Smith and Jones*—The Girl in Boxcar Number Three" 2-11-71; *Young Maverick*—"Hearts O'Gold" 12-12-79.

Martinson, Richard. Writer. Films: "Branded a Coward" 1935 (story).

Marton, Andrew (1904-1/7/92). Director. Films: "Gentle Annie" 1944; "The Wild North" 1952; "Africa—Texas Style!" 1967-U.S./Brit. (& sp.).

Marton, Pierre. Screenwriter. Films: "Skin Game" 1971.

Marvin, Joseph. *see* Merino, Jose.

Marx, Samuel (1902-3/2/92). Producer. Films: "Northwest Rangers" 1942; "Apache Trail" 1943; "Kiss of Fire" 1955.

Mascott, Laurence. Screenwriter. Films: "Ten Days to Tulara" 1958.

Masella, Fulvio. Writer. Films: "My Name Is Nobody" 1973-Ital. (story).

Masini, Luigi. Screenwriter. Films: "Deat at Owell Rock" 1967-Ital.

Maslansky, Paul (1933-). Producer. Films: "The Gun and the Pulpit" TVM-1974.

Mason, Leslie. Screenwriter. Films: "Senor Americano" 1929; "The Wagon Master" 1929; "The Fighting Legion" 1930; "Mountain Justice" 1930; "Sons of the Saddle" 1930; "The Man from Monterey" 1933.

Mason, Lucky. Screenwriter. Films: "Parade of the West" 1930.

Mason, Mildred. Writer. Films: "Men of the Mountain" 1915 (story); "The Trapper's Revenge" 1915 (story).

Mason, Noel. Director. Films: "Yankee Don" 1931.

Mason, Sarah Y. Screenwriter. Films: "One Hour of Love" 1927.

Mason, Scott. Screenwriter. Films: "Ride Him, Cowboy" 1932.

Massaccesi, Scandariato. Screenwriter. Films: "Bounty Hunter in Trinity" 1972-Ital.

Massaccessi, Aristide (Jo D'Amato). Director. Films: "Red Coat" 1975-Ital. (& sp.).

Massi, Stelvio (Newman Rostel). Director. Films: "Halleluja to Vera Cruz" 1973-Ital.

Masters, E. Lanning. Writer. Films: "The Valley of Bravery" 1926 (story).

Matassi, Enzo. Director. Films: "Once Upon a Time in the Wild, Wild West" 1969-Ital.

Mate, Rudolph (1898-10/27/64). Director. Films: "Branded" 1951; "The Siege at Red River" 1954; "The Far Horizons" 1955; "The Violent Men" 1955; "The Rawhide Years" 1956; "Three Violent People" 1956.

Mathis, June (1889-7/26/27). Screenwriter. Films: "The Trail of the Shadow" 1917; "The Claim" 1918; "The Trail to Yesterday" 1918; "The Desert Flower" 1925.

Mathison, Melissa (1949-). Screenwriter. Films: "Son of the Morning Star" TVM-1991.

Matofsky, Harvey (1933-1/3/94). Producer. Films: "Zandy's Bride" 1974.

Mattei, Bruno (Werner Knox, Vincent Dawn). Director. Films:

"White Apache" 1984-Ital./Span.; "Scalps" 1986-Ital./Ger. (& sp.).

Mattela, Raifaela. Screenwriter. Films: "Ace High" 1967-Ital./Span.

Matthews, David. Screenwriter. "Cody of the Pony Express" 1950-serial.

Matthews, Dorcas. Director. Films: "Refuge" 1915.

Mattison, Frank S. Director. Films: "The Better Man Wins" 1922 (& sp.); "The Lone Wagon" 1923; "The Last White Man" 1924; "Kit Carson Over the Great Divide" 1925 (& sp.); "Buffalo Bill on the U.P. Trail" 1926; "Code of the Northwest" 1926 (& story); "Daniel Boone Thru the Wilderness" 1926; "King of the Herd" 1927.

Mattoli, Mario. Director. Films: "For a Few Dollars Less" 1966-Ital.

Mattox, Walt. Producer. Films: "White Stallion" 1947; "Deadline" 1948; "Fighting Mustang" 1948; "Sunset Carson Rides Again" 1948; "Battling Marshal" 1950.

Matzen, Madeline. Screenwriter. Films: "Bulldog Pluck" 1927; "The Fighting Hombre" 1927.

Maurer, Norman (1926-11/23/86). Director. Films: "The Outlaws Is Coming!" 1965 (& prod./story).

Mauri, Roberto (Robert Johnson). Director. Films: "Colorado Charlie" 1965-Ital./Span.; "Shotgun" 1969-Ital. & (sp.); "Sartana in the Valley of Death" 1970-Ital. (& sp.); "Wanted Sabata" 1970-Ital. (& sp.); "Death Is Sweet from the Soldier of God" 1972-Ital. (& sp.); "He Was Called the Holy Ghost" 1972-Ital. (& sp.); "Animal Called Man" 1973-Ital. (& sp.); "Gunmen and the Holy Ghost" 1973-Ital. (& sp.).

Maurizzo, Giorgio (George Mc-Roots). Films: "Apahe Woman" 1975-Ital. (& sp.).

Maxwell, E.C. Screenwriter. Films: "The Old Code" 1928.

Maxwell, Paul. see Bianchini, Paolo.

May, Karl Friedrich. Writer. Films: "Treasure of Silver Lake" 1963-Fr./Ger./Yugo. (story); "Among Vultures" 1964-Ger./Ital./Fr./Yugo. (story); "Apache Gold" 1965-Ger. (story); "The Desperado Trail" 1965-Ger./Yugo. (story); "Flaming Frontier" 1965-Ger./Yugo. (story); "Pyramid of the Sun God" 1965-Ger./Ital./Fr. (story); "Rampage at Apache Wells" 1965-Ger./Yugo. (story); "Last of the Renegades" 1966-Fr./Ital./Ger./Yugo. (story).

Mayberry, Russ. Director. TV:

Alias Smith and Jones—The Night of the Red Dog" 11-4-71; *Paradise*—"Home Again" 9-16-89, "Orphan Train" 10-28-89.

Mayer, Gerald (1919-). Director. Films: "Inside Straight" 1951; "The Marauders" 1955. ¶TV: *Gunsmoke*—"The Wake" 12-10-60, "Big Man" 3-25-61, "The Squaw" 11-11-61; *Shane* 1966; *Bonanza*—"Showdown at Tahoe" 11-19-67, "Justice Deferred" 12-17-67; *Cimarron Strip*—"Sound of a Drum" 2-1-68, "The Blue Moon Train" 2-15-68; *Nichols* 1971.

Mayer, Louis B. (1885-10/29/57). Producer. Films: "The Eternal Struggle" 1923.

Mayes, Wendell. Screenwriter. Films: "From Hell to Texas" 1958; "The Hanging Tree" 1959; "North to Alaska" 1960; "The Stalking Moon" 1969; "The Revengers" 1972-U.S./Mex.

Maynard, Ken (1895-3/23/73). Director. Films: "Senor Americano" 1929 (prod. only); "The Wagon Master" 1929 (prod. only); "The Fighting Legion" 1930 (& prod.); "Lucky Larkin" 1930 (prod. only); "Mountain Justice" 1930 (prod. only); "Parade of the West" 1930 (prod. only); "Sons of the Saddle" 1930 (prod. only); "King of the Arena" 1933; "The Trail Drive" 1933 (prod. only); "Strawberry Roan" 1933 (prod. only); "The Fiddlin' Buckaroo" 1934 (& prod.); "Gun Justice" 1934; "Honor of the Range" 1934; "Smoking Guns" 1934 (prod./story only); "Wheels of Destiny" 1934 (prod. only); "Heir to Trouble" 1935 (story only); "Western Frontier" 1935 (story only); "Song of the Cabellero" 1939 (prod. only).

Mayo, Melvin. Director. Films: "None So Blind" 1916.

Mazzuca, Joseph. Director. TV: *The Big Valley*—"The Lady from Mesa" 4-3-67, "A Noose Is Waiting" 11-13-67, "The Buffalo Man" 12-25-67, "The Good Thieves" 1-1-68, "The Secret" 1-27-69.

Meadows, Herb. Screenwriter. Films: "The Redhead from Wyoming" 1953; "Count Three and Pray" 1955; "Stranger on Horseback" 1955; "The Lone Ranger" 1956. ¶TV: *The Man from Blackhawk* 1959-60 (prod.).

Meagher, Edward J. Screenwriter. Films: "Tracked in the Snow Country" 1925; "Night Cry" 1926 (story only); "Burning Brides" 1928; "The Overland Telegraph" 1929.

Meals, A.R. Director. Films: "The Unknown Rider" 1929.

Medak, Peter. Director. Films: "Zorro, the Gay Blade" 1981.

Medford, Don (1920-). Director. Films: "The Hunting Party" 1971-Brit./Ital./Span. ¶TV: *The Rifleman*—"The Mind Reader" 6-30-59, "Obituary" 10-20-59, "The Vision" 3-22-60, "The Lariat" 3-29-60, "Meeting at Midnight" 5-17-60, "The Illustrator" 12-13-60, "The Silent Knife" 12-20-60; *The Dick Powell Show*—"Colossus" 3-12-63; *Cimarron Strip*—"The Battleground" 9-28-67; *Lancer*—"Warburton's Edge" 2-4-69.

Medford, Harold (1911-10/26/77). Screenwriter. Films: "Smoky" 1966.

Meehan, Elizabeth. Screenwriter. Films: "Northwest Outpost" 1947.

Meehan, Lew (1890-8/10/51). Screenwriter. Films: "The Ranger and the Law" 1921; "The Masked Avenger" 1922; "Silver Spurs" 1922.

Meins, Gus (1893-8/4/40). Director. Films: "The Californian" 1937; "Roll Along, Cowboy" 1937.

Melford, Frank. Producer. Films: "The Cowboy Star" 1936 (sp. only); "Massacre River" 1949; "Rogue River" 1950; "Fort Defiance" 1951.

Melford, George (1877-4/25/61). Director. Films: "Arizona Bill" 1911 (& sp.); "The Bugler of Battery B" 1912; "The Attack at Rocky Pass" 1913; "The Invaders 1913; "The Last Blockhouse" 1913; "The Brand" 1914 (& sp.); "Tennessee's Pardner" 1916; "The Cost of Hatred" 1917; "Nan of Music Mountain" 1917; "On the Level" 1917; "The Sunset Trail" 1917; "Told in the Hills" 1919; "The Round Up" 1920; "Salomy Jane" 1923; "The Flame of the Yukon" 1926; "Whispering Smith" 1926; "The Boiling Point" 1932; "Cowboy Counsellor" 1933; "The Dude Bandit" 1933; "Man of Action" 1933.

Mellone, Amedeo. Screenwriter. Films: "Seven Dollars on the Red" 1968-Ital./Span.

Melson, John. Screenwriter. Films: "Savage Pampas" 1966-U.S./Span./Arg.

Meltzer, Lewis (1910-2/23/95). Screenwriter. Films: "Texas" 1941 (& story); "Comanche Territory" 1950; "Along the Great Divide" 1951; "Shark River" 1953.

Melville, Wilbert. Director. Films: "The Mexican Spy" 1913.

Mendez, Fernando. Director. Films: "The Legend of a Bandit" 1945-Mex.

Mendez, Jose Briz (Gilbert Lee Kay). Director. Films: "The White Comanche" 1967-Ital./Span./U.S. (& sp.).

Menzies, William Cameron (1896-3/5/57). Director. Films: "Drums in the Deep South" 1951.

Merchant, Jay. Director. Films: "A Battle Against Odds" 1921.

Merchant, Joaquin Romero. *see* Romero Marchant, Joaquin.

Merchant, Rafael Romero. *see* Romero Marchent, Rafael

Meredith, Sean. Screenwriter. Films: "James A. Michener's Texas" TVM-1995.

Meredyth, Bess (1890-7/13/69). Screenwriter. Films: "The Mystery of Yellow Aster Mine" 1913; "The Trey O'Hearts" 1914-serial; "The Ghost Wagon" 1915; "Pay Me!" 1917; "The Red, Red Heart" 1918"The Fighting Breed" 1921; "Rose of the Golden West" 1927; "Mark of Zorro" 1940 (adapt. only).

Meredyth, F.A. Screenwriter. Films: "A 45 Calibre Mystery" 1917.

Merighi, Ferdinando. Screenwriter. Films: "They Called Him Trinity" 1972-Ital./Span.

Merino, Jose Luis (Joseph Marvin). Director. Films: "Duel in the Eclipse" 1967-Span.; "Kitosch, the Man Who Came from the North" 1967-Ital./Span. (& sp.); "Machine Gun Killers" 1968-Ital./Span. (sp. only); "More Dollars for the MacGregors" 1970-Ital./Span. (& sp.); "Zorro, Rider of Vengeance" 1971-Span./Ital. (& sp.).

Merlich, Jack. Writer. Films: "The Gun and the Pulpit" TVM-1974 (story).

Merlin, Milton. Screenwriter. Films: "Henry Goes Arizona" 1939; "The Kid from Texas" 1939 (story).

Merolle, Sergio. Director. Films: "Cost of Dying" 1968-Ital./Fr.

Merrick, George M. Screenwriter. Films: "The Terror of Bar X" 1927; "Cyclone of the Saddle" 1935; "Fighting Caballero" 1935; "Pals of the Range" 1935 (& prod.); "Rough Riding Ranger" 1935 (& prod.); "Custer's Last Stand" 1936-serial (prod. only).

Merrick, Monte. Screenwriter. Films: "8 Seconds" 1994.

Merrill, Keith. Director. Films: "The Great American Cowboy" 1974 (& prod.); "Windwalker" 1980.

Merritt, Helen. Screenwriter. Films: "Opitsah" 1912.

Mersereau, Jack. Screenwriter. Films: "Whispering Canyon" 1926; "Texas Trail" 1937; "Hidden Gold" 1940.

Merton, Roger. Screenwriter.

Films: "Down the Wyoming Trail" 1939; "The Golden Trail" 1940; "Rainbow Over the Range" 1940; "Roll, Wagons, Roll" 1940; "King of the Stallions" 1942 (story only).

Merwin, Bannister. Director. Films: "A Cowboy's Stratagem" 1912 (& sp.); "The Red Man's Burden" 1912 (& sp.).

Metzenni, Leo. Screenwriter. Films: "Last Ride to Santa Cruz" 1969-Ger./Fr.

Metzler, Robert. Screenwriter. Films: "Riders of the Purple Sage" 1941; "Sundown Jim" 1942.

Meyer, Cleve. Screenwriter. Films: "Code of the Range" 1927.

Meyer, Jeffrey M. Screenwriter. Films: "Conagher" TVM-1991.

Meyer, Marc. *see* Bazzoni, Luigi.

Meyer, Nicholas (1945-). Screenwriter. Films: "Sommersby" 1993 (& story).

Meyers, Henry. Screenwriter. Films: "Destry Rides Again" 1939.

Michaelian, Michael. Screenwriter. Films: "Miracle in the Wilderness" TVM-1991.

Michaels, Lorne (1945-). Screenwriter. Films: "Three Amios" 1986 (& prod.).

Michaels, Richard. Director. Films: "Charlie Cobb: Nice Night for a Hanging" TVM-1977. ¶TV: *Big Hawaii* 1977.

Michener, James A. (1907-). Writer. Films: "James A. Michener's Texas" TVM-1995 (story).

Michili, Ornella. Screenwriter. Films: "Silver Saddle" 1978-Ital.

Middleton, George E. Director. Films: "The Lily of Poverty Flat" 1915; "The Heart of Juanita" 1919; "Just Squaw" 1919; "The Flame of Hellgate" 1920.

Middleton, Roy. Screenwriter. Films: "Calibre 38" 1919.

Middleton, T.P. Writer. Films: "The Castle Ranch" 1915 (story).

Miehe, Ulf. Screenwriter. Films: "Yankee Dudler" 1973-Ger./Span.

Mighels, Philip Verrill. Writer. "If Only Jim" 1921 (story).

Migliorini, Romano. Screenwriter. Films: "Bandidos" 1967-Ital.; "Miss Dynamite" 1972-Ital./Fr.

Miles, John Anthony. Screenwriter. Films: "Trail of Hate" 1922.

Milestone, Lewis (1895-9/25/80). Director. Films: "Kangaroo" 1952. ¶TV: *Have Gun Will Travel*—"Hey Boy's Revenge" 4-12-58.

Milicevic, Djordje. Screenwriter. Films: "Iron Will" 1994.

Milius, John (1944-). Screenwriter. Films: "Jeremiah Johnson" 1972; "The Life and Times of Judge Roy Bean" 1972; "Geronimo: An American Legend" 1993 (& story).

Milland, Oscar. Screenwriter. Films: "The Reward" 1965.

Milland, Ray (1908-3/10/86). Director. Films: "A Man Alone" 1955.

Millard, Stuart (1929-). Director. Films: "Little Big Man" 1971 (prod. only); "When the Legends Die" 1972 (& prod.); "Rooster Cogburn" 1975.

Millarde, Harry (1885-11/2/31). Director. Films: "Rose of the West" 1919; "Sacred Silence" 1919.

Miller, Arthur. Screenwriter. Films: "The Misfits" 1961.

Miller, Ashley (1867-11/19/49). Director. Films: "Joyce of the North Woods" 1913.

Miller, Bill (1887-11/12/39). Director. Films: "The Fighting Ranger" 1922.

Miller, Charles. Director. Films: "The Flame of the Yukon" 1917; "The Law of the Yukon" 1920; "The Man She Brought Back" 1922.

Miller, David (1909-4/14/92). Director. Films: "Billy the Kid" 1941; "Lonely Are the Brave" 1962.

Miller, Edward G. *see* Mulargia, Edoardo.

Miller, George (1943-). Director. Films: "The Man from Snowy River" 1982-Australia.

Miller, James M. Screenwriter. Films: "Testimony of Two Men" TVM-1977.

Miller, Jennifer. Screenwriter. Films: "Testimony of Two Men" TVM-1977.

Miller, Marvin (1913-2/8/85). Producer. Films: "Man and Boy" 1971.

Miller, Robert Alan. Screenwriter. Films: "The Westward Trail" 1948.

Miller, Robert Ellis (1927-). Director. TV: *The Virginian*—"Vengeance Is the Spur" 2-27-63, "To Make This Place Remember" 9-25-63.

Miller, Ron. Producer. Films: "Ride a Northbound Horse" 1969; "The Wild Country" 1971; "The Castaway Cowboy" 1974; "Hot Lead and Cold Feet" 1978; "The Apple Dumpling Gang Rides Again" 1979.

Miller, Ronald. Screenwriter. Films: "Rose Marie" 1954.

Miller, Seton I. (1902-3/29/74). Producer. Films: "The Lone Star Ranger" 1930 (sp. only); "California" 1946.

Miller, Winston (1911-6/21/94). Screenwriter. Films: "Vigilantes Are Coming" 1936-serial (story only); "The Painted Stallion" 1937-serial; "Carolina Moon" 1940; "Ride, Tenderfoot, Ride" 1940; "The Medico of Painted Springs" 1941; "Prairie Stranger" 1941; "The Royal Mounted Patrol" 1941; "Heart of the Rio Grande" 1942; "Man from Cheyenne" 1942; "Song of Texas" 1943; "My Darling Clementine" 1946; "Fury at Furnace Creek" 1948; "Relentless" 1948; "Station West" 1948; "Rocky Mountain" 1950; "The Last Outpost" 1951; "The Vanquished" 1953; "The Bounty Hunter" 1954 (& story); "The Boy from Oklahoma" 1954; "The Far Horizons" 1955; "Run for Cover" 1955; "Tension at Table Rock" 1956; "Female Artillery" TVM-1973 (prod. only). ¶TV: *The Virginian* 1962-70 (prod.); *Little House on the Prairie* 1974-82 (prod.).

Millhauser, Bertram (1892-12/1/58). Director. Films: "The Challenge" 1916 (sp. only); "The Phantom Foe" 1920-serial; "The Smoking Trail" 1924; "The Texans" 1938 (sp. only); "River's End" 1940 (prod. only).

Milligan, Bill. Writer. Films: "Lightning Guns" 1950 (story).

Milne, Peter. Screenwriter. Films: "God's Country and the Woman" 1937 (story only); "Rancho Grande" 1940 (& story).

Milton, A.R. Screenwriter. Films: "Buffalo Gun" 1961 (& prod.).

Milton, George. *see* Sayre, George & Raison, Milton.

Minardi, Ofelia. Screenwriter. Films: "Halleluja to Vera Cruz" 1973-Ital.

Mindlin, Frederick Arthur. Writer. Films: "Out of the West" 1926 (story); "Tom and His Pals" 1926 (story).

Miner, Allen H. Director. Films: "Ghost Town" 1956; "Black Patch" 1957 (& prod.); "The Ride Back" 1957. ¶TV: *Wagon Train*—"The Charles Maury Story" 5-7-58, "The Doctor Willoughby Story" 11-5-58, "The Flint McCullough Story" 1-14-59, "The Hunter Malloy Story" 1-21-59, "The Ella Lindstrom Story" 2-4-59, "The Elizabeth McQueeney Story" 10-28-59, "The Ricky and Laura Bell Story" 2-24-60, "The Maggie Hamilton Story" 4-6-60, "The Sam Pulaski Story" 11-4-63,

"The Kitty Pryer Story" 11-18-63, "The Story of Cain" 12-16-63, "The Stark Bluff Story" 4-6-64, "The Last Circle Up" 4-27-64, "The Story of Hector Heatherington" 12-20-64.

Miner, Worthington (1900-12/11/82). Producer. TV: *Frontier* 1955-56.

Mintz, Sam. Screenwriter. Films: "The Gay Defender" 1927; "Shootin' Irons" 1927; ; "Avalanche" 1928; "Stairs of Sand" 1929; "The Santa Fe Trail" 1930 (& prod.).

Miraglia, Emilio P. (Hal Brady). Director. Films: "Shoot Joe, and Shoot Again" 1972-Ital. (& sp.).

Miret, Pedro. Screenwriter. Films: "Lucky Johnny: Born in America" 1973-Ital./Mex.

Mirisch, Andrew. Writer. Films: "Desperado: Badlands Justice" TVM-1989 (story); "Desperado: The Outlaw Wars" TVM-1989 (story).

Mirisch, Walter M. (1921-). Producer. Films: "Cavalry Scout" 1951; "Fort Osage" 1952; "Hiawatha" 1952; "Rodeo" 1952; "Wild Stallion" 1952; "Wichita" 1955; "The First Texan" 1956; "The Oklahoman" 1957; "The Tall Stranger" 1957; "Fort Massacre" 1958; "Man of the West" 1958; "Cast a Long Shadow" 1959; "The Gunfight at Dodge City" 1959; "The Spikes Gang" 1974. ¶TV: *Wichita Town* 1959-60.

Mitchell, Bruce (1880-9/26/52). Director. Films: "The Stranger of the Hills" 1922; "The Hellion" 1924; "Tricks" 1925; "The Battling Buckaroo" 1927; "Blind Man's Bluff" 1927; "Danger Ahead" 1927; "Dangerous Double" 1927; "Ridin' Wild" 1927; "The Scrappin' Fool" 1927; "Sky-High Saunders" 1927 (& sp.); "Boss of the Rancho" 1928; "The Brand of Courage" 1928; "Framed" 1928; "The Getaway Kid" 1928; "The Gold Claim" 1928; "Hidden Money" 1928; "The Looters" 1928; "The Payroll Roundup" 1928; "The Phantom Flyer" 1928 (& sp.); "The Valiant Rider" 1928; "Beyond the Smoke" 1929; "Born to the Saddle" 1929; "The Danger Line" 1929; "In Line of Duty" 1929; "Forty-Five Calibre Echo" 1932.

Mitchell, Howard M. (1887-10/4/58). Director. Films: "Petticoats and Politics" 1918; "The Crusader" 1922; "Man's Size" 1923; "Romance Rance" 1924.

Mitchell, Sidney. Screenwriter. Films: "Smoke Lightning" 1933.

Mix, Tom (1880-10/12/40). Director. Films: "A Child of the Prairies" 1913 (story only); "The Law and the Outlaw" 1913 (story only); "Local Color" 1913 (& story); "The Sheriff and the Rustler" 1913 (story only); "Cactus Jake, Heart-Breaker" 1914; "Jimmy Hayes and Muriel" 1914; "The Man from the East" 1914 (& story); "The Mexican" 1914; "A Militant School Ma'am" 1914; "The Moving Picture Cowboy" 1914 (& story); "The Ranger's Romance" 1914 (& story); "The Real Thing in Cowboys" 1914; "The Rival Stage Lines" 1914; "Saved by a Watch" 1914 (& sp.); "The Scapegoat" 1914 (& story); "The Sheriff's Reward" 1914 (& story); "The Telltale Knife" 1914 (& story); "The Way of the Redman" 1914 (& story); "Why the Sheriff Is a Bachelor" 1914 (& story); "An Arizona Wooing" 1915; "Athletic Ambitions" 1915; "The Auction Sale of Run-Down Ranch" 1915; "Bad Man Bobbs" 1915; "Bill Haywood, Producer" 1915 (& story); "The Brave Deserve the Fair" 1915 (& story); "Cactus Jim's Shopgirl" 1915; "The Chef at Circle G" 1915; "A Child of the Prairie" 1915 (& story); "The Child, the Dog, and the Villain" 1915; "The Conversion of Smiling Tom" 1915; "The Foreman of the Bar-Z Ranch" 1915; "Forked Trails" 1915; "Getting a Start in Life" 1915; "The Girl and the Mail Bag" 1915; "The Gold Dust and the Squaw" 1915; "The Grizzly Gulch Chariot Race" 1915; "Harold's Bad Man" 1915; "The Heart of the Sheriff" 1915 (& sp.); "Her Slight Mistake" 1915; "How Weary Went Wooing" 1915; "The Impersonation of Tom" 1915; "A Lucky Deal" 1915 (& sp.); "The Man from Texas" 1915 (& story); "Ma's Girls" 1915 (& story); "A Matrimonial Boomerang" 1915; "Mrs. Murphy's Cooks" 1915 (& story); "Never Again" 1915 (& story); "On the Eagle Trail" 1915; "The Outlaw's Bride" 1915; "Pals in Blue" 1915 (& sp.); "The Race for a Gold Mine" 1915; "The Range Girl and the Cowboy" 1915 (& story); "Roping a Bride" 1915; "Sagebrush Tom" 1915 (& story); "Saved by Her Horse" 1915; "The Stagecoach Driver and the Girl" 1915 (& sp.); "The Stagecoach Guard" 1915 (& story); "The Taking of Mustang Pete" 1915; "The Tenderfoot's Triumph" 1915; "With the Aid of the Law" 1915; "An Angelic Attitude" 1916; "Along the Border" 1916 (& story); "A Bear of a Story" 1916 (& story); "The Canby Hill Outlaws" 1916 (& story); "A Close Call" 1916 (& story); "A Corner in Water" 1916 (& story); "The Cowpuncher's Peril" 1916 (& story); "Crooked Trails" 1916 (& story); "The Desert Calls Its

Own" 1916; "An Eventful Evening" 1916; "The Girl of Gold Gulch" 1916 (& story); "Going West to Make Good" 1916 (& story); "The Golden Thought" 1916; "In the Days of Daring" 1916 (& story); "Legal Advice" 1916 (& story); "Local Color" 1916 (& story); "Making Good" 1916 (& story); "The Man Within" 1916; "A Mistake in Rustlers" 1916 (& story); "Mistakes Will Happen" 1916 (& story); "A Mix-Up in Movies" 1916 (& story); "The Passing of Pete" 1916 (& story); "The Pony Express Rider" 1916 (& story); "The Raiders" 1916 (& story); "Roping a Sweetheart" 1916 (& story); "The Sheriff's Blunder" 1916 (& story); "The Sheriff's Duty" 1916 (& story); "Shooting Up the Movies" 1916 (& story); "Starring in Western Stuff" 1916 (& story); "Taking a Chance" 1916 (& story); "The Taming of Groucho Bill" 1916 (& story); "Tom's Sacrifice" 1916 (& story); "Tom's Strategy" 1916 (& story); "Too Many Chefs" 1916 (& story); "Trilby's Love Disaster" 1916 (& story); "Twisted Trails" 1916; "A Western Masquerade" 1916 (& story); "When Cupid Slipped" 1916 (& story); "Hearts and Saddles" 1917 (& story); "The Luck That Jealousy Brought" 1917; "The Saddle Girth" 1917 (& story); "A Soft Tenderfoot" 1917 (& sp.); "Tom and Jerry Mix" 1917 (& sp.); "Slim Higgins" 1919 (& story); "The Daredevil" 1920; "A Child of the Prairie" 1925 (& story).

Mizrani, Hy. Screenwriter. Films: "The Animals" 1971.

Moberg, Vilhelm (1898-8/8/73). Writer. Films: "The New Land" 1973-Swed. (story).

Moder, Dick. Director. TV: *Zane Grey Theater* 1956; *Johnny Ringo* 1959; *The Rifleman*—"Dead Cold Cash" 11-22-60, "The Promoter" 12-6-60; *Bonanza*—"Cut-Throat Junction" 3-18-61.

Moder, Mike. TV: *Wild Wild West*—"The Night of the Death Masks" 1-26-68, "The Night of the Fugitives" 11-8-68, "The Night of the Cossacks" 3-21-69, "The Night of the Tycoons" 3-28-69.

Moffa, Paolo (John Byrd). Director. Films: "Bury Them Deep" 1968-Ital. (& sp.); "I Am Sartana, Your Angel of Death" 1969-Ital./Fr. (prod. only).

Moffat, Edward Stewart. Writer. Films: "Revenge" 1918 (story).

Moffat, Ivan. Screenwriter. Films: "Giant" 1956; "They Came to Cordura" 1959.

Moffett, John. Screenwriter. Films: "Rhythm on the Range" 1936.

Moffitt, Jefferson. Screenwriter. Films: "In the Days of Daniel Boone" 1923-serial; "The Oregon Trail" 1923-serial; "The Cowboy and the Flapper" 1924 (story only).

Moffitt, Jack. Screenwriter. Films: "Melody Ranch" 1940; "Ramrod" 1947.

Molla, Jose Luis Martinez. Screenwriter. Films: "A Bullet for Sandoval" 1970-Ital./Span.

Mollica, Antonio (Tony Mulligan). Director. Films: "Born to Kill" 1967-Ital. (& sp.).

Mollo, Gumersindo. Screenwriter. Films: "God Forgives—I Don't" 1966-Ital./Span.

Molteni, Ambrogio. Screenwriter. Films: "Last Gun" 1964-Ital.; "Three Graves for a Winchester" 1966-Ital.

Molter, Bennett A. Screenwriter. Films: "The Sea Gull" 1914.

Momplet, Antonio. Director. Films: "Terrible Sheriff" 1963-Span./Ital.

Monaghan, Jay. Writer. Films: "Bad Men of Tombstone" 1949 (story).

Mondello, Luigi. Producer. Films: "Rattler Kid" 1968-Ital./Span.; "Raise Your Hands, Dead Man ... You're Under Arrest" 1971-Ital./Span.

Mong, William V. (1875-12/11/40). Director. Films: "Told in the Rockies" 1915 (sp. only); "Birds of a Feather" 1916 (& story); "Wild Sumac" 1917.

Monicada, Santiago. Screenwriter. Films: "Awkward Hands" 1968-Span./Ital.; "Sartana Kills Them All" 1970-Ital./Span.; "Cut-Throats Nine" 1973-Span./Ital.

Montagne, Edward J. Screenwriter. Films: "Billy the Kid" 1911; "Sunlight's Last Raid" 1917; "Vengeance and the Woman" 1917-serial; "The Dawn of Understanding" 1918; "Channing of the Northwest" 1922; "The Last of the Duanes" 1924 (prod. only); "Flaming Frontier" 1926.

Montagne, Edward J. Producer. Films: "The Shakiest Gun in the West" 1968; "High Noon, Part II: The Return of Will Kane" TVM-1980. ¶TV: *The Tall Man* 1960-62 (exec. prod.).

Montague, John. Screenwriter. Films: "Get Your Man" 1921; "Straight from the Shoulder" 1921.

Montaigue, Josef. Writer. Films: "Range War" 1939 (story).

Montana, Monte. Producer. Films: "Gunsmoke on the Guadalupe" 1935; "Gun Smoke" 1936.

Montefiore, Luigi (George Eastman). Screenwriter. Films: "Ben and Charlie" 1970-Ital.; "Keoma" 1975-Ital./Span.

Montemurro, Francesco (Jean Monty). Director. Films: "Zorro, the Navarra Marquis" 1969-Ital./Span. (& sp.).

Monter, Luis. *see* Montero, Roberto.

Montero, Roberto Bianchi (Luis Monter). Director. Films: "Man from Oklahoma" 1965-Ital./Span./Ger.; "Seven Pistols for a Gringo" 1967-Ital./Span. (sp. only); "Sheriff Won't Shoot" 1967-Ital./Fr./Brit. (& sp.); "Two Sides of the Dollar" 1967-Fr./Ital.; "Death Is Sweet from the Soldier of God" 1972-Ital. (sp. only); "Durango Is Coming, Pay or Die" 1972-Ital./Span.; "Thunder Over El Paso" 1972-Ital./Span.

Montgomery, Frank E. Director. Films: "A Frontier Girl's Courage" 1911; "The Cowboy's Adopted Child" 1911 (& sp.); "In the Days of Gold" 1911 (story only); "The Night Herder" 1911 (& sp.); "The Bandit's Mask" 1912; "Big Rock's Last Stand" 1912; "A Broken Spur" 1912; "A Crucial Test" 1912 (& sp.); "Darkfeather's Strategy" 1912; "The End of the Romance" 1912; "The Massacre of Santa Fe Trail" 1912; "The Shrinking Rawhide" 1912; "Tenderfoot Bob's Resignation" 1912; "A Forest Romance" 1913; "An Indian's Honor" 1913; "The Fuse of Death" 1914; "Kidnapped by Indians" 1914; "Priest or Medicine Man?" 1914; "The Vanishing Tribe" 1914; "The Western Border" 1915 (sp. only).

Montgomery, James. Writer. Films: "Riding High" 1943 (story).

Montgomery, Rutherford. Writer. Films: "Mustang" 1959 (story).

Monty, Jean. *see* Montemurro, Francesco.

Mooch, Donal. *see* Forester, Frank.

Moody, H.G. Director. Films: "The Range Patrol" 1923; "Scars of Hate" 1923; "The Vow of Vengeance" 1923; "Beaten" 1924.

Moody, Ralph (1888-9/16/71). Writer. Films: "The Wild Country" 1971 (story).

Moody, William Vaughn (1869-1910). Writer. Films: "The Great Divide" 1915 (story); "The Great Divide" 1925 (story); "The Great Divide" 1929 (story); "Woman Hungry" 1931 (story).

Moomaw, L.H. Director. Films: "The Golden Trail" 1920.

Moore, Albert. *see* Zurli, Guido.

Moore, Brian. Screenwriter. Films: "Black Robe" 1991-Can./Australia.

Moore, Charles. Director. Films: "Treachery Rides the Trail" 1949-short.

Moore, Daniel. Screenwriter. Films: "The Last of the Mohicans" 1936.

Moore, Harold James. Director. Films: "Powder River Gunfire" 1948-short.

Moore, Irving J. Director. TV: *Lawman* 1958; *Maverick*—"Dodge City or Bust" 12-11-60, "The Bold Fenian Men" 12-18-60, "Flood's Folly" 2-19-61, "Dade City Dodge" 9-18-61, "The Golden Fleecing" 10-8-61, "Epitaph for a Gambler" 2-11-62, "The Maverick Report" 3-4-62; *Temple Houston* 1963; *Wild Wild West*—"The Night of the Glowing Corpse" 10-29-65, "The Night of the Red-Eyed Madman" 11-26-65, "The Night of the Howling Light" 12-17-65, "The Night the Dragon Screamed" 1-14-66, "The Night of the Grand Emire" 1-28-66, "The Night of the Puppeteer" 2-25-66, "The Night of the Burning Diamond" 4-8-66, "The Night of the Sudden Plague" 4-22-66, "The Night of the Golden Cobra" 9-23-66, "The Night of the Raven" 9-30-66, "The Night of the Watery Death" 11-11-66, "The Night of the Ready-Made Corpse" 11-25-66, "The Night of the Tottering Tontine" 1-6-67, "The Night of the Vicious Valentine" 2-10-67, "The Night of the Deadly Bubble" 2-24-67, "The Night of the Bogus Bandits" 4-7-67, "Night of the Bubbling Death" 9-8-67, "The Night of the Jack O'Diamonds" 10-6-67, "The Night of Montezuma's Hordes" 10-27-67, "The Night of the Circus of Death" 11-3-67, "The Night of the Death-Maker" 2-23-68, "The Night of the Big Blackmail" 9-27-68, "The Night of the Doomsday Formula" 10-4-68, "The Night of the Juggernaut" 10-11-68, "The Night of the Avaricious Actuary" 12-6-68, "The Night of the Janus" 2-15-69, "The Night of the Plague" 4-4-69; *Laredo*—"Quarter Past Eleven" 3-24-66, "Road to San Remo" 11-25-66; *Gunsmoke*—"Stage Stop" 11-26-66, "Noose of Gold" 3-4-67, "Ladies from St. Louis" 3-25-67, "Wonder" 12-18-67, "Baker's Dozen" 12-25-67, "The Gunrunners" 2-5-68, "The Night Riders" 2-24-69, "Lijah" 11-8-71, "No Tomorrow" 1-3-72, "The Fugitives" 10-23-72, "Eleven Dollars" 10-30-72, "Arizona Midnight" 1-1-73, "The Child Between" 12-24-73, "Like Old Times" 1-21-74; *The Guns of Will Sonnett*—"Meeting at Devil's Fork" 10-27-67; *Here Come the Brides*—"Next Week, East Lynne" 10-17-69; *Dirty Sally* 1974; *The Quest*—"The Seminole Negro Indian Scouts" 1976; *The Life and Times of Grizzly Adams* 1977; *The Young Pioneers*—4-16-78; *How the West Was Won*—"Hillary" 2-26-79.

Moore, Lola D. Screenwriter. Films: "The Clean-Up Man" 1928.

Moore, Lucky. *see* Croccolo, Carlo.

Moore, Michael. Director. Films: "An Eye for an Eye" 1966; "The Fastest Guitar Alive" 1967; "Buckskin" 1968. ¶TV: *Hondo*—"Hondo and the War Hawks" 10-20-67, "Hondo and the Commancheros" 11-10-67, "Hondo and the Rebel Hat" 12-29-67; *Bonanza*—"False Witness" 10-22-67.

Moore, Simon. Screenwriter. Films: "The Quick and the Dead" 1995.

Moore, Vin (1878-12/5/49). Director. Films: "Brakin' Loose" 1925; "Just Cowboys" 1925; "Shootin' Wild" 1925; "Too Many Buck" 1925; "Barely Reasonable" 1926; "The Big Game" 1926; "Desperate Dan" 1926; "Fade Away Foster" 1926; "The Hen Punchers of Piperock" 1926; "The Hero of Piperock" 1926; "Let Loose" 1926; "A Man's Size Pet" 1926; "One Wild Time" 1926; "Piperock Goes Wild" 1926; "The Rescue" 1926; "When East Meets West" 1926; "Cows Is Cows" 1927; "Flaming Snow" 1927; "The Piperock Blaze" 1927; "The Pride of Peacock" 1927; "The Rest Cure" 1927; "A Strange Inheritance" 1927; "Tied Up" 1927; "Too Much Progress for Piperock" 1927; "When Oscar Went Wild" 1927; "Beauty and Bullets" 1928 (story only); "The Red Rider" 1934-serial (sp. only); "Rustlers of Red Dog" 1935-serial (sp. only).

Mora, Philippe. Director. Films: "Mad Dog Morgan" 1975-Australia (& sp.).

Morandi, Armando. Director. Films: "Patience Has a Limit, We Don't" 1974-Span./Ital.

Morandi, Fernando. Screenwriter. Films: "The Big Gundown"

1966-Ital. (story only); "Stranger in Paso Bravo" 1968-Ital.

Morante, Milburn (1887-1/28/64). Director. Films: "Hearts O' the Range" 1921; "Bucking the Truth" 1926; "Chasing Trouble" 1926; "The Escape" 1926.

Morayta, Miguel. Screenwriter. Films: "Guns for San Sebastian" 1967-U.S./Fr./Mex./Ital.

Mordini, Gino. Producer. Films: "Nephews of Zorro" 1969-Ital.; "Patience Has a Limit, We Don't" 1974-Span./Ital.

More, Julian. Screenwriter. Films: "The Valley of Gwangi" 1969.

Moreau, Emile. Writer. Films: "The Midnight Stage" 1919 (story).

Moreland, Wes. *see* Westmoreland, Forrest.

Moreno, David. Screenwriter. Films: "Coffin for the Sheriff" 1965-Ital./Span.

Morgan, Byron (1889-5/22/63). Screenwriter. Films: "Way Out West" 1930 (& story); "The Kid from Texas" 1939 (story only).

Morgan, George. Screenwriter. Films: "The Sheriff's Trap" 1915; "Bandits Beware" 1921; "The Cactus Kid" 1921; "Crossed Clues" 1921; "The Movie Trail" 1921; "Out O' Luck" 1921; "Who Was That Man?" 1921; "The Big Ranger" 1922; "Desperation" 1922 (story only); "Matching Wits" 1922; "Perils of the Yukon" 1922-serial; "The Trail of the Wolf" 1922; "Romance and Rustlers" 1925; "Fangs of Destiny" 1927; "Galloping Thunder" 1927; "One Glorious Scrap" 1927; "Burning the Wind" 1928; "The Clean-Up Man" 1928; "Plunging Hoofs" 1928; "The Two Outlaws" 1928; "King of the Rodeo" 1929; "Smilin' Guns" 1929; "Wild Blood" 1929; "The Avenger" 1931; "Cyclone Kid" 1931; "Headin' for Trouble" 1931; "Quick Trigger Lee" 1931; "The Devil Horse" 1932-serial; "The Red Rider" 1934-serial; "The Silent Code" 1935; "Deadwood Dick" 1940-serial; "Human Targets" 1932.

Morgan, J.P. Director. Films: "Quick Trigger Lee" 1931.

Morgan, John. Screenwriter. Films: "Trailing North" 1933.

Morgan, Marjorie. Screenwriter. Films: "Marie-Ann" 1978-Can.

Morgan, William. Director. Films: "Sierra Sue" 1941; "Sunset in Wyoming" 1941; "Bells of Capistrano" 1942; "Cowboy Serenade" 1942; "Heart of the Rio Grande"

1942; "Home in Wyomin'" 1942; "Stardust on the Sage" 1942.

Morheim, Lou. Producer. Films: "Wild Women" TVM-1970 (& sp.); "The Hunting Party" 1971-Brit./Ital./Span. (& sp./story); "A Cry in the Wilderness" TVM-1974. ¶TV: *The Big Valley* 1965-69.

Moroni, Mario. Director. Films: "Saguaro" 1968-Ital. (sp. only); "Mallory Must Not Die" 1971-Ital. (& sp.).

Morosco, Oliver (1876-8/25/45). Writer. Films: "The Half-Breed" 1922 (story).

Morosco, Walter (1899-12/30/48). Producer. Films: "The Gay Caballero" 1940; "The Cowboy and the Blonde" 1941.

Morris, Edmund. Screenwriter. Films: "The Savage Guns" 1961-U.S./Span.

Morris, Fred Lyon. *see* Batzella, Luigi.

Morris, Gordon (1899-4/7/40). Writer. Films: "Under the Pampas Moon" 1935 (story).

Morris, Howard (1925-). Director. TV: *Laredo*—"That's Noway, Thataway" 1-20-66.

Morris, Richard. Screenwriter. Films: "Take Me to Town" 1953.

Morrison, Robert E. Producer. Films: "Seven Men from Now" 1956; "Gun the Man Down" 1957; "Escort West" 1959.

Morrissey, Paul (1939-). Director. Films: "Lonesome Cowboys" 1968.

Morrow, Frank. Director. Films: "Let Him Buck" 1924; "Reckless Riding Bill" 1924.

Morrow, Honore. Writer. Films: "Seven Alone" 1974 (story).

Morrow, Vic (1932-7/23/82). Director. Films: "Man Called Sledge" 1971-Ital./U.S. (& sp.).

Morrow, William. Screenwriter. Films: "Buck Benny Rides Again" 1940.

Morse, Beatrice. Screenwriter. Films: "Who Knows?" 1918.

Morse, Hollingsworth (1910-1/23/88). Director. TV: *Broken Arrow* 1956; *Zorro*—"The Gay Caballero" 1-22-59, "Tornado Is Missing" 1-29-59, "Zorro Versus Cupid" 2-5-59, "The Missing Father" 2-26-59, "Please Believe Me" 3-5-59, "The Brooch" 3-12-59, "The Hound of the Sierras" 3-26-59, "Manhunt" 4-2-59, "The Man from Spain" 4-9-59, "Treasure for the King" 4-16-59, "Exposing the Tyrant" 4-23-59, "Zorro

Takes a Dare" 4-30-59, "An Affair of Honor" 5-7-59, "Invitation to Death" 5-21-59, "The Captain Regrets" 5-28-59, "Masquerade for Murder" 6-4-59, "Long Live the Governor" 6-11-59, "Finders Keepers" 7-2-59; *Laramie*—"The Killer Legend" 12-12-61, "The Unvanquished" 3-12-63, "Edge of Evil" 4-2-63; *Bonanza*—"Elegy for a Hangman" 1-20-63; *F Troop* 1965; *Laredo*—"The Legend of Midas Mantee" 9-16-66; *The Men from Shiloh* 1970-71; *The Oregon Trail* 1977; *Young Maverick*—"Half-Past Noon" 1-30-80.

Morse, John H. Director. TV: *The Lone Ranger*—"Damsels in Distress" 6-8-50, "Man Without a Gun" 6-16-50, "Pardon for Curley" 6-22-50, "White Man's Magic" 7-13-50, "Trouble for Tonto" 7-20-50, "Sheriff of Gunstock" 7-27-50, "The Whimsical Bandit" 8-31-50, "Double Jeopardy" 9-7-60, "Million Dollar Wallpaper" 9-14-50, "Danger Ahead" 10-12-50, "Crime in Time" 10-19-50, "Drink of Water" 10-26-50, "Bankers Choice" 11-23-50, "Desert Adventure" 11-30-50, "Bad Medicine" 12-7-50, "Letter of the Law" 1-4-51, "The Silent Voice" 1-11-51, "The Outcast" 1-18-51, "Two Gold Lockets" 2-15-51, "The Hooded Men" 2-22-51, "Special Edition" 9-25-52, "Desperado at Large" 10-2-52, "Through the Wall" 10-9-52, "Jeb's Gold Mine" 10-16-52, "Frame for Two" 10-23-52, "Ranger in Danger" 10-30-52, "Delayed Action" 11-6-52, "Word of Honor" 11-27-52, "Best Laid Plans" 12-25-52, "The Devil's Bog" 2-5-53, "Sinner by Proxy" 3-5-53, "Stage for Mademoiselle" 3-12-53, "Black Gold" 4-9-53, "The Durango Kid" 4-16-53, "The Deserter" 4-23-53, "Triple Cross" 5-21-53, "Death in the Forest" 6-4-53, "The Woman from Omaha" 7-2-53, "Stage to Estacado" 7-23-53, "Prisoner in Jeopardy" 8-20-53, "Diamond in the Rough" 8-27-53, "The Red Mark" 9-3-53; *Sky King* 1951.

Morse, Terry O. (1906-5/19/84). Director. Films: "Don Ricardo Returns" 1946; "The Bells of San Fernando" 1947.

Morsella, Fulvio. Screenwriter. Films: "For a Few Dollars More" 1965-Ital./Ger./Span.; "Once Upon a Time in the West" 1968-Ital.; "Duck, You Sucker!" 1971-Ital.; "Genius" 1975-Ital./Fr./Ger. (& prod.).

Mortimer, Edmund (1875-5/21/44). Director. Films: "Against All Odds" 1924; "The Desert Outlaw" 1924; "The Arizona Romeo" 1925 (& sp.); "Gold and the Girl" 1925; "The

Man from Red Gulch" 1925; "The Prairie Pirate" 1925; "Satan Town" 1926.

Morty, Frank. Director. Films: "Mary of the Mines" 1912; "The Sheriff of Stony Butte" 1912; "The Sheriff's Adopted Child" 1912; "The Claim Jumper" 1913; "An Indian's Gratitude" 1913; "The Land of Dead Things" 1913.

Moser, James E. Screenwriter. Films: "Wings of the Hawk" 1953.

Moss, Charles. Screenwriter. Films: "Dirty Little Billy" 1972.

Moss, Frank L. Screenwriter. Films: "The Vanquished" 1953; "Apache Territory" 1958 (adapt. only).

Moullet, Luc. Director. Films: "A Girl Is a Gun" 1970-Fr. (& prod./sp.).

Mowery, William Byron. Writer. Films: "Heart of the North" 1938 (story).

Moxey, John Llewellyn (1920-). Director. Films: "Bounty Man" TVM-1972; "Hardcase" TVM-1972. ¶TV: *Kung Fu*—"The Squaw Man" 11-1-73, "Empty Pages of a Dead Book" 1-10-74, "Night of the Owls, Day of the Doves" 2-14-74, "The Passion of Chen Yi" 2-28-74.

Muir, Jean (1911-). Writer. Films: "Northwest Stampede" 1948 (story).

Mulargia, Edoardo (Edward G. Miller, Edward Muller). Director. Films: "Go with God, Gringo" 1966-Ital./Span. (& sp.); "Blood at Sundown" 1967-Span./Ital.; "Cjamango" 1967-Ital.; "Don't Wait, Django ... Shoot!" 1969-Ital.; "Shango" 1969-Ital. (& sp.); "The Reward's Yours, the Man's Mine" 1970-Ital. (& sp.). "Brother Outlaw" 1971-Ital. (& sp.); "Man Called Django" 1971-Ital.

Mulford, Clarence E. (1895-1970). Writer. Films: "The Deadwood Coach" 1924 (story); "Hopalong Cassidy" 1935 (story); "Bar 20 Rides Again" 1936 (story); "Call of the Prairie" 1936 (story); "The Eagle's Brood" 1936 (story); Hopalong Cassidy Returns" 1936 (story); "Three on the Trail" 1936 (story); "Trail Dust" 1936 (story); "Borderland" 1937 (story); "Heart of the West" 1937 (story); "Hills of Old Wyoming" 1937 (story); "Hopalong Rides Again" 1937 (story); "North of the Rio Grande" 1937 (story); "Texas Trail" 1937 (story); "Bar 20 Justice" 1938 (story); "Cassidy of Bar 20" 1938 (story); "Heart of Arizona" 1938 (story); "Partners of the Plains" 1938 (story); "Pride of the West" 1938

(story); "Sunset Trail" 1938; "Silver on the Sage" 1939 (story); "Border Patrol" 1943 (story); "Lost Canyon" 1943 (story).

Mulhauser, James (1889-6/15/39). Screenwriter. Films: "Hidden Gold" 1933.

Mullally, Don. Writer. Films: "The Desert Flower" 1925 (story).

Muller, Edward G. *see* Mulargia, Edoardo.

Mulligan, Robert (1925-). Director. Films: "The Stalking Moon" 1969.

Mulligan, Ted. *see* Esteba, Manuel.

Mulligan, Tony. *see* Mollica, Antonio.

Mullin, Eugene. Screenwriter. Films: "Onawanda" 1909; "The Deerslayer" 1913.

Murdock, Perry. Screenwriter. Films: "Big Calibre" 1935.

Murfin, Jane (1892-8/10/55). Screenwriter. Films: "The Silent Call" 1921; "Stand Up and Fight" 1939.

Murillo, Mary. Screenwriter. Films: "The Heart of Wetona" 1919; "Moonshine Valley" 1922.

Murphy, Audie (1924-5/28/71). Producer. Films: "A Time for Dying" 1971.

Murphy, C.B. (1881-6/11/42). Writer. Films: "Jack's Pals" 1915 (story).

Murphy, Emmett. Screenwriter. Films: "Canyon Crossroads" 1955; "Valerie" 1957.

Murphy, Geoff. Director. Films: "Young Guns II" 1990.

Murphy, Joseph P. Screenwriter. Films: "The Kid from Santa Fe" 1940 (story only); "Law of the Wolf" 1941.

Murphy, Martin. Director. Films: "Bought and Fought For" 1920; "The Smoke Signal" 1920; "A Tough Tenderfoot" 1920.

Murphy, Patrick J. Director. Films: "Squares" 1972 (& prod.).

Murphy, Ralph Francis (1895-2/10/67). Director. Films: "Red Stallion in the Rockies" 1949; "Stage to Tucson" 1950. ¶TV: *Broken Arrow* 1956.

Murphy, Richard (1912-5/19/93). Screenwriter. Films: "The Apache Kid" 1941; "Back in the Saddle" 1941; "The Singing Hill" 1941 (story only); "The Cyclone Kid" 1942; "Jesse James, Jr." 1942 (& story); "Broken Lance" 1954.

Murray, Henry. Director. Films: "One He Man" 1920.

Murray, Jean. Writer. Films: "Roll on, Texas Moon" 1946 (story).

Murray, Ken (1903-10/12/88). Director. Films: "The Marshal's Daughter" 1953 (prod. only). ¶TV: *El Coyote Rides*—Pilot 1958.

Musolino, Vincenzo (Glen Vincent Davis). Screenwriter. Films: "Go with God, Gringo" 1966-Ital./Span.; "Blood at Sundown" 1967-Span./Ital.; "Cjamango" 1967-Ital.; "May God Forgive You ... But I Won't' 1968-Ital. (& sp.); "Don't Wait, Django ... Shoot!" 1969-Ital. (& prod.); "Quintana: Dead or Alive" 1969-Ital./Span. (& dir./prod.).

Mussetto, Giambattista. Screenwriter. Films: "Bandidos" 1967-Ital.

Musson, Bennet (1866-2/17/46). Screenwriter. Films: "White Oak" 1921.

Muzzy, Bertha Sinclair. Writer. Films: "The Taming of the West" 1925 (story).

Myers, Roy. Screenwriter. Films: "War on the Plains" 1912; "Ridin' Wild" 1922 (& story).

Myerson, Alan. Director. TV: *Gun Shy* 1983; *Zorro and Son* 1983.

Myles, Norbert. Director. Films: "The Daughter of Dawn" 1920 (& sp.); "Walloping Wallace" 1924.

Myton, Fred (1887-6/6/55). Screenwriter. Films: "Fighting for Love" 1917; "Fighting Mad" 1917 (story only); "Follow the Girl" 1917; "The Gunman's Gospel" 1917; "Desert Gold" 1919; "The Gray Wolf's Ghost" 1919; "A Man in the Open" 1919; "Fighting Cressy" 1920; "The Spoilers" 1923; "Man of the Forest" 1926; "The Mysterious Rider" 1927; "Hello Cheyenne" 1928; "A Horseman of the Plains" 1928; "The Great Divide" 1929; "Smoke Bellew" 1929; "White Eagle" 1932; "The King of the Wild Horses" 1933; "Border Phantom" 1937; "Doomed at Sundown" 1937 (story only); "The Gambling Terror" 1937; "Gun Lords of Stirrup Basin" 1937; "Moonlight on the Range" 1937; "The Roaming Cowboy" 1937; "Trail of Vengeance" 1937; "The Trusted Outlaw" 1937; "Desert Patrol" 1938; "Gunsmoke Trail" 1938; "Knight of the Plains" 1938; "The Terror of Tiny Town" 1938 (& story); "Two-Gun Justice" 1938; "Code of the Fearless" 1939; "Rollin' Westward" 1939; "Six-Gun Rhythm" 1939; "Pioneers of the Frontier" 1940; "Prairie Schooners" 1940; "The Return of Wild Bill" 1940; "Texas Stagecoach" 1940; "Two-Fisted Rangers" 1940; "Billy the Kid Wanted" 1941; "Billy the

Kid's Roundup" 1941; "The Lone Rider in Frontier Fury" 1941; "The Pinto Kid" 1941; "White Eagle" 1941-serial (story only); "Wildcat of Tucson" 1941; "The Lone Prairie" 1942; "Prairie Gunsmoke" 1942; "Black Hills Express" 1943; "Death Valley Manhunt" 1943 (story only); "The Kid Rides Again" 1943; "Law of the Saddle" 1943; "Riders of the Northwest Mounted" 1943; "Oath of Vengeance" 1944; "Thundering Gun Slingers" 1944; "Wyoming Hurricane" 1944; "Prairie Rustlers" 1945; "Shadows of Death" 1945; "Stagecoach Outlaws" 1945; "Gentlemen with Guns" 1946; "Prairie Badmen" 1946; "Western Pacific Agent" 1950; "Whistling Hills" 1951; "The Gunman" 1952.

Nablo, James Benson. Writer. Films: "Raw Edge" 1956 (story).

Nachmann, Kurt. Screenwriter. Films: "Halleluja and Sartana Strikes Again" 1972-Ger./Ital.

Nadel, Arthur H. (1921-2/22/90). Director. TV: *Law of the Plainsman* 1959-60 (assoc.prod.); *The Rifleman*—"The Wanted Man" 9-25-62, "The Assailants" 11-12-62, "The Most Amazing Man" 11-26-62, "Gun Shy" 12-10-62, "Conflict" 12-24-62, "The Sixteenth Cousin" 1-28-63, "Hostages to Fortune" 2-4-63, "End of the Hunt" 2-18-63, "The Bullet" 2-25-63, "Requiemn at Mission Springs" 3-4-63; *Bonanza*—"The Boss" 5-19-63, "Warbonnet" 12-26-71; *The Big Valley*—"Lost Treasure" 9-12-66, "Target" 10-31-66, "The Velvet Trap" 11-7-66, "Hide the Children" 12-19-66; *Hondo*—"Hondo and the Mad Dog" 10-27-67; *The High Chaparral*—"The Badge" 12-18-70.

Nagrom, Hugh. Screenwriter. Films: "The Crimson Canyon" 1928.

Napolitano, Joe. TV: *Adventures of Brisco County, Jr.*—"Deep in the Heart of Dixie" 11-5-93.

Narizzano, Silvio (1928-). Director. Films: "Blue" 1968.

Narzisa, Gianni. Director. Films: "Djurado" 1966-Ital./Span. (& sp.).

Nash, N. Richard (1913-). Screenwriter. Films: "The Rainmaker" 1956.

Nassour, Edward (1917-12/15/62). Director. Films: "The Beast of Hollow Mountain" 1956 (& prod.).

Nassour, William. Producer. Films: "The Beast of Hollow Mountain" 1956.

Natale, Roberto. Screenwriter. Films: "A Long Ride from Hell" 1968-Ital.; "Hate Thy Neighbor" 1969-Ital.

Natteford, Jack Francis. Screenwriter. Films: "Cyclone Jones" 1923 (story only); "Fighter's Paradise" 1924; "That Wild West" 1924; "Wild West" 1925-serial; "Call of the Klondike" 1926 (story only); "Moran of the Mounted" 1926; "Lightning" 1927; "Clearing the Trail" 1928; "Untamed Justice" 1929; "Border Romance" 1930; "Fighting Thru" 1930; "Arizona Terror" 1931; "Clearing the Range" 1931; "Hard Hombre" 1931; "The Two Gun Man" 1931 (& story); "Wild Horse" 1931; "Gold" 1932; "The Last of the Mohicans" 1932-serial; "My Pal, the King" 1932; "Spirit of the West" 1932 (story only); "The California Trail" 1933 (story only); "Cowboy Counsellor" 1933; "The Dude Bandit" 1933; "Fighting with Kit Carson" 1933-serial; "Hidden Gold" 1933; "Brand of Hate" 1934; "A Demon for Trouble" 1934; "The Crimson Trail" 1935; "The Rider of the Law" 1935; "The Lonely Trail" 1936; "The Oregon Trail" 1936; "Roarin' Lead" 1936; "The Three Mesquiteers" 1936; "Boots and Saddles" 1937; "Heart of the Rockies" 1937; "Rootin' Tootin' Rhythm" 1937; "Yodelin' Kid from Pine Ridge" 1937 (& story); "Billy the Kid Returns" 1938; "Gold Mine in the Sky" 1938; "Heroes of the Hills" 1938 (story only); "Rawhide" 1938; "Shine on Harvest Moon" 1938; "Colorado Sunset" 1939 (story only); "Come On, Rangers" 1939; "Days of Jesse James" 1939 (story only); "The Kansas Terrors" 1939; "Rough Riders' Round-Up" 1939; "Southward Ho!" 1939 (story only); "Wyoming Outlaw" 1939 (& story); "Heroes of the Saddle" 1940; "One Man's Law" 1940; "Pioneers of the West" 1940; "Trail of Kit Carson" 1945 (& story); "Badman's Territory" 1946; "Rustler's Roundup" 1946; "Trail to San Antone" 1947; "Black Bart" 1948; "Return of the Badmen" 1948 (& story); "The Last Bandit" 1949 (story only); "Rustlers" 1949; "The Return of Jesse James" 1950; "Cattle Drive" 1951; "Blackjack Ketchum, Desperado" 1956; "Kid Rodelo" 1966-U.S./Span.; "The Ride to Hangman's Tree" 1967 (& story).

Naughton, Edmund. Writer. Films: "McCabe and Mrs. Miller" 1971 (story).

Navarro, Agustin. Director. Films: "Shots Ring Out!" 1965-Ital./Sp.; "Ruthless Colt of the Gringo" 1967-Ital./Span. (sp. only).

Navarro, Jesus. Screenwriter. Films: "Gunfight at High Noon" 1963-Span./Ital.; "Coyote" 1964-Span./Ital.; "Two Gunmen" 1964-Span./Ital.

Navarro, Jose Luis. Screenwriter. Films: "Massacre at Fort Grant" 1963-Span.; "Fury of the Apaches" 1966-Span./Ital.; "Challenge of the Mackennas" 1969-Ital./Span.; "Raise Your Hands, Dead Man ... You're Under Arrest" 1971-Ital./Span.

Nayfack, Nicholas (1909-3/31/58). Producer. Films: "The Devil's Doorway" 1950; "Vengeance Valley" 1951; "Escape from Fort Bravo" 1953; "Gun Glory" 1957.

Nazarro, Ray (1902-9/8/86). Director. Films: "Outlaws of the Rockies" 1945; "Song of the Prairie" 1945; "Texas Panhandle" 1945; "Cowboy Blues" 1946; "The Desert Horseman" 1946; "Lone Star Moonlight" 1946; "Galloping Thunder" 1946; "Gunning for Vengeance" 1946; "Heading West" 1946; "Roaring Rangers" 1946; "Singing on the Trail" 1946; "Terror Trail" 1946; "That Texas Jamboree" 1946; "Throw a Saddle on a Star" 1946; "Two-Fisted Stranger" 1946; "Last Days of Boot Hill" 1947; "Law of the Canyon" 1947; "The Lone Hand Texan" 1947; "Over the Santa Fe Trail" 1947; "West of Dodge City" 1947; "Blazing Across the Pecos" 1948; "Buckaroo from Powder River" 1948; "Phantom Valley" 1948; "Quick on the Trigger" 1948; "Singing Spurs" 1948; "Six-Gun Law" 1948; "Smoky Mountain Melody" 1948; "Song of Idaho" 1948; "Trail to Laredo" 1948; "West of Sonora" 1948; "The Blazing Trail" 1949; "Challenge of the Range" 1949; "El Dorado Pass" 1949; "Home in San Antone" 1949; "Laramie" 1949; "Renegades of the Sage" 1949; "South of Death Valley" 1949; "Frontier Outpost" 1950; "Hoedown" 1950; "Outcast of Black Mesa" 1950; "The Palomino" 1950; "Streets of Ghost Town" 1950; "Texas Dynamo" 1950; "Trail of the Rustlers" 1950; "Al Jennings of Oklahoma" 1951; "Bandits of El Dorado" 1951; "Cyclone Fury" 1951; "Fort Savage Raiders" 1951; "Indian Uprising" 1951; "The Kid from Amarillo" 1951; "Cripple Creek" 1952; "Junction City" 1952; "Laramie Mountains" 1952; "Montana Territory" 1952; "The Rough, Tough West" 1952; "Gun Belt" 1953; "Kansas Pacific" 1953; "The Black Dakotas" 1954; "The Lone Gun" 1954; "Southwest Passage" 1954; "Top Gun" 1955; "The White Squaw" 1956; "Domino Kid" 1957; "The Hired Gun" 1957; "The Phantom Stagecoach" 1957; "Apache Territory"

1958; "Return to Warbow" 1958. ¶TV: *Fury* 1950-55; *The Gene Autry Show*—"The Million Dollar Fiddle" 10-1-55, "The Golden Chariot" 10-29-55; *Annie Oakley*—"The Waco Kid" 10-28-56, "The Saga of Clement O'Toole" 11-4-56.

Nebenzal, Seymour (1899-9/25/61). Producer. Films: "Heaven Only Knows" 1947.

Needham, Hal (1931-). Director. Films: "The Villain" 1979.

Negulesco, Jean (1900-7/18/93). Director. Films: "Cliff Edwards and His Buckaroof" 1941-short; "Roaring Guns" 1944-short.

Neider, Charles. Writer. Films: "One-Eyed Jacks" 1961 (story).

Neidig, William J. Writer. Films: "Tracked to Earth" 1922 (story).

Neilan, Marshall (1891-10/26/58). Director. Films: "The Country That God Forgot" 1916 (& story); "The Jaguar's Claws" 1917; "Heart of the Wilds" 1918; "M'Liss" 1918; "Bob Hampton of Placer" 1921 (& prod.).

Neill, James (1860-3/15/31). Director. Films: "Where the Trail Divides" 1914.

Neill, R. William (1887-12/14/46). Director. Films: "Flare-Up Sal" 1918; "The Inner Voice" 1920; "The Cowboy and the Countess" 1926; "The Fighting Buckaroo" 1926; "A Man Four-Square" 1926; "Arizona Wildcat" 1927; "The Avenger" 1931.

Neilson, James (1918-12/9/79). Director. Films: "The Adventures of Bullwhip Griffin" 1967; "Return of the Gunfighter" TVM-1967. ¶TV: *Wagon Train*—"The Kitty Angel Story" 1-7-59; *The Rifleman*—"The Blowout" 10-13-59, "The Coward" 12-22-59; *Law of the Plainsman* 1959; *Have Gun Will Travel*—"An International Afffair" 4-2-60; *Bonanza*—"The Mission" 9-17-60, "The Hopefuls" 10-8-60, "The Savage" 12-3-60, "The Wagon" 10-5-70.

Neitz, Alvin J. (Alan James) (1890-12/30/52). Director. Films: "Fighting Back" 1917; "The Learnin' of Jim Benton" 1917 (story only); "The Medicine Man" 1917 (sp. only); "Boss of the Lazy Y" 1918 (sp. only); "The Gun Woman" 1918 (story only); "Keith of the Border" 1918; "The Law's Outlaw" 1918 (sp. only); "Paying His Debt" 1918 (sp. only); "The Pretender" 1918 (sp. only); "Wolves of the Border" 1918 (story only); "The Girl Who Dared" 1920 (sp. only); "The Lone Hand" 1920 (story only); "Three Gold Coins" 1920; "Crossing Trails" 1921 (sp. only); "Outlawed"

1921 (& sp.); "Western Hearts" 1921 (sp. only); "Back Fire" 1922 (& sp.); "The Firebrand" 1922; "Gun Shy" 1922; "Dangerous Trails" 1923; "Salty Saunders" 1923 (sp. only): "The Secret of the Pueblo" 1923 (sp. only); "Wolves of the Border" 1923; "Battlin' Buckaroo" 1924 (& sp.); "Border Women" 1924; "Call of the Mate" 1924; "The Cowboy and the Flapper" 1924; "Crashin' Thru" 1924; "Cyclone Buddy" 1924 (& sp.); "Down by the Rio Grande" 1924; "Fighter's Paradise" 1924; "The Man from God's Country" 1924; "That Wild West" 1924; "The Valley of Vanishing Men" 1924 (story only); "Girl of the West" 1925; "The Mystery Box" 1925-serial (sp./story only); "Warrior Gap" 1925; "Bad Man's Bluff" 1926; "Beyond All Odds" 1926 (& sp.); "The Fighting Peacemaker" 1926; "A Six Shootin' Romance" 1926 (prod. only); "Thundering Speed" 1926; "Born to Battle" 1927; "Loco Luck" 1927 (story only); "Lure of the West" 1928 (& sp.); "Breed of the West" 1930 (& sp.); "Canyon Hawks" 1930; "Firebrand Jordan" 1930; "Trails of Danger" 1930 (& sp./story); "Flying Lariats" 1931 (& sp.); "Hell's Valley" 1931 (& sp.); "Pueblo Terror" 1931; "Red Fork Range" 1931 (& sp.); "Tombstone Canyon" 1931; "Tex Takes a Holiday" 1932 (& sp.); "Come on Tarzan" 1933 (& sp.); "Drum Taps" 1933; "Fargo Express" 1933 (& sp.); "King of the Arena" 1933 (& sp.); "Lariats and Sixshooters" 1933; "The Lone Avenger" 1933 (& sp.); "The Phantom Thunderbolt" 1933; "Strawberry Roan" 1933; "The Trail Drive" 1933 (& sp.); "Gun Justice" 1934; "Honor of the Range" 1934; "Smoking Guns" 1934; "Wheels of Destiny" 1934; "When a Man Sees Red" 1934 (& sp.); "Arizona Trails" 1935; "Desert Mesa" 1935; "Swifty" 1935; "Valley of Wanted Men" 1935; "Lucky Terror" 1936 (& sp.); "The Painted Stallion" 1937-serial; "Wild Horse Round-Up" 1937; "Call of the Rockies" 1938; "Flaming Frontier" 1938-serial; "Land of Fighting Men" 1938; "Two-Gun Justice" 1938; "West of Rainbow's End" 1938; "Trigger Smith" 1939; "The Law Rides Again" 1943; "Wild Horse Stampede" 1943; "Outlaw Trail" 1944 (story only); "Mule Train" 1950 (story only); "Silver Canyon" 1951 (story only).

Nelson, Dick. Screenwriter. Films: "One More Train to Rob" 1971; "Shootout in a One-Dog Town" TVM-1974.

Nelson, Don. Screenwriter. Films: "Hot Lead and Cold Feet" 1978.

Nelson, Gary. Director. Films: "Molly and Lawless John" 1972; "Santee" 1973. ¶TV: *Shane* 1966.

Nelson, Gene (1920-). Director. TV: *The Rifleman*—"First Wage" 10-9-61, "The Decision" 11-6-61, "Knight Errant" 11-13-61, "The Long Goodbye" 11-27-61, "A Friend in Need" 12-25-61, "The Quiet Fear" 1-22-62, "Sporting Chance" 1-29-62; *Gunsmoke*—"Malachi" 11-13-65; *Laredo*—"Enemies and Brothers" 2-17-67; *Lancer*—"Blood Rock" 10-1-68, "Glory" 12-10-68.

Nelson, Grant. Screenwriter. Films: "Zorro's Black Whip" 1944-serial.

Nelson, Jack. Director. Films: "The Covered Trail" 1924; "Beyond the Rockies" 1926; "The Dead Line" 1926; "The Devil's Gulch" 1926; "The Dude Cowboy" 1926; "The Fighting Boob" 1926 (& sp.); "Hair Trigger Baxter" 1926; "The Valley of Bravery" 1926; "Bulldog Pluck" 1927; "The Fighting Hombre" 1927; "The Mystery Rider" 1928-serial; "The Boy and the Bad Man" 1929; "Dangerous Days" 1929; "The Kid Comes Through" 1929; "Orphan of the Wagon Trails" 1929; "Waif of the Wilderness" 1929; "Alias the Bandit" 1930; "The Battling Kid" 1930; "The Danger Claim" 1930; "The Last Stand" 1930; "The Pony Express Kid" 1930; "The Post of Honor" 1930; "Six-Gun Justice" 1930; "Son of Courage" 1930; "Two Gun Caballero" 1931 (& sp.); "Border Guns" 1934; "The Border Menace" 1934; "Rawhide Terror" 1934 (sp. only).

Nelson, James. Director. Films: "Night Passage" 1957.

Nelson, O. Arthur. Writer. Films: "Howlin' Jones" 1913 (story); "The Noisy Six" 1913 (story); "The Pote Lariat of the Flying A" 1914 (story); "The Grizzly Gulch Chariot Race" 1915 (story).

Nelson, Ralph (1916-12/21/87). Director. Films: "Duel at Diablo" 1966 (& prod.); "Soldier Blue" 1970; "The Wrath of God" 1972 (& prod./sp.).

Nelson, Sam (1896-5/1/63). Director. Films: "Outlaws of the Prairie" 1937; "Cattle Raiders" 1938; "Colorado Trail" 1938; "Law of the Plains" 1938; "Rio Grande" 1938; "South of Arizona" 1938; "West of Cheyenne" 1938; "West of Santa Fe" 1938; "The Man from Sundown" 1939; "North of the Yukon" 1939; "Overland with Kit Carson" 1939-serial; "The Stranger from Texas" 1939; "Texas Stampede" 1939; "The Thun-

dering West" 1939; "Western Caravans" 1939; "Bullets for Rustlers"
1940; "Konga, the Wild Stallion"
1940; "Pioneers of the Frontier" 1940;
"Prairie Schooners" 1940; "Outlaws
of the Panhandle" 1941; "The Avenging Rider" 1943; "Sagebrush Law"
1943.

Nemec, Dennis. Screenwriter.
Films: "The Avenging Angel" TVM-
1995.

Nemours, Jean. Screenwriter.
Films: "The Legend of Frenchie
King" 1971-Fr./Ital./Span./Brit.

Nesmith, Michael (1943-).
Screenwriter. Films: "Timerider"
1983.

Neufeld, Sigmund. Producer.
Films: "Bulldog Courage" 1935;
"Code of the Mounted" 1935; "His
Fighting Blood" 1935; "Red Blood of
Courage" 1935; "Timber War" 1935;
"Trails of the Wild" 1935; "Aces and
Eights" 1936; "Border Caballero"
1936; "Ghost Patrol" 1936; "Light-
ning Bill Carson" 1936; "The Lion's
Den" 1936; "Roarin' Guns" 1936;
"The Traitor" 1936; "Six-Gun
Rhythm" 1939; "Arizona Gang-
busters" 1940; "Billy the Kid in
Texas" 1940; "Billy the Kid Out-
lawed" 1940; "Billy the Kid's Gun
Justice" 1940; "Frontier Crusader"
1940; "Gun Code" 1940; "Riders of
Black Mountain" 1940; "The Sage-
brush Family Trails West" 1940;
"Texas Renegades" 1940; "Billy the
Kid in Santa Fe" 1941; "Billy the Kid
Wanted" 1941; "Billy the Kid's Fight-
ing Pals" 1941; "Billy the Kid's Range
War" 1941; "Billy the Kid's Roundup"
1941; "The Lone Rider Ambushed"
1941; "The Lone Rider Crosses the
Rio" 1941; "The Lone Rider Fights
Back" 1941; "The Lone Rider in
Frontier Fury" 1941; "The Lone Rider
in Ghost Town" 1941; "The Lone
Rider Rides On" 1941; "Outlaws of
the Rio Grande" 1941; "The Texas
Marshal" 1941; "Along the Sundown
Trail" 1942; "Billy the Kid Trapped"
1942; "Billy the Kid's Smoking Guns"
1942; "Border Roundup" 1942; "Law
and Order" 1942; "The Lone Rider
and the Bandit" 1942; "The Lone
Rider in Cheyenne" 1942; "The Mysterious Rider" 1942; "Outlaws of
Boulder Pass" 1942; "Overland Stagecoach" 1942; "Prairie Pals" 1942;
"Raiders of the West" 1942; "Rolling
Down the Great Divide" 1942; "Sheriff of Sage Valley" 1942; "Texas Justice" 1942; "Texas Man Hunt" 1942;
"Cattle Stampede" 1943; "Fugitive of
the Plains" 1943; "The Kid Rides
Again" 1943; "Law of the Saddle"
1943; "Raiders of Red Gap" 1943;

"The Renegade" 1943; "Western Cy-
clone" 1943; "Wild Horse Rustlers"
1943; "Wolves of the Range" 1943;
"Blazing Frontier" 1944; "Death
Rides the Plains" 1944; "Devil Rid-
ers" 1944; "The Drifter" 1944; "Fron-
tier Outlaws" 1944; "Fuzzy Settles
Down" 1944; "Oath of Vengeance"
1944; "Rustlers' Hideout" 1944;
"Thundering Gun Slingers" 1944;
"Valley of Vengeance" 1944; "Wild
Horse Phantom" 1944; "Border Badmen" 1945; "Fighting Bill Carson"
1945; "Gangster's Den" 1945; "His
Brother's Ghost" 1945; "Prairie
Rustlers" 1945; "Shadows of Death"
1945; "Stagecoach Outlaws" 1945;
"Gentlemen with Guns" 1946;
"Ghost of Hidden Valley" 1946;
"Lightning Raiders" 1946; "Outlaw
of the Plains" 1946; "Overland Riders" 1946; "Prairie Badmen" 1946;
"Terrors on Horseback" 1946; "Western Pacific Agent" 1950; "Three Desperate Men" 1951; "Last of the Desperados" 1955; "Frontier Gambler"
1956; "The Three Outlaws" 1956;
"The Wild Dakotas" 1956. ¶TV:
Hawkeye and the Last of the Mohicans
1957 (& dir.).

Neufeld, Jr., Sigmund. Director. TV: *The Chisholms* 1980.

Neumann, Kurt (1908-8/21/
58). Director. Films: "My Pal, the
King" 1932; "The Dude Goes West"
1948; "Bad Men of Tombstone" 1949;
"The Kid from Texas" 1950; "Cattle
Drive" 1951; "Hiawatha" 1952; "The
Desperados Are in Town" 1956 (&
prod./sp.); "My Pal, the King" 1932;
"Mohawk" 1956; "Mohawk" 1956;
"Apache Warrior" 1957 (story/sp.
only); "The Deerslayer" 1957 (&
prod./sp.).

Neumann, Sam. Screenwriter.
Films: "I Killed Geronimo" 1950;
"Buffalo Bill in Tomahawk Territory"
1952; "Jesse James Versus the Daltons" 1954.

Neville, John T. Screenwriter.
Films: "Winners of the Wilderness"
1927; "The Dawn Trail" 1930; "The
Ranger's Code" 1933 (story only);
"The Sundown Rider" 1933 (story
only); "Battle of Greed" 1934; "Ivory-
Handled Gun" 1935; "Outlawed
Guns" 1935; "The Lion's Den" 1936;
"Rebellion" 1936; "Ridin' On" 1936;
"The Traitor" 1936; "Blazing Sixes"
1937; "Drums of Destiny" 1937;
"Empty Holsters" 1937; "The Glory
Trail" 1937; "Old Louisiana" 1937
(story only); "Raw Timber" 1937.

Nevin, David. Writer. Films:
"Dream West" TVM-1986 (story).

Nevins, Frank J. Writer. Films:
"Rock Island Trail" 1950 (story).

Newell, Gordon. Writer. Films:
"The California" 1937 (adapt.).

Newfield, Sam (Peter Stewart,
Sherman Scott) (1900-11/10/64). Di-
rector. Films: "Branded a Coward"
1935; "Bulldog Courage" 1935;
"Code of the Mounted" 1935;
"Northern Frontier" 1935; "Timber
War" 1935; "Trails of the Wild" 1935;
"Undercover Men" 1935; "Aces and
Eights" 1936; "Border Caballero"
1936; "Ghost Patrol" 1936; "Light-
ning Bill Carson" 1936; "The Lion's
Den" 1936; "Roarin' Guns" 1936;
"Roarin' Lead" 1936; "The Traitor"
1936; "Arizona Gunfighter" 1937;
"Bar Z Bad Men" 1937; "Boothill
Brigade" 1937; "Doomed at Sundown" 1937; "The Fighting Deputy"
1937; "The Gambling Terror" 1937;
"Gun Lords of Stirrup Basin" 1937;
"Guns in the Dark" 1937; "A Law-
man Is Born" 1937; "Lightnin' Crandall" 1937; "Melody of the Plains"
1937; "Moonlight on the Range"
1937; "Ridin' the Lone Trail" 1937;
"Trail of Vengeance" 1937; "Code of
the Rangers" 1938; "Colorado Kid"
1938; "Desert Patrol" 1938; "Durango Valley Raiders" 1938; "The
Feud Maker" 1938; "Gunsmoke
Trail" 1938; "Knight of the Plains"
1938; "Lightning Carson Rides
Again" 1938; "Paroled to Die" 1938;
"Phantom Ranger" 1938; "The
Rangers' Roundup" 1938; "Six-Gun
Trail" 1938; "Songs and Bullets"
1938; "The Terror of Tiny Town"
1938; "Thunder in the Desert" 1938;
"Code of the Cactus" 1939; "Fighting
Mad" 1939; "Fighting Renegade"
1939; "Flaming Lead" 1939; "Fron-
tier Scout" 1939; "Outlaw's Paradise"
1939; "Six-Gun Rhythm" 1939;
"Straight Shooter" 1939; "Texas
Wildcats" 1939; "Trigger Fingers"
1939; "Trigger Pals" 1939; "Arizona
Gangbusters" 1940; "Billy the Kid in
Texas" 1940; "Billy the Kid Out-
lawed" 1940; "Billy the Kid's Gun
Justice" 1940; "Death Rides the
Range" 1940; "Frontier Crusader"
1940; "Gun Code" 1940; "Riders of
Black Mountain" 1940; "The Sage-
brush Family Trails West" 1940;
"Texas Renegades" 1940; "Billy the
Kid in Santa Fe" 1941; "Billy the Kid
Wanted" 1941; "Billy the Kid's Fight-
ing Pals" 1941; "Billy the Kid's Range
War" 1941; "Billy the Kid's Roundup"
1941; "The Lone Rider Ambushed"
1941; "The Lone Rider Crosses the
Rio" 1941; "The Lone Rider Fights
Back" 1941; "The Lone Rider in
Frontier Fury" 1941; "The Lone Rider
in Ghost Town" 1941; "The Lone
Rider Rides On" 1941; "Outlaws of
the Rio Grande" 1941; "The Texas

Marshal" 1941; "Along the Sundown Trail" 1942; "Billy the Kid Trapped" 1942; "Billy the Kid's Smoking Guns" 1942; "Border Roundup" 1942; "Law and Order" 1942; "The Lone Rider and the Bandit" 1942; "The Lone Rider in Cheyenne" 1942; "The Mysterious Rider" 1942; "Outlaws of Boulder Pass" 1942; "Overland Stagecoach" 1942; "Prairie Pals" 1942; "Raiders of the West" 1942; "Rolling Down the Great Divide" 1942; "Texas Man Hunt" 1942; "Sheriff of Sage Valley" 1942; "Texas Justice" 1942; "Cattle Stampede" 1943; "Fugitive of the Plains" 1943; "The Kid Rides Again" 1943; "Raiders of Red Gap" 1943; "The Renegade" 1943; "Western Cyclone" 1943; "Wild Horse Rustlers" 1943; "Wolves of the Range" 1943; "Blazing Frontier" 1944; "Death Rides the Plains" 1944; "Devil Riders" 1944; "The Drifter" 1944; "Frontier Outlaws" 1944; "Fuzzy Settles Down" 1944; "Oath of Vengeance" 1944; "Rustlers' Hideout" 1944; "Thundering Gun Slingers" 1944; "Valley of Vengeance" 1944; "Wild Horse Phantom" 1944; "Border Badmen" 1945; "Fighting Bill Carson" 1945; "Gangster's Den" 1945; "His Brother's Ghost" 1945; "Prairie Rustlers" 1945; "Shadows of Death" 1945; "Stagecoach Outlaws" 1945; "Gentlemen with Guns" 1946; "Ghost of Hidden Valley" 1946; "Lightning Raiders" 1946; "Outlaw of the Plains" 1946; "Overland Riders" 1946; "Prairie Badmen" 1946; "Terrors on Horseback" 1946; "Western Pacific Agent" 1950; "Skipalong Rosenbloom" 1951; "Three Desperate Men" 1951; "Outlaw Women" 1952; "Last of the Desperadoes" 1955; "Frontier Gambler" 1956; "The Three Outlaws" 1956; "The Wild Dakotas" 1956; "Flaming Frontier" 1958-Can.; "Wolf Dog" 1958 (& prod.). ¶TV: *Hawkeye and the Last of the Mohicans* 1957.

Newman, Ben Ali. Screenwriter. Films: "Davy Crockett at the Fall of the Alamo" 1926.

Newman, David (1937-). Screenwriter. Films: "There Was a Crooked Man" 1970; "Bad Company" 1972.

Newman, Joseph M. (1909-). Director. Films: "Northwest Rangers" 1942; "The Outcasts of Poker Flat" 1952; "Pony Soldier" 1952; "Kiss of Fire" 1955; "Fort Massacre" 1958; "The Gunfight at Dodge City" 1959; "A Thunder of Drums" 1961.

Newman, Randy (1944-). Screenwriter. Films: "Three Amigos" 1986.

Newman, Walter (1920-10/14/93). Screenwriter. Films: "The True Story of Jesse James" 1957; "The Magnificent Seven" 1960; "Cat Ballou" 1965.

Newmeyer, Fred. Director. Films: "Rodeo Rhythm" 1942.

Newton, Douglas. Writer. Films: "The Brute" 1927 (story).

Nibbelink, Phil. Director. Films: "An American Tail: Fievel Goes West" 1991.

Nibley, Sloan. Screenwriter. Films: "Bells of San Angelo" 1947; "On the Old Spanish Trail" 1947; "Springtime in the Sierras" 1947; "Eyes of Texas" 1948; "The Gay Ranchero" 1948; "Night Time in Nevada" 1948; "Under California Stars" 1948; "Down Dakota Way" 1949; "The Far Frontier" 1949; "The Golden Stallion" 1949; "Susanna Pass" 1949; "Bells of Coronado" 1950; "Surrender" 1950; "Twilight in the Sierras" 1950; "In Old Amarillo" 1951; "Pals of the Golden West" 1951 (story only); "Spoilers of the Plains" 1951; "Springfield Rifle" 1952 (story only); "Thunder Over Arizona" 1956; "Hostile Guns" 1967 (& story).

Niblo, Fred (1874-11/11/48). Director. Films: "Partners Three" 1919; "Mark of Zorro" 1920; "Way Out West" 1930.

Nichols, Dudley (1895-1/4/60). Screenwriter. Films: "Three Rogues" 1931; "Robbers' Roose" 1933; "The Arizonian" 1935; "Stagecoach" 1939; "Rawhide" 1951; "The Big Sky" 1952; "Return of the Texan" 1952; "The Tin Star" 1957; "The Hangman" 1959; "Heller in Pink Tights" 1960; "Stagecoach" TVM-1986 (story only).

Nichols, Jr., George (1897-11/13/39). Director. Films: "Man of Conquest" 1939.

Nicholson, Jack (1937-). Director. Films: "Ride in the Whirlwind" 1966 (prod./sp. only); "The Shooting" 1966; "Goin' South" 1978.

Nickell, Paul. Director. TV: *Bonanza*—"Crucible" 4-8-62; *The Virginian*—"The Small Parade" 2-20-63.

Nicol, Alex (1919-). TV: *Wild Wild West*—"The Night of the Legion of Death" 11-24-67, "The Night of the Arrow" 12-29-67, "The Night of the Pelican" 12-27-68.

Nigh, William (1881-11/27/55). Director. Films: "A Yellow Streak" 1915 (& sp.); "The Blue Streak" 1917 (& sp.); "Fear-Bound" 1925 (& sp.); "The Law of the Range" 1928; "Fighting Thru" 1930; "Border Devils" 1932; "The Night Rider" 1932; "Without Honor" 1932; "North of

Nome" 1936; "The Law Commands" 1937; "Rose of the Rio Grande" 1938; "The Kid from Kansas" 1941; "Beauty and the Bandit" 1946; "The Gay Cavalier" 1946; "South of Monterey" 1946; "Riding the California Trail" 1947.

Night, Eugenia. Writer. Films: "Untamed Frontier" 1952 (story).

Nimrod, Brent. Screenwriter. Films: "The Female Bunch" 1971.

Noble, Hollister. Writer. Films: "Drums in the Deep South" 1951 (story).

Noble, John W. Director. Films: "The Gray Towers Mystery" 1919 (& sp.); "Buffalo Bill's Last Fight" 1927.

Nobles, Milton. Writer. Films: "The Price of Pride" 1917 (story).

Noel, Joseph. Writer. Films: "Whispering Sage" 1927 (story).

Nolte, William L. Screenwriter. Films: "Gun Play" 1935; "Big Boy Rides Again" 1935; "The Silver Bullet" 1935 (story only); "Sundown on the Prairie" 1939; "Saddle Mountain Roundup" 1941; "Land of Hunted Men" 1943 (story only); "Two Fisted Justice" 1943; "Law of the Lash" 1947; "Square Dance Jubilee" 1949 (story only).

Norden, Eric. Screenwriter. Films: "Stagecoach to Fury" 1956 (& story); "Apache Warrior" 1957; "Copper Sky" 1957; "The Quiet Gun" 1957; "Ride a Violent Mile" 1957; "Cattle Empire" 1958.

Nordlinger, Victor. Director. Films: "The Love Deputy" 1926; "Pep of the Lazy J" 1926; "The Saddle Tramp" 1926; "The Show Cowpuncher" 1926.

Norfleet, Hal C. Screenwriter. Films: "Smilng Jim" 1922.

Norman, Marc. Screenwriter. Films: "Oklahoma Crude" 1973; "Zandy's Bride" 1974.

Norris, Frank (1870-1902). Writer. Films: "Desert Gold" 1914 (story).

Norris, Stephen. Screenwriter. Films: "Phantom Patrol" 1936.

North, Edmund H. (1911-8/28/90). Screenwriter. Films: "Colorado Territory" 1949; "Only the Valiant" 1951; "The Outcasts of Poker Flat" 1952; "Destry" 1954; "The Far Horizons" 1955; "The Proud Ones" 1956; "Cowboy" 1958.

North, Robert (1884-8/13/76). Producer. Films: "The Girl of the Golden West" 1923; "The Great Divide" 1929; "Hurricane Smith" 1942; "In Old California" 1942; "In Old Oklahoma" 1943.

Norton, Grace. Screenwriter. Films: "Deep in the Heart of Texas" 1942.

Norton, Roy. Writer. Films: "The Plunderer" 1915 (story); "The Mediator" 1916 (story); "The Plunderer" 1924 (story).

Norton, William. Screenwriter. Films: "The Scalphunters" 1968; "Sam Whiskey" 1969; "The Hunting Party" 1971-Brit./Ital./Span.; "September Gun" TVM-1983.

Nosler, Lloyd. Director. Films: "The Man from Death Valley" 1931 (& sp.); "Single-Handed Sanders" 1932; "Son of the Border" 1933; "Dawn Rider" 1935 (story only).

Nostro, Nick. *see* Iquino, Ignacio.

Nugent, Elliott (1899-8/9/80). Director. Films: "My Brother, the Outlaw" 1951.

Nugent, Frank S. (1908-12/29/65). Screenwriter. Films: "Fort Apache" 1948; "The Three Godfathers" 1948; "She Wore a Yellow Ribbon" 1949; "Two Flags West" 1950 (story only); "Wagonmaster" 1950; "They Rode West" 1954; "The Tall Men" 1955; "The Searchers" 1956; "Gunman's Walk" 1958; "Two Rode Together" 1961; "Incident at Phantom Hill" 1966.

Nyby, Christian (1913-9/17/93). Director. Films: "Young Fury" 1965. ¶TV: *The Roy Rogers Show*—"Loaded Guns" 4-15-53, "Fishing for Fingerprints" 10-28-56, "Mountain Pirates" 11-4-56, "His Weight in Wildcats" 11-11-56, "Tossup" 12-2-56, "Deadlock at Dark Canyon" 1-6-57; *Zane Grey Theater* 1956; *Gunsmoke*—"Young Man with a Gun" 10-20-56, "Tail to the Wind" 10-17-59, "The Gunmen" 1-23-60, "Coventry" 3-17-62, "Hammerhead" 12-26-64; *Wagon Train*—"The Steve Campden Story" 5-13-59, "The Jenny Tannen Story" 6-24-59; *Bonanza*—"The Newcomers" 9-26-59, "The Julia Bulette Story" 10-17-59, "The Magnificent Adah" 11-14-59, "The Truckee Strip" 11-21-59, "The Hanging Posse" 11-28-59, "The Sisters" 12-12-59, "The Last Hunt" 12-19-59, "El Toro Grande" 1-2-60, "The Spanish Grant" 2-6-60, "The Stranger" 2-27-60, "The Avenger" 3-19-60, "The Frenchman" 12-10-61, "The Law Maker" 3-11-62, "The Dowry" 4-29-62, "The Quest" 9-30-62, "The Beginning" 11-25-62, "Gallagher Sons" 12-9-62, "The Jury" 12-30-62, "The Actress" 2-24-63, "The Prime of Life" 12-29-63, "Thanks for Everything, Friend" 10-11-64, "The Scapegoat" 10-25-64, "Napoleon's

Children" 4-16-67; *Rawhide*—"Incident at Cactus Wells" 10-12-62, "Incident of the Prodigal Son" 10-19-62, "Incident at Sugar Creek" 11-23-62, "Incident at Quivira" 12-14-62, "Incident of the Gallows Tree" 2-22-63, "Incident of the Pale Rider" 3-15-63, "Incident of the White Eyes" 5-3-63, "Incident of Iron Bull" 10-3-63, "Incident of the Wnderer" 2-27-64, "Incident at Zebulon" 3-5-64, "Incident at Hourglass" 3-12-64, "Incident of the Banker" 4-2-64, "Incident of the Gilded Goddess" 4-30-64, "Incident of the Gilded Goddess" 4-30-64, "Incidet at Seven Fingers" 5-7-64; *Lancer*—"Jelly" 11-19-68, "Devil's Blessing" 4-22-69, "Jelly Hoskins' American Dream" 11-11-69, "The Lorelei" 1-27-70.

Nye, Ned. Writer. Films: "Thundering Romance" 1924 (story); "Gold and Grit" 1925 (story).

Oaks, Theresa. Writer. Films: "Lady from Cheyenne" 1941 (story).

Obon, Raymond. Screenwriter. Films: "Bullet for Billy the Kid" 1963.

O'Brien, John. Director. Films: "The Angel of Contention" 1914; "Sierra Jim's Reformation" 1914; "Big Jim's Heart" 1915; "An Obstinate Sheriff" 1915 (story only); "Daring Days" 1925; "The Outlaw's Daughter" 1925; "Jim Hood's Ghost" 1926; "The Little Warrior" 1926; "Montana of the Ranges" 1926; "Mountain Molly" 1926; "Outlaw Love" 1926; "Queen of the Hills" 1926.

O'Brien, Liam. Screenwriter. Films: "The Redhead and the Cowboy" 1951; "The Awakening Land" TVM-1978.

O'Brien, Robert. Screenwriter. Films: "Fancy Pants" 1950.

O'Brien, Willis (1886-11/8/62). Writer. Films: "The Beast of Hollow Mountain" 1956 (story).

O'Connall, Joe. Screenwriter. Films: "Border Feud" 1947.

O'Connolly, James (1926-). Director. Films: "The Valley of Gwangi" 1969.

O'Connor, Mary. Screenwriter. Films: "A Yankee from the West" 1915; "Girl of the Timber Claims" 1917.

O'Connor, William. Director. Films: "Cheyenne Tornado" 1935.

O'Darsa, Ted. *see* Sabastello, Dario.

O'Day, Peggy. Writer. Films: "Whistling Jim" 1925 (story).

O'Dea, John. Screenwriter. Films: "Jack McCall, Desperado" 1953; "Robbers' Roost" 1955.

O'Dell, Garry. Writer. Films: "Ridin' Eash" 1925 (story).

Odlum, Jerome. Writer. Films: "Last Frontier Uprising" 1947 (story).

O'Donnell, Joseph. Screenwriter. Films: "Bulldog Courage" 1935; "His Fighting Blood" 1935; "Timber War" 1935; "Trails of the Wild" 1935; "Border Caballero" 1936; "Ghost Patrol" 1936 (story only); "Lightning Bill Carson" 1936; "Roarin' Guns" 1936; "Vengeance of Rannah" 1936; "Wildcat Trooper" 1936; "Fighting Texan" 1937; "North of the Rio Grande" 1937; "Texas Trail" 1937; "Whistling Bullets" 1937; "Wild Horse Round-Up" 1937; "Land of Fighting Men" 1938; "Lightning Carson Rides Again" 1938; "Phantom Ranger" 1938 (& story); "Six-Gun Trail" 1938; "Songs and Bullets" 1938; "The Adventures of the Masked Phantom" 1939; "The Gentleman from Arizona" 1939; "Flaming Lead" 1939; "Straight Shooter" 1939; "Arizona Gangbusters" 1940; "Billy the Kid in Texas" 1940; "Gun Code" 1940; "Riders of Black Mountain" 1940; "Texas Renegades" 1940; "Billy the Kid in Santa Fe" 1941; "King of the Texas Rangers" 1941-serial; "The Lone Rider Fights Back" 1941; "The Lone Rider in Ghost Town" 1941; "The Lone Rider Rides On" 1941; "King of the Mounties" 1942-serial; "Cattle Stampede" 1943; "Daredevils of the West" 1943-serial; "Raiders of Red Gap" 1943; "The Renegade" 1943; "Wild Horse Rustlers" 1943; "Wolves of the Range" 1943; "Death Rides the Plains" 1944; "Devil Riders" 1944; "Frontier Outlaws" 1944; "Land of the Outlaws" 1944; "Law of the Valley" 1944; "Rustlers' Hideout" 1944; "Tucson Raiders" 1944; "Valley of Vengeance" 1944; "Royal Mounted Rides Again" 1945-serial; "The Scarlet Horseman" 1946-serial; "Return of the Lash" 1947; "Check Your Gun" 1948; "Coyote Canyon" 1949-short; "South of Santa Fe" 1949-short; "Cactus Caravan" 1950-short; "The Fargo Phantom" 1950-short; "Gold Strike" 1950-short; "Ready to Ride" 1950-short; "Nevada Badmen" 1951; "Oklahoma Justice" 1951; "Prairie Roundup" 1951; "Stagecoach Driver" 1951; "The Man from Black Hills" 1952.

Ogden, George Washington. Writer. Films: "Winner Takes All" 1918 (story).

O'Hanlon, James. Screenwriter. Films: "Calamity Jane" 1953; "Murieta" 1965-Span./U.S.

O'Hara, Mary (1885-10/14/80).

Screenwriter. Films: "Braveheart" 1925; "My Friend Flicka" 1943 (story only); "Green Grass of Wyoming" 1948 (story only).

O'Herlihy, Michael (1929-). Director. Films: "Smith" 1969; "Young Pioneers" TVM-1976; "Young Pioneers' Christmas" TVM-1976; "Peter Lundy and the Medicine Hat Stallion" TVM-1977; "I Married Wyatt Earp" TVM-1983. ¶TV: *Bronco* 1958; *Maverick—*"The Art Lovers" 10-1-61, "Poker Face" 1-7-62; *Rawhide—*"A Man Called Mushy" 10-23-64, "Damon's Road" 11-13-64 & 11-20-64, "The Meeting" 12-25-65, "Mrs. Harmon" 4-16-65; *The Guns of Will Sonnett—*"Look for the Hound Dog" 1-26-68, "Alone" 2-9-68; *Bret Maverick—*"The Vulture Also Rises" 3-16-82; *Gunsmoke—*"Blue Heaven" 9-26-64, "Big Man, Big Target" 11-28-64, "Bad Lady from Brookline" 5-1-65, "The Tarnished Badge" 11-11-74; *The Quest—*"The Freight Train Rescue" 12-29-76.

Ojeda, Manuel R. Screenwriter. Films: "The Last Rebel" 1961-Mex.

Olcott, Peggene. Screenwriter. Films: "Fighting Jack" 1926 (story only); "Saddle Jumpers" 1927.

Olcott, Sidney (1872-12/16/49). Director. Films: "Her Indian Mother" 1910 (& sp.); "The Indian Scout's Revenge" 1910 (& sp.); "The Mystery of Pine Creek Camp" 1913; "The Brand" 1914; "Wolfe, or the Conquest of Quebec" 1914 (& sp.); "God's Country and the Law" 1922; "Ranson's Folly" 1926.

Olds, John N. *see* Bava, Mario.

O'Leary, J.R. Writer. Films: "True Western Hearts" 1914 (story).

Olin, Ken. Director. Films: "White Fang 2: Myth of the White Wolf" 1994.

Oliver, Guy (1878-9/1/32). Director. Films: "The Coyote" 1915.

Oliver, James. Screenwriter. Films: "Thunder Town" 1946.

Olmsted, Harry F. Writer. Film: "Arizona Gunfighter" 1937 (story); "Boothill Brigade" 1937 (story); "Gun Lords of Stirrup Basin" 1937 (story); "A Lawman Is Born" 1937 (story); "Outlaws of the Prairie" 1937 (story); "Colorado Kid" 1938 (story); "Durango Valley Raiders" 1938 (story); "The Feud Maker" 1938 (story); "Paroled to Die" 1938 (story); "Stagecoach War" 1940 (story & sp.).

Olsen, Rolf. Director. Films: "Last Ride to Santa Cruz" 1969-Ger./Fr.

Olsen, Theodore V. (1932-). Writer. Films: "The Stalking Moon" 1969 (story); "Soldier Blue" 1970 (story).

Olson, James P. Writer. Films: "Bar Z Bad Men" 1937 (story).

O'Malley, David. Director. Films: "The Adventures of Frontier Fremont" 1976 (sp. only); "Guardian of the Wilderness" 1976; "The Incredible Rocky Mountain Race" TVM-1977.

O'Neal, Charles. Screenwriter. Films: "Return of the Badmen" 1948; "Montana" 1950.

O'Neal, Sean. *see* Fidani, Demofilo.

O'Neil, Maurice G. Director. Films: "A Tenderfoot Goes West" 1937 (& prod.).

O'Neill, Ella. Screenwriter. Films: "Battling with Buffalo Bill" 1931-serial; "Heroes of the West" 1932-serial; "Clancy of the Mounted" 1933-serial; "Gordon of Ghost City" 1933-serial; "The Red Rider" 1934-serial; "The Roaring West" 1935-serial; "Rustlers of Red Dog" 1935-serial; "Rustlers' Roundup" 1935; "The Phantom Rider" 1936-serial; "Flaming Frontier" 1938-serial.

O'Neill, George (1898-5/24/40). Screenwriter. Films: "Sutter's Gold" 1936; "Yellow Dust" 1936 (story only); "High, Wide and Handsome" 1937.

O'Neill, Simon. Screenwriter. Films: "One After Another" 1968-Span./Ital.

O'Reilly, Tex. Writer. Films: "On the High Card" 1921 (story).

Orkow, Harrison. Screenwriter. Films: "Alaska" 1944.

Orlebeck, Les. Director (1907-8/2/70). Films: "Pioneers of the West" 1940; "Gauchos of El Dorado" 1941; "Outlaws of the Cherokee Trail" 1941; "Pals of the Pecos" 1941; "Prairie Pioneers" 1941; "Saddlemates" 1941; "West of Cimarron" 1941; "Shadows on the Sage" 1942.

Orloff, Arthur E. Screenwriter. Films: "Cheyenne Takes Over" 1947; "Wild Country" 1947; "Code of the Silver Sage" 1950; "The Missourians" 1950; "Buckaroo Sheriff of Texas" 1951; "Thunder in God's Country" 1951; "Desperadoes' Outpost" 1952; "The Last Musketeer" 1952; "South Pacific Trail" 1952; "Trail Guide" 1952; "El Paso Stampede" 1953; "Gun Belt" 1953 (story only); "Red River Shore" 1953; "Five Guns to Tombstone" 1961.

Ormond, Ron (1911-5/11/81). Director. Films: "Dead Man's Gold" 1948 (prod./story only); "Frontier Revenge" 1948 (prod. only); "Mark of the Lash" 1948 (& prod./sp.); "The Dalton Gang" 1949 (prod. only); "Outlaw Country" 1949 (prod./sp. only); "Red Desert" 1949 (prod./sp. only); "Rimfire" 1949 (prod./sp. only); "Son of Billy the Kid" 1949 (prod./sp. only); "Son of a Badman" 1949 (prod./sp. only); "Square Dance Jubilee" 1949 (prod./sp. only); "Colorado Ranger" 1950 (prod./sp. only); "Crooked River" 1950 (prod./sp. only); "The Daltons' Women" 1950 (prod./sp. only); "Fast on the Draw" 1950 (prod./sp. only); "Hostile Country" 1950 (prod./sp. only); "King of the Bullwhip" 1950 (& prod.); "Marshal of Heldorado" 1950 (prod./sp. only); "West of the Brazos" 1950 (prod./sp. only); "The Thundering Trail" 1951 (& prod.); "The Vanishing Outpost" 1951 (& prod.); "The Black Lash" 1952 (& prod.); "The Frontier Phantom" 1952 (& prod.); "Outlaw Women" 1952 (& prod.); "Frontier Woman" 1956; "The Naked Gun" 1956 (prod./sp. only).

Ormont, James. Screenwriter. Films: "Baffled" 1924; "Courage" 1924 (story only); "Crossed Trail" 1924 (story only); "A Desperate Adventure" 1924 (story only); "A Two Fisted Tenderfoot" 1924; "Western Vengeance" 1924; "Border Intrigue" 1925 (story only); "The Ridin' Streak" 1925; "The Dude Cowboy" 1926 (story only); "The Fighting Boob" 1926; "Hair Trigger Baxter" 1926 (story only); "The Valley of Bravery" 1926.

Ornitz, Samuel (1891-3/10/57). Screenwriter. Films: "Men of America" 1933; "Three Faces West" 1940.

O'Rourke, Frank (1916-4/27/89). Writer. Films: "The Bravados" 1958 (story); "The Professionals" 1966 (story); "The Great Bank Robbery" 1969 (story).

Orr, Gertrude. Screenwriter. Films: "The Flying Horseman" 1926; "Call of the Yukon" 1938.

Orr, William T. (1917-). Producer. TV: *Cheyenne* 1955-63 (exec. prod.); *Colt .45* 1957-62 (exec. prod.); *Sugarfoot* 1957-60 (exec. prod.); *Maverick* 1957-62; *Bronco* 1958-60 (exec. prod.); *The Texan* 1958-60 (exec. prod.); *Lawman* 1958-62 (exec. prod.); *The Alaskans* 1959-60; *The Dakotas* 1963 (exec. prod.); *F Troop* 1965-67.

Orsatti, Frank. Director. TV: *Outlaws—*"Primer" 1-10-87, "Potboiler" 2-28-87, "Hardcase" 3-28-87.

Orsatti, Victor M. Producer. Films: "Domino Kid" 1957; "The Hired Gun" 1957; "Apache Territory" 1958. ¶TV: *The Texan* 1958-60.

Ortas, Jose. Screenwriter. Films: "Death on High Mountain" 1969-Ital./Span.

Orth, Marion. Screenwriter. Films: "White Gold" 1927; "Romance of the Rio Grande" 1929.

Ortosolli, Daniel. Screenwriter. Films: "God in Heaven … Arizona on Earth" 1972-Span./Ital.

Osborne, Hugh R. Screenwriter. Films: "Nugget Nell" 1919.

Osborne, Kent. Director. Films: "Cain's Way" 1969 (& prod.).

Osmon, Leighton. Screenwriter. Films: "The Jaguar's Claws" 1917; "The Claim" 1918.

Ostroff, Howard. Screenwriter. Films: "The Wackiest Wagon Train in the West" 1976.

O'Sullivan, Tony (-7/4/20). Director. Films: "A Gambler's Honor" 1913.

O'Sullivan, William J. Producer. Films: "King of the Mounties" 1942-serial; "Daredevils of the West" 1943-serial; "Hellfire" 1949; "The Showdown" 1950; "A Perilous Journey" 1953; "The Outcast" 1954.

Oswald, Gerd (1916-5/22/89). Director. Films: "The Brass Legend" 1956; "Fury at Showdown" 1957; "Valerie" 1957. ¶TV: *Black Saddle* 1959; *Rawhide*—"Incident of the Deserter" 4-29-60, "The Testing Post" 11-30-65; *Bonanza*—"Five Sundowns to Sunup" 12-5-65, "Destiny's Child" 1-30-66, "The Oath" 11-20-66, "A Christmas Story" 12-25-66, "The Unseen Wound" 1-29-67, "A Woman in the House" 2-19-67; *Temple Houston* 1963; *Shane* 1966; *Daniel Boone*—"The Ballad of Sidewinder and Cherokee" 9-14-67; *Nichols* 1971-72.

Othile, Frank W. Screenwriter. Films: "99 Wounds" 1931.

Otto, Henry (1877-8/3/52). Director. Films: "The Silent Way" 1914; "The Castle Ranch" 1915; "Reformation" 1915; "The Senor's Silver Buckle" 1915; "Wild Life" 1918.

Overholser, Wayne D. (Lee Leighton) (1906-). Writer. Films: "Star in the Dust" 1956 (story); "Cast a Long Shadow" 1959 (story).

Overholt, Miles. Writer. Films: "The Meddler" 1925.

Owen, Seena (1894-8/15/66). Screenwriter. Films: "The Great Man's Lady" 1942.

Owens, Richard. Director. Films: "Judge Roy Bean" 1970-Fr.

Oxford, Buckleigh Fritz. Screenwriter. Films: "Tiger Thompson" 1924; "Bustin' Thru" 1925; "The Cowby Musketeer" 1925; "The Demon" 1926; "A Regular Scout" 1926 (story only); "The Tough Guy" 1926; "Painted Post" 1928; "The Lariat Kid" 1929 (story only).

Packer, Peter (1905-2/13/87). Producer. Films: "Seventh Cavalry" 1956 (sp. only). ¶TV: *My Friend Flicka* 1955-56; *Man Without a Gun* 1958-59; *Law of the Plainsman* 1959-60.

Padget, Calvin J. *see* Ferroni, Giorgio.

Padilla, Miguel. Writer. Films: "Passion" 1954 (story).

Padilla, Robert. Writer. Films: "The Great Gundown" 1977 (story).

Pagano, Ernest (1900-4/29/53). Screenwriter. Films: "Frontier Gal" 1945 (& prod.).

Pagano, Joe (1906-3/23/81). Screenwriter. Films: "The Leather Burners" 1943; "Adventures in Silverado" 1948; "Thunder in the Pines" 1948 (story only); "Yaqui Drums" 1956.

Page, Adrian. Screenwriter. Films: "Pioneer Justice" 1947.

Pakula, Alan J. (1928-). Director. Films: "The Stalking Moon" 1969 (prod. only); "Comes a Horseman" 1978.

Palli, Vincenzo G. Screenwriter. Films: "Death on High Mountain" 1969-Ital./Span.

Panaccio, Elo. Director. Films: "Death Played the Flute" 1972-Ital./Span. (& sp.).

Panama, Norman (1914-). Director. Films: "Callaway Went Thataway" 1951 (& prod./sp.); "The Jawhawkers" 1959 (prod. only).

Pan Cosmatos, George. Director. Films: "Tombstone" 1993.

Paolella, Domenico. Director. Films: "Hate for Hate" 1967-Ital. (& sp.); "Execution" 1968-Ital./Fr. (& sp.).

Paramore, Edward E. (1895-5/1/56). Screenwriter. Films: "The Virginian" 1929; "The Border Legion" 1930; "The Santa Fe Trail" 1930; "Fighting Caravans" 1931; "Rocky Mountain Mystery" 1935; "The Three Godfathers" 1936; "Man of Conquest" 1939; "The Oklahoma Kid" 1939 (& story); "Twenty Mule Team" 1940; "Tombstone, the Town Too Tough to Die" 1942; "The Virginian" 1946.

Paredes, America. Writer. Films: "The Ballad of Gregorio Cortez" 1983 (story).

Paris, Jerry (1925-3/31/86). Director. Films: "Evil Roy Slade" TVM-1972. ¶TV: *Sheriff Who?*—Pilot 9-5-67.

Park, Ida May (1880-6/13/54). Director. Films: "The Grand Passion" 1918 (& sp.).

Parker, Albert (1887-8/10/74). Director. Films: "Arizona" 1918; "The Knickerbocker Buckaroo" 1919.

Parker, Ben. Director. Films: "The Shepherd of the Hills" 1964 (& sp.).

Parker, Fess (1927-). Director. TV: *Daniel Boone*—"Then Who Will They Hang from the Yardarm if Willy Gets Away?" 2-8-68, "The Plague That Came to Ford's Run" 10-31-68, "Hannah Comes Home" 12-25-69, "An Angel Cried" 1-8-70.

Parker, Gilbert (1860-1932). Writer. Films: "Pierre of the Plains" 1914 (story); "Over the Border" 1922 (story).

Parker, Lem B. Director Films: "A Western Romance" 1913.

Parker, Norton S. (1901-7/5/69). Screenwriter. Films: "The Lady from Hell" 1926 (story only); "Courage of the West" 1937; "Border Wolves" 1938; "The Last Stand" 1938; Outlaw Express" 1938; "Western Trails" 1938; "Stage to Chino" 1940 (story only); "Three Men from Texas" 1940; "Young Bill Hickok" 1940; "The Bandit Trail" 1941; "Cyclone on Horseback" 1941; "In Old Colorado" 1941; "Six Gun Gold" 1941; "Come On, Danger!" 1942; "Fighting Frontier" 1943; "Rio Grande Raiders" 1946; "Coyote Canyon" 1949-short (story only); "South of Santa Fe" 1949-short (story only); "Devil's Canyon" 1953 (story only).

Parker, William. Screenwriter. Films: "Guilty" 1916; "Anything Once" 1917; "Revenge" 1918; "Bare-Fisted Gallagher" 1919; "Ten Scars Make a Man" 1924-serial (dir. only).

Parkhill, Forbes. Screenwriter. Films: "Blazing Guns" 1935; "Alias John Law" 1935; "No Man's Range" 1935; "Brand of the Outlaws" 1936; "The Law Rides" 1936 (story only); "Stand Up and Fight" 1939 (story only).

Parks, Jr., Gordon (1948-4/3/79). Director. Films: "Thomasine and Bushrod" 1974.

Parks, Johnson. Screenwriter. Films: "In Old Montana" 1939.

Parks, Michael (1938-). Director. Films: "The Return of Josey Wales" 1987.

Parolini, Gianfranco (Frank Kramer). Director. Films: "Left Handed Johnny West" 1965-Span./Ital. (& sp.); "Sartana" 1968-Ital./Ger. (& sp.); "Sabata" 1969-Ital. (& sp.); "Adios, Sabata" 1970-Ital./Span. (& sp.); "The Bounty Hunters" 1970-Ital. (& sp.); "Return of Sabata" 1972-Ital./Fr./Ger. (& sp.); "God's Gun" 1976-Ital./Israel (& sp.).

Parriott, James D. Screenwriter. Films: "The Legend of the Golden Gun" TVM-1979.

Parrish, Randall. Writer. Films: "Bob Hampton of Placer" 1921 (story).

Parrish, Robert (1916-12/4/95). Director. Films: "The San Francisco Story" 1952; "Saddle the Wind" 1958; "The Wonderful Country" 1959; "A Town Called Hell" 1971-Span./Brit.

Parrott, Charles (Charley Chase) (1893-6/20/40). Director. Films: "Wild West Love" 1914.

Parrott, James (1898-5/10/39). Screenwriter. Films: "Way Out West" 1937.

Parry, Robert. *see* Selander, Lesley.

Parsons, Agnes. Screenwriter. Films: "Riding with Death" 1921; "The Fast Mail" 1922.

Parsons, Buck. Writer. Films: "The Lone Bandit" 1934 (story).

Parsons, Harriet (1906-1/2/83). Director. Films: "Meet Roy Rogers" 1941-short (& prod.).

Parsons, J. Palmer. Writer. Films: "White Gold" 1927 (story).

Parsons, Lindsley (1905-10/9/92). Producer. Films: "Sagebrush Trail" 1933 (sp. only); "Randy Rides Alone" 1934 (sp. only); "The Trail Beyond" 1934 (sp. only); "Desert Trail" 1935 (sp. only); "Lawless Range" 1935 (sp. only); "The Man from Utah" 1935 (sp. only); "Paradise Canyon" 1935 (sp./story only); "Rainbow Valley" 1935 (sp. only); "Westward Ho" 1935 (sp./story only); "The Oregon Trail" 1936 (sp./story only); "Headin' for the Rio Grande" 1937; "Arizona Days" 1937 (story only); "Riders of the Rockies" 1937 (story only); "Tex Rides with the Boy Scouts" 1937 (story only); "Trouble in Texas" 1937 (story only); "Frontier Town" 1938 (sp. only); "Panamint's Bad Man" 1938 (story only); "Rollin' Plains" 1938 (sp. only); "Utah Trail" 1938 (story only); "Oklahoma Terror" 1939 (& story); "Alaska" 1944; "Trail of the Yukon" 1949; "The Wolf Hunters" 1949; "Snow Dog" 1950; "Call of the Klondike" 1950; "Sierra Passage" 1951; "Northwest Territory" 1951; "Desert Pursuit" 1952; "Fangs of the Arctic" 1953; "Jack Slade" 1953; "Northern Patrol" 1953; "The Return of Jack Slade" 1955; "Dragoon Wells Massacre" 1957; "Oregon Passage" 1958.

Partos, Frank (1901-12/23/56). Screenwriter. Films: "Heritage of the Desert" 1932; "Rose of the Rancho" 1936.

Pas, Tonio. Screenwriter. Films: "Thunder Over El Paso" 1972-Ital./Span.

Pascal, Ernest L. (1896-11/4/66). Screenwriter. Films: "Last of the Duanes" 1930; "Fair Warning" 1931; "Under the Pampas Moon" 1935; "Canyon Passage" 1946.

Passadore, E. Screenwriter. Films: "Return of Clint the Strange" 1971-Ital./Span.

Passalacqua, Pino. Screenwriter. Films: "Jesse James' Kid" 1966-Span./Ital.

Pasternak, Joe (1901-9/13/91). Producer. Films: "Destry Rides Again" 1939; "The Kissing Bandit" 1948.

Pastore, Sergio. Director. Films: "Chrysanthemums for a Bunch of Swine" 1968-Ital. (& sp.).

Pate, Michael. Writer. Films: "Escape from Fort Bravo" 1953 (story).

Paton, Stuart (1883-12/16/44). Director. Films: "The Border Raiders" 1918; "The Devil's Trail" 1919; "The Terror of the Range" 1919-serial; "The Conflict" 1921; "Man to Man" 1922; "Wolf Law" 1922; "The Love Brand" 1923; "The Night Hawk" 1924; "Baited Trap" 1926; "The Lady from Hell" 1926; "The Wolf Hunters" 1926; "Fangs of Destiny" 1927; "The Bullet Mark" 1928; "The Four-Footed Ranger" 1928; "In Old Cheyenne" 1931; "Mounted Fury" 1931; "The Mystery Trooper" 1931-serial; "The Silent Code" 1935; "Thunderbolt" 1935.

Patrick, John. Screenwriter. Films: "Daniel Boone, Trail Blazer" 1957.

Patrizi, Massimo. Screenwriter. Films: "The Price of Power" 1969-Ital./Span.

Patten, Lewis B. (1924-5/22/81). Writer. Films: "Red Sundown" 1956 (story); "Death of a Gunfighter" 1969 (story); "Don't Turn the Other Cheek" 1974-Ital./Ger./Span. (story).

Patterson, J. Wesley. Screenwriter. Films: "The Outlaw Tamer" 1934.

Patterson, John D. Director. Films: "The Legend of Earl Durand" 1974 (& prod.); "Independence" TVM-1987. ¶TV: *Bonanza*—"Hallie" 2-9-82; *Bret Maverick*—"The Eight Swords of Cyrus and Other Illusions of Grandeur" 3-23-83.

Patullo, George. Screenwriter. Films: "The Angel of Contention" 1914; "The Gunman" 1914 (story only); "The Horse Wrangler" 1914 (story only).

Paul, Byron. Director. TV: *Have Gun Will Travel*—"The Poker Friend" 11-12-60; *Gunsmoke*—"The Imposter" 5-13-61; *Empire*—"A House in Order" 3-5-63.

Paul, Val (1886-3/23/62). Director. Films: "Hearts Up" 1920 (& sp.); "Sundown Slim" 1920; "West Is West" 1920; "Good Men and True" 1922; "The Kick Back" 1922; "Canyon of the Fools" 1923; "Crashin' Thru" 1923; "Desert Driven" 1923; "The Miracle Baby" 1923.

Paylow, Clark (1919-9/25/85). Writer. Films: "Cowboy Commandos" 1943 (story).

Payne, John (1912-12/6/89). Producer. TV: *The Restless Gun* 1957-59 (exec. prod.).

Payne, Stephen. Writer. Films: "Swifty" 1935 (story).

Pazailori, Fulvio. Screenwriter. Films: "Blood Calls to Blood" 1968-Ital.

Peabody, Jack. Screenwriter. Films: "The Big Trail" 1930.

Peacocke, Capt. Leslie T. Screenwriter. Films: "Whatever the Cost" 1918; "The Heart of Juanita" 1919 (story only).

Pearce, Richard. Director. Films: "Heartland" 1980.

Pearl, Edith Cash. Screenwriter. Films: "The Purple Hills" 1961; "The Broken Land" 1962.

Pearsall, Richard D. Writer. Films: "Pinto Canyon" 1940 (story).

Pearson, Barry. Screenwriter. Films: "Sally Fieldgood & Co." 1975-Can.

Pearson, Humphrey. Writer. Films: "Men of America" 1933 (story); "Ruggles of Red Gap" 1935 (adapt.).

Pearson, W.B. Screenwriter. Films: "The Devil's Own" 1916; "Love's Lariat" 1916; "Roped In" 1917; "Hell's Crater" 1918 (& dir.).

Peck, Jr., Charles K. Screenwriter. Films: "Seminole" 1953.

Peck, Charles Mortimer. Screenwriter. Films: "The Kill-Joy" 1917 (story only); "The Law of the Great Northwest" 1918; "The Arizona Catclaw" 1919; "The One Way Trail" 1920.

Peckinpah, Sam (1925-12/28/84). Director. Films: "The Deadly Companions" 1961; "Ride the High Country" 1962; "The Glory Guys" 1965 (sp. only); "Major Dundee" 1965 (& sp.); "Villa Rides" 1968 (sp. only); "The Wild Bunch" 1969 (& sp.); "The Ballad of Cable Hogue" 1970 (& prod.); "Junior Bonner" 1972; "Pat Garrett and Billy the Kid" 1973. ¶TV: *Broken Arrow* 1956; *The Rifleman*—"The Marshal" 10-21-58, "The Boarding House" 2-24-59, "The Baby Sitter" 12-15-59; *Klondike* 60-61; *The Westerner*—1960 (prod.), "Jeff" 9-30-60, "Brown" 10-21-60, "The Courting of Libby" 11-11-60, "Hand on theGun" 12-23-60, "The Painting" 12-30-60.

Peeples, Samuel A. Screenwriter. Films: "Advance to the Rear" 1964. ¶TV: *Overland Trail* 1960 (prod.); *The Tall Man* 1960-62 (prod.).

Peerce, Larry (1935-). TV: *Branded*—"Seward's Folly" 10-17-65, "The Richest Man in Boot Hill" 10-31-65, "$10,000 for Durango" 11-28-65, "A Proud Town" 12-19-65, "The Wolfers" 1-9-66; *Wild Wild West*—"The Night of the Braine" 2-17-67.

Peil, Paul Leslie. Screenwriter. Films: "Frontier Woman" 1956; "Yaqui Drums" 1956 (story only); "Gunsmoke in Tucson" 1958.

Peletier, Jr., Louis. Screenwriter. Films: "Cowboy from Brooklyn" 1938 (story); "Two Guys from Texas" 1948 (story only); "Smith" 1969.

Pelley, William Dudley. Writer. Films: "A Case of Law" 1917 (story); "The Sawdust Trail" 1924 (story); "Courtin' Wildcats" 1929 (story).

Pelusi, Richard. Screenwriter. Films: "Mad at the Moon" 1992.

Pembroke, Percy. Director. Films: "Cactus Trails" 1927.

Pembroke, Scott (1890-2/21/51). Director. Films: "Galloping Thunder" 1927; "The Terror of Bar X" 1927; "Gypsy of the North" 1928; "The Lawless Nineties" 1936 (story only); "The Oregon Trail" 1936.

Pendexter, Hugh. Writer. Films: "A Daughter of the West" 1919 (story).

Penn, Arthur (1922-). Director. Films: "The Left-Handed Gun" 1958; "Little Big Man" 1971; "The Missouri Breaks" 1976.

Penn, Cynthia. Screenwriter. Films: "The Son of Sontag" 1925.

Penn, Leo. Director. Films: "Testimony of Two Men" TVM-1977. ¶TV: *Laredo*—"A Question of Guilt" 3-10-67; *Gunsmoke*—"Slocum" 10-21-68, "The Prisoner" 3-17-69; *Bonanza*—"Yonder Man" 12-8-68, "The Weary Willies" 9-27-70, "The Power of Life and Death" 10-11-70, "Shadow of a Hero" 2-21-71, "The Iron Butterfly" 11-28-71, "A Home for Jamie" 12-19-71, "Shanklin" 2-13-72, "Search in Limbo" 2-20-72, "New Man" 10-10-72, "The Twenty-Sixth Grave" 10-31-72; *Lancer*—"Blind Man's Bluff" 9-23-69, "Zee" 9-30-69; *Little House on the Prairie* 1974; *Sara* 1976; *Bret Maverick*—"The Not So Magnificent Six" 3-2-82, "Faith, Hope and Clarity" 4-13-82 & 4-20-82.

Penney, Edmund. Screenwriter. Films: "The Ballad of Cable Hogue" 1970.

Penney, Joseph. Director. Films: "Back to God's Country" 1953.

Peon, Ramon. Director. Films: "The Devil's Godmother" 1938-Mex.

Peoples, David Webb. Screenwriter. Films: "Unforgiven" 1992.

Peple, Edward. Writer. Films: "The Love Route" 1915 (story).

Peple, Howard Henry. Writer. Films: "The Bachelor Daddy" 1922 (story).

Perelli, Luigi. Director. Films: "They Call Him Veritas" 1972-Ital./Span.

Perez, Marcel. Director. Films: "The Better Man Wins" 1922 (& sp.); "Duty First" 1922; "West vs. East" 1922; "Pioneers of the West" 1927 (& sp.).

Perez, Paul. Screenwriter. Films: "Smoky" 1933; "One Man Justice" 1937; "Two-Fisted Sheriff" 1937; "Flaming Frontier" 1938-serial.

Perez, Raul. Screenwriter. Films: "The Great Divide" 1929; "The Last of the Mohicans" 1936.

Peri, Enzo. Director. Films: "Death Walks in Laredo" 1966-Ital./Span. (& sp.).

Perkins, Kenneth. Writer. Films: "Romance Land" 1923 (story); "Ride Him, Cowboy" 1932 (story); "The Unknown Cavalier" 1926 (story); "Relentless" 1948 (story); "Desert Pursuit" 1952 (story); "Tumbleweed" 1953 (story); "Riding Shotgun" 1954 (story).

Perkins, Lynn. Screenwriter. Films: "King of the Forest Rangers" 1946-serial; "The Phantom Rider" 1946-serial.

Perlberg, William (1899-10/31/68). Producer. Films: "The Tin Star" 1957.

Perrin, Nat. Screenwriter. Films: "Rose of the Rancho" 1936.

Perrored, Filippo. Screenwriter. Films: "Anything for a Friend" 1973-Ital.

Perry, Ben L. Screenwriter. Films: "Terror in a Texas Town" 1958.

Perry, Eleanor (1914-3/14/81). Screenwriter. Films: "The Man Who Loved Cat Dancing" 1973 (& prod.).

Perry, Frank (1930-8/29/95). Director. Films: "Doc" 1971 (& prod.); "Rancho Deluxe" 1975.

Pescatori, Pino. Screenwriter. Films: "Garter Colt" 1967-Ital./Span./Ger.

Pesce, P.J. Director. Films: "Garter Colt" 1967-Ital./Span./Ger.

Peters, Lucy. Screenwriter. Films: "A Broken Spur" 1912.

Petersson, Harold G. Screenwriter. Films: "Treasure of Silver Lake" 1963-Fr./Ger./Yugo.; "Apache Gold" 1965-Ger.; "The Desperado Trail" 1965-Ger./Yugo.; "Last of the Renegades" 1966-Fr./Ital./Ger./Yugo.; "Thunder at the Border" 1967-Ger./Yugo.

Petitclerc, Denne Bart. Screenwriter. Films: "Red Sun" 1971-Fr./Ital./Span.; "Bonanza: Under Attack" TVM-1995. ¶TV: *Shane* 1966 (prod.).

Petracca, Joseph (1914-9/28/63). Screenwriter. Films: "The Proud Ones" 1956; "The Proud Rebel" 1958; "The Jayhawkers" 1959; "Guns of the Timberland" 1960.

Petrie, Daniel (1920-). Director. Films: "Hec Ramsey" TVM-1972; "The Gun and the Pulpit" TVM-1974.

Petrilli, Vittorio. Screenwriter. Films: "Great Silence" 1968-Ital./Fr.

Petroff, Hamil. Director. Films: "California" 1963 (& prod.).

Petroni, Giulio. Director. Films: "Death Rides a Horse" 1967-Ital. (& sp.); "Blood and Guns" 1968-Ital./Span. (& sp.); "A Sky Full of Stars for a Roof" 1968-Ital.; "Night of the Serpent" 1969-Ital. (& sp.); "Sometimes Life Is Hard, Right Providence?" 1972-Ital./Fr./Ger. (& sp.).

Pettito, Tony. Screenwriter. Films: "Comin' at Ya" 1981-Ital.

Pettus, Ken. Screenwriter. Films: "Incident at Phantom Hill" 1966; "Land Raiders" 1969-U.S./Span. (& story).

Pevney, Joseph (1920-). Director. Films: "The Lady from Texas" 1951; "The Plunderers" 1960 (& prod.); "The Night of the Grizzly" 1966. ¶TV: *Wagon Train*—"The Vivian Carter Story" 3-11-59, "The Sister Rita Story" 3-25-59, "The Felezia Kingdom Story" 11-18-59, "The Amos Gibbon Story" 4-20-60, "The Saul Bevins Story" 4-12-61, "The Widow O'Rourke Story" 10-7-63, "The Myra Marshall Story" 10-21-63, "The Cassie Vance Story" 12-23-63, "The Fenton Canaby Story" 12-30-63, "The Grover Allen Story" 2-3-64, "The Melanie Craig Story" 2-17-64, "The Ben Engel Story" 3-16-64; *The Big Valley*—"The Brawlers" 12-15-65; *Laredo*—"Scourge of San Rosa" 1-20-67; *The High Chaparral*—"Tornado Frances" 10-11-68, "The Promised Land" 10-25-68, "Pale Warrior" 12-11-70; *Bonanza*—"The Last Vote" 10-20-68, "The Lady and the Mountain Lion" 2-23-69, "The Gold-Plated Rifle" 1-10-71, "The Buffalo Soldiers" 11-22-68, "A Way of Justice" 12-13-68, "Shadow of the Wind" 1-10-69, "The Last Hundred Miles" 1-24-69, "Kingdom of Fear" 4-4-71, "Easy Come, Easy Go" 12-12-71, "Customs of the Country" 2-6-72; *Sara* 1976; *How the West Was Won*—"The Slavers" 4-23-79; *Father Murphy*—"The Father Figure" 10-5-82, "Outrageous Fortune" 11-9-82, "John Michael Murphy, R.I.P." 12-7-82, "The Matchmakers" 6-10-83.

Peyser, John (1916-). Director. Films: "Four Rode Out" 1969-Ital./Span./U.S. ¶TV: *Sergeant Preston of the Yukon* 1955; *Law of the Plainsman* 1959; *The Rifleman*—"A Case of Identity" 1-19-60; *Bonanza*—"The Lady from Baltimore" 1-14-62.

Phelps, Win. TV: *Adventures of Brisco County, Jr.*—"Crystal Hawks" 11-12-93.

Philips, Lee (1927-). Director. Films: "Wanted: The Sundance Woman" TVM-1976 ¶TV: *Kung Fu*—"The Raiders" 1-24-74.

Phillip, Alex. Writer. Films: "Fighting Playboy" 1937 (story).

Phillipp, Harald. Director. Films: "Rampage at Apache Wells" 1965-Ger./Yugo. (& sp.); "Half Breed" 1966-Ger./Yugo./Ital.

Phillips, Arthur. Screenwriter. Films: "Riding High" 1943.

Phillips, Bill. Screenwriter. Films: "El Diablo" CTVM-1990.

Phillips, Gordon. Screenwriter. Films: "Desert Justice" 1936; "Gun Grit" 1936.

Phillips, Henry Wallace. Writer.

Films: "By Proxy" 1918 (story); "The Fly God" 1918 (story); "The Red Haired Cupid" 1918 (story).

Phillips, Michael. Writer. Films: "Salome, Where She Danced" 1945 (story).

Piccioni, Fabio. Screenwriter. Films: "Finders Killers" 1969-Ital.

Pichel, Irving (1891-7/13/54). Director. Films: "Hudson Bay" 1941; "Santa Fe" 1951.

Picker, Sidney. Producer. Films: "Marshal of Laredo" 1945; "Wagon Wheels Westward" 1945; "California Gold Rush" 1946; "Santa Fe Uprising" 1946; "Sheriff of Redwood Valley" 1946; "Stagecoach to Denver" 1946; "Sun Valley Cyclone" 1946; "Homesteaders of Paradise Valley" 1947; "The Marshal of Cripple Creek" 1947; "Oregon Trail Scouts" 1947; "Robin Hood of Texas" 1947; "Rustlers of Devil's Canyon" 1947; "Saddle Pals" 1947; "Vigilantes of Boomtown" 1947; "Oklahoma Annie" 1952; "Toughest Man in Arizona" 1952; "Untamed Heiress" 1954; "Carolina Cannonball" 1955; "Law That Rifle Down" 1955; "Santa Fe Passage" 1955; "Stranger at My Door" 1956.

Pickett, Elizabeth. Screenwriter. Films: "Redskin" 1929.

Pickford, Mary (1904-5/29/79). Producer. Films: "The Gay Desperado" 1936.

Pierce, Charles B. (1938-). Director. Films: "Winterhawk" 1975 (& prod./sp.); "The Winds of Autumn" 1976 (& prod.); "Grayeagle" 1977 (& prod./sp.).

Pierce, Frank Richardson. Writer. Films: "The Miracle Baby" 1923 (story); "Renegades of the West" 1932 (story).

Pierce, Grace Adele. Screenriter. Films: "The Angel of the Desert" 1913 (story only); Anne of the Mines" 1914.

Pierotti, Mario. *see* Craig, Dean.

Pierotti, Piero (Peter E. Stanley) (1912-5/4/70). Director. Films: "Lost Treasure of the Incas" 1965-Ger./Ital./Fr./Span. (& sp.); "Heads or Tails" 1969-Ital./Span. (& sp.); "Zorro, the Navarra Marquis" 1969-Ital./Span. (sp. only).

Pierro, Ugo. Writer. Films: "Navajo Joe" 1966-Ital./Span. (story).

Piersall, Richard. Writer. Films: "Riders from Nowhere" 1940 (story).

Pierson, Carl. Director. Films: "The New Frontier" 1935; "Paradise Canyon" 1935; "The Singing Vagabond" 1935.

Pierson, Frank. Screenwriter. Films: "Cat Ballou" 1965. ¶TV: *Have Gun Will Travel* 1957-63 (prod.); *Nichols* 1971-72 (prod.).

Piffath, Rod. Writer. Films: "Hot Lead and Cold Feet" 1978 (story).

Piggott, William S. Screenwriter. Films: "Lone Hand Wilson" 1920.

Pilcher, Jay. Screenwriter. Films: "Code of the Wilderness" 1924; "Baree, Son of Kazan" 1925; "Steele of the Royal Mounted" 1925.

Pillsbury, Sam. Director. Films: "Into the Badlands" TVM-1991.

Pinchon, Edgecumb. Writer. Films: "Daniel Boone" 1936 (story).

Pine, F.A.E. Screenwriter. Films: "The Cowboy Cop" 1926; "Red Hot Hoofs" 1926; "Tom and His Pals" 1926; "Wild to Go" 1926; "Cyclone of the Range" 1927; "Lightning Lariats" 1927; "The Outlaw Dog" 1927.

Pine, Howard. Producer. Films: "The Man from Bitter Ridge" 1955; "Ride a Crooked Trail" 1958.

Pine, Philip (1925-). Director. Films: "Posse from Heaven" 1975 (& prod./sp.).

Pine, William H. (1896-4/29/55). Producer. Films: "Albuquerque" 1948; "El Paso" 1949; "The Eagle and the Hawk" 1950; "The Last Outpost" 1951; "Passage West" 1951; "Those Redheads from Seattle" 1953; "The Vanquished" 1953; "The Far Horizons" 1955; "Run for Cover" 1955.

Pink, Sidney W. (Rudolf Zehetgruber) (1916-). Director. Films: "Finger on the Trigger" 1965-Span./Ital./U.S. (& prod./sp.); "The Christmas Kid" 1966-Span./Ital. (& prod.); "The Tall Women" 1966-Austria/Ital./Span. (& prod.); "The Bang Bang Kid" 1968-U.S./Span./Ital. (prod. only).

Pino, Conchita. Screenwriter. Films: "Magniicent Brutes of the West" 1965-Ital./Span./Fr.

Pintoff, Ernest (1931-). Director. TV: *The Kowboys*—Pilot 7-13-70; *Young Dan'l Boone* 1977.

Pinzauti, Mario. Director. Films: "Ringo, It's Massacre Time" 1970-Ital. (& sp.); "Let's Go and Kill Sartana" 1972-Ital./Span.

Pirosh, Robert (1910-12/25/89). Producer. TV: *Laramie* 1959-63.

Pischin, Otto. Screenwriter. Films: "Last Ride to Santa Cruz" 1969-Ger./Fr.

Pitt, Arthur. Director. Films: "Sundance and the Kid" 1975.

Pittman, Frank. Producer. TV: *Tombstone Territory* 1957-60; *Bat Masterson* 1958-61.

Pittman, Michael. Director. TV: *Cheyenne* 1955; *Colt .45* 1957; *Sugarfoot* 1957; *Lawman* 1958.

Pittman, Montgomery (1917-6/26/62). Director. Films: "Slim Carter" 1957 (sp. only); "Money, Women and Guns" 1958 (sp. only). ¶TV: *The Rifleman*—"The Sister" 11-25-58; *Maverick*—"Island in the Swamp" 11-30-58, "Pappy" 9-13-59, "A Cure for Johnny Rain" 12-20-59.

Pittorru, Fabio. Screenwriter. Films: "Macho Killers" 1977-Ital.

Pivar, Ben (1901-3/28/63). Producer. Films: "Man from Montreal" 1940 (& story); "The Kid from Kansas" 1941; "Men of the Timberland" 1941; "Road Agent" 1941.

Pizor, William. Producer. Films: "Two Gun Caballero" 1931; "The Galloping Kid" 1932; "The Texan" 1932; "Arizona Cyclone" 1934; "Carrying the Mail" 1934-short; "Desert Man" 1934; "The Lone Rider" 1934; "Pals of the Prairie" 1934-short; "Pals of the West" 1934-short; "The Sundown Trail" 1934; "West of the Law" 1934-short.

Plympton, George H. Screenwriter. Films: "Dead Shot Baker" 1917; "The Tenderfoot" 1917; "The Home Trail" 1918; "Tucson Jennie's Heart" 1918; "The Canyon Holdup" 1919; "The Trials of Texas Thompson" 1919; "A Broadway Cowboy" 1920; "The Deputy's Double Cross" 1921; "Double Crossers" 1921; "The Fightin' Actor" 1921; "The Man Trackers" 1921; "That Girl Montana" 1921; "The Wild Wild West" 1921; "Perils of the Yukon" 1922-serial; "The Steel Trail" 1923-serial; "Western Fate" 1924; "Blood and Steel" 1925; "Galloping Vengeance" 1925; "The Range Terror" 1925; "The Texas Bearcat" 1925; "The Stolen Ranch" 1926; "Blazing Days" 1927; "Hard Fists" 1927; "One Glorious Scrap" 1927; "Beauty and Bullets" 1928; "Burning the Wind" 1928; "Born to the Saddle" 1929; "Grit Wins" 1929; "Harvest of Hate" 1929 (& story); "Hoofbeats of Vengeance" 1929 (& story); "The Smiling Terror" 1929; "The Indians Are Coming" 1930-serial; "Battling with Buffalo Bill" 1931-serial; "The One Way Trail" 1931; "Heroes of the West" 1932-serial; "The Last Frontier" 1932-serial; "Gordon of Ghost City" 1933-serial; "The Red Rider" 1934-serial; "The Roaring West" 1935-serial; "Rustlers of Red Dog" 1935-serial; "Cavalry" 1936; "The Crooked Trail" 1936; "The Phantom Rider" 1936-serial; "Arizona Gunfighter" 1937; "Bar Z Bad Men" 1937; "Boothill Brigade" 1937; "Doomed at Sundown" 1937; "The Gambling Terror" 1937; "Gun Lords of Stirrup Basin" 1937; "The Gun Ranger" 1937; "The Idaho Kid" 1937; "A Lawman Is Born" 1937; "The Red Rope" 1937; "Trail of Vengeance" 1937; "The Trusted Outlaw" 1937; "Durango Valley Raiders" 1938; "The Feud Maker" 1938; "Flaming Frontier" 1938-serial; "Paroled to Die" 1938; "The Rangers' Roundup" 1938; "Songs and Bullets" 1938 (& story); "Thunder in the Desert" 1938; "Whirlwind Horseman" 1938; "Mesquite Buckaroo" 1939; "The Oregon Trail" 1939-serial; "Smoky Trails" 1939; "Texas Wildcats" 1939; "Trigger Pals" 1939 (& story); "Trailing Double Trouble" 1940 (story only); "Winners of the West" 1940-serial; "Billy the Kid's Fighting Pals" 1941; "Outlaws of the Rio Grande" 1941; "Riders of Death Valley" 1941-serial; "Gangster's Den" 1945; "Last of the Redmen" 1947; "The Vigilante" 1947-serial; "Cody of the Pony Express" 1950-serial (story only); "Roar of the Iron Horse" 1950-serial; "Son of Geronimo" 1952-serial; "Gunfighters of the Northwest" 1954-serial; "Riding with Buffalo Bill" 1954-serial; "Blazing the Overland Trail" 1956-serial; "Perils of the Wilderness" 1956-serial.

Pocock, Roger. Writer. Films: "A Man in the Open" 1919 (story); "Brand of Cowardice" 1925 (story).

Poe, James (1923-1/24/80). Screenwriter. Films: "Last Train from Gun Hill" 1959.

Poe, Jeanne. Screenwriter. Films: "Bulldog Courage" 1922.

Poggi, Franco. Screenwriter. Films: "Holy Water Joe" 1971-Ital.

Poitier, Sidney (1924-). Director. Films: "Buck and the Preacher" 1972.

Poland, Joseph F. Screenwriter. Films: "The Taming of Texas Pete" 1913 (story only); "The Golden Spurs" 1915; "His Father's Rifle" 1915; "Blind Hearts" 1921; "Man's Size" 1923; "Romance Land" 1923; "Three Who Paid" 1923; "The Night Hawk" 1924; "The Silent Rider" 1927; "Sagebrush Troubador" 1935; "The Lawless Nineties" 1936 (& story); "The Old Corral" 1936; "Silver Spurs" 1936; "Winds of the Wasteland" 1936; "Range Defenders" 1937; "The Trigger Trio" 1937 (& story); "Cattle Raiders" 1938; "Renfrew on the Great White Trail" 1938; "Overland with Kit Carson" 1939-serial; "King of the Royal Mounted" 1940-serial; "King of the Texas Rangers" 1941-serial; "King of the Mounties" 1942-serial; "Daredevils of the West" 1943-serial; "Zorro's Black Whip" 1944-serial; "Conquest of Cheyenne" 1946; "Stage to Mesa City" 1947; "Black Hills" 1948; "Cody of the Pony Express" 1950-serial (story only); "Law of the Panhandle" 1950; "Stage to Blue River" 1951; "Texas Lawmen" 1951; "Canyon Ambush" 1952; "Dead Man's Trail" 1952; "Fargo" 1952; "Texas City" 1952; "Texas Bad Man" 1953.

Poll, Martin (1922-). Producer. Films: "The Man Who Loved Cat Dancing" 1973; "My Heroes Have Always Been Cowboys" 1991.

Pollack, Sidney (1930-). Director. Films: "The Scalphunters" 1968; "Jeremiah Johnson" 1972; "The Electric Horseman" 1979.

Pollard, Harry W. (1879-7/6/34). Director. Films: "The Loaded Door" 1922; "Trimmed" 1922.

Pollexfen, Jack. Screenwriter. Films: "The Secret of Convict Lake" 1951 (story only); "Captain John Smith and Pocahontas" 1953; "Five Bold Women" 1960.

Polonsky, Abraham (1910-). Director. Films: "Tell Them Willie Boy Is Here" 1969 (& sp.).

Pond, Elmer S. *see* Clifton, Elmer.

Ponicsan, Darryl. Screenwriter. Films: "The Girl Called Hatter Fox" TVM-1977.

Ponte, Rick. Writer. Films: "Samurai Cowboy" 1993 (story).

Ponti, Carlo (1913-). Producer. Films: "Heller in Pink Tights" 1960.

Poole, Richard. Writer. Films: "The Peacemaker" 1956 (story).

Porter, Edwin S. (1870-4/30/41). Director. Films: "The Great Train Robbery" 1903; "The Life of a Cowboy" 1907; "The House of Cards" 1909; "Pony Express" 1909; "The Cowpuncher's Glove" 1910 (& sp.); "The Luck of the Roaring Camp" 1910 (& sp.); "More Than His Duty" 1910; "Ononko's Vow" 1910 (& sp.); "Ranson's Folly" 1910 (& sp.); "Riders of the Plains" 1910; "A Western Romance" 1910 (& sp.); "The White Red Man" 1911.

Porter, Sidney. Writer. Films: "Jimmy Hayes and Muriel" 1914 (story).

Porter, Verne Hardin. Screenwriter. Films: "Winner Takes All" 1918.

Portis, Charles (1933-). Writer. Films: "True Grit" 1969 (story).

Post, Charles A. (1897-12/20/52). Screenwriter. Films: "Near the Rainbow's End" 1930; "Single-Handed Sanders" 1932.

Post, Ted (1925-). Director. Films: "The Peacemaker" 1956; "The Legend of Tom Dooley" 1959; "Hang 'Em High" 1968; "Yuma" TVM-1971; "The Bravos" TVM-1972 (& sp.); "Stagecoach" TVM-1986. ¶TV: *Gunsmoke*—"Doc's Revenge" 6-9-56, "How to Die for Nothing" 6-23-56, "Prairie Happy" 7-7-56, "Mr. and Mrs. Amber" 8-4-56, "Unmarked Grave" 8-18-56, "Alarm at Pleasant Valley" 8-25-56, "Brush at Elkader" 9-15-56, "Custer" 9-22-56, "The Roundup" 9-29-56, "Indian White" 10-27-56, "How to Cure a Friend" 11-10-56, "Greater Love" 12-1-56, "No Indians" 12-8-56, "Spring Term" 12-15-56, "Gone Straight" 2-9-57, "Skid Row" 2-23-57, "Cain" 3-9-57, "The Bureaucrat" 3-16-57, "Chester's Murder" 3-30-57, "Big Girl Lost" 4-20-57, "Crack-Up" 9-14-57, "Potato Road" 10-12-57, "Romeo" 11-9-57, "Kitty Lost" 12-21-57, "Joe Phy" 1-4-58, "Buffalo Man" 1-11-58, "Claustrophobia" 1-25-58, "Dirt" 3-1-58, "Joke's on Us" 3-15-58, "Laughing Gas" 3-29-58, "Widow's Mite" 5-10-58, "Chester's Hanging" 5-17-58, "Carmen" 5-24-58, "The Gentleman" 6-7-58, "Stage Holdup" 10-25-58, "Land Deal" 11-8-58, "Snakebite" 12-20-58, "Passive Resistance" 1-17-59, "Sky" 2-14-59, "Buffalo Hunter" 5-2-59, "The Choice" 5-9-59, "Print Asper" 5-23-59, "Cheyennes" 6-13-59, "False Witness" 12-12-59, "The Cook" 12-17-60, "Old Fool" 12-24-60, "Bless Me Till I Die" 4-11-61, "Chester's Dilemma" 5-20-61, "The Love Of Money" 5-27-61, "Old Yellow Boots" 10-7-61, "Chesterland" 11-18-61, "Half Straight" 2-17-62, "The Widow" 3-24-62, "Shona" 2-9-63, "Blind Man's Bluff" 2-23-63; *Rawhide*—"Incident of the Widowed Dove" 1-30-59, "Incident of the Town in Terror" 3-6-59, "Incident of the Curious Street" 4-10-59, "Incident of the Dust Flower" 3-4-60, "Incident of the Last Chance" 6-10-60, "Incident at Rojo Canyon" 9-30-60, "Incident at Dragoon Crossing" 10-21-60, "Incident of the Slavemaster" 11-11-60, "Incident at Poco Tiempo" 12-9-60, "Incident of the Buffalo Soldier" 1-1-61, "Incident at the Top of the World" 1-27-61, "Incident Near the Promised Land" 2-3-61, "Incident of the Fish Out of the Water" 2-17-61, "Incident of His Brother's Keeper" 3-31-61, "Incident of the

Lost Idol" 4-28-61, "Incident Before Black Pass" 5-19-61, "Incident at Rio Salado" 9-29-61, "Incident of the Portrait" 10-5-62, "Incident of the Travellin' Man" 10-17-63, "Incident of the Rawhiders" 11-14-63, "Incident of the Geisha" 12-19-63, "Incident at Ten Trees" 1-2-64, "Incident of the Rusty Shotgun" 1-9-64, "Incident of the Dowry Dundee" 1-23-64; *The Rifleman*—"Tension" 10-27-59, "Sins of the Father" 4-19-60, "Nora" 5-24-60, "Seven" 10-11-60; *Wagon Train*—"The Larry Hanify Story" 1-27-60, "The Tracy Sadler Story" 3-9-60, "The Countess Baranof Story" 5-11-60, "The Eleanor Culhane Story" 5-17-61, "Wagon to Fort Anderson" 6-7-61; *The Westerner*—"Treasure" 11-18-60; *Laramie*—"The Accusers" 11-14-61; *Alcoa Premiere*—"Second Chance" 3-13-62; *The Virginian*—"Throw a Long Rope" 10-3-62.

Postal, Florence. Screenwriter. Films: "The Big Trail" 1930.

Potel, Victor (1889-3/8/47). Director. Films: "The Action Craver" 1927.

Potter, Henry C. (1904-8/31/77). Director. Films: "Cowboy and the Lady" 1938.

Povare, Jon. Screenwriter. Films: "Down the Long Hill" TVM-1987.

Povare, Ruth. Screenwriter. Films: "Down the Long Hill" TVM-1987.

Powell, Charles Arthur. Screenwriter. Films: "The Great Adventures of Wild Bill Hickok" 1938-serial; "Panamint's Bad Man" 1938; "Home on the Prairie" 1939.

Powell, Frank. Director. Films: "The Tenderfoot's Triumph" 1910; "An Indian's Loyalty" 1913; "The Tenderfoot's Money" 1913; "Heart of the Sunset" 1918; "The Forfeit" 1919 (& sp.); "The Unbroken Promise" 1919 (& sp.).

Powell, John Wesley. Writer. Films: "Ten Who Dared" 1960 (story).

Powell, Norman S. Director. Films: "Gunsmoke: The Long Ride" TVM-1993 (prod. only); "Gunsmoke: One Man's Justice" TVM-1994 (prod. only). ¶TV: *The Big Valley*—"Ladykiller" 10-16-67, "Shadow of a Giant" 1-29-68, "Town of No Exit" 4-7-69.

Powell, Paul (1881-7/2/44). Director. Films: "Girl of the Timber Claims" 1917; "The Crimson Challenge" 1922; "Death Valley" 1927; "Kit Carson" 1928 (sp. only).

Powers, Francis (1865-5/10/40).

Director. Films: "The Arrow Maiden" 1915; "As in the Days of Old" 1915 (& sp.); "Shadows of Conscience" 1921 (sp. only).

Powers, Katharyn. Screenwriter. Films: "Rodeo Girl" TVM-1980.

Powers, P.A. Producer. Films: "Marked Men" 1919; "The Outcasts of Poker Flat" 1919; "Riders of Vengeance" 1919; "The Kick Back" 1922.

Pradeaux, Maurizio. Director. Films: "Ramon the Mexican" 1966-Ital./Span. (& sp.); "Thunder Over El Paso" 1972-Ital./Span.

Prades, Jaime. Producer. Films: "Savage Pampas" 1966-U.S./Span./Arg.

Prager, Stanley (1917-1/18/72). Director. Films: "The Bang Bang Kid" 1968-U.S./Span./Ital.

Praskins, Leonard (1898-10/2/68). Screenwriter. Films: "Secrets" 1933; "Call of the Wild" 1935; "The Big Bonanza" 1944 (story only); "Three Violent People" 1956 (story only).

Pratt, Jack (1878-12/24/38). Director. Films: "Who Knows?" 1918.

Prebble, John (1915-). Writer. Films: "White Feather" 1955 (story).

Preece, Larry. Director. TV: *The Monroes*—"Incident at Hanging Tree" 10-12-66, "Range War" 12-21-66.

Preece, Michael. Director. TV: *Sara* 1976; *Young Riders*—"Good Night Sweet Charlotte" 1-4-92.

Preminger, Otto (1905-4/23/86). Director. Films: "River of No Return" 1954.

Prentiss, Gregory. Screenwriter. Films: "The Culpepper Cattle Company" 1972.

Presnell, Robert (1894-2/12/69). Screenwriter. Films: "Massacre" 1934; "Hurricane Smith" 1942; "The Big Bonanza" 1944 (story only); "The Michigan Kid" 1947.

Presnell, Jr., Robert (1914-6/14/86). Screenwriter. Films: "The Rawhide Years" 1956.

Price, Charles. Screenwriter. Films: "The Road to Fort Alamo" 1966-Fr./Ital.

Price, Frank. Producer. TV: *The Tall Man* 1960-62; *The Virginian* 1962-70.

Price, Myriam S. Screenwriter. Films: "The Naked Man" 1987-Mex.

Price, Paton. Director. TV: *Maverick*—"Red Dog" 3-5-61,

Prichard, Hesketh. Writer. Films: "Don Q, Son of Zorro" 1925 (story).

Prichard, Kate. Writer. Films: "Don Q, Son of Zorro" 1925 (story).

Prindle, Don. Screenwriter. Films: "The Ugly Ones" 1966-Ital./Span.

Printzlau, Olga (1893-7/8/62). Screenwriter. Films: "The Ring of Destiny" 1915; "Two Men of Sandy Bar" 1916; "Lawless Love" 1918; "The Bachelor Daddy" 1922.

Prinz, LeRoy (1894-9/15/83). Director. Films: "Bob Wills and His Texas Playboys" 1944-short.

Prochnik, Leon. Screenwriter. Films: "Four Eyes and Six-Guns" TVM-1992.

Proietti, Biagio. Screenwriter. Films: "Cost of Dying" 1968-Ital./Fr.

Prosperi, Franco. Screenwriter. Films: "White Apache" 1984-Ital./Span.

Pryor, Charles A. Director. Films: "The Tonopah Stampede for Gold" 1913.

Pryor, Richard (1941-). Screenwriter. Films: "Blazing Saddles" 1974.

Puccini, Gianni. Director. Films: "Fury of Johnny Kid" 1967-Span./Ital.

Puente, Jose Vincent. Screenwriter. Films: "Trinity Sees Red" 1971-Ital./Span.

Puenzo, Luis. Director. Films: "Old Gringo" 1989 (& sp.).

Puglia, Kidia. Screenwriter. Films: "Seven Nuns in Kansas City" 1973-Ital.

Pugliese, Alberto. Producer. Films: "A Pistol for Ringo" 1965-Ital./Span.; "The Return of Ringo" 1966-Ital./Span.; "The Ruthless Four" 1968-Ital./Ger.

Pupillo, Massimo (Max Hunter). Director. Films: "Django Kills Softly" 1968-Ital.

Purcell, Gertrude (1896-5/1/63). Screenwriter. Films: "Destry Rides Again" 1939; "In Old California" 1942.

Purdom, Herbert. Screenwriter. Films: "The Dalton Girls" 1957.

Purdy, Julia M. Writer. Films: "The Stolen Treaty" 1913 (story).

Putnam, Nina Wilcox. Screenwriter. Films: "It's a Bear" 1919; "The Fourth Horseman" 1933 (story only).

Pyle, Denver (1920-). Director. TV: *Dirty Sally* 1974.

Pyne, Daniel. Screenwriter. Films: "The Return of Desperado" TVM-1988.

Pyper, George W. Screenwriter. Films: "The Shootin' Kid" 1920;

"Ghost City" 1923-serial; "The Riddle Rider" 1924-serial; "A Daughter of the Sioux" 1925; "The Fighting Ranger" 1925-serial (story only); "The Fighting Sheriff" 1925 (story only); "Fort Frayne" 1925; "The Man from Lone Mountain" 1925; "Moccasins" 1925; "Range Justice" 1925 (story only); "Riders of Mystery" 1925; "Ridin' Comet" 1925; "Scar Hanan" 1925; "A Two-Fisted Sheriff" 1925; "Warrior Gap" 1925; "Wolves of the Road" 1925; "Baited Trap" 1926; "Avenging Fangs" 1927; "The Silent Hero" 1927; "Son of the Golden West" 1928; "The Drifter" 1929; "Outlawed" 1929.

Questi, Giulio. Director. Films: "Django Kill" 1967-Ital./Span. (& prod.).

Quigley, Robert. Screenwriter. Films: "The Land of Missing Men" 1930; "At the Ridge" 1931; "Near the Trail's End" 1931 (story only); "Shotgun Pass" 1931; "Fighting for Justice" 1932; "Man of Action" 1933; "Rusty Rides Alone" 1933; "Gun Justice" 1934.

Quillan, Joseph (1884-11/16/52). Screenwriter. Films: "Son of Paleface" 1952.

Quillen, Thomas. Director. Films: "Pursuit" 1975.

Quine, Richard (1920-6/10/89). Director. Films: "Talent for Loving" 1969-Brit./Span.

Quintana, Gene. Screenwriter. Films: "Comin' at Ya" 1981-Ital.

Raboch, Al. Director. Films: "Rocky Rhodes" 1934; "The Crimson Trail" 1935.

Raccioppi, Antonio. Screenwriter. Films: "Apache Woman" 1975-Ital.

Rachmil, Lewis J. (1909-2/18/84). Producer. Films: "The Devil's Playground" 1946; "Dangerous Venture" 1947; "Fool's Gold" 1946; "Hoppy's Holiday" 1947; "The Marauders" 1947; "Unexpected Guest" 1947; "Borrowed Trouble" 1948; "The Dead Don't Dream" 1948; "False Paradise" 1948; "Silent Conflict" 1948; "Sinister Journey" 1948; "Strange Gamble" 1948; "Gun Fury" 1953; "They Rode West" 1954; "The Violent Men" 1955; "Reprisal!" 1956.

Rackin, Martin (1918-4/15/76). Screenwriter. Films: "Distant Drums" 1951; "The Big Land" 1957; "Fort Dobbs" 1958 (prod. only); "The Horse Soldiers" 1959 (& prod.); "North to Alaska" 1960; "Stagecoach" 1966 (prod. only); "Rough Night in Jericho" 1967 (prod. only); "Two

Mules for Sister Sara" 1970; "The Revengers" 1972-U.S./Mex. (prod. only); "Nevada Smith" TVM-1975 (& prod.).

Radnitz, Brad. Screenwriter. Films: "The Wackiest Wagon Train in the West" 1976.

Radnitz, Robert B. (1925-). Producer. Films: "...And Now Miguel" 1966.

Rafill, Stewart. Director. Films: "Across the Great Divide" 1976 (& sp.).

Rafkin, Alan (1938-). Director. Films: "The Ride to Hangman's Tree" 1967; "The Shakiest Gun in the West" 1968.

Ragaway, Martin A. Screenwriter. Films: "Lost in Alaska" 1952.

Raimi, Sam (1959-). Director. Films: "The Quick and the Dead" 1995.

Raine, Norman Reilly (1895-7/19/71). Screenwriter. Films: "God's Country and the Woman" 1937; "Virginia City" 1940; "Woman of the North Country" 1952.

Raine, William MacLeod. Writer. Films: "Bringing in the Law" 1914 (story); "Forked Trails" 1915 (story); "Ridgeway of Montana" 1915 (story); "Pure Grit" 1923 (story); "The Man from Wyoming" 1924 (story); "Ridgeway of Montana" 1924 (story); "A Man Four-Square" 1926 (story); "The Man from Bitter Ridge" 1955 (story)."An Arizona Wooing" 1915 (story); "Burning the Wind" 1928 (story); "Three Young Texans" 1954 (story).

Raisbeck, Kenneth. Screenwriter. Films: "The Gay Defender" 1927.

Raison, Milton (George Milton) (1904-1/20/82). Screenwriter. Films: "Murder on the Yukon" 1940; "West of Carson City" 1940 (& story); "Tumbledown Ranch in Arizona" 1941; "Billy the Kid's Smoking Guns" 1942; "Rolling Down the Great Divide" 1942; "Sheriff of Sage Valley" 1942; "The Renegade" 1943 (story only); "Wild Horse Phantom" 1944; "Border Badmen" 1945; "His Brother's Ghost" 1945; "Terrors on Horseback" 1946; "Western Pacific Agent" 1950 (story only); "Old Oklahoma Plains" 1952; "The Homesteaders" 1953; "Old Overland Trail" 1953; "Topeka" 1953.

Rakoff, Alvin (1927-). Director. TV: *Hudson's Bay*—"The Celebration" 4-5-58.

Ralston, Rudy. Producer. Films: "Arizona Manhunt" 1951; "Buckaroo

Sheriff of Texas" 1951; "The Dakota Kid" 1951; "Desperadoes' Outpost" 1952; "Thundering Caravans" 1952; "Wild Horse Ambush" 1952; "Down Laredo Way" 1953; "El Paso Stampede" 1953; "Marshal of Cedar Rock" 1953; "Red River Shore" 1953; "Savage Frontier" 1953; "Shadows of Tombstone" 1953; "The Phantom Stallion" 1954; "Gunfire at Indian Gap" 1957; "Hell's Crossroads" 1957; "The Last Stagecoach West" 1957; "The Lawless Eighties" 1958. ¶TV: *Stories of the Century* 1955.

Ramirez, Pedro L. Director. Films: "None of the Three Were Called Trinity" 1974-Span.

Ramrus, Al. Screenwriter. Films: "Goin' South" 1978.

Rankin, William. Writer. Films: "The Harvey Girls" 1946 (story).

Ranous, William (1857-4/1/15). Director. Films: "Western Courtship" 1908 (sp. only); "Hiawatha" 1909; "Yellow Bird" 1912 (& sp.).

Rapf, Harry. Producer. Films: "The Bad Man of Brimstone" 1938; "Let Freedom Ring" 1939.

Rapf, Matthew. Screenwriter. Films: "The Bad Man of Brimstone" 1938 (story only); "The Adventures of Gallant Bess" 1948; "Hardcase" TVM-1972 (prod. only). ¶TV: *Jefferson Drum* 1958-59 (exec. prod.); *Two Faces West* 1960-61 (prod.); *Iron Horse* 1966-68 (exec. prod.).

Rapf, Maurice. Writer. Films: "Call of the Canyon" 1942 (story).

Rapoport, I.C. Screenwriter. Films: "I Married Wyatt Earp" TVM-1983.

Rathmell, John. Screenwriter. Films: "In Old Santa Fe" 1934 (story only); "The Law of the Wild" 1934-serial (story only); "The Miracle Rider" 1935-serial; "The Phantom Empire" 1935-serial; "Vigilantes Are Coming" 1936-serial; "Ghost Town Gold" 1937; "Riders of the Whistling Skull" 1937; "Trapped" 1937; "Two Gun Law" 1937; "Zorro Rides Again" 1937-serial; "The Painted Desert" 1938; "Starlight Over Texas" 1938; "Fighting Mad" 1939; "Renegade Trail" 1939; "Song of the Buckaroo" 1939; "Southward Ho!" 1939 (story only); "Bullets for Rustlers" 1940; "The Range Busters" 1940; "Underground Rustlers" 1941 (story only).

Rauh, Stanley. Writer. Films: "The Cisco Kid and the Lady" 1939 (story).

Raumaker, Herman C. Director. Films: "Night Cry" 1926.

Ravetch, Irving (1915-). Screen-

writer. Films: "The Outriders" 1950; "Vengeance Valley" 1951; "The Lone Hand" 1953 (story only); "Run for Cover" 1955 (story only); "Ten Wanted Men" 1955 (story only); "Hud" 1963 (& prod.); "Hombre" 1967 (& prod.); "The Cowboys" 1972; "The Spikes Gang" 1974.

Rawles, Carrie E. Screenwriter. Films: "General Custer at Little Big Horn" 1927 (story only); "The Little Big Horn" 1927.

Rawlings, Jr., Richard M. Director. TV: *Paradise*—"Twenty-Four Hours" 5-3-91.

Rawlins, John (1902-). Director. Films: "Men of the Timberland" 1941; "Overland Mail" 1942-serial; "The Arizona Ranger" 1948; "Massacre River" 1949; "Rogue River" 1950; "Fort Defiance" 1951; "Shark River" 1953 (& prod.).

Rawlins, Phil. Director. TV: *The High Chaparral*—"The Lost Ones" 11-21-69, "The Little Thieves" 12-26-69, "The Long Shadow" 1-2-70, "The Guns of Johnny Rondo" 2-6-70, "Wind" 10-9-70, "A Matter of Vengeance" 11-27-70, "Sangre" 2-26-71.

Ray, Albert (1884-2/5/44). Director. Films: "Call of the West" 1930; "Everyman's Law" 1936; "Undercover Man" 1936; "Lawless Land" 1937; "Arizona Wildcat" 1938 (story only); "Desperate Trails" 1939 (& prod.); "Oklahoma Frontier" 1939.

Ray, Bernard B. (Franklin Shamray, Raymond Samuels, Ray Bernard) (1898-12/11/64). Director. Films: "Mystery Ranch" 1932 (& prod. only); "Girl Trouble" 1933 (& prod.); "Arizona Nights" 1934 (& prod.); "The Cactus Kid" 1934; "Loser's End" 1934 (& prod.); "Mystery Ranch" 1934 (& prod.); "Nevada Cyclone" 1934 (& prod.); "Potluck Pards" 1934 (& prod.); "Rainbow Riders" 1934 (prod. only); "Rawhide Mail" 1934 (& prod.); "Ridin' Gent" 1934-short (prod. only); "Terror of the Plains" 1934 (prod. only); "West on Parade" 1934 (& prod.); "Born to Battle" 1935; "Coyote Trails" 1935 (& prod.); "The Laramie Kid" 1935 (prod. only); "Rio Rattler" 1935 (& prod.); "North of Arizona" 1935 (prod. only); "Ridin' Thru" 1935; "Silent Valley" 1935; "The Silver Bullet" 1935 (& prod.); "Skull and Crown" 1935 (prod. only); "Texas Jack" 1935 (& prod.); "Tracy Riders" 1935; "Trigger Tom" 1935 (prod. only); "The Unconquered Bandit" 1935 (prod. only); "Wolf Riders" 1935 (prod. only); "Ambush Valley" 1936 (& prod.); "Caryl of the Moun-

tains" 1936 (& prod.); "Fast Bullets" 1936 (prod. only); "Pinto Rustlers" 1936 (prod. only); "Ridin' On" 1936 (& prod.); "Roamin' Wild" 1936 (& prod.); "Santa Fe Bound" 1936; "Vengeance of Rannah" 1936 (& prod.); "Santa Fe Rides" 1937 (& prod.); "The Silver Trail" 1937 (& prod.); "Smoky Trails" 1939; "Law of the Wolf" 1941 (prod. only); "Buffalo Bill Rides Again" 1947; "Hollywood Barn Dance" 1947 (& story); "Buffalo Bill in Tomahawk Territory" 1952 (& prod.).

Ray, Nicholas (1911-6/16/79). Director. Films: "The Lusty Men" 1952; "Johnny Guitar" 1954; "Run for Cover" 1955; "The True Story of Jesse James" 1957.

Raye, Randall. Screenwriter. Films: "Great Stagecoach Robbery" 1945.

Rayfiel, David. Screenwriter. Films: "Valdez Is Coming" 1971.

Raymaker, Herman C. (1893-3/6/44). Director. Films: "Tracked in the Snow Country" 1925 (& sp.); "Under the Tonto Rim" 1928; "Trailing the Killer" 1932.

Raynor, William. Screenwriter. Films: "Snow Dog" 1950; "Northwest Territory" 1951; "Yukon Manhunt" 1951; "Yukon Gold" 1952; "Fangs of the Arctic" 1953; "Son of Belle Star" 1953; "Yukon Vengeance" 1954.

Rea, Gennard. Screenwriter. Films: "West of Rainbow's End" 1938; "Where the West Begins" 1938.

Reade, Charles. Screenwriter. Films: "Ranson's Folly" 1910.

Reardon, M.S. Screenwriter. Films: "Three Friends" 1912.

Rebuas, Harry. Screenwriter. Films: "Out West with the Peppers" 1940.

Rector, Josephine. Screenwriter. Films: "Broncho Billy's Reason" 1913.

Redford, William. see Squittieri, Pasquale.

Reece, Cornelius. Writer. Films: "The Cowboy Star" 1935 (story).

Reed, Carol (1906-4/25/76). Director. Films: "Flap" 1970.

Reed, Frank. see Ciorciolini, Marcello.

Reed, James. see Malatesta, Guido.

Reed, Tom (1901-8/17/61). Screenwriter. Films: "Hell's Heroes" 1930; "Law and Order" 1932; "The Spoilers" 1942; "The Untamed Breed" 1948; "Back to God's Country" 1953.

Reel, Jr., Frederick. Director.

"The Border Rider" 1924; "The Desert Secret" 1924; "The Last Man" 1924; "Eyes of the Desert" 1926; "Gasoline Cowboy" 1926.

Reese, John. Writer. Films: "Good Day for a Hanging" 1958 (story); "The Young Land" 1959 (story).

Reeve, Arthur B. Writer. Films: "The Return of the Riddle Rider" 1927-serial (story).

Reeves, Steve (1926-). Screenwriter. Films: "A Long Ride from Hell" 1968-Ital.

Regan, Jayne. Screenwriter. Films: "Terror of the Plains" 1934.

Regan, Willy S. *see* Garrone, Sergio.

Reggiani, Franco. Screenwriter. Films: "Django Strikes Again" 1987-Ital./Span./Ger.

Regnoli, Piero (Italo Alfaro). Director. Films: "And They Smelled the Strange, Exciting, Dangerous Scent of Dollars" 1973-Ital. (& sp.).

Reicher, Frank (1875-1/19/65). Director. Films: "The Love Mask" 1916; "The Claim" 1918; "The Only Road" 1918.

Reid, Cliff (1890-8/22/59). Producer. Films: "West of the Pecos" 1934; "Annie Oakley" 1935; "The Arizonian" 1935; "Powdersmoke Range" 1935; "Yellow Dust" 1936; "The Law West of Tombstone" 1938; "The Girl and the Gambler" 1939; "Mexican Spitfire Out West" 1940.

Reid, Hal (1860-5/22/20). Director. Films: "At Cripple Creek" 1912 (& sp.); "The Deerslayer" 1913; "Hearts and Horses" 1913; "A Rose of Old Mexico" 1913.

Reid, Wallace (1891-1/18/23). Director. Films: "Hearts and Horses" 1913; "A Hopi Legend" 1913 (& sp.); "The Mystery of Yellow Aster Mine" 1913; "A Rose of Old Mexico" 1913.

Reinecker, Herbert. Screenwriter. Films: "Winnetou and Shatterhand in the Valley of Death" 1968-Ger./Yugo./Ital.

Reinhardt, Gottfried (1911-7/19/94). Producer. Films: "Big Jack" 1949.

Reiniger, Lotte (1899-6/19/81). Screenwriter. Films: "The Girl of the Golden West" 1942-Ital.

Reinl, Harald. Director. Films: "Treasure of Silver Lake" 1963-Fr./Ger./Yugo.; "Apache Gold" 1965-Ger.; "The Desperado Trail" 1965-Ger./Yugo.; "The Last Tomahawk" 1965-Ger./Ital./Span.; "Last of the Renegades" 1966-Fr./Ital./Ger./Yugo.; "Winnetou and Shatterhand

in the Valley of Death" 1968-Ger./Yugo./Ital.

Reis, Irving (1906-7/3/53). Director. Films: "New Mexico" 1951.

Reisner, Allen. Director. TV: *Rawhide*—"Incident of the Boomerang" 3-24-61; *Gunsmoke*—"Song for Dying" 2-13-65, "South Wind" 11-27-65, "By Line" 4-9-66, "Muley" 1-21-67, "Old Friend" 2-4-67; *Branded*—"A Destiny Which Made Us Brothers" 1-23-66, "Nice Day for a Hanging" 2-6-66, "Call to Glory" 2-27-66, 3-6-66 & 3-13-66; *The High Chaparral*—"The Fillibusteros" 10-22-67; *Lancer*—"Goodbye, Lizzie" 4-28-70; *Kung Fu*—"Nine Lives" 2-15-73.

Reisner, Dean. Screenwriter. Films: "Skipalong Rosenbloom" 1951; "The Man from Galveston" 1964; "Stranger on the Run" TVM-1967; "The Intruders" TVM-1970.

Remington, Colt. Screenwriter. Films: "Crossed Trails" 1948.

Remington, Frederic. Writer. Films: "John Ermine of the Yellowstone" 1917 (story).

Remis, Manuel Martinez. Screenwriter. Films: "Secret of Captain O'Hara" 1965-Span.; "Between God, the Devil and a Winchester" 1968-Ital./Span.; "Quinta: Fighting Proud" 1969-Ital./Span.; "Reverend Colt" 1970-Ital./Span.

Renaldo, Duncan (Renault Duncan) (1904-9/3/80). Screenwriter. Films: "Don Ricardo Returns" 1946; "The Bells of San Fernando" 1947 (& prod.).

Repp, Ed Earl. Screenwriter. Films: "The Man from Hell" 1934 (story only); "The Roaring West" 1935-serial (story); "Cherokee Strip" 1937; "The Devil's Saddle Legion" 1937; "Empty Holsters" 1937 (story only); "The Old Wyoming Trail" 1937; "Outlaws of the Prairie" 1937; "Prairie Thunder" 1937; "Call of the Rockies" 1938; "Cattle Raiders" 1938; "West of Cheyenne" 1938; "Rawhide Rangers" 1941; "The Lone Prairie" 1942 (story only); "Oklahoma Outlaws" 1943-short; "Saddles and Sagebrush" 1943; "Silver City Raiders" 1943; "Six Gun Gospel" 1943; "Wagon Wheels West" 1943-short; "The Last Horseman" 1944; "Roaring Guns" 1944-short; "Trigger Trail" 1944; "The Vigilantes Ride" 1944; "Texas Panhandle" 1945; "The Fighting Frontiersman" 1946; "Galloping Thunder" 1946; "Gunning for Vengeance" 1946; "Heading West" 1946; "Terror Trail" 1946; "The Lone Hand Texan" 1947; "Prairie Raiders" 1947;

"The Stranger from Ponca City" 1947; "The Tioga Kid" 1948; "Challenge of the Range" 1949; "Rider from Tucson" 1950; "Storm Over Wyoming" 1950; "Gunplay" 1951; "Law of the Badlands" 1951; "Saddle Legion" 1951; "The Kid from Broken Gun" 1952.

Resner, Lawrence. Screenwriter. Films: "Gun Battle at Monterey" 1957.

Retchin, Norman. Screenwriter. Films: "Ride Out for Revenge" 1957 (& prod.).

Revier, Harry. Director. Films: "The Challenge of Chance" 1919; "Heart of the North" 1921.

Rey, Gonzalo Asensio. Screenwriter. Films: "Seven for Pancho Villa" 1966-Span.

Reyher, Ferdinand. Screenwriter. Films: "Two in Revolt" 1936.

Reynolds, Clarke (1918-8/18/94). Screenwriter. Films: "Shotgun" 1955; "Gunmen from Laredo" 1959; "Man Called Gringo" 1964-Ger./Span.; "Gunfighters of Casa Grande" 1965-U.S./Span; "Son of a Gunfighter" 1966-U.S./Span.; "Shalako" 1968-Brit./Fr. (story only); "The Desperados" 1969 (story only).

Reynolds, Don. *see* Savino, Renato.

Reynolds, Gene (1925-). Director. TV: *Wanted—Dead or Alive*—"The Cure" 9-28-60; *F Troop* 1965.

Reynolds, Lynn (1891-2/25/27). Director. Films: "The Range Rider" 1910; "The Mexican" 1914 (sp. only); "The End of the Rainbow" 1916 (& sp.); "Broadway, Arizona" 1917 (& sp.); "The Greater Law" 1917; "Up or Down?" 1917 (& sp.); "Ace High" 1918 (& sp.); "Fame and Fortune" 1918; "Mr. Logan, U.S.A." 1918 (& sp.); "Western Blood" 1918 (& sp.); "Treat 'Em Rough" 1919 (& sp.); "Bullet Proof" 1920 (& sp.); "Overland Red" 1920 (& sp.); "The Texan" 1920 (& sp.); "Big Town Round-Up" 1921 (& sp.); "The Night Horsemen" 1921 (& sp.); "Trailin'" 1921 (& sp.); "Arabia" 1922 (& sp.); "For Big Stakes" 1922 (& sp.); "Just Tony" 1922 (& sp.); "Sky High" 1922 (& sp.); "Up and Going" 1922 (& sp.); "Brass Commandments" 1923; "The Gunfighter" 1923 (& sp.); "The Huntress" 1923; "The Deadwood Coach" 1924 (& sp.); "Last of the Duanes" 1924; "Durand of the Bad Lands" 1925 (& sp.); "The Rainbow Trail" 1925 (& sp.); "Riders of the Purple Sage" 1925; "The Buckaroo Kid" 1926 (& sp.); "Chip of the Flying U" 1926 (& sp.); "The Man in the Saddle" 1926; "The Texas Streak" 1926 (& sp.); "Hey! Hey! Cowboy" 1927 (& sp.); "The Silent Rider" 1927.

Reynolds, Sheldon (Ralph Gideon). Director. Films: "A Place Called Glory" 1966-Span./Ger.

Rhine, Larry. Screenwriter. Films: "Chip of the Flying U" 1939.

Rhodes, Eugene Manlove. Writer. Films: "West Is West" 1920 (story); "The Wallop" 1921 (story); "The Mysterious Witness" 1923 (story); "Four Faces West" 1948 (story).

Rhodes, James. Writer. Films: "At the Ridge" 1931 (story).

Rhodes, Michael. Director. TV: *Paradise*—"Founder's Day" 11-10-88.

Ribera, Dan. Screenwriter. Films: "Three Swords of Zorro" 1963-Ital./Span.

Ricci, Tonino. Director. Films: "Bad Kids of the West" 1967-Ital.; "Great Treasure Hunt" 1967-Ital./ Span. (& sp.); "Showdown for a Badman" 1972-Ital. (sp. only).

Rich, David Lowell (1923-). Director. Films: "The Plainsman" 1966; "The Daughters of Joshua Cabe Return" TVM-1975; "Bridger" TVM-1976 (& sp.); "Ransom for Alice!" TVM-1977. ¶TV: *Zane Grey Theater* 1956; *Maverick*—"Yellow River" 2-8-59; *Johnny Ringo* 1959; *Black Saddle* 1959; *Law of the Plainsman* 1959; *Wagon Train*—"The Tiburcio Mendez Story" 3-22-61; *Laredo*—"Yahoo" 9-30-65.

Rich, John (1925-). TV: *Gunsmoke*—"How to Kill a Woman" 11-30-57, "Twelfth Night" 12-28-57, "The Cabin" 2-22-58, "Dooley Surrenders" 3-8-58, "Bottleman" 3-22-58, "Texas Cowboys" 4-5-58, "Amy's Good Deed" 4-12-58, "Hanging Man" 4-19-58, "Innocent Broad" 4-26-58, "The Big Con" 5-3-58, "Hard Luck Henry" 10-23-67, "Deadman's Law" 1-8-68, "O'Quillian" 10-28-68, "The Long Night" 2-17-69; *The Rifleman*—"A Time for Singing" 3-8-60, "The Pitchman" 10-18-60; *Bonanza*—"The Mill" 10-1-60, "The Trail Gang" 11-26-60, "The Conquistadors" 10-1-67, "Judgment at Olympus" 10-8-67.

Richards, Dick (1936-). Director. Films: "The Culpepper Cattle Company" 1972 (& story).

Richards, Hal. Screenwriter. Films: "The Peacemaker" 1956.

Richards, Jackson. Screenwriter. Films: "Trailing the Killer" 1932.

Richards, Marc. Screenwriter.

Films: "The Five Man Army" 1969-Ital.

Richards, Robert L. Screenwriter. Films: "Kansas Raiders" 1950; "Winchester '73" 1950.

Richards, Sylvia. Screenwriter. Films: "Tomahawk" 1951; "Rancho Notorious" 1952 (story only).

Richardson, Don. Director. TV: *Laramie*—"Wolf Cub" 11-21-61; *The Virginian*—"Jennifer" 11-3-65; *Bonanza*—"Little Girl Lost" 11-3-68, "Sweet Annie Laurie" 1-5-69, "A Lawman's Lot Is Not a Happy One" 10-5-69, "A Darker Shadow" 11-23-69, "For a Young Lady" 12-27-70; *Lancer*—"The Last Train for Charlie Poe" 11-26-68, "The Black McGloins" 1-21-69, "Angel Day and Her Sunshine Girls" 2-25-69, "The Knot" 3-18-69, "The Man Without a Gun" 3-25-69; *The High Chaparral*—"Lady Fair" 11-14-69, "The Legacy" 11-28-69, "Jelks" 1-23-70, "Mi Casa, Su Casa" 2-20-70, "Only the Bad Come to Sonora" 10-2-70, "The Forge of Hate" 11-13-70; *The Oregon Trail* 1977.

Richardson, Gladwell. Writer. Films: "Fighting for Justice" 1932 (story).

Richardson, Sy. Screenwriter. Films: "Posse" 1993.

Richardson, Tony (1928-11/15/91). Director. Films: "Ned Kelly" 1970-Brit. (& sp.).

Richmond, Ted (1912-). Producer. Films: "Six-Gun Rhythm" 1939 (story only); "Trigger Pals" 1939 (story only); "Singin' in the Corn" 1946; "King of the Wild Horses" 1947; "Thunderhoof" 1948; "Kansas Raiders" 1950; "The Cimarron Kid" 1951; "Bronco Buster" 1952; "Column South" 1953; "Rails into Laramie" 1954; "Count Three and Pray" 1955; "Advance to the Rear" 1964; "Return of the Seven" 1966-Span.; "Villa Rides" 1968; "Red Sun" 1971-Fr./Ital./Span.

Richter, Conrad (1890-10/30/68). Writer. Films: "The Sea of Grass" 1947 (story); "The Light in the Forest" 1958 (story).

Ricketts, Thomas (1853-1/19/39). Director. Films: "The Belle of the Bar Z Ranch" 1912; "The Ghost of the Hacienda" 1913; "Calamity Anne's Love Affair" 1914; "Her Fighting Chance" 1914; "Jim" 1914; "The Buzzard's Shadow" 1915.

Ricks, Archie (1896-1/10/62). Director. Films: "In Broncho Land" 1926.

Ridgely, Richard. Director. Films: "A Tale of Old Tucson" 1914; "Ranson's Folly" 1915 (& sp.).

Rigal, Arturo. Screenwriter. Films: "Sign of Zorro" 1964-Ital./Span.

Rigby, Gordon. Screenwriter. Films: "Tiger Rose" 1929; "Under a Texas Moon" 1930; "Captain Thunder" 1931; "The Golden West" 1932; "Smoke Lighting" 1933.

Rigby, L.G. Screenwriter. Films: "Rustlin' for Cupid" 1926; "Wings of the Storm" 1926; "The Frontiersman" 1927; "Nevada" 1927; "The Rainbow" 1929.

Riggs, Lynn. Writer. Films: "The Plainsman" 1936; "Oklahoma!" 1955.

Rigsby, Howard (1909-). Writer. Films: "The Last Sunset" 1961 (story).

Rinaldo, Frederic I. (1914-6/22/92). Screenwriter. Films: "The Wistful Widow of Wagon Gap" 1947.

Rinehart, Mary Roberts (1876-9/22/58). Writer. Films: "The Cave on Thunder Cloud" 1915 (story); "Aflame in the Sky" 1927 (story).

Ringoold, Fred. *see* Cerchio, Fernando.

Ripley, Clements. Screenwriter. Films: "Gold Is Where You Find It" 1938 (story only); "Buffalo Bill" 1944; "Roaring Guns" 1944-short (story only); "Old Los Angeles" 1948 (& story).

Rister, Claude. Screenwriter. Films: "The One Way Trail" 1931 (story only); "Tombstone Canyon" 1932; "The Prescott Kid" 1934; "Trapped" 1937 (story only).

Ritchey, Will M. (1882-1/14/37). Screenwriter. Films: "When the Range Called" 1914 (story only); "Told in the Hills" 1919; "North of the Rio Grande" 1922; "The Flame of the Yukon" 1926; "The Last Frontier" 1926; "Whispering Smith" 1926; "Jim the Conqueror" 1927.

Ritchie, Michael (1939-). Director. TV: *The Big Valley*—"Teacher of Outlaws" 2-2-66, "Under a Dark Sea" 2-9-66, "Barbary Red" 2-16-66.

Ritchie, Robert Welles. Writer. Films: "Two Moons" 1920 (story).

Ritt, Martin (1920-12/8/90). Director. Films: "The Outrage" 1964; "Hombre" 1967 (& prod.); "Hud" 1967 (& prod.).

River, W.L. Screenwriter. Films: "The Great Man's Lady" 1942.

Rivera, Manuel. Screenwriter. Films: "White Comnanche" 1967-Ital./Span./U.S.

Rivero, Rodrigo. Screenwriter. Films: "The Christmas Kid" 1966-Span./Ital.

Rivkins, Allen. Screenwriter. Films: "The Road to Denver" 1955; "Timberjack" 1955.

Rix, George. Screenwriter. Films: "Ghost City" 1921.

Roach, Hal (1892-11/2/92). Producer. Films: "The King of the Wild Horses" 1924 (& story); "Black Cyclone" 1925 (sp. only); "The Devil Horse" 1926 (story only); "Men of the North" 1930 (& dir.); "Dudes Are Pretty People" 1942.

Roach, Jr., Hal (1920-3/29/72). Director. Films: "Dudes Are Pretty People" 1942; "Calaboose" 1943; "Prairie Chickens" 1943.

Roach, Joseph Anthony. Screenwriter. Films: "The Cyclone" 1920; "The Daredevil" 1920; "Shod with Fire" 1920; "Fighting for Justice" 1924; "Where the Worst Begins" 1925; "Hoof Marks" 1927; "The Bullet Mark" 1928; "Heroes of the West" 1932-serial; "Jaws of Justice" 1933; "Somewhere in Sonora" 1933; "The Ferocious Pal" 1934.

Roan, Tom. Screenwriter. Films: "The Painted Trail" 1928.

Robbie, Seymour. Director. TV: *F Troop* 1965; *The High Chaparral*—"The Kinsman" 1-28-68, "Tiger by the Tail" 2-25-68; *Bonanza*—"Blood Tie" 2-18-68; *Big Hawaii* 1977.

Robbins, Budd. Screenwriter. Films: "Kid Vengeance" 1976-Ital./U.S./Israel.

Robbins, Jerome C. (1918-). Producer. Films: "The Iron Sheriff" 1957.

Robbins, Jesse. Director. Films: "Shootin' Mad" 1918; "Red Blood and Yellow" 1919; "The Son of a Gun" 1919 (& sp.).

Robe, Mike. Director. Films: "Son of the Morning Star" TVM-1991; "Return to Lonesome Dove" TVM-1993.

Roberson, James. Director. Films: "The Giant of Thunder Mountain" 1991.

Roberts, Ben (1916-5/12/84). Screenwriter. Films: "The Legend of the Lone Ranger" 1981.

Roberts, Charles. Director. Films: "Fighting Hero" 1934 (story only); "Fighting Pioneers" 1935 (sp. only); "Rhythm Wrangles" 1937-short (& sp.); "Prairie Papas" 1938-short (sp. only); "A Western Welcome" 1938-short (sp. only); "Sagebrush Serendade" 1939-short (& sp.); "Corralling a School Marm" 1940-short; "Mexican Spitfire Out West" 1940 (& story); "The Musical Bandit" 1941-short (& sp.); "Range Rhythm" 1942-short (& sp.); "Cactus Capers" 1942-short; "Cactus Cut-Up" 1949-short.

Roberts, Charles E. Writer. Films: "Oklahoma Annie" 1952 (story).

Roberts, Elizabeth Maddox (1886-1941). Writer. Films: "The Great Meadow" 1931.

Roberts, Jack. Screenwriter. Films: "Triple Justice" 1940 (story only).

Roberts, John. Screenwriter. Films: "It Happened Out West" 1937.

Roberts, Kenneth (1885-1957). Writer. Films: "Northwest Passage" 1940 (story).

Roberts, Marguerite (1904-2/17/89). Screenwriter. Films: "Honky Tonk" 1941; "The Sea of Grass" 1947; "Ambush" 1950; "Five Card Stud" 1968; "True Grit" 1969; "Shoot Out" 1971.

Roberts, Meade (1931-2/10/92). Screenwriter. Films: "Blue" 1968.

Roberts, Richard Emery. Writer. Films: "The Last Frontier" 1955 (story); "The Second Time Around" 1961 (story).

Roberts, Stanley (1917-4/22/82). Screenwriter. Films: "Code of the Rangers" 1938; "Heroes of the Hills" 1938 (& story); "Land of Fighting Men" 1938 (story only); "Pals of the Saddle" 1938; "Phantom Ranger" 1938 (story only); "Prairie Moon" 1938; "Red River Range" 1938; "West of Rainbow End" 1938; "Where the West Begins" 1938 (& story); "Colorado Sunset" 1939; "The Night Riders" 1939; "Three Texas Steers" 1939; "Under Western Skies" 1945 (& story); "Curtain Call at Cactus Creek" 1950 (story only).

Roberts, Victor. Screenwriter. Films: "Cowboy Grit" 1925; "Range Buzzards" 1925; "Stampede Thunder" 1925; "West of Arizona" 1925.

Roberts, William. Screenwriter. Films: "The Sheepman" 1958 (adapt. only); "The Magnificent Seven" 1960; "One More Train to Rob" 1971 (story only); "Posse" 1975; "The Legend of the Lone Ranger" 1981.

Roberts, William L. Writer. Films: "Hell's Oasis" 1920 (story).

Robertson, Cliff (1925-). Director. Films: "J.W. Coop" 1971 (& prod./sp.).

Robertson, E.C. Screenwriter. Films: "Buzzy Rides the Range" 1940; "Buzzy and the Phantom Pinto" 1941.

Robins, Sam (Steve Braxton). Screenwriter. Films: "Range War" 1939; "Bad Man from Red Butte" 1940; "The Masked Rider" 1941 (story only); "Law and Order" 1942; "The Lone Rider and the Bandit" 1942; "The Mysterious Rider" 1942; "Outlaws of Boulder Pass" 1942; "Overland Stagecoach" 1942; "Texas Justice" 1942.

Robinson, Casey (1903-12/6/79). Screenwriter. Films: "Renegades of the West" 1932; "Two Flags West" 1950 (& prod.); "A Bullet Is Waiting" 1954.

Robson, Mark (1913-6/20/78). Director. Films: "Roughshod" 1949.

Rocco, Gian Andrea. Director. Films: "Garter Colt" 1967-Ital./Span./Ger. (& sp.).

Roche, Arthur Somers. Screenwriter. Films: "Trail's End" 1922.

Rock, Phillip. Writer. Films: "Escape from Fort Bravo" 1953 (story).

Rodat, Robert. Screenwriter. Films: "Tall Tales: The Unbelievable Adventures of Pecos Bill" 1995.

Roddick, Virginia. Screenwriter. Films: "The Walking Hills" 1949.

Rodgers, Richard (1902-12/30/79). Writer. Films: "Oklahoma!" 1955 (story).

Rodney, Earle (1888-12/16/32). Screenwriter. Films: "The Cow-Catcher's Daughter" 1931-short.

Rodney, Eugene B. (1898-11/26/85). Producer. Films: "Relentless" 1948.

Rodney, Col. George B. Writer. Films: "Frontier Justice" 1936 (story).

Rodriguez, Carlos. Screenwriter. Films: "One After Another" 1968-Span./Ital.

Rodriguez, Ismael. Director. Films: "Daniel Boone, Trail Blazer" 1957.

Roe, Vingie E. Writer. Films: "The Primal Lure" 1916 (story); "Wild Honey" 1918 (story); "The Crimson Challenge" 1922 (story); "North of the Rio Grande" 1922 (story); "The Splendid Road" 1925 (story); "A Perilous Journey" 1953 (story).

Roeca, Sam. Screenwriter. Films: "Sierra Passage" 1951; "The Tall Texan" 1953; "The Outlaw's Daughter" 1954; "Hidden Guns" 1956; "Raiders of Old California" 1957.

Rogell, Albert (1901-4/7/87). Director. Films: "The Mask of Lopez" 1923; "The Dangerous Coward" 1924; "The Fighting Sap" 1924; "Galloping Gallagher" 1924; "Lightning Romance" 1924; "North of Nevada" 1924; "The Silent Stranger" 1924; "Thundering Hoofs" 1924; "The Circus Cyclone" 1925 (& sp.); "Cyclone Cavalier" 1925; "The Knockout Kid" 1925; "The Man from the West" 1926; "Red Hot Leather" 1926; "Senor Daredevil" 1926; "The Unknown Cavalier" 1926; "Wild Horse Stampede" 1926; "The Devil's Saddle" 1927; "The Fighting Three" 1927; "Grinning Guns" 1927; "Men of Daring" 1927; "The Overland Stage" 1927; "Red Raiders" 1927; "Rough and Ready" 1927; "Somewhere in Sonora" 1927; "The Western Rover" 1927; "The Western Whirlwind" 1927 (& story); "The Canyon of Adventure" 1928; "The Glorious Trail" 1928; "Phantom City" 1928; "The Shepherd of the Hills" 1928; "The Upland Rider" 1928; "The California Mail" 1929; "Cheyenne" 1929; "Rider of Death Valley" 1932; "In Old Oklahoma" 1943; "Heaven Only Knows" 1947; "Northwest Stampede" 1948 (& prod.). ¶TV: *My Friend Flicka* 1955.

Rogell, Sid (1900-11/15/73). Producer. Films: "Nevada" 1944; "Guns of Hate" 1948.

Rogers, Cameron. Writer. Films: "Belle Starr" 1941 (story).

Rogers, Charles R. (1892-3/29/57) Producer. Films: "The Devil's Saddle" 1927 (sp. only); "Red Raiders" 1927; "Border Patrol" 1928; "The Shepherd of the Hills" 1928; "The Royal Rider" 1929; "The Fighting Parson" 1930-short (dir. only); "Way Out West" 1937 (sp./story only); "The Parson and the Outlaw" 1957.

Rogers, Gregory. Writer. Films: "Jaws of Steel" 1927 (story); "Tracked by the Police" 1927 (story).

Rogers, Howard Emmet. Writer. Films: "Billy the Kid" 1941 (story).

Rogers, John W. Producer. Films: "Law and Order" 1953; "Ride Clear of Diablo" 1953; "War Arrow" 1953; "Black Horse Canyon" 1954.

Rogers, Roy (1912-). Producer. TV: *The Roy Rogers Show* 1951-57.

Rogers, Will (1879-8/15/35). Writer. Films: "The Ropin' Fool" 1921 (story).

Roland, Gilbert (1905-5/15/94). Screenwriter. Films: "King of the Bandits" 1947.

Roland, Jurgen. Director. Films: "Pirates of the Mississippi" 1963-Ger./Ital./Fr.

Roley, Sutton. Director. TV: *Wagon Train*—"The Earl Packer Story" 1-4-61; *Gunsmoke*—"Aunt Thede" 12-19-64; *Rawhide*—"Encounter at Boot Hill" 9-14-65, "Duel at Daybreak" 11-16-65; *The Big Valley*—"The River Monarch" 4-6-66; *Bonanza*—"To Bloom for Thee" 10-16-66.

Rolfe, Sam (1924-7/10/93). Screenwriter. Films: "The Naked Spur" 1953; "Pillars of the Sky" 1956; "Hardcase" TVM-1972; "This Was the West That Was" TVM-1974; "Law of the Land" TVM-1976.

Roli, Mino. Screenwriter. Films: "The Tall Women" 1966-Austria/Ital./Span.; "Beyond the Law" 1968-Ital.; "Matalo!" 1971-Ital./Span.; "On the Third Day Arrived the Crow" 1972-Ital./Span.; "Carambola" 1974-Ital.; "Carambola's Philosophy: In the Right Pocket" 1975-Ital.

Rollens, Jack. Writer. Films: "A Roaring Adventure" 1925 (story).

Roman, Lawrence. Screenwriter. Films: "Drums Across the River" 1954; "The Man from Bitter Ridge" 1955; "Day of the Bad Man" 1958.

Roman, Michael Martinez. Screenwriter. Films: "Duel in the Eclipse" 1967-Span.

Romano, Antonio. Director. Films: "Savage Gringo" 1966-Ital.; "Winchester Does Not Forgive" 1968-Ital. (sp. only).

Romero, Eddie. Director. Films: "Cavalry Command" 1963-U.S./Phil. (& sp.).

Romero Marchent, Joaquin L. (Joaquin Romero Hernandez). Director. Films: "Gunfight at High Noon" 1963-Span./Ital. (& sp.); "Magnificent Three" 1963-Span./Ital.; "Shadow of Zorro" 1963-Span./Ital. (& sp.); "Coyote" 1964-Span./Ital. (& sp.); "Seven Guns from Texas" 1964-Span./Ital. (& prod./sp.); "Seven Hours of Gunfire" 1964-Span./Ital. (& sp.); "Hands of a Gunman" 1965-Ital./Span. (sp. only); "Kill Them All and Come Back Alone" 1967-Ital./Span. (sp. only); "Awkward Hands" 1968-Span./Ital. (sp. only); "Dollars for a Fast Gun" 1968-Ital./Span.; "Hour of Death" 1968-Span./Ital. (& sp.); "I Do Not Forgive ... I Kill!" 1968-Span./Ital. (& sp.); "Two Crosses at Danger Pass" 1968-Ital./Span. (sp. only); "Dead Are Countless" 1969-Ital./Span. (sp. only); "Sartana Kills Them All" 1970-Ital./Span. (sp. only); "Cut-Throats Nine" 1973-Span./Ital. (& sp.).

Romero Marchent, Rafael. Director. Films: "Gunfight at High Noon" 1963-Span./Ital. (sp. only); "Shadow of Zorro" 1963-Span./Ital. (sp. only); "Hands of a Gunman" 1965-Ital./Span.; "Woman for Ringo" 1966-Ital./Span. (& sp.); "Ringo, the Lone Rider" 1967-Ital./Span.; "Awkward Hands" 1968-Span./Ital.; "Cry for Revenge" 1968-Ital./Span. (& sp.); "Hour of Death" 1968-Span./Ital. (sp. only); "One Against One ... No Mercy" 1968-Span./Ital.; "Two Crosses at Danger Pass" 1968-Ital./Span. (& sp.); "Dead Are Countless" 1969-Ital./Span.; "Sartana Kills Them All" 1970-Ital./Span.; "Prey of Vultures" 1973-Span./Ital. (& sp.).

Rondeau, Charles R. Director. TV: *The Dakotas* 1963; *Temple Houston* 1963; *Bonanza*—"Calamity Over the Comstock" 11-3-63; *Rawhide*—"A Time for Waiting" 1-22-65; *F Troop* 1965; *Laredo*—"A Prince of a Ranger" 12-9-66, "Oh Careless Love" 12-23-66, "The Bitter Yen of General Ti" 2-3-67; *Gunsmoke*—"Mad Dog" 1-14-67; *Wild Wild West*—"The Night of the Tartar" 2-3-67, "The Night of the Colonel's Ghost" 3-10-67, "The Night of the Wolf" 3-31-67, "The Night of the Sabatini Death" 2-2-69; *Cimarron Strip*—"Knife in the Darkness" 1-25-68.

Ronson, Arthur. Screenwriter. Films: "The Honor of the Mounted" 1914.

Root, Lynn. Screenwriter. Films: "Wild and Woolly" 1937.

Root, Wells (1900-3/8/93). Screenwriter. Films: "The Storm" 1930; "Bold Caballero" 1936 (& sp.); "Man of Conquest" 1939 (& story); "The Bad Man" 1941; "Texas Across the River" 1966.

Ropes, Bradford. Screenwriter. Films: "Gaucho Serenade" 1940; "Rancho Grande" 1940; "Ridin' on a Rainbow" 1941 (& story); "Hands Across the Border" 1943; "Man from Music Mountain" 1943; "Cowboy and the Senorita" 1944 (story only); "Swing in the Saddle" 1944; "Song of Arizona" 1946 (story only); "Pirates of Monterey" 1947 (story only); "The Arizona Cowboy" 1950; "Redwood Forest Trail" 1950.

Rosati, Guiseppe. Director. Films: "Twenty Paces to Death" 1970-Ital./Span. (sp. only); "Those Dirty Dogs!" 1973-U.S./Ital./Span. (& sp.).

Rose, Jack. Screenwriter. Films: "The Paleface" 1948; "Talent for Loving" 1969-Brit./Span.; "The Duchess and the Dirtwater Fox" 1976.

Rose, Reginald (1921-). Screenwriter. Films: "Man of the West" 1958; "Stranger on the Run" TVM-1967 (story only).

Rosebrook, Jeb. Screenwriter. Films: "Junior Bonner" 1972; "I Will Fight No More Forever" TVM-1975; "The Mystic Warrior" TVM-1984; "The Gambler, Part III—The Legend Continues" TVM-1987.

Rosen, Philip E. (1888-10/22/51). Director. Films: "The Double Hold-Up" 1919; "The Jay Bird" 1920; "Roarin' Dan" 1920; "The Sheriff's Oath" 1920; "West Is Best" 1920; "Alias the Bad Man" 1931; "Arizona Terror" 1931; "Branded Men" 1931; "The Pocatello Kid" 1931; "Range Law" 1931; "The Two Gun Man" 1931; "The Gay Buckaroo" 1932; "Klondike" 1932; "A Man's Land" 1932; "Texas Gun Fighter" 1932; "The Vanishing Frontier" 1932; "Whistlin' Dan" 1932; "Young Blood" 1932; "West of the Pecos" 1934; "Roaring Timber" 1937; "Queen of the Yukon" 1940; "In Old New Mexico" 1945.

Rosenberg, Aaron (1912-9/1/79). Producer. Films: "Winchester '73" 1950; "Cattle Drive" 1951; "Bend of the River" 1952; "Gunsmoke" 1953; "The Man from the Alamo" 1953; "Wings of the Hawk" 1953; "Saskatchewan" 1954; "The Far Country" 1955; "Man Without a Star" 1955; "Backlash" 1956; "Walk the Proud Land" 1956; "Night Passage" 1957; "The Badlanders" 1958; "The Reward" 1965; "Smoky" 1966. ¶TV: *Daniel Boone* 1964-70 (exec. prod.).

Rosenberg, Frank P. Producer. Films: "The Secret of Convict Lake" 1951; "Return of the Texan" 1952; "One-Eyed Jacks" 1961.

Rosenberg, Jeanne. Screenwriter. Films: "White Fang" 1991.

Rosenberg, Meta. Producer. TV: *Nichols* 1971-72 (exec. prod.); *Bert Maverick* 1981-82 (exec. prod.).

Rosenberg, Stuart (1925-). Director. Films: "Pocket Money" 1972; "My Heroes Have Always Been Cowboys" 1991. ¶TV: *Rawhide*—"The Gray Rock Hotel" 5-21-65.

Rosener, George (1879-3/29/45). Screenwriter. Films: "The Great Adventures of Wild Bill Hickok" 1938-serial; "Fighting Mad" 1939.

Rosenwald, Francis. Screenwriter. Films: "The Dead Don't Dream" 1948; "Red Stallion in the Rockies" 1949.

Ross, Arthur. Screenwriter. Films: "The Stand at Apache River" 1953.

Ross, Dick. Director. Films: "The Persuaders" 1957 (& prod./sp.).

Ross, Frank (1904-2/18/90). Producer. Films: "A Lady Takes a Chance" 1943.

Ross, Lillian Bos. Writer. Films: "Zandy's Bride" 1974 (story).

Ross, Nat. Director. Films: "The Galloping Kid" 1922; "Jaws of Steel" 1922; "Never Let Go" 1922; "Plain Grit" 1922; "Ridin' Wild" 1922; "Tracked Down" 1922; "Unmasked" 1922; ; "The Payroll Thief" 1923; "Pure Grit" 1923; "The Rustlin' Buster" 1923; "Stolen Gold" 1923; "Western Skies" 1923; "Down in Texas" 1924; "Gold Digger Jones" 1924; "The Man from Guntown" 1935 (prod only); "The Outlaw Deputy" 1935 (prod. only).

Ross, Rita. Screenwriter. Films: "Fighting Mustang" 1948.

Rossati, Nello (Ted Archer). Director. Films: "Django Strikes Again" 1987-Ital./Span./Ger. (& sp.).

Rosseau, Victor. Screenwriter. Films: "The Devil's Tower" 1928.

Rossen, Robert (1908-2/18/66). Director. Films: "Desert Fury" 1947 (sp. only); "They Came to Cordura" 1959 (& sp.).

Rossetti, Franco. Director. Films: "The Avengers" 1966-Ital. (sp. only); "Django" 1966-Ital./Span. (sp. only); "Ringo and His Golden Pistol" 1966-Ital. (sp. only); "Texas, Adios" 1966-Ital./Span. (sp. only); "Big Ripoff" 1967-Span./Ital. (& sp.); "Rita of the West" 1967-Ital. (sp. only); "Get the Coffin Ready" 1968-Ital. (sp. only); "Chuck Moll" 1970-Ital. (sp. only); "The Dirty Outlaws" 1971-Ital. (& prod./sp.).

Rosso, Salvatore. Director. Films: "Stranger in Paso Bravo" 1968-Ital.

Rosson, Arthur (1887-6/17/60). Director. Films: "Bloodhounds of the North" 1913 (story only); "A Case of Law" 1917; "Headin' South" 1918; "The Coming of the Law" 1919 (& sp.); "Rough-Riding Romance" 1919; "Fighting Streak" 1922 (& sp.); "Blasted Hopes" 1924; "The Measure of a Man" 1924; "The Burning Trail" 1925; "The Meddler" 1925; "Ridin' Pretty" 1925; "Ridin' Through" 1925; "The Taming of the West" 1925; "The Last Outlaw" 1927; "Set Free" 1927; "The Long, Long Trail" 1929; "Points West" 1929; "The Winged Horseman" 1929; "The Concentratin' Kid" 1930; "The Mounted Stranger" 1930 (& sp.); "Trailin' Trouble" 1930 (& sp./story); "Flaming Guns" 1932; "Wide Open Spaces" 1932-short;

"Hidden Gold" 1933; "Boots of Destiny" 1937 (& sp.); "Trailing Trouble" 1937.

Rosson, Richard. Director. Films: "Shootin' Irons" 1927.

Rostel, Newman. see Massi, Stelvio.

Rothafel, Robert C. Screenwriter. Films: "The Roaring West" 1935-serial.

Rothchild, Julius. Writer. Films: "American Maid" 1917 (story).

Rouse, Russell (1913-10/2/87). Director. Films: "Fastest Gun Alive" 1956 (& sp.); "Thunder in the Sun" 1959 (& sp.).

Rousseau, Louis. Screenwriter. Films: "Fuzzy Settles Down" 1944; "Fight Bill Carson" 1945; "Lonesome Trail" 1945; "Riders of the Dawn" 1945; "Rockin' in the Rockies" 1945 (story only); "Gunning for Vengeance" 1946 (story only); "Lone Star Moonlight" 1946; "Moon Over Montana" 1946; "West of the Alamo" 1946; "Over the Santa Fe Trail" 1947; "Under Colorado Skies" 1947; "Prince of the Plains" 1949.

Rousseau, Victor (1879-4/5/60). Writer. Films: "West of the Rainbow's End" 1926 (story).

Rowe, Arthur. Screenwriter. Films: "The Magnificent Seven Ride" 1972.

Rowland, E.G. see Castellari, Enzo.

Rowland, Roy (1910-6/29/95). Director. Films: "Boy's Ranch" 1946; "The Outriders" 1950; "The Moonlighter" 1953; "Many Rivers to Cross" 1955; "Gun Glory" 1957; "Man Called Gringo" 1964-Ger./Span.; "Gunfighters of Casa Grande" 1965-U.S./Span.

Royal, Charles Francis. Screenwriter. Films: "The Courageous Avenger" 1935; "Western Courage" 1935 (story only); "Guns in the Dark" 1937; "Lightnin' Crandall" 1937; "Outlaws of the Orient" 1937; "Phantom of Santa Fe" 1937; "Ridin' the Lone Trail" 1937; "Colorado Kid" 1938; "Colorado Trail" 1938; "The Old Barn Dance" 1938; "Rio Grande" 1938; "Outpost of the Mounties" 1939; "The Taming of the West" 1939; "Texas Stampede" 1939; "Trouble in Sundown" 1939 (story only); "Lone Star Raiders" 1940 (story only); "The Man from Tumbleweeds" 1940; "North from the Lone Star" 1941; "A Tornado in the Saddle" 1942.

Royle, Edwin Milton. Writer. Films: "The Squaw Man" 1914 (story); "The Squaw Man's Son" 1917 (son); "The Squaw Man" 1918 (story); "The Squaw Man" 1931 (story).

Royal, Lloyd. Producer. Films: "Jesse James' Women" 1954; "Frontier Woman" 1956; "Natchez Trace" 1960.

Rubel, James L. Writer. Films: "The Medico of Painted Springs" 1941 (story); "Prairie Stranger" 1941 (story); "Thunder Over the Prairie" 1941 (story).

Ruben, Albert. Screenwriter. Films: "Journey Through Rosebud" 1972.

Ruben, J. Walter. Director. Films: "The Last Outlaw" 1927; "Open Range" 1927; "Shootin' Irons" 1927; "Avalanche" 1928 (sp. only); "Under the Tonto Rim" 1928 (sp. only); "The Vanishing Pioneer" 1928 (sp. only); "Stairs of Sand" 1929; "Sunset Pass" 1929; "The Bad Man of Brimstone" 1938 (& story); "Twenty Mule Team" 1940 (prod. only); "The Bad Man" 1941 (prod. only).

Rubin, Daniel N. Screenwriter. Films: "The Texan" 1930.

Rubin, Stanley. Producer. Films: "Destry" 1954; "River of No Return" 1954; "The Rawhide Years" 1956. ¶TV: *Hotel De Paree* 1959-60.

Rubio, Miguel. Screenwriter. Films: "Trinity Sees Red" 1971-Ital./Span.

Rude, Dick. Screenwriter. Films: "Straight to Hell" 1987-Brit.

Rudolph, Alan (1943-). Screenwriter. Films: "Buffalo Bill and the Indians, or Sitting Bull's History Lesson" 1976.

Rudolph, Oscar (1911-2/1/91). Director. Films: "The Wild Westerners" 1962 ¶TV: *The Lone Ranger—* "Texas Draw" 11-4-54.

Ruggles, Wesley (1889-1/8/72). Director. Films: "Cimarron" 1931; "Arizona" 1940 (& prod.).

Runnell, Ruth. Screenwriter. Films: "Racketeer Round-Up" 1934.

Rush, Charles O. Director. Films: "When Romance Rides" 1922.

Rush, Dick. Director. Films: "Playing Double" 1923. ¶TV: *Brave Eagle* 1955-56 (exec. prod. only).

Ruskin, Harry (1894-11/16/69). Screenwriter. Films: "Barbary Coast Gent" 1944.

Rusoff, Lou. Screenwriter. Films: "Apache Woman" 1955; "The Oklahoma Woman" 1956.

Russell, Albert (1876-4/3/46). Director. Films: "Double Danger" 1920; "Fight It Out" 1920; "'In Wrong' Wright" 1920; "Marryin' Marion" 1920; "The Moon Riders" 1920-serial (& sp.); "A Pair of Twins" 1920; "Tipped Off" 1920; "The Trail of the Hound" 1920; "The Driftin' Kid" 1921; "Kickaroo" 1921; "The White Horseman" 1921-serial (& sp.); "The Call of Courage" 1922; "Matching Wits" 1922; "Trickery" 1922; "The Verdict" 1922; "The Lone Fighter" 1923.

Russell, Bing (1928-). Screenwriter. Films: "An Eye for an Eye" 1966.

Russell, John. Writer. Films: "The Iron Horse" 1924 (story).

Russell, L. Case. Writer. Films: "Red Love" 1925 (story).

Russell, William D. Director. Films: "Best of the Badmen" 1951. ¶TV: *Gunsmoke—* "The Cover Up" 1-12-57, "The Photographer" 4-6-57, "Moon" 5-11-57, "The Man Who Would Be Marshal" 6-15-57.

Ruthven, Madeleine. Screenwriter. Films: "Spoilers of the West" 1928; "Wyoming" 1928.

Ryan, Dan. Screenwriter. Films: "Death Valley Outlaws" 1941; "West of Cimarron" 1941.

Ryan, Mrs. James A. Screenwriter. Films: "The Song of the Wildwood Flute" 1910.

Ryan, Marah Ellis. Writer. Films: "That Girl Montana" 1921 (story).

Ryan, Tim. Screenwriter. Films: "Bowery Buckaroos" 1947.

Rydell, Mark (1934-). Director. Films: "The Cowboys" 1972 (& prod.). ¶TV: *Gunsmoke—* "Hung High" 11-14-64, "Chief Joseph" 1-30-65, "The Lady" 3-27-65, "Twenty Miles from Dodge" 4-10-65, "Ten Little Indians" 10-9-65, "Outlaw's Woman" 12-11-65, "Death Watch" 1-8-66, "Snap Decision" 9-17-66, "The Mission" 10-8-66, "Gunfighter, R.I.P." 10-22-66; *Wild Wild West—* "The Night of the Whirring Death" 2-18-66.

Ryerson, Florence. Screenwriter. Films: "Blazing Days" 1927 (story only); "Call of the West" 1930; "Henry Goes Arizona" 1939; "The Kid from Texas" 1939.

Ryter, Frederick. Writer. Films: "The Man from New Mexico" 1932 (story).

Saal, William. Producer. Films: "Between Fighting Men" 1932; "Dynamite Ranch" 1932; "Come On Tarzan" 1933; "Drum Taps" 1933;

"Fargo Express" 1933; "The Lone Avenger" 1933; "The Phantom Thunderbolt" 1933.

Sabatello, Dario (Ted O'Darsa). Producer. Films: "Seven Guns for the MacGregors" 1965-Ital./Span.; "Up the MacGregors!" 1967-Ital./Span.

Sabello, Julio. Writer. Films: "Down by the Rio Grande" 1924 (story).

Sackheim, Jerry (1905-5/13/79). Screenwriter. Films: "Saddle Pals" 1947; "Young Jesse James" 1960.

Sackheim, William (1919-). Screenwriter. Films: "Barricade" 1950; "Column South" 1953; "Border River" 1954. ¶TV: *Empire* 1962-63 (prod.).

Sacks, Ruth Buchanan. Writer. Films: "A Woman's Man" 1920 (story).

Saeta, Eddie. Director. TV: *Hondo—* "Hondo and the Gladiators" 12-15-67.

Sagal, Boris (1923-5/22/81). Director. Films: "Guns of Diablo" 1964; "Hitched" TVM-1973; "The Oregon Trail" TVM-1976; "The Awakening Land" TVM-1978. ¶TV: *Dundee and the Culhane—* "The Turn the Other Cheek Brief" 9-6-67; *Cimarron Strip—* "Nobody" 12-7-67.

St. Clair, Arthur. Screenwriter. Films: "Boss of Bullion City" 1941; "Road Agent" 1941 (story only); "King of the Stallions" 1942; "Stagecoach Buckaroo" 1942 (story only); "Gunman's Code" 1946 (story only); "The Prairie" 1947; "Rimfire" 1949.

St. Clair, Malcolm (1897-6/1/52). Director. Films: "Montana Moon" 1930.

St. John, Adele Rogers (1894-8/10/88). Screenwriter. Films: "Arizona Wildcat" 1927 (story only); "Broncho Twister" 1927 (story only); "The Great Man's Lady" 1942.

St. Joseph, Ellis. Writer. Films: "Reno" 1939 (story).

St. Laire, Arthur. Screenwriter. Films: "Along the Sundown Trail" 1942.

Sais, Marin (1890-12/31/71). Writer. Films: "Barb Wire" 1922 (story).

Sale, Richard (1911-3/4/93). Director. Films: "Northwest Outpost" 1947 (sp. only); "The Dude Goes West" 1948 (sp. only); "Ticket to Tomahawk" 1950 (& sp.); "The White Buffalo" 1977 (sp. only). ¶TV: *Yancy Derringer* 1958-59 (& prod.); *The High Chaparral—* "Sudden Country" 11-5-67.

Salerno, Vittorio. Screenwriter.

Films: "Cry for Revenge" 1968-Ital./
Span.; "Pistol for a Hundred Coffins"
1968-Ital./Span.; "Blood at Sundown" 1969-Ital./Ger.; "Dead Are
Countless" 1969-Ital./Span.

Salkow, Sidney (1909-). Director. Films: "Rhythm on the Range"
1936 (sp. only); "The Pathfinder"
1952; "Jack McCall, Desperado"
1953; "Sitting Bull" 1954 (& sp.);
"Robbers' Roost" 1955 (& sp.); "Gun
Brothers" 1956; "Gun Duel in Durango" 1957; "The Iron Sheriff"
1957; "Blood on the Arrow" 1964;
"The Quick Gun" 1964; "The Great
Sioux Massacre" 1965 (& story).
¶TV: *Bronco* 1958; *Maverick*—"Marshal Maverick" 3-11-62, "The Troubled Heir" 4-1-62.

Salkowitz, Sy. Screenwriter.
Films: "Nakia" TVM-1974.

Salle, Michael. Director. Films:
"Riders of the Pony Express" 1949.

Salt, Waldo (1914-3/7/87).
Screenwriter. Films: "Rachel and the
Stranger" 1948.

Salter, Harry (1898-3/5/84).
Screenwriter. Films: "The Sage Hen"
1921.

Salter, Marck. Screenwriter.
Films: "Shoot the Living ... Pray for
the Dead" 1972-Ital.

Salvador, Jimmy. Director.
Films: "Dalton That Got Away"
1960.

Salvi, Erminio. Director. Films:
"Three Graves for a Winchester"
1966-Ital. (& sp.); "Wanted Johnny
Texas" 1971-Ital. (& sp.).

Salvioni, Giorgio. Screenwriter.
Films: "Alive or Preferable Dead"
1969-Span./Ital.

Samuels, Harry. *see* Webb,
Harry S.

Samuels, Henri. *see* Webb,
Harry S.

Samuels, Lesser (1894-12/22/
80). Screenwriter. Films: "Great Day
in the Morning" 1956.

Samuels, Raymond. *see* Ray,
Bernard B.

Sandler, Barry. Screenwriter.
Films: "The Duchess and the Dirtwater Fox" 1976 (& story).

Sandefur, Duke. Screenwriter.
Films: "Ghost Town" 1988.

Sandoz, Mari. Writer. Films:
"Cheyenne Autumn" 1964 (story).

Sandrich, Mark. Director.
Films: "Buck Benny Rides Again"
1940 (& prod.). ¶TV: *Lawman* 1958.

Sanford, Harry. Screenwriter.
Films: "Apache Uprising" 1966 (&
story).

Sanford, John. Screenwriter.
Films: "Honky Tonk" 1941.

Sanford, Joseph. Producer.
Films: "Law and Order" 1940; "Rag-
time Cowboy Joe" 1940; "Son of
Roaring Dan" 1940.

Sanforth, Clifford. Screenwriter. Films: "The Adventures of the
Masked Phantom" 1939.

Sangster, Jimmy (1927-). Producer. Films: "The Savage Guns"
1961-U.S./Span. ¶TV: *Young Dan'l
Boone* 1977.

Sanpietro, Jaime. Screenwriter.
Films: "Bandidos" 1991-Mex.

Sansone, Alfonso. Producer.
Films: "Day of Anger" 1967-Ital./
Ger.; "Death Rides a Horse" 1967-
Ital.; "Beyond the Law" 1968-Ital.;
"It Can Be Done ... Amigo" 1971-
Ital./Fr./Span.

Santell, Alfred (1895-6/19/81).
Director. Films: "The Man Who
Played Square" 1925; "Romance of
the Rio Grande" 1929; "The Arizona
Kid" 1930.

Santi, Giancarlo. Director.
Films: "Big Showdown" 1972-Ital./
Fr.

Santiago, Cirio H. Producer.
Films: "Cavalry Command" 1963-
U.S./Phil.; "Arizona Kid" 1974-Ital./
Phil.

Santini, Gino. Screenwriter.
Films: "Twenty Thousand Dollars for
Seven" 1968-Ital.

Santley, Joseph (1889-8/8/71).
Director. Films: "Melody Ranch"
1940; "Down Mexico Way" 1941;
"Call of the Canyon" 1942.

Santoni, Dino. Screenwriter.
Films: "Chrysanthemums for a
Bunch of Swine" 1968-Ital.

Santschi, Tom (1880-4/9/31).
Director. Films: "How Callahan
Cleaned Up Little Hell" 1915; "The
Test" 1914.

Sanz, Ricardo. Producer. Films:
"Relentless Four" 1966-Span./Ital.;
"Ringo, the Lone Rider" 1967-Ital./
Span.; "Awkward Hands" 1968-
Span./Ital.; "I Do Not Forgive ... I
Kill!" 1968-Span./Ital.

Sapinsley, Alvin. Screenwriter.
Films: "Invitation to a Gunfighter"
1964.

Saraceno, Carol. Director. TV:
Bonanza—"The Burning Sky" 1-28-
68.

Sarafian, Richard C. (1927-).
Director. Films: "Terror at Black
Falls" 1962 (& prod.); "Man in the
Wilderness" 1971-U.S./Span.; "The
Man Who Loved Cat Dancing" 1973.

¶TV: *Cheyenne* 1955; *Bronco* 1958;
Lawman 1958; *Maverick*—"The Forbidden City" 3-26-61; *The Dakotas*
1963; *Bonanza*—"The Waiting
Game" 12-8-63; *Gunsmoke*—"Eliab's
Alm" 2-27-65, "Vengeance" 10-2-67
& 10-9-67, "A Noose for Dobie Price"
3-4-68; *Wild Wild West*—"The Night
of the Inferno" 9-17-65, "The Night
of a Thousand Eyes" 10-22-65; *The
Big Valley*—"Winner Lose All" 10-27-
65; *The Guns of Will Sonnett*—"Of
Lasting Summers and Jim Sonnett"
10-6-67, "Message at Noon" 10-13-67,
"A Son for a Son" 10-20-67.

Sarecky, Barney (1895-8/10/68).
Screenwriter. Films: "The Devil
Horse" 1932-serial; "Fighting with
Kit Carson" 1933-serial; "Mystery
Mountain" 1934-serial (story only);
"The Miracle Rider" 1935-serial;
"Zorro's Fighting Legion" 1939-ser-
ial; "Adventures of Red Ryder" 1940-
serial; "King of the Royal Mounted"
1940-serial; "The Phantom Rider"
1946-serial; "Buffalo Bill Rides
Again" 1947; "Code of the Saddle"
1947 (prod. only); "Flashing Guns"
1947 (prod. only); "Gun Talk" 1947
(prod. only); "Land of the Lawless"
1947 (prod. only); "Law Comes to
Gunsight" 1947 (prod. only); "Prairie
Express" 1947; "Six Gun Serenade"
1947 (prod. only); "Song of the
Wasteland" 1947 (prod. only); "Trailing Danger" 1947 (prod. only); "Back
Trail" 1948 (prod. only); "The Fighting Ranger" 1948 (prod. only);
"Frontier Agent" 1948 (prod. only);
"Gunning for Justice" 1948; "Overland Trails" 1948 (prod. only); "The
Sheriff of Medicine Bow" 1948 (prod.
only); "Triggerman" 1948 (prod.
only); "Crashing Thru" 1949 (prod.
only); "Hidden Danger" 1949 (prod.
only); "Law of the West" 1949 (prod.
only); "Range Justice" 1949 (prod.
only); "Shadows of the Wst" 1949
(prod. only); "Trail's End" 1949
(prod. only); "West of El Dorado"
1949 (prod. only).

Sarecky, Louis. Screenwriter.
Films: "Kansas Cyclone" 1941 (story
only); "North to the Klondike" 1942.

Sargent, Alvin. Screenwriter.
Films: "The Stalking Moon" 1969.

Sargent, Eppes Winthrop.
Screenwriter. Films: "Capturing Bad
Bill" 1915; "Her Slight Mistake" 1915.

Sargent, G.L. Director. Films:
"Tucson Jennie's Heart" 1918.

Sargent, Joseph (1925-). Direc-
tor. Films: "Friendly Persuasion"
TVM-1975 (& prod.). ¶TV: *Gun-
smoke*—"Uncle Sunday" 12-15-62,
"Tell Chester" 4-20-63, "Daddy
Went Away" 5-11-63, "Double Entry"

1-2-65, "The New Society" 5-22-65, "The Storm 9-25-65, "Clayton Thaddeus Greenwood" 10-2-65; *Bonanza*—"The Cheating Game" 2-9-64.

Sargent, P.D. Director. Films: "Battling King" 1922.

Sargent, Richard (1937-7/8/94). Director. TV: *Gunsmoke*—"Chester's Indian" 5-12-62.

Sarver, Charles. Screenwriter. Films: "Wolf Law" 1922.

Sasdy, Peter (1934-). Director. Films: "Welcome to Blood City" 1977-Brit./Can.

Sauber, Harry. Screenwriter. Films: "Riders of the Golden Gulch" 1932.

Saul, Oscar (1913-). Screenwriter. Films: "The Secret of Convict Lake" 1951; "The Second Time Around" 1961; "Major Dundee" 1965; "Man and Boy" 1971; "Deaf Smith and Johnny Ears" 1972-Ital. (& story).

Savage, Jr., Les. Screenwriter. Films: "Hills of Utah" 1951 (story only); "Black Horse Canyon" 1954 (story only); "The White Squaw" 1956; "Return to Warbow" 1958.

Savage, Paul. Screenwriter. Films: "Cutter's Trail" TVM-1970; "The Wild Country" 1971; "The Daughters of Joshua Cabe" TVM-1972; "Mackintosh & T.J." 1975; "The New Daughters of Joshua Cabe" TVM-1976 (& prod.); "Bonanza: The Next Generation" TVM-1988.

Savalas, Telly (1924-1/22/94). Screenwriter. Films: "Pancho Villa" 1975-Span.

Savino, Renato (Don Reynolds). Director. Films: "Vengeance" 1968-Ital./Ger. (prod./sp. only); "Gold of the Heroes" 1971-Ital./Fr. (& sp.); "Hey Amigo! A Toast to Your Death!" 1971-Ital. (sp. only); "His Name Was King" 1971-Ital. (& sp.).

Savona, Leopoldo (Leo Coleman). Director. Films: "Rojo" 1966-Ital./Span.; "Killer Kid" 1967-Ital. (& sp.); "God Will Forgive My Pistol" 1969-Ital. (& sp.); "Apocalypse Joe" 1970-Ital./Span. (& sp.); "Pistol Packin' Preacher" 1972-Ital./Fr. (& sp.).

Saxon, Mary Ann. Screenwriter. Films: "Squares" 1972.

Saxton, Charles. Screenwriter. Films: "Desperate Chance" 1926 (story only); "Road Agent" 1926 (story only); "The Concentratin' Kid" 1930.

Sayre, George Wallace (George Milton) (1903-10/23/62). Screenwriter. Films: "Code of the Mounted" 1935; "Song of the Trail" 1936; "Song of the Trail 1936; "Billy the Kid's Smoking Guns" 1942; "Rolling Down the Great Divide" 1942; "Sheriff of Sage Valley" 1942; "Fugitive of the Plains" 1943; "The Renegade" 1943 (story only); "Alaska" 1944; "Wild Horse Phantom" 1944; "Border Badmen" 1945; "His Brother's Ghost" 1945; "Terrors on Horseback" 1946.

Sayre, Joel (1901-9/9/79). Screenwriter. Films: "Annie Oakley" 1935.

Scandariato, Romano. Screenwriter. Films: "Go Away! Trinity Has Arrived in Eldorado" 1972-Ital.

Scanlan, Joseph L. Director. TV: *Paradise*—"The Holstered Gun" 11-3-88, "Ghost Dance" 11-24-88; *Young Riders*—"A Tiger's Tale" 12-28-91, "Song of Isiah" 1-18-92; *Adventures of Brisco County, Jr.*—"Hard Rock" 2-4-94, "Bad Luck Betty" 4-29-94, "High Treason" Part Two 5-20-94.

Scarborough, Dorothy. Writer. Films: "The Wind" 1928 (story).

Scarborough, George. Writer. Films: "West of Chicago" 1922 (story).

Scardamagali, Elio. Producer. Films: "Arizona Colt" 1965-Ital./Fr./Span.; "Johnny Hamlet" 1966-Ital. (& sp.); "A Bullet for Sandoval" 1970-Ital./Span.

Scardamaglia, Franco. Screenwriter. Films: "The Moment to Kill" 1968-Ital./Ger.

Scardapane, Dario. Screenwriter. Films: "Posse" 1993.

Scavolini, Romano. Screenwriter. Films: "John the Bastard" 1967-Ital.

Scavolini, Sauro. Screenwriter. Films: "Johnny Yuma" 1966-Ital. (& story); "10,000 Dollars Blood Money" 1966-Ital.; "My Horse, My Gun, Your Widow" 1972-Ital./Span.; "Man Called Blade" 1977-Ital.

Schaefer, Armand (1898-9/26/67). Director. Films: "Hurricane Horseman" 1931; "Lightning Warrior" 1931-serial; "Battling Buckaroo" 1932; "The Cheyenne Cyclone" 1932; "Law and Lawless" 1932; "The Reckless Rider" 1932; "Wyoming Whirlwind" 1932; "The Fighting Texans" 1933; "Fighting with Kit Carson" 1933-serial; "Outlaw Justice" 1933; "Sagebrush Trail" 1933; "Terror Trail" 1933; "The Law of the Wild" 1934-serial; "Mystery Mountain" 1934-serial (sp. only); "The Miracle Rider" 1935-serial; "The Phantom Empire" 1935 (sp. only); "The Singing Vagabond" 1935 (prod. only); "The Old Corral" 1936 (prod. only); "Git Along, Little Dogies" 1937 (prod. only); "Rootin' Tootin' Rhythm" 1937 (prod. only); "Yodelin' Kid from Pine Ridge" 1937 (prod. only); "Call of the Yukon" 1938 (prod. only); "In Old Monterey" 1939 (prod. only); "Jeepers Creepers" 1939 (prod. only); "Wagons Westward" 1940 (prod. only); "Arkansas Judge" 1941 (prod. only); "Girl from Alaska" 1942 (prod. only); "My Pal Trigger" 1946; "Sioux City Sue" 1946 (prod. only); "The Last Round-Up" 1947 (prod. only); "Trail to San Antone" 1947 (prod. only); "Twilight on the Rio Grande" 1947 (prod. only); "Loaded Pistols" 1948 (prod. only); "The Strawberry Roan" 1948 (prod. only); "The Big Sombrero" 1949 (prod. only); "The Cowboy and the Indians" 1949 (prod. only); "Riders in the Sky" 1949 (prod. only); "Riders of the Whistling Pines" 1949 (prod. only); "Rim of the Canyon" 1949 (prod. only); "Sons of New Mexico" 1949 (prod. only); "Beyond the Purple Hills" 1950 (prod. only); "The Blazing Sun" 1950 (prod. only); "Cow Town" 1950 (prod. only); "Indian Territory" 1950 (prod. only); "Mule Train" 1950; "Gene Autry and the Mounties" 1951 (prod. only); "Hills of Utah" 1951 (prod. only); "Silver Canyon" 1951 (prod. only); "Texans Never Cry" 1951 (prod. only); "Valley of Fire" 1951 (prod. only); "Whirlwind" 1951 (prod. only); "Apache Country" 1952 (prod. only); "Barbed Wire" 1952 (prod. only); "Blue Canadian Rockies" 1952 (prod. only); "Night Stage to Galveston" 1952 (prod. only); "The Old West" 1952 (prod. only); "Wagon Team" 1952 (prod. only); "Goldtown Ghost Raiders" 1953 (prod. only); "Last of the Pony Riders" 1953 (prod. only); "On Top of Old Smoky" 1953 (prod. only); "Pack Train" 1953 (prod. only); "Saginaw Trail" 1953 (prod. only); "Winning of the West" 1953 (prod. only). ¶TV: *The Gene Autry Show* 1950-55 (exec. prod.); *The Range Rider* 1951-53 (exec. prod.); *Buffalo Bill, Jr.* 1955-56 (exec. prod.).

Schaefer, George (1920-). Director. Films: "The Girl Called Hatter Fox" TVM-1977 (& prod.).

Schaefer, Jack (1907-1/24/91). Writer. Films: "Shane" 1953 (story); "The Silver Whip" 1953 (story); "Tribute to a Badman" 1956 (story); "Trooper Hook" 1957 (story); "Advance to the Rear" 1964 (story); "Monte Walsh" 1970 (story).

Schaefer, Robert. Screenwriter. Films: "Raiders of Tomahawk Creek" 1950 (story only); "The Lone Ranger and the Lost City of Gold" 1958.

Schaefer, Rosaline. Writer. Films: "Jesse James" 1939 (story).

Schamoni, Peter. Director. Films: "Montana Trap" 1976-Ger.

Schary, Dore (1905-7/7/80). Producer. Films: "Westward the Women" 1951; "Bad Day at Black Rock" 1955; "The Last Hunt" 1956.

Schayer, E. Richard (1881-3/13/56). Screenwriter. Films: "A Man's Country" 1919; "The Westerners" 1919; "The Killer" 1921; "Man of the Forest" 1921; "The Ramblin' Kid" 1923; "Hook and Ladder" 1924; "Ride for Your Life" 1924; "Ridgeway of Montana" 1924; "The Sawdust Trail" 1924; "The Calgary Stampede" 1925 (story only); "The Hurricane Kid" 1925; "The Frontier Trail" 1926; "Rustlers' Ranch" 1926; "The Scrappin' Kid" 1926; "The Seventh Bandit" 1926; "The Terror" 1926; "The Law of the Range" 1928; "Destry Rides Again" 1932; "My Pal, the King" 1932 (story); "Davy Crockett, Indian Scout" 1950; "The Iroquois Trail" 1950; "Indian Uprising" 1951 (& story); "The Texas Rangers" 1951; "Cripple Creek" 1952; "Gun Belt" 1953; "The Lone Gun" 1954; "Top Gun" 1955; "Gun Brothers" 1956; "Gun Fight" 1961; "Arizona Raiders" 1965 (story only).

Scheerer, Robert. Director. TV: *Paradise*—"Devil's Canyon" 12-1-88, "A Private War" 1-5-89, "A Matter of Honor" Part One 4-8-89, "Hour of the Wolf" 4-29-89.

Schenck, Aubrey (1908-). Producer. Films: "Red Stallion in the Rockies" 1949; "Wyoming Mail" 1950; "Outlaw's Son" 1957; "Fort Bowie" 1958; "Born Reckless" 1959 (& sp.).

Schenck, George. Screenwriter. Films: "More Dead Than Alive" 1968; "Barquero" 1970.

Schenck, Joseph M. (1877-10/22/61). Producer. Films: "Go West" 1925.

Schenck, Stephen. Screenwriter. Films: "Welcome to Blood City" 1977-Brit./Can.

Schepisi, Fred (1939-). Director. Films: "Barbarosa" 1982.

Schertzinger, Victor (1890-10/26/41). Director. Films: "The Son of His Father" 1917; "Playing the Game" 1918; "The Lady of Red Butte" 1919; "The Sheriff's Son" 1919; "Frivolous Sal" 1925; "The Golden Strain" 1925; "Redskin" 1929.

Schlank, Morris R. Director. Films: "Code of the Range" 1927.

Schlesinger, John (1926-). Director. TV: *Cliffhangers*—"The Secret Empire" 1979.

Schlesinger, Leon (1883-12/25/49). Producer. Films: "The Big Stampede" 1932; "Haunted Gold" 1932; "Ride Him, Cowboy" 1932; "The Man from Monterey" 1933; "Somewhere in Sonora" 1933; "The Telegraph Trail" 1933.

Schlom, Herman (1904-11/2/83). Producer. Films: "Nevada" 1944; "Wanderer of the Wasteland" 1945; "West of the Pecos" 1945; "Sunset Pass" 1946; "Code of the West" 1947; "Thunder Mountain" 1947; "Under the Tonto Rim" 1947; "Wild Horse Mesa" 1947; "The Arizona Ranger" 1948; "Gun Smugglers" 1948; "Guns of Hate" 1948; "Indian Agent" 1948; "Western Heritage" 1948; "Brothers in the Saddle" 1949; "Masked Raiders" 1949; "The Mysterious Desperado" 1949; "Rustlers" 1949; "Stagecoach Kid" 1949; "Border Treasure" 1950; "Dynamite Pass" 1950; "Rider from Tucson" 1950; "Riders of the Range" 1950; "Rio Grande Patrol" 1950; "Storm Over Wyoming" 1950; "Best of the Badmen" 1951; "Gunplay" 1951; "Hot Lead" 1951; "Law of the Badlands" 1951; "Overland Telegraph" 1951; "Pistol Harvest" 1951; "Saddle Legion" 1951; "Desert Passage" 1952; "The Half-Breed" 1952; "Road Agent" 1952; "Target" 1952; "Trail Guide" 1952. ¶TV: *My Friend Flicka* 1955-56.

Schmidt, H.C. Writer. Films: "Young Whirlwind" 1928 (story).

Schmoeller, David. Screenwriter. Films: "Ghost Town" 1988 (story only).

Schneer, Charles (1920-). Screenwriter. Films: "Red River" 1948; "The Furies" 1950; "Westward the Women" 1951; "Good Day for a Hanging" 1958; "Land Raiders" 1969-U.S./Span.; "The Valley of Gwangi" 1969 (prod. only).

Schneider, Herman. Screenwriter. Films: "The Naked Dawn" 1955.

Schneider, Nina. Screenwriter. Films: "The Naked Dawn" 1955.

Schock, G. Screenwriter. Films: "A Fistful of Dollars" 1964-Ital./Ger./Span.

Schoedack, Ernest B. (1893-12/79). Director. Films: "Outlaws of the Orient" 1937.

Schofield, Paul. Screenwriter. Films: "Just Pals" 1920; "The Rose of Nome" 1920; "The Last Trail" 1921;

"The Primal Law" 1921; "Lights of the Desert" 1922; "West of Chicago" 1922; "Shadows of the North" 1923; "Sunset Range" 1935; "Wells Fargo" 1937.

Scholl, Jack (1903-3/25/88). Director. Films: "Frontier Days" 1945-short; "Law of the Badlands" 1945-short (& sp.); "Space Cooley, King of Western Swing" 1945-short.

Schorr, William (1901-6/18/89). Producer. Films: "The Indian Fighter" 1955.

Schrader, Marie. Writer. Films: "So This Is Arizona" 1922 (story).

Schrock, Raymond L. (1892-12/12/50). Screenwriter. Films: "The Trail of the Upper Yukon" 1915 (story only); "The She Wolf" 1919; "I Am the Law" 1922; "The Long Chance" 1922; "Kindled Courage" 1923; "Shootin' for Love" 1923 (& story); "Forty-Horse Hawkins" 1924; "Hook and Ladder" 1924 (story only); "Ride for Your Life" 1924; "Ridgeway of Montana" 1924; "The Ridin' Kid from Powder River" 1924; "The Sawdust Trail" 1924; "The Calgary Stampede" 1925 (story); "The Hurricane Kid" 1925; "Let 'Er Buck" 1925; "The Saddle Hawk" 1925; "Spook Ranch" 1925; "The Taming of the West" 1925; "Burning the Wind" 1928; "The Winged Horseman" 1929; "Wild Bill Hickok Rides" 1942; "Daughter of the West" 1949.

Schroeder, Doris. Screenwriter. Films: "The Sage Brush Girl" 1915; "The Girl Who Wouldn't Quit" 1918; "The Call of the Canyon" 1923; "To the Last Man" 1923; "Hopalong Cassidy" 1935; "Bar 20 Rides Gain" 1936; "Call of the Prairie" 1936; "The Eagle's Brood" 1936; "Three on the Trail" 1936; "Heart of the West" 1937; "Wall Street Cowboy" 1939 (story only); "Bullet Code" 1940; "Legion of the Lawless" 1940; "Oklahoma Renegades" 1940; "Prairie Law" 1940; "Texas Terrors" 1940; "Gangs of Sonora" 1941; "Kansas Cyclone" 1941; "A Missouri Outlaw" 1941; "The Phantom Cowboy" 1941; "Two-Gun Sheriff" 1941; "Arizona Terrors" 1942; "Jesse James, Jr." 1942; "Pirates of the Prairie" 1942; "The Sombrero Kid" 1942 (story only); "Stagecoach Express" 1942 (story); "Westward Ho" 1942; "Bandits of the Badlands" 1945; "Days of Buffalo Bill" 1946; "Death Valley" 1946; "The Devil's Playground" 1946; "Fool's Gold" 1946; "Dangerous Venture" 1947; "False Paradise" 1948; "Sinister Journey" 1948; "Strange Gamble" 1948; "The Gay Amigo" 1949.

Schubert, Bernard. Screenwriter. Films: "The Barrier" 1937; "Silver Queen" 1942; "Bruckskin Frontier" 1943.

Schulberg, B.P. (1892-2/25/57). Producer. Films: "The Virginian" 1923; "The Mysterious Rider" 1927; "Shootin' Irons" 1927.

Schulman, Arnold. Screenwriter. Films: "Cimarron" 1960.

Schultz, Carl. Director. Films: "Bullseye!" 1986-Australia.

Schuster, Harold (1902-7/19/86). Director. Films: "My Friend Flicka" 1943; "Jack Slade" 1953; "The Return of Jack Slade" 1955; "Dragoon Wells Massacre" 1957.

Schuyler, Philip. Screenwriter. Films: "Headin' Westward" 1928; "Law of the Mounted" 1928; "West of the Rockies" 1929.

Schwabacher, Leslie. Writer. Films: "Trail of the Mounties" 1947 (story).

Schwalb, Ben. Producer. Films: "Dig That Uranium" 1956; "Cole Younger, Gunfighter" 1958; "Quantrill's Raiders" 1958; "King of the Wild Stallions" 1959; "Gunfight at Comanche Creek" 1964.

Schwartz, Elroy. Producer. Films: "The Wackiest Wagon Train in the West" 1976 (& sp.).

Schwartz, Marvin. Producer. Films: "The War Wagon" 1967; "100 Rifles" 1969; "Kid Blue" 1973.

Schwartz, Sherwood. Screenwriter. Films: "The Wackiest Wagon Train in the West" 1976.

Schwarz, Jack (Jack Seeman). Producer. Films: "Buffalo Bill Rides Again" 1947; "Hollywood Barn Dance" 1947; "Border Outlaws" 1950; "The Fighting Stallion" 1950; "I Killed Geronimo" 1950; "Cattle Queen" 1951; "Gold Raiders" 1951.

Schweitzer, S.S. Screenwriter. Films: "The Deerslayer" TVM-1978; "Donner Pass: The Road to Survival" TVM-1978.

Scola, Kathryn. Screenwriter. Films: "Lady from Cheyenne" 1941.

Scott, Adrian (1912-12/25/72). Screenwriter. Films: "The Parson of Panamint" 1941.

Scott, Betty. Writer. Films: "Pardon My Gun" 1930 (story).

Scott, DeVallon. Screenwriter. Films: "Conquest of Cochise" 1953; "The Black Dakotas" 1954; "They Rode West" 1954; "The Maverick Queen" 1956.

Scott, Ewing. Director. Films: "Hollywood Cowboy" 1937; "Hollywood Cowboy" 1937 (& sp.); "Park Avenue Logger" 1937 (sp. only); "Hollywood Roundup" 1938; "Headin' East" 1947.

Scott, Lester F. Producer. Films: "Walloping Wallace" 1924; "Border Romance" 1930.

Scott, Randolph (1903-3/2/87). Producer. Films: "Buchanan Rides Alone" 1958; "Comanche Station" 1960.

Scott, Sherman. see Newfield, Sam.

Scullin, George. Writer. Films: "Gunfight at the O.K. Corral" 1957 (story).

Scully, Mary Alice. Screenwriter. Films: "Whispering Canyon" 1926; "A Hero on Horseback" 1927.

Sears, Fred F. (1912-11/30/57). Director. Films: "Desert Vigilante" 1949; "Across the Badlands" 1950; "Horsemen of the Sierras" 1950; "Lightning Guns" 1950; "Raiders of Tomahawk Creek" 1950; "Bonanza Town" 1951; "Pecos River" 1951; "Prairie Roundup" 1951; "Ridin' the Outlaw Trail" 1951; "Snake River Desperadoes" 1951; "The Hawk of Wild River" 1952; "The Kid from Broken Gun" 1952; "Smoky Canyon" 1952; "Ambush at Tomahawk Gap" 1953; "The Nebraskan" 1953; "Massacre Canyon" 1954; "The Outlaw Stallion" 1954; "Overland Pacific" 1954; "Apache Ambush" 1955; "Wyoming Renegades" 1955; "Fury at Gunsight Pass" 1956; "Utah Blaine" 1957; "Badman's Country" 1958.

Seastrom, Victor (1879-1/3/60). Director. Films: "The Wind" 1928.

Seaton, George (1911-7/28/79). Director. Films: "The Tin Star" 1957 (prod. only); "Showdown" 1973 (& prod.).

Sebares, Manuel. Screenwriter. Films: "Two Thousand Dollars for Coyote" 1965-Span.; "Django, A Bullet for You" 1966-Span./Ital.; "Few Dollars for Django" 1966-Ital./Span.; "Relentless Four" 1966-Span./Ital.; "Woman for Ringo" 1966-Ital./Span.; "Hour of Death" 1968-Span./Ital.; "If You Shoot ... You Live!" 1974-Span.

Secchi, Toni (Tony Dry). Director. Films: "Calibre .38" 1971-Ital. (& sp.).

Sedgwick, Edward (1892-5/7/53). Director. Films: "Rough and Ready" 1918 (sp. only); "Bar Nothin'" 1921; "The Rough Diamond" 1921 (& sp.); "The Bearcat" 1922; "Do and Dare" 1922 (& sp.); "Blinky" 1923 (& prod.); "Dead Game" 1923 (& sp.); "Out of Luck" 1923 (& sp.); "The Ramblin' Kid" 1923; "Romance Land" 1923; "Shootin' for Love" 1923 (& story); "Single-Handed" 1923 (& sp.); "The Thrill Chaser" 1923 (& sp.); "Broadway or Bust" 1924; "Forty-Horse Hawkins" 1924 (& sp.); "Hook and Ladder" 1924 (& story); "Ride for Your Life" 1924; "The Ridin' Kid from Powder River" 1924; "The Sawdust Trail" 1924; "The Hurricane Kid" 1925; "Let 'Er Buck" 1925 (& sp.); "The Saddle Hawk" 1925 (& sp.); "Two-Fisted Jones" 1925; "Flaming Frontier" 1926 (& story); "The Bugle Call" 1927.

Seeling, Charles R. Director. Films: "The Jack Rider" 1921; "The Vengeance Trail" 1921; "Western Firebrands" 1921; "Across the Border" 1922 (& sp.); "The Cowboy King" 1922; "Rounding Up the Law" 1922; "Cyclone Jones" 1923; "End of the Rope" 1923; "$1,000 Reward" 1923; "The Avenger" 1924; "The Eagle's Claw" 1924; "Big Stunt" 1925.

Seeman, Jack. see Schwarz, Jack.

Seff, Manuel (1895-9/22/69). Screenwriter. Films: "The Three Godfathers" 1936.

Segall, Harry (1897-11/25/75). Screenwriter. Films: "The Outcasts of Poker Flat" 1937.

Seid, Sylvia Bernstein. Screenwriter. Films: "The Lariat Kid" 1929.

Seidelman, Arthur Allan. Director. Films: "Poker Alice" TVM-1987.

Seiler, Lewis (1891-1/8/64). Director. Films: "The Cowboys" 1924; "The Great K & A Train Robbery" 1926; "No Man's Gold" 1926; "The Last Trail" 1927; "Outlaws of Red River" 1927; "Tumbling River" 1927; "Men Without Law" 1930 (story only); "Frontier Marshal" 1934; "Heart of the North" 1938.

Seiter, William A. (1892-7/26/64). Director. Films: "Allegheny Uprising" 1939; "Susannah of the Mounties" 1939; "A Lady Takes a Chance" 1943; "Belle of the Yukon" 1944 (& prod.). ¶TV: *The Alaskans* 1959-60.

Seitz, George B. (1888-7/8/44). Director. Films: "Galloping Hoofs" 1924-serial; "Leatherstocking" 1924-serial; "Way of a Man" 1924-serial (& sp.); "The Vanishing American" 1925; "Wild Horse Mesa" 1925; "Desert Gold" 1926; "The Last Frontier" 1926; "Jim the Conqueror" 1927; "The Thrill Hunter" 1933; "Treason" 1933; "The Fighting Ranger" 1934; "The Last of the Mohicans" 1936; "Out West with the Hardys" 1938; "Kit Carson" 1940; "Pierre of the Plains" 1942. ¶TV: *The*

Lone Ranger—"Enter the Lone Ranger" 9-15-49, "The Lone Ranger Fights On" 9-22-49, "The Lone Ranger's Triumph" 9-29-49, "Legion of Old Timers" 10-6-49, "Rustler's Hideout" 10-13-49, "War Horse" 10-20-49, "Pete and Pedro" 10-27-49, "The Renegades" 11-3-49, "The Tenderfeet" 11-10-49, "Greed for Gold" 1-19-50, "Man of the House" 1-26-50, "Barnaby Boggs, Esquire" 2-2-50, "Gold Train" 3-16-50, "Pay Dirt" 3-23-50, "Billie the Great" 3-30-50, "A Matter of Courage" 4-27-50, "Rifles and Renegades" 5-4-50, "Bullets for Ballots" 5-11-50, "The Black Hat" 5-18-50, "Devil's Pass" 5-25-50, "Spanish Gold" 6-1-50, "Eye for an Eye" 6-29-60, "The Beeler Gang" 8-10-50, "The Star Witness" 8-17-50, "The Black Widow" 8-24-50, "Mission Bells" 9-21-50, "Dead Man's Chest" 9-28-50, "Outlaw's Revenge" 10-5-50, "Thieves' Money" 11-2-50, "The Squire" 11-9-50, "One Jump Ahead" 12-14-50, "Lady Killer" 12-21-50, "Paid in Full" 12-28-50, "Backtrail" 1-25-51, "Behind the Law" 2-1-51, "Trouble at Black Rock" 2-8-51, "Mr. Trouble" 3-8-51, "The Gentleman from Julesburg" 6-11-53.

Selander, Lesley (Robert Parry) (1900-12/5/79). Director. Films: "Boss Rider of Gun Creek" 1936; "Ride 'Em Cowboy" 1936; "The Barrier" 1937; "Empty Saddles" 1937; "Hopalong Rides Again" 1937; "Left-Handed Law" 1937; "Sandflow" 1937; "Smoke Tree Range" 1937; "Bar 20 Justice" 1938; "Cassidy of Bar 20" 1938; "The Frontiersman" 1938; "Heart of Arizona" 1938; "The Mysterious Rider" 1938; "Partners of the Plains" 1938; "Pride of the West" 1938; "Sunset Trail" 1938; "Heritage of the Desert" 1939; "Range War" 1939; "Renegade Trail" 1939; "Silver on the Sage" 1939; "Cherokee Strip" 1940; "Hidden Gold" 1940; "Knights of the Range" 1940; "The Light of Western Stars" 1940; "Santa Fe Marshal" 1940; "Stagecoach War" 1940; "Three Men from Texas" 1940; "Doomed Caravan" 1941; "Pirates on Horseback" 1941; "Riders of the Timberline" 1941; "The Round Up" 1941; "Stick to Your Guns" 1941; "Wide Open Town" 1941; "Bandit Ranger" 1942; "Thundering Hoofs" 1942; "Undercover Man" 1942; "Bar 20" 1943; "Border Patrol" 1943; "Buckskin Frontier" 1943; "Colt Comrades" 1943; "Lost Canyon" 1943; "Red River Robin Hood" 1943; "Riders of the Deadline" 1943; "Bordertown Trail" 1944; "Call of the Rockies" 1944; "Cheyenne Wildcat" 1944; "Firebrands of Arizona" 1944; "Forty Thieves" 1944; "Lumberjack" 1944; "Sheriff of Las Vegas" 1944; "Sheriff of Sundown" 1944; "Stagecoach to Monterey" 1944; "Great Stagecoach Robbery" 1945; "Phantom of the Plains" 1945; "Trail of Kit Carson" 1945; "Out California Way" 1946; "Belle Starr's Daughter" 1947; "Last Frontier Uprising" 1947; "The Red Stallion" 1947; "Robin Hood of Texas" 1947; "Saddle Pals" 1947; "Guns of Hate" 1948; "Indian Agent" 1948; "Panhandle" 1948; "Brothers in the Saddle" 1949; "Masked Raiders" 1949; "The Mysterious Desperado" 1949; "Rustlers" 1949; "Stampede" 1949; "Dakota Lil" 1950; "The Kangaroo Kid" 1950; "Rider from Tucson" 1950; "Riders of the Range" 1950; "Rio Grande Patrol" 1950; "Short Grass" 1950; "Storm Over Wyoming" 1950; "Cavalry Scout" 1951; "Gunplay" 1951; "Law of the Badlands" 1951; "Overland Telegraph" 1951; "Pistol Harvest" 1951; "Saddle Legion" 1951; "Desert Passage" 1952; "Fort Osage" 1952; "The Raiders" 1952; "Road Agent" 1952; "Trail Guide" 1952; "Cow Country" 1953; "Fort Vengeance" 1953; "War Paint" 1953; "Arrow in the Dust" 1954; "The Yellow Tomahawk" 1954; "Fort Yuma" 1955; "Shotgun" 1955; "Tall Man Riding" 1955; "The Broken Star" 1956; "Quincannon, Frontier Scout" 1956; "Outlaw's Son" 1957; "Revolt at Fort Laramie" 1957; "Tomahawk Trail" 1957; "The Lone Ranger and the Lost City of Gold" 1958; "Convict Stage" 1965; "Fort Courageous" 1965; "Town Tamer" 1965; "War Party" 1965; "The Texican" 1966-U.S./Span.; "Fort Utah" 1967; "Arizona Bushwhackers" 1968. ¶TV: *Cowboy G-Men* 1952-53 (& prod.); *Laramie*—"Ladies Day" 10-3-61, "Siege at Jubilee" 10-10-61, "Deadly Is the Night" 11-7-61, "The Perfect Gift" 1-2-62, "The Runaway" 1-23-62, "The Confederate Express" 1-30-62, "The Runt" 2-20-62, "The Dynamiters" 3-6-62, "The Replacement" 3-27-62, "The Turn of the Wheel" 4-3-62, "War Hero" 10-2-62, "The Long Road Back" 10-23-62, "The Sunday Shoot" 11-13-62, "Beyond Justice" 11-27-62, "No Place to Run" 2-5-63, "The Renegade Brand" 2-26-63, "The Violent Ones" 3-5-63, "The Last Battleground" 4-16-63.

Self, William. Producer. Films: "From Noon to Three" 1976; "The Shootist" 1976. ¶TV: *Hotel De Paree* 1959-60.

Selig, William M. (1864-7/16/48). Producer. Films: "The Galloping Devil" 1920; "The Last Chance" 1921.

Sellers, Ollie. Director. Films: "The Able-Minded Lady" 1922.

Sellers, William. Screenwriter. Films: "The Gunfighter" 1950.

Sellier, Jr., Charles E. Producer. Films: "The Brothers O'Toole" 1973; "The Life and Times of Grizzly Adams" 1975; "The Adventures of Frontier Fremont" 1976; "Guardian of the Wilderness" 1976 (& story); "The Capture of Grizzly Adams" TVM-1982 (story only); "Desperado" TVM-1987; "Desperado: Avalanche at Devil's Ridge" TVM-1988; "Longarm" TVM-1988; "The Return of Desperado" TVM-1988; "Desperado: Badlands Justice" TVM-1989; "Desperado: The Outlaw Wars" TVM-1989. ¶TV: *The Life and Times of Grizzly Adams* 1977-78 (exec. prod.).

Selman, David. Director. Films: "The Prescott Kid" 1934 (& prod.); "The Westerner" 1934; "Fighting Shadows" 1935; "Gallant Defender" 1935; "Justice of the Range" 1935; "The Revenge Rider" 1935; "Riding Wild" 1935; "Square Shooter" 1935; "The Cowboy Star" 1936; "The Mysterious Avenger" 1936; "Secret Patrol" 1936; "Texas Trail" 1937.

Selpin, Herbert. Director. Films: "Water for Canitoga" 1939-Ger.

Seltzer, Charles Alden. Writer. Films: "Fame and Fortune" 1918 (story); "Riddle Gawne" 1918; "The Trail to Yesterday" 1918; "Square Deal Sanderson" 1919 (story only); "Firebrand Trevison" 1920 (story); "Rough Shod" 1922 (story only); "Silver Spurs" 1936 (story only).

Seltzer, Frank N. Producer. Films: "Terror in a Texas Town" 1958.

Seltzer, Walter (1914-). Producer. Films: "Will Penny" 1968; "The Last Hard Men" 1976.

Selwyn, Edgar (1875-2/13/44). Writer. Films: "Pierre of the Plains" 1914 (story); "Heart of the Wilds" 1918 (story); "The Kid from Texas" 1939 (prod. only); "Pierre of the Plains" 1942 (story & prod.).

Selznick, David O. (1902-6/22/65). Producer. Films: "The Conquerors" 1932; "Crossfire" 1933; "Scarlet River" 1933; "Duel in the Sun" 1946 (& sp.).

Semon, Lawrence (1889-10/8/28). Director. Films: "Guns and Greasers" 1918 (& sp.).

Senensky, Ralph. Director. TV: *The Big Valley*—"By Fires Unseen" 1-5-66; *Wild Wild West*—"The Night of the Druid's Blood" 3-25-66, "The Night of the Big Blast" 10-7-66; *The High Chaparral*—"The Terrorist"

12-17-67; *How the West Was Won—*"The Scavengers" 3-12-79; *Young Maverick—*"Makin' Tracks" 1-9-80; *Big Bend Country—*Pilot 8-27-81.

Sennett, Mack (1880-11/5/60). Director. Films: Films: "The Tourists" 1912; "Suzanna" 1922 (sp. only).

Seone, Aldo. Screenwriter. Films: "Paid in Blood" 1972-Ital.

Seone, Jose-Maria. Screenwriter. Films: "Rojo" 1966-Ital./Span.

Sequi, Mario (Anthony Wileys). Director. Films: "The Tramplers 1965-Ital.

Sergeyeff, Sergey. Screenwriter. Films: "Trumpin' Trouble" 1926; "The Galloping Gobs" 1927 (story only).

Serling, Rod (1924-6/28/75). Screenwriter. Films: "Saddle the Wind" 1958. ¶TV: *The Loner* 1965-66 (creator).

Serrao, A.E. Screenwriter. Films: "Hurrican Horseman" 1926.

Service, Robert W. (1874-9/11/58). Writer. Films: "The Shooting of Dan McGrew" 1915 (story); "The Trail of '98" 1929 (story).

Seton, Ernest Thompson (1860-1946). Writer. Films: "King of the Grizzlis" 1970 (story).

Seven, Johnny (1930-). Director. Films: "Navajo Run" 1966 (& prod.).

Seward, Edmond (1891-2/12/54). Screenwriter. Films: "Bowery Buckaroos" 1947.

Sgarro, Nicholas. Director. TV: *Paradise—*"Treasure" 5-6-89, "The Return of Johnny Ryan" 12-2-89.

Shaff, Monroe. Screenwriter. Films: "Headin' East" 1936 (story only); "California Frontier" 1938; "Hollywood Roundup" 1938; "Law of the Texan" 1938 (& prod.); "The Overland Express" 1938; "The Stranger from Arizona" 1938 (& prod.).

Shaffer, Anthony (1926-). Screenwriter. Films: "Sommersby" 1993 (story only).

Shaftel, Josef. Director. Films: "The Naked Hills" 1956 (& prod./sp.).

Shamray, Franklin. *see* Ray, Bernard B.

Shane, Maxwell (1905-10/25/83). Screenwriter. Films: "Three Hours to Kill" 1954.

Shane, Ted. Writer. Films: "The Desert Rider" 1929 (story).

Shanner, John Herman. Screenwriter. Films: "Goin' South" 1978.

Shannon, Robert T. Screen-

writer. Films: "Sons of the Pioneers" 1942 (& story).

Shapiro, Richard. Screenwriter. Films: "The Great Scout and Cathouse Thursday" 1976.

Sharp, Alan. Screenwriter. Films: "The Hired Hand" 1971; "Ulzana's Raid" 1972; "Billy Two Hats" 1973-Brit.

Sharp, Alex. Screenwriter. Films: "Vengeance" 1964.

Sharp, Mordaunt. Screenwriter. Films: "The Barrier" 1937.

Shaw, Frank. Screenwriter. Films: "The Frisco Kid" 1979.

Shaw, Run Run (1907-). Producer. Films: "Stranger and the Gunfighter" 1973-Ital./Span./Hong Kong.

Shawkey, James. Screenwriter. Films: "Frontier Days" 1934.

Shea, Cornelius. Writer. Films: "The Rejected Lover's Luck" 1913 (story); "The Rustler's Reformation" 1913 (story); "Sallie's Sure Shot" 1913 (story); "The Schoolmarm's Shooting Match" 1913 (story); "The Stolen Moccasins" 1913 (story); "Taming a Tenderfoot" 1913 (story); "The Auction Sale of Run-Dawn Ranch" 1915 (story); "The Girl and the Mail Bag" 1915 (story); "The Gold Dust and the Squaw" 1915 (story); "The Impersonation of Tom" 1915 (story); "On the Eagle Trail" 1915 (story); "The Outlaw's Bride" 1915 (sp.); "The Race for a Gold Mine" 1915 (story); "Saved by Her Horse" 1915 (story); "The Tenderfoot's Triumph" 1915 (story); "The Luck That Jealousy Brought" 1917 (story).

Shear, Barry (1923-6/13/79). Director. Films: "Deadly Trackers" 1973. ¶TV: *Alias Smith and Jones—*"The Root of It All" 4-1-71, "The Day They Hanged Kid Curry" 9-16-71, "The Reformation of Harry Briscoe" 11-11-71, "Dreadful Sorry, Clementine" 11-18-71, "The Bounty Hunter" 12-9-71; *The Quest—*"The Captive" 9-22-76.

Sheck, Joseph T. Screenwriter. Films: "Waterhole No. 3" 1967 (& prod.).

Sheekman, Arthur (1892-1/12/78). Screenwriter. Films: "Rose of the Rancho" 1936.

Sheldon, Forrest. Director. Films: "Black Gold" 1924; "False Trails" 1924 (sp. only); "Buckin' the West" 1924 (sp. only); "Pot Luck Pards" 1924 (story only); "Rainbow Rangers" 1924 (& sp.); "Always Ridin' to Win" 1925; "Border Vengeance" 1925; "Don X" 1925 (& sp.);

"The Empty Saddle" 1925 (story only); "The Knockout Kid" 1925 (sp. only); "Stampedin' Trouble" 1925; "Ahead of the Law" 1926; "The Grey Vulture" 1926 (sp. only); "Lawless Trails" 1926 (& sp.); "The Man from Oklahoma" 1926; "The Dawn Road" 1930 (story only); "Between Fighting Men" 1932 (& sp.); "Dynamite Ranch" 1932; "The Lone Rider" 1930 (sp. only); "Law of the Rio Grande" 1931; "The Sign of the Wolf" 1931-serial; "The Texas Ranger" 1931 (sp. only); "Hell Fire Austin" 1932 (& sp./story); "The Lone Avenger" 1933 (sp./story only); "The Phantom Thunderbolt" 1933 (sp. only); "The Fighting Trooper" 1934 (sp. only); "Wilderness Mail" 1935; "Riders of the Sage" 1939 (story only); "Texas Stampede" 1939 (story only); "Pioneer Days" 1940 (story only); "The Silver Trail" 1937 (sp. only).

Sheldon, Frank. Writer. Films: "The Pal from Texas" 1939 (story).

Sheldon, James. Director. TV: *Gunsmoke—*"Fingered" 11-23-57, "Tapes for Old Jeb" 10-16-65; *Zane Grey Theater—*"Man of Fear" 3-14-58; *The Virginian—*"The Brazen Bell" 10-17-62.

Sheldon, Norman. Director. Films: "Two Gun Law" 1937 (story only); "Alias Billy the Kid" 1946 (story only); "The El Paso Kid" 1946 (sp. only); "Border Fence" 1951 (& sp.).

Sheldon, Sidney (1917-). Screenwriter. Films: "Annie Get Your Gun" 1950; "Pardners" 1956.

Shepard, Sam (1943-). Director. Films: "Silent Tongue" 1993 (& sp.).

Shepherd, Scott. Director. TV: *Young Riders—*"The Presence of Mine Enemies" 11-9-91.

Sher, Jack (1913-8/23/88). Screenwriter. Films: "Shane" 1953; "Walk the Proud Land" 1956; "The Wild and the Innocent" 1959 (& dir.); "Female Artillery" TVM-1973 (story only).

Sherdeman, Ted (1909-8/22/87). Screenwriter. Films: "Lust for Gold" 1949; "Riding Shotgun" 1954 (prod. only); "...And Now Miguel" 1966.

Sheridan, John. Writer. Films: "When California Was Wild" 1915 (story).

Sherin, Edwin (1930-). Director. Films: "Valdez Is Coming" 1971.

Sherman, Arthur. Screenwriter. Films: "Shadow Valley" 1947.

Sherman, George (1908-3/15/

91). Director. Films: "Wild Horse Rodeo" 1937; "Heroes of the Hills" 1938; "Outlaws of Sonora" 1938; "Overland Stage Raiders" 1938; "Pals of the Saddle" 1938; "The Purple Vigilantes" 1938; "Red River Range" 1938; "Rhythm of the Saddle" 1938; "Riders of the Black Hills" 1938; "Santa Fe Stampede" 1938; "Colorado Sunset" 1939; "Cowboys from Texas" 1939; "In Old Monterey" 1939 (story only); "The Kansas Terrors" 1939; "Mexicali Rose" 1939; "New Frontier" 1939; "The Night Riders" 1939; "Rovin' Tumbleweeds" 1939; "South of the Border" 1939; "Three Texas Steers" 1939; "Wyoming Outlaw" 1939; "Covered Wagon Days" 1940; "Frontier Vengeance" 1940 (prod. only); "Ghost Valley Raiders" 1940 (& prod.); "Lone Star Raiders" 1940; "One Man's Law" 1940 (& prod.); "Rocky Mountain Rangers" 1940; "Texas Terrors" 1940 (& prod.); "The Trail Blazers" 1940; "The Tulsa Kid" 1940 (& prod.); "Under Texas Skies" 1940; "The Apache Kid" 1941 (& prod.); "Death Valley Outlaws" 1941 (& prod.); "Desert Bandit" 1941 (& prod.); "Kansas Cyclone" 1941 (& prod.); "The Missouri Outlaw" 1941 (& prod.); "The Phantom Cowboy" 1941 (& prod.); "Two-Gun Sheriff" 1941 (& prod.); "Wyoming Wildcat" 1941 (& prod.); "Arizona Terrors" 1942 (& prod.); "The Cyclone Kid" 1942 (& prod.); "Jesse James, Jr." 1942 (& prod.); "The Sombrero Kid" 1942 (& prod.); "Stagecoach Express" 1942 (& prod.); "Renegades" 1946; "Last of the Redmen" 1947; "Black Bart" 1948; "Relentless" 1948; "River Lady" 1948; "Calamity Jane and Sam Bass" 1949 (& story); "Red Canyon" 1949; "Comanche Territory" 1950; "Tomahawk" 1951; "The Battle at Apache Pass" 1952; "The Lone Hand" 1953; "War Arrow" 1953; "Border River" 1954; "Dawn at Socorro" 1954; "Chief Crazy Horse" 1955; "Count Three and Pray" 1955; "The Treasure of Pancho Villa" 1955; "Comanche" 1956; "Reprisal!" 1956; "The Hard Man" 1957; "The Last of the Fast Guns" 1958; "Ten Days to Tulara" 1958 (& prod.); "For the Love of Mike" 1960 (& prod.); "Hell Bent for Leather" 1960; "The Comancheros" 1961; "Murieta" 1965-Span./U.S.; "Smoky" 1966; "Big Jake" 1971. ¶TV: *Rawhide*—"Incident of the Dog Days" 4-17-59, "Incident of a Burst of Evil" 6-26-59; *Daniel Boone* 1964-70 (prod.).

Sherman, Harry A. (1884-9/25/52). Producer. Films: "The Light of the Western Stars" 1930; "Hopalong Cassidy" 1935; "Bar 20 Rides Again"

1936; "Call of the Prairie" 1936; "The Eagle's Brood" 1936; "Hopalong Cassidy Returns" 1936; "Three on the Trail" 1936; "Trail Dust" 1936; "The Barrier" 1937; "Borderland" 1937; "Heart of the West" 1937; "Hills of Old Wyoming" 1937; "Hopalong Rides Again" 1937; "North of the Rio Grande" 1937; "Rustler's Valley" 1937; "Texas Trail" 1937; "Bar 20 Justice" 1938; "Cassidy of Bar 20" 1938; "The Frontiersman" 1938; "Heart of Arizona" 1938; "In Old Mexico" 1938; "The Mysterious Rider" 1938; "Partners of the Plains" 1938; "Pride of the West" 1938; "Sunset Trail" 1938; "Heritage of the Desert" 1939; "Law of the Pampas" 1939; "The Llano Kid" 1939; "Range War" 1939; "Renegade Trail" 1939; "Silver on the Sage" 1939; "Cherokee Strip" 1940; "Hidden Gold" 1940; "Knights of the Range" 1940; "The Light of Western Stars" 1940; "Santa Fe Marshal" 1940; "The Showdown" 1940; "Stagecoach War" 1940; "Three Men from Texas" 1940; "Border Vigilantes" 1941; "Boss of Bullion City" 1941; "Doomed Caravan" 1941; "In Old Colorado" 1941; "Outlaws of the Desert" 1941; "The Parson of Panamint" 1941; "Pirates on Horseback" 1941; "Riders of the Timberline" 1941; "The Round Up" 1941; "Secrets of the Wastelands" 1941; "Stick to Your Guns" 1941; "Twilight on the Trail" 1941; "Wide Open Town" 1941; "American Empire" 1942; "Silver Queen" 1942; "Tombstone, the Town Too Tough to Die" 1942; "Undercover Man" 1942; "Bar 20" 1943; "Border Patrol" 1943; "Buckskin Frontier" 1943; "Colt Comrades" 1943; "False Colors" 1943; "Hoppy Serves a Writ" 1943; "The Kansan" 1943; "The Leather Burners" 1943; "Lost Canyon" 1943; "Riders of the Deadline" 1943; "The Woman of the Town" 1943; "Buffalo Bill" 1944; "Forty Thieves" 1944; "Lumberjack" 1944; "Mystery Man" 1944; "Texas Masquerade" 1944; "Ramrod" 1947; "Four Faces West" 1948.

Sherman, Robert M. Producer. Films: "The Missouri Breaks" 1976.

Sherman, Teddi. Screenwriter. Films: "Four Faces West" 1948; "The Man from Bitter Ridge" 1955; "Tennessee's Partner" 1955.

Sherman, Vincent (1906-). Director. Films: "Heart of the North" 1938 (sp. only); "Lone Star" 1952 (sp. only); "The Second Time Around" 1961. ¶TV: *Alias Smith and Jones*—"Miracle at Santa Marta" 12-30-71.

Sherry, John. Screenwriter. Films: "The Last Challenge" 1967 (& story).

Shert, Antonio. Screenwriter. Films: "Eye for an Eye" 1972-Ital./Span./Mex.

Sherwood, John. Director. Films: "Raw Edge" 1956.

Shipman, Barry (1912-8/12/94). Screenwriter. Films: "The Painted Stallion" 1937; "Zorro Rides Again" 1937-serial; "The Lone Ranger" 1938-serial; "The Lone Ranger Rides Again" 1939-serial; "Frontier Vengeance" 1940; "Lone Star Raiders" 1940; "Rocky Mountain Rangers" 1940; "The Trail Blazers" 1940; "Prairie Pioneers" 1941; "Code of the Outlaw" 1942; "The Phantom Plainsmen" 1942; "Raiders of the Range" 1942; "Lumberjack" 1944; "Out California Way" 1946 (story only); "Roaring Rangers" 1946; "Riders of the Lone Star" 1947; "Smoky River Serenade" 1947; "Swing the Western Way" 1947; "Singing Spurs" 1948; "Six-Gun Law" 1948; "Smoky Mountain Melody" 1948; "Song of Idaho" 1948; "Trail to Laredo" 1948; "West of Sonora" 1948; "The Blazing Trail" 1949; "Home in San Antone" 1949; "Laramie" 1949; "Across the Badlands" 1950; "Frontier Outpost" 1950; "Hoedown" 1950; "Horsemen of the Sierras" 1950; "Outcast of Black Mesa" 1950; "Raiders of Tomahawk Creek" 1950; "Streets of Ghost Town" 1950; "Texas Dynamo" 1950; "Bandits of El Dorado" 1951; "Bonanza Town" 1951; "Cyclone Fury" 1951; "Fort Savage Raiders" 1951; "The Kid from Amarillo" 1951; "Pecos River" 1951; "Snake River Desperadoes" 1951; "Junction City" 1952; "The Kid from Broken Gun" 1952; "Laramie Mountains" 1952; "Montana Territory" 1952; "The Rough, Tough West" 1952; "Smoky Canyon" 1952; "Untamed Heiress" 1954; "Carolina Cannonball" 1955; "Law That Rifle Down" 1955; "Stranger at My Door" 1956; "Gunfire at Indian Gap" 1957; "Hell's Crossroads" 1957; "The Last Stagecoach West" 1957.

Shipman, Nell (1892-1/23/70). Writer. Films: "Outwitted by Billy" 1913.

Shirreffs, Gordon D. (1914-). Writer. Films: "The Lonesome Trail" 1955 (story); "Oregon Passage" 1958 (story); "A Long Ride from Hell" 1968-Ital. (story).

Sholem, Lee (1900-). Director. Films: "The Redhead from Wyoming" 1953; "The Stand at Apache River" 1953; "Sierra Strange" 1957. ¶TV: *Cheyenne* 1955; *Colt .45* 1957; *Sugarfoot* 1957; *Bronco* 1958; *Lawman* 1958; *Maverick*—"Last Wire from

Stop Gap" 10-16-60, "A Bullet for the Teacher" 10-30-60, "The Money Machine" 4-8-62, "One of Our Trains Is Missing" 4-22-62.

Shonteff, Lindsay. Director. Films: "The Last Gunfighter" 1961-Can. (& prod./sp.).

Shor, Sol. Screenwriter. Films: "The Lone Ranger Rides Again" 1939; "Zorro's Fighting Legion" 1939-serial; "Adventures of Red Ryder" 1940-serial; "King of the Royal Mounted" 1940-serial; "Jesse James Rides Again" 1947-serial; "Son of Zorro" 1947; "The Adventures of Frank and Jesse James" 1948-serial; "Dangers of the Canadian Mounted" 1948-serial; "Sons of Adventure" 1948; "Ghost of Zorro" 1949-serial; "The James Brothers of Missouri" 1950-serial.

Shores, Lynn. Director. Films: "Rebellion" 1936; "The Glory Trail" 1937.

Short, Luke (1908-8/18/75). Writer. Films: "Ramrod" 1947 (story); "Albuquerque" 1948 (story); "Blood on the Moon" 1948 (story); "Coroner Creek" 1948 (story); "Station West" 1948 (story); "Ambush" 1950 (story); "Silver City" 1951 (story); "Vengeance Valley" 1951 (story); "Ride the Man Down" 1952 (story); "Hell's Outpost" 1954 (story); "The Hangman" 1959 (story).

Shpetner, Stan. Screenwriter. Films: "The Legend of Tom Dooley" 1959 (& prod.); "Two Rode Together" 1961.

Shrake, Bud. Screenwriter. Films: "J.W. Coop" 1971; "Kid Blue" 1973; "Tom Horn" 1980.

Shryack, Dennis. Screenwriter. Films: "The Good Guys and the Bad Guys" 1969 (& prod.); "Pale Rider" 1985.

Shuken, Phil. Screenwriter. Films: "Plunderers of Painted Flats" 1959.

Shumate, Harold. Screenwriter. Films: "The Call of Courage" 1925 (story only); "The Outlaw's Daughter" 1925; "West of Broadway" 1926; "Black Jack" 1927; "The Circus Ace" 1927 (story only); "Outlaws of Red River" 1927; "Whispering Sage" 1927; "Heritage of the Desert" 1932; "Ridin' for Justice" 1932; "Wild Horse Mesa" 1932; "Crossfire" 1933; "Man of the Forest" 1933; "Scarlet River" 1933; "Son of the Border" 1933; "The Westerner" 1934; "Home on the Range" 1935; "Square Shooter" 1935; "End of the Trail" 1936; "Dodge City Trail" 1937; "Man

of Conquest" 1939 (story only); "South of the Rio Grande" 1939 (story only); "Konga, the Wild Stallion" 1940; "Trail of the Vigilantes" 1940; "When the Daltons Rode" 1940; "Badlands of Dakota" 1941 (story only); "The Parson of Panamint" 1941; "The Round Up" 1941; "Men of Texas" 1942 (& story); "Ride 'Em, Cowboy" 1942; "The Kansan" 1943; "Abilene Town" 1946; "Renegades" 1946 (story only); "Blood on the Moon" 1948 (adapt. only); "Saddle Tramp" 1950; "The Lady from Texas" 1951 (story only); "Little Big Horn" 1951 (story only); "The Half-Breed" 1952.

Shyer, Charles (1941-). Screenwriter. Films: "Goin' South" 1978.

Shyer, Melville. Screenwriter. Films: "The Man from Hell" 1934; "Dead Man's Trail" 1952.

Sibelius, Johanna. Screenwriter. Films: "Among Vultures" 1964-Ger./Ital./Fr./Yugo.

Siciliano, Mario (Marlon Sirko). Director. Films: "Cowards Don't Pray" 1968-Ital./Span. (& prod./sp.); "Halleluja and Sartana Strikes Again" 1972-Ger./Ital.; "Trinity and Sartana Are Coming" 1972-Ital.

Sickner, Roy N. Writer. Films: "The Wild Bunch" 1969 (story).

Sidney, George (1911-). Director. Films: "The Harvey Girls" 1946; "Annie Get Your Gun" 1950.

Sidney, Scott (1872-7/20/28). Director. Films: "Desert Gold" 1914; "The Deserter" 1916; "Her Own People" 1917.

Siegel, Don (1912-4/20/91). Director. Films: "The Duel at Silver Creek" 1952; "Flaming Star" 1960; "Stranger on the Run" TVM-1967; "Death of a Gunfighter" 1969; "Two Mules for Sister Sara" 1970; "The Shootist" 1976. ¶TV: *The Legend of Jesse James* 1965-66 (prod.).

Siegel, Lionel E. Screenwriter. Films: "Run, Simon, Run" TVM-1970.

Siegel, Sol C. (1903-82). Producer. Films: "Boots and Saddles" 1937; "Come On, Cowboys" 1937; "Gunsmoke Ranch" 1937; "Heart of the Rockies" 1937; "Public Cowboy No. 1" 1937; "Range Defenders" 1937; "Springtime in the Rockies" 1937; "The Trigger Trio 1937; "Wild Horse Rodeo" 1937; "Zorro Rides Again" 1937-serial; "The Lone Ranger" 1938-serial; "The Old Barn Dance" 1938; "The Purple Vigilantes" 1938; "Under Western Stars" 1938; "Man of Conquest" 1939; "The Dark Command" 1940; "Melody

Ranch" 1940; "Three Faces West" 1940; "Broken Lance" 1954; "Alvarez Kelly" 1966.

Siegmann, George (1882-6/22/28). Director. Films: "A Yankee from the West" 1915.

Silver, Arthur (1910-4/26/95). Producer. TV: *Cheyenne* 1955-63; *Bronco* 1958-60; *Maverick* 1960-61.

Silver, Pat. Writer. Films: "Land Raiders" 1969-U.S./Span. (story).

Silverman, Stanley H. Screenwriter. Films: "Gun Fever" 1958.

Silvernail, Clarke. Screenwriter. Films: "Shadow Ranch" 1930 (& story).

Silverstein, David. Screenwriter. Films: "The Kid from Kansas" 1941.

Silverstein, Elliot (1927-). Director. Films: "Cat Ballou" 1965; "A Man Called Horse" 1970. ¶TV: *The Westerner*—"Going Home" 12-16-60.

Silvestri, Alberto. Screenwriter. Films: "Yankee" 1967-Ital./Span.; "If One Is Born a Swine ... Kill Him" 1968-Ital. (prod. only).

Silvestre, Dario. see Girolami, Marino.

Simmonds, Leslie. Producer. Films: "Bulldog Courage" 1935; "Aces and Eights" 1936; "Border Caballero" 1936; "Lightning Bill Carson" 1936; "The Lion's Den" 1936; "Roarin' Guns" 1936; "The Traitor" 1936.

Simmons, Michael. Screenwriter. Films: "Landrush" 1946; "South of the Chisholm Trail" 1947.

Simmons, Richard Alan. Screenwriter. Films: "War Paint" 1953; "Three Hours to Kill" 1954; "The Yellow Tomahawk" 1954; "King and Four Queens" 1956; "Outlaw's Son" 1957; "Lock, Stock and Barrel" TVM-1971 (& prod.); "Skin Game" 1971 (story only); "Hitched" TVM-1973 (& prod.).

Simon, S. Sylvan (1910-5/17/51). Director. Films: "The Kid from Texas" 1939; "Bad Bascomb" 1946; "Lust for Gold" 1949 (& prod.).

Simonelli, Gianni (George Simonelli). Screenwriter. Films: "Gunmen of the Rio Grande" 1964-Fr./Ital./Span.; "Left Handed Johnny West" 1965-Span./Ital.; "Two Gangsters in the Wild West" 1965-Ital./Span. (& sp.); "Two Sergeants of General Custer" 1965-Ital./Span. (& sp.); "Johnny Yuma" 1966-Ital.; "Man with the Golden Pistol" 1966-Span./Ital.; "One Hundred Thousand Dollars for Ringo" 1966-Ital./Span.; "Two Sons of Ringo" 1966-Ital.; "Any Gun Can Play" 1968-Ital./

Span.; "I Do Not Forgive ... I Kill!" 1968-Span./Ital.; "I'll Sell My Skin Dearly" 1968-Ital.; "Sartana Does Not Forgie" 1968-Span./Ital.; "Return of Clint the Stranger" 1971-Ital./Span.; "Have a Good Funeral, My Friend ... Sartana Will Pay" 1972-Ital.; "I Am Sartana, Trade Your Guns for a Coffin" 1972-Ital.; "Return of Halleluja" 1972-Ital./Ger.; "Sting of the West" 1972-Ital./Span.; "Watch Out Gringo! Sabata Will Return" 1972-Ital./Span.; "Dick Luft in Sacramento" 1974-Ital.

Simpson, S.E. Director. Films: "Darkfeather's Strategy" 1912.

Sinatra, Frank (1915-). Producer. Films: "White Stallion" 1947 (story only); "Johnny Concho" 1956; "Sergeants 3" 1962.

Sinclair, Bertrand. Writer. Films: "Shotgun Jones" 1914 (story).

Sinclair, Harold. Writer. Films: "The Horse Soldiers" 1959 (story).

Sinclair, Richard. Director. TV: *Bronco* 1958; *Lawman* 1958; *The Alaskans* 1959.

Sinclair, Robert B. (1905-1/3/70). Director. TV: *Maverick*—"A Stage of Siege" 1-1-61,

Singer, Alexander (1932-). Director. Films: "Captain Apache" 1971-Brit./Span. ¶TV: *Lancer*—"Foley" 10-15-68; *Alias Smith and Jones*—"How to Rob a Bank in One Hard Lesson" 9-23-71, "Everything Else You Can Steal" 12-16-71, "The McCreedy Bust—Going, Going Gone" 1-13-72, "The Biggest Game in the West" 2-3-72, "The Long Chase" 9-16-72, "High Lonesome Country" 9-23-72, "The McCreedy Feud" 9-30-72, "The Clementine Incident" 10-7-72, "McGuffin" 12-9-72.

Siodmak, Curt (1902-). Screenwriter. Films: "Frisco Sal" 1945.

Siodmak, Robert (1900-3/10/73). Director. Films: "Pyramid of the Sun God" 1965-Ger./Ital./Fr.; "Custer of the West" 1967-U.S./Span.

Sirens, Bob. Screenwriter. Films: "Billy the Kid" 1962-Span.

Sirk, Douglas (1900-1/14/87). Director. Films: "Take Me to Town" 1953; "Taza, Son of Cochise" 1954.

Sirko, Marlon. *see* Siciliano, Mario.

Sisk, Robert. Producer. Films: "The Last Outlaw" 1936; "Two in Revolt" 1936; "Border Cafe" 1937; "The Outcasts of Poker Flat" 1937; "Bad Lands" 1939; "Reno" 1939; "Gentle Annie" 1944; "Boy's Ranch" 1946; "Across the Wide Missouri"

1951; "The Man Behind the Gun" 1952. ¶TV: *Wyatt Earp* 1955-61 (exec. prod.).

Skarstedt, Vance. Screenwriter. Films: "Man or Gun" 1958 (& prod.).

Skouras, Plato. Producer. Films: "Apache Warrior" 1957; "Sierra Baron" 1958; "Villa!" 1958.

Slater, Barney (1923-11/29/78). Screenwriter. Films: "Three Violent People" 1956 (story only); "The Tin Star" 1957 (story only); "Cahill, United States Marshal" 1973 (story only). ¶TV: *MacKenzie's Raiders* 1958-59 (prod.).

Slatter, Arthur. Screenwriter. Films: "A Hero on Horseback" 1927.

Slavin, George F. Screenwriter. Films: "The Fighting Stallion" 1950 (story only); "The Nevadan" 1950; "Red Mountain" 1951 (& story); "City of Badmen" 1953; "Smoke Signal" 1955; "The Halliday Brand" 1957.

Sloan, Robert. Writer. Films: "Cowboy from Brooklyn" 1938 (story).

Sloane, Everett (1909-8/6/65). Director. TV: *Lawman*—"Shadow Witness" 11-15-59.

Sloane, Paul H. (1893-11/15/63). Director. Films: "Pardners" 1917 (sp. only); "The Texans" 1938 (sp. only); "The Lone Cowboy" 1934 (& sp.); "Geronimo" 1940 (& sp.).

Sloane, Robert. Screenwriter. Films: "Two Guys from Texas" 1948 (story only).

Sloman, Edward (1883-9/29/72). Director. Films: "The Legend of the Poisoned Pool" 1915; "Lone Star" 1916; "Snap Judgment" 1917; "Put Up Your Hands" 1919; "The Westerners" 1919; "The Sagebrusher" 1920; "The Eagle's Feather" 1923; "Caught" 1931; "The Conquering Horde" 1931; "Gun Smoke" 1931.

Small, Bernard. Producer. Films: "The Iroquois Trail" 1950; "Indian Uprising" 1951.

Small, Edward (1891-1/25/77). Producer. Films: "The Last of the Mohicans" 1935; "Kit Carson" 1940; "Davy Crockett, Indian Scout" 1950; "The Texas Rangers" 1951; "Cripple Creek" 1952; "Gun Belt" 1953; "The Lone Gun" 1954; "Overland Pacific" 1954; "Southwest Passage" 1954; "Top Gun" 1955.

Smalley, Phillips (1865-5/2/39). Director. Films: "When a Girl Loves" 1919.

Smight, Jack (1926-). Director. TV: *Our American Heritage*—"Destiny West" 1-24-60.

Smith, Alson Jesse. Writer. Films: "The Lawless Eighties" 1958 (story).

Smith, Bernard (1905-). Producer. Films: "How the West Was Won" 1962; "Cheyenne Autumn" 1964.

Smith, Charles B. (1920-12/26/88). Screenwriter. Films: "Apache Rifles" 1964.

Smith, Clifford S. (1886-9/17/37). Director. Films: "The Gringo" 1914; "Cash Parrish's Pal" 1915; "The Conversion of Frosty Blake" 1915; "The Darkening Trail" 1915; "Keno Bates—Liar" 1915; "Mr. Silent Haskins" 1915; "The Roughneck" 1915; "The Ruse" 1915; "The Scourge of the Desert" 1915; "The Taking of Luke McVane" 1915; "The Apostle of Vengeance" 1916; "The Aryan" 1916; "The Devil Dodger" 1917; "The Learnin' of Jim Benton" 1917; "The Medicine Man" 1917; "One Shot Ross" 1917; "Boss of the Lazy Y" 1918; "By Proxy" 1918; "Cactus Crandall" 1918; "Faith Endurin'" 1918; "The Fly God" 1918; "The Girl of Hell's Agony" 1918; "Keith of the Border" 1918; "The Law's Outlaw" 1918; "Paying His Debt" 1918; "The Pretender" 1918; "The Red Haired Cupid" 1918; "The Silent Rider" 1918; "Untamed" 1918; "Wolves of the Border" 1918; "The She Wolf" 1919; "The Cyclone" 1920; "The Girl Who Dared" 1920; "The Lone Hand" 1920; "Three Gold Coins" 1920; "Crossing Trails" 1921; "The Stranger in Canyon Valley" 1921; "Western Hearts" 1921 (& sp.); "Wild Bill Hickok" 1923; "Daring Danger" 1922; "The Back Trail" 1924; "Daring Chances" 1924; "Fighting Fury" 1924; "Ridgeway of Montana" 1924; "Singer Jim McKee" 1924; "The Western Wallop" 1924; "Bustin' Thru" 1925; "The Call of Courage" 1925; "Don Dare Devil" 1925; "Flying Hoofs" 1925; "The Red Rider" 1925; "Ridin' Thunder" 1925; "A Roaring Adventure" 1925; "The Sign of the Cactus" 1925; "The White Outlaw" 1925; "Arizona Sweepstakes" 1926; "The Demon" 1926; "The Desert's Toll" 1926; "The Fighting Peacemaker" 1926; "The Man in the Saddle" 1926; "The Phantom Bullet" 1926; "The Ridin' Rascal" 1926; "Rustlers' Ranch" 1926; "The Scrappin' Kid" 1926; "The Set-Up" 1926; "A Six Shootin' Romance" 1926; "Sky High Coral" 1926; "The Terror" 1926; "Loco Luck" 1927; "Open Range" 1927; "Spurs and Saddles" 1927; "The Valley of Hell" 1927; "The Three Outcasts" 1929; "Riders of the Golden Gulch" 1932;

"The Texan" 1932; "Devil's Canyon" 1935; "Five Bad Men" 1935; "Wild West Days" 1937-serial.

Smith, David. Director. Films: "Baree, Son of Kazan" 1918; "The Dawn of Understanding" 1918; "Pioneer Trails" 1923; "Code of the Wilderness" 1924; "Baree, Son of Kazan" 1925; "Steele of the Royal Mounted" 1925.

Smith, Earl E. Director. Films: "Winterhawk" 1975 (sp. only); "The Winds of Autumn" 1976 (sp. only); "Shadow of Chikara" 1978 (& prod./sp.).

Smith, Frank Leon. Screenwriter. Films: "Go Get 'Em Garringer" 1919; "Ruth of the Range" 1923-serial; "Galloping Hoofs" 1924 (story only); "Idaho" 1925-serial (story).

Smith, Garret. Writer. Films: "Honest Hutch" 1920 (story).

Smith, George. Screenwriter. Films: "The Hawk of Powder River" 1948.

Smith, Hal. Screenwriter. Films: "Black Eagle" 1948; "Thunderhoof" 1948.

Smith, Hamilton. Screenwriter. Films: "The Man in Irons" 1915 (story only); "American Maid" 1917.

Smith, Harold Jacob (1912-12/28/70). Screenwriter. Films: "The McMasters" 1970.

Smith, Howard. Screenwriter. Films: "Land of the Silver Fox" 1928.

Smith, Mathilda. Screenwriter. Films: "Ridin' Wild" 1925.

Smith, Noel Mason. Director. Films: "Clash of the Wolves" 1925; "Trailin' West" 1936; "Blazing Sixes" 1937; "The California Mail" 1937; "Cherokee Strip" 1937; "Guns of the Pecos" 1937; "Cattle Town" 1952.

Smith, Paul Gerard (1895-4/4/68). Screenwriter. Films: "Wild Bill Hickok Rides" 1942; "Moonlight and Cactus" 1944.

Smith, R. Cecil. Screenwriter. Films: "The Law of the North" 1918; "Playing the Game" 1918; "Smashing Barriers" 1919-serial; "The Valley of Doubt" 1920.

Smith, Robert. Screenwriter. Films: "The Lonely Man" 1957.

Smith, Steven Phillip. Screenwriter. Films: "The Long Riders" 1980.

Smith, Vernon. Screenwriter. Films: "Call of the Prairie" 1936; "Three on the Trail" 1936.

Smith, W.M. Screenwriter. Films: "Cotton and Cattle" 1921; "A

Cowboy Ace" 1921; "Flowing Gold" 1921; "Out of the Clouds" 1921 (story only); "Rustlers of the Night" 1921; "The Range Pirate" 1921; "The Trail to Red Dog" 1921.

Smith, Wallace (1888-1/31/37). Screenwriter. Films: "West of Broadway" 1926 (story only); "Beau Bandit" 1930; "The Gay Desperado" 1936.

Smith, William. Screenwriter. Films: "The Silver Horde" 1930.

Smithee, Alan. Director. Films: "Call of the Wild" TVM-1993.

Smollen, Bradley. Screenwriter. Films: "Steelheart" 1921; "The Fighting Guide" 1922.

Snell, Earle (1886-5/6/65). Screenwriter. Films: "The Heart of Juanita" 1919 (story only); "Just Squaw" 1919; "The Flame of Hellgate" 1920; "Alias the Bad Man" 1931; "Branded Men" 1931; "Range Law" 1931; "The Two Gun Man" 1931; "Tombstone Canyon" 1932; "Fargo Express" 1933; "Branded a Coward" 1935; "Stone of Silver Creek" 1935; "Everyman's Law" 1936; "King of the Royal Mounted" 1936; "Rogue of the Range" 1936; "Sunset of Power" 1936; "Wild Brian Kent" 1936; "Desert Phantom" 1937; "It Happened Out West" 1937; "Secret Valley" 1937; "Western Gold" 1937; "Days of Jesse James" 1939; "Covered Wagon Days" 1940; "Oklahoma Renegades" 1940; "Rocky Mountain Rangers" 1940; "West of Pinto Basin" 1940; "Gauchos of El Dorado" 1941; "The Kid's Last Ride" 1941; "Tonto Basin Outlaws" 1941 (story only); "Trail of the Silver Spurs" 1941; "Wrangler's Roost" 1941 (story only); "Riding the Wind" 1942; "Rock River Renegades" 1942; "Thunder River Feud" 1942 (& story); "Prairie Chickens" 1943; "Colorado Pioneers" 1945; "Phantom of the Plains" 1945; "Wagon Wheels Westward" 1945; "Alias Billy the Kid" 1946; "Conquest of Cheyenne" 1946; "Santa Fe Uprising" 1946; "Sheriff of Redwood Valley" 1946; "Stagecoach to Denver" 1946; "Sun Valley Cyclone" 1946; "Along the Oregon Trail" 1947; "Homesteaders of Paradise Valley" 1947; "The Last Round-Up" 1947; "The Marshal of Cripple Creek" 1947; "Oregon Trail Scouts" 1947; "Robin Hood of Texas" 1947; "Rustlers of Devil's Canyon" 1947; "Vigilantes of Boomtown" 1947; "Carson City Raiders" 1948; "Desert Vigilante" 1949; "El Dorado Pass" 1949; "Ranger of Cherokee Strip" 1949 (story only); "Renegades of the Sage" 1949; "South of Death Valley" 1949;

"Valley of Fire" 1951 (story only); "The Desperados Are in Town" 1956.

Solinas, Franco. Screenwriter. Films: "The Big Gundown" 1966-Ital. (story only); "A Bullet for the General" 1966-Ital.; "Blood and Guns" 1968-Ital./Span.; "The Mercenary" 1968-Ital./Span. (story only).

Sollazzo, Amadeo. Screenwriter. Films: "Two Sons of Ringo" 1966-Ital.; "Two R-R-Ringos from Texas" 1967-Ital.; "Ciccio Forgives, I Don't" 1968-Ital.

Sollima, Sergio. Director. Films: "The Big Gundown" 1966-Ital. (& sp.); "Face to Face" 1967-Ital. (& sp.); "Run Man, Run" 1967-Ital./Fr. (& sp.).

Soloman, David. Director. Films: "Kentucky Days" 1923.

Solomon, Louis. Screenwriter. Films: "Mark of the Renegade" 1951.

Solvay, Paolo. *see* Batzella, Luigi.

Somerville, Roy. Screenwriter. Films: "The Challenge of Chance" 1919; "Eastward Ho!" 1919; "The Orphan" 1920.

Sontag, George. Writer. Films: "The Folly of a Life of Crime" 1915 (story).

Soria, Julio. Screenwriter. Films: "Three from Colorado" 1967-Span.

Sorrentino, Elido. Screenwriter. Films: "Sheriff of Rock Spring" 1971-Ital.; "Seven Nuns in Kansas City" 1973-Ital. (prod. only).

Sowders, Edward. Director. Films: "Finger Prints" 1920; "A Sagebrush Gentleman" 1920.

Spalding, Harry (Henry Cross). Screenwriter. Films: "The Firebrand" 1962; "Young Guns of Texas" 1963; "One Little Indian" 1973.

Spangler, Larry G. Director. Films: "The Last Rebel" 1971-Ital./U.S./Span.; "The Legend of Nigger Charley" 1972 (prod./sp. only); "A Knife for the Ladies" 1973 (& prod.); "The Soul of Nigger Charley" 1973 (& prod./story); "Joshua" 1977 (& prod./sp.).

Sparks, Robert. Producer. Films: "Go West, Young Lady" 1941; "Station West" 1948. ¶TV: *Have Gun Will Travel* 1957-63; *The Travels of Jaimie McPheeters* 1963-64.

Sparr, Robert. Director. Films: "More Dead Than Alive" 1968. ¶TV: *Lawman* 1958; *The Alaskans* 1959; *Bonanza*—"The Countess" 11-19-61; *Wild Wild West*—"The Night of the Eccentrics" 9-16-66, "The Night of the Flying Pie Plate" 10-21-66, "The Night of the Bottomless Pit" 11-4-66, "The Night of the Green Terror" 11-18-66, "The Night of the Feathered Fury" 1-13-67; *The High Chaparral*—"The Widow from Red Rock" 11-26-67.

Spataro, Diego. Producer. Films: "Hero Called Allegria" 1971-Ital. (sp. only); "Go Away! Trinity Has Arrived in Eldorado" 1972-Ital.; "Showdown for a Badman" 1972-Ital.

Spaziani, Renzo. *see* Bianchi, Mario.

Spear, Gil. Screenwriter. Films: "High Pockets" 1919.

Spearman, Frank Hamilton. Writer. Films: "Medicine Bend" 1916 (story); "Whispering Smith" 1916 (story); "Nan of Music Mountain" 1917 (story); "Whispering Smith" 1926 (story); "Whispering Smith Speaks" 1935; "Whispering Smith" 1948 (story).

Spears, Raymond. Writer. Films: "The Bar C Mystery" 1926 (story).

Specht, Jack. Writer. Films: "Ole Rex" 1961 (story).

Speirs, Jack. Screenwriter. Films: "King of the Grizzlies" 1970.

Spelling, Aaron (1928-). Producer. Films: "Guns of the Timberland" 1960 (& sp.); "One Foot in Hell" 1960 (sp./story only); "The Over-the-Hill Gang" TVM-1969; "Run, Simon, Run" TVM-1970; "The Trackers" TVM-1971 (& story); "Yuma" TVM-1971; "Bounty Man" TVM-1972. ¶TV: *Zane Grey Theater* 1956-61; *Wagon Train*—"The Conchita Vasquez Story" 3-18-59 (dir.); *Johnny Ringo* 1959-60; *Daniel Boone* 1964-70 (exec. prod.); *The Guns of Will Sonnett* 1967-69; *Rango* 1967.

Spence, Ralph (1890-12/21/49). Screenwriter. Films: "Way Out West" 1930; "Plainsman and the Lady" 1946 (story only).

Spencer, Brenton. Director. TV: *Hawkeye*—"Vengeance Is Mine" 2-23-95, "The Bounty" 5-3-95.

Spencer, Jeanne. Screenwriter. Films: "The Shootin' Fool" 1920; "Some Shooter" 1920.

Spencer, Norman. Director. Films: "Rainbow's End" 1935.

Spencer, Richard V. Screenwriter. Films: "Custer's Last Fight" 1912; "The Claim Jumper" 1913; "Desert Gold" 1914; "The Gringo" 1914; "In the Cow Country" 1914; "The Deserter" 1916; "The Hidden Spring" 1917; "The Promise" 1917; "Under Handicap" 1917.

Sperling, Milton (1912-8/88). Producer. Films: "The Return of the Cisco Kid" 1939 (sp. only); "Pursued" 1947; "South of St. Louis" 1949; "Distant Drums" 1951; "Blowing Wild" 1953; "Captain Apache" 1971-Brit./Span.

Spicer, Bryan. Director. TV: *Adventures of Brisco County, Jr.*—Pilot 8-27-93, "Ned Zed" 3-13-94.

Spielman, Ed. Screenwriter. Films: "Kung Fu" TVM-1972 (& story).

Spina, Sergio. Screenwriter. Films: "Mercenary" 1968-Ital./Span.

Spitfire, Dick. *see* Fidani, Demofilo.

Springer, Norman. Writer. Films: "Frontier Days" 1934 (story).

Springsteen, R.G. (1904-12/9/89). Director. Films: "Colorado Pioneers" 1945; "Marshal of Laredo" 1945; "Phantom of the Plains" 1945; "Wagon Wheels Westward" 1945; "California Gold Rush" 1946; "Conquest of Cheyenne" 1946; "Home on the Range" 1946; "The Man from Rainbow Valley" 1946; "Santa Fe Uprising" 1946; "Sheriff of Redwood Valley" 1946; "Stagecoach to Denver" 1946; "Sun Valley Cyclone" 1946; "Along the Oregon Trail" 1947; "Homesteaders of Paradise Valley" 1947; "The Marshal of Cripple Creek" 1947; "Oregon Trail Scouts" 1947; "Rustlers of Devil's Canyon" 1947; "Under Colorado Skies" 1947; "Vigilantes of Boomtown" 1947; "Renegades of Sonora" 1948; "Son of God's Country" 1948; "Sundown in Santa Fe" 1948; "Death Valley Gunfighter" 1949; "Hellfire" 1949; "Navajo Trial Raiders" 1949; "Sheriff of Wichita" 1949; "The Arizona Cowboy" 1950; "Covered Wagon Raid" 1950; "Frisco Tornado" 1950; "Hills of Oklahoma" 1950; "Singing Guns" 1950; "Oklahoma Annie" 1952; "Toughest Man in Arizona" 1952; "A Perilous Journey" 1953; "Cole Younger, Gunfighter" 1958; "King of the Wild Stallions" 1959; "Showdown" 1963; "Bullet for a Badman" 1964; "He Rides Tall" 1964; "Taggart" 1964; "Black Spurs" 1965; "Apache Uprising" 1966; "Johnny Reno" 1966; "Waco" 1966; "Hostile Guns" 1967; "Red Tomahawk" 1967. ¶TV: *Wanted—Dead or Alive*—"Competition" 1-31-59, "The Corner" 2-21-59, "Angels of Vengeance" 4-18-59; *Gunsmoke*—"Brother Whelp" 11-7-59, "Box O'Rocks" 12-5-59; *Rawhide*—"Incident of the Music Maker" 5-20-60, "Incident of the Night Visitor" 11-4-60, "Incident on the Road to Yesterday" 11-18-60, "Incident of the Broken Word" 1-20-61, "Incident Near Gloomy River" 3-17-61, "Incident in the Middle of Nowhere" 4-7-61, "Incident of the Blackstorms" 5-26-61, "Incident of the Wager on Payday" 6-16-61; *Laredo*—"A Question of Discipline" 10-28-65, "A Matter of Policy" 11-11-65, "The Land Grabbers" 12-9-65, "The Last of the Caesars—Absolutely" 12-2-66; *Wagon Train*—"The Jane Hawkins Story" 11-30-60, "The Sam Spicer Story" 10-28-63, "The Eli Bancroft Story" 11-11-63; *Bonanza*—"The Reluctant Rebel" 11-21-65, "The Trouble with Jamie" 3-20-66, "The Genius" 4-3-66, "The Fighters" 4-24-66, "The Last Mission" 5-8-66; *The Monroes*—"Killer Cougar" 2-1-67; *Daniel Boone*—"Bitter Mission" 3-30-67.

Squittieri, Pasquale (William Redford). Director. Films: "Django Challenges Sartana" 1970-Ital.; "Vengeance Is a Dish Served Cold" 1971-Ital./Span. (& sp.).

Stabile, Ed. Director. Films: "Plainsong" 1982 (& sp.).

Stabler, Robert (1918-11/21/88). Producer. Films: "The Black Whip" 1956; "Copper Sky" 1957 (& story); "Ride a Violent Mile" 1957; "Blood Arrow" 1958; "Cattle Empire" 1958; "The Incredible Rocky Mountain Race" TVM-1977; "Last of the Mohicans" TVM-1977.

Stafford, Babe. Director. Films: "The Cow-Catcher's Daughter" 1931-short.

Stafford, H.G. Screenwriter. Films: "An Indian Legend" 1912; "Mary of the Mines" 1912; "The Vengenace of Fate" 1912; "The Green Shadow" 1913; "A Slave's Devotion" 1913; "The Law of the Range" 1914.

Stallings, Laurence (1895-2/28/68). Screenwriter. Films: "Billy the Kid" 1930; "Song of the West" 1930 (story only); "The Man from Dakota" 1940; "Northwest Passage" 1940; "Salome, Where She Danced" 1945; "The Three Godfathers" 1948; "She Wore a Yellow Ribbon" 1949.

Stanford, Harry. Writer. Films: "Waco" 1966 (story).

Stanlaws, Penrhyn. Director. Films: "Over the Border" 1922.

Stanley, George C. Director. Films: "The Little Sheriff" 1914.

Stanley, Jack. Screenwriter. Films: "Black Arrow" 1944-serial.

Stanley, Paul. Director. TV: *Have Gun Will Travel*—"The Monster of Moon Ridge" 2-28-59; *Laredo*—"Lazyfoot, Where Are You?" 9-16-65, "Jinx" 12-2-65, "The Heroes of San

Gill" 12-23-65, "A Very Small Assignment" 3-17-66; *The High Chaparral*—"Gold Is Where You Leave It" 1-21-68; *Wild Wild West*—"The Night of the Spanish Curse" 1-3-69; *Gunsmoke*—"Phoenix" 9-20-71, "My Brother's Keeper" 11-15-71, "Drago" 11-22-71, "Survival" 1-10-72.

Stanley, Peter E. *see* Pierotti, Piero.

Stanton, Richard. Director. Films: "Shorty Escapes Marriage" 1914; "Durand of the Bad Lands" 1917; "North of '53" 1917; "One Touch of Sin" 1917; "Rough and Ready" 1918 (& sp.); "McGuire of the Mounted" 1923.

Stanton, Whitney J. Writer. Films: "Red River Robin Hood" 1943 (story).

Stanush, Claude. Writer. Films: "The Lusty Men" 1952 (story).

Star, Ben. Screenwriter. Films: "Texas Across the River" 1966.

Starr, Helen. Screenwriter. Films: "Lone Larry" 1917.

Starr, Irving. Producer. Films: "Tombstone Canyon" 1932; "Border Brigands" 1935; "Stone of Silver Creek" 1935.

Starr, James A. Screenwriter. Films: "Rough Waters" 1930.

Starrett, Jack (1936-3/27/89). Director. Films: "Cry Blood, Apache" 1970; "Mr. Horn" TVM-1979.

Statter, Arthur. Screenwriter. Films: "Honest Hutch" 1920; "The Galloping Kid" 1922; "Step on It!" 1922; "Trimmed" 1922; "Renegade Holmes, M.D." 1925 (story only); "Cyclone of the Range" 1927; "Galloping Fury" 1927; "Painted Ponies" 1927; "The Danger Rider" 1928; "The Flyin' Cowboys" 1928; "The Rawhide Kid" 1928; "A Trick of Hearts" 1928.

Staub, Ralph (1899-10/22/69). Director. Films: "Romance of the West" 1935-short; "Prairie Moon" 1938; "Western Jamboree" 1938; "Chip of the Flying U" 1939; "Danger Ahead" 1940; "Sky Bandits" 1940; "Yukon Flight" 1940; "My Pal Ringeye" 1947-short (& prod.).

Steck, H. Tipton. Screenwriter. Films: "By Indian Post" 1919; "Gun Law" 1919; "The Last Outlaw" 1919; "Marked Men" 1919; "The Outcasts of Poker Flat" 1919; "The Rider of the Law" 1919; "Sting of the Lash" 1921.

Stedman, Marshal (1874-12/16/43). Director. Films: "Between Love and the Law" 1912; "The Brand Blotter" 1912; "The Cattle Rustlers" 1912;

"So-Jun-Wah and the Tribal Law" 1912.

Steeber, Max. Writer. Films: "The Gun Hawk" 1963 (story); "Apache Uprising" 1966 (story).

Steele, Rufus. Writer. Films: "The Divorcee" 1917 (story).

Stegani, Giorgio (George Finlay). Director. Films: "Adios Gringo" 1965-Ital./Fr./Span. (& sp.); "Blood for a Silver Dollar" 1965-Ital./Fr. (sp. only); "Beyond the Law" 1968-Ital. (& sp.); "Blood at Sundown" 1969-Ital./Ger.; "Gentleman Killer" 1969-Span./Ital. (& sp.).

Steinbeck, John (1902-12/20/68). Screenwriter. Films: "Viva Zapata!" 1952.

Steinberg, Norman. Screenwriter. Films: "Blazing Saddles" 1974.

Stemmle, Robert A. Screenwriter. Films: "Pyramid of the Sun God" 1965-Ger./Ital./Fr.; "Old Shatterhand" 1968-Ger./Yugo./Fr./Ital.

Steno (Stefano Vanzina) (1915-3/12/88). Director. Films: "Heroes of the West" 1964-Span./Ital. (& sp.); "Twins from Texas" 1964-Ital./Span.

Stephens, Peter. Director. Films: "Mustang" 1959.

Stephens, William. Producer. Films: "Thunder in the Pines" 1948; "Deputy Marshal" 1949.

Stephenson, Timothy. Screenwriter. Films: "Manchurian Avenger" 1985.

Stern, Alfred. Producer. Films: "The Rangers Take Over" 1942; "Bad Men of Thunder Gap" 1943; "Border Buckaroos" 1943; "Fighting Valley" 1943; "West of Texas" 1943; "Boss of Rawhide" 1944; "Outlaw Roundup" 1944; "The Pinto Bandit" 1944; "Trail of Terror" 1944.

Stern, Leonard. Screenwriter. Films: "Lost in Alaska" 1952.

Stern, Sandor (1936-). Screenwriter. Films: "True Grit" TVM-1978 (& prod.).

Stern, Steven Hilliard (1937-). Director. Films: "Draw" CTMV-1984; "Black Fox" TVM-1995.

Stern, Stewart (1922-). Screenwriter. Films: "Thunder in the Sun" 1959.

Sterne, Elaine. Screenwriter. Films: "The Inner Voice" 1920.

Sterret, Walter. Screenwriter. Films: "The Invaders" 1929; "The Oklahoma Kid" 1929.

Stevens, Gay. Screenwriter. Films: "A Buckaroo Broadcast" 1938-short.

Stevens, George (1904-3/8/75).

Director. Films: "Annie Oakley" 1935; "Shane" 1953 (& prod.); "Giant" 1956 (& prod.).

Stevens, Leslie (1924-). Screenwriter. Films: "The Left-Handed Gun" 1958. ¶TV: *Stoney Burke* 1962-63 (prod.); *The Virginian* 1962-70 (exec. prod.); *The Men from Shiloh* 1970-71 (prod.).

Stevens, Louis (1900-9/29/63). Screenwriter. Films: "The Texas Rangers" 1936; "The Border Legion" 1940; "Colorado" 1940; "The Massacre River" 1949; "Streets of Laredo" 1949 (story only); "Cimarron Kid" 1951 (& prod.); "Santa Fe" 1951 (story only); "Horizons West" 1952; "Border River" 1954; "Gun Duel in Durango" 1957; "Flaming Frontier" 1958-Can.; "Wolf Dog" 1958-Can.

Stevens, Mark (1922-). Director. Films: "Gun Fever" 1958 (& sp.); "Sunscorched" 1966-Span./Ger. (& sp.). ¶TV: *Wagon Train*—"The John Darro Story" 11-6-57, "The Luke O'Malley Story" 1-1-58, "The Annie MacGregor Story" 2-5-58, "The Major Adams Story" 4-23-58 & 4-30-58, "The Cassie Tanner Story" 6-4-58, "The John Wilbot Story" 6-11-58, "The Monte Britton Story" 6-18-58, "The Last Man" 2-11-59.

Stevenson, Robert (1905-4/30/86). Director. Films: "Old Yeller" 1957. ¶TV: *Gunsmoke*—"The Killer" 5-26-56, "The Preacher" 6-16-56, "Dutch George" 6-30-56, "Chester's Mail Order Bride" 7-14-56, "Cara" 7-28-56; *Zorro*—"Shadow of Doubt" 1-9-58, "Garcia Stands Accused" 1-16-58, "Slaves of the Eagle" 1-23-58,

Stevenson, Robert Lewis (1850-94). Writer. Films: "Adventures in Silverado" 1948 (story); "The Treasure of Lost Canyon" 1952 (story).

Stewart, Douglas C. Screenwriter. Films: "Seven Alone" 1974; "Against a Crooked Sky" 1975.

Stewart, Elinore Randall. Writer. Films: "Heartland" 1980 (story).

Stewart, Peter. *see* Newfield, Sam.

Stewart, Ramona. Writer. Films: "Desert Fury" 1947 (story).

Stoliar, Steve. Director. TV: *Legend*—"Knee-High Noon" 5-23-95.

Stoloff, Benjamin (1896-9/7/60). Director. Films: "The Canyon of Light" 1926; "The Circus Ace" 1927; "Silver Valley" 1927; "A Horseman of the Plains" 1928; "Three Rogues" 1931; "Destry Rides Again" 1932; "The Red Stallion" 1947 (prod. only).

Stone, Ezra (1917-3/3/94). Director. TV: *Laredo*—"The Sweet Gang" 11-4-66, "The Short, Happy Fatherhood of Reese Bennett" 1-27-67, "The Other Cheek" 2-10-67.

Stone, Harold. Screenwriter. Films: "The Soul of Nigger Charley" 1973.

Stone, Irving (1903-8/26/89). Writer. Films: "Arkansas Judge" 1941 (story).

Stone, John (1888-6/3/61). Screenwriter. Films: "The Heart Buster" 1924; "Gold and the Girl" 1925; "Hearts and Spurs" 1925; "The Lucky Horseshoe" 1925; "The Man Who Played Square" 1925; "The Timber Wolf" 1925; "The Canyon of Light" 1926; "The Great K & A Train Robbery" 1926; "Hard-Boiled" 1926; "A Man Four-Square" 1926; "No Man's Gold" 1926; "Three Bad Men" 1926 (prod. only); "Arizona Bound" 1927; "Arizona Wildcat" 1927; "Broncho Twister" 1927; "Drums of the Desert" 1927; "The Last Outlaw" 1927; "The Last Trail" 1927; "Nevada" 1927; "Open Range" 1927; "Daredevil's Reward" 1928; "Wild and Woolly" 1937 (prod. only); "Arizona Wildcat" 1938 (prod. only); "The Cisco Kid and the Lady" 1939 (prod. only); "Shooting High" 1940 (prod. only); "Wild Heritage" 1958.

Stone, LeRoy. Screenwriter. Films: "Eyes of the Forest" 1923.

Stone, Jr., N.B. Screenwriter. Films: "Man with the Gun" 1955; "Ride the High Country" 1962.

Stonehouse, Ruth (1892-5/12/41). Writer. Films: "Rough Going" 1925 (story).

Storey, Thomas L. Director. Films: "Queen of the Northwoods" 1929-serial; "Two in Revolt" 1936 (story only).

Storm, Barry. Writer. Films: "Lust for Gold" 1949 (story).

Storm, Jerome. Director. Films: "The Man from Nowhere" 1915; "A Desert Wooing" 1918; "A California Romance" 1923; "The Law of Fear" 1928; "Tracked" 1928; "Courtin' Wildcats" 1929; "The Yellowback" 1929.

Story, Thomas L. Director. Films: "The Last Frontier" 1932-serial.

Stothart, Herbert. Writer. Films: "Rose Marie" 1936 (story); "Rose Marie" 1954 (story).

Stowers, Frederick. Screenwriter. Films: "The Coast of Opportunity" 1920.

Stratton, Bill. Screenwriter.

Films: "The Last Days of Frank of Jesse James" TVM-1986; "Gunsmoke: The Long Ride" TVM-1993.

Strauss, Theodore. Screenwriter. Films: "I Will Fight No More Forever" TVM-1975.

Strawn, Arthur. Screenwriter. Films: "Road Agent" 1941; "Bad Men of Tombstone" 1949; "Hiawatha" 1952.

Strayer, Frank R. (1891-2/3/64). Director. Films: "The Lure of the Wild" 1925; "Go West, Young Lady" 1941; "Senorita from the West" 1945.

Stresa, Nino. Screenwriter. Films: "Buffalo Bill, Hero of the Far West" 1964-Ital./Ger./Fr.; "Colorado Charlie" 1965-Ital./Span.; "Man and a Colt" 1967-Span./Ital.; "All Out" 1968-Ital./Span.; "Beast" 1970-Ital. (& sp.); "Sabata the Killer" 1970-Ital./Span.; "Man Called Django" 1971-Ital.

Striker, Frank. Writer. Films: "The Lone Ranger" 1938-serial (story); "The Lone Ranger Rides Again" 1939-serial (story).

Stringer, Arthur. Writer. Films: "The Prairie Wife" 1925 (story); "Buck Benny Rides Again" 1940 (story).

Strock, Herbert L. (1918-). Director. Films: "Rider on a Dead Horse" 1962. ¶TV: *Cheyenne* 1955; *Colt .45* 1957; *Sugarfoot* 1957; *Bronco* 1958; *The Alaskans* 1959; *Maverick*— "The Town That Wasn't There" 10-2-60.

Stromberg, Hunt (1894-8/23/68). Producer. Films: "Soft Shoes" 1925 (sp. only); "Rose Marie" 1936; "Northwest Passage" 1940.

Strong, Harrington. Writer. Films: "Saddle Mates" 1928 (story).

Strumwasser, Jack. Screenwriter. Films: "Bar Nothin'" 1921 (& story); "To a Finish" 1921; "Catch My Smoke" 1922; "The Crusader" 1922; "Iron to Gold" 1922; "Pardon My Nerve!" 1922; "Rough Shod" 1922; "The Yosemite Trail" 1922; "Bucking the Barrier" 1923; "The Buster" 1923; "Snowdrift" 1923.

Stuart, Angela. Writer. Films: "Northwest Outpost" 1947 (story).

Stuart, Colin. Writer. Films: "The Legend of Walks Far Woman" TVM-1982 (story).

Stuart, Dorrell. Screenwriter. Films: "Hellfire" 1949.

Stuart, Malcolm. Producer. Films: "The Great Bank Robbery" 1969; "The Call of the Wild" TVM-1976.

Stuart, Mel. Director. Films:

"The Chisholms" TVM-1979. ¶TV: *The Chisholms* 1980.

Stuart, William L. (1912-1/11/88). Producer. TV: *Maverick* 1961-62.

Sturdy, John Rhodes. Writer. Films: "The Cariboo Trail" 1950 (story).

Sturgeon, Rollin. Director. Films: "When California Was Young" 1912; "The Angel of the Desert" 1913; "Polly at the Ranch" 1913; "The Little Angel of Canyon Creek" 1914; "The Sea Gull" 1914; "A Child of the North" 1915; "Love and Law" 1915; "The Sage Brush Girl" 1915; "Unclaimed Goods" 1918; "The Sundown Trail" 1919.

Sturges, John (1911-8/18/92). Director. Films: "The Walking Hills" 1949; "The Capture" 1950; "Escape from Fort Bravo" 1953; "Bad Day at Black Rock" 1955; "Backlash" 1956; "Gunfight at the O.K. Corral" 1957; "The Law and Jake Wade" 1958; "Last Train from Gun Hill" 1959; "The Magnificent Seven" 1960 (& prod.); "Sergeants 3" 1962; "The Hallelujah Trail" 1965; "Hour of the Gun" 1967 (& prod.); "Joe Kidd" 1972; "Chino" 1973-Ital./Span./Fr.

Sullivan, Alan. Writer. Films: "Get Your Man" 1921 (story).

Sullivan, C. Gardner (1884-9/4/65). Screenwriter. Films: "Army Surgeon" 1912; "The Invaders" 1912; "Days of '49" 1913; "A Shadow of the Past" 1913; "The Tell Tale Hat Band" 1913; "The Bargain" 1914; "Last of the Line" 1914; "The Passing of Two-Gun Hicks" 1914; "Shorty and the Fortune Teller" 1914; "The Word of His People" 1914; "The Man from Oregon" 1915; "On the Night Stage" 1915; "Pinto Ben" 1915; "The Roughneck" 1915; "The Ruse" 1915; "Satan McAllister's Heri" 1915; "The Aryan" 1916; "The Bugle Call" 1916; "The Dawn Maker" 1916; "The Return of Draw Egan" 1916; "The Border Wireless" 1918; "Branding Broadway" 1918; "Selfish Yates" 1918; "Hell's Hinges" 1919; "The Lady of Red Butte" 1919; "Wagon Tracks" 1919; "Tumbleweeds" 1925; "White Gold" 1927 (prod. only); "Union Pacific" 1939; "Jackass Mail" 1942 (story only).

Sullivan, Francis William. Writer. Films: "The Wilderness Trail" 1919 (story).

Sullivan, Joseph. Director. Films: "The Fall of Black Hawk" 1912.

Sullivan, Tim. Director. Films: "Run Home Slow" 1965 (& prod.).

Summers, E. Lynn. Screenwriter. Films: "When Thieves Fall Out" 1914; "Roping a Bride" 1915 (story only); "The Man Within" 1916 (story only).

Summers, Richard. Writer. Films: "The San Francisco Story" 1952 (story).

Summerville, Slim (1892-1/5/46). Director. Films: "Ranch Romeos" 1922.

Sussman, Barth Jules. Screenwriter. Films: "Stranger and the Gunfighter" 1973-Ital./Span./Hong Kong.

Sutter, Larabie. Writer. Films: "The White Squaw" 1956 (story).

Sutton, T. Shelley. Screenwriter. Films: "The Golden Bullet" 1917.

Swabacher, Les J. Screenwriter. Films: "Vigilantes Are Coming" 1936-serial; "Northwest Trail" 1945; "Where the North Begins" 1947.

Swackhamer, E.W. (1927-12/5/94). Director. Films: "Man and Boy" 1971; "The Return of Desperado" TVM-1988; "Desperado: Badlands Justice" TVM-1989; "Desperado: The Outlaw Wars" TVM-1989. ¶TV: *Here Come the Brides*—"Here Come the Brides" 9-25-68, "And Jason Makes Five" 10-9-68, "Man of the Family" 10-16-68, "After a Dream Comes Mourning" 1-1-69, "The Log Jam" 1-8-69, "The Eyes of London Bob" 11-28-69, "The Fetching of Jenny" 12-5-69; *The Outcasts* 1968-69 (& prod.); *Bonanza*—"Stallion" 11-14-72.

Swan, Mark. Screenwriter. Films: "Andy and the Redskins" 1914.

Swanson, Neil H. Writer. Films: "Allegheny Uprising" 1939 (story); "Unconquered" 1947 (story).

Swanton, Harold. Screenwriter. Films: "Ballad of Josie" 1968.

Swarthout, Glendon F. (1918-9/23/92). Writer. Films: "Seventh Cavalry" 1956 (story); "They Came to Cordura" 1959 (story); "The Shootist" 1976 (story).

Swarthout, Miles Hood. Screenwriter. Films: "The Shootist" 1976.

Swerling, Jo (1897-). Screenwriter. Films: "The Westerner" 1940; "A Lady Takes a Chance" 1943 (story only).

Swerling, Jr., Jo. Producer. Films: "Sam Hill: Who Killed the Mysterious Mr. Foster?" TVM-1971; "This Was the West That Was" TVM-1974.

Swickard, Charles (1868-5/12/29). Director. Films: "The Renegade" 1915; "Mixed Blood" 1916; "The Plow Woman" 1917; "The Light of Western Stars" 1918; "The Last Straw" 1920; "The Third Woman" 1920.

Swift, David (1919-). TV: *Wagon Train*—"The Juan Ortega Story" 10-8-58; *The Rifleman*—"The Angry Gun" 12-23-58.

Swift, Don. Screenwriter. Films: "Thunder Mountain" 1935; "Whispering Smith Speaks" 1935; "The Mine with the Iron Door" 1936; "Wild Brian Kent" 1936.

Swope, Jr., Herbert B. Producer. Films: "The True Story of Jesse James" 1957; "The Bravados" 1958; "The Fiend Who Walked the West" 1958.

Syson, Michael. Writer. Films: "Eagle's Wing" 1979-Brit./Span. (story).

Szwarc, Jeannot (1936-). Director. TV: *The Men from Shiloh* 1970; *Alias Smith and Jones*—"Exit from Wickenberg" 1-28-71.

Tabet, Andre. Screenwriter. Films: "Sign of Zorro" 1964-Ital./Span.

Taffel, Bess. Screenwriter. Films: "Badman's Territory" 1946.

Taggert, Brian. Screenwriter. Films: "The Mark of Zorro" TVM-1974.

Tait, Don. Screenwriter. Films: "One More Train to Rob" 1971; "The Castaway Cowboy" 1974 (& story); "The Apple Dumpling Gang" 1975; "The Apple Dumpling Gang Rides Again" 1979.

Talbot, Monroe. Screenwriter. Films: "The Last of the Clintons" 1935 (story only); "Rustlers' Paradise" 1935 (story only); "Wagon Trail" 1935; "Wild Mustang" 1935 (story only); "Ghost Town" 1936 (story only); "Hair-Trigger Casey" 1936; "Wildcat Saunders" 1936 (story only); "Aces Wild" 1937; "Lure of the Wasteland" 1939; "Lightning Strikes West" 1940 (story only).

Tallevi, Fabio. Screenwriter. Films: "Great Treasure Hunt" 1967-Ital./Span.

Talmadge, Richard (1896-1/25/81). Director. Films: "Yankee Don" 1931 (prod. only); "The Devil Horse" 1932-serial; "Jeep-Herders" 1949; "Border Outlaws" 1950 (& prod.); "I Killed Wild Bill Hickok" 1956. ¶TV: *El Coyote Rides*—Pilot 1958.

Talman, William (1915-8/30/68). Screenwriter. Films: "Joe Dakota" 1947.

Tanchuck, Nat. Screenwriter. Films: "I Killed Geronimo" 1950; "Buffalo Bill in Tomahawk Territory" 1952.

Tansey, John. Director. Films: "Romance of the West" 1930 (& sp.); "Riders of the Rio" 1931 (& prod.).

Tansey, Robert Emmett (1897-6/17/51). Director. Films: "Riders of the Rio" 1931 (prod. only); "The Galloping Kid" 1932 (& sp.); "Arizona Cyclone" 1934 (& sp.); "Carrying the Mail" 1934-short; "Desert Man" 1934 (& sp.); "The Lone Rider" 1934; "Pals of the Prairie" 1934-short (& sp.); "Pals of the West" 1934-short (& sp.); "The Sundown Trail" 1934; "The Way of the West" 1934 (& prod.); "West of the Law" 1934-short; "Courage of the North" 1935 (& prod./sp.); "Law of the 45's" 1935 (sp. only); "The New Frontier" 1935 (sp. only); "Paradise Canyon" 1935 (sp. only); "Timber Terrors" 1935 (& prod./sp.); "Westward Ho" 1935 (sp. only); "Men of the Plains" 1936 (sp. only); "The Oregon Trail" 1936 (sp./story only); "Pinto Rustlers" 1936 (sp. only); "Roamin' Wild" 1936 (sp. only); "Song of the Gringo" 1936 (sp. only); "Danger Valley" 1937 (sp. only); "God's Country and the Man" 1937 (sp. only); "Headin' for the Rio Grande" 1937 (sp. only); "Hittin' the Trail" 1937 (sp. only); "Riders of the Dawn" 1937 (story only); "Riders of the Rockies" 1937 (sp. only); "Romance of the Rockies" 1937 (sp. only); "Sing, Cowboy, Sing" 1937 (sp. only); "Stars Over Arizona" 1937 (sp. only); "Trouble in Texas" 1937 (sp. only); "Where Trails Divide" 1937 (sp. only); "Gun Packer" 1938 (prod./sp. only); "Gunsmoke Trail" 1938; "Man's Country" 1938 (prod./sp. only); "Mexicali Kid" 1938 (prod./sp. only); "The Painted Trail" 1938 (prod./sp. only); "West of Rainbow's End" 1938 (story only); "Where the Buffalo Roam" 1938 (sp. only); "Wild Horse Canyon" 1938 (prod./sp. only); "Across the Plains" 1939 (sp. only); "Drifting Westward" 1939 (sp. only); "The Man from Texas" 1939 (sp. only); "Overland Mail" 1939 (prod./sp. only); "Trigger Smith" 1939 (prod./sp. only); "Westbound Stage" 1939 (story only); "Arizona Frontier" 1940 (story only); "Cowboy from Sundown" 1940 (sp. only); "The Golden Trail" 1940 (sp. only); "Rainbow Over the Range" 1940 (sp. only); "Rhythm of the Rio Grande" 1940 (sp. only); "Take Me Back to Oklahoma" 1940 (sp. only); "The Driftin' Kid" 1941 (& prod./sp.); "Dynamite Canyon" 1941 (& prod./sp.); "Lone Star Law Men" 1941 (& prod./sp.); "Riding the Sunset Trail" 1941 (& prod./sp.); "Rollin' Home to Texas"

1941 (sp. only); "Silver Stallion" 1941 (sp. only); "Wanderers of the West" 1941 (prod. only); "Arizona Roundup" 1942 (& prod./sp.); "Texas to Bataan" 1942; "Trail Riders" 1942; "Western Mail" 1942 (& prod./sp.); "Where Trails End" 1942 (& prod./sp.); "Blazing Guns" 1943 (& prod.); "The Haunted Ranch" 1943; "The Law Rids Again" 1943; "Two Fisted Justice" 1943; "Wild Horse Stampede" 1943 (prod. only); "Arizona Whirlwind" 1944 (& prod.); "Death Valley Rangers" 1944 (& prod./sp.); "Outlaw Trail" 1944 (& prod.); "Sonora Stagecoach" 1944 (& prod./story); "Westward Bound" 1944 (& prod.); "Song of Old Wyoming" 1945 (& prod.); "Wildfire" 1945; "The Caravan Trail" 1946 (& prod.); "Colorado Serenade" 1946 (& prod.); "Driftin' River" 1946 (& prod.); "God's Country" 1946; "Romance of the West" 1946 (& prod.); "Stars Over Texas" 1946 (& prod.); "Tumbleweed Trail" 1946 (& prod.); "Wild West" 1946 (& prod.); "White Stallion" 1947; "Prairie Outlaws" 1948 (& prod.); "Riders of the Dusk" 1949 (sp. only); "The Fighting Stallion" 1950 (& prod.); "Badman's Gold" 1951 (& prod./sp.); "Cattle Queen" 1951 (& story).

Tansey, Ruth. Director. Films: "Romance of the West" 1930 (& sp.).

Taradash, Daniel (1913-). Screenwriter. Films: "Rancho Notorious" 1952.

Tarantini, Michele Massimo. Screenwriter. Films: "Arizona" 1970-Ital./Span.; "Trinity Plus the Clown and a Guitar" 1975-Ital./Austria/Fr.

Tarshis, Harold. Screenwriter. Films: "The Concentratin' Kid" 1930; "Trailin' Trouble 1930; "Adventures of Don Coyote" 1947.

Tashlin, Frank (1913-5/5/72). Director. Films: "The Paleface" 1948 (sp. only); "Son of Paleface" 1952 (& sp.); "The Shakiest Gun in the West" 1968 (story only).

Tasker, Robert (1898-12/7/44). Screenwriter. Films: "Home in Wyomin'" 1942.

Tatelman, Harry. Producer. Films: "Incident at Phantom Hill" 1966 (& story). ¶TV: *Colt .45* 1957-62; *Sugarfoot* 1957-60; *The Alaskans* 1959-60.

Taurog, Norman (1899-4/7/81). Director. Films: "Rhythm on the Range" 1936; "Pardners" 1956; "Tickle Me" 1965.

Taylor, Belle. Screenwriter. Films: "The Broken Doll" 1910; "Iola's Promise" 1912.

Taylor, C.B. Screenwriter. Films: "Thunder at the Border" 1967-Ger./Yugo.

Taylor, Charles. Director. Films: "The Half-Breed" 1926 (& sp.).

Taylor, Don (1920-). Director. Films: "Something for a Lonely Man" TVM-1968; "The Five Man Army" 1969-Ital.; "Wild Women" TVM-1970; "Honky Tonk" TVM-1974; "The Great Scout and Cathouse Thursday" 1976; "September Gun" TVM-1983. ¶TV: *Johnny Ringo* 1959; *The Rifleman*—"Outlaw's Inheritance" 6-16-59, "The Jailbird" 5-10-60, "The Lost Treasure of Canyon Town" 2-28-61; *Have Gun Will Travel*—"Tiger" 11-28-59, "One Came Back" 12-26-59; *Wild Wild West*—"The Night of the Casual Killer" 10-15-65, "The Night of the Double-Edged Knife" 11-12-65; *The Big Valley*—"Deathtown" 10-28-68.

Taylor, Edward C. Director. Films: "Across the Great Divide" 1915 (& sp.).

Taylor, Eric (1897-9/8/52). Screenwriter. Films: "North of the Great Divide" 1950; "Heart of the Rockies" 1951; "Pals of the Golden West" 1951; "South of Caliente" 1951; "Colorado Sundown" 1952.

Taylor, Grant. Writer. Films: "Terror Trail" 1933 (story).

Taylor, Henry. Screenwriter. Films: "Breed of the West" 1930; "Canyon Hawks" 1930; "Firebrand Jordan" 1930 (prod. only); "Trails of Danger" 1930 (story only); "Flying Lariats" 1931 (prod./story only); "Red Fork Range" 1931 (& story).

Taylor, Jud (1940-). Director. TV: *Shane* 1966; *Sara* 1976.

Taylor, Lawrence. Screenwriter. Films: "White Eagle" 1941-serial.

Taylor, Philip John. Screenwriter. Films: "Lust in the Dust" 1985.

Taylor, R.O. Director. Films: "The Return of Josey Wales" 1987 (& sp.).

Taylor, Ray (1888-2/15/52). Director. Films: "The Ridin' Kid from Powder River" 1924; "Fighting with Buffalo Bill" 1926-serial; "The Trial of Trickery" 1926; "Barrymore Tommy" 1927; "The Courage of Collins" 1927; "An Exciting Day" 1927; "The Menace of the Mounted" 1927; "The Plumed Rider" 1927; "A Ranger's Romance" 1927; "Whispering Smith Rides" 1927-serial; "Beauty and Bullets" 1928; "The Border Wildcat" 1928; "The Clean-Up Man" 1928; "The Crimson Canyon" 1928; "Greased Lighting" 1928; "Quick Triggers" 1928; "The Scarlet Arrow" 1928-serial; "The Vanishing Rider" 1928-serial; "Perilous Paths" 1929; "A Rider of the Sierras" 1929; "The Ridin' Demon" 1929; "Battling with Buffalo Bill" 1931-serial; "The One Way Trail" 1931; "Heroes of the West" 1932-serial; "Clancy of the Mounted" 1933-serial; "Gordon of Ghost City" 1933-serial; "The Fighting Trooper" 1934; "Ivory-Handled Gun" 1935; "Outlawed Guns" 1935; "The Roaring West" 1935-serial; The Three Mesquiteers" 1935; "The Throwback" 1935; "The Cowboy and the Kid" 1936; "The Phantom Rider" 1936-serial; "Silver Spurs" 1936; "Sunset of Power" 1936; "Vigilantes Are Coming" 1936-serial; "Boss of Lonely Valley" 1937; "Drums of Destiny" 1937; "The Mystery of the Hooded Horsemen" 1937; "The Painted Stallion" 1937-serial; "Ray Timber" 1937; "Sudden Bill Dorn" 1937; "Tex Rides with the Boy Scouts" 1937; "Flaming Frontier" 1938-serial; "Frontier Town" 1938; "Hawaiian Buckaroo" 1938; "Panamint's Bad Man" 1938; "Rawhide" 1938; "Bad Man from Red Butte" 1940; "Law and Order" 1940; "Pony Post" 1940; "Ragtime Cowboy Joe" 1940; "Riders of Pasco Basin" 1940; "West of Carson City" 1940; "Winners of the West" 1940-serial; "Boss of Bullion City" 1941; "Bury Me Not on the Lone Prairie" 1941; "Law of the Range" 1941; "Man from Montana" 1941; "Rawhide Rangers" 1941; "Riders of Death Valley" 1941-serial; "Fighting Bill Fargo" 1942; "Stagecoach Buckaroo" 1942; "Cheyenne Roundup" 1943; "The Lone Star Trail" 1943; "Boss of Boomtown" 1944; "Raiders of Ghost City" 1944-serial (& prod.); "The Daltons Ride Again" 1945; "Royal Mounted Rides Again" 1945-serial; "The Scarlet Horseman" 1946-serial; "Border Feud" 1947; "Cheyenne Takes Over" 1947; "The Fighting Vigilantes" 1947; "Ghost Town Renegades" 1947; "Law of the Lash" 1947; "The Michigan Kid" 1947; "Pioneer Justice" 1947; "Range Beyond the Blue" 1947; "Return of the Lash" 1947; "Shadow Valley" 1947; "Stage to Mesa City" 1947; "The Vigilantes Return" 1947; "West to Glory" 1947; "Wild Country" 1947; "Black Hills" 1948; "Check Your Guns" 1948; "Dead Man's Gold" 1948; "Frontier Revenge" 1948 (& sp.); "Gunning for Justice" 1948; "The Hawk of Powder River" 1948; "Mark of the Lash" 1948; "The Return of Wildfire" 1948; "The Tioga Kid" 1948; "Tornado Range" 1948;

"The Westward Trail" 1948; "Crashing Thru" 1949; "Hidden Danger" 1949; "Law of the West" 1949; "Outlaw Country" 1949; "Range Justice" 1949; "Shadows of the West" 1949; "Son of a Badman" 1949; "Son of Billy the Kid" 1949; "West of El Dorado" 1949.

Taylor, Rex. Screenwriter. Films: "Leave It to Susan" 1919; "Bells of San Juan" 1922.

Taylor, Richard G. Screenwriter. Films: "Ambush at Cimarron Pass" 1958.

Taylor, Robert Lewis (1912-). Writer. Films: "Guns of Diablo" 1964 (story).

Taylor, Rod (1929-). Producer. Films: "Chuka" 1967.

Taylor, Roderick. Screenwriter. Films: "Wild Horses" TVM-1985; "The Gambler, Part III—The Legend Continues" TVM-1987.

Taylor, S.E.V. Screenwriter. Films: "The Greaser's Gauntlet" 1908; "The Kentuckian" 1908; "The Red Girl" 1908; "Comata, the Sioux" 1909; "The Indian Runner's Romance" 1909; "Leather Stocking" 1909; "The Mended Lute" 1909; "The Gold Seekers" 1910; "In Old California" 1910; "In the Border States" 1910; "The Man" 1910; "A Mohawk's Way" 1910; "Over Silent Paths" 1910; "A Romance of the Western Hills" 1910; "The Thread of Destiny" 1910; "The Twisted Trails" 1910; "Unexpected Help" 1910; "The Squaw's Love" 1911; "In the Aisles of the Wild" 1912; "Under Burning Skies" 1912; "The Yaqui Cur" 1913; "Scarlet Days" 1919; "In the North Woods" 1921; "The Mohican's Daughter" 1922 (& dir.); "Breed of the Sunsets" 1928 (story only); "King Cowboy" 1928 (story only).

Taylor, Sam (1896-3/6/58). Screenwriter. Films: "The Gray Towers Mystery" 1919.

Taylor, Theodore. Screenwriter. Films: "Showdown" 1973.

Taylor, William Desmond (1872-2/1/22). Director. Films: "Sir Galahad of Twilight" 1914; "Ben Blair" 1916; "Davy Crockett" 1916; "The Parson of Panamint" 1916; "Jack and Jill" 1917; "The World Apart" 1917.

Tazil, Zara. Screenwriter. Films: "Lawless Borders" 1935; "The Reckless Buckaroo" 1935; "Blazing Justice" 1936; "Outlaws of the Range" 1936.

Tedesco, Guy J. Writer. Films: "Requiem for a Gunfighter" 1965 (story).

Teed, Tom. Writer. Films: "Red Stallion in the Rockies" 1949 (story).

Tejedor, Darturo. Screenwriter. Films: "If You Want to Live … Shoot!" 1967-Ital./Span.

Telfer, Jay. Screenwriter. Films: "Kid Vengeance" 1976-Ital./U.S./Israel.

Telford, Frank (1914-5/19/87). Producer. TV: *The Outlaws* 1960-62 (exec. prod.); *Wide Country* 1962-63; *Destry* 1964.

Templeton, George. Director. Fims: "Trailin' West" 1949; "High Lonesome" 1950 (prod. only); "The Sundowners" 1950. ¶TV: *Rawhide*— "Incident on the Road Back" 2-24-61, "Incident of the Phantom Burglar" 4-14-61, "The Sendoff" 10-6-61, "The Lost Tribe" 10-27-61, "Inside Man" 11-3-61, "Incident of the Woman Trap" 1-26-62, "The Devil and the Deep Blue" 5-11-62.

Tennand, Andy. Director. TV: *Adventures of Brisco County, Jr.*—"The Orb Scholar" 9-3-93, "Brisco for the Defense" 10-22-93.

Terry, G.N. Writer. Films: "The Race War" 1915 (story).

Tessari, Duccio (1927-9/6/94). Director. Films: "A Fistful of Dollars" 1964-Ital./Ger./Span. (sp. only); "A Pistol for Ringo" 1965-Ital./Span. (& sp./story); "The Return of Ringo" 1966-Ital./Span. (& sp.); "Train fur Durango" 1967-Ital./Span. (sp. only); "Alive or Preferable Dead" 1969-Span./Ital. (& sp.); "Don't Turn the Other Cheek" 1974-Ital./Ger./Span.; "Zorro" 1974-Ital./Fr. (& sp.); "Tex and the Lord of the Deep" 1985-Ital. (& prod.).

Tetford, Charles L. Screenwriter. Films: "Pony Express Days" 1940-short; "Valley of Hunted Men" 1942 (story only).

Tetzlaff, Ted (1903-). Director. Films: "The Treasure of Lost Canyon" 1952; "The Young Land" 1959.

Thalberg, Irving (1899-9/14/36). Producer. Films: "Winners of the Wilderness" 1927.

Thalberg, Sylvia. Screenwriter. Films: "Montana Moon" 1930 (& story).

Thayer, Otis B. Director. Films: "The Bully of Bingo Bulch" 1911 (& story); "The Telltale Knife" 1911 (& story); "The Cowboy's Best Girl" 1912; "A Cowboy's Mother" 1912; "Driftwood" 1912; "An Equine Hero" 1912; "The Horseshoe" 1912; "The Scapegoat" 1912 (& story); "Two Men and a Girl" 1912; "The Whiskey Runners" 1912; "The Greater Barrier"

1915; "Told in the Rockies" 1915; "Miss Arizona" 1919; "The Desert Scorpion" 1920; "Out of the Depths" 1921; "Riders of the Range" 1923 (& sp.); "Tracy the Outlaw" 1928.

Theil, Sidney. Screenwriter. Films: "The Maverick" 1952; "The Homesteaders" 1953; "Rebel City" 1953; "Vigilante Terror" 1953.

Thew, Harry F. Screenwriter. Films: "Rimrock Jones" 1918; "What Am I Bid?" 1919 (& story); "Tiger Rose" 1929; "Song of the West" 1930.

Thiel, Nick. Screenwriter. Films: "White Fang" 1991.

Thiele, William J. (1890-9/7/75). Director. TV: *The Lone Ranger*— "Dan Reid's Fight for Life" 11-18-54, "The Sheriff's Wife" 8-18-55.

Thoeren, Robert. Writer. Films: "Big Jack" 1949 (story).

Thom, James Alexander. Writer. Films: "Tecumseh: The Last Warrior" TVM-1995 (story).

Thomas, Augustus. Director. Films: "Arizona" 1913; "Colorado" 1915 (story only); "Arizona" 1918 (story only); "In Mizzoura" 1919 (story only); "Rio Grande" 1920 (story only).

Thomas, Danny (1914-2/6/90). Producer. TV: *The Guns of Will Sonnett* 1967-69 (exec. prod.); *Rango* 1967 (exec. prod.).

Thomas, Elton. see Fairbanks, Sr., Douglas.

Thomas, Faith. Writer. Films: "Rock River Renegades" 1942 (story).

Thomas, Jack. Screenwriter. Films: "Lone Texan" 1959; "Thirteen Fighting Men" 1960.

Thomas, Jerry. Producer. Films: "Border Feud" 1947; "Cheyenne Takes Over" 1947; "The Fighting Vigilantes" 1947; "Ghost Town Renegades" 1947; "Law of the Lash" 1947; "Pioneer Justice" 1947; "Range Beyond the Blue" 1947; "Return of the Lash" 1947; "Shadow Valley" 1947; "Stage to Mesa City" 1947; "West to Glory" 1947; "Black Hills" 1948; "Check Your Guns" 1948; "The Hawk of Powder River" 1948; "The Tioga Kid" 1948; "Tornado Range" 1948; "The Westward Trail" 1948; "Ride, Ryder, Ride" 1949; "Roll, Thunder, Roll" 1949; "Cowboy and the Prizefighter" 1950 (& sp.); "The Fighting Redhead" 1950 (& sp.); "Law of the Panhandle" 1950.

Thomas, Ted. Writer. Films: "King of the Wild Horses" 1947 (story).

Thomas, Vincent. see Gicca Palli, Enzo.

Thomas, William C. Producer. Films: "Albuquerque" 1948; "El Paso" 1949; "The Eagle and the Hawk" 1950; "The Last Outpost" 1951; "Passage West" 1951; "Those Redheads from Seattle" 1953; "The Vanquished" 1953; "The Far Horizons" 1955; "Run for Cover" 1955.

Thompson, Charles. Director. Films: "The Movie Trail" 1921.

Thompson, Franklin. Screenwriter. Films: "Standing Tall" TVM-1978.

Thompson, Frederick A. (1870-1/23/25). Director. Films: "The Danger Trail" 1917.

Thompson, Garfield. Screenwriter. Films: "By Right of Possession" 1917; "Vengeance and the Woman" 1917-serial.

Thompson, Harlan. Producer. Films: "Ruggles of Red Gap" 1935; "Rose of the Rancho" 1936; "Bad Men of Missouri" 1941.

Thompson, J. Lee (1914-). Director. Films: "Mackenna's Gold" 1969; "The White Buffalo" 1977.

Thompson, Kay. Screenwriter. Films: "The Girl and the Law" 1920; "A Son of the North" 1920.

Thompson, Keene (1886-7/11/37). Screenwriter. Films: "Border Women" 1924; "The Virginian" 1929; "Caught" 1931; "Fighting Caravans" 1931.

Thompson, Robert C. Producer. Films: "The Mark of Zorro" TVM-1974; "Hearts of the West" 1975. ¶TV: *The Travels of Jaimie McPheeters* 1963-64.

Thompson, Robert W. Screenwriter. Films: "The Dangerous Days of Kiowa Jones" TVM-1966.

Thompson, Thomas (1933-10/29/82). Screenwriter. Films: "Saddle the Wind" 1958 (story only); "Cattle King" 1963.

Thompson, William C. Director. Films: "The Irish Gringo" 1935 (& prod./sp.).

Thornby, Robert T. (1888-3/6/53). Director. Films: "When California Was Young" 1912 (sp. only); "The Outlaw" 1913; "Old California" 1914 (story only); "Lawless Love" 1918; "Fighting Cressy" 1920; "The Fox" 1921; "That Girl Montana" 1921; "The Sagebrush Trail" 1922; "West of Broadway" 1926.

Thornton, E.J. Screenwriter. Films: "The Judgement Book" 1935.

Thorp, Raymond W. Films: "Jeremiah Johnson" 1972.

Thorpe, Jerry (1930-). Director. Films: "Day of the Evil Gun" 1968 (& prod.); "Lock, Stock and Barrel" TVM-1971; "Kung Fu" TVM-1972 (& prod.). ¶TV: *Kung Fu* 1972-75 (prod.), "King of the Mountain" 10-14-72, "Dark Angel" 11-11-72, "Blood Brother" 1-18-73, "An Eye for an Eye" 1-25-73, "The Well" 9-27-73, "The Chalice" 10-11-73, "My Brother, My Executioner" 10-12-74.

Thorpe, Richard (1896-5/1/91). Director. Films: "Battling Buddy" 1924; "Bringin' Home the Bacon" 1924; "Fast and Fearless" 1924; "Hard Hitten' Hamilton" 1924; "Rarin' to Go" 1924; "Rip Roarin' Roberts" 1924; "Rough Ridin'" 1924; "Thundering Romance" 1924; "Walloping Wallace" 1925; "The Desert Demon" 1925; "Double Action Daniels" 1925; "Full Speed" 1925; "Galloping On" 1925; "Gold and Grit" 1925; "On the Go" 1925; "Quicker'n Lightnin'" 1925; "Saddle Cyclone" 1925; "A Streak of Luck" 1925; "Tearin' Loose" 1925; "The Bandit Buster" 1926 (& sp.); "The Bonanza Buckaroo" 1926; "Comin an' Going" 1926; "The Dangerous Dub" 1926; "Deuce High" 1926; "Double Daring" 1926; "Easy Going" 1926; "The Fighting Cheat" 1926; "Rawhide" 1926; "Riding Rivals" 1926; "Roaring Rider" 1926; "Speedy Spurs" 1926; "Trumpin' Trouble" 1926; "Twin Triggers" 1926; "Twisted Triggers" 1926; "Between Dangers" 1927 (& sp.); "The Cyclone Cowboy" 1927; "The Desert of the Lost" 1927; "The Galloping Gobs" 1927; "The Interferin' Gent" 1927; "The Meddlin' Stranger" 1927; "The Obligin' Buckaroo" 1927; "Pals in Peril" 1927; "Ride 'Em High" 1927; "The Ridin' Rowdy" 1927; "Roarin' Broncs" 1927; "Skedaddle Gold" 1927; "Soda Water Cowboy" 1927; "Tearin' into Trouble" 1927; "White Pebbles" 1927; "The Ballyhoo Buster" 1928; "The Cowboy Cavalier" 1928; "Desperate Courage" 1928; "The Flying Buckaroo" 1928; "Saddle Mates" 1928; "The Valley of Hunted Men" 1928; "The Vanishing West" 1928-serial; "Border Romance" 1930; "The Dude Wrangler" 1930; "The Lone Defender" 1930-serial; "Under Montana Skies" 1930; "The Utah Kid" 1930; "Wings of Adventure" 1930; "Wild Horse" 1931; "Twenty Mule Team" 1940; "Wyoming" 1940; "The Bad Man" 1941; "Apache Trail" 1943; "Big Jack" 1949; "Vengeance Valley" 1951; "How the West Was Won" 1962; "Four for Texas" 1964; "The Last Challenge" 1967 (& prod.).

Thourlby, William. Producer. Films: "Vengeance" 1964.

Tidyman, Ernest (1928-7/14/84). Screenwriter. Films: "High Plains Drifter" 1973.

Tilighman, William. Director. Films: "The Bank Robbery" 1908.

Tilton, Deborah. Screenwriter. Films: "Samurai Cowboy" 1993.

Tilton, Edwin Booth. (1859-1/16/26). Screenwriter. Films: "While Justice Waits" 1922.

Tinker, Mark. Director. Films: "Bonanza: Under Attack" TVM-1995.

Tinkle, J. Lon. Writer. Films: "The Alamo: 13 Days to Glory" TVM-1987 (story).

Tinling, James (1898-5/14/67). Director. Films: "The Last Trail" 1933; "Under the Pampas Moon" 1935; "Last of the Duanes" 1941; "Riders of the Purple Sage" 1941; "Lone Star Ranger" 1942; "Sundown Jim" 1942.

Tinney, Claus. Director. Films: "Prairie in the City" 1971-Ger. (& prod./sp.).

Tiomkin, Dimitri (1899-11/11/79). Producer. Films: "Mackenna's Gold" 1969.

Titus, Harold. Writer. Films: "The Last Straw" 1920 (story).

Todaro, Armando. Producer. Films: "Carambola" 1974-Ital.; "Carambola's Philosophy: In the Right Pocket" 1975-Ital.

Todd, Lucas. Writer. Films: "Fury at Showdown" 1957 (story).

Todd, Ruth. Writer. Films: "Cornered" 1932 (story).

Tokar, Norman (1920-4/6/79). Films: "Savage Sam" 1963; "The Apple Dumpling Gang" 1975.

Tombragel, Maurice. Screenwriter. Films: "Men of the Timberland" 1941; "Road Agent" 1941; "Thunder in the Pines" 1948; "Colorado Ranger" 1950; "Crooked River" 1950; "The Daltons' Women" 1950; "Fast on the Draw" 1950; "Hostile Country" 1950; "Marshal of Heldorado" 1950; "West of the Brazos" 1950; "Lawless Cowboys" 1951; "Man from Sonora" 1951; "The Frontier Phantom" 1952; "Night Raiders" 1952; "The Dalton Girls" 1957; "Fort Bowie" 1958.

Torrado, Ramon. Director. Films: "Shoot to Kill" 1963-Span.; "Cavalry Charge" 1964-Span. (& sp.).

Torres, Miguel Contreras. Director. Films: "Pancho Villa Returns" 1950-Mex. (& prod./sp.); "The Last Rebel" 1961-Mex. (& prod./sp.).

Tors, Ivan (1916-6/4/83). Producer. Films: "Africa—Texas Style!" 1967-U.S./Brit.

Tortelli, Luci. Screenwriter. Films: "Grandsons of Zorro" 1968-Ital.

Totheroh, Dan (1894-12/3/76). Writer. Films: "Yellow Dust" 1936 (story).

Totman, Wellyn. Screenwriter. Films: "God's Country and the Man" 1921; "The Nevada Buckaroo" 1931; "Rider of the Plains" 1931; "The Ridin' Fool 1931; "Sunrise Trail" 1931; "Broadway to Cheyenne" 1932; "Fighting Champ" 1932; "Galloping Thru" 1932; "Hidden Valley 1932; "The Man from Arizona" 1932; "Riders of the Desert" 1932; "Son of Oklahoma" 1932 (story only); "Texas Pioneers" 1932; "Vanishing Men" 1932; "Young Blood" 1932; "Crashing Broadway" 1933; "The Fighting Texans" 1933; "Lucky Larrigan" 1933; "Son of the Border" 1933 (& story); "The Miracle Rider" 1935-serial.

Totten, Robert (1937-1/27/95). Director. Films: "Death of a Gunfighter" 1969; "Ride a Northbound Horse" 1969; "The Wild Country" 1971; "Pony Express Rider" 1976 (sp. only); "The Sacketts" TVM-1979. ¶TV: *The Dakotas* 1963; *Temple Houston* 1963; *The Virginian*—"The Secret of Brynmar Hall" 4-1-64; *Bonanza*—"A Natural Wizard" 12-12-65; *Gunsmoke*—"My Father's Guitar" 2-12-66, "My Father, My Son" 4-23-66, "Prime of Life" 5-7-66, "The Good People" 10-15-66, "The Wrong Man" 10-29-66, "The Newcomes" 12-3-66, "Saturday Night" 1-7-67, "Mail Drop" 1-28-67, "Mistaken Identity" 3-18-67, "Nitro!" 4-8-67 & 4-15-67, "The Wreckers" 9-11-67, "A Hat" 10-16-67, "Major Glory" 10-30-67, "Blood Money" 1-22-68, "Hill Girl" 1-29-68, "The First People" 2-19-68, "Waco" 12-9-68, "Stryker" 9-29-69, "A Matter of Honor" 11-17-69, "Stark" 9-28-70, "Jenny" 12-28-70, "Murdock" 2-8-71, "The Lost" 9-13-71; *The Monroes*—"War Arrow" 11-2-66; *Kung Fu*—"The Tong" 11-15-73, "The Hoots" 12-13-73; *The Texas Wheelers* 1974.

Tourjansky, Viachetslav (1891-8/13/76). Director. Films: "The Adventurer" 1928.

Tourneur, Jacques (1904-12/19/77). Director. Films: "Canyon Passage" 1946; "Stars in My Crown" 1950; "Way of a Gaucho" 1952; "Stranger on Horseback" 1955; "Wichita" 1955; "Great Day in the Morning" 1956. ¶TV: *Northwest Passage*—"Surprise Attack" 10-5-58, "Break Out" 10-19-58, "The Hostage" 11-2-58, "The Assassin" 11-16-58, "The Vulture" 12-28-58; *G.E. Theater*—"Aftermath" 4-17-60; *The Alaskans* 1959-60; *Bonanza*—"Denver McKee" 10-15-60.

Tourneur, Maurice (1873-8/4/61). Director. Films: "The Last of the Mohicans" 1920.

Towne, Robert (1936-). Screenwriter. Films: "Villa Rides" 1968.

Townley, Jack (1897-10/15/60). Director. Films: "The Avenger" 1931 (story only); "The Last Outlaw" 1936 (sp. only); "Prairie Papas" 1938-short (& sp.); "Home on the Prairie" 1939; "Mexican Spitfire Out West" 1940 (sp. only); "Vengeance of the West" 1942 (story only); "The Yellow Rose of Texas" 1944; "Bells of Rosarita" 1945 (sp. only); "Utah" 1945 (sp. only); "My Pal Trigger" 1946 (sp. only); "The Last Round-Up" 1947 (sp. only); "Riders of the Whistling Pines" 1949 (sp. only); "The Blazing Sun" 1950 (sp. only); "Oklahoma Annie" 1952 (sp./story only); Untamed Heiress" 1954 (story only).

Townley, Robert. Director. Films: "Honeymoon Ranch" 1920 (& sp.); "West of the Rio Grande" 1921 (& sp.); "Partners of the Sunset" 1922.

Townsend, Leo. Screenwriter. Films: "White Feather" 1955.

Trader, Joseph. *see* Zabalza, Jose Maria.

Trampe, Ray. Screenwriter. Films: "Wild West Days" 1937-serial.

Trapnell, Charles. Producer. TV: *Lawman* 1958-62; *The Alaskans* 1959-60; *Maverick* 1959-61.

Traub, Joe. Screenwriter. Films: "Romance of the West" 1935-short.

Traven, B. (1890-3/26/69). Writer. Films: "The Treasure of the Sierra Madre" 1948 (story).

Traxler, Ernest. Director. Films: "Go Get 'Em Garringer" 1919.

Trell, Max. Screenwriter. Films: "New Mexico" 1951.

Tremayne, W.A. Screenwriter. Films: "Wards Claim" 1914.

Trendle, George W. (1885-5/10/72). Producer. TV: *The Lone Ranger* 1949-57.

Trenker, Luis (1893-4/13/90). Director. Films: "Kaiser von Kalifornien" 1936-Ger. (& prod./sp.).

Trevelyan, Michael. Screenwriter. Films: "Daring Danger" 1932.

Trevey, Ken (1930-7/8/92). Screenwriter. Films: "The Hanged Man" TVM-1974; "Banjo Hackett: Roamin' Free" TVM-1976.

Trevino, Jesus. Director. TV: *Hawkeye*—"The Traitor" 2-2-95, "The Visit" 5-24-95.

Trifone, Fabrizio. Screenwriter. Films: "Fighting Fists of Shanghai Joe" 1973-Ital.

Trimble, Larry (1885-2/8/54). Director. Films: "Billy the Kid" 1911; "Indian Romeo and Juliet" 1912; "The Deerslayer" 1913; "Getting Some" 1920 (sp. only); "The Silent Call" 1921; "Sundown" 1924.

Trivas, Victor (1896-4/12/70). Screenwriter. Films: "The Secret of Convict Lake" 1951.

Trivers, Barry (1907-8/17/81). Screenwriter. Films: "Arizona Wildcat" 1938; "River's End" 1940.

Troisio, Antonio. Screenwriter. Films: "The Magnificent Bandits" 1969-Ital./Span.; "The White, the Yellow, and the Black" 1974-Ital./Span./Fr.

Troell, Jan (1931-). Director. Films: "The New Land" 1973-Swed. (& sp.); "Zandy's Bride" 1974.

Trosper, Guy (1911-12/20/63). Screenwriter. Films: "The Devil's Doorway" 1950; "Inside Straight" 1951; "The Americano" 1955; "Many Rivers to Cross" 1955; "Thunder in the Sun" 1959 (story only); "One-Eyed Jacks" 1961.

Trotti, Lamar (1900-8/23/52). Screenwriter. Films: "The Country Beyond" 1936; "Ramona" 1936; "Drums Along the Mohawk" 1939; "Brigham Young—Frontiersman" 1940; "Belle Starr" 1941; "Hudson Bay" 1941; "The Ox-Bow Incident" 1943 (& prod.); "Yellow Sky" 1948 (& prod.).

Trueblood, Guerdon. Screenwriter. Films: "The Last Hard Men" 1976.

Trumbo, Christopher. Screenwriter. Films: "Nakia" TVM-1974 (& story).

Trumbo, Dalton (1905-9/10/76). Screenwriter. Films: "The Last Sunset" 1961; "Lonely Are the Brave" 1962.

Tryon, Glenn (1899-4/18/70). Director. Films: "The Law West of Tombstone" 1938; "Calaboose" 1943 (prod. only).

Tu Lung Li. Screenwriter. Films: "Kung Fu Brothers in the Wild West" 1973-Ital./Hong Kong.

Tuchetto, Bruno. Films: "Adios Gringo" 1965-Ital./Fr./Span.

Tuchock, Wanda (1898-2/10/85). Screenwriter. Films: "Billy the Kid" 1930; "The Llano Kid" 1939.

Tucker, George L. (1872-6/20/21). Director. Films: "Behind the Stockade" 1911 (& sp.).

Tucker, Melville. Producer. Films: "Along the Oregon Trail" 1947; "Under Colorado Skies" 1947; "California Firebrand" 1948; "Son of God's Country" 1948; "Sundown in Santa Fe" 1948; "The Timber Trail" 1948; "Law of the Golden West" 1949; "Outcasts of the Trail" 1949; "Pioneer Marshal" 1949; "Prince of the Plains" 1949; "Ranger of Cherokee Strip" 1949; "San Antone Ambush" 1949; "South of Rio" 1949; "The Missourians" 1950; "The Old Frontier" 1950; "Singing Guns" 1950; "Under Mexicali Stars" 1950; "The Vanishing Westerner" 1950; "Rodeo King and the Senorita" 1951; "Silver City Bonanza" 1951; "Thunder in God's Country" 1951; "Utah Wagon Train" 1951; "Drums Across the River" 1954.

Tully, Richard Walton. Writer. Films: "Rose of the Rancho" 1914 (story); "Rose of the Rancho" 1936 (story).

Tunberg, William. Screenwriter. Films: "War Paint" 1953 (story only); "Garden of Evil" 1954 (story only); "Massacre" 1956 (story only); "Old Yeller" 1957; "Savage Sam" 1963.

Tupper, Tristan. Screenwriter. Films: "Klondike" 1932.

Turley, Jack. Screenwriter. Films: "Peter Lundy and the Medicine Hat Stallion" TVM-1977.

Turnbull, Margaret. Writer. Films: "Jack and Jill" 1917 (story).

Turner, Brad. Director. TV: Hawkeye—Pilot 9-14-94 & 9-21-94, "The Siege" 10-12-94, "Amnesty" 2-9-95, "Fly With Me" 3-29-95, "The Return" 5-10-95.

Turner, Otis. Director. Films: "Dad's Girls" 1911 (& sp.); "George Warrington's Escape" 1911; "The Rose of Old St. Augustine" 1911; "Tribal Law" 1912; "A Frontier Providence" 1913; "The Mediator" 1916 (& sp.).

Turner, Ramon C. Screenwriter. Films: "Colt Is the Law" 1965-Ital./Span.

Tuttle, Bud. Screenwriter. Films: "Underground Rustlers" 1941.

Tuttle, Burl R. Screenwriter. Films: "Man Rustlin'" 1926; "Son of Oklahoma" 1932; "Circle Canyon" 1934; "'Neath the Arizona Skies" 1934.

Tuttle, Frank (1892-1/6/63). Director. Films: "Dude Ranch" 1931.

Tuttle, Gene. Screenwriter. Films: "Rodeo Rhythm" 1942.

Tuttle, Ted. Writer. Films: "The Pecos Kid" 1935 (story).

Tuttle, Wilbur C. Screenwriter. Films: "Fight It Out" 1920 (story only); "Hell's Oasis" 1920; "Fools of Fortune" 1922; "Peaceful Peters" 1922 (story only); "The Sheriff of Sun-Dog" 1922 (story only); "The Law Rustlers" 1923 (story only); "Spawn of the Desert" 1923 (story only); "The Prairie Pirate" 1925 (story only); "Rustlers' Ranch" 1926 (story only); "Man in the Rough" 1928 (story only); "Driftin' Sands" 1928 (story only); "The Cheyenne Kid" 1933 (story only); "The Red Rider" 1934 (story only); "Rocky Rhodes" 1934 (story only); "Lawless Valley" 1938 (story only); "Henry Goes Arizona" 1939 (story only); "The Fargo Kid" 1940 (story only).

Twist, John Stuart (1898-2/11/76). Screenwriter. Films: "The Big Diamond Robbery" 1929; "The Yellowback" 1929; "West of the Pecos" 1934; "Annie Oakley" 1935; "The Last Outlaw" 1936; "Yellow Dust" 1936; "The Outcasts of Poker Flat" 1937; "The Law West of Tombstone" 1938; "Reno" 1939; "Colorado Territory" 1949; "Dallas" 1950; "Fort Worth" 1951; "The Big Trees" 1952; "The Man Behind the Gun" 1952; "A Distant Trumpet" 1964.

Tynan, James J. Screenwriter. Films: "The Cowboy Kid" 1928; "The Girl-Shy Cowboy" 1928.

Tyron, Glen. Director. Films: "Two in Revolt" 1936.

Tyrone, Madge. Screenwriter. Films: "Rio Grande" 1920.

Uger, Alan. Screenwriter. Films: "Blazing Saddles" 1974.

Ullman, Daniel B. (Elwood Ullman) (1903-10/11/85). Screenwriter. Films: "Teacher's Pest" 1939-short; "Yes, We Have No Bonanza" 1939-short; "Phony Express" 1943-short; "Red Desert" 1949 (& story); "Sqaure Dance Jubilee" 1949; "Cherokee Uprising" 1950; "Silver Raiders" 1950; "Outlaws of Texas" 1950; "Cavalry Scout" 1951; "The Longhorn" 1951; "Montana Desperado" 1951; "Fort Osage" 1952; "Hiawatha" 1952; "Kansas Territory" 1952; "Montana Incident" 1952; "Waco" 1952; "Wagons West" 1952; "Wild Stallion" 1952; "Wyoming Roundup" 1952; "The Fighting Lawman" 1953; "Fort Vengeance" 1953; "Kansas Pacific" 1953; "The Marksman" 1953; "Star of Texas" 1953; "The Forty-Niners" 1954; "Two Guns and a Badge" 1954; "At Gunpoint" 1955; "Seven Angry Men" 1955; "Wichita" 1955; "Can-

yon River" 1956; "Dig That Uranium" 1956; "The First Texan" 1956; "Badlands of Montana" 1957 (& prod./sp.); "Last of the Badmen" 1957 (& story); "The Oklahoman" 1957; "Cattle Empire" 1958 (story only); "Good Day for a Hanging" 1958; "Face of a Fugitive" 1959; "The Gunfight at Dodge City" 1959; "The Outlaws Is Coming!" 1965; "Tickle Me" 1965.

Ullman, Elwood. see Ullman, Daniel B.

Ulmer, Edgar G. (John Warner) (1904-9/30/72). Director. Films: "Thunder Over Texas" 1934; "The Naked Dawn" 1955.

Underwood, Ron. Director. Films: "City Slickers" 1991.

Unland, Ethel C. Writer. Films: "The Good Indian" 1913 (story); "How Betty Made Good" 1913 (story).

Unsell, Eve. Screenwriter. Films: "The Long Trail" 1917; "Captain Fly-By-Night" 1922; "The Golden Strain" 1925; "The Yankee Senor" 1926.

Upton, William. TV: Bonanza— "My Son, My Son" 1-19-64.

Uris, Leon (1924-). Screenwriter. Films: "Gunfight at the O.K. Corral" 1957.

Uris, Michael. Writer. Films: "Plainsman and the Lady" 1946 (story).

Vadnay, Laszlo. Writer. Films: "Girl Rush" 1944 (story).

Vainstok, Vladimir. Director. Films: "Armed and Dangerous" 1977-Sov. (& prod.).

Vajda, Ernest (1887-4/3/54). Screenwriter. Films: "Manhattan Cowboy" 1928.

Valdez, Luis. Director. Films: "The Cisco Kid" CTMV-1994 (& sp.).

Vale, Travers (1865-1/10/27). Director. Films: "The Abandoned Well" 1913; "Western Pluck" 1926.

Valenza, M.R. Vitelli. Screenwriter. Films: "Django and Sartana Are Coming ... It's the End" 1970-Ital.; "One Damned Day at Dawn ... Django Meets Sartana" 1971-Ital.; "Fistful of Death" 1971-Ital.; "Stranger That Kneels Beside the Shadow of a Corpse" 1971-Ital.

Valerii, Tonino. Director. Films: "Taste for Killing" 1966-Ital./Span.; "Day of Anger" 1967-Ital./Ger. (& sp.); "The Price of Power" 1969-Ital./Span.; "Massacre at Fort Holman" 1972-Ital./Fr./Span./Ger. (& sp.); "My Name Is Nobody" 1973-Ital.

Van, Beatrice. Screenwriter. Films: "Penny of Top Hill Trail" 1921; "Crashin' Thru" 1923.

Van, Wally (1885-5/9/74). Director. Films: "Rough Going" 1925.

Van Buren, A. Screenwriter. Films: "The Captain of the Gray Horse Troop" 1917.

Vance, Louis Joseph. Screenwriter. Films: "The Mainspring" 1917 (story only); "Wild Honey" 1918.

Vance, Stan. *see* Vancini, Florestano.

Vancini, Florestano (Stan Vance). Director. Films: "Long Days of Vengeance" 1967-Ital./Span.

Van Dyke, W.S. (1890-2/5/43). Director. Films: "The Land of Long Shadows" 1917 (& sp.); "Men of the Desert" 1917 (& sp.); "Open Places" 1917 (& sp.); "The Range Boss" 1917 (& sp.); "The Lady of the Dugout" 1918 (& sp.); "The Avenging Arrow" 1921-serial; "White Eagle" 1922-serial; "Hearts and Spurs" 1925; "Ranger of the Big Pines" 1925; "The Timber Wolf" 1925; "The Trail Rider" 1925; "The Gentle Cyclone" 1926; "War Paint" 1926; "California" 1927; "Winners of the Wilderness" 1927; "Riders of the Dark" 1928 (sp. only); "Spoilers of the West" 1928; "Wyoming" 1928; "Rose Marie" 1936; "Stand Up and Fight" 1939.

Vane, Norman Thaddeus. Screenwriter. Films: "Shadow of the Hawk" 1976.

Van Eyes, Otto. Screenwriter. Films: "Big Jack" 1949.

Van Loan, Charles E. Writer. Films: "Buck Parvin and the Movies" 1915 (story); "Buck's Lady Friend" 1915 (story); "Buckshot John" 1915; "Man-Afraid-of-His Wardrobe" 1915 (story); "This Is the Life" 1915 (story).

Van Loan, H.H. Screenwriter. Films: "The Great Redeemer" 1920; "Fightin' Mad" 1921 (story only); "The Sagebrush Trail" 1922; "Danger Patrol" 1928.

Van Marter, George. Screenwriter. Films: "Four Guns to the Border" 1954; "Thunder Pass" 1954 (story only).

Van Peebles, Mario. Director. Films: "Posse" 1993.

Van Pelt, Ernest. Director. Films: "Avenging Fangs" 1927.

Van Riper, Kay. Screenwriter. Films: "Out West with the Hardys" 1938.

Van Upp, Helen. Screenwriter. Films: "The Wolverine" 1921.

Van Winkle, Joseph. Screenwriter. Films: "The Gatling Gun" 1972.

Vanzi, Luigi (Vance Lewis). Director. Films: "A Stranger in Town" 1966-U.S./Ital.; "The Stranger Returns" 1967-U.S./Ital./Ger./Span.; "Stranger in Japan" 1969-Ital./U.S./Jap.

Vanzina, Stefano. *see* Steno.

Vari, Giuseppe (Joseph Warren). Director. Films: "Deguello" 1966-Ital. (& sp.); "Django, Last Killer" 1967-Ital.; "Poker with Pistols" 1967-Ital.; "Death Rides Alone" 1968-Ital./Span.; "Hole in the Forehead" 1968-Ital./Span.; "Shoot the Living ... Pray for the Dead" 1971-Ital.; "Thirteenth Is a Judas" 1971-Ital. (& sp.).

Vazquez, Ricardo. Screenwriter. Films: "Seven for Pancho Villa" 1966-Span.

Veiller, Anthony (1903-6/27/65). Producer. Films: "Colorado Territory" 1949; "Dallas" 1950; "Along the Great Divide" 1951; "Fort Worth" 1951.

Veitch, Anthony Scott. Writer. Films: "The Kangaroo Kid" 1950 (story).

Vejar, Michael. Director. TV: *Legend*—"Legend on His President's Secret Service" 5-2-95, "The Gospel According to Legend" 6-12-95.

Vekroff, Perry N. (1880-1/4/37). Director. Films: "Perils of the Yukon" 1922-serial; "The White Messenger" 1922; "The Stranger Rider" 1925 (story only).

Venturelli, Douglas. Screenwriter. Films: "China 9, Liberty 37" 1978-Ital./Span./U.S.

Venturini, Edward T. Director. Films: "The Old Fool" 1923; "In Old Mexico" 1938; "The Llano Kid" 1939.

Veo, Carlo. Screenwriter. Films: "The Man Who Killed Billy the Kid" 1967-Span./Ital. (story only); "Those Dirty Dogs!" 1973-U.S./Ital./Span.

Verneuil, Henri (Achod Malakian). Director. Films: "Guns for San Sebastian" 1967-U.S./Fr./Mex./Ital.

Vernon, Bobby. Screenwriter. Films: "The Lone Cowboy" 1934.

Verucci, Franco. Screenwriter. Films: "Two Sides of the Dollar" 1967-Fr./Ital.; "Sheriff Won't Shoot" 1967-Ital./Fr./Brit.

Victor, David. Screenwriter. Films: "Trooper Hook" 1957; "The Bravos" TVM-1972 (story only).

Victor, Mark. Screenwriter. Films: "Death Hunt" 1981.

Vidal, Gore (1925-). Writer. Films: "The Left-Handed Gun" 1958 (story).

Vidor, Charles (1900-6/4/59). Director. Films: "The Arizonian" 1935; "The Desperadoes" 1943.

Vidor, Elizabeth Hill. Writer. Films: "The Texas Rangers" 1936 (story).

Vidor, King (1895-11/1/82). Director. Films: "The Sky Pilot" 1921; "Billy the Kid" 1930; "The Texas Rangers" 1936 (& prod./story); "Northwest Passage" 1940; "Duel in the Sun" 1946; "Man Without a Star" 1955.

Viertel, Peter (1920-). Writer. Films: "Roughshod" 1949 (story).

Vietri, Franco. Screenwriter. Films: "For a Book of Dollars" 1973-Ital./Span.

Vighi, Vittorio. Screenwriter. Films: "Terrible Sheriff" 1963-Span./Ital.; "Shots Ring Out!" 1965-Ital./Span.; "Ringo and Gringo Against All" 1966-Ital./Span.

Vigne, Daniel. Screenwriter. Films: "Sommersby" 1993 (story only).

Vignola, Robert (1882-10/25/53). Director. Films: "Arizona Bill" 1911.

Villalobos, Reynaldo. Director. Films: "Conagher" TVM-1991.

Villasenor, Victor. Screenwriter. Films: "The Ballad of Gregorio Cortez" 1983.

Villert, Michele. Screenwriter. Films: "Adios Gringo" 1965-Ital./Fr./Span.

Vincent, James. Director. Films: "Gold and the Woman" 1916.

Vincenzoni, Luciano. Screenwriter. Films: "For a Few Dollars More" 1965-Ital./Ger./Span.; "The Good, the Bad, and the Ugly" 1966-Ital.; "Death Rides a Horse" 1967-Ital.; "The Mercenary" 1968-Ital./Span."Duck, You Sucker!" 1971-Ital.; "Cipolla Colt" 1975-Ital./Ger.

Vining, Danile. Screenwriter. Films: "Wild Horses" TVM-1985.

Vitelli, Mila. Screenwriter. Films: "Anything for a Friend" 1973-Ital.

Vittes, Louis. Screenwriter. Films: "Pawnee" 1957; "Showdown at Boot Hill" 1958; "Villa!" 1958; "The Oregon Trail" 1959 (& story).

Vladimirov, Vladimir. Screenwriter. Films: "Armed and Dangerous" 1977-Sov.

Vlahos, John. Screenwriter. Films: "Tonto Basin Outlaws" 1941;

"Underground Rustlers" 1941; "Wrangler's Roost" 1941; "Rock River Renegades" 1942; "Thunder River Feud" 1942.

Vlamos, John. Director. Films: "Fugitive Valley" 1941.

Vogel, Virgil (1918-). Director. Films: "Law of the Land" TVM-1976; "Desperado" TVM-1987; "Longarm" TVM-1988. ¶TV: *Wagon Train*—"The Mary Ellen Thomas Story" 12-24-58, "The Old Man Charvanaugh Story" 2-18-59, "The Swift Cloud Story" 4-8-59, "The Duke LeMay Story" 4-29-59, "Chuck Wooster, Wagonmaster" 5-20-59, "The Andrew Hale Story" 6-3-59, "The Rodney Lawrence Story" 6-10-59, "The Steele Family" 6-17-59, "The Cappy Darrin Story" 11-11-59, "The Colonel Harris Story" 1-13-60, "The Clayton Tucker Story" 2-10-60, "The Benjamin Burns Story" 2-17-60, "The Jonas Murdock Story" 4-13-60, "Trial for Murder" 4-27-60 & 5-4-60, "The Dr. Swift Cloud Story" 5-25-60, "The Allison Justice Story" 10-19-60, "The Bleymier Story" 11-16-60, "The Jeremy Dow Story" 12-28-60, "The Sam Elder Story" 1-18-61, "Path of the Serpent" 2-8-61, "The Beth Pearson Story" 2-22-61, "The Jed Polke Story" 3-1-61, "The Nellie Jefferson Story" 4-5-61, "The Duke Shannon Story" 4-26-61, "The Chalice" 5-24-61, "The Ah Chong Story" 6-14-61, "The Molly Kincaid Story" 9-16-63, "The Gus Morgan Story" 9-30-63, "The Sandra Cummings Story" 12-2-63, "The Michael Malone Story" 1-6-64, "The Jed Whitmore Story" 1-13-64, "The Kate Crawley Story" 1-27-64, "The Trace McCloud Story" 3-2-64, "The Wipping" 3-23-64, "The Santiago Quesada Story" 3-30-64, "The Zebedee Titus Story" 4-20-64; *Laramie* 1959; *Bonanza*—"Devil on Her Shoulder" 10-17-65, "Her Brother's Keeper" 3-6-66; *The Big Valley*—"The Murdered Party" 11-17-65, "Into the Widow's Web" 3-23-66, "By Force and Violence" 3-30-66, "Tunnel of Gold" 4-20-66, "Last Train to the Fair" 4-27-66, "Legend of a General" 9-19-66 & 9-26-66, "Caesar's Wife" 10-3-66, "Pursuit" 10-10-66, "The Martyr" 10-17-66, "The Great Safe Robbery" 11-21-66, "A DAy of Terror" 12-12-66, "Day of the Comet" 12-26-66, "Wagonload of Dreams" 1-2-67, "Image of Yesterday" 1-9-67, "Down Shadow Street" 1-23-67, "Brother Love" 2-20-67, "Court Martial" 3-6-67, "Turn of a Card" 3-20-67, "Cage of Eagles" 4-24-67, "Joaquin" 9-11-67, "Ambush" 9-18-67, "A Flock of Trouble" 9-25-67,

"Night in a Small Town" 10-9-67, "The Disappearance" 11-6-67, "Explosion!" 11-20-67 & 11-27-67, "Four Days to Furnace Hill" 12-4-67, "Night of the Executioners" 12-11-67, "Days of Wrath" 1-8-68, "Fall of a Hero" 2-5-68, "The Emperor of Rice" 2-12-68, "Run of the Savage" 3-11-68, "The Challenge" 3-18-68, "They Called Her Delilah" 9-30-68, "Presumed Dead" 10-7-68, "The Jonah" 11-11-68, "Hell Hath No Fury" 11-18-68, "The Long Ride" 11-25-68, "The Prie" 12-16-68, "Top of the Stairs" 1-6-69, "Joshua Watson" 1-20-69, "Alias Nellie Handley" 2-24-69, "The Royal Road" 3-3-69, "The Battle of Mineral Springs" 3-24-69, "The Other Face of Justice" 3-31-69, "Danger Road" 4-21-69; *Here Come the Brides*—"Hosanna's Way" 10-31-69, "Land Grant" 11-21-69, "To the Victor" 2-27-70; *The High Chaparral*—"Trail to Nevermore" 10-31-69, "New Hostess in Town" 3-20-70, "Too Many Chiefs" 3-27-70; *The Oregon Trail* 1977; *Young Riders*—"The Initiation" 11-25-91.

Vogeler, Volker. Director. Films: "Yankee Dudler" 1973-Ger./Span. (& sp.); "Valley of the Dancing Widows" 1974-Span./Ger. (& sp.).

Vohrer, Alfred (1918-2/86). Director. Films: "Among Vultures" 1964-Ger./Ital./Fr./Yugo.; "Flaming Frontier" 1965-Ger./Yugo.; "Thunder at the Border" 1967-Ger./Yugo.

Von Ronkle, Rip. Screenwriter. Films: "Hannah Lee" 1953.

Von Theumer, Ernst. Screenwriter. Films: "Ballad of a Gunman" 1967-Ital./Ger.

Vorhaus, Bernard (1898-). Director. Films: "Three Faces West" 1940; "Hurricane Smith" 1942.

Wadde, C.C. Writer. Films: "So This Is Arizona" 1922 (story).

Waggner, George (1894-12/11/84). Director. Films: "Cowboy Millionaire" 1935; "Black Bandit" 1938; "Ghost Town Riders" 1938; "Guilty Trails" 1938; "Outlaw Express" 1938; "Prairie Justice" 1938; "Western Trails" 1938; "Honor of the West" 1939; "The Phantom Stage" 1939; "Wolf Call" 1939; "Badlands of Dakota" 1941 (prod. only); "Men of Texas" 1942 (prod. only); "Sin Town" 1942; "Frisco Sal" 1945 (& prod.); "The Gunfighters" 1947; "The Fighting Kentuckian" 1949 (& sp.); "Bitter Creek" 1954 (sp. only); "Pawnee" 1957 (& sp.); "Man from God's Country" 1958 (sp. only). ¶TV: *Screen Director's Playhouse*—"Arroyo" 10-26-55; *Cheyenne* 1955; *Colt .45*

1957; *Sugarfoot* 1957; *Wagon Train*—"The John Cameron Story" 10-2-57, "The Cliff Grundy Story" 12-25-57; *Bronco* 1958; *Lawman* 1958; *Northwest Passage*—"Fight at the River" 9-14-58, "War Sign" 11-30-58, "The Secret of the Cliff" 1-9-59, "Death Rides the Wind" 1-23-59; *Maverick*—"The Sheriff of Duck 'n' Shoot" 9-27-59, "You Can't Beat the Percentage" 10-4-59, "The Cactus Switch" 1-15-61; *The Alaskans* 1959-60.

Wald, Jerry (1912-7/13/62). Producer. Films: "The Lusty Men" 1952.

Waldman, Frank (1920-9/5/90). Screenwriter. Films: "Dirty Dingus Magee" 1970.

Waldman, Tom (1922-7/23/85). Screenwriter. Films: "Dirty Dingus Magee" 1970.

Waldron, John A. Screenwriter. Films: "The Cow-Catcher's Daughter" 1931-short.

Wales, Robert. Screenwriter. Films: "Bullseye!" 1986-Australia.

Walker, Drake. Writer. Films: "Buck and the Preacher" 1972 (story).

Walker, H.M. Writer. Films: "The Fighting Parson" 1930-short (story).

Walker, Robert G. Director. Films: "My Pal" 1925 (story only); "The Kid from Arizona" 1931 (sp. only); "The Three Outcasts" 1929 (sp. only); "Tex Takes a Holiday" 1932 (sp. only); "Dangers of the Canadian Mounted" 1948-serial (sp. only). ¶TV: *The Range Rider* 1951; *The Roy Rogers Show*—"The Set-Up" 1-20-52, "The Treasure of Howling Dog Canyon" 1-27-52, "The Train Robbery" 2-3-52, "Badman's Brother" 2-10-52, "The Outlaw's Girl" 2-17-52, "Outlaws' Town" 3-1-52, "The Unwilling Outlaw" 3-8-52, "Dead Men's Hills" 3-15-52, "Ghost Gulch" 3-30-52, "Ride in the Death Wagon" 4-6-52, "Perils from the Past" 4-13-52, "Shoot to Kill" 4-27-52, "The Hermit's Secret" 5-1-52, "Haunted Mine of Paradise Valley" 5-18-52, "Ghost Town Gold" 5-25-52, "The Double Crosser" 6-1-52, "Carnival Killer" 6-8-52, "Death Medicine" 9-7-52, "Outlaw's Return" 9-28-52, "Huntin' for Trouble" 10-5-52, "The Feud" 11-16-52, "Go for Your Gun" 11-23-52, "The Mayor of Ghost Town" 11-30-52, "Blind Justice" 12-14-52, "The Knockout" 12-28-52, "The Run-A-Round" 2-22-53, "The Silver Fox Hunt" 4-19-53, "The Mingo Kid" 4-26-53, "The Long Chance" 5-24-53, "Money to Burn" 6-28-53, "The Milliner from Medicine Hate" 10-11-53, "Gun

Trouble" 11-22-53, "M Stands for Murder" 12-6-53, "Phantom Rustlers" 4-25-54, "Doc Stevens' Traveling Store" 7-25-54, "The Hijackers" 10-24-54, "Violence in Paradise Valley" 11-2-55; *The Adventures of Rin Rin Tin* 1954; *The Gene Autry Show*—"The Portrait of White Cloud" 10-15-55, "Go West, Young Lady" 11-19-55; *The Adventures of Champion* 1955; *Buffalo Bill, Jr.* 1955.

Wallace, C.R. Director. Films: "Trooper O'Neil" 1922; "West of Chicago" 1922.

Wallace, Charles A. Screenwriter. Films: "Stage to Thunder Rock" 1964; "Yuma" TVM-1971.

Wallace, Earl W. Screenwriter. Films: "Wild and Wooly" TVM-1978 (& prod.); "Last Ride of the Dalton Gang" TVM-1979; "The Wild Women of Chastity Gulch" TVM-1982; "Gunsmoke: The Last Apache" TVM-1990; "Gunsmoke: To the Last Man" TVM-1991.

Wallace, Irving (1916-6/29/90). Screenwriter. Films: "Gun Fury" 1953; "The Gambler from Natchez" 1954; "The Burning Hills" 1956.

Wallace, Richard (1894-11/3/51). Director. Films: "A Texas Steer" 1927.

Wallace, Tommy Lee. Screenwriter. Films: "El Diablo" CTVM-1990.

Wallace, William. Director. Films: "Western Speed" 1922.

Waller, Manuel. Screenwriter. Films: "Bullets Don't Argue" 1964-Ital./Ger./Span.

Wallerstein, Herb (1926-9/28/85). Director. TV: *Here Come the Brides*—"A Dream That Glitters" 2-26-69, "The Legend of Big Foot" 11-14-69; *Wild Wild West*—"The Night of the Diva" 3-7-69; *Gunsmoke*—"P.S. Murry Christmas" 12-27-71, "Phoebe" 2-21-72, "The River" 9-11-72 & 9-18-72, "Horse Fever" 12-18-72; *Barbary Coast*—"An Iron-Clad Plan" 10-31-75, "Mary Had More Than a Little" 1-2-76; *The Oregon Trail* 1977.

Wallis, Hal B. (1898-10/5/86). Producer. Films: "Cowboy from Brooklyn" 1938; "Gold Is Where You Find It" 1938; "Santa Fe Trail" 1940; "They Died with Their Boots On" 1941; "Desert Fury" 1947; "The Furies" 1950; "Red Mountain" 1951; "The Rainmaker" 1956; "Gunfight at the O.K. Corral" 1957; "Last Train from Gun Hill" 1959; "Four for Texas" 1964; "The Sons of Katie Elder" 1965; "Five Card Stud" 1968; "True Grit" 1969; "Shoot Out" 1971; "Rooster Cogburn" 1975.

Walsh, Bill (1914-1/27/75). Producer. Films: "Davy Crockett, King of the Wild Frontier" 1955; "Westward Ho the Wagons" 1956 (sp. only); "Davy Crockett and the River Pirates" 1956; "Scandalous John" 1971 (& sp.).

Walsh, Raoul (1892-12/31/80). Director. Films: "Blue Blood and Red" 1916 (& sp.); "Evangeline" 1919 (& sp.); "In Old Arizona" 1929; "The Big Trail" 1930 (& story); "The Dark Command" 1940; "They Died with Their Boots On" 1941; "Cheyenne" 1947; "Pursued" 1947; "Silver River" 1948; "Colorado Territory" 1949; "Along the Great Divide" 1951; "Distant Drums" 1951; "The Lawless Breed" 1952; "Gun Fury" 1953; "Saskatchewan" 1954; "The Tall Men" 1955; "King and Four Queens" 1956; "The Sheriff of Fractured Jaw" 1958-Brit.; "A Distant Trumpet" 1964.

Walsh, Ray. Screenwriter. Films: "Santa Fe Pete" 1925.

Walter, Eugene. Writer. Films: "Boots and Saddles" 1916 (story).

Walters, R. Martin. Director. Films: "Marie-Ann" 1978-Can.

Wanamaker, Sam (1919-12/18/93). Director. Films: "Catlow" 1971-Span. ¶TV: *Cimarron Strip*—"Broken Wing" 9-21-67; *Lancer* 1968-71 (prod.), "The High Riders" 9-24-68.

Wandberg, Warren D. Screenwriter. Films: "Sierra Passage" 1951.

Wanger, Walter (1894-11/18/68). Producer. Films: "Stagecoach" 1939; "Canyon Passage" 1946; "Fort Vengeance" 1953; "Kansas Pacific" 1953.

Wanzer, Orville. Director. Films: "The Devil's Mistress" 1968 (& sp.).

Ward, Bill. Director. Films: "Ballad of a Gunfighter" 1964 (& prod./sp.).

Ward, Brad. Writer. Films: "A Lawless Street" 1955 (story).

Ward, Jonas. Writer. Films: "Buchanan Rides Alone" 1958 (story).

Ward, Luci. Screenwriter. Films: "Cherokee Strip" 1937; "Land Beyond the Law" 1937; "Call the Mesquiteers" 1938 (adapt. only); "Man from Music Mountain" 1938; "Overland Stage Raiders" 1938; "Panamint's Bad Man" 1938; "Red River Range" 1938; "Santa Fe Stampede" 1938 (& story); "The Arizona Kid" 1939 (& story); "Colorado Sunset" 1939 (story only); "The Kansas Terrors" 1939 (story only); "Mexicali Rose" 1939 (story only); "New Fron-

tier" 1939; "Beyond the Sacramento" 1940; "Bad Men of the Hills" 1942; "Lawless Plainsmen" 1942; "The Lone Star Vigilantes" 1942; "Vengeance of the West" 1942; "Calling Wild Bill Elliott" 1943; "The Fighting Buckaroo" 1943; "Law of the Northwest" 1943; "Cowboy from Lonesome River" 1944; "Raiders of Ghost City" 1944-serial; "Riding West" 1944; "Sundown Valley" 1944; "Badman's Territory" 1946; "Black Bart" 1948; "Return of the Badmen" 1948 (& story); "Cheyenne Cowboy" 1949-short; "The Last Bandit" 1949 (story only); "Rustlers" 1949; "Six Gun Music" 1949-short; "Blackjack Ketchum, Desperado" 1956; "The Ride to Hangman's Tree" 1967 (& story).

Ward, Robert. Screenwriter. Films: "Cattle Annie and Little Britches" 1981 (& story).

Ward, Rollo. Screenwriter. Films: "Rainbow's End" 1935.

Warde, Ernest C. (1874-9/9/23). Director. Films: "Prisoner of the Pines" 1918; "A Man in the Open" 1919; "The Midnight Stage" 1919; "A White Man's Chance" 1919; "The Coast of Opportunity" 1920; "The Trail of the Axe" 1922; "Ruth of the Range" 1923-serial.

Ware, Clyde. Screenwriter. Films: "The Silent Gun" TVM-1969; "The Alamo: 13 Days to Glory" TVM-1987; "Bad Jim" 1990 (& dir.).

Ware, F.H. Screenwriter. Films: "The Shootin' Fool" 1920.

Ware, Hadden. Screenwriter. Films: "Some Shooter" 1920.

Warhol, Andy (1927-2/22/87). Director. Films: "Lonesome Cowboys" 1968 (& prod./sp.).

Warner, Jack L. (1892-9/9/78). Producer. Films: "Santa Fe Trail" 1940; "Dirty Little Billy" 1972.

Warner, John. *see* Ulmer, Edgar G.

Warnick, Ed. Director. Films: "Manchurian Avenger" 1985.

Warren, Charles Marquis (1912-8/11/90). Director. Films: "Streets of Laredo" 1949 (sp. only); "Little Big Horn" 1951 (& sp.); "Oh! Susanna" 1951 (sp. only); "Only the Valiant" 1951 (story only); "The Redhead and the Cowboy" 1951 (story only); "Hellgate" 1952 (& sp./story); "Springfield Rifle" 1952; "Woman of the North Country" 1952 (story only); "Arrowhead" 1953 (& sp.); "Pony Express" 1953 (sp. only); "Seven Angry Men" 1955; "The Black Whip" 1956; "Tension at Table Rock" 1956; "Copper Sky" 1957; "Ride a Violent Mile" 1957 (& story); "Trooper Hook" 1957 (& sp.); "Blood Arrow" 1958; "Cattle Empire" 1958; "Day of the Evil Gun" 1968 (sp. only); "Charro!" 1969 (& prod./sp.). ¶TV: *Gunsmoke* 1955-56 (prod.), "Matt Gets It" 9-10-55, "Hot Spell" 9-17-55, "Word of Honor" 10-1-55, "Home Surgery" 10-8-55, "Obie Tater" 10-15-55, "Night Incident" 10-29-55, "Smoking Out the Nolans" 11-5-55, "Kite's Reward" 11-12-55, "The Hunter" 11-26-55, "The Queue" 12-3-55, "General Parsley Smith" 12-10-55, "Magnus" 12-24-55, "The Reed Survives" 12-31-55, "Professor Lute Bone" 1-7-56, "No Handcuffs" 1-21-56, "Reward for Matt" 1-28-56, "Robin Hood" 2-4-56, "Yorky" 2-18-56, "20-20" 2-25-56, "Reunion '78" 3-3-56, "Helping Hand" 3-17-56, "Tap Day for Kitty" 3-24-56, "The Pest Hole" 4-14-56, "The Big Broad" 4-28-56, "Hack Prine" 5-12-56, "Cooter" 5-19-56; *Rawhide*—1959-66 (exec. prod), "Incident with an Executioner" 1-23-59, "Incident at Barker Springs" 2-20-59, "Incident West of Lano" 2-27-59, "Incident of the Golden Calf" 3-13-59, "Incident at Dangerfield Dip" 10-2-59, "Incident of the Blue Fire" 12-11-59, "Incident of the Challenge" 10-14-60; *Gunslinger* 1961 (prod.); *The Virginian*—"It Tolls for Thee" 11-21-62; *Iron Horse* 1966-68 (prod.).

Warren, Giles R. Director. Films: "A Texas Steer" 1915.

Warren, Jerry (1923-8/21/88). Producer. Films: "Bullet for Billy the Kid" 1963.

Warren, Joseph. *see* Vari, Giuseppe.

Warren, Michael. Screenwriter. Films: "Hawmps!" 1976.

Waters, Frank. Writer. Films: "River Lady" 1948 (story).

Waters, John (1893-5/5/65). Director. Films: "Born to the West" 1926; "Forlorn River" 1926; "Man of the Forest" 1926; "Arizona Bound" 1927; "Drums of the Desert" 1927; "The Mysterious Rider" 1927; "Nevada" 1927; "The Vanishing Pioneer" 1928; "The Overland Telegraph" 1929; "Sioux Blood" 1929.

Watkin, Lawrence Edward (1901-). Screenwriter. Films: "The Great Locomotive Chase" 1956 (& prod.); "The Light in the Forest" 1958; "Ten Who Dared" 1960.

Watson, Joseph K. (1887-5/16/42). Screenwriter. Films: "Cherokee Strip" 1937; "Land Beyond the Law" 1937.

Watson, Robert. Screenwriter.

Films: "Secret Patrol" 1936; "Stampede" 1936.

Watson, W.W. Screenwriter. Films: "The Oregon Trail" 1939-serial.

Watt, Nate (1889-5/26/68). Director. Films: "The Galloping Devil" 1920; "Hopalong Cassidy Returns" 1936; "Trail Dust" 1936; "Hills of Old Wyoming" 1937; "North of the Rio Grande" 1937; "Rustler's Valley" 1937 (sp. only); "Pride of the West" 1938 (sp. only); "Law of the Pampas" 1939; "Frontier Vengeance" 1940; "Oklahoma Renegades" 1940; "Cheyenne Cowboy" 1949-short; "Six Gun Music" 1949-short. ¶TV: *Judge Roy Bean*—"Ad Sid, Cowboy" 1-1-56, "Gunman's Bargain" 1-1-56, "The Hidden Truth" 1-1-56, "The Judge's Dilemma" 1-1-56, "The Katcina Doll" 1-1-56, "Outlaw's Son" 1-1-56, "The Reformer" 1-1-56, "Deliver the Body" 6-1-56, "The Hypnotist" 6-1-56, "Terror Rides the Trail" 6-1-56.

Watters, William. *see* Hall, Sr., Arch.

Wayne, John (1907-6/11/79). Producer. Films: "Angel and the Badman" 1947; "The Fighting Kentuckian" 1949; "Hondo" 1953; "Track of the Cat" 1954; "The Alamo" 1960 (& dir.).

Wayne, Michael (1934-). Producer. Films: "McLintock" 1963; "Big Jake" 1971; "Cahill, United Staters Marshal" 1973; "The Train Robbers" 1973.

Weaver, Dennis (1924-). Director. TV: *Gunsmoke*—"Love Thy Neighbor" 1-28-61, "Little Girl" 4-1-61, "Hard Virtue" 5-6-61, "Marry Me" 12-23-61.

Weaver, John V.A. Screenwriter. Films: "A Man from Wyoming" 1930.

Webb, Harry S. (Harry Samuels). Director. Films: "Coyote Fangs" 1924; "Ridin' West" 1924; "Border Vengeance" 1925; "Cactus Trails" 1925; "Canyon Rustlers" 1925; "Desert Madness" 1925; "Double Fisted" 1925; "The Empty Saddle" 1925 (prod. only); "The Mystery of Lost Ranch" 1925; "Santa Fe Pete" 1925; "Silent Sheldon" 1925; "Starlight, the Untamed" 1925; "The Man from Oklahoma" 1926; "Starlight's Revenge" 1926; "West of the Rainbow's End" 1926; "The Golden Stallion" 1927; "Phantom of the North" 1929; "Untamed Justice" 1929; "Bar L Ranch" 1930; "Beyond the Rio Grande" 1930; "Phantom of the Desert" 1930 (& prod.); "Ridin' Law" 1930 (& prod.); "Westward Bound" 1930 (& prod.); "The Mystery

Trooper" 1931-serial; "The Sign of the Wolf" 1931-serial (& prod.); "West of Cheyenne" 1931; "The Cactus Kid" 1934; "Loser's End" 1934 (story only); "Fighting Hero" 1934; "Terror of the Plains" 1934; "Born to Battle" 1935; "The Laramie Kid" 1935; "North of Arizona" 1935; "Ridin' Thru" 1935; "Tracy Rides" 1935; "Trigger Tom" 1935; "The Unconquered Bandit" 1935; "Wolf Riders" 1935; "Fast Bullets 1936; "Pinto Rustlers" 1936; "Santa Fe Bound" 1936; "The Great Adventures of Wild Bill Hickok" 1938-serial (prod. only); "El Diablo Rides" 1939 (prod. only); "Feud of the Range" 1939 (& prod.); "Mesquite Buckaroo" 1939 (& prod.); "The Pal from Texas" 1939 (& prod.); "Riders of the Sage" 1939 (& prod.); "Smoky Trails" 1939 (prod. only); "The Cheyenne Kid" 1940; "Covered Wagon Trails" 1940; "The Kid from Santa Fe" 1940 (prod. only); "Land of the Six Guns" 1940 (prod. only); "Pinto Canyon" 1940; "Pioneer Days" 1940; "Riders from Nowhere" 1940 (prod. only); "Wild Horse Range" 1940 (prod. only); "Wild Horse Valley" 1940 (prod. only).

Webb, Ira. Director. Films: "El Diablo Rides" 1939; "King of the Bullwhip" 1940 (sp. only); "Wild Horse Valley" 1940; "Mark of the Lash" 1948 (sp. only); "Dead Man's Gold" 1948 (story only); "Outlaw Country" 1949 (sp. only); "Son of a Badman" 1949 (sp. only); "Son of Billy the Kid" 1949 (sp. only).

Webb, James R. (1910-9/27/74). Screenwriter. Films: "Bad Man of Deadwood" 1941; "Jesse James at Bay" 1941; "Nevada City" 1941; "Sheriff of Tombstone" 1941 (story only); "South of Santa Fe" 1942; "South of St. Louis" 1949; "Montana" 1950; "Raton Pass" 1951; "The Big Trees" 1952; "The Iron Mistress" 1952; "The Charge at Feather River" 1953; "Apache" 1954; "Vera Cruz" 1954; "The Big Country" 1958; "How the West Was Won" 1962; "Cheyenne Autumn" 1964.

Webb, Millard (1893-4/21/35). Screenwriter. Films: "Tiger Rose" 1923.

Webb, Robert D. (1903-4/18/90). Director. Films: "White Feather" 1955; "Love Me Tender" 1956; "The Proud Ones" 1956; "Guns of the Timberland" 1960.

Webber, Ethel. Screenwriter. Films: "The Mediator" 1916.

Weber, Lois (1881-11/13/39). Director. Films: "When a Girl Loves" 1919 (& sp.).

Webster, George H. Director. Films: "Blazing the Way" 1920.

Webster, M. Coates. Screenwriter. Films: "Home in Wyomin'" 1942; "Sons of the Pioneers" 1942; "Klondike Kate" 1943 (& story); "Song of Arizona" 1946; "Under Nevada Skies" 1946 (story only); "Renegades of Sonora" 1948; "Navajo Trail Raiders" 1949; "The Wyoming Bandit" 1949; "Covered Wagon Raid" 1950; "Frisco Tornado" 1950; "Gunmen of Abilene" 1950; "Salt Lake Raiders" 1950; "Desert of Lost Men" 1951; "Night Riders of Montana" 1951; "Rough Riders of Durango" 1951; "Wells Fargo Gunmaster" 1951; "Captive of Billy the Kid" 1952; "Leadville Gunslinger" 1952; "Montana Belle" 1952 (story only); "Thundering Caravans" 1952; "Marshal of Cedar Rock" 1953 (story only).

Webster, Nicholas (1922-). Director. TV: *The Big Valley*—"A Passage of Saints" 3-10-69; *Bonanza*—"The Luck of Pepper Shannon" 11-22-70, "Heritage of Anger" 9-19-72; *The Chisholms* 1980.

Weed, Marlene. Screenwriter. Films: "The Red, White and Black" 1970.

Weeks, George W. (1885-11/16/53). Producer. Films: "Rogue of the Rio Grande" 1930; "The Range Busters" 1940; "Trailing Double Trouble" 1940; "West of Pinto Basin" 1940; "Fugitive Valley" 1941; "The Kid's Last Ride" 1941; "Saddle Mountain Roundup" 1941; "Tonto Basin Outlaws" 1941; "Trail of the Silver Spurs" 1941; "Tumbledown Ranch in Arizona" 1941; "Underground Rustlers" 1941; "Wrangler's Roost" 1941; "Arizona Stagecoach" 1942; "Boot Hill Bandits" 1942; "Rock River Renegades" 1942; "Texas to Bataan" 1942; "Thunder River Feud" 1942; "Trail Riders" 1942; "Black Market Rustlers" 1943; "Bullets and Saddles" 1943; "Cowboy Commandos" 1943; "The Haunted Ranch" 1943; "Land of Hunted Men" 1943; "Two Fisted Justice" 1943.

Weems, Walter. Screenwriter. Films: "Wide Open Spaces" 1932-short.

Weil, Richard. Writer. Films: "Singin' in the Corn" 1946 (story).

Weiland, Paul. Director. Films: "City Slickers II: The Legend of Curly's Gold" 1994.

Weinstein, Marvin R. Director. Films: "Running Target" 1956 (& sp.).

Weis, Don (1922-). Director.

TV: *Wagon Train*—"The Nels Stack Story" 10-23-57; *Barbary Coast*—"Funny Money" 9-8-75, "Crazy Cats" 9-15-75.

Weisbart, David (1915-7/21/67). Producer. Films: "The Charge at Feather River" 1953; "The Command" 1953; "Thunder Over the Plains" 1953; "The Boy from Oklahoma" 1954; "Tall Man Riding" 1955; "Love Me Tender" 1956; "These Thousand Hills" 1959; "Flaming Star" 1960; "Rio Conchos" 1964. ¶TV: *Custer* 1967 (exec. prod.).

Weisberg, Brenda. Screenwriter. Films: "King of the Wild Horses" 1947.

Weiss, Allan. Screenwriter. Films: "Four for Texas" 1964; "The Sons of Katie Elder" 1965.

Weiss, Louis. Producer. Films: "Cavalier of the West" 1931; "Border Devils" 1932; "The Night Rider" 1932; "Without Honor" 1932; "The Cowboy and the Bandit" 1935; "Cyclone of the Saddle" 1935; "Fighting Caballero" 1935; "The Ghost Rider" 1935; "Pals of the Range" 1935; "Rough Riding Ranger" 1935; "The Silent Code" 1935.

Welch, Lester (1906-3/6/85). Producer. Films: "Gunfighters of Casa Grande" 1965-U.S./Span.; "Son of a Gunfighter" 1966-U.S./Span.

Welch, Robert L. Producer. Films: "The Paleface" 1948; "Fancy Pants" 1950; "Son of Paleface" 1952 (& sp.).

Welles, Halsted. Screenwriter. Films: "3:10 to Yuma" 1957; "The Hanging Tree" 1959; "A Time for Killing" 1967.

Welles, Mel (Mark Welles) (1930-). Director. Films: "Requiem for a Bounty Hunter" 1970-Ital. (& sp.).

Wellman, Paul I. (1898-9/17/66). Writer. Films: "Cheyenne" 1947 (story); "The Iron Mistress" 1952 (story); "Apache" 1954 (story); "Jubal" 1956 (story); "The Comancheros" 1961.

Wellman, William A. (1896-12/9/75). Director. Films: "The Man Who Won" 1923; "Circus Cowboy" 1924; "Not a Drum Was Heard" 1924; "The Vagabond Tril" 1924; "The Conquerors" 1932; "Call of the Wild" 1935; "Robin Hood of El Dorado" 1936 (& sp.); "The Great Man's Lady" 1942 (& prod.); "The Ox-Bow Incident" 1943; "Buffalo Bill" 1944; "Yellow Sky" 1948; "Across the Wide Missouri" 1951; "Westward the Women" 1951; "Track of the Cat" 1954.

Wells, Alexander J. Screenwriter. Films: "The Rawhide Trail" 1958.

Wells, Elmer N. Screenwriter. Films: "Pierre of the North" 1913.

Wells, Jack. Director. Films: "Human Targets" 1918.

Wells, Raymond (1880-8/9/41). Director. Films: "Fighting Back" 1917; "Fighting for Love" 1917 (& story); "The Gunman's Gospel" 1917; "The Law of the Great Northwest" 1918; "Man Above the Law" 1918; "Death Valley" 1927 (story only).

Wells, Robert. Director. Films: "The Ranger of Pike's Peak" 1919; "Winning a Bride" 1919.

Wells, Simon. Director. Films: "An American Tail: Fievel Goes West" 1991.

Wells, William K. Screenwriter. Films: "Captain Thunder" 1931.

Welsch, Gloria. Screenwriter. Films: "Dead Man's Gold" 1948.

Welsch, Howard. Producer. Films: "The Daltons Ride Again" 1945; "The Michigan Kid" 1947; "The Vigilantes Return" 1947; "Montana Belle" 1952 (& story); "Rancho Notorious" 1952; "The San Francisco Story" 1952; "A Bullet Is Waiting" 1954.

Welsh, Phillip. Writer. Films: "The Vagabond Soldier" 1914 (story).

Wendkos, Paul (1922-). Director. Films: "Face of a Fugitive" 1959; "Guns of the Magnificent Seven" 1969; "Cannon for Cordoba" 1970. ¶TV: *Law of the Plainsman* 1959; *The Rifleman*—"Six Years and a Day" 1-3-61, "None So Blind" 3-19-62; *The Big Valley*—"Young Marauders" 10-6-65, "Hermitage" 10-20-65.

Wendlandt, Horst. Producer. Films: "Apache Gold" 1965-Ger.; "The Desperado Trail" 1965-Ger./Yugo.; "Flaming Frontier" 1965-Ger./Yugo.; "Rampage at Apache Wells" 1965-Ger./Yugo. (& sp.); "Half Breed" 1966-Ger./Yugo./Ital.; "Last of the Renegades" 1966-Fr./Ital./Ger./Yugo.; "Thunder at the Border" 1967-Ger./Yugo.; "Buddy Goes West" 1981-Ital.

Wentz, Roby. Screenwriter. Films: "Heroes of the Alamo" 1938.

Werker, Alfred (1896-7/28/75). Director. Films: "Ridin' the Wind" 1925; "Kit Carson" 1928; "The Pioneer Scout" 1928; "The Sunset Legion" 1928; "Last of the Duanes" 1930; "Fair Warning" 1931; "The Gay Caballero" 1932; "Wild and Woolly" 1937; "Pirates of Monterey" 1947; "Devil's Canyon" 1953; "The Last

Posse" 1953; "Three Hours to Kill" 1954; ; "At Gunpoint" 1955; "Canyon Crossroads" 1955; "Rebel in Town" 1956.

Werner, Peter. Director. Films: "Outlaws" TVM-1986; "Substitute Wife" TVM-1994.

Wertmuller, Lina (Nathan Wich) (1926-). Director. Films: "Belle Starr Story" 1968-Ital. (& sp.).

West, James. Screenwriter. Films: "California" 1963.

West, Jessamyn (1902-2/23/84). Writer. Films: "Friendly Persuasion" 1956 (story); "The Big Country" 1958 (adapt.); "Friendly Persuasion" TVM-1975 (story).

West, John. *see* Jevne, Jack.

West, Joseph. Screenwriter. Films: "Black Bandit" 1938; "Ghost Town Riders" 1938; "Guilty Trails" 1938; "Prairie Justice" 1938; "Honor of the West" 1939; "Oklahoma Terror" 1939; "The Phantom Stage" 1939; "Wolf Call" 1939; "Queen of the Yukon" 1940.

West, Langdon. Director. Films: "The Colonel's Daughter" 1915.

West, Mae (1892-11/22/80). Screenwriter. Films: "My Little Chickadee" 1940.

West, Raymond (1886-9/23). Director. Films: "The Quakeress" 1913.

West, Roland (1885-3/31/52). Director. Films: "The Siren" 1917.

West, Victor. Screenwriter. Films: "Bandit Queen" 1950 (& story); "Border Rangers" 1950; "Gunfire" 1950; "Train to Tombstone" 1950.

West, Wilton. Writer. Films: "The Crimson Trail" 1935 (story); "The Riding Avenger" 1936 (story).

Westmoreland, Forrest (Wes Moreland). Producer. Films: "The Devil's Mistress" 1968.

Weston, Ed. Screenwriter. Films: "The Fighting Parson" 1933.

Weston, Garnett. Screenwriter. Films: "Nevada" 1935; "Pony Soldier" 1952 (story only).

Westover, Clyde C. Screenriter. Films: "Sunset Sprague" 1920; "Bar Nothin'" 1921 (story only).

Westrate, Edwin. Screenwriter. Films: "Renegade Girl" 1946; "Jesse James Versus the Daltons" 1954 (story only).

Wharton, Theodore. Director. Films: "The Adventures of Buffalo Bill" 1914; "The Moon Riders" 1920-serial (sp. only).

Whatley, Roger. Screenwriter.

Films: "Drums of Destiny" 1937 (& story).

Wheeler, Leonard. Director. Films: "Four Hearts" 1922 (& sp.).

Whelan, Tim (1893-8/12/57). Director. Films: "Badman's Territory" 1946; "Rage at Dawn" 1955; "Texas Lady" 1955.

Whitaker, Herman. Writer. Films: "Three Bad Men" 1926 (story); "Three Rogues" 1931 (story).

Whitcomb, Cynthia. Screenwriter. Films: "Buffalo Girls" TVM-1995.

Whitcomb, Daniel F. Screenwriter. Films: "Sunset Jones" 1921; "Another Man's Boots" 1922; "Peaceful Peters" 1922; "The Sheriff of Sun-Dog" 1922; "At Devil's Gorge" 1923; "Battling Bates" 1923; "Spawn of the Desert" 1923; "The Sting of the Scorpion" 1923; "Sun Dog Trails" 1923; "Blasted Hopes" 1924; "The Desert Hawk" 1924; "Notch Number One" 1924.

Whitcomb, Dean. *see* Corbucci, Bruno.

Whitcomb, Ritchie. Screenwriter. Films: "Three Pals" 1916.

White, Alexander. Screenwriter. Films: "The Thundering Trail" 1951; "The Vanishing Outpost" 1951.

White, Andy. Producer. Films: "Africa—Texas Style!" 1967-U.S./Brit. (sp. only). ¶TV: *Tombstone Territory* 1957-60; *Bat Masterson* 1958-61; *Redigo* 1963; *The Loner* 1965-66; *Cowboy in Africa* 1967-68.

White, Eddy. Producer. Films: "The Sombrero Kid" 1942 (story only); "The Sundown Kid" 1942; "Black Hills Express" 1943; "Bordertown Gunfighters" 1943; "California Joe" 1943; "Canyon City" 1943; "Carson City Cyclone" 1943; "Days of Old Cheyenne" 1943; "Dead Man's Gulch" 1943; "Death Valley Manhunt" 1943 (& story); "The Big Bonanza" 1944; "Tucson Raiders" 1944; "Down Dakota Way" 1949; "Sunset in the West" 1950; "Carson City" 1952.

White, Edward J. Producer. Films: "Fugitive from Sonora" 1937; "Outlaws of Pine Ridge" 1942; "The Man from the Rio Grande" 1943; "Mojave Firebrand" 1944; "Outlaws of Santa Fe" 1944; "San Fernando Valley" 1944; "Along the Navajo Trail" 1945; "Bells of Rosarita" 1945; "Heldorado" 1946; "Home in Oklahoma" 1946; "Rainbow Over Texas" 1946; "Roll on, Texas Moon" 1946; "Song of Arizona" 1946; "Under Nevada Skies" 1946; "Apache Rose" 1947; "Bells of San Angelo" 1947;

"On the Old Spanish Trail" 1947; "Springtime in the Sierras" 1947; "Eyes of Texas" 1948; "The Gay Ranchero" 1948; "Grand Canyon Trail" 1948; "Night Time in Nevada" 1948; "Under California Stars" 1948; "The Far Frontier" 1949; "The Golden Stallion" 1949; "Susanna Pass" 1949; "Bells of Coronado" 1950; "North of the Great Divide" 1950; "Trail of Robin Hood" 1950; "Trigger, Jr." 1950; "Twilight in the Sierras" 1950; "Heart of the Rockies" 1951; "In Old Amarillo" 1951; "Pals of the Golden West" 1951; "South of Caliente" 1951; "Spoilers of the Plains" 1951; "Colorado Sundown" 1952; "The Last Musketeer" 1952; "Old Oklahoma Plains" 1952; "South Pacific Trail" 1952; "Iron Mountain Trail" 1953; "Old Overland Trail" 1953. ¶TV: *Frontier Doctor* 1958-59.

White, Jack. Screenwriter. Films: "Three Troubledoers" 1946-short; "Pals and Gals" 1954-short.

White, Jules (1900-4/30/85). Director. Films: "Whoops, I'm an Indian" 1936-short (prod. only); "Back to the Woods" 1937-short (prod. only); "Yes, We Have No Bonanza" 1939-short; "Rockin' Through the Rockies" 1940-short (& prod.); "Pals and Gals" 1954-short (& prod.); "Short in the Frontier" 1954-short (& prod).

White, Leslie T. Writer. Films: "The Americano" 1955 (story).

White, Malcolm S. Writer. Films: "Do It Now" 1924 (story).

White, Peter. Screenwriter. Films: "Colt Is the Law" 1965-Ital./Span.).

White, Philip Graham. Screenwriter. Films: "The Gay Buckaroo" 1932; "Local Bad Man" 1932; "Spirit of the West" 1932; "Trailing Trouble" 1937.

White, Robert M. *see* Balcazar, Jaime J.

White, Stewart Edward. Writer. Films: "The Call of the North" 1914 (story); "The Westerners" 1919 (story only); "The Call of the North" 1921 (story); "The Killer" 1921 (story); "Under a Texas Moon" 1930; "Mystery Ranch" 1932 (story).

White, William Patterson. Writer. Films: "Pardon My Nerve!" 1922 (story).

Whitefield, Nellie. Screenwriter. Films: "Ace of Cactus Range" 1924.

Whitehead, Peter. Writer. Films: "Colorado Pioneers" 1945 (story); "Two-Fisted Stranger" 1946 (story).

Whitman, Dr. Marcus. Writer. Films: "The Oregon Trail" 1923-serial (story); "The Oregon Trail" 1939-serial (story).

Whitman, S.E. Writer. Films: "Captain Apache" 1971-Brit./Span. (story).

Whitney, C.V. (1899-12/13/92). Producer. Films: "The Searchers" 1956.

Whittaker, Charles E. (1877-1/4/53). Screenwriter. Films: "Under Western Skies" 1926.

Whorf, Richard (1906-12/14/66). Producer. Films: "The Burning Hills" 1956; "Shoot-Out at Medicine Bend" 1957. ¶TV: *Gunsmoke*—"Never Pester Chester" 11-16-57, "Cows and Cribs" 12-7-57, "Doc's Reward" 12-14-57, "Kitty Caught" 1-18-58, "Sunday Supplement" 2-8-58, "Wild West" 2-15-58, "Matt for Murder" 9-13-58, "The Patsy" 9-20-58, "Gunsmuggler" 9-27-58, "Letter of the Law" 10-11-58, "Thoroughbreds" 10-18-58, "Lost Rifle" 11-1-58, "Lynching Man" 11-15-58, "How to Kill a Friend" 11-22-58, "Grass" 11-29-58, "Robber and Bridegroom" 12-13-58, "Gypsum Hills Feud" 12-27-58, "Milly" 11-25-61; *Rawhide*—"Incident of the Tumbleweed Wagon" 1-9-59, "Incident at Alabaster Plain" 1-16-59, "Crossing at White Feather" 12-7-65; *Have Gun Will Travel*—"Lady on the Stagecoach" 1-17-59, "Treasure Trail" 1-24-59, "Gold and Brimstone" 6-20-59; *Law of the Plainsman* 1959-60; *Wagon Train*—"Princess of a Lost Tribe" 11-2-60; *Wild Wild West*—"The Night of the Fatal Trap" 12-24-65.

Whytock, Grant. Producer. Films: "Apache Rifles" 1964; "The Quick Gun" 1964; "Arizona Raiders" 1965; "40 Guns to Apache Pass" 1967.

Wiard, William (1928-7/2/87). Director. Films: "Scott Free" TVM-1976; "Tom Horn" 1980. ¶TV: *The Monroes*—"Gun Bound" 1-25-67, "Ghosts of Paradox" 3-15-67; *Daniel Boone*—"The Secret Code" 12-14-67, "Orlando, the Prophet" 2-29-68, "The Far Side of Fury" 3-7-68, "The Fleeing Nuns" 10-24-68, "Big, Black and Out There" 11-14-68, "A Pinch of Salt" 5-1-69, "A Bearskin for Jamie Blue" 11-27-69, "The Kidnaping" 1-22-70, "The Landlords" 3-5-70, "Readin', Ritin', and Revolt" 3-12-70, "How to Become a Goddess" 4-30-70; *Bonanza*—"Anatomy of a Lynching" 10-12-69, "The Night Virginia City Died" 9-13-70, "A Matter of Faith" 9-20-70, "A Single Pilgrim" 1-3-71, "Winter Kill" 3-28-71, "Bush-

wacked" 10-3-71, "The Rattlesnake Brigade" 12-5-71; *The High Chaparral*—"The Lieutenant" 2-27-70, "A Matter of Survival" 10-16-70; *Sara* 1976; *Bret Maverick*—"The Yellow Rose" 12-22-81, "A Night at the Red Ox" 3-23-82.

Wich, Nathan. *see* Wertmuller, Lina.

Wiesenthal, Sam. Producer. Films: "Tension at Table Rock" 1956.

Wilbur, Crane (1886-10/18/73). Screenwriter. Films: "Ride, Cowboy, Ride" 1939-short; "The Red Stallion" 1947; "The Lion and the Horse" 1952.

Wilder, John. Screenwriter. Films: "Law of the Land" TVM-1976 (& prod.); "Return to Lonesome Dove" TVM-1993. ¶TV: *Centennial* 1978-79 (exec. prod.).

Wilder, Laura Ingalls (1867-1957). Writer. Films: "Little House on the Prairie" TVM-1974 (story).

Wilder, Margaret Buell. Screenwriter. Films: "Pirates of Monterey" 1947.

Wilder, Myles. Screenwriter. Films: "Seven Guns to Mesa" 1958 (& story).

Wilder, W. Lee (1904-82). Director. Films: "Yankee Fakir" 1947 (& prod.).

Wildes, Newlin B. Writer. Films: "Heart of the Rio Grande" 1942 (story).

Wileys, Anthony. *see* Sequi, Mario.

Wilhite, Marvin. Screenwriter. Films: "That Devil Quemado" 1925.

Wilkes, Anne Tupper. Screenwriter. Films: "Arms and the Gringo" 1914.

Wilkinson, Richard Hill. Writer. Films: "Rustlers of the Badlands" 1945 (story).

Willat, Irvin (1890-4/17/76). Director. Films: "The Law of the North" 1918; "A Daughter of the Wolf" 1919; "Rustling a Bride" 1919; "The Siren Call" 1922; "The Wanderer of the Wasteland" 1924; "The Cavalier" 1928 (prod. only); "Heritage of the Desert" 1924; "North of '36" 1924; "The Enchanted Hill" 1926; "The Luck of Roaring Camp" 1937; "Old Louisiana" 1937; "Under Strange Flags" 1937.

Willets, Gilson (1869-5/26/22). Screenwriter. Films: "The Escape of Jim Dolan" 1913; "Buffalo Hunting" 1914 (story only); "In the Days of the Thundering Herd" 1914; "The Heart of Texas Ryan" 1917; "Hands Up" 1918-serial (story only); "Ruth of the Range" 1923-serial.

Williams, B.L. Writer. Films: "Dishwash Dick's Counterfeit" 1913 (story).

Williams, C. Jay. Director. Films: "Lo, the Poor Indian" 1914.

Williams, Earle (1880-4/25/27). Director. Films: "Bring Him In" 1921.

Williams, Elmo (1913-). Director. Films: "The Tall Texan" 1953; "The Cowboy" 1954.

Williams, George. Writer. Films: "The Canyon of Missing Men" 1930 (story).

Williams, George. Screenwriter. Films: "War Party" 1965.

Williams, Guinn "Big Boy" (1900-6/6/62). Screenwriter. Films: "The Jack Rider" 1921; "The Vengeance Trail" 1921 (story only); "Red Blood and Blue" 1925 (story only); "Danger Trails" 1935 (story only).

Williams, John T. Screenwriter. Films: "The Law vs. Billy the Kid" 1954.

Williams, Lester. *see* Berke, William.

Williams, Lorraine. Screenwriter. Films: "The Cowboy" 1954.

Williams, Rebecca Yancey. Writer. Films: "The Vanishing Virginian" 1941 (story).

Williams, Robert. Screenwriter. Films: "Ridin' Down the Canyon" 1942 (story only); "Dead Man's Gold" 1943; "Overland Mail Robbery" 1943; "Beneath Western Skies" 1944; "Bordertown Trail" 1944; "Call of the Rockies" 1944; "Hidden Valley Outlaws" 1944; "Pride of the Plains" 1944; "Lone Texas Ranger" 1945; "Marshal of Laredo" 1945; "Trail to Vengeance" 1945; "California Gold Rush" 1946; "The Lawless Breed" 1946; "Adventures of Don Coyote" 1947; "Bandits of Dark Canyon" 1947; "Saddle Pals" 1947; "The Bold Frontiersman" 1948; "The Denver Kid" 1948; "Desperadoes of Dodge City" 1948; "Marshal of Amarillo" 1948; "Oklahoma Badlands" 1948; "Son of God's Country" 1948; "The Timber Trail" 1948; "Death Valley Gunfighter" 1949; "Frontier Marshal" 1949; "Pioneer Marshal" 1949; "Ranger of Cherokee Strip" 1949; "Sheriff of Wichita" 1949; "The Old Frontier" 1950; "Stage to Tucson" 1950; "Under Mexical Stars" 1950; "The Vanishing Westerner" 1950; "Silver City Bonanza" 1951; "Duel at Apache Wells" 1957; "The Saga of Hemp Brown" 1958.

Williams, Robert Creighton.

Screenwriter. Films: "He Rides Tall" 1964; "Taggart" 1964.

Williams, Spencer. (1893-12/13/69) Screenwriter. Films: "Harlem Rides the Range" 1939.

Williams, Sumner. Screenwriter. Films: "An Eye for an Eye" 1966.

Williams, Thames (1927-10/23/90). Screenwriter. Films: "Brimstone" 1949.

Williams, Whitney. Writer. Films: "Moonlight on the Range" 1937 (story).

Williamson, Birger E. Producer. Films: "Swing, Cowboy, Swing" 1944; "Trouble at Melody Mesa" 1944.

Williamson, Bob. Screenwriter. Films: "King's Creek Law" 1923; "Headin' Through" 1924; "Huntin' Trouble" 1924 (dir. only); "The Ghost Rider" 1925; "A Ropin' Ridin' Fool" 1925.

Williamson, Fred (1937-). Director. Films: "Boss Nigger" 1974 (prod./sp. only); "Adios Amigo" 1975 (& prod./sp.).

Williamson, R.E. Director. Films: "Wanderer of the West" 1927.

Williamson, Robin. Director. Films: "Prince of the Plains" 1927.

Williamson, Thames (1894-). Screenwriter. Films: "Cheyenne" 1947; "The Savage Horde" 1950 (story only); "A Bullet Is Waiting" 1954 (& story).

Williamson, Thomas. Screenwriter. Films: "The Last Bandit" 1949.

Willingham, Calder (1922-2/19/95). Screenwriter. Films: "One-Eyed Jacks" 1961; "Little Big Man" 1971.

Willingham, Mary. Screenwriter. Films: "Bullet for a Badman" 1964; "Arizona Raiders" 1965; "Gunpoint" 1966; "40 Guns to Apache Pass" 1967.

Willingham, Willard. Screenwriter. Films: "Bullet for a Badman" 1964; "Arizona Raiders" 1965; "Gunpoint" 1966; "40 Guns to Apache Pass" 1967.

Willis, F. McGrew. Screenwriter. Films: "Across the Desert" 1915; "In the Sunset Country" 1915; "On the Border" 1915 (story only); "The Valley of Regeneration" 1915; "The Beckoning Trail" 1916; "The End of the Game" 1919; "The Forty-Niners" 1932; "When a Man Rides Alone" 1933 (story only).

Willis, Richard. Screenwriter. Films: "Big Rock's Last Stand" 1912.

Willis, Walter. Director. Films: "A Pair of Hellions" 1924.

Wills, Ross B. Screenwriter. Films: "Spoilers of the West" 1928; "Wyoming" 1928.

Wilsie, Honore. Writer. Films: "The Red, Red Heart" 1918 (story).

Wilson, Ben (1876-8/25/30). Director. Films: "When the Cartridges Failed" 1914 (& sp.); "The Sheriff of Pine Mountain" 1916; "The Broken Spur" 1921; "The Man from Texas" 1921; "The Sheriff of Hope Eternal" 1921; "Back to Yellow Jacket" 1922; "The Marshal of Moneymint" 1922 (prod. only); "One-Eighty Apache" 1922; "Spawn of the Desert" 1923 (& prod.); "Branded a Bandit" 1924 (prod. only); "Days of '49" 1924-serial; "Lash of the Whip" 1924 (prod. only); "Notch Number One" 1924; "A Daughter of the Sioux" 1925; "Fort Frayne" 1925; "The Fugitive" 1925; "The Human Tornado" 1925; "The Man from Lone Mountain" 1925; "Renegade Holmes, M.D." 1925; "Ridin' Comet" 1925; "Romance and Rustlers" 1925; "Scar Hanan" 1925; "Tonio, Son of the Sierras" 1925; "A Two-Fisted Sheriff" 1925; "White Thunder" 1925; "The Fighting Stallion" 1926; "The Sheriff's Girl" 1926; "West of the Law" 1926; "The Wolf Hunters" 1926 (prod. only); "Wolves of the Desert" 1926; "The Mystery Brand" 1927; "The Range Riders" 1927; "Riders of the West" 1927; "Saddle Jumpers" 1927; "Western Courage" 1927; "A Yellow Streak" 1927; "The Old Code" 1928; "The Saddle King" 1929; "Thundering Thompson" 1929.

Wilson, Carey (1889-2/1/62). Screenwriter. Films: "Broken Chains" 1922.

Wilson, Jr., Charles J. Screenwriter. Films: "Cheyenne's Pal" 1917; "Swede Hearts" 1917; "Beyond the Shadows" 1918; "Wild Life" 1918.

Wilson, Cherry. Writer. Films: "The Branded Sombrero" 1928 (story); "The Saddle Buster" 1932 (story); "The Throwback" 1935 (story); "Empty Saddles" 1937 (story); "Sandflow" 1937 (story).

Wilson, Elizabeth. Screenwriter. Films: "Cave of Outlaws" 1951; "Invitation to a Gunfighter" 1964.

Wilson, Fred. *see* Girolami, Marino.

Wilson, Gerald. Screenwriter. Films: "Lawman" 1971; "Chato's Land" 1972.

Wilson, Harry Leon (1867-1939). Writer. Films: "Ruggles of Red Gap" 1918 (story); "Ruggles of Red Gap" 1923 (story); "Ruggles of Red Gap" 1935 (story); "Fancy Pants" 1950 (story).

Wilson, Hugh. Director. Films: "Rustler's Rhapsody" 1985 (& sp.).

Wilson, Jerome N. Screenwriter. Films: "A Woman's Man" 1920.

Wilson, Michael (1915-4/9/78). Screenwriter. Films: "Bar 20" 1943; "Border Patrol" 1943; "Colt Comrades" 1943; "Forty Thieves" 1944; "Friendly Persuasion" 1956.

Wilson, Richard (1915-9/24/91). Director. Films: "Ricochet Romance" 1954 (prod. only); "Man with the Gun" 1955 (& sp.); "Invitation to a Gunfighter" 1964 (& prod./sp.).

Wilson, Ted. Writer. Films: "The Devil's Playground" 1946 (story).

Wilson, Warren. Producer. Films: "Twilight on the Prairie" 1944 (& story); "Under Western Skies" 1945.

Wilstach, Frank J. Writer. Films: "The Plainsman" 1936 (story).

Wincer, Simon. Director. Films: "Lonesome Dove" TVM-1989; "Quigley Down Under" 1990; "Lightning Jack" 1994-Australia (& prod.).

Winch, Frank. Writer. Films: "Buffalo Bill" 1944 (story).

Windemere, Fred. Director. Films: "Three in Exile" 1925; "Morganson's Finish" 1926.

Winder, Michael. Screenwriter. Films: "Welcome to Blood City" 1977-Brit./Can.

Windom, Lawrence. Director. Films: "Ruggles of Red Gap" 1918; "It's a Bear" 1919.

Windust, Bretaigne (1906-3/18/60). Director. Films: "Face to Face" 1952 ("The Bride Comes to Yellow Sky" segment). ¶TV: *Wagon Train*— "The Greenhorn Story" 10-7-59, "The Estaban Zamora Story" 10-21-59, "The St. Nicholas Story" 9-23-59.

Winehouse, Irwin. Screenwriter. Films: "Powder River Gunfire" 1948-short.

Wing, Marie. Writer. Films: "Wade Brent Pays" 1914 (story).

Wing, Ward. Writer. Films: "The Overland Telegraph" 1929 (story).

Wing, William E. Screenwriter. Films: "Polly at the Ranch" 1913 (story only); "Spell of the Primeval" 1913 (story only); "The Puny Soul of Peter Rand" 1915 (story only); "The

Desert Calls Its Own" 1916; "The Return" 1916 (story only); "Before the White Man Came" 1920; "Vanishing Trails" 1920-serial; "Vengeance and the Girl" 1920; "The Fighting Stranger" 1921 (story only); "The Lash Chance" 1921 (story only); "The Struggle" 1921; "The Riddle Rider" 1924-serial; "No Man's Law" 1925; "Sand Blind" 1925; "Vic Dyson Pays" 1925 (story only); "Beyond the Rockies" 1926; "Born to Battle" 1926; "Hands Across the Border" 1926; "The Masquerade Bandit" 1926; "The Two-Gun Man" 1926.

Winkler, Irwin (1931-). Producer. Films: "Blue" 1968.

Winner, Michael (1935-). Director. Films: "Lawman" 1971 (& prod.); "Chato's Land" 1972 (& prod.).

Winstatt, C.B. Writer. Films: "The Charmed Arrow" 1914 (story).

Winston, Ron. Director. TV: *Branded*—"A Taste of Poison" 5-2-65.

Winters, Sally. Screenwriter. Films: "The Texas Terror" 1926; "Headin' Westward" 1928; "Manhattan Cowboy" 1928 (& story); "On the Divide" 1928; "Code of the West" 1929; "The Cowboy and the Outlaw" 1929; "The Fighting Terror" 1929; "The Invaders" 1929 (story only); "The Last Roundup" 1929; "The Lone Horseman" 1929 (story only); "The Man from Nevada" 1929 (story only); "'Neath Western Skies" 1929; "The Oklahoma Kid" 1929 (story only); "Pioneers of the West" 1929; "Riders of the Rio Grande" 1929; "A Texas Cowboy" 1929; "Breezy Bill" 1930; "Call of the Desert" 1930; "The Canyon of Missing Men" 1930; "Covered Wagon Trails" 1930; "Hunted Men" 1930; "The Man from Nowhere" 1930; "Near the Rainbow's End" 1930; "The Oklahoma Sheriff" 1930; "Parting of the Trails" 1930.

Wire, Harold C. Screenwriter. Films: "Royal Mounted Rides Again" 1945-serial; "The Yellow Mountain" 1954 (story only).

Wisbar, Frank (1899-3/17/67). Director. Films: "The Prairie" 1947; "Madonna of the Desert" 1948 (story only); "Rimfire" 1949 (sp. only). ¶TV: *Fireside Theater*—"Man of the Comstock" 11-3-53.

Wisberg, Aubrey (1909-3/14/90). Screenwriter. Films: "Heaven Only Knows" 1947 (story only); "Captain John Smith and Pocahontas" 1953 (& prod.).

Wise, Robert (1914-). Director. Films: "Blood on the Moon" 1948; "Two Flags West" 1950; "Tribute to a Badman" 1956.

Wisher, William. Screenwriter. Films: "Desperado: The Outlaw Wars" TVM-1989.

Wister, Owen (1860-1938). Writer. Films: "A Western Romance" 1910 (story); "The Virginian" 1914 (story); "The Virginian" 1923 (story); "The Virginian" 1929 (story); "The Virginian" 1946 (story).

Withey, Chester (1887-10/6/39). Director. Films: "Madame Bo-Peep" 1917 (& sp.).

Witney, William H. (1910-). Director. Films: "The Painted Stallion 1937-serial; "The Trigger Trio" 1937; "Zorro Rides Again" 1937-serial; "The Lone Ranger" 1938-serial; "The Lone Ranger Rides Again" 1939-serial; "Zorro's Fighting Legion" 1939-serial; "Adventures of Red Ryder" 1940-Serial; "Heroes of the Saddle" 1940; "King of the Royal Mounted" 1940-serial; "King of the Texas Rangers" 1941-serial; "King of the Mounties" 1942-serial; "Outlaws of Pine Ridge" 1942; "Heldorado" 1946; "Home in Oklahoma" 1946; "Roll on, Texas Moon" 1946; "Apache Rose" 1947; "Bells of San Angelo" 1947; "On the Old Spanish Trail" 1947; "Springtime in the Sierras" 1947; "Eyes of Texas" 1948; "The Gay Ranchero" 1948; "Grand Canyon Trail" 1948; "Night Time in Nevada" 1948; "Under California Stars" 1948; "Down Dakota Way" 1949; "The Far Frontier" 1949; "The Golden Stallion" 1949; "Susanna Pass" 1949; "Bells of Coronado" 1950; "North of the Gret Divide" 1950; "Sunset in the West" 1950; "Trail of Robin Hood" 1950; "Trigger, Jr." 1950; "Twilight in the Sierras" 1950; "Heart of the Rockies" 1951; "In Old Amarillo" 1951; "Pals of the Golden West" 1951; "South of Caliente" 1951; "Spoilers of the Plains" 1951; "Border Saddlemates" 1952; "Colorado Sundown" 1952; "The Last Musketeer" 1952; "Old Oklahoma Plains" 1952; "South Pacific Trail" 1952; "Down Laredo Way" 1953; "Iron Mountain Trail" 1953; "Old Overland Trail" 1953; "Shadows of Tombstone" 1953; "The Outcast" 1954; "Santa Fe Passage" 1955; "Stranger at My Door" 1956; "The Long Rope" 1961; "Apache Rifles" 1964; "Arizona Raiders" 1965; "40 Guns to Apache Pass" 1967. ¶TV: *Sky King* 1951; *Zorro*—"Welcome to Monterey" 10-9-58, "Zorro Rides Alone" 10-16-58, "Horse of Another Color" 10-23-58, "The Senorita Makes a Choice" 10-30-58, "Rendezvous at Sundown" 11-6-58, "The New Order" 11-13-58, "The Runaways" 1-8-59, "The Iron Box" 1-15-

59, "The Legend of Zorro" 2-12-59, "Spark of Revenge" 2-19-59; *Bonanza*—"The Lonely House" 10-15-61, "Tax Collector" 2-18-61, "The Gift" 4-1-61, "The Burma Rarity" 10-22-61, "The Auld Sod" 2-4-62, "The Jacknife" 2-18-62, "The Gamble" 4-1-62, "The Deserter" 10-21-62, "The Wild One" 10-4-64, "Between Heaven and Earth" 11-15-64, "Lothario Larkin" 4-25-65, "The Lonely Runner" 10-10-65, "Ride the Wind" 1-16-66 & 1-23-66, "Peace Officer" 2-6-66, "Horse of a Different Hue" 9-18-66, "Tommy" 12-18-66, "Sense of Duty" 9-24-67, "The Sure Thing" 11-12-67; *The Virginian*—"The Devil's Children" 12-5-62, "Say Goodbye to All That" 1-23-63, "Man of Violence" 12-25-63, "A Man Called Kane" 5-6-64, "Man of the People" 12-23-64; *Laramie*—"Broken Honor" 4-9-63, "The Marshals" 4-30-63; *Wagon Train*—"The Robert Harrison Clarke Story" 10-14-63, "The Bleeker Story" 12-9-63; *Wild Wild West*—"Night of the Deadly Bed" 9-24-65, "The Night of the Sudden Death" 10-8-65; *Branded*—"McCord's Way" 1-30-66, "The Ghost of Murrieta" 3-20-66, "The Assassins" 3-27-66 & 4-3-66; *Laredo*—"The Treasure of San Diablo" 2-17-66, "A Taste of Money" 4-28-66, "One Too Many Voices" 11-18-66, "Hey Diddle Diddle" 2-24-67; *Hondo*—"Hondo and the Singing Wire" 9-22-67, "Hondo and the Apache Kid" 10-13-67, "Hondo and the Death Drive" 12-1-67; *The High Chaparral*—"The Firing Wall" 12-31-67, "Survival" 1-14-68, "The Stallion" 9-20-68, "The Deceivers" 11-15-68.

Witt, Paul Junger (1943-). Director. TV: *Here Come the Brides* 1968-70 (prod.), "Letter of the Law" 10-30-68, "One Good Lie Deserves Another" 2-12-69, "The Crimpers" 3-5-69, "The Deadly Trade" 4-16-69, "The Soldier" 10-10-69, "A Wild Colonial Boy" 10-24-69, "Absalom" 3-20-70.

Wittliff, William D. Screenwriter. Films: "Barbarosa" 1982 (& prod.); "Red Headed Stranger" 1987 (& prod./dir.); "Lonesome Dove" TVM-1989.

Wizan, Joe (1935-). Producer. Films: "Jeremiah Johnson" 1972; "Junior Bonner" 1972.

Wohl, Burton. Screenwriter. Films: "Rio Lobo" 1970 (& story).

Wolbert, William. Director. Films: "By Right of Possession" 1917; "The Captain of the Gray Horse Troop" 1917; "The Divorcee" 1917; "Sunlight's Last Raid" 1917; "Cavanaugh of the Forest Rangers" 1918; "The Home Trail" 1918.

Wolf, Jack. Screenwriter. Films: "The Man from the Desert" 1915.

Wolford, Nelson. Writer. Films: "A Time for Killing" 1967 (story).

Wolford, Shirley. Writer. Films: "A Time for Killing" 1967 (story).

Wolfson, P.J. Screenwriter. Films: "Allegheny Uprising" 1939 (& prod.); "The Twinkle in God's Eye" 1955.

Wood, Frank. Screenwriter. Films: "The Redman's View" 1909.

Wood, Harry. Writer. Films: "The Bullet Mark" 1928 (story).

Wood, John. *see* Iquino, Ignacio.

Wood, Sam. Director. Films: "The Mine with the Iron Door" 1924; "Rangers of Fortune" 1940; "Ambush" 1950.

Wood, T.J. Producer. Films: "The Tall Texan" 1953.

Wood, Ward. Screenwriter. Films: "Posse from Heaven" 1975 (& prod.).

Wood, William. Screenwriter. Films: "Friendly Persuasion" TVM-1975. ¶TV: *Big Hawaii* 1977 (prod.).

Woodbury, Herbert A. Writer. Films: "Riders in the Sky" 1949 (story).

Woodhouse, J. Stewart. Screenwriter. Films: "Playing Double" 1923.

Woodman, Ruth. Screenwriter. Films: "Last of the Pony Riders" 1953.

Woods, Clee. Writer. Films: "Flying Hoofs" 1925 (story).

Woods, Frank E. Screenwriter. Films: "Fools of Fate" 1909; "The Honor of the Family" 1909; "The Mountaineer's Honor" 1909; "The Tenderfoot's Triumph" 1910; "The Mountain Rat" 1913; "Strongheart" 1914; "Beauty and the Bad Man" 1925.

Woods, Walter (1881-12/7/42). Screenwriter. Films: "The Trap That Failed" 1915; "D'Arcy of the Northwest Mounted" 1916; "Smashing Through" 1918; "Ruggles of Red Gap" 1923; "The Pony Express" 1925 (& story); "Sutter's Gold" 1936.

Woolf, Edgar Allan (1881-12/9/43). Screenwriter. Films: "The Kid from Texas" 1939.

Woolnough, Jeff. Director. TV: *Hawkeye*—"The Quest" 11-23-94, "Hester" 4-26-95.

Wormser, Richard. Screenwriter. Films: "Plainsman and the Lady" 1946; "Powder River Rustlers" 1949; "Rustlers on Horseback" 1950; "The Showdown" 1950 (story only); "Vigilante Hideout" 1950; "Fort Dodge Stampede" 1951; "Captive of Billy the Kid" 1952; "The Half-Breed" 1952; "A Perilous Journey" 1953; "The Outcast" 1954.

Worne, Duke (1888-10/13/33). Director. Films: "The Blue Fox" 1921-serial; "Blue Blood and Red" 1922; "Giants of the Open" 1922; "King of the Forest" 1922; "Nan of the North" 1922-serial; "Rustlers of the Redwoods" 1922; "Timberland Treachery" 1922; "Better Than Gold" 1923; "The Doomed Sentinels" 1923; "A Fight for a Mine" 1923; "God's Law" 1923; "The Guilty Hand" 1923; "Hard to Beat" 1923; "Hearts of Oak" 1923; "Knights of the Timber" 1923; "Do It Now" 1924; "Marry in Haste" 1924; "The Silent Hero" 1927; "Danger Patrol" 1928; "Bride of the Desert" 1929.

Worsley, Wallace (1878-3/26/44). Director. Films: "The Goddess of Lost Lake" 1918.

Worthing, George. Writer. Films: "Lightning Lariats" 1927 (story).

Worthington, William (1872-4/9/41). Director. Films: "D'Arcy of the Northwest Mounted" 1916; "The Man Who Took a Chance" 1917; "The Ghost of the Rancho" 1918; "The Beautiful Gambler" 1921; "Tracked to Earth" 1922; "Out of the Silent North" 1923; "Kindled Courage" 1923; "Beauty and the Bad Man" 1925.

Worts, George Frank. Writer. Films: "Where the Worst Begins" 1925 (story).

Wrather, Jack (1918-11/12/84). Producer. Films: "The Lone Ranger and the Lost City of Gold" 1958.

Wright, Charles. Screenwriter. Films: "Cupid Rides the Range" 1939-short.

Wright, Francis M. Writer. Films: "The Man from the West" 1913 (story).

Wright, Fred E. Director. Films: "The Kill-Joy" 1917.

Wright, Gilbert. Screenwriter. Films: "The Californian" 1937; "Springtime in the Rockies" 1937; "Wild Horse Rodeo" 1937 (story only); "Ranch House Romeo" 1939-short; "Utah" 1945 (story only).

Wright, Harold Bell (1872-1944). Writer. Films: "The Mine with the Iron Door" 1924 (story); "When a Man's a Man" 1924 (story); "A Son of His Father" 1925 (story); "The Winning of Barbara Worth" 1926 (story); "The Shepherd of the Hills" 1928 (story); "When a Man's a Man" 1935 (story); "The Mine with the Iron Door" 1936 (story); "Wild Brian Kent" 1936 (story); "The Californian" 1937 (story); "It Happened Out West" 1937 (story); "Secret Valley" 1937 (story); "Western Gold" 1937 (story); "The Sherpherd of the Hills" 1941 (story); "The Shepherd of the Hills" 1964 (story).

Wright, Herbert J. Screenwriter. Films: "Shadow of the Hawk" 1976.

Wright, Mack V. (1895-8/14/65). Director. Films: "The Broncho Kid" 1920; "The Great Round Up" 1920; "The Lone Ranger" 1920; "Masked" 1920; "Ransom" 1920; "The Red Hot Trail" 1920; "Thieves' CLothes" 1920; "The Lost Trail" 1926 (sp. only); "Arizona Days" 1928 (sp. only); "West of Santa Fe" 1928 (sp. only); "Wolf Tracks" 1929 (& sp.); "Haunted Gold" 1932; "The Man from Monterey" 1933; "Somewhere in Sonora" 1933; "Comin' Round the Mountain" 1936; "Roarin' Lead" 1936; "The Singing Cowboy" 1936; "Vigilantes Are Coming" 1936-serial; "Winds of the Wasteland" 1936; "The Big Show" 1937 (sp. only); "Hit the Saddle" 1937; "Range Defenders" 1937; "Riders of the Whistling Skull" 1937; "Rootin' Tootin' Rhythm" 1937; "The Great Adventures of Wild Bill Hickok" 1938-serial; "Wells Fargo Days" 1944-short.

Wright, Tenny (1885-9/13/71). Director. Films: "The Fightin' Comeback" 1927; "Hoof Marks" 1927; "The Big Stampede" 1932; "The Telegraph Trail" 1933.

Wright, William H. Producer. Films: "Stars in My Crown" 1950; "The Naked Spur" 1953; "A Distant Trumpet" 1964; "The Sons of Katie Elder" 1965 (sp. only).

Wright, William Lord. Writer. Films: "Ace of Spades" 1925-serial (story); "Plunging Hoofs" 1928 (story); "Harvest of Hate" 1929 (story); "Hoofbeats of Vengeance" 1929 (story).

Wurlitzer, Rudolph. Screenwriter. Films: "Pat Garrett and Billy the Kid" 1973.

Wurtzel, Sol M. (1890-4/9/58). Producer. Films: "The Country Beyond" 1936; "Ramona" 1936; "Fair Warning" 1937; "Frontier Marshal" 1939; "Lucky Cisco Kid" 1940; "Viva Cisco Kid" 1940; "Last of the Duanes" 1941; "Ride On, Vaquero" 1941; "Riders of the Purple Sage" 1941;

"Romance of the Rio Grande" 1941; "Lone Star Ranger" 1942; "Sundown Jim" 1942; "Tucson" 1949.

Wyatt, Nate. Director. Films: "Bordertown" 1937.

Wyler, John. *see* Ciani, Sergio.

Wyler, Robert (1900-1/16/71). Screenwriter. Films: "Friendly Persuasion" 1956; "The Big Country" 1958.

Wyler, William (1902-7/27/81). Director. Films: "The Crook Buster" 1925; "Don't Shoot" 1926; "The Fire Barrier" 1926; "The Gunless Bad Man" 1926; "Lazy Lightning" 1926; "Martin of the Mounted" 1926; "The Pinnacle Rider" 1926; "Ridin' for Love" 1926; "The Stolen Ranch" 1926; "Blazing Days" 1927; "Border Cavalier" 1927; "Desert Dust" 1927; "Galloping Justice" 1927; "Gun Justice" 1927; "Hard Fists" 1927; "The Haunted Homestead" 1927; "The Home Tril" 1927; "The Horse Trader" 1927; "The Lone Star" 1927; "The Ore Raiders" 1927; "The Phantom Outlaw" 1927; "Shooting Straight" 1927; "The Silent Partner" 1927; "The Square Shooter" 1927; "Straight Shootin'" 1927; "Tenderfoot Courage" 1927; "The Two Fister" 1927; "Thunder Riders" 1928; "Hell's Heroes" 1930; "The Storm" 1930; "The Westerner" 1940; "Friendly Persuasion" 1956 (& prod.); "The Big Country" 1958 (& prod.).

Wylie, Philip (1902-10/25/71). Writer. Films: "Fair Warning" 1937 (story).

Wynn, Tracy Keenan. Screenwriter. Films: "The Quest" TVM-1976.

Xydias, Anthony J. Producer. Films: "Wolf Tracks" 1923; "Heroes of the Alamo" 1938.

Yanok, George. Screenwriter. Films: "Go West, Young Girl" TVM-1978 (& prod.).

Yarbrough, James P. Director. *Bonanza*—"The Ape" 12-17-60; *Rawhide*—"Gold Fever" 5-4-62; *The Guns of Will Sonnett* 1967-69.

Yarbrough, Jean (1900-8/2/75). Director. Films: "A Buckaroo Broadcast" 1938-short; "Molly Cures a Cowboy" 1940-short; "Twilight on the Prairie" 1944; "Under Western Skies" 1945; "Lost in Alaska" 1952; "Yaqui Drums" 1956; "The Over-the-Hill Gang" TVM-1969. ¶TV: *Cheyenne* 1955; *Gunsmoke*—"The Tragedian" 1-23-60, "Colleen So Green" 4-2-60, "No Chip" 12-3-60; *Laramie*—"Dragon at the Door" 9-26-61; *Bonanza*—"Home from the Sea" 5-1-

66; *The Guns of Will Sonnett*—"First Love" 11-3-67, "The Favor" 11-10-67, "And a Killing Rode into Town" 12-1-67, "Sunday in Paradise" 12-15-67, "End of the Rope" 1-12-68, "And He Shall Lead the Children" 1-19-68, "The Warriors" 3-1-68, "A Fool and His Money" 3-8-68, "Reunion" 9-27-68, "Chapter and Verse" 10-11-68, "Pariah" 10-18-68, "Joby" 11-1-68, "The Straw Man" 11-8-68, "A Difference of Opinion" 11-15-68, "Meeting in a Small Town" 12-6-68, "The Fearless Man" 12-13-68, "Where There's Hope" 12-20-68, "Join the Army" 1-3-69, "Time Is the Rider" 1-10-69, "Robber's Roost" 1-17-69, "A Town in Terror" 2-7-69 & 2-14-69, "Jim Sonnett's Lady" 2-21-69, "One Angry Juror" 3-7-69, "The Marriage" 3-14-69.

Yates, George Worthing (1900-6/6/75). Screenwriter. Films: "The Lone Ranger" 1938-serial; "The Last Outpost" 1951; "Those Redheads from Seattle" 1953.

Yates, Hal. Screenwriter. Films: "Bandits and Ballads" 1939-short; "West of the Rockies" 1941-short.

Yates, Herbert J. (1880-2/3/66) Producer. Films: "Northwest Outpost" 1947; "Surrender" 1950; "Belle Le Grand" 1951; "Black Hills Ambush" 1952; "Border Saddlemates" 1952; "Johnny Guitar" 1954; "Jubilee Trail" 1954; "The Phantom Stallion" 1954; "A Man Alone" 1955; "The Road to Denver" 1955; "Timberjack" 1955; "The Twinkle in God's Eye" 1955; "The Vanishing American" 1955; "The Maverick Queen" 1956.

Yeo Ban Yee. Director. Films: "Kung Fu Brothers in the Wild West" 1973-Ital./Hong Kong.

Yordan, Philip (1913-). Screenwriter. Films: "Bad Men of Tombstone" 1949; "Drums in the Deep South" 1951; "Blowing Wild" 1953; "Broken Lance" 1954 (story only); "Johnny Guitar" 1954; "The Last Frontier" 1955; "The Man from Laramie" 1955; "Gun Glory" 1957 (story only); "The Bravados" 1958; "The Fiend Who Walked the West" 1958; "Day of the Outlaw" 1959; "Custer of the West" 1967-U.S./Span. (prod. only); "Bad Man's River" 1971-Span./Ital./Fr.; "Captain Apache" 1971-Brit./Span. (& prod.).

Yost, Dorothy. Screenwriter. Films: "Youth Must Have Love" 1922; "The Footlight Ranger" 1923; "Kentucky Days" 1923; "Broadway or Bust" 1924; "Romance Ranch" 1924; "Wings of the Storm" 1926; "Smoky" 1946; "Loaded Pistols" 1948; "The Strawberry Roan" 1948; "The Cow-

boy and the Indians" 1949; "Saginaw Trail" 1953.

Yost, Robert (1886-4/10/67). Screenwriter. Films: "The Arizona Raiders" 1936; "Arizona Mahoney" 1936; "Desert Gold" 1936; "Drift Fence" 1936; "Born to the West" 1937; "Forlorn River" 1937; "Thunder Trail" 1937; "Carson City Kid" 1940; "Young Buffalo Bill" 1940; "The Phantom Plainsmen" 1942 (& story); "Sunset Serenade" 1942 (story only); "Canyon City" 1943; "Overland Mail Robbery" 1943; "Thundering Trails" 1943 (& story).

Young, Carroll. Screenwriter. Films: "Overland Telegraph" 1951 (story only); "Apache Warrior" 1957 (& story); "The Deerslayer" 1957.

Young, Clarence Upson. Screenwriter. Films: "The Law West of Tombstone" 1938 (& story); "Bad Lands" 1939; "The Girl and the Gambler" 1939; "Son of Roaring Dan" 1940; "North to the Klondike" 1942; "Badman's Territory" 1946; "Riding the California Trail" 1947; "Albuquerque" 1948; "Showdown at Abilene" 1956 (story only); "Gunfight in Abilene" 1967 (story only).

Young, Collier (1908-12/25/80). Producer. Films: "The Halliday Brand" 1957. ¶TV: *Wild Wild West* 1965-69.

Young, Frank H. Screenwriter. Films: "Ghost Guns" 1944; "Partners of the Trail" 1944; "Range Law" 1944; "Gun Smoke" 1945; "The Navajo Trail" 1945 (story only); "Stranger from Santa Fe" 1945; "Border Bandits" 1946; "The Haunted Mine" 1946; "Trigger Fingers" 1946; "Flashing Guns" 1947; "Song of the Drifter" 1948.

Young, Gordon Ray. Writer. Films: "Tall in the Saddle" 1944 (story); "Born to the Saddle" 1953 (story).

Young, Howard Irving (1893-2/24/52). Screenwriter. Films: "Sacred Silence" 1919.

Young, Howard J. Writer. Films: "The Pitfall" 1915 (story).

Young, Nedrick (1914-9/16/68). Writer. Films: "Passage West" 1951 (story).

Young, Robert M. Director. Films: "The Ballad of Gregorio Cortez" 1983.

Young, Robert R. Screenwriter. Films: "Waterhole No. 3" 1967.

Young, Roger. Director. Films: "Geronimo" TVM-1993.

Young, Terence (1915-9/7/94). Director. Films: "Red Sun" 1971-Fr./Ital./Span.

Young, Waldemar (1878-8/30/38). Screenwriter. Films: "The Sundown Trail" 1919; "The Great Divide" 1925; "The Flaming Forest" 1926; "Tide of Empire" 1929; "Girl of the Golden West" 1930; "The Plainsman" 1936.

Young, Zella. Screenwriter. Films: "Wings of Adventure" 1930.

Young Deer, James. Director. Films: "Under Both Flags" 1910; "Yaqui Girl" 1911; "The Unwilling Bride" 1912.

Younger, A.P. Screenwriter. Films: "The Galloping Kid" 1922; "The Lone Hand" 1922.

Youngstein, Max E. Producer. Films: "The Dangerous Days of Kiowa Jones" TVM-1966; "Welcome to Hard Time" 1967; "Young Billy Young" 1969.

Yust, Larry. Director. Films: "Testimony of Two Men" TVM-1977.

Zabalza, Jose Maria (Harry Freeman, Joseph Trader). Director. Films: "Damned Pistols of Dallas" 1964-Span./Ital./Fr.; "Adios Cjamango" 1969-Ital./Span. (& sp.); "Rebels of Arizona" 1969-Span. (& sp.).

Zagor, Michael. Screenwriter. Films: "The Man from Galveston" 1964.

Zanuck, Darryl F. (1902-12/22/79). Producer. Films: "Call of the Wild" 1935; "White Fang" 1936; "Jesse James" 1939; "The Return of Frank James" 1940; "Western Union" 1941; "Viva Zapata!" 1952.

Zapponi, Bernardino. Screenwriter. Films: "The Magnificent Bandits" 1969-Ital./Span.

Zeanile, Marcello. Director. Films: "Seven Nuns in Kansas City" 1973-Ital.

Zeglio, Primo (Anthony Green, Anthony Greepy, Omar Hopkins). Director. Films: "Man from the Cursed Valley" 1964-Ital./Span.; "Two Gunmen" 1964-Span./Ital. (& sp.); "Relentless Four" 1966-Span./Ital.; "Killer Goodbye" 1969-Ital./Span. (& sp.); "Sheriff of Rock Spring" 1971-Ital.

Zehetgruber, Rudolf. *see* Pink, Sidney.

Zeliff, Seymour (1886-1/17/53). Director. Films: "The Mysterious Witness" 1923.

Zellner, Lois. Screenwriter. Films: "The Gamesters" 1920; "Frivolous Sal" 1925.

Zemeckis, Robert (1952-). Director. Films: "Back to the Future, Part III" 1990.

Zibaso, Werner P. Screenwriter. Films: "Pirates of the Mississippi" 1963-Ger./Ital./Fr.; "Massacre at Marble City" 1964-Ger./Ital./Fr.

Zieff, Howard (1943-). Director. Films: "Hearts of the West" 1975.

Ziegler, Henry. Screenwriter. Films: "The Green Shadow" 1913.

Zimbalist, Sam. Producer. Films: "Tribute to a Badman" 1956.

Zimet, Julian. Screenwriter. Films: "Sierra Sue" 1941; "Heldorado" 1946; "The Strawberry Roan" 1948 (story only).

Zimm, Maurice. Screenwriter. Films: "Good Day for a Hanging" 1958.

Zingarelli, Italo (Ike Zingar-

mann). Producer. Films: "Gunmen of the Rio Grande" 1964-Fr./Ital./Span. (& sp.); "Johnny Yuma" 1966-Ital.; "Hate for Hate" 1967-Ital.; "The Five Man Army" 1969-Ital.; "They Call Me Trinity" 1970-Ital.; "Trinity Is Still My Name" 1974-Ital.

Zinneman, Fred (1907-). Director. Films: "High Noon" 1952; "Oklahoma!" 1955.

Zivelli, Joseph E. Director. Films: "Wanderer of the West" 1927.

Zodorow, John. Screenwriter. Films: "Kate Bliss and the Ticker Tape Kid" TVM-1978 (& story).

Zuckerman, George. Screenwriter. Films: "Ride Clear of Diabloe" 1953; "Dawn at Socorro" 1954; "Taza, Son of Cochise" 1954; "The Yellow Mountain" 1954; "The Brass Legend" 1956 (story only).

Zugsmith, Albert (1910-). Producer. Films: "Raw Edge" 1956; "Red Sundown" 1956; "Star in the Dust" 1956; "Man in the Shadow" 1957.

Zukor, Adolph (1873-6/10/76). Producer. Films: "The Border Legion" 1924; "The Wanderer of the Wasteland" 1924; "The Light of Western Stars" 1925; "The Pony Express" 1925; "The Vanishing American" 1925; "Desert Gold" 1926; "Man of the Forest" 1926; "Jesse James" 1927; "Nevada" 1927; "Open Range" 1927; "Under the Tonto Rim" 1928; "Sunset Pass" 1933; "Under the Tonto Rim" 1933.

Zurli, Guido (Albert Moore). Director. Films: "Thompson 1880" 1966-Ital./Ger.; "Son of Zorro" 1973-Ital./Span. (sp. only).